INTERNATIONAL LITERARY MARKET PLACE™

ILMP 2005

International Literary Market Place™
37th Edition

Publisher
Thomas H. Hogan

Vice President, Content
Dick Kaser

Director, ITI Reference Group
Owen O'Donnell

Managing Editor
Karen Hallard

Associate Editors
Kevin Araujo; Kathryn Eaton; Mary-Anne Lutter

Tampa Operations:

Production Manager, Tampa Editoral
Debbie James

Project Coordinator, Tampa Editorial
Carolyn Victor

Associate Project Coordinator, Tampa Editorial
Paula Watts

Data Entry Clerk, Tampa Editorial
Barbara Lauria

INTERNATIONAL LITERARY MARKET PLACE™

ILMP 2005

The Directory of the International Book Publishing Industry

OVER 180 COUNTRIES COVERED

Published by

Information Today, Inc.
143 Old Marlton Pike
Medford, NJ 08055-8750
Phone: (609) 654-6266
Fax: (609) 654-4309
E-mail (Orders): custserv@infotoday.com
Web site: http://www.infotoday.com
Copyright 2004, Information Today, Inc. All Rights Reserved

ISSN 0074-6827
ISBN 1-57387-205-9
Library of Congress Catalog Card Number 77-70295

COPYRIGHT © 2004 INFORMATION TODAY, INC. All rights reserved. No part of this publication may be reproduced, stored in a retrieval system, or transmitted, in any form or by any means, electronic, mechanical, photocopy, recording or otherwise without the prior written permission of the publisher.

Information Today, Inc. uses reasonable care to obtain accurate and timely information. However, Information Today, Inc. disclaims any liability to any party for any loss or damage caused by errors or omissions in *International Literary Market Place*™ whether or not such errors or omissions result from negligence, accident or any other cause.

Information Today, Inc.
143 Old Marlton Pike
Medford, NJ 08055-8750
  Phone: 800-300-9868 (Customer Service)
               800-409-4929 (Editorial)
Fax: 609-654-4309
E-mail (orders): custserv@infotoday.com
Web Site: www.infotoday.com

Printed in the United States of America

CONTENTS

Preface vii
Editorial Revision Form ix
Copyright Conventions xi
The ISBN System xiii
Abbreviations xxii

PUBLISHING
Publishers 1
Type of Publication Index 787
Subject Index 889
Literary Agents 1129
International Publishing Services 1145
Translation Agencies & Associations 1147

MANUFACTURING
Complete Book Manufacturing 1153
Prepress Services Index 1169
Prepress Services 1175
Printing, Binding & Book Finishing Index 1191
Printing, Binding & Book Finishing 1215
Manufacturing Materials Index 1233
Manufacturing Materials 1235
Manufacturing Services & Equipment Index 1243
Manufacturing Services & Equipment 1245

BOOK TRADE INFORMATION
Book Clubs 1251
Book Trade Organizations 1259
Major Book Dealers 1297
Book Trade Reference Books & Journals 1357

LITERARY ASSOCIATIONS & PRIZES
Literary Associations & Societies 1395
Literary Prizes 1411

BOOK TRADE CALENDAR
Alphabetical Index of Sponsors 1457
Alphabetical Index of Events 1463
Calendar of Book Trade & Promotional Events 1467

LIBRARY RESOURCES
Major Libraries 1489
Library Associations 1557
Library Reference Books & Journals 1575

INDEXES
Industry Yellow Pages 1595

Preface

Since 1965, *International Literary Market Place (ILMP)* and its companion *Literary Market Place*, have covered the world of book publishing. These directories provide detailed information on the global book publishing industry. This edition of *ILMP* includes over 16,500 entries in over 180 countries. Publishers account for 10,276 of these entries.

Organization & Content
The six areas of coverage into which *ILMP* is arranged are as follows: Publishing, Manufacturing, Book Trade Information, Literary Associations & Prizes, Book Trade Calendar and Library Resources. Within most chapters, companies are sorted first by their country, then by key words in the company name. Sorting preference is determined by the entrant.

Pertinent information regarding each country represented - such as capital, language, population, currency, trade and copyright restrictions - can be found at the beginning of that country's listings in the Publishers section. The basic content of company entries includes - but is not limited to - address, telecommunications data, key personnel, a descriptive annotation and assorted statistics.

There are exceptions to this arrangement. International Publishing Services, located within the Publishing chapter, contains U.S. and Canadian companies that do a significant amount of international business and wish to advertise their services to users of *ILMP*. Also, those U.S. and Canadian book manufacturing companies that do 10% or more of their business overseas are included in the appropriate sections within the Manufacturing chapter.

Compilation
ILMP is updated throughout the year via a number of methods. A questionnaire is mailed to every current listing to corroborate and update the information contained on our database. All returned mailers are edited for the next product release. If a reply is not received, public sources are researched to determine the status of the listee.

Information on new listings is gathered using a similar method. *ILMP* editors identify possible new listings through their daily research or as a result of nominations from the organization itself or from third parties. A questionnaire is then sent to gather the essential listing information. Unless we receive information directly from the organization, the new listing will not be included in the *ILMP* database.

Updated information or suggestions for new listings can also be submitted by using the form that follows this preface.

Simply fill in the information requested and send the form to:

International Literary Market Place
630 Central Avenue
New Providence, NJ 07974
United States of America
Fax: 908-219-0192

An updating method using Internet technology is also available for *ILMP* listings:

You can use the *Literary Market Place* web site to update an *ILMP* listing. **Literarymarketplace.com** allows you the opportunity to provide new information for a listing by clicking on the option to Update or Correct Your Entry. The Feedback option on the home page of the web site can be used to suggest new entries as well.

Once information regarding a suggested new entry or a correction to an existing listing has been submitted, our editors verify the data with the organization to ensure the accuracy of the update.

Related Services
International Literary Market Place, along with its companion publication *Literary Market Place*, is now available through the World Wide Web at **www.literarymarketplace.com**. Designed to give users simple, logical access to the information they require, the site offers the choice of searching for data alphabetically, geographically, by type, or by subject. Continuously updated by Information Today, Inc.'s team of editors, this is a truly enhanced version of the *ILMP* and *LMP* databases, incorporating features that make "must have" information easily available.

Your feedback is important to us. We strongly encourage you to contact us with comments on this 2005 edition of *ILMP*, as well as suggestions and comments for future editions. Our editorial office can be reached by phone at 1-800-409-4929 or 908-286-1090, or by e-mail at khallard@infotoday.com. Most importantly, thanks are due to those entrants who took the time to respond to our questionnaires.

Return this form to:
International Literary Market Place
Information Today, Inc.
630 Central Avenue
New Providence, NJ 07974, USA
Fax: 908-219-0192

INTERNATIONAL LITERARY MARKET PLACE™
EDITORIAL REVISION FORM

Company Name:_____

The company listing is found on page number:_____

☐ Please check here if you are nominating this organization for a new listing in the directory

General Information

Address:_____

City:_____ State/Province:_____ Postal Code:_____

Phone:_____ Fax:_____

E-mail:_____ Web Site:_____

Brief Description:_____

Personnel

☐ Addition   ☐ Deletion   ☐ Correction

First Name:_____ Last Name:_____ Title:_____

☐ Addition   ☐ Deletion   ☐ Correction

First Name:_____ Last Name:_____ Title:_____

☐ Addition   ☐ Deletion   ☐ Correction

First Name:_____ Last Name:_____ Title:_____

☐ Addition   ☐ Deletion   ☐ Correction

First Name:_____ Last Name:_____ Title:_____

(continued on back)

Other Information

Indicate other information to be added to or corrected in this listing; please be as specific as possible, noting erroneous data to be deleted.

_____
_____
_____
_____
_____
_____
_____
_____

Verification

Data for this listing will not be updated without the following information (*indicates mandatory information)

*Your First Name:_____   *Your Last Name:_____

Organization Name:_____

*Address:_____

*City:_____   *State/Province:_____   *Postal Code:_____

*Phone:_____   E-mail:_____

*Indicate if you are a: ☐ Representative of this Organization ☐ User of this directory ☐ Other

If other, please specify:_____

**Thank you for helping Information Today, Inc. maintain the most up-to-date information available.
Please return by fax to: 908-219-0192, or visit www.literarymarketplace.com and
click on the option to Update or Correct Your Entry under Free Services.**

Copyright Conventions

The Universal Copyright Convention was sponsored by Unesco in 1952. It states that 'Each signatory country extends to foreign works covered by UCC the same protection which such country extends to works of its own nationals published within its own borders.'

The Berne Convention is a system of international copyright which is maintained among countries which have become signatories of the International Copyright Union for the Protection of Literary and Artistic Works. This Union plan, which was first agreed upon at Berne, Switzerland, in 1886, has been subject to later revisions.

The basic principle of the agreement is that any work properly copyrighted in its country of origin has protection in every Union country. Any work originating in a non-Union country, if it is simultaneously published in a Union country, has the same standing as it would if it had originated in a Union country. Different countries have different relationships under one or more of the revisions (Berlin, 1908; Rome, 1928; Brussels, 1948; Stockholm, 1968; and Paris, 1971).

The Florence Agreement, also known as the 'free flow of book', is a Unesco-sponsored international agreement aimed at easing the flow of books and other scientific, educational and cultural materials, through the elimination or reduction of tariffs and other barriers.

The Buenos Aires Convention: In most Latin-American countries, compliance with the copyright law of the country of first publication protects the work in other countries of the Buenos Aires Convention (1910). To secure copy-right, each work must carry a notice to the effect that any use of the book or article will not be permitted without the consent of the copyright owner, and that copyright is reserved in English or any other language; for complete safety it is advised to add 'All rights reserved'. A later revision of the Buenos Aires Convention was made at the Washington Conference (Pan-American Copyright Convention) of 1946 which goes into greater detail than the Buenos Aires Convention.

See the General Information for each country in the Publishers Section for country specific copyright information.

The ISBN System

Background

The question of the need and feasibility of an international numbering system for books was first discussed at the third International Conference on Book Market Research and Rationalization in the Book Trade held in November 1966 in Berlin. At this time a number of publishers and book distributors in Europe were considering the use of computers in order processing and inventory control; and it was evident that a prerequisite of an efficient automated system was a unique and simple identification number for a published item.

The system which fulfilled this requirement and which became known as the International Standard Book Number (ISBN) System developed out of the book numbering system introduced into the United Kingdom in 1967.

In a report to the British Publishers Association, Professor F.G. Foster of the London School of Economics stated that there was '...a clear need of the introduction into the book trade of standard numbering...and substantial benefits would accrue to all parties therefrom'. After further study and deliberation, a detailed plan for standard numbering was produced. At the same time, the Technical Committee on Documentation of the International Standards Organization (ISO/TC 46) set up a working party (with the British Standards Institution acting as secretariat) to investigate the possibility of adapting the British system for international use. A meeting was held in London in 1968 with representatives from Denmark, France, Federal Republic of Germany, Eire, the Netherlands, Norway, the United Kingdom, the United States of America and an observer from Unesco. Other countries contributed written suggestions and expressions of interest. A report of the meeting was circulated to all countries belonging to the ISO. Comments on this report and subsequent proposals were considered at meetings held in Berlin and Stockholm in 1969.

As a result of these meetings there emerged ISO Recommendations 2108 which sets out the principles and procedures for international standard book numbering. The purpose of the ISO Recommendations is to coordinate and standardize internationally the use of book numbers so that an International Standard Book Number (ISBN) identifies one title or edition of a title from one specific publisher and is unique to that edition.

The ISBN applies in the main to books - for which the system was originally created - but, by extension, it may be used for any item produced by publishers or collected by libraries.

How the International Standard Book Number (ISBN) is Built Up

Every International Standard Book Number (ISBN) consists of ten digits; and whenever it is printed it is preceded by the letters ISBN. (Note: In those countries where the Latin alphabet is not used, an abbreviation in the characters of the local alphabet may be used in addition to the Latin letters ISBN.)

The ten-digit number is divided into four parts of variable length, each part when printed being separated by a hyphen or space. (Note: Experience suggests that the hyphen is preferable to the space.)

The four parts are as follows:

Part 1. Group Identifier
This part identifies the national, geographic or other similar grouping of publishers.

Part 2. Publisher's Prefix
This part identifies a particular publisher within a group.

Part 3. Title Identifier
This part identifies a particular title or edition of a title published by a particular publisher.

Part 4. Check Digit
This is a single digit at the end of the ISBN which provides an automatic check on the correctness of the ISBN.

Group Identifier
Group identifiers are allocated by the International ISBN Agency and a publisher wishing to participate in the ISBN system must belong to a recognized ISBN group. Groups are determined by national, geographic, language or other pertinent considerations. Experience has shown that groups based on national or geographic consideration are the most satisfactory. The following group identifiers are in use at present:

0 and 1	Australia, English-speaking Canada, Gibraltar, Ireland, Namibia, New Zealand, Puerto Rico, South Africa, Swaziland, UK, USA, Zimbabwe
2	France, French-speaking Belgium, French-speaking Canada, Luxembourg, French-speaking Switzerland
3	Austria, Germany, German-speaking Switzerland
4	Japan
5	Kazakhstan (also 9965), Moldova (also 9975), Russia
7	China (People's Republic of)
80	Czech Republic, Slovakia
81	India (also 93)
82	Norway
83	Poland
84	Spain
85	Brazil
86	Slovenia (also 961)
87	Denmark
88	Italy, Italian-speaking Switzerland
89	Republic of Korea
90	Netherlands, Flemish-speaking Belgium
91	Sweden
92	International Publishers (Unesco, EU); European Community Organizations
93	India (also 81)
950	Argentina (also 987)
951	Finland (also 952)
952	Finland (also 951)
953	Croatia
954	Bulgaria
955	Sri Lanka
956	Chile
957	Taiwan, China (also 986)
958	Colombia
959	Cuba
960	Greece
961	Slovenia (also 86)
962	Hong Kong (People's Republic of China) (also 988)

THE ISBN SYSTEM

963	Hungary	9946	Korea (People's Democratic Republic)	9981	Morocco (also 9954)
964	Iran	9947	Algeria (also 9961)	9982	Zambia
965	Israel	9948	United Arab Emirates	9983	Gambia
966	Ukraine	9949	Estonia (also 9985)	9984	Latvia
967	Malaysia (also 983)	9950	Palestine	9985	Estonia (also 9949)
968	Mexico (also 970)	9951	Kosovo	9986	Lithuania (also 9955)
969	Pakistan	9952	Azerbaijan	9987	Tanzania (also 9976)
970	Mexico (also 968)	9953	Lebanon	9988	Ghana (also 9964)
971	Philippines	9954	Morocco (also 9981)	9989	Macedonia
972	Portugal (also 989)	9955	Lithuania (also 9986)	99901	Bahrain
973	Romania	9956	Cameroon	99902	Gabon (reserved)
974	Thailand	9957	Jordan	99903	Mauritius
975	Turkey	9958	Bosnia and Herzegovina	99904	Netherlands Antilles, Aruba
976	Caribbean Community (CARICOM): Antigua and Barbuda, Bahamas, Barbados, Belize, Bermuda, British Virgin Islands, Cayman Islands, Dominica, Dominican Republic, Grenada, Guyana, Haiti, Jamaica, Montserrat, St. Kitts and Nevis, St. Lucia, St. Maarten, St. Vincent and the Grenadines, Trinidad and Tobago, Turks and Caicos Islands	9959	Libya	99905	Bolivia
		9960	Saudi Arabia	99906	Kuwait
		9961	Algeria (also 9947)	99908	Malawi
		9962	Panama	99909	Malta (also 99932)
		9963	Cyprus	99910	Sierra Leone
		9964	Ghana (also 9988)	99911	Lesotho
		9965	Kazakhstan (also 5)	99912	Botswana
977	Egypt	9966	Kenya	99913	Andorra (also 99920)
978	Nigeria	9967	Kyrgyz Republic	99914	Suriname
979	Indonesia	9968	Costa Rica (also 9977)	99915	Maldives
980	Venezuela	9970	Uganda	99916	Namibia
981	Republic of Singapore (also 9971)	9971	Republic of Singapore (also 981)	99917	Brunei Darussalam
982	South Pacific: Cook Islands, Fiji, Kiribati, Marshall Islands, Micronesia (Federated States of), Nauru, New Caledonia, Niue, Palau, Solomon Islands, Tokelau, Tonga, Tuvalu, Vanuatu, Western Samoa	9972	Peru	99918	Faroe Islands
		9973	Tunisia	99919	Benin
		9974	Uruguay	99920	Andorra (also 99913)
		9975	Moldova (also 5)	99921	Qatar
		9976	Tanzania (also 9987)	99922	Guatemala (also 99939)
983	Malaysia (also 967)	9977	Costa Rica (also 9968)	99923	El Salvador
984	Bangladesh	9978	Ecuador	99924	Nicaragua
985	Belarus	9979	Iceland	99925	Paraguay
986	Taiwan, China (also 957)	9980	Papua New Guinea	99926	Honduras
987	Argentina (also 950)				
988	Hong Kong (People's Republic of China) (also 962)				
989	Portugal (also 972)				

99927	Albania (also 99943)
99928	Georgia (also 99940)
99929	Mongolia
99930	Armenia (also 99941)
99931	Seychelles
99932	Malta (also 99909)
99933	Nepal
99934	Dominican Republic
99935	Haiti
99936	Bhutan
99937	Macau
99938	Srpska
99939	Guatemala (also 99922)
99940	Georgia (also 99928)
99941	Armenia (also 99930)
99942	Sudan
99943	Albania (also 99927)
99944	Ethiopia

Publisher's Prefix
The publisher's prefix designates the publisher of a given book. Publishers with a large output of books are assigned a short publisher's prefix; publishers with a small output of books are assigned a longer publisher's prefix.

Title Identifier
The title identifier is assigned to a particular title or edition of a title by the publisher from within the range of numbers assigned to him and which will depend upon the length of his publisher's prefix. Title identifiers are normally assigned by the publisher himself. Publishers who assign their own title identifiers may use them to identify titles in the publishing house throughout the planning stages.

Check Digit
The 'check digit' is the last digit in an ISBN and is computed as the result of an elaborate calculation on the other nine digits. This calculation is performed almost instanta-neously by an electronic computing device, and is a means of detecting incorrectly transcribed numbers. The check digit is calculated on a modulus 11 with weights 10-2, using X in lieu of 10 where ten would occur as a check digit. This means that each of the first nine digits on the ISBN - i.e. excluding the check digit itself - is multiplied by a number ranging from 10 to 2; and the sum of the products thus obtained, plus the check digit, must be divisible, without remainder, by 11. For example:

	Group Identifier		Publisher's Prefix	
ISBN	0	8	4	3 6
Weight	10	9	8	7 6
Products	0+	72+	32+	21+ 36+

	Title Number		Check Digit	
ISBN	1	0	7 2	7
Weight	5	4	3 2	
Products	5+	0+	21+	4+ 7+

Total: 198

As 198 can be divided by 11 without remainder 0 8436 1072 is a valid International Standard Book Number.

The number of digits in each part, and how to recognize them in an ISBN
The number of digits in each of the identifying parts 1, 2 and 3 is variable, though the total number of digits contained in these parts is always 9. These nine digits together with the check digit bring the total number of digits in an ISBN to ten.

The number of digits in the group identifier will vary according to the likely output of books in a group. Thus, groups with an expected large output will get numbers of one or two digits; and publishers with an expected large output will get numbers of two or three digits.

Exceptionally, a one-digit number may be assigned to a publisher, but it will be appreciated that the assignment of one-digit publisher identifiers greatly reduces the range of possible identifiers in the group. For ease of reading, the four parts of the ISBN are divided by spaces or hyphens. These spaces or hyphens, however, are not retained in a computer which depends upon the special distribution of ranges of numbers for the recognition of the parts.

Scope of the ISBN

For the purposes of the ISBN system books and other items to be numbered include:

Printed books and pamphlets

Mixed media publications

Other similar media including educational films/ videos and transparencies

Books on cassettes

Microcomputer software (educational only)

Electronic publications
— machine-readable tapes (designed to produce readable printout)
— CD-ROM etc

Micro-form publications

Braille publications

Atlases & Maps

Except:
Ephemeral printed materials such as diaries, calendars, advertising matter and the like

Art prints and art folders without title page and text

Sound recordings

Serial publications

Principles and procedures to be observed by the publisher numbering his own publications

A publisher must ensure that a competent person is responsible for the assignment of ISBN and the application of the pertinent regulations. A publisher will be assigned a publisher identifier (publisher's prefix) by the group agency which will determine the range of title identifiers available to him. The number of title identifiers will depend upon the length of the publisher identifier assigned to him. The publisher should ensure that the group agency has as much information as possible about his back lists of books still available; and present and future publication programmes in order that a suitable publisher identifier can be assigned. A publisher is responsible for assigning title identifiers to the individual items he publishes.

A publisher may wish to incorporate an existing non-classifying identification system into his ISBN allocation. This may be arranged provided that such incorporation does not alter the fundamental characteristics of the ISBN system or reduce the amount of numbers available. For example: the publisher must not incorporate digits other than numerals which cause the resulting ISBN to be longer than or shorter than ten digits, nor must the publisher attempt to build in special meanings or hierarchical order to groups of numbers, if by so doing he reduces the amount of available numbers in the range allocated to him.

Non-participating publishers

If by choice, or for any other reason, a publisher does not accept responsibility for assigning ISBN to his publications, two alternatives are open to the group agency.

1. The group agency can allocate a block of numbers for miscellaneous publishers and number all titles within that block irrespective of the publisher. In such a case the resulting ISBN will not identify the publisher of a specific title. (It is strongly recommended that this procedure should be reserved for publishers who only publish an occasional title and who are never likely to be in a position to assume the responsibility for numbering themselves.)

2. The group agency can assume responsibility for assigning a publisher identifier, a block of ISBNs

THE ISBN SYSTEM

associated with the publisher identifier and a number to each publication as well as informing the publisher before publication of the number assigned. In such a case, if the publisher agrees to do so, the ISBN can be printed in the book. It is expected that such a publisher will eventually assume full responsibility for assigning his own ISBN.

Application of ISBN

General
A separate ISBN must be assigned to every different edition of a book; but NOT to an unchanged impression or unchanged reprint of the same book in the same format and by the same publisher. Price changes do not need new ISBN.

Facsimile reprints
A separate ISBN must be assigned to a facsimile reprint produced by a different publisher.

Books in different formats
A separate ISBN must be assigned to the different formats in which a particular title is published. For example: a hardback edition and a paperback edition each receives a separate ISBN. On the same principle, a microform edition receives a separate ISBN.

Looseleaf publications
If a publication appears in looseleaf form, an ISBN is allocated to identify an edition at a given time. Individual issues of additions or replacement sheets will likewise be given an ISBN.

Multi-volume works
An ISBN must be assigned to the whole set of volumes of a multi-volume work, as well as to each individual volume in the set.

Back stock
A publisher is required to number his back stock and publish the ISBN in his catalogues. He must also print the ISBN in the first available reprint of an item from his back stock.

Collaborative publications
A publication issued as a coedition or joint imprint with other publishers is assigned an ISBN by the publisher in charge of distribution. Books sold or distributed by agents According to the principles of the ISBN system, a particular edition published by a particular publisher receives only one ISBN; this ISBN must be retained no matter where or by whom the book is distributed or sold.

A book imported by an exclusive distributor or sole agent from an area not yet in the ISBN system and for which, therefore, no ISBN has been assigned may be assigned an ISBN by the exclusive distributor.

A book imported by an exclusive distributor or sole agent to which a new title-page, bearing the imprint of the exclusive distributor, has been added in place of the title page of the original publisher, is to be given a new ISBN by the exclusive distributor or sole agent. The ISBN of the original publisher is also to be given as a related ISBN.

A book imported by several distributors from an area not yet in the ISBN system and for which, therefore, no ISBN has been assigned may be assigned an ISBN by the group agency responsible for those distributors.

Publishers with more than one place of publication
A publisher operating in a number of places which are listed together in the imprint of a book will assign only one ISBN to the book. A pub-lisher operating separate and distinct offices or branches in different places may have a publisher identifier for each office or branch. Nevertheless, each book published is to be assigned only one ISBN, the assignment being made by the office or branch responsible for publication.

Register of ISBNs
Every publisher must keep a register of ISBNs that have been assigned to published and forthcoming books. The register is to be kept in numerical sequence giving ISBN, author, title and edition (where appropriate).

ISBNs are not to be re-used under any circumstances
An ISBN once allocated must not under any circumstances be re-used. This is of the utmost importance to avoid confusion. It is recognized that, owing to clerical errors, numbers will be incorrectly assigned. If this happens, the number must be deleted from the list of usable numbers and must not be assigned to another title. Every publisher will have sufficient numbers in his range for the loss of these numbers to be insignificant. Publishers should advise the group agency of the numbers thus deleted and of the titles to which they were erroneously assigned.

Guidelines for ISBN assignment to software

An ISBN is used to identify a specific software product. If there is more than one version (perhaps versions adapted for different machines, carrier media or language version), each version must have a different ISBN. When a software product is updated, revised or otherwise amended and the changes are sufficiently substantial for the product to be called a new edition (and thus probably the subject of a new launch, or marketing push) then a new ISBN must be allocated. A relaunch of an existing product, even in new packaging, where there is no basic difference in the performance of the new and the old product, does NOT justify a new ISBN, and the original ISBN must be used.

When software is accompanied by a manual, useful only as an adjunct to the software, and the software needs the manual before it can be operated, and the two items are always sold as a package, one ISBN must be used to cover both items. When two or more items in a software package (as above) can be used separately, or are sold separately as well as together, then
(i) the package as a whole must have an ISBN
(ii) each item in the package must have its own ISBN.

ISBNs should be allocated to a software product independent of its physical form, eg, if software is only available from a remote database form whence it is downloaded to the customer.

As well as identifying the product itself, an ISBN identifies the publisher or manufacturer; it should not be used to identify a distributor or wholesaler.

Printing of the ISBN

General
The ISBN must appear on the item itself. This is essential for the efficient running of the system. Printing of ISBN on books In the case of books, the ISBN must appear whenever possible:

On the reverse of the title page, or, if this is not possible, on the base of the title page, or, if this too is not possible, at some other conspicuous location in the book.

On the base of the spine.

On the back of the cover in 9-point type or larger.

On the back of the dust jacket, and on the back of any other protective case or wrapper.

The ISBN should always be printed in type large enough to be easily legible (i.e. not smaller than 9 point).

Printing of ISBN on books in machine readable coding
In the last few years there has been much work done on machine-readable representations of the ISBN. The rapid, worldwide extension of bar code scanning has brought into prominence the agreement reached between the International Article Numbering Association (EAN) and the International ISBN Agency, which allows the ISBN to be translated into an EAN bar code.

All EAN bar codes start with a national identifier **except** those on books and periodicals. The agreement replaces the usual national identifier with a special 'Bookland' identifier represented by the digits 978 for books and 977 for periodicals. The 978 Bookland/EAN prefix is followed by the first nine digits of the ISBN. The check digit of the ISBN is dropped and replaced by a check digit calculated according to the EAN rules.

Optional 5-digit add-on code
There is an optional 5-digit add-on code which can be used for additional information. In the publishing industry it can be used for price information which may have the following formats:

a) Five-digit bar code indicating the price with human readable numbers above the bar code or
b) Five-digit bar code indicating the price with no human readable numbers.

Administration of the ISBN System

General
The administration of the ISBN system is carried on at three levels. These are the international, group and publisher levels.

International administration
The international administration of the system is in the hands of the International Standard Book Number Agency which has an Advisory Panel representing the ISO and the publishing and library world. The address of the International Agency is:

International ISBN Agency
Staatsbibliothek zu Berlin
Preussischer Kulturbesitz
10772 Berlin
Germany

The principal functions of the International Agency are:

To supervise the use of the system

To approve the definition and structure of groups

To allocate identifiers to groups

To advise groups on the setting up and functioning of group agencies

To advise group agencies on the allocation of publisher identifiers

To promote the worldwide use of the system

In addition, the International Agency also offers the following services. It will:

Provide a group agency with lists of ISBNs (with computer-generated check digits) for the use of publishers in the group

Provide international registers of publishers, prefixes and publishers' names

Provide from information supplied by group agencies a computer printout of lists of publishers' prefixes, names and locations

Provide from information supplied by group agencies a computer printout of invalid or duplicate ISBNs

Group administration
Groups are administered by Group Agencies. Within the group there may be several national agencies, eg. group 0/1 has separate agencies in USA, United Kingdom, Canada, Australia, etc, with the main agency for the whole group in the UK.

The functions of a group agency are:

To manage and administer the affairs of the group

To handle relations with the International ISBN Agency on behalf of all the publishers in the group

To decide, in consultation with trade organizations and publishers, the publisher identifier ranges required

To allocate publishers' prefixes to publishers eligible to join the group and to maintain a register of publishers and their prefixes

To decide, in consultation with trade organizations and publishers, which publishers shall assign numbers to their own titles and which publishers shall have numbers assigned to their titles by the group agency

To provide technical advice and assistance to the publishers and to ensure that standards and approved procedures are observed in the group

To make available a manual of instruction for publishers

To make available computer printouts of ISBNs to publishers numbering their own books with check digits already calculated (Such printouts may be obtained from the International Agency on request)

To validate all ISBNs assigned by publishers numbering their own books and keep a register of them

To inform publishers of any invalid or duplicate ISBNs assigned by them

To assign numbers to all publications from those publishers who do not assign their own ISBNs and advise the publishers concerned of ISBNs assigned upon request

To achieve, thereby, total numbering in the group

To arrange with book listing and bibliographic agencies for the publication of ISBNs with the titles to which they refer

To arrange with publishers for the numbering of their back lists and for the publication of these in appropriate trade lists and bibliographies

To maintain liaison with all elements of the book trade and introduce new publishers to the system

To assist the trade in the use of the ISBN in computer systems

The national agencies are:

Albania
Ms. Violeta Viso, Biblioteka Kombetare, Agjensia Kombetare e ISBN, Sheshi "Skenderbe", Tirana

Algeria
Mlle. Hayet Gounni, Bibliotheque Nationale d'Algerie, BP 127, Hamma-el Annassers, Alger

Andorra
Sr. Pilar Burgues Monserrat, Andorran Standard Book Num-bering Agency, Biblioteca Nacional, Placeta Sant Esteve s/n, Andorra la Vella

Argentina
Claudia Rodriguez, Camara Argentina del Libro, Agencia Argentina ISBN, Avenida Belgrano 1580, 1093 Buenos Aires

Armenia
Dr. Hovhannes Bekmezyan, National Book Chamber of Armenia, ISBN Agency, G. Kochar St. 21, 375009 Yerevan

Australia
Ms. Maria Watt, ISBN Agency, C3, 85 Turner St, Port Melbourne, Vic 3207

Austria
Lea Raffl, Hauptverband des Osterreichischen Buchhandels, Grunangergasse 4, 1010 Vienna

Azerbaijan
Tatyana Zaytceva, Khazar University, 11, Mehseti St., Baku AZ1096

Bahrain
Mr. Jamal Dawood Salman, Directorate of Publication & Press, Ministry of Information, PO Box 253, Manama

Bangladesh
Mr. Golam Mostofa, National Library of Bangladesh, Directorate of Archives & Libraries, ISBN Agency, 32, Justice S. M. Morshed Sarani, Sher-e-Bangla Nagar (Agargaon), Dhaka 1207

Belarus
Mr. Anatoli I. Voronko, National Book Chamber of Belarus, ISBN Agency, 31a V Khoryzhey Str, 220002 Minsk

Belgium (Flemish-speaking)
Mr. Maarten van den Heuvel, Bureau ISBN, Centraal Boekhuis, Postbus 360, 4100 AJ Culemborg

Belgium (French-speaking)
Ms. Joelle Aernoudt, AFNIL (Agence Francophone pour la Numerotation Internationale du Livre), 35 rue Gregoire de Tours, 75006 Paris

THE ISBN SYSTEM

Benin
Adio Nourou Akadiri, Agence Nationale ISBN, Bibliotheque Nationale, BP 401, Porto-Novo

Bhutan
Mr. Sonam Kinga, The Centre for Bhutan Studies, ISBN Agency, Post Box 111, Thimphu

Bolivia
Sra. Marlene Perez, Camara Boliviana del Libro, Agencia ISBN, Calle Capitan, Ravelo, No. 2116, Casilla 682, La Paz

Bosnia and Herzegovina
Mrs. Nevenka Hajdarovic, National and University Library of Bosnia and Herzegovina, ISBN Centre, Zmaja od Bosne 8b, 71000 Sarajevo

Botswana
Ms. Galetshege Tshupoeng, Botswana National Library Service, Private Bag 0036, Gaborone

Brazil
Ms. Celia Ribeiro Zaher, Fundacao Biblioteca Nacional Agencia Brasileira do ISBN, Av Rio Branco, n. 219/31 – 1 andar, Centro - Rio de Janeiro – RJ 20040-008

Brunei Darussalam
Mr. Haji Abu Bakar Bin Haji Zainal, Pusat Kebangsaan ISBN, Dewan Bahasa Dan Pustaka, Jalan Elizabeth II, Bandar Seri Begawan BB3510, Negara

Bulgaria
Ms. Tatjana Dermendzieva, National Library St Cyril and St Methodiuos, National ISBN Agency, Boulevard V Levski 88, 1037 Sofia

Cameroon
Agence ISBN, Bibliotheque Nationale, Yaounde

Canada (English-speaking)
Ms. Dawna Gallagher, National Library of Canada, Canadian ISBN Agency, 395 Wellington St, Ottawa, Ontario K1A 0N4

Canada (French-speaking)
Mme. Lucie Martel, ISBN/BNQ, Bibliotheque nationale du Quebec, 2275, rue Holt, Montreal, Quebec H2G 3H1

Caribbean Community
Ms. Maureen Newton, Caribbean Community Secretariat, Documentation Centre, Bank of Guyana Bldg, PO Box 10827, Georgetown, Guyana

Chile
Jaime Pizarro Carrasco, Agencia Chilena ISBN, Camara Chilena del Libro AG, Avda Libertador Bernardo O'Higgins 1370, Oficina 502, Santiago de Chile

China (People's Republic of)
Mr. Li Lu, China ISBN Agency, China Bar Code Agency, 85 Dongsinan Street, Beijing 100703

Colombia
Sra. Sandra Del Mar Sacanamboy Franco, Agencia Colombiana del ISBN, Camara Colombiana del Libro, Carrera 17A No 37-27, Santafe de Bogota

Costa Rica
Marie Elena Alpizar Vargas, Departamento Unidad Tecnica, Biblioteca Nacional, Ave 3 calles 15 y 17, APDO 10008-1000 San Jose

Croatia
Ms. Jasenka Zajec, Hrvatski ured za ISBN, Nacionalna i sveucilisna knjizica, Hrvatske bratske zajednice 4, HR-10000 Zagreb

Cuba
Sra. Rosa Amelia Lay Portuondo, Camara Cubana del Libro, Agencia Cubana del ISBN, Calle 15 No 602 esq C, Vedado, Ciudad Havana

Cyprus
Mr. Antonis Maratheftis, Cyprus Library, Eleftheria Square, 1011 Nicosia

Czech Republic
Mr. Antonin Jerabek, Narodni knihovna Eeske republiky, Narodni agentura ISBN v CR, Klementinum 190, 110 01 Prague 1

Denmark
Ms. Randi Diget Hansen, Dansk Biblioteks Center, Tempovej 7-11, 2750 Ballerup

Dominican Republic
Sra. Iris Pineda, Agencia Domenicana de ISBN, Biblioteca Nacional Pedro Henriquez Urena, Calle Cesar Nicolas Penson No 91, Plaza de la Cultura, Santo Domingo

Ecuador
Sr. Patricio Mena, Agencia Ecuatoriana del ISBN, Av Eloy Alfaro N29-61 e Inglaterra, Edif Eloy Alfaro Piso N° 9, Quito

Egypt
Prof. Mohammed Galal Ghandour, National Library and Archives, Corniche El Nil-Boulac, Cairo

El Salvador
Sra. Doris Elizabeth Siliezar Orellana, Biblioteca Nacional, Agencia ISBN, Av Monsenor. Oscar A. Romero, y 4a Calle Oriente N° 124, San Salvador

Estonia
Ms. Mai Valtna, Estonian ISBN Agency, National Library of Estonia, Tonismagi 2, 15189 Tallinn

Ethiopia
Mr. Solomon Mulugeta, ISBN Agency, National Archives and Library of Ethiopia, PO Box 717, Addis Ababa

European Community Organizations
Ms. Madeleine Kiss, Office for official publications for the European Community, Authors Service Unit, ISBN Agency, 2, rue Mercier, 2985 Luxembourg, Luxembourg

Faroe Islands
Mr. Erhard Jacobsen, Foroya Landsbokasavn, Faroese ISBN office, J.C. Svabosgotu 16, PO Box 61, FR-110 Torshavn

Finland
Ms. Maarit Huttunen, Finnish ISBN Agency, Helsinki University Library, National Library of Finland, PO Box 26, (Teollisuuskatu 23), 00014 University of Helsinki

France
Ms. Joelle Aernoudt, AFNIL (Agence Francophone pour la Numerotation Internationale du Livre), 35, rue Gregoire de Tours, 75006 Paris

Gambia
Mr. Abdou Wally Mbye, The Chief Librarian, Gambia National Library, R.G. Pye Lane, Banjul

Georgia
Mrs. Nino Simonishvili, Georgian Parliament I. Chavchavadze National Library, ISBN Centre, 5 Gudiashvili st., 380007 Tbilisi

Germany
Ms. Anke Lehr, MVB Marketing- und Verlagsservice des Buchhandels GmbH, ISBN-Agentur fur die Bundesrepublik Deutschland, Postfach 10 04 42, 60004 Frankfurt am Main

Ghana
Mr. Omari Mensah Tenkorang, Ghana Library Board, George Padmore, Research Library on African Affairs, PO Box 2970, Accra

Gibraltar
Mrs. G. Finlayson, The John Mackintosh Hall, Knightsfield Holdings Ltd., 308 Main St, PO Box 939, Gibraltar

Greece
Dr. G. Zachos, National Library of Greece, National Centre of ISBN, Panepistimiou 32, 10679 Athens

Guatemala
Sra. Silvia Regina De Leon, Agencia ISBN, Gremial de Editores de Guatemala, Ruta 6, 9-21 zona 4, Edificio Camara de Industria 8vo nivel, Ciudad Guatemala

Haiti
Ms. Nadege Constant, Bibliotheque Nationale d'Haiti, 193, Rue du Centre, Port-au-Prince

THE ISBN SYSTEM

Honduras
Sr. Remo Jose Flores Escobar, Biblioteca Nacional, Agencia ISBN de Honduras, Barrio El Centro, Avda Cervantes, 1 cuadra al Sur Hotel Prado, Tegucigalpa, MDC

Hong Kong (People's Republic of China)
Ms. Chow Kam-sheung, Leisure and Cultural Services Department, Books Registration Office, Room 805, 8/F, Lai Chi Kok Government Offices, 19 Lai Wan Rd, Lai Chi Kok, Kowloon

Hungary
Ms. Susanne Berke, Magyar ISBN Iroda, Orszagos Szechenyi Konyvtar, Budavari Palota F epulet, H-1827 Budapest

Iceland
ISBN Agency Iceland, National and University Library of Iceland, Arngrimsgotu 3, 107 Reykjavik

India
Dr. Suresh Chand, Raja Rammohun Roy, National Agency for ISBN, Government of India, Ministry of Human Resource Development, A2/ W4, Curzon Road Barracks, New Delhi 110001

Indonesia
Dra. Sauliah Saleh, Directorate of Legal Deposit, National Library of Indonesia, Jl Salemba Raya 28, PO Box 3624, Jakarta 10002

International Publishers (Unesco, EU)
Ms. Maha Bulos, UNESCO, Division of Arts and Cultural Enterprise, 1, rue Miollis, 75732 Paris Cedex 15, France

Iran
Mr. Vahraz Nowruzpur Deilami, Iran Book House, Iran ISBN Agency, 1178 Enqelab St, 13156 Tehran

Ireland (Republic of)
United Kingdom agency

Israel
Ms. Anna Sela, Israeli ISBN Group Agency, Israeli Center for Libraries, Baruch Hirsh 22, POB 801, Bnei Brak 51108

Italy
Mr. Michele Costa, Editrice Bibliografica SpA, Via Bergonzoli, 1/5, 20127 Milan

Japan
Mr. Iwao Sekiguchi, Japan ISBN Agency, c/o Japan Publishers Bldg, 6 Fukuro machi Shinjuku-ku, Tokyo 162-0828

Jordan
Mr. Mamoun Tharwat Talhouni, The Department of the National Library, ISBN Agency, PO Box 6070, Amman 11118

Kazakhstan
Ms. K. M. Mukhataeva, Book Chamber of Kazakhstan, ISBN Agency, Ulica Puskina 2, Almaty 480016

Kenya
Kenya National Library Services, ISBN Agency, PO Box 30573-00100 GPO, Nairobi

Korea (Democratic People's Republic)
Mr. Jean Bahng. Korea Science and Encyclopedia Publishing House, ISBN DPR Korea Agency, PO Box 73, Pyongyang

Korea (Republic of)
Ms. Nam-Sook Kim, The National Library of Korea, Korea ISBN Agency, 60-1 Banpo-Dong, Seocho-Gu, Seoul 137-702

Kuwait
Mrs. Wafa'a H. Al-Sane, National Library of Kuwait, ISBN Agency, PO Box 26182, 13122 Safat

Kyrgyz Republic
Ms. Mambetkazieva Mairam Orozbaevna,. ISBN Agency, National Book Chamber, Sovetskaya 170a, p/b 806, 720000 Bischek

Latvia
Ms. Laimdota Pruse, ISBN/ISMN Agency, Anglikaou Street 5, Riga 1816 LV

Lebanon
Ms. Rita Akl, Ministry of Culture, ISBN Agency, Bristol Street, Hamra, Hatab Bldg, 6th Floor, Beirut

Lesotho
Ms. Mamothepane Kotele, ISBN Agency, The National University of Lesotho Library, PO Roma 180, Lesotho

Libya
Mr. Saleh M. Najim, National Library of Libya, PO Box 9127, Benghazi

Lithuania
Ms. Dalia Smoriginiene, Martynas Mazvydas, National Library of Lithuania, Gediminas av.51, 01504 Vilnius

Luxembourg
Mr. Andre-Nicolas Schoup, Bibliotheque nationale Grand-Duche de Luxembourg, 37, bd F-D Roosevelt, L-2450 Luxembourg

Macau
Mr. Tang Va Chio, Agencia do ISBN, Biblioteca Central de Macau, Av Conselheiro Ferreira de Almeida, no. 89A-B, Macau

Macedonia
Ms. Zlata Talaganova, Narodna i Univerzitetska Biblioteka, "Sv. Kliment Ohridski", ISBN Agencija, Bul. Goce Delcev, 6, 1000 Skopje

Malawi
Mr. Stanley S. Gondwe, Malawi National ISBN Agency, National Archives of Malawi, Mkulichi Rd, PO Box 62, Zomba

Malaysia
Mr. Zulkefli Abdul Samad, National Library of Malaysia, National Depository Centre, ISBN National Centre, 232 Jalan Tun Razak, 50572 Kuala Lumpur

Maldives
Mr. Mohammed Waheed, Ministry of Education, Ghaazee Bldg, Ameeru Ahmed Magu, Male 20-05

Malta
Mr. Emanuel Debattista, Publishers Enterprises Group (PEG) Ltd, PEG Bldg, UB7 Industrial Estate, San Gwann SGN 09

Mauritius
Ms. Sadhna Ramlallah, Editions de l'Ocean Indien, Stanley, Rose Hill

Mexico
Alfredo Toral Azuela, Agencia ISBN Mexico, Calle Dinamarca 84, 2° piso, Colonia Juarez, Delegacion Cuauhtemoc, 06600 Mexico, DF

Moldova
Ms. Valentina Chitoroaga, Chambre Nationale du Livre, Agence ISBN, bd Stefan cel Mare, 180, Office 202, 2004 Chisinau

Mongolia
Ms. Tsagaach, Mongolian Book Publishers' Association, Amar Str., Building #1, Room 306, Central Post Box 5, Ulan Bator

Morocco
Mme. Meryem Moussaid, Agence Marocaine de l'ISBN, Bibliotheque Generale et Archives, Service du depot legal, Av Ibn Battouta, BP 1003, Rabat

Namibia
Mr. Werner Hillebrecht, National Library of Namibia, Private Bag 13349, Windhoek

Nepal
Mr. Krishna Mani Bhandary, Tribhuvan University, Central Library, ISBN National Agency, Kirtipur, Kathmandu

Netherlands
Mr. Maarten van den Heuvel, Centraal Boekhuis, Postbus 360, 4100 AJ Culemborg

Netherlands Antilles
Mrs. Navisella Ignacio, Bureau Intellectual Property, Berg Carmelweg 10A, Willenstad- Curacao

New Zealand
Ms. Joy Grove, ISBN Agency, National Library of New Zealand, PO Box 1467, Wellington

THE ISBN SYSTEM

Nicaragua
Sra. Maribel Otero, Agencia Nacional ISBN, Palacio Nacional de la Cultura, Apartado Postal 101, Managua

Nigeria
Dr. I. Oketunji, National Bibliographic Control Dept, National Library of Nigeria, Nigerian ISBN Agency, 4 Wesley St, PMB 12626, Lagos

Norway
Ms. Ingebjorg Rype, ISBN-kontoret Norge, Katalogseksjonen, Bibliografiske tjenester, Nasjonalbiblioteket, avdeling Oslo, Postboks 2674, Solli, 0203 Oslo

Pakistan
Mr. Syed Ghyour Hussain, National Library of Pakistan, Constitution Ave, Islamabad 44000

Palestine
Prof. Mohammed S. Dajani, Palestine ISBN Agency, PO Box 4414, Al-Bireh Palestine

Panama
Guadalupe G. de Rivera, Agencia Panamena del ISBN, Biblioteca Nacional de Panama, San Francisco, Via Porras, Parque Recreativo y Cultural Omar, Apartado Postal 7906, Zona 9, Panama

Papua New Guinea
Mr. Chris Kelly Meti, Bibliographical Services Librarian, Papua New Guinea ISBN Agency, National Library Service, PO Box 734, Waigani, NCD

Paraguay
Sr. Francisco Perez Maricevich, Viceministerio de Cultura, Agencia ISBN, Humaita 145, Calle Independencia Nacional y Nuestra Senora, Asuncion

Peru
Sra. Alejandrina Garcia Caballero, Biblioteca Nacional del Peru, Av Abancay 4ta Cdra S/N, Lima

Philippines
Ms. Leonila DA. Tominez, The National Library of the Philippines, Standard Book Numbering Agency, PO Box 2926, Remita Manila 1000

Poland
Ms. Hanna Zawado, National Library, Bibliographic Institute, al Niepodleglosci 213, 02-086 Warsaw

Portugal
Ms. Conceicao Tome, Associacao Portuguesa de Editores e Livreiros, Av Estados Unidos da America, 97-6° Esq, 1700-167 Lisbon

Qatar
Mr. Sami Abdel Jawad, National Library, ISBN group agency, PO Box 205, Doha

Romania
Ms. Mihaela Laura Stanciu, Biblioteca Nationala a Romaniei, Centrul National de Numerotare Standardizata, (ISBN, ISMN, ISSN, CIP), Str Ion Ghica 4, sector 3, 79708 Bucharest

Russia
Mr. Boris Lenski, Russian Book Chamber, Russian ISBN Agency, Kremlevskaja nab 1/9, 109019 Moscow

Saudi Arabia
Mr. Musaed A. Al-Swailem, King Fahd National Library, Book Registration & Numbering Dept, PO Box 7572, Riyadh 11472

Serbia & Montenegro
Ms. Stanka Jovicic, Jugoslovenski Bibliografsko-Informacijski Institut, ISBN Agency, Terazije 26, 11000 Belgrade

Seychelles
Ms. Pamela Denousse, Ministry of Local Government Sports & Culture, National Library, Victoria, PO Box 45, Mahe

Sierra Leone
Sallieu Turay, Sierra Leone Library Board, ISBN Agency, PO Box 326, Freetown

Singapore (Republic of)
Ms. Annick Wong, National Library Board, Library Supply Centre, 3 Changi South St 2, Tower B, #03-00, Singapore 486548

Slovakia
Ms. Erika Poloncova, Slovak ISBN Group Agency, Slovak National Library, Nam J.C. Hronskeho 1, 03601 Martin

Slovenia
Ms. Alenka Kanic, National and University Library, Turjaska 1, p.p. 259, 1000 Ljubljana

South Africa
Ms. Magret Kibido, The National Library of South Africa, ISN Agency, PO Box 397, Pretoria 0001

South Pacific
Ms. Joan Yee, Regional ISBN Centre, The University of the South Pacific Library, PO Box 1168, Suva, Fiji

Spain
Sra. Pilar Gomez Font, Agencia Espanola del ISBN, Calle Santiago Rusinol, 8, 28040 Madrid

Sri Lanka
Mr. M.S.U. Amarasiri, National Library and Documentation Services Board, No 14, Independence Ave, Colombo

Sudan
Mr. Yassin Mohammed Abdalla, National Library, ISBN Agency, PO Box 6279, Khartoum

Suriname
Mr. E. Hogenboom, Publishers Association Suriname, Standard Book Numbering Agency, Domineestr 32 boven, PO Box 1841, Paramaribo

Swaziland
Ms. M. R. Mavuso, University of Swaziland Libraries, Private Bag 4, Kwaluseni

Sweden
Ms. Anna Hulten, The Royal Library, Swedish National ISBN Agency, Legal Deposits, Box 5039, 102 41 Stockholm

Switzerland (French-speaking)
Ms. Joelle Aernoudt, AFNIL (Agence Francophone pour la Numerotation Internationale du Livre), 35, rue Gregoire de Tours, 75006 Paris

Switzerland (German-speaking)
Ms. Stefanie Nubling, ISBN-Agentur Schweiz, c/o Schweizer Buchhandler- und Verleger-Verband (SBVV), Alderstrasse 40, Postfach, 8034 Zurich

Switzerland (Italian-speaking)
Mr. Michele Costa, Editrice Bibliografica SpA, Via Bergonzoli, 1/5, 20127 Milan, Italy

Taiwan, China
Ms. Li-chien Lee, National Central Library, 20 Chung Shan South Rd, Taipei 100

Tanzania
M.S. Mkenga, Tanzania Library Services Board, National Bibliographic Agency, PO Box 9283, Dar es Salaam

Thailand
Ms. Wilawan Supphansaen, National Library of Thailand, Samsen Rd., Bangkok 10300

Tunisia
Ms. Ben Sedrine Nabiha, National ISBN Agency, Bibliotheque Nationale, Service de la Documentation et de l'Information, 20 Souk El Attarine, BP 42, 1008 Tunis

Turkey
Mr. Fikret Komser, ISBN Turkiye Ajansy, Kultur ve Turizm Bakanlyoy, Kutuphaneler ve Yayymlar, Genel Mudurlugu, Necatibey Cad 55, 06440 Syhhyye Ankara

Uganda
Mr. Martin Okia, Uganda Publishers and Booksellers Association, PO Box 7732, Kampala

Ukraine
Ms. Iryna Pogorelovs'ka, Knyzkova Palata Ukrainy, National ISBN Agency, 27, Yuri Gagarin Ave, 02660 Kiev

United Arab Emirates
Ministry of Information and Culture, Copyright Section, ISBN Agency, PO Box 17, Abu Dhabi

United Kingdom & Ireland (Republic of)
Ms. Stella Griffiths, ISBN Agency, Midas House, 3rd Floor, 62 Goldsworth Road, Woking GU21 6LQ

United Nations see *International Publishers*

United States of America
Paula Kurdi, R.R. Bowker Co., LLC, International Standard Book Numbering, United States Agency, 630 Central Ave., New Providence, NJ 07974

Uruguay
Julio Castro, Biblioteca Nacional, Seccion Bibliografia Nacional - Agencia ISBN, 18 de julio 1790, 11200 Montevideo

Venezuela
Sra. Angela Negrin, Agencia Venezolana del ISBN, Parque Central, Torre Este, piso 3, Caracas 1011

Zambia
Dr. H. Mwacalimba, Booksellers & Publishers Association of Zambia, The ISBN Secretariat, c/o University of Zambia Library, PO Box 32379, Lusaka

Zimbabwe
Director, National Archives of Zimbabwe, Causeway, Private Bag 7729, Harare

ISBN and ISSN

In addition to the International Standard Book Number System, a complementary numbering system for serial publications has also been established.

A serial is defined as any publication issued in successive parts, usually bearing numerical or chronological designations and intended to be continued indefinitely.

Serials include periodicals, yearbooks and monographic series.

The International Standard Serial Number system (ISSN) is administered by the ISSN International Centre, whose address is:

ISSN International Centre
20, rue Bachaumont
75002 Paris
France

Publishers of serials should apply to the ISSN International Centre or to their National Serials Data Centre, if there is one, for ISSNs for their serial publications.

Certain publications, such as yearbooks, annuals, monographic series, etc, should be assigned an ISSN for the serial title (which will remain the same for all the parts or individual volumes of the serial) and an ISBN for each individual volume.

Both ISSN and ISBN, when they are assigned, must be given on the publication and clearly identified.

(The preceding information is mainly from the ISBN User's Manual, compiled by the International ISBN Agency, Staatsbibliothek zu Berlin, Preussischer Kulturbesitz, Berlin, Germany.)

Abbreviations

+	Publisher's indication of interest in buying/selling international rights or editions
†	Organizations that are international in scope
§	Publications that are international in scope
◊	Organizations with publishing activities
‡	United nations agencies with publishing activities
☆	Prizes with no geographical restriction placed upon recipients
AB	aktiebolag (=public limited company)
AE	anonymous etaireia
AG	Aktiengesellschaft (=public limited company)
al	aleja
Apdo	apartado (=post-box)
ApS	anpartsselskab (=private limited company)
A/S	(Norwegian) aksjeselskap. (Swedish) aaktieselskab (=limited company)
AS	anonim sirketi
ASBL	association sans but lucratif (=non-profit-making society)
Av	(Spanish) avenida
Ave	(English, French) avenue. (Portuguese) avenida
Bldg	Building
Blvd	(Bulgarian, Romanian) bulevard. (English, French) boulevard
BP	boite postale (=post-box)
BV	besloten vennootschap (=private limited company)
C	compagnia (=company)
CA	compania anonima (=public limited company)
CEDEX	Courrier d'enterpise a distribution exceptionnelle
CFA	Communaute financiere africaine
CFP	comptoirs fracais du Pacifique
Cia	companhia, compania (=company)
Cie	compagnie (=company)
Co	(English) company, county. (German) Kompanie
c/o	care of
CP	(Italian) casetta postale. (Portuguese) caixa postal, (=post-box)
CV	commanditaire vennootschap (=limited partnership)
Dept	department
Dir	Director
EE	eterorruthmos etaireia
eV	einetragener Verein (=registered society)
ext	extension
GmbH	Gesellschaft mit beschrankter Haftung (=private limited company)
Inc	incorporated
ISBN	international standard book number
Jl	jalan (=street)
KG	Kommanditgesellschaft (=partnership)
KK	kabushiki kaisha (=public limited company)
Lda	limitida (=limited)
Ltd	limited
Ltda	limitada (=limited)
Man Dir	Managing Director
Nachf	Nachfolger(s) (=successor(s))
nam	namesti (=square)
NV	naamloze vennootschap (=public limited company)
OE	omorruthmos etaireia of oficina (=office)
Off	office
Oy	osakeyhitio (=limited company)
pA	per Adresse (=care of)
Pl	(Bulgarian) ploshtad. (English, French) place. (Polish) plac. (Russian) ploshchad. (Spanish) plaza
PL	postriokero (=post-box)
PLC	public limited company
PMB	private mail bag
PO	Post Office
Prof	Professor
Pty	proprietary
PVBA	personenvennootschap met beperkte aansprakelijkheid (=private limited company)
Pvt	private
Rd	Road
SA	(French) societe anonyyme. (Portuguese) sociedade anonima.(Spanish) sociedad anonima (=public limited company)
Sarl	societe a responsabilite limitee (=private limited company)
SAS	societa in accomandita semplice (=limited partnership)
SCA	sociedad en comandita por acciones (=limited partner ship)
S de RL	sociedad de responsabilidad limitada (=private limited company)
Sdn Bhd	sendirian berhad (=private limited company)
SL	sociedad de responsabilidad limitada (=private limited company)
SNC	societa in nome collettivo (=partnership)
SpA	societa per azioni (=public limited company)
SPRL	societe de personnes a responsabilite (=private limited company)
SRL	(Italian) societa a responsabilita limita. (Spanish) sociedad de responsabilida limitada. (=private limited company)
St	Saint, street
STD	subscriber trunk dialing
Str	(Danish) straede. (Dutch) straat. (German) Strasse. (Icelandic) straeti. (Italian) strada. (Romanian) strada (=street)
Sq	square
Tel	telephone number
u	utca (=street)
UCC	Universal Copyright Convention
ul	(Bulgarian) ulitsa. (Czech) ulice. (Polish) ulica. (Romanian) ulita. (Russian) ulitsa. (Serbocroatian, Slovak, Slovene) ulica. (=street)
UK	United Kingdom
USA	United States of America
VEB	volkseigener Betrieb (=people's enterprise)
VZW	vereniging zonder winstoogmerk (=non-profit-making society)

A limited company is a corporation owned by shareholders (or stockholders) who may contribute capital to the company but are not other-wise generally liable for its debts.

A public company may invite anyone to become a shareholder, and its
shares (or stock) are usually traded on a stock exchange.

A private, or proprietary, company has a restricted number of shareholders and its shares are not traded on a stock exchange.

The owners of a partnership or proprietorship are generally liable for its debts, but a limited partnership has some owners who only contribute capital and are not otherwise liable for debts.

Publishing

Publishers

This section covers book publishers throughout the world, with the exception of U.S. and Canadian publishers, which can be found in the companion publication, *Literary Market Place*. Publishers and their imprints are listed alphabetically within their country of business. General information for each country can be found preceding the entries for that country.

+ following a publisher's name indicates those who are involved in the buying or selling of international rights.

Immediately following this section are indexes that list publishers by type of publication and by subjects.

Afghanistan

General Information

Capital: Kabul
Language: Pushtu and Dari Afghan
Religion: Sunni Muslim with approximately 1 million Shiite Muslim
Population: 16.1 million
Bank Hours: 0800-1200, 1300-1600 Saturday-Wednesday; 0800-1300 Thursday
Shop Hours: 0800-about 1800 Saturday-Thursday
Currency: 100 puls = 2 krans = 1 afghani
Copyright: Florence (see Copyright Conventions, pg xi)

Book Publishing Institute
Herat
Founded: 1970 (by cooperation of Government Press and citizens of Herat)
Subjects: Fiction, History, Religion - Other

Franklin Book Programs Inc
PO Box 332, Kabul

Government Press
Kabul
Tel: 26851
Founded: 1870
Under supervision of Ministry of Information & Culture.
Subjects: Ethnicity, History, Regional Interests

Ministry of Education, Department of Educational Publications
PO Box 717, Kabul
Tel: (0873) 32076 *Fax:* (0873) 15051

Pushtu Toulana, Afghan Academy
Alikhan St, Kabul
Tel: 20350

Albania

General Information

Capital: Tirane
Language: Albanian
Religion: Islamic, Orthodox, Roman Catholic
Population: 3.3 million
Bank Hours: 0730-2330 Monday-Saturday
Shop Hours: 0900-1200 and 1600-2000; one day per week is holiday
Currency: 100 qintars = 1 lek
Export/Import Information: Importation of books is through State Trading Organization, Nd. Shperndarjes Te (or NST) Librit, Blvd K e Pezes, Tirana. Correspondence should be in English, French, German or Italian. Copies of correspondence to Albanian Legation in Rome. Some import licenses but no strict exchange controls.
Copyright: Berne (see Copyright Conventions, pg xi)

Botimpex Publications Import-Export Agency
Rr "Naim Frasheri" P 84/ Sh 2/ Ap 37, Tirana
Tel: (042) 34023 *Fax:* (042) 26886
E-mail: botimpex@albaniaonline.net; botimpex@icc-al.org; ebega@albmail.com
Web Site: pages.albaniaonline.net/botimpex/
Key Personnel
Dir: Dr Estref Bega *E-mail:* ebega@albmail.com
Founded: 1991
Subjects: Biography, Fiction, History, Literature, Literary Criticism, Essays, Poetry
ISBN Prefix(es): 99927-628; 99927-823
Number of titles published annually: 11 Print

Fan Noli Verlag Rexhep Hida+
Bulev, Shqip e Re, Pallati 33/4/8, Tirana
Tel: (042) 61673
Founded: 1991
Subjects: Fiction, Nonfiction (General)
Total Titles: 670 Print

NL SH+
Rruga Muhamet Gjollesha, Tirana
Tel: (042) 34207 *Fax:* (042) 34207
Key Personnel
Dir: Hilmi Brace
Subjects: Accounting, Advertising, Aeronautics, Aviation, Agriculture, Americana, Regional, Animals, Pets, Anthropology, Antiques, Archaeology, Architecture & Interior Design, Art, Astronomy, Biblical Studies, Biography, Biological Sciences, Business, Career Development, Chemistry, Chemical Engineering, Child Care & Development, Cookery, Crafts, Games, Hobbies, Developing Countries, Drama, Theater, Earth Sciences, Economics, Education, Electronics, Electrical Engineering, Energy, Engineering (General), English as a Second Language, Finance, Foreign Countries, Gardening, Plants, Geography, Geology, Government, Political Science, History, Humor, Labor, Industrial Relations, Language Arts, Linguistics, Law, Library & Information Sciences, Literature, Literary Criticism, Essays, Management, Marketing, Mathematics, Mechanical Engineering, Medicine, Nursing, Dentistry, Microcomputers, Military Science, Music, Dance, Mysteries, Native American Studies, Nonfiction (General), Philosophy, Photography, Physical Sciences, Physics, Poetry, Psychology, Psychiatry, Public Administration, Publishing & Book Trade Reference, Radio, TV, Science (General), Science Fiction, Fantasy, Securities, Self-Help, Social Sciences, Sociology, Sports, Athletics, Technology, Theology, Veterinary Science, Women's Studies
Total Titles: 9,999 Print
Branch Office(s)
Rruga Kavajes, NR 116, Tirana *Tel:* (042) 47129; (042) 47130
Distributed by Zina Bunjaj
Distributor for Klodiana Peci
Showroom(s): Tirana *Tel:* (042) 47130

SHBLSH, *imprint of* State Textbook Publishing House

Shtepia Botuese Enciklopedike (Encyclopaedia Publishing House)
Rr Muhamet Gjollesha, Tirana
Tel: (042) 28064 *Fax:* (042) 28064
Key Personnel
Gen Dir: Arben Xoxa
Founded: 1991
Subjects: Labor, Industrial Relations, Regional Interests

State Textbook Publishing House+
Rruga e Kavajes, Tirana
Tel: (042) 22331 *Fax:* (042) 22331
Key Personnel
Dir: Teuta Mati *E-mail:* tmati@tbph.gov.al
Founded: 1967 (STPH was created to prepare all school textbooks for the pre-university system)
Over 800 textbook titles & wishes to have connections with other publishing houses which specialize for schools.
Subjects: Accounting, Animals, Pets, Art, Biological Sciences, Business, Communications, Earth Sciences, Education, Electronics, Electrical Engineering, Energy, Engineering (General), English as a Second Language, Government,

ALBANIA

Political Science, History, Literature, Literary Criticism, Essays, Mathematics, Medicine, Nursing, Dentistry, Psychology, Psychiatry, Radio, TV, Science (General), Social Sciences, Sociology, Sports, Athletics, Technology
Total Titles: 700 Print
Imprints: SHBLSH
Branch Office(s)
STPH Sector Computer *Tel:* (042) 26177

Algeria

General Information

Capital: Algiers (El Djazair)
Language: Arabic. French is the language of business and administration
Religion: Islamic
Population: 26.7 million
Bank Hours: 0900-1500 or 1600 Saturday-Wednesday
Shop Hours: 0900-1200, 1500-1900 Monday-Saturday
Currency: 100 centimes = 1 Algerian dinar
Export/Import Information: Books may be imported or exported only by or with permission of SNED State Monopoly, 3 blvd Zirout Yousef, BP 49, Alger Strasbourg. There are also quota restrictions. Permission to import usually entitles holder to obtain necessary foreign exchange; strict controls are in effect. Documentation formalities are rigidly enforced.
Copyright: UCC (see Copyright Conventions, pg xi)

Les Editions Algeriennes En-Nahdha+
2 rue Larbi Ben M'Hidi, 16000 Alger
Tel: (021) 737627 *Fax:* (021) 737627
Fax on Demand: (021) 479424
E-mail: info@ennahdha.com
Key Personnel
Chief Executive: Omar Mimouni *Tel:* (213) 61 55 20 62 *E-mail:* omimouni2000@yahoo.com
Founded: 1946
Vice President of National Syndicate of Book Business.
Membership(s): Association of Algerian Editors.
Subjects: History
Number of titles published annually: 15 Print
Total Titles: 150 Print
Parent Company: Les Editions Algeriennes En-Nahdha
Associate Companies: Editions Mimouni
Subsidiaries: Mimomultimedia (Canada)
Bookshop(s): Avenue du 1er Novembre, Laghouat *Tel:* (029) 90 40 85
Book Club(s): Association del Editeurs Algeriens
Orders to: 37 rue Amar El Kama, Alger

Chihab, see SARL DAR-Echihab

SARL DAR-Echihab
10, ave Brahim Gharafa, BEO, 16009 Alger
Tel: (02) 626727; (02) 626734 *Fax:* (02) 574632
ISBN Prefix(es): 9961-63
Subsidiaries: Chihab 2000
Showroom(s): 11, ave Brahim Gharafa, 16009 Alger
Bookshop(s): Ave de l'independence n 10, Batna

Enterprise Nationale du Livre (ENAL)+
3, blvd Ziroud Youcef, Algiers
Tel: (021) 737494; (021) 735841 *Fax:* (021) 735841
Telex: 53845 Sneda *Cable:* SNEDA ALGER
Key Personnel
Dir General: Seghir Benamar

Editorial: Abdel Kader M'Silti; Abdel Krim Saighi
Founded: 1983 (SNED 1966)
Subjects: Biography, Fiction, History, Nonfiction (General), Philosophy, Poetry, Regional Interests, Religion - Other, Science (General), Social Sciences, Sociology, Sports, Athletics, Travel

Angola

General Information

Capital: Luanda
Language: Portuguese (official), several African languages also in common use
Religion: Christian (mainly Roman Catholic)
Population: 8.9 million
Currency: 100 iwei = 1 new kwanza
Export/Import Information: No tariff on books and advertising. Very restricted issuance of import licenses. Advertising matter is currently given considerably lower priority. Exchange controls.

Biblioteca Nacional de Angola (Angola National Library)
Ave Commandante Jika, Luanda
Mailing Address: CP 2915, Luanda
Tel: (02) 322 070 *Fax:* (02) 323 979

Antigua & Barbuda

General Information

Capital: St John's
Language: English (official) and local dialects
Religion: Predominantly Angelican; other Protestant sects; some Roman Catholic
Population: 64,246
Currency: 2.70 East Caribbean dollars = $1 US

FT Caribbean (BVI) Ltd
PO Box 1037, Saint John's
Tel: 462-3392; 462-3692 *Fax:* 462-3492
E-mail: ftcarib@candw.ag
Key Personnel
Publisher: Edna Fortescue
Founded: 1978
Specialize in Caribbean economic-business & tourism publications.
ISBN Prefix(es): 976-8033
Total Titles: 1 Print
Branch Office(s)
PO Box 675, Saint George's, Grenada, Contact: Yvonne Warren *Tel:* 444-4930 *Fax:* 444-3391 *E-mail:* warrenp@caribsurf.com (Caribbean South)
19 Mercers Rd, London N19 4PH, United Kingdom, Man Editor: Lindsay Maxwell *Tel:* (020) 7281-5746 *Fax:* (020) 7281-7157 *E-mail:* ftcaribbean@btinternet.com (international)

Argentina

General Information

Capital: Buenos Aires
Language: Spanish
Religion: Roman Catholic
Population: 33 million
Bank Hours: 1000-1500 Monday-Friday
Shop Hours: 0900-1900 Monday-Saturday
Currency: 100 centavos = 1 nuevo peso argentino
Export/Import Information: No import licenses required. Import duties are assessed ad valorem. However, no import duties on books or similar material.
Copyright: UCC, Berne, Buenos Aires (see Copyright Conventions, pg xi)

Editorial Abaco de Rodolfo Depalma SRL+
Tucuman 1429 Piso 4°, 1050 Buenos Aires
Tel: (011) 4371-1675 *Fax:* (011) 4371-5802
E-mail: info@abacoeditorial.com.ar
Web Site: www.abacoeditorial.com.ar
Key Personnel
Man Dir & Editorial: Rodolfo Depalma
Production: Susana P Garcia de Gigena
Founded: 1975
Subjects: Economics, History, Journalism, Law, Philosophy, Psychology, Psychiatry, Public Administration, Social Sciences, Sociology
ISBN Prefix(es): 950-569
Number of titles published annually: 20 Print
Total Titles: 150 Print

Abeledo-Perrot SAE e I+
Lavalle 1280/1328, 1048 Buenos Aires
Tel: (011) 4124-9750 *Fax:* (011) 4371-5156
E-mail: editorial@abeledo-perrot.com
Key Personnel
Man Dir: Emilio Jose Perrot *E-mail:* eperrot@abeledo-perrot.com
General Manager: Carlos Alberto Pazos *E-mail:* cpazos@abeledo-perrot.com
Founded: 1901
Subjects: Criminology, Law, Philosophy, Public Administration
ISBN Prefix(es): 950-20
Total Titles: 17 CD-ROM

Editorial Abril SA+
Moreno 1617, 1093 Buenos Aires
Tel: (011) 3752450; (011) 3752451
Telex: 22630 Ryela
Key Personnel
Man Dir, Editor, Sales & Publicity: Roberto M Ares
Rights & Permissions: Alberto Cervetto
Founded: 1961
Editorial Huemul SA is the division of the company producing secondary & primary school textbooks.
Subjects: Fiction, Nonfiction (General)
ISBN Prefix(es): 950-10
Parent Company: Bramihuemul

Academia Argentina de Letras (Argentine Academy of Letters)
Sanchez de Bustamante 2663, 1425 Buenos Aires
Tel: (011) 4802-3814; (011) 4802-7509; (011) 4802-5161 *Fax:* (011) 4-8028340
E-mail: aaldespa@fibertel.com.ar; aaladmin@fibertel.com.ar; aalbibl@fibertel.com.ar
Founded: 1931
Specialize in Literature, Philology & Linguistics.
Subjects: Language Arts, Linguistics, Literature, Literary Criticism, Essays
ISBN Prefix(es): 950-585
Number of titles published annually: 4 Print

Editorial Acme SA+
Santa Magdalena 635, 1277 Buenos Aires
Tel: (011) 4328-1508; (011) 4328-1662
Fax: (011) 4328-9345
E-mail: acme@redynet.com.ar
Key Personnel
Man Dir: Emilio I Gonzalez
Founded: 1949
Subjects: Biography, Fiction, How-to
ISBN Prefix(es): 950-565

Ada Korn Editora SA+
Uruguay 651, floor 8 H, 1015 Buenos Aires
Tel: (011) 4374-6199 *Fax:* (011) 4374-9699
E-mail: adakorn@datamarkets.com.ar
Key Personnel
President: Ada Korn
Founded: 1984
Subjects: Drama, Theater, Fiction, Nonfiction (General), Science (General)
ISBN Prefix(es): 950-9540
Number of titles published annually: 3 Print
Total Titles: 50 Print

Aguilar Altea Taurus Alfaguara SA de Ediciones
Beazley 3860, 1437 Buenos Aires
Tel: (011) 4912-7220 *Fax:* (011) 4912-7440
E-mail: info@alfaguara.com.ar
Web Site: www.alfaguara.com.ar
Key Personnel
President & General Manager: Esteban Fernandez Rosado
Editorial Dir: Juan Martini
Founded: 1946
Subjects: Economics, Literature, Literary Criticism, Essays, Philosophy
ISBN Prefix(es): 950-511
Parent Company: Grupo Santillana Argentina

Libreria Akadia Editorial+
Paraguay 2078, 1121 Buenos Aires
Tel: (011) 4961-8614; (011) 4964-2230
Fax: (011) 4961-8614
E-mail: akadia@arnet.com.ar
Key Personnel
President: Jose Patlallan
Dir: Daniel Patlallan
Founded: 1967
Specialize in medical books.
Membership(s): Argentina Book Association.
Subjects: Health, Nutrition, Medicine, Nursing, Dentistry
ISBN Prefix(es): 950-9020

Editorial Albatros SACI+
Torres Las Plazas, J Salguero 2745, Piso 5º, oficina 51, 1425 Buenos Aires
Tel: (011) 4807-2030 *Fax:* (011) 4807-2010
E-mail: info@edalbatros.com.ar
Web Site: www.edalbatros.com.ar
Key Personnel
President: Andrea Ines Canevaro
Vice President, Executive: Gustavo Gabriel Canevaro
Founded: 1945
Subjects: Agriculture, Animals, Pets, Astrology, Occult, Economics, Electronics, Electrical Engineering, Environmental Studies, Gardening, Plants, Health, Nutrition, Medicine, Nursing, Dentistry, Social Sciences, Sociology, Sports, Athletics, Veterinary Science
ISBN Prefix(es): 950-24
Distributed by Artemis Distribuciones (Guatemala); Centro Libros Book Shop (Puerto Rico); Daisy Sel S Kuan Lau (Nicaragua); Distribuidora Lewis (Panama); Distribuidora Luongo SA (Argentina); Edaf (Spain); Edaf y Morales SA (Mexico); Editorial La Celba (El Salvador); La Familia Distribuidora de Libros SA (Peru); Gaierna SRL (Argentina); Lectorum Publications (United States); Libreria Amenguai (Dominican Republic); Libreria Lehmann SA (Costa Rica); Libreria Libertad (Chile); Libro Shop (Argentina); Libros Sin Fronteras (United States); Litexsa Venezolana (Venezuela); Mr Books (Ecuador); Multicor SRL (Uruguay); Panamericana Libreria y Papeleria (Colombia)
Bookshop(s): Libreria Editorial Albatros SACI, J Salguero 2745, 1425 Buenos Aires

Alfagrama SRL ediciones
Bolivar 547, Piso 2A, 1066 Buenos Aires
Tel: (011) 4342-2452; (011) 4345-2299
Fax: (011) 4345-5411
E-mail: libros@alfagrama.com.ar
Web Site: www.alfagrama.com.ar
Key Personnel
Contact: Alfredo Nunez
Subjects: Disability, Special Needs, Gay & Lesbian, Library & Information Sciences, Publishing & Book Trade Reference, Science (General), Technology, Women's Studies
ISBN Prefix(es): 987-95615

Alianza Editorial de Argentina SA+
Av Belgrano 355, Piso 10º, 1092 Buenos Aires
Tel: (011) 4342-4426; (011) 4342-9029
Fax: (011) 4342-4426; (011) 4342-9025
E-mail: gconosur@satlink.com
Key Personnel
General Manager: Jorge Laforque
Founded: 1985
Subjects: Anthropology, Fiction, History, Literature, Literary Criticism, Essays, Philosophy, Psychology, Psychiatry, Social Sciences, Sociology
ISBN Prefix(es): 84-206; 950-40
Parent Company: Alianza Editorial SA, Juan Ignacio Luca de Tena, 15, 28027 Madrid, Spain
Showroom(s): Av Cordoba 2064, 1120 Buenos Aires
Bookshop(s): Av Cordoba 2064, 1120 Buenos Aires

Amorrortu Editores SA+
Paraguay 1225, Piso 7, 1057 Buenos Aires
Tel: (011) 4816-5812; (011) 4816-5869
Fax: (011) 4816-3321
E-mail: info@amorrortueditores.com
Web Site: www.amorrortueditores.com
Key Personnel
President: Horacio de Amorrortu
Founded: 1967
Subjects: Anthropology, Economics, Education, Philosophy, Psychology, Psychiatry, Regional Interests, Religion - Other, Social Sciences, Sociology
ISBN Prefix(es): 950-518; 84-610

Editorial Argentina Plaza y Janes SA
Lambare 893, 1185 Buenos Aires
Tel: (011) 4862-6769; (011) 4862-6785
Fax: (011) 4864-4970
Key Personnel
Man Dir: Jorge Perez
Sales Dir: Ernesto Pena
Subjects: Fiction, Nonfiction (General)
ISBN Prefix(es): 950-644

Argentine Bible Society+
Tucuman 352/58, 1049 Buenos Aires
Tel: (011) 4312-5787; (011) 4312-8558
Fax: (011) 4312-3400
E-mail: socbiblicaarg@biblica.org
Web Site: www.biblesociety.org
Key Personnel
General Secretary: Marcelo Figuero
General Manager: Juan Terranova
Subjects: Biblical Studies
ISBN Prefix(es): 950-711; 950-99044
Branch Office(s)
Centro Regional de las Americas, 1989 NW 88 Court, Miami, FL 33177, United States
Obispo Salguero 141, 5000 Cordoba
Avda Francia 1129, 2000 Rosario

Asociacion Bautista Argentina de Publicaciones+
Ave Rivadavia 3464, 1203 Buenos Aires
Tel: (011) 4863-8924 *Fax:* (011) 4863-6745
Key Personnel
Assistant Manager: Emanuel Benavidez
Founded: 1911
Subjects: Religion - Other
ISBN Prefix(es): 950-841; 950-9074
Branch Office(s)
Tucuman 351, 5000 Cordoba
San Martin 1572, 2000 Rosario, Santa Fe

Asociacion Educacionista Argentina, see Editorial Stella

Editorial Astrea de Alfredo y Ricardo Depalma SRL+
Lavalle 1208, 1048 Buenos Aires
Tel: (011) 4382-1880 *Toll Free Tel:* 800-345-278732 *Fax:* (011) 4382-4203
E-mail: info@astrea.com.ar
Web Site: www.astrea.com.ar
Key Personnel
Man Dir: Alfredo Depalma
Sales Dir: Ricardo Depalma
Founded: 1968
Subjects: Economics, Government, Political Science, History, Law, Philosophy, Social Sciences, Sociology
ISBN Prefix(es): 950-508
Number of titles published annually: 65 Print
Total Titles: 900 Print
Bookshop(s): Libreria Astrea

Editorial Atlantida SA+
Azopardo 579, 3 Piso, 1307 Buenos Aires
Tel: (011) 4331-4591; (011) 4331-4599
Fax: (011) 3313341
Web Site: www.atlantida.com.ar
Telex: 21163 *Cable:* EDIATLAN
Key Personnel
Executive Dir: Alfredo Vercelli
Editorial Dir: Jorge Naveiro
Founded: 1918
Subjects: Fiction, Nonfiction (General)
ISBN Prefix(es): 950-08
U.S. Office(s): 31 West 57 St, 6th floor, New York, NY 10019, United States, Contact: Maria Campbell
Bookshop(s): Galerias Pacifico, San Martin 760, Local 5215, 1004 Buenos Aires *Tel:* (011) 3116411; Nuevo Centro Shopping, D Quiros 1400, Local 2241, 5000 Cordoba *Tel:* (051) 891440
Shipping Address: Rio Cuarto 1907, 1292 Buenos Aires
Warehouse: Rio Cuarto 1907, 1292 Buenos Aires

AZ Editora SA+
Paraguay 2351, 1121 Buenos Aires
Tel: (011) 4961-4036; (011) 4961-4037; (011) 4961-4038; (011) 4961-0088 *Fax:* (011) 4961-0089
E-mail: correo@az-editora.com
Web Site: www.az-editora.com.ar
Key Personnel
President: Dante Omar Villalba
Vice President: Luis Alberto Villone
Technical Dir: Luis Mendez Davila
Founded: 1976
Subjects: Economics, History, Law, Psychology, Psychiatry
ISBN Prefix(es): 950-534

ARGENTINA

La Azotea Editorial Fotografica SRL
Paraguay 1480, 1061 Buenos Aires
Tel: (011) 4811-0931 *Fax:* (011) 4811-0931
E-mail: azotea@laazotea.com.ar
Web Site: www.laazotea.com.ar
ISBN Prefix(es): 950-9536

Beas Ediciones SRL+
Inclan 3945, 1258 Buenos Aires
Tel: (011) 4923-4030; (011) 4924-5337
 Fax: (011) 4924-0217
Key Personnel
President: Hugo S Beas
Commercial Dir: Jorge Luis Sanchez
Founded: 1992
Subjects: Fiction, Humor, Nonfiction (General), Self-Help
ISBN Prefix(es): 950-834
Parent Company: Circulo del Buen Lecetor SRL, Argentina
Associate Companies: Circulo del Buen Lector SA de CV, Mexico

Beatriz Viterbo Editora+
Espana 1150, 2000 Rosario-Santa Fe
Tel: (0341) 4487521 *Fax:* (0341) 4261919
Key Personnel
Contact: Adriana Astutti *E-mail:* aastutti@arnet.com.ar; Sandra Contreras
Founded: 1991
Subjects: Drama, Theater, Fiction, Literature, Literary Criticism, Essays, Nonfiction (General), Poetry
ISBN Prefix(es): 950-845; 950-99766
Distributed by Fernando Garcia Cambeiro e Hijos

Revista Biblica, *imprint of* Editorial Guadalupe

Bonum Editorial SACI+
Av Corrientes 6687, 1427 Buenos Aires
Tel: (011) 4554-1414 *Fax:* (011) 4554-1414
E-mail: produccion@editorialbonum.com.ar
Web Site: www.editorialbonum.com.ar *Cable:* BONUM
Key Personnel
Dir Commerce: Martin Gremmelspacher
Founded: 1960
Membership(s): Argentina Book Association, Foreign Trade.
Subjects: Drama, Theater, Education, Literature, Literary Criticism, Essays, Music, Dance, Nonfiction (General), Philosophy, Psychology, Psychiatry, Religion - Catholic, Religion - Other, Securities, Self-Help, Theology
ISBN Prefix(es): 950-507
Bookshop(s): Maipu 869, 1006 Buenos Aires *Fax:* (011) 4314-0888

Bosco Don Ediciones Argentina, see Ediciones Don Bosco Argentina

Ediciones Botella al Mar
Luis Agote 2280, Piso 7°, 1425 Buenos Aires
Tel: (011) 4803-8246
E-mail: edicionesbotellaalmar@hotmail.com
ISBN Prefix(es): 950-513

Editorial Cangallo SACI+
Av Belgrano 609, 1092 Buenos Aires
Tel: (011) 4331-0204; (011) 4331-8848
Key Personnel
Man Dir: Norberto del Hoyo
President: Rosa del Valle Cardozo
Founded: 1968
Subjects: Business, Economics, Law
ISBN Prefix(es): 950-543

Editorial Caymi SACI
15 de Noviembre de 1889 N° 1149, 1130 Buenos Aires
Tel: (011) 4304-2474 *Fax:* (011) 4304-2474
Founded: 1945
Subjects: Animals, Pets, Astrology, Occult, Automotive, Cookery, Gardening, Plants, Medicine, Nursing, Dentistry, Science Fiction, Fantasy, Self-Help, Sports, Athletics
ISBN Prefix(es): 950-501

Centro Editor de America Latina SA
Tucuman 1736, 1050 Buenos Aires
Tel: (011) 4371-2411 *Cable:* Centroedit
Key Personnel
Man Dir: Jose Boris Spivacow
Sales Dir: Aldo Antonio Sangoi
Founded: 1966
Subjects: Art, Biography, Education, History, How-to, Literature, Literary Criticism, Essays, Psychology, Psychiatry, Science (General), Social Sciences, Sociology
ISBN Prefix(es): 950-25

Cesarini Hermanos+
Sarmiento 3219/31, C1196 AA1 Buenos Aires
Tel: (011) 4861-1152 *Fax:* (011) 4861-1152
E-mail: cesarinihnos@movi.com.ar
Key Personnel
Associate Manager: Osvaldo Cesarini
Founded: 1940
Membership(s): Argentina Book Association.
Subjects: Environmental Studies, Music, Dance, Nonfiction (General), Technology
ISBN Prefix(es): 950-526

Cientifica Interamericana SACI, Editorial
Marcelo T de Alvear 2147, 1122 Buenos Aires
Tel: (011) 4822-8883 *Fax:* (011) 4827-0486
E-mail: edit@interame.satlink.net
Key Personnel
President: Mauricio Modai
ISBN Prefix(es): 950-9428

Editorial Ciudad Nueva de la Sefoma+
Lezica 4358, 1202 Buenos Aires
Tel: (011) 4981-4885 *Fax:* (011) 4981-4885
E-mail: ciudadnueva@ciudadnueva.org.ar
Web Site: www.ciudadnueva.org.ar
Key Personnel
Manager: Alejandro Frere
Editor: Carlos Mana
Founded: 1964
Subjects: Biography, Education, Religion - Catholic, Securities, Theology
ISBN Prefix(es): 950-586
Parent Company: Citta Nuova Editrice (for associate companies), Italy
Distributed by Ciudad Nueva (Chile, Uruguay, Paraguay, Colombia, Mexico)

Editorial Claretiana+
Lima 1360, 1138 Buenos Aires
Tel: (011) 4305-9597; (011) 4305-9510
 Fax: (011) 4305-6552
E-mail: editorial@editorialclaretiana.com.ar
Web Site: www.editorialclaretiana.com.ar *Cable:* EDITORIAL CLARETIANA
Key Personnel
Man Dir, Editorial, Rights & Permissions: Gustavo Larrazabal
Manager: Eduardo Righetti
Publicity: Jose Luis Perez
Founded: 1956
Subjects: Religion - Catholic, Theology
ISBN Prefix(es): 950-512

Editorial Claridad SA+
Viamonte 1730, Piso 1°, 1055 Buenos Aires
Tel: (011) 4371-5546 *Fax:* (011) 4375-1659
E-mail: editorial@heliasta.com.ar
Web Site: www.heliasta.com.ar *Cable:* CLARIDAD BAIRES
Key Personnel
President: Dr Ana Maria Cabanellas
Vice President: Dr Guillermo Cabanellas
Founded: 1922
Subjects: Biography, Government, Political Science, History, Law, Philosophy, Poetry
ISBN Prefix(es): 950-620
Subsidiaries: Editorial Heliasta SRL

Club de Lectores+
Av de Mayo 624, 1084 Buenos Aires
Tel: (011) 4342-6251; (011) 4342-3955
Key Personnel
Man Dir: Mercedes Fontenla
Sales: Carlos A Alvano
Publicity: Cesar Tomas Fontenla
Founded: 1938
Subjects: History, Philosophy, Psychology, Psychiatry, Religion - Other, Social Sciences, Sociology
ISBN Prefix(es): 950-9034
Bookshop(s): Libreria Accion, Av de Mayo 624, 1084 Buenos Aires; Libreria Universitaria Fontis, Av de Mayo 624, 1084 Buenos Aires

Coleccion Juridica Bco de Datos en Computacion, *imprint of* Editorial Zeus SRL

Libreria del Colegio SA+
Humberto I 531, 1103 Buenos Aires
Tel: (011) 4300-5400; (011) 4362-1222
 Fax: (011) 4362-7364
E-mail: edsudame@satlink.com *Cable:* LIBRECOL
Key Personnel
Contact: Javier Lopez Llovet
Founded: 1830
Subjects: Education
ISBN Prefix(es): 950-548
Parent Company: Editorial Sudamericana SA

Colmegna SA
San Martin 2546, 3000 Sante Fe
Tel: (042) 523102; (042) 557345 *Fax:* (042) 4557345
Key Personnel
President: Jose Luis Anessi
Manager: Guillermo Goatherd
Founded: 1889
Subjects: Literature, Literary Criticism, Essays, Poetry
ISBN Prefix(es): 950-535

Concilium, *imprint of* Editorial Guadalupe

Ediciones Corregidor SAICI y E+
Rodriguez Pena 452, 1020 Buenos Aires
Tel: (011) 4374-5000; (011) 4374-4959
 Fax: (011) 4374-5000
E-mail: corregidor@corregidor.com
Web Site: www.corregidor.com
Key Personnel
Dir: Manuel Pampin *E-mail:* manuel.pampin@corregidor.com
Founded: 1970
Subjects: Drama, Theater, Economics, Literature, Literary Criticism, Essays, Music, Dance, Poetry, Cinema
ISBN Prefix(es): 950-05
Number of titles published annually: 50 Print
Total Titles: 3,000 Print
Warehouse: Pasaje Berg 4060, Lanus Oeste, 1826 Buenos Aires

Cosmopolita SRL
Piedras 744, 1070 Buenos Aires
Tel: (011) 4361-8925; (011) 4361-8049
 Fax: (011) 4361-8049; (011) 4361-8925
Key Personnel
Man Dir: Eva Ruth F de Rapp
Founded: 1940

Subjects: Agriculture
ISBN Prefix(es): 950-9069

Critica+
Independencia, 1668 Buenos Aires 1100
Tel: (011) 4382-4045; (011) 4382-4043
 Fax: (011) 4383-3793
E-mail: info@grijalbo.com.ar
Key Personnel
General Manager: Felipe Munde
 E-mail: fmunoz@grijalbo.com.ar
Subjects: Fiction, Nonfiction (General)
ISBN Prefix(es): 950-28; 987-9317
Parent Company: Grijalbo Mondadori SA

Studia Croatica
Matienzo 2530, 1426 Buenos Aires
Tel: (011) 4771-4954 *Fax:* (011) 4771-4954
E-mail: webmasters@studiacroatica.com
ISBN Prefix(es): 987-95467

Depalma SRL+
Talcahuano 494, 1013 Buenos Aires
Tel: (011) 5382-8806 *Fax:* (011) 5382-8888
E-mail: info@depalma.ssdnet.com.ar
Key Personnel
Man Dir, Production: Roberto Suardiaz
General Manager: Alberto Evaristo Baron
International Marketing Manager: Nicolas von der Pahlen
Founded: 1944
Also distributor of Iberiamerican Juridical books.
Subjects: Business, History, Law, Social Sciences, Sociology
ISBN Prefix(es): 950-14
Showroom(s): Lavalle 1302, Buenos Aires

Diana Argentina SA, Editorial
Beauchef 559, 1424 Buenos Aires
Tel: (011) 4922-5035; (011) 4922-5036
 Fax: (011) 4922-5035; (011) 4922-5036
E-mail: to_dianaarg@sinectis.com.ar
Key Personnel
General Dir: Jorge Baez Arganaraz
Subjects: Accounting, Animals, Pets, Art, Biography, Business, Communications, Computer Science, Economics, Education, Engineering (General), History, Journalism, Language Arts, Linguistics, Literature, Literary Criticism, Essays, Marketing, Medicine, Nursing, Dentistry, Music, Dance, Philosophy, Photography, Religion - Other, Self-Help, Sports, Athletics, Travel
ISBN Prefix(es): 987-96980
Parent Company: Casa Amtriz

Diario la Voz del Interior
Tte Gral Peron 1628, Piso 2, 1037 Buenos Aires
Tel: (011) 4382-2267 *Fax:* (011) 3822508
E-mail: info@nueva.com.ar
Key Personnel
Dir: Cuesta Carlos Enrique
ISBN Prefix(es): 950-879; 950-884

Editorial Ruy Diaz SAEIC+
Elpidio Gonzalez 5562/66, 1407 Buenos Aires
Tel: (011) 4567-4918; (011) 4567-2865
 Fax: (011) 4567-4918
E-mail: editorial@ruydiaz.com.ar
Web Site: www.ruydiaz.com.ar *Cable:* EDIRUY
Key Personnel
President: Rafael Juan Zucotti
Man Dir: Gustavo H Zuccotti
Founded: 1966
Membership(s): Argentina Book Association.
Subjects: Cookery, Education, Law
ISBN Prefix(es): 950-9023; 987-516
Branch Office(s)
Casilla de Correo 46, Suc 6, 1406 Buenos Aires

Ediciones Don Bosco Argentina+
Don Bosco 4069, 1206 Buenos Aires
Tel: (011) 4981-7314; (011) 4981-1388
 Fax: (011) 4958-1506
E-mail: e.d.b.sofrasa@interlink.com.ar
Key Personnel
Contact: Roque R Cella
Founded: 1941
Membership(s): Camara del Libro.
Subjects: Accounting, Drama, Theater, Education, History, Journalism, Radio, TV, Religion - Catholic
ISBN Prefix(es): 950-514
Distributed by Centro Salesiano de Estudios
Distributor for Edebe
Bookshop(s): Don Bosco 4069, 1206 Capital Federal
Orders to: Don Bosco 4069, 1206 Capital Federal

Ediciones del Eclipse+
Julian Alvarez 843, 1414 Buenos Aires
Tel: (011) 4771-3583 *Fax:* (011) 4771-3583
E-mail: info@deleclipse.com
Web Site: www.deleclipse.com
Key Personnel
President: Maria Del Rosario Charquero
Subjects: Literature, Literary Criticism, Essays, Psychology, Psychiatry
ISBN Prefix(es): 987-9011; 950-99530

Edicial SA+
Rivadavia 761, 1002 Buenos Aires
Tel: (011) 4342-8481; (011) 4342-8482; (011) 4342-8483 *Fax:* (011) 4342-8481
E-mail: edicial@edicial.com.ar
Key Personnel
President: Juan A Musset
Founded: 1931
Subjects: Communications, Language Arts, Linguistics, Literature, Literary Criticism, Essays, Philosophy, Regional Interests
ISBN Prefix(es): 950-506
U.S. Office(s): Distribooks, 8220 N Christiana Ave, Skokie, IL 60076-2911, United States
Showroom(s): Palacio del Libro International, Suipacha 1136, 1008 Buenos Aires

Editorial Kapelusz SA, see Kapelusz Editora SA

Editorial Universitaria de Buenos Aires, see EUDEBA (Editorial Universitaria de Buenos Aires)

EDIUM, see Editorial Idearium de la Universidad de Mendoza (EDIUM)

Emece Editores SA+
Independencia 1668, 1100 Buenos Aires
Tel: (011) 4382-4045; (011) 4382-4043
 Fax: (011) 4383-3793
E-mail: info@eplaneta.com.ar; pasiusis@planeta.com.ar
Web Site: www.emece.com.ar
Key Personnel
President: Ing Alfredo del Carril *E-mail:* acarril@emece.com.ar
General Director: Francisco F del Carril
 E-mail: fcarril@emece.com.ar
Editorial Director: Bonifacio P del Carril
 E-mail: bcarril@emece.com.ar
Editorial: Eduardo Garcia Belsunce
 E-mail: edicion@emece.com.ar
Sales Dir, Export: Carlos A Bustillo
 E-mail: cbustillo@emece.com.ar
Editorial Dept: Stella Maris Rozas
 E-mail: srozas@emece.com.ar
Administration: Marcos I Fantin
Founded: 1939
Subjects: Art, Biography, Fiction, History, Literature, Literary Criticism, Essays, Mysteries, Nonfiction (General)

ISBN Prefix(es): 950-04
Number of titles published annually: 120 Print
Associate Companies: Emece Editores SA, Mallorca 237 Entlo, 1a, 08008 Barcelona, Spain, Contact: Siprid Kraus *Tel:* (03) 215-1199 *Fax:* (03) 215-4636; Emece Mexicana SA, de CV Vito Alessio Robles 140, Col Florida CP, 01030 Mexico, DF, Mexico, Contact: Iuan Mozo *Tel:* (05) 661-7590 *Fax:* (05) 661-4110 *E-mail:* emece@podernet.com.ar; Emece/Urano SA, av Francisco Bilbao, 2809 Santiago de Chile, Chile, Contact: Ricardo Ulasteliga *Tel:* (02) 341-6731 *Fax:* (02) 225-3896 *E-mail:* emc-uran@entelchile.net; Av Uruguay 1579, Montevideo, Uruguay, Contact: Reinaldo Rodriguez *Tel:* (02) 42-9358 *Fax:* (02) 42-9359 *E-mail:* pero@adinet.com.uy
U.S. Office(s): Sanford J Greenburger Associates Inc, 55 Fifth Ave, New York, NY 10003, United States, Contact: Carol Frederick *Tel:* 212-206-5600 *Fax:* 212-463-8718; 212-687-9281

Errepar SA+
Parana 725, 1017 Buenos Aires
Tel: (011) 4370-2002 *Fax:* (011) 4307-9541
E-mail: clientes@errepar.com
Web Site: www.errepar.com
Key Personnel
Vice President: Dr Francisco Canada
International Rights Contact: Veronica Parada; Irene Acero
Subjects: Astrology, Occult, Cookery, Economics, Education, Religion - Catholic, Religion - Hindu, Religion - Other, Self-Help
ISBN Prefix(es): 950-739; 950-9524; 987-01

Espasa-Calpe Argentina SA+
Independencea 1668, 1100 Buenos Aires
Tel: (011) 4382-4043; (011) 4382-4045
 Fax: (011) 4383-3793
E-mail: info@eplaneta.com.ar
Key Personnel
Dir General: Guillermo Schavelzon
Founded: 1929
ISBN Prefix(es): 950-852
Parent Company: Grupo Planeta
Subsidiaries: Seix Barral; Destino; Ariel; Deusto; Austral

Angel Estrada y Cia SA
Bolivar 462/66, 1066 Buenos Aires
Tel: (011) 4344-5500 *Fax:* (011) 4331-6527
E-mail: editocom@estrada.com.ar
Web Site: www.estrada.com.ar
Telex: 17990 Estra
Key Personnel
President: Zsolt Arardy
Director: Tomas de Estrada
Publishing Manager: Marcela Iraola
Founded: 1869
Subjects: Education, How-to
ISBN Prefix(es): 950-01

EUDEBA (Editorial Universitaria de Buenos Aires)+
Av Rivadavia 1573, C1033AAF Buenos Aires
Tel: (011) 4383-8025 *Fax:* (011) 4383-2202
E-mail: eudeba@eudeba.com
Web Site: www.eudeba.com.ar
Key Personnel
President: Alicia Rosalia Wigdorovitz de Camilloni
Manager of Institutional Relations: Martin Unzue
 E-mail: institucionales@eudeba.com.ar
Publishing Manager: Victor Palaces
 E-mail: geditorial@eudeba.com.ar
Commercial Manager: Gustavo Kogan
 E-mail: ventas@eudeba.com.ar
Founded: 1958
Subjects: Accounting, Archaeology, Architecture & Interior Design, Art, Astrology, Occult, Chemistry, Chemical Engineering, Drama, The-

ARGENTINA

ater, Economics, Education, Geography, Geology, History, Law, Literature, Literary Criticism, Essays, Mathematics, Medicine, Nursing, Dentistry, Music, Dance, Philosophy, Physics, Psychology, Psychiatry, Science (General), Theology, Veterinary Science
ISBN Prefix(es): 950-23
Number of titles published annually: 150 Print; 5 CD-ROM
Bookshop(s): Pasaje El Fundador-Loca, 9 Obispo Trejo, 29 Cordoba, 5000 Codigo

Ediciones Librerias Fausto+
Av Corrientes 1316, 1043 Buenos Aires
Tel: (011) 4372-4919 *Fax:* (011) 4372-3914
E-mail: fausto@fausto.com
Web Site: www.fausto.com
Key Personnel
President: Rafael Pedro Zorrilla
Manager: Jose Luis Retes
ISBN Prefix(es): 950-653
Branch Office(s)
Corrientes 1243, 1715 Santa Fe
Galerias Pacifico, 1311 Santa Fe
Bookshop(s): Libreria Fausto

Ediciones de la Flor SRL+
Gorriti 3695, 1172 Buenos Aires
Tel: (011) 4963-7950 *Fax:* (011) 4963-5616
E-mail: edic-flor@datamarkets.com
Web Site: www.edicionesdelaflor.com.ar
Key Personnel
Dir: Daniel Divinsky *Tel:* (011) 4963-1460
Man Dir: Ana M Miler
Publicity & Advertising Dir, Rights & Permissions: Daniel Borenstein
Founded: 1967
Subjects: Biography, Drama, Theater, Fiction, History, Humor, Literature, Literary Criticism, Essays, Philosophy, Psychology, Psychiatry, Social Sciences, Sociology
ISBN Prefix(es): 950-515
Number of titles published annually: 40 Print
Total Titles: 500 Print

Fundacion Editorial de Belgrano
Federico Lacroze 1959, Piso 4°, 1426 Buenos Aires
Tel: (011) 4772-4014 *Fax:* (011) 4775-8788
Key Personnel
President: Avelino J Porto
Subjects: Architecture & Interior Design, Economics, Government, Political Science, Law, Literature, Literary Criticism, Essays, Psychology, Psychiatry, Radio, TV, Social Sciences, Sociology
ISBN Prefix(es): 950-577; 987-95823

Ediciones de Arte Gaglianone
Cnel M Chilavert 1136/1146, 1437 Buenos Aires
Tel: (011) 4923-2579; (011) 4923-0150
 Fax: (011) 4923-0150; (011) 4923-2579
E-mail: ediciones@gaglianone.com.ar
Key Personnel
President: Jose Horacio Gaglianone
General Manager: Oscar A Aimar
Editor: Patricio Lopez Tobares
Accounting & Finances: Gustavo Portela
Subjects: Music, Dance
ISBN Prefix(es): 950-720; 950-9004

Editorial Galerna SRL+
Lambare 893, 1185 Buenos Aires
Tel: (011) 4867-1661 *Fax:* (011) 4862-5031
E-mail: gventas@hg.com.ar *Cable:* GALERNA
Key Personnel
Dir: Hugo Benjamin Levin; Juan Jose D'AAbtibua
Founded: 1967
Afiliados a la Camara Argentina del Libro.
Membership(s): Argentina Book Association.
Subjects: Drama, Theater, History, Humor, Literature, Literary Criticism, Essays, Poetry, Social Sciences, Sociology, Theology
ISBN Prefix(es): 950-556
Subsidiaries: Librogal SRL
Bookshop(s): Septimo Rayo, Callao 729, Buenos Aires; Libreria Galerna, Corrientes 1776, Mar del Plata, Buenos Aires; Ramon L Falcon 7115, Loc 305, Buenos Aires; Rivadavia 3050, Loc 21, Mar del Plata, Buenos Aires; Nazarre 3175, Loc 119/20, Buenos Aires; Gueemes 369, Loc 50, Haedo

Gram Editora
Cochabamba 1652, 1148 Buenos Aires
Tel: (011) 4304-4833; (011) 4305-8397
 Fax: (011) 4304-5692
E-mail: grameditora@infovia.com.ar
Web Site: www.grameditora.com.ar
Key Personnel
Dir: Manuel Herrero Montes
Founded: 1925
Subjects: Computer Science, Education, Religion - Catholic, Religion - Other
ISBN Prefix(es): 950-530
Branch Office(s)
Libreria Marista, Av Callao 226, 1148 Buenos Aires *Tel:* (011) 374-3114 *Fax:* (011) 374-3146

Grupo Editorial Planeta, see Editorial Planeta Argentina SAIC

Grupo Editorial Planets, see Seix Barral

Editorial Guadalupe+
Mansilla 3865, 1425 Buenos Aires
Tel: (011) 4826-8587 *Fax:* (011) 4826-8587
E-mail: ventas@editorialguadalupe.com.ar
Web Site: www.editorialguadalupe.com.ar
Key Personnel
Dir: Lorenzo Goyeneche
Man Dir, Production: Mario V Keiner
Publicity Dir: Osvaldo Lopez
Founded: 1895
Membership(s): Argentina Book Association.
Subjects: Anthropology, Education, History, Language Arts, Linguistics, Literature, Literary Criticism, Essays, Music, Dance, Philosophy, Psychology, Psychiatry, Religion - Catholic, Social Sciences, Sociology, Theology
ISBN Prefix(es): 950-500
Imprints: Revista Biblica; Concilium
Branch Office(s)
Libreria Verbo Divino, Velez Sarsfield 76-5000 Cordoba
Bookshop(s): Libreria Guadalupe, Mansilla 3865, 1425 Buenos Aires; Libreria Verbo Divino, Velez Sarsfield 76, 5000 Cordoba

Editorial Heliasta SRL
Viamonte 1730 Piso 1, 1055 Buenos Aires
Tel: (011) 4371-5546 *Fax:* (011) 4375-1659
E-mail: editorial@heliasta.com.ar
Web Site: www.heliasta.com.ar
ISBN Prefix(es): 950-9065; 950-885

Editorial Hemisferio Sur SA+
Pasteur 743, 1028 Buenos Aires
Tel: (011) 49529825 *Fax:* (011) 49528454
E-mail: informe@hemisferiosur.com.ar
Web Site: www.hemisferiosur.com.ar
Key Personnel
President & Man Dir, Licensing: Adolfo Julian Pena
Founded: 1966
Subjects: Agriculture, Animals, Pets, Biological Sciences, Gardening, Plants, Science (General), Veterinary Science, Wine & Spirits
ISBN Prefix(es): 950-504

Editorial Huemul SA, see Editorial Abril SA

Libreria Huemul SA+
Ave Santa Fe 2237, 1123 Buenos Aires
Tel: (011) 4822-1666; (011) 4825-2290
 Fax: (011) 822-1666
Key Personnel
President & Manager: Antonio Rego
Sales, Publicity, Rights & Permissions: Carlos L Sanchez
Founded: 1941
ISBN Prefix(es): 950-571; 84-8201

Editorial Idearium de la Universidad de Mendoza (EDIUM)
Aristides Villanueva 773, 5500 Mendoza
Tel: (0261) 420-2017; (0261) 420-0740
 Fax: (0261) 420-1100
E-mail: umimen@um.edu.ar
Web Site: www.um.edu.ar/um/
Key Personnel
Dir: Dr Juan Carlos Menghini
Manager: Jose Miguel Ciarcia
Founded: 1979
Subjects: Architecture & Interior Design, Computer Science, Economics, Education, Electronics, Electrical Engineering, Engineering (General), Environmental Studies, History, Language Arts, Linguistics, Law, Mathematics, Medicine, Nursing, Dentistry, Philosophy, Physics, Social Sciences, Sociology, Technology
ISBN Prefix(es): 950-624
Distributed by Abeledo-Perrot

INCYTH, see Instituto Nacional de Ciencia y Tecnica Hidrica (INCYTH)

Inter-Medica+
Junin 917, Piso 1 A, 1113 Buenos Aires
Tel: (011) 4961-9234 *Fax:* (011) 4961-5572
E-mail: info@inter-medica.com.ar
Web Site: www.inter-medica.com.ar
Key Personnel
President: Jorge Modyeievsky
Vice President: Sonia M B de Modyeievsky
General Manager: Tatiana Modyeievsky Bakenroth; Eduardo Modyeievsky Bakenroth; Daniel Sergio
Founded: 1959
Subjects: Veterinary Science
ISBN Prefix(es): 950-555
Branch Office(s)
Editorial Intervet SA, Junin 917-1 A, Capital 1113

Juegos & Co SRL+
Av Corrientes 1312, Piso 8, 1043 Buenos Aires
Tel: (011) 4374-7903; (011) 4371-1825
 Fax: (011) 4372-3829
E-mail: juegosyc@impsat1.com.ar
Web Site: www.demente.com
Key Personnel
Dir: Jaime Poniachik
Editor: Diego Uribe
Founded: 1980
Membership(s): Argentine Association of Magazine Publishers.
Subjects: Mathematics
ISBN Prefix(es): 950-765
Associate Companies: Zugarto Ediciones, Madrid, Spain

Juris Editorial+
Moreno 1580, 2000 Rosario
Tel: (0341) 4267301; (0341) 4267302 *Fax:* (0341) 4267301; (0341) 4267302
E-mail: editorialjuris@arnet.com.ar
Web Site: www.editorialjuris.com
Key Personnel
International Contact: Luis Maesano
Founded: 1952
Subjects: Criminology, Law

PUBLISHERS ARGENTINA

ISBN Prefix(es): 950-817; 950-99649
Number of titles published annually: 25 Print

Kapelusz Editora SA
San Jose 831, 1076 Buenos Aires
Tel: (011) 5236-5000 *Fax:* (011) 5236-5050
E-mail: editorial@kapelusz.com.ar
Web Site: www.kapelusz.com.ar
Telex: 18342 Ekasa *Cable:* Kapelusz
Key Personnel
President: Tomas Castle
Vice President: Juan Silva Baptist
Dir: Ivan Dario Pineda
Sales Manager: Hernando S Ferreres
Publicity: Carlos O Otero
Founded: 1905
Subjects: Education, Psychology, Psychiatry
ISBN Prefix(es): 950-13
Subsidiaries: Editorial Cincel SA; Editorial Kapelusz Colombiana SA; Editorial Kapelusz Mexicana SA; Editorial Kapelusz SA; Editorial Kapelusz Venezolana SA
Bookshop(s): Corrientes 999, Buenos Aires

Editorial Kier SACIFI+
Ave Santa Fe 1260, 1059 Buenos Aires
Tel: (011) 4811-0507 *Fax:* (011) 4811-3395
E-mail: ediciones@kier.com.ar
Web Site: www.kier.com.ar
Key Personnel
President: Hector Pibernus
Vice President: Alfonso Sergio Pibernus
Man Dir: Osvaldo Pibernus
Sales Dir: Sergio F Pibernus
Founded: 1907
Specialize in medicine.
Subjects: Anthropology, Astrology, Occult, Health, Nutrition, Parapsychology, Religion - Buddhist, Religion - Hindu, Religion - Islamic, Religion - Jewish, Religion - Other, Self-Help
ISBN Prefix(es): 950-17
Number of titles published annually: 40 Print
Total Titles: 800 Print
Bookshop(s): Libreria Kier, Ave Santa Fe 1260, 1059 Buenos Aires

Laffont Ediciones Electronicas SA
Av Reg Patricios 929, 1265 Buenos Aires
Tel: (011) 4302-8668 *Fax:* (011) 4301-2525
E-mail: info@laffont.com.ar
Web Site: www.laffont.com.ar
Key Personnel
Contact: Dr Julio Laffont
Membership(s): Camara del Libro.
Subjects: Art, Education, Geography, Geology, History, Science (General)
ISBN Prefix(es): 987-9220; 987-95410

Ediciones Larousse Argentina SA
Valentin Gomez 3530, 1191 Buenos Aires
Tel: (011) 4865-9581; (011) 4865-9582; (011) 4865-9583 *Toll Free Tel:* 800-333-5757
  Fax: (011) 4865-9581; (011) 4865-9582; (011) 4865-9583 *Toll Free Fax:* 800-333-5757
E-mail: editorial@aique.com.ar; comercial@aique.com.ar
Web Site: www.larousse.com.ar
Telex: 0121783 *Cable:* Editlarousse
Key Personnel
President: Dominique Bertin
ISBN Prefix(es): 950-538

Latina SA, see Ediciones Preescolar SA

La Ley SA Editora e Impresora+
Tucuman 1471, 1050 Buenos Aires
Tel: (011) 4378-4841 *Fax:* (011) 4372-0953
E-mail: atcliente1@laley.com.ar
Web Site: www.la-ley.com.ar
Telex: 17465 Laley
Key Personnel
President: Juan C Milberg
Vice President: Enrique J Algorta
General Dir: Enrique J Algorta Gaona
Commercial Manager: Manuel E Schkolnik
Production: Roberto Pedretti
Founded: 1935
Subjects: Economics, History, Law, Philosophy
ISBN Prefix(es): 950-527

Libres, *imprint of* Ediciones Macchi

Librograf Editora+
Chacabuco 1185/87, 1069 Buenos Aires
Tel: (011) 4300-3670; (011) 4300-1466
  Fax: (011) 4300-3670
Key Personnel
Contact: Adriana Arribas; Eduardo Rosales
Founded: 1968
Subjects: Cookery, Education
ISBN Prefix(es): 950-848; 950-99827

Ediciones Lidiun
Patagones 2459, 1282 Buenos Aires
Tel: (011) 4942-9002 *Fax:* (011) 4942-9162
E-mail: info@ateneo.com
Web Site: www.ateneo.com
Founded: 1970
Subjects: Animals, Pets, Health, Nutrition, Outdoor Recreation, Psychology, Psychiatry, Religion - Other, Sports, Athletics
ISBN Prefix(es): 950-524

Lopez Libreros Editores S R L
Av Cordoba 2370, 1120 Buenos Aires
Tel: (011) 4963-9646
Key Personnel
Man Dir: Dr Pablo A Lopez; Josefina A Lopez
Founded: 1927
Subjects: Medicine, Nursing, Dentistry
ISBN Prefix(es): 950-505

Editorial Losada SA+
Corrientes 1551, 1042 Buenos Aires
Tel: (011) 4373-4006; (011) 4375-5001
  Fax: (011) 4373-4006; (011) 4375-5001
E-mail: administra@editoriallosada.com
  Cable: EDILOSADA
Key Personnel
President: Jose Juan Fernandez Reguera
Vice President: Dr Moretti Luis Angel
Secretary: Mabel Peremarti
Founded: 1938
Membership(s): Camara Argentina del Libro.
Subjects: Biography, Drama, Theater, Education, Fiction, History, Law, Philosophy, Poetry, Psychology, Psychiatry
ISBN Prefix(es): 950-03

Ediciones LR SA+
Sarmiento 835, 1041 Buenos Aires
Tel: (011) 4326-3725; (011) 4326-3826
Telex: 22087 Elerre
Key Personnel
President: Bautista L Tello
Founded: 1981
Membership(s): Camara Argentina de Publicaciones.
ISBN Prefix(es): 950-604
Parent Company: Libreria Rodriguez SA
Associate Companies: LR Distribuidora SA
Distributor for LR Distribuidora SA
Warehouse: Boedo 377, 1206 Buenos Aires

Ediciones Macchi+
Alsina 1535/37, 1088 Buenos Aires
Tel: (011) 4375-1195 *Fax:* (011) 4375-1870; (011) 4374-2506
E-mail: info@macchi.com.ar
Web Site: www.macchi.com
Key Personnel
President: Raul Luis Macchi
Founded: 1947
ISBN Prefix(es): 950-537
Imprints: Libres
Bookshop(s): Ave Cordoba 2015, 1120 Bueno Aires *Tel:* (011) 4961-8355

Macchi Grupo Editors SA, see Ediciones Macchi

Marymar Ediciones SA+
Chile 1432, 1098 Buenos Aires
Tel: (011) 4381-9083
Key Personnel
President: Isay Klasse
Vice President: Saul Chernicoff
Founded: 1960
Also book packager.
Subjects: Architecture & Interior Design, Economics, Education, Environmental Studies, Fiction, Film, Video, Government, Political Science, History, Library & Information Sciences, Music, Dance, Philosophy, Psychology, Psychiatry, Science (General), Social Sciences, Sociology, Technology
ISBN Prefix(es): 950-503

Editorial Medica Panamericana SA+
Marcelo T de Alvear 2145, 1122 Buenos Aires
Tel: (011) 4821-5520; (011) 4821-0175
  Fax: (011) 4821-1214
E-mail: info@medicapanamericana.com
Web Site: www.medicapanamericana.com.ar
Key Personnel
President: Hugo Brik
Founded: 1953
Subjects: Biological Sciences, Medicine, Nursing, Dentistry, Psychology, Psychiatry
ISBN Prefix(es): 950-06
Branch Office(s)
Carrera 7a A N° 69-19, Santa Fe de Bogota DC, Colombia
Alberto Alcocer 24, 28036 Madrid, Spain
Calzada de Tlalpan N°5022, Colonia La Joya, 14090 Mexico DF, Mexico
Edificio Polar, Torre Oeste, Piso 6, Oficina 6-C, Plaza Venezuela, Urbanizacion Los Caobos, Parroquia El Recreo, Municipio Libertador, Distrito Federal, Venezuela

Ediciones Medicas SA
Cerrito 512 Piso 2, 1010 Buenos Aires
Tel: (011) 4384-0750 *Fax:* (011) 4384-0750
E-mail: emsa@havasmedimedia.com.ar
Key Personnel
Dir: Juan Jose Vallory
ISBN Prefix(es): 987-97055; 987-9492

Ediciones Minotauro SA
Independencia 1668, 1100 Ciudad Autonoma de Bs As
Tel: (011) 4382-4043; (011) 4382-4045
  Fax: (011) 4383-3793
E-mail: sansaldi@eplaneta.com.ar
Web Site: www.edicionesminotauro.com
Founded: 1955
Subjects: Fiction, Science Fiction, Fantasy
ISBN Prefix(es): 950-547
Number of titles published annually: 15 Print
Total Titles: 15 Print
Parent Company: Grupo Editorial Planeta SAIC
Distributed by Grupo Editorial Planeta
Warehouse: Interbook
Distribution Center: Interbook

Instituto Nacional de Ciencia y Tecnica Hidrica (INCYTH)
Empalme Ruta 205 KM 2.5, Lomas de Zamora, 1832 Buenos Aires
Tel: (011) 4295-1503 *Fax:* (011) 4800094

ARGENTINA

Key Personnel
President: Dr Mario Rodolfo de Marco Naon
Subjects: Computer Science, Earth Sciences, Geography, Geology, Law, Library & Information Sciences, Mathematics, Technology
ISBN Prefix(es): 950-634

Instituto de Publicaciones Navales+
Division of Centro Naval - Argentina
Cordoba 354, 1054 Buenos Aires
Tel: (011) 4311-0042; (011) 4311-0043
E-mail: ipn@web-mail.com.ar; ipn@fibertel.com.ar
Web Site: www.centronaval.org.ar
Key Personnel
President: Carlos Frasch
Manager: Jorge Bergallo
Founded: 1961
Specialize in strategy, naval history, international relations & maritime issues.
Membership(s): Argentina Book Association.
Subjects: Biography, Maritime, Military Science, Sports, Athletics, International Relations, Narrative, Nautical Sports, Sailing, Strategics
ISBN Prefix(es): 950-9016; 950-899
Number of titles published annually: 7 Print
Total Titles: 155 Print
Distributed by Tuskets Editores

Editorial Norte SA+
Jose Marmol 2131, 1255 Buenos Aires
Tel: (011) 4921-1440 *Fax:* (011) 4921-1440
Key Personnel
Dir General: Alejandro I Lamarque
Founded: 1961
Specializes in marketing.
Subjects: Education
ISBN Prefix(es): 950-27; 950-598

Ediciones Nueva Vision SAIC+
Tucuman 3748, 1189 Buenos Aires
Tel: (011) 4863-1461; (011) 4863-5050
Fax: (011) 4863-5980
E-mail: ednuevavision@ciudad.com.ar
Key Personnel
Man Dir: Haydee P de Giacone
Sales Manager: Anibal Victor Giacone
Founded: 1954
Subjects: Architecture & Interior Design, Art, Drama, Theater, Psychology, Psychiatry, Social Sciences, Sociology
ISBN Prefix(es): 950-602

Oikos+
Rivadavia 1823, Piso 9, 1033 Buenos Aires
Tel: (011) 4951-9489; (011) 4951-8129
E-mail: postmaster@atlas.edu.ar
Key Personnel
President: Mario C Fuschini Mejia
Founded: 1975
Subjects: Earth Sciences, Geography, Geology, Social Sciences, Sociology
ISBN Prefix(es): 950-601
Bookshop(s): Hipolito Yrigoyen 1970, 1089 Buenos Aires

Editorial Paidos SAICF
Defensa, 599, 1°, 1065 Buenos Aires
Tel: (011) 4331-2275 *Fax:* (011) 4343-0954
E-mail: direccion@editorialpaidos.com.ar
Web Site: www.paidosargentina.com.ar
Key Personnel
Man Dir, Rights & Permissions: Maria Gottheil
Founded: 1945
Subjects: Child Care & Development, Communications, Education, Environmental Studies, Government, Political Science, Philosophy, Psychology, Psychiatry, Self-Help, Social Sciences, Sociology, Women's Studies
ISBN Prefix(es): 950-12
Subsidiaries: Ediciones Paidos Iberica SA (Mexico & Spain)

Editora Patria Grande
Rivadavia 6369, 1406 Buenos Aires
Tel: (011) 4631-6446
Key Personnel
General Manager, Rights & Permissions: Washington Uranga
Editorial: Carlos J Duran
Sales: Elsa S de Fernandez
Production: Carlos D Arnedillo
Publicity: Duilio Lopez
Founded: 1974
Subjects: Poetry, Religion - Other
ISBN Prefix(es): 950-546
Branch Office(s)
Casilla de Correo 5, Suc 8, 1408 Buenos Aires
Bookshop(s): Libreria Didaje, Jose Cubas 3543, Buenos Aires

Pearson Educacion de Argentina
Avenida Regimiento Patricios 1959, 1266 Buenos Aires
Tel: (011) 4309 6100 *Fax:* (011) 4309 6199
Key Personnel
President - Southern Cone: Juan Carlos Cavin
Manager, Finance & Administration: Ernesto Merlo
Manager, Argentinean ELT/School: Diane Repetto
Publisher, Manager Professional/Trade: Guillermo Rivas
Publisher, Manager College: Esteban Lo Presti

Editorial Planeta Argentina SAIC+
Av Independencia 1668, 1100 Buenos Aires
Tel: (011) 4382-4045; (011) 4382-4043
Fax: (011) 4383-3793
E-mail: info@eplaneta.com.ar; lpasiusis@planeta.com.ar
Key Personnel
Executive President: Julio Perez Vega
General Dir: Guillermo Schavelzon
Editorial Manager: Leandro de Sagastizabal
Editorial Manager: Ricardo Sabanes
Founded: 1983
Subjects: Biography, Environmental Studies, Fiction, Health, Nutrition, History, How-to, Literature, Literary Criticism, Essays, Nonfiction (General), Parapsychology, Psychology, Psychiatry, Religion - Other
ISBN Prefix(es): 950-742; 950-9216; 950-49
Parent Company: Planeta Internacional SA, Barcelona, Spain
Subsidiaries: Ariel; Destino; Deusto; Espese Calpe; Montiuez Rica; Seix Berral; Teures de Teay

Plaza & Janes, see Editorial Argentina Plaza y Janes SA

Editorial Pleamar
Pena 3161, Piso 7 B, 1425 Buenos Aires
Tel: (011) 485-6597
Key Personnel
Man Dir: Andres Alfonso Bravo
Founded: 1965
Subjects: Government, Political Science, Social Sciences, Sociology
ISBN Prefix(es): 950-583

Editorial Plus Ultra SA
Callao 575, 1022 Buenos Aires
Tel: (011) 4374-2973; (011) 4374-5092
Fax: (011) 4374-2973
E-mail: plus_ultra@epu.virtual.ar.net *Cable:* Plusultra
Key Personnel
President: Rafael Roman Picon
Man Dir: Lorenzo Marengo
Editorial: Carlos Alberto Loprete; Jose Isaacson
Sales: Ricardo Errea
Production: Renato Gardoni
Publicity: Lily Sosa de Newton

Founded: 1964
Subjects: Economics, Education, Government, Political Science, History, Law, Literature, Literary Criticism, Essays, Philosophy, Psychology, Psychiatry, Social Sciences, Sociology
ISBN Prefix(es): 950-21

Editorial Polemos SA+
Moreno 1785 5° piso, 1093 Buenos Aires
Tel: (011) 4383-5291 *Fax:* (011) 4382-4181
E-mail: editorial@polemos.com.ar
Web Site: www.polemos.com.ar
Key Personnel
President: Juan Carlos Stagnaro
Founded: 1990
Subjects: Behavioral Sciences, Medicine, Nursing, Dentistry, Psychology, Psychiatry, Science (General), Social Sciences, Sociology, Psychoanalysis
ISBN Prefix(es): 987-9165; 987-99545

Biblioteca Popular Judia
Larrea 744, 1030 Buenos Aires
Tel: (011) 4961-4534 *Fax:* (011) 4963-7056
E-mail: cjl@mayo.com.ar *Cable:* WORLDGRESS BAIRES
Key Personnel
Editorial: Roberto Brzostowski; Pedro Olschansky
ISBN Prefix(es): 987-99868
Parent Company: Congreso Judio Latinoamericano

Ediciones Preescolar SA+
Argerich 1928, 1416 Buenos Aires
Tel: (011) 4581-3182 *Fax:* (011) 4581-3182
Key Personnel
Editorial: Juan Carlos Orgueira
Founded: 1971 (1984)
Incorporating Latina SA.
Subjects: Cookery, Education, Health, Nutrition, Sports, Athletics
ISBN Prefix(es): 950-9574

Editorial Quetzal-Domingo Cortizo+
Barragan 740, 1408 Buenos Aires
Tel: (011) 4641-5639
E-mail: profika@ciudad.com.ar
Founded: 1952
Subjects: Art, Biography, Drama, Theater, Literature, Literary Criticism, Essays, Music, Dance, Poetry
ISBN Prefix(es): 950-590; 987-97723

Ricordi Americana SAEC
Tte Gral J D Peron 1558, Piso 2°, 1037 Buenos Aires
Tel: (011) 4371-9841; (011) 4371-9843
Fax: (011) 4372-3459
E-mail: ricordi@sminter.com.ar
Telex: 1222580 for Ricordi *Cable:* Ricordamericana
Key Personnel
President, General Manager: Renzo Valcarenghi
Dir & Deputy Manager: Ernesto R Larcade
Marketing: Claudio Firmenich
Founded: 1924
Subjects: Education, Music, Dance
ISBN Prefix(es): 950-22
Associate Companies: Ricordi Brasileira S/A, Rua Conselheiro Nebias 1136, 01203 Sao Paulo SP, Brazil; G e C Ricordi SpA, Italy; G Ricordi & Co, Paseo de la Reforma 481-A, 06500 Mexico DF, Mexico

Ediciones La Rocca+
Talcahuano 467, 1013 Buenos Aires
Tel: (011) 4382 8526 *Fax:* (011) 4384 5774
E-mail: ed-larocca@sinectis.com
Key Personnel
Dir: Alfonso La Rocca

Founded: 1985
Subjects: Law
ISBN Prefix(es): 950-9714; 987-517

San Pablo+
Riobamba 230, 1025 Buenos Aires
Tel: (011) 5555-2400; (011) 555-2401 *Fax:* (011) 5555-2425
E-mail: sobicain@san-pablo.com.ar
Web Site: www.san-pablo.com.ar
Key Personnel
Man Dir: P Arcangel Cadenas
Founded: 1931
Subjects: Biblical Studies, Education, Health, Nutrition, Human Relations, Language Arts, Linguistics, Psychology, Psychiatry, Religion - Catholic, Self-Help, Theology
ISBN Prefix(es): 950-861
Distributed by Paulinas (Brazil); San Pablo (Brazil)
Distributor for San Pablo (Columbia, Chile, Spain)

Editorial Santiago Rueda
Bayaca 51, 1406 Buenos Aires
Tel: (011) 4611-9174
Key Personnel
Man Dir: Enrique S Rueda
Founded: 1940
Subjects: Literature, Literary Criticism, Essays
ISBN Prefix(es): 950-564; 987-98745

Seix Barral+
Av da Independencia 1668, 1100 Buenos Aires
Tel: (011) 4382-4043; (011) 4382-4045; (011) 4381-8285 *Fax:* (011) 4383-3793
E-mail: editorial@seix-barral.es
Web Site: www.seix-barral.es
Key Personnel
General Dir: Guillermo Schavelzon
Founded: 1950
Subjects: Literature, Literary Criticism, Essays
ISBN Prefix(es): 950-742; 950-9216; 950-49

Sigmar, *imprint of* Editorial Sigmar SACI

Editorial Sigmar SACI+
Av Belgrano 1580, 7 Piso, 1089 Buenos Aires
Tel: (011) 4381-2844; (011) 4381-2241 *Fax:* (011) 4383-5633
E-mail: editorial@sigmar.com.ar
Web Site: www.sigmar.com.ar *Cable:* SIGMAR
Key Personnel
President & Man Dir: Robert G Chwat
 E-mail: rchwat@sigmar.com.ar
Founded: 1941
Membership(s): Argentina Book Association.
ISBN Prefix(es): 950-11
Number of titles published annually: 100 Print
Total Titles: 1,200 Print
Imprints: Sigmar
Distributor for Albatros (Argentina & Latin America)

Editorial Sopena Argentina SACI e I
Maza 2138/40, 1240 Buenos Aires
Tel: (011) 4912-2383 *Fax:* (011) 4912-2383
E-mail: edsopena@elsitio.net
Key Personnel
President: Roberto Omar Antonio
Dir: Marta A J Olsen; Leopoldo Costa Urruty
Manager: Hipolito Oscar Dhers
Subjects: Ethnicity, Government, Political Science, Health, Nutrition, History, How-to, Language Arts, Linguistics, Literature, Literary Criticism, Essays
ISBN Prefix(es): 950-542

Editorial Stella
Viamonte 1984, 1056 Buenos Aires
Tel: (011) 4374-0346 *Fax:* (011) 4374-8719
E-mail: admin@editorialstella.com.ar
Web Site: www.editorialstella.com.ar
Founded: 1941
Membership(s): Asociacion Educacionista Argentina.
Subjects: Nonfiction (General)
ISBN Prefix(es): 950-525

Editorial Sudamericana SA+
Division of Random House-Mondadori
Humberto 1º 555, C1103ACK Buenos Aires
Tel: (011) 4300-5400 *Fax:* (011) 4362-7364
E-mail: info@edsudamericana.com.ar
Web Site: www.edsudamericana.com.ar *Cable:* LIBRECOL
Key Personnel
President: Javier Lopez Llovet
Editor: Gloria Lopez Llovet de Rodrigue
Sales Dir: Francisco La Falce
Publicity Dir: Ana Maria Muchnik
Rights & Permissions: Susana Kaluzynski
Founded: 1939
Subjects: Biography, Fiction, History, Literature, Literary Criticism, Essays, Nonfiction (General), Philosophy, Psychology, Psychiatry
ISBN Prefix(es): 950-07; 950-37
Parent Company: Editorial Sudamericana
Associate Companies: Random House-Mondadori, Edificio del Comercio, Momjitas 392, Piso 11 Of. 1101/1102, Comuna de Santiago, Chile *Tel:* (02) 782-8200 *Fax:* (02) 782-8210 *E-mail:* sudchile@edsudamericana.com.ar; Editorial Sudamericana Uraguaya, ConcepcionArenal 1769, 11800 Montevideo, Uruguay *Tel:* (02) 203 3668 *Fax:* (02) 203 3668
Subsidiaries: Editorial Sudamericana Chilena

Theoria SRL Distribuidora y Editora+
Av Rivadavia 1255, Piso 4 407, 1033 Buenos Aires
Tel: (011) 4381-0131 *Fax:* (011) 4381-0131
E-mail: edicionestheoria@ciudad.com.ar
Key Personnel
Man Dir: Jorge O Orus
Sales Dir: Jose Luis Menendez
Founded: 1954
Subjects: Anthropology, Biography, Genealogy, Government, Political Science, History, Literature, Literary Criticism, Essays, Military Science, Religion - Catholic
ISBN Prefix(es): 950-99711; 987-9048

Tipografica Editora Argentina
Lavalle 1430, Piso 1, 1048 Buenos Aires
Tel: (011) 4373-2581 *Fax:* (011) 4775-2521
E-mail: bernardosm@sinectis.com.ar
Key Personnel
President: Pedro G San Martin
Founded: 1946
Subjects: Anthropology, Archaeology, History, Law
ISBN Prefix(es): 950-521

Instituto Torcuato Di Tella
Minones 2177, piso 1, 1428 Buenos Aires
Tel: (011) 4783-8680; (011) 4784-0084 *Fax:* (011) 4783-3061
E-mail: postmaster@itdtar.edu.ar
Web Site: www.itdt.edu *Cable:* INSTELLA BAIRES
Key Personnel
President: Guido Di Tella
Founded: 1958
Subjects: Economics, Government, Political Science, History, Social Sciences, Sociology
ISBN Prefix(es): 950-621

Editorial Troquel SA+
Pichincha 969, 1219 Buenos Aires
Tel: (011) 4308-3638; (011) 4308-3637 *Fax:* (011) 4941-3110
E-mail: info@troquel.com.ar
Web Site: www.troquel.com.ar *Cable:* TROQUELSA
Key Personnel
President: Gustavo Ressia
Founded: 1954
Subjects: Literature, Literary Criticism, Essays, Psychology, Psychiatry, Religion - Other, Technology
ISBN Prefix(es): 950-16

Editorial Universidad SRL+
Rivadavia 1225, 1003 Buenos Aires
Tel: (011) 4382-9022; (011) 4382-6850 *Fax:* (011) 4381-2005
E-mail: univers@nat.com.ar
Web Site: www.nat.com.ar/universidad
Key Personnel
Partner: Raul Caracciolo; Alejandro lo Iacono; Rafael del Buono
Founded: 1970
Membership(s): Camara Argentina del Libro.
Subjects: Economics, Law, Social Sciences, Sociology
ISBN Prefix(es): 950-679; 950-9072
Branch Office(s)
Facultad de Derecho, UBA
Bookshop(s): Talcahuano 487, 1013 Buenos Aires

Universidad Nacional de la Patagonia, see Editoria Universitaria de la Patagonia

Editoria Universitaria de la Patagonia
Ciudad Universitaria Rm 4, Comodoro Rivadavia, 9000 Chubut
Tel: (02967) 428834; (02967) 424969
E-mail: rcesar@unpbib.edu.ar
Key Personnel
Dir: Romeo Cesar
Founded: 1993
Subjects: Agriculture, Biological Sciences, Fiction, Geography, Geology, History, Philosophy
ISBN Prefix(es): 950-763

Javier Vergara Editor SA+
Paseo Colon 221, Piso 6, 1399 Buenos Aires
Tel: (011) 4343-7510; (011) 4343-7706 *Fax:* (011) 4334-0173
E-mail: ediciones-b-arg@ciudad.com.ar
Key Personnel
President: Javier Vergara
Vice President & Rights: Gabriela Cruz de Vergara
Editorial Dir: Trinidad Vergara
Sales Dir: Ricardo Bianchini
Publicity Manager: Marilen Stengel
Founded: 1975
Subjects: Biography, Business, Fiction, History, Music, Dance, Nonfiction (General), Psychology, Psychiatry, Self-Help
ISBN Prefix(es): 950-15
Branch Office(s)
Rancagua 549, Casilla Postale 10471, Santiago, Chile *Tel:* (02) 2049583 *Fax:* (02) 2096929
Carrera 53 A No 81-24, Bodega Entre Rios, Bogota, Colombia *Tel:* (01) 2507297 *Fax:* (01) 2506005
Ctra Boadilla del Monte, KM 5800, Poligono Industrial Ventorro del Cano, 28925 Alcorcon, Madrid, Spain *Tel:* (01) 6332395 *Fax:* (01) 6332312
Kansas 161, Col Ampliacion Napoles, Delegacion Benito Juarez, CP 03840 Mexico, DF, Mexico *Tel:* (05) 6829636 *Fax:* (05) 6829511
Edificio Yolanda Local Norte, Calle Madrid con Av Trieste, California Sur, Estado Miranda, Caracas, Venezuela *Tel:* (02) 228854 *Fax:* (02) 228854
Warehouse: Vieytes 1534, 1275 Buenos Aires

Manrique Zago Ediciones SRL
Av San Martin 7210, 1419 Buenos Aires

Tel: (011) 4382-8880; (011) 4501-1497; (011) 4383-2611 *Fax:* (011) 4502-7937
E-mail: mzago@lvd.com.ar
Key Personnel
Dir: Manrique Zago
Subjects: Art, Ethnicity
ISBN Prefix(es): 950-9517; 987-509

Victor P de Zavalia SA+
Alberti 835, 1223 Buenos Aires
Tel: (011) 942-1274; (011) 942-3046 *Fax:* (011) 942-5706
Key Personnel
Man Dir: Victor H de Zavalia
Sales Dir: Ricardo L de Zavalia
Founded: 1950
Subjects: Law
ISBN Prefix(es): 950-572

Editorial Zeus SRL+
Balcarce 730, Rosario, 2000 Santa Fe
Tel: (0341) 449-5585 *Fax:* (0341) 425-4259
E-mail: editorialzeus@citynet.net.ar
Web Site: www.editorial-zeus.com.ar
Key Personnel
President & Editor: Gustavo Luis Caviglia
Founded: 1970
Subjects: Law
ISBN Prefix(es): 950-664
Imprints: Coleccion Juridica Bco de Datos en Computacion

Armenia

General Information

Capital: Yerevan
Language: Armenian (officially) and Kurdish
Religion: Predominantly Christian (Armenian Apostolic Church)
Population: 3.4 million
Bank Hours: Generally open for short hours between 0930-1230 Monday-Friday
Shop Hours: Generally 0900-1800 Monday-Friday; often open weekends
Currency: 100 kopeks = 1 rubl
Export/Import Information: According to Ukrainian quotas and customs duties, companies engaged in trade should register with the Ukraine Ministry of Foreign Economic Relations. Licenses for export and import are also required for trade with Russia.

Ajstan Publishers+
Isaakjana 28, 37509 Erevan
Tel: (01) 528520
Key Personnel
Dir: D M Sarkissian
Editor in Chief: V K Sanbekian
Founded: 1921
Subjects: Agriculture, Government, Political Science, Law, Literature, Literary Criticism, Essays, Military Science, Science (General)
ISBN Prefix(es): 5-540

Arevik (Little Sun)+
Terjan Str 91, 375009 Erevan
Tel: (02) 524561 *Fax:* (02) 520536
E-mail: arevikp@freenet.am; arevick@netsys.am
Web Site: www.arevik.am
Key Personnel
President: David Hovhannes
Founded: 1986
Membership(s): Armenian Publishers' Association.
Subjects: Chemistry, Chemical Engineering, Crafts, Games, Hobbies, Education, English as a Second Language, Fiction, Gardening, Plants, Geography, Geology, History, Humor, Language Arts, Linguistics, Mathematics, Natural History, Poetry, Science Fiction, Fantasy
ISBN Prefix(es): 5-8077
Number of titles published annually: 28 Print
Total Titles: 2,000 Print

Australia

General Information

Capital: Canberra
Language: English
Religion: Predominantly Christian
Population: 17.6 million
Bank Hours: 1000-1500 Monday-Thursday; 1000-1700 Friday
Shop Hours: 0900-1700 Monday-Saturday
Currency: 100 cents = 1 Australian dollar
Export/Import Information: No tariffs on books. Most books, especially of literary or educational nature, free of sales tax. No import licenses for books; no seditious literature permitted.
Copyright: UCC, Berne (see Copyright Conventions, pg xi)

ABC Books (Australian Broadcasting Corporation)+
GPO Box 9994, Sydney, NSW 2001
Tel: (02) 8333 3959 *Fax:* (02) 8333 3999
E-mail: abcbooks@abc.net.au
Web Site: abcshop.com.au
Key Personnel
General Manager: Grahame Grassby
Publisher: Stuart Neal *E-mail:* neal.stuart@abc.net.au
Subjects: Fiction, Nonfiction (General)
ISBN Prefix(es): 0-7333
Number of titles published annually: 95 Print; 50 Audio
Parent Company: ABC Enterprises
Ultimate Parent Company: Australian Broadcasting Corporation
Distributed by Allen & Unwin Pty Ltd
Orders to: Allen & Unwin Pty Ltd, 83 Alexander St, Crows Nest, NSW 2065, Liz Bray *Tel:* (02) 8425 0100 *Fax:* (02) 9906 2218 *E-mail:* frontdesk@allen-unwin.net.au

Aboriginal Studies Press+
GPO Box 553, Canberra, ACT 2601
Tel: (02) 6246 1226 *Fax:* (02) 6261 4285
E-mail: sales@aiatsis.gov.au
Web Site: www.aiatsis.gov.au
Key Personnel
Principal: Steve Larkin
Dir, ASP: Rhonda Black *E-mail:* rhonda.black@aiatsis.gov.au
Deputy Dir ASP: Gabby Lhuede
Subjects: Anthropology, Archaeology, Art, Biography, Biological Sciences, Education, Ethnicity, History, Language Arts, Linguistics, Music, Dance, Regional Interests
ISBN Prefix(es): 0-85575
Parent Company: Australian Institute of Aboriginal & Torres Strait Islander Studies

Academic Press, *imprint of* Elsevier Australia

Access Press, *imprint of* Access Press

Access Press+
PO Box 446, Bassendean, WA 6054
Tel: (08) 9379 3188 *Fax:* (08) 9379 3199
Key Personnel
Publicity & Rights & Permission: John Harper-Nelson
Founded: 1978
Standard publishing contract but also specialize in small print runs privately funded.
Subjects: Biography, Genealogy, History, Literature, Literary Criticism, Essays, Nonfiction (General), Poetry
ISBN Prefix(es): 0-949795
Number of titles published annually: 14 Print
Total Titles: 90 Print
Parent Company: Reeve Pty Ltd as trustee for Reeve Unit Trust
Ultimate Parent Company: Reeve Etc
Imprints: Access Press

ACER Press+
347 Camberwell Rd, Camberwell, Victoria 3124
Tel: (03) 9277 5555; (03) 9835 7447 (customer service) *Toll Free Tel:* (800) 338 402 (customer service) *Fax:* (03) 9277 5500; (02) 9835 7499 (customer service)
E-mail: sales@acer.edu.au
Web Site: www.acer.edu.au
Key Personnel
Man Ed: Joy Whitton
Publishing Manager: Anne Peterson
Founded: 1930
Subjects: Education, Human Relations, Psychology, Psychiatry
ISBN Prefix(es): 0-86431; 0-85563
Parent Company: Australian Council for Educational Research, 19 Prospect Hill Rd, Private Bag 55, Camberwell, Victoria 3124
Distributed by Stylus Publishing (USA)

ACHPER Inc (Australian Council for Health, Physical Education & Recreation)
214 Port Rd, Hindmarsh, SA 5007
Mailing Address: PO Box 304, Hindmarsh, SA 5007
Tel: (08) 8340 3388 *Fax:* (08) 8340 3399
E-mail: achper@achper.org.au
Web Site: www.achper.org.au
Key Personnel
Executive Dir: Jeff Emmel
National President: Dr Colvin
National Vice President: Ms Sheehan
Contact: Felicity Vanderheul
E-mail: membership@achper.org.au
Founded: 1955
Specialize in Community Fitness & Movement Sciences, Dance, Health Education, Physical Education, Recreation, Sports.
Subjects: Education, Sports, Athletics
ISBN Prefix(es): 0-909120; 0-9595612; 1-86352
Branch Office(s)
73 Wakefield St, 1st floor, Adelaide, SA 5000, Matt Schmidt *E-mail:* info@achpersa.com.au
PO Box 57, Claremont, WA 6010, Denyse Passmore *E-mail:* denyse@achperwa.asn.au
PO Box 84, Croydon, NSW 2132, Julie Percival *E-mail:* achperns@ozemail.com.au
PO Box 789, Jamieson, ACT 2614, Jodie Sindeberry *E-mail:* ihellyer@dynoamite.com.au
C1-117 Canning St, Launceston, Tas 7250, Peter Daniel
GPO BOX 412C, Melbourne, Victoria 3001, Mary Wilson *E-mail:* achvic@unite.com.au
PO Box 8141, Woolloongabba, Qld 4102, Jill Duffield *E-mail:* achqld@ecn.net.au
Bookshop(s): Achper Healthy Lifestyles Bookshop, Emma Price *E-mail:* bookshop@achper.org.au

Acorn Press, *imprint of* Rainbow Book Agencies Pty Ltd

ACP Publishing Pty Ltd+
54-58 Park St, Sydney, NSW 1028
Tel: (02) 9282 8000 *Fax:* (02) 9267 4361
Web Site: www.acp.com.au
Key Personnel
Publisher: Richard Walsh
Subjects: Cookery

PUBLISHERS

AUSTRALIA

ISBN Prefix(es): 0-949892; 1-86396; 0-949128; 0-9598059
Parent Company: Australian Consolidated Press
Imprints: The Australian Women's Weekly; Home Library
Branch Office(s)
Arnoul Media Services Pty Ltd, 45 Ward St, North Adelaide, SA 5006 *Tel:* (08) 8361 9999 *Fax:* (08) 8361 9990
Bowengate Office Park, 2nd floor, Corner Bowen Bridge Rd & Campbell St, Bowen Hills, Qld 4006 *Tel:* (07) 3000 8500 *Fax:* (07) 3000 8555
73 Atherton Rd, Oakleigh, Victoria 3166 *Tel:* (03) 9567 4200 *Fax:* (03) 9563 4554
102-108 Toorak Rd, South Yarra, Victoria 3141 *Tel:* (03) 9823 6333 *Fax:* (03) 9823 6300
Foreign Rep(s): Melanie Franklin (Asia & the Pacific, Europe, USA); Christian Hyland (Asia & the Pacific, Europe, USA); Michael Sport (Asia & the Pacific, Europe, USA)

Addison Wesley, *imprint of* Pearson Education Australia

The Advancement Centre
9 Brett Ave, Wentworthville, NSW 2145
Tel: (02) 9896 2311 *Fax:* (02) 9368 323
Subjects: Education, Psychology, Psychiatry
ISBN Prefix(es): 0-9586212
Distributed by University of NSW

Aeolian Press
PO Box 303, Claremont, WA 6010
Tel: (08) 9761 2772 *Fax:* (08) 9761 4151
Founded: 1985
Subjects: Art, Poetry, Australian Art, Italian Classic Text & Illustration
ISBN Prefix(es): 1-875306
Distributor for Edizioni Tallone (Australia); Edizioni Valdonega (Australia)

Aerospace Publications Pty Ltd
PO Box 1777, Fyshwick, ACT 2609
Tel: (02) 6280 0111 *Fax:* (02) 6280 0007
E-mail: mail@ausaviation.com.au
Web Site: www.ausaviation.com.au
Subjects: Aeronautics, Aviation
ISBN Prefix(es): 0-9587978; 1-875671

AHB Publications+
24/14 Lansell Rd, Toorak, Victoria 3142
Subjects: Foreign Countries
Distributor for Random House (Australia)

AIFS, see Australian Institute of Family Studies (AIFS)

Aletheia Publishing
18 Willow St, Albany Creek, Qld 4035
Tel: (07) 3855 2056
E-mail: aletheia@powerup.com.au
Key Personnel
Contact: David Holden
Founded: 1992
Subjects: Biblical Studies, History, Religion - Protestant, Religion - Other, Theology
ISBN Prefix(es): 0-9587113; 0-9578052
Total Titles: 3 Print

Allen & Unwin Pty Ltd+
83 Alexander St, Crows Nest, NSW 2065
Mailing Address: PO Box 8500, St Leonards, NSW 1590
Tel: (02) 8425 0100 *Fax:* (02) 9906 2218
E-mail: frontdesk@allenandunwin.com
Web Site: www.allenandunwin.com
Key Personnel
Man & Publishing Dir: Patrick Gallagher
Sales & Marketing Dir: Paul Donovan
Rights & Export Manager: Angela Namoi
Head of Publicity: Andrew Hawkins
Finance & Distribution Dir: Peter Eichorn
National Sales Manager: Lou Johnson
Children's Publishing Dir: Rosalind Price
Academic Publisher: Elizabeth Weiss
Academic & Professional Marketing Manager: Carolyn Crowther
Founded: 1976
Membership(s): Australian Publishers Association (APA); Publish Australia (PA); Australian Multimedia Industry Association (AMIA).
Subjects: Alternative, Art, Asian Studies, Behavioral Sciences, Business, Cookery, Earth Sciences, Economics, Education, Ethnicity, Fiction, Gay & Lesbian, Government, Political Science, Health, Nutrition, History, Labor, Industrial Relations, Literature, Literary Criticism, Essays, Nonfiction (General), Science (General)
ISBN Prefix(es): 1-86448; 1-86508; 1-74114
Number of titles published annually: 250 Print
Subsidiaries: Osborne House
Branch Office(s)
406 Albert St, East Melbourne, Victoria
One John St, Kingswood, Adelaide, SA
One Park Rd, Milton, Brisbane 4064
Distributor for Osborne House
Warehouse: ADS, PO Box 520, 9 Pioneer Ave, Tuggerah, NSW 2259 *Tel:* (02) 43901300 *Fax:* (02) 43901333
Orders to: ADS, PO Box 520, 9 Pioneer Ave, Tuggerah, NSW 2259 *Tel:* (02) 43901300 *Fax:* (02) 43901333

AMCS, see Australian Marine Conservation Society Inc (AMCS)

AMPCO, see Australasian Medical Publishing Company Ltd (AMPCO)

Anchor, *imprint of* Random House Australia

Anchor, *imprint of* Transworld Publishers Pty Ltd

Robert Andersen & Associates Pty Ltd+
433 Wellington St, Clifton Hill, Melbourne, Victoria 3068
Tel: (03) 9489 3968 *Fax:* (03) 9482 2416
E-mail: 100357.354@compuserve.com
Key Personnel
Man Dir: Bob Andersen
Subjects: Education
ISBN Prefix(es): 0-949133

Anderson, *imprint of* Random House Australia

Michelle Anderson Publishing+
PO Box 6032, Chapel St N, South Yarra, Victoria 3141
Tel: (03) 9826 9028 *Fax:* (03) 9826 8552
E-mail: mapubl@bigpond.net.au
Web Site: www.michelleandersonpublishing.com
Key Personnel
Publisher, Rights & Permissions: Michelle Anderson
Founded: 1965
Membership(s): Australian Publishers Association.
Subjects: Health, Nutrition, Philosophy, Psychology, Psychiatry, Babies & Motherhood, Bushwalking, Cycling
ISBN Prefix(es): 0-85572
Number of titles published annually: 15 Print
Total Titles: 70 Print
Distributed by Bookwise International (Australia); Deep Books UK (UK); Peter Hyde & Associates (South Africa)
Foreign Rep(s): Choicemaker (Korea); Prava: Provida (Russia); Lennart Sane (Sweden)
Foreign Rights: Thomas Schluck (Germany); Susan Schulman (USA)
Warehouse: Matrae P/L, 568 Geelong Rd, West Footscray, Melbourne, Victoria

Angel Publications
5 Lithgow St, Goulburn, NSW 2580
Tel: (02) 4821 1463
Key Personnel
Contact: Steven Shackel *E-mail:* shack@goulburn.net.au
Founded: 1982
Subjects: Astrology, Occult, Fiction, Parapsychology, Philosophy, Self-Help
ISBN Prefix(es): 0-9593419

Ansay Pty Ltd+
19-25 Beeson St, Leichhardt, NSW 2040
Mailing Address: PO Box 90, Leichhardt, NSW 2040
Tel: (02) 5602044 *Fax:* (02) 5694585
Key Personnel
Man Dir: Philip Lindsay
Editorial, Production & Publicity: H E Lindsay
Sales, Rights & Permissions: P S Lindsay
Founded: 1972
Subjects: Education, Fiction
ISBN Prefix(es): 0-909245
Parent Company: A L Lindsay & Co Pty Ltd
Imprints: Dollar Books

Anzea Publishers Ltd+
3-5 Richmond Rd, Homebush West, NSW 2140
Tel: (02) 7631211 *Fax:* (02) 7643201
Key Personnel
Head of Company: Jeffrey Blair
Subjects: Religion - Other
ISBN Prefix(es): 0-85892
Imprints: Lancer; Scripture Union
Divisions: Boronia Book Agencies; Emu Book Agencies; Waverley House

APACE, see Appropriate Technology Development Group (Inc) WA

APACE Aid Inc, *imprint of* Appropriate Technology Development Group (Inc) WA

Appropriate Technology Development Group (Inc) WA
One Johannah St, North Fremantle, WA 6159
Tel: (08) 9336 1262 *Fax:* (08) 9430 5729
E-mail: apace@argo.net.au
Web Site: www.argo.net.au/apace
Key Personnel
President: Richard Cooke
Coordinator: Tony Freeman
Founded: 1983
Not for profit community group - environmental.
Subjects: Alternative, Environmental Studies, Technology, Appropriate Technology, Bush Regeneration, Revegetation
ISBN Prefix(es): 0-9590309
Number of titles published annually: 5 Print
Associate Companies: Apace Aid Inc
Imprints: APACE Aid Inc

Aquila Press
Anglican Youthworks, Level 2, St Andrews House, 464 Kent St, Sydney South, NSW 1235
Mailing Address: PO Box A287, Sydney South, NSW 1235
Tel: (02) 8268 3333 *Fax:* (02) 8268 3357
E-mail: sales@youthworks.asn.au
Web Site: www.youthworks.net.au
Key Personnel
Chief Executive Officer: Alan Stewart
Founded: 1994
Subjects: Biblical Studies, Religion - Protestant
ISBN Prefix(es): 1-875861
Parent Company: Anglican Press Australia
Imprints: Christian Education Publications

Arcadia, *imprint of* Australian Scholarly Publishing

Argyle-Pacific, *imprint of* Austed Publishing Co

Edward Arnold (Australia) Pty Ltd+
12 Strathalbyn St, Kew East, Victoria 3102
Mailing Address: PO Box 885, Kew, Victoria 3101
Tel: (03) 9859 9011 *Fax:* (03) 9859 9141
Key Personnel
Man Dir: Malcolm Edwards
General Manager: R Bartlett
Publishing: Anita Ray
Production: Jane Hazell
Marketing: Penny Doust
Tertiary: Louise Cook
Founded: 1966
Acts as agent for Edward Arnold (UK), Taylor & Francis & Blackie & Sons (secondary only).
Membership(s): Australian Book Publishers Association.
Subjects: Accounting, Asian Studies, Behavioral Sciences, Career Development, Computer Science, Cookery, Geography, Geology, Government, Political Science, Health, Nutrition, Law, Mathematics, Nonfiction (General), Psychology, Psychiatry, Technology
ISBN Prefix(es): 0-7131; 0-7267
Parent Company: Hodder & Stoughton (Australia) Pty Ltd
Ultimate Parent Company: Hodder & Stoughton Ltd, United Kingdom
Warehouse: Hodder & Stoughton Pty Ltd, 10-16 South St, Rydalmere, NSW 2116
Orders to: Hodder & Stoughton (Australia) Pty Ltd, PO Box 386, Rydalmere, NSW 2116

Arrow, *imprint of* Random House Australia

Art Gallery of South Australia Bookshop
North Terrace, Adelaide, SA 5000
Tel: (08) 8207 7029 *Fax:* (08) 8207 7069
E-mail: agsa.bookshop@saugov.sa.gov.au
Web Site: www.artgallery.sa.gov.au
Key Personnel
Head of Company: Ron Radford
Bookshop Manager: Letitia Ashworth
   E-mail: ashworth.letitia@saugov.sa.gov.au
Subjects: Art
ISBN Prefix(es): 0-7308

Art Gallery of Western Australia+
Perth Cultural Centre, 47 James St, Perth, WA 6000
Mailing Address: Perth Business Centre, PO Box 8363, Perth, WA 6849
Tel: (08) 9492 6600 *Fax:* (08) 9492 6655
E-mail: admin@artgallery.wa.gov.au
Web Site: www.artgallery.wa.gov.au
Key Personnel
Dir: Alan R Dodge
Chief Curator: Gary Dufour
Dir, Strategic & Commercial Programs: Keith Lord
Manager Information Services: Joyce Carter
   Tel: (08) 9492 6622
Founded: 1895
Exhibition catalogues.
Subjects: Art
ISBN Prefix(es): 0-7309; 0-7244; 0-7307
Total Titles: 22 Print

Art on the Move
GPO Box M937, Perth, WA 6000
Tel: (08) 9227 7505 *Fax:* (08) 9227 5304
E-mail: artmoves@highway1.com.au
Key Personnel
Dir: Paul Thompson
Founded: 1996

Subjects: Architecture & Interior Design, Art, Marketing
ISBN Prefix(es): 0-9585326; 0-9578242; 0-9581859

Artemis Publishing, *imprint of* Rainbow Book Agencies Pty Ltd

Artmoves Inc+
27 Burwood Ave, Hawthorn East, Victoria 3123
Tel: (03) 9882 8116 *Fax:* (03) 9882 8162
E-mail: artmoves@bigpond.com
Key Personnel
Contact: Helen Vivian
Founded: 1987
Subjects: Art, History, Women's Studies
ISBN Prefix(es): 0-646

Ashling Books+
26 Hewlett Court, Florey, ACT 2615
Tel: (02) 6259 1027
Key Personnel
Man Dir & International Rights: Edward J Murtagh
Founded: 1992
Subjects: Fiction, How-to, Poetry, Religion - Catholic, Self-Help
ISBN Prefix(es): 0-9585244

Ashton Egan, *imprint of* Egan Publishing Pty Ltd

Ashwood House, *imprint of* Dellasta Publishing

Ashwood House Medical, *imprint of* Dellasta Publishing

Athena Press+
PO Box 1497, Potts Point, NSW 2011
Tel: (02) 9357 3720 *Fax:* (02) 9357 3720
Key Personnel
Contact: Dr Marlene J Norst
Subjects: Biography, Ethnicity, History
ISBN Prefix(es): 0-9587113

Auslib Press Pty Ltd+
PO Box 622, Blackwood, SA 5051
Tel: (08) 8278 4363 *Fax:* (08) 8278 4000
E-mail: info@auslib.com.au
Web Site: www.auslib.com.au
Key Personnel
Man Dir: Judith Bundy
Editorial & Sales Manager: Dr Alan Bundy
Founded: 1984
Specialize in Library & Information Science Titles, Information Literacy Titles, Literary Directories, Mailing Labels for Australian & New Zealand Libraries.
Subjects: Education, Library & Information Sciences
ISBN Prefix(es): 1-875145; 0-9589895
Number of titles published annually: 4 Print
Total Titles: 47 Print

Ausmed Publications Pty Ltd+
275-277 Mt Alexander Rd, Ascot Vale, Victoria 3032
Mailing Address: PO Box 4086, Parksville, Victoria 3052
Tel: (03) 9375 7311 *Fax:* (03) 9375 7299
E-mail: ausmed@ausmed.com.au
Web Site: www.ausmed.com.au
Key Personnel
Head of Company & Dir: Cynthea Wellings
   E-mail: cwelling@ausmed.com.au
General Manager: Natalie Angove
   E-mail: nangove@ausmed.com.au
Man Editor: Bernadette Keane *E-mail:* bkeane@ausmed.com.au
Founded: 1987

Specialize in books & conferences for nurses & other workers in related health fields.
Subjects: Behavioral Sciences, Ethnicity, Health, Nutrition, Medicine, Nursing, Dentistry, Social Sciences, Sociology, Allied Health, Clinical Issues
ISBN Prefix(es): 0-9587113; 0-646; 0-9587171
Total Titles: 24 Print

Aussie Books
Unit 6, 30 Lensworth St, Coopers Plains, Qld 4108
Mailing Address: PO Box 383, Archerfield, Qld 4108
Tel: (07) 3345 4253 *Fax:* (07) 3344 1582
E-mail: sildale@yahoo.com
Web Site: www.treasureenterprises.com
Key Personnel
Dir: David A Cooper
Founded: 1977
Supplier of Detection & Treasure Hunting Equipment.
Subjects: Earth Sciences, Geography, Geology, History
ISBN Prefix(es): 0-947336
Parent Company: Sildale Pty Ltd
Distributor for Hesperian Press

Aussies Afire Publishing
PO Box 954, Port Macquarie, NSW 2444
Tel: (02) 6581 0654 *Fax:* (02) 6581 0745
Web Site: www.gracechurchpm.org.au
Key Personnel
Head of Company: Kerry Medway
   E-mail: kerry@gracechurchpm.org.au
Founded: 1989
Subjects: Humor, Regional Interests, Religion - Protestant
ISBN Prefix(es): 0-646
Number of titles published annually: 1 Print
Total Titles: 5 Print

Austed Publishing Co+
PO Box 8025, Subiaco East, WA 6008
Tel: (08) 9203 6044 *Fax:* (08) 9203 6055
E-mail: net@austed.com.au
Web Site: www.austed.com.au
Key Personnel
Man Dir: W B R Banks
Head of Company: K Chesson *E-mail:* kc@austed.com.au
Founded: 1983
Subjects: Accounting, Animals, Pets, Education, Fiction, Mathematics
ISBN Prefix(es): 1-86307; 0-9592597
Imprints: Argyle-Pacific; Churchill House

Australasian Medical Publishing Company Ltd (AMPCO)+
26-32 Pyrmont Bridge Rd, Level 2, Pyrmont, NSW 2009
Mailing Address: Locked Bag 3030, Strawberry Hills, NSW 2012
Tel: (02) 9562 6666 *Fax:* (02) 9562 6699
E-mail: medjaust@ampco.com.au
Web Site: www.mja.com.au
Key Personnel
Chief Executive: Dr Martin Van Der Weyden
Advertising Manager: Peter Butterfield
Media Coordinator: Stephanie Elliott
Founded: 1913
Publisher of *The Medical Journal of Australia* & *Medical Directory of Australia*.
Distributor of medical publications.
Membership(s): ABP, commercial & publishing arm of the Australian Medical Association.
Subjects: History, Medicine, Nursing, Dentistry
ISBN Prefix(es): 0-85557
Parent Company: Australian Medical Association Limited

Australasian Textiles & Fashion Publishers
19-21 Broadbeach Rd, Jan Juc, Victoria 3228

PUBLISHERS AUSTRALIA

Mailing Address: PO Box 286, Belmont, Victoria 3216
Tel: (03) 5261 3966 *Fax:* (03) 5261 6950
Web Site: www.atfmag.com
Key Personnel
Publisher: Rosemary Boston *E-mail:* roseboston@atfmag.com
Dir: Stan Boston *E-mail:* sboston@atfmag.com
Managing Editor: James Boston
Associate Editor: Jack Finlay *E-mail:* jfinlay@atfmag.com
Subjects: Fashion, Textiles
ISBN Prefix(es): 0-9590875

Australian Academic Press Pty Ltd+
32 Jeays St, Bowen Hills, Qld 4006
Tel: (07) 3257 1176 *Fax:* (07) 3252 5908
E-mail: info@australianacademicpress.com.au
Web Site: www.australianacademicpress.com.au
Key Personnel
Man Dir: Stephen May
Founded: 1987
Specialize in book production; also acts as book packager. Independent publisher for the behavioral sciences.
Subjects: Behavioral Sciences, Psychology, Psychiatry
ISBN Prefix(es): 1-875378

Australian Academy of Science
Ian Potter House, Gordon St, Canberra, ACT 2601
Mailing Address: GPO Box 783, Canberra, ACT 2601
Tel: (02) 6247 5777 *Fax:* (02) 6257 4620
E-mail: eb@science.org.au; aas@science.org.au
Web Site: www.science.org.au
Key Personnel
Publications: Maureen Swanage *E-mail:* maureen.swanage@science.org.au
Founded: 1956
Subjects: Biological Sciences, Chemistry, Chemical Engineering, Environmental Studies, Geography, Geology, Mathematics
ISBN Prefix(es): 0-85847

Australian Association for the Study of Religion, *imprint of* Rainbow Book Agencies Pty Ltd

Australian Broadcasting Authority
Darling Park, Level 15, 201 Sussex St, Sydney, NSW 2000
Mailing Address: PO Box Q500, Queen Victoria Bldg, Sydney, NSW 1230
Tel: (02) 9344 7700 *Toll Free Tel:* 800 22 6667 (Australia only) *Fax:* (02) 9334 7799
E-mail: info@aba.gov.au
Web Site: www.aba.gov.au
Key Personnel
Chairman: Prof David Flint
Publisher: Anne Hewer
Manager Media & Public Relations: Donald Robertson
Founded: 1992
Subjects: Communications, Broadcasting
ISBN Prefix(es): 0-642
Branch Office(s)
Blue Bldg, Benjamin Offices, Chan St, Belconnen, Canberra, ACT 2617 *Tel:* (02) 6256 2800 *Fax:* (02) 6253 3277

Australian Broadcasting Corporation, see ABC Books (Australian Broadcasting Corporation)

Australian Chart Book Pty Ltd
PO Box 148, Turramurra, NSW 2074
Tel: (02) 9489 4786 *Fax:* (02) 9487 2089
Web Site: www.austchartbook.com.au
Key Personnel
Contact: David Kent *E-mail:* davidkent@austchartbook.com.au
Founded: 1970

Australian Film Television & Radio School
Corner Epping & Balaclava Roads, North Ryde, NSW 2113
Mailing Address: PO Box 126, North Ryde, NSW 1670
Tel: (02) 9805 6611 *Fax:* (02) 9805 1275
E-mail: info_nsw@aftrs.edu.au
Web Site: www.aftrs.edu.au
Key Personnel
Publisher & Training Officer: Meredith Quinn *E-mail:* meredith.quinn@syd.aftrs.edu.au
Founded: 1973
Subjects: Film, Video, Radio, TV
ISBN Prefix(es): 1-876351
Branch Office(s)
5 Trumpeter St, Battery Point, Tas 7004, Representative: Craig Kirkwood *Tel:* (03) 6223 8703 *Fax:* (03) 6224 6143 *E-mail:* info_tas@aftrs.edu.au
Judith Wright Centre of Contemporary Arts, Centre Brunswick & Berwick St, Level 2, PO Box 1480, Fortitude Valley, Qld 4006, Manager: Alex Daw *Tel:* (07) 3257 7646 *Fax:* (07) 3257 7641 *E-mail:* info_qld@aftrs.edu.au
92 Adelaide St, Fremantle, WA 6160, Tom Lubin *Tel:* (08) 9335 1055 *Fax:* (08) 9335 1283 *E-mail:* info_wa@aftrs.edu.au
SAFS Studios, 3 Butler Dr, Hendon, SA 5014, Representative: Ann Walton *Tel:* (08) 8244 0357 *Fax:* (08) 8244 5608 *E-mail:* info_sa@aftrs.edu.au
144 Moray St, 1st floor, PO Box 1008, South Melbourne, Victoria 3205, Manager: Simon Britton *Tel:* (03) 9690 7111 *Fax:* (03) 9690 1283 *E-mail:* info_vic@aftrs.edu.au
Distributed by Allen & Unwin

Australian Institute of Criminology
74 Leichhardt St, Griffith, ACT 2603
Mailing Address: GPO Box 2944, Caberra, ACT 2601
Tel: (02) 6260 9200 *Fax:* (02) 6260 9201
E-mail: aicpress@aic.gov.au
Web Site: www.aic.gov.au
Key Personnel
Acting Dir: Dr Toni Makkai *Tel:* (02) 6260 9205 *E-mail:* toni.makkai@aic.gov.au
Executive Officer, Research: Leanne Huddy *Tel:* (02) 6260 9255 *E-mail:* leanne.huddy@aic.gov.au
Founded: 1976
Subjects: Criminology
ISBN Prefix(es): 0-642
U.S. Office(s): Criminal Justice Press, PO Box 249, Monsey, NY 10952, United States
Orders to: CanPrint Information Services, PO Box 7456, Canberra MC, ACT 2610 *Toll Free Tel:* 300 889 873 *Fax:* (02) 6293 8333 *E-mail:* sales@infoservices.com.au

Australian Institute of Family Studies (AIFS)
300 Queen St, Melbourne, Victoria 3000
Tel: (03) 9214 7888 *Fax:* (03) 9214 7839
E-mail: publications@aifs.org.au
Web Site: www.aifs.org.au
Key Personnel
Marketing Manager: Catherine Rosenbrock *Tel:* (03) 9214 7804 *E-mail:* cathr@aifs.org.au
Founded: 1980
Undertake research & factors affecting family stability & well-being; Australian government statutory authority.
Subjects: Behavioral Sciences, Criminology, Disability, Special Needs, Economics, Human Relations, Social Sciences, Sociology, Women's Studies
ISBN Prefix(es): 0-642; 1-876513

Number of titles published annually: 3 Print; 1 CD-ROM
Total Titles: 12 Print; 4 CD-ROM

Australian Large Print Pty Ltd, see Bolinda Publishing Pty Ltd

Australian Marine Conservation Society Inc (AMCS)
PO Box 3139, Yeronga, Qld 4104
Tel: (07) 3848 5235 *Toll Free Tel:* 800 066 299 *Fax:* (07) 3892 5814
E-mail: amcs@amcs.org.au
Web Site: www.amcs.org.au
Key Personnel
Dir: E J Hegerl
National Coordinator: Kate Davey *E-mail:* katedavey@amcs.org.au
Subjects: Biological Sciences, Earth Sciences, Environmental Studies, Geography, Geology, Maritime, Natural History
Branch Office(s)
c/o Conservation Council of South Australia, 120 Wakefield St, Adelaide, SA 5000, Contact: John Emmett *Tel:* (08) 8223 5155 *E-mail:* affadavid@hotmail.com
Penneshaw, Kangaroo Island, SA 5222, Contact: John Lavers *Tel:* (08) 8553 1072 *E-mail:* echidna@kin.net.au
PO Box 2415, Fitzroy, Victoria 3065, Contact: Michelle Barret-Dean *E-mail:* amcsmelbourne@hotmail.com.au
PO Box 404, Wynnum, Qld 4178, Contact: Michael Lusis *Tel:* (07) 3822 6824 *E-mail:* lusisfam@bigpond.com.au
2 Delhi St, City West Lotteries House, West Perth, WA 6005, Secretary: Dennis Beros *Tel:* (08) 9420 7209 *Fax:* (08) 9486 7833 *E-mail:* amcswa@iinet.net.au
Great Oceans Rd, Victoria, Contact: Terry Gunn *Tel:* (03) 5263 1392

Australian National University Press, *imprint of* A S Wilson Inc

Australian Rock Art Research Association
3 Buxton St, Elsternwick, Victoria 3185
Mailing Address: PO Box 216, Caulfield South, Victoria 3162
Tel: (03) 9523 0549 *Fax:* (03) 9523 0549
E-mail: auraweb@hotmail.com
Web Site: mc2.vicnet.net.au/home/aura/web/index.html
Key Personnel
Dir & International Rights: Robert Bednarik *E-mail:* robertbednarik@hotmail.com
Founded: 1983
Books, Periodicals, Academic Textbooks & Conference Proceedings.
Subjects: Anthropology, Archaeology, Art
ISBN Prefix(es): 0-646
Number of titles published annually: 3 Print
Distributed by Piedra Pintada Books (USA); ANH Publications (Australia)

Australian Scholarly, *imprint of* Australian Scholarly Publishing

Australian Scholarly Publishing+
PO Box 299, Kew, Victoria 3101
Tel: (03) 98175208 *Fax:* (03) 8176431
E-mail: aspic@ozemail.com.au
Key Personnel
Publisher: Nicholas Walker
Senior Editor: Dr Diane Carlyle
Founded: 1991
Subjects: Environmental Studies, Geography, Geology, Government, Political Science, History, Nonfiction (General), Publishing & Book Trade Reference, Social Sciences, Sociology, Wine & Spirits
ISBN Prefix(es): 1-875606

AUSTRALIA

Imprints: Arcadia; Australian Scholarly
Distribution Center: Kirby Book Co, 7 Help St, Suite 704, Chatswood, NSW 2064

The Australian Women's Weekly, *imprint of* ACP Publishing Pty Ltd

Australia's Best Garden Guide Series, *imprint of* Hyland House Publishing Pty Ltd

Autonomous Learning Publications & Specialists, *imprint of* Hawker Brownlow

Avon, *imprint of* Random House Australia

Axiom Publishers & Distributors
One Union St, Unit 2, Stepney, SA 5069
Tel: (08) 83627052 *Fax:* (08) 83629430
E-mail: axiompub@camtech.net.au
Key Personnel
Contact: John Gallehawk
ISBN Prefix(es): 0-947338; 0-9594164; 1-86476

Babel Handbooks, *imprint of* Nimrod Publications

Babysitters Club, *imprint of* Scholastic Australia Pty Ltd

Bahloo Publishers Real-Life Education, *imprint of* R J Cleary Publishing

Ballantine, *imprint of* Random House Australia

Bandicoot Books
PO Box 373, Margate, Tas 7054
Tel: (03) 6267 2530 *Fax:* (03) 6267 1223
Web Site: www.bandicootbooks.com
Key Personnel
Contact: Marion Isham *E-mail:* ishams@ozemail.com.au
Subjects: Animals, Pets, Fiction, Foreign Countries, History, Language Arts, Linguistics, Mysteries, Poetry
ISBN Prefix(es): 0-9586536
Distributed by Roots & Wings Books (US & Canada)

Bantam Books, *imprint of* Random House Australia

Bantam, *imprint of* Transworld Publishers Pty Ltd

Bay Books, *imprint of* Murdoch Books

Bayda Books
PO Box 178, East Brunswick, Victoria 3057
Tel: (0613) 9387-2799 *Fax:* (0613) 9387-2799
Web Site: www.bayda.com.au
Key Personnel
Manager: Yuri Tkacz *E-mail:* ytkacz@bigpond.net.au
Founded: 1976
Specialize in books in Russian & Ukrainian. Also acts as mail order book supplier & library supplier.
Total Titles: 11 Print; 3 Audio
Distributor for Lastivka Press

Joycelyn Bayne
2 Lee St, Fulham Gardens, SA 5024
Mailing Address: PO Box 59, Brooklyn Park, SA 5022
Tel: (08) 8356 1748
Subjects: History
ISBN Prefix(es): 0-7316

BBC Worldwide, *imprint of* Random House Australia

Beazer Publishing Company Pty Ltd
PO Box 150, Paynesville, Victoria 3880
Tel: (03) 5156 0556 *Fax:* (03) 5156 0556
E-mail: info@beazerpublishing.com
Web Site: www.beazerpublishing.com
Key Personnel
Contact: Margaret Beazer
Founded: 1994
Subjects: Earth Sciences, Environmental Studies, Law, Science (General)
ISBN Prefix(es): 1-876435
Total Titles: 8 Print; 1 Audio

BEC Publications, *imprint of* Hawker Brownlow

Barbara Beckett Publishing Pty Ltd
14 Hargrave St, Paddington, NSW 2021
Tel: (02) 93312871 *Fax:* (02) 93603106
Key Personnel
Publisher: Barbara Beckett
Founded: 1994
Subjects: Art, Cookery
ISBN Prefix(es): 1-875891
Book Club(s): Doubleday Australia

Bellcourt Books
63 Gray St, Hamilton, Victoria 3300
SAN: 902-4646
Tel: (03) 5572 1310 *Fax:* (03) 5572 1310
E-mail: bellcourt@ansonic.com.au
Key Personnel
Contact: Guy Stephens
Founded: 1983
Independent bookshop.

Beri Publishing+
36 Alfred Rd, Burwood, Victoria 3125
Tel: (03) 9809 1434 *Fax:* (03) 9809 1434
E-mail: beripub@ozemail.com.au
Key Personnel
Head of Company: Nola Schlegel
Founded: 1991
Subjects: Education
ISBN Prefix(es): 0-9587113; 0-646; 0-9577233

Bernal Publishing+
4 Frank St, Box Hill South, Victoria 3128
Tel: (0613) 9808-3775 *Fax:* (0613) 9888-7572
E-mail: sales@bernalpublishing.com
Web Site: www.bernalpublishing.com
Key Personnel
Man Editor: Robert Martin
Founded: 1991
Subjects: Agriculture, Biography, History, Non-fiction (General), Farming (Commercial Chick Sexing)
ISBN Prefix(es): 0-646

Robert Berthold Photography
11 Wolfe Rd, North Ryde, NSW 2113
Tel: (02) 9887 3986 *Fax:* (02) 9887 3986
Key Personnel
Head of Company: Robert Berthold
Subjects: Biological Sciences, Environmental Studies, Maritime, Natural History, Outdoor Recreation, Photography, Physics, Science (General), Sports, Athletics
ISBN Prefix(es): 0-646

Better Homes & Gardens, *imprint of* Murdoch Books

Beyond Bullying Association, *imprint of* Rainbow Book Agencies Pty Ltd

Bible Society in Australia National Headquarters+
30 York Rd, Ingleburn, NSW 2565
Tel: (02) 9829 9001 *Fax:* (02) 9829 9020
E-mail: customer.service@bible.org.au; sdadm@boble.org.au
Web Site: www.biblesociety.com.au
Key Personnel
Marketing Manager: Gregory N Page
E-mail: greg.page@bbla.org.au
Founded: 1817
Specialize in Bibles & related publications.
Membership(s): United Bible Societies.
Subjects: Biblical Studies, Religion - Catholic, Religion - Protestant, Theology
ISBN Prefix(es): 0-647
Bookshop(s): 2-6 Albert St, Blackburn, Victoria 3130 *Tel:* (03) 9877 9233 *Fax:* (03) 9877 8399; 212 Main St, Lilydale, Victoria 3140 *Tel:* (03) 9735 0410 *Fax:* (03) 9735 2013; Locked Bag 3, Minto, NSW 2566 *Fax:* (02) 9829 4685 *E-mail:* bsdirect@bible.org.au; 95 Bathurst St, Sydney, NSW 2000 *Tel:* (02) 9267 6862 *Fax:* (02) 9267 7415 *E-mail:* shop@biblesociety.com.au

Bio Concepts Publishing
Unit 9/783 Kingsford Smith Dr, Eagle Farm, Qld 4009
Mailing Address: PO Box 1492, Eagle Farm, Qld 4009
Tel: (07) 3868-0699 *Fax:* (07) 3868-0600
E-mail: info@bioconcepts.com.au
Web Site: www.bioconcepts.com.au
Key Personnel
President: Henry Osiecki
Sales Manager: Mary Waldie
Subjects: Alternative, Health, Nutrition, Self-Help, Sports, Athletics
ISBN Prefix(es): 1-875239

Birchgrove Books
18 Louisa Rd, Birchgrove, NSW 2041
Tel: (02) 9810 5040 *Fax:* (02) 9810 6053
E-mail: 100406.343@compuserve.com
ISBN Prefix(es): 0-646

Black Dog Books+
15 Gertrude St, Fitzroy, Victoria 3065
Tel: (03) 9419 9406 *Fax:* (03) 9419 1214
E-mail: dog@bdb.com.au
Web Site: www.bdb.com.au
Key Personnel
Contact: Andrew Kelly *E-mail:* andrew@bdb.com.au
ISBN Prefix(es): 1-876372

Black Swan, *imprint of* Random House Australia

Black Swan, *imprint of* Transworld Publishers Pty Ltd

Blackbooks Co-operative for Aborigines Ltd
11-13 Mansfield St, Glebe, NSW 2037
Tel: (0612) 9660 2396 *Fax:* (0612) 9660 1924
E-mail: tranby@tranby.com.au
Web Site: www.tranby.com.au
Key Personnel
Head of Company: Kevin Cook
Founded: 1982
Specialize in Aboriginal & Torres Strait Islands.
Orders to: Allbooks Distribution, 16 Darghan St, Glebe, NSW 2037

Blackstone, *imprint of* Pascoe Publishing Pty Ltd

Blackstone Press Pty Ltd
500 Oxford St, 18th floor, Bondi Junction, NSW 2022
Tel: (02) 9389 7677
E-mail: c.l.e.@laams.com.au

PUBLISHERS AUSTRALIA

Subjects: Law
ISBN Prefix(es): 1-875114

Blackwell Publishing Asia+
Formerly Blackwell Scientific Publications (Australia) Pty Ltd
550 Swanston St, Carlton South, Victoria 3053
Mailing Address: PO Box 378, Carlton South, Victoria 3053
Tel: (03) 8359 1011 *Fax:* (03) 8359 1120
E-mail: info@blackwellpublishingasia.com.au
Web Site: www.blacksci.co.uk
Key Personnel
Chief Executive, Man Dir: Mark Robertson
Marketing & Operations Dir: Neil Walsh
Publishing & Finance Dir: Jane Watson
Customer Service: Robert Turner
Founded: 1971
Subjects: Computer Science, Earth Sciences, Engineering (General), Mathematics, Medicine, Nursing, Dentistry, Physical Sciences, Physics, Psychology, Psychiatry, Science (General)
ISBN Prefix(es): 0-86793
Parent Company: Blackwell Science Ltd, United Kingdom
Subsidiaries: Blackwell Science KK
U.S. Office(s): Blackwell Publishing Inc, Commerce Pl, 350 Main St, Malden, MA 02148, United States *Tel:* 781-388-8200 *Fax:* 781-388-8210
Distributor for American Society for Microbiology; American Psychiatric Press Inc; Garland Publishers; Jones & Bartlett; Springer Verlag (Australia & New Zealand only)
Warehouse: 26 Albert St, Brunswick, Victoria 3056

Blackwell Scientific Publications (Australia) Pty Ltd, see Blackwell Publishing Asia

Horst Blaich Pty Ltd
24 John St, Bayswater, Victoria 3153
Tel: (03) 9720 2658 *Fax:* (03) 9762 4225
ISBN Prefix(es): 1-86347

Joan Blair
15 Antrim St, Kiama, NSW 2533
Mailing Address: PO Box 432, Kiama, NSW 2533
Tel: (02) 4232 1642
Key Personnel
Author & Publisher: Joan Blair
Founded: 1986
Subjects: Human Relations, Self-Help
ISBN Prefix(es): 1-86252
Distributed by ROSE Education & Training (Australia)

Bloomings, *imprint of* Bloomings Books

Bloomings Books+
7 Newry St, Richmond, Victoria 3121
Tel: (03) 9427 1234 *Fax:* (03) 9427 9066
E-mail: sales@bloomings.com.au
Web Site: www.bloomings.com.au
Key Personnel
Publisher: Warwick Forge *E-mail:* warwick@bloomings.com.au
Founded: 1994
Publish, distribute & wholesale horticulture & natural history books.
Subjects: Gardening, Plants, Natural History
ISBN Prefix(es): 1-876473
Total Titles: 12 Print
Imprints: Bloomings; Rodale; Timber

Blubber Head Press
81 Salamanca Place, 1st floor, Hobart Tasmania 7000
Mailing Address: PO Box 475, Sandy Bay, Tas 7006

Tel: (03) 6223 8644 *Fax:* (03) 6223 8644
E-mail: books@astrolabebooks.com.au
Web Site: www.astrolabebooks.com.au
Key Personnel
Proprietor: Michael Sprod *E-mail:* michael@astrolabebooks.com.au
Founded: 1978
Subjects: History, Regional Interests, Travel
ISBN Prefix(es): 0-908528
Bookshop(s): Astrolabe Antiquarian Booksellers, 81 Salamanca Place, 1st floor, Hobart, Tasmania 7004

Board of Studies
117 Clarence St, Sydney, NSW 2000
Mailing Address: GPO Box 5300, Sydney, NSW 2001
Tel: (02) 9367 8111 *Fax:* (02) 9367 8484
E-mail: customerliason@boardofstudies.nsw.edu.au
Web Site: www.boardofstudies.nsw.edu.au
Key Personnel
President: Prof Gordon Stanley *Tel:* (02) 9367 8176
General Manager: Dr John Bennett *Tel:* (02) 9367 8169
Membership(s): NSW Government Dept.
Subjects: Education
ISBN Prefix(es): 0-7305; 0-7310

Boat Books Group
31 Albany St, Crows Nest, NSW 2065
Tel: (02) 94391133 *Fax:* (02) 94398517
E-mail: boatbook@boatbooks-aus.com.au
Key Personnel
Contact: Philip Brook
Founded: 1973
Subjects: Nautical Titles (recreational & professional)
Branch Office(s)
Brisbane *E-mail:* boatbks@bluesky.net.au
Melbourne *E-mail:* boatbks@ozemail.com.au

Boinkie Publishers
PO Box 27, Brighton-Le-Sands, NSW 2216
Tel: (02) 588-7010 *Fax:* (02) 9311-3428
ISBN Prefix(es): 0-9587468

Bolinda, *imprint of* Bolinda Publishing Pty Ltd

Bolinda Audio, *imprint of* Bolinda Publishing Pty Ltd

Bolinda Press, *imprint of* Bolinda Publishing Pty Ltd

Bolinda Publishing Pty Ltd+
Formerly Australian Large Print Pty Ltd
17 Mohr St, Tullamarine, Victoria 3043
Tel: (03) 9338 0666 *Fax:* (03) 9335 1903
Web Site: www.bolinda.com
Key Personnel
Dir: Philip Walshe
Marketing Manager: Rebecca Walshe
Founded: 1985
Specialize in unabridged audio books & large-print publishing.
Subjects: Disability, Special Needs, Fiction, Non-fiction (General)
ISBN Prefix(es): 0-947072; 1-86340; 1-74030; 1-876584; 1-74093; 1-74094
Number of titles published annually: 12 Print; 120 Audio
Imprints: Bolinda; Bolinda Audio; Bolinda Press
U.S. Office(s): Bolinda Publishing Inc, PO Box 307, Shelton, CT 06484, United States *Tel:* 203-924-2434 *Fax:* 203-924-2599 *E-mail:* usa@bolinda.com
Distributor for Center Point Publishing; Clipper Audio; Clipper Large Print; Mills & Boon; Thorndike Press

Herbert Bolles
130 Warks Hill Rd, Kurrajong Heights, NSW 2758
Tel: (02) 4567 7350 *Fax:* (02) 4567 7350
E-mail: bolles@pnc.com.au
ISBN Prefix(es): 0-646

Boobook Publications
PO Box 238, Tea Gardens, NSW 2324
Tel: (049) 97 0811 *Fax:* (049) 97 1089
Key Personnel
Head of Company: Ian Hoyle; Sally Hoyle
Founded: 1981
Subjects: Sports, Athletics
ISBN Prefix(es): 0-908121

Book Agencies of Tasmania+
5 Cleve Court, Howrah, Tas 7018
Mailing Address: PO Box 327, Rosny Park, Tas 7018
Tel: (03) 6247 7405 *Fax:* (03) 6247 1116
E-mail: bookagencies@trump.net.au
Key Personnel
Manager: Graeme Thurlow
Founded: 1982
Subjects: Regional Interests
Number of titles published annually: 2 Print
Total Titles: 15 Print

Book Collectors' Society of Australia
678 Victoria Rd, Unit 150, Ryde, NSW 2112
Tel: (02) 9807 5489 *Fax:* (02) 9807 5489
Key Personnel
President: Neil Radford
Secretary: Jeff Bidgood *E-mail:* bidgood@bigpond.net.au
Founded: 1944
ISBN Prefix(es): 0-646; 0-9586761; 0-9587263; 0-9589220
Number of titles published annually: 5 Print

The Book Company Publishing Pty Ltd
Austlink Corporate Park, One Minna Close, Belrose, Sydney, NSW 2085
Tel: (02) 94863711 *Fax:* (02) 94863722
E-mail: sales@thebookcompany.com.au
Web Site: www.thebookcompany.com.au
Key Personnel
Chief Operating Officer: Andrew G Steele-Smith *Tel:* (0402) 214 218 *E-mail:* andrewss@thebookcompany.com.au
Publisher: Glenn Johnstone
Founded: 1986
Specialize in innovative childrens' novelty books & adult stationery items.
Number of titles published annually: 200 Print

Book Lures Inc, *imprint of* Hawker Brownlow

Bookman Health
Level 9, Trak Centre, 443-449 Toorak Rd, Toorak, Victoria 3142
Tel: (03) 9521 3250 *Toll Free Tel:* 800 060 555 *Fax:* (03) 9826 1744
E-mail: sales@bookman.com.au
Web Site: www.bookman.com.au

Books & Writers, *imprint of* Wild & Woolley

Boolarong Press
35 Hamilton Rd, Moorooka, Qld 4105
Mailing Address: PO Box 308, Moorooka, Qld 4105
Tel: (07) 3848 8200 *Fax:* (07) 3848 8077
Key Personnel
Head of Company: Lester Padman
General Manager, Sales & Publicity: R J Keirnan
Editorial: M Weaver
Production: C L Padman

AUSTRALIA

Founded: 1977
Subjects: Art, Biography, Business, History, Management, Nonfiction (General)
ISBN Prefix(es): 0-86439; 0-908175
Parent Company: Artists Associated Pty Ltd

Boombana Publications+
PO Box 118, Mount Nebo, Qld 4520
Tel: (07) 3289 8106 *Fax:* (07) 3289 8107
Web Site: www.boombanapublications.com
Key Personnel
Contact: Jean-Claude Lacherez *E-mail:* j.lacherez@uq.net.au
Founded: 1992
Subjects: Language Arts, Linguistics, Literature, Literary Criticism, Essays, Nonfiction (General)
ISBN Prefix(es): 0-9586685

M J Bowen
18 Ranfurlie Drive, Glen Waverley, Victoria 3150
Tel: (03) 9561 3425 *Fax:* (03) 9882 9405
Key Personnel
Dir: M J Bowen
ISBN Prefix(es): 0-7316

Boxtree, *imprint of* Pan Macmillan Australia Pty Ltd

David Boyce Publishing+
44 Regent St, Redfern, NSW 2016
Tel: (02) 6997484
Key Personnel
Owner, Publisher & Sales Dir: David Boyce
  E-mail: david@boyces.com
Founded: 1975
Specialize in automotive manuals for workshops & software.
Subjects: Automotive, Technology
ISBN Prefix(es): 0-909682
Distributor for Robert Bosch

Louis Braille Audio
31-51 Commercial Rd, South Yarra, Victoria 3141
Mailing Address: PO Box 860, Hawthorn, Victoria 3122
Tel: (03) 9864 9645 *Fax:* (03) 9864 9646
E-mail: lba.sales@visionaustralia.org.au
Web Site: www.louisbrailleaudio.com
Key Personnel
Managing Dir: Rose Blustein *E-mail:* rose.blustein@visionaustralia.org.au
Publishing & Rights Manager: Edwina Kenrick
  Tel: (03) 9864 9615 *E-mail:* edwina.kenrick@visionaustralia.org.au
Founded: 1993
Subjects: Biography, Fiction, History, Travel
ISBN Prefix(es): 0-7320; 0-86764
Total Titles: 258 Print; 258 Audio
Parent Company: Vision Australia Foundation Library
Ultimate Parent Company: Vision Australia Foundation

Bridge To Peace Publications+
149 Dartford Rd, Thornleigh, NSW 2120
Tel: (02) 9875 1912
E-mail: books@bridgetopeace.com.au; adesso@bridgetopeace.com.au
Web Site: www.bridgetopeace.com.au
Key Personnel
General Manager: Jim Scarano
Founded: 1997
Specialize in internet e-mail orders for all books published.
Subjects: Alternative, History, How-to, Human Relations, Nonfiction (General), Philosophy, Psychology, Psychiatry, Self-Help, Alexander Technique, Italian Culture, Yoga, Meditation & Personal Development

ISBN Prefix(es): 0-9587094; 0-9577615; 0-9581323; 0-9752107
Subsidiaries: Adesso Studio
Branch Office(s)
Paul Laccona, 341 Farleigh Terrace, Marietta, GA 30068, United States

Bridgeway Publications+
12 Christina Pl, Belmont, Qld 4153
Mailing Address: GPO Box 2547, Brisbane, Qld 4001
Tel: (07) 3390 4323 *Fax:* (07) 3390 4323
E-mail: info@bridgeway.org.au
Web Site: www.bridgeway.org.au
Key Personnel
Executive Dir: Don Fleming
  E-mail: donfleming@bridgeway.org.au
Founded: 1988
Non-profit organization which sends sponsored Christian reference materials to churches & institutions in needy countries.
Subjects: Biblical Studies, Religion - Protestant, Theology
ISBN Prefix(es): 0-947342
Total Titles: 15 Print
Distributed by AMG Publishers (USA); Copperbelt Christian Publications (Zambia); Horizon Publishers (India); Riverside World Inc (USA)
Shipping Address: Harvest Products, PO Box 108, Upper Gravatt, Qld 4122, Contact: Gordon Cowell *Tel:* (07) 3849 1812 *Fax:* (07) 3849 1820 *E-mail:* harvest@tpgi.com.au
Warehouse: Harvest Products, PO Box 108, Upper Gravatt, Qld 4122, Contact: Gordon Cowell *Tel:* (07) 3849 1812 *Fax:* (07) 3849 1820 *E-mail:* harvest@tpgi.com.au
Orders to: Harvest Products, PO Box 108, Upper Gravatt, Qld 4122, Contact: Gordon Cowell *Tel:* (07) 3849 1812 *Fax:* (07) 3849 1820 *E-mail:* harvest@tpgi.com.au

E J Brill, Robert Brown & Associates+
Formerly Robert Brown & Associates Australia Pty Ltd
154 Bentinck St, Bathhurst, NSW 2795
Tel: (063) 318577 *Fax:* (063) 321273
Key Personnel
Man Editor: Robert Brown
Subjects: Natural History, Travel
ISBN Prefix(es): 0-949267; 0-909197; 1-86173; 1-86273
Total Titles: 24 Print

R A Broadberh, *imprint of* Universal Press Pty Ltd

Broadway Books, *imprint of* Random House Australia

Broadway Dela Corte, *imprint of* Transworld Publishers Pty Ltd

Brookfield Press
871 Upper Brookfield Rd, Upper Brookfield, Qld 4069
Mailing Address: PO Box 738, Kenmore, Qld 4069
Tel: (07) 3374 1053 *Fax:* (07) 3374 2059
Key Personnel
Dir: Frank Stacey *E-mail:* frank.stacey@csiro.au
Subjects: Earth Sciences, Geography, Geology, Physics

Brooks Waterloo, *imprint of* John Wiley & Sons Australia, Ltd

Budget Books Pty Ltd, see Reed for Kids

Bureau of Resource Sciences
PO Box E11, Kingston, ACT 2604

Tel: (02) 6272 4282 *Fax:* (02) 6272 4747
Key Personnel
Dir: Ian Lambert *E-mail:* ian@mailpc.brs.gov.au
Subjects: Agriculture, Biological Sciences, Science (General), Veterinary Science
ISBN Prefix(es): 0-642; 0-644

Butterworths Australia Ltd
Member of The LexisNexis Group
Tower 2, 475-495 Victoria Ave, Chatswood, NSW 2067
Mailing Address: Level 9, Locked Bag 2222, Chatswood Delivery Centre, Chatswood NSW 2067
Tel: (02) 9422 2189 *Toll Free Tel:* 800 772 772
  Fax: (02) 9422 2406
E-mail: orders@butterworths.com.au; customer.relations@lexisnexis.com.au
Web Site: www.butterworths.com.au
Key Personnel
CEO & Man Dir: Tony Kinnear
Publishing Dir: James Broadfoot
Finance Dir: Philip Cauwood
Sales & Marketing Dir: Catherine Yeomans
Human Resources Manager: Rachel Sutton
Founded: 1910
A division of Reed International Books Australia Pty Ltd (ABN 7000 1002 357).
Subjects: Accounting, Business, Law
ISBN Prefix(es): 0-409
Parent Company: Reed Elsevier Australia Pty Ltd
Ultimate Parent Company: Reed Elsevier plc, 25 Victoria St, London SW1H 0EX, United Kingdom
Associate Companies: Butterworth & Co (Publishers) Ltd UK; Butterworth Publishers (Pty) Ltd, South Africa; Butterworths Canada Ltd; Butterworth & Co (Asia) Pte Ltd, India; Butterworths (Ireland) Ltd; Butterworths Asia, Singapore; Butterworths of New Zealand Ltd; Guiffre Editore SpA, Italy; Editions du Juris-Classeur, France; Malayan Law Journal Sdn Bhd, Malaysia; Wydawnictwa Prawnicze PWN, Poland; Verlag Stampfli, Switzerland; Lexis-Nexis USA
Branch Office(s)
St George Centre, 60 Marcus Clarke St, Canberra, ACT 2600
Adelaide Chambers, 122 Pirie St, Adelaide, SA 5000
461 Bourke St, Melbourne, Victoria 3000
44 St George's Terrace, Perth, WA 6000
286 Montague Rd, West End, Qld 4101

Cairns Art Society Inc
PO Box 992, Cairns, Qld 4870
Tel: (07) 4039 1122
E-mail: cas@internetnorth.com.au
Key Personnel
President: Mr K Ryan
Founded: 1931
ISBN Prefix(es): 0-7316

Cambridge University Press
477 Williamstown Rd, Port Melbourne, Victoria 3207
Mailing Address: Private Bag 31, Port Melbourne, Victoria 3207
Tel: (03) 8671 1400 *Fax:* (03) 9676 9966
E-mail: info@cambridge.edu.au; customerservice@cambridge.edu.au
Web Site: www.cambridge.edu.au
Key Personnel
Dir: Kim Harris
Subjects: Education
ISBN Prefix(es): 0-521
Parent Company: Cambridge University Press, United Kingdom

PUBLISHERS — AUSTRALIA

U.S. Office(s): Cambridge University Press, 40 W 20 St, New York, New York, NY 10011-4211, United States
Distributor for Currency Press (Australia); Stanford University Press (Australia & New Zealand)

Rod Campbell Books, *imprint of* Pan Macmillan Australia Pty Ltd

Canadian Conference of Catholic Bishops, *imprint of* Rainbow Book Agencies Pty Ltd

Candlelight Trust T/A Candlelight Farm
Box 1125, Midland Business Centre, WA 6936
Tel: (08) 92944141 *Fax:* (08) 92944141
Key Personnel
Editorial Manager: Ross Mars *E-mail:* rossmars@yahoo.com
Subjects: Agriculture, Education, Environmental Studies, Gardening, Plants
ISBN Prefix(es): 0-9587626
Total Titles: 4 Print

Jonathon Cape, *imprint of* Random House Australia

Captain Jonas Publications
Rosslyn Crannog, Mail Service 60, Mackay, Qld 4740
Tel: (07) 4956 5022 *Fax:* (07) 4956 2633
E-mail: aarfw@ozemail.com.au
Key Personnel
Manager: Anthony G Wheeler

Carter's (Antiques & Collectibles) P/L
PO Box 7246, Baulkham Hills BC, NSW 2153
Tel: (02) 8850 4600 *Fax:* (02) 8850 4100
E-mail: info@carters.com.au
Web Site: www.carters.com.au
Key Personnel
Contact: Trent McVey *E-mail:* trent@carters.com.au
Founded: 1980
Subjects: Antiques, Collectibles
ISBN Prefix(es): 1-876079
Number of titles published annually: 2 Print
Total Titles: 2 Print
Subsidiaries: Carter's Publications - New Zealand Ltd

Casket Publications
Macquarie University, NSW 2109
Tel: (02) 9805 8878; (02) 9481 9145 *Fax:* (02) 9875 5382
Key Personnel
Contact: Prof D B Waterson
Founded: 1992
Self publishing: research tools. Queensland political biographical retailers.
Subjects: Biography, History
ISBN Prefix(es): 0-646
Total Titles: 2 Print
Branch Office(s)
20 Angophora Place, Pennant Hills, Sydney, NSW 2120 *Tel:* 9481 9145 *Fax:* 9875 5382

Cassel PLC, *imprint of* Hawker Brownlow

Catchfire Press Inc
PO Box 2101, Dangar, NSW 2309
Tel: (02) 4951 8859
E-mail: catchfire@idl.com.au
Web Site: www.cust.idl.com.au/catchfire
Key Personnel
Convenor: Zenovia Doratis
Treasurer: Jackie Jools

Catholic Institute of Sydney+
99 Albert Rd, Strathfield, NSW 2135
Tel: (02) 9752 9500 *Fax:* (02) 9746 6022
E-mail: cisinfo@cis.catholic.edu.au
Web Site: www.cis.catholic.edu.au
Key Personnel
President: Rev Dr Gerard Kelly *Tel:* (02) 9752 9510
Subjects: Biblical Studies, History, Philosophy, Religion - Catholic, Theology
ISBN Prefix(es): 0-908224

Cavendish Publishing, *imprint of* Cavendish Publishing Pty Ltd

Cavendish Publishing Pty Ltd+
45 Beach St, Coogee, NSW 2034
Tel: (02) 9664 0909 *Fax:* (02) 9664 5420
E-mail: info@cavendishpublishing.com
Web Site: www.cavendishpublishing.com.au
Key Personnel
Chief Executive Officer: Mr Sonny Leong *Tel:* (020) 7278 8000 *E-mail:* sonnyleong@cavendishpublishing.com
Specialize in Law & Medicine.
Subjects: Law, Medicine, Nursing, Dentistry
ISBN Prefix(es): 1-85941; 1-876213; 1-876905
Total Titles: 400 Print
Ultimate Parent Company: Cavendish Publishing Ltd, The Glass House, Wharton St, London WC1X 9PX, United Kingdom
Imprints: Cavendish Publishing

Centenary of Technical Education in Bairnsdale Group
32 Grant St, Bairnsdale, Victoria 3875
Tel: (03) 5152-4556
Key Personnel
Editorial Manager: Lorna Prendergast
Subjects: History
ISBN Prefix(es): 0-9587113

Centre for Comparative Literature & Cultural Studies
Monash University, Clayton Campus, Clayton, Victoria 3168
Tel: (03) 9905 4000; (03) 9905 3059 *Fax:* (03) 9905 4007
Web Site: www.arts.monash.edu/au/cclcs
Key Personnel
Editorial Manager: C G Worth *E-mail:* chris.worth@arts.monash.edu.au
Subjects: Ethnicity, Literature, Literary Criticism, Essays
ISBN Prefix(es): 0-7326; 0-86746; 0-909835

Centre for Creative Learning, *imprint of* Hawker Brownlow

Centre Publications+
PO Box 359, Warwick, Qld 4370
Tel: (03) 8700149
Key Personnel
Man Dir: Robert Snow
Founded: 1974
Subjects: Education, Health, Nutrition
ISBN Prefix(es): 0-909698
Associate Companies: THE Foundation; The Yoga Education Centre, 226 Moggill Rd, Taringa, Qld 4068

Century, *imprint of* Random House Australia

Chalkface Press Pty Ltd+
PO Box 23, Cottesloe, Perth, WA 6011
Tel: (08) 9385 1923 *Fax:* (08) 9385 1923
E-mail: info@chalkface.net.au; sales@wooldridges.com.au (orders)
Web Site: www.chalkface.net.au
Key Personnel
Dir: Bronwyn Mellor; Stephen Mellor
Founded: 1987
Membership(s): Australian Publishers Association.
ISBN Prefix(es): 1-875136
Distributed by English & Media Centre (UK)
Distributor for English & Media Centre (UK)
Foreign Rep(s): Gould Media (USA)

Channel 4, *imprint of* Pan Macmillan Australia Pty Ltd

Chapter & Verse, *imprint of* Wellington Lane Press Pty Ltd

Chatto & Windus, *imprint of* Random House Australia

Childerset Publishers+
16 Tunba Court, Cooroy, Qld 4563
Mailing Address: PO Box 1107, Noosaville DC 4566
Tel: (074) 425510 *Fax:* (074) 425512
E-mail: tessgsp@ozemail.com.au
Key Personnel
Man Dir: David Ridyard
Founded: 1970
ISBN Prefix(es): 0-909405; 0-949130

China Books
234 Swanston St, 2nd Floor, Melbourne, Victoria 3000
Tel: (03) 9663 8822 *Fax:* (03) 9663 8821
E-mail: info@chinabooks.com.au
Web Site: www.chinabooks.com.au
Key Personnel
Man Dir: Ian Fox; Tony McGlinchey
Founded: 1989
Book importer, wholesaler & retailer/specialist.
Subjects: Asian Studies, Language Arts, Linguistics, China, Chinese Studies
ISBN Prefix(es): 0-646
Bookshop(s): 81 Enmore Rd, Enmore, NSW 2042 *Tel:* (02) 9557 2701 *Fax:* (02) 9661 8727 *E-mail:* chinabooks@hotkey.net.au

Chingchic Publishers
83 River Walk Ave, Robina, Qld 4226
E-mail: chingchic@winshop.com.au
Web Site: www.chingchic.com
Key Personnel
Proprietor: Judy Eather
Manager, Author & Historian: Charles E Eather
Founded: 1993
Subjects: Aeronautics, Aviation
ISBN Prefix(es): 0-646; 0-9586746; 0-949756
Total Titles: 2 CD-ROM

Chiron Media
PO Box 6069, Mooloolah, Qld 4553
Tel: (074) 947311 *Fax:* (074) 947890
E-mail: chiron@acslink.net.au
Key Personnel
Contact: Helen Penridge
Founded: 1990
Subjects: Animals, Pets, Environmental Studies, Government, Political Science, Public Administration, Veterinary Science
ISBN Prefix(es): 0-9586784
Parent Company: Penridge Information Pty Ltd

CHOICE Magazine+
57 Carrington Rd, Marrickville, NSW 2204
Tel: (02) 9577 3399 *Fax:* (02) 9577 3377
E-mail: ausconsumer@choice.com.au
Web Site: www.choice.com.au
Key Personnel
Publisher: Keren Lavelle
General Manager: Norm Crothers

AUSTRALIA

Founded: 1960
Membership(s): Australian Publishers' Association, Publish Australia.
Subjects: Architecture & Interior Design, Automotive, Health, Nutrition, House & Home, Self-Help, Travel
ISBN Prefix(es): 0-947277; 0-9591120; 0-9596536; 1-920705
Parent Company: Australian Consumers' Association

Christian Education Publications, imprint of Aquila Press

Christian Literature Crusade
Division of CLC Publications
125 New Rd, West Pennant Hills, NSW 2120
Tel: (02) 9875 1330 Fax: (02) 9481 8304
Key Personnel
Contact: K T Ridley
ISBN Prefix(es): 0-9595552
U.S. Office(s): PO Box 1449, Fort Washington, PA 19034-8449, United States

Christian Research Association, imprint of Rainbow Book Agencies Pty Ltd

Church Archivists Press
PO Box 130, Virginia, Qld 4014
Tel: (07) 3865 0466 Fax: (07) 3865 0458
Key Personnel
Dir: Leo J Ansell E-mail: ANSELL@staff.nudgee.com
Founded: 1980 (Known as Church Archives Society Press until 1992)
Subjects: Biography, Computer Science, Genealogy, History, Poetry, Theology
ISBN Prefix(es): 1-876194
Total Titles: 75 Print

Churchill House, imprint of Austed Publishing Co

Churchill Livingstone, imprint of Elsevier Australia

CIS Publishers
22 Salmon St, Port Melbourne, Victoria 3027
Tel: (03) 92467131 Fax: (03) 3470175
E-mail: samone.underwood@reeducation.com.au
Key Personnel
Man Dir: Elio Guarnuccio
Subjects: Education
ISBN Prefix(es): 0-949919; 1-875633; 1-86391; 1-74070

Classroom Magazine, imprint of Scholastic Australia Pty Ltd

R J Cleary Publishing+
PO Box 939, Darlinghurst, NSW 2010
Tel: (02) 2643750
Key Personnel
Man Dir: R J Cleary
Founded: 1969
Subjects: Film, Video, Regional Interests
ISBN Prefix(es): 0-85567
Imprints: Bahloo Publishers Real-Life Education; Education; Success Education

Cole Publications
5 Cooba St, Canterbury, Victoria 3126
Tel: (03) 9830 4242 Fax: (03) 9830 4242
Key Personnel
Head of Company: Merron Cullum
Editorial Manager: Cole Turnley
Founded: 1868
Subjects: Humor

ISBN Prefix(es): 0-909900
Parent Company: Alterns Pty Ltd

Commonwealth Scientific & Industrial Research Organisation, see CSIRO Publishing (Commonwealth Scientific & Industrial Research Organisation)

Companion Travel Guide Books+
19 Kilmorey St, Busby, NSW 2168
Tel: (02) 9608-1169 Fax: (02) 9608-1169
E-mail: 6LEI937764@aol.com
Key Personnel
International Rights: G R Leitner
Founded: 1990
Subjects: Travel, Latin America
ISBN Prefix(es): 0-646; 0-9587498
Distributed by Hunter Publishing Inc (USA, Canada, Central America, Caribbean)

Constitutional Publishing Co Pty Ltd
622 Hay St, Perth, WA 6000
Mailing Address: GPO Box D152, Perth, WA 6001
Tel: (08) 9421 6216 Fax: (08) 9221 1572
Key Personnel
Customer Service: Roger L Day
ISBN Prefix(es): 0-646

Cookery Book
31 Albany St, Crows Nest, NSW 2065
Tel: (02) 9439 3144 Fax: (02) 9439 3405
E-mail: answers@cookerybook.com.au
Web Site: www.cookerybook.com.au
Key Personnel
Man Dir: John T Ivimey
Founded: 1985
Australia's only exclusive distributor of cookery books for the professional chef & the home cook.
Subjects: Cookery, Wine & Spirits, Culinary Arts
Total Titles: 3,200 Print
Parent Company: Ivimey & Associates Pty Ltd
Branch Office(s)
9 Axon St, Subiaco, WA 6008, Jennie Ivimey
Tel: (08) 9382 2122 Fax: (08) 9381 3256

Coolabah Publishing
5 Coolabah Close, Tamworth, NSW 2340
Tel: (02) 6766 4420 Fax: (02) 6766 1058
E-mail: narnia@mpx.com.au
Key Personnel
International Rights: Patrick O'Connor
Founded: 1991
Subjects: Education, Aboriginal
ISBN Prefix(es): 1-876400

Corgi, imprint of Random House Australia

Corgi, imprint of Transworld Publishers Pty Ltd

Cornford Press
6 Salisbury Crescent, Launceston, Tas 7250
Tel: (03) 6331 9658 Fax: (03) 6331 9658
E-mail: info@cornfordpress.com
Web Site: www.cornfordpress.com
Key Personnel
Managing Editor: Tim Thorne
Founded: 1989
Subjects: Biography, Poetry, Travel
ISBN Prefix(es): 0-9577565; 0-9581960
Number of titles published annually: 3 Print
Total Titles: 10 Print
Distributor for CACTI

Cornucopia Press
PO Box 27, Subiaco, WA 6008
Tel: (08) 9388 1965 Fax: (09) 3817341
E-mail: cornucop@aoi.com.au

Key Personnel
Principal: David Noel
Founded: 1982
Subjects: Agriculture, Gardening, Plants, Trees, Tree Crops, Useful Horticulture
ISBN Prefix(es): 0-9593205; 0-947260
Imprints: R*O*D Books
Subsidiaries: Personal Publishing Press Services
Showroom(s): Tree Crops Centre, 208 Nicholson Rd, Subiaco, WA 6008

Coronet, imprint of Hodder Headline Australia

Covenanter Press
159 Bourke St, Dapto, NSW 2530
Mailing Address: PO Box 636, Lithgow, NSW 2790
Tel: (02) 4257 9188 Fax: (02) 6351 4611
Web Site: www.covenanterpress.com.au
Key Personnel
Sales Manager: Don Burgess E-mail: don.burgess@prc.org.au
Founded: 1967
Publisher of Christian books.
Subjects: History, Religion - Protestant, Theology
ISBN Prefix(es): 0-908189
Number of titles published annually: 2 Print
Total Titles: 50 Print
Parent Company: Presbyterian Reformed Church of Australia

Craftsman House, imprint of Fine Art Publishing Pty Ltd

Crawford House Publishing Pty Ltd+
PO Box 50, Belair, SA 5052
Tel: (08) 8370 0300; (08) 8370 3555 (orders)
Fax: (08) 8370 0344; (08) 8370 3566 (orders)
Web Site: www.crawfordhouse.com.au
Key Personnel
Man Dir: Anthony L Crawford
E-mail: tonycraw@bigpond.net.au
Editorial Manager: David H Barrett
E-mail: chpdavid@chp.com.au
Secretary: Jennifer Crawford E-mail: frontdesk@chp.com.au
Founded: 1989
Subjects: Anthropology, Asian Studies, Biography, Government, Political Science, History, Maritime, Natural History, Science Fiction, Fantasy, Self-Help, Social Sciences, Sociology, Travel, Wine & Spirits
ISBN Prefix(es): 1-86333
Number of titles published annually: 15 Print
Total Titles: 82 Print
Imprints: Pants on Fire
Distributed by University of Hawaii Press

Creative Learning Consultants, imprint of Hawker Brownlow

Creative Learning Press, imprint of Hawker Brownlow

Crista International+
PO Box 8096, Bundall, Qld 9726
Tel: (07) 5537 2956 Fax: (07) 5537 2956
Key Personnel
Principal: Helen Derrington
Founded: 1994
How-to publishing for consultants & sales professionals.
Subjects: Business, How-to, Marketing, Self-Help
ISBN Prefix(es): 0-9587262

Critical Thinking Press & Software, imprint of Hawker Brownlow

Crossroad Distributors Pty Ltd
9 Euston St, Rydalmere, NSW 2116
Tel: (02) 8845 7744 Fax: (02) 8845 7755

PUBLISHERS

E-mail: custserv@crossroad.com.au
Subjects: Biblical Studies, Child Care & Development, Human Relations, Religion - Protestant, Self-Help, Theology

Crown Publishing Group, *imprint of* Random House Australia

Crystal Publishing+
6 Park St, Saint Kilda, Victoria 3182
Tel: (03) 9525 4549
E-mail: minx@alphalink.com.au
Key Personnel
President: Beryl K Rohan
Founded: 1980
Specialize in Economics & Sociology.
Subjects: Economics, Government, Political Science, Philosophy, Social Sciences, Sociology
ISBN Prefix(es): 0-9593859

CSIRO Publishing (Commonwealth Scientific & Industrial Research Organisation)+
150 Oxford St, Collingwood, Victoria 3066
Mailing Address: PO Box 1139, Collingwood, Victoria 3066
Tel: (03) 9662 7500 *Fax:* (03) 9662 7555
E-mail: publishing@csiro.au
Web Site: www.publish.csiro.au
Telex: 30236
Key Personnel
General Manager: Paul Reekie *Tel:* (03) 9662 7650
Founded: 1926
Subjects: Agriculture, Biological Sciences, Chemistry, Chemical Engineering, Environmental Studies, Natural History, Physical Sciences, Physics, Science (General), Technology
ISBN Prefix(es): 0-643; 0-52285; 0-52163
Number of titles published annually: 50 Print
Distributed by Antipodes Books & Beyond Ltd (USA & Canada); Eurospan (UK, Europe, Middle East & North Africa); Manaaki Whenua Press (New Zealand); Publishers Marketing Services Pte Ltd (Singapore, Malaysia & Brunei)

Currency Press Pty Ltd+
201 Cleveland St, Redfern, NSW 2016
Mailing Address: PO Box 2287, Strawberry Hills, NSW 2012
Tel: (02) 9319 5877 *Fax:* (02) 9319 3649
E-mail: enquiries@currency.com.au
Web Site: www.currency.com.au
Key Personnel
Chairman: Nicholas Parsons
Publisher: Victoria Chance
Sales & Marketing Dir: Deborah Franco
  E-mail: franco@currency.com.au
Founded: 1971
Specialize in performing arts.
Subjects: Drama, Theater, Film, Video, Music, Dance
ISBN Prefix(es): 0-86819
Number of titles published annually: 30 Print
Total Titles: 450 Print
Distributor for Nick Hern Books (Australia); Oberon Books (Australia)
Distribution Center: Antipodes Books & Beyond Ltd, 9707 Fairway Ave, Silver Springs, MD 20910-3001, United States *Tel:* 301-602-9519 *Fax:* 301-565-0160 *E-mail:* antipodes@antipodesbooks.com *Web Site:* www.antipodes.com

Curriculum Associates Inc, *imprint of* Hawker Brownlow

Curriculum Corporation+
Casselden Pl, Level 5, 2 Lonsdale St, Melbourne, Victoria 3000
Mailing Address: PO Box 177, Carlton South, Victoria 3053
Tel: (03) 9207 9600 *Fax:* (03) 9639 1616
E-mail: sales@curriculum.edu.au
Web Site: www.curriculum.edu.au *Cable:* EDUCATION CANBERRA
Key Personnel
Chief Executive Officer: Bruce Wilson
  E-mail: bruce.wilson@curriculum.edu.au
Executive Dir: David Francis
Publishing Manager: Esther Grounds
Sales & Marketing Dir: Sandra Hay
  E-mail: sandra.hay@curriculum.edu.au
Business Development Manager: Martin Murley
  E-mail: martin.murley@curriculum.edu.au
Production Manager: Bernie Handley
  E-mail: bernie.handley@curriculum.edu.au
General Manager, Curriculum Operations: Keith Gove *E-mail:* keith.gove@curriculum.edu.au
General Manager, Curriculum Programs: Pamela Macklin *E-mail:* pamela.macklin@curriculum.edu.au
Founded: 1990
Specialize in curriculum & education support material.
Subjects: Education
ISBN Prefix(es): 1-86366
Parent Company: Australian Ministers for Education
Orders to: PO Box 177, Carlton South, Victoria 3053

Eleanor Curtain Publishing+
906 Malvem Rd, Armadale, Victoria 3143
Tel: (03) 9822 0344 *Fax:* (03) 9824 8851
Key Personnel
Man Dir: Eleanor Curtain *E-mail:* ecurtain@ozemail.com.au
International Rights: Jane Curtain
Subjects: Education, Literature, Literary Criticism, Essays, Poetry
ISBN Prefix(es): 1-875327
Distributed by Horwitz Martin
Distributor for Heinemann Education (US); Stenhouse

Cygnet Books, *imprint of* University of Western Australia Press

Cygnet Young Fiction, *imprint of* University of Western Australia Press

D&B Marketing Pty Ltd
479 St Kilda Rd, Melbourne, NSW 3004
Tel: (03) 9828 3333 *Fax:* (03) 9828 3300
E-mail: csc.austral@dnb.com.au
Web Site: www.dnb.com.au
Key Personnel
Public Relations: Chris Gray
Founded: 1887
Subjects: Business, Finance
ISBN Prefix(es): 0-9593441
Parent Company: D&B (Australia) Pty Ltd
Divisions: Riddell Publishing

Dabill Publications
PO Box 707, Wollongong, NSW 2520
Tel: (02) 4228 8836 *Fax:* (02) 4226 9367
Web Site: www.dabill.com.au
Key Personnel
Author: Tim Cattell *E-mail:* tim@dabill.com.au
Business Manager: Frances Cattell
Founded: 1980
Subjects: Economics, Education, Environmental Studies, Geography, Geology, Social Sciences, Sociology

Dagraja Press+
3 Verco St, Hackett, ACT 2602
Tel: (02) 6247 0782; (02) 6262 7533
E-mail: granorab@ozemail.com.au

AUSTRALIA

Key Personnel
Owner: Mr Graeme Barrow
Founded: 1977
Specialize in bushwalking guides & local history.
Subjects: History
ISBN Prefix(es): 0-9587552
Number of titles published annually: 1 Print
Total Titles: 4 Print
Distributed by MacStyle Media

Dandy Lion Publications, *imprint of* Hawker Brownlow

Dangaroo Press+
GPO Box 1209, Sydney, NSW 2001
Tel: (02) 49545938 *Fax:* (02) 49546531
Key Personnel
Sales Manager: Allan Rich
Founded: 1978
Subjects: Art, Ethnicity, Literature, Literary Criticism, Essays, Nonfiction (General), Poetry, Social Sciences, Sociology, Women's Studies
ISBN Prefix(es): 1-871049; 1-875523

D'Artagnan Publishing+
PO Box 107, Burnside, SA 5066
Tel: (08) 2726718
Key Personnel
Head of Business: Hazel I Barrett
Writer: Elizabeth Whitbread
Founded: 1982
Membership(s): Australian Journalist Association.
Subjects: Animals, Pets, Art, Romance
ISBN Prefix(es): 0-9593142; 1-875201; 1-8752010

D'Assis Books+
44 Tristania Dr, Marcus Beach, Qld 4573
Mailing Address: PO Box 1189, Noosa Heads, Qld 4567
Tel: (07) 5448 2145 *Fax:* (07) 5447 5200
ISBN Prefix(es): 0-646
Orders to: Gemcraft, 14 Duffy St, Burwood, Melbourne, Victoria 3125
Warwick Page Eagle Heights Relaxation Retreat, 168 McDonell Rd, Eagle Heights, Mount Harborite, Qld 4271 *Tel:* (075) 545-3903 *Fax:* (075) 545-2426
Bhudens, PO Box 163, West Burleigh, Qld
  Tel: (075) 534 9200 *Fax:* (073) 302 2998

Deakin University Press+
Pigdons Rd, Geelong, Victoria 3217
Tel: (03) 5227 8144 *Fax:* (03) 5227 2020
E-mail: lynnew@deakin.edu.au
Web Site: www.deakin.edu.au
Telex: 35625
Key Personnel
Chief Executive: Ed Brumby
Manager: Marie Kelly
Manager, Sales: David Oswell *E-mail:* doswell@deakin.edu.au
Founded: 1979
Membership(s): Australian Book Publishers Association, National Book Council.
Subjects: Anthropology, Business, Environmental Studies, Mathematics, Medicine, Nursing, Dentistry, Women's Studies
ISBN Prefix(es): 0-949823; 0-86828; 0-7300
Total Titles: 356 Print
Parent Company: Learning Resources Services Deakin University

Del Rey, *imprint of* Random House Australia

Dell, *imprint of* Transworld Publishers Pty Ltd

Dell Publishing, *imprint of* Random House Australia

Dellasta Publishing+
10 Worrall St, Burwood, Victoria 3125

AUSTRALIA

Mailing Address: PO Box 777, Mount Waverley, Victoria 3149
Tel: (03) 9888 9188 *Fax:* (03) 9888 7806
E-mail: dellasta@publishaust.net.au
Web Site: www.dellasta.com.au
Key Personnel
Man Dir: Christian Esterhuyse
Customer Service: Irene Horwood
Founded: 1986
Membership(s): Publish Australia.
Subjects: Education, Environmental Studies, Geography, Geology, Language Arts, Linguistics, Mathematics, Science (General)
ISBN Prefix(es): 0-947138; 1-875627; 1-875640
Imprints: Ashwood House; Ashwood House Medical
Divisions: Ashwood Medical; Ashwood House Medical
Distributor for Green Submarine (UK); Learning Resources Inc (USA); Ver Lag An Der Ruhr (Germany)
Orders to: PO Box 777, Mount Waverley, Victoria 3149

Demonvamp Publications
24 Kiah St, Glen Waverley, Victoria 3150
Tel: (03) 9802 3875
Key Personnel
Publisher: W H Brook
ISBN Prefix(es): 1-86252

Department of Energy (NSW)+
Level 17, 227 Elizabeth St, Sydney, NSW 2001
Mailing Address: G PO Box 3889, Sydney, NSW 2001
Tel: (02) 8281 7777 *Fax:* (02) 8281 7799
E-mail: information@deus.nsw.gov.au
Web Site: www.doe.nsw.gov.au
Key Personnel
Dir General: Brian Steffen
Marketing: Peter Walker
Subjects: Earth Sciences

Department of Mineral Resources (NSW), see Department of Energy (NSW)

Department of Primary Industries, Queensland
Primary Industries Bldg, 1st floor, Publishing Services, 80 Ann St, Brisbane, Qld 4000
Mailing Address: GPO Box 46, Brisbane, Qld 4001
Tel: (07) 3239 3772 *Fax:* (07) 3239 6509
E-mail: books@dpi.qld.gov.au
Web Site: www.dpi.qld.gov.au
Subjects: Agriculture, Animals, Pets, Gardening, Plants
ISBN Prefix(es): 0-7242
Orders to: DPI Publications, Primary Industries Bldg, Brisbane, Qld 4000

Desbooks, *imprint of* Rainbow Book Agencies Pty Ltd

Desbooks Pty Ltd
56 Wales St, Thornbury, Victoria 3071
Tel: (03) 9484 2465 *Fax:* (03) 9484 3877
E-mail: desb@alphalink.com.au
Key Personnel
Contact: Hugh McGinlay
Founded: 1981
Subjects: Religion - Other, Theology
ISBN Prefix(es): 0-949824
Imprints: Wisdom Press

Desert Pea Press, *imprint of* The Federation Press

Deva Wings Publications+
PO Box 322, Daylesford, Victoria 3460
Tel: (03) 5348 1414 *Fax:* (03) 5348 1414
E-mail: devawings@netconnect.com.au
Web Site: www.spacountry.net.au/devawings
Key Personnel
Contact: Arjuna Govindamurti
Founded: 1994
Subjects: Human Relations, Nonfiction (General), Psychology, Psychiatry, Self-Help
ISBN Prefix(es): 0-9587202

Dharma Publishing, *imprint of* Windhorse Books

Dollar Books, *imprint of* Ansay Pty Ltd

Doubleday, *imprint of* Random House Australia

Doubleday, *imprint of* Transworld Publishers Pty Ltd

Dragon Press+
PO Box 209, Scarborough, WA 6019
Tel: (09) 9341 2004
Key Personnel
Contact: Bryn Griffiths
Founded: 1989
Subjects: Literature, Literary Criticism, Essays, Maritime, Poetry
ISBN Prefix(es): 1-875662
Parent Company: Dragon International
Imprints: Platypus Press Australia
Showroom(s): 9 The Glebe, Bishopston, Gower, Swansea, United Kingdom

Dryden Press, *imprint of* Elsevier Australia

Dryden Press
Imprint of Harcourt Australia Pty Ltd
PO Box 46, Darlinghurst, NSW 2010
Tel: (02) 331-4571 *Fax:* (02) 398-9782
Key Personnel
Contact: Ian R Stubbin
Subjects: Business, History, Travel
ISBN Prefix(es): 0-909162

Dubois Publishing
10 Grafton St, Chippendale, NSW 2008
Tel: (02) 92111178 *Fax:* (02) 92111868
Key Personnel
Publisher & Author: Bob Wood *Tel:* (02) 65671407
Distributor: Ron Wood *E-mail:* books@elt.com.an
Subjects: Mathematics
Total Titles: 1 Print
Distributed by Melting Pot Press

Dun & Bradstreet Marketing Pty Ltd, see D&B Marketing Pty Ltd

Dynamo House P/L+
4-10 Yorkshire St, Richmond, Victoria 3121
Mailing Address: PO Box 110, Richmond, Victoria 3121
Tel: (03) 9427 0955; (03) 9428 3636 *Fax:* (03) 9429 8036
E-mail: info@dynamoh.com.au
Web Site: www.dynamoh.com.au
Key Personnel
Publisher: Stefan Mager
Founded: 1979
Subjects: Astrology, Occult, Health, Nutrition, Humor, Alternative Therapies & Philosophies, Aromatherapy, Reflexology
ISBN Prefix(es): 0-949266; 1-876100; 0-949383
Subsidiaries: Dynamo Press
Distributed by Aromaland Inc (USA); Asiapac Books (Singapore); Milk & Honey, Inc. (USA)

EA Books+
2 Ernest St, Level 4, Crows Nest, NSW 2065
Mailing Address: PO Box 588, Crows Nest, NSW 1585
Tel: (02) 9438 1533 *Fax:* (02) 9438 5934
E-mail: eabooks@engaust.com.au
Web Site: www.engaust.com.au
Key Personnel
General Manager: Bruce Roff *E-mail:* broff@engaust.com.au
Editor: Dietrich Georg *E-mail:* dgeorg@engaust.com.au
Editorial: Bob Jackson *E-mail:* bjackson@engaust.com.au; Nathan Menser *E-mail:* nmenser@engaust.com.au; Paul Woolnough *E-mail:* pwoolnough@engaust.com.au
Advertising Manager: Terry Marsden *E-mail:* tmarsden@engaust.com.au
Advertising Sales: Maria Mamone *E-mail:* mmamone@engaust.com.au
Subscriptions: Pam Chenery *E-mail:* jmcgregor@engaugst.com.au
Founded: 1919 (I E Aust, 1976 E A Books)
Subjects: Chemistry, Chemical Engineering, Civil Engineering, Electronics, Electrical Engineering, Mechanical Engineering, Railway Engineering
ISBN Prefix(es): 0-85825
Number of titles published annually: 5 Print
Parent Company: Institution of Engineers Australia, 11 National Circuit, Barton, ACT 2600
Associate Companies: Chemical Engineering in Australia Magazine; Engineering World Magazine; Engineers Australia Magazine
Imprints: IE Aust Publications

Ebury Press, *imprint of* Random House Australia

The Edge of It, *imprint of* Feakle Press

Edubook, *imprint of* Egan Publishing Pty Ltd

Education, *imprint of* R J Cleary Publishing

Educational Advantage+
29 Meninya St, Moama, NSW 2731
Mailing Address: PO Box 1068, Echuca, Victoria 3564
Tel: (03) 5480 9466 *Fax:* (03) 5480 9462
E-mail: joe@mathsmate.net
Web Site: www.mathsmate.net
Key Personnel
Manager: Joanna Tutos
Contact: Joseph B Wright
Founded: 1995
Subjects: Education, Mathematics
ISBN Prefix(es): 1-876081
Total Titles: 46 Print
Associate Companies: Learning Cycles USA; Math's Mate USA
Foreign Rep(s): Kathy Frick (USA); Trish Kidd (New Zealand)

Educational Assessment Service Inc, *imprint of* Hawker Brownlow

Educational Impressions, *imprint of* Hawker Brownlow

Educational Insights, *imprint of* Hawker Brownlow

Educational Supplies Pty Ltd (The Dominie Group)
8 Cross St, Brookvale, NSW 2100
Mailing Address: PO Box 33, Brookvale, NSW 2100
Tel: (02) 99050201 *Fax:* (02) 99055209
Key Personnel
Man Dir: Ross Martin *E-mail:* ross@educationalsuppliesptyltd.com.au
Founded: 1951
ISBN Prefix(es): 1-86251; 0-909268; 0-949029

PUBLISHERS

AUSTRALIA

Edwina Publishing+
20 Willandra Ave, Canterbury, Victoria 3126
Tel: (03) 9836 3810 *Fax:* (03) 9830 1356
Web Site: www.edwinapublishing.com
Key Personnel
President: Christopher J Venn
Author: Susan L Venn
Founded: 1991
Subjects: Art
ISBN Prefix(es): 0-646
Total Titles: 3 Print

Egan Publishing Pty Ltd+
8 Waverley St, East Brighton, Victoria 3187
Tel: (03) 5923451 *Fax:* (03) 95931026
Key Personnel
Head of Company: Cecilia Egan
Founded: 1986
Subjects: Animals, Pets, Cookery, Crafts, Games, Hobbies, Fiction, Gardening, Plants
ISBN Prefix(es): 0-947272; 0-9593542; 0-9581361
Imprints: Edubook; Ashton Egan

Egmont, *imprint of* Random House Australia

Elephas Books Pty Ltd+
1/18 Mooney St, Bayswater, WA 6053
Tel: (08) 9370 1461 *Fax:* (08) 9341 8952
Key Personnel
Head of Company: Alan Falkson; Rume Karlson
Founded: 1989
Specialize in How-to & informational titles, also acts as importer & distributor of small press titles through Practical Books subsidiary.
Subjects: How-to, Library & Information Sciences
ISBN Prefix(es): 1-875273
Parent Company: The Firs
Imprints: Wilbur

David Ell Press Pty Ltd+
226 Crown St, Darlington, NSW 2010
Tel: (02) 5551634 *Fax:* (02) 5557067
Key Personnel
Head of Company: David Ell
Man Editor: Kathryn Lamberton
Founded: 1978
Subjects: Art, Crafts, Games, Hobbies
ISBN Prefix(es): 0-908197
Imprints: Ellsyd Press (paperbacks & children's)
Subsidiaries: Ellsyd Press Pty Ltd; Longueville Publications
Orders to: Tower Books, 2 Sydenham Rd, Brookvale, NSW 2100

Ellsyd Press, *imprint of* David Ell Press Pty Ltd

Elsevier Australia+
30-52 Smidmore St, Marrickville, NSW 2204
Mailing Address: Locked Bag 16, St Peters, NSW 2044
Tel: (029) 5178999 *Toll Free Tel:* 1-800 263 951 (within Australia); 0-800 170 165 (to Australia from New Zealand) *Fax:* (029) 5172249
Toll Free Fax: 0-800 170 160 (from Australia to New Zealand)
E-mail: service@elsevier.com.au
Web Site: www.elsevier.com.au
Key Personnel
Man Dir: Brian Brennan *Fax:* (02) 95506007 *E-mail:* bbrennan@harcourt.com.au
Financial Controller & Operations Manager: Jim Robinson *Fax:* (02) 95506007 *E-mail:* jrobinson@harcourt.com.au
General Manager College Division: Paul Barry *Fax:* (02) 95506007 *E-mail:* pbarry@harcourt.com.au
TPC General Manager: Dianne Lissner *Fax:* (02) 95506007 *E-mail:* dlissner@harcourt.com.au
General Manager STM Division: Anneke Baeten *Fax:* (02) 95506007 *E-mail:* abaeten@harcourt.com.au
Founded: 1972
Also several divisions: college, medical, psychological testing & professional/trade.
Subjects: Business, Education, Mathematics, Medicine, Nursing, Dentistry, Psychology, Psychiatry, Science (General), Social Sciences, Sociology, Veterinary Science
ISBN Prefix(es): 0-7295
Total Titles: 8,000 Print; 65 CD-ROM
Parent Company: Harcourt Inc, 6277 Sea Harbor Dr, Orlando, FL 32887, United States
Associate Companies: Harcourt Brace Japan Inc, Ichibancho Central Bldg, 22-1, Ichibancho, Chiyoda-ku, Tokyo 102, Japan; Academic Press Ltd, Harcourt Place, 32 Jamestown Road, London NW1 7BY, United Kingdom; Bailliere Tindall Ltd, Harcourt Place, 32 Jamestown Road, London NW1 7BY, United Kingdom; Harcourt Publishers Ltd, Harcourt Place, 32 Jamestown Road, London NW1 7BY, United Kingdom; Academic Press Inc, 1250 Sixth Ave, San Diego, CA 92101, United States; Harcourt Inc, 6277 Sea Harbor Dr, Orlando, FL 32821, United States; W B Saunders Co, The Curtis Center, Independence Sq, Philadelphia, PA 19106-3399, United States; Holt Rinehart & Winston Inc, 1627 Woodland Ave, Austin, TX 78741, United States; Harcourt College Publishers, 301 Commerce St, Suite 3700, Fort Worth, TX 78741, United States; The Psychological Corporation, 555 Academic Court, San Antonio, TX 78204-0952, United States
Imprints: Academic Press; Churchill Livingstone; Dryden Press; Harcourt Brace; Holt, Rinehart and Winston; Industrial Press; Mayfield Publishing; Morgan Kaufmann; Mosby; The Psychological Corporation; W B Saunders/Bailliere Tindall; Saunders College; Singular Press; Technomic Publishing
Branch Office(s)
Level 3, 71 Queens Rd, Melbourne, Victoria 3004
236 Dominion Rd, Mt Eden, Auckland 3, New Zealand
Distributor for Mayfield (Australia & New Zealand); Technomic Publishing (Australia & New Zealand)

Elton Publications+
57 Camden St, Wembly Downs, WA 6019
Tel: (08) 9 446 1328 *Fax:* (08) 9 445 8229
E-mail: elton@iinet.net.au
Web Site: www.elton.iinet.net.au
Key Personnel
Contact: Richard Lyon
Founded: 1994
Blackline Masters books which are used by teachers; educational, internet, Australia, Aborigines.
Membership(s): Copyright Agency Ltd.
Subjects: History, Culture, Wildlife
ISBN Prefix(es): 0-646; 1-876486
Number of titles published annually: 8 Print; 1 E-Book
Total Titles: 49 Print; 6 E-Book
Distributed by Chalkies n Kids Dominie; Dominie; Holding Educational Aids; Narnia Bookshop; Wooldridges

Emerald City Books+
21 Redmyre Rd, Strathfield, NSW 2135
Tel: (02) 7641115 *Fax:* (02) 7641115
E-mail: emeraldcitybooks@hotmail.com
Key Personnel
Dir: Ken Preece
Founded: 1995
Subjects: Biological Sciences, Business, Chemistry, Chemical Engineering, Computer Science, Economics, Mathematics, Physics, Science (General)
ISBN Prefix(es): 1-876133

Emmaus Productions, *imprint of* Rainbow Book Agencies Pty Ltd

Emperor Publishing+
55 Oxford St, Darlinghurst, NSW 2010
Tel: (02) 9261 4055 *Fax:* (02) 9264 9435
E-mail: pa@oxfordsquare.com.au
Key Personnel
Head of Company & Dir: Phil Birnbaum
Founded: 1989
Subjects: Anthropology, Biography, Foreign Countries, Humor, Nonfiction (General), Photography, Travel
ISBN Prefix(es): 0-7316
Total Titles: 2 Print

Encyclopaedia Britannica (Australia) Inc
90 Mount St, Level 1, North Sydney, NSW 2060
Tel: (02) 9923 5600 *Fax:* (02) 9929 3758
Web Site: www.britannica.com.au
Telex: 23044 Enbrit
Key Personnel
Man Dir: David Campbell
General Manager, Sales & Marketing: James Buckle
Subjects: Art, Biological Sciences, Geography, Geology, Science (General)
ISBN Prefix(es): 0-909263
Parent Company: Encyclopaedia Britannica Inc, Britannica Centre, 310 South Michigan Ave, Chicago, IL 60604, United States
Associate Companies: Encyclopaedia Britannica International Ltd, UK

Enrich, *imprint of* Hawker Brownlow

Enterprise Publications+
3 Stanford-Smith St, Klemzig, SA 5087
Tel: (08) 8261 9528 *Fax:* (08) 8261 9528
Founded: 1972
Membership(s): Fellow of Royal Photographic Society (FRPS).
Subjects: History, Maritime, Natural History, Outdoor Recreation, Photography, Regional Interests
ISBN Prefix(es): 0-85913
Distributed by State Mutual Books (USA)

Envirobook+
38 Rose St, Annandale, NSW 2038
Tel: (02) 9518 6154 *Fax:* (02) 9518 6156
E-mail: trekaway@sia.net.au
Telex: 271206
Key Personnel
Man Dir: Patrick Thompson
Subjects: Environmental Studies, Natural History, Outdoor Recreation, Aboriginal Children
ISBN Prefix(es): 0-85881
Number of titles published annually: 15 Print
Total Titles: 30 Print

ERA Picture Books, *imprint of* Era Publications

Era Publications+
220 Grange Rd, Flinders Park, SA 5025
Mailing Address: PO Box 231, Brooklyn Park, SA 5032
Tel: (08) 8352 4122 *Fax:* (08) 8234 0023
E-mail: admin@erapublications.com; service@erapublications.com
Web Site: www.erapublications.com
Key Personnel
Chief Executive Officer & Man Dir: Dr Rodney Martin *E-mail:* rod@erapublications.com
Founded: 1971
Primary school educational materials.
Subjects: Education, Nonfiction (General), Primary/Elementary School Literature
ISBN Prefix(es): 1-86374; 1-74120; 0-947212; 0-908507
Total Titles: 250 Print; 1 CD-ROM; 28 Audio

Parent Company: R D Martin Pty Ltd
Imprints: ERA Picture Books; Magic Bean
Distributed by Ragged Bears (UK, Picture Books)
Distributor for Gareth Stevens Inc; Moonlight (Australia); Tessloff
Foreign Rep(s): The Choice Maker InterAustralia Co (Korea); Daniel Doglioli (Italy); Martina Oepping (France)

Escutcheon Press
37 Cornelian Rd, Pearl Beach, NSW 2256
Tel: (02) 4344 2304 *Fax:* (02) 4341 1248
Key Personnel
Contact: R E Summers
ISBN Prefix(es): 1-875862; 0-9588066

Essien, *imprint of* Hudson Publishing

Experimental Art Foundation
Lion Arts Centre, N Terrace & Morphett St, Adelaide, SA 5000
Mailing Address: PO Box 8091, Station Arcade, Adelaide, SA 5000
Tel: (08) 8211 7505 *Fax:* (08) 8211 7323
E-mail: eaf@eaf.asn.au
Web Site: www.eaf.asn.au
Key Personnel
Director: Melentie Pandilovski
Administrator: Julie Lawton
Founded: 1974
Subjects: Art, Literature, Literary Criticism, Essays, Philosophy
ISBN Prefix(es): 0-949836; 0-9596729
Associate Companies: Otis Rush Magazine & Little Esther Books

Extraordinary People Press+
27 Meymott St, Randwick, NSW 2031
Tel: (02) 9326 6609 *Fax:* (02) 9399 6587
E-mail: info@extraordinarypeoplepress.com
Web Site: www.extraordinarypeoplepress.com
Key Personnel
Commissions Editor: Katrina Fox
 E-mail: katfox@easynet.co.uk
International Rights: K Butler
Founded: 1997
Subjects: Behavioral Sciences, Gay & Lesbian, Health, Nutrition, Human Relations, Nonfiction (General), Psychology, Psychiatry, Self-Help, Social Sciences, Sociology
ISBN Prefix(es): 0-9529482
Bookshop(s): Turnaround, Unit 3, Olympia Trading Estate, Cobury Rd, Wood Crear, London N22, United Kingdom

Fairfield Press, *imprint of* Rainbow Book Agencies Pty Ltd

Family Circle, *imprint of* Murdoch Books

Family Health Publications+
88 Broadway, Suite 1, Nedlands, WA 6009
Mailing Address: PO Box 3100, Nedlands, WA 6009
Tel: (08) 9389 8777 *Fax:* (08) 9389 8444
Web Site: www.familyhealth.info
Key Personnel
President: Allan Borushek *E-mail:* allan@calorieking.com
Founded: 1972
Subjects: Health, Nutrition
ISBN Prefix(es): 0-947091
U.S. Office(s): Allan Borushek & Associates Inc, 1760 Monrovia Ave, PO Box 1616, Costa Mesa, CA 92628, United States *Tel:* 949-642-8500 *Fax:* 949-642-8900

Family Reading Publications
B100 Ring Rd, Ballarat, Victoria 3350
Tel: (03) 5334 3244 *Fax:* (03) 5334 3299
E-mail: info@familyreading.com.au
Web Site: www.familyreading.com.au
Key Personnel
Contact: Colin Handreck *E-mail:* colin.handreck@familyreading.com.au; Ian Ruddick
Founded: 1976
Wholesale distributor - Christian books.
Distributor for Baker Book House; Christian Focus Publications (Australia); J Countryman; Harvest House Publishing; Intervarsity Press (Australia); Thomas Nelson; Tommy Nelson; Word Publishing; Zondervan (Australia)

Fawcett, *imprint of* Random House Australia

Feakle Press
126 Lennox St, Newtown, NSW 2042
Tel: (02) 9557 3248
Key Personnel
International Rights: Colleen Burke
Founded: 1992
Subjects: Poetry
ISBN Prefix(es): 0-646
Imprints: The Edge of It; Wildlife in Newtown

Fearon Teacher Aids, *imprint of* Hawker Brownlow

The Federation Press+
71 John St, Leichhardt, NSW 2040
Mailing Address: PO Box 45, Annandale, NSW 2038
Tel: (02) 9552-2200 *Fax:* (02) 9552-1681
E-mail: info@federationpress.com.au
Web Site: www.federationpress.com.au
Key Personnel
Dir: Christopher Holt; Diane Young *E-mail:* d.young@federationpress.com.au
Founded: 1988
Legal & social issues publisher.
Subjects: Business, Environmental Studies, Law, Academic Texts
ISBN Prefix(es): 1-86287
Total Titles: 300 Print
Imprints: Desert Pea Press; Hawkins Press
Distributed by Dunmore Press (New Zealand); Willan Publishing UK (Australiasia)
Distributor for Criminal Justice Press US; Dunmore Press (New Zealand)

Fernfawn Publications+
83 Weekes Rd, Moggill, Qld 4070
Mailing Address: PO Box 1010, Kenmore, Qld 4069
Tel: (07) 3202 6157 *Fax:* (07) 3202 6157
Key Personnel
Head of Company: Jarvis L Finger
Founded: 1992
Subjects: Education, Humor, Law, Management
ISBN Prefix(es): 0-646

Finch Publishing+
PO Box 120, Lane Cove, NSW 2066
Tel: (02) 9418 6247 *Fax:* (02) 9418 8878
E-mail: info@finch.com.au
Web Site: www.finch.com.au
Key Personnel
Publisher: Rex Finch
Dir: Vicki Finch
Marketing Coordinator: Julian Sheedy
Editor: Sean Doyle
Founded: 1992
Subjects: Child Care & Development, Communications, Education, Human Relations, Nonfiction (General), Psychology, Psychiatry, Self-Help, Social Sciences, Sociology, Women's Studies, Parenting, Relationships, Mens Studies, Social Issues, Children's Health
ISBN Prefix(es): 1-876451
Number of titles published annually: 10 Print
Total Titles: 17 Print
Distributed by Double & Newman Pty Ltd (Territory: Asia); Simon & Schuster (Territory: Australia); Southern Publishers Group (Territory: New Zealand); Pearson Education South (Territory: South Africa); Deep Books (Territory: UK)

Fine Art Publishing Pty Ltd+
42 Chandos St, St Leonards, NSW 2065
Tel: (02) 99668400 *Fax:* (02) 99660355
E-mail: info@gbpub.com.au
Web Site: www.gbpub.com.au *Cable:* IMPRINT SYDNEY
Key Personnel
Publisher: Sam Ure Smith
Editor: Dinah Dysart; Leon Paroissien
Editorial Manager: Hannah Fink
Founded: 1963
Art & Australia, quarterly journal, company also produces books for other publishers.
Subjects: Art
ISBN Prefix(es): 0-86917; 1-877004
Imprints: Craftsman House
Divisions: Craftsman House (Book Division)

The Five Mile Press Pty Ltd
950 Stud Rd, Rowville, Victoria 3178
Mailing Address: PO Box 177, Ferntree Gully, Victoria 3156
Tel: (03) 8756 5500 *Fax:* (03) 8756 5588
E-mail: publishing@fivemile.com.au
Web Site: www.fivemile.com.au
Key Personnel
Man Dir: David Horgan
Subjects: Regional Interests
ISBN Prefix(es): 0-86788; 1-875971; 1-86503

Flactem
1429A Toorak Rd, Camberwell, Victoria 3124
Tel: (03) 9889 6855 *Fax:* (03) 98888948
Key Personnel
Contact: Judith Paphazy
ISBN Prefix(es): 0-646

Flora Publications International Pty Ltd+
371 Queen St, 8th Floor, Brisbane, Qld 4001
Mailing Address: GPOB 2927, Brisbane, Qld 4001
Tel: (07) 3229 6366 *Fax:* (07) 3378 7102
E-mail: info@flora.com.au
Key Personnel
President & International Rights: Paul Niederer
Founded: 1995
Subjects: Gardening, Plants, Outdoor Recreation, Horticulture
ISBN Prefix(es): 1-876060
Associate Companies: Infomedia Publishing Pty Ltd, Brisbane, Qld
Imprints: Infomedia

Florilegium+
PO Box 644, Rozelle, NSW 2039
Tel: (02) 95558589 *Fax:* (02) 98184409
E-mail: florileg@ozemail.com.au
Key Personnel
Manager: Gilbert Teague
Founded: 1989
Membership(s): ABPA, NIAA.
Subjects: Gardening, Plants
ISBN Prefix(es): 0-9586498; 1-876314

Fodor, *imprint of* Random House Australia

Forge, *imprint of* Pan Macmillan Australia Pty Ltd

Foundation for Critical Thinking, *imprint of* Hawker Brownlow

Fraser Publications+
PO Box 215, Rutherglen, Victoria 3685

PUBLISHERS

Tel: (018) 039845 *Fax:* (057) 261775
E-mail: fraspub@albury.net.au
Key Personnel
Manager: Ian C Fraser
Founded: 1987
Subjects: Health, Nutrition, Medicine, Nursing, Dentistry, Self-Help
ISBN Prefix(es): 0-9588384

Free Spirit Publishing Inc, *imprint of* Hawker Brownlow

Oliver Freeman Editions, *imprint of* Prospect Media Pty Ltd

Fremantle Arts Centre Press
25 Quarry St, Fremantle, WA 6160
Mailing Address: PO Box 158, North Fremantle, WA 6159
Tel: (08) 9430 6331 *Fax:* (08) 9430 5242
E-mail: facp@iinet.net.au
Web Site: facp.iinet.net.au
Key Personnel
Publisher: Ray Coffey
General Manager: Clive Newman
Founded: 1976
Subjects: Art, Biography, Education, Fiction, History, Literature, Literary Criticism, Essays, Poetry
ISBN Prefix(es): 1-86368; 0-949144; 0-949206; 1-920731
Number of titles published annually: 35 Print
Total Titles: 250 Print
Imprints: Sandcastle Books
Distributed by Penguin Books (NZ) Ltd (New Zealand); Penguin Books Australia Ltd (Australia)
Foreign Rep(s): International Specialized Book Services (North America)
Distribution Center: International Specialized Book Service, 5804 NE Hassala St, Portland, OR 97213-3644, United States, Contact: Tamma Greenfield *Tel:* 503-287-3093 *Fax:* 503-280-8832 *E-mail:* orders@isbs.com
Web Site: www.isbs.com (US distribution only)

Freshet Press+
2 Lyttleton Ave, Castlemaine, Victoria 3450
Tel: (03) 53483085
Key Personnel
International Rights: J Richards
Founded: 1982
Subjects: Gardening, Plants, Literature, Literary Criticism, Essays, Philosophy, Poetry, Psychology, Psychiatry, Religion - Other, Social Sciences, Sociology
ISBN Prefix(es): 0-9593361

Full Circle Publications Co-Operative
12 Cornell St, Camberwell, Victoria 3124
Tel: (03) 9830 4253
ISBN Prefix(es): 0-9587113
Distributor for Australian Council for Educational Research
Bookshop(s): Politics & Prose Bookstore, 5015 Connecticut Ave NW, Washington, DC 20008, United States *Tel:* 202-364-1919

Galations Group, *imprint of* Rainbow Book Agencies Pty Ltd

Galley Press Publishing+
50 Arthur St, Surry Hills, NSW 2010
Tel: (02) 9698 9262 *Fax:* (02) 9360 1968
E-mail: isbin@ozemail.com.au
Key Personnel
Contact: Tony Markidis
Founded: 1992
Also acts as bookshop & infoserver, stop distribution service.
Subjects: Fiction, Poetry, Sports, Athletics

ISBN Prefix(es): 1-875701
Total Titles: 15 Print
Associate Companies: Home Grown Book Distribution Co-op Ltd; Isbin Bookspider

Gamco Industries Inc, *imprint of* Hawker Brownlow

Gangan Publishing+
PO Box 522, Strawberry Hills, NSW 2012
Tel: (02) 9280 2120 *Fax:* (02) 9280 2130
E-mail: books@gangan.com
Web Site: www.gangan.com
Key Personnel
Publisher: Gerald Ganglbauer *Tel:* (0411) 156 309 *E-mail:* gerald@gangan.com
Founded: 1984
Subjects: Fiction, Literature, Literary Criticism, Essays, Poetry, Regional Interests, Contemporary literature from Australia & Austria
ISBN Prefix(es): 1-86336
Imprints: Gangaroo
Orders to: Brodtrager & Partner OEG, Rainleiten 62, A-8045 Graz, Austria, Guenter Brodtrager *Tel:* (0316) 670 4090 *Fax:* (0316) 670 4096 *E-mail:* gbrodtrager@greenbrains.com

Gangaroo, *imprint of* Gangan Publishing

Garr Publishing+
Palm Court, 464 The Entrance Rd, Erina Heights, NSW 2260
Tel: (02) 4367 7762 *Fax:* (02) 4367 7223
E-mail: garrpublishing@mail2me.com.au
Web Site: www.garrpublishing.com.au
Key Personnel
Contact: R Symington *Tel:* (02) 4367 7223
Founded: 1994
An all Australian Enterprise, whose aim is to introduce, establish & market Australian works to the national & international markets. Specialize in fiction based on fact (Australian authors).
Subjects: Fiction
Number of titles published annually: 2 CD-ROM; 6 Online; 4 E-Book
Total Titles: 4 Print; 6 CD-ROM; 8 Online; 6 E-Book; 5 Audio
Subsidiaries: Softmail Computing

Garradunga Press
1/33 Jensen St, Manoora, Qld 4870
Tel: (0409) 320 619 (mobile) *Fax:* (07) 4032 5918
E-mail: bolton@iig.com.au
Key Personnel
Contact: Colleen Rowe
Specialize in travel.
Subjects: Travel
ISBN Prefix(es): 0-646

John Garratt Publishing+
32 Glenvale Crescent, Private Bag 400, Mulgrave, Victoria 3170
Tel: (03) 9545 3111 *Toll Free Tel:* 300 650 878 *Fax:* (03) 9545 3222
E-mail: sales@johngarratt.com.au
Web Site: www.johngarratt.com.au
Key Personnel
Man Dir: Garry Eastman *E-mail:* garryeastman@johngarratt.com.au
Founded: 1995
Importation & marketing of overseas religious titles.
Membership(s): CBAA.
Subjects: Religion - Other
ISBN Prefix(es): 1-875938; 1-920682; 1-920721
Number of titles published annually: 5 Print
Total Titles: 20 Print

AUSTRALIA

Distributor for Emmas Publications; General Synod of the Anglican Church of Australia
Book Club(s): Sophia Booknet

Germinal Press
PO Box 345, Toowong, Qld 4066

Gifted Children Information Centre, *imprint of* Hawker Brownlow

Ginninderra Press
PO Box 53, Charnwood, ACT 2615
Tel: (02) 6258 9060 *Fax:* (02) 6258 9069
Web Site: www.ginninderrapress.com.au
Key Personnel
Publisher: Stephen Matthews *E-mail:* stephenmatthews@ginninderrapress.com.au
Founded: 1996
Subjects: Biography, Disability, Special Needs, Education, Fiction, Health, Nutrition, History, Library & Information Sciences, Music, Dance, Poetry
ISBN Prefix(es): 1-876259; 0-9586825; 1-74027
Number of titles published annually: 40 Print
Total Titles: 200 Print
Imprints: Indigo; Mockingbird

Global Business Network, *imprint of* Prospect Media Pty Ltd

Gnostic Editions
12 Miller Ave, Kew, Victoria 3101
Mailing Address: PO Box 410, Kew, Victoria 3101
Tel: (03) 9853 1401 *Fax:* (03) 9853 1481
E-mail: mail@gnoticeditions.com
Key Personnel
Dir: Ian Watchorn *E-mail:* ian@ianwatchorn.com
Contact: Robyn Lambert
Founded: 1992
Associate companies located in Brazil, Portugal, Spain, Thailand & United Kingdom.
Subjects: Alternative, Anthropology, Archaeology, Astrology, Occult, Human Relations, Mysteries, Parapsychology, Philosophy, Psychology, Psychiatry, Religion - Other, Self-Help, Theology
ISBN Prefix(es): 0-646
Number of titles published annually: 2 Print
Total Titles: 10 Print
Parent Company: Nous Editores, Calle Mina Nº 209, Col Tetela del Monte, CP 62130, Cuernavaca Morelos DF, Mexico
Associate Companies: Anubis Publishers International (Canada)

Gould Genealogy
Unit 4, 247 Milne Rd, Modbury North, SA 5092
Mailing Address: PO Box 675, Modbury, SA 5092
Tel: (08) 8396 1110 *Fax:* (08) 8396 1163
E-mail: inquiries@gould.com.au
Web Site: www.gould.com.au
Key Personnel
Contact: Alan Phillips *E-mail:* alan@gould.com.au
Founded: 1976
Subjects: Genealogy, History
ISBN Prefix(es): 0-947284

Graffiti Publications+
69 Forest St, Castlemaine, Victoria 3450
Mailing Address: PO Box 2328, Castlemaine, Victoria 3450
Tel: (03) 5472 3805
E-mail: graffiti@netcon.net.au
Web Site: www.graffitipub.com.au
Key Personnel
Dir: Larry O'Toole
Founded: 1976
Subjects: Automotive, Crafts, Games, Hobbies

ISBN Prefix(es): 0-949398
Total Titles: 16 Print
Distributed by Celebrity Books (New Zealand); MotorBooks International
Distributor for The Rodder's Journal; Tex Smith Library
Foreign Rep(s): Motorbooks International (North America)

Grainger Museum
Information Division, University of Melbourne, Melbourne, Victoria 3010
Tel: (03) 8344 5270 *Fax:* (03) 9349 1707
E-mail: grainger@unimelb.edu.au
Web Site: www.lib.unimelb.edu.au/collections/grainger
Telex: AA 35185
Key Personnel
Curator: Rosemary Florrimell
Founded: 1938
Subjects: Music, Dance

Granrott Press
The Old Rectory, Lule Rd, Clarendon, SA 5157
Mailing Address: PO Box 6, Clarendon, SA 5157
Tel: (08) 8383 6081 *Fax:* (08) 8383 6067
Key Personnel
Dir: N Hjorth
Founded: 1984
Family business that was founded based on the need to cross boundaries of an autobiographical book with feminine based visual arts.
Subjects: Art, Theology, Women's Studies
ISBN Prefix(es): 0-9590720
Total Titles: 4 Print

Grass Roots, *imprint of* Grass Roots Publishing

Grass Roots Publishing
Formerly Night Owl Publishers Pty Ltd
PO Box 117, Seymour, Victoria 3661
Tel: (03) 5794 7256 *Fax:* (03) 5794 7285
Key Personnel
Head of Company: David A Miller
Production: Meg Miller
Founded: 1973
ISBN Prefix(es): 0-9595244; 0-9590152; 0-947065; 0-9580894; 1-876321
Imprints: Grass Roots

Great Western Press Pty Ltd+
PO Box 482, Chatswood, NSW 2067
Tel: (02) 4124 394 *Fax:* (02) 9144 5566
Key Personnel
Man Dir: John Isaacs *E-mail:* jisaacssydney@aol.com
Sales: Anne Isaacs
Rights & Permissions: Robert Elliott
Founded: 1974
Subjects: How-to, Romance, Science (General), Autobiographies, Memoirs
ISBN Prefix(es): 0-86901
Number of titles published annually: 2 Print
Total Titles: 57 Print
Associate Companies: Pymble Trading Pty Ltd
Imprints: GWP
Shipping Address: ACP Customs Services Pty Ltd, PO Box 148, Rosebery, NSW 2018, Contact: Geoff Dickson *Tel:* (02) 9669 0966 *Fax:* (02) 9669 0999 *E-mail:* acpcustoms@att.net.au
Warehouse: Unit 3, 809-821 Botany Rd, Rosebery, NSW 2018, Contact: Peter Reid

Greater Glider Productions Australia Pty Ltd+
Book Farm, 8 Rees Lane, Maleny, Qld 4552
Tel: (07) 5494 3000 *Fax:* (07) 5494 3284
Key Personnel
Publishing Dir: Jill Morris *E-mail:* jillmorris@greaterglider.com.au
Manager: Cheryl Wickes
Founded: 1983
Membership(s): Australian Publishers Association.
Subjects: Education, Health, Nutrition, Natural History, Science (General)
ISBN Prefix(es): 0-947304
Foreign Rep(s): Australia for Kids (Roots & Wings) (USA); The Choicemaker (Korea); Portfolio Children's Books (UK)
Foreign Rights: The Choicemaker (Korea); Quarter Marketing (South Africa)
Bookshop(s): Peace of Green, Maple St, Maleny 4552
Book Club(s): Choice Magazine; Scholastic; Wilderness Society

Gregory's, *imprint of* Universal Press Pty Ltd

Griffin, *imprint of* Pan Macmillan Australia Pty Ltd

GWP, *imprint of* Great Western Press Pty Ltd

Halbooks Publishing+
PO Box 224, Coogee, NSW 2034
Tel: (02) 9326 4250 *Fax:* (02) 9326 4250
E-mail: sean@iotaproductions.com.au
Key Personnel
Contact: Alan Halbish
Also acts as print broker & literary agent.
ISBN Prefix(es): 0-9585807; 0-9578908

Hale & Iremonger Pty Ltd+
76-82 Chapel St, Marrickville, NSW 2204
Mailing Address: PO Box 205, 2015 Alexandria, NSW
Tel: (02) 9560 0470 *Fax:* (02) 9550 0097
E-mail: info@haleiremonger.com
Web Site: www.haleiremonger.com
Key Personnel
Marketing Manager: Matthew Harrigan *E-mail:* matthew@haleiremonger.com
Publisher & General Manager: Sylvia Hale *E-mail:* sylvia@haleiremonger.com
Founded: 1977
Membership(s): Australian Publishers Association, Australian Booksellers Association.
Subjects: Asian Studies, Biography, Business, Career Development, Child Care & Development, Genealogy, Government, Political Science, Health, Nutrition, History, Management, Nonfiction (General), Philosophy, Psychology, Psychiatry, Public Administration, Self-Help, Women's Studies
ISBN Prefix(es): 0-86806; 0-908094; 0-949818
Number of titles published annually: 10 Print
Total Titles: 200 Print
Distributed by Forrester Books 2 (New Zealand); Pacific Island Books (USA); Roundhouse Publishing Group (UK & Western Europe)

F H Halpern+
2/75 Gardenvale Rd, Elsternwick, Victoria 3185
Tel: (03) 9596 1436 *Fax:* (03) 9596 1436
Key Personnel
Contact: F H Halpern
Subjects: History, Travel
ISBN Prefix(es): 0-7223; 0-7316
Branch Office(s)
Melbourne

Kerri Hamer+
347 Maroubra Rd, Maroubra, NSW 2035
Tel: (02) 9349 5170 *Fax:* (02) 9349 5170
Key Personnel
Publisher & Author: Kerri Hamer *E-mail:* khamer@oakhill.nsw.edu.au
Subjects: Behavioral Sciences, Communications, Education, How-to, Human Relations, Psychology, Psychiatry, Self-Help, Social Sciences, Sociology
ISBN Prefix(es): 0-646

Hamish Hamilton, *imprint of* Penguin Group (Australia)

Hamlyn Childrens, *imprint of* Random House Australia

Geoffrey Hamlyn-Harris
5 Garden St, Stanthorpe, Qld 4380
Tel: (07) 4681 1450 *Fax:* (07) 4681 1450
Key Personnel
Proprietor & Author: Geoffrey Hamlyn-Harris *Fax:* (076) 811450
Subjects: Drama, Theater, Fiction, Nonfiction (General), Poetry, Science Fiction, Fantasy
ISBN Prefix(es): 0-9592203
Total Titles: 7 Print; 7 Online; 1 Audio

Hampden Press+
51 Hampden Rd, Five Dock, NSW 2046
Mailing Address: PO Box 134, Five Dock, NSW 2046
Tel: (02) 9351 9070 *Fax:* 9351 9323
E-mail: j.higgs@cchs.usyd.edu.au
Key Personnel
Publisher: Saul Kamerman *E-mail:* saulk@bigpond.com
Subjects: Child Care & Development, Medicine, Nursing, Dentistry, Psychology, Psychiatry
ISBN Prefix(es): 1-875648

H&H Publishing
6 Southern Court, Forest Hill, Victoria 3131
Tel: (03) 98774428 *Fax:* (03) 98774222
Key Personnel
Contact: Malcolm Raymond Harris *E-mail:* malh@melbpc.com.au
Founded: 1981
Subjects: Civil Engineering, Mechanical Engineering
ISBN Prefix(es): 0-646

Harcourt Brace, *imprint of* Elsevier Australia

Hargreen Publishing Co
430 William St, Melbourne, Victoria 3000
Tel: (03) 9329 9714 *Fax:* (03) 9329 5295
E-mail: em@execmedia.com.au
Key Personnel
Chief Executive: Michael Haratsis, Sr
Editorial & Production: Rick Navarro
Founded: 1972
Specialize in Australian history.
Subjects: Education, History, Nonfiction (General)
ISBN Prefix(es): 0-949905; 0-9596696
Parent Company: Scotshouse Corp Pty Ltd

Harlequin Books
Unit 2/3 Gibbes St, Chatswood, NSW 2067
Mailing Address: Locked Bag 2, Chatswood, NSW 2067
Tel: (02) 9415 9230 *Fax:* (02) 9417 5232
E-mail: bhobbs@romance.net.au
Web Site: www.eharlequin.com.au
Key Personnel
Man Dir: Nancy Peters
ISBN Prefix(es): 0-949162; 0-949489
Parent Company: Harlequin Enterprises

HarperCollins Publishers (Australia) Pty Ltd+
25 Ryde Rd, Pymble, NSW 2073
Mailing Address: PO Box 321, Pymble, NSW 2073
Tel: (02) 9952 5000 *Fax:* (02) 9952 5555
Web Site: www.harpercollins.com.au
Key Personnel
Man Dir: Brian Murray
Finance Dir: Malcolm Boyd
Commercial Dir: Lil Velis

PUBLISHERS

AUSTRALIA

Publishing Dir: Shona Martyn
Sales Dir: Robert Gorman
Publishing Manager: James Herd
Marketing Dir: Jim Demetriou
Publicity Manager: Christine Farmer
Production Manager: Jill Donald
Art Dir: Russell Jeffrey
IT Manager: Richard Beath
Manager, Multimedia & Internet Services: Laura Tricker
Rights Manger: Airlie Lawson
ISBN Prefix(es): 0-7322
Parent Company: HarperCollins Publishers Group
Associate Companies: Bay Books; Angus & Robertson Publishers; Collins Dove; HarperCollins Publishers India (P) Ltd, India; HarperCollins Ltd, Hong Kong; HarperCollins Publishers - Japan, Japan; HarperCollins Publishers, New Zealand; Golden Press, New Zealand; HarperCollins Publishers Asia Pte Ltd, Singapore; HarperCollins Publishers (SA) (Pty) Ltd, South Africa; HarperCollins General Books, United Kingdom; Fontana, United Kingdom; Grafton Books, United Kingdom; Thorsons Times Books, United Kingdom; Marshall Pickering, United Kingdom; Bartholomew, United Kingdom; HarperCollins; Zondervan; Collins Inc; Scott Foresman
Distribution Center: Yarrawa Rd, PO Box 264, Moss Vale NSW 2577 *Tel:* (02) 4860 2900 *Fax:* (02) 4860 2990

HarperCollinsReligious
Imprint of HarperCollinsPublishers Australia
25 Ryde St, Pymble, NSW 2073
Mailing Address: PO Box 321, Pymble, NSW 2073
Tel: (011) 6222900 *Fax:* (011) 6223553
E-mail: fiona.mclennan@harpercollins.com.au
Web Site: www.harpercollinsreligious.com.au
Key Personnel
Permissions: Annette Renshaw *E-mail:* annette.renshaw@harpercollins.com.au
Rights: Airlie Lawson *E-mail:* airlie.lawson@harpercollins.com.au
Founded: 1962
Subjects: Biblical Studies, Fiction, Nonfiction (General)
ISBN Prefix(es): 0-00; 0-00

Hartys Creek Press
PO Box 342, Wauchope, NSW 2446
Tel: (02) 6587 1100
Key Personnel
Contact: Lois Higgins
Subjects: Art, Environmental Studies, Geography, Geology, Humor, Travel
ISBN Prefix(es): 0-646
Publication(s): *Antartica Alphabetically*; *Australia Alphabetically*; *Log Book of an Antarctic Journey*

Roland Harvey Studios+
9 Delta St, Port Melbourne, Victoria 3207
Tel: (03) 9836 6655 *Fax:* (03) 9836 6652
E-mail: sales@rolandharvey.com.au
Key Personnel
Publisher: Roland Harvey
Contact: Dinah Lewis
Founded: 1978
Membership(s): ABPA.
ISBN Prefix(es): 0-949714
Imprints: Periscope Press
Warehouse: Unit 1, 13 Downarh St, Braeside, Victoria 3195

Hat Box Press
3 Huntingfield Drive, Hoppers Crossing, Victoria 3029
Tel: (03) 9749 2510

Key Personnel
Contact: Bronwen Hickman *E-mail:* bronwenh@vicnet.net.au
Subjects: Fiction, History, Literature, Literary Criticism, Essays, Short stories by Mary Gaunt
ISBN Prefix(es): 0-9590422
Number of titles published annually: 1 Print

Hawker Brownlow+
1123a Nepean Highway, Highett, Victoria 3190
Mailing Address: PO Box 580, Moorabbin, Victoria 3189
Tel: (03) 9555 1344 *Toll Free Tel:* 800-334-603 *Fax:* (03) 9553 4538 *Toll Free Fax:* 800-150-445
E-mail: orders@hbe.com.au
Web Site: www.hbe.com.au
Key Personnel
Man Dir: David Brownlow
General Manager: Elaine Brownlow
 E-mail: ebrownlow@hbe.com.au
Founded: 1981
Subjects: Asian Studies, Human Relations, Mathematics, Technology
ISBN Prefix(es): 1-86299; 1-86401; 0-947326; 1-74025; 1-74101
Parent Company: Hawker Brownlow Education
Imprints: Autonomous Learning Publications & Specialists; BEC Publications; Book Lures Inc; Cassel PLC; Centre for Creative Learning; Creative Learning Consultants; Creative Learning Press; Critical Thinking Press & Software; Curriculum Associates Inc; Dandy Lion Publications; Educational Assessment Service Inc; Educational Impressions; Educational Insights; Enrich; Fearon Teacher Aids; Foundation for Critical Thinking; Free Spirit Publishing Inc; Gamco Industries Inc; Gifted Children Information Centre; The Learner's Dimensions; The Learning Works; Michael Grinder & Associates; Modern Learning Press; New Horizons for Learning; Ohio Psychology Press; Perfection Learning Corporation; Personal Power Press International Inc; Prufrock Press; Skylight Publishing Inc; Star Teaching; Sterling Publishing Co Inc; Sundance Inc; Teacher Created Materials; Trillium Press; United Educational Services (DDK); Zephyr Press
Subsidiaries: Learner's World

Hawkins Press, *imprint of* The Federation Press

Hayes Publishing Co
52 Dewar Terrace, Sherwood, Qld 4075
Tel: (07) 3379 4137 *Fax:* (07) 3379 4137
Key Personnel
Contact: P C Hayes *E-mail:* p.hayes@minmet.uq.edu.au
Subjects: Engineering (General)
ISBN Prefix(es): 0-9589197
Number of titles published annually: 1 Print
Total Titles: 1 Print
Orders to: Koala Books of Canada, 14327-95A Ave, Edmonton, AB T5N 0B6, Canada *Tel:* (780) 452 5149

Hayward Books, *imprint of* In-Tune Books

Headline, *imprint of* Hodder Headline Australia

Headline Feature, *imprint of* Hodder Headline Australia

Headline Review, *imprint of* Hodder Headline Australia

Heinemann, *imprint of* Reed Educational Publishing Australia

Heinemann Library
22 Salmon St, Port Melbourne, Victoria 3207
Tel: (03) 92467131
ISBN Prefix(es): 0-949919; 1-875633; 1-86391; 1-74070
Parent Company: Reed Educational & Professional Publishing
Ultimate Parent Company: Reed Elsevier

William Heinemann, *imprint of* Random House Australia

Hema Maps Pty Ltd+
25 McKechnie Drive, Eight Mile Plains, Qld 4113
Mailing Address: PO Box 4365, Eight Mile Plains, Qld 4113
Tel: (07) 3340 0000 *Fax:* (07) 3340 0099
E-mail: manager@hemamaps.com.au
Web Site: www.hemamaps.com
Key Personnel
Man Dir: Henry Boegheim
Founded: 1983
Membership(s): IMTA.
Subjects: Travel
ISBN Prefix(es): 1-875610; 1-875992; 1-86500
Distributed by Brettschneider GmbH (Germany); Cartotheque (France); T B Clarke (Overseas) Pty Ltd; Craenen Cartografie (Belgium); Estate Publications (United Kingdom); Freytag & Berndt u Artaria (Austria); Geocentre (Germany); Gordon & Gotch (PNG) Pty Ltd (Papua New Guinea); Hema Maps NZ Ltd (New Zealand); Inteligentni Turisticke Mapy (Czech Republic); ITMB Publishing Ltd (Canada); Jana Seta (Latvia); Kartbutiken (Sweden); Magellan Buchversand (Germany); Map Co Trading (Singapore); Map House Co Ltd (Tokyo); Map Link Inc (USA); Namdo Net (South Korea); Nilsson & Lamm (Holland); OLF (Switzerland); Scanvik Books (Denmark)
Distributor for AA-New Zealand; AA-UK; Ausmap; Australian Geographic; Berndtson & Berndtson; Boiling Billy; Cartographics; CMA New South Wales; Collins; DOLA; Forestry Maps-NSW; Mapland; Nelles Maps; Periplus; Rand McNally; Sunmap; Tasmap; Universal Maps; Vicmaps; Westprint (all Australia)

Henry Holt, *imprint of* Pan Macmillan Australia Pty Ltd

Heresy Press, *imprint of* Prospect Media Pty Ltd

Hihorse Publishing Pty Ltd+
59 Princess St, Williamstown, Victoria 3016
Tel: (03) 9397 3084 *Fax:* (03) 9397 3084
E-mail: hihorse@c031.aone.net.au
Key Personnel
Contact: Patricia Kovac
Founded: 1995
Subjects: Alternative, Astrology, Occult, Parapsychology, Self-Help, Aromatherapy, Meditation, Crystal Healing
ISBN Prefix(es): 0-909223
Associate Companies: Gemcraft Pty Ltd, 14 Duffy St, Burwood, Victoria 3125, Afghanistan

Histec Publications
c/o B E Lloyd & Associates, 13 Connor St, East Brighton, Victoria 3187
Tel: (03) 9592 3787 *Fax:* (03) 9592 2823
Web Site: www.histec.com
Key Personnel
Dir: Dr Brian E Lloyd *E-mail:* belloyd@projectx.com.au
Founded: 1987
Subjects: Biography, Engineering (General), History, Labor, Industrial Relations, Regional Interests, Social Sciences, Sociology
ISBN Prefix(es): 0-9587705

Number of titles published annually: 2 Print; 1 CD-ROM
Total Titles: 20 Print; 3 CD-ROM
Parent Company: B E Lloyd & Associates Histec Nominees Pty Ltd

Hodder, *imprint of* Hodder Headline Australia

Hodder Headline Australia+
Level 22, 207 Kent Street, Sydney, NSW 2000
Tel: (02) 82480800; (02) 43901300 (customer service) *Fax:* (02) 82480810
E-mail: Auspub@hha.com.au (Australian publishing); hsales@alliancedist.com.au; adscs@alliancedist.com.au (customer service)
Web Site: www.hha.com.au
Key Personnel
Man Dir: Malcolm Edwards
Sales & Marketing Dir: Mary Drum
Publishing Dir: Lisa Highton
Founded: 1958
Also distributor of group product agents for Piatkus (UK).
ISBN Prefix(es): 0-340; 0-450; 0-7336
Number of titles published annually: 120 Print
Total Titles: 1,500 Print
Parent Company: Hodder Headline UK, United Kingdom
Ultimate Parent Company: W H Smith
Imprints: New English Library; Sceptre; Teach Yourself; Coronet; Headline; Headline Feature; Headline Review; Hodder
Distributor for Hodder Headline plc UK; Lion

Holt, Rinehart and Winston, *imprint of* Elsevier Australia

Home Library, *imprint of* ACP Publishing Pty Ltd

Homestead Books
29 Lisbeth Ave, Donvale, Victoria 3111
Tel: (03) 9873 7202 *Fax:* (03) 9873-0542
E-mail: service@theruralstore.com.au
Web Site: www.theruralstore.com.au
Key Personnel
Proprietor: Jim Lowden *E-mail:* jim@theruralstore.com.au

Horan Wall & Walker+
162 Goulburn St, Darlinghurst NSW 2010
Mailing Address: PO Box 996, Darlinghurst NSW 2010
Tel: (02) 8268 8268 *Fax:* (02) 8268 8267
E-mail: info@hww.com.au
Web Site: www.hww.com.au
Key Personnel
Man Dir: Stephen Wall
Founded: 1974
Subjects: Cookery, Crafts, Games, Hobbies, Finance, Real Estate, Travel, Entertainment, Leisure
ISBN Prefix(es): 0-9590027; 0-9599177; 1-875700
Parent Company: HWW Pty Ltd
Associate Companies: Australian Property Monitors

Hospitality Books
7 Regent St, Ryde, NSW 2112
Mailing Address: PO Box 3007, Putney, NSW 2112
Tel: (02) 9809 5793 *Fax:* (02) 9809 4884
Web Site: www.hospitalitybooks.com.au
Key Personnel
Head of Company & Dir: Maureen Puckeridge *E-mail:* sales@hospitalitybooks.com.au
Founded: 1987
Publish "how-to" books on professional bartending, waiting, the Australian Wine Guide & Hospitality Core Units.
Membership(s): Copyright Agency Ltd.
Subjects: How-to, Wine & Spirits, Food & Beverage Service, Hospitality Industry
ISBN Prefix(es): 0-9587113; 0-957703
Total Titles: 4 Print

Hudson Publishing+
Division of NS Hudson Publishing Services P/L
89 Stevenson St, Kew, Victoria 3101
Mailing Address: PO Box 2088, Kew, Victoria 3101
Tel: (03) 9853 7753 *Fax:* (03) 9853 7290
E-mail: hudson@c031.aone.net.au
Key Personnel
Head of Company, Editorial Dir & Manager: Nick Hudson
Founded: 1985
Membership(s): Australian Publishers Association.
Subjects: Literature, Literary Criticism, Essays, Nonfiction (General)
ISBN Prefix(es): 0-949873
Total Titles: 50 Print
Imprints: Essien
Distributed by Jenny Nagle Addenda Publishing Sales & Marketing Services (New Zealand)
Warehouse: Peribo P/L, 50 Beaumont Rd, Mount Kuring Gai, NSW 2080 *Tel:* (02) 9457 0011 *Fax:* (02) 9457 0022 (national distributor)
Orders to: Peribo P/L, 50 Beaumont Rd, Mount Kuring Gai, NSW 2080 *Tel:* (02) 9457 0011 *Fax:* (02) 9457 0022 (national distributor)

Hungry Minds Australia, *imprint of* John Wiley & Sons Australia, Ltd

Hunter Books
PO Box 3362, Weston Creek, ACT 2611
Subjects: Fiction
ISBN Prefix(es): 0-646

Hunter House Publications+
8 Swan St, Hinton, NSW 2321
Tel: (02) 4930 5992 *Fax:* (02) 4930 5993
E-mail: wf&mc@hunterlink.net.au
Key Personnel
Author & Publisher: Cynthia Hunter
Founded: 1991
Specialize in history research.
Subjects: History
ISBN Prefix(es): 0-646; 1-876388
Number of titles published annually: 1 Print
Total Titles: 5 Print

Hutchinson, *imprint of* Random House Australia

Hyland House Publishing Pty Ltd+
50 Pin Oak Crescent, Flemington, Victoria 3031
Mailing Address: PO Box 122, Flemington, Victoria 3031
Tel: (03) 9376 4461 *Fax:* (03) 9376 4461
E-mail: hyland3@netspace.net.au
Key Personnel
Man Dir: Michael Schoo
Founded: 1976
Subjects: Animals, Pets, Asian Studies, Gardening, Plants, How-to, Nonfiction (General), Organizational Histories
ISBN Prefix(es): 0-908090; 0-947062; 1-875657; 1-86447
Associate Companies: Australian Book Distribution Group
Imprints: Australia's Best Garden Guide Series; Hylanders
Warehouse: Australian Book Group, Calway St, Drouin, Victoria 3818 *Tel:* (03) 5625 4290 *Fax:* (03) 5625 4272
Distribution Center: Gazelle Book Services, White Cross Mills, Hightown, Lancaster LA1 4XS, United Kingdom, Contact: Trevor Witcher *Tel:* (01524) 68765 *Fax:* (01524) 63232 (UK)
Orders to: Australian Book Group, Calway St, Drouin, Victoria 3818 *Tel:* (03) 5625 4290 *Fax:* (03) 5625 4272

Hylanders, *imprint of* Hyland House Publishing Pty Ltd

IAD, see Institute of Aboriginal Development (IAD Press)

IE Aust Publications, *imprint of* EA Books

Illert Publications+
2/3 Birch Crescent, East Corrimal, NSW 2518
Tel: (02) 4283 3009 *Fax:* (02) 4283 3009
E-mail: illert@keira.hotkey.net.au
Key Personnel
Editorial Manager: C Illert
Subjects: Anthropology, Asian Studies, Biological Sciences, Computer Science, Education, Environmental Studies, Genealogy, History, Language Arts, Linguistics, Mathematics, Natural History, Physics, Science (General), Technology
ISBN Prefix(es): 0-949357; 0-9597201

The Images Publishing Group Pty Ltd+
Images House, 6 Bastow Pl, Mulgrave, Victoria 3170
Tel: (03) 9561 5544 *Fax:* (03) 9561 4860
E-mail: books@images.com.au
Web Site: www.imagespublishinggroup.com
Key Personnel
Dir: Alessina Rose Brooks; Paul Alan Latham
Founded: 1983
Subjects: Accounting, Advertising, Architecture & Interior Design, Art, Biography, Civil Engineering, Engineering (General), Fashion
ISBN Prefix(es): 1-875498; 0-9589598; 1-876907; 1-920744
Number of titles published annually: 40 Print
Parent Company: Images Australia Pty Ltd
Distributed by ACC UK; ACC US; Antique Collectors' Club (Europe & USA); Bookwise International (Australia); Gingko Bookspan; Nippan IPS (Asia); Anthony Rudkin Associates (Middle East excluding Israel, Malta, Cypress, Turkey & Iran)

In-Tune Books+
PO Box 193, Avalon Beach, NSW 2107
Tel: (02) 9974 5981 *Fax:* (02) 9974 4552
Web Site: www.haywardbooks.com.au
Key Personnel
Manager: Malcolm Cohan *E-mail:* mcohan@ozemail.com.au
Founded: 1984
Subjects: Alternative, Art, Philosophy, Self-Help
ISBN Prefix(es): 0-9577024; 0-9577025; 0-9590439
Imprints: Hayward Books
Distributed by Alternate Books (South Africa); HarperCollins (New Zealand)
Distribution Center: WORDS Distributing Co, 7900 Edgewater Dr, Oakland, CA 94621, United States
World Leisure Marketing, Unit 11, Newmarket Court, Newmarket Dr, Derby DE24 8NW, United Kingdom *Tel:* (01332) 573 737 *Fax:* (01332) 573 399

Incunabula Press
608 Canning St, North Carlton, Victoria 3054
Tel: (03) 9381 1559
Key Personnel
Contact: John Ryrie *E-mail:* jryrie@pgrad.unimelb.edu.au
Founded: 1990
Specialize in handmade books in a limited edition of 20 to 30 copies, letterpress & printmaking.

Subjects: Art, Poetry
Total Titles: 10 Print

Indigo, *imprint of* Ginninderra Press

Indra Publishing+
142 Ryans Rd, Eltham North, Victoria 3095
Mailing Address: PO Box 7, Briar Hill, Victoria 3088
Tel: (03) 9439 7555 *Fax:* (03) 9439 7555
Web Site: www.indra.com.au
Key Personnel
Dir: Ian James Fraser *E-mail:* ian@indra.com.au
Founded: 1987
Membership(s): Australian Publisher's Association.
Subjects: Asian Studies, Biography, Disability, Special Needs, Ethnicity, Fiction, Foreign Countries, Literature, Literary Criticism, Essays, Romance, Women's Studies, Asia, Australia, Pacific
ISBN Prefix(es): 0-9587718; 0-9585805; 0-9578735; 1-9207870
Number of titles published annually: 6 Print; 1 Audio
Total Titles: 34 Print; 3 Audio
Distributed by Australian Book Group P/L (Australia); Gazelle Book Services Ltd (Europe); Horizon Books Pte Ltd (Southeast Asia); International Specialized Book Services (USA & Canada)
Foreign Rep(s): ISBS Corp (Canada, USA)
Foreign Rights: Alice Gruenfelder Literary Agency (Europe)

Industrial Press, *imprint of* Elsevier Australia

Infomedia, *imprint of* Flora Publications International Pty Ltd

Inner City Books, *imprint of* Rainbow Book Agencies Pty Ltd

Instauratio Press
PO Box 36, Yarra Junction, Victoria 3797
Tel: (03) 59666217 *Fax:* (03) 59666447
E-mail: catholic@scservnet.com
Key Personnel
Head of Company: Andrina McLean
Founded: 1982
Subjects: Religion - Catholic
ISBN Prefix(es): 0-9587113; 0-646
Subsidiaries: St Benedict Book Centre
Branch Office(s)
Instauratio Press, Box 1789, Post Falls, ID 83854, United States
Distributor for The Angelus Press (USA); Neumann Books (USA); Tan Books (USA)

Institute of Aboriginal Development (IAD Press)+
3 South Terrace, Alice Springs, NT 0871
Mailing Address: PO Box 2531, Alice Springs, NT 0871
Tel: (08) 8951 1311 *Fax:* (08) 8952 2527
E-mail: ozlit@netspace.net.au
Web Site: home.vicnet.au/~ozlit/iadpress.html
Key Personnel
Dir: Eileen Shaw
Publisher: Josie Douglas
Founded: 1969 (Aboriginal community controlled, publishing arm of Institute for Aboriginal Development)
Indigenous publishing house producing works by Aboriginal & Torres Strait Islander peoples of Australia.
Membership(s): APA (Australian Publishers Association) & Publish Australia.
Subjects: Anthropology, Art, Biography, Education, History, Language Arts, Linguistics, Literature, Literary Criticism, Essays, Natural History, Nonfiction (General), Regional Interests, Dictionaries, Language & Bilingual Books, Literature
ISBN Prefix(es): 0-949659; 1-86465; 1-9596206
Number of titles published annually: 10 Print; 1 E-Book; 1 Audio
Total Titles: 55 Print; 1 CD-ROM; 3 E-Book; 3 Audio
Imprints: Jukurrpa Books
U.S. Office(s): ISBS International Specialized Book Services, 5804 NE Massalo St, Portland, OR 97213-3644, United States, Contact: Tamma Greenfield *Tel:* 503-287-3093 *Fax:* 503-280-8882 *E-mail:* tamma@isbs.com

INT Press+
386 Mt Alexander Rd, Ascot Vale, Victoria 3032
Tel: (03) 9326 2416 *Fax:* (03) 9326 2413
E-mail: sales@intpress.com.au
Web Site: www.intpress.com.au
Key Personnel
International Rights: Luiai Rizzo
Founded: 1981
Subjects: English as a Second Language, Ethnicity
ISBN Prefix(es): 1-86310
Associate Companies: INT Press Distribution Pty Ltd
Bookshop(s): The LOTE INT Bookshop

Intext Book Company Pty Ltd
825 Glenferrie Rd, Hawthorn, Victoria 3122
Tel: (03) 9819-4500 *Fax:* (03) 9819-4511
E-mail: customerservice@intextbook.com.au
Web Site: www.intextbook.com.au
Key Personnel
Man Dir: Jillian Taylor *E-mail:* jillian@intextbook.com.au
Founded: 1982
Specialize in foreign languages other than English; distribution & promotion.
Subsidiaries: Language International Bookshop
Distributor for ALC Press (Japan); Alma Edizione (Italy); Bonacci (Italy); Cheng & T sui (USA); Cle International; Duerr Kessler (Germany); Diesterweg (Germany); Difusion (Spain); Duden (Germany); Edelsa (Spain); Ediciones SM (Spain); European School Books (UK); Gallimard (France); Giunti (Italy); Guerra (Italy); Hachette Livre International (France); Hatier/Didier (France); Klett (Germany); Kumon (Japan); Langenscheidt Texts & Dictionaries (Germany); Larousse (France); Menschenkinder (Germany); Nathan (France); Nihongo Journal (Japan); Ravensburger (Germany); Robert (France); SGEL (Spain); Santillana (Spain); Senmon Kyouiku (Japan); Soleil (Canada); The Japan Times (Japan); Vut Caps (Australia)

Inwardpath Publishers
76 McArthur Rd, Ivanhoe, Victoria 3079
Tel: (03) 9499 3405 *Fax:* (03) 9497 5656
Subjects: Philosophy, Esoteric, New Age
ISBN Prefix(es): 0-9585722
Distributor for Specialist Publications (Australia & Territories)
Foreign Rep(s): Four Corners (England)

Island Press Co-operative
29 Park Rd, Woodford, NSW 2778
Tel: (02) 4758 6635
E-mail: isphaw@hermes.net.au
Key Personnel
Man Dir: Philip Hammial
Founded: 1970
Subjects: Poetry
ISBN Prefix(es): 0-909771
Number of titles published annually: 4 Print
Total Titles: 45 Print

Jabiru Press
13 Ferdinand Ave, Balwyn North, Victoria 3104
Tel: (03) 9609 3535 *Fax:* (03) 9857 9110
Key Personnel
Contact: Dick Johnson *E-mail:* djohnson@netspace.net.au
ISBN Prefix(es): 0-908104

James Nicholas Publishers Pty Ltd
PO Box 244, Albert Park, Victoria 3206
Tel: (03) 9690 5955 (customer service); (03) 9696 5545 (editorial office) *Fax:* (03) 9699 2040
E-mail: info@jamesnicholaspublishers.com.au; info@jnponline.com
Web Site: www.jamesnicholaspublishers.com.au; www.jnponline.com
Key Personnel
Publisher & Editor: Ms Rea Zajda
Founded: 1978
Subjects: Business, Communications, Education, Government, Political Science, Health, Nutrition, Management, Marketing, Medicine, Nursing, Dentistry, Social Sciences, Sociology
ISBN Prefix(es): 1-875408
Total Titles: 10 Print

Jared Publishing
PO Box 51, Mitcham, Victoria 3132
Tel: (03) 9874 2415

Jarrah Publications+
42 Chisholm Circle, Heritage Estate, Armadale, WA 6112
Mailing Address: PO Box 1041, Kelmscott Delivery Centre, Kelmscott, WA 6997
Tel: (08) 9495 4569 *Fax:* (08) 9495 4569
Key Personnel
Head of Company: W F Vormair
Sales Dir & International Rights: Willy Frank
Author: Jean Vormair
Editor & International Rights: Jan Margaret
Founded: 1987
Partnership specializing in fantasy & contemporary issues.
Subjects: Fiction, Human Relations, Romance, Science Fiction, Fantasy
ISBN Prefix(es): 0-9587113; 0-646
Total Titles: 2 Print

Jenelle Press
PO Box 656, Gladesville, NSW 2111
Tel: (02) 4281531 *Fax:* (02) 4284144
Key Personnel
Head of Company: Mark Robert Mannering
Subjects: Education
ISBN Prefix(es): 1-875734

Jesuit Publications+
Unit of Society of Jesus
PO Box 553, Richmond, Victoria 3121
Tel: (03) 9427 7311 *Fax:* (03) 9428 4450
E-mail: jespub@jespub.jesuit.org.au
Web Site: www.jesuitpublications.com.au
Key Personnel
Dir: Christopher Gleeson
Publisher: Andrew Hamilton
Business Manager: Mark Dowell *E-mail:* mark@jespub.jesuit.org.au
Marketing: Kirsty Grant
Production: Geraldine Battersby; Irene Hunter
Founded: 1988
Subjects: Poetry, Religion - Catholic, Religion - Protestant, Religion - Other, Theology
ISBN Prefix(es): 0-9586796
Divisions: Aurora Books; Australian Catholics; Eureka Street; Madonna

Jesuit Publications/Aurora Books, *imprint of* Rainbow Book Agencies Pty Ltd

Jika Publishing+
3 Witney Way, Bundoora, Victoria 3083

AUSTRALIA

Tel: (03) 9467 3295 *Fax:* (03) 9467 1770
E-mail: jordanca@alphalink.com.au
Subjects: Drama, Theater, Poetry
ISBN Prefix(es): 0-9587113; 0-646

JL Publications+
Division of Submariner Publication, P/C
26 Highgate Gue, Ashburton, Victoria 3147
Mailing Address: PO Box 387, Ashburton, Victoria 3147
Tel: (03) 98860200 *Fax:* (03) 98860200
E-mail: jlpubs@c031.aone.net.au
Key Personnel
Contact: John Lippmann
Subjects: Scuba Diving Safety
Total Titles: 12 Print
Distributed by Aqua Quest Publications (New York)

Michael Joseph, *imprint of* Penguin Group (Australia)

Journeys, *imprint of* Lonely Planet Publications Pty Ltd

Joval Publications
PO Box 618, Bacchus Marsh, Victoria 3340
Tel: (053) 674593
Key Personnel
Contact: John Reid
Founded: 1986
Subjects: History, Photography, Poetry
ISBN Prefix(es): 0-9588112

Jukurrpa Books, *imprint of* Institute of Aboriginal Development (IAD Press)

Kangaroo Press, *imprint of* Simon & Schuster (Australia) Pty Ltd

Kangaroo Press+
Imprint of Simon & Schuster Australia
PO Box 6125, Dural Delivery Centre, NSW 2158
Tel: (02) 6541502 *Fax:* (02) 6541338
Key Personnel
Publisher: David Rosenberg
Publicity Manager: Priscilla Rosenberg
Founded: 1981
Subjects: Biography, Crafts, Games, Hobbies, Gardening, Plants, History, Natural History, Nonfiction (General), Regional Interests, Sports, Athletics, Transportation, Travel
ISBN Prefix(es): 0-949924; 0-86417
Imprints: Roo Books

Gregory Kefalas Publishing
5a Byron St, Campsie, NSW 2194
Tel: (02) 9789 6049 *Fax:* (02) 97876181
Subjects: Automotive
ISBN Prefix(es): 0-9586798

Ken Fin, *imprint of* Social Club Books

Killara Press+
MS 660, Proston, Qld 4613
Tel: (07) 5499-7717 *Fax:* (07) 4168-0244
Key Personnel
Contact: Sylvia Seiler *E-mail:* seiler@elr.com.au
Founded: 1991
Writing & publishing.
Subjects: Disability, Special Needs, Fiction, Human Relations
ISBN Prefix(es): 0-9585731

Kingfisher Books+
51 Henry St, Hawthorn, Victoria 3122
Tel: (03) 9819 9100 *Fax:* (03) 9819 0977
Founded: 1989

Subjects: Maritime
ISBN Prefix(es): 0-9593999

Kingsclear Books+
36 Kingsclear Rd, Alexandria, NSW 2015
Mailing Address: PO Box 335, Alexandria, NSW 1435
Tel: (02) 95574367 *Fax:* (02) 95572337
E-mail: kingsclear@wr.com.au
Web Site: www.kingsclearbooks.com.au
Key Personnel
Chief Executive Officer & Dir Sales & Production: Catherine Warne
Founded: 1983
Specialize in local history, alternative health, tourism & true crime.
Subjects: Criminology, Health, Nutrition, History, Travel
ISBN Prefix(es): 0-908272
Number of titles published annually: 6 Print
Total Titles: 40 Print
Imprints: Kingsclear Books Pty Ltd
Subsidiaries: Atrand Pty Ltd
Distributed by Envirobooks
Shipping Address: Tower Books, 2/19 Rodborough Rd, Frenchs Forest, NSW 2086, Contact: Dale Druckman *Tel:* (02) 9975-5586 *Fax:* (02) 9975-5599
Warehouse: Federation Press, 71 John St, Leichhardt, NSW 2040, Contact: John Xenos *Tel:* (09552) 2200

Kingsclear Books Pty Ltd, *imprint of* Kingsclear Books

Knopf Publishing, *imprint of* Random House Australia

Kookaburra Technical Publications Pty Ltd
6 Colvin Court, Glen Waverley, Victoria 3150
Tel: (03) 9560 0841 *Fax:* (03) 9545 1121
Web Site: members.dcsi.net.au/jtboundy/hkookafo.htm
Key Personnel
Head of Company: Geoff Pentland
Customer Service: Jenny Martin
Founded: 1963
Specialize in reference books for modelers & historians.
Subjects: Aeronautics, Aviation
ISBN Prefix(es): 0-85880

Kurlana Publishing
PO Box 481, North Adelaide, SA 5006
Tel: (08) 3886619
Founded: 1988
Subjects: Psychology, Psychiatry
ISBN Prefix(es): 0-9587998

Lancer, *imprint of* Anzea Publishers Ltd

Landarc Publications
46 McIlwraith St, North Carlton, Victoria 3054
Tel: (03) 93801276 *Fax:* (03) 93801276
E-mail: carmar@bigpond.com
Key Personnel
Manager: Carolyn Pike
Founded: 1981
Subjects: Gardening, Plants
ISBN Prefix(es): 0-9587100; 0-9594220
Total Titles: 3 Print

Lansdowne Publishing Pty Ltd+
PO Box 48, Milson's Point, NSW 2061
Tel: (02) 9240 9222 *Fax:* (02) 9241 4818
E-mail: sales@lanspub.com.au
Key Personnel
Chief Executive: Steven Morris
Publisher: Deborah Nixon

Publicity & Office Manager: Valerie Sadlier
Tel: (02) 9240 9201 *E-mail:* valerie@lanspub.com.au
Production Manager: Sally Davies
Subjects: Animals, Pets, Cookery, Gardening, Plants, Health, Nutrition, History, Mythology
ISBN Prefix(es): 1-86302; 0-947116; 0-949708
Parent Company: Kirin Publishing Pty Ltd

Laurel Press+
850 Huon Rd, Ferntree, Tas 7054
Mailing Address: PO Box 132, Sandy Bay, Tas 7006
Tel: (03) 6239 1139 *Fax:* (03) 6239 1139
Key Personnel
Head of Company: Chris Bell *E-mail:* chrisjen@southcom.com.au
Founded: 1990
Publisher of on-going large-format fine editions.
Subjects: Natural History, Photography
ISBN Prefix(es): 0-646
Total Titles: 2 Print

Law Book Co Information Services+
50 Waterloo Rd, North Ryde, NSW 2113
Mailing Address: PO Box 24, Toronto Dominion Centre, Toronto, ON M5K 1A1, Canada
Tel: (02) 99366444 *Fax:* (02) 98882229
Telex: 27995 Asbook *Cable:* Asbook
Key Personnel
Publishing Manager: E Costigan; A M O'Neill
National Sales Manager: B Crane
Marketing Manager: C Simmons
Manager, Editorial: Y Stewart
Founded: 1898
Subjects: Accounting, Business, Criminology, Environmental Studies, Finance, Labor, Industrial Relations, Law, Medicine, Nursing, Dentistry, Real Estate
ISBN Prefix(es): 0-455
Parent Company: Thomson Corporation Publishing Ltd, United Kingdom
Ultimate Parent Company: The Thomson Corp, Suite 2706, Toronto Dominion Bank Tower, Toronto, ON M5K 1A1, Canada
Subsidiaries: Centre for Professional Development; Newsletter Information Services
Branch Office(s)
Thomson International Publishing Group, Metro Center, One Station Place, Stamford, CT 06902, United States
Bookshop(s): 4/167 Phillip St, Sydney, NSW 2000; 560 Lonsdale St, Melbourne, Victoria 3000; 1/40 Queen St, Brisbane, Qld 4000; 77 St Georges Terr, 13th Floor, Perth, WA 6000
Warehouse: 50 Waterloo Rd, North Ryde, NSW 2113
Orders to: 50 Waterloo Rd, North Ryde, NSW 2113

LBC Information Services, see Law Book Co Information Services

The Learner's Dimensions, *imprint of* Hawker Brownlow

The Learning Works, *imprint of* Hawker Brownlow

Sandra Lee Agencies
23 Arthur St, Brighton, Victoria 3186
Mailing Address: PO Box 32, Brighton, Victoria 3186
Tel: (03) 9592 5235 *Fax:* (03) 9592 7608
E-mail: winston@ozonline.com.au
Key Personnel
Marketing: Sandra Lewin-Smith
Founded: 1970
Subjects: Cookery
ISBN Prefix(es): 0-7316

Legal Books, *imprint of* Prospect Media Pty Ltd

PUBLISHERS — AUSTRALIA

Let's Go, *imprint of* Pan Macmillan Australia Pty Ltd

Levanter Publishing & Associates+
2 Bowlers Ave, Bexley, NSW 2207
Tel: (02) 9371 7824
Key Personnel
Head of Company: David Ehrlich
Sales Manager: Claudine Auger
Editor: Frank Hariri
Founded: 1991
Subjects: Fiction, Romance
ISBN Prefix(es): 0-646
Showroom(s): Flat 5, No 3, Rockley St, Bondi, NSW 2026
Warehouse: Flat 5, No 3, Rockley St, Bondi, NSW 2026
Orders to: Flat 5, No 3, Rockley St, Bondi, NSW 2026

Libra Books Pty Ltd
GPO Box 10, Hobart, Tas 7001
Tel: (03) 6230 2656 *Fax:* (03) 6225 0900
Key Personnel
Head of Company: Bert Wicks E-mail: bwicks@trump.net.au
Founded: 1972
ISBN Prefix(es): 0-909619

Library of Australian History
17 Mitchell St, North Sydney, NSW 2060
Mailing Address: PO Box 795, North Sydney, NSW 2059
Tel: (02) 9929 5087 *Fax:* (02) 9929 5087
E-mail: grdxxx@ozemail.com.au
Key Personnel
Editorial Manager: Keith Johnson
Founded: 1977
Subjects: Genealogy, History, Regional Interests, Australian History & Reference, Family History
ISBN Prefix(es): 0-908120; 0-9579524
Subsidiaries: Genealogical Research Directory
U.S. Office(s): 130 E Montecito Ave, No 120, Sierra Madre, CA 91024-1924, United States, John Poole Tel: 626-792-1339 E-mail: grdusa@earthlink.net

Life Planning Foundation of Australia, Inc
341 Queen St, Ground floor, Melbourne, Victoria 3000
Tel: (03) 9670 4417 *Fax:* (03) 9640 0094
E-mail: lifeclub@vicnet.net.au
Web Site: www.life.org.au
Key Personnel
Executive Dir: John Vial
Founded: 1974
Subjects: Finance, Health, Nutrition, Human Relations, Nonfiction (General), Self-Help
ISBN Prefix(es): 0-9590567

Lineup, *imprint of* Troll Books of Australia

Linking-Up Publishing+
99 First Ave, Five Dock, NSW 2046
Mailing Address: PO Box W28, Wareemba, NSW 2046
Tel: (02) 9712 5576 *Fax:* (02) 9712 1963
Key Personnel
Contact: Julian Raimundo
Subjects: Psychology, Psychiatry
ISBN Prefix(es): 0-646
Distributor for Castalia Publishing; Chevron Corp; Taylor Publishing

Little Hills Press Pty Ltd+
18 Bearing Rd, Seven Hills, NSW 2147
Tel: (02) 9838 4373 *Fax:* (02) 9838 7929
E-mail: lhills@bigpond.net.au
Web Site: www.littlehills.com
Key Personnel
Chief Executive & Sales: Charles C Burfitt
Founded: 1981
Subjects: Crafts, Games, Hobbies, Fashion, Nonfiction (General), Travel
ISBN Prefix(es): 0-949773; 1-86315
Total Titles: 59 Print
Imprints: Mount
Distributed by Cimino Publishing (USA); Pelican (USA); Ulysses Books (Canada); World Leisure Marketing (UK)
Distributor for Berndston & Berndston Maps; Camerapix; Firefly; Formac Publishing; Four Courts; Gault Millau; Gracewing; Hunter Publications; Kuemmerly & Frey Maps; Marcopolo; John Muir; Pallas Athena; Penton Overseas Inc; Scepter (USA & UK); Sinag-Tala (Philippines); Ulysses Travel Publishers; World Leisure Marketing

Little Red Apple Publishing+
PO Box 67, Thornleigh, NSW 2120
Tel: (02) 9430 6867
E-mail: littleredapple@hotmail.com
Key Personnel
Contact: Rosa Solomon
Founded: 1988
Specialize in novels, plays, Aboriginal myths & legends. Network for author, publisher & artists.
Subjects: Biography, Child Care & Development, Disability, Special Needs, Education, Fiction, History, Human Relations, Humor, Nonfiction (General), Poetry, Religion - Catholic, Religion - Other, Romance, Plays
ISBN Prefix(es): 0-9587113; 1-875329
Number of titles published annually: 10 Print
Total Titles: 26 Print
Distributor for Il Castello; Ripostes
Distribution Center: PO Box K152, Haymarket, NSW 1240

Living Books, *imprint of* Random House Australia

Local Consumption Publications
42 Forbes St, Newtown (Sydney), NSW 2042
Mailing Address: PO Box 116, Wentworth Bldg, Sydney University, Sydney, NSW 2006
Tel: (02) 9519-7503 *Fax:* (02) 95197503
Key Personnel
Contact: Stephen Muecke E-mail: stephen.muecke@uts.edu.au
ISBN Prefix(es): 0-949793

Lonely Planet Publications Pty Ltd+
ABN 36 005 607 983, Locked Bag 1, Footscray, Victoria 3011
Tel: (03) 8379 8000 *Fax:* (03) 8379 8111
E-mail: talk2us@lonelyplanet.com.au
Web Site: www.lonelyplanet.com.au
Key Personnel
Dir: Maureen Wheeler; Tony Wheeler
Publisher: Sue Galley; Rob van Dreisum; Susan Keogh; Sally Steward; Paul Smitz
Rights & Permissions: Annalisa Guidici
Production: Graham Imeson
Promotions & Publicity: Anna Bolger
Co-General Manager: Steve Hibbard
Founded: 1973
Phrasebooks, travel literature, walking & diving guides & pictorials.
Subjects: Travel
ISBN Prefix(es): 0-908086; 0-86442; 1-86450; 1-74079; 1-74104
Imprints: Journeys; Pisces
Branch Office(s)
Lonely Planet, One rue du Dahomey, 75011 Paris, France Tel: (01) 55 25 33 00 Fax: (01) 55 25 33 01 E-mail: bip@lonelyplanet.fr
Lonely Planet, 72-82 Rosebery Ave, Clerkenwell, London EC1R 4RW, United Kingdom Tel: (020) 7841 9000 Fax: (020) 7841 9001 E-mail: go@lonelyplanet.co.au
U.S. Office(s): Lonely Planet Publications Inc, 150 Linden St, Oakland, CA 94607, United States Tel: 510-893-8555 Fax: 510-893-8563 E-mail: info@lonelyplanet.com

Lonestone Press, *imprint of* Oceans Enterprises

Barry Long Books+
PO Box 574, Mullumbimby, NSW 2482
E-mail: contact@barrylongbooks.com
Web Site: www.barrylongbooks.com
Key Personnel
International Rights: Clive Tempest Tel: (01823) 430061 Fax: (01823) 430062 E-mail: clive.tempest@btinternet.com
Founded: 1994
Non-profit educational company.
Specialize in the work of spiritual teacher Barry Long.
Subjects: Religion - Other, Self-Help
ISBN Prefix(es): 0-9508050; 1-899324
Number of titles published annually: 2 Print
Total Titles: 20 Print
Parent Company: The Barry Long Foundation International, Box 5277, Gold Coast MC, Qld 4217, Contact: Sara Koh
Branch Office(s)
BCM Box 876, London WC1N 3XX, United Kingdom, Contact: Clive Tempest Tel: (01823) 430061 Fax: (01823) 430062 E-mail: contact@barrylongbooks.com Web Site: www.barrylongbooks.com
U.S. Office(s): 6230 Wilshire Blvd, Suite 251, Los Angeles, CA 90048, United States, Contact: Simon Warwick Smith Tel: 707-939-9212 Fax: 707-938-3515
Distributed by Brumby Books (Australia); Deep Books (UK & Ireland); New Leaf Distributing Co (US & Canada); Peaceful Living (New Zealand)
Orders to: Bookworld Services, 1933 Whitfield Park Loop, Sarasota, FL 34243, United States E-mail: sales@bookworld.com Web Site: www.bookworld.com

Longman, *imprint of* Pearson Education Australia

Lothian Books, see Thomas C Lothian Pty Ltd

Thomas C Lothian Pty Ltd+
Level 5, 132 Albert Rd, South Melbourne, Victoria 3205
Tel: (03) 9694 4900 *Fax:* (03) 9645 0705
E-mail: books@lothian.com.au
Web Site: www.lothian.com.au
Key Personnel
Man Dir & Publishing: Peter Lothian E-mail: peter_lothian@lothian.com.au
Sales & Marketing Dir: Bruce Hilliard E-mail: bruce_hilliard@lothian.com.au
Founded: 1888
Membership(s): Australian Publishers Association.
Subjects: Biography, Business, Health, Nutrition, Nonfiction (General), Self-Help, Sports, Athletics, Australiana
ISBN Prefix(es): 0-85091; 0-7344
Number of titles published annually: 110 Print
Total Titles: 800 Print
Distributed by Forrester Books (New Zealand); Phambili Agencies CC (South Africa); Ragged Bears (Children); Roundhouse Publishing GRP (Adult); Star Bright Books USA; STP/Times Publishing Group (Singapore); Vanwell Publishing (Canada)
Distributor for Barron's; Lothian Publishing Co; North South Books
Distribution Center: MDS

David Lovell Publishing, *imprint of* Rainbow Book Agencies Pty Ltd

Lowden Publishing Co
29 Lisbeth Ave, Donvale, Victoria 3111
Tel: (03) 9873 7202 *Fax:* (03) 9873 0542
E-mail: service@theruralstore.com.au
Web Site: www.theruralstore.com.au
Key Personnel
Man Dir: Jim Lowden *E-mail:* jim@theruralstore.com.au
Founded: 1969
Subjects: Biography, History, Religion - Other, Transportation
ISBN Prefix(es): 0-909706
Associate Companies: The Rural Store (Agricultural Booksellers)

Lucasville Press
Lukis House, 1a Dalzell Rd, Raaf Base, Point Cook, Victoria 3030
Tel: (03) 9395 1446
Key Personnel
Head of Company: S Campbell-Wright
Founded: 1987
Specialize in Australian history.
Subjects: Biography, Genealogy, History
ISBN Prefix(es): 0-9587113; 0-646

MacLennan & Petty Pty Ltd+
152 Bunnerong Rd, Suite 405, Eastgardens, NSW 2036
Tel: (02) 9349 5811 *Fax:* (02) 9349 5911
E-mail: macpetty@zip.com.au
Key Personnel
Man Dir & International Rights Contact: Pamela Petty
Special Projects Dir: Rod Mead *E-mail:* rmead@maclennanpetty.com.au
Founded: 1988
Specialize in human services.
Subjects: Disability, Special Needs, Education, Health, Nutrition, Medicine, Nursing, Dentistry
ISBN Prefix(es): 0-86433
Number of titles published annually: 10 Print
Total Titles: 55 Print
Distributed by APAC Publishers (Southeast Asia); F A Davis (United States); Jessica Kingsley Publishing Co; Springer Publishing Co (Europe & UK)
Distributor for Adis Press (New Zealand); Aspen Publishers Inc (US); Brookes Publishing Co (United States); F A Davis; Health Press (United Kingdom); Health Professions Press (United States); Icon Learning Systems (United States); Isis Medical Media (United Kingdom); J & S Publishing (United States); Love Publishing Co; MacLennan & Petty (Australia); Merit Publishing (United Kingdom); Paul H Brookes; Pavilion Publishers (United Kingdom); Quay Books (Div of Mark Allen Publishing) (United Kingdom); Roeher Institute (Canada); Slack Inc (United States); Springhouse Publishing (United States); Springhouse (United States); Whurr Publishers (United Kingdom); York Press (United States)

Macmillan, *imprint of* Pan Macmillan Australia Pty Ltd

Macmillan Education Australia+
Level 4, 627 Chapel St, South Yarra, Victoria 3141
Tel: (03) 9825 1025 *Fax:* (03) 9825 1010
E-mail: mea@macmillan.com.au
Web Site: www.macmillan.com.au
Key Personnel
Man Dir: Shane Armstrong *E-mail:* shane.armstrong@macmillan.com.au
Sales Dir: Peter Huntley *E-mail:* peter.huntley@macmillian.com.au
Marketing Manager: Christine Powers *E-mail:* christine.powers@macmillan.com.au
Senior Sales Coordinator: Vicky Cheong *E-mail:* vicky.cheong@macmillan.com.au
Founded: 1896
Subjects: Accounting, Behavioral Sciences, Economics, Education, Geography, Geology, Government, Political Science, History, Management, Mathematics, Physics, Science (General), Social Sciences, Sociology
ISBN Prefix(es): 0-7329; 0-7330
Parent Company: Macmillan Publishers Australia Pty Ltd
Branch Office(s)
Level 2, St Martins Tower, 31 Market St, Sydney, NSW 2000 *Tel:* (02) 9264 0522 *Fax:* (02) 9264 0770 *E-mail:* measyd@macmillan.com.au
Warehouse: Macmillan Distribution Services Pty Ltd, 56 Parkwest Dr, Derrimut, Victoria 3030, Man Dir: Andy Palmer *Tel:* (03) 9825 1000 *Fax:* (03) 9825 3210 *E-mail:* mds@macmillan.com.au *Web Site:* www.ozemail.com.au/~mds/; www.macmillan.com.au

Macmillan Publishers Australia Pty Ltd+
Subsidiary of Macmillan Publishers (UK) Ltd
627 Chapel St, Level 4, South Yarra, Victoria 3141
Tel: (03) 9825 1000 *Fax:* (03) 9825 1015
Web Site: www.panmacmillan.com.au
Key Personnel
Man Dir: Ross Gibb *E-mail:* ross.gibb@macmillan.com.au
Sales/Trade Manager: Laurie Giles
College Sales Manager: Harry Khoury
Customer Service: Younia Jarmam
Founded: 1968
Subjects: Education, Engineering (General), Literature, Literary Criticism, Essays, Military Science, Psychology, Psychiatry, Science (General), Social Sciences, Sociology
ISBN Prefix(es): 0-02; 0-08; 0-9585743; 1-876832
Subsidiaries: Australian National University Press
Sales Office(s): Melbourne
Sydney
Warehouse: 2-A Lord St, Botany, NSW 2019

Macquarie Library, *imprint of* Pan Macmillan Australia Pty Ltd

The Macquarie Library Pty Ltd
Macquarie University, Sydney, NSW 2109
Tel: (02) 9805 9800 *Fax:* (02) 9888 2984
E-mail: alison@dict.mq.edu
Key Personnel
Publisher: Richard Tardif
Founded: 1980
ISBN Prefix(es): 0-949757; 1-876429
Parent Company: Kirin Publishing Pty Ltd
Orders to: Gary Allen Pty Ltd, 9 Cooper St, Smithfield, Sydney, NSW 2164

Magabala Books Aboriginal Corporation+
PO Box 668, Broome, WA 6725
Tel: (08) 9192 1991 *Fax:* (08) 9193 5254
E-mail: info@magabala.com
Web Site: www.magabala.com
Key Personnel
Publishing Manager: Bruce Sims
Administration Manager: Jill Walsh
Management Committee Chairperson: Arnhem Hunter
Founded: 1987
Specialize in indigenous publishing.
Subjects: Anthropology, Art, Biography, Drama, Theater, Fiction, Human Relations, Literature, Literary Criticism, Essays, Natural History, Nonfiction (General), Philosophy, Religion - Other
ISBN Prefix(es): 1-875641; 0-9588101
Warehouse: Discount Freight Express, PO Box 260, Bentley, WA 6102

Magic Bean, *imprint of* Era Publications

Magpie Books
PO Box 2038, Brighton, Victoria 3186
Tel: (0613) 9592 9931 *Fax:* (0613) 9592 2045
E-mail: admin01@magpiebooks.com.au
Web Site: www.magpiebooks.com.au
Founded: 1980
Publisher of price guides for the second hand book trade.
Subjects: Publishing & Book Trade Reference

Magpie Publications
PO Box 3427, Weston Creek, ACT 2611
Tel: (06) 2509442
Key Personnel
Contact: T A Orchard
Specialize in Philately.
Subjects: Philatey & Postal History
ISBN Prefix(es): 0-9587862; 1-875579

Magpies Magazine Pty Ltd
13 Frome St, Grange, Qld 4051
Mailing Address: PO Box 98, Grange, Qld 4051
Tel: (07) 3356 4503 *Fax:* (07) 3356 4649
E-mail: james@magpies.net.au
Web Site: www.magpies.net.au
Key Personnel
Editor: Ray Turton
Founded: 1986
Subjects: Library & Information Sciences
ISBN Prefix(es): 1-875249

Mammoth UK, *imprint of* Random House Australia

Margaret Hamilton Books Pty Ltd+
Imprint of Scholastic Australia
76-80 Railway Crescent, Lisarow, NSW 2250
Mailing Address: PO Box 579, Gosford, NSW 2250
Tel: (02) 4328 3555 *Toll Free Tel:* 800-021-233 *Fax:* (02) 4323 3827 *Toll Free Fax:* 800-789-948
E-mail: customer_service@scholastic.com.au
Web Site: www.scholastic.com.au
Key Personnel
Dir: Margaret Hamilton
Sr Editor: Margrete Lamond *Tel:* (02) 9413 8343
Founded: 1988
ISBN Prefix(es): 0-947241; 1-876289
Ultimate Parent Company: Scholastic Inc

Margin Magazines, *imprint of* Mulini Press

Marketing Focus
26 Central Rd, Kalamunda, WA 6076
Tel: (08) 92571777 *Fax:* (08) 92571888
Web Site: www.marketingfocus.net.au
Key Personnel
Head of Company & Man Dir: Barry Ross Urquhart *E-mail:* urquhart@marketingfocus.net.au
Founded: 1978
Marketing & strategic planning consultant.
Subjects: Business, Marketing
ISBN Prefix(es): 0-9586558

Marque Publishing Co Pty Ltd
470 Pacific Highway, Wyoming, NSW
Mailing Address: PO Box 1896, Gosford, NSW 2250
Tel: (02) 4322 4803 *Fax:* (02) 4329 1475
E-mail: books@marque.com.au
Web Site: www.marque.com.au

Key Personnel
Editorial Dir: Ewan Kennedy
Business Manager: Alistair Kennedy
Founded: 1987
Specialize in motoring books.
Subjects: Transportation
ISBN Prefix(es): 0-947079
Distributed by Bookworks Pty Ltd

Tracy Marsh Publications Pty Ltd+
1/79 Osmond Terrace, Norwood SA 5067
Tel: (08) 8363 1248 *Fax:* (08) 8363 1352
Web Site: www.tracymarsh.com
Key Personnel
Chief Executive: Tracy Marsh *E-mail:* tracy@tracymarsh.com
Co-Editions Manager: Jane Moseley
Founded: 1984
Subjects: Crafts, Games, Hobbies, Travel
ISBN Prefix(es): 1-875899; 0-9590174

Horwitz Martin Education+
Horwitz House, 55 Chandos St, St Leonards, NSW 2065
Mailing Address: PO Box 5555, St Leonards, NSW 2065
Tel: (02) 9901 6100 *Fax:* (02) 9901 6166
Key Personnel
General Manager: Stephen Wilson
 E-mail: stephenw@horwitz.com.au
Founded: 1958
Educational publishing company
Specialize in elementary textbook & literacy materials.
Subjects: Education, Literature, Literary Criticism, Essays, Literacy
ISBN Prefix(es): 0-7253; 0-7252; 0-7255
Number of titles published annually: 120 Print
Total Titles: 500 Print
Parent Company: Horwitz Publications Pty Ltd

Matthias Media
42 Gardeners Rd, Suite 1, Kingsford, NSW 2032
Mailing Address: PO Box 225, Kingsford, NSW 2032
Tel: (02) 3100813; (02) 9663-1478 (overseas)
 Toll Free Tel: 800 814 360 *Fax:* (02) 9663-3265; (02) 9663-3265
E-mail: info@matthiasmedia.com.au
Web Site: www.matthiasmedia.com.au
Key Personnel
Man Dir & International Rights: Ian Carmichael
Founded: 1988
Subjects: Education, Religion - Protestant, Christianity, Bible, Evangelicalism, Ministry
ISBN Prefix(es): 1-875245
Parent Company: St Matthias Press

Mayfield Publishing, *imprint of* Elsevier Australia

Mayne Publishing+
MS 422, Clifton, Qld 4361
Tel: (07) 4697 3228 *Fax:* (07) 4697 3228
Web Site: www.maynepublishing.com.au
Key Personnel
Contact: C Mayne
Founded: 1993
Subjects: Behavioral Sciences, Cookery, Crafts, Games, Hobbies, Fiction, Government, Political Science, Health, Nutrition, How-to, Self-Help
ISBN Prefix(es): 0-646; 0-9578142

Yvonne McBurney
Educational Material Aid, 140L Obley Rd, MS3, Dubbo, NSW 2830
Tel: (02) 68873608
Key Personnel
Dir: Yvonne McBurney
Founded: 1976
Subjects: History, Regional Interests
ISBN Prefix(es): 0-908053
Warehouse: 140L Obley Rd MS3, Dubbo, NSW 2830 *Tel:* (068) 873608

McGraw-Hill Australia Pty Ltd+
Subsidiary of The McGraw-Hill Companies
82 Waterloo Rd, North Ryde, NSW 2113
Mailing Address: Locked bag 2233, Business Centre, North Ryde, NSW 1670
Tel: (02) 9900 1800; (02) 9900 1806 (customer service); (02) 9900 1802 (customer service) *Fax:* (02) 9878 8280 (customer service)
E-mail: cservice_sydney@mcgraw-hill.com.au
Web Site: www.mcgraw-hill.com.au
Key Personnel
General Manager: Yasminka Nemet
 E-mail: yasminka_nemet@mcgraw-hill.com
Publishing Manager, Science, Humanities & Vocational Education & Training: Michael Tully
 E-mail: michael_tully@mcgraw-hill.com
Sponsoring Editor, Business Publishing: Alisa Brackley du Bois
 E-mail: alisa_brackleydebois@mcgraw-hill.com
Marketing Coordinator, Business: Paula McGuinness *Tel:* (02) 9900 1890 *Fax:* (02) 9878 8881
 E-mail: cherie_cadongan@mcgraw-hill.com
Marketing Coordinator, Medical: Sam McGown
 Tel: (02) 9900 1836 *Fax:* (02) 9878 8881
 E-mail: sam_mcgown@mcgraw-hill.com
Editorial Assistant: Eiko Bron *Tel:* (02) 9900 1905 *Fax:* (02) 9878 8881 *E-mail:* eiko_bron@mcgraw-hill.com
Founded: 1964
Subjects: Accounting, Advertising, Aeronautics, Aviation, Anthropology, Architecture & Interior Design, Art, Automotive, Behavioral Sciences, Biological Sciences, Chemistry, Chemical Engineering, Child Care & Development, Computer Science, Criminology, Disability, Special Needs, Earth Sciences, Economics, Education, Electronics, Electrical Engineering, Engineering (General), English as a Second Language, Environmental Studies, Film, Video, Geography, Geology, Health, Nutrition, Journalism, Labor, Industrial Relations, Language Arts, Linguistics, Management, Maritime, Marketing, Mathematics, Mechanical Engineering, Medicine, Nursing, Dentistry, Philosophy, Photography, Physical Sciences, Physics, Psychology, Psychiatry, Social Sciences, Sociology, Sports, Athletics
ISBN Prefix(es): 0-07; 0-697; 0-256
Associate Companies: McGraw-Hill Book Co NZ Ltd, 56-60 Cawley St, Level 8, Ellerslie, Auckland, New Zealand, Contact: Max Loveridge
 Tel: (09) 526 6200 *Fax:* (09) 526 6216
Imprints: PressXpress
Branch Office(s)
Melbourne Office, 8 Yarra St, Hawthorn, Victoria 3122, PTR State Manager: Nick Dallas
 Tel: (03) 9819 0511 *Fax:* (03) 9819 0524
Brisbane Office, 588 Boundary St, Spring Hill, Qld 4000, Professional Division State Manager: Brent Pattison *Tel:* (07) 3835 1166 *Fax:* (07) 3831 7119
Distributed by Amacom (American Mangement); Active Path (Wrox); American Education Publishing; Appleton & Lange; ASQ (American Society of Quality); Barnell Loft Ltd; Benziger Publishing Co; Brown & Benchmark; William C Brown; Business Week Books; Certification Press; Charles E Merrill; Citrix Press; Clearway Exam Questions (HSC); Clearway Textbooks; CommerceNet Press; Computing McGraw-Hill; Contemporary Publications/NTC; Corel Press; Custom Publications; Dushkin Publishing Group; J D Edwards; Fine Arts Press; Friends of Ed; Glencoe/McGraw; Harvard Business School Press; International Marine; Irwin Publishers; Richard D Irwin; James Town Publishers/NTC; Keats Publishing/NTC; Learning Triangle Press; London House; MacMillan/McGraw-Hill School; Mayfield Publishing Co; McGraw-Hill Canada; Tata McGraw-Hill India; McGraw-Hill Italy; McGraw-Hill Microsoft Press; McGraw-Hill Singapore; McGraw-Hill UK; McGraw-Hill USA; Metric Schaum; New Holland Publishers; NTC (National Textbook Co); Oracle Press; Osborne; Platts (USA); Possum Press; Prmis; Quicken Press; Quilt Digest Press/NTC; Ragged Mountain Press; Rebol Press; Republic of Texas Press; RSA Press; Sapphire Books; Schaum; Science Research Associates (SRA); Tab Books; Terrific Science Press; Visual Education Corp (School); Webster Publishing; Windcrest; Wordware Publishing; Wright Group/McGraw-Hill; Wrox Press; Xebec/McGraw-Hill
Distributor for Alfred Waller (UK); Amacom - American Management (USA); Barnell Loft Ltd (USA); Benziger Publishing Co (USA); Brown & Benchmark; William C Brown; Clearway Textbooks; Custom Publications ((USA) part of McGraw); Charles E Merrill (USA); Clearway Exam Questions-HSC; Dushkin Publishing Group; Glencoe/McGraw (USA); Harvard Business School Press (USA); International Marine (USA); Irwin Professional PRO (USA); Irwin Publishers (USA); Richard D Irwin (USA); London House (USA); Webster Publishing; MacMillan/McGraw-Hill School (USA); McGraw-Hill Canada (Canada); McGraw-Hill Italy (Italy); McGraw-Hill Singapore (Singapore); Tata McGraw-Hill India (India); McGraw-Hill (UK); McGraw-Hill USA (USA); Metric Schaum (Singapore); Osborne (USA); Possum Press (Australia); Primis; Ragged Mountain Press ((USA) part of McGraw); Republic of Texas Press (USA); Sapphire Books (Australia); Schaum (USA); Science Research Associates SRA (USA); Tab Books (USA); Wordware Publishing (USA); Wrox Press; Windcrest

J M McGregor Pty Ltd+
PO Box 40, Double Bay, NSW 2028
Tel: (02) 9135 1923
Key Personnel
Man Dir: Malcolm McGregor
Founded: 1968
Subjects: Crafts, Games, Hobbies, Education, Photography
ISBN Prefix(es): 0-85921
Subsidiaries: J M McGregor NZ Ltd

Media East Press
PO Box 363, Kingsford, NSW 2032
Tel: (02) 9349 6683 *Fax:* (02) 9349 6683
Key Personnel
Man Dir: Thomas E King
Founded: 1977
Award-winning editorial agency/book publisher specializing in golf venues & travel destinations.
Membership(s): Australian Society of Travel Writers & Australian Society of Authors.
Subjects: Nonfiction (General), Travel
Total Titles: 5 Print
Parent Company: Media East Pty Ltd

Melbourne Institute of Applied Economic & Social Research
University of Melbourne, 6th floor, Parkville, Victoria 3010
Tel: (03) 8344 2100 *Fax:* (03) 8344 2111
E-mail: melb-inst@unimelb.edu.au
Web Site: www.melbourneinstitute.com
Key Personnel
Dir & Prof: Peter Dawkins *Tel:* (03) 8344 7915
 E-mail: p.dawkins@unimelb.edu.au
Deputy Dir & Associate Prof: David Johnson
 Tel: (03) 8344 7485 *E-mail:* d.johnson@unimelb.edu.au
Founded: 1963

AUSTRALIA

Specialize in Economic & Social research, publishing working papers, newsletters & reports.
Subjects: Economics, Social Sciences, Sociology
Parent Company: The University of Melbourne, 3010
Orders to: Blackwell Publishers Journals, 108 Cowley Rd, PO Box 805, Oxford OX4 1FH, United Kingdom *Tel:* (01865) 244083 *Fax:* (01865) 381381 *E-mail:* jnlinfo@blackwellpublishers.co.uk *Web Site:* www.blackwellpublishers.co.uk (Only for Australian Economic Review)

Melbourne University Press+
268 Drummond St, Carlton South, Victoria 3053
Mailing Address: PO Box 1167, Carlton, Victoria 3053
Tel: (03) 9342 0300 *Fax:* (03) 9342 0399
E-mail: mup-info@unimelb.edu.au
Web Site: www.mup.unimelb.edu.au
Key Personnel
Dir: Louise Adler *E-mail:* adlerl@unimelb.edu.au
General Manager: Ross Wallis *Tel:* (03) 9420305 *E-mail:* rwallis@unimelb.edu.au
Marketing Manager: John Denithorne *E-mail:* johnad@unimelb.edu.au
Comm Editor (General Nonfiction): Sybil Nolan
Founded: 1922
Subjects: Biography, History, Literature, Literary Criticism, Essays, Natural History, Nonfiction (General), Psychology, Psychiatry, Travel
ISBN Prefix(es): 0-522; 0-734
Number of titles published annually: 50 Print; 2 CD-ROM; 10 E-Book
Total Titles: 600 Print; 3 CD-ROM; 1 E-Book
Parent Company: The University of Melbourne
Imprints: Miegunyah Press
Warehouse: Palgrave Macmillan, 627 Chapel St, South Yarra, Victoria 3141 *Tel:* (03) 9825 1113 *Fax:* (03) 9825 1010 *E-mail:* customer.service@macmillan.com.au *Web Site:* www.macmillan.com
Orders to: Palgrave Macmillan, 627 Chapel St, South Yarra, Victoria 3141 *Tel:* (03) 9825 1113 *Fax:* (03) 9825 1010 *E-mail:* customer.service@macmillan.com.au *Web Site:* www.macmillan.com

Melting Pot Press+
10 Grafton St, Chippendale, NSW 2008
SAN: 901-1005
Tel: (02) 9211 1660 *Fax:* (02) 9211 1868
E-mail: books@elt.com.au
Key Personnel
Dir: Ron Wood *Tel:* (02) 9211 1178; Rita Yip *Tel:* (02) 9212 1882
Founded: 1983
Specialize in distributing & publishing English Language Teaching (ELT) titles.
Subjects: English as a Second Language
ISBN Prefix(es): 0-947103
Total Titles: 3 Print; 3 Audio
Distributor for Academic English Press; Catt Publishing; Dubois Publishing; Migsico-Piscean Productions; Leigh Slater

Melway Publishing Pty Ltd
32 Ricketts Rd, Mount Waverley, Victoria 3149
Tel: (03) 9585 9888 *Fax:* (03) 9585 9800
E-mail: melway@ausway.com
Web Site: www.ausway.com
Key Personnel
Dir: Murray Godfrey *E-mail:* murray@ausway.com
Founded: 1966
Membership(s): IMTA
Subjects: Publishing & Book Trade Reference
Total Titles: 2 Print; 2 CD-ROM
Parent Company: Ausway Publishing Pty Ltd
Associate Companies: Sydway Publishing Pty Ltd, PO Box 693, Coogee, NSW 2034, Contact: Murray Godfrey *Tel:* (03) 9585 9808 *Fax:* (03) 9585 9800 *E-mail:* murray@ausway.com

Michael Grinder & Associates, *imprint of* Hawker Brownlow

Miegunyah Press, *imprint of* Melbourne University Press

Mimosa Publications Pty Ltd+
8 Yarra St, Hawthorn, Victoria 3122
Tel: (03) 9819 0511 *Fax:* (03) 9819 0524
E-mail: info@mimosa.pub.com.au
Key Personnel
International Marketing & Publishing Dir: Sue Donovan
Man Dir: John Gilder
Founded: 1980
Subjects: English as a Second Language, Language Arts, Linguistics, Mathematics, Poetry, Science (General), Reading
ISBN Prefix(es): 0-7327
Parent Company: Tribune Co
Associate Companies: Mimosa Education Inc, 50 South Steele St, Suite 755, Denver, CO 80209, United States
Subsidiaries: Dragon Media P/L
Divisions: Mimosa Shortland

Minerva, *imprint of* Random House Australia

Mission Publications of Australia
19 Cascade St, Lawson, NSW 2783
Tel: (02) 4759 1003 *Fax:* (02) 4759 1101
E-mail: missionpublaust@bigpond.com
Founded: 1960
Specialize in Easy English Christian Literature.
Subjects: Religion - Other
ISBN Prefix(es): 0-909448; 1-86288
Associate Companies: Aborigines Inland Mission & United Aborigines Mission

Mockingbird, *imprint of* Ginninderra Press

Modern Learning Press, *imprint of* Hawker Brownlow

Moon-Ta-Gu Books
10A East Parade, Leura, NSW 2780
Tel: (02) 6336 0317 *Fax:* (02) 6336 1319
E-mail: wtba@ozemail.com.au
Key Personnel
Contact: Erle Montaigue
Subjects: Health, Nutrition, Self-Help, Martial Arts
ISBN Prefix(es): 0-949132

Moonlight Publishing
PO Box 5, Golden Square, Victoria 3555
Tel: (03) 5447 8221
E-mail: moonlight@impulse.net.au
Key Personnel
Manager: Chris Spencer *E-mail:* chris_spencer@bssc.edu.au
Founded: 1989
Subjects: Music, Dance
ISBN Prefix(es): 1-876187; 0-9586515
Total Titles: 60 Print; 1 Audio
Imprints: Windwood

Morgan Kaufmann, *imprint of* Elsevier Australia

Mosby, *imprint of* Elsevier Australia

K & Z Mostafanejad+
PO Box 118, Geraldton, WA 6531
Tel: (08) 9923 3741 *Fax:* (08) 9923 3741
Key Personnel
Head of Company: Karola Mostafanejad
Sales Manager: Zaim Mostafanejad
Founded: 1989
Subjects: Mathematics, Science (General), Science Fiction, Fantasy
ISBN Prefix(es): 0-646

Mostly Unsung+
PO Box 20, Gardenvale, Victoria 3186
Tel: (03) 9555 5401 *Fax:* (03) 9555 5401
E-mail: milhis@alphalink.com.au
Key Personnel
Head of Company: Neil C Smith
Founded: 1990
Subjects: History, Military Science, Regional Interests
ISBN Prefix(es): 1-876179
Total Titles: 35 Print
U.S. Office(s): c/o Anzar Services Inc, PO Box 274, Lexington, VA 24450, United States

Mount, *imprint of* Little Hills Press Pty Ltd

Mountain House Press
370 Wallace Rd, The Channon, NSW 2480
Tel: (02) 6688 6318 *Fax:* (02) 6688 6318
Key Personnel
Contact: Margery J Kemp *E-mail:* kkemp@nor.com.au
Subjects: Art, Photography, Poetry
ISBN Prefix(es): 0-9586639

Mouse House Press
30 Kinkead St, Evatt, ACT 2617
Tel: (02) 93512612 *Fax:* (02) 93512606
E-mail: s.juan@edfac.usyd.edu.au
Key Personnel
Contact: M L Beggs
Subjects: Behavioral Sciences, Health, Nutrition
ISBN Prefix(es): 1-875397

Mulavon Press Pty Ltd+
131 Ryedale Rd, West Ryde, NSW 2114
Tel: (02) 9808 3662 *Fax:* (02) 9552 1608
Key Personnel
Contact: Rebecca Pinchin
Subjects: Environmental Studies, Natural History, Nonfiction (General), Outdoor Recreation, Australia Flora & Fauna
ISBN Prefix(es): 0-85899

Mulini Press+
PO Box 82, Jamison Centre, Canberra, ACT 2614
Tel: (02) 6251 2519 *Fax:* (02) 6251 2519
Key Personnel
Dir: Victor Crittenden
Founded: 1965
Also specializes in Early Australian history.
Subjects: Biography, Gardening, Plants, History, Literature, Literary Criticism, Essays, Poetry
ISBN Prefix(es): 0-949910; 0-9598414
Number of titles published annually: 10 Print
Total Titles: 80 Print
Imprints: Margin Magazines

Murdoch Books+
Pier 8/9, 23 Hickson Rd, Millers Point, Sydney, NSW 2000
Mailing Address: GPO Box 1203, Sydney, NSW 2001
Tel: (02) 8220 2000 *Fax:* (02) 8220 2020
Web Site: www.mm.com.au
Key Personnel
International Sales Dir: Mark Newman *E-mail:* markn@mm.com.au
Chief Executive Officer & Publisher: Anne Wilson *E-mail:* annew@mm.com.au
Founded: 1989
General nonfiction illustrated publisher.
Subjects: Domestic & Decorative Arts

ISBN Prefix(es): 0-86411; 0-74045
Total Titles: 800 Print
Parent Company: Murdoch Magazines Pty Ltd
Imprints: Bay Books; Better Homes & Gardens; Family Circle
Warehouse: Unit 2, 8A Ethel Ave, Brookvale, NSW 2100

Museum of Victoria
GPO Box 666E, Melbourne, Victoria 3001
Tel: (03) 8341 7777 *Fax:* (03) 9651 6321
Web Site: www.museum.vic.gov.au
Key Personnel
Productions Manager: Teresa Paterson
    E-mail: tpater@mov.vic.gov.au
Subjects: Education, History

Narkaling Inc+
39 Helena St, Midland, WA 6936
Mailing Address: PO Box 1409, Midland, WA 6936
Tel: (08) 9274 8022 *Fax:* (08) 9274 8362
E-mail: info@narkaling.com.au
Web Site: www.narkaling.com.au
Key Personnel
Executive Dir: Marion Slany
Administrative Officer: Erika Troy
Founded: 1997
Non-profit organization which provides educational sources to people with reading difficulties: adults, teenagers & children.
Subjects: Fiction, Nonfiction (General)
ISBN Prefix(es): 0-86457
Number of titles published annually: 40 Audio
Total Titles: 300 Audio

National Association of Forest Industries Ltd
PO Box E89, Kingston, ACT 2604
Tel: (02) 6285 3833 *Fax:* (02) 6285 3855
E-mail: enquiries@nafi.com.au
Web Site: www.nafi.com.au
ISBN Prefix(es): 1-86346

National Gallery of Australia+
Parkes Pl, Canberra, ACT 2601
Mailing Address: GPO Box 1150, Canberra, ACT 2601
Tel: (02) 6240 6501; (02) 6240 6502 *Fax:* (06) 6240 6427
E-mail: information@nga.gov.au
Web Site: www.nga.gov.au
Telex: 61500 *Cable:* NGA CANBERRA
Key Personnel
Publications Manager: Jane Arms *E-mail:* jane.arms@nga.gov.au
Editorial: Alistair McGhie
Rights & Permissions: Leanne Handreck
    E-mail: copyright@nga.gov.au
Founded: 1982
Subjects: Art
ISBN Prefix(es): 0-642

National Gallery of Victoria
180 St Kilda Rd, Melbourne, Victoria 3004
Mailing Address: PO Box 7259, Melbourne, Victoria 8004
Tel: (03) 8620 2212 *Fax:* (03) 8620 2535
E-mail: enquiries@ngv.vic.gov.au
Web Site: www.ngv.vic.gov.au
Key Personnel
Dir: Gerard Vaughan
Publications Manager: Philip Jago *Tel:* (03) 9208 0275 *E-mail:* philip.jago@ngv.vic.gov.au
Founded: 1861
Specialize in large collections of art for the state of Victoria, Australia.
Subjects: Art, Fashion
ISBN Prefix(es): 0-86459
Number of titles published annually: 10 Print
Total Titles: 75 Print

Distributed by Bookwise International (Australia & New Zealand)
Bookshop(s): The Gallery Shop *Tel:* (03) 9208 0310 *Fax:* (03) 9208 0201 *E-mail:* gallery.shop@ngv.vic.gov.au

National Library of Australia
Parkes Pl, Canberra, ACT 2600
Tel: (02) 6262 1111 *Fax:* (02) 6257 1703
E-mail: www@nla.gov.au
Web Site: www.nla.gov.au
Telex: AA62100
Key Personnel
Publications Dir: Dr Paul Hetherington *Tel:* (02) 6262 1474 *E-mail:* phetheri@nla.gov.au
Manager, Publications: Nicola Mackay-Sim
    E-mail: nmackays@nla-gov.au
Editor: Paul Cliff
Founded: 1960
ISBN Prefix(es): 0-642

Navarine Publishing
PO Box 1275, Woden, ACT 2606
Tel: (02) 62824602
Key Personnel
Contact: Graeme Broxam *E-mail:* gjbroxam@bigpond.com.au
Founded: 1992
Membership(s): Roebuck Society.
Subjects: Genealogy, History, Maritime, Nonfiction (General), Regional Interests, Transportation
ISBN Prefix(es): 0-9586561
Number of titles published annually: 2 Print
Total Titles: 8 Print
Associate Companies: The Roebuck Society, PO Box 1275, Woden, ACT 2606
Distributor for Roebuck Society

New American Library, *imprint of* Penguin Group (Australia)

New Creation Publications Ministries & Resource Centre
936 Ackland Hill Rd, Coromandel Valley, SA 5051
Mailing Address: PO Box 403, Blackwood, SA 5051
Tel: (08) 8270 1497; (08) 8270 1861 *Fax:* (08) 8270 4003
E-mail: ministry@newcreation.org.au
Web Site: www.newcreation.org.au
Key Personnel
Dir, Ministry: Martin Bleby
General Manager: John David Skewes
    E-mail: john@newcreation.org.au
Founded: 1974
Christian publishing.
Subjects: Biblical Studies, Fiction, Human Relations, Theology
ISBN Prefix(es): 0-86408; 0-949851
Number of titles published annually: 10 Print
Total Titles: 390 Print
Imprints: Troubadour Press

New Endeavour Press+
PO Box 1596, Strawberry Hills, NSW 2012
Tel: (02) 3182384 *Fax:* (02) 3103613
Key Personnel
Head of Company: Philippe Tanguy
Founded: 1989
Specialize in quality Australian fiction, poetry & art books.
Subjects: Anthropology, Art, Fiction, Humor, Journalism, Language Arts, Linguistics, Poetry
ISBN Prefix(es): 1-875505
Associate Companies: New South Wales University Press

New English Library, *imprint of* Hodder Headline Australia

New Era Publications Australia Pty Ltd
Subsidiary of New Era Publications International
Level 1, 61-65 Wentworth Ave, Surry Hills, NSW 2010
Tel: (02) 9211 0692 *Fax:* (02) 9211 0686
E-mail: books@newerapublications.com
Web Site: www.newerapublications.com
Key Personnel
Executive Dir: Gabi Lumsden *Tel:* (02) 9211 0691
Founded: 1969
Also specialize in L Ron Hubbard books.
Subjects: Fiction, Self-Help
ISBN Prefix(es): 0-9586577
Total Titles: 16 Print; 17 Audio
Distributed by Victorian Wholesalers

New Horizons for Learning, *imprint of* Hawker Brownlow

New Music Articles, see NMA Publications

Newman Centre Publications
Cardinal Newman Catechist Centre, One Chetwynd Rd, Merrylands, NSW 2160
Tel: (02) 9637 9406 *Fax:* (02) 9637 3351
Key Personnel
Contact: Rev Fr B J H Tierney
Founded: 1974
Subjects: Education, Fiction, Philosophy, Religion - Catholic, Catholic Catechism
ISBN Prefix(es): 0-909615; 0-9587535

Night Owl Publishers Pty Ltd, see Grass Roots Publishing

Nimaroo Publishers
PO Box 2046, Wollongong, NSW 2500
Tel: (042) 292297
Key Personnel
Manager & Publicity: Stephen Standish
Editorial: P Balnaves
Sales: T Balnaves
Production: M Standish
Rights & Permissions: N Standish
Founded: 1978
Subjects: Business, Science (General)
ISBN Prefix(es): 0-9596525
Branch Office(s)
11 Airds Rd, Lower Templestone, Victoria 3107

Nimrod Publications+
Dept of English, University of Newcastle, Newcastle, NSW 2308
Tel: (02) 4957 5562; (02) 4921 5173 *Fax:* (02) 4957 5562
E-mail: nimrod@hunterlink.com.au
Founded: 1964
Subjects: Language Arts, Linguistics, Literature, Literary Criticism, Essays, Poetry, Science Fiction, Fantasy
ISBN Prefix(es): 0-909242 (Nimrod & Babel)
Imprints: Babel Handbooks
Subsidiaries: Babel Handbooks

NMA Publications
PO Box 5034, Burnley, Victoria 3121
Tel: (03) 9428 2405
Web Site: www.rainerlinz.net/NMA/
Key Personnel
Publisher: R G Linz *E-mail:* rlinz@alphalink.com.au
Founded: 1982
Subjects: Literature, Literary Criticism, Essays, Music, Dance
ISBN Prefix(es): 0-9587113; 0-646; 0-9577549
Total Titles: 1 Print
Distributed by Frog Peak Music (USA)

NSW Agriculture
161 Kite St, Orange, NSW 2800

Mailing Address: Locked Bag 21, Orange, NSW 2800
Tel: (02) 6391 3100 *Fax:* (02) 6391 3336
E-mail: nsw.agriculture@agric.nsw.gov.au
Web Site: www.agric.nsw.gov.au
Key Personnel
Publisher: Geof Murray
U.S. Office(s): Florida Science Source Inc, PO Box 927, Lake Alfred, FL 33850-0927, United States

Ocean Press+
Hasta 1a Victoria Street Bookshop, 360 Victoria St, North Melbourne, Victoria 3051
Mailing Address: GPO Box 3279, Melbourne, Victoria 3001
Tel: (03) 9326 4280 *Fax:* (03) 9329 5040
E-mail: edit@oceanpress.com.au; info@oceanbooks.com.au
Web Site: www.oceanbooks.com.au
Key Personnel
President: David Deutschmann
Founded: 1989
Subjects: Biography, Developing Countries, Environmental Studies, Government, Political Science, History, Social Sciences, Sociology, Women's Studies
ISBN Prefix(es): 1-875284; 1-876175
Total Titles: 60 Print
U.S. Office(s): Ocean Press, Old Chelsea Station, PO Box 1186, New York, NY 10113-1186, United States *Tel:* 718-246-4160 *E-mail:* info@oceanbooks.com.au
Warehouse: LPC Warehouse, 4029 W George St, Chicago, IL 60641, United States *E-mail:* ftg@lpcgroup.com
Distribution Center: LPC Group, 1436 W Randolph St, Chicago, IL 60607, United States
Orders to: LPC, 1436 W Randolph St, Chicago, IL 60607, United States
Returns: LPC, 4029 W George St, Chicago, IL 60641, United States

Oceans Enterprises+
303 Commercial Rd, Yarram, Victoria 3971
Tel: (03) 5182 5108 *Fax:* (03) 5182 5823
Web Site: www.oceans.com.au
Key Personnel
Contact: Peter Stone *E-mail:* peter@oceans.com.au
Founded: 1982
Specialize in marine, military & history publications, commercial & sport scuba diving.
Subjects: History, Maritime, Military Science, Sports, Athletics, Travel
ISBN Prefix(es): 0-9586657
Imprints: Lonestone Press
Subsidiaries: Lonestone Press
Distributed by Gary Allen PL, Sydney

Anne O'Donovan Pty Ltd+
PO Box 5073, Glenferrie South, Victoria 3122
Tel: (03) 9819 5372 *Fax:* (03) 9818 6849
E-mail: odonovan@netspace.net.au
Key Personnel
Head of Company: Anne O'Donovan
Founded: 1978
Subjects: Cookery, Finance, Health, Nutrition, Music, Dance, Nonfiction (General), Self-Help
ISBN Prefix(es): 1-876026; 0-908476
Distributed by Penguin Books Australia Ltd (Australia)
Warehouse: Penguin Books, 487 Maroondah Hwy, Ringwood, Victoria 3134
Orders to: Penguin Books, 487 Maroondah Hwy, Ringwood, Victoria 3134

Off the Shelf Publishing+
32 Thomas St, Lewisham, NSW 2049
Tel: (02) 9560 3058 *Fax:* (02) 9564 0758
E-mail: offshelf@ozemail.com.au

Key Personnel
Publisher: Gillian Souter
Co-Proprietor: John Souter
Founded: 1991
Specialize in illustrated international craft & leisure books.
Subjects: Crafts, Games, Hobbies, Travel
ISBN Prefix(es): 0-646; 0-9586682; 1-876779
Total Titles: 20 Print
Distributed by Australian Book Group in Australia (Australia)

Ohio Psychology Press, *imprint of* Hawker Brownlow

Oidium Books+
PO Box 191, Corio, Victoria 3214
Tel: (052) 757045
E-mail: tecnilab@ozemail.com.au
Key Personnel
Contact: Richard Turner
Founded: 1985
Subjects: Health, Nutrition
ISBN Prefix(es): 0-9589510

Ollif Publishing+
41 Galston Rd, Hornsby, NSW 2077
Mailing Address: PO Box 439, Hornsby, NSW 2077
Tel: (02) 9477-3496
Key Personnel
President: Lorna Ollif
Founded: 1965
Subjects: Biography, Fiction, History
ISBN Prefix(es): 0-9599183
Number of titles published annually: 1 Print
Total Titles: 6 Print
Distributed by NSW Military Historical Society

Omnibus Books+
52 Fullarton Rd, Norwood, SA 5067
Tel: (08) 8363 2333 *Fax:* (08) 8363 1420
E-mail: omnibus@scholastic.com.au
Key Personnel
Publisher: Dyan Blacklock
General Manager: Dyan Blacklock
Senior Editor: Penny Matthews
Founded: 1980
Subjects: Fiction, Nonfiction (General), Poetry
ISBN Prefix(es): 0-86896; 1-86291; 0-949641
Number of titles published annually: 25 Print
Total Titles: 238 Print
Parent Company: Scholastic Australia Ltd, Railway Terrace, Lisarow, Gosford, NSW
Shipping Address: Scholastic Australia Ltd, Railway Terrace, Lisarow, Gosford, NSW
Warehouse: Scholastic Australia Ltd, Railway Terrace, Lisarow, Gosford, NSW

On The Stone+
252 Durham St, Bathurst, NSW 2795
Tel: (02) 6334 3442 *Fax:* (02) 6334 3009
Web Site: www.onthestone.com.au
Key Personnel
Man Dir: Marje Prior *E-mail:* m.prior@onthestone.com
Subjects: Asian Studies, Regional Interests
ISBN Prefix(es): 0-9585719

Online Information Resources
42 Waller Crescent, Campbell, ACT 2612
Mailing Address: PO Box 57, Ainslie, ACT 2602
Tel: (03) 6257 9177 *Fax:* (03) 6257 9030
Key Personnel
Dir: Sherrey Quinn
Subjects: Library & Information Sciences
ISBN Prefix(es): 0-646

Open Training & Education Network, see OTEN (Open Training & Education Network)

Openbook Publishers+
205 Halifax St, Adelaide, SA 5000
Mailing Address: GPO Box 1368, Adelaide, SA 5001
Tel: (08) 8223 5468 *Fax:* (08) 8223 4552
E-mail: openbook@peg.apc.org; service@openbook.com.au
Web Site: www.openbook.com.au
Key Personnel
General Manager: Chris Pfeiffer *E-mail:* chrisp@openbook.com.au
Editorial & Rights & Permission: John Pfitzner *E-mail:* johnp@openbook.com.au
Founded: 1913
Subjects: Education, Religion - Protestant, Religion - Other
ISBN Prefix(es): 0-85910
Number of titles published annually: 20 Print
Total Titles: 200 Print

Oriental Publications+
18 Market St, Adelaide, SA 5000
Tel: (08) 8212 6055 *Fax:* (08) 8410 0863
E-mail: oriental@dove.mtx.net.au
Key Personnel
Dir: Tiny Bruzzone
Subjects: Antiques, Art, Asian Studies, Cookery, Language Arts, Linguistics, Religion - Buddhist, Religion - Hindu, Religion - Islamic
ISBN Prefix(es): 0-9587113

Orin Books
PO Box 2089, St Kilda, West Victoria 3182
Tel: (03) 9534 5680; (03) 9534 4746 *Fax:* (03) 9527 6995
Key Personnel
Man Dir: S E Shifrin
Membership(s): Australian Publishers Association.
Subjects: Humor
ISBN Prefix(es): 1-875230; 0-9588190; 0-9588648; 0-9592263

OTEN (Open Training & Education Network)+
51 Wentworth Rd, Strathfield, NSW 2135
Tel: (02) 9715 8000; (02) 9715 8222 (sales) *Fax:* (02) 9715 8111; (02) 9715 8174 (sales)
E-mail: oten.courseinfo@tafensw.edu.au
Web Site: www.oten.edu.au
Key Personnel
Dir: Greeme Dobbs
Founded: 1994
Specialize in college textbooks & video cassettes.
Membership(s): Australian Publishers Association.
Subjects: Accounting, Aeronautics, Aviation, Agriculture, Automotive, Business, Child Care & Development, Civil Engineering, Computer Science, Disability, Special Needs, Electronics, Electrical Engineering, English as a Second Language, Fashion, Finance, Management, Maritime, Marketing, Microcomputers, Real Estate
Parent Company: New South Wales Technical & Further Education Commission

Outback Books, *imprint of* Outback Books - CQU Press

Outback Books - CQU Press
PO Box 1615, Rockhampton, Qld 4701
Tel: (07) 4923 2520 *Fax:* (07) 4923 2525
E-mail: cqupress@cqu.edu.au
Web Site: www.outbackbooks.com
Key Personnel
Dir: Prof David Myers *E-mail:* d.myers@cqu.edu.au
Founded: 1993
Specialize in subjects about country heritage, regional history, South Pacific & Australiana.
Subjects: Biography, History, Nonfiction (General), Regional Interests

ISBN Prefix(es): 1-875998; 1-876780
Imprints: Outback Books; South Pacific Books

Outdoor Press Pty Ltd+
PO Box 866, Shepparton, Victoria 3632
Tel: (03) 5790 5226 *Fax:* (03) 5790 5393
Web Site: www.goldexpeditions.com.au
Key Personnel
Manager: Douglas M Stone *Tel:* (0438) 369919
 E-mail: dougstone@goldexpeditions.com.au
Founded: 1976
Specialize in gold & gemstone guides to Australia.
Subjects: Gold & Gemstones
Total Titles: 4 Print

Owl Books, *imprint of* Pan Macmillan Australia Pty Ltd

Owl Publishing
22 Rooding St, Brighton, Victoria 3186
Tel: (03) 95966064 *Fax:* (03) 95966942
E-mail: owlbooks@bigpond.com
Key Personnel
Publisher: Helen Nickas
Founded: 1992
Subjects: Ethnicity, Literature, Literary Criticism, Essays, Poetry
ISBN Prefix(es): 0-9586390
Number of titles published annually: 1 Print
Total Titles: 15 Print

Oxfam Community Aid Abroad
Affiliate of Oxfam International
156 George St, 1st floor, Fitzroy, Victoria 3065
Tel: (03) 9289 9444 *Fax:* (03) 9419 5895
E-mail: enquire@caa.org.au
Web Site: www.caa.org.au
Key Personnel
Publications Coordinator: Sarah Lowe
 E-mail: sarahlo@caa.org.au
Specialize in overseas aid & development.
Subjects: Economics, Education, Environmental Studies, Foreign Countries, Genealogy, Government, Political Science, Health, Nutrition, Women's Studies
ISBN Prefix(es): 0-9587791; 0-9599636; 0-875870
Associate Companies: Oxfam Great Britain
Distributed by Oxfam Great Britain

Jill Oxton Publications Pty Ltd+
PO Box 283, Park Holme, SA 5043
Tel: (08) 2762722 *Fax:* (08) 3743494
E-mail: jill@jilloxtonxstitch.com
Web Site: www.jilloxtonxstitch.com
Key Personnel
Contact: Jill Oxton
Founded: 1989
Publishing cross stitch & beading charted designs.
Subjects: Crafts, Games, Hobbies
ISBN Prefix(es): 0-9587576
Number of titles published annually: 4 Print
Total Titles: 50 Print

Pacific Publications (Australia) Pty Ltd
35-51 Mitchell St, McMahons Point, NSW 2060
Tel: (02) 9464 3300 *Fax:* (02) 9464 3375
Web Site: pacificpubs.com.au
Key Personnel
Publisher: Geoff Husey
Founded: 1930
Papua New Guinea Handbook.
Subjects: Agriculture, Regional Interests
ISBN Prefix(es): 0-85807
Parent Company: Seven Network Ltd
Branch Office(s)
Pacific Publications Brisbane, Centro on James, 10B, 23 James St, Fortitude Valley, Qld 4006
Pacific Publications Melbourne, 160 Harbour Esplanade, Docklands, Victoria
Orders to: Robert Brown & Associates, 7 Atherton St, Buranda, Qld 4102

Pademelon Press+
7/3 Packard Ave, Castle Hill, NSW 2154
Mailing Address: PO Box 6500, Baulkham Hills BC, NSW 2153
Tel: (02) 9634-4655 *Fax:* (02) 9680-4634
E-mail: info@pademelonpress.com.au
Web Site: www.pademelonpress.com.au
Key Personnel
Dir & International Rights: Rodney Kenner
Founded: 1990
Specialize in early childhood teacher resource & reference books.
Subjects: Child Care & Development, Education
ISBN Prefix(es): 1-876138
Number of titles published annually: 4 Print
Total Titles: 15 Print
Parent Company: Pademelon Press Pty Ltd
Distributed by Gryphon House Inc (USA & Canada only)
Distributor for Building Blocks; Child Care Information Exchange; Gryphon House; High/Scope Press; National Association for the Education of Young Children; New Horizons; Our Kids Press; Redleaf Press; School-Age Notes; Teacher's College Press; Teaching Strategies; William Publishing Co (all restricted to Australia & New Zealand)
Foreign Rep(s): Gryphon House Inc (Canada, USA)

Charles Paine Pty Ltd
204 Clarence St, Sydney, NSW 2000
Tel: (02) 9890 1388 *Fax:* (02) 9890 1915
ISBN Prefix(es): 0-909687

Pali Text Society, *imprint of* Windhorse Books

Palm Beach Press
40 Ocean Rd, Palm Beach, NSW 2108
Tel: (02) 6646 1622 *Fax:* (02) 9946 1515
Key Personnel
Contact: Nat Young *E-mail:* nato@hor.com.au
Founded: 1976
Subjects: Surfing
ISBN Prefix(es): 0-9591816

Palms Press
87 Newport Rd, Dora Creek, NSW 2264
Tel: (02) 4973 1236
Key Personnel
Contact: H K Garland
Subjects: Environmental Studies, History, How-to, Humor, Public Administration
ISBN Prefix(es): 0-9593041

Pan, *imprint of* Pan Macmillan Australia Pty Ltd

Pan Macmillan Australia Pty Ltd+
Level 18, St Martins Tower, 31 Market St, Sydney, NSW 2000
Tel: (02) 9285 9100 *Fax:* (02) 9285 9100
E-mail: pansyd@macmillan.com.au (general); panpublicity@macmillan.com.au (publicity)
Web Site: www.panmacmillan.com.au
Key Personnel
Publishing Dir: James Fraser *E-mail:* james.fraser@macmillan.com.au
Sales Dir, Melbourne Office: Peter Phillips
 Tel: (03) 9825 1000 *Fax:* (03) 9825 1015
 E-mail: peter.phillips@macmillan.com.au
Product Department Manager, Melbourne Office: Andrew Farrell *Tel:* (03) 9825 1000 *Fax:* (03) 9825 1015 *E-mail:* andrew.farrell@macmillan.com.au
Founded: 1983
Submissions must include a short cover letter (1 or 2 pages), along with a detailed chapter outline for nonfiction or a synopsis of the plot for fiction. See web site for additional submission information. No children's picture books, short story collections or poetry.
Subjects: Biography, Fiction, Health, Nutrition, Humor, Literature, Literary Criticism, Essays, Nonfiction (General), Self-Help, Travel
ISBN Prefix(es): 0-330; 0-7329
Parent Company: Macmillan Ltd, United Kingdom
Imprints: Boxtree; Rod Campbell Books; Channel 4; Forge; Griffin; Henry Holt; Let's Go; Macmillan; Macquarie Library; Owl Books; Pan; Pancake; Papermac; Picador; Priddy & Bicknell; Sidgwick & Jackson; St Martins; Sun; Tor Books
Branch Office(s)
Level 4, 627 Chapel St, South Yarra, Victoria 3141 *Tel:* (03) 9825 1000 *Fax:* (03) 9825 1015 *E-mail:* panmel@macmillan.com.au *Web Site:* www.panmacmillan.com.au
Warehouse: Macmillan Distribution Services Pty Ltd, 56 Parkwest Dr, Derrimut, Victoria 3030, Man Dir: Andy Palmer *Tel:* (03) 9825 1000 *Fax:* (03) 9825 3210 *E-mail:* mds@macmillan.com.au *Web Site:* www.ozemail.com.au/~mds; www.macmillan.com.au

Pan Pacific Publications, *see* Peter Pan Publications

Pancake, *imprint of* Pan Macmillan Australia Pty Ltd

Pandani Press
17 Derwentwater Ave, Sand Bay, Tas 7005
Tel: (03) 6225 1956
E-mail: pandani@iprimus.com.au
Key Personnel
Head of Company: Sue Backhouse
Subjects: Art, Natural History
ISBN Prefix(es): 0-9587113; 0-85901
Total Titles: 1 Print

Panorama Books, *imprint of* St George Books

Pantheon, *imprint of* Random House Australia

Pants on Fire, *imprint of* Crawford House Publishing Pty Ltd

Papermac, *imprint of* Pan Macmillan Australia Pty Ltd

Papyrus Publishing
c/o Post Office, Scarsdale, Victoria 3351
Tel: (03) 5342 2394 *Fax:* (03) 5342 2423
E-mail: editor@papyrus.com.au
Web Site: www.papyrus.com.au
Key Personnel
Contact: Herbert Stein
Founded: 1991
Subjects: Ethnicity, Fiction, Literature, Literary Criticism, Essays, Poetry
ISBN Prefix(es): 1-875934

Parabel Place+
67 Exeter Rd, North Croydon, Victoria 3136
Tel: (03) 9727 1894 *Fax:* (03) 9727 1857
Key Personnel
Head of Company: Brigitte Lambert
Founded: 1991
Membership(s): Society of Women Writers (Victoria Branch) Australia.
Subjects: Cookery, Women's Studies
ISBN Prefix(es): 0-9586591

AUSTRALIA

Pascal Press+
655 Parramutta Rd, Leichhardt, NSW 2040
Mailing Address: PO Box 250, Glebe, NSW 2037
Tel: (02) 8585 4044 *Fax:* (02) 8585 4001
E-mail: contact@pascalpress.com.au; info@pascalpress.com.au
Web Site: www.pascalpress.com.au
Key Personnel
Man Dir: Matthew B Sandblom *Tel:* (0612) 8585 4024 *Fax:* (0612) 8585 4024
 E-mail: matthew@pascalpress.com.au
Primary Publisher: Katy Pike *Tel:* (0612) 9518 6777 *Fax:* (0612) 9518 6888
Founded: 1989
Specialize in school publishing.
Membership(s): Australian Publishers Association.
Subjects: Education
Total Titles: 1,000 Print; 16 CD-ROM; 50 Online; 50 E-Book; 20 Audio
Parent Company: S D & M Software Pty Ltd
Subsidiaries: Blake Education Pty Ltd; Video Education Australia
Distributed by Nelson Thomes (United Kingdom); Sundance (United States)
Distributor for Wild Daisies (New Zealand)
Shipping Address: TLD Distribution, 15-23 Hellen Ave, Moorebank, NSW 2170, Contact: Chris Stasis *Tel:* (0612) 8585 4044 *Fax:* (0612) 8585 4001

Pascoe Publishing Pty Ltd+
30 Gambler St, Apollo Bay, Victoria 3233
Mailing Address: PO Box 42, Apollo Bay, Victoria 3233
Tel: (03) 5237 9227 *Fax:* (03) 5237 6559
Web Site: www.bruce-pascoe.pho-online.net
Key Personnel
Dir: Bruce Pascoe *E-mail:* pascoe@vicnet.net.au
Dir & International Rights: Lyn Harwood
Founded: 1983
Subjects: Fiction, History, Literature, Literary Criticism, Essays, Social Sciences, Sociology, Australian Literary Fiction
ISBN Prefix(es): 0-947087; 0-9592104
Number of titles published annually: 4 Print
Total Titles: 110 Print
Imprints: Blackstone; Seaglass
Subsidiaries: Koori Tours

Kevin J Passey+
468 David St, Albury, NSW 2640
Mailing Address: PO Box 971, Albury, NSW 2640
Tel: (060) 216 933 *Fax:* (060) 412 950
Key Personnel
Head of Company: Kevin J Passey
Founded: 1986
Membership(s): Australian Institute of History & Arts, Australian Writers Guild, History-Bushranging; also acts as a script writer.
Subjects: History, Regional Interests
ISBN Prefix(es): 0-9588470

Pavillion, *imprint of* Random House Australia

PCE Press
35 Amelia St, Fortitude Valley, Qld 4006
Mailing Address: PO Box 1508, Fortitude Valley, Qld 4006
Tel: (07) 3252 1114 *Fax:* (07) 3852 1564
E-mail: webmaster@pcq.org.au
Web Site: www.pcq.org.au
Key Personnel
Dir: Rev J C Nicol *E-mail:* director@pcq.org.au
Publications Department of the Presbyterian Church of Queensland.
Subjects: Religion - Protestant

Pearson Education Australia+
Unit 4, Level 2, 14 Aquatic Drive, Frenchs Forest, NSW 2086
Mailing Address: LMB 507, Frenchs Forest, NSW 1640
Tel: (02) 9454 2200 *Fax:* (02) 9453 0089
E-mail: firstname.lastname@pearsoned.com.au
Web Site: www.pearson.com.au
Key Personnel
Man Dir: Pat Evans
Financial Controller: Ted Impey
General Manager, Humanities & Sciences: David Barnett
General Manager, Professional & Vocational Education: Gillian May
General Manager, Business & Economics: Michael Page
General Manager, Computer, Trade & Reference: Paul Summers
Educational Publishers.
Subjects: Accounting, Anthropology, Behavioral Sciences, Biological Sciences, Business, Child Care & Development, Communications, Computer Science, Criminology, Economics, Education, Engineering (General), Fiction, Government, Journalism, Labor, Industrial Relations, Language Arts, Linguistics, Law, Library & Information Sciences, Management, Mathematics, Medicine, Nursing, Dentistry, Science (General), Social Sciences, Sociology
ISBN Prefix(es): 1-74091; 1-74103
Number of titles published annually: 500 Print
Parent Company: Pearson Plc
Imprints: Prentice Hall; Addison Wesley; Longman
Branch Office(s)
Suite B, Level 2, 57 Coronation Drive, Milton, Qld 4000 *Tel:* (07) 3236 5901 *Fax:* (07) 3236 5907 (Queensland & Northern Territory)
95 Coventry St, South Melbourne, Victoria 3205 (Victoria & Tasmania)
PO Box 353, Mitcham S/C, Torrens Park 5062 (South Australia)
177 Great Eastern Hwy, Belmont 6104 *Tel:* (08) 9477 1539 *Fax:* (08) 9466 1547 (Western Australia)

Penguin, *imprint of* Penguin Group (Australia)

Penguin Group (Australia)+
250 Camberwell Rd, Camberwell, Victoria 3124
Mailing Address: PO Box 701, Hawthorn, Victoria 3122
Tel: (613) 9811 2400 *Fax:* (613) 9811 2620
Web Site: www.penguin.com.au
Key Personnel
Chief Executive Officer: P Field
Publishing Dir: Robert Sessions *Tel:* (613) 9811 2468 *Fax:* (613) 9811 2621 *E-mail:* robert.sessions@au.penguingroup.com
Sales Dir: P Blake
Mgr Rts: Peg McColl
Founded: 1946
Subjects: Biography, Cookery, Fiction, Humor, Literature, Literary Criticism, Essays, Nonfiction (General), Science Fiction, Fantasy, Self-Help, Travel
ISBN Prefix(es): 0-14; 0-670; 1-872031; 0-86914
Parent Company: Pearson Australia Group Pty Ltd
Ultimate Parent Company: Pearson plc (London)
Associate Companies: Pearson Education; Penguin Group Canada, 10 Alcorn Ave, Suite 300, Toronto, ON M4V 3B2, Canada; Penguin Books (NZ) Ltd, New Zealand; Penguin Books India Pvt Ltd, India; Penguin Books (South Africa) (Pty) Ltd, South Africa
Imprints: Hamish Hamilton; Michael Joseph; New American Library; Penguin; Puffin; Viking; Signet; Frederick Warne
Divisions: Penguin Adult, Penguin Children
Branch Office(s)
Penguin Group (USA) Inc, 375 Hudson St, New York, NY 10014-3657, United States

Perfection Learning Corporation, *imprint of* Hawker Brownlow

Peribo Pty Ltd
58 Beaumont Rd, Mount Kuring-gai, NSW 2080
Tel: (02) 4457 0011 *Fax:* (02) 9457 0022
E-mail: peribo@bigpond.com
Key Personnel
Chairman: Edward Coffey
Founded: 1981
ISBN Prefix(es): 1-86322

Periscope Press, *imprint of* Roland Harvey Studios

Personal Power Press International Inc, *imprint of* Hawker Brownlow

Peter Pan Publications+
Formerly Pan Pacific Publications
PO Box 342, Moorooka, Qld 4105
Tel: (07) 3848 0350 *Fax:* (07) 3848 4945
E-mail: paramountbooks@optusnet.com.au
Web Site: www.peterpan.ziby.net
Key Personnel
Man Dir: Donald Jefferies
Founded: 1982
Also distributors.
Subjects: Regional Interests, Religion - Other
ISBN Prefix(es): 0-9596931
Number of titles published annually: 1 Online; 1 E-Book
Total Titles: 5 Print; 1 Online
Parent Company: Donald Jefferies (Q) Pty Ltd
Subsidiaries: Paramount Books

Phoenix Education Pty Ltd+
102 Charles St, Putney, NSW 2112
Mailing Address: PO Box 3141, Putney, NSW 2112
Tel: (02) 9809 3579; (03) 9699 8377 *Fax:* (02) 9808 1430; (03) 9699 9242
E-mail: service@phoenixeduc.com
Web Site: www.phoenixeduc.com
Key Personnel
Dir: Barney Rivers
Founded: 1991
Subjects: Language Arts, Linguistics, Mathematics
ISBN Prefix(es): 1-876580
Number of titles published annually: 20 Print
Total Titles: 200 Print

Picador, *imprint of* Pan Macmillan Australia Pty Ltd

Pimlico, *imprint of* Random House Australia

Pinchgut Press
6 Oaks Ave, Cremorne, NSW 2090
Tel: (02) 9908-2402 *Fax:* (02) 9960-4689
Key Personnel
Chief Executive & Dir: Marjorie Pizer
Art Dir: Judy Lane
Founded: 1947
Small independent publisher.
Subjects: Poetry, Self-Help
ISBN Prefix(es): 0-9598913; 0-949625
Total Titles: 17 Print

Pinevale Publications+
Pike Rd, Emerald Creek, Mareeba, Qld 4880
Mailing Address: PO Box 822, Mareeba, Qld 4880
Tel: (07) 93-3169
Key Personnel
Publisher & Editor: Glenville Pike
Founded: 1981
Subjects: Biography, History, Travel

ISBN Prefix(es): 0-9593783; 1-875375
Number of titles published annually: 2 Print
Total Titles: 23 Print
Distribution Center: 45 Pike Rd, Emerald Creek, Mareeba, Qld *Tel:* (07) 933169
Orders to: 45 Pike Rd, Emerald Creek, Mareeba, Qld *Tel:* (07) 933169

Pioneer Design Studio Pty Ltd+
31 North Rd, Lilydale, Victoria 3140
Tel: (03) 9735 5505
Key Personnel
Head of Company: Derrick I Stone
Sales Manager: Carolyn R Stone
Subjects: Environmental Studies, Gardening, Plants, History
ISBN Prefix(es): 0-909674

Pisces, *imprint of* Lonely Planet Publications Pty Ltd

Plantagenet Press+
PO Box 934, Fremantle, WA 6160
Tel: (09) 4304466 *Fax:* (09) 4305217
E-mail: 100240.3406rogergarwood@compuserve.com
Key Personnel
Dir: Trish Ainslie
Founded: 1989
Also acts as distributor.
Subjects: Fiction, History, Humor, Journalism, Nonfiction (General)
ISBN Prefix(es): 0-646; 1-875968
Book Club(s): Lucky Book Club

Platypus Press Australia, *imprint of* Dragon Press

Playbox Theatre Co+
113 Sturt St, Southbank, Victoria 3006
Tel: (03) 9685 5100 *Fax:* (03) 9685 5112
E-mail: playbox@netspace.net.au
Web Site: www.playbox.com.au
Key Personnel
General Manager: Jill Smith
Development, presentation & promotion of new Australian plays & playwrights.
Subjects: Drama, Theater
ISBN Prefix(es): 0-7326
Number of titles published annually: 12 Print
Distributed by Currency Press
Distributor for Currency Press

Playlab Press
7 Pender St, The Gap, Qld 4061
Tel: 3236 1396 *Fax:* 3236 1026
E-mail: cluster@thehub.com.au
Key Personnel
Project Officer: Louise Terry
Founded: 1972
Subjects: Drama, Theater, History, Humor, Literature, Literary Criticism, Essays, Music, Dance, Women's Studies, Australian, Youth, Comedy
ISBN Prefix(es): 0-908156

Jurriaan Plesman
17/54-56 Beach Rd, Bondi Beach, NSW 2026
Tel: (02) 9130 6202 *Fax:* (02) 9130 6202
E-mail: jurplesman@hotmail.com
Subjects: Behavioral Sciences, Criminology, Health, Nutrition, How-to, Medicine, Nursing, Dentistry, Psychology, Psychiatry, Self-Help, Social Sciences, Sociology
ISBN Prefix(es): 1-86252

Plum Press+
PO Box 419, Toowong, Qld 4066
Tel: (07) 3870 2964 *Fax:* (07) 3870 2860
E-mail: tom@justasktom.com
Web Site: www.justasktom.com

Key Personnel
Head of Company: Neil Flanagan *E-mail:* neilfl@squirrel.com.au
Founded: 1989
Subjects: Management
ISBN Prefix(es): 0-9587113

Pluto Press Australia Pty Ltd+
PO Box 617, North Melbourne, Victoria 2038
Tel: (02) 9692 5111; (03) 9328 3811 *Fax:* (02) 9692 5192; (03) 9329 9939
E-mail: pluto@plutoaustralia.com
Web Site: www.plutoaustralia.com
Key Personnel
Man Dir: Sean Kidney
Founded: 1984
Subjects: Environmental Studies, Government, Political Science, History, Labor, Industrial Relations, Social Sciences, Sociology, Women's Studies
ISBN Prefix(es): 0-949138; 1-86403
Parent Company: Social Change Media
Associate Companies: Social Change On-Line
Divisions: University of NSW Press
Orders to: University of NSW Press, 45 Beach St, Coogee 2031 *Tel:* (02) 9664 0999 *Fax:* (02) 9664 5420

The Polding Press+
322 Lonsdale St, Melbourne, Victoria 3000
Tel: (03) 9639 0844 *Fax:* (03) 9639 0879
E-mail: manager@catholicbookshop.com.au
Web Site: www.catholicbookshop.com.au
Founded: 1968
Subjects: Biography, History, Religion - Other
ISBN Prefix(es): 0-85884
Bookshop(s): Central Catholic Library Bookshop, 322 Lonsdale St, Melbourne, Victoria 3000 *Tel:* (03) 9639 0844

Pollitecon Publications
PO Box 324, Five Dock, NSW 2046
Tel: (02) 9713 7608 *Fax:* (02) 9713 1004
Web Site: members.ozemail.com.au/~vbivell
Key Personnel
Publisher: Victor Bivell *E-mail:* vbivell@vcjournal.com.au
Founded: 1992
Subjects: Anthropology, Ethnicity, Foreign Countries, History, Literature, Literary Criticism, Essays, Regional Interests, Social Sciences, Sociology, Macedonians of Greece, Human Rights
ISBN Prefix(es): 0-9586789
Total Titles: 6 Print

Power Publications+
Power Institute, Mills Bldg, A26, University of Sydney, Sydney, NSW 2006
Tel: (02) 9351 6904 *Fax:* (02) 9351 7323
E-mail: power.publications@arts.usyd.edu.au
Web Site: www.power.arts.usyd.edu.au/institute
Key Personnel
Dir: Prof Roger Benjamin
Managing Editor: Victoria Dawson
Founded: 1987
Subjects: Art, Film, Video
ISBN Prefix(es): 0-909952

Prentice Hall, *imprint of* Pearson Education Australia

Press for Success+
One Ensign Lane, East Perth, WA 6004
Mailing Address: PO Box 8142, Perth Business Center, WA 6849
Tel: (08) 9221 6166 *Fax:* (08) 9221 6166
E-mail: press4@press4success.com.au
Web Site: www.press4success.com.au
Key Personnel
Dir: Jill Yelland
Founded: 1993

Membership(s): International Type Designers Association A Type 1.
Subjects: Architecture & Interior Design, Art, Business, How-to
ISBN Prefix(es): 0-646; 0-9577374
Parent Company: Yelland & Associates Pty Ltd
Associate Companies: Yelland INK

PressXpress, *imprint of* McGraw-Hill Australia Pty Ltd

Price Publishing+
Unit 2, 40 Benelong Rd, Cremorne, NSW 2090
Tel: (02) 9904 9811
E-mail: pricesys@localnet.com.au
Founded: 1994
Subjects: Education, Microcomputers, Learning & Training
ISBN Prefix(es): 0-646

Priddy & Bicknell, *imprint of* Pan Macmillan Australia Pty Ltd

Priestley Consulting+
12 Trinidad St, Kawana Island, Qld 4575
Tel: (07) 4937179 *Fax:* (07) 54458288
E-mail: adpriestley@ozemail.com.au
Key Personnel
Contact: Andrew Priestly *E-mail:* adpriestly@ozemail.com.au
Subjects: Advertising, Child Care & Development, Education, Marketing, Self-Help, Social Sciences, Sociology
ISBN Prefix(es): 0-9587298

Primary English Teaching Association
PO Box 3106, Marrickville, NSW 2204
Tel: (02) 9565 1277 *Fax:* (02) 9565 1070
E-mail: info@peta.edu.au
Web Site: www.peta.edu.au
Key Personnel
Executive Dir: Peter O'Brien
Founded: 1972
ISBN Prefix(es): 0-909955; 1-875622

Prospect, *imprint of* Prospect Media Pty Ltd

Prospect Media Pty Ltd+
Level 1, 7173 Lithgow St, St Leonards, NSW 2065
Tel: (02) 9349 6077 *Fax:* (02) 9439 5411
E-mail: prospect@prospectmedia.com.au
Web Site: www.prospectmedia.com.au
Key Personnel
Man Dir & Publisher: Oliver Freeman
Finance Manager: Vicky Mahadeva
Managing Editor: Jenny Berich
Senior Editor: Carolyn Stott
Marketing Manager: Matthew Langman
Sales Manager: Sue Howard
Founded: 1987
Membership(s): Australian Publishers Association; Publish Australia.
Subjects: Accounting, Business, Computer Science, Environmental Studies, Finance, Law
ISBN Prefix(es): 1-86316; 0-947309; 0-949553
Total Titles: 40 Print
Parent Company: Oliver Freeman Pty Ltd
Imprints: Oliver Freeman Editions; Global Business Network; Heresy Press; Legal Books; Prospect
Subsidiaries: Australian Business Network Pty Ltd
Divisions: Legal Books; Legal Publications; Prospect
Bookshop(s): Legal Publications, 121 William St, Melbourne, Victoria 3000
Book Club(s): ABN Bookclub
Shipping Address: Mezzanine Level, G10 Bldg, 60-70 Elizabeth St, Sydney, NSW 2000
Orders to: Mezzanine Level, G10 Bldg, 60-70 Elizabeth St, Sydney, NSW 2000

AUSTRALIA

Protestant Publications
7 Park St, Peakhurst, NSW 2210
Tel: (02) 9868 4591 *Fax:* (02) 9868 7953
Key Personnel
Contact: D Shelton
Founded: 1945
Subjects: History, Religion - Catholic, Religion - Protestant
ISBN Prefix(es): 0-949926

Prufrock Press, *imprint of* Hawker Brownlow

The Psychological Corporation, *imprint of* Elsevier Australia

Puffin, *imprint of* Penguin Group (Australia)

Quakers Hill Press+
6 Caper Pl, Quakers Hill, NSW 2763
Tel: (02) 9626 6112 *Fax:* (02) 9626 9846
E-mail: dayp@mpx.com.au
Key Personnel
Publisher: Peter Day
Founded: 1993
Subjects: Biography, Fiction, History, Mathematics, Nonfiction (General), Philosophy
ISBN Prefix(es): 1-876192

Queen Victoria Museum & Art Gallery Publications
Division of Launceston City Council
2 Wellington St, Launceston, Tas 7250
Tel: (03) 6323 3777 *Fax:* (03) 6323 3776
E-mail: library@qvmag.tas.gov.au
Web Site: www.qvmag.tas.gov.au
Key Personnel
Editor: Mr Chris B Tassell E-mail: chris.tassell@qvmag.tas.gov.au
Publications Coordinator: Kaye Dimmack
  E-mail: kaye.dimmack@qvmag.tas.gov.au
Founded: 1891
Operated as a department of Launceston City Council.
Subjects: Anthropology, Archaeology, Art, Biological Sciences, Earth Sciences, History, Natural History, Physical Sciences
ISBN Prefix(es): 0-7246
Number of titles published annually: 1 Print
Total Titles: 27 Print

Queensland Art Gallery
Melbourne St, South Brisbane, Qld 4101
Mailing Address: PO Box 3686, South Brisbane, Qld 4101
Tel: (07) 3840 7333; (07) 3840 7303 *Fax:* (07) 3844 8865; (07) 3840 7350
E-mail: gallery@qag.qld.gov.au
Web Site: www.qag.qld.gov.au
Key Personnel
Manager Gallery Shop: Linda Mehan
  E-mail: linda.mehan@qag.qld.gov.au
Gallery Dir: Doug Hall
Senior Editor: Ian Were E-mail: ian.were@qag.qld.gov.au
Subjects: Art, Asian Studies
Number of titles published annually: 6 Print
Total Titles: 15 Print
Distributed by James Bennett Pty Ltd; DAP; IDEA; Thames & Hudson Australia Pty Ltd; Timezone 8; Worldwide Books; YBP Library Services
Orders to: Gallery Shop, South Brisbane, Qld, Contact: Peter Beiers *Tel:* (07) 38 40 713 2 *Fax:* (07) 38 40 714 9 E-mail: peter.beiers@qag.qld.gov.au Web Site: www.gallerystore.com.au

R & R Publications Pty Ltd+
12 Edward St, Brunswick, Victoria 3056
Mailing Address: PO Box 254, Carlton North, Victoria 3054
Tel: (03) 9381 2199 *Toll Free Tel:* 800 063 296 *Fax:* (03) 9381 2689
Key Personnel
Publisher & International Rights: Richard Carroll
  E-mail: richardc@bigpond.net.au
Founded: 1989
Book packagers; Specializes in cooking, drinking & lifestyles.
Subjects: Cookery, Crafts, Games, Hobbies, Gardening, Plants, Health, Nutrition, How-to, Sports, Athletics, Wine & Spirits, Lifestyle
ISBN Prefix(es): 1-875655; 1-74022
Number of titles published annually: 60 Print
Total Titles: 140 Print; 4 CD-ROM

R*O*D Books, *imprint of* Cornucopia Press

Radiating Books
6 Sapphire Crescent, Coffs Harbour, NSW 2450
Tel: (066) 536 280 *Fax:* (066) 514 970
Key Personnel
Head of Company: Helen Seccombe
Membership(s): OMCE (Organization for Management of Cultural Endeavour).
ISBN Prefix(es): 0-646

Rainbow Book Agencies Pty Ltd+
303 Arthur St, Fairfield, Victoria 3078
Tel: (03) 9481 6611 *Fax:* (03) 9481 2371
E-mail: rba@rainbowbooks.com.au; custserv@rainbowbooks.com.au; despatch@rainbowbooks.com.au (warehouse)
Web Site: www.rainbowbooks.com.au
Key Personnel
Dir: Rob Humphrys E-mail: rob.humphrys@rainbowbooks.com.au
Founded: 1985
National distribution to the religious & mind, body & spirit trade in Australia.
Subjects: Religion - Other
ISBN Prefix(es): 1-875138
Imprints: Acorn Press; Artemis Publishing; Australian Association for the Study of Religion; Beyond Bullying Association; Canadian Conference of Catholic Bishops; Christian Research Association (CRA); Desbooks; Emmaus Productions; Fairfield Press; Galations Group; Inner City Books; Jesuit Publications/Aurora Books; David Lovell Publishing; Templegate Publishers; Word of Life Distributors Pty Ltd
Distributed by Ateliers Et Presses de Taize; Australian Thelogical Forum (Australia); Carpe Diem Books (South Africa); Cluster Publications (South Africa); Columba Publications (Ireland); Comsoda Communications (Australia); Darton Longman & Todd (UK); Dominican Publications (Ireland); Eclipse Music; Emmanuel Community (Australia); Emmaus Productions (Australia); Gujarat Sahitya Prakash (India); Joshua Press (Canada); David Lovell Publishing (Australia); Maryknoll Productions (USA); Medical Mission Sisters (USA); Leigh Newton; Oregan Catholic Press (USA); Paraclete Press (USA); Pastoral Press (USA); Pauline Books & Media (UK); Random House NY (religious titles only); Redemptorist Publications; Regina Press-Malhame; Resources for Christian Living (USA); Editions du Signe (France); Spectrum Publications; Templeton Foundation Press (USA); Tanya Wittwer & Leigh Newton
Distributor for Ateliers et Presses de Taize; INTJ Books; Liguori Publication/Triumph Books; Liturgy Training Publications; Merciful Love Music (UK); Orbis Books; Our Sunday Visitor; Paulist Press; Resource Publications; St Anthony Messenger Press/Franciscan Communications; St Valdimir's Seminary Press (SVS Press); World Library Publications

Raincloud Productions
6 Castlereagh Crescent, Macquarie, ACT 2614
Tel: (02) 6251 1765
Key Personnel
Head of Company: Craig Dent
Founded: 1989
Subjects: Photography, Poetry
ISBN Prefix(es): 0-7316
Orders to: PO Box 451, Albury, NSW 2640

Rainforest Publishing+
8 Napier St, Paddington, NSW 2021
Tel: (02) 93313004 *Fax:* (02) 93805729
E-mail: rod.ritchie@sfine.arts.sa.edu.au
Key Personnel
Head of Company: Rod Ritchie
Founded: 1985
Subjects: Environmental Studies, History
ISBN Prefix(es): 0-947134
Distributed by Tower Books

Rams Skull Press
12 Fairyland Rd, Kuranda, Qld 4881
Tel: (07) 4093 7474 *Fax:* (07) 4051 4484
E-mail: ramskull@tpg.com.au
Key Personnel
Publisher: Ron Edwards
Founded: 1950
Subjects: Alternative, Cookery, Crafts, Games, Hobbies, Folklore
Number of titles published annually: 20 Print
Total Titles: 130 Print

Random House, *imprint of* Random House Australia

Random House Australia+
Subsidiary of Bertelsmann AG
20 Alfred St, Milson's Point, NSW 2061
Tel: (02) 8923 9863 *Fax:* (02) 9753 3944
E-mail: randomhouse@randomhouse.com.au
Key Personnel
Man Dir: Margaret Seale
Head of Publishing, Random House: Jane Palfreyman
Sales & Marketing Dir: Carol Davidson
Deputy Man Dir: Margaret Seale
Publisher, Bantam Doubleday: Fiona Henderson
Children's Publisher: Linsay Knight
Illustrated - Managing Editor: Jude McGee
Head of Publicity: Karen Reid
Rights & Permission: Nerrilee Weir
Business Man: Andrew Leake
Production Man: Lisa Hanrahan
Agencies: Andersen Press; Everyman's Library; TSR; Pavillion; Robinson; Virgin; World Book International, BBC.
Membership(s): APA Australia.
Subjects: Fiction, Nonfiction (General)
ISBN Prefix(es): 0-09; 1-74051; 0-7352; 0-7593
Associate Companies: Random House NZ, 18 Poland Road, Glenfield, Auckland, New Zealand *Tel:* (09) 444 7197 *Fax:* (09) 444 7524; Random House South Africa, Endulini, East Wing, 5A Jubilee Road, Parktown 2193, South Africa *Tel:* (011) 484 3538 *Fax:* (011) 484 6180; Random House UK, 20 Vauxhall Bridge Rd, London SWIV 2SA, United Kingdom *Tel:* (020) 8840 8400 *Fax:* (020) 8840 8408; Random House, Inc, 201 E 50th St, New York, NY 10022, United States *Tel:* (212) 940-7478 *Fax:* (212) 572-6045
Imprints: Anchor; Anderson; Arrow; Avon; Ballantine; Bantam Books; BBC Worldwide; Black Swan; Broadway Books; Jonathon Cape; Century; Chatto & Windus; Corgi; Crown Publishing Group; Del Rey; Dell Publishing; Doubleday; Ebury Press; Egmont; Fawcett; Fodor; Hamlyn Childrens; William Heinemann; Hutchinson; Knopf Publishing; Living Books; Mammoth UK; Minerva; Pantheon; Pavillion; Pimlico; Random House; Ravette; Red Fox; Rider; Robinson; Running Press; Secker &

Warburg; Sesame Street; Vermillion; Vintage; Virgin
Shipping Address: 16 Dalmore Dr, Scoresby, Victoria 3179 *Tel:* (03) 9753 4511 *Fax:* (03) 9753 3944
Warehouse: 16 Dalmore Dr, Scoresby, Victoria 3179
Orders to: 16 Dalmore Dr, Scoresby, Victoria 3179 *Tel:* (03) 97534511 *Fax:* (03) 94533944

Rangging Yeshe Publications, *imprint of* Windhorse Books

Rankin Publishers
PO Box 500, Sumner Park, Qld 4074
Tel: (07) 3376 9115 *Fax:* (07) 3376 9360
E-mail: info@rankin.com.au
Web Site: www.rankin.com.au
Key Personnel
Proprietor & International Rights: Robert Rankin
Founded: 1980
Subjects: Outdoor Recreation, Photography, Physics, Science (General), Australiana
ISBN Prefix(es): 0-9592418

Ravette, *imprint of* Random House Australia

Rawlhouse Publishing
PO Box 145, West Perth, WA 6005
Tel: (08) 9321 8951 *Fax:* (08) 9481 1914
E-mail: info@rawlhouse.com
Web Site: www.rawlinsons.com
Key Personnel
Dir & Editor: I A Baillie
Founded: 1983
Construction cost reference books.
ISBN Prefix(es): 0-9587406; 0-9587853
Total Titles: 2 Print

RD Press, *imprint of* Reader's Digest (Australia) Pty Ltd

Reader's Digest (Australia) Pty Ltd+
26-32 Waterloo St, Surry Hills, Sydney, NSW 2010
Mailing Address: GPO Box 4353, Sydney, NSW 2001
Tel: (02) 96906935 *Fax:* (02) 96906390
Cable: READIGEST SYDNEY
Key Personnel
Man Dir: William Toohey
Editorial, Condensed Books: Joshua Shrubb
Editorial, General Books: Margaret Fraser
Publisher, Catalog & Trade Books: Robert Sarsfield
Founded: 1946
Subjects: Education
ISBN Prefix(es): 0-86438; 0-909486; 0-949819; 0-86449; 0-9577023
Parent Company: The Reader's Digest Association Inc, PO Box 235, Pleasantville, NY 10570, United States
Imprints: RD Press; Reader's Digest Condensed Books
Book Club(s): Reader's Digest Condensed Books
Orders to: Hodder Headline Australia, PO Box 386, Rydalmere, NSW 2116

Reader's Digest Condensed Books, *imprint of* Reader's Digest (Australia) Pty Ltd

Ready-Ed Publications+
11/17 Foley St, Balcatta, WA 6021
Mailing Address: PO Box 276, Greenwood, WA 6024
Tel: (08) 9349 6111 *Fax:* (08) 9349 7222
E-mail: info@readyed.com.au
Web Site: www.readyed.com.au
Key Personnel
International Rights: Tim Lowson *E-mail:* tim@readyed.com.au
Founded: 1984
Subjects: Education
ISBN Prefix(es): 1-83697

The Real Estate Institute of Australia+
16 Thesiger Court, Deakin, ACT 2600
Mailing Address: PO Box 234, Deakin, West ACT 2600
Tel: (02) 6282 4277 *Fax:* (02) 6285 2444
E-mail: reia@reiaustralia.com.au
Web Site: www.reiaustralia.com.au
Key Personnel
Chief Executive Officer: Bryan Stevens *E-mail:* bryan.stevens@reiaustralia.com.au
Public Affairs Manager: Alison Verhoeven *E-mail:* alison.verhoeven@reiaustralia.com.au
Research Manager: David Wesney *E-mail:* david.wesney@reiaustralia.com.au
Finance Manager: Trevor Smith *E-mail:* trevor.smith@reiaustralia.com.au
Publisher: Sandra Green
Subjects: Accounting, Advertising, Business, Finance, Management, Marketing, Real Estate, Self-Help
ISBN Prefix(es): 0-909784
Imprints: REIA; RIAL
Distributor for Dearborn Trade (Australia & New Zealand)

Red Fox, *imprint of* Random House Australia

Reed Educational Publishing Australia+
Division of Reed Educational & Professional Publishing
22 Salmon St, Port Melbourne, Victoria 3207
Mailing Address: PO Box 460, Port Melbourne, Victoria 3207
Tel: (03) 9245 7188 *Fax:* (03) 9245 7265
E-mail: admin@reededucation.com.au; customerservice@reededucation.com.au
Web Site: www.reededucation.com.au
Key Personnel
Man Dir: David O'Brian *Tel:* (03) 92457103 *Fax:* (03) 92457173 *E-mail:* david.obrian@reededucation.com.au
Founded: 1982
Subjects: Art, Chemistry, Chemical Engineering, Environmental Studies, Geography, Geology, Health, Nutrition, History, Mathematics, Physics
ISBN Prefix(es): 0-7312; 0-85859
Total Titles: 5,000 Print; 50 CD-ROM; 20 Audio
Imprints: Heinemann

Reed for Kids
Formerly Budget Books Pty Ltd
17 Redwood Drive, Dingly, Victoria 3172
Tel: (03) 5516111 *Fax:* (03) 95517490
Key Personnel
Man Dir: Robert Ungar
ISBN Prefix(es): 0-86801; 0-947192; 0-908505; 0-7323

Regency Publishing+
Division of Regency Institute TAFE
Days Rd, Regency Park, SA 5010
Tel: (08) 8348 4599 Toll Free *Tel:* 800 649 898 (ext 4599) *Fax:* (08) 8348 4400
E-mail: regencypublishing@regency.tafe.sa.edu.au
Web Site: www.regencypublishing.com.au; www.tafe.sa.edu.au/institutes/regency/regency-publishing/main.htm
Key Personnel
Manager: Mimma Trimboli *E-mail:* mimma.trimboli@regency.tafe.sa.edu.au
Educational textbooks specifically related to the vocational training sector.
Subjects: Cookery, Engineering (General), Health, Nutrition, Wine & Spirits, Cosmetology, Food Processing, Hairdressing, Hospitality Operations & Management, Recreation, Sport & Tourism
ISBN Prefix(es): 1-86418
Total Titles: 120 Print; 2 CD-ROM

REIA, *imprint of* The Real Estate Institute of Australia

RIAL, *imprint of* The Real Estate Institute of Australia

RIC Publications Pty Ltd+
4 Bendsten Pl, Balcatta, WA 6021
Mailing Address: PO Box 332, Greenwood, WA 6924
Tel: (09) 9240 9888 *Fax:* (09) 9240 1513
E-mail: mail@ricgroup.com.au
Web Site: www.ricgroup.com.au
Key Personnel
Man Dir: Peter Woods *E-mail:* peter@ricgroup.com.au
Founded: 1986
Subjects: Education
ISBN Prefix(es): 1-86400; 1-86311
Number of titles published annually: 90 Print
Total Titles: 800 Print
Subsidiaries: Prim Ed Publishing PM Ltd
Branch Office(s)
Prim-Ed Publishing Limited, Bosheen New Ross, County Wexford, Ireland
Prim Ed Publishing (UK) Limited, 5A Kelsey Close, Attleborough Field, Nuneaton CVII 6RS, United Kingdom

Rider, *imprint of* Random House Australia

RLCP, *imprint of* University of New South Wales Press Ltd

RMIT Press, *imprint of* RMIT Publishing

RMIT Publishing+
Level 3, 449 Swanston St, Melbourne, Victoria 3000
Mailing Address: PO Box 12058, A'Beckett St, Melbourne, Victoria 8006
Tel: (03) 9925 8100 *Fax:* (03) 9925 8134
E-mail: info@rmitpublishing.com.au
Web Site: www.rmitpublishing.com.au
Key Personnel
Training Liaison Officer: Judy Benson
Membership(s): Australian Publishers Association National Book Council; also acts as distributor.
Subjects: Accounting, Business, Child Care & Development, Engineering (General), Fashion, Language Arts, Linguistics, Management, Travel
ISBN Prefix(es): 0-86459; 0-7306
Imprints: RMIT Press; TAFE Publications

Robert Brown & Associates Australia Pty Ltd, see E J Brill, Robert Brown & Associates

Tom Roberts (Pat Roberts)+
241 West Beach Rd, Richmond, SA 5033
Tel: (08) 8143 7578
Key Personnel
Owner & Dir: Pat Roberts
Founded: 1971
Specialize in Equestrian Control.
Subjects: Animals, Pets, Family History, Horse Training & Educating, War, World War II Diaries
ISBN Prefix(es): 0-9599413
Total Titles: 6 Print
Branch Office(s)
Western International Inc, 1875 Oddie Blvd, Sparks, NV 89431-6238, United States
Tel: 775-359-4400 *Fax:* 775-359-4439

AUSTRALIA

Distributed by Rom Kerrigan; Western International Inc (USA)
Orders to: Western International Inc, 1875 Oddie Blvd, Sparks, NV 89431-6238, United States
Tel: 775-359-4400 *Fax:* 775-359-4439

Robinson, *imprint of* Random House Australia

Robinson's, *imprint of* Universal Press Pty Ltd

Rodale, *imprint of* Bloomings Books

Roo Books, *imprint of* Kangaroo Press

Royal Society of New South Wales
157 Gloucester St, Sydney, NSW 2000
Mailing Address: PO Box 1525, Macquarie Centre, NSW 2113
Tel: (02) 9887 4448 *Fax:* (02) 9887 4448
E-mail: info@nsw.royalsoc.org.au
Web Site: nsw.royalsoc.org.au
Founded: 1821
Subjects: Chemistry, Chemical Engineering, Environmental Studies, Geography, Geology, Mathematics, Medicine, Nursing, Dentistry, Physics, Science (General)
ISBN Prefix(es): 0-9598274

Royal Society of Victoria Inc
9 Victoria St, Melbourne, Victoria 3000
Tel: (03) 9663 5259 *Fax:* (03) 9663 2301
E-mail: sciencevictoria@org.au; rsvinc@vicnet.net.au
Web Site: www.sciencevictoria.org.au
Key Personnel
Executive Officer: Camilla van Megen
Founded: 1854
Learned scientific organization.
Subjects: Science (General)
Number of titles published annually: 1 Print

Rumsby Scientific Publishing
PO Box Q355, QVB, Sydney, NSW 2000
Tel: (02) 98076184 *Fax:* (02) 98076184
Subjects: Mathematics
ISBN Prefix(es): 0-646; 0-7316

Running Press, *imprint of* Random House Australia

Ruskin Rowe Press+
28 Ruskin Rowe, Avalon Beach, NSW 2107
Tel: (02) 9918-8810 *Fax:* (02) 9918-8884
Key Personnel
Author & International Rights: Dr Jan Roberts
Founded: 1996
Subjects: Architecture & Interior Design, Art, Biography, Education, History, Nonfiction (General), Regional Interests, Women's Studies
ISBN Prefix(es): 0-9587095

St Clair Press+
PO Box 287, Rozelle, NSW 2039
Tel: (02) 9818 1942 *Fax:* (02) 9418 1923
E-mail: stclair@australis.net.au
Web Site: www.stclairpress.com.au
Key Personnel
Dir: Bruce Watson
Subjects: Education
ISBN Prefix(es): 0-949898
Total Titles: 63 Print
Distributor for Broadview Press (Restrictions in Australia); Carcanet (Australia); Seren (Australia); University of Hull (Australia); University of Wales (Australia)

St George Books
125 St George's Terrace, Perth, WA 6000
Tel: (08) 9482 9051 *Fax:* (08) 9482 9043
Key Personnel
Publications Manager: Simon Waight *Tel:* (08) 9482 9043 *E-mail:* simon.waight@wanews.com.au
Founded: 1980
Subjects: Nonfiction (General), Regional Interests
ISBN Prefix(es): 0-86778; 0-949864; 0-909699
Total Titles: 40 Print; 1 CD-ROM
Parent Company: West Australian Newspapers Holdings Ltd
Imprints: Panorama Books; WA Newspaper
Distributor for Orin Books (Western Australia)

St Joseph Publications+
Provincial House, 34 Liverpool Rd, Croydon, NSW 2132
Tel: (02) 99297344 *Fax:* (02) 91303678; (02) 99297994
E-mail: sosjelt@internet-australia.com
Key Personnel
Contact: Sister Marie Levey; Sister Bernadette O'Sullivan
Founded: 1981
Subjects: Education, History, Music, Dance, Religion - Catholic
ISBN Prefix(es): 1-875933; 0-9592316; 0-9579976
Total Titles: 30 Print
Showroom(s): Mary MacKillof Place, 7 Mount St, North Sydney, NSW 2060

St Martins, *imprint of* Pan Macmillan Australia Pty Ltd

St Pauls Publications+
60-70 Broughton Rd, Strathfield, NSW 2135
Mailing Address: PO Box 906, Strathfield, NSW 2135
Tel: (02) 9746 2288 *Fax:* (02) 9746 1140
E-mail: publications@stpauls.com.au; info@stpauls.com.au; sales@stpauls.com.au
Web Site: www.stpauls.com.au
Key Personnel
Head of Company: Bruno Colombari
Founded: 1953
Membership(s): Christian Bookselling Association of Australia (CBAA).
Subjects: Biblical Studies, Biography, Education, Human Relations, Nonfiction (General), Religion - Catholic, Social Sciences, Sociology, Theology
ISBN Prefix(es): 0-949080; 0-909986; 1-875570; 1-876295
Distributed by Alba House (US); Editions Mediaspaul (Canada); St Pauls Distribution (Ireland); St Pauls Publishing (United Kingdom)

Saltwater Publications
8 Wattle Ave, Mount Martha, Victoria 3934
Mailing Address: PO Box 160, Mount Martha, Victoria 3934
Tel: (03) 5974 1959 *Fax:* (03) 5974 1959
Key Personnel
Contact: Richard Hawkins
Founded: 1983
Subjects: Maritime, Outdoor Recreation, Boating guides
ISBN Prefix(es): 0-9592578

Sandcastle Books, *imprint of* Fremantle Arts Centre Press

W B Saunders/Bailliere Tindall, *imprint of* Elsevier Australia

Saunders College, *imprint of* Elsevier Australia

Sceptre, *imprint of* Hodder Headline Australia

Scholastic Australia Pty Ltd
76-80 Railway Crescent, Lisarow, NSW 2250
Mailing Address: PO Box 579, Gosford, NSW 2250
Tel: (02) 4328 3555 *Toll Free Tel:* 800-021-233 *Fax:* (02) 4323 3827 *Toll Free Fax:* 800-789-948
E-mail: customerservice@scholastic.com.au
Web Site: www.scholastic.com.au
Key Personnel
Man Dir: Ken A Jolly
Publishing, Rights & Permissions: David Harris
Corporate Communications Manager: Leanie Sweeney
Founded: 1968
Subjects: Education
ISBN Prefix(es): 0-86896; 1-86388; 1-86504; 0-9689600
Parent Company: Scholastic Inc, 557 Broadway, New York, NY 10012-3999, United States
Associate Companies: Margaret Hamilton Books; Omnibus Books, 335 Linley Rd, Malvern, SA
Tel: (08) 8363 2333 *Fax:* (08) 8363 1420
Imprints: Classroom Magazine; Babysitters Club
Branch Office(s)
1091 Toorak Rd, Hartwell, Victoria 3124
2/350 Lytton Rd, Morningside, Qld 4170
52 Fullarton Rd, Norwood 5067
Book Club(s): Arrow; Lucky; Star; Teachers Bookshelf; Wombat
Shipping Address: Railway Crescent, Lisarow, via Gosford, NSW 2250

Science Press+
Unit 16, 102 Edinburgh Rd, Marrickville, NSW 2204
Tel: (02) 9516 1122 *Fax:* (02) 9550 1915
Key Personnel
Man Dir: William Boden
General Manager: Robert Koo
Marketing Manager: Barry Brown
Founded: 1945
Subjects: Education
ISBN Prefix(es): 0-85583

Scripture Union, *imprint of* Anzea Publishers Ltd

Scroll Publishers
12 Redwood St, Upper Coomera, Qld 4210
Mailing Address: PO Box 112, Oxenford, Qld 4210
Tel: (07) 5573 0835 *Fax:* (07) 5529 9155
Subjects: Alternative
ISBN Prefix(es): 0-646

Seaglass, *imprint of* Pascoe Publishing Pty Ltd

Seanachas Press
PO Box 169, Maroubra, NSW 2035
Tel: (02) 6299 5434
Key Personnel
Contact: Peter Gibson
Founded: 1993
Subjects: Genealogy, History, Family History
ISBN Prefix(es): 0-9586638

Secker & Warburg, *imprint of* Random House Australia

See Australia Guides P/L+
Valley Farm Rd, Healesville, Victoria 3777
Tel: (03) 5962 5723 *Fax:* (03) 5962 4718
E-mail: sag@minopher.net.au
Key Personnel
Dir: Greg Dunnett
Founded: 1990
Subjects: Travel
ISBN Prefix(es): 0-9586439

PUBLISHERS

AUSTRALIA

Sesame Street, *imprint of* Random House Australia

The Sheringa Book Committee
Lake Hamilton Station, PMB 73, Port Lincoln, SA 5607
Tel: (086) 878750
Key Personnel
Head of Company: William Nosworthy
Subjects: History
ISBN Prefix(es): 0-7316

Sidgwick & Jackson, *imprint of* Pan Macmillan Australia Pty Ltd

Signet, *imprint of* Penguin Group (Australia)

Simon & Schuster Australia, *imprint of* Simon & Schuster (Australia) Pty Ltd

Simon & Schuster (Australia) Pty Ltd+
Division of Simon & Schuster Inc
PO Box 507, East Roseville, NSW 2069
Tel: (02) 9415 9900 *Fax:* (02) 9417 3188 (customer service); (02) 9417 4292 (editorial); (02) 9417 1087 (publicity)
E-mail: cservice@simonandschuster.com.au; rights.dept@simonandschuster.com.au
Web Site: www.simonsays.com; www.simonandschuster.com.au
Key Personnel
Man Dir: Jon Attenborough
Founded: 1987
Subjects: Alternative, Animals, Pets, Anthropology, Child Care & Development, Cookery, Crafts, Games, Hobbies, Health, Nutrition, History, House & Home, How-to, Management, Natural History, Nonfiction (General), Outdoor Recreation, Self-Help
ISBN Prefix(es): 0-7318; 0-86417 (Kangaroo Press)
Number of titles published annually: 70 Print
Total Titles: 700 Print
Ultimate Parent Company: Viacom Inc, 1515 Broadway, New York, NY 10036, United States
Associate Companies: Simon & Schuster UK Ltd, Africa House, 64-78 Kingsway, London WC2B 6AH, United Kingdom *Tel:* (020) 7316 1900 *Fax:* (020) 7316 0032
Imprints: Kangaroo Press; Simon & Schuster Australia
Distributed by The Search Press (craft only - UK & Europe)
Distributor for AA Publishing; Australian Women's Weekly; Duncan Baird; Kyle Cathie; Finch Publishing; Gaia Books; Jenman Group; National Geographic; Ten Speed Press

Single X Publications+
PO Box 227, Glenside, SA 5065
Tel: (08) 8127 0827
Key Personnel
Editor & Author: Michael X Savvas
  E-mail: msavvas@usa.net
Founded: 1994
Subjects: Biography, Self-Help, Sports, Athletics, Travel, Motivational

Singular Press, *imprint of* Elsevier Australia

Skills Publishing
PO Box 514, Hazelbrook, NSW 2779
Tel: (02) 4759 2844 *Fax:* (02) 4759 3721
E-mail: aww@skillspublish.com.au
Web Site: www.skillspublish.com.au
Key Personnel
Publisher: Art Burrows
Man Dir: Steven Burrows
Founded: 1985
Publisher of books & magazines in woodworking, metalworking, home construction & renovation.
Subjects: Crafts, Games, Hobbies, House & Home, How-to
ISBN Prefix(es): 0-646

Skylight Publishing Inc, *imprint of* Hawker Brownlow

Slouch Hat Publications+
PO Box 174, Rosebud, Victoria 3939
Tel: (03) 5986-6437 *Fax:* (03) 5986-6312
E-mail: slouchat@surf.net.au
Web Site: www.slouch-hat.com.au
Key Personnel
Contact: Ron Austin
Founded: 1989
Subjects: History, Military Science
ISBN Prefix(es): 0-9585296; 0-9579752

Social Club Books
6-10 Keele St, Collingwood, Victoria 3066
Mailing Address: PO Box 2937, Fitzroy, Melbourne, Victoria 3065
Tel: (03) 9473 5555 *Fax:* (03) 9417 5574
E-mail: info@scb.com.au
Web Site: www.scb.com.au
Key Personnel
Man Dir: Ken Finlayson *E-mail:* kenf@scb.com.au
Founded: 1983
Subjects: Astrology, Occult, Cookery, Gardening, Plants
Imprints: Ken Fin

Social Science Press+
Imprint of Thomson Learning
102 Dodds St, Southbank, Victoria 3006
Tel: 800-654-831 *Fax:* 800-641-823
E-mail: newtext@thomsonlearning.com.au
Web Site: www.thomsonlearning.com.au/higher/index.asp
Founded: 1980
Subjects: Education
ISBN Prefix(es): 0-949218; 1-876033

Somerset Publications
PO Box 8, Samford, Qld 4520
Tel: (07) 3425 1857 *Fax:* (07) 3425 1857
E-mail: info@crabbetarabian.com; crabbetarabian@hotkey.net.au
Web Site: www.crabbetarabian.com; www.hotkey.net.au/~crabbetarabian
Key Personnel
Editor: Joan Flynn; Coralie Gordon
Founded: 1987
Specialize in books & magazines on Arabian horses.
Subjects: Arabian Horses
ISBN Prefix(es): 0-947256
Parent Company: Limbale Pty Ltd
Distributed by J A Allen & Co; Alexander Heriot; Silver Monarch POB (USA)
Distributor for J A Allen & Co (UK); Alexander Heriot (UK); Borden Publishing (USA); Gordon & Gotch

South Australian Government-Department of Education, Employment & Training
Curriculum Resources Unit, Banksia Ave, Seacombe Gardens, SA 5047
Tel: (08) 8377 0399 *Fax:* (08) 8377 0341
Key Personnel
Managing Editor: Pamela Ball
Founded: 1974
Membership(s): Australian Publishers Association.
Subjects: Education
ISBN Prefix(es): 0-7243; 7-308
Bookshop(s): The Shop, The Orphanage Teachers Centre, 181 Coodwood Rd, Millswood, SA 5034
Orders to: Curriculum Resources Australia, PO Box 33, Campbelltown, SA 5074 *Tel:* (08) 8373 6077 *Fax:* (08) 8234 5086

South Head Press
1102 Windsong, 212 Marine Parade, Labrador, Qld 4215
Mailing Address: PO Box 59, Southport, Qld 4215
Tel: (07) 5526 4670
Key Personnel
Head of Company: John Millett
  E-mail: johnmarion@telstra.com
Founded: 1964
Subjects: Poetry
ISBN Prefix(es): 0-909185; 0-901760

South Pacific Books, *imprint of* Outback Books - CQU Press

Southern Cross PR & Press Services
Arakoon, Via Tenterfield, NSW 2372
Tel: (02) 6737 5436 *Fax:* (02) 6737 5436
Key Personnel
Contact: Joan Starr
ISBN Prefix(es): 0-9588021

Spacevision Publishing+
12 Fry's Track, Newborough, Victoria 3825
Tel: (03) 5127 2398
Key Personnel
Head of Company: A E Allison
Founded: 1994
Subjects: Mysteries
ISBN Prefix(es): 0-646

Spaniel Books+
PO Box 167, Paddington, NSW 2021
Tel: (02) 9360 9985 *Fax:* (02) 9331 4653
E-mail: spanielbooks@hotmail.com
Key Personnel
Contact: Michael Giffin
Founded: 1995
Subjects: Literature, Literary Criticism, Essays, Theology
ISBN Prefix(es): 0-9579568

Specialist Publications
One Edwin St, Mortlake, NSW 2137
Tel: (02) 9736 2191 *Fax:* (02) 9736 2663
Web Site: www.specialist.com.au
Key Personnel
Contact: John Brooks *E-mail:* john@specialist.com.au
ISBN Prefix(es): 0-9588973; 1-86434

Spectrum Publications+
PO Box 75, Richmond, Victoria 3121
Tel: (03) 9429 1404 *Fax:* (03) 9428 9407
E-mail: spectpub@ozemail.com.au
Web Site: www.ozemail.com.au/~spectpub
Key Personnel
Man Dir: Peter Henry Rohr
Sales Manager: Maria Peters
Founded: 1974
Membership(s): Australian Publishers Association.
Subjects: Biography, Education, Gay & Lesbian, History, Music, Dance, Nonfiction (General), Psychology, Psychiatry, Religion - Buddhist, Religion - Catholic, Religion - Hindu, Religion - Islamic, Religion - Jewish, Religion - Protestant, Religion - Other, Self-Help, Theology, Australiana, Grief, Inspirational
ISBN Prefix(es): 0-86786; 0-909837
Number of titles published annually: 10 Print
Total Titles: 70 Print

41

AUSTRALIA

Spellbound Promotions
7 Market St, Woolgoolga, NSW 2456
Tel: (066) 542133 *Fax:* (066) 541258
E-mail: Jodiadv@oncs.com.au
Key Personnel
Manager: Ron Blackmore
Founded: 1987
Publishing, Promotion, Typesetting, Editing & Cover Design
Privately owned company.
ISBN Prefix(es): 1-876005
Total Titles: 3 Print; 3 Audio
Distributed by Crown Publishing (Taiwan)
Foreign Rep(s): Crown Publishing (Taiwan)

Spinifex Press+
504 Queensberry St, North Melbourne, Victoria 3051
Mailing Address: PO Box 212, North Melbourne, Victoria 3051
Tel: (03) 9329-6088 *Fax:* (03) 9329-9238
E-mail: women@spinifexpress.com.au
Web Site: www.spinifexpress.com.au
Key Personnel
Dir: Susan Hawthorne *E-mail:* hawsu@spinifexpress.com.qu; Renate Klein
Founded: 1991
Specialize in feminist publishing.
Membership(s): APA.
Subjects: Alternative, Art, Asian Studies, Astrology, Occult, Astronomy, Developing Countries, Disability, Special Needs, Economics, Education, Environmental Studies, Fiction, Gay & Lesbian, Health, Nutrition, Literature, Literary Criticism, Essays, Nonfiction (General), Poetry, Social Sciences, Sociology, Technology, Travel, Women's Studies, Feminism
ISBN Prefix(es): 1-875559; 1-876756
Number of titles published annually: 10 Print
Total Titles: 150 Print
Foreign Rights: Arts & Licensing International Inc (China, Hong Kong, Malaysia, Taiwan); Best Literary & Rights Agency (Korea); Bestun Korea Literary Agency (Korea); BookCosmos (Korea); The Harris/Elon Agency (Israel); Imprima Korea Agency (Korea); International Editors' Co (Argentina, Spain); Iris Agency (Greece); Vanessa Kling & Michele Kanonidis (France); Literarische Agentur (Germany); Natoli, Stefan & Oliva (Italy); Pikarski Literary Agency (Israel); Read n' Right Agency (Greece); Tuttle Mori Agency (Japan); Eric Yang Agency (Korea); Tatjana Zoldnere (Latvia)
Distribution Center: Macmillan Distribution Services, 627 Chapel St, Level 4, South Yarra, Victoria 3141 *Toll Free Tel:* 300 135 113 *Toll Free Fax:* 300 135 103 *E-mail:* customer.service@macmillan.com.au (Australia)
Addenda, PO Box 78-224, GrayLynn, Auckland, New Zealand *Tel:* (09) 8367471 *Fax:* (09) 8367401 *E-mail:* addenda@addenda.co.nz
A Star Distributor, One Tannery Rd, No 04-01, Cencon 1 347719 *Tel:* 6746 3165 *Fax:* 6745 6729 *E-mail:* astargp@mbox3.singnet.com.sg
Fernwood Books Ltd, PO Box 1981, Peterborough, ON K9J 7X7, Canada *Tel:* 705-743-8990 *Fax:* 705-743-8353 *E-mail:* lgray@broadviewpress.com (Canada - trade & academic orders)
Gazelle, Falcon House, Queen Sq, Lancaster LA1 1RN, United Kingdom *E-mail:* sales@gazellebooks.co.uk
Independent Publishers Group, Order Department, 814 N Franklin St, Chicago, IL 60610, United States *Tel:* 312-337-0747 *Fax:* 312-337-5985 *E-mail:* frontdesk@ipgbook.com *Web Site:* www.ipgbook.com
Missing Link, Westerstr 114-116, 28199 Bremen, Germany *Tel:* (0421) 50 43 48 *Fax:* (0421) 50 43 16 *E-mail:* info@missing-link.de (Europe bookshops only))

Standards Association of Australia
PO Box 458, North Sydney, NSW 2060
Tel: (02) 99634231 *Fax:* (02) 9746 8450
Telex: AA26514
Key Personnel
Chief Executive: Ross Wraight
Founded: 1922
Subjects: Chemistry, Chemical Engineering, Civil Engineering, Communications, Electronics, Electrical Engineering, Engineering (General), Mechanical Engineering, Technology
ISBN Prefix(es): 0-7262

Star Teaching, *imprint of* Hawker Brownlow

State Library of NSW Press+
Macquarie St, Sydney, NSW 2000
Tel: (02) 92731568 *Fax:* (02) 92731259
E-mail: helene@ilanet.slnsw.gov.au
Web Site: www.sl.nsw.gov.au
Key Personnel
Manager: Judith Kelly *E-mail:* jkelly@ilanet.slnsw.gov.au
Founded: 1988
Membership(s): Australian Publishers Association.
Subjects: Art, Biography, Ethnicity, Genealogy, History, Literature, Literary Criticism, Essays, Natural History, Nonfiction (General), Social Sciences, Sociology, Women's Studies
ISBN Prefix(es): 0-7305; 0-7310
Parent Company: Library Council of NSW
Distributed by Peribo Pty Ltd (Australia/NZ/PNG)

State Library of Victoria
328 Swanston St, Melbourne, Victoria 3000
Tel: (03) 8664 7000 *Fax:* (03) 9639 2175
E-mail: abirkenbeil@slv.vic.gov.au
Web Site: www.slv.vic.gov.au
Key Personnel
Publisher: Rob Blackmore
ISBN Prefix(es): 0-9585959; 0-9750153

State Publishing Unit of State Print SA+
282 Richmond Rd, Netley, SA 5037
Mailing Address: PO Box 210, Plympton, SA 5038
Tel: (08) 9226 4677 *Fax:* (08) 9226 4726
Key Personnel
General Manager: Tony Fitzsimmons
Founded: 1986
Also acts as Agents.
Subjects: History, Regional Interests
ISBN Prefix(es): 0-7243

Sterling Publishing Co Inc, *imprint of* Hawker Brownlow

Ian Stewart Marine Publications
PO Box 5154, Rockingham Beach, WA 6168
Tel: (08) 9593 1331 *Fax:* (08) 9593 1331
Key Personnel
Dir: Ian Graham Stewart
Founded: 1992
Subjects: Maritime, Shipping
Total Titles: 2 Print
Distributed by Anthony Cooke (UK & Europe); Cordillera Press (Canada & US)
Distributor for Carmania Press

Stirling Press
69 Paringa/Pde, Old Noarlung, SA 5168
Mailing Address: PO Box 39, Old Noarlung, SA 5168
Tel: (08) 327-1166 *Fax:* (08) 9327-1166
E-mail: stirl@ozemail.com.au
Subjects: Business, Health, Nutrition, Self-Help
ISBN Prefix(es): 0-949142
Showroom(s): 100 King William Rd, Hyde Park, SA 5034

Strucmech Publishing
1A Southey St, Sandringham, Victoria 3191
Tel: (03) 95989245 *Fax:* (03) 95989245
Key Personnel
Author & Manager: Alan K Hosking
Founded: 1984
Subjects: Civil Engineering, Applied structural design
ISBN Prefix(es): 0-9586580

Success Education, *imprint of* R J Cleary Publishing

Summer Institute of Linguistics, Australian Aborigines Branch
60 Vanderlin Dr, Berrimah, NT 5788
Tel: (08) 8922 5700 *Fax:* (08) 8922 5717
E-mail: sildarwin@taunet.net.au
Founded: 1961
Subjects: Anthropology, Education, Language Arts, Linguistics, Australian Aboriginal & Torres Strait Islander Languages
ISBN Prefix(es): 0-86892
Parent Company: Summer Institute of Linguistics, Attn: Academic Publications, 7500 W Camp Wisdom Rd, Dallas, TX 75326, United States

Sun, *imprint of* Pan Macmillan Australia Pty Ltd

Sundance Inc, *imprint of* Hawker Brownlow

Systex
2 Ayres Rd, Saint Ives, NSW 2075
Tel: (02) 9944 2668
Key Personnel
Head of Company: Peter Burke
ISBN Prefix(es): 0-646

T & A, *imprint of* Turton & Armstrong Pty Ltd Publishers

Tabletop Press+
2 Lambell Close, Palmerston, ACT 2913
Tel: (06) 6242 0995 *Fax:* (06) 6242 0674
Key Personnel
Head of Company: Klaus Hueneke
Founded: 1985
Also acts as distributor.
Subjects: Geography, Geology, History, Photography, Regional Interests
ISBN Prefix(es): 0-9590841; 0-9587049
Distributed by Evirobook; Tower Books

TAFE Publications, *imprint of* RMIT Publishing

Tamarind Publications
PO Box 624, Warner's Bay, NSW 2282
Tel: (02) 467934 *Fax:* (02) 659515
E-mail: sigi@hunterlink.net.au
Key Personnel
Principal: Pauline Clare Egan
Founded: 1996
Subjects: Philosophy, Poetry, Religion - Buddhist
ISBN Prefix(es): 0-9586836
Number of titles published annually: 1 Print
Total Titles: 2 Print

Tarka Publishing+
8 William St, North Sydney, NSW 2060
Tel: (02) 9955 2074 *Fax:* (02) 9925 0664
Key Personnel
Head of Company & Dir: Ann Howard *E-mail:* lnchoward9@aol.com
Founded: 1990
Subjects: History, Poetry, Women's Studies, Juvenile Migration
ISBN Prefix(es): 0-9585843
Number of titles published annually: 1 Print

PUBLISHERS

AUSTRALIA

Total Titles: 12 Print
Distributed by Bay Books; Lothian; Tower Books
Book Club(s): Doubleday

Teach Yourself, *imprint of* Hodder Headline Australia

Teacher Created Materials, *imprint of* Hawker Brownlow

Technomic Publishing, *imprint of* Elsevier Australia

Templegate Publishers, *imprint of* Rainbow Book Agencies Pty Ltd

Terania Rainforest Publishing
Terania Creek Rd, The Channon, NSW 2480
Tel: (02) 6688 6204 *Fax:* (02) 6688 6227
E-mail: terania@nrg.com.au
Key Personnel
Contact: Nan J Nicholson
Founded: 1985
Subjects: Environmental Studies, Gardening, Plants, Natural History, Botany, Rainforest
ISBN Prefix(es): 0-9589436
Total Titles: 5 Print
Distributed by Frith & Frith (Australia); Tower Books (Australia)

Tertiary Press+
12-50 Norton Rd, Croydon, Victoria 3136
Tel: (03) 9726 1505 *Fax:* (03) 9726 1706
E-mail: tertiarypress@swin.edu.au
Web Site: www.tertiarypress.com.au
Key Personnel
Manager: Cathy Grundy *Tel:* (03) 9726 1674
  E-mail: cgrundy@swin.edu.au
Founded: 1995
Subjects: Accounting, Business, Child Care & Development, Computer Science, Economics, Human Relations, Management, Marketing, Microcomputers, Technology
ISBN Prefix(es): 1-875794; 1-875886; 0-86458
Number of titles published annually: 35 Print; 2 CD-ROM; 1 Audio
Total Titles: 200 Print
Parent Company: Swinburne University of Technology
Foreign Rep(s): Educational Books Ltd (New Zealand)

Text, *imprint of* The Text Publishing Company Pty Ltd

The Text Publishing Company Pty Ltd+
171 Latrobe St, Melbourne, Victoria 3000
Tel: (03) 9272 4700 *Fax:* (03) 9926 4854
E-mail: books@textmedia.com.au
Web Site: www.textpublishing.com.au
Key Personnel
Publisher: Michael Heyward *Tel:* (03) 9272 4716
Publicist: Emily Booth
Founded: 1990
Subjects: Biography, Fiction, History, Humor, Literature, Literary Criticism, Essays, Nonfiction (General), Political Science
ISBN Prefix(es): 1-875847; 1-876485; 1-877008; 1-86372
Number of titles published annually: 40 Print
Total Titles: 105 Print
Associate Companies: The Text Media Group Pty Ltd
Imprints: Text
Distributed by Archetype Book Agents; Penguin Books Australia
Foreign Rights: Agencia Litterari BMSR (Brazil); Antonella Antonelli Agencia (Italy); Agencia Litteraria Carmen Balcells (Portugal, Spain); Bardon-Chinese Media Agency (China, Taiwan); Eliane Benisti Agency (France); Paul & Peter Fritz (Germany); Caroline van Gelderen (Netherlands); Graal Ltd (Poland); International Copyright Agency (Romania); Katai & Bolza (Hungary); Korea Copyright Centre (Korea); Leonhardt & Hoier (Scandinavia); Lutyens & Rubinstein (UK); Tuttle-Mori Agency (Japan); Andrew Nurnberg Associates (Baltic States); Witherspoon Associates Inc (USA)
Warehouse: Peguin Books Australia, 30 Centre Rd, Scoresby, Victoria 3179 *Tel:* (03) 9811 2555 *Fax:* (03) 9811 8309
Orders to: Peguin Books Australia, 30 Centre Rd, Scoresby, Victoria 3179 *Tel:* (03) 9811 2555 *Fax:* (03) 9811 8309

Thames & Hudson (Australia) Pty Ltd
Portside Business Park, 11 Central Blvd, Fishermans Bend, Victoria 3207
Tel: (03) 9646 7788 *Fax:* (03) 9646 8790
E-mail: thaust@thaust.com.au
Key Personnel
Man Dir: Peter Shaw
Customer Service Manager: Elizabeth Ioannidis
Founded: 1968 (Wholly owned subsidiary of Thames & Hudson UK)
Distribute books for Thames & Hudson UK & other publishers.
Subjects: Archaeology, Architecture & Interior Design, Art, Fashion, Foreign Countries, History, Literature, Literary Criticism, Essays, Music, Dance, Natural History, Photography, Travel
ISBN Prefix(es): 0-500
Subsidiaries: Thames & Hudson
Distributor for AA Gallery of New South Wales; AA Gallery of Queensland; AA Gallery of South Australia; Abrams (Australia); Boothe-Clibborn Editions; British Museum Press (Australia); Craftsman House (Australia); Flammarion (Australia); Lawrence King (Australia); MOMA (Australia); National Gallery of Australia (Australia); Rizzoli/Universe; RotoVision; SCALO (Australia); SKIRA (Australia); Tate Gallery (Australia); Vision On

The Jacaranda Press, *imprint of* John Wiley & Sons Australia, Ltd

Thin Rich Press+
70 Gairloch St, Applecross, WA 6153
Mailing Address: PO Box 650, Claremont, WA 6010
Tel: (08) 9364 4799 *Fax:* (08) 9316 3338
Key Personnel
Head of Company: M Smallbone
Subjects: Human Relations, Humor, Philosophy, Poetry, Religion - Buddhist, Self-Help
ISBN Prefix(es): 0-646

Thornbill Press
4 Thornbill Crescent, Coromandel Valley, SA 5051
Tel: (08) 2705172
Key Personnel
Head of Company: Graeme Webster
Subjects: Law, Literature, Literary Criticism, Essays
ISBN Prefix(es): 0-9586973
Parent Company: Thornbill Professional Services Pty Ltd (ACN 050 019 915)

Caroline Thornton+
18 Doonan Rd, Nedlands, WA 6009
Tel: (08) 9386 1555 *Fax:* (08) 9389 5162
Founded: 1988
Subjects: History
ISBN Prefix(es): 0-7316

Thorpe-Bowker+
Division of R R Bowker LLC
85 Turner St, Bldg C3, Port Melbourne, Victoria 3207
Tel: (03) 8645 0300 *Fax:* (03) 8645 0333
E-mail: yoursay@thorpe.com.au
Web Site: www.thorpe.com.au
Key Personnel
General Manager: Richard Siegersma *Tel:* (03) 8645 0374 *E-mail:* richards@thorpe.com.au
Founded: 1921
Bibliographic & library reference publisher.
Membership(s): ABA, APA, ALIA.
Subjects: Business, Library & Information Sciences, Publishing & Book Trade Reference
ISBN Prefix(es): 0-909532; 1-875589; 1-86452
Distributor for Bowker; R R Bowker; Whitaker

Three Sisters Publications Pty Ltd
PO Box 104, Winmalee, NSW 2777
Tel: (047) 588138
Key Personnel
Principal Officer: Margaret Baker
Founded: 1983
Subjects: Archaeology, Biological Sciences, Gardening, Plants, Geography, Geology, History, Natural History
ISBN Prefix(es): 0-9590203

Threshold Publishing
PO Box 60, Croydon, Victoria 3136
Tel: (03) 9724 9067 *Fax:* (03) 9724 9067
Key Personnel
Manager: Adrian Anderson *E-mail:* adrian@alphalink.com.au
Founded: 1992
ISBN Prefix(es): 0-646

Timber, *imprint of* Bloomings Books

Time Life Australia Pty Ltd
Level 10, 77 Pacific Hwy, North Sydney, NSW 2060
Mailing Address: PO Box 3814, Sydney, NSW 2001
Tel: (02) 1300 364 437 *Toll Free Tel:* 300 364 437 *Fax:* (02) 9957 2773
E-mail: tlservice@timelife.com
Web Site: www.timelife.com.au
Key Personnel
Man Dir: Bonita L Boezeman
Founded: 1961
Subjects: Books, Music, Videos & Direct Marketing
ISBN Prefix(es): 0-8094
Parent Company: Time Warner Inc
Subsidiaries: Record Clubs of Australia
Branch Office(s)
Time Life Inc, 5 Ottho Heldringstr, 1066 AZ Amsterdam, Netherlands *Tel:* (020) 48 74 293 *Web Site:* www.timelife.nl
U.S. Office(s): Time Life, PO Box 85060, Richmond, VA 32285-5060, United States *Tel:* 804-261-1300 *Web Site:* www.timelife.com
Distributed by Collins New Zealand; Hodder Headline Australia
Book Club(s): The Softback Preview

Tirian Publications
116 Queens Cliff Rd, Queenscliff, NSW 2096
Tel: (02) 9908 1196 *Fax:* (02) 9907 1196
E-mail: Tirian@bigpond.com; infoweb@tirian.com
Web Site: www.users.bigpond.com/tirian
Subjects: Education
ISBN Prefix(es): 0-9586056

Tom Publications+
153 McDonald St, Yoodanna, WA 6060
Tel: (08) 9444 4570
Key Personnel
Contact: Radmila Mijatovic
Membership(s): WA Writers.

43

AUSTRALIA

Subjects: Ethnicity, Fiction, Nonfiction (General), Poetry, Romance, Migrants
ISBN Prefix(es): 1-87515; 0-9594810; 1-875715

Tomorrow Publications+
33 Mitchell St, Merewether, NSW 2291
Mailing Address: PO Box 313, Merewether, NSW 2291
Tel: (02) 4961 2115
E-mail: tomorrowtrading@hotmail.com
Key Personnel
Contact: Paula Morrow
Subjects: Alternative, Fiction, Health, Nutrition, How-to, Science Fiction, Fantasy, Self-Help
ISBN Prefix(es): 0-646

Tor Books, *imprint of* Pan Macmillan Australia Pty Ltd

Tower Books
17 Rodborough Rd, Unit 2, French's Forest, NSW 2086
Tel: (02) 9975 5566 *Fax:* (02) 9975 5599
E-mail: info@towerbooks.com.au
Web Site: www.towerbooks.com.au
Key Personnel
Contact: Dale Druckman

Transpareon Press+
PO Box 4, Hornsby, NSW 2077
Tel: (02) 99874570 *Fax:* (02) 99874570
Key Personnel
Dir: Frances Wheelhouse
Founded: 1970
Membership(s): Australian Book Publishers Association.
Subjects: Agriculture, Anthropology, Biography, History, Regional Interests, Science (General), Women's Studies, Australian History, Biographies, Medicine
ISBN Prefix(es): 0-908021

Transworld Publishers Pty Ltd+
20 Alfred St S, Milsons Point, NSW 2061
Tel: (02) 9954 9966 *Fax:* (02) 9954 4562
Key Personnel
Man Dir & Chief Executive Officer: Geoff Rumpf
Deputy Man Officer Finance & Operations: Greg Little
Publisher: Shona Martyn
National Sales Manager: Chris Raine
Head Publicity & Promotions: Maggie Hamilton
Founded: 1980
Subjects: Fiction, Health, Nutrition, Humor, Non-fiction (General), Romance, Science Fiction, Fantasy, Self-Help
ISBN Prefix(es): 0-552; 0-86824; 0-7338; 0-86451; 0-947189; 1-86359
Parent Company: Bertelsmann AG
Associate Companies: Transworld Publishers, United Kingdom; Bantam Doubleday Dell Inc, 1540 Broadway, New York, NY 19936, United States
Imprints: Bantam; Corgi; Doubleday; Dell; Anchor; Broadway Dela Corte; Black Swan
U.S. Office(s): Bantam Doubleday Dell, 1540 Broadway, New York, NY 10036, United States
Distributed by Transworld Publishers (New Zealand)
Distributor for Avon; Potentials Unlimited; Ravette; Running Press; Workman
Book Club(s): Doubleday Book & Music Clubs

Travelog, *imprint of* Universal Press Pty Ltd

Trillium Press, *imprint of* Hawker Brownlow

Troll Books of Australia+
20 Barcoo St, East Roseville, NSW 2069
Tel: (02) 9417 2699 *Fax:* (02) 9417 1599
E-mail: webmaster@troll.com
Web Site: www.troll.com
Key Personnel
Chief Executive: Terry T Hughes
Founded: 1997
Subjects: Fiction, Nonfiction (General), Science (General), Activity, Teacher Resources with Specialist Materials on early reading & reading recovery
ISBN Prefix(es): 1-875675
Parent Company: Troll Communications LLC, 100 Corporate Dr, Mahwah, NJ 07430, United States
Imprints: Lineup; Watermill
Branch Office(s)
Auckland, New Zealand

Tropicana Press+
7 Sheoak Pl, Alfords Point, NSW 2234
Mailing Address: PO Box 385, Padstow, NSW 2211
Tel: (02) 9543 7728
Key Personnel
Contact: R B Shaw *E-mail:* rsshaw@netspace.net.au
Subjects: Fiction
ISBN Prefix(es): 0-9581418

Troubadour Press, *imprint of* New Creation Publications Ministries & Resource Centre

Troubadour Press
Imprint of New Creation Publications Ministries & Resource Center
PO Box 403, Blackwood, SA 5051
Tel: (08) 8270 1861 *Fax:* (08) 8270 4003
E-mail: newcreat@camtech.net.au
Key Personnel
Head of Company: Geoffrey Bingham
ISBN Prefix(es): 1-875653

Tudor Australia Press
14 Tudor St, Dulwich, SA 5065
Tel: (08) 8332 8884
Key Personnel
Manager: Andrew G Peake *E-mail:* agpeake@senet.com.au
Founded: 1984
Subjects: Geography, Geology, History
ISBN Prefix(es): 0-9589177; 0-9599599
Number of titles published annually: 2 Print
Total Titles: 3 Print

Turton & Armstrong Pty Ltd Publishers+
21 Lister St, Wahroonga, NSW 2076
Tel: (02) 9489 6719 *Fax:* (02) 9489 6719
E-mail: turtarm@attglobal.net
Key Personnel
Dir: Paul T Armstrong
Founded: 1977
Non-fiction book publisher.
Subjects: Aeronautics, Aviation, Automotive, Biography, Crafts, Games, Hobbies, History, Maritime, Music, Dance, Nonfiction (General), Transportation, Special Interest & Motor Racing
ISBN Prefix(es): 0-908031
Number of titles published annually: 6 Print
Total Titles: 40 Print
Imprints: T & A
Distributed by Bookworks Pty Ltd
Orders to: Bookworks PLC, 56 Bonds Rd, Punchbowl, NSW 2196 *Tel:* (02) 9740 6766 *E-mail:* sales@bookworks.com.au

UBD, *imprint of* Universal Press Pty Ltd

Unichurch Publishing
Level 9, 222 Pit St, Sydney, NSW 2000
Mailing Address: PO Box A2178, Sydney South, NSW 1235
Tel: (02) 8267 4308 *Fax:* (02) 9267 4716
E-mail: insights@nsw.uca.org.au
Web Site: www.nsw.uca.org.au/cu/publishing.htm
Key Personnel
Unit Manager, Editor: Marjorie Lewis-Jones
ISBN Prefix(es): 0-908525

United Educational Services (DDK), *imprint of* Hawker Brownlow

Uniting Church Press, *imprint of* Uniting Education

Uniting Education
PO Box 1245, Collingwood, Victoria 3066
Tel: (03) 9416 4262 *Fax:* (03) 9416 4264
E-mail: contact@unitinged.org.au
Web Site: www.unitinged.org.au
Key Personnel
Dir: John Emmett *E-mail:* john@unitinged.org.au
Books Manager: Hugh McGinlay
Founded: 1914
Specialize in Christian Education Resources.
Subjects: Education, Human Relations, Religion - Protestant, Theology
ISBN Prefix(es): 0-85819; 1-86407
Imprints: Uniting Church Press
Distributed by National Christian Education Council (UK)
Orders to: Rainbow Books, 303 Arthur St, Fairfield, Victoria 3068 *Tel:* (03) 9481 6611 *Fax:* (03) 9481 2371 *E-mail:* rainbowb@axs.com.au

Unity Press
6A Ortana Rd, Lindfield, NSW 2070
Tel: (02) 4671342 *Fax:* (02) 9736-2663
Key Personnel
Dir: Nevill Drury; Anna Voigt
Subjects: Anthropology, Art, Astrology, Occult, Health, Nutrition, Music, Dance, Mysteries, Parapsychology, Philosophy, Poetry, Psychology, Psychiatry, Religion - Buddhist, Religion - Other, Self-Help, Women's Studies
ISBN Prefix(es): 0-9589759
Parent Company: Voigt Drury Publishing Pty Ltd

Universal Press Pty Ltd+
One Waterloo Rd, Macquarie Park, NSW 2113
Tel: (02) 9857 3700 *Toll Free Tel:* 800 021 987 *Fax:* (02) 9888 9074 *Toll Free Fax:* 800 636 197
E-mail: unipress@unipress.com.au
Key Personnel
Sales & Marketing Manager: Kim Mouret
Founded: 1950
Large range of D I Y Service, repair car manuals for popular imported & Australian produced vehicles; also list of automotive technical vehicles & automotive technical publications for trade education.
Subjects: Automotive, Travel, Automotive Publications, Maps, Street Directories & Guides
ISBN Prefix(es): 0-85566; 0-7319; 0-949164
Imprints: R A Broadberh; Gregory's; Robinson's; Travelog; UBD
Distributor for Berlitz; Fielding Worldwide; Geographer's A-Z; Michelin; National Geographic Society (maps only); Rand McNally; Replogle Globes

University of New South Wales Press Ltd+
Cliffbrook Campus, 45 Beach St, Coogee, NSW 2034
Mailing Address: University of New South Wales, Sydney, NSW 2052
Tel: (02) 9664 0900 *Fax:* (02) 9664 5420
E-mail: info.press@unsw.edu.au
Web Site: www.unswpress.com.au
Key Personnel
Man Dir: Dr Robin Derricourt *Tel:* (02) 9664 0905 *E-mail:* r.derricourt@unsw.edu.au

Publishing Manager: John Elliot *E-mail:* john.elliot@unsw.edu.au
Marketing Manager: Nella Softerboek *E-mail:* nella.s@unsw.edu.au
Founded: 1962
Membership(s): Australian Publishers Association.
Subjects: Architecture & Interior Design, Biography, Biological Sciences, Child Care & Development, Earth Sciences, Engineering (General), Environmental Studies, Gardening, Plants, Government, Political Science, History, Natural History, Nonfiction (General), Public Administration, Science (General), Social Sciences, Sociology, Technology, Women's Studies
ISBN Prefix(es): 0-86840; 0-947205
Number of titles published annually: 50 Print
Total Titles: 350 Print
Imprints: UNSW Press; RLCP
Sales Office(s): University & Reference Publishers Services UNIREPS, University of New South Wales, Sydney, NSW 2052
Distributed by Addenda Ltd; Apac Publishers Services Pte Ltd; Eurospan (UK); United Publishers Services Ltd; University & Reference Publishers Services UNIREPS; University of British Columbia Press; University of Washington Press
Distributor for Auckland University Press; Broadview; Brookings Institution Press; Canterbury University Press; Cavendish Publishing; CSIRO Publishing; Currency Press; Deakin University Press; Edinburgh University Press; C Hurst & Co; Indiana University Press; McGill-Queen's University Press; Pandanus Books; Pluto Press Australia; Reaktion Books; Rivers Oram (Pandora); Signal Books; Singapore University Press; Editions Tom Thompson; University of Otago Press; University of Washington Press
Bookshop(s): UNSW Bookshop, Sydney, NSW 2052
Warehouse: UNSW Press, Govett St, Randwick, NSW 2031

University of Newcastle
Callaghan Campus, University Drive, Callaghan, NSW 2308
Tel: (02) 4921 5000
Web Site: www.newcastle.edu.au
ISBN Prefix(es): 0-7259; 1-920701

University of Queensland Press+
Unit of The University of Queensland
Staff House Rd, St Lucia, Qld 4067
Mailing Address: PO Box 6042, Saint Lucia, Qld 4067
Tel: (07) 3365 2127; (07) 3377 7244; (07) 3365 2440 (sales) *Fax:* (07) 3365 7579
E-mail: uqp@uqp.uq.edu.au
Web Site: www.uqp.uq.edu.au
Key Personnel
General Manager: Greg Bain
Managing Editor: Madonna Duffy *E-mail:* editor@uqp.uq.edu.au
Rights Manager: Dinah Johnson *Tel:* (07) 3365 7244 *E-mail:* dinah@uqp.uq.edu.au
Founded: 1948
Publisher of quality literary works of fiction & nonfiction
Also specialize in Black Australian writings, Aboriginal studies & social & political issues, reference books.
Subjects: Biography, Fiction, History, Literature, Literary Criticism, Essays, Nonfiction (General), Poetry, Sports, Athletics, Travel
ISBN Prefix(es): 0-7022
Number of titles published annually: 60 Print
Imprints: UQP
Branch Office(s)
International Specialised Book Services, Inc, 5804 NE Hassalo St, Portland, OR 97213-3640, United States *Tel:* 503-287-3093 *Fax:* 503-380-8832

Distributed by Penguin Books Australia Ltd
Foreign Rep(s): Literary Agent (France); Lora Fountain (France, Italy, Belgium & Germany)
Foreign Rights: Inter Australia Company (Korea)

University of Western Australia Press+
35 Stirling Highway, Crawley, WA 6009
Tel: (08) 9380 3670 *Fax:* (08) 9380 1027
E-mail: uwap@cyllene.uwa.edu.au
Web Site: www.uwapress.uwa.edu.au
Key Personnel
Dir: Dr Jenny Gregory *E-mail:* jag@cyllene.uwa.edu.au
Marketing Manager: Anastasia Stachewicz *E-mail:* ana@cyllene.uwa.edu.au
Sales Manager: J Brown *E-mail:* jbrown@cyllene.uwa.edu.au
Founded: 1954
Subjects: Biography, Fiction, History, Literature, Literary Criticism, Essays, Natural History, Nonfiction (General), Regional Interests, Science Fiction, Fantasy, Social Sciences, Sociology, Women's Studies
ISBN Prefix(es): 1-875560; 1-876268; 1-920694
Number of titles published annually: 30 Print
Imprints: Cygnet Books; Cygnet Young Fiction
U.S. Office(s): ISBS, 5824 NE Hassalo St, Portland, OR 97213-3644, United States *Tel:* 503-287-3093 *Fax:* 503-280-8832 *E-mail:* orders@isbn.com *Web Site:* www.isbs.com
Distributed by Addenda Ltd; Eurospan; ISBS Inc; United Publishing Services (UPS) (Japan)
Distributor for Centre for Studies in WA History, University of Western Australia; Westerly Centre, University of Western Australia

UNSW Press, *imprint of* University of New South Wales Press Ltd

UQP, *imprint of* University of Queensland Press

The Useful Publishing Co+
2/795 Beaufort St, Mount Lawley, Perth, WA 6050
Tel: (08) 9370 4577 *Fax:* (08) 9370 2540
Key Personnel
Contact: Murray Davey
Founded: 1992
Subjects: Career Development, Finance, Nonfiction (General)
ISBN Prefix(es): 1-875693
Associate Companies: Davey Business Accountants Pty Ltd

VCTA Publishing+
Imprint of Macmillan Education Australia
Level 1, 102 Victoria Rd, Carlton, Victoria 3053
Tel: (03) 94199622 *Fax:* (03) 94191205
E-mail: vcta@vcta.asn.au
Web Site: www.vcta.asn.au
Key Personnel
Dir: Robert Taylor
Publishing Manager: Susan Watson
Production Editor: Maree Keating
Founded: 1953
Subjects: Accounting, Business, Career Development, Communications, Economics, Finance, Law, Regional Interests
ISBN Prefix(es): 0-86859; 0-909715

Veritas Press
PO Box 1653, Bundaberg, Qld 4670
Fax: (071) 529256
E-mail: copytype@interworx.com.au
Key Personnel
President & Author: J West
General Manager & Editor: Rob Giles
Founded: 1987
Subjects: Anthropology, Archaeology, Astrology, Occult, Health, Nutrition, Medicine, Nursing, Dentistry, Poetry, Science (General), Expose books in Science & Medicine
ISBN Prefix(es): 0-9588131
Subsidiaries: Whale Books
Distributed by Lilly Books (USA); Veritas Publishing (Australia); Whales Books (UK)
Distributor for Random House (Australia)

Vermillion, *imprint of* Random House Australia

Victorian Arts Centre Trust
100 Saint Kilda Rd, Melbourne, Victoria 3004
Mailing Address: PO Box 7585, Melbourne, Victoria 8004
Tel: (03) 9281 8000 *Fax:* (03) 9281 8282
Web Site: www.artscentre.net.au
Telex: Vicart AA 39141
Key Personnel
Chief Executive Officer: Tim Jacobs

Viking, *imprint of* Penguin Group (Australia)

Villamonta Publishing Services Inc+
2 Downes Pl, Geelong, Victoria 3220
Tel: (03) 5229 2029 *Fax:* (03) 5222 5399
E-mail: villapub@ozemail.com.au
Key Personnel
Executive Officer: Charles Lucas
Founded: 1993
Subjects: Disability, Special Needs, Law
ISBN Prefix(es): 0-9587635
Total Titles: 14 Print

Vintage, *imprint of* Random House Australia

Virgin, *imprint of* Random House Australia

Vista Publications+
PO Box 76, St Kilda, Victoria 3182
Tel: (03) 9534 8881 *Fax:* (03) 9534 9711
E-mail: vistaof@mbox.com.au
Key Personnel
Editorial Dir: Christine Mitchell
International Rights: Eva Fabian
Founded: 1996
Publishing nonfiction books (small company).
Membership(s): Victorian Writers' Centre.
Subjects: Biography, Education, Environmental Studies, Government, Political Science, Health, Nutrition, History, How-to, Nonfiction (General), Poetry, Social Sciences, Sociology, Community Development, Peace
ISBN Prefix(es): 0-9586496; 0-9592816; 1-876370
Total Titles: 18 Print

Vital, *imprint of* Vital Publications

Vital Publications
PO Box 101, North Essendon, Melbourne, Victoria 3041
Tel: (03) 9379-1219 *Fax:* (03) 9379-0015
E-mail: vitalpubs@churchesofchrist.org.au; aceditor@ozemail.com.au
Key Personnel
Marketing Representative: Don Smith
Contact: Nigel Pegram
Religious publications.
Subjects: Biblical Studies, Education, Religion - Other
ISBN Prefix(es): 0-909116; 1-875915
Number of titles published annually: 3 Print
Parent Company: National Council Churches of Christ
Imprints: Vital

WA Newspaper, *imprint of* St George Books

Wakefield Crime Classics, *imprint of* Wakefield Press Pty Ltd

AUSTRALIA

Wakefield Press Pty Ltd+
Wakefield Press Distribution, One The Parade West, Kent Town, SA 5067
Mailing Address: PO Box 2266, Kent Town, SA 5071
Tel: (08) 8362 8800 *Fax:* (08) 8362 7592
E-mail: info@wakefieldpress.com.au
Web Site: www.wakefieldpress.com.au
Key Personnel
Dir: Michael Bollen; Stephanie Johnston
 E-mail: stephanie@wakefieldpress.com.au
Founded: 1989
Subjects: Art, Biography, Cookery, Fiction, History, Literature, Literary Criticism, Essays, Mysteries, Travel
ISBN Prefix(es): 1-86254; 0-949268
Number of titles published annually: 30 Print
Total Titles: 600 Print
Imprints: Wakefield Crime Classics
Distributor for AATE Interface Series (Australia); Akashic Books (USA); Allison & Busby (UK); Arsenal Pulp Press (Canada); Avocado Press (New Zealand); Bookends Books (Australia); Bookhappy Books (USA); Calypso Press (Australia); City of Adelaide (Australia); Conway's Collectables (Australia); Council Oak Books (USA); Cybersell Online (Australia); Davam Place (Australia); Delafon Press (Australia); Department of Environment (Australia); Department of Transport (Australia); DFK Management (Australia); Dilettante Press (USA); E&E Productions (Australia); ECW Press (Canada); Ellipsis (UK); Encounter Books (USA); Girl Press Books (USA); David R Godine (USA); Headpress (UK); The Gerald & Mark Hoberman Collection (UK & USA); Kensington West Productions (UK); Key Porter Books (Canada); Lythrum Press (Australia); Macleay Press (Australia); Tracy Marsh (Australia); Metro Publications (UK); Mosaic Press (Canada); Prospect Books (UK); Rakennusteito (Finland); RDR Books (USA); RDV Books (USA); Santa Monica Press (USA); Scout Outdoor Centre (Australia); Select Books (USA); Serif (UK); Splash Publishing (Australia); State Records of South Australia; Still Life Cards (Australia); Suhas (Australia); surfBrains.com Books (New Zealand); Tomahawk Press (UK); Uglytown (USA); Voice (Australia); Wakefield Press (Australia); Welcome Rain Publishers (USA); Whereabouts Press (USA)
Foreign Rep(s): Airlift Book Company (UK, Europe); Independent Publishers Group (North America)
Foreign Rights: Eliane Benisti (France); Peng Cheng (China); Fritz Agency (Germany); Mirah Hong (Korea); Gundhild Lenz-Mulligan (UK, Scandinavia); Daniela Micura (Italy); Maru de Monserrat (Spain); Michele Rubin (North America); Flavio Sala (Brazil)
Orders to: Wakefield Press Distribution, One The Parade West, Kent Town, SA 5067, Contact: John Inverarity *Tel:* (08) 8362 8800 *Fax:* (08) 8362 7592 *E-mail:* warehouse@wakefieldpress.com.au

Frederick Warne, *imprint of* Penguin Group (Australia)

The Watermark Press+
3-A Llewellyn St, Balmain, NSW 2041
Mailing Address: PO Box 63, Balmain, NSW 2041
Tel: (02) 9818 5677 *Fax:* (02) 9818 5581
E-mail: books@nsw.bigpond.net.au
Key Personnel
Head of Company: Simon Blackall
Founded: 1983
Subjects: Animals, Pets, Architecture & Interior Design, Cookery, Crafts, Games, Hobbies, Gardening, Plants, Humor, Military Science, Nonfiction (General), Travel, Wine & Spirits
ISBN Prefix(es): 0-949284

Watermill, *imprint of* Troll Books of Australia

Franklin Watts Australia
31/56 O'Riordan St, Alexandria, NSW 2015
Tel: (02) 8338 8800 *Fax:* (02) 8338 8881
E-mail: info@wattspub.com.au
Web Site: www.wattspub.com.au
Key Personnel
General Manager: Tony Watts
ISBN Prefix(es): 0-86415
Parent Company: Watts Publishing Group Ltd, 96 Leonard St, London EC2A 4XD, United Kingdom
Ultimate Parent Company: Scholastic Library Publishing
Associate Companies: Children's Press; Grolier Educational Inc; Grolier Electronic Publishing Inc; Orchard, United Kingdom; Orchard Books, United Kingdom; Franklin Watts, United Kingdom
Divisions: Grolier Educational Australia

Weather Press+
PO Box 107, Boronia, Victoria 3155
Tel: (03) 9762-1647
Key Personnel
International Rights: Philip Johns
Subjects: Fiction

Weatherlight Press, *imprint of* Windhorse Books

WebsterWorld Pty Ltd
36-38 Wattle Rd, Brookvale, NSW 2100
Tel: (02) 9939 5505 *Fax:* (02) 9939 8355
E-mail: webpub@websterpublishing.com
Web Site: www.websterpublishing.com; www.websterworld.com; www.websterselearning.com
Founded: 1985
ISBN Prefix(es): 1-86398; 0-947302

Wellington Lane Press Pty Ltd+
120 Wycombe Rd, Neutral Bay, NSW 2089
Tel: (02) 99040962 *Fax:* (02) 99040962
Key Personnel
Publisher: Carol Dettmann *E-mail:* dettmann@ozemail.com.au
Founded: 1976
Subjects: Art, Photography, Regional Interests
ISBN Prefix(es): 0-908022; 0-947322
Imprints: Chapter & Verse

Wellness Australia+
Box 519, Subiaco, WA 6904
Tel: (08) 9387 6134 *Fax:* (08) 9383 7323
E-mail: info@workteams.com
Key Personnel
Head of Company & Dir: Grant Donovan
 E-mail: grant@workteams.com
Founded: 1988
Subjects: Health, Nutrition, Management, Psychology, Psychiatry
ISBN Prefix(es): 1-875139
Subsidiaries: Workplace Global Network

Wilbur, *imprint of* Elephas Books Pty Ltd

Wild & Woolley+
17 Military Rd, Watsons Bay, NSW 2030
Mailing Address: PO Box W76, Watsons Bay, NSW 2030
Tel: (02) 9337 6844 *Fax:* (02) 9337 6822
E-mail: pwoolley@fastbooks.com.au
Web Site: www.booksandwriters.net
Key Personnel
President & Man Dir: Pat Woolley
Founded: 1974
Specialize in prints for self-publishers.
Membership(s): APA.
ISBN Prefix(es): 0-909331; 1-74018

Imprints: Books & Writers
Divisions: Fast Books In Print

Wild Publications Pty Ltd
389 Malvern Rd, South Yarra, Victoria 3141
Mailing Address: PO Box 415, Prahran, Victoria 3181
Tel: (03) 9826-8482 *Fax:* (03) 9826-3787
E-mail: management@wild.com.au
Web Site: www.wild.com.au
Key Personnel
Dir: Chris Baxter
Founded: 1981
Publisher of *Wild Magazine* & *Rock Magazine*
Specialize in rockclimbing & hiking magazines & guidebooks to Australia.
Subjects: Sports, Athletics, Canoeing, Caving, Cross-Country Skiing, Hiking, Rock Climbing
Parent Company: Hamilton Foulser Pty Ltd; Wild Holdings Pty Ltd
Distributed by Macstyle (Australia)

Wildlife in Newtown, *imprint of* Feakle Press

Wildscape Australia
Division of Thunderhead Photographics Pty Ltd
6 Ardmore Park, Kuranda, Qld 4872
Mailing Address: PO Box 549, Kuranda, Qld 4872
Tel: (07) 4093 7171 *Fax:* (07) 4093 8897
Key Personnel
Manager: Debbie Jarver
Contact: Peter Jarver *E-mail:* jarver@ozemail.com.au
Founded: 1979
Specialize in books of photographs taken by Peter Jarver.
Subjects: Photography of landscapes, skyscapes, Top End, Central Australia & Queensland
ISBN Prefix(es): 0-9589067
Total Titles: 5 Print

Wileman Publications+
Chidon Court, One Cronin Ave, Main Beach, Qld 4217
Tel: (07) 312770
E-mail: wileman@onthenet.com.au
Key Personnel
International Rights: Bud Wileman
Subjects: Art, Behavioral Sciences, Criminology, Education, English as a Second Language, How-to, Human Relations, Language Arts, Linguistics, Law, Parapsychology, Psychology, Psychiatry, Self-Help, Social Sciences, Sociology
ISBN Prefix(es): 0-949026
Distributed by Barnes & Noble (North America)

John Wiley & Sons, *imprint of* John Wiley & Sons Australia, Ltd

John Wiley & Sons Australia, Ltd+
33 Park Rd, 3rd Floor, Milton, Qld 4064
Mailing Address: PO Box 1226, Milton, Qld 4064
Tel: (07) 3859 9755 *Fax:* (07) 3859 9715
E-mail: brisbane@johnwiley.com.au
Web Site: www.johnwiley.com.au
Key Personnel
Man Dir: Peter C Donoughue
Dir Finance & Administration: Andrew Betts
General Manager, School: Peter Van Noorden
General Manager, Higher Education: Lucy Russell
General Manager, Distribution: Jim Dwyer
Manager, Contracts & Licensing: Julie Barnett
Information Services: Heather Linaker
Founded: 1954
Membership(s): Australian Publishers Association.
Subjects: Education, Nonfiction (General)

ISBN Prefix(es): 0-395; 0-471; 0-393; 1-740; 1-876; 0-7314; 0-7016
Parent Company: John Wiley & Sons Inc, 111 River St, Hoboken, NJ 07030, United States
Associate Companies: John Wiley & Sons Canada Ltd, Canada; John Wiley & Sons (Asia) Pte Ltd, Singapore, Singapore; John Wiley & Sons Ltd, United Kingdom
Imprints: The Jacaranda Press; Wrightbooks; John Wiley & Sons; Hungry Minds Australia; Brooks Waterloo
Branch Office(s)
Level 3, 2 Railway Parade, Camberwell 3124 *Tel:* (03) 9811-1333 *Fax:* (03) 9811-1344 *E-mail:* melbourne@johnwiley.com.au
Suite 4A, 113 Wicks Rd, North Ryde, NSW 2113 *Tel:* (02) 9856-0200 *Fax:* (02) 9805 1597 *E-mail:* sydney@johnwiley.com.au
Distributor for Houghton Mifflin; W W Norton
Warehouse: Australian Center, 33 Windorah St, Stafford 4053 *Tel:* 3354-8455 *Fax:* 3352-7109
Distribution Center: Australian Distribution Centre

A S Wilson Inc+
PO Box 296, Jannali, NSW 2226
Tel: (02) 9528 8977
Key Personnel
President: Charles M Iossi
Agent, McMahon Publishers: Brian McMahon
Founded: 1994 (Acquired from Maxwell MacMillan Australia Pty Ltd)
High School study guides, trade & tertiary titles.
ISBN Prefix(es): 0-02; 0-08
Total Titles: 60 Print
Parent Company: c/o Ennis Cavuoto & Co, 7 Main St, Glen Rock, NJ 07632, United States
Imprints: Australian National University Press
Shipping Address: Elsevier Science, Locked Bag 16, Marricksville, NSW 2204 *Tel:* (02) 517 8999 *Fax:* (02) 517 2249

Windhorse Books+
Rear 139 Wells St, Newtown, NSW 2042
Mailing Address: PO Box 574, Newtown, NSW 2042
Tel: (02) 9519 8826 *Fax:* (02) 9519 8826
E-mail: books@windhorse.com.au
Web Site: www.windhorse.com.au
Key Personnel
Contact: Dh Ratnajyoti
Founded: 1994
Subjects: Asian Studies, Human Relations, Poetry, Psychology, Psychiatry, Religion - Buddhist, Self-Help, Women's Studies, Specialize in Buddhism & Meditation
Imprints: Dharma Publishing; Pali Text Society; Rangging Yeshe Publications; Weatherlight Press; Windhorse Publications

Windhorse Publications, *imprint of* Windhorse Books

Windward Publications+
RMB 206 Woodhill Mountain Rd, Via Berry, NSW 2535
Tel: (02) 4464 1977 *Fax:* (02) 4464 1906
E-mail: sales@windward.com.au
Web Site: www.windward.com.au
Key Personnel
Contact: David Colfelt *E-mail:* dc@windward.com.au
Founded: 1984
Subjects: Maritime, Travel, Great Barrier Reef, Whitsunday Islands
ISBN Prefix(es): 0-9590830; 0-9586989

Windwood, *imprint of* Moonlight Publishing

Winetitles
Imprint of Wine Publishers Pty Ltd
97 Carrington St, Adelaide, SA 5000
Mailing Address: PO Box 6015, Halifax St, SA 5000
Tel: (08) 8233 4799 *Fax:* (08) 8233 4790
E-mail: admin@winetitles.com.au
Web Site: www.winetitles.com.au
Key Personnel
Publisher: Paul Clancy *E-mail:* pclancy@winetitles.com.au
Dir: Fran Clancy *E-mail:* fclancy@winetitles.com.au
Publish two magazines: *Australian Viticulture* & *The Australian & New Zealand Wine Industry Journal.* Also annual wine industry directory, books on viticulture & oenology & an annual wine industry yearbook. Designs & builds websites for wineries.
Subjects: Agriculture, Wine & Spirits, Wine & Viticulture Industries
ISBN Prefix(es): 1-875130
Number of titles published annually: 5 Print
Total Titles: 25 Print; 1 CD-ROM

Wisdom Press, *imprint of* Desbooks Pty Ltd

Wizard Books Pty Ltd+
PO Box 304, Ballarat, Victoria 3353
Tel: (03) 5332 3435 *Fax:* (03) 5331 1488
E-mail: admin@wizardbooks.com.au
Web Site: www.wizardbooks.com.au
Key Personnel
Dir & International Rights: Richard McRoberts
Dir: Valerie McRoberts
Founded: 1991
Membership(s): Australian Publishers Association (APA).
Subjects: Drama, Theater, Education, Literature, Literary Criticism, Essays, Science (General)
ISBN Prefix(es): 1-875739; 1-876367
Distributed by Claire Publications (UK); EPB (Singapore)

Women's Health Advisory Service+
PO Box 689, Camden, NSW 2570
Tel: (02) 4655 8855 *Fax:* (02) 4655 8699
Web Site: www.whas.com.au
Key Personnel
Head of Company: Jacqui Comley
Author: Sandra Cabot *E-mail:* sandracabot@whas.com.au
Founded: 1990
Subjects: Health, Nutrition, Women's Studies, Weight loss
ISBN Prefix(es): 0-646
Total Titles: 10 Print
Associate Companies: Health Direction Pty Ltd; SCB International
U.S. Office(s): SCB International Inc *Tel:* 602-860-4299
Distributed by Ten Speed Press

Woodlands Publications
9 Bryant St, Tighes Hill, NSW 2297
Tel: (02) 4969 3961 *Fax:* (02) 4962 3162
E-mail: woodlands@whopres.com.au
Web Site: www.woodlandspublications.com
Key Personnel
Contact: A N Bendeich
Founded: 1982
Subjects: Business, Career Development, Communications, Education, Finance, Travel
ISBN Prefix(es): 1-875457; 0-9593057

Word of Life Distributors Pty Ltd, *imprint of* Rainbow Book Agencies Pty Ltd

Workaway Guides
PO Box 206, Tugun, Qld 4224
E-mail: workaway@bigpond.com
Web Site: www.users.bigpond.com/workaway
Key Personnel
Contact: Karen Halliday

Worsley Press+
11 Lintel Court, Hastings, Victoria 3915
Tel: (03) 5979-1112 *Fax:* (03) 5979-1112
E-mail: info@worsleypress.com
Web Site: www.worsleypress.com
Key Personnel
Owner, Publisher & International Rights: Gordon Woolf *E-mail:* gordon@worsleypress.com
Founded: 1991
Specialize in books on publication production.
Subjects: Business, How-to, Publishing & Book Trade Reference
ISBN Prefix(es): 1-875750
Number of titles published annually: 3 Print
Total Titles: 10 Print
Distributed by Eyelevel Books (UK); Florida Academic Press (North America)

Wrightbooks, *imprint of* John Wiley & Sons Australia, Ltd

Wrightbooks Pty Ltd+
Imprint of John Wiley & Sons Australia Ltd
PO Box 270, Elsternwick, Victoria 3185
Tel: (03) 9532 7082 *Toll Free Tel:* 800 777 474 *Fax:* (03) 9532 7082 *Toll Free Fax:* 800 802 258
E-mail: custservice@johnwiley.com.au
Web Site: www.wrightbooks.com.au
Key Personnel
Man Dir: Geoff Wright
Publisher: Lesley A Beaumont
Founded: 1988
Membership(s): ABPA.
Subjects: Business, Career Development, Finance, Management, Real Estate, Self-Help
ISBN Prefix(es): 0-947351; 1-875857; 1-876627
Total Titles: 90 Print

Yanagang Publishing
41 Beaufort Rd, Croydon, Victoria 3136
Tel: (03) 9870-3052 *Fax:* (03) 9876-1853
E-mail: gallerywithoutwalls@hotmail.com
Key Personnel
Contact: Dindy Vaughan
Subjects: Art, Environmental Studies, Music, Dance, Poetry
ISBN Prefix(es): 0-9588046; 0-9577974; 0-9577975
Number of titles published annually: 2 Print
Orders to: PO Box 668, Ringwood, Qld 3134

Zephyr Press, *imprint of* Hawker Brownlow

Zoe Publishing Pty Ltd+
PO Box 77, Tugun, Qld 4224
Tel: (07) 5534 1522 *Fax:* (07) 5534 1502
E-mail: zoemkt@onthenet.com.au
Key Personnel
Contact: Tim McClymont
Founded: 1995
Subjects: Child Care & Development, Health, Nutrition, Parenting & Mother & Child Health Guide
ISBN Prefix(es): 0-9586581

Austria

General Information

Capital: Vienna
Language: German, small Croat & Slovene speaking minorities

AUSTRIA

Religion: Predominantly Roman Catholic, some Protestant and Muslim
Population: 8.1 million
Bank Hours: 0800-1230, 1330-1500 Monday-Wednesday, Friday; 0800-1230, 1300-1730 Thursday
Shop Hours: 0800-1800 Monday-Friday; 0800-1200 or 1300 Saturday
Currency: 100 Eurocents = 1 Euro; 13.7603 schillings = 1 Euro
Export/Import Information: Import licenses not required for books. No exchange controls. 10% VAT on books.
Copyright: UCC, Berne, Florence (see Copyright Conventions, pg xi)

Aarachne Verlag+
Vergengasse 6, RH 14, 1220 Vienna
Tel: (01) 2855353 *Fax:* (01) 2855353
E-mail: spinne@aarachne.at
Web Site: www.aarachne.at
Key Personnel
Manager: Ernst Petz
Marketing: Astrid Rossbacher
Founded: 1992
Subjects: Drama, Theater, Ethnicity, Fiction, Human Relations, Journalism, Literature, Literary Criticism, Essays, Mysteries, Science Fiction, Fantasy
ISBN Prefix(es): 3-85255

Abakus Verlag GmbH+
Pezoltgasse 50, 5020 Salzburg
Tel: (0662) 632076 *Fax:* (0662) 8044137
Founded: 1979
Subjects: Environmental Studies, Language Arts, Linguistics, Mathematics
ISBN Prefix(es): 3-7044

Aeneas Verlagsgesellschaft GmbH+
Hauptstr 38, 2340 Moedling
Tel: (02236) 25422
Key Personnel
Manager: Johanna Theurer; Hermann Theurer
Founded: 1989
ISBN Prefix(es): 3-85065

Agens-Werk, Geyer & Reisser, Druck und Verlagsgesellschaft mbH
Arbeitergasse 1-7, 1051 Vienna
Tel: (01) 5445641-46 *Fax:* (01) 5445641-46
E-mail: prepress@agens-werk.at
Key Personnel
Man Dir: Friedrich Geyer
ISBN Prefix(es): 3-7033; 3-85202

Akademische Druck-u Verlagsanstalt Dr Paul Struzl GmbH+
Auersperggasse 12, 8010 Graz
Mailing Address: Postfach 598, 8011 Graz
Tel: (0316) 3644 *Fax:* (0316) 3644-24
E-mail: info@adeva.com
Web Site: www.adeva.com *Cable:* ADEVA GRAZ
Key Personnel
General Manager: Dr Hubert C Konrad
 Tel: (0316) 936 44-50 *E-mail:* konrad@adeva.com
 Editor: Dr Christine Brandstaetter *Tel:* (0316) 36 44-34 *E-mail:* bradstaetter@adeva.com; Gerhard Lechner *Tel:* (0316) 36 44-45 *E-mail:* lechner@adeva.com
Founded: 1949
Specializes in Facsimile.
Subjects: Anthropology, Archaeology, Art, Biography, Language Arts, Linguistics, Military Science, Music, Dance, Regional Interests
ISBN Prefix(es): 3-201; 3-900144
Number of titles published annually: 10 Print
Total Titles: 2,000 Print
Subsidiaries: Codices Selecti

Alekto Verlag GmbH+
St Veiter Ring 22, 9020 Klagenfurt
Mailing Address: Postfach 502, 9020 Klagenfurt
Tel: (0463) 591180 *Fax:* (0463) 593217
E-mail: bali@bali.co.at
Key Personnel
Man Dir: Stefan Zefferer *E-mail:* stefan.zefferer@bali.co.at
Manager & Marketing Dir: Harry Haberl *E-mail:* harry.haberl@bali.co.at
Founded: 1986
Specialize in Austrian Literature.
Subjects: History, Poetry, Politics
ISBN Prefix(es): 3-900743; 3-902202
Total Titles: 200 Print; 5 CD-ROM; 5 E-Book
Foreign Rep(s): VG Dr Glas

Amalthea-Verlag
Subsidiary of Buchverlage Langen-Mueller/Herbig
Am Heumarkt 19, 1030 Vienna
Tel: (01) 712 35 60 *Fax:* (01) 713 89 95
E-mail: amalthea.verlag@amalthea.at
Web Site: www.amalthea.at
Key Personnel
Geschref: Dr Herbert Fleissner
International Rights: Dorothea Esthermann
Founded: 1917
Membership(s): Buchverlage Ullstein Langen Mueller/Herbig, Germany.
Subjects: Art, Fiction, Music, Dance
ISBN Prefix(es): 3-85002
Associate Companies: Ullstein Langen Mueller

Andreas und Andreas Verlagsbuchhandel+
Hans-Seebachstr 10, 5023 Salzburg
Tel: (0662) 6575-0 *Fax:* (0662) 6575-5 *Cable:* ANDREASVERLAG SALZBURG
Key Personnel
Publisher: Ingrid Andreas; Wolf-Dietrich Andreas
Dir: Franz Pemwieser
Founded: 1956
Subjects: Fiction
ISBN Prefix(es): 3-85012
Branch Office(s)
Andreas und Andreas Verlagsbuchhandel Zweigniederlassing, 8228 Freilassingy, Germany
Andreas und Andreas Verlagsanstal, 9490 Vaduz, Liechtenstein
Oskar Andreas Nachfolger Herzog & Co, Reise- und Versandbuchhande, Parhamerpl 9, 1170 Vienna

Annette Betz, *imprint of* Verlag Carl Ueberreuter GmbH

Verlag Der Apfel+
Matteottipl 1, 1160 Vienna
Tel: (01) 52 661 52 *Fax:* (01) 52 287 18
Key Personnel
Man Dir: Thomas C Cubasch
Founded: 1984
Subjects: Art, History, Literature, Literary Criticism, Essays, Music, Dance, Arts Restoration & Conservation, Musicology
ISBN Prefix(es): 3-85450
Number of titles published annually: 20 Print
Total Titles: 80 Print

Astor-Verlag, Willibald Schlager+
Rosentalgasse 5/1/5, 1140 Vienna
Tel: (01) 9144281 *Fax:* (01) 9144281
Key Personnel
Owner: Willi Schlager *E-mail:* willi.schlager@chello.at
Founded: 1975
Subjects: Biography, Fiction, Humor, Literature, Literary Criticism, Essays, Regional Interests
ISBN Prefix(es): 3-900277

Autorensolidaritat - Verlag der Interessengemeinschaft osterreichischer Autorinnen und Autoren
Literaturhaus, Seidengasse 13, 1070 Vienna
Tel: (01) 526 20 44-13 *Fax:* (01) 526 20 44-55
E-mail: ig@literaturhaus.at
Key Personnel
President: Milo Dor
Man Dir: Gerhard Ruiss
Founded: 1982
Subjects: Publishing & Book Trade Reference
ISBN Prefix(es): 3-419

Verlag Alexander Bernhardt
Vomperberg, 6134 Vomp/Tirol
Tel: (05242) 62131-0 *Fax:* (05242) 72801
Key Personnel
Contact: Siegfried Bernhardt
Founded: 1945
Subjects: Philosophy
ISBN Prefix(es): 3-87860
Associate Companies: Verlag der Stiftung Gralsbotschaft GmbH, Lenzhalde 15, 70192 Stuttgart, Germany *E-mail:* info@gral.de *Web Site:* www.gral.de
U.S. Office(s): Grail Foundation of America, 2081 Partridge Lane, Binghamton, NY 13903, United States, Richard H Gehl
Grail Movement of America, 7204 Lucern Court, Charlotte, NC 28277, United States, Emanuel O'Biorah
Orders to: Verlag der Stiftung Gralsbotschaft GmbH, Schuckerstr 8, 71254 Ditzingen, Germany

Bethania Verlag+
Theresiengasse 33, 1180 Vienna
Tel: (01) 6672216
Key Personnel
Contact: Helene Mirtl
Founded: 1982
Subjects: Biological Sciences, Chemistry, Chemical Engineering, Philosophy, Physical Sciences, Science (General)
ISBN Prefix(es): 3-900085

Annette Betz Verlag im Verlag Carl Ueberreuter+
Alser Str 24, 1091 Vienna
Mailing Address: Postfach 306, 1091 Vienna
Tel: (01) 40 444-172 *Fax:* (01) 40 444-5
Web Site: www.annettebetz.com; www.ueberreuter.at
Telex: 114802 *Cable:* UEBER A
Key Personnel
Man Dir: Dr Fritz Panzer; Dr Richard Starkel
Editorial: Irmgard Harrer
Contact: Dr Susanne Czeitschner *Tel:* (01) 40 444-165 *E-mail:* czeitschner@ueberreuter.at
Founded: 1962
ISBN Prefix(es): 3-219
Parent Company: Verlag Carl Ueberreuter
Shipping Address: Dr Franz Hain Verlagsausciferung, Dr Otto-Neurath-Gasse 5, 1220 Vienna *Tel:* (01) 2826565 *Fax:* (01) 2825282
Warehouse: Dr Franz Hain Verlagsausciferung, Dr Otto-Neurath-Gasse 5, 1220 Vienna

Bibliothek der Provinz, see Richard Pils Publication PN°1

Der Baum Wolfgang Biedermann Verlag+
Apollogasse 14/1, 1070 Vienna
Tel: (01) 526 2720
Key Personnel
President & Publisher: Wolfgang Bedermann
Subjects: Literature, Literary Criticism, Essays
ISBN Prefix(es): 3-901133

Boehlau Verlag GmbH & Co KG+
Sachsenplatz 4-6, 1201 Vienna

Mailing Address: Postfach 87, 1201 Vienna
Tel: (01) 330 24 27 *Fax:* (01) 330 24 32
E-mail: boehlau@boehlau.at
Web Site: www.boehlau.at
Telex: 114506 Spriw A
Key Personnel
Man Dir: Dr Peter Rauch *E-mail:* peter.rauch@boehlau.at
Editorial: Dr Eva Reinhold-Weisz *E-mail:* eva.reinholdweisz@boehlau.at
Press: Elisabeth Dechant *E-mail:* elisabeth.dechant@boehlau.at
Production: Ulrike Dietmayer *E-mail:* ulrike.dietmayer@boehlau.at
Marketing Sales: Roland Tomrle *E-mail:* roland.tomrle@boehlau.at
Founded: 1947
Subjects: Art, Government, Political Science, History, Language Arts, Linguistics, Law, Science (General), Social Sciences, Sociology, Women's Studies
ISBN Prefix(es): 3-205
Associate Companies: Boehlau-Verlag GmbH & Cie, Cologne, Germany
Orders to: Springer Verlagsauslieferung, Postfach 8, 1201 Vienna *Tel:* (01) 3302415

Bohmann Druck und Verlag GmbH & Co KG
Leberstr 122, 1110 Vienna
Tel: (01) 74095 114 *Fax:* (01) 74095 111
E-mail: g.huber.zv@bohmann.at
Web Site: www.bohmann.co.at
Key Personnel
President Supervisory Board: Dr Rudolf Bohmann
Manager: Dr Gabriele Ambros
Founded: 1936
Subjects: Automotive, Business, Computer Science, Environmental Studies, Transportation, Travel
ISBN Prefix(es): 3-901983

Braintrust Marketing Services Ges mbH Verlag
Schopenhauerstr 36, 1180 Vienna
Tel: (01) 40416-0 *Fax:* (01) 40416-33
E-mail: braintrust@magnet.at
Web Site: www.braintrust.at
Key Personnel
Man Dir: Thomas Stern *E-mail:* stern@braintrust.at
Dir: Christian Seifert *E-mail:* seifert@braintrust.at
Founded: 1989
Subjects: Career Development, Education, Management
ISBN Prefix(es): 3-901116

Christian Brandstaetter Verlagsgesellschaft mbH+
Schwarzenbergstr 5, 1015 Vienna
Tel: (01) 512 15 43 *Fax:* (01) 512 15 43-231
E-mail: cbv@oebv.co.at
Web Site: www.brandstaetter-verlag.at
Key Personnel
Publisher: Dr Christian Brandstaetter
Manager: Mag Walter Amon; Dr Robert Sedlacek
Founded: 1982
Subjects: Architecture & Interior Design, Art, Biography, Photography, Regional Interests
ISBN Prefix(es): 3-85447; 3-206; 3-85498
Total Titles: 236 Print
Parent Company: Oesterreichischer Bundesverlag GmbH

BSE Verlag Dr Bernhard Schuttengruber+
Klosterwiegasse 52, 8010 Graz
Tel: (0316) 839600; (0316) 283170
Founded: 1984
Subjects: History, Poetry
ISBN Prefix(es): 3-900542

Buchkultur Verlags GmbH Zeitschrift fuer Literatur & Kunst
Huetteldorferstr 26, 1150 Vienna
Tel: (01) 7863380 *Fax:* (01) 7863380-10
E-mail: office@buchkultur.net
Web Site: www.buchkultur.net
Key Personnel
Geschf: Michael Schnepf
Founded: 1989
Subjects: Communications, Journalism, Literature, Literary Criticism, Essays, Publishing & Book Trade Reference, Regional Interests
ISBN Prefix(es): 3-901052
Branch Office(s)
Birkenstr 7, 85774 Unterfoehring, Germany
Fax: (089) 958216-92

Fachverlag fur Burgerinformation, Eigenvelag+
Grabenstr 117, 8010 Graz
Tel: (0316) 686727 *Fax:* (0316) 6867274
E-mail: fachverlag@sime.com
Key Personnel
Manager: Alfred Steingruber
Founded: 1986
Subjects: Public Administration
ISBN Prefix(es): 3-85363

Camera Austria+
Lendkai 1, 8020 Graz
Tel: (0316) 81 55 50-0 *Fax:* (0316) 81 55 50-9
E-mail: office@camera-austria.at
Web Site: www.camera-austria.at
Key Personnel
Publisher: Manfred Willmann
Editor: Christine Frisinghelli; Maren Luebbke
Founded: 1980
Subjects: Art, Photography
ISBN Prefix(es): 3-900508; 3-9501098

Carinthia Verlag
Voelkermarkter Ring 25, 9020 Klagenfurt
Tel: (0463) 50 12 20-220 *Fax:* (0463) 50 12 20-214
Web Site: www.verlag.carinthia.com
Key Personnel
Dir: Karin Waldner *Tel:* (0463) 50 12 20-210
  E-mail: karin.waldner@carinthia.com
Founded: 1893
Subjects: Archaeology, Art, Cookery, History, Religion - Other
ISBN Prefix(es): 3-85378; 3-900184
Number of titles published annually: 20 Print
Total Titles: 120 Print

CEEBA Publications Antenne d'Autriche+
2340 Saint Gabriel, Moedling
Tel: (02236) 803115 *Fax:* (02236) 8033
E-mail: svd@steyler.at
Web Site: www.ceeba.at
Key Personnel
Man Dir, Editorial: Dr Hermann Hochegger
  E-mail: hochegger@steyler.at
Founded: 1965
Specialize in paperback, rituals. Also a study center for traditional culture of Black Africa & Haiti.
Subjects: Agriculture, Anthropology, Art, Ethnicity, Health, Nutrition, History, Language Arts, Linguistics, Literature, Literary Criticism, Essays, Psychology, Psychiatry, Religion - Other, Social Sciences, Sociology
ISBN Prefix(es): 3-902011
Number of titles published annually: 4 Print
Total Titles: 2 Print
Parent Company: CEEBA, Bandundu, Kongo
Foreign Rep(s): Antenne d'Antride

Compass-Verlag GmbH
Matznergasse 17, 1141 Vienna
Mailing Address: Postfach 160, 1141 Vienna
Tel: (01) 981 16-113; (01) 981 16-114 *Fax:* (01) 981 16-118; (01) 981 16-108
E-mail: hfu@compass.at; ssc@compass.at; office@compass.at
Web Site: www.compass.at; www.cmd.at
Key Personnel
Man Dir: Werner Futter; Horst Dolezal
Sales Dir: Michael Bayer *E-mail:* mba@compass.al
Founded: 1867
Specialize in Internet databases.
Membership(s): OeAVV, EAVV.
Subjects: Business, Economics, Finance
ISBN Prefix(es): 3-85041
Number of titles published annually: 4 Print; 2 CD-ROM
Total Titles: 4 Print
Subsidiaries: Comp Almanach Kft

Cura Verlag GmbH
Beatrixgasse 32, 1037 Vienna
Mailing Address: Postfach 49, Vienna
Tel: (01) 7136480 *Fax:* (01) 7126258; (01) 7126219
Key Personnel
Man Dir: Brigitte Podoschek
Publicity Manager: Eva M Plattner
Subjects: Education, Regional Interests, Religion - Other
ISBN Prefix(es): 3-7027

Czernin Verlag Ltd+
Kupkagasse 4, 1080 Vienna
Tel: (01) 403 35 63 *Fax:* (01) 403 35 63-15
E-mail: office@czernin-verlag.com
Web Site: www.czernin-verlag.com
Key Personnel
Publisher: Hubertus Czernin *E-mail:* hoz@czernin-verlag.com
Production: Klaus Gadermaier
  E-mail: gadermaier@czernin-verlag.com
Marketing & Press: Benedikt Foeger
  E-mail: foeger@czernin-verlag.com
Founded: 1999
Subjects: Cookery, Film, Video, History, Law, Literature, Literary Criticism, Essays, Poetry
ISBN Prefix(es): 3-7076
Number of titles published annually: 15 Print
Total Titles: 120 Print

DachsVerlag GmbH+
Praterstra 25/92, 1020 Vienna
Tel: (01) 285 22 05-0 *Fax:* (01) 285 22 05-15
E-mail: office@dachs.at
Web Site: www.dachs.at
Key Personnel
Man Dir: Dr Hubert Hladej *E-mail:* hladej.sen@dachs.at
Founded: 1921
Subjects: Art, Education, Ethnicity, Literature, Literary Criticism, Essays, Music, Dance, Psychology, Psychiatry, Social Sciences, Sociology
ISBN Prefix(es): 3-900763; 3-85191

Danubia Werbung und Verlagsservice
Viehmarktgasse 4, 1030 Vienna
Tel: (01) 792666 *Fax:* (01) 792666443
Key Personnel
Man Dir: N Schnabl
Publicity Dir: Dr P Wasservogel
Founded: 1952
Subjects: Art, Fiction, Science (General)
ISBN Prefix(es): 3-7006; 3-85044

dbv-Druck Beratungs-und Verlags GmbH Verlag fur die Technische Universitaet Graz+
Geidorfguertel 20, 8010 Graz
Tel: (0316) 38 30 33 *Fax:* (0316) 38 30 43
E-mail: office@dbv.at
Web Site: www.dbv.at

Key Personnel
Man Dir: Gerhard E Erker
Founded: 1976
ISBN Prefix(es): 3-7041

Denkmayr GmbH Druck & Verlag+
Reslweg 3, 4020 Linz
Mailing Address: Postfach 14, 4020 Linz
Tel: (0732) 654511 *Fax:* (0732) 65451117
E-mail: denkmayr.linz@magnet.at
Key Personnel
Contact: Ernst Denkmayr
International Rights: Regina Noebauer
Founded: 1989
Subjects: Poetry, Regional Interests, Self-Help
ISBN Prefix(es): 3-901838; 3-901123

Verlag Harald Denzel, Auto- und Freizeitfuehrer+
Maximilianstr 9, 6020 Innsbruck
Tel: (0512) 586880 *Fax:* (0512) 586880
E-mail: denzel-verlag@web.de
Web Site: members.telering.at/denzel-verlag
Key Personnel
Contact: Harald Denzel
Founded: 1952
Subjects: Geography, Geology, Outdoor Recreation, Travel, Illustrated Guide Books
ISBN Prefix(es): 3-85047

Franz Deuticke Verlagsgesmbh+
Schwarzenbergstr 5, 1015 Vienna
Tel: (01) 512 15 44 280 *Fax:* (01) 512 15 44 289
E-mail: info@deuticke.at
Web Site: www.deuticke.at
Key Personnel
Manager: Dr Martina Schmidt *Tel:* (01) 512 15 44-300 *Fax:* (01) 512 15 44-289 *E-mail:* schmidt@deuticke.at
Marketing & Sales: Silvia Wahrstaetter *Tel:* (01) 512 15 44-274 *E-mail:* wahrstaetter@deuticke.at
Press & Public Relations: Friederike Rumschoettel *Tel:* (01) 512 15 44-258 *Fax:* (01) 512 15 44-289 *E-mail:* rumschoettel@deuticke.at
Founded: 1878
Specialize in psychology.
Subjects: Literature, Literary Criticism, Essays, Mysteries, Nonfiction (General), Philosophy, Regional Interests, Science (General)
ISBN Prefix(es): 3-7005; 3-216
Total Titles: 629 Print
Orders to: Osterr Schulbuchzentrum, Postfach 133, 2355 Wiener Neudorf *Fax:* (2236) 63535243

Development News Ltd
Pragerstr 92, Stg 4, Vienna
Tel: (0222) 3880324 *Toll Free Tel:* (0222) 3880324
Key Personnel
Man Dir & Publisher: Dr Yemi D Ogunyemi
Editorial Manager: Simon Adewale Ebine
Publications Manager: Willy Bruckner
Publicity Executive: Pius Eyitayo Ogunyemi
Sales Executive: T A Ogunyemi
Founded: 1983
Also promotes Nigerian/African literatures through seminars, lectures, symposia, conferences, book presentations & writing workshops.
Subjects: Agriculture, Animals, Pets, Anthropology, Child Care & Development, Communications, Developing Countries, Education, English as a Second Language, Ethnicity, Fiction, Government, Political Science, History, Journalism, Literature, Literary Criticism, Essays, Nonfiction (General), Poetry, Regional Interests, Religion - Other, Social Sciences, Sociology, Women's Studies

ISBN Prefix(es): 978-2843
U.S. Office(s): Diaspora Press of America, 91 Ames St, Box C340, Boston, MA 02124-3033, United States

Diotima Presse+
Bachgasse 22, 3200 Obergrafendorf
Tel: (043) 2747-8528 *Fax:* (043) 2747-8528
E-mail: buecher4web@diotimapresse.com
Web Site: www.diotimapresse.com
Founded: 2000
Handcrafted books with mainly original illustrations.
Subjects: Philosophy, Poetry
Number of titles published annually: 6 Print
Total Titles: 23 Print

Ludwig Doblinger (Bernhard Herzmansky) Musikverlag KG
Dorotheergasse 10, 1010 Vienna
Tel: (01) 515 03-0 *Fax:* (01) 515 03-51
E-mail: music@doblinger.at
Web Site: www.doblinger.at
Key Personnel
Man Dir: Helmuth Pany
Sales Manager: Peter Pany *E-mail:* peter.pany@doblinger.at
Rights & Licensing: Christine Prindl
Advertising Manager: Dr Christian Heindl *E-mail:* christian.heindl@doblinger.at
Founded: 1876
Specializes in music-notes & books.
Subjects: Music, Dance
ISBN Prefix(es): 3-900695; 3-900035
Distributor for Musikwissenschaftlicher Verlag Wien (MWV)
Bookshop(s): Musikhaus Doblinger, Vienna

Doecker Verlag GmbH & Co KG+
Hintzerstr 11/3, 1030 Vienna
Mailing Address: Postfach 91, 1030 Vienna
Tel: (01) 7159200 *Fax:* (01) 715920076
E-mail: doecker@ping.at
Key Personnel
Man Dir, Production & Rights & Permissions: Ulrike Doecker
Editorial: Peter Horn
Sales, Publicity: Petra Hartlieb
Founded: 1980
Subjects: Archaeology, Biography, Education, Fiction, Film, Video, History, Journalism, Labor, Industrial Relations, Outdoor Recreation, Women's Studies
ISBN Prefix(es): 3-85115

Literature Verlag Droschl+
Alberstr 18, 8010 Graz
Tel: (0316) 32-64-04 *Fax:* (0316) 32-40-71
E-mail: droschl@droschl.com; literaturverlag@droschl.com
Web Site: www.droschl.com
Key Personnel
Contact: Dr Rainer Gotz *E-mail:* rainer@droschl.com
Founded: 1978
Publishing honor for contemporary European literature
Books & Audio CD's.
Subjects: Art, Drama, Theater, Literature, Literary Criticism, Essays, Poetry
ISBN Prefix(es): 3-85420
Number of titles published annually: 18 Print
Total Titles: 300 Print; 5 Audio
Imprints: Edition Neue Text

Edition Neue Text, *imprint of* Literature Verlag Droschl

Edition S der OSD+
Rennweg 16, 1037 Vienna
Tel: (01) 61077-315 *Fax:* (01) 61077-419

E-mail: office@verlagoesterreich.at
Telex: 131 805 *Cable:* OESTAATSDRUCK WIEN
Key Personnel
Man Dir: Dr Manfred A Schmid
Founded: 1985
Subjects: Criminology, Fiction, Film, Video, History, Human Relations, Literature, Literary Criticism, Essays, Maritime, Parapsychology
ISBN Prefix(es): 3-7046; 3-85201
Parent Company: Oesterreichische Staatsdruckerei

Ennsthaler GesmbH & Co KG+
Stadtplatz 26, 4400 Steyr
Tel: (07252) 52053-10 *Fax:* (07252) 52053-16
E-mail: buero@ennsthaler.at
Web Site: www.ennsthaler.at
Founded: 1880
Subjects: Cookery, Health, Nutrition, History, Medicine, Nursing, Dentistry, Poetry, Regional Interests, Religion - Catholic, Theology
ISBN Prefix(es): 3-85068

Edition Ergo Sum+
Berggasse 31, 2391 Kaltenleutgeben
Tel: (02238) 77078 *Fax:* (02238) 77076
E-mail: apverlag@magnet.at
Key Personnel
Owner: Anna Pichler
Owner & International Rights: Heinz Lasta
Founded: 1989
Subjects: Environmental Studies, Fiction, Nonfiction (General), Philosophy, Poetry
ISBN Prefix(es): 3-901087; 3-902008
Distributed by Dessauer; EDIS

Evangelischer Presseverband in Osterreich
Ungargasse 9, 1030 Vienna
Tel: (01) 712 54 61 *Fax:* (01) 712 54 75
E-mail: epv@evang.at
Key Personnel
Man Dir: Paul Weiland
Founded: 1925
ISBN Prefix(es): 3-85073
Warehouse: Ungargasse 12, 1030 Vienna

Fassbaender Verlag
Lichtgasse 10, 1150 Vienna
Tel: (01) 8923546 *Fax:* (01) 8923546-22
E-mail: mail@fassbaender.com
Web Site: www.fassbaender.com
Key Personnel
Executive: Ernst Becvar *Tel:* (01) 8923546-12 *E-mail:* becvar-senior@inode.at
Founded: 1987
Specialize in Literature, Literary Criticism.
Subjects: History, Language Arts, Linguistics, Science (General)
ISBN Prefix(es): 3-900538; 3-900338
Number of titles published annually: 5 Print
Total Titles: 70 Print

Ferdinand Berger und Sohne
Wienerstr 80, 3580 Horn
Tel: (02982) 4161-332 *Fax:* (02982) 4161-382
E-mail: druckerei.office@berger.at
Web Site: www.berger.at
Telex: 78613 *Cable:* BERGER HORN
Key Personnel
Man Dir: Peter Berger *E-mail:* peter.jun@berger.at
Founded: 1868
Subjects: Anthropology, Archaeology, Art, Natural History
ISBN Prefix(es): 3-85028
Branch Office(s)
Pulverturmasse 3, 1090 Vienna *Tel:* (01) 313 35-0 *Fax:* (01) 313 35-19

Folio Verlagsgesellschaft mbH+
Gruengasse 9, 1050 Vienna

Tel: (01) 5813708-0 *Fax:* (01) 5813708-20
E-mail: office@folioverlag.com; folio@thing.at; folio@dialogon.at
Web Site: www.folioverlag.com/books.php
Founded: 1992
ISBN Prefix(es): 3-85256
Number of titles published annually: 30 Print
Total Titles: 130 Print
Branch Office(s)
Mitterweg 16a, 39100 Bozen, Italy *Tel:* (0471) 971323 *Fax:* (0471) 971603

Fremdenverkehrs Aktiengessellschaft+
Formerly Waren-Erzeugungs-und Handelgesellschaft GmbH
Schwarzstr 15, Postfach 6, 5024 Salzburg
Tel: (0662) 88861011 *Fax:* (0662) 8886202
Telex: 633588 *Cable:* BERGLANDBUCH SALZBURG
Key Personnel
Man Dir: Alfred Schulz
Founded: 1929
Subjects: Fiction, History, Regional Interests, Science (General)
ISBN Prefix(es): 3-7023
Orders to: Morawa & Co, Hackingerstr 52, A-1140

Freytag-Berndt und Artaria, Kartographische Anstalt+
Brunner-Str 69, 1231 Vienna
Tel: (01) 869 90 90-83 *Fax:* (01) 869 90 90-61
E-mail: office@freytagberndt.at
Telex: 133526
Key Personnel
Chairman: Bernd Mahr
Man Dir: Christian Halbwachs
Sales Manager: Wolfgang Kaiser
Founded: 1770
Subjects: Geography, Geology
ISBN Prefix(es): 3-85084; 3-7079
Bookshop(s): Wilhelm-Greil Str 15, 6020 Innsbruck; Kohlmarkt 9, 1010 Vienna; Schottenfeldgasse 62, Postfach 169, 1070 Vienna

Georg Fromme und Co
Arbeitergasse 1-7, 1051 Vienna
Tel: (01) 5445641 *Fax:* (01) 544564166
Telex: 111969
Key Personnel
Man Dir: Friedrich Geyer
Founded: 1748
Subjects: Science (General)
ISBN Prefix(es): 3-85086

Edition Dr Heinrich Fuchs
Thimiggasse 82, 1180 Vienna
Tel: (01) 4792381 *Fax:* (01) 4792381
E-mail: edition.h.fuchs@aon.at
Subjects: Art
ISBN Prefix(es): 3-85390

Gangan Verlag+
Rainleiten 62, 8045 Graz
Tel: (0316) 670 4090 *Fax:* (0316) 670 4096
Web Site: www.gangan.com
Key Personnel
Publisher: Gerald Ganglbauer *E-mail:* gerald@gangan.com
Distributor: Guenter Brodtrager *E-mail:* gbrodtrager@greenbrains.com
Editor: Rudi Krausmann
Founded: 1985
Subjects: Literature, Literary Criticism, Essays
ISBN Prefix(es): 3-900530
Number of titles published annually: 2 E-Book
Total Titles: 24 Print; 12 E-Book
Imprints: GanGAROO (The OZlit Collection)
Subsidiaries: Gangan Books Australia
Branch Office(s)
15 Naranja Way, Portola Valley, CA 94028, United States, Contact: Janet Wells

GanGAROO, *imprint of* Gangan Verlag

Gerold & Co
Rathausstr 5, 1010 Vienna
Tel: (01) 532 0102 *Fax:* (01) 532 01 02-15; (01) 532 01 02-22
E-mail: office@gerold.at
Web Site: www.gerold.at
Telex: 847136157 Gerol; 76157 *Cable:* Geroldbuch Vienna
Key Personnel
Man Dir: Hans Neusser
Subjects: Language Arts, Linguistics, Philosophy
ISBN Prefix(es): 3-900190

Verlag fuer Geschichte und Politik
Neulinggasse 26/12, 1030 Vienna
Tel: (01) 712 62 58 0 *Fax:* (01) 712 62 58 19
E-mail: office@oldenbourg.at
Key Personnel
Man Dir: Dr Erika Ruedegger
Sales Dir: Gerda Adler
Publicity & Advertising: Dr Ursula Huber *E-mail:* ursula.huber@oldenbourg.co.at
Founded: 1947
Subjects: Economics, Government, Political Science, History, Social Sciences, Sociology
ISBN Prefix(es): 3-7028
Associate Companies: Verlag Oldenbourg

Verlag Lynkeus/H Hakel Gesellschaft+
Traisengasse 17/28, 1200 Vienna
Tel: (01) 7342294
Key Personnel
Man Dir: Emmerich Kolovic
Founded: 1988
Subjects: Biography, Fiction, Humor, Literature, Literary Criticism, Essays, Poetry
ISBN Prefix(es): 3-900924

Globus Buchvertrieb
Seilerstatte 22/1, 1010 Vienna
Tel: (01) 513 96 92 0 *Fax:* (01) 513 96 92 9
Key Personnel
General Manager: Hans Jauker; H Zaslawski
Founded: 1945
Firms are also general representatives & distributors.
Subjects: Government, Political Science
ISBN Prefix(es): 3-85364

Alois Goschl & Co
Trummelhofgasse 12, 1190 Vienna
Tel: (01) 321180 *Fax:* (01) 651899
Key Personnel
Proprietor: Hiltraud Lechner
Founded: 1949
Subjects: Health, Nutrition, Psychology, Psychiatry, Veterinary Science
ISBN Prefix(es): 3-85096

Edition Graphischer Zirkel
Langegasse 14/44, 1080 Vienna
Tel: (01) 0277346615
Subjects: Art, Fiction, Literature, Literary Criticism, Essays, Poetry, Travel
ISBN Prefix(es): 3-900308

Graz Stadtmuseum
Sackstr 18, 8010 Graz
Tel: (0316) 822580 *Fax:* (0316) 822580-6
Web Site: homepage.sime.com
Key Personnel
Dir: Dr Guenther Dienes
Subjects: Art, History, Regional Interests
ISBN Prefix(es): 3-900764
Total Titles: 275 Print

Guthmann & Peterson Liber Libri, Edition+
Elsslergasse 17, 1130 Vienna
Tel: (01) 877 04 26 *Fax:* (01) 876 40 04
E-mail: verlag@guthmann-peterson.de
Web Site: www.guthmann-peterson.de
Key Personnel
Man Dir: W Peterson
Founded: 1988
Subjects: Developing Countries, Government, Political Science, Literature, Literary Criticism, Essays, Science (General), Social Sciences, Sociology
ISBN Prefix(es): 3-900782; 3-85306; 3-85481
Divisions: Edition Garamond

Hand-Presse
Hottingergasse 41, 6020 Innsbruck
Tel: (0512) 87975
Key Personnel
Owner: Hans Augustin
ISBN Prefix(es): 3-900862

Haymon-Verlag GesmbH+
Kochstr 10, 6020 Innsbruck
Tel: (0512) 576300 *Fax:* (0512) 576300-14
E-mail: office@haymonverlag.at
Web Site: www.haymonverlag.at
Key Personnel
Man Dir & Rights & Permissions: Dr Michael Forcher *E-mail:* michael.forcher@haymonverlag.at
Sales & International Rights: Valerie Besl *Tel:* (0512) 567300-16 *E-mail:* valerie.besl@haymonverlag.at
Sales: Gerhard Roedlach *Tel:* (0512) 576300-11 *E-mail:* gerhard.roedlach@haymonverlag.at
Production: Dr Benno Peter *Tel:* (0512) 576300-15 *E-mail:* bennopeter@haymonverlag.at
Founded: 1982
Subjects: Architecture & Interior Design, Art, Biography, Cookery, Criminology, Fiction, History, Literature, Literary Criticism, Essays, Mysteries, Philosophy, Social Sciences, Sociology
ISBN Prefix(es): 3-85218
Number of titles published annually: 25 Print
Total Titles: 350 Print

Helbling Verlags-Gesellschaft mbH
Kaplanstr 9, 6063 Rum/Innsbruck
Mailing Address: Postfach 12, 6063 Rum/Innsbruck
Tel: (0512) 262333-0 *Fax:* (0512) 262333-111
E-mail: office@helbling.co.at
Web Site: www.helbling.com
Key Personnel
President: Markus Spielmann
International Rights: Klaus Mayerl *E-mail:* k.mayerl@helbling.co.at
Founded: 1946
Specialize in choral music books.
Subjects: Education, English as a Second Language, Music, Dance, Choral Music
ISBN Prefix(es): 3-85061; 3-900590

Verlag Herder & Co, see Verlag Kerle im Verlag Herder & Co

Hermagoras/Mohorjeva+
Viktringer ring 26, 9020 Klagenfurt, Celovec
Tel: (0463) 56515 21 *Fax:* (0463) 514189
E-mail: office@mohorjeva.at
Web Site: www.mohorjeva.at
Telex: 422801
Key Personnel
Man Dir: Dr Anton Koren
Sales & Publicity: Karl Boehm; Janko Ferk
Editorial & Production: Franz Kattnig
Founded: 1851
Specializes in books in Slovenian & German.
ISBN Prefix(es): 3-85013; 3-900119

AUSTRIA

Parent Company: Mohorjeva Druzba/Hermagoras Gesellschaft
Subsidiaries: Korotan Import-Export GmbH

Herold Business Data AG+
Guntramsdorfer Str 105, 2340 Moedling
Tel: (02236) 401-0 *Fax:* (02236) 401-8
E-mail: kundendienst@herold.at
Web Site: www.herold.co.at
Telex: 114336 herol a
Key Personnel
Manager: Yon M Martinsen
Founded: 1918
Subjects: Marketing
ISBN Prefix(es): 3-85110

Herold Druck-und Verlagsgesellschaft mbH+
Faradaygasse 6, 1032 Vienna
Tel: (01) 795 94 *Fax:* (01) 795 94-115
Telex: 111760 Wspro
Key Personnel
Man Dir: Franz Hoermann; Leopold Kurz
Founded: 1893
Subjects: Art, History, Religion - Catholic
ISBN Prefix(es): 3-7008; 3-9500004; 3-901628

Johannes Heyn GmbH & Co KG
Kramergasse 2-4, 9020 Klagenfurt
Tel: (0463) 54 2 49 *Fax:* (0463) 54 2 49-41
E-mail: buch@heyn.at
Web Site: www.heyn.at
Telex: 042401; 422401 *Cable:* Heyn Klagenfurt
Key Personnel
Editor: Bernhard Koessler
Founded: 1868
Subjects: Art, Biography, Fiction, History, How-to, Music, Dance, Poetry, Science (General)
ISBN Prefix(es): 3-85366; 3-7084
Bookshop(s): Buchhandlung Johannes Heyn

Edition E Hilger
Dorotheergasse 5, 1010 Vienna
Tel: (01) 512 53 15-0 *Fax:* (01) 513 91 26
E-mail: hilger@hilger.at
Key Personnel
Man Dir & Production: Ernst Hilger
Sales & Publicity: Monica Zimmermann
Founded: 1973
Subjects: Art
ISBN Prefix(es): 3-900318

Verlag Hoelder-Pichler-Tempsky+
Frankgasse 4, 1090 Vienna
Tel: (01) 401 36-139 *Fax:* (01) 401 36-128
E-mail: hpt@hpt.co.at
Key Personnel
Man Dir: Gustav Gloeckler
Founded: 1690
Subjects: Mathematics, Philosophy, Physics
ISBN Prefix(es): 3-7004; 3-209
Subsidiaries: hpt Verlagsges mbH & Co KG
Warehouse: Jochen-Rindt-Str 11, Postfach 107, 1232 Vienna

Dr Verena Hofstaetter
Steinfeldgasse 5, 1190 Vienna
Tel: (01) 370 33 02 *Fax:* (01) 370 59 34
E-mail: verlag@vh-communications.at
Subjects: Communications, Film, Video, Marketing, Social Sciences, Sociology
ISBN Prefix(es): 3-900936

Hollinek Bruder & Co mbH Gesellschaftsdruckerei & Verlagsbuchhandring+
Luisenstr 20, 3002 Purkersdorf
Tel: (02231) 67365 *Fax:* (02231) 67365
E-mail: hollinek@via.at
Key Personnel
Man Dir: R Hollinek
Founded: 1872
Subjects: Law
ISBN Prefix(es): 3-85119

IAEA - International Atomic Energy Agency
Division of Conference & Document Services, PO Box 100, 1400 Vienna
Tel: (01) 2600-0; (01) 2600-22530 *Fax:* (01) 2600-7
E-mail: official.mail@iaea.org
Web Site: www.iaea.org/worldatom/Books
Telex: 112645 ATOM A
Key Personnel
Dir General: Dr Mohamed ElBaradei
Head, Publishing Section: Manfred F Boemeke
 E-mail: m.f.boemeke@iaea.org
Founded: 1957
Serves as the worlds central intergovernmental forum for scientific & technical cooperation in the nuclear field.
International Organization.
Subjects: Agriculture, Biological Sciences, Chemistry, Chemical Engineering, Energy, Environmental Studies, Geography, Geology, Health, Nutrition, Law, Physical Sciences, Physics, Technology, Veterinary Science, Nuclear Science
ISBN Prefix(es): 92-0
Number of titles published annually: 40 Print; 5 CD-ROM
Total Titles: 2,000 Print; 3 CD-ROM

Ibera VerlagsgesmbH+
Hegelgasse 15, 1010 Vienna
Tel: (01) 513 19 72 *Fax:* (01) 513 19 72-28
E-mail: presse@ibera.at
Web Site: www.ibera.at
Key Personnel
Manager: Brigitte Strobele *E-mail:* strobele@ibera.at
Press: Simon Hoeller *E-mail:* hoeller@ibera.at
Sales: Matthias Strobele *E-mail:* sales@ibera.at
Subjects: Nonfiction (General)
ISBN Prefix(es): 3-900436; 3-85052
Distributed by Herold Verlagsauslieferung GmbH (Germany); Mohr-Morawa

IG Autorinnen Autoren (Austrian Author's Association)
im Literaturhaus, Seidengasse 13, 1070 Vienna
Tel: (01) 526 20 44-13 *Fax:* (01) 526 20 44-55
E-mail: ig@literaturhaus.at
Web Site: www.literaturhaus.at/lh/ig
Key Personnel
President: Milo Dor
Vice President: Peter Turrini; Anna Mitgutsch
Man Dir: Gerhard Ruiss *Tel:* (01) 526 20 44-35
Founded: 1971
Subjects: Publishing & Book Trade Reference
ISBN Prefix(es): 3-900419

IIASA, see International Institute for Applied Systems Analysis (IIASA)

Innverlag + Gatt+
Hunoldstr 12, 6020 Innsbruck
Tel: (0512) 34 53 31 *Fax:* (0512) 34 12 90
E-mail: innverlag@tirol.com; info@innverlag.at
Web Site: www.innverlag.at *Cable:* INNVERLAG INNSBRUCK
Key Personnel
Production: Klaus Hagleitner
Sales: Manfred Hagleitner
Founded: 1947
Subjects: History, Public Administration, Sports, Athletics
ISBN Prefix(es): 3-85123
Bookshop(s): Kommissions-Reise & Versandbuchhandlung, Innsbruck

Interessengemeinschaft oesterreichischer Autorinnen und Autoren, see IG Autorinnen Autoren

International Atomic Energy Agency, see IAEA - International Atomic Energy Agency

International Institute for Applied Systems Analysis (IIASA)
Schlossplatz 1, 2361 Laxenburg
Tel: (02236) 807 433 *Fax:* (02236) 71313
E-mail: info@iiasa.ac.at; publications@iiasa.ac.at
Web Site: www.iiasa.ac.at
Founded: 1972
Subjects: Computer Science, Energy, Environmental Studies, Management, Mathematics, Science (General)
ISBN Prefix(es): 3-7045

Verlag Jungbrunnen - Wiener Spielzeugschachtel GesellschaftmbH+
Rauhensteingasse 5, 1010 Vienna
Tel: (01) 512-1299 *Fax:* (01) 512-1299-75
E-mail: office@jungbrunnen.co.at
Key Personnel
Man Dir, Editorial: Hildegard Gaertner
Rights & Permissions: Christina Krajicek
Founded: 1923
Subjects: Developing Countries, Fiction, Human Relations
ISBN Prefix(es): 3-7026

Junius Verlags- und Vertriebs GmbH
Brunnengasse 3, 1160 Vienna
Tel: (01) 4921272
Key Personnel
President & Publisher: Mat Dillinger
ISBN Prefix(es): 3-900370

Jupiter Verlagsgesellschaft mbH
Robertgasse 2, 1020 Vienna
Tel: (01) 21422940 *Fax:* (01) 2160720
Telex: 111563
Key Personnel
Manager: Dr Hans Georg Zeiner
ISBN Prefix(es): 3-900063

Juridica Verlag GmbH
Kohlmarkt 16, 1010 Vienna
Tel: (01) 533 37 47-0 *Fax:* (01) 533 37 47-196
E-mail: juridica@manz.at
Web Site: www.juridica.at
Key Personnel
Manager: Grete Grill; Werner Sopper
ISBN Prefix(es): 3-85131

Kaerntner Druck- und Verlags-GmbH
Viktringer Ring 28, 9010 Klagenfurt
Tel: (0463) 5866 *Fax:* (0463) 5866-321
E-mail: info@kaerntner-druckerei.at
Web Site: www.kaerntner-druckerei.at
Telex: 422415
Key Personnel
Contact: Wolbert Ebner *Tel:* (0463) 5855-261 *Fax:* (0463) 5866-111 *E-mail:* wolbert.ebner@kaerntner-druckerei.at
Founded: 1949
ISBN Prefix(es): 3-85391
Bookshop(s): Kaerntner Buchhandlung, Neuer Platz 11, 9020 Klagenfurt; Universitaetsstr 90, 9020 Klagenfurt; 8-Mai-Platz 3, 9500 Villach; Joh-Offner-Str 11, 9400 Wolfsberg

Karolinger Verlag GmbH & Co KG+
Staudgasse 12, 1180 Vienna
Tel: (0222) 4302093 *Fax:* (0222) 4302093
Key Personnel
Man Dir, Sales: Jean-Jacques Langendorf
Editorial: Dr Peter Weiss
Publicity: Cornelia Langendorf
Rights & Permissions: Hans Hofinger
Founded: 1980

PUBLISHERS

AUSTRIA

Subjects: Fiction, Government, Political Science, History, Literature, Literary Criticism, Essays
ISBN Prefix(es): 3-85418
Number of titles published annually: 6 Print
Total Titles: 82 Print
Distributed by Brockhaus Commission

Verlag Kerle im Verlag Herder & Co+
Wollzeile 33, 1010 Vienna
Tel: (01) 5121413-60 *Fax:* (01) 5121413-65
E-mail: vertriebsbuero@herder.at *Cable:* HERDERBUCH VIENNA
Key Personnel
Man Dir: Prof Erich M Wolf
Editorial: Dr Evelyn Kapaun
Sales: Susanne Pratscher
Advertising, Rights: Helga Thiele
Founded: 1886
ISBN Prefix(es): 3-210; 3-85303
Associate Companies: Verlag Herder GmbH & Co KG, Germany; Herder Editrice e Libreria, Italy; Editorial Herder SA, Spain; Herder AG, Switzerland
Subsidiaries: Herder Kiado
Bookshop(s): Herder & Co, Wollzeile 33, 1010 Vienna
Warehouse: Herder, Viktor Kaplanstr 9, 2201 Gerasdorf

Johann Kliment KG Musikverlag
Kolingasse 15, 1090 Vienna
Tel: (01) 317 51 47 *Fax:* (01) 310 08 27
E-mail: office@kliment.at
Web Site: www.kliment.at
Founded: 1928
ISBN Prefix(es): 3-85139
Bookshop(s): Neuer Markt 8, 39210 Zwettl

Horst Knapp Finanznachrichten
Lisztstr 10, 1037 Vienna
Mailing Address: PO Box 97, 1037 Vienna
Tel: (01) 7154460-0 *Fax:* (01) 7154460-22
Key Personnel
Owner: Horst Knapp
Subjects: Business, Economics, Finance, Government, Political Science
ISBN Prefix(es): 3-900068

Edition Koenigstein+
Anzengrubergasse 50, 3400 Klosterneuburg
Tel: (02243) 26046 *Fax:* (02243) 26046
E-mail: edition.koenigstein@aon.at
Web Site: members.aon.at/edition_koenigstein
Key Personnel
Master of Arts: Georg Koenigstein
Contact: Christine Koenigstein
Founded: 1987
Specialize in fine editions & poetry.
Subjects: Art, Poetry
ISBN Prefix(es): 3-901495
Number of titles published annually: 5 Print
Total Titles: 49 Print

Verlag A F Koska
Esterhazygasse 35, 1060 Vienna
Tel: (0222) 5874344
Key Personnel
Manager: Prof Alfred F Koska
ISBN Prefix(es): 3-85334

Kremayr & Scheriau Verlag+
Wahringerstr 76, 1090 Vienna
Tel: (01) 713 8770-10 *Fax:* (01)713 8770-20
E-mail: m.scheriau@kremayr-scheriau.at
Key Personnel
Man Dir: Dr Maria Seifert *Tel:* (01) 713 8770-12 *Fax:* (01) 713 8770-20 *E-mail:* maria.seifert@bertelsmann.de
Founded: 1950
Subjects: Art, History, Music, Dance, Nonfiction (General)

ISBN Prefix(es): 3-218
Parent Company: Bertelsmann AG, Germany
Bookshop(s): Buchhandlung uend Zeitschriftenvertrieb Kremayr und Scheriau, Niederhofstr 37, 1121 Vienna
Book Club(s): Buchgemeinschaft Donauland Kremayr & Scheriau
Orders to: Dr Otto-Neurath-Gasse 5, 1220 Vienna

Kuemmerly und Frey Verlags GmbH
Nikolsdorfergasse 8, 1050 Vienna
Tel: (01) 545 14 45 *Fax:* (01) 545 10 80-83
E-mail: kuemmerly-frey@xpoint.at
Subjects: Travel
ISBN Prefix(es): 3-900382
Associate Companies: J Fink-Kuemmerly und Frey Verlag GmbH, Germany; Kuemmerly und Frey, Switzerland (Geographischer Verlag)

Verlag Lafite+
Hegelgasse 13/22, 1010 Vienna
Tel: (01) 5126869 *Fax:* (01) 51268699
Key Personnel
Contact: Prof Dr Diederichs-Lafite
Founded: 1962
Specialize in music.
Publisher of the *Austrian Music Magazine*.
Subjects: Journalism, Music, Dance
ISBN Prefix(es): 3-85151
Associate Companies: Internationale Schonberg Gesellschaft, Vienna

Landesverlag, *imprint of* Niederosterreichisches Pressehaus Druck- und Verlagsgesellschaft mbH

Langenscheidt-Verlag GmbH
Sulzengasse 2, 1232 Vienna
Tel: (01) 6887133 *Fax:* (01) 68014140
Telex: 131912
Membership(s): Langenscheidt Group, Germany.
ISBN Prefix(es): 3-208
Parent Company: Langenscheidt KG, Germany

Gerda Leber Buch-Kunst-und Musikverlag Proscenium Edition+
Wallnerstr 4, 1010 Vienna
Tel: (01) 5332858; (01) 6390025
Key Personnel
Contact: Dr Gerda Leber-Hageneau
Founded: 1965
Subjects: Drama, Theater, Music, Dance
ISBN Prefix(es): 3-900217; 3-900297

Leopold Stocker Verlag+
Hofgasse 5, 8011 Graz
Mailing Address: Postfach 189, 8011 Graz
Tel: (0316) 82 16 36 *Fax:* (0316) 83 56 12
E-mail: stocker-verlag@stocker-verlag.com
Web Site: www.stocker-verlag.com *Cable:* STOCKERVERLAG GRAZ
Key Personnel
Publisher: Wolfgang Dvorak-Stocker
Founded: 1917
Subjects: Agriculture, Cookery, Gardening, Plants, Government, Political Science, History, Military Science, Wine & Spirits
ISBN Prefix(es): 3-7020
Associate Companies: Buecherquelle Buchhandlungs GmbH

Leykam Buchverlagsges mbH
Stempfergasse 3, 8010 Graz
Tel: (0316) 8076-531 *Fax:* (0316) 8076-539
E-mail: verlag@leykam.com
Web Site: www.leykam.com; www.leykamverlag.at
Telex: 032209 *Cable:* LEYKAM GRAZ
Key Personnel
Man Dir: Klaus Brunner *Tel:* (0316) 2800-204 *E-mail:* klaus.brunner@leykam.com

Founded: 1585
Subjects: Art, Fiction
ISBN Prefix(es): 3-7011

Linde Verlag Wien GmbH+
Scheydgasse 24, 1211 Vienna
Tel: (01) 24630-0 *Fax:* (01) 24630-23
E-mail: office@lindeverlag.at; presse@lindeverlag.at
Web Site: www.linde-verlag.at
Key Personnel
Manager: Dr Oskar Mennel *Tel:* (01) 24630-10 *E-mail:* oskar.mennel@lindeverlag.at
Editor: Dr Eleonore Breitegger *Tel:* (01) 278 05 26-21 *Fax:* (01) 278 05 26-51 *E-mail:* redaktion@lindeverlag.at
Public Relations: Christine Reisinger *Tel:* (01) 278 05 26-30 *Fax:* (01) 278 05 26-53 *E-mail:* presse@lindeverlag.at
Sales: Sabine Purger *Tel:* (01) 278 05 26-83 *Fax:* (01) 278 05 26-53 *E-mail:* sabine.purger@lindeverlag.at
Advertising: Gertraud Reznicek *Tel:* (01) 278 05 26-62 *Fax:* (01) 278 05 26-53 *E-mail:* gertraud.reznicek@lindeverlag.at
Founded: 1925
Subjects: Accounting, Business, Communications, Economics, How-to, Labor, Industrial Relations, Law, Management, Marketing
ISBN Prefix(es): 3-85122; 3-7073
Number of titles published annually: 120 Print; 3 CD-ROM
Total Titles: 300 Print; 20 CD-ROM

Literas-Verlag GmbH
Fischerstrand 9, 1220 Vienna
Tel: (01) 269 22 07 *Fax:* (01) 269 22 07
Telex: 116529 Icpfa
Founded: 1981
Subjects: Psychology, Psychiatry
ISBN Prefix(es): 3-85429
Associate Companies: Facultas Verlag

Loecker Verlag+
Annagasse 5, 1015 Vienna
Tel: (01) 512 02 82 *Fax:* (01) 512 02 82-22
E-mail: lverlag@loecker.at
Web Site: www.loecker.at
Key Personnel
General Manager: Erhard Loecker
Rights & Permissions: Dr Alexander Lellek
Founded: 1974
Subjects: Architecture & Interior Design, Art, History, Literature, Literary Criticism, Essays, Photography
ISBN Prefix(es): 3-85409
Bookshop(s): Antiquariat Loecker un Woegenstein, Annagasse 5, 1010 Vienna; Loecker GmbH, Gluckgasse 3, 1010 Vienna

LOG-Internationale Zeitschrift fuer Literatur+
Donaustadtstr 30/16, 1220 Vienna
Tel: (01) 2313433 *Fax:* (01) 2313433
Key Personnel
Publisher: Leo Detela; Prof Wolfgang Mayer Koenig
Founded: 1978
Subjects: Art, Drama, Theater, Language Arts, Linguistics, Literature, Literary Criticism, Essays, Poetry
ISBN Prefix(es): 3-900647
Orders to: Eigenauslieferung

Mangold Kinderbucher+
Saint Peter Hauptstr 28, 8042 Graz-St Peter
Tel: (0316) 475613 *Fax:* (0316) 475613
Cable: MANGOLDVERLAG
Key Personnel
Man Dir: Bernhard Lernpeiss
Founded: 1977
ISBN Prefix(es): 3-900301; 3-901282

AUSTRIA

MANZ'sche Verlags- und Universitaetsbuchhandlung GMBH
Kohlmarkt 16, 1010 Vienna
Tel: (01) 531 61-161 *Fax:* (01) 531 61-181
E-mail: verlag@manz.at
Web Site: www.manz.at
Telex: 75310631
Key Personnel
Management: Dr Kristin Hanusch-Linser; Lucas Schneider-Manns-Au
Founded: 1849
Specialize in law books in Europe.
Subjects: Economics, Law
ISBN Prefix(es): 3-214; 3-7067
Distributor for Amt der Europaeischen Gemeinschaften; Auslieferung fuer Oesterreich
Bookshop(s): Kohlmarkt 16, Postfach 163, 1014 Vienna; FRIC, Technische Fachbuchhandlung, Wiedner Hauptstr 13, 1040 Vienna
Warehouse: Siebenbrunnengasse 21, 1050 Vienna
Orders to: Siebenbrunnengasse 21, 1050 Vienna

Wilhelm Maudrich KG+
Lazarettgasse 1, 1096 Vienna
Tel: (01) 4024712 *Fax:* (01) 4085080
E-mail: medbook@maudrich.com
Web Site: www.maudrich.com
Telex: 135177 *Cable:* MAUDRICH VERLAG VIENNA
Key Personnel
Man Dir: Dr Heinz Pinker; Prof Gerhard Grois
Founded: 1929
Subjects: Medicine, Nursing, Dentistry, Psychology, Psychiatry
ISBN Prefix(es): 3-85175
Distributed by Stein und Co (Germany); Verlag Hans Huber (Switzerland)
Distributor for Point Verlag (Austria, Germany & Switzerland)
Bookshop(s): Spitalgasse 21a, 1096 Vienna
Tel: (01) 4024712 *Fax:* (01) 4085080

Medien & Recht+
Danhausergasse 6, 1040 Vienna
Tel: (01) 5052766 *Fax:* (01) 5052766-15
E-mail: verlag@medien-recht.ccom
Web Site: www.medien-recht.com
Key Personnel
University Prof: Dr Heinz Wittmann *E-mail:* h.wittmann@medien-recht.com
Founded: 1985
Subjects: Communications, Computer Science, Journalism, Law
ISBN Prefix(es): 3-900741
Parent Company: Medien & Recht Verlags GmbH

Merbod Verlag+
Herrengasse 2, 2700 Wiener Neustadt
Mailing Address: Postfach 201, 2700 Wiener Neustadt
Tel: (02622) 81724 *Fax:* (02622) 817244
Key Personnel
Contact: Peter Zumpf
Founded: 1989
Specializes in: Local listings & authors.
Subjects: Fiction, History, Humor, Literature, Literary Criticism, Essays, Nonfiction (General), Poetry
ISBN Prefix(es): 3-900844
Total Titles: 45 Print

Metrica Fachverlag u Versandbuchhandlung Ing Bartak+
Neugebaeudestr 18-12-8, 1110 Vienna
Tel: (01) 769 51 60 *Fax:* (01) 769 51 60
Key Personnel
Publisher: Ing Werner H Bartak
Founded: 1978
Subjects: Energy, Engineering (General), Technology
ISBN Prefix(es): 3-900368; 3-900329

Milena Verlag+
Lange Gasse 51/10, 1080 Vienna
Tel: (01) 402 59 90 *Fax:* (01) 408 88 58
E-mail: frauenverlag@milena-verlag.at
Key Personnel
Contact: Karin Ballauff; Martina Kopf
Founded: 1980
Subjects: Biography, Fiction, Gay & Lesbian, History, Library & Information Sciences, Literature, Literary Criticism, Essays, Nonfiction (General), Philosophy, Social Sciences, Sociology, Women's Studies
ISBN Prefix(es): 3-900399; 3-85286
Total Titles: 160 Print
Orders to: Mohr Z-G, Sulzengasse 2, 1230 Vienna *Tel:* (01) 68014-231 *Fax:* (01) 68014-140
E-mail: momo@mohr-morawa.co.at

Thomas Mlakar Verlag
Michlbauerweg 1, 8755 Saint Peter ob Judenburg
Tel: (03579) 2258 *Fax:* (03579) 2258
E-mail: mlakar-media@gmx.at
Founded: 1970
Subjects: Fashion, History, Literature, Literary Criticism, Essays, Natural History
ISBN Prefix(es): 3-900289

Modulverlag+
Mahlerstr 3, 1010 Vienna
Tel: (01) 5129892 *Fax:* (01) 5129893
Key Personnel
Contact: Dr Berthold Schwanzer
Founded: 1973
Specialize in architecture-marketing research.
Subjects: Architecture & Interior Design, Art, Marketing
ISBN Prefix(es): 3-900507
Distributor for Visual Reference Publications Inc (USA for Austria, retail books)

Moedling, *imprint of* Verlag St Gabriel

Verlag Monte Verita+
Hahngasse 15, 1090 Vienna
Tel: (01) 5487080 *Fax:* (01) 5487081
Web Site: www.anares.org
Key Personnel
Publisher: Peter Stipkovics
Founded: 1982
Subjects: History, Literature, Literary Criticism, Essays, Philosophy
ISBN Prefix(es): 3-900434

Otto Mueller Verlag
Ernst-Thunstr 11, 5020 Salzburg
Mailing Address: Postfach 167, 5021 Salzburg
Tel: (0662) 881974-0 *Fax:* (0662) 872387
E-mail: otto.muellerverlag@salzburg.co.at *Cable:* MULLER VERLAG
Key Personnel
Man Dir, Sales & Publicity: Arno Kleibel
Founded: 1937
Subjects: History, Literature, Literary Criticism, Essays, Poetry, Psychology, Psychiatry, Religion - Other, Theology
ISBN Prefix(es): 3-7013

Mueller-Speiser Wissenschaftlicher Verlag
Mitterweg 6, 5081 Anif/Salzburg
Tel: (06246) 73166 *Fax:* (06246) 73166
E-mail: verlag@mueller-speiser.at
Web Site: www.mueller-speiser.at
Key Personnel
Contact: Ursula Mueller-Speiser
Founded: 1989
Subjects: Drama, Theater, Music, Dance, Philosophy, Religion - Other, Theology, General Religion & Musicscience/Musicethnology
ISBN Prefix(es): 3-85145
Total Titles: 78 Print

Paul Neff Verlag KG+
Hackingerstr 52, 1140 Vienna
Tel: (01) 94061115 *Fax:* (01) 947641288 *Cable:* Neffverlag
Key Personnel
Man Dir: Dagmar Stecher-Konsalik
Founded: 1829
Subjects: Art, Biography, Fiction, Music, Dance
ISBN Prefix(es): 3-7014
Parent Company: Hestia-Verlag GmbH, Germany

Verlag Neues Leben
Thueringerberg 77, 6721 Thueringerberg
Tel: (05579) 31 96
Key Personnel
Man Dir: Dr Rudolf Ingrisch
Founded: 1946
Subjects: Biography, Drama, Theater, Economics, Medicine, Nursing, Dentistry
ISBN Prefix(es): 3-85335

Edition Neues Marchen+
Kloster, 8413 St Georgen a d Stiefing
Tel: (03184) 2417 *Fax:* (03183) 7400
Key Personnel
Owner: Folke Tegetthoff
Founded: 1990
Subjects: Poetry
ISBN Prefix(es): 3-85325

Neufeld-Verlag und Galerie
Schillerstr 7, 6890 Lustenau
Tel: (05577) 46 57
Telex: 59162 *Cable:* Neufeld
Key Personnel
Man Dir: K G Loepfe
Editorial, Rights & Permissions: Ivo Loepfe
Founded: 1962
ISBN Prefix(es): 3-900651
Parent Company: Loepfe KG
Branch Office(s)
Nordstr 227, 8037 Zurich, Switzerland

Wolfgang Neugebauer Verlag GmbH
Kalvarienguertel 62, 8020 Graz
Tel: (05522) 747 70 *Fax:* (05522) 747 70
E-mail: wnverlag@utanet.at
Key Personnel
Man Dir: Wolfgang Neugebauer
Founded: 1975
Subjects: History, Language Arts, Linguistics, Literature, Literary Criticism, Essays, Theology
ISBN Prefix(es): 3-85376
Total Titles: 100 Print
Bookshop(s): Buchandlung Bayer, Inh W Neugebauer Verlag GmbH, Kreuzgasse 6, 6800 Feldkirch *E-mail:* bayer.buch@utanet.at
Orders to: Kreuzgasse 6, 6800 Feldkirch

Dr Waltraud Neuwirth Selbstverlag (Dr Waltraud Neuwirth Self Publishing House)
Barawitzkagasse 27/1/4/31, 1190 Vienna
Tel: (01) 3207323 *Fax:* (01) 3200225
E-mail: waltraud.neuwith@eunet.at
Founded: 1976
ISBN Prefix(es): 3-900282

Niederosterreichisches Pressehaus Druck- und Verlagsgesellschaft mbH+
Gutenbergstr 12, 3100 Saint Poelten
Tel: (02742) 802-1412 *Fax:* (02742) 802-1431
E-mail: verlag@np-buch.at
Web Site: www.np-buch.at
Telex: 015512
Key Personnel
Man Dir: Herwig Bitsche *Tel:* (02742) 802-1410 *E-mail:* h.bitsche@np-buch.at
Publicity: Johanna Stromberger *E-mail:* j.stromberger@np-buch.at
Marketing: Roswitha Wonka
Founded: 1889

PUBLISHERS — AUSTRIA

Subjects: Biography, Cookery, Health, Nutrition, History, Human Relations, Humor, Nonfiction (General), Outdoor Recreation, Travel, Wine & Spirits
ISBN Prefix(es): 3-85214; 3-85326; 3-85236
Number of titles published annually: 40 Print
Total Titles: 200 Print
Imprints: Landesverlag; NP Buchverlag
Orders to: Mohr Morawa, Buchvertrieb GmbH, Sulzengasse 2, 1232 Vienna *Tel:* (01) 680 14-0 *Fax:* (01) 688 71-30 *E-mail:* momo@mohr-morawa.co.at

NOI - Verlag
Morresstr 13, 9020 Klagenfurt, Oostenrijk
Tel: (0463) 224722 *Fax:* (0463) 224744
E-mail: office@noisapil.com
Key Personnel
Owner: Dr Dietfried Schoenemann
Subjects: Education, Environmental Studies, Ethnicity, Health, Nutrition, History, Social Sciences, Sociology
ISBN Prefix(es): 3-900453

NP Buchverlag, *imprint of* Niederosterreichisches Pressehaus Druck- und Verlagsgesellschaft mbH

Obelisk-Verlag+
Falkstr 1, 6020 Innsbruck
Tel: (0512) 58 07 33 *Fax:* (0512) 58 07 33 13
E-mail: obelisk-verlag@utanet.at
Web Site: www.obelisk-verlag.at
Key Personnel
Proprietor: Helga Buchroithner
Founded: 1946
ISBN Prefix(es): 3-85197

OEAW, see Verlag der Oesterreichischen Akademie der Wissenschaften (OEAW)

oebv & hpt Verlagsgesellschaft mbH & Co KG+
Frankgasse 4, 1090 Vienna
Tel: (01) 40136-0 *Fax:* (01) 40136-185
E-mail: office@oebvhpt.at
Web Site: www.oebvhpt.at
Key Personnel
Contact: Werner Brunner
International Rights: Hubert W Krenn
Marketing Manager: Herwig Arlt *Tel:* (01) 400 90-91 *Fax:* (01) 400 90-40 *E-mail:* vertrieb@oebvhpt.at
Advertising: Martina Moosleitner *Tel:* (01) 400 90-11 *Fax:* (01) 400 90-40 *E-mail:* werbung@oebvhpt.at
Founded: 1985
Subjects: Education, Mysteries, Nonfiction (General), Romance
ISBN Prefix(es): 3-85128
Divisions: Neuer Breitschopf Verlag; Ed Boesskraut & Bernardi; Kurz & Bundigi, hpt Extra
Orders to: Mohr-Morawa, Sulzeng 2, 1230 Vienna *Tel:* (01) 684614-0

Verlag Oesterreich GmbH+
Kandlgasse 21, 1070 Vienna
Tel: (01) 61077-0 *Fax:* (01) 61077-419
E-mail: office@verlagoesterreich.at
Web Site: www.verlagoesterreich.at
Key Personnel
Manager: Peter Wittmann *Tel:* (01) 610771401 *Fax:* (01) 610771419 *E-mail:* wittmann@verlagoesterreich.at
Membership(s): Haupt Verband des Osterr Buchhandels & Deutscher Borsevrerein Frankfurt.
ISBN Prefix(es): 3-7046
Total Titles: 1,000 Print; 20 CD-ROM; 1 Online; 1 E-Book
Bookshop(s): Jurbooks, Wollzeile 16, 1010 Vienna, Contact: Gert Weiss *Tel:* (01) 5124885 *Fax:* (01) 5120663 *E-mail:* buchhandlung@verlagoesterreich.at

Oesterreichische Staatsdruckerei (Austrian State Printing Office)
Rennweg 16, 1037 Vienna
Tel: (01) 20666-302 *Fax:* (01) 20666-100
E-mail: zach@staatsdruckerei.at
Web Site: www.oesd.co.at
Key Personnel
Dir: Aribert Schwarzmann
ISBN Prefix(es): 3-7046; 3-85201

Oesterreichische Verlagsanstalt GmbH
Arbeitergasse 1-7, 1051 Vienna
Tel: (01) 5445641-46 *Fax:* (01) 5445641-46
E-mail: prepress@agens-werk.at
Key Personnel
Man Dir: Friedrich Geyer
ISBN Prefix(es): 3-7033; 3-85202

Verlag der Oesterreichischen Akademie der Wissenschaften (OEAW) (Austrian Academy of Sciences Press)+
Postgasse 7, 1010 Vienna
Mailing Address: Postfach 471, 1010 Vienna
Tel: (01) 512 9050; (01) 51581-3401 *Fax:* (01) 51581-3400
E-mail: verlag@oeaw.ac.at
Web Site: verlag.oeaw.ac.at
Key Personnel
Manager: Mag Herwig Stoeger *Tel:* (01) 51581-3405 *E-mail:* herwig.stoeger@oeaw.ac.at
Founded: 1973
Subjects: Archaeology, Asian Studies, Biography, Biological Sciences, History, Language Arts, Linguistics, Law, Physical Sciences, Science (General), Social Sciences, Sociology
ISBN Prefix(es): 3-7001
Number of titles published annually: 80 Print; 3 Audio
Total Titles: 20 Audio
Distributed by Rinson Books (Japan); University of Washington Press (USA)

Verlag des Oesterreichischen Gewerkschaftsbundes GmbH
Altmannsdorfer Str 154-156, 1231 Vienna
Tel: (01) 662 32 96 *Fax:* (01) 662 32 96-63 85
E-mail: office@oegbverlag.at
Web Site: www.verlag-oegb.co.at
Telex: 1311326
Key Personnel
Man Dir: Friedrich Loew
Editor-in-Chief: Fritz Fadler
Founded: 1947
Subjects: Career Development, Government, Political Science, History, Labor, Industrial Relations, Law
ISBN Prefix(es): 3-7035
Subsidiaries: Elbemuhl GmbH; EDV GmbH; Printex GmbH; Pichler GmbH
Book Club(s): Buechergilde Gutenberg

Oesterreichischer Agrarverlag, Druck- und Verlags- GmbH+
Achauer Str 49A, 2335 Leopoldsdorf bei Wien
Tel: (02235) 404-440 *Fax:* (02235) 404-459
E-mail: buch@agrarverlag.at
Web Site: www.agrarverlag.at
Telex: 14030 *Cable:* AGRARVERLAG
Key Personnel
Man Dir: Dr Wolfgang Brandstetter
Founded: 1945
Subjects: Agriculture, Environmental Studies, Fiction
ISBN Prefix(es): 3-7040
Subsidiaries: Hugo H Hitschmann Verlag
Warehouse: Hennersdorfer Str 32/6, 2333 Leopoldsdorf
Orders to: Ing H Fischer/AV Buchhandlung, Linzerstr 32, 1141 Vienna *Fax:* (01) 951501-289

Oesterreichischer Bundesverlag Gmbh
Schwarzenbergstr 5, 1015 Vienna
Tel: (01) 5262091-0 *Fax:* (01) 526209111
E-mail: oebz@oebv.co.at
Web Site: www.oebv.at
Telex: 79246
Key Personnel
Contact: Dr Othmar Spachinger
International Rights: Wilbirg Stoger
Founded: 1772
Subjects: Biological Sciences, Career Development, Chemistry, Chemical Engineering, Education, English as a Second Language, History, Language Arts, Linguistics, Music, Dance, Nonfiction (General), Philosophy, Sports, Athletics
ISBN Prefix(es): 3-215

Oesterreichischer Gewerbeverlag GmbH
Herrengasse 10, 1014 Vienna
Mailing Address: Postfach 182, 1014 Vienna
Tel: (01) 535 9404 *Fax:* (01) 5330768030
E-mail: gewerbeverlag@tbxa.telecom.at
Key Personnel
Man Dir, Sales, Publicity: Franz Scharetzer
Editorial, Rights & Permissions: Dr Josef Peter Ortner
Production: Heinz Stuiber
Founded: 1945
Subjects: Career Development, English as a Second Language
ISBN Prefix(es): 3-85207
Parent Company: Oesterreichischer Bundesverlag GmbH

Oesterreichischer Jagd -und Fischerei-Verlag
Wickenburggasse 3, 1080 Vienna
Tel: (01) 405 16 36-39 *Fax:* (01) 405 16 36-36
E-mail: verlag@jagd.at
Web Site: www.jagd.at
Key Personnel
Publisher: Dr Peter Lebersorger
ISBN Prefix(es): 3-85208

Oesterreichischer Kunst und Kulturverlag+
Freundgasse 11, 1040 Vienna
Tel: (01) 587 85 51 *Fax:* (01) 587 85 52
E-mail: office@kunstundkulturverlag.at
Key Personnel
Contact: Dr Michael Martischnig
Founded: 1981
Subjects: Antiques, Architecture & Interior Design, Communications, Engineering (General), History, Nonfiction (General), Regional Interests, Social Sciences, Sociology
ISBN Prefix(es): 3-85437
Total Titles: 350 Print; 3 CD-ROM; 3 Audio

Oesterreichisches Katholisches Bibelwerk
Stiftsplatz 8, 3400 Klosterneuburg
Mailing Address: Postfach 48, 3400 Klosterneuburg
Tel: (02243) 2938 *Fax:* (02243) 2939
Telex: (61) 3222523
Key Personnel
Man Dir, Editorial, Rights & Permissions: Dr Norbert Hoeslinger
Sales: Elisabeth Csencsics
Publicity: Erika Pruckmoser
Founded: 1966
Membership(s): AMB & WCBFA (World Catholic Federation for the Biblical Apostolate)
Subjects: Religion - Other
ISBN Prefix(es): 3-85396
Bookshop(s): Singerstr 7, 1010 Vienna

AUSTRIA

Verlag Oldenbourg+
Neulinggasse 26/12, 1030 Vienna
Tel: (01) 712 62 58 *Fax:* (01) 712 62 58-19
E-mail: office@oldenbourg.at
Key Personnel
Sales Dir: Gerda Adler
Publicity & Advertising: Dr Ursula Huber
    E-mail: ursula.huber@oldenbourg.co.at
Mag: Veronika Weidenholzer *E-mail:* veronika.weidenholzer@oldenbourg.co.at
Founded: 1957
Subjects: Engineering (General), History, Philosophy, Science (General), Social Sciences, Sociology
ISBN Prefix(es): 3-7029
Parent Company: R Oldenbourg Verlag GmbH, Germany
Associate Companies: Verlag fuer Geschichte und Politik

Verlag Orac im Verlag Kremayr & Scheriau+
Waehringer Str 76/8, 1090 Vienna
Tel: (01) 713 87 70 *Fax:* (01) 713 87 70-20
E-mail: office@kremayr-scheriau.at
Web Site: www.kremayr-scheriau.at
Key Personnel
Publisher: Prof Leo Mazakarini
Program Development: Dr Michal Scheriau
Production: Claudia Rinne
Press & Public Relations: Astrid Lefenda
Founded: 1946
Subjects: Cookery, Economics, Environmental Studies, Government, Political Science, Health, Nutrition, Management, Nonfiction (General)
ISBN Prefix(es): 3-7015; 3-85368
Parent Company: Kremayr & Scheriau
Orders to: Dr Otto Neurath-Gasse 5, 1220 Vienna, Contact: Dr Franz Hain *Tel:* (01) 282 65 65 *Fax:* (01) 282 52 82 *E-mail:* office@hain.at

Verlag des Osterr Kneippbundes GmbH+
Kunigundenweg 10, 8700 Leoben
Tel: (03842) 21682; (03842) 21718; (03842) 24094 *Fax:* (03842) 2171832
E-mail: office@kneippverlag.com
Web Site: www.kneippverlag.com
Key Personnel
Manager: Waltraud Ruth
Founded: 1985
Specializing in Health & Medicine.
Subjects: Alternative, Child Care & Development, Cookery, Health, Nutrition, Medicine, Nursing, Dentistry, Outdoor Recreation, Philosophy, Psychology, Psychiatry, Sports, Athletics
ISBN Prefix(es): 3-900696; 3-901794; 3-902191
Distributed by B&M Medien Service (Switzerland); Knoe (Germany); Morawa (Austria); Weltbild
Distributor for Kneipp-Verlag Bad Woerishofen

Osterreichischer Alpenverein Sektion Weiner Lehrer, see Wienerland Zeitung & Verlag

Osterreichischer Wirtschaftsverlag Druck-und Verlagsgesellschaft mbH
Nikolsdorfer Gasse 7-11, 1051 Vienna
Tel: (01) 546 64-0 *Fax:* (01) 546 64-215
E-mail: office@oewv.at
Key Personnel
Man Dir: Robert Graf
ISBN Prefix(es): 3-85212

Passagen Verlag GmbH+
Walfischgasse 15-14, 1010 Vienna
Tel: (01) 513 77 61 *Fax:* (01) 512 63 27
E-mail: office@passagen.at
Web Site: www.passagen.at
Key Personnel
Publisher: Dr Peter Engelmann
    E-mail: engelmann@passagen.at
Founded: 1987
Subjects: Architecture & Interior Design, Art, Economics, Government, Political Science, Literature, Literary Criticism, Essays, Philosophy, Theology
ISBN Prefix(es): 3-900767; 3-85165
Total Titles: 600 Print
Orders to: Bugrim Verlagsauslieferung, Saalburgstr 3, 12099 Berlin, Germany, Contact: Herr Lindemann *Tel:* (030) 6068457 *Fax:* (030) 6063476 *E-mail:* bugrim@t-online.de *Web Site:* www.bugrim.de

E Perlinger Naturprodukte Handelsgesellschaft mbH+
Itter 300, 6300 Woergl
Tel: (05332) 524 40 *Fax:* (05332) 516 79
E-mail: engelberts.naturprodukte@tirol.com
Telex: 051205 Teltaz *Cable:* Perlinger Verlag Woergl
Key Personnel
Man Dir: Engelbert Perlinger
Founded: 1977
Subjects: Astrology, Occult, Ethnicity, Medicine, Nursing, Dentistry
ISBN Prefix(es): 3-85399

Verlag Sankt Peter
Erzabtei St Peter, 5010 Salzburg
Mailing Address: Postfach 113, 5010 Salzburg
Tel: (0662) 842166-82 *Fax:* (0662) 842166-80
E-mail: verlag-st.peter@magnet.at
Web Site: www.stift-stpeter.at
Telex: 063094
Key Personnel
Man Dir: Dr R Rinnerthaler
    E-mail: rinnerthaler@hotmail.com
Founded: 1946
Subjects: Art, Regional Interests, Religion - Other
ISBN Prefix(es): 3-900173

Pichler Verlag GmbH & Co KG
Imprint of Styria Pichler Verlag GmbH & Co KG
Lobkowitzplatz 1, 1010 Vienna
Tel: (01) 203 28 28-0 *Fax:* (01) 203 28 28-6875
E-mail: office@styriapichler.at
Web Site: www.styriapichler.at
Key Personnel
Dir: Michael Hlatky *Tel:* (01) 2032828-6870
    E-mail: michael.hlatky@pichlerverlag.at
Public Relations: Dr Barbara Brunner *Tel:* (01) 624673955 *E-mail:* barbara.brunner@utanet.at
Founded: 1793
ISBN Prefix(es): 3-85431
Bookshop(s): Wipplingerstr 37, 1010 Vienna; Favoritenstr 42, 1040 Vienna

Richard Pils Publication PN°1+
Grosswolfgers 29, 3970 Weitra
Tel: (0043) 2856 3794 *Fax:* (0043) 2856 3792
E-mail: verlag@bibliothekderprovinz.at
Web Site: www.bibliothekderprovinz.at
Key Personnel
Contact: Richard Pils
Founded: 1989
Subjects: Art, Cookery, Drama, Theater, Fiction, Literature, Literary Criticism, Essays, Photography, Poetry
ISBN Prefix(es): 3-900878; 3-85252
Number of titles published annually: 50 Print
Total Titles: 700 Print

Pinguin-Verlag, Pawlowski GmbH+
Lindenbuehelweg 2, 6020 Innsbruck
Tel: (0512) 281183-0 *Fax:* (0512) 293243
Web Site: www.worldport.at *Cable:* PINGUINVERLAG INNSBRUCK
Key Personnel
Man Dir: Hella Pawlowski; Olaf Pawlowski
Founded: 1945
Subjects: Art, Astrology, Occult, Cookery, Foreign Countries, Geography, Geology, Nonfiction (General), Physical Sciences, Travel
ISBN Prefix(es): 3-7016
Distributor for Readers Digest; Verlag Frankfurt

Georg Prachner KG+
Kaerntner Str 30, 1010 Vienna
Tel: (01) 512 85 49-0 *Fax:* (01) 512-01-58
Key Personnel
Man Dir: O G Prachner
Founded: 1931
Subjects: Agriculture, Art, Fiction, History
ISBN Prefix(es): 3-85367
Divisions: Prachner GmbH, Verlag und Grosshandel

Progress-Verlag Dr Micolini's Witwe
Glacisstr 57, 8010 Graz
Tel: (0316) 829508 *Fax:* (0316) 829508
Cable: Micolini Graz
Founded: 1934
ISBN Prefix(es): 3-85237

Promedia Verlagsges mbH+
Wickenburggasse 5/12, 1080 Vienna
Tel: (01) 405 27 02 *Fax:* (01) 405 71 59 22
E-mail: promedia@mediashop.at
Web Site: www.mediashop.at
Key Personnel
Contact: Hannes Hofbauer
Founded: 1982
Subjects: Anthropology, Architecture & Interior Design, Biography, Developing Countries, Foreign Countries, Government, Political Science, History, Nonfiction (General), Travel, Women's Studies
ISBN Prefix(es): 3-900478; 3-85371
Number of titles published annually: 20 Print
Total Titles: 200 Print
Distribution Center: Mohr Morawa Buchvertrieb Ges mbH, Sulzeng 2, 1230 Vienna *Tel:* (01) 68 0 14-5 *Fax:* (01) 68 0 14-140
Prolit Verlagsauslieferung, Siemensstr 16, 35463 Fernwald, Germany *Tel:* (0641) 94393-23 *Fax:* (0641) 94393-29
Scheidegger & Co bei AVA, Centralweg 16, 8910 Affoltern, Switzerland *Tel:* (01) 762 42 10 *Fax:* (061) 272 94 76 *E-mail:* buchundinfo@ava.ch

Prugg Verlag
Haydngasse 10, 7000 Eisenstadt
Tel: (02682) 2114
ISBN Prefix(es): 3-85238

Verlag Anton Pustet+
Bergstr 12, 5020 Salzburg
Tel: (0662) 87 35 07-55 *Fax:* (0662) 87 35 07-79
E-mail: buch@verlag-anton-pustet.at
Web Site: www.verlag-anton-pustet.at
Key Personnel
Rights & Permissions: M A Mona Muery-Leitner
    Tel: (0662) 87 35 07-54
Contact: Dr Roman Hoellbacher *Tel:* (0662) 87 35 07-53
Founded: 1598
Subjects: Architecture & Interior Design, Art, Cookery, History, Philosophy, Psychology, Psychiatry, Theology, Travel
ISBN Prefix(es): 3-7025
Total Titles: 90 Print

Reinhold Schmidt Verlag
Kastanienweg 9, 2362 Biedermannsdorf
Tel: (02236) 72469 *Fax:* (02236) 73784
Key Personnel
Editor-in-Chief: Herbert Schwestka
ISBN Prefix(es): 3-900124

Resch Verlag+
Maria-Eich-Str 77, 82166 Graefelfing
Tel: (089) 8 54 65-0 *Fax:* (089) 8 54 65-11
E-mail: info@resch-verlag.com

Web Site: www.resch-verlag.com
Key Personnel
Publisher: Dr Ingo Resch
Contact: Prof P Andreas Resch, PhD; Mag Priska Kapferer
Founded: 1974
Subjects: Parapsychology, Physics, Science (General), Theology, Ethics
ISBN Prefix(es): 3-85382

Residenz Verlag GmbH+
Gaisbergstr 6, 5025 Salzburg
Tel: (0662) 641986-0 *Fax:* (0662) 643548
E-mail: info@residenzverlag.at
Web Site: www.residenzverlag.at
Key Personnel
Man Dir: Hernig Bitsche *E-mail:* h.bitsche@np-buch.at
Sales Manager: Roswitha Wonka
Foreign Rights & Permissions: Ingrid Fuehrer *E-mail:* ingrid.fuehrer@oebv.co.at
Editorial: Dr Astrid Graf *E-mail:* astrid.graf@oebv.co.at
Founded: 1956
Subjects: Art, Drama, Theater, Film, Video, Music, Dance, Poetry, Contemporary Literature
ISBN Prefix(es): 3-7017
Number of titles published annually: 25 Print
Total Titles: 350 Print
Parent Company: Niederoesterreichisches Pressehaus, Saint Poelten

Rhombus Verlag
Matteottipl 1, 1160 Vienna
Tel: (01) 526 61 52 *Fax:* (01) 522 87 18
Key Personnel
Man Dir: Thomas C Cubasch
Subjects: Literature, Literary Criticism, Essays, Avant Garde & Experimental Literature
ISBN Prefix(es): 3-85394
Number of titles published annually: 1 Print
Total Titles: 20 Print

Ritter Druck und Verlags KEG+
Hagenstr 3, 9020 Klagenfurt
Tel: (0463) 42631 *Fax:* (0463) 42631-77
E-mail: office@ritterbooks.at
Web Site: www.ritterbooks.com
Key Personnel
Contact: Karin Ritter
Founded: 1980
Subjects: Architecture & Interior Design, Art, Literature, Literary Criticism, Essays, Music, Dance, Art Theory, Exhibition
ISBN Prefix(es): 3-85415

Verlag Roeschnar+
Beethovenstr 4, 9065 Pfaffendorf
Tel: (0463) 740513 *Fax:* (0463) 740817
E-mail: roesch@eunet.at
Web Site: members.eunet.at/roesch
Key Personnel
Publishing Manager: Renate Peball
Founded: 1876
Subjects: Poetry
ISBN Prefix(es): 3-900735; 3-85277

Roetzer Druck GmbH & Co KG
Bundesstr 50, 7001 Eisenstadt
Tel: (02682) 2473 *Fax:* (02682) 65008
E-mail: roetzeredition@wellcom.at
Key Personnel
Man Dir: Rainer Roetzer
Founded: 1969
Subjects: Physics
ISBN Prefix(es): 3-85253

Verlag St Gabriel+
Gabrielerstr 171, 2340 Moedling
Tel: (02236) 803-225 *Fax:* (02236) 24483
E-mail: zeitschriften.stgabriel@steyler.at@steyler.at
Web Site: www.steyler.at
Key Personnel
Man: Elisabeth Birklhuber *Tel:* (02236) 803163 *E-mail:* ltg.verlag@steyler.at
Contact: Gerd Milcke *E-mail:* bur.verlag@steyler.at
Founded: 1901
Subjects: Religion - Catholic, Theology
ISBN Prefix(es): 3-85264
Number of titles published annually: 8 Print
Total Titles: 40 Print
Parent Company: Missionshaus Sankt Gabriel
Ultimate Parent Company: Gesellschaft des Gottlichen Wortes, Provinz Osterreich
Imprints: Moedling
Distributed by Rex-Verlag; Steyler Verlag
Bookshop(s): Missions Buch Handlung St Gabriel, Contact: Mr Queder *Tel:* (02236) 47834 *Fax:* (02236) 803273; Stephansplatz 6, 1010 Vienna *Tel:* (01) 5122105 *Fax:* (01) 5122105
Distribution Center: Verlagsauslieferungen, 1220 Vienna, Ms Korecky *Tel:* (01) 282656524 *Fax:* (01) 2825282 *E-mail:* office@hain.at

Verlag der Salzburger Druckerei
Bergstr 12, 5020 Salzburg
Tel: (0662) 873507-56 *Fax:* (0662) 873507-62
E-mail: verlag@salzburger-druckerei.at
ISBN Prefix(es): 3-85338

Salzburger Kulturvereinigung
Waagplatz 1a Trakl-Haus, 5010 Salzburg
Mailing Address: Postfach 42, 5010 Salzburg
Tel: (0662) 845346 *Fax:* (0662) 842665
E-mail: kulturvereinigung@salzburg.co.at
Web Site: www.salzburg.com/kulturvereinigung
Key Personnel
Manager: Dr Heinz Klier
Classic concerts with orchestras.
Subjects: Music, Dance
ISBN Prefix(es): 3-85259

Salzburger Nachrichten Verlagsgesellschaft mbH & Co KG
Karolingerstr 40, 5020 Salzburg
Tel: (0662) 8373-0; (0662) 8373-210 *Fax:* (0662) 8373-210
E-mail: anzeigen@salzburg.com
Web Site: www.salzburg.com
Telex: 633383
Key Personnel
Publisher & Man Dir: Dr Maximillian Dasch
Man Dir: Ramon Torra
Editor-in-Chief: Ronald Barazon
Subjects: Architecture & Interior Design, Drama, Theater, History, Music, Dance, Regional Interests
ISBN Prefix(es): 3-85304

Verlag fuer Sammler+
St Peter Hauptstr 35e, 8042 Graz
Tel: (0316) 47 22 30 *Fax:* (0316) 67 39 87
E-mail: ssu@literaturhaus.at
Web Site: www.literaturhaus.at/buch/verlagsportraits/sammler.html
Key Personnel
Owner: Uta Gratzl
Founded: 1968
Subjects: Art, History, Natural History, Social Sciences, Sociology
ISBN Prefix(es): 3-85365
Showroom(s): Koeroesistr 17/4, 8010 Graz

Sankt Hermagoras Bruderschaft, see Hermagoras/Mohorjeva

Paul Sappl, Schulbuch- und Lehrmittelverlag
Eichelwang 15, 6330 Kufstein
Tel: (05372) 64300 *Fax:* (05372) 64300-17
Telex: 5119115
Founded: 1953
ISBN Prefix(es): 3-85263
Branch Office(s)
Stolberggasse 31-33, 1050 Vienna

Dr A Schendl GmbH und Co KG
Geblergasse 95, 1170 Vienna
Tel: (01) 484 17 85-0 *Fax:* (01) 484 17 85-15
E-mail: info@schendl.at
Web Site: www.schendl.at
Key Personnel
Dir: Martin Oegg
Founded: 1965
Also acts as packager, warehouse, promoter.
Subjects: Economics, Ethnicity, Geography, Geology, History, Literature, Literary Criticism, Essays, Music, Dance, Natural History
ISBN Prefix(es): 3-85268

Schlager Verlag, see Astor-Verlag, Willibald Schlager

Andreas Schnider Verlags-Atelier
Peterstalerstr 127, 8042 Graz-St Peter
Tel: (0316) 471302 *Fax:* (0316) 4713024
E-mail: bookstore@net.burger.at
Key Personnel
Owner: Andreas Schnider
Founded: 1989
Subjects: Archaeology, Architecture & Interior Design, Art, Computer Science, Education, Electronics, Electrical Engineering, Fiction, Government, Political Science, History, Law, Literature, Literary Criticism, Essays, Photography, Poetry, Psychology, Psychiatry, Religion - Catholic, Religion - Other, Theology, Veterinary Science
ISBN Prefix(es): 3-900993; 0-902020
Branch Office(s)
Attila Mudrok, Vak u 6, H-2500 Grztergom
U.S. Office(s): Roy Mittelman, 607 West End Ave, New York, NY 10024, United States *Tel:* 212-769-3323 *Fax:* 212-769-2325

Schubert & Franzke Gesellschaft mbH
Kranzbichlerstr 57, 3100 Saint Poelten
Tel: (02742) 78 501-0 *Fax:* (02742) 78 501-15
E-mail: office@schubert-franzke.com
Web Site: www.map2web.cc/schubert-franzke
Key Personnel
Manager: Josef Scheibenreif *E-mail:* j.scheibenreif@schubert-franzke.com
Sales & Marketing: Peter Labas *E-mail:* p.labas@schubert-franzke.com
ISBN Prefix(es): 3-7056; 3-900938

Verlagsbuero Karl Schwarzer
Ziegelofengasse 27/1/2, 1050 Vienna
Tel: (01) 548 31 15-0 *Fax:* (01) 548 31 15-39
E-mail: verlagsbuero@schwarzer.at
Web Site: www.schwarzer.at
ISBN Prefix(es): 3-900392

Verlag Josef Otto Slezak+
Wiedner Hauptstr 40-42, 1040 Vienna
Tel: (01) 587 02 59 *Fax:* (01) 587 02 59
E-mail: verlag.slezak@aon.at
Web Site: www.byronny.at/index.html
Key Personnel
Sales Manager: Ilse Slezak
Contact: Josef Otto Slezak
Founded: 1960
Specialize in railway books.
Membership(s): Oesterreichische Verkehrswissenschaftliche Gesellschaft.
Subjects: Foreign Countries, History, Transportation
ISBN Prefix(es): 3-85416; 3-900134
Number of titles published annually: 4 Print

Total Titles: 50 Print
Distributed by Minirex (Switzerland)

SN-Verlag, see Salzburger Nachrichten Verlagsgesellschaft mbH & Co KG

Springer-Verlag Wien+
Sachsenplatz 4-6, 1200 Vienna
Mailing Address: PO Box 89, 1201 Vienna
Tel: (01) 3302415 *Fax:* (01) 3302426
E-mail: books@springer.at (orders); journals@springer.at (orders)
Web Site: www.springer.at
Key Personnel
Dir, Ed, Art, Cultural Studies: Rudolf Siegle
  E-mail: siegle@springer.at
Founded: 1924
Subjects: Anthropology, Architecture & Interior Design, Art, Biological Sciences, Business, Chemistry, Chemical Engineering, Civil Engineering, Communications, Computer Science, Economics, Education, Electronics, Electrical Engineering, Engineering (General), Environmental Studies, Law, Mathematics, Mechanical Engineering, Medicine, Nursing, Dentistry, Philosophy, Physics, Psychology, Psychiatry, Science (General), Technology
ISBN Prefix(es): 3-211
Associate Companies: Springer-Verlag New York Inc, 175 Fifth Ave, New York, NY 10010, United States
Distributor for Birkhaaeuser; Boehlau; L Mueller; Springer; Steinkopff
Bookshop(s): Minerva Wissenschaftliche Buchhandlung GmbH, Sachsenplatz 4-6, 1200 Vienna

J Steinbrener OHG+
Im Eichbuchl 1, 4780 Scharding
Tel: (07712) 2038 *Fax:* (07712) 2038-20
E-mail: steinbrener@aon.at
Founded: 1855
Subjects: Religion - Other
ISBN Prefix(es): 3-85296
Associate Companies: J Steinbrener OHG Zweigneiderlassung Neuhaus, Wagnerstr 21, Neuhaus, Germany

Dr Paul Struzl GmbH, see Akademische Druck-u Verlagsanstalt Dr Paul Struzl GmbH

Studien Verlag Gmbh+
Amraser Str 118, 6020 Innsbruck
Tel: (0512) 395045 *Fax:* (0512) 395045-15
E-mail: order@studienverlag.at
Web Site: www.studienverlag.at
Key Personnel
Contact: Martin Kofler
Founded: 1984
Publishing company for scientific books.
Subjects: Communications, Education, History, Journalism, Language Arts, Linguistics, Literature, Literary Criticism, Essays, Music, Dance, Philosophy, Science (General), Women's Studies
ISBN Prefix(es): 3-901160; 3-7065
Number of titles published annually: 80 Print
Total Titles: 1,000 Print

Verlag Styria+
Imprint of Styria Pichler Verlag GmbH & Co KG
Schoenaugasse 64, 8010 Graz
Tel: (0316) 8063 7601 *Fax:* (0316) 8063 7004
E-mail: office@styriapichler.at
Web Site: www.verlagstyria.com *Cable:* STYRIAVERLAG GRAZ
Key Personnel
Man Dir: Dietmar Sternad *Tel:* (0316) 8063 7001
  E-mail: dietmar.sternad@styriapichler.at
Sales: Isabella Scheuringer *E-mail:* isabella.scheuringer@styriapichler.at

Founded: 1869
Subjects: Biography, Education, History, Journalism, Philosophy, Religion - Other
ISBN Prefix(es): 3-222; 3-7012
Number of titles published annually: 70 Print
Associate Companies: Verlag Corinthion, Volkermarkter Ring 25, 9020 Ulapenfurt
Branch Office(s)
Verlag Styria Koeen, Rodenberg 18, Kuerten-Bechen
Bookshop(s): Buchhandlung Styria, Albrechtgasse 5, 8010 Graz; Buchhandlung und Antiquariat Moser, Herrengasse 23, 8010 Graz

Suedwind - Buchwelt GmbH
Baumgasse 79, 1034 Vienna
Tel: (01) 798 83 49 *Fax:* (01) 798 83 75
E-mail: versand@suedwind.at
Web Site: www.suedwind.at
Key Personnel
Contact: Barbara Hosp
Founded: 1984
Subjects: Government, Political Science, Nonfiction (General)
ISBN Prefix(es): 3-900592
Total Titles: 25 Print

Edition Tau u Tau Type Druck Verlags-und Handels GmbH+
Biriczweg 1, Postfach 19, 7202 Bad Sauerbrunn
Tel: (02625) 32000 *Fax:* (02625) 320003
Key Personnel
Publisher: Erich Greistorfer
Production Dir: Peter Feigl
Contact: Klaus Kopinitsch
Founded: 1988
Subjects: Biography, Nonfiction (General), Religion - Other
ISBN Prefix(es): 3-900977; 3-901997

Thanhaeuser Edition
Wallseerstr 6, 4100 Ottensheim
Mailing Address: Postfach 9, 4100 Ottensheim
Tel: (07234) 83800 *Fax:* (07234) 83800
E-mail: thanhaeuser@bibliotheca-selecta.de
Key Personnel
Contact: Christian Thanhaeuser; Irmgard Thanhaeuser
Founded: 1989
Subjects: Poetry
ISBN Prefix(es): 3-900986
Total Titles: 40 Print

Edition Thurnhof KEG
Wiener Str 2, 3580 Horn
Tel: (02982) 629-54 *Fax:* (02982) 3333
E-mail: edition@thurnhof.at
Web Site: www.thurnhof.at
Key Personnel
Publisher: Toni Kurz *E-mail:* toni.kurz@eunet.at
Founded: 1983
Subjects: Art, Poetry
ISBN Prefix(es): 3-900678
Divisions: Galerie-Thurnhof
Branch Office(s)
Druckerei & Atelier, 3580 Muehlfeld 43

Trauner Verlag
Koeglstr 14, 4021 Linz
Tel: (0732) 77 82 41-212 *Fax:* (0732) 77 82 41-400
E-mail: office@trauner.at
Web Site: www.trauner.at
Key Personnel
Man Dir: Rudolf Trauner
Founded: 1946
Subjects: Cookery, Medicine, Nursing, Dentistry, Science (General)
ISBN Prefix(es): 3-85320

Edition Tusch+
Heigerleinstr 36-40, 1160 Vienna
Tel: (01) 485 40 01 *Fax:* (01) 485 40 01-15
E-mail: citypost@cpz.at
Telex: 116262 Tusch *Cable:* EDITUSCH VIENNA
Key Personnel
Man Dir: Anton Tusch
Editorial: Wolfgang Prager
Founded: 1972
Subjects: Architecture & Interior Design, Art, Ethnicity
ISBN Prefix(es): 3-85063

Tyrolia Verlagsanstalt GmbH
Exlgasse 20, 6020 Innsbruck
Tel: (0512) 2233-510 *Fax:* (0512) 2233-512
E-mail: pgh@tyrolia.at
Web Site: www.tyrolia.at
Telex: 053620 *Cable:* TYROLIA VERLAG INNSBRUCK
Key Personnel
Dir: Dr Schiemer
Founded: 1888
Subjects: Nonfiction (General), Religion - Other, Travel
ISBN Prefix(es): 3-7022
Bookshop(s): Tyrolia, Exlgasse 20, Postfach 220, 6020 Innsbruck

Verlag Carl Ueberreuter, see Annette Betz Verlag im Verlag Carl Ueberreuter

Verlag Carl Ueberreuter GmbH+
Alser Str 24, 1091 Vienna
Mailing Address: Postfach 306, 1091 Vienna
Tel: (01) 40 444-172 *Fax:* (01) 40 444-5
E-mail: office-v@ueberreutes.at
Web Site: www.ueberreuter.de
Key Personnel
Holding: Ing Michael Salzer
Editorial: Britta Groiss; Irmgard Harrer; Gudula Jungeblodt; Dr Alfred Schierer; Thomas Zauner
Production: Maria Schuster
Publicity: Iris Seidenstricker
Sales: Petra Thomsen
Rights & Permissions: Dr Sibylle Goeller
  Tel: (01) 40444173 *E-mail:* goeller@ueberreuter.at
Man Dir: Dr Fritz Panzer
Contact: Monika Reisenbauer *Tel:* (01) 40444-171
  E-mail: reisenbauer@ueberreuter.at
Founded: 1548
Subjects: Animals, Pets, Art, Astrology, Occult, Biography, Economics, Fiction, Government, Political Science, Health, Nutrition, History, Music, Dance, Nonfiction (General), Science (General), Science Fiction, Fantasy
ISBN Prefix(es): 3-220
Number of titles published annually: 140 Print
Total Titles: 800 Print
Imprints: Annette Betz
Subsidiaries: Annette Betz Verlag
Foreign Rights: A C E R; A R T Dialog (Czech Republic); Akcali; Ball & Co; Bettiua & Julia Nibbe; China Consult (China & Taiwan); Ashley Grayson (USA); Hercules (China & Taiwan); Imprima Korea (Korea); Iris; Liu Media (China); Onon L J Pren (Japan); Margit Schaleck; Shing-Shang (Taiwan); Tuttle Mori (Japan)
Shipping Address: BTG Spedition & Logistik GmbH, Neudorfstr 114, 2353 Guntramsdorf
Warehouse: BTG Spedition & Logistik GmbH, Neudorfstr 114, 2353 Guntramsdorf

Universal Edition AG
Karlsplatz 6, 1010 Vienna
Tel: (01) 337 23-0 *Fax:* (01) 337 23-400
E-mail: office@universaledition.com
Web Site: www.universaledition.com *Cable:* MUSIKEDITION VIENNA

PUBLISHERS — AUSTRIA

Key Personnel
Man Dir: Johann Juranek; Marion von Hartlieb
Sales, Marketing & Public Relations: Ferdinand Walcher *E-mail:* walcher@universaledition.com
Founded: 1901
Subjects: Music, Dance
ISBN Prefix(es): 3-7024
Subsidiaries: Urtext Edition-Musikverlag GmbH KG (jointly owned with B Schott's Soehne, Germany)

Urban und Schwarzenberg GmbH
Postfach 102, 1096 Vienna
Tel: (01) 4052731 *Fax:* (01) 405272441
Key Personnel
Manager: Gunter Royer
Founded: 1866
Subjects: Medicine, Nursing, Dentistry, Physics, Psychology, Psychiatry
ISBN Prefix(es): 3-85327
Parent Company: Williams & Wilkins Ltd, 428 East Preston St, Baltimore, MD 21202, United States
Associate Companies: Urban und Schwarzenberg GmbH, Verlag fuer Medizin, Germany

Edition Va Bene+
Max-Kahrer-G 32, 3400 Klosterneuburg
Mailing Address: Reichsratsstr 17, 1010 Vienna
Tel: (02243) 22 159; (0664) 1616356 (mobile) *Fax:* (02243) 22 159
E-mail: edition@vabene.at
Web Site: www.vabene.at
Key Personnel
Owner: Dr Walter Weiss
Founded: 1991
Subjects: Anthropology, Asian Studies, Communications, Developing Countries, Ethnicity, Foreign Countries, Health, Nutrition, Literature, Literary Criticism, Essays, Philosophy, Physical Sciences, Poetry, Religion - Catholic, Romance, Science (General), Theology, Travel
ISBN Prefix(es): 3-85167
Total Titles: 160 Print
Warehouse: Dr Franz Hain, Dr Otto Neurath-Gasse 5, 1220 Vienna *Tel:* (01) 28265650 *Fax:* (01) 2825282

Verband der Wissenschaftlichen Gesellschaften Oesterreichs (VWGOe)
Lindengasse 37, 1070 Vienna
Tel: (01) 932166; (01) 934756 *Fax:* (01) 5262054
Key Personnel
Man Dir: Dr Rainer Zitta
Founded: 1954
Subjects: Archaeology, Business, Education, History, Mathematics, Music, Dance, Philosophy, Physical Sciences
ISBN Prefix(es): 3-85369

Verein Gruppe Wespennest, *imprint of* Wespennest - Zeitschrift fuer brauchbare Texte und Bilder

Verlag Veritas Mediengesellschaft mbH+
Hafenstr 1-3, 4020 Linz
Tel: (0732) 776451; (0732) 776450 *Fax:* (0732) 776451-283
Key Personnel
Man Dir: Christl Manfred
Chief Editor: M Griessner *Tel:* (0732) 776451732 *E-mail:* mgriessner@veritas.co.at
Sales & Publicity: Meraner Manfred
Founded: 1945
Subjects: Cookery, Education, Health, Nutrition, Outdoor Recreation, Regional Interests
ISBN Prefix(es): 3-85329; 3-7058; 3-85214
Total Titles: 450 Print; 5 CD-ROM; 20 Audio
Parent Company: Cornelsen, Germany
Subsidiaries: Ehrenwirth Verlag; Salzburger Jugend-Verlag

Bookshop(s): Buchhandlung Veritas, Harrachstr 5, 4020 Linz
Warehouse: Wertpraesent, Boschstr 31, 4600 Weis
Tel: (7242) 696-0

Verlag Anton Schroll & Co+
Spengergasse 37, 1051 Vienna
Tel: (01) 5445641-46 *Fax:* (01) 544564166
E-mail: prepress@agens-werk.at *Cable:* Schrollverlag Vienna
Key Personnel
Man Dir: Friedrich Geyer
Founded: 1884
Subjects: Art, History, Travel
ISBN Prefix(es): 3-7031
Branch Office(s)
Anton Schroll & Co GmbH, Germany

Verlag Wilhelm Braumuller Universitats-Verlagsbuchhandlung GmbH
Servitengasse 5, 1092 Vienna
Tel: (01) 319 11 59 *Fax:* (01) 310 28 05
E-mail: office@braumueller.at
Web Site: www.braumueller.at
ISBN Prefix(es): 3-7003

Vorarlberger Verlagsanstalt Aktiengesellschaft
Schwefel 81, 6850 Dornbirn
Tel: (05572) 24 6 97-0 *Fax:* (05572) 24 6 97-78
E-mail: office@vva.at
Web Site: www.vva.at
Key Personnel
Contact: Karl-Heinz Milz *E-mail:* kh.milz@vva.at; Marlene Sutter
Founded: 1920
Subjects: Geography, Geology, History, Regional Interests
ISBN Prefix(es): 3-85430

VWGOe, see Verband der Wissenschaftlichen Gesellschaften Oesterreichs (VWGOe)

Universitaetsverlag Wagner GmbH
Andreas-Hoferstr 13, 6010 Innsbruck
Mailing Address: Postfach 165, 6010 Innsbruck
Tel: (0512) 597721 *Fax:* (0512) 582209
E-mail: mail@uvw.at
Cable: UNIVERSITAETSVERLAG WAGNER INNSBRUCK
Key Personnel
Man Dir: Gottfried Grasl
Contact: Dr Blaas Mercedes *E-mail:* mercedes.blaas@uvw.at
Founded: 1554
Subjects: Archaeology, Automotive, Geography, Geology, History, Language Arts, Linguistics, Science (General)
ISBN Prefix(es): 3-7030

Verlag Mag Wanzenbock+
Landstrasser Hauptstr 88/6, 1030 Vienna
Tel: (01) 7148542 *Fax:* (01) 7135814
Key Personnel
Dir: Hans Wanzenbock *E-mail:* johann.wanzenboeck@chello.at
Founded: 1990
Subjects: English as a Second Language
ISBN Prefix(es): 3-901682
Number of titles published annually: 2 Print
Total Titles: 1 Print
Orders to: Oebz, Iz Noe Sued Str 1, OBJ 34, 2355 Wiener Neudorf, Contact: Mrs Prinz *Tel:* (02263) 63535 *Fax:* (02263) 63535243

Waren-Erzeugungs-und Handelsgesellschaft GmbH, see Fremdenverkehrs Aktiengessellschaft

Weilburg Verlag
Fleschgasse 34, 1130 Vienna

Tel: (02622) 29538 *Fax:* (02622) 2953822
Key Personnel
Owner & Man Dir: Helmut Dresel
Sales: Selbst Liefert
Subjects: Art, Poetry
ISBN Prefix(es): 3-900100; 3-85246

Dr Otfried Weise Verlag Tabula Smaragdina+
Anton-Langer-Gasse 46/2/5, 1130 Vienna
Tel: (01) 804 2974 *Fax:* (01) 961 8287
E-mail: tabula@smaragdina.at
Web Site: smaragdina.at
Key Personnel
Man Dir: Otfried Weise
Founded: 1991
Subjects: Astrology, Occult, Health, Nutrition, Nonfiction (General)
ISBN Prefix(es): 3-9802471; 3-931138

Herbert Weishaupt Verlag+
Hauptplatz 27, 8342 Gnas
Tel: (03151) 8487 *Fax:* (03151) 84874
E-mail: verlag@weishaupt.at
Web Site: www.weishaupt.at
Key Personnel
Contact: Herbert Weishaupt; Annemarie Weishaupt
Founded: 1980
Subjects: Aeronautics, Aviation, Maritime, Military Science, Natural History, Nonfiction (General), Regional Interests, Travel
ISBN Prefix(es): 3-7059; 3-900310
Number of titles published annually: 35 Print; 1 CD-ROM; 1 Audio
Total Titles: 320 Print

Verlag Welsermuehl+
Maria-Theresiastr 41, 4600 Wels
Tel: (07242) 231-0 *Fax:* (07242) 23118
Telex: 25586 *Cable:* WELSERMUHLDRUCK WELS
Key Personnel
Dir: Karl Pramendorfer
Founded: 1928
ISBN Prefix(es): 3-85339
Branch Office(s)
Kufsteinerstr 8, 81679 Munich, Germany

Verlag Galerie Welz Salzburg
Sigmund-Haffner Gasse 16, 5020 Salzburg
Tel: (0662) 841771; (0662) 840990 *Fax:* (0662) 84177120
E-mail: office@galerie-welz.at
Web Site: www.galerie-welz.at
Key Personnel
Publisher: Franz Eder
Sales: Hannes Lueftenegger
Subjects: Art
ISBN Prefix(es): 3-85349

Wespennest - Zeitschrift fuer brauchbare Texte und Bilder+
Rembrandtstr 31/4, 1020 Vienna
Tel: (01) 332 66 91 *Fax:* (01) 333 29 70
E-mail: office@wespennest.at
Web Site: www.wespennest.at
Key Personnel
Managing Editor: Walter Famler
Contact: Friederike Schwabel
Founded: 1969
Literary essayistic cultural magazine, quarterly publication.
Subjects: Literature, Literary Criticism, Essays
ISBN Prefix(es): 3-85458
Imprints: Verein Gruppe Wespennest
Distributed by Deutsche Verlagsanstalt

Wiener Dom-Verlag GmbH
Spiegelgasse 3/D, 1014 Vienna
Mailing Address: Postfach 152, 1014 Vienna
Tel: (01) 5123503 *Fax:* (01) 5123503-30

AUSTRIA

Web Site: www.buchwirtschaft.at
Telex: 111760
Key Personnel
Man Dir: Franz Pollhammer
  E-mail: pollhammer@domverlag.at
Founded: 1946
Subjects: Religion - Catholic
ISBN Prefix(es): 3-85351
Divisions: Kunsthandlung
Bookshop(s): Rathausplatz 10, 3390 Melk; Bahnstr 1, 2130 Mistelbach; Stephansplatz 5, 1010 Vienna; Favoritenstr 115, 1100 Vienna; Domgasse 3, 2700 Wiener Neustadt

Wienerland Zeitung & Verlag
Formerly Osterreichischer Alpenverein Sektion Weiner Lehrer
Pammessergasse 13, 2103 Langenzersdorf
Mailing Address: Postfach 33, 2103 Langenzersdorf
Tel: (02244) 3536 *Fax:* (02244) 3536-4
E-mail: wienerland@asn.or.at
Telex: 75211689 avw a
Key Personnel
Contact: Peterka Fritz
Founded: 1973
Subjects: Travel
ISBN Prefix(es): 3-900451

Wieser Verlag+
Ebentaler Str 34b, 9020 Klagenfurt/Celovec
Tel: (0463) 37036 *Fax:* (0463) 37635
E-mail: office@wieser-verlag.com
Web Site: www.wieser-verlag.com
Key Personnel
Publisher: Lojze Wieser
Founded: 1987
Subjects: Biography, Drama, Theater, Fiction, Government, Political Science, Literature, Literary Criticism, Essays, Poetry
ISBN Prefix(es): 3-85129

Kunstverlag Wolfrum
Augustinerstr 10, 1010 Vienna
Tel: (01) 512 53 98-0 *Fax:* (01) 512 53 98-57
E-mail: your-welcome@wolfrum.at
Web Site: www.wolfrum.at/html/wolfrum.htm
Telex: 75311081 Wolb *Cable:* WITWOLF VIENNA
Key Personnel
Man Dir: Monika Engel
Founded: 1919
Subjects: Art
ISBN Prefix(es): 3-900178

WUV/Facultas Universitaetsverlag
Mountain Lane 5, 1090 Vienna
Tel: (01) 310 53 56 *Fax:* (01) 319 70 50
E-mail: verlage@facultas.at
Web Site: www.wuv-verlag.at
Telex: 116529 Icpfa
Key Personnel
Manager: Thomas Stauffer *E-mail:* stauffer@facultas.at
Marketing: Christine Bernert *E-mail:* bernert@facultas.at
Publisher: Dr Michael Huter *E-mail:* huter@facultas.at
Editor: Dr Sigrid Neulinger *E-mail:* neulinger@facultas.at
Founded: 1962
Subjects: Art, Behavioral Sciences, Communications, History, Language Arts, Linguistics, Law, Medicine, Nursing, Dentistry, Nonfiction (General), Philosophy, Psychology, Psychiatry, Science (General), Social Sciences, Sociology, Women's Studies, Specialize in scientific literature
ISBN Prefix(es): 3-85076; 3-85114
Associate Companies: Facultas Universitaetsverlag

WUV/Service Fachverlag+
Berggasse 5, 1090 Vienna
Tel: (01) 310 53 56 *Fax:* (01) 319 70 50
E-mail: verlag@facultas.at
Web Site: www.wuv-verlag.at/WUV
Telex: 135720 hwusv
Key Personnel
Publishing Dir: Dr Christin Draexler
Founded: 1981
Subjects: Accounting, Business, Career Development, Economics, Finance, Law, Management, Marketing
ISBN Prefix(es): 3-85428
Bookshop(s): Universitat Buchhandlung, Doblinger Hauptstr 7A/12, 1190 Vienna
Orders to: Augasse 2-6, 1090 Vienna
  Tel: (01) 317 91 62 *Fax:* (01) 317 91 62-45
  E-mail: wuv-buchhandlung@facultas.at

Zirkular - Verlag der Dokumentationsstelle fuer neuere oesterreichische Literatur
Silk Lane 13, 1070 Vienna
Tel: (01) 526 20 44-0 *Fax:* (01) 526 20 44-30
E-mail: info@literaturhaus.at
Web Site: www.literaturhaus.at
Key Personnel
Founder: Dr Heinz Lunzer *Tel:* (01) 526 20 44-17
  E-mail: hl@literaturhaus.at
President: Dr Uwe Baur
Founded: 1979
Subjects: Biography, Literature, Literary Criticism, Essays
ISBN Prefix(es): 3-900467

Paul Zsolnay Verlag GmbH+
Prinz-Eugenstr 30, 1040 Vienna
Mailing Address: Postfach 142, 1040 Vienna
Tel: (01) 50576610 *Fax:* (01) 505766110
E-mail: info@zsolnay.at
Web Site: www.zsolnay.at *Cable:* ZSOLNAYVERLAG WIEN
Key Personnel
Man Dir: Stephan Joss; Michael Krueger
Rights & Permissions: Annette Lechner
Sales Manager: Felicitas Feilhauer
Editorial Dir: Herbert Ohrlinger
Production: Stefanie Schelleis
Contact: Bettina Woergoetter *Tel:* (01) 5057661-14
Founded: 1923
Subjects: Biography, Fiction, History, Nonfiction (General), Poetry
ISBN Prefix(es): 3-552; 3-223; 3-85190
Number of titles published annually: 40 Print
Total Titles: 500 Print
Parent Company: Carl Hanser GmbH & Co, Vilshofenerstr 10, 81679 Munich, Germany
Orders to: Dr Franz Hain, Dr Otto-Neurath-Gasse 5, 1220 Vienna *Tel:* (01) 2826565 *Fax:* (01) 2825282
Verlegerdienst Muenchen, Gutenbergstr 1, 82205 Gilching, Germany, Contact: Evelyne Weindl *Tel:* (08105) 388-122 *Fax:* (08105) 388-100
E-mail: weindl@verlegerdienst.de

Azerbaijan

General Information
Capital: Baku
Language: Azerbaijani
Religion: Predominantly Muslim (Shiite and Sunni); also Christian (mainly Russian Orthodox & Armenian Apostolic)
Population: 7.5 million
Bank Hours: Generally open for short hours between 0930-1230 Monday-Friday

Shop Hours: Generally 0900-1800 Monday-Friday; often open weekends
Currency: 1 kopeks = 1 rubl
Export/Import Information: According to Ukrainian quotas & customs duties, companies engaged in trade should register with the Ukraine Ministry of Foreign Economic Relations. Licenses for export & import are also required for trade with Russia.
Copyright: UCC (see Copyright Conventions, pg xi)

Azernesr
Gusi Gadzieva 4, 370005 Baku
Tel: (012) 925015
Key Personnel
Dir: A Mustafazade
Editor-in-Chief: A Guseinzade
Founded: 1924
Subjects: Agriculture, Fiction, Government, Political Science, Science (General), Technology
ISBN Prefix(es): 5-552

Sada, Literaturno-Izdatel'skij Centr+
Ul Bol'saja Krepostnaja, 28, 370004 Baku
Tel: (012) 927564 *Fax:* (012) 929843
Key Personnel
Contact: Guliev Tarlan
Subjects: Accounting, Asian Studies, Astrology, Occult, Business, Child Care & Development, Disability, Special Needs, Drama, Theater, Earth Sciences, Economics, Education, English as a Second Language, Finance, History, Humor, Language Arts, Linguistics, Management, Marketing, Music, Dance, Mysteries, Natural History
ISBN Prefix(es): 5-86874
Parent Company: National Peace Fund

Bahrain

General Information
Capital: Manama
Language: Arabic (English also widely spoken)
Religion: Muslims of the Shiite & Sunni sects
Population: 551,000
Bank Hours: 0730-1200 Saturday-Wednesday; 0730-1100 Thursday
Currency: 1000 Fils = 1 Bahrain dinar
Export/Import Information: Generally books dutied at 10%, most schoolbooks free of duty; none on advertising matter. No import license required but no obscene literature permitted & for books (not for advertising) a Chamber of Commerce certificate is mandatory. No exchange controls.

Arab Communicators
PO Box 551, Manama
Tel: (0973) 254 258 *Fax:* (0973) 531 837
Key Personnel
Publisher & Editor-in-Chief: Ahmed A Fakhri
Publisher: Hamed A Abul
Founded: 1981
Parent Company: ArabConsult
Subsidiaries: Arabvision; Arabad

Al Hilal Publications
Government Ave, Manama
Mailing Address: PO Box 224, Manama
Tel: 231122
Telex: 8981 Hilal
Key Personnel
Contact: Mr Silveira Haydn
Bookshop(s): Al Hilal Bookshop

Bangladesh

General Information

Capital: Dhaka
Language: Bengali (English widely used commercially)
Religion: Predominately Muslim with some Hindu
Population: 129.2 million
Bank Hours: 0900-330 Saturday-Wednesday; 0900-1100 Thursday
Shop Hours: 1000-2030 Saturday-Thursday
Currency: 100 pisha = 1 taka (Tk)
Export/Import Information: No tariff on books and advertising matter. Import licenses required for all imports.
Copyright: UCC (see Copyright Conventions, pg xi)

Academic Publishers+
2/7 Nawab-Habibullah Rd, Dhaka 1000
Tel: (02) 507355; (02) 507366 *Fax:* (02) 863060
Key Personnel
Joint Man Dir: Habibur Rahman
Founded: 1982
Subjects: Social Sciences, Sociology
ISBN Prefix(es): 984-08

Adeyle Brothers & Co
60 Patuatuly, Dhaka 1100
Tel: (02) 233508
ISBN Prefix(es): 984-402

Ankur Prakashani+
38/4 Bangla Bazar, Dhaka 1100
Tel: (02) 250132 *Fax:* (02) 9567730
E-mail: ankur@bangla.net
Founded: 1986
Also acts as a library supplier & importer of reference books.
Subjects: Anthropology, Asian Studies, Economics, Education, Fiction, Government, Political Science, Literature, Literary Criticism, Essays, Nonfiction (General)
ISBN Prefix(es): 984-464; 984-8010
Distributor for Narosa (India); Prints India
Orders to: 40/1 Purana Paltan, Dhaka 1000

Bangladesh Government Press, Ministry of Establishment, Government of the Peoples Republic of Bangladesh
Tejgaon, Dhaka 1209
Tel: (02) 606 316 *Fax:* (02) 8113095
E-mail: adab@bdonline.com
ISBN Prefix(es): 984-01

Bangladesh Publishers+
45 Patuatuli Rd, Dhaka 1100
Tel: (02) 233135
Key Personnel
Dir: Maya Rani Ghosal
Founded: 1952
Membership(s): Book Sellers & Publication Association of Bangladesh, Pranab Math (a philanthropic organization that helps in free education). Also acts as distributor of books & periodicals of both local & foreign countries.
Subjects: Accounting, Drama, Theater, Economics, Physics, Public Administration, Religion - Hindu
ISBN Prefix(es): 984-8012
Associate Companies: Ratan & Sons
Bookshop(s): 38/19/B Banglabazar, 2nd floor, Dhaka 1100

Boighar
110-286 Bipani Bitan, Chittagong
Tel: (031) 252745
ISBN Prefix(es): 984-423

Chalantika
14 Banglabazar, 1st floor, Dhaka 1100
Tel: (02) 257345 *Fax:* (02) 7115691
ISBN Prefix(es): 984-8019

Gatidhara+
38/2-ka Banglabazar, Dhaka 1100
Tel: (02) 7392077 (press); (02) 7113117 (res); (02) 7115630 (res); (02) 7117515 (showroom); (02) 7118273 (showroom) *Fax:* (02) 9134617; (02) 9566456
E-mail: akter@aitlbd.net; gatidara@bdonline.com
Key Personnel
Publisher & Chief Executive: Sikder Abul Bashar
Founded: 1988
Also acts as distributor & exporter.
Membership(s): Publishers Association; Publishers Guild.
Subjects: Behavioral Sciences, Child Care & Development, Drama, Theater, Education, Fiction, Health, Nutrition, Humor, Literature, Literary Criticism, Essays, Poetry, Religion - Islamic
ISBN Prefix(es): 984-461
Subsidiaries: Gatidhara Computers
Bookshop(s): 38/2 Banglabazar, Dhaka 1100
Book Club(s): National Book Center; National Library
Warehouse: Kumarpatty Rd, Jhalakati 8400
Orders to: 38/4 Banglabazar, Dhaka 1100

Gono Prakashani, Gono Shasthya Kendra+
14/E Dhanmondhi R/A, Dhaka 1205
Tel: (02) 500406; (02) 839366 *Fax:* (02) 863567; (02) 833182
E-mail: gk.mail@drik.bgd.toolnet.org *Cable:* GRAM GORO, DHAKA
Key Personnel
Man Dir: Mr Shafio Khan
Editor: Mr Bazlur Rahim
Chairman & President Editorial Board: Dr Zafrullah Chowdhury
Founded: 1978
Subjects: Child Care & Development, Health, Nutrition, Medicine, Nursing, Dentistry, Self-Help, Social Sciences, Sociology
ISBN Prefix(es): 984-431
Parent Company: Gonoshasthaya Kendra Trust
Associate Companies: Gonoshasthaya Pharmaceutical, Ltd; Gonoshasthaya Antibiotic Ltd
Subsidiaries: Gono Mudran (printing company)
Distributed by Baulman Prakason (Kolkata, India)
Showroom(s): Gono Prakashani Aziz Cooperative Market Shahbagh, Dhaka
Bookshop(s): Gono Prakashani Aziz Cooperative Market Shahbagh, Dhaka
Shipping Address: Gono Prakashani Po Mirzanaga, Nayarhat, 1344 Dhaka
Warehouse: Gono Prakashani Po Mirzanagar, Nayarhat, Dhaka 1344
Orders to: Gono Prakashani Po Mirzanagar, Nayarhat, Dhaka 1344

Mullick Bros
3/1 Bangla Bazar, Dhaka 1100
Tel: (02) 280728
Subjects: Education
ISBN Prefix(es): 984-411; 984-8272

Agamee Prakashani+
36 Banglabazar, Dhaka 1100
Tel: (02) 711-1332; (02) 711-0021 *Fax:* (02) 9562018; (02) 7123945
E-mail: agamee@bdonline.com
Web Site: www.agameeprakashani-bd.com *Cable:* AGAMEE
Key Personnel
Chief Executive Officer: Osman Gani *Tel:* (02) 189219024 *Fax:* (02) 9340856 *E-mail:* bfdr@bdonline.com
Founded: 1986
Membership(s): Bangladesh Publishers & Book Sellers Association; Dhaka Chamber of Commerce & Industry; FBCCI; Bangladesh Publishers Council.
Subjects: Fiction, Government, Political Science, Journalism, Literature, Literary Criticism, Essays, Music, Dance, Philosophy, Poetry, Science (General), Social Sciences, Sociology, Women's Studies
ISBN Prefix(es): 984-401
Number of titles published annually: 70 Print
Total Titles: 802 Print
Distributed by Phuthipatra (Kalkata)
Distributor for Muktadhara (USA)
Book Club(s): Bangladesh Book Club (Bangladesh)

The University Press Ltd+
Red Crescent Bldg, 114 Motijheel C/A, Dhaka 1000
Mailing Address: GPO Box 2611, Dhaka 1000
Tel: (02) 861208; (02) 255789 *Fax:* (02) 8332112
E-mail: upl@bangla.net; upl@bttb.net.bd
Telex: 642460 bhlbj *Cable:* DUNIPRESS
Key Personnel
Man Dir & Publisher: Mr Mohiuddin Ahmed
Senior Manager Editorial: Badiuddin Nazir
Sales Manager: M A Halim
Production Executive: Abdar Rahman
Founded: 1975
Specializes in publishing, selling & importing.
Subjects: Agriculture, Anthropology, Archaeology, Architecture & Interior Design, Art, Biography, Economics, Education, Environmental Studies, Finance, Geography, Geology, Government, Political Science, History, Management, Military Science, Public Administration, Publishing & Book Trade Reference, Religion - Islamic, Technology, Travel, Women's Studies
ISBN Prefix(es): 984-05
Number of titles published annually: 70 Print
Total Titles: 500 Print
Branch Office(s)
146 Dampara, Chittagong & 86 K D Ghose Rd, Khulna
Distributed by Intermediate Technology (UK); Manohar Publishers & Distributors (New Delhi, India); Oxford University Press (Pakistan); Paragon Enterprise (India); ZED Books (UK)
Distributor for Intermediate Technology (UK); Manohar Publishers & Distributors (India); Oxford University Press (UK, Pakistan & India); ZED Books (UK)
Distribution Center: Government New Market, Gulshan, Banani, Hotel Sonargaon, Zia International Airport, Dhaka

Barbados

General Information

Capital: Bridgetown
Language: English
Religion: Anglican
Population: 263,000
Bank Hours: 0800-1500 Monday-Thursday; 0800-1750 Friday
Shop Hours: 0800-1600 Monday-Friday; 0800-1200 Saturday
Currency: 100 cents = 1 Barbados dollar
Export/Import Information: No tariff on books. Import license covering exchange required; no obscene literature permitted.
Copyright: Berne, UCC (see Copyright Conventions, pg xi)

Business Tutors
124 Chancery Lane, Christ Church
Tel: (246) 428-5664 *Fax:* (246) 429-4854
E-mail: pchad@caribsurf.com
Subjects: Astrology, Occult, Business, Disability, Special Needs, Management, Microcomputers, Self-Help
ISBN Prefix(es): 976-8084
Subsidiaries: P & R Chad Ltd

Carib Research & Publications Inc
PO Box 556, Bridgetown
Tel: 438-0580
Key Personnel
Chief Executive: Dr Farley Brathwaite
Founded: 1986
Also acts as agent for Antilles Publications.
Subjects: Regional Interests
ISBN Prefix(es): 976-8051
Associate Companies: Antilles Publications

Belarus

General Information

Capital: Minsk
Language: Belarussian
Religion: Predominantly Christian (mostly Roman Catholic & Eastern Orthodox)
Population: 10.4 million
Bank Hours: Generally open for short hours between 0930-1230 Monday-Friday
Shop Hours: Generally 0900-1800 Monday-Friday; often open weekends
Currency: 100 kopeks = 1 rubl
Export/Import Information: According to Ukrainian quotas & customs duties, companies engaged in trade should register with the Ukraine Ministry of Foreign Economic Relations. Licenses for export & import are also required for trade with Russia.
Copyright: UCC (see Copyright Conventions, pg xi)

Belarus (The Belorussia)
Prospect Maserova, 11, 220600 Minsk
Tel: (0172) 238742 *Fax:* (0172) 238731
Key Personnel
Dir: V L Dubovsky
Editor-in-Chief: L N Teterina
Founded: 1921
Subjects: Art, Economics, Government, Political Science, Medicine, Nursing, Dentistry, Music, Dance
ISBN Prefix(es): 5-338; 985-01

Belaruskaya Encyklapedyya (Byelossian Encyclopaedia)
vul Akademichnaya, 15A, 220072 Minsk
Tel: 2840600; 2841767 *Fax:* 2840983
Key Personnel
Editor-in-Chief: Genadz P Pashkou
Founded: 1967
Subjects: Agriculture, Archaeology, Architecture & Interior Design, Art, Biography, Biological Sciences, Cookery, Crafts, Games, Hobbies, Drama, Theater, Education, Fiction, Finance, Health, Nutrition, History, House & Home, Language Arts, Linguistics, Law, Literature, Literary Criticism, Essays, Mathematics, Medicine, Nursing, Dentistry, Natural History, Parapsychology, Photography, Physics, Poetry, Religion - Other, Science (General), Sports, Athletics
ISBN Prefix(es): 5-85700; 985-11

Interdigest Publishing House+
vul Zaharava 24, k 20, 220005 Minsk
Mailing Address: 24 Zakharov Ave, Off 20, 172, 220005 Minsk
Tel: 331888; 333418 *Fax:* 133073; 333180
Key Personnel
President: Anatoli Kudrjavtsev
Vice President: Vladimir Sivchik
Founded: 1991
Subjects: Animals, Pets, Automotive, Biography, Career Development, Child Care & Development, Criminology, Fiction, Health, Nutrition, Music, Dance, Nonfiction (General), Women's Studies
ISBN Prefix(es): 985-10
Total Titles: 25,000 Print
Associate Companies: TOO Echo, Smolensk, Russian Federation; Digest & Kolm, Kaliningrad, Russian Federation
Distributed by TOO Echo (Smolensk, Russia)
Distributor for TOO Echo (Smolensk, Russia)
Showroom(s): 34, Skaryna Ave, Off 25, 220005 Minsk
Bookshop(s): 124, Partizanski Prospect, Minsk
Shipping Address: 3, Ingenernaja, Minsk
Warehouse: 3, Ingenernaja, Minsk

Kavaler Publishers+
7 Ignatenko St, 220035 Minsk
Tel: (0172) 2506485; (0172) 548198 *Fax:* (0172) 238041
E-mail: Kavaler@inbox.ru
Key Personnel
Dir & Publisher: Constantine Khotyanovsky
Deputy Dir: Svetlana Morozova
Founded: 1991
All editions are prize winners of the annual national contests *Art of the Book*.
Membership(s): Belarusian Association of Book Publishers & Book Distributors; Belarusian Union of Artists.
Subjects: Advertising, Business, English as a Second Language, Fiction, History, Nonfiction (General), Poetry, Wine & Spirits, German as a Second Language
ISBN Prefix(es): 985-6427
Number of titles published annually: 8 Print
Total Titles: 70 Print
Book Club(s): Minsk Book Exhibition-Sale Club Belakk

Izdatelstvo Mastatskaya Litaratura
Maserava prospect 11, 220600 Minsk
Tel: (0172) 236131 *Fax:* (0172) 269112; (0172) 236184
Key Personnel
Dir: S A Andreyuk
Editor-in-Chief: N S Kusenkov
Founded: 1972
Subjects: Fiction, Literature, Literary Criticism, Essays
ISBN Prefix(es): 5-340; 985-02

Narodnaya Asveta+
prasp Malerava 11, 220600 Minsk
Tel: 2236131 *Fax:* 2236184
E-mail: ngpna@asveta.belpak.minsk.by
Key Personnel
Dir: I Laptenok
Founded: 1951
Subjects: Biological Sciences, Economics, Environmental Studies, Geography, Geology, History, Mathematics
ISBN Prefix(es): 5-341; 985-03; 985-12

Publishing Center of Belarus State University+
Division of BSU
Krasnoarmejskaja 6, Minsk
Tel: (0172) 227 18 08 *Fax:* (0172) 226 01 75
E-mail: pubcentre@org.bsu.unibee.by
Key Personnel
Dir: Alexandre Nechaj
Founded: 1997
Subjects: Computer Science, Education, Law, Mathematics, Physics, Science (General)
Total Titles: 20 Print
Parent Company: BSU

Belgium

General Information

Capital: Brussels
Language: Dutch in the north, French in the south. Brussels is officially bilingual. German in eastern Belgium
Religion: Predominantly Roman Catholic, some Protestant
Population: 10.2 million
Bank Hours: Main towns: 0900-1200/1300 & 1400-1530/1600: Monday-Friday
Shop Hours: 0900-1900 with variations
Currency: 100 Eurocents = 1 Euro; 40.3399 Belgian francs = 1 Euro
Export/Import Information: Member of the European Economic Community. No import license required, just Model A form of notice declaration of payment. No exchange controls. 6% VAT on books.
Copyright: UCC, Berne, Florence (see Copyright Conventions, pg xi)

Abimo+
Beukenlaan 8, 9250 Waasmunster
Tel: (052) 462407 *Fax:* (052) 461962
E-mail: info@abimo-uitgeverij.com
Web Site: www.abimo-uitgeverij.com
Key Personnel
Publisher: K David *E-mail:* k.david@planetinternet.be
Founded: 1993
Membership(s): Vlaamse Uitgevers Vereniging.
Subjects: Drama, Theater, Earth Sciences, Education, Foreign Countries, Specialize in Geography
ISBN Prefix(es): 90-75905; 90-801767; 90-5932

Academia-Bruylant+
Subsidiary of Bruylant
Grand'Place 29, 1348 Louvain-la-Neuve
Tel: (010) 45 23 95 *Fax:* (010) 45 44 80
E-mail: academia.bruylant@skynet.be
Web Site: www.academia-bruylant.be
Key Personnel
President: Jean Vandeveld
Founded: 1987
Membership(s): ADEB.
Subjects: Accounting, Anthropology, Journalism, Law, Physical Sciences, Religion - Islamic, Social Sciences, Sociology
ISBN Prefix(es): 2-87209
Total Titles: 500 Print

Academia Press+
Eekhout 2, 9000 Ghent
Tel: (09) 233.80.88 *Fax:* (09) 233.14.09
E-mail: info@academiapress.be
Web Site: www.academiapress.be
Key Personnel
International Rights: Peter Laroy
Founded: 1989
Scientific Publishers.
Subjects: Business, Economics, Journalism, Psychology, Psychiatry, Science (General), Social Sciences, Sociology
ISBN Prefix(es): 90-382
Parent Company: J Story-Scientia Scientia bvba, Van Duyseplein 8, 9000 Ghent

Uitgeverij Acco
Brusselstr 153, 3000 Leuven

Tel: (016) 62 80 41 *Fax:* (016) 62 80 01
E-mail: uitgeverij@acco.be
Web Site: www.acco.be
Key Personnel
Dir: Herman Peeters *Tel:* (016) 62 80 10
  E-mail: herman.peeters@acco.be
Founded: 1960
Subjects: Criminology, Economics, Education, History, Language Arts, Linguistics, Law, Mathematics, Medicine, Nursing, Dentistry, Philosophy, Psychology, Psychiatry, Religion - Other, Science (General), Social Sciences, Sociology
ISBN Prefix(es): 90-334
Imprints: De Horstink
Subsidiaries: Acco; Broadcast Book Services (UK & Ireland)
Orders to: Tiensestr 134-136, 3000 Leuven

Actualquarto+
Allee des Bouleaux, 20, 6280 Gerpinnes
Tel: (071) 21 61 53 *Fax:* (071) 21 77 13
Key Personnel
Man Dir & Sales, Rights & Permission: Michel Paunet
Editorial: Jean Delahaut
Founded: 1970
Subjects: Education

Centre Aequatoria
Stationsstraat 48, 3360 Lovenjoel
Tel: (016) 46 44 84
E-mail: info@abbol.com
Web Site: www.aequatoria.be; www.abbol.com
Key Personnel
Dir: Honore Vinck *E-mail:* vinck.aequatoria@skynet.be
Documentaliste: Guillaume Essalo
Founded: 1980
Promotes research on Central African humanities preference for Central African authors.
Subjects: Anthropology, Biography, Ethnicity, History, Language Arts, Linguistics, Regional Interests, Social Sciences, Sociology
Branch Office(s)
BP 276, Mbandaka, Congo
U.S. Office(s): The Missionaries of the S Heart (Aequatoria), 305 S Lake St, PO Box 270, Aurora, IL 60507, United States *Fax:* 630-892-3071 *E-mail:* mscusafin@ibm.net (only for payments of subscriptions to Annales Aequatoria)
Distributed by Editions St Paul (Zaire)

Alamire vzw, Music Publishers+
Division of Musica VZW
Toekomstlaan 5B, 3910 Neerpelt
Tel: (011) 610 510 *Fax:* (011) 610 511
E-mail: info@alamire.com
Web Site: www.alamire.com
Key Personnel
Dir: Herman Baeten *E-mail:* herman.baeten@alamire.com
Marketing: Annelies Van Boxel *E-mail:* annelies.vanboxel@alamire.com
Founded: 1978
Specialize in early music facsimiles.
Subjects: Library & Information Sciences, Music, Dance
ISBN Prefix(es): 90-6853

Altina+
Dirk Lippens Vredestraat 34, 8400 Ostende
Tel: (059) 80-16-51 *Fax:* (059) 51-27-17
Key Personnel
President & International Rights: Dirk Lippens *Tel:* (059) 703324
Author: Christiane Beerlandt *Tel:* (059) 70 3324
Administration: Davina Doom *Tel:* (059) 80 1651
Founded: 1996
Publish works of Belgian author Christiane Beerlandt

Audio.
Subjects: Alternative, Astrology, Occult, Health, Nutrition, Music, Dance, Nonfiction (General), Philosophy, Psychology, Psychiatry, Self-Help, Philosophy of Joyful Life, Original Fairy Tales, Psychological Causes for Disease, Self Knowledge & realization, Physical Immortality, Health & Nutrition
ISBN Prefix(es): 90-75849
Number of titles published annually: 10 Print; 1 Audio
Total Titles: 25 Print; 3 Audio

Amnesty International VZW
Kerkstraat 156, 2060 Antwerp
Tel: (03) 271 16 16 *Fax:* (03) 235 78 12
E-mail: amnesty@aivl.be
Web Site: www.aivl.be
Telex: 32079
Key Personnel
Dir: Jane Brocatus *E-mail:* janb@aivl.be
Contact: Katrien Scholiers *E-mail:* promotie@aivl.be
ISBN Prefix(es): 90-70895

Libraire Ancienne Noel Anselot
18 rue de Transinne, 6890 Redu
Tel: (061) 656091 *Fax:* (061) 656091
Key Personnel
Man Dir: Andre de Rache
Founded: 1954
Subjects: Art, Biography, Poetry
ISBN Prefix(es): 2-8015

Artel
2 Place Baudouin-ler, 5004 Namur, Bouge
Tel: (081) 21 37 00 *Fax:* (081) 21 23 72
E-mail: erasme@skynet.be
Key Personnel
General Manager: Joseph Ponet
Editorial Dir: Francoise Dury
Subjects: Biological Sciences, Environmental Studies, Government, Political Science, History, Mathematics, Religion - Catholic, Social Sciences, Sociology, Theology
ISBN Prefix(es): 2-87374
Parent Company: Editions Erasme SA
Divisions: Ciaco editeur
Distributed by GM Diffusion (Switzerland); Liber-T (Canada); Presses de Belgique
Distributor for Bit-IIo; Feuilles familales

NV Artis-Historia+
One rue Carli, 1140 Brussels 1
Tel: (02) 2409200 *Fax:* (02) 2480818
E-mail: info@artis-historia.be
Web Site: www.artis-historia.be
Key Personnel
Chief Executive, Editing & Marketing Dir: Christian Kremer
Founded: 1948 (Companies merged to form Artis-Historia in 1976)
Subjects: Art, Cookery, Crafts, Games, Hobbies, Geography, Geology, History, Music, Dance, Natural History, Travel
ISBN Prefix(es): 2-87391; 90-5657; 90-940163
Total Titles: 180 Print
Parent Company: Vicindo
Ultimate Parent Company: Belgian Post Group
Divisions: Artoria

Assimil NV
Rue du Congres 13, 1000 Brussels
Tel: (02) 5114502 *Fax:* (02) 5129138
E-mail: contact@assimil.be
Web Site: www.assimil.be
Key Personnel
Dir: S Peters
Editorial: E Defraene; R Deblomme
Founded: 1939
Membership(s): VBVB-VUNB; CBL-ADEB.

Subjects: Language Arts, Linguistics, Language Study Method
ISBN Prefix(es): 90-70077; 90-74996

Aurelia Books PVBA
Museumlaan 17, 9831 Sint-Martens Latem
Tel: (091) 82 55 82 *Fax:* (091) 82 72 47
Key Personnel
Dir: A d'Oosterlynck
Sales & Publicity: L Bullaert
Founded: 1972
Subjects: Medicine, Nursing, Dentistry, Regional Interests, Religion - Other
ISBN Prefix(es): 90-70827

NV Uitgeverij Altiora Averbode+
Abdijstraat 1, 3271 Averbode
Mailing Address: PO Box 54, 3271 Averbode
Tel: (013) 780156 *Fax:* (013) 776837
E-mail: averbode.publ@verbode.be
Key Personnel
Dir: R Biemans *Tel:* (013) 780102 *Fax:* (013) 776837 *E-mail:* dir@verbode.be
Editor: N C Vranckx *Tel:* (013) 780170 *Fax:* (013) 780179
Production: I Willems *Tel:* (013) 780140 *Fax:* (013) 780310
Founded: 1934
Subjects: Education, Religion - Other, Novels
ISBN Prefix(es): 90-317; 2-87394

Maison d'Editions Baha'ies ASBL
rue du Trone, 205, 1050 Brussels
Tel: (02) 647 07 49 *Fax:* (02) 646 21 77
E-mail: meb@swing.be
Web Site: www.adeb.irisnet.be
Key Personnel
Dir: Louis Henuzet
Founded: 1970
Membership(s): Association of Belgian Publishers.
Subjects: Biography, History, Law, Philosophy, Religion - Other
ISBN Prefix(es): 2-87203

Bakermat NV
Wollemarkt 18, 2800 Mechelen
Tel: (015) 42 05 08 *Fax:* (015) 42 05 73
E-mail: info@bakermat.com
Web Site: www.bakermat.com
Key Personnel
General Dir: Jos Baekens
Founded: 1991
ISBN Prefix(es): 90-5461; 90-5924

Bartleby & Co+
15, Rue des Pretres, 1000 Brussels
Tel: (02) 538 10 51
E-mail: bartleby@skynet.be
Key Personnel
President: Thorsten Baensch
Founded: 1996
Specialize in artist books & limited edition prints.
Subjects: Art, Literature, Literary Criticism, Essays
ISBN Prefix(es): 2-930279
Number of titles published annually: 3 Print
Total Titles: 15 Print

Bibliotheque des Signes, *imprint of* Editions Delta SA

Editions Gerard Blanchart & Cie SA+
Ave Ernest Masoin, 15, 1090 Brussels
Tel: (02) 4783706 *Fax:* (02) 4786429
Key Personnel
President: Charles Blanchart *E-mail:* charles.blanchart@chello.be
Production, Rights & Permissions: Therese Chantrenne
Founded: 1958
Specialize in railways & animals.

Subjects: Animals, Pets, Art, Biblical Studies, Photography, Religion - Catholic, Religion - Protestant, Religion - Other, Transportation
ISBN Prefix(es): 2-87202; 90-74760
Total Titles: 13 Print

Editions Blanco SA+
61/17 Ch des Deux-Maisons, 1200 Brussels
Tel: (02) 7720320 *Fax:* (02) 7706429
Key Personnel
Administrator & General Dir: Guy Leblanc
Founded: 1987
ISBN Prefix(es): 2-87297; 90-73106

Blitz, *imprint of* De Schaar/Geknipt Papier

De Boeck et Larcier SA+
Fond Jean-Paques, 4, 1348 Louvain-la-Neuve
Tel: (010) 48 2500 *Fax:* (010) 48 2519
E-mail: acces+cde@deboeck.be
Web Site: www.larcier.be/larcier.html
Key Personnel
Man Dir: Goerges Hoyos
Editor: Olivier Cruysmans *Tel:* (010) 48 26 19 *Fax:* (010) 48 26 50 *E-mail:* olivier.cruysmans@larcier.be
Editor, School Books: Francoise Goethals
Editor, University Books: Michel Jezierski
Assistant Editor: Anne Eloy *Tel:* (010) 48 26 20 *Fax:* (010) 48 26 50 *E-mail:* anne.eloy@larcier.be; Patricia Keunings *Tel:* (010) 48 26 13 *Fax:* (010) 48 26 50 *E-mail:* patricia.keunings@larcier.be
Founded: 1918
Subjects: Education, English as a Second Language, Language Arts, Linguistics, Literature, Literary Criticism, Essays
ISBN Prefix(es): 2-8011
Parent Company: Groupe de Boeck SA
Associate Companies: Acces+ SPRL; De Boeck & Larcier SA
Distributed by Editions Belin (France); G M Diffusion (Suisse); Litec (France); Editions du Renouveau Pedagogique (Canada)
Showroom(s): Rue des Minimes 39, 1000 Brussels *Tel:* (02) 548 07 11 *Fax:* (02) 513 90 09
Orders to: Acces Plus SPRL, Fond Jean-Paques 4, 1348 Louvain-La-Neuve

Bourdeaux-Capelle SA
359 rue St-Jacques, 5500 Dinant
Tel: (082) 222283; (082) 222277 *Fax:* (082) 226378
Key Personnel
Dir: Michel Bourdeaux
Founded: 1913
Subjects: Language Arts, Linguistics

Brepols, *imprint of* Brepols Publishers NV

Brepols Publishers NV+
Begijnhof 67, 2300 Turnhout
Tel: (014) 448020 *Fax:* (014) 428919
E-mail: info@brepols.net
Web Site: www.brepols.net
Key Personnel
Chairman: J L de Cartier de Marchienne
General Manager: Paul De Jongh *Tel:* (014) 44-80-21 *E-mail:* paul.dejongh@brepols.net
Commercial Manager: Hans Deraeve *Tel:* (014) 44-80-22 *E-mail:* hans.deraeve@brepols.net
Publishing Manager: Johan Van der Beke *Tel:* 212-737-0518 *Fax:* 212-288-7044 *E-mail:* johan.van.der.beke@brepols.net; Chris Vanden Borre *Tel:* (014) 44-80-27 *E-mail:* chris.vandenborre@brepols.net; Roland Demeulenaere *Tel:* (050) 368822 *Fax:* (050) 371457 *E-mail:* roland.demeulenaere@brepols.net; Simon Forde *Tel:* (020) 7284-4359, (014) 44-80-25 *Fax:* (020) 7267-8764 *E-mail:* simon.forde@brepols.net; Luc Jocque *Tel:* (050) 368820 *Fax:* (050) 371457 *E-mail:* luc.jocque@brepols.net; Christophe Lebbe *Tel:* (014) 44-80-26 *E-mail:* christophe.lebbe@brepols.net; Roel Vander Plaetse *Tel:* (050) 368821 *Fax:* (050) 371457 *E-mail:* roel.vander.plaetse@brepols.net
Production Manager: Jean Verstraete *Tel:* (014) 44-80-28 *E-mail:* jean.verstraete@brepols.net
Marketing Manager: Patrick Daemen *Tel:* (014) 44-80-31 *E-mail:* patrick.daemen@brepols.net
Administration & IT Manager: Wim Borgers *Tel:* (014) 44-80-39 *E-mail:* wim.borgers@brepols.net
Customer Care Manager: Ann Duchene *Tel:* (014) 44-80-34 *E-mail:* ann.duchene@brepols.net
Founded: 1796
International academic publishers.
Subjects: Archaeology, Architecture & Interior Design, Art, Asian Studies, Biblical Studies, History, Language Arts, Linguistics, Literature, Literary Criticism, Essays, Native American Studies, Philosophy, Religion - Other
ISBN Prefix(es): 2-503; 90-5622; 2-85006; 90-72100
Number of titles published annually: 240 Print; 5 CD-ROM; 5 Online
Total Titles: 5,000 Print
Parent Company: Brepols Group NV
Imprints: Brepols; Corpus Christianorum; Harvey Miller
Warehouse: Tieblokken 67, Gate C, 2300 Turnhout
Distribution Center: David Brown Book Distribution (USA)
Marston Book Services (UK)
Sogedin (France)

Vanden Broele NV+
Lieven Bauwensstr 33, 8200 Brugge
Tel: (050) 456 177 *Fax:* (050) 456 199
E-mail: graphic.group@vandenbroele.be
Web Site: www.vandenbroele.be
Key Personnel
Dir: E de Jonghe
Founded: 1957
Subjects: Government, Political Science, Law, Public Administration, Social Sciences, Sociology
ISBN Prefix(es): 90-5753; 90-6267; 90-5946

Etablissements Emile Bruylant SA+
rue de la Regence 67, 1000 Brussels
Tel: (02) 512 98 45 *Fax:* (02) 511 72 02
E-mail: info@bruylant.be
Web Site: www.bruylant.be
Key Personnel
President & Dir: Jean Vandeveld *Tel:* (02) 512 98 42 *Fax:* (02) 511 94 77 *E-mail:* jean@bruylant.be
Founded: 1838
Publisher & bookseller of law books & law periodicals.
Subjects: Government, Political Science, Law
ISBN Prefix(es): 2-8027
Number of titles published annually: 90 Print
Total Titles: 1,600 Print
Associate Companies: Academia-Bruylant, Grand-Place, 29, 1348 Louvain-la-Neuve *Tel:* (010) 45 23 95 *Fax:* (010) 45 44 80 *Web Site:* www.academia-bruylant.be
Distributed by Arts, Lettres et Techniques; Dokumente Verlag; Dott A Giuffre Editore; Um Fieldgen Buchhandlung; Grande Librairie Specialisee Fendri Ali; LGDJ - Montchrestien; Librairie Ernster; Librairie Le Point; Libraria Ferin; Licosa - Libreria Commissionaria Sansoni; Marcial Pons; Martinus Nijhoff; Miura Shoten Booksellers Ltd; La Nuova Italia Bibliografica; Promoculture; Sochepress; Editions Zoe
Distributor for Editorial Aranzadi; BECK'sche Verlag; Matthew Bender & Co Inc; Butterworths; Cambridge University Press; Cujas; Dalloz Sirey; Editions Legislatives et Administratives; Forum Europeen de la Communication (FEC); A Giuffre Editore; GLN Joly Editions; Helbing & Lichtenhan; Carl Heymanns Verlag; Juris-Classeur; Kluwer Law & Taxation; Kluwer Law International; LGDJ - Montchrestien; Litec; Lloyd's of London; MANZ'sche Verlag; Martinus Nijhoff; Nomos Verlag; Nouvelles Editions Fiduciaires; Pedone; Oxford University Press; Sakkoulas; Staempfli; Sweet & Maxwell; Themis; West Publishing Co; Wiley Law

Campinia Media VZW+
Kleinhoefstr 4, 2440 Geel
Tel: (014) 59 09 59 *Fax:* (014) 59 03 44
E-mail: info@campiniamedia.be
Web Site: www.campiniamedia.be
Key Personnel
Dir: Erik Borgmans *E-mail:* erik.borgmans@campiniamedia.be
Contact: Eveline Loos
Founded: 1983
Subjects: Agriculture, Behavioral Sciences, Biological Sciences, Computer Science, Language Arts, Linguistics, Physics, Science (General), Social Sciences, Sociology
ISBN Prefix(es): 90-356

Caramel, *imprint of* Caramel, Uitgeverij

Caramel, Uitgeverij+
Pagodenlaan 7, 1020 Brussels
Tel: (02) 2452427 *Fax:* (02) 2558493
E-mail: caramel@skynet.be
Key Personnel
Contact: Yvan Meyers *E-mail:* yvan.meyers@caramel.de
International Rights: Dirk Mennes *Tel:* (02) 263 2046 *E-mail:* production@caramel.de
Founded: 1993
Also acts as packager.
Subjects: Crafts, Games, Hobbies, Fiction
ISBN Prefix(es): 90-5562; 90-5828
Number of titles published annually: 250 Print
Imprints: Caramel

Carmelitana VZW+
Burgstr 92, 9000 Ghent
Tel: (09) 225.48.36 *Fax:* (09) 224.06.01
E-mail: boekhandel@carmelitana.be
Web Site: www.carmelitana.be
Key Personnel
President: Jos Rymen
Editor: F Lodewijckx
Founded: 1941
Subjects: Religion - Other
ISBN Prefix(es): 90-70092; 90-76671

Carto BVBA
Pagodenlaan 241, 1020 Brussels
Tel: (02) 2680345 *Fax:* (02) 2680345 *Cable:* Cartopress
Key Personnel
Man Dir: Michiel Plaizier
Founded: 1950
Subjects: Education, Geography, Geology, History, Travel
ISBN Prefix(es): 90-74437
Subsidiaries: Carpress, International Press Agency; European Cartographic Institute; Cremers (Schoollandkaarten) PVBA; Cremers Cartographic Institute

Cartoeristiek (Federatie van Belgische Autobus- en Autocarondernemers) (BAAV)+
Motestraat 41, 8800 Roeselare
Tel: (051) 226060 *Fax:* (051) 229273
Key Personnel
Contact: Luc Glorieux
Secretary: Mrs Riet Espeel *E-mail:* riet.espeel@busworld.org

Subjects: Travel
ISBN Prefix(es): 90-71408

Cartoon Creation, see IMPS SA

Editions Casterman SA+
rue Royale, 132-boite 2, 1000 Brussels
Tel: (02) 209 83 00 *Fax:* (02) 209 83 01
Web Site: www.casterman.com
Key Personnel
Man Dir: Frederic Morel
General Manager: Louis Delas
Dir, Production: Moline France
International Dir: Willy Insipidity
Marketing: Simon Casterman
International Rights Manager: Fabiana Angelini
Founded: 1780
ISBN Prefix(es): 2-203; 2-542
Parent Company: Editions Flammarion
Ultimate Parent Company: RCS Group

Editions du CEFAL+
Affiliate of UDC Consortium
Blvd Frere-Orban 31, 4000 Liege
Tel: (04) 254 25 20 *Fax:* (04) 254 24 40
E-mail: cefal.celes@skynet.be
Web Site: www.cefal.com
Key Personnel
Dir: Jacques Burlet
Founded: 1993
Membership(s): French Editor UDC Consortium; Editions de l'Universite de Liege.
Subjects: Library & Information Sciences, Specialize in Para-Literary - school books
ISBN Prefix(es): 2-87130
Number of titles published annually: 30 Print
Total Titles: 80 Print
Distributor for Editions de l'Universite de Liege (Belgium)
Distribution Center: Alterdis, 5, rue du Marechal Leclerc, 28600 Luisant, France
Edipresse, 945 ave Beaumont, Nontical, Canada

Centrale d'Impression et d'Achats en Cooperative, see CIACO

Centre d'action Laique, see Espace de Libertes

Centre de Recherches Culturelles Africanistes, see Centre Aequatoria

Centre International de Recherches 'Primitifs Flamands' ASBL+
One parc du Cinquantenaire, 1040 Brussels
Tel: (02) 7396866 *Fax:* (02) 7320105
Key Personnel
President & Rights & Permissions: H Pauwels
Scientific Editor & Sales: H Mund
  E-mail: helene.mund@kikirpa.be; C Stroo
  E-mail: cyriel.stroo@kikirpa.be
Founded: 1950
Specialize in Flemish Painting XV Century.
Subjects: Art
ISBN Prefix(es): 2-87033

Centre National Infor-Jeunes (CNIJ) (Centre of Information for Youth)
2, impasse des Capucins bte 8, 5000 Namur
Tel: (081) 22 08 72 *Fax:* (081) 22 82 64
Key Personnel
Dir: Georges Vallee
Membership(s): ERYICA (European Youth Information & Counselling Agency).
ISBN Prefix(es): 2-8091

Editions de la Chambre de Commerce et d'Industrie SA (ECCI)+
Palais de Congres, Esplanade de l'Europe, 2, 4020 Liege
Tel: (04) 344-50-88 *Fax:* (04) 343-05-53

E-mail: lvenanzi@ecci.be
Web Site: www.ecci.be
Founded: 1998
Subjects: Accounting, Business, Law
ISBN Prefix(es): 2-930287; 90-76924
Number of titles published annually: 15 Print
Total Titles: 50 Print
Distribution Center: Patrimoine, Rue du Noyer, 7030 Brussels
Soficom, 15, rue du Docteur Lancereaux, 75008 Paris, France *Tel:* (01) 42 56 45 71 *Fax:* (01) 42 56 45 72 *E-mail:* soficom@soficom-diffusion.com
UNIVERS, Senc, 845, rue Marie-Victorin, Saint-Nicolas (Levis), PQ G7A 3S8, Canada *Tel:* 418-831-7474 *Fax:* 418-831-4021 *E-mail:* d.univers@videotron.ca

Editions Chanlis
52 rue de Lennery, 5650 Walcourt
Tel: (071) 326394
Key Personnel
Man Dir: Pierre Magain
Sales: M Nowak
Founded: 1968
Subjects: Antiques, Archaeology, Art, Crafts, Games, Hobbies, History, Military Science
ISBN Prefix(es): 2-87039

Chantecler, *imprint of* Zuid-Nederlandse Uitgeverij NV/Central Uitgeverij

Editions Chantecler+
Vluchtenburgstraat 7, Aartselaar 2630
Tel: (03) 8 70 44 00 *Fax:* (03) 8 77 21 15
Telex: 31739 Zuidb
Key Personnel
Man Dir: Jan Vande Velden
Editorial: Bart Clinckemalie
Production: Eric Feyten
Rights & Permissions: Wilfried Wuyts
Founded: 1947
Subjects: Fiction, Nonfiction (General)
ISBN Prefix(es): 2-8034; 90-243; 90-447
Parent Company: Zuidnederlandse Uitgeverij NV
Imprints: Pre-Ecole

La Charte Editions juridiques
rue Guimard 19/2, 1040 Brussels
Tel: (02) 512 29 49 *Fax:* (02) 512 26 93
E-mail: info@lacharte.be
Web Site: www.lacharte.be
Key Personnel
Dir Editor-Legal: Rik Carton
Dir Editor-Educational: Jean-Paul Steevens
Founded: 1948
Subjects: Government, Political Science, Language Arts, Linguistics, Law, Social Sciences, Sociology
ISBN Prefix(es): 2-87403

CIACO+
Chez Erasme 2, pl Baudoin-ler, 5004 Bouge-Namur
Tel: (018) 213700 *Fax:* (018) 212372
Key Personnel
Dir: Gerard Lambert
Founded: 1983
ISBN Prefix(es): 2-87085
Subsidiaries: Artel SC

CIEFR (Centre International d'Etudes de la Formation Religieuse), see Editions Lumen Vitae ASBL

Uitgeverij Clavis+
Vooruitzichtstr 42, 3500 Hasselt
Tel: (011) 28 68 68 *Fax:* (011) 28 68 69
E-mail: info@clavis.be
Web Site: www.clavis.be

Key Personnel
Man Dir, Editorial: Philippe Werck
Licensing Manager: Sigrid Werck
Rights & Permissions: Tina Troonbeeckx
Production: Lisette Aerts
Promotion: Tanja Appeltants *E-mail:* tanja@clavis.be
Financial Dir: Jos Rens
Editorial: Mark Lens; Hilde Vanmechelen
Founded: 1981
Subjects: Fiction, Nonfiction (General)
ISBN Prefix(es): 90-6822; 90-5933; 90-77106; 90-448; 90-77060
Total Titles: 560 Print
Imprints: Mozaiek
Bookshop(s): Poespas, Kapelstr 38, 3500 Hasselt

Coach & Bus Federation, see Cartoeristiek (Federatie van Belgische Autobus- en Autocarondernemers) (BAAV)

Coalition of the Flemish North South Movement, see Koepel van de Vlaamse Noord - Zuidbeweging 11.11.11

Editions Complexe SPRL+
24, rue de Bosnie, 1060 Brussels
Mailing Address: 43, rue Entrepreneurs, 75015, Paris, France
Tel: (02) 538 88 46 *Fax:* (02) 538 88 42
Telex: 64507 Patica
Key Personnel
Man Dir, Publicity: Danielle Vincken
Man Dir, Editorial: Andre Versaille
Founded: 1971
Subjects: History, Literature, Literary Criticism, Essays, Science (General)
ISBN Prefix(es): 2-87027; 2-8048
Associate Companies: Nouvelle Diffusion SPRL DPI

Concraid+
Parc de la Sablonniere bte 707, 7000 Mons
Tel: (065) 34-72-34 *Fax:* (065) 34-72-34
Key Personnel
General Dir: E Preud'homme
Founded: 1983
Membership(s): ADEB; Specialize in Finance, Stockmarket & Health.
ISBN Prefix(es): 2-87189

Conservart SA+
Chee Alsemberg 975, 1180 Brussels
Tel: (02) 3322538 *Fax:* (02) 3322840
E-mail: conservart@skynet.be
Key Personnel
General Dir: Jean-Claude Echement
Subjects: Architecture & Interior Design, Art, Chemistry, Chemical Engineering, Literature, Literary Criticism, Essays, Photography
ISBN Prefix(es): 2-930022

Uitgeverij Contact NV
Capucienenlaan 49, 9300 Aalst
Tel: (03) 4572024 *Fax:* (03) 4581327
Key Personnel
Dir: A J H Binneweg
Founded: 1946
Subjects: Art, Crafts, Games, Hobbies, Education, Literature, Literary Criticism, Essays, Sports, Athletics
ISBN Prefix(es): 90-73185

Corpus Christianorum, *imprint of* Brepols Publishers NV

Creadif
67 Rue de la Regence, 1000 Brussels
Tel: (02) 512 98 45 *Fax:* (02) 511 72 02
Key Personnel
Dir: Jean Vandeveld

Founded: 1974
Publisher of law books.
Subjects: Business, Economics, Ethnicity, Geography, Geology, History, Law, Travel
ISBN Prefix(es): 2-8022

Cremers (Schoollandkaarten) PVBA
Pagodenlaan 241, 1020 Brussels
Tel: (02) 2680345 *Fax:* (02) 2680345 *Cable:* Cartopress
Key Personnel
Dir: Michiel Plazier
Founded: 1950
Subjects: Ethnicity, Geography, Geology, History, Travel
ISBN Prefix(es): 90-74437
Parent Company: Carto BVBA

Le Cri Editions+
One Rue Victor Greyson, 1050 Brussels
Tel: (02) 6466533 *Fax:* (02) 6466607
E-mail: lecri@skynet.be
Key Personnel
Dir: Lutz Christian
Founded: 1981
Subjects: Biography, History, Literature, Literary Criticism, Essays
ISBN Prefix(es): 2-87106

Cultura
Hoenderstr 22, 9230 Wetteren
Tel: (032) 093691595 *Fax:* (032) 093695925
E-mail: info@cultura-net.com
Web Site: www.cultura-net.com; www.cultura.be
Key Personnel
President: Rene De Meester, Sr
Vice President: Jan De Meester, Jr
Specialize in numismatic publications.
ISBN Prefix(es): 90-74623

Le Daily-Bul
rue Daily Bul 29, 7100 La Louviere
Tel: (064) 222973 *Fax:* (064) 222973
Key Personnel
Man Dir: Andre Balthazar
Founded: 1957
Subjects: Art, Literature, Literary Criticism, Essays, Poetry
ISBN Prefix(es): 2-930136

Daphne Diffusion SA
Poortakkerstraat, 29, 9051 Ghent
Tel: (09) 221 45 91 *Fax:* (09) 220 16 12
E-mail: info@daphne.be
Telex: 11659
Key Personnel
General Manager: Francois Dubrulle
Administrator & Sales Manager: Pierre Dubrulle
Subjects: Travel
ISBN Prefix(es): 2-504

Davidsfonds Uitgeverij NV+
Blijde-Inkomststr 79-81, 3000 Leuven
Tel: (016) 310600 *Fax:* (016) 310608
E-mail: informatie@davidsfonds.be
Web Site: www.davidsfonds.be
Key Personnel
Dir: Rudi Teirlinck
Subjects: Art, Fiction, History
ISBN Prefix(es): 90-6152; 90-6565
Number of titles published annually: 110 Print
Distributor for NBCC (Netherlands)
Bookshop(s): Blijde-Inkomststr 79-81, 3000 Leuven
Warehouse: Distributiecentrum AGORA, De Vunt 5, 3220 Holsbeek

Editions De Boeck-Larcier SA+
rue des Minimes 39, 1000 Brussels
Tel: (02) 548 07 11 *Fax:* (02) 513 90 09
Web Site: www.deboeck.be
Key Personnel
President: Christian De Boeck *E-mail:* christian.deboeck@deboeck.be
Dir: Georges Hoyos *E-mail:* georges.hoyos@deboeck.be
University Publications: Michel Jezierski *E-mail:* michel.jezierski@deboeck.be
Educational Publishing: Francoise Goethals *E-mail:* francoise.goethals@deboeck.be
Press Officer: Nora Jezierski-Ramakers *E-mail:* nora.jezierski@deboeck.be
Law: Patricia Wilhelm
R/D: Genevieve Dieu
Founded: 1883
Subjects: Accounting, Anthropology, Art, Behavioral Sciences, Biological Sciences, Business, Chemistry, Chemical Engineering, Communications, Economics, Education, English as a Second Language, Environmental Studies, Finance, Geography, Geology, Government, Political Science, Health, Nutrition, Human Relations, Language Arts, Linguistics, Law, Management, Marketing, Mathematics, Medicine, Nursing, Dentistry, Philosophy, Physical Sciences, Psychology, Psychiatry, Science (General), Social Sciences, Sociology
ISBN Prefix(es): 2-8041
Parent Company: Groupe De Boeck SA
Associate Companies: Acces Plus SPRL
Divisions: De Boeck Universite; De Boeck-Wesmael, Larcier; Dessain; Duculot; Didacta
Showroom(s): Acces Plus SPRL, Fond Jean-Paques 4, 1348 Louvain-la-Neuve *Tel:* (010) 482500 *Fax:* (010) 482519
Bookshop(s): Acces Plus SPRL, Fond Jean-Paques 4, 1348 Louvain-la-Neuve *Tel:* (010) 482500 *Fax:* (010) 482519
Shipping Address: Acces Plus SPRL, Fond Jean-Paques 4, 1348 Louvain-la-Neuve *Tel:* (010) 482500 *Fax:* (010) 482519
Warehouse: Acces Plus SPRL, Fond Jean-Paques 4, 1348 Louvain-la-Neuve *Tel:* (010) 482500 *Fax:* (010) 482519
Orders to: Acces Plus SPRL, Fond Jean-Paques 4, 1348 Louvain-la-Neuve *Tel:* (010) 482500 *Fax:* (010) 482519 *E-mail:* acces+cde@deboeck.be

DEF (De Blauwe Vogel) NV/SA+
Jan Carlierstraat, 1, Bus, 3800 Sint-Truiden
Tel: (011) 685751-2 *Fax:* (011) 67-21-70
Telex: 39810
Key Personnel
Contact: Willy-Paul Carlier
Founded: 1929
Subjects: Travel
ISBN Prefix(es): 90-72432

Maison d'Editions Claude Dejaie+
1154 chaussee de Dinant, 5100 Namur-Wepian
Tel: (081) 460748
Key Personnel
Dir: M Claude M Dejaie
Founded: 1972
Subjects: Art, Literature, Literary Criticism, Essays, Philosophy
ISBN Prefix(es): 2-87157

Editions Delta SA (Delta Publications)+
416, ave Louise, 1050 Brussels
Tel: (02) 217 55 55 *Fax:* (02) 217 93 93
E-mail: editions.delta@skynet.be
Key Personnel
Man Dir: Georges-Francis Seingry
Founded: 1976
Specialize in European public affairs & art books.
Subjects: Art, Biography, Public Administration
ISBN Prefix(es): 2-8029
Number of titles published annually: 8 Print
Parent Company: Euro-references
Imprints: Bibliotheque des Signes
Distributed by Bernan (USA); Cedar Media House; LGDJ-Montchrestien
Foreign Rep(s): Bernan; Cedar Media; LGDJ Montchretien

Deltas, *imprint of* Zuid-Nederlandse Uitgeverij NV/Central Uitgeverij

Dessain - Departement de De Boeck & Larcier SA+
rue Des Minimes, 39, 1000 Brussels
Tel: (02) 548 07 11 *Fax:* (02) 513 90 09
E-mail: adeb@adeb.be
Web Site: www.adeb.irisnet.be
Key Personnel
President: Christian De Boeck *E-mail:* christiandeboeck@deboeck.be
Dir: Georges Hoyos *E-mail:* georges.hoyos@deboeck.be
Editor, Scholarly Books: Francoise Goethals
Founded: 1719
Subjects: Education, Geography, Geology, Mathematics, Natural History, Physics, Religion - Catholic, Science (General)
ISBN Prefix(es): 2-8041; 2-502
Parent Company: Groupe De Boeck SA
Associate Companies: De Boeck & Larcier SA - Acces Plus Sprl
Warehouse: Acces Plus SPRL, Fond Jean-Paques 4, 1348 Louvain-la-Neuve *Tel:* (010) 482500 *Fax:* (010) 482519
Orders to: Access Plus SPRL, Fond Jean-Paques 4, 1348 Louvain *Tel:* (010) 482500 *Fax:* (010) 482519

Dexia Bank+
Activites culturelles, RC 1/0, Blvd Pacheco 44, 1000 Brussels
Tel: (02) 222 54 89 *Fax:* (02) 222 57 52
E-mail: cultureline@dexia.be
Web Site: www.dexia.be/culture
Key Personnel
Contact: Renaud Gahide
Founded: 1860
Subjects: Art, Genealogy, Geography, Geology, History, Music, Dance, Photography
ISBN Prefix(es): 90-5066; 2-87193
Number of titles published annually: 10 Print
Total Titles: 90 Print; 8 E-Book
Distributed by Exhibitions International

Diligentia-Uitgeverij
Schrijnwerkerstr 11, 9240 Zele
Tel: (052) 44 45 11 *Fax:* (052) 44 45 22
E-mail: diligentia.book@planetinternet.be
Key Personnel
Contact: C Van den broeck
Founded: 1908
ISBN Prefix(es): 90-70978

Documenta CV
21, Rue des Drappiers, 1050 Brussels
Tel: (02) 5102313 *Fax:* (02) 5102497
Key Personnel
President: Philippe de Buck van Overstraeten
Manager: Christian Franzen
Founded: 1986
Subjects: Business, Economics, Electronics, Electrical Engineering, Management, Technology
ISBN Prefix(es): 2-930096; 90-75062
Distributed by Academia
Distributor for Academia; Mim

Duculot, see De Boeck et Larcier SA

Editions Dupuis SA+
Rue Destree 52, 6001 Marcinelle
Tel: (071) 600 500 *Fax:* (071) 600 599
E-mail: info@dupuis.com
Web Site: www.dupuis.com

Key Personnel
Dir General: Jean Deneumostier
Editorial Dir: Philippe Vandooren
Sales Dir: Philippe Buck
Finance: Stephane Desmet
Rights & Permissions: Jean-Philippe Doutrelugne
Dir Audiovisual & Development: Leon Perahia
Founded: 1898
Subjects: Humor
ISBN Prefix(es): 90-314; 2-8001; 90-6574
Parent Company: Groupe Jean Dupuis SA
Associate Companies: Editions Dupuis France SA; Mediatoon SA

Easy Computing NV
Bourdon 100, 1180 Brussels
Tel: (02) 346 52 52 *Fax:* (02) 346 01 20
E-mail: info@easycomputing.com
Web Site: www.easycomputing.com
Key Personnel
Contact: F Wiener *Tel:* (02) 3401521
E-mail: fwiener@easycomputing.com
Founded: 1989
Subjects: Computer Science, Electronics, Electrical Engineering, Microcomputers
ISBN Prefix(es): 90-5167; 90-456; 2-87208
Total Titles: 100 Print; 70 CD-ROM
Subsidiaries: Easy Computing bv
Distributor for Micro Application

ECCI, see Editions de la Chambre de Commerce et d'Industrie SA (ECCI)

Ecobooks
Heerbaan 132, 1840 Steenhuffel
Tel: (052) 37 11 38 *Fax:* (052) 37 11 51
E-mail: ecobooks@ping.be
Key Personnel
Contact: Mevr M Muylaert
International Rights: Hugo Vanderstadt
Subjects: Ecology, Sustainability
ISBN Prefix(es): 90-75855

Ediblanchart sprl+
Ave Ernest Masoin, 15, 1090 Brussels
Tel: (02) 4783706 *Fax:* (02) 4786429
Key Personnel
President & Administrator: Charles Blanchart
  E-mail: charles.blanchart@chello.be
Founded: 1962
Subjects: Animals, Pets, Transportation, Railways, Flowers
ISBN Prefix(es): 2-87202
Number of titles published annually: 2 Print
Total Titles: 9 Print

Editest, SPRL+
16 rue de Chambery, 1040 Brussels
Tel: (02) 6476284 *Fax:* (02) 7325629
Key Personnel
Dir: B Evrard
Specialize in psychological tests.
Subjects: Psychology, Psychiatry
ISBN Prefix(es): 2-8000

Uitgeverij de Eenhoorn+
Vlasstraat 17, 8710 Wielsbeke
Tel: (056) 60 54 60 *Fax:* (056) 61 69 81
E-mail: info@eenhoorn.be
Web Site: www.eenhoorn.be
Key Personnel
Man Dir & International Rights: Bart Desmyter
  E-mail: bart.desmyter@eenhoorn.be
Founded: 1990
Subjects: Fiction
ISBN Prefix(es): 90-73913; 90-5838
Number of titles published annually: 50 Print
Imprints: Medaillon

EMPC, see Editions Medicales et Paramedicales de Charleroi (EMPC)

Editions les Eperonniers
62B rue St Catherine, 1370 Jodoigne
Tel: (010) 813614 *Fax:* (010) 815386
Key Personnel
President: Lysiane D'Haeyere-Antoine
Subjects: Literature, Literary Criticism, Essays, Philosophy, Science (General)
ISBN Prefix(es): 2-87132; 2-87015; 2-87159

EPO Publishers, Printers, Booksellers+
Lange Pastoorstr 25-27, 2600 Berchem-Antwerp
Tel: (03) 2396874 *Fax:* (03) 2184604
E-mail: publishers@epo.be
Web Site: www.epo.be
Key Personnel
Man Dir: Jos Hennes
Publisher: Hugo Franssen
Sales: Kris Van Kersschaever
Founded: 1978
Subjects: Anthropology, Biography, Communications, Developing Countries, Fiction, History, Journalism, Literature, Literary Criticism, Essays, Nonfiction (General), Psychology, Psychiatry, Social Sciences, Sociology
ISBN Prefix(es): 90-6445; 2-87262
Branch Office(s)
Chaussee de Haecht L55, 1030 Brussels
Tel: (02) 215 6651 *Fax:* (02) 215 6604
E-mail: editions@epo.be
Distributed by De Geus (The Netherlands)
Distributor for Coutinho (The Netherlands); De Geus (The Netherlands)
Bookshop(s): Groene Waterman, Wolstr 7, 2000 Antwerp; Librairie Internationale, Ave LeMonnier 171, 1000 Brussels
Book Club(s): Komma's en Punten

Esco BVBA
Venusstraat 31, 2000 Antwerp
Tel: (03) 2223800 *Fax:* (03) 2223838
Key Personnel
Contact: Jan Fremeijer
ISBN Prefix(es): 90-6415

Editions Espace de Libertes, *imprint of* Espace de Libertes

Espace de Libertes+
Formerly Centre d'action Laique
av Arnaud Fraiteur, ULB, Bd du Triomphe, Campus de la Plane, CP 236, 1050 Brussels
Tel: (02) 6276860 *Fax:* (02) 6266861
Key Personnel
Collections Dir: Patrice Dartevelle
  E-mail: espace@cal.ulb.ac.be
Founded: 1979
Membership(s): A D E B.
Subjects: Biography, Government, Political Science, History, Philosophy, Religion - Other, Social Sciences, Sociology
ISBN Prefix(es): 2-930001
Imprints: Editions Espace de Libertes

EVO, see Les Editions Vie ouvriere ASBL

Facet NV+
Willem Linnigstr 13, 2060 Antwerp
Tel: (03) 227 40 28 *Fax:* (03) 227 37 92
E-mail: facet@village.uunet.be
Web Site: www.mijnweb.nu/be021988
Key Personnel
Publisher: Walter A P Soethoudt
Founded: 1986
Specialize in children's books.
ISBN Prefix(es): 90-5016

Garant Publishers Ltd
Somersstr 13-15, 2018 Antwerp
Tel: (03) 231 29 00 *Fax:* (03) 233 26 59
E-mail: uitgeverij@garant.be
Web Site: www.garant.be

Key Personnel
Dir: Huug Van Gompel *E-mail:* huug.vangompel@garant.be
Publisher: Liesbeth Driesen
Promotion: Werner Peeters
Founded: 1990
Subjects: Economics, Education, Social Sciences, Sociology
ISBN Prefix(es): 90-441
Number of titles published annually: 120 Print
Total Titles: 1,500 Print
Associate Companies: Maklu Publishers
Distributed by Central Books; Coronet Books

Uitgevery Gelbis NV+
Cockerillaai 30, 2000 Antwerp
Tel: (03) 2410202 *Fax:* (03) 2410200
E-mail: gelbis.boeken@lequana.com
Key Personnel
Contact: Leo van der Linden
Founded: 1982
Subjects: Automotive, Travel
ISBN Prefix(es): 90-71288
Divisions: GelbiStudio; Gelbis Boekhandel

Geocart Uitg Cartogr AG Claus BVBA+
Breedstr 94, 9100 Sint-Niklaas
Tel: (03) 760 14 60 *Fax:* (03) 760 15 28
E-mail: site@geocart.be
Web Site: www.geocart.be
Key Personnel
Algemene Dir: Egide Van Eyck
Founded: 1972
Specialize in cartography.
ISBN Prefix(es): 90-6736
Subsidiaries: Girault Gilbert, BVBA
Divisions: Geocart Information System
Warehouse: Libricart, Breedstr 94, 9100 Sint-Niklaas

Georeto-Geogidsen
Rozenstr 11, 3723 Kortessem
Tel: (011) 37 52 54 *Fax:* (011) 37 52 54
E-mail: georeto@pandora.be
Web Site: www.geogidsen.be
Key Personnel
Contact: P Diriken
Founded: 1991
Subjects: Geography, Geology, History, Outdoor Recreation
Number of titles published annually: 4 Print
Total Titles: 45 Print

Girault Gilbert bvba+
50, Rue de l'Association, 1000 Brussels
Tel: (02) 2171430; (02) 2175880 *Fax:* (02) 2173375
Key Personnel
President: Egide Van Eyck
Founded: 1928 (Reconstituted: 1956)
ISBN Prefix(es): 2-87273
Warehouse: Libricart, Breedstr 94, 9100 Sint-Niklaas

Glenat Benelux SA+
131 rue Saint-Lambert, 1200 Brussels
Tel: (02) 7612640 *Fax:* (02) 7612645
E-mail: glenat@glenat.be
Web Site: www.glenat.com
Key Personnel
Dir, Editor & International Rights: Paul Herman
Administrative Delegate: Dominique Leblan
Founded: 1985
Subjects: Antiques, Art, Automotive, Crafts, Games, Hobbies, Humor, Regional Interests, Wine & Spirits, Comics
ISBN Prefix(es): 2-87176; 90-6969
Subsidiaries: Glenat France
Distributor for Vent D'Ouest

Bookshop(s): Slumberland, 20 rue des sables, 1000 Brussels; Slumberland, 131 rue Saint-Lambert, 1200 Brussels; Slumberland, 3 Louvain-la-Neuve

Globe, *imprint of* Roularta Books NV

Globe, *imprint of* Scoop Infotex NV

Graton Editeur NV+
Av du Perou, 1000 Brussels
Tel: (02) 6756 666 *Fax:* (02) 6756 363
E-mail: graton.sa@skynet.be
Key Personnel
Executive: Ph Graton
Founded: 1981
Subjects: Film, Video, Journalism, Photography, Sports, Athletics, Motorracing, Comic Strips
ISBN Prefix(es): 90-70816; 2-87098
Divisions: Kurz & Bundigi, hpt Extra
Distributed by Diffulivre (Switzerland); Dupuis (Belgium); Hachette (France); Mediavision (USA); Seven Island (Germany)

Groeninghe NV
Lange Steenstr 2, 8500 Kortrijk
Tel: (056) 22 40 77 *Fax:* (056) 22 82 86
Web Site: www.groeninghe.com
Key Personnel
General Dir: Robert Timperman
Founded: 1924
Subjects: Archaeology, Art, History
ISBN Prefix(es): 90-71868
Parent Company: Groeninghe Printers
Associate Companies: Groeninghe Bookbinders
Showroom(s): Budastr 64, 8500 Kortrijk

Den Gulden Engel, *imprint of* Uitgeverij Houtekiet

Hadewijch, *imprint of* Uitgeverij Houtekiet

Imprimerie Hayez SPRL
Rue Fernand Brunfaut 19, 1080 Brussels
Tel: (02) 413 02 00 *Fax:* (02) 411 23 78
E-mail: com@hayez.be
Web Site: www.hayez.be
Telex: 63467 Hayez
Key Personnel
Man Dir: Frederic Hayez *E-mail:* fh@hayez.be; Maximilien Hayez *E-mail:* mh@hayez.be
Founded: 1780
Subjects: History, Medicine, Nursing, Dentistry, Philosophy, Poetry, Religion - Other, Science (General), Sports, Athletics
ISBN Prefix(es): 2-87126

Heideland-Orbis NV
Santvoortbeekln 21-23, 2100 Deurne
Tel: (03) 3600211 *Fax:* (03) 3600212
Telex: 3600212 *Cable:* 33649
Key Personnel
Dir: C van Baelen
Editorial Manager: R Fransen
Production: H Leduc
Founded: 1969
ISBN Prefix(es): 90-291

Uitgeverij Helios NV
Kapelsestr 222, 2080 Kapellen
Tel: (03) 6645320
Telex: 32242 Anvers Dnb
Key Personnel
Man Dir: J Pelckmans
Founded: 1976
ISBN Prefix(es): 90-333
Associate Companies: Uitgeverij De Nederlandsche Boekhandel

Helyode Editions (SA-ADN)+
Coccinelle Edition, Chaussee d'Alsemberg, 1180 Brussels
Tel: (02) 3444934 *Fax:* (02) 3475534
Key Personnel
General Dir: Patrice le Hodey
Dir: Marie Vernofstede
Founded: 1991
Specialize in cartoons.
Subjects: Fiction, History, Humor
ISBN Prefix(es): 2-87353; 90-5415
Subsidiaries: Memoire D'Europe

Van Hemeldonck NV+
Van Hemeldonckstr, 5, 2350 Vosselaar
Tel: (014) 611034 *Fax:* (014) 620288
E-mail: booksell@innet.be
Key Personnel
President: Johan Van Hemeldonck
Vice President: Georges Aerts
Founded: 1932
Specialize in large prints.
ISBN Prefix(es): 90-5274
Associate Companies: Grootdruk-Uitgevery Eindhoven BV, Netherlands

Editions Hemma+
106, rue de Chevron, 4987 Chevron
Tel: (086) 43 01 01 *Fax:* (086) 43 36 40
Web Site: www.hemma.be
Key Personnel
Dir: Albert Hemmerlin
Founded: 1952
Subjects: Crafts, Games, Hobbies, Fiction, Mysteries, Science Fiction, Fantasy
ISBN Prefix(es): 2-8006
Subsidiaries: Editions Diffusion Hemma; Hemma Verlag GmbH; Hemma Joven SA
Distributed by Dar Almoufid (Lebanon); Diffusion Transat SA (Switzerland); Impato (Switzerland); Les Presses D-Or (Canada) Inc (Canada); Messageries du Livre (Luxembourg); Socadis Inc (Canada)

De Horstink, *imprint of* Uitgeverij Acco

Uitgeverij Houtekiet
Subsidiary of Veen, Bosch & Keuning Uitgevers NV
Vrijheidstraat 33, 2000 Antwerp
Tel: (03) 2381296 *Fax:* (03) 2388041
E-mail: info@houtekiet.com
Web Site: www.boekenwereld.com
Telex: 43272beka
Key Personnel
Dir: Marij Bertram
Publisher: Leo de Haes
Marketing & Sales: Hendrik de Leeuw
Publicity: Melanie Elst *E-mail:* melanie.elst@houtekiet.com
Sales: Thea Bon; Ingrid Kee; Petra Wildvank
ISBN Prefix(es): 90-5067; 90-5240; 90-70876
Imprints: Hadewijch; Den Gulden Engel

Huis Van Het Boek
Hof ter Schriecklaan 17, 2600 Berchem, Antwerp
Tel: (03) 230 89 23 *Fax:* (03) 281 22 40
E-mail: info@boek.be
Web Site: www.boek.be
Key Personnel
Dir: Dorian Van Der Brempt *E-mail:* dorian.van.der.brempt@vbvb.be
Founded: 1929
Professional organization for booksellers, distributors & editors.
Subjects: Literature, Literary Criticism, Essays, Publishing & Book Trade Reference
ISBN Prefix(es): 90-72103; 90-77165; 90-940004

IMPS SA+
Formerly Cartoon Creation
85 rue du Cerf, 1332 Genval
Tel: (02) 6520220 *Fax:* (02) 6520160
Key Personnel
Dir General: Hendrik Coysman
Founded: 1984
Licensor of the Smurfs.
ISBN Prefix(es): 2-87345

Infoboek NV
Lil 51, 2450 Meerhout
Tel: (014) 369292 *Fax:* (014) 369293
E-mail: info@infoboek.be
Web Site: www.infoboek.com
Key Personnel
Dir: W Verhaert
Founded: 1971
Subjects: Crafts, Games, Hobbies, Education, Language Arts, Linguistics, Literature, Literary Criticism, Essays, Music, Dance, Philosophy, Religion - Other, Sports, Athletics
ISBN Prefix(es): 90-5535

Infotex NV
Forelstraat 22, 9000 Ghent
Tel: (09) 265 64 23 *Fax:* (09) 225 84 06
Telex: 11228
Key Personnel
Man Dir: J van Haverbeke
ISBN Prefix(es): 90-6334
Bookshop(s): Boekhandel Het Volk

Institut Royal des Relations Internationales
(Royal Institute for International Relations)
Rue de Namur 69, 1000 Brussels
Tel: (02) 2234114 *Fax:* (02) 2234116
E-mail: info@irri-kiib.be
Web Site: www.irri-kiib.be
Key Personnel
President: Vte E Davignon
Dir General: Claude Misson
Founded: 1947
Research institute.
Subjects: Developing Countries, Economics, Foreign Countries, Government, Political Science, Law
ISBN Prefix(es): 2-9600353
Number of titles published annually: 5 Print
Total Titles: 2 Print

International Institute of Catechetics & Pastoral Studies, see Editions Lumen Vitae ASBL

International Peace Information Service, see IPIS vzw (International Peace Information Service)

Intersentia Uitgevers NV
Churchilllaan 108, 2900 Schoten-Antwerp
Tel: (03) 680 15 50 *Fax:* (03) 658 71 21
E-mail: mail@intersentia.be
Web Site: www.intersentia.com
Key Personnel
Publisher, Law: Kris Moeremans *E-mail:* k.moeremans@intersentia.be
Founded: 1996
Academic publishing house specializing in Belgian, Dutch, European & international law & economics.
Subjects: Accounting, Finance, Law, Human Rights, European Law
ISBN Prefix(es): 90-5095
Number of titles published annually: 70 Print; 3 CD-ROM
Total Titles: 420 Print; 2 Online
Distributed by Aditya Books (India); James Bennett Pty Ltd (Australia); Gaunt Inc (North America); Hart Publishing (UK); Mare Nostrum (France, Italy, Spain & Portugal); Verlag Oesterreich (Austria & Czech Republic); Schulthess Verlag (Germany & Switzerland)
Distributor for Hart Publishing

Invader, *imprint of* Zuid-Nederlandse Uitgeverij NV/Central Uitgeverij

IPIS vzw (International Peace Information Service)+
98a Italielei, 2000 Antwerp
Tel: (03) 225 00 22; (03) 225 21 96 *Fax:* (03) 231 0151
E-mail: info@ipisresearch.be
Web Site: www.ipisresearch.be
Key Personnel
Dir: Johan Peleman *E-mail:* johan@ipisresearch.be
Research: An Yrankx *E-mail:* an@ipisresearch.be
Founded: 1981
Specialize in world security & human rights, conflict areas, arms trade & international relations.
Membership(s): NGO.
Subjects: Developing Countries, Foreign Countries, Government, Political Science, Military Science, Nonfiction (General)
ISBN Prefix(es): 90-70316; 90-71247

IRRI-KIIB, see Institut Royal des Relations Internationales

Uitgeverij J van In+
Nijverheidsstr 92/5, 2160 Wommelgem
Tel: (03) 4805511 *Fax:* (03) 4807664
Key Personnel
Man Dir & Rights & Permissions: Dr Laurent Woestenburg
Editorial: Ludo Camps
Production: Danielle Brabants
Publicity: Fred Caluwe
Founded: 1833
Firm is part of Educational Book Publishing division of V N U BV, Netherlands.
Subjects: Education, Language Arts, Linguistics, Law
ISBN Prefix(es): 90-306
Subsidiaries: Van In J Editions
Divisions:

Editions Juridiques Kluwer a Deurne Anvers
Kouterveld, 2, 1831 Diegem
Tel: (02) 300 3000 *Fax:* (03) 360-04
E-mail: custumer.kejb@wkb.be
Web Site: www.editionskluwer.be
Telex: 33649
Key Personnel
Dir: B Houdmont
Manager: B Houdmont; G VanPeel
Publisher: A Knops; D Lefebvre; D Vanhove
Logistic Manager: A Geladi
Founded: 1977
Subjects: Economics, Law
ISBN Prefix(es): 90-6321; 2-87377
Parent Company: Wolters Kluwer Belgie NV
Ultimate Parent Company: Wolters Kluwer NV, Netherlands
Imprints: E Story-Scientia; Service

Die Keure+
Oude Gentweg 108, 8000 Brugge
Tel: (050) 47 12 72 *Fax:* (050) 34 37 68
E-mail: info@diekeure.be
Web Site: www.diekeure.be
Key Personnel
Dir: Jean Paul Steevens
Founded: 1948
Subjects: Education
ISBN Prefix(es): 90-6200; 90-5751; 90-5958

King Baudouin Foundation
Rue Brederodestr 21, 1000 Brussels
Tel: (02) 511 18 40 *Fax:* (02) 511 52 21
E-mail: proj@kbs-frb.be
Web Site: www.kbs-frb.be
Key Personnel
Man Dir: Luc Tayart de Borms
Improve living conditions for the population taking economic, social, scientific & cultural factors into account.
Subjects: Agriculture, Architecture & Interior Design, Economics, Labor, Industrial Relations, Social Sciences, Sociology
ISBN Prefix(es): 90-5130; 2-87212

Kluwer Rechtswetenschappen Belgie, see Editions Juridiques Kluwer a Deurne Anvers

KnackBibliotheek/Radio 1, *imprint of* Roularta Books NV

Koepel van de Vlaamse Noord - Zuidbeweging 11.11.11 (Coalition of the Flemish North South Movement)+
Vlasfabriekstraat 11, 1060 Brussels
Tel: (02) 536-11-13 *Fax:* (02) 536-19-10
E-mail: info@11.be
Web Site: www.11.be
Key Personnel
Education Coordinator: Bart Demedts *Tel:* (02) 536-11-14 *Fax:* (02) 536-19-02 *E-mail:* bart.demedts@11.be
Founded: 1966
Specialize in Third World affairs.
Subjects: Anthropology, Child Care & Development, Cookery, Developing Countries, Economics, Geography, Geology, Government, Political Science, Health, Nutrition, Journalism, Labor, Industrial Relations, Literature, Literary Criticism, Essays, Travel
ISBN Prefix(es): 90-71665
Distributed by Jan Van Arkel (Netherlands); Van Haelewyck-Uitgeverij (Belgium)
Distributor for Kit (Netherlands); Jan Mets (Netherlands); Novib (Netherlands)
Orders to: Eric Vander Borght *Tel:* (02) 536 1122 *E-mail:* eric.vanderborght@ncos.ngonet.be

Koninklijke Vlaamse Academie van Belgie voor Wetenschappen en Kunsten (Dutch-Speaking Royal Belgian Academy of Sciences, Letters & Fine Arts)
Paleis der Academien, Hertogsstr 1, 1000 Brussels
Tel: (02) 550 23 23 *Fax:* (02) 550 23 25
E-mail: info@kvab.be
Web Site: www.kvab.be
Key Personnel
Permanent Secretary: Niceas Schamp *E-mail:* niceas.schamp@kvab.be
Publications: Gilbert Reynders *Tel:* (02) 550 23 32 *E-mail:* gilbert.reynders@kvab.be
Founded: 1938
Membership(s): International Academic Association.
Subjects: Art, Music, Dance, Philosophy, Science (General)
ISBN Prefix(es): 90-6569
Orders to: Brepols Publishers IGP, Begynhof 67, 2300 Turnhout *Tel:* (014) 448 020 *Fax:* (014) 428 919 *E-mail:* info@brepols.com *Web Site:* www.brepols.net/publishers

De Krijger+
Dorpsstraat, 144, 9420 Erpe-Mere
Tel: (053) 808449 *Fax:* (053) 808453
E-mail: de.krijger@primemedia.be
Key Personnel
Owner: Vammabost Koem
Founded: 1987
Subjects: Military Science
ISBN Prefix(es): 90-72547; 90-5868
Number of titles published annually: 15 Print
Total Titles: 68 Print

Editions Labor
Quai du Commerce 29, 1000 Brussels
Tel: (02) 250-06-70 *Fax:* (02) 217-71-97
E-mail: labor@labor.be
Web Site: www.labor.be
Telex: 25532 Labor
Key Personnel
President: Th Vanderworst
Assistant Dir: Fabienne Herc *E-mail:* herc@labor.be
General Services: Jean-Pierre Van Mullem *E-mail:* vanmullen@labor.be
Founded: 1927
Subjects: Biography, Economics, Education, History, Philosophy, Poetry, Psychology, Psychiatry, Science (General), Social Sciences, Sociology
ISBN Prefix(es): 2-8040

Editions Lampe d'Or ASBL, see Ligue pour la lecture de la Bible

Uitgeverij Lannoo NV+
Kasteelstr 97, 8700 Tielt
Tel: (051) 42 42 11 *Fax:* (051) 40 11 52
E-mail: lannoo@lannoo.be
Web Site: www.lannoo.com
Key Personnel
President: Matthias Lannoo
Man Dir: Luc Demeester
Editorial Dir: Lieven Sercu
Founded: 1909
Subjects: Architecture & Interior Design, Art, Biography, Cookery, Economics, Gardening, Plants, Government, Political Science, Health, Nutrition, History, House & Home, Management, Nonfiction (General), Photography, Poetry, Religion - Catholic, Self-Help, Travel, Greeting Cards & Staty
ISBN Prefix(es): 90-209
Associate Companies: Bakermat NV, Mechelen; Distrimedia NV, Tielt; Touring Lanno NV, Brussels
Subsidiaries: ASDU International; Lannoo Campus; Editions Racine; Uitgeverij Terra Lannoo
Divisions: Lannoo Publishers; Lannoo Graphics
Distributed by Terra (Netherlands); Vilo (France & Canada)
Distributor for Academic Service (Netherlands); ANWB (Netherlands); Apress (Germany); Averbode (Belgium); Bakermat Uitgevers (Belgium); Beta Plus (Belgium); D-Publications (Belgium); Lonely Planet (UK); Microsoft Press (Ireland); Editions Moulinsart (Belgium); Nieuwezilds (Netherlands); O'Reilly (UK); Racine (Belgium); Sdu (Netherlands); Terra (Netherlands); Touring Lannoo (Belgium); Wiley (UK)
Warehouse: DistriMedia nv, Meulebeeksesteenweg 20, 8700 Tielt

Lansman Editeur (Lansman Publisher)+
65, rue Royale, 7141 Carnieres-Morlanwelz
Tel: (064) 23-78-40 *Fax:* (064) 44-31-02; (064) 23-78-49
E-mail: info@lansman.org
Web Site: www.lansman.org
Key Personnel
Dir: Emile Lansman
Press, Bookshop: Caroline Cullus
Founded: 1989
Specialize in theatre in French language (plays & research books).
Subjects: Art, Drama, Theater, Education, Literature, Literary Criticism, Essays
ISBN Prefix(es): 2-87282
Number of titles published annually: 35 Print
Total Titles: 450 Print
Distributor for Le bruit des Autres (outside France); Cahiers de Theatre Jeu (Europe); Solitaires Intempestifs (outside France)
Distribution Center: Casteilla SA, 10 rue Leon Foucault, 78180 Montigny-le-Bretonneux, France *Tel:* (01) 30 14 19 30 *Fax:* (01) 34 60 31 32 *E-mail:* casteilla@wanadoo.fr

Diffusion Dimedia Inc, 539, Blvd Lebeau, Saint-Laurent, PQ H4N 1S2, Canada *Tel:* 514-336-3941 *Fax:* 514-331-3916 *E-mail:* general@dimedia.qc.ca

Larcier-Department of De Boeck & Larcier SA
Rue des Minimes 39, 1000 Brussels
Mailing Address: Fond Jean-Pacques 4, 1348 Louvain-la-Neuve
E-mail: deboeck.larcier@deboeck.be
Web Site: www.larcier.be
Key Personnel
Chairman of the Board: Christian de Boeck
  Tel: (010) 10-48 26 21 *Fax:* (010) 10-48 26 50
  E-mail: christian.deboeck@deboeck.be
Man Dir: Bernard Houdmont
Dir: Georges Hoyos *Tel:* (010) 10-48 26 04
  Fax: (010) 10-48 26 50 *E-mail:* georges.hoyos@deboeck.be
Group Editorial Dir: Yann Delalande
Founded: 1839
Subjects: Law
ISBN Prefix(es): 2-8044
Parent Company: Groupe De Boeck SA
Associate Companies: De Boeck & Larcier SA-Acces Plus SPRL
Distributed by LITEC (France only)
Orders to: Acces Plus SPRL, Fond Jean-Paques 4, 1348 Louvain-La-Neuve

Claude Lefrancq Editeur+
chaussee d'Alsemberg, 1180 Brussels
Tel: (02) 344-49-34 *Fax:* (02) 347-55-34
E-mail: claude.lefrancq@skynet.be
Key Personnel
Chairman & Man Dir: R Demartin
Editor: Claude Lefrancq
Founded: 1995
Subjects: Anthropology, Biography, Film, Video, Humor, Literature, Literary Criticism, Essays, Mysteries, Romance
ISBN Prefix(es): 2-87153; 90-71987; 90-75388

Editions Lessius ASBL+
Division of South Belgian Area of the Company of Jesus
Blvd Saint-Michel, 24, 1040 Brussels
Tel: (02) 739 34 90 *Fax:* (02) 739 34 91
E-mail: info@editions-lessius.be
Web Site: www.adeb.irisnet.be/annuaire/lessius.htm
Key Personnel
Dir: Daniel Dideberg *Tel:* (02) 739 34 92
  E-mail: d.dideberg@iet.be
Dir of Collection: Rene Lafontaine; Benoit Malvaux; Jacques Scheuer; Jean-Pierre Sonnet
Communication Manager: Nathalie Dubois
  Tel: (02) 739 34 93 *E-mail:* nath.dubois@skynet.be
Founded: 1997
Specialize in exegetic Biblical commentaries; essays (language, philosophy, theology, psychology, art, law); meditation & pray; biography; & meeting between religions.
Subjects: Art, Biblical Studies, Biography, Language Arts, Linguistics, Law, Literature, Literary Criticism, Essays, Philosophy, Religion - Catholic, Religion - Hindu, Religion - Jewish, Social Sciences, Sociology, Theology
ISBN Prefix(es): 2-87299
Number of titles published annually: 12 Print
Total Titles: 120 Print
Distributed by Editions du Cerf

Leuven University Press+
Blijde Inkomstraat 5, 3000 Leuven
Tel: (016) 32 53 45 *Fax:* (016) 32 53 52
E-mail: university.press@upers.kuleuven.ac.be; universitaire.pers@upers.kuleuven.ac.be
Web Site: www.lup.be
Key Personnel
Dir: Hilde Lens-Gielis *E-mail:* hilde.gielis@upers.kuleuven.ac.be
Publisher: Beatrice Van Eeghem
Public Relations & Marketing: Ineke Deckers
  E-mail: ineke.deckers@upers.kuleuven.ac.be; Patricia Di Constanzo *E-mail:* patricia.dicostanzo@upers.kuleuven.ac.be
Accounting: Regine Vanswijgenhoven
  E-mail: regine.vanswijgenhoven@upers.kuleuven.ac.be
Founded: 1971
Membership(s): International Association of Scholarly Publishers.
Subjects: Agriculture, Archaeology, Biological Sciences, Criminology, Economics, Education, Environmental Studies, Geography, Geology, Government, Political Science, History, Language Arts, Linguistics, Law, Literature, Literary Criticism, Essays, Mathematics, Medicine, Nursing, Dentistry, Music, Dance, Philosophy, Physical Sciences, Physics, Psychology, Psychiatry, Science (General), Social Sciences, Sociology, Theology
ISBN Prefix(es): 90-6186; 90-5867
Number of titles published annually: 100 Print; 1 Audio
Total Titles: 1,400 Print; 5 CD-ROM; 3 Audio
Distribution Center: Coronet Books, 311 Bainbridge St, Philadelphia 19147, United States
Orders to: Coronet Books, 311 Bainbridge St, Philadelphia 19147, United States

Liberica, *imprint of* Zuid-Nederlandse Uitgeverij NV/Central Uitgeverij

Ligue pour la lecture de la Bible+
Formerly Editions Lampe d'Or ASBL
Subsidiary of Scripture Union
Ave Giele, 23, 1090 Brussels
Tel: (02) 427-92-77 *Fax:* (02) 428-82-06
E-mail: llb_ibb@freegates.be
Key Personnel
Man Dir: J Makkink
Founded: 1955
Subjects: Religion - Other
ISBN Prefix(es): 2-87001
Number of titles published annually: 3 Print
Distributed by Lique pour la Lecture de la Bible France; Lique pour la Lecture de la Bible Quebec, Canada; Maison de la Bible Suisse
Distributor for Ligue pour la Lecture de la Bible France; Ligue pour la Lecture de la Bible Suisse

Editeurs de Litterature Biblique+
Chaussee de Tubize, 479, 1420 Braine-l'Alleud
Tel: (02) 384-54-02; (02) 384-52-12 *Fax:* (02) 384-98-66
E-mail: elbpub@elbeurope.org
Web Site: www.elbeurope.org
Key Personnel
Dir: Joel Rousseau
Founded: 1959
Subjects: Crafts, Games, Hobbies, Education, Music, Dance, Philosophy, Religion - Other, Sports, Athletics
ISBN Prefix(es): 2-8045
Branch Office(s)
Biblical Publications, 22 W 569 Winthrop, Glen Ellyn, IL 60139, United States

Uitgeverij Loempia+
Mechelsesteenweg, 123, 2018 Antwerp
Tel: (03) 2184292
Key Personnel
Man Dir: Jef Meert
Founded: 1983
ISBN Prefix(es): 90-6771

Les Editions du Lombard SA+
Subsidiary of Sofidar
7 av Paul-Henri-Spaak, 1060 Brussels
Tel: (02) 5266811 *Fax:* (02) 5204405
E-mail: info@lombard.be
Web Site: www.lelombard.com
Telex: 23097 *Cable:* LOMBARBEL BRUSSELS
Key Personnel
General Manager: Francois Pernot
Editorial Manager: Yves Sente
Public Relations: Anne-Marie De Coster
  E-mail: annemarie.decoster@lelombard.be
Licensing, Rights, Press: Jean-Philippe Buysschaert *E-mail:* jeanphilippe.buysschaert@edlbm.be
Rights & Permissions: Sophie Castille
Founded: 1946
Subjects: Fiction, History, Humor, Science Fiction, Fantasy
ISBN Prefix(es): 2-8036; 2-87389
Subsidiaries: Citel & Dargaud; Dargaud Benelux; Dargaud Marina; Dargaud Suisse
Branch Office(s)
15-27 rue Moussorgski, 75018 Paris, France
  Tel: (01) 53 26 32 32 *Fax:* (01) 53 26 32 40
Orders to: MDS, ZI de la Gaudree, 91417 Cedex, Dourdan, France *Tel:* (01) 60818700 *Fax:* (01) 64593063

La Longue Vue+
Division of RVJ Editions
Dreve Pittoresque 92, 1640 Rhode Saint-Genese
Tel: (02) 358 23 93 *Fax:* (02) 358 17 37
E-mail: longuevue@skynet.be
Key Personnel
Dir, Editions: Charles de Trazegnies *Tel:* (02) 358 23 93
Founded: 1984
Specialize in Belgian literature & translation; also acts as a translation agency.
Subjects: Biblical Studies, Fiction, Literature, Literary Criticism, Essays, Philosophy, Poetry
ISBN Prefix(es): 2-87121
Total Titles: 100 Print
Distributed by Nord-Sud Diffusion (Belgium); Casteilla-Chiron (France)

Editions Lumen Vitae ASBL+
Division of CIEFR Centre Lumen Vitae
184-186 rue Washington, 1050 Brussels
Tel: (02) 3490399; (02) 3490370 *Fax:* (02) 3490385
E-mail: international@lumenvitae.be
Web Site: www.catho.be/lumen
Key Personnel
Publishing Dir: Henri Derroitte
Secretary & International Rights: Gabriella Tihon-Gyorffy *E-mail:* gabriella.tihon@lumenvitae.be
Founded: 1935
Subjects: Biblical Studies, Education, Religion - Catholic, Theology
ISBN Prefix(es): 2-87324
Number of titles published annually: 25 Print
Total Titles: 100 Print
Distributed by Cerf (France & Switzerland); Novalis (Canada & USA)

Maklu+
Somersstraat 13-15, 2018 Antwerp 1
Tel: (03) 231-29-00 *Fax:* (03) 233-26-59
E-mail: info@maklu.be
Web Site: www.maklu.be
Key Personnel
Dir: Bert Boerwinkel; Huug Van Gompel
  E-mail: huug.vangompel@maklu.be
Publisher: Stephan Svacina
Promotion: Werner Peeters
Founded: 1972
Also acts as wholesaler (Dutch books).
Specialize in law books & dictionaries.
Subjects: Economics, Government, Political Science, Law, Management, Social Sciences, Sociology
ISBN Prefix(es): 90-6215

Number of titles published annually: 80 Print
Total Titles: 800 Print
Associate Companies: Garant Publishers Ltd
Subsidiaries: Maklu bv
Distributed by Bayliss (London); Gaunt & Sons (USA); Juridik & Samhaelle (Sweden); Nomos Verlag (Germany); Schulthess Verlag (Switzerland)

Manteau, *imprint of* Standaard Uitgeverij

Marabout+
Ave de l'Energie, 30, 4432 Alleur
Tel: (04) 246 3863; (04) 4146 3815 *Fax:* (04) 246 3635
Key Personnel
President: Jacques Firmin
Financial Dir: Andre Palmans
Dir: Jean Arache
Foreign Rights: Michele Boschis
Founded: 1949
Subjects: Animals, Pets, Astrology, Occult, Behavioral Sciences, Career Development, Child Care & Development, Computer Science, Cookery, Crafts, Games, Hobbies, English as a Second Language, Gardening, Plants, Genealogy, Health, Nutrition, History, Human Relations, Humor, Medicine, Nursing, Dentistry, Self-Help
ISBN Prefix(es): 2-501
Parent Company: Hachette
Distributed by Diffulivre Suisse; Hachette Canada; Hachette Livre France; Tous Pays

Mardaga, Pierre, Editeur
Hayen 11, 4140 Sprimont
Tel: (04) 3684242 *Fax:* (04) 3684240
Key Personnel
Dir & Rights & Permissions: Pierre Mardaga
Founded: 1938
1600 titles on catalogue.
Subjects: Architecture & Interior Design, Education, Human Relations, Language Arts, Linguistics, Music, Dance, Philosophy, Psychology, Psychiatry
ISBN Prefix(es): 2-87009; 2-8047
Number of titles published annually: 45 Print

Medaillon, *imprint of* Uitgeverij de Eenhoorn

Editions Medicales et Paramedicales de Charleroi (EMPC)
rue Saint-Charles, 9, 6061 Montignies-sur-Sambre
Tel: (071) 324689 *Fax:* (071) 324689
Key Personnel
General Dir: Chantal Zanella
ISBN Prefix(es): 2-87133

Editions Memor
Rue Gustave Biot 23-25, 1050 Brussels
Tel: (02) 644-04-43 *Fax:* (02) 644-04-43
Web Site: www.memor.cjb.net
Key Personnel
Dir: John F Ellyton *E-mail:* john.ellyton@skynet.be
Founded: 1995
Specialize in general Collection Couleurs Teenagers, Transparences Adults.
Subjects: Fiction, Literature, Literary Criticism, Essays
ISBN Prefix(es): 2-930133
Number of titles published annually: 8 Print
Total Titles: 3 Print
Foreign Rep(s): Alterdis (France)

Mercatorfonds NV+
Meir 85, 2000 Antwerp
Tel: (03) 2027260 *Fax:* (03) 2311319
E-mail: artbooks@mercatorfonds.be
Web Site: www.mercatorfonds.be

Key Personnel
Publisher: Jan Martens *E-mail:* jm@mercatorfonds.be
Founded: 1965
Publisher of fine art books & illustrated historical studies.
Subjects: Architecture & Interior Design, Art, History
ISBN Prefix(es): 90-6153
Number of titles published annually: 10 Print

Michelin Editions des Voyages
33 quai de Willebroek, 1000 Brussels
Tel: (02) 274 45 03 *Fax:* (02) 274 43 62
E-mail: kontakt@viamichelin.com
Web Site: www.viamichelin.com *Cable:* PNEUMICLIN
Key Personnel
Dir: Robert Van Keerberghen *E-mail:* robert-vankeerberghen@be.michelin.com
Founded: 1913
Subjects: Travel, Tourist Guides
Parent Company: Michelin Editions Des Voyages
Ultimate Parent Company: Manufacture Francaise Des Pneumatiques Michelin
U.S. Office(s): Michelin Travel Publications & Michelin Tire Corporation, One Parkway S, Greenville, SC 29615, United States

Harvey Miller, *imprint of* Brepols Publishers NV

Mozaiek, *imprint of* Uitgeverij Clavis

Nauwelaerts Edition SA+
Eglise St Sulpice 19, 1320 Beauvechain
Tel: (010) 86 67 37 *Fax:* (010) 86 16 55
Key Personnel
Man Dir: Stephane Rouget
Founded: 1934
Subjects: Economics, History, Literature, Literary Criticism, Essays, Medicine, Nursing, Dentistry, Philosophy, Psychology, Psychiatry, Social Sciences, Sociology, Theology
ISBN Prefix(es): 2-8038
Associate Companies: Vander Publishing

Nouvelle Diffusion SPRL DPI, see Editions Complexe SPRL

Les Nouvelles Editions Marabout SA, see Marabout

Petraco-Pandora NV+
Indiestr 21, 2000 Antwerp
Tel: (03) 2338770 *Fax:* (03) 2333399
Founded: 1988
Subjects: Art, Catalogues, Monographs, Catalogue Raisonne
ISBN Prefix(es): 90-5325
Number of titles published annually: 30 Print
Total Titles: 180 Print

Paradox Express - Manuscripten, *imprint of* Paradox Pers vzw

Paradox Pers vzw+
Leopoldstraat 55/1, 2000 Antwerp
Tel: (03) 2318873 *Fax:* (03) 2386605
E-mail: paradox@glo.be; paradoxpers@belgacom.be
Key Personnel
Dir: Dirk Claus
Founded: 1960
Subjects: Fiction, Philosophy, Poetry
ISBN Prefix(es): 90-72533
Number of titles published annually: 10 Print
Imprints: Paradox Express - Manuscripten
Distributed by EPO (Belgium)

Parasol NV+
Mechelse Steenweg 434, 2650 Edegem
Tel: (03) 460 1880 *Fax:* (03) 460 1881
E-mail: info@parasol.be
Web Site: www.parasol.be
Key Personnel
Man Dir: Wilfried Wuyts *Fax:* (03) 460 1888
  E-mail: ww@parasol.be
Founded: 1994
Specialize in children's books ; publish in Dutch & French.
ISBN Prefix(es): 90-5593; 90-5888
Number of titles published annually: 60 Print
Total Titles: 300 Print

Parsifal BVBA
Gulden Vlieslaan 67, 8000 Brugge
Tel: (050) 339516 *Fax:* (050) 333386
E-mail: info@parsifal.be
Web Site: www.parsifal.be
Key Personnel
Chief Executive, Rights & Permissions: Christian Vandekerkhove
Production: Erna Droesbeke
Founded: 1974
Subjects: Astrology, Occult, Parapsychology, Philosophy
ISBN Prefix(es): 90-6458; 2-87259
Associate Companies: Editions Verrycken
Branch Office(s)
Steenhouwersvest, 2000 Antwerp *Tel:* (03) 2316039
Bookshop(s): Librairie Verrycken, Weigstr 30, 2000 Antwerp (jointly owned with Editions Verrycsen); Occult Bookshop, Hoogstr 68, B-2000 Antwerp

La Part de L'Oeil+
Rue du Midi, 144, 1000 Brussels
Tel: (02) 514 18 41 *Fax:* (02) 514 18 41
E-mail: lapartdeloeil@brunette.brucity.be
Key Personnel
Contact: Lucien Massaert
International Rights Contact: Karine Barbareau
Founded: 1985
La Part de L'Oeil is a theoretical arts review published in French.
Subjects: Art, Language Arts, Linguistics, Literature, Literary Criticism, Essays, Philosophy, Poetry, Psychology, Psychiatry
ISBN Prefix(es): 2-930174
Number of titles published annually: 4 Print
Total Titles: 32 Print
Distributed by La Federation Diffusion (France, Quebec & Switzerland); La Part de l'Oeil (Belgium); UD-Union Distribution (France, Quebec & Switzerland)
Foreign Rep(s): Karine Barbareau

Uitgeverij Peeters Leuven (Belgie) (Peeters Publishers & Booksellers)+
Bondgenotenlaan 153, 3000 Leuven
Tel: (016) 23 51 70 *Fax:* (016) 22 85 00
E-mail: peeters@peeters-leuven.be
Web Site: www.peeters-leuven.be
Key Personnel
Dir: Mr P Peeters
Founded: 1857
Publish books & journals in English, French, German & Dutch. Publish original research as well as bibliographic data, reviews & reference material.
Subjects: Archaeology, Art, Asian Studies, Biblical Studies, History, Language Arts, Linguistics, Literature, Literary Criticism, Essays, Philosophy, Religion - Other, Theology, Classical Studies, Ethics, History of Art, Medieval Studies, Oriental Studies
ISBN Prefix(es): 2-87723; 90-6831; 90-429; 2-8017
Number of titles published annually: 150 Print; 2 CD-ROM; 50 Online

Total Titles: 3,500 Print; 50 Online
Subsidiaries: Peeters
Distribution Center: Book Representation & Distribution Ltd, 244a London Rd, Hadleigh-Essex SS7 2DE, United Kingdom *Tel:* (17) 02-552912 *Fax:* (17) 02-556095 *E-mail:* sales@bookreps.com
The David Brown Book Co, PO Box 511, Oakville, CT 06679, United States, Contact: I Stevens *E-mail:* david.brown.bk.co@snet.net *Web Site:* www.davidbrownbookco.com
VRIN, 6 Place de la Sodonne, 75005 Paris, France *Tel:* (01) 43540347 *Fax:* (01) 43544818 *E-mail:* contact@vrin.fr

Pelckmans NV, De Nederlandsche Boekhandel+
Kapelsestraat 222, 2950 Kapellen
Tel: (03) 660 27 00 *Fax:* (03) 660 27 01
E-mail: uitgeverij@pelckmans.be
Web Site: www.pelckmans.be
Key Personnel
General Director: Jan en Rudi Pelckmans
Founded: 1892
Subjects: Geography, Geology, History, Language Arts, Linguistics, Literature, Literary Criticism, Essays, Mathematics, Philosophy, Religion - Catholic
ISBN Prefix(es): 90-289

Uitgeverij Pelckmans NV
Kapelsestr 222, 2950 Kapellen
Tel: (03) 6602700 *Fax:* (03) 66022701
E-mail: uitgeverij@pelckmans.be
Web Site: www.pelckmans.be
Telex: 32242 Anvers Dnb
Key Personnel
Man Dir: J Pelckmans; R Pelckmans
Founded: 1892
Subjects: History, Philosophy, Religion - Other, Social Sciences, Sociology
ISBN Prefix(es): 90-289
Associate Companies: Uitgeverij Helios; Uitgeverij Patmos
Bookshop(s): Sint Jacobsmarkt 7, 2000 Antwerp

Poeziecentrum+
Vrydagmarkt 36, 9000 Gent
Tel: (09) 225 22 25 *Fax:* (09) 225 90 54
E-mail: info@poeziecentrum.be
Web Site: www.poeziecentrum.be
Key Personnel
Man Dir: Willy Tibergien
Founded: 1980
Subjects: Poetry
ISBN Prefix(es): 90-5655; 90-70968
Number of titles published annually: 10 Print

Le Pole Nord ASBL
Rue du Nord, 66, 1000 Brussels
Tel: (02) 2184576 *Fax:* (02) 2184576
E-mail: pole.nord@skynet.be
Key Personnel
President: Anny Frenay
Secretary: Charlotte Goetz
Founded: 1983
Also acts as Scientific Research Association.
Subjects: History, French Revolution, Jean-Paul Marat
ISBN Prefix(es): 2-930040
Distributed by Pole Nord Asbl

Pre-Ecole, *imprint of* Editions Chantecler

Preschool, *imprint of* Zuid-Nederlandse Uitgeverij NV/Central Uitgeverij

Presses agronomiques de Gembloux ASBL+
2, Passage des Deportes, 5030 Gembloux
Tel: (081) 62 22 42 *Fax:* (081) 62 22 42
E-mail: pressesagro@fsagx.ac.be
Web Site: www.bib.fsagx.ac.be/presses/

Key Personnel
Dir: Mr B Pochet
Founded: 1964
Specialize also in chemistry & the food industry.
Subjects: Agriculture, Biological Sciences, Environmental Studies, Mathematics, Technology
ISBN Prefix(es): 2-87016
Number of titles published annually: 3 Print
Total Titles: 30 Print
Foreign Rep(s): Lavoisier (Canada, France)

Presses Universitaires de Bruxelles asbl
Ave Paul Heger, 42, 1000 Brussels
Mailing Address: CP 149, 1000 Brussels
Tel: (02) 649 97 80 *Fax:* (02) 647 79 62
E-mail: editions@admin.ulb.ac.be
Web Site: www.ulb.ac.be/ulb/docs/pub.html
Key Personnel
President: Thierry Lambrecht
Man Dir: Jeannine De Backer *E-mail:* jdbacker@ulb.ac.be
Sales: Henri De Smet
Founded: 1958
Subjects: Architecture & Interior Design, Economics, Engineering (General), Medicine, Nursing, Dentistry, Philosophy, Science (General)
ISBN Prefix(es): 2-500

Presses Universitaires de Liege
Domaine Universi du Sart-Tilman, Batiment 87, bte 27, 4000 Liege
Tel: (041) 562218
Founded: 1969
Subjects: Government, Political Science, Law, Medicine, Nursing, Dentistry, Social Sciences, Sociology
ISBN Prefix(es): 2-87014
Branch Office(s)
7, Place du 20-Aout Bat A1, 04000 Leige
Tel: (041) 420080

Presses Universitaires de Namur ASBL
Rempart de la Vierge 13, 5000 Namur
Tel: (081) 72 48 84 *Fax:* (081) 72 49 12
E-mail: pun@fundp.ac.be
Web Site: www.pun.be
Key Personnel
Dir: Rene Robaye
Editor: Myriam Despineux *Tel:* (081) 72 48 86 *E-mail:* myriam.despineux@fundp.ac.be
Public Relations: Stephanie Herfurth *Tel:* (081) 72 48 85 *E-mail:* stephanie.herfurth@fundp.ac.be
Founded: 1977
Membership(s): ADEB (Association des Editeurs Belges).
ISBN Prefix(es): 2-87037
Number of titles published annually: 15 Print

Prodim SPRL+
184, Blvd General Jacques, 1050 Brussels
Tel: (02) 640 59 70 *Fax:* (02) 640 59 91
E-mail: prodim.books@prodim.be
Web Site: www.prodim.be
Key Personnel
President: Mdme Nile Patrick
Founded: 1968
Physiotherapy.
Membership(s): ADEB.
Subjects: Medicine, Nursing, Dentistry
ISBN Prefix(es): 2-87017
Subsidiaries: de Visscher
Distributor for Jibena (Belgium); Similia (Belgium)
Foreign Rep(s): Nile Patrick

Production et Diffusion de Medias SPRL, see Prodim SPRL

Henri Proost & Co, Pvba
Everdongenlaan 23, 2300 Turnhout
Tel: (014) 40 08 11 *Fax:* (014) 42 87 94
Web Site: www.proost.be
Telex: 33185
Key Personnel
Man Dir: Herman Peeters *E-mail:* herman.peeters@proost.be
Sales Dir: Jan Jacobs
Subjects: Cookery, Gardening, Plants, History, Religion - Other, Travel
ISBN Prefix(es): 90-6150
Subsidiaries: Bedford Editions Ltd; Salamander Books Ltd

Publications des Facultes Universitaires Saint Louis+
Blvd du Jardin Botanique 43, 1000 Brussels
Tel: (02) 211 78 94 *Fax:* (02) 211 79 97
Web Site: www.fusl.ac.be
Key Personnel
Man Dir: Francois Ost
Sales & Publicity: Marie-Francoise Thoua *E-mail:* thoua@fusl.ac.be
Founded: 1973
Subjects: Economics, History, Law, Philosophy, Psychology, Psychiatry, Social Sciences, Sociology, Theology
ISBN Prefix(es): 2-8028

Editions Racine+
Rue du Chatelain 49, 1050 Brussels
Tel: (02) 646 44 44 *Fax:* (02) 646 55 70
E-mail: info@racine.be
Web Site: www.racine.be
Key Personnel
Dir: Emmanuel Brutsaert
Founded: 1993
Specialize also in nature.
Subjects: Architecture & Interior Design, Art, History, Nonfiction (General)
ISBN Prefix(es): 2-87386
Total Titles: 160 Print
Parent Company: Lannoo
Ultimate Parent Company: Lannoo
Distributed by Lannoo (Belgium); Vilo (France); Altera Diffusion (Begium)

Rainbow Grafics Intl - Baronian Books SC+
63 rue Charles Legrelle, 1040 Brussels
Tel: (02) 7348114 *Fax:* (02) 7325764
Key Personnel
Man Dir: Mdme Anne Lous Baronian
Editorial Dir: Jehn Baptiste Lous Baronian
Specialize in International Co-Production.

Reader's Digest SA
blvd Paepsem 20, 1070 Brussels
Tel: (02) 5268111 *Fax:* (02) 5268112
Telex: 21876
Key Personnel
Man Dir: J H Beauduin
Founded: 1947
Subjects: Education, Geography, Geology, History, Sports, Athletics, Travel
ISBN Prefix(es): 90-70818; 2-87101

La Renaissance du Livre+
14/1 Rue de Paris, 7500 Tournai
Tel: (069) 89 15 55 *Fax:* (069) 89 15 50
Web Site: www.larenaissancedulivre.com
Founded: 1923
Subjects: Art, History
ISBN Prefix(es): 2-8041; 2-87148; 2-8046
Distributed by Exhibitions International (Dutch-speaking Belgium & Netherlands); Vivendi Universal Publishing (French-speaking Belgium & Grand Duchy)

Roularta Books NV+
meiboomlaan 33, 8800 Roeselare

Tel: (051) 266967 *Fax:* (051) 266680
E-mail: info@roularta.be
Web Site: www.roulartabooks.be
Key Personnel
President: Jan Ingelbeen
Business Mgr: Lieve Claeys
Founded: 1988
Subjects: Architecture & Interior Design, Art, Business, Economics, Gardening, Plants, Literature, Literary Criticism, Essays, Management, Marketing, Nonfiction (General), Sports, Athletics, Travel
ISBN Prefix(es): 90-5466; 90-72411; 90-940073
Imprints: Globe; KnackBibliotheek/Radio 1

Scaillet, SA+
Rue de Marchienne 203, 6110 Montigny-le-Tilleul
Tel: (071) 516335 *Fax:* (071) 511795
Key Personnel
Administrative Delegate: Andre Scaillet
Founded: 1984
Also acts as a printing office.
Subjects: History
ISBN Prefix(es): 2-930002

Schaar, *imprint of* De Schaar/Geknipt Papier

De Schaar/Geknipt Papier+
Penitentenstr 24, 9000 Ghent
Tel: (09) 225 5414 *Fax:* (09) 225 9724
E-mail: geknipt@skynet.be
Key Personnel
International Rights: Carla Wauben
Contact: Paul D'Haene
Founded: 1989
Subjects: Comics
ISBN Prefix(es): 90-5775; 90-73619
Imprints: Blitz; Schaar; Scissors

Paul Schiltz
3 Place Rotenberg, 4700 Eupen
Tel: (087) 553271
Key Personnel
Man Dir: Paul Schiltz
Founded: 1963
Subjects: Medicine, Nursing, Dentistry
ISBN Prefix(es): 2-87058

Schott Freres SA (Editeurs de Musique)
30 rue Saint-Jean, 1000 Brussels
Tel: (02) 5123980 *Fax:* (02) 5142845
Key Personnel
Man Dir: Jean-Jacques Junne
Founded: 1823
Subjects: Music, Dance
Associate Companies: Schott Freres Sarl, France

Scissors, *imprint of* De Schaar/Geknipt Papier

Scoop Infotex NV+
Subsidiary of VUM Group
Forelstr 22, 9000 Ghent
Tel: (09) 2056430 *Fax:* (09) 2056449
E-mail: scoop@infotex.be
Key Personnel
Delegate Dir: Johan De Koning
Editor: Leen Van Troys *E-mail:* leen.vantroys@infotex.be
Founded: 1991
Subjects: Biography, Business, Career Development, Economics, Government, Political Science, History, Journalism, Literature, Literary Criticism, Essays, Management, Marketing, Travel
ISBN Prefix(es): 90-5312; 90-900261; 90-940062
Number of titles published annually: 30 Print; 1 CD-ROM
Imprints: Globe

Service, *imprint of* Editions Juridiques Kluwer a Deurne Anvers

Uitgeverij De Sikkel NV+
Nijverheidsstr 8, 2390 Oostmalle
Tel: (03) 312 86 30 *Fax:* (03) 311 77 39
E-mail: informatie@deboeck.be
Web Site: www.desikkel.be
Key Personnel
Man Dir: Bart Hye *Tel:* (03) 3128643
 E-mail: bhye@desikkel.be
Contact: Bieke Berhaers *E-mail:* bberhaers@desikkel.be; Patrick Vandevelde *Tel:* (03) 3128644 *E-mail:* pvandevelde@desikkel.be
Founded: 1919
Membership(s): Flemish Publishers Association.
Subjects: Education, English as a Second Language
ISBN Prefix(es): 90-260
Parent Company: De Pioen, Oostmalle
Distributor for Dijkstra (Groningen); Ediciones SM (Madrid); Panta Rhei; Spruyt; Verpleegkundig fonds (Leiden); Von Mantgem en de Does; UBS (Oegstgeest); De Vey-Mestdagh (Middelburg); Westermann Lernspiel (Braunschweig)
Bookshop(s): De Pioen, Oostmalle

Snoeck-Ducaju en Zoon NV
Begijnhoflaan 464, 9000 Ghent
Tel: (09) 267.04.11 *Fax:* (09) 267.04.60
E-mail: sdz@sdz.be
Web Site: www.sdz.be
Telex: 12765
Key Personnel
Algemene Dir: S Snoeck
Founded: 1782
Subjects: Literature, Literary Criticism, Essays
ISBN Prefix(es): 90-70481; 90-5349

Sonneville Press (Uitgeverij) VTW
Karel De Stoutelaan 142, 8000 Brugge
Tel: (050) 321112
Key Personnel
Dir: J Sonneville
Founded: 1987
Subjects: Art, Education, Ethnicity, Geography, Geology, Government, Political Science, History, Language Arts, Linguistics, Law, Literature, Literary Criticism, Essays, Music, Dance, Philosophy, Religion - Other, Social Sciences, Sociology, Sports, Athletics, Travel
ISBN Prefix(es): 90-5149

Stafeto, *imprint of* Vlaamse Esperantobond VZW

Standaard Uitgeverij+
Belgielei 147a, 2018 Antwerp
Tel: (03) 285 72 00 *Fax:* (03) 285 72 99
E-mail: info@standaarduitgeverij.be
Web Site: www.standaarduitgeverij.be
Key Personnel
Man Dir: Eric Willems
Editorial Dir: Johan de Koning; Diane Devriendt
Publisher: Wim Verheije
Editorial Dir: Jacques Germonprez
Founded: 1906
Subjects: Biography, Fiction, Humor, Poetry
ISBN Prefix(es): 90-02
Parent Company: PCM Algemene Boeken bv, Nieuwekade 1, 3511 RV Utrecht, Netherlands
Imprints: Manteau
Warehouse: Libridis-Bulkmagazijn Temse, Schoenstr 6, 9140 Temse
Orders to: Libridis-Bulkmagazijn Temse, Schoenstr 6, 9140 Temse

Stichting Kunstboek bvba+
Legeweg 165, 8020 Oostkamp
Tel: (050) 461910 *Fax:* (050) 461918

Key Personnel
Contact: Jaak van Damme; Karel Puype
Founded: 1992
Subjects: Architecture & Interior Design, Art, Crafts, Games, Hobbies, Gardening, Plants, History, Music, Dance
ISBN Prefix(es): 90-74377; 90-5856

Stichting Ons Erfdeel VZW
Murissonstr 260, 8930 Rekkem
Tel: (056) 41 12 01 *Fax:* (056) 41 47 07
E-mail: info@onserfdeel.be
Web Site: www.onserfdeel.be
Key Personnel
Man Dir & Chief Editor: Luc Devoldere
Head, Administration: Bernard Viaene
 E-mail: adm@onserfdeel.be
Founded: 1970
Specialize in promoting cultural cooperation among all speakers of the Dutch language & increase awareness of Flemish & Dutch culture abroad. Publish & distribute a range of periodicals & other publications, both in Dutch & other languages.
Subjects: Art, Ethnicity, Language Arts, Linguistics, Literature, Literary Criticism, Essays, Regional Interests
ISBN Prefix(es): 90-70831; 90-75862
Branch Office(s)
Rijvoortshoef 265, 4941 VJ Raamsdonksveer, Netherlands *Tel:* (0162) 513425 *Fax:* (0162) 519227

E Story-Scientia, *imprint of* Editions Juridiques Kluwer a Deurne Anvers

Editions Techniques et Scientifiques SPRL
37 rue Borrens, 1050 Brussels
Tel: (02) 6401040 *Fax:* (02) 6400739
Key Personnel
Man Dir: A Louis
Founded: 1919
Subjects: Ethnicity, Geography, Geology, History, Law, Mathematics, Science (General), Technology, Travel
ISBN Prefix(es): 2-87004

Toneelfonds J Janssens BVBA+
Te Boelaerlei 107, 2140 Borgerhout-Antwerp
Tel: (03) 366 44 00 *Fax:* (03) 366 45 01
E-mail: info@toneelfonds.be
Web Site: www.toneelfonds.be
Key Personnel
Dir: Jessica Janssens *E-mail:* jessica.janssens@toneelfonds.be
Founded: 1880
Publisher of plays & brochures. Also acts as literary agent for playwrights.
Subjects: Drama, Theater
ISBN Prefix(es): 90-385
Number of titles published annually: 100 Print

Toulon Uitgeverij
Sportstr 35, 8400 Oostende
Tel: (059) 800927
Key Personnel
Dir: P A Toulon
Subjects: Education
ISBN Prefix(es): 90-70270

UCL, see Presses Universitaires de Louvain-UCL

UGA Editions (Uitgeverij)
Stijn Streuvelslaan 73, 8501 Courtrai
Tel: (056) 36 32 00 *Fax:* (056) 35 60 96
E-mail: publ@uga.be
Web Site: www.uga.be *Cable:* UGA
Key Personnel
Dir: L Deschildre
Editorial, Sales: Patrick van Assche *E-mail:* pva@uga.be

Founded: 1948
Also acts as packager.
Subjects: History, Language Arts, Linguistics, Law, Public Administration, Social Sciences, Sociology
ISBN Prefix(es): 90-6768
Branch Office(s)
CAD, rue Guimard, 19 - Boite 2, 1040 Brussels
Tel: (02) 512 09 75 *Fax:* (02) 512 26 93

Uitgeverij Averbode NV (Averbode Publishers)+
Abdijstraat 1, 3271 Averbode
Tel: (013) 780 184 *Fax:* (013) 780 183
E-mail: educational@verbode.be
Web Site: www.averbode.com
Key Personnel
Business Unit Manager: Patrick Hermans
 E-mail: patrick.hermans@verbode.be
Rights & License Assistant: Ann Vanoppen
Founded: 1993
Subjects: Education, Religion - Catholic, Educational youth magazines, teacher support materials
ISBN Prefix(es): 90-317
Number of titles published annually: 40 Print
Total Titles: 250 Print

Uitgeverij De Garve
Groene Poortdreef 27, 8200 Sint Michiels Brugge
Tel: (050) 400050 *Fax:* (050) 388099
E-mail: info@degarve.be
Web Site: www.degarve.be
Key Personnel
Dir: G Barbiaux
Founded: 1909
Subjects: Biography, Government, Political Science, Language Arts, Linguistics, Law, Mathematics, Music, Dance, Physics, Social Sciences, Sociology
ISBN Prefix(es): 90-5148
Parent Company: Drukkerij PVBA G Barbiaux

Unistad Verspreiding CV+
Jan Moorkensstr 46, 2600 Berchem
Tel: (03) 2307725 *Fax:* (03) 2307725
Key Personnel
Dir: Rob Claes
Editorial: Bennie Callebaut
Founded: 1984
Subjects: Religion - Other
ISBN Prefix(es): 90-70276; 90-6721
Parent Company: Citta Nuova Editrice, Italy

Universitaire Pers Leuven, see Leuven University Press

Presses Universitaires de Louvain-UCL
Place de l'Universite Catholique de Louvain, 1, 1348 Louvain-la-Neuve
Tel: (010) 47 40 30 *Fax:* (010) 47 25 31
Web Site: www.ucl.ac.be
Telex: UCL AC 59516
Key Personnel
Dir: Jacqueline Tulkens
Membership(s): ADEB.
Subjects: Science (General)
ISBN Prefix(es): 2-87200; 90-06; 2-930344

Editions de l'Universite de Bruxelles+
26, ave Paul-Heger, CP 163, 1000 Brussels
Tel: (02) 650 37 99 *Fax:* (02) 650 37 94
E-mail: editions@admin.ulb.ac.be
Web Site: www.editions-universite-bruxelles.be
Key Personnel
President: Robert Tollet
Editorial Manager: Michele Mat *Tel:* (02) 650 37 97 *E-mail:* mmat@admin.ulb.ac.be
Secretary: Betty Prevost *E-mail:* bprevost@admin.ulb.ac.be
Founded: 1972

Subjects: Economics, Government, Political Science, History, Law, Mathematics, Medicine, Nursing, Dentistry, Philosophy, Social Sciences, Sociology
ISBN Prefix(es): 2-8004
Number of titles published annually: 20 Print
Total Titles: 260 Print
Distributed by Somabec (Canada)

Imprimeur - Editeur Vaillant-Carmanne SA
20 Zevenputtenstr, 3690 Zutendaal
Tel: (011) 612452 *Fax:* (011) 612451
Key Personnel
Man Dir: G Dengis
Founded: 1838
Subjects: Education, Government, Political Science, History, Law, Medicine, Nursing, Dentistry, Religion - Other, Science (General)
ISBN Prefix(es): 2-87021

Marc Van de Wiele bvba+
Jakobinessenstr 5, 8000 Brugge
Tel: (050) 333805 *Fax:* (050) 346457
Key Personnel
Contact: M van de Wiele
Founded: 1979
Subjects: Art, History
ISBN Prefix(es): 90-6966; 90-76297
Bookshop(s): Antiquariaat Marc Van de Wiele, St Salvator Keru Hof 7, 8000 Brugge; Zeewindstr 4, 8300 Knouue-Heist

Vander Editions, SA
321 Ave des Volontaires, 1150 Brussels
Tel: (02) 7629804 *Fax:* (02) 7620662
Key Personnel
Man Dir: Willy Vandermeulen
Editorial Dir: Stephane Rouget
Founded: 1880
Subjects: Economics, Government, Political Science, Law, Psychology, Psychiatry, Science (General), Social Sciences, Sociology
ISBN Prefix(es): 2-8008
Associate Companies: Nauwelaerts Edition SA

VBVB, see Huis Van Het Boek

Les Editions Vie ouvriere ASBL
rue Anderlecht 4, 1000 Brussels
Tel: (02) 5125090 *Fax:* (02) 5145231
Key Personnel
Chief Executive: Andre Samain
Founded: 1958
Subjects: Economics, History, Photography, Psychology, Psychiatry, Religion - Other, Social Sciences, Sociology
ISBN Prefix(es): 2-87003

Vita+
Speelstraat 14, 9750 Zingem
Tel: (09) 3842114 *Fax:* (09) 1842114
Key Personnel
Contact: Eric De Preester
Founded: 1964
Subjects: Alternative, Crafts, Games, Hobbies, Health, Nutrition, Literature, Literary Criticism, Essays, Philosophy, Poetry, Theology
ISBN Prefix(es): 90-73323
Number of titles published annually: 3 Print
Total Titles: 22 Print

Vlaamse Esperantobond VZW+
Frankrijklei 140, 2000 Antwerp
Tel: (03) 2343400 *Fax:* (03) 2335433
E-mail: esperanto@agoranet.be
Key Personnel
General Dir: Paul Peeraerts *E-mail:* pp@fel.agoranet.be
Founded: 1979
Subjects: Education, Fiction, Language Arts, Linguistics, Poetry

ISBN Prefix(es): 90-71205; 90-77066
Total Titles: 10 Print
Imprints: Stafeto
U.S. Office(s): Esperanto League of North America, PO Box 1129, El Cerrito, CA 94530-1129, United States

C De Vries Brouwers BVBA
Haantjeslei 80, 2018 Antwerp
Tel: (03) 2374180 *Fax:* (03) 2377001
Key Personnel
Dir: I de Vries
Founded: 1946
Subjects: History
ISBN Prefix(es): 90-6174; 90-5927

VUB Brussels University Press+
Waversesteenweg 1077, 1160 Brussels
Tel: (02) 629 35 90 *Fax:* (02) 629 26 94
E-mail: vubpress@vub.ac.be
Web Site: www.vubpress.org
Key Personnel
General Manager: Kris Van Scharen
 E-mail: kvschare@vub.ac.be
Founded: 1987
Specialize in scientific publications.
Subjects: Communications, Environmental Studies, Government, Political Science, History, Philosophy, Science (General), Social Sciences, Sociology, Women's Studies
ISBN Prefix(es): 90-5487
Number of titles published annually: 30 Print
Total Titles: 400 Print

Wereldwijd Mediahuis VzW+
Hoogstr 139, 1000 Brussels
Tel: (02) 3-2162935 *Fax:* (02) 3-2377757
E-mail: wereldwijd@wereldwijd.ngonet.be
Key Personnel
Dir: Agnes Van Speybroeck
Founded: 1970
Membership(s): VBVB.
Subjects: Developing Countries
ISBN Prefix(es): 90-76421

Editions Luce Wilquin+
rue d'Atrive 48, 4280 Avin
Tel: (019) 69 98 13 *Fax:* (019) 69 98 13
E-mail: wilquin.bouquin@skynet.be
Web Site: www.wilquin.com
Founded: 1992
Subjects: Art, Fiction, History, Literature, Literary Criticism, Essays, Romance
ISBN Prefix(es): 2-88161; 2-88253
Number of titles published annually: 20 Print
Total Titles: 170 Print

Wolters Kluwer Belgie NV
Ragheno Business Park, Motstraat 30, 2800 Mechelen
Tel: (015) 36 10 00
Key Personnel
Man Dir: Daniel Lefebvre
Founded: 1964
Subjects: Accounting, Business, Economics, Labor, Industrial Relations, Law, Social Sciences, Sociology
ISBN Prefix(es): 90-5334; 90-5754
Parent Company: Wolters Kluwer Belgium NV
Ultimate Parent Company: Wolters Kluwer NV

Wolters Plantyn Educatieve Uitgevers
Santvoortbeeklaan 21-25, 2600 Deurne
Tel: (03) 360 03 37 *Fax:* (03) 360 03 30
E-mail: klantendienst@woltersplantyn.be
Web Site: www.woltersplantyn.be
Founded: 1959
Educational publishers.
Subjects: Computer Science, Economics, Education, Language Arts, Linguistics, Mathematics,

Physics, Psychology, Psychiatry, Science (General)
ISBN Prefix(es): 90-309; 90-301
Parent Company: Wolters Kluwer Belgie NV
Ultimate Parent Company: Wolters Kluwer NV, Netherlands
Orders to: Zeutestr 5, 2800 Mechelen

Zuid En Noord VZW
Hanebergstraat 75, 3581 Beringen
Tel: (011) 34 4991
Web Site: www.schrijversnet.nl
Key Personnel
Algemene directie: Edith Oeyen
Subjects: Biography, Literature, Literary Criticism, Essays, Poetry, Romance
ISBN Prefix(es): 90-72087; 90-5684

Zuid-Nederlandse Uitgeverij NV/Central Uitgeverij+
Vluchtenburgstr 7, 2630 Aartselaar
Tel: (03) 8774400 *Fax:* (03) 8772115
Telex: 31739 Zuidb
Key Personnel
Man Dir: Jan Vande Velden
Publisher: Bart Clinckemalie
Production: Eric Feyten
Sales Dir: Wilfried Wuyts
Founded: 1946
Subjects: Animals, Pets, Child Care & Development, Crafts, Games, Hobbies, English as a Second Language, Gardening, Plants, Humor
ISBN Prefix(es): 2-8034; 90-243; 90-447
Imprints: Chantecler; Deltas; Invader; Liberica; Preschool
Subsidiaries: Editions Chantecler; Centrale Uitgeverij; Invader Ltd; Liberica

Benin

General Information
Capital: Porto-Novo
Language: French
Religion: About 15% Christian (mostly Roman Catholic), 13% Islamic, remainder traditional beliefs
Population: 4.5 million
Bank Hours: 0800-1000, 1500-1600 Monday-Friday
Shop Hours: 0800-1300, 1500-1900 Monday-Saturday. Larger ones close Monday, some open for a few hours Sunday morning
Currency: 100 centimes = CFA franc
Export/Import Information: Import license required but issued automatically for imports from EEC countries. Exchange controls for non-franc zone.
Copyright: Berne (see Copyright Conventions, pg xi)

Les Editions du Flamboyant
Immeuble EYEBIYI, Carre 236, BP 08-271, Cotonou
Tel: 310220 *Fax:* 312079
E-mail: IPEC@leland.bj
Key Personnel
Contact: Oscar de Souza
Founded: 1997
ISBN Prefix(es): 2-909130; 99919-41

Logos de l'Office, *imprint of* Office National d'Edition de Presse et d'Imprimerie (ONEPI)

Office National d'Edition de Presse et d'Imprimerie (ONEPI)
PO Box 1210, Cotonou
Tel: 300299; 301152 *Fax:* 303463
Key Personnel
Administrator: Innocent Adjaho
Founded: 1975
Imprints: Logos de l'Office

ONEPI, see Office National d'Edition de Presse et d'Imprimerie (ONEPI)

Bermuda

General Information
Capital: Hamilton
Language: English & some Portuguese
Religion: Predominantly Anglican
Population: 60,213
Bank Hours: 0930-1500 Monday-Thursday; 0930-1500, 1630-1800 Friday
Shop Hours: 0900-1700 Monday-Saturday
Currency: 100 cents = 1 Bermuda dollar. US currency circulates
Export/Import Information: No tariff on books and advertising matter. No import license. Exchange controls on imports valued over $100.
Copyright: Berne (see Copyright Conventions, pg xi)

The Bermudian Publishing Co
PO Box HM283, Hamilton HM AX
Tel: 295-0695 *Fax:* 295-8616
E-mail: info@thebermudian.com
Web Site: www.thebermudian.com *Cable:* BERPUBLISH
Key Personnel
Publisher: Tina Stevenson
Founded: 1930
Publish magazines.
Subjects: Business, Fiction, Social Sciences, Sociology, Sports, Athletics, Specializes in Bermuda
ISBN Prefix(es): 976-8143
Warehouse: Addendum Lane, Pitts Bay Rd, Pembroke

Bolivia

General Information
Capital: Sucre
Religion: Predominantly Roman Catholic
Population: 7.3 million
Bank Hours: 0900-1200, 1400-1630 Monday-Friday
Shop Hours: 0900-1200, 1400-1800 Monday-Friday; 0900-1200 Saturday
Currency: 100 centavos = 1 Boliviano
Export/Import Information: Member of the Latin American Free Trade Association. No tariffs on books, except for 10% luxury bindings. No import licenses, except for textbooks, but no pornography allowed. No advertising that includes imitation money, stamps, etc, allowed. No exchange controls.
Copyright: UCC, Berne, Buenos Aires (see Copyright Conventions, pg xi)

Los Amigos del Libro Ediciones+
Member of Distripress
Calle Heroinas, No E-0311, esquina Espana, Cochabamba
Mailing Address: Apdo Aereo 450, Cochabamba
Tel: (04) 254114 *Fax:* (04) 251140
Web Site: www.librosbolivia.com
Key Personnel
President & Man Dir: Werner Guttentag *E-mail:* gutten@amigol.bo.net
Sales Dir: Ingrid Guttentag *E-mail:* gutten@amigol.bo.net
Foreign Sales Manager: Eva Guttentag
Production: Norma de Rivero; Rita Arze
Founded: 1945
Member of Distripress.
Subjects: Regional Interests, All aspects of Bolivia
ISBN Prefix(es): 84-8370; 99905-45
Number of titles published annually: 1,250 Print
Total Titles: 600 Print
Parent Company: Los Amigos del Libro, Cochabamba
Subsidiaries: Bio Bibliografia Boliviana
Branch Office(s)
La Paz
Santa Cruz
Distributed by Fondo de Cultura Economica (Argentina & Chile)
Distributor for Time; Newsweek; Fondo de Cultura Economica; Serres
Bookshop(s): Libreria los Amigos del Libro, Casilla 450 Avenida Ayacucho, S-0156 Cochabamba

Editorial Don Bosco
Av 16 de Julio 1899, Casilla de Correo 4458, La Paz
Tel: (02) 357755; (02) 371149 *Fax:* (02) 362822
Cable: EDEBE-LA PAZ
Key Personnel
Dir: Gramaglia Magliano; R P Giorgio
Subjects: Chemistry, Chemical Engineering, History, Literature, Literary Criticism, Essays, Mathematics, Philosophy, Physics, Religion - Catholic, Science (General)

Gisbert y Cia SA
Calle Comercio 1270, Plaza Murillo La Paz, La Paz
Mailing Address: Casilla Postal 195, La Paz
Tel: (02) 20 26 26 *Fax:* (02) 20 29 11
E-mail: libgis@ceibo.entelnet.bo
Web Site: www.sonnegocios.com *Cable:* GISBERCIA
Key Personnel
President: Javier Gisbert
Manager: Antonio Schulczewski; Maria del Carmen Schulczewski
Founded: 1907
Subjects: History, Law
Number of titles published annually: 2 Print
Distributor for Pearson Education

Universidad Autonoma Tomas Frias, Div de Extension Universitaria
Casilla 36, Av Civica y Serrudo, Potosi
Tel: (062) 2-73-28; (062) 2-73-00 *Fax:* (062) 2-66-63; (062) 2-31-96
E-mail: rector@rect.nrp.edu.bo
Web Site: www.unam.mx/udal/afiliacion/Bolivia/frias.htm
Subjects: History, Literature, Literary Criticism, Essays

Universidad Mayor de San Andres, Editorial Universitaria
Avda Villazon 1995, Casilla 4787, La Paz
Tel: (02) 359491
Key Personnel
Contact: David Barrientos Zapata

Bosnia and Herzegovina

General Information

Capital: Sarajevo
Language: Bosnian, Servian, Croatian
Religion: Predominantly Sunni Muslim, also Serbian Orthodox and Roman Catholic
Population: 4.4 million
Currency: 100 convertible pfenniga = 1 convertible marka (KM)
Copyright: UCC, Berne (see Copyright Conventions, pg xi)

Bemust (Bemust Printing House, Publishing & Trade Company)
Put Famosa 38, 71000 Sarajevo
Tel: (033) 414-050; (061) 173780 *Fax:* (033) 414-050
E-mail: bemust@bih.net.ba
Subjects: Education, Geography, Geology, History, Law, Philosophy, Poetry, Regional Interests, Religion - Islamic, Technology
ISBN Prefix(es): 9958-725

IP Oslobodenje
Dzemala Bijedica 185, 71000 Sarajevo
Tel: (033) 276900; (033) 468054
E-mail: info@oslobodjenje.com.ba
Web Site: www.oslobodjenje.com.ba
Telex: 41148; 41136
Key Personnel
Dir: Ivica Lovric
ISBN Prefix(es): 86-319; 9958-719; 99938-678

Veselin Maslesa
Obla Kulina bana 4, 71000 Sarajevo
Tel: (033) 667735; (033) 667736 *Fax:* (033) 668351; (033) 667738
E-mail: sapublishing@bihart.com
Telex: 41154 Yu Vesmas *Cable:* Vesmas Maslesa
Key Personnel
Man Dir, Editorial, Rights & Permissions: Alija Velic
Founded: 1950
Subjects: Fiction, Government, Political Science, Philosophy, Science (General)
ISBN Prefix(es): 86-21
Branch Office(s)
Zagreb, Croatia
Skopje, The Former Yugoslav Republic of Macedonia
Belgrade, Serbia and Montenegro

Sarajevo Publishing, see Veselin Maslesa

Svjetlost
Muhameda Kantardzica 3, 71000 Sarajevo
Tel: (033) 442634; (033) 200066 *Fax:* (033) 443435
E-mail: ipsvjet@bih.net.ba
Telex: 41326 Yu Ikpres *Cable:* Svjetlost Sarajevo
Key Personnel
Man Dir: Abdulah Jesenkovic
Sales Dir: Rizvanbegovic Enver
Editorial: Miodrag Bogicvic
Subjects: Business, Science (General)
ISBN Prefix(es): 86-81903; 9958-9701
Branch Office(s)
Subiceva 65, Zagreb, Croatia
Obilicev venac 10, Belgrade, Serbia and Montenegro

Botswana

General Information

Capital: Gaborone
Language: English (official) & Setswana (national)
Religion: Traditional African
Population: 1.3 million
Bank Hours: 0830-1300 Monday-Friday; 0830-1100 Saturday
Shop Hours: 0800-1300, 1400-1700 or 1800 Monday-Saturday
Currency: 100 thebe = 1 pula
Export/Import Information: No import license required; no obscene literature. Exchange controls.

The Botswana Society
Uni-Span Bldg, Lot 54, International Commerce Park, Kgale View, Gaborone
Mailing Address: PO Box 71, Gaborone
Tel: 3919673 *Fax:* 3919745
E-mail: botsoc@botsnet.bw
Web Site: www.botswanasociety.com
Key Personnel
Editor: Dr Ian Taylor
Executive Secretary: Trevor Burnett
Founded: 1968
Subjects: Archaeology, Art, Earth Sciences, Environmental Studies, Government, Political Science, History, Language Arts, Linguistics, Law, Music, Dance, Natural History, Regional Interests
ISBN Prefix(es): 99912-60

Heinemann Botswana
PO Box 10103, Village Post Office, Gaborone
Tel: 372305 *Fax:* 371832
Key Personnel
Man Dir: Lesedi Seitei
ISBN Prefix(es): 99912-63
Parent Company: Heinemann Publishers Ltd, Oxford, United Kingdom
Ultimate Parent Company: Reed Elsevier plc, 25 Victoria St, London SW1H 0EX, United Kingdom

Maskew Miller Longman
PO Box 1083, Gaborone
Tel: 322969 *Fax:* 322682
E-mail: longman@info.bw
Key Personnel
Man Dir: Joe Chalashika
Sales & Marketing Manager: Carlson Moilwa
Publishing Manager: Michelle Aarons
Subjects: English as a Second Language, Fiction, Geography, Geology, History, Language Arts, Linguistics, Literature, Literary Criticism, Essays, Poetry, Travel
ISBN Prefix(es): 99912-66; 99912-73
Parent Company: Pearson Education
Ultimate Parent Company: Pearson Plc, United Kingdom

Morula Press, Business School of Botswana
PO Box 402492, Gaborone
Tel: (0267) 353499 *Fax:* (0267) 304809
Key Personnel
Contact: Mr A Briscoe
Founded: 1994
Subjects: Business, Law
ISBN Prefix(es): 99912-902; 99912-909; 99912-912; 99912-952; 99912-968; 99912-969; 99912-991; 99912-992

National Library Service
Private Bag 0036, Gaborone
Tel: 352288; 352397 *Fax:* 301149
E-mail: vmaje@gov.bw
ISBN Prefix(es): 99912-0

Sygma Publishing
PO Box 753, Gaborone
Tel: 351371 *Fax:* 372531
E-mail: sygma@info.bw
Key Personnel
International Rights: Mary-Anne Lovera

Brazil

General Information

Capital: Brasilia
Language: Portuguese
Religion: Predominantly Roman Catholic
Population: 157 million
Bank Hours: Generally 1000-1500 Monday-Friday
Shop Hours: 0900-1700 Monday-Friday (many open much later); 0900-1400 Saturday
Currency: 100 centavos = 1 real
Export/Import Information: Member of the Latin American Free Trade Association. No tariffs on books & advertising, but luxury bindings & children's picture books are dutied. Import licenses & deposits required; exchange controls operate.
Copyright: UCC, Berne, Buenos Aires, Florence (see Copyright Conventions, pg xi)

A & A & A Edicoes e Promocoes Internacionais Ltda+
R Jose Lemos, 82, 25725-020 Petropolis-RJ
Tel: (024) 221-1467 *Fax:* (024) 221-3669
Key Personnel
President: Gianvittore Calvi
General Dir: Lucilla Martinez
Founded: 1977
Membership(s): National Syndication of Book Publishers.
Subjects: Child Care & Development, Cookery, Education, Library & Information Sciences, Public Administration, Science Fiction, Fantasy
ISBN Prefix(es): 85-7210
Subsidiaries: IPE Amarelo Criacao Multimidia Ltda
Branch Office(s)
Gian Calvi & Asun Balzola & Assn, Calle de Clara del Rey, 39 Ofic 708, 28002 Madrid, Spain
Showroom(s): Livraria Amais, Rua Real Grandeza, 314 Botafogo

A Laser, *imprint of* Centro de Estudos Juridicosdo Para (CEJUP)

Abril SA
Av Otaviaro Alves de Lima, 4400, 02909-900 Sao Paulo-SP
Tel: (011) 877-1190 *Fax:* (011) 877-1640
Web Site: abril.com.br
Telex: 21-34716
Key Personnel
Contact: Sir Roberto Civita
Founded: 1983
Subjects: Cookery, Science (General)
ISBN Prefix(es): 85-86476
Parent Company: Editora Abril SA Sao Paulo
Associate Companies: Time-Life Inc, Alexandria, VA, United States

Action Editora Ltda+
Avenida das Americas, 3333 sala 817, 22631-003 Rio de Janeiro-RJ
Tel: (021) 3325-7229 *Fax:* (021) 3325-7229
Web Site: www.editora.com.br

PUBLISHERS
BRAZIL

Key Personnel
Dir: Carlos Lorch
Business Manager: Raimundo Carlos Bezerra
Founded: 1986
Specialize in military history, natural history, aviation.
Membership(s): SNEL (Sindicato Nacional de Editores de Livros).
Subjects: Aeronautics, Aviation, History, Military Science, Sports, Athletics
ISBN Prefix(es): 85-85654
Number of titles published annually: 8 Print
Total Titles: 60 Print
Distributed by Howell Press (USA)

Addison Wesley, *imprint of* Pearson Education Do Brasil

Affonso & Reichmann Editores Associados+
Rua do Ouvidor 161/1302, 20040-030 Rio de Janeiro
Tel: (021) 507-1270 *Fax:* (021) 507-1270
Key Personnel
Dir: Renato Reichmann *E-mail:* rrre@lb.com
Contact: Aluisia Affonso *E-mail:* aaff@ar.inf
Subjects: STM
ISBN Prefix(es): 85-87148
Number of titles published annually: 18 Print

Agalma Psicanalise Editora Ltda+
Av Anita Garibaldi, 1815, Centro Medico Empresarial, Bloco 'B' Saia 401, 40170-130 Salvador-Bahia
Tel: (071) 332-8776 *Fax:* (071) 245-7883
E-mail: pedidos@agalma.com.br
Web Site: www.agalma.com.br
Key Personnel
Contact: Marcus Do Rio Teixeira
Founded: 1991
Membership(s): National Syndicate of Book Publishers of Brazil (SNEL).
Subjects: Anthropology, Child Care & Development, Nonfiction (General), Philosophy, Psychology, Psychiatry, Romance
ISBN Prefix(es): 85-85458
Distributor for Editions De L'Association Freudienne

AGIR S/A Editora+
Rua dos Invalidos, 198 - Centro, 20231-020 Rio de Janeiro-RJ
Tel: (021) 221-6424 *Fax:* (021) 252-0410
E-mail: info@agireditora.com.br
Web Site: www.visualnet.com.br/cmaya/cm-ft-01.htm *Cable:* AGIRSA
Key Personnel
President: Jose de Paula Machado
Editorial: Regina Lemos
Founded: 1944
Subjects: Architecture & Interior Design, Art, Biography, Communications, Cookery, Drama, Theater, Education, Fiction, History, Literature, Literary Criticism, Essays, Philosophy, Social Sciences, Sociology
ISBN Prefix(es): 85-220; 85-85076
Distributor for Armand Collin; Ed Nathan; Ed Seuil; HarperCollins; Random House
Bookshop(s): Livraria Agir, Rua Mexico, 98-B, 20031-141
Book Club(s): Circulo do Livro

Editora Agora Ltda+
Rua Itapicuru 613 7° Andar, 05006-000 Perdizes-SP
Tel: (011) 38723322 *Fax:* (011) 38727476
E-mail: agora@editoraagora.com.br
Web Site: www.gruposummus.com.br/agora
Key Personnel
Editor: Edith M Elek
Founded: 1979
Subjects: Astrology, Occult, Health, Nutrition, Psychology, Psychiatry, Self-Help
ISBN Prefix(es): 85-7183

Aide Editora e Comercio de Livros Ltda
Rua Bela, 740, Sao Cristovao, 20930-380 Rio de Janeiro-RJ
Tel: (021) 2589-9926 *Fax:* (021) 2589-9926
E-mail: aideeditora@radnet.com.br
Web Site: www.radnet.com.br/aideeditora
Key Personnel
President: Ruy de Castro
Editor: Joao Virgilio de Castro *Tel:* (0371) 5724958
Founded: 1976
Membership(s): SNEL.
Subjects: Law
ISBN Prefix(es): 85-321
Total Titles: 5 Print

Livraria Alema Ltda Brasileitura+
Rua Dr Amadeu da Luz, Blumenau 89010 160
Tel: (047) 326-4558 *Fax:* (0473) 3263062
Key Personnel
Executive: Juergen Konig
Founded: 1989
ISBN Prefix(es): 85-85415; 85-7324
Subsidiaries: Editora EKO/Disbribuidora Alema

Editora Alfa Omega Ltda+
Rua Lisboa, 489, 05413-000 Sao Paulo-SP
Tel: (011) 3062-6400; (011) 3062-6690
 Fax: (011) 3083-0746
E-mail: alfaomega@alfaomega.com.br
Web Site: www.alfaomega.com.br
Telex: 011 22888 XPSPBR
Key Personnel
Editorial Dir: Fernando Celso De C Mangariello
Founded: 1973
Subjects: Anthropology, Behavioral Sciences, Biography, Economics, History, Law, Management, Philosophy, Social Sciences, Sociology
ISBN Prefix(es): 85-295
Divisions: Alfa Omega Data; Distribuidora Alfa Omega e Disque Livros; Estudio Alfa Omega

Livraria Francisco Alves Editora SA+
Rua Urguaiana, 94-13 andar-Centro, 20050-091 Rio de Janeiro-RJ
Tel: (021) 221-3198 *Fax:* (021) 242-3438
Founded: 1854
Membership(s): Sindicato Nacional de Editores de Livros.
Subjects: Astrology, Occult, Criminology, Fiction, Literature, Literary Criticism, Essays, Nonfiction (General), Science (General), Science Fiction, Fantasy
ISBN Prefix(es): 85-265
Warehouse: Rua Luis de Camoes 100, Rio de Janeiro-RJ

Antenna Edicoes Tecnicas Ltda+
Ave Marechal Floriano, 151-1°-Andar, 20080-005 Rio de Janeiro-RJ
Tel: (021) 2223-2442 *Fax:* (021) 2263-8840
E-mail: antenna@anep.com.br
Web Site: www.anep.com.br
Key Personnel
Man Dir: Maria Beatriz Affonso Penna
Publicity: Sergio Porto
Founded: 1926
Subjects: Computer Science, Electronics, Electrical Engineering, Microcomputers, Technology
ISBN Prefix(es): 85-7036
Number of titles published annually: 5 Print
Total Titles: 60 Print
Bookshop(s): Lojas do Livro Electronico, Ave Mal Floriano 151, 20080-005 Rio de Janeiro-RJ
Book Club(s): SNEL-Sind Nac Editors Livros, Ave Rio Branco 37, 20090-003 Rio de Janeiro-RJ *Tel:* (021) 2233-6481 *Fax:* (021) 2253-8502
E-mail: snel@snel.org.br

Editora Antroposofica Ltda+
Rua da Fraternidade, 174, 04738-020 Sao Paulo-SP
Tel: (011) 5687-9714; (011) 5686-4550
 Fax: (011) 2479714
E-mail: editora@antroposofica.com.br
Web Site: www.sab.org.br/edit; www.antroposofica.com.br
Key Personnel
General Manager & International Rights: Jacira S Cardoso *E-mail:* jacira.c@zaz.com.br
Founded: 1981
Specializes in therapy & anthroposophy.
Membership(s): Brazilian House of Books.
Subjects: Agriculture, Child Care & Development, Cookery, Disability, Special Needs, Economics, Education, Health, Nutrition, Medicine, Nursing, Dentistry, Philosophy, Psychology, Psychiatry, Anthroposophy, Therapy
ISBN Prefix(es): 85-7122
Number of titles published annually: 15 Print
Total Titles: 140 Print
Parent Company: Livraria Antroposofica
Ultimate Parent Company: Sociedade Antroposofica no Brasil

Ao Livro Tecnico Industria e Comercio Ltda+
Rua Sa Freire, 40, Sao Cristovao, Rio de Janeiro 20930-430
Tel: (021) 580-6230; (021) 580-1168 *Fax:* (021) 580-9955
E-mail: contatos@editoraolivrotecnico.com.br
Web Site: www.editoraolivrotecnico.com.br
Cable: LITECNICO
Key Personnel
Man Dir: Reynaldo Max Paul Bluhm
Editorial, Production, Sales, Rights & Permissions, Publicity: Gisela Bluhm
Founded: 1933
Membership(s): IPA.
Subjects: Education, Language Arts, Linguistics, Sports, Athletics
ISBN Prefix(es): 85-215
Associate Companies: Sociedade Distribuidora de Livros Ltda (Sodilivro)
Subsidiaries: DISAL (Distribuidores Associados de Livros Ltda); SODILIVRO (Sociedade Distribuidora de Livros Ltda)
Warehouse: Rua Sa Freire, 40

Editora Aquariana Ltda+
R Pamplona, 935-Cj 11, 01405-001 Sao Paulo-SP
Tel: (011) 288 7139 *Fax:* (011) 283 0476
E-mail: aquariana@ground.com.br
Key Personnel
Executive Director: Jose Carlos Rolo Venancio *E-mail:* jcvenancio@ground.com.br
Founded: 1988
Membership(s): the Brazilian Association of Publishers.
Subjects: Alternative, Environmental Studies, Management, Marketing, Self-Help, Occult, Health & New Science
ISBN Prefix(es): 85-7217
Parent Company: Editora Ground Ltda
Associate Companies: Editora Ground Ltda, R Lacedomonia, 68, Sao Paulo-SP, Contact: Jose Carlos Venancio *Tel:* (011) 5031 1500 *Fax:* (011) 5031 3462 *E-mail:* editora@ground.com.br

M J Bezerra de Araujo Editora Ltda
Rua Haddoc Lobo, 72, Sala 507 e-508, 20260-132 Rio de Janeiro-RJ
Tel: (021) 5024435 *Fax:* (021) 5024435
Key Personnel
Dir & President: Maria Jose Bezerra de Araujo
ISBN Prefix(es): 85-85767

Branch Office(s)
Alameda Santos 734, Apt 02, Jardim Paulista, Sao Paulo, SP CEP 01418-100
Warehouse: Rua Haddock Lobo 17B, Estacio, RJ, Bradesco AG 2013-3, Conta 9958-9

Arquivo Nacional
Rua Azeredo Coutinho, 77-3º Andar, Centro, 20230-170 Rio de Janeiro-RJ
Tel: (021) 232-6938 *Fax:* (021) 224-4525
E-mail: arqnacdg@rio.com.br
ISBN Prefix(es): 85-7009

Ars Poetica Editora Ltda+
Av Irai, 79, Cj 114-B, 04082-001 Sao Paulo-SP
Tel: (011) 2405598 *Fax:* (011) 5312648
Key Personnel
Contact: Ubiratan Ramos-Mascarenhas
Founded: 1991
Subjects: Anthropology, Archaeology, Biography, Language Arts, Linguistics, Poetry, Psychology, Psychiatry, Religion - Protestant, Sports, Athletics, Theology
ISBN Prefix(es): 85-85470

Artes e Oficios Editora Ltda+
Rua Henrique Dias, 201, 90035-100 Porto Alegre
Tel: (051) 311 0832; (051) 311 5442 *Fax:* (051) 311 0832
E-mail: artesofi@pro.via-rs.com.br
Key Personnel
Contact: Sergio Boeck-Ludtke
Founded: 1991
Subjects: Biography, Fiction, Human Relations, Humor, Journalism, Psychology, Psychiatry, Romance, Travel
ISBN Prefix(es): 85-7421; 85-87239
Branch Office(s)
Rua Eudoro Berlink, 988 Auxiliadora, 90450-160 Porto Alegre *Tel:* (051) 3317387 *Fax:* (051) 3317387

Editora Artes Medicas Ltda+
R Dr Cesario Motta Jr, 63, 01221-020 Sao Paulo-SP
Tel: (011) 221-9033 *Fax:* (011) 223-6635
E-mail: artesmedicas@artesmedicas.com.br
Web Site: www.artesmedicas.com.br *Cable:* LEAM
Key Personnel
Man Dir: Henrique Hecht
Editorial, Production: M Hecht
Sales: C dos Santos
Publicity: J Hecht
Founded: 1964
Subjects: Medicine, Nursing, Dentistry
ISBN Prefix(es): 85-7404

ARTMED Editora+
Av Jeronimo de Ornelas 670, 90040-340 Porto Alegre-RS
Tel: (051) 33303444 *Fax:* (051) 3302378
E-mail: artmed@artmed.com.br
Web Site: www.artmed.com.br
Key Personnel
President: Henrique L Kiperman
Vice President: Celso Kiperman
International Rights Manager & Permissions: Angelo I Castrogiovanni *E-mail:* angelo@artmed.com.br
Founded: 1973
Membership(s): Brazilian Book Association; Publishers Club of Southern Rio Grande.
Subjects: Architecture & Interior Design, Behavioral Sciences, Biological Sciences, Child Care & Development, Civil Engineering, Computer Science, Economics, Education, Health, Nutrition, Management, Marketing, Medicine, Nursing, Dentistry, Psychology, Psychiatry, Science (General), Sports, Athletics, Technology, Veterinary Science

ISBN Prefix(es): 85-7307
Number of titles published annually: 90 Print; 3 CD-ROM
Total Titles: 893 Print; 11 CD-ROM
Associate Companies: Bookman Companhia Editora Ltda, Patio Revista Pedagogica
Branch Office(s)
Av Reboucas, 1073, 05414-020 Sao Paulo-SP
Tel: (011) 3062 3757 *Fax:* (011) 3062 2487
Bookshop(s): Rua General Vitorino 277, 90020 Porto Alegre-RS, Dir: Celso Kiperman
Tel: (051) 32251579
Warehouse: Artomed Aeditora Ltda, Rua Ernesto Alves 150, Porto Alegre-RS 90000-000
Tel: (051) 32251579
Distribution Center: Artomed Aeditora Ltda, Rua Ernesto Alves 150, Porto Alegre-RS 90000-000
Tel: (051) 32251579

Associacao Arvore da Vida
Rua Tuiuti, 1372, Tatuape, 03081-000 Sao Paulo-SP
Tel: (011) 2185399 *Fax:* (011) 2181401
E-mail: editora@eavida.com.br
Key Personnel
Dir: Ildeu R Dos Santos
Contact: Andre Dong
Founded: 1981
Membership(s): Camara Brasileira de Livros.
Subjects: Biblical Studies
ISBN Prefix(es): 85-7304
Divisions: Jornal Arvore Da Vida
Book Club(s): Sindicato Nacional de Editores (SNEL)

Associacao Palas Athena do Brasil+
Rua Serra de Paracaina, 240, 01522-020 Cambuci-Sao Paulo SP
Tel: (011) 3209-6288 *Fax:* (011) 3277-8137
E-mail: grafica@palasathena.org; editora@palasathena.org
Web Site: www.palasathena.org
Key Personnel
Contact: Basilio Pawlowicz
Founded: 1972
Subjects: Anthropology, Philosophy, Psychology, Psychiatry, Religion - Other
ISBN Prefix(es): 85-7242
Orders to: R Jose Bento 384, 01523-030 Sao Paulo-SP

Editora Atheneu Ltda+
Rua Jesuino Pascoal, 30, 01224-050 Sao Paulo-SP
Tel: (011) 220-9186 *Fax:* (011) 221-3389
E-mail: atheneau@nutecnet.com.br
Web Site: www.atheneu.com.br *Cable:* ZIGADAG
Key Personnel
Man Dir & Editorial Dir: Paulo Rezinski
Sales Dir: Alexandre Massa
Production Dir: Prado Orimar
Founded: 1928
Subjects: Medicine, Nursing, Dentistry, Psychology, Psychiatry
ISBN Prefix(es): 85-7379
Subsidiaries: Editora Atheneu Cultura
Branch Office(s)
Rua Domingos Vieira 319 Conj 1.104, Santa Efigenia, Belo Horizonte 30150-240
E-mail: atheneu@u-net.com.br

Editora Atica SA
Rua Barao de Iguape 110, 01507-900 Sao Paulo-SP
Tel: (011) 278 93 22 *Fax:* (011) 277 41 46
Telex: 32969 Edat *Cable:* BOMLIVRO
Key Personnel
Edit Dir: Sr Renato Jose Laporta Filho Pimazzoni *E-mail:* rpimazzoni@atica.com.br
Publicity Dir: Vera Elena Hoexter Esau
Contact: Nelson Dos Reis
Founded: 1965

Subjects: Literature, Literary Criticism, Essays, Regional Interests
ISBN Prefix(es): 85-08
Branch Office(s)
Rua Barao de Uba 173, Praca da Bandeira, 20260 Rio de Janeiro-RJ

Editora Atlas SA+
Rue Conselheiro Nebias, 1384, Campos Elisios, 01203-904 Sao Paulo-SP
Tel: (011) 3357-9144
E-mail: edatlas@editora-atlas.com.br
Web Site: www.edatlas.com.br; www.atlasnet.com.br *Cable:* ATLASEDITA
Key Personnel
Vice President: Luiz Herrmann, Jr
Editorial & Marketing Dir: A B Brandao
Production: S Gerencer
Founded: 1944
Subjects: Accounting, Business, Economics, Finance, Law, Management, Marketing
ISBN Prefix(es): 85-224
Branch Office(s)
Amazonas
Brazilia
Bahia
Ceara
Goias
Minas Gerais
Parana
Pernambuco
Rio Grande do Sul
Santa Catarina
Bookshop(s): Livraria Atlas Ltda, Rua Pedroso Alvarenga, 1285 - Itaim, 04531-012 Sao Paulo
Tel: (011) 881-8799

Berkeley Brasil Editora Ltda+
AV Raimundo Pereira De Magalhaes, 3305, 3 Andar, 05145-200 Sao Paulo-SP
Tel: (011) 839-5525 *Fax:* (011) 261-1342
E-mail: berkeley@siciliano.com.br
Key Personnel
President: Osvaldo Siciliano, Jr
Executive Vice President: Ricardo Reinprecht
Founded: 1986
Specialize in computer & business books.
Subjects: Business, Computer Science, Microcomputers, Technology
ISBN Prefix(es): 85-7251

Bertrand Brasil, *imprint of* Editora Bertrand Brasil Ltda

Editora Bertrand Brasil Ltda+
Subsidiary of Distribuidora Record de Servicos de Imprensa SA
Rua Argentina, 171, Sao Cristoras, 20921-380 Rio de Janeiro-RJ RJ
Mailing Address: CP 884, 20001-970 Rio de Janeiro-RJ
Tel: (021) 2585 2000 *Fax:* (021) 2585 2085
E-mail: record@record.com.br
Web Site: www.record.com.br
Key Personnel
President: Sergio Abreu Da Cruz Machado *E-mail:* smachado@record.com.br
Rights & Permissions: Rosemary Alves *E-mail:* rosemary@bertrandbrasil.com.br
Founded: 1951 (as Difusao Editorial SA (DIFEL)
Subjects: Anthropology, Astrology, Occult, Behavioral Sciences, Biography, Cookery, Drama, Theater, Education, Fiction, Geography, Geology, Government, Political Science, Literature, Literary Criticism, Essays, Nonfiction (General), Poetry, Religion - Buddhist, Religion - Hindu, Religion - Jewish, Romance, Self-Help, Women's Studies
ISBN Prefix(es): 85-286
Number of titles published annually: 80 Print
Total Titles: 1,000 Print
Imprints: Bertrand Brasil; Difel

PUBLISHERS

BRAZIL

Branch Office(s)
R do Paraiso 139, 7° andar, 04103-000 Sao Paulo-SP *Tel:* (011) 3171-1540 *Fax:* (011) 3285-0251

Editora Betania S/C+
Rua Padre Pinto, 2435 Venda Nova, 31510-000 Belo Horizonte-MG
Tel: (031) 3451-1122 *Fax:* (031) 3451-1638
E-mail: betanhdv@prover.com.br
Web Site: www.editorabetania.com.br
Key Personnel
Dir: Luiz Dirceu dos Arjos *E-mail:* director@editorabetania.com.br
Founded: 1967
Subjects: Religion - Other
Imprints: Temos Grafica Propria

Bloch Editores SA
Rua do Russell, 766-10° Andar, 22210-010 Rio de Janeiro-RJ
Tel: (021) 555-4167 *Fax:* (021) 555-4069
E-mail: blocheditores@ieg.com.br
Key Personnel
Contact: Anna Maria de O. Renhack
Publicity: Expedito Jose Chaves Grossi
ISBN Prefix(es): 85-258

Editora Edgard Blucher Ltda
Rua Pedroso Alvarenga 1245, 04531-012 Sao Paulo-SP
Tel: (011) 852-5366 *Fax:* (011) 852 2707
E-mail: eblucher@uol.com.br *Cable:* BLUCHERLIVRO
Key Personnel
Man Dir: Edgard Blucher
Founded: 1966
Subjects: Biological Sciences, Earth Sciences, Electronics, Electrical Engineering, Engineering (General), Management, Mathematics, Physics, Science (General), Technology
ISBN Prefix(es): 85-212

Editora Brasil-America (EBAL) SA+
Rua General Almerio de Moura 302/320, 20921-060 Rio de Janeiro-RJ
Tel: (021) 5800303 *Fax:* (021) 5801637
Key Personnel
Man Dir: Luba Aizen
Editorial: Naumim Aizen
Dir: Paulo Adolfo Aizen
Production: Fernando Albagli
Founded: 1945
Subjects: Film, Video, Children & Young People's Books
ISBN Prefix(es): 85-272

Editora do Brasil SA+
Rua Conselheiro Nebias, 887, 01203-001 Sao Paulo-SP
Tel: (011) 222 0211 *Fax:* (011) 222 5583 *Cable:* EDITABRAS
Key Personnel
President: Dr Carlos Costa
Superintendent: Luis Roberto Netto
Founded: 1943
Subjects: Education, History, Psychology, Psychiatry, Social Sciences, Sociology
ISBN Prefix(es): 85-10
Branch Office(s)
Rua do Resende 89, 20231 Rio de Janeiro-RJ
Tel: (021) 224-8123

Instituto Brasileiro de Informacao em Ciencia e Tecnologia
SAS Qd 5, Lote 6, Bloco H - 5° andar, 70070-914 Brasilia-DF
Tel: (061) 217-6360; (061) 217-6350 *Fax:* (061) 226-2677
E-mail: webmaster@ibict.br
Web Site: www.ibict.br

Telex: (061) 2481
ISBN Prefix(es): 85-7013

Editora Brasiliense SA+
Rua Airi, 22, Tatuape, 03310-010 Sao Paulo-SP
Tel: (011) 6198-1488 *Fax:* (011) 6198-1488
E-mail: brasilienseedit@uol.com.br
Web Site: www.editorabrasiliense.com.br
Cable: EDIBRASA
Key Personnel
Man Dir & Editor: Teresa B Lima; Yolanda Prado
Production: Celia Rogalsky
Founded: 1943
Subjects: Education, Literature, Literary Criticism, Essays, Social Sciences, Sociology
ISBN Prefix(es): 85-11; 85-206
Bookshop(s): Livraria Brasiliense Editora SA, Rua Emilia Marengo, 216-Tatuape, 03336-000 Sao Paulo-SP *Tel:* (011) 6675-0188 *Fax:* (011) 6675-0188 *E-mail:* brasilienseedit@editorabrasiliense.com.br

Brasilivros Editora e Distribuidora Ltda
Rua Conselheiro Ramalho, 701, Matriz Loja 22, 01325-001 Sao Paolo
Tel: (011) 3284-8155 *Fax:* (011) 2850305; (011) 2856406
Key Personnel
Executive: Juarez Cordeiro de Oliveira

Brinque Book Editora de Livros Ltda+
Av Dr Guilherme Dumot Villares, 2352 1 andar, 05640-004 Sao Paulo-SP
Tel: (011) 8428142 *Fax:* (011) 8432235
E-mail: brinquebook@infantil.net
Key Personnel
President: Suzana Taves de Sanson
Founded: 1990
Specialize in Children's Literature.
Membership(s): SNEL, FNLIJ & CBL.
Subjects: Cookery, Music, Dance
ISBN Prefix(es): 85-7412

Cadence Publicacoes Internacionais Ltda+
Rua Visconde Inhauma 134, Sala 1532, 20091-000 Rio de Janeiro-RJ
Tel: (021) 2637885 *Fax:* (021) 2830812
E-mail: cadence@mtecnet.com.br
Key Personnel
Associate Manager: Reinaldo C Palmeira
Executive Secretary: Geni Celia Miranda
Founded: 1980
Subjects: Science (General), Technology
Parent Company: Cadence

Callis Editora Ltda+
Rua Afonso Bras 203, 04511-010 Sao Paulo-SP
Tel: (011) 3842-2066 *Fax:* (011) 3849-5882
E-mail: editorial@callis.com.br; callis@callis.com.br
Web Site: www.callis.com.br
Key Personnel
President: Miriam Gabbai
Founded: 1987
Subjects: Art, Computer Science, Cookery, Microcomputers, Military Science, Nonfiction (General)
ISBN Prefix(es): 85-85642; 85-7416

Camara Dos Deputados Coordenacao De Publicacoes (Chamber of Deputies, Coordination of Publications)
Division of Chamber of Deputies
Praca dos Tres Poderes, 70160-900 Brasilia-DF
Tel: (061) 216-0000 *Fax:* (061) 318-2190
E-mail: publicacoes.cedi@camara.gov.br
Web Site: www.camara.gov.br
Key Personnel
Coordination of Publications Dir: Nelda Raulino
Librarian: Andrea Perna *Tel:* (061) 318-6864
E-mail: andrea.perna@camara.gov.br

Founded: 1971
Produces & distributes Chamber of Deputies printed publications. Created primarily to satisfy the printing needs of Chamber of Deputies, today has contributed to disseminate Brazilian legislative information around the country & the world.
Subjects: Government, Political Science, Public Administration
ISBN Prefix(es): 85-7365
Number of titles published annually: 60 Print
Total Titles: 781 Print

Editora Caminho Suave Ltda
rua Fagundes 157, 01508-030 Sao Paulo-SP
Tel: (011) 2733377 *Fax:* (011) 2783537
Key Personnel
Contact: Branca Alves de Lima
ISBN Prefix(es): 85-85473

Instituto Campineiro de Ensino Agricola Ltda
Rua Romoaldo Andreazzi, 425, Jd do Trevo, 13036-100 Campinas-SP
Tel: (019) 3272-2280 *Fax:* (019) 3272-6004
E-mail: icea@icea.com.br
Web Site: www.icea.com.br
Key Personnel
Contact: Gervasio de Souza Cavalcanti
Founded: 1955
Subjects: Agriculture
ISBN Prefix(es): 85-7121

Editora Campus Ltda+
Rua Sete de Setembro, 111, 16 Andar, 20050-002 Centro Rio de Janeiro RJ
Tel: (021) 3970-9300 *Fax:* (021) 2507-1991
E-mail: info@elsevier.com
Web Site: www.campus.com.br
Key Personnel
Publishing Manager: Ricardo Redisch *E-mail:* ricardo@campus.com.br
Production Dir: Daniel Sant'Anna
Rights & Permissions: Emilia Fernandez
Founded: 1976
Subjects: Art, Civil Engineering, Communications, Computer Science, Economics, Electronics, Electrical Engineering, Engineering (General), Environmental Studies, Government, Political Science, Health, Nutrition, History, Microcomputers, Nonfiction (General), Physics, Psychology, Psychiatry, Science (General), Social Sciences, Sociology, Travel
ISBN Prefix(es): 85-7001; 85-352
Number of titles published annually: 190 Print
Parent Company: Elsevier Science
Ultimate Parent Company: Reed Elsevier plc
Branch Office(s)
Rua da Consolacao 348/10, Andar-Conj 102, Sao Paulo-SP 01302-000 *Fax:* (011) 259 9944

Alzira Chagas Carpigiani+
Av Gethsemani, 85, 05625-090 Sao Paulo
Mailing Address: Caixa Postal 3702, Cep 01060-970, Sao Paulo SP
Tel: (011) 849-0189 *Fax:* (011) 227-3384
E-mail: kerredit@uol.com.br
Key Personnel
Executive: Alzira Chagas Carpigiani
Founded: 1997
Subjects: Literature, Literary Criticism, Essays, Religion - Protestant, Romance
Subsidiaries: Kerr Editorial Ltda
Divisions: Rua Maua 960-Casa 10

Centro de Estudos Juridicosdo Para (CEJUP)+
Travessa Rui Barbosa 726, 66053-260 Belem-PA
Tel: (091) 225-0355 *Fax:* (091) 241-3184
Key Personnel
Contact: Gengis Freire de Souza
Founded: 1979

Membership(s): Associacao Nacional de Livrarias (ANL) & Sindicato Nacional de Livrarias (SNL).
Subjects: Biological Sciences, Criminology, Drama, Theater, Education, Fiction, Law, Science Fiction, Fantasy, Social Sciences, Sociology
ISBN Prefix(es): 85-338
Imprints: Off Set; A Laser
Branch Office(s)
Av Rio Branco, 37 Sala 601, CEP 20040-004 Rio de Janeiro, RJ
Bookshop(s): Assis de Vasconcelos, N 498, CEP 66017-070 Belem PA

Centro Editor de Psicologia Aplicada Ltda, see CEPA - Centro Editor de Psicologia Aplicada Ltda

CEPA - Centro Editor de Psicologia Aplicada Ltda
Rua Senador Dantas 118, GR 901 a 920, 20031-201 Rio de Janeiro-RJ
Tel: (021) 2220-6545 *Fax:* (021) 2262-2717
E-mail: psicocepa@psicocepa.com.br
Web Site: www.psicocepa.com.br *Cable:* EDICEPA
Key Personnel
Man Dir: Antonio Rodrigues, Jr
Founded: 1952
Subjects: Psychology, Psychiatry
ISBN Prefix(es): 85-7043

Editora Cidade Nova+
Rua Jose Ernesto Tozzi, 198, 06730-000 Vargen Grande Paulista-SP
Tel: (011) 4158-2252 *Fax:* (011) 4158-2252
E-mail: editoria@cidadenova.org.br
Web Site: www.cidadenova.org.br
Key Personnel
President Dir: Ekkehard Andreas Schneider
Man Dir: Olavo de Freitas
Publisher & Editor: Klaus Brueschke
Founded: 1960
Subjects: Biblical Studies, Religion - Catholic, Social Sciences, Sociology, Theology
ISBN Prefix(es): 85-7112; 85-89736
Parent Company: Citta Nuova Editrice, Italy
Branch Office(s)
Rua Arthur da Silva Bernardes, 769, Loja 34, 80320-300 Curitiba-PR
Av Assis Brasil, 115, Sala 308, 50020-036 Recife-PE
U.S. Office(s): City New Press, 206 Skillman Ave, Brooklyn, NY 11211, United States
Living City, PO Box 837, New York, NY, United States
Showroom(s): Av Arthur da Silva Bernardes 769, Loja 34, 80320-300 Curitiba-PR; Av Assis Brasil, 115, Sala 308, 50010-036 Recife-PE; Rua Domingos de Moraes, 348 Loja 46, 04009-000 Sao Paulo-SP

Codice Comercio Distriduicao e Casa Editorial Ltda+
Rua Simoes Pinto, 120, Sao Paulo
Tel: (011) 5031-8033
E-mail: codice@codicenet.com.br
Key Personnel
Contact: Eduardo Augusto-Serverino
Founded: 1991

Comissao Nacional de Energia Nuclear (CNEN)
Rua General Severiano, 90 Terreo, Botafogo, 22294-900 Rio de Janeiro-RJ
Tel: (021) 2295-9596 *Fax:* (021) 2295-8696
E-mail: macedo@cnen.gov.br
Web Site: www.cnen.gov.br
Key Personnel
President: Odair Dias Goncalves
  E-mail: presidencia@cnen.gov.br
Founded: 1970
Acts as the Brazilian national center for the International Nuclear Information System (INIS) & for the Energy Technology Data Exchange (ETDE).
Subjects: Energy, Engineering (General), Environmental Studies, Nuclear Energy
ISBN Prefix(es): 85-344

Editora Companhia das Letras/Editora Schwarcz Ltda+
Rua Bandeira Paulista, 702, cj 72, 04532-002 Sao Paulo-SP
Tel: (011) 3707-3500 *Fax:* (011) 3707-3501
E-mail: editora@companhiadasletras.com.br
Web Site: www.companhiadasletras.com.br
Key Personnel
Editor: Luiz Schwarcz
Foreign Rights Manager: Ruth Lanna
  E-mail: ruth.lanna@companhiadasletras.com.br
Founded: 1986
Subjects: Anthropology, Biblical Studies, Biography, Cookery, Fiction, History, Humor, Literature, Literary Criticism, Essays, Philosophy, Photography, Poetry
ISBN Prefix(es): 85-7164; 85-85095; 85-85466
Number of titles published annually: 150 Print
Distributed by Jorge Zahar (Rio de Janeiro)
Distributor for Jorge Zahar (Sao Paulo)
Foreign Rights: Carmen Balcells for Rubem Fonseca (Europe); Melanie Jackson for Rubem Fonseca & Patricia Melo (USA); Ray-Guede Mertin (Europe); Anne Marie Vallat for Milton Hatoum (Spain)

Companhia Editora Naciona, see Cia Editora Nacional

Concordia Editora Ltda
Av Sao Pedro, 633, Bairro Sao Geraldo, 90230-120 Porto Alegre-RS
Tel: (051) 3342 2699 *Fax:* (051) 3342 2699
E-mail: pedido@editoraconcordia.com.br; editora@editoraconcordia.com.br
Web Site: www.editoraconcordia.com.br
  Cable: CONCORDIA
Key Personnel
Man Dir: Martinho Krebs
Sales & Publicity: Walter Eidam
Founded: 1923
Subjects: Music, Dance, Religion - Other, Theology
Parent Company: Igreja Evangelica Luterana do Brasil
Branch Office(s)
Ave Getulio Vargas 4388, Sao Leopoldo-RS

Conquista, Empresa de Publicacoes Ltda
Av 28 de Setembro, 174, V Isabel, 20551-031 Rio de Janeiro-RJ
Tel: (021) 228-6752 *Fax:* (021) 228-5709
Key Personnel
Dir: Nilde Hersen Aragao da Fonseca; Leonardo Hersen da Costa
Sales Dir: Antonio da Silva Aragao da Fonseca
Founded: 1951
Subjects: Art, Cookery, Literature, Literary Criticism, Essays
ISBN Prefix(es): 85-7066
Bookshop(s): Livraria Conquista

Consultor Assessoria de Planejamento Ltda
Rua General Gurjao, 479, 20931-040 Rio de Janeiro-RJ
Tel: (021) 5893030 *Fax:* (021) 580-2163
Key Personnel
Contact: Sra Andreia Niskier Chelman; Selmado Amaral
Founded: 1988
Subjects: Education, Literature, Literary Criticism, Essays
ISBN Prefix(es): 85-85206; 85-7434

Editora Contexto (Editora Pinsky Ltda)+
Rua Acopiara 199, 05083-110 Sao Paulo-SP
Tel: (011) 3832-5838 *Fax:* (011) 3832-1043
E-mail: contexto@editoracontexto.com.br
Web Site: www.editoracontexto.com.br
Key Personnel
Executive: Jaime Pinsky *E-mail:* pinsky@editoracontexto.com.br
Founded: 1987
Membership(s): Camara Brasileira do Livro.
Subjects: Economics, Education, Health, Nutrition, History
ISBN Prefix(es): 85-7244; 85-85134
Number of titles published annually: 30 Print
Total Titles: 20 Print

Editora Crescer Ltda+
Rua Do Ouro 104, Conj 501-Serra, 30220-000 Belo Horizonte-MG
Tel: (031) 221-9335 *Fax:* (031) 3227-0729
E-mail: crescer@crescer.com.br
Web Site: www.crescer.com.br
Key Personnel
Executive: Clara Feldman
Founded: 1983
Subjects: Human Relations, Self-Help
ISBN Prefix(es): 85-85615

Editora Cultura Medica Ltda+
Rua Sao Francisco Xavier, 111 - Tijuca, 20550-010 Rio de Janeiro-RJ
Tel: (021) 2567-3888 *Fax:* (021) 2569-5443
E-mail: atendimento@culturamedica.com.br
Web Site: www.culturamedica.com.br
Key Personnel
Man Dir: Ezequiel Feldman
Founded: 1966
Subjects: Medicine, Nursing, Dentistry, Biomedicine
ISBN Prefix(es): 85-7006
Orders to: Rua Lucio de Mendonca, 37, Apt 401, 20470-040 Rio de Janeiro-RJ

Difel, *imprint of* Editora Bertrand Brasil Ltda

Editorial Dimensao Ltda+
Rua Santo Cristo, 201, 20220-301 Rio de Janeiro-RJ
Tel: (021) 233-2764 *Fax:* (021) 233-2570
E-mail: memoria@ig.com.br
Key Personnel
Contact: Gilberto Gusmao Andrade
Founded: 1985
Membership(s): the Brazilian House of Books.
Subjects: Law, Psychology, Psychiatry
ISBN Prefix(es): 85-86163

Editora e Distribuidora Irradiacao Cultural Ltda
Rua Visconde de Santa Isabel 46-Fundos, 20560-120 Rio de Janeiro-RJ
Tel: (021) 5773522 *Fax:* (021) 5771249
Key Personnel
Dir, President: Stelio De Andrade Soares
Founded: 1980
ISBN Prefix(es): 85-85677

Livraria Duas Cidades Ltda
Rua Bento Freitas 158, 01220-000 Sao Paulo-SP
Tel: (011) 220 4702 *Fax:* (011) 220-5813
Key Personnel
Man Dir: Jose Petronillo de Santa Cruz
Sales Dir: Mitsuro Nagata
Publicity Dir: Mara Valles
Founded: 1956
Subjects: Literature, Literary Criticism, Essays, Philosophy, Psychology, Psychiatry, Religion - Other, Social Sciences, Sociology

ISBN Prefix(es): 85-235
Branch Office(s)
Ave Rio Branco 9, Sala 116, Centro, 20090 Rio de Janeiro-RJ

Dumara Distribuidora de Publicacoes Ltda+
Rua Barata Ribeiro 17 - SI 202, 22011-000 Rio de Janeiro-RJ
Tel: (021) 5420248 *Fax:* (021) 2750294
Key Personnel
Contact: Alberto Jak Schprejer; Ari Roitman
Founded: 1989
Subjects: Anthropology, Drama, Theater, Fiction, Social Sciences, Sociology
ISBN Prefix(es): 85-7316

E P U Editora Pedagogica e Universitaria Ltd
Rua Joaquim Floriano, 72-6 andar Conjuntos 65/68, 04534-000 Sao Paulo-SP
Tel: (011) 3168-6077 *Fax:* (011) 3078-5803
E-mail: epu@epu.com.br
Web Site: www.epu.com.br
Key Personnel
Executive: Wolfgang Knapp *E-mail:* knapp@epu.com.br
Founded: 1952
Subjects: Education, Medicine, Nursing, Dentistry, Philosophy, Psychology, Psychiatry
ISBN Prefix(es): 85-12

EBAL, see Editora Brasil-America (EBAL) SA

Edicon Editora e Consultorial Ltda
Rua Herculano de Freitas, 181, Cerqueira Cesar, 01308-020 Sao Paulo-SP
Tel: (011) 3255-1002 *Fax:* (011) 3255-9822
E-mail: edicon@edicon.com.br
Web Site: www.edicon.com.br
Key Personnel
Executive: Valentina Ljubschenko
Founded: 1981
Subjects: Antiques, Art, Astrology, Occult, Drama, Theater, Earth Sciences, Education, Gay & Lesbian, Mathematics, Philosophy, Physics, Poetry, Romance, Science Fiction, Fantasy
ISBN Prefix(es): 85-290

Edipro-Edicoes Profissionais Ltda+
Rua 1 de Agosto, 2-51, 17010-011 Bauru
Tel: (014) 232-3375 *Fax:* (014) 232-4684
Key Personnel
Contact: Jair Lot-Viera
Subjects: Law
ISBN Prefix(es): 85-7283

Companhia Editora Forense+
Av Erasmo Braga, 299-2º andar, 20020-000 Rio de Janeiro-RJ
Tel: (021) 2533-5537 *Fax:* (021) 2533-5537
E-mail: forense@forense.com.br
Web Site: www.forense.com.br
Key Personnel
President: Regina Bilac Pinto
Vice President: Francisco Bilac Pinto
Founded: 1904
Subjects: Biography, Cookery, Criminology, Education, Health, Nutrition, History, Law, Music, Dance, Nonfiction (General), Philosophy, Psychology, Psychiatry, Religion - Buddhist, Romance, Self-Help, Social Sciences, Sociology, Sports, Athletics, Travel, Women's Studies
ISBN Prefix(es): 85-309
Number of titles published annually: 360 Print
Imprints: Editora Gryphus
Subsidiaries: Companhia Forense de Artes Graficas (printing plant)

Branch Office(s)
Rua Guajajaras, 337 Lj 3, Barro Preto-MG, 30180-100 Belo Horizonte *Tel:* (031) 222-2184
Rua Senador Feijo, 137, Centro-SP, 01006-001 Sao Paulo *Tel:* (011) 3105-0111

Editora Koinonia Ltda, see Koinonia Comunidade Edicoes Ltda (Editora Koinonia Ltda)

Editora 34, see 34 Literatura S/C Ltda

EDUSC - Editora da Universidade do Sagrado Coracao (Sacred Heart University Press)+
Rua Irma Arminda, 10-50, 17011-160 Bauru-SP
Tel: (014) 3235-7111 *Fax:* (014) 3235-7219
E-mail: edusc@usc.br
Web Site: www.edusc.com.br
Key Personnel
President: Sr Jacinta Turolo Garcia
Publisher: Dr Luiz Eugenio Vescio
 E-mail: lpelegrin@usc.br
Founded: 1996
Subjects: Biological Sciences, Child Care & Development, Education, Health, Nutrition, History, Journalism, Law, Literature, Literary Criticism, Essays, Philosophy, Psychology, Psychiatry, Religion - Catholic, Science (General), Social Sciences, Sociology, Brazilian originals
ISBN Prefix(es): 85-7460
Number of titles published annually: 80 Print
Distribution Center: Rio de Janeiro
Sao Paulo

EFE Tres D-Pub Juridicas Ltda
Rua Torres Galvao, 35, 1 andar, 59032-160 Natal RN
Tel: (084) 2233394 *Fax:* (084) 2232263
E-mail: f3dsat@truenetrn.com.br
Key Personnel
Contact: Manoel Digesio de Costa

Editora Elevacao+
Affiliate of Brazilian Book Chamber
Av Rudge, 938, Bom Retiro, 01134-000 Sao Paulo-SP
Tel: (011) 3358-6868; (011) 3358-6875; (011) 3358-6869 *Fax:* (011) 3331-5803
E-mail: info@elevacao.com.br
Web Site: www.elevacao.com.br
Key Personnel
Contact: Marcus Alexandre Pineze
 E-mail: mpineze@uol.com.br
Founded: 1998
Subjects: Biblical Studies, Biography, Business, Communications, Education, Health, Nutrition, Human Relations, Parapsychology, Philosophy, Poetry, Religion - Other, Romance, Self-Help, Sports, Athletics, Theology
Number of titles published annually: 84 Print; 2 Audio
Total Titles: 35 Print; 2 Audio
Distributed by Distribooks Inc

Emporio de Promocoes Artistica Cultural e Editora Ltda+
Rua Ceara 184, 01243-010 Sao Paulo-SP
Tel: (011) 8262992 *Fax:* (011) 661135
Key Personnel
Contact: Luiz Bueno D'Horta
Founded: 1989
Membership(s): CBL.
ISBN Prefix(es): 85-85431

Empresa Brasileira de Pesquisa Agropecuaria (Embrapa Publishing House)+
Parque Estacao Biologica-PqEB S/N, Edificio Sede, Plano Piloto, 70770-901 Brasilia DF
Tel: (061) 348-4113 *Fax:* (061) 347-1041
E-mail: webmaster@sct.embrapa.br
Web Site: www.embrapa.br

Key Personnel
President & Dir: Clayton Campanhola
 E-mail: presid@sede.embrapa.br
Subjects: Agriculture, Biological Sciences, Earth Sciences, Economics, Journalism, Social Sciences, Sociology, Technology, Veterinary Science
ISBN Prefix(es): 85-7383

Escrituras Editora e Distribuidora de Livros Ltda+
Rua Maestro Callia, 123, Vila Mariana, 04012-100 Sao Paulo-SP
Tel: (011) 5082-4190 *Fax:* (011) 5082-4190
E-mail: escrituras@escrituras.com.br
Web Site: www.escrituras.com.br
Key Personnel
Executive Editor: Raimundo Nonato Rocha Gadelha
ISBN Prefix(es): 85-86303

Editora Expressao e Cultura-Exped Ltda
Est dos Bandeirantes, 1700, 22710-113 Rio de Janeiro-RJ
Tel: (021) 445-0333 *Fax:* (021) 445-0996
Telex: 33280
Key Personnel
Publisher: Gilberto Huber
Dir & Editor: Ferdinando Bastos de Souza
Editorial Manager: Paulo Schvinger
Founded: 1967
Subjects: Education, Literature, Literary Criticism, Essays
ISBN Prefix(es): 85-208
Parent Company: Grupo Gilberto Huber
Associate Companies: Ebid-Editora Paginas Amarelas SA
Orders to: CP 20030, Rio de Janeiro-RJ

FAE, see Fundacao de Assistencia ao Estudante

Editora FCO Ltda+
Av do Conturno, 2205, 30110-070 Belo Horizonte-MG
Tel: (031) 2131288 *Fax:* (031) 2243825
Key Personnel
Contact: Sr Lucio Fernando Borges
Founded: 1994
Subjects: Civil Engineering, Education, Engineering (General), Management

FEI, *imprint of* Editora Gaia Ltda

Livraria Martins Fontes Editora Ltda+
Rua Conselheiro Ramalho 330, 01325-000 Sao Paulo-SP
Tel: (011) 3241-3677 *Fax:* (0800) 11-605-6867
E-mail: info@martinsfontes.com.br
Web Site: www.martinsfontes.com.br *Cable:* CABOGRAMA
Key Personnel
Contact: Waldir Martins Fontes
Founded: 1960
Subjects: Art, Education, English as a Second Language, History, Law, Nonfiction (General), Philosophy, Psychology, Psychiatry, Social Sciences, Sociology
ISBN Prefix(es): 85-336

Editora Forense Universitaria Ltda+
Rua Sa Freire, 25, 20930-430 Rio de Janeiro-RJ
Tel: (011) 580-0776 *Fax:* (011) 589-2084
E-mail: foruniv@unisys.com.br
Key Personnel
Dir: Regina Bilac Pinto
Founded: 1973
Membership(s): National Book Publishers of Rio de Janeiro, Brasil.
Subjects: Economics, Government, Political Science, Language Arts, Linguistics, Law, Philos-

ophy, Psychology, Psychiatry, Social Sciences, Sociology
ISBN Prefix(es): 85-218
Bookshop(s): Livraria Forense Universitaria Lg Sao Francisco, Lg Sao Francisco, 20, 01005-010 Sao Paulo-SP, Paulo Abrantes *Tel:* (011) 31040396
Warehouse: Rua Sa Freire, 25, 20930-430 Rio De Janeiro-RJ

Scott Foresman, *imprint of* Pearson Education Do Brasil

Formato Editorial ltda+
Av Marques de Sao Vicente, 1697-Barra Funda, 01139-904 San Paulo-SP
Tel: (011) 3613-3000 *Fax:* (011) 3611-3308
E-mail: falecom@formatoeditorial.com.br
Web Site: www.formatoeditorial.com.br
Key Personnel
Dir: Jose de Alencar Mayrink *E-mail:* alencar@formatoeditorial.com.br; Claudia Pereira-Rezende *Tel:* (031) 4211777 *E-mail:* claudia@graficaformato.com.br
Editor: Sonia Marta Junqueira *Tel:* (031) 4218544 *E-mail:* soniajunqueira@formatoeditorial.com.br
Founded: 1986
Membership(s): Camara Brasileira do Livro & Fundacao Nacional do Livro Infantil e Juvenil.
Subjects: Education, Literature, Literary Criticism, Essays
ISBN Prefix(es): 85-7208
Number of titles published annually: 35 Print
Total Titles: 268 Print

Livraria Freitas Bastos Editora SA+
Avenida Londre, 381 Bonsucesso, 21041-030 Rio de Janeiro-RJ
Tel: (021) 290-9949 *Fax:* (021) 290-9949
E-mail: fbastos@netfly.com.br; freitasbastos@freitasbastos.com.br *Cable:* ETIEL
Key Personnel
President: Isaac Delgado Abulafia *E-mail:* isaac@netfly.com.br
Founded: 1917
Membership(s): the Association of Brazilian Publishers.
Subjects: Accounting, Law
ISBN Prefix(es): 85-353

Editora FTD SA
Rua Manoel Dutra, 225, Bairro Bela Vista, 01328-010 Sao Paulo-SP
Tel: (011) 3284-8500 *Fax:* (011) 3283-5011
E-mail: ftd@dial.ta.com.br
Web Site: www.ftd.com.br
Key Personnel
Man Dir: Joao Tissi
Contact: Romeu Rossi
Founded: 1897
ISBN Prefix(es): 85-322
Branch Office(s)
Rua Agenor Meira 4/67, Bauro, Sao Paulo-SP
Rua Lavras 235, Carmo Sion, Belo Horizonte-MG
Ave Goias 1146, Goiania-GO
Ave Tiradentes 963, Maringa
Rua Andre Cavalcanti 78, Rio de Janeiro-GB
Ave Joana Angelica 963, Salvador-BA
Rua Mal Deodoro 887, Curitiba-PR
Ave do Imperador 1203, Fortaleza-CE
Ave Rio Branco 185, Londrina-PR
Rua Martins Junior 39, Recife-PE
Rua Prof Baltazar 12, Vitoria-ES

Fundacao Cultural Avatar
R Pereira Nunes, 141 - Inga, 24210-430 Niteroi-RJ
Tel: (021) 621-0217 *Fax:* (021) 2621-0217
E-mail: fcavatar@nitnet.com.br
Web Site: www.nitnet.com.br/~fcavatar
Key Personnel
President: Prof Tania Goncalves de Araujo
Dir, Administration & Financial: Dr Jayme Treiger
Dir, Culture: Prof Ruth Machado Barbosa
Subjects: Asian Studies, Astrology, Occult, Biography, Education, Philosophy, Psychology, Psychiatry, Religion - Other
ISBN Prefix(es): 85-7104

Fundacao de Assistencia ao Estudante
SAS Quadra 1- BI/A Sl 806, 70729-000 Brasilia-DF
Tel: (061) 223-9329 *Fax:* (061) 226-6270
Key Personnel
Man Dir: Rubens Jose de Castro Albuquerque
Editorial Dir: Luiz Pasquale Filho
Sales Dir: Avari de Campos
Production Manager: Maria Aparecida de Oliveira
Publicity Manager: Geni Hirata
Rights & Permissions: Jose Ribeiro de Castro Neto
Founded: 1967
276 bookshops throughout Brazil.
ISBN Prefix(es): 85-222

Fundacao Instituto Brasileiro de Geografia e Estatistica (IBGE - CDDI/DECOP) (Brasilian Institute of National Statistics & Geography)
Rua General Canabarro, 706, Bairro Maracana, 20271-201 Rio de Janeiro
Tel: (021) 569-2043 *Fax:* (021) 234-6189
Web Site: www.ibge.gov.br
Telex: (021) 2139128
Key Personnel
President: Sergio Besserman Vianna *Fax:* (021) 220-5943
Senior Technician: Raul Aloysio Telles Ribeiro *Tel:* (021) 569-2043 *E-mail:* raultri@ibge.gov.br
Founded: 1936
Subjects: Economics, Geography, Geology, Mathematics
ISBN Prefix(es): 85-240
Bookshop(s): Av Franklin Roosevet, 146 lj.A, 20021 Castelo-RJ
Orders to: IBGE - CDDI/DECOP/DICOM, Rua General Canabarro 666, Bloco B - 2/Andar, 20271-200 Rio de Janerio-RJ, Contact: Carlos Lessa *Tel:* (021) 569-2043 *Fax:* (021) 234-8480 *E-mail:* atandicddi@ibge.gov.br

Fundacao Joaquim Nabuco-Editora Massangana+
Av Dezessete de agosto, 2187 Casa Forte 52061-540
Tel: (081) 3441-5500 *Fax:* (081) 3441-5600
E-mail: editora@fundaj.gov.br
Web Site: www.fundaj.gov.br
Telex: 081 1180
Key Personnel
Dir General: Leonardo Dantas Silva
Founded: 1978
Subjects: Anthropology, Economics, Education, History, Social Sciences, Sociology
ISBN Prefix(es): 85-7019

Fundacao Sao Paulo, EDUC+
Rua Ministro Godoi, 1213, 05015-001 Sao Paulo-SP
Tel: (011) 3873-3359 *Fax:* (011) 38733359
E-mail: educsp@puc001.pucsp.ansp.br
Key Personnel
Dir: Maria do Carmo Guedes
Vice Dir: Maria Eliza Mazzilli Pereira
Founded: 1984
Membership(s): CBL, ABEU, ABEC.
Subjects: Anthropology, Biological Sciences, Communications, Disability, Special Needs, Economics, Education, English as a Second Language, Geography, Geology, Government, Political Science, History, Humor, Language Arts, Linguistics, Law, Literature, Literary Criticism, Essays, Mathematics, Medicine, Nursing, Dentistry, Music, Dance, Philosophy, Psychology, Psychiatry, Social Sciences, Sociology, Theology
ISBN Prefix(es): 85-283
Total Titles: 230 Print; 1 Audio
Parent Company: Pontificia Universidade Catolica de Sao Paulo
Ultimate Parent Company: Funda cao Cultural Sao Paulo
Bookshop(s): Espaco EDUC, Rua Monte Alegre, 984 *Tel:* (011) 36708297 *Fax:* (011) 38733359
Orders to: Livraria Cultura, Avenida Paulista, 2073, Conj Nacional Cerqueira Cesar, 01310-300 Sao Paulo-SP, Contact: Ana Regina *Tel:* (011) 2854033 *Fax:* (011) 2854457
E-mail: livro@livcultura.com.br

Editora Gaia Ltda+
Rua Pirapitingui, 111, 01508-020 Sao Paulo-SP
Tel: (011) 2777999 *Fax:* (011) 2778141
E-mail: gaia@dialdata.com.br
Key Personnel
Prof: Carlos Alberto Pereira de Oliveira
Founded: 1989
Subjects: Cookery, Environmental Studies, Health, Nutrition, Self-Help
ISBN Prefix(es): 85-85351
Parent Company: Global Editora E Distribuidora Ltda
Associate Companies: Editora Ground Ltda
Imprints: FEI

Editora Gente Livraria e Editora Ltda+
Rua Pedro Soares de Almeida 114, 05029-030 Sao Paulo-SP
Tel: (011) 3675 2505 *Fax:* (011) 3675 0430
E-mail: gentedit@mandic.com.br
Key Personnel
Editor: Rosely Boschini
Founded: 1976
Subjects: Philosophy, Psychology, Psychiatry
ISBN Prefix(es): 85-7312

Global Editora e Distribuidora Ltda+
Rua Pirapitingui, 111, Liberdade, 01508-020 Sao Paulo-SP
Tel: (011) 2777999 *Fax:* (011) 2778141
E-mail: global@dialdata.com.br
Key Personnel
Man Dir, Sales: Luis Alves, Jr
Editorial, Production, Rights & Permissions: Jose Venancio
Founded: 1973
Subjects: Anthropology, Biography, Education, Fashion, Health, Nutrition, History, Music, Dance, Poetry, Romance, Social Sciences, Sociology
ISBN Prefix(es): 85-260
Associate Companies: Editora Ground Ltda; Editora Gaia Ltda
Imprints: Parma; Prol; Sao Paulo Editora
Subsidiaries: Centro Editorial Latino Americano Ltda

Editora Globo SA+
Av Jaguare, 1485, 05346-902 Sao Paulo-SP
Tel: (011) 3767-7886 *Fax:* (011) 3767-7870
E-mail: wcarelli@edgloblo.com.br
Web Site: www.editoraglobo.com.br
Telex: 81574
Key Personnel
General Dir: Ricardo Alberto Fischer
Editorial Dir: Flavio Barros Pinto
Sales Dir: Fernando Alberto Costa
Founded: 1954
Subjects: Biography, Business, Cookery, Drama, Theater, Economics, Education, Environmental Studies, Fiction, History, How-to, Humor, Journalism, Language Arts, Linguistics, Law, Literature, Literary Criticism, Essays, Medicine,

Nursing, Dentistry, Music, Dance, Mysteries, Poetry, Science (General), Self-Help, Sports, Athletics, Travel
ISBN Prefix(es): 85-250; 85-217
Branch Office(s)
Rua Itapiru, 1209, 20251 Rio de Janeiro
Warehouse: Alameda Tocantins, 679 Alphaville Barueri, Sao Paulo

Edicoes Graal Ltda+
CP 128, 06801-970 Embau-SP
Tel: (011) 7961-0006 *Fax:* (011) 7961-0006
Key Personnel
Man Dir, Editorial & Publicity Dir & Rights & Permissions: Fernando Gasparian
Sales & Production Dir: Marcus F Gasparian
Founded: 1977
Subjects: Economics, Education, History, Medicine, Nursing, Dentistry, Philosophy, Psychology, Psychiatry, Social Sciences, Sociology
ISBN Prefix(es): 85-7038
Associate Companies: Editora Paz e Terra

Ordem do Graal na Terra
CP 128, 06801-970 Embu-SP
Tel: (011) 4781-0006 *Fax:* (011) 4781-0006 (ext 217)
E-mail: graal@graal.org.br
Web Site: www.graal.org.br
Key Personnel
President: Harald Schuler
Distribution Mgr: Paulo Nobre *Tel:* (011) 4781 1671 *Fax:* (011) 4781 1671
E-mail: nobrebooks@graal.org.br
Founded: 1947
Subjects: Philosophy, Religion - Other, Self-Help, New-Age, Spiritualism
ISBN Prefix(es): 85-7279
Number of titles published annually: 3 Print
Total Titles: 55 Print
U.S. Office(s): Nobre Books Distributor, 5117 Black Diamond Court, Raleigh, NC 27604, United States *Tel:* 919-212-6211
E-mail: nobrebooks@graal.org.br
Bookshop(s): Av Sao Luiz, 192-lj14, Sao Paulo, SP 01046-000 *Tel:* (011) 259-7646
Shipping Address: Biblio Distribution, 15200 NBN Way, Blue Ridge Summit, PA 17214, United States
Warehouse: Biblio Distribution, 15200 NBN Way, Blue Ridge Summit, PA 17214, United States
Distribution Center: Biblio Distribution, 15200 NBN Way, Blue Ridge Summit, PA 17214, United States
Orders to: Biblio Distribution, 15200 NBN Way, Blue Ridge Summit, PA 17214, United States
Returns: Biblio Distribution, 15200 NBN Way, Blue Ridge Summit, PA 17214, United States

Editora e Grafica Carisio Ltda, Minas Editora+
Av Batalhao Maua, 1055, 38440-000 Araguari-MG
Tel: (034) 2413557 *Fax:* (034) 2413310
Key Personnel
Contact: Publio Carisio de Paula
Founded: 1984
Subjects: Fiction, Religion - Other, Self-Help
ISBN Prefix(es): 85-86030

Grafica Editora Primor Ltda+
Rua Presidente Dutra 2611, 21535-500 Rio de Janeiro
Tel: (021) 4744966
Key Personnel
Man Dir: Sergio Jacques Waissman; Simao Waissman
Sales & Publicity: Miguel Paixao
Production: Paulo Duante
Founded: 1969
Subjects: Art, Education

ISBN Prefix(es): 85-7024
Parent Company: Editora Primor Ltda

Editora Ground Ltda+
Rua Lacedemonia, 68, 04634-020 Sao Paulo-SP
Tel: (011) 5031-1500 *Fax:* (011) 5031-3462
E-mail: editora@ground.com.br; vendas@ground.com.br; marketing@ground.com.br
Web Site: www.ground.com.br
Key Personnel
Executive & Publisher: Jose Carlos Rolo Venancio *E-mail:* jcvenancio@ground.com.br
Founded: 1973
Subjects: Asian Studies, Astrology, Occult, Environmental Studies, Health, Nutrition, Philosophy
ISBN Prefix(es): 85-7187
Associate Companies: Editora Aquariana Ltda, Rua Lacedemonia, 68, Sao Paulo *E-mail:* aquariana@ground.com.br

Editora Gryphus, imprint of Companhia Editora Forense

Editora Guanabara Koogan SA+
Travessa do Ouvidor 11, 1º AO 8º Andares, 20040-040 Rio de Janeiro-RJ
Tel: (021) 3970-9450 *Fax:* (021) 2252-2732
E-mail: gbk@editoraguanabara.com.br
Web Site: www.editoraguanabara.com.br
Key Personnel
Dir: Joao Pedro Lorch; Mauro Koogan Lorch
Rights & Permissions: Christina Noren
Founded: 1930
Subjects: Biological Sciences, Environmental Studies, Medicine, Nursing, Dentistry, Veterinary Science
ISBN Prefix(es): 85-277; 85-226

Enio Matheus Guazzelli e Cia Ltd, see Livraria Pioneira Editora/Enio Matheus Guazzelli e Cia Ltd

Editora Harbra Ltda+
Rua Joaquim Tavora, 779, Vila Mariana, 04015-001 Sao Paulo-SP
Tel: (011) 5084-2403; (011) 5084-2482; (011) 5571-1122; (011) 5549-2244; (011) 5571-0276 *Fax:* (011) 5575-6876; (011) 5571-9777
E-mail: editorial@harbra.com.br
Web Site: www.harbra.com.br
Key Personnel
Dir: Julio Esteban Emod-Eghy *Tel:* (011) 50842482 *E-mail:* emod@harbra.com.br
Founded: 1986
Subjects: Behavioral Sciences, Biography, Biological Sciences, Computer Science, Earth Sciences, Management, Physical Sciences, Science (General), Self-Help, Social Sciences, Sociology
ISBN Prefix(es): 85-294
Total Titles: 250 Print; 1 CD-ROM; 1 Audio
Branch Office(s)
Rua 70, No 687 Qd 127 Lt 05, 74055-120 Goiania *Tel:* (062) 212-9875; (062) 225-8632 *Fax:* (062) 212-9874
Rua do Riachuelo 453, Loja 7, 50050-400 Recife *Tel:* (081) 3221-0700; (081) 3222-2808 *Fax:* (081) 3221-3655
Rua Conde de Bomfim 944-A (Tijuca), 20520-000 Rio de Janeiro *Tel:* (021) 572-4668; (021) 238-4670 *Fax:* (021) 572-8576
Rua Guajajaras 1148, 30180-100 Belo Horizonte *Fax:* (031) 3275-4016
Distributor for editora Edgard Blucher; editora Universidade de Brasilia

Hemus Editora Ltda+
Rua da Gloria 312, 01510-000 Sao Paulo-SP
Tel: (011) 279-9911 *Fax:* (011) 279-9721
Telex: 32005 Edil *Cable:* HETEC

Key Personnel
President: Rachel Behar
Man Dir: Maxim Behar
Founded: 1965
Subjects: Archaeology, Architecture & Interior Design, Astrology, Occult, Career Development, Civil Engineering, Electronics, Electrical Engineering, Law, Philosophy
ISBN Prefix(es): 85-289

Horus Editora Ltda+
Rua dos Ingleses, 222 cj 121, 01329-902 Sao Paulo-SP
Tel: (011) 288-7681 *Fax:* (011) 288-7681
E-mail: horus@horuseditora.com.br
Web Site: www.horuseditora.com.br
Key Personnel
President: Juan Ferre' Serrano
Manager: Roberto Ferre' Serrano
Founded: 1977
Also acts as distributor.
Subjects: Astrology, Occult, Music, Dance, Psychology, Psychiatry, Religion - Buddhist, Religion - Catholic, Religion - Hindu, Religion - Islamic, Religion - Jewish, Religion - Other, Theology
ISBN Prefix(es): 85-86204

Livro Ibero-Americano Ltda
Hermenegildo de Barros, 40-Gloria, 20241-040 Rio de Janeiro-RJ
Tel: (021) 2221 2026 *Fax:* (021) 2252 8814
Web Site: www.livroiberoamericano.com.br
Cable: NEBRIJA
Key Personnel
Man Dir: Sir Joao Francisco J Gomes
Founded: 1946
Subjects: Agriculture, Art, Electronics, Electrical Engineering, History, Language Arts, Linguistics, Philosophy, Photography, Psychology, Psychiatry, Religion - Other
ISBN Prefix(es): 85-7032
Branch Office(s)
Rua Conselheiro Crispiniano 29 - 1 pav, Sao Paulo-SP

IBGE - CDDI/DECOP, see Fundacao Instituto Brasileiro de Geografia e Estatistica (IBGE - CDDI/DECOP)

IBICT, see Instituto Brasileiro de Informacao em Ciencia e Tecnologia

IBRASA (Instituicao Brasileira de Difusao Cultural Ltda)+
Rua Treze De Maio, 365/367, 01327-000 Sao Paulo-SP
Tel: (011) 3107 41 00 *Fax:* (011) 3107 35 13
E-mail: editora.ibrasa@uol.com.br
Web Site: www.ibrasa.com.br
Key Personnel
Man Dir: Jorge Leite
Founded: 1958
Subjects: Economics, Education, Government, Political Science, Health, Nutrition, History, Literature, Literary Criticism, Essays, Medicine, Nursing, Dentistry, Parapsychology, Philosophy, Psychology, Psychiatry, Science (General), Social Sciences, Sociology, Sports, Athletics, Physical education
ISBN Prefix(es): 85-348
Bookshop(s): IBREX - Distribuidora de Livros e Material de Escritorio Ltda
Orders to: IBREX Ltda, Rua Treze de Maio 361, 01327-000 Sao Paulo-SP

Icone Editora Ltda+
Rua das Palmeiras, 213, 01226-010 Sao Paulo-SP
Tel: (011) 826-7074; (021) 826-9510 *Fax:* (011) 826-9510

Key Personnel
President: Luiz Carlos Fanelli
Vice President: Tatiana Fanelli
Founded: 1985
Membership(s): Brazilian House of Books, National Syndication of Books, Brazilian Association of Books & Collections; also acts as distributor.
Subjects: Agriculture, Astrology, Occult, Biography, Crafts, Games, Hobbies, Law, Medicine, Nursing, Dentistry, Science (General), Sports, Athletics, Technology
ISBN Prefix(es): 85-274; 85-85503
Divisions: Editorial, Production, Publication & Distribution Departments

Iglu Editora Ltda
Rua Duilio 386, Lapa, 05043-020 Sao Paulo-SP
Tel: (011) 3873-0227 *Fax:* (011) 3873-0227
Key Personnel
Contact: Julio Igliori Netto
Founded: 1987
Subjects: Economics, Education, Health, Nutrition, Law
ISBN Prefix(es): 85-7494

Iluminuras - Projetos e Producoes Editoriais Ltda+
Rua Oscar Freire 1233, 01426-001 Sao Paulo-SP
Tel: (011) 3068-9433 *Fax:* (011) 3082-5317
Key Personnel
Contact: Beatriz Costa; Sir Samuel Leon
Founded: 1987
ISBN Prefix(es): 85-85219

Imago Editora Importacao e Exportacao Ltda+
Rua Santos Rodrigues, nº 201-A, Estacio, 20250-430 Rio de Janeiro-RJ
Tel: (021) 2502-9092 *Fax:* (021) 2502-5435
E-mail: imago@imagoeditora.com.br
Web Site: www.imagoeditora.com.br
Key Personnel
President: Jayme Salomao
Executive Dir: Eduardo Salomao
Founded: 1967
Membership(s): SNEL, CBL.
Subjects: Biblical Studies, Biography, Drama, Theater, Fiction, Film, Video, Health, Nutrition, History, How-to, Language Arts, Linguistics, Literature, Literary Criticism, Essays, Mysteries, Nonfiction (General), Philosophy, Psychology, Psychiatry, Religion - Other, Romance, Science Fiction, Fantasy, Self-Help
ISBN Prefix(es): 85-312

Editora Index Ltda+
Av Rio Branco, 45 - S1 1707, Centro, 20090-003 Rio de Janeiro-RJ
Tel: (021) 516 2336 *Fax:* (021) 253 3507
E-mail: editoraindex@ax.ibase.org.br
Key Personnel
President: Jose Paulo M Soares; Christina Ferrao
Founded: 1982
Membership(s): Chealsea Arts Club (London).
Subjects: Art, Environmental Studies, History
ISBN Prefix(es): 85-7083
Associate Companies: Editora Libris
Warehouse: Rua Sacadura Cabral 81 gr 804, Rio de Janeiro 20221

Instituicao Brasileira de Difusao Cultural Ltda (IBRASA), see IBRASA (Instituicao Brasileira de Difusao Cultural Ltda)

Editora Interciencia Ltda
Av Presidente Vargas, 435 - S/Lj 604, 20077-900 Rio de Janeiro-RJ
Tel: (021) 242-2861 *Fax:* (021) 242-7787
Key Personnel
Man Dir & Rights & Permissions: Edson G S Nascimento
Publicity: Nize Nascimento
Founded: 1969 (1975 as publisher)
Subjects: Science (General)
ISBN Prefix(es): 85-7193

Interlivros Edicoes Ltda
Rua Comandante Coelho 1085, 21250-510 Rio de Janeiro-RJ
Tel: (021) 3913134 *Fax:* (021) 3521005
E-mail: interlivros@ibm.net
Key Personnel
Executive: Abel Simoes de Morais
Subjects: Biological Sciences, Health, Nutrition, Medicine, Nursing, Dentistry, Psychology, Psychiatry
ISBN Prefix(es): 85-7236; 85-85891

Irmaos Vitale S/A Industria e Comercio
Rua Franca Pinto, 42, vila Mariana, 04704-000 Sao Paulo-SP
Tel: (011) 5574-7001 *Fax:* (011) 5574-7388
E-mail: irmaos@vitale.com.br
Web Site: www.vitale.com.br
ISBN Prefix(es): 85-7407; 85-85188
Parent Company: Irmaos Vitale S/A Ind E Comercio
Subsidiaries: Casa Vitale
Divisions: Edicoes musicais e Instrumentos musicais (Nacionais e importados)

ISAEC, see Editora Sinodal

JUERP, see Junta de Educacao Religiosa e Publicacoes da Convencao Batista Brasileira (JUERP)

Junta de Educacao Religiosa e Publicacoes da Convencao Batista Brasileira (JUERP)+
Rua Silva Vale, 781, 21370-360 Rio de Janeiro-RJ
Tel: (021) 2690772 *Fax:* (021) 2690296
E-mail: juerp@openlink.com.br
Web Site: www.juerp.org.br *Cable:* BATISTAS
Key Personnel
General Superintendent: Dr Claudio Mazzoni
Editorial & Rights & Permissions: Prof Joelcio Barreto
Marketing: Dr Oswaldo Paiao, Jr
Production: Dr Samuel Justino
Founded: 1907
Membership(s): Association of Brazilian Christian Publishers & Association of Brazilian Baptist Publishers.
Subjects: Religion - Other
ISBN Prefix(es): 85-350
Branch Office(s)
Filial Juerp, Ave Sao Joao 816/820, 01036-100 Sao Paulo-SP
Trav Padre Prudencio 61, 66000 Belem-PA
Rua Bahia 360 - Sobre loja, 30000 Belo Horizonte-MG
SDS Bl G - loja 17 - Conj Baracat, 70302 Brasilia-DF
Rua Treze de Maio 2659, 79100 Camop Grande-MS
Rua Rui Barbosa 139, 69007 Manaus-AM
Rua do Hospicio 187, 50000 Reclife-PE
Juerp Suese, Rua Silva Vale, 781 - Cavalcante, 21370-360 Rio de Janeiro-RJ
Av Sao Pantaleao 195, LJS A E B, Centro, 65015 Sao Kyis-MA
Abba Press Editora, Rua do Mar, 20 Interlagos, 04654-060 Sao Paulo-SP
Rua Barao de Itapemirim 208, 29000 Vitoria-ES
Bookshop(s): Ave Nil Pecanha 411, 25000 Caxais-RJ; Rua XV de Novembro 49, 24000 Niteroi-RJ; Rua Otavio Tarquinio 178, 26000 Nova Iguacu-RJ; Rua Cel Vicente 614, 90000 Porto Alegre-RS; Rua fo Rosario 141/216, Centro, 20041 Rio de Janeiro-RJ; Rua Mariz e Barris 39, Praca da Bandeira, 20270 Rio de Janeiro-RJ; Ave Viscondede Sao Lourenco 6, 40000 Salvador-BA

Koinonia Comunidade Edicoes Ltda (Editora Koinonia Ltda)
SCLN 203 - Bl 1, 1 Andar, 70833-510 Brasilia-DF
Tel: (061) 322-4458 *Fax:* (061) 3228377
Key Personnel
Contact: Divino Soares da Silva
Founded: 1992
Subjects: Biblical Studies, Religion - Protestant
ISBN Prefix(es): 85-85810
Divisions: Gravadora Koinonia Music
Bookshop(s): Praca Carlos Gomes, 01501-040 Sao Paulo-SP *Tel:* (011) 606-2644; Rua 4 N 906-Sector Central CEP, 74025-020 Gioania-GO

Editora Kuarup Ltda+
rua Diamantina, 381, 91040-460 Porto Alegre-RS
Tel: (051) 361-5522 *Fax:* (051) 361-3550
E-mail: kuarup@conex.com.br
Key Personnel
Director: Adalberto Felix Souto
Editor: Vera Miranda Ritter-Souto
Founded: 1983
Subjects: Astrology, Occult, Education, Religion - Other
ISBN Prefix(es): 85-269

Francisco J Laissue Livraria
Prace Olavo Bilac 28, 201, 20041 Rio de Janeiro
Tel: (021) 509-7298
Founded: 1947
Bookshop specializing in Portuguese, Spanish, French & English.
Subjects: African American Studies, Anthropology, Archaeology, Asian Studies, Astrology, Occult, Religion - Buddhist, Religion - Hindu, Religion - Islamic, Religion - Jewish
Foreign Rep(s): Editorial Kier (Argentina)

Lake-Livraria Editora Allan Kardec+
Rua Assuncao, 45, Bras, 03005-020 Sao Paulo-SP
Tel: (011) 229-0526; (011) 229-1227; (011) 227-1396; (011) 229-0937; (011) 229-4592; (011) 229-0514 *Fax:* (011) 229-0935; (011) 227-5714
E-mail: lake@lake.com.br
Web Site: www.lake.com.br
Key Personnel
Contact: Roberto Francisco-Ferrero
Founded: 1937
ISBN Prefix(es): 85-7360

LDA Editores Ltda+
Rua Dias da Rocha Filho 1253, Unidade 03, 80410-510 Curitiba PR
Tel: (041) 362-9173 *Fax:* (041) 262-3439
E-mail: lda.editores@uol.com.br
Key Personnel
Executive: Lionel de Almeida
Founded: 1991
Subjects: Architecture & Interior Design, Biography, Cookery, History, Journalism, Literature, Literary Criticism, Essays, Philosophy, Travel
Imprints: Peninsula

Editora Leitura Ltda
Rua Pedra Bonita, 870, Belo Horizonte-MG 30430-390
Tel: (031) 3371-4902 *Fax:* (031) 3714902
E-mail: leitura@editoraleitura.com.br
Web Site: www.editoraleitura.com.br
Subjects: Education
ISBN Prefix(es): 85-7358

PUBLISHERS — BRAZIL

Libreria Editora Ltda+
Rua Taquaritinga, 137/139, Mooca, 03170-010 Sao Paulo-SP
Tel: (011) 608-5411 *Fax:* (011) 948-1615
E-mail: portal@libreria.com.br; libreria@libreria.com.br
Web Site: www.libreria.com.br
Key Personnel
Dir Coml: Fiorentino S Mario
Founded: 1974
Membership(s): the Association of Brazilian Publishers; Association of Brazilian Distributors.
Subjects: Cookery, English as a Second Language, Geography, Geology, Language Arts, Linguistics, Natural History, Globes
ISBN Prefix(es): 85-85900

Editora Lidador Ltda+
Rua Hilario Ribeiro 154, Pca da Bandeira, 20270-180 Rio de Janeiro-RJ
Tel: (021) 2569-0594 *Fax:* (021) 2204-0684
E-mail: lidador@infolink.com.br
Key Personnel
Publicity Manager: Ruy Carvalho
Founded: 1960
Subjects: Communications, Economics, Education, Erotica, Fiction, Human Relations, Music, Dance, Parapsychology, Social Sciences, Sociology
ISBN Prefix(es): 85-7003
Number of titles published annually: 9 Print
Distributed by Topbook

Waldir Lima Editora
Rua 24 de Maio, 347, 20950-090 Rio de Janeiro-RJ
Tel: (05521) 581-5000 *Fax:* (05521) 581-3586
E-mail: geapo@ccaa.com.br
Web Site: www.ccaa.com.br
Key Personnel
Dir-General, Rights & Permissions: Waldyr Lima
Editorial, Research & Planning Dir: Rosane Roale
Sales, Production & Publicity Dir: Rogerio Gama
Founded: 1967
Specialize in English, Portuguese & Spanish language instruction.
Subjects: Education, English as a Second Language, Language Arts, Linguistics
ISBN Prefix(es): 85-341
Total Titles: 2,000,000 Print
U.S. Office(s): CCLS Publishing House, 3181 Coral Way, Miami, FL 33145, United States
Showroom(s): Publishing House, 3181 Coral Way, Miami, FL 33145, United States
Orders to: Publishing House, 3181 Coral Way, Miami, FL 33145, United States

LISA (Livros Irradiantes SA)
Rua Major Sertorio, 772, 01222-000 Sao Paulo-SP
Tel: (011) 2563755 *Fax:* (011) 2575776
E-mail: lerlisalivros@ig.com.br
Key Personnel
Man Dir: Leonidio Balbino da Silva
Sales Dir: Francisco de Paula Oliveira Filho
Founded: 1965
Subjects: Education
ISBN Prefix(es): 85-257

Livraria Dos Advogados Editora Ltda
Rua Riachuelo, 201, 3º andar, Sao Paulo-SP
Tel: (011) 3107-3979 *Fax:* (011) 3107-6878
E-mail: lael@lael.com.br
Web Site: www.lael.com.br
Subjects: Law

Livraria Editora Infobook SA+
Rua do Mercado 34 Sala 1501, 20010-120 Rio de Janeiro-RJ
Tel: (021) 263-3807 *Fax:* (021) 263-3807
Key Personnel
Contact: Virginia Maria Reeve Andrea
Founded: 1993
Subjects: Computer Science, Management
ISBN Prefix(es): 85-85588; 85-7331

Livraria Kosmos Editora Ltda
Rua do Rosario 155, 20041-005 Rio de Janeiro-RJ
Tel: (021) 2224-8616 *Fax:* (021) 2221-4582
E-mail: livro-rio@kosmos.com.br
Web Site: www.kosmos.com.br *Cable:* EIKOS
Key Personnel
Man Dir: Stefan Geyerhahn; Luiz C Poppi
Founded: 1935
Subjects: Engineering (General), History, Language Arts, Linguistics, Music, Dance, Travel
ISBN Prefix(es): 85-7096

Livraria Nobel S/A+
Rua Pedroso Alvarenga, 1046 9 andar, Sao Paulo CEP 04531-004
Tel: (011) 3933-2822; (011) 3933-2811
Fax: (011) 3218-2833; (011) 3931-3988
E-mail: ary@editoranobel.com.br
Web Site: www.livnobel.com.br
Founded: 1943
Subjects: Advertising, Agriculture, Animals, Pets, Architecture & Interior Design, Biography, Business, Cookery, Economics, Gardening, Plants, Health, Nutrition, House & Home, Romance, Self-Help, Sports, Athletics, Technology, Travel
ISBN Prefix(es): 85-279; 85-213; 85-7553
Number of titles published annually: 80 Print
Total Titles: 230 Print
Imprints: Marco Zero; Studio Nobel
Subsidiaries: Editora Marco Zero; Editora Studio Nobel
Distributor for Harper Collins; Heinemann

Livros Irradiantes SA, *see* LISA (Livros Irradiantes SA)

Oficina de Livros Ltda+
Rua Tupinanbas, 360, 30120-070 Belo Horizonte
Tel: (061) 386-2355 *Toll Free Tel:* 800-644-3002
Fax: (061) 386-9248
E-mail: nicanorsena2001@aol.com.br
Key Personnel
President: Bernardino Jose Monteiro Moniz
Commercial Dir: Geraldo Alberto Alvares
Editor: Antonio Roberto Bertelli
Founded: 1987
Subjects: Literature, Literary Criticism, Essays, Social Sciences, Sociology
ISBN Prefix(es): 85-85170
Branch Office(s)
Rua Genebra, 135-9 andar, 01316 Sao Paulo-SP
Tel: (011) 379872

Editora Logosofica
Rua Coronel Oscar Porto, 818, Paraiso, 04003-004 Sao Paulo-SP
Tel: (011) 8851476; (011) 8856574 *Fax:* (011) 8879480
Key Personnel
Man Dir, Editorial: Jose Antonio Antonini
Author: Carlos Bernardo Gonzalez Pecotche
Sales: Alayde Thereza Melloni
Production: Darcio Giavoni
Founded: 1964
Membership(s): Brazilian Book Association.
Subjects: Behavioral Sciences, Education, Philosophy
ISBN Prefix(es): 85-7097
Branch Office(s)
Argentina
Mexico
Uruguay
U.S. Office(s): Centro de Estudos Logosoficos, 50 Woodfall Rd, Belmont, MA 02178, United States
Bookshop(s): SHCG - Norte, Area de Escolas Q704, 70000 Brasilia-DF; Rua Piaui 74 2, 30000 Belo Horizonte-MG; Rua General Polidoro 36, 22280 Rio de Janeiro-RJ

Longman, *imprint of* Pearson Education Do Brasil

Edicoes Loyola SA+
Rua 1822 No 347, 04216-000 Sao Paulo-SP
Tel: (011) 69141922 *Fax:* (011) 61634275
E-mail: editorial@loyola.com.br
Web Site: www.loyola.com.br
Key Personnel
Dir: Fidel Garcia Rodriguez *E-mail:* fidel@loyola.com.br
Editorial & Rights & Permissions: Marcos Marcionilo
Founded: 1965
Also acts as book packager.
Subjects: Anthropology, Art, Biblical Studies, Communications, Computer Science, Drama, Theater, Economics, Education, History, Law, Literature, Literary Criticism, Essays, Management, Philosophy, Psychology, Psychiatry, Religion - Other, Self-Help, Social Sciences, Sociology
ISBN Prefix(es): 85-15
Parent Company: Seas Edicoes Loyola
Divisions: Loyola Multimidia

LTC-Livros Tecnicos e Cientificos Editora S/A+
Travessa do Ouvidor, 11, 6th Andar-Parte, 20040-040 Rio de Janeiro-RJ
Tel: (021) 2221-7106; (021) 224-5877 *Fax:* (021) 252-2732; (021) 2221-5744
Key Personnel
Dir: Joao Pedro Lorch; Mauro Koogan Lorch
Rights & Permissions: Christina Noren
E-mail: norenltc@unisys.com.br
Founded: 1968
Subjects: Chemistry, Chemical Engineering, Computer Science, Economics, Engineering (General), Management, Mathematics, Physics, Technology
ISBN Prefix(es): 85-216

LTR Editora Ltda
Rua Jaguaribe, 585, 01224-001 Sao Paulo-SP
Mailing Address: CP 2112, 01224-001 Sao Paulo-SP
Tel: (011) 3667-1101 *Fax:* (011) 3825-6695
E-mail: ltr@ltr.com.br
Web Site: www.ltr.com.br/web/home.asp
Key Personnel
Man Dir: Vbiratan de Freitas Mesquita
Sales: Vbiratan de Freitas Mesquita
Founded: 1937
Subjects: Law
ISBN Prefix(es): 85-7322
Branch Office(s)
Guanabara Palace Hotel, Av Pres Vargas, 392, Rio de Janeiro-RJ *Tel:* (021) 2220-4744 *Fax:* (021) 2533-1393

Editora Lucre Comercio e Representacoes+
Av. Paulista, 1159-Cj 507, 01311-200 Sao Paulo-SP
Tel: (019) 287-8593 *Fax:* (019) 287 8593
E-mail: lucre@mute.net.br
Key Personnel
Contact: Eduardo Montalban
Founded: 1996
Subjects: Career Development, Economics, Finance, Management

Madras Editora+
Rua Paulo Goncalves, 88, 02403-020 Sao Paulo-SP
Tel: (011) 6959-1127 *Fax:* (011) 6959-3090
E-mail: editor@madras.com.br
Web Site: www.madras.com.br
Key Personnel
President: Wagner Veneziani Costa
Founded: 1991
Books for University students, professional people esoteric ones, self-help, mysticism, freemasonry. Distribute for self & 30 publishing houses throughout Brazil.
Subjects: Astrology, Occult, Self-Help
ISBN Prefix(es): 85-7374
Total Titles: 300 Print
Imprints: WVC
Foreign Rights: H Katia Schumer (Brazil)

Makron Books do Brasil Editora Ltda+
Rua Tabapua 1348, 04533-044 Sao Paulo-SP 20689
Tel: (011) 829-6879 *Fax:* (011) 829-8947
E-mail: makron@books.com.br
Web Site: www.makron.com.br
Key Personnel
President: Milton Assumplao *Fax:* (011) 8294970
  E-mail: milton@makron.com.be
Founded: 1985
Subjects: Business, Computer Science
ISBN Prefix(es): 85-346

Editora Manole Ltda+
Avenida Ceci, 672, 06460-120 Barueri-SP
Tel: (011) 4196-6000 *Fax:* (011) 4196 6007
E-mail: manole@virtual-net.com.br
Web Site: www.manole.com.br
Key Personnel
Editorial, Production, Rights & Permissions: Dinu Manole
Sales: Carlos Telles
Publicity: Ilma Manole
Production: Amarylis Manle
Founded: 1969
Subjects: Cookery, Crafts, Games, Hobbies, Health, Nutrition, Medicine, Nursing, Dentistry, Sports, Athletics, Veterinary Science
ISBN Prefix(es): 85-204
Total Titles: 120 Print
Distributed by Dina Livros

Editora Mantiqueira de Ciencia e Arte+
Av Eduardo Moreira da Cruz 295, 12460-000 Campos do Jordao-SP
Tel: (0122) 621832 *Fax:* (0122) 622126
Key Personnel
Executive: Antonio Fernando Costella
Subjects: Animals, Pets, Art, Communications, Fiction, History, Journalism, Poetry, Travel
ISBN Prefix(es): 85-85681

Editora Manuais Tecnicos de Seguros Ltda
Rua Brigadeiro Galvao 288, 01151-00 Sao Paulo-SP
Tel: (011) 8260844 *Fax:* (011) 8250833
Key Personnel
Contact: Christina Roncarati
Founded: 1970
Subjects: Securities
ISBN Prefix(es): 85-85549

Marco Zero, *imprint of* Livraria Nobel S/A

Editora Marco Zero Ltda+
Rua da Balsa, 559, 02910-000 Sao Paulo-SP
Tel: (011) 876-2822 *Fax:* (011) 257-2744
E-mail: marcozero@mutecnet.com.br
Key Personnel
International Rights: Maria Jose Silveria
Founded: 1980
Subjects: Biography, Child Care & Development, Cookery, How-to, Literature, Literary Criticism, Essays, Mysteries, Nonfiction (General), Travel
ISBN Prefix(es): 85-279
Parent Company: Nobel
Associate Companies: Studio Nobel

McKids, *imprint of* Editora Mundo Cristao

Editora Meca Ltda
Rua Araujo 81, 01220-020 Sao Paulo-SP
Tel: (011) 2599049; (011) 2599034; (011) 2575346 *Fax:* (011) 2570312
E-mail: editora_meca@uol.com.br
Web Site: www.editorameca.com.br *Cable:* CABOGRAMA
Key Personnel
Man Dir & Editor: Cosmo Juvela
Sales: Anna Maria Santos Brasil
Publicity: Marcos Juvela
Rights & Permissions: Guarany Gallo
Founded: 1970
Subjects: English as a Second Language, Parapsychology
Imprints: Jogos Pedagogicos
Warehouse: Rio de Janeiro, 51 Campos Eliseos, Sao Paulo-SP

Medicina Panamericana Editora Do Brasil Ltda+
Rua Santa Isabel 265, 012221-010 Sao Paulo-SP
Tel: (011) 222-0366 *Fax:* (011) 222-0542
Key Personnel
Executive: Nivacir Carlos Emmerick
Founded: 1950
Subjects: Medicine, Nursing, Dentistry
ISBN Prefix(es): 85-303
Parent Company: Editorial Medica Panamericana SA, Buenos Aires, Argentina
Subsidiaries: RJ/MG/RS

Medsi - Editora Medica e Cientifica Ltda
Rua Visconde de Cairu, 165, 20270-050 Rio de Janeiro-RJ
Tel: (021) 5694342 *Fax:* (021) 2646392
Key Personnel
Dir: Jackson Alves de Oliveira
Founded: 1981
Subjects: Medicine, Nursing, Dentistry
ISBN Prefix(es): 85-7199; 85-85019
Branch Office(s)
Rua Dr Cesario Motta Jr, 179, CEP 01221-020 Sao Paulo, SP

Editora Melhoramentos Ltda+
Subsidiary of Companhia Melhoramentos de Sao Paulo
Rua Tito, 479, 05051-000 Sao Paulo-SP
Tel: (011) 3874 0854 *Fax:* (011) 3874 0855
E-mail: blerner@melhoramentos.com.br
Web Site: melhoramentos.com.br
Key Personnel
Publishing Dir: Breno Lerner *E-mail:* blerner@melhoramentos.com.br
Contact: Alfredo Weiszflog *E-mail:* aweiszfl@melhoramentos.com.br
Founded: 1915
Specialize in reference books.
Subjects: Archaeology, Art, Cookery, English as a Second Language, History, Literature, Literary Criticism, Essays
ISBN Prefix(es): 85-06
Total Titles: 1,200 Print; 20 CD-ROM; 8 Audio
Distributed by ACME; Atlantida; Capeletti; Emece; L Rodrigues; SEP; Sigmar; Volcano Press
Distributor for Disney

Memorias Futuras Edicoes Ltda+
Rua Pereira da Silva 322, 22221-140 Rio de Janeiro-RJ
Tel: (021) 2053549 *Fax:* (021) 2252518
E-mail: memorias@br.homeshopping.com.br
Key Personnel
Contact: Hedy Costa de Oliveira
Founded: 1982
Subjects: Fiction
ISBN Prefix(es): 85-287

Editora Mercado Aberto Ltda+
Rua Dona Margarida, 894, Bairro Navegantes, 90240-610 Porto Alegre RS
Tel: (051) 3337-4833 *Fax:* (051) 3337-4905
E-mail: mercado@mercadoaberto.com.br
Web Site: www.mercadoaberto.com.br
Key Personnel
Executive: Roque Jacoby
Founded: 1977
Subjects: Anthropology, Education, Fiction, Health, Nutrition, History, Literature, Literary Criticism, Essays, Romance
ISBN Prefix(es): 85-280

Mercuryo Jovem, *imprint of* Editora Mercuryo Ltda

Editora Mercuryo Ltda+
Alameda dos Guaramomis, 1267, 04076-012 Sao Paulo-SP
Tel: (011) 5531-8222 *Fax:* (011) 5093-3265
E-mail: diretoraeditorial@mercuryo.com.br
Web Site: www.mercuryo.com.br
Key Personnel
Editor: Julia Barany
Founded: 1987
Subjects: Art, Biblical Studies, Biography, Fiction, History, Human Relations, Literature, Literary Criticism, Essays, Mysteries, Nonfiction (General), Parapsychology, Psychology, Psychiatry, Religion - Other, Science Fiction, Fantasy, Self-Help
ISBN Prefix(es): 85-7272
Number of titles published annually: 10 Print
Total Titles: 190 Print
Imprints: Unicornio Azul; Mercuryo Jovem

MG Editores Associados Ltda
Rua Primavera, 261, 01435-050 Sao Paulo-SP
Tel: (011) 8890861 *Fax:* (011) 8858646
Key Personnel
Contact: Flavio Gikovate
Subjects: Behavioral Sciences, Education
ISBN Prefix(es): 85-7255

Ministerio da Marinha Diretoria de Hidrografia Navegacao
Rua Barao de Jaceguai, s/n Ponta da Areia, 24048-900 Niteroi-RJ
Tel: (021) 719-2626 (ext 147) *Fax:* (021) 719-4989
E-mail: 01@dhm.mar.mil.sr
Telex: 2133858/213220
Key Personnel
Bilingual Assistant: Jose Mauro F Lopes
  E-mail: 122@bhm.mar.mil.sr
ISBN Prefix(es): 85-7293

Editora Moderna Ltda+
Rua Padre Adelino, 758, 03303-904 Sao Paulo-SP
Tel: (011) 609-0130 *Fax:* (011) 608-3055
E-mail: moderna@moderna.com.br
Web Site: www.moderna.com.br
Key Personnel
President & Man Dir: Ricardo Arissa Feltre
  Tel: (011) 60901369 *E-mail:* ricardo@moderna.com.br
Man Editor: Geraldo Fernandes
Founded: 1968
Subjects: Education, Fiction, Health, Nutrition, History, Literature, Literary Criticism, Essays, Mathematics, Social Sciences, Sociology, Women's Studies

ISBN Prefix(es): 85-16
Total Titles: 1,515 Print; 12 CD-ROM
Subsidiaries: Rio Grande Do Sul
Branch Office(s)
Rua Sen Furtado 31, 20270 Rio de Janeiro-RJ

Modulo Editora e Desenvolvimento Educacional Ltda
Rua Albano Reis, 1093, Born Retiro, 80520-530 Curitiba
Tel: (041) 2530077 *Fax:* (041) 2530103
E-mail: moduloed@moduloeditora.com.br
Web Site: www.moduloeditora.com.br
Key Personnel
Contact: Fausto Luiz Charneski
Founded: 1991
Subjects: Education, Geography, Geology, History, Mathematics, Science (General), Sports, Athletics
ISBN Prefix(es): 85-7397; 85-85764

Editora Mundo Cristao+
Rua Antonio Carlos Tacconi 79, 04810-020 Sao Paulo-SP
Tel: (011) 5668-1700 *Fax:* (011) 5666-4829
E-mail: editora@mundocristao.com.br
Web Site: www.mundocristao.com.br
Key Personnel
President: Mark L Carpenter
Founded: 1965
Subjects: Biblical Studies, Biography, Child Care & Development, Fiction, Religion - Protestant, Theology
ISBN Prefix(es): 85-7325
Imprints: Nexo; McKids

Musa Editora Ltda
Rua Monte Alegre, 1276, 05014-001 Perdizes-SP
Tel: (011) 62-2586 *Fax:* (011) 62-2586
E-mail: musaeditora@vol.com.br
Key Personnel
Executive: Ana Candida Costa
ISBN Prefix(es): 85-85653

Musimed Edicoes Musicais Importacao E Exportacao Ltda+
SCRS 505, Bloco A, Loja 65, 70350-510 Brasilia-DF
Mailing Address: CP 09693, Ag Central, 70001-970 Brasilia-DF
Tel: (061) 244-9799 *Fax:* (061) 226-0478
E-mail: cartas@musimed.com.br
Web Site: www.musimed.com.br
Key Personnel
Dir: Bohumil Med *E-mail:* bohumil@brnet.com.br
Purchasing Manager: Joselita Soares
Founded: 1984
Specialize in sheet music & music books.
Subjects: Music, Dance
ISBN Prefix(es): 85-7092; 85-85886
Total Titles: 23 Print
Showroom(s): SDS Ed Venaneio IV, Sobreloja, loja-14 Brasilia
Orders to: MusiMed Edicioes Musicias, SDS Edicioes Vanancio IV, Sobreloja, loja 14 Brasilia, Purchasing Managaer: Joselita Soares

Cia Editora Nacional
Rua Joli 294, 03016-020 Sao Paulo-SP
Tel: (011) 2912355 *Fax:* (011) 2918614
Cable: EDITORA
Key Personnel
Man Dir, Rights & Permissions: Jorge Antonio Miguel Yunes
Editorial: Paulo Marti
Founded: 1925
Subjects: Business, Education, Fiction, History, Philosophy, Psychology, Psychiatry, Science (General), Social Sciences, Sociology, Technology

ISBN Prefix(es): 85-04
Branch Office(s)
Aracatuba
Bauru
Belem
Belo Horizonte
Edificio Venancio VI - DS bloco 0 - lojas 13 e 17, Brasilia
Campo Grande
Caruaru
Cuiaba
Curitiba
Fortaleza
Goiania
Manaus
Natal
Porto Alegre
Presidente Prudente
Recife
Ribeirao Preto
Rio de Janeiro, Ave Lobo Junior 1011, Bairro Penha, Rio de Janeiro
Sa Luis
Salvador
Sao Jose do Rio Preto
Teresina
Vila Velho

Companhia Editora Nacional
Rua Joli, 294, 03016-020 Sao Paulo-SP
Tel: (011) 6099-7799 (ext 246) *Fax:* (011) 6694-5338
Web Site: www.ibep-nacional.com.br
Key Personnel
Editor: Mr Mauro Aristides *E-mail:* mauro@ibep-nacional.com.br
Founded: 1925
ISBN Prefix(es): 85-342
Number of titles published annually: 50 Print
Total Titles: 500 Print
Parent Company: Instituto Brasileiro de Edicoes Pedagogicas (IBEP)

Nexo, *imprint of* Editora Mundo Cristao

Editora Nova Aguilar SA+
Rua Dona Mariana, 205-Casa 01, Botafogo, 22280-020 Rio de Janeiro-RJ
Tel: (021) 537-7189; (021) 537-8275
Telex: 34695 Enfs *Cable:* AGUILAR
Key Personnel
President: Sebastiao Lacerda
Man Dir: Carlos Augusto Lacerda
Founded: 1958
ISBN Prefix(es): 85-210
Parent Company: Editora Nova Fronteira SA
Branch Office(s)
Ave Pedro Bueno 1509-1511, Jabaquara, 04342 Sao Paulo SP

Editora Nova Alexandria Ltda+
Rua Dionisio da Costa, 141, 04117-110 Sao Paulo-SP
Tel: (011) 5571-5637 *Fax:* (011) 5571-5637
E-mail: novaalexandria@novaalexandria.com.br
Web Site: www.novaalexandria.com.br
Key Personnel
Associate: Luiz Baggio-Neto *E-mail:* lbaggio@novaalexandria.com.br
Founded: 1992
Subjects: Biography, Cookery, Education, Fiction, History, Literature, Literary Criticism, Essays, Philosophy, Poetry, Romance, Sports, Athletics
ISBN Prefix(es): 85-7492
Number of titles published annually: 18 Print
Total Titles: 136 Print

Editora Nova Era, *imprint of* Distribuidora Record de Servicos de Imprensa SA

Editora Nova Fronteira SA+
Rua Bambina, 25, 22251-050 Rio de Janeiro-RJ
Tel: (021) 25 37 87 70; (021) 22 66 51 84
Fax: (021) 22 86 67 55
Web Site: www.novafronteira.com.br
Key Personnel
General Dir & International Rights: Carlos Augusto Lacerda *E-mail:* caml@novafronteira.com.br
Foreign Rights Dir: Carlos Barbosa
Sales: Elson M da Rocha
Founded: 1965
Subjects: Art, Astrology, Occult, Astronomy, Biography, Biological Sciences, Business, Education, Fiction, Health, Nutrition, History, Language Arts, Linguistics, Literature, Literary Criticism, Essays, Mysteries, Natural History, Nonfiction (General), Philosophy, Poetry, Psychology, Psychiatry, Publishing & Book Trade Reference, Regional Interests, Romance, Science (General), Self-Help, Social Sciences, Sociology, Theology
ISBN Prefix(es): 85-209
Number of titles published annually: 90 Print
Total Titles: 1,200 Print
Associate Companies: Lexikon Informatica Ltd

Editora Objetiva Ltda+
Rua Cosme Velho, 103, 22241-090 Rio de Janeiro-RJ
Tel: (021) 2556-7824 *Fax:* (021) 2556-3322
Web Site: www.objetiva.com.br
Key Personnel
Publisher: Roberto Feith
Foreign Rights Acquisitions Manager: Alessandra Blocker *E-mail:* aless.blocker@ibm.net
Subjects: Behavioral Sciences, Biography, Fiction, Human Relations, Humor, Nonfiction (General), Science (General), Self-Help
Number of titles published annually: 60 Print

Off Set, *imprint of* Centro de Estudos Juridicosdo Para (CEJUP)

Olho D'Agua Comercio e Servicos Editoriais Ltda+
Rua Dr Homem de Melo, 1036, 05007-002 Sao Paulo-SP
Tel: (011) 2631287 *Fax:* (011) 2631287
E-mail: editora@olhodaguo.com.br
Key Personnel
Executive: Jorge Claudio Noel Ribeiro, Jr
Founded: 1991
Subjects: Behavioral Sciences, Education, Journalism, Literature, Literary Criticism, Essays, Psychology, Psychiatry, Social Sciences, Sociology, Theology
ISBN Prefix(es): 85-85428
Distributed by Distribuidora Loyola

Oliveira Rocha-Comercio e Servics Ltda+
Av Bernardino de Campos, 327, cj 24, 04004-050 Sao Paulo-SP
Tel: (011) 2845527; (011) 2886440 *Fax:* (011) 2845362; (011) 2842096
E-mail: dialetic@virtual.net.com.br
Key Personnel
Contact: Valdir Oliveira Rocha
Founded: 1995
Subjects: Law
ISBN Prefix(es): 85-86208

Organizacao Andrei Editora Ltda+
Rua Conselheiro Nebias, 1071, 01203-002 Sao Paulo-SP
Tel: (011) 223-5111 *Fax:* (011) 221-0246
E-mail: diretoria@editora-andrei.com.br
Web Site: www.editora-andrei.com.br
Key Personnel
Executive: Edmundo Andrei
Founded: 1955
Subjects: Medicine, Nursing, Dentistry, Veterinary Science, Acupuncture, Homeopathy

Number of titles published annually: 30 Print
Total Titles: 650 Print; 3 CD-ROM

Editora Ortiz SA
Av Julio de Castilhos, 159 - SI 801, 90030-131 Porto Alegre-RS
Tel: (051) 225-3026 *Fax:* (051) 225-3026
Key Personnel
President: Airton Ortiz
Founded: 1982
Subjects: Accounting, Agriculture, Business, Economics, Finance, Management, Marketing, Public Administration
ISBN Prefix(es): 85-85279

Edit Palavra Magica+
Rua Americo Brasiliense, 1205/1, Centro, Ribeirao Preto SP 14015-050
Tel: (016) 610-0204 *Fax:* (016) 625-4583
E-mail: editora@palavramagica.com.br
Web Site: www.palavramagica.com.br
Key Personnel
Dir: Galeno Amorim *E-mail:* galeno@palavramagica.com.br
Assistant Dir: Mariana Carla Magri *E-mail:* mariana@palavramagica.com.br
Man Dir, Financial: Luiz Antonio Ferraro *E-mail:* ferraro@palavramagica.com.br
Secretary: Maria Ivone Rodrigues dos Santos *E-mail:* ivone@palavramagica.com.br
Founded: 1995
Subjects: Behavioral Sciences, Earth Sciences, Human Relations, Regional Interests, Religion - Catholic, Religion - Other, Romance, Social Sciences, Sociology
ISBN Prefix(es): 85-85997

Pallas Editora e Distribuidora Ltda+
Rua Frederico de Albuquerque, 56, 44 Higienopolis, 21050-840 Rio de Janeiro-RJ
Tel: (021) 270-0186 *Fax:* (021) 590-6996; (21) 5618007
E-mail: pallas@alternex.com.br
Web Site: www.pallaseditora.com.br
Key Personnel
Man Dir: Antonio Carlos Fernandes
Editorial, Rights & Permissions: Cristina Fernandes Warth
Sales: Antonio Carlos Fernandes
Founded: 1975
SNEL - Sindicets Notional des Editores de Livros.
Subjects: African American Studies, Anthropology, Art, Biography, Ethnicity, Human Relations, Music, Dance, Philosophy, Religion - Catholic, Religion - Other, Self-Help, Social Sciences, Sociology, Theology, Afro-Brasilian religions, culture, history, social sciences
ISBN Prefix(es): 85-347
Number of titles published annually: 30 Print
Total Titles: 200 Print

Parma, *imprint of* Global Editora e Distribuidora Ltda

Paulinas Editorial+
Rua Pedro de Toledo, 164, 04039-000 Sao Paulo SP
Tel: (011) 50855199 *Fax:* (011) 50855198
E-mail: editora@paulinas.org.br
Subjects: Biblical Studies, Biography, Child Care & Development, Communications, Education, Human Relations, Psychology, Psychiatry, Religion - Catholic, Self-Help, Social Sciences, Sociology, Theology
ISBN Prefix(es): 85-356; 85-7311

Paulus Editora+
Rua Francisco Cruz, 229, 04117-091 Sao Paulo SP
Tel: (011) 50843066; (011) 5757362 *Fax:* (011) 5703627
E-mail: dir.editorial@paulus.org.br
Web Site: www.paulus.com.br
Telex: 1139464 Pssp *Cable:* PAULINOS
Key Personnel
Man Dir, Publicity & Production: Arno Brustolin
Editorial & Rights & Permissions: Zolferino Tonon
Sales: A C D'Elboux
Founded: 1931
Bookshops throughout Brazil.
Subjects: Biblical Studies, Education, How-to, Music, Dance, Philosophy, Psychology, Psychiatry, Religion - Catholic, Religion - Other, Self-Help, Social Sciences, Sociology, Theology
ISBN Prefix(es): 85-05; 85-349
Bookshop(s): Praca da Se 180, Sao Paulo; Rua Mexico 111-B, Rio de Janeiro

Editora Paz e Terra+
Rua do Triunfo, 177, Sta Ifigenia, 01212-010 Sao Paulo-SP
Tel: (011) 3337-8399 *Fax:* (011) 223-6290
E-mail: vendas@pazeterra.com.br
Web Site: www.pazeterra.com.br
Key Personnel
General Manager, Sales & Editorial: Fernando Gasparian
Production, Publicity & Rights & Permissions: Marcus F Gasparian
Founded: 1966
Subjects: Drama, Theater, Government, Political Science, Literature, Literary Criticism, Essays, Philosophy, Regional Interests, Social Sciences, Sociology
ISBN Prefix(es): 85-219
Subsidiaries:
Bookshop(s): Livraria Argumento, Rua Oscar Freire 608, San Paulo-SP; Rua Dias Ferreira 199, Rio de Janeiro-RJ; Livraria e Editora Livre, Rua Armando Penteado 44, Sao Paulo-SP

Pearson Education Do Brasil
Rua Emilio Goeldi, 747 Lapa, Sao Paulo 05065-110
Tel: (011) 3611 0740 *Fax:* (011) 3611 0444
E-mail: firstname.lastname@pearsoned.com.br
Telex: 2121799
Key Personnel
Interim General Manager/Commercial Dir: Jaime Carneiro
Finance Dir: Solange Beletatti
Promotion Manager ELT: Marco Malossi
Marketing Manager ELT: Helena Nagano
Administrative Assistant: Claudia Fisher
Representative, Higher Education: Luiz Henrique
Founded: 1996
Subjects: Accounting, Behavioral Sciences, Biological Sciences, Business, Economics, Engineering (General), Marketing, Technology
ISBN Prefix(es): 85-7054; 85-87675
Number of titles published annually: 20 Print
Parent Company: Pearson Plc
Imprints: Addison Wesley; Longman; Scott Foresman; Prentice Hall
Branch Office(s)
Belo Horizonte, Rua Silva Jardim 235, Sao Paulo 30150-010
Foreign Rights: Roger Trimer

Jogos Pedagogicos, *imprint of* Editora Meca Ltda

Peninsula, *imprint of* LDA Editores Ltda

Editora Perspectiva
Ave Brigadeiro Luis Antonio, 3025/3035, 01401-000 Sao Paulo-SP
Tel: (011) 8858388 *Fax:* (011) 3885-8388
E-mail: editora@editoraperspectiva.com.br
Web Site: www.editoraperspectiva.com.br
Key Personnel
Man Dir: Jaco Guinsburg
Founded: 1965
Subjects: Drama, Theater, Economics, Education, History, Human Relations, Music, Dance, Philosophy, Psychology, Psychiatry, Religion - Other, Social Sciences, Sociology
ISBN Prefix(es): 85-273

Petit Editora e Distribuidora Ltda+
Rua Atuai, 383 5 V Esperanca, 03646-000 Sao Paulo-SP
Tel: (011) 698 4162; (011) 691 7165 *Fax:* (011) 292 4616
E-mail: petit@dialdata.com.br
Web Site: www.petit.com.br
Key Personnel
Contact: Flavio Machado
Founded: 1982
Subjects: Religion - Other
ISBN Prefix(es): 85-7253

Pia Sociedade Filhas De Sao Paulo, see Paulinas Editorial

Editora Pini Ltda
Rua Anhaia, 964, 01130-900 Sao Paulo-SP
Tel: (011) 224-8811 *Fax:* (011) 224-0314; (011) 224-8541
E-mail: construcao@pini.com.br
Web Site: www.piniweb.com
Telex: 11-37803
Key Personnel
Contact: Ricardo Bertagnon
Founded: 1948
ISBN Prefix(es): 85-7266
Bookshop(s): R Vitoria, 486/496, 01210 Sao Paulo-SP; Rua Gentil de Moura, 128, 04278 Sao Paulo-SP

Livraria Pioneira Editora/Enio Matheus Guazzelli e Cia Ltd+
Praca Dirceu de Lima 313, 02515-050 Sao Paulo-SP
Tel: (011) 858-3199 *Fax:* (011) 858-0443
E-mail: pioneira@virtual-net.com.br
Key Personnel
Editor & Rights & Permissions: Liliana Guazzelli
Dir, Finance: Roberto Guazzelli
Founded: 1960
Subjects: Accounting, Advertising, Agriculture, Architecture & Interior Design, Astrology, Occult, Behavioral Sciences, Business, Computer Science, Economics, Education, History, Language Arts, Linguistics, Management, Mysteries, Photography, Psychology, Psychiatry, Social Sciences, Sociology
ISBN Prefix(es): 85-221
Associate Companies: Disal, Distribuidores Associados de Livros Ltda

Prentice Hall, *imprint of* Pearson Education Do Brasil

Casa Editora Presbiteriana SC+
Rua Miguel Telles Junior, 382/394, Cambuci, 01540-040 Sao Paulo-SP
Tel: (011) 270-7099 *Fax:* (011) 279-1255
E-mail: cep@cep.org.br
Web Site: www.cep.org.br
Key Personnel
Editor: Claudio A B Marra
Founded: 1948
Subjects: History, Religion - Other
ISBN Prefix(es): 85-86886

Primor Editora Ltda, see Grafica Editora Primor Ltda

PUBLISHERS   BRAZIL

Editora Primor Ltda+
Rodovia Presidente Dutra 2611, 21535-500 Rio de Janeiro-RJ
Tel: (021) 4744966
Telex: 22150 *Cable:* Primor
Subjects: Fiction, Humor, Nonfiction (General)
ISBN Prefix(es): 85-7024
Subsidiaries: Grafica Editora Primor SA

Prol, *imprint of* Global Editora e Distribuidora Ltda

Proton Editora Ltda
Ave Reboucas 3819, 05401-450 Sao Paulo-SP
Tel: (011) 2103616; (011) 8147922; (011) 8159708 *Fax:* (011) 8159920
Key Personnel
President: Norberto R Keppe
Man Dir: Claudia S Pacheco
Founded: 1976
Subjects: Medicine, Nursing, Dentistry, Psychology, Psychiatry, Science (General)
ISBN Prefix(es): 85-7072; 85-85001

Ediouro Publicacoes, SA+
Rua Nova Jerusalem, 345, 21042-230 Rio de Janeiro-RJ
Tel: (021) 5606122 *Fax:* (011) 55893300
E-mail: ediourolivrosp@openlink.com.br; livros@ediouro.com.br
Web Site: www.ediouro.com.br
Key Personnel
President: Jorge Carneiro
Editor: Paul Christoph, Jr
Subjects: Animals, Pets, Biography, How-to, Journalism, Literature, Literary Criticism, Essays, Mysteries, Science Fiction, Fantasy
ISBN Prefix(es): 85-00

Editora de Publicacoes Medicas Ltda
Rua do Russel, 404-grs 901/2-parte, 22210 Rio de Janeiro-RJ
Tel: (021) 2654047; (021) 2253516 *Fax:* (021) 2613749
Key Personnel
Man Dir: Jose Maria de Sousa e Melo
Editorial: Dr Almir Lourenco da Fonseca
Sales & Publicity: Jose Ayrton de Souza Avila
Production: Edson de Oliveira Vilar
Founded: 1959
Subjects: Medicine, Nursing, Dentistry
Branch Office(s)
Rua Borges Lagoa 426, Sao Paulo
Book Club(s): Club do Livro Cientifico

Qualitymark Editora Ltda+
R Teixeira Junior, 441, Sao Cristovao, 20921-400 Rio de Janeiro-RJ
Tel: (021) 3860-8422 *Fax:* (021) 3860-8424
E-mail: quality@qualitymark.com.br
Web Site: www.qualitymark.com.br
Key Personnel
Contact: Saidual Rahman Mahomed
Founded: 1991
Promote events dealing with seminars & lectures.
Subjects: Career Development, Economics, Education, Environmental Studies, Finance, Labor, Industrial Relations, Management, Medicine, Nursing, Dentistry, Nonfiction (General), Public Administration, Self-Help
ISBN Prefix(es): 85-7303; 85-85360

Raboni Editora Ltda+
Rua Sampaio Vidal, 629, Jardim Chapadao, 13090-070 Campinas-SP
Mailing Address: CP 140, 13001-970 Campinas-SP
Tel: (019) 32428433 *Fax:* (019) 32428505
E-mail: raboni@raboni.com.br
Web Site: www.raboni.com.br
Key Personnel
Dir: Stella Castro *E-mail:* stella@raboni.com.br
Contact: Regis Castro
Founded: 1991
Publish & distribute Catholic books worldwide.
Subjects: Religion - Catholic
ISBN Prefix(es): 85-7345

Editora Record, *imprint of* Distribuidora Record de Servicos de Imprensa SA

Distribuidora Record de Servicos de Imprensa SA+
Rua Argentina 171, Sao Cristovao, 20921-380 Rio de Janeiro-RJ
Tel: (021) 2585-2000 *Fax:* (021) 2580-4911
E-mail: record@record.com.br
Web Site: www.record.com.br
Key Personnel
Chairman, President & General Manager: Sergio C Machado
Vice President, Operations: Sonia M Sardim, Jr
Editorial Dir: Luciana Villas Boas
Founded: 1942
Subjects: Biography, Business, Fiction, History, Nonfiction (General), Philosophy
ISBN Prefix(es): 85-01; 85-20
Number of titles published annually: 320 Print
Total Titles: 2,003 Print
Imprints: Editora Nova Era; Editora Record; Editora Rosa dos Tempos
Subsidiaries: Editora Bertrand Brazil Ltd; Editora Jose Olympio Ltd
Divisions: Bertrand Brasil, Difel, Civilizacao Brasileira
Branch Office(s)
Paraiso 139, 7 audar, 04103-000 Sao Paulo-SP, Contact: Francinete Zerbetto *Tel:* (011) 3286-0802 *Toll Free Tel:* (011) 0800-212380

Rede Das Artes (Boccato Editores Collector's)+
Rua Graham Bell 355, 04737-030 Sao Paulo-SP
Tel: (011) 246-5556 *Fax:* (011) 246-5556
Key Personnel
Executive: Andre Boccato
Founded: 1993
Subjects: Art, Cookery, Gardening, Plants, Health, Nutrition, Photography, Sports, Athletics, Travel, Wine & Spirits
ISBN Prefix(es): 85-85657

Editora Resenha Tributaria Ltda
Rua Quatinga, 12, 04140-020 Sao Paulo-SP
Tel: (011) 5772822 *Fax:* (011) 5772526
Key Personnel
Man Dir: Vaner Bicego
Editorial Dir: Valdyr Rezende Xavier
Commercial Dir: Jose Figueira da Cruz
Subjects: Education, Law
ISBN Prefix(es): 85-236

Editora Revan Ltda+
Av Paulo de Frontin, 163, Rio Comprido, 20260-010 Rio de Janeiro-RJ
Tel: (021) 25027495 *Fax:* (021) 22736873
E-mail: editor@revan.com.br
Web Site: www.revan.com.br
Key Personnel
Contact: Dr Ing Renato Guimaraes-Cupertino
Founded: 1983
Subjects: Anthropology, Art, Behavioral Sciences, Biography, Computer Science, Criminology, Fiction, Military Science, Science (General), Self-Help, Social Sciences, Sociology
ISBN Prefix(es): 85-7106
Number of titles published annually: 40 Print
Total Titles: 300 Print

Livraria Editora Revinter Ltda+
Rua do Matoso 170, Tijuca, 20270-131 Rio de Janeiro-RJ
Tel: (021) 2563-9700 *Fax:* (021) 2563-9701
E-mail: livraria@revinter.com.br
Web Site: www.revinter.com.br
Key Personnel
Contact: Sergio Duarte Dortas
Subjects: Medicine, Nursing, Dentistry
ISBN Prefix(es): 85-7309
Distributor for Churchill Livingstone; Lippincott; Mosby; W B Saunders; Georg Thieme

RHJ Livros Ltda+
Rua Cuiaba, 415, Prado, 30410-140 Belo Horizonte-MG
Tel: (031) 3334-1566 *Fax:* (031) 3332-5823
Web Site: www.editorarhj.com.br
Key Personnel
Dir: Rafael Borges de Andrade
Founded: 1974
Membership(s): SNEL-457.
Subjects: Literature, Literary Criticism, Essays
ISBN Prefix(es): 85-7153

Editora Rideel Ltda+
Alameda Afonso Schmidt No 879, Santa Terezinha, 02450-001 Sao Paulo-SP
Tel: (011) 6977-8344 *Fax:* (011) 6976-7415
E-mail: rideel@virtual-net.com.br
Web Site: www.rideel.com.br
Key Personnel
Man Dir, Editorial: Italo Amadio
Production: Roberto Amadio
Founded: 1970
Subjects: Cookery, History, Language Arts, Linguistics, Medicine, Nursing, Dentistry, Religion - Other
ISBN Prefix(es): 85-339
Bookshop(s): Al Afonso Schmidt, No 877, Sta Terezinha, 02450-001 Sao Paulo-SP

Livraria Roca Ltda+
Rua Dr Cesario Mota Jr 73, 01221-020 Sao Paulo-SP
Tel: (011) 221-8609; (011) 221-6814 *Fax:* (011) 3331-8653
E-mail: edroca@uol.com.br
Web Site: www.editoraroca.com.br
Key Personnel
Contact: Casimiro Paya Piqueres
Founded: 1973
Subjects: Medicine, Nursing, Dentistry, Veterinary Science
ISBN Prefix(es): 85-7241
Associate Companies: Livraria Paya Ltda

Editora Rocco Ltda+
Rua Rodrigo Silva 26-4 andar, 20011-040 Rio de Janeiro-RJ
Tel: (021) 2507-2000 *Fax:* (021) 2507-2244
E-mail: rocco@rocco.com.br
Web Site: www.rocco.com.br
Key Personnel
Contact: Paulo Roberto Rocco
Founded: 1975
Subjects: Anthropology, Biography, Communications, Management, Science (General), Self-Help, Social Sciences, Sociology, Women's Studies
ISBN Prefix(es): 85-325
Warehouse: Av Brasil, 10-600, 21012-351 Rio de Janeiro-RJ

Editora Rosa dos Tempos, *imprint of* Distribuidora Record de Servicos de Imprensa SA

Salamandra Consultoria Editorial SA+
Av Nilo Pecanha 155, Grupo 301, 20027-900 Rio de Janeiro-RJ
Tel: (021) 2406306 *Fax:* (021) 2404775; (021) 5331622
E-mail: salprod@openlink.com.br

Key Personnel
Contact: Sir Geraldo Jordao Pereira
Founded: 1982
Subjects: Art
ISBN Prefix(es): 85-281

Livraria Santos Editora Comercio e Importacao Ltda+
Rua Dona Brigida, 691/701, 04111-081 Sao Paulo-SP
Tel: (011) 574-1200 *Fax:* (011) 573-8774
E-mail: editorasantos@terra.com.br
Key Personnel
Contact: Rui Santos
Founded: 1974
Subjects: Medicine, Nursing, Dentistry, Veterinary Science
ISBN Prefix(es): 85-7288
Number of titles published annually: 60 Print
Total Titles: 510 Print

Editora Santuario+
Rua Padre Claro Monteiro 342, 12570-000 Sao Paulo-SP
Tel: (012) 3104-2000 *Fax:* (012) 565 2141
E-mail: vendas@redemptor.com.br
Web Site: www.redemptor.com.br
Key Personnel
Administrative Manager: Padre Luis Rodrigues Batista
Founded: 1900
Specialize in graphics.
Subjects: Literature, Literary Criticism, Essays, Religion - Catholic
ISBN Prefix(es): 85-7200; 85-7265
Parent Company: Congregacao do Santissimo Redentor
Bookshop(s): Praca Nossa Senhora Aparecida 292, Aparecida-SP

Sao Paulo Editora, *imprint of* Global Editora e Distribuidora Ltda

Saraiva SA, Livreiros Editores+
Ave Marques de Sao Vicente 1697, 01139-904 Sao Paulo-SP
Tel: (011) 861-3344 *Fax:* (011) 861-3308
E-mail: diretoria.editora@editorasaraiva.com.br
Web Site: www.editorasaraiva.com.br
Telex: 1126789 *Cable:* ACADEMICA
Key Personnel
President: Jorge Eduardo Saraiva
Man Dir: Ruy Mendes Gono1alves; Jose Luiz M A Prosper; Wander Soares
Editorial Dir, Education: Antonio Alexandre Faccioli
Editorial Dir, Law: Juarez de Oliveira
Sales Dir: Nilson Lepera
Founded: 1914
17 Branches in Sao Paulo.
Subjects: Accounting, Business, Economics, Education, Finance, Law, Management, Marketing, Mathematics, Philosophy, Psychology, Psychiatry, Securities
ISBN Prefix(es): 85-02
Subsidiaries: Saraiva Data-Informatica
Branch Office(s)
Ave Marechal Rondon 2231, Rio de Janeiro-RJ
Rua Celia de Souza 571, Belo Horizonte
Ave Princesa Isabel 1555, Curitiba
Ave Chicago 307, Porto Alegre

Sarvier - Editora de Livros Medicos Ltda
Rua Dr Amancio de Carvalho 459, 04012-090 Sao Paulo-SP
Tel: (011) 571-4570 *Fax:* (011) 571-3439
Key Personnel
Man Dir: Fernando Silva Xavier
Founded: 1965
Subjects: Medicine, Nursing, Dentistry
ISBN Prefix(es): 85-7378

Karin Schindler Representante de Direitos Autorais
CP 19051, 04505-970 Sao Paulo SP
Tel: (011) 241-9177 *Fax:* (011) 241-9077
Key Personnel
Executive: Karin Schindler *E-mail:* kschind@terra.com.br

Editora Scipione Ltda+
Praca Carlos Gomes, 46, 01501-040 Sao Paulo-SP
Tel: (011) 2392255 *Fax:* (011) 31053526
E-mail: info@scipione.com.br
Web Site: www.scipione.com.br
Key Personnel
General Dir: Luis Esteves Sallum
General Marketing: Maria Jose Rosolino
General Editorial: Aurelio Goncalves Filho
Founded: 1983
Specialize in books pre-school to second grade & also in technical & professional books.
Membership(s): Brazilian Book Association; National Book Foundation for Children & Juveniles.
Subjects: Astronomy, Biological Sciences, Chemistry, Chemical Engineering, Education, Environmental Studies, Fiction, Geography, Geology, History, Literature, Literary Criticism, Essays, Mathematics, Mysteries, Nonfiction (General), Physics, Religion - Other, Romance, Science (General)
ISBN Prefix(es): 85-262
Branch Office(s)
S P R Teodoro da Silva, 1004 Rio de Janeiro-RJ
Av Visconde de Suassuna, 634 Recife-PE
Rua da Independecia, 21/13, Salvador-BA
Rua Gago Coutinho, 238, Lapa, Sao Paulo-SP
Distributor for Allca XX/Scipione Culture - Collection Archivos (South America)
Showroom(s): Rua Fagundes, 01508-030 Sao Paulo-SP
Warehouse: Via BR 116, 84 - km 291, 6 - Itapecerica da Serra, Sao Paulo-SP

Seculo XXI Editora e Comercio de Livros
Rua Marcos Moreira, 119, Sala 201, 91350-040 Porto Alegre-RS
Tel: (051) 3614459 *Fax:* (051) 3614459
E-mail: sewloxxi@poa-online.com.br
Key Personnel
Contact: Carlos Mauricio Igreja do Prado
Founded: 1993
ISBN Prefix(es): 85-86371

Selecoes Eletronicas Editora Ltda+
Ladeira Do Faria 23, 20221-380 Rio de Janeiro-RJ
Tel: (021) 2539268 *Fax:* (021) 2638840
Key Personnel
Man Dir: Maria B A Penna
Editorial: Gilberto A Penna, Jr
Publicity: Helio N Santos
Founded: 1960
Subjects: Computer Science, Electronics, Electrical Engineering, Microcomputers, Technology
ISBN Prefix(es): 85-7037
Associate Companies: Antenna Edicoes Tecnicas Ltda

Selinunte Editora Ltda+
Ave Miguel Stefano 183 Cj 01, 04301-010 Sao Paulo-SP
Tel: (011) 2760318
Key Personnel
Editorial Dir: Roberto Wilson
Administrative Dir, Financial: Arnaldo Majer
Founded: 1987
Membership(s): The Brazilian House of Books.
Subjects: Literature, Literary Criticism, Essays
ISBN Prefix(es): 85-85538

SELTRON, see Selecoes Eletronicas Editora Ltda

Siciliano SA+
Ave Raimundo Pereira de Magalhaes 3305, 05145-200 Sao Paulo-SP
Tel: (011) 8395500; (011) 8319911 *Fax:* (011) 8328616
Telex: 1180677
Key Personnel
Contact: Oswaldo Siciliano
Founded: 1952
Subjects: Literature, Literary Criticism, Essays
ISBN Prefix(es): 85-267
Divisions: Editorial, Livraria, Distribuidora de revistas

Editora Sinodal+
Rua Amadeo Rossi 467, 93001-970 Sao Leopoldo-RS
Mailing Address: CP 11, 93001-970 Sao Leopoldo-RS
Tel: (051) 590-2366 *Fax:* (051) 590-2664
E-mail: editora@editorasinodal.com.br
Web Site: www.editorasinodal.com.br
Telex: 511219 Xpsl *Cable:* SINODAL
Key Personnel
General Dir: Eloy Teckemeier *E-mail:* diretor@editorasinodal.com.br
Publishing Manager: Joao Artur M da Silva *E-mail:* editor@editorasinodal.com.br
Manager, Production: Silvio J dos Santos *E-mail:* grafica@editorasinodal.com.br
Manager, Vendas: Asciepiades Pomme *E-mail:* gerentedevendas@editorasinodal.com.br
Founded: 1949
Subjects: Education, Music, Dance, Religion - Other, Social Sciences, Sociology, Theology
ISBN Prefix(es): 85-233
Parent Company: Instituicao Sinodal de Assistencia, Educacao e Cultura (ISAEC)
Associate Companies: Colegio Sinodal
Subsidiaries: Escola Superior de Teologia
Showroom(s): Rua Buenos Aires, 123 Sao Paulo-SP
Bookshop(s): Editora Sinodal-Livraria; Livraria Volante

Sobrindes Linha Grafica E Editora Ltda+
Sig Sul Quadra 2 Lote 460, 70610-400 Brasilia-DF
Tel: (061) 2247778; (061) 2247706; (061) 2247756 *Fax:* (061) 2241895
E-mail: linhagrafica@conectanet.com.br
Subjects: Fiction, History, Journalism, Religion - Other
ISBN Prefix(es): 85-7238

Sociedade Distribuidora de Livros Ltda (Sodilivro)+
Rua Sa Freire 36/40, Parte, Sao Cristovao, 20930-430 Rio de Janeiro RJ
Tel: (021) 580-1168; (021) 580-6230 *Fax:* (021) 580-5868
Key Personnel
Executive: Reynaldo Max Paul Bluhm
ISBN Prefix(es): 85-215
Parent Company: Ao Livro Tecnico Ind e Com Ltda

Spala Editora Ltda
Rua Lauro Muller, 116-31 Andar S1 3101, 22290-160 Rio de Janeiro-RJ
Tel: (021) 542-9995 *Fax:* (021) 542-4738
Telex: (021) 2664093
Key Personnel
Contact: Luis Fernando Freire
Founded: 1974
Subjects: Architecture & Interior Design, Art, Biography
ISBN Prefix(es): 85-7048
Subsidiaries: Spala Publicidade; Spala Comunicacoes

Studio Nobel, *imprint of* Livraria Nobel S/A

Livraria Sulina Editora+
Av Borges de Medeieros 1030-1036, 90000 Porto Alegre RS
Mailing Address: CP 357, 90000 Porto Alegre
Tel: (051) 254765; (051) 250287
E-mail: sulina@sulina.com.br *Cable:* ZIPASUL
Key Personnel
President: Vilson Nailon Noen
Editor: Luis Gomes
Founded: 1946
Subjects: Law, Psychology, Psychiatry, Science (General)
ISBN Prefix(es): 85-205
Parent Company: Organizacao Sulina de Representacoes SA, Rua Cel Gennino 290, 90010-350 Porto Alegre, RS
Subsidiaries: Editora Sulina
Showroom(s): Rua Deuetrio Ribeiro, 990 202 Porta Alegre
Bookshop(s): Livraria Sulina, Rua Riachuelo, 1218 Porta Alegre

Summus Editorial Ltda+
Rua Itapicuru 613 7° andar, 05006-000 Perdizes-SP
Tel: (011) 38723322 *Fax:* (011) 38727476
E-mail: summus@summus.com.br
Web Site: www.summus.com.br
Key Personnel
Dir: Raul Wassermann
Founded: 1974
Subjects: Advertising, Behavioral Sciences, Business, Communications, Education, Film, Video, Human Relations, Journalism, Marketing, Music, Dance, Psychology, Psychiatry, Radio, TV, Self-Help, Sports, Athletics, Women's Studies
ISBN Prefix(es): 85-323

Edicoes Tabajara
Rua dos Andradas 1774, 90000 Porto Alegre-RS
Tel: (0512) 241073; (0512) 247724
Key Personnel
Assistant Manager: Maria Azambuja
Subjects: Drama, Theater, Education, Language Arts, Linguistics, Mathematics, Science (General), Social Sciences, Sociology
Branch Office(s)
Rua Santa Ifigenia 72, Sao Paulo

Talento Publicacoes Editora e Grafica Ltda
Rua Desembargador Joaquim Celidonio 33, 01413-060 Sao Paulo-SP
Tel: (011) 3816-1718 *Fax:* (011) 2823752
E-mail: talento@talento.com.br
Web Site: www.talento.com.br
Key Personnel
Contact: Robert Henry Lennard Seadon
Subjects: Advertising, Communications
ISBN Prefix(es): 85-85062

Livros Tecnicos e Cientificos Editora Ltda, see LTC-Livros Tecnicos e Cientificos Editora S/A

Temos Grafica Propria, *imprint of* Editora Betania S/C

Tempus Editores
Rua Viana do Castelo, 8 Cave Esq, Bairro Sao Joao, 2775 Carcavelos, Portugal
Mailing Address: Apartado 2422, 1111 Lisbon Codex
Tel: (021) 4535000 *Fax:* (021) 4426482
Key Personnel
Contact: Paula Santos
Founded: 1994
Subjects: Law, Literature, Literary Criticism, Essays, Romance
ISBN Prefix(es): 972-8198

Thex Editora e Distribuidora Ltda+
Rua da Lapa 180, Conj 804/806, 20021-180 Rio de Janeiro-RJ
Tel: (021) 2221-4458 *Fax:* (021) 2252-9338
Fax on Demand: (021) 252-9338
E-mail: atendimento@thexeditora.com.br
Web Site: www.thexeditora.com.br
Key Personnel
International Rights: Thex Correa da Silva
  E-mail: thex@domain.com.br
Founded: 1992
Subjects: Earth Sciences, Economics, Education, Fiction, Human Relations, Literature, Literary Criticism, Essays, Marketing, Mysteries, Poetry, Self-Help, Social Sciences, Sociology
ISBN Prefix(es): 85-85575
Number of titles published annually: 10 Print
Total Titles: 50 Print

34 Literatura S/C Ltda+
Rua Hungria, 592, 01455-000 Sao Paulo-SP
Tel: (011) 3816-6777 *Fax:* (011) 3816-0078
Web Site: www.rattapallax.com/editora34.htm
Key Personnel
Contact: Beatriz Bracher
Founded: 1992
Subjects: Anthropology, Drama, Theater, Fiction, Literature, Literary Criticism, Essays, Music, Dance, Philosophy, Poetry, Romance, Science Fiction, Fantasy, Technology
ISBN Prefix(es): 85-85490; 85-7326
Branch Office(s)
Rua Massaca, 276 Alto de Pinheiros, 05465-050 Sao Paulo-SP *Tel:* (011) 2609738 *Fax:* (011) 8321041

Totalidade Editora Ltda+
Rua Eng Alcides Barbosa 29, Jardim America, 01430-010 Sao Paulo-SP
Tel: (011) 3064 3688 *Fax:* (011) 3081 9503
E-mail: totail@terra.com.br
Web Site: www.totalidade.com.br
Key Personnel
Contact: Elisa Guerra Malta Campos
Founded: 1989
Membership(s): Brazilian House of Books, National Syndication of Book Publishers, Astrological-Psychological Institute, English Huber School of Astrology, Seven Ray Institute & University of the Seven Rays & Meditation Mount.
Subjects: Art, Astrology, Occult, Psychology, Psychiatry, Self-Help
ISBN Prefix(es): 85-85293

Triom Centro de Estudos Marina e Martin Hawey Editorial e Comercial Ltda+
Rua Aracari, 218, 01453-020 Sao Paulo-SP
Tel: (011) 3168-8380 *Fax:* (011) 3845-0966
E-mail: info@triom.com.br
Web Site: www.triom.com.br
Key Personnel
Contact: Ruth Cunha-Cintra
Founded: 1991
Bookstore, publishing house.
Subjects: Alternative, Astrology, Occult, Music, Dance, Women's Studies
ISBN Prefix(es): 85-85464
Number of titles published annually: 5 Print
Total Titles: 40 Print; 2 Audio

Editora UNESP+
Praca Da Se, 108, 01001-900 Sao Paulo-SP
Tel: (011) 3242-7171 *Fax:* (011) 3242-7172
E-mail: feu@editora.unesp.br
Web Site: www.editora.unesp.br
Key Personnel
Dir: Jose Castilho Marques *E-mail:* castilho@editora.unesp.br
Executive Editor: Jezio H B Gutierre
  E-mail: jezio@editora.unesp.br
Founded: 1987
Membership(s): Camara Brasileira do Livro; Associacao Brasileira das Editoras Universitarias; Associacao Brasileira de Direitos Reprograficos; Asociacion de Editoriales de America Latina y el Caribe.
Subjects: Anthropology, Education, Government, Political Science, History, Philosophy, Psychology, Psychiatry, Social Sciences, Sociology
ISBN Prefix(es): 85-7139
Number of titles published annually: 100 Print
Parent Company: State University of Sao Paulo
Bookshop(s): Alameda Santos, 647, 01419-901 Sao Paulo-SP, Contact: Sandra Pedro
Tel: (011) 252 0630 *Fax:* (011) 252 0631
E-mail: livraria@editora.unesp.br

Unicornio Azul, *imprint of* Editora Mercuryo Ltda

Editora Universidade de Brasilia
SCS Quadra 2, Bloco C, No 78, 2° andar, Ed OK, 70300-500 Brasilia-DF
Tel: (061) 226-6874 *Fax:* (061) 323-1017
E-mail: editora@unb.br
Web Site: www.editora.unb.br
Telex: 611083 Unbs *Cable:* UNIVERBRASILIA EDITORA
Key Personnel
Chairman: Antonio A Briquet de Lemos
President: Alexandre Lima
Editorial Dir & Rights & Permissions: Airton Lugarinho
Production: Elmano Rodrigues Pinheiro
Founded: 1962
Subjects: Government, Political Science, Human Relations, Physical Sciences, Social Sciences, Sociology
ISBN Prefix(es): 85-230
Branch Office(s)
Escritorio de Representacao da Universidade de Brasilia, Ave Presidente Vargas 542 - 1309, 20210 Rio de Janeiro-RJ *Tel:* (021) 2636959
Rua Joao Adolfo 118 - 6° andar - sala 608, 01050 Sao Paulo-SP *Tel:* (011) 321413
Bookshop(s): SCS, Ed Anapolis, 70300 Brasilia-DF
Book Club(s): Clube do Livro da Universidade de Brasilia
Warehouse: Subsolo ICC-SUL, CP 04551, 70919 Brasilia-DF

Editora da Universidade de Sao Paulo+
Ave Prof Luciano Gualberto Travessau 374, 6 andar, 05508-900 Sao Paulo-SP
Tel: (011) 8184160; (011) 8138837 *Fax:* (011) 221-6988
Telex: 36950 *Cable:* RUSPAULO
Key Personnel
President: Sergio Miceli Pessoa De Barros
Chairman: Heitor Ferraz
Publishing Dir: Plinio Martins Filho
Founded: 1962
Specialize in academic text.
Subjects: Anthropology, Art, Literature, Literary Criticism, Essays, Medicine, Nursing, Dentistry, Philosophy, Science (General), Social Sciences, Sociology
ISBN Prefix(es): 85-314
Bookshop(s): Antigo Predio da Reitoria, Avenida Prof Luciano Gualberto, Travessa J, n 374, Cidade Universitaria, 05508 Sao Paulo-SP; Centro de Convivencia da Reitoria, Rua da Reitoria, 74, Cidade Universitaria, 05508 Sao Paulo-SP; Faculdade de Educacao, Avenida da Universidade, Travessa 11, n 251, Cidade Universitaria, 05508 Sao Paulo; FFLCH, Departamento de Historia e Geografia, Avenida Prof Lineu Prestes, n 338, Cidade Universitaria, 05508 Sao Paulo-SP; Instituto de Ciencias Biomedicas, Avenida Prof Lineu Prestes, 1524. Cidade Universitaria, 05508 Sao Paulo-SP; Instituto de Biociencias, Rua do Matao, 277; Es-

cola Politecnica Avenida Prof Almeida Prado, Travessa 2, n 128, 05508 Sao Paulo; Faculdade de Medicina de Ribeirao Preto Predio da Biblioteca, Avenida Bandeirantes, n 3900, 14049 Ribeirao Preto-SP; Escola Superior de Agricultura "Luis de Queiroz", Avenida Padua Dias, n 11, 13400 Piracicaba-SP

Editora Universidade Federal do Rio de Janeiro+
Forum de Ciencia e Cultura Avenida Pasteur, 250-Urca, Praia Vermelha, 22290-902 Rio de Janeiro
Tel: (021) 2542-7640 *Fax:* (021) 2295-0346
E-mail: livraria@editora.ufrj.br
Web Site: www.editora.ufrj.br; www.ufrj.br *Cable:* 22924
Key Personnel
Contact: Heloisa Buarque de Hollanda
Founded: 1986
Subjects: Anthropology, Architecture & Interior Design, Art, Economics, Education, History, Language Arts, Linguistics, Library & Information Sciences, Management, Physical Sciences, Social Sciences, Sociology
ISBN Prefix(es): 85-7108

Livraria e Editora Universitaria de Direito Ltda
Rua Benjamin Constant, 171, 1, andar, 01005-000 Sao Paulo-SP
Tel: (011) 3105-6374 *Fax:* (011) 3104-0317
Key Personnel
Man Dir, Production: Armando Luiz Almeida Martins
Editorial Dir: Pedro Gellindo Sommavilla
Sales Dir: Armando des Santos Mesquita Martins
Founded: 1968
Subjects: Law
ISBN Prefix(es): 85-7456

Fundacao Getulio Vargas+
Praia de Botafogo, 190-14º andar-Botafog, 22250-900 Rio de Janeiro-RJ
Tel: (021) 2559-5542; (021) 2559-5543; (021) 2559-5544 *Toll Free Tel:* 800-217777 *Fax:* (021) 2559-5532
E-mail: editora@fgv.br
Web Site: www.fgv.br
Telex: 36811 *Cable:* FUGEVAR
Key Personnel
Man Dir: Francisco de Castro Azevedo
Sales Dir: Juarez Nery de Souza
Subjects: Accounting, Business, Economics, Education, Marketing, Psychology, Psychiatry, Public Administration, Social Sciences, Sociology
ISBN Prefix(es): 85-225

Editora Vecchi SA
Rua do Resende 144, Esplanda do Senado, 20234 Rio de Janeiro-RJ
Tel: (021) 2444522
Telex: 32756 *Cable:* Vekieditora
Key Personnel
Dir-Superintendent: Delman Bonatto
Founded: 1913
Subjects: Astrology, Occult, Biography, Cookery, Philosophy, Religion - Other

Editora Verbo Ltda
Av Antonio Augusto Aguiar 148-6º, 1069 019 Lisbon
Tel: (021) 380 1100 *Fax:* (021) 386-5397
E-mail: verbo@virtual-net.com.br
Web Site: www.editorialverbo.pt *Cable:* Verbo
Founded: 1966
Subjects: Art, Education, Geography, Geology, History, Psychology, Psychiatry, Religion - Other, Social Sciences, Sociology
ISBN Prefix(es): 85-7230

Editora Vida Crista Ltda+
R Carlos Meira, 396 - Penha, 03605-010 Sao Paulo-SP
Tel: (011) 6647-7788 *Toll Free Tel:* 800-11-5074 *Fax:* (011) 6647-7125
E-mail: editora@vidacrista.com.br
Web Site: www.vidacrista.com.br
Key Personnel
Executive: Alan Leite
Founded: 1977
Subjects: Religion - Protestant
ISBN Prefix(es): 85-7163

Editora Vigilia Ltda
Rua Felipe dos Santos 508, Lourdes, 30180-160 Belo Horizonte-MG
Tel: (031) 3372744; (031) 3372363 *Fax:* (031) 3372834
Founded: 1960
Subjects: Education, Philosophy
ISBN Prefix(es): 85-259

Vozes Editora Ltda
Rua Frei Luis, 100, 25689-900 Petropolis-RJ
Tel: (024) 237 5112 *Fax:* (024) 231 4676
E-mail: editorial@vozes.com.br
Web Site: www.vozes.com.br *Cable:* VOZES
Key Personnel
Man Dir: Stephan Ottenbreit
Founded: 1901
Subjects: Communications, Language Arts, Linguistics, Philosophy, Psychology, Psychiatry, Public Administration, Religion - Other, Social Sciences, Sociology
ISBN Prefix(es): 85-326
Branch Office(s)
Rua Sergope, 120 Bairro Funcionarios, Belo Horizonte
Rua Tupis, 114, Belo Horizonte
SCLR/Norte, Q-704, bl A, N 16, Brasilia
Rua Barao de Jaguara, 1164, Campinas
Rua Dr Faivre, 1271, Curitiba
Rua Voluntarios da Patria, 41, Curitiba
Av Osmar Cunha, 183 Loja 15, Florianopolis
Rua Major Facundo, 730, Fortaleza
Rua 3, n 291, Goiania
Rua Espirito Santo, 963, Juiz de Fora
Rua Piaui, 72 Loja 1, Londrina
Rua Ramiro Barcelos, 386, Porto Alegre
Rua Riachuelo, 1280, Porto Alegre
Rua do Principe, 482, Recife
Rua Benedito Hipolito 1, Rio de Janeiro
Rua Senador Dantos, 118-I, Rio de Janeiro
Rua Carlos Gomes, 698-A, Salvador
Rua Luis Coelho, 295, Sao Paulo
Rua Senador Feijo, 168, Sao Paulo
Haddock Lobo, 360, Sao Paulo

WVC, *imprint of* Madras Editora

Jorge Zahar Editor+
Rua Mexico 31, Sobreloja Centro, 20031-144 Rio de Janeiro-RJ
Tel: (021) 2240-0226 *Fax:* (021) 2262-5123
E-mail: jze@zahar.com.br
Web Site: www.zahar.com.br
Key Personnel
General Manager: Jorge Zahar, Jr; Ana Cristina Zahar
Editorial: Mariana Zahar Ribeiro
  E-mail: mzahar@zahar.com.br
Founded: 1957
Subjects: Anthropology, Art, Behavioral Sciences, Biography, Economics, Education, Finance, History, Human Relations, Literature, Literary Criticism, Essays, Management, Marketing, Music, Dance, Philosophy, Psychology, Psychiatry, Science (General), Social Sciences, Sociology
ISBN Prefix(es): 85-7110; 85-85061
Number of titles published annually: 40 Print
Total Titles: 600 Print

Warehouse: Rua Cotia 35 (Rocha), 20960 Rio de Janeiro-RJ *Tel:* (021) 2218-3700 *Fax:* (021) 2581-2205 *E-mail:* comercial@zahar.com.br
Distribution Center: Companhia das Letias

Zip Editora Ltda
Rua Filomena Nunes 162, Olaria, 21021 Rio de Janeiro-RJ
Mailing Address: CP 20095, 21021 Rio de Janeiro-RJ
Tel: (021) 2807272
Key Personnel
Man Dir: Jan Rais
Marketing: Paul Margittai
Founded: 1978

Brunei Darussalam

General Information

Capital: Bandar Seri Begawan
Language: Malay, English & Chinese
Religion: Predominantly Sunni Muslim
Population: 369,000
Bank Hours: 0900-1200, 1400-1500 Monday-Friday; 0900-1100 Saturday
Shop Hours: 0730-1930 or 2000 Monday-Saturday in Bandar Seri Begawan, Tuesday-Sunday in Seria, Wednesday-Monday in Kuala Belait
Currency: 100 sen = 1 Brunei dollar
Export/Import Information: No tariff on books. No obscene literature allowed. Import licenses not required. No exchange controls.

Leong Brothers
52 Jl Bunga Kuning, Seria
Mailing Address: PO Box 164, Seria 7001
Tel: (03) 22381 *Fax:* (03) 222223
Telex: BU 3338 *Cable:* Leong

Bulgaria

General Information

Capital: Sofia
Language: Bulgarian
Religion: Bulgarian Orthodox & Islamic
Population: 8.9 million
Bank Hours: 0800-1200 Monday-Friday
Shop Hours: 0900-1230, 1300-1800 Monday-Saturday
Currency: 100 stotinki = 1 lev
Export/Import Information: Books imported by the foreign trade organization 'Hemus', pl Slavejkov 11, Sofia. Exchange controls. 18% VAT on books.
Copyright: UCC, Berne (see Copyright Conventions, pg xi)

Abagar Pablioing+
ul Golas 18, 1111 Sofia
Tel: (02) 702826 *Fax:* (02) 702926
E-mail: abagar@gti.bg
Key Personnel
Contact: Maria Arabadjieva
Founded: 1990
Subjects: Art, Fiction, History, Mathematics, Mysteries, Physical Sciences, Publishing & Book Trade Reference, Science (General), Science Fiction, Fantasy
ISBN Prefix(es): 954-584; 954-8004

Divisions: Abanas Ltd; Abhadon Ltd
Showroom(s): 55 Neofit Rilsui Str, Sofia 1000
Bookshop(s): Rousse Str, Rostislav Bluskov 1; Kjustendil Str, Tzar Osvoboditel 1; 55 Neofit Rilsui Str

Abagar, Veliko Tarnovo+
98 Nikola Gabrovski St, 5000 Veliko Tarnovo
Tel: (062) 43936; (062) 47814 *Fax:* (062) 46993
Key Personnel
General Manager: Marian Kenarov
Founded: 1991
Membership(s): Bulgarian Book Publishers Association.
Subjects: Art, Education, Fiction, Health, Nutrition, History, Science (General)
ISBN Prefix(es): 954-427
Distributed by Damian Jacob (Sofia); Hermes (Plovdiv)
Showroom(s): 47N Tzarigradsko shose Str, Sofia

AECD, imprint of Agencija Za Ikonomicesko Programirane i Razvitie

Agencija Za Ikonomicesko Programirane i Razvitie+
ul Aksakov 31, Sofia 1000
Tel: (02) 9816597 *Fax:* (02) 466110
E-mail: aecd@sf.cit.bg
Key Personnel
Vice President: Ms Mariel Nenova
International Rights: Ana-Maria Yankova
Head of Publications: Mr Ventsislav Voikov
Founded: 1991
Subjects: Economics
ISBN Prefix(es): 954-567
Imprints: AECD

Agency for Economic Coordination & Development, see Agencija Za Ikonomicesko Programirane i Razvitie

Aleks Print Publishing House+
ul Kavala 22, et 1, ap 1, 9000 Varna
Tel: (052) 823147 *Fax:* (052) 823147
E-mail: dstankov@ultranet.bg
Key Personnel
Contact: Anelia Stankova
Founded: 1992
Subjects: Romance, Science (General), Science Fiction, Fantasy, Travel
ISBN Prefix(es): 954-8261
Parent Company: Aleks Print & Tourism, Krali Marko 3, Varna
Bookshop(s): Alex Print & Tourism, Krali Marko 3, Varna 9000

Aleks Soft+
kv Banisora, ul ohrid, bl 32-36, vh A, et 5, 1000 Sofia
Tel: (02) 328855 *Fax:* (02) 328855
E-mail: info@alexsoft.net
Key Personnel
General Manager: Alexander Alexandrov
Founded: 1994
Subjects: Computer Science, Microcomputers
ISBN Prefix(es): 954-656
Parent Company: Aleks Soft Ltd

Andina Publishing House
ul Car Simeon I 10, 9000 Varna
Tel: (052) 630902
Key Personnel
Contact: Panko Anchev
ISBN Prefix(es): 954-432
Distributor for Longman (UK); Penguin (UK)

Antroposofsko Izdatelstvo Dimo R Daskalov OOD
ul M Stanev 61-A, 6000 Stara Zagora
Mailing Address: PO Box 255, 6000 Stara Zagora
Tel: (042) 54481
Key Personnel
Contact: Dr Dimitar Dimchev
Founded: 1991
Subjects: Astrology, Occult, Biblical Studies, Education, Philosophy, Science (General), Social Sciences, Sociology
ISBN Prefix(es): 954-495

Aratron, IK+
pl Slavejkov 11, et 6, 1000 Sofia
Mailing Address: PO Box 1587, 1000 Sofia
Tel: (02) 9807455 *Fax:* (02) 958-19-31
E-mail: aratron@techno-link.com
Key Personnel
President: Dobrin Vassilev
Founded: 1993
Specialize in New Age Books.
Subjects: Astrology, Occult, Business, Health, Nutrition, How-to, Nonfiction (General), Parapsychology, Psychology, Psychiatry, Self-Help
ISBN Prefix(es): 954-626

Izdatelstvo na Balgarskata Akademija na Naukite
ul Akad Georgi Boncev - bl 6, 1113 Sofia
Tel: (02) 720922; (02) 9793449; (02) 9793441 *Fax:* (02) 704054
Telex: 32123 Izdban
Key Personnel
Editor-in-Chief: Todor Rangelov
Sales & Publicity Manager: Maria Arabadjieva
Production Manager: Peter Tsanev
Founded: 1869
Publishing House of the Bulgarian Academy of Sciences.
Subjects: Science (General)
ISBN Prefix(es): 954-430
Bookshop(s): ul Rakovski 135, 1000 Sofia; ul V Kolarov 19, 4000 Plovdiv

Bilblioteka Nov den - Sajuz na Svobodnite Demokrati (Union of Free Democrats)+
Zk Mladost 4, bl 468, vh B, et 3, ap 41, Sofia 1715
Tel: (02) 773982; (02) 9814280 *Fax:* (02) 327972
Key Personnel
President & Editor: Prof Ivan Kaltchev
 E-mail: ivan_kaltchev@yahoo.com
Founded: 1991
Specialize in theoretical books only.
Membership(s): Union of Bulgarian Foundations.
Subjects: Ethnicity, History, Philosophy, Religion - Other
ISBN Prefix(es): 954-8575
Number of titles published annually: 4 Print
Total Titles: 24 Print
Parent Company: Research Center for Direct Democracy
Imprints: Dimiter Blagoev; LIK
Subsidiaries: Bulgarian Philosophical Association
Distributed by Filvest; Dimiter Blagoev
Distributor for LIK
Bookshop(s): 15, Tzar Osvoboditel Blvd, Sofia 1000, Sacho Savov *Tel:* (02) 85-81, code 003592
Book Club(s): Abagar, 47, Tzar Osvoboditel Blvd, Sofia 1000, Stefan Vlakhov *Tel:* (02) 46-31, code 003592

Bulgarski Houdozhnik Publishers+
6 Shipka Str, et 1, 1504 Sofia
Tel: (02) 467285; (02) 43351; (02) 43278 *Fax:* (02) 467285
Key Personnel
Dir: Bouyan Filchev *E-mail:* filchev@bulnet.bg
Founded: 1952 (reformation 1991)
ISBN Prefix(es): 954-406
Subsidiaries: Union of Bulgarian Artists

Bulgarski Pissatel+
6 Septemvri 35, 1000 Sofia
Tel: (02) 875873; (02) 873454; (02) 874527 *Fax:* (02) 872495
Key Personnel
Dir: Gertcho Atanasov
Publishing House of the Union of Bulgarian Writers.
Subjects: Fiction
ISBN Prefix(es): 954-443

Bulvest 2000 Ltd+
ul Serdika 13, vh A, et 3, 1000 Sofia
Tel: (02) 9833286; (02) 9833169 *Fax:* (02) 9815464
E-mail: bulvest@internet-bg.net
Key Personnel
President: Vladimir Topencharov
Founded: 1990
Subjects: Education, Fiction, Science (General)
ISBN Prefix(es): 954-18; 954-8112

Ciela Publishing House+
Member of Wolters Kluwer Group
80-A Patriarh Evtimii Blvd, 1463 Sofia
Tel: (02) 951 63 76; (02) 954 93 97; (02) 951 66 97 *Fax:* (02) 954 93 97
E-mail: ciela@bulnet.bg
Web Site: www.ciela.net
Telex: 24 611
Key Personnel
President: Vesselin Todorov *Tel:* (02) 954 93 98
 E-mail: vtodorov@ciela.net
Editor-in-Chief, Head of Law Editorial Dept: Yavor Mihaylov *Tel:* (02) 986 33 11; (02) 980 18 68
Publicity Manager: Violeta Igova *Tel:* (02) 986 33 11; (02) 980 18 68
Founded: 1990
Membership(s): Bulgarian Book Publishers Association.
Subjects: Accounting, Business, Economics, Education, Fiction, Finance, Law, Medicine, Nursing, Dentistry, Nonfiction (General), Psychology, Psychiatry, Publishing & Book Trade Reference, Technology
ISBN Prefix(es): 954-649
Number of titles published annually: 39 Print
Total Titles: 487 Print
Associate Companies: Ciela Consultancy, Ciela Printing House
Distributed by New Star; Sofi-R

DA-Izdatelstvo Publishers+
ul Patriarh Evtimij 26, Sofia 1000
Tel: (02) 988 1208 *Fax:* (02) 986 6290
Key Personnel
Dir: Aleko Djankov *E-mail:* alekoda@aster.net
Founded: 1996
Subjects: Fiction, History, Medicine, Nursing, Dentistry, Psychology, Psychiatry, Transportation

Hristo G Danov State Publishing House+
ul Stojan Calakov 1, 4025 Plovdiv
Tel: (032) 632552; (032) 265421 *Fax:* (032) 260560
Key Personnel
Dir: Nacho Hristoskov
Editorial: Dimitur Stoilov
Founded: 1855
Subjects: Fiction, Poetry
ISBN Prefix(es): 954-442

Darzhavno Izdatelstvo Zemizdat+
ul Georgi Benkovski 14, 1000 Sofia
Tel: (02) 9867895 *Fax:* (02) 442319
Key Personnel
Dir: Petar Angelov
Chief Editor: Emil Krustev
Founded: 1949
State Agricultural Publishing House.

Subjects: Agriculture, Cookery, Crafts, Games, Hobbies, Environmental Studies, Nonfiction (General), Science (General)
ISBN Prefix(es): 954-05

DATAMAP - Europe+
22 Shandor Petiofi St, 1606 Sofia
Tel: (02) 510090 *Fax:* (02) 510090
E-mail: datamap@mail.techno-linek.com
Key Personnel
President: Chaudor Dinev
Founded: 1991
Specialize in digital & printed maps, atlases & catalogues.
ISBN Prefix(es): 87-17
Total Titles: 25 Print; 2 CD-ROM
Associate Companies: Datamap Review Ltd, Sofia, Contact: Christo Assenor *Tel:* (02) 510090 *Fax:* (02) 510090

Dimiter Blagoev, *imprint of* Bilblioteka Nov den - Sajuz na Svobodnite Demokrati (Union of Free Democrats)

Dolphin Press Group Ltd+
PO Box 296, Bourgas 8000
Tel: (056) 45085 *Fax:* (056) 48481
Web Site: www.dolphin-press.com
Key Personnel
Chairman: Valentin Fortunov *Tel:* (088) 206 530
    E-mail: valentin.fortunov@unacs.bg
Founded: 1990
Subjects: Business, Career Development, Economics, Finance, Law, Management, Marketing, Public Administration
ISBN Prefix(es): 954-721
Subsidiaries: AB-Direct, Ltd; Eurobook, Ltd
Bookshop(s): 17 Botev St, Bourgas 8000
Book Club(s): The Golden Dolphin

EA EOOD+
43 San Stefano St, 5800 Pleven
Tel: (064) 22827 *Fax:* (064) 22528
E-mail: ea@famahold.com
Key Personnel
President: V Velikova
Editor-in-Chief: M Phillipova
Sales Manager: Y Raikova
Founded: 1991
Membership(s): the Bulgarian Publishers Association.
Subjects: Behavioral Sciences, Biography, Economics, Fiction, Literature, Literary Criticism, Essays, Philosophy, Poetry, Psychology, Psychiatry, Romance, Psychoanalysis
ISBN Prefix(es): 954-450
Bookshop(s): Pleven, V Levski St 161

EnEffect, Center for Energy Efficiency
One, Christo Smirnensky Blvd, 3rd floor, 1164 Sofia
Mailing Address: PO Box 43, 1606 Sofia
Tel: (02) 963 17 14; (02) 963 07 23; (02) 963 21 69 *Fax:* (02) 963 25 74
E-mail: eneffect@mail.orbitel.bg
Web Site: www.eneffect.bg
Key Personnel
Executive Dir: Dr Zdravko Genchev
Founded: 1992
Subjects: Energy, Environmental Studies

Eurasia Academic Publishers+
Lyulin bl 332, vh-b, ap 40, 1336 Sofia
Mailing Address: Lyulin 332 B-25, 1336 Sofia
Tel: (02) 241523
E-mail: eurasia@realsci.com
Web Site: www.biblio.hit.bg
Key Personnel
President: Plamen Gradinarov
Founded: 1990
Subjects: Asian Studies, Education, History, Natural History, Philosophy, Psychology, Psychiatry, Religion - Buddhist, Religion - Hindu
ISBN Prefix(es): 954-628

Evrazija, see Eurasia Academic Publishers

Factor-Alias+
Zk Mladost 1, bl 62, vh 1, ap 27, Sofia 1784
Tel: (02) 747-891
E-mail: factoral@omega.bg
Key Personnel
President: Bakalova Rossitza
Founded: 1997
Subjects: Education, English as a Second Language, Fiction, Western Fiction
Orders to: 12-14 Demkogly St, Rm 508, Sofia 1000

Fama+
ul Aksakov 10, ul Canko Cerkovski 23, 1000 Sofia
Tel: (02) 881175; (02) 657006 *Fax:* (02) 657006
Key Personnel
Editor: Maria Koeva; Igor Shemtov
Founded: 1992
Subjects: Literature, Literary Criticism, Essays
ISBN Prefix(es): 954-597

Foi-Commerce+
PO Box 775, 1000 Sofia
Tel: (02) 227116 *Fax:* (02) 227116
E-mail: foi@nlcv.net
Key Personnel
President: Markov Krassimir
Founded: 1990
Subjects: Accounting, Business, Computer Science, Library & Information Sciences, Mathematics, Science (General)
ISBN Prefix(es): 954-16

Fondacija Zlatno Kljuce+
Zk Mladost 1A, bl 523, vh 5, ap 115, Sofia 1729
Tel: (02) 760-671; (02) 623517 *Fax:* (02) 623517
E-mail: ynfirst@mat.bg
Key Personnel
President & International Rights: Mr M Tsvetanov
Founded: 1991
Promotion & subsidizing of miscellaneous pieces of art-created by & addressed to children; puppet theatre.
Membership(s): ASIFA.
Subjects: Art, Child Care & Development, Drama, Theater, Education
ISBN Prefix(es): 954-90237

Galaktika Publishing House+
ul Aleksandar Djakovic 25V, 9000 Varna
Tel: (052) 225077; (052) 241132; (052) 241156; (052) 604716; (052) 604715 *Fax:* (052) 234750
Key Personnel
General Dir: Assya Kadreva
Publicity Manager: Dimitrichka Telezarova
Founded: 1960
Subjects: Economics, Literature, Literary Criticism, Essays, Science Fiction, Fantasy
ISBN Prefix(es): 954-418

Gea-Libris Publishing House+
Al Batenberg 16b, Sofia 1000
Mailing Address: PO Box 365, Sofia 1000
Tel: (02) 9863171; (02) 9864604 *Fax:* (02) 9866900
E-mail: emilgea@techno-link.com
Web Site: www.gea-libris.search.bg
Key Personnel
Editor-in-Chief: Svetla Evstatieva
Dir: Emil Krastev
Computer & Design: Galina Krasteva
International Rights Contact: Milena Kardeleva
Founded: 1990
Subjects: Animals, Pets, Biological Sciences, Chemistry, Chemical Engineering, Economics, Environmental Studies, Fiction, Gardening, Plants, Geography, Geology, Health, Nutrition, Mathematics, Physical Sciences, Science (General), zoology, botany
Total Titles: 500 Print
Branch Office(s)
Gea-Libris-Varna, Boucher Str No 5, Contact: Anton Apostolov *Tel:* (052) 250452; (052) 824369

Global Kontakts Balgarija
34 Vladajska St, 1606 Sofia
Tel: (02) 540636 *Fax:* (02) 528790
Key Personnel
Man Dir: Maxim Behar *E-mail:* max@mbox.cit.bg
Founded: 1997
Subjects: Advertising
ISBN Prefix(es): 954-90246

Heliopol
zk Mladost 1, bl 29, vh7, 1750 Sofia
Tel: (02) 746850; (02) 718513
E-mail: heliopol@heliopol.bg
ISBN Prefix(es): 954-578

Hermes Publishing House+
16 Dobry Voynikov St, 4000 Plovdiv
Tel: (032) 630630 *Fax:* (032) 634095
E-mail: hermes@plovdiv.techno-link.com
Web Site: www.hermesbooks.com
Key Personnel
President: Stoyo Vartolomeev
International Rights: Victoria Petrova
Founded: 1991
Membership(s): Bulgarian Bookpublishers Association.
Subjects: Education, Fiction, Health, Nutrition, Nonfiction (General), Romance
ISBN Prefix(es): 954-459; 954-26
Subsidiaries: Hermes Publishers
Book Club(s): Friends of Hermes; Connoisseurs of the Book

Heron Press Publishing House+
18 Oborishte St, 1504 Sofia
Tel: (02) 443368 *Fax:* (02) 443368
E-mail: heron_press@attglobal.net
Key Personnel
Contact: Ilia Petrov
Founded: 1993
Subjects: Fiction, Geography, Geology, History, Mathematics, Medicine, Nursing, Dentistry, Natural History, Nonfiction (General), Physical Sciences, Physics, Science (General)
ISBN Prefix(es): 954-580
Book Club(s): Association of Bulgarian Publishers

Hriker+
Banichora, 17-A, vh b, et 5 ap 65, 1233 Sofia
Tel: (02) 319-217
Key Personnel
Contact: Ms Nevena Konstantinova Keremedchieva
Founded: 1994
Subjects: Art, Ethnicity, Literature, Literary Criticism, Essays, Philosophy, Poetry
ISBN Prefix(es): 954-8498
Number of titles published annually: 12 Print
Total Titles: 61 Print
Book Club(s): Club of Modern Bulgarian Poetry

Publishing House Hristo Botev+
ul Slavjanska 38 vh A et 1, 1000 Sofija
Tel: (02) 9870810
Key Personnel
Dir: Ivan Dinkov
Founded: 1944

Subjects: Biography, Fiction, Government, Political Science, History, Literature, Literary Criticism, Essays, Philosophy, Social Sciences, Sociology
ISBN Prefix(es): 954-445

Interpres+
1343, Ljulin-2 bl 214-d-102, 1343 Sofia
Mailing Address: PO Box 18, 1582 Sofia
Tel: (02) 517915 *Fax:* (02) 517915
E-mail: interpres@bis.bg; intrpres@usa.net
Key Personnel
President: Mariana Evlogieva
Founded: 1992
Subjects: Advertising, Business, Crafts, Games, Hobbies, Education, Human Relations, Humor, Language Arts, Linguistics, Literature, Literary Criticism, Essays
ISBN Prefix(es): 954-664

Izdatelstvo Ja
ul Preslav 19, Jambol 8600
Tel: (046) 26166; (046) 20077
ISBN Prefix(es): 954-615

Izdatelstvo Lettera (Lettera Publishers)+
ul Rhodope No 62, 4000 Plovdiv
Mailing Address: PO Box 802, 4000 Plovdiv
Tel: (032) 600 930 *Fax:* (032) 600 940
E-mail: lettera@plovdiv.techno-link.com; office@lettera.bg
Web Site: www.lettera.bg
Key Personnel
President: Nadya Furnadzhieva
Founded: 1991
Membership(s): EEPG (European Educational Publishers Group); ICC (International Certificate Conference); ABK (Association of Bulgarian Publishers).
Subjects: Education, English as a Second Language, Fiction, Humor, Language Arts, Linguistics, Mathematics
ISBN Prefix(es): 954-516
Distributed by Damian Yakov
Showroom(s): 10 Svetoslav Terter Str, 1124 Sofia
Tel: (02) 944 14 52
Bookshop(s): 10 Svetoslav Terter Str, 1124 Sofia

Pejo K Javorov Publishing House+
52 Dondukov Blvd, 1000 Sofia
Tel: (02) 875201; (02) 880137; (02) 876765 *Fax:* (02) 875592
Key Personnel
Man Dir: Julia Bouchkova
Founded: 1945
State owned publisher.
Subjects: Cookery, Fiction, History, Humor, Nonfiction (General), Poetry
ISBN Prefix(es): 954-525

Kibea Publishing Co+
Mailing Address: PO Box 70, 1336 Sofia
Tel: (02) 24 10 20; (02) 925 01 52 *Fax:* (02) 925 07 48
E-mail: kibea@internet-bg.net; office@kibea.net
Web Site: www.kibea.net
Key Personnel
Publisher: Dimitar Zlatarev
Founded: 1991
Subjects: Alternative, Anthropology, Art, Astrology, Occult, Biography, Cookery, Fiction, Foreign Countries, Health, Nutrition, History, How-to, Human Relations, Nonfiction (General), Parapsychology, Philosophy, Poetry, Psychology, Psychiatry, Religion - Buddhist, Religion - Other, Self-Help
ISBN Prefix(es): 954-474
Total Titles: 300 Print
Bookshop(s): Kibea Books & Health Centre
Book Club(s): Friends of Kibea Club

Kolibri Publishing Group
Ul Solunska 40, Sofia 1000
Tel: (02) 988-87-81; (02) 955-84-81; (02) 955-91-990 *Fax:* (02) 813625
E-mail: colibri@inet.bg; colibry@bgnet.bg
Key Personnel
President: Raymond Wagenstein
Editor: Zhechka Georgieva
Founded: 1990
Subjects: Fiction, Literature, Literary Criticism, Essays, Nonfiction (General)
ISBN Prefix(es): 954-529
Distributor for Abrams, Thames & Hudson; Larousse; Robert; Taschen; etc; Random House Group
Bookshop(s): 2 Levski St, Sofia 1000

Kralica MAB (Queen Mab)+
Mladost 1, bl 29A, vh 2 ap 21, Sofia 1750
Tel: (02) 767357 *Fax:* (02) 767357
E-mail: mab@slovar.org
Web Site: www.slovar.org/mab
Key Personnel
President: Mariana Aretova
Senior Editor: Nikolay Aretov *E-mail:* naretov@yahoo.com
Founded: 1992
Subjects: Astrology, Occult, Cookery, Literature, Literary Criticism, Essays, Mysteries, Parapsychology, Philosophy, Psychology, Psychiatry, Theology
ISBN Prefix(es): 954-533
Number of titles published annually: 20 Print
Total Titles: 110 Print

LIK, imprint of Bilblioteka Nov den - Sajuz na Svobodnite Demokrati (Union of Free Democrats)

LIK Izdanija+
ul Nikolaj Gogol 16, 1504 Sofia
Tel: (02) 9443181; (02) 943400; (02) 9434748 *Fax:* (02) 9434400; (02) 9434748; (02) 9443181
E-mail: lik@ttm.bg
Key Personnel
President: Liuben Kosarev
Founded: 1993
Subjects: Anthropology, Education, Health, Nutrition, History, Literature, Literary Criticism, Essays, Mathematics, Philosophy, Psychology, Psychiatry, Social Sciences, Sociology
ISBN Prefix(es): 954-607

Litera Prima+
Drouzhba-2, Bl 418, Entr 2, App 46, 1528 Sofia
Mailing Address: PO Box 38, 1528 Sofia
Tel: (02) 9731698; (02) 9745575
E-mail: mmihales@vmei.acad.bg
Key Personnel
Contact: Marin Naydenov *Fax:* (02) 9731698 *E-mail:* mmihalev@vmei.acad.bg
Founded: 1993
Subjects: Anthropology, Archaeology, Astronomy, Mysteries, Natural History, Parapsychology, Physical Sciences, Science (General)
ISBN Prefix(es): 954-8163; 954-738

Makros 2000 - Plovdiv+
Bul Nezavisimost 119, zk Izgrev, 4019 Plovdiv
Tel: (032) 620770
Key Personnel
President & Owner: Georgi Stanchev Nikolov
Founded: 1991
Subjects: Art, Astronomy, Biography, Biological Sciences, Business, Chemistry, Chemical Engineering, Computer Science, Economics, Education, Electronics, Electrical Engineering, Geography, Geology, History, Literature, Literary Criticism, Essays, Management, Mathematics, Medicine, Nursing, Dentistry, Microcomputers, Music, Dance, Philosophy, Physical Sciences, Physics, Psychology, Psychiatry, Science (General), Social Sciences, Sociology
ISBN Prefix(es): 954-561
Bookshop(s): Makros 2000, Tsar Assen 16, Plovdiv 4000

Mateks, see MATEX

MATEX+
ul Han Omurtag 10, Sofia 1000
Tel: (02) 430177
E-mail: mmk_fte@uacg.acad.bg
Key Personnel
President: Mihail Konstantinov
Manager: Emil Enchev
Founded: 1991
Subjects: Cookery, Education, Electronics, Electrical Engineering, Fiction, Health, Nutrition, Mathematics, Nonfiction (General), Science Fiction, Fantasy
ISBN Prefix(es): 954-508
Associate Companies: ELMA Publishing House, Sofia
Subsidiaries: BIAR

Medicina i Fizkultura EOOD
pl Slavejkov 11, Sofia 1000
Tel: (02) 871308; (02) 884068 *Fax:* (02) 871308
Subjects: Biological Sciences, Geography, Geology, Health, Nutrition, Medicine, Nursing, Dentistry, Sports, Athletics
ISBN Prefix(es): 954-420

Mladezh IK+
ul Car Kalojan 10, 1000 Sofia
Tel: (02) 882137 *Fax:* (02) 876135
Key Personnel
Dir: Stanimir Ilchev
Founded: 1945
Youth Publishing House.
Subjects: Fiction, Government, Political Science, Philosophy, Social Sciences, Sociology
ISBN Prefix(es): 954-413

Musica EOOD, see Musica Publishing House Ltd

Musica Publishing House Ltd+
11 Slaveikov Sq, 1000 Sofia
Tel: (02) 877 963; (02) 892 642 *Fax:* (02) 877 963
E-mail: musicaph@abv.bg
Web Site: www.geocities.com/musicapublishinghouse
Key Personnel
President: Neli Koulaksazova
Founded: 1975
Membership(s): Bulgarian Book Publishing Association.
Subjects: Art, Biography, Child Care & Development, Education, Music, Dance, Poetry, Publishing & Book Trade Reference
ISBN Prefix(es): 954-405

Naouka i Izkoustvo, Ltd+
11 Slaveikov, et 5, 1080 Sofia
Tel: (02) 9874790; (02) 9872496 *Fax:* (02) 9872496
E-mail: nauk_izk@sigma-bg.com
Key Personnel
Dir: Loreta Poushkarova
Founded: 1948
Bulgarian & foreign scientific literature in the fields of philosophy, psychology, linguisitics, history, dictionaries & language learning materials.
Subjects: Art, Business, Economics, History, Language Arts, Linguistics, Law, Mathematics, Philosophy, Physics, Psychology, Psychiatry, Science (General), Social Sciences, Sociology
ISBN Prefix(es): 954-02

BULGARIA

Narodna Kultura+
One Angel Kunchev, 1000 Sofia
Tel: (02) 9878063; (02) 9872722; (02) 9871684
E-mail: peepcult@intemet-bg.net
Web Site: web.narodnakultura.hit.bg
Key Personnel
Dir: Petar Manolov
Founded: 1944
Subjects: Literature, Literary Criticism, Essays, Poetry
ISBN Prefix(es): 954-04

Narodna Kultura
ul Angel Kanchev 1, 1000 Sofia
Mailing Address: PO Box 421, 1000 Sofia
Tel: (02) 981 4739 *Fax:* (02) 981 4739
E-mail: peepcult@internet-bg.net
Web Site: www.geocities.com/narodna_kultura
Key Personnel
Dir: Alexander Donev
Founded: 1944
Subjects: Social Sciences, Sociology
ISBN Prefix(es): 954-04

Publishing House Narodno delo OOD+
Bul Hristo Botev 3, Varna 9000
Mailing Address: PO Box 59, Varna 9000
Tel: (052) 230241; (052) 288516
Key Personnel
Contact: Mr Konstantin Paskalev
Founded: 1990
Subjects: Advertising, Maritime, Regional Interests, Travel
ISBN Prefix(es): 954-627
Branch Office(s)
Bourgas
Dobritch
Rouse
Shoumen
Sofia
Orders to: Festival & Congress Centre, Varna

Nauka i Izkustovo EOOD, see Naouka i Izkoustvo, Ltd

New Man Publishers, *imprint of* Nov Covek Publishing House

Nov Covek Publishing House+
28 Antim I St, 1303 Sofia
Tel: (02) 9863766 *Fax:* (02) 9863772
E-mail: newman@mbox.cit.bg; vogda@stratec.net
Key Personnel
President: Rumen Papratilov
Founded: 1990
Produces & distributes theological, reference & sociological literature.
Membership(s): International Literature Associates, Bulgarian Book Publishers Association.
Subjects: Biblical Studies, Child Care & Development, History, Human Relations, Philosophy, Psychology, Psychiatry, Social Sciences, Sociology, Theology
ISBN Prefix(es): 954-407
Imprints: New Man Publishers

Universitetsko Izdatelstvo 'Kliment Ochridski'
Blvd Carigradsko Sose 125, bl 4, 1113 Sofia
Tel: (02) 71288; (02) 71265; (02) 704271; (02) 71151 *Fax:* (02) 704271
E-mail: gzisha@ns.sclg.uni-sofia.bg
Key Personnel
Dir: Dimitaz Tomov
Subjects: Science (General)
ISBN Prefix(es): 954-07

Pensoft Publishers+
Akad G Bonchevstr, Bldg 6, 1113 Sofia
Tel: (02) 716451 *Fax:* (02) 704508
E-mail: pensoft@mbox.infotel.bg; orders@pensoft.net; info@pensoft.net

Web Site: www.pensoft.net
Key Personnel
Man Dir: Dr Lyubomir D Penev, PhD
Publisher-in-Chief: Sergei I Golovatch
Founded: 1993
Also acts as book supplier for East European books.
Subjects: Agriculture, Archaeology, Biological Sciences, Business, Earth Sciences, Environmental Studies, Finance, History, Language Arts, Linguistics, Mathematics, Natural History, Physics, Religion - Other, Science (General), Botany, Zoology
ISBN Prefix(es): 954-642
Number of titles published annually: 60 Print
Total Titles: 160 Print
Divisions: Pensoft-Moscow
Branch Office(s)
Institute for Problems of Ecology & Education, Leninsky pr 33, V-71 Moscow, Russian Federation, Dr Sergei Golovatch *E-mail:* spol@orc.ru
Web Site: www.pensoft.net
Distributed by Coronet Books Inc (USA); DA Information Services; Goecke & Evers Antiquariat (Germany); Kabourek; NHBS-Natural History Book Service
Distributor for Academic Publishing House-Sofia; Heron Press
Orders to: Coronet Books Inc, 311 Bainbridge St, Philadelphia, PA 19147, United States *Tel:* 215-925-2762 *Fax:* 215-925-1912 *E-mail:* jeffgolds@aol.com *Web Site:* www.coronetbooks.com

Pet Plus+
142 Rakovski St, 1000 Sofia
Tel: (02) 9874188
E-mail: editor@545plus.com; petplus@bnc.bg
Web Site: www.545plus.com
Key Personnel
President: Petyo Hristov
Founded: 1990
Specialize in books with cassette.
Membership(s): Association of the Bulgarian Editors.
Subjects: Biography, Literature, Literary Criticism, Essays, Poetry, Religion - Other
ISBN Prefix(es): 954-462
Total Titles: 2 Print
Book Club(s): Association of Book Publications

Prohazka I Kacarmazov+
ul Vasil Levski 50, Sofia 1000
Tel: (02) 654969 *Fax:* (02) 654969
E-mail: eto@einet.bg
Subjects: Education, Language Arts, Linguistics, Literature, Literary Criticism, Essays, Poetry, Social Sciences, Sociology
ISBN Prefix(es): 954-603

Prosveta Publishers AS+
117, Bul Carigradsko Sose, 1184 Sofia
Tel: (02) 760651; (02) 9743696; (02) 761182 *Fax:* (02) 764451
E-mail: prosveta@intech.bg
Key Personnel
President: Joana Tomova
Founded: 1945
Specialize in school textbooks.
Subjects: Education
ISBN Prefix(es): 954-01
Bookshop(s): 39 Ivan Assen II Str, Sofia

Prozoretz, see Prozoretz Ltd Publishing House

Prozoretz Ltd Publishing House (Izdatelsica Kushta Prozoretz)+
117, Tzarigradsko Shousse Blvd, 1784 Sofia
Tel: (02) 765171; (02) 746053 *Fax:* (02) 746053
E-mail: prozor@tea.bg

Key Personnel
Man Dir: Joana Tomova
Subjects: English as a Second Language, Fiction, Health, Nutrition, Philosophy, Poetry, Religion - Other, Self-Help
ISBN Prefix(es): 954-733
Bookshop(s): 39 Ivan Assen II Str, Sofia

Rakla+
Zk Borovo, bl 222 A, vh D, et 6, ap 112, Sofia 1680
Tel: (02) 580-569
E-mail: grigorit@yahoo.com
Key Personnel
Senior Manager: Velichka Bojinova *E-mail:* rakla.net@usa.net
Founded: 1993
Membership(s): Union of Bulgarian Journalists.
Subjects: Cookery, Gardening, Plants, History
ISBN Prefix(es): 954-90251

Regalia 6 Publishing House+
PO Box 172, 1700 Sofia
Tel: (02) 754111 *Fax:* (02) 566573
E-mail: vpruu@dir.bg
Key Personnel
Contact: Raicho Ushatov
Founded: 1991
Publication of school aids & supplementary materials for all levels of education, compiled by the specialists in the corresponding areas.
Subjects: Career Development, Computer Science, Crafts, Games, Hobbies, Education, English as a Second Language, Mathematics, Science (General)
ISBN Prefix(es): 954-8147

Reporter+
113 Tzarigradsko chausse, 1184 Sofia
Tel: (02) 760834; (02) 761084; (02) 769028 *Fax:* (02) 745114
E-mail: reporter@techno-link.com
Key Personnel
Manager: Krum Blagov *E-mail:* reporter@mail.techno-link.com
Founded: 1990
Nonfiction & fiction Bulgarian & foreign literature, planners & calendars.
Subjects: Advertising, Biography, Child Care & Development, Fiction, Health, Nutrition, Nonfiction (General)
ISBN Prefix(es): 954-8102
Number of titles published annually: 12 Print
Total Titles: 30 Print

Sanra Book Trust
ul Dragan Cankov 18, 1421 Sofia
Mailing Address: PO Box 47, 1408 Sofia
Tel: (02) 665124; (02) 9549481 *Fax:* (02) 9549871
Key Personnel
Contact: Sasho Ranguelov
Founded: 1993
Subjects: English as a Second Language
ISBN Prefix(es): 954-662

Seven Hills Publishers+
ul Veliko Tarnovo 13, Plovdiv 4000
Mailing Address: PO Box 976, Plovdiv 4000
Tel: (032) 262235 *Fax:* (032) 262235
Key Personnel
President: Valeri Nichevski
Vice President: Evelina Proeva
Founded: 1993
Subjects: Art, Business, English as a Second Language, Language Arts, Linguistics, Law, Medicine, Nursing, Dentistry, Psychology, Psychiatry
ISBN Prefix(es): 954-669

Sibi+
4 Slaveikov Sq, 1000 Sofia
Tel: (02) 9870141 *Fax:* (02) 9875709
E-mail: sibi@ind.interner-bg.bg
Key Personnel
President: Mr Vassil Tashev
Vice President & International Rights: Mrs Natalia Goudjeva
Founded: 1990
Sibi has own bookshops in major Bugarian cities.
Subjects: Labor, Industrial Relations, Law
ISBN Prefix(es): 954-8150; 954-730
Bookshop(s): City Court of Plovdiv, 6 Septemvri St 168, 4000 Plovdiv; Sibi Specialize Bookshop, Supreme Administrative Court Building, Stambolijski Blvd 18, 1000 Sofia
Shipping Address: 1799 Sofia, Mladost-2, bl 227, vh 5, et 2, ap 96
Warehouse: Mladost-2, bl 227, vh 5, et 2, ap 96, 1799 Sofia
Orders to: Mladost-2, bl 227, vh 5, et 2, ap 96, 1799 Sofia

Sila & Zivot
ul Dimitar Blagoev St, vh. 3, 8001 Burgas
Mailing Address: PO Box 609, 8001 Burgas
Tel: (056) 20965
E-mail: silajivot@bse.bg
Key Personnel
Publisher: Milka Kraleva
Founded: 1992
Specialize in books & music of Peter Deunov (1864-1944).
Subjects: Astrology, Occult, Biblical Studies, Child Care & Development, Education, Music, Dance, Parapsychology, Philosophy, Self-Help, Theology
ISBN Prefix(es): 954-8146

Sinodalno Izdatelstvo na Balgarskata pravoslavna carkva
ul Oboriste 4, 1000 Sofia
Tel: (02) 875611; (02) 875245
Synodal Publishing House.
Subjects: Religion - Other
ISBN Prefix(es): 954-8398

Sita-MB+
ul Vasil Drumev 47, vhA ap21, Varna 9002
Tel: (092) 872285
Founded: 1992
Subjects: Communications, Human Relations, Labor, Industrial Relations, Management
ISBN Prefix(es): 954-518

Slance, see Sluntse Publishing House

Slavena+
Radko Dimitriev St No 59A, 9000 Varna
Tel: (052) 602465; (052) 225935 *Fax:* (052) 225935
E-mail: slavena@triada.bg
Web Site: www.slavena.net
Key Personnel
Contact: Nasko Yakimov
Founded: 1990
Subjects: Art, Crafts, Games, Hobbies, Economics, Education, History, Law, Literature, Literary Criticism, Essays, Science (General)
ISBN Prefix(es): 954-579

Sluntse Publishing House+
11 Slaveykov Sq, 1000 Sofia
Mailing Address: PO Box 694, 1000 Sofia
Tel: (02) 988 37 97 *Fax:* (02) 987 14 05
E-mail: info@sluntse.com
Web Site: www.sluntse.com
Key Personnel
President: Nadia Kabakchieva
Founded: 1937

Subjects: Astrology, Occult, Biography, Child Care & Development, Education, Fiction, Foreign Countries, Gardening, Plants, Health, Nutrition, House & Home, Human Relations, Marketing, Native American Studies, Nonfiction (General), Publishing & Book Trade Reference, Romance, Autobiography, Memoirs, Letter & Beauty
ISBN Prefix(es): 954-8023; 954-742

Srebaren lav+
ul Plovdivsko pole, bl2 vhA ap3, 1756 Sofia
Tel: (02) 752298
Founded: 1991
Subjects: Literature, Literary Criticism, Essays
ISBN Prefix(es): 954-571

Svetra Publishing House+
Major Thompson St, Bl 12, entr 2, 1407 Sofia
Tel: (02) 62 27 39; (02) 983 45 42 *Fax:* (02) 23 49 66
E-mail: svetlev@cybernet.bg
Key Personnel
President: Nickolay Svetlev
Founded: 1993
Subjects: Advertising, Art, Biblical Studies, Fiction, Literature, Literary Criticism, Essays, Poetry, Science Fiction, Fantasy
ISBN Prefix(es): 954-8430
Warehouse: 83A Simeon St, 1000 Sofia *Tel:* (02) 834541

Technica+
Slaveikov One Sq, 1000 Sofia
Tel: (02) 987 1283 *Fax:* (02) 987 4906
E-mail: technica@netel.bg; sales@technica-bg.com
Web Site: www.technica-bg.com
Key Personnel
Manager: Nina Deneva *E-mail:* deneva@technica-bg.com
Editorial Manager: Evelina Kachakova
Founded: 1958
Subjects: Science (General)
ISBN Prefix(es): 954-03

Tehnika EOOD, see Technica

TEMTO
Bul Gen Skobelev 35, Sofia 1463
Tel: (02) 524-924
E-mail: temto@sf.icn.bg
Key Personnel
President: Temenouga Todorova
Programmer: Kiril Voykov
Artist: Monika Voykova
Founded: 1991
Subjects: Advertising, Agriculture, Architecture & Interior Design, Computer Science, Health, Nutrition, Mathematics, Microcomputers, Poetry, Psychology, Psychiatry, Advertising, Programming
ISBN Prefix(es): 954-9566

Todor Kableshkov University of Transport+
158 Geo Milev St, 1574 Sofia
Tel: (02) 9709335; (02) 9709384; (02) 9709478 *Fax:* (02) 9709407
E-mail: office@vtu.bg
Web Site: www.vtu.bg
Key Personnel
Rector: Nencho Nenov, PhD *Tel:* (02) 97 09 406 *Fax:* (02) 97 09 242 *E-mail:* rector@vtu.bg
Vice Rector, Educational Activities: Detelin Vasilev, PhD *Tel:* (02) 97 09 406 *Fax:* (02) 97 09 407 *E-mail:* dvasilev@vtu.bg
Vice Rector, Research & International Relations: Rusko Valkov, PhD *Tel:* (02) 97 09 335 *Fax:* (02) 97 09 325 *E-mail:* rvalkov@vtu.bg
Founded: 1922

Subjects: Advertising, Behavioral Sciences, Business, Civil Engineering, Communications, Economics, Electronics, Electrical Engineering, Engineering (General), Mechanical Engineering, Transportation
ISBN Prefix(es): 954-12
Number of titles published annually: 45 Print
Parent Company: Ministry of Education & Science

Trud - Izd kasta+
15 Dunav Str, 1000 Sofia 1000
Tel: (02) 9814110; (02) 9878261; (02) 9872924 *Fax:* (02) 467565
E-mail: book@cybernet.bg
Web Site: www.trud.bg
Key Personnel
President: Nikola Kitsevski *Tel:* (02) 9214157
Founded: 1994
Subjects: Biography, Fiction, History, Humor, Mysteries, Western Fiction
ISBN Prefix(es): 954-528
Number of titles published annually: 40 Print
Total Titles: 500 Print
Parent Company: Media Holding, 119 Ekzarh Joseph, 1000 Sofia
Ultimate Parent Company: WAZ- Germany
Branch Office(s)
Trud Publishing House, Contact: Krasimir Mirchev *Tel:* (02) 987-29-24

Ivan Vazov Publishing House
ul. Georgi Benkovski 14, Sofia 1000
Tel: (02) 878481; (02) 871572 *Fax:* (02) 878416
Founded: 1948
Subjects: Biography, Fiction, Government, Political Science, History, Humor, Literature, Literary Criticism, Essays, Nonfiction (General), Poetry, Science (General)
ISBN Prefix(es): 954-604

Voenno Izdatelstvo
ul Ivan Vazov 12, Sofia 1000
Tel: (02) 9802766; (02) 9804186; (02) 9802779 *Fax:* (02) 881568
Subjects: History, Military Science, Social Sciences, Sociology
ISBN Prefix(es): 954-509

Zunica+
Zk Bakston, bl 10, et 11, ap 48, Sofia 1618
Tel: (02) 551-977
Subjects: Art, Drama, Theater, Fiction, Humor, Mysteries, Poetry, Romance, Science Fiction, Fantasy
ISBN Prefix(es): 954-9604

Burundi

General Information

Capital: Bujumbura
Language: French & Kirundi (Swahili & French commercially)
Religion: About half Roman Catholic; others follow traditional animist beliefs
Population: 6.0 million
Bank Hours: Normally closed for cash transactions in afternoon but open for all other business morning & afteroon
Shop Hours: 0800-1200, 1400-1630 Monday-Friday; 0800-1200 Saturday
Currency: 100 centimes = 1 Burundi franc
Export/Import Information: Import license required over value of 20,000 Burundi francs.

Government Printer (INABU)
BP 991, Bujumbura
Tel: (02) 22214; (02) 24046

Editions Intore+
5 Av de France, Bujumbura
Mailing Address: BP 2524, Bujumbura
Tel: (02) 225167
Key Personnel
Edition Dir: Dr Andre Birabuza
 E-mail: anbirabuza@yahoo.fr
Founded: 1992
Subjects: Developing Countries, Ethnicity, History, Journalism, Literature, Literary Criticism, Essays, Philosophy, Social Sciences, Sociology
ISBN Prefix(es): 2-9506222
Divisions: Binensuel Intore; Librairie Papeterie Intore

Les Presses Lavigerie
5 Av de l'Uprona, BP 1640 Bujumbura
Tel: (02) 22368 *Fax:* (02) 220318
E-mail: lpl~bujumbura@cbinf.com
Key Personnel
Contact: Geiss Anton *Tel:* (02) 228508

Cameroon

General Information

Capital: Yaounde
Language: French & English (officially bilingual)
Religion: Christian, Islamic, traditional
Population: 12.7 million
Bank Hours: East: 0800-1130, 1430-1630 Monday-Friday; West: 0800-1330 Monday-Friday
Shop Hours: 0800-1200, 1430-1730 (earlier closing in West) Monday-Friday; 0800-1200 Saturday
Currency: 100 centimes = 1 CFA franc
Export/Import Information: Member of Customs & Economic Union of Central Africa. Import license, entitling holder to provision for necessary foreign exchange, required if value of import is over 500,000 CFA francs.
Copyright: UCC, Berne, Florence (see Copyright Conventions, pg xi)

CAW Series, imprint of Editions Buma Kor & Co Ltd

Centre d'Edition et de Production pour l'Enseignement et la Recherche (CEPER)+
BP 808, Yaounde
Tel: (023) 221323
Telex: 838 KN *Cable:* Cepmae Yaounde
Key Personnel
Dir General: Jean Claude Fouth
Sales Manager: Thomas Victor Mang Ngouni
Production Manager: Sonny Ekono
Contact: Theophile Maurice
Founded: 1967
Subjects: History, Nonfiction (General), Science (General), Social Sciences, Sociology, Technology
ISBN Prefix(es): 2-7405

CEPER, see Centre d'Edition et de Production pour l'Enseignement et la Recherche (CEPER)

Editions CLE+
BP 1501, Ave Marechal Foch, Yaounde
Tel: (0237) 22-35-54 *Fax:* (0237) 23-27-09
E-mail: edition@iccnet.cm *Cable:* CLE YAOUNDE
Key Personnel
Dir: Mr Comlan Prosper
Founded: 1963
Subjects: Drama, Theater, Fiction, How-to, Literature, Literary Criticism, Essays, Poetry, Religion - Protestant, Social Sciences, Sociology
ISBN Prefix(es): 2-7235
Distributed by CEC (Brussels); Editions ZOE (Geneva); L'Harmattan (Paris); Presence Africaine (Paris)
Distributor for CEDA (Ivory Coast); Editions Reynald Goulet (Quebec, Canada); Modulo Editeur (Quebec, Canada)
Bookshop(s): Librairie CLE, BP 1501, Yaounde

Editions Buma Kor & Co Ltd+
Box 727, Yaounde
Tel: (023) 22 48 99 *Fax:* (023) 23 29 03
Telex: 8438 KN
Key Personnel
Man Dir, Rights & Permissions: B D Buma Kor
Founded: 1977
Also act as representatives for Oxford University Press, Oxford, England.
Subjects: Drama, Theater, Economics, Fiction, Mathematics, Nonfiction (General), Poetry, Religion - Protestant, Self-Help
Parent Company: Buma Kor & Co (Sarl)
Associate Companies: Speedymint Centres
Imprints: CAW Series
Bookshop(s): Librairie Bilingue/The Bilingual Bookshop

Presses Universitaires d'Afrique+
BP 71636, Yaounde
Tel: (023) 22 00 30 *Fax:* (023) 22 23 25
Founded: 1986
Membership(s): Cameroon Publisher Association.
Subjects: Economics, Education, Finance, Law, Literature, Literary Criticism, Essays, Public Administration, Social Sciences, Sociology, Theology
ISBN Prefix(es): 2-912086
Parent Company: L'Africaine D'Edition et de Services (AES)
Distributed by Editions CLE (West Africa); Librarie de France

Editions Semences Africaines+
BP 5329, Yaounde Nlongkak
Tel: (023) 224058
Key Personnel
Man Dir, Production: Philippe-Louis Ombede
Editorial, Rights & Permissions: Martin King Mbida
Sales: Lea Ombede
Founded: 1974
Subjects: Drama, Theater, Fiction, History, Poetry, Regional Interests, Religion - Other
ISBN Prefix(es): 2-907553

Cape Verde

General Information

Capital: Praia
Language: Portuguese (official), French & English are also widely spoken
Religion: Predominantly Roman Catholic
Population: 398,000
Currency: 100 centavos = 1 Cape Verde escudo = $0.82 US
Export/Import Information: Member of the Economic Community of the West African States (ECWAS); Member of the ACP

Centro de Documentacao e Informao para o Desenvolvimento
CP 120, Praia
Tel: 613969 *Fax:* 1527
Telex: 6037 CV

Chad

General Information

Capital: N'Djamena
Language: French & Arabic
Religion: Islamic in north, traditional and some Christian in south
Population: 5.2 million
Bank Hours: 0700-1200 Monday-Saturday
Shop Hours: 0700 or 0800-1200 or 1230. 1600-1900 Monday-Saturday; some close Monday
Currency: 100 centimes = 1 CFA franc
Export/Import Information: No tariff on books. Consumption tax on children's picture-books & advertising. Import licenses required except for imports from the European Econimic Community & the Franc Zone.
Copyright: Berne (see Copyright Conventions, pg xi)

Government Printer (Imprimerie National Du Tchad)
BP 453, N'Djamena

Chile

General Information

Capital: Santiago
Language: Spanish
Religion: Roman Catholic
Population: 14 million
Bank Hours: 0900-1400 Monday-Friday
Shop Hours: 1000-1900 Monday-Friday; 1000-1800 Saturday-Sunday
Currency: 100 centavos = 1 Chilean peso
Export/Import Information: Member of Latin American Integration Association (ALADI). 19% VAT on books, 11% tariff.
Copyright: UCC, Berne, Buenos Aires (see Copyright Conventions, pg xi)

Alfabeta Impresores Ltda
Lira 140, Santiago
Tel: (02) 6397765 *Fax:* (02) 6391752
Key Personnel
Contact: Jaime Vicente Martinez

Arrayan Editores
Bernarda Morin 435, Providencia, Santiago
Tel: (02) 4314200 *Fax:* (02) 2741041
E-mail: web@arrayan.cl
Web Site: www.arrayan.cl
Key Personnel
President: Ramon Luis Undurraga Laso
Manager: Pablo Marinkovic
Editor: Juan Andres Pina Riquelme
Founded: 1982
Subjects: Accounting, Anthropology, Archaeology, Art, Astronomy, Biography, Biological Sciences, Chemistry, Chemical Engineering, Communications, Computer Science, Drama, Theater, Economics, Education, Engineering (General), Environmental Studies, Ethnicity, Geography, Geology, History, Journalism, Language Arts, Linguistics, Literature, Literary Criticism, Essays, Marketing, Mathematics, Medicine, Nursing, Dentistry, Music, Dance, Mythology, Philosophy, Physical Sciences, Psychology, Psychiatry, Radio, TV, Regional Interests, Self-Help, Social Sciences, Sociology, Sports, Athletics, Technology, Travel, Veterinary Science, Customs, Design, Folklore, Religion, Zoology
ISBN Prefix(es): 956-240

PUBLISHERS

Ediciones Bat+
Silvina Hurtado 1841-C, Providencia, Santiago
Tel: (02) 2743171 *Fax:* (02) 2250261
Key Personnel
Manager: Jose Cayuela Arzac
Founded: 1988
Subjects: Biography, History, Literature, Literary Criticism, Essays
ISBN Prefix(es): 956-7022

Editorial Andres Bello/Editorial Juridica de Chile+
Avda Ricardo Lyon 946, Providencia, Santiago
Tel: (02) 2049900; (02) 4619500 *Fax:* (02) 2253600
Web Site: www.editorialjuridica.cl
Telex: 240901 Edjur *Cable:* EDIBEL
Key Personnel
General Manager: Julio Serrano Lamas
 E-mail: julio_serrano@entelchile.net
Dir: Ana Maria Garcia B
Publisher: Pilar de Iruarrizaga B; Karem Duffoo C
Founded: 1947
Subjects: Art, Education, History, Law, Literature, Literary Criticism, Essays, Medicine, Nursing, Dentistry
ISBN Prefix(es): 85-613
Bookshop(s): Libreria Andres Bello (under Major Booksellers)
Book Club(s): Clubs de Lectores 'Andres Bello'

Bibliografica Internacional SA
Monjitas 308, Santiago
Tel: (02) 6394057 *Fax:* (02) 6397693
Key Personnel
Manager: Ramon Trepat-Pinilla
ISBN Prefix(es): 956-7240; 956-8090

Cesoc Ltda+
Esmeralda 636, Santiago
Tel: (02) 6391081; (02) 6336992 *Fax:* (02) 6325382
E-mail: cesoc@bellsouth.cl
Key Personnel
Manager: Julio Silva Solar
Founded: 1984
ISBN Prefix(es): 956-211
U.S. Office(s): Para Textor, 6 Avery St, Saratoga Springs, NY 12866, United States *Tel:* (518) 587-3774 *Fax:* (518) 581-1859

Cetal Ediciones
Abtao 576, Cerro Concepcion, Valparaiso
Tel: (032) 213360 *Fax:* (032) 214851
Key Personnel
Manager: Pedro Berho Arteagotia
Founded: 1984
Services in technology.
Subjects: Environmental Studies
ISBN Prefix(es): 956-209

Ediciones Cieplan
Francisco Noguera 217, piso 4, depto 40, Providencia, Santiago
Tel: (02) 2323212; (02) 2324558; (02) 6333836 *Fax:* (02) 3340312
E-mail: cieplan@ctcreuna.cl
Key Personnel
President: Pablo Pinera
Subjects: Developing Countries, Economics, Public Administration, Technology
ISBN Prefix(es): 956-204

Congregacion Paulinas - Hijas de San Pablo
Vicuna Mackenna 6299, La Florida, Santiago
Tel: (02) 221 2832 *Fax:* (02) 221 2832
E-mail: paulinasedit@entelchile.net
Key Personnel
Sister Superior: Hortensia Lizama
Dir: Veronica Pinto Pasten
Subjects: Religion - Catholic, Theology
ISBN Prefix(es): 956-7433
Bookshop(s): Libreria San Pablo (under Major Booksellers); Centro Catequistico, Cienfuegos 60, Casilla, 3429 Santiago
Orders to: Centro Catequistico Cienfuegos 60, Casilla, 3429 Santiago *Tel:* (02) 6964650 *Fax:* (02) 6990327

Corporacion de Promocion Universitaria
Av Miguel Claro No 1460, Providencia, CP 664 1209 Casilla 11 Correo 28, Santiago
Tel: (02) 2749022 *Fax:* (02) 2741828
ISBN Prefix(es): 956-229

Editorial Cuarto Propio
Keller 1175, Providencia, Santiago
Tel: (02) 204 7645 *Fax:* (02) 204 7622
E-mail: cuartopropio@cuartopropio.cl
Web Site: www.cuartopropio.cl
Key Personnel
General Manager: Marisol Vera
Founded: 1987
Membership(s): Chilean Chamber of the Book.
Subjects: Fiction, Nonfiction (General), Poetry, Women's Studies
Distributed by Paratextos (USA)
Distributor for Editorial Biblos (Argentina); Editorial La Marca (Argentina)
Bookshop(s): Libros sin Frontera, PO Box 2085, Olympia, WA 98507-2085, United States
Orders to: Paratextos, 6 Avery St, Saratoga Springs, NY 12866, United States

Editorial Cuatro Vientos (Cuatro Vientos Publishing House)+
Av Jaime Guzman Errazuriz 3293, Santiago
Mailing Address: Casilla 131 Correo 29, Santiago
Tel: (02) 2258381; (02) 269 5343 *Fax:* (02) 3413107
E-mail: 4vientos@netline.cl
Web Site: www.cuatrovientos.net
Key Personnel
Manager: Dr Francisco Huneeus
Commercial Manager: Renato Valenzuela
Founded: 1980
Membership(s): The Chilean Association of Publishers.
Subjects: Nonfiction (General), Psychology, Psychiatry
ISBN Prefix(es): 956-242
Number of titles published annually: 12 Print
Total Titles: 120 Print
Distributed by Edin (Argentina); Editorial Andres Bello (Chile); Editorial Universitaria (Chile)
Distributor for Be-Uve-Drais (Chile); Editorial Nuevo Extremo (Argentina); Editorial Troquel (Argentina); Luz De Luna (Argentina)

Dolmen Ediciones SA, see J.C. Saez Editor

Edeval (Universidad de Valparaiso)
Errazuriz 2190, mesa central: 56-32-507000, Valparaiso
Tel: (02) 250792 *Fax:* (02) 252125
E-mail: rrpp@uv.cl
Web Site: www.uv.cl
Key Personnel
International Rights: Arturo Salas Caceres
Founded: 1961
Subjects: Criminology, Economics, Government, Political Science, History, Human Relations, Labor, Industrial Relations, Law, Maritime, Philosophy, Publishing & Book Trade Reference, Social Sciences, Sociology
ISBN Prefix(es): 956-200
Bookshop(s): Libreria Andres Bello, Huerfanos, 1158 Santiago

Instituto Geografico Militar
Dieciocho N° 369, Santiago
Tel: (02) 4606863 *Fax:* (02) 4608294
E-mail: clientes@igm.cl
Web Site: www.igm.cl
Telex: 441677 16M C2
Key Personnel
Brig General: Enrique Gillmore Callejas
Contact: Mercedes Lucar
Founded: 1992
Specialized in cartography & topography of national territory.
Subjects: Earth Sciences, Geography, Geology
ISBN Prefix(es): 956-202
Total Titles: 30 Print; 2 CD-ROM

Grijalbo Mondadori SA
Monjitas 392, Piso 11, Oficinas 1101-1102, Santiago
Tel: (02) 782-8200 *Fax:* (02) 782-8210
E-mail: editorial@randomhouse-mondadori.cl
Web Site: www.grijalbo.com
Key Personnel
Contact: Gian Carlo Corte Truffello
ISBN Prefix(es): 956-258
Parent Company: Ediciones Grijalbo SA
Ultimate Parent Company: Random House Mondadori

Ediciones Mil Hojas Ltda
Av Antonio Varas 1480, Providencia, Santiago
Tel: (02) 2743172 *Fax:* (02) 2250261
Key Personnel
Dir: David R Turkieltaub
Founded: 1991
Subjects: Anthropology, Art, Astrology, Occult, Education, Self-Help, Sports, Athletics, Travel
ISBN Prefix(es): 956-7741
Subsidiaries: Abanico Libros Ltda

Editorial Juridica de Chile, see Editorial Andres Bello/Editorial Juridica de Chile

Libreria Libertad SA
Rosas No 1281, Santiago
Tel: (02) 698 8773 *Fax:* (02) 672 6314
Key Personnel
Manager: Alejandro Melo
Founded: 1967
ISBN Prefix(es): 956-7348

Ediciones y Publicidad Melquiades
Bandera 341 of 352, Casilla 144/12, Santiago
Tel: (02) 2731545 *Fax:* (02) 2266602 *Cable:* 240984
Key Personnel
Editor: Arturo Navarro
Founded: 1987
Subjects: Government, Political Science, Literature, Literary Criticism, Essays, Social Sciences, Sociology
ISBN Prefix(es): 956-231

Museo Chileno de Arte Precolombino
Bandera 361, Casilla 3687, Santiago
Tel: (02) 6887078; (02) 6972779 *Fax:* (02) 6972779
E-mail: bibmchap@ctcreuna.cl
Web Site: www.precolombino.cl
Specialize in Pre-Colombian Art.
Subjects: Archaeology, Art
ISBN Prefix(es): 84-89332; 956-243

Norma de Chile
Providencia 1760 Oficina 502, Santiago
Tel: (02) 236 3355 *Fax:* (02) 236 3362
Web Site: www.norma.com
Key Personnel
Manager: Elsy Salzar *E-mail:* esalazar@carvajal.cl
Contact: Octavio Alvarez Piedrahita

Subjects: Art, Literature, Literary Criticism, Essays, Management, Marketing, Science Fiction, Fantasy, Self-Help
ISBN Prefix(es): 956-7250

Editora Nueva Generacion+
Casilla 22, Covero 30 Santiago
Tel: (02) 2183974 *Fax:* (02) 2182281
Key Personnel
Manager: Pablo Huneeus
Founded: 1982
Subjects: Cookery, Human Relations, Humor, Social Sciences, Sociology
ISBN Prefix(es): 956-226

Editorial Patris SA+
Jose Miguel Infante 132, Providencia, Santiago
Tel: (02) 2351343 *Fax:* (02) 2351343
E-mail: edit.patris@entelchile.net
Web Site: www.patris.cl
Key Personnel
Contact: German B Pumpin
Founded: 1974
Subjects: Religion - Other
ISBN Prefix(es): 956-246
Distributor for Edit Patris (Argentina)
Bookshop(s): Libreria Patris (Nazareth), Providencia, 1001 Santiago

Pehuen Editores Ltda+
Maria Luisa Santander 537, Providencia, Santiago
Tel: (02) 2049399 *Fax:* (02) 2049399
E-mail: pehuen@cmet.net
Key Personnel
Dir: Jorge T Barros
General Manager: Alicia Z Cerda
Sales Manager: J Sebastian Barros
Founded: 1983
Subjects: Biography, Literature, Literary Criticism, Essays, Philosophy, Poetry, Social Sciences, Sociology
ISBN Prefix(es): 956-16
Subsidiaries: Temuco

Planeta SA+
Santa Lucia 360, Piso 7, Santiago
Tel: (02) 6962374 *Fax:* (02) 6957260
Telex: 242514 EPCMI
Key Personnel
General Manager: Bartolo Ortiz Henriquez
ISBN Prefix(es): 956-247
Parent Company: Planeta Internacional SA
Subsidiaries: Inversiones Planeta SA

Editorial Planeta Chilena, see Planeta SA

Pontificia Universidad Catolica de Chile+
Av Libertador Bernardo O'Higgins 340 of 311, Santiago
Mailing Address: Casilla 114-D, Santiago
Tel: (02) 2224516 (ext 2417) *Fax:* (02) 2225515
Web Site: www.puc.cl
Telex: 240395
Key Personnel
Dir & Editor: Gabriela Echeverria-Duco *Tel:* (02) 6862424 *E-mail:* gechever@vra.puc.cl
Founded: 1981
50% University textbooks & 50% all reader.
Subjects: Art, Biological Sciences, Economics, Education, Engineering (General), History, Literature, Literary Criticism, Essays, Philosophy, Psychology, Psychiatry, Religion - Other, Agronomy
ISBN Prefix(es): 956-14
Total Titles: 15 Print
Foreign Rep(s): Alfaomega Grupo Editor SA de CV (Argentina, Colombia, Mexico); Alfaomega Grupo Editor, S A de C V (Argentina, Colombia, Mexico)

Proa SA+
Mac Iver 140, Casilla 9935 Dir Postal, Santiago
Tel: (02) 633 65 34; (02) 633 98 54 *Fax:* (02) 633 98 54
E-mail: proa@eutelchile.net
Key Personnel
Manager: Jose Luis Benavente; Guillermo Varas Valdes
Founded: 1954
Specialize in importing Reproductive Art.
Subsidiaries: Libreria Noray

Publicaciones Lo Castillo SA
Perez Valenzuela No 1620, Providencia, Santiago
Tel: (02) 235 2606 *Fax:* (02) 235 2007
Key Personnel
General Manager: Alvaro Perez
Editor: Bartolome Yankovic
Founded: 1982
Subjects: Education, House & Home, Journalism, Travel
ISBN Prefix(es): 956-237
Imprints: Revista DATO

Publicaciones Nuevo Extremo
Bombero Adolfo Ossa 1067, Santiago
Tel: (02) 698 1523; (02) 697 2337 *Fax:* (02) 697 2545
E-mail: nexxtremo@entelchile.net
Key Personnel
Managing Dir: Eduardo G Castillo
ISBN Prefix(es): 956-7063

Red Internacional Del Libro+
El Vergel 2882, of 11, Providencia, Santiago
Tel: (02) 2238100 *Fax:* (02) 2254269
E-mail: ril@rileditores.com
Web Site: www.rileditores.com
Key Personnel
Legal Representative: Ricardo Diaz Ramirez
Publisher: Daniel Calabrese; Eleonora Finkelstein
Sales: Emilio Campos
Founded: 1991
Subjects: Education, Literature, Literary Criticism, Essays, Poetry
ISBN Prefix(es): 956-284; 956-7159

Ediciones Rehue Ltda
Argomedo 40, Santiago
Tel: (02) 6344653; (02) 6341804 *Fax:* (02) 6351096
Key Personnel
Dir: Anibal Pastor Ninez
ISBN Prefix(es): 956-228

Revista DATO, *imprint of* Publicaciones Lo Castillo SA

J.C. Saez Editor+
Formerly Dolmen Ediciones SA
Elretiro 4853, Santiago Vitacura
Tel: (02) 3260104
E-mail: jcsaezc@jcsaezeditor.cl
Web Site: www.jcsaezeditor.cl
Key Personnel
General Manager: Juan Carlos Saez Contreras
 E-mail: jcsaezc@vtr.net
Founded: 2002
Subjects: Education, Literature, Literary Criticism, Essays
ISBN Prefix(es): 956-7802

Publicaciones Tecnicas Mediterraneo+
Elidoro Yanez 2541, Providencia, Santiago
Tel: (02) 251 62 57; (02) 233 82 72 *Fax:* (02) 231 06 94
E-mail: msalinero@entelchile.net
Key Personnel
Manager: Ramon Alvarez Minder
Founded: 1981
Membership(s): Chilean Book Association.

Subjects: Medicine, Nursing, Dentistry
ISBN Prefix(es): 956-220

Texido Ltda, see Editorial Texido Ltda

Editorial Texido Ltda+
Av Einstein 921, Recoleta, Santiago
Tel: (02) 6224652 *Fax:* (02) 6224660
Founded: 1969
Subjects: Gardening, Plants, Human Relations, Nonfiction (General)
ISBN Prefix(es): 956-273
Associate Companies: Comercial Distribuidora Librimundi Ltda; Altima Ltda

Ediciones de la Universidad de la Frontera
Av Francisco Salazar, 01145 Temuco
Mailing Address: Casilla 54-D, Temuco
Tel: (045) 325000 *Fax:* (045) 325116
ISBN Prefix(es): 956-236

Universidad de Valparaiso, see Edeval (Universidad de Valparaiso)

Editorial Universitaria SA+
Maria Luisa Santander, 0447 Providencia, Santiago
Tel: (02) 487 0700 *Fax:* (02) 487 0702
E-mail: comunicaciones@universitaria.cl
Web Site: www.universitaria.cl/index.pl *Cable:* EDUNSA
Key Personnel
Man Dir: Rodrigo Castro
Editor: Braulio Fernandez
Founded: 1947
Subjects: Literature, Literary Criticism, Essays, Science (General), Social Sciences, Sociology
ISBN Prefix(es): 84-8340; 956-11
Subsidiaries: Talleres Graficos; Texto Libro
Distributed by Axius (Argentina); Contemporanea de Ediciones (Venezuela); Ediciones Coliguee (Argentina); Ericiencia (Ecuador); Maria Ester Garcia (Paraguay); Librerias Faustos (Argentina); Zulema Medina (Uruguay)
Showroom(s): Sala Matte, Av Libertador B O'Higgins, 1050 Santiago *Fax:* (02) 6956387
Bookshop(s): Latorre 2500, Local 4, Antofagasta *Fax:* (055) 494 864; El Roble 510, Chillan *Fax:* (042) 216 443; Bernardo O'Higgins 770, Local 33, Concepcion *Fax:* (041) 250 867; Cordovez 470, La Serena *Fax:* (051) 224 685; Cochrane 545, Osorno *Fax:* (064) 232 613; Av Dag Hammarskjold S/N, Santiago *Tel:* (02) 210 2477; Av Libertador B O'Higgins 1040, Santiago *Tel:* (02) 487 0991; (02) 487 0990; Av Libertador Bernardo O'Higgins 1050, Santiago *Tel:* (02) 487 0983 *Fax:* (02) 487 0972; Avda Providencia 2110, Santiago; Uno Sur 1111, Talca *Tel:* (071) 213 803; Diego Portales 861, Temuco *Fax:* (045) 215 330; Picarte 461, Local 1, Valdivia *Fax:* (063) 212 645; Esmeralda 1132, Valparaiso *Fax:* (032) 257 573
Shipping Address: Ricardo Matte Perez 04310, Casilla 10220, Providencia, Santiago *Tel:* (02) 2233765 *Fax:* (02) 2099455 (02) 2049058
Orders to: Ricardo Matte Perez 04310, Casilla, 10220 Providencia, Santiago *Tel:* (02) 2233765 *Fax:* (02) 2049058

Ediciones Universitarias de Valparaiso+
12 De Febrero 187, Valparaiso
Tel: (032) 273087; (02) 6332230 *Fax:* (032) 273429
Telex: 230389 Ucval Cl
Key Personnel
Manager: Karlheinz H Laage
Founded: 1970
Subjects: Art, Education, Engineering (General), History, Law, Literature, Literary Criticism, Essays, Music, Dance, Philosophy, Science (General), Social Sciences, Sociology, Technology
ISBN Prefix(es): 956-17

Parent Company: Universidad Catolica de Valparaiso, 12 De Febrero 187, Valparaiso
Branch Office(s)
Moneda 673 - 8 piso, Santiago *Tel:* (02) 633233

Zig-Zag SA+
Los Conquistadores 1700, piso 17 of 17B, Providencia, Santiago
Tel: (02) 335 7477 *Fax:* (02) 335 7545
E-mail: zigzag@rdc.cl
Web Site: www.zigzag.cl
Key Personnel
General Manager: Francisco Perez Frugone
Publishing Manager: Jose Manuel Zanartu
Founded: 1934
Distribuidor en Chile de otros sellos editoriales.
Subjects: Literature, Literary Criticism, Essays
ISBN Prefix(es): 956-12
Distributor for Editorial Atlantida (Argentina); Editorial Voluntad (Colombia)
Showroom(s): Compania 2752, Santiago
Orders to: Compania 2752, Santiago

China

General Information

Capital: Beijing
Language: Principally Northern Chinese (Mandarin). Local dialects spoken in the south & southeast
Religion: Confucianism, Buddhism & Daoism with small Muslim & Christian minorities
Population: 1.2 billion
Shop Hours: Generally 0900-1900 every day
Currency: 100 fen = 10 jiao = 1 yuan
Export/Import Information: Foreign trade is a state monopoly. The foreign distributor for Chinese publications is Guoji Shudian, PO Box 399, Beijing. The importing organization is Waiwen Shudian, PO Box 88, Beijing.
Copyright: UCC, Berne (see Copyright Conventions, pg xi)

Agricultural Publishing House, see China Agriculture Press

Anhui Children's Publishing House+
One Yuejin Rd, Hefei, Anhui 230063
Tel: (0551) 2849306 *Fax:* (0551) 2849306
E-mail: ahsebwsh@mail.hf.ah.cn
Web Site: www.ahse.cn
Key Personnel
President: Jianwei Liu
Chief Editor: Zhirun Zhu
Rights: Li Wang
Founded: 1984
Subjects: Child Care & Development
ISBN Prefix(es): 7-5397
Number of titles published annually: 300 Print
Total Titles: 2,509 Print

Anhui People's Publishing House+
381 Jinzhailu, Hefei, Anhui Providence 230063
Tel: (0551) 257134; (0551) 2653673 *Cable:* 1344
Key Personnel
Dir: Mr Guo Minggang
Founded: 1952
Subjects: Accounting, Advertising, Behavioral Sciences, Economics, Government, Political Science, History, Law, Philosophy, Social Sciences, Sociology
ISBN Prefix(es): 7-212

Aviation Industry Press+
14 Xiaoguan Dongli, Anwai, Beijing 100029
Mailing Address: PO Box 9817, Beijing 100029
Tel: (010) 64918415 *Fax:* (010) 64922211

Key Personnel
Dir General, Editorial Dept: Tiejun Zhang
Founded: 1985
Subjects: Aeronautics, Aviation, Computer Science, Economics, English as a Second Language, Mechanical Engineering
ISBN Prefix(es): 7-80046

Beijing Ancient Books Publishing House+
6 Beisanhuan Zhonglu, Beijing 100011
Tel: (010) 2016699 313; (010) 2013122
Fax: (010) 2012339
E-mail: geo@bph.com.cn *Cable:* 8909
Key Personnel
Rights Dir: Ms Jackie Huang
Founded: 1979
ISBN Prefix(es): 7-5300
Parent Company: Beijing Publishing House

Beijing Arts & Crafts Publishing House
30 Shatan Houjie, Beijing 100006
Tel: (010) 65230677; (010) 4031811
Key Personnel
President: Wang Zhen
Vice President: Wu Peng
Subjects: Art
ISBN Prefix(es): 7-80526
Subsidiaries: Beijing Stars Advertisement Co

Beijing Education Publishing House+
6 Beisanhuan Zhonglu, Beijing 100011
Tel: (010) 2016699-268; (010) 62013122
Fax: (010) 2012339
E-mail: geo@bph.com.cn *Cable:* 8909
Key Personnel
Rights Dir: Ms Jackie Huang
Founded: 1983
Subjects: Education
ISBN Prefix(es): 7-5303
Parent Company: Beijing Publishing House

Beijing Fine Arts & Photography Publishing House+
6 Beisanhuan Zhonglu, Beijing 100011
Tel: (010) 2016699; (010) 62016699-315
Fax: (010) 2012339
E-mail: geo@bph.com.cn *Cable:* 8909
Key Personnel
Rights Dir: Ms Jackie Huang
Founded: 1983
ISBN Prefix(es): 7-80501
Parent Company: Beijing Publishing House

Beijing Juvenile & Children's Books Publishing House+
6 Beisanhuan Zhonglu, Beijing 100011
Tel: (010) 2016699-350; (010) 62013122
Fax: (010) 2012339
E-mail: geo@bph.com.cn *Cable:* 8909
Key Personnel
Rights Dir: Ms Jackie Huang
Founded: 1983
Subjects: Child Care & Development, Education, Self-Help
ISBN Prefix(es): 7-5301
Parent Company: Beijing Publishing House

Beijing Medical University Press+
Beijing Medical University, 38 Xue Yuan Rd, Beijing 100083
Tel: (010) 62092249 *Fax:* (010) 62029848
E-mail: bmupress@public.fhnet.cn.net
Web Site: www.bjmu.edu.cn
Key Personnel
Dir: Dr Lin An *E-mail:* cbi@mail.bjmu.edu.cn
Contacts: Yin-dao Lu; Dipl Ing Zheng-bao Lu
Tel: (010) 62092405
Founded: 1989
Subjects: Biological Sciences, Environmental Studies, Health, Nutrition, Medicine, Nursing, Dentistry, Psychology, Psychiatry

ISBN Prefix(es): 7-81034
Number of titles published annually: 180 Print; 4 CD-ROM
Total Titles: 950 Print; 2 CD-ROM

Beijing Publishing House+
6 Beisanhuan Zhonglu, Beijing 100011
Tel: (010) 62003964 *Fax:* (010) 62012339; (010) 62016699
E-mail: geo@bph.com.cn; public@bphg.com.cn
Web Site: www.bph.com.cn *Cable:* 8909
Founded: 1956
Subjects: Agriculture, Antiques, Architecture & Interior Design, Art, Behavioral Sciences, Biography, Business, Child Care & Development, Computer Science, Cookery, Drama, Theater, Economics, Education, Engineering (General), English as a Second Language, Fiction, Finance, History, How-to, Human Relations, Language Arts, Linguistics, Law, Literature, Literary Criticism, Essays, Management, Marketing, Medicine, Nursing, Dentistry, Nonfiction (General), Philosophy, Physics, Poetry, Science (General), Self-Help, Social Sciences, Sociology, Western Fiction, Women's Studies
ISBN Prefix(es): 7-200

Beijing University Press+
Haidianqu, Beijing 100871
Tel: (010) 62752033 *Fax:* (010) 2564095
E-mail: psj@pup.pku.edu.cn
Key Personnel
President: Peng Songjian
Founded: 1979
Subjects: Biological Sciences, Chemistry, Chemical Engineering, Computer Science, Economics, Education, English as a Second Language, Finance
ISBN Prefix(es): 7-301

CFERT, see China Foreign Economic Relations & Trade Publishing House

Chemical Industry Press+
Huixinli No 3, Chaoyang District, Beijing 100029
Tel: (010) 64918054; (010) 4213641; (010) 4234411 *Fax:* (010) 64918054
Web Site: www.cip.com.cn
Key Personnel
President: Feng Peizong
Rights Manager: Liang Hong *E-mail:* liangh@cip.com.cn
Founded: 1953
Subjects: Agriculture, Biological Sciences, Chemistry, Chemical Engineering, Civil Engineering, Communications, Education, Electronics, Electrical Engineering, Energy, Engineering (General), Environmental Studies, Health, Nutrition, Mechanical Engineering, Medicine, Nursing, Dentistry, Technology, Transportation
ISBN Prefix(es): 7-5025
Number of titles published annually: 1,000 Print
Total Titles: 10,000 Print
Divisions: The Applied Chemistry & Agricultural Reader Publishing Center; Beijing Progress Periodical; The Environmental Science & Engineering Publishing Center; The Fine Chemical Publishing Center; The Industrial Equipment & Information Engineering Publishing Center; The Material Science & Engineering Publishing Center; The Modern Biotech & Medical Sci-Tech Publishing Center; The Multi-Media Publishing Center; The Textbook Publishing Center
Bookshop(s): Chemical Bookstore

Chengdu Maps Publishing House+
Longquanyi, Chengdu, Sichuan 610100
Tel: (028) 485 2177; (028) 445 3030
E-mail: ccph@public.cd.sc.cn *Cable:* 9570
Key Personnel
President: Yao Rusong

Founded: 1985
Membership(s): Sichuan Surveying & Mapping Bureau & Sichuan News Publishing Bureau.
Subjects: Advertising, Communications, Computer Science, Earth Sciences, Education, Foreign Countries, Geography, Geology, Travel
ISBN Prefix(es): 7-80544
Divisions: Mapping Dept, Printing Factory
Distributor for China Cartography Publishing House
Shipping Address: Chengdu Cartography Publishing House, 29 Yikuan N Rd, 3rd Section, Wholesale Dept., Chengdu, Sichuan, PR China

China Agriculture Press+
2 Nongzhanguan North Rd, Chaoyang Dist, Beijing 100026
Tel: (010) 5005665 *Fax:* (010) 5005894
E-mail: fcap@bj.col.com.cn
Key Personnel
President: Cai Shenglin
International Rights: Hui Xu
Founded: 1958
Specialize in agricultural, scientific & technological books.
Subjects: Agriculture, Animals, Pets, Biological Sciences, Gardening, Plants, Technology, Veterinary Science
ISBN Prefix(es): 7-109
Subsidiaries: Rural Readings Press

China Braille Publishing House
39 Chengnei St, Lu Gou Qiao, Beijing 100072
Tel: (010) 6382 5214; (010) 6381 7417
Fax: (010) 6383 3585
Key Personnel
President: Song Jianmin
Founded: 1953
Production of books & magazines in braille & tapes for the blind.
Membership(s): Press & Publication Administration; specialize in braille books; also acts as China Library for the Blind.
Subjects: Animals, Pets, Art, Child Care & Development, Crafts, Games, Hobbies, Disability, Special Needs, Economics, Education, English as a Second Language
ISBN Prefix(es): 7-5002
Subsidiaries: Beijing Hengji Co
Book Club(s): China Library for the Blind; Reading Club

China Cartographic Publishing House+
3 Baizhifang Xijie, Xuanwu Dist, Beijing 100054
Tel: (010) 6356 4947 *Fax:* (010) 6352 9403
E-mail: fanyi@chinamap.com *Cable:* 1955
Key Personnel
President: Wang Jixian
International Rights: Fan Yi
Founded: 1954
Subjects: Earth Sciences, Geography, Geology, Transportation, Travel
ISBN Prefix(es): 7-5031; 7-900048

China Film Press+
22 Beisanhuan Donglu, Beijing 100013
Tel: (010) 4216761; (010) 4219917 *Fax:* (010) 4219489
Telex: 222669 CFP CN *Cable:* 8468 BEIJING
Key Personnel
Editor-in-Chief: Cui Junyan
Founded: 1956
Membership(s): International Film Exchange; specialize in film.
Subjects: Advertising, Art, Biography, Career Development, Crafts, Games, Hobbies, Drama, Theater, Fashion, Fiction, Film, Video, History, Law, Literature, Literary Criticism, Essays, Marketing, Outdoor Recreation, Photography
ISBN Prefix(es): 7-106

Subsidiaries: Beijing Film Book; Shanghai Film Services Co
Bookshop(s): China Film Bookshop

China Foreign Economic Relations & Trade Publishing House+
28 Donghouxiang, Andingmenwai Dajie, Main Bldg, Room 309, Beijing 100710
Tel: (010) 64248236; (010) 64219742; (010) 64245686 *Fax:* (010) 64219392
E-mail: cfertph@263.net
Web Site: www.caitec.org.cn/cfertph/indexv3.htm
Key Personnel
President: Yan Weijing *E-mail:* yanweijing@263.net
Vice President: Song Dongjin
Founded: 1980
Business Books & Magazines.
Subjects: Accounting, Business, Economics, English as a Second Language, Finance, Government, Political Science, Management, Marketing
ISBN Prefix(es): 7-80004

China Forestry Publishing House+
7 Liuhai Hutong, Xichengqu District, Beijing 100009
Tel: (010) 6013117; (010) 661884477 *Fax:* (010) 66180373
E-mail: cfph@public3.bta.net.cn *Cable:* 1010
Key Personnel
Vice Editor-in-Chief: Chen Li
Subjects: Agriculture, Animals, Pets, Biological Sciences, Chemistry, Chemical Engineering, Economics, Gardening, Plants
ISBN Prefix(es): 7-5038
Distributed by University of British Columbia Press (UBC Press) (North America)

China Labour Publishing House+
One Huixin Dongjie Chaoyangqu, Beijing 100029
Tel: (010) 64911180; (010) 4910488
Key Personnel
President: Yunqi Tang
Editor-in-Chief: Wang Jianxin
Deputy Editor-in-Chief: Mengxin Zhang
Sales Dir: Hongrui Li
Production Dir: Yongguang Xie
Publicity Dir: Zhang Jiasheng
Rights & Permissions: Chao Zhou
Founded: 1980
Subjects: Business, Labor, Industrial Relations
ISBN Prefix(es): 7-5045

China Light Industry Press+
6 Dongchanganjie St, Beijing 100740
Tel: (010) 65271562 *Fax:* (010) 65121371 *Cable:* 1508
Key Personnel
President: Zhao Ti-Qing
Founded: 1954
Subjects: Art, Cookery, Fashion, Film, Video, House & Home, Language Arts, Linguistics, Wine & Spirits
ISBN Prefix(es): 7-5019

China Machine Press (CMP)+
22 Baiwanzhuang Rd, Beijing 100037
Tel: (010) 88379973 *Fax:* (010) 68320405 (orders)
E-mail: cjhui@mail.machineinfo.gov.cn
Web Site: www.cmpbook.com; www.machineinfo.gov.cn
Telex: 222557 STIP CN
Key Personnel
President: Wang Wenbin
Vice President: Li Qi
Sales: Tang Xiaoming
Production: Cheng Jingning
Publicity: Xu Tong
Rights & Permissions, I D D Dir: Chen Jianhui

Founded: 1952
Subjects: Architecture & Interior Design, Automotive, Business, Computer Science, Electronics, Electrical Engineering, Management, Mechanical Engineering, Microcomputers, Technology, Foreign Languages, Telecommunications
ISBN Prefix(es): 7-111
Number of titles published annually: 3,000 Print; 130 CD-ROM
Associate Companies: Jingfeng Printing Company of China Machine Press, 88 Liuzhuangzi, Fengtai District, Beijing 100071 *Tel:* (010) 63793671; The Printing Company of China Machine Press, 4 Ganjiakou, Haidian District, Beijing 100037 *Tel:* (010) 68353476
Subsidiaries: Huazhang Graphics & Information Co
Bookshop(s): Jigong Bookstore *Tel:* (010) 88379641
Warehouse: Huaxiang, Beijing 100071

China Materials Management Publishing House+
25 Yuetan Beijie, Xichengqu District, Beijing 100834
Tel: (010) 68392913; (010) 68392825 *Fax:* (010) 8392911 *Cable:* 1444
Key Personnel
President: Fan Xiyi
General Editor: Zhang Lizhong
Founded: 1981
Subjects: Automotive, Behavioral Sciences, Business, Economics, Human Relations, Management, Marketing
ISBN Prefix(es): 7-5047
Book Club(s): China Copyright Association

China Ocean Press+
Subsidiary of State Oceanic Administration
8 Da Hui Si Rd, Haidian District, Beijing 100081
Tel: (010) 62112880-888 *Fax:* (010) 62112880-617
E-mail: zbs@oceanpress.com.cn
Web Site: www.oceanpress.com.cn
Key Personnel
President: Gai Guangsheng
Editor-in-Chief: Miss Yang Suihua
Dir, International Dept: Miss Yang Qing
Tel: (010) 62173322, ext 212
Founded: 1978
Publish mainly in English, other languages available; specialize in marine science & technology.
Subjects: Biography, Biological Sciences, Chemistry, Chemical Engineering, Civil Engineering, Computer Science, Earth Sciences, Environmental Studies, Geography, Geology, Management, Maritime, Mechanical Engineering, Physical Sciences, Physics, Real Estate, Religion - Buddhist, Religion - Islamic, Religion - Jewish, Science (General), Social Sciences, Sociology, Technology
ISBN Prefix(es): 7-5027
Number of titles published annually: 10 Print
Total Titles: 300 Print

China Oil & Gas Periodical Office+
One Lou, 2 Qu Anhuali, Andingmenwai, Beijing 100011
Tel: (010) 64219111
Key Personnel
Editor-in-Chief: Zhaoren Li
Distribution Manager: Baoguo Wu
Founded: 1994
Subjects: Energy
ISBN Prefix(es): 7-5021

China Pictorial Publishing House
33 Chegongzhuang Xilu, Haidian District, Beijing 100044

Tel: (010) 68412392; (010) 68414896; (010) 68412665 *Fax:* (010) 68413023
E-mail: wangjingtang@hotmail.com
Web Site: www.china-pictorial.com *Cable:* CHINAPIC 3973
Key Personnel
Contact: Li Lian
Founded: 1985
ISBN Prefix(es): 7-80024

China Social Sciences Publishing House+
A158 Gulou Xidajie, Beijing 100720
Tel: (010) 64031534 *Fax:* (010) 64074509
Key Personnel
Dir, Social Sciences: Wang Baochun
Dir, Reader Services: Wana Shan
Dir: Cui Yaqin
Founded: 1978
Specialize in the task of editing & publishing monographs, reference books, teaching materials & basic reading materials in the fields of philosophy & social sciences as well as Chinese translations of major foreign works, publisher for Social Sciences in China (Journal of Cass) & periodicals for several research institutes.
Subjects: Philosophy, Social Sciences, Sociology
ISBN Prefix(es): 7-5004
Bookshop(s): A62 Jianguomennei Dajie, Benjing 100005; 31 Book-Town Haidian Dajie, Bejing 10080

China Textile Press+
Subsidiary of China National Textile Industry Council (CNTIC)
No 6, Dongzhimen Nandajie, Beijing 100027
Tel: (010) 64168240 *Fax:* (010) 64168225
Web Site: www.c-textilep.com
Key Personnel
President: Chen Zhishan
Administrative Vice President: Li Lingshen
Editor-in-Chief: Zheng Qun
Copyright Manager: Li Jing *E-mail:* jing_lg@163.com
Textile & clothing technology, arts & crafts, business & management, culture & life style.
Membership(s): The Publishers Association of China.
Subjects: Business, Crafts, Games, Hobbies, Management
ISBN Prefix(es): 7-5064

China Theatre Publishing House+
A81 Dazhongsi Nancun, Haidianqu, Beijing 100086
Tel: (010) 62244207; (010) 62244208
Key Personnel
President: Li Haichuan
Founded: 1957
Subjects: Crafts, Games, Hobbies, Drama, Theater, Education, Fiction, History, Literature, Literary Criticism, Essays, Nonfiction (General)
ISBN Prefix(es): 7-104

China Tibetology Publishing House+
131 Beisihuandonglu, Beijing 100101
Tel: (010) 64917618; (010) 64932942 *Fax:* (010) 4917619
Key Personnel
Dir: Tendzin Sr
Editor-in-Chief: Liao Zugui
Specialize in Tibetan studies.
Subjects: Anthropology, Archaeology, Asian Studies, Economics, Education, Religion - Buddhist, Social Sciences, Sociology
ISBN Prefix(es): 7-80057
Orders to: China International Book Trading Corporation, PO Box 399, Beijing 100080

China Translation & Publishing Corp+
4 Taipingqiao Dajie, Xichengqu District, Beijing 100810
Tel: (010) 66168196; (010) 66168647 *Fax:* (010) 6022734
E-mail: ctpc@public.bta.net.cn
Key Personnel
Contact: Xu Jihong
International Rights & Deputy General Manager: Hsuan-chin Chou
Subjects: Economics, Education, Management
ISBN Prefix(es): 7-5001

China Youth Publishing House+
21 Dongsi Shiertiao, Beijing 100708
Tel: (010) 64033812; (010) 64032266 *Fax:* (010) 4031803 *Cable:* 4357
Key Personnel
President: Cai Yun
Editor: Kan Daolong
Contact: Mr Bingbin Bi
Founded: 1950
Subjects: Education, Language Arts, Linguistics, Literature, Literary Criticism, Essays, Science (General), Social Sciences, Sociology
ISBN Prefix(es): 7-5006

Chinese Literature Press+
24 Baiwanzhuang Rd, Beijing 100037
Tel: (010) 68326678 *Fax:* (010) 68326678
E-mail: chinalit@public.east.cn.net
Key Personnel
Commissioning Editor: Zhang Shaoning
Contact: Shen Jieying
Founded: 1951 (English); 1964 French)
Subjects: Art, Fiction, Poetry
ISBN Prefix(es): 7-5071
Parent Company: China International Publishing Group
Orders to: China International Book Trading Corp (CIBTC), PO Box 399, Beijing 100044

Chinese Pedagogics Publishing House+
24 Baiwanzhuanglu Rd, Beijing 100037
Mailing Address: PO Box 399, Beijing 10004
Tel: (010) 68326333 *Fax:* (010) 8317390
Telex: 222475 FLP CN *Cable:* FOLAPRESS BEIJING
Key Personnel
President & Chief Executive: Shan Ying
Tel: (010) 68994599
Editor-in-Chief: Jia Yinhuai
Sales (Overseas Dept Sinolingua) & Publicity: Hui Han
Rights & Permissions: Ling Yu
Founded: 1985
Specialize in teaching Chinese as a foreign language.
Membership(s): China International Publishing Group.
Subjects: Education, Language Arts, Linguistics
ISBN Prefix(es): 7-80052
Total Titles: 300 Print; 30 Audio
Parent Company: Foreign Languages Press
Associate Companies: China International Book Trading Corporation, 35 Chegong-zhuang Xilu, Beijing 100044 *Fax:* (010) 68412023 *E-mail:* om@mail.cibtc.com.cn
Branch Office(s)
CBT China Book Trading GmbH, Max-Planck Str 6-A, 63322 Rodermark, Germany *Fax:* (0674) 95271 *E-mail:* chinabook@aol.com
Cypress Book Co Ltd, 10 Swinton St, London WC1X 9NX, United Kingdom *Fax:* (020) 7833 0220
U.S. Office(s): Cypress Books (US) Co Inc, 450 Third St, Unit 4B, San Francisco, CA 94124, United States
Distributed by China Books & Periodicals
Shipping Address: China International Book Trading Corporation, 35 Chegong-zhuang Xilu, Beijing 100044 *Fax:* (010) 68412023 *E-mail:* om@mail.cibtc.com.cn; CBT China Book Trading GmbH, Max-Planck Str 6-A, 63322 Rodermark, Germany *Fax:* (0674) 95271 *E-mail:* chinabook@aol.com
Warehouse: China International Book Trading Corporation, 35 Chegong-zhuang Xilu, Beijing 100044 *Fax:* (010) 68412023 *E-mail:* om@mail.cibtc.com.cn
CBT China Book Trading GmbH, Max-Planck Str 6-A, 63322 Rodermark, Germany *Fax:* (0674) 95271 *E-mail:* chinabook@aol.com
Orders to: Cypress Book Co (UK) Ltd, 10 Swinton St, London WC1X 9NX, United Kingdom *Fax:* (020) 7837 7768
CBT China Book Trading GmbH, Max-Planck Str 6-A, 63322 Rodermark, Germany *Tel:* (0674) 95271 *E-mail:* chinabook@aol.com
Cypress Books (US) Co Inc, 450 Third St, Unit 4B, San Francisco, CA 94124, United States

Chongqing University Press+
No 174 Shapingba Zhengjie, Chongqing 400030
Tel: (023) 65111125 *Fax:* (023) 65106879
E-mail: chenxy@cqup.com.cn
Web Site: www.cqup.com.cn
Key Personnel
Dir: Zhang Gesheng
Founded: 1985
Subjects: Language Arts, Linguistics, Management, Science (General), Social Sciences, Sociology, Technology
ISBN Prefix(es): 7-5624
Number of titles published annually: 500 Print
Total Titles: 4,000 Print

CITIC Publishing House+
Ta Yuan Diplomatic Office Bldg, No 14, Liangmahe St, Chaoyang District, Beijing 100600
Tel: (010) 85323366 *Fax:* (010) 85322508
E-mail: g-office@citic.com.cn; mail@citicpub.com
Web Site: www.citic.com.cn; www.publish.citic.com
Telex: 210026 CITIC CN
Key Personnel
Chairman: Wang Jun
Vice Chairman & President: Kong Dan
Chief Editor: Li Debao
Senior Revisor: Gong Yuang
Senior Editor: He Peihui
Founded: 1988
Specialize in both copyright transactions & co-publication of books with foreign publishers, bookdealers or any other relevant groups or individuals, & launching joint ventures on business in publication & distribution.
Subjects: Accounting, Business, Economics, Finance, How-to, Law, Management, Marketing, Nonfiction (General)
ISBN Prefix(es): 7-80073
Parent Company: China International Trust & Investment Corporation (Holdings)
Associate Companies: CITIC Representative Office in Japan, 3/F, The Landic Third Akasaka Bldg, 2-3-2, Akasaka, Minato-Ku, Tokyo 107-0052, Japan *Tel:* (03) 35842636 *Fax:* (03) 35056235 *E-mail:* citic.tyo@nifty.com; CITIC Representative Office in New York, 350 Albany St, New York, NY 10280, United States *Tel:* 212-945-4068 *Fax:* 212-945-0273 *E-mail:* citicny@msn.com; CITIC Representative Office in Europe, HongKongstr 5, 3047 BR Rotterdam, Netherlands *Tel:* (010) 4626 588 *Fax:* (010) 2624 768

CMP, see China Machine Press (CMP)

Cultural Relics Publishing House+
Affiliate of Chinese Administration For Cultural Heritage
29 Wusi Dajie, Beijing 100009
Tel: (010) 64048057 *Fax:* (010) 64010698
E-mail: web@wenwu.com
Web Site: www.wenwu.com

Key Personnel
International Division: Mr Zhao Lihua *Tel:* (010) 64048057
Founded: 1957
Subjects: Anthropology, Antiques, Archaeology, Art, Asian Studies, History
ISBN Prefix(es): 7-5010
Divisions: International Division
Orders to: International Division, 29 Wusi Dajie, Beijing 100009

CWPP, see Water Resources and Electric Power Press (CWPP)

Dalian Maritime University Press+
One Linghai Rd, Dalian 116026
Tel: (0411) 84729480; (0411) 84728394 *Fax:* (0411) 84727996
E-mail: dmup@dmupress.com; cbs@dmupress.com
Web Site: www.dmupress.com
Key Personnel
Dir: Yuan Linxin
Founded: 1987
Subjects: Communications, Computer Science, Economics, Electronics, Electrical Engineering, English as a Second Language, Management, Maritime, Science (General)
ISBN Prefix(es): 7-5632

Dolphin Books+
24 Baiwanzhanglu, Beijing 100037
Tel: (010) 68326332 *Fax:* (010) 8317390
Telex: 222475 Flp *Cable:* FOLAPRESS BEIJING
Key Personnel
Dir: Jiang Cheng'an
Publicity & Production: Zhangyun He
Founded: 1986
Specialize in illustrated children's books.
ISBN Prefix(es): 7-80051; 7-80138
Parent Company: Foreign Languages Press
U.S. Office(s): Cypress Book (US) Co Inc, 3450 Third St, Unit 4B, San Francisco, CA 94124, United States *Tel:* (415) 821-3582
Shipping Address: China International Book Trading Corporation, 35 Chegong-zhuang Zilu, Beijing 100044
Warehouse: China International Book Trading Corporation, 35 Chegong-zhuang Zilu, Beijing 100044
Orders to: Cypress Book Co (UK) Ltd, 10 Swinton St, London WC1X 9NX, United Kingdom
Cypress Book (US) Co Inc, 3450 Third St, Unit 4B, San Francisco, CA 94124, United States *Tel:* 415-821-3582

East China Normal University Press+
N Zhongshan Rd 3663, Shanghai 200062
Tel: (021) 62232613 *Fax:* (021) 62864922
E-mail: lxb@ecnu.edu.cn
Web Site: www.ecnu.edu.cn
Key Personnel
President: Wang Jianpan
Editor: Jin Qin Xiang
Author: Kuan Guang Ye
Founded: 1957
ISBN Prefix(es): 7-5617
Subsidiaries: Da Hua Industry & Trade Co

East China University of Science & Technology Press
130 Meilong Rd, Shanghai 200237
Tel: (021) 64132885 *Fax:* (021) 64250735
Web Site: www.ecust.edu.cn *Cable:* 9006
Key Personnel
President: Wang Xingyu
Founded: 1986
Subjects: Agriculture, Computer Science, Education, Engineering (General), English as a Second Language, Environmental Studies, Finance, Technology
ISBN Prefix(es): 7-5628

Education Science Publishing House
46 Beisanhuan Zhonglu, Beijing 100088
Tel: (010) 62102454; (010) 62013803 *Fax:* (010) 62012454
E-mail: esph@public.net.china.com.cn
Key Personnel
International Rights: Ms Li Bin *Tel:* (010) 62003353
Founded: 1980
Subjects: Education, English as a Second Language, Human Relations, Military Science, Natural History, Science Fiction, Fantasy
ISBN Prefix(es): 7-5041
Total Titles: 1,866 Print; 12 Audio
Parent Company: Yan-Li Gin
Ultimate Parent Company: Xu-Chang Fa

Electronics Industry Publishing House
PO Box 173, Wanshoulu, Beijing 100036
Tel: (010) 68253874; (010) 68233825 *Fax:* (010) 86106821-4062
Key Personnel
President: Mr Liang Xiang Feng
International Rights: Mr Huang Zhi Yu
Subjects: Communications, Computer Science, Electronics, Electrical Engineering, Microcomputers, Radio, TV
ISBN Prefix(es): 7-5053

Encyclopedia of China Publishing House+
17 Fuchengmen Bei Dajie, Beijing 100037
Tel: (010) 68315610 *Fax:* (010) 68316510
E-mail: ygh@bj.col.com.cn *Cable:* ECPH
Key Personnel
President: Shan Jifu
Founded: 1978
Subjects: Art, Education, Fiction, Technology
ISBN Prefix(es): 7-5000
Subsidiaries: Knowledge Publishing House

First Edition, *imprint of* Jinan Publishing House

Foreign Language Teaching & Research Press+
No 19, Xisanhuabeilu, Beijing 100081
Tel: (010) 68420958; (010) 68420959 *Fax:* (010) 68420956
Key Personnel
President: Li Pengyi
Vice President, Sales & Publishing Manager: Zhao Wenyan
Assistant President & Head of the Inter-area & International Cooperation Dept: Yu Chunchi
Chief, General Editorial Office: Lei Hang
Chief, First Editorial Section: Wang Weiguo
Chief, Second Editorial Section: Cai Jianfeng
Chief, Third Editorial Section: Xu Jianzhong
Chief, Fourth Editorial Section: Xu Chunjian
Editorial Manager, Publicity & Rights & Permissions: Zheng Jiande
Head, Inter-Area & International Cooperation Dept: Yu Chanchi
Chief, Finance Section: Ge Jusheng
Founded: 1979
Subjects: English as a Second Language, Foreign Countries, History, Language Arts, Linguistics, Literature, Literary Criticism, Essays, Social Sciences, Sociology, Western Fiction
ISBN Prefix(es): 7-5600; 7-900626

Foreign Languages Press+
24 Baiwanzhuang Rd, Xicheng District, Beijing 100037
Tel: (010) 68995852; (010) 68996188
E-mail: flpcn@public3.bta.net.cn
Web Site: www.flp.com.cn
Telex: 222475 FLP CN *Cable:* FOLAPRESS BEIJING
Key Personnel
President: Xu Mingqiang
Vice President: Li Zhengno
Over Seas Dept Dir & Rights & Permissions: Sun Haiyu
Founded: 1952
Published Languages (in addition to Chinese): Arabic, Bengali, English, French, German, Hindi, Indonesian, Italian, Japanese, Korean, Myanmar, Portuguese, Russian, Spanish, Swahili, Urdu, & Vietnamese.
Subjects: Anthropology, Archaeology, Art, Biography, Cookery, Drama, Theater, Economics, Geography, Geology, Government, Political Science, History, Law, Literature, Literary Criticism, Essays, Medicine, Nursing, Dentistry, Philosophy, Science (General), Sports, Athletics, Travel
ISBN Prefix(es): 7-119
Total Titles: 1,500 Print; 40 Audio
Parent Company: China International Publishing Group
Imprints: Phoenix
Subsidiaries: Dolphin Books; Sinolingua
U.S. Office(s): Cypress Book Co Inc, 3450 Third St, Suite 4B, San Francisco, CA, United States *Tel:* 415-821-3582
Orders to: Cypress Book (US) Co Inc, 3450 Third St, Suite 4B, San Francisco, CA 94124, United States
Cypress Book Co (UK) Ltd, 10 Swinton St, London WC1X 9NX, United Kingdom

Fudan University Press+
579 Guoquanlu, Shanghai 200433
Tel: (021) 5484906-2842 *Fax:* (021) 65104812; (021) 65642840
E-mail: fupirc@fudan.edu.cn
Key Personnel
President: Zhiwei Xu
Dir: Xianghua Lin
Founded: 1981
Subjects: Accounting, Advertising, Art, Asian Studies, Behavioral Sciences, Biography, Biological Sciences, Business, Chemistry, Chemical Engineering, Communications, Computer Science, Economics, Education, Electronics, Electrical Engineering, English as a Second Language, Finance, Genealogy, Geography, Geology, Government, Political Science, Health, Nutrition, History, How-to, Human Relations, Language Arts, Linguistics, Law, Library & Information Sciences, Literature, Literary Criticism, Essays, Management, Marketing, Mathematics, Microcomputers, Natural History, Philosophy, Photography, Physical Sciences, Physics, Poetry, Psychology, Psychiatry, Public Administration, Regional Interests, Religion - Buddhist, Science (General), Securities, Social Sciences, Sociology, Technology, Women's Studies, Comprehensive
ISBN Prefix(es): 7-309; 7-900606

Fujian Children's Publishing House+
59 Deguixiang, Fuzhou, Fujian Province 350001
Fax: (0591) 7539070
E-mail: fcph@163.net
Subjects: Art, Education, Humor, Literature, Literary Criticism, Essays
ISBN Prefix(es): 7-5395
Total Titles: 320 Print

Fujian Science & Technology Publishing House+
59 Deguixiang, Fuzhou, Fujian 350001
Tel: (0591) 7538745; (0591) 7538623 *Fax:* (0591) 7538472
Founded: 1979
Subjects: Agriculture, Communications, Computer Science, Electronics, Electrical Engineering, Health, Nutrition, Medicine, Nursing, Dentistry, Science (General), Technology, Transportation
ISBN Prefix(es): 7-5335
Total Titles: 300 Print
Parent Company: Fujian General Publishing House

PUBLISHERS   CHINA

Geological Publishing House+
10 Lou, 7 Qu, Hepingli, Beijing 100083
Tel: (010) 62351944 *Fax:* (010) 6024523
Telex: 22531 MGMRC
Key Personnel
Man Dir & Rights & Permissions: Ma Qingyang
Editor-in-Chief: Shen Shurong
Sales Manager: Xu Yixiao
Production Manager: Wei Hongzhen
Founded: 1954
Subjects: Geography, Geology
ISBN Prefix(es): 7-116
Bookshop(s): Geological Bookshop, Xisi, Beijing

Guangdong Science & Technology Press+
13-14F/11 Shuiyin Rd, Guangzhou, Guangdong 510075
Tel: (020) 87768688; (020) 87618770 (Directorial Office); (020) 87769412 (Foreign Cooperation Editorial Office) *Fax:* (020) 87764169
E-mail: gdkjwb@ns.guangzhou.gb.com.cn
Web Site: www.xwcbj.gd.gov.cn *Cable:* 3934
Key Personnel
President: Ouyang Lian
International Rights: Yunfei (Violet) Ding
Founded: 1979
Subjects: Agriculture, Architecture & Interior Design, Computer Science, Cookery, English as a Second Language, Gardening, Plants, Mathematics, Medicine, Nursing, Dentistry
ISBN Prefix(es): 7-5359; 7-900341

Guizhou Education Publishing House
289 Zhonghua Beilu, Guiyang, Guizhou Province 550001
Tel: (0851) 627904; (0851) 524211
Key Personnel
President: Jize Zhang
Founded: 1990
Subjects: Art, Chemistry, Chemical Engineering, Child Care & Development, Economics, Education, Gardening, Plants, History, Human Relations
ISBN Prefix(es): 7-80583

Heilongjiang Science & Technology Press+
41 Jianshejie Nangangqu, Harbin, Heilongjiang Province 150001
Tel: (0451) 3635613 *Fax:* (0451) 3642127
Key Personnel
President: Xiao Erbin
International Rights: Liu Zhong
Founded: 1979
Subjects: Advertising, Agriculture, Architecture & Interior Design, Business, Communications, Economics, Electronics, Electrical Engineering, Health, Nutrition, How-to, Management, Marketing, Medicine, Nursing, Dentistry, Photography, Physical Sciences, Science (General), Technology, Transportation, Veterinary Science
ISBN Prefix(es): 7-5388

Henan Science & Technology Publishing House+
66 Jingwu Rd, Zhengzhou, Henan Province 450002
Tel: (0371) 5727616; (0371) 5721756-643 *Fax:* (0371) 5727616
E-mail: hnkj565@public2.zz.ha.cn *Cable:* 5171
Key Personnel
President & Rights Contact: Li Jing-lin
Editor-in-Chief: Yuan Yuan *Tel:* (0371) 5727616
Rights Contact: Ms Liu Xin
Founded: 1980
Specialize in scientific & technological subjects.
Subjects: Architecture & Interior Design, Biological Sciences, Chemistry, Chemical Engineering, Gardening, Plants, Mechanical Engineering, Medicine, Nursing, Dentistry, Physical Sciences, Living
ISBN Prefix(es): 7-5349
Total Titles: 300 Print

Parent Company: News & Publishing Bureau of Henan Province, Hong Kong
Ultimate Parent Company: News & Publicity Bureau of China

HEP, *imprint of* Higher Education Press

Higher Education Press+
4 Dewai Dajie, Xicheng District, Beijing 100011
Tel: (010) 58581862 *Fax:* (010) 82085552
Web Site: www.hep.edu.cn; www.hep.com.cn
Cable: 7559
Key Personnel
President: Liu Zhipeng
Vice President & Editor-in-Chief: Zhang Zengshun
Dir, International Cooperation Division: Li Min
 E-mail: limin@hep.com.cn
Founded: 1954
Publications for textbooks & references in higher education, vocational & adult educational.
Subjects: Agriculture, Architecture & Interior Design, Biological Sciences, Civil Engineering, Computer Science, Cookery, Education, Engineering (General), English as a Second Language, Finance, Gardening, Plants, Geography, Geology, History, Language Arts, Linguistics, Management, Psychology, Psychiatry, Science (General), Social Sciences, Sociology, Technology, Travel, Women's Studies
ISBN Prefix(es): 7-04; 7-900076
Number of titles published annually: 4,000 Print
Total Titles: 12,000 Print
Parent Company: Ministry of Education
Imprints: HEP
Subsidiaries: Beijing Kewen Higher Education Co Ltd
Divisions: Shanghai Office

IAP, *see* International Academic Publishers (IAP)

Inner Mongolia Science & Technology Publishing House+
4 Nanyiduan, Hadajie, Chifengshi, Inner Mongolia 024000
Tel: (0476) 82222 942 *Cable:* 5536
Key Personnel
President: Edensanbu
Founded: 1982
Subjects: Agriculture, Astronomy, Electronics, Electrical Engineering, Mathematics, Microcomputers, Physics, Publishing & Book Trade Reference, Science (General), Veterinary Science
ISBN Prefix(es): 7-5380

International Academic Publishers (IAP)
Xizhimenwai Dajie, Beijing Exhibition Centre, Beijing 100044
Tel: (010) 8316677-530 *Fax:* (010) 4015664
Telex: 22313 CPC CN
Key Personnel
Dir: Lu Bohua
Founded: 1988
Subjects: Agriculture, Biological Sciences, Chemistry, Chemical Engineering, Computer Science, Electronics, Electrical Engineering, Engineering (General), Medicine, Nursing, Dentistry, Technology
ISBN Prefix(es): 1-58868

International Culture Publishing Corp+
40 Andingmennei Dajie, Beijing 100009
Tel: (010) 64013415 *Fax:* (010) 64013437
Founded: 1984
ISBN Prefix(es): 7-80049

Jiangsu Juveniles & Children's Publishing House
14F Phoenix Palace Hotel, 47 Hunan Rd, Nanjing, Jiangsu 210009

Tel: (025) 83242938 *Fax:* (025) 83242350
E-mail: susao@publicl.ptt.js.en
Key Personnel
Rights Contact: Xiaohong Wu
Publish books for children under 15 years old including picture books, literature & parenting books.
ISBN Prefix(es): 7-5346

Jiangsu People's Publishing House+
156 Zhongyanglu, Jiangsu, Nanjing 210009
Tel: (025) 86634309 *Fax:* (025) 83379766
Web Site: www.book-wind.com
Telex: 0512
ISBN Prefix(es): 7-214

Jiangsu Science & Technology Publishing House+
47 Hunan Road, Nanjing, Jiangsu 210009
Tel: (025) 83273033 *Fax:* (025) 83273111
E-mail: cnjsstph@publicl.ptt.js.cn
Web Site: www.jskjpub.com
Key Personnel
President: Ming Xiu Hu
International Dept: Helen Deng; LianMin Sun
Founded: 1978
Subjects: Chemistry, Chemical Engineering, Computer Science, Earth Sciences, Engineering (General), Environmental Studies, Geography, Geology, Health, Nutrition, Physical Sciences, Science (General), Technology
ISBN Prefix(es): 7-5345

Jilin Science & Technology Publishing House+
A22 Tongzhijie, Changchun, Jilin 130021
Tel: (0431) 5635185 *Fax:* (0431) 5635185
E-mail: jlkjcbs@public.ec.jl.cn
Key Personnel
Rights Director: Frank Young
 E-mail: frankyoung@sina.com
Founded: 1984
Publishing house.
Subjects: Accounting, Advertising, Agriculture, Animals, Pets, Anthropology, Architecture & Interior Design, Astronomy, Automotive, Biography, Biological Sciences, Business, Career Development, Chemistry, Chemical Engineering, Child Care & Development, Civil Engineering, Computer Science, Cookery, Electronics, Electrical Engineering, Engineering (General), English as a Second Language, Environmental Studies, Health, Nutrition, House & Home, How-to, Management, Marketing, Mathematics, Mechanical Engineering, Medicine, Nursing, Dentistry, Microcomputers, Outdoor Recreation, Photography, Physical Sciences, Physics, Science (General), Science Fiction, Fantasy, Sports, Athletics, Technology, Travel, Veterinary Science
ISBN Prefix(es): 7-5384
Number of titles published annually: 200 Print
Total Titles: 500 Print

Jinan Publishing House+
251 Jingqilu, Jinan, Shandong 250001
Tel: (0531) 6913006
Key Personnel
President: Weng Cheng
Founded: 1988
Subjects: Agriculture, Cookery, Economics, Education, Medicine, Nursing, Dentistry, Nonfiction (General), Social Sciences, Sociology
ISBN Prefix(es): 7-80572; 7-80629
Imprints: First Edition

Juvenile & Children's Publishing House
1538 Yan'an Road W, Shanghai 200052
Tel: (021) 62823025 *Fax:* (021) 62526963
Web Site: www.jcph.com
ISBN Prefix(es): 7-5324

Knowledge Press+
17 Fuchengmen Beidajie, Beijing 100037
Tel: (010) 68315610 *Fax:* (010) 68316510
E-mail: ecphtdb@public3.bta.net.cn *Cable:* ECPH
Key Personnel
President: Zhai Defang
Subjects: Civil Engineering, Health, Nutrition, Human Relations, Science (General), Social Sciences, Sociology
ISBN Prefix(es): 7-5015

Kunlun Publishing House+
3A Maowu Hutong, Xishiku, Beijing 100034
Tel: (010) 6732721 *Fax:* (010) 62183683; (010) 66847703
Key Personnel
President: Cheng Bu-tao
Vice President: Fan Chuan-xin; Zhu Ya-nan
Founded: 1951
Subjects: Biography, Literature, Literary Criticism, Essays, Military Science, Nonfiction (General), Social Sciences, Sociology
ISBN Prefix(es): 7-80040
Parent Company: The Cultural Dept of the General Political Dep
Bookshop(s): 36 Middle North Sanhuan Rd, Beijing 100084

Language Publishing House+
51 Nanxiaojie Chaonei, Beijing 100010
Tel: (010) 65130349; (010) 65241766
Key Personnel
President: Li Xingjian
Founded: 1980
Subjects: Communications
ISBN Prefix(es): 7-80126

Lanzhou University Press+
216 Tianshuilu, Lanzhou, Gansu 730000
Mailing Address: General Edition Office, 308 Tianshui Rd, Lanzhou, Gansu 730000
Tel: (0931) 8843000-3514 *Fax:* (0931) 8615095
E-mail: press@lzu.edu.cn
Key Personnel
Chairman: Prof Li Ji-Jun *Tel:* (0931) 891-1282 *Fax:* (0931) 891-1282 *E-mail:* lijj@lzu.edu.cn
President: Mr Yu Zejun
Vice President: Mr Lei Hongchang; Mrs Rao Hui
General Editor: Mr Zhang Kefei
Founded: 1985
Subjects: Behavioral Sciences, Economics, Education, Government, Political Science, History, Law, Philosophy, Physics, Psychology, Psychiatry, Social Sciences, Sociology
ISBN Prefix(es): 7-311
Bookshop(s): 268 Tianshui Rd, Lanzhou University, Lanzhou, Gansu 730000

The Law Publishing House
17 Denglai Hutong, Guangneidajie, Xuanwuqu, Beijing 100073
Tel: (010) 63266796; (010) 63266790
Key Personnel
Executive Dir, Editorial: Lan Ming-Liang
Sales: Wang Jia-jing
Production, Publicity: Ling Yu-jie
Rights & Permissions: Jiang Xou Yuan
Founded: 1980
Also acts as book packager.
Subjects: Law
ISBN Prefix(es): 7-5036

Liaoning People's Publishing House+
108 Beiyi Malu, Hepingqu, Shenyang, Liaoning 110001
Tel: (024) 3864674; (024) 3863316 *Fax:* (024) 371472 *Cable:* 3652
Key Personnel
Chief Executive: Ren Huiying
Editorial Dir: Li Fan
Sales: Li Wenshan

Founded: 1951
Subjects: Economics, History
ISBN Prefix(es): 7-205
Subsidiaries: Liao-Shen Publishing House

Metallurgical Industry Press (MIP)+
39 Songzhuyuan Beixiang, Beiheyuan Dajie, Beijing 100009
Tel: (010) 64013877; (010) 64015599 *Fax:* (010) 64013877
Telex: 222753 CMMI CN *Cable:* 3658
Key Personnel
President: Qing Qiyun
Sales: Yang Jin
Editor-in-Chief: Yang Chuanfu; Liu Shan
Founded: 1953
Subjects: Chemistry, Chemical Engineering, Computer Science, Earth Sciences, Electronics, Electrical Engineering, Engineering (General), Environmental Studies, Geography, Geology, Management, Mathematics, Mechanical Engineering, Technology
ISBN Prefix(es): 7-5024

MIP, see Metallurgical Industry Press (MIP)

Modern Press
504 Anhuali, Andingmenwai, Beijing 100011
Tel: (010) 4215031-383 *Fax:* (010) 4214540 *Cable:* 1200
Key Personnel
President: Lou Ming
ISBN Prefix(es): 7-80028

Morning Glory Press+
35 Chegongzhuang Xilu, Beijing 100044
Tel: (010) 68411973; (010) 68433187 *Fax:* (010) 68412023; (010) 68485739
E-mail: zh@mail.cibtc.com.cn; zh1@mail.cibtc.com.cn *Cable:* CIBTC BEIJING
Key Personnel
Contact: Ms Zheng Wenlei
Founded: 1982
Copyright transfer; purchase of entire editions.
Subjects: Art, Cookery, History, Photography
ISBN Prefix(es): 7-5054
Parent Company: China International Book Trading Corporation

Nanjing University Press+
Nanjing University, 22 Hankoulu Rd, Nanjing, Jiangsu 210093
Tel: (025) 83593450; (025) 83303347
Web Site: press.nju.edu.cn
Key Personnel
President: Shi Huirong
Founded: 1984
Subjects: Biography, Biological Sciences, Chemistry, Chemical Engineering, Computer Science, Earth Sciences, Economics, English as a Second Language, Environmental Studies
ISBN Prefix(es): 7-305

National Defence Industry Press+
23 Zizhuyuan Nanlu, Beijing 100044
Tel: (010) 68412244; (010) 6842577 *Fax:* (010) 68413125; (010) 68427707
E-mail: ndip@public3.bta.net.cn
Key Personnel
President: You Dong Zhang
Foreign Rights: Chen Bin *E-mail:* chenbin@public3.bta.net.cn
Founded: 1954
Subjects: Aeronautics, Aviation, Automotive, Computer Science, Electronics, Electrical Engineering, Microcomputers, Military Science, Science (General), Technology
ISBN Prefix(es): 7-118; 7-88704

The Nationalities Publishing House+
14 Hepingli Beijie, Beijing 100013

Tel: (010) 64212794; (010) 64212031
Founded: 1953
ISBN Prefix(es): 7-105
Bookshop(s): The Nationalities Culture Bookshop, 5 Hepingli Beijie, Beijing 100013

New Times Press+
23 Zizhuyuan Nanlu, Beijing 100044
Tel: (010) 68412244 *Fax:* (010) 68413125
Key Personnel
Foreign Rights: Chen Bin *E-mail:* chenbin@public3.bta.net.ca
Founded: 1980
Subjects: Education, Electronics, Electrical Engineering, English as a Second Language, Science (General), Technology
ISBN Prefix(es): 7-5042

Patent Documentation Publishing House
6 Xituchenglu, Jimenquiao Haidianqu, Beijing 100088
Tel: (010) 62362813; (010) 2026893 *Fax:* (010) 2019307
Subjects: Law, Science (General), Technology
ISBN Prefix(es): 7-80011

Peking Union Medical College & Beijing Medical University Press, see Beijing Medical University Press

The People's Communications Publishing House+
10 Hepingli St (E), Beijing 100013
Tel: (010) 64214479 *Fax:* (010) 64213713 *Cable:* 3652
Key Personnel
Contact: Gao Zhendu
Founded: 1952
Subjects: Automotive, Civil Engineering, Communications, Film, Video, Transportation, Shipbuilding & Repair
ISBN Prefix(es): 7-114

People's Education Press+
55 Sha Tan Hou St, Beijing 100009
Tel: (010) 6402 4555 *Fax:* (010) 6401 0370
E-mail: yaod@pep.com.cn (English); dongyj@pep.com.cn (Japanese)
Web Site: www.pep.com.cn/yingwenban; www.pep.com.cn/index.htm
Key Personnel
Editor-in-Chief: Wei Guodong
Dir: Han Shaoxiang
Founded: 1950
Subjects: Disability, Special Needs
ISBN Prefix(es): 7-900055
Number of titles published annually: 300 Print
Total Titles: 1,400 Print

People's Fine Arts Publishing House+
32 Beizongbu Hutong, Beijing 100735
Tel: (010) 65122375 *Fax:* (010) 65122370
Key Personnel
President: Yunhe Chen
Vice President: Youyuan Zhang
Founded: 1951
Membership(s): China Publishing Association.
Subjects: Art, Biography, History, Photography
ISBN Prefix(es): 7-102
Book Club(s): Art Books Research Association

People's Health Publishing House, see People's Medical Publishing House (PMPH)

People's Literature Publishing House
166 Chaonei Dajie, Beijing 100705
Tel: (010) 65138394 *Fax:* (010) 65138394
Founded: 1951
Subjects: Literature, Literary Criticism, Essays, Nonfiction (General), Poetry, Cultural history & studies; current events

ISBN Prefix(es): 7-02
Branch Office(s)
Shanghai

People's Medical Publishing House (PMPH)+
10 Tian Tanxili, Beijing 100050
Tel: (010) 67015812; (010) 67028822 *Fax:* (010) 67025429 *Cable:* 0427
Key Personnel
President: Dong Mianguo
Deputy Editor-in-Chief: Zhang Yuankang
Sales Dir: Yao Lingi
Production: Wang Duzhong
Head, Centre: Mr Liu Yiqing
Founded: 1953
Division of Ministry of Public Health.
Subjects: Health, Nutrition, Medicine, Nursing, Dentistry
ISBN Prefix(es): 7-117
Bookshop(s): 92 Dongdan Beidajie, Beijing

The People's Posts & Telecommunication Publishing House
27 Dongchanganjie, Beijing 100700
Tel: (010) 65139968; (010) 65138129 *Fax:* (010) 65138139
Key Personnel
President: Niu Tianjia
Founded: 1953
Subjects: Communications, Computer Science, Crafts, Games, Hobbies, Electronics, Electrical Engineering
ISBN Prefix(es): 7-115

People's Sports Publishing House+
8 Tiyuguanlu Rd, Beijing 100061
Tel: (010) 67117673 *Fax:* (010) 67116129
E-mail: cbszbs@sohu.com
Key Personnel
Chief Executive: Liu Meng
Rights & Permissions: He Yang
Founded: 1954
Subjects: Crafts, Games, Hobbies, Sports, Athletics
ISBN Prefix(es): 7-5009
Number of titles published annually: 440 Print; 70 Audio
Total Titles: 3,800,000 Print; 70,000 Audio
Bookshop(s): Wu Huan Bookshops

Petroleum Industry Publishing House, see China Oil & Gas Periodical Office

Phoenix, *imprint of* Foreign Languages Press

PMPH, see People's Medical Publishing House (PMPH)

Popular Science Press
32 Baishiqiao Lu, Haidianqu, Beijing 100081
Tel: (010) 62178877
Telex: 5198
Key Personnel
President: Wen Zuning
Vice President: Gu Lizhi; Wu Zhijing
Editor-in-Chief: Jin Tao
ISBN Prefix(es): 7-110

Printing Industry Publishing House+
2 Cuiweilu Fuxingmenwai, Beijing 100036
Tel: (010) 68218367 *Fax:* (010) 8214683
E-mail: capt@public3.bta.net.cn
Key Personnel
President: Shen Haixiang
Founded: 1981
Subjects: Chemistry, Chemical Engineering, Electronics, Electrical Engineering, Engineering (General), Management, Mechanical Engineering, Photography, Technology
ISBN Prefix(es): 7-80000

Qi Lu Press
39 Shengli Dajie, Jingjiulu, Jinan, Shandong 250001
Tel: (0531) 6910055-4920 *Fax:* (0531) 2906811 *Cable:* 0427
Key Personnel
Dir: Meng Fan-Hai; Li Xin
Editorial: Zhao Bing-Nan; Sun Yan-Cheng
Founded: 1979
ISBN Prefix(es): 7-5333
Branch Office(s)
76 Jing-Shi Rd, Jinan

Qingdao Publishing House+
77 Xuzhoulu Qingdao, Shandong 266071
Tel: (0532) 5814611; (0532) 362524 *Fax:* (0532) 515240
Key Personnel
President: Xu Cheng
Subjects: Accounting, Advertising, Aeronautics, Aviation, Agriculture, Alternative, Animals, Pets, Anthropology, Antiques, Archaeology, Architecture & Interior Design, Art, Asian Studies, Astrology, Occult, Astronomy, Automotive, Behavioral Sciences, Biblical Studies, Biography, Biological Sciences, Business
ISBN Prefix(es): 7-5436
Showroom(s): Cui Zifan Art Gallery

Science Press+
16 Donghuangchenggen N St, Beijie, Beijing 100717
Tel: (010) 6401643; (010) 64019823 *Fax:* (010) 64010642
Key Personnel
President: Mr Wang Jixiang
Dir, International Sales & Marketing: Shi Xiong Zhao
Founded: 1954
Subjects: Animals, Pets, Archaeology, Biological Sciences, Chemistry, Chemical Engineering, Computer Science, Earth Sciences, Electronics, Electrical Engineering, Environmental Studies, Gardening, Plants, Law, Mathematics, Medicine, Nursing, Dentistry, Natural History, Physics, Science (General), Technology
ISBN Prefix(es): 7-03
Number of titles published annually: 500 Print; 20 Audio
Total Titles: 5,000 Print
Subsidiaries: Science Press New York Ltd
U.S. Office(s): 84-04 58 Ave, Elmhurst, NY 11373, United States, Contact: Mr Zhang Ju
Tel: 718-476-0238 *Fax:* 718-476-0273

SDX (Shenghuo-Dushu-Xinzhi) Joint Publishing Co
166 Chaoyangmennei Dajie, Beijing 100010
Tel: (010) 555159 *Fax:* (010) 5138378 *Cable:* 1003
Key Personnel
President: Shen Changwen
Vice President: Dong Xiuyu
Rights & Permissions: Yang Jin; Ze Wei
Founded: 1932
Subjects: Biography, Economics, Government, Political Science, History, Literature, Literary Criticism, Essays, Management, Philosophy, Psychology, Psychiatry, Social Sciences, Sociology
ISBN Prefix(es): 7-108

Shandong Education Publishing House+
321 Jing Ba Weigi Rd, Jinan, Shandong Province 250001
Tel: (0531) 2092661; (0531) 2092663 *Fax:* (0531) 2092661
E-mail: sdjys@sjs.com.cn
Web Site: www.sjs.com.cn *Cable:* 0427
Key Personnel
Vice President: Yang Wen Hui *Tel:* (0531) 2016904

Dir: Wang Hongxin
Chief Editor: Xie Rongdai
Editor-in-Chief: Sun Yong Da *Tel:* (0531) 2907274
Founded: 1982
Subjects: Child Care & Development, Education, Fiction
ISBN Prefix(es): 7-5328
Parent Company: Shandong General Publication Bureau, 39 Shengli Dajie, Jingjiulu Shandong, Jinan 250001
Orders to: 39 Shengli St, Jinan, Shandong

Shandong Fine Arts Publishing House+
269 Jingsilu Rd, Jinan, Shandong 250001
Tel: (0531) 6910055 *Fax:* (021) 6911563 *Cable:* 0427
Key Personnel
Dir & Editor-in-Chief: Liu Zhenqing
Deputy Dir: Jingchun Wang
Deputy General Editorial: Yarbo Jiang; Ying Wang
Founded: 1984
Books, commercial printing, engineering & architectural services, newspapers.
ISBN Prefix(es): 7-5330
Parent Company: Shandong General Publication Bureau
Bookshop(s): Fine Arts Bookshop, Bldg No 1, Shunhe Commercial St, Jinan

Shandong Friendship Publishing House+
Formerly Shandong People's Publishing House
39 Shengli Dajie, Jinan, Shandong 250001
Tel: (0531) 2060055-7302 *Fax:* (0531) 2909354
E-mail: friendpub@sina.com
Web Site: www.sdpress.com.cn
Key Personnel
President: Yaping Li
Dir: Lui Tongshun
Deputy Dir: Chun Han
Deputy Editor-in-Chief: Yang Qizhang; Zhao Zhiping
Founded: 1986
Elt materials, travel, biography, fiction, lifestyle, chinese culture.
Subjects: Fashion, Fiction, Travel, Comics/cartoons, lifestyle
ISBN Prefix(es): 7-209; 7-80551; 7-80642
Parent Company: Shandong General Publication House, 39 Shengli Dajie, Jinan, Shandong 250001

Shandong Literature & Art Publishing House+
39 Shengli Dajie, Jinan, Shandong 250001
Tel: (0531) 6910055 *Fax:* (0531) 613584 *Cable:* 0427
Key Personnel
Dir: Guo Zhenming
Editor-in-Chief: Wang Shuguo
Founded: 1984
Subjects: Drama, Theater, Literature, Literary Criticism, Essays, Music, Dance
ISBN Prefix(es): 7-209; 7-80551; 7-80642
Parent Company: Shandong General Publications Bureau
Showroom(s): 85 Culture Market, 46 Maarshan Rd, Jinan, Shandong PC 25001 *Tel:* (0531) 6915710
Warehouse: 85 Culture Market, 46 Maarshan Rd, Jinan, Shandong PC 25001 *Tel:* (0531) 6915710
Orders to: 85 Culture Market, 46 Maarshan Rd, Jinan, Shandong PC 25001 *Tel:* (0531) 6915710

Shandong People's Publishing House, see Shandong Friendship Publishing House

Shandong Science & Technology Press+
16 Yuhan Rd, Jinan, Shandong Province 250002

Tel: (0531) 6915110 *Fax:* (0531) 2023898
E-mail: li_yujn@sina.com *Cable:* 0067
Key Personnel
President: Xie Rongdai
Dir of International Cooperation: Li Yu
Founded: 1978
Subjects: Agriculture, Architecture & Interior Design, Business, Earth Sciences, Economics, Education, Electronics, Electrical Engineering, Energy, Engineering (General), English as a Second Language, Environmental Studies, Mechanical Engineering, Medicine, Nursing, Dentistry, Technology, Computers, Foreign Language Study
ISBN Prefix(es): 7-5331
Parent Company: Shandong General Publishing House, 39 Shengli Dajie St, Jinan, Shandong 250001

Shandong University Press+
Shanda Nanlu, 27, Jinan, Shandong 250100
Tel: (0531) 8902601
E-mail: hustpub@blue.hust.edu.cn
Key Personnel
Vice President: Li Qiuping
Founded: 1980
Subjects: Accounting, Architecture & Interior Design, Behavioral Sciences, Business, Chemistry, Chemical Engineering, Communications, Computer Science, Economics, Electronics, Electrical Engineering, Energy, Engineering (General), English as a Second Language, Environmental Studies, Finance, Geography, Geology, History, Human Relations, Library & Information Sciences, Management, Mathematics, Mechanical Engineering, Microcomputers, Philosophy, Physical Sciences, Physics, Public Administration, Science (General), Technology
ISBN Prefix(es): 7-5607

Shanghai Calligraphy & Painting Publishing House+
237 Hengshan Lu, Shanghai 200031
Tel: (021) 64311905 *Fax:* (021) 3207505
E-mail: shcpph@online.sh.cn *Cable:* 5600
Key Personnel
President: Zhu Junbo
Founded: 1960
Subjects: Antiques, Art, Biography, Fashion, Photography, Culural Studies, Lifestyles
ISBN Prefix(es): 7-80635; 7-80512
Bookshop(s): Shanghai

Shanghai College of Traditional Chinese Medicine Press+
530 Linglinglu, Shanghai 200032
Tel: (021) 64175039 *Fax:* (021) 64175039
Key Personnel
President: Hong Jiahe
Founded: 1985
Subjects: Asian Studies, Behavioral Sciences, Health, Nutrition, Science (General)
ISBN Prefix(es): 7-81010

Shanghai Educational Publishing House+
123 Yong Fu Rd, Shanghai 200031
Tel: (021) 64 37 71 65 *Fax:* (021) 64 33 99 95
E-mail: wuyiyang@public2.sta.net.cn *Cable:* 3413
Key Personnel
Chief Executive, Production & International Rights: Chen He
Editorial: Bao Nan Ling
Adjoint Dir Editorial: M Zhang Wen-Jie
Founded: 1958
Subjects: Child Care & Development, Education, English as a Second Language, History, Microcomputers, Physics, Science (General), Social Sciences, Sociology
ISBN Prefix(es): 7-5320
Distributor for Xin Hua Book Store (Peoples Republic of China)

Shanghai Far East Publishers
357 Xianxia Rd, Shanghai 200336
Tel: (021) 62247733-661 *Fax:* (021) 62414469
E-mail: ydbook@ydbook.com
Web Site: www.ydbook.com
Key Personnel
Vice Chief Editor: Zhang Anping
 E-mail: anping@ydbook.com
Editor: Zhao Jin
Subjects: Accounting, Animals, Pets, Art, Biography, Business, Career Development, Child Care & Development, Communications, Economics, English as a Second Language, Film, Video, Health, Nutrition, Humor, Literature, Literary Criticism, Essays, Management, Nonfiction (General), Psychology, Psychiatry, Social Sciences, Sociology, Travel, Women's Studies
Parent Company: Shanghai Century Publishing Group

Shanghai Foreign Language Education Press+
295 Zhongshan Bei Yi Lu, Shanghai 200083
Tel: (021) 65425300; (021) 65422896 *Fax:* (021) 65609540
Web Site: www.sflep.com
Key Personnel
President: Zhuang Zhixiang
International Rights: Zhang (John) Hong
 E-mail: johnhzhang@sflep.com
Founded: 1979
Subjects: Business, Education, English as a Second Language, Language Arts, Linguistics, Literature, Literary Criticism, Essays
ISBN Prefix(es): 7-81009
Bookshop(s): 564 Dalian Xi Rd, Shanghai 200083

Shanghai People's Fine Arts Publishing House
D Bldg, No 33, Lane 672, Changle Road, Shanghai 200040
Tel: (021) 54044520 *Fax:* (021) 54032331
E-mail: finearts@shi63.net
Key Personnel
Rights Manager: Summer Shao; Qian Simon
Established publisher with 50 years publishing history on fine arts, visual arts (architecture, design, photography) & children's books.
Subjects: Architecture & Interior Design, Art, Photography
ISBN Prefix(es): 7-5322

Shanghai Scientific & Technical Publishers+
450 Ruijin Er Rd, Shanghai 200020
Tel: (021) 64736055; (021) 64184881; (021) 64174349 *Fax:* (021) 64730679
E-mail: gjb@sstp.cn
Web Site: www.sstp.com.cn; www.sstp.cn
Telex: 33384 Cpts
Key Personnel
President: Wu Zhiren
Editor-in-Chief: Hu Dawei
Sales: Wang Feng-ying
Founded: 1956
Subjects: Agriculture, Engineering (General), Medicine, Nursing, Dentistry, Science (General), Technology
ISBN Prefix(es): 7-5323
Bookshop(s): SSTP Bookshop, 50 Ruijin Rd, Shanghai 200020

Shanghai Scientific & Technological Literature Press
2 Wukanglu, Shanghai 200031
Tel: (021) 64370782 *Cable:* 2115
Key Personnel
Chief Executive: Shu Feng Xiang
Editorial: Wen Jun Chi
Sales: Yi Liang Zhao
Production & Publicity: Cheng Qing Qu
Rights & Permissions: Jian Yue Sun
Founded: 1978
Subjects: Agriculture, Engineering (General), Medicine, Nursing, Dentistry, Science (General)
ISBN Prefix(es): 7-5439
Parent Company: Science & Technology Commission of Shanghai Municipality, 30 Fu Zhou Rd, Shanghai

Sichuan Science & Technology Publishing House+
3 Yandaojie, Chengdu, Sichuan 610012
Tel: (028) 664982; (028) 662 5025 *Fax:* (028) 6654063 *Cable:* CHENGDU 1555
Key Personnel
President: Li Guangwei
International Rights: Luo Xiaoyan
Subjects: Agriculture, Crafts, Games, Hobbies, Fashion, Health, Nutrition, Medicine, Nursing, Dentistry, Science (General), Technology
ISBN Prefix(es): 7-5364

Sichuan University Press+
29 Wangjianglu, Chengdu, Sichuan 610064
Tel: (028) 583875-62529
Key Personnel
President: Wang Jintrou
Founded: 1985
Subjects: Accounting, Antiques, Computer Science, Economics, History, Marketing, Mathematics
ISBN Prefix(es): 7-5614

South China University of Science & Technology Press+
Wushan Guangzhou, Guangdong 510641
Tel: (020) 87113489; (020) 87113484 *Cable:* 7003
Key Personnel
President: Zhou Shaohua
Founded: 1985
Subjects: Agriculture, Biological Sciences, Chemistry, Chemical Engineering, Civil Engineering, Computer Science, Economics, Education, Electronics, Electrical Engineering
ISBN Prefix(es): 7-5623

Southwest China Jiaotong University Press+
Jiulidi, Chengdu, Sichuan 610031
Tel: (028) 784160-763 *Fax:* (028) 24377
E-mail: swju@swjtu.edu.cn
Telex: 600072 SWJUCN *Cable:* 6445
Key Personnel
President: Fan Ziliang
Vice President: Zhang Xue
Editor-in-Chief: Zhu Yonglin
Founded: 1985
Membership(s): Sichuan Publishers Association.
Subjects: Civil Engineering, Computer Science, Electronics, Electrical Engineering, Engineering (General), Management, Mathematics, Mechanical Engineering, Publishing & Book Trade Reference, Science (General), Transportation
ISBN Prefix(es): 7-81022
Divisions: Division of Audiovisual Publication, SWJU Press
Bookshop(s): SWJUP Readers Service, Chengdu, Sichuan

Tianjin Science & Technology Publishing House+
Unit of Bureau of Publications
189 Zhangzizhonglu Lu Hepingqu, Hepinggu, Tianjin 300020
Tel: (022) 7312749 *Fax:* (022) 27312755
E-mail: tjstp@public.tpt.tj.on
Key Personnel
Dir: Wang Shu-Ze *Tel:* (022) 27301162
Editor-in-Chief: Kou Xiu-Rong *Tel:* (022) 27306821
Editor: Wu Chun-Li
Founded: 1979
Subjects: Agriculture, Architecture & Interior Design, Biological Sciences, Chemistry, Chemical

Engineering, Child Care & Development, Computer Science, Cookery, Electronics, Electrical Engineering, Engineering (General), English as a Second Language, Gardening, Plants, Health, Nutrition, Mathematics, Medicine, Nursing, Dentistry, Microcomputers, Physical Sciences, Science (General), Technology
ISBN Prefix(es): 7-5308
Number of titles published annually: 300 Print
Total Titles: 1,000,000 Print

Tomorrow Publishing House+
39 Shengli Dajie, Jinan, Shandong 250001
Tel: (0531) 206 0055 *Fax:* (0531) 290 2094
E-mail: tomorrow@sdpress.com
Web Site: www.tomorrowpub.com *Cable:* 0427
Key Personnel
President & Editor-in-Chief: Liu Haiqi
Dir, Rights Section: David Fu
Founded: 1984
ISBN Prefix(es): 7-5332
Parent Company: Shandong General Press
Associate Companies: Shandong Xinhua Book Store

Tsinghua University Press+
Tsinghua University, Haidiangu District, Beijing 100084
Tel: (010) 62783933; (010) 62594726 *Fax:* (010) 62770278
E-mail: right-tup@mail.tsinghua.edu.cn
Telex: 22617 QHTSC CN *Cable:* 1331 BEIJING
Key Personnel
President: Wang Minfu
Editor-in-Chief: Zhang Zhaoqi
Founded: 1980
Subjects: Architecture & Interior Design, Chemistry, Chemical Engineering, Civil Engineering, Computer Science, Education, Electronics, Electrical Engineering, Engineering (General), English as a Second Language, Mathematics, Technology, Computers: Educational Software, Operating Systems, Programming Languages & Software
ISBN Prefix(es): 7-302
Number of titles published annually: 250 Print
Total Titles: 700 Print

Universidade de Macau, Centro de Publicacoes
(University of Macau, Publications Centre)
Av Padre Tomas Pereira, S J, Taipa, Macau
Tel: 397 4504 *Fax:* 397 4506
E-mail: pub_grp@umac.mo
Web Site: www.umac.mo
Key Personnel
Head: Dr Raymond Wong
Founded: 1993
Subjects: Art, Economics, Education, Government, Political Science, History, Literature, Literary Criticism, Essays, Management, Public Administration, Social Sciences, Sociology
ISBN Prefix(es): 972-97631; 972-96791; 972-97050; 972-97834
Number of titles published annually: 10 Print
Total Titles: 71 Print

Water Resources and Electric Power Press (CWPP)+
6 Sanlihelu, Fuxingmenwai, Beijing 100044
Tel: (010) 898031 *Fax:* (010) 68353010
  Cable: BEIJING 81605
Key Personnel
President: Mr Tang Xinhua
Vice President: Mr Liu Fengtong
Editor-in-Chief: Mr Jin Yan
International Cooperation Office & Project Manager: Ms Fang Ping
Founded: 1956
Subjects: Civil Engineering, Electronics, Electrical Engineering, Energy, Engineering (General), Environmental Studies
ISBN Prefix(es): 7-120

Bookshop(s): CWPP Retail Dept, 6 Sanlihe Rd, Beijing 100044
Orders to: International Cooperation Div, 6 Sanlihe Rd, Beijing 100044

World Affairs Press+
A31 Waijiaobujie, Beijing 100005
Tel: (010) 65232695 *Fax:* (010) 5133181
E-mail: wap@bj.col.com.cn
Key Personnel
President: Mr An Guozheng
Founded: 1934
Subjects: Biography, Developing Countries, Fiction, Foreign Countries, Government, Political Science, History, Journalism, Social Sciences, Sociology
ISBN Prefix(es): 7-5012
Imprints: World Affairs Printing House

World Affairs Printing House, *imprint of* World Affairs Press

World Books Publishing Corporation+
137 Chaonei Dajie, Beijing 100010
Tel: (010) 64016320 *Fax:* (010) 4016320
E-mail: wpc@china.kw.co.cn
ISBN Prefix(es): 7-5062
Branch Office(s)
Beijing World Publishing Corp

Writers' Publishing House+
10 Nongzhanguan Nanli, Wenliandalou, Beijing 100026
Tel: (010) 65004079; (010) 65389244 *Fax:* (010) 65930761
E-mail: wrtspub@public.bta.net.cn
Web Site: www.zuojiachubanshe.com
Founded: 1953
A state enterprise publishing reprints of Chinese literature.
Subjects: Fiction, Poetry, Romance, Essay
ISBN Prefix(es): 7-5063
Number of titles published annually: 200 Print

Wuhan University Press+
Luojiashan, Wuhan, Hubei 430072
Tel: (027) 7870651; (010) 82001239 *Fax:* (027) 712661; (10) 82001248
Telex: 5678
Key Personnel
President: Xiong Yulian
Vice President: Li Haojie; Wang Wen-Hao
Founded: 1981
Subjects: Biological Sciences, Chemistry, Chemical Engineering, Computer Science, Economics, English as a Second Language, Government, Political Science, History, Law, Library & Information Sciences, Mathematics, Social Sciences, Sociology
ISBN Prefix(es): 7-307; 7-900634
Subsidiaries: Edit Computer Company; Wuhan University

Xiamen University Press
Xiamen University, Xiamen, 422 Siming Nanlu, Fujian 361005
Tel: (0592) 2186128
E-mail: chbanshe@jingxian.xmu.edu.cn; xmdx@fjbook.com
Key Personnel
Dir: Jiang Dongming
Chief Editor: Chen Fulang
Founded: 1985
ISBN Prefix(es): 7-5615

Xi'an Cartography Publishing House+
124 Youyi Donglu, Xi'an, Shaanxi 710054
Tel: (029) 7898962
Key Personnel
President: Xu Guohua
International Rights: Huang Meihua
Founded: 1985
Subjects: Earth Sciences, Environmental Studies, Geography, Geology, Nonfiction (General)
ISBN Prefix(es): 7-80545
Distributor for China Cartography Publishing House

Xi'an Maps Publishing House, see Xi'an Cartography Publishing House

Xinhua Publishing House+
Division of Xinhua News Agency
57 Xuanwumen Xidajie, Beijing 100803
Tel: (010) 3073880 *Fax:* (010) 3073880
E-mail: nianzh@xinhuanet.com
Telex: 22316 Xnabj *Cable:* 1631
Key Personnel
Dir: Qiu Yongsheng
Editor-in-Chief & Deputy Dir: Zhang Shoudi
Deputy Dir: Juo Bomin
Founded: 1979
Subjects: Biography, Economics, Ethnicity, Government, Political Science, Journalism, Social Sciences, Sociology, People's Republic of China Year Book
ISBN Prefix(es): 7-5011
Bookshop(s): China Journalism Bookstore

Yunnan University Press+
Yinghua Campus of Yunnan University, No 2 Cuihu Rd N, Kunming 650091
Tel: (0871) 5032001; (0871) 5031057 *Fax:* (0871) 5162823
Web Site: www.ynup.com
Key Personnel
President: Shi Weida *Tel:* (0871) 5033890
  E-mail: wds@ynup.com
Vice President: Zhang Yonghong *Tel:* (0871) 5032152 *E-mail:* zyh@ynup.com
Copyright Dir: Xiong Xiaoxia *E-mail:* helenx@ynup.com
Founded: 1988
Publishing house of Yunnan University. Over 1,700 titles published covering a wide variety of academic fields.
Subjects: Anthropology, Art, Business, Career Development, English as a Second Language, Ethnicity, Management, Marketing, Outdoor Recreation, Photography, Public Administration, Self-Help, Social Sciences, Sociology, Travel
ISBN Prefix(es): 7-81068
Number of titles published annually: 125 Print; 10 CD-ROM
Total Titles: 150 Print; 10 CD-ROM
Parent Company: Yunnan University

Zhejiang Education Publishing House+
347 Tiyuchanglu, Hangzhou, Zhejiang 310006
Tel: (0571) 5170300; (0571) 85103298
  Fax: (0571) 5176944
E-mail: zjjy@zjcb.com *Cable:* 2403
Key Personnel
Vice President: Shao Rouyu *E-mail:* shaory@zjcb.com
Founded: 1983
Subjects: Education, English as a Second Language
ISBN Prefix(es): 7-5338
Parent Company: Zhejiang General Publishing House

Zhejiang University Press+
20 Yugu Rd, Hangzhou, Zhejiang 310027
Tel: (0571) 88273066 *Fax:* (0571) 88273066
E-mail: zupress@zju.edu.cn
Web Site: www.zjupress.com
Key Personnel
President: Han Zhaoxiong
International Rights: You Jianzhong
Founded: 1984

Subjects: Accounting, Agriculture, Art, Biological Sciences, Business, Chemistry, Chemical Engineering, Civil Engineering, Computer Science, Education, History, How-to, Science (General), Technology, Computers, Electronic Media, Natural Sciences, Teaching Methods & Materials
ISBN Prefix(es): 7-308

Zhong Hua Book Co
38 Taipingqiao Xili, Fengtai District, Beijing 100073
Tel: (010) 63458226 *Fax:* (010) 63458226
Web Site: www.zhbc.com
Founded: 1912
Also distribution.
Subjects: Anthropology, Fiction, History, Language Arts, Linguistics, Literature, Literary Criticism, Essays, Poetry, Travel
ISBN Prefix(es): 7-101
Number of titles published annually: 800 Print
Total Titles: 20,000 Print

Colombia

General Information

Capital: Bogota
Language: Spanish (English widely used in business)
Religion: Roman Catholic
Population: 34.3 million
Bank Hours: 0900-1500 Monday-Friday
Shop Hours: 0900-1230, 1430-1830 Monday-Saturday
Currency: 100 centavos = 1 Colombian peso
Export/Import Information: Member of Latin American Free Trade Association. Value added taxes on all imports; no sales tax on books. Ad valorem: none generally on books except on books bound in leather or similar materials, on photonovels of thrillers, detective stories, etc., on horoscopes, children's picture books, atlases & advertising catalogues. No import license for books. Exchange license from Banco de la Republica required.
Copyright: UCC, Berne, Buenos Aires (see Copyright Conventions, pg xi)

ACPO, see Dosmil Editora

Amazonas Editores Ltda
Carrera 11 No 94-02 Ofc 121, 47009 Bogota, DC
Tel: (091) 6180256; (091) 2182760 *Fax:* (091) 6180326
Key Personnel
Legal Representative: Ferrer Lucia Montano
Founded: 1991
Distribuidor de libros de otras Editoriales Colombianas.
Subjects: Archaeology, Architecture & Interior Design, Art, Environmental Studies, Government, Political Science, History, Poetry
ISBN Prefix(es): 958-95493
Distributor for Cridtina Uribe Editores; El Sello Editorial; Fondo FEN Colombia
Book Club(s): Camara Colombiana del Libro

Asociacion Instituto Linguistico de Verano
Calle 13 No 8-38, of 409, Apdo Aereo 27744, Bogota DC
Tel: (01) 2821047; (01) 3416185
E-mail: sil_colombia@sil.org
Web Site: www.sil.org/americas/colombia
Founded: 1962
All queries regarding activities in Colombia should be directed to the following: SIL International, Americas Area Office, 7500 W Camp Wisdom Rd, Dallas, TX 75236, USA. Tel: 972-708-7333, Fax: 972-708-7324.
Subjects: Language Arts, Linguistics
ISBN Prefix(es): 958-21

Bedout Editores SA+
Calle 61 No 51-04, Apdo Aereo 760, Medellin, Antioquia
Tel: (04) 5112900 *Fax:* (04) 2517946 *Cable:* BEDOUT
Key Personnel
President: Campuzano R Ilbgnacio
Manager: Mario Gutierrez
Founded: 1889
Subjects: Education, Literature, Literary Criticism, Essays, Social Sciences, Sociology
ISBN Prefix(es): 84-8274; 958-03
Divisions: Editora Beta SA
Branch Office(s)
Calle 13 No 21-51, Local 5, Bucaramanga
Tel: (076) 352171
Calle 25N No 3 bis-35, 200 piso, Cali *Tel:* (02) 672367
Calle 39 No 233-25, Santa Fe de Bogota DC
Tel: (01) 2445232

Cekit SA+
Calle 22, No 8-22, Piso 2, Pereira, Risaralda
Tel: (06) 3253033; (06) 3348179; (06) 3348189 *Fax:* (06) 3348020
E-mail: comercial@cekit.com.co
Web Site: www.cekit.com.co
Key Personnel
Contact: William Rojas
Founded: 1985
Specialize in learning material for the study of electronics.
Subjects: Electronics, Electrical Engineering
ISBN Prefix(es): 958-657
Branch Office(s)
Cekits Carrera 17 No 53-48, Piso 2, Bogota

CELAM, see Consejo Episcopal Latinoamericano (CELAM)

Centro Regional para el Fomento del Libro en America Latina y el Caribe (Regional Center for the Promotion of Books in Latin America & the Caribbean)
Calle 70 No 9-52, Bogota DC
Tel: (01) 212 6056; (01) 249 5141; (01) 321 7501; (01) 540 2071; (01) 312 5690 *Fax:* (01) 255 4614
E-mail: cerlalc@impsat.net.co; info@cerlalc.org; libro@cerlalc.org
Web Site: www.cerlalc.org
Key Personnel
Dir: Carmen Bravo
Founded: 1971
Subjects: Law, Literature, Literary Criticism, Essays, Editing, lecture promotion, production & circulation
ISBN Prefix(es): 92-9057; 958-671

CERLALC, see Centro Regional para el Fomento del Libro en America Latina y el Caribe

CIAT - Centro Internacional de Agricultura Tropical
Recta Cali-Palmira, km 17, Apdo Aereo 6713, Cali
Tel: (02) 445-0000 *Fax:* (02) 445-0073
E-mail: ciat@cgiar.org
Web Site: www.ciat.cgiar.org
Telex: 05769CIAT CO
Key Personnel
Contact: Luis Alberto Garcia *E-mail:* l.garcia-ciat@cgiar.org
Specialize in Investigation of Tropical Agriculture.
ISBN Prefix(es): 958-9183; 9972-856

CINEP, see Fundacion Centro de Investigacion y Educacion Popular (CINEP)

Consejo Episcopal Latinoamericano (CELAM)+
Transversal 67, Ave Boyaca No 173-71, Bogota
Tel: (01) 6670050; (01) 6706416
E-mail: editora@celam.org; celam@celam.org; itepal@celam.org
Web Site: www.celam.org
Key Personnel
Dir: Eduardo Pena Vanegas
Founded: 1970
Subjects: Biblical Studies, Child Care & Development, Education, Nonfiction (General), Philosophy, Regional Interests, Religion - Catholic, Theology
ISBN Prefix(es): 958-625

Ediciones Cultural Colombiana Ltda
Calle 72, No 16-15/21, Apdo Aereo 6307, Bogota
SAN: 001-6462
Tel: (01) 2116090 *Fax:* (01) 2176570 *Cable:* CULBIANA
Key Personnel
Man Dir: Jose Porto
Editorial: Jose Porto Vazquez
Sales Dir: Hernando Salazar
Production: Maximilian Nicolas
Founded: 1951
ISBN Prefix(es): 84-8273; 958-9013
Bookshop(s): Libreria Cultural Colombian

Ediciones Culturales Ver Ltda+
Calle 37 No 16-64, Apdo Aereo 51095, Bogota
Tel: (01) 2859362; (01) 2859204 *Fax:* (01) 2859362
Telex: 45805
Key Personnel
Manager: Gaspar Alfonso Bacca
Founded: 1989
Membership(s): The House of Books.
Subjects: Education
ISBN Prefix(es): 958-9204

Derecho Penal y Criminologia, *imprint of* Universidad Externado de Colombia

Dosmil Editora
Carrera 39A, No 15-11, Bogota DC
Tel: (01) 2694800
Telex: 45623 Accpo *Cable:* Radiofonicas Bogota
Key Personnel
Man Dir: Hernando Bernal A
Editorial: Javier Martinez Naranjo
Sales & Rights & Permissions: Luis Felipe Delgado; Manuel Hoyos
Founded: 1947 (ACPO - Editora Dosmil 1964)
Formerly Accion Cultural Popular ACPO - Editora Dosmil.
Subjects: Art, Literature, Literary Criticism, Essays, Regional Interests, Social Sciences, Sociology
ISBN Prefix(es): 84-8275

Ecoe Ediciones Ltda
Calle 32 bis No 17-22, Bogota
Tel: (01) 2889821; (01) 2889871 *Fax:* (01) 3201377
E-mail: correo@ecoeediciones.com
Web Site: www.ecoeediciones.com
ISBN Prefix(es): 958-648

Editorial Educativo Ltda, see Fondo Educativo Interamericano SA

PUBLISHERS

COLOMBIA

El Ancora Editores+
Ave 25c, No 3-99, Bosque Izquierdo, Bogota
Tel: (01) 283 9040; (01) 342 6224; (01) 283 9235 *Fax:* (01) 283 9235
E-mail: ancoraed@elancoraeditores.com
Web Site: www.elancoraeditores.com
Key Personnel
Man Dir: Patricia Hoher
Editorial, Rights & Permissions: Felipe Escobar Uribe
Founded: 1980
Subjects: Art, Economics, History, Humor, Journalism, Literature, Literary Criticism, Essays, Poetry, Social Sciences, Sociology
ISBN Prefix(es): 958-9044; 84-8277; 958-36; 958-96577; 958-8048

Escala Ltda
Calle 30 No 17-70, Bogota
Tel: (01) 2878200 *Fax:* (01) 2325148
Key Personnel
Contact: Ana Medina De Serna
Founded: 1962
Subjects: Architecture & Interior Design, Art, Engineering (General)
ISBN Prefix(es): 958-9082
Branch Office(s)
Ave San Antonio No 79 Of 101 Napoles, Mexico, DF, Mexico *Tel:* 5633672
Edif Tacagua piso 19 Apdo 19Q, Parque Central Ave Lecuna, Caracas, Venezuela
Apoquinto 4900 of 147-148 las Condes, Santiago de Chile *Tel:* 2466111

Eurolibros Ltda+
Affiliate of Camara de Comercio de Bogota
Calle 40 No 20-27, Bogota
Tel: (01) 2886400; (01) 3401837 *Fax:* (01) 2886400
Telex: 3 40 18 11; 3 40 18 37
Key Personnel
Legal Representative: Carlos Roberto Jimenez
E-mail: carlosji@latino.net.co
Founded: 1983
Membership(s): Camara Colombiana de la Industria Editorial.
Subjects: Education, Outdoor Recreation, Religion - Catholic
ISBN Prefix(es): 958-9417
Number of titles published annually: 2 Print
Total Titles: 12 Print
Associate Companies: Libros Leo Ltda
Distributed by Oriente (Argentina)

Universidad Externado de Colombia+
Calle 12 0-46 Este, Bogota
Tel: (01) 3428984; (01) 3420288 (ext 3151) *Fax:* (01) 3424948
E-mail: publicaciones@uexternado.edu.co
Web Site: www.uexternado.edu.co
Key Personnel
Dir: Conrado Zuluago
Founded: 1886
Subjects: Criminology, Education, Finance, Government, Political Science, Law, Management, Mathematics, Social Sciences, Sociology
ISBN Prefix(es): 958-616
Imprints: Derecho Penal y Criminologia; Informativo; Juridica
Bookshop(s): Calle 12 N° 1-17 Este, Bloque A Primer Piso, Bogota *Tel:* (01) 342 0288 (ext 3152)

Fondo Educativo Interamericano SA+
Calle 36 No 22-33, Apdo Aereo 29696, Bogota
Tel: (01) 3382577; (01) 3382877 *Fax:* (01) 2852891; (01) 2320191
E-mail: eeducativa@epm.net.co; educapyv@multi.net.co
Telex: 45581 *Cable:* ADIWES BOGOTA
Key Personnel
Man Dir: Alvaro Toledo

Founded: 1970
ISBN Prefix(es): 958-610; 84-89220

Fundacion Centro de Investigacion y Educacion Popular (CINEP)+
Carrera 5a No 33A-08, Apdo Aereo 25916, Bogota
Tel: (01) 2456181 *Fax:* (01) 2879089
E-mail: info@cinep.org.co
Web Site: www.cinep.org.co
Key Personnel
Man Dir & Rights & Permissions: Francisco de Roux
Production, Publicity & Publications Manager: Helena Gardeazabal
Founded: 1959
Specialize in social science.
Subjects: Economics, Regional Interests, Social Sciences, Sociology
ISBN Prefix(es): 958-644; 958-9027

Fundacion Universidad de la Sabana Ediciones INSE+
Calle 70 No 12-08, Apdo Aereo 53753, Bogota
Tel: (01) 6760867
E-mail: susabana@col1.telcom.com.co
Founded: 1987
Subjects: Biological Sciences, Economics, Management, Philosophy, Religion - Catholic
ISBN Prefix(es): 958-12
Bookshop(s): Sede del Puente del Comon-Chiacundina-marca

Ediciones Gamma+
Calle 85, No 18-32, Piso 5, Bogota
Tel: (01) 6227054; (01) 6227076 *Fax:* (01) 6227129
E-mail: diners@cable.net.co
Key Personnel
Contact: Gustavo Casadiego
Founded: 1978
Subjects: Travel
ISBN Prefix(es): 958-95108; 958-95237; 958-8177; 958-9308
Parent Company: Diners Club of Colombia

Editora Guadalupe Ltda
Carrera 42 No 10-57, Apdo Aereo 29765, Bogota
Tel: (01) 2690788; (01) 2690211 *Fax:* (01) 2685308
Key Personnel
Man Dir & Editorial: Marco A Moreno H
Sales: Mario E Joya Hernandez
Production: Jose Adel Lopez Q
Founded: 1969
Membership(s): the Columbian Booksellers Association.
Subjects: Literature, Literary Criticism, Essays, Science (General), Technology
ISBN Prefix(es): 958-608

Editorial Hispanoamerica+
Carrera 56 B, No 45-27, Bogota DC
Tel: (01) 2216694 *Fax:* (01) 2213020
Key Personnel
Contact: Alvaro Pinzon
ISBN Prefix(es): 958-9104; 958-658

Imprenta de la Universidad Nacional
Ciudad Universitaria Edif 561, Apdo Aereo 37855, Bogota
Tel: (01) 2666965; (01) 2699111 *Fax:* (01) 2441035
ISBN Prefix(es): 958-628

Informativo, *imprint of* Universidad Externado de Colombia

Instituto Caro y Cuervo+
Carrera 11 No 64-37, Apdo Aereo 51502, Bogota

Tel: (01) 3456004 *Fax:* (01) 2170243; (01) 3422121
E-mail: direcciongeneral@caroycuervo.gov.co
Web Site: www.caroycuervo.gov.co
Key Personnel
Dir: Ignacio Chaves
Founded: 1942
Subjects: Education, Language Arts, Linguistics
ISBN Prefix(es): 958-611
Bookshop(s): Libreria Yerbabuena; Libreria Cuervo

Juridica, *imprint of* Universidad Externado de Colombia

Editorial Juventud Colombiana Ltda
Calle 58 N° 19-41, Apdo Aereo 53694, Bogota
Tel: (01) 2557485; (01) 2490543 *Fax:* (01) 2557416
Key Personnel
Man Dir: Cecilia De Huidobro
ISBN Prefix(es): 958-23
Parent Company: Editorial Juventud SA, Spain

Kapelusz Ltda Editorial+
Calle 37 N° 25-10, Bogota DC
Tel: (01) 2442035; (01) 3350031 *Fax:* (01) 3350042
Telex: 3350042 *Cable:* Kapelusz
Key Personnel
Man Dir, Sales & Rights & Permissions: Diego Tenorio
Founded: 1964
Subjects: Education, Physics, Psychology, Psychiatry
ISBN Prefix(es): 958-9010

LEGIS - Editores SA+
Av El Dorado 81-10, Apdo Aereo 8646-9888, Bogota
Tel: (01) 4255255 *Fax:* (01) 4255317
E-mail: scliente@legis.com.co
Telex: 43300 Legis *Cable:* LEGISLACION
Key Personnel
Man Dir: Mauricio Serna Melendez
Founded: 1952
Subjects: Economics, Law, Management, Marketing
ISBN Prefix(es): 958-653
Subsidiaries: Legislacion Economica Srl; URB Industrial la Urbina
Orders to: CRA 16, No 98-62, Bogota

Lerner Ediciones
Calle 8A, No 68A-41, Apdo Aereo 8304, Bogota
Mailing Address: PO Box 8304, Bogota
Tel: (01) 2628200; (01) 2624224 *Fax:* (01) 2624459
Telex: 43195 *Cable:* Edilerner
Key Personnel
Man Dir: Jack A Grimberg Possin
Editorial: Juan Francisco di Domenico
Sales: Diego Jaramillo
Founded: 1959
Subjects: History, Literature, Literary Criticism, Essays, Medicine, Nursing, Dentistry
ISBN Prefix(es): 958-95013; 958-9135
Bookshop(s): Libreria y Distribuidora Lerner Ltda

Libiosy Libres, Editorial+
Ave Americas No 64A-39, Apdo Aereo 006642, Bogota
Tel: (01) 2907145; (01) 2907862; (01) 2886188 *Fax:* (01) 2696830
Key Personnel
Man Dir, Sales, Publicity: Alberto Umana Carrizosa
Editorial: M C Jimero
Production: Jose B Restreps
ISBN Prefix(es): 958-9253; 958-9008

Libros, *imprint of* RAM Editores

COLOMBIA

Editorial Libros y Libres SA+
Ave Americus No 64A-39, Apdo Aero 006642, Bogota DC, Cundinamarca
Tel: (01) 2907145; (01) 2907862; (01) 2886188 *Fax:* (01) 2696830
E-mail: edilibro@colomsat.net.co
Key Personnel
General: Rivero Samuel Diaz
Founded: 1985
Subjects: Behavioral Sciences, Biological Sciences, Earth Sciences, Education, Science (General), Social Sciences, Sociology
ISBN Prefix(es): 958-9253; 958-9008

Lito Technion Ltda
Calle 21 No 43A-23, Apdo Aereo 80085, Bogota
Tel: (01) 2443502; (01) 2443177; (01) 2441538
Telex: 41456
Key Personnel
Man Dir: Benjamin Bursztyn V
Editorial: Samuel Bursztyn V
Sales: Ricardo Herrera G
Production: German Arias G
Publicity: Yonatan Bursztyn V
Founded: 1980
ISBN Prefix(es): 958-9007

McGraw-Hill Colombia+
Carrerall, No 93-46, Bogota
Tel: (01) 6003800 *Fax:* (01) 6003811
Web Site: www.mcgraw-hill.com.co
Telex: 43306 MNLACO
Key Personnel
Dir General: Carlos G Marquez H
  E-mail: cmarquez@attmail.com
Professional Division Manager: Martha Edna Suarez
College Division Manager: Luis Fernando Pinzon
Education Division Manager: Hector Zulauga
Controller: Luis Fernando Garavito
Production Manager: Consuelo Ruiz
Founded: 1974
Colombia, Venezuela, Ecuador, Peru & Bolivia.
Subjects: Accounting, Biological Sciences, Business, Chemistry, Chemical Engineering, Economics, Engineering (General), Physics, Psychology, Psychiatry, Social Sciences, Sociology, Technology
ISBN Prefix(es): 958-600; 84-8278
Parent Company: The McGraw-Hill Companies, 1221 Avenue of the Americas, New York, NY 10020, United States
Subsidiaries: McGraw-Hill Interamericana de Venezuela
Distributor for Houghton Mifflin; Microsoft Press; Harvard Business
Warehouse: Calle 22 No 90-27

Migema Ediciones Ltda
Calle 32 No 19-22, Bogota
Tel: (01) 2873158; (01) 2858538 *Fax:* (01) 2858538; (01) 2858224
E-mail: emigema@cc-net.net
Key Personnel
Legal Representative: Miguel Angel Torres Campos
ISBN Prefix(es): 958-681
Orders to: Calle 33A N 18-2D, Bogota

Instituto Misionerao Hijas De San Pablo+
Carrera 9A No 13 27, Santafe de Bogota DC, Cundinamarca
Tel: (01) 2435885; (01) 6 71 89 74 *Fax:* (01) 670 6378
Key Personnel
Editorial Dir: Lucero Patino
Superior Provincial: Yermy Castano
Founded: 1948
Subjects: Communications, Education, Philosophy, Women's Studies
ISBN Prefix(es): 958-9335

Branch Office(s)
Barranquilla (two)
Bogota
Cali
Cucuta
Manizales
Medellin
Bookshop(s): Carrera No 32A 161A 04, Apdo Aereo 6291, Santafe de Bogota Cundinamarca; Carrera 13 No 72-41, Bogota

Ediciones Monserrate+
Calle 122 No 53A-29, Bogota
Tel: (01) 253 1347; (01) 253 3033 *Fax:* (01) 253 9517
E-mail: comercial@edimonserrate.com
Web Site: www.edimonserrate.com
Key Personnel
Man Dir & Editorial: P Enrique Fajardo
Sales: Maria Consuelo de Fajardo
Founded: 1977
Subjects: Law
ISBN Prefix(es): 958-95014

Editorial Norma SA
Calle 29N No 6A-40, Cali
Tel: (02) 660 1901 *Fax:* (02) 661 5278
Web Site: www.norma.com
Telex: 45584 NORMA *Cable:* Edinorma
Key Personnel
President: Fernando Gomez Campo *Tel:* (02) 660 1901 (ext 2740) *E-mail:* fernando.gomez@norma.com
Editorial Dir, Trade Division: Maria del Mar Ravassa
Editorial Dir, Textbook Division: Bernardo Pena
Editorial Dir, Periodicals Division: Maria C Posada
Editorial Dir, International Division: Gustavo Adolfo Carvajal
ISBN Prefix(es): 958-04
Parent Company: Carvajal SA
Branch Office(s)
Barranquilla
Bogota
Bucaramanga
Cartagena
Cucuta
Ibaque
Manizales
Medellin
Neiva

Editorial Oveja Negra Ltda+
Carrera 14 N° 79-17, Apdo Aereo 23940, Bogota
Tel: (01) 5309678 *Fax:* (01) 2577900
Key Personnel
Editor: Jose Vicente Katarain
Commercial Manager: Leyla Bibiana Cangrejo; Victor Hugo Cangrejo
Founded: 1977
Subjects: Biography, Business, Humor, Literature, Literary Criticism, Essays, Poetry, Social Sciences, Sociology
ISBN Prefix(es): 958-06

Editorial Panamericana (Panamericana Publishing)+
Calle 12 No 34-20, Apdo Aereo No 6210, Santafe de Bogota DC
Tel: (01) 360 30 77; (01) 277 01 00; (01) 3649000 (ext 213); (03) 5603831; (03) 5603832; (03) 5603833 *Fax:* (01) 2373805
E-mail: panaedit@panamericanaeditorial.com
Web Site: www.panamericanaeditorial.com
Key Personnel
Marketing Manager: Fernando Rojas
  E-mail: frojas@panamericanaeditorial.com
Editor: Mireya Fonseca *E-mail:* mfonseca@panamericanaeditorial.com; Gabriel Silva *E-mail:* gsilva@panamericanaeditorial.com
Founded: 1993

Publish books of science & culture.
Subjects: Biography, Business, Communications, Drama, Theater, English as a Second Language, Fashion, History, Literature, Literary Criticism, Essays, Poetry, Religion - Other, Self-Help, Sports, Athletics
ISBN Prefix(es): 958-30
Number of titles published annually: 180 Print
Total Titles: 2,100 Print
Parent Company: Panamericana Editorial Ltda

Pearson Educacion de Colombia LTDA+
Imprint of Prentice Hall - Pearson
Carrera 65B No 14-32, Bogota
Tel: (0571) 420 1955 *Fax:* (0571) 420 2168
Key Personnel
President: Mauricio Mikan *E-mail:* mauricio.mikan@pearsoned.com
Man Dir, Columbia: Antonio Ballesteros
Manager, Operations: Hector Franco
Publisher & Manager, Escolar Division: Oscar E Rodriguez
Publisher & Manager, College Division: Carlos E Bermudez
Publisher & Manager, Professional/Trade: Liliana Gonzalez
Founded: 1999
Educational texts in Spanish language.
Subjects: Computer Science, Education
ISBN Prefix(es): 958-9498
Number of titles published annually: 40 Print
Parent Company: Pearson Plc

Procultura SA
Ave 25C No 3-97, Apdo Aereo 044700, Bogota
Tel: (01) 2818254
Key Personnel
Manager: Ana Cristina Mejia
General Secretary: Lelia Arango
Founded: 1980
Nueva Biblioteca Colombiana de Cultura.
Subjects: Economics, History, Literature, Literary Criticism, Essays, Poetry
ISBN Prefix(es): 958-9043

RAM Editores+
Calle 20 Sur No 60-24, Bogota DC, Cundinamarca
Tel: (01) 2623067
Key Personnel
Man Dir: Jaime Ramirez Palmar
Sales: Luz Helena S de Ramirez
Production: Bernarda Sabogal Rodriguez
Founded: 1983
Also acts as book packager.
Subjects: Astrology, Occult, Crafts, Games, Hobbies, Fashion, Health, Nutrition, Regional Interests, Self-Help
ISBN Prefix(es): 958-9063
Imprints: Libros

Editorial Santillana SA+
Calle 80, No 10-23, Bogota
Tel: (01) 635 12 00 *Fax:* (01) 236 93 82
E-mail: alfaquar@latino.net.co
Web Site: www.santillana.com.co
Key Personnel
President: Gonzalo Arboleda
General Manager: Francisco Abbad
Founded: 1988
Membership(s): Colombia Book Association
Also acts as distributor.
Subjects: Animals, Pets, Antiques, Art, Cookery, Management, Science Fiction, Fantasy, Self-Help
ISBN Prefix(es): 958-24

Siglo XXI Editores de Colombia Ltda
Carrera 14 No 80-44, Bogota DC
Tel: (01) 6110787 *Fax:* (01) 6110757
Key Personnel
Man Dir: Santiago Pombo Vejarano
Contact: Lina Maria Perez Gaviria

PUBLISHERS / COLOMBIA

Founded: 1976
Subjects: Anthropology, Architecture & Interior Design, Art, Fiction, Government, Political Science, History, Language Arts, Linguistics, Philosophy, Psychology, Psychiatry, Social Sciences, Sociology
ISBN Prefix(es): 958-606
Parent Company: Siglo XXI de Espana Editores SA, Spain
Associate Companies: Siglo XXI Editores SA de CV, Mexico

Susaeta Ediciones
Carrera 43A No 49B Sur-45, Apdo Aereo 1742-596, Envigado
Tel: (01) 2884422; (01) 2885500 *Fax:* (01) 881472
E-mail: mdsusaet@medellin.impsat.net.co
Key Personnel
Contact: William Armando Rodriguez
ISBN Prefix(es): 958-07

Tercer Mundo Editores S A, *imprint of* Tercer Mundo Editores SA

Tercer Mundo Editores SA+
Transversal 2A No 67-27, Bogota, Cundinamarca
Tel: (01) 2551539; (01) 2550737; (01) 2551695 *Fax:* (01) 2125976
E-mail: tmundo@polcola.com.co
Telex: 42192 *Cable:* TERCER MUNDO
Key Personnel
President: Santiago V Pombo
Editorial Dir: Maria Teresa Barajas
Founded: 1961
Editing, printing & distribution of book, mainly in Colombia & Latino America, with or without the company's name. Administration, management & city's studies.
Membership(s): Tercer Mundo Distribuidores S A.
Subjects: Anthropology, Astrology, Occult, Economics, Education, Environmental Studies, Government, Political Science, History, Literature, Literary Criticism, Essays, Psychology, Psychiatry, Science Fiction, Fantasy, Self-Help, Social Sciences, Sociology, Technology, Women's Studies
ISBN Prefix(es): 958-601
Number of titles published annually: 60 Print
Total Titles: 500 Print
Imprints: Tercer Mundo Editores S A
Divisions: Tercer Mundo Editores, Grafica
Distributed by Alfaomega Grupo Editor SA de CV (Mexico & Central America); Centro de Investigacion Para el Desarrollo Cid; Dolmen Ediciones SA (Chile); Edisa, Ediciones Y Disribuciones Del Istmo SA (Costa Rica); La Familia (Peru); Latin American Book Source Inc (United States); Libri Mundi (Equador); Presa Peyran Editores CA (Venezuela)
Distributor for Tercer Mundo Distribuidores SA
Bookshop(s): Libreria Tercer Mundo, Carrera 7 No 16-91, Bogota, Clara Cortes
Tel: (01) 3340504 *Fax:* (01) 2125976
E-mail: tmundolib@polcola.com.co (Bolivia)
Book Club(s): Libreria Tercer Mundo, CRA 13 No 44-70, Sandra Guerrero
E-mail: tmundolib@polcola.com.co
Shipping Address: Calle 69 No 6-46, Bogota

UNISUR, see Universidad Nacional Abierta y a Distancia

Universidad de Antioquia, Division Publicaciones+
Calle 67 No 53-108, Ciudad Universitaria, Bloque 28, oficina 233, Medellin
Mailing Address: Apdo Aereo 1226, Medellin
Tel: (04) 210 50 10 *Fax:* (04) 210 50 12
E-mail: direccion@editorialudea.com; comunicaciones@editorialudea.com
Web Site: www.editorialudea.com
Key Personnel
Dir & Professor: Jorge Juan Franco
  E-mail: j_franco64@hotmail.com
Founded: 1984
Specialize in scientific & cultural texts, not only from the institution, but also from other intellectual & academic environments.
Membership(s): The University Editorial Association of Columbia - ASEUC; The Asociancion of Editorials.
Subjects: Art, Drama, Theater, Education, History, Journalism, Literature, Literary Criticism, Essays, Medicine, Nursing, Dentistry, Music, Dance, Philosophy, Poetry, Social Sciences, Sociology
ISBN Prefix(es): 958-9021; 958-655
Number of titles published annually: 80 Print; 1 CD-ROM
Total Titles: 79 Print

Universidad de los Andes Editorial
Carrera 1 No 19-27, Edificio Au 106, Bogota
SAN: 005-2027
Tel: (01) 3394949; (01) 3394999 *Fax:* (01) 3394949 (ext 2158)
E-mail: infeduni@uniandes.edu.co
Web Site: ediciones.uniandes.edu.co
Telex: 42343 *Cable:* UNAND
Key Personnel
Dir: Martha Helena Esguerra Perez
  E-mail: maesguer@uniandes.edu.co
Founded: 1958
Subjects: Economics
ISBN Prefix(es): 958-695
Distributed by Libreria Uniandes (Colombia)

Universidad Nacional Abierta y a Distancia
Calle 53 No 14-39, Apdo Aereo 42891, Bogota
Tel: (01) 212 0159; (01) 346 0088 *Fax:* (01) 522 3497
E-mail: unisur12@gaitana.interred.net.co
Key Personnel
Contact: Jesus Emilio Martinez Henao
Founded: 1981
Subjects: Accounting, Agriculture, Biological Sciences, Business, Chemistry, Chemical Engineering, Communications, Computer Science, Economics, Environmental Studies, Film, Video, Finance, Management, Mathematics, Philosophy, Physics, Science (General), Social Sciences, Sociology
ISBN Prefix(es): 958-651
Bookshop(s): Cread Jose Acevedo y Gomex, Autopista Sur No 16-38, Bogota

Universidad Nacional Centro Editorial
Ciudad Universitaria, Torre Activa 602, Apdo Aereo 14490, Bogota
Tel: (01) 2448640
Key Personnel
Editor: Santiago Mutis Duran
ISBN Prefix(es): 958-17

Editorial Universitaria de America Ltda
Calle 41 No 20-39, Apdo Aereo 51820, Bogota
Tel: (01) 2566948; (01) 3201097 *Fax:* (01) 3201097
ISBN Prefix(es): 958-613

Carlos Valencia Editores+
Ave 25C No 3-99, Apdo Aereo 5832, 56882, Bogota
Tel: (01) 2839040; (01) 3426224 *Fax:* (01) 2839235
E-mail: ancoraed@elancoraeditores.com
Key Personnel
Man Dir: Patricia Hoher
Editorial, Rights & Permissions: Felipe Escobar Uribe
Founded: 1976
Specialize in literature for children & juveniles.
Subjects: Art, Economics, Government, Political Science, Regional Interests, Social Sciences, Sociology
ISBN Prefix(es): 958-9044; 84-8277; 958-36; 958-96577; 958-8048

Vertice Ltda
Apdo Aereo 71137, Bogota
Tel: (01) 2437113
Key Personnel
General Manager: Jesus Antonio Villa Posse
Founded: 1980
ISBN Prefix(es): 84-8281

Villegas Editores Ltda
Ave 82 No 11-50, Bogota
Tel: (01) 6161788 *Fax:* (01) 6160020
E-mail: villedi@cable.net
Web Site: www.villegaseditores.com
Key Personnel
President & Editor: Benjamin Villegas
Subjects: Art, Cookery, Photography
ISBN Prefix(es): 958-8160; 958-9393

Editorial Voluntad SA+
Carrera 7 No 24-89 Pisos 21 & 24, Bogota
Tel: (01) 241 04 44 *Fax:* (01) 241 04 39
E-mail: voluntad@voluntad.com.co
Web Site: www.voluntad.com.co
Key Personnel
Man Dir: Gaston de Bedout-Arbelaez
Editorial Dir: William Gomez
Administration Dir: Hector Hurtado
Sales & Publicity Dir: Jairo Roldan
Founded: 1930
Subjects: Art, Communications, Cookery, Crafts, Games, Hobbies, Journalism, Language Arts, Linguistics, Music, Dance, Sports, Athletics
ISBN Prefix(es): 958-02
Branch Office(s)
Carrera 43B No 80-60, Barranquilla
  Tel: (095) 378 0955 *Fax:* (095) 373 5117
  E-mail: volbar01@voluntad.com.co
Zona Norte, Carrera 43B No 22A Bis 12, Bogota
  Tel: 368 3168; 368 3169; 268 3371 *Fax:* 368 3168; 368 3169; 268 3371 *E-mail:* volbog03@andinet.com
Zona Sur, Calle 1 No 29-15, Bogota *Tel:* 247 1617; 562 3390 *E-mail:* volbog01@andinet.com
Carrera 34 No 51-79, Bucaramanga
  Tel: (0976) 577 232 *Fax:* (0976) 573 502
  E-mail: volbuc01@andinet.com
Avenida 5a B Norte N, 21-69, Cali *Tel:* (092) 660 1069; (092) 660 1070; (092) 660 1071; (092) 667 3207; (092) 660-0653; (092) 661 5929 *E-mail:* volcali@voluntad.com.co
Carrera 60 A No 30-47, Cartagena *Tel:* (0956) 534 387; (0956) 531 254; (0956) 531 230; (0956) 531 296 *Fax:* (0956) 534 387; (0956) 531 254; (0956) 531 230; (0956) 531 296 *E-mail:* volcar01@voluntad.com.co
Avenida 2 E N 17 A 35, Cucuta *Tel:* (097) 571 9984 *Fax:* (097) 583 3132 *E-mail:* volcuc01@telecom.com.co
Carrera 8 No 17 B 44, Duitama *Tel:* (098) 760 3273 *Fax:* (098) 763 0999 *E-mail:* voldui01@telecom.com.co
Calle 18 No 7-21 Piso 1, Ibague *Tel:* (098) 262 3895; (098) 263 5548; (098) 263 0899 *Fax:* (098) 262 3895; (098) 263 5548; (098) 263 0899 *E-mail:* vollba01@telecom.com.co
Calle 36 No 77-36, Medellin *Tel:* (094) 411 5916; (094) 411 5897; (094) 413 1665 *Fax:* (094) 411 5767 *E-mail:* volmed01@voluntad.com.co
Carrera 6a No 27-36, Monteria *Tel:* (0947) 82 1266 *Fax:* (0947) 82 1266 *E-mail:* volmon01@telecom.com.co

Calle 8a No 12-25, Neiva *Tel:* (0988) 715 276 *Fax:* (0988) 715 276 *E-mail:* edivolnei@multiphone.net.co
Carrera 21 A No 17-10, Pasto *Tel:* (0927) 214 128 *E-mail:* volpas01@etb.net.co
Calle 32 Bis No 13-09 piso 2, Pereira *Tel:* (096) 336 0095 *Fax:* (096) 266156 *E-mail:* volper01@epm.net.co
Carrera 21B No 21-65, Santa Marta *Tel:* (095) 420 1601 *Fax:* (095) 420 1661 *E-mail:* volsma01@celcaribe.net.co
Carrera 26 No 19-50, Sincelejo *Tel:* (095) 281 8916; (095) 281 7050 *E-mail:* volunsjo@telecom.com.co
Carrera 5a No 14-69 Piso 1, Valledupar *Tel:* (0955) 742 153 *Fax:* (0955) 708 717 *E-mail:* volva101@teleupar.net.co
Calle 39 B No 27-86 piso 2, Villavicencio *Tel:* (098) 670 4921 *Fax:* (098) 664 17 42 *E-mail:* volvil01@andinet.com

Ediciones Alfred y Cia Wild Ltda
Calle 82 No 12A-35 Piso 2, Bogota
Tel: (01) 6218000 *Fax:* (01) 6114338
E-mail: info@galeriaalfredwild.com
Web Site: www.galeriaalfredwild.com
Key Personnel
Legal Representative: Alfred Wild Toro
ISBN Prefix(es): 958-95327; 958-96323
Subsidiaries: Casa Poblana (3 almacenes)

The Democratic Republic of the Congo

General Information

Capital: Kinshasa
Language: Officially French
Religion: Most follow traditional African beliefs; some Catholic and Protestant
Population: 39 million
Shop Hours: 0800-1200, 1500-1800 Monday-Friday; 0800-1200 Saturday
Currency: 100 makutu = 1 zaire
Export/Import Information: No tariff, but for books not of educational, scientific or cultural use there is a revenue tax; children's picture books and atlases are also taxed. Small quantities of advertising matter free. Statistical Tax on all imports. Goods subject to duty also subject to Turnover Tax of percentage of CIF value and customs and statistical tax. No import licences for books. Exchange controls.
Copyright: Berne, Florence (see Copyright Conventions, pg xi)

CDPZ, see Connaissance et Pratique du Droit Zairos (CDPZ)

Centre de Recherche, et Pedagogie Appliquee
BP 8815, Kinshasa 1
Key Personnel
Dir: P Detienne *Tel:* (012) 22248
Adminstration: J Vannuffelen
Founded: 1959
Subjects: Accounting, Education, Geography, Geology, Language Arts, Linguistics, Mathematics, Medicine, Nursing, Dentistry, Physical Sciences
Distributor for L'Epiphamie

Shipping Address: 1142 11e Rue, Limete, Kinshasa
Warehouse: 1142 11e Rue, Limete, Kinshasa
Orders to: 1142 11e Rue, Limete, Kinshasa

Centre de Vulgarisation Agricole
BP 4008, Kinshasa 2
Tel: (012) 71165 *Fax:* (012) 21351
Key Personnel
Dir General: Kimpianga Mahaniah
Publications: Ntanama Kamba
Subjects: Agriculture, Environmental Studies, Gardening, Plants, Health, Nutrition
Branch Office(s)
1920 Roosevelt Dr, Apt 52, Northfield, MN, United States
Distributed by Inades Formation (Zaire)

Centre Protestant d'Editions et de Diffusion (CEDI)+
BP 11398, Kinshasa 1
Key Personnel
Man Dir: Henry Dirks
Founded: 1935
Subjects: Biography, Fiction, Poetry, Religion - Other
Bookshop(s): CEDI Bookshop

Connaissance et Pratique du Droit Zairos (CDPZ)+
BP 5502, Kinshasa, Gombe
Key Personnel
Editor: Dibunda Kabuinji
Founded: 1987
Subjects: Law
Total Titles: 6 Print; 6 Online
Associate Companies: Societe d'Etudes Juridiques du Congo (SEJC)
Imprints: Reper Toire General be Jurisprubence be la Cour Supreme be Justice; Revue Analytiqu ebe Jurisprubencebu Congo; Revue Juritique bu Congo
Bookshop(s): One rue Limete, Kinshasa/Masina-Petro Congo, Republique Democratique du Congo
Warehouse: One, rue Limete, Kinshasa-Masina/Petro Congo

Facultes catholiques de Kinshasa
c/o Prof Dr L Bertsch S J, Ave de l'Universite 2, Kinshasa-Limete
Mailing Address: BP 1534, Kinshasa-Limete
Tel: (0243) 88 46 965 *Fax:* (0243) 88 46 965
E-mail: facakin@yahoo.fr

Facultes Catoliques de Kinshasa
2, Ave de l'Universite, 1534 Kinshasa
Tel: (088) 46 965 *Fax:* (088) 46 965
E-mail: facakin@ic.cd
Web Site: www.cenco.cd/facultescath/
Key Personnel
Dir: Prof Abbe Waswandi Kakule
Editorial: Prof Abbe Mukuna Wa Mutanda; Prof Abbe Atal; Prof Pere Leon de Saint Moulin; Prof Mweze
Founded: 1957
Subjects: Anthropology, Art, Biblical Studies, Communications, Computer Science, Economics, Government, Political Science, History
Bookshop(s): Librarie Saint Paul, Kinshasa-Limete
Orders to: SEDIP (Service de Diffusion des Publications), Kinshasa-Limete

Presses Universitaires du Zaiire (PUZ)
Blvd du 30 Juin 4113, Kinshasa 1
Mailing Address: BP 1682, Kinshasa 1
Tel: 30652
Telex: 21394 Bce Es *Cable:* PUZ Enseignement

Key Personnel
Man Dir, Rights & Permissions: Mumbanza mwa Bawele
Editorial: Kabongo Kabongo
Sales: Nsolo Abeyingi
Production: Kawumbu Kabemba
Publicity: Bisimwa Nabintu
Founded: 1972
Subjects: Biography, Economics, Education, Ethnicity, Foreign Countries, History, Law, Literature, Literary Criticism, Essays, Medicine, Nursing, Dentistry, Philosophy, Poetry, Psychology, Psychiatry, Religion - Other, Science (General), Social Sciences, Sociology, Technology
Parent Company: Enseignement Superieu, Universitaire et Recherche Scientifique, BP 1682, Kinshasa-Gombe
Imprints: PUZ
Branch Office(s)
Lubumbashi
Bookshop(s): Librairie des Presses Universitaires; Librairie Universitaire de l'ISP/Kawanga; Librairie du 'Groupe du Mukuba', Lubumbashi

PUZ, *imprint of* Presses Universitaires du Zaiire (PUZ)

Reper Toire General be Jurisprubence be la Cour Supreme be Justice, *imprint of* Connaissance et Pratique du Droit Zairos (CDPZ)

Revue Analytiqu ebe Jurisprubencebu Congo, *imprint of* Connaissance et Pratique du Droit Zairos (CDPZ)

Revue Juritique bu Congo, *imprint of* Connaissance et Pratique du Droit Zairos (CDPZ)

Saint-Paul+
10, rue Limete, BP 127, Kinshasa
Key Personnel
President: Charles Djunju-Simba
International Rights: M Claude Lechat
Founded: 1989
Subjects: Communications, Drama, Theater, Fiction, Literature, Literary Criticism, Essays
ISBN Prefix(es): 2-7414
Distributed by Mediaspaul

Costa Rica

General Information

Capital: San Jose
Language: Spanish
Religion: Roman Catholic
Population: 3.2 million
Bank Hours: 0900-1500 Monday-Friday
Shop Hours: 0800-1200, 1400-1800 Monday-Saturday (some close Saturday afternoon)
Currency: 100 centimos = 1 Costa Rican colon
Export/Import Information: No import licenses, but statistical recording prior to importation necessary. Imports over a certain value must be registered with Banco Central to be eligible for foreign exchange allocation.
Copyright: Berne, UCC, Buenos Aires (see Copyright Conventions, pg xi)

Academia de Centro America+
Apdo 6347, 1000 San Jose
Tel: 283-1847 *Fax:* 283-1848
E-mail: info@academiaca.or.cr; rherrera@acedmiaca.or.cr

PUBLISHERS — COSTA RICA

Key Personnel
President: Eduardo Lizano
Subjects: Agriculture, Business, Economics, Environmental Studies, Finance, Health, Nutrition, Labor, Industrial Relations
ISBN Prefix(es): 9977-21

Asamblea Legislativa, Biblioteca Monsenor Sanabria
Apdo 1013, 1000 San Jose
Tel: 223-2396 *Fax:* 243-2400
E-mail: jvolio@congreso.aleg.go.cr; vvargas@congreso.aleg.go.cr; epaniagu@congreso.aleg.go.cr
Subjects: Economics, Education, Social Sciences, Sociology
ISBN Prefix(es): 9977-916

CATIE, see Centro Agronomico Tropical de Investigacion y Ensenanza (CATIE)

CCCCA, see Confederacion de Cooperativas del Caribe y Centro America (CCCCA)

Centro Agronomico Tropical de Investigacion y Ensenanza (CATIE)
Apdo 7170, 150 Turrialba
Tel: 556-6431 *Fax:* 556-1533
E-mail: comunicacion@catie.ac.cr
Web Site: www.catie.ac.cr
Telex: 8005 CATIE CR *Cable:* CATIE TURRIALBA
Key Personnel
Editor: Eli Rodriguez *E-mail:* erodrigu@catie.ac.cr
Founded: 1942
Research & Higher Educational Center
Specialize in scientific investigation & techniques of Tropical America, Research & Training of Tropical Agriculture & Natural Resouces.
Subjects: Agriculture, Biological Sciences, Developing Countries, Economics, Education, Engineering (General), Environmental Studies, Gardening, Plants, How-to, Natural History, Social Sciences, Sociology, Technology
ISBN Prefix(es): 9977-57; 9977-951

Confederacion de Cooperativas del Caribe y Centro America (CCCCA)+
400 mts este contiguo a Kilates, del Edificio el ICE en Tibas, Apdo 3658, San Jose
Tel: 2404592 *Fax:* 2333122
E-mail: ccocca@sol.racsa.co.cr
Key Personnel
Executive Director: Felix J Cristia
Subjects: Finance, Public Administration
ISBN Prefix(es): 9977-82
Subsidiaries: Sistema de Informacion Cooperativa (REDI-COOP)
Branch Office(s)
CCC-CA/Oficina Subrregional, PO Box 360707, San Juan 00936-0707, Puerto Rico

Editorial Costa Rica
Apdo 10010, 1000 San Jose
Tel: 253-5354 *Fax:* 253-5091
E-mail: ventas@editorialcostarica.com; difusion@editorialcostarica.com
Web Site: www.editorialcostarica.com
Key Personnel
Management: Habib Succar *E-mail:* editocr@racsa.co.cr
Sales: Enilda Campos Barrantes
Production: Dennis Mesen Segura
Publicity Manager: Gustavo Adolfo Gonzalez Mederas
Founded: 1959
Subjects: Regional Interests
ISBN Prefix(es): 84-8361; 9977-23

Editorial DEI (Departamento Ecumenico de Investigaciones)+
Apdo 390-2070, Sabanilla, Montes de Oca, San Jose
Tel: 253-0229; 253-9124 *Fax:* 2531541
E-mail: publicaciones@dei-cr.org
Web Site: www.dei-cr.org
Telex: 3472 ADEI
Key Personnel
General Manager: Jose Duque
Founded: 1977
Subjects: Economics, Government, Political Science, History, Theology, Women's Studies
ISBN Prefix(es): 9977-904; 9977-83
Imprints: Revista Pasos
Bookshop(s): Libreria Horizonte, Apdo 447-2070, San Jose

Fundacion Omar Dengo
Apdo 1032-2050, San Jose
Tel: 257 6263 *Fax:* 2221654
E-mail: info@fod.ac.cr
Web Site: www.fod.ac.cr
Key Personnel
President: Alfonso Gutierrez Cerdas
Founded: 1987
ISBN Prefix(es): 9977-11

Departamento Ecumenico de Investigaciones, see Editorial DEI (Departamento Ecumenico de Investigaciones)

EDUCA, see Editorial Universitaria Centroamericana (EDUCA)

Asocicion Escuela Para Todos+
Apdo 4757, 1000 San Jose
Tel: 2255438; 2255338; 2340530; 2341339 *Fax:* 2243014
Key Personnel
President: Manuela Tattenbach
Founded: 1963
ISBN Prefix(es): 9977-51

EUNA, see Editorial Universidad Nacional (EUNA)

Ediciones FLACSO Costa Rica
Del Automercado los Yoses, 400 mts al sur y 200 al oeste, 1000 San Jose
Mailing Address: Apdo 11747, 1000 San Jose
Tel: 2346890 *Fax:* 2256779
ISBN Prefix(es): 9977-68; 84-89401

Garcia Hermanos Imprenta y Litografia
Apdo 10015, 1000 Santa Ana, San Jose
Tel: 2202003; 2212223 *Fax:* 2310675
E-mail: info@novanet.co.cr
Web Site: www.novanet.co.cr
Key Personnel
Contact: Juan Carlos Caamano Umana *E-mail:* jcc@novanet.co.cr
ISBN Prefix(es): 9977-38

IICA, see Instituto Interamericano de Cooperacion para la Agricultura (IICA)

Imprenta y Litografia Trejos SA
Apdo 10-096, 1000 San Jose
Tel: 2242411 *Fax:* 2241528
Key Personnel
President: Alvaro Trejos
ISBN Prefix(es): 9977-54

INCAE, see Insituto Centroamericano de Administracion de Empresas (INCAE)

Insituto Centroamericano de Administracion de Empresas (INCAE)
Del Vivero Procesa No 1, 2 Km al Oeste, La Garita, Alajuela
Tel: 433-9908; 433-9961; 437-2305 *Fax:* 433-9989; 433-9983
E-mail: incaecr@mail.incae.ac.cr
Web Site: www.incae.ac.cr
Key Personnel
Chief Marketing: Sonia Jimenez *E-mail:* jimenezs@mail.incae.ac.cr
ISBN Prefix(es): 9977-71

Instituto Interamericano de Cooperacion para la Agricultura (IICA)
PO Box 55-2200, San Isidro de Coronado, San Jose
Tel: (0506) 216-0222 *Fax:* (0506) 216-0233
E-mail: iicahq@iica.ac.cr
Web Site: www.iica.int
Key Personnel
Dir, Information & Communication: Jorge Sariego *E-mail:* jsariego@iica.ac.cr
Subjects: Agriculture, Computer Science, Developing Countries, Earth Sciences, Environmental Studies, Marketing, Technology, Veterinary Science, Women's Studies
ISBN Prefix(es): 956-212

Jose Alfonso Sandoval Nunez+
100 mts este de la Municipalidad, Residencia El Carmen San Pedro de Montes de Oca, San Jose
Tel: 2252331; 8-326-426
E-mail: asandova@alpha.emate.ucr.ac.cr; k_sanny@hotmail.com
Subjects: Education, Mathematics
ISBN Prefix(es): 9968-9882
Total Titles: 5 Print

Juricom+
De la Pops Curridabat, 100 mts sur, Apdo 4387, 1000 San Jose
Tel: 2836942 *Fax:* 2253800
E-mail: juricom@sol.racsa.co.cr
Key Personnel
Contact: Alejandra Linner de Silva
Founded: 1996
Subjects: Law
ISBN Prefix(es): 9968-769

Libreria Imprenta y Litografia Lehmann SA
Apdo 10011, San Jose
Tel: 2231212
Telex: 2540 Lill Eh
Key Personnel
Man Dir: Antonio Lehmann Struve
Publicity: Orlando Mora
Founded: 1894
Subjects: Fiction, Nonfiction (General)
ISBN Prefix(es): 9977-949

Litografia Artex, SA+
Apdo 7111, 1000 Heredia
Tel: 2373144 *Fax:* 2379568
Key Personnel
Contact: Gilbert Campos Gamboa
Founded: 1971
Subjects: Advertising, Medicine, Nursing, Dentistry, Poetry, Religion - Catholic
ISBN Prefix(es): 9977-86

Litografia e Imprenta LIL SA
Apdo 75, 1100 Tibas
Tel: 2350011; 2213622 *Fax:* 2407814
Key Personnel
Contact: Mario Salazar Fonseca
Founded: 1974
ISBN Prefix(es): 9977-47

Museo Historico Cultural Juan Santamaria
Apdo 785, 4050 Alajuela

Tel: 441-4775; 442-1838 *Fax:* 441-6926
E-mail: mhcjscr@racsa.co.cr
Web Site: www.museojuansantamaria.go.cr
Key Personnel
Dir: Raul Aguilar
Founded: 1980
Subjects: Genealogy, History
ISBN Prefix(es): 9977-953

Editorial Nacional de Salud y Seguridad Social Ednass
Caja Costarricense de Seguridad Social, Apdo 10105, 1000 San Jose
Tel: 231-2214 *Fax:* 232-7451
E-mail: cendeiss@info.ccss.sa.cr
Key Personnel
Contact: Gerardo Campos Gamboa
Founded: 1988
Subjects: Behavioral Sciences, Biological Sciences, Health, Nutrition, Medicine, Nursing, Dentistry, Public Administration, Social Sciences, Sociology
ISBN Prefix(es): 9977-984
Number of titles published annually: 10 Print
Total Titles: 2 Print

Revista Pasos, *imprint of* Editorial DEI (Departamento Ecumenico de Investigaciones)

Editorial Porvenir
300 este de la escuela Franklin D Roosevelt, Barrio La Granja, San Pedro
Mailing Address: Apdo 447-2050, Montes de Oca
Tel: 224-8119; 224-1052; 225-3115 *Fax:* 283-8893; 224-8119
E-mail: porvenir@racsa.co.cr
Telex: 3220 CECADE CR
Key Personnel
President: William Reuben
Dir: Victoria Paris
Founded: 1979
Subjects: Economics, History, Law, Psychology, Psychiatry, Social Sciences, Sociology
ISBN Prefix(es): 9977-944; 9968-764

Ediciones Promesa+
Contiguo a Taco Bell, Barrio Dent, Apdo 4300, San Jose
Tel: 253-3759; 225-1511; 283-3033 *Fax:* 225-1286
E-mail: edicionespromesa@hotmail.com
Key Personnel
President: Helena Ospina *E-mail:* helenaospina@hotmail.com
Manager: Erika Chinchilla
Founded: 1982
Publishing, video, CD & documentation cultural center
Cultural project interrelating the arts.
Membership(s): Camara Costarricense del Libro.
Subjects: Anthropology, Art, Behavioral Sciences, Biography, Child Care & Development, Drama, Theater, Education, Fashion, Film, Video, History, Human Relations, Language Arts, Linguistics, Literature, Literary Criticism, Essays, Music, Dance, Philosophy, Poetry, Psychology, Psychiatry, Religion - Catholic, Self-Help, Social Sciences, Sociology, Theology, Women's Studies
ISBN Prefix(es): 9977-947; 9968-41
Number of titles published annually: 24 Print; 6 Audio
Total Titles: 85 Print; 2 E-Book; 20 Audio
Parent Company: Promotora de Medios de Comunicacion SA
Associate Companies: Electronic Engineering, PO Box 4300, 1000 San Jose, Contact: Helena Maria Fonseca
U.S. Office(s): Ma Rosa Noda, 9022 SW 123 Court 0-109, Miami, FL 33186, United States, Contact: Maria Rosa Noda *Tel:* 305-279-9997 *E-mail:* mrnoda@un.int

Showroom(s): Edificio Electronic Engineering, Frente a Rectoria, Universidad de Costa Rica, Carretera a Sabanilla, 1000 San Jose, Contact: Helena Maria Fonseca *Tel:* (305) 283-3033 *Fax:* (305) 225-1286 *E-mail:* hf@eecrica.com *Web Site:* www.eecrica.com
Bookshop(s): Libreria Universal, Libreria Lehmann, San Jose

Editorial Tecnologica de Costa Rica+
Apdo 159, 7050 Cartago
Tel: 552-5333 ext 2297 *Fax:* 552-5354; 551-5348
E-mail: editec@itcr.ac.cr
Web Site: www.itcr.ac.cr
Key Personnel
Dir: Mario Castillo-Mendez
Founded: 1978
Membership(s): EULAC (Association of University Publishers of Latin American & the Caribbean).
Subjects: Science (General), Technology
ISBN Prefix(es): 9977-66; 84-89400

Editorial Texto Ltda+
Apdo 2988, 1000 San Jose
Tel: 2316643 *Fax:* 2962429
Key Personnel
President: Frank Thomas Gallardo
  E-mail: gallardo@sol.racsa.co.cr
Vice President: Renee Echeverria Rodriguez de Luz
Founded: 1963
Private Company
Online translating from Spanish to English & vice versa.
Subjects: Animals, Pets, Real Estate, Regional Interests
ISBN Prefix(es): 9977-29
Total Titles: 8 Print

UICN, see Union Mundial para la Naturaleza (UICN), Oficina Regional para Mesoamerica

Union Mundial para la Naturaleza (UICN), Oficina Regional para Mesoamerica
Apdo 146-2150, San Jose
Tel: 241-0101 *Fax:* 240-9934
E-mail: correo@iucn.org
Web Site: www.iucn.org/places/orma
Key Personnel
Contact: Dr Enrique J Lahmann
Founded: 1988
Subjects: Biological Sciences, Developing Countries, Environmental Studies, Coastal Zone Management, Wetlands, Gender & Development, Nature Conservation, Sustainable Development, Wildlife Management, Forest Management
ISBN Prefix(es): 9968-743
Branch Office(s)
IUCN Canada, 555 Rene Levesque Blvd W, Suite 500, Montreal, PQ H2Z 1B1, Canada *Tel:* 514-287-9704 *Fax:* 514-287-6987 *E-mail:* canada@iucn.org *Web Site:* www.iucn.org/places/canada
IUCN Laguna Lachua National Park Project Office, 7a, av 6-80, Zona 13, Guatemala, Guatemala *Tel:* (0247) 35214 *Fax:* (0247) 35214 *E-mail:* proy.lachua@starnet.net.gt
IUCN Manglares del Pacifico de Guatemala Project Office, 7a, av 6-80, Zona 13, Guatemala, Guatemala *Tel:* (0247) 35213 *Fax:* (0247) 35213 *E-mail:* proy.manglares@starnet.net.gt
UICN Oficina Regional para America del Sur, Av De Los Shyris 2680 y Gaspar de Villarroel, Edificio Mita-Cobadelsa, Penthouse, PH, Casilla 17-17-626, Quito, Ecuador *Tel:* (02) 2261-075 *Fax:* (02) 2261-075 (ext 230) *E-mail:* samerica@sur.iucn.org *Web Site:* www.sur.iucn.org (South America)
U.S. Office(s): IUCN US Multilateral Office, 1630 Connecticut Ave NW, 3rd floor, Washington, DC 20009-1053, United States *Tel:* 202-387-4826 *Fax:* 202-387-4823 *E-mail:* postmaster@iucnus.org *Web Site:* www.iucn.org/places/usa

Editorial de la Universidad de Costa Rica+
Imprint of University of Costa Rica
Ciudad Universitaria Rodrigo Facio, 2060 Montes de Oca
Tel: 207-5006; 207-5837 *Fax:* 224-9367
E-mail: direccion@editorial.ucr.ac.cr
Web Site: www.editorial.ucr.ac.cr
Telex: 2544 Unicori
Key Personnel
Dir: Fernando Duran
Administrative Coordinator: Ruben Chacon
  Tel: 207-5624 *E-mail:* administracion@editorial.ucr.ac.cr
Founded: 1975
Subjects: Agriculture, Anthropology, Archaeology, Architecture & Interior Design, Art, Behavioral Sciences, Biological Sciences, Career Development, Civil Engineering, Computer Science, Cookery, Earth Sciences, Economics, Education, Energy, Engineering (General), English as a Second Language, Environmental Studies, Government, Political Science, Health, Nutrition, History, Language Arts, Linguistics, Law, Management, Natural History, Physical Sciences, Poetry, Public Administration, Science (General), Social Sciences, Sociology, Sports, Athletics
ISBN Prefix(es): 9977-67
Total Titles: 40 Print; 1 CD-ROM

Editorial Universidad Estatal a Distancia (EUNED)
Apdo 474-2050, San Pedro de Montes De Oca, San Jose
Tel: 234-7954; 253-2121 (ext 2440) *Fax:* 257-5042; 234-9138
E-mail: editoria@uned.ac.cr
Web Site: www.uned.ac.cr/ejecutiva/editorial/
Telex: 3003 *Cable:* UNED
Key Personnel
President, Rights & Permissions: Dr Alberto Canas Escalante
Editorial Dir: Rene Muinos Gual
Sales Dir: Hernan Mora Gonzalez
Production: Carlos Zamora-Murillo
Publicity: Annie Umana Campos
Founded: 1977
Subjects: Agriculture, Economics, Education, Government, Political Science, History, Medicine, Nursing, Dentistry, Philosophy
ISBN Prefix(es): 9977-64; 84-8362; 9968-31
Showroom(s): Calle 11, Ave 12-14, San Jose *Fax:* 331601
Bookshop(s): Libreria UNED; Calle 11, Ave 12-14, San Jose

Editorial Universidad Nacional (EUNA)
Apdo 86, 3000 Heredia
Tel: 277-3204; 277-3825 *Fax:* 277-3204
E-mail: editoria@una.ac.cr
Web Site: www.una.ac.cr/euna
Key Personnel
Contact: Sr Francisco Carballo
Founded: 1978
Membership(s): EULAC-CERLAC.
Subjects: Education, History, Literature, Literary Criticism, Essays, Poetry
ISBN Prefix(es): 9977-65
Number of titles published annually: 45 Print
Total Titles: 250 Print
Distributed by ACAL

Universidad para la Paz (University for Peace)
Apdo 138, 6100 Ciudad Colon, San Jose
Tel: 205-9000; 249-1511 (ext 20) *Fax:* 249-1929
E-mail: info@upeace.org
Web Site: www.upeace.org
ISBN Prefix(es): 9977-925

Editorial Universitaria Centroamericana (EDUCA)+
Ciudad Universitaria Rodrigo Facio, Apdo 64, 2060 San Jose
Tel: 2258740 *Fax:* 2340071
E-mail: educacr@sol.racsa.co.cr
Telex: 3011 COSUCA
Key Personnel
Dir: Sebastian Vaquerano
Sales: Anita de Formoso
Founded: 1969
Subjects: History, Poetry, Regional Interests, Romance, Social Sciences, Sociology
ISBN Prefix(es): 9977-30; 84-8360

Cote d'Ivoire

General Information

Capital: Yamoussoukro
Language: French (officially) and several African languages
Religion: Traditional, 20% Islamic, 20% Christian (mostly Roman Catholic)
Population: 13.5 million
Bank Hours: 0800-1200, 1500-1900 Monday-Friday
Shop Hours: 0800-1200, 1530-1830 or 1900 Monday-Friday; 0800-1200, 1430-1730 Saturday
Currency: 100 centimes = 1 CFA franc
Export/Import Information: Member of West African Economic Community. No tariff on books; single copies free but most advertising subject to customs duty, fiscal duty and VAT. No import licenses required for imports from EEC or Franc Zone.
Copyright: Berne, Florence (see Copyright Conventions, pg xi)

Universite d'Abidjan+
BP V 34, Abidjan 01
Tel: 441285 *Fax:* 434254
E-mail: puci@africaonline.co.ci
Telex: 3469
Key Personnel
Publications Dir: Alain Poiri
Founded: 1964
Subjects: Biography, Communications, Developing Countries, Economics, Environmental Studies, Law, Microcomputers, Public Administration, Social Sciences, Sociology
ISBN Prefix(es): 2-7166
Number of titles published annually: 50 Print

Akohi Editions
13 BP 585, Abidjan 13
Tel: 24 39 54 79 *Fax:* 24 39 75 58
Key Personnel
President: Bosson Brou Evariste *Tel:* 24 39 58 01; 05 99 25 52
Founded: 1995
Subjects: Drama, Theater, Human Relations, Literature, Literary Criticism, Essays, Music, Dance, Poetry
ISBN Prefix(es): 2-9507542; 2-910569
Total Titles: 10 Print
Parent Company: Editions Akohi
Associate Companies: Biennale Internationale des Arts Lettres et du Tourisme, 13 BP, 585 Abidjan, Contact: Bosson Brou Evariste *Tel:* 24 39 58 01; 24 99 25 52; 24 39 40 37
Subsidiaries: Imprimerie Akohi
Divisions: Akohi Diffusion
Distributed by Ed Passerelle Abidjan
Distributor for Ed Baudhouat Abidjan; Ed Passerelle Abidjan
Showroom(s): Librairie Akohi *Tel:* 05 99 25 52

Book Club(s): Association des Editeurs-Ivoiriens, Contact: Mariam Sy Diawara *Tel:* 35 35 35 *Fax:* 39 75 58; Association des Ecrivains, Contact: Josetti Abondio *Tel:* 24 39 10 37
Shipping Address: Abobo, 2e Arret Sotra, 500M apres Brigade Gendarmerie Route, Anyama, Contact: Bosson Brou Evariste Kowouka

CEDA, see Centre d'Edition et de Diffusion Africaines

Centre de Publications Evangeliques
BP 900, Abidjan 08
Tel: 444805 *Fax:* 445817
Key Personnel
Dir: Jules Ouoba
Founded: 1970
Subjects: Biblical Studies, Nonfiction (General), Religion - Protestant, Religion - Other
ISBN Prefix(es): 2-910307

Centre d'Edition et de Diffusion Africaines
17 rue des Carrossiers, Abidjan 04
Mailing Address: 04 BP 541, Abidjan 04
Tel: 21 24 65 10; 21 24 65 11 *Fax:* 21 25 05 67
E-mail: infos@ceda-ci.com
Web Site: www.ceda-ci.com
Key Personnel
Editorial Dir: Marie Agathe Amoikon
Dir: Mr Venance Kacou
Founded: 1961
Distributors on behalf of INADES, the National University of the Ivory Coast & the Bibliotheque nationale.
Subjects: Biography, History, Law, Nonfiction (General), Philosophy, Regional Interests, Science (General), Social Sciences, Sociology
ISBN Prefix(es): 2-86394

Heritage Publishing Co+
BP 54, Cidex 3 Abidjan-Riviera
Tel: 433056 *Fax:* 433056
Key Personnel
Contact: Tah Asongwed
Founded: 1993
Subjects: Biography, Developing Countries, Fiction, Government, Political Science, Language Arts, Linguistics, Nonfiction (General)
ISBN Prefix(es): 2-910021
Imprints: HP
U.S. Office(s): Heritage Publshing Company, 1015 Stirling Rd, Silver Spring, MD 20901, United States *Tel:* 301-593-6450
Distributed by Waterville Publishing House (Ghana)
Distributor for Three Dimensional Publishing (USA)

HP, *imprint of* Heritage Publishing Co

NEI, see Les Nouvelles Editions Ivoiriennes (NEI)

Les Nouvelles Editions Ivoiriennes+
One blvd de Marseille, 01 Abidjan
Mailing Address: 01 BP 1818, 01 Abidjan
Tel: 21 24 07 66; 21 24 08 25 *Fax:* 21 24 24 56
E-mail: edition@nei-ci.com
Web Site: www.nei-ci.com
Telex: 22564 Nea CI
Key Personnel
Commercial Dir: M Oze G Roger
Founded: 1972
Subjects: Art, Drama, Theater, History, Literature, Literary Criticism, Essays, Religion - Other
ISBN Prefix(es): 2-7236
Parent Company: Les Nouvelles Editions Africaines du Senegal, 10, rue Amadou Assane-Ndoye, BP 260, Dakar, Senegal
Associate Companies: Togo

Les Nouvelles Editions Ivoiriennes (NEI)+
Subsidiary of Hachette Livre International
One blvd de Marseille, 01 Abidjan
Mailing Address: 01 BP 1818, Abidjan 01
Tel: 21 24 92 12; 21 24 07 66; 21 24 08 25 *Fax:* 21 24 24 56
Key Personnel
Dir General: Guy Lambin
Founded: 1992
Subjects: Art, Literature, Literary Criticism, Essays, Poetry
ISBN Prefix(es): 2-910190; 2-911725; 2-84487
Distributed by EDICEF (France)
Distributor for Classiques Hachette sur Cote d'Ivoire; Hachette Livres

PUCI, see Universite d'Abidjan

Croatia

General Information

Capital: Zagreb
Language: Croatian
Religion: Predominantly Roman Catholic & Eastern Orthodox
Population: 4.8 million
Bank Hours: 0700-1900 Monday-Friday; 0700-1200 Saturday; 0800-1600 in the small towns
Shop Hours: 0800-1900 Monday-Friday & 0800-1300 Saturday
Currency: kuna, divisible into 100 lipa
Export/Import Information: Firms trade freely with foreign partners in accordance with international agreements & treaties, and with measures which are in line with the principles & demands of the World Trade Organization.
Copyright: UCC, Berne (see Copyright Conventions, page xi)

AGM doo+
Mihanoviceva 28, 10000 Zagreb
Tel: (01) 4856309; (01) 4856307 *Fax:* (01) 4856316
E-mail: agm@agm.hr
Web Site: www.agm.hr
Key Personnel
Dir: Janislav Saban *E-mail:* janislav.saban@agm.hr
Subjects: Art, Drama, Theater, History, Literature, Literary Criticism, Essays, Nonfiction (General), Philosophy, Social Sciences, Sociology
ISBN Prefix(es): 953-174

ALFA dd za izdavacke, graficke i trgovacke poslove+
Nova Ves 23/a, 10000 Zagreb
Tel: (01) 4666 066; (01) 4666 077 *Fax:* (01) 4666 258
E-mail: alfa-zg@zg.tel.hr
Key Personnel
Manager: Miro Petric
Editor: Bozidar Petrac
Public Relations & Marketing: Ana Maria Bogisic
Founded: 1971
Subjects: Cookery, Education, Fiction, Gardening, Plants, Government, Political Science, Literature, Literary Criticism, Essays, Poetry, Religion - Catholic
Bookshop(s): Krjizara (bookshop), ALFA, Importanne Centar, 1000 Zagreb
Shipping Address: Platana bb, 10000 Zagreb
Warehouse: Platana bb, 10000 Zagreb

ArTresor naklada+
Amruseva, 9, 10000 Zagreb
Tel: (01) 487 2917 *Fax:* (01) 487 2916
E-mail: artresor@zg.tel.hr

Key Personnel
Manager: Silva Tomanic Kis
Founded: 1996
Subjects: History, Language Arts, Linguistics, Literature, Literary Criticism, Essays, Philosophy, Poetry
ISBN Prefix(es): 953-6522

Drzavna Uprava za Zastitu Prirode i Okolisa (State Directorate for the Protection of Nature & Environment)
Ulica Grada Vukovara 78/111, 10000 Zagreb
Tel: (01) 613 3444 *Fax:* (01) 611 2073
E-mail: duzo@ring.net
Web Site: www.mzopu.hr
Key Personnel
Dir: Ante Kutle, MD
Founded: 1991
Subjects: Environmental Studies
ISBN Prefix(es): 953-97087; 953-6793

Durieux d o o+
Sulekova 23, 10000 Zagreb
Tel: (01) 23 00 337; (01) 23 21 178 *Fax:* (01) 23 00 337
E-mail: durieux@durieux.hr
Web Site: www.durieux.hr
Key Personnel
President: Drazen Toncic
Editor: Nenad Popovic
Founded: 1990
Subjects: Drama, Theater, Fiction, History, Literature, Literary Criticism, Essays, Philosophy, Poetry
ISBN Prefix(es): 953-188

Faust Vrani+
Kersovanijev Trg 1, 10000 Zagreb
Tel: (01) 231 3646; (01) 2332 302 *Fax:* (01) 231 3646; (01) 2332 302
E-mail: pontes@pontes.com
Key Personnel
Dir: Valerij Juresic
Editor: Katarina Mazuran *E-mail:* katarina.mazuran@pontes.com
Founded: 1995
Specialize in new literature, promotion of Croatian literature & new authors from abroad.
Membership(s): Croatian Independent Publishers.
Subjects: Fiction, Journalism, Literature, Literary Criticism, Essays, Music, Dance, Philosophy, Poetry, Science Fiction, Fantasy
ISBN Prefix(es): 953-6804
Number of titles published annually: 8 Print
Total Titles: 5 Print

Filozofski Fakultet Sveucilista u Zagrebu
Ivana Lucica 3, 10000 Zagreb
Tel: (01) 6120111 *Fax:* (01) 6156879
E-mail: tajnik_fakultet@ffzg.hr
Web Site: www.ffzg.hr
Key Personnel
Editor & Author: Ms Jadranka Brncic
E-mail: jbrncic@mudrac.ftzg.hr
Subjects: History, Language Arts, Linguistics, Literature, Literary Criticism, Essays, Social Sciences, Sociology
ISBN Prefix(es): 86-80279; 953-175

Globus-Nakladni zavod
Vlaska 109, 10000 Zagreb
Tel: (01) 462 8400 *Fax:* (01) 462 8400 *Cable:* GLOBUS ZAGREB
Key Personnel
President & Editor: Tomislav Pusek
Founded: 1969
Subjects: Art, Fiction, Government, Political Science, History, Philosophy, Social Sciences, Sociology
ISBN Prefix(es): 86-343; 953-167

Graficki zavod Hrvatske
Radnicka Cesta 210, 10000 Zagreb
Tel: (01) 2404 444; (01) 240 7166 *Fax:* (01) 240 4444
Telex: 21606 Yu Gzh *Cable:* GZH ZAGREB
Key Personnel
Man Dir: Zdravko Zidovec
Editor: Branko Matan
Sales: Vilma Lopuh
Rights & Permissions: Maja Kotur
Production: Boro Brekalo
Founded: 1874
Subjects: Art, Biography, Fiction
ISBN Prefix(es): 86-399; 953-6009

Izdavacka Delatnost Hrvatske Akademije Znanosti I Umjetnosti
Zrinski trg 11, 10000 Zagreb
Tel: (01) 49 22 373; (01) 48 72 902 *Fax:* (01) 48 19 979
E-mail: stross@mahazu.hazu.hr
Key Personnel
Man Dir: Gordana Poletto Ruzic
Founded: 1861
Subjects: Education, Government, Political Science, History, Medicine, Nursing, Dentistry, Philosophy, Science (General)
ISBN Prefix(es): 86-407; 953-154

Hrvatsko filozofsko drustvo (Croatian Philosophy Society)+
Ivana Lucica 3 (FF), 10000 Zagreb
Tel: (01) 612 0156 *Fax:* (01) 617 0682
E-mail: filozofska-istrazivanja@zg.tel.hr
Key Personnel
President: Milan Polio
Vice President: Dubravka Kuzina
Founded: 1957
Subjects: Ethnicity, Philosophy, Psychology, Psychiatry, Social Sciences, Sociology
ISBN Prefix(es): 86-81173; 953-164
Divisions: Journal Filozofska Istrazivanja/Synthesis Philosophica
Warehouse: Krcka 1, 10000 Zagreb

Informator dd+
Gunduliceva 19, 10000 Zagreb
Tel: (01) 4852 665; (01) 4852 668 *Fax:* (01) 4852 673
E-mail: informator@informator.hr
Web Site: www.informator.hr
Telex: 21264 *Cable:* YU INF
Key Personnel
Manager: Dr Ivo Buric
Editor-in-Chief: Jasna Vukoja
Sales Manager: Milan Jerbic
Subjects: Economics, Finance, Government, Political Science, Law, Marketing, Social Sciences, Sociology
ISBN Prefix(es): 86-301; 953-170
Bookshop(s): M Visnsic, 7800 Banja Luka, Bosnia and Herzegovina; Vojv, Putnika 16B, 71000 Sarajevo, Bosnia and Herzegovina; Kej M Pijade 8, 21000 Novi Sad; Trg Lava Mirskog 3, 54000 Osijek; Dj Djakovica 30, 51000 Rijeka; Ilica 24, 41000 Zagreb
Warehouse: Janka Gredelja 3, 41000 Zagreb
Orders to: Odjel Prodaje Knjiga, Ilica 24, 41000 Zagreb *Tel:* (041) 433666

Knjizevni Krug Split
Ispod Ure 3/11, 21000 Split
Tel: (021) 342 226; (021) 361 081 *Fax:* (021) 342 226
E-mail: bratislav.lucin@public.srce.hr
Key Personnel
President: Prof Nenad Cambi, PhD
Vice President: Prof Ivo Petrinovic, PhD
Editor: Prof Bratislav Lucin
Founded: 1979
Subjects: Archaeology, Drama, Theater, History, Language Arts, Linguistics, Law, Literature, Literary Criticism, Essays, Maritime, Poetry
ISBN Prefix(es): 86-7397; 953-163

Krscanska sadasnjost
Marulicev trg 14, 10000 Zagreb
Tel: (01) 48 28 219; (01) 48 28 222 *Fax:* (01) 48 28 227
E-mail: ks@zg.tel.hr
Web Site: www.ks.hr
Also acts as a press agency.
Subjects: Art, Biblical Studies, Religion - Other, Theology
ISBN Prefix(es): 86-397; 953-151

Leksikografski Zavod Miroslav Krleza (The Miroslav Krleza Lexicographic Institute)
Frankopanska 26, 10000 Zagreb
Tel: (01) 4800 492; (01) 4800 494 *Fax:* (01) 4800 399
E-mail: lzmk@lzmk.hr
Web Site: www.lzmk.hr
Key Personnel
Dir: Vlaho Bogisic *Tel:* (01) 4800 398
E-mail: vlaho.bogisic@lzmk.hr; Tomislav Ladan *Tel:* (01) 4800 398 *E-mail:* tomislav.ladan@lzmk.hr
Assistant Dir: Damir Boras *Tel:* (01) 4800 424 *E-mail:* damir.boras@lzmk.hr; Ankica Karacic *Tel:* (01) 4800 319 *E-mail:* ankica.karacic@lzmk.hr; Zdenka Ozic *Tel:* (01) 4800 392 *E-mail:* zdenka.ozic@lzmk.hr; Tomislav Virovic *Tel:* (01) 4800 353 *E-mail:* tomislav.virovic@lzmk.hr
Contact: Vedrana Martinovic *Tel:* (01) 4800 331
E-mail: vedrana.martinovic@lzmk.hr
Founded: 1950
ISBN Prefix(es): 953-6036

Masmedia+
Baruna Trenka 13, 10000 Zagreb
Tel: (01) 457-7400 *Fax:* (01) 457 7769
E-mail: masmedia@zg.tel.hr; mm@masmedia.hr
Web Site: www.masmedia.hr
Key Personnel
President: Stjepan Andrasic *E-mail:* stjepan.andrasic@zg.tel.hr
Contact: Romina Belak
Founded: 1990
Subjects: Business, Economics, Finance, Management, Marketing
ISBN Prefix(es): 953-157
Associate Companies: Andratom; Creditreform; GBMA; Rimedia
Subsidiaries: Masmedia-Split
U.S. Office(s): Associated Book Publishers Inc, PO Box 5657, Scottsdale, AZ 85261-5657, United States
Distributed by Associated Book Publishers
Distributor for Braun Verlag; Euredit (Europages) BDI; Gentner Verlag; Herold
Bookshop(s): Masmedia Rijeka, Dolac 9A, 51000 Rijeka
Book Club(s): Croatian Book Clubs

Matica hrvatska+
Matice hrvatske 2, Strossmayerov trg 4, 10000 Zagreb
Tel: (01) 4878-360; (01) 4878-354; (01) 4878-362 *Fax:* (01) 4819-319
E-mail: matica@matica.hr
Web Site: www.matica.hr
Key Personnel
President: Igor Zidic
International Rights: Vera Cicin-Sain
Founded: 1842
Publisher of Biweekly Newspaper *Vijenac*.
Subjects: Agriculture, Archaeology, Art, Drama, Theater, History, Language Arts, Linguistics, Literature, Literary Criticism, Essays, Medicine, Nursing, Dentistry, Natural History,

Nonfiction (General), Philosophy, Poetry, Regional Interests, Science (General), Social Sciences, Sociology
ISBN Prefix(es): 86-401; 86-7807
Bookshop(s): Maticina 2, 10000 Zagreb

Mladost d d Izdavacku graficku i informaticku djelatnost
Borongajska 69, 10000 Zagreb
Tel: (01) 215-853; (01) 229-811 *Fax:* (01) 239-5336
Telex: 21263 yu mladzg *Cable:* IRO ZAGREB
Key Personnel
Man Dir: Branko Juricevic
Import-Export Dir: Branko Vukovic
Publisher: Josip Fruk
Production Manager: Stipan Medak
Marketing Manager: Eduard Osredecki
Founded: 1948
Subjects: Art, Crafts, Games, Hobbies, Fiction, History, How-to, Music, Dance, Philosophy, Poetry, Science (General), Social Sciences, Sociology, Sports, Athletics
ISBN Prefix(es): 86-05; 953-152
Book Club(s): Mladost's Book Fans Club

Muzicka Naklada
Nikole Tesle 10/I, 41000 Zagreb
Tel: (01) 424 099; (01) 424 019
Telex: 22430
Key Personnel
Dir: Rajko Latinovic
Founded: 1952
Publish music editions & scores.
Subjects: Music, Dance
ISBN Prefix(es): 86-80637

Naklada Ljevak doo
Palmoticeva 30/1, 10000 Zagreb
Tel: (01) 4804-000 *Fax:* (01) 4804-001
E-mail: naklada-ljevak@zg.hinet.hr
Web Site: www.naklada-ljevak.hr
Telex: 21449 Yu Ikpnzg *Cable:* Izdavacko Naprijed
Key Personnel
Dir: Nives Tomasevic
Subjects: Art, Economics, Fiction, Government, Political Science, History, Philosophy, Psychology, Psychiatry, Science (General), Social Sciences, Sociology
ISBN Prefix(es): 86-349; 953-178
Bookshop(s): Cetinska bb, 21, 21 310 Omis
Tel: (021) 757-344 *Fax:* (021) 757-345
E-mail: knjizara-ljevak-omis@zg.htnet.hr;
Trg bana Jelacica 17, 10 000 Zagreb *Tel:* (01) 4812-992; (01) 4812-963 *Fax:* (01) 4812-970
E-mail: knjizara-ljevak@zg.htnet.hr

Narodne Novine
Odjel oglasa i pretplate, Ulica Kralja Drzislava 14, 10000 Zagreb
Tel: (01) 4501-310 *Fax:* (01) 4501-348; (01) 4501-349
E-mail: e-pretplata@nn.hr
Web Site: www.nn.hr
Key Personnel
Dir: Ilija Dautovic
Subjects: Career Development, Law, Science (General)
ISBN Prefix(es): 86-337; 953-6053

Nasa Djeca Publishing+
Gunduliseva 40, 10000 Zagreb
Tel: (01) 485 6056; (01) 485 6046 *Fax:* (01) 485 6613
E-mail: nasa-djeca@zg.tel.hr
Key Personnel
Dir: Prof Drago Kozina
Secretary, Editorial Office: Verica Ozimec
Founded: 1951
Also publish children's periodical *Radost*.

Subjects: Literature, Literary Criticism, Essays, Poetry
ISBN Prefix(es): 86-7037; 953-171
Number of titles published annually: 30 Print

Edit Niro (Novinska-izdavacka radna organizacija)
Ulica kralja Zvonimira 20a, 51 000 Rijeka
Tel: (051) 672 119; (051) 672 112 *Fax:* (051) 672 151
E-mail: niro-edit@ri.tel.hr
Key Personnel
Dir: Ennio Machin
ISBN Prefix(es): 86-7127; 953-6150
Bookshop(s): Korzo Narodne Revolucije 37, 51000 Rijeka

Otokar Kersovani
Janeza Trdine 2/11, 51000 Rijeka
Tel: (051) 338 558; (051) 338 016 *Fax:* (051) 331 690
E-mail: otokar-kersovani@ri.tel.hr *Cable:* Otokar Kersovani
Key Personnel
Man Dir & Editor-in-Chief: Tomislav Pilepic
Founded: 1954
Subjects: Biography, Fiction
ISBN Prefix(es): 86-385; 953-153
Branch Office(s)
Mehmed-pase Soholovica 24, Sarajevo, Bosnia and Herzegovina
Slavise Vajiera-Cice 3, Rijeka
Biankinijeva, 11 Zagreb
Zrmanjska 2/a, Belgrade, Serbia and Montenegro
Nade Tomic 15, Nis, Serbia and Montenegro

Prosvjeta
Berislaviceva 10, Zagreb
Tel: (01) 4872 477 *Fax:* (01) 366 5309 *Cable:* Prosvjeta Zagreb
Key Personnel
Dir: Branislav Celap
Subjects: Business, Journalism
ISBN Prefix(es): 86-353; 953-6279
Bookshop(s): trg Bratstva i Jedinstva 5, Zagreb

Prosvjeta (Novinsko-izdavacko i Stamparsko)
Nazorova 25, 43000 Bjelovar
Tel: (043) 245 222; (043) 245 223 *Fax:* (043) 245 220 *Cable:* Nisp Prosvjeta Bjelovar
Key Personnel
Dir: Branimir Premuzic *Tel:* (043) 245 224
Production: Ivan Ninic
ISBN Prefix(es): 86-80823; 953-6340
Branch Office(s)
Mose Pijade 31, Zagreb

Skolska Knjiga
Masarykova 28, 10000 Zagreb
Tel: (01) 48 30 491; (01) 48 30 511 *Fax:* (01) 48 30 506
E-mail: skolska@skolskaknjiga.hr
Web Site: www.skolskaknjiga.hr
Telex: 21894 *Cable:* SKOLSKA KNJIGA ZAGREB
Key Personnel
President: Ante Zuzul
Founded: 1950
Subjects: Art, Biography, Education, Engineering (General), History, How-to, Medicine, Nursing, Dentistry, Music, Dance, Philosophy, Poetry, Psychology, Psychiatry, Science (General), Social Sciences, Sociology
ISBN Prefix(es): 86-03; 953-0
Bookshop(s): Knjizara Skolska knjiga *Tel:* (01) 48 30 488; Knjizara Skolske knjige, Bogoviceva 1/a, 41000 Zagreb *Tel:* (01) 48 10 989

Privlacica Slavonska Naklada+
Ruzina 5 a, 32100 Vinkovci

Tel: (032) 306 068; (032) 306 069; (032) 306 070 *Fax:* (032) 331735
E-mail: privlacica@vk.tel.hr
Key Personnel
Contact: Martin Grgurovac
ISBN Prefix(es): 953-156

Sveucilisna tiskara doo
Trg marsala Tita 14, 10000 Zagreb
Tel: (01) 4564430; (01) 4564428 *Fax:* (01) 4564427
Key Personnel
Editor: Vera C Sain; Nikola Petrak
Publishing service of Zagreb University.
Subjects: Ethnicity, Language Arts, Linguistics, Literature, Literary Criticism, Essays, Science (General)
ISBN Prefix(es): 86-7819; 86-329; 953-6231

Tehnicka Knjiga
Jurisiceva 10, 10000 Zagreb
Tel: (01) 481 0818 *Fax:* (01) 481 0821 *Cable:* Tehnoknjiga
Key Personnel
Man Dir, Chief Editor: Zvonimir Vistricka
Founded: 1947
Subjects: Engineering (General), Literature, Literary Criticism, Essays, Science (General)
ISBN Prefix(es): 86-7059; 953-172
Bookshop(s): Knjizara Tehnicka Knjiga, Masarykova 17; Antikvarijat, Zagreb; Gunduliceva 19, Zagreb

Vitagraf+
Slogin kula 12, 51000 Rijeka
Tel: (051) 215087; (051) 338489
Toll Free Tel: (051) 322880 *Fax:* (051) 212622
E-mail: vitagraf@ri.hinet.hr
Key Personnel
President: Prof Boze Mimica
Author: Ivan Sokolic; Jeurem Brkovic; Lujo Margetic; Zjonimie Dusper
Founded: 1990
Specialize in Numismatic, History, Vine Books, Gastronomy Guide.
Subjects: Cookery, Crafts, Games, Hobbies, History, Radio, TV, Wine & Spirits
ISBN Prefix(es): 953-6059

Znaci Vremena, Institut Za Istrazivanje Biblije
Marulevec 82 E, 42243 Marulevec
Tel: (042) 729 977 *Fax:* (042) 729 977
Key Personnel
Dir: Karlo Lenart
Subjects: Archaeology, Biblical Studies, Health, Nutrition, Human Relations, Religion - Protestant, Theology
ISBN Prefix(es): 86-425; 953-183

Znanje d d+
Zvonimira 17, Ulica Kralja 10000 Zagreb 1000
Tel: (01) 4551500 *Fax:* (01) 4553-652
E-mail: znanje@zg.tel.hr *Cable:* ZNANJE ZAGREB
Key Personnel
President: Zarko Sepetavc
Vice President: Branko Jazbec
Founded: 1946
Subjects: Textbooks
ISBN Prefix(es): 86-313; 953-195; 953-6124; 953-6473
Divisions: Printing House
Branch Office(s)
Riva 8, Rijeka
Znanje d o o Mostar, Stjepana Radica 76E, 88000 Mostar, Bosnia and Herzegovina
Osijek, Vukovarska 71, 31000 Osijeck
Showroom(s): Vojnoviceva, 42 Zagreb
Bookshop(s): AG Matos stationary & bookstore, Frankopanska 5; I G Kovacic stationary & bookstore, Marticeva 12; Miroslav Krleza bookstore, Trg bana J Jelacica 17; Tin Ujevic second-hand bookstore, Zrinjevac 16; Znanje

stationary & book store, Llica 17; Znanje stationary & bookstore, Ozaljska 102; Znanje stationary/paper shop, Gajeva 2

Cuba

General Information

Capital: Havana
Language: Spanish
Religion: Predominantly Roman Catholic
Population: 10.8 million
Bank Hours: 0800-1200, 1415-1615 Monday-Friday; 0800-1200 Saturday
Currency: 100 centavos = 1 Cuban peso
Export/Import Information: Control of all import & export by Ministry of Foreign Trade; books imported & exported by Ediciones Cubanas, Apdo 605, Havana. No commercial advertising permitted in Cuba; brochures etc must be sent to the appropriate foreign trade organization. Exchange controlled by National Bank of Cuba.
Copyright: UCC, Florence (see Copyright Conventions, pg xi)

Apocalipis Digital+
Calle 47 No 869, 3er Piso, Apto 6 entre 26 y Sta Ana, Plaza de la Revolucion, Havana
Tel: (07) 816625
E-mail: adigital@tinored.cu; adigital@colombus.cu
Key Personnel
President: Pedro E Garcia
Founded: 1987
Membership(s): Comicion Nacional de Proteccion de Datos.
Subjects: Computer Science, Microcomputers
ISBN Prefix(es): 959-231

Editorial Capitan San Luis+
Av 25 No 3406 entre 34 y 36, La Habana, Playa
Tel: (07) 2034475 *Fax:* (07) 332070
Key Personnel
Dir: Carlos Morales Quevedo
Founded: 1989
Subjects: Government, Political Science, Literature, Literary Criticism, Essays
ISBN Prefix(es): 959-211
Warehouse: Ave 41 No 1410 entre 14 y 18, Playa, La Havana

Casa de las Americas
Calle 3 3/4 y G, Vedado CP 10400, Plaza de la Revolucion, Havana
Tel: (07) 327271; (07) 323588 *Fax:* (07) 327272
Telex: 511019
Key Personnel
Dir: Abel Martinez
Founded: 1960
Subjects: Art, Ethnicity, Social Sciences, Sociology
ISBN Prefix(es): 959-04

Casa Editora Abril+
Prado 553 esq a Tte Rey, CP 10200 Habana Vieja, Havana
Tel: (07) 8627871; (07) 8624359 *Fax:* (07) 335282
E-mail: eabril@jcc.org.cu
Web Site: www.almamater.cu
Key Personnel
Dir: Mario Vizcaino Serrat
Sub-Dir: Silvio Gutierrez Perez
Publisher: Eduardo Jimenez Garcia
Founded: 1980
Subjects: Advertising, Film, Video, History, Humor, Journalism, Literature, Literary Criticism, Essays, Microcomputers, Philosophy, Poetry, Science Fiction, Fantasy
ISBN Prefix(es): 959-210

Editorial de Ciencias Sociales
Calle 14, No 4104, entre 41 y 43, Playa, Ciudad de la Havana
Tel: (07) 2036090; (07) 333441 *Fax:* (07) 2304801
E-mail: nuevomil@icl.cult.cu
Key Personnel
Dir: Ricardo Garcia Pampin
Founded: 1967
Subjects: Social Sciences, Sociology
ISBN Prefix(es): 959-06
Orders to: Ediciones Cubanas, Obispo y Bernaza, La Habana Vieja

Editorial Cientifico Tecnica+
Calle 14, No 4104 entre 41 y 43, Playa, Havana 10400
Tel: (07) 2036090 *Fax:* (07) 333441
E-mail: nuevomil@icl.cult.cu
Key Personnel
Dir: Isidro Fernandez Rodriguez
Founded: 1965
Subjects: Engineering (General), Science (General)
ISBN Prefix(es): 959-05

Editora Cultura Popular, *imprint of* Editora Politica

Editorial Gente Nueva+
O'Reilly No 4 esq a Tacon, Habana Vieja, CP 10100 Havana
Tel: (07) 833-7676 *Fax:* (07) 33-8187
E-mail: gentenueva@icl.cult
Key Personnel
Dir: Elenia Rodriguez Oliva
Founded: 1967
ISBN Prefix(es): 959-08

Holguin, Ediciones
Arias No 144, esq a Fomento, CP 80100, Holguin
Tel: (024) 424974
E-mail: promotoraliteraria@baibrama.cult.cu
Founded: 1986
Subjects: Art, Biography, Drama, Theater, History, Literature, Literary Criticism, Essays, Poetry
ISBN Prefix(es): 959-221
Book Club(s): SCAL (Sociedad Cabana de Amigos del Libro)

IDICT, see Instituto de Informacion Cientifica y Tecnologica (IDICT)

Instituto de Informacion Cientifica y Tecnologica (IDICT)+
Prado entre Dragones y San Jose, CP 10200 La Habana, Habana Vieja
Tel: (07) 862-6531; (07) 860-3411 *Fax:* (07) 862-6531
E-mail: andresdt@idict.cu; comercial@idict.cu
Web Site: www.idict.cu
Subjects: Career Development, Library & Information Sciences, Technology
ISBN Prefix(es): 959-234

ISCAH Fructuoso Rodriguez
Carretera de Tapaste y Autopista Nacional, San Jose de las Lajas, Havana 32700
Tel: (07) 62936 *Fax:* (07) 330942
Key Personnel
Contact: Julian Garcia Gomex *E-mail:* julian@reduniv.edu.cu
Subjects: Agriculture, Alternative, Economics, Education, Environmental Studies, Management, Sports, Athletics, Veterinary Science
ISBN Prefix(es): 959-232

Editorial Letras Cubanas+
O'Reilly No 4 esq Tacon, Habana Vieja, La Habana, Havana 10100
Tel: (07) 862-6864 *Fax:* (07) 33-8187
E-mail: elc@icl.cult.cu
Telex: 511881
Key Personnel
Dir: Juan Nicolas Padron Barquin; Daniel Garcia Santos
Sub-Dir: Basilia Papastamatiu; Esther Acosta Testa
Founded: 1977
Membership(s): Instituto Cubano del Libro.
Subjects: Art, Drama, Theater, Fiction, Literature, Literary Criticism, Essays, Poetry, Romance, Science Fiction, Fantasy
ISBN Prefix(es): 959-10
Number of titles published annually: 70 Print
Total Titles: 70 Print
Distribution Center: Ediciones Cubanas Empresa de Comercio Exterior de Publicaciones, Obispo 527 esq, a Bernaza, La Habana 10100, Dir: Jorge Paz *Tel:* (07) 631989; (07) 338942 *Fax:* (07) 338943 *E-mail:* edicuba@artsoft.cult.cu

Editorial Oriente+
Santa Lucia No 356, CP 90100 Santiago de Cuba
Tel: (0226) 22496; (0226) 28096 *Fax:* (0226) 86111
E-mail: edoriente@cultstgo.cult.cu
Telex: 061170
Key Personnel
President: Aida Bahr
Editorial: Consuel Muniz
Production: Sergio Daquin
Publicity: Ana Maria Rodriguez
Rights & Permissions: Omar Betancourt
Founded: 1971
Subjects: African American Studies, Cookery, Crafts, Games, Hobbies, Fiction, Health, Nutrition, History, House & Home, Literature, Literary Criticism, Essays, Poetry, Self-Help, Sports, Athletics
ISBN Prefix(es): 959-11
Total Titles: 821 Print
Parent Company: Vicepresidencia Editorial
Ultimate Parent Company: Instituto Cubano del Libro

Editora Politica+
Calle Belascoain No 864, esq a Desague, Municipio Centro Habana, CP 10300 Havana
Tel: (07) 79 8553-59 *Fax:* (07) 811024
E-mail: editora@ns.cc.cu; edit63@enet.cu
Web Site: www.pcc.cu/pccweb/publicaciones/editorapolitica.php
Telex: 1380
Key Personnel
Dir: Santiago Dorquez Perez
Chief Editor: Anolan Aguila
Founded: 1963
Subjects: Biography, Economics, Education, Government, Political Science, Health, Nutrition, History, Human Relations, Law, Philosophy, Poetry, Psychology, Psychiatry, Religion - Catholic, Religion - Other, Science (General), Social Sciences, Sociology
ISBN Prefix(es): 959-01
Associate Companies: Editora Cultura Popular
Imprints: Editora Cultura Popular
Showroom(s): Pabelloo Medios de Difusion EX-POCUBA, Tienda 11 y Paseo
Bookshop(s): Centro Internacional de Prensa, Calle 23 esq O Vedado

Pueblo y Educacion Editorial (PE)+
Ave 3A No 4605 entre 46 y 60, Playa, Havana 11300
Tel: (07) 20021490 *Fax:* (07) 2040844
E-mail: epe@ceniai.inf.cu
Key Personnel
Dir: Catalina Lajud
Sub-Dir: Juan Alberto Andino
Founded: 1971
Subjects: Computer Science, Education, Literature, Literary Criticism, Essays, Psychology, Psychiatry, Science (General), Social Sciences, Sociology, Sports, Athletics, Technology
ISBN Prefix(es): 959-13
Number of titles published annually: 476 Print
Total Titles: 8 Print
Distributed by Ediciones Cubanas Empresa de Comercio Exterior de Publicaciones

Union de Escritores y Artistas de Cuba (Union of Writers & Artists of Cuba)+
Calle 17 No 354,e/ G y H, Vedado, Plaza de la Revolucion, Havana CP 10400
Tel: (07) 324551; (07) 324252; (07) 324553; (07) 553113 *Fax:* (07) 333158
Telex: 051156364
Key Personnel
Dir: Daniel Garcia Santos
Production: Jose Raul Garrido
Publicity: Emilio Comas Paret
Founded: 1961
Rights & Permissions, National Center of Author Rights, Linea y G, Vedado.
Subjects: Art, Literature, Literary Criticism, Essays, Regional Interests

Cyprus

General Information

Capital: Nicosia
Language: Greek & Turkish (English widely spoken)
Religion: Greek Orthodox & Islamic (among Turks)
Population: 716,000
Bank Hours: 0830-1200 Monday-Saturday
Shop Hours: Winter: 0800-1300, 1430-1700 Monday-Friday; 0730-1300 Saturday. Summer: 0730-1300, 1600-1830 Monday-Friday. Closed Wednesday afternoon (both winter & summer)
Currency: 100 cents = 1 Cyprus pound
Export/Import Information: No tariffs on books or advertising matter. No import license specially required. Exchange control administered by Central Bank of Cyprus.
Copyright: UCC, Berne, Florence (see Copyright Conventions, pg xi)

Action Publications
PO Box 24676, Lefkosia
Tel: (022) 818884 *Fax:* (022) 873634
Key Personnel
President: Tony Christodoulou
Vice President: Mickey Christodoulou
Production Dir: Dina Wilde
Founded: 1971
Subjects: Travel, Airline
ISBN Prefix(es): 9963-7587
Parent Company: Action Public Relations & Publishing Ltd
Subsidiaries: Action Media
Orders to: 6 Kondilakis St, 1090 Lefkosia

Air Larko Panorama ALP
11 Nicos Antonlades, Paphos 8046
Tel: (06) 236181 *Fax:* (06) 245046
ISBN Prefix(es): 9963-574

ALITHIA Publishing Co
Pindarou & Androkleous, Nicosia 1060
Tel: (022) 463040 *Fax:* (022) 463945 *Cable:* ALITHIA
ISBN Prefix(es): 9963-586

Andreou Chr Publishers
64A Regenas, Nicosia
Tel: (022) 666877 *Fax:* (022) 666878
E-mail: andzeou2@cytanet.com.cy
Founded: 1979
Specialize in Cypress History, Literature, Biography & Bibliographies.
Subjects: Biography, History, Literature, Literary Criticism, Essays, Regional Interests
ISBN Prefix(es): 9963-563
Associate Companies: Practorion Vivliou; Chr Andreou Co Ltd
Bookshop(s): Rigenis 64a, Nicosia; Rigenis 67A, Nicosia *Fax:* (02) 666563

James Bendon Ltd
PO Box 56484, 3307 Limassol
Fax: (025) 632352
E-mail: books@jamesbendon.com
Web Site: www.jamesbendon.com
Key Personnel
President: James Bendon
Vice President: Rida Bendon
Founded: 1988
Subjects: Crafts, Games, Hobbies, History
ISBN Prefix(es): 9963-579; 9963-7624
Distributor for Christie's Robson Lowe

Chrysopolitissa Publishers
27 Al Papadiamanti, 2400 Nicosia
Tel: (022) 353929 *Fax:* (022) 353929
Key Personnel
Dir: Rina Catselli *E-mail:* rina@spidernet.com.cy
Founded: 1973
Subjects: Drama, Theater, Literature, Literary Criticism, Essays
ISBN Prefix(es): 9963-559
Number of titles published annually: 4 Print
Showroom(s): 9 Othello's St, 2018 Nicosia; MAM, C Paleologos St, No 10, Nicosia
Bookshop(s): Kypriaka Themata, PO Box 3835, Nicosia; MAM, PO Box 21722, Nicosia

Cyprus Telecommunications Authority (CYTA)
Telecommunications Str, Strovolos, TK 24929, 1396 Nicosia
Tel: (022) 701000 *Fax:* (022) 497155
E-mail: enquiries@cyta.com.cy
Web Site: www.cyta.com.cy
Telex: 2288 CYTA ENAC CY
Key Personnel
Chairman: Mr Stathis Papadakis
Vice Chairman: Markos Drakos
General Manager: Nicos M Timotheou
Deputy General Manager: Mr Photios Savvides
Assistant General Manager, Operations: Christos C Chappas
Assistant General Manager, Administration: Michael I Economides
ISBN Prefix(es): 9963-43

CYTA, see Cyprus Telecommunications Authority (CYTA)

Kenek Ltd
PO Box 4611, Nicosia
Tel: (022) 365842 *Fax:* (022) 475150
ISBN Prefix(es): 9963-596

KY KE M+
PO Box 4108, Nicosia
Tel: (022) 450302 *Fax:* (022) 463624
Telex: 4022
Key Personnel
President: Nicos Koutsou
Vice President: Soula Zavou
Founded: 1983
ISBN Prefix(es): 9963-562

Kyrenia Municipality+
PO Box 5182, Nicosia
Tel: (022) 351460
Key Personnel
Editor: Rina Catselli
ISBN Prefix(es): 9963-559
Associate Companies: Chrysopolitissa Publishers
Showroom(s): 9 Othello's St, Nicosia
Bookshop(s): Kypriaka Themata, PO Box 3835, Nicosia

MAM (The House of Cyprus & Cyprological Publications)+
Leoforos Konstantinou Palaiologou 19, 1015 Nicosia
Tel: (022) 753536 *Fax:* (022) 375802
E-mail: mam@mam.com.cy
Web Site: www.mam.com.cy
Key Personnel
Secretary: Mr Mikis A Michaelides
Founded: 1965
Specialize in all kinds of publications on Cyprus & in all publications by Cypriots. Supplying all over the world to bookstores, libraries & anyone interested in these types of publications.
Subjects: Ethnicity, Cyprus
ISBN Prefix(es): 9963-625
Bookshop(s): MAM Kypriakes Ekdoseis, Stoa tou Vivliou ap 16, Odos Pesmazoglon 5, 105 64 Athens, Greece
Book Club(s): Cyprus Bibliophiles Association

The Moufflon Book & Art Centre, see Romantic Cyprus Publications

Nikoklis Publishers+
PO Box 3697, Nicosia
Tel: (022) 456544 *Fax:* (022) 360668
Key Personnel
Editor: Ellada Sophocleous
Founded: 1978
Subjects: Ethnicity, Travel
ISBN Prefix(es): 9963-566

Omilos Pnevmatikis Ananeoseos
29 Ionon, Nicosia 1096
Tel: (022) 775854 *Fax:* (022) 311931
Subjects: Literature, Literary Criticism, Essays
ISBN Prefix(es): 9963-552
Orders to: Omerou 1, Egomi, Nicosia 2407

Pierides Foundation
4, Zennonos Kitieos, 6023 Larnaka
Mailing Address: PO Box 25, Larnaka
Tel: (02) 444486 *Fax:* (02) 466412
Telex: 4498
Key Personnel
Administration: M Polyvia
ISBN Prefix(es): 9963-560

POLTE (Pancyprian Organization of Tertiary Education)
c/o Higher Technical Institute, Nicosia
Tel: (022) 305030 *Fax:* (022) 494953
Key Personnel
President: Costas Neocleous
ISBN Prefix(es): 9963-564

Romantic Cyprus Publications
PO Box 2375, Nicosia
Fax: (022) 445155
ISBN Prefix(es): 9963-571
Bookshop(s): One Bophoulis St, PO Box 2375, Nicosia

Czech Republic

General Information

Capital: Prague
Language: Czech (official)
Religion: Predominantly Christian (mostly Roman Catholic)
Population: 10.4 million
Currency: 100 halerue = 1 koruna
Export/Import Information: 5% VAT on books.
Copyright: UCC, Berne (see Copyright Conventions, pg xi)

Academia
Legerova 61, 120 00 Prague 2
Tel: (02) 24 941 976 *Fax:* (02) 24 212 582
E-mail: academia@academia.cz
Web Site: www.academia.cz *Cable:* ACADEMY BOOKS PRAGUE
Key Personnel
Dir: Alexander Tomsky *Tel:* (02) 24 942 584 *Fax:* (02) 24 941 982 *E-mail:* director@academia.cz
Founded: 1953
Subjects: Archaeology, Chemistry, Chemical Engineering, Economics, Engineering (General), Geography, Geology, History, Language Arts, Linguistics, Mathematics, Philosophy, Physics
ISBN Prefix(es): 80-200
Bookshop(s): nam Svobody 13, Brno *Tel:* (05) 42 217 954 *E-mail:* knihy.brno@academia.cz; Zamecka 2, Ostrava *Tel:* (069) 596 114 578; (069) 596 114 580; (069) 596 116 692 *Fax:* (069) 596 123 097; Vaclavske nam 34, Prague *Tel:* (02) 24 223 511 *E-mail:* knihy.vaclavskenam@academia.cz; Narodni trida 7, Prague *Tel:* (02) 24 240 547 *E-mail:* knihy.narodni@academia.cz; Na Florenci 3, Prague *Tel:* (02) 24 814 621 *E-mail:* knihy.naflorenci@academia.cz

Albatros AS+
Member of Bonton Group
Pankraci 30, 140 00 Prague 4
Tel: (02) 34633261 *Fax:* (02) 34633262
E-mail: albatros@bonton.cz
Web Site: www.albatros.cz *Cable:* ALBATROS PRAHA
Key Personnel
Man Dir: Martin Slavik *E-mail:* martin.slavik@bonton.cz
Editorial Dir: Ondrej Muller *Tel:* (02) 24810850
Foreign Rights: Katerina Nicajasova *Tel:* (02) 34633271 *E-mail:* katerina.nicajasova@bonton.cz
Founded: 1949
ISBN Prefix(es): 80-00
Total Titles: 8,700 Print; 2 CD-ROM
Bookshop(s): Krizikova, Thamova 22, Prama 8 *Tel:* (02) 24814725
Book Club(s): KMC (Young Readers' Club), Contact: Ludmila Hobova *Tel:* (02) 2319739 *Fax:* (02) 2311178
Warehouse: 252 16 Nucice *Tel:* (0311) 678754 *Fax:* (0311) 670525

AMA nakladatelstvi+
Gen Svobody 636, Trebic
Tel: (0618) 265 84 *Fax:* (0618) 228 31
E-mail: rstudio@login.cz
Key Personnel
Contact: Karel Karmasin
Founded: 1990
Specialize in desktop publishing & prepress technology.
Subjects: Radio, TV
ISBN Prefix(es): 80-900232
Associate Companies: Ar Nakladatelstvi
Orders to: Eliscina 24, 67401 Trebic

Amosium Servis
Hladnovska 119 b, 712 00 Ostrava
Tel: (069) 624 55 01
Key Personnel
Dir: Karel Janak
Founded: 1990
ISBN Prefix(es): 80-85498

Atlantis sro+
PS 374, Ceska 15, 602 00 Brno
Tel: (05) 422 132 21 *Fax:* (05) 422 132 21
E-mail: atlantis-brno@volny.cz
Web Site: www.volny.cz/atlantis/
Key Personnel
Publisher & International Rights: Jana Uhdeova
Founded: 1989
Subjects: Biography, History, Literature, Literary Criticism, Essays
ISBN Prefix(es): 80-7108

AULOS sro
Kosarkovo nab. 1, 118 00 Prague 1
Tel: (02) 536863 *Fax:* (02) 90004536
E-mail: aulos@volny.cz
Key Personnel
Editor: Zdenek Krenek
Founded: 1992
Subjects: Fiction, Literature, Literary Criticism, Essays, Philosophy, Poetry
ISBN Prefix(es): 80-901261; 80-901895; 80-86184
Showroom(s): Michalska 21, 110 00 Prague 1
Bookshop(s): Michalska 21, 110 00 Prague 1
Shipping Address: Michalska 21, 110 00 Prague 1, Czech Republic
Warehouse: Michalska 21, Prague 1, 110 00 Czech Republic

Aurora
Opletalova 8, 110 00 Prague 1
Tel: (02) 24 21 43 26; (02) 24 21 46 24 *Fax:* (02) 24 21 43 26
E-mail: eaurora@eaurora.cz
Web Site: www.eaurora.cz
Key Personnel
Owner: Eva Michalkova
Editor: Katerina Zavadova *E-mail:* zavadova@eaurora.cz
Founded: 1993
Subjects: Art, Fiction, Humor, Military Science, Nonfiction (General), Outdoor Recreation, Philosophy, Poetry
ISBN Prefix(es): 80-85974; 80-901603; 80-7299
Number of titles published annually: 50 Print
Total Titles: 75 Print

AVCR Historicky ustav
Prosecka 76, 190 00 Prague 9
Tel: (02) 868 821 21; (02) 838 813 73 *Fax:* (02) 887 513
E-mail: panek@hiu.cas.cz
Key Personnel
Dir, Productions: Dr Pavla Vosahlikova
Founded: 1921
Subjects: History
ISBN Prefix(es): 80-85268; 80-7286

Aventinum Nakladatelstvi spol sro+
Nikoly Vapcarova 3274, 14300 Prague, Modrany 4
Tel: (02) 4021907; (02) 4019069; (02) 40193056 *Fax:* (02) 4018534
Key Personnel
Man Dir: Zdenek Pavlik
Founded: 1990
Specialize in illustrated books.
Subjects: Animals, Pets, Art, Astrology, Occult, Biological Sciences, Gardening, Plants, Natural History
ISBN Prefix(es): 80-7151; 80-85277

Babtext Nakladatelska Spolecnost+
Zirovnicka 2, 106 00 Prague 10
Tel: (02) 435 992 *Fax:* (02) 768992; (02) 61221868
Key Personnel
Contact: Hilar Baburek
Founded: 1990
Subjects: Economics, Law
ISBN Prefix(es): 80-900178; 80-901444; 80-85816

Bakalar spol sro+
Rusna 417, 321 03 Plzen
Tel: (019) 523197
Key Personnel
Dir & President: Katerina Rubasova
Founded: 1991
Bachelor Ltd.
ISBN Prefix(es): 80-901213

Barollet Publishers Inc, see Baronet

Baronet+
Krizikova 16, 186 00 Prague 8
Tel: (02) 22310115 *Fax:* (02) 22310118
E-mail: baronet.odbyt@volny.cz
Web Site: www.baronet-knihy.cz; www.baronet.cz
Key Personnel
Publishing Dir: Mr Milan Soska, PhD
Founded: 1993
Specialize in historical romances, horoscopes & English/American fiction.
Subjects: Fiction, Military Science, Nonfiction (General), Romance, Science Fiction, Fantasy
ISBN Prefix(es): 80-7214; 80-85621; 80-85890; 80-900765; 80-901068

Barrister & Principal+
Rybkova 23 Budova C 16, 602 00 Brno
Tel: (05) 45211015 *Fax:* (05) 45210607
E-mail: barrister@barrister.cz
Web Site: www.barrister.cz
Key Personnel
Manager: Ivo Lukas *E-mail:* lukas@barrister.cz
Founded: 1994
Subjects: Archaeology, Economics, Education, Government, Political Science, History, Journalism, Language Arts, Linguistics, Philosophy, Poetry, Psychology, Psychiatry, Religion - Catholic, Social Sciences, Sociology, Theology
ISBN Prefix(es): 80-85947; 80-86598
Number of titles published annually: 20 Print
Total Titles: 5 Print

Brody+
Nakladatelství krásných knih, Spanelska 6/742, 121 11 Prague 2
Tel: (02) 22252077 *Fax:* (02) 22252077
E-mail: brody@draha.czcom.cz
Key Personnel
Contact: Dita Horakova
Founded: 1995
Specialize in publishing books on the Far East & Russian Avant-Garde for reference markets in all areas of humanities.
Subjects: Art, Fiction, Literature, Literary Criticism, Essays, Nonfiction (General), Philosophy
ISBN Prefix(es): 80-86112; 80-902113

Canis Vydavatelstvi a Nakladatelstvi+
Korunni 9, 120 00 Prague 2
Tel: (02) 251096
Key Personnel
Editor & Publisher: Dr M Cisarovsky
Founded: 1990
ISBN Prefix(es): 80-900820
Associate Companies: Canis centrum, Vrsovicka 7/27, Prague 10
Divisions: Manesova 48

PUBLISHERS   CZECH REPUBLIC

Ceska Biblicka Spolecnost (Czech Bible Society)
Nahorni 12, 182 00 Prague 8
Tel: (02) 84 693 925 *Fax:* (02) 84 693 933
E-mail: cbs@dumbible.cz
Web Site: www.dumbible.cz
Key Personnel
Contact: Pavel Kral
Founded: 1990
Membership(s): United Bible Societies.
Subjects: Biblical Studies, Theology
ISBN Prefix(es): 80-85810; 80-900881

Ceska Expedice+
Jihozapadni III, 14, 141 00 Prague 4
Tel: (02) 727 612 04
Key Personnel
Contact: Jaromir Horec
Founded: 1989
Subjects: History, Literature, Literary Criticism, Essays, Poetry, Russie Subcarpatig
ISBN Prefix(es): 80-85281

Cesky Filmovy ustav, see Narodni filmovy archiv

Chvojkova nakladatelstvi
Smilovskeho 3, 120 00 Prague 2
Mailing Address: Machova 22, 101 00 Prague 10
Tel: (02) 717 430 23
Tel: (02) 225 169 65; (02) 717 430 23 *Fax:* (02) 225 169 65
Key Personnel
Contact: Jiri Chvojka
Subjects: Alternative, Astrology, Occult, History, Parapsychology, Psychology, Psychiatry
ISBN Prefix(es): 80-900239; 80-901270; 80-901622; 80-86183

Cinema+
Seifertova 47, 130 00 Prague 3
Tel: (02) 627 83 95-6 *Fax:* (02) 627 72 39
E-mail: schur@comp.cz
Key Personnel
International Rights: Roland Schuer
Founded: 1991
Subjects: Film, Video
ISBN Prefix(es): 80-85933; 80-901675

Columbus+
Nad Kolcavkov 8, 190 00 Prague 9
Tel: (02) 683 10 17; (02) 683 47 65; (02) 74771407 *Fax:* (02) 683 10 17; (02) 683 08 28
E-mail: columbus@alpha-net.cz
Key Personnel
Contact: Ivo Smoldas
Founded: 1991
Subjects: Biography, Geography, Geology, History, Parapsychology
ISBN Prefix(es): 80-85928; 80-901578; 80-901696; 80-901727; 80-7249

Concordia+
Belohorska 99, 169 00 Prague 6
Tel: (02) 355241; (02) 7929747 *Fax:* (02) 7929747
Key Personnel
Executive: Ales Pech
Founded: 1990
Subjects: Literature, Literary Criticism, Essays
ISBN Prefix(es): 80-900124; 80-901389; 80-85997

Diderot sro
Jecna 12, 12000 Prague 2
Tel: (02) 55707711; (02) 55707703 *Fax:* (02) 55707700
E-mail: redakce@diderot.cz; obchod@bp.diderot.cz
Web Site: www.diderot.cz

Key Personnel
Contact: Martina Fialkova
Founded: 1988
Private publishing organization.
ISBN Prefix(es): 80-86613; 80-902555; 80-902723
Total Titles: 2 Print; 1 CD-ROM
Branch Office(s)
Moravian Branch, Sevcovska 1156, Ziln 76001
  Tel: (067) 34156 *Fax:* (067) 779493

Dimenze 2 Plus 2 Praha+
Soukenicka 21, 110 00 Prague 1
Tel: (02) 231 11 41 *Fax:* (02) 231 11 41
Web Site: www.dub.cz/dimenze.html
Key Personnel
President: Tomas Pfeiffer
Founded: 1990
Subjects: Health, Nutrition, Philosophy
ISBN Prefix(es): 80-85238

Divadelni Ustav (Theatre Institute Prague)+
Subsidiary of Ministry of Culture, Czech Republic
Celetna 17, 110 00 Prague 1
Tel: (02) 24809111 *Fax:* (02) 24811452
E-mail: divadelni.ustav@czech-theatre.cz
Web Site: www.divadelni-ustav.cz
Key Personnel
Dir: Ondrej Cerny *Tel:* (02) 22315966
Contact: Paula Kucharova *Tel:* (02) 24809192
  E-mail: pavla.kucharova@theatre.cz
Founded: 1960
Subjects: Drama, Theater, Theatre plays
ISBN Prefix(es): 80-7008
Number of titles published annually: 10 Print
Bookshop(s): Prospero Bookshop
  Tel: (02) 24809156 *Fax:* (02) 24809156
  E-mail: prospero@divadlo.cz *Web Site:* www.divadlo.cz/prospero

Doplnek+
Bratislavska 48/50, 602 00 Brno
Tel: (05) 452-424-55 *Fax:* (05) 452-424-55
E-mail: doplnek@doplnek.cz
Web Site: www.doplnek.cz
Key Personnel
Contact: Jan Sabata *E-mail:* sabata@sky.cz
Founded: 1991 (Founded in Bruo, Czech Republic)
Specialize in publishing of books with subject specialties.
Membership(s): The Association of Czech Booksellers & Publishers.
Subjects: Biography, Economics, Education, Environmental Studies, History, Humor, Journalism, Law, Literature, Literary Criticism, Essays, Psychology, Psychiatry, Science Fiction, Fantasy, Social Sciences, Sociology
ISBN Prefix(es): 80-7239; 80-85765; 80-901102
Number of titles published annually: 35 Print
Total Titles: 200 Print
Subsidiaries: Jan Sabata
Distributor for Jan Sabata
Foreign Rep(s): Andrew Nurberg Associate (Czech Republic); Thomas Perry (USA)
Bookshop(s): Zerotinovo nam 9, 60200 Brno
  Tel: (05) 42128382

Erika spol sro+
Jarnikova 1894, 148 00 Prague 4
Mailing Address: PO Box 27, 148 00 Prague 4
Tel: (02) 7950452 *Fax:* (02) 7929351
Key Personnel
Contact: Jan Suchl
Founded: 1990
Subjects: Health, Nutrition, Nonfiction (General)
ISBN Prefix(es): 80-900091; 80-85612; 80-7190
Orders to: Spira, Horska 10, 46014 Liberec

Euromedia Group-Odeon+
V Jamw 1, 111 21 Prague 1

Fax: (02) 241 623 28
E-mail: odeon@euromedia.cz *Cable:* ODEON PRAHA
Key Personnel
Man Dir: Ing Jiri Havlik
Editorial Rights & Permissions (Fiction): Dr Jiri Nasinec
Editorial Rights & Permissions (Art): Dr Milada Motlova
Publicity: Eva Svobodova
Production: Zdenek Suska
Founded: 1953
Publishing House of Literature & Art.
Subjects: Art, Biography, Fiction, Poetry
ISBN Prefix(es): 80-207
Bookshop(s): Na Florenci 3, 11586 Prague 1
Book Club(s): Odeon Book Club (Klub Ctenaru)

Exemplare, *imprint of* Granit sro

Galaxie, vydavatelelstvi a nakladatelstvi+
Petrska 29, 110 00 Prague 1
Tel: (02) 2317801; (02) 2317875 *Fax:* (02) 2311351
Key Personnel
Man Partner & Editor-in-Chief: Milan Pavek
Subjects: Education, Ethnicity, Fiction, Literature, Literary Criticism, Essays
ISBN Prefix(es): 80-85204

Grada Publishing+
U Pruhonu 22, 170 00 Prague 7
Tel: (02) 20386401; (02) 20386402 *Fax:* (02) 20386400
E-mail: info@gradapublishing.cz; obchod@gradapublishing.cz
Web Site: www.gradapublishing.cz; www.grada.cz
Key Personnel
Marketing: Zdenek Jaros *E-mail:* jaros@gradapublishing.cz
Foreign Rights: Magdalena Brenkova
  E-mail: brenkova@gradapublishing.cz
Founded: 1993
Subjects: Computer Science, Economics, Law, Technology, Medicine
ISBN Prefix(es): 80-7169; 80-85424; 80-85623; 80-900250; 80-247
Total Titles: 850 Print

Granit sro+
Stefanikova 43, 150 00 Prague 5
Tel: (02) 27 018 361 *Fax:* (02) 27 018 361
E-mail: info@granit-publishing.cz
Web Site: www.granit-publishing.cz
Key Personnel
Dir: Lubomir Mlcoch *Tel:* (02) 57018361
Founded: 1992
Subjects: Animals, Pets, Biological Sciences, Crafts, Games, Hobbies, Education, Gardening, Plants, Geography, Geology, Health, Nutrition, Natural History, Science (General)
ISBN Prefix(es): 80-85805; 80-7296; 80-901195; 80-901443
Number of titles published annually: 12 Print
Total Titles: 80 Print
Imprints: Exemplare

Galerie Hlavniho Mesta Prahy
Mickiewiczova 3, 160 00 Prague 6
Tel: (02) 3332 1200 *Fax:* (02) 3332 3664
E-mail: ghmp@volny.cz
Web Site: www.citygalleryprague.cz
Key Personnel
Dir: Jaroslav Fatka
Founded: 1963
ISBN Prefix(es): 80-7010

Horacek Ladislav-Paseka
Chopinova 4, 120 00 Prague 2
Tel: (02) 222 710 751-3; (02) 222 718 886
  Fax: (02) 22718886

CZECH REPUBLIC

E-mail: paseka@paseka.cz
Web Site: www.paseka.cz
Key Personnel
Publisher: Ladislav Horacek
Dir: Vladimir Pistorius
Founded: 1989
Subjects: Art, Biography, Fiction, History, Literature, Literary Criticism, Essays, Poetry
ISBN Prefix(es): 80-85192; 80-7185

Josef Hribal+
Na Vaclavce 10/1202, 150 21 Prague 5
Mailing Address: PO Box 210, 150 21 Prague 5
Tel: (02) 542731
Key Personnel
Contact: Zdenek Hribal
Founded: 1893
Subjects: Economics, Law, Nonfiction (General)
ISBN Prefix(es): 80-900132; 80-900892; 80-901381

Infoa+
Nova 141, 789 72 Dubicko
Tel: (0583) 449 091 *Fax:* (0583) 456 810
E-mail: infoa@infoa.cz
Web Site: www.infoa.cz
Key Personnel
Dir: Stanislav Sojak *Tel:* (0583) 456 811
Founded: 1992
Private company with its own distribution network in the Czech Republic, Slovakia & Poland.
Specialize in foreign languages.
ISBN Prefix(es): 80-7240; 86-85836; 80-86323; 88-901005; 1-900702
Total Titles: 250 Print
Branch Office(s)
Komenskeho 59, 90901 Skalica, Slovakia, Dir: Pavol Rehus *Tel:* (0801) 646172 *Fax:* (0801) 646172
Distributor for Express Publishing (Distribution rights for the Czech Republic & Slovakia)

Inspirace+
Volsinach 11, 100 00 Prague 10
Tel: (02) 7356615
Key Personnel
Contact: Alois Myslik
Founded: 1990
Subjects: Philosophy, Religion - Other
ISBN Prefix(es): 80-900119

ISE, see Institut Pro Stredoevropskou Kulturu A Politiku (ISE)

Iuventus+
Nedvezska 6, 100 00 Prague 10
Tel: (02) 7817314
Key Personnel
President: Dr Josef Smolka, CSC
Founded: 1990
Subjects: Government, Political Science
ISBN Prefix(es): 80-7123

Nakladatelstvi Jan Vasut+
Vitkova 10, 18621 Prague 8
Tel: (02) 22319 319 *Fax:* (02) 2481 1059
E-mail: vasut@mbox.vol.cz
Web Site: www.vasut.cz
Key Personnel
Publisher: Jan Vasut *Tel:* (02) 22 318 707
  E-mail: jan.vasut@vasut.cz
Foreign Rights: Milena Taralezkovova
Founded: 1990
Subjects: Cookery, Crafts, Games, Hobbies, Humor, Sports, Athletics
ISBN Prefix(es): 80-7236
Warehouse: Grada Bohemia sro, Luzna 591, Prague 6 *Tel:* (02) 20121360

Jednota Ceskych Matematiku A Fysiku
Zitna 25, 117 10 Prague 1
Tel: (02) 222 111 54; (02) 220 907 08; (02) 220 907 09
E-mail: jcmf@math.cas.cz; predseda@jcmf.cz
Web Site: www.jcmf.cz
ISBN Prefix(es): 80-246; 80-7184; 80-7015
Bookshop(s): Celetna 18, 116 36 Prague 1
  Tel: (02) 24491448 *Fax:* (02) 24491671

Nakladatelstvi Jota spol sro+
Krenova 19, Budova 1A, 602 00 Brno
Tel: (05) 37 014 203 *Fax:* (05) 37 014 213
E-mail: jota@jota.cz; books@bm.cesnet.cz
Web Site: www.jota.cz
Key Personnel
Contact: Marcel Nekvinda
Founded: 1990
Subjects: Alternative, Biography, Crafts, Games, Hobbies, Health, Nutrition, History, Military Science, Outdoor Recreation, Science Fiction, Fantasy
ISBN Prefix(es): 80-85617; 80-900281; 80-7217

Kalich SRO
Jungmannova 9, 111 21 Prague 1
Mailing Address: PO Box 220
Tel: (02) 24947505; (02) 24220296 *Fax:* (02) 24947504; (02) 24220296
E-mail: kalichpub@volny.cz
Key Personnel
Dir: Ema Snelia
Manager: Juan Vasin
Founded: 1922
Subjects: History, Philosophy, Religion - Catholic, Religion - Jewish, Religion - Protestant, Religion - Other, Social Sciences, Sociology, Theology
ISBN Prefix(es): 80-7017; 80-7072

Jan Kanzelsberger Praha
Jana Masaryka 56, 120 00 Prague 2
Tel: (02) 22 51 42 40; (02) 22 52 02 64 *Fax:* (02) 22 51 15 73
E-mail: masarykova@volny.cz
Founded: 1990
Subjects: Biography, Language Arts, Linguistics
ISBN Prefix(es): 80-900095; 80-85387; 80-900184
Branch Office(s)
Vaclavske nam 42, 110 00 Prague *Tel:* (02) 24217335 *Fax:* (02) 24221243
Bookshop(s): Knihkupectvi Orbis, Scobarova 5, 130 00 Prague

Karmelitanske Nakladatelstvi+
Kostelni Vydoi 58, Daeice 38001
Tel: 384 420 295 *Fax:* 384 420 295
E-mail: vydri@karmelitanske-nakladatelstvi.cz; zasilky@kna.cz
Web Site: www.karmelitanske-nakladatelstvi.cz; www.kna.cz
Key Personnel
Dir: Jan Fatka *Tel:* 220 181 350 *Fax:* 220 181 390 *E-mail:* fatka@kna.cz
Founded: 1991
Subjects: Biblical Studies, Biography, History, Poetry, Religion - Catholic, Theology
ISBN Prefix(es): 80-7192; 80-7195; 80-85527
Total Titles: 530 Print; 150 Audio
Branch Office(s)
Thakurova 3, 160 00 Prague 6 *Tel:* 220 181 350 *Fax:* 220 181 390
Bookshop(s): Mirove nam 15, Litomioice *Tel:* 416 732 458 *E-mail:* jonas@kna.cz; F Prochazky 101, Nova Paka *Tel:* 493 721 967 *E-mail:* nova.paka@kna.cz; Wurmova 6, Olomouc *Tel:* 587 405 336 *E-mail:* velehrad@kna.cz; Puchmajerova 10, Ostrava *Tel:* 596 121 463 *Fax:* 596 121 463 *E-mail:* caritas@kna.cz; Prokopova 19, Plzeo *Tel:* 377 237 253 *E-mail:* usvit@kna.cz; Jindoisska 23, Prague 1 *Tel:* 224 212 376 *E-mail:* sv.jindrich@kna.cz; Kolejni 4, Prague 6 *Tel:* 220 181 714 *E-mail:* sv.vojtech@kna.cz; Hradeanske namisti 16, Prague 1 *Tel:* 220 392 185 *E-mail:* sv.vit@kna.cz; Marianske nam 200, Uherske Hradisti *Tel:* 572 557 842 *E-mail:* uh.hradiste@kna.cz

Karolinum, nakladatelstvi (The Karolinum Press)+
Ovocny trh 3/5, 116 36 Prague 1
Tel: (02) 24491276 *Fax:* (02) 24212041
E-mail: cupress@ruk.cuni.cz; cupress@cuni.cz
Web Site: www.cupress.cuni.cz
Key Personnel
Dir: Jaroslav Jirsa *E-mail:* jaroslav.jirsa@ruk.cuni.cz
Production: Nadezda Lemochova *Tel:* (02) 24 491 271 *E-mail:* nadezda.lemochova@ruk.cuni.cz; Kamila Schullerova *Tel:* (02) 24 491 272 *E-mail:* kamila.schullerova@ruk.cuni.cz
Distribution: Jaroslava Stribrska *Tel:* (02) 24491275 *E-mail:* jaroslava.stribrska@ruk.cuni.cz
Editor: Renata Camska *Tel:* (02) 24 491 266 *E-mail:* renata.camska@ruk.cuni.cz; Zdenka Lubenova *Tel:* (02) 24 491 273; Milada Motlova *Tel:* (02) 24 491 266 *E-mail:* milada.motlova@ruk.cuni.cz; Petr Valo *Tel:* (02) 24 491 268 *E-mail:* petr.valo@ruk.cuni.cz; Jana Velova *Tel:* (02) 24 491 274 *E-mail:* jana.velova@ruk.cuni.cz
Foreign Rights: Martin Janecek *Tel:* (02) 24 491 269 *E-mail:* martin.janecek@ruk.cuni.cz
Promotion: Milan Susta *Tel:* (02) 24 491 265 *E-mail:* milan.susta@ruk.cuni.cz
Founded: 1990
Publishing House of Charles University, Prague.
Subjects: Architecture & Interior Design, Art, Business, Economics, Education, Fiction, Foreign Countries, History, Language Arts, Linguistics, Law, Mathematics, Medicine, Nursing, Dentistry, Philosophy, Physical Sciences, Religion - Other, Science (General), Social Sciences, Sociology, Political science
ISBN Prefix(es): 80-7066; 80-7184; 80-246
Bookshop(s): Celetna 18, 11636 Prague 1

Kartografie Praha
Ostrovni 30, 11000 Prague 1
Tel: (02) 21969411 *Fax:* (02) 21969428
E-mail: info@kartografie.cz
Web Site: www.kartografie.cz
Telex: 121471 guvs c *Cable:* GEOKART
Key Personnel
Man Dir: Miroslav Miksovsky
Editor-in-Chief: Ales Hasek
Founded: 1954
Geodetic & Cartographic Enterprise in Prague.
ISBN Prefix(es): 80-7011
Orders to: Artia, Foreign Trade Corporation, Ve Smeckach 30, 11127 Prague 1

Knihovna A Tiskarna Pro Nevidome
Ve Smeckach 15, 115 17 Prague 1
Tel: (02) 22 21 04 92; (02) 22 21 15 23 *Fax:* (02) 22 21 04 94
E-mail: ktn@ktn.cz
Web Site: www.ktn.cz
Key Personnel
Dir: Dr Josef Doksansky
Subjects: Biography, Fiction, Humor, Mysteries, Poetry, Psychology, Psychiatry, Religion - Other, Science Fiction, Fantasy
ISBN Prefix(es): 80-7061

Konias+
Waltrova 26, 318 14 Plzen
Tel: (019) 28 06 90 *Fax:* (019) 28 06 90
E-mail: konias@literaplzen.cz
Key Personnel
Contact: Miroslav Moravek
Founded: 1990

Subjects: Travel
ISBN Prefix(es): 80-900167; 80-901379

Konsultace spol sro+
Bilkova 8, 110 00 Prague 1
Tel: (02) 2310363 *Fax:* (02) 2310363
Key Personnel
Publisher (Oberengstringen): Antonin Pasek
Publisher (Zurich): Sarka Pasek
Dir: Antonin Seda
Founded: 1990
Subjects: Government, Political Science, History, Humor, Philosophy, Poetry
ISBN Prefix(es): 80-7124
Associate Companies: Consultation Verlag, Oberengstringen, Switzerland
Orders to: S Pasek, Consultation, Regensdorfestr 175, 8049 Zurich, Switzerland

Kosik
Hajecka 184, Chyne, 253 01 Hostivice
Tel: (02) 670929 *Fax:* (02) 2359403
Key Personnel
Contact: Jiri Kosik
ISBN Prefix(es): 80-900248; 80-902007

Svet Kridel+
PO Box 147, 350 02 Cheb
Tel: (0166) 43475 *Fax:* (0166) 23395
Key Personnel
Contact: Arnost Moucha
Subjects: Aeronautics, Aviation
ISBN Prefix(es): 80-85280

Labyrint+
Dittrichova 5, 120 00 Prague 2
Mailing Address: PO Box 52, Jablonecka 715, 190 00 Prague 9
Tel: (02) 24 922 422 *Fax:* (02) 24 922 422
E-mail: labyrint@wo.cz
Web Site: www.labyrint.net
Key Personnel
Contact: Joachim Dvorak
Founded: 1992
Subjects: Art, Fiction, Library & Information Sciences, Poetry
ISBN Prefix(es): 80-85935
Number of titles published annually: 10 Print; 1 E-Book
Total Titles: 100 Print; 2 E-Book
Subsidiaries: RAKETA (Children's books)

Libri spol sro (Libri Ltd)+
Na Hutmance 7, 158 00 Prague 5
Tel: (02) 5161 3113; (02) 5161 2302 *Fax:* (02) 5161 1013
E-mail: libri@libri.cz
Web Site: www.libri.cz
Key Personnel
Manager: Marie Honzakova
Founded: 1993
Original Czech encyclopedia, popularization.
Membership(s): Federation of Czech Publishers & Booksellers.
Subjects: Archaeology, Architecture & Interior Design, Economics, Foreign Countries, Geography, Geology, History, Literature, Literary Criticism, Essays, Social Sciences, Sociology
ISBN Prefix(es): 80-901579; 80-85983; 80-7277
Number of titles published annually: 50 Print
Total Titles: 300 Print; 3 CD-ROM; 25 E-Book

Lidove Noviny Publishing House+
Jana Masaryka 56, 120 00 Prague 2
Tel: (02) 225 223 50; (02) 222 510 845 *Fax:* (02) 225 240 12; (02) 222 514 012
E-mail: nln@nln.cz; nln@iol.cz
Web Site: www.nln.cz
Key Personnel
Editor-in-Chief: Eva Pleskova *Tel:* 603 810 506
E-mail: pleskova@nln.cz

Founded: 1993
Subjects: Archaeology, Art, Biography, Fiction, History, Language Arts, Linguistics, Nonfiction (General), Poetry, Science (General), Social Sciences, Sociology, Travel
ISBN Prefix(es): 80-7106
Number of titles published annually: 100 Print; 2 CD-ROM
Total Titles: 10 CD-ROM

Josef Lukasik A Spol sro+
Snopkova 481/3, 142 00 Prague 4
Tel: (02) 471 22 19; (02) 83 22 84; (0603) 95 52 55
Key Personnel
Contact: Marie Lukasikova
Founded: 1939
Subjects: Humor, Mysteries, Nonfiction (General), Romance
ISBN Prefix(es): 80-900303; 80-901763; 80-902508

Luxpress VOS+
Maliiska 6, 170 00 Prague 7
Tel: (02) 203 972 60 *Fax:* (02) 203 972 60
E-mail: ibs.czech@iol.cz
Founded: 1990
Subjects: Health, Nutrition, Human Relations, Religion - Other
ISBN Prefix(es): 80-7130

Lyra Pragensis Obecne Prospelna Spolecnost
Karlova 2, 110 00 Prague 1
Tel: (02) 222 202 89 *Fax:* (02) 222 212 67
Web Site: lyra-pragensis.scena.cz
Founded: 1967
Subjects: Drama, Theater, Fiction, Music, Dance, Philosophy, Poetry, Religion - Buddhist
ISBN Prefix(es): 80-7059
Subsidiaries: Spolecnost pratel kultury slova

Mariadan+
Klobouncnicka 7, 140 00 Prague 4
Tel: (02) 41 40 83 91
Key Personnel
Contact: Marie Jehlickova-Gucklerova
Founded: 1990
Subjects: Archaeology, Art, Astronomy, Earth Sciences, Fiction, Foreign Countries, History, Medicine, Nursing, Dentistry, Science Fiction, Fantasy
ISBN Prefix(es): 80-900304
Imprints: Tesinska
Distribution Center: Bookshop Kanzelberger, Vaclavske namesti, Prague 1

Maxdorf Ltd+
Na Sejdru 247, 142 00 Prague 4
Tel: (02) 444 710 37; (02) 41 011 680; (02) 41 011 681 *Fax:* (02) 41 710 245
E-mail: info@maxdorf.cz
Web Site: www.maxdorf.cz
Key Personnel
Editor-in-Chief: Jan Hugo *E-mail:* hugo@maxdorf.cz
Founded: 1993
Publishing house of scientific & professional literature.
Subjects: Art, Health, Nutrition, History, Medicine, Nursing, Dentistry, Science (General), Specialize in medicine, monograhies & handbooks
ISBN Prefix(es): 80-85800; 80-85912
Number of titles published annually: 40 Print
Total Titles: 105 Print; 1 E-Book

Melantrich, akc spol
Vaclavske nam 36, 112 12 Prague 1
Tel: (02) 24227258 *Fax:* (02) 24213176
Telex: 121422 *Cable:* Melantrich

Key Personnel
Man Dir: Petr Zantovsky
Sales Dir: K Volesky
Editorial: Dr K Houba
Production: M Nevole
Founded: 1898
Subjects: Biography, Philosophy, Poetry
ISBN Prefix(es): 80-7023
Bookshop(s): Na prikope 3, Prague 1; Jilska 9, Prague 1

Mendelova zemedelska a lesnicka univerzita v Brne (Mendel University of Agriculture & Forestry Brno)
Zemedelska 1, 613 00 Brno
Tel: (05) 4513 1111; (05) 4513 2678 *Fax:* (05) 4513 5008
Web Site: www.mendelu.cz
Key Personnel
Contact: Dr Jiri Potacek *E-mail:* potacek@mendelu.cz
Founded: 1992
Subjects: Agriculture, Animals, Pets, Biological Sciences, Earth Sciences, Economics, Physical Sciences
ISBN Prefix(es): 80-7157
Number of titles published annually: 70 Print; 30 Audio
Total Titles: 400 Print; 2,000 Audio

Mlada fronta+
Division of Mlada fronta a s
Mezi Vodami 1952/9, 143 00 Prague 4
Tel: (02) 25 276 281 *Fax:* (02) 25 276 278
Web Site: www.mf.cz
Key Personnel
Dir: Dr Jiri Kolecko
Editor-in-Chief: Vlastimil Fiala *E-mail:* fiala@mf.cz
Founded: 1945
Subjects: Art, Astronomy, Biography, Fiction, History, Nonfiction (General), Philosophy, Poetry, Science (General), Science Fiction, Fantasy, Travel
ISBN Prefix(es): 80-204
Number of titles published annually: 100 Print
Total Titles: 6,500 Print

Nakladatelstvi Momcilova, imprint of Pavla Momcilova

Pavla Momcilova+
V Zahradach 146, Cestlice, 251 01 Ricany
Tel: (02) 726 809 19 *Fax:* (02) 726 809 19
E-mail: momcilova@volny.cz
Key Personnel
Publisher: Pavla Momcilova
Founded: 1990
Subjects: Child Care & Development, Cookery, Education, Health, Nutrition, Medicine, Nursing, Dentistry, Poetry, Self-Help
ISBN Prefix(es): 80-900140; 80-901137; 80-85936
Total Titles: 52 Print
Imprints: Nakladatelstvi Momcilova
Warehouse: PEMIC, Ostrava 71900, Vratimovska 101, Contact: Mr Petr Michalek *Tel:* (02) 95683169

Editio Moravia-Moravske hudebni vydavatelstvi+
Sosnova 18, 637 00 Brno
Tel: (05) 41220025
E-mail: emdl@vtx.cz *Cable:* CS-61300 BRNO 13
Key Personnel
Publishing Dir: Dr Jaromir Dlouhy
Marketing Manager: Mag Martin Dlouhy
Founded: 1990
Specialize in music literature for schools.
Subjects: Education, Music, Dance
ISBN Prefix(es): 80-85322

CZECH REPUBLIC

Moravska Galerie v Brno
Prazak Palace, Husova 18, 66226 Brno
Tel: (05) 42 211 464; (05) 42 215 753 *Fax:* (05) 42 215 758
E-mail: m-gal@moravska-galerie.cz
Web Site: www.moravska-galerie.cz
Key Personnel
Acting Dir: Katerina Tlachova
Marketing: Pavla Teglova
Administration: Simona Smolova
Founded: 1873
Exhibition Catalogues; Bulletin of Moravian Gallery.
Subjects: Architecture & Interior Design, Art, Photography, Applied Art
ISBN Prefix(es): 80-7027
Total Titles: 30 Print

Narodni filmovy archiv+
Formerly Cesky Filmovy ustav
Malesicka 12, 130 00 Prague 3
Mailing Address: Bartolomejska 11, 110 00 Prague 1
Tel: (02) 71 770 500; (02) 71 770 502-9
 Fax: (02) 71 770 501
E-mail: nfa@nfa.cz
Key Personnel
President: Vladimir Opela
Founded: 1970
Subjects: Film, Video
ISBN Prefix(es): 80-7004

Narodni Knihovna CR (The National Library of the Czech Republic)+
c/o The National Library of the Czech Republic, Klementinum 190, 110 01 Prague 1
Tel: (02) 2810 13 316; (02) 2810 13 317
 Fax: (02) 216 632 61; (02) 2810 13 333
E-mail: sekret.ur@nkp.cz; mirosovsky.ivo@cdh.nkp.cz
Web Site: www.nkp.cz
Key Personnel
Head, Publishing Division: Milena Redinova, PhD
 E-mail: redinova.milena@cdh.nkp.cz
The publishing division manages & coordinates publishing activities of the National Library in the areas of librarianship, bibliography & scientific information. The division is responsible for editorial planning, production, sales & shipping.
Membership(s): Conference of European National Librarians (CENL); Czech Association of Booksellers & Publishers; Czech Association of Librarian & Information Professionals; International Federation of Library Associations & Institutions (IFLA); Lique des Bibliotheques Europeennes de Recherche (LIBER).
Subjects: Library & Information Sciences
ISBN Prefix(es): 80-7050
Number of titles published annually: 32 Print; 2 CD-ROM; 1 Online
Total Titles: 94 Print; 2 CD-ROM; 1 Online
Imprints: National Library of the Czech Republic
Distributed by National Library of the Czech Republic
Shipping Address: National Library of the Czech Republic, Publishing Division, Central Depository Hostivar, Sodomkova 2, 102 00 Prague 10
 Tel: (02) 2810 13 230
Orders to: National Library of the Czech Republic, Publishing Division, Central Depository Hostivar, Sodomkova 2, 102 00 Prague 10
Returns: National Library of the Czech Republic, Publishing Division, Central Depository Hostivar, Sodomkova 2, 102 00 Prague 10

Narodni Muzeum
Vaclavske namisti 68, 115 79 Prague 1
Tel: (02) 24497111; (02) 24226488 *Fax:* (02) 22246047
E-mail: ais@nm.anet.cz
Web Site: www.nm.cz
Key Personnel
Dir: Dipl Ing Milan Placek *Tel:* (02) 24497235
 Fax: (02) 24224940 *E-mail:* milan.placek@nm.cz; Dr Milan Stloukal; Lukas Viktora
 E-mail: lukas.viktora@nm.cz
Founded: 1818
Subjects: Animals, Pets, Anthropology, Archaeology, Art, Asian Studies, Biological Sciences, Drama, Theater, Earth Sciences, History, Music, Dance, Natural History, Science (General), Sports, Athletics
ISBN Prefix(es): 80-7036

Nase vojsko, nakladatelstvi a knizni obchod+
Vitezne nam 4, 16000 Prague 6
Tel: (02) 243 130 71; (02) 243 112 04; (02) 249 171 47 *Fax:* (02) 243 112 04
E-mail: info@nasevojsko.com; info@nasevojsko.cz
Web Site: www.nasevojsko.com
Key Personnel
Dir: Jakub Cisar
Editorial: Dr Zdenka Alanova
Sales: Miroslav Ambros
Rights & Permissions: Marie Kutilkkova
Founded: 1945
Subjects: History, Humor, Maritime, Military Science, Mysteries, Nonfiction (General), Philosophy
ISBN Prefix(es): 80-206
Warehouse: Ostrovni 32, Prague 1

National Library of the Czech Republic, *imprint of* Narodni Knihovna CR

Nava+
Hankova 6, 301 33 Plzen
Tel: (019) 7235633; (019) 7235721; (019) 7223294; (019) 7223251; (019) 7235509
 Fax: (019) 223143
Key Personnel
Contact: Ota Rubner
Founded: 1990
Specializes in children's books.
Subjects: Fiction, History, Humor
ISBN Prefix(es): 80-85254; 80-7211

NLN Ltd, see Lidove Noviny Publishing House

Cesky normalizacni institut (Czech Standards Institute)
Biskupsky dvur 5, 110 02 Prague 1
Tel: (02) 21 80 21 11 *Fax:* (02) 21 80 23 10
E-mail: info@csni.cz
Web Site: www.csni.cz *Cable:* NORMALIZACE PRAHA
Key Personnel
Contact: Jan Jelinek; Otakar Kunc; Ms Bures ova Zdenka
Founded: 1922
Membership(s): CEN; CENELEC; ETSi; IEC; ISO.
Subjects: Automotive, Chemistry, Chemical Engineering, Electronics, Electrical Engineering, Engineering (General), Environmental Studies, Mechanical Engineering, Medicine, Nursing, Dentistry
ISBN Prefix(es): 80-85111; 80-7283
Bookshop(s): Prodejna norem, Hornomecholupska 40, 102 04 Prague 10 *Tel:* (02) 71 96 17 70 *Fax:* (02) 74 86 69 51; (02) 71 96 20 43 *E-mail:* odbyt@csni.cz; Prodejna norem, Biskupsky dvur c 5, 110 02 Prague 1 *Fax:* (02) 74 86 69 51; (02) 71 96 20 43 *E-mail:* odbyt@csni.cz

Nakladatelstvi Olympia AS+
Klimentska 1246/1, 110 15 Prague 1
Tel: (02) 224 810 146 *Fax:* (02) 222 312 137
E-mail: olympia@mbox.vol.cz
Telex: 121717 *Cable:* OLYMPIA PRAGUE
Key Personnel
Man Dir: Karel Zelnicek
Dir: Alexander Zurman
Sales Dir: Zdenek Pobuda
Publicity & Advertising: Monika Charvatova
Editor: Josef Smatlak
Founded: 1954
Publishing house of sports & tourism.
Subjects: Sports, Athletics, Travel
ISBN Prefix(es): 80-7033
Bookshop(s): Opletalova 59, Prague 1

Omnipress Praha+
Na Sypcine 9, 147 00 Prague 4
Tel: (02) 61211406 *Fax:* (02) 61211856
E-mail: dcf.clock@omnipress.cz
Web Site: www.omnipress.cz
Key Personnel
Contact: Dr Metodej K Chytil *E-mail:* m.chytil@omnipress.cz
Founded: 1990
Subjects: Communications, Medicine, Nursing, Dentistry, Philosophy, Science (General)
ISBN Prefix(es): 80-900153
Associate Companies: Omikron Desk-Top Publishing
Orders to: PO Box 106, 140 00 Prague

P & R Centrum Vydavateistvi a Nakladateistvi
Pod Barvirkou 14, 150 00 Prague 5
Tel: (02) 542901 *Fax:* (02) 51554485
E-mail: olda@katapult.cz
Key Personnel
Publisher: Milan Nestaval
Founded: 1990
Also a music agency.
Subjects: Language Arts, Linguistics, Literature, Literary Criticism, Essays, Music, Dance
ISBN Prefix(es): 80-85333
Imprints: P R Centrum
Divisions: Zborovska 60
Bookshop(s): Belgicka 36, 120 00 Prague 2

P R Centrum, *imprint of* P & R Centrum Vydavateistvi a Nakladateistvi

Portal, *imprint of* Portal spol sro

Portal spol sro+
Klapkova 2, 182 00 Prague 8
Tel: (02) 83028111 *Fax:* (02) 83028112
E-mail: naklad@portal.cz
Web Site: www.portal.cz
Key Personnel
Dir: Jaroslav Kuchar
Rights: Dominik Dvorak *Tel:* (02) 83028111 (ext 602) *E-mail:* dvorak@portal.cz
Founded: 1990
Membership(s): Association of Catholic Publishers & Booksellers.
Subjects: Child Care & Development, Communications, Disability, Special Needs, Education, Human Relations, Psychology, Psychiatry, Religion - Catholic
ISBN Prefix(es): 80-7178; 80-85282
Number of titles published annually: 90 Print
Total Titles: 450 Print
Imprints: Portal
Foreign Rep(s): Artforum sro (Slovak Republic)
Bookshop(s): Dominikanske nam 8, 602 00 Brno *Tel:* (05) 42213140 *E-mail:* brno@studovna.cz; Jindrisska 30, 11000 Prague 1 *Tel:* (02) 24213415 *E-mail:* praha@studovna.cz; Klapkova 2, 182 00 Prague 8 *Tel:* (02) 83028203 *E-mail:* obchod@portal.cz; Kostelni nam 2, Ostrava *Tel:* (05) 95136508 *Fax:* (05) 95136508

Pragma 4+
V Hodkoviekach 2/20, 147 00 Prague 4
Tel: 241 768 565; 241 768 566; 603 205 099
 Fax: 241 768 561
E-mail: pragma@pragma.cz

PUBLISHERS CZECH REPUBLIC

Web Site: www.pragma.cz
Key Personnel
Business Manager: Ivan Marinec
Contact: Robert Nemec
Founded: 1989
Specialize in US publishers.
Subjects: Business, Health, Nutrition, Philosophy, Self-Help
ISBN Prefix(es): 80-7205; 80-85213
Total Titles: 480 Print; 20 Audio
Parent Company: Pragma
Distributed by Kanzelsberger

Prazske nakladatelstvi Pluto
Kremencova 1, 110 00 Prague 1
Tel: (02) 249 301 89; (02) 43 25 05 *Fax:* (02) 249 301 89
Key Personnel
Owner: Jiri Polacek; Leontina Polackova
Founded: 1990
Subjects: Art, History, Travel
ISBN Prefix(es): 80-900192; 80-901224; 80-901544; 80-86435; 80-902183

PressArt Nakladatelstvi+
Aloisina vyhlidka 628/100, 460 05 Liberec
Tel: (048) 29377 *Fax:* (048) 27958
Key Personnel
President: Jiri Oplt
Vice President: Petr Bartos
Founded: 1990
Subjects: Advertising, Business, Drama, Theater
ISBN Prefix(es): 80-900367
Parent Company: PressART
Associate Companies: Bohemia Union
Subsidiaries: M-Print; Eurotip
Divisions: Exportabt, Innlandabt

Pressfoto Vydavatelstvi Ceske Tiskove Kancelare
Zirovnicka 2389, 106 00 Prague 10
Tel: (02) 727 700 10 *Fax:* (02) 727 700 10
Telex: 122908 ctKC
Founded: 1963
Subjects: History, Regional Interests
ISBN Prefix(es): 80-7046

Prostor, nakladatelstvi sro+
Tynska 21, 110 00 Prague 1
Tel: (02) 224 826 688 *Fax:* (02) 242 441 694
E-mail: prostor@ini.cz
Web Site: www.prostor-nakladatelstvi.cz
Key Personnel
International Rights: Sylva Kurdiovska
Foreign Rights Agent: Kristin Olson *Tel:* (02) 222 580 048 *Fax:* (02) 222 582 042 *E-mail:* kolson@vol.cz
Founded: 1990
Specialize in Czech & German history.
Membership(s): Svaz ceskych knihkupcu a nakladatelu
Subjects: Biography, Fiction, Government, Political Science, History, Nonfiction (General), Philosophy, Photography
ISBN Prefix(es): 80-7260
Number of titles published annually: 25 Print
Total Titles: 210 Print

Psychoanalyticke Nakladatelstvi+
Vinohradska 71, 120 00 Prague 2
Tel: (02) 33340305; (02) 545 97 12; (02) 627 1855 *Fax:* (02) 312 03 05
Key Personnel
Assistant Professor: Jiri Kocourek, PhD *E-mail:* kocourek@serverpha.czcom.cz
Founded: 1992
Subjects: Education, Medicine, Nursing, Dentistry, Psychology, Psychiatry, Psychoanalysis, Psychotherapy, Scientific & Popular
ISBN Prefix(es): 80-901601; 80-86123
Number of titles published annually: 10 Print

Total Titles: 40 Print
Branch Office(s)
Vitezne nam 10, 16000 Prague 6
Distributed by Grada, Mata, Kolporter

Verlag Harry Putz+
Oldichova 89/28, 460 03 Liberec
Mailing Address: PO Box 89, 460 31 Liberec
Tel: (048) 515 21 20; (048) 510 32 75 *Fax:* (048) 510 32 75
E-mail: harrputz@mbox.vol.cz
Subjects: Language Arts, Linguistics
ISBN Prefix(es): 80-901119; 80-902165

Simon Rysavy
Ceska 31, 602 00 Brno
Tel: (05) 42 212 052; (05) 42 213 849 *Fax:* (05) 42 216 633
E-mail: info@rysavy.cz
Web Site: www.itn.cz/rysavy-books; www.rysavy.cz
ISBN Prefix(es): 80-86137; 80-902143

SEVT, see Statisticke a evidencni vydavatelstvi tiskopisu (SEVT)

Slon Sociologicke Nakladatelstvi+
Jilska 1, 110 00 Prague 1
Tel: (02) 222 220 025 *Fax:* (02) 222 220 025
E-mail: redakce@slon-knihy.cz
Web Site: www.slon-knihy.cz
Key Personnel
Contact: Alena Miltova
Founded: 1991
Subjects: Anthropology, Government, Political Science, History, Philosophy, Psychology, Psychiatry, Social Sciences, Sociology
ISBN Prefix(es): 80-85850; 80-901059; 80-901424; 80-86429
Number of titles published annually: 17 Print
Total Titles: 146 Print

Sofiprin+
PO Box 1006, 111 21 Prague 1
Tel: (0602) 30 87 21 *Fax:* (02) 758280
Key Personnel
Dir: Jiri Horak
Foreign Relations Officer: Jan Spousta
Founded: 1991
ISBN Prefix(es): 80-85391

Statisticke a evidencni vydavatelstvi tiskopisu (SEVT)
Pekarova 4, 181 06 Prague 8
Tel: 233 551 711; 283 090 352 *Fax:* 233 543 918
E-mail: sevt@sevt.cz
Web Site: www.sevt.cz
Key Personnel
Head of Production: Jarmila Frysova *Tel:* 283 090 339 *E-mail:* frysova@sevt.cz
General Manager: Jaroslav Cizek
Publishing House of Statistics & Data.
ISBN Prefix(es): 80-7049

Statni Vedecka Knihovna Usti Nad Labem
W Churchilla 3, 401 34 Usti Nad Labem
Tel: (047) 5200045; (047) 5209126 *Fax:* (047) 5200045
E-mail: library@svkul.cz
Web Site: www.svkul.cz
Key Personnel
Library Dir: Mr Brozek Ales *E-mail:* brozeka@svkul.cz
Founded: 1945
Subjects: Library & Information Sciences
ISBN Prefix(es): 80-7055

Institut Pro Stredoevropskou Kulturu A Politiku (ISE)
Vysehradska 2, 128 00 Prague 2

Tel: (02) 249 168 60 *Fax:* (02) 249 168 60
E-mail: panevropa@iol.cz
ISBN Prefix(es): 80-85241; 80-86130

Svepomoc
Senovazne nam 10, 113 28 Prague 1
Tel: (02) 24223446; (02) 24223450 *Fax:* (02) 24223439
Publishing House of the Central Cooperative Council.
ISBN Prefix(es): 80-7063

NS Svoboda spol sro+
Jungmannova 12, 113 03 Prague 1
Mailing Address: K Safine 145, 149 00 Prague 4
Tel: (02) 24 22 98
Tel: (02) 449 132 58; (02) 23 06 14 *Fax:* (02) 449 132 58
E-mail: nssvobod@centrum.cz
Key Personnel
Dir: Stefan Szerynski
Rights & Permissions: Michal Bencok
Founded: 1970
Publishing house in state ownership.
Subjects: Finance, History, Management, Marketing, Mysteries, Nonfiction (General)
ISBN Prefix(es): 80-205
Book Club(s): Friends of Antiquity; Readers Club of Svoboda

Svoboda Servis GmbH+
Jungmannova 12, 113 03 Prague 1
Tel: (02) 449 132 58; (02) 230614 *Fax:* (02) 449 132 58
E-mail: nssvoboda@centrum.cz
Key Personnel
Dir: Stefan Szerynski
Foreign Rights Representative: Michal Bencok *Tel:* (02) 24009277 *Fax:* (02) 22247383 *E-mail:* ak.bencok@cmail.cz
Founded: 1994
Subjects: Business, Management, Mysteries, Philosophy, Science Fiction, Fantasy
ISBN Prefix(es): 80-205
Number of titles published annually: 4 Print
Total Titles: 30 Print

SystemConsult+
Bartolomejska 89, CZ 530 02 Pardubice
Tel: (040) 466 501 585 *Fax:* (040) 466 501 585
E-mail: system.consult@tiscali.cz
Web Site: www.systemconsult.cz
Key Personnel
Contact: Ivo Machacka
Founded: 1990
Specialize in Computer Dictionaries (German-Czech, English-Czech), Road-Transport Techniques & Automotive Industry Dictionaries (German-English-Czech), Travel Dictionaries (English & German) & Road Transport, Traffic Signs in Europe.
Subjects: Business, Computer Science, History, Transportation, Travel
ISBN Prefix(es): 80-900344; 80-85629
Number of titles published annually: 5 Print; 1 CD-ROM
Total Titles: 50 Print; 2 CD-ROM

Tesinska, *imprint of* Mariadan

Touzimsky & Moravec
Pod Lazni 12, 140 00 Prague 4
Tel: (02) 612 13 631; (02) 612 12 458 *Fax:* (02) 612 12 458
Key Personnel
Contact: Michal Moravec
Subjects: Science Fiction, Fantasy, Western Fiction
ISBN Prefix(es): 80-900955; 80-900137; 80-85773; 80-7264

CZECH REPUBLIC

Trizonia
U Sipku 15, 15400 Prague 5
Tel: (02) 5816502
Telex: Trizonia Prag 2
Key Personnel
President: Dr Jindrich Jirka
Founded: 1990
Subjects: Economics, Law
ISBN Prefix(es): 80-900953; 80-900117; 80-85573

Evzen Uher, Musikverlag UHER+
Kollarova 404, 686 01 Uherske Hradiste
Tel: (0632) 40376
Key Personnel
Contact: Evzen Uher
Founded: 1990
Subjects: Music, Dance
ISBN Prefix(es): 80-900136; 80-901386

Univerzity Karlovy, see Karolinum, nakladatelstvi

Ladislav Vasicek+
Pellicova 17, 602 00 Brno
Key Personnel
Contact: Ladislav Vasicek
Founded: 1990
Subjects: Poetry
ISBN Prefix(es): 80-900164
Bookshop(s): Ing Vasicek, Kr Pole Berkova 46, 61200 Brno
Orders to: Kvetinarska 1, 600 00 Brno

Vitalis sro+
U Zelezne lavky 568/10, 118 00 Prague 1
Tel: (02) 57530732 *Fax:* (02) 57531974
E-mail: info@vitalis-verlag.com
Web Site: www.vitalis-verlag.com
Key Personnel
Publisher: Dr Harald Salfellner
Sales Manager: Dr Gabriela Salfellner
Founded: 1992
Specialize in Bohemica.
Subjects: Biography, Cookery, Fiction, Foreign Countries, Poetry
ISBN Prefix(es): 80-85938; 80-901621; 80-901370; 80-7253
Number of titles published annually: 40 Print
Total Titles: 300 Print
Warehouse: LKG, Potzschauer Weg, 04579 Espenhain, Germany
Orders to: LKG, Potzschauer Weg, 04579 Espenhain, Germany

Vodnar
Radlicka 2, 150 00 Prague 5
Tel: (02) 51563603 *Fax:* (02) 51563603
E-mail: naklvodnar@volny.cz
Web Site: www.volny.cz/naklvodnar
Key Personnel
Contact: Vladimir Kvasnicka
Founded: 1990
Subjects: Astrology, Occult, Philosophy
ISBN Prefix(es): 80-85255; 80-86226
Number of titles published annually: 10 Print

Volvox Globator Nakladatelstvi & vydavatelstvi
One Pluku 7, 186 00 Prague 8
Tel: 224 236 268 *Fax:* 224 217 721
E-mail: volvox@volvox.cz
Web Site: www.volvox.cz
Key Personnel
Contact: Vit Houska
Founded: 1990
ISBN Prefix(es): 80-7207; 80-85769; 80-900906; 80-901226
Bookshop(s): Knihkupectvi VOLVOX GLOBATOR s literarni kavarnou, Stitneho 16, 130 00 Praque 3

Votobia sro+
Lazecka 70a, 771 00 Olomouc
Mailing Address: PO Box 214, 771 00 Olomouc
Tel: (068) 522 46 21 *Fax:* (068) 523 18 90
E-mail: votobia@mbox.vol.cz
Key Personnel
Contact: Tomas Koudela
Founded: 1991
Subjects: Alternative, Art, Astrology, Occult, Biography, Computer Science, Cookery, History, Literature, Literary Criticism, Essays, Music, Dance, Philosophy, Poetry, Religion - Buddhist
ISBN Prefix(es): 80-7198; 80-85619; 80-85885; 80-900614
Bookshop(s): Riegrova 33, 77100 Olomouc

Vydavatelstvi Cesky Geologicky Ustav
Klarov 3, 118 21 Prague 1
Tel: 257 089 411 *Fax:* 257 531 376
E-mail: sekret@cgu.cz
Web Site: www.cgu.cz
Founded: 1919
Subjects: Chemistry, Chemical Engineering, Earth Sciences, Geography, Geology, Physical Sciences
ISBN Prefix(es): 80-7075
Branch Office(s)
Leitnerova 22, 658 69 Brno *Tel:* 543 429 200 *Fax:* 543 212 370

Vysehrad spol sro+
Vita Nejedleho 15, 130 00 Prague 3
Tel: 224 221 703 *Fax:* 224 221 703
E-mail: info@ivysehrad.cz
Web Site: www.ivysehrad.cz
Key Personnel
Dir: Pravomil Novak *E-mail:* novak@ivysehrad.cz
Founded: 1934
Specialize in Christian-oriented books.
Subjects: Ethnicity, Philosophy, Poetry, Public Administration, Religion - Other, Science (General)
ISBN Prefix(es): 80-7021

Denmark

General Information

Capital: Copenhagen
Language: Danish (English and German widely spoken). Faeroese in the Faroes. Greenlandic in Greenland
Religion: Evangelical Lutheran
Population: 5.2 million
Bank Hours: 0930-1600 Monday-Friday; open until 1800 Thursday
Shop Hours: 0800 or 0900-1700 or 1730 Monday-Thursday; open until 1900 Friday; open until 1300 or 1700 Saturday
Currency: 100 ore = 1 krone
Export/Import Information: Denmark is a member of the European Union, Faroes and Greenland are not. No tariff on books except children's picture-books from non-EU. No import licenses required. Importers must use longest of alternative credit terms in contract, otherwise no exchange controls. 25% VAT on books.
Copyright: UCC, Berne, Florence (see Copyright Conventions, pg xi)

Aarhus Universitetsforlag (Aarhus University Press)+
Langelandsgade 177, 8200 Aarhus N
Tel: 89425370 *Fax:* 89425380
E-mail: unipress@au.dk
Web Site: www.unipress.dk
Key Personnel
Man Dir: Claes Hvidbak *Tel:* 89425377
E-mail: ch@unipress.au.dk
Marketing Coordinator & Editor: Sanne Lind Hansen *Tel:* 89425376 *E-mail:* slh@unipress.au.dk
Editor: Carsten Fenger-Gren *Tel:* 89425379 *E-mail:* cfg@unipress.au.dk; Anette Juul Hansen *Tel:* 89425374 *E-mail:* ajh@unipress.au.dk; Pernille Pennington *Tel:* 89425373 *E-mail:* pp@unipress.au.dk
English Editor: Mary Waters Lund *Tel:* 89425375 *E-mail:* mwl@unipress.au.dk
Founded: 1985
Membership(s): International Association of Scholarly Publishers.
Subjects: Anthropology, Archaeology, Asian Studies, Biblical Studies, Drama, Theater, Language Arts, Linguistics, Literature, Literary Criticism, Essays, Philosophy, Psychology, Psychiatry, Religion - Other, Social Sciences, Sociology, Theology
ISBN Prefix(es): 87-7288; 87-7934
Number of titles published annually: 40 Print
Total Titles: 650 Print
Distributed by David Brown Book Co (USA & Canada); Lavis Marketing (UK & Ireland)
Distributor for Aalborg University Press; Jutland Archaeological Society
Warehouse: Katrinebjergvej 89B, 8200 Aarhus N

Academic Press, see Akademisk Forlag A/S

Agertofts Forlag A/S+
Hinbjerg 9, 2690 Karlsunde
Tel: 4615 1248 *Fax:* 4615 2404
Key Personnel
Man Dir: Ejnar Agertoft
Founded: 1986
ISBN Prefix(es): 87-88014; 87-89970; 87-7878
Bookshop(s): The Children's Bookshop, Kobmagergade 50, 1150 Copenhagen K

Akademisk Forlag A/S+
PO Box 54, 1002 Copenhagen K
Tel: 33 43 40 80 *Fax:* 33 43 40 99
E-mail: akademisk@akademisk.dk
Web Site: www.akademisk.dk
Key Personnel
Man Dir: Helle Lehrmann Madsen
Marketing: Gitte Kolbaek Jensen
Founded: 1962
Subjects: Economics, Education, Engineering (General), History, Language Arts, Linguistics, Law, Medicine, Nursing, Dentistry, Philosophy, Psychology, Psychiatry, Science (General), Social Sciences, Sociology
ISBN Prefix(es): 87-500
Subsidiaries: Akademisk Forlag

Alinea A/S+
Ewaldsgade 9, 2200 Copenhagen N
Mailing Address: Postboks 599, 2200 Copenhagen N
Tel: 33 69 46 66 *Fax:* 33 69 46 60
E-mail: alinea@alinea.dk; skoleservice@alinea.dk
Web Site: www.alinea.dk
Key Personnel
Administrative Dir: Ebbe Dam Nielsen
E-mail: edn@alinea.dk
Founded: 1996
ISBN Prefix(es): 87-23
Parent Company: Egmont Aschehoug

Alma+
Kaalundsvej 13, 3400 Hillerod
Tel: 48 25 54 41 *Fax:* 48 25 20 41
Key Personnel
Chief Executive: Susanne Vebel
Founded: 1984
Specialize in picture books.
Subjects: Fiction
ISBN Prefix(es): 87-7243; 87-985145

PUBLISHERS

DENMARK

Shipping Address: Stabrand Spedition, Billedvej 8, Frihavnen, 2100 Copenhagen O
Warehouse: Jernholmen 29, 2650 Hvidovre
Orders to: DBK, Siljangade 2-8, Box 1731, 2300 Copenhagen S

Forlaget alokke AS+
Porskaervej 15, Nim, 8700 Horsens
Tel: 75671119 *Fax:* 75671074
E-mail: alokke@get2net.dk
Key Personnel
President: Bertil Toft Hansen
Founded: 1977
Membership(s): Danish Publishers Association.
Subjects: Advertising, English as a Second Language
ISBN Prefix(es): 87-592; 87-87777

Amanda
Rathsacksvej 7, 1862 Frederiksberg C
Tel: 3379-0110 *Fax:* 33790011
E-mail: forlag@dansklf.dk
Key Personnel
Editorial Dir: Emborg Uhd Gert
ISBN Prefix(es): 87-89537

Forlaget Apostrof ApS+
Berggreensgade 24, 2100 Copenhagen O
Mailing Address: Postboks 2580, 2100 Copenhagen O
Tel: 3920 8420 *Fax:* 3920 8453
E-mail: info1@apostrof.dk
Web Site: www.apostrof.dk
Key Personnel
Publisher: Mia Thestrup *E-mail:* mt@apostrof.dk; Ole Thestrup *E-mail:* ot@apostrof.dk
Founded: 1980
Specialize in psychology books, children's books & quality children's books.
Subjects: Psychology, Psychiatry
ISBN Prefix(es): 87-591; 87-88002
Number of titles published annually: 30 Print
Total Titles: 400 Print
Warehouse: Dbks Forlagsekspedition, Mimersuej 4, 4600 Koge

Arkitektens Forlag
Overgaden oven Vandet 10, 1, 1415 Copenhagen K
Tel: 32836970 *Fax:* 32836940
E-mail: eksp@arkfo.dk; red@arkfo.dk
Web Site: www.arkfo.dk
Key Personnel
Dir: Kim Dirckinck-Holmfeld
Founded: 1949
Subjects: Architecture & Interior Design
ISBN Prefix(es): 87-7407

Arnkrone Forlaget A/S
Fuglebaekvej 4, 2770 Kastrup
Tel: 32507000 *Fax:* 32522652
Key Personnel
Man Dir: J Juul Rasmussen
Founded: 1941
Subjects: Art, Ethnicity, Medicine, Nursing, Dentistry
ISBN Prefix(es): 87-87007

Aschehoug Dansk Forlag A/S+
Division of Egmont
8, Landemaerket, 1119 Copenhagen K
Mailing Address: PO Box 2179, 1017 Copenhagen K
Tel: 33305522; 33305822 *Fax:* 33305823
E-mail: info@ash.egmont.com
Web Site: www.aschehoug.dk
Key Personnel
Man Dir: Henrik Kristensen
Publishing Dir: Anette Wad
Founded: 1977

Subjects: Biography, Cookery, Fiction, Health, Nutrition, How-to, Maritime
ISBN Prefix(es): 87-11; 87-429; 87-7512
Total Titles: 900 Print
Imprints: Sesam

Atuakkiorfik A/S Det Greenland Publishers+
Hans Egedesvej 3, 3900 Nuuk (Greenland)
Mailing Address: Postboks 840, 3900 Nuuk (Greenland)
Tel: 32 21 22 *Fax:* 32 25 00
E-mail: henri@atuakkiorfik.gl
Web Site: www.atuakkiorfik.gl
Key Personnel
Man Dir: Nukaaraq Eugenius
Manager: Ove-Karl Berthelsen
Editor: Pauline Abelsen *E-mail:* pa@atuakkiorfik.gl
Founded: 1956
Also acts as educational book publisher, public relations.
Subjects: Art, Education, Fiction, Nonfiction (General)
ISBN Prefix(es): 87-558
Number of titles published annually: 35 Print

Bibelselskabets Forlag og Det Kgl Vajsenhus' Forlag, see Det Danske Bibelselskab

Bierman og Bierman I/S
Vestergade 126, 7200 Grindsted
Tel: 75 32 02 88 *Fax:* 75 32 15 48
E-mail: mail@bierman.dk
Web Site: www.bierman.dk
Key Personnel
Man Dir: Bo Lorentzen; Tom Selmer-Petersen
Founded: 1968
Subjects: Management

Bogan's Forlag+
8, Kastaniebakken, 3540 Lynge
Tel: 48188055 *Fax:* 48188769
Key Personnel
Owner & Publisher: Evan Bogan
Founded: 1974
Subjects: Astrology, Occult, Health, Nutrition, Humor, Nonfiction (General), Science (General)
ISBN Prefix(es): 87-87533; 87-7466; 87-7525
Number of titles published annually: 30 Print
Total Titles: 250 Print
Imprints: My Best Book
Warehouse: DBK, Siljangade 6, 2300 Copenhagen S *Tel:* 32697788 *Fax:* 32697789

Bogfabrikken Fakta ApS
Jacob Dannefaerdsvej 6 B/1, 1973 Frederiksberg C
Tel: 3537 3533 *Fax:* 3537 3299
Subjects: Crafts, Games, Hobbies, Environmental Studies, Fashion, Nonfiction (General), Science (General), Transportation
ISBN Prefix(es): 87-7771
Parent Company: K D - Consult A/S

Bogklubben for Laeger, *imprint of* Gyldendalske Boghandel - Nordisk Forlag A/S

Bogklubben for Sygeplejersker, *imprint of* Gyldendalske Boghandel - Nordisk Forlag A/S

Bonnier Publications A/S+
Strandboulevarden 130, 2100 Copenhagen
Tel: 3917 2000 *Fax:* 3929 0199
Web Site: www.bonnierpublications.com
Key Personnel
Man Dir: Michael Cordsen
Marketing: Jesper Buchvald
Founded: 1966

Subjects: Criminology, Fiction, Military Science, Western Fiction
ISBN Prefix(es): 82-535
Parent Company: Bonnier AB
Branch Office(s)
Kirkegatan 20, 4, 0153 Oslo, Norway *Tel:* 2240 1200

Bonniers Specialmagasiner A/S Bogdivisionen+
Strandboulevarden 130, 2100 Copenhagen 0
Tel: 39295500 *Fax:* 39172300
Telex: 15712 bonmag dk
Key Personnel
Publisher: Jette Juliusson
Founded: 1989
Subjects: Fiction, Nonfiction (General)
ISBN Prefix(es): 87-7741
Parent Company: Bonnier Publication A/S
Subsidiaries: Autour Du Fil, Editions Bonnier; Bonniers Blade OG Boker
Book Club(s): Bogklubben 12 Boger A/S (jointly owned with Lindhardt Ringhof) & Munksgaard
Warehouse: Bonniers Boger, Islevdalvej 148, 2610 Rodovre

Borgens Forlag A/S+
Valbygardsvej 33, 2500 Valby
Tel: 36 15 36 15 *Fax:* 36 15 36 16
E-mail: post@borgen.dk
Web Site: www.borgen.dk
Key Personnel
Man Dir: Niels Borgen *E-mail:* nborgen@borgen.dk
Editorial Dir: Helle Borgen *E-mail:* hborgen@borgen.dk
Production: Dennis Stovring *E-mail:* dstovring@borgen.dk
Rights & Permissions Manager: Mette Nymark *E-mail:* mnymark@borgen.dk
Founded: 1948
Subjects: Alternative, Animals, Pets, Art, Astrology, Occult, Behavioral Sciences, Child Care & Development, Crafts, Games, Hobbies, Education, Environmental Studies, Fiction, Health, Nutrition, How-to, Human Relations, Humor, Literature, Literary Criticism, Essays, Music, Dance, Nonfiction (General), Philosophy, Poetry, Psychology, Psychiatry, Regional Interests, Religion - Other, Self-Help
ISBN Prefix(es): 87-418; 87-21; 87-7895; 87-982973
Number of titles published annually: 250 Print; 5 Audio
Total Titles: 2,000 Print; 10 Audio
Subsidiaries: Hekla; Maaholms Forlag; Sommer & Sorensen; Forlaget Vindrose A/S
Book Club(s): Borgens Bogklub
Orders to: DBK-Logistik Service, Mimersvej 4, 4600 Koge

Bornegudstjeneste-Forlaget+
25 Korskaervej, 7000 Fredericia
Tel: 75934455 *Fax:* 75924275
E-mail: lohse@imh.dk
Key Personnel
Dir: Finn Andersen
Founded: 1868
ISBN Prefix(es): 87-87828; 87-89682

Borsen Forlag
Montergade 19, 1140 Copenhagen K
Tel: 33 32 01 02 *Fax:* 33 12 24 45
E-mail: redaktionen@borsen.dk
Web Site: www.borsen.dk
Key Personnel
Editor-in-Chief & Chief Executive Officer: Leif Beck Fallesen
Chief Sub-Editor: Bent Sorenson
Subjects: Management
ISBN Prefix(es): 87-7553; 87-7664; 87-7901; 87-88184; 87-90790; 87-91157

DENMARK

Ca Luna Forlaget+
Frischsvej 40a, 1 sal, 8600 Silkeborg
Tel: 86 82 86 88; 26 20 24 68 *Fax:* 86 82 86 64
E-mail: caluna@caluna.dk
Web Site: www.caluna.dk
Founded: 1995
Specialize in New Age books.
Subjects: New Age
ISBN Prefix(es): 87-90312
Total Titles: 10 Print

Carit Andersens Forlag A/S
Affiliate of Mercantila Publishers A/S
18 Upsalagade, 2100 Copenhagen
Tel: 35436222 *Fax:* 35435151
E-mail: info@mercantila.dk
Web Site: www.caritandersen.dk
Key Personnel
Publisher: Erik Albrechtsen
Founded: 1982
Subjects: Fiction, Nonfiction (General)
ISBN Prefix(es): 87-424

Forlaget Carlsen A/S+
Krogshojvej 32, 2880 Bagsvaerd
Tel: 4444 3233 *Fax:* 4444 3633
E-mail: carlsen@carlsen.dk
Web Site: www.carlsen.dk
Key Personnel
Man Dir: Jesper Holm
Founded: 1942
Subjects: Humor
ISBN Prefix(es): 87-562; 87-456; 87-7529
Number of titles published annually: 300 Print; 3 CD-ROM; 75 Audio
Total Titles: 2,000 Print; 8 CD-ROM; 120 Audio
Parent Company: Bonniers Forlagene A/S
Ultimate Parent Company: Bonnier Media ATS
Imprints: Carlsen Comics
Subsidiaries: Carlsen Book Production
Book Club(s): Bogklubben Rasmus & Den Faktyrlige Boklub
Warehouse: Holme Forlags Service, Lise Lundvej 4, 4791 Borre *Tel:* 55812252 *Fax:* 55 812078
Holme Forlag Service APS
Semil Forlag NE A/S

Carlsen Comics, *imprint of* Forlaget Carlsen A/S

Forlaget Centrum (Central Publishers)+
Imprint of Bonnier
St Kongensgade 92, 3, 1264 Copenhagen K
Tel: 33 32 12 06 *Fax:* 33 32 12 07
E-mail: info@forlaget-centrum.dk
Web Site: www.forlaget-centrum.dk
Key Personnel
Publisher: Lisbeth Moller-Madsen
Founded: 1979
Subjects: Fiction, Nonfiction (General)
ISBN Prefix(es): 87-583; 87-87123; 87-87810

Cicero-Chr Erichsens
Vester Voldgade 83, 2, 1552 Copenhagen V
Tel: 3316-0308 *Fax:* 33160307
E-mail: info@cicero.dk
Web Site: www.cicero.dk *Cable:* BOGERICH
Key Personnel
Dir: Alis Caspersen; Niels Gudbergsen
Editor: Marie Louise Valeur Jaques; Anders Mejlbjerg
Founded: 1902
Subjects: Fiction, Mysteries
ISBN Prefix(es): 87-7714; 87-555

Copenhagen, *imprint of* Spektrum Forlagsaktieselskab

Copenhagen Business School Press
Virginiavej 11, 2000 Copenhagen F
Tel: 38153960 *Fax:* 38153962
E-mail: cbspress@cbs.dk
Web Site: www.cbspress.dk
Key Personnel
Man Dir & Marketing Manager: Axel Schultz-Nielsen *E-mail:* asn.press@cbs.dk
Marketing Coordinator: Hanne Thorninger Ipsen *E-mail:* hti.press@cbs.dk

Dafolo Forlag+
Division of Dafolo A/S
Dafolo A/S, Suderbovej 22-24, 9900 Frederikshavn
Tel: 9620 6666 *Fax:* 9842 9711
E-mail: dafolo@dafolo.dk
Web Site: www.dafolo.dk; www.dafaloforlag.dk
Key Personnel
Man Dir: Michael Schelde *E-mail:* ms@dafolo.dk
Administrative Dir: Jorgen Ulrik Jensen
Founded: 1960
Specialize in elementary textbooks.
Subjects: Education, Foreign Countries, History
ISBN Prefix(es): 87-7794; 87-7281; 87-7320; 87-7846; 87-89460; 87-982569; 87-984669

Dahlgaard Media BV
c/o KD - Consults A/S, Jakob Dannefaerds Vej 6B, 1973 Frederiksberg C
Tel: 3537 3533 *Fax:* 3537 3299
Subsidiaries: Bogfabrikken Fakta ApS

The Danish Literature Centre
Kongens Nytorv 3, 1022 Copenhagen
Mailing Address: Postboks 9012, 1022 Copenhagen
Tel: 33744500 *Fax:* 33744565
E-mail: danlit@danlit.dk
Web Site: www.literaturenet.dk
Key Personnel
Chief Sub-Editor: Annette Bach
Founded: 1990
Promotion of Danish literature abroad & foundation for translation grants.
Subjects: Drama, Theater, Fiction, Literature, Literary Criticism, Essays, Poetry

Danmarks Forvaltningshojskole Forlaget
Lindevangs Alle 6-12, 2000 Frederiksberg
Tel: 38 14 52 00 *Fax:* 38 14 53 45
E-mail: dhf@dhfnet.dk; dspa@dspa.dk
Web Site: www.dkdfh.dk
Key Personnel
Dir: Inge Maerkdahl
ISBN Prefix(es): 87-7392

Dansk Biblioteks Center (Danish Bibliographic Centre)+
Tempovej 7-11, 2750 Ballerup
Tel: 44 86 77 77 *Fax:* 44 86 78 91
E-mail: dbc@dbc.dk
Web Site: www.dbc.dk
Key Personnel
Man Dir: Mogens Brabrand Jensen *Tel:* 44 86 77 00 *E-mail:* mbj@dbc.dk
Editor: Kirsten Waneck *E-mail:* kwh@dbc.dk
Secretary: Ann Sogaard Jensen *E-mail:* aj@dbc.dk
Founded: 1991
Subjects: Library & Information Sciences
ISBN Prefix(es): 87-552

Dansk Historisk Handbogsforlag ApS
Buddingevej 87 A, 2800 Lyngby
Tel: 45 93 48 00 *Fax:* 45 93 47 47
E-mail: genos@worldonline.dk
Key Personnel
Owner, Man Dir: Henning Jensen
Founded: 1976
Subjects: Biography, Ethnicity, Genealogy, History, Law, Regional Interests
ISBN Prefix(es): 87-85207; 87-88742; 87-90222
Parent Company: Tordenskjold Forlag ApS
Subsidiaries: Juridisk Forlag

Dansk Psykologisk Forlag
Kongevejen 155, 2830 Virum
Tel: 3538 1665 *Fax:* 3538 1655
E-mail: salg@dpf.dk; dk-psych@dpf.dk
Web Site: www.dpf.dk
Key Personnel
Man Dir: Hans Gerhardt *E-mail:* hg@dpf.dk
Chief Editor: Lone Berg Jensen *E-mail:* lbj@dpf.dk
Membership(s): European Test Publishers Group.
Subjects: Psychology, Psychiatry
ISBN Prefix(es): 87-7706; 87-87580

Dansk Teknologisk Institut, Forlaget
Gregersensvej, 2630 Taastrup
Tel: 42 99 66 11 *Fax:* 42 99 54 36
E-mail: info@teknologisk.dk
Telex: 33416 ti dk *Cable:* TEKNOLOGISK
Key Personnel
Contact: Ulrik Spanager *Tel:* 72 20 20 07 *E-mail:* ulrik.spanager@teknologisk.dk
Subjects: Crafts, Games, Hobbies, Labor, Industrial Relations
ISBN Prefix(es): 87-7511; 87-7756

Det Danske Bibelselskab+
50 Frederiksborggade, 1360 Copenhagen K
Tel: 33 12 78 35 *Fax:* 33 93 21 50
E-mail: bibelselskabet@bibelselskabet.dk
Web Site: www.bibelselskabet.dk
Key Personnel
General Secretary: Rev Tine Lindhardt
Publishing Secretary International Rights: Lene Trap-Lind *E-mail:* lene@bibelselskab.dk
Founded: 1814
ISBN Prefix(es): 87-7523; 87-7524

Djof Publishing Jurist-og Okonomforbundets Forlag
17, Lyngbyvej, 2100 Copenhagen O
Mailing Address: Postboks 2702, 2100 Copenhagen O
Tel: 39 13 55 00 *Fax:* 39 13 55 55
E-mail: fl@djoef.dk
Web Site: www.djoef-forlag.dk
Key Personnel
President: Rolf Tvedt
Founded: 1959
Membership(s): IUS-Nordica, Nordic Legal Publishers Group.
Subjects: Economics, Finance, Law, Social Sciences, Sociology
ISBN Prefix(es): 87-574; 87-629
Subsidiaries: Handelshojskolens Forlag; Nyt Juridisk Forlag
Distributed by Enfield Publishing (US)
Orders to: Enfield Publishing (US)

Egmont International Holding A/S
Vognmagergade 11, 1148 Copenhagen K
Tel: 33 30 55 50 *Fax:* 33 32 19 02
E-mail: egmont@egmont.com
Web Site: www.egmont.com
Key Personnel
Vice President, Corporate Communications: Sascha Amarasinha *Tel:* 33 30 51 40 *E-mail:* sas@egmont.com
ISBN Prefix(es): 87-982380

Egmont Lademann A/S, see Aschehoug Dansk Forlag A/S

Egmont Serieforlaget A/S
Vognmagergade 11, 1148 Copenhagen K
Tel: 70 20 50 35 *Fax:* 33 30 57 60; 36 18 58 90
E-mail: abonnement@tsf.egmont.com
Web Site: www.serieforlaget.dk
Key Personnel
Marketing Dir: Jesper Christiansen
ISBN Prefix(es): 87-89601

Christian Ejlers' Forlag aps+
Solvgade 38/3, 1307 Copenhagen K
Mailing Address: Postboks 2228, 1307 Copenhagen K
Tel: 3312 2114 *Fax:* 3312 2884
E-mail: liber@ce-publishers.dk
Web Site: www.ejlers.dk
Key Personnel
Publisher: Christian Ejlers
Founded: 1967
Subjects: Architecture & Interior Design, Art, Biography, Cookery, Education, History, Law, Nonfiction (General)
ISBN Prefix(es): 87-7241
Number of titles published annually: 20 Print; 1 CD-ROM; 1 Audio
Total Titles: 100 Print; 3 CD-ROM; 3 Audio

FADL's Forlag A/S+
Blegdamsvej 30, 2200 Copenhagen N
Tel: 35 35 62 87 *Fax:* 35 36 62 29
E-mail: forlag@fadl.dk
Web Site: forlag.fadl.dk
Key Personnel
Man Dir: Jan Frejlev *E-mail:* jan@fadl.dk
Founded: 1962
Membership(s): STM.
Subjects: Biological Sciences, Medicine, Nursing, Dentistry
ISBN Prefix(es): 87-7437; 87-7749

Forlaget for Faglitteratur A/S
Vandkunsten 6, 1467 Copenhagen K
Tel: 33137900 *Fax:* 33145156
Subjects: Medicine, Nursing, Dentistry, Technology
ISBN Prefix(es): 87-573

Faktor Funf, *imprint of* Kaleidoscope Publishers Ltd

Ficcion Espanola, *imprint of* Kaleidoscope Publishers Ltd

Fiction Factory, *imprint of* Kaleidoscope Publishers Ltd

Fiction Francaise, *imprint of* Kaleidoscope Publishers Ltd

Foreningen af danske Laegestuderendes Forlag, see FADL's Forlag A/S

Forlaget Forum (Forum Publishers)
Imprint of Gyldendalske Boghandel - Nordisk Forlag A/S
Kobmagergade 62 4 sal, 1019 Copenhagen K
Mailing Address: PO Box 2252, 1019 Copenhagen K
Tel: 33411830 *Fax:* 33411831
E-mail: kontakt@forlagetforum.dk
Web Site: www.forlagetforum.dk *Cable:* FORUMBOOKS COPENHAGEN
Key Personnel
Man Dir: Werner Svendsen
Editor, Juvenile & Children: Lotte Nyholm
Founded: 1940
Subjects: Fiction, History, Humor, Mysteries
ISBN Prefix(es): 87-553
Divisions: Spektrum Publishers

Forum Publishers, *imprint of* Gyldendalske Boghandel - Nordisk Forlag A/S

Fremad A/S, *imprint of* Gyldendalske Boghandel - Nordisk Forlag A/S

Fremad A/S
Imprint of Gyldendalske Boghandel - Nordisk Forlag A/S
Kobmagergade 62, 1150 Copenhagen K
Tel: 33 41 18 10 *Fax:* 33 41 18 11
Web Site: www.fremad.dk *Cable:* Bogfremad
Key Personnel
Man Dir: Niels Kolle *E-mail:* niels_koelle@gyldendal.dk
Founded: 1912
Subjects: Astronomy, Business, Child Care & Development, Economics, Fiction, Health, Nutrition, History, Language Arts, Linguistics, Mathematics, Science (General), Social Sciences, Sociology, Political science
ISBN Prefix(es): 87-557
Bookshop(s): Boghandelen Fremad, Frederikssundsvej 168, Bronshoj, 2700 Copenhagen

J Frimodt Forlag+
Korskaervej 25, 7000 Fredericia
Tel: 75934455 *Fax:* 75924275
E-mail: lohse@imh.dk
Key Personnel
Man Dir: Finn Andersen
Subjects: Fiction, Religion - Protestant
ISBN Prefix(es): 87-7446
Associate Companies: Lohses Forlag

Forlaget FSR A/S (ITID A/S), see Forlaget Thomson A/S

Gads Forlag
Klosterstraede 9, 1157 Copenhagen K
Tel: 7766 6000 *Fax:* 7766 6001
E-mail: kuneservice@gads-forlag.dk
Web Site: www.gads-forlag.dk *Cable:* BOGGAD
Key Personnel
Man Dir: Peter Hartman
International Rights: Lars Boesgaard
Founded: 1855
Subjects: Biological Sciences, Cookery, Crafts, Games, Hobbies, Economics, Education, English as a Second Language, Environmental Studies, Gardening, Plants, History, Mathematics, Natural History, Nonfiction (General), Physics, Travel
ISBN Prefix(es): 87-12; 87-13; 87-557
Associate Companies: Alinea A/S; Systime A/S
Bookshop(s): G E C Gads Boglader A/S GADs, Antikvariat Fiolstr 31-33, Copenhagen

Forlaget GMT+
Havet 66 A, 8585 Glaesborg
Tel: 86386095
Key Personnel
Publishers: Hans Jorn Christensen; Erik Bjorn Olsen
Founded: 1971
Subjects: Education, Fiction, Government, Political Science, History, Philosophy, Psychology, Psychiatry, Social Sciences, Sociology
ISBN Prefix(es): 87-7330

Greenland Publishers, see Atuakkiorfik A/S Det Greenland Publishers

Grevas Forlag
Auningvej 33, Sdr Kastrup, 8544 Morke
Tel: 86997065 *Fax:* 86997265
Key Personnel
Sales & Man Dir: Luise Hemmer Pihl
Founded: 1966
Subjects: Art, Biography, Fiction, Poetry
ISBN Prefix(es): 87-7235

Gyldendalske Boghandel - Nordisk Forlag A/S
Klareboderne 3, 1001 Copenhagen K
Mailing Address: PO Box 11, 1001 Copenhagen K
Tel: 33755555 *Fax:* 33755556
E-mail: gyldendal@gyldendal.dk
Web Site: www.gyldendal.dk
Telex: 15887 Gyldaldk *Cable:* GYLDENDALSKE
Key Personnel
Dir: Per Hedeman
Man Dir: Stig Andersen
Literary Dir: Johannes Riis
Marketing Manager: Tine Smedegaard Andersen
Sales Dir: Jan H Schmith
Rights & Permissions, Juveniles: Louise Langhoff Koch
Rights & Permissions, Adult Fiction & Nonfiction: Esthi Kunz; Ingelise Korsholm
Founded: 1770
Subjects: Art, Biography, Education, Fiction, History, How-to, Medicine, Nursing, Dentistry, Music, Dance, Philosophy, Poetry, Psychology, Psychiatry, Science (General), Social Sciences, Sociology
ISBN Prefix(es): 87-01; 87-00; 87-02
Imprints: Bogklubben for Laeger; Bogklubben for Sygeplejersker; Forum Publishers; Fremad A/S; Host & Son Publishers Ltd; Munksgaard Danmark; Paedagogisk Bogklub; Hans Reitzels Forlag; Rosinante; Samlerens Forlag A/S; Spektrum Forlagsaktieselskab
Subsidiaries: G-B-Forlagene A/S; Gyldendal Akademisk A/S; Gyldendals Akademiske Bogklubber
Book Club(s): Gyldendals Baby Bogklub; Gyldendals Bogklub; Gyldendals Bornebogklub; Gyldendals Junior Bogklub; Klassikere (Gyldendals Bogklubber); Laerer Bogklubben; Samlerens Bogklub

P Haase & Sons Forlag A/S+
Loevstraede 8, 2 tv, 1152 Copenhagen K
Tel: 33 18 10 80 *Fax:* 33 11 59 59
E-mail: haase@haase.dk
Web Site: www.haase.dk
Key Personnel
Man Dir: Michael Haase *E-mail:* mh@haase.dk
Foreign Rights: Nina Jensen *E-mail:* nj@haase.dk
Founded: 1877
Subjects: Education, Fiction, Health, Nutrition, Humor, Maritime, Nonfiction (General)
ISBN Prefix(es): 87-559
Imprints: Rasmus Naver

Edition Wilhelm Hansen AS
Bornholmsgade 1, 1266 Copenhagen K
Tel: 33 11 78 88 *Fax:* 33 14 81 78
E-mail: ewh@ewh.dk
Web Site: www.ewh.dk; www.wilhelm-hansen.dk
Cable: MUSIKHANSEN
Key Personnel
Man Dir: Tine Birger Christensen *E-mail:* tbc@ewh.dk
Sales: Tina Andersen *Tel:* 33 70 15 05 *E-mail:* ta@ewh.dk
Promotion: Marlene S Ottosen *Tel:* 33 70 15 11 *E-mail:* mo@ewh.dk; Eline W Sigfusson *Tel:* 33 70 15 09 *E-mail:* ews@ewh.dk
Production (education): Rene Jensen *Tel:* 33 70 15 06 *E-mail:* rj@ewh.dk
Founded: 1857
Subjects: Art, Education, Music, Dance
ISBN Prefix(es): 87-7455; 87-598
Parent Company: Music Sales Ltd, 8/9 Frith St, London W1V 5TZ, United Kingdom

Hekla Forlag+
Valbygaardsvej 33, 2500 Valby
Tel: 36 15 36 15 *Fax:* 36 15 36 16
E-mail: post@borgen.dk
Web Site: www.borgen.dk
Key Personnel
Publisher: Helle Borgen
Founded: 1979
Subjects: Fiction, Nonfiction (General)
ISBN Prefix(es): 87-7474

DENMARK

Number of titles published annually: 5 Print
Total Titles: 20 Print
Parent Company: Borgens Forlag A/S
Orders to: DBK-Logistik Service, Mimersvej 4, 4600 Koge

Hernovs Forlag+
Norrebakken 25, 2820 Gentofte
Tel: 32963314 *Fax:* 32960446
E-mail: admin@hernov.dk
Web Site: www.hernov.dk
Key Personnel
Managing Editor: Else Hernov
Founded: 1941
Membership(s): Independent Danish Publishers.
Subjects: Fiction, Nonfiction (General)
ISBN Prefix(es): 87-7215; 87-590
Subsidiaries: Vinimport ApS
Warehouse: DBK-Dansk Boghandleres Kommissionsanstalt, Siljangade 6, 2300 Copenhagen S

Forlaget Hjulet
Bakkegardsalle 9 kld, 1804 Frederiksberg C
Tel: 31310900 *Fax:* 31310900
E-mail: aloa@gte2net.dk
Key Personnel
Contact: Vagn Plenge
Founded: 1976
Subjects: Cookery, Developing Countries, Fiction, Literature, Literary Criticism, Essays, Travel
ISBN Prefix(es): 87-87403; 87-89213
Subsidiaries: Foerlaget Hjule

Holkenfeldt 3
Fuglevadsvej 71, 2800 Lyngby
Tel: 931221 *Fax:* 938241
Key Personnel
Man Dir: Kay Holkenfeldt
Subjects: Nonfiction (General)
ISBN Prefix(es): 87-90368; 87-7720; 87-89906

Host & Son Publishers Ltd, *imprint of* Gyldendalske Boghandel - Nordisk Forlag A/S

Host & Son Publishers Ltd+
Imprint of Gyldendalske Boghandel - Nordisk Forlag A/S
Kobmagergade 62, 1018 Copenhagen
Mailing Address: PO Box 2212, 1018 Copenhagen K
Tel: 33382888 *Fax:* 33382898
E-mail: host@euroconnect.dk *Cable:* BOOKHOST
Key Personnel
Man Dir: Erik C Lindgren
Editorial, Reference Books: Kirsten Fasmer; Hans Kristian Harbo
Editorial, Juvenile Books: Christel Amundsen
Editorial, Young Adults: Anne Morch-Hansen; Nanna Gyldenkaerne
Founded: 1836
Subjects: Crafts, Games, Hobbies, Environmental Studies, Fiction, History, Regional Interests
ISBN Prefix(es): 87-14
Warehouse: NBC, Bokvej 10-12, 4690 Haslev

Forlaget Hovedland+
Elsdyrvej 4, 8270 Hojbjerg
Tel: 86276500 *Fax:* 86276537
E-mail: mail@hovedland.dk
Web Site: www.hovedland.dk
Key Personnel
Publisher: Steen Piper
Founded: 1984
Subjects: Biography, Crafts, Games, Hobbies, Economics, Environmental Studies, Fiction, History, Humor, Literature, Literary Criticism, Essays, Mysteries, Nonfiction (General), Philosophy, Self-Help, Social Sciences, Sociology, Sports, Athletics, Theology
ISBN Prefix(es): 87-7739; 87-88589

IBIS
Norrebrogade 68B, 2200 Copenhagen N
Tel: 35358788 *Fax:* 35350696
E-mail: ibis@ibis.dk
Web Site: www.ibis.dk
Telex: 1585 0 wus dk
Key Personnel
Editorial Dir, Rights & Permissions: Virginia Allen Jensen
Founded: 1972
ISBN Prefix(es): 87-87804
Parent Company: International Children's Book Service (ICBS)
Branch Office(s)
Odensegade 4B, 8000, Aarhus C *Tel:* 86181412
E-mail: aarhus@ibis.dk

Ingenioeren/Boger (Engineering Books Danish Technical Press)+
Skelbaekgade 4, 1705 Copenhagen V
Mailing Address: Postboks 373, 1503 Copenhagen V
Tel: 63 15 17 00 *Fax:* 63 15 17 33
E-mail: info@nyttf.dk
Web Site: www.bog.ing.dk
Key Personnel
Man Dir: Per Westergaard
Manager, Book Dept: Henrik Larsen *E-mail:* hl@nyttf.dk
Founded: 1948
Subjects: Business, Computer Science, Engineering (General)
ISBN Prefix(es): 87-571; 87-88939; 87-987965
Number of titles published annually: 80 Print; 4 CD-ROM; 3 E-Book
Parent Company: Ingenioeren A/S
Book Club(s): Ingenioeren/Bogklubben

Interpresse A/S+
Ronnegade 1/5, 2100 Copenhagen
Tel: 39160200 *Fax:* 39272402
Key Personnel
Man Dir: Haahon W Isachsen
Founded: 1954
Subjects: Fiction, Film, Video, Humor
ISBN Prefix(es): 87-456; 87-7529; 87-90008
Parent Company: Semic International AB, Sweden
Shipping Address: Bent Bagger Spedition, Peder Skrams Gade 11, 1054 Copenhagen K

IT-og Telestyrelsen
Formerly Statens Information (Danish Information Service)
Holsteinsgade 63, 2100 Copenhagen O
Tel: 35 45 00 00 *Fax:* 35 45 00 10; 33 37 92 99
E-mail: itst@itst.dk
Web Site: www.denmark.dk; www.si.dk
Key Personnel
Head, Media Center: Hugo Prestegaard
Also acts as agent for official government publications.
Subjects: Environmental Studies, Government, Political Science, Library & Information Sciences, Public Administration
ISBN Prefix(es): 87-503; 87-601

Jespersen og Pio, see Lindhardt og Ringhof Forlag A/S

Kaleidoscope Publishers Ltd+
3 Klareboderne, 1001 Copenhagen K
Tel: 33755555 *Fax:* 33755544
E-mail: gujbt@gyldendal.dk
Web Site: www.kaleidoscope.publishers.dk; www.gyldendal.dk *Cable:* GYLDENDALSKE

BOOK

Key Personnel
Publisher: Jens Bendtsen *Tel:* 33755509
E-mail: jens_bendtsen@gyldendal.dk
Founded: 1983
Subjects: Education, English as a Second Language, Film, Video, Language Arts, Linguistics, Literature, Literary Criticism, Essays
ISBN Prefix(es): 87-7565; 87-431
Parent Company: Gyldendal
Imprints: Faktor Funf; Ficcion Espanola; Fiction Factory; Fiction Francaise
Subsidiaries: Fiction Factory International Ltd/ APS
Warehouse: Baekvej
Gyldendal
Haslev

Forlaget Klematis A/S+
Ostre Skovvej 1, 8240 Risskov
Tel: 86175455 *Fax:* 86175959
E-mail: klematis@klematis.dk; production@klematis.dk
Web Site: www.klematis.dk
Key Personnel
President: Claus Dalby
Editor: Mette Jorgensen
Founded: 1987
Specialize in children's books, craft, fiction & nonfiction.
Subjects: Crafts, Games, Hobbies, Fiction, Nonfiction (General)
ISBN Prefix(es): 87-7721; 87-7905
Shipping Address: JEURO Danmark, Baggeskaervej 6, 7400 Herning, Contact: M Stausholm
Warehouse: D B K, Siljangade 6-8, 2300 Copenhagen S

Kraks Forlag AS
Virumgardsvej 21, 2830 Virum
Tel: 95 65 00 *Fax:* 95 65 55
E-mail: krak@krak.dk
Web Site: www.krak.dk
Key Personnel
Administration Dir: Ove Leth-Sorensen
Founded: 1770
Subjects: Regional Interests
ISBN Prefix(es): 87-7225

Lindhardt og Ringhof Forlag A/S+
Frederiksborggade 1, 1360 Copenhagen K
Tel: 33 69 50 00 *Fax:* 33695001
E-mail: lr@lrforlag.dk
Web Site: www.lrforlag.dk *Cable:* ELETEREDIT
Key Personnel
Dir: Morten Hesseldahl
Dir, Sales & Marketing: Michael Bach-Marklund
Founded: 1971
Subjects: Fiction, Nonfiction (General)
ISBN Prefix(es): 87-595; 87-7560
Parent Company: Bonniers & Stockholm
Divisions: Jespersen og Pio
U.S. Office(s): Maria B Campbell Associates, United States
Book Club(s): Bogklubben 12 Boger (part owner)

Lohse Forlag+
Korskaervej 25, 7000 Fredericia
Tel: 7593 4455 *Fax:* 7592 4275
E-mail: lohse@imh.dk
Web Site: www.lohse.dk
Key Personnel
Dir: Finn Andersen
Founded: 1868
Subjects: Biblical Studies, Fiction, Religion - Other
ISBN Prefix(es): 87-564
Associate Companies: J Frimodts Forlag

Mallings ApS
Forlaget Carlsen, Krogshujvej 32, 2880 Bagsvaerd

Tel: 4444 3233 *Fax:* 4444 3633
E-mail: carlsen@carlsen.dk
Telex: 15817 Jmco *Cable:* Mallingbook
Key Personnel
Man Dir, Editorial, Rights & Permissions:
    Joachim Malling
Owner: Hannah Malling
Production: Michael Malling
Publicity: Dorthe Malling
Founded: 1975
Subjects: Education
ISBN Prefix(es): 87-7333

Mellemfolkeligt Samvirke+
Borgergade 14, 1300 Copenhagen K
Tel: 7731 0000 *Fax:* 7731 0101
E-mail: ms@ms.dk
Web Site: www.ms.dk
Subjects: Developing Countries, Education, Ethnicity, Foreign Countries, Publishing & Book Trade Reference, Travel
ISBN Prefix(es): 87-7028; 87-7907
Bookshop(s): Verdensbutikken *E-mail:* butik@ms.dk *Web Site:* www.verdensbutikken.dk

Mercantila Publishers A/S
18 Upsalagade, 2100 Copenhagen
Tel: 35436222 *Fax:* 35435151
E-mail: info@mercantila.dk
Web Site: www.mercantila.dk
Key Personnel
Man Dir: Erik Albrechtsen
Founded: 1986
The guides to food transport are reference books with basic information about transporting perishables.
Subjects: Transportation, Food & Food Transport
ISBN Prefix(es): 87-89010
Associate Companies: Carit Andersens Forlag A/S

MIKRO, *imprint of* Wisby & Wilkens

Forlaget Modtryk AMBA+
Anholtsgade 4-6, 8000 Aarhus C
Tel: 8731 7600 *Fax:* 8731 7601
E-mail: forlaget@modtryk.dk
Web Site: www.modtryk.dk
Telex: Mod
Key Personnel
Man Dir, Rights & Permissions (Textbooks): Ilse Norr *E-mail:* in@modtryk.dk
Sales: Niels Jorn Jensen *E-mail:* njj@modtryk.dk
Production: Henning Morck Jensen *E-mail:* hmj@modtryk.dk
Founded: 1972
Subjects: Fiction, Mysteries, Nonfiction (General)
ISBN Prefix(es): 87-87458; 87-7394; 87-87620; 87-87817; 87-88135

Munksgaard Danmark, *imprint of* Gyldendalske Boghandel - Nordisk Forlag A/S

Museum Tusculanum Press+
University of Copenhagen, Njalsgade 92, 2300 Copenhagen S
Tel: 35 32 91 09 *Fax:* 35 32 91 13
E-mail: mtp@mtp.dk
Web Site: www.mtp.dk
Key Personnel
Dir & Man Dir: Marianne Alenius *Tel:* 35 32 91 10 *E-mail:* alenius@mtp.dk
Marketing & Promotion Manager: Nana Klitgaard *Tel:* 35 32 91 10 *E-mail:* nana@mtp.dk
Founded: 1975
Subjects: Anthropology, Antiques, Archaeology, Art, Asian Studies, Foreign Countries, History, Language Arts, Linguistics, Literature, Literary Criticism, Essays, Philosophy, Religion - Other, Social Sciences, Sociology, Women's Studies
ISBN Prefix(es): 87-980131; 87-88073; 87-7289

Number of titles published annually: 50 Print
Total Titles: 600 Print
Distributed by Gazelle Book Service Ltd (Europe, excluding Scandinavia & Germany); ISBS International Specialized Bookservices (USA & Canada)

My Best Book, *imprint of* Bogan's Forlag

Rasmus Naver, *imprint of* P Haase & Sons Forlag A/S

New Era Publications International ApS+
Subsidiary of New Era Publications Private Ltd
Store Kongensgade 55, 1264 Copenhagen K
Tel: 33736666 *Fax:* 33736633
E-mail: books@newerapublications.com
Web Site: www.newerapublications.com
Key Personnel
Man Dir: Ruth Lanciai
Senior Vice President: Thomas Bucher; Christiane Dumas
Publicity Dir & Foreign Rights Dir: Stephen Shinn
Founded: 1969
Subjects: Art, Education, Management, Philosophy, Science Fiction, Fantasy, Self-Help
ISBN Prefix(es): 87-7336; 87-87347; 87-7816; 87-7968
Subsidiaries: New Era Publications Australia Pty Ltd; New Era Publications Deutschland GmbH; New Era Publications Italia Srl; New Era Publications Japan Inc; New Era Publications Group; Continental Publications Pty Ltd; New Era Publications UK Ltd

Nyt Nordisk Forlag Arnold Busck A/S+
Kobmagergade 49, 1150 Copenhagen K
Tel: 33733575 *Fax:* 33733576
E-mail: nnf@nytnordiskforlag.dk
Web Site: www.nytnordiskforlag.dk
Key Personnel
Man Dir: Ole Arnold Busck
Dir: Jesper Toft Fensrig
Founded: 1896
Subjects: Art, Biography, Fiction, History, How-to, Medicine, Nursing, Dentistry, Music, Dance, Philosophy, Psychology, Psychiatry, Religion - Other, Science (General), Social Sciences, Sociology
ISBN Prefix(es): 87-17
Subsidiaries: Det Schonbergske Forlag A/S; Haandbog for Bygningsindustrien, HFB
Bookshop(s): Arnold Busck International Boghandel A/S *Tel:* 33733500 *Fax:* 33733535; Birkerod Boghandel & Kontorforsyning Arnold Busck A/S, Hovedgaden 37, 3460 Birkerod; Arnold Busck Antiquarian A/S, Fiolstraede 24, 1171 Copenhagen K *Tel:* 33733545 *Fax:* 33733587; Arnold Busck Boghandel A/S, Ballerup Centret, PO Box 604, 2750 Ballerup *Tel:* 44979009 *Fax:* 44682327; Arnold Busck Boghandel A/S, Stengade 51, PO Box 167, 3000 Helsingor *Tel:* 49210128 *Fax:* 49210111; Arnold Busck Boghandel A/S, Bredgade 18, 7400 Herning *Tel:* 97120299 *Fax:* 97120521; Arnold Busck Boghandel A/S, Norregade 13, 7500 Holstebro *Tel:* 97423433 *Fax:* 97427722; Arnold Busck Boghandel A/S, Norregade 5, 4600 Koge *Tel:* 56650254 *Fax:* 56636005; Arnold Busck Boghandel A/S, Vestergade 54, 5000 Odense C *Tel:* 66126803 *Fax:* 66114670; Arnold Busck Boghandel A/S, Perlegade 8, 6400 Sonderborg *Tel:* 74423800 *Fax:* 74432240; Arnold Busck Boghandel A/S, Haderslev, Apotekergade 4, 6100 Haderslev *Tel:* 74522703 *Fax:* 74530582; Arnold Busck Boghandel, Nakskov, Sondergade 24, 4900 Nakskov *Tel:* 54923246; Arnold Busck Boghandel, Nykobing F, Lilletorv, 4800 Nykobing F *Tel:* 54850255; Arnold Busck Boghandel, Randers, Radhusstraede 2, 8900 Randers *Tel:* 86420113 *Fax:* 86409113; Bornenes Boghandel ApS, Kobmagergade 50, 1150 Copenhagen K *Tel:* 33154466 *Fax:* 33931460; Arnold Busck Boghandel, Maribo, Ostergade 5, 4930 Maribo *Tel:* 53881244 *Fax:* 53881525
Orders to: Nordisk Bog Center, Baekvej 2, 4690 Haslev *Tel:* 56364010 *Fax:* 56364038

Olivia, *imprint of* Politikens Forlag A/S

Paedagogisk Bogklub, *imprint of* Gyldendalske Boghandel - Nordisk Forlag A/S

Palle Fogtdal A/S
Ostergade 22, 1100 Copenhagen K
Tel: 3315 3915 *Fax:* 3393 3505
Key Personnel
Man Dir: Palle Fogtdal
ISBN Prefix(es): 87-7248

Joergen Paludan Forlag ApS
Straedet 4, Borsholm, 3100 Hornbaek
Tel: 4975-1536 *Fax:* 4975-1537
E-mail: paludans.forlag@mobilixnet.dk
Key Personnel
Man Dir: Joergen Paludan
Subjects: Economics, Education, Government, Political Science, History, Nonfiction (General), Psychology, Psychiatry, Self-Help
ISBN Prefix(es): 87-7230

Politiken, *imprint of* Politikens Forlag A/S

Politikens Forlag A/S+
Vestergade 26, 1456 Copenhagen K
Tel: 33 47 07 07 *Fax:* 33 47 07 08
E-mail: politikensforlag@pol.dk
Web Site: www.politikensforlag.dk
Key Personnel
Publisher-Olivia: Kirsten Skaarup *E-mail:* kirsten.skaarup@pol.dk
Administrative Dir: Karsten Blauert
Founded: 1986
Subjects: Alternative, Cookery, Crafts, Games, Hobbies, Health, Nutrition, Psychology, Psychiatry, Self-Help
ISBN Prefix(es): 87-89019; 87-90181; 87-7963
Imprints: Olivia; Politiken
Warehouse: D B K Bogdistribution, Siljangade 2-8, 2300 Copenhagen S

Politisk Revy+
Nansensgade 70/st, 1366 Copenhagen K
Tel: 33 91 41 41 *Fax:* 33 91 51 15
E-mail: politiskrevy@forlagene.dk
Web Site: www.forlagene.dk/politiskrevy
Key Personnel
Publisher: Johannes Sohlman *E-mail:* sohlman@danbbs.dk
Founded: 1963
Small press, Independent publisher.
Subjects: Fiction, Government, Political Science, Literature, Literary Criticism, Essays, Nonfiction (General), Philosophy, Photography, Poetry, Psychology, Psychiatry, Social Sciences, Sociology
ISBN Prefix(es): 87-7378; 87-85186
Number of titles published annually: 12 Print
Total Titles: 250 Print
Warehouse: Nordisk Bogcenter A/S, Baekvej 2, Haslev 4690

Polyteknisk Boghandel & Forlag+
Anker Engelunds Vej 1, Bygn 101 A, 2800 Lyngby
Tel: 77 42 43 44 *Fax:* 77 42 43 54
E-mail: forlag@poly.dtu.dk
Web Site: www.polyteknisk.dk
Key Personnel
Dir: Lotte Lonver *E-mail:* lotte@poly.dtu.dk

DENMARK

Founded: 1962
Subjects: Engineering (General), Science (General)
ISBN Prefix(es): 87-502

C A Reitzel Boghandel & Forlag A/S+
Norregade 20, 1165 Copenhagen K
Tel: 33 12 24 00 *Fax:* 33 14 02 70
E-mail: info@careitzel.dk
Web Site: www.careitzel.dk
Key Personnel
Man Dir: Svend Olufsen
Founded: 1819
Subjects: Human Relations, Literature, Literary Criticism, Essays, Nonfiction (General), Philosophy, Science (General)
ISBN Prefix(es): 87-421; 87-7421; 87-7876; 87-87504

Hans Reitzel Publishers Ltd+
Ostergade 13, 1008 Copenhagen K
Mailing Address: PO Box 1073, 1008 Copenhagen K
Tel: 33382800 *Fax:* 33382808
E-mail: hrf@hansreitzel.dk
Web Site: www.hansreitzel.dk *Cable:* REITZELBOOKS
Key Personnel
Publishing Dir: Hanne Salomonsen *Tel:* 3338 2813 *E-mail:* hs@hansreitzel.dk
Founded: 1949
Subjects: Education, Philosophy, Psychology, Psychiatry, Social Sciences, Sociology
ISBN Prefix(es): 87-412
Total Titles: 350 Print
Parent Company: Gyldendalske Boghandel
Ultimate Parent Company: Nordisk Forlag Ltd, United Kingdom
Warehouse: Nordisk Bog Center, Bcekvej 10-12, 4690 Haslev

Hans Reitzels Forlag, *imprint of* Gyldendalske Boghandel - Nordisk Forlag A/S

Rhodos, International Science & Art Publishers
Holtegaard Horsholmvej 17, 3050 Humlebaek K
Tel: 32543020 *Fax:* 32543022
E-mail: rhodos@rhodos.com
Web Site: www.rhodos.dk *Cable:* SCIENCEBOOKS
Key Personnel
Man Dir: Ruben Blaedel
ISBN Prefix(es): 87-7245; 87-7496

Rosenkilde & Bagger
Kronprinsensgade 3, 1114 Copenhagen K
Mailing Address: PO Box 111, 2920 Charlottenlund
Tel: 33157044 *Fax:* 33937007
E-mail: r-b@rosenkilde-bagger.dk
Web Site: www.rosenkilde-bagger.dk
Key Personnel
Proprietor: Hans Bagger; Soren Bagger
Founded: 1941
Also has a rare book department.
Subjects: Science (General)
ISBN Prefix(es): 87-423

Rosinante, *imprint of* Gyldendalske Boghandel - Nordisk Forlag A/S

Samfundslitteratur+
Rosenorns Alle 9-11, 1970 Frederiksberg C
Tel: 38153880 *Fax:* 35357822
E-mail: samfundslitteratur@sl.cbs.dk; slforlag@sl.cbs.dk
Web Site: www.samfundslitteratur.dk
Key Personnel
Man Dir: Mogens Eliasson *Tel:* 35356399 *E-mail:* me@sl.cbs.dk

Editorial Dir, Rights & Permissions: Birgit Vra
Tel: 35356399 *E-mail:* bv@sl.cbs.dk
Founded: 1967
Publishers at Copenhagen Business School.
Subjects: Accounting, Advertising, Business, Communications, Developing Countries, Economics, Education, English as a Second Language, Environmental Studies, Finance, History, Journalism, Language Arts, Linguistics, Management, Marketing, Public Administration, Religion - Protestant, Social Sciences, Sociology
ISBN Prefix(es): 87-593; 87-7313; 87-87322
Total Titles: 600 Print; 3 CD-ROM
Parent Company: Samfundslitterator
Distributor for The World Bank (Denmark)
Bookshop(s): Dalgas Have 15, 2000 Frederiksberg C; Rosenorns Alle 11, 1970 Frederiksberg C; RUC, Bygn 01, Marbjergvej 35, 4000 Roskilde
Book Club(s): Erhverislitteratur

Samlerens Forlag A/S, *imprint of* Gyldendalske Boghandel - Nordisk Forlag A/S

Samlerens Forlag A/S+
Imprint of Gyldendalske Boghandel - Nordisk Forlag A/S
Kobmagergade 62, 4, 1019 Copenhagen K
Mailing Address: Postboks 2252, 1019 Copenhagen K
Tel: 3341 1800 *Fax:* 3341 1801
E-mail: samleren@samleren.dk
Web Site: www.samleren.dk
Key Personnel
Dir: Torben Madsen *E-mail:* torben_madsen@samleren.dk
Foreign Rights: Ingelise Korsholm
Founded: 1943
Subjects: Fiction, Government, Political Science, History, Literature, Literary Criticism, Essays
ISBN Prefix(es): 87-568
Total Titles: 150 Print

Scan-Globe A/S
25 Ulvevej, 4622 Havdrup
Tel: 46 18 54 00 *Fax:* 46 18 52 70
E-mail: info@scanglobe.dk
Telex: 40275
Key Personnel
Man Dir: Mr Per Lund-Hansen
Founded: 1963
Subjects: Geography, Geology
ISBN Prefix(es): 87-87343; 87-90468; 87-91154

Scandinavia Publishing House+
Drejervej 15-3, 2400 Copenhagen NV
Tel: 35 31 03 30 *Fax:* 35 31 03 34
E-mail: info@scanpublishing.dk
Web Site: www.scanpublishing.dk
Key Personnel
President & Publisher: Jorgen Vium Olesen *E-mail:* jvo@scanpublishing.dk
Editor & Secretary: Jytte Larsen *Tel:* 35 31 03 31 *E-mail:* jytte@scanpublishing.dk
Sales & Marketing: Anthony Hoglind
Founded: 1979
Specialize in education & religion.
Subjects: Biblical Studies, Biography, Education, Theology
ISBN Prefix(es): 87-7247; 87-87732
Total Titles: 323 Print
Book Club(s): Den Kristne Bogklub, Contact: Bo Nielsen *Tel:* 35 31 03 36

Det Schonbergske Forlag A/S+
Subsidiary of Nyt Nordisk Forlag Arnold Busck A/S
Landemaerket 5, 1119 Copenhagen K
Tel: 33 73 35 85 *Fax:* 33 73 35 76
E-mail: Schoenberg@nytnordiskforlag.dk

BOOK

Web Site: www.nytnordiskforlag.dk *Cable:* SCHOENBOOK
Key Personnel
Dir: Joakim Werner
Production Manager: Arvid Honore
Sales Manager: Max-Erik Reinhold
Founded: 1857
Subjects: Art, Biography, Career Development, Fiction, History, Humor, Philosophy, Poetry, Psychology, Psychiatry, Travel
ISBN Prefix(es): 87-570
Divisions: Woeldike

Schultz Information+
Herstedvang 12, 2620 Albertslund
Tel: 43632300 *Fax:* 43631969
E-mail: schultz@schultz.dk
Web Site: www.schultz.dk
Key Personnel
Man Dir: Henrik Christiansen
Division Manager: Gert Eriksen *E-mail:* ge@schultz.dk
Contact: Anette Klubien
Founded: 1661
Specialize in law information.
Subjects: Business, Environmental Studies, Law, Nonfiction (General)
ISBN Prefix(es): 87-569; 87-609
Parent Company: J H Schultz Holding A/S
Ultimate Parent Company: J H Schultz-Fondeu
Associate Companies: Schultz Interactive Information A/S; J H Schultz Grafisk A/S *Fax:* 4635329; Synergi Data A/S
Bookshop(s): Schultz Boghandel, Herstedvang 4, 2620 Albertslund *Tel:* 33734747 *Fax:* 43155772 *E-mail:* boghandel@schultz.dk

Sesam, *imprint of* Aschehoug Dansk Forlag A/S

Forlaget Sesam
Aschehoug Dansk Forlag A/S, Vognmagergade 7, 1120 Copenhagen K
Tel: 3330-5044; 3330-5522 *Fax:* 3391-3878
E-mail: aschehoug@ash.egmont.com
Key Personnel
Publishing Dir: Per Kolle *Fax:* 3330-5824
ISBN Prefix(es): 87-7258; 87-7324; 87-7801
Divisions: Aschehoug, Egmont

A/S Skattekartoteket
Palaegade 4, 1022 Copenhagen K
Mailing Address: Postboks 9026, 1022 Copenhagen K
Tel: 33117874 *Fax:* 33938025
E-mail: magnus@cddk.dk
Key Personnel
Man Dir: Peter Taarnhoj
Subjects: Public Administration
ISBN Prefix(es): 87-87451; 87-7762
Parent Company: CD-Danmark A/S

Sommer & Sorensen
Valbygaardsvej 33, 2500 Valby
Tel: 36153615 *Fax:* 36153616
Key Personnel
Dir: Niels Borgen
Editorial Dir: Jens Christiansen
Contact: Mette Nymark
Subjects: Fiction
ISBN Prefix(es): 87-7499; 87-90189
Number of titles published annually: 5 Print
Total Titles: 10 Print
Parent Company: Borgens Forlag A/S

Spektrum Forlagsaktieselskab, *imprint of* Gyldendalske Boghandel - Nordisk Forlag A/S

Spektrum Forlagsaktieselskab+
Imprint of Gyldendalske Boghandel - Nordisk Forlage A/S
Snaregade 4, 1250 Copenhagen K

Mailing Address: PO Box 2252, 1019 Copenhagen K
Tel: 33 14 77 14 *Fax:* 33 14 77 91
Key Personnel
Man Dir: Werner Svendsen
Founded: 1990
Subjects: Nonfiction (General)
ISBN Prefix(es): 87-7763
Imprints: Copenhagen

Square Dance Partners Forlag+
Hasselvej 18, 2830 Virum
Tel: 45 83 99 83
Key Personnel
President & International Rights Contact: Margot Gunzenhauser *E-mail:* mgunz@worldonline.dk
Founded: 1987
Specialize in the publishing of books, tapes & CD's dealing with traditional style American square & contra dancing, related dance forms & their music.
Subjects: Crafts, Games, Hobbies, How-to, Music, Dance
ISBN Prefix(es): 87-982674
Total Titles: 4 Print
U.S. Office(s): K-113 Pennswood Village, 1382 Newtown-Langhorne Rd, Newtown, PA 18940, United States, Contact: Dorothy Gunzenhauser *Tel:* 215-579-2298 *E-mail:* deg@tradenet.net
Distributed by Barn Dance Publications Ltd (UK)

Statens Information (Danish Information Service), see IT-og Telestyrelsen

Strandbergs Forlag+
Vedbaek Strandvej 475, 2950 Vedbaek
Tel: 4589 4760 *Fax:* 4589 4701
E-mail: strandberg.publishing@get2net.dk
Key Personnel
Publisher: Hans Joergen Strandberg
Founded: 1861
Also book packager.
Subjects: Ethnicity, Humor
ISBN Prefix(es): 87-7717; 87-87200
Parent Company: Strandberg

Strubes Forlag og Boghandel ApS
Damhus Blvd 65, 2610 Rodovre
Tel: 36721750 *Fax:* 36721752 *Cable:* STRABEBOOKS
Key Personnel
Man Dir: Jonna Strube

Syddansk Universitetsforlag (University Press of Southern Denmark)+
Campusvej 55, 5230 Odense M
Tel: 66 15 79 99 *Fax:* 66 15 81 26
E-mail: press@forlag.sdu.dk
Web Site: www.universitypress.dk
Key Personnel
Man Dir: Thomas Kaarsted *E-mail:* thk@forlag.sdu.dk
Founded: 1966
Subjects: Archaeology, Fiction, History, Literature, Literary Criticism, Essays, Medicine, Nursing, Dentistry, Philosophy, Technology
ISBN Prefix(es): 87-7492; 87-7838

Systime+
Skt Pauls Gade 25, 8000 Aarhus C
Tel: 70 12 11 00 *Fax:* 70 12 11 05
E-mail: systime@systime.dk
Web Site: www.systime.dk
Key Personnel
Man Dir: P H Mikkelsen
Editor: Stefan Emkjaer; Birte Annette Noerregaard; Christine Ohlenschlaeger; Claes Soenderriis
Rights & Permissions: Inga-Lill Amini
Founded: 1980
Specialize in educational materials.

Subjects: Accounting, Chemistry, Chemical Engineering, Computer Science, Economics, English as a Second Language, Film, Video, Geography, Geology, History, Mathematics, Philosophy, Physics, Religion - Other, Technology
ISBN Prefix(es): 87-616; 87-7351; 87-7783; 87-87454
Total Titles: 100 Print
Parent Company: GEC Gad

Teaterforlaget Drama
Nygade 15, 6300 Grasten
Tel: 70 25 11 41 *Fax:* 74 65 20 93
E-mail: drama@drama.dk
Web Site: www.drama.dk
Key Personnel
Dir: Liselotte Lunding *E-mail:* 11@drama.dk
Founded: 1977
Specialize in drama & theatre, books & manuscripts.
Subjects: Drama, Theater
Associate Companies: Teater Hjornet; International Teater Boghandel, Vesterbrogade 175, 1800 Frederisberg *Tel:* 33222247 *Fax:* 33225847 *E-mail:* drama@dats.dk

Forlaget Thomson A/S+
Formerly Forlaget FSR A/S (ITID A/S)
Nytorv 5, 1450 Copenhagen K
Tel: 33 74 07 00 *Fax:* 33 12 16 36
E-mail: thomson@thomson.dk
Web Site: www.thomson.dk
Key Personnel
Administrative Dir: Thomas Hegelund
Chief Sales & Marketing: Per Holst-Hansen
Subjects: Accounting, Business, Education, Law
ISBN Prefix(es): 87-619; 87-7747; 87-88109; 87-980953
Parent Company: The Thomson Corporation

Tiderne Skifter Forlag A/S+
Laederstraede 5, 1, 1201 Copenhagen K
Tel: 33 18 63 90 *Fax:* 33 18 63 91
E-mail: tiderneskifter@tiderneskifter.dk
Web Site: www.tiderneskifter.dk
Key Personnel
Man Dir: Claus Clausen
Founded: 1973
Subjects: Ethnicity, Fiction, Literature, Literary Criticism, Essays, Photography
ISBN Prefix(es): 87-7445; 87-7973
Number of titles published annually: 40 Print
Total Titles: 1,000 Print
Orders to: Nordisk Bog Center, Baekvej 10-12, 4690 Haslev *Tel:* 56364000 *Fax:* 56384038

Unitas Forlag+
Peter Bangs Vej 1D, 2000 Frederiksberg
Tel: 36166481 *Fax:* 38116481
E-mail: forlag@unitas.dk
Web Site: forlag.unitas.dk
Key Personnel
Publisher: Peder Gundersen *E-mail:* pg@forlag.unitas.dk
Founded: 1914
Subjects: Biblical Studies, Biography, Fiction, Religion - Protestant, Theology
ISBN Prefix(es): 87-7517
Parent Company: YMCA/YWCA

Vandrer mod Lysets Forlag Aps
Solvgade 10, 6 sal, 1307 Copenhagen K
Tel: 3315 7815 *Fax:* 3315 8030
Web Site: www.vandrer-mod-lyset.dk
Key Personnel
Dir: Boerge Broennum
Publisher: Mrs Konny Falck
ISBN Prefix(es): 87-87871; 87-980350

Forlaget Vindrose A/S+
Valbygardsvej 33, 2500 Valby

Tel: 36153615 *Fax:* 36153616
E-mail: post@borgen.dk
Web Site: www.borgen.dk
Key Personnel
Publisher: Jens Christiansen
Man Dir: Niels Borgen
Rights & Permissions Manager: Mette Nymark *E-mail:* mnymark@borgen.dk
Production: Dennis Stovring
Founded: 1980
Subjects: Fiction, Poetry, Science (General), Social Sciences, Sociology
ISBN Prefix(es): 87-7456
Number of titles published annually: 20 Print
Total Titles: 200 Print
Parent Company: Borgens Forlag A/S
Warehouse: DBK-Logistik Service, Mimersvej 4, 4600 Koge
Orders to: D B K-bogdistribution, Siljangade 2-8, 2300 Copenhagen S

Wisby & Wilkens+
Vesterled 45, 8300 Odder
Mailing Address: PO Box 98, 8464 Galten
Tel: 7023 4622 *Fax:* 7043 4722
E-mail: mail@bogshop.dk
Web Site: www.wisby-wilkens.com; www.bogshop.dk
Key Personnel
Dir: Jacob Wisby
Founded: 1986
Membership(s): Danish Publishers Association.
Subjects: Crafts, Games, Hobbies, Fiction, Humor, Literature, Literary Criticism, Essays, Nonfiction (General), Outdoor Recreation, Science Fiction, Fantasy
ISBN Prefix(es): 87-89190; 87-89191; 87-7046
Number of titles published annually: 24 Print
Total Titles: 200 Print
Imprints: MIKRO
Distributor for Grandview USA (Scandinavia)
Warehouse: DBK, Siljangade 2, 2300 Copenhagen S

Forlaget Woldike K/S
c/o Det Schonbergske Forlag, 5 Landemaerket, 1119 Copenhagen K
Tel: 33 73 35 85
Founded: 1969
Subjects: Fiction, Nonfiction (General)
ISBN Prefix(es): 87-7233

Dominican Republic

General Information

Capital: Santo Domingo
Language: Spanish
Religion: Predominantly Roman Catholic
Population: 7.5 million
Bank Hours: 0830-1230 Monday-Friday; some open 0830-1130 Saturday
Shop Hours: 0800-1200, 1400 or 1500-1800 Monday-Friday; some open Saturday
Currency: 100 centavos = 1 Dominican Republic peso. US currency is widely used
Export/Import Information: No import licenses required for books. Exchange license and approval from Central Bank required.
Copyright: UCC, Berne, Buenos Aires (see Copyright Conventions, pg xi)

Editorama SA
Calle Eugenio Contreras No 54, Los Trinitarios, Santo Domingo

DOMINICAN REPUBLIC

Mailing Address: Apartado Postal 2074, Santo Domingo
Tel: 596-6669; 596-4274 *Fax:* 594-1421
E-mail: editorama@codetel.net.do
Web Site: www.editorama.com
Key Personnel
Dir: Juan R Quinones
Founded: 1970
ISBN Prefix(es): 9977-88

Editora Listin Diario
Calle Paseo de los Periodistas, No 52, Ensanche Miraflores, Santo Domingo 1455
Tel: (0809) 686-6688 *Fax:* (0809) 686-6595
Telex: (809) 346-0206 *Cable:* LISTIN
Key Personnel
President: Eduardo Pellerano

Pontificia Universidad Catolica Madre y Maestra+
Departamento de Puplicaciones, Autopista Duparte, km 1 1/2, Santiago de los Caballeros
SAN: 004-5527
Tel: (809) 5801962; (809) 5350111 *Fax:* (809) 5824549; (809) 5350053
Web Site: www.pucmmsti.edu.do
Telex: 3461032 PUCMM
Key Personnel
Editorial: Carmen Perez de Cabral
Founded: 1962
Membership(s): University Editorial Association of Latin America & the Caribbean.
Subjects: Accounting, Agriculture, Archaeology, Architecture & Interior Design, Biblical Studies, Biography, Biological Sciences, Business, Career Development, Chemistry, Chemical Engineering, Civil Engineering, Communications, Developing Countries, Drama, Theater, Economics, Education, Electronics, Electrical Engineering, Energy, Engineering (General), English as a Second Language, Environmental Studies, Geography, Geology, Government, Political Science, Health, Nutrition, History, Language Arts, Linguistics, Law, Library & Information Sciences, Literature, Literary Criticism, Essays, Management, Marketing, Mathematics, Mechanical Engineering, Medicine, Nursing, Dentistry, Philosophy, Physical Sciences, Physics, Poetry, Regional Interests, Religion - Catholic, Social Sciences, Sociology, Technology, Theology
ISBN Prefix(es): 84-89548
Warehouse: Economato Universitario, PUCMM

Sociedad Editorial Americana+
Ramon Santana No 2-B, esquina Benito Moncion Gazcue, Santo Domingo
Tel: 689 7813 *Fax:* 688 9378 *Cable:* FRANKLIN FRANCO
Key Personnel
President: Franklin Franco
Founded: 1975
Subjects: Economics, History, Law, Literature, Literary Criticism, Essays, Philosophy, Social Sciences, Sociology
ISBN Prefix(es): 99934-0
Total Titles: 2 CD-ROM
Parent Company: Credilibros, Apdo 559, Calle Ramon Santana 2B, Santo Domingo

Editora Taller+
Calle Juan vallenilla esq Jauncio Dolores, Zona Industrial de Herrera, Apdo 1, 190 Santo Domingo
SAN: 002-2136
Tel: 531-7975 *Fax:* 531-7979
E-mail: editora.taller@codetel.net.do
Key Personnel
Contact: Lourdes Cuello
Founded: 1971
Subjects: Economics, History, Literature, Literary Criticism, Essays

ISBN Prefix(es): 84-8400; 99934-846
Distributor for Editora Vicens Vives
Orders to: Vicente Celestino Duarte, No 2

Ecuador

General Information

Capital: Quito
Language: Spanish
Religion: Predominantly Roman Catholic
Population: 10.9 million
Bank Hours: 0900-1330 Monday-Friday
Shop Hours: 0930-1300, 1500-1900 Monday-Friday; 0930-1300 Saturday
Currency: 100 centavos = 1 sucre
Export/Import Information: Member of the Latin American Free Trade Association. Books and most advertising catalogues not dutiable. No import licenses or exchange controls for books.
Copyright: UCC, Buenos Aires (see Copyright Conventions, pg xi)

Ediciones Abya-Yala+
Ave 12 de Octubre 1430 y Wilson, Casilla 17-12-719 Quito
Tel: (02) 2506251; (02) 2506247 *Fax:* (02) 2506255
E-mail: editorial@abyayala.org
Web Site: www.abyayala.org
Key Personnel
Dir: Padre Juan Bottasso *E-mail:* jbottasso@abyayala.org
Dir General: P Xavier Herran
Founded: 1975
Membership(s): Quito Book Association.
Subjects: Anthropology, Environmental Studies, Language Arts, Linguistics, Theology
ISBN Prefix(es): 9978-04; 9978-22
Total Titles: 1,060 Print; 2 CD-ROM; 900 E-Book

Biblioteca Ecuatoriana Aurelio Espinosa Polit'
Jose Nogales 220 y Francisco Arcos, Cotocollao, Quito
Tel: (02) 492190 *Fax:* (02) 493928
Key Personnel
Dir: Rev Julian G Bravo
Founded: 1929
Specialize in all publications by Ecuadorians &/or about Ecuador.
Subjects: Ecuador
ISBN Prefix(es): 9978-971

Centro De Educacion Popular
Av America 3584, Quito
Mailing Address: Casilla Postal 17-08-8604, Quito
Tel: (02) 525 521 *Fax:* (02) 542 818
E-mail: cedep@fmlaluna.com
Web Site: www.jacomenet.com/laluna/cedep.html
Key Personnel
Dir: Diego Landazuri
Founded: 1978
Subjects: Communications, Economics
ISBN Prefix(es): 9978-00

Centro de Planificacion y Estudios Sociales (CEPLAES)
Av 6 de Diciembre y Alpallana, Quito
Tel: (02) 548-547 *Fax:* (02) 566-207
E-mail: ceplaes@ceplaes.ec
Key Personnel
Executive Dir: Alexandra Ayala Marin
Founded: 1978

Subjects: Agriculture, Anthropology, Child Care & Development, Education, Health, Nutrition, Social Sciences, Sociology, Women's Studies
ISBN Prefix(es): 9978-93

Centro Internacional de Estudios Superiores de Comunicacion para America Latina, see CIESPAL (Centro Internacional de Estudios Superiores de Comunicacion para America Latina)

CEPLAES, see Centro de Planificacion y Estudios Sociales (CEPLAES)

CIDAP
Calle Hermano Miguel 3-23, La Escalinata, Cuenca
Tel: (07) 829-451; (07) 828-878 *Fax:* (07) 831-450
E-mail: ciesa@pi.pro.ec
Key Personnel
Dir: Claudio Malo Gonzalez
Subjects: Art, Crafts, Games, Hobbies
ISBN Prefix(es): 84-89420; 9978-85

CIESPAL (Centro Internacional de Estudios Superiores de Comunicacion para America Latina)
Av Diego de Almagro N32-133 y Andrade Marin, Quito
Mailing Address: Apdo 17-01-584, Quito
Tel: (02) 2524177 *Fax:* (02) 2502487
E-mail: publicaciones@ciespal.net
Web Site: www.ciespal.net
Telex: 2474 Ciespl *Cable:* Ciespal
Key Personnel
Dir: Dr Edgar Jaramillo
Dir, Orders: Jorge Jarrin
Founded: 1959
Subjects: Biography, Communications, Journalism, Publishing & Book Trade Reference, Radio, TV, Technology
ISBN Prefix(es): 9978-55

Corporacion de Estudios y Publicaciones
Acuna 168 y Agama, 17-21-00186 Quito, Casilla
Tel: (02) 221-711 *Fax:* (02) 226-256
E-mail: cep@accessinter.net
Founded: 1963
Subjects: Law, Public Administration
ISBN Prefix(es): 9978-86

Corporacion Editora Nacional
Roca 230 y Tamayo, Casilla 17-12-88, Quito
Tel: (02) 554358; (02) 554558; (02) 554658 *Fax:* (02) 566340
E-mail: cen@accessinter.net
Key Personnel
President: Ernesto Alban Gomez
Founded: 1978
Editorial corporation with non-profits.
Subjects: Archaeology, Biography, Economics, Education, Geography, Geology, Government, Political Science, History, Law, Literature, Literary Criticism, Essays, Philosophy, Social Sciences, Sociology
ISBN Prefix(es): 9978-84; 9978-958
Total Titles: 332 Print

Ediciones Legales SA
Unit of Corporacion Myl
Polonia N31-134 y Vancouver, Quito
Mailing Address: Apdo 1703-186, Quito
Tel: (02) 250-7729 *Fax:* (02) 250-8490
E-mail: edicioneslegales@corpmyl.com
Web Site: www.edicioneslegales.com
Key Personnel
President: Manuel Mejia Dalmau
General Manager: Ernesto Alban Gomez
Founded: 1989
Subjects: Law

ISBN Prefix(es): 9978-81
Total Titles: 28 Print; 2 CD-ROM

Libresa S A+
Murgeon 346 y Uloa, Quito
Tel: (02) 230925; (02) 525581 Fax: (02) 502992
E-mail: libresa@interactive.net.ec
Key Personnel
President: Fausto Coba Estrella
General: Jaime Pena Novoa
Founded: 1979
Subjects: Education, Literature, Literary Criticism, Essays, Philosophy
ISBN Prefix(es): 9978-80; 9978-952
Associate Companies: Delibresa, Librerias Espanolas

Pontificia Universidad Catolica del Ecuador, Centro de Publicaciones
Ave 12 de Octubre y Carrion, Quito
Tel: (02) 2991700; (02) 2565627
E-mail: wjimenez@puceuio.puce.edu.ec
Web Site: www.puce.edu.ec
Key Personnel
Dir: Dr Marco Vinicio Rueda
Founded: 1946
Subjects: Anthropology, Archaeology, Art, Economics, Government, Political Science, History, Law, Literature, Literary Criticism, Essays, Philosophy, Science (General), Social Sciences, Sociology, Theology
ISBN Prefix(es): 9978-77

Pudeleco/Publicaciones de Legislacion
Reina Victoria 447 y Roca, Primer Piso Office 1-C, Quito
Tel: (02) 543273 Fax: (02) 2543607
E-mail: pudeleco@uio.satnet.net
Key Personnel
Manager: Ramiro Arias Gerente
ISBN Prefix(es): 9978-966

SECAP
Jose Arizaga entre Londres y Jorge Drom, Casilla 2221, Quito
Tel: (02) 446248 Fax: (02) 448644
Subjects: Agriculture, Automotive, Education, Library & Information Sciences, Public Administration
ISBN Prefix(es): 9978-64

Universidad Central del Ecuador, Departamento de Publicaciones
Avda America y A Perez, Quito
Mailing Address: Apdo 3291, Quito
Tel: (02) 2234 722 Fax: (02) 2236 367; (02) 2521 925
Web Site: www.ucentral.edu.ec
Key Personnel
Academic Dir: Tiberio Juado Cevallos

Egypt (Arab Republic of Egypt)

General Information

Capital: Cairo
Language: Arabic (English and French widely used)
Religion: Predominantly Muslim (of the Sunni sect)
Population: 56.4 million

Bank Hours: Generally 0830-1230 Monday-Thursday; 1000-1200 Saturday
Shop Hours: 0830-1330, 1630-1900 Monday-Saturday
Currency: 1,000 milliemes = 100 piastres = 5 tallaris = 1 Egyptian pound
Export/Import Information: Exchange rate set by individual banks. No longer government monopoly but some book importing done by Foreign Trade Company, Misr Import & Export Co, 6 Adly St, Cairo.
Copyright: Berne, Florence (see Copyright Conventions, pg xi)

Al Ahram Establishment
6 Al-Galaa' St, Cairo
Tel: (02) 748248 Fax: (02) 745888
E-mail: ahram@ahram.org.eg
Telex: 20185-92544
Key Personnel
Editor-in-Chief: Ibrahim Nafei
General Manager: Hany Tolba
Production: Fathi Al Charkawi
Rights & Permissions: Mrs Nawal El Mahallawi
Founded: 1875
Also translation agency, printer, distributor, importer, exporter; member of Distripreso STM.
Subjects: Human Relations, Science (General)
ISBN Prefix(es): 977-13
Associate Companies: Al Ahram Commercial Press; Al Ahram Agency for Distribution
Subsidiaries: Al Ahram Center for Strategic & Political Studies; Al Ahram Center for Scientific Translation & Publishing; Al Ahram Center for Microfilm & Organization; Al Ahram Center for Computer & Management; Al Ahram Advertising Agency; Al Ahram Org 8 Information Technology Center; Al Ahram Commercial Press; Al Ahram Press Agency
Bookshop(s): Al Ahram Bookshop, 165 Mohamed Faird St, Cairo
Book Club(s): Al Ahram Book Club; ARL (Al-Ahram Research Library)

American University in Cairo Press+
113 Sharia Kasr el Aini, Cairo 11511
Tel: (02) 797 6926; (02) 797 6895 (orders)
Fax: (02) 794 1440
E-mail: aucpress@aucegypt.edu
Web Site: aucpress.com
Telex: 92224 Aucai un Cable: VICTORIOUS
Key Personnel
Dir: Mark Linz Tel: (02) 797-6888 E-mail: linz@aucegypt.edu
Associate Dir, Finance & Administration: Laila Ghali Tel: (02) 797-6890 E-mail: lailag@aucegypt.edu
Man Editor: Neil Hewison Tel: (02) 797-6892 E-mail: rnh@aucegypt.edu
Marketing Manager: Atef el-Hoteiby Tel: (02) 797-6981 E-mail: ahoteiby@aucegypt.edu
Sales & Distribution Manager: Tahany el-Shammaa Tel: (02) 797-6895 E-mail: tahanys@aucegypt.edu
Promotion Manager: Nabila Akl Tel: (02) 797-6896 E-mail: akl@aucegypt.edu
Managing Publications Services: Miriam Naim Atef Fahmi Tel: (02) 797-6937 E-mail: miriam@aucegypt.edu
Rights & Permissions Coordinator: Hala Ganayni Tel: (02) 797-6889 E-mail: halag@aucegypt.edu
Founded: 1960
Membership(s): AAUP.
Subjects: Anthropology, Architecture & Interior Design, Art, Earth Sciences, History, Language Arts, Linguistics, Literature, Literary Criticism, Essays, Social Sciences, Sociology
ISBN Prefix(es): 977-424
U.S. Office(s): 420 Fifth Ave, New York, NY 10018-2729, United States Tel: 212-730-8800 Fax: 212-730-1600 E-mail: ct_aucpress@aucnyo.edu

Distributed by Columbia University Press
Orders to: Books International, PO Box 605, Hendon, VA 20172, United States Tel: 703-661-1570 Fax: 703-661-1501 E-mail: bimail@presswarehouse.com (North America)
Eurospan (EDS), 3 Henrietta St, London WC2E 8LU, United Kingdom Tel: (020) 7240 0856 Fax: (020) 7379 0609 E-mail: orders@edspubs.co.uk Web Site: www.eurospan.co.uk (UK & Europe)
Rassan Trading Co Pty Ltd, PO Box 44, Kingsway West, NSW 2208, Australia Tel: (02) 9159 4411 Fax: (02) 9502 2711 (Australasia & Far East)

Al Arab Publishing House+
23 Faggalah St, Cairo
Tel: (02) 908027
Key Personnel
Man Dir: Prof Saladin Boustany, PhD
Sales Manager: George G Edde
Founded: 1900
Specialize in modern, contemporary & out-of-print Arabic monographs & periodicals.
Subjects: Developing Countries, Economics, Fiction, Government, Political Science, History, Journalism, Language Arts, Linguistics, Law, Literature, Literary Criticism, Essays, Philosophy, Poetry, Psychology, Psychiatry, Religion - Islamic, Religion - Other, Social Sciences, Sociology

Cairo University Press
Al-Giza, Cairo
Tel: (02) 846144
ISBN Prefix(es): 977-223

CEDEJ, see Centre d'Etudes et Documentation Economique Juridique et Sociale (CEDEJ)

Centre d'Etudes et Documentation Economique Juridique et Sociale (CEDEJ)
2, Sikkat al-Fadl, Qasr al-Nil, Cairo
Mailing Address: PO Box 392, Muhhamad Farid, Cairo
Tel: (02) 392 87 11; (02) 392 87 16; (02) 392 87 39; (02) 704641 Fax: (02) 392 87 91
E-mail: cedej@idsc.net.eg
Web Site: www.cedej.org.eg
Key Personnel
Dir: Philippe Fargues
Founded: 1970
ISBN Prefix(es): 2-905838

Dar Al-Kitab Al-Masri+
33 Kasr El Nile St, 11511 Cairo
Mailing Address: PO Box 156 Atabah, 11511 Cairo
Tel: (02) 742168; (02) 754301; (02) 744657 Fax: (02) 3924657
E-mail: info@daralkitab-online.com Cable: KITAMISR
Key Personnel
President & Man Dir: El-Zein Hassan E-mail: hlelzein@datum.com.eg
Founded: 1929
Also distributor & printer.
Membership(s): Time Life Time Warner.
Subjects: Education, Regional Interests
ISBN Prefix(es): 977-238
Parent Company: Dar Al-Kitab Al-Lubnani
Associate Companies: Dar Al-Kitab Al-Lubnani, Madame Kuri St in front of Hotel Bristol, PO Box 11, 8330 Beirut, Lebanon Tel: (01) 735731, (01) 735732 Fax: (01) 351433
Branch Office(s)
Cairo
Paris, France
Beirut, Lebanon
Casablanca, Morocco
Madrid, Spain
Geneva, Switzerland

EGYPT (ARAB REPUBLIC OF EGYPT)

Dar Al-Matbo at Al-Gadidah
5 Saint Mark St, Alexandria
Tel: (03) 4825508 *Fax:* (03) 4833819
Subjects: Agriculture, Animals, Pets, Library & Information Sciences, Social Sciences, Sociology
ISBN Prefix(es): 977-207

Dar al-Nahda al Arabia
32 Abdel Khalek Sarwat St, Cairo
Founded: 1960
Also distributor.
Subjects: Law, Literature, Literary Criticism, Essays
ISBN Prefix(es): 977-04

Dar Al-Thakafia Publishing+
32 Sabry Abou-Alam St, Cairo
Tel: (02) 42718 *Fax:* (02) 4034694
E-mail: nassar@hotmail.com
Key Personnel
President: Mohamed Youssef Elguindi
Founded: 1968
Publishes Arabic books in a variety of disciplines including comparative literature & regional political issues.
Subjects: Child Care & Development, Computer Science, History, Theology, Religion
ISBN Prefix(es): 977-221

Dar El Shorouk+
8 Sebaweh El Masry St, Rabaa El Adawia, Nasr City, Cairo
Tel: (02) 4023399; (02) 4037567 *Fax:* (02) 3934814
E-mail: dar@shorouk.com
Web Site: www.shorouk.com
Telex: 93091 Shrok *Cable:* SHOROUK
Key Personnel
Chief Executive, Editorial, Rights & Permissions: Ibrahim El Moallim
Sales: Ahmad El Sawy
Production: Ahmed El Zayadi
Children's Books: Amira Aboulmadg
Founded: 1976
Subjects: Behavioral Sciences, Biography, Business, Computer Science, Education, English as a Second Language, Fiction, History, Law, Literature, Literary Criticism, Essays, Management, Mysteries, Nonfiction (General), Poetry, Psychology, Psychiatry, Religion - Islamic
ISBN Prefix(es): 977-09
Associate Companies: Shorouk Press
Subsidiaries: Shorouk Bookshop
Bookshop(s): The First Mall, 25 Giza St, Giza; One Soliman Pasha Sq, Cairo

The Egyptian Society for the Dissemination of Universal Culture and Knowledge (ESDUCK)
1081 Corniche El Nil, Garden City, Cairo
Mailing Address: PO Box 21, Cairo
Tel: (02) 35425079; (02) 3542 0295 *Fax:* (02) 3540295 *Cable:* ESDUCK
Key Personnel
Executive Manager: Dr Amin El-Gamal
Production: Amal Kilany
Rights & Permissions: Inas Effat
Founded: 1953
Co-publisher with local & American firms. Also translation agency.

Elias Modern Publishing House+
One Kenisset El-Rum el Kathulik St, Cairo 11271
Tel: (02) 5903756; (02) 5939544 *Fax:* (02) 5880091
E-mail: eliasmph@gega.net
Web Site: www.eliaspublishing.com
Key Personnel
Man Dir: Laura Kfoury
Founded: 1913
Subjects: Language Arts, Linguistics, Literature, Literary Criticism, Essays, Poetry
ISBN Prefix(es): 977-5028
Subsidiaries: Elias Modern Press

ESDUCK, see The Egyptian Society for the Dissemination of Universal Culture and Knowledge (ESDUCK)

General Egyptian Book Organization+
Corniche el-Nil - Ramlet Boulac, Cairo 11221
Tel: (02) 5799635; (02) 5775228; (02) 5775367; (02) 5775436; (02) 5775545; (02) 5775000; (02) 5775109 *Fax:* (02) 5765058; (02) 5799635
E-mail: info@egyptianbook.org
Web Site: www.egyptianbook.org
Telex: 93932bookun *Cable:* GEBO
Key Personnel
Chairman: Dr Mohamed Samir Sarhan
General Manager, Marketing: Mr Samir Saad
Founded: 1961
26 Branches throughout Egypt.
ISBN Prefix(es): 977-01
Bookshop(s): International Book Centre, 3, 26th July St, Cairo *Tel:* (02) 5788431

Dar Al Hilal Publishing Institution
16 Mohamed Ezz Al-Arab St, Cairo 11511
Tel: (02) 362 5450 *Fax:* (02) 362 5469
Telex: 92703 Hilal *Cable:* Al Mussawar Cairo
Key Personnel
Chairman of the Board & Editor-in-Chief: Makram Muhammad Ahmed
Founded: 1892
Subjects: Fiction, Nonfiction (General)
ISBN Prefix(es): 977-07

Lehnert & Landrock Bookshop
44 Sherif St, Cairo 11511
Tel: (02) 3927606 *Fax:* (02) 3934421
Key Personnel
Manager: Dr E Lambelet
Founded: 1924
Subjects: Archaeology, History, Travel
ISBN Prefix(es): 977-243
Number of titles published annually: 2 Print

Dar Al Maaref+
1119 Courniche EL Nil, Cairo
Tel: (02) 759411; (02) 759552 *Fax:* (02) 5744999
E-mail: maaref@idsc.gov.eg
Telex: 92199 Marefun *Cable:* Damaref
Key Personnel
Chairman & Man Dir: Ragab Al-Banna
Founded: 1890
Also co-publishers, importers & exporters.
Subjects: Education, Regional Interests, Science (General)
ISBN Prefix(es): 977-02
Subsidiaries: Dar Al-Maaref Liban Sarl
Bookshop(s): Alexandria; El Arish; Assiut; Asswan; Cairo; Ismailia; Mansoura; Qena; Shebin El kom; Sohage; Suez; Tanta; Zagazig

Middle East Book Centre
45 Kasr Al-Nil St, Cairo
Tel: (02) 910980
Key Personnel
Man Dir: Dr A M Mosharrafa
Sales Manager: A Ismail
Founded: 1954
Subjects: Biography, Fiction, History, Language Arts, Linguistics, Literature, Literary Criticism, Essays, Philosophy, Poetry, Regional Interests, Religion - Other, Science (General), Social Sciences, Sociology

Senouhy Publishers
54 Sharia Abdel-Khalek, Tharwat, Cairo
Key Personnel
Man Dir: Leila A Fadel
Founded: 1956
Subjects: History, Nonfiction (General), Poetry, Regional Interests, Religion - Other

Sphinx Publishing Co
3 Shawarby St, 3rd Floor, Cairo
Tel: (02) 392 4616 *Fax:* (02) 391 8802
E-mail: sphinx@intouch.com
Telex: 93927
Key Personnel
Man Dir: Habib Sayegh
Founded: 1958
Part of Librairie du Liban Group, Lebanon.
Subjects: Education
Parent Company: Pearson Plc

Ummah Press+
24 Degla St-Flat 9, Off Shehab St, Mohandiseen, Cairo
Tel: (02) 337-8556
E-mail: ghurabh@internetegypt.com
Key Personnel
President: Ahmad El Shazly
Publishing & Translation Service.
Subjects: Business, Economics, Government, Political Science, Journalism, Regional Interests, Religion - Islamic

El Salvador

General Information

Capital: San Salvador
Language: Spanish
Religion: Predominantly Roman Catholic
Population: 5.6 million
Bank Hours: 0900-1200, 1345-1530 Monday-Friday
Shop Hours: 0800-1200, 1400-1800 Monday-Friday; 0800-1200 Saturday
Currency: 100 centavos = 1 Salvadorean colon
Export/Import Information: Member of the Central American Common Market. No import licenses but exchange license from Exchange Control Department of Central Reserve Bank required, if goods coming from outside Central America. Commercial banks authorize certain import payments.
Copyright: UCC, Berne, Buenos Aires, Florence (see Copyright Conventions, pg xi)

Clasicos Roxsil Editorial SA de CV+
4A Ave Sur N° 2-3, La Libertad, Santa Tecla
Tel: 228-1832; 288-2646; 229-6742 *Fax:* 228-1212
Key Personnel
Manager: Rosa Serrano de Lopez
Chief Editorial Dept: Roxana Beatriz Lopez
E-mail: roxanabe@navegante.com.sv
Founded: 1976
Subjects: Biography, Literature, Literary Criticism, Essays, Poetry
ISBN Prefix(es): 84-89541; 84-89899; 99923-24
Number of titles published annually: 10 Print
Total Titles: 130 Print
Distributor for Fondo Editorial UNESCO (El Salvador)
Book Club(s): Club de Lectores de Clasicos Roxsil, Marco Antonio Barraza

UCA Editores+
Blvd Los Proceres, San Salvador
Tel: 210-6600 *Fax:* 210-6655
E-mail: info@uca.edu.sv
Web Site: www.uca.edu.sv
Key Personnel
Dir: Rodolfo Cardenal SJ
Sub Dir: Carolina Cordova
Founded: 1975

Subjects: Philosophy, Religion - Other, Social Sciences, Sociology, Theology
ISBN Prefix(es): 99923-34
Number of titles published annually: 10 Print
Bookshop(s): Libreria UCA (under Major Booksellers)
Orders to: Distribuidora de Publicaciones de la Universidad Centroamericana, Universidad Centroamericana Jose Simeon Canas, Apdo 01-575, Autopista Sur, Jardinesde Guadalupe, San Salvador

Editorial Universitaria de la Universidad de El Salvador
Ciudad Universitaria, Apdo de Correos 3110, San Salvador
Tel: 2558826 *Fax:* 254208
Key Personnel
Dir: Armando Herrara
Contact: Francisco Guzman Argueta
Founded: 1923
Subjects: Gardening, Plants, Government, Political Science, Literature, Literary Criticism, Essays, Philosophy, Poetry, Regional Interests, Social Sciences, Sociology
ISBN Prefix(es): 84-89540

Estonia

General Information

Capital: Tallinn
Language: Estonian, Russian, Finnish & English
Religion: Evangelical Lutheran
Population: 1.5 million
Currency: 100 cents = 1 kroon (eek); 8 eek = 1 dem
Export/Import Information: No export/import duties. 18% VAT on books (except educational & medical).
Copyright: Berne (see Copyright Conventions, pg xi)

Academic Library of Tallinn Pedagogical University (Tallinna Pedagoogikaulikooli Akadeemiline Raamatukogu)
Formerly Estonian Academic Library
10 Raevala Ave, 15042 Tallinn
Tel: (02) 6659 401 *Fax:* (02) 6659 400
E-mail: ear@ear.ee
Web Site: www.ear.ee
Key Personnel
Head Librarian: Andres Kollist *E-mail:* andres.kollist@ear.ee
Learned Secretary: Aita Kraut *Tel:* (02) 6659 404 *E-mail:* aita.kraut@ear.ee
Founded: 1946
Subjects: Biological Sciences, Ethnicity, Geography, Geology, History, Library & Information Sciences, Exhibition Catalogues, Yearbooks
Number of titles published annually: 6 Print; 1 CD-ROM
Parent Company: Tallinn Pedagogical University, Narva St 25, 10120 Tallinn

Eesti Entsuklopeediakirjastus (Estonian Encyclopaedia Publishers)+
Narva mnt 4, 10117 Tallinn
Tel: 6999 620 *Fax:* 6999 621
E-mail: ene@ene.ee
Web Site: www.ene.ee
Key Personnel
Chairman of the Board: Hardo Aasmae
International Rights: Aili Saks
Founded: 1991 (as the successor of former Encyclopedia Editorial Board, founded 1963)
Specialize in reference books for all age groups.
Membership(s): Estonian Publishers Association.
Subjects: Agriculture, Art, Astronomy, Biography, Biological Sciences, Earth Sciences, Economics, Geography, Geology, History, Military Science, Music, Dance, Natural History, Nonfiction (General), Philosophy, Physical Sciences, Science (General), Social Sciences, Sociology, Sports, Athletics, Technology
ISBN Prefix(es): 5-89900; 9985-70
Number of titles published annually: 40 Print
Total Titles: 240 Print
Bookshop(s): A&O Reference Book Shop

Eesti Piibliselts+
Member of United Bible Societies
Kaarli pst 9, 10119 Tallinn
Tel: 631 1671 *Fax:* 631 1438
E-mail: eps@eps.ee
Web Site: www.eps.ee
Key Personnel
Head of Publications: Sra Tarmo Lilleoja *E-mail:* tarmo@eps.ee
Founded: 1813
Specialize in Estonian bibles, new testaments & portions, bible related literature.
Subjects: Biblical Studies, History
ISBN Prefix(es): 9985-889; 9985-9027
Number of titles published annually: 4 Print; 1 CD-ROM
Total Titles: 2 Print

Eesti Rahvusraamatukogu (National Library of Estonia)
Tonismagi 2, 15189 Tallinn
Tel: 630 7611 *Fax:* 631 1410
E-mail: nlib@nlib.ee
Web Site: www.nlib.ee
Key Personnel
Dir General: Tiiu Valm *Tel:* 630 7600 *E-mail:* tiiu.valm@nlib.ee
Marketing Manager: Triin Soone *Tel:* 630 7271 *E-mail:* triin@nlib.ee
Founded: 1918
Information services on humanities & social sciences; exhibition & conference service; book binding & conservation; photocopying; publishing.
Membership(s): CDNL, CENL, EIA, IALL, IAML, IFLA, International Council of Archives, International Paper Conservation Institute & LIBER.
Subjects: Art, History, Law, Library & Information Sciences, Music, Dance, Specialize in information services, exhibition & conference services, preservation, publishing for Parliament & other libraries. Specialize in dictionaries & reference books
ISBN Prefix(es): 9985-803; 9985-9217; 9985-9265; 9985-9334
Number of titles published annually: 50 Print; 13 CD-ROM; 2 E-Book
Total Titles: 13 CD-ROM; 8 E-Book

Estonian Academic Library, see Academic Library of Tallinn Pedagogical University

Estonian Academy Publishers (Eesti Teaduste Akadeemia Kirjastus)
Unit of Estonian Academy of Sciences
Kohtu Stz 6, 10130 Tallinn
Tel: 645 4504 *Fax:* 646 6026
E-mail: niine@kirj.ee
Web Site: www.kirj.ee
Key Personnel
Dir: Ulo Niine
Executive Editor: Virve Kurnitski *Tel:* 645 4156 *E-mail:* virve@kirj.ee
Marketing Manager: Asta Tikerpae *E-mail:* asta@kirj.ee
Founded: 1994
Subjects: Science (General)
ISBN Prefix(es): 9985-50
Number of titles published annually: 30 Print
Total Titles: 360 Print; 8 Online

Estonian ISBN Agency
Tonismaegi 2, 15189 Tallinn
Tel: 630 7372 *Fax:* 631 1200
E-mail: eraamat@nlib.ee
Web Site: www.nlib.ee
Key Personnel
Contact: Mai Valtna
Parent Company: National Library of Estonia

Ilmamaa+
Vanemuise 19, 51014 Tartu
Tel: (07) 427 290 *Fax:* (07) 427 320
E-mail: ilmamaa@ilmamaa.ee
Web Site: www.ilmamaa.ee
Key Personnel
Chairman: Hando Runnel
Dir: Mart Jagomagi *E-mail:* mj@ilmamaa.ee
Founded: 1993
Subjects: Fiction, History, Literature, Literary Criticism, Essays, Nonfiction (General), Philosophy, Poetry
ISBN Prefix(es): 9985-821; 9985-878; 9985-77
Number of titles published annually: 30 Print; 6 Online
Total Titles: 105 Print; 23 Online

Kirjastus Kunst (Kunst Publishers)+
Lai t 34, 10133 Tallinn
Tel: 6411764; 6411766 *Fax:* 6411762
E-mail: kunst.myyk@mail.ee
Web Site: www.kirjastused.com/kunst
Key Personnel
Editorial Dir: Katre Oim
Marketing: Asta Pajumaee
Design: Tiiu Allikvee
Finance: Marika Kirbits
Foreign Rights Manager: Eve Kork *Tel:* (02) 6411363
Founded: 1957
Specialize in Art.
Subjects: Architecture & Interior Design, Art, Biography, Fiction, History
ISBN Prefix(es): 5-89920; 9949-407
Number of titles published annually: 40 Print
Total Titles: 8 Print

Koolibri+
Lehola 8 / Hiiu 38, 11620 Tallinn
Tel: 651 5300 *Fax:* 651 5301
E-mail: koolibri@koolibri.ee
Web Site: www.koolibri.ee
Key Personnel
Dir: Kalle Kaljurand *Tel:* 651 5325 *E-mail:* kalle@koolibri.ee; Ants Lang *Tel:* 651 5302 *E-mail:* ants@koolibri.ee
Assistant Dir: Valve Kruusma *Tel:* 651 5303 *E-mail:* valve@koolibri.ee
Publicity Manager: Maire Tanna *Tel:* 651 5318 *E-mail:* maire@koolibri.ee
ISBN Prefix(es): 9985-0
Total Titles: 300 Print

Kupar Publishers+
Pamu mnt 67a, 10134 Tallinn
Tel: (02) 628 6173; (02) 628 6175 *Fax:* (02) 646 2076
E-mail: kupar@netexpress.ee
Key Personnel
Chairman: Mihkel Mutt
Man Dir: Ivo Sandre
Editor-in-Chief: Marilin Lips
Founded: 1987
Subjects: Fiction, Human Relations, Parapsychology, Social Sciences, Sociology, Western Fiction
ISBN Prefix(es): 9985-61
Bookshop(s): Kupar, Lossi 9, Poltsamaa; Kupar, Harju 1, EE0001 Tallinn

ESTONIA

Mats Publishers Ltd+
Laki 15, EE 12915 Tallinn
Tel: (02) 6563589
Key Personnel
President & Man Dir: Heido Ots
Founded: 1991
Subjects: Automotive, History, House & Home, Transportation
ISBN Prefix(es): 9985-51
Number of titles published annually: 10 Print
Total Titles: 30 Print
Imprints: Mats Tallinn

Mats Tallinn, *imprint of* Mats Publishers Ltd

AS Medicina+
Laki 26, 12915 Tallinn
Tel: (06) 567660 *Fax:* (06) 567620
E-mail: medicina@hot.ee
Web Site: medicina.co.ee
Key Personnel
Man Dir: Kaja Uska
Founded: 1993
Membership(s): the Estonian Book Publishers Association.
Subjects: Medicine, Nursing, Dentistry
ISBN Prefix(es): 9985-829
Parent Company: Kustannus Oy Duodecim, Helsinki, Finland

Olion Publishers+
Laki 26, 12915 Tallinn
Tel: 655 0175 *Fax:* 655 0173
E-mail: olion@not.ee
Key Personnel
Dir: Hulle Unt
Editor-in-Chief: Veiko Talts *Tel:* 644 4347
Founded: 1989
Subjects: Biography, Business, Economics, Education, Fiction, History, Law, Nonfiction (General), Philosophy, Social Sciences, Sociology, Western Fiction
ISBN Prefix(es): 5-460; 9985-66
Number of titles published annually: 40 Print

Oue Eesti Raamat
Laki tn 26, Tallinn 12915
Tel: 658 7885; 658 7886; 658 7887; 658 7889
   Fax: 658 7889
E-mail: helgi.gailit@mail.ee
Web Site: www.eestiraamat.ee
Key Personnel
Dir: Anne Kask *E-mail:* anne.kask.003@mail.ee
Rights & Contract Manager: Georg Grunberg
   E-mail: georg.grynberg@mail.ee
Founded: 1964
Subjects: Biography, Fiction, Poetry
ISBN Prefix(es): 9985-65
Number of titles published annually: 50 Print

Perioodika+
Voorimehe 9, PO Box 3648, Tallinn 10507
Tel: 644 1262 *Fax:* 644 2484
E-mail: perioodika@hot.ee
Key Personnel
Manager, Editorial Board: Ivar Sinimets
Dir: Uuno Sillajoe
Founded: 1973
Subjects: Astrology, Occult, Cookery, Romance, Women's Studies
ISBN Prefix(es): 5-7979
Number of titles published annually: 30 Print
Total Titles: 90 Print

Sinisukk+
Tueri 9, Tallinn 11314
Tel: 656 1872 *Fax:* 656 1872
E-mail: sinisukk@vorguvara.ee
Key Personnel
President & International Rights: Marie Edala
   E-mail: marie@sinisukk.ee

Founded: 1992
Subjects: Animals, Pets, Astrology, Occult, Biography, Child Care & Development, Cookery, Crafts, Games, Hobbies, Fiction, Film, Video, Gardening, Plants, House & Home, How-to, Nonfiction (General), Psychology, Psychiatry, Self-Help
ISBN Prefix(es): 9985-73; 9985-812
Number of titles published annually: 180 Print
Total Titles: 212 Print

Tael Ltd
Ruutli 6, Tallinn EE0001
Tel: (02) 6314162 *Fax:* (02) 6314162
E-mail: tael@teleport.ee
Key Personnel
Publisher: Vladimir Sokolovski
Founded: 1991
Subjects: Archaeology
Total Titles: 1 Print

TEA Kirjastus (Tea Publishers)+
Liivalaia 28, 10118 Tallinn
Tel: 644 9253; 645 9206 *Fax:* 645 9208
E-mail: info@tea.ee
Web Site: www.tea.ee
Key Personnel
President: Mrs Silva Tomingas *E-mail:* silva.tomingas@tea.ee
General Manager: Mr Olavi Valner
International Rights Manager: Kersti Neiman
   E-mail: kersti.neiman@tea.ee
Founded: 1992
Publishing & design of books & dictionaries on diskettes. Subject specialties include textbooks, practice books & grammar books.
ISBN Prefix(es): 9985-71; 9985-843; 9985-9003; 9985-9029
Number of titles published annually: 50 Print; 1 CD-ROM; 3 Audio
Total Titles: 130 Print; 1 CD-ROM; 10 Audio
Branch Office(s)
Parnu, Sirje Manna *Tel:* (02) 4476303
TARTU, Botooni 9 *Tel:* (02) 7307959 *Fax:* (02) 7307970
Bookshop(s): 27 Narva Mnt, Tallinn, Contact: Mrs Ene Tiidelepp *Tel:* (02) 6426019

Tuum+
Harju 1, 10146 Tallinn
Tel: 627 6427; (051) 41 290 *Fax:* 641 8054
E-mail: enelier@yahoo.com
Key Personnel
Contact: Piret Viires
Founded: 1992
Subjects: Human Relations, Literature, Literary Criticism, Essays, Natural History, Philosophy, Poetry, Psychology, Psychiatry, Science Fiction, Fantasy
ISBN Prefix(es): 9985-802

Valgus Publishers+
Tulika 19, Tallinn 10613
Tel: 650 5025; (050) 59 958 *Fax:* 650 5104
E-mail: info@kirjastusvalgus.ee
Key Personnel
Dir: Ants Sild
Founded: 1965
Subjects: Agriculture, Animals, Pets, Archaeology, Architecture & Interior Design, Biological Sciences, Child Care & Development, Cookery, Crafts, Games, Hobbies, Electronics, Electrical Engineering, Engineering (General), English as a Second Language, Gardening, Plants, Geography, Geology, Health, Nutrition, Medicine, Nursing, Dentistry, Science (General), Handbooks, Healthcare, Popular-science
ISBN Prefix(es): 5-440; 9985-68

Ethiopia

General Information

Capital: Addis Ababa
Language: Amharic (official), English also widely used
Religion: Ethiopian Orthodox
Population: 51.1 million
Bank Hours: 0830-1230, 1430-1730 Monday-Friday; 0830-1230 Saturday
Shop Hours: Addis Ababa: 0900-1300, 1500-2000 Monday-Saturday. Asmara: 0800-1300, 1600-2000 Monday-Friday
Currency: 100 cents = 1 birr
Export/Import Information: No tariff on books, but additional taxes. Advertising subject to customs and same taxes. No import license required but Exchange Payment License necessary.
Copyright: No copyright conventions signed

Addis Ababa University Press
PO Box 1176, Addis Ababa
Tel: (01) 239746; (01) 239800 (ext 227) *Fax:* (01) 239729
E-mail: aau.pres@telecom.net.et *Cable:* AA UNIV
Key Personnel
General Editor & Dir: Prof Darge Wole
Assistant General Dir: Messelech Habte
Founded: 1968
Publishing House of the Addis Ababa University.
Membership(s): Ethiopian Publishers Association; African Association of Science Editors; APNET; ABC.
Subjects: Biography, Chemistry, Chemical Engineering, Geography, Geology, Health, Nutrition, History, Language Arts, Linguistics, Literature, Literary Criticism, Essays, Science (General), Technology, Botany, Climatology, Diary, Hydrology, Public Health
Total Titles: 15 Print
Associate Companies: James Currey Publishers, United Kingdom; Illinois University Press, IL, United States; Lund University Press, Sweden; Norwegian University of Science & Technology, Norway

ENI, see Ethiopian Nutrition Institute (ENI)

Ethiopian Nutrition Institute (ENI)
PO Box 5654, Addis Ababa
Tel: (01) 151600 *Fax:* (01) 754744 *Cable:* NUTRITION
Key Personnel
Dir: Dr Zewdie Wolde-Gebriel
Parent Company: Ministry of Health
Divisions: Medical, Laboratory, Training, Food Science & Technology

Government Printer
Government Printing Press, Addis Ababa
Mailing Address: PO Box 1241, Addis Ababa

Fiji

General Information

Capital: Suva
Language: Fijian & Hindi. English widely spoken
Religion: Christian (mainly Methodist) with large minority of Hindus
Population: 800,000
Bank Hours: 1000-1500 Monday-Thursday; 1000-1600 Friday

Shop Hours: 0800-1630 or later Monday-Friday; early closing Wednesday or Saturday
Currency: 100 cents = 1 Fiji dollar
Export/Import Information: No tariffs on books and advertising. No import licenses. Exchange control by Reserve Bank of Fiji; no specific Exchange license required and authorized banks perform transaction upon application.
Copyright: Berne, UCC (see Copyright Conventions, pg xi)

Islands Business International Ltd
46 Gordon St, Suva
Mailing Address: PO Box 12718, Suva
Tel: 312 040 *Fax:* 301 423
E-mail: 75070.2637@compuserve.com
Telex: 2350
Key Personnel
Man Dir: Godfrey Scoullar
Publisher: Robert Keith-Reid
Editor: Peter Lomas
Senior Writer: Vasiti Waqa
Advertising Manager: Ganga Gounder
Circulation Manager: Davina Hughes
ISBN Prefix(es): 982-206
Publication(s): *Fiji Islands Business*

Library Service of Fiji
Government Bldgs, Suva
Mailing Address: PO Box 2526, Suva
Tel: 311224; 315 344; 315303 *Fax:* 314 994; 314 994
Key Personnel
Chief Librarian: Humesh Prasad
Founded: 1964
Oversees the management of public, government department & school libraries in Fiji. Operates 37 government department libraries, 28 school media centers & 5 mobile libraries
Listing & information service.
Branch Office(s)
Nausori Library, Nausori *Tel:* 476387 *Fax:* 400048
Northern Regional Library, Ministry of Education, Labasa *Tel:* 812894 *Fax:* 814770
Raki Raki Branch Library, PO Box 1, Raki Raki *Tel:* 694153 *Fax:* 694855
Savu Savu Branch Library, Savu Savu *Tel:* 850154 *Fax:* 850154
Tavua Branch Library, Tauna *Tel:* 694153 *Fax:* 681390
Western Regional Library, PO Box 150, Lautokia *Tel:* 660091 *Fax:* 668195

Lotu Pacifika Productions
Government Bldgs, Suva
Mailing Address: PO Box 2401, Suva
Tel: 301314 *Fax:* 301183 *Cable:* LOTUPAK
Key Personnel
Manager: Seru L Verebalavu
Founded: 1973
Subjects: Cookery, Education, Ethnicity, Poetry, Religion - Other

University of the South Pacific+
PO Box 1168, Suva
Tel: (033) 13900 *Fax:* (033) 01305
Web Site: www.usp.ac.fj
Telex: 2276 usp fj *Cable:* UNIVERSITY SUVA
Founded: 1968
Subjects: Education, Environmental Studies, Natural History, Regional Interests
ISBN Prefix(es): 982-302; 982-03; 982-01

Finland

General Information

Capital: Helsinki
Language: Finnish and Swedish (officially bilingual); English and German spoken widely
Religion: Predominantly Evangelical Lutheran
Population: 5.2 million
Bank Hours: 0915-1615 Monday-Friday
Shop Hours: 0900-1700 or later Monday-Friday; 0900-1600 (1400 in summer) Saturday
Currency: 100 Eurocents = 1 Euro; 5.94573 markkas = 1 Euro
Export/Import Information: Member of the European Union. 12% VAT on books. No import licenses required on books. No exchange controls.
Copyright: UCC, Berne, Florence (see Copyright Conventions, pg xi)

AB Svenska Laromedel-Editum+
Rusthaellargatan 1, 02270 Esbo
Tel: (09) 8043188 *Fax:* (09) 8043257
Key Personnel
Chief Executive: Jan-Peter Kullberg
Founded: 1971
Subjects: Education, Fiction, Nonfiction (General)
ISBN Prefix(es): 951-553
Showroom(s): Kyruoesplanaden 9, 65100 Vasa

Abo Akademis forlag - Abo Akademi University Press
Tavastgatan 30 C, 20700 Abo
Tel: (02) 215 3292 *Fax:* (02) 215 4490
E-mail: forlaget@abo.fi
Web Site: www.abo.fi/stiftelsen/forlag
Key Personnel
Secretary: Inger Hassel
Founded: 1987
Subjects: Science (General), Doctoral Dissertations
ISBN Prefix(es): 951-9498; 952-9616; 951-765
Number of titles published annually: 20 Print
Orders to: Oy Tibo-Trading Ab, PO Box 33, 21601 Pargas *Tel:* (02) 454 9200 *Fax:* (02) 454 9220 *E-mail:* tibo@tibo.net *Web Site:* www.tibo.net

Akateeminen Kustannusliike Oy+
Arkadiankatu 12 A 5, 00100 Helsinki
Tel: (09) 434 2320
Web Site: www.spes.fi
Key Personnel
Manager: Tapani Mattila
Sales: Ulla-Riitta Tuulenmaki
Founded: 1927
Subjects: History, Language Arts, Linguistics, Religion - Protestant
ISBN Prefix(es): 951-9023

Art House Group
Bulevardi 19 C, 00120 Helsinki
Tel: (09) 9800 2500 *Fax:* (09) 693 3762
ISBN Prefix(es): 951-884; 951-96086; 951-96135

Atena Kustannus Oy+
PL 436, 40101 Jyvaskyla
Tel: (014) 620192 *Fax:* (014) 620190
E-mail: atena@atenakustannus.fi
Web Site: www.atenakustannus.fi
Key Personnel
Contact: Pekka Maekelae
Founded: 1986
Subjects: History, Nonfiction (General)
ISBN Prefix(es): 951-9362; 951-796

Basam Books Oy+
Hameentie 155 A 7, 00561 Helsinki
Mailing Address: PL 42, 00561 Helsinki
Tel: (09) 7579 3839 *Fax:* (09) 7579 3838
E-mail: bs@basambooks.com
Web Site: www.basambooks.com
Key Personnel
Man Dir & International Rights: Batu Samaletdin
Founded: 1993
Subjects: Fiction, Literature, Literary Criticism, Essays, Philosophy, Poetry, Psychology, Psychiatry
ISBN Prefix(es): 952-9842; 952-5534

Building Information Ltd
Formerly Finnish Building Centre Ltd
Runeberginkatu 5, 00101 Helsinki
Mailing Address: PO Box 1004, 00101 Helsinki
Tel: (09) 549 5570 *Fax:* (09) 5495 5320
E-mail: rakennustieto@rakennustieto.fi
Web Site: www.rakennustieto.fi
Key Personnel
Man Dir: Markku Salmi *Tel:* (09) 5495 5333 *E-mail:* markku.salmi@rakennustieto.fi
Assistant Man Dir: Heimo Salo *Tel:* (09) 5495 5395 *E-mail:* heimo.salo@rakennustieto.fi
Subjects: Architecture & Interior Design, Building & Construction
Total Titles: 8 CD-ROM; 2 Online; 1 E-Book
Parent Company: The Building Information Foundation RTS, Helsinki
Associate Companies: Helsinki Building Centre *Tel:* (09) 5495 5426 *Fax:* (09) 5495 5420; Lappeenranta Building Centre, Raatimiehenkatu 20, 53100 Lappeenranta *Tel:* (05) 415 0990 *Fax:* (05) 415 2600; Kuopio Building Centre, Kauppakatu 40-42, 70110 Kuopio *Tel:* (017) 261 6109 *Fax:* (017) 261 8666; Oulu Building Centre, Uusikatu 32, 90100 Oulu *Tel:* (08) 311 6122 *Fax:* (08) 377 334; Tampere Building Centre, Satakunnankatu 18, 33210 Tampere *Tel:* (03) 212 6961 *Fax:* (03) 212 6989
Foreign Rep(s): Latvian Building Centre Ltd (LBC) (Latvia); Estonian Building Centre (Estonia); Moscow Construction Centre ZAO (Russia); St Petersburg Construction Centre Ltd (Russia)
Bookshop(s): The Building Bookshop, Helsinki *Tel:* (09) 5495 5400 *Fax:* (09) 5495 5340

Docendo Finland Oy+
Vapaaherrantie 2, 40100 Jyvaskyla
Tel: (014) 339 7700 *Fax:* (014) 339 7755
E-mail: info@docendo.fi
Web Site: www.docendo.fi
Key Personnel
Man Dir: Sahlman Mika
Founded: 1990
Subjects: Civil Engineering, Computer Science, Engineering (General), Microcomputers
ISBN Prefix(es): 952-9823; 952-5159; 951-96321; 951-846
Parent Company: Werner Soderstrom Oy

Kustannus Oy Duodecim (Duodecim Medical Publications Ltd)+
Kalevankatu 11 A, 00100 Helsinki
Mailing Address: PO Box 713, 00101 Helsinki
Tel: (09) 618851 *Fax:* (09) 61885400
E-mail: etunimi.sukunimi@duodecim.fi
Web Site: www.duodecim.fi
Key Personnel
Secretary: Raija Orndahl *E-mail:* raija.orndahl@duodecim.ti
Man Dir: Pekka Mustongn *E-mail:* pekka.mustongn@duodecim.ti
Information Officer: Annakaisa Tavast *E-mail:* annakaisa.tavast@duodecim.fi
Founded: 1984
Membership(s): the Finnish Book Publishers Association.
Subjects: Medicine, Nursing, Dentistry, Psychology, Psychiatry
ISBN Prefix(es): 951-656; 951-8917; 951-9347

FINLAND

Number of titles published annually: 15 Print
Associate Companies: AS Medicina, Gonsiori 29, Tallinn, Estonia *Tel:* (06) 484 679

Edita Publishing Oy+
Siltasaarenkatu 14, 00043 Helsinki
Mailing Address: PL 700, 00043 Edita
Tel: (020) 450 00 *Fax:* (020) 450 2396
E-mail: etunimi.sukunimi@edita.fi
Web Site: www1.edita.fi
Telex: 123458 Vapk
Key Personnel
Dir-General: Mikko Suotsalo *E-mail:* mikko.suotsalo@edita.fi
Dir, Publication: Leo Eskola *E-mail:* leo.eskola@edita.fi
Editorial Dir: Lauri Veijola *E-mail:* lauri.veijola@edita.fi; Timo Lepisto *Tel:* (020) 450 2355 *E-mail:* timo.lepisto@edita.fi
Marketing Dir & Rights & Permissions: Pauli Niemi-Jaskari *E-mail:* pauli.niemi-jaskari@edita.fi
Founded: 1859
ISBN Prefix(es): 951-37; 951-859; 951-860; 951-861
Bookshop(s): Annankatu 44, 00100 Helsinki; Etelaeesplanadi 4

Ekenas Tryckeri AB
PB 26, 10601 Ekenaes
Tel: (019) 222 800 *Fax:* (019) 222 815
E-mail: leif.rex@eta.fi
Key Personnel
Man Dir: Sven Sundstroem
Founded: 1881
Subjects: Government, Political Science, History
ISBN Prefix(es): 951-9000; 951-9001

Fenix-Kustannus Oy+
PL 11, 02211 Espoo
Tel: (09) 420 8190 *Fax:* (09) 420 8045
Key Personnel
Chief Executive, Rights & Permissions: Reima T A Luoto *E-mail:* reima.luoto@matkailutoimittajat.fi
Editorial: Kalevi Viljanen
Sales: Tapio Vaekevaeinen
Production: Matti Saarinen
Founded: 1993
Subjects: Nonfiction (General)
ISBN Prefix(es): 951-862

Finnish Building Centre Ltd, see Building Information Ltd

Finnish Lawyers' Publishing Co, see Kauppakaari Oyj

Forsamlingsforbundets Forlags AB+
Bangatan 29 A, 00120 Helsingfors
Mailing Address: PO Box 285, 00121 Helsingfors
Tel: (09) 61261546 *Fax:* (09) 603963
E-mail: bokhandel@ff-forlag.fi
Key Personnel
Man Dir: Leif Westerling *E-mail:* leif.westerling@ff-forlag.fi
Sales: Asa Nordstrom
Founded: 1920
Subjects: Biblical Studies, Psychology, Psychiatry, Religion - Protestant
ISBN Prefix(es): 951-550
Distributor for Verbum-Sweden

Frenckellin Kirjapaino Oy (Frenckell Printing Works)
Niittyrinne 4, 02270 Espoo
Tel: (09) 887 3611 *Fax:* (09) 887 3670
E-mail: etunimi.sukunimi@frenckell.fi
Web Site: www.frenckell.fi

Key Personnel
Chief Executive Officer: Berndt von Frenckell *Tel:* (09) 887 3622
Marketing Manager: Jari Mikola *Tel:* (09) 887 3627 *E-mail:* jari.mikola@frenckell.fi
Sales Manager: Harri Nikulainen *Tel:* (09) 887 3625 *E-mail:* harri.nikulainen@frenckell.fi; Lauri Silvennoinen *Tel:* (09) 887 3631 *E-mail:* lauri.silvennoinen@frenckell.fi
Founded: 1642
ISBN Prefix(es): 951-9417; 951-95311

Gummerus Publishers+
Arkadiankatu 23 B, 00100 Helsinki
Mailing Address: PO Box 749, 00101 Helsinki
Tel: (09) 584 301 *Fax:* (09) 5843 0200
E-mail: publisher@gummerus.fi
Web Site: www.gummerus.fi
Key Personnel
Man Dir: Ilkka Kylmala
Publishing Manager, Nonfiction: Risto Vaisanen
Publishing Manager, Ajatus Kirjat (Nonfiction): Jan Erola
Publishing Manager, Foreign Fiction: Anna Baijars
Publishing Manager, Dictionaries: Virpi Kalliokuusi
Rights & Permissions: Paula Peltola
Founded: 1872
Subjects: Fiction, Nonfiction (General)
ISBN Prefix(es): 951-20
Parent Company: Gummerus Oy

Herattaja-yhdistys Ry
PL 21, 62101 Lapuan
Tel: (06) 438 8911 *Fax:* (06) 438 7430
E-mail: jormakka@nic.fi
Key Personnel
Executive Dir: Jouko Kuusinen
Founded: 1892
Subjects: Biblical Studies, History, Literature, Literary Criticism, Essays, Poetry, Religion - Protestant, Theology
ISBN Prefix(es): 951-878; 951-9012; 951-9013; 951-9014

Kaantopiiri Oy+
Meritullinkatu 21, 00170 Helsinki
Tel: (09) 622 9970 *Fax:* (09) 135 1872
E-mail: like@likekustannus.fi
Web Site: www.likekustannus.fi
Key Personnel
Editor & Foreign Rights: Saara Karvinen *Tel:* (09) 68746077
Founded: 1987
Specialize in literature by women in Third World countries.
Subjects: Fiction, Foreign Countries, Literature, Literary Criticism, Essays, Nonfiction (General), Women's Studies
ISBN Prefix(es): 951-8989
Parent Company: Like Kustannus Oy

Karas-Sana Oy+
Kaisaniemenkatu 8, 4 krs, 00100 Helsinki
Tel: (09) 6815 5600 *Fax:* (09) 6815 5611
E-mail: toimitus@sana.fi
Web Site: www.karas-sana.fi/sana
Key Personnel
Man Dir: Hans Krause *E-mail:* hans.krause@karas-sana.fi
Publishing Manager: Paivi Karri *E-mail:* paivi.karri@karas-sana.fi
Founded: 1974
Subjects: Human Relations, Religion - Protestant, Self-Help
ISBN Prefix(es): 951-655; 951-851
Number of titles published annually: 15 Print
Total Titles: 172 Print; 1 Audio
Parent Company: Kansan Raamattuseuran Saeaetioe, PO Box 48, Vivamo SF-08101 Lohja

BOOK

Karisto Oy+
Paroistentie 2, 13600 Hameenlinna
Tel: (03) 63 151 *Fax:* (03) 616 1565
E-mail: kustannusliike@karisto.fi
Web Site: www.karisto.fi
Key Personnel
Man Dir: Simo Moisio
Publishing Dir, Editorial & Foreign Rights: Pirkko Mikkola *Tel:* (03) 631 5210
Founded: 1900
Subjects: Fiction, Nonfiction (General)
ISBN Prefix(es): 951-23
Warehouse: Kirjavalitys Oy, Hakakalliontie 10, 05800 Hyvinkaeae

Kauppakaari Oyj
Uudenmaankatu 4-6A, 00120 Helsinki
Tel: (020) 442 4730 *Fax:* (020) 442 4723
E-mail: etunimi.sukunimi@talentum.fi
Web Site: www.talentum.fi/kirjat
Key Personnel
Publishing Dir: Mr Tuomo Rasanen
Sales Secretary: Ms Taija Haapaniemi
Founded: 1958
Subjects: Business, Law
ISBN Prefix(es): 951-640; 952-14; 951-8986; 951-762
Bookshop(s): Lakipiste, Uudenmaankatu 4-6A, 00120 Helsinki *Tel:* (09) 54212230 *Fax:* (09) 54212223

Kirja-Leitzinger+
Kytoesuontie 8 D 47, 00300 Helsinki
Tel: (09) 588 3377 *Fax:* (09) 588 3373
E-mail: leitzinger@luukku.com
Key Personnel
Man Dir: Antero Leitzinger
Founded: 1993
Subjects: Asian Studies, Ethnicity, Foreign Countries, Genealogy, Government, Political Science, History, Music, Dance, Travel
ISBN Prefix(es): 952-9752
Total Titles: 15 Print

Kirjatoimi+
Ketarantie 4, 33680 Tampere
Mailing Address: PL 94, 33101 Tampere
Tel: (03) 360 0000 *Fax:* (03) 360 0454
E-mail: kirjatoimi@sdafin.org *Cable:* KIRJATOIMI
Key Personnel
Man Dir & Chief Editor: Kalliokoski Klaus
Office Manager: Kallman Maarit *E-mail:* wellwoma@sdafin.org
Founded: 1897
Subjects: Health, Nutrition, Religion - Protestant
ISBN Prefix(es): 951-629
Parent Company: Seventh-Day Adventist Church in Finland

Kirjayhtyma Oy
Urho Kekkosen Katu 4-6E, 00100 Helsinki
Tel: (09) 6937641 *Fax:* (09) 69376366
E-mail: oppimateriaauit@tammi.net *Cable:* KIRJAYHTYMAe
Key Personnel
Man Dir: Olli Arrakoski
Publishing Dir, Textbooks: Tuija Nurmiranta
Publishing Dir, Fiction & Nonfiction: Jaakko Tapaninen
Contact: Haarala Paeivi
Founded: 1958
Subjects: Fiction, Nonfiction (General)
ISBN Prefix(es): 951-26
Parent Company: Tammi Publishers
Bookshop(s): Kirjava Satama, Urho Kekkosen Katu 4-6E, 00100 Helsinki
Warehouse: Libri-Logistiikka Oy, Hakakalliontie 10, 05800 Hyvinkaa
Orders to: Libri-Logistiikka Oy, Hakakalliontie 10, 05800 Hyvinkaa

PUBLISHERS

FINLAND

Koala-Kustannus Oy (Greenbay House Publishing Ltd)+
Kulosaarentie 8 C 20, 00570 Helsinki
Tel: (050) 408 1590 *Fax:* (09) 6845034
E-mail: info@koalakustannus.fi
Web Site: www.koalakustannus.fi
Key Personnel
Man Dir & International Rights: Lassi Eskola
E-mail: lassi.eskola@koalakustannus.fi
Founded: 1997
Membership(s): Finnish Book Publishers Association.
Subjects: Aeronautics, Aviation, Film, Video, History, Maritime, Military Science, Music, Dance, Nonfiction (General), Sports, Athletics
ISBN Prefix(es): 952-5186
Number of titles published annually: 20 Print; 1 CD-ROM
Total Titles: 40 Print

Kustannus Oy Kolibri+
Office Center, Lautatarhankatu 6A, 00581 Helsinki
Mailing Address: PL 399, 00101 Helsinki
Tel: (09) 774 5310 *Fax:* (09) 701 9351
E-mail: susanna.frankenhaeuser@kolibrikustannus.fi
Key Personnel
Man Dir: Rauno Malmstrom
Founded: 1989
Subjects: Nonfiction (General), Wine & Spirits
ISBN Prefix(es): 951-576; 952-16

Rakentajain Kustannus Oy (Building Publications Ltd)+
Rahakamarinportti 3A, 00240 Helsinki
Tel: (09) 142855 *Fax:* (09) 5032542
Key Personnel
Chief Executive Officer: Pertti Sarmala
Publishing Dir: Eeva Kalin
Founded: 1916
Specialize in books on all fields & levels of construction.
Subjects: Architecture & Interior Design, How-to
ISBN Prefix(es): 951-676
Bookshop(s): Fredrikinkatu 53, 00100 Helsinki

Kustannus Oy Semic
PL 317, 33101 Tampere
Tel: (03) 273 8111 *Fax:* (031) 243 8287
E-mail: minna.alanko@egmont-kustannus.fi
Telex: Semic
Key Personnel
Chief Executive & Publicity: Pentti Molander
Editorial, Production: Marjaana Tulosmaa
Founded: 1971
ISBN Prefix(es): 951-9112; 951-876; 951-95793; 951-95794; 951-95231; 951-95232
Parent Company: Semic International AB, Sweden

Kustannus Oy Uusi Tie+
Opistotie 1, 12310 Ryttylae
Tel: (019) 77 920 *Fax:* (019) 779 2300
E-mail: uusitie@uusitie.com
Web Site: www.uusitie.com
Key Personnel
Editor-at-Large: Vuokko Vanska
Sales: Raimo Raukko
Founded: 1965
Subjects: Fiction, Religion - Other, Theology
ISBN Prefix(es): 951-619

Kustannuskiila Oy
Vuorikatu 21-23, 70100 Kuopio
Mailing Address: PL 68, 70101 Kuopio
Tel: (017) 303 111 *Fax:* (017) 303 242
E-mail: anneli-siimes@savonsanomat.fi
Telex: 42111 Sasan
Key Personnel
President, Editorial, Production, Publicity & Sales: Juhani Pitkaenen *E-mail:* juhani.pitkaenen@savonsanomat.fi
Founded: 1964
Subjects: History
ISBN Prefix(es): 951-657
Parent Company: Savon Sanomat

Kustannusosakeyhtio Tammi (Tammi Publishers)
Urho Kekkosen katu 4-6 E, 00100 Helsinki
Mailing Address: PL 410, 00101 Helsinki
Tel: (09) 6937 621 *Fax:* (09) 6937 6266
E-mail: tammi@tammi.net
Web Site: www.tammi.net *Cable:* TAMMI
Key Personnel
Man Dir: Pentti Molander
Manager, Children's & Juvenile: Terttu Toiviainen
Literary Dir: Jaakko Tapaninen *E-mail:* jaakko.tapaninen@tammi.net
Founded: 1943
Subjects: Fiction, Nonfiction (General)
ISBN Prefix(es): 951-30; 951-31
Number of titles published annually: 400 Print
Parent Company: Bonnier Media AB, Sweden
Associate Companies: Libri-Logistiikka Oy
Subsidiaries: Kirjayhtymae Oy; Kirjasuomi Oy; Kustannus Oy Kolibri; Oy Opifer Ltd; Oy Satusiivet-Sagovingar AB
Bookshop(s): Kirjava Satama, Urho Kekkosen katu 4-6 E, 00100 Helsinki
Book Club(s): ExLibris; Lasten Parhaat Kirjat
Warehouse: Libri-Logistiikka Oy, Hakakalliontie 10, 05800 Hvyinkaa
Orders to: Libri-Logistiikka Oy, Hakakalliontie 10, 05800 Hvyinkaa

Kuva ja Sana+
PL 86, 00381 Helsinki
Tel: (09) 477 4920 *Fax:* (09) 4774 9250
E-mail: kuva.sana@patmos.fi
Key Personnel
Chief Executive Officer, President, Editor-in-Chief, Rights & Permissions: Leo Meller
Production, Publicity: Olli Palen
Founded: 1942
Subjects: Government, Political Science, Religion - Other, Social Sciences, Sociology
ISBN Prefix(es): 951-9024; 951-9072; 951-9073; 951-9203; 951-585
Associate Companies: Patmos International
Subsidiaries: Ideakustannus
Bookshop(s): Christian Center, Harjukatu 2, 00500 Helsinki

Lasten Keskus Oy
Saerkiniementie 7 A, 00210 Helsinki
Tel: (09) 6877 450 *Fax:* (09) 6877 4545
E-mail: tilaukset@lastenkeskus.fi
Web Site: www.lastenkeskus.fi *Cable:* LASTEN KESKUS
Key Personnel
Man Dir: Pertti Rosenholm *Tel:* (09) 6877 4540
Manager: Maisa Tonteri *Tel:* (09) 6877 4542
Manager Children's Books & Juveniles: Arja Kanerva *Tel:* (09) 6877 4535
Founded: 1974
Subjects: Biblical Studies, Child Care & Development, Crafts, Games, Hobbies, Education, Human Relations, Religion - Protestant
ISBN Prefix(es): 951-627; 951-626
Associate Companies: Suomen Kirkko-Mediat Oy
Subsidiaries: Pentella Oy
Bookshop(s): Lasten Kirjakauppa, Fredrikinkatu 61, 00100 Helsinki (Children's Bookstore)

Oy LIKE Kustannus (Like Publishing Ltd)+
Meritullinkatu 21, 00170 Helsinki
Tel: (09) 622 9970 *Fax:* (09) 135 1372
E-mail: like@like.fi
Web Site: www.likekustannus.fi
Key Personnel
Man Dir: Hannu Paloviita *E-mail:* hannu.paloviita@likekustannus.fi
Founded: 1987
The leading independent publishing house in Finland. Publishes a cultural magazine, circulation 700,000 copies.
Subjects: Fiction, Nonfiction (General), Science Fiction, Fantasy
ISBN Prefix(es): 951-578; 951-8929; 951-96078; 952-471
Number of titles published annually: 100 Print
Total Titles: 600 Print
Bookshop(s): Like Kirjakauppe, Vuorikatu 5, 00100 Helsinki, Contact: Otto Sallinen *Tel:* (09) 2600288

Otava Publishing Co Ltd+
Affiliate of Otava Books & Magazines Group Ltd
Uudenmaankatu 10, 00120 Helsinki
Mailing Address: PO Box 134, 00121 Helsinki
Tel: (09) 19961
E-mail: etunimi.sukunimi@otava.fi
Web Site: www.otava.fi *Cable:* OTAVA HELSINKI
Key Personnel
Chairman: Olli Reenpaa
Man Dir: Antti Reenpaa
Publishing Dir, General Books: Leena Majander
Publishing Dir, Educational Books: Jukka Vahtola
Publishing Manager, General Nonfiction: Liisa Steffa
Publishing Manager, Translated Fiction: Minna Castren
Publishing Manager, Children's Books: Katriina Kauppila
Publishing Manager, Special Books: Eva Reenpaa
Publishing Manager, Otava Education/Humanities & Arts Dept: Helena Ruuska
Publishing Manager, Otava Education/Modern Languages Dept: Laura Paivanen
Publishing Manager, Otava Education/Science Dept: Teuvo Sankila
Publishing Manager, Otava Education/Basic Education: Juha Vuorinen
Publishing Manager, Reference Books: Irja Hamalainen
Publishing Manager, Handbooks: Heli Hottinen
Foreign Rights Manager, Selling: Eila Mellin *Tel:* (09) 1996 445 *Fax:* (09) 1996 440
E-mail: eila.mellin@otava.fi
Founded: 1890
Subjects: Architecture & Interior Design, Art, Fiction, History, How-to, Nonfiction (General)
ISBN Prefix(es): 951-1
Subsidiaries: Otavan Kirjapaino Oy (Otava Book Printing Ltd); Suuri Suomalainen Kirjakerho Oy (The Great Finnish Book Club Ltd); Yhtyneet Kuvalehdet Oy (United Magazines Ltd)

Paiva Osakeyhtio+
Lukiokatu 15, 13101 Hameenlinna
Mailing Address: PL 10, 13101 Hameenlinna
Tel: (03) 644 6110 *Fax:* (03) 612 2109
E-mail: paiva@paiva.fi
Web Site: www.paiva.fi
Key Personnel
Man Dir: Merja Pitkanen *Tel:* (03) 644 6111
E-mail: merja.pitkanen@paiva.fr
Founded: 1962
Subjects: Religion - Protestant, Religion - Other
ISBN Prefix(es): 951-622

Pohjoinen
Lekatie 1, 90150 Oulu
Mailing Address: PL 170, 90401 Oulu
Tel: (08) 5377 111 *Fax:* (08) 5377 572
E-mail: pohjoinen@kaleva.fi
Web Site: www.kaleva.fi

FINLAND

Key Personnel
Publishing Manager: Peerit Tahtinen *Tel:* (08) 5377 570 *E-mail:* peerit.tahtinen@kaleva.fi
Founded: 1964
ISBN Prefix(es): 951-749; 951-9099; 951-9152
Parent Company: Kirjapaino Osakeyhito Kaleva

Rakennusalan Kustantajat RAK+
Kaupintie 13, 00440 Helsinki
Tel: (09) 503 2540 *Fax:* (09) 503 2542
E-mail: info@sarmala.com
Web Site: www.sarmala.com
Key Personnel
Publisher: Pertti Sarmala
Founded: 1991
ISBN Prefix(es): 952-9687; 951-664

Rakennustieto Oy (Building Information Ltd)+
Runeberginkatu 5, 00100 Helsinki
Mailing Address: PL 1004, 00101 Helsinki
Tel: (09) 549 5570 *Fax:* (09) 5495 5320
E-mail: rakennustieto@rakennustieto.fi
Web Site: www.rakennustieto.fi
Key Personnel
Man Dir: Markku Salmi
Assistant Man Dir: Heimo Salo
Founded: 1974
Subjects: Architecture & Interior Design
ISBN Prefix(es): 951-682
Parent Company: Rakennustietosaeaetio - Building Information Foundation RTS

Recallmed Oy+
Valkjarventie 45, 01800 Klaukkala
Tel: (09) 8797177 *Fax:* (09) 8797088
E-mail: recallmed@racallmed.fi
Key Personnel
Publishing Dir: Timo Saarinen
Chairman of the Board: Dr Bruno Taajamaa
Founded: 1981
Subjects: Biography, Medicine, Nursing, Dentistry, Music, Dance, Sports, Athletics
ISBN Prefix(es): 951-9221; 951-847

Sairaanhoitajien Koulutussaatio+
Sitratori 5, 00420 Helsinki
Tel: (09) 5666788 *Fax:* (09) 531504
Key Personnel
Executive Dir: Paivi Huopalahti
Financial Manager: Raija Jarvio
Chief Editor: Maija Tupala
Founded: 1944
Subjects: Medicine, Nursing, Dentistry
ISBN Prefix(es): 951-8963; 951-9105

Schildts Forlags AB+
Rusthallargatan 1, 02270 Esbo
Mailing Address: PO Box 86, 02271 Esbo
Tel: (09) 88 70 400 *Fax:* (09) 804 32 57
E-mail: schildts@schildts.fi
Web Site: www.schildts.fi *Cable:* BOKSCHILDT
Key Personnel
Man Dir: Mr Johan Johnson *Tel:* (09) 88 70 40 17 *E-mail:* jjohnson@schildts.fi
Rights & Permissions: Helen Svensson *Tel:* (09) 88 70 40 33 *E-mail:* helens@schildts.fi
Marketing Dir: Elisabeth Jansson *Tel:* (09) 88 70 40 20 *E-mail:* bettan@schildts.fi
Founded: 1913
Subjects: Art, Biography, Fiction, History, Music, Dance, Philosophy, Poetry
ISBN Prefix(es): 951-50
Associate Companies: Pagina
Orders to: Foerlagssystem Finland Ab *Tel:* (09) 88 70 40 52 *Fax:* (09) 88 70 40 55

Scriptum Forlags AB
Handelsesplanaden 23 A, 65100 Vasa
Fax: (06) 3242 210
E-mail: scriptum@svof.fi
Web Site: www.svof.fi/scriptum

Key Personnel
Chairman: Vivan Lygdback *Tel:* (06) 3242 226 *E-mail:* vivan.lygdback@svof.fi
Founded: 1987
Subjects: Archaeology, Fiction, Poetry, Essays
ISBN Prefix(es): 951-8902; 952-5496
Number of titles published annually: 9 Print
Total Titles: 100 Print

Soderstroms Forlag
Georgsgatan 29 A, 2 van, 00101 Helsingfors
Mailing Address: PB 870, 00101 Helsingfors
Tel: (09) 6841 8620 *Fax:* (09) 6841 8621
E-mail: soderstrom@soderstrom.fi
Web Site: www.soderstrom.fi *Cable:* SOeDERSTROeMS
Key Personnel
Man Dir: Marianne Bargum *Tel:* (09) 6841 8644 *E-mail:* marianne.bargum@soderstrom.fi
Editorial Dir: Tapani Ritamaki *Tel:* (09) 6841 8616 *E-mail:* ritamaki@soderstrom.fi
Editorial Dir, School Books: Kenneth Nykvist *Tel:* (09) 6841 8633 *E-mail:* nykvist@soderstrom.fi
Information & Marketing: Susanna Sucksdorff *Tel:* (09) 6841 8622 *E-mail:* sucksdorff@soderstrom.fi
Founded: 1891
Subjects: Art, Biography, Fiction, History, How-to, Philosophy, Poetry, Psychology, Psychiatry, Religion - Other, Science (General)
ISBN Prefix(es): 951-52
Total Titles: 30 Print
Orders to: Foerlagssystem Finland Ab *Tel:* (09) 8870 4052 *Fax:* (09) 8870 4055

Suomalaisen Kirjallisuuden Seura (Finnish Literature Society)
Hallituskatu 1, 00170 Helsinki
Mailing Address: PL 259, 00171 Helsinki
Tel: (09) 131231 *Fax:* (09) 1312 3219
Key Personnel
Secretary-General-Dir: Tuomas M S Lehtonen
Publisher: Paivi Vallisaari *Tel:* (09) 131 23 210 *E-mail:* paivi.vallisaari@finlit.fi
Founded: 1831
Subjects: Anthropology, History, Language Arts, Linguistics, Literature, Literary Criticism, Essays
ISBN Prefix(es): 951-717; 951-746
Number of titles published annually: 100 Print
Total Titles: 1,500 Print

Suomen Matkailuliitto ry (The Finish Travel Association)
Atomitie 5 C, 00370 Helsinki
Tel: (09) 622 6280 *Fax:* (09) 654 358
E-mail: matkailuliitto@matkailuliitto.org
Web Site: www.matkailuliitto.org
Founded: 1887
Subjects: Travel
ISBN Prefix(es): 951-838

Suomen Pipliaseura RY+
Kauppiaankatu 7, 00161 Helsinki
Mailing Address: PL 173, 00161 Helsinki
Tel: (09) 612 9350 *Fax:* (09) 612 935 11
E-mail: info@bible.fi; etunimi.sukunimi@bible.fi
Web Site: www.bible.fi
Founded: 1812
Specialize in Bibles, fund raising for Bible Society & development of teaching methods of the Bible.
Subjects: Biblical Studies
ISBN Prefix(es): 951-9010; 951-577

SV-Kauppiaskanava Oy+
Kruunuvuorenkatu 5A, 00160 Helsinki
Tel: (09) 10 53010 *Fax:* (09) 10 5336238
E-mail: kaija.tynkkynen@k-kauppasuitto.fi
Web Site: www.k-kauppasliitto.fi

Key Personnel
Man Dir: Rinta Perttu
Publishing Manager: Tommi Tanhuanpaa *Tel:* (09) 105336218 *Fax:* (09) 105336206 *E-mail:* tommi.tanhuanpaa@k-kauppasliitto.fi
Founded: 1912
Publishing House of the Finnish Retailers Association
Groceries, food, shoes, clothes, sports equipment, builders' & agricultural supplies.
Subjects: Cookery, Crafts, Games, Hobbies, House & Home
ISBN Prefix(es): 951-635

Svenska Oesterbottens Litteraturfoerening
Stagnas Vagen 85, 66640 Maxmo
Tel: (06) 3450286
Key Personnel
Contact: Gun Anderssen
Subjects: Poetry
ISBN Prefix(es): 951-95007

Tietotoeos Publishing Co
PL 22, 02881 Veikkola
Tel: (09) 2564475 *Fax:* (09) 8136361
E-mail: tt@jkttietoteos.fi
Web Site: www.jkttietoteos.fi
Key Personnel
Man Dir: Jyrki K Talvitie *E-mail:* jyrki.talvitie@tt.inet.fi
Founded: 1948
Subjects: Economics, Travel
ISBN Prefix(es): 951-9035; 951-8919

Ursa ry+
Raatimiehenkatu 3A2, 00140 Helsinki
Tel: (09) 684 0400 *Fax:* (09) 6840 4040
E-mail: ursa@ursa.fi
Web Site: www.ursa.fi
Key Personnel
Publications Dir: Markku Sarimaa *Tel:* (09) 6840 4060 *E-mail:* markku.sarimaa@ursa.fi
Founded: 1921
Subjects: Earth Sciences, Physical Sciences, Science (General)
ISBN Prefix(es): 951-9269; 952-5329

Osuuskunta Vastapaino+
Yliopistonkatu 60 A, 33100 Tampere
Tel: (03) 214 6246 *Fax:* (03) 214 6646
E-mail: vastapaino@vastapaino.fi
Web Site: www.vastapaino.fi
Key Personnel
Man Dir: Teijo Makkonen *E-mail:* teijo.makkonen@vastapaino.fi
Founded: 1981
Subjects: Behavioral Sciences, Education, History, Journalism, Literature, Literary Criticism, Essays, Philosophy, Social Sciences, Sociology, Women's Studies
ISBN Prefix(es): 951-9066; 951-768
Number of titles published annually: 25 Print
Total Titles: 180 Print

Watti-Kustannus Oy
Meritullinkatu 11 C, 00170 Helsinki
Tel: (09) 1356878 *Fax:* (09) 1356437
ISBN Prefix(es): 951-95945

Weilin & Goos Oy+
Kappelitie 8, 02200 Espoo
Mailing Address: PL 123, 02201 Espoo
Tel: (09) 4377 603 *Fax:* (00) 4377 334
E-mail: asiakaspalvelu@wg.fi
Web Site: www.wg.fi
Key Personnel
President: Koskinen Olle
Publishing Dir: Juhani Mikola
Editorial Manager, Nonfiction: Kuosmanen Riitta-Liisa
Information Officer: Irmeli Kotkavuori
Founded: 1872

Subjects: Animals, Pets, Art, Health, Nutrition, History, Nonfiction (General)
ISBN Prefix(es): 951-35
Parent Company: WSOY Group
Subsidiaries: Bertmark Media AB

Werner Soederstrom Osakeyhtio (WSOY)+
Division of SanomaWSOY Corporation
Bulevardi 12, 00120 Helsinki
Mailing Address: PO Box 222, 00121 Helsinki
Tel: (09) 61 681 *Fax:* (09) 616 3566
Key Personnel
Man Dir: Jorma Kaimio *E-mail:* jorma.kaimio@wsoy.fi
Foreign Rights Manager: Sirkku Klemola
 E-mail: sirkku.klemola@wsoy.fi
Literary Dir: Touko Siltala *E-mail:* touko.siltala@wsoy.fi
Educational Division: Hannu Laukkanen
 E-mail: hannu.laukkanen@wsoy.fi
Founded: 1878
Subjects: Education, Fiction, Nonfiction (General)
ISBN Prefix(es): 951-0
Associate Companies: Rautakirja Oy, Koivuvaarankuja 2, 01640 Vantaa *Tel:* (00) 85281 *Fax:* (00) 8533281; WS Bookwell, Teollisuustie 4, 06100 Porvoo *Tel:* (019) 21941 *Fax:* (019) 219 4802
Subsidiaries: Ajasto Osakeyhtio; Bertmark A/S; Bertmark Media AB; Bertmark Norge AS; Bertmarks Forlag AB; Weilin & Goos Oy
Book Club(s): Uudet Kirjat

WSOY, see Werner Soederstrom Osakeyhtio (WSOY)

Yliopistopaino/Helsinki University Press+
Teollisuuskatu 23B, University of Helsinki, 00014 Helsinki
Mailing Address: PO Box 26, University of Helsinki, 00014 Helsinki
Tel: (09) 7010 230; (09) 7010 2360 *Fax:* (09) 7010 2370
E-mail: sst@yopaino.yliopistopaino.helsinki.fi
Web Site: www.yliopistopaino.helsinki.fi
Key Personnel
Chief Executive: Reino Lantto
Dir of Publishing: Minna Laukkanen
Founded: 1987
Subjects: Behavioral Sciences, Biological Sciences, Communications, Drama, Theater, Education, Environmental Studies, Gay & Lesbian, Health, Nutrition, History, Journalism, Language Arts, Linguistics, Literature, Literary Criticism, Essays, Mathematics, Medicine, Nursing, Dentistry, Music, Dance, Psychology, Psychiatry, Social Sciences, Sociology, Theology, Travel, Women's Studies
ISBN Prefix(es): 951-570; 951-95164; 952-442
Parent Company: Helsinki University

Yritystieto Oy - Foretagsdata AB
PO Box 148, 00181 Helsinki
Tel: (00) 648292 *Fax:* (00) 648250
Key Personnel
Publisher: Boerje Thilman
Founded: 1972
Subjects: Business
ISBN Prefix(es): 951-9102

France

General Information

Capital: Paris
Language: French (regional dialects), Basque in the Basque country of the southwest, Breton in Brittany, Catalan in Roussillon, Corsican in Corsica, Dutch along parts of border with Belgium, German in Alsace, Occitan in south; most people in these minority linguistic groups also speak French
Religion: Predominantly Roman Catholic
Population: 59.3 million
Bank Hours: 0900-1200, 1400-1600 Monday-Friday. Some closed Monday.
Shop Hours: 0900-1930 Monday-Saturday. Many closed Monday
Currency: 100 Eurocents = 1 Euro; 6.55957 French francs = 1 Euro
Export/Import Information: Member of the European Economic Community. 5.5% VAT on books. Import licenses not required. There is a control of the book trade based on a number of legal and regulating provisions applying to the import of pirated publications, articles and writings that offend against morality and public order, publications harmful to youth, writings forbidden by the Minister for the Interior; the customs official must submit articles subject to control for examination by the General Information Service of the Ministry of the Interior.
Copyright: UCC, Berne, Buenos Aires, Florence (see Copyright Conventions, pg xi)

ABES, see Agence Bibliographique de l'Enseignement Superieur

Academie Nationale de Reims
17 rue du Jard, 51100 Reims
Tel: (0326) 910449 *Fax:* (0326) 910449
E-mail: academie.nationale.reims@wanadoo.fr
Key Personnel
Secretary General: Patrick Demouy *Tel:* (0326) 479819 *E-mail:* patrick.demouy@laposte.net
Administrative Secretary: Philippe Petit-Stervinou
Founded: 1841
Founded by Cardinal Gousset, archeveque de Reims.
Subjects: Biography, Communications, History
Total Titles: 500 Print
Foreign Rep(s): Champagne

Editions Accarias, see L'Originel - Editions Accarias

Editions ACLA+
5 bis, rue Saint Paul, 75004 Paris
Tel: (01) 48 04 00 75 *Fax:* (01) 42 77 72 98
Telex: 613814
Key Personnel
Man Dir: Thierry Schimpff
Founded: 1980
Subjects: Sports, Athletics
ISBN Prefix(es): 2-86519

ACR Edition+
20 ter, rue de Bezons, 92400 Courbevoie, Paris
Tel: (01) 47 88 14 92 *Fax:* (01) 43 33 38 81
E-mail: acredition@acr-edition.com
Web Site: www.acr-edition.com
Key Personnel
Man Dir, Rights & Permissions: A Rafif
Editorial: Mrs M P Kerbrat
Founded: 1983
Membership(s): Syndicat de L'Edition Groupe Art.
Subjects: Art
ISBN Prefix(es): 2-86770
Foreign Rep(s): Artbook International (London)

Actes-Graphiques+
67 ter Cours Fauriel, 42010 Saint-Etienne Cedex 2
Mailing Address: BP 81, 42010 Saint-Etienne Cedex 2
Tel: (04) 77 21 23 80; (06) 09 42 21 19 *Fax:* (04) 77 25 39 28
Web Site: www.actes-graphiques.com
Key Personnel
Dir: Georges Callet *E-mail:* georges.callet@free.fr
Founded: 1994
Subjects: Geography, Geology, Government, Political Science, Humor, Literature, Literary Criticism, Essays, Mysteries, Photography, Regional Interests, Religion - Catholic, Religion - Other
ISBN Prefix(es): 2-910868
Subsidiaries: Le Henaff-Action Graphique
Distributor for Action Graphique; Le Henaff

Editions Actes Sud+
BP 38, 13633 Arles Cedex
Tel: (04) 90 49 86 91 *Fax:* (04) 90 96 95 25
E-mail: contact@actes-sud.fr
Web Site: www.actes-sud.fr
Key Personnel
President: Hubert Nyssen
Man Dir: Francoise Nyssen
Editorial: Bertrand Py
Rights: Franck Benalloul
Foreign Rights: Elisabeth Beyer *Tel:* (04) 90 49 56 66 *E-mail:* e.beyer@actes-sud.fr
Financial Dir: Jean Paul Capitani
Founded: 1978
Subjects: Biography, Drama, Theater, Literature, Literary Criticism, Essays, Poetry
ISBN Prefix(es): 2-7427; 2-86869; 2-86943; 2-7274; 2-85376; 2-901567
Number of titles published annually: 300 Print
Imprints: Babel (paperback); Solin (nonfiction: essays, biographies & foreign literature); Travel Aventure; Cactus
Subsidiaries: Actes Sud Junior (Children books & literature); Babel (paperback); Sinbad (Arabv literatures & Islam); Solin (nonfiction: essays, biographies & foreign literature)
Branch Office(s)
18 rue Seguier, 75006 Paris *Tel:* (01) 55 42 63 00 *Fax:* (01) 55 42 63 01 *E-mail:* accueil.paris@actes-sud.fr
Distributor for Andre Dimanche; Lemeac; Paris-Musees
Bookshop(s): 47, rue du Docteur Fanton, 13200 Arles *Tel:* (04) 90495677 *E-mail:* librairie@actes-sud.fr; Le Mejan, Pl Nina Berberova, 13200 Arles *E-mail:* mejan@actes-sud.fr
Orders to: U D Union Distributors Flammarion, 2A Delta, 29-31 ave Guynemer, BP 403, Chevilly Lorue, 94152 Rungis Cedex

Action Artistique de la Ville de Paris
25 rue Saint-Louis-en-l'Ile, 75004 Paris
Tel: (01) 43 25 30 30 *Fax:* (01) 43 25 17 69
E-mail: aavp@club-internet.fr
Also specializes in Urbanism.
Subjects: Architecture & Interior Design, Art, History
ISBN Prefix(es): 2-905118; 2-913246
Total Titles: 70 Print
Distributor for CiD

ADPF Publications
6, rue Ferrus, 75683 Paris Cedex 14
Tel: (01) 43 13 11 00 *Fax:* (01) 43 13 11 25
Web Site: www.france.diplomatie.fr; www.adpf.asso.fr
Key Personnel
International Rights: Anne Parian
Service Communication: Anne du Parquet
Founded: 1996
Subjects: Art, Biography, Literature, Literary Criticism, Essays, Philosophy, Photography, Poetry
ISBN Prefix(es): 2-911127

Adrian+
12 rue Bachaumont, 75002 Paris
Tel: (01) 42 36 44 29 *Fax:* (01) 42 36 44 29
Key Personnel
Publisher: Paul Adrian
Specialize in spectacles of circus, cinema or variety.

ISBN Prefix(es): 2-900107
Total Titles: 9 Print

Adverbum SARL+
La Fresquiere, 04340 Meolans-Revel
Tel: (04) 92 81 28 81 *Fax:* (04) 92 81 37 11
E-mail: info@adverbum.fr
Web Site: www.adverbum.fr
Key Personnel
Manager: Michel Mirale
Founded: 1989
Subjects: Anthropology, Behavioral Sciences, Biblical Studies, Health, Nutrition, How-to, Language Arts, Linguistics, Medicine, Nursing, Dentistry, Religion - Catholic
ISBN Prefix(es): 2-907653; 2-911328; 2-914338; 2-911220
Number of titles published annually: 18 Print
Total Titles: 120 Print
Imprints: Editions Desiris; Editions Gregoriennes; Atelier Perrousseaux Editeur; Editions le Sureau

Agence Bibliographique de l'Enseignement Superieur
Unit of French Ministry for Higher Education
25, rue Guillaume Dupuytren, BP 4367, 34196 Montpellier Cedex 5
Tel: (04) 67 54 84 10 *Fax:* (04) 67 54 84 14
E-mail: nom@abes.fr
Web Site: www.abes.fr
Key Personnel
Dir: Sabine Barral *E-mail:* barral@abes.fr
Librarian: Anne Brigant *E-mail:* brigant@abes.fr
Founded: 1994
Membership(s): GFII, ADBS, IFLA, EUSIDIC & AFUGI.
Subjects: Library & Information Sciences
ISBN Prefix(es): 2-912292
Total Titles: 2 CD-ROM
Imprints: CCNPS
Branch Office(s)
Repertoire des bibliotheque
Distributed by Bibliopolis

Editions Al Liamm
venelle Poulbriken, 29200 Brest
Tel: (0298) 02 10 84
Key Personnel
Man Dir: Ronan Huon
Founded: 1949
This is a non-commercial organization specializing in the Breton Language.
Subjects: Drama, Theater, Education, Fiction, Literature, Literary Criticism, Essays, Poetry
ISBN Prefix(es): 2-7368; 2-902427
Parent Company: Association Al Liamm, 2 Venelle Poulbriquen, 29200 Brest
U.S. Office(s): Schoenhof's Foreign Books, Catalogue Dept, 76A Mount Auburn St, Cambridge, MA 02138, United States *Tel:* 617-5478855 *Fax:* 617-5478551
Stephen Griffin, 9 Irvington Rd, Medford, MA, United States
Orders to: R Huon L Vennelle Poulbriquen, 29200 Brest

Editions Albatros, see Editions Copernic

Alliance Biblique Universelle, *imprint of* Societe Biblique Francaise

Alsatia SA
4 pl de la Reunion, 68100 Mulhouse Cedex
Mailing Address: BP 66, 68051 Mulhouse
Tel: (03) 89 45 21 53 *Fax:* (03) 89 45 18 98
Key Personnel
Man Dir: Eric de Valence
Sales, Publicity, Advertising, Rights & Permissions: Virginie Poussier
Founded: 1896
Subjects: Biography, Education, History, How-to, Medicine, Nursing, Dentistry, Poetry, Religion - Other
ISBN Prefix(es): 2-7032
Bookshop(s): Librairie Alsatia, 31 pl de la Cathedrale, 67000 Strasbourg; Librairie Union, 28 rue des Tetes, 68000 Colmar; 26 rue Charles de Gaulle, 68130 Altkirch; 108 ruede la Republique, 68500 Guebwiller

Editions Alternatives+
5 rue de Pontoise, 75005 Paris
Tel: (01) 43 29 88 64 *Fax:* (01) 43 29 02 70
E-mail: info@editionsalternatives.com
Web Site: www.editionsalternatives.com
Key Personnel
President: Gerard Aime *Tel:* (01) 46 33 49 22
Founded: 1975
Subjects: Alternative, Architecture & Interior Design, Art, House & Home, How-to, Music, Dance, Photography
ISBN Prefix(es): 2-86227
Orders to: CDE, 17 rue de Tournon, 75006 Paris

Editions ALTESS+
4 rue des Petits Hotels, espace Harmonie, 75010 Paris
Tel: (01) 47 70 78 79 *Fax:* (01) 47 70 78 77
E-mail: eliaur@club-internet.fr
Web Site: www.ifrance.com/3eMillenaire/altess/index.htm
Key Personnel
Contact: Alain-Rene Gelineau
Founded: 1990
Subjects: Biography, Health, Nutrition, Poetry, Psychology, Psychiatry, Religion - Other, Spirituality; personal development
ISBN Prefix(es): 2-84243; 2-905219
Number of titles published annually: 15 Print
Total Titles: 160 Print
Distributed by LAVAL Distribution (Quebec Canada)
Distributor for Editions Voici la Clef (Here's the Key) (France)
Showroom(s): Espace Harmonie, 4 rue des Petits Hotels, 75010 Paris *Tel:* (01) 47 70 78 79 *Fax:* (01) 47 70 78 77
Warehouse: ALTESS-AR Gelineau, 95 Residence Vincennes, 77330 Ozoir-la-Ferriere *Tel:* (01) 64 40 35 89 *Fax:* (01) 64 40 27 57
Orders to: ALTESS-AR Gelineau, 95 Residence Vincennes, 77330 Ozoir-la-Ferriere *Tel:* (01) 64 40 35 89 *Fax:* (01) 64 40 27 57

Editions Alzieu+
BP 3045, 38816 Grenoble Cedex 1
Tel: (04) 76 51 09 51 *Fax:* (04) 76 51 09 51
E-mail: admin@editions-alzieu.com
Web Site: www.editions-alzieu.com
Key Personnel
Dir: Claude Alzieu
Founded: 1991
ISBN Prefix(es): 2-910717; 2-914093
Distributed by Brepols

Editions de l'Amateur+
25 rue Ginoux, 75015 Paris
Tel: (01) 45 77 08 05 *Fax:* (01) 45 79 97 15
Key Personnel
President-Dir General: Nuria Boussac
Subjects: Art
ISBN Prefix(es): 2-85917; 2-84647

Editions d'Amerique et d'Orient, Adrien Maisonneuve+
11 rue St-Sulpice, 75006 Paris
Tel: (01) 43 26 86 35 *Fax:* (01) 43 54 59 54
E-mail: maisonneuve@maisonneuve-adrien.com
Key Personnel
Man Dir: Jean Maisonneuve
Founded: 1926
Subjects: Art, Ethnicity, History, Philosophy, Religion - Other, Social Sciences, Sociology
ISBN Prefix(es): 2-7200
Imprints: Librairie D'Amerique Et D'Orient

Editions Amez+
One Sq de l'Aiguillage, 67100 Strasbourg
Tel: (03) 88 84 56 56 *Fax:* (03) 88 84 56 84
Key Personnel
Associate Editor: Christine Vanet
Founded: 1991
Subjects: Art
ISBN Prefix(es): 2-909242

L'Amitie par le Livre+
13 ave du 60 Ri, 25001 Cedex, Besancon
Mailing Address: BP 1031, 25001 Cedex, Besancon
Tel: (03) 81820894 *Fax:* (03) 81820894
Key Personnel
Dir General: Gerard Varin
Founded: 1930
Subjects: Biography, Education, Humor, Literature, Literary Criticism, Essays, Natural History, Photography, Poetry
ISBN Prefix(es): 2-7121

Editions Amphora SA+
14 rue de l'Odeon, 75006 Paris
Mailing Address: 27 rue Saint Andre des Arts, 75006 Paris
Tel: (01) 43 29 03 04; (01) 43 26 10 87 *Fax:* (01) 43 29 49 49; (01) 40 46 85 76
Web Site: www.ed-amphora.fr
Key Personnel
Man Dir & Publicity: Bernard Dubois
Founded: 1954
Subjects: Crafts, Games, Hobbies, Sports, Athletics
ISBN Prefix(es): 2-85180
Distributed by Dimedia (Canada); OLF Diffusion (Switzerland); Presses De Belgique (Belgium)

Editions Amrita SA+
Les Cheyroux, 24580 Plazac-Rouffignac
Tel: (05) 53 50 79 54 *Fax:* (05) 53 50 80 20
E-mail: amrita.editions@perigord.com
Key Personnel
PDG: Anne Meurois-Givaudan
Founded: 1984
Subjects: Art, Astrology, Occult, Health, Nutrition, How-to, Parapsychology, Philosophy, Religion - Other
ISBN Prefix(es): 2-904616; 2-911022

L'Anabase+
284 rue de Croisades, Les Jardins du Ponant, 11 bat H, 34280 La Grande-Motte
Tel: (04) 67561338 *Fax:* (01) 34858073
Key Personnel
Contact: Christian Molinier
Founded: 1991
Subjects: Literature, Literary Criticism, Essays, Philosophy, Psychology, Psychiatry, Social Sciences, Sociology
ISBN Prefix(es): 2-909535
Bookshop(s): Librairie Roudil, 53, rue Saint Jacques, 75005 Paris

Anako Editions+
236 Ave Victor Hugo, 94120 Fontenay-Sous-Bois
Tel: (01) 43 94 92 88 *Fax:* (01) 43 94 02 45
E-mail: anako.editions@anako.com
Web Site: www.anako.com
Key Personnel
Dir: Patrick Bernard
Sales & Administration: Jean-Marie Gehin
Founded: 1988
Subjects: Anthropology, Photography, Travel
ISBN Prefix(es): 2-907754

PUBLISHERS — FRANCE

Editions l'Ancre de Marine+
11 rue au Coq, 27400 Louviers
Tel: (02) 32 25 45 97
E-mail: service-clients@ancre-de-marine.com
Web Site: www.ancre-de-marine.com
Key Personnel
Dir: Bertrand de Queretain
Founded: 1985
Subjects: History, Maritime, Regional Interests
ISBN Prefix(es): 2-905970; 2-84141
Number of titles published annually: 20 Print
Total Titles: 200 Print
Parent Company: Syndicat National de l'edition
Imprints: Cifonit Figle
Distributed by Edilarge Ouest France

Editions d'Annabelle+
8 rue d'Anjou, 75008 Paris
Mailing Address: 11, rue Tronchet, 75008 Paris
Tel: (01) 47420161 *Fax:* (01) 47424214
Key Personnel
Manager: Lydia Rolland
Founded: 1991
Subjects: Animals, Pets
ISBN Prefix(es): 2-909660
Branch Office(s)
93 rue du Fg St, Monore, 75008 Paris
Bookshop(s): Sofedis, 29 rue St, Sulpice 6e, Paris
Warehouse: Sodis

Annales de l'Est, *imprint of* Presses Universitaires de Nancy

Annales du Bac, *imprint of* Librairie Vuibert

l'ANRT, see Atelier National de Reproduction des Theses

Edition Anthese+
30 ave Jean-Jaures, 94117 Arcueil Cedex
Tel: (01) 46 56 06 67 *Fax:* (01) 49 85 09 92
Telex: 202382 F
Key Personnel
Man Dir: Claude Draeger
Sales: Fransoise Benoit-Latour
Press: Cristina Campodonico
Founded: 1983
Subjects: Architecture & Interior Design, Art, Biography
ISBN Prefix(es): 2-904420; 2-912257
Orders to: Generale du Livre, 13 rue Ernest Cressou, 75014 Paris

Editions Anthropos+
49 rue Hericarte, 75015 Paris
Tel: (01) 45781292 *Fax:* (01) 45750567
Key Personnel
Man Dir: Maurice Guini
Manager: Pierre Guini
Founded: 1964
Subjects: Anthropology, Economics, Government, Political Science, History, Military Science, Philosophy, Social Sciences, Sociology
ISBN Prefix(es): 2-7157; 2-7178; 2-7178
Orders to: Editions Anthropos, Librairie des Sciences de l'Homme, 15 rue Lacepede, Paris 75005 *Tel:* (01) 45352247

APRD, see Association pour la Recherche et l'Information demographiques (APRD)

L'Arbalete
8 rue Paul-Bert, 69150 Decines
Tel: (04) 72933434 *Fax:* (04) 72933400
Subjects: Art, Literature, Literary Criticism, Essays
ISBN Prefix(es): 2-902375

Editions Arcam
40 rue de Bretagne, 75003 Paris

Tel: (01) 42729312
E-mail: phreatiq@multimania.com
Key Personnel
Man Dir: Lorris Murail
Editorial, Sales, Production & Publicity: Gerard Murail
Founded: 1971
Subjects: Art, Poetry
ISBN Prefix(es): 2-86476

L'Arche Editeur
86, rue Bonaparte, 75006 Paris
Tel: (01) 46 33 46 45 *Fax:* (01) 46 33 56 40
E-mail: contact@arche-editeur.com
Web Site: www.arche-editeur.com
Key Personnel
Dir: Rachel Rudolf
Stage Rights: Katharina Bismarck *Tel:* (01) 46 33 63 26
Bookstore Dept: Laurence Dorveaux *Tel:* (01) 46 33 57 47 *E-mail:* commande@arche-editeur.com
Founded: 1947
Publishes some of the most famous dramatic authors of the 19th & 20th centuries, also contemporary texts. Essays on art, music, cinema & philosophy.
Membership(s): SNE (Syndicate National de L'Edition).
Subjects: Art, Biography, Drama, Theater, Literature, Literary Criticism, Essays, Music, Dance, Philosophy, Psychology, Psychiatry, Social Sciences, Sociology
ISBN Prefix(es): 2-85181
Number of titles published annually: 15 Print
Total Titles: 436 Print
Foreign Rep(s): Claude M Diffusion (Canada)

Editions de l'Archipel+
34 rue des Bourdonnais, 75001 Paris
Tel: (01) 55 80 77 40 *Fax:* (01) 55 80 77 41
E-mail: ecricom@wanadoo.fr
Key Personnel
Dir: Jean-Daniel Belfond
Founded: 1991
Subjects: Biography, Fiction, Literature, Literary Criticism, Essays
ISBN Prefix(es): 2-84187; 2-909241
Number of titles published annually: 80 Print
Total Titles: 300 Print
Divisions: Editions Ecriture; Presses du Chatelet
Foreign Rep(s): Chloe Ataroff (USA); Arabella Cruse (Netherlands & Scandinavia); Anna Droumeva (Bulgaria, Romania, Serbia and Montenegro); Catherine Fragou-Rassinier (Greece); Laura Grandi (Italy); Judit Hermann (Croatia, Hungary); Jackie Huang (China); Asli Karasuil (Turkey); Pauline Kim (Korea); Eva Koralnik (Germany); Efrat Lev (Israel); Corinne Quentin (Japan); Ingrida Sniedze (Baltic States); Maria Strarz-Kanska (Poland); Ludmilla Sushkova (Russia); Petra Tobiskova (Czech Republic, Slovenia); Anne-Marie Vallat (Spain)

Architecture-Modelisme, *imprint of* Editions l'Instant Durable

Publications Aredit+
357 blvd Gambetta, 59200 Tourcoing
Tel: (03) 20 26 79 81
Telex: 130372 F
Key Personnel
Editor: Emile Keirsbilk
Editorial, Publicity: Yves Catteloin
Subjects: Fiction, Military Science, Romance, Science Fiction, Fantasy, Western Fiction
ISBN Prefix(es): 2-7346; 2-7311

Editions de l'Armancon+
24, rue de l'Hotel-de-Ville, 21390 Precy-sous-Thil

Mailing Address: BP 14, 21390 Precy-sous-Thil
Tel: (03) 80 64 41 87 *Fax:* (03) 80 64 46 96
Web Site: www.editions-armancon.fr
Key Personnel
Dir: Gerard Gautier
Founded: 1987
Subjects: Art, Biography, Cookery, History, Literature, Literary Criticism, Essays, Photography, Regional Interests, Wine & Spirits
ISBN Prefix(es): 2-906594; 2-84479
Number of titles published annually: 10 Print
Total Titles: 110 Print

Armand Colin Drott, *imprint of* Editions Dalloz Sirey

Armenia Editions+
Chemin des Veufs, 13112 La Destrousse
Tel: (06) 08 22 71 50 *Fax:* (06) 08 27 85 94
Key Personnel
Contact: Elisabeth Tavitian
Founded: 1991
Membership(s): American Booksellers Association.
Subjects: Architecture & Interior Design, Art, Biography, Cookery, History, Language Arts, Linguistics, Literature, Literary Criticism, Essays, Music, Dance, Poetry, Regional Interests, Religion - Other, Romance, Theology, Travel, Armenian Art, Armenian History, Armenian Literature, Religion-Apostolic
ISBN Prefix(es): 2-88421

Arnette+
224, blvd Saint-Germain, 75007 Paris
Tel: (01) 45496500 *Fax:* (01) 45491288
Telex: 270150F TXFRA 690
Key Personnel
General Dir: Gil Raveux
Founded: 1915
Subjects: Medicine, Nursing, Dentistry
ISBN Prefix(es): 2-7184
Parent Company: Blackwell Scientific Publications, United Kingdom
U.S. Office(s): Blackwell Scientific Publication, Boston, MA, United States
Orders to: One rue d Lille, 75007 Paris *Tel:* (01) 44860770 *Fax:* (01) 44860766

Editions Art & Metiers Du Livre+
110, ave de Villiers, 75017 Paris
Tel: (01) 42 27 32 36 *Fax:* (01) 47 63 25 52
E-mail: infos@faton.fr
Web Site: www.art-metiers-du-livre.com
Key Personnel
Dir: Louis Faton
Publicity: Marie Garrigue
Founded: 1994
Subjects: Art, Presse-edition
ISBN Prefix(es): 2-911071
Total Titles: 3 Print

Art Creation Realisation, see ACR Edition

Arthaud, *imprint of* Flammarion SA

Artprice+
BP 69, 69270 Saint-Romain-au-Mont-d'Or
Tel: (04) 72 421 706 *Fax:* (04) 78 220 606
Web Site: www.artprice.com
Key Personnel
Dir General: Jacques Madina
ISBN Prefix(es): 2-909711
Parent Company: Groupe Serveur

ASA Editions
18, rue Laffitte, 75009 Paris
Tel: (01) 47 70 42 90 *Fax:* (01) 47 70 42 98
E-mail: info@asaeditions.fr
Web Site: www.asaeditions.fr

147

FRANCE

Key Personnel
Administrative & Sales Manager: Marc Wiltz
Dir Commercial/Export: Catherine Sas
ISBN Prefix(es): 2-911589

L'Asiatheque, see Langues & Mondes-L'Asiatheque

Editions Assimil SA
13 rue Gay-Lussac, 94431 Chennevieres-sur-Marne Cedex
Mailing Address: BP 25, 94331 Chennevieres-sur-Marne Cedex
Tel: (01) 45 76 87 37 *Fax:* (01) 45 94 06 55
E-mail: contact@assimil.com
Web Site: www.assimil.com
Key Personnel
Dir & Editorial: J L Cherel
Sales, Advertising: J P Vandenhende
Production: A Blanquet
Founded: 1929
Subjects: Language Arts, Linguistics
ISBN Prefix(es): 90-74996; 2-7005; 88-86968
Bookshop(s): Boutique Assimil, 11, rue des Pyramides, 75001 Paris *Tel:* (01) 42 60 40 66 *Fax:* (01) 40 20 02 17

L'Association
16 rue de la Pierre-Levee, 75011 Paris
Tel: (01) 43558587 *Fax:* (01) 43558621
E-mail: lassocia@club-internet.fr
Key Personnel
President: Jean-Christophe Menu
Founded: 1990
ISBN Prefix(es): 2-909020; 2-84414

Association pour la Recherche et l'Information demographiques (APRD)
Universite de Paris-Sorbonne, 191 rue Saint-Jacques, 75005 Paris
Tel: (01) 44321400 *Fax:* (01) 40462588
Key Personnel
Chairman & President: Gerard-Francois Dumont *E-mail:* Gerard-Francois.Dumont@paris4.sorbonne.fr
Founded: 1976
Subjects: Social Sciences, Sociology
ISBN Prefix(es): 2-86419
Total Titles: 27 Print

Editions de l'Atelier+
12 ave Soeur Rosalie, 75013 Paris
Tel: (01) 44089515 *Fax:* (01) 44089500
Key Personnel
President: Daniel Prin
Editor: Bernard Stephan
Foreign Rights: Valerie Francois
Sales Manager: Patrick Merrant
Founded: 1939
Subjects: Biblical Studies, Biography, Economics, Government, Political Science, History, Religion - Catholic, Social Sciences, Sociology
ISBN Prefix(es): 2-7082

Atelier National de Reproduction des Theses
9 rue Auguste Angellier, 59046 Lille Cedex
Tel: (03) 20 30 86 73 *Fax:* (03) 20 54 21 95
E-mail: anrt@univ-lille3.fr
Web Site: www.anrtheses.com.fr
Key Personnel
Dir: Elisabeth Fichez
Founded: 1971
Reproduction sur micro-fiches et numerisation de theses universitaires soutenues en France.
Subjects: Art, Geography, Geology, History, Language Arts, Linguistics, Law, Literature, Literary Criticism, Essays, Philosophy, Psychology, Psychiatry, Social Sciences, Sociology
ISBN Prefix(es): 2-284; 2-7295
Distributed by Presses du Septentrion (Universite Lille III at Villeneuve d'Ascq)

Ateliers et Presses de Taize+
71250 Taize-Communaute
Tel: (03) 85 50 30 50 *Fax:* (03) 85 50 30 55
E-mail: editions@taize.fr
Web Site: www.taize.fr
Key Personnel
Contact: Reynold Gallusser
Founded: 1959
Subjects: Religion - Catholic, Religion - Protestant
ISBN Prefix(es): 2-85040
Number of titles published annually: 2 Print
Imprints: Les Presses de Taize

Editions Atlantica Seguier+
Rue du Loustalot, Blvd du BAB, 64600 Anglet
Tel: (05) 59 52 84 00 *Fax:* (05) 59 52 84 01
E-mail: atlantica@atlantica.fr
Web Site: www.atlantica.fr
Key Personnel
Literary Dir: Marie-Helene Saphore *Tel:* (05) 59 52 84 07 *E-mail:* mhs@atlantica.fr
Founded: 1992
Subjects: Art, Biography, Drama, Theater, Fiction, Literature, Literary Criticism, Essays
ISBN Prefix(es): 2-84049

Editions Atlas
89 rue de la Boetie, 75008 Paris
Tel: (01) 40 74 38 38 *Fax:* (01) 45 61 19 85
E-mail: contact@editionsatlas.fr
Web Site: www.editionsatlas.fr
Telex: 642481F
Key Personnel
Contact: Patrick Lemarchand
ISBN Prefix(es): 2-7312
Branch Office(s)
1186, rue de Cocherel, Evreux *Tel:* (032) 29 29 29 *E-mail:* serviceclients@editionsatlas.fr

ATP - Packager+
ZA les Vignettes, 63405 Chamalieres Cedex
Mailing Address: BP 75, 63405 Chamalieres Cedex
Tel: (0473) 19 58 80 *Fax:* (0473) 195899
E-mail: atp.chamalieres@wanadoo.fr
Key Personnel
Dir: Herve Chaumeton
International Rights: Isabelle Leyris-Chambon *Tel:* 473195896
Founded: 1984
Subjects: Aeronautics, Aviation, Animals, Pets, Archaeology, Automotive, Cookery, Earth Sciences, Gardening, Plants, Health, Nutrition, History, House & Home, Natural History, Outdoor Recreation, Wine & Spirits
Number of titles published annually: 100 Print

Aubanel Editions+
93-95, rue Vendome, 69006 Lyon
Tel: (04) 78 94 61 42; (04) 78 94 21 73
Key Personnel
Man Dir: Laurent Theodore-Aubanel
Founded: 1744
Subjects: Fiction, Psychology, Psychiatry, Regional Interests, Travel
ISBN Prefix(es): 2-7006
Branch Office(s)
4, rue Pedro Meylan, 1208 Geneva, Switzerland *Tel:* (022) 7365110 *Fax:* (022) 7352402

Editions de l'Aube+
Le Moulin de Chateau, 84240 La-Tour-d'Aigues
Tel: (04) 90 07 46 60 *Fax:* (04) 90 07 53 02
Key Personnel
Man Dir: Jean Viard
Literary Dir: Marion Hennebert
Founded: 1987
Subjects: Cookery, Economics, Environmental Studies, Foreign Countries, Literature, Literary Criticism, Essays, Mysteries, Philosophy, Social Sciences, Sociology
ISBN Prefix(es): 2-87678
Distributed by Editions Zoe (Switzerland)

Aubie, *imprint of* Flammarion SA

Editions Aubier-Montaigne SA
26, rue Racine, 75278 Paris Cedex 06
Tel: (01) 40 51 31 00 *Fax:* (01) 43 29 21 48
Key Personnel
Man Dir: Mrs M Aubier-Gabail
Sales Manager, Rights & Permissions: Patrice Mentha
Founded: 1924
Subjects: Education, History, Language Arts, Linguistics, Philosophy, Poetry, Psychology, Psychiatry, Religion - Other, Social Sciences, Sociology
ISBN Prefix(es): 2-7007
Parent Company: Flammarion et Cie

Etudes Augustiniennes, see Institut d'Etudes Augustiniennes

Editions d'Aujourd'hui (Les Introuvables)
c/o L'Harmattan, 5-7 rue de l'Ecole-Polytechnique, 75005 Paris
Tel: (01) 43547910 *Fax:* (01) 43298620
Key Personnel
Man Dir: Odette Charriere
Founded: 1974
Subjects: Drama, Theater, Ethnicity, Fiction, Film, Video, Human Relations, Literature, Literary Criticism, Essays, Music, Dance, Poetry
ISBN Prefix(es): 2-7307; 2-85775
Distributed by UNIVERS (Canada)
Bookshop(s): 16 rue des ecoles, 75005 Paris *Tel:* (01) 40 46 79 11; (01) 40 46 79 20

Aurore Editions D'Art, *imprint of* Editions Cercle d'Art SA

Autrement Editions
77 rue du Faubourg Saint-Antoine, 75011 Paris
Tel: (01) 44 73 80 00 *Fax:* (01) 44 73 00 12
E-mail: contact@autrement.com
Web Site: www.autrement.com
Key Personnel
President, Chief Executive Officer & Dir, Publication: Henry Dougier *E-mail:* henry.dougier@autrement.com
Sales & Transfer of Rights: Anne-Marie Bellard *E-mail:* commercial@autrement.com
Founded: 1975
Subjects: Anthropology, Behavioral Sciences, Fiction, Foreign Countries, History, Literature, Literary Criticism, Essays, Natural History, Nonfiction (General), Philosophy, Psychology, Psychiatry, Regional Interests, Social Sciences, Sociology, Travel
ISBN Prefix(es): 2-86260; 2-7467
Total Titles: 700 Print
Distributed by Editions du le Seuil

Autres Temps+
97, ave de la Gouffonne, 13009 Marseille
Tel: (0491) 26 80 33 *Fax:* (0491) 41 11 01
Key Personnel
Contact: Gerard Blua
Founded: 1990
Subjects: Literature, Literary Criticism, Essays
ISBN Prefix(es): 2-908805; 2-911873; 2-84521
Total Titles: 200 Print
Imprints: Litterature Generale

Editions Philippe Auzou+
24-32 rue des Amandiers, 75020 Paris
Tel: (01) 40338400 *Fax:* (01) 47972008
Telex: Auzou Sofradif 220686 F

Key Personnel
Man Dir: M Philippe Auzou
Dir: M van Gendt; J Gerlag
Founded: 1978
Subjects: Art
ISBN Prefix(es): 2-7338
Subsidiaries: A Diffusion-Sofradif

Editions l'Avant-Scene de Prette Technique+
6 rue Git-le-Coeur, 75006 Paris
Tel: (01) 46342820 *Fax:* (01) 43545014
Key Personnel
Man Dir: Jacques Leclere
Founded: 1949
Subjects: Drama, Theater, Film, Video, Music, Dance
ISBN Prefix(es): 2-907468
Warehouse: 6 Mail Nord, 5350 Boynes

Babel, *imprint of* Editions Actes Sud

Bac en Poche, *imprint of* Librairie Vuibert

Editions J B Bailliere
2, cite Paradis, 75010 Paris
Tel: (01) 55 33 69 00 *Fax:* (01) 55 33 68 07
Telex: Livrcom 201326 F
Key Personnel
Dir General: Dr Philippe Le Due
Rights & Permissions: Arlette Hertig
Advertising: Marika Papageoriou
Founded: 1802
Subjects: Agriculture, Labor, Industrial Relations, Medicine, Nursing, Dentistry, Technology
ISBN Prefix(es): 2-7008

La Baleine, *imprint of* Editions du Seuil

Editions Balland+
33 rue Saint-Andre des Arts, 75006 Paris
Tel: (01) 43 25 74 40 *Fax:* (01) 46 33 56 21
E-mail: info@balland.fr
Web Site: www.balland.fr
Key Personnel
Publisher: Jean-Jacque Auj-ier
Sales: Jean-Paul Hirsch
Founded: 1966
Subjects: Biography, Fiction, Film, Video, Humor
ISBN Prefix(es): 2-7158

La Bartavelle
39, rue des Tanneries, 42190 Charlieu
Tel: (02) 37821450 *Fax:* (02) 37821463
Key Personnel
Publications Dir: Eric Ballandras
Subjects: Literature, Literary Criticism, Essays, Photography
ISBN Prefix(es): 2-87744

Editions A Barthelemy+
Domaine de Fontvert, 84132 Le Pontet Cedex
Mailing Address: BP 50, 84132 Le Pontet Cedex
Tel: (04) 90 03 60 00 *Fax:* (04) 90036009
E-mail: infos@editions-barthelemy.com
Web Site: www.editions-barthelemy.com
Key Personnel
Editor: Alain Barthelemy; Odile Barthelemy
Founded: 1978
Subjects: Cookery, Health, Nutrition, Regional Interests, Travel
ISBN Prefix(es): 2-87923

Societe Nouvelle Rene Baudouin+
10, rue de Nesle, 75006 Paris
Tel: (01) 43290050 *Fax:* (01) 43257241
Key Personnel
President: Alain Levy *E-mail:* al.levy@wanadoo.fr
Founded: 1974
Remainder dealer.

Subjects: Antiques, Art, Cookery
ISBN Prefix(es): 2-86396
Total Titles: 4 Print
Divisions: Le Dernier Terrain Vague; Levy; Editions Charles Moreau

Bayard Editions, *imprint of* Bayard Presse

Bayard Presse+
3, rue Bayard, 75008 Paris
Tel: (01) 44 35 60 60 *Fax:* (01) 44 35 61 61
Web Site: www.bayardpresse.com
Key Personnel
President: Alain Cordier
Dir: Frederic Boyer
Sales & Marketing Dir: Anne Duchemin
Dir, Communication: Emmanuelle Duthu *Tel:* (01) 44 35 60 73
  E-mail: communication@bayard-presse.com
Founded: 1873
Specialize in Essays, Adult Books.
Subjects: Art, Education, Religion - Other
ISBN Prefix(es): 2-227; 2-7009; 2-7470
Number of titles published annually: 60 Print
Imprints: Bayard Editions; Centurion
Orders to: Sofedis, The Soufflot, 75005 Paris

Editions des Beatitudes, Pneumatheque+
Burtin, 41600 Nouan le Fuzelier
Tel: (02) 54 88 21 18 *Fax:* (02) 54 88 97 73
E-mail: edd.etrangers@wandadoo.com
Web Site: www.editions-beatitudes.fr
Key Personnel
Foreign Rights Manager: Laurence de Feydean
Founded: 1984
Subjects: Religion - Catholic
ISBN Prefix(es): 2-905480; 2-84024

Beauchesne Editeur+
72 rue des Saints-Peres, 75007 Paris
Tel: (01) 45 48 80 28 *Fax:* (01) 42 22 59 79
Key Personnel
Contact: Mr Jean Pierre Druaud
Editorial: Mdme Francoise Druaud
Founded: 1851
Subjects: Biography, Government, Political Science, History, Human Relations, Journalism, Literature, Literary Criticism, Essays, Religion - Other, Social Sciences, Sociology, Theology
ISBN Prefix(es): 2-7010
Total Titles: 800 Print; 1 CD-ROM; 1 Audio
Distributed by O L F S A (Suisse)
Distributor for Anne Sigier France (Belgique & Luxembourg); Anne Sigier (Canada)

Editions Belin+
8, rue Ferou, 75278 Paris Cedex 06
Tel: (01) 55 42 84 00 *Fax:* (01) 43 25 18 29
E-mail: contact@edition-belin.fr
Web Site: www.editions-belin.com
Key Personnel
President: Marie Claude Brossollet
Documentation: Soraya Eghbal-Dupouey
Marketing: Emmanuel Fouquet
Rights & Permissions: Anne Vignau
  E-mail: anne.vignau@editions-belin.fr
Founded: 1777
Subjects: Art, Education, Gardening, Plants, Literature, Literary Criticism, Essays, Poetry, Science (General)
ISBN Prefix(es): 2-7011
Number of titles published annually: 150 Print; 5 CD-ROM; 10 Audio
Total Titles: 2,000 Print; 40 Audio
Subsidiaries: Editions Herscher; Pour la Science SARL
Shipping Address: Editions Belin, 4 rue Ferdinand de Lesseps, 91420 Morangis
Warehouse: Editions Belin, 4 rue Ferdinand de Lesseps, 91420 Morangis *Tel:* (01) 69090097 *Fax:* (01) 69348198

Societe d'Edition Les Belles Lettres+
95 Blvd Raspail, 75006 Paris
Tel: (01) 44398420 *Fax:* (01) 45449288
E-mail: courrier@lesbelleslettres.com
Web Site: www.lesbelleslettres.com
Key Personnel
President & Man Dir: Michel Desgranges
International Rights: Marie Jose D'Hoop
Founded: 1919
Subjects: Education, Fiction, History, Language Arts, Linguistics, Literature, Literary Criticism, Essays, Philosophy, Religion - Other, Classical studies
ISBN Prefix(es): 2-251
Imprints: Manitoba; Sortileges
Bookshop(s): Librairie Guillaume Bude, Paris

Berg International Editeur+
129 blvd Saint-Michel, 75005 Paris
Tel: (01) 43267273 *Fax:* (01) 46339499
Cable: BERGEDIT PARIS
Key Personnel
Man Dir: Georges Nataf
Contact: Marie Gougaud
Founded: 1969
Subjects: Anthropology, History, Literature, Literary Criticism, Essays, Philosophy, Religion - Islamic, Religion - Jewish, Religion - Other
ISBN Prefix(es): 2-900269; 2-911289
Orders to: Press Universitairs de France, 14 Ave du Boisdel' Epi, 91003 Evry

Berger-Levrault Editions SAS
5, rue Andre Ampere, 54250 Champigneulles
Mailing Address: BP 79, 54250 Champigneulles
Tel: (03) 83 38 83 83 *Fax:* (03) 83 38 86 10; (03) 83 38 37 12
E-mail: ble@berger-levrault.fr
Web Site: www.berger-levrault.fr
Telex: 270797 F
Key Personnel
President Dir General: Alain Sourisseau
Dir General: Gilles Brochen
Founded: 1676
Subjects: Architecture & Interior Design, Art, Ethnicity, History, Social Sciences, Sociology
ISBN Prefix(es): 2-7013
Parent Company: Berger-Levrault Imprimerie, Nancy
Branch Office(s)
3, rue Ferrus, 75014 Paris *Tel:* (01) 40644232 *Fax:* (01) 40644230 *E-mail:* ble@berger-levrault.fr
Bookshop(s): Librairie Berger-Levrault, 23 pl Broglie, F-67000 Strasbourg

Editions Bertout
6 rue Gutenberg, 76810 Luneray
Mailing Address: BP 7, 76810 Luneray
Tel: (02) 35 04 69 68 *Fax:* (02) 35 04 69 65
Web Site: www.editionsbertout.com
Key Personnel
Dir: Florence Bertout
Founded: 1934
Subjects: Cookery, Genealogy, History, Regional Interests
ISBN Prefix(es): 2-86743
Imprints: La Memoire Normande

Editions Bertrand-Lacoste
36 rue Saint-Germain-l'Auxerrois, 75041 Paris Cedex 01
Tel: (01) 53 40 53 53 *Fax:* (01) 42 33 82 47
E-mail: contact@bertrand-lacoste.fr
Web Site: www.bertrand-lacoste.fr
Founded: 1980
Subjects: Accounting, Computer Science, Economics, Law
ISBN Prefix(es): 2-7399; 2-7352

FRANCE

La Bibliotheque des Arts+
3, Place de l'Odeon, 75006 Paris
Tel: (01) 46331818 *Fax:* (01) 40469596
Key Personnel
Chairman: Francois Daulte
Founded: 1954
Subjects: Architecture & Interior Design, Art, Literature, Literary Criticism, Essays, Poetry, Travel
ISBN Prefix(es): 2-85047; 2-88453
Distributor for Ides & Calendes

Bibliotheque Nationale de France (National Library of France)+
58, rue de Richelieu, 75084 Paris Cedex 02
Tel: (01) 53 79 59 59; (01) 53 79 81 75; (01) 53 79 87 94 *Fax:* (01) 53 79 81 72
E-mail: commercial@bnf.fr
Web Site: www.bnf.fr
Key Personnel
President: Jean-Noel Jeanneney
Head, Publications & Sales: Christopher Beslon *Tel:* (01) 53 79 88 01 *E-mail:* christopher.beslon@bnf.fr
Publishing department of the French National Library.
Subjects: History, Library & Information Sciences, Literature, Literary Criticism, Essays
ISBN Prefix(es): 2-7177
Number of titles published annually: 30 Print
Total Titles: 500 Print
Foreign Rep(s): Sevil (World)

Societe Biblique Francaise+
5 Ave des Erables, 95400 Villiers-le-Bel
Mailing Address: BP 47, 95400 Villiers-le-Bel
Tel: (01) 39945051 *Fax:* (01) 39905351
E-mail: contacts@alliance-biblique-fr.org
Web Site: www.la-bible.net
Key Personnel
Editorial: Elsbeth Scherrer *E-mail:* elsbethscherrer@wanadoo.fr
Sales & Production: Pascal Dubs
Founded: 1818
Membership(s): United Bible Societies/Alliance Biblique Universelle.
Subjects: Religion - Catholic, Religion - Protestant
ISBN Prefix(es): 2-85300
Total Titles: 140 Print
Imprints: Alliance Biblique Universelle
U.S. Office(s): American Bible Society, 1865 Broadway, New York, NY 10023-9980, United States
Distributed by CERF; Excelsis; Oberlin
Distributor for Brepols; CERF; CLC; Desclee de Brower; Farel; Vie et Sante

Adam Biro Editions+
28, rue de Sevigne, 75004 Paris
Tel: (01) 44 59 84 59 *Fax:* (01) 44 59 87 17
Key Personnel
Editor: Adam Biro
Editor & Publicity: Laurence Golstennel
Author: Daniel Arasse; Bernard Comment; Georges Didi-Huberman; Ernst Gombrich; Tzvetan Todorov
Founded: 1987
Subjects: Antiques, Architecture & Interior Design, Art, Fashion, Photography
ISBN Prefix(es): 2-87660
Number of titles published annually: 20 Print
Total Titles: 285 Print
Distributor for Office du Livre (Switzerland); Presse de Belgique (Beligum)
Warehouse: Vilo, 21 Leval 11 ave Arago, Morangis
Orders to: Vilo, 25 rue Ginoux, 75015 Paris

William Blake & Co+
15, rue Maubec, 33037 Bordeaux Cedex
Mailing Address: BP 4, 33037 Bordeaux Cedex
Tel: (05) 56 31 42 20 *Fax:* (05) 56 31 45 47
E-mail: editions.william.blake@wanadoo.fr
Web Site: www.editions-william-blake-and-co.com
Key Personnel
Publications Dir: Jean-Paul Michel
Founded: 1976
Subjects: Architecture & Interior Design, Art, Literature, Literary Criticism, Essays, Philosophy, Photography, Poetry
ISBN Prefix(es): 2-84103; 2-905810
Imprints: L'Invention du Lecteur; La Pharmacie de Platon
Distributor for Arts & Arts

Librairie Scientifique et Technique Albert Blanchard, see Librairie Scientifique et Technique Albert Blanchard

Blay Foldex
40-48 rue des Meuniers, 93108 Montreuil Cedex
Tel: (01) 49 88 92 10 *Fax:* (01) 49 88 92 09
Founded: 1934
Subjects: How-to
Parent Company: Langenscheidt Publishing Group, Munich, Germany

Blondel La Rougery SARL
268, rue de Brement, 93561 Rosny-Sous-Bois Cedex
Tel: (01) 48 94 94 52 *Fax:* (01) 48 94 94 38
Key Personnel
Chairman: J Barbotte
Founded: 1902
Subjects: Advertising, Foreign Countries, Geography, Geology, How-to, Public Administration, Transportation
ISBN Prefix(es): 2-903862

De Boccard Edition-Diffusion
11, rue de Medicis, 75006 Paris
Tel: (01) 43 26 00 37 *Fax:* (01) 43 54 85 83
Key Personnel
Man Dir: Dominique Chaulet
Manager: Jean-Bernard Chaulet
Founded: 1866
Subjects: Archaeology, Art, Asian Studies, History, Religion - Other
ISBN Prefix(es): 2-7018

Editions Andre Bonne+
29 rue Marceau, 94200 Ivry-sur-Seine
Tel: (01) 45150061 *Fax:* (01) 45218175
Key Personnel
Dir General: Annet-Georges Aupois
Dir, Literature: Alain Armand-Villoy
Subjects: Art, Biography, Crafts, Games, Hobbies, History, Literature, Literary Criticism, Essays, Poetry, Travel
ISBN Prefix(es): 2-7019

Bookmaker+
12, rue Servandoni, 75006 Paris
Tel: (01) 43 54 84 34 *Fax:* (01) 43 54 71 02
E-mail: bookmake@club-internet.fr
Key Personnel
Editor: Jean-Loup Chiflet
Founded: 1985
Specialize in packaging.
Subjects: Art, Astronomy, Gardening, Plants, Bookart & Artist's Books, Edutainment, Picture Books
ISBN Prefix(es): 2-906986

Bordas, *imprint of* Editions Bordas

Editions Bordas+
89, blvd Auguste Blanqui, 75013 Paris
Tel: (01) 44395445 *Fax:* (01) 44394350
Web Site: www.editions-bordas.com
Key Personnel
General Manager: Jean Lissarrague
Man Dir: Dominique Desmottes; Didier Tetaud
Editorial, Trade: Philippe Fournier-Bourdier
Editorial, School: Alain Cardona
Sales, France: Jean-Michel Angenault
Sales, Export: Alain Guilermin
Production: Francoise Barbera
Publicity, Trade: Dominique de Romanet
Publicity, School: Isabelle Brunelin
Rights & Permissions: Mireille Debenne
Founded: 1946
Subjects: Education, Nonfiction (General)
ISBN Prefix(es): 2-04; 2-7294; 2-7109
Parent Company: Groupe de la Cite, 20 ave Hoche, F-75008 Paris
Imprints: Bordas; Pedagogie Modern; Technique et Vulgarisation
Subsidiaries: Societe Gauthier-Villars; Privat SA; Dunod Editeur SA (all France); Bordas-Dunod Bruxelles
Bookshop(s): Librairie Dunod, 30 rue St-Sulpice, 75006 Paris; Librairie Beranger, Liege, Belgium
Warehouse: Route d'Etampes, 45330 Malesherbes *Tel:* (01) 38349249 *Fax:* (01) 38347385
Orders to: 11 rue Gossin, 92543 Montrouge Cedex *Tel:* (01) 46565266 *Fax:* (01) 46560476

Pierre Bordas & Fils, Editions
25 rue Saint Sulpice, 75006 Paris
Tel: (01) 43 25 04 51 *Fax:* (01) 43 25 47 84
E-mail: pierre.bordas.filsd@wanadoo.fr
Key Personnel
Man Dir: Nicole Bordas
Editorial, Rights & Permissions: Pierre Bordas
Founded: 1978
Subjects: Art, Cookery, Crafts, Games, Hobbies, Education, Environmental Studies, Literature, Literary Criticism, Essays, Poetry, Travel
ISBN Prefix(es): 2-86311
Distribution Center: NQL, 78 Bd Saint Michel, 75280 Paris Cedex 06

Presses Universitaires de Bordeaux (PUB)+
Universite Michel de Montaigne Bordeaux 3, Domaine Universitaire, 33607 Pessac cedex
Tel: (05) 57 12 44 22 *Fax:* (05) 57 12 45 34
E-mail: pub@montaigne.u-bordeaux.fr
Web Site: www.pub.montaigne.u-bordeaux.fr
Key Personnel
Dir General: Bernard Gilbert *Tel:* (05) 5712 4421
Dir Commercial: Antoine Poli *Tel:* (05) 5712 4634
Founded: 1983
Subjects: Anthropology, Education, Environmental Studies, Geography, Geology, History, Law, Literature, Literary Criticism, Essays, Philosophy, Wine & Spirits
ISBN Prefix(es): 2-86781
Orders to: CID, 131 blvd Saint-Michel, 75005 Paris *Tel:* (01) 43 54 47 15 *Fax:* (01) 43 54 80 73 *E-mail:* cid@msh-paris.fr
Nord-Sud, 150, rue Berthelot, 1190 Brussels, Belgium *Tel:* (02) 343 10 13 *Fax:* (02) 343 42 91
University of Exeter Press, Reed Hall, Streatham Drive, Exeter EX4 4QR, United Kingdom *Tel:* (01392) 263066 *Fax:* (01392) 263064 *E-mail:* uep@exeter.ac.uk *Web Site:* www.ex.ac.uk/uep/

Bornemann, *imprint of* Editions Sang de la Terre

Editions Bornemann
62, rue Blanche, 75009 Paris
Tel: (01) 42 82 74 44 *Fax:* (01) 48 74 14 88
Key Personnel
Manager: Pierre C Lahaye
Founded: 1829
Subjects: Animals, Pets, Art, Environmental Studies, How-to, Sports, Athletics
ISBN Prefix(es): 2-85182

PUBLISHERS   FRANCE

Bottin SA
4, rue Andre Boulle, 94941 Creteil Cedex 9
Tel: (01) 49 81 56 56 *Fax:* (01) 49 81 56 76
Telex: 262 407 F
Key Personnel
President: Jean Paul Devai
Founded: 1796
Subjects: Agriculture, Business, Finance, Human Relations, Medicine, Nursing, Dentistry, Sports, Athletics
ISBN Prefix(es): 2-7039
Parent Company: Editions du Juris-Classeur
Ultimate Parent Company: Reed Elsevier plc

Christian Bourgois, see Presses de la Cite

Christian Bourgois Editeur
116 rue du bac, Paris 75007
Tel: (01) 45 44 09 13 *Fax:* (01) 45 44 87 86
E-mail: bourgois-editeur@wanadoo.fr
Web Site: www.christianbourgois-editeur.fr
Key Personnel
Contact: Dominique Bourgois *E-mail:* dominique.bourgois2@wanadoo.fr
Subjects: Fiction, Essays, Music
ISBN Prefix(es): 2-267

Editions Colin Bourrelier, see Armand Colin, Editeur

Bragelonne+
15 rue Girard, 93100 Montreuil
Tel: (01) 48 18 19 70; (01) 48 18 19 71 *Fax:* (01) 48 18 02 47
E-mail: info@bragelonne.fr
Web Site: www.bragelonne.fr
Key Personnel
Senior Editor: Stephane Marsan *E-mail:* s.marsan@bragelonne.fr; Alain Nevant *Tel:* (01) 4818 1971 *E-mail:* a.nevant@bragelonne.fr
Founded: 2000
Subjects: Crafts, Games, Hobbies, Fiction, Film, Video, History, Humor, Literature, Literary Criticism, Essays, Mysteries, Radio, TV, Science Fiction, Fantasy
ISBN Prefix(es): 2-914370
Number of titles published annually: 16 Print
Total Titles: 8 Print
Foreign Rights: L'Agebce de l'Est (Bulgaria, Croatia, Czech Republic, Estonia, Germany, Latvia, Lithuania, Poland, Slovak Republic, Slovenia)
Distribution Center: Harmonia Mundi, Mas de Vert, BP 150, 13631 Arles Cedex, Frederic Salbans *Tel:* (04) 9049 9049 *Fax:* (04) 9049 9614 *E-mail:* fsalbans@harmoniamundi.com

Editions Breal
One rue de Rome, 93561 Rosny-sous-Bois Cedex
Tel: (01) 48 12 22 22 *Fax:* (01) 48 12 22 39
E-mail: infos@editions-breal.fr
Web Site: www.editions-breal.fr
Key Personnel
Man Dir: Jean-Michel Zunquin
Founded: 1969
Subjects: Accounting, Advertising, Biological Sciences, Communications, Computer Science, Economics, Electronics, Electrical Engineering, History, Language Arts, Linguistics, Law, Management, Marketing, Mathematics, Philosophy, Physical Sciences, Physics
ISBN Prefix(es): 2-85394; 2-84291
Associate Companies: ABC Editions
Bookshop(s): Librairie Des Prepas, 34 rue Serpente, 75006 Paris
Orders to: Breal Diffusion, Bat No 9, 20 rue Escoffier, 94671 Charenton Cedex

Emgleo Breiz+
10 rue de Quimper, 29200 Brest
Tel: (02) 98 44 89 42 *Fax:* (02) 98 02 68 17

E-mail: andrelemercier@hotmail.com; brud.nevez@wanadoo.fr
Web Site: emgleo.breiz.online.fr
Key Personnel
Man Dir, Rights & Permissions: M le Mercier
Sales: Miss Allain
Production: M le Gall
Publicity: M Keravel
Founded: 1954
ISBN Prefix(es): 2-900828; 2-911210

Editions Jacques Bremond+
Le Clos de la Cournilhe, 30210 Remoulins-sur-Gardon
Tel: (04) 66 57 45 61; (06) 78 51 48 15 *Fax:* (04) 66 37 27 40
E-mail: editions-jacques-bremond@wanadoo.fr
Key Personnel
Chairman: Jacques Bremond
Founded: 1975
Subjects: Drama, Theater, Literature, Literary Criticism, Essays, Poetry
ISBN Prefix(es): 2-910063; 2-903108; 2-915519
Number of titles published annually: 10 Print
Total Titles: 300 Print

Alain Brethes Editions+
7, rue du Port, 44470 Thouare-sur-Loire
Mailing Address: 3, rue de la Liberte Le Parc, 78280 Guyancourt
Tel: (02) 40 77 35 11; (02) 51 13 04 55
Key Personnel
Editor: Alain Brethes
Subjects: Astrology, Occult, Health, Nutrition, Human Relations, Philosophy, Psychology, Psychiatry
ISBN Prefix(es): 2-906803

Editions BRGM+
3 Ave Claude-Guillemin, 45060 Orleans Cedex 02
Mailing Address: PO Box 6009, 45060 Orlcans Cedex 02
Tel: (02) 38 64 30 28 *Fax:* (02) 38 64 36 82
E-mail: editions@brgm.fr
Web Site: editions.brgm.fr
Key Personnel
Dir: Florence Jaudin *Tel:* (02) 38 64 31 61 *E-mail:* f.jaudin@brgm.fr
Founded: 1962
BRGM is the Office of Geological & Mineral Research in France & French Geological Survey.
Subjects: Earth Sciences, Environmental Studies, Geography, Geology
ISBN Prefix(es): 2-7159; 2-901709
Number of titles published annually: 20 Print
Total Titles: 800 Print; 80 E-Book; 3 Audio
Parent Company: BRGM, 39-43 quai Andre Citroen, 75739 Paris Cedex 15

Brud Nevez
6 rue Beaumarchais, 29200 Brest
Tel: (02) 98 44 89 42 *Fax:* (02) 98 02 68 17
Key Personnel
Man Dir: M Le Mercier
Subjects: Education, Fiction, Geography, Geology, Language Arts, Linguistics, Literature, Literary Criticism, Essays, Maritime, Poetry, Travel
ISBN Prefix(es): 2-86775
Divisions: Ar Skol Vrezoneg, Engelo Breiz, Liogam

Editions Buchet-Chastel Pierre Zech Editeur+
18 rue de Conde, 75006 Paris
Tel: (01) 44 32 05 60 *Fax:* (01) 44 32 05 61
E-mail: buchet.chastel@wanadoo.fr
Web Site: www.theatre-contemporain.net/editions/buchet/buchet.htm
Key Personnel
Dir: Pierre Zech
Founded: 1986

Subjects: Art, Biblical Studies, Crafts, Games, Hobbies, Education, Photography, Religion - Catholic, Theology
ISBN Prefix(es): 2-7020; 2-283
Imprints: Le Seneve; Le Temps apprivoise; Lethielleux
Subsidiaries: Marque le Temps Apprivoise

Editions du Buot
chez Acte 3 212, rue Saint-Maur, 75010 Paris
Tel: (01) 53388110 *Fax:* (01) 53388119
Founded: 1975
Subjects: Art, Travel
ISBN Prefix(es): 2-908480

Bureau des Longitudes
Formerly IMC Editions
3, rue Mazarine, 75006 Paris
Tel: (01) 43 26 59 02 *Fax:* (01) 43 26 80 90
E-mail: contact@bureau-des-longitudes.fr
Web Site: www.bureau-des-longitudes.fr
Key Personnel
President: Suzanne Debarbat
Vice President: Francois Barlier
Founded: 1795
Subjects: Earth Sciences, Science (General), Space Science

Cactus, *imprint of* Editions Actes Sud

Editions du Cadratin+
Division of MCP Sarl
13, rue Lafayette, 75009 Paris
Tel: (01) 42 81 52 23 *Fax:* (01) 42 82 17 01
Key Personnel
Editor: Marie-Claude Dufourneaud
Founded: 1979
Subjects: Art, History, Literature, Literary Criticism, Essays
ISBN Prefix(es): 2-86549

Editions des Cahiers Bourbonnais+
rue de l'Horloge, 03140 Charroux
Tel: (0470) 568 061 *Fax:* (0470) 568 080
Web Site: www.cahiers-bourbonnais.com
Key Personnel
Dir: Jean-Pierre Petit *E-mail:* j-p.petit@cahiers-bourbonnais.com
Founded: 1957
Subjects: Agriculture, Archaeology, Art, Business, History, Literature, Literary Criticism, Essays, Poetry, Publishing & Book Trade Reference
ISBN Prefix(es): 2-85370

Editions Cahiers d'Art
14 rue du Dragon, 75006 Paris
Tel: (01) 45487673 *Fax:* (01) 45449850
E-mail: cahiersart@aol.com
Key Personnel
Man Dir: Yves de Fontbrune
Founded: 1926
Subjects: Art
ISBN Prefix(es): 2-85117

Cahiers du Cinema+
9, passage de la Boule-Blanche, 75012 Paris
Tel: (01) 53 44 75 75 *Fax:* (01) 43 43 95 04
Key Personnel
Dir General: Claudine Paquot; Serge Toubiana
Contact: Pierre Zins
Founded: 1951
Subjects: Drama, Theater
ISBN Prefix(es): 2-86642

Les Cahiers Fiscaux Europeens Sarl+
51 Ave Reine Victoria, 06000 Nice
Tel: (04) 93 53 89 39 *Fax:* (04) 93 53 66 28
E-mail: auteurs@fontaneau.com
Key Personnel
Man Dir: Simone Branca
Founded: 1968
Subjects: Economics

ISBN Prefix(es): 2-85444
Parent Company: Societe d'Etudes Juridiques Internationales et Fiscales, Nice
Subsidiaries: CFE Belgique

Cahiers Rouges, *imprint of* Societe des Editions Grasset et Fasquelle

Editions Calmann-Levy SA+
3 rue Auber, 75009 Paris
Tel: (01) 47 42 38 33 *Fax:* (01) 47 42 77 81
Key Personnel
President & Man Dir: Denis Bourgeois
    E-mail: dbourgeois@calmann_levy.fr
Sales Dir: Marc Grinsztajn
Rights & Permissions: Heidi Warneke
    E-mail: hwarneke@calmann_levy.fr
Founded: 1836
Subjects: Biography, Economics, Fiction, History, Humor, Philosophy, Psychology, Psychiatry, Science Fiction, Fantasy, Social Sciences, Sociology, Sports, Athletics
ISBN Prefix(es): 2-7021
Orders to: Hachette Distribution, ZA de Coignieres, One Avenue Gutenberg, 78316 Maurepas Cedex

Editions Canal+
8 av du Maine, 75015 Paris
Tel: (01) 42222730 *Fax:* (01) 42223025
Key Personnel
Man Dir: Richard Ducousset
Editorial Dir: Herve Desinge
Public Relations: Soraya Devisscher
Rights & Permissions: Joschi Guitton
Founded: 1991
Subjects: Humor, Nonfiction (General), Sports, Athletics
ISBN Prefix(es): 2-911493

Canal+ Editions, *see* Editions Canal

Editions Canope+
20 Bd Gambetta, 63400 Chamalieres
Tel: (04) 73 93 82 90 *Fax:* (04) 73 39 33 00
Key Personnel
Dir: Marcel Antonio
Founded: 1984
Subjects: Art, Biography, History, Regional Interests
ISBN Prefix(es): 2-906320
Number of titles published annually: 2 CD-ROM
Total Titles: 30 Print

La Capitelle, *imprint of* Editions Casteilla

Editions Caracteres+
7, rue de l'Arbalete, 75005 Paris
Tel: (01) 43 37 96 98 *Fax:* (01) 43 37 26 10
E-mail: caracteres2000@aol.com
Web Site: www.editions-caracteres.fr
Key Personnel
Contact: Bruno Durocher
Founded: 1950
Subjects: Philosophy, Poetry
ISBN Prefix(es): 2-85446
Distributed by Alterdis

Editions Didier Carpentier
7 rue Saint-Lazare, 75009 Paris
Tel: (01) 48780072 *Fax:* (01) 42829199
Key Personnel
Manager: Didier Carpentier
Founded: 1982
Subjects: Crafts, Games, Hobbies, House & Home
ISBN Prefix(es): 2-84167; 2-906962
Total Titles: 250 Print

Editions Casteilla+
10, rue Leon Foucault, 78184 Saint-Quentin en Yvelines Cedex
Tel: (01) 30 14 19 30 *Fax:* (01) 34 60 31 32
E-mail: info@casteilla.fr
Web Site: www.casteilla.fr
Key Personnel
Manager: Marinus Visser *Tel:* (01) 30141945
    E-mail: visser@chiron.as
Founded: 1950
Specialize in textbooks, vocational training.
Subjects: Art, Economics, Law, Vocational Training
ISBN Prefix(es): 2-7135
Number of titles published annually: 100 Print
Total Titles: 800 Print
Parent Company: VisLand SA
Imprints: La Capitelle; Desforges; Educalivre; Techniplus

Editions Casterman+
36, rue du Chemin-Vert, 75011 Paris
Tel: (01) 55 28 12 00 *Fax:* (01) 55 28 12 60
Web Site: www.casterman.com
Telex: 200001 F Edicast
Key Personnel
President: Didier Platteau
Dir: Jacques Simon
Sales Dir: Simon Casterman
Publicity, Advertising Dir: Odile Mardon
Rights & Permissions: Ivan Noerdinger
Founded: 1780 (Tournai; 1857 Paris)
Subjects: Antiques, Archaeology, Architecture & Interior Design, Art, Cookery, Fiction, History, How-to
ISBN Prefix(es): 90-303
Subsidiaries: Districast

Le Castor Astral+
53, rue Carnot, 33130 Begles
Mailing Address: BP 11, 33038 Bordeaux Cedex
Tel: (01) 48 40 14 95 *Fax:* (01) 48 45 97 52
E-mail: swproduction@magic.fr
Key Personnel
Man Editor: Marc Torralba
Founded: 1975
Subjects: Literature, Literary Criticism, Essays
ISBN Prefix(es): 2-85920

CCNPS, *imprint of* Agence Bibliographique de l'Enseignement Superieur

CELSE, *see* Compagnie d'Editions Libres, Sociales et Economiques (CELSE)

Cemagref Editions+
Parc de Tourvoie, 92163 Antony Cedex
Mailing Address: BP 44, 92163 Antony Cedex
Tel: (01) 4096 61 21 *Fax:* (01) 4096 60 36
E-mail: info@cemagref.fr
Web Site: www.cemagref.fr
Key Personnel
Regional Dir: Gerard Sachon
Dir General: Patrick Ravarde
Dir: M Nicolas de Menthiere *Tel:* (01) 40 96 61 87 *Fax:* (01) 40 96 61 39 E-mail: nicolas.dementhiere@cemagref.fr
Chief of Service: Mdme Odile Hologne *Tel:* (01) 40 96 60 96 E-mail: odile.hologne@cemagref.fr
Subjects: Agriculture, Earth Sciences, Engineering (General), Environmental Studies, Mechanical Engineering
ISBN Prefix(es): 2-85362

Editions Cenomane+
33-39 rue des Ponts Neufs, 72000 Le Mans
Tel: (02) 43242157 *Fax:* (02) 43771916
Key Personnel
Dir General: Alain Mala
Founded: 1986
Subjects: Art, History, Literature, Literary Criticism, Essays, Military Science, Regional Interests, Transportation
ISBN Prefix(es): 2-905596
Number of titles published annually: 5 Print
Total Titles: 100 Print

Cent Pages
27, rue Nicolas-Chorier, 38009 Grenoble Cedex
Mailing Address: BP 291, 38009 Grenoble Cedex
Tel: (04) 38 12 16 20 *Fax:* (04) 38 12 16 29
E-mail: editions@editions-centpages.fr
Web Site: www.editions-centpages.fr
Key Personnel
Literary Dir: Gadet Olivier
    E-mail: aministrateur@editions-centpages.fr
ISBN Prefix(es): 2-906724
Distributed by Les Belles Lettres

Center Technique Industriel de la Fonderie, *see* CTIF (Center Technique Industriel de la Fonderie)

Centre de Formation et de Perfectionnement des Journalistes, *see* Les Editions du CFPJ (Centre de Formation et de Perfectionnement des Journalistes) - Sarl Presse et Formation

Centre de Librairie et d'Editions Techniques (CLET)
c/o Dunod, 15 rue Gossin, 92543 Montrouge Cedex
Tel: (01) 40926500 *Fax:* (01) 40926550
Telex: 634916
Key Personnel
Man Dir: Binnen Dyke
Editorial & Sales: Philippe Gualino
Founded: 1975
Subjects: Accounting, Economics, Finance, Law, Management
ISBN Prefix(es): 2-85354
Bookshop(s): Librairie CLET, 15 rue Gossin, 92543 Montrouge

Centre de Recherche d'Etude et de Documentation en Economie de la Sante, *see* CREDES - Centre de Recherche d'Etude et de Documentation en Economie de la Sante

Centre National de Documentation Pedagogique (CNDP)+
29, rue d'Ulm, 75230 Paris Cedex 05
Tel: (01) 55 43 60 00 *Fax:* (01) 55 43 60 01
Web Site: www.cndp.fr/cndp_reseau
Key Personnel
Dir: Alain Coulon
Publisher of multimedia works under direction of the Minister of Education.
Subjects: Education
ISBN Prefix(es): 2-240
Bookshop(s): 13, rue du Four, 75006 Paris
Tel: (01) 46 34 54 80 *Fax:* (01) 46 34 82 01
Distribution Center: 4, ave du Futuroscope Teleport 1, BP 80158, 86961 Futuroscope Cedex
Tel: (05) 49 49 78 09

Centre national de la recherche scientifique editions, *see* CNRS Editions

Centre pour l'Innovation et la Recherche en Communication de l'Entreprise (CIRCE)+
20 rue de l'Arcade, 75008 Paris
Tel: (01) 49 24 96 76
Key Personnel
Dir: Claude Lutz
Founded: 1988
Subjects: Drama, Theater, Fiction, Literature, Literary Criticism, Essays, Nonfiction (General), Philosophy, Poetry
ISBN Prefix(es): 2-9505426
Orders to: Harmonia Mundi, Le Mas de Vert, 13200 Arles

PUBLISHERS

Centre Technique National d'Etudes et de Recherches sur les Handicaps et les Inadaptations, see CTNERHI - Centre Technique National d'Etudes et de Recherches sur les Handicaps et les Inadaptations

Centurion, *imprint of* Bayard Presse

CEP Editions
17 rue d'Uzes, 75002 Paris
Tel: (01) 42961550 *Fax:* (01) 48243489
Telex: 680 876 f
Key Personnel
President: Christian Bregou
Subjects: Architecture & Interior Design, Technology
ISBN Prefix(es): 2-281
Associate Companies: Editions du Moniteur
Subsidiaries: Librairie Larousse
Branch Office(s)
rue d'Uzes, 75002 Paris *Tel:* (01) 42961550

Cepadues Editions SA+
111, rue Nicolas Vauquelin, 31100 Toulouse
Tel: (05) 61 40 57 36 *Fax:* (05) 61 41 79 89
E-mail: cepadues@cepadues.com
Web Site: www.cepadues.com
Key Personnel
President: Jean-Claude Joly
Dir: Annie Joly
Sales Manager & International Rights: Jean-Pierre Marson
Founded: 1969
Specialize in scientific & technical books.
Subjects: Aeronautics, Aviation, Computer Science, Education, Mathematics, Mechanical Engineering, Science (General), Technology, Transportation
ISBN Prefix(es): 2-85428
Total Titles: 200 Print

Editions Cercle d'Art SA+
10, rue Sainte-Anastase, 75003 Paris
Tel: (01) 48 87 92 12 *Fax:* (01) 48 87 47 79
E-mail: info@officieldesarts.com
Web Site: www.officieldesarts.com/cercledart/
Telex: 206685 Cerdart
Key Personnel
Man Dir: Philippe Monsel
Founded: 1950
Subjects: Art
ISBN Prefix(es): 2-7022
Imprints: Diagonales; Aurore Editions D'Art

CERDIC-Publications+
11 Rue Jean Sturm, 67520 Nordheim
Tel: (0388) 877107 *Fax:* (0388) 877125
E-mail: cerdic@wanadoo.fr
Key Personnel
Man Dir: Marie Zimmerman
Founded: 1968
Subjects: History, Law, Religion - Catholic, Religion - Islamic, Religion - Jewish, Religion - Protestant, Religion - Other, Social Sciences, Sociology, Women's Studies
ISBN Prefix(es): 2-85097
Total Titles: 1 Print

Editions du Cerf
29 bd La Tour-Maubourg, 75340 Paris Cedex 07
Tel: (01) 44 18 12 12 *Fax:* (01) 45 56 04 27
Web Site: www.editionsducerf.fr
Key Personnel
General Dir: P Moity
Editorial Dir: D Barrios-Delgado; F D Boespflug; B Lauret; N J Sed
Sales Dir, Publicity & Advertising: P Marion
Rights & Permissions: Mrs F de Chassey
Founded: 1929
Subjects: Biblical Studies, History, Philosophy, Religion - Other, Social Sciences, Sociology
ISBN Prefix(es): 2-204
Distributed by Fides; Labor & Fides Medialogue; Novalis; Saint Paul
Warehouse: 3 Chemin de Prunais, 94350 Villiers sp Marne

CF, *imprint of* References cf

CF, see References cf

CFAG, *imprint of* Compagnie Francaise des Arts Graphiques SA

Chadwyck-Healey France (CHF)+
50 rue de Paradis, 75010 Paris
Tel: (01) 44 83 81 81 *Fax:* (01) 44 83 81 83
Key Personnel
Man Dir: Jean-Pierre Sakoun
Sales: Charles Myara
Founded: 1985
Publisher of CD-ROMs.
ISBN Prefix(es): 2-86976
Parent Company: Chadwyck-Healey Ltd, United Kingdom
Associate Companies: Chadwyck-Healey, Spain
U.S. Office(s): Chadwyck-Healey Inc, 1101 King St, Alexandria, VA 22314, United States

Editions du Chalet+
15-27, rue de Poussorgski, 75018 Paris
Tel: (01) 53263335 *Fax:* (01) 53263336
Telex: 202036 F (Begedis SA)
Key Personnel
Publishing Manager: Bernard Le Bras
Founded: 1946
Subjects: Biblical Studies, Religion - Catholic, Religion - Other, Theology
ISBN Prefix(es): 2-7023
Associate Companies: Editions Desclee et Cie; Editions Gamma; Nouvelles Editions Mame; Editions Universitaires
Orders to: Begedis, 11 rue Duguay-Trouin, 75006 Paris
Arc-en-Ciel International, ZI Tournai Ouest, 7713 Marquain, Belgium (Foreign)

Editions Jacqueline Chambon+
route de Sauve, 30900 Nimes
Tel: (04) 23 23 27 *Fax:* (04) 26 55 02
Founded: 1988
Subjects: Art, Literature, Literary Criticism, Essays, Philosophy, Photography
ISBN Prefix(es): 2-87711
Total Titles: 150 Print
Shipping Address: Harmonia Mundi, BP 150, 13631 Arles Cedex *E-mail:* webmaster@harmoniamundi.com
Orders to: Harmonia Mundi, BP 150, 13631 Arles Cedex

Champ Libre, *imprint of* Ivrea

Editions Champ Vallon+
01420 Seyssel
Tel: (04) 50 56 15 51 *Fax:* (04) 50 56 15 64
E-mail: info@champ-vallon.com
Web Site: www.champ-vallon.com
Key Personnel
Editor: Patrick Beaune
International Rights: Myriam Monteiro-Braz
E-mail: myriam.monteiro@champ-vallon.com
Founded: 1980
Subjects: Biography, Fiction, History, Literature, Literary Criticism, Essays, Philosophy, Poetry, Psychology, Psychiatry, Social Sciences, Sociology
ISBN Prefix(es): 2-87673; 2-903528
Total Titles: 440 Print

FRANCE

Distributed by Presses Universitaires de France; Union Diffusion
Foreign Rights: Marion Colas

Champs Dominos, *imprint of* Flammarion SA

Librairie des Champs-Elysees/Le Masque+
17, rue Jacob, 75006 Paris
Tel: (01) 44 41 74 50; (01) 44 41 74 00 *Fax:* (01) 43 26 91 04
Web Site: www.lemasque.com
Key Personnel
Dir General: Isabelle Laffont
Editorial Dir: Helene Bihery
Founded: 1927
Subjects: Criminology, Mysteries
ISBN Prefix(es): 2-7024
Parent Company: Hachette Livre
Imprints: Editions du Masque; Club des Masques

Philippe Chancerel Editeur
17, route de Meulan, 78480 Verneuil-sur-Seine
Tel: (01) 39 65 69 18
Telex: 314235 F
Key Personnel
Chairman: Philippe Chancerel
Founded: 1960
Subjects: Crafts, Games, Hobbies, Humor, Sports, Athletics
ISBN Prefix(es): 2-907390
Associate Companies: Chancerel Publishers Ltd, United Kingdom

Editions Chardon Bleu+
29 rue Charton, 69600 Oullins
Mailing Address: BP 3050, 14018 Caen Cedex 02
Tel: (04) 72 39 02 13 *Fax:* (04) 72 39 04 03
E-mail: chardonbleued@aol.com
Web Site: www.chardonbleu.com
Key Personnel
Responsible: Claude Four; Dominique Isnard
Founded: 1983
ISBN Prefix(es): 2-86833
Orders to: BP 3050, 14018 Caen Cedex

Editions du Chariot+
BP 14, 28190 Saint Georges S/Eure
Tel: (02) 37258989 *Fax:* (02) 37258900
E-mail: edchariot@aol.com
Web Site: www.editions-du-chariot.com
Key Personnel
Publisher & Editor: Liliane Genin-Muchery
Tel: (02) 37258662
Founded: 1927
Subjects: Astrology, Occult, Parapsychology
ISBN Prefix(es): 2-85371

Editions Charles-Lavauzelle SA+
BP 8, 87350 Panazol
Tel: (05) 55584500 *Fax:* (05) 55584543
Key Personnel
Man Dir: Jean Claude Mazaud
Publicity & Production: Henri Chabrier
Founded: 1830
Subjects: Law, Military Science, Sports, Athletics
ISBN Prefix(es): 2-7025
Branch Office(s)
20 rue de Saint Petersbourg, 75008 Paris Cedex
Tel: (01) 43874230

Chasse Maree
Abri du Marin, rue Henri Barbusse, 29177 Douarnenez Cedex
Tel: (02) 98 92 66 33 *Fax:* (02) 98 92 04 34
E-mail: chasse-maree@glenat.com
Web Site: www.chasse-maree.com
Key Personnel
Dir: Jacques Glenat
Dir General: Olivier Blanche
Founded: 1981

Subjects: Art, Crafts, Games, Hobbies, History, How-to, Maritime, Music, Dance
ISBN Prefix(es): 2-903708; 2-914208

Editions du Chene+
Quai de Grenelle, 75905 Paris Cedex 15
Tel: (01) 43 92 30 00 *Fax:* (01) 43 92 33 81
Key Personnel
Man Dir: Isabelle Jendron
Rights & Co-Editions Manager: Sherri Aldis
Editorial Dir: Philippe Pierrelee
Founded: 1941
Specializes in illustrated books.
Subjects: Architecture & Interior Design, Art, Cookery, Travel
ISBN Prefix(es): 2-85108
Number of titles published annually: 65 Print
Parent Company: Hachette Livre SA
Imprints: Editions du Chene, EPA
Orders to: Hachette Livre SA, 43, Quai de Grenelle, 75905 Paris Cedex 15

Le Cherche Midi Editeur+
23 rue du Cherche-Midi, 75006 Paris
Tel: (01) 42 22 71 20 *Fax:* (01) 45 44 08 38
E-mail: infos@cherche-midi.com
Web Site: www.cherche-midi.com
Key Personnel
President, General Binding: Philippe Heracles
General Dir: Jean Orizet
Founded: 1978
Subjects: Aeronautics, Aviation, Animals, Pets, Astrology, Occult, Biography, Cookery, Fiction, History, Humor, Journalism, Literature, Literary Criticism, Essays, Nonfiction (General), Poetry, Romance, Science (General), Social Sciences, Sociology, Sports, Athletics, Transportation
ISBN Prefix(es): 2-86274; 2-7491
Distributed by Servidis for Switzerland; ADP for Canada; Dilibel for Belgium
Foreign Rights: Chantal Galtier Roussel (Brazil, China, Eastern Europe, Greece, Japan); Patricia Berg (Australia, Africa, UK, Germany, Israel, Italy, Netherlands & Scandinavia, South Africa, South America, Spain & Portugal, Turkey, USA)

CHF, see Chadwyck-Healey France (CHF)

Editions Chiron+
10, rue Leon-Foucault, 78184 Montigny-le-Bretonneux
Tel: (01) 30141930 *Fax:* (01) 34603132
E-mail: chiron@wanadoo.fr
Key Personnel
Chairman: Denys Ferrando-Durfort
Promotion & Foreign Rights: Chantal Ferrando-Durfort
Founded: 1906
Subjects: Aeronautics, Aviation, Automotive, Health, Nutrition, How-to, Music, Dance, Outdoor Recreation, Psychology, Psychiatry, Sports, Athletics
ISBN Prefix(es): 2-7027

Chotard et Associes Editeurs
One av Edouard-Belin, 92856 Rueil-Malmaison
Tel: (01) 41 29 96 05 *Fax:* (01) 41 29 98 15
Key Personnel
Man Dir: Nicole Boinet
Founded: 1969
Subjects: Economics, Engineering (General), Management, Marketing, Psychology, Psychiatry, Social Sciences, Sociology
ISBN Prefix(es): 2-7127
Orders to: Sofedis, 29 rue St Sulpice, 75006 Paris

Chronique Sociale+
7, rue du Plat, 69288 Lyon Cedex 02
Tel: (04) 78372212 *Fax:* (04) 78420318
E-mail: chroniquesociale@wanadoo.fr
Web Site: www.chroniquesociale.com
Key Personnel
Commercial Dir: Andre Soutrenon
Founded: 1920
Subjects: Human Relations, Philosophy, Psychology, Psychiatry, Religion - Other, Self-Help, Social Sciences, Sociology
ISBN Prefix(es): 2-85008
Number of titles published annually: 25 Print
Total Titles: 550 Print
Distributor for Couleurs Savoirs (Brussels); Beauchemin (Canada); Presses Universite Laval (PUL) (Canada)

Cicero Editeurs+
6, rue de la Sorbonne, 75005 Paris
Tel: (01) 43544757 *Fax:* (01) 40517385
Founded: 1989
Subjects: Art, Drama, Theater, Literature, Literary Criticism, Essays, Music, Dance
ISBN Prefix(es): 2-908369
Orders to: Klincksieck, 18 rue de Lille, 75007 Paris

Cifonit Figle, *imprint of* Editions l'Ancre de Marine

CILF, see Counseil International de la Langue Francaise

Cimaise sarl
95 rue Vieille du Temple, 75003 Paris
Tel: (01) 45437045 *Fax:* (01) 45437045
Key Personnel
Publication Dir: Nartine Arnault-tran
Founded: 1953
Art magazine (contemporary art).

Cirad+
Avenue Agropolis, 34398 Montpellier Cedex 5
Tel: (04) 67 61 58 00 *Fax:* (04) 67 61 55 47
Web Site: www.cirad.fr
Key Personnel
Head, Publication Unit: Martine Seguier-Guis *Tel:* (0467) 61 44 86 *E-mail:* seguier@cirad.fr
Promotion & Export: Christiane Jacquet *E-mail:* christiane.jacquet@cirad.fr
Founded: 1985
Subjects: Agriculture, Veterinary Science, Tropical Agronomy, Scientific & Technical Books
ISBN Prefix(es): 2-87614
Total Titles: 250 Print; 50 CD-ROM

CIRCE, see Centre pour l'Innovation et la Recherche en Communication de l'Entreprise (CIRCE)

Editions Circonflexe+
12 rue de la Montagne Sainte Genevieve, 75005 Paris
Tel: (01) 46 34 77 77 *Fax:* (01) 43 25 34 67
E-mail: info@circonflexe.fr
Web Site: www.circonflexe.fr
Telex: 200128
Key Personnel
Dir: Paul Fustier
Commercial Dir: Benoit Rouillard
Founded: 1989
Subjects: Art, Education, Fiction, History, Humor, Language Arts, Linguistics
ISBN Prefix(es): 2-87833
Parent Company: Info Media Communication
Orders to: Dilisco, 122 rue Marcel Hartmann, 92400 Ivry sur Seine

Editions Citadelles & Mazenod+
33 rue de Naples, 75008 Paris
Tel: (01) 53043060 *Fax:* (01) 45220427
E-mail: info@citadelles-mazenod.com
Web Site: www.citadelles-mazenod.com
Key Personnel
President & Dir General: Francois de Waresquiel
Editorial Manager: Agnes de Gorter *Tel:* (01) 53043064 *E-mail:* a.degorter@citadelles-mazenod.com
Commercial Manager: Ludovic du Ranquet *Tel:* (01) 53043066 *E-mail:* l.duranquet@citadelles-mazenod.com
Foreign Rights: Clair Morizet *Tel:* (01) 53043070 *E-mail:* c.morizet@citadelles-mazenod.com
Founded: 1936
Specialize in architecture & art.
Subjects: Architecture & Interior Design, Art
ISBN Prefix(es): 2-85088
Number of titles published annually: 12 Print
Total Titles: 80 Print
Distributed by Hachette Diffusion International; Dilibel (Belgium); Diffulivre (Switzerland); Hachette Canada Inc (Canada); CELF

Editions de la Cite, *imprint of* Editions Ouest-France

CLD+
42 avenue des Platanes, 37172 Chambray-les-Tours cedex
Mailing Address: BP 203, 37172 Chambray-les-Tours cedex
Tel: (02) 47282068 *Fax:* (02) 47288548
Key Personnel
Man Dir, Editorial: Michel Magat
Deputy Manager: Michel Jacquet
Production: Emmanuel Magat
Founded: 1961
Subjects: Architecture & Interior Design, Ethnicity, History, Regional Interests, Religion - Other, Travel
ISBN Prefix(es): 2-85443
Total Titles: 300 Print

Cle International+
27 rue de la Glaciere, 75013 Paris
Tel: (01) 45 87 44 00 *Fax:* (01) 45 87 44 10
E-mail: cle@vuef.fr
Web Site: www.cle-inter.com
Key Personnel
Dir: Jean-Luc Wollensack
Sales Dir: Dominique Richard
Editorial Dir: Michele Grandmangin
Founded: 1973
Subjects: Education, Language Arts, Linguistics
ISBN Prefix(es): 2-19; 2-09
Showroom(s): Espace Luxembourg, 103 Boulevard Saint-Michel, 75005 Paris *Tel:* (01) 53104120 *Fax:* (01) 45874425

CLET, see Centre de Librairie et d'Editions Techniques (CLET)

CLET, *imprint of* Dunod Editeur

Climapoche, *imprint of* SEDIT (Societe d'Etudes et de Diffusion des Industries Thermiques et Aerauliques)

Editions Climats+
470 chemin des Pins, 34170 Castelnau-le-Lez
Tel: (04) 99 58 30 91; (04) 67 45 37 90 *Fax:* (04) 99 58 30 92
E-mail: contact@editions-climats.com
Web Site: www.editions-climats.com
Key Personnel
Man Editor: Alain Martin
Founded: 1988
Subjects: Film, Video, Literature, Literary Criticism, Essays, Music, Dance, Mysteries
ISBN Prefix(es): 2-84158; 2-907563
Shipping Address: Harmonia Mundi, BP 150, 13631 Arles Cedex *Tel:* (04) 90499049 *Fax:* (04) 90499614

Warehouse: Harmonia Mundi, BP 150, 13631 Arles Cedex
Orders to: Harmonia Mundi, BP 150, 13631 Arles Cedex *Tel:* (04) 90499049 *Fax:* (04) 90499614

Club J G, *imprint of* Sarl Editions Jean Grassin

CNDP, see Centre National de Documentation Pedagogique (CNDP)

CNE, see Comite National d'Evaluation (CNE)

CNRS Editions+
15 rue Malebranche, 75005 Paris
Tel: (01) 53 10 27 00 *Fax:* (01) 53 10 27 27
Web Site: www.cnrseditions.fr
Key Personnel
Man Dir: Danielle Saffar *Tel:* (01) 53 10 27 15 *E-mail:* danielle.saffar@cnrseditions.fr
Publicity & Advertising Manager: Liliane Bruneau *Tel:* (01) 53 10 27 11 *E-mail:* liliane.bruneau@cnrseditions.fr
Editorial: Pascal Rouleau *E-mail:* pascal.rouleau@cnrseditions.fr
Founded: 1986
Specializes in scientific books.
Subjects: Archaeology, Art, Astrology, Occult, Biological Sciences, Chemistry, Chemical Engineering, Communications, Economics, Education, Environmental Studies, Ethnicity, Geography, Geology, History, Language Arts, Linguistics, Law, Literature, Literary Criticism, Essays, Mathematics, Music, Dance, Philosophy, Physics, Psychology, Psychiatry, Religion - Other, Science (General), Social Sciences, Sociology
ISBN Prefix(es): 2-222; 2-271
Number of titles published annually: 100 Print
Total Titles: 2 CD-ROM
Parent Company: Centre National de la Recherche Scientifique

Codes Rousseau
BP 93, 85103 Les Sables d'Olonne Cedex
Tel: (02) 51 23 11 00 *Fax:* (02) 51 21 31 02
E-mail: info@codes-rousseau.fr
Web Site: www.codes-rousseau.fr
Key Personnel
President: Mr C Czajka
Dir General: M Goepp
Subjects: Education, Electronics, Electrical Engineering, Law, Transportation
ISBN Prefix(es): 2-7095
Parent Company: Bertelsmann A G
Subsidiaries: La Baule; Les Editions du Bateau, Les Editions; Rousseau Diffusion, Sables d'Olonne

Armand Colin, Editeur
21, rue Montparnasse, 75298 Paris cedex 6
Tel: (01) 44395447 *Fax:* (01) 44394343
E-mail: infos@armand-colin.com
Web Site: www.armand-colin.com/pr/infosf.html
Telex: Acolin 201269 F
Key Personnel
Man Dir: Jean-Max Leclerc
Sales Dir: Remy Bourrelier
Publicity & Advertising: Yvette Dardenne
Rights & Permissions: Antoine Bonfait *E-mail:* abonfait@her.fr
Editor: Armand Colin
General Manager: Alain Cardona *E-mail:* acardona@vuef.fr
Founded: 1870
Incorporates publications of former separate company, Editions Armand Colin Bourrelier.
Subjects: Education, Geography, Geology, History, Literature, Literary Criticism, Essays, Philosophy, Psychology, Psychiatry, Social Sciences, Sociology

ISBN Prefix(es): 2-200
Orders to: BP 107, 75663 Paris Cedex 14

College de Philosophie, *imprint of* Societe des Editions Grasset et Fasquelle

Editions du Comite des Travaux Historiques et Scientifiques (CTHS)+
One rue Descartes, 75005 Paris Cedex
Tel: (01) 55 55 97 64 *Fax:* (01) 55 55 97 60
E-mail: cths.ventes@recherche.gouv.fr
Web Site: www.cths.fr
Key Personnel
President: Leon Pressouyre
Vice President: Bruno Delmas
Secretary: Olivier Guyotjeannin; Pierre Pinon
Founded: 1834
Subjects: Archaeology, Art, Ethnicity, Geography, Geology, History
ISBN Prefix(es): 2-7355
Shipping Address: Distique, 5 rue du Marechal Leclerc, 28600 Luisant

Comite National d'Evaluation (CNE)
43, rue de la Procession, 75015 Paris
Tel: (01) 55 55 60 97 *Fax:* (01) 55 55 63 94
Web Site: www.cne-evaluation.fr
Key Personnel
Publisher: Francine Sarrazin *Tel:* (01) 55 55 63 63 *E-mail:* francine.sarrazin@cne-evaluation.fr
President: Gilles Bertrand *Tel:* (01) 55 55 69 80 *E-mail:* pdtcne@cne-evaluation.fr
Deputy General: Jolivet Jean-Wolf *E-mail:* sgcne@cne-evaluation.fr
Founded: 1986
Subjects: Education
Number of titles published annually: 15 Print; 15 E-Book
Total Titles: 230 Print; 165 E-Book
Divisions: Service Publications

Communication Par Livre (CPL)
3, square du Croisic, 75015 Paris
Mailing Address: 28 rue Vaneau, 75007 Paris
Tel: (01) 42733047 *Fax:* (01) 42733047
Key Personnel
General Dir: Philippe Leclerc
Founded: 1989
Subjects: Advertising, Architecture & Interior Design, Art, History, Real Estate
ISBN Prefix(es): 2-908867

Editions Comp'Act+
157, Carre Curial, 73000 Chambery
Tel: (04) 79 85 27 85 *Fax:* (04) 79 85 29 34
E-mail: contact@editionscompact.com
Web Site: www.editionscompact.com
Key Personnel
Literary Dir: Henri Poncet
Founded: 1986
Subjects: Literature, Literary Criticism, Essays, Photography, Poetry
ISBN Prefix(es): 2-87661
Number of titles published annually: 30 Print

Compagnie d'Editions Libres, Sociales et Economiques (CELSE)
10 rue Leon Coqniet, 75821 Paris Cedex 17
Mailing Address: BP 106, 75821 Paris Cedex 17
Tel: (01) 42674123 *Fax:* (01) 42274020
E-mail: celse@celsedit.com
Web Site: www.celsedit.com
Key Personnel
Dir General: Marc Lamoussiere
Founded: 1957
Subjects: Transportation
ISBN Prefix(es): 2-85009
Total Titles: 72 Print

Compagnie Europeenne de Publication, see CEP Editions

Compagnie Francaise des Arts Graphiques SA+
47 rue des Murs, 45300 Ecrennes
Tel: (05) 46243925
Key Personnel
President: V P Victor-Michel
Founded: 1939
Subjects: Art, Drama, Theater, Music, Dance
ISBN Prefix(es): 2-85001
Imprints: CFAG
Orders to: 129 Ave Achille Peretti, 92200 Neuilly sur Seine

Compagnie 12+
210, rue du Faubourg-Saint-Antoine, 75012 Paris
Tel: (01) 43 70 99 00 *Fax:* (01) 43 70 80 88
Founded: 1981
ISBN Prefix(es): 2-903866; 2-221
U.S. Office(s): Company 12 Inc, 190 E 56 St, New York, NY 10017, United States
Orders to: 22, rue des Canettes, 75006 Paris

Editions de Compostelle+
BP 7, 77890 Beaumont-du-Gatinais
Tel: (01) 64299404
Key Personnel
Contact: Francois-Xavier Chaboche
Founded: 1988
Subjects: Human Relations, Parapsychology, Philosophy, Religion - Other, Theology
ISBN Prefix(es): 2-907449
Total Titles: 10 Print

Le Conseiller Juridique Pour Tous, *imprint of* Editions du Puits Fleuri

Continent Europe, *imprint of* Editions Hermes Science Publications

Cooperative Regionale de l'Enseignement Religieux (CRER)
22 blvd Jacques-Millot, 49008 Angers Cedex 01
Mailing Address: BP 848, 49008 Angers Cedex 01
Tel: (02) 41689140 *Fax:* (02) 41689141
E-mail: crer49@wanadoo.fr
Key Personnel
Man Dir: Michel Pourrias
Founded: 1968
Subjects: Religion - Other
ISBN Prefix(es): 2-85733

Editions Copernic
25 rue Barque, 75015 Paris
Tel: (01) 40 61 97 67 *Fax:* (01) 40 61 96 33
Key Personnel
Man Dir: Bertrand Sorlot
Sales, Production, Rights & Permissions, Publicity: Jeanne Bordeau
Founded: 1976
Subjects: Film, Video, History, Philosophy, Religion - Other, Science Fiction, Fantasy
ISBN Prefix(es): 2-85984
Associate Companies: Editions Albatross, Publeditec

Editions Coprur+
34 rue du Wacken, 67000 Strasbourg
Tel: (03) 88 14 72 41 *Fax:* (03) 88 14 72 39
E-mail: coprur@editions-coprur.fr
Key Personnel
Dir: Bernard Sadoun
Founded: 1871
Subjects: History, Natural History, Regional Interests
ISBN Prefix(es): 2-84208; 2-903297
Number of titles published annually: 25 Print
Total Titles: 300 Print

Corsaire Editions+
One rue Royale, 45000 Orleans
Tel: (02) 38 53 15 00 *Fax:* (02) 38 54 08 92
E-mail: corsaire.editions@wanadoo.fr
Web Site: www.corsaire-editions.com
Key Personnel
President: Gilbert Trompas
Founded: 1994
Subjects: Biography, Biological Sciences, Earth Sciences, History, Humor, Literature, Literary Criticism, Essays, Poetry, Social Sciences, Sociology
ISBN Prefix(es): 2-910475
Distributed by Diffusion Transat (Switzerland)

Editions Jose Corti+
11 rue de Medicis, 75006 Paris
Tel: (01) 43 26 63 00; (01) 43 26 80 48 *Fax:* (01) 40 46 89 24
E-mail: corti@noos.fr
Web Site: www.jose-corti.fr
Key Personnel
Man Dir: Bertrand Fillaudeau
Editorial: Fabienne Raphoz-Fillaudeau
Publicity, Rights & Permissions: Isabelle Dibie
Founded: 1938
Subjects: Fiction, Literature, Literary Criticism, Essays, Poetry
ISBN Prefix(es): 2-7143
Total Titles: 799 Print
Orders to: Edition du Seuil, 27 rue Jacob, 75006 Paris

Council of Europe Publishing+
Division of Council of Europe
Palais de l'Europe, 67075 Strasbourg Cedex
Tel: (0388) 41 25 81 *Fax:* (0388) 41 39 10
E-mail: publishing@coe.int
Web Site: book.coe.int
Telex: 870943F
Key Personnel
Commercial Manager: Sophie Lobey *Tel:* (0388) 412263 *E-mail:* sophie.lobey@coe.int
Rights & Permissions Manager: Charalambos Papadopoulos *Tel:* (0388) 412952 *E-mail:* charalambos.papadopoulos@coe.int
Editorial Manager: Annick Pachod *Tel:* (0388) 412249 *E-mail:* annick.pachod@coe.int; Francine Raveney *Tel:* (0388) 415114 *E-mail:* francine.raveney@coe.int
Founded: 1949
Official publisher of the Council of Europe & reflects many different aspects of the Council's work, addressing the main challenges facing European society & the world today. Our catalogue of over 1500 titles in French & English includes topics ranging from international law, human rights, ethical & moral issues, society, environment, health, education & culture.
Subjects: Law, Medicine, Nursing, Dentistry, Social Sciences, Sociology, Human Rights, Criminology, Sociology, Nature, Consumer Protection, Education, Sports, Culture, Social Security, Youth, Local Authorities
ISBN Prefix(es): 92-871
Number of titles published annually: 120 Print
Total Titles: 1,500 Print
Distributed by Manhattan Publishing Co
Foreign Rep(s): Akademika A/S Universitetsbokhandel; Akateeminen Asta Liimen (Finland); Bersy (Switzerland); Bookshop Jean de Lannoy (Belgium); De Lindeboom Int Publikaties/Inor (Netherlands); Euro Information Service (Hungary); European Bookshop SA (Belgium); Glowna Ksiegarnia Naukowa im B Prusa (Poland); Hunter Publications (Australia); Kauffmann Bookshop (Greece); Libreria Commissionaria Sansoni (Italy); Livraria Portugal (Portugal); Manhattan Publishing Co (USA); Mundi-Prensa Libros SA (Spain); Munksgaard Book & Subscription Service (Denmark); Renouf Publishing Co Ltd (Canada); TSO (UK); UNO Verlag (Austria, Germany)

Shipping Address: T S O, 51 Nine Elms Lane, London SW8 5DR, United Kingdom *Tel:* (020) 7873 8200
Returns: Mundi-Prensa Libros SA, Castell6 37, E-28001 Madrid, Spain *Fax:* (01) 575 3998 *E-mail:* libreria@mundiprensa.es *Web Site:* www.mundiprensa.es

Counseil International de la Langue Francaise
11 rue de Navarin, 75009 Paris
Tel: (01) 48787395 *Fax:* (01) 48784928
E-mail: cilf@cilf.org
Web Site: www.cilf.org
Key Personnel
Secretary-General: Hubert Joly
Founded: 1968
Specialize in multilingual scientific dictionaries.
Subjects: Agriculture, Architecture & Interior Design, Language Arts, Linguistics, Medicine, Nursing, Dentistry, Public Administration
ISBN Prefix(es): 2-85319

Editions Courrier du Livre
65 rue Claude Bernard, 75005 Paris
Tel: (01) 43 36 41 05 *Fax:* (01) 43 31 07 45
E-mail: info@tredaniel-courrier.com
Web Site: www.tredaniel.com/
Subjects: Environmental Studies, Gardening, Plants, Health, Nutrition, Philosophy, Religion - Other, Sports, Athletics
ISBN Prefix(es): 2-7029

CPL, see Communication Par Livre (CPL)

CREDES - Centre de Recherche d'Etude et de Documentation en Economie de la Sante
One rue Paul-Cezanne, 75008 Paris
Tel: (01) 53 93 43 00 *Fax:* (01) 53 93 43 50
Web Site: www.credes.fr
Key Personnel
Chair: Francois Joliclerc
Dir: Domenica Polton
Founded: 1985
ISBN Prefix(es): 2-87812

Editeurs Crepin-Leblond
14, rue du Patronage Laique, 52000 Chaumont
Tel: (03) 25 03 87 48 *Fax:* (03) 25 03 87 40
E-mail: crepin-leblond@graphycom.com
Web Site: www.graphycom.com
Key Personnel
Man Dir: Jean Bletner
Publicity: Laurent Picart *Tel:* (032) 5038749; Francoise Pelletier *Tel:* (032) 5038749; Christophe Inoux *Tel:* (032) 5038645 *Fax:* (032) 5038652
Founded: 1952
Subjects: Animals, Pets, Environmental Studies, Sports, Athletics
ISBN Prefix(es): 2-7030

CRER, see Cooperative Regionale de l'Enseignement Religieux (CRER)

Editions Criterion+
11 rue Duguay-Trouin, 75006 Paris
Tel: (01) 45443834 *Fax:* (01) 45499392
Key Personnel
Dir General: Pierre-Marie Dumont
Founded: 1990
Subjects: Biography, History, Literature, Literary Criticism, Essays, Social Sciences, Sociology
ISBN Prefix(es): 2-903702; 2-7413; 2-903701; 2-902105

CTHS, see Editions du Comite des Travaux Historiques et Scientifiques (CTHS)

CTIF (Center Technique Industriel de la Fonderie)
44 ave de la Division Leclerc, 92318 Sevres Cedex
Tel: (01) 41 14 63 00 *Fax:* (01) 45 34 14 34
E-mail: contact@ctif.com
Web Site: www.ctif.com
Key Personnel
Contact: Michel Guiny *E-mail:* guiny_mi@ctif.com
Subjects: Technology
ISBN Prefix(es): 2-7119

CTNERHI - Centre Technique National d'Etudes et de Recherches sur les Handicaps et les Inadaptations
236 Bis rue de Tolbiac, 75013 Paris
Tel: (01) 45 65 59 00 *Fax:* (01) 45 65 44 94
E-mail: ctnerhi@club-internet.fr
Web Site: perso.club-internet.fr/ctnerhi
Key Personnel
President: Marc Dupont
Dir: Marc Maudinet
Subjects: Disability, Special Needs, Psychology, Psychiatry, Social Sciences, Sociology
ISBN Prefix(es): 2-87710
Distributed by Presses Universitaires de France

Editions Cujas+
4/8, rue de la Maison Blanche, 75013 Paris
Mailing Address: BP 417, 75626 Paris Cedex 13
Tel: (01) 44 24 24 36; (01) 44 24 24 37 *Fax:* (01) 44 24 24 38
E-mail: cujas@cujas.fr
Web Site: www.cujas.fr
Telex: 200513
Key Personnel
Man Dir: Pierre Joly
Founded: 1946
Subjects: Economics, Education, Government, Political Science, History, Law, Social Sciences, Sociology
ISBN Prefix(es): 2-254
Bookshop(s): Cujjas Librairie, 2 rue de Rouen, 92000 Nanterre

Culture et Bibliotheque pour Tous
212, rue Lecourbe, 75015 Paris
Tel: (01) 45 33 07 07 *Fax:* (01) 45 33 45 76
E-mail: uncbpt.services@wanadoo.fr
Key Personnel
Publication Dir: Marie-Francoise Cathala
Founded: 1943
Monthly periodicals.
Subjects: Biography, Fiction, History, Human Relations, Literature, Literary Criticism, Essays, Mysteries, Publishing & Book Trade Reference, Romance

Les Editions Roger Dacosta+
19 blvd Raspail, 75007 Paris
Tel: (01) 45441491
Key Personnel
Man Dir: Marie-Madeleine Dacosta
Sales Dir: Isabelle Dacosta
Founded: 1912
Subjects: Medicine, Nursing, Dentistry
ISBN Prefix(es): 2-85128

DAFSA
117 quai de Valmy, 75010 Paris
Tel: (01) 44 37 26 00 *Fax:* (01) 44 37 26 35
E-mail: dorra.medjani@dri-wefa.com
Web Site: www.dafsa.fr
Telex: 640472 Daf Doc
Key Personnel
Chairman: Pierre Cabon
Man Dir: Yves Wilmors
Subjects: Economics, Finance
ISBN Prefix(es): 2-270

Dalloz, *imprint of* Editions Dalloz Sirey

PUBLISHERS FRANCE

Editions Dalloz Sirey+
31-35, rue Froidevaux, 75685 Paris Cedex 14
Tel: (01) 40 64 54 54 *Fax:* (01) 40 64 54 60
E-mail: ventes@dalloz.fr
Web Site: www.dalloz.fr
Telex: 206446 F
Key Personnel
President: Charles Vallee *Tel:* (01) 40655436
Chief Executive Officer: Philippe Chagnon
 Tel: (01) 40645434
Dir General: Nathalie De Baudry D'Asson
Marketing: Nathalie Thouny *Tel:* (01) 40645438
Foreign Rights: Muriel Funel *Tel:* (01) 40645420
Founded: 1845 (Sirey, 1845 Dalloz)
Administration Office: 35 rue Tournefort, 75240 Paris, Cedex 05. Tel: (01) 40515454
Online publishing.
Subjects: Advertising, Economics, Finance, Law, Marketing
ISBN Prefix(es): 2-247
Total Titles: 2,000 Print; 50 CD-ROM; 10 E-Book
Parent Company: Havas Vivendi
Imprints: Armand Colin Drott; Dalloz; Delmas; Sirey
Distributor for Groupe Revue Fiduciaire
Bookshop(s): 14 rue Soufflot, 75005 Paris; 22 rue Soufflot, 75005 Paris
Distribution Center: Livredis, 11-15 Rue Pierre Rig-Aud, 94854 Ivry S/Jeine

Librairie D'Amerique Et D'Orient, *imprint of* Editions d'Amerique et d'Orient, Adrien Maisonneuve

Editions Dangles SA-Edilarge SA+
18, rue Lavoisier, 03945801 Saint Jean-de-Braye
Mailing Address: BP 30 039, 03945801 Saint Jean-de-Braye
Tel: (02) 38864180 *Fax:* (02) 38837234
E-mail: dangles@wanadoo.fr
Web Site: www.editions-dangles.com
Key Personnel
Man Dir, Rights & Permissions: J Y Anstet Dangles
Sales: Alain Queant
Contact: Berangere Lemaiitre
Founded: 1926
Subjects: Medicine, Nursing, Dentistry, Parapsychology, Psychology, Psychiatry
ISBN Prefix(es): 2-7033
Branch Office(s)
30 rue des Freres Lumiere, 94260 Fresnes

Dargaud+
15/27 rue Moussorgski, 75018 Paris
Tel: (01) 53 26 32 32 *Fax:* (01) 53 26 32 00
E-mail: contact@dargaud.fr
Web Site: www.dargaud.fr
Key Personnel
President & Publisher: Claude de Saint Vincent
Editorial: Guy Vidal
Rights & Permissions: Sophie Castille
 E-mail: castille@dargaud.fr
Dir, Commercial & International: Eric de Moutlivault
Founded: 1943
Subjects: Fiction, Humor, Mysteries, Science Fiction, Fantasy, Western Fiction, Comics
ISBN Prefix(es): 2-205
Parent Company: Sofidar
Subsidiaries: Citel Video; Dargaud Benelux; Dargaud Publishing International; Dargard Suisse; Delta Verlag; Editions Blake et mortimer; Editions du Lombard; Grijalbo-Dargaud; Hodder-Dargaud; Marina Productions; Millesime Productions
Distributor for Blake et Mortimer; Lombard
Orders to: MDS, ZI de la Gaudree, 91417 Dourdan Cedex *Tel:* (01) 60818700 *Fax:* (01) 64593063

Editions du Dauphin+
43-45, rue Tombe-Issoire, 75014 Paris
Tel: (01) 43 27 79 00 *Fax:* (01) 43 27 76 31
Key Personnel
Publishing Manager: Anne Tromelin
Founded: 1935
Subjects: Fiction, How-to, Psychology, Psychiatry
ISBN Prefix(es): 2-7163
Subsidiaries: Editions Jacqueline Renard
Distribution Center: Diffedit, 96 bd du Montparnasse, 75014 Paris, Contact: Francois Bera
 Tel: (0144) 107575 *Fax:* (0144) 107580

Michel De Maule Editions+
41, rue de Richelieu, 75001 Paris
Tel: (01) 42 97 93 56; (01) 42 97 93 48 *Fax:* (01) 42 97 94 90
Key Personnel
President: Hubert de Bouville
Founded: 1997
Specialize in Latin & Greek publications.
ISBN Prefix(es): 2-87623
Parent Company: Editions Tum

De Vecchi Editions SA
52, rue Montmartre, 75002 Paris
Mailing Address: 29 rue Gustave-Eiffel, Zlle Val, 91420 Morangis
Tel: (01) 69 34 12 01; (01) 44 76 88 88 *Fax:* (01) 64 48 24 97; (01) 44 76 88 89
Key Personnel
Dir: J M Gosselin
Founded: 1971
Subjects: Animals, Pets, Astrology, Occult, Business, Health, Nutrition, How-to, Outdoor Recreation, Parapsychology, Sports, Athletics
ISBN Prefix(es): 2-7328; 2-85177

Nouvelles Editions Debresse
17 rue Duguay-Trouin, 75006 Paris
Tel: (01) 45481047
Key Personnel
Man Dir: Pierre Moulin
Editorial, Sales & Publicity: Vincent Moulin
Founded: 1933
Subjects: Astrology, Occult, Fiction, History, Poetry, Religion - Other, Social Sciences, Sociology
ISBN Prefix(es): 2-7164

Decanord
30 rue de Verlinghem, 59130 Lambersart Cedex
Mailing Address: BP 139, 59832 Lambersart Cedex
Tel: (03) 20 09 90 60 *Fax:* (03) 20 09 92 75
Key Personnel
General Dir: Luc Jonghmans
Founded: 1948
Subjects: Religion - Catholic
ISBN Prefix(es): 2-903898

Editions La Decouverte+
9 bis, rue Abel-Hovelacque, 75013 Paris
Tel: (01) 44 08 84 01 *Fax:* (01) 44 08 84 17
E-mail: ladecouverte@ladecouverte-syros.com
Web Site: www.editionsladecouverte.fr
Key Personnel
Man Dir: Francois Geze
Foreign Rights Manager: Delphime Ribouchon
Founded: 1959
Membership(s): SNE.
Subjects: Communications, Developing Countries, Economics, Fiction, Foreign Countries, History, Philosophy, Social Sciences, Sociology
ISBN Prefix(es): 2-7071
Parent Company: Vivendi Universal Publishing
Subsidiaries: Le Monde-Editions

Editions Delcourt+
54, rue d'Hauteville, 75010 Paris
Tel: (01) 56 03 92 20 *Fax:* (01) 56 03 92 30
Web Site: www.editions-delcourt.fr
Key Personnel
Dir: Guy Delcourt
International Rights: Catherine Cropsal
Founded: 1986
ISBN Prefix(es): 2-906187; 2-84055; 2-84789
Distributed by Diffulivre (Switzerland); Evadix Logistics (Benelux); Flammarion; Flammarion-Casterman (Benelux); Flammarion Export (Switzerland); OLF (Switzerland); Union-Distribution; Vertige Graphic

La Delirante
8, rue des Ecoles Rondil SA, 75005 Paris
Tel: (01) 43 54 47 97 *Fax:* (01) 43 54 06 97
Key Personnel
President: Patrick Genevaz
Founded: 1967
Subjects: Drama, Theater, Literature, Literary Criticism, Essays, Poetry
ISBN Prefix(es): 2-85745

Delmas, *imprint of* Editions Dalloz Sirey

Editions Delmas
31-35 rue Froidevaux, 75685 Paris Cedex 14
Tel: (08) 20 80 00 17 *Fax:* (01) 40 64 89 90
E-mail: delmas@dalloz.fr
Web Site: www.editions-delmas.com
Key Personnel
Man Dir: Charles Vallee
Dir Sales: Philippe Nani
Publicity: Monique Remillieux
International Rights: Christian Roblin
Founded: 1947
Subjects: Accounting, Economics, Law, Public Administration, Real Estate, Securities
ISBN Prefix(es): 2-247; 2-7034
Parent Company: Editions Dalloz Sirey

Jean-P Delville Editions+
40 rue du Four, 75006 Paris
Tel: (01) 42 22 72 90 *Fax:* (01) 42 22 65 62
E-mail: editions.delville@wanadoo.fr
Key Personnel
Man Dir: Jean-Pierre Delville
Founded: 1976
Subjects: Aeronautics, Aviation, Automotive, Cookery, History, How-to
ISBN Prefix(es): 2-85922

Editions du Demi-Cercle+
29 rue Jean-Jacques-Rousseau, 75001 Paris
Tel: (01) 42330685 *Fax:* (01) 42330862
Key Personnel
Manager: Veronique Hartmann
Founded: 1987
Subjects: Archaeology, Architecture & Interior Design, Environmental Studies
ISBN Prefix(es): 2-907757

Editions Denoel+
9, rue de Cherche-Midi, 75006 Paris
Tel: (01) 44 39 73 73 *Fax:* (01) 44 39 73 90
E-mail: denoel@denoel.fr *Cable:* Edepege
Key Personnel
Man Dir: Olivier Rubinstein
Rights & Permissions: Marie-Fransoise Bothorel; Juliette Moreau
Foreign Rights: Marie Ledereg
Founded: 1932
Subjects: Art, Economics, Fiction, Government, Political Science, History, Philosophy, Psychology, Psychiatry, Science Fiction, Fantasy
ISBN Prefix(es): 2-207
Parent Company: Editions Gallimard, 5, rue Sebastien-Bottin, 75328 Paris Cedex 07
Associate Companies: Mercure de France

Dervy, *imprint of* Dervy Editions

Dervy Editions+
204, blvd Raspail, 75014 Paris
Tel: (01) 42 79 25 21 *Fax:* (01) 42 78 25 39
E-mail: contact@dervy.fr
Key Personnel
Manager: Bernard Renaud de la Faverie
Founded: 1946
Subjects: History, Human Relations, Psychology, Psychiatry, Religion - Other, Social Sciences, Sociology, Free Masonry, Personnel Development, Spiritualities
ISBN Prefix(es): 2-85076; 2-84454
Number of titles published annually: 40 Print
Total Titles: 600 Print
Parent Company: SFPI
Imprints: Dervy
Subsidiaries: CQFDL
Warehouse: Dilisco, Parc Mure 2, Batiment 4.4, 128 Ave Jean Jaures, BP 102, 94208 Ivry Sur Seine

Desclee de Brouwer SA+
76 bis, rue des Sts-Peres, 75007 Paris
Tel: (01) 45 49 61 92 *Fax:* (01) 42 22 61 41
E-mail: direction@descleedebrouwer.com
Web Site: www.descleedebrouwer.com
Key Personnel
President: Marc Leboucher
General Manager: Etienne Leroy
Founded: 1877
Subjects: History, Literature, Literary Criticism, Essays, Religion - Other, Social Sciences, Sociology, Theology
ISBN Prefix(es): 2-220; 2-7045
Divisions: (Social Sciences) Epi

Desclee Editions
11, rue Duguay-Trouin, 75006 Paris
Tel: (01) 45443834 *Fax:* (01) 45499392
Cable: Desclee Marquain
Key Personnel
Literary Dir: A Paul
Founded: 1872
Subjects: Literature, Literary Criticism, Essays, Philosophy, Religion - Other
ISBN Prefix(es): 2-7189
Associate Companies: Editions Desclee; Droquet & Ardant; Editions Gamma, Belgium; Mame
Divisions: Groupe Mame

Desforges, *imprint of* Editions Casteilla

Editions Desiris, *imprint of* Adverbum SARL

Dessain et Tolra SA+
21, rue du Montparnasse, 75283 Paris Cedex 06
Tel: (01) 44 39 44 00 *Fax:* (01) 44 39 43 43
Telex: 260776F
Key Personnel
Dir: Marie-Pierre Levallois
General Manager: Philippe Fournier-Bourdier
Editorial Manager: Jean Gueret
Founded: 1964
Subjects: Architecture & Interior Design, Art, Crafts, Games, Hobbies, How-to
ISBN Prefix(es): 2-249; 2-04
Bookshop(s): Diff-edi, 96 BD DU Montparnasse, 75680 Paris Cedex 14

Editions Desvigne
10, rue Leon Foucault, 78184 Saint-Quentin Yvelines Cedex
Tel: (01) 30 14 19 30 *Fax:* (01) 34 60 31 32
E-mail: info@casteilla.fr
Web Site: www.casteilla.fr
Key Personnel
President: Visser Marinus *Tel:* (01) 30141945
Fax: (01) 30141946
Subjects: Education
ISBN Prefix(es): 2-7037

Total Titles: 800 Print
Ultimate Parent Company: Editions Casteilla

Les Editions des Deux Coqs d'Or+
43 Quai de Grenelle, 75905 Cedex 15
Tel: (01) 43923334 *Fax:* (01) 43923338
Telex: 650780 Deucodo *Cable:* Deucodo Paris
Key Personnel
Man Dir: Frederique de Buron
Editor: Christine Foulquies
Art Manager: Maryvonne Denizet
Rights & Permissions: Monique Lantelme
Founded: 1949
Membership(s): the Syndicat National de L'Edition Francaise.
Subjects: Animals, Pets, Fiction, History, Religion - Catholic, Religion - Other
ISBN Prefix(es): 2-01; 2-7192; 2-906017
Parent Company: Hachette Livre SA
Warehouse: Centre de Distribution du Livre, Z A de Coignieres-Maurepas, 1 avenue Gutenberg, 78316 Maurepas Cedex
Orders to: Hachette Livre, 43 Quai de Grenelle, 75905 Paris Cedex 15

Deux Coqs d'Or, *imprint of* Hachette Jeunesse Image

Institut pour le Developpement Forestier
(Institute for Forestry Development)
23 ave Bosquet, 75007 Paris
Tel: (01) 40622280 *Fax:* (01) 45559854
E-mail: paris@association-idf.com
Key Personnel
President: Roland Martin
Founded: 1960
Subjects: Agriculture, Environmental Studies
ISBN Prefix(es): 2-904740

Les Devenirs Visuels+
56 rue du Faubourg Poissonniere, 75010 Paris
Tel: (01) 47 70 60 02 *Fax:* (01) 47 70 60 03
Key Personnel
Contact: Claive Rius
Founded: 1987
Specialize in packaging.
Subjects: Economics, Geography, Geology, Physical Sciences
ISBN Prefix(es): 2-910745

Diagonales, *imprint of* Editions Cercle d'Art SA

Editions de la Difference+
47 rue de la Villette, 75019 Paris
Tel: (01) 53 38 85 38 *Fax:* (01) 42 45 34 94
E-mail: editions-de-la-difference@wanadoo.fr
Web Site: www.ladifference.fr
Key Personnel
Dir: Colette Lambrichs; Joaquim Vital
Press: Frederique Martinie
Administration: Parcidio Gonclaves
Founded: 1976
Subjects: Art, Literature, Literary Criticism, Essays, Poetry
ISBN Prefix(es): 2-7291

Le Dilettante+
9-11 rue du Champ-de-l'Alouette, 75013 Paris 13e
Tel: (01) 43-37-98-98 *Fax:* (01) 43-37-06-10
E-mail: info@ledilettante.com
Web Site: www.ledilettante.com
Key Personnel
President: Dominique Gaultier *E-mail:* gaultier@ledilettante.com
Founded: 1985
Subjects: Literature, Literary Criticism, Essays, Science (General)
ISBN Prefix(es): 2-84263; 2-905344
Branch Office(s)
Impasse du Ferradou, 11170 Montolieu

Dilicom
20, rue des Grands-Augustins, 75006 Paris
Tel: (01) 43254335 *Fax:* (01) 43297688
E-mail: dilicom@edilectre.fr
Web Site: www.dilicom.net
Key Personnel
President: Dominique Maillotte
Dir General: Bernard de Freminville

Editions Dis Voir+
3, rue Beautreillis, 75004 Paris
Tel: (01) 48 87 07 09 *Fax:* (01) 48 87 07 14
E-mail: disvoir@aol.com
Web Site: www.disvoir.com
Key Personnel
Dir General & Editor: Daniele Riviere
E-mail: daniele.riviere@free.fr
Founded: 1986
Subjects: Architecture & Interior Design, Art, Fiction, Film, Video, Literature, Literary Criticism, Essays, Music, Dance, Philosophy
ISBN Prefix(es): 2-906571; 2-914563
Total Titles: 100 Print; 55 Online
U.S. Office(s): DAP, 636 Broadway, 12th floor, New York, NY, United States *Tel:* 212-473-5119 *Fax:* 212-673-2887
Distributed by CELF (South America, Italy, Spain, Japan, Germany, Greece, Portugal); Central Books (UK); DAP (USA); Dimedia (Canada); Exhibitions International (Netherlands); Manic Ex-Poseur/BAM (Australia); NORD-SUD (Belgium); Onslow Books (Scandinavia); Sevil (France)

Disney Hachette Edition+
10 rue du Colisee, 75008 Paris
Tel: (01) 53898500 *Fax:* (01) 45632201
Key Personnel
President: Pierre Sissmann
Dir: Catherine Teissandier
Founded: 1992
Subjects: Child Care & Development
ISBN Prefix(es): 2-230
Parent Company: The Walt Disney Company France/Hachette Groupe Livre
Shipping Address: Centre de distribution du Livre, One ave Gutenberg, 78316 Maurepas
Warehouse: Centre de distribution du Livre, One ave Gutenberg, 78316 Maurepas
Orders to: Hachette - Service Commercial, 79 blvd St Germain, 75006 Paris

Societe de Documentation et d'Analyses Financieres, see DAFSA

La Documentation Francaise+
29 Quai Voltaire, 75007 Paris Cedex 07
Tel: (01) 40 15 70 00 *Fax:* (01) 40 15 72 30
E-mail: contact@ladocumentationfrancaise.fr
Web Site: www.ladocfrancaise.gouv.fr
Telex: 204826 Docfran Paris
Key Personnel
Man Dir: Sophie Moati *E-mail:* s-moati@ladocfrancaise.gouv.fr
Sales, Promotion: Alain-Marie Bassy *Tel:* (01) 40 15 70 80 *E-mail:* am-bassy@ladocfrancaise.gouv.fr; Sophie Seyer *E-mail:* s-seyer@ladocfrancaise.gouv.fr
Publicity: Laura Esterhazy
Foreign Rights: Francoise Bacnus *E-mail:* f-bacnus@ladocfrancaise.gouv.fr; Bernard Meunier *E-mail:* b-meunier@ladocfrancaise.gouv.fr
Founded: 1945
Publications of the General Secretary's Office of the French Government.
Membership(s): Syndicat National de l'Edition.
Subjects: Art, Economics, Environmental Studies, Government, Political Science, Law, Management, Technology
ISBN Prefix(es): 2-11
Number of titles published annually: 500 Print; 3 CD-ROM; 200 E-Book

PUBLISHERS   FRANCE

Total Titles: 6,000 Print; 5 CD-ROM; 500 E-Book
Foreign Rep(s): Distribuidora Bertrand (Portugal); DPLU Inc (Canada); Jean de Lannoy (Belgium, Luxembourg); Librairie Kauffmann SA (Greece); Licosa (Italy); Maruzen Co (Japan); Mundi Prensa Libros SA (Spain); Servidis SA (Switzerland)
Bookshop(s): 165 rue Garibaldi, 69401 Lyon Cedex 03 *Tel:* (01) 78 63 23 02 *Fax:* (01) 78 63 32 24 *E-mail:* docfr2@easynet.fr; 29 quai Voltaire, 75007 Paris *Tel:* (01) 40 15 71 10 *Fax:* (01) 40 15 67 83 *E-mail:* libparis@ladocumentationfrancaise.fr
Orders to: 124 rue Henri Barbusse, 93308 Aubervilliers Cedex, Contact: Charles Mbanda *Tel:* (01) 40 15 68 74 *Fax:* (01) 40 15 68 01 *E-mail:* libauber@ladocumentationfrancaise.fr

Doin Editeurs+
1, av Edouard-Belin, 92500 Ruel Malmaison
Tel: (01) 34 63 33 33 *Fax:* (01) 34 65 39 85
Key Personnel
President: M Jean-Francois Roure; M Thierry Verret
Founded: 1874
Subjects: Biological Sciences, Chemistry, Chemical Engineering, Earth Sciences, Education, Health, Nutrition, How-to, Medicine, Nursing, Dentistry, Psychology, Psychiatry, Science (General), Social Sciences, Sociology
ISBN Prefix(es): 2-7040
Parent Company: Groupe Lamarre
Warehouse: Editions Maisonneuve, 386 route de Paris, Sainte-Ruffine, 57162 Moulins-les-Metz
Orders to: Tothemes, 47 rue Saint-Andre-des-Arts, 75006 Paris

Les Dossiers d'Aquitaine
5, impasse Bardos, 33800 Bordeaux
Tel: (05) 56 91 84 98 *Fax:* (05) 56 91 64 92
E-mail: ddabx@wanadoo.fr
Web Site: www.ddabordeaux.com
Key Personnel
President: Andre Desforges
Founded: 1978
Publisher.
Subjects: Biography, History, How-to, Literature, Literary Criticism, Essays, Poetry, Publishing & Book Trade Reference
ISBN Prefix(es): 2-905212; 2-84622
Number of titles published annually: 50 Print
Total Titles: 200 Print

Draeger Editeur, see Edition Anthese

Dreamland Editeur+
60, rue Blanche, 75009 Paris
Tel: (01) 53 20 46 66 *Fax:* (01) 53 20 46 67
E-mail: dreamland@nous.fr
Subjects: Art, Film, Video, Radio, TV
ISBN Prefix(es): 2-910027; 2-84808
Total Titles: 70 Print; 33 E-Book
Distribution Center: Vilo

Editions Droguet et Ardant
11 rue Duguay-Trouin, 75006 Paris
Tel: (01) 45 44 38 34 *Fax:* (01) 45 49 93 92
Telex: 580934
Key Personnel
Man Dir: Robert Ardant
Publicity Dir: Suzanne Ardant
Subjects: Religion - Catholic
ISBN Prefix(es): 2-7041

B Drouaud Editions, see Editions J H Paillet et B Drouaud

Du May+
20, rue de la Saussiere, 92100 Boulogne-Billancourt
Tel: (01) 46992424 *Fax:* (01) 48255692
Key Personnel
Dir General: Jacques Peron
Founded: 1986
ISBN Prefix(es): 2-84102

Dunod Editeur+
5 rue Laromiguiere, 75005 Paris
Tel: (01) 40 46 49 02 *Fax:* (01) 40 46 49 90
E-mail: infos@dunod.com
Web Site: www.dunod.com
Key Personnel
President: Charles Vallee
General Manager: Philippe Chagnon
Assistant General Manager: Pierre-Andre Michel
Editorial, Information & Electronics: Jean-Luc Sensi
Editorial, Reference: Eileen Lignot
Marketing: Marc Laforge
Rights & Permissions: Maryvonne Vitry
Technical Education: Francoise Menasce
Founded: 1800
Subjects: Computer Science, Economics, Education, Electronics, Electrical Engineering, Film, Video, Language Arts, Linguistics, Literature, Literary Criticism, Essays, Management, Microcomputers, Photography, Psychology, Psychiatry, Science (General)
ISBN Prefix(es): 2-10
Parent Company: Editions Bordas, 17 rue Remy Dumoncel, BP 50, 75661 Paris Cedex 14
Imprints: CLET; Gauthier-Villars; Privat-Garnier; PSI; Radio; Editions Techniques et Scientifiques Francaises (ETSF)
Subsidiaries: Classiques Garnier
U.S. Office(s): Gauthier-Villars North America Inc, 875-81 Massachusetts Ave, Cambridge, MA 02139, United States
Showroom(s): 5 rue Mabillon, 75006 Paris
Bookshop(s): Librairie des Arts et Metiers, 33 rue Reaumur, 75003 Paris; Librairie Dauphine, Place du Marechal de Lattre de Tasigny, 75016 Paris; Librairie Saint-Sulpice, 30 rue St Sulpice, 75006 Paris
Warehouse: Route d'Etampes, 45330 Malesherbes
Orders to: 11 rue Gossin, 92543 Montrouge Cedex

Duo, Harlequin, *imprint of* Harlequin SA

Editions J Dupuis+
57, blvd de la Villette, 75010 Paris
Tel: (01) 44 84 40 80 *Fax:* (01) 44 84 40 99
Web Site: www.dupuis-entertainment.com
Key Personnel
President & General Manager: Jean-Manuel Bourgois
Founded: 1898
Subjects: Humor
ISBN Prefix(es): 90-314; 2-8001
Parent Company: Editions Dupuis SA, Belgium

Editions de l'Eclat+
23 rue d'Anjou, 75008 Paris
Tel: (01) 45 77 04 04 *Fax:* (01) 45 75 92 51
E-mail: eclat@lyber-eclat.net
Web Site: www.lyber-eclat.net
Key Personnel
General Dir: Michel Valensi
Founded: 1985
Subjects: Philosophy, Religion - Islamic, Religion - Jewish
ISBN Prefix(es): 2-84162; 2-905372
Total Titles: 160 Print
Distributed by Caravelle (Belgium); Dimedia (Canada); Harmonia Mundi (France); Zoe (Switzerland)

Editions de l'Ecole
11 rue de Sevres, 75278 Paris Cedex 06
Tel: (01) 42 22 94 10 *Fax:* (01) 45 48 04 99
E-mail: edl@ecoledesloisirs.com
Web Site: www.ecoledesloisirs.fr
Telex: Ecolois 205735 F *Cable:* LIBRECOLE
Key Personnel
Man Dir: Jean Fabre
Export Sales Manager, Rights & Permissions: S Sevray
Publicity & Advertising: Jean Delas
Subjects: Education
ISBN Prefix(es): 2-211
Divisions: Pastel A

Editions de l'Ecole des Hautes Etudes en Sciences Sociales (EHESS)+
Unit of E HESS
54 blvd Raspail, 75006 Paris
Tel: (01) 49 54 25 25 *Fax:* (01) 45 44 93 11
E-mail: editions@ehess.fr
Web Site: www.ehess.fr
Key Personnel
President: M Jacques Revel *Tel:* (01) 49 54 25 01 *Fax:* (01) 49 54 24 96 *E-mail:* preside@ehess.fr
Founded: 1959
Subjects: Anthropology, Asian Studies, Economics, History, Social Sciences, Sociology
ISBN Prefix(es): 2-7132
Number of titles published annually: 15 Print
Total Titles: 650 Print
Orders to: CID, 131 blvd St Michel, 75005 Paris

Editions et Publications de l'Ecole Lacanienne (EPEL)+
29, rue Madame, 75006 Paris
Tel: (01) 45 49 29 36; (01) 45 44 24 00 *Fax:* (01) 45 44 22 85
E-mail: epel.paris@wanadoo.fr
Web Site: www.ecole-lacanienne.net/popup-epel.html
Key Personnel
Dir: Jean Allouch *E-mail:* jallouch@noos.fr
Founded: 1990
Subjects: Philosophy, Psychology, Psychiatry
ISBN Prefix(es): 2-908855

Ecole Nationale Superieure des Beaux-Arts+
14, rue Bonaparte, 75006 Paris
Tel: (01) 47035000 *Fax:* (01) 47035080
E-mail: info@ensba.fr
Web Site: www.ensba.fr
Key Personnel
Dean: Alfred Pacquement
Editor: Pascale Le Thorel-Daviot *E-mail:* pascale.lethoreldaviot@ensba.fr
Subjects: Art
ISBN Prefix(es): 2-84056; 2-903639
Number of titles published annually: 15 Print; 1 CD-ROM
Total Titles: 100 Print
Parent Company: Ministry of Culture
Bookshop(s): 13, quai Malaquais, 75006 Paris

EDHIS, see Editions d'Histoire Sociale (EDHIS)

EDICEF - Editions Classiques d'Expression Francaise, see Hachette Livre International

Editions Edisud+
La Calade, 3120 Route d'Avignon, 13090 Aix-en-Provence
Tel: (04) 42 21 61 44 *Fax:* (04) 42 21 56 20
E-mail: info@edisud.com
Web Site: www.edisud.com
Key Personnel
Man Dir, Sales, Production: Charly-Yves Chaudoreille
Editorial: Anne-Marie Lapillonne
Rights & Permissions: Marie-Noelle Boudon
Founded: 1971
Subjects: Agriculture, Anthropology, Archaeology, Architecture & Interior Design, Art, Cookery, Energy, Environmental Studies, Ethnicity,

Gardening, Plants, Geography, Geology, History, How-to, Music, Dance, Outdoor Recreation, Regional Interests, Sports, Athletics, Wine & Spirits
ISBN Prefix(es): 2-85744; 2-7449

Institute Editeur
63, rue Edouard-Vaillant, 92300 Levallois-Perret
Tel: (01) 40 87 17 17 *Fax:* (01) 40 87 17 18
Key Personnel
Dir: Claudine Muller
Founded: 1989
Subjects: Advertising, Architecture & Interior Design, Electronics, Electrical Engineering, History, Management
ISBN Prefix(es): 2-907904
Imprints: Histoire D'Entreprises

Les Editeurs Reunis+
11, rue de la Montagne-Sainte-Genevieve, 75005 Paris
Tel: (01) 43 54 74 46; (01) 43 54 43 81 *Fax:* (01) 43 25 34 79
Founded: 1932
The company acts as sole agent for YMCA Press in publishing a comprehensive list of Russian books in the original Russian.
Subjects: Literature, Literary Criticism, Essays, Religion - Other
ISBN Prefix(es): 2-85065

Edition1+
43 Quai de Grenelle, 75905 Paris Cedex 15
Tel: (01) 43923587 *Fax:* (01) 43923585
Key Personnel
Publisher, Editor, Man Dir & Right & Permissions: Rene Guitton
Editor: Isabelle Brossard
Founded: 1979
Subjects: Biography, Literature, Literary Criticism, Essays, Nonfiction (General), Self-Help, Sports, Athletics
ISBN Prefix(es): 2-86391
Parent Company: Hachette Group

Les Editions de Minuit SA+
7, rue Bernard-Palissy, 75006 Paris
Tel: (01) 44 39 39 20 *Fax:* (01) 45 44 82 36
E-mail: contact@leseditionsdeminuit.fr
Web Site: www.leseditionsdeminuit.fr
Key Personnel
President & Dir General: Irene Lindon *Tel:* (01) 44 39 39 22
Founded: 1942
Subjects: Fiction, Literature, Literary Criticism, Essays, Philosophy, Social Sciences, Sociology
ISBN Prefix(es): 2-7073
Number of titles published annually: 20 Print
Total Titles: 600 Print
Distributed by La Cite - L'Age d'Homme (Switzerland); Dimedia Inc (Canada)
Bookshop(s): Compagnie, 58 rue des Ecoles, 75005 Paris
Orders to: Le Seuil, 27 rue Jacob, 75006 Paris *Tel:* (01) 43547486

Editions d'Organisation+
61 blvd Saint-Germain, 75240 Paris Cedex 05
Tel: (01) 44 41 11 11 *Fax:* (01) 44 41 11 85
E-mail: service-lecteurs@editions-organisation.com
Web Site: www.editions-organisation.com
Key Personnel
President: Serge Eyrolles
General Manager: Jean Pierre Tissier
Founded: 1952
Subjects: Business, Computer Science, Electronics, Electrical Engineering, Engineering (General), House & Home, How-to, Law, Management, Social Sciences, Sociology
ISBN Prefix(es): 2-7081

Number of titles published annually: 550 Print
Parent Company: Groupe Eyrolles SA, 57 blvd Saint Germain, 75240 Paris Cedex 05
Bookshop(s): Librairie Eyrolles, Paris *Tel:* (01) 44 41 11 74; Librairie Des Entreprises, 79 ave de la Republique, ESCP Hall Blondeau, 75543 Paris Cedex 11 *Tel:* (01) 43 38 26 71; Librairie De Provence, 31 Cours Mirabeau, 13100 Aix-en-Provence *Tel:* (042) 42 26 07 23; Librairie Des Entreprises, One rue de la Liberation, Centre HEC-ISA, Jouy-en-Josas *Tel:* (01) 39 67 94 59; Librarie Des Entreprises, Av Bernard Hirsch, BP 105, 95021 Cergy Pontoise Cedex *Tel:* (01) 30 38 14 52

Les Editions du CFPJ (Centre de Formation et de Perfectionnement des Journalistes) - Sarl Presse et Formation+
Affiliate of CFPJ
35 rue du Louvre, 75002 Paris
Tel: (01) 44 82 20 00 *Fax:* (01) 44 82 20 01
Web Site: www.cfpj.com
Key Personnel
General Dir: Daniele Granet
Founded: 1988
Subjects: Communications, Journalism
ISBN Prefix(es): 2-85900; 2-902734
Imprints: Presse et Formation

Editions du Chene, EPA, *imprint of* Editions du Chene

Editions du Conseil de l'Europe, see Council of Europe Publishing

Editions ELOR
10 rue du Chandelier, 56350 Saint-Vincent-sur-Oust
Tel: (02) 99 91 22 80 *Fax:* (02) 99 91 34 45
E-mail: edit.elor@wanadoo.fr
Web Site: www.elor.com
Key Personnel
Dir: Jacqueline Frain
Founded: 1976
Subjects: Crafts, Games, Hobbies, Religion - Catholic
ISBN Prefix(es): 2-907524; 2-912214
Imprints: Editions de Iorme Rond
Distributed by Duquesne Diffusion

Les Editions ESF+
2 rue Maurice Hartmann, 92133 Issy-les-Moulineaux Cedex
Mailing Address: BP 62, 92133 Issy-les-Moulineaux Cedex
Tel: (02) 37 29 69 20 *Fax:* (02) 37 29 69 35
E-mail: info@esf-editeur.fr
Web Site: www.esf-editeur.fr
Key Personnel
President: Dominique Prat
Man Dir: Vincent Wackenheim
Founded: 1947
Subjects: Business, Communications, Economics, Education, Finance, Law, Management, Marketing, Microcomputers, Psychology, Psychiatry, Technology
ISBN Prefix(es): 2-7101
Parent Company: Reed Business Information
Warehouse: PRAT, Zi de Comhre, 28481 Thiron
Orders to: Presses de Belgique, Belgium
Dimedia, Canada
CDE, 17 rue de Tournon, 75006 Paris
Servidis, Switzerland

Editions Grund+
60 rue Mazarine, 75006 Paris
Tel: (01) 53103600 *Fax:* (01) 43294986
E-mail: grund@grund.fr
Web Site: www.grund.fr *Cable:* GRUND PARIS
Key Personnel
President: Alain Grund

Sales: Yannick Lemonnier
Chief Editor: Monique Souchon
Public Relations: Chantal Janisson *Tel:* (01) 53103612 *E-mail:* chantal.janisson@grund.fr
Founded: 1880
Subjects: Animals, Pets, Art, Environmental Studies, How-to, Travel
ISBN Prefix(es): 2-7000; 2-85205
Number of titles published annually: 180 Print
Associate Companies: Editions Alpina; Editions Guy Le Prat

Editions Litteraires et Linguistiques de l'Universite de Grenoble III, see ELLUG (Editions Litteraires et Linguistiques de l'Universite de Grenoble III)

Editions Recherche sur les Civilisations (ERC)
Unit of ADPF
6, rue Ferrus, 75683 Paris Cedex 14
Tel: (01) 43 13 11 00 *Fax:* (01) 43 13 11 25
E-mail: erc.edit@adpf.asso.fr
Web Site: www.france.diplomatie.fr; www.adpf.asso.fr
Key Personnel
Editorial Dir: Hina Descat
Contact: Guillaume Desanges
Founded: 1980
Subjects: Anthropology, Archaeology, Ethnicity, History, Social Sciences, Sociology
ISBN Prefix(es): 2-86538
Total Titles: 268 Print

Editions rue d'Ulm
45 rue d'Ulm, 75005 Paris
Tel: (01) 44 32 30 29 *Fax:* (01) 44 32 36 86
E-mail: ulm-editions@ens.fr
Web Site: www.presses.ens.fr
Key Personnel
Man Dir: Laure Leveille
Editorial: Frederique Matonti
Sales: Angustinee Belsoeur
Production: Pascale Lehec
Founded: 1975
Subjects: Archaeology, Economics, History, Literature, Literary Criticism, Essays, Philosophy, Science (General), Social Sciences, Sociology
ISBN Prefix(es): 2-7288
Bookshop(s): 29, rue d'Ulm, 75005 Paris *Tel:* (01) 44 32 29 70 *Fax:* (01) 44 32 29 72

Editions Techniques et Scientifiques Francaises (ETSF), *imprint of* Dunod Editeur

Editions Terrail/Finest SA
25, rue Ginoux, 75015 Paris
Tel: (01) 45 77 08 05 *Fax:* (01) 45 79 97 15
Key Personnel
Dir, Editorial: Jean-Francois Gonthier
Dir, Ventes & Marketing: Erik Boursier
Specialize in art books.
Subjects: Archaeology, Architecture & Interior Design, Art
ISBN Prefix(es): 2-87939
Parent Company: Groupe Bayard Presse

Editions Unes+
BP 205, 83006 Draguignan cedex
Tel: (04) 94673158 *Fax:* (04) 94673175
Key Personnel
Contact: Jean-Pierre Sintive
Founded: 1981
Subjects: Library & Information Sciences, Literature, Literary Criticism, Essays, Poetry
ISBN Prefix(es): 2-87704
Branch Office(s)
Raphaille Dedourge, 15 rue ar Maire, 75003 Cedex Paris *Tel:* (01) 42 77 25 82 *E-mail:* raphaellededourge2@compuses.com

Editions Verticales, *imprint of* Editions du Seuil

EDJA, *imprint of* Editions Juridiques Africaines

EDP Sciences+
Subsidiary of Societe Francaise de Physique
17, ave du Hoggar, Parc d'Activities de Courtaboeuf, 91944 Les Ulis Cedex A
Mailing Address: BP 112, 91944 Les Ulis Cedex A
Tel: (01) 69 18 75 75 *Fax:* (01) 69 28 84 91
E-mail: edps@edpsciences.org
Web Site: www.edpsciences.org
Key Personnel
Man Dir & Publications Manager: Jean-Marc Quilbe *E-mail:* quilbe@edpsciences.org
Founded: 1920
Services for electronic publications, web site development & printing.
Subjects: Astronomy, Engineering (General), Mathematics, Mechanical Engineering, Physics, Science (General), Technology, Life Sciences
ISBN Prefix(es): 2-86883; 2-902731
Number of titles published annually: 45 Print
Total Titles: 20 E-Book
U.S. Office(s): 875-81 Massachusetts Ave, Cambridge, MA 02139, United States, Contact: Doug Wright *Tel:* 617-395-4070 *Fax:* 617-354-6875 *E-mail:* dwright@pcgplus.com

Educalivre, *imprint of* Editions Casteilla

EHESS, see Editions de l'Ecole des Hautes Etudes en Sciences Sociales (EHESS)

Electre
35 rue Gregoire-de-Tours, 75006 Paris
Tel: (01) 44 41 28 00 *Fax:* (01) 44 41 28 65
E-mail: biblio@electre.com
Web Site: www.electre.com
Key Personnel
Man Dir: Jean-Marie Doublet
Dir Development: Pascal Fouche
Founded: 1983
Subjects: Library & Information Sciences
ISBN Prefix(es): 2-7654

Elf Exploration Production+
Ave Larribau, 64018 Pau Cedex
Tel: (05) 59 83 65 80 *Fax:* (05) 59 83 58 11
E-mail: contact_ep@cgt-totalfina-elf.org
Web Site: www.cgt-totalfina-elf.org
Key Personnel
Editor: Jean-Francois Raynaud
Founded: 1967
Subjects: Earth Sciences, Geography, Geology
ISBN Prefix(es): 2-901026; 2-85843
Book Club(s): France Edition; Syndicate National de L'Edition; Unipresse

Ellebore Editions
18, Impasse Mousset, 75560 Paris Cedex 12
Mailing Address: PO Box 01, 75560 Paris Cedex 12
Tel: (01) 40 01 09 49 *Fax:* (01) 40 01 09 94
E-mail: ellebore@wfi.fr; info@ellebore.fr
Web Site: www.wfi.fr/ellebore
Telex: 213907 Parac
Key Personnel
Manager: Jean-Paul Barriolade
Founded: 1980
Subjects: Health, Nutrition, Psychology, Psychiatry
ISBN Prefix(es): 2-86898

Ellipses - Edition Marketing SA
32, rue Bargue, 75740 Paris Cedex 15
Tel: (01) 45 67 74 19 *Fax:* (01) 47 34 67 94
E-mail: infos@editions-ellipses.com
Web Site: www.editions-ellipses.fr
Key Personnel
Man Dir: Jean-Pierre Benezet
Founded: 1973
Subjects: Medicine, Nursing, Dentistry, Science (General)
ISBN Prefix(es): 2-7298

ELLUG (Editions Litteraires et Linguistiques de l'Universite de Grenoble III) (University Stendhal-Grenoble III Press)+
Universite Stendhal, 1180 ave Centrale-Domaine Universitaire, 38400 Saint Martin d'Heres
Mailing Address: BP 25, 38040 Grenoble Cedex 9
Tel: (04) 76 82 43 72; (04) 76 82 77 74 *Fax:* (04) 76 82 41 85
E-mail: ellug@u-grenoble3.fr
Web Site: www-ellug.u-grenoble3.fr/ellug
Key Personnel
Man Dir: Pierre Morere
Editor: Elisabeth Greslou *E-mail:* elisabeth.greslou@u-grenoble3.fr
Founded: 1978
Membership(s): International Association of Scholarly Publishers.
Subjects: Antiques, Communications, Language Arts, Linguistics, Literature, Literary Criticism, Essays
ISBN Prefix(es): 2-902709; 2-84310
Number of titles published annually: 10 Print
Total Titles: 120 Print
Distribution Center: CID, 131 bd Saint Michel, Paris 75005 *Tel:* (01) 43 54 47 15 *Fax:* (01) 43 54 80 73 *E-mail:* cid@msh_paris.fr *Web Site:* www.u-grenoble3.fr

Elsevier SAS (Editions Scientifiques et Medicales Elsevier)
2, rue Linois, 75724 Paris Cedex 15
Tel: (01) 45589110 *Fax:* (01) 45589419
Web Site: www.elsevier.fr
Key Personnel
President & Dir-General: Catherine Lucet
Finance Dir: Patrick Regnier
Founded: 1984
Subjects: Mathematics, Medicine, Nursing, Dentistry, Physics
ISBN Prefix(es): 2-84299; 2-906077

EM Inter, *imprint of* Editions Lavoisier

Encres Vives
2, allee des Allobroges, 31770 Colomiers
Tel: (05) 62740787
E-mail: encres@mygale.org
Key Personnel
Dir: Michel Cosem
Founded: 1960
Subjects: Poetry
ISBN Prefix(es): 2-85550

Encyclopedia Universalis France SA+
18 rue de Tilsitt, 75809 Paris Cedex 17
Tel: (01) 45 72 72 72 *Fax:* (01) 45 72 03 43
E-mail: contact@universalis.fr
Web Site: www.universalis.fr
Key Personnel
President: Giuseppe Annoscia
Editorial: Bernard Couvelaire
Financial Manager: Herve Rouanet
Export Manager: Speranta Gallage *Tel:* (01) 45 72 72 52 *E-mail:* sgallage@universalis.fr
Production Manager: Dominique Reyren
Founded: 1968
ISBN Prefix(es): 2-85229

L'encyclopedie Poetique, *imprint of* Sarl Editions Jean Grassin

Les Encyclopedies du Patrimoine
2 rue de Valois, 75001 Paris
Tel: (01) 42 60 66 63 *Fax:* (01) 42 60 66 73
Web Site: www.culture.gouv.fr
Key Personnel
Dir: Wanda Diebolt
ISBN Prefix(es): 2-911200

Editions Entente+
12, rue Honore-Chevalier, 75006 Paris
Tel: (01) 55 42 84 00 *Fax:* (01) 40 49 01 02
Key Personnel
Man Dir: Edouard Esmerian
Founded: 1975
Publish *La Gazette du Livre* (La Tribune des Petits Editeurs).
Membership(s): Association des Petits Editeurs Francophones.
Subjects: Cookery, Developing Countries, Economics, Education, Energy, Environmental Studies, Human Relations, Literature, Literary Criticism, Essays, Poetry, Science (General), Technology
ISBN Prefix(es): 2-7266
Total Titles: 102 Print; 1 Audio
Distributor for l'Athanor; Editions d'En-Bas; Robert Jauze; Jacques Laget; Lierre & Coudrier; Mamamelis; Le Nid; La Pleine Lune; Le Signet
Bookshop(s): Librairie Entente12 rue Honore-Chevalier, 75006 Paris

Histoire D'Entreprises, *imprint of* Institute Editeur

EPA (Editions Pratiques Automobiles)+
Imprint of Editions du Chene
43 Quai de Grenelle, 75905 Paris Cedex 15
Tel: (01) 43 92 30 00 *Fax:* (01) 43 92 33 81
Web Site: www.editionsduchene.fr
Key Personnel
President: Fatine Layt
Man Dir: Isabelle Jendron
Editorial Dir: Philippe Pierrelee
Rights Manager: Sherri Aldis
Founded: 1972
Subjects: Aeronautics, Aviation, Architecture & Interior Design, Automotive, Cookery, History, Maritime, Military Science, Sports, Athletics, Transportation, Wine & Spirits
ISBN Prefix(es): 2-85120
Parent Company: Hachette Livre

Epanouissement, *imprint of* Jouvence Editions

Editions de l'Epargne+
18-24 rue Cabanis, 12 villa Lourcine, 75014 Paris
Tel: (01) 44 16 95 80 *Fax:* (01) 44 16 95 99
Key Personnel
Man Dir: Dominique Therond
Founded: 1957
Subjects: Architecture & Interior Design, Art, Economics, Finance, History, How-to, Law
ISBN Prefix(es): 2-85015

EPEL, see Editions et Publications de l'Ecole Lacanienne (EPEL)

ERC, see Editions Recherche sur les Civilisations (ERC)

L'Ere Nouvelle+
BP 171, 06407 Cannes Cedex
Tel: (04) 93 99 30 13
E-mail: lerenouvelle@wanadoo.fr
Web Site: assoc.wanadoo.fr/lerenouvelle/pub
Key Personnel
Dir: Pierre Lance *E-mail:* pierre.lance@wanadoo.fr
Founded: 1980
Subjects: Energy, Health, Nutrition, Philosophy, Psychology, Psychiatry, Social Sciences, Sociology
ISBN Prefix(es): 2-905825

Editions Eres+
11 rue des Alouettes, 31520 Ramonville
Tel: (05) 61 75 15 76 *Fax:* (05) 61 73 52 89
E-mail: eres@edition-eres.com
Web Site: www.edition-eres.com
Key Personnel
President & Dir General: Jean Sacrispeyre
Founded: 1980
Subjects: Criminology, Law, Philosophy, Psychology, Psychiatry, Social Sciences, Sociology
ISBN Prefix(es): 2-86586; 2-7492
Number of titles published annually: 60 Print

Editions Errance
7 rue Jean du Bellay, 75004 Paris
Tel: (01) 43 26 85 82 *Fax:* (01) 43 29 34 88
Key Personnel
Editor: Frederic Lontcho
Founded: 1982
Subjects: Archaeology, History
ISBN Prefix(es): 2-87772; 2-903442

Editions Eska
12, rue du Quatre Septembre, 75002 Paris
Tel: (01) 42 86 55 73 *Fax:* (01) 42 60 45 35
E-mail: eska@multimediart.fr
Web Site: www.sybex.fr
Key Personnel
Sales Dir: Patricia Fousweray
Subjects: Aeronautics, Aviation, Economics, Engineering (General), Labor, Industrial Relations, Law, Management, Medicine, Nursing, Dentistry
ISBN Prefix(es): 2-86911; 2-7472
Distributor for Presses Universitaires du Quebec (Canada)

Editions Espaces 34+
BP 2080, 34025 Montpellier Cedex
Tel: (04) 67 84 11 23 *Fax:* (04) 67 84 00 74
E-mail: chesp34@club-internet.fr
Web Site: www.editions-espaces34.fr
Key Personnel
President: Laurent Chevallier
Subjects: Biological Sciences, Drama, Theater, Literature, Literary Criticism, Essays, Mathematics, Medicine, Nursing, Dentistry, Social Sciences, Sociology
ISBN Prefix(es): 2-907293; 2-84705
Total Titles: 110 Print

L'Esprit Du Temps+
115 ave Anatole France, 33491 Le Bouscat Cedex
Mailing Address: BP 107, 33491 Le Bouscat Cedex
Tel: (0556) 02 84 19 *Fax:* (0556) 02 91 31
E-mail: espritemp@aol.com
Web Site: www.psy-book.net
Key Personnel
Manager: Eleonore Brenot
Literary Dir: Philippe Brenot
Founded: 1989
Subjects: Literature, Literary Criticism, Essays, Medicine, Nursing, Dentistry, Psychology, Psychiatry, Psychoanalysis, Reviews
ISBN Prefix(es): 2-908206; 2-913062; 2-84795
Number of titles published annually: 30 Print
Total Titles: 250 Print
Orders to: PUF, 14 ave du Bois de l'Epiue, BP 90, 91003 Evry Cedex

Editions de L'Est+
Rue Theophraste-Renaudot, 54185 Heillecourt Cedex
Tel: (03) 83598054 *Fax:* (03) 83598072
Telex: 961749F
Key Personnel
President: Pascal Chipot
Dir General: Gerard Gabriel
ISBN Prefix(es): 2-86955

Institut d'Ethnologie du Museum National d'Histoire Naturelle
Service des Publications Scientifiques, 57, rue Cuvier, 75231 Paris Cedex 05
Tel: (01) 40 79 48 38 *Fax:* (01) 40 79 38 58
E-mail: diff.pub@mnhn.fr
Web Site: www.mnhn.fr/publication
Key Personnel
Head: Philippe Bouchet
Founded: 1925
Subjects: Archaeology, Ethnicity, Language Arts, Linguistics
ISBN Prefix(es): 2-85653; 2-85265
Number of titles published annually: 1 Print
Total Titles: 125 Print

ETSF, see Editions Techniques et Scientifiques Francaises

Institut d'Etudes Augustiniennes
3 rue de l'Abbaye, 75006 Paris
Tel: (01) 43 54 80 25 *Fax:* (01) 43 54 39 55
E-mail: iea@wanadoo.fr
Key Personnel
Man Dir: Jean-Claude Fredouille
Contact: Claudine Croyere
Founded: 1954
Subjects: Antiques, Archaeology, History, Philosophy, Religion - Catholic, Theology
ISBN Prefix(es): 2-85121
Shipping Address: Brepols Steen Weg op Tielen 68, 2300 Turnhout, Belgium *Tel:* (014) 40 27 00 *Fax:* (014) 42 89 19 *E-mail:* publishers@brepols.com
Warehouse: Brepols Steen Weg op Tielen 68, 2300 Turnhout, Belgium *Tel:* (014) 40 27 00 *Fax:* (014) 42 89 19 *E-mail:* publishers@brepols.com
Orders to: Brepols Steen Weg op Tielen 68, 2300 Turnhout, Belgium *Tel:* (014) 40 27 00 *Fax:* (014) 42 89 19 *E-mail:* publishers@brepols.com

Institut d'Etudes Slaves IES+
9, rue Michelet, 75006 Paris
Tel: (01) 43 26 50 89; (01) 43 26 79 18 *Fax:* (01) 43 26 16 23
E-mail: etudes.slaves@paris4.sorbonne.fr
Web Site: www.etudes-slaves.paris4.sorbonne.fr
Key Personnel
Dir: Pierre Gonneau
Founded: 1920
Subjects: History, Language Arts, Linguistics, Literature, Literary Criticism, Essays, Slavic Studies
ISBN Prefix(es): 2-7204

l'Europeenne, *imprint of* Editions de Septembre

L'Expansion Scientifique Francaise
15, rue Saint-Benoit, 75006 Paris
Tel: (01) 45 48 42 60 *Fax:* (01) 45 44 81 55
E-mail: expansionscientifiquefrancaise@wanadoo.fr
Web Site: www.expansionscientifique.com
Key Personnel
Man Dir: Pierre Bergeaud
Founded: 1925
Subjects: Biological Sciences, Medicine, Nursing, Dentistry
ISBN Prefix(es): 2-7046
Bookshop(s): Librairie des Facultes de Medecine et de Pharmacie, 174 blvd St-Germain, 75297 Paris Cedex 06 *Tel:* (01) 45 48 54 48

Editions Eyrolles+
61 blvd Saint-Germain, 75240 Paris Cedex 05
Tel: (01) 44 41 11 11 *Fax:* (01) 44 41 11 85
E-mail: service-lecteurs@editions-eyrolles.com
Web Site: www.editions-eyrolles.com
Telex: Eyrotp 203385 F

Key Personnel
Man Dir: Jean-Pierre Tissier
Editorials: Eric Sulpice; Jean-Jacques Brisebarre
Foreign Rights: Marlyne Tolentino *Tel:* (01) 44 41 11 16 *Fax:* (01) 44 41 46 00
E-mail: foreignrights@eyrolles.com
Contact: Miguel Tejedor
Founded: 1918
Subjects: Architecture & Interior Design, Computer Science, Crafts, Games, Hobbies, Earth Sciences, Electronics, Electrical Engineering, Management, Mechanical Engineering, Physical Sciences
ISBN Prefix(es): 2-212
Parent Company: Ecole Speciale des Travaux Publics
Associate Companies: Editions d'Organisation
Distributor for Microsoft Press France

Falguiere 36, see Galerie Esther Woerdehoff

Editions Fallois
22 rue La Boetie, 75008 Paris
Tel: (01) 42669195 *Fax:* (01) 49240637
Founded: 1987
Subjects: Literature, Literary Criticism, Essays
ISBN Prefix(es): 2-87706
Orders to: Hachette Export, 58 rue Jean Bleuzen, 92178 Vanves Cedex

Editions Pierre Fanlac+
12 Rue du Professeur-Peyrot, 24002 Perigueux Cedex
Mailing Address: BP 2043, 24002 Perigueux Cedex
Tel: (05) 53-53-41-90 *Fax:* (05) 53-08-05-85
E-mail: info@fanlac.com
Web Site: www.fanlac.com
Key Personnel
Dir General: Bernard Tardien
Founded: 1943
Subjects: Art, Cookery, Literature, Literary Criticism, Essays, Photography, Poetry, Regional Interests, Travel
ISBN Prefix(es): 2-86577; 2-85122
Number of titles published annually: 10 Print
Branch Office(s)
31 rue Faidherbe, 75011 Paris *Tel:* (01) 43-67-51-32 *Fax:* (01) 40-09-94-00
Distribution Center: Fanlac Editions

Editions Farel+
BP 20, 77421 Marne-la-Vallee Cedex 2
Tel: (01) 64 68 46 44 *Fax:* (01) 64 68 39 90
E-mail: lire@editionsfarel.com
Web Site: www.editionsfarel.com
Key Personnel
Dir: D Steven Dixon
Founded: 1978
Subjects: Religion - Protestant
ISBN Prefix(es): 2-86314
Number of titles published annually: 20 Print
Total Titles: 220 Print
Distributed by Le Bon Livre (Belgium); Diffusion Emmaues (Switzerland); Inter-livres LLB (Canada)
Distributor for G-Lu Publishing House; Janz Team/Peniel

Editions Fata Morgana+
Fontfroide le Haut, 34980 Saint-Clement
Tel: (04) 67 54 40 40 *Fax:* (04) 67 04 14 91
E-mail: davidini@wanadoo.fr
Web Site: perso.wanadoo.fr/fatamorgana
Key Personnel
President: Roy Bruno
International Rights: David Massabuau
Founded: 1966
Subjects: Art, Asian Studies, Literature, Literary Criticism, Essays, Philosophy, Religion - Catholic, Religion - Hindu, Religion - Islamic, Religion - Jewish, Religion - Other

ISBN Prefix(es): 2-85194
Subsidiaries: Fakir Press; Bibliotheque Artistique & Litteraire
Distributed by DPLU (Canada); L'Age-D'Homme (Switzerland); Nouvelle Diffusion (Belgium)
Bookshop(s): Librairie Freecyb, 41 rue Basfroi, Paris, Jean-Francois Poupelin
E-mail: yanndortin@freecyb.com *Web Site:* freecyb.com
Orders to: Les Belles Lettres, 95 Bd Raspail, 75006 Paris *Tel:* (01) 44-39-84-20 *Fax:* (01) 45-44-92-88

Librairie Artheme Fayard+
75, rue des Saints-Peres, 75279 Paris Cedex 6
Tel: (01) 45498200 *Fax:* (01) 42224017
Web Site: www.editions-fayard.fr
Telex: 264918 trace
Key Personnel
President & Man Dir: Claude Durand
Publicity: Caroline Gutmann
Advertising Dir: Frederique Larvor
Rights & Permissions: Martine Bertea
  E-mail: rights@editions-fayard.fr
Founded: 1854
Subjects: Biography, Fiction, History, Music, Dance, Philosophy, Religion - Other, Science (General), Social Sciences, Sociology, Technology
ISBN Prefix(es): 2-213
Parent Company: Hachette

FBT de R Editions
31, quai de la Tournelle, 75005 Paris
Tel: (01) 41 15 19 69; (06) 07 68 33 71 *Fax:* (01) 41 15 19 69
Key Personnel
President: Francoise Thiam
Founded: 1995
Subjects: Art, Criminology, Economics, Fiction, Foreign Countries, Government, Political Science, Human Relations, Literature, Literary Criticism, Essays, Travel
ISBN Prefix(es): 2-911064

Federation d'Activities Culturelles, Fac Editions
30, rue Madame, 75006 Paris
Tel: (01) 45 48 76 51 *Fax:* (01) 42 22 22 31
Key Personnel
General Dir: Max Huot De Longchamp
Subjects: Philosophy, Religion - Catholic, Theology
ISBN Prefix(es): 2-903422
Imprints: Paroisse & Famille
Distributor for CLD

Federation Francaise de la Randonnee Pedestre+
14, rue Riquet, 75019 Paris
Tel: (01) 44 89 93 90 *Fax:* (01) 40 35 85 48
E-mail: info@ffrp.asso.fr
Web Site: asp.ffrp.asso.fr
Key Personnel
President: Maurice Bruzek
Founded: 1947
Subjects: Outdoor Recreation, Sports, Athletics
ISBN Prefix(es): 2-85699
Shipping Address: IGN, lamp des Landes, 41200 Villefranche s/cher
Warehouse: IGN, lamp des Landes, 41200 Villefranche s/cher
Orders to: IGN, lamp des Landes, 41200 Villefranche s/cher

Editions Des Femmes+
6, rue de Mezieres, 75006 Paris Cedex 6
Tel: (01) 42 22 60 74 *Fax:* (01) 42 22 62 73
E-mail: info@desfemmes.fr
Web Site: www.desfemmes.fr

Key Personnel
Proprietor & Man Dir: Antoinette Fouque
General Manager: Marie-Claude Grumbach
Founded: 1974
Subjects: Art, Biography, Drama, Theater, Fiction, History, Literature, Literary Criticism, Essays, Photography, Poetry
ISBN Prefix(es): 2-7210
Number of titles published annually: 5 Print; 2 Audio
Total Titles: 450 Print; 100 Audio
Distributor for Sonjis

Editions du Feu Nouveau+
3, rue du Chateau, 60390 Troussures
Tel: (01) 44844797
Key Personnel
Man Dir: Henri Caffarel
Founded: 1946
Subjects: Literature, Literary Criticism, Essays, Religion - Catholic, Religion - Other
ISBN Prefix(es): 2-85017
Shipping Address: SOFEDIS (Diffuseur), 29 rue Saint-Sulpice, 75006 Paris

Figures, *imprint of* Societe des Editions Grasset et Fasquelle

Editions Filipacchi-Sonodip+
151 rue Anatole-France, Immeuble Europa, 92534 Levallois-Perret Cedex
Tel: (01) 41 34 90 69; (01) 41 34 90 55 *Fax:* (01) 41 34 90 70
Key Personnel
Manager, Editorial: Marie-Francoise Acdouard
Founded: 1970
Subjects: Cookery, House & Home, Photography, Travel
ISBN Prefix(es): 2-85018

Editions First+
33 Ave de la Republique, 5e etage, 75011 Paris
Tel: (01) 40 21 46 46 *Fax:* (01) 55 43 25 20
E-mail: firstinfo@efirst.com
Web Site: www.efirst.com
Key Personnel
Editorial Dir: Henri Bovet
Production & Administration: Jean Fontanieu
Rights: Stephanie Koch
Founded: 1985
Subjects: Computer Science, Health, Nutrition, Humor, Marketing
ISBN Prefix(es): 2-87691

Librairie Fischbacher, International Art Book Distribution (import-export)
33, rue de Seine, 75006 Paris
Tel: (01) 43 26 84 87 *Fax:* (01) 43 26 48 87
Key Personnel
Dir, Production, Publicity, Rights & Permissions: Marie-Colette Galand
Sales: P Diani-Garel
Founded: 1850
Membership(s): the Library of Fine Arts; specialize in original art.
Subjects: Art, History, Music, Dance, Philosophy, Religion - Protestant, Social Sciences, Sociology, Theology
ISBN Prefix(es): 2-7179
Parent Company: Librairie Fischbacher SA

Editions Fivedit
96 rue du Faubourg-Poissonniere, 75010 Paris
Mailing Address: BP 146, 74941 Annecy Le Vieux Cedex
Tel: (04) 50 66 33 78 *Fax:* (04) 50 23 33 08
E-mail: fivedit.sa@wanadoo.fr
Key Personnel
Man Dir: Rene Fivel-Demoret
Founded: 1976
Subjects: How-to, Travel

ISBN Prefix(es): 2-904394
Total Titles: 30 Print
Branch Office(s)
Distribution Ulysse, 4176 Saint Denis, Montreal, PQ, Canada
Distributed by Vivendi Universal Publishing Services
Distributor for APCA Bienvenue a la Ferme; Gites de France; Logis de Belgique; Logis de France; Logis D' Italia; Tables et Auberges de France

Flammarion SA+
26 rue Racine, 75006 Paris
Tel: (01) 40513008; (01) 4053127 *Fax:* (01) 43250118; (01) 43292148
Telex: flamedit 205641 *Cable:* 205146
Key Personnel
Chairman: Charles-Henri Flammarion
Man Dir: Danielle Nees
Sales Manager: Alain Flammarion
Publicity, Advertising: Catherine Bachelez
Rights & Permissions: Renata Morteo
Press: Francine Brobeil *Fax:* (01) 40 51 31 29
  E-mail: fbr@flammarion.fr
Founded: 1875
Subjects: Architecture & Interior Design, Art, Fiction, Gardening, Plants, House & Home, Literature, Literary Criticism, Essays, Medicine, Nursing, Dentistry, Nonfiction (General), Wine & Spirits
ISBN Prefix(es): 2-257
Associate Companies: Pygnalion
Imprints: Arthaud; Aubie; Champs Dominos; GF; Glacial; Fluide; J'ailu; Librio; Medecine-Sciences; Pere Castor
Subsidiaries: Aubie; Beau Arts SA; Delagrave; Editions Aubier, Flammarion Canada; Flammarion 4; Flammarion Presse; Flammarion 2; Flammarion Switzerland; Flammarion USA Inc; J'ai Lu; Union-Distribution
U.S. Office(s): Flammarion USA Inc, 200 Park Ave S, Suite 1406, New York, NY 10003, United States *Tel:* 212-777-6888 *Fax:* 212-777-3438
Distributed by Abbeville (USA); Thames & Hudson (UK)
Distributor for Abbeville; Actes Sud; Assouline; Bibliotheque de l'Image; CNAC; Delcourt; Flohic; Hoebeke; Horay; Le Petit Fute; Pygnalion; Revue du Vin de France; Zulma
Bookshop(s): Flammarion 4, 19 Rue Visconti, 75006 Paris
Warehouse: UD-Union Distribution, 06 rue Petit le roy, Chevilly-Larue, 94152 Rungis Cedex
Tel: (01) 41802020 *Fax:* (01) 46875104
Orders to: UD-Union Distribution, 106 rue Petit le roy, Chevilly-Larue, 94152 Rungis Cedex
Tel: (01) 41802020 *Fax:* (01) 46875180

FLE, see Hachette francais langue etrangere - FLE

Editions Fleurus+
11 rue Duguay-Trovin, 75006 Paris
Tel: (01) 45 44 38 34 *Fax:* (01) 45 49 93 92
Telex: 201650 F
Key Personnel
Man Dir: Pierre-Marie Dumont
Eitorial Dir: Christophe Savoure
Editorial: Janine Boudineau
Sales Dir: Dominique Delage
Foreign Rights: Euriel Donval; Chantal Hourcade
Founded: 1944
Subjects: Architecture & Interior Design, Art, Crafts, Games, Hobbies, Fiction, Psychology, Psychiatry, Religion - Other, Social Sciences, Sociology
ISBN Prefix(es): 2-215

Fleuve No ite Editions, see Presses de la Cite

Fluide, *imprint of* Flammarion SA

FRANCE

Folklore Comtois
Musee des Maisons Comtoises, 25360 Nancray
Tel: (03) 81 55 29 77 *Fax:* (03) 81 55 23 97
Key Personnel
President: Jean Louis Clade
Vice President: Pierre Bourgin
Subjects: Agriculture, Architecture & Interior Design, History, House & Home

Editions Foucher
Subsidiary of Hachette
58 rue Jean Bleuzen, 92178 Vanves Cedex
Tel: (01) 41 23 65 60 *Fax:* (01) 41 23 65 03
E-mail: contact@editions-foucher.fr
Web Site: www.editions-foucher.fr
Key Personnel
President: Christine Breiteinstein
General Manager: Daniel Segala
Founded: 1936
Subjects: Accounting, Economics, Education, Medicine, Nursing, Dentistry, Public Administration
ISBN Prefix(es): 2-216
Total Titles: 1,000 Print

Editions Fragments
5, rue de Charonne, 75011 Paris
Tel: (01) 47 00 76 48 *Fax:* (01) 47 00 22 04
E-mail: art@fragmentseditions.com
Web Site: www.fragmentseditions.com
Key Personnel
Dir: Francois de Villandry
Publishing Coordinator: Julie Alinquant
Press & Public Relations: Sophie Godard
Founded: 1989
Specialize in contemporary art.
Subjects: Art, Photography
ISBN Prefix(es): 2-908066
Number of titles published annually: 7 Print
Total Titles: 80 Print
Distributed by Goutal-Darly (Europe); Vilo (China, Europe, Japan, Korea, North America, South America)
Warehouse: Zone Industrielle Leval, 11 ave Arago, 91420 Morangis
Orders to: Vilo Diffusion, 25 rue Ginoux, 75015 Paris

Institut Francais de Recherche pour l'Exploitation de la Mer (IFREMER) (French Research Institute for Exploitation of the Sea)
155, rue Jean-Jacques Rousseau, 92138 Issy-les-Moulineaux Cedex
Mailing Address: BP 70, 29280 Plouzane Cedex
Tel: (02) 98 22 40 13 *Fax:* (02) 98 22 45 86
E-mail: editions@ifremer.fr
Web Site: www.ifremer.fr
Key Personnel
Chief Executive Officer: Jean-Francois Minster
Editorial & Promotion: Courtay Nelly
  E-mail: nelly.courtay@ifremer.fr
Founded: 1984
Specialize in scientific & technical publications.
Subjects: Environmental Studies, Maritime, Outdoor Recreation, Technology, Transportation
ISBN Prefix(es): 2-905434; 2-84433
Total Titles: 4 CD-ROM; 40 Audio
Orders to: ALT Brest Service Logistique, 3, rue Edouard Belin BP 23, 29801 Brest Cedex 9
Tel: (02) 98 02 42 34 *Fax:* (02) 98 41 49 43
E-mail: logistique.brest@alt.sa.com (for booksellers)
INRA Editions, RD 10, 78026 Versailles Cedex
Tel: (01) 30 83 34 06 *Fax:* (01) 30 83 34 49
E-mail: intra.editions@versailles.inra.fr (mail order)

Association Francaise de Normalisation+
11, ave Francis de Pressense, 93571 Saint-Denis La Plaine Cedex
Tel: (01) 41 62 80 00 *Fax:* (01) 49 17 90 00
Web Site: www.afnor.fr

Key Personnel
Dir, Publication & General Manager: Alan Bryden
Administrator & International Rights: Gildas Bourdais
Subjects: Management
ISBN Prefix(es): 2-12

France Edition Office de Promotion Internationale
Association d'editeurs, 115, Blvd Saint-Germain, 75006 Paris
Tel: (01) 44 41 13 13 *Fax:* (01) 46 34 63 83
E-mail: info@franceedition.com
Web Site: bief.org
Key Personnel
President: Liana Levi
General Secretary: Marc Franconie
  E-mail: franconie@franceedition.com
Managing Dir: Jean-Guy Boin *E-mail:* jgboin@franceedition.com
Specialize in all subjects.
Branch Office(s)
France Edition Vietnam, Mlle Ho Thi Ngoc Lan, 30 rue Dinh Ngaug, Hanoi, Viet Nam
Tel: (04) 826 48 62 *Fax:* (04) 825 34 11
E-mail: lanfevn@hn.vnn.vn
U.S. Office(s): France Edition Inc, 853 Broadway, New York, NY 10003-4703, United States, Contact: Lucinda Karter *Tel:* 212-254-4540 *Fax:* 212-254-4540 *Web Site:* www.frenchpubagency.com
Foreign Rights: France Edition Inc

Editions France-Empire+
13, rue Le Sueur, 75116 Paris
Tel: (01) 45 00 33 00 *Fax:* (01) 45 00 20 77
E-mail: france-empire@france-empire.fr
Web Site: www.france-empire.fr
Key Personnel
Contact: Jean-Louis Giral
Founded: 1945
ISBN Prefix(es): 2-7048
Parent Company: Desquenne et Giral
Bookshop(s): Librairie France-Empire, 30 rue Washington, 75008 Paris

France-Loisirs
123 blvd de Grenelle, 75015 Paris
Tel: (01) 45 68 60 00 *Fax:* (01) 42 73 14 38
Web Site: www.franceloisirs.com
Telex: 202 459 f
Key Personnel
Publicity: A Cinar
Subjects: Art, Literature, Literary Criticism, Essays
ISBN Prefix(es): 2-7242; 2-7441

Les Editions Franciscaines SA
9, rue Marie-Rose, 75014 Paris
Tel: (01) 45407351 *Fax:* (01) 40447504
E-mail: editions-franciscaines@wanadoo.fr
Key Personnel
President: Michel Deleu
Founded: 1932
Specialize in books.
Subjects: Religion - Catholic, Theology, Franciscan Spirituality
ISBN Prefix(es): 2-85020
Number of titles published annually: 5 Print
Total Titles: 105 Print
Distributed by Alliances Service (Belgium); Univers (Canada)
Distributor for Franciscan Printing Press

Association Frank+
c/o Frank Books, BP 29, 94301 Vincennes Cedex
Tel: (01) 43656405 *Fax:* (01) 48596668
Key Personnel
President: David Applefield *E-mail:* david@paris-anglo.com
Founded: 1990
A special group called Lawyers for Literature functions as honorary publishers for Frank, The Literary Journal.
Subjects: Drama, Theater, Fashion, Fiction, How-to, Labor, Industrial Relations, Literature, Literary Criticism, Essays, Poetry
ISBN Prefix(es): 2-908171
Associate Companies: Anglophone SA
U.S. Office(s): Mosaic Press, 85 River Rock Drive, No 202, Buffalo, NY, United States
Distributed by Houghton-Mifflin (UK)

Futuribles SARL+
55, rue de Varenne, 75007 Paris
Tel: (01) 53 63 37 70 *Fax:* (01) 42 22 65 54
E-mail: revue@futuribles.com
Web Site: www.futuribles.com
Key Personnel
General Dir: Hugues de Jouvenel *Tel:* (01) 53 63 37 73 *E-mail:* hjouvenel@futuribles.com
International Rights & General Secretary: Corinne Roels *Tel:* (01) 53 63 37 71
Founded: 1975
Publish a monthly independent transdisciplinary policy oriented journal.
Subjects: Developing Countries, Economics, Environmental Studies, Government, Political Science, Labor, Industrial Relations, Management, Social Sciences, Sociology, Technology
ISBN Prefix(es): 2-84387
Number of titles published annually: 11 Print
Total Titles: 300 Print
Associate Companies: Association Futuribles International

Les Editions Gabalda et Cie
18, rue Pierre et Marie Curie, 75005 Paris
Tel: (01) 43 26 53 55 *Fax:* (01) 43 25 04 71
E-mail: editions@gabalda.com
Web Site: www.gabalda.com
Key Personnel
Proprietor: J Gabalda
Founded: 1845
Subjects: Religion - Other, Theology
ISBN Prefix(es): 2-85021
Parent Company: Librarie Lecoffre

Editions Jacques Gabay+
151 bis, rue Saint-Jacques, 75005 Paris
Tel: (01) 43 54 64 64 *Fax:* (01) 43 54 87 00
E-mail: infos@gabay.com
Web Site: www.gabay.com
Key Personnel
Man Dir: Jacques Gabay
Founded: 1987
Subjects: Astronomy, Chemistry, Chemical Engineering, Economics, Mathematics, Philosophy, Physical Sciences, Physics, Science (General)
ISBN Prefix(es): 2-87647
Total Titles: 230 Print
Imprints: Oblong

Editions Galilee+
9, rue de Linne, 75005 Paris
Tel: (01) 43 31 23 84 *Fax:* (01) 45 35 53 68
E-mail: editions.galilee@free.fr
Key Personnel
Man Dir: Michel Delorme
Founded: 1971
Subjects: Art, History, Literature, Literary Criticism, Essays, Philosophy, Poetry, Psychology, Psychiatry, Social Sciences, Sociology
ISBN Prefix(es): 2-7186
Shipping Address: 128 ave du Marechalde Laltre-de-Tattiguy, 77400 Lagny
Warehouse: 128 ave du Marechalde Laltre-de-Tattiguy, 77400 Lagny
Orders to: Sodis, BP 142, 77403 Lagny sur Marne *Tel:* (01) 45 31 16 06

Editions Gallimard
5, rue Sebastien-Bottin, 75328 Paris Cedex 07

Tel: (01) 49 54 42 00 *Fax:* (01) 45 44 94 03
Web Site: www.gallimard.fr
Telex: GALLIM 204121F *Cable:* Enerefene Paris 044
Key Personnel
President: Antoine Gallimard
Editorial Dir: Teresa Cremisi
Sales Dir: Bruno Caillet
Rights & Permissions: Prune Berge; Anne Solange Noble
Editor: Jean-Loup Champion; Francoise Cibiel; Colline Faure-Poiree; Yvon Girard; Gustavo Guerrero; Veronique Jacob; Christine Jordis; Bernard Lortholary; Jean Mattern; Patrick Raynal; Eric Vigne
Art Dir: Jacques Maillot
Export: Jean-Charles Grunstein
Founded: 1911
Subjects: Art, Biography, Fiction, History, Music, Dance, Philosophy, Poetry
ISBN Prefix(es): 2-07
Subsidiaries: Editions Denoel; Editions Gallimard Jeunesse; Editions Gallimard Images (Canada); Editions Mercure de France; Schoenhof's Foreign Books (USA); Les Editions de la Table Ronde
Distributed by Centre de Diffusion de l'Edition; France Export Diffusion; La SODIS
Bookshop(s): Le Divan, 203, rue la convention, 75015 Paris *Tel:* (01) 53 68 90 68 *Fax:* (01) 42 50 84 68; Librairie Delamain, 155, rue Saint Honore, 75001 Paris *Tel:* (01) 42 61 48 78 *Fax:* (01) 40 15 91 69; Librairie des Facultes, Strasbourg; Librairie Gallimard, 15 blvd Raspail, 75007 Paris *Tel:* (01) 45 48 24 84 *Fax:* (01) 42 84 16 97; Librairie Kleber, 1, rue des Francs Bourgeois, 67000 Strasbourg *Tel:* (03) 88 15 78 88 *Fax:* (03) 88 15 78 80; Librairie de Paris, 7, 9, 11 Place de Clichy, 75017 Paris *Tel:* (01) 45 22 47 81 *Fax:* (01) 40 08 08 50

Editions Gamma
Les Comptoirs de Bonneuil, 60120 Bonneui-les-Eaux
Tel: (03) 44806868 *Fax:* (03) 44806860
Telex: 202036 (Begedis SA)
Key Personnel
President: Bernard Ramspaxher
Editor: Jean Nicolas Moreau
Founded: 1963
Subjects: Social Sciences, Sociology
ISBN Prefix(es): 2-7130
Parent Company: Gedit SA Tournai
Associate Companies: Editions Desclee et Cie, Paris; Editions du Chalet, Paris; Nouvelles Editions Mame, Paris; Editions Universitaires, Paris; Desclee Editeurs, Belgium; Editions Gamma, Belgium
Orders to: Begedis, 11 rue Duquay-Trouin, 75006 Paris
Arc-en-Ciel International, 2 I Tournai Ouest, B-7713 Marquain, Belgium (Foreign)

Gammaprim+
78, rue de Dunkerque, 75009 Paris
Tel: (01) 49959492 *Fax:* (01) 40230134
E-mail: fgosselin@gammaprim.fr
Key Personnel
Editor: Franck Gosselin
Founded: 1982
Subjects: Biological Sciences, Chemistry, Chemical Engineering, Economics, Geography, Geology, History, Literature, Literary Criticism, Essays, Mathematics, Philosophy, Physics
ISBN Prefix(es): 2-903908; 2-84391
Distributed by Sodis; Sofedis
Warehouse: Sodis, 128 ave du Mal de lattre de Tassigny, 77400 Lagny Sur Marne
Orders to: Sodis, 128 ave du Mal de Lattre de Tassigny, 77400 Lagny sur Marne

Editions Ganymede+
PO Box 12, 77220 Presles-en-Brie
Tel: (01) 48945232 *Fax:* (02) 64 42 86 68
E-mail: rozeille.hatem@wanadoo.fr
Web Site: www.hatem.com
Key Personnel
Dir & International Rights: Frank Hatem
Founded: 1973
Subjects: Philosophy, Physics, Psychology, Psychiatry, Science (General)
ISBN Prefix(es): 2-9500999; 2-85824

Editions du Garde-Temps+
106, rue Vieille-du-Temple, 75003 Paris
Tel: (01) 44788477 *Fax:* (01) 44788479
E-mail: studio-magnet@calva.net
Key Personnel
Contact: Michel Le Louarn
Founded: 1995
Subjects: Travel
ISBN Prefix(es): 2-9509273; 2-913545
Warehouse: Vilo, 25 rue Gihoux, 75737 Paris Cedex 15, Contact: Sophie Praquin *Tel:* (01) 45770805 *Fax:* (01) 45799715

Imprimerie Librairie Gardet
Unit of Edimontagne
La Mollard, 74400 Chamonix
Tel: (04) 50 53 67 47 *Fax:* (04) 50 53 67 47
E-mail: edimontagne@wanadoo.fr
Key Personnel
Editor: Jacques Gendrault
Founded: 1836
Subjects: Art, Crafts, Games, Hobbies, Education, History, Regional Interests
ISBN Prefix(es): 2-7049
Total Titles: 70 Print

Gauthier-Villars, *imprint of* Dunod Editeur

Gautier Languereau, *imprint of* Hachette Jeunesse Image

Librairie Generale Francaise SA
43, Quai de Grenelle, 75905 Paris Cedex 15
Tel: (01) 43 92 30 00 *Fax:* (01) 43 92 35 90
The above is the Head Office. Editorial & production are run from Le Livre de Poche.
ISBN Prefix(es): 2-253

Editions Gerard de Villiers
43 Quai de Grenelle, 75905 Paris Cedex 15
Tel: (01) 43 92 30 00 *Fax:* (01) 43 92 35 80
Web Site: www.editionsgerarddevilliers.com
Telex: 204434
Key Personnel
President & Dir General: M Gerard de Villiers
Editorial Dir: Christine de Grandmaison
Founded: 1988
Subjects: Fiction, Mysteries
ISBN Prefix(es): 2-7386

Paul Geuthner Librairie Orientaliste+
12, rue Vavin, 75006 Paris
Tel: (01) 43 29 75 64 *Fax:* (01) 46 34 71 30
E-mail: geuthner@geuthner.com
Web Site: www.geuthner.com *Cable:* LIBORIENT PARIS
Key Personnel
Man Dir: Marc F Seidl-Geuthner
Founded: 1901
Subjects: Anthropology, Antiques, Art, Biblical Studies, Biography, Foreign Countries, Geography, Geology, History, Law, Music, Dance, Philosophy, Religion - Buddhist, Religion - Catholic, Religion - Hindu, Religion - Islamic, Religion - Jewish, Religion - Protestant, Social Sciences, Sociology
ISBN Prefix(es): 2-7053

GF, *imprint of* Flammarion SA

GIPPE, see Groupement d'Information Promotion Presse Edition (GIPPE)

Gippe-Les Amoureux des Livres, *imprint of* Groupement d'Information Promotion Presse Edition (GIPPE)

Editions Jean Paul Gisserot+
10, rue Gracieuse, 75005 Paris
Tel: (01) 43 31 80 04 *Fax:* (01) 43 31 88 15
E-mail: editions@editions-gisserot.com
Web Site: www.editions-gisserot.com
Key Personnel
Dir: Thibault Chattard *E-mail:* thibault.chattard@editions-gisserot.com
Founded: 1988
Subjects: Aeronautics, Aviation, Animals, Pets, Anthropology, Archaeology, Architecture & Interior Design, Art, Astronomy, Biography, Cookery, Education, English as a Second Language, Foreign Countries, Gardening, Plants, Genealogy, History, How-to, Humor, Maritime, Music, Dance, Natural History, Regional Interests, Religion - Catholic, Religion - Protestant, Travel, Wine & Spirits
ISBN Prefix(es): 2-87747
Number of titles published annually: 50 Print
Total Titles: 560 Print
Subsidiaries: Telegiss Distribution (France)
Shipping Address: TeleGiss Distribution, Z I de Saint Eloi, 29800 Plouedern *Tel:* (02) 9821 3663 *Fax:* (02) 9821 5631
Orders to: TeleGiss Distribution, Z I de Saint Eloi, 29800 Plouedern *Tel:* (02) 9821 3663 *Fax:* (02) 9821 5631
Returns: TeleGiss Distribution, Z I de Saint Eloi, 29800 Plouedern *Tel:* (02) 9821 3663 *Fax:* (02) 9821 5631

Glacial, *imprint of* Flammarion SA

Editions Glenat+
6, rue du Lieutenant Chanaron, BP 177, 38008 Grenoble Cedex
Tel: (04) 76 88 75 75 *Fax:* (04) 76 88 75 70
Web Site: www.glenat.com
Telex: 320030 glenat
Key Personnel
President & Joint Man Dir: Jacques Glenat
Editorial: Dominique Burdot; Jean-Claude Camano
Sales (Export): Christine Glenat
Production: Francis Bernard
Rights & Permissions: Jean-Brice Roux
Founded: 1974
Subjects: Cookery, Fiction, Humor, Science Fiction, Fantasy, Sports, Athletics, Travel, Comic Books
ISBN Prefix(es): 2-7234
Subsidiaries: Glenat-Benelux; Glenat-Images; Glenat Espagne
Bookshop(s): Glenat-Librairie, 16 Lafayette, 75009 Paris *Tel:* (01) 42469881

Editions Jacques Grancher+
98, rue de Vaugirard, 75006 Paris
Tel: (01) 42 22 64 80 *Fax:* (01) 45 48 25 03
E-mail: info@grancher.com
Web Site: www.grancher.com *Cable:* SCE DE VENTE/LIBRAIRIES 5480317
Key Personnel
Man Dir: Jacques Grancher
Editor: Michel Grancher *E-mail:* m.grancher@worldonline.fr; Philippe Grancher *E-mail:* grancher@worldonline.fr
Founded: 1952
Subjects: Astrology, Occult, Cookery, Health, Nutrition, How-to, Humor, Military Science, Nonfiction (General), Parapsychology, Psychology, Psychiatry, Religion - Catholic, Religion - Is-

lamic, Religion - Jewish, Religion - Protestant, Religion - Other, Travel
ISBN Prefix(es): 2-7339
Number of titles published annually: 40 Print
Total Titles: 400 Print
Distributed by Hachette
Distribution Center: Hachette

Grand Angle, *imprint of* Editions l'Instant Durable

Les Grandes Anthologies, *imprint of* Sarl Editions Jean Grassin

Editions Grandir (To Grow)+
Rue des 3 Ponts, 30000 Nimes
Tel: (04) 66 84 01 19 *Fax:* (04) 66 26 14 50
Key Personnel
Manager: Rene Turc
Founded: 1978
Subjects: Art, Fiction, Physical Sciences
ISBN Prefix(es): 2-84166; 2-904292
Total Titles: 350 Print

Granit Editions
24, rue de Varize, 75016 Paris
Tel: (01) 40 71 98 75 *Fax:* (01) 46 51 30 06
Key Personnel
Dir: Francois Xavier Jaujard
ISBN Prefix(es): 2-86281
Orders to: Distique, 5 rue du Marechal Leclerc, 28600 Luisant

Sarl Editions Jean Grassin
Place de Port-en-Dro, 56342 Carnac-Plage
Mailing Address: BP 75, 56342 Carnac Cedex
Tel: (02) 97 52 93 63 *Fax:* (02) 97 52 83 90
E-mail: j.grassin@wanadoo.fr
Web Site: www.editions-grassin.com
Key Personnel
Man Dir: Jean Grassin
Founded: 1957
Subjects: History, Literature, Literary Criticism, Essays, Poetry
ISBN Prefix(es): 2-7055
Imprints: Club J G; L'encyclopedie Poetique; Les Grandes Anthologies; Sequences
Book Club(s): Poetes Presents

Editions Gregoriennes, *imprint of* Adverbum SARL

GRET, *see* Groupe de Recherche et d'Echanges Technologiques (GRET)

Groupe de Recherche et d'Echanges Technologiques (GRET)
211-213 rue La Fayette, 75010 Paris
Tel: (01) 40 05 61 61 *Fax:* (01) 40 05 61 10
E-mail: gret@gret.org; librairie@gret.org
Web Site: www.gret.org
Key Personnel
President: Herve Bichat
Dir: Serge Allou
Founded: 1976
Subjects: Agriculture, Anthropology, Developing Countries, Finance, Journalism, Technology
ISBN Prefix(es): 2-86844
Total Titles: 110 Print
Distribution Center: CELF

Groupe des Editions du Rocher
6 place St-Sulpice, 75279 Paris Cedex 06
Tel: (01) 40 46 54 00 *Fax:* (01) 40 46 91 36
Key Personnel
President: Jean-Paul Bertrand *E-mail:* jpb@post.club-internet.fr

Groupe Express-Expansion
17, rue de l'Arrivee, 75733 Paris Cedex 15
Tel: (01) 53 91 10 63 *Fax:* (01) 53 91 10 06
Web Site: www.groupe-expansion.com
Telex: 205581 f
Key Personnel
President & Man Dir: Jean-Louis Servan-Schreiber
General Manager: Damien Dufour *Tel:* (01) 40 60 44 12 *Fax:* (01) 40 60 41 29
Publicity, International Advertising Dir: Vincent Perrote
Subjects: Architecture & Interior Design, Economics, Education, Government, Political Science, Law, Literature, Literary Criticism, Essays, Science (General), Social Sciences, Sociology, Technology
ISBN Prefix(es): 2-904833
Parent Company: Socpresse

Groupe Hatier International+
Subsidiary of Groupe Alexandre Hatier
31 rue de Fleurus, 75006 Paris
Tel: (01) 44 39 28 00 *Fax:* (01) 45 44 84 54
E-mail: hatier@intl.com
Key Personnel
Man Dir: Patrick C Dubs *Fax:* (01) 44 39 28 16 *E-mail:* pdubs@hatier.intl.com
Promotion: Nathalie Hernandez *Tel:* (01) 44 39 28 14 *Fax:* (01) 42 84 03 19 *E-mail:* nhernandez@hatier-intl.com
Specialize in export & textbook publishing for French & Arabic speaking countries. Educational materials, maps.
ISBN Prefix(es): 2-7473
Number of titles published annually: 60 Print
Total Titles: 300 Print
Ultimate Parent Company: Hachette SA
Distributor for Editions Didier

Groupe Revue Fiduciaire+
Formerly La Villeguerin
100 rue La Fayette, 75010 Paris Cedex 10
Tel: (01) 47 70 42 42 *Fax:* (01) 48 24 12 93
E-mail: courrier@grouperf.com
Web Site: www.grouperf.com
Key Personnel
Dir General: Yves-Robert De la Villeguerin
ISBN Prefix(es): 2-86521
Associate Companies: Societe Europeenne de Presse Fiscale, Juridique
Orders to: 45 rue Victor Hugo, 93507 Pantin *Tel:* (01) 48 40 01 11

Groupement d'Information Promotion Presse Edition (GIPPE)
60, rue Dombasle, 75015 Paris
Tel: (01) 45 32 12 75
E-mail: gippe@free.fr
Web Site: gippe.free.fr
Key Personnel
General Secretary: Rene Froment
Founded: 1987
Subjects: Literature, Literary Criticism, Essays
ISBN Prefix(es): 2-9508635
Parent Company: Les Amoureux des Livres-Gippe (Publisher)
Imprints: Gippe-Les Amoureux des Livres

Librairie Guenegaud
Subsidiary of P M C
10, rue de l'Odeon, 75006 Paris
Tel: (01) 43260791 *Fax:* (01) 40468872
E-mail: libraire.guenegaud@wanadoo.fr
Key Personnel
Man Dir: Philippe Barrault
Founded: 1910
Subjects: Biography, Genealogy, History, Outdoor Recreation, Regional Interests, Romance
ISBN Prefix(es): 2-85023
Number of titles published annually: 10 Print

Total Titles: 95 Print
Associate Companies: La Societe et le High Life

Guide Franck, *imprint of* Editions Franck Mercier

Guide Pratique, *imprint of* Les Presses du Management

Guides Gallimard, *imprint of* Societe Nouveaux Loisirs

Editions d'Art Albert Guillot
4 rue de Seze, 69006 Lyon
Tel: (04) 78521026
Subjects: Art
ISBN Prefix(es): 2-85096

Hachette Education+
43 Quai de Grenelle, 75905 Paris Cedex 15
Tel: (01) 43923000; (01) 43923797 *Fax:* (01) 43923575
Web Site: www.hachette-education.com
Key Personnel
Dir: Isabelle Jeuge-Maynart
Founded: 1826
Specialize in CD-ROMs & reference books.
Subjects: Education, French as a Second Language
ISBN Prefix(es): 2-01
Total Titles: 4,000 Print
Parent Company: Hachette Livre, 43 Quai de Grenelle, Paris 75905
Ultimate Parent Company: Lagardere Groupe
Subsidiaries: Edicef; Sylemma-Andrieu; Hachette Diffusion Internationale
Showroom(s): Espace Enseignant, 8 rue Haute Jenille, 75006 Paris

Hachette francais langue etrangere - FLE+
58, rue Jean-Bleuzen, 92178 Vanves Cedex
Tel: (01) 43 92 30 00 *Fax:* (01) 43 92 39 20
E-mail: fle@hachette-livre.fr
Web Site: www.fle.hachette-livre.fr
Key Personnel
Publishing Dir: Anne Reberioux *Tel:* (01) 46 62 10 58 *E-mail:* anneberioux@hachette.lane.fr
ISBN Prefix(es): 2-01
Number of titles published annually: 50 Print; 4 Audio
Total Titles: 50 Print
Parent Company: Hachette Livre SA, Paris

Hachette Jeunesse, *imprint of* Hachette Jeunesse Image

Hachette Jeunesse Image+
43 quai de Grenelle, 75905 Paris Cedex 15
Tel: (01) 43923000 *Fax:* (01) 43923030
Web Site: www.hachettejeunesse.com
Key Personnel
Dir: Frederique de Buron
Editorial Dir: Emmanuelle Massonaud
International Rights Manager: Evelyne Dil
Founded: 1885
Subjects: Nonfiction (General), Picture & Character Books
ISBN Prefix(es): 2-01; 2-217
Parent Company: Hachette Livre SA
Imprints: Hachette Jeunesse; Gautier Languereau; Deux Coqs d'Or
Warehouse: Centre de Distribution du Livre, Z A Coignieres-Maurepas, One ave Gutenberg, 78316 Maurepas Cedex

Hachette Jeunesse Roman+
43 Quai de Grenelle, 75905 Paris Cedex 15
Tel: (01) 43923000 *Fax:* (01) 43923222
Cable: HACHECI-PARIS 25
Key Personnel
Dir: Catherine Tessandier
International Rights Manager: Monique Lantelme

Founded: 1856
Parent Company: Hachette

Hachette Livre+
43 Quai de Grenelle, 75905 Paris Cedex 15
Tel: (01) 43923000 *Fax:* (01) 43923030
Key Personnel
Chief Executive Officer: Arnaud Nourry
Founded: 1826
Book publishing.
Subjects: Architecture & Interior Design, Art, Economics, Education, Engineering (General), Fiction, Government, Political Science, History, Language Arts, Linguistics, Nonfiction (General), Philosophy, Science (General), Self-Help, Social Sciences, Sociology, Sports, Athletics, Travel
ISBN Prefix(es): 2-01
Number of titles published annually: 5,000 Print
Ultimate Parent Company: Lagardere Groupe
Subsidiaries: Hachette Pratique (General Interest); Hachette Litteratures (General Interest); Editions du Chene (General Interest)

Hachette Livre International+
Formerly EDICEF - Editions Classiques d'Expression Francaise
58 rue Jean Bleuzen, 92178 Vanves Cedex
Tel: (01) 55 00 11 00 *Fax:* (01) 55 00 11 60
Key Personnel
Dir General, Africa & Indian Ocean: Laurent Loric
Subjects: Economics, Education, English as a Second Language, Environmental Studies, Law, Literature, Literary Criticism, Essays, Mathematics, Physics
ISBN Prefix(es): 2-84129; 2-85069
Parent Company: Hachette Livre SA
Associate Companies: EDICEF; Hatier International
Subsidiaries: NEI (Nouvelles Editions Ivoiriennes)
Distributor for EDICEF; Hatier International

Hachette Pratiques+
43 Quai de Grenelle, 75905 Paris Cedex 15
Tel: (01) 43923238 *Fax:* (01) 43923030
Key Personnel
Dir: Jean Arcache *E-mail:* jarcache@hachette-livre.fr
Editorial: Pierre Baron
Publicity: Cecile Boyer
Foreign Rights: Monique Lanthelme
Coeditions & Foreign Rights: David Inman
Founded: 1826
Subjects: Animals, Pets, Astrology, Occult, Biography, Cookery, Crafts, Games, Hobbies, Fashion, Gardening, Plants, Health, Nutrition, Management, Sports, Athletics, Wine & Spirits
ISBN Prefix(es): 2-01
Warehouse: Hachette Distribution, ZA Coignietires, One avenue Gutenberg, 78316 Maurepas Cedex

Editions Viviane Hamy+
89 rue du Faubourg Saint Antoine, 75011 Paris
Tel: (01) 53171600 *Fax:* (01) 53171609
E-mail: information@viviane-hamy.fr
Web Site: www.viviane-hamy.fr/0000.html
Key Personnel
Contact: Viviane Hamy; Frederic Martin *E-mail:* frederic.martin@viviane-hamy.fr
Founded: 1990
Subjects: Literature, Literary Criticism, Essays
ISBN Prefix(es): 2-87858
Number of titles published annually: 12 Print
Total Titles: 120 Print
Distributed by Flammarion

Harlequin SA
83-85 blvd Vincent-Auriol, 75013 Paris
Tel: (01) 42166363 *Fax:* (01) 45828694
Key Personnel
Man Dir: Frederique Sarfati
Editorial Manager: Anne Coquet
Founded: 1978
Subjects: Astrology, Occult, Romance
ISBN Prefix(es): 2-280; 2-86259
Parent Company: Hachette SA
Imprints: Duo, Harlequin

L'Harmattan+
5-7 rue de l'Ecole-Polytechnique, 75005 Paris
Tel: (01) 40 46 79 11; (01) 40 46 79 20 *Fax:* (01) 43 25 82 03
E-mail: harmat@worldnet.fr
Web Site: www.editions-harmattan.fr
Key Personnel
Man Editor: Denis Pryen
Foreign Relations: Armelle Riche
Founded: 1975
Subjects: Developing Countries, Foreign Countries, Language Arts, Linguistics, Literature, Literary Criticism, Essays, Science (General), Social Sciences, Sociology
ISBN Prefix(es): 2-7384; 2-85802
Total Titles: 1,400 Print
Subsidiaries: Diffusion Nord-Sud (Belgium); L'Harmattan Hongrie; L'Harmattan Inc (Canada); L'Harmattan Italia SRL; L'Age d'Homme
Distributed by Distribution de Livres Univers (Canada)
Bookshop(s): 16 rue des Ecoles, 75005 Paris *Tel:* (01) 40467911 *Fax:* (01) 43298620

Harmonia Mundi, *imprint of* Lettres Vives Editions

Editions Hatier SA+
8, rue d'Assas, 75278 Paris Cedex 06
Tel: (01) 49 54 49 54 *Fax:* (01) 40 49 00 45
E-mail: enseignants@editions-hatier.fr
Web Site: www.editions-hatier.fr
Telex: 202732 F
Key Personnel
Man Dir: Bernard Foulon
Sales & Distribution: Fabienne Fera *Tel:* (01) 49 54 48 04 *Fax:* (01) 49 54 49 71 *E-mail:* ffera@editions-hatier.fr
Foreign Rights: Anne Risaliti *Tel:* (01) 49 54 48 99 *Fax:* (01) 49 54 47 30 *E-mail:* arisaliti@editions-hatier.fr
Human Resources Dir: Alain Bergdoll *Fax:* (01) 49 54 49 51 *E-mail:* drh@editions-hatier.fr
Founded: 1880
Subjects: Architecture & Interior Design, Biological Sciences, Economics, Education, English as a Second Language, Environmental Studies, Self-Help
ISBN Prefix(es): 2-218
Parent Company: Groupe Hachette Livre
Imprints: Rageot Editeur
Bookshop(s): 59 blvd Raspail, 75006 Paris, Contact: Christian Reynaud *Tel:* (05) 49 91 80 50 *E-mail:* creynaud@editions-hatier.fr

Pierre Hautot Editions
36, rue du Bac, 75007 Paris
Tel: (01) 42 61 10 15 *Fax:* (01) 49 27 00 06
Telex: 214293
Founded: 1952
Subjects: Art

Editions Hazan+
Imprint of Hachette Illustrated
64 Quai Marcel Cachin, 94290 Villeneuve-le-Roi
Mailing Address: BP 26, 94290 Villeneuve-le-Roi
Tel: (01) 49 61 92 08; (01) 49 61 90 90 *Fax:* (01) 45 97 83 47; (01) 45 97 83 45
Telex: 250769
Key Personnel
Dir: Jean-Francois Barrielle
Rights Manager: Sherri Aldis
Founded: 1945
Subjects: Architecture & Interior Design, Art
ISBN Prefix(es): 2-85025; 2-7198
Bookshop(s): Editions Fernand Hazan, 35-37 rue de Seine, 75006 Paris
Distribution Center: Diffulivre Suisse
Dilibel Belgique
Hachette Canada
Hachette Diffusion Internationale
Hachette-Livre

Editions Herault
13, ruede Langeais, BP 345, 49300 Cholet
Tel: (02) 41554590 *Fax:* (02) 41586228
Key Personnel
General Manager: Andre Hubert Herault
Founded: 1971
Subjects: Biography, Genealogy, History, Regional Interests
ISBN Prefix(es): 2-7407; 2-903851
Parent Company: Farre, BP 345, 49305 Cholet Cedex

Hermann editeurs des Sciences et des Arts SA+
293 rue Lecourbe, 75015 Paris
Tel: (01) 45 57 45 40 *Fax:* (01) 40 60 12 93
E-mail: hermann.sa@wanadoo.fr
Key Personnel
Man Dir: Pierre Beres
Foreign Rights: Nissa Bernard
Founded: 1870
Subjects: Art, Chemistry, Chemical Engineering, Mathematics, Medicine, Nursing, Dentistry, Physics, Science (General), Technology
ISBN Prefix(es): 2-7056
Number of titles published annually: 50 Print
Total Titles: 1,000 Print
Subsidiaries: Pierre Beres; Richard Masse (music); La Palme
Showroom(s): 6 rue de la Sorbonne, 75005 Paris
Bookshop(s): 6 rue de la Sorbonne, 75005 Paris

Hermes Science, *imprint of* Editions Lavoisier

Editions Hermes Science Publications+
8, Quai du Marche-neuf, 75004 Paris
Tel: (01) 53 10 15 20 *Fax:* (01) 53 10 15 21
E-mail: hermes@iway.fr
Web Site: www.hermes-science.com; www.editions-hermes.fr
Key Personnel
Man Dir: M Menasce
Marketing Dir: M Philippe
Founded: 1981
Membership(s): French Publishers Association.
Subjects: Chemistry, Chemical Engineering, Civil Engineering, Electronics, Electrical Engineering, Engineering (General), Geography, Geology, Health, Nutrition, Language Arts, Linguistics, Law
ISBN Prefix(es): 2-86601; 2-7462
Number of titles published annually: 300 Print; 150 Online; 150 E-Book
Total Titles: 1,200 Print; 1 CD-ROM; 15 Online; 15 E-Book
Associate Companies: Hermes Science Publishing Ltd, 120 Pentonville Rd, N1 9JN Oxford, United Kingdom, Contact: Sami Menasce *Tel:* (020) 78 431920 *Fax:* (020) 78 376348 *E-mail:* hermes_science@BTinternet.com
Imprints: Continent Europe
Distributed by Editions Continent Europe

Editions de l'Herne
41, rue de Verneuil, 75007 Paris
Tel: (01) 42 61 25 60 *Fax:* (01) 42 60 10 00
E-mail: lherne@freesurf.fr

FRANCE

Key Personnel
Chairman, Rights & Permissions: Constantin Tacou
Director: Laurence Tacou
Editorial, Press Agent: Alexandre Tacou
Founded: 1964
Subjects: Art, Fiction, Government, Political Science, Philosophy, Poetry, Social Sciences, Sociology
ISBN Prefix(es): 2-85197

Herscher+
8 rue Ferou, 75278 Paris Cedex 06
Tel: (08) 25 82 01 11 *Fax:* (01) 43 25 18 29
E-mail: contact@editions-belin.fr
Web Site: www.editions-belin.fr
Key Personnel
President: Marie-Claude Brossollet
Subjects: Art
ISBN Prefix(es): 2-7335
Total Titles: 1,200 Print; 50 Audio
Parent Company: Editions Belin
Bookshop(s): 8, rue Ferou, 75278 Paris Cedex 6
  Tel: (01) 55 42 84 55 *Fax:* (01) 55 42 84 58
Shipping Address: 4 rue Ferdinand de Lesseps, 91420 Morangis
Warehouse: 4 rue Ferdinand de Lesseps, 91420 Morangis

Editions Hervas
123, ave Philippe-Auguste, 75011 Paris
Tel: (01) 43 79 10 95 *Fax:* (01) 43 79 77 10
ISBN Prefix(es): 2-903118; 2-84334

Editions d'Histoire Sociale (EDHIS)
23 rue de Valois, 75001 Paris
Tel: (01) 42614778
Key Personnel
Man Dir: Anne Centner
Founded: 1967
Subjects: Economics, Foreign Countries, History, Social Sciences, Sociology
ISBN Prefix(es): 2-7156
Bookshop(s): 144 Galerie de Valois, Paris

Editions Hoebeke+
12 rue du Dragon, 75006 Paris
Tel: (01) 42 22 83 81 *Fax:* (01) 45 44 04 96
Key Personnel
Dir: Lionel Hoebeke
Dir, Commercial/Export: Mdme Aline Goujon
Subjects: Art, Fiction, Humor, Photography
ISBN Prefix(es): 2-905292; 2-84230

Editions Honore Champion
7, quai Malaquais, 75006 Paris
Tel: (01) 46340729 *Fax:* (01) 46346406
E-mail: champion@honorechampion.com
Web Site: www.honorechampion.com
Key Personnel
Man Dir: Michel Slatkine
Subjects: History, Comparative Literature, Freemasonry, French Literature, Grammar, Jewish Studies, Lexicography, Linguistics, Music
ISBN Prefix(es): 2-85203; 2-7453

Pierre Horay Editeur
22 bis, passage Dauphine, 75006 Paris
Tel: (01) 43 54 53 90 *Fax:* (01) 43 54 63 50
E-mail: editions@horay-editeur.fr
Web Site: www.horay-editeur.fr
Key Personnel
Man Dir & Rights & Permissions: Sophie Horay
Founded: 1946
Subjects: Art, Biography, Fiction, History, How-to, Music, Dance
ISBN Prefix(es): 2-7058
Orders to: Flammarion, 26 rue Racine, 75006 Paris

Editions Humblot, *imprint of* Presses Universitaires de Nancy

IBE, *imprint of* UNESCO Publishing

Ici et Ailleurs-Vents d'Ailleurs
4, allee des Argelas-la-Gavotte, 13790 Chateauneuf-le-Rouge
Tel: (04) 42533087 *Fax:* (04) 42533097
E-mail: info@kaona.com
Web Site: www.kaona.com
Key Personnel
General Dir: Gilles Colleu *E-mail:* gcolleu@kaona.com
International Rights: Jutta Hepka
  E-mail: jhepka@kaona.com
Assistant: David Barrel *E-mail:* dbarrel@kaona.com; Sebastian Mengin *E-mail:* smengin@kaona.com
Founded: 1995
Publisher of multimedia & Caribbean literature.
Subjects: Literature, Literary Criticism, Essays
ISBN Prefix(es): 2-911412

Editions Ifremer, see Institut Francais de Recherche pour l'Exploitation de la Mer (IFREMER)

IGN, see Institut Geographique National IGN

IIEP, *imprint of* UNESCO Publishing

Image/Magie+
4, rue Diderot, 92150 Suresnes
Tel: (01) 66 80 34 02 *Fax:* (01) 66 80 34 56
Key Personnel
Editor: Jean-Paul Menges
Subjects: Art, Photography, Travel
ISBN Prefix(es): 2-907059

Editions Imago+
7, rue Suger, 75006 Paris
Tel: (01) 46 33 15 33 *Fax:* (01) 60 23 87 51
E-mail: info@editions-imago.fr
Web Site: www.editions-imago.fr
Key Personnel
Dir General: Thierry Auzas
Subjects: Anthropology, History, Literature, Literary Criticism, Essays, Philosophy, Psychology, Psychiatry, Social Sciences, Sociology, Ethnology, Fine Arts, Religions, Romance
ISBN Prefix(es): 2-902702; 2-911416
Number of titles published annually: 20 Print
Total Titles: 200 Print
Distributed by Diffusion Dimedia Inc (Canada); Nouvelle Diffusion (Belgium); Office du Livre (Switzerland); Presses Universitaires de France
Distribution Center: Union-Distribution, 6 avenue de l'Europe, 45300 Sermaises *Tel:* (02) 38 39 00 43 *Fax:* (02) 38 39 03 08

IMC Editions, see Bureau des Longitudes

IMEC+
9 rue Bleue, 75009 Paris
Tel: (01) 53 34 23 23 *Fax:* (01) 43-79-46-87
E-mail: bibliotheque@imec-archives.com
Web Site: www.imec-archives.com
Key Personnel
General Manager: Olivier Corpet *E-mail:* olivier.corpet@imec-archives.com
Founded: 1989
Preserves & manages archives & studies linked to the writing & book world of the 20th century allowing academic researches in intellectual, artistic & literary domains.
Subjects: History of literature & publications
ISBN Prefix(es): 2-908295
Number of titles published annually: 4 Print
Total Titles: 30 Print

Branch Office(s)
l'abbaye d'Ardenne, St Germain-La-Blanche-Herbe, F-14280 Caen, Contact: Catherine Girerd *Tel:* (02) 31 29 37 37 *Fax:* (02) 31 29 36 36 *E-mail:* ardenne@imec-archives.com

Indigo & Cote-Femmes Editions+
4 rue de la Petite Pierre, 75011 Paris
Tel: (01) 43 79 74 79 *Fax:* (01) 43 79 46 87
E-mail: indigo.cote-femmes.edition@wanadoo.fr
Web Site: www.indigo-cf.com
Key Personnel
Dir: Milagros Palma
Founded: 1989
Subjects: Anthropology, Art, Biography, Literature, Literary Criticism, Essays, Women's Studies
ISBN Prefix(es): 2-907883; 2-911571; 2-914378
Number of titles published annually: 20 Print

Editions Infrarouge+
79 rue Vitruve, 75020 Paris
Tel: (01) 44 93 45 64 *Fax:* (01) 49 95 08 74
E-mail: editionsinfrarouge@libertysurf.fr; editions.infrarouge@caramail.com
Web Site: www.chez.com/editinfrarouge
Key Personnel
President: Yves Soubrillard *E-mail:* yves.soubrillard@libertysurf.fr
Literature Dir: Isabelle Soubrillard
Founded: 1996
Subjects: Drama, Theater, Fiction, Humor, Literature, Literary Criticism, Essays, Religion - Other, Science Fiction, Fantasy, Social Sciences, Sociology, Novels
ISBN Prefix(es): 2-908614
Number of titles published annually: 6 Print
Total Titles: 50 Print

INRA Editions (Institut National de la Recherche Agronomique)+
RD10, Route de St Cyr, 78026 Versailles Cedex
Tel: (01) 30833406 *Fax:* (01) 30833449
E-mail: inra_editions@versailles.inra.fr
Web Site: www.inra.fr/editions
Key Personnel
Service Dir: Claudine Geynet
International Rights: Christiane Colon
Founded: 1946
Subjects: Agriculture, Biological Sciences, Earth Sciences, Economics, Environmental Studies, Geography, Geology, Health, Nutrition, Social Sciences, Sociology, Veterinary Science
ISBN Prefix(es): 2-7380; 2-85340
Number of titles published annually: 25 Print
Distributed by Backhuys Publishers (Germany, Netherlands, Scandinavia); De Lannoy (Benelux); Dokumente Verlag (Germany); DPLU (Canada); Estem (France); Interscientia (Italy); Librairie Albert le Brand (Switzerland); Librairie Antoine (Lebanon); Librairie Internationale (Morocco); Librairie le Point (Lebanon); Mundi-Prensa Libros (Spain); Patri Moine (Benelux); Le Triangle Universitaire (Morocco)

Editions INSERM+
Member of STM Group
101 rue de Tolbiac, 75654 Paris Cedex 13
Tel: (01) 44 23 60 82 *Fax:* (01) 44 23 60 69
Web Site: www.inserm.fr
Key Personnel
Man Dir, Editorial, Rights & Permissions: Stephanie Lux *E-mail:* lux@tolbiac.inserm.fr
Contact: Brigitte Durrande *E-mail:* durrande@tolbiac.inserm.fr
Founded: 1970
Subjects: Biological Sciences, Health, Nutrition, Medicine, Nursing, Dentistry, Social Sciences, Sociology, Biomedical Research, Public Health
ISBN Prefix(es): 2-85598
Total Titles: 2 Print

PUBLISHERS

FRANCE

Parent Company: Institut National de la Sante et de la Recherche Medicale
Distributed by Lavoisier (France)

Editions l'Instant Durable+
PO Box 234, 63007 Clermont-Ferrand Cedex 1
Tel: (04) 73 91 13 87 *Fax:* (04) 73 91 13 87
E-mail: art@instantdurable.com
Web Site: www.instantdurable.com
Key Personnel
Publisher: Alain de Bussac
Founded: 1983
Membership(s): SNE (Syndicat National de L'Edition - Paris).
Subjects: Architecture & Interior Design, Art
ISBN Prefix(es): 2-86404
Imprints: Architecture-Modelisme; Grand Angle

Institut de Recherche Scientifique pour le Developpement, see IRD Editions

Institut Geographique National IGN
136, bis rue de Grenelle, 75700 Paris O7 SP
Tel: (01) 43988000 *Fax:* (01) 43988400
Web Site: www.ign.fr
Key Personnel
Man Dir: J F Carrez
Sales: J P Grelot
Production: J Moschetti
Publicity: A C Ferrari
Rights & Permissions: C Dupre
Founded: 1940
ISBN Prefix(es): 2-85595

InterEditions+
5, rue Laromiguiere, 75005 Paris
Tel: (01) 40 46 35 00 *Fax:* (01) 40 46 49 95
Key Personnel
Man Dir: Lidy Arslan
Rights & Permissions: Valere Talamon
Publicity: Veronique Bernier
Founded: 1976
Subjects: Biological Sciences, Business, Chemistry, Chemical Engineering, Computer Science, Management, Mathematics, Medicine, Nursing, Dentistry, Physics, Psychology, Psychiatry
ISBN Prefix(es): 2-10; 2-7296; 2-225; 2-294

Les Editions Interferences
4 rue Cesar Franck, 75015 Paris
Tel: (01) 45 67 33 56
E-mail: interferences@editions-interferences.com
Web Site: www.editions-interferences.com
Key Personnel
Translator: Sophie Benech
Publisher-Bookseller: Alain Benech
Founded: 1992
Subjects: Literature, Literary Criticism, Essays
ISBN Prefix(es): 2-909589
Distribution Center: maison Belin, 8 rue Ferou, 75006 Paris *Tel:* (01) 55 42 84 00 *Fax:* (01) 55 42 84 30 *Web Site:* www.editions-belin.com

International Art Books Distribution, see Librairie Fischbacher, International Art Book Distribution (import-export)

Institut International de la Marionnette
7 pl Winston Churchill, 08000 Charleville-Mezieres
Tel: (03) 24 33 72 50 *Fax:* (03) 24 33 72 69
E-mail: institut@marionnette.com
Web Site: www.marionnette.com
Key Personnel
President: Jacques Felix
Dir: Lucile Bodson
Founded: 1981
Subjects: Art, Drama, Theater
ISBN Prefix(es): 2-9505282

L'Invention du Lecteur, *imprint of* William Blake & Co

Editions de Iorme Rond, *imprint of* Editions ELOR

IRD Editions
213 rue La Fayette, 75480 Paris Cedex 10
Tel: (01) 48 03 76 06 *Fax:* (01) 48 02 79 09
E-mail: editions@paris.ird.fr
Web Site: www.editions.ird.fr *Cable:* ORSTOM PARIS
Key Personnel
Dir: Thomas Mourier *E-mail:* mourier@paris.ird.fr
Editorial: Elisabeth Lorne
Founded: 1962
Subjects: Archaeology, Biological Sciences, Developing Countries, Earth Sciences, Environmental Studies, Geography, Geology, Health, Nutrition, History, Science (General), Social Sciences, Sociology, Technology, Ecology
ISBN Prefix(es): 2-7099
Number of titles published annually: 35 Print; 2 CD-ROM
Total Titles: 830 Print; 5 CD-ROM
Shipping Address: IRD Editions-Diffusion, 32 ave Henri-Varagnat, 93143 Bondy Cedex, Contact: Alain Morliere *Tel:* (01) 48 02 56 49 *Fax:* (01) 48 02 79 09 *E-mail:* diffusion@bondy.ird.fr
Web Site: www.bondy.ird.fr

Isoete
123 rue Emile Zola, 50100 Cherbourg
Tel: (0233) 533409 *Fax:* (0233) 534731
Key Personnel
Dir: Alain Fleury
Founded: 1984
Subjects: History, Literature, Literary Criticism, Essays, Photography, Regional Interests
ISBN Prefix(es): 2-905385; 2-913920
Distributor for Distique

Ivrea+
27, rue de Sommerard, 75005 Paris
Tel: (01) 43 26 06 21 *Fax:* (01) 43 26 11 68
Key Personnel
Contact: Valentin Lorenzo
International Rights: Dodart Jacques *E-mail:* jacques.dodart@liane.net
Founded: 1970
Subjects: History, Literature, Literary Criticism, Essays, Military Science, Poetry, Social Sciences, Sociology
ISBN Prefix(es): 2-85184
Imprints: Champ Libre
Warehouse: SODIS, 128 ave du Marechal de Lattre de Tassigny, BP 142, 77400 Lagny
Orders to: CDE, 17 rue de Tounon, 75006 Paris

Editions du Jaguar
57 bis rue d'Auteuil, 75016 Paris
Tel: (01) 44301970 *Fax:* (01) 44301979
Telex: 651 105F
Key Personnel
General Manager & Foreign Rights: Danielle Ben Yahmed
Vice President: Jany Lecreux-Cournot
Press: Arlette Gelbert
Founded: 1985
Subjects: Art, Cookery, Geography, Geology, Government, Political Science, Health, Nutrition, History, How-to, Human Relations, Regional Interests, Religion - Islamic, Social Sciences, Sociology, Travel
ISBN Prefix(es): 2-86950; 2-85258

Editions J'ai Lu
Subsidiary of Flammarion et Cie
84 rue de Grenelle, 75007 Paris
Tel: (01) 44 39 34 70 *Fax:* (01) 44 39 32 60
E-mail: ajasmin@jailu.com
Web Site: www.flammarion.com
Telex: Jailu 202765
Founded: 1958
Subjects: Fiction, Science Fiction, Fantasy
ISBN Prefix(es): 2-277; 2-290

J'ailu, *imprint of* Flammarion SA

Editions Jannink, SARL
127 rue de la Galciere, 75013 Paris
Tel: (01) 45 89 14 02 *Fax:* (01) 45 89 14 02
E-mail: jannink@noos.fr
Web Site: www.editionsjannink.com
Key Personnel
Dir: Baudouin Jannink
Literary Dir: Marie Caroline Aubert
Commercial Dir: Antoine Soriano
Production: Claire Bonnevie
Founded: 1977
Subjects: Art, History, Adult books; contemporary art
ISBN Prefix(es): 2-902462
Number of titles published annually: 6 Print
Total Titles: 70 Print
Associate Companies: SIPEL

Editions Jean-Claude Lattes+
17 rue Jacob, F-75006 Paris
Tel: (01) 44417400 *Fax:* (01) 43253047
E-mail: jpeguillam@editions-jclattes.fr
Key Personnel
Man Dir: Isabelle Laffont *Fax:* (01) 43 26 91 04
Editorial: Laurent Laffont *Fax:* (01) 43 26 91 04
Foreign Rights: Eva Bredin *Tel:* (01) 44 41 74 34 *Fax:* (01) 43 26 91 04 *E-mail:* ebredin@editions-jclattes.fr
Founded: 1968
General trade publisher.
Subjects: Fiction, Nonfiction (General)
ISBN Prefix(es): 2-7096
Number of titles published annually: 100 Print
Total Titles: 1,250 Print
Parent Company: Hachette Livre
Ultimate Parent Company: Hachette/Lagardere

Editions du Jeu de Paume
One Place de la Concorde, Jardin des Tuileries, 75001 Paris
Tel: (01) 47 03 13 25 *Fax:* (01) 42 61 26 10
Key Personnel
Dir General: Regis Durand
Editor & International Rights: Francoise Bonnefoy *E-mail:* francoisebonnefoy@jeudepaume.org
Founded: 1991
Specialize in exhibitions catalogues.
Subjects: Art, Film, Video, Photography
ISBN Prefix(es): 2-915704
Number of titles published annually: 5 Print
Total Titles: 80 Print

Joly Editions+
31 rue Falguiere, 75741 Paris Cedex 15
Tel: (01) 56 54 16 00 *Fax:* (01) 56 54 16 46
E-mail: loic.even@eja.fr
Web Site: www.editions-joly.com
Key Personnel
Manager: Nathalic Jouven
Subjects: Law, Securities
ISBN Prefix(es): 2-907512
Parent Company: EJA
Distributed by EJA

Le Jour, Editeur+
Division of Sogides
Immeuble Paryseine 3, alle de la Seine, 94854 Ivry Cedex
Tel: (01) 49591189 *Fax:* (01) 49591196
Web Site: www.edjour.com

Key Personnel
Contact: H Laurent *E-mail:* hlaurent@sogides.com
Subjects: Animals, Pets, Astrology, Occult, Career Development, Health, Nutrition, How-to, Medicine, Nursing, Dentistry, Psychology, Psychiatry, Women's Studies
ISBN Prefix(es): 2-89041
Branch Office(s)
955 rue Amherst, Montreal, PQ H2L 3K4, Canada, Contact: Pierre Lesperance
Tel: 514-523-1182 *Fax:* 514-597-0370
E-mail: edhomme@sogides.com
Foreign Rights: Chantal Galtier-Roussel

Jouvence Editions+
Formerly Editions Trois Fontaines
BP 7, 74161 St Julien-en-Genevois
Tel: (04) 50 43 28 60 *Fax:* (04) 50 43 29 24
E-mail: info@editions-jouvence.com
Web Site: www.editions-jouvence.com
Key Personnel
Manager & International Rights: Nelly Irniger
Founded: 1991
Subjects: Cookery, Earth Sciences, Education, Health, Nutrition, How-to, Human Relations, Medicine, Nursing, Dentistry, Philosophy, Psychology, Psychiatry, Self-Help, Social Sciences, Sociology, Sports, Athletics
ISBN Prefix(es): 2-88353; 2-909206
Imprints: Epanouissement; Pratique Sante; Sante Spiritualite
Distributor for Carthame editions

Jupiter, *imprint of* Les Editions LGDJ-Montchrestien

Editions Juridiques Associees, see Les Editions LGDJ-Montchrestien

Editions Juridiques Africaines
44 rue Poliveau, 75005 Paris
Tel: (01) 43370401 *Fax:* (01) 43370401
Founded: 1987
Subjects: Foreign Countries, Law
ISBN Prefix(es): 2-87838
Imprints: EDJA
Divisions:

Editions Juridiques et Techniques Lamy SA
21-23 rue des Ardennes, 75935 Paris cedex 19
Tel: (01) 44721200 *Fax:* (01) 44721389
Telex: 214398
Key Personnel
President: Jean-Marc Detailleur
Sales: Jean-Luc Cretal; Eric Forein
Publicity: Jean-Pierre Benedi
Founded: 1949
Subjects: Law, Social Sciences, Sociology
ISBN Prefix(es): 2-7212
Parent Company: Wolters Kluwer NV

Jurif (Societe d' Etudes Juridiques Internationales et Fiscales), see Les Cahiers Fiscaux Europeens Sarl

Editions du Juris-Classeur
141 rue de Javel, 75747 Paris Cedex 15
Tel: (01) 45 58 92 00 *Fax:* (01) 45 58 94 00
E-mail: editorial@juris-classeur.com; relations-clients@juris-classeur.com
Web Site: www.juris-classeur.fr
Key Personnel
President: Martin Desprez
Editorial Dir: Bernard Bonjean; Christophe Veyrin Forrer
Marketing: Bruno DeClementi
Subjects: Law
ISBN Prefix(es): 2-7110
Parent Company: LexisNexis Group

Ultimate Parent Company: Reed Elsevier plc
Warehouse: 14 rue de la Passerelle, 31200 Toulouse Cedex

Editions Juris Service
12 Quai Andre Lassagne, 69001 Lyon
Tel: (04) 72 10 10 01 *Fax:* (04) 78 28 93 83
E-mail: info@editionsjuris.com
Web Site: www.editionsjuris.com
Key Personnel
President: Philippe Chagnon
Founded: 1983
Specialize in tourism & law, non-profit sector, real estate joint ownership, liberal professions.
Subjects: Communications, Law, Management, Real Estate
ISBN Prefix(es): 2-907648; 2-910992
Number of titles published annually: 5 Print
Total Titles: 70 Print; 2 CD-ROM

Kailash Editions+
69 rue Saint-Jacques, 75005 Paris
Tel: (01) 43.29.52.52 *Fax:* (01) 46.34.03.29
E-mail: kailash@imaginet.fr
Key Personnel
Dir: Raj de Condappa
Founded: 1991
Subjects: Anthropology, Archaeology, Art, Asian Studies, Biography, History, Literature, Literary Criticism, Essays, Travel, Specialize in Asia & Indian continent
ISBN Prefix(es): 2-909052; 2-84268
Distributor for Kwokon
Bookshop(s): Librairie Kailash, 69 rue Saint-Jacques, 75005 Paris

Editions Kaleidoscope+
11 Rue de Sevres, 75006 Paris
Tel: (01) 45 44 07 08 *Fax:* (01) 45 44 53 71
E-mail: infos@editions-kaleidoscope.com
Web Site: www.editions-kaleidoscope.com
Key Personnel
President: Isabel Finkenstaedt
Founded: 1988
ISBN Prefix(es): 2-87767
Warehouse: Ecole des loisirs, Lotissment de la Butte, 11 rue Gutenberg, 91620 Nozay
Orders to: L'Ecole des Loisirs, 11 rue de Sevres, 75006 Paris

Karger, *imprint of* Librairie Luginbuhl

Karthala Editions-Diffusion+
22-24 Blvd Arago, 75013 Paris
Tel: (01) 43 31 15 59 *Fax:* (01) 45 35 27 05
E-mail: karthala@wanadoo.fr
Telex: 250303 Public Paris
Key Personnel
Man Dir, Editorial, Rights & Permissions, & Production: Robert Ageneau
Publicity: Farida Benbelaid
Founded: 1980
Subjects: Anthropology, Asian Studies, Developing Countries, Economics, Education, Geography, Geology, Literature, Literary Criticism, Essays, Religion - Catholic, Religion - Islamic, Religion - Protestant, Social Sciences, Sociology, Travel
ISBN Prefix(es): 2-86537; 2-84586
Branch Office(s)
Editions Hurthbise, 7360 Blvd Newtian, La Salle, PQ H8N 1X2, Canada
Distributor for Codesria; CRA; Haho; Hurthbise; Inades; Institut Royal des Tropiques; Jasor

Editions Klincksieck
8 rue de la Sorbonne, 75005 Paris
Tel: (01) 43.54.59.53 *Fax:* (01) 43.25.25.53
Key Personnel
Joint Man Dir: Alain Baudry
Founded: 1842

Subjects: Archaeology, Art, History, Language Arts, Linguistics, Literature, Literary Criticism, Essays, Music, Dance, Science (General), Social Sciences, Sociology
ISBN Prefix(es): 2-252
Associate Companies: Aux Amateurs De Livres

Eric Koehler+
6 rue du Mail, 75002 Paris
Tel: (01) 49 27 06 37; (01) 44 55 37 50 *Fax:* (01) 47 03 39 86; (01) 40 20 99 74
Founded: 1987
Subjects: Photography
ISBN Prefix(es): 2-7107; 2-907220

Editions Lacour-Olle+
25 blvd Amiral Courbet, 30000 Nimes
Tel: (04) 66 67 30 30 *Fax:* (04) 66 21 11 23
E-mail: c.lacour@editions-lacour.com
Web Site: www.editions-lacour.com
Key Personnel
Contact: Christian Lacour
Founded: 1791
Subjects: Astrology, Occult, Cookery, Parapsychology, Regional Interests, Religion - Catholic, Religion - Protestant, Religion - Other
ISBN Prefix(es): 2-86971; 2-84149; 2-84406; 2-84692; 2-84691

L'Adret editions+
Route de Soueiche, Encausse-les-Thermes, 31160 Aspet
Key Personnel
Man Dir: Jean Mandion
Founded: 1983
Subjects: History, Regional Interests
ISBN Prefix(es): 2-904458

Laffitte Reprints
25, cours d'Estienne d'Orves, 13225 Marseille Cedex 02
Mailing Address: BP 1903, Marseille Cedex 02
Tel: (04) 91 59 80 40 *Fax:* (04) 91 54 25 65
Key Personnel
President: Jeanne Laffitte *E-mail:* editions@jeanne-laffitte.com
Founded: 1980
Subjects: Ethnicity, History, Regional Interests
ISBN Prefix(es): 2-85203; 2-86276; 2-7348; 2-86604
Distributed by CELF; Editions Jeanne Laffitte (France)

Editions Robert Laffont+
24 ave Marceau, 75381 Paris Cedex 08
Tel: (01) 53 67 14 00 *Fax:* (01) 53 67 14 14
Web Site: www.laffont.fr
Telex: 260 808
Key Personnel
Pres & Dir General: Leonello Brandolini
Founded: 1987
Subjects: Fiction
ISBN Prefix(es): 2-221; 2-87645
Associate Companies: Bellitz Fixot

Editions Jacques Lafitte - Who's Who in France
16, rue Camille Pelletan, 92300 Levallois-Perret
Tel: (0141) 272 830 *Fax:* (0141) 272 840
E-mail: whoswho@whoswho.fr
Web Site: www.whoswho.fr
Key Personnel
President: Antoine Hebrard *E-mail:* antoine.hebrard@whoswho.fr
Dir General: Eleonore de Dampierre
E-mail: eleonore.de.dampierre@whoswho.fr
Publicity: Marion Poussielgue
E-mail: mpoussielgue@whoswho.fr
Founded: 1951
Subjects: Biographical Dictionary

PUBLISHERS   FRANCE

ISBN Prefix(es): 2-85784
Number of titles published annually: 1 Print; 1 Online

Michel Lafon Publishing+
7-13 blvd Paul-Emile Victor, 92521 Neuilly Cedex
Tel: (01) 41 43 85 85 *Fax:* (01) 46 24 00 95
Key Personnel
Publisher: Pierre Fery-Zendel; Michel Lafon
Publicity: Nathalie Ladurantie
Rights & Permissions: Patricia Nadal
Founded: 1983
Subjects: Biography, Cookery, Drama, Theater, Fiction, Film, Video, History, Sports, Athletics, Autobiography, Testimony, Thriller
ISBN Prefix(es): 2-84098; 2-908652; 2-7499

Librairie Leonce Laget
76 rue de Seine, 75006 Paris
Tel: (01) 43 29 90 04 *Fax:* (01) 43 26 89 68
E-mail: liblaget@wanadoo.fr
Web Site: www.franceantiq.fr/slam/laget/uk.htm
Cable: LIBLAGET PARIS 110
Key Personnel
President: Veronique Delvaux
Founded: 1955
Subjects: Architecture & Interior Design, Art, Career Development, Crafts, Games, Hobbies, History
ISBN Prefix(es): 2-85204

Editions Lamarre SA
One, av Edouard Belin, 92856 Rueil-Malmaison Cedex
Mailing Address: BP 60, 78141 Velizy Cedex
Tel: (01) 41 29 99 99 *Fax:* (01) 41 29 95 13
Key Personnel
Dir: Marie-Laure Dechatre *Tel:* (01) 41 29 76 76 *E-mail:* mldechatre@groupeliaisons.fr
Sales Manager: Thierry de Puniet de Parry
Marketing: Nelly Couret *Tel:* (01) 41 29 77 03 *E-mail:* ncouret@groupeliaisons.fr
Commercial: Philippe Hamel *Tel:* (01) 41 29 96 89 *E-mail:* phamel@groupeliaisons.fr
Founded: 1957
Subjects: Medicine, Nursing, Dentistry
ISBN Prefix(es): 2-85030

Langues & Mondes-L'Asiatheque+
Cite Veron 11, 75018 Paris
Tel: (01) 42 62 04 00 *Fax:* (01) 42 62 12 34
E-mail: info@asiatheque.com
Web Site: www.asiatheque.com
Key Personnel
General & Editorial Dir: Mdme Christiane Thiollier
Editorial Dir: Alain Thiollier
Editorial Assistant: Elizabeth Eldin
Founded: 1973
Specialize in material for learning of foreign languages & books about cultures & civilizations of the whole world.
Subjects: Asian Studies, Cookery, Education, Foreign Countries, Language Arts, Linguistics, Literature, Literary Criticism, Essays, Religion - Buddhist, Religion - Hindu, Self-Help
ISBN Prefix(es): 2-911053; 2-901795; 2-915255
Total Titles: 130 Print; 23 Audio
Distributor for Presses Universitaires de France (PUF); Union Distribution Flammarion (UD)

Editions Fernand Lanore Sarl+
One rue Palatine, 75006 Paris
Tel: (01) 43256661 *Fax:* (01) 43296981
Key Personnel
Dir: Francois Sorlot
Founded: 1920
Subjects: Education, History, Language Arts, Linguistics, Outdoor Recreation, Philosophy, Religion - Other, Travel
ISBN Prefix(es): 2-85157

Editions du Laquet+
Rue Droite, 46600 Martel
Tel: (05) 65 37 43 54 *Fax:* (05) 65 37 43 55
E-mail: contact@editions-dulaquet.fr
Web Site: editions-dulaquet.fr
Key Personnel
Sales Manager: Dominique Barbier
Founded: 1990
Subjects: Art, Cookery, Drama, Theater, Fiction, Literature, Literary Criticism, Essays, Travel
ISBN Prefix(es): 2-910333; 2-84523
Number of titles published annually: 25 Print
Total Titles: 170 Print

Editions Larousse+
21 rue du Montparnasse, 75283 Paris Cedex 06
Tel: (01) 44 39 44 00 *Fax:* (01) 44 39 43 43
Web Site: www.larousse.fr
Telex: 250828 LAROUS PARIS *Cable:* Liblarous 43 Paris
Key Personnel
Chairman & Man Dir: Christian Bregou
Foreign Rights Dir: Evelyne Le Bourse
Founded: 1852
Subjects: Animals, Pets, Art, Child Care & Development, Cookery, Gardening, Plants, History, Language Arts, Linguistics, Medicine, Nursing, Dentistry, Music, Dance, Psychology, Psychiatry, Regional Interests, Science (General), Self-Help, Social Sciences, Sociology, Sports, Athletics, Technology
ISBN Prefix(es): 2-03
Parent Company: Vivendi Universal Publishing
Subsidiaries: Ediciones Larousse Argentina SA; Ediciones Larousse Colombiana Ltda; Ediciones Larousse SA; Editions Francaises Inc; Editora Larousse do Brazil; Larousse-Belgique; Larousse (Suisse) SA

Editions Le Laurier
19, Passage Jean Nicot, 75007 Paris
Tel: (01) 45 51 55 08 *Fax:* (01) 45 51 81 83
E-mail: editions@lelaurier.fr
Web Site: www.lelaurier.fr
Key Personnel
Manager: Nicolas Macarez
Founded: 1981
Subjects: Religion - Catholic
ISBN Prefix(es): 2-86495; 2-910095

Editions Lavoisier+
Formerly Editions Tec & Doc - Lavoisier
11 rue Lavoisier, 75008 Paris 08
Tel: (01) 47 40 67 00 *Fax:* (01) 47 40 67 88
E-mail: edition@tec-et-doc.com
Web Site: www.tec-et-doc.com
Key Personnel
Man Dir: Patrick Fenouil
Import Manager: Romuald Verrier
Editorial: Jean-Marc Bocabeille; Philippe Zawieja
Marketing & Publicity: Christine Cardinal *E-mail:* cardinal@lavoisier.fr
Founded: 1947
Subjects: Agriculture, Biological Sciences, Chemistry, Chemical Engineering, Cookery, Electronics, Electrical Engineering, Engineering (General), Environmental Studies, Geography, Geology, Labor, Industrial Relations, Maritime, Medicine, Nursing, Dentistry, Technology, New Communication & Information Technologies
ISBN Prefix(es): 2-85206; 2-7430
Number of titles published annually: 100 Print
Imprints: EM Inter; Hermes Science; Tec & Doc
Branch Office(s)
Intercept Ltd, PO Box 716, Andover, Hants SP10 1YG, United Kingdom *Tel:* (01264) 334748 *Fax:* (01264) 334058 *E-mail:* intercept@andover.co.uk
U.S. Office(s): Lavoisier Publishing Inc, Springer Verlag Customer Services, PO Box 2485, Secaucus, NJ 07096-2485, United States *Fax:* 201-348-4505 *E-mail:* orders@springer-ny.com
Shipping Address: 14 rue de Provigny, 94236 Cachan Cedex *Tel:* (01) 47406700 *Fax:* (01) 47406702

Editions Universitaires LCF
Passage des Graves, 33000 Bordeaux Cedex
Tel: (05) 56 51 51 37 *Fax:* (05) 56 51 51 37
Key Personnel
Dir: Alain Yagues
Founded: 1989
Subjects: Health, Nutrition, History, Law, Wine & Spirits
ISBN Prefix(es): 2-908193

Editions Francis Lefebvre
42 rue de Villiers, 92532 Levallois, Cedex
Tel: (01) 41 05 22 00; (08) 36 70 00 14; (01) 41 05 22 06 *Fax:* (01) 41 05 36 80
Telex: 649470
Key Personnel
Dir: J Icart
Contact: Y Chareton
Subjects: Law
ISBN Prefix(es): 2-85115; 2-85786

Editions Legislatives+
80, ave de la Marne, 92546 Montrouge Cedex
Tel: (01) 40 92 36 36 *Fax:* (01) 46 56 00 15
E-mail: infocom@editions-legislatives.fr
Web Site: www.editions-legislatives.fr
Telex: 632855F
Key Personnel
General Dir: Pierre-Paul Richard
Dir, Foreign Relations: Michel Blanc
Founded: 1947
Subjects: Agriculture, Business, Career Development, Economics, Environmental Studies, Labor, Industrial Relations, Law, Library & Information Sciences, Medicine, Nursing, Dentistry, Real Estate
ISBN Prefix(es): 2-85086

Editions Dominique Leroy+
3, rue Docteur Andre Ragot, BP 313, 89103 Sens Cedex
Tel: (03) 86 64 15 24 *Fax:* (03) 86 64 15 24
Web Site: www.enfer.com
Key Personnel
Man Dir: Dominique Leroy *E-mail:* domleroy@enfer.com
Founded: 1970
Subjects: Art, Erotica, Fiction, Humor, Literature, Literary Criticism, Essays
ISBN Prefix(es): 2-86688
Number of titles published annually: 4 CD-ROM; 12 E-Book
Total Titles: 110 Print; 10 CD-ROM; 42 E-Book
Imprints: Vertiges Bulles
Bookshop(s): Librairie Curiosa - MBD, Contact: Daniele Masson *E-mail:* curiosa@enfer.com

Lethielleux, *imprint of* Editions Buchet-Chastel
Pierre Zech Editeur

P Lethielleux Editions+
54, rue Michel-Ange, 75016 Paris
Tel: (01) 44 32 05 60 *Fax:* (01) 44 32 05 61
Telex: ELITA 283155 F
Key Personnel
Dir: M Pierre Zech
International Rights: Sophie Zech
Subjects: Biblical Studies, Religion - Catholic, Theology
ISBN Prefix(es): 2-249; 2-283
Parent Company: Pierre Zech Editeur

Letouzey et Ane Editeurs
87, blvd Raspail, 75006 Paris
Tel: (01) 45 48 80 14 *Fax:* (01) 45 49 03 43

E-mail: letouzey@tree.tr
Key Personnel
General Dir: Florence Letouzey-Dumont
Founded: 1885
Subjects: Biblical Studies, Biography, History, Religion - Catholic, Religion - Islamic, Religion - Other
ISBN Prefix(es): 2-7063
Number of titles published annually: 10 Print
Distributor for L'Annee Canonique

Lettres Modernes Minard
10 rue de Valence, 75005 Paris
Tel: (01) 43 36 25 83 *Fax:* (02) 31 84 48 09
E-mail: editorat.lettresmodernes@wanadoo.fr
Key Personnel
Contact: Dominique Alice Minard
Founded: 1954
Subjects: Film, Video, Literature, Literary Criticism, Essays
ISBN Prefix(es): 2-256
Number of titles published annually: 20 Print
Shipping Address: Minard Distribution, 45 rue de Saint Andre, 14123 Fleury Sur Orne
  Tel: (02) 31 84 47 06 *Fax:* (02) 31 84 48 09
  E-mail: minarddistribution@wanadoo.fr
Warehouse: Minard Distribution, 45 rue de Saint Andre, 14123 Fleury Sur Orne
  Tel: (02) 31 84 47 06 *Fax:* (02) 31 84 48 09
  E-mail: minarddistribution@wanadoo.fr
Orders to: Minard Distribution, 45 rue de Saint Andre, 14123 Fleury Sur Orne
  Tel: (02) 31 84 47 06 *Fax:* (02) 31 84 48 09
  E-mail: minarddistribution@wanadoo.fr

Lettres Vives Editions+
Campu Magnu, 20213 Castellare-di-Casinca
Mailing Address: PO Box 7, 20213 Folelli
Tel: (04) 95 36 40 93 *Fax:* (04) 95 36 59 92
E-mail: lettresvives@mic.fr
Key Personnel
Editor: Claire Tievant
Founded: 1981
Subjects: Literature, Literary Criticism, Essays, Poetry
ISBN Prefix(es): 2-903721; 2-914577
Number of titles published annually: 5 Print
Total Titles: 120 Print
Imprints: Harmonia Mundi

Liana Levi Editions+
One Paul Painleve Pl, 75005 Paris
Tel: (01) 43 26 29 61 *Fax:* (01) 46 33 69 56
Key Personnel
Man Dir: Liana Levi *E-mail:* llevi@club-internet.fr
Rights & Permissions: Colette Fradin
Foreign Rights: Sylvie Mouches
Editor: Stephanie Neumayer
Founded: 1983
Subjects: Art, Fiction, History, Nonfiction (General)
ISBN Prefix(es): 2-86746

Les Editions LGDJ-Montchrestien+
31 rue Falguiere, 75741 Paris Cedex 15
Tel: (01) 56 54 16 00 *Fax:* (01) 56 54 16 49
Web Site: www.lgdj.fr/lgdj/accueil.php
Key Personnel
Man Dir: Vincent Marty
Man Dir & Sales Manager, Rights & Permissions: Nathalie Jouven
Sales Manager: Piene Coustols
Founded: 1836
Subjects: Economics, Government, Political Science, History, Law, Public Administration, Social Sciences, Sociology
ISBN Prefix(es): 2-275
Parent Company: Petites Affiches
Imprints: Jupiter; Navarre
Distributed by Bruylant; Patrimoine
Distributor for L'Abecedaire parlementaire; Academia; AENGDE; ATOL; Bruylant; City & York; Comite pour l'histoire economique et financiere de la France; Delta; Edition Formation Entreprise; Georg; Imprimerie Nationale; MB Edition; Pantheon-Assas Paris II; Presses Universitaires de la Faculte de droit de Clermont; Presses Universitaires de Laval; SCHULTHESS; Staempfli
Bookshop(s): 20 rue Soufflot, 75005 Paris
  Tel: (01) 46 33 89 85 *Fax:* (01) 40 51 81 85
  E-mail: librairie-lgdj@eja.fr
Orders to: 160 rue Saint-Jacques, 75005 Paris

L'Harmattan Paris, *imprint of* Revue Espaces et Societes

Editions John Libbey Eurotext+
Subsidiary of John Libbey Co Ltd
127, ave de la Republique, 92120 Montrouge
Tel: (01) 46 73 06 60 *Fax:* (01) 40 84 09 99
E-mail: contact@john-libbey-eurotext.fr
Web Site: www.john-libbey-eurotext.fr
Key Personnel
Dir, Publications: Gilles Cahn *Tel:* (01) 46 73 06 79 *E-mail:* gilles.cahn@jle.com
Dir, Marketing: Perrine Sentilhes *Tel:* (01) 46 73 01 35 *E-mail:* perrine.sentilhes@jle.com
Advertising Dir: Anne Coche *Tel:* (01) 46 73 06 77 *E-mail:* anne.coche@jle.com
Editorial & Development Manager: Marie-Anne Lambert *Tel:* (01) 46 73 06 70 *E-mail:* marie-anne.lambert@jle.com
Founded: 1986
Subjects: Agriculture, Economics, Environmental Studies, Medicine, Nursing, Dentistry, Life Sciences
ISBN Prefix(es): 2-7420

Editions Librairie-Galerie Racine+
Formerly Editions Saint-Germain-des-Pres SA
23 rue Racine, 75006 Paris
Tel: (01) 43269724 *Fax:* (01) 43269724
E-mail: lgr@librairie-galerie-racine.com
Key Personnel
Editorial: Jean Breton
Publicity: Philippe Heracles
Founded: 1969
Subjects: Poetry
ISBN Prefix(es): 2-243; 2-84328

Librairie Luginbuhl
36 blvd de Latour-Maubourg, 75007 Paris
Tel: (01) 45 51 42 58 *Fax:* (01) 45 56 07 80
E-mail: liblug@club-internet.fr
Key Personnel
Contact: Jean Luginbuhl
Subjects: Medicine, Nursing, Dentistry
Imprints: Karger

Librairie Scientifique et Technique Albert Blanchard
9, Rue de Medicis, 75006 Paris
Tel: (01) 43 26 90 34 *Fax:* (01) 43 29 97 31
E-mail: librairie.blanchard@wanadoo.fr
Web Site: www.blanchard75.fr
Key Personnel
Contact: Laurent Debruyne
Subjects: Astronomy, Chemistry, Chemical Engineering, Earth Sciences, Mathematics, Natural History, Philosophy, Physics, Science (General)
ISBN Prefix(es): 2-85367
Number of titles published annually: 3 Print
Total Titles: 1,721 Print

Librarie Maritime Outremer
17 rue Jacob, 75006 Paris
Tel: (04) 91 54 79 40 *Fax:* (04) 91 54 79 49
E-mail: webmaster@librairie-outremer.com
Web Site: www.librairie-outremer.com
Telex: 205652 JCLates

Key Personnel
Man Editor: Pierre Gutelle
Rights & Permissions: Emilie Levi
Founded: 1839
Subjects: Maritime, Sports, Athletics
ISBN Prefix(es): 2-7070
Parent Company: Editions Jean-Claude Lattes

Libraries Techniques SA, see LiTec (Librairies Techniques SA)

Librio, *imprint of* Flammarion SA

Le Lierre et Le Coudrier+
83, rue Lamarck, 75018 Paris
Mailing Address: PO Box 54, 75861 Paris Cedex 18
Tel: (01) 42550027 *Fax:* (01) 42570497
ISBN Prefix(es): 2-907975; 2-9502146
Associate Companies: La Lonave-vue, 363 b, Chaunic de Waterloo, 1060 Bruyelle, Belgium

Lignes De Vie, *imprint of* Editions de Septembre

Ligue pour la Lecture de la Bible, see LLB France (Ligue pour la Lecture de la Bible)

Editions des Limbes d'Or FBT de R Editions
49, av de la Reistance, 92370 Chaville
Tel: (01) 41151969 *Fax:* (01) 41151969
Key Personnel
President: Francoise Thiam
Founded: 1995
Subjects: Art, Criminology, Economics, Fiction, Foreign Countries, Government, Political Science, Human Relations, Literature, Literary Criticism, Essays, Travel
ISBN Prefix(es): 2-911064

LiTec (Librairies Techniques SA)+
141, rue de Javel, 75747 Paris
Tel: (01) 45 58 92 70 *Fax:* (01) 45 58 94 00
E-mail: libraries@juris-classeur.com
Web Site: www.lexisnexis.fr
Key Personnel
Dir: Alexandre Guegan
Sales Manager: Marie Oneissi
Founded: 1927
Subjects: Accounting, Government, Political Science, Labor, Industrial Relations, Law
ISBN Prefix(es): 2-7111
Parent Company: Editions du Juris-Classeur
Ultimate Parent Company: Reed Elsevier plc/LexisNexis
Branch Office(s)
26 rue Soufflot, 75005 Paris *Tel:* (01) 43 29 07 71 *Fax:* (01) 40 51 83 72 *E-mail:* librairie@soufflot@juris-classeur.com
U.S. Office(s): 27 Place Dauphine, 75001 Paris *Tel:* (01) 43 26 60 90 *Fax:* (01) 46 34 22 98 *E-mail:* librairie.dauphine@juris-classeur.com
Warehouse: Zone Artisanale-Route de Niort, 85205 Fontenay le Comte Cedex

Editions Lito
41, rue de Verdun, 94503 Champigny-sur-Marne Cedex
Mailing Address: BP 363, 94503 Champigny-sur-Marne, Cedex
Tel: (01) 45161700 *Fax:* (01) 48820085
E-mail: annick.cabrelli@editionslito.com
Key Personnel
Man Dir, Editorial, Rights & Permissions: Pierre Rosdahl
Founded: 1958
Subjects: Crafts, Games, Hobbies, Nonfiction (General)
ISBN Prefix(es): 2-244
Subsidiaries: Lito Editrice

Litterature Generale, *imprint of* Autres Temps

Le Livre de Paris+
58, rue Jean Bleuzen, 92178 Vanves Cedex
Tel: (01) 41 23 60 00 *Fax:* (01) 41 45 34 42
E-mail: ldpsiege@hachette-livre.fr
Web Site: www.livredeparis.com
Key Personnel
General Dir: Patrice Burckel de Tell
International Rights Contact: Monica Mondardini
Founded: 1935
Membership(s): the Syndicat National de L'Edition.
Subjects: Art, How-to
ISBN Prefix(es): 2-245
Imprints: Livres de Paris; Quillet; Tout L'Univers

Le Livre de Poche-L G F (Librairie Generale Francaise)+
43, Quai de Grenelle, 75905 Paris Cedex 15
Tel: (01) 43923000 *Fax:* (01) 43923590
Web Site: www.livredepoche.com; www.hachette.com
Key Personnel
Man Dir & Dir, Foreign Rights & International Development: Dominique Goust
Founded: 1953
Subjects: Biography, Drama, Theater, Environmental Studies, Fiction, Government, Political Science, History, Language Arts, Linguistics, Literature, Literary Criticism, Essays, Philosophy, Poetry, Science (General), Science Fiction, Fantasy, Social Sciences, Sociology
ISBN Prefix(es): 2-253
Parent Company: Hachette

Livre des Vacances, *imprint of* Librairie Vuibert

Livres de Paris, *imprint of* Le Livre de Paris

Les Livres du Dragon d'Or+
60, rue Mazarine, 75006 Paris
Tel: (01) 53 10 36 37 *Fax:* (01) 53 10 36 39
E-mail: dragondor@gruend.fr
Key Personnel
Man Dir: Nathalie Perrin
Founded: 1989
Specialize in license publishing & book packaging for the international market.
ISBN Prefix(es): 2-87881
Number of titles published annually: 10 Print
Total Titles: 100 Print
Parent Company: Editions Gruend
Orders to: Editions Gruend, 60, rue Mazarine, Paris 75006 *Tel:* (01) 53 10 36 00 *Fax:* (01) 43 29 49 86 *Web Site:* www.grund.fr

LLB France (Ligue pour la Lecture de la Bible)+
51 Blvd Gustave-Andre, 26007 Valence, Cedex
Mailing Address: BP 728, 26007 Valence, Cedex
Tel: (04) 75 56 02 68 *Fax:* (04) 75 56 02 97
E-mail: contact@llbfrance.com
Web Site: www.llbfrance.com
Key Personnel
President: Pierre Berthoud
General Dir: Marc Deroeux
Editor: Eric Denimal *E-mail:* eric.denimal@llbfrance.com
Founded: 1946
Subjects: Archaeology, How-to, Religion - Protestant, Theology
ISBN Prefix(es): 2-85031
U.S. Office(s): Scripture Union, Suite 115, 150 Shafford Ave, Wayne, PA 19087, United States
Distributed by Cedis; CLC; Vida (France)

Lonely Planet
71 bis, blvd du Cardinal-Lemoine, 75005 Paris
Tel: (01) 44 32 06 20 *Fax:* (01) 46 34 72 55
E-mail: 100560.415@compuserve.com
Web Site: www.lonelyplanet.fr
Key Personnel
General Dir: Zahia Hafs
Founded: 1992
Subjects: Travel
ISBN Prefix(es): 2-84070
Parent Company: Lonely Planet Publications, Australia
U.S. Office(s): Autre Filiale de Lonely Planet-Aux E-U Cette Fois, 150 Linden St, Oakland, CA 94607, United States *Tel:* 510-893-8555 *Fax:* 510-893-8563 *E-mail:* miriam@lonelyplanet.com *Web Site:* www.lonelyplanet.com
Orders to: Vilo Diffusion, 25 rue Ginoux, 75015 Paris

Editions Loubatieres+
10 bis rue de l'Europe, 31190 Portet-sur Garonne Cedex
Mailing Address: BP 27, 31122 Portet-sur Garonne Cedex
Tel: (05) 61 72 83 53 *Fax:* (05) 61 72 83 50
E-mail: loubatieres@club-internet.fr
Key Personnel
Dir: Francis Loubatieres
Founded: 1970
Subjects: Art, Geography, Geology, History, Regional Interests, Travel
ISBN Prefix(es): 2-86266
Divisions: Librairie Loubatieres

LPM, see Les Presses du Management

LT Editions-Jacques Lanore+
15, rue Soufflot, 75254 Paris Cedex 05
Tel: (01) 44 41 89 30 *Fax:* (01) 44 41 89 39
E-mail: lanore@lanore.com
Web Site: www.lanore.com
Key Personnel
Contact: A M Tabaste
Subjects: Architecture & Interior Design, Career Development, Child Care & Development, Cookery, Health, Nutrition, House & Home, Law, Technology, Travel
ISBN Prefix(es): 2-86268
Parent Company: Groupe Flammarion
Bookshop(s): Librarie-Editions J Lanore, 4 rue de Tournon, 75006 Paris *Tel:* (01) 43 29 43 50

LT Editors, see LT Editions-Jacques Lanore

Lumiere Biblique series, *imprint of* Les Editions de la Source Sarl

Editions Josette Lyon+
Division of Editions La Maisnie
19, rue Saint-Severin, 75005 Paris
Tel: (01) 40 44 81 60 *Fax:* (01) 45 42 30 99
E-mail: editions.josette.lyon@wanadoo.fr
Web Site: www.editions-josette-lyon.com
Key Personnel
Man Dir: Sophie Gillot
Founded: 1986
Subjects: Health, Nutrition
ISBN Prefix(es): 2-906757; 2-84319

Editions Lyonnaises d'Art et d'Histoire
2, Quai Claude Bernard, 69007 Lyon 07
Tel: (04) 78 72 49 00 *Fax:* (04) 78 69 00 48
Web Site: www.achatlyon.com/editionslyonnaises
Key Personnel
General Dir: Corinne Poirieux
Founded: 1995
Subjects: Archaeology, Biography, Genealogy, History, How-to, Literature, Literary Criticism, Essays
ISBN Prefix(es): 2-84147
Distributor for Ed Nichel Chomarer; Ed Nichel Repnier

Macula+
6, rue Coetlogon, 75006 Paris
Tel: (01) 45 48 58 70 *Fax:* (01) 45 44 45 89
Key Personnel
Dir: Jean Clay
Founded: 1980
Subjects: Antiques, Art, Film, Video, History, Literature, Literary Criticism, Essays, Photography, Psychology, Psychiatry
ISBN Prefix(es): 2-86589
Total Titles: 58 Print

Magnard
20 rue Berbier-du-Mets, 75647 Paris Cedex 13
Tel: (01) 44 08 85 85 *Fax:* (01) 44 08 49 79
Web Site: www.magnard.fr
Telex: 202294 F
Key Personnel
Contact: Jean-Manuel Bourgois
Founded: 1933
Subjects: Education
ISBN Prefix(es): 2-210
Subsidiaries: Dilisco (Diffusion du Livre Scolaire)

Maison de la Revelation+
46 av de la Liberation, 33740 Ares
Mailing Address: BP 16, 33740 Ares
Tel: (05) 56602477 *Fax:* (05) 56931631
Key Personnel
President: Dominique Mottas
Author: Michel Potay
Founded: 1974
Subjects: Philosophy, Religion - Other
ISBN Prefix(es): 2-901821

La Maison des Instituteurs, see Editions MDI (La Maison des Instituteurs)

Editions de la Maison des Sciences de l'Homme, Paris
54, blvd Raspail, 75270 Paris Cedex 06
Tel: (01) 49 54 20 30; (01) 49 54 20 31 *Fax:* (01) 49 54 21 33
E-mail: public@msh-paris.fr
Web Site: www.editions.msh-paris.fr
Telex: 203104 F
Key Personnel
Dir: Maurice Aymard
Head of Services: F Kahn *E-mail:* kahn@msh-paris.fr
Production: R Arcier; S Farraut; Jacky Thowmine
Founded: 1975
Specializes in French-German Programs.
Subjects: Anthropology, Archaeology, Economics, History, Music, Dance, Psychology, Psychiatry, Social Sciences, Sociology
ISBN Prefix(es): 2-7351; 2-901725
Orders to: CID, 131 blvd St-Michel, F-75005 Paris

La Maison du Dictionnaire+
98 Bd du Montparnasse, 75014 Paris
Tel: (01) 43 22 12 93 *Fax:* (01) 43 22 01 77
E-mail: contact@lmdd.com
Web Site: www.lmdd.com
Key Personnel
Man Dir: Michel Feutry
Founded: 1976
Specialize in software aides, electronic dictionaries & CD-ROMs.
ISBN Prefix(es): 2-85608
Branch Office(s)
DPLU, 5165 Ouest Rue Sherbrooke, Montreal, PQ H4A 1T6, Canada
U.S. Office(s): International Book Distributor Ltd, 24 Hudson St, Kinderhook, NY 12106, United States

Adrien Maisonneuve, see Editions d'Amerique et d'Orient, Adrien Maisonneuve

FRANCE

Editions Adrien Maisonneuve
Librairie d'Amerique et d'Orient, 11 rue Saint Sulpice, 75006 Paris
Tel: (01) 43 26 19 50 *Fax:* (01) 43 54 59 54
E-mail: maisonneuve@maisonneuve-adrien.com
Web Site: www.maisonneuve-adrien.com
Key Personnel
Dir General: Jean Maisonneuve
ISBN Prefix(es): 2-7200

Maisonneuve Editeur
26, Av de l'Europe, 78141 Velizy Cedex
Mailing Address: BP 60, 78141 Velizy Cedex
Tel: (01) 34 63 33 33 *Fax:* (01) 34 65 39 70
Key Personnel
Man Dir: Andre G Maisonneuve
Founded: 1959
Subjects: Health, Nutrition, Medicine, Nursing, Dentistry
ISBN Prefix(es): 2-7160

Maisonneuve et Larose+
15 rue Victor-Cousin, 75005 Paris
Tel: (01) 44414930 *Fax:* (01) 43257741
E-mail: servedit1@wanadoo.fr
Key Personnel
President: Ms France Roque
Man Dir: Alain Jauson
Founded: 1835 (& 1860 respectively, merged 1961)
Subjects: Agriculture, Animals, Pets, Astrology, Occult, Language Arts, Linguistics, Regional Interests, Religion - Jewish
ISBN Prefix(es): 2-7068
Distributed by Belles Lettres; Servedit
Distributor for Ecole Francais d'Extreme Orient

Editions Maloine+
23, rue de l'Ecole de Medecine, 75006 Paris
Tel: (01) 43 25 60 45; (01) 43 29 54 50 *Fax:* (03) 44 23 02 27
E-mail: vpc@vigot.fr
Web Site: www.vigotmaloine.fr
Telex: 203215 F
Key Personnel
President, Man Dir, Rights & Permissions: Daniel Vigot
Dir: Christian Vigot
Sales, Publicity & Advertising: Thierry de Puniet
Production, Publicity & Advertising: Jean Phillipart
Founded: 1881
Subjects: Medicine, Nursing, Dentistry, Veterinary Science
ISBN Prefix(es): 2-224

Editions Mango+
4, rue Caroline, 75017 Paris
Tel: (01) 55 30 40 50 *Fax:* (01) 55 30 40 50
E-mail: mango@editions-mango.fr
Web Site: www.editions-mango.fr
Key Personnel
Dir General: Hugues de Saint Vincent
International Rights: Sophie Thunierelle
Founded: 1990
Subjects: Art, Child Care & Development, Crafts, Games, Hobbies, Gardening, Plants, Health, Nutrition, House & Home, How-to, Microcomputers, Outdoor Recreation, Sports, Athletics, Wine & Spirits
ISBN Prefix(es): 2-7404; 2-84270
Parent Company: Editions Fleurus
Distributed by SODIS

Manitoba, *imprint of* Societe d'Edition Les Belles Lettres

Editions Marcus
25, rue Ginoux, 75015 Paris
Tel: (01) 45770404 *Fax:* (01) 45759251
Telex: 643841
Key Personnel
Man Dir: Patrick Arfi
Sales: Mrs Gaubert
Founded: 1963
Subjects: Travel
ISBN Prefix(es): 2-7131

La Marge+
4 rue Emmanuel Arene, 20000 Ajaccio, Corsica
Tel: (04) 95512367 *Fax:* (04) 95500900
Key Personnel
Dir: Jean Jacques Colonna d'Istria
Founded: 1986
ISBN Prefix(es): 2-86523

Editions Marie-Noelle+
7, rue de la Liberte, 39700 Orchamps
Tel: (03) 81877500; (03) 84812891 *Fax:* (03) 81875669
Key Personnel
General Dir: Michel Siegwart
Founded: 1993
Subjects: Fiction, Literature, Literary Criticism, Essays, Science Fiction, Fantasy
ISBN Prefix(es): 2-910186

Editions Maritimes et D'Outremer, *imprint of* Editions Ouest-France

Martelle
3, rue des Vergeaux, 80005 Amiens Cedex 1
Mailing Address: BP 0540, 80005 Amiens Cedex 1
Tel: (03) 22 71 54 54 *Fax:* (03) 22 92 89 33
Telex: 145306
Key Personnel
Contact: M Cochard
Founded: 1990
Subjects: Regional Interests
ISBN Prefix(es): 2-87890
Bookshop(s): Centre Amiens, 2 le Fleure, 94 rue St Lazare, Paris

Editions de la Martiniere
2, rue Christine, 75006 Paris
Tel: (01) 40 51 52 00 *Fax:* (01) 40 51 52 05
E-mail: coedition@lamartiniere.fr
Web Site: www.lamartiniere.fr
Key Personnel
President: Herve De La Martiniere
General Dir: Olivier d' Arrouzat
Editorial: Philippe Gadesaude
Foreign Rights: Marianne Lassandro
ISBN Prefix(es): 2-8307

Editions Marval+
30 rue de Charonne, 75011 Paris
Tel: (01) 48 07 50 40 *Fax:* (01) 48 07 01 08
E-mail: info@marval.com
Web Site: www.marval.com
Key Personnel
Manager: Yves-Marie Marchand
  E-mail: ymarval@noos.fr
Founded: 1942 (New company 1999)
Subjects: Art, Photography
ISBN Prefix(es): 2-86234
Total Titles: 180 Print
Ultimate Parent Company: Vilo
Distribution Center: CELF *Tel:* (01) 43 47 30 03 *Fax:* (01) 43 47 59 43
Edipress, 945, ave Beaumont, Montreal, PQ H3N 1W3, Canada (Canada)
Nouvelle Diffusion, 24, rue de Bosnie, 1060 Bruxelles, Belgium *Tel:* (2) 538 88 46 *Fax:* (2) 538 88 42 (Belgium)
OLF, ZI 3 Corminboeuf, 1701 Fribourg, Switzerland *Tel:* (26) 46 75 111 *Fax:* (26) 46 75 444 (Switzerland)
Vilo, 25, rue Ginoux, 75015 Paris *Tel:* (01) 45 77 08 05 *Fax:* (01) 45 79 97 15

Le Masque, see Librairie des Champs-Elysees/Le Masque

Editions du Masque, *imprint of* Librairie des Champs-Elysees/Le Masque

Club des Masques, *imprint of* Librairie des Champs-Elysees/Le Masque

Editions Charles Massin et Cie
16-18 rue de l'Amiral Mouchez, 75686 Paris Cedex 14
Tel: (01) 45 65 48 55 *Fax:* (01) 45 65 47 00
E-mail: info@massin.fr
Web Site: www.massin.fr
Telex: 4264918 Trace
Founded: 1910
Subjects: Architecture & Interior Design, Art, House & Home
ISBN Prefix(es): 2-7072

Masson Editeur+
21, rue Camille Desmoulins, Issy Les Moulineaux, 92789 Paris Cedex 9
Tel: (01) 73 28 16 34 *Fax:* (01) 73 28 16 49
E-mail: infos@masson.fr
Web Site: www.masson.fr; www.e2med.com
Telex: Massoned 260946 *Cable:* GEMAS PARIS 025
Key Personnel
Chairman & Dir, Publication: Daniel Rodriguez
Foreign Rights Manager: Gail Markham
  Tel: (01) 44 09 68 58 *Fax:* (01) 44 09 58 56
  E-mail: gmarkham@mmi.tm.fr
Founded: 1804
Publish medicine & health care-related subjects & 50 journals in paper & on-line versions; dictionaries.
Subjects: Medicine, Nursing, Dentistry, Psychology, Psychiatry, Veterinary Science
ISBN Prefix(es): 2-225; 2-294
Number of titles published annually: 200 Print
Total Titles: 3,000 Print
Ultimate Parent Company: Groupe MediMedia
Subsidiaries: Masson SpA; Masson SA
Distributed by Havas Diffusion International; Havas Services Suisse; Livredis; O L F; Presses de Belgique; Somabec

Masson-Williams et Wilkins+
3-5, rue Laromiguiere, 75005 Paris
Tel: (01) 40466000 *Fax:* (01) 40466126
E-mail: pradel@lsicom.fr
Key Personnel
Contact: Mariette Guena; Ray Pitt
Founded: 1988
Subjects: Biological Sciences, Medicine, Nursing, Dentistry
ISBN Prefix(es): 2-907516; 2-84360
Parent Company: Wolters Kluwer NV

Matrice
71, rue des Camelias, 91270 Vigneux
Tel: (01) 69 42 13 02 *Fax:* (01) 69 40 21 57
Key Personnel
President: Jacques Pain
Founded: 1984
Subjects: Human Relations
ISBN Prefix(es): 2-905642
Showroom(s): Casteilla, 10, rue Leon-Foucault, 78180 Montigny le Bretonneux *Tel:* (01) 30 14 19 30

Maxima Laurent du Mesnil Editeur+
192, bd Saint-Germain, 75007 Paris
Tel: (01) 44397400 *Fax:* (01) 45484688
E-mail: edition@maxima.fr
Web Site: www.maxima.fr
Key Personnel
President & General Dir: Laurent du Mesnil du Buisson

Dir: Stephane Derville *E-mail:* sderville@maxima.fr
Founded: 1990
Subjects: Business, Career Development, Economics, Finance, Human Relations, Law, Management, Marketing
ISBN Prefix(es): 2-84001
Number of titles published annually: 20 Print; 5 E-Book
Total Titles: 250 Print; 20 E-Book
Associate Companies: Editions Francis Lefebvre
Distributed by Interforum-Editis

Editions MDI (La Maison des Instituteurs)
56-60 rue de la Glaciere, 75640 Paris 13
Tel: (01) 45 87 52 11 *Fax:* (01) 45 87 51 97
E-mail: serviceclient@mdi-editions.com; mpetit@vuef.fr
Web Site: www.mdi-editions.com
Telex: MDI Edit 698094 F
Key Personnel
Man Dir: Marc Baudry
Export Dir: Daniel Beaudat
Founded: 1954
Subjects: Education, Geography, Geology, History, Science (General)
ISBN Prefix(es): 2-223
Parent Company: Editions Bordas

Medecine-Sciences, *imprint of* Flammarion SA

Editions Medianes+
72 rue d'Amiens, 76000 Rouen
Tel: (02) 35 88 85 71 *Fax:* (02) 35 15 28 44
E-mail: medianesconseil@wanadoo.fr
Key Personnel
Dir General: Jean-Marie Tiercelin
Contact: Christian de Chanteloup
Founded: 1989
Membership(s): SNE.
Subjects: Art, Biography, Drama, Theater, History, Literature, Literary Criticism, Essays, Photography, Regional Interests
ISBN Prefix(es): 2-908345

Editions Mediaspaul+
48, rue du Four, 75006 Paris
Tel: (01) 45 48 71 93 *Fax:* (01) 42 22 47 46
E-mail: mediaspaul.com@wanadoo.fr
Founded: 1981
Subjects: Biblical Studies, Religion - Catholic, Theology
ISBN Prefix(es): 2-7122
Bookshop(s): 16 rue de la Visitation, 71600 Paray Le Monial *Tel:* (03) 85 81 08 93 *Fax:* (03) 85 81 08 93
Warehouse: BP 26, 62 rue de Chanteloup, 91291 Arpajon Cedex *Tel:* (01) 64 90 87 40 *Fax:* (01) 64 90 96 09 *E-mail:* media.arp@wanadoo.fr

Medius Editions
204, blvd Raspail, 75014 Paris
Tel: (01) 42 79 25 21 *Fax:* (01) 42 78 25 39
E-mail: contact@dervy.fr
Key Personnel
Manager: Bernard Renaud de la Faverie
Subjects: Astrology, Occult, Psychology, Psychiatry, Bach Flowers, Feng Shui, Reiki, Self Medicine, Yi King Chakras
ISBN Prefix(es): 2-85327
Number of titles published annually: 12 Print
Total Titles: 120 Print
Warehouse: Dilisco, Parc Mure 2, Batiment 4.4, 128 Ave Jean Jaures, BP 102, 94208 Ivry Sur Seine

Editions Memo+
4, rue des Olivettes Passage Douard, 44000 Nantes
Tel: (02) 40 47 98 19 *Fax:* (02) 40 47 98 21
Key Personnel
General Dir: Mdme Christine Morault
Founded: 1993
Subjects: Art
ISBN Prefix(es): 2-910391

Editions Memoire des Arts+
BP 4553, 69244 Lyon Cedex 04
Tel: (04) 78 83 22 62 *Fax:* (04) 72 19 48 74
Key Personnel
General Dir: Alain Vollerin *E-mail:* alain.vollerin@wanadoo.fr
Founded: 1991
Subjects: Art
ISBN Prefix(es): 2-912544

La Memoire Normande, *imprint of* Editions Bertout

Editions Menges
6, rue du Mail, 75002 Paris
Tel: (01) 44 55 37 50 *Fax:* (01) 40 20 99 74
E-mail: info@editions-menges.com
Web Site: www.editions-menges.com
Telex: Cflglm 630385
Key Personnel
Manager, Admin & Finance: Carl Van Eiszner
Editorial Dir & Foreign Rights: Isabelle de Tinguy
Sales Manager: Guillaume Dopffer
Public Relations: Carole Brianchon
Founded: 1975
Subjects: Cookery, Gardening, Plants, Health, Nutrition, Sports, Athletics
ISBN Prefix(es): 2-85620
Parent Company: Editions Sand
Distributed by Vivendi Universal Publishing Services

Editions Franck Mercier+
One bis rue du Forum, 74013 Annecy, cedex
Mailing Address: BP 404, 74013 Annecy cedex
Tel: (04) 50 57 16 50 *Fax:* (01) 450579301
E-mail: franck@mercier.com.ch
Key Personnel
Contact: Franck Mercier
Founded: 1985
Subjects: Geography, Geology, How-to, Outdoor Recreation, Sports, Athletics, Travel
ISBN Prefix(es): 2-86868
Total Titles: 120 Print
Imprints: Guide Franck

Mercure de France SA
26, rue de Conde, 75006 Paris
Tel: (01) 55 42 61 90 *Fax:* (01) 43 54 49 91
E-mail: mercure@mercure.fr
Web Site: www.gallimard.fr
Key Personnel
Production Dir: Brigitte Duverger
Foreign Rights & Permissions: Nicole Boyer
Editor: Nicolas Brehal; Jean-Marc Roberts
Founded: 1891
Subjects: Astrology, Occult, Biography, Fiction, History, Literature, Literary Criticism, Essays, Philosophy, Poetry
ISBN Prefix(es): 2-7152
Parent Company: Editions Gallimard
Associate Companies: Editions Denoel Sarl

Editions A M Metailie+
5 rue de Savoie, 75006 Paris
Tel: (01) 55 42 83 00 *Fax:* (01) 55 42 83 04
E-mail: presse@metailie.info
Web Site: www.metailie.info
Key Personnel
Man Dir & Editor: Anne Marie Metailie *E-mail:* presse@metailie.info
Manager: Jocelyne Valle
Literary Dir: P Dibie; P Leglise-Costa
Communication & Foreign Rights: Marie Descourtieux
Founded: 1979
Subjects: Anthropology, Fiction, Literature, Literary Criticism, Essays, Mysteries, Social Sciences, Sociology
ISBN Prefix(es): 2-86424
Total Titles: 550 Print
Warehouse: Seuil, 13 ave du General Leclere, 91120 L Ballainvilliers, Longjumeau
Orders to: Seuil, 27 rue Jacob, 75261 Paris Cedex 06

Editions Albin Michel+
22, rue Huyghens, 75014 Paris Cedex 14
Tel: (01) 42 79 10 00 *Fax:* (01) 43 27 21 58
Web Site: www.albin-michel.fr
Key Personnel
President: Francis Esmenard
Vice President: Richard Ducousset
General Secretary: Agnes Fruman *E-mail:* afrumen@aldin-michel.fr; Thierry Pfister
Man Dir: Alexis Esmenard; Henri Esmenard; Patrice Gueriy
Sales Dir: Jean-Yves Bry
Dir, Advertising & Promotion: Sylvie Hoare
Foreign Rights: Jacqueline Favero
Subsidiary Rights: Marie Dormann
Dir, Foreign Dept: Tony Cartano
Public Relations: Regine Billot; Florence Godfernaux
Children's Books: Marion Jablonski
Foreign Rights (Children's books): Aurelie Lapautre
Founded: 1902
Subjects: Art, Biography, Child Care & Development, Cookery, Fiction, History, How-to, Humor, Literature, Literary Criticism, Essays, Music, Dance, Nonfiction (General), Philosophy, Religion - Other, Social Sciences, Sociology
ISBN Prefix(es): 2-226

Michelin Editions des Voyages
46, ave de Breteuil, 75324 Paris Cedex 07
Tel: (01) 45 66 12 34 *Fax:* (01) 45 66 11 63
Telex: 270 789 F
Key Personnel
Contact: M Alain Arnaud
Founded: 1900
Subjects: Travel
ISBN Prefix(es): 2-06
Associate Companies: Elastika Michelin, Greece; Michelin Asia Co PTE Ltd, Singapore; Michelin Asia Ltd, Hong Kong; Michelin Companhia Luso Pneu LDA Portugal; Michelin Reifenwerke, Austria; Michelin Reifenwerke, Germany; Michelin Travel Publications; Michelin Tyre PLC, United Kingdom; Nihon Michelin Tire KK, Japan; S A Belge du Pneumatique Michelin, Belgium; SA des Pneumatiques Michelin, Switzerland; SAFE de Neumaticos Michelin, Spain; S P A Michelin Italiana, Italy; Ste Canadienne des Pneus Michelin

Microsoft Press France
18, ave du Quebec, 91957 Courtaboeuf Cedex
Tel: (0825) 827 829 *Fax:* (01) 64 46 06 60
E-mail: msfrance@microsoft.com
Web Site: www.microsoft.com/france
Founded: 1992
Subjects: Computer Science
ISBN Prefix(es): 2-84082

Mille et Une Nuits+
37, rue du Four, 75006 Paris
Tel: (01) 45 49 82 00 *Fax:* (01) 45 49 79 96
E-mail: info1001nuits@editions-fayard.fr
Web Site: www.1001nuits.com
Key Personnel
President: Monsieur Maurizio Medico
International Rights: Monsieur Olivier Rubinstein

Founded: 1993
Subjects: Literature, Literary Criticism, Essays
ISBN Prefix(es): 2-84205; 2-910233

Librairie Minard
45 rue de St-Andre, 14 123 Fleury/Orne
Tel: (02) 31844706 *Fax:* (02) 31844809
Key Personnel
Man Dir: Michel J Minard
Contact: Daniele Minard
Founded: 1978
Subjects: Film, Video, Literature, Literary Criticism, Essays
ISBN Prefix(es): 2-85210
Distributor for Lettres Modernes

Editions Minerva
Subsidiary of La Martiniere Groupe
7 rue d'Assas, 75014 Paris
Tel: (01) 53 63 31 60 *Fax:* (01) 45 49 17 60
Web Site: www.lamartiniere.fr
Key Personnel
President: Herve De La Martiniere
ISBN Prefix(es): 2-8307

Presses Universitaires du Mirail+
Universite Toulouse-Le Mirail, 5 allees Antonio Machado, 31058 Toulouse cedex 1
Tel: (0561) 503808 *Fax:* (0561) 503800
E-mail: pum@univ-tlse2.fr
Web Site: www.crlmidipyrenees.asso.fr/editeurs/pum.htm
Key Personnel
Dir, Science: Wilfrid Rotge *Tel:* 561503805
Founded: 1987
University press that publishes books written mainly by academics.
Subjects: Geography, Geology, History, Language Arts, Linguistics, Literature, Literary Criticism, Essays, Philosophy, Psychology, Psychiatry, Social Sciences, Sociology, Women's Studies
ISBN Prefix(es): 2-85816
Number of titles published annually: 30 Print
Total Titles: 600 Print; 1 CD-ROM; 1 E-Book
Imprints: PUM Toulouse

Miroir Sprint Publications, see Les Editions Vaillant-Miroir-Sprint Publications

Editions Modernes Media+
12, rue Haudriettes, 75003 Paris
Tel: (01) 44 54 90 42 *Fax:* (01) 44 54 90 47
E-mail: ed.mod.media@wanadoo.fr
Key Personnel
Literary Dir: A M Marina Mediavilla
Founded: 1972
Subjects: Education, Language Arts, Linguistics, Literature, Literary Criticism, Essays, Philosophy
ISBN Prefix(es): 2-85398

Gerard Monfort Editeur Sarl+
BP 20, 27800 Brionne
Tel: (01) 40 27 95 54 *Fax:* (01) 40 27 95 60
E-mail: contact@gerard-monfort.com
Web Site: www.gerard-monfort.com
Founded: 1960
Subjects: Art, History, Literature, Literary Criticism, Essays, Specialize in Art History
ISBN Prefix(es): 2-85226

Editions du Moniteur+
17, rue d'Uzes, 75108 Paris Cedex 02
Tel: (01) 40 13 33 72 *Fax:* (01) 40 41 08 87
E-mail: clients@editionsdumoniteur.fr
Web Site: www.editionsdumoniteur.com
Telex: 680876 F
Key Personnel
President: Jacques Guy *Tel:* (01) 40 13 32 31
Man Dir: Frederic Lenne *Tel:* (01) 40 13 34 34
Commercial Manager: Florence Delouche *Tel:* (01) 40 13 37 34
Editor: Jean-Marc Joannes *Tel:* (01) 40 13 32 62
Founded: 1981
Subjects: Architecture & Interior Design, Law, Technology, Construction/Building
ISBN Prefix(es): 2-281; 2-7327; 2-902302
Number of titles published annually: 30 Print; 1 CD-ROM
Total Titles: 160 Print; 4 CD-ROM
Bookshop(s): Librairies du Moniteur, 15 rue d'Uzes, 75002 Paris; 7 pl de l'Odeon, 75006 Paris
Distribution Center: Interforum

Editions Paul Montel
11, rue Gossin, 92543 Montrouge Cedex
Tel: (01) 46565266
Key Personnel
Man Dir: Marc Vigier
Dir: Guy de Dampierre
Sales: Yves-Louis Walle
Subjects: Film, Video, Photography
ISBN Prefix(es): 2-7075

Muller Edition+
BP 122, 92134 Issy-les-Moulineaux Cedex
Tel: (01) 40 90 09 65 *Fax:* (01) 47 76 33 97
E-mail: courrier@muller-edition.com
Web Site: www.muller-edition.com
Key Personnel
President: Joseph Muller
Founded: 1990
Subjects: Archaeology, History, How-to, Military Science
ISBN Prefix(es): 2-904255
Total Titles: 500 Print; 300 E-Book
Distributed by Editions Picard; Goutiere diffusioer; Histoire et documents
Distributor for Editions Bertout; Editions Jean Curutchet; Editions des Ecrivains Associes; Editions Domens; Editions Etoile De La Pensee; Editions L' Harmattan; Editions Charles Lavauzelle; Martelle; Ouest-France
Distribution Center: Muller, 123 av Publo Picasso, Nanterre, 2 etage, Porte 3024

Editions de la Reunion des Musees Nationaux+
49, rue Etienne Marcel, 75039 Paris Cedex 01
Tel: (01) 40 13 49 66 *Fax:* (01) 40 13 49 73
E-mail: editions@rmn.fr
Web Site: www.rmn.fr
Key Personnel
Dir: J J Lugbull
Founded: 1931
Subjects: Antiques, Archaeology, Architecture & Interior Design, Art, Ethnicity, History
ISBN Prefix(es): 2-7118
Branch Office(s)
Reumusnat Paris *Fax:* (01) 42225073 (Telex: Rm 200115 F)
Distributed by Editions du Seuie
Bookshop(s): Grand Louvre, 75001 Paris; Librairie du Musee d'Orsay, 60ter rue de Lille, 75001 Paris
Warehouse: Centre de Distribution de la R M N, 1-31, allee du 12 fevrier 1934, 77186 Noisiel

Editions Maurice Nadeau, Les Lettres Nouvelles+
135, rue Saint-Martin, 75194 Paris Cedex 04
Tel: (01) 48 87 75 87 *Fax:* (01) 48 87 13 01
Key Personnel
President: Bernard Coutaz
Manager: Maurice Nadeau
Subjects: Literature, Literary Criticism, Essays
ISBN Prefix(es): 2-86231
Parent Company: Societe D'Editions Litteraires et Scientifiques (SELIS)
Orders to: Harmonia Mundi, 13200 Arles

Nanga
BP 62, 22430 Erquy
Tel: (02) 96 72 32 16 *Fax:* (02) 96 72 08 48
E-mail: nanga@nanga.fr; nangaw@wanadoo.fr
Web Site: www.nanga.info
Key Personnel
Publisher: Jerome Feugereux *E-mail:* jerome@feugereux.com
Founded: 1991
Subjects: Art, Earth Sciences, Literature, Literary Criticism, Essays, Poetry
ISBN Prefix(es): 2-909152
Number of titles published annually: 4 Print; 2 E-Book
Total Titles: 20 Print; 3 E-Book

Editions Fernand Nathan
Subsidiary of Vivendi Universal Publishing
9, rue Mechain, 75014 Paris
Tel: (01) 45 87 50 00; (0825) 00 11 67 *Fax:* (01) 43 37 53 00
Web Site: www.nathan.fr
Telex: Nataned 204525 F *Cable:* NATHANED PARIS
Key Personnel
Dir General: Catherine Lucet
Executive Vice President: Jean-Paul Baudouin
Elementary Dir: Arnaud Langlois-Meurinne
Educational Dir: Michel Legrain
Educational Aids & University Dir: Philippe Merlet
Dir, Children's Books: Marc Baudry
Languages Dir: Marc Gudimard
Sales Dir: Alain Carita; Patrick de Porcaro
Marketing Dir: Emilie Carelli
Finance Dir: Serge Grand
Rights & Permissions: Evelyne Mathiaud *Tel:* (01) 45 87 51 54 *Fax:* (01) 45 87 57 80 *E-mail:* emathiaud@nathan.fr
Founded: 1881
Specialize in Children & Pedagogy.
Subjects: Education, History, Philosophy, Psychology, Psychiatry, Science (General), Social Sciences, Sociology
ISBN Prefix(es): 2-09
Subsidiaries: CLE; Retz; Le Robert

Nathan International
9, rue Mechain, 75014 Paris
Tel: (01) 45 87 50 00 *Fax:* (01) 45 87 57 57
Web Site: www.nathan.fr
Telex: 201426
ISBN Prefix(es): 2-288
Parent Company: Vivendi Universal Publishing

Centre National de la Photographie+
11, rue Berryer, Hoetel Salomon de Rothschild, 75008 Paris
Tel: (01) 53 76 12 31 *Fax:* (01) 53 76 12 33
E-mail: centre.national.de.la.photographie@wanadoo.fr
Web Site: www.cnp-photographie.com
Key Personnel
Dir: Regis Durand *Tel:* (01) 53 76 86 66
Commercial Dir: Benoit Rivero
Publishing Manager: Maurice Lecomte *Tel:* (01) 53 76 86 76
Production Manager: Annie Girard *Tel:* (01) 53 76 86 77 *E-mail:* a.girard@cnp-photo.com
Founded: 1982
Subjects: Photography
ISBN Prefix(es): 2-86754

Institut National de Recherche Pedagogique INRP
29 rue d'Ulm, 75230 Paris Cedex 05
Tel: (01) 46 34 90 00 *Fax:* (01) 46 54 32 01
Web Site: www.inrp.fr *Cable:* INATREP
Key Personnel
Dir: Emannual Fraisse
Sec Gen: Martine Muller *E-mail:* sg@inrp.fr
Founded: 1879
Subjects: Education

ISBN Prefix(es): 2-7342
Parent Company: Ministere de l'Education Nationle, 110 rue de Grenelle, 75357 Paris

Navarre, *imprint of* Les Editions LGDJ-Montchrestien

NEF, see Nouvelles Editions Francaises

NEL, *imprint of* Nouvelles Editions Latines

Nil Editions+
24, Ave Marceau, 75381 Paris Cedex 08
Tel: (01) 53 67 14 00 *Fax:* (01) 53 67 14 90
Web Site: www.laffont.fr; www.nil-editions.fr
Key Personnel
President: Nicole Lattes
International Rights: Celine Chiflet
Foreign Rights: Olga Begin *E-mail:* obegin@robert-laffont.fr; Renata de La Chapelle *E-mail:* rdelachapelle@robert-laffont.fr; Benita Edzard *E-mail:* bedzard@robert-laffont.fr; Gwenael Gouiffes *E-mail:* ggouiffes@robert-laffont.fr; Camille Schyrr *E-mail:* cschyrr@robert-laffont.fr
Founded: 1993
Subjects: Biography, Fiction, Literature, Literary Criticism, Essays, Philosophy, French literature, Spirituality
ISBN Prefix(es): 2-84111
Orders to: Edition du Sevil, BP 281, 911621 Longjumeau Cedex *Tel:* (01) 64 48 49 63

Librairie A-G Nizet Sarl+
41, rue de l'Auberdiere, 37510 Saint Genouph
Tel: (02) 47 45 50 41 *Fax:* (02) 47 45 50 15
E-mail: librairie-a.g-nizet@wanadoo.fr
Key Personnel
Man Dir & General Manager: Daniel Nizet
Founded: 1945
Also acts as Bookseller.
Membership(s): Edition Syndication, Group "Scholarship".
Subjects: Drama, Theater, Literature, Literary Criticism, Essays
ISBN Prefix(es): 2-7078
Number of titles published annually: 6 Print
Total Titles: 762 Print
Distributed by D P L U (North America); L'Age d'homme (Switzerland); Nord-Sud (Benelux)
Distributor for France Tosho

Librairie F de Nobele
35 rue Bonaparte, 75006 Paris
Tel: (01) 43 26 08 62 *Fax:* (01) 40 46 85 96
E-mail: librairie.f.de.nobele@wanadoo.fr *Cable:* Denobelef Paris 110
Key Personnel
Man Dir: F de Nobele
Founded: 1885
Subjects: Art
ISBN Prefix(es): 2-85189

Noir Sur Blanc+
One rue Garnier, 92200 Neuilly sur Seine
Tel: (01) 41 43 72 70 *Fax:* (01) 41 43 72 71
E-mail: noirsurblanc@noirsurblanc.com
Web Site: www.noirsurblanc.com
Key Personnel
Literary Dir: Jan Michalski
Dir: Vera Michalski
Founded: 1990
Subjects: Biography, Cookery, Drama, Theater, Fiction, Literature, Literary Criticism, Essays
ISBN Prefix(es): 2-88250
Parent Company: Editions Noir sur Blanc

Editions Nord-Sud (North-South Editions)
Imprint of Nord-Sud Verlag
2, rue Racine, 78100 Saint-Germain-en-Laye
Tel: (01) 39 21 90 40 *Fax:* (01) 39 21 90 42
E-mail: nord-sud@editions-nord-sud.com
Web Site: www.ldj.tm.fr/editeurs/editeurs/nordsud.htm
Key Personnel
President: Davy Sidjanski
Dir: Didier Teyras
Founded: 1981

Editions Norma+
149, rue de Rennes, 75006 Paris
Tel: (01) 45 48 70 96 *Fax:* (01) 45 48 05 84
E-mail: norma@freesurf.fr
Key Personnel
Manager: Maiite Hudry
Founded: 1991
Subjects: Architecture & Interior Design, Art, Drama, Theater, Foreign Countries, History, House & Home, Regional Interests, 20th Century Decorative Arts
ISBN Prefix(es): 2-909283
Warehouse: ETAI, 20 rue de la Saussiere, 92100 Boulogne *Tel:* (01) 46992424

Editions Mare Nostrum
12 bis, rue Jeanne d'Arc, 66000 Perpignan
Tel: (04) 68 51 17 50 *Fax:* (05) 61 41 15 43
E-mail: mare.nost@wanadoo.fr
Telex: 34421415
Key Personnel
President: Philippe Salus
Treasurer: Henri Taverner
Founded: 1990
Subjects: Literature, Literary Criticism, Essays, Philosophy, Poetry, Religion - Jewish
ISBN Prefix(es): 2-908476
Warehouse: Taye, 28110 Luce
Orders to: Taye, 28110 Luce

Nouvelle Cite+
37, Ave de la Marne, 92120 Montrouge
Tel: (01) 40927085 *Fax:* (01) 40921168
Key Personnel
Man Dir, Rights & Permissions: Henri-Louis Roche
Sales: Christian Charnay
Founded: 1963
Subjects: Education, Literature, Literary Criticism, Essays, Religion - Other
ISBN Prefix(es): 2-85313

Nouvelles Editions Fiduciaires
2 bis, rue de Villiers, 92 300 Levallois Perret
Tel: (01) 46 39 47 13; (01) 46 39 47 00 *Fax:* (01) 47 58 00 63
Key Personnel
Dir: Sophie Robert
Founded: 1980
Subjects: Economics, Law, Management
ISBN Prefix(es): 2-86544

Nouvelles Editions Francaises+
152, rue de Picpus, 75583 Paris Cedex 12
Tel: (01) 44 74 16 00 *Fax:* (01) 44 04 98 03
Key Personnel
Man Dir: Eliane Allegret
Founded: 1843
Subjects: Art, History, House & Home
ISBN Prefix(es): 2-7079

Nouvelles Editions Latines+
One, rue Palatine, 75006 Paris
Tel: (01) 43 54 77 42 *Fax:* (01) 43 29 69 81
E-mail: info@editions-nel.com
Web Site: www.editions-nel.com
Key Personnel
Man Dir: Jean Sorlot
Founded: 1928
Subjects: Fiction, History, Poetry, Religion - Other, Travel

ISBN Prefix(es): 2-7233; 2-85147
Imprints: NEL

La Nuee Bleue - Dernieres Nouvelles d'Alsace
3 rue saint Pierre-le-Jeune, 67000 Strasbourg
Tel: (03) 88 15 77 27 *Fax:* (03) 88 75 16 21
E-mail: nuee-bleue@sdv.fr
Web Site: www.sdv.fr/nuee-bleue/
ISBN Prefix(es): 2-7165

Oblong, *imprint of* Editions Jacques Gabay

Editions Obsidiane+
11, rue Andre Gateau, 89100 Sens
Tel: (03) 86965218 *Fax:* (03) 86870112
E-mail: genevieve.bigant@wanadoo.fr
Key Personnel
Manager: Francois Boddaert
Founded: 1985
Subjects: Literature, Literary Criticism, Essays, Poetry
ISBN Prefix(es): 2-904469; 2-911914
Number of titles published annually: 10 Print
Total Titles: 200 Print
Distributed by Les Belles-Lettres
Distribution Center: Farandole Diffusion (Belgium)
Librairie Gallimard a Montreal (Canada)

Editions Odile Jacob+
15, rue Soufflot, 75005 Paris
Tel: (01) 44 41 64 84 *Fax:* (01) 44 41 64 99; (01) 43 29 88 77
Web Site: www.odilejacob.fr
Key Personnel
President: Odile Jacob
Rights & Permissions: Claire Teeuwissen *Tel:* (01) 44 41 64 80
Founded: 1985
Subjects: Biography, Economics, Fiction, Government, Political Science, History, How-to, Law, Philosophy, Psychology, Psychiatry, Science (General), Social Sciences, Sociology
ISBN Prefix(es): 2-7381
Number of titles published annually: 120 Print
Imprints: Poches Odile Jacob

OGC Michele Broutta Editeur
31 rue des Bergers, 75015 Paris
Tel: (01) 45779371 *Fax:* (01) 40590432
Key Personnel
Man Dir: Michele Broutta *E-mail:* m.broutta@wanadoo.fr
Founded: 1970
Subjects: Art, Library & Information Sciences
ISBN Prefix(es): 2-900332; 2-902886

L' Olivier, *imprint of* Editions du Seuil

Editions Omnibus+
12 ave d'Italie, 75013 Paris
Tel: (01) 44 16 05 00 *Fax:* (01) 44 16 05 05
E-mail: omnibus@psb-editions.com
Web Site: www.omnibus.tm.fr
Telex: preci 204 807 f
Key Personnel
Man Dir: Georges Leser
Dir, Literature: Jean-Louis Festjens
International Rights: Florence De Bourgues
Founded: 1993
Subjects: Humor
ISBN Prefix(es): 2-258; 2-285; 2-84119
Parent Company: Presses/Solar

Editions Ophrys+
5 allee du Torrent, 05000 Gap
Tel: (04) 92 53 85 72 *Fax:* (04) 92 51 78 65
E-mail: edition.ophrys@ophrys.fr; infos@ophrys.fr
Web Site: www.ophrys-editions.com

FRANCE

Key Personnel
Man Dir, Publicity & Advertising: Mrs B Monnier
Founded: 1934
Subjects: Earth Sciences, Education, English as a Second Language, Genealogy, Geography, Geology, History, Language Arts, Linguistics, Regional Interests, Self-Help, Social Sciences, Sociology, Travel
ISBN Prefix(es): 2-7080
Bookshop(s): Succursale de Paris, 10 rue de Nesle, 75006 Paris *Tel*: (01) 44 41 63 75 *Fax*: (01) 46 33 15 97
Orders to: 10 rue de Nesle, 75006 Paris *Tel*: (01) 44 41 63 75 *Fax*: (01) 46 33 15 97 *E-mail*: ophrys4@wanadoo.fr

Opsys Operating System
3 rue Paul-Valerien-Perrin, 38172 Seyssinet-Pariset
Tel: (04) 76 84 34 20; (04) 76 84 34 34 *Fax*: (04) 76 84 34 21
E-mail: opsys@opsys.fr
Web Site: www.opsys.fr
Key Personnel
President & Dir General: Alain Gagne
 E-mail: agagne@opsys.fr
Commercial Dir: Thierry Ponset
 E-mail: tponset@opsys.fr
Operations Dir: Jean-Pierre Schmitt
 E-mail: jpschmitt@opsys.fr
Development Dir: Joseph Ramblas
 E-mail: jramblas@opsys.fr
Research Dir: Jacques Kergomard
 E-mail: jkergomard@opsys.fr
Subjects: Library & Information Sciences

Editions de l'Orante+
6 rue du General-Bertrand, 75007 Paris
Tel: (01) 47 83 55 02 *Fax*: (01) 45 66 00 16
Key Personnel
Man Dir: Jacques Lafarge
Founded: 1940
Membership(s): Syndicat National de l'Edition.
Subjects: History, Philosophy, Poetry, Religion - Other
ISBN Prefix(es): 2-7031
Total Titles: 80 Print

Organisation for Economic Co-operation & Development OECD+
2, rue Andre Pascal, 75775 Paris Cedex 16
Tel: (01) 45 24 82 00 *Fax*: (01) 45 24 85 00
E-mail: sales@oecd.org
Web Site: www.oecd.org/bookshop; www.sourceoecd.org
Key Personnel
Sales Manager: Toby Green *Tel*: (01) 45 24 94 15 *Fax*: (01) 45 24 19 50 *E-mail*: toby.green@oecd.org
International Rights: Laurence Gerrer *Tel*: (01) 45 24 13 90 *Fax*: (01) 45 24 13 91 *E-mail*: laurence.gerrer@oecd.org
Founded: 1960
OECD is a forum for governments of 30 market democracies that work together to address the economic, social & governance challenges of the globalising work economy, as well as to exploit its opportunities.
Specialize in economic co-operation & development.
Subjects: Economics
ISBN Prefix(es): 92-64; 92-821
Number of titles published annually: 250 Print; 12 CD-ROM; 250 Online; 250 E-Book
Total Titles: 12 CD-ROM; 250 Online; 250 E-Book
Branch Office(s)
OECD Berlin Centre, Albrechtstr 9, 3 OG, 10117 Berlin-Mitte, Germany *Tel*: (030) 2888 353 *Fax*: (030) 2888 35 45 *E-mail*: berlin.contact@oecd.org *Web Site*: www.oecd.org/deutschland (Austria, Germany & Switzerland)
OECD Mexico Centre, av Presidente Mazaryk 526, Colonia, Polanco, 11560 Mexico DF, Mexico *Tel*: (0525) 281 3810 *Fax*: (0525) 280 0480 *E-mail*: mexico.contact@oecd.org *Web Site*: www.rtn.net/nixlocdel (Latin America)
OECD Tokyo Centre, Nippon Press Center Bldg, 2-2-1, 3rd floor, Uchisaiwaicho, Chiyoda-ku, Tokyo 100-0011, Japan *Tel*: (03) 5532 0021 *Fax*: (03) 5532 0035 *E-mail*: centre@oecdtokyo.org *Web Site*: www.oecdtokyo.org (Asia)
U.S. Office(s): OECD Washington Center, 2001 "L" St NW, Suite 650, Washington, DC 20036-4922, United States *Tel*: 202-785-6323 *Fax*: 202-785-0350 *E-mail*: washington.contact@oecd.org *Web Site*: www.oecdwash.org
Distributor for European Conference of Ministers of Transport; International Energy Agency; Nuclear Energy Agency
Foreign Rep(s): ADECO - Van Diermen Editions Techniques (Switzerland); Akademibokhandeln (Sweden); Akademika AS (Norway); Anvil Publishing Inc (Philippines); Ars Polona (Poland); Bernan Associates (USA); Bokabud Mals og Menninga (Iceland); Bookwell (India); CADOC (Algeria); Charlesworth China (China); Co-operative Bookshop Ltd (Malaysia); DA Information Services (Australia); Dandy Booksellers (UK); Data Beuro (UK); La Documentation Francaise (France); Dunya Infotel AS (Turkey); Dynapresse Marketing SA (Switzerland); Euro Info Service (Hungary); Federal Publications Inc (Canada); GAD Direct (Denmark); GV Zalozba doo (Slovenia); Librairie Internationale (Morocco); Izdatelstvo VES MIR (Russia); JSC MK-Periodica (Russia); Librairie Kauffmann (Greece); KINS Inc (Korea); Jean De Lannoy (Belgium); Legislation Direct (New Zealand); Liberalia (Chile); Les Editions la Liberte Inc (Canada); Librotrade Kft (Hungary); De Lindeboom Internationale Publikaties bv (Netherlands); MERIC-The Middle East Readers' Information Center (Egypt); Miller Distributors Ltd (Malta); Mundi-Prensa Barcelona (Spain); Mundi-Prensa Libros SA (Spain); Overseas Press (India); Librairie Payot SA (Switzerland); PDII-LIPI (Indonesia); Livraria Portugal (Portugal); PrioInfo AB (Sweden); Les Publications Gouvernementales (Canada); Renouf Publishing Co Ltd (Canada); Libreria Commissionaria Sansoni (Italy); J H Schultz Information (Denmark); SDU Uitgevers Externe Fondsen (Netherlands); SLOVART GTG sro (Slovak Republic); The Stationery Office (UK); Suksit Siam Co Ltd (Thailand); Suomalainen Kirjakauppa Oy (Finland); Swindon Book Co Ltd (Hong Kong); Systematics Studies Ltd (Caribbean, Trinadad & Tobago); Tycoon Information Inc (China); UNO Verlag GmbH (Germany); World Publications SA (Argentina); Xunhasaba (Vietnam)
Distribution Center: Extenza-Turpin, 56 Industrial Park Drive, Pembroke, MA 02359, United States *Tel*: 781-829-8973 *Fax*: 781-829-9052 *E-mail*: oecdna@extenza-turpin.com
OECD Turpin Distribution Services Ltd, Stratton Business Park, Pegasus Drive, Biggleswade, Beds SG18 8QB, United Kingdom *E-mail*: books@extenza-turpin.com *Web Site*: www.extenza-turpin.com

Librairie Orientaliste, see Paul Geuthner Librairie Orientaliste

L'Originel - Editions Accarias+
cite Industrielle, 75011 Paris
Mailing Address: passage de la Folie-Regnault, 75011 Paris
Tel: (01) 43 48 73 07 *Fax*: (01) 43 48 73 07
E-mail: originel-accarias@club-internet.fr
Key Personnel
Dir: Jean-Louis Accarias
Founded: 1980
Subjects: Philosophy, Religion - Buddhist, Religion - Hindu, Religion - Other, Social Sciences, Sociology
ISBN Prefix(es): 2-86316
Shipping Address: Dilisco, 128 bis avenue Jean Jaures, 94200 Ivry-sur-Seine
Orders to: Dilisco, 128 bis avenue Jean Jaures, 94200 Ivry-sur-Seine

Ouest Editions
immeuble du Petit port, One, rue de La Noe, 44071 Nantes Cedex 3
Tel: (02) 40 14 34 34 *Fax*: (02) 40 14 36 36
Key Personnel
Dir General: Yves Suaudeau
Founded: 1989
Subjects: Accounting, Biological Sciences, Chemistry, Chemical Engineering, Civil Engineering, Earth Sciences, Economics, Geography, Geology, History, Regional Interests
ISBN Prefix(es): 2-908261
Distributed by Alena Libert Inc (Canada); Boinemouth (UK); Chinon Diffusion (Europe); Continental Books

Editions Ouest-France+
Subsidiary of Sofiouest
13 rue du Breil, 35063 Rennes Cedex
Mailing Address: CS 26339, 35063 Rennes Cedex
Tel: (02) 99 32 58 27 *Fax*: (02) 99 32 58 30
Web Site: www.edilarge.com
Key Personnel
Dir General: Servane Biguais
Founded: 1975
Subjects: Cookery, History, Science (General), Travel, Creative Leisures
ISBN Prefix(es): 2-7373; 2-85882
Number of titles published annually: 150 Print
Total Titles: 1,800 Print
Parent Company: Ouest France
Imprints: Editions de la Cite; Editions Maritimes et D'Outremer

Editions J H Paillet et B Drouaud+
73 rue de La Varenne, 41120 Cellettes
Tel: 54704303
Key Personnel
Editor: Jean-Hubert Paillet; Brigitte Drouaud
Founded: 1989
Subjects: Literature, Literary Criticism, Essays
ISBN Prefix(es): 2-9504241; 2-909565

Editions du Papyrus
17, bd Rouget de Lisle, 93189 Montreuil
Tel: (01) 48 57 27 05 *Fax*: (01) 48 57 26 79
E-mail: papyrus@netfly.fr
Web Site: www.editions-papyrus.com
Founded: 1986
Subjects: Law
ISBN Prefix(es): 2-86541

Editions Paradigme
14 Quai Saint Laurent, 45000 Orleans
Tel: (02) 38 70 84 44 *Fax*: (02) 38 70 56 76
Web Site: paradigme.com; cpuniv.com
Key Personnel
President & Editor: Bernard Legrand
 E-mail: blegrand@wanadoo.fr
Founded: 1983
Specialize in erudition & law.
Subjects: Energy, Geography, Geology, History, Law, Literature, Literary Criticism, Essays, Philosophy, Erudition
ISBN Prefix(es): 2-86878; 2-911377
Total Titles: 170 Print
Parent Company: FAB

Editions Pardes+
9 rue Jules Dumesnil, 45390 Puiseaux
Mailing Address: BP 47, 45390 Puiseaux
Tel: (02) 38 33 53 28 *Fax:* (02) 38 33 58 99
Web Site: perso.wanadoo.fr/mackadam/livre/
Editeurs/pardes.htm
Key Personnel
Man Editor: Georges Gondinet
Founded: 1982
Subjects: Archaeology, Astrology, Occult, Health, Nutrition, History, Religion - Buddhist, Religion - Hindu, Social Sciences, Sociology
ISBN Prefix(es): 2-86714

Editions Parentheses
72, cours Julien, 13006 Marseille
Tel: (0495) 08 18 20 *Fax:* (0495) 08 18 24
Key Personnel
General Dir: Varoujan Arzoumanian
Dir: Patrick Bardon
Founded: 1978
Subjects: Anthropology, Architecture & Interior Design, Art, Ethnicity, Music, Dance
ISBN Prefix(es): 2-86364
Total Titles: 150 Print
Distribution Center: Diffusion Dimedia, 539 blvd Lebeau, Ville Saint-Laurent, ON N4N 1S2, Canada
Harmonia Mundi, Mas de Vert, BP 150, 13631 Arles Cedex *Tel:* (0490) 49 90 49 *Fax:* (0490) 49 96 14
Nouvelle Diffusion, 24, rue de Bosnie, 1060 Brussels, Belgium
Office du Livre, Route de Villars 101, 1701 Fribourg, Switzerland

Association Paris-Musees+
28, rue Notre Dame des Victoires, 75002 Paris
Tel: (01) 44 58 99 19 *Fax:* (01) 47 03 36 44
Key Personnel
Publisher: Arnauld Pontier
Distribution: Emmanuelle Sarrazin
Founded: 1985
Specialize in art-exhibition's catalogues & children's books.
Subjects: Architecture & Interior Design, Art, Fashion, History, Photography
ISBN Prefix(es): 2-87900
Foreign Rights: Cecile Capelle (Worldwide)

Paroisse & Famille, *imprint of* Federation d'Activities Culturelles, Fac Editions

Le Parvis des Arts, *imprint of* Presses Universitaires de Nancy

Payot & Rivages+
Formerly Editions Rivages
106, Blvd Saint-Germain, 75006 Paris
Tel: (01) 44413990 *Fax:* (01) 44413969
E-mail: editions@payotrivages.com
Key Personnel
Man Dir: Jean-Francois Lamuniere
Foreign Rights: Marie-Martine Serrano-Lavau
Founded: 1984
Subjects: Anthropology, Biography, Cookery, Fiction, History, Humor, Language Arts, Linguistics, Literature, Literary Criticism, Essays, Mysteries, Nonfiction (General), Philosophy, Religion - Other, Science Fiction, Fantasy, Social Sciences, Sociology, Technology, Transportation, Travel, Contemporary History, Cultural Studies, Ethnology, Fantasy, Modern History, Political Science, Sexuality Short Stories, Thriller
ISBN Prefix(es): 2-7436; 2-903059; 2-86930
Parent Company: Eol Rivagei
Orders to: Le Seuil, 27 rue Jacod, 75006 Paris

Pearson Education/CampusPress, *imprint of* Pearson Education France

Pearson Education France+
47 bis, rue des Vinargriers, 75010 Paris
Tel: (01) 7274 9000 *Fax:* (01) 4804 5361 (sales); (01) 4887 7130 (finance); (01) 4205 2217
E-mail: infos@pearsoned.fr
Web Site: www.pearsoneducation.fr
Key Personnel
President: Helene Dennery
Vice President, Finance & Operations: Patricia Gasquet
Editor, CampusPress Man Dir: Patrick Ussunet
Editor, Village Mondail Man Dir: Geoff Staines
Founded: 1995
Publisher of computer books.
Subjects: Business, Computer Science, Education, Finance, Microcomputers
ISBN Prefix(es): 2-7440
Total Titles: 300 Print
Parent Company: Pearson Education
Ultimate Parent Company: Pearson Plc
Imprints: Pearson Education/CampusPress; Pearson Education/Les Echos; Pearson Education/Les Echos.fr Press

Pearson Education/Les Echos, *imprint of* Pearson Education France

Pearson Education/Les Echos.fr Press, *imprint of* Pearson Education France

Pedagogie Modern, *imprint of* Editions Bordas

Editions Pedone+
13 rue Soufflot, 75005 Paris
Tel: (01) 43 54 05 97 *Fax:* (01) 46 34 07 60
E-mail: editions-pedone@wanadoo.fr
Web Site: www.franceedition.org/Pedone
Key Personnel
Man Dir: Denis Pedone
Founded: 1837
Subjects: Agriculture, Earth Sciences, Economics, Engineering (General), Law, Management, Maritime, Air Law, Criminal Philosophy, Diplomatic History, International Law, International Relations, Penal Sciences, Philosophy of the Right, Right European, Right of the Sea
ISBN Prefix(es): 2-233

Peeters-France
52 Blvd Saint-Michel, 75006 Paris
Tel: (01) 40 51 81 05 *Fax:* (01) 40 51 89 20
Web Site: www.peeters-leuven.be
Key Personnel
Editor: Vladimir Randa
Specialize in Classical Studies, Eastern Studies, Egyptology, History of Art, Medicine, Oriental Studies & Ethics, Patristics.
Subjects: Anthropology, Archaeology, Biblical Studies, History, Language Arts, Linguistics, Literature, Literary Criticism, Essays, Philosophy, Theology
ISBN Prefix(es): 2-87723; 90-6831; 90-429
Number of titles published annually: 120 Print; 2 CD-ROM
Parent Company: Peeters, Bondgenoten Laan 153, 3000 Leuven, Belgium
U.S. Office(s): Peeters Academic Publishers Inc, 6 Ash Lane, Dudley, MA 07517, United States, Contact: Catherine Cornille *Fax:* 508-949-0557 *E-mail:* peeters@charter.net
Distributed by BR&D
Bookshop(s): Bondgenotenlaan 153, 3000 Leuven, Belgium, I Huenaerts *Tel:* (016) 23 51 70 *Fax:* (016) 22 85 00 *E-mail:* peeters@peeters-leuven.be; Grand rue 56, 1348 Louvain-la-Neuve, Belgium
Shipping Address: Kolonel Begaultlaan 61, 3000 Leuven, Belgium *Tel:* (016) 24 40 00 *Fax:* (016) 22 85 00 *E-mail:* peeters@peeters-leuven.be
Warehouse: Kolonel Begaultlaan 61, 3000 Leuven, Belgium
Orders to: Bondgenotenlaan 153, 3000 Leuven, Belgium, I Huenaerts *Tel:* (016) 23 51 70 *Fax:* (016) 22 85 00 *E-mail:* peeters@peeters-leuven.be

PEMF, see Editions Publications de l'Ecole Moderne Francaise sa (PEMF)

Pere Castor, *imprint of* Flammarion SA

Atelier Perrousseaux Editeur, *imprint of* Adverbum SARL

La Pharmacie de Platon, *imprint of* William Blake & Co

Editions Phebus
12 rue Gregoire de Tours, 75006 Paris
Tel: (01) 46 33 36 36 *Fax:* (01) 43 25 67 69
E-mail: phebedit@wanadoo.fr
Web Site: www.phebus-editions.com
Key Personnel
Man Dir: Jean-Pierre Sicre
Founded: 1976
Subjects: Art, Literature, Literary Criticism, Essays
ISBN Prefix(es): 2-85940
Orders to: SEUIL Diffusion, 27 rue Jacob, 75006 Paris

Editions A et J Picard SA
82, rue Bonaparte, 75006 Paris
Tel: (01) 43 26 97 78 *Fax:* (01) 43 26 42 64
E-mail: livres@librairie-picard.com
Web Site: www.abebooks.com/home/libpicard/
Telex: Bsc Picaredit 305551 F
Key Personnel
Man Dir: Chantal Pasini-Picard
Founded: 1869
Subjects: Antiques, Archaeology, Architecture & Interior Design, Art, Education, Ethnicity, History, Language Arts, Linguistics, Literature, Literary Criticism, Essays, Music, Dance, Religion - Other
ISBN Prefix(es): 2-7084

Editions Jean Picollec+
47, rue Auguste Lancon, 75013 Paris
Tel: (01) 45 89 73 04 *Fax:* (01) 45 89 40 72
E-mail: jean.picollec@noos.fr
Key Personnel
Publisher & Man Dir: Jean Picollec
Publishing Consultant: Helene Simon
Public Relations & Sales: Corinne Saulneron
Founded: 1979
Specialize in reference books & documents - Celtic World.
Subjects: Biography, Ethnicity, Fiction, Government, Political Science, History, Literature, Literary Criticism, Essays, Nonfiction (General), Regional Interests, Travel
ISBN Prefix(es): 2-86477
Number of titles published annually: 12 Print
Total Titles: 25 Print
Distributed by Age d'Homme (Switzerland); Nouvelle Diffusion (Belgium)
Foreign Rep(s): L'age d'Homme (Switzerland); Nouvelle Diffusion (Belgium)
Foreign Rights: Arabella Cruse (Scandinavia); Laura Dail (North America); Catherine Fragou (Greece); Patricia Pasqualini (Central & Eastern Europe)
Distribution Center: Alterdis, 5, Rue du Marechal-Leclerc, 28600 Luisant *Tel:* (02) 37 30 57 00 *Fax:* (02) 37 30 57 12
Orders to: CED, 73 quai Auguste Deshaies, 94200 Ivry-Sur-Seine *Tel:* (01) 46 58 38 40 *Fax:* (01) 46 71 25 59

FRANCE

Editions Philippe Picquier+
Le Mas De Vert, BP 150, 13631 Arles
Tel: (04) 90496156 *Fax:* (04) 90499614
Key Personnel
Dir: Philippe Picquier
Founded: 1986
Subjects: Literature, Literary Criticism, Essays
ISBN Prefix(es): 2-87730
Orders to: Harmonia Mundi Diffusion Livres, Le Mas de Vert BP 150, 13631 Arles Cedex

Editions Pierron+
2, rue Gutenberg, 57206 Sarreguemines
Mailing Address: BP 80609, 57206 Sarreguemines
Tel: (03) 87 95 10 89 *Fax:* (03) 87 95 60 95
E-mail: editions@pierron.fr
Web Site: www.editions-pierron.com
Telex: 860495 F
Key Personnel
Dir: Jeannie Jung-Pierron
Subjects: Education, History
ISBN Prefix(es): 2-7085
Parent Company: Pierron Entreprise SA

Editions Christian Pirot+
13 rue Maurice-Adrien, 37540 Saint-Cyr-Sur-Loire
Tel: (02) 47 54 54 20; (06) 70 06 87 78 *Fax:* (02) 47 51 57 96
E-mail: contact@friendship-first.com
Web Site: www.friendship-first.com
Key Personnel
Dir: Christian Pirot
Founded: 1979
Subjects: Biography, Cookery, Fiction, Literature, Literary Criticism, Essays, Music, Dance, Poetry, Travel
ISBN Prefix(es): 2-86808
Number of titles published annually: 12 Print
Total Titles: 160 Print
Branch Office(s)
Diffusion Canada, Diffusion DIMEDIA, 539 Blvd Libeau, Ville Saint Laurent, Quebec, ON H4N 1S2, Canada *Tel:* 514-336-3941 *Fax:* 514-331-3916 *E-mail:* dimedia@infopuq.uquebec.ca
U.S. Office(s): Diffusion USA, University Press of the South, 5500 Prytania St, Suite 421, New Orleans, LA 70115, United States *Tel:* 504-866-2791 *Fax:* 504-866-2750 *E-mail:* unprsouth@aol.com
Distributed by Harmonia Mundi Diffusion; University Press of the South (USA)
Orders to: Harmonia Mundi Diffusion, BP 150, 13631 Arles Cedex *Tel:* (04) 90499049 *Fax:* (04) 90499614

Jean-Michel Place+
3, rue Lhomond, 75005 Paris
Tel: (01) 44 32 05 90 *Fax:* (01) 44 32 05 91
E-mail: place@jmplace.com
Web Site: www.jmplace.com
Founded: 1973
Subjects: Anthropology, Art, Literature, Literary Criticism, Essays, Philosophy, Photography, Publishing & Book Trade Reference
ISBN Prefix(es): 2-85893

Plon-Perrin
76, rue Bonaparte, 75006 Paris
Tel: (01) 44 41 35 00 *Fax:* (01) 44 41 35 02
Key Personnel
Man Dir: Xavier de Bartillat
Foreign Rights: Sylvie Breguet
ISBN Prefix(es): 2-259

Editions Plume+
26, rue Racine, 75278 Paris Cedex 06
Tel: (01) 40 51 31 00 *Fax:* (01) 43 14 02 01
Key Personnel
Director: Nathalie Peillard
Editor & Publicity: Catherine Laulhere-Vigneau
Chief of Manufacturing: Julie Rouart
Author: Michel Boujut; Frederic Mitterand; Isabel Munoz
Founded: 1989
Subjects: Drama, Theater, Fashion, Film, Video, Music, Dance, Photography
ISBN Prefix(es): 2-84110; 2-908034
Orders to: Harmonia Mundi, Petite Route de Saint Gilles, Mas de Vert, 13200 Arles

Poches Odile Jacob, *imprint of* Editions Odile Jacob

POF, see Publications Orientalistes de France (POF)

Point Hors Ligne Editions
28, rue Barbet de Jouy, 75007 Paris
Tel: (01) 43544964 *Fax:* (01) 43253032
Subjects: Psychology, Psychiatry
ISBN Prefix(es): 2-904821

Les Editions du Point Veterinaire+
9, rue Alexandre, BP 233, 94702 Maisons-Alfort Cedex
Tel: (01) 45 17 02 25 *Fax:* (01) 42 07 93 88
Web Site: www.pointveterinaire.com
Key Personnel
President: Patrick Join-Lambert
International Rights: Christine Graffard-Lenormand
Subjects: Animals, Pets, Veterinary Science
ISBN Prefix(es): 2-86326

Editions POL+
33, rue Saint-Andre-des-Arts, 75006 Paris
Tel: (01) 43 54 21 20 *Fax:* (01) 43 54 11 31
Web Site: www.pol-editeur.fr
Key Personnel
President: Paul Otchakovsky-Laurens
Founded: 1983
Subjects: Drama, Theater, Fiction, Literature, Literary Criticism, Essays, Poetry
ISBN Prefix(es): 2-86744
Foreign Rep(s): Gallimard/La Caravelle (Belgium); Gallimard Limitee (Canada); Gallimard/Office du Livre (Switzerland); SODIS (France)
Orders to: Sodis, BP 142, 77403 Lagny sur Maine Cedex

Pole de Recherche pour l'Organisation et la Diffusion de l'Information Geographique, see PRODIG

Polytechnica SA+
49, rue Hericart, 75015 Paris
Tel: (01) 45 78 12 92 *Fax:* (01) 45 75 05 67
Key Personnel
President: Daniel Loizeau
Promotion & International Rights: Isabelle Doal
Founded: 1992
Subjects: Agriculture, Biological Sciences, Chemistry, Chemical Engineering, Electronics, Electrical Engineering, Energy, Engineering (General), Health, Nutrition, Mechanical Engineering, Physical Sciences, Physics, Science (General), Technology
ISBN Prefix(es): 2-7178; 2-84054
Distributor for AIA; CIIA; INA

Editions du Centre Pompidou+
75191 Paris Cedex 04
Tel: (01) 44 78 12 33 *Fax:* (01) 44 78 12 05
Web Site: www.centrepompidou.fr
Key Personnel
President: Jean-Jacques Aillagon
Head of Publications & Sales: Martin Bethenod
Deputy Manager: Philippe Bidaine
Sales Manager & Foreign Rights: Benoit Collier
Founded: 1977
Subjects: Architecture & Interior Design, Art, Film, Video, Gay & Lesbian
ISBN Prefix(es): 2-85850; 2-84426
Distributed by Art Data (Great Britain); Flammarion (Canada); Flammarion Export (Greece, Turkey, Syria); Idea Books (Holland); Union Distribution (France, Belgium & Switzerland); Yohan (Japan)
Distributor for BPI
Foreign Rep(s): Richard Bowen (Denmark, Finland, Norway, Sweden); Phillip Galgiani (USA)
Orders to: Service Commercial, 75191 Paris Cedex 04

Pratique Sante, *imprint of* Jouvence Editions

Editions Pratiques Automobiles, see EPA (Editions Pratiques Automobiles)

Le Pre-aux-clercs+
12, ave D'Italie, 75013 Paris
Tel: (01) 44 16 05 00 *Fax:* (01) 44 16 05 05
Key Personnel
Chairman: Jerome Talamon
Vice President: Jean Manuel Bourgois
Dir General Adjoint: Fabienne Delmote
Rights & Permissions: Frederique Polet
Founded: 1963
Subjects: Art, Biography, Fiction, Health, Nutrition, History, How-to, Human Relations, Literature, Literary Criticism, Essays, Music, Dance, Mysteries, Nonfiction (General), Poetry, Romance
ISBN Prefix(es): 2-7144; 2-84228
Parent Company: Masson

Presence Africaine Editions+
25bis, rue des Ecoles, 75005 Paris
Tel: (01) 43 54 13 74; (01) 43 54 15 88 *Fax:* (01) 43 25 96 67
E-mail: presaf@club-internet.fr
Web Site: www.letissu.com *Cable:* PRESAFRIC PARIS
Key Personnel
Dir, Publicity, Rights & Permissions: Mrs Yande Christiane Diop
Press Relations: R J Agonse
Manufacturing: D Alliot
Founded: 1947
Subjects: Fiction, History, Philosophy, Poetry, Religion - Other
ISBN Prefix(es): 2-7087
Distributed by Nord-Sud (Benelux); Zoe (Switzerland)

Presse et Formation, *imprint of* Les Editions du CFPJ (Centre de Formation et de Perfectionnement des Journalistes) - Sarl Presse et Formation

Presses, *imprint of* Presses de la Cite

Presses de la Cite+
Imprint of Belfond
12 Ave d'Italie, 75627 Paris Cedex 13
Tel: (01) 44160500 *Fax:* (01) 44160505
Web Site: www.pressesdelacite.com
Telex: preci 204 807 f *Cable:* SVENNIL PARIS
Key Personnel
Man Dir: Georges Leser
General Dir: Pierre Dutilleul
Founded: 1947
Subjects: Biography, Fiction, History, Mysteries, Nonfiction (General), Romance, Science Fiction, Fantasy, Family Saga, Horror, Humor, Mystery & Detective, Thriller, Science Fiction
ISBN Prefix(es): 2-258
Total Titles: 300 Print
Parent Company: Havas

Ultimate Parent Company: Vivendi
Imprints: Presses; Solar

Presses de la Renaissance+
Subsidiary of Havas
12, Ave de Italie, 75627 Paris Cedex 13
Tel: (01) 55 43 27 50 *Fax:* (01) 55 43 27 60
Web Site: www.presses-renaissance.com
Key Personnel
Man Dir: Pierre Dutilleul
Literary Manager: Alain Noel *Tel:* (01) 44 16 05 96 *E-mail:* alainoel@aol.com
Rights Manager: Delphina Ribouchon *Tel:* (01) 44 08 84 35 *Fax:* (01) 44 08 84 05
Founded: 1997
Subjects: Biography, Philosophy, Spirituality, Novels, Documents & Testimonials
ISBN Prefix(es): 2-85616
Total Titles: 40 Print
Ultimate Parent Company: Vivendi

Presses de la Sorbonne Nouvelle/PSN
Universite Paris III, 13, rue Santeuil, 75231 Paris Cedex 05
Tel: (01) 45874027; (01) 45874168 *Fax:* (01) 45877854; (01) 45874175
E-mail: n.carbon@univ-paris3.fr
Web Site: www.univ-paris3.fr
Key Personnel
General Dir: Pierre Vilar
Founded: 1982
Subjects: Drama, Theater, History, Language Arts, Linguistics, Literature, Literary Criticism, Essays
ISBN Prefix(es): 2-87854
Number of titles published annually: 20 Print
Total Titles: 20 Print
Distributor for Cid (France)
Bookshop(s): CID, 131 Blvd St Michel, 75005 Paris, Contact: Michel Zumkir *Tel:* (01) 43544745 *Fax:* (01) 43548073 *E-mail:* cid@msh-paris.fr

Presses de l'Ecole Nationale des Ponts et Chaussees+
Unit of Ponts Formation Edition SA
28, rue des Saints-Peres, 75343 Paris Cedex 07
Tel: (01) 44 58 27 40 *Fax:* (01) 44582744
Web Site: www.enpc.fr
Key Personnel
Dir: Guy Coronio *Tel:* (01) 44582460 *E-mail:* coronio@enpc.fr
Marketing: Laurent Deschryver *Tel:* (01) 44582832 *E-mail:* laurent.deschryver@mail.enpc.fr
Founded: 1977
Specialize in scientific, technical & professional subjects.
Membership(s): Syndicat National de l'Edition.
Subjects: Civil Engineering, Computer Science, Earth Sciences, Real Estate, Transportation
ISBN Prefix(es): 2-85978
Total Titles: 200 Print; 2 CD-ROM
Distributed by Geodif

Presses de Sciences Politiques+
44 rue du Four, 75006 Paris
Tel: (01) 44 39 39 60 *Fax:* (01) 45 48 04 41
Web Site: www.sciences.po.fr
Telex: Scipol 201002 F
Key Personnel
Man Dir, Sales: Louis Bodin
Editorial, Rights & Permissions: Mireille Perche
Periodicals: Josee Cabillon
Public Relations: Christelle Michel-Flandin
Founded: 1975
Subjects: Economics, Government, Political Science, History, Social Sciences, Sociology
ISBN Prefix(es): 2-7246

Les Presses de Taize, *imprint of* Ateliers et Presses de Taize

Les Presses d'Ile-de-France Sarl+
54 Ave Jean-Jaures, 75940 Paris Cedex 19
Tel: (01) 44 52 37 24 *Fax:* (01) 42 38 09 87
E-mail: scouts@scouts-france.fr
Web Site: www.scouts-france.fr
Key Personnel
Man Dir: Pierre Tremeau
Manager: Bernard Le Roux
Founded: 1929
Subjects: Crafts, Games, Hobbies, Music, Dance, Outdoor Recreation, Religion - Catholic
ISBN Prefix(es): 2-7088

Les Presses du Management+
41, rue Greneta, 75002 Paris
Tel: (01) 53 00 11 71 *Fax:* (01) 53 00 10 08
Key Personnel
Contact: Jacques Descubes Marie
Founded: 1989
Subjects: Business, Career Development, Economics, How-to, Management, Marketing, Psychology, Psychiatry, Self-Help
ISBN Prefix(es): 2-87845
Parent Company: Editions Michel Lafon
Imprints: Guide Pratique; Turbo
Orders to: 7, rue de Malte, 75011 Paris

Presses-Pocket, see Presses de la Cite

Presses Universitaires de Caen
14032 Caen Cedex
Tel: (02) 31 56 62 20 *Fax:* (02) 31 56 62 25
E-mail: puc@mrsh.unicaen.fr
Web Site: www.unicaen.fr/mrsh/puc
Key Personnel
Dir, University Press: Michel Zuinghedau
Founded: 1984
Subjects: Accounting, Antiques, Biological Sciences, Geography, Geology, History, Language Arts, Linguistics, Literature, Literary Criticism, Essays, Philosophy, Social Sciences, Sociology
ISBN Prefix(es): 2-84133; 2-905461

Presses Universitaires de France (PUF)+
6, Ave Reille, 75685 Paris Cedex 14
Tel: (01) 58 10 31 00 *Fax:* (01) 58 10 31 82
E-mail: puf.com@puf.com
Web Site: www.puf.com
Key Personnel
President & Dir General: Michel Prigent *Tel:* (01) 53 10 00 07 *Fax:* (01) 53 10 41 79
Dir: Eric Amaudry *Tel:* (01) 43 26 7741 *Fax:* (01) 46 33 21 94; Bruno Clerc *Tel:* (01) 44 41 17 20 *Fax:* (01) 46 33 61 21
Sales Dir: Jean-Pierre Giband *Tel:* (01) 60 87 30 00 *Fax:* (01) 60 79 20 45
Technical Dir: Bruno Clerc
Dir, Development: Dominique Morel *Tel:* (01) 55 02 20 61
Publicity, Advertising: Alain Papillaud *Tel:* (01) 44 41 39 39 *Fax:* (01) 43 54 78 87
Foreign Rights: Marion Colns *E-mail:* colas@puf.com
Press: Dominique Reymond *Tel:* (01) 58 10 31 80
Editorial: Jean-Christophe Brochier *E-mail:* brochier@puf.com
Founded: 1921
Administration & Editorial offices are located at the above main address; Public Relations & Publicity departments are at 90 Blvd St-Germain, 75005 Paris.
Subjects: Art, Biography, Engineering (General), Geography, Geology, Government, Political Science, History, Human Relations, Law, Medicine, Nursing, Dentistry, Music, Dance, Philosophy, Psychology, Psychiatry, Religion - Other, Social Sciences, Sociology
ISBN Prefix(es): 2-13
Bookshop(s): Librairie generale des PUF, 49, Bd Saint Michel, 75005 Paris, Contact: Dominique Morel *Tel:* (01) 44 41 81 20 *Fax:* (01) 43 54 64 81 (Under Major Booksellers); La Pochotheque, 17 rue Soufflot, F-75005 Paris *Tel:* (01) 43267741 *Fax:* (01) 46332196
Orders to: 14 Ave du Bois de l'Epine, BP 90, 91003 Evry Cedex, Contact: Jean-Pierre Giband *Tel:* (01) 60 87 30 00 *Fax:* (01) 60 79 20 45

Presses Universitaires de Grenoble+
1041, rue de Residences, 38400 Saint-Martin-d'Heres 9
Mailing Address: BP 47, 38040 Grenoble Cedex 9
Tel: (04) 76 82 56 51; (04) 76 82 56 52 *Fax:* (04) 76 82 78 35
E-mail: pug@pug.fr
Web Site: www.pug.fr
Telex: Unisog 980910
Key Personnel
General Manager: Bernard Wirbel *E-mail:* bernard.wirbel@pug.fr
Editorial Manager: Rene Bourgeois *Fax:* rene.bourgeois@pug.fr
Finance Manager: Corine Desbenoit *E-mail:* corine.desbenoit@pug.fr
Sales Manager: Barbara Muller *E-mail:* barbara.muller@pug.fr
Manufacturing: Muriel Girard *E-mail:* muriel.girard@pug.fr
Founded: 1972
Subjects: Accounting, Chemistry, Chemical Engineering, Communications, Economics, History, Language Arts, Linguistics, Law, Literature, Literary Criticism, Essays, Management, Marketing, Mathematics, Psychology, Psychiatry, Social Sciences, Sociology, Sports, Athletics, Economics, Europe, French Language, Political Science
ISBN Prefix(es): 2-7061
Number of titles published annually: 45 Print
Total Titles: 1,000 Print
Imprints: PUG
Orders to: Sofedis, 11 rue Soufflot, 75005 Paris *Tel:* 01 53102526

Presses Universitaires de Lyon+
80, Blvd de la Croix-Rousse, BP 4371, 69242 Lyon Cedex 04
Tel: (04) 78 29 39 39 *Fax:* (04) 78 29 39 41
Web Site: sites.univ-lyon2.fr/pul
Key Personnel
Man Dir: Andre Pelletier *E-mail:* andre.pelletier@univ-lyon2.fr
Sales & Marketing: Norbert Fauvet *E-mail:* norbert.fauvet@univ-lyon2.fr
Founded: 1976
Membership(s): Syndicat National de l'Edition
Subjects: Economics, Government, Political Science, History, Human Relations, Language Arts, Linguistics, Law, Literature, Literary Criticism, Essays, Management
ISBN Prefix(es): 2-7297
Distributor for Editions W a Macon; Editions Lyonnaises d'Art et d'Histoire a'Lyon

Presses Universitaires de Nancy+
42-44 ave de la Liberation, 54014 Nancy Cedex
Mailing Address: BP 3347, 54014 Nancy Cedex
Tel: (03) 83 96 84 30 *Fax:* (03) 83 96 84 39
E-mail: pun@univ-nancy2.fr
Web Site: www.univ-nancy2.fr/PUN
Key Personnel
Chairman: Jean-Marie Bonnet
Man Dir: Alain Trognon
General Manager: Jeanne Weill
Editorial Manager: Daniele Silvy-Leligois
Sales: Sophie Izorche
Publicity, Rights & Permissions: Daniele Silvy-Leligois
Founded: 1976
Subjects: Communications, Drama, Theater, Economics, Education, Geography, Geology, Gov-

ernment, Political Science, History, Language Arts, Linguistics, Law, Literature, Literary Criticism, Essays, Philosophy, Psychology, Psychiatry, Religion - Other, Social Sciences, Sociology
ISBN Prefix(es): 2-86480
Associate Companies: Editions Serpenoise, BP 89, 57140 Metz-Woippy
Imprints: Annales de l'Est; Editions Humblot; Le Parvis des Arts
Warehouse: Sodis-128, ave de Lattre de Tassigny, 77400 Lagny-Sur-Marne
Orders to: Sofedis, 29 rue Saint-Sulpice, 75006 Paris

Presses Universitaires de Strasbourg
Palais Universitaire, 9, place de l'Universite, 67084 Strasbourg Cedex
Tel: (03) 88 25 97 21 *Fax:* (03) 88 35 65 23
E-mail: info@pu-strasourg.com
Web Site: www.pu-strasbourg.com
Key Personnel
President: Lucien Braun
Founded: 1920
Subjects: Art, History, Literature, Literary Criticism, Essays, Philosophy, Social Sciences, Sociology
ISBN Prefix(es): 2-86820

Presses Universitaires du Septentrion+
Rue du Barreau, 59654 Villeneuve d'Ascq, Cedex
Mailing Address: BP 199, 59654 Villeneuve d'Ascq, Cedex
Tel: (03) 20 41 66 80 *Fax:* (03) 20 41 66 90
E-mail: septentrion@septentrion.com
Web Site: www.septentrion.com
Key Personnel
Editorial & Production: Jerome Vaillant
Sales, Publicity, Rights & Permissions: Jean-Gabriel Caby
Founded: 1971
Subjects: History, Language Arts, Linguistics, Law, Literature, Literary Criticism, Essays, Philosophy, Psychology, Psychiatry, Social Sciences, Sociology
ISBN Prefix(es): 2-284; 2-85939; 2-7295; 2-86531; 2-907170

Privat-Garnier, *imprint of* Dunod Editeur

PRODIG+
191, rue Saint-Jacques, 75005 Paris
Tel: (01) 44 32 14 81; (01) 42 34 56 21 *Fax:* (01) 43 29 63 83
E-mail: prodig@univ-paris1.fr
Web Site: prodig.univ-paris1.fr/umr
Key Personnel
Dir: Jean Louis Chaleard *E-mail:* jl.chaleard@wanadoo.fr
Contact: Beatrice Velard *E-mail:* bvelard@univ-paris1.fr
Founded: 1947
Subjects: Geography, Geology, Library & Information Sciences
ISBN Prefix(es): 2-901560
Parent Company: Centre national de la recherche scientifique (CNRS)
Associate Companies: Universite de Paris One; Universite de Paris Four; Universite de Paris Seven

Propos de Campagne+
Allee de Provence, 04100 Manosque
Tel: (04) 92 77 03 51 *Fax:* (04) 92 77 09 36
E-mail: ProposdeC@aol.com
Web Site: www.lisez.com/propos
Key Personnel
Publications Dir: Samuel Autexier
Founded: 1993
Revue d art et de Poesie.

Subjects: Art, Poetry
ISBN Prefix(es): 2-912144

Editions Prosveta
BP 12, 83601 Frejus Cedex
Tel: (04) 94 19 33 33 *Fax:* (04) 94 19 33 34
E-mail: international@prosveta.com
Web Site: www.prosveta.com
Telex: 970809F
Key Personnel
President: Marcel Cieutat
Author: Mikhael Aivanhov
Founded: 1976
Subjects: Education, Philosophy, Religion - Other
ISBN Prefix(es): 2-85566
U.S. Office(s): Prosveta USA, PO Box 49614, Los Angeles, CA 90049, United States

PSI, *imprint of* Dunod Editeur

PUB, see Presses Universitaires de Bordeaux (PUB)

Publi-Fusion+
Village Artisanal de Regourd, 46000 Cahors
Tel: (05) 65220303 *Fax:* (05) 65220322
Key Personnel
Contact: Jean-Claude Delmas
Founded: 1987
Subjects: Automotive, Literature, Literary Criticism, Essays
ISBN Prefix(es): 2-907265

Publi Union, *imprint of* Editions Village Mondial

Editions Publications de l'Ecole Moderne Francaise sa (PEMF)+
Parc d'activites de l'Argile, 06376 Mouans Sartoux Cedex
Tel: (04) 92 28 42 84 *Fax:* (04) 92 28 42 99
Key Personnel
Man Dir & Editorial: Robert Poitrenaud
Man Dir: Norbert Jouve
Founded: 1986
ISBN Prefix(es): 2-87785; 2-84526

Publications de l'Universite de Rouen
One, rue Lavoisier, 76821 Mont-Saint-Aignan Cedex
Tel: (02) 35 14 63 43 *Fax:* (02) 35 14 65 38
Key Personnel
Man Dir: Henry Decaens
Communications: Patricia Lanoe
Founded: 1968
Subjects: Geography, Geology, History, Law, Literature, Literary Criticism, Essays, Psychology, Psychiatry
ISBN Prefix(es): 2-87775
Orders to: CID, 131 Blvd St-Michel, 75005 Paris

Publications Orientalistes de France (POF)+
14, Ave du Garric, 15000 Aurillac
Tel: (04) 71 43 23 78 *Fax:* (04) 71 43 23 78
E-mail: sieffert@pofjapon.com
Web Site: www.pofjapon.com
Key Personnel
Dir: Simone Sieffert
Founded: 1973
Subjects: Drama, Theater, History, Language Arts, Linguistics, Literature, Literary Criticism, Essays, Music, Dance, Poetry, Social Sciences, Sociology
ISBN Prefix(es): 2-7169
Orders to: Distique, 5, rue du Mal Leclerc, 28600 Luisant

Publisud Editions+
15 rue des Cinq-diamants, 75013 Paris
Tel: (01) 45 80 78 50 *Fax:* (01) 45 89 94 15

E-mail: publisud@compuserve.com; edipublsud@wanadoo.fr
Key Personnel
Man Editor: Marybel Boix
Founded: 1980
ISBN Prefix(es): 2-86600

PUF, see Presses Universitaires de France (PUF)

PUG, *imprint of* Presses Universitaires de Grenoble

Editions du Puits Fleuri+
22 Ave Fontainebleau, 77850 Hericy
Tel: (01) 64 23 61 46 *Fax:* (01) 64 23 69 42
Key Personnel
Literary Dir: Emile Guchet
Founded: 1981
Subjects: How-to, Law
ISBN Prefix(es): 2-86739
Imprints: Le Conseiller Juridique Pour Tous
Showroom(s): Amphora, 14 rue de l'Odeon, 75006 Paris

PUM Toulouse, *imprint of* Presses Universitaires du Mirail

PUS, see Presses Universitaires du Septentrion

PYC Edition+
16-18 Pl de La Chapelle, 75018 Paris
Tel: (01) 53 26 48 00 *Fax:* (01) 53 26 48 01
E-mail: info@pyc.fr
Web Site: www.pyc.fr
Key Personnel
Man Dir: Pierre Benichou
Founded: 1934
Subjects: Energy, Mechanical Engineering
ISBN Prefix(es): 2-85330; 2-911008

Editions Pygmalion+
70 Ave de Breteuil, 75007 Paris
Tel: (01) 45 67 40 77 *Fax:* (01) 47 34 51 52
E-mail: pygmalion@pygmalion.fr
Key Personnel
General Manager: Gilles Haeri
Sales & Foreign Rights: Sylvie Goguel
Founded: 1974
Subjects: Archaeology, Art, Biography, Fiction, History, Literature, Literary Criticism, Essays, Parapsychology
ISBN Prefix(es): 2-85704
Total Titles: 500 Print
Warehouse: Union Distribution, 106 rue Petit Leroy, Cherilly-La rue, 94152 Rungis Cedex
Distribution Center: Flammarion, 26 rue Racine, 75278 Paris Cedex 06, Marketing Dir: Patrick Du Fant *Tel:* (01) 40513100

Quillet, *imprint of* Le Livre de Paris

Radio, *imprint of* Dunod Editeur

Rageot Editeur, *imprint of* Editions Hatier SA

Rageot Editeur+
6, rue d'Assas, 75006 Paris
Tel: (01) 45 48 07 31 *Fax:* (01) 42 22 68 01
E-mail: rageotediteur@editions-hatier.fr
Web Site: www.rageotediteur.fr
Key Personnel
Dir: Caroline Westberg
Manager: Arnaud Nourry
Founded: 1941
ISBN Prefix(es): 2-7002
Orders to: Librairie Hatier SA, 8 rue d'Assas, 75006 Paris *Tel:* (01) 30 66 20 66 *Fax:* (01) 49 54 49 71 *Web Site:* www.editions-hatier.com

Editions Ramsay
60, rue Saint Andres des Arts, 75006 Paris

PUBLISHERS — FRANCE

Tel: (01) 53 10 02 80 *Fax:* (01) 53 10 02 88
Key Personnel
Man Dir: Jean-Claude Gawsewitch
Rights & Permissions: Zeline Guena
Founded: 1976
Subjects: Drama, Theater, Fiction, History, Literature, Literary Criticism, Essays, Nonfiction (General)
ISBN Prefix(es): 2-84114

Realisations pour l'Enseignement Multilingue International (REMI)
70, rue du Theatre, 75015 Paris
Tel: (01) 45 75 78 49 *Fax:* (01) 45 79 06 66
Key Personnel
Man Dir: Mrs D Holtzer
Founded: 1966
ISBN Prefix(es): 2-85134

Refclim, *imprint of* SEDIT (Societe d'Etudes et de Diffusion des Industries Thermiques et Aerauliques)

References cf
26340 Saint Nazaire le Desert
Tel: (04) 75 27 52 59 *Fax:* (04) 75 27 52 59
Key Personnel
Publisher: Bernard Dermineur
Founded: 1984
Subjects: Art, Genealogy, History, Library & Information Sciences
ISBN Prefix(es): 2-908302
Total Titles: 20 Print; 3 CD-ROM
Imprints: CF
Bookshop(s): Librarie la Stravaganza, 32 rue Traversiere, 75012 Paris *Tel:* (01) 43 45 80 83 *Fax:* (01) 43 45 50 96

REMI, see Realisations pour l'Enseignement Multilingue International (REMI)

Les Editions Albert Rene+
26, Ave Victor Hugo, 75116 Paris
Tel: (01) 45 00 41 41 *Fax:* (01) 40 67 95 12
E-mail: rene.cominfo@editions-albert-rene.com
Web Site: www.editions-albert-rene.com
Telex: 613160 F
Key Personnel
Dir: Sylvie Uderz
Founded: 1979
Subjects: Humor
ISBN Prefix(es): 2-86497
Distributed by Hachette
Orders to: Les Presses de la Cite, 8 rue Garanciere, 75006 Paris

Editions Revue EPS+
11, Ave of Tremblay, 75012 Paris
Tel: (01) 41 74 82 82 *Fax:* (01) 43 98 37 38
E-mail: revue@revue-eps.com
Web Site: www.revue-eps.com
Key Personnel
President: Jean Eisenbeis
Subjects: Education, Sports, Athletics
ISBN Prefix(es): 2-86713

Revue Espaces et Societes+
Universite de Toulouse-Le-Mirail, 5, allee A Machado, 31058 Toulouse Cedex
Tel: (0551) 60 35 70 *Fax:* (0551) 60 49 58
E-mail: jjaquin@espacesetsocietes.com
Web Site: www.espacesetsocietes.com
Key Personnel
Dir: Jean Remy *E-mail:* jremy@espacesetsocietes.com
Head Writer: Maurice Blanc *E-mail:* mblanc@espacesetsocietes.com
Editorial: Joelle Jacquin *E-mail:* jjacquin@espacesetsocietes.com
Founded: 1968
2 or 3 installments/year in 16 x 24 cm format (about 600 pages/year).
Subjects: Anthropology, Environmental Studies, Social Sciences, Sociology
Imprints: L'Harmattan Paris
Distributed by L' Harmattan

Revue Noire
8 rue Cels, 75014 Paris
Tel: (01) 43 20 92 00 *Fax:* (01) 43 22 92 60
E-mail: redaction@revuenoire.com
Web Site: www.revuenoire.com
Key Personnel
President: Michelle Rakotoson
Dir, Publications & Editor: Jeau Loup Pivin *Tel:* (01) 43 20 78 38
Editor: Simon Njami *Tel:* (01) 43 20 79 56
Distribution & Web Dir: N'Gone Fall *Tel:* (01) 43 20 82 34
Art Dir: Pascal Martin St Leon *Tel:* (01) 43 20 83 02
Editor Member: Bruno Tilliette
Administration Dir: Gwendal Vaillant *Tel:* (01) 43 20 80 07 *E-mail:* order@revuenoire.com
Founded: 1991
Subjects: African American Studies, Architecture & Interior Design, Art, Fashion, Literature, Literary Criticism, Essays, Music, Dance, Photography, Poetry
ISBN Prefix(es): 2-909571
Parent Company: Revue Noire Sarl
Distributed by Editions Hazan Distribution (France, Belgium, Switzerland, Canada)
Distributor for DAP

Editions Rivages, see Payot & Rivages

Yves Riviere Editeur+
117 rue Vieille-du-Temple, 75003 Paris
Tel: (01) 42 74 77 84 *Fax:* (01) 42 78 12 65
E-mail: yvestri@mail.club.internet.fr
Founded: 1971
Specialize in catalogues & reference books, art posters & prints signed & numbered.
Subjects: Art
ISBN Prefix(es): 2-85666
Total Titles: 75 Print

Le Robert
27, rue de la Glaciere, 75640 Paris Cedex 13
Tel: (01) 45 87 43 00 *Fax:* (01) 45 35 76 06
Web Site: www.lerobert.com.fr
Telex: Dicorob 240763 F
Key Personnel
President, Man Dir: Bertrand Eveno
Publicity: Denis A Fasse
Technical Manager: Jacques Pierre
Export Manager: Michel Terrier
Founded: 1951
ISBN Prefix(es): 2-85036

Editions Rombaldi SA
58 rue Jean Bleuzen, 92178 Vanves Cedex
Tel: (01) 41 23 65 00 *Fax:* (01) 46 45 34 42
Telex: 631 253
Key Personnel
President: Etienne Vendroux
Commercial Dir & Production Manager: Henri Kaufman
Commercial Dir: Francis Petit
Founded: 1920
Subjects: Cookery, Crafts, Games, Hobbies, Humor
ISBN Prefix(es): 2-231

Guide Rosenwald
10 rue Vineuse, 75784 Paris Cedex 16
Tel: (01) 44 30 81 00 *Fax:* (01) 44 30 81 11
E-mail: info@rosenwald.com
Web Site: www.rosenwald.com
Key Personnel
Editor: Afif Ben Yedder *E-mail:* benyedder@icpublications.com
Founded: 1887
Subjects: Health, Nutrition, Medicine, Nursing, Dentistry
ISBN Prefix(es): 2-907749
Number of titles published annually: 5 Print; 5 CD-ROM; 5 Online
Total Titles: 20 Print; 20 CD-ROM; 20 Online
Parent Company: I C Publications

Editions Roudil SA
8, rue des Ecoles, 75005 Paris
Tel: (01) 43 54 47 97 *Fax:* (01) 43 54 06 97
Key Personnel
Man Dir: Henry Roudil
Founded: 1954
Subjects: Fiction, History, Philosophy
ISBN Prefix(es): 2-85044

Editions du Rouergue+
Parc Saint-Joseph, BP 3522, 12035 Rodez Cedex 9
Tel: (05) 65.77.73.70 *Fax:* (05) 65.77.73.71
E-mail: info@lerouergue.com
Web Site: www.lerouergue.com
Key Personnel
Contact: Danielle Dastugue; Anne Marcy
Founded: 1986
Subjects: Cookery, Fiction, Gardening, Plants, Health, Nutrition, How-to, Romance, Wine & Spirits
ISBN Prefix(es): 2-84156; 2-905209

Editions Saint-Germain-des-Pres SA, see Editions Librairie-Galerie Racine

Editions Saint-Michel SA+
Fougerolles, La Reserve de Gamillon Saint-Michel-de-Boulogne, 07200 Saint-Michel-de-Boulogne
Tel: (04) 75 87 10 50 *Fax:* (04) 75 87 10 61
Key Personnel
Contact: Guy Dupuis
Subjects: Astrology, Occult, Behavioral Sciences, Medicine, Nursing, Dentistry, Parapsychology
ISBN Prefix(es): 2-902450

Editions Saint-Paul SA+
3, rue de la Porte de Buc, 78000 Versailles
Mailing Address: BP 652, 78006 Versailles
Tel: (01) 39 67 16 00 *Fax:* (01) 30 21 41 95
Key Personnel
Man Dir: M Lerozier
Dir, Religous Edition: M Larive
Founded: 1879
Subjects: Philosophy, Religion - Other, Theology
ISBN Prefix(es): 2-85049
Total Titles: 150 Print
Subsidiaries: Editions Saint-Paul SA
Distributed by CERF

Editions Salvator Sarl+
103, rue Notre-Dame-des-Champs, 75006 Paris
Tel: (01) 53 10 38 38 *Fax:* (01) 53 10 38 39
E-mail: salvator.editions@wanadoo.fr
Founded: 1924
Subjects: Human Relations, Religion - Other
ISBN Prefix(es): 2-7067

Salvy Editeur+
33 rue Saint Andre des Arts, 75006 Paris
Tel: (01) 43 25 74 40 *Fax:* (01) 46 33 56 21
Key Personnel
President: Gerard-Julien Salvy
Founded: 1989
Subjects: Literature, Literary Criticism, Essays
ISBN Prefix(es): 2-905899

Editions Sand et Tchou SA
6 rue du Mail, 75002 Paris
Tel: (01) 44 55 37 50 *Fax:* (01) 40 20 99 74
E-mail: info@editions-menges.com
Key Personnel
Man Dir: Carl van Eiszner
Rights & Permissions: Isabelle de Tinguy
Founded: 1979
Subjects: Astrology, Occult, Biography, Fiction, Health, Nutrition, How-to, Music, Dance, Psychology, Psychiatry, Social Sciences, Sociology
ISBN Prefix(es): 2-7107
Subsidiaries: Editions Menges

Editions Sang de la Terre+
62, rue Blanche, 75009 Paris
Tel: (01) 42 82 08 16 *Fax:* (01) 48 74 14 88
E-mail: editeur@sangdelaterre.com
Web Site: www.sangdelaterre.com
Key Personnel
Publications Dir: Dominique Bigourdan
Editor: Karine Reysset
Founded: 1986
Subjects: Agriculture, Animals, Pets, Cookery, Crafts, Games, Hobbies, Environmental Studies, Gardening, Plants, Health, Nutrition, How-to
ISBN Prefix(es): 2-86985
Imprints: Bornemann
Subsidiaries: 670 Bornemann

Sante Spiritualite, *imprint of* Jouvence Editions

Editions Le Sarment+
75, rue des Sts-Peres, 75279 Paris Cedex 06
Tel: (01) 45 49 82 00 *Fax:* (01) 42 22 40 17
E-mail: cremond@editions-fayard.fr
Web Site: www.editions-fayard.fr
Key Personnel
Man Dir: Jean-Claude Didelot
Assistant Editor: Odile Level
Responsable Commercial: Christophe Remond *E-mail:* cremond@editions-fayard.fr
Founded: 1980
Subjects: Religion - Catholic
ISBN Prefix(es): 2-86679
Number of titles published annually: 30 Print
Parent Company: Librairie Artheme Fayard

Sauramps Medical+
11 blvd Henri IV, 34000 Montpellier
Tel: (04) 67 63 68 80 *Fax:* (04) 67 52 59 05
E-mail: sauramps.medical@livres-medicaux.com
Web Site: www.livres-medicaux.com
Key Personnel
Man Dir: Dominique Torreilles
Founded: 1985
Subjects: Medicine, Nursing, Dentistry, Gynecology-Obstetrics, Orthopaedic Surgery, Radiology
ISBN Prefix(es): 2-905030; 2-84023
Number of titles published annually: 35 Print
Total Titles: 500 Print
Distributed by Lidel (Portugal); SODIS (France); Somabec (Canada); Vivendi (Belgium)
Bookshop(s): Librairie Sauramps Medical (under Major Booksellers); 30, rue Godefroy Cavaignac, 75011 Paris, Contact: George Lauret *Tel:* (01) 40092771 *Fax:* (01) 40038071

Editions Scala+
Passage Lhomme, 26 rue de Charonne, 75011 Paris
Tel: (01) 49 29 42 25 *Fax:* (01) 49 29 99 33
E-mail: editions.scala@wanadoo.fr
Web Site: www.ldj.tm.fr/editeurs/editeurs/scala.htm
Key Personnel
Contact: Chantal Desmazieres
Founded: 1980
Subjects: Antiques, Art

ISBN Prefix(es): 2-86656
Total Titles: 110 Print

SEDIT (Societe d'Etudes et de Diffusion des Industries Thermiques et Aerauliques)
Domaine de St-Paul, 102 Route de Limours - Bat 16_, 78471 St-Remy-les-Chevreuse Cedex
Tel: (01) 30 85 20 10 *Fax:* (01) 30 85 20 38
E-mail: sedit@costic.com
Web Site: www.costic.com
Key Personnel
Contact: Armel Jegou; Odette Guibert
ISBN Prefix(es): 2-236
Imprints: Refclim; Climapoche

Editions Seghers
Imprint of Editions Robert Laffont
24 Ave Marceau, 75008 Paris
Tel: (01) 53 67 14 00 *Fax:* (01) 53 67 14 14
Web Site: www.laffont.fr/seghers
Key Personnel
President & Man Dir: Leonello Brandolini
Literary Manager: Alain Beiastein
Rights & Permissions: Beatrix Vernet *Tel:* (01) 53 67 14 89 *E-mail:* bvernet@robert.laffont.fr
Founded: 1944
Subjects: Poetry
ISBN Prefix(es): 2-232
Orders to: Inter Forum, 46 route de Sermaires, BP 11, 45337 Nalesherbes Cedex *Tel:* (02) 38 32 71 00

Selection du Reader's Digest SA
5/7 Ave Louis Pasteur, 92220 Bagneux
Mailing Address: BP 101, 92225 Bagneux Cedex
Tel: (01) 46748484 *Fax:* (01) 46748580
E-mail: serviceclients@readersdigest.tm.fr
Web Site: www.selectionclic.com/srd/; www.rd.com/international/shared/?countryid=fr
Cable: Readigest Paris
Key Personnel
President & Dir General: Patricia Killen
Founded: 1947
Subjects: Architecture & Interior Design, Art, Economics, Environmental Studies, Fiction, History, How-to, Medicine, Nursing, Dentistry, Science (General), Social Sciences, Sociology, Technology, Travel
ISBN Prefix(es): 2-7098

Editions Selection J Jacobs SA+
66 rue Falguiere, 75015 Paris
Subjects: Art, How-to, Technology
ISBN Prefix(es): 2-7174

Le Seneve, *imprint of* Editions Buchet-Chastel Pierre Zech Editeur

Sepia Editions
6 Ave du Gouverneur General Binger, 94100 St-Maur
Tel: (01) 43 97 22 14 *Fax:* (01) 43 97 32 62
E-mail: sepia@editions-sepia.com
Web Site: www.editions-sepia.com
Key Personnel
Dir: Patrick Merand
Founded: 1987
Specialize in Africa.
Subjects: Archaeology, Art, Ethnicity, Fiction, Foreign Countries, Social Sciences, Sociology
ISBN Prefix(es): 2-84280; 2-907888

Editions de Septembre+
34 rue de l'Abbe-Groult, 75015 Paris
Tel: (01) 53 68 96 20 *Fax:* (01) 53 68 96 21
Key Personnel
Dir: Christophe Roux; Jean-Luc Simonin
Editor: Rodolphe Fouano; Alain Vuyet
Founded: 1990
Membership(s): SNE.
Subjects: Biography, Fiction, Humor, Journalism, Literature, Literary Criticism, Essays, Science (General), Social Sciences, Sociology
ISBN Prefix(es): 2-87914
Imprints: l'Europeenne; Lignes De Vie
Divisions: Atelier Graphique des Editions de Septembre; Septembre Communication

Sequences, *imprint of* Sarl Editions Jean Grassin

Editions Le Serpent a Plumes
20 rue des Petits Champs, 75002 Paris
Tel: (01) 55 35 95 85 *Fax:* (01) 42 61 17 46
E-mail: contact@serpentaplumes.com
Key Personnel
Dir, Editorial: Pierre Astier
Sales: Xavier Belrose
Production: Sylvia Lohr
Rights: Laure Pecher
Founded: 1988
Subjects: Fiction, Foreign Countries, Literature, Literary Criticism, Essays
ISBN Prefix(es): 2-908957; 2-84261
Distributed by CDE; Foliade-La Caravelle; Gallimard Export; Gallimard Ltee; Office du Livre; SODIS

Servedit+
15, rue Victor-Cousin, 75005 Paris
Tel: (01) 44 41 49 30 *Fax:* (01) 43 25 77 41
E-mail: servedit@wanadoo.fr
Key Personnel
President: Alain Jauson
ISBN Prefix(es): 2-86877

Service des Publications Scientifiques du Museum National d'Histoire Naturelle
57 rue Cuvier, 75231 Paris Cedex 05
Tel: (01) 40 79 48 38 *Fax:* (01) 40 79 38 40
E-mail: diff.pub@mnhn.fr
Web Site: www.mnhn.fr/publication
Key Personnel
Dir: Philippe Bouchet
Founded: 1802
Subjects: Earth Sciences, Environmental Studies, Natural History, Also bilingual
ISBN Prefix(es): 2-85653; 2-86515
Number of titles published annually: 314 Print
Warehouse: Bibliotheque Centrale du Museum National d, 38 rue Geoffroy, Saint Hilaire, 75005 Paris
Orders to: Universal Book Services, Dr Backhuys, PO Box 321, 2300 AH Leiden, Netherlands (Only for the memoires collection/series, except geology)

Service Hydrographique et Oceanographique de la Marine (SHOM)
3 avenue Octave Greard, Paris 7eme
Mailing Address: BP 5, 00307 Armees
Tel: (01) 44 38 41 16
Web Site: www.shom.fr
Key Personnel
Off Manager: Ica Bessero
ISBN Prefix(es): 2-218

Service Technique pour l'Education
19 blvd Poissonniere, 75002 Paris
Tel: (01) 45084756
Key Personnel
Man Dir: Mrs Gradvohl
Founded: 1962
Subjects: Art, Biography, Education, Fiction, History, Music, Dance, Philosophy, Poetry, Religion - Jewish, Religion - Other
ISBN Prefix(es): 2-901041

Editions du Seuil+
27 rue Jacob, 75006 Paris
Tel: (01) 40 46 50 50 *Fax:* (01) 40 46 43 00
E-mail: contact@seuil.com
Web Site: www.seuil.com *Cable:* EDISEUIL

PUBLISHERS
FRANCE

Key Personnel
Chairman: Claude Cherki
General Manager: Pascal Flamand
Chairman & Editorial Advisor: Olivier Cohen
Chairman & Advisor: Francoise Peyrot
Marketing Manager: Ludovic Girod
   E-mail: lgirod@seuil.com
Executive Dir: Marie-France Fontaine
Publicity: Nathalie Cordier
Production: Daniel Glorel
Rights & Permissions Manager: Mireille Reissoulet *Tel:* (01) 40465103 *E-mail:* mreissou@sevil.com
Editorial: Vincent Bardet; Jacques Binsztok; Evelyne Cazade; Rene de Ceccatty; Richard Figuier; Anne Freyer; Louis Gardel; Martine van Geertruyden; Jean-Luc Giribone; Jean-Claude Guillebaud; Claude Henard; Jean-Marc Levy-Leblond; Thierry Marchaisse; Annie Morvan; Maurice Olender; Christelle Paris; Robert Pepin; Denis Roche; Jean-Louis Schlegel; Michel Winock
Founded: 1935
Subjects: Art, Biography, Fiction, Government, Political Science, History, How-to, Literature, Literary Criticism, Essays, Music, Dance, Philosophy, Photography, Poetry, Psychology, Psychiatry, Religion - Other, Science (General), Social Sciences, Sociology
ISBN Prefix(es): 2-02
Parent Company: Editions de l'Olivier
Imprints: La Baleine; L' Olivier; Editions Verticales
Subsidiaries: Societe d'Editions Scientifiques; Boreal (Montreal, Canada); College de France
Distributor for Alliage; L'Ane; Arlea; Autrement; Baleine; Belin; Bibliotheque Nationale de France; Boreal; Bourgois; Cahiers Cinema du; Callicephale; Cause Freudienne; Corti; Esprit; Genre Humain; Hoebeke; Les 400 coups; L'Homme; Liana Levi; O Jacob; A M Metailie; Maison des Roches; Milan; Minuit; Mollat; Montparnasse Editions Video; Navarin; Noir sur Blanc; Olivier; Panoramiques; Payot-Rivages; Phebus; Raisons d'Agir; RMN; Regard; Sept Video Arte; Taize; Textuel; Thames & Hudson; Verticales
Orders to: 13 rue du General Leclerc, Ballainvilliers, 91160 Longjumeau

SHOM, see Service Hydrographique et Oceanographique de la Marine (SHOM)

Siloe - Kerdore+
4, rue Souchu-Serviniere, BP 939, 53009 Laval Cedex
Tel: (02) 43532601 *Fax:* (02) 43535601
E-mail: siloe-kerdore@wanadoo.fr
Key Personnel
Man Dir: Michel Thierry
Founded: 1982
Subjects: Geography, Geology, History, How-to, Literature, Literary Criticism, Essays, Photography, Regional Interests, Religion - Catholic, Travel, Wine & Spirits
ISBN Prefix(es): 2-905259; 2-84231
Total Titles: 250 Print
Branch Office(s)
18 rue des Carmelites, 44000 Nantes *Tel:* (02) 40 98 61 10
La Rinjardiene, 44370 Varades, Contact: Yves Brien *Tel:* (0240) 98 61 10 *Fax:* (0240) 98 61 10
Distribution Center: Litteral Diffusion, ZI du bois Imberk, BP 11, 85280 La Ferriere

Editions Andre Silvaire Sarl+
20 rue Domat, 75005 Paris
Tel: (01) 43 26 72 34 *Fax:* (01) 55 42 16 69
Founded: 1944

Subjects: Drama, Theater, Fiction, Literature, Literary Criticism, Essays, Philosophy, Poetry, Social Sciences, Sociology
ISBN Prefix(es): 2-85055

Sirey, *imprint of* Editions Dalloz Sirey

Slavonic, see Institut d'Etudes Slaves IES

Societe des Editions Grasset et Fasquelle+
61 rue des Sts-Peres, 75006 Paris
Tel: (01) 44392200 *Fax:* (01) 42226418
E-mail: editorial@grasset.fr
Web Site: www.grasset.fr
Telex: 615887
Key Personnel
Chairman: Jean-Claude Fasquelle
Man Dir: Yves Berger; Manuel Carcassonne; Jean-Paul Enthoven
Sales: Jean-Pierre Pigeard
General Manager, Publicity & Advertising: Denis Bourgeois
Production: Jean-Pierre Decaens
Administrative Dir: Denis Lepeu
Rights & Permissions: Marie-Helene d'Ovidio
Public Relations: Claude Dalla-Torre; Joelle Faure; Martine Savary
Founded: 1907
Subjects: Fiction, Literature, Literary Criticism, Essays, Nonfiction (General), Philosophy
ISBN Prefix(es): 2-246
Imprints: Figures; College de Philosophie; Cahiers Rouges
U.S. Office(s): c/o Sanford & Greenburger Associates, 55 Fifth Ave, 15th floor, New York, NY 10003, United States

Societe des Editions Privat SA+
10, rue des Arts, 31000 Toulouse
Mailing Address: BP 828, 31080 Toulouse Cedex
Tel: (05) 34 31 81 81; (05) 34 31 81 88 *Fax:* (05) 34 31 64 44
E-mail: editionsprivat@wanadoo.fr
Key Personnel
Dir: Dominique Porte
Publicity & Press Relations: Anne-Marie Bagieu
Editor: Veronique Sucere
Foreign Rights: Chantal Galtier Roussel
Founded: 1839
Subjects: Regional Interests, Patrimony, Health, National & International, Southern History
ISBN Prefix(es): 2-7089
Number of titles published annually: 70 Print
Parent Company: Laboratories Pierre Fabre, Le Carla-Burlats, 81106 Castres Cedex

Societe d'Etudes et de Diffusion des Industries Thermiques et Aerauliques, see SEDIT (Societe d'Etudes et de Diffusion des Industries Thermiques et Aerauliques)

Societe d'Etudes Juridiques Internationales et Fiscales, see Les Cahiers Fiscaux Europeens Sarl

Societe Francaise des Imprimeries Administratives Centrales, see Sofiac (Societe Francaise des Imprimeries Administratives Centrales)

Societe Mathematique de France - Institut Henri Poincare
11 rue Pierre-et-Marie-Curie, 75231 Paris Cedex 05
Tel: (01) 44 27 67 96 *Fax:* (01) 40 46 90 96
E-mail: smf@dma.ens.fr
Web Site: smf.emath.fr
Key Personnel
President: M Waldschmidt
Secretary General: Claire Ropartz

Founded: 1872
Subjects: Mathematics
Number of titles published annually: 20 Print
Bookshop(s): Maison de la SMF, BP 67, 13276 Marseille Cedex 9, C Munusami *Tel:* (0491) 833025 *Fax:* (0491) 411751 *E-mail:* smf@smf.univ-mrs.fr

Societe Nouveaux Loisirs+
5, rue Sebastien-Bottin, 75328 Paris cedex 07
Tel: (01) 49 54 42 00 *Fax:* (01) 45 44 94 03
Web Site: www.gallimard.fr
Key Personnel
Dir of Development: Ghislain de Compreignac
International Rights: Hedwige Pasquet
Founded: 1992
Subjects: Architecture & Interior Design, Art, Environmental Studies, Geography, Geology, History, How-to, Regional Interests
ISBN Prefix(es): 2-7424
Parent Company: Editions Gallimard
Associate Companies: Gallimard Jeunesse
Imprints: Guides Gallimard
Distributed by Dohosna (Japan); Dumont (Germany); Everytian (UK); Knopf (USA); Owl Publishing (China, Taiwan); SM-Acento (Spain); Standard (Netherlands); TCI (Italy)

Sofiac (Societe Francaise des Imprimeries Administratives Centrales)+
3, rue Ferrus, 75014 Paris Cedex
Tel: (01) 40 64 42 42 *Fax:* (01) 40 64 42 40
E-mail: ble@berger-levrault.fr
Web Site: www.editions.berger-levrault.fr
Key Personnel
President: Bruno Declementi
Publisher: Veronique Fastrez
Subjects: Accounting, Business, Law, Public Administration
ISBN Prefix(es): 2-85130
Parent Company: Groupe Berger-Levrault
Orders to: 5, rue Andre Ampere, BP 79, 54250 Champigneulles *Tel:* (03) 83 38 83 83 *Fax:* (03) 83 38 37 12

Solar, *imprint of* Presses de la Cite

Solin, *imprint of* Editions Actes Sud

Editions Soline+
10, blvd de la paix, 92400 Courbevoie
Tel: (01) 43 33 74 24 *Fax:* (01) 43 33 67 37
E-mail: contact@soline.fr
Web Site: perso.wanadoo.fr/soline
Key Personnel
Manager: Nicole Pialet
Founded: 1988
Subjects: Automotive, Fashion, Gardening, Plants, House & Home, Wine & Spirits
ISBN Prefix(es): 2-87677
Total Titles: 90 Print
Distributed by VILO
Warehouse: 19-23 rue Pierre Curie, 92400 Courbevoie

Somogy editions d'art+
57, rue de la Roquette, 75011 Paris
Tel: (01) 48 05 70 10 *Fax:* (01) 48 05 71 70
E-mail: somogy@magic.fr
Key Personnel
Man Dir: Nicolas Neumann
Editorial: Veronique le Dosseur
International Rights: Jana Navratil-Nanent
Founded: 1937
Subjects: Antiques, Archaeology, Architecture & Interior Design, Art, Biography, Photography
ISBN Prefix(es): 2-84598; 2-85056

Publications de la Sorbonne
212, rue Saint-Jacques, 75005 Paris
Tel: (01) 43 25 80 15 *Fax:* (01) 43 54 03 24

E-mail: publisor@univ-paris1.fr
Web Site: www.univ-paris1.fr/recherche/rubrique46.html
Key Personnel
Dir: Elisabeth Mornet
Founded: 1971
Subjects: Archaeology, Art, Economics, Geography, Geology, Government, Political Science, History, Law, Literature, Literary Criticism, Essays, Philosophy, Social Sciences, Sociology
ISBN Prefix(es): 2-85944
Number of titles published annually: 25 Print
Total Titles: 25 Print
Orders to: Diffusion CID, 131 blvd Saint Michel, 75005 Paris *Tel:* (01) 43 54 47 15 *Fax:* (01) 40 51 02 80 *E-mail:* cid@msh-paris.fr

Association d'Editions Sorg
54 rue de l'Est, 92100 Boulogne
Tel: (01) 48252524 *Fax:* (01) 46052563
Key Personnel
Chairman & International Rights: Jacques Sorg
Founded: 1986
Subjects: Aeronautics, Aviation, Fiction, History, Humor, Philosophy
ISBN Prefix(es): 2-906794

Sortileges, *imprint of* Societe d'Edition Les Belles Lettres

Editions SOS (Editions du Secours Catholique)
11, rue de Cambrai Batiment 28, 2E Etage, 75019 Paris
Tel: (01) 40 35 44 65 *Fax:* (01) 40 35 42 73
Key Personnel
Man Dir: Maurice Herr
Publicity & Advertising: Georges Fanucchi
Founded: 1949
Subjects: History, Philosophy, Religion - Other, Social Sciences, Sociology
ISBN Prefix(es): 2-7185

Souffles+
85 rue Gabriel-Peri, 92120 Montrouge
Tel: (01) 42 31 07 20 *Fax:* (01) 42310729
Key Personnel
President: Thomas Jallaud
Founded: 1987
Subjects: Literature, Literary Criticism, Essays
ISBN Prefix(es): 2-87658

Les Editions de la Source Sarl
5 rue de la Source, 75016 Paris
Tel: (01) 45 25 30 07
Key Personnel
Man Dir: Rev Father Dom Gozier
All Other Offices: Rev Father Dom Balladur
Founded: 1927
Subjects: Biblical Studies, Religion - Other, Theology
ISBN Prefix(es): 2-900005
Imprints: Lumiere Bibliaue series
Bookshop(s): Librairie Sainte Marie, 5 rue de la Source, 75016 Paris
Orders to: Office General du Livre, 14 bis rue Jean-Ferrandi, 75006 Paris *Tel:* (01) 45 48 38 28

Spectres Familiers
29, rue Barthelemy, 13001 Marseille
Tel: (0491) 912645 *Fax:* (0491) 909951
Key Personnel
Literature Dir: Emmanuel Ponsart
Subjects: Literature, Literary Criticism, Essays, Poetry
ISBN Prefix(es): 2-909097

Spengler Editeur+
130 blvd Saint Germain, 75006 Paris
Tel: (01) 49 70 15 55 *Fax:* (01) 49 70 15 50
Founded: 1992
Subjects: Fiction, Literature, Literary Criticism, Essays
ISBN Prefix(es): 2-909997
Distributed by Prologue (Canada)

Editions Spratbrow+
27 rue Adrien-Weil, 59770 Marly
Mailing Address: BP 1, 59301 Valenciennes Cedex
Tel: (03) 27 33 62 58; (03) 27 41 12 14 *Fax:* (03) 27 45 29 99
E-mail: sjbv.cdi@wanadoo.fr
Key Personnel
President: Francoise Begrand
Founded: 1990
Subjects: Education, English as a Second Language, Language Arts, Linguistics, Self-Help
ISBN Prefix(es): 2-903891
Distributed by Groupe Deboeck a Louvin (Belgium)
Distributor for Santillana (France)
Warehouse: 27 rue Weil, 59770 Marly

Editions Springer France+
One, rue Paul Cezanne, 75008 Paris
Tel: (01) 5393 3647 *Fax:* (01) 53933729
Web Site: www.springer-paris.fr
Founded: 1986
Subjects: Astronomy, Chemistry, Chemical Engineering, Civil Engineering, Computer Science, Earth Sciences, Economics, Electronics, Electrical Engineering, Engineering (General), Mathematics, Mechanical Engineering, Medicine, Nursing, Dentistry, Physics, Psychology, Psychiatry
ISBN Prefix(es): 2-287; 3-540
Parent Company: Springer-Verlag GmbH & Co KG, Heidelberger Platz 3, 14197 Berlin, Germany

Editions Stil
22, blvd Saint-Denis, 75010 Paris
Tel: (01) 48009224; (06) 85024238 *Fax:* (01) 48009336
Key Personnel
Editor: Alain Villain
Founded: 1971
Subjects: Art, Literature, Literary Criticism, Essays, Music, Dance
ISBN Prefix(es): 2-85254

Editions Stock+
31 rue de Fleurus, 75006 Paris
Tel: (01) 49543655 *Fax:* (01) 49543662
Web Site: www.editions-stock.fr/
Key Personnel
President: Claude Durand
Rights & Permissions: Fabienne Roussel
Founded: 1708
Subjects: Biography, Child Care & Development, Fiction, Film, Video, Literature, Literary Criticism, Essays, Nonfiction (General), Poetry, Social Sciences, Sociology
ISBN Prefix(es): 2-234
Parent Company: Librairie Hachette
Branch Office(s)
US Office: Bureau du Livre Francais, 583 Broadway, New York, New York, NY 10003, United States

Editions Subervie
Parc des Moutiers, 12032 Rodez Cedex 09
Tel: (05) 65 67 20 17 *Fax:* (05) 65 67 36 38
E-mail: contact@subervie.com
Web Site: www.subervie.com
Key Personnel
Contact: Jo Subevio
ISBN Prefix(es): 2-85644; 2-911381

SUD+
62 rue Sainte, BP 38, 13484 Marseille Cedex 20
Tel: (0491) 336068 *Fax:* (0491) 336068
Key Personnel
Man Dir: Yves Broussard
Founded: 1970
Subjects: Literature, Literary Criticism, Essays, Poetry
ISBN Prefix(es): 2-86446

Editions Sud Ouest
6, rue de la Merci, 33000 Bordeaux
Mailing Address: BP 130, 33036 Bordeaux Cedex
Tel: (0556) 44 68 21 *Fax:* (0556) 44 40 83
E-mail: contact@editions-sudouest.com
Web Site: www.editions-sudouest.com
Key Personnel
Contact: Catherine Dubourg *Tel:* (0556) 003508 *E-mail:* c.dubourg@sudouest.com
Founded: 1988
Subjects: Cookery, History, How-to, Outdoor Recreation, Regional Interests
ISBN Prefix(es): 2-87901
Number of titles published annually: 60 Print
Total Titles: 500 Print
Parent Company: Groupe Sud-Ouest, 8 rue de Cheverus, 33000 Bordeaux
Distributor for Editions Jean Paul Gisserot
Warehouse: Rando SA, Queeynes, 33000 Bordeaux

Editions le Sureau, *imprint of* Adverbum SARL

Sybex+
Immeuble Polaris, 76 ave Pierre Brossolette, 92247 Malakoff Cedex
Tel: (01) 55 58 40 00 *Fax:* (01) 49 65 04 10
E-mail: contact@sybex.fr
Web Site: www.sybex.fr
Key Personnel
President: Francois-Xavier Chaussonniere
Founded: 1976
Subjects: Microcomputers
ISBN Prefix(es): 2-7361; 2-902414
Parent Company: Sybex Inc, 1151 Marina Village Parkway, Alameda, CA 94501, United States
Foreign Rep(s): Woodslane Pty Limited (Australia & New Zealand); Acorn Publishing Co (Korea); BPB Publications (Bangladesh, India, Pakistan); Express Trains Distributors Computer (Caribbean & Latin America); Firefly Books Ltd (Canada); International Sybex (UK, Europe & Middle East, North Africa); Intersoft (South Africa); Lidel Edicoes Tecnicas Lda (Portugal); Livraria Cultura (Brazil); Sulcor Investindo (Indonesia); TransQuest Publishers Pte Ltd (Hong Kong, Singapore & Malaysia, Thailand)

Les Editions de la Table Ronde
7 rue Corneille, 75006 Paris
Tel: (01) 40 46 70 70 *Fax:* (01) 40 46 71 01
E-mail: editionslatableronde@wanadoo.fr
Key Personnel
President & Dir General: Denis Tillinac
Publisher: Olivier Frebourg
Rights & Permissions: Marie-Therese Caloni
Founded: 1944
Subjects: Biography, Fiction, History, Nonfiction (General), Psychology, Psychiatry, Religion - Other
ISBN Prefix(es): 2-7103
Associate Companies: Editione la Palatine

Editeurs Tacor International
13 rue Saint-Honore, 78000 Versailles
Mailing Address: BP 1, 78170 La Celle-Saint Cloud
Tel: (01) 39 18 29 39 *Fax:* (01) 30 82 43 90
Key Personnel
Man Dir: Annette Riis-Zahrai
Founded: 1988

PUBLISHERS
FRANCE

Subjects: Human Relations, Religion - Other, Social Sciences, Sociology
ISBN Prefix(es): 2-907308

Editions Tallandier+
18, rue Dauphine, 75006 Paris
Tel: (01) 40 46 43 88 *Fax:* (01) 40 46 43 98
Web Site: www.tallandier.com
Founded: 1865
Subjects: Art, Fiction, Geography, Geology, History
ISBN Prefix(es): 2-235
Warehouse: BP 65, 45390 Puiseaux
Orders to: BP 65, 45390 Puiseaux

Editions Tardy SA+
11 rue Duguay-Trouin, 75006 Paris
Tel: (01) 45 44 38 34 *Fax:* (01) 45 49 93 92
Telex: 205781
Key Personnel
Man Dir, Rights & Permissions: Pierre Penet
Dir: Pierre-Marie Dumont
Founded: 1938
Subjects: Religion - Catholic, Religion - Other
ISBN Prefix(es): 2-7105
Warehouse: 48 rue Galande, 75005 Paris

Taride Editions+
Division of ULISSE Edition
15 rue Mansart, 75009 Paris
Tel: (01) 48 78 40 74 *Fax:* (01) 48 78 40 77
Web Site: www.taride.com
Key Personnel
Man Dir: Pierre-Alain Imhof
General Manager: Frederique Imhof
Founded: 1852
Subjects: Cookery, Geography, Geology, Travel
ISBN Prefix(es): 2-7106

Editions Tarmeye+
Roudon, 43520 Mazet Saint Voy
Tel: (0471) 650153 *Fax:* (0471) 650154
Key Personnel
Publisher: Jacqueline Tartar; Jean-Marc Tartar
Founded: 1986
Subjects: Humor
ISBN Prefix(es): 2-906029

Tec & Doc, *imprint of* Editions Lavoisier

Editions Tec & Doc - Lavoisier, see Editions Lavoisier

Editions Technip SA+
27 rue Ginoux, 75737 Paris Cedex 15
Tel: (01) 45 78 33 80 *Fax:* (01) 45 75 37 11
E-mail: info@editionstechnip.com
Web Site: www.editionstechnip.com
Key Personnel
President & Dir General: Jean-Pierre Sabbagh
Sales Manager: Corinne Herran
Founded: 1956
Specialize in the publishing of scientific & technical books on the oil & gas industry.
Subjects: Automotive, Chemistry, Chemical Engineering, Computer Science, Earth Sciences, Electronics, Electrical Engineering, Energy, Engineering (General), Mathematics, Technology
ISBN Prefix(es): 2-7108
Number of titles published annually: 20 Print
Total Titles: 1,000 Print; 3 CD-ROM
Parent Company: Institut Francais du Petrole, 1-4, ave de Bois Preau, 92852 Rueil-Malmaison Cedex
Bookshop(s): Brown Book Shop, 1517 San Jacinto, Houston, TX 77002, United States *Tel:* 713-652-3937 *Fax:* 713-652-1914 *E-mail:* info@brownbookshop.com; J A Majors Co, 8961 Interchange Dr, Houston, TX 77054, United States *Tel:* 713-662-3984 *Fax:* 713-662-9627 *E-mail:* houston@majors.com; DeMille

Technical Books, 120 Eighth Ave SW, Calgary, AB T2P 1B3, Canada *Tel:* 403-264-7411 *Fax:* 403-262-1445 *E-mail:* sales@calgary.mcnallyrobison.ca
Distribution Center: DA Information Services, 648 Whitehorse Rd, Mitcham, Victoria 3132, Australia *Tel:* (03) 9210 7777 *Fax:* (03) 9210 7788 *E-mail:* service@dadirect.com.au
Enfield Publishing & Distribution Co, PO Box 699, May St, Enfield, NH 03748, United States *Tel:* 603-632-7377 *Fax:* 603-632-5611 *E-mail:* info@enfieldbooks.com *Web Site:* www.enfieldbooks.com
Hikari Book Trading Co Ltd, Nagatani Bldg, Room 201, 26 Sakamachi, Shinjuku-ku, Tokyo 160 *Tel:* (03) 3353 5201 *Fax:* (03) 3353 5203 *E-mail:* yoshikal@sepia.ocn.ne.jp
PF Book, jl Dr Setia Budhi 274, Bandung 40143, Indonesia *Tel:* (022) 2011149 *Fax:* (022) 2012840 *E-mail:* pfbook@bandung.wasantara.net.id
Presses Internationales Polytechnique, 1170 Beaumont, Mont-Royal, PQ H3P 3E5, Canada *Tel:* 514-340-3286 *Fax:* 514-340-5882 *E-mail:* pip@polymlt.ca *Web Site:* www.polymlt.ca/pub/
Progressive International Agencies (Pvt) Limited, 174-X, Block 2, PECH Society, Off Tarig Rd, PO Box Nº=8069, Karachi 75400, Pakistan *Tel:* (021) 452 5544-6 *Fax:* (021) 2454 6687 *E-mail:* gaziani@super.net.pk
Shankar's Book Agency Private Ltd, 133, Lenin Sarani, Kolkata 700 013, India *Tel:* (033) 246 8993 *Fax:* (033) 246 3257 *E-mail:* davinder@vsnl.com
Shankar's Book Agency Private Ltd, 103, Munish Plaza, 20, Ansari Rd, Darya Ganj, New Delhi 110 002, India *Tel:* (011) 3279 967 *Fax:* (012) 6322 806 *E-mail:* sbapld@de12.vsnl.net.in

Techniplus, *imprint of* Editions Casteilla

Technique et Vulgarisation, *imprint of* Editions Bordas

Editions Techniques et Scientifiques Francaises
Imprint of Dunod Editeur
5 rue Laromiguiere, 75005 Paris
Tel: (01) 40 46 35 00 *Fax:* (01) 40 46 49 95
E-mail: infos@dunod.com
Web Site: www.dunod.com
Telex: pgv230472f
Key Personnel
President: Charles Vallee
ISBN Prefix(es): 2-85535

Le Temps apprivoise, *imprint of* Editions Buchet-Chastel Pierre Zech Editeur

10/18+
Imprint of Havas Poche
12 avenue d'Italie, 75013 Paris
Tel: (01) 44 16 05 00 *Fax:* (01) 44 16 05 03
E-mail: editeur@10-18.fr; commercial@10-18.fr
Web Site: www.10-18.fr
Telex: 204807F
Key Personnel
Publisher: Jean-Claude Dubost
Editor: Pauline de Margerie
Founded: 1961
Quality paperbacks.
Membership(s): Vivendi Universal Publishing Group.
Subjects: Fiction, Government, Political Science, Literature, Literary Criticism, Essays, Mysteries, International fiction & mysteries (mostly historical crime)
ISBN Prefix(es): 2-264

Librairie Pierre Tequi et Editions Tequi+
82 Le Roc Saint-Michel, 53150 Saint-Cenere

Tel: (02) 43.01.01.81 *Fax:* (02) 43.02.25.52
E-mail: pierre.tequi@wanadoo.fr
Web Site: www.librairietequi.com
Key Personnel
General Manager: Pierre Lemaire
Literary Manager: G Cerbelaud Salagnac
Founded: 1845
Subjects: Education, Philosophy, Religion - Catholic, Social Sciences, Sociology, Theology
ISBN Prefix(es): 2-7403; 2-85244
Bookshop(s): S A Vander (Belgium); Iris Diffusion (Canada); Editions Saint-Augustin (Switzerland)

Terre Vivante+
Domaine de Raud, 38710 Mens
Tel: (04) 76 34 80 80 *Fax:* (04) 76 34 84 02
E-mail: infos@terrevivante.org
Web Site: www.terrevivante.org
Key Personnel
Man Dir: Claude Aubert
Founded: 1980
Subjects: Agriculture, Cookery, Energy, Gardening, Plants, Health, Nutrition, House & Home, Technology
ISBN Prefix(es): 2-904082; 2-914717
Total Titles: 2 Print; 60 Audio

Editions Thames & Hudson+
12, rue de Seine, 75006 Paris
Tel: (01) 56240450 *Fax:* (01) 56240458
E-mail: thameshudson@wanadoo.fr
Web Site: www.thameshudson.fr
Key Personnel
Dir: Thomas Neurath
Editor: Helene Borraz *E-mail:* h.borraz.thameshudson@wanadoo.fr; Frederique Popet *E-mail:* f.popet.thameshudson@wanadoo.fr
Ed: Anne Levine *E-mail:* a.levine.thameshudson@wanadoo.fr
Publicity: Perrine Auclair *E-mail:* p.auclair.thameshudson@wanadoo.fr
Founded: 1989
Subjects: Archaeology, Architecture & Interior Design, Art, Fashion, Photography, Religion - Jewish
ISBN Prefix(es): 2-87811
Parent Company: Thames & Hudson Londres
Orders to: Hazan *Tel:* (01) 49619207 *Fax:* (01) 45978347

Editions Theatrales+
38, rue du Faubourg Saint-Jacques, 75014 Paris
Tel: (01) 53 10 23 00 *Fax:* (01) 53 10 23 01
E-mail: info@editionstheatrales.fr
Web Site: www.editionstheatrales.fr
Key Personnel
Dir: J P Engelbach
Founded: 1990
Subjects: Drama, Theater
ISBN Prefix(es): 2-907810; 2-84260
Distributed by Distique
Distributor for CNDP collection Theatre Aujourd-hui; Theatre du Soleil

Alain Thomas Editeur+
18 passage Foubert, 75013 Paris
Tel: (01) 45 88 28 03 *Fax:* (01) 45 88 49 24
Web Site: alainthomasimages.com
Key Personnel
Editor: Alain Thomas *E-mail:* alain-thomas@wanadoo.fr
Founded: 1991
Subjects: Photography, Travel, Western Fiction
ISBN Prefix(es): 2-9503864
Total Titles: 3 Print
Parent Company: Alain Thomas Images
Distributed by Centre Cartographique (in Belgium only)

Editions Tiresias Michel Reynaud+
21, rue Letort, 75018 Paris

FRANCE

Mailing Address: BP 249, 75866 Paris Cedex 18
Tel: (01) 42 23 47 27 *Fax:* (01) 42 23 73 27
E-mail: editions.tiresias@club-internet.fr
Web Site: www.editions-tiresias.fr.tc
Key Personnel
Contact: Michel Reynaud
Founded: 1990
Subjects: Biography, History, Literature, Literary Criticism, Essays
ISBN Prefix(es): 2-908527
Branch Office(s)
12 rue de Nombonnet, 28160 Unverre

TOP Editions+
Member of Casteilla
10, rue Leon-Foucault, 78184 Montigny-le-Bretonneux
Tel: (01) 30 14 19 30 *Fax:* (01) 34 60 31 32
E-mail: info@editionschiron.com
Web Site: www.editionschiron.com
Key Personnel
Dir General: Marinus Visser
Founded: 1982
Subjects: Accounting, Career Development, Communications, Finance, How-to, Management, Marketing, Securities
ISBN Prefix(es): 2-87731
Number of titles published annually: 25 Print
Total Titles: 75 Print

Tout L'Univers, *imprint of* Le Livre de Paris

Transedition ASBL
11 rue d'Odessa, 75014 Paris
Tel: (01) 43211080 *Fax:* (01) 43211079
Key Personnel
Man Dir, Editorial: Marc Dachy
Sales: Anne Barres
Production: Paule Pousseele
Publicity: Stephanie Gregoire
Rights & Permissions: Jacques Bekaert
Founded: 1972
Subjects: Art, Literature, Literary Criticism, Essays
ISBN Prefix(es): 2-8025
Associate Companies: Montfaucon Research Center, 8 rue d'Anjou, 75008 Paris
Subsidiaries: Editions Luna-Park

Transeuropeennes/RCE+
c/o Maison de l'Europe, Hotel de Coulanges, 35, rue des Francs Bourgeois, 75004 Paris
Tel: (01) 55 07 88 90 *Fax:* (01) 55 07 97 38
E-mail: te.revue@transeuropeennes.org; contact@transeuropeennes.org
Web Site: www.transeuropeennes.org
Key Personnel
Editor-in-Chief: Ghislaine Glasson Deschaumes
Man Dir: Gaele de la Brosse
Distribution Manager: Yacine Saadi
Founded: 1993
Comprehensive & interdisciplinary review.
Subjects: Art, Drama, Theater, Foreign Countries, History, Literature, Literary Criticism, Essays, Philosophy, Photography, Social Sciences, Sociology
ISBN Prefix(es): 2-912002
Number of titles published annually: 3 Print
Total Titles: 14 Print

Travel Aventure, *imprint of* Editions Actes Sud

Editions Trois Fontaines, *see* Jouvence Editions

Turbo, *imprint of* Les Presses du Management

Ulisse Editions+
15 rue Mansart, 75009 Paris
Tel: (01) 48 78 40 74 *Fax:* (01) 48 78 40 77
Web Site: www.ulisseditions.com

Key Personnel
Managing Editor: Gerard Boulanger
Founded: 1990
Subjects: Architecture & Interior Design, Art, Crafts, Games, Hobbies, House & Home, Sports, Athletics, Travel
ISBN Prefix(es): 2-907601; 2-84415; 2-921403

UNESCO Publishing+
Imprint of UNESCO Publishing
7 place de Fontenoy, 75352 Paris 07-SP
Tel: (01) 45 68 10 00 *Fax:* (01) 45 67 16 90
E-mail: publishing.promotion@unesco.org
Web Site: www.upo.unesco.org
Telex: 204461; 270602
Key Personnel
Dir General: Koichiro Matsuura
Chief, Promotion & Sales: Chandran Nair
Chief Publisher: Michiko Tanaka
Promotion: Cristina Laje
Founded: 1946
Subjects: Art, Communications, Education, Human Relations, Science (General), Social Sciences, Sociology
ISBN Prefix(es): 92-3
Imprints: IBE; IIEP
Distributed by Bernan Associate (USA); Stationery Office Books (UK)

Universitas
Subsidiary of Buchverlage Langen-Mueller/Herbig
62 ave de Suffren, 75015 Paris
Tel: (01) 45 67 18 38 *Fax:* (01) 45 66 50 70
E-mail: info@universitas.fr
Key Personnel
Dir: Andrew Brown
Founded: 1989
Subjects: History, Language Arts, Linguistics, Literature, Literary Criticism, Essays, Philosophy
ISBN Prefix(es): 2-7400

Publications de l'Universite de Pau
Av de l'Universite, 64000 Pau
Tel: (05) 59923347 *Fax:* (05) 59923275
Web Site: www.univ-pau.fr
Key Personnel
Dir: Bertrand Rouge
Man Dir: Alain Andreucci
Founded: 1992
Subjects: Art, Geography, Geology, Language Arts, Linguistics, Law, Literature, Literary Criticism, Essays, Photography, Poetry, Social Sciences, Sociology
ISBN Prefix(es): 2-908930

La Vague a l'ame+
BP 22, 38701 La Tronche Cedex
Tel: (04) 76470784
Key Personnel
President: Georges Elisee
Founded: 1980
Subjects: Cookery, Drama, Theater, Humor, Photography, Poetry, Religion - Catholic, Travel
ISBN Prefix(es): 2-84063

Editions Vague Verte+
271 rue du Haut, 80460 Woignarue
Tel: (03) 22 30 72 50 *Fax:* (03) 22 26 58 73
E-mail: edlavagueverte@wanadoo.fr
Web Site: perso.wanadoo.fr/editionslavagueverte
Key Personnel
Dir: Jimmy Grandsire
Founded: 1989
Subjects: Art, Biography, Earth Sciences, Environmental Studies, History, Literature, Literary Criticism, Essays, Mysteries, Natural History, Poetry, Regional Interests, Travel
ISBN Prefix(es): 2-908227
Number of titles published annually: 25 Print

Les Editions Vaillant-Miroir-Sprint Publications
146 rue du Faubourg-Poissoniere, 75010 Paris
Tel: (01) 42819103
Telex: f 281353f
Key Personnel
International Sales Manager: Alain Lesaint
Subjects: Humor, Sports, Athletics
ISBN Prefix(es): 2-7325

Editions Van de Velde+
La Haute Limougere, BP 22, 37230 Fondettes
Tel: (02) 47 49 43 43 *Fax:* (02) 47 49 43 49
Key Personnel
Dir: Francis Van de Velde
Copyrights: Ursula Van de Velde *Tel:* (02) 47 49 43 40
Founded: 1898
Subjects: Music, Dance
ISBN Prefix(es): 2-85868; 2-86299
Number of titles published annually: 20 Print
Total Titles: 197 Print
Distributor for Konemann Music Budapest
Distribution Center: Van De Velde, 37230 Fondettes *E-mail:* vandevelde.musique@wanadoo.fr

Gerard Varin, *see* L'Amitie par le Livre

Vents d'Ouest+
31-33 rue Ernest Renan, 92130 Issy-les-Moulineaux
Tel: (01) 41 46 11 46 *Fax:* (01) 40 93 05 58
Web Site: www.ventsdouest.com
Key Personnel
Contact: Estelle Revelant *E-mail:* estelle.revelant@glenat.com
International Rights: Annick Briard
Subjects: Humor, Science Fiction, Fantasy
ISBN Prefix(es): 2-86967; 2-7493

Editions Verdier
234, rue du Faubourg-Saint-Antoine, 75012 Paris
Tel: (04) 68 24 05 75; (01) 43 79 20 45 *Fax:* (04) 68 24 00 89; (01) 43 79 84 20
E-mail: contact@editions-verdier.fr
Web Site: www.editions-verdier.fr
Key Personnel
Dir, Literature: Gerard Bobillier
Founded: 1979
Subjects: Literature, Literary Criticism, Essays, Philosophy, Religion - Islamic, Religion - Jewish
ISBN Prefix(es): 2-86432
Number of titles published annually: 25 Print
Total Titles: 400 Print
Distributed by SODIS

Editions de Vergeures+
23 ave Villemain, 75014 Paris
Tel: (01) 45 43 82 60 *Fax:* (01) 45 43 81 40
Key Personnel
Manager: Robert Cauchuix
Founded: 1979
Subjects: Art, How-to
ISBN Prefix(es): 2-7309; 2-909175

Vertiges Bulles, *imprint of* Editions Dominique Leroy

Editions Vigot Universitaire
23 rue de l'Ecole de Medecine, 75006 Paris
Tel: (01) 43 29 54 50 *Fax:* (01) 46 34 05 89
E-mail: vpc@vigot.fr
Web Site: www.vigotmaloine.fr
Telex: 201708 F
Key Personnel
Man Dir: Daniel Vigot
Founded: 1890
Subjects: Medicine, Nursing, Dentistry, Sports, Athletics, Veterinary Science

ISBN Prefix(es): 2-7114
Bookshop(s): Librairie Vigot Maloine *Tel:* (01) 43 25 60 45

Editions Village Mondial+
47 bis, rue des Vinaigriers, 75010 Paris
Tel: (01) 72 74 90 00 *Fax:* (01) 42 05 22 17
E-mail: infos@pearsoned.fr
Web Site: www.pearsoneducation.fr
Key Personnel
President: Geoffrey Staines
Founded: 1995
Specialize in higher education textbooks.
Subjects: Economics, Finance, Human Relations, Management, Marketing
ISBN Prefix(es): 2-84211; 2-7440
Total Titles: 100 Print
Parent Company: Pearson Education France
Imprints: Publi Union

La Villeguerin, see Groupe Revue Fiduciaire

Editions Vilo SA
25 rue Ginoux, 75015 Paris
Tel: (01) 45 77 08 05 *Fax:* (01) 45 79 97 15
Telex: 200305 F *Cable:* Edivilo Paris
Key Personnel
Man Dir: Mme Larfillon
Subjects: Architecture & Interior Design, Art, Automotive, History, Language Arts, Linguistics, Literature, Literary Criticism, Essays, Nonfiction (General), Religion - Other, Sports, Athletics, Travel
ISBN Prefix(es): 2-7191

Editions VM+
61 bd Saint-Germain, 75240 Paris Cedex 05
Tel: (01) 44 41 11 11 *Fax:* (01) 44 41 11 85
Founded: 1965
Subjects: Photography
ISBN Prefix(es): 2-86258
Parent Company: Groupe Eyrolles
Bookshop(s): La Photo Librairie, 49 Ave de Villiers, 75017 Paris

La Voix du Regard
11 rue Henri Martin, 94200 Ivry-sur-Seine, Paris
Tel: (01) 46 70 88 69 *Fax:* (01) 46 70 88 69
E-mail: voixduregard@9online.fr
Key Personnel
President: Jocelyn Maixent *E-mail:* jocelyn.maixent@wanadoo.fr
International Rights: Pauline Jacquey
Founded: 1991
Subjects: Art, Drama, Theater, Fiction, Film, Video, Literature, Literary Criticism, Essays, Photography, Poetry, Radio, TV
ISBN Prefix(es): 2-9517982

Librairie Philosophique J Vrin+
6 place de la Sorbonne, 75005 Paris
Tel: (01) 43 54 03 47 *Fax:* (01) 43 54 48 18
E-mail: contact@vrin.fr
Web Site: www.vrin.fr
Key Personnel
Man Dir: Anne-Marie Arnaud
Founded: 1920
Publisher & Bookseller of New Books, Bookseller of Secondhand Books.
Subjects: History, Philosophy, Psychology, Psychiatry, Religion - Other, *Specializes in philosophy*
ISBN Prefix(es): 2-7116
Number of titles published annually: 50 Print; 1 CD-ROM
Total Titles: 1,500 Print
Bookshop(s): Philosophy, Law, Religion, Literature, Art & History, 75005 Paris

Librairie Vuibert+
20 rue Berbier-du-Mets, 75647 Paris Cedex 13
Tel: (01) 44 08 49 00 *Fax:* (01) 44 08 49 39
Web Site: www.vuibert.com
Telex: 201005 F Vuibpar *Cable:* VUIBERT PARIS
Key Personnel
President: Philippe Sylvestre
Founded: 1877
Subjects: Biological Sciences, Chemistry, Chemical Engineering, Earth Sciences, Economics, Law, Mathematics, Physics
ISBN Prefix(es): 2-7117
Imprints: Annales du Bac; Bac en Poche; Livre des Vacances

Galerie Lucie Weill-Seligmann
6 rue Bonaparte, 75006 Paris
Tel: (01) 43 54 71 95 *Fax:* (01) 40 51 82 88
Key Personnel
President: France Faure-Seligmann
Founded: 1930
Book Club(s): Nouveau Cercle Parisien du Livre

Editions Weka
249, rue de Crimee, 75935 Paris Cedex 19
Tel: (01) 53 35 16 16; (01) 53 35 17 17 *Fax:* (01) 53 35 17 01
E-mail: infos@weka.fr
Web Site: www.weka.fr
Telex: 210 504 f
Key Personnel
General Man: Robert Christian
Editorial: Philippe Dorenlot
Commercial (Sales Direct Marketing): Jean-Pierre Chauvet
Founded: 1979
Subjects: Computer Science, Electronics, Electrical Engineering, Labor, Industrial Relations, Law, Management, Social Sciences, Sociology
ISBN Prefix(es): 2-7337
Parent Company: Weka-Verlag, Postfach 1180, 8901 Kissing, Germany
Associate Companies: Weka Presse, 82 rue Curial, 75935 Paris
U.S. Office(s): Weka Publishing Inc, 97 Indian Field Rd, Greenwich, CT 06830, United States
50 Main St, Suite 1000, White Plains, NY 10606, United States

Galerie Esther Woerdehoff
36 rue Falguiere, 75015 Paris
Tel: (01) 43 21 44 83 *Fax:* (01) 43 21 45 03
E-mail: galerie@ewgalerie.com
Web Site: www.ewgalerie.com

YMCA-Press
11 rue de la Montagne Ste-Genevieve, 75005 Paris
Tel: (01) 43 54 74 46 *Fax:* (01) 43 25 34 79
See also Les Editeurs Reunis.
Subjects: Literature, Literary Criticism, Essays, Religion - Other
ISBN Prefix(es): 2-85065

Editions Philateliques Yvert et Tellier
37 rue des Jacobins, 80036 Amiens Cedex 1
Tel: (03) 22914171 *Fax:* (03) 22912454
Telex: 145010f
Subjects: Sports, Athletics
ISBN Prefix(es): 2-86814

French Guiana

General Information

Capital: Cayenne
Language: French and Creole
Religion: Roman Catholic
Population: 133,000
Bank Hours: 0700-1130, 1400-1600 Monday-Friday
Shop Hours: 0800-1300, 1500-1800 Monday-Friday
Currency: 100 centimes = 1 French franc
Export/Import Information: Overseas department of France, which is a member of the European Economic Community. Tariff as for France. See France for domiciliation of documents. No import licenses required. Same exchange restrictions as France.
Copyright: Berne, UCC (see Copyright Conventions, pg xi)

Guy Delabergerie Editions Sarl
BP 682, 97303 Cayenne
Tel: 311162 *Fax:* 311759
ISBN Prefix(es): 2-906262
Warehouse: ZI du Larivot Lot, Dalmuzin Haugar Briot, 97351 Matoury

French Polynesia

General Information

Capital: Papeete
Language: French (official) & Polynesian languages
Religion: Mainly Protestant & Roman Catholic
Population: 199,031
Bank Hours: 0730-1530 Monday-Friday; some 0730-1130 Saturday
Shop Hours: 0730-1100, 1400-1700 Monday-Friday; 0730-1130 Saturday
Currency: 100 centimes = 1 CFA franc
Export/Import Information: No tariff on books other than children's picture books; advertising matter subject to customs duty, import duty, although catalogues generally considered printed books. Advertising subject to Statistical Tax. Miscellaneous tax of 2% of customs value on books and advertising. No import license required. Exchange controls.

Ancre de Polynesie, *imprint of* Simone Sanchez

Scoop/Au Vent des Iles+
BP 5670, 98716 Pirae, Tahiti
Tel: 50 95 95 *Fax:* 50 95 97
E-mail: contact@tahiti-books.com
Web Site: www.tahiti-books.com
Key Personnel
Manager: Robert Christian
Founded: 1992
Membership(s): Ligne Editoriale Rattachee au Pacifique Sud, Pacific Islands Book Council.
Subjects: Biography, Cookery, Fiction, Geography, Geology, History, How-to, Literature, Literary Criticism, Essays, Mysteries, South Pacific
ISBN Prefix(es): 2-909790
Imprints: Nouvelles du Pacifique

Collection Moemoea, *imprint of* Simone Sanchez

Haere Po Editions+
BP 1958, 8713 Papeete Tahiti
Tel: 582636 *Fax:* 582333
E-mail: haerepotahiti@mail.pf
Key Personnel
Man Dir: L Shan
Founded: 1981

Subjects: Anthropology, Earth Sciences, Ethnicity, History, Language Arts, Linguistics, Natural History, Travel
ISBN Prefix(es): 2-904171

Nouvelles du Pacifique, *imprint of* Scoop/Au Vent des Iles

Simone Sanchez
BP 13973, Punaauia, Tahiti
Tel: (0689) 533260
Key Personnel
Contact: Simone Sanchez
Founded: 1993
Subjects: Fiction, History, Regional Interests
ISBN Prefix(es): 2-910256
Imprints: Ancre de Polynesie; Collection Moemoea

Scoop, see Scoop/Au Vent des Iles

Gambia

General Information

Capital: Banjul
Language: English
Religion: Predominantly Islamic
Population: 1,026,000
Bank Hours: 0800-1300 Monday-Thursday; 0800-1000 Friday-Saturday
Shop Hours: 0800 or 0900-1200, 1400-1700 Monday-Thursday; 0800 or 0900-1200, 1500-1700 Friday; 0800 or 0900-1200 Saturday
Currency: 100 butut = 1 dalasi
Export/Import Information: No tariff on books. Import tax on all. No import license required. National Trading Corporation has no monopoly. Exchange controls.
Copyright: Berne (see Copyright Conventions, pg xi)

Government Printer
PO Box 898, Printing Dept, Banjul
Tel: 227399
Telex: 2204
ISBN Prefix(es): 9983-86

Georgia

General Information

Capital: Tbilisi
Language: Georgian
Religion: Predominantly Georgian Orthodox
Population: 5.6 million
Currency: 100 tetri = 1 lari; 1 dollar = 2.23 lari
Export/Import Information: Customs duty for import, 12% to 20% of VAT.

Merani Publishing House
42, Shota Rustaveli Ave, 380008 Tbilisi
Tel: (032) 996492; (032) 935396; (032) 935554; (032) 935514 *Fax:* (032) 932996
Key Personnel
President & Dir: G E Gvertfsiteli
Editor-in-Chief: G I Alhazishvili
Commercial Manager: E G Gamezardashvili
Founded: 1925
Subjects: Regional Interests
ISBN Prefix(es): 5-515; 99928-947; 99928-946; 99928-16; 99928-948; 99928-949; 99928-950

Sakartvelo Publishing House
5 Marjanishvili St, Tbilisi
Tel: 954201; 952927
Key Personnel
Dir: D A Tcharkviani
Chief Editor: V R Djavakhadze
Founded: 1921
Subjects: Agriculture, Government, Political Science, Science (General), Social Sciences, Sociology
ISBN Prefix(es): 5-529; 99928-29

Germany

General Information

Capital: Berlin
Language: German. Sorbian speaking minority. Danish spoken by a Danish minority in South Schleswig, North Frisian in North Frisian Islands
Religion: Predominately Protestant and Roman Catholic
Population: 82.7 million
Bank Hours: 0900-1300, 1430-1600 Monday-Friday
Shop Hours: 0900-1830 Monday-Friday; 0900-1400 Saturday
Currency: 100 Eurocents = 1 Euro; 1.95583 Deutsche marks = 1 Euro
Export/Import Information: Member of the European Economic Community. No tariff on books except children's picture books from non-EEC. None on advertising to be distributed free, if exporter's country grants reciprocal treatment, otherwise charged. Import turnover tax on books and advertising. Also, 7% VAT on books. No import license required. No exchange controls.
Copyright: UCC, Berne, Florence (see Copyright Conventions, pg ix)

A Francke Verlag (Tubingen und Basel)+
Hans-Graessel-weg 13, 81375 Munich
Mailing Address: Postfach 701067, 81310 Munich
Tel: (089) 718 747 *Fax:* (089) 7142039
E-mail: info@iudicium.de
Web Site: www.geist.de
Key Personnel
Publisher: Gunter Narr
Manufacturing: Horst Schmid
Founded: 1831
Subjects: Drama, Theater, Economics, Government, Political Science, Literature, Literary Criticism, Essays, Philosophy, Psychology, Psychiatry, Social Sciences, Sociology, Theology
ISBN Prefix(es): 3-7720
Associate Companies: Gunter Narr Verlag
Branch Office(s)
Gerbergasse 48, 4001 Basel, Switzerland

Abakus Musik Barbara Fietz
Haversbach 1, 35753 Greifenstein
Tel: (06478) 2250 *Fax:* (06478) 1355
E-mail: hotline@abakus-musik.de
Web Site: www.abakus-musik.de
Key Personnel
Man Dir: Barbara Fietz *Tel:* (06478) 911060
Man Dir, Production: Siegfried Fietz
Founded: 1974
Specialize in musical & notebook publications.
Membership(s): JFPI; Borsenverein; DMV.
Subjects: Music, Dance, Religion - Other
ISBN Prefix(es): 3-88124
Total Titles: 100 E-Book; 250 Audio
Distributed by BMK Wartburg Vertriebsges mbH (Austria); Herder AG Basel (Switzerland)

ABC der Deutschen Wirtschaft, Verlagsgesellschaft mbH
Berliner Allee 8, 64295 Darmstadt
Mailing Address: Postfach 100264, 64202 Darmstadt
Tel: (06151) 38920 *Fax:* (06151) 33164; (06151) 389280
E-mail: info@abconline.de
Web Site: www.abconline.de
Key Personnel
Man Dir: Margit Selka
Publisher of industrial reference directories.
ISBN Prefix(es): 3-87000
Number of titles published annually: 3 Print
Total Titles: 5 Print
Associate Companies: ABC Europe Production; Industrischow Verlags GmbH

Accedo Verlagsgesellschaft mbH+
Verkehrsnummer 10004, 78202 Munich
Tel: (089) 935714 *Fax:* (089) 9294109
E-mail: accedoverlag@web.de
Web Site: www.accedoverlag.de
Key Personnel
Manager: Dr Manfred Holler *E-mail:* holler@econ.uni-hamburg.de
Marketing: Dr Barbara Klose-Ullmann
Founded: 1988
Subjects: Art, Economics, Geography, Geology, Government, Political Science, History, Management, Medicine, Nursing, Dentistry, Philosophy, Science (General), Social Sciences, Sociology, Art history, Medicine
ISBN Prefix(es): 3-89265
Total Titles: 50 Print
Associate Companies: Verlag Holler
Imprints: Homo Oeconomicus
Distributor for Verlag Holler

Achterbahn AG Buch+
Achterbahn AG, Werftbahnstr 8, 24143 Kiel
Tel: (0431) 7028-200 *Fax:* (0431) 7028-228
E-mail: info@achterbahn.de
Web Site: www.achterbahn.de
Key Personnel
Publisher: Christian Dreller
Manager: Jens Nieswand
Rights: Hans Kettwig
Founded: 1991
Subjects: Humor
ISBN Prefix(es): 3-928950; 3-89719
Warehouse: KVA Verlagsauslieferung, Speckenbeker Weg 116, 24113 Kiel

Joh van Acken GmbH & Co KG
Magdeburger Str 5, 47800 Krefeld
Mailing Address: Postfach 105, 47701 Krefeld
Tel: (02151) 44 00-0 *Fax:* (02151) 44 00-11
E-mail: verlag@vanacken.de
Web Site: www.spendengrusskarten.de/willkommen.html
Key Personnel
Publisher & International Rights: Ulrich Kaltenmeier
Founded: 1890
Subjects: Regional Interests
ISBN Prefix(es): 3-923140

F A Ackermanns Kunstverlag GmbH
Meglinger Str 60, 81477 Munich
Mailing Address: Postfach 71 01 08, 81451 Munich
Tel: (089) 78580826 *Fax:* (089) 78580828
E-mail: info@ackermann-kalender.de
Web Site: www.ackermann-kalender.de *Cable:* KUNSTACKERMANN MUNICH
Key Personnel
Man Dir: Michael G Kathan
Founded: 1806
Specialize in calendars.
Subjects: Art, Photography

ISBN Prefix(es): 3-8173; 3-87002
Number of titles published annually: 100 Print

Addison Wesley Verlag, see Pearson Education Deutschland GmbH

Adyar Edition, *imprint of* Aquamarin Verlag

Adyar Verlag, *imprint of* Aquamarin Verlag

Aerogie-Verlag+
Fliessstr 20/21, 12526 Berlin
Tel: (030) 6 76 32 00 *Fax:* (030) 6 76 32 00
Key Personnel
Man Dir: Gerd Otto
Founded: 1990
Specialize in Environmental Energy.
Subjects: Energy, Engineering (General), Environmental Studies, Science (General), Transportation
ISBN Prefix(es): 3-910142
Associate Companies: Ingenieurbuero fuer Windenergie und Schadstofffreie Energetik

Aethera, *imprint of* Verlag Freies Geistesleben

The African Literature Club+
Ladenburgerstr 50, 69120 Heidelberg
Mailing Address: Postfach 1320, 69193 Schriesheim
Tel: (06221) 411861 *Fax:* (06221) 411861
Key Personnel
Man Dir: Jerry Bedu-Addo *E-mail:* jbeduaddo@aol.com
Founded: 1982
Book publication & distribution.
Subjects: Africa
ISBN Prefix(es): 3-927198
Associate Companies: Timbuktu, Ladenburgerstr 50, 69120 Heidelberg
Branch Office(s)
Books on African Studies, PO Box BT, 328, Tema, Ghana *Tel:* (022) 206135 *Fax:* (022) 206134 *E-mail:* beaddo@ghana.com
Book Club(s): African Literature Club, Ladenburgerstr 50, Heidelberg 69120, Contact: Eva Groppenbaecher *Tel:* (06221) 411861 *Fax:* (06221) 473946 *E-mail:* evagroppe@aol.com

Agentur des Rauhen Hauses Hamburg GmbH
Beim Bruederhof 8, 22844 Norderstedt
Tel: (040) 53 53 88-0 *Fax:* (040) 53 53 88-43
E-mail: kundenservice@agentur-rauhes-haus.de
Web Site: www.agentur-rauhes-haus.de
Key Personnel
Man Dir: Willi Kohlmann
Rights & Permissions: Hans-Heinrich Holm
Cataloging: Ms Schrom
Founded: 1842
Subjects: Religion - Protestant, Religion - Other, Theology
ISBN Prefix(es): 3-7600
Divisions: Reise-und Versandbuchhandlung des Rauhen Hauses

AGIS Verlag GmbH
Ooser Luisenstr 23, 76532 Baden-Baden
Mailing Address: Postfach 22 20, 76492 Baden-Baden
Tel: (07221) 95 75-0 *Fax:* (07221) 6 68 10
E-mail: info@agis-verlag.de
Web Site: www.agis-verlag.de *Cable:* AGIS BADEN BADEN
Key Personnel
Man Dir: Karl G Fischer; Karin Grochowiak
Media consulting.
Subjects: Art, Philosophy, Science (General)
ISBN Prefix(es): 3-87007

Ahriman-Verlag GmbH+
Stuebeweg 60, 79108 Freiburg
Mailing Address: Postfach 6569, 79041 Freiburg
Tel: (0761) 502303 *Fax:* (0761) 502247
E-mail: ahriman@t-online.de
Web Site: www.ahriman.com
Key Personnel
Man Dir: Edeltraud Rudow *E-mail:* thanilo@t-online.de
Founded: 1983
Subjects: Government, Political Science, History, Psychology, Psychiatry, Religion - Other, Science (General)
ISBN Prefix(es): 3-922774; 3-89484
Total Titles: 1 Print; 1 CD-ROM; 20 Audio

aid infodienst - Verbraucherdienst, Ernaehrung, Landwirtschaft eV
Friedrich-Ebert-Str 3, 53177 Bonn - Bad Godesberg
Tel: (0228) 8499-0 *Fax:* (0228) 8499-177
E-mail: aid@aid.de
Web Site: www.aid.de
Key Personnel
Man Dir: Dr Margret Buening-Fesel

Air Gallery Edition, Helmut Kreuzer
Goethestr 8, 85435 Erding
Mailing Address: Postfach 1526, 85425 Erding
Tel: (08122) 84487 *Fax:* (08122) 84487
Key Personnel
President: Helmut Kreuzer
Founded: 1988
Subjects: Aeronautics, Aviation
ISBN Prefix(es): 3-9802101; 3-9805934

Aisthesis Verlag+
Oberntorwall 21 (Eingang Mauerstr), 33602 Bielefeld
Tel: (0521) 172604 *Fax:* (0521) 172812
E-mail: aisthesis@bitel.net
Web Site: www.aisthesis.de
Key Personnel
Man Dir, Rights & Permissions: Dr Detlev Kopp; Dr Michael Vogt
Founded: 1985
Subjects: Art, History, Literature, Literary Criticism, Essays, Philosophy, Science (General)
ISBN Prefix(es): 3-925670; 3-89528

Akademie Schloss Solitude, see Merz & Solitude - Akademie Schloss Solitude

Akademie Verlag GmbH+
Palisadenstr 40, 10243 Berlin
Tel: (030) 4 22 00 60 *Fax:* (030) 422 00 657
E-mail: info@akademie-verlag.de
Web Site: www.akademie-verlag.de
Key Personnel
Man Dir: Dr Gerd Giesler *E-mail:* giesler@akademie-verlag.de
Founded: 1946
Membership(s): the Association of German Booksellers.
Subjects: History, Language Arts, Linguistics, Literature, Literary Criticism, Essays, Philosophy, Social Sciences, Sociology
ISBN Prefix(es): 3-05; 3-922251
Parent Company: R Oldenbourg Verlag Muenchen, Rosenheimerstr 145, 81671 Munich
Distribution Center: Publisher Service Munich, PO Box 1280, 82197 Munich *Fax:* (08105) 388 100
Orders to: Verlegerdienst Muenchen, Gutenbergstr 1, 82205 Gilching

akg-images gmbh+
Formerly Archiv fuer Kunst & Geschichte Bilderdienst & Verlagsgesellschaft mbH
Teutonenstr 22, 14129 Berlin
Tel: (030) 80485200 *Fax:* (030) 80485500
E-mail: info@akg.de; info@akg-images.com
Web Site: www.akg-images.com
Key Personnel
Contact: Kathrin Goepel
Founded: 1945
Picture library, collection, documentation.
Subjects: Art, History, Photojournalism
ISBN Prefix(es): 3-88912
Associate Companies: akg-images Ltd, London, United Kingdom; akg-images SAR, Paris, France

M Akselrad+
Hauptstr 190, 69117 Heidelberg
Tel: (06221) 183030 *Fax:* (06221) 181223
E-mail: makselrad@gmx.net
Key Personnel
Dir: Michael Akselrad
Founded: 1972
Subjects: Literature, Literary Criticism, Essays, Nonfiction (General)
ISBN Prefix(es): 3-921265

Alba Fachverlag GmbH & Co KG+
Willstaetterstr 9, 40549 Duesseldorf
Mailing Address: Postfach 11 01 50, 40501 Duesseldorf
Tel: (0211) 5 20 13-0 *Fax:* (0211) 5 20 13-28
E-mail: oepnv@alba.verlag.de
Web Site: www.alba-verlag.de
Telex: 8585536
Key Personnel
Publishing Dir: Robert Braun
Man Dir, Rights & Permissions: Alf Teloeken *Tel:* (0211) 5 20 13-10 *E-mail:* at@alba-verlag.de
Manager: Tim Teloeken *Tel:* (0211) 5 20 13-12 *E-mail:* teloeken@alba-verlag.de
Sales, Publicity: Willi Lennartz; Cornelia Honekamp
Production: P Gerens
Founded: 1951
Subjects: Crafts, Games, Hobbies, Film, Video, Outdoor Recreation
ISBN Prefix(es): 3-87094
Associate Companies: Alba Publikation Alf Teloeken GmbH und Co KG; Schwesterngesellschaft: Alba Fachverlag GmbH & Co KG

Albarello Verlag GmbH+
Dornaperstr 23, 42327 Wuppertal
Tel: (0202) 2058 8279 *Fax:* (0202) 2058 80534
Web Site: www.vier-v.de
Founded: 2001

Verlag Karl Alber GmbH+
Hermann-Herder-Str 4, 79104 Freiburg im Breisgau
Tel: (0761) 27 17-436 *Fax:* (0761) 27 17-212
E-mail: info@verlag-alber.de
Web Site: www.verlag-alber.de
Key Personnel
Man Dir: Lukas Trabert
Founded: 1939
Subjects: History, Philosophy
ISBN Prefix(es): 3-495
Number of titles published annually: 30 Print
Total Titles: 400 Print
Parent Company: Verlag Herder
Orders to: Verlagsauslieferung Koch, Neff & Oetinger, Schockenriedstr 39, Postfach 800620, 70565 Stuttgart

Albert Nauck & Co
Luxemburgerstr 449, 50939 Cologne
Tel: (0221) 94373-0 *Fax:* (0221) 94373-901
Key Personnel
Contact: A Gallus; J Kuth
ISBN Prefix(es): 3-87574

Albino Verlag, *imprint of* Bruno Gmuender Verlag GmbH

E Albrecht Verlags-KG+
Freihamer Str 2, 82166 Graefelfing
Mailing Address: Postfach 11 40, 82153 Graefelfing
Tel: (089) 85853-0 *Fax:* (089) 85853199
E-mail: av@albrecht.de
Key Personnel
Man Dir & Publisher: Hansgeorg Albrecht
Publisher: Oliver Albrecht
Founded: 1927
Subjects: Career Development, Sports, Athletics
ISBN Prefix(es): 3-87014

Verlag und Antiquariat Frank Albrecht
Panoramastr 4, 69198 Schriesheim
Tel: (06203) 65713 *Fax:* (06203) 65311
E-mail: albrecht@antiquariat.com
Web Site: www.antiquariat.com
Key Personnel
Publisher: Frank Albrecht
Founded: 1985
Membership(s): PEN International & German Antiques.
Subjects: Government, Political Science, History, Literature, Literary Criticism, Essays
ISBN Prefix(es): 3-926360
Total Titles: 1 Print

Alexander Verlag Berlin+
Postfach 191824, 14008 Berlin
Tel: (030) 3021826 *Fax:* (030) 3029408
E-mail: info@alexander-verlag.com
Web Site: www.alexander-verlag.com
Key Personnel
Owner: Alexander Wewerka *E-mail:* wewerka@alexander-verlag.com
Founded: 1983
Subjects: Drama, Theater, Film, Video, Literature, Literary Criticism, Essays, Music, Dance
ISBN Prefix(es): 3-923854; 3-89581
Total Titles: 85 Print; 8 CD-ROM; 3 Audio
Distributed by AVA-Buch 2000 (Switzerland); AS Verlagsservice Holler (Austria)
Orders to: Sova, Friesstr 20-24, 60388 Frankfurt am Main, Contact: Brigitte Platteel *Tel:* (069) 410211 *Fax:* (069) 410280 *E-mail:* sovaffm@t-online.de

Alibaba Verlag GmbH+
Nordendstr 20, 60318 Frankfurt am Main
Tel: (069) 590097 *Fax:* (069) 559855
E-mail: alibaba@alibaba-verlag.de
Web Site: www.alibaba-verlag.de
Key Personnel
International Rights: Anne Teuter
Contact: Abraham Teuter
Founded: 1980
Subjects: Art, Literature, Literary Criticism, Essays
ISBN Prefix(es): 3-922723; 3-927926; 3-86042
Imprints: Krimi-Reihe
Distributed by Sova

Alkor-Edition Kassel GmbH+
Heinrich-Schuetz-Allee 35, 34131 Kassel
Tel: (0561) 3105-282 *Fax:* (0561) 37755
E-mail: alkor-edition@baerenreiter.com
Web Site: www.alkor-edition.com
Key Personnel
Man Dir: Barbara Scheuch-Voetterle
Founded: 1934
Subjects: Music, Dance
ISBN Prefix(es): 3-920018
Distributed by Baerenreiter Ltd (Great Britain, Ireland, New Zealand & Australia); Baerenreiter Music Corporation (Canada & US); Editio Baerenreiter Praha (Slovakian & Czech Republic); Casa Musicale Sonzogno (Italy); Faber Music Distribution (Great Britain, Ireland, New Zealand & Australia); Hartai Music Agency (Hungary); Muziekhandel Albersen & Co (Netherlands); Polskie Wydawnictwo Muzyczne (PWM) (Germany & Austria); SEEMSA (Spain & Portugal); Zamp (Croatia & Slovenia)
Distributor for Editio Baerenreiter Praha (Germany, Austria & Switzerland); Baerenreiter Verlag Kassel (Basel, London, New York, Prag) (Worldwide); Gustav Bosse Verlag Kassel (Worldwide); Dilia Prag (Germany, Austria, Switerland, Benelux countries, Scandinavia); Faber Music London (Germany, Austria & Switzerland); Henle Verlag Muenchen (Worldwide); Henschel Verlag fuer Musik Berlin (Worldwide); Editions Henry Lemoine Paris (Germany, Austria & Switzerland); Musikwissenschaftlicher Verlag Wien (Worldwide with the exception of Austria); Polskie Wydawnictwo Muzyczne (PWM) (Germany & Austria); Slowakischer Musikfonds Bratislava (Germany, Austria, Switerland, Benelux countries); Strauss Edition Wien (Worldwide); Sueddeutscher Musikverlag Heidelberg (Worldwide); Tschechischer Musikfonds Praha (Germany, Austria, Switzerland, Benelux countries, Scandinavia, Spain & Portugal)

Alouette Verlag+
Uferstr 41, 22113 Oststeinbek
Tel: (040) 712 23 53 *Fax:* (040) 713 41 88
E-mail: webmaster@alouette-verlag.de
Web Site: www.alouette-verlag.de
Key Personnel
President & Publisher: Juergen F Boden *E-mail:* juergen.boden@alouette-verlag.de
Editor: Elke Emshoff
Art Dir: Petra Horn
Founded: 1983
Book & film publishers
Specialize in nature-oriented picture & text books (pictorials with profound text matter) mainly about North America, the Arctic & Siberia, TV documentaries & cultural books.
Subjects: Natural History, Travel, Foreign Cultures
ISBN Prefix(es): 3-924324
Number of titles published annually: 2 Print; 2 Audio
Total Titles: 20 Print; 4 Audio

Alpha Literatur Verlag/Alpha Presse
August-Siebertstr 9, 60323 Frankfurt
Tel: (069) 555325 *Fax:* (069) 955130-99
Key Personnel
Man Dir: Dr Gisela Philipps
Founded: 1969
Subjects: Drama, Theater, Poetry
ISBN Prefix(es): 3-924510

ALS-Verlag GmbH+
Voltastr 3, 63128 Dietzenbach
Mailing Address: Postfach 1440, 63114 Dietzenbach
Tel: (06074) 82 16-0; (06074) 82 16-50 (orders) *Fax:* (06074) 2 73 22
E-mail: info@als-verlag.de
Web Site: www.als-verlag.de
Key Personnel
Man Dir: Juergen Hils
Founded: 1967
Subjects: Art, Crafts, Games, Hobbies, Education, Environmental Studies, How-to, Outdoor Recreation
ISBN Prefix(es): 3-89135; 3-921366
Imprints: Dietzenbach

Altberliner Verlag GmbH+
Neue Schoenhauser Str 8, 10178 Berlin (Mitte)
Tel: (030) 284 992-0 *Fax:* (030) 284 992-20
E-mail: presse@altberliner.de
Web Site: www.altberliner.de
Key Personnel
Owner: Dr Stephan Schmidt
Owner & Dir: Renate Nickl
Founded: 1945
Subjects: Developing Countries, Fiction, Literature, Literary Criticism, Essays, Mysteries
ISBN Prefix(es): 3-357
Branch Office(s)
Zentuerstr 19, 80798 Munich *Tel:* (089) 1 23 62-59 *Fax:* (089) 12 779 954 *E-mail:* vertrieb@altberliner.de

Anneliese Althoff, see Asso Verlag

Aluminium-Verlag Marketing & Kommunikation GmbH
Aachener Str 172, 40223 Duesseldorf
Fax: (0211) 15 91-379
E-mail: info@alu-verlag.de
Web Site: www.alu-verlag.de
Key Personnel
Man Dir: Werner Lenzen *Tel:* (0211) 15 91-370 *E-mail:* w.lenzen@alu-verlag.de
Sales Manager: Anne Tappen *Tel:* (0211) 15 91-371 *E-mail:* a.tappen@alu-verlag.de
Seminar & Advertising Manager: Christiane Czech *Tel:* (0211) 15 91-372 *E-mail:* c.czech@alu-verlag.de
Founded: 1953
Subjects: Earth Sciences
ISBN Prefix(es): 3-87017
Number of titles published annually: 3 CD-ROM
Total Titles: 17 Print; 3 CD-ROM

Anabas-Verlag Guenter Kaempf GmbH & Co KG+
Friesstr 20-24, 60388 Frankfurt
Tel: (069) 94 21 98 71 *Fax:* (069) 94 21 98 72
E-mail: info@anabas-verlag.com
Key Personnel
Man Dir: Guenter Kaempf
Founded: 1966
Membership(s): Borsenverein des Deutschen Buchandles, Hessischer Buchhandler- und Verlegerverband.
Subjects: Art, History, Poetry, Travel
ISBN Prefix(es): 3-87038
Number of titles published annually: 10 Print
Total Titles: 315 Print
Foreign Rep(s): Pierre Bachofner (Switzerland); Seth Meyer-Bruhns (Austria)
Orders to: Sozialistische Verlagsauslieferung GmbH, Friesstr 20-22, 60388 Frankfurt am Main *Tel:* (069) 410211 *Fax:* (069) 410280 *E-mail:* sovaffm@t-online.de

Angelika und Lothar Binding
Gaisbergstr 68, 69115 Heidelberg
Tel: (06221) 20955 *Fax:* (06221) 181846
E-mail: Angelika.Binding@gmx.net
Web Site: www.binding-singles.de
Key Personnel
Owner: Angelika Binding *E-mail:* angelika.binding@gmx.net; Lothar Binding
Founded: 1984
Subjects: Music, Dance
ISBN Prefix(es): 3-9804710
Total Titles: 2 Print

Anrich Verlag GmbH+
Werderstr 10, 69469 Weinheim
Mailing Address: Postfach 100154, 69441 Weinheim
Tel: (06201) 6007-0 *Fax:* (06201) 17464
Key Personnel
Man Dir: Gerold Anrich *E-mail:* g.anrich@beltz.de
Founded: 1970
Membership(s): Arbeitsgemeinschaft von Jugend Buchverlegern in Der Brd eV.
ISBN Prefix(es): 3-920110; 3-89106

Antex Verlag-Hans Joachin Schuhmacher+
Am Gabelsee, 15306 Falkenhagen
Tel: (033603) 40410 *Fax:* (033603) 40400

Key Personnel
Publisher: Hajo Schuhmacher
Sales: Heidi Schuhmacher
Author: Tina Rau
Founded: 1988
ISBN Prefix(es): 3-9801871

Antiqua-Verlag GmbH
Dorneckstr 3a, 79793 Wutoeschingen-Horheim
Tel: (07746) 2273 *Fax:* (07746) 2260
Key Personnel
Manager: Ottfried Ludwig
Founded: 1977
Subjects: Geography, Geology, Medicine, Nursing, Dentistry
ISBN Prefix(es): 3-88210

Antiquariats-Union Vertriebs GmbH & Co KG
Luener Rennbahn 14, 21339 Lueneburg
Tel: (04131) 983504 *Fax:* (04131) 9835595
E-mail: webmaster@restauflagen.de
Web Site: www.restauflagen.de
Key Personnel
Contact: Jens Harelberg *E-mail:* harelberg@antiquariats-union.de
Number of titles published annually: 15 Print
Total Titles: 70 Print

Anzeigenverwaltung & Herstellung, *imprint of* Johann Wolfgang Goethe Universitat

AOL-Verlag Frohmut Menze
Waldstr 18, 77839 Lichtenau-Scherzheim
Tel: (07227) 95 88-0 *Fax:* (07227) 95 88-95
E-mail: info@aol-verlag.de; bestellung@aol-verlag.de
Web Site: www.aol-verlag.de
Key Personnel
Man Dir: Frohmut Menze *Fax:* (07227) 95 88-22 *E-mail:* frohmut.menze@aol-verlag.de
Advertising: Ute Hettel *Fax:* (07227) 95 88-21 *E-mail:* ute.hettel@aol-verlag.de
Sales: Thomas Hofmann *Tel:* (07227) 95 88-94 *E-mail:* thomas.hofmann@aol-verlag.de; Gisela Korn *Tel:* (07227) 95 88-31 *E-mail:* gisela.korn@aol-verlag.de
Subjects: Advertising, Art, Biological Sciences, Career Development, Chemistry, Chemical Engineering, Child Care & Development, Computer Science, Drama, Theater, Education, Energy, English as a Second Language, Environmental Studies, Fiction, Film, Video, Foreign Countries, Government, Political Science, Health, Nutrition, History, Literature, Literary Criticism, Essays, Management, Mathematics, Natural History, Nonfiction (General), Outdoor Recreation, Physical Sciences, Physics, Science (General), Sports, Athletics, Transportation
ISBN Prefix(es): 3-89111

Verlag APHAIA Svea Haske, Sonja Schumann GbR
Radickestr 44, 12489 Berlin-Treptow
Tel: (030) 813 39 98 *Fax:* (030) 813 39 98
E-mail: info@aphaia-verlag.de
Web Site: www.aphaia-verlag.de
Key Personnel
Contact: Svea Haske; Sonja Schumann
Founded: 1986
Subjects: Art, Literature, Literary Criticism, Essays, Music, Dance, Poetry, Bookart, Literature, Lyrics, Music
ISBN Prefix(es): 3-926677
Number of titles published annually: 5 Print
Total Titles: 125 Print
Distributor for Friedrich Nolte Verlag; Paian Verlag
Orders to: Aphaia Verlag, Berlin-Treptow

Apollo-Verlag Paul Lincke GmbH
Weihergarten 5, 55116 Mainz
Mailing Address: Postfach 3640, 55026 Mainz
Tel: (06131) 246300 *Fax:* (06131) 246861
E-mail: apollo@schott-musik.de
Key Personnel
Contact: Dr Christian Sprang
Subjects: Music, Dance
ISBN Prefix(es): 3-920030
Sales Office(s): SMD Schott Music Distribution GmbH, Carl Zeissstr 1, 55129 Mainz

Aquamarin Verlag+
Muehlenstr 43, 85567 Grafing
Tel: (08092) 9444 *Fax:* (08092) 1614
E-mail: aquamarin-verlag@t-online.de
Key Personnel
Man Dir: Dr Peter Michel
Founded: 1980
Subjects: Art, Astrology, Occult, Parapsychology, Philosophy, Religion - Buddhist, Religion - Hindu, Science (General)
ISBN Prefix(es): 3-922936; 3-89427
Imprints: Adyar Edition; Adyar Verlag; Sulamith Wulfing Edition; Sulamith Wulfing Verlag
U.S. Office(s): Bluestar, 160 Camino Don Miguel, Orinda, CA 94563, United States, Contact: Petra Michel *Tel:* 925-386-0440 *Fax:* 925-386-0386 *Web Site:* www.bluestar.com
Foreign Rep(s): Dr Fiuliana Bernardi (Italy)
Foreign Rights: Katia Schume (Portugal, South America, Spain)

arani-Verlag GmbH+
Gneisenaustr 23, 10961 Berlin
Mailing Address: Postfach 610494, 10928 Berlin
Tel: (030) 691-7073 *Fax:* (030) 691-4067
Key Personnel
Man Dir: Volker Spiess
Founded: 1947
Subjects: History, Regional Interests, Religion - Jewish, Judaica
ISBN Prefix(es): 3-7605
Associate Companies: Haude und Spenersche Verlagsbuchhandlung; Wissenschaftsverlag Volker Spiess GmbH
Orders to: VAH-Jager Verlagsauslieferungen, Miraustr 54, 13509 Berlin

Arbeiterpresse Verlags- und Vertriebsgesellschaft mbH+
Postfach 500105, 45055 Essen
Tel: (0201) 6462106 *Fax:* (0201) 6462108
E-mail: vertrieb@arbeiterpresse.de
Web Site: www.arbeiterpresse.de
Key Personnel
Contact: Wolfgang Zimmermann *E-mail:* wz@arbeiterpresse.de
Founded: 1979
Subjects: Government, Political Science, History, Labor, Industrial Relations, Social Sciences, Sociology
ISBN Prefix(es): 3-88634
Number of titles published annually: 4 Print
Total Titles: 32 Print
U.S. Office(s): Mehring Books, PO Box 48377, Oak Park, MI 48237, United States *Tel:* 967-2924 *Fax:* 967-3023 *E-mail:* inquiries@mehring.com

Arbeitsgruppe LOK Report eV
Sigmaringerstr 26, 10713 Berlin
Tel: (030) 86 40 92 63 *Fax:* (030) 86 40 92 64
E-mail: redaktion@lok-report.de
Web Site: www.lok-report.de
Key Personnel
Chief Editor: Martin Stertz
Founded: 1972
Specialize in transport, railways, locomotive, German & Eastern European railways
Publish monthly railway magazine *Lok Report*.
Subjects: Transportation, Locomotives, Railways
ISBN Prefix(es): 3-921980

Number of titles published annually: 2 Print
Total Titles: 6 Print

Arcadia Verlag GmbH+
Johnsallee 23, 20148 Hamburg
Tel: (040) 4141000 *Fax:* (040) 41410041
E-mail: contact@sikorski.de
Web Site: www.sikorski.de
Key Personnel
Man Dir: Dagmar Sikorski; Prof Hans-Wilfred Sikorski
Rights & Permissions: Karl-Hermann Adrio
Founded: 1935
Subjects: Drama, Theater, Music, Dance
ISBN Prefix(es): 3-920033
Parent Company: Buehnen-und Musikverlage Dr Sikorski KG

Archiv fuer Kunst & Geschichte Bilderdienst & Verlagsgesellschaft mbH, see akg-images gmbh

ARCult Media+
Affiliate of ERICarts - European Institute for Comparative Cultural Research
Dahlmannstr 26, 53113 Bonn
Tel: (0228) 211059 *Fax:* (0228) 217493
E-mail: info@arcultmedia.de
Web Site: www.arcultmedia.de; www.kulturforschung.de; www.ericarts.org
Key Personnel
Dir: Dr Andreas Joh Wiesand
Contact: Ingo Bruenglinghaus
Founded: 1969
Publications & research documents in all fields of the arts & culture industries.
Subjects: Art, Developing Countries, Drama, Theater, Journalism, Management, Music, Dance, Outdoor Recreation, Publishing & Book Trade Reference, Radio, TV, Social Sciences, Sociology, Women's Studies
ISBN Prefix(es): 3-930395
Total Titles: 55 Print; 2 CD-ROM; 5 Online
Branch Office(s)
Vienna, Austria
Berlin
Distributed by C H Beck (Munich); Leske & Budrich (Opladen); Sam's Books (Services for Arts Management)

Ardey-Verlag GmbH
An den Speichern 6, 48157 Muenster
Tel: (0251) 4132-0 *Fax:* (0251) 4132-20
Web Site: www.ardey-verlag.de
Key Personnel
Man Dir: Bodo Strotötte
Publisher: Ulrich Grabowsky
Founded: 1951
Subjects: Architecture & Interior Design, Art, Geography, Geology, History, Literature, Literary Criticism, Essays, Nonfiction (General), Regional Interests, Religion - Other
ISBN Prefix(es): 3-87023
Orders to: CVK, Kammeratsheide 66, 33609 Bielefeld

Arena Verlag GmbH+
Rottendorferstr 16, 97074 Wuerzburg
Mailing Address: Postfach 5169, 97001 Wuerzburg
Tel: (0931) 79 644-0 *Fax:* (0931) 79 644-13
Key Personnel
Man Dir: Juergen Weidenbach
Publicity: Dirk Meyer
Sales Dir: Albrecht Oldenbourg
Production: Winfried Popp
Foreign Rights: Monika Obrist *Tel:* (0931) 73644-62 *E-mail:* monika.obrist@arena-verlag.de
Founded: 1949
Subjects: Fiction, Nonfiction (General)
ISBN Prefix(es): 3-401; 3-88155
Number of titles published annually: 500 Print
Total Titles: 2,000 Print

GERMANY

Parent Company: Georg Westermann GmbH & Co, Georg-Westermann-Allee 66, 38104 Braunschweig
Imprints: Edition Buecherbar im Arena Verlag; Ensslin Verlag im Arena Verlag
Warehouse: VSB Verlagsservice Braunschweig GmbH, Georg-Westermann-Allee 66, 38104 Braunschweig

Argon Verlag GmbH+
Unit of S Fischer Verlag
Neuenburgerstr 17, 10969 Berlin
Tel: (030) 25 37 38-0 *Fax:* (030) 25 37 38-99
E-mail: info.argon@fischerverlage.de
Web Site: www.fischerverlage.de
Key Personnel
Editor-in-Chief: Hans Christian Rohr *Tel:* (030) 25 37 38-24 *E-mail:* christian.rohr@fischerverlage.de
Founded: 1952
Subjects: Fiction, Nonfiction (General)
ISBN Prefix(es): 3-87024; 3-930088
Orders to: S Fischer Verlag, 60591 Frankfurt/Main *Tel:* (069) 60620 *Fax:* (069) 6062214 *E-mail:* verkauf@fischerverlage.de

Argument-Verlag+
Eppendorfer Weg 95a, 20259 Hamburg
Tel: (040) 401800-0 *Fax:* (040) 401800-20
E-mail: verlag@argument.de
Web Site: www.argument.de
Key Personnel
Contact: Bettina Fischer; Wolfgang Fritz Haug; Frigga Haug
Founded: 1959
Subjects: Fiction, Gay & Lesbian, Government, Political Science, Philosophy, Science Fiction, Fantasy, Social Sciences, Sociology, Women's Studies
ISBN Prefix(es): 3-88619; 3-920037
Divisions: Redaktion

Aries-Verlag Paul Johannes Muller+
Ringstr 32a, 83355 Grabenstaett
Mailing Address: Postfach 166, 83355 Grabenstaett
Tel: (08661) 8209 *Fax:* (08661) 985980
Key Personnel
Owner: Paul J Mueller *E-mail:* pjm@aires-verlag.de
Founded: 1965
Subjects: Architecture & Interior Design, Art
ISBN Prefix(es): 3-920041

Ariston, *imprint of* Heinrich Hugendubel Verlag GmbH

Arkana Verlag Tete Boettger Rainer Wunderlich GmbH+
Hainbundstr 17, 37085 Goettingen
Mailing Address: Postfach 1140, 37001 Goettingen
Tel: (0551) 41709 *Fax:* (0551) 43868
Key Personnel
Owner: Mr T Boettger *E-mail:* teteboettger@t-online.de
Founded: 1981
Subjects: Art, History, Science (General), History of Science
ISBN Prefix(es): 3-923257

Arnoldsche Verlagsanstalt GmbH (Arnoldsche Art Publishers)+
Liststr 9, 70180 Stuttgart
Tel: (0711) 645618-0 *Fax:* (0711) 645618-79
E-mail: art@arnoldsche.com
Web Site: www.arnoldsche.com
Key Personnel
International Rights: Dieter Zuehlsdorff
Marketing, Distribution & Public Relations: Dirk Allgaier *Tel:* (0711) 645618-20 *E-mail:* allgaier@arnoldsche.com
Founded: 1988
Subjects: Antiques, Architecture & Interior Design, Art, Fashion, Photography, Specialize in jewelry, glass, porcelain, Asian art & Non-European Art
ISBN Prefix(es): 3-925369; 3-89790
Number of titles published annually: 15 Print
Total Titles: 80 Print
Associate Companies: Forum fuer Europaeische Kunst und Kultur, Stuttgart
U.S. Office(s): Antique Collectors' Club Ltd, 51 Market St, Industrial Park, Wappings Falls, NY 12590, United States *Tel:* 845-297-0003 *Fax:* 845-297-0068

Ars Edition GmbH+
Friedrichstr 9, 80801 Munich
Mailing Address: Postfach 430151, 80731 Munich
Tel: (089) 3810060 *Fax:* (089) 381006-58
Key Personnel
Man Dir: Marcel Nauer
Man Dir, Rights & Permissions: Sabine Lippert
Production: Gregor Schulze
Public Relations: Birgit Welzel
Founded: 1896
Subjects: Art, Child Care & Development, Cookery, Crafts, Games, Hobbies, Fiction, House & Home, Nonfiction (General), Romance
ISBN Prefix(es): 3-7607
Subsidiaries: Ars Edition

Ars Vivendi Verlag+
Bauhof 1, 90556 Cadolzburg
Mailing Address: Postfach 9, 90553 Cadolzburg
Tel: (09103) 719 29 0 *Fax:* (09103) 719 59 19
E-mail: ars@arsvivendi.com
Web Site: www.arsvivendi.com
Key Personnel
Owner: Norbert Treuheit
Founded: 1988
Subjects: Cookery, Nonfiction (General), Travel
ISBN Prefix(es): 3-927482; 3-931043; 3-89716

Art Directors Club Verlag GmbH
Leibnizstr 65, 10629 Berlin-Charlottenburg
Tel: (030) 59 00 31 0 *Fax:* (030) 59 00 31 0
E-mail: adc@adc.de
Web Site: www.adc.de
Key Personnel
Manager: Elly Koszytorz; Susann Schronen *Tel:* (030) 59 22 31 0-21 *Fax:* (030) 59 22 31 0-21 *E-mail:* susann.schronen@adc.de
Project Manager: Astrid Hegenauer *Tel:* (030) 59 00 31 0-21 *Fax:* (030) 59 00 31 0-21 *E-mail:* astrid.hegenauer@adc.de
Project Management Events/Seminars: Katrin Puelacher *Tel:* (030) 59 00 31 0-21 *Fax:* (030) 59 00 31 0-21 *E-mail:* katrin.puelacher@adc.de
Founded: 1964
Art Directors Club is only licenser.
Subjects: Advertising, Communications
ISBN Prefix(es): 3-87439
Orders to: Universitaetsdruckerei und Verlag Hermann Schmidt Mainz, Robert-Kochstr 8, 55214 Mainz *Tel:* (06131) 506030 *Fax:* (06131) 506080

Artcolor+
Ostenallee 78, 59071 Hamm
Tel: (02381) 980190 *Fax:* (02381) 9801999
Key Personnel
Rights & Permissions: Christof Kaplanek
Contact: Wilhelm Spindelndreier
Founded: 1987
Specialize in postcards, books, travel & pictures.
Subjects: Art, Cookery, Photography, Regional Interests, Travel
ISBN Prefix(es): 3-89743; 3-923166

BOOK

Associate Companies: Eggenkamp Verlagsgesellschaft mbH
Distributed by Buchzentrum (Switzerland); Olten (Switzerland); Schweizer (Switzerland)
Warehouse: Verlagsservice Braunschweig, Westermannallee 66, 38104 Braunschweig *Tel:* (0531) 708646

Arun-Verlag+
Ortsstr 28, 07407 Engerda
Tel: (036743) 233-0 *Fax:* (036743) 233-17
E-mail: info@arun-verlag.de
Web Site: www.arun-verlag.de
Key Personnel
Publisher: Stefan Ulbrich
Founded: 1989
Subjects: Astrology, Occult, Native American Studies, Philosophy, Religion - Other
ISBN Prefix(es): 3-927940; 3-935581
Total Titles: 50 Print

Roland Asanger Verlag GmbH
Boedldorf 3, 84178 Kroening
Tel: (08744) 7262 *Fax:* (08744) 967755
E-mail: verlag@asanger.de
Web Site: www.asanger.de
Key Personnel
Publisher: Dr Gerd Wenninger
Founded: 1987
Subjects: Environmental Studies, Health, Nutrition, Psychology, Psychiatry, Social Sciences, Sociology
ISBN Prefix(es): 3-89334
Distributed by Herder AG Basel
Distribution Center: Publishing House Service Southwest *Tel:* (07254) 507-0 *Fax:* (07254) 507-24 *E-mail:* verlagsservicesw@tonline.de
Orders to: Verlagsservice Suedwest, Boschstr 2, 68753 Waghaeusel *Tel:* (07254) 507 13 *Fax:* (07254) 507 24 *E-mail:* verlagsservice-sw@t-online.de

Aschendorffsche Verlagsbuchhandlung GmbH & Co KG+
Soester Str 13, 48135 Muenster
Tel: (0251) 690101 *Fax:* (0251) 690143
E-mail: buchverlag@aschendorff.de
Web Site: www.aschendorff.de/buch
Telex: 892555
Key Personnel
Contact: Dr Eduard Huffer; Dr Jurgeu Beuedikt Huffer
Founded: 1720
Membership(s): VGS - Verlagsgesellschaft mbH & Co KG.
Subjects: History, Language Arts, Linguistics, Philosophy, Psychology, Psychiatry, Regional Interests, Religion - Other, Theology
ISBN Prefix(es): 3-402
Number of titles published annually: 80 Print; 2 CD-ROM

Asclepios Edition Lothar Baus+
Zum Lappentascher Hof 65, 66424 Homburg/Saar
Tel: (06841) 71863
Web Site: www.asclepiosedition.de
Key Personnel
Contact: Lothar Baus *E-mail:* lotharbaus@web.de
Founded: 1985
Specialize in Goethe-Studies, Friedrich Nietzsche & Stoic Philosophie.
Subjects: Biography, Literature, Literary Criticism, Essays, Philosophy
ISBN Prefix(es): 3-925101; 3-935288

Asgard-Verlag Dr Werner Hippe GmbH
Einsteinstr 10, 53757 Sankt Augustin
Mailing Address: Postfach 1465, 53732 Sankt Augustin
Tel: (02241) 3164-0 *Fax:* (02241) 316436
E-mail: service@asgard.de

Key Personnel
Man Dir: Stefan Maus; Uwe Schliebusch
Founded: 1947
Subjects: Government, Political Science, Health, Nutrition, Medicine, Nursing, Dentistry, Public Administration, Social Sciences, Sociology
ISBN Prefix(es): 3-537
Subsidiaries: Siegler & Co Verlag fur Zeitarchive GmbH

Assimil GmbH
Hinter den Hagen 1, 52388 Noervenich
Mailing Address: Postfach 47, 52386 Noervenich
Tel: (02426) 94000 *Fax:* (02426) 4862
E-mail: kontakt@assimil.com
Web Site: www.assimil.com
Founded: 1988
Specialize in textbooks-foreign languages.
Subjects: Language Arts, Linguistics
ISBN Prefix(es): 3-89625

Asso Verlag+
Martin-Heix-Platz 3, 46045 Oberhausen
Tel: (0208) 802356 *Fax:* (0208) 809882
Key Personnel
Contact: Anneliese Althoff
Founded: 1970
Subjects: Labor, Industrial Relations, Poetry, Regional Interests, Social Sciences, Sociology
ISBN Prefix(es): 3-921541
Warehouse: Lothringerstr 64, 46045 Oberhausen

Verlag Atelier im Bauernhaus Fischerhude Wolf-Dietmar Stock+
In der Bredenau 6, 28870 Ottersberg-Fischerhude
Tel: (04293) 491; (04293) 493 *Fax:* (04293) 1238
Key Personnel
Publisher: Wolf-Dietmar Stock
Rights & Permissions: Hans-Guenther Pawelzik
Founded: 1976
Subjects: Art, Fiction, Regional Interests
ISBN Prefix(es): 3-88132
Orders to: VVA, An der Autobahn, 33310 Guetersloh

Atelier Verlag Andernach (AVA)+
Antel 74, 56626 Andernach
Tel: (02632) 44432 *Fax:* (02632) 31383
Key Personnel
Man Dir, Rights & Permissions: Fritz Werf
Founded: 1966
Subjects: Art, Poetry
ISBN Prefix(es): 3-921042

AUE-Verlag GmbH+
Postfach 1108, 74215 Moeckmuehl
Tel: (06298) 1328 *Fax:* (06298) 4298
E-mail: aue-verlag@web.de
Web Site: www.aue-verlag.com
Key Personnel
Manager: Thomas Gauger
Founded: 1919
Subjects: Crafts, Games, Hobbies, Education, Religion - Protestant, Religion - Other
ISBN Prefix(es): 3-87029
Divisions: Redaktion

Auer Verlag GmbH+
Heilig-Kreuzstr 16, 86609 Donauwoerth
Mailing Address: Postfach 1152, 86601 Donauwoerth
Tel: (0906) 73-240 *Fax:* (0906) 73177; (0906) 73178
E-mail: info@auer-verlag.de
Web Site: www.auer-verlag.de *Cable:* AUER DONAUWORTH
Key Personnel
Man Dir: Herr Buechler *Tel:* (0906) 73242
Contact: Tanja Auernhamer *Tel:* (0906) 73152 *E-mail:* auernhamer@auer-verlag.de
Founded: 1875

Membership(s): TR-Verlagsunion GmbH.
Subjects: Education, History, Mathematics, Music, Dance, Psychology, Psychiatry, Religion - Catholic, Science (General), Sports, Athletics, Theology
ISBN Prefix(es): 3-403; 3-87904
Number of titles published annually: 100 Print; 20 CD-ROM; 5 Audio
Total Titles: 1,800 Print; 60 CD-ROM; 20 Audio
Branch Office(s)
Westenhellweg 126, 44137 Dortmund *Tel:* (0231) 5844830 *Fax:* (0231) 58448320
August-Bebelstr 43, 04275 Leipzig *Tel:* (0341) 3026270 *Fax:* (0341) 3026271

Aufbau Taschenbuch Verlag GmbH
Neue Promenade 6, 10178 Berlin
Mailing Address: Postfach 193, 10105 Berlin
Tel: (030) 283 94-0 *Fax:* (030) 283 94 100
E-mail: info@aufbau-verlag.de
Web Site: www.aufbau-verlag.de
Key Personnel
Program Manager: Rene Strien
Manager: Peter Dempewolf
International Rights: Astrid Poppenhusen
 Tel: (030) 283 94 212 *E-mail:* poppenhusen@aufbau-verlag.de
Contact: Barbara Stang
Rights & Permissions: Kathrin Schulz
Founded: 1994
Subjects: Fiction, Film, Video, Government, Political Science, Literature, Literary Criticism, Essays, Poetry, Romance
ISBN Prefix(es): 3-7466
Number of titles published annually: 150 Print
Total Titles: 500 Print
Shipping Address: Mohr Morawa, Buchvertrieb Gesellschaft mbH, Postfach 260, A-1101 Vienna, Austria; Buecher Balmer Verlagsauslieferung, Neugasse 12, CH-6301 Zurich, Switzerland
Warehouse: Libri-Distributions GmbH, August-Schanzstr 33, 60433 Frankfurt
Orders to: Libri-Distributions GmbH, August-Schanzstr 33, 60433 Frankfurt

Aufbau-Verlag GmbH+
Neue Promenade 6, 10178 Berlin
Mailing Address: Postfach 193, 10105 Berlin
Tel: (030) 28 394-0 *Fax:* (030) 28 394-100
E-mail: info@aufbau-verlag.de
Web Site: www2.aufbauverlag.de
Key Personnel
Program Manager: Rene Strien
Manager: Peter Dempewolf
International Rights: Astrid Poppenhusen
 Tel: (030) 28394212 *E-mail:* poppenhussen@aufbau-verlag.de
Contact: Barbara Stang
Rights & Permissions: Kathrin Schulz
Founded: 1945
Subjects: Fiction, Film, Video, Government, Political Science, Literature, Literary Criticism, Essays, Mysteries, Poetry, Romance
ISBN Prefix(es): 3-351
Number of titles published annually: 80 Print; 20 Audio
Total Titles: 400 Print
Shipping Address: Mohr Morawa, Buchvertrieb Gesellschaft mbH, Postfach 260, 1101 Vienna, Austria; Buecher Balmer Verlagsauslieferung, Neugasse 12, 6301 Zurich, Switzerland
Warehouse: Libri-Distributions-GmbH, August-Schanz-Str 33, 60433 Frankfurt
Orders to: Libri-Distributions-GmbH, August-Schanz-Str 33, 60433 Frankfurt

Aufstieg-Verlag GmbH
Isarweg 37, 84028 Landshut
Tel: (0871) 54112 *Fax:* (0871) 54112
Web Site: www.aufstieg-verlag.de

Key Personnel
Man Dir & International Rights: Gisela Werner
Founded: 1947
Subjects: Cookery, Fiction, Foreign Countries, History, Humor
ISBN Prefix(es): 3-7612; 3-920235

August Guese Verlag GmbH
Am Spitzacker 10, 61184 Karben
Tel: (06039) 48 01 10 *Fax:* (06039) 48 01 48
E-mail: info@guese.de
Web Site: www.guese.de
Key Personnel
Man Dir: Johannes Guese
Founded: 1954
Subjects: Gardening, Plants
ISBN Prefix(es): 3-87278

J J Augustin Verlag GmbH
Am Fleth 36-37, 25348 Glueckstadt
Mailing Address: Postfach 1106, 25342 Glueckstadt
Tel: (04124) 20 44-46 *Fax:* (04124) 47 09
Key Personnel
President & International Rights: Walter Pruess
Founded: 1920
Subjects: Asian Studies, Literature, Literary Criticism, Essays, Religion - Islamic, Science (General)
ISBN Prefix(es): 3-87030

Augustinus-Verlag Wurzburg Inh Augustinerprovinz
Grabenberg 2, 97070 Wuerzburg
Tel: (0931) 3097-400 *Fax:* (0931) 3097-401
E-mail: verlag@augustiner.de
Web Site: www.augustiner.de
Key Personnel
Publishing Dir: Eric Englert
Contact: Jrina Nebel
Founded: 1922
Subjects: Religion - Other
ISBN Prefix(es): 3-7613
Bookshop(s): Buch und Kumst, Dominikanerplarz 4, 97070 Wuerzburg

Augustus Verlag+
Hilblestr 54, 80636 Munich
Tel: (089) 9271-0 *Fax:* (089) 9271-168
Web Site: www.droemer-weltbild.de
Key Personnel
Publisher: Dr Hans-Peter Uebleis
Man Dir: Ralf Mueller
Marketing: Christian Tesch
Founded: 1989
Subjects: Animals, Pets, Architecture & Interior Design, Crafts, Games, Hobbies, Gardening, Plants, Photography
ISBN Prefix(es): 3-8043
Parent Company: Verlagsgruppe Droemer Weltbild
Orders to: VVA-Bertelsmann Distribution GmbH, Postfach 7600, 33310 Guetersloh

Aulis Verlag Deubner & Co KG+
Antwerpener Str 6-12, 50672 Cologne
Tel: (0221) 9514540 *Fax:* (0221) 518443
E-mail: info@aulis.de
Web Site: www.aulis.de
Key Personnel
Publisher: Wolfgang Deubner
Founded: 1950
Subjects: Biological Sciences, Chemistry, Chemical Engineering, Geography, Geology, History, Mathematics, Nonfiction (General), Physics, Science (General)
ISBN Prefix(es): 3-7614

Aussaat Verlag+
Andreas-Braem-Str 18/20, 47506 Neukirchen-Vluyn

Mailing Address: Postfach 101265, 47497 Neukirchen-Vluyn
Tel: (02845) 392222 *Fax:* (02845) 33689
E-mail: info@neukirchener-verlag.de
Web Site: www.aussaat-verlag.de
Key Personnel
Man Dir: Klaus Guenther
Sales Manager: Christoph Siepermann
  E-mail: vertrieb@neukirchener-verlagshaus.de
Founded: 1978
Subjects: Biblical Studies, Education, Fiction, Religion - Protestant, Religion - Other, Theology
ISBN Prefix(es): 3-7615
Number of titles published annually: 50 Print
Total Titles: 400 Print
Parent Company: Verlagsgesellschaft des Erziehungsvereins mbH
Divisions: Edition Sonnenweg, Friedrich Bahn Verlag

Verlag der Autoren GmbH & Co KG+
Schleusenstr 15, 60327 Frankfurt am Main
Mailing Address: Postfach 111 963, 60054 Frankfurt am Main
Tel: (069) 23 85 74-0 *Fax:* (069) 24 27 76 44
E-mail: buch@verlag-der-autoren.de
Web Site: www.verlag-der-autoren.de *Cable:* AUTORENVERLAG FRANKFURT
Key Personnel
Contact: Brigitte Pfannmoeller *Tel:* (069) 23857441; Annette Reschke *Tel:* (069) 23857423
Founded: 1969
One of Germany's theatre & film agencies, publishing a line of titles on theatre & film.
Subjects: Drama, Theater, Film, Video
ISBN Prefix(es): 3-920983; 3-88661
Number of titles published annually: 8 Print
Total Titles: 190 Print
Foreign Rep(s): International Editors (Argentina, South America, Spain); Marton Agency of New York (USA); Orion Library Agency of Tokyo (Japan); Rosica Colin Ltd (Canada, London)
Orders to: Edition Text und Kritik, Levelingstr 6a, 81673 Munich, Contact: Mrs Ingmann *Tel:* (089) 432929 *Fax:* (089) 433997 *E-mail:* etk.muenchen@t-online.de

Autovision Verlag Guenther & Co+
Kronprinzenstr 54, 22587 Hamburg
Tel: (040) 810327 *Fax:* (040) 87932995
Web Site: www.autovision-verlag.de
Key Personnel
Publisher: Dieter Guenther
Founded: 1992
Subjects: Automotive, Technology
ISBN Prefix(es): 3-9802766
Orders to: VAL, Luener Dennbahn 16, 21339 Luneburg

AVA, see Atelier Verlag Andernach (AVA)

Aviatic Verlag GmbH+
Kolpingring 16, 82041 Oberhaching
Tel: (089) 613890-0 *Fax:* (089) 613890-10
E-mail: aviatic@aviatic.de
Web Site: www.aviatic.de
Key Personnel
Manager: Peter Pletschacher
Founded: 1985
Specialize in aeronautics.
Subjects: Aeronautics, Aviation
ISBN Prefix(es): 3-925505
Total Titles: 35 Print
Distributed by Schiffer Publishing (USA)

AvivA Britta Jurgs GmbH
Emdener Str 33, 10551 Berlin
Tel: (030) 39 73 13 72 *Fax:* (030) 39 73 13 71
E-mail: aviva@txt.de
Web Site: www.aviva-verlag.de

Key Personnel
Publisher: Jurgs Britta
Founded: 1997
Subjects: Art, Literature, Literary Criticism, Essays, Women's Studies
ISBN Prefix(es): 3-932338

Axel Juncker Verlag Jacobi KG
Member of The Langenscheidt Group
Mies-van-der-Rohestr 1, 80807 Munich
Mailing Address: Postfach 401120, 80711 Munich
Tel: (089) 360960 *Fax:* (089) 36096222
Telex: 5215379 lkgmd
Key Personnel
Man Dir: Karl Ernst Tielebier-Langenscheidt; Andreas Langenscheidt
Founded: 1902
Sales & promotion through Langenscheidt KG.
ISBN Prefix(es): 3-558
Orders to: Langenscheidt KG, Neusserstr 3, 80807 Munich

AZ Bertelsmann Direct GmbH
Division of Bertelsmann Services Group
Unit of Avarto AG
Carl-Bertelsmann-Str 161S, 33311 Guetersloh
Tel: (05241) 805438 *Fax:* (05241) 8066962
E-mail: az@bertelsmann.de
Web Site: www.az.bertelsmann.de
Founded: 1966
International full-service direct marketing.
Subjects: Business, Marketing
ISBN Prefix(es): 3-573

Babel Verlag Kevin Perryman
Lorenz Paulstr 4, 86920 Denklingen
Mailing Address: PO Box 1, 86920 Denklingen
Tel: (08243) 961691 *Fax:* (08243) 961614
E-mail: info@babel-verlag.de
Web Site: www.babel-verlag.de
Key Personnel
Publisher: Kevin Perryman
Founded: 1983
Specializes in poetry, bilingual poetry & translations.
Subjects: Poetry
ISBN Prefix(es): 3-931798
Number of titles published annually: 2 Print
Total Titles: 39 Print
Distribution Center: GVA, Goettingen

J P Bachem Verlag GmbH+
Ursulaplatz 1, 50668 Cologne
Tel: (0221) 1619-0 *Fax:* (0221) 1619-159
E-mail: info@bachem-verlag.de
Web Site: www.bachem-verlag.de
Telex: 8881128 *Cable:* BACHEMHAUS COLOGNE
Key Personnel
Dir: Dipl Kfm Lambert Bachem
Publisher: Reinhard Metz
Founded: 1818
Subjects: Regional Interests
ISBN Prefix(es): 3-7616
Parent Company: Bachem Publishing Group

Dr Bachmaier Verlag GmbH+
Kagerstr 8B, 81669 Munich
Tel: (089) 685120 *Fax:* (089) 685120
E-mail: contact@verlag-drbachmaier.de
Web Site: www.verlag-drbachmaier.de
Key Personnel
Man Dir: Dr Peter Bachmaier
Contact: Barbara Bachmaier
Also acts as Bookseller.
Subjects: History, Literature, Literary Criticism, Essays, Poetry, Science (General), Science Fiction, Fantasy
ISBN Prefix(es): 3-931680
Number of titles published annually: 7 Print

Total Titles: 34 Print
Foreign Rights: Dr Doglioli (Italy)

Badenia Verlag und Druckerei GmbH+
Rudolf-Freytag-Str 6, 76189 Karlsruhe
Tel: (0721) 95 45-0 *Fax:* (0721) 95 45-125
E-mail: verlag@badeniaverlag.de
Web Site: www.badeniaverlag.badeniaonline.de
Key Personnel
Publisher: Angelika Schmidt
Founded: 1874
Subjects: Regional Interests, Travel
ISBN Prefix(es): 3-7617

Badischer Landwirtschafts-Verlag GmbH
Friedrichstr 43, 79098 Freiburg
Mailing Address: Postfach 209, 79002 Freiburg
Tel: (0761) 271330 *Fax:* (0761) 2713372
E-mail: redaktion@blv-freiburg.de *Cable:* BBZ FRBG
Key Personnel
Assistant Editor-in-Chief: Richard Briskowski
Rights: Manfred Zimper
Founded: 1947
Subjects: Agriculture
ISBN Prefix(es): 3-9801818

Baedeker, *imprint of* Mairs Geographischer Verlag

Hans A Baensch, see Mergus Verlag GmbH Hans A Baensch

Baerenreiter-Spieltexte, *imprint of* Otto Teich

Baha'i Verlag GmbH+
Eppsteiner Str 89, 65719 Hofheim
Tel: (06192) 22921 *Fax:* (06192) 22936
E-mail: info@bahai-verlag.de
Web Site: www.bahaipublishers.org
Key Personnel
Man Dir, Rights & Permissions: F Ardalan
Founded: 1925
Subjects: Religion - Other
ISBN Prefix(es): 3-87037

Bahnsport Aktuell Verlag GmbH
Birkenweiherstr 14, 63505 Langenselbold
Tel: (06184) 9233-30 *Fax:* (06184) 9233-50
E-mail: mce-aktuell@mce-online.de
Founded: 1971

Baken-Verlag Walter Schnoor+
Kastanienallee 16, 25548 Kellinghusen
Tel: (04822) 1671; (04192) 1784 *Cable:* BAKEN
Key Personnel
Owner: Uwe Jens Schnoor
Founded: 1951
Subjects: Environmental Studies, History, Regional Interests
ISBN Prefix(es): 3-7622
Bookshop(s): Buecherstube, Maienbeeck 4, 24576 Bad Bramstedt

Edition Balance Marion Guenther Bonsack+
Brunnenstr 12, 99867 Gotha
Tel: (03621) 750061 *Fax:* (0721) 151315156
E-mail: info@edition-balance.de
Web Site: www.edition-balance.de
Key Personnel
International Rights: Henry Guenther
Founded: 1990
Subjects: Art
ISBN Prefix(es): 3-928440
Associate Companies: Atelier Buchkunst, Brunenstr 12, 99867 Gotha

C Bange GmbH & Co KG+
Marienplatz 12, 96142 Hollfeld
Mailing Address: Postfach 1160, 96139 Hollfeld
Tel: (09274) 94130 *Fax:* (09274) 94132

PUBLISHERS — GERMANY

E-mail: service@bange-verlag.de
Web Site: www.bange-verlag.de
Key Personnel
Manager: Thomas Appel
Assistant Manager: Kerstin Lange
Founded: 1871
Subjects: Education, Fiction
ISBN Prefix(es): 3-8044
Number of titles published annually: 20 Print
Total Titles: 850 Print
Imprints: Bange Lernhilfen; Koenigs Erlaeuterungen; Koenigs Lektueren; Kon & Bundig

Bange Lernhilfen, *imprint of* C Bange GmbH & Co KG

Bank-Verlag GmbH+
Wendelinstr 1, 50933 Cologne
Mailing Address: Postfach 450209, 50877 Cologne
Tel: (0221) 54 90-0 *Fax:* (0221) 54 90-120
E-mail: bank-verlag@bank-verlag.de
Web Site: www.bank-verlag.de
Key Personnel
Manager: Helmut Gsanger
Founded: 1961
Subjects: Business, Economics, Finance, Law, Management, Securities
ISBN Prefix(es): 3-00

Dr Richard Bar di animali
Kopernikusplatz 36, 90459 Nurnberg
Tel: (0911) 951 9490 *Fax:* (0911) 951 9489
E-mail: di.animali@web.de
Web Site: www.zivilist.it
ISBN Prefix(es): 3-00

Barenreiter-Verlag Karl-Votterle GmbH & Co KG+
Heinrich-Schuetz-Allee 35, 34131 Kassel
Tel: (0561) 3105-0 *Fax:* (0561) 3105-176
E-mail: info@baerenreiter.com
Web Site: www.baerenreiter.com
Key Personnel
Man Dir: Leonhard Scheuch *E-mail:* lscheuch@baerenreiter.com; Barbara Scheuch-Voetterle *E-mail:* bscheuch@baerenreiter.com
Dir, Finances: Anne Schaefer *E-mail:* schaefer@baerenreiter.com
Publishing Dir: Dr Wendelin Goebel *E-mail:* goebel@baerenreiter.com
Dir, Sales & Marketing: Christine Husemann *E-mail:* husemann@baerenreiter.com
Sales Manager: Uta Dangelmaier *E-mail:* dangelmaier@baerenreiter.com; Dr Christiane Loskant *E-mail:* loskant@baerenreiter.com; Corinne Votteler *E-mail:* votteler@baerenreiter.com; Petra Woodfull-Harris *E-mail:* pwoodfull-harris@baerenreiter.com
Product Information: Ilse-Lore Krummel-Laartz *E-mail:* krummel-laartz@baerenreiter.com
International Rights: Thomas Tietze
Founded: 1923
Subjects: Music, Dance
ISBN Prefix(es): 3-7618
Associate Companies: Baerenreiter Verlag Basel
Subsidiaries: Gustav Bosse Verlag; KGA, Verlags-Service GmbH; Sueddeutscher Musikverlag, Alkor-Edition, Henschel Verlag Fuer Musik
Branch Office(s)
Basel, Switzerland
Prague, Czech Republic
London, United Kingdom
New York, NY, United States
U.S. Office(s): Music Associates of America, 224 King St, Englewood, NJ 07631, United States, Contact: George Strum *Tel:* 201-569-2898 *Fax:* 201-569-7023
Distributed by Barenreiter Ltd (UK); Baerenreiter Verlag Basel AG (Switzerland)

Bookshop(s): Neuwerk-Buch-und Musikalienhandlung
Shipping Address: KGA-technischer Betrieb, Brandaustr 10, 34127 Kassel
Warehouse: KGA-technischer Betrieb, Brandaustr 10, 34127 Kassel
Orders to: KGA, Postfach 102180, 34021 Kassel

Verlag Dr Albert Bartens KG
Lueckhoffstr 16, 14129 Berlin
Mailing Address: Postfach 380250, 14112 Berlin
Tel: (030) 803 56 78 *Fax:* (030) 803 20 49
E-mail: info@bartens.com
Web Site: www.bartens.com
Key Personnel
Editor: Dr Juergen Bruhns
Founded: 1951
Subjects: Agriculture, Economics, Energy, Technology
ISBN Prefix(es): 3-87040

Otto Wilhelm Barth-Verlag KG
Hilblestr 54, 80636 Munich
Tel: (089) 9271-0 *Fax:* (089) 9271-168
Key Personnel
Man Dir: Peter Lohmann; Andreas Wiedmann
Sales: Wolfgang Radaj
Editor: Graf Eckhard
Rights & Permissions: Barbara Fankhauser
Founded: 1924
Subjects: Astrology, Occult, Philosophy, Religion - Other
ISBN Prefix(es): 3-502; 3-89304
Parent Company: Scherz Verlag AG, Marktgasse 25 Postf 66, 3000 Bern, Switzerland
Associate Companies: Scherz Verlag GmbH, Munich

Bartkowiaks Forum Book Art
Koernerstr 24, 22301 Hamburg
Tel: (040) 2793674 *Fax:* (040) 2704397
E-mail: info@forumbookart.de
Web Site: www.forumbookart.com
Key Personnel
Man Dir: Heinz Stefan Bartkowiak
Founded: 1988
Subjects: Art
ISBN Prefix(es): 3-9802935

Basilisken-Presse+
Hirschberg 5, 35037 Marburg
Mailing Address: Postfach 561, 35017 Marburg
Tel: 06421 15188
Key Personnel
Owner, Rights & Permissions: Armin Geus
Founded: 1976
Specialize in medicine, nursing & history of science.
Subjects: Art, History, Medicine, Nursing, Dentistry
ISBN Prefix(es): 3-925347; 3-9800020

BasisDruck Verlag GmbH
Schliemannstr 23, 10437 Berlin
Tel: (030) 445 76 80 *Fax:* (030) 445 95 99
E-mail: basisdruck@onlinehome.de
Web Site: www.basisdruck.de
Key Personnel
Man Dir: Michael Kukutz
Founded: 1990
Subjects: Government, Political Science, History
ISBN Prefix(es): 3-86163

Bassermann Verlag+
Neumarkter Str 28, 81673 Munich
Tel: (089) 41 360
E-mail: vertrieb.verlagsgruppe@randomhouse.de
Web Site: www.randomhouse.de/bassermann
Key Personnel
Publisher: Stefan Ewald *E-mail:* stefan.ewald@bertelsmann.de

Foreign Rights: Silke Bruenink *Tel:* (089) 43 72-26 48 *Fax:* (089) 43 72-27 47 *E-mail:* silke.bruenink@bertelsmann.de
Founded: 1843
Subjects: Cookery, Crafts, Games, Hobbies, Gardening, Plants, Nonfiction (General), Outdoor Recreation
ISBN Prefix(es): 3-8094

Bastei Luebbe Taschenbuecher, *imprint of* Verlagsgruppe Luebbe GmbH & Co KG

Bastei Luebbe Taschenbuecher+
Imprint of Verlagsgruppe Luebbe GmbH & Co KG
Scheidtbachstr 23-31, 51469 Bergisch Gladbach
Mailing Address: Postfach 200180, 51431 Bergisch Gladbach
Tel: (02202) 121-293; (02202) 121-544 *Fax:* (02202) 121-927
E-mail: bastei.luebbe@luebbe.de
Web Site: www.luebbe.de
Key Personnel
Man Dir: Karlheinz Jungbeck
Founded: 1963
Subjects: Fiction, Nonfiction (General)
ISBN Prefix(es): 3-404
Total Titles: 500 Print

Bastei Verlag, *imprint of* Verlagsgruppe Luebbe GmbH & Co KG

Bastei Verlag+
Imprint of Verlagsgruppe Luebbe GmbH & Co KG
Scheidtbachstr 23-31, 51431 Bergisch Gladbach
Mailing Address: Postfach 200180, 51431 Bergisch Gladbach
Tel: (02202) 121-0 *Fax:* (02202) 121-936
E-mail: info@bastei.de
Web Site: www.bastei.de *Cable:* SCHEIDTBACHSTR 23-31
Key Personnel
Man Dir: Karlheinz Jungbeck
Founded: 1949
Subjects: Fiction, Science Fiction, Fantasy, Western Fiction
ISBN Prefix(es): 3-404
Number of titles published annually: 80 Print
Associate Companies: Gustav Luebbe Verlag

Verlag Hermann Bauer Gmbh & Co KG+
Kronenstr 2-4, 79100 Freiburg
Mailing Address: Postfach 167, 79001 Freiburg
Tel: (0761) 7082-0 *Fax:* (0761) 701811
E-mail: info@hermann-bauer.de
Telex: 772821
Key Personnel
Man Dir: Friedrich Kirner
Rights & Permissions: Petra Danner
Sales Manager: Wilfried Hille
Editorial: Katin Vial
Founded: 1937
Subjects: Astrology, Occult, Health, Nutrition, Parapsychology, Philosophy
ISBN Prefix(es): 3-7626
Imprints: Kutz und praktisch; Esotere Taschenbuch
Subsidiaries: Ebertin-Verlag

Baumann GmbH & Co KG+
E-C-Baumann-Str 5, 95326 Kulmbach
Tel: (09221) 949413 *Fax:* (09221) 949352
E-mail: service@baumann-online.de
Web Site: www.baumann-online.de
Key Personnel
Dir: Helmut Korndoerfer
Sales: Walter Ruisinger
Founded: 1902
ISBN Prefix(es): 3-922091
Subsidiaries: Coburger Tageblatt; Filialbetrieb Naila

GERMANY

Dr Wolfgang Baur Verlag Kunst & Alltag+
Poignring 24c, 82515 Wolfratshausen
Tel: (08171) 217514 *Fax:* (08171) 217515
E-mail: verlag@kunstalltag.de
Web Site: www.kunstalltag.de
Key Personnel
Owner: Dr Wolfgang Baur
Founded: 1977
Subjects: Art, Environmental Studies, Ethnicity, Humor, Philosophy, Poetry, Science (General)
ISBN Prefix(es): 3-88410
Imprints: Edition Jonas; Edition U

Bautz Traugott
Eisenacher Str 15, 37412 Herzberg
Tel: (05521) 57 00; (05521) 55 88 *Fax:* (05521) 16 73; (05521) 57 80
E-mail: bautz@bautz.de
Web Site: www.bautz.de
Key Personnel
Contact: Traugott Bautz
Founded: 1971
Subjects: Regional Interests, Theology
ISBN Prefix(es): 3-88309

Bauverlag GmbH+
Avenwedderstr 55, 33311 Guetersloh
Tel: (05241) 802119 *Fax:* (05241) 809582
E-mail: info@bauverlag.de
Web Site: www.bauverlag.de *Cable:* BAUVERLAG WALL&U14FF
Key Personnel
Dir: Stefan Ruehling; Ulrike Mattern
Founded: 1929
Subjects: Architecture & Interior Design, Civil Engineering, Energy, Environmental Studies
ISBN Prefix(es): 3-7625
Parent Company: Emap
Imprints: LBO-Dienst
Branch Office(s)
Nikolsburger Str 11, 10717 Berlin

Bayerische Akademie der Wissenschaften
(Bavarian Academy of Sciences & Humanities)
Marstallplatz 8, 80539 Munich
Tel: (089) 23031-0 *Fax:* (089) 23031-100
E-mail: webmaster@badw.de; presse@badw.de
Web Site: www.badw.de
Key Personnel
President: Noeth Heinrich
Secretary General: Monika Stoermer
Librarian: Heldegard Glaser *Tel:* (089) 23037746
 E-mail: glaser@bsb.badw-muencher.de
Founded: 1759
Subjects: Science (General)
ISBN Prefix(es): 3-7696
Number of titles published annually: 130 Print
Orders to: CH Beck'sche Verlags Buchhandlung, Postfach 400340, 80703 Munich, Contact: Oscar Beck *Tel:* (089) 381890 *Fax:* (089) 38189/381398

Bayerische Verlagsanstalt GmbH+
Laubanger 23, 96052 Bamberg
Mailing Address: Postfach 2709, 96018 Bamberg
Tel: (0951) 967120 *Fax:* (0951) 96712235
Key Personnel
Man Dir: Helmut Treml
Founded: 1949
Subjects: Economics, Literature, Literary Criticism, Essays, Regional Interests
ISBN Prefix(es): 3-87052
Parent Company: Sankt Otto-Verlag GmbH
Bookshop(s): Goerres Buchhandlung, Langestr 24, 96047 Bamberg

Bayerischer Schulbuch-Verlag GmbH
Rosenheimer Str 145, 81671 Munich
Mailing Address: Postfach 801360, 81613 Munich
Tel: (089) 450510 *Fax:* (089) 45051-200
Key Personnel
Dir: Hartmut Koeppelmann; Roland Mayr
Subjects: Biological Sciences, Business, Chemistry, Chemical Engineering, English as a Second Language, Environmental Studies, Geography, Geology, History, Literature, Literary Criticism, Essays, Mathematics, Music, Dance, Philosophy, Physics
ISBN Prefix(es): 3-7627
Warehouse: Bayerischer Schulbuch-Verlag, Ohmstr 10, 85757 Karlsfeld

BdWi, see Bund demokratischer Wissenschaftlerinnen und Wissenschafler eV (BdWi)

be.bra verlag GmbH+
KulturBrauerei Haus S, Schoenhauser Allee 37, 10435 Berlin
Tel: (030) 440 23-810 *Fax:* (030) 440 23-819
E-mail: post@bebraverlag.de
Web Site: www.bebraverlag.de
Key Personnel
Publisher: Ulrich Hopp
Press Manager: Regine Buczek *Tel:* (030) 440 23-812
Sales Managers: Antje Steinriede *Tel:* (030) 440 23-813
Founded: 1994
Membership(s): Borsenverein des Deutschen Buchhandels.
Subjects: Architecture & Interior Design, Government, Political Science, Regional Interests
ISBN Prefix(es): 3-930863; 3-89809
Number of titles published annually: 20 Print
Total Titles: 46 Print

Beacon Verlag Koerber OHG
Birkenthal 13, 67098 Bad Duerkheim
Mailing Address: Postfach 1161, 67085 Bad Duerkheim
Tel: (06322) 2056 *Fax:* (06322) 2056 *Cable:* BEACON-DUERKHEIM
Key Personnel
Editor: Mrs Ortrun Scheumann
Founded: 1949
Subjects: Language Arts, Linguistics
ISBN Prefix(es): 3-920075

Ludwig Bechauf Verlag
Friedrichstr 48, 33615 Bielefeld
Tel: (0521) 130648 *Fax:* (0521) 139347
Key Personnel
Owner: Wilfried Carlmeyer
Founded: 1893
Subjects: Theology
ISBN Prefix(es): 3-8076

Bechtermuenz Verlag
Hilblestr 54, 80636 Munich
Tel: (089) 9271 312 *Fax:* (0821) 70 04-179
ISBN Prefix(es): 3-86047; 3-8289; 3-89350; 3-927117
Parent Company: Weltbild Verlag GmbH

Bechtle Graphische Betriebe und Verlagsgesellschaft GmbH und Co KG
Zeppelinstr 116, 73730 Esslingen
Mailing Address: Postfach 100209, 73702 Esslingen
Tel: (0711) 9310-0
Key Personnel
Manager, International Rights: Otto W Bechtle; Dr Christine Bechtle-Koberg
Manager: Ulrich Gottlieb
Founded: 1868
Subjects: Biography
ISBN Prefix(es): 3-7628
Subsidiaries: Rotenberg Verlag GmbH

Beck & Gluckler Verlag GmbH & Co KG+
Maximilianstr 30, 79100 Freiburg im Breisgau
Tel: (0761) 701530 *Fax:* (0761) 701580
Key Personnel
Man Dir, Rights & Permissions: Jutta Beck
Founded: 1985
ISBN Prefix(es): 3-89470
Shipping Address: Prolit Verlagsauslieferung, Siemensstr 16, 35463 Fernwald-Annerod
Warehouse: Prolit Verlagsauslieferung, Siemensstr 16, 35463 Fernwald-Annerod
Orders to: Prolit Verlagsauslieferung, Siemensstr 16, 35463 Fernwald-Annerod *Tel:* (0641) 943930 *Fax:* (0641) 9439393

Verlag C H Beck oHG+
Wilhelmstr 9, 80801 Munich
Mailing Address: Postfach 400340, 80703 Munich
Tel: (089) 38189-0 *Fax:* (089) 38189-402
E-mail: info.lsw@beck.de; bestellung@beck.de (orders)
Web Site: www.beck.de
Telex: 5215085 beck d
Key Personnel
Dir: Dr Hans D Beck; Wolfgang Beck
Editorial, Fiction, Humanities: Dr Detlef Felueu
Rights & Permissions: Susanne Simor
 Tel: (089) 38189-228 *Fax:* (089) 38189-699
 E-mail: susanne.simor@beck.de
Editorial Law & Taxation Economy: Burkail Schulz
Founded: 1763
Subjects: Anthropology, Archaeology, Art, Economics, History, Language Arts, Linguistics, Law, Literature, Literary Criticism, Essays, Management, Music, Dance, Nonfiction (General), Philosophy, Social Sciences, Sociology, Theology
ISBN Prefix(es): 3-406
Associate Companies: Verlag Franz Vahlen GmbH
Branch Office(s)
Palmengartenstr 14, 60325 Frankfurt am Main

Edition Monika Beck
Schwedenhof/Am Roemermuseum, 66424 Homburg/Saar
Tel: (06848) 72152 *Fax:* (06848) 72159
E-mail: info@mathbeck.de
Web Site: www.mathbeck.de/edmb
Key Personnel
Man Dir & Proprietor: Mathias Beck
 E-mail: mathiasbeck@mathbeck.de
Editorial & Publicity Dir: Susanna Eckenfels
Founded: 1967
Edition for Contemporary Art.
Subjects: Art
ISBN Prefix(es): 3-924360
Number of titles published annually: 8 Print
Total Titles: 248 Print
Parent Company: Mathias Beck Kulturmanagement Ltd

Beerenverlag
Morfelder Landstr 109, 60598 Frankfurt
Tel: (069) 61009551 *Fax:* (069) 61009560
Key Personnel
Manager: Bernard Rensinghoff
Art Dir: Thomas Majevszky
Editorial: Andreas Golm
Founded: 1992
Subjects: Fiction, Humor, Poetry, Travel
ISBN Prefix(es): 3-929198
Imprints: Kleine Reike; Rudi der Bar ist las
Distributed by Harrassourk Verlag

M P Belaieff, *imprint of* C F Peters Musikverlag GmbH & Co KG

Verlag Beleke KG+
Kronprinzenstr 13, 45128 Essen
Tel: (0201) 8130-0 *Fax:* (0201) 8130-108

E-mail: info@beleke.de
Web Site: www.beleke.de
Key Personnel
Owner & Man Dir: Norbert Beleke
Man Dir: Heike Bogott
International Rights: Dr Michael Platzkoester
    Tel: (0201) 8130-118 *Fax:* (0201) 8130-130
    E-mail: mplatzkoester@beleke.de
Founded: 1964
Membership(s): Verband Deutscher Auskunfts und Verzeichnismedien eV; European Association of Directory & Database Publishers; Boersenverein des Deutschen Buchhandels eV.
Subjects: Biography, Business, Criminology, Medicine, Nursing, Dentistry, Nonfiction (General), Regional Interests
ISBN Prefix(es): 3-8215
Associate Companies: ELVIKOM Film-Verlag GmbH, Essen; Hansisches Verlagskontor, Postfach 2051, 23508 Luebeck *Tel:* (0451) 703101 *Fax:* (0451) 7031281; NOBEL-Verlag GmbH, Postfach 103952, 45039 Essen; ntv neue television FILM-TV-PRODUKTION GmbH, Essen; Das Rathaus Verlagsgesellschaft mBH & Co KG; Verlag Schmidt-Roemhild, Luebeck
Showroom(s): Hohe Str 56, 44139 Dortmund 1; Redaktionsbuero Duesseldorf, Berliner Allee 30, 40212 Duesseldorf; Drei-Lilien-Platz 1, 65183 Wiesbaden; Verlag Schmidt-Roemhild, Prinzregentenstr 42, 10715 Berlin; Verlag Schmidt-Roemhild, Mengstr 16, 23552 Luebeck

Edition Belletriste, *imprint of* Weidler Buchverlag Berlin

Belser Wissenschaftlicher Dienst+
Gartenstr 1, 72218 Wildberg
Mailing Address: Postfach 126, 72215 Wildberg
Tel: (07054) 2475 *Fax:* (07054) 2639
E-mail: 101553.3467@compuserve.com
Web Site: www.belser.com
Key Personnel
General Manager: Dr Rolf D Schmid *Tel:* (079) 63763 *Fax:* (079) 63764 *E-mail:* rolf.schmid@belser.com
Founded: 1989
Subjects: Drama, Theater, Labor, Industrial Relations, Library & Information Sciences, Poetry, Psychology, Psychiatry, Religion - Catholic, Social Sciences, Sociology, Women's Studies, Microform Publisher, Electronic Publications
ISBN Prefix(es): 3-628
Total Titles: 100 CD-ROM; 15,000 E-Book
Associate Companies: Belser Wissenschaftlicher Dienst Ltd, Maple Dr, Boyle, Co Roscommon, Ireland *Tel:* (079) 63763 *Fax:* (079) 63764

Julius Beltz GmbH & Co KG+
Werderstr 10, 69469 Weinheim
Tel: (06201) 60070
E-mail: info@beltz.de
Web Site: www.beltz.de
Key Personnel
Man Dir: Joachim Radmer; Dr Manfred Beltz Ruebelmann
Marketing: Eckhard Mueller
Rights: Charlotte Larat
Marketing: Rosemarie Bornholt *Tel:* (06201) 6007-433 *Fax:* (06201) 6007-493 *E-mail:* r.bornholt@beltz.de
Founded: 1841
Membership(s): VGS - Verlagsgesellschaft mbH & Co KG.
Subjects: Science (General)
ISBN Prefix(es): 3-407
Subsidiaries: Beltz Athenaeum Verlag, Anrich Verlag; Deutscher Studien Verlag; PsychologieVerlagsUnion
Warehouse: Koch, Neff & Oetinger Verlagsauslieferung, 70551 Stuttgart *Tel:* (0711) 7899 20 30 *Fax:* (0711) 7899 10 10 *E-mail:* order@kno-va.de

Petra Bornhauber Benleo Verlag+
Bahnstr 16, 50126 Bergheim
Tel: (02271) 4782-0 *Fax:* (02271) 4782-20
Web Site: www.benleo.de
Key Personnel
International Rights: Petra Bornhauber
Founded: 1996
ISBN Prefix(es): 3-9805061

Bergmoser & Holler Verlag AG
Karl-Friedrich-Str 76, 52072 Aachen
Mailing Address: Postfach 50 04 04, 52088 Aachen
Tel: (0241) 93888-10 *Fax:* (0241) 93888-134
E-mail: kontakt@buhv.de
Web Site: www.buhv.de
Key Personnel
Man Dir: Josef Bergmoser
Founded: 1971
ISBN Prefix(es): 3-88997
U.S. Office(s): ci Publishing Inc, 230 Fifth Ave NE, Hickory, NC 28601, United States

Bergstadtverlag Wilhelm Gottlieb Korn GmbH Wuerzburg+
Hermann-Herder-Str 4, 79104 Freiburg im Breisgau
Mailing Address: Postfach 4201, 73745 Freiburg im Breisgau
Tel: (0711) 4406-193 *Fax:* (0711) 4406-199
Key Personnel
Dir: Dr Joachim Bensch
Founded: 1732
Subjects: Art, Biography, History, Literature, Literary Criticism, Essays, Poetry, Regional Interests, Travel
ISBN Prefix(es): 3-87057

Bergverlag Rother GmbH+
Haidgraben 3, 85521 Ottobrunn
Tel: (089) 608669-0 *Fax:* (089) 608669-69
E-mail: bergverlag@rother.de
Web Site: www.rother.de
Key Personnel
Manager: Dr Christian Halbwachs
    E-mail: halbwachs@freytagberndt.at
Founded: 1920
Specialize in Alpine literature, documents & guidebooks.
Subjects: Nonfiction (General), Outdoor Recreation, Sports, Athletics, Travel
ISBN Prefix(es): 3-7633
Number of titles published annually: 50 Print; 1 CD-ROM
Total Titles: 300 Print; 13 CD-ROM
Parent Company: Freytag-Berndt u Artaria KG, Brunner Str 63, 1231 Vienna, Austria
Distributed by Cordee (UK)

Berliner Debatte Wissenschafts Verlag, GSFP-Gesellschaft fur Sozialwissen-schaftliche Forschung und Publizistik mbH & Co KG
Erich-Weinert-Str 19, 10439 Berlin
Tel: (030) 44651355 *Fax:* (030) 44651358
E-mail: web@berlinerdebatte.de
Web Site: www.berlinerdebatte.de
Key Personnel
Manager: Dr Rainer Land; Dr Erhard Crome
Founded: 1992
Subjects: Government, Political Science, History, Philosophy, Social Sciences, Sociology
ISBN Prefix(es): 3-929666; 3-931703; 3-936382
Orders to: Bugrim, Saalburgstr 3, 12099 Berlin

Berliner Handpresse Wolfgang Joerg und Erich Schonig
Prinzessinenstr 20, 10969 Berlin
Tel: (030) 6148728; (030) 6142605
Key Personnel
Publisher: Wolfgang Joerg

Founded: 1961
Subjects: Art, Fiction

Berliner Wissenschafts-Verlag GmbH (BWV)+
Axel-Springer-Str 54b, 10117 Berlin
Tel: (030) 84 17 70-0 *Fax:* (030) 84 17 70-21
E-mail: bwv@bwv-verlag.de
Web Site: www.bwv-verlag.de
Key Personnel
Man Dir: Dr Volker Schwarz
Manager: Brigitta Weiss
Founded: 1962
Subjects: Business, Economics, Environmental Studies, Government, Political Science, History, Law, Library & Information Sciences, Management, Marketing, Mathematics, Medicine, Nursing, Dentistry, Music, Dance, Philosophy, Public Administration, Publishing & Book Trade Reference, Real Estate, Theology
ISBN Prefix(es): 3-87061; 3-8305
Parent Company: Nomos Verlagsgesellschaft GmbH, Waidseestr 3-5, 76530 Baden-Baden, Baden Baden
Imprints: Ostrecht
Warehouse: Nomos Verlagsgesellschaft, Waldseestr 3-5, 75630 Baden-Baden
Orders to: Nomos Verlagsgesellschaft, Waldseestr 3-5, 76530 Baden-Baden

Bernard und Graefe Verlag+
Heilsbachstr 26, 53123 Bonn
Tel: (0228) 64830 *Fax:* (0228) 6483109
E-mail: 101336.245@compuserve.com
Key Personnel
Man Dir: Manfred Sadlowski
Rights & Permissions (Sales): Jung Horst
Founded: 1918
Subjects: Military Science
ISBN Prefix(es): 3-7637

Berndtson & Berndtson GmbH Verlag-Publishing+
Lindach 4, 82256 Fuerstenfeldbruck
Tel: (08141) 222 580 *Fax:* (08141) 902 41
E-mail: sales@berndtson.com
Web Site: www.berndtson.com
Key Personnel
Man Dir: Kerstin Borch *E-mail:* kborch@berndtson.com; Markus Borch
Founded: 1988
Publish laminated international road & city maps & other specialized cartography. Also produces cartography-related marketing products.
Membership(s): Borsenverein des Deutschen Buchhandels, Verkehrsnummer: 10404.
Subjects: Geography, Geology, Travel, Tourism
ISBN Prefix(es): 3-928855; 3-929811; 3-89707
Total Titles: 180 Print
Associate Companies: Frog Map Co, 14031 80 Ave, Seminole, FL 33776, United States, Contact: Lisa Bohart

Bernecker Mediagruppe
Unter dem Schoeneberg 1, 34212 Melsungen
Tel: (05661) 731-0 *Fax:* (05661) 731-111
Web Site: www.bernecker.de
Key Personnel
Manager: Conrad Fischer *E-mail:* fischer@bernecker.de
Assistant Editor-in-Chief: Mr Roennfranz
Founded: 1869
ISBN Prefix(es): 3-87064
Subsidiaries: A Bernecker GmbH & Co Druckerei KG; Agentur Bernecker Media Ware GmbH

C Bertelsmann Verlag GmbH
Neumarkterstr 28, 81673 Munich 80
Mailing Address: Postfach 800360, 81603 Munich
Tel: (089) 41360; (1805) 990505 (hotline for literature & nonfiction) *Fax:* (089) 4372-2812

E-mail: vertrieb.verlagsgruppe@randomhouse.de
Web Site: www.randomhouse.de
Telex: 523259 vbm ve d
Key Personnel
Press Dir: Margrit Schoenberger
Founded: 1835
Membership(s): TR- Verlagsunion GmbH.
Subjects: Art, Biography, Fiction, Government, Political Science, Nonfiction (General)
ISBN Prefix(es): 3-570
Parent Company: Verlagsgruppe Bertelsmann GmbH
Associate Companies: Verlagsgruppe Bertelsmann GmbH
U.S. Office(s): Bettina Schrewe Literary Scouting, 101 Fifth Ave, Suite 11B, New York, NY 10003, United States (US Scout)

Bertelsmann Lexikon Verlag GmbH
Avenwedderstr 55, D-33311 Gutersloh
Mailing Address: Postfach 800360, 81603 Munich
Tel: (05241) 800 *Fax:* (05241) 73075
E-mail: vertrieb.verlagsgruppe@bertelsmann.de
Web Site: www.lexiconverlag.de/lexiconverlag.html
Telex: 933646 *Cable:* BERTELSMANN GUTERSLOH
Key Personnel
President & Chief Executive Officer: Dr Mark Woessner
Division President, Bertelsmann Publishing Group International: Bernhard von Minckwitz
Division President: Frank Woessner
Division President, Electronic Media: Manfred Lahnstein
Division President, Printing & Manufacturing: Dr Gunter Thielen
Vice Chairman & Chief Executive Officer, Gruner & Jahr AG: Gerd Schulte-Hillen
Chairman & Chief Executive Officer, Bertelsmann Music Group (BMG), New York: Dr Michael Dornemann
Subjects: Anthropology, Art, Biography, Business, Career Development, Communications, Economics, Fiction, Film, Video, Foreign Countries, History, How-to, Law, Management, Marketing, Medicine, Nursing, Dentistry, Radio, TV, Technology, Travel
ISBN Prefix(es): 3-570
Parent Company: Bertelsmann HG
Associate Companies: Bertelsmann Inc, 1540 Broadway, New York, NY 10036, United States
Divisions: International Book & Record Clubs; Book Germany; Bertelsmann Publishing Group International Printing & Manufacturing; Bertelsmann Music Group, Electronic Media; Gruner + Jahr; Book Germany
U.S. Office(s): Bettina Schrewe Literary Scouting, 101 Fifth Ave, Suite 11B, NY 10003, United States (US Scout)
Book Club(s): Bertelsmann Club; Bertelsmann Club Vertrieb; Buchgemeinschaft Donauland, Kremayr & Scheriau; Buch-und Schallplattenfreunde; Deutsche Buch-Gemeinschaft; Deutscher Buecherbund; EBG Buch & Musik; Hallo RTL; Ring der Musikfreunde; Club Top 13; Doubleday Australia, Australia; ECI voor Boeken en Platen, Belgium; France Loisirs Belgique, Belgium; Doubleday Book & Music Clubs; Quebec Loisirs; France Loisirs, France; Librarie Papeterie Marigny et Joly, France; Setradis, France; SGED, France; Bookclub of Ireland; Euroclub Italia, Italy; Librum, Italy; ECI voor Boeken en Platen, Netherlands; Eurobook, Netherlands; Grambo BV, Netherlands; Nederlandse Lezerskring Boek en Plaat, Netherlands; Doubleday New Zealand, New Zealand; Circulo de Leitores, Portugal; Circulo de Lectores, Spain; France Loisirs Suisse, Switzerland; Book Club Associates, United Kingdom; Doubleday Book & Music Club, New York, NY,

United States; Magyar Konyvklub, Budapest, Hungary; Magyar Konyvklub, Budapest, Hungary

Verlag Bertelsmann Stiftung (Bertelsmann Foundation Publishers)+
Carl-Bertelsmannstr 256, 33311 Gutersloh
Mailing Address: Postfach 103, 33311 Gutersloh
Tel: (05241) 8181197 *Fax:* (05241) 8181931
E-mail: sabine.klemm@bertelsmann.de
Web Site: www.bertelsmann-stiftung.de/verlag
Key Personnel
Publisher: Annette Sanders
Subjects: Education, Government, Political Science
ISBN Prefix(es): 3-89204
Number of titles published annually: 50 Print
Total Titles: 308 Print
Orders to: Brooking Institution Press, 1775 Massachusetts Ave NW, Washington, DC 20036, United States *Fax:* 202-797-2960

W Bertelsmann Verlag GmbH & Co KG
Auf dem Esch 4, 33619 Bielefeld
Mailing Address: Postfach 100633, 33506 Bielefeld
Tel: (0521) 911-01-0 *Fax:* (0521) 911 01-79
E-mail: service@wbv.de
Web Site: www.wbv.de; www.berufsbildung.de; www.berufe.net
Key Personnel
Dir: Thomas Kellersohn *Tel:* (0521) 91101-38
E-mail: thomas.kellersohn@wbv.de
Founded: 1864
Subjects: Career Development, Education, Foreign Countries, Labor, Industrial Relations, Law, Management, Public Administration, Science (General), Social Sciences, Sociology, Vocational Training
ISBN Prefix(es): 3-7639
Distributor for Bundesanstalt fuer Arbeit; Bundesinstitut fuer Berufsbildung; Deutsches Institute fuer Erwachsenenbildung

BertelsmannSpringer Science & Business Media GmbH, see Springer Science+Business Media GmbH & Co KG, Berlin

Verlag Beruf und Schule Belz KG+
Albert-Schweitzer-Ring 45, 25524 Itzehoe
Mailing Address: Postfach 2008, 25510 Itzehoe
Tel: (04821) 40140 *Fax:* (04821) 4941
E-mail: info@vbus.de
Web Site: www.verlag-beruf-schule.de
Key Personnel
Contact: Renate Golpon
Founded: 1970
Subjects: Career Development, Chemistry, Chemical Engineering, Computer Science, Humor, Mathematics, Poetry, Publishing & Book Trade Reference
ISBN Prefix(es): 3-88013
Imprints: Edition Heitere Poetik
Divisions: Edition Heitere Poetik; Buchdienst B & S
Orders to: VVA Bertelsmann Distribution GmbH, Postfach 7777, 33310 Guetersloh

Betzel Verlag GmbH+
Postfach 1905, 31569 Nienburg
Tel: (05021) 91 48 69 *Fax:* (05021) 91 48 68
E-mail: betzelverlag@proximedia.de
Key Personnel
Man Dir, Rights & Permissions: Anita Kubicek
Formerly Gruppe Hinterhaus.
Subjects: Art, Drama, Theater, Fiction, Philosophy, Poetry
ISBN Prefix(es): 3-921818; 3-929017

Beust Verlag GmbH+
Fraunhoferstr 13, 80469 Munich

Tel: (089) 230895-0 *Fax:* (089) 230895-131
E-mail: mail@beustverlag.de
Founded: 1994
Subjects: Child Care & Development, Psychology, Psychiatry
ISBN Prefix(es): 3-89530
Subsidiaries: Gaia Text Publishing

Beuth Verlag GmbH
Burggrafenstr 6, 10787 Berlin
Tel: (030) 26010 *Fax:* (030) 26011260
E-mail: info@beuth.de
Web Site: www.beuth.de; www.mybeuth.de
Telex: 183622 bvb d; 185730 bvb d *Cable:* DEUTSCHNORMEN BERLIN
Key Personnel
Man Dir: Georg Gruetzner; Claudia Michalski
Publicity Dir: Peter Anthony
Founded: 1924
Specialize in technical & scientific literature.
Subjects: Architecture & Interior Design, Chemistry, Chemical Engineering, Communications, Electronics, Electrical Engineering, Energy, Engineering (General), Environmental Studies, Health, Nutrition, Management, Mathematics, Mechanical Engineering, Physics, Securities, Technology, Theology, Transportation
ISBN Prefix(es): 3-410
Parent Company: DIN Deutsches Institut fuer Normung eV
Orders to: Osterreichisches Normungsinstitut, Heinestr 38, 1021 Vienna 2, Austria (in Austria)
Schweizerische Normenvereinigung, Muehlebachstr 54, 8008 Zurich, Switzerland (in Switzerland)

Bewusster Leben, *imprint of* Koenigsfurt Verlag, Evelin Buerger et Johannes Fiebig

Joachim Beyer Verlag+
Langgasse 25, 96142 Hollfeld
Tel: (09274) 95051 *Fax:* (09274) 95053
E-mail: info@beyerverlag.de
Web Site: www.derschachladen.de
Key Personnel
Owner: Joachim Beyer
Founded: 1972
Subjects: Crafts, Games, Hobbies
ISBN Prefix(es): 3-88805; 3-921202; 3-89168

Bezugsbedingungen, *imprint of* Johann Wolfgang Goethe Universitat

Biblio Verlag
Subsidiary of Zeller Verlag GmbH & Co
Auf dem Busch 2, 49143 Bissendorf
Tel: (05402) 641720 *Fax:* (05402) 641722
E-mail: info@militaria-biblio.de; biblio-verlag@t-online.de
Web Site: www.militaria-biblio.de
Subjects: Archaeology, Art, History, Language Arts, Linguistics, Law, Military Science, Philosophy, Religion - Other
ISBN Prefix(es): 3-7648

Bibliographisches Institut & F A Brockhaus AG+
Duden Route 6, 68167 Mannheim
Mailing Address: Postfach 10 03 11, 68003 Mannheim
Tel: (0621) 3901-01 *Fax:* (0621) 3901-3 91
Web Site: www.brockhaus.de *Cable:* BIFAB
Key Personnel
Man Dir: Albrecht Kiel; Andreas Langenscheidt; Dr Florian Langenscheidt; Dr Karl-Josef Schmidt; Dr Michael Wegner
Sales: Rosita Throm
Publicity Manager: Hans Gareis
Sales Dir, Rights & Permissions: Claus Greuner
Public Relations: Anja zum Hingst

Product Informations: Michaela Thuerling
 Tel: (0621) 3901-650 *Fax:* (0621) 3901-633
Pressing & Public Work: Klaus Holoch
 Tel: (0621) 3901-385 *Fax:* (0621) 3901-395
Personnel: Wolf of Zobeltitz *Tel:* (0621) 3901-267
Founded: 1805
Publishers of the Duden Series of Dictionaries, Brockhaus und Meyer Series of Encyclopedias.
Subjects: Engineering (General), Geography, Geology, Language Arts, Linguistics, Medicine, Nursing, Dentistry, Science (General)
ISBN Prefix(es): 3-411
Associate Companies: Thueringer Verlagsauslieferung Langenscheidt KG, Langenscheidtstr 10, 99867 Gotha; Mohr MORAWA, Sulzengasse 2, 1232 Vienna, Austria; Schweizer Buchzentrum, Postfach 522, 4600 Olten, Switzerland
Subsidiaries: Bibliographisches Institut GmbH (Mannheim); Dr Helmuth Buecking GmbH (Mannheim); Brockhaus Direkt Gmbh (Mannheim); Suedbuch-Vertriebgesellschaft mbH (Mannheim); Thueringer Verlagsausliferung Langenscheidt SK (Mannheim); Bibliographisches Institut & F A Brockhaus (Salzburg, Austria); VBH-Verlagsbuchhandelsgesellschaft mbH (Salzburg, Austria); Bibliographisches Institut & F A Brockhaus AG (Zug, Switzerland); Suedbuch Vertrieb AG (Zurich, Switzerland)

Bibliographisches Institut GmbH+
Subsidiary of Bibliographisches Institut und F A Brockhaus AG
Querstr 18, 04103 Leipzig
Mailing Address: Postfach 100130, 04001 Leipzig
Tel: (0341) 97 86-30 *Fax:* (0341) 97 86-5 60
Key Personnel
Man Dir: Dieter Baer
Dir, Rights & Permissions: Dr Karl-Josef Schmidt; Dr Michael Wegner
Founded: 1826
ISBN Prefix(es): 3-323

Bibliomed - Medizinische Verlagsgesellschaft mbH
Stadtwaldpark 10, 34202 Melsungen
Mailing Address: Postfach 1150, 34202 Melsungen
Tel: (05661) 73440 *Fax:* (05661) 8360
E-mail: info@bibliomed.de
Web Site: www.bibliomed.de
Key Personnel
Man Dir: Uta Meurer
Dir: Dr Annette Beller
Editorial: Markus Boucsein
Sales, Rights & Permissions: Harald Horchler
Founded: 1977
Subjects: Medicine, Nursing, Dentistry
ISBN Prefix(es): 3-89556
Total Titles: 8 CD-ROM
Imprints: Krankenpflegeforschung; Melsunger Medizinische Mitteilungen

Bibliothek Klassischer Texte, *imprint of* Wissenschaftliche Buchgesellschaft

Bibliothek Natur & Wissenschaft, *imprint of* Verlag Natur & Wissenschaft Harro Hieronimus & Dr Jurgen Schmidt

Edition Bielefelden Kunstverein, *imprint of* Pendragon Verlag

Bielefelder Verlagsanstalt GmbH & Co KG Richard Kaselowsky+
Ravensbergerstr 10 F, 33602 Bielefeld
Mailing Address: Postfach 100653, 33506 Bielefeld
Tel: (0521) 595 514 *Fax:* (0521) 595 518
E-mail: kontakt@bva-bielefeld.de
Web Site: www.bva-bielefeld.de
Key Personnel
Publishing Dir: Hans-Joerg Kaiser *Tel:* (0521) 510-514
Books & Maps: Ralph Plum *Tel:* (0521) 521-510
Public Services: Miriam Flacke *Tel:* (0521) 595 542
Founded: 1946
Publish books & maps for cyclists (travel guides) & in Germany bicycle report books.
Membership(s): Borsenverein.
Subjects: How-to, Outdoor Recreation, Travel
ISBN Prefix(es): 3-87073
Total Titles: 170 Print
Parent Company: E Gundlach GmbH & Co KG
Distributed by Mairs Geographischer Verlag

Biermann Verlag GmbH
Otto-Hahn-Str 7, 50997 Cologne
Tel: (02236) 376-0 *Fax:* (02236) 376-999
E-mail: info@biermann.net
Web Site: www.biermann-online.de
Key Personnel
Contact: Dr Hans Biermann
Man Dir: Ernst-Uwe Kopperf
Leader: Christoph Dusse *Tel:* (02236) 376-202 *Fax:* (02236) 376-203 *E-mail:* du@biermann-verlag.de
Editor: Bernd Schunk *Tel:* (02236) 376-400 *Fax:* (02236) 376-401 *E-mail:* sk@biermann-verlag.de
CVD Print: Axel Viola *Tel:* (02236) 376-402 *Fax:* (02236) 376-403 *E-mail:* av@biermann-verlag.de
Graphics: Heike Dargel *Tel:* (02236) 376-151 *E-mail:* hd@biermann-verlag.de
Marketing: Jan-Hendrik Wiedemann *Tel:* (02236) 376-300 *Fax:* (02236) 376-301 *E-mail:* wi@biermann-verlag.de
EDP: Thomas Narres *Tel:* (02236) 376-260 *Fax:* (02236) 376-261 *E-mail:* it@biermann-verlag.de
Founded: 1989
Subjects: Medicine, Nursing, Dentistry
ISBN Prefix(es): 3-924469; 3-930505

Bild und Heimat Verlagsgesellschaft GmbH
Zwickauerstr 68, 08468 Reichenbach
Mailing Address: Postfach 1143, 08461 Reichenbach
Tel: (03765) 78 15-0 *Fax:* (03765) 1 22 45
Key Personnel
Man Dir & Owner: Harald Guenther; Stephan Treuleben
Man Dir: Sven Hoefgen
Founded: 1964
ISBN Prefix(es): 3-7310
Parent Company: Treuleben & Bischof Beteiligungsgesellschaft, Planegg

Bild und Text, *imprint of* Wilhelm Fink GmbH & Co Verlags-KG

Bildarchiv Preussischer Kulturbesitz bpk+
Maerkisches Ufer 16-18, 10179 Berlin (Mitte)
Tel: (030) 278 792 0 *Fax:* (030) 278 792 39
E-mail: bildarchiv@bpk.spk-berlin.de
Web Site: www.bildarchiv-bpk.de
Key Personnel
Man Dir, Rights & Permissions: Dr Karl H Puetz
Founded: 1965
Subjects: Photography, Prussian picture archives
Parent Company: Stiftung Preussischer Kulturbesitz

BW Bildung und Wissen Verlag und Software GmbH+
Suedwestpark 82, 90449 Nuremberg
Mailing Address: Postfach 820150, 90252 Nuremberg
Tel: (0911) 96 76-175 *Fax:* (0911) 96 76-189
E-mail: info@bwverlag.de
Web Site: www.bwverlag.de
Key Personnel
Man Dir & International Rights Contact: L Lodter; U Sippel
Contact for Orders: Thomas Preuss *E-mail:* thomas.preuss@bwverlag.de
Contact: Silke Radzuweit *Tel:* (0911) 9676158 *E-mail:* silke.radzuweit@bwverlag.de
Founded: 1975
Specialist publishers for initial & further training, occupation & employment.
Membership(s): Stock Exchange of German Booksellers, Bavarian Booksellers & Publishers Association.
Subjects: Career Development, Education
ISBN Prefix(es): 3-8214

Bindernagelsche Buchhandlung
Kaiserstr 72, 61169 Friedberg
Mailing Address: Postfach 100153, 61141 Friedberg
Tel: (06031) 7323-0 *Fax:* (06031) 734949
Key Personnel
Owner: Karl C Herrmann
Founded: 1834
Subjects: Regional Interests
ISBN Prefix(es): 3-87076

Birkner & Co Zweigniederlassung Mecklenburg-Vorpommern
Winsbergring 38, 22525 Hamburg
Mailing Address: Postfach 540750, 22507 Hamburg
Tel: (040) 85308502 *Fax:* (040) 85308381
Key Personnel
Man Dir: Dr Christoph Dunnrath
Contact: Stefan Otto
Founded: 1904
Also acts as Internationale Zellstoff- und Papierindustrie.
ISBN Prefix(es): 3-923543; 3-929467
Parent Company: Dumrath & Fassnacht Komm Gesellschaft

BKV-Brasilienkunde Verlag GmbH
Sunderstr 15, 49497 Mettingen
Mailing Address: Postfach 1220, 49494 Mettingen
Tel: (05452) 4598 *Fax:* (05452) 4357
E-mail: brasilien@T-Online.de
Web Site: www.brasilienkunde.de; home.t-online.de/home/Brasilien
Key Personnel
Man Dir, Rights & Permissions: P O Gogolok
Founded: 1979
Subjects: Ethnicity, Foreign Countries, Regional Interests, Religion - Other, Social Sciences, Sociology
ISBN Prefix(es): 3-88559
Imprints: Aspekter der Brasilienkunde; BTB

Blackwell Wissenschafts-Verlag GmbH+
Kurfuerstendamm 57, 10707 Berlin
Tel: (030) 32 79 06-0 *Fax:* (030) 32 79 06-10
E-mail: verlag@blackwell.de
Web Site: www.blackwis.de
Key Personnel
Man Dir: Elisabeth Kukla *Tel:* (030) 32 79 06-16
Marketing Manager: Christine Laufer *Tel:* (030) 32 79 06-11 *E-mail:* christine.laufer@blackwell.de
Foreign Rights & Permissions: Axel Ader *Tel:* (030) 32 79 06-12 *E-mail:* rights@blackwell.de
Founded: 1989
Integration in 1994 of the Scientific Program of Paul Parey Publishers (Berlin/Hamburg) & 1996 Integration of the Professional List of Paul Parey Publishers (Berlin/Hamburg).
Subjects: Agriculture, Animals, Pets, Biological Sciences, Environmental Studies, Gardening, Plants, Medicine, Nursing, Dentistry, Natural

History, Nonfiction (General), Physical Sciences, Veterinary Science
ISBN Prefix(es): 3-89412; 3-8263
Parent Company: Blackwell Science, Ltd, Osney Mead, Oxford OX2 OEL
Imprints: Parey Buchverlag
Subsidiaries: Blackwell Wissenschafts-Verlag
U.S. Office(s): Blackwell Science Inc, Commerce Place, 350 Main St, Malden, MA 02148, United States
Orders to: Koch, Neff & Oetinger, Schockenriedstr 39, 70565 Stuttgart

Edition Klaus Blahak Dr Fredric Kroll+
Lange Reihe 102, 20099 Hamburg
Tel: (049) 761-244-73 *Fax:* (049) 761-244-73
Key Personnel
Contact: Stefan Blahak; Dr Fredric Kroll
 Tel: (049) 761-243-77
Founded: 1976
Subjects: Biography, Literature, Literary Criticism, Essays
ISBN Prefix(es): 3-88179
Total Titles: 10 Print
Publication(s): Biography of Klaus Mann; German Literature in Exile, 1933-1949
Distributed by MaennerschwarmSkript Verlag

Blanvalet VerlagGmbH+
Neumarkter Str 18, 81673 Munich
Mailing Address: Postfach 800360, 81603 Munich
Tel: (089) 41360; (089) 4372-0 (literature hotline) *Fax:* (089) 4372-2812
E-mail: vertrieb.verlagsgruppe@randomhouse.de
Web Site: www.blanvalet-verlag.de
Telex: 529965 wg vmn d *Cable:* Bertelsmann Muenchen
Founded: 1935
Subjects: Biography
ISBN Prefix(es): 3-7645
Parent Company: Verlagsgruppe Bertelsmann GmbH
U.S. Office(s): Bettina Schrewe Literary Scouting, 101 Fifth Ave, Suite 11B, New York, NY 10003, United States (US Scout)

Verlag Die Blaue Eule
Annastr 74, 45130 Essen
Tel: (0201) 8 77 69 63 *Fax:* (0201) 8 77 69 64
E-mail: info@die-blaue-eule.de
Web Site: www.die-blaue-eule.de
Key Personnel
Publisher: Dr W L Hohmann
Contact: Eva Wunsch
Founded: 1983
Galeria.
Subjects: Art, Education, History, Language Arts, Linguistics, Music, Dance, Mythology, Philosophy, Psychology, Psychiatry, Science (General), Social Sciences, Sociology, Theology
ISBN Prefix(es): 3-924368; 3-89206; 3-89924
Total Titles: 1,000 Print
Distributed by Engros Buchhandlung Dessauer; Freihofer AG Verlagsauslieferung Wissenschaft

Die Blauen Buecher (The Blue Book), *imprint of* Karl Robert Langewiesche Nachfolger Hans Koester KG

Blaukreuz-Verlag Wuppertal+
Freiligrathstr 27, 42289 Wuppertal
Mailing Address: Postfach 200252, 42202 Wuppertal
Tel: (0202) 6200370 *Fax:* (0202) 6200381
E-mail: bkv@blaukreuz.de
Web Site: www.blaukreuz.de
Key Personnel
Publisher: Horst Westmeier *E-mail:* westmeier@blaukreuz.de
Founded: 1892
Subjects: Health, Nutrition, Human Relations, Literature, Literary Criticism, Essays, Self-Help, Addiction & Assistance
ISBN Prefix(es): 3-920106; 3-89175
Number of titles published annually: 7 Print
Total Titles: 70 Audio
Parent Company: Blaues Kreuz in Deutschland eV, Wuppertal
Distributed by Blaukreuz-Verlag Bern (Switzerland); BMK Wartburg Vertriebsges.mbH (Austria)
Distributor for Nicol-Verlag Kassel
Distribution Center: Chris Media GmbH, Staufenberg

Bleicher Verlag GmbH+
Weilimdorfestr 76, 70839 Gerlingen
Mailing Address: Postfach 10 01 23, 70826 Gerlingen
Tel: (07156) 43 08-0 *Fax:* (07156) 43 08-27
E-mail: info@bleicher-verlag.de
Web Site: www.bleicher-verlag.de
Key Personnel
Dir: Rainer Abel
Publisher, Editorial: Ev Marie Bartolitius
Publisher, Editorial, Rights & Permissions: Thomas Bleicher
Sales: Klaus Vahlbruch
Press Relations: Edda Bournot
Founded: 1968
Subjects: Fiction, Government, Political Science, History, Social Sciences, Sociology
ISBN Prefix(es): 3-88350; 3-7953; 3-7988; 3-921097
Number of titles published annually: 20 Print
Subsidiaries: Hoffmann Verlag GmbH

BLISTA, see Deutsche Blinden-Bibliothek

Eberhard Blottner Verlag GmbH+
Silberbachstr 9, 65232 Taunusstein
Mailing Address: Postfach 1104, 65219 Taunusstein
Tel: (06128) 2 36 00 *Fax:* (06128) 21180
E-mail: blottner@blottner.de
Web Site: www.blottner.de *Cable:* BLOTTNERTAUNUSSTEIN
Key Personnel
Publisher, Rights & Permissions: Eberhard Blottner
Marketing: Britta Blottner
Founded: 1988
Subjects: Architecture & Interior Design, Crafts, Games, Hobbies, Earth Sciences, Environmental Studies, House & Home
ISBN Prefix(es): 3-89367
Total Titles: 28 Print
Associate Companies: Blottner Fachverlag GmbH & Co KG

BLT, *imprint of* Verlagsgruppe Luebbe GmbH & Co KG

BLV Verlagsgesellschaft mbH+
Lothstr 29, 80797 Munich
Tel: (089) 127050 *Fax:* (089) 12705354
E-mail: blv.verlag@blv.de
Web Site: www.blv.de *Cable:* BLV VERLAG
Key Personnel
Man Dir, Book Division: Hartwig Schneider
Marketing & Distribution Manager: Michael Wellbrock
Editorial, Nature: Wilhelm Eisenreich
Editorial, Sports: Juergen Kemmler
Foreign Rights: Undine Hoegl *Tel:* (089) 12705-417 *Fax:* (089) 12705-415 *E-mail:* undine.hoegl@blv.de; Hannelore Koenig *Tel:* (089) 12705-416 *Fax:* (089) 12705-415 *E-mail:* hannelore.koenig@blv.de
Book Trade: Karin Herbschleb *E-mail:* karin.herbschleb@blv.de
Warehouse & Specialty Shop: Helga Weingartner *E-mail:* helga.weingartner@blv.de
Delivery Trade: Eva Bednarek *E-mail:* eva.bednarek@blv.de
Founded: 1946
Membership(s): TR-Verlagsunion GmbH.
Subjects: Agriculture, Animals, Pets, Astronomy, Gardening, Plants, Natural History, Outdoor Recreation, Sports, Athletics, Travel
ISBN Prefix(es): 3-405
Number of titles published annually: 80 Print
Total Titles: 600 Print
Imprints: VUA (agricultural titles)
Subsidiaries: DLV Deutscher Landwirtschaftsverlag GmbH
Branch Office(s)
BLV Verlagsgesellschaft mbH, Verlagsbuero Berlin, Gurtelstr 29a-30, 10247 Berlin
Distributed by Athesia Buch GmbH (Italy)
Distributor for Ceres Verlag
Warehouse: BLV Auslieferung, Rotwandweg 2, 82024 Taufkirchen

Verlag Erwin Bochinsky GmbH & Co KG+
Muenchener Str 45, 60329 Frankfurt am Main
Tel: (069) 27 13 78 90 *Fax:* (069) 27 13 78 94
Web Site: www.bochinsky.de
Key Personnel
Man Dir: Helmut Amberg; Thilo M Kramny
Founded: 1952
Specialize in musical instruments (acoustic & electronic).
Membership(s): Europiano.
Subjects: Electronics, Electrical Engineering, Music, Dance, Nonfiction (General)
ISBN Prefix(es): 3-920112; 3-923639
Parent Company: PPVMEDIEN GmbH, Dachauer Str 376, 85232 Feldgeding

Bock und Herchen Verlag
Reichenbergerstr 11e, 53604 Bad Honnef
Mailing Address: Postfach 11 45, 53581 Bad Honnef
Tel: (02224) 57 75 *Fax:* (02224) 7 83 10
E-mail: buh@bock-net.de
Web Site: www.b-u-b.de
Key Personnel
Man Dir, Rights & Permissions: Prof Karl Heinrich Bock
Founded: 1977
Subjects: Library & Information Sciences, Science (General)
ISBN Prefix(es): 3-88347

Boehlau-Verlag GmbH & Cie+
Ursulaplatz 1, 50668 Cologne
Tel: (0221) 91 39 0-0 *Fax:* (0221) 91 39 0-32
E-mail: vertrieb@boehlau.de
Web Site: www.boehlau.de *Cable:* BOHLAU, COLOGNE
Key Personnel
Man Dir: Dr Peter Rauch *E-mail:* peter.rauch@boehlau.at
Sales & Distribution: Joachim Bischofs
 Tel: (0221) 91390-16
Founded: 1951
Subjects: Anthropology, Archaeology, Art, Education, History, Journalism, Language Arts, Linguistics, Social Sciences, Sociology, Women's Studies
ISBN Prefix(es): 3-412
Number of titles published annually: 180 Print
Total Titles: 1,800 Print
Associate Companies: Boehlau Verlag GmbH, Sachsenplatz 4-6, 1201 Vienna, Austria
 Tel: (01) 3024270 *Fax:* (01) 3302432
 E-mail: boehlau@boehlau.at *Web Site:* www.boehlau.at
Branch Office(s)
Boehlau Verlag GmbH & Cie, Eisfeld 5, 99423 Weimar
Orders to: Koch, Neff und Oetinger & Co, Postfach 800620, 70506 Stuttgart

Verlag Hermann Boehlaus Nachfolger Weimar GmbH & Co+
Prellerstr 2a, 99423 Weimar
Mailing Address: Postfach 2260, 99403 Weimar
Tel: (03643) 8508-90; (03643) 8508-91
Fax: (03643) 8508-92
Key Personnel
Editor & International Rights: Gunter Lauterbach
Founded: 1624
Subjects: Architecture & Interior Design, Art, Foreign Countries, History, Law, Literature, Literary Criticism, Essays, Poetry, Science (General), Theology
ISBN Prefix(es): 3-7400
Orders to: Verlagsaurlieferung Karlstr 10, Postfach 546, 72488 Sigmaringen

Klaus Boer Verlag+
Vokartstr 30, 80634 Munich
Tel: (089) 13938099 *Fax:* (089) 13938098
E-mail: boerv@online.de
Web Site: www.boerverlag.de
Key Personnel
Owner: Klaus Boer
Founded: 1984
Subjects: Art, History, Literature, Literary Criticism, Essays, Philosophy
ISBN Prefix(es): 3-924963
Orders to: Buchvertrieb Grimmstr, Saalburgstr 3, 12099 Berlin

Edition Boiselle+
Wormsestr 30, 67346 Speyer
Tel: (06232) 629662 *Fax:* (06232) 629664
E-mail: info@edition-boiselle.de
Web Site: www.edition-boiselle.de
Key Personnel
Man Dir: Gabriele Boiselle
Founded: 1990
Subjects: Calendars, Equestrian
ISBN Prefix(es): 3-927589
Sales Office(s): Kraemer Pferdesportversandhaus, 68764 Hockenheim *Tel:* (0180) 5949400 *Fax:* (06205) 949488 *E-mail:* info@kraemer-pferdesport.de *Web Site:* www.kraemer-pferdesport.de
Distributed by Buecher Zentrum (Austria); Edition Boiselle (UK, US, France & Spain); Islandpferdehof Plarenga (Switzerland); Mias Ridsport (Sweden)

Bolanz Verlag fur Alle
Friedrichstr, Moltkestr 11/1, 88046 Friedrichshafen
Mailing Address: Postfach 2528, 88015 Friedrichshafen
Tel: (07541) 33 6 99 *Fax:* (07541) 32467
Specialize in calendars.
ISBN Prefix(es): 3-927744; 3-932640
Bookshop(s): Christliche Buchhandlung Buecherecke, Ailingerstr 11, 88046 Friedrichshafen; Christliche Buchhandlung Buecherecke, Zeppelinstr 2, 88212 Ravensburg; Christliche Buchhandlung Buecherecke, Ambrosius-Blaresstr 3, 78532 Tuttlingen

CB-Verlag Carl Boldt
Baseler Str 80, 12205 Berlin
Mailing Address: Postfach 45 02 07, 12172 Berlin
Tel: (030) 833 70 87 *Fax:* (030) 833 91 25
E-mail: cb-verlag@t-online.de
Key Personnel
Contact: Wolf P Gesellius
Founded: 1904
Subjects: Law, Medicine, Nursing, Dentistry
ISBN Prefix(es): 3-920731

Bollmann-Bildkarten-Verlag GmbH & Co KG
Lilienthalplatz 1, 38108 Braunschweig
Tel: (0531) 332069 *Fax:* (0531) 353064
E-mail: info@bollmann-bildkarten.de
Web Site: www.bollmann-bildkarten.de
Key Personnel
Man Dir, Rights & Permissions: Friedrich Bollmann
Founded: 1948

Dr Bolte KG, see Polyglott-Verlag

Bonifatius GmbH Druck-Buch-Verlag+
Karl-Schurzstr 26, 33100 Paderborn
Mailing Address: Postfach 1280, 33042 Paderborn
Tel: (05251) 153 0 *Fax:* (05251) 153 104
E-mail: mail@bonifatius.de
Web Site: www.bonifatius.de
Key Personnel
Manager: Rainer Beseler; Gerd Geliner
Founded: 1869
Subjects: Art, Literature, Literary Criticism, Essays, Music, Dance, Theology
ISBN Prefix(es): 3-87088; 3-00; 3-89710
Imprints: Kontur; Creator

Bonsai-Centrum
Mannheimerstr 401, 69123 Heidelberg-Weiblingen
Tel: (06221) 8491-0 *Fax:* (06221) 849130
E-mail: info@bonsai-centrum.de
Web Site: www.bonsai-centrum.de
Key Personnel
President, Publisher & Author: Paul Lesniewicz
Subjects: Gardening, Plants
ISBN Prefix(es): 3-924982; 3-9800345

Richard Boorberg Verlag GmbH & Co
Scharrstr 2, 70563 Stuttgart
Tel: (0711) 73 85-0 *Fax:* (0711) 73 85-100
Web Site: www.boorberg.de
Key Personnel
Manager: Dr Berndt Oesterhelt
Administration: Markus Ott
Production: Werner Frasch
Sales: Hermann Ruckdeschel
International Rights: Roderich Dohse
Founded: 1927
Subjects: Law
ISBN Prefix(es): 3-415
Subsidiaries: Josef Moll Verlag GmbH & Co
Branch Office(s)
Berlin
Hanover
Levelingstr 6a, 81673 Munich *Tel:* (089) 43 60 00-0 *Fax:* (089) 4 36 15 64
Weimar

Boosey & Hawkes Music Publishers LTD, London+
Luetzowufer 26, 10787 Berlin
Tel: (030) 25001300 *Fax:* (030) 25001399
E-mail: musikverlag@boosey.com
Web Site: www.boosey.com/publishing
Key Personnel
Chief Executive: Richard Holland
Manager: W Jacobs
Founded: 1838
Subjects: Music, Dance
ISBN Prefix(es): 3-7931
Parent Company: Boosey & Hawkes Music Publishers Ltd, London
Branch Office(s)
Boosey & Hawkes Pty Ltd, Unit 12/6 Campbell St, Artarmon, NSW 2076, Australia *Tel:* (02) 9439 4144 *Fax:* (02) 9439 2912 *E-mail:* info@boosey.au.com
Buffet Crampon Limited, 8-17, Toyo-4, Koto-ku, Tokyo 135-0016, Japan *Tel:* (05632) 5511 *Fax:* (05632) 5527 *E-mail:* tokyo@boosey.com
Boosey & Hawkes Music Publishers LTD, 295 Regent St, London W1B 2JH, United Kingdom *Tel:* (020) 7580 2060 *Fax:* (020) 7637 7109 *E-mail:* composers@boosey.com
U.S. Office(s): Boosey & Hawkes New York Inc, 35 East 21 St, New York, NY 10010-6216, United States *Tel:* 212-358-5300 *Fax:* 212-358-5301 *E-mail:* info.ny@boosey.com
Bookshop(s): 10623 Berlin *Tel:* (030) 31100310

Born-Verlag+
Leuschnerstr 72-74, 34134 Kassel
Mailing Address: Postfach 420220, 34071 Kassel
Tel: (0561) 4095107 *Fax:* (0561) 4095112
E-mail: info.born@ec-jugend.de
Web Site: www.born-buch.de
Key Personnel
Publishing Manager: Claudia Siebert
    E-mail: siebert.born@ec-jugend.de
Founded: 1898
Subjects: Religion - Catholic, Religion - Protestant
ISBN Prefix(es): 3-87092

Borntraeger Verlagsbuchhandlung, *imprint of* Gebrueder Borntraeger Science Publishers

Gustav Bosse GmbH & Co KG+
Heinrich-Schutz-Allee 35, 34131 Kassel
Mailing Address: Postfach 101420, 34014 Kassel
Tel: (0561) 31 05-0 *Fax:* (0561) 31 05-2 40
E-mail: info@bosse-verlag.de
Web Site: www.bosse-verlag.de
Key Personnel
Man Dir: Barbara Scheuch-Voetterle; Leonhard Scheuch
Rights & Permissions: Thomas Tietze
Editor: Berthold Kloss
Founded: 1912
Subjects: Education, Music, Dance
ISBN Prefix(es): 3-7649
Parent Company: Verlag Baerenreiter, Kassel
Distributed by Barenreiter Ltd (UK); Barenreiter Verlag Basel AG (Switzerland)
Warehouse: KGA-Technischer Betrieb, Brandaustr 10, 34127 Kassel
Orders to: KGA, Postfach 102180, 34021 Kassel

Bote & Bock Musikalienhandelsgesellschaft mbH+
Lutzowufer 26, 10787 Berlin
Tel: (030) 2500-1300 *Fax:* (030) 2500-1399
E-mail: musikverlag@boosey.com
Key Personnel
Contact: Regina Steinhauber *Tel:* (030) 3110013-14
Founded: 1838
Primarily a music store.
Subjects: Music, Dance
ISBN Prefix(es): 3-7931

Bouvier Verlag+
Am Hof 28, 53113 Bonn
Mailing Address: Postfach 1268, 53002 Bonn
Tel: (0228) 72901124 *Fax:* (0228) 637909
E-mail: verlag@books.de
Web Site: www.bouvier-online.de
Key Personnel
Publishing Dir & International Rights: Peter Parusel
Sales, Press: Elisabeth Keuthen-Nuechel
Sales, President: Sabine Taeffner
Manager & Publishing Dir: Thomas Grundmonn
Founded: 1828
Subjects: Government, Political Science, Regional Interests, Science (General)
ISBN Prefix(es): 3-416
Orders to: Koch, Neff, Oetinger & Co, Schockenriedstr 39, 70565 Stuttgart *Tel:* (0711) 78991120 *Fax:* (0711) 78991155

Verlag Brandenburger Tor GmbH
Wittestr 30 K, 13509 Berlin

Tel: (030) 8557511 *Fax:* (030) 85605332
E-mail: info@verlag-brandenburger-tor.de
Key Personnel
Publisher: Klaus-Juergen Holzapfel; Andreas Holzapfel
Founded: 1973
Subjects: Government, Political Science
Subsidiaries: Verlag Brandenburger Tor
Orders to: NDV Neue Darmstaedter Verlagsanstalt, Postfach 1560, 53585 Bad Honnef *Tel:* (022241) 3232 *Fax:* (022241) 78639 *E-mail:* ndv@ndvverlag.de

Brandenburgisches Verlagshaus, *imprint of* Verlagsgruppe Dornier GmbH

Brandenburgisches Verlagshaus in der Dornier Medienholding GmbH+
Dircksenstr 48, 10178 Berlin
Tel: (030) 28447-112; (030) 28447-113
Fax: (030) 28447-123
E-mail: info@dornier-verlage.de
Web Site: www.dornier-verlage.de
Key Personnel
Man Dir: Dr Juergen A Bach; Peter Gutsch
Founded: 1956
Subjects: Biography, Engineering (General), Foreign Countries, History, Management, Maritime, Military Science, Nonfiction (General), Regional Interests, Travel
ISBN Prefix(es): 3-89488
Parent Company: Dormier Medienholding GmbH

Brandes & Apsel Verlag GmbH+
Scheidswaldstr 33, 60385 Frankfurt am Main
Tel: (069) 957 301 86 *Fax:* (069) 957 301 87
E-mail: brandes-apsel@doodees.de
Web Site: www.brandes-apsel-verlag.de
Founded: 1986
Subjects: Anthropology, Developing Countries, Education, Ethnicity, Fiction, Government, Political Science, Human Relations, Literature, Literary Criticism, Essays, Poetry, Psychology, Psychiatry, Social Sciences, Sociology, Dance, Psychoanalysis, Theater, Self Psychology
ISBN Prefix(es): 3-925798; 3-86099
Number of titles published annually: 40 Print
Total Titles: 300 Print
Orders to: Prolit Verlagsauslieferung, Siemensstr 16, 35463 Fernwald-Annerod *Tel:* (0641) 94393-22, (0641) 94393-23 *Fax:* (0641) 94393-29

Oscar Brandstetter Verlag GmbH & Co KG+
Wilhelminenstr 1a, 65193 Wiesbaden
Mailing Address: Postfach 1708, 65007 Wiesbaden
Tel: (0611) 9 91 20-0 *Fax:* (0611) 3 08 37 85
E-mail: brandstetter-verlag@t-online.de
Web Site: www.brandstetter-verlag.de
Key Personnel
Man Dir: Guenther H Froehlen
Founded: 1862
Subjects: Chemistry, Chemical Engineering, Communications, Computer Science, Economics, Electronics, Electrical Engineering, Engineering (General), Language Arts, Linguistics, Law, Medicine, Nursing, Dentistry, Physical Sciences, Technology
ISBN Prefix(es): 3-87097
Shipping Address: Koch, Neff & Oetinger & Co, Verlagsauslieferung Smlt, 70551 Stuttgart, Contact: Erika Vogelmann *Tel:* (0711) 78992123 *Fax:* (0711) 78991010
Warehouse: Koch, Neff & Oetinger & Co, Verlagsauslieferung Smlt, 70551 Stuttgart, Contact: Erika Vogelmann *Tel:* (0711) 78992123 *Fax:* (0711) 78991010
Orders to: Koch, Neff & Oetinger & Co, Verlagsauslieferung Smlt, 70551 Stuttgart, Contact: Erika Vogelmann *Tel:* (0711) 78992123 *Fax:* (0711) 78991010

Aspekter der Brasilienkunde, *imprint of* BKV-Brasilienkunde Verlag GmbH

Brasilienkunde Verlag GmbH, see BKV-Brasilienkunde Verlag GmbH

Breitkopf & Hartel+
Walkmuehlstr 52, 65195 Wiesbaden
Mailing Address: Postfach 1707, 65007 Wiesbaden
Tel: (0611) 450080 *Fax:* (0611) 4500859; (0611) 4500860; (0611) 4500861
E-mail: info@breitkopf.com
Web Site: www.breitkopf.com; www.breitkopf.de
Cable: BREITKOPFS WIESBADEN
Key Personnel
Man Dir: Gottfried Moeckel; Lieselotte Sievers
International Rights: Vivian Rehman
Tel: (0611) 45008 36 *Fax:* (0611) 45008 60
E-mail: rehman@breitkopf.de
UK Sales Representative: Robin Winter
Tel: (01263) 768732 *Fax:* (01263) 768733
E-mail: sales@breitkopf.com
Founded: 1719
Music publisher.
Subjects: Music, Dance
ISBN Prefix(es): 3-7651
Branch Office(s)
22 rue Chauchat, 75009 Paris, France, Contact: Mr Farid Aich *Tel:* (01) 48 01 01 33 *Fax:* (01) 48 01 01 66 *E-mail:* breitkopf.aich@wanadoo.fr
Deutscher Verlag fuer Musik, Bauhofstr 3-5, 04103 Leipzig *Tel:* (0341) 997190 *Fax:* (0341) 9971930 *E-mail:* leipzig@breitkopf.com
Obere Waldstr 30, 65232 Taunusstein *Tel:* (06128) 9663 0 *Fax:* (06128) 9663 50; (06128) 966360 *E-mail:* sales@breitkopf.com
Broome Cottage, The Street, Suffield Norwich NR 11 7EQ, United Kingdom, Contact: Robin Winter *Tel:* (01263) 768732 *Fax:* (01263) 768733 *E-mail:* sales@breitkopf.com

Breklumer Buchhandlung und Verlag
Kirchenstr 1, 25821 Breklum
Tel: (04671) 910020 *Fax:* (04671) 910030
E-mail: verlag@breklumer.de
Web Site: www.breklumer.de *Cable:* BREKLUMER VERLAG BREKLUM
Key Personnel
Publisher: Manfred Siegel
Founded: 1875
Subjects: Religion - Other
ISBN Prefix(es): 3-7793

Joh & Sohn Brendow Verlag GmbH+
Gutenbergstr 1, 47443 Moers
Tel: (02841) 809-0 *Fax:* (02841) 97761-30
E-mail: info@brendow-verlag.de
Web Site: www.brendow.de
Key Personnel
Man Dir: Friedr-Wilh Seinsche
Founded: 1849
Subjects: Religion - Other
ISBN Prefix(es): 3-87067

Verlag Das Brennglas+
Roettbacherstr 61, 97892 Kreuzwertheim
Tel: (09342) 915843 *Fax:* (09342) 915843
E-mail: info@das-brennglas.com
Web Site: www.brennglas.com
Founded: 1981
Subjects: Art, Literature, Literary Criticism, Essays
ISBN Prefix(es): 3-924243

Brigg Verlag Franz-Joset Buchler KG
Zusamstr 9, 86165 Augsburg
Tel: (0821) 78094660 *Fax:* (0821) 78094661
Key Personnel
Man Dir: Franz-Josef Buechler
Founded: 1950
Subjects: Poetry, Regional Interests
ISBN Prefix(es): 3-87101

Verlag Ekkehard & Ulrich Brockhaus GmbH & Co KG
Am Wolfshahn 31, 42117 Wuppertal
Tel: (0202) 44 74 74; (0172) 2 55 59 61
Fax: (0202) 42 82 82
E-mail: mail@verlag-brockhaus.de
Web Site: www.verlag-brockhaus.de
Subjects: Genealogy, Cultural History
ISBN Prefix(es): 3-930132

F A Brockhaus GmbH
Dudenstr 6, 68167 Mannheim
Tel: (0621) 3901-01 *Fax:* (0621) 3901-391
Web Site: www.brockhaus.de
Key Personnel
Contact: Dieter Baer; Dr Karl-Josef Schmidt; Dr Michael Wegner
Founded: 1805
Parent Company: Bibliographisches Institut & F A Brockhaus AG, Mannheim

Brockhaus/Kommission GmbH
Kreidlerstr 9, 70806 Kornwestheim
Tel: (07154) 1327-0 *Fax:* (07154) 1327-13
Key Personnel
Man Dir: Dr Wolfgang Berg; Steffen Goehler
Founded: 1805
Subjects: Geography, Geology
ISBN Prefix(es): 3-87103

R Brockhaus Verlag+
Bodenborn 43, 58452 Witten
Tel: (02302) 930 93 800 *Fax:* (02302) 930 93 801
E-mail: info@brockhaus-verlag.de
Web Site: www.brockhaus-verlag.de
Key Personnel
Chief Executive Officer & Publisher: Erhard Diehl
Editorial: Hans-Werner Durau
International Rights: Christina Schneider
Founded: 1853
Membership(s): Stiftung Christliche Medien.
Subjects: Biography, Fiction, Music, Dance, Psychology, Psychiatry, Religion - Other, Theology
ISBN Prefix(es): 3-417
Associate Companies: Oncken Verlag KG
Subsidiaries: R Brockhaus Verlag AG

F Bruckmann Munchen Verlag & Druck GmbH & Co Produkt KG+
Innsbrucker Ring 15, 81637 Munich
Mailing Address: Postfach 80 02 40, 81602 Munich
Tel: (089) 13 06 99 11 *Fax:* (089) 13 06 99 10
E-mail: info@bruckmann.de
Web Site: www.bruckmann-verlag.de *Cable:* BRUCKMANNKOGE MUNICH
Key Personnel
Editor & Publishing Manager: Dr Joerg D Stiebner
Editor: Michael Wellbrock
Sales Manager: Dr Klaus Beckschulte *Tel:* (089) 13 06 99 48 *E-mail:* klaus.beckschulte@bruckmann.de; Andreas von Bleichert *Tel:* (089) 13 06 99 49 *E-mail:* andreas.vonbleichert@bruckmann.de
Marketing Manager: Thilo Heller *Tel:* (089) 89 13 06 99 45 *E-mail:* thilo.heller@bruckmann.de
Manager, Magazines & Periodicals: Dr Regine Hahn *Tel:* (089) 13 06 99 17 *E-mail:* regine.hahn@bruckmann.de
Sales: Maria Elisabeth Jantzer
Publicity: Barbara Aschenberner
Production: Helmut Huber
Sales & Trade Service: Nina Baier *Tel:* (089) 13 06 99 14 *E-mail:* nina.baier@bruckmann.de

de; Angelika Maerz *Tel:* (089) 13 06 99 15
  E-mail: angelika.maerz@bruckmann.de
Customer Service: Sabine Korb *Tel:* (089) 13 06
  99 15 *E-mail:* sabine.korb@bruckmann.de
Press: Carola Schindler *Tel:* (089) 13 06 99 27
  E-mail: carola.schindler@bruckmann.de
Product Management: Martina Appich
  E-mail: martina.appich@geranova.de; Sabine
  Klingan *E-mail:* sabine.klingan@bruckmann.de;
  Sonya Mayer *E-mail:* sonya.mayer@geranova.
  de
Founded: 1858
Membership(s): TR - Verlagsunion GmbH.
Subjects: Art, Film, Video, Gardening, Plants, History, Humor, Outdoor Recreation, Regional Interests, Science (General), Travel
ISBN Prefix(es): 3-7654

Bruecke-Verlag Kurt Schmersow
Arnekenstr 22-25, 31134 Hildesheim
Tel: (05121) 91 92 0 *Fax:* (05121) 91 92 20
E-mail: buchhaltung@bruecke-verlag.de
Web Site: www.bruecke-verlag.de
Key Personnel
Owner: Gerda Niemz
Founded: 1920
ISBN Prefix(es): 3-87105

Bruehlsche Uni-Druckerei Verlag, der Giessener Anzeiger GmbH & Co KG
Am Urnenfeld 12, 35396 Giessen
Mailing Address: Postfach 100451, 35334 Giessen
Tel: (0641) 95040 *Fax:* (0641) 9504100
Telex: 482859 bruel
Key Personnel
Manager & International Rights: Dr Wolfgang Maass
ISBN Prefix(es): 3-922300

BRUEN-Verlag, Gorenflo
Weserstr 22, 65428 Ruesselsheim
Mailing Address: Postfach 1356, 65403 Ruesselsheim
Tel: (06142) 61434 *Fax:* (06142) 61259
E-mail: 0614261434-1@t-online.de
Key Personnel
Man Dir: R Gorenflo
Founded: 1987
Subjects: Art, Fiction, History, Nonfiction (General), Poetry, Regional Interests
ISBN Prefix(es): 3-926759

Brunnen-Verlag GmbH+
Gottlieb-Daimler Str 22, 35398 Giessen
Tel: (0641) 6059-0 *Fax:* (0641) 6059-100
E-mail: info@brunnen-verlag.de
Web Site: www.brunnen-verlag.de
Key Personnel
Man Dir: Detlef Holtgrefe
Editorial: Eva-Maria Busch; Irmgard Froese-Schreer; Renate Huebsch; Helmut Jablonski; Petra Luetjen
International Rights & Editorial: Ralf Tibusek
  E-mail: ralf.tibusek@brunnen-verlag.de
Sales Manager: Reinhard Engeln
  E-mail: reinhard.engeln@brunnen-verlag.de
Founded: 1919
Subjects: Religion - Other, Theology
ISBN Prefix(es): 3-7655
Number of titles published annually: 120 Print
Total Titles: 800 Print
Associate Companies: Brunnen Verlag, Basel, Switzerland
Distribution Center: ChrisMedia *Tel:* (06406) 8346-100 *E-mail:* bestellung@chrismedia24.de

BTB, *imprint of* BKV-Brasilienkunde Verlag GmbH

Buch- und Kunstverlag Kleinheinrich+
Koenigsstr 42, 48143 Muenster
Tel: (0251) 4840193 *Fax:* (0251) 4840194
Key Personnel
International Rights: Dr Josef Kleinheinrich
Founded: 1986
Subjects: Art, Literature, Literary Criticism, Essays
ISBN Prefix(es): 3-926608; 3-930754

Bucharchiv, *see* Deutsches Bucharchiv Muenchen, Institut fur Buchwissenschaften

Verlag C J Bucher GmbH+
Paul-Heysestr 28, 80336 Munich
Tel: (089) 51480 *Fax:* (089) 5148-2229
Key Personnel
Man Dir: Axel Schenck
Sales & Publicity: Alexander Herrmann
Production: Angelika Kerscher
Publisher: Christian Strasser
Rights & Permissions: Bettina Breitling
Publicity: Michael Then
Founded: 1956
Subjects: Art, Nonfiction (General), Photography, Travel
ISBN Prefix(es): 3-7658
Associate Companies: Paul List Verlag; Suedwest Verlag; W Ludwig Verlag
Orders to: Koch, Neff, Oetinger & Co Verlagsauslieferung GmbH, Schockenriedstr 39, 70506 Stuttgart

Buchhaendler-Vereinigung GmbH, *see* MVB Marketing- und Verlagsservice des Buchhandels GmbH

Buchhandlung Holl & Knoll KG, Verlag Alte Uni
Brettenerstr 30, 75031 Eppingen
Tel: (07262) 4417 *Fax:* (07262) 7942
E-mail: alteuni@aol.com
Key Personnel
Contact: Karl Knoll
Founded: 1986
Subjects: Language Arts, Linguistics, Regional Interests
ISBN Prefix(es): 3-926315

Buchheim-Verlag
Biersackstr 23, 82340 Feldafing
Tel: (08157) 1221 *Fax:* (08157) 3143
Key Personnel
Owner & International Rights: Lothar-Guenther Buchheim
Founded: 1951
Subjects: Art
ISBN Prefix(es): 3-7659

BuchMarkt Verlag K Werner GmbH
  (Bookmarket)
Sperberweg 4a, 40668 Meerbusch
Tel: (02150) 9191-0 *Fax:* (02150) 919191
E-mail: redaktion@buchmarkt.de
Web Site: www.buchmarkt.de
Key Personnel
Dir, International Rights: Christian Von Zittwitz
Founded: 1966
Publishers of the trade magazine Buchmart for the booktrade.
Subjects: Publishing & Book Trade Reference
ISBN Prefix(es): 3-920518

C C Buchners Verlag GmbH & Co KG
Laubanger 8, 96052 Bamberg
Mailing Address: Postfach 1269, 96003 Bamberg
Tel: (0951) 96 501-0 *Fax:* (0951) 61-774
E-mail: service@ccbuchner.de
Web Site: www.ccbuchner.de
Key Personnel
Dir, Rights & Permissions: Gunnar Gruenke
Founded: 1832
Subjects: Earth Sciences, Government, Political Science, History, Regional Interests
ISBN Prefix(es): 3-7661

Buchverlag Junge Welt GmbH
Oranienburgerstr 65, 10117 Berlin
Tel: (030) 231079 0 *Fax:* (030) 2826989
E-mail: bvjw.berlin@t-online.de
Web Site: www.buchverlagjw.com
Key Personnel
Manager: Dr Thomas Seng; Eberhard Tackenberg
Founded: 1991
Subjects: Education, Science (General), Technology
ISBN Prefix(es): 3-7302

Buchverlage Langen-Mueller/Herbig+
Thomas-Wimmer-Ring 11, 80539 Munich
Tel: (089) 2 90 88-0
E-mail: info@herbig.net
Web Site: www.herbig.net
Key Personnel
Man Dir: Dr Herbert Fleissner
International Rights: Frauke Hoppen *E-mail:* f. hoppenaherbig@net
Subjects: Cookery, Economics, Fiction, Health, Nutrition, Parapsychology, Self-Help
ISBN Prefix(es): 3-7766; 3-7844
Subsidiaries: Amalthea; Bechtle; F A Herbig Verlagsbuchhandlung GmbH; Langen Mueller; Mary Hahn; Nymphenburger; Signum; Terra Magica; Universitas; Wirtschaftsverlag
Warehouse: Vereinigte Verlagsauslieferung, Guetersloh

Edition Buecherbaer im Arena Verlag, *see* Arena Verlag GmbH

Edition Buecherbar im Arena Verlag, *imprint of* Arena Verlag GmbH

Buchergilde Gutenberg Verlagsgesellschaft mbH
Untermainkai 66, 60329 Frankfurt am Main
Mailing Address: Postfach 160165, 60064 Frankfurt am Main
Tel: (069) 27 39 08-0 *Fax:* (069) 27 39 08-26;
  (069) 27 39 08-25
E-mail: service@buechergilde.de
Web Site: www.buechergilde.de
Key Personnel
Man Dir, Editorial, Rights & Permsissions: Mario Frueh
Sales & Publicity: Carol Mueller
Production: Grit Fischer
Founded: 1924
Primarily a Book Club, but also a publisher.
Subjects: Art, Government, Political Science, History, Literature, Literary Criticism, Essays
ISBN Prefix(es): 3-7632
Book Club(s): Buechergilde Gutenberg

Buechse der Pandora Verlags-GmbH+
Schulstr 20, 35579 Wetzlar, OT Steindorf
Mailing Address: Postfach 2820, 35538 Wetzlar OT Steindorf
Tel: (06441) 911312 *Fax:* (06441) 911314 *Cable:* 35579 WETZLAR-STEINDORF
Key Personnel
Man Dir: Peter Grosshaus
Founded: 1977
Subjects: Art, Education, Literature, Literary Criticism, Essays, Philosophy
ISBN Prefix(es): 3-88178
Orders to: Rotation Verlagsauslieferung, Mehringdamm 51, 10961 Berlin

Bund demokratischer Wissenschaftlerinnen und Wissenschafler eV (BdWi)+
Gisselbergstr 7, 35037 Marburg
Tel: (06421) 2 13 95 *Fax:* (06421) 2 46 54

E-mail: verlag@bdwi.de
Web Site: www.bdwi.de
Key Personnel
Manager: Dr Rainer Rilling
Founded: 1993
Subjects: Government, Political Science, Psychology, Psychiatry, Social Sciences, Sociology, Women's Studies
ISBN Prefix(es): 3-924684
Associate Companies: Informationsstelle Wissenschaft und Frieden (IWIF), 53113 Bonn *Tel:* (0228) 210744 *Fax:* (0228) 214924; Informationsdienst Wissenschaft und Frieden ev, Reuterstr 44, 5300 Bonn 1 *Tel:* (0228) 213334 *Fax:* (0228) 214924
Imprints: Forum Wissenschaft Studien; Internationale Studien zen Fatigkeititleone; Sammlung; Schriftenfeibe Wissenschaft und Frieden
Branch Office(s)
BdWi Bonn ev, Reuterstr 44, 53115 Bonn 1 *Tel:* (0228) 219946 *Fax:* (0228) 214924
Orders to: Bugtiur-Verlagsanslieferung, Sodelburgstr 3, 12099 Berlin

Bund Deutscher Schriftsteller (German Writers Association)
Romerstr 2, 63128 Dietzenbach
Tel: (06074) 47566 *Fax:* (06074) 47540
Web Site: www.bund-deutscher-schriftsteller.de
Founded: 1997
Membership(s): World Writers Association, London
Also acts as Literary Agent.
ISBN Prefix(es): 3-00
Total Titles: 2 Print
Publication(s): *Authors Yearbook*; *Register of German Authors*

Bund fuer deutsche Schrift und Sprache
Postfach 1145, 38711 Seesen
Tel: (05381) 46355 *Fax:* (05381) 46355
E-mail: verwaltung@bfds.de
Web Site: www.bfds.de
Key Personnel
Man Dir: Helmut Delbanco
Founded: 1918
ISBN Prefix(es): 3-930540

Bund-Verlag GmbH+
Heddernheimer Landstr 144, 60439 Frankfurt am Main
Tel: (069) 79 50 10 0 *Fax:* (069) 79 50 10 10
E-mail: kontakt@bund-verlag.de
Web Site: www.bund-verlag.de
Key Personnel
Man Dir: Christian Paulsen
Sales: Tamara Kellberg
Production: Birgit Gast; Inga Tomalla
Rights & Permissions: Dr Angermund Schroeder
Founded: 1947
Subjects: Economics, Fiction, Finance, Government, Political Science, Law, Poetry
ISBN Prefix(es): 3-7663

Bundes-Verlag GmbH
Bodenborn 43, 58452 Witten
Tel: (02302) 930 93-0
E-mail: info@bundesverlag.de
Web Site: www.bundes-verlag.de
Key Personnel
Man Dir: Erhard Diehl
Founded: 1887
Subjects: Religion - Catholic
ISBN Prefix(es): 3-926417

Bundesanzeiger Verlagsgesellschaft
Amsterdamerstr 192, 50735 Cologne
Mailing Address: Postfach 10 05 34, 50445 Cologne
Tel: (0221) 9 76 68-0 *Fax:* (0221) 9 76 68-278
E-mail: vcotiicb@bundesanzeiger.de
Web Site: www.bundesanzeiger.de
Key Personnel
Man Dir: Rainier Diesem
Contact: Birgit Drehsen
Founded: 1948
Subjects: Government, Political Science, History, Law, Regional Interests
ISBN Prefix(es): 3-88784; 3-89817
Subsidiaries: Deutscher Bundesverlag

Burckhardthaus-Laetare Verlag GmbH+
Schumannstr 161, 63069 Offenbach
Tel: (069) 8400030 *Fax:* (069) 84000333
Key Personnel
Publisher & Manager: Andre Juenger
Rights & Permissions: Alexandra Cordes
Founded: 1918
Subjects: Education, Psychology, Psychiatry, Religion - Other
ISBN Prefix(es): 3-7664

Aenne Burda Verlag
Am Kestendamm 2, 77652 Offenburg
Mailing Address: Postfach 1160, 77601 Offenburg
Tel: (0781) 843322 *Fax:* (0781) 843386
Telex: 752804 *Cable:* BURDAMODEN OFFENBURG
Founded: 1949
Subjects: Cookery, Crafts, Games, Hobbies
ISBN Prefix(es): 3-920158; 3-88978
Subsidiaries: Burda Patterns Inc; Dipa SA; ZVB Zeitschriften Vertriebs AB

Ulrich Burgdorf/Homeopathic Publishing House+
Tegeler Weg 8, 37085 Goettingen
Tel: (0551) 796050 *Fax:* (0551) 796955
E-mail: Burgdorf-Verlag@t-online.de
Web Site: www.burgdorf-verlag.de
Key Personnel
Contact: Dons Scheleper
Founded: 1979
Subjects: Philosophy, Photography, Psychology, Psychiatry
ISBN Prefix(es): 3-922345

Kartographischer Verlag Busche GmbH
Schleefstr 1, 44287 Dortmund
Tel: (0231) 4 44 77-0 *Fax:* (0231) 4 44 77-77
E-mail: info@kvbusche.de
Web Site: www.kvbusche.de
Key Personnel
Man Dir, Publicity: Juergen Ruediger Klaffka
Editorial: Barbara Roemer
Marketing Management: Ulrike Rudolph
Tel: (05221) 775-275
Founded: 1972
Subjects: Travel
ISBN Prefix(es): 3-88584; 3-921143; 3-89764
Parent Company: Busche KG

Anita und Klaus Buscher B & B Verlag+
Erika-Koth-Str 56, 67435 Neustadt-Konigsbach
Tel: (06321) 968485 *Fax:* (06321) 968486
Key Personnel
Man Dir: Anita Buscher
Founded: 1988
ISBN Prefix(es): 3-927419

Helmut Buske Verlag GmbH+
Richardstr 47, 22081 Hamburg
Mailing Address: Postfach 760244, 22052 Hamburg
Tel: (040) 2999580 *Fax:* (040) 29995820
E-mail: info@buske.de
Web Site: www.buske.de
Key Personnel
Man Dir: Manfred Meiner
Publishing Dir: Michael Hechinger *Tel:* (040) 299958-25
Rights, Marketing: Johannes Kambylis *Tel:* (040) 299958-23 *E-mail:* kambylis@buske.de
Founded: 1959
Subjects: Language Arts, Linguistics
ISBN Prefix(es): 3-87118; 3-87548
Ultimate Parent Company: Felix Meiner Verlag GmbH

Verlag Busse und Seewald GmbH+
Ahmserstr 190, 32052 Herford
Mailing Address: Postfach 1344, 32003 Herford
Tel: (05221) 77 5-0 *Fax:* (05221) 77 52 04
E-mail: info@busse-seewald.de
Web Site: www.busse-seewald.de
Key Personnel
Manager: Michael Best; Harald Busse
Sales & Advertising: Regina Benecke
Rights & Permissions: Ulrike Rudolph
Tel: (05221) 775-275
Founded: 1947
Subjects: Architecture & Interior Design, Maritime, Nonfiction (General), Outdoor Recreation, Regional Interests, Travel, Wine & Spirits
ISBN Prefix(es): 3-512; 3-87120
Associate Companies: Buchdruckerei und Verlag Busse; Westdeutsche Verlagsanstalt GmbH
Distributor for DSV-Verlag (Germany, Austria, Switzerland)

Butzon & Bercker GmbH+
Hoogeweg 71, 47623 Kevelaer
Mailing Address: Postfach 215, 47623 Kevelaer
Tel: (02832) 929-130 *Fax:* (02832) 929-139
E-mail: service@butzonbercker.de
Web Site: www.butzonbercker.de *Cable:* BUTZONBERCKER
Key Personnel
Dir: Dr Edmund J Bercker; Klaus Bercker
Editorial: Pit Stenmans
Sales: Helga Behr
Publicity: Helmut Kaiser
Rights & Permissions: Anne Moore
Founded: 1870
Subjects: Religion - Catholic, Theology
ISBN Prefix(es): 3-7666
Distributor for Lahn (Limburg); Styria (Graz/Cologne)

BVB, see Bayerische Verlagsanstalt GmbH

BWV, see Berliner Wissenschafts-Verlag GmbH (BWV)

Caann Verlag, Klaus Wagner
Am Anger 11, 85570 Ottenhofen
Tel: (08121) 9 32 71 *Fax:* (08121) 9 32 78
E-mail: info@caann-verlag.de
Web Site: www.caann-verlag.de
Key Personnel
Man Dir: Klaus Wagner
Founded: 1969
Subjects: Nonfiction (General), Philosophy, Social Sciences, Sociology
ISBN Prefix(es): 3-87121

Cadmos Verlag GmbH+
Luener Rennbahn 14, 21339 Lueneburg
Tel: (04131) 981 666 *Fax:* (04131) 981 668
E-mail: cadmos-verlag@tonline.de
Web Site: www.cadmos.de
Key Personnel
Publisher: Hans J Schmidtke
Founded: 1986
Subjects: Dogs, Equestrian, Horses
ISBN Prefix(es): 3-925760; 3-86127
Number of titles published annually: 50 Print; 2 Audio
Total Titles: 150 Print; 8 Audio
Foreign Rep(s): Hans Schmidtke

Verlag Georg D W Callwey GmbH & Co+
Streitfeldstr 35, 81673 Munich
Tel: (089) 4360050 *Fax:* (089) 436005113
Web Site: www.callwey.de *Cable:* CALLWEYVERLAG
Key Personnel
Man Dir: Amos Kotte
Editorial: Dr Stefan Granzow
Rights & Permissions, Publicity & Sales: Jens-Peter Arndt
Rights & Permissions: Dorothea Montigel
Publicity: Andreas Hagenkord
Founded: 1884
Subjects: Architecture & Interior Design, Crafts, Games, Hobbies, Gardening, Plants, House & Home, How-to
ISBN Prefix(es): 3-7667

Calwer Verlag GmbH+
Balingerstr 31, 70567 Stuttgart
Mailing Address: Postfach 810293, 70519 Stuttgart
Tel: (0711) 167 22-0 *Fax:* (0711) 167 22 77
E-mail: info@calwer.com
Web Site: www.calwer.com
Key Personnel
Dir: Dr Berthold Brohm *E-mail:* brohm@calwer.com; Joachim Hinderer *E-mail:* hinderer@calwer.com
Marketing: Beatrice Basgier *E-mail:* basgier@calwer.com
Production: Karin Klopfer *E-mail:* klopfer@calwer.com
Rights: Susanne Hien *E-mail:* hien@calwer.com
Founded: 1836
Subjects: Education, Religion - Other, Theology
ISBN Prefix(es): 3-7668
Orders to: Brockhans Kommission, Kreidlestr 9, 70806 Kornwestheim *Fax:* (07154) 13 27 13

Campus Verlag GmbH+
49 Kurfuerstenstr, 60486 Frankfurt am Main
Tel: (069) 976 516-0 *Fax:* (069) 976 516-78
E-mail: info@campus.de
Web Site: www.campus.de
Key Personnel
Executive Dir, Publisher & Rights & Permissions: Thomas Carl Schwoerer *Tel:* (069) 976 516-43 *E-mail:* schwoerer@campus.de
Foreign Rights: Franziska Stadler *Tel:* (069) 976 516-15 *E-mail:* stadler@campus.de
Editor-in-Chief: Britta Kroker *Tel:* (069) 976 516-56 *E-mail:* kroker@campus.de
Editor-in-Chief, Science: Adalbert Hepp *Tel:* (069) 976 516-52 *E-mail:* hepp@campus.de
Sales Dir: Andreas Horn *Tel:* (069) 976 516-14 *E-mail:* horn@campus.de
Production: Klaus Schoeffner *Tel:* (069) 976 516-64; Ulrich Begemeier *Tel:* (069) 976 516-66
Advertising: Markus J Karsten *Tel:* (069) 976 516-32
Publicity: Margit Knauer *Tel:* (069) 976 516-21
Founded: 1975
Specialize also in cultural studies.
Subjects: Business, Career Development, Economics, Government, Political Science, History, Management, Philosophy, Social Sciences, Sociology, Women's Studies
ISBN Prefix(es): 3-593
Number of titles published annually: 240 Print; 10 Audio
Orders to: Brockhaus Commission, Kreidlestr 9, 70806 Kornwestheim *Tel:* (07154) 1327-76 *Fax:* (07154) 1327-13 *E-mail:* bestell@brocom.de *Web Site:* www.brocom.de

Campusbooks Medien AG+
Bonner Platz 4, 80803 Munich
Tel: (089) 18921730 *Fax:* (089) 18921731
E-mail: info@campusbooks.de
Web Site: www.campusbooks.de/partner_main.html
Key Personnel
Dir Business Development: Juergen Reuter
Founded: 2000
Bookseller for corporate customers & publishing house for theses & magazines.
Number of titles published annually: 10 Print

Dr Cantz'sche Druckerei GmbH & Co+
Senefelderstr 12, 73760 Ostfildern
Tel: (0711) 4405-0; (0711) 4405-121 (Marketing & Sales) *Fax:* (0711) 4405-111
E-mail: bklein@jfink.de
Web Site: www.jfink.de
Key Personnel
Publisher & International Rights: Annette Kulenkanpff
Publisher: Bernd Barde
Man Dir & Sales Dir: Markus Hartmann
Founded: 1980
Distributor of Art Books.
Subjects: Architecture & Interior Design, Art, Photography
ISBN Prefix(es): 3-89322; 3-922608
U.S. Office(s): DAP (Distributed Art Publishers), 636 Broadway, Rm 1200, New York, NY 10012, United States *Tel:* 212-627-1999 *Fax:* 212-627-9484
Distributed by Thames & Hudson Ltd (London)
Distributor for Guggenheim Museum; Skira Editore (Milano)
Orders to: Cantz Verlag, Senefelderstr 12, 73760 Ostfildern-Ruit
Koch, Neff, Oetinger & Co, Postfach 800620, 70565 Stuttgart

Carl-Auer-Systeme Verlag+
Weberstr 2, 69120 Heidelberg
Tel: (06221) 64380 *Fax:* (06221) 643822
E-mail: info@carl-auer.de
Web Site: www.carl-auer.de
Key Personnel
Man Dir: Dr Fritz B Simon
Program & Production: Beate Ch Ulrich *Tel:* (06221) 6438-15 *E-mail:* ulrich@carl-auer.de
Publishing: Klaus W Muller *Tel:* (06221) 6438-16 *E-mail:* mueller@carl-auer.de
Sales: Johannes Altrock *Tel:* (06221) 6438-20 *E-mail:* altrock@carl-auer.de
Publicity: Francoise Jaouiche *Tel:* (06221) 6438-17 *E-mail:* jaouiche@carl-auer.de
Founded: 1989
Subjects: Child Care & Development, Human Relations, Management, Philosophy, Psychology, Psychiatry
ISBN Prefix(es): 3-927809; 3-931574; 3-89670
Total Titles: 110 Print; 90 Audio

Fachverlag Hans Carl GmbH+
Andernacher Str 33a, 90411 Nuremberg
Mailing Address: Postfach 990153, 90268 Nuremberg
Tel: (0911) 95285-0 *Fax:* (0911) 95285-48; (0911) 95285-71; (0911) 95285-61
E-mail: info@hanscarl.com
Web Site: www.hanscarl.com
Key Personnel
Man Dir, Editorial: Dr Karl-Ullrich Heyse *Tel:* (0911) 95285-22 *Fax:* (0911) 95285-60 *E-mail:* heyse@hanscarl.com
Man Dir: Wolfgang Illguth *Tel:* (0911) 95285-20 *E-mail:* illguth@hanscarl.com
Board: Michael Schmitt *E-mail:* m.schmitt@hanscarl.com
Founded: 1861
Subjects: Art, Chemistry, Chemical Engineering, Fiction, History, Outdoor Recreation, Philosophy, Poetry, Regional Interests, Science (General), Wine & Spirits
ISBN Prefix(es): 3-418
Bookshop(s): Fachbuchhandlung Hans Carl, Wolf-Dieter Schoyerer *Tel:* (0911) 9528531 *E-mail:* fachbuchhandlung@hanscarl.com

Carl Link Verlag-Gesellschaft mbH Fachverlag fur Verwaltungsrecht
Freisinger Str 3, 85716 Unterschleissheim
Tel: (089) 36007 0 *Fax:* (089) 36007 3310
E-mail: info@carllink.de
Web Site: www.carllink.de
Key Personnel
Man Dir & International Rights: Dr Wilhelm Warth
Founded: 1884
Subjects: Law
ISBN Prefix(es): 3-556
Parent Company: Carl Link
Associate Companies: Bueromarkt, Kronach; Carl Link Druck GmbH, Kronach
Bookshop(s): Buchdienst, Gueterstr 7, 96317 Kronach
Warehouse: Carl Link Bueromarkt, Gueterstr 7, 96317 Kronach

Carlsen Verlag GmbH+
Voelckersstr 14-20, 22765 Hamburg
Mailing Address: Postfach 500380, 22703 Hamburg
Tel: (040) 39 804 0 *Fax:* (040) 39 804 390
Key Personnel
Dir: Klaus Humann; Klaus Kaempfe-Burghardt
Editorial: Anne Bender; Barbara Koenig; Frank Kuehne; Ulrike Schuldes; Katja Schultze
Sales: Ann Oelkers
Production: Wiebke Duesedau
Advertising: Marianne Ohmann
Public Relations: Cornelia Berger
Press Manager: Katrin Hogrebe *E-mail:* katrin.hogrebe@carlsen.de
Foreign Rights: Erdmut Gross
Founded: 1953
Specialize in children's books & comics.
Subjects: Fiction, Humor
ISBN Prefix(es): 3-551
Parent Company: Bonnier Media Holding GmbH, Hamburg
Associate Companies: ARS Edition; Piper Verlag; Thienemann Verlag

CartoTravel Verlag GmbH & Co KG+
Auf der Krautweide 24, 65812 Bad Soden/Taunus
Tel: (06196) 6096-0 *Fax:* (06196) 27450
E-mail: info@cartotravel.de
Web Site: www.cartotravel.de *Cable:* ADACVERLAG
Key Personnel
Man Dir: Thomas Haupka; Thomas Mueller
Founded: 1958
Also carry magazines & travel guides.
Subjects: Automotive, Travel
ISBN Prefix(es): 3-87003; 3-8264

Catia Monser Eggcup-Verlag
Werstener Feld 235, 40591 Duesseldorf
Tel: (0211) 215122 *Fax:* (0211) 215122
E-mail: cmonserev@aol.com
Web Site: members.aol.com/CMonserEV
Key Personnel
Contact: Catia Monser
Founded: 1992
Subjects: Disability, Special Needs, Health, Nutrition, Human Relations, Medicine, Nursing, Dentistry, Mysteries
ISBN Prefix(es): 3-930004

Centaurus-Verlagsgesellschaft GmbH
Bugstr 7-9, 79336 Herbolzheim
Tel: (07643) 93 39-0 *Fax:* (07643) 93 39-11
E-mail: info@centaurus-verlag.de
Web Site: www.centaurus-verlag.de

Key Personnel
Manager: Petra Sanft; Britta Schulz
Founded: 1983
Membership(s): The Stock Exchange of German Booksellers.
Subjects: Criminology, Education, History, Law, Psychology, Psychiatry, Religion - Other, Social Sciences, Sociology, Women's Studies
ISBN Prefix(es): 3-89085; 3-8255

Chancerel International Publishers Ltd+
Rotebuhlstr 77, Stuttgart 70178
Tel: (049711) 6672 5728 *Fax:* (049711) 6672 2004
E-mail: tvandree@klett-mail.de
Web Site: www.chancerel.com
Key Personnel
Man Dir: W D B Prowse
Founded: 1976
Specialize in language teaching materials: English (British & American), German, French, Spanish, Italian & Japanese.
Subjects: Education, Language Arts, Linguistics
ISBN Prefix(es): 0-905703; 1-899888; 1-903749
Parent Company: Klett Languages London Ltd
Ultimate Parent Company: Ernst Klett Sprachen GmbH
Distributed by BEBC (UK)

Verlag fur chemische Industrie H Ziolkowsky GmbH
Beethovenstr 16, 86150 Augsburg
Mailing Address: Postfach 10 25 65, 86015 Augsburg
Tel: (0821) 325-830 *Fax:* (0821) 325-8323
Key Personnel
Contact: Bernd Ziolkowsky
ISBN Prefix(es): 3-87846

Chiron-Verlag Reinhardt Stiehle+
Staeudach 6/1, 72074 Tuebingen
Tel: (07071) 8884150 *Fax:* (07071) 8884151
E-mail: info@chironverlag.de
Web Site: www.chironverlag.de
Key Personnel
President & Publisher: Reinhardt Stiehle
Founded: 1985
Membership(s): The Stock Exchange of German Booksellers.
Subjects: Astrology, Occult
ISBN Prefix(es): 3-925100
Orders to: Brockhaus Commission, Kreidlerstrasse 9, 70806 Kornwestheim

Chmielorz GmbH Verlag+
Marktplatz 13, 65183 Wiesbaden
Mailing Address: Postfach 22 29, 65183 Wiesbaden
Tel: (0611) 360980 *Fax:* (0611) 36098-17
E-mail: tme@chmielorz.de
Web Site: www.chmielorz.de
Key Personnel
Man Dir: Thomas Mueller-Eggergluess
Founded: 1949
Publish professional magazines (trade press), handbooks, loose-leaf books (law commentaries), CD-ROMs, databases.
Subjects: Business, Civil Engineering, Cookery, Earth Sciences, Economics, Fiction, Geography, Geology, Health, Nutrition, Law, Medicine, Nursing, Dentistry, Public Administration, Publishing & Book Trade Reference, Social Sciences, Sociology, Sports, Athletics, Cinema, Film Industry, Food, International Law, Movies, Sport (Trade, Industry)
ISBN Prefix(es): 3-87124
Branch Office(s)
Druckhaus Chmielorz, Ostring 13, 65205 Wiesbaden-Nordenstadt, Carsten Augsburger *Tel:* (06122) 7709-01 *Fax:* (06122) 7709-181 *E-mail:* dc@chmielorz.de
Distributor for EuBuCo-Verlag; mhp-Verlag

Chorus-Verlag
Wichernweg 22 A, 81737 Munich
Tel: (089) 634 999 60 *Fax:* (089) 634 999 61
Web Site: www.chorus-verlag.de
Key Personnel
Dir: Martin van der Koelen *Tel:* (089) 63499960 *E-mail:* mvdk@chorus-verlag.de
Founded: 1995
Subjects: Art, Specialize in museum catalogues & catalog raisonnes
ISBN Prefix(es): 3-931876; 3-926663
Total Titles: 60 Print
Distributed by Arteko Galeria de Arte (Spain); AVA-Buch 2000 Verlagsauslieferung (Switzerland); Bugrim Verlagsauslieferung (Germany & Austria); Continent Books (Benelux); Joker Art Diffusion (France); Hurtado de Ediciones (Spain)

Chr Belser AG fur Verlagsgeschaefte und Co KG+
Pfizerstr 5-7, 70184 Stuttgart
Mailing Address: Postfach 100561, 70004 Stuttgart
Tel: (0711) 2191-0 *Fax:* (0711) 2191-330 *Cable:* BELSERVERLAG
Key Personnel
Publisher: Dr Herbert Fleissner
Manager: Axel Meffert
Rights & Permissions: Andrea Ahlers
Publicity: Renate Palmer
Production: Ulrich Dotzauer
Founded: 1835
Subjects: Art, History, Music, Dance, Nonfiction (General), Religion - Other, Theology, Travel
ISBN Prefix(es): 3-7630
Parent Company: Chr Belser AG Zuerich
Subsidiaries: Amalthea; Bechtle; Kronos; Langen Mueller; Lentz; Mahnert-Lueg; Mary Hahn; Meyster; Nymphenburger; Reich; Universitas; USM Soft Media; Wirtschaftsverlag
Warehouse: VVA, An der Autobahn, 33310 Gutersloh

Christian Verlag GmbH+
Amalienstr 62, 80799 Munich
Tel: (089) 381803-17; (089) 381803-31 *Fax:* (089) 38180381
E-mail: info@christian-verlag.de
Web Site: www.christian-verlag.de
Key Personnel
Manager: Martin Dort; Johannes Heyne
Chief Editor: Florentine Schwabbauer
Sales & Advertising: Barbara Thieme *Tel:* (089) 38 18 03-30 *Fax:* (089) 38 18 03-81; Dr Ingeborg Kluge *Tel:* (089) 38 18 03-17; Susanne Pietsch *Tel:* (089) 38 18 03-31
Editorial Rights: Claudia Bitz; Tanja Germann
Public Relations: Gudrun Schroeder *Tel:* (089) 2 01 40 10 *Fax:* (089) 2 01 40 11 *E-mail:* g.schroeder.muc@t-online.de
Founded: 1979
Subjects: Architecture & Interior Design, Cookery, Gardening, Plants, Nonfiction (General), Photography, Wine & Spirits
ISBN Prefix(es): 3-88472

Hans Christians Druckerei und Verlag GmbH & Co KG+
Behringstr 28 a, 22765 Hamburg
Tel: (040) 35 60 06-0 *Fax:* (040) 35 60 06-26
E-mail: verlag@christians.de
Web Site: www.christians.de *Cable:* CHRISTIANS DRUCK
Key Personnel
Man Dir: Susanne Liebelt *Tel:* (040) 35 60 06-11 *E-mail:* susanne.liebelt@christians.de
Manager: Martin Lind *Tel:* (040) 35 60 06-27 *E-mail:* martin.lind@christians.de
Public Relations, Rights & Permissions: Sabine Bayer *Tel:* (040) 35 60 06-15 *E-mail:* sabine.bayer@christians.de
Sales: Petra Jehnichen *Tel:* (040) 35 60 06-35 *E-mail:* petra.jehnichen@christians.de
Founded: 1740
Subjects: Architecture & Interior Design, Art, Biography, Communications, Cookery, Education, Ethnicity, Gardening, Plants, Geography, Geology, History, Music, Dance, Natural History, Nonfiction (General), Outdoor Recreation, Photography, Regional Interests, Religion - Jewish, Social Sciences, Sociology, Travel
ISBN Prefix(es): 3-7672
Distributor for CCV; Eylers; Verlag Gronenberg; Land & Meer Verlag; Verlag fuer Medienliteratur; Verlag Robert Wenzel
Warehouse: Vull-Service GmbH, Werftbahnstr 8, 24143 Kiel *Tel:* (0431) 702 82 70 *Fax:* (0431) 702 82 99

Christliche Verlagsgesellschaft mbH+
Molkestr 1, 35683 Dillenburg
Tel: (02771) 8302-0 *Fax:* (02771) 8302-30
E-mail: info@cv-dillenburg.de
Web Site: www.cb-buchshop.de
Key Personnel
Editorial, Publicity, Production: Hartmut Jaeger
Sales: Bernd-Udo Flick
Rights & Permissions: Mirko Merten
Founded: 1957
Subjects: Religion - Other
ISBN Prefix(es): 3-89436
Subsidiaries: Christliche Buecherstuben GmbH
Distributed by CB Medienvertrieb (Germany); Schwengeler Verlag (Switzerland)
Distributor for CLV; Daniel Verlag; KEB; Leuchtturm Verlag; Media C; Schwengeler; 3L Verlag
Bookshop(s): Lennestr 25, 58762 Altena; Molkestr 1, 35683 Dillenburg; Friedrichsstr 10, Duesseldorf; Rosenallee, 52249 Eschweiler; Dreikoenigstr 21, 47799 Krefeld 1; Poststr 24, 4780 Lippstadt; Muensterstr 27, 4670 Luenen; Lindauerstr 8, 87700 Memmingen; Am Koenigshof 43, 40822 Mettman; Hofgarten 4, 52249 Neunkirchen; Im Kobbenrod 3, 58840 Plettenberg; Harschbacherstr 12, 56316 Raubach; Koenigstr 20, Rendsburg; Alte Poststr 7, 57072 Siegen 1; Zwingergasse 1, 74889 Sinsheim; Kirchstr 19, 52531 Uebach-Palenberg; Neustadtstr 12, 58791 Werdohl; Schwelmerstr 48, 42389 Wuppertal 22

Christliches Verlagshaus GmbH+
Motorstr 36, 70499 Stuttgart
Mailing Address: Postfach 311141, 70471 Stuttgart
Tel: (0711) 830000 *Fax:* (0711) 830010
Key Personnel
Man Dir: Armin Jetter
Founded: 1872
Subjects: Literature, Literary Criticism, Essays, Religion - Other
ISBN Prefix(es): 3-7675
Subsidiaries: Anker Buch und Medien GmbH; Druckhaus West GmbH

Christophorus-Verlag GmbH+
Subsidiary of Verlag Herder GmbH & Co KG
Hermann-Herderstr 4, 79104 Freiburg im Breisgau
Tel: (0761) 27170 *Fax:* (0761) 2717352
Key Personnel
Man Dir: Dr Klaus-Christoph Scheffels
International Rights: Norbert Landa
Founded: 1935
Subjects: Crafts, Games, Hobbies, How-to, Outdoor Recreation
ISBN Prefix(es): 3-419
Book Club(s): Bertelsmann; Weltbild
Shipping Address: Koch, Neff & Oetinger, Schockenriedstr 39, 70565 Stuttgart

Warehouse: Koch, Neff & Oetinger, Schockenriedstr 39, 70565 Stuttgart
Orders to: Koch, Neff & Oetinger, Schockenriedstr 39, 70565 Stuttgart

Christusbruderschaft Selbitz ev, Abt Verlag
Wildenberg 23, 95152 Selbitz
Mailing Address: Postfach 1260, 95147 Selbitz
Tel: (09280) 68-34 *Fax:* (09280) 68-68
E-mail: info@verlag-christusbruderschaft.de
Web Site: www.verlag-christusbruderschaft.de
Key Personnel
International Rights: Sr Baerbel Quarg
Founded: 1953
Subjects: Art, Poetry, Religion - Protestant, Theology
ISBN Prefix(es): 3-928745

Cicero Presse Verlag & Antiquariat
25980 Morsum/Sylt
Tel: (04651) 890305 *Fax:* (04651) 890885
E-mail: ciceropresse@t-online.de
Web Site: www.zvab.com
Founded: 1965
Membership(s): International League of Antiquarian Booksellers (ILAB) & Verband Deutscher Antiquare (VDA).
ISBN Prefix(es): 8-9120
Total Titles: 20 Print

Marianne Cieslik+
Theodor-Heuss-Str 185, 52428 Juelich
Tel: (02461) 51222; (02461) 57661 *Fax:* (02461) 52772
Key Personnel
Owner: Marianne Cieslik
    E-mail: verlagmariannecieslik@t-online.de
Manager: Jurgen Cieslik
Founded: 1975
Publishers for collector books & magazines (dolls, toys, teddy bears).
Subjects: Crafts, Games, Hobbies, Price guides
ISBN Prefix(es): 3-921844

Claassen Verlag GmbH+
Paul-Heyssstr 28, 80336 Munich
Tel: (089) 5148-0 *Fax:* (089) 5148-2229
E-mail: info@ullstein-heyne-list.de
Web Site: www.claassen-verlag.de
Telex: 927108
Key Personnel
Man Dir: Hubertus Meyer-Burckhardt; Christian Strasser
Founded: 1934
Subjects: Biography, Fiction, Literature, Literary Criticism, Essays, Nonfiction (General)
ISBN Prefix(es): 3-546
Parent Company: Gebrueder Gerstenberg GmbH & Co

Claudius Verlag+
Birkerstr 22, 80636 Munich
Tel: (089) 12172-123 *Fax:* (089) 12172-138
E-mail: info@claudius.de
Web Site: www.claudius.de
Key Personnel
Dir: Hartmut Joisten *Tel:* (089) 12172112
Publisher: Dr Manuel Zelger *Tel:* (089) 12172136
    E-mail: mzelger@epv.de
International Rights: Antje Fritsch-Brown
    Tel: (089) 12172132 *E-mail:* afritsch@epv.de
Founded: 1954
Subjects: Developing Countries, Humor, Religion - Protestant, Religion - Other, Self-Help, Theology
ISBN Prefix(es): 3-532
Number of titles published annually: 30 Print
Total Titles: 300 Print
Parent Company: Evangelischer Presseverband fuer Bayern eV
Bookshop(s): Claudius Versandbuchhandlung, Contact: Regine Zendrek *Tel:* (089) 12172119 *Fax:* (089) 12172138 *E-mail:* vsb@epv.de

CMA Edition+
Roter Brach Weg 54b, 93049 Regensburg
Tel: (0941) 23939; (0941) 34003; (08458) 8960
    Fax: (08458) 8960; (0941) 34003
Key Personnel
Contact: Christine Adlhoch; Dietrich Leisching
Founded: 1984
Subjects: Biography, Poetry
ISBN Prefix(es): 3-9801025

Charles Coleman Verlag GmbH & Co KG
Stolberger Str 84, 50933 Cologne
Mailing Address: Postfach 41 09 49, 50869 Cologne
Tel: (0221) 5497-0 *Fax:* (0221) 5497-326
E-mail: coleman@rudolf.mueller.de
Web Site: www.coleman-verlag.de; www.rudolf-mueller.de
Key Personnel
Man Dir: Rudolf M Bleser; Dr Christoph Mueller
Founded: 1894
Subjects: Career Development, Engineering (General), Mechanical Engineering
ISBN Prefix(es): 3-87128
Parent Company: Verlagsgesellschaft Rudolf Mueller GmbH, Stolbergerstr 84, 50933 Cologne

Collection b, *imprint of* Deutsche Bibelgesellschaft

Columbus Verlag Paul Oestergaard GmbH+
Am Bahnhof 2, 72505 Krauchenwies
Tel: (07576) 96 03-0 *Fax:* (07576) 96 03-29
E-mail: info@columbus-verlag.de
Web Site: www.columbus-verlag.de *Cable:* COLUMBUS-VERLAG
Key Personnel
Publisher: Torsten Oestergaard
Founded: 1909
Subjects: Astronomy, Geography, Geology, House & Home, Globes
ISBN Prefix(es): 3-87129
Subsidiaries: Leipziger Globusmanufaktur
Orders to: Columbus Haus, an der Station 2, 72505 Krauchenwies

ComMedia & Arte Verlag Bernd Mayer+
Am Hang 27, 74626 Bretzfeld
Mailing Address: Postfach 1117, 74622 Bretzfeld
Tel: (07945) 950719 *Fax:* (07945) 950718
Key Personnel
Owner: Bernd Mayer
Founded: 1982
Subjects: Fiction, Gay & Lesbian
ISBN Prefix(es): 3-924244
Orders to: Rotation, Mehringdamm 51, 10000 Berlin *Tel:* (030) 6927934 *Fax:* (030) 6942006

Compact Verlag GmbH+
Zuericherstr 29, 81476 Munich
Tel: (089) 7451610 *Fax:* (089) 756095
E-mail: info@compactverlag.de
Web Site: www.compactverlag.de
Key Personnel
Publisher, Manager & International Rights: Friedrich Niendieck
Man Dir: Bernd Steier
Foreign Rights: Sandra Brack *Tel:* (089) 74516183 *E-mail:* sandra.brack@compactverlag.de
Founded: 1976
Specialize in nonfiction books.
Subjects: Business, Cookery, Crafts, Games, Hobbies, Education, English as a Second Language, Gardening, Plants, Health, Nutrition, History, House & Home, How-to, Law, Nonfiction (General), Real Estate, Travel
ISBN Prefix(es): 3-8174
Number of titles published annually: 180 Print
Total Titles: 1,000 Print
Warehouse: CDC GmbH, Rotwandweg 1, 82024 Taufkirchen-Potzham

Concordia-Buchhandlung & Verlag+
Bahnhofstr 8, 08056 Zwickau
Mailing Address: Postfach 200226, 08002 Zwickau
Tel: (0375) 21 28 50 *Fax:* (0375) 29 80 80; (0375) 21 28 50
E-mail: concordia@t-online.de
Web Site: www.concordiabuch.de
Key Personnel
Business Associate: Dr Gottfried Herrmann
Founded: 1990
Subjects: Religion - Other, Theology
ISBN Prefix(es): 3-910153

Connection Medien GmbH+
Hauptstr 5, 84494 Niedertaufkirchen
Tel: (08639) 98 34-0 *Fax:* (08639) 1219
E-mail: seminare@connection.de
Web Site: www.connection.de; www.seminar-connection.de
Key Personnel
Contact: Wolf Schneider *E-mail:* schneider@connection.de
Founded: 1985
Subjects: Human Relations, Parapsychology, Religion - Buddhist, Religion - Other, Self-Help
ISBN Prefix(es): 3-928248
Number of titles published annually: 5 Print
Parent Company: Connection Medien GmbH
Divisions: Satzstudio, Seminar-und organisation, Vertrieb

Copernicus, *imprint of* Springer Science+Business Media GmbH & Co KG

Coppenrath Verlag+
Subsidiary of Verlag Wolfgang Hoelker
Hafenweg 30, 48155 Muenster
Tel: (0251) 41411-0 *Fax:* (0251) 4141120
E-mail: info@coppenrath.de
Web Site: www.coppenrath.de
Key Personnel
Man Dir: Wolfgang Hoelker
Production: Wolfgang Foerster
Publicity: Tomas Rensing
Sales: Hubert Bergmoser
Rights & Permissions: Anette Riedel
Founded: 1768
Subjects: Architecture & Interior Design, Art, Nonfiction (General)
ISBN Prefix(es): 3-88547; 3-8157
Divisions: Edition Spiegelburg
Warehouse: Coppenrath-Hoelker Distribution, 48612 Horstmar *Tel:* (02558) 98818 *Fax:* (02558) 98819

Copress Verlag+
Imprint of Stiebner Verlag GmbH
Nymphenburgerstr 86, 80636 Munich
Tel: (089) 1257414 *Fax:* (089) 12162282
E-mail: verlag@stiebner.com
Web Site: www.stiebner.com *Cable:* COPRESS MUNCHEN
Subjects: Health, Nutrition, History, Outdoor Recreation, Sports, Athletics
ISBN Prefix(es): 3-7679; 3-8307

Corian-Verlag Heinrich Wimmer
Bernhard-Monath-Str 28, 86405 Meitingen
Mailing Address: Postfach 1169, 86400 Meitingen
Tel: (08271) 5951 *Fax:* (08271) 6931

GERMANY

E-mail: 082716941-0001@t-online.de; 101374.1022@compuserve.com
Key Personnel
Man Dir: Heinrich Wimmer
Founded: 1983
Subjects: Film, Video, Science Fiction, Fantasy
ISBN Prefix(es): 3-89048

Cornelsen und Oxford University Press GmbH & Co
Johannisbergerstr 74, 14197 Berlin
Tel: (030) 827936-0 *Fax:* (030) 827936-36
Web Site: www.cornelsen.de
Telex: 184968 cvk b
Key Personnel
Dir: Jesus Lezcano; Alfred Predhumean
Founded: 1971
Subjects: Education
ISBN Prefix(es): 3-8109
Subsidiaries: Cornelsen Verlag GmbH & Co

Cornelsen Verlag GmbH & Co OHG+
Mecklenburgischestr 53, 14197 Berlin
Tel: (030) 897 85-0 *Fax:* (030) 897 85-299
E-mail: c-mail@cornelsen.de
Web Site: www.cornelsen.com
Key Personnel
Man Dir: Hans-Joerg Duellmann; Wolf-Rudiger Feldmann; Walter Funken; Alfred Gruener; Martin Hueppe
International Relations & Foreign Rights: Holger Behm *Tel:* (030) 897 85-341 *E-mail:* holger.behm@cornelsen.de
Founded: 1946
Textbook publisher in all areas of learning.
Membership(s): European Educational Publishers Group (EEPG); Association of German Booksellers.
Subjects: Accounting, Advertising, Biological Sciences, Career Development, Chemistry, Chemical Engineering, Communications, Economics, Education, English as a Second Language, Geography, Geology, History, Management, Marketing, Mathematics, Physical Sciences, Physics, Technology
ISBN Prefix(es): 3-464
Total Titles: 8,000 Print; 100 CD-ROM; 150 Audio
Parent Company: Cornelsen Verlagsholding GmbH & Co
Associate Companies: ALL-Group, Bucharest, Romania; Cornelsen Experimenta, Berlin; Cornelsen Verlagskontor GmbH Co KG; CS Druck Cornelsen Stuertz, Berlin; Nakladatelstri Fraus, Plzen, Czech Republic; Kamp Schulbuchverlag Due sseldorf, PZV Berlin; VERITAS, Linz, Austria
Subsidiaries: Cornelsen Verlag Scriptor; Sauerlaender Verlage AG
Orders to: CVK Cornelsen Verlagskontor, Kammerratsheide 66, 33609 Bielefeld

Cornelsen Verlag Scriptor GmbH & Co KG+
Subsidiary of Cornelsen Verlag
Mecklenburgische Str 53, 14197 Berlin
Tel: (030) 89 7858700 *Fax:* (030) 89 7858799
E-mail: c-mail@cornelsen.de
Web Site: www.cornelsen.de
Key Personnel
General Manager: Alfred Gruener; Horst Linder
Founded: 1973
Subjects: Education
ISBN Prefix(es): 3-589
Orders to: CVK Cornelsen Verlagskontor, Kammerratsheide 66, 33598 Bielefeld

Corona Verlag+
Saselbekstr 35, 22393 Hamburg
Tel: (040) 6424144 *Fax:* (040) 64221023
Key Personnel
Publisher: Halina Kamm
Editor: Joachim Stiller

Founded: 1990
Subjects: Music, Dance, Psychology, Psychiatry, Esoteric, Meditation, Natural Science
ISBN Prefix(es): 3-928084; 3-934438
Total Titles: 100 Print; 100 CD-ROM; 100 Audio

J G Cotta'sche Buchhandlung Nachfolger GmbH+
Rotebuehlstr 77, 70178 Stuttgart
Mailing Address: Postfach 106016, 70049 Stuttgart
Tel: (0711) 6672-1256 *Fax:* (0711) 6672-2031
E-mail: info@klett-cotta.de
Web Site: www.klett-cotta.de
Telex: 7222232 klet d
Key Personnel
Publisher: Michael Klett
Man Dir: Rainer Just *E-mail:* r.just@klett-cotta.de
Foreign Relations: Derrik Jenkins
Foreign Rights: Roland Knappe *E-mail:* r.knappe@klett-cotta.de
Founded: 1659
Subjects: Child Care & Development, Education, Fiction, History, Human Relations, Literature, Literary Criticism, Essays, Management, Nonfiction (General), Philosophy, Poetry, Psychology, Psychiatry, Science (General)
ISBN Prefix(es): 3-12; 3-7681; 3-608; 3-7885; 3-7835
Total Titles: 3,000 Print
Parent Company: Ernst Klett AG
Imprints: Pfeiffer bei Klett-Cotta
Warehouse: BDK Bucherdienst GmbH, Kolnerstr 248, Cologne

Creator, imprint of Bonifatius GmbH Druck-Buch-Verlag

Verlag CSA Rosemarie Schneider+
Limesstr 16, 61389 Schmitten-Oberreifenberg
Tel: (06082) 970116 *Fax:* (06082) 970123
E-mail: csa-europa@csa-activ.de
Web Site: www.csa-activ.de
Key Personnel
Owner: Rosemarie Schneider
Senior Partner: Brigitte K Schneider
Founded: 1978
Subjects: Education, Psychology, Psychiatry, Religion - Other, Self-Help
ISBN Prefix(es): 3-922779
U.S. Office(s): Rosemarie Schneider, 66 Indian Springs, 49305 Highway 74, Palm Desert, CA 92260, United States

CTL-Presse Clemens-Tobias Lange
Borselstr 9-11, 22765 Hamburg
Tel: (040) 39902223 *Fax:* (040) 39902224
E-mail: ctl@europe.com
Web Site: www.ctl-presse.de
Founded: 1989
Subjects: Art, Photography, Poetry, Artist's Books, Literature
Number of titles published annually: 2 Print
Total Titles: 79 Print

Daco Verlag Guenter Blase oHG+
Christophstr 40-42, 70180 Stuttgart
Tel: (0711) 96421-0 *Fax:* (0711) 96421-10
E-mail: info@daco-verlag.de
Web Site: www.daco-verlag.de
Key Personnel
Publishing Dir, Rights & Permissions: Stephan Goetz
Founded: 1943
Subjects: Art
ISBN Prefix(es): 3-87135
Imprints: Hanfstaengl-Verlag; Nadif

Daedalus Verlag+
4622 Amtsgericht, 48145 Muenster
Tel: (0251) 231355 *Fax:* (0251) 232631

E-mail: info@daedalus-verlag.de
Web Site: www.daedalus-verlag.com
Key Personnel
Publisher, Rights & Permissions: Joachim Herbst
Founded: 1984
Subjects: Communications, Government, Political Science, Nonfiction (General), Psychology, Psychiatry, Social Sciences, Sociology
ISBN Prefix(es): 3-89126

Dagmar Dreves Verlag+
Spangenbergstr 29, 21337 Lueneburg
Tel: (04131) 248100 *Fax:* (04131) 248102
Key Personnel
Manager: Horst Ernst
Founded: 1989
Subjects: Mysteries, Nonfiction (General), Parapsychology
ISBN Prefix(es): 3-924532; 3-936269
Bookshop(s): Dagmar Dreves Verlag, Knoopstr 8, Hamburg 21073
Warehouse: Dagmar Dreves Verlag, Knoopstr 8, 21073 Hamburg
Orders to: Dagmar Dreves Verlag, Knoopstr 8, 21073 Hamburg

Dana Verlag
Campemoorweg 8, 49565 Bram
Tel: (05468) 1813 *Fax:* (05468) 239
Key Personnel
Contact: Wolfgang Sewald; Gonda Sewald
Founded: 1988
Subjects: Science Fiction, Fantasy
ISBN Prefix(es): 3-9801976; 3-931335

Dareschta Consulting und Handels GmbH+
Bahnhofstr 41, 65185 Wiesbaden
Tel: (0611) 9310992 *Fax:* (0611) 3082096
Key Personnel
International Rights: Beatrix Siebel
Founded: 1988
Subjects: Anthropology, Biological Sciences, Medicine, Nursing, Dentistry, Psychology, Psychiatry, Religion - Catholic, Religion - Protestant, Social Sciences, Sociology, Women's Studies
ISBN Prefix(es): 3-89379; 3-9801744

Verlag Darmstaedter Blaetter Schwarz und Co
Haubachweg 5, 64285 Darmstadt
Tel: (06151) 48196
Key Personnel
Man Dir: Dr Guenther Schwarz
Founded: 1967
Subjects: Language Arts, Linguistics, Philosophy, Psychology, Psychiatry, Religion - Jewish, Social Sciences, Sociology
ISBN Prefix(es): 3-87139

Das Arsenal, Verlag fuer Kultur und Politik GmbH+
Tegeler Weg 97, 10589 Berlin
Tel: (030) 3441827; (030) 34651361 *Fax:* (030) 34651362
Key Personnel
Man Dir: Dr Peter Moses-Krause
Publisher: Jutta Siegert
Founded: 1977
Membership(s): Stock Exchange of German Booksellers.
Subjects: Art, Drama, Theater, Fiction, History, Philosophy
ISBN Prefix(es): 3-921810; 3-931109
Orders to: Bugrim, Saalburgstr 3, 12099 Berlin

Data Becker GmbH & Co KG+
Merowingerstr 30, 40223 Duesseldorf
Mailing Address: Postfach 102044, 40011 Duesseldorf
Tel: (0211) 9331 800; (0211) 9334 900 (orders) *Fax:* (0211) 9331 444; (0211) 9334 999 (orders)

E-mail: info@databecker.de
Web Site: www.databecker.de
Key Personnel
President: Harald Becker
President & Marketing: Dr Achim Becker
Founded: 1981
Subjects: Computer Science, Microcomputers
ISBN Prefix(es): 3-8158; 3-89011

Datacom Buchverlag GmbH+
Zum Biotop 15, 50127 Bergheim
Tel: (02271) 6080 *Fax:* (02271) 608290
Key Personnel
International Rights: Klaus Lipinski
Founded: 1984
Subjects: Communications
ISBN Prefix(es): 3-89238
Associate Companies: Datacom Zeidschriften-Verlag GmbH

Verlag Werner Dausien+
Burgallee 67, 63454 Hanau
Tel: (06181) 92810 *Fax:* (06181) 5070932
Key Personnel
Man Dir, Rights & Permissions: Werner Dausien
Founded: 1949
Subjects: Art, How-to, Music, Dance
ISBN Prefix(es): 3-7684
Associate Companies: Verlag Mueller und Kiepenheuer
Divisions: Verlag Fuer Zahnmedizin

DBV, *imprint of* Don Bosco Verlag

R v Decker's Verlag, G Schenck GmbH, see Huthig GmbH & Co KG

Degener & Co, Manfred Dreiss Verlag+
Nuernbergerstr 27, 91413 Neustadt an der Aisch
Tel: (09161) 886039 *Fax:* (09161) 886057
E-mail: degener@degener-verlag.com
Web Site: www.degener-verlag.com
Key Personnel
Contact: Manfred Dreiss
Founded: 1910
Subjects: Genealogy, History, Military Science, Regional Interests
ISBN Prefix(es): 3-7686
Associate Companies: Verlag Bauer & Raspe; Heinz Reise-Verlag
Distributor for Bauer & Raspe; Heinz-Reise-Verlag
Distribution Center: Stuttgarter Verlagskoutor, SVK-VA, PO Box 106016, 70049 Stuttgart
Orders to: Verlag Degener & Co, Nurnbergerstr 27, 91413 Neustadt

Verlag Horst Deike KG+
Robert-Bosch-Str 18, 78467 Konstanz
Mailing Address: Postfach 100452, 78404 Konstanz
Tel: (07531) 81550 *Fax:* (07531) 815581
E-mail: info@deike-verlag.de
Web Site: www.deike-verlag.de
Key Personnel
President: Wolfgang Deike
Founded: 1923
Subjects: Art, Literature, Literary Criticism, Essays, Music, Dance
ISBN Prefix(es): 3-87142
Subsidiaries: Deike AG
U.S. Office(s): Horst Deike KG Verlag, 463 State St, Santa Barbara, CA, United States

Delius, Klasing und Co+
Siekerwall 21, 33602 Bielefeld
Tel: (0521) 55 90 *Fax:* (0521) 55 91 13
E-mail: info@delius-klasing.de
Web Site: www.delius-klasing.de
Telex: 0932934 Dekla *Cable:* BUCHKLASING BIELEFELD

Key Personnel
Dir: Konrad-Wilhelm Delius; Kurt Delius
Production: Hermann Ludewig
Publicity: Susanne Lange
Rights & Permissions: Petra Trueltzsch
Founded: 1911
Subjects: Automotive, Maritime, Outdoor Recreation
ISBN Prefix(es): 3-7688
Associate Companies: Edition Maritim Hamburg; Moby Dick Kiel
Distributed by Ermatingen; Lechner & Sohn (Austria); Neptun Verlag; Schweiz
Orders to: Delius Klasing Verlag GmbH, Siekerwall 21, 33602 Bielefeld

Delius Klasing Verlag+
Siekerwall 21, 33602 Bielefeld
Tel: (0521) 55 90 *Fax:* (0521) 55 91 13
E-mail: info@delius-klasing.de
Web Site: www.delius-klasing.de *Cable:* BUCHKLASING BIELEFELD
Key Personnel
Librarian: Baerbel Schubel
Publisher: Kurt Delius
Sales & Publicity Manager: Susanne Lange
Rights & Permissions: Petra Trueltzsch
Producer: Hermann Ludewig
Founded: 1911
Subjects: Maritime
ISBN Prefix(es): 3-87412
Parent Company: Delius, Klasing und Co
Associate Companies: Edition Maritim Hamburg; Moby Dick Verlag Uiel
Distributed by Ermatingeni; Lechner & Sohn (Austria); Neptun Verlag; Schweiz

Delphin Verlag GmbH+
Emil-Hoffmannstr 1, 50996 Cologne
Mailing Address: Postfach 501863, 50978 Cologne
Tel: (02236) 39990 *Fax:* (02236) 399997
Telex: 8886642/2236364kvg
Key Personnel
Man Dir: Guenter Goebel; Juergen Naumann
Founded: 1962
ISBN Prefix(es): 3-7735; 3-8184; 3-88971
Parent Company: Naumann & Goebel Verlagsgesellschaft mbH
Associate Companies: Daumueller Werbeges mbH; Delphin AG; Naturalis Verlags und Vertriebsgesellschaft mbH; Neuer Pawlak Verlag GmbH; Tigris Verlag GmbH; V & M Verlags & Medienges Koeln mbH; VEMAG Verlags- und Medien AG; Verlag 'Das persoenliche Geburtstagsbuch' GmbH

Delp'sche Verlagsbuchhandlung
Kegetstr 11, 91438 Bad Windsheim
Mailing Address: Postfach 140, 91424 Bad Windsheim
Tel: (09841) 9030 *Fax:* (09841) 90315
Telex: 61524
Key Personnel
Man Dir: Heinrich Delp
Founded: 1961
Subjects: Art, Regional Interests
ISBN Prefix(es): 3-7689

Delta, *imprint of* Egmont EHAPA Verlag GmbH

Engelbert Dessart Verlag KG, see Siebert Verlag GmbH

Verlag Harri Deutsch+
Graefstr 47, 60486 Frankfurt am Main
Tel: (069) 77015860 *Fax:* (069) 77015869
E-mail: verlag@harri-deutsch.de
Web Site: www.harri-deutsch.de/verlag
Key Personnel
Man Dir: Martin Kegel

Dir, Rights & Permissions: Harri Deutsch
Editor: Bernd Mueller
Production: Torsten Hellbusch
Founded: 1960
Subjects: Biological Sciences, Chemistry, Chemical Engineering, Earth Sciences, Economics, Electronics, Electrical Engineering, Engineering (General), Mathematics, Natural History, Physical Sciences, Physics, Sports, Athletics
ISBN Prefix(es): 3-87144; 3-8171
Subsidiaries: Verlag Harri Deutsch AG
Bookshop(s): Naturwissenschaftliche Fachbuchhandlung Harri Deutsch, Graefstr 47/51, 60486 Frankfurt am Main

Deutsche Bibelgesellschaft+
Balingerstr 31, 70567 Stuttgart
Tel: (0711) 7181-0 *Fax:* (0711) 7181-250
E-mail: infoabt@dbg.de
Web Site: www.dbg.de
Telex: 7255299 Bibl d *Cable:* BIBELHAUS STUTTGART
Key Personnel
Dir & International Rights: Dr Volkmar J Loebel
Dir: Rev Jan A Buehner, PhD
Founded: 1812 (1981)
German Bible Society.
Subjects: Biblical Studies
ISBN Prefix(es): 3-438
Imprints: Collection b
U.S. Office(s): American Bible Society, New York, NY, United States *Fax:* 212-408-1456
Web Site: www.americanbible.org

Deutsche Bibliothek der Wissenschaften/German Library of Sciences, *imprint of* Frankfurter Literaturverlag GmbH

Die Deutsche Bibliothek/Deutsche Buecherei Leipzig
Adickesallee 1, 60322 Frankfurt am Main
Tel: (069) 1525-0 *Fax:* (069) 1525-1010
E-mail: info@dbf.ddb.de
Web Site: www.ddb.de
Key Personnel
Dir: Dr Elisabeth Niggemann
Contact: Kathrin Ansorge *Tel:* (069) 15251004 *E-mail:* ansorge@dbf.ddb.de
Founded: 1912
Deutsches Buch-und Schriftmuseum.
Subjects: Literature, Literary Criticism, Essays
ISBN Prefix(es): 3-922051; 3-933641
Branch Office(s)
Deutsche Buecherei Leipzig, Deutscher Platz 1, 04103 Leipzig *Tel:* (0341) 22710 *Fax:* (0341) 2271444
Distributed by Buchhaendler-Vereinigung GmbH

Deutsche Blinden-Bibliothek+
Am Schlag 8, 35037 Marburg
Mailing Address: Postfach 1160, 35001 Marburg
Tel: (06421) 6060 *Fax:* (06421) 606259
E-mail: info@blista.de
Web Site: www.blista.de
Key Personnel
Man Dir: Juergen Hertlein *Tel:* (06421) 606101 *E-mail:* hertlein@blista.de
Library Dir, Publishing Manager & International Rights: Rainer F V Witte *Tel:* (06421) 606103 *Fax:* (06421) 606269 *E-mail:* witte@blista.de
Founded: 1916
German Library for the Blind.
ISBN Prefix(es): 3-89642
Parent Company: Deutsche Blindenstudienanstalt eV (DBSTA)
Divisions: Archiv und Internat Dokumentation zzuum Blinden-und Sehbehindertenwesen; Bibliographic Centre; Deutsche Blindenhoerbuecherei (aufgesprochene Literatur/talking books); Emil-Krueckmann-Bibliothek (Blindenschift/Braille)

Deutsche Gesellschaft fuer Eisenbahngeschichte eV
Kleinsorgenring 14, 59457 Werl
Tel: (02922) 84970 *Fax:* (02922) 84927
E-mail: info@dgeg.de
Web Site: www.dgeg.de
Key Personnel
Contact: Guenter Krause
Founded: 1967
Subjects: Transportation
ISBN Prefix(es): 3-921700

Deutsche Gesellschaft fuer Luft-und Raumfahrt Lilienthal Oberth eV
Godesberger Allee 70, 53175 Bonn
Tel: (0228) 30 80 5-0 *Fax:* (0228) 30 80 5-24
E-mail: geschaeftsstelle@dglr.de
Web Site: www.dglr.de
Key Personnel
Secretary General: Hans Luttgen
ISBN Prefix(es): 3-922010; 3-932182

Deutsche Hochschulschriften/German University Studies, *imprint of* Frankfurter Literaturverlag GmbH

Deutsche Landwirtschafts-Gesellschaft VerlagsgesGmbH+
Eschborner Landstr 122, 60489 Frankfurt
Tel: (069) 24 788-451 *Fax:* (069) 24 788-484
E-mail: dlg-verlag@dlg-frankfurt.de
Web Site: www.dlg-verlag.de
Telex: veber 413185 dig.ffm
Key Personnel
President & International Rights: Karin Scheller
Marketing Manager: Stefan Pierre-Louis
 Tel: (069) 24 788-466 *E-mail:* s.pierrelouis@dlg-frankfurt.de
Founded: 1952
Subjects: Agriculture, Health, Nutrition, Travel
ISBN Prefix(es): 3-7690
Number of titles published annually: 15 Print
Total Titles: 350 Print
Parent Company: DLG eV
Distributed by Verlagsunion Agrar
Distribution Center: SuedOst Verlags Service, Am Steinfeld 4, 94065 Waldkirchen
Returns: SuedOst Verlags Service, Am Steinfeld 4, 94065 Waldkirchen

Verlag Deutsche Unitarier+
Birkenstr 4, 88214 Ravensburg
Tel: (0751) 625 96 *Fax:* (0751) 672 01
E-mail: verlag@unitarier.de
Web Site: www.unitarier.de
Key Personnel
Publisher: Micha Ramm
Founded: 1950
Membership(s): International Association for Religious Freedom (IARF); International Council of Unitarians & Universalists (ICUU).
Subjects: Philosophy, Religion - Other
ISBN Prefix(es): 3-922483
Total Titles: 15 Print
Parent Company: Deutsche Unitarier Religionsgemeinschaft eV, Hamburg

Deutsche Verlags-Anstalt GmbH (DVA)+
Koeniginstr 9, 80539 Munich
Tel: (089) 45554-0 *Fax:* (089) 45554-100; (089) 45554-111
E-mail: info@dva.de; buch@dva.de
Web Site: www.dva.de
Telex: 7111193DVA d *Cable:* DEVA STUTTGART
Key Personnel
Man Dir: Juergen Horbach *E-mail:* juergen.horbach@dva.de; Dr Ulrich Quiel
Marketing: Susanne Lange *E-mail:* susanne.lange@dva.de
Publisher: Michael Neher
Rights & Licenses: Susanne Seggewiss
 E-mail: susanne.seggewiss@dva.de
Advertising: Ulrike Bachmann *E-mail:* ulrike.bachmann@dva.de
Public Relations: Markus Desaga *E-mail:* markus.desaga@dva.de; Christine Liebl
 E-mail: christine.liebl@dva.de
Founded: 1831
Subjects: Architecture & Interior Design, Astronomy, Biography, Earth Sciences, Fiction, Government, Political Science, History, Literature, Literary Criticism, Essays, Music, Dance, Philosophy, Poetry, Psychology, Psychiatry, Science (General)
ISBN Prefix(es): 3-421
Parent Company: Verlagsgruppe, Frankfurter Allgemeine Zeitung GmbH, Frankfurt am Main
Subsidiaries: Engelhorn Verlag GmbH; Julius Hoffmann Verlag GmbH; Manesse Verlag GmbH
U.S. Office(s): Del Commune Enterprises, Inc, 285 W Broadway, Suite 310, New York, NY 10013, United States *Tel:* 212-226-6664 *Fax:* 212-965-9294
Warehouse: Verlegerdienst Muenchen, Gutenbergstr 1, 82205 Gilching

Deutscher Adressbuch-Verlag fuer Wirtschaft und Verkehr GmbH
c/o Dumrath & Fassnacht KG (GmbH & Co), Winsbergring 38, 22525 Hamburg
Tel: (040) 85308-410 *Fax:* (040) 85308-385
E-mail: info@businessdeutschland.de
Web Site: www.businessdeutschland.de
Key Personnel
Man Dir & Publisher: Klaus Boller
Editorial: Helmut Kolb
Production & Publicity: Hans Zimmer
Founded: 1923
The German Directory Publishing Company for Industry & Commerce.
Membership(s): German & European Book Publishers Association.
Subjects: Business
ISBN Prefix(es): 3-87148
Parent Company: De Te Medien GmbH/alle Gelbe Seiten Verlage

Deutscher Aerzte-Verlag GmbH+
Dieselstr 2, 50859 Cologne
Tel: (02234) 7011-0 *Fax:* (02234) 7011-398; (02234) 7011-475
E-mail: zielinka@aerzteverlag.de
Web Site: www.aerzteverlag.de
Key Personnel
Man Dir: Hermann Dinse
Man Dir & International Rights: Dieter Weber
Founded: 1949
Subjects: Medicine, Nursing, Dentistry
ISBN Prefix(es): 3-7961
Subsidiaries: CEDIP Verlags GmbH; J F Lehmanns Med Buchhandlung GmbH; Otto Spatz GmbH & Co KG; Schwarzeck-Verlag GmbH

Deutscher Apotheker Verlag Dr Roland Schmiedel GmbH & Co (German Pharmacists Publishers)+
Birkenwaldstr 44, 70191 Stuttgart
Mailing Address: Postfach 101061, 70009 Stuttgart
Tel: (0711) 2582-0 *Fax:* (0711) 2582-290
E-mail: service@deutscher-apotheker-verlag.de
Web Site: www.deutscher-apotheker-verlag.de
Key Personnel
Man Dir: Dr Klaus G Brauer; Andre Caro; Dr Christian Rotta
International Rights: Sabine Koerner
Marketing Manager: Siegmar Bauer
 E-mail: sbauer@deutscher-apotheker-verlag.de
Founded: 1861
Subjects: Medicine, Nursing, Dentistry, Pharmacy
ISBN Prefix(es): 3-7692
Subsidiaries: S Hirzel Verlag GmbH & Co; Medpharm Scientific Publishers; Franz Steiner Verlag Wiesbaden GmbH; Wissenschaftliche Verlagsgesellschaft mbH
Distributor for American Society of Hospital Pharmacists; Drug Intelligence Publications (Europe); Pharmaceutical Press (London, UK); United States Pharmacopeial Convention Inc (USA)
Foreign Rights: Sabine Koerner

Deutscher Betriebswirte-Verlag GmbH+
Bleichstr 20-22, 76593 Gernsbach
Mailing Address: Postfach 1332, 76586 Gernsbach
Tel: (07224) 9397-151 *Fax:* (07224) 9397-905
E-mail: info@betriebswirte-verlag.de
Web Site: www.betriebswirte-verlag.de
Telex: 78915 dbv d *Cable:* DBV GERNSBACH
Key Personnel
Man Dir: Dr Casimir Katz; Christel Katz
Editor, Rights & Permissions, Publicity: Regina Meier
Founded: 1926
Subjects: Business, Economics, Public Administration
ISBN Prefix(es): 3-921099; 3-88640

Deutscher Drucker Verlagsgesellschaft mbH & Co KG (German Printer Publishing House)
Riedstr 25, 73760 Ostfildern
Mailing Address: Postfach 4125, 73744 Ostfildern
Tel: (0711) 448170 *Fax:* (0711) 442099
E-mail: info@publish.de
Web Site: www.publish.de
Key Personnel
Man Dir: Martin Metzger *E-mail:* m.metzger@publish.de
Information for professionals, dealing with all aspects of digital workflow. Print communication, colour publishing & packaging.
ISBN Prefix(es): 3-920226
Parent Company: Ebner Verlag
Foreign Rep(s): Babel Marketing (UK); Ebner Publishing (USA); Andrew Karning (Scotland)

Deutscher EC-Verband
Leuschnerstr 74, 34134 Kassel
Tel: (0561) 40950 *Fax:* (0561) 4095112
E-mail: info.dv@ec-jugend.de
Web Site: www.ec-jugend.de
Key Personnel
Man Dir: Rolf Trauernicht
Subjects: Religion - Catholic, Religion - Protestant

Deutscher Fachverlag GmbH
Mainzer Landstr 251, 60326 Frankfurt am Main
Tel: (069) 7595-01 *Fax:* (069) 75952999
E-mail: info@dfv.de
Web Site: www.dfv.de
Key Personnel
Man Dir: Klaus Kottmeier; Peter Russ; Michael Schellenberger
Manager: Joerg Hintz
Founded: 1946
Sportswear International New York.
Subjects: Advertising, Agriculture, Business, Communications, Engineering (General), Fashion, Marketing, Nonfiction (General)
ISBN Prefix(es): 3-87150
Associate Companies: Manstein Zeitschnfton Verlag, Perchtoldsdorf B Wein, Austria; Edizioni Ecomarket SpA, 1-20121 Milan
Subsidiaries: Verlag Alfred Strothe GmbH & Co

Deutscher Gemeindeverlag GmbH
Hebruhlstr 69, 70549 Stuttgart
Tel: (0711) 78630 *Fax:* (0711) 7863400
Founded: 1925
Subjects: Government, Political Science
ISBN Prefix(es): 3-555

Parent Company: Verlag W Kohlhammer GmbH
Branch Office(s)
Rudolf-Leonhardstr 28, 01097 Dresden
 Tel: (0351) 5022685 *Fax:* (0351) 5670664
Gustav-Freytag Str 59, 99096 Erfurt *Tel:* (0361) 3735379 *Fax:* (0361) 3460537
Postfach 1465, 30014 Hannover *Tel:* (0511) 327029 *Fax:* (0511) 320143
Postfach 1865, 24017 Kiel *Tel:* (0431) 554857 *Fax:* (0431) 554944
Schleinufes 14, 39104 Magdeburg *Tel:* (0391) 597080 *Fax:* (0391) 5970813
Postfach 261134/55057, Mainz *Tel:* (06131) 891540 *Fax:* (06131) 891624
Sellostr 19, 14471 Potsdam *Tel:* (0331) 964670 *Fax:* (0331) 964672 (German Municipality Publishing Company)
Postfach 040204, 19026 Schwerin *Tel:* (0385) 616105 *Fax:* (0385) 616146
Warehouse: Verlagsvertrieb Stuttgart GmbH, Hepbruehlstr 69, 76565 Stuttgart

Deutscher Instituts-Verlag GmbH+
Subsidiary of Koelner Universitaetsverlag GmbH
Gustav-Heinemann Ufer 84-88, 50968 Cologne
Mailing Address: Postfach 510670, 50942 Cologne
Tel: (0221) 49 81-0 *Fax:* (0221) 49 81
E-mail: div@iwkoeln.de
Web Site: www.divkoeln.de
Key Personnel
Man Dir, Rights & Permissions: Dr Franz Josef Link *Tel:* (0221) 49 81-410 *Fax:* (0221) 49 81-501; Ulrich Brodersen *Tel:* (0221) 49 81-420 *Fax:* (0221) 49 81-501
Marketing: Michael Opferkuch *Tel:* (0221) 49 81-285 *Fax:* (0221) 49 81-286
Man Dir, Rights & Permissions: Axel Rhein *Tel:* (0221) 49 81-510 *Fax:* (0221) 49 81-533 *E-mail:* geisler@iwkoeln.de
Founded: 1951
Subjects: Developing Countries, Economics, Labor, Industrial Relations
ISBN Prefix(es): 3-602; 3-931206; 3-88054
Number of titles published annually: 100 Print
Total Titles: 148 Print
Parent Company: Institut der Deutschen Wirtschaft, Cologne (German Economics Institute)
Subsidiaries: Alpha Omega GmbH; Berolino.pr GmbH; Edition Agrippa GmbH; Rheinsitemedia GmbH

Deutscher Klassiker Verlag
Lindenstr 29-35, 60325 Frankfurt am Main
Mailing Address: Postfach 101945, 60019 Frankfurt am Main
Tel: (069) 75601-0 *Fax:* (069) 75601-522
Web Site: www.suhrkamp.de
Key Personnel
Publisher: Ulla Unseld-Berkewicz
Man Dir: Philip Roeder *Tel:* (069) 75601-500 *E-mail:* roeder@suhrkamp.de
Rights & Permissions: Dr Petra Hardt
Founded: 1981
ISBN Prefix(es): 3-618
Parent Company: Insel Verlag
Associate Companies: Suhrkamp Verlag; Suhrkamp Verlag AG, Switzerland

Deutscher Kunstverlag GmbH
Nymphenburger Str 84, 80636 Munich
Mailing Address: Postfach 190354, 80603 Munich
Tel: (089) 121516-0 *Fax:* (089) 121516-10; (089) 121516-16
E-mail: vertrieb@deutscher-kunstverlag.ccn.de
Key Personnel
Man Dir: Albert Hirmer; Juergen Kleidt
Rights & Permissions: Rudolf Winterstein
Founded: 1921
Subjects: Art
ISBN Prefix(es): 3-422
Orders to: Koch, Neff, Oetinger & Co, Schockenriedstr 39, Postfach 800620, 70565 Stuttgart
Buch 2000, Affoltern 8910, Switzerland

Deutscher Literatur-Verlag
Muehlenstieg 16-22, 22041 Hamburg
Mailing Address: Postfach 701009, 22010 Hamburg
Tel: (040) 682895-0 *Fax:* (040) 68289550
E-mail: info@kelter.de
Web Site: www.kelter.de
Telex: 213126
Key Personnel
Man Dir: Gerhard Melchert; Otto Melchert
Sales: Richard de Vries
Founded: 1905
ISBN Prefix(es): 3-87152
Associate Companies: Martin Kelter Verlag GmbH & Co, Muehlenstieg 16-22, 22041 Hamburg; Mero-Druck GmbH & Co KG
Orders to: Martin Kelter Verlag GmbH & Co

Deutscher Psychologen Verlag GmbH (DPV)
Oberer Lindweg 2, 53129 Bonn
Tel: (0228) 987310 *Fax:* (0228) 641023
E-mail: service@bdp-verband.org
Web Site: www.bdp-verband.org
Key Personnel
Man Dir: Jan Frederichs *Tel:* (0228) 19873118 *E-mail:* dpv@bdp-verband.org
Founded: 1984
Subjects: Psychology, Psychiatry
ISBN Prefix(es): 3-925559; 3-931589
Number of titles published annually: 5 Print
Total Titles: 65 Print
Parent Company: Berufsverband Deutscher Psychologinnen und Psychologen eV
Warehouse: Deutscher Psychologen Verlag, Verlagsauslieferung, Holzwiesenstr 2, 72127 Kusterdingen, Jan Frederichs

Deutscher Sparkassenverlag GmbH
Am Wallgraben 115, 70565 Stuttgart
Mailing Address: Postfach 70547, 70565 Stuttgart
Tel: (0711) 782-0 *Fax:* (0711) 782-16 35
E-mail: webredaktion@dsv-gruppe.de
Web Site: www.dsv-gruppe.de
Key Personnel
Man Dir: Bernd Kobarg
Founded: 1947
Membership(s): Boersenverein des Deutschen Buchhandels; Suedwestdeutsches Zeitschriftenverleger-Verband; Verband der Verlage und Buchhandlungen; Specialize in Literature on Banking Business Management.
ISBN Prefix(es): 3-09
Associate Companies: Deutsche Sparkassen-Datendienste GmbH; AM-Werbegesellschaft mbH

Deutscher Studien Verlag+
Werderstr 10, 69469 Weinheim
Tel: (06201) 60070
E-mail: info@beltz.de
Web Site: www.beltz.de
Key Personnel
Man Dir: Dr Manfred Beltz Ruebelmann; Joachim Radmer
Contact: Rosemarie Bornholt *Tel:* (06201) 6007 433 *E-mail:* r.bornholt@beltz.de
Rights: Charlotte Larat
Subjects: Psychology, Psychiatry, Social Sciences, Sociology
ISBN Prefix(es): 3-89271
Parent Company: Julius Beltz GmbH
Warehouse: Koch, Neff & Detringer, Verlagsauslieferung, 70551 Stuttgart *Tel:* (0711) 7899 20 30 *Fax:* (0711) 7899 10 10

Deutscher Taschenbuch Verlag GmbH & Co KG (dtv)+
Friedrichstr 1a, 80801 Munich
Mailing Address: Postfach 400422, 80704 Munich
Tel: (089) 38167-0 *Fax:* (089) 346428
E-mail: verlag@dtv.de
Web Site: www.dtv.de
Key Personnel
Man Dir: Wolfgang Balk
Finance Dir: Markus Angst
Rights & Permissions: Constance Chory; Elke Feistauer
Founded: 1961
Subjects: Art, Astronomy, Behavioral Sciences, Biography, Child Care & Development, Education, Fiction, Government, Political Science, Health, Nutrition, History, Humor, Law, Literature, Literary Criticism, Essays, Music, Dance, Nonfiction (General), Philosophy, Poetry, Psychology, Psychiatry, Religion - Other, Science (General), Science Fiction, Fantasy, Self-Help, Social Sciences, Sociology
ISBN Prefix(es): 3-423
Orders to: Koch, Neff, Oetinger & Co, Schockenriedstr 39, 70506 Stuttgart *Tel:* (0711) 78603322

Deutscher Universitats-Verlag
Unit of GWV Fachverlage GmbH
Abraham-Lincoln-Str 46, 65189 Wiesbaden
Tel: (0611) 7878-0 *Fax:* (0611) 7878-400
Web Site: www.duv.de; www.gwv-fachverlage.de
Key Personnel
General Manager: Dr Hans-Dieter Haenel
Man Dir: Dr Heinz Weinheimer
Editorial: Ute Wrasmann *E-mail:* ute.wrasmann@gwv-fachverlage.de
Founded: 1968
Subjects: Economics, Science (General), Social Sciences, Sociology
ISBN Prefix(es): 3-8244
Parent Company: Springer Science & Business Media
Distribution Center: VVA Bertelsmann Distribution, Postfach 7777, 33310 Guetersloh

Deutscher Verlag fur Grundstoffindustrie GmbH+
Ruedigerstr 14, 70469 Stuttgart
Mailing Address: Postfach 301120, 70451 Stuttgart
Tel: (0711) 8931-0 *Fax:* (0711) 8931-298
E-mail: kunden.service@thieme.de
Web Site: www.thieme.de
Key Personnel
Editor: Christoph Iven *E-mail:* christoph.iven@thieme.de
Foreign Rights: Barbara Pfeifer *Tel:* (0711) 8931184 *E-mail:* barbara.pfeifer@thieme.de
Contact: Martin Spencker
Founded: 1960
Subjects: Chemistry, Chemical Engineering, Earth Sciences, Energy, Engineering (General), Environmental Studies, Geography, Geology, Mechanical Engineering, Nonfiction (General), Technology
ISBN Prefix(es): 3-342
Number of titles published annually: 3 Print
Total Titles: 90 Print
Parent Company: Georg Thieme Verlag KG

Deutscher Verlag fur Kunstwissenschaft GmbH+
Charlottenstr 13, 10969 Berlin
Tel: (030) 25913864; (030) 25913865 *Fax:* (030) 25913537
Key Personnel
Man Dir: Holger Beer
Publishing Dir: Andreas A Catsch
Founded: 1964
Subjects: Art

ISBN Prefix(es): 3-87157
Parent Company: Springer-Verlag
Associate Companies: Gebr Mann Verlag, Charlottenstr 13, 10969 Berlin
Orders to: Koch, Neff, Oetinger & Co Verlagsauslieferung GmbH, Schockenriedstr 39, Postfach 800620, 70565 Stuttgart

Deutscher Wanderverlag Dr Mair & Schnabel & Co+
Gutenbergstr 13, 73760 Ostfildern
Tel: (0711) 455005 *Fax:* (0711) 4569952
Key Personnel
Publisher: Rudolf K Fr Schnabel
Founded: 1978
Subjects: Outdoor Recreation, Travel
ISBN Prefix(es): 3-8134

Deutscher Wirtschaftsdienst John von Freyend GmbH+
Imprint of Wolters Kluwer Deutschland GmbH
Marienburger Str 22, 50968 Cologne
Tel: (0221) 93763-0 *Fax:* (0221) 93763-99
E-mail: box@dwd-verlag.de
Web Site: www.dwd-verlag.de
Key Personnel
Sales, Rights & Permissions Dir: Peter John von Freyend
Editorial & Publicity: Michael Rieck
Editorial: Dr Reinhardt Spindler
Founded: 1949
Membership(s): The Stock Exchange of German Publishers.
Subjects: Business, Career Development, Communications, Energy, Environmental Studies, Finance, Management, Technology
ISBN Prefix(es): 3-87156
Subsidiaries: VWV Verlag fuer Wirtschaft und Verwaltung GmbH; Weltforum Verlag fuer Politik und Auslandskunde GmbH; Kontaplan Werbegesellschaft mbH

Deutsches Bucharchiv Muenchen, Institut fur Buchwissenschaften
Salvatorplatz 1, 80333 Munich
Tel: (089) 291951-90; (089) 291951-91
Fax: (089) 291951-95
E-mail: kontakt@bucharchiv.de
Web Site: www.bucharchiv.de
Key Personnel
Dir: Prof Ludwig Delp *Tel:* (089) 790 11 90
Founded: 1948
Membership(s): Boersenverein des Deutschen Buchhandels eV.
Subjects: Communications, Journalism, Library & Information Sciences, Publishing & Book Trade Reference
ISBN Prefix(es): 3-447
Total Titles: 72 Print
Distributed by Otto Harrassowitz Verlag

Deutsches Jugendinstitut (DJI) (German Youth Institute)
Nockherstr 2, 81541 Munich
Tel: (089) 62306-0 *Fax:* (089) 62306-265
E-mail: dji@dji.de
Web Site: www.dji.de
Key Personnel
Man Dir: Dr Thomas Rauschenbach
Editorial, Publicity & Rights: Hans-Hermann Schwarzer
Sales & Production: Maria-Anne Weber
Sales: Natascha Wolf *E-mail:* nwolf@dji.de
Founded: 1963
Subjects: Education, Social Sciences, Sociology
ISBN Prefix(es): 3-87966; 3-935701

Dharma Edition, Tibetisches Zentrum+
Hermann Balkstr 106, 22147 Hamburg
Tel: (040) 6443585 *Fax:* (040) 6443515
E-mail: tz@tibet.de
Web Site: www.tibet.de
Key Personnel
President: Axel Prosch
Publisher: Rolf Kraemer
Founded: 1979
Subjects: Religion - Buddhist
ISBN Prefix(es): 3-927862
Bookshop(s): Tsongkang Buddhistische Buecher *Tel:* (040) 6449828 *E-mail:* tk@tibet.de

Edition Dia+
Fidicinstr 9, 10965 Berlin
Tel: (030) 6235021; (030) 6235022 *Fax:* (030) 6235023
E-mail: info@editiondia.de
Web Site: www.editiondia.de
Key Personnel
Man Dir: Helmut Lotz *E-mail:* lotz@editiondia.de
Man Dir, International Rights: Kai Precht
Founded: 1984
Subjects: Biography, Cookery, Gay & Lesbian, Nonfiction (General)
ISBN Prefix(es): 3-86034

Diagonal-Verlag GbR Rink-Schweer+
Alte Kasselerstr 43, 35039 Marburg
Mailing Address: Postfach 1248, 35002 Marburg
Tel: (06421) 681936 *Fax:* (06421) 681944
E-mail: info@diagonal-verlag.de
Web Site: www.diagonal-verlag.de
Key Personnel
Publisher: Steffen Rink *E-mail:* rink@diagonal-verlag.de; Thomas Schweer *E-mail:* schweer@diagonal-verlag.de
Founded: 1988
Specialize in science of religion.
Subjects: Literature, Literary Criticism, Essays, Poetry, Religion - Other, Science (General)
ISBN Prefix(es): 3-927165
Total Titles: 35 Print

Dialog-Verlag GmbH
Haidkoppelweg 24a, 21465 Reinbek
Tel: (040) 7111424 *Fax:* (040) 7101267
Founded: 1982
Subjects: Regional Interests, Travel
ISBN Prefix(es): 3-923707

Die Andere Bibliothek, *imprint of* Eichborn AG

Die Verlag H Schafer GmbH+
Industriestr 16, 61381 Friedrichsdorf
Tel: (06172) 95830 *Fax:* (06172) 71288
E-mail: dieverlag@t-online.de
Key Personnel
Man Dir: Peter Vollrath-Kuhne
Founded: 1923
Subjects: Economics, Government, Political Science, Law, Management, Radio, TV
ISBN Prefix(es): 3-920826
Associate Companies: Menschund Leben Verlagsgesellschaft, Postfach 2243, 61292 Bad Homburg

Diederichs, *imprint of* Heinrich Hugendubel Verlag GmbH

Diesterweg, Moritz Verlag+
Heddrichstr 108-110, 60596 Frankfurt am Main
Mailing Address: Postfach 701161, 60561 Franfurt am Main
Tel: (069) 42081-0 *Fax:* (069) 42081-200
Web Site: www.diesterweg.de
Key Personnel
Man Dir: Ralf Meier; Karl Slipek
Founded: 1860
Subjects: Education, Language Arts, Linguistics, Social Sciences, Sociology
ISBN Prefix(es): 3-425
Distributed by European Book Co (USA); IBIS (USA)
Warehouse: Sigloch GmbH, Zeppelinstr 35, D-74653 Kuenzelsau
Orders to: Schroedel Verlag, Hildesheimerstr 202-206, D-30517 Hannover

Sammlung Dieterich Verlagsgesellschaft mbH
Gerichtsweg 28, 04103 Leipzig
Mailing Address: Postfach 101563, 04015 Leipzig
Tel: (0341) 9954600 *Fax:* (0341) 9954620
E-mail: info@aufbau-verlag.de
Web Site: www.aufbau-verlag.de
Key Personnel
Man Dir: Peter Birgit; Peter Dempewolf
Founded: 1991
Subjects: Literature, Literary Criticism, Essays, Philosophy
ISBN Prefix(es): 3-7350
Parent Company: Leipziger Verlags- und Vertriebsgesellschaft mbH
Associate Companies: Gustav Kiepenheuer Verlag Leipzig und Weimar GmbH
Shipping Address: Mohr-Morava Buchrertrieb Gesellschatt mbH, Sulzengasse 2, 1101 Vienna, Austria; Pegasus-Stichting, Uitgeverijen-Boekhandel, Rhijuvis Feithstr 28, PO Box 59687, 1054 PZ Amsterdam, Netherlands; Verlaapauslieferung Balmer, Bosch 41, Huenenberg, 6331 Olten, Switzerland

Dieterichsche Verlagsbuchhandlung Mainz+
Beuthenstr 17, 55131 Mainz
Tel: (06131) 573276 *Fax:* (06131) 571061
E-mail: DVB~mainz@t-online.de
Key Personnel
Publisher: Prof Alfred Klemm, PhD
Founded: 1766
Subjects: Art, Asian Studies, History, Literature, Literary Criticism, Essays, Philosophy, Poetry, Religion - Other
ISBN Prefix(es): 3-87162
Number of titles published annually: 3 Print
Orders to: A Eipper, Kirchensteig 12, 71126 Gaeufelden
GVA Postfach 2021, 37010 Gottingen *Tel:* (0551) 487177 *Fax:* (0551) 41392

Maximilian Dietrich Verlag+
Weberstr 36, 87700 Memmingen
Mailing Address: Postfach 1636, 87686 Memmingen
Tel: (08331) 2853 *Fax:* (08331) 490364
Telex: ueber 54524 mzdruk d
Key Personnel
Man Dir: Curt Visel
Sales: Jurgen Schweitzer
Founded: 1946
Subjects: Biography, Human Relations, Regional Interests
ISBN Prefix(es): 3-87164
Subsidiaries: Edition Curt Visel

Dietrich zu Klampen Verlag+
Hermannshof Voelksen Roese 21, 31832 Springe
Tel: (5041) 801133 *Fax:* (5041) 801336
E-mail: info@zuklampen.de
Web Site: www.dan4u.de/zuklampen
Key Personnel
Owner: Dietrich zu Klampen
Publisher: Dr Rolf Johannes
Founded: 1983
Subjects: Government, Political Science, Philosophy, Poetry, Psychology, Psychiatry, Science (General), Social Sciences, Sociology
ISBN Prefix(es): 3-924245; 3-933156

Verlag J H W Dietz Nachf GmbH+
Dreitehnmorgenweg 24, 53129 Bonn
Tel: (0228) 23 80 83 *Fax:* (0228) 23 41 04
E-mail: info@dietz-verlag.de
Web Site: www.dietz-verlag.de
Key Personnel
Manager: Dr Gerhard Fischer

Dir, Sales: Hilde Holthamp *E-mail:* hilde.holtkamp@dietz-verlag.de
Editorial, Rights & Permissions: Daniela Mueller *E-mail:* daniela.mueller@dietz-verlag.de
Founded: 1881
Subjects: Developing Countries, Environmental Studies, Government, Political Science, History, Nonfiction (General), Social Sciences, Sociology
ISBN Prefix(es): 3-8012; 3-87831
Foreign Rep(s): Elisabeth Anintah-Hirt (Austria)
Distribution Center: Beat Eberle buch 2000 Verlagsauslieferung AVA, Centralweg 16, Postfach 27, 8910 Affoltern am Albis, Switzerland *Tel:* (04117) 62 42 60 *Fax:* (04117) 62 42 10 (Switzerland)
Far Eastern Book Sellers, PO Box 72, Kanda, Tokyo, Japan (Japan)
LIBRI Distributions GmbH, Postfach 10 14 34, 60014 Frankfurt *Tel:* (069) 95 42 22 24 *Fax:* (069) 54 20 13 (Germany & Austria)

Dietz Verlag Berlin GmbH+
Weydingerstr 14-16, 10178 Berlin
Mailing Address: Postfach 273, 10124 Berlin
Tel: (030) 24 00 92 90 *Fax:* (030) 24 00 95 90
E-mail: info@dietzverlag.de
Web Site: www.dietzverlag.de
Key Personnel
Man Dir: Dr Reinhard Semmelmann
Sales Dir: Hartmut Goetze
Editorial, Rights & Permissions: Christine Krauss
Founded: 1945
Subjects: Biography, Government, Political Science, History, Social Sciences, Sociology
ISBN Prefix(es): 3-320
Shipping Address: Bugrim Verlagsauslieferung, Saalburgstr 3, 12099 Berlin
Warehouse: Bugrim Verlagsauslieferung, Saalburgstr 3, 12099 Berlin
Orders to: Bugrim Verlagsauslieferung, Saalburgstr 3, 12099 Berlin

Dietzenbach, *imprint of* ALS-Verlag GmbH

Digital Publishing+
Tumblingerstr 32, 80337 Munich
Tel: (089) 747482-0 *Fax:* (089) 74792308
E-mail: info@digitalpublishing.de
Web Site: www.digitalpublishing.de
Key Personnel
International Market: Elsa Blume
Public Relations Manager: Sina Wolf
Founded: 1994
Independent publisher.
ISBN Prefix(es): 3-89477; 3-930947
Total Titles: 65 CD-ROM
Distributor for M8 das medieu team (Bookstores/Germany)

Dipa-Verlag GmbH+
Friesstr 20-24, 60388 Frankfurt
Tel: (069) 95732044 *Fax:* (069) 576128
Key Personnel
Man Dir, Rights & Permissions: Gerd Hofmann
Founded: 1948
Subjects: Education, Fiction, Government, Political Science, History, Nonfiction (General)
ISBN Prefix(es): 3-7638

Discordia Verlagsgesellschaft mbH
Wiehlerstr 5, 51545 Waldbroel
Tel: (02291) 911024 *Fax:* (02291) 911925
Founded: 1978
ISBN Prefix(es): 3-922733

Edition Diskord
Schwaerzlocherstr 104/b, 72070 Tuebingen
Tel: (07071) 40102 *Fax:* (07071) 44710
E-mail: ed.diskord@t-online.de
Web Site: www.edition-diskord.de

Key Personnel
Man Dir: Gerd Kimmerle
Founded: 1985
Subjects: Biography, History, Philosophy, Psychology, Psychiatry, Social Sciences, Sociology, Women's Studies
ISBN Prefix(es): 3-89295

Divyanand Verlags GmbH+
Saegestr 37, 79737 Herrischried
Tel: (07764) 93 97-0 *Fax:* (07764) 93 97-39
E-mail: info@sandila.de
Web Site: www.sandila.de
Key Personnel
Man Dir: Gerlinde Gloeckner
Founded: 1987
Specialize in Spirituality.
Subjects: Parapsychology, Philosophy, Religion - Other, Self-Help
ISBN Prefix(es): 3-926696
Number of titles published annually: 2 Print
Total Titles: 23 Print
U.S. Office(s): 129 Juneberry Court, San Jose, CA 95136, United States

DJI, *see* Deutsches Jugendinstitut (DJI)

DLV Deutscher Landwirtschaftsverlag GmbH
(German Agriculture Publishing House)
Subsidiary of BLV Verlagsgesellschaft mbH
Kabelkamp 6, 30179 Hannover
Mailing Address: Postfach 14 40, 30014 Hannover
Tel: (0511) 678 06-0 *Fax:* (0511) 678 06-110
E-mail: dlv.hannover@dlv.de
Web Site: www.dlv.de
Key Personnel
Man Dir: Hans-Peter Kliemann; Bernd Kuhrmeier; Hans Mueller
Founded: 2001
Subjects: Agriculture, Animals, Pets, Environmental Studies, Gardening, Plants, Country Life with Garden, Nature, Environment, Beekeeping/Apiculture & Folk Music, Farming, Forestry, Hunting
ISBN Prefix(es): 3-331
Ultimate Parent Company: Landbuch-Verlagsgesellschaft mbH, Hannover
Branch Office(s)
Berliner Str 112A, 13189 Berlin *Tel:* (030) 29 39 74-50 *Fax:* (030) 29 39 74-59 *E-mail:* dlv.berlin@dlv.de
Lothstr 29, 80797 Munich *Tel:* (089) 12 70 5-1 *Fax:* (089) 1 27 05-355 *E-mail:* dlv.muenchen@dlv.de

Christoph Dohr
Kasselberger Weg 120, 50769 Cologne
Tel: (0221) 70 70 02 *Fax:* (0221) 70 43 95
E-mail: info@dohr.de
Web Site: www.dohr.de
Key Personnel
Contact: Christoph Dohr
Founded: 1990
Music publisher.
Subjects: Music, Dance
ISBN Prefix(es): 3-925366
Number of titles published annually: 80 Print
Total Titles: 1,100 Print

Dolling und Galitz Verlag GmbH+
Grosse Bergstr 253, 22767 Hamburg
Tel: (040) 3893515 *Fax:* (040) 38904945
E-mail: doellingundgalitzverlag@compuserve.com
Web Site: www.doellingundgalitz.com
Key Personnel
Editor: Dr Peter Dolling; Dr Robert Galitz
Press: Brita Reimers
Manager: Sabine Niemann
Founded: 1986

Subjects: Architecture & Interior Design, Art, History, Literature, Literary Criticism, Essays, Music, Dance, Photography, Religion - Jewish, Religion - Other
ISBN Prefix(es): 3-926174; 3-930802; 3-933374; 3-935549
Warehouse: Siemensstra 16, 35463 Fernwald (Annerod) *Fax:* 06419439329
Orders to: PROLIT Verlagsauslieferung

agenda Verlag Thomas Dominikowski+
Hammer Str 223, 48153 Muenster
Tel: (0251) 79 96 10 *Fax:* (0251) 79 95 19
E-mail: info@agenda.de
Web Site: www.agenda.de
Key Personnel
Publisher: Thomas Dominikowski
International Rights: Michael Alfs
Founded: 1992
Subjects: Developing Countries, Environmental Studies, Government, Political Science, History, Journalism, Regional Interests, Social Sciences, Sociology, Women's Studies
ISBN Prefix(es): 3-929440; 3-89688

Domino Verlag, Guenther Brinek GmbH
Menzinger Str 13, 80638 Munich
Tel: (089) 179130
E-mail: info@domino-verlag.de
Web Site: www.domino-verlag.de
Key Personnel
Manager: Guenther Brinek
Founded: 1964
Subjects: Drama, Theater
ISBN Prefix(es): 3-926123

Domowina Verlag GmbH
Tuchmacherstr 27, 02625 Bautzen
Tel: (03591) 5770 *Fax:* (03591) 577243
E-mail: domowinaverlag@t-online.de
Web Site: www.buchhandel.de/domowinaverlag
Key Personnel
Man Dir: Ludmila Budar *Tel:* (03591) 577 241
Marketing & Management: Manja Bujnowska *Tel:* (03591) 577 262
Press: Mirana Mieth *Tel:* (03591) 577 256 *E-mail:* Werbung.LND@t-online.de
Publications & Bookshop: Dr Ruth Thiemann *Tel:* (03591) 422 32
Founded: 1958
Subjects: Ethnicity, Scientific, Technical Literature
ISBN Prefix(es): 3-7420

Don Bosco Verlag+
Sieboldstr 11, 81669 Munich
Tel: (089) 48008300 *Fax:* (089) 48008309
Web Site: www.donbosco.de
Key Personnel
Dir: Alfons Friedrich
Editorial: Reinhold Storkenmaier
Sales: Gerhard Sacher
Founded: 1948
Subjects: Education, Religion - Other
ISBN Prefix(es): 3-7698
Imprints: DBV
Branch Office(s)
Rixdorferstr 15, 51063 Cologne
Kaulbachstr 63a, 805369 Munich

Donat Verlag+
Borgfelder Heerstr 29, 28357 Bremen
Tel: (0421) 274886 *Fax:* (0421) 275106
E-mail: donatverlag@excite.de
Key Personnel
Publisher: Helmut Donat
Founded: 1988
Membership(s): Bvrsenverein des Deutschen Buchhandels.
Subjects: Art, Government, Political Science, History, Regional Interests, Religion - Jewish

ISBN Prefix(es): 3-924444; 3-931737; 3-934836
Number of titles published annually: 35 Print
Total Titles: 220 Print

Verlagsgruppe Dornier GmbH (Publishing Group Dornier)+
Liebknechtstr 33, 70565 Stuttgart
Tel: (0711) 78803-0 *Fax:* (0711) 78803-10
E-mail: info@verlagsgruppe-dornier.de
Web Site: www.verlagsgruppe-dornier.de
Cable: EDILEIP
Key Personnel
Man Dir: Olaf Carstens; Roland Grimmelsmann
Parent Company: Verlagsgruppe Dornier, Dircksenstr 48, 10178 Berlin, Sabine Schubert
Associate Companies: Cross Publishing House, Postfach 80 06 69, 70506 Stuttgart *Tel:* (0711) 788 03-0; Kreuz Verlag, Breitwiesenstr 30, 70565 Stuttgart *Tel:* (0711) 78803-91 *Fax:* (0711) 78803-10 *E-mail:* info@kreuzverlag.de *Web Site:* www.kreuzverlag.de (religion, self-help, spiritual giftbooks); Theseus Verlag, Dircksenstr 48, 10178 Berlin, Contact: Ursula Richard *Tel:* (030) 28447-100 *Fax:* (030) 28447-103 *E-mail:* theseus@dornier-verlage.de *Web Site:* www.theseus-verlage.de (Buddhist publisher); Urania Verlag, Berlin (parenting, home improvement, arts & crafts)
Imprints: Brandenburgisches Verlagshaus (military history); EA Seemann Verlag (art, photography); Edition Leipzig (regional art, architecture & history books (Saxonia), official publisher of books on Meissen porcelaine); Henschel Verlag (performing arts: theater, cinema, music, ballet); Alf Luechow Verlag (advaita, spiritual health, self-help)
Orders to: Leipziger Kommissions und Grossbuchhandelsgesellschaft mbH, Poetzschauer Weg, 04579 Espenhain

DPV, see Deutscher Psychologen Verlag GmbH (DPV)

Drei Brunnen Verlag GmbH & Co
Heusee 19, 73655 Pluederhausen
Tel: (0711) 86020 *Fax:* (0711) 860229
E-mail: mail@drei-brunnen-verlag.de
Web Site: www.drei-brunnen-verlag.de
Key Personnel
Man Publisher: Emmerich Mueller
Publisher: Dieter Rath
Contact: Thomas Mueller
Founded: 1950
Subjects: Outdoor Recreation, Travel
ISBN Prefix(es): 3-7956
Number of titles published annually: 10 Print
Total Titles: 60 Print
Shipping Address: Geo Center, Schockenriedstr 44, 70565 Stuttgart
Orders to: Geo Center, Schockenriedstr 44, 70565 Stuttgart

Drei Eichen Verlag Manuel Kissener+
Bahnhofstr 36, 97762 Hammelburg
Mailing Address: Postfach 1147, 97754 Hammelburg
Tel: (09732) 9142-0 *Fax:* (09732) 9142-20
E-mail: info@drei-eichen.de
Web Site: www.drei-eichen.de
Key Personnel
Owner: Manuel Kissener
Founded: 1931
Subjects: Philosophy, Science Fiction, Fantasy, Self-Help
ISBN Prefix(es): 3-7699
Number of titles published annually: 10 Print
Total Titles: 200 Print
Imprints: Edition Kima; Politik und Spiritualitaet

Drei Ulmen Verlag GmbH+
Schleissheimer Str 274, 80809 Munich
Tel: (089) 3087911; (089) 3088343
Key Personnel
Publisher: Dr Hermann Schreiber
Founded: 1985
Membership(s): Small Publishers Study Group.
Subjects: Biography, Literature, Literary Criticism, Essays, Travel
ISBN Prefix(es): 3-926087
Associate Companies: AVA-GmbH, Seeblickstr 46, 82211 Herrsching

Dreisam Ratgeber in der Rutsker Verlag GmbH+
Schreberstr 2, 51105 Cologne
Tel: (0221) 921635-0 *Fax:* (0221) 921635-24
E-mail: kontakt@hayit.com
Web Site: www.hayit.com
Key Personnel
International Rights: Ertay Hayit *E-mail:* hayit@hayit.com
Editorial: Cornelia Auschra *Tel:* (0221) 921635-13 *E-mail:* cornelia.auschra@hayit.com; Mike Gahn *E-mail:* mike@hayit.com; Ute Hayit *Tel:* (0221) 921635-11 *E-mail:* ute.hayit@hayit.com; Simone Kruger-Naujoks *Tel:* (0221) 921635-22 *E-mail:* simone-naujoks@hayit.com
Founded: 1988
Subjects: Biological Sciences, Career Development, Cookery, Economics, Education, Environmental Studies, Health, Nutrition, Human Relations, Law, Medicine, Nursing, Dentistry, Psychology, Psychiatry, Religion - Islamic
ISBN Prefix(es): 3-89607

Cecilie Dressler Verlag GmbH & Co KG+
Poppenbuetteler Chaussee 53, 22397 Hamburg
Mailing Address: Postfach 658230, 22374 Hamburg
Tel: (040) 607909-03 *Fax:* (040) 6072326
E-mail: dressler@vsg-hamburg.de
Web Site: www.cecilie-dressler.de
Key Personnel
Man Dir & Sales: Thomas Huggle
Man Dir, Rights & Permissions: Silke Weitendorf
Editorial: Ursula Heckel
Publicity: Katja Muissus
International Rights: Renate Reichstein *Tel:* (040) 607909-13 *Fax:* (040) 607909-51 *E-mail:* lizenzen@vsg-hamburg.de
Press: Judith Richter *Tel:* (040) 607909-65 *Fax:* (040) 607909-40 *E-mail:* presse@vsg-hamburg.de; Frauke Wedler *Tel:* (040) 607909-23 *Fax:* (040) 607909-40 *E-mail:* presse@vsg-hamburg.de
Internet Editor: Svenja David *Tel:* (040) 607909-48 *Fax:* (040) 607909-51 *E-mail:* internetredaktion@vsg-hamburg.de
Marketing: Dr Juergen Huebner *Tel:* (040) 607909-55 *Fax:* (040) 607909-50 *E-mail:* werbung@vsg-hamburg.de
Founded: 1928
Subjects: Fiction
ISBN Prefix(es): 3-7915
Associate Companies: Atrium Verlag
Warehouse: Runge Verlagsauslieferung, Bergstr 2, 33803 Steinhagen

Verlagsgruppe Droemer Knaur GmbH & Co KG+
Hilblestr 54, 80636 Munich
Tel: (089) 9271-0 *Fax:* (089) 9271-168
E-mail: info@droemer-knaur.de
Web Site: www.droemer-knaur.de *Cable:* DROEMERVERLAG
Key Personnel
Publisher & Man Dir: Dr Hans Peter Uebleis
Commercial Man Dir: Ralf Mueller
Man Dir Sales & Marketing: Christian Tesch
Public Relations: Susanne Klein
Rights: Renate Abrasch
Sales: Iris Haas
Founded: 1901
Also known as Droemer Knaur Verlag.
Subjects: Biography, Business, Cookery, Erotica, Fiction, How-to, Humor, Mysteries, Nonfiction (General), Science (General), Self-Help, Wine & Spirits, Anthology, Fairy Tales, Family Saga, Fantasy, Food/Drink, Horror, Movie or Television, Thriller
ISBN Prefix(es): 3-426
Parent Company: Verlagsgruppe Droemer Weltbild GmbH & Co KG
Associate Companies: Augustus Verlag; Knaur Taschenbuecher; Midena Verlag; Pattloch Verlag; Schneekluth Verlag GmbH
Imprints: MenSana
Shipping Address: VVA Bertelsmann Distribution

Droste Verlag GmbH
Martin-Luther-Platz 26, 40212 Duesseldorf
Tel: (0211) 8605228 *Fax:* (0211) 3230098
Telex: 8582495 dv d *Cable:* DROSTEVERLAG DUSSELDORF
Key Personnel
Chairman & Man Dir: Clemens Bauer
Man Dir: Dieter Reichel
Publishing Dir: Dr Manfred Lotsch
Editorial: Heidemarie Alertz
Production, Publicity: Helmut Schwanen
Founded: 1711
Subjects: Art, Economics, Government, Political Science, History, Humor, Social Sciences, Sociology
ISBN Prefix(es): 3-7700
Subsidiaries: Wilhelm Knapp Verlag
Warehouse: Xantheuerstr 3a, 41460 Neuss

Karl Elser Druck GmbH
Kisslingweg 35, 75417 Muehlacker
Tel: (07041) 805-41 *Fax:* (07041) 805-50
E-mail: info@elserdruck.de
Web Site: www.elserdruck.de
Key Personnel
Man Dir & International Rights: Brigitte Wetzel-Haendle
Man Dir: Else Haendle
Founded: 1890
Also acts as newspaper & printing office.
Subjects: Biography, Fiction, Regional Interests
ISBN Prefix(es): 3-7987
Associate Companies: Karl Elser Druck GmbH
Bookshop(s): Buch-Elser, Bahnhofstr 62, 75417 Muehlacker

Druckerei u Verlagsanstalt Bayerland GmbH
Konrad-Adenauerstr 19, 85221 Dachau
Mailing Address: Postfach 1868, 85208 Dachau
Tel: (08131) 7 20 66 *Fax:* (08131) 73 53 99
E-mail: zentrale@bayerland-amperbote.de
Web Site: www.bayerland.de
Key Personnel
Contact: Klaus Kiermeier
ISBN Prefix(es): 3-89251; 3-922394; 3-9800040
Number of titles published annually: 20 Print
Total Titles: 250 Print

Druffel-Verlag+
Landsbergerstr 57, 82266 Inning
Tel: (08143) 992160 *Fax:* (08143) 992241; (08143) 992161
Key Personnel
Publisher: Dr Gert Suedholt
Founded: 1952
Subjects: Government, Political Science, History
ISBN Prefix(es): 3-8061

DRW-Verlag Weinbrenner-GmbH & Co+
Fasanenweg 18, 70771 Leinfelden-Echterdingen
Tel: (0711) 75 91-0 *Fax:* (0711) 75 91-333
E-mail: info@weinbrenner.de
Web Site: www.drw-verlag.de; www.weinbrenner.de
Key Personnel
Dir: Karl-Heinz Weinbrenner

Business Manager: Bernhard Driehaus
Founded: 1874
Subjects: Nonfiction (General), Physical Sciences, Regional Interests
ISBN Prefix(es): 3-87181; 3-87422
Subsidiaries: BIT-Verlag Weinbrenner; Verlagsanstalt Alexander Koch GmbH
Divisions: Fachbuch Service
Orders to: Koch, Neff & Oetinger Verlagsauslieferung, Schockenriedstr 39, 70565 Stuttgart

DSI Data Service & Information
Xantener Str 51a, 47495 Rheinberg
Tel: (049) 2843 3220 *Fax:* (049) 2843 3230
E-mail: dsi@dsidata.com
Web Site: www.dsidata.com
Key Personnel
Manager: Dr Wilhelm Hennerkes
Contact: Konrad Wilms *E-mail:* konrad.wilms@dsidata.com
Founded: 1985
Electronic preparation & publishing of national & international statistical information (numerical databases) on CD-ROM & on the internet.
Subjects: Economics, Social Sciences, Sociology
Distributor for Bernan; Enerdata SA; European Union; International Bank for Reconstruction & Development; Organization for Economic Co-Operation & Development; Smartal Solutions Ltd
Foreign Rep(s): ABE Marketing (Poland); Albertina Data SRO (Czech Republic, Slovak Republic); Albertina Incone Praha (Czech Republic); BH Sistemas de Informacao (Portugal); Diaz de Santos SA (Spain); Edutech (United Arab Emirates); Far Eastern Booksellers (Kyokuto Shoten) (Japan); Greendata (Spain); IBS Buke SDN BHD (Malaysia); Info Access & Distribution Pte Ltd (Singapore); Info Technology Supply Ltd (UK); Kaiga Kyozai Center (Japan); Kinokuniya Co Ltd (Japan); Kyobo Book Centre (Korea); Leader Books SA (Greece); Licosa SpA (Italy); Logiser SA (Portugal); LUSODOC (Portugal); Maruzen Co, IRN Import (Books) (Japan); Mundi-Prensa Libros SA (Spain); Paradox Libros (Spain); RoweCom Espana (Spain); Sistemas Documentales SL (Spain)

dtv, see Deutscher Taschenbuch Verlag GmbH & Co KG (dtv)

Verlag Duerr & Kessler GmbH+
Sieglarer Str 2, 53842 Troisdorf
Tel: (0180) 304 14 20 *Fax:* (02241) 39 76 190
E-mail: info@wolfverlag.de
Web Site: www.wolfverlag.de
Key Personnel
Publisher: Franz Symes *E-mail:* fsymes@by-1.de
Marketing: Alexandra Ried *Tel:* (02241) 39 76-806 *E-mail:* aried@by-1.de
Founded: 1953
Subjects: Education, Language Arts, Linguistics
ISBN Prefix(es): 3-8181

Dumjahn Verlag
Immenhof 12, 55128 Mainz
Tel: (06131) 330810 *Fax:* (06131) 330811
E-mail: eisenbahn@dumjahn.de
Web Site: www.dumjahn.de
Founded: 1974
Specialize in railway.
Membership(s): Borsenverein des Deutschen Buchhandels.
Subjects: Publishing & Book Trade Reference, Transportation, Travel
ISBN Prefix(es): 3-921426; 3-88992
Number of titles published annually: 2 Print; 2 E-Book

Total Titles: 18 Print
Bookshop(s): Versandbuchhandlung und Antiquariat Horst-Werner Dumjahn, Immenhof 12, 55128 Mainz

DuMont monte Verlag GmbH & Co KG+
Neven DuMont Haus, Amsterdamer Str 192, 50735 Cologne
Tel: (0221) 224-1823 *Fax:* (0221) 224-1812
E-mail: info@dumontmonte.de
Web Site: www.dumontmonte.de
Telex: 8882975 dbeb d
Key Personnel
Manager: Dieter Eickel *Tel:* (0221) 224-2931 *E-mail:* eickel@dumontmonte.de
Sales Manager: Anke Hardt *Tel:* (0221) 224-1964 *E-mail:* hardt@dumontmonte.de; Jan Scherberich *Tel:* (0221) 224-1821 *E-mail:* scherberich@dumontmonte.de
Founded: 1998
Subjects: Architecture & Interior Design, Art, Cookery, Crafts, Games, Hobbies, Gardening, Plants, House & Home, How-to
ISBN Prefix(es): 3-8320
Total Titles: 75 Print
Parent Company: Dumont

DuMont Reiseverlag GmbH & Co KG+
Amsterdamer Str 192, 50735 Cologne
Mailing Address: Postfach 101045, 50450 Cologne
Tel: (0221) 224-1839 *Fax:* (0221) 224-1855
E-mail: info@dumontreise.de
Web Site: www.dumontreise.de
Telex: 8882 975 dbeb d
Key Personnel
Man Dir: Uwe Distelrath; Andreas von Stedman
Marketing Manager: Udo Zimmermann *Tel:* (0221) 224-1894 *E-mail:* zimmermann@dumontreise.de
Sales Manager: Katharina Hokema *Tel:* (0221) 224-1833 *E-mail:* hokema@dumontreise.de
Public Relations: Angelika Trippe *Tel:* (0221) 224-1835 *E-mail:* trippe@dumontreise.de
Rights: Yvonne Paris
Founded: 1956
Subjects: Archaeology, Art, Cookery, Gardening, Plants, Travel
ISBN Prefix(es): 3-8320
Orders to: BDK Buecherdienst, Koelner 87 248, 50859 Cologne

Duncker und Humblot GmbH+
Carl-Heinrich-Becker-Weg 9, 12165 Berlin
Mailing Address: Postfach 410329, 12113 Berlin
Tel: (030) 79 00 06-0 *Fax:* (030) 79 00 06-31
E-mail: info@duncker-humblot.de
Web Site: www.duncker-humblot.de
Key Personnel
Publisher & International Rights: Prof H C Norbert Simon, PhD *Tel:* (030) 790006-19 *Fax:* (030) 790006-43 *E-mail:* verlag@duncker-humblot.de
Marketing: Ingrid Buehrig *Tel:* (030) 790006-30 *Fax:* (030) 790006-53 *E-mail:* werbung@duncker-humblot.de
Founded: 1798
Subjects: Asian Studies, Biography, Criminology, Developing Countries, Economics, Environmental Studies, Finance, Government, Political Science, History, Law, Literature, Literary Criticism, Essays, Marketing, Military Science, Philosophy, Science (General), Social Sciences, Sociology, Theology
ISBN Prefix(es): 3-428
Number of titles published annually: 350 Print
Total Titles: 9,300 Print
Subsidiaries: Speyer & Peters GmbH; Berliner Buchdruckerei Union Gmb

Dustri-Verlag Dr Karl Feistle+
Bajuwarenring 4, 82041 Oberhaching-Munich

Mailing Address: Postfach 1351, 82032 Deisenhofen-Munich
Tel: (089) 61 38 61-0 *Fax:* (089) 613 54 12
E-mail: info@dustri.de
Web Site: www.dustri.de
Key Personnel
Dir: Frank Feistle; Joerg Feistle *Tel:* (089) 61 38 61-30 *E-mail:* joerg.feistle@dustri.de
Founded: 1965
Subjects: Medicine, Nursing, Dentistry
ISBN Prefix(es): 3-87185

Klaus D Dutz+
Lingener Str 7, 48155 Muenster
Mailing Address: Postfach 5725, 48031 Muenster
Tel: (0251) 65514 *Fax:* (0251) 661692
E-mail: dutz.nodus@t-online.de
Key Personnel
Contact: Klaus D Dutz
Founded: 1987
Subjects: Film, Video, Language Arts, Linguistics, Philosophy, Science (General)
ISBN Prefix(es): 3-89323
Subsidiaries: Stichting Neerlandistiek VU; Stichting Uitgeverij De Keltische Draak

DVA, see Deutsche Verlags-Anstalt GmbH (DVA)

DVG-Deutsche Verlagsgesellschaft mbH+
Postfach 1180, 32352 Preubisch Oldendorf
Tel: (08031) 15643 *Fax:* (08031) 380662
Key Personnel
Contact: Waldemar Schuetz
Founded: 1969
Subjects: Government, Political Science, History, Military Science
ISBN Prefix(es): 3-920722
Associate Companies: Verlag fuer Aussergewoehnliche Perspektiven
Orders to: VAP Verlagsauslieferung, Mindenerstr 34, 32361 Preussisch Oldendorf

DVS-Verlag GmbH, see Verlag fur Schweissen und Verwandte Verfahren

Ebenhausen bei Muenchen, *imprint of* Verlag Langewiesche-Brandt KG

Ebersberg, *imprint of* Eironeia-Verlag

Echo Verlag+
Postfach 1704, 37007 Goettingen
Tel: (0551) 796824 *Fax:* (0551) 74035
E-mail: clages.echoverlag@t-online.de
Web Site: www.echoverlag.de
Key Personnel
Man Dir, Rights & Permissions: Andrea Clages
Founded: 1985
Membership(s): The Stock Exchange of German Booksellers; Land Association Lower Saxony.
Subjects: Animals, Pets, Environmental Studies
ISBN Prefix(es): 3-9801216; 3-926914

Echter Wurzburg Frankische Gesellschaftsdruckerei und Verlag GmbH+
Dominikanerplatz 8, 97070 Wuerzburg
Tel: (0931) 66068-0 *Fax:* (0931) 66068-23
E-mail: info@echterverlag.de
Web Site: www.echter-verlag.de *Cable:* ECHTERVERLAG
Key Personnel
Dir: Gerhard Schaefer *Tel:* (0931) 6671-220 *Fax:* (0931) 6671-295 *E-mail:* g.schaefer@echter.de; Albrecht Siedler *Tel:* (0931) 6671-216 *Fax:* (0931) 6671-295 *E-mail:* a.siedler@echter.de
Publisher: Thomas Haeussner *Tel:* (0931) 6671-158 *Fax:* (0931) 6671-151 *E-mail:* th.haeussner@echter.de
Founded: 1900

Subjects: Art, Biblical Studies, Fiction, History, Regional Interests, Religion - Catholic, Religion - Other, Theology, Wine & Spirits
ISBN Prefix(es): 3-429
Total Titles: 600 Print

Ecomed Verlagsgesellschaft AG & Co KG+
Justus-Von-Liebig Str 1, 86899 Landsberg
Tel: (08191) 1250 *Fax:* (08191) 125492
E-mail: info@ecomed.de
Web Site: www.ecomed.de
Key Personnel
Publishing Manager: Udo Graf *Tel:* (08191) 125208
Foreign Rights Manager: Gerlinde Stanglmeier *Tel:* (08191) 125571 *E-mail:* g.stanglmeier@ecomed.de
Marketing: Gerhard Heinzmann *Tel:* (08191) 125399
Product Management: Manuela Czech *Tel:* (08191) 125420; Bernhard Gall *Tel:* (08191) 125564; Dr Iris Korn *Tel:* (08191) 125191; Susanne Kuehbandner *Tel:* (08191) 125500; Dr Norbert Schueller *Tel:* (08191) 125804
Sales: Nina Karlsdorfer *Tel:* (08191) 125800
Customer Service: Gabriele Honzu *Tel:* (08191) 125152
Founded: 1979
Subjects: Biological Sciences, Chemistry, Chemical Engineering, Engineering (General), Environmental Studies, Gardening, Plants, Labor, Industrial Relations, Medicine, Nursing, Dentistry, Technology, Transportation
ISBN Prefix(es): 3-609
Total Titles: 700 Print
Parent Company: verlag moderne industrie AG

Econ Taschenbuchverlag+
Subsidiary of Econ Verlag GmbH
Kaiserswertherstr 282, 40474 Duesseldorf
Tel: (0211) 43596
Key Personnel
Chief Executive Officer & Publisher: Dr Dietrich Oppenberg
Marketing & Sales: Felicitas Wendt
Rights & Permissions: Herbert Borgartz
Founded: 1951
Publishing group comprised of: Econ-Verlag GmbH; Econ Taschenbuch Verlag GmbH. The group forms part of the newspaper publishing concern Rheinisch-Westfaelische Verlagsgesellschaft mbH, Pressehaus NRZ, Sachsenstr 30, 45128 Essen
Representative: Christina McInerney International Ltd, 730 Fifth Ave, Suite 402, New York, NY 10019, USA.
Subjects: Career Development, Computer Science, Economics, Health, Nutrition, Mysteries, Nonfiction (General), Self-Help
Associate Companies: Groethe str 43, 80336 Munich
Warehouse: VVA, Guetersloh

Econ Verlag GmbH+
Paul-Heyse-Str 28, 80336 Munich
Tel: (089) 5148-0 *Fax:* (089) 5148-2229
Web Site: www.econ-verlag.de *Cable:* ECON-VERLAG
Key Personnel
Chief Executive Officers & Publishers: Heinrich Meyer; Christian Strasser
Marketing: Herbert Borgartz
Rights & Permissions: Felicitas Wendt
Founded: 1950
Subjects: Economics, Fiction, Nonfiction (General), Science (General)
ISBN Prefix(es): 3-430; 3-612; 3-547
Subsidiaries: Econ Taschenbuch Verlag GmbH; Marion von Schroeder Verlag GmbH
U.S. Office(s): Jane Starr, Planetarium Station, PO Box 907, New York, NY 10024, United States

Distributor for Stiftung Warentest GmbH (Berlin/Germany)
Warehouse: VVA, An der Autobahn, 33310 Guetersloh

Ede Vau Verlag GmbH
Halskestr 3-5, 47877 Willich
Tel: (02154) 490080 *Fax:* (02154) 490081
E-mail: evvgmbh@t-online.de
Key Personnel
Manager: Horst Stuhlweissenburg
Founded: 1989
ISBN Prefix(es): 3-89428

Edition Aragon-Verlagsgesellschaft mbH+
Neumarkt 7-9, 47441 Moers
Mailing Address: Postfach 1110, 47407 Moers
Tel: (02841) 16561 *Fax:* (02841) 24336
Key Personnel
President & Publisher: Willi Klauke
Founded: 1984
Subjects: Art, Drama, Theater, Travel
ISBN Prefix(es): 3-89535
Distributed by AVA b+i (Switzerland)
Orders to: Prolit, Siemensstr 18a, 35463 Fernwald/Annerod

Edition Tranvia, see Verlag Walter Frey

editionLuebbe, *imprint of* Verlagsgruppe Luebbe GmbH & Co KG

Egmont EHAPA Verlag GmbH+
Wallstr 59, 10179 Berlin
Mailing Address: Postfach 040740, 10064 Berlin
Tel: (030) 24008-0 *Fax:* (030) 24008-599
Web Site: www.ehapa.de
Key Personnel
Man Dir: Frank Knau
International Rights: Peter M Schmitz
Public Relations Manager: Marion Egenberger *E-mail:* kontakt@ehapa.de
Founded: 1951
Children's magazines.
Subjects: Humor, Comics
ISBN Prefix(es): 3-7704; 3-89343; 3-928108
Number of titles published annually: 200 Print
Total Titles: 1,000 Print
Parent Company: Egmont Holding GmbH
Imprints: Delta
Subsidiaries: Cultfish Entertainment (Teen Label)
Divisions: OU Character Kids (Comic Magazine & Juvenile Journals); OU Disney Kids (Disney Publication); Egmont Manga & Anime Europe (Manga)

Egmont Franz Schneider Verlag GmbH+
Schleissheimer Str 267, 80809 Munich
Tel: (089) 3 58 11-6 *Fax:* (089) 3 58 11-7 55
E-mail: postmaster@schneiderbuch.de
Web Site: www.schneiderbuch.de
Telex: 05215804
Key Personnel
Man Dir: Rehne Herzig
Marketing: Hans-Juergen Schneider
Account: Matthias Allendorff
Production: Karl-Heinz Bezold
Publicity: Dr Andrea Hilbk
Founded: 1913
Specialize in Disney books, Television/Film related books.
Subjects: Fiction, Film, Video, History, Nonfiction (General), Science Fiction, Fantasy
ISBN Prefix(es): 3-505
Number of titles published annually: 150 Print
Total Titles: 700 Print
Parent Company: Egmont

Egmont Pestalozzi-Verlag+
Schleissheimer Str 267, 80809 Munich

Mailing Address: Postfach 460725, 80915 Munich
Tel: (089) 35811-862 *Fax:* (089) 5811-869
Telex: 629766 Pevau *Cable:* PESTALOZZI ERLANGEN
Key Personnel
Man Dir: Rehne Herzig
Editorial, Rights & Permissions: Sibylle Lehmann
Founded: 1844
Subjects: Crafts, Games, Hobbies
ISBN Prefix(es): 3-614; 3-87624
Subsidiaries: Boje-Verlag
Distributed by Groupe de la Cite (France); Gutenberghus (Scandinavia); Arnoldo Mondadori (Italy); Simon & Schuster (USA)

Egmont vgs verlagsgesellschaft mbH+
Gertrudenstr 30-36, 50667 Cologne
Mailing Address: Postfach 101251, 50452 Cologne
Tel: (0221) 20811-0 *Fax:* (0221) 20811-66
E-mail: info@vgs.de
Web Site: www.vgs.de
Key Personnel
Man Dir: Dr Bernward Malaka *E-mail:* b.malaka@vgs.de
Man Dir & Publisher: Michael Schweins
Communications: Dr Juergen Puetz *E-mail:* j.puetz@vgs.de
Sales: Andrea Rueller
Advertising: Ingrid Reisner
Editorial Dir: Kurt-Juergen Heering; Stefanie Koch
Press Manager: Simone Altheim
Founded: 1970
Market-leading TV tie-in publisher in the German-speaking territory; popular nonfiction on health subjects, illustrated books.
Subjects: Animals, Pets, Art, Asian Studies, Biography, Crafts, Games, Hobbies, Fiction, Film, Video, Foreign Countries, Gardening, Plants, Health, Nutrition, History, House & Home, Music, Dance, Mysteries, Natural History, Nonfiction (General), Outdoor Recreation, Radio, TV, Science Fiction, Fantasy, Travel
ISBN Prefix(es): 3-8025
Number of titles published annually: 120 Print
Total Titles: 500 Print
Parent Company: Egmont Holding GmbH (Berlin)
Warehouse: Cornelsen Verlagskontor, Kammerratsheide 66, 33609 Bielefeld
Orders to: Cornelsen Verlagskontor, Kammerratsheide 66, 33609 Bielefeld

Ehrenwirth Verlag, *imprint of* Verlagsgruppe Luebbe GmbH & Co KG

Ehrenwirth Verlag+
Imprint of Verlagsgruppe Luebbe GmbH & Co KG
Scheidtbachstr 23-31, 51469 Bergisch Gladbach
Mailing Address: Postfach 200180, 51431 Bergisch Gladbach
Tel: (02202) 121-330 *Fax:* (02202) 121-920
E-mail: ehrenwirth@luebbe.de
Web Site: www.luebbe.de
Key Personnel
Man Dir: Karlheinz Jungbeck
Founded: 1945
Subjects: Fiction, How-to, Nonfiction (General)
ISBN Prefix(es): 3-431
Number of titles published annually: 25 Print

Ehrenwirth Verlag GmbH+
Scheidtbachstr 23-31, 51469 Bergisch Gladbach
Tel: (02202) 121-0 *Fax:* (02202) 121 920
Web Site: www.ehrenwirth.de
Key Personnel
Man Dir: Karlheinz Jungbeck
Founded: 1945
Membership(s): TR-Verlagsunion GmbH.

Subjects: Biography, Crafts, Games, Hobbies, Fiction, History, How-to, Poetry, Psychology, Psychiatry, Social Sciences, Sociology
ISBN Prefix(es): 3-431
Parent Company: Veritas-Verlag und Handelsgesellschaft mbH, Linz, Austria
Orders to: Verlegerdienst Muenchen, Postfach 1280, 82205 Gilching

Eichborn AG+
Kaiserstr 66, 60329 Frankfurt
Tel: (069) 256003-0 *Fax:* (069) 256003-30
E-mail: rights@eichborn.de; vertrieb@eichborn.de
Web Site: www.eichborn.de
Key Personnel
Chief Executive: Matthias Kierzek
Publishing Dir: Dr Wolfgang Hoeruer; Matthias Bischoff
Production: Ulrike Bettermann
Sales & Publicity: Ute Hollmann
Founded: 1980
Subjects: Fiction, History, Humor, Literature, Literary Criticism, Essays, Mysteries, Nonfiction (General)
ISBN Prefix(es): 3-8218
Number of titles published annually: 200 Print; 30 Audio
Imprints: Die Andere Bibliothek
Foreign Rights: ACER (Latin America, Portugal, Spain); Agence Hoffman (Belgium, France); Hercules Business & Culture Development GmbH (China, Taiwan); Imrie & Dervis Literary Agency (UK, Greece); International Literatuur Bureau BV (Belgium, Netherlands); Leonhardt & Hoier (Denmark, Finland, Iceland, Norway, Sweden); Onk Agency Ltd (Turkey); Orion Literary Agency (Japan); Pikarski Ltd Literary Agency (Israel); Studio Nabu (Italy); Writers House LLC (USA)

Eiland-Verlag Sylt Frank Roseman
Friesische Str 53, 25980 Westerland
Tel: (04651) 936212 *Fax:* (04651) 936214
E-mail: info@eiland-verlag.de
Web Site: www.eiland-verlag.de
Founded: 1975
ISBN Prefix(es): 2-922753

EinfallsReich Verlagsgesellschaft MbH+
Breitenkamp 43, 37619 Kirchbrak
Tel: (05533) 2017
Founded: 1987
Subjects: Art, Environmental Studies, Fiction, Humor, Literature, Literary Criticism, Essays, Music, Dance, Nonfiction (General), Travel
ISBN Prefix(es): 3-926207

Einfuehrungen, *imprint of* Wissenschaftliche Buchgesellschaft

Eironeia-Verlag
Sonnhalde 37, 79194 Gundelfingen
Tel: (0761) 581617 *Fax:* (0761) 3603474529
Key Personnel
Man Dir: Thomas Ebersberg
Founded: 1987
Subjects: History, Human Relations, Literature, Literary Criticism, Essays, Philosophy
ISBN Prefix(es): 3-926607
Imprints: Ebersberg; Th Kirchbaum, K

Eisenbahn-Kurier Verlag, see EK-Verlag GmbH

EK-Verlag GmbH+
H-V Stephanstr 15, 79100 Freiburg
Mailing Address: Postfach 500111, 79027 Freiburg
Tel: (0761) 70310-31 *Fax:* (0761) 70310-50
Key Personnel
Man Dir: Rudolf Wesemann
Man Dir & Production: Wolfgang Schumacher

Editorial & Publicity: Klaus Eckert
Editorial: Ingo Seifert
Sales: Karin Klemm
Rights & Permissions: Hansjuergen Wenzel
Founded: 1966
Subjects: Film, Video, Transportation
ISBN Prefix(es): 3-88255

Elefanten Press Verlag GmbH, see Espresso Verlag GmbH

Elektor-Verlag, *imprint of* Elektor-Verlag GmbH

Elektor-Verlag GmbH+
Susterfeldstr 25, 52072 Aachen
Tel: (0241) 889090 *Fax:* (0241) 8890988
E-mail: redaktion@elektor.de
Web Site: www.elektor.de
Key Personnel
Man Dir: M M F Landman
Publications Man: A Schommers
Marketing Man: G Klein
Founded: 1972
Membership(s): German Association of Book Distributors.
Subjects: Electronics, Electrical Engineering, Engineering (General), Environmental Studies, Microcomputers, Nonfiction (General), Physical Sciences, Technology, Travel
ISBN Prefix(es): 3-921608; 3-928051
Parent Company: Elektuur BV
Imprints: Elektor-Verlag

Verlag Heinrich Ellermann GmbH & Co KG+
Poppenbuetteler Chaussee 53, 22397 Hamburg
Mailing Address: Postfach 658220, 22374 Hamburg
Tel: (040) 607909-08 *Fax:* (040) 607909-59
E-mail: ellermann@vsg-hamburg.de
Web Site: www.ellermann.de
Key Personnel
Press: Frauke Wedler *Tel:* (040) 607909-23 *Fax:* (040) 607909-40 *E-mail:* wedler@vsg-hamburg.de
Marketing: Dr Juergen Huebner *Tel:* (040) 607909-55 *Fax:* (040) 607909-50 *E-mail:* marketing@vsg-hamburg.de; Susanne Weiss *Tel:* (040) 607909-777 *Fax:* (040) 607909-50 *E-mail:* vertrieb@vsg-hamburg.de
Advertising: Katja Muissus *Tel:* (040) 607909-30 *Fax:* (040) 607909-40 *E-mail:* werbung@vsg-hamburg.de
Rights & Licensing: Renate Reichstein *Tel:* (040) 607909-13 *Fax:* (040) 607909-51 *E-mail:* lizenzen@vsg-hamburg.de
Founded: 1934
ISBN Prefix(es): 3-7707
Parent Company: Koesel-Verlag GmbH & Co
Orders to: Moderne Industrie Verlagsservice, Landsberg

Ellert & Richter Verlag GmbH+
Grosse Brunnenstr 116-120, 22763 Hamburg
Tel: (040) 39 84 77-0 *Fax:* (040) 39 84 77-23
E-mail: info@ellert-richter.de
Web Site: www.ellert-richter.de
Key Personnel
International Rights: Marita Ellert-Richter
Founded: 1979
Subjects: Architecture & Interior Design, Art, Foreign Countries, Gardening, Plants, History, Nonfiction (General), Travel
ISBN Prefix(es): 3-89234
Warehouse: Runge GmbH, Bergstr 2, 4803 Steinhagen *Web Site:* www.rungeva.de

Elpis Verlag GmbH+
Rohrbacherstr 20, 69115 Heidelberg
Tel: (06221) 165789
Key Personnel
Dir: Lothar Faas; Dr Manfred Thiel

Founded: 1977
Subjects: Philosophy, Poetry, Religion - Islamic, Theology
ISBN Prefix(es): 3-921806
Number of titles published annually: 2 Print

Elsevier GmbH/Urban & Fischer Verlag+
Karlstr 45, 80333 Munich
Mailing Address: Postfach 201930, 80019 Munich
Tel: (089) 5383-0 *Fax:* (089) 5383-939
E-mail: info@elsevier-deutschland.de
Web Site: www.elsevier.de
Key Personnel
Man Dir: Angelika Lex
Rights & Permissions: Cathrin Korz *E-mail:* c.korz@elsevier.com
Founded: 1866
Subjects: Health, Nutrition, Medicine, Nursing, Dentistry, Science (General)
ISBN Prefix(es): 3-437
Number of titles published annually: 220 Print
Parent Company: Reed Elsevier GmbH, Munich
Branch Office(s)
Urban & Partner Wydawnictno Medyene nl, Curie-Skldowskiei 55/61, Instytut Elektrotechniki 50, 950 Wroclaw, Poland
Urban & Schwarzenberg GesmbH, Frankgasse 4, 1096 Vienna, Austria
Bookshop(s): Oscar Rothacker Versandbuchhandlung GmbH, Fraunhoferstr 10, 82152 Martinsried
Shipping Address: Servicecenter Fachverlage, Holzwiesenstr 2, 72127 Kusterdingen

N G Elwert Verlag+
Reitgasse 7-9, Pilgrimstein 30, 35037 Marburg
Tel: (06421) 17090 *Fax:* (06421) 15487
E-mail: elwertmail@elwert.de
Web Site: www.elwert.de *Cable:* ELWERT MARBURG
Key Personnel
Man Dir: Rudolph Braun-Elwert
Founded: 1726
Subjects: History, Law, Literature, Literary Criticism, Essays, Religion - Other, Social Sciences, Sociology
ISBN Prefix(es): 3-7708
Bookshop(s): N G Elwert Universitaetsbuchhandlung GmbH & Co KG, Reitgasse 7-9, Pilgrimstein 30, 35037 Marburg/Lahn

Gholam Emami
Fritz-von-Rothstr 25, 90249 Nurnberg
Mailing Address: Postfach 810451, 90249 Nurnberg
Tel: (0911) 288356 *Fax:* (0911) 288356
ISBN Prefix(es): 3-9801145

Emons Verlag+
Luetticher Str 38, 50674 Cologne
Tel: (0221) 56977-0 *Fax:* (0221) 524937
E-mail: info@emons-verlag.de
Web Site: www.emons-verlag.de
Key Personnel
Publisher: Hejo Emons *E-mail:* emons@emons-verlag.de
Press: Dr Britta Schmitz *E-mail:* schmitz@emons-verlag.de
Sales: Dorothee Junck *E-mail:* junck@emons-verlag.de
Founded: 1984
Subjects: Film, Video, Mysteries
ISBN Prefix(es): 3-924491; 3-89705
Total Titles: 120 Print

Encyclopedia Britannica
Rosenstr 12/13, 48143 Munster
Tel: (0251) 48 227-0 *Fax:* (0251) 48 227-27
E-mail: lexikadienst@aol.com

Web Site: www.britannica.de
Key Personnel
Contact: Hans-Dieter Blatter

Engel & Bengel Verlag+
Haardtweg 3, 67273 Bobenheim
Tel: (06353) 8107 *Fax:* (06353) 507057
E-mail: verlag@engelundbengel.de
Web Site: www.engelundbengel.de
Founded: 1990
Subjects: Animals, Pets, Disability, Special Needs, Fiction, How-to, Human Relations
ISBN Prefix(es): 3-928129
Orders to: Verlag Koch, Neff & Oetinger, Stuttgart
Koehler & Volckmar, Cologne

Engelhorn Verlag GmbH+
Koniginstr 9, 80539 Munich
Tel: (089) 45554-0 *Fax:* (089) 45554-111
Telex: uber 71 11193-DVA
Key Personnel
Publisher: Jurgen Horbach
Founded: 1860
Subjects: Biography
ISBN Prefix(es): 3-87203
Parent Company: Deutsche Verlags-Anstalt GmbH

Englisch Verlag GmbH+
Toepferstr 14, 65191 Wiesbaden
Tel: (0611) 9 427 2-0 *Fax:* (0611) 9 42 72 30
E-mail: info@englisch-verlag.de
Web Site: www.englisch-verlag.de
Key Personnel
Publisher: Iring F Englisch *E-mail:* iring.englisch@englischverlag.de
Program Management: Britta Sopp *Tel:* (0611) 9 42 72-15 *E-mail:* programm@englischverlag.de
Sales: Alexander Leidl *Tel:* (0611) 9 42 72-11 *E-mail:* alexander.leidl@englischverlag.de
Press: Sandra Will *Tel:* (0611) 9 42 72-17 *E-mail:* presse@englischverlag.de
Founded: 1973
Membership(s): Boersenverein des Deutschen Buchhandels.
Subjects: Art, Crafts, Games, Hobbies, How-to
ISBN Prefix(es): 3-8241
Number of titles published annually: 80 Print
Total Titles: 300 Print
Foreign Rep(s): Schweizer Buchzentrum (Switzerland); Dr Franz Hain (Austria)
Warehouse: VVA Vereinigte Verlagsauslieferung, 33310 Guetersloh, Contact: Ms Riediger *Tel:* (05241) 803893 *Fax:* (05241) 46750
Orders to: VVA Bertelsmann Distribution, Postfach 7777, 33310 Guetersloh

Verlag Peter Engstler
Oberwaldbehrungen 10, 97645 Ostheim/Rhoen
Tel: (09774) 858490 *Fax:* (09774) 858491
E-mail: engstler-verlag@t-online.de
Web Site: www.engstler-verlag.de
Key Personnel
Contact: Peter Engstler
Founded: 1988
Subjects: Art, Fiction, Government, Political Science, Literature, Literary Criticism, Essays, Poetry
ISBN Prefix(es): 3-929375; 3-9801770; 3-9802826

Enke, *imprint of* Georg Thieme Verlag KG

Ensslin Jugendbuchverlag, see Ensslin und Laiblin Verlag GmbH & Co KG

Ensslin und Laiblin Verlag GmbH & Co KG+
Harretstr 6, 72800 Eningen
Tel: (07121) 98 98 0 *Fax:* (07121) 98 98 44
E-mail: ensslin-verlag@t-online.de
Web Site: www.ensslin-verlag.de *Cable:* BUCHHAUS REUTLINGEN
Key Personnel
Man Dir, Rights & Permissions: Ariane Hanfstein *Tel:* (07121) 989822
Sales Dir: Joachim Hanfstein *Tel:* (01721) 989825
Production: Birgit Weber *Tel:* (07121) 989831
Public Relations, Advertising: Friederike Tiemann *Tel:* (07121) 989829
Founded: 1818
Specialize in children's & juvenile literature & in highly qualified teaching materials for pre-school & elementary school children. A special focus of the program is on "playing & learning" educational aids like the "Ensslin-Lernpuck®" or the "New learning games" (NELS) which enable children to exercise topics of various subjects at their very own pace. A new kind of educational aid are the "Duesenberg-Kids" - funny comics combined with detailed information & activity-tips which encourage children to have self-confidence & sense of responsibility.
Membership(s): Association of Children's Books.
Subjects: Education, Fiction, Literature, Literary Criticism, Essays, Nonfiction (General), Science Fiction, Fantasy
ISBN Prefix(es): 3-7709
Total Titles: 180 Print
Warehouse: Libri Distributions GmbH, August-Schanz-Str 33, 60433 Frankfurt *Tel:* 069 95422219 *Fax:* 069 542013

Ensslin Verlag im Arena Verlag, *imprint of* Arena Verlag GmbH

EOS Verlag der Benefiktiner der Erzabtei St. Ottilien+
86941 St Ottilien
Tel: (08193) 71261 *Fax:* (08193) 6844
E-mail: mail@eos-verlag.de
Web Site: www.eos-verlag.de
Key Personnel
Man Dir: P Walter Sedlmeier
Founded: 1885
Subjects: Art, Fiction, History, Religion - Other, Theology
ISBN Prefix(es): 3-88096; 3-920289
Subsidiaries: Druckerei
Divisions: Satz, Repro, Druckerei, Buchbiudeve
Bookshop(s): Klosterladen, Erzabtei St Ottilien, 86941 Sankt Ottilien

Eppinger-Verlag OHG
Stauffenbergstr 18, 74523 Schwaebisch Hall
Tel: (0791) 95061-0 *Fax:* (0791) 95061-41
E-mail: info@eppinger-verlag.de *Cable:* EPPINGER-VERLAG SCHWAEBISCH HALL
Key Personnel
Man Dir: Hans Paul Eppinger
Founded: 1970
Subjects: Business, Career Development, Developing Countries, Economics, Foreign Countries, Management, Regional Interests, Technology
ISBN Prefix(es): 3-87176

Erasmus Grasser-Verlag GmbH
Bachtal 6, 86978 Hohenfurch
Tel: (08861) 241900 *Fax:* (08861) 241901
Key Personnel
Manager: Wolfgang Vogelsgesang
Founded: 1974
ISBN Prefix(es): 3-925967

Eremiten-Presse und Verlag GmbH
Fortunastr 11, 40235 Duesseldorf
Mailing Address: Postfach 170143, 40082 Duesseldorf
Tel: (0211) 66 05 90 *Fax:* (0211) 698 94 70
Key Personnel
Man Dir: Friedolin Reske; Jens D Olsson
Founded: 1949
Subjects: Art, Fiction, Poetry
ISBN Prefix(es): 3-87365

Eres Editions-Horst Schubert Musikverlag
Haupstr 35, 28865 Lilienthal
Mailing Address: Postfach 1220, 28859 Lilienthal
Tel: (04298) 1676 *Fax:* (04298) 5312
E-mail: info@eres-musik.de
Web Site: www.eres-musik.de
Key Personnel
Man Dir: Horst Schubert
Founded: 1946
Subjects: Music, Dance
ISBN Prefix(es): 3-87204

ERF-Verlag GmbH+
Berliner Ring 62, 35576 Wetzlar
Tel: (06441) 9570 *Fax:* (06441) 957120
E-mail: info@erf.de
Web Site: www.erf.de
Key Personnel
Chairman: Ulrich Ruesch
Chairman & Dir: Juergen Werth
Head Sales & Distribution: Lars Kissner
Founded: 1978
Specialize in audio & video.
Subjects: Music, Dance, Religion - Other
ISBN Prefix(es): 3-89562
Parent Company: Evangeliums-Rundfunk eV
Branch Office(s)
Vienna, Austria
Zurich, Switzerland
U.S. Office(s): Trans World Radio, Cary, NC, United States

Ergebnisse Verlag GmbH+
Abendrothsweg 58, 20251 Hamburg
Tel: (040) 4801027 *Fax:* (040) 4801592
Key Personnel
Editor: Dietrich Lueders; Wolfgang Schwibbe; Michael Wildt
Sales, Rights & Permissions: Dr Thomas Neumann
Sales, Advertising & Publicity: Inge Busch
Founded: 1978
Subjects: Health, Nutrition, History, Medicine, Nursing, Dentistry, Psychology, Psychiatry, Regional Interests
ISBN Prefix(es): 3-87916
Orders to: PNV Petersen und Nieswand Vertriebsservice GmbH, Werftbahnstr 8, 24143 Kiel

Ergon Verlag Dr H J Dietrich+
Grombuehlstr 7, 97080 Wurzburg
Tel: (0931) 280084 *Fax:* (0931) 282872
E-mail: service@ergon-verlag.de
Web Site: www.ergon-verlag.de
Key Personnel
Press: Brigitte Miebach-Schrader *E-mail:* miebach-schrader@ergon-verlag.de
Contact: Dr Hans-Juergen Dietrich *E-mail:* dr.dietrich@ergon-verlag.de
ISBN Prefix(es): 3-928034; 3-932004; 3-933563
Distribution Center: Hora-Verlags-Gesellschaft m.b.H., Hackhofergasse 8-10, Postfach 24, 1195 Vienna-Nussdorf, Austria *Tel:* (0222) 67 15 80 *Fax:* (0222) 37 63 93
Schweizer Buchzentrum, 4601 Olten 1, Switzerland *Tel:* (062) 209 25 25 *Fax:* (062) 209 26 27

Erlanger Verlag Fuer Mission und Okumene (Erlanger Publishing House for Missions & Ecumerics)+
Hauptstr 2, 91564 Neuendettelsau
Mailing Address: Postfach 68, 91561 Neuendettelsau
Tel: (09874) 9 17 00 *Fax:* (09874) 9 33 70
E-mail: verlagsleitung@erlanger-verlag.de
Web Site: www.erlanger-verlag.de

Key Personnel
Director: Dr Johannes Triebel
Founded: 1897
Subjects: Asian Studies, Developing Countries, Religion - Islamic, Religion - Other, Theology, Specialize in African studies
ISBN Prefix(es): 3-87214
Total Titles: 106 Print
Parent Company: Evang Luth Church in Bavaria, Germany

Ernst Kabel Verlag GmbH+
Imprint of Piper Verlag Gmbh
Georgeustr 4, 80799 Munich
Mailing Address: Postfach 430861, 80731 Munich
Tel: (089) 381801-0 *Fax:* (089) 338704
E-mail: info@piper.de
Web Site: www.piper.de
Key Personnel
Publisher: Victor Niemann
Man Dir: Hartmyt Jedicke
Editorial: Bettiva Feldweg
Founded: 1977
Specialize in gift books.
Subjects: Biography, Fiction, Nonfiction (General), Psychology, Psychiatry, Self-Help
ISBN Prefix(es): 3-8225
Number of titles published annually: 25 Print
Ultimate Parent Company: Bounier Media Holding GmbH
Orders to: Koch Neff Ogtinger & Co, Schockenriedstr 39, 7055A Stuttgart

Ernst, Wilhelm & Sohn, Verlag Architektur und technische Wissenschaft GmbH & Co+
Buhringstr 10, 13086 Berlin
Tel: (030) 47031-200 *Fax:* (030) 47031-270
E-mail: info@ernst-und-sohn.de
Web Site: www.wiley.vch.de/ernstsohn
Key Personnel
Dir: Dagmar Stehle
Editorial, Rights & Permissions: Monika Herr
Founded: 1851
Subjects: Architecture & Interior Design, Civil Engineering, Technology
ISBN Prefix(es): 3-433
Parent Company: Wiley-VCH Verlag GmbH, Boschstr 12, 69469 Weinheim
Shipping Address: VSW GmbH, Postfach 1355, 68745 Waghaeusel
Warehouse: Wiley-VCH Verlag GmbH, Boschstr 12, 69469 Weinheim

Ertraege der Forschung zur Forschung-, *imprint of* Wissenschaftliche Buchgesellschaft

Verlagsgesellschaft des Erziehungsvereins GmbH+
Andreas-Braem-Str 18-20, 47506 Neukirchen-Vluyn
Tel: (02845) 392-0 *Fax:* (02845) 392392
E-mail: info@neukirchener-verlag.de
Web Site: www.neukirchener-verlag.de *Cable:* VERLAGSHAUS NEUKIRCHEN VLUYN
Key Personnel
Man Dir: Jochen Boeckler; Dr Rudolf Weth
Publishing Manager: Dr Volker Hampel
  E-mail: verlagsleitung@neukirchener-verlag.de
Sales Representative: Stefan Schubert
  E-mail: schubert@neukirchener-verlag.de
Lecturer: Ekkehard Starke *E-mail:* letkorat@neukirchener-verlag.de
Production: Hans Hegner *E-mail:* herstellung@neukirchener-verlag.de; Karin Jacobs *E-mail:* herstellung@neukirchener-verlag.de; Volker Kuschnik *E-mail:* herstellung@neukirchener-verlag.de
Advertising: Christoph Siepermann
  E-mail: vertrieb@neukirchener-verlag.de
Dispatch Bookshop: Angelika Boos *Tel:* (02845) 392-218 *E-mail:* vsb@neukirchener-verlag.de
Subjects: Religion - Protestant, Theology
ISBN Prefix(es): 3-7615; 3-7887; 3-7621; 3-7673; 3-7958
Associate Companies: Aussaat Verlag; Kalenderverlag des Erziehungsvereins; Neukirchener Verlag

Verlag am Eschbach GmbH+
Im Alten Rathaus, Haupstr 37, 79427 Eschbach/Markgraeflerland
Tel: (07634) 1088 *Fax:* (07634) 3796
E-mail: vertrieb@verlag-am-eschbach.de
Web Site: www.verlag-am-eschbach.de
Key Personnel
Gesellschafter-Geschaeftsfuehrers: Heribert Mohr; Martin Schmeisser; Juergen Schwarz
Founded: 1979
Subjects: Art, Religion - Catholic, Religion - Protestant
ISBN Prefix(es): 3-88671

Esogetics GmbH+
Hildastr 8, 76646 Bruchsal
Tel: (07251) 8001-40 *Fax:* (07251) 8001-55
E-mail: info-de@esogetics.com
Web Site: www.esogetics.com
Key Personnel
Man Dir: Sophocles Amanatidis *E-mail:* sa@esogetics.com; Markus Wunderlich
Founded: 1988
Subjects: Health, Nutrition, Medicine, Nursing, Dentistry, Science (General)
ISBN Prefix(es): 3-925806
Total Titles: 2 Print
Foreign Rep(s): Techiche Nuove, Hay
Foreign Rights: Techiche Nuove, Hay (Spain)

Esotere Taschenbuch, *imprint of* Verlag Hermann Bauer Gmbh & Co KG

Verlag Esoterische Philosophie GmbH
Goedekeweg 8, 30419 Hannover
Tel: (0511) 755331 *Fax:* (0511) 755334
E-mail: info@esoterische-philosophie.de
Web Site: www.esoterische-philosophie.de
Key Personnel
Man Dir: Baerbel Ackermann
Art Dir: Matthias Winter
Founded: 1984
Specialize in translations of English literature.
Subjects: Anthropology, Astrology, Occult, Parapsychology, Philosophy, Religion - Buddhist, Religion - Other, Science (General), Cosmology, Science of Religions
ISBN Prefix(es): 3-924849

Espresso Verlag GmbH+
Formerly Elefanten Press Verlag GmbH
Am Treptower Park 28-30, 12435 Berlin
Tel: (030) 5333 4444 *Fax:* (030) 5333 4159
E-mail: info@espresso-verlag.de
Web Site: www.espresso-verlag.de
Key Personnel
Manager: Maruta Schmidt
Sales Manager: Martina Hayo
Public Relations & Rights: Claudia Schulz
Founded: 1977
Subjects: Art, Developing Countries, Government, Political Science, History, Humor, Literature, Literary Criticism, Essays, Mysteries, Photography, Social Sciences, Sociology, Women's Studies
ISBN Prefix(es): 3-88520
Total Titles: 200 Print

Esslinger Verlag J F Schreiber GmbH+
Marktplatz 19, 73728 Esslingen
Mailing Address: Postfach 10 03 25, 73703 Esslingen
Tel: (0711) 310594-6 *Fax:* (0711) 310594-77; (0711) 310594-65
E-mail: esslinger@klett-mail.de
Key Personnel
Man Dir: Franz Scharetzer
Man Dir & Publishing Dir: Mathias Berg
Editor, Publicity: Sabine Frankholz
Editor: Urte Fiutak
Founded: 1831
Children's book publisher.
Specialize in nostalgic children's books, reprints & fairy tales.
ISBN Prefix(es): 3-480; 3-87286
Parent Company: Ernst Klett Information

Eulen Verlag+
Einsteinstr 167, 81675 Munich
Tel: (089) 47 07 77 44 *Fax:* (089) 47 07 77 42
E-mail: info@eulenverlag.de
Web Site: www.eulen-verlag.de
Key Personnel
Owner & Publisher: Harald Glaeser
Founded: 1983
Subjects: Art, Crafts, Games, Hobbies, Outdoor Recreation, Photography, Regional Interests, Travel
ISBN Prefix(es): 3-89102
Total Titles: 125 Print
Warehouse: Libri Distributions Gmbh, August-Schanzstr 33, 60433 Frankfurt am Main

Eulenhof-Verlag Wolfgang Ehrhardt Heinold+
Appener Weg 3b, 20251 Hamburg
Tel: (040) 490005-14 *Fax:* (040) 490005-15
E-mail: w.e.heinold@eulenhof.de
Web Site: www.eulenhof.de
Key Personnel
Man Dir: Iris Wolf *Tel:* (0171) 4181248
Founded: 1981
Specialize in information on children's media.
Membership(s): Borsenverein des Deutschen Buchhandels & Arbeitskreis Fur Jugendliteratur EV.
Subjects: Library & Information Sciences
ISBN Prefix(es): 3-88710
Number of titles published annually: 1 Print
Total Titles: 3 Print
Associate Companies: Eulenhof Institut, WE Heinold Beratungs Gesellschaft mbH, Contact: Wolfgang Ehrhardt Heinold *Tel:* (040) 4900050 *Fax:* (040) 49000515 *E-mail:* eulenwolf@compuserve.com
Branch Office(s)
Nuernbergerstr 25, 86609 Donauwoerth
Tel: (0906) 2461-17 *Fax:* (0906) 2461-16
E-mail: m.j.bock@eulenhof.de

Europ Export Edition GmbH
Berliner Allee 8, 64295 Darmstadt
Mailing Address: Postfach 100264, 64202 Darmstadt
Tel: (06151) 38920 *Fax:* (06151) 38 92 80
E-mail: info@abconline.de
Web Site: www.abconline.de
Key Personnel
Publisher: Margit Selka
Founded: 1958
ISBN Prefix(es): 3-87208
Foreign Rep(s): Export Edition SA (France, Italy, Switzerland)

Verlag Europa-Lehrmittel GmbH & Co KG+
Nourney, Vollmer GmbH & Co KG, Duesselberger Str 23, 42781 Haan-Gruiten
Mailing Address: Postfach 21 60, 42765 Haan-Gruiten
Tel: (02104) 6916-0 *Fax:* (02104) 6916-27
E-mail: info@europa-lehrmittel.de
Web Site: www.europa-lehrmittel.de
Key Personnel
General Manager, Rights & Permissions: Joachim Nourney
Editor: Armin Steinmueller
Sales: Wolfgang Baldauf
Founded: 1948

Subjects: Automotive, Computer Science, Economics, Electronics, Electrical Engineering, Geography, Geology, Physics
ISBN Prefix(es): 3-8085

Europa Union Verlag GmbH+
Holtorfer Str 35, 53229 Bonn
Mailing Address: Postfach 33 01 49, 53203 Bonn
Tel: (0228) 7 29 00 0
E-mail: Service@euverlag.de
Web Site: www.europa-union-verlag.de
Key Personnel
Man Dir, Rights & Permissions: Gisbert Karsten
Sales: Rainer Mertens; Wolfgang Schuefer
Founded: 1959
Subjects: Government, Political Science
ISBN Prefix(es): 3-7713
Subsidiaries: Verlag fur Internationale Politik GmbH
Warehouse: VVA, Postfach 7777, 33310 Guetersloh

Europa Verlag GmbH+
Neuer Wall 10, 20354 Hamburg
Tel: (040) 355434-0 *Fax:* (040) 355434-66
E-mail: info@europaverlag.de
Web Site: www.europaverlag.de *Cable:* EUROPAVERLAG
Key Personnel
Manager: Vito von Eichborn
Editorial Dir, Sales & International Rights: Gisela Anna Stuempel
International Rights: Peter Hahn
  E-mail: lizenzen@europaverlag.de
Publisher Reader: Dr Edgar Bracht; Afra Margaretha
Press: Eva Betzwieser *E-mail:* presse@europaverlag.de
Programmer: Aenne Glienke
Production: Frank Wagner *E-mail:* herstellung@europaverlag.de
Founded: 1933
Subjects: Biography, Fiction, Government, Political Science, Literature, Literary Criticism, Essays, Mysteries, Nonfiction (General), Philosophy
ISBN Prefix(es): 3-203
Parent Company: Europaverlag GmbH Muenich
Subsidiaries: Europaverlag GmbH
Foreign Rep(s): Tom Franke (Germany); Gabriele Funcke (Germany); Barbara Haab (Switzerland); Mareile Handrich (Germany); Peter Handrich (Germany); Juergen Niemeier (Germany); Guenther Poelking-Henkel (Germany); Achim Reigel (Germany); Raimund Thomas (Germany); Guenter Weber (Germany); Okkar Wuthe (Austria)
Distribution Center: Dr Franz Hain GmbH Verlagsauslieferungen, Dr Otto Neurathstr 3-5, 1220 Vienna, Austria *Tel:* (0282) 65 65-24 *Fax:* (0282) 65 65-75
Koch, Neff & Oetinger Co GmbH, Schockenriedstr 39, 70565 Stuggart *Tel:* (0711) 7899-20 36 *Fax:* (0711) 7899-10 10
Schweizer Buchzentrum, 4601 Olten, Switzerland *Tel:* (062) 209 23-44 *Fax:* (062) 209 27 60

Europaeische Verlagsanstalt GmbH & Rotbuch Verlag GmbH & Co KG+
Bei den Muehren 70, 20457 Hamburg
Tel: (040) 450194-0 *Fax:* (040) 450194-50
E-mail: info@rotbuch.de
Web Site: www.rotbuch.de; www.europaeische-verlagsanstalt.de
Key Personnel
Publisher: Dr Sabine Groenewold *E-mail:* info@sabine-groenewold-verlage.de
Editor: Irlen Kauser
International Rights: Helge Juergens *Tel:* (040) 450194-31
Lektorat - Literature: Olaf Irlenkaeuser
  E-mail: irlenkaeuser@rotbuch.de
Lektorat - Special Book: Christina Knuellig
  E-mail: knuellig@rotbuch.de
Foreign Rights: Andrea Schlotfeldt *Tel:* (040) 450194-13 *E-mail:* rechte@sabine-groenewold-verlage.de
Founded: 1946
Subjects: Anthropology, Architecture & Interior Design, Biography, Criminology, Government, Political Science, History, Literature, Literary Criticism, Essays, Philosophy
ISBN Prefix(es): 3-434; 3-88022
Total Titles: 600 Print; 2 CD-ROM
Subsidiaries: Rotbuch Verlag; Syndikat Autoren und Verlagsgesellschaft
Foreign Rep(s): Rolf-Peter Baacke (Germany); Richard Bhend (Switzerland); Fina Bothur (Germany); Fritz Denke (Germany); Karlheinz Flessenkemper (Germany); Edwin Gantert (Germany); Stefan Moedritscher (Austria); Guenther Raunjak (Austria); Juergen Stelling (Germany); Verena Suery (Switzerland)

Verlag Europaeische Wehrkunde+
Steintorwall 17, 32052 Herford
Tel: (0228) 340884 *Fax:* (040) 79713304
Key Personnel
Publisher: Peter Tamm
Manager: Lothar Lichtenheldt
Associate Companies: Verlagsgruppe Koehler/Mittler, Steintorwall 17, 32052 Herford
Branch Office(s)
Austr 19, 53179 Bonn *Tel:* (0228) 530962-64 *Fax:* (0228) 230102

Evangelische Haupt-Bibelgesellschaft und von Cansteinsche Bibelanstalt+
Ziegelstr 30, 10117 Berlin
Tel: (030) 28878850-0 *Fax:* (030) 28878850-8
E-mail: kontakt@ehbg.de
Web Site: www.ehbg.de
Key Personnel
Church President: Helge Klasson
Man Dir & Pastor: Friedrich Delius
  E-mail: delius@ehbg.de
Founded: 1814
Subjects: Literature, Literary Criticism, Essays
ISBN Prefix(es): 3-7461

Evangelische Verlagsanstalt GmbH+
Blumenstr 76, 04155 Leipzig
Tel: (0341) 71141-0 *Fax:* (0341) 7114150
E-mail: info@eva-leipzig.de
Web Site: www.eva-leipzig.de *Cable:* EVAVERLAG LEIPZIG
Key Personnel
Dir: Ulrich Roebbelen
Founded: 1946
Subjects: Biblical Studies, Biography, Fiction, Religion - Protestant, Religion - Other, Theology
ISBN Prefix(es): 3-374
Total Titles: 270 Print
Bookshop(s): Buchhandlung an der Thomaskirche, Burgstr 1, 04109 Leipzig; C L Ungelenk Nachfolger, Kreuzstr 7, 01067 Dresden *Tel:* (0351) 4969804
Warehouse: Leipziger Kommissions- und Grosbuchhandelsgesellschaft, Potzschauer Weg, 04579 Espenhain
Orders to: Leipziger Kommissions- und Grossbuchhandelsgesellschaft, Potzchauer Weg, 04579 Espenhain

Evangelischer Presseverband fuer Baden eV
Vorholzstr 7, 76137 Karlsruhe
Mailing Address: Postfach 2280, 76010 Karlsruhe
Tel: (0721) 93 27 50 *Fax:* (0721) 9 32 75 20
Key Personnel
Manager: Herwig Schelling
Subjects: Religion - Protestant
ISBN Prefix(es): 3-87210
Subsidiaries: Hans Thoma Verlag

Evangelischer Presseverband fuer Bayern eV+
Birkerstr 22, 80636 Munich
Tel: (089) 121 72-0 *Fax:* (089) 121 72-138
E-mail: info@epv.de
Web Site: www.epv.de
Telex: 523718
Key Personnel
Dir: Hartmut Joisten
Publisher: Dr Manuel Zelger
International Rights: Antje Fritsch-Brown
  Tel: (089) 121 72-132 *E-mail:* afritsch@epv.de
Founded: 1932
Bavarian Evangelical Press Union.
Subjects: Philosophy, Theology
ISBN Prefix(es): 3-583
Total Titles: 60 Print

EVT Energy Video Training & Verlag GmbH
Borsigallee 37, 60388 Frankfurt
Tel: (069) 431575 *Fax:* (069) 4950974
Key Personnel
Author: Marianne Uhl
International Rights: Karsten Schloberg
  E-mail: kschloberg@aol.com
Founded: 1991
Subjects: Alternative, Astrology, Occult, Medicine, Nursing, Dentistry, Music, Dance, Parapsychology, Psychology, Psychiatry, Self-Help, Esoteric, Healing, Meditation
ISBN Prefix(es): 3-930255

Exil Verlag+
Rheinstr 20, 60325 Frankfurt
Tel: (069) 751102 *Fax:* (069) 751547
E-mail: fs7a020@uni-hamburg.de
Key Personnel
Publisher: Edita Koch *Tel:* (069) 751102
Founded: 1981
Publisher of books about German theater in exile 1933-1945 & a journal about literature, arts, theater, film & science of Germans in exile 1933-1945.
Total Titles: 36 Print
Distributed by Otto Harrassowitz

expert verlag GmbH, Fachverlag fuer Wirtschaft & Technik+
Wankelstr 13, 71272 Renningen
Tel: (07159) 92 65-0 *Fax:* (07159) 92 65-20
E-mail: expert@expertverlag.de
Web Site: www.expertverlag.de
Key Personnel
Publisher: Elmar Wippler
Editor: Dr Arnulf Krais *Tel:* (07159) 92 65-12
  E-mail: krais@expertverlag.de
Advertising: Rainer Paulsen *Tel:* (07159) 92 65-16 *E-mail:* paulsen@expertverlag.de
Press: Christa Beran *Tel:* (07159) 92 65-16
  E-mail: presse@expertverlag.de
Founded: 1979
Subjects: Electronics, Electrical Engineering, Energy, Environmental Studies, Management, Mechanical Engineering
ISBN Prefix(es): 3-8169
Number of titles published annually: 100 Print
Total Titles: 800 Print
Distributed by Baufachverlag (Switzerland); Lindeverlag (Austria); Schweizer Baudokumentation (Switzerland)
Distribution Center: Dessauer Engros Buchhandlung, 8046 Zurich, Switzerland *Tel:* (01) 466 96 66 *Fax:* (01) 466 96 69 *E-mail:* dessauer@dessauer.ch
Dr Franz Hain Verlagsauslieferungen, Dr Otto Neurath Gasse 5, 1220 Vienna, Austria *Tel:* (01) 2 82 65 65 *Fax:* (01) 2 82 52 82 *E-mail:* office@hain.at

Expolibri GmbH
Buchwebung & Austellungen Gerichtsweg 26, 7010 Leipzig
Tel: (0341) 2113 231 *Fax:* (0341) 2115 996

Key Personnel
Man Dir: Marion Renker
Founded: 1991

Extent Verlag und Service Wolfgang M Flamm+
Pestalozzistr 64, 10627 Berlin-Charlottenburg
Mailing Address: Postfach 120429, 10594 Berlin
Tel: (030) 3279805-0; (030) 3279805-11
 Fax: (030) 3279805-35
E-mail: extent@t-online.de
Key Personnel
International Rights: Flamm Wolfgang-Martin
Founded: 1987
Subjects: Art, Astrology, Occult, Communications, Fashion, Human Relations, Literature, Literary Criticism, Essays, Music, Dance
ISBN Prefix(es): 3-926671
Imprints: Pixel Transfer Design Studio

Fabel-Verlag Gudrun Liebchen+
Kirchenstr 6, 97657 Sandberg
Tel: (09701) 1463 *Fax:* (09701) 1463
Key Personnel
Dir: Gudrun Liebchen
Founded: 1989
Subjects: Drama, Theater, Environmental Studies, Literature, Literary Criticism, Essays, Nonfiction (General), Poetry
ISBN Prefix(es): 3-9802142

Fabylon-Verlag+
Forststr 10-12, 80997 Munich
Tel: (0172) 8211847 *Fax:* (089) 8110882
E-mail: fabylon@t-online.de
Web Site: www.fabylonzeitspur.de
Key Personnel
Publisher, Editor, Rights & Permissions: Gerald Jambor
Publisher & Authoress: Uschi Zietsch-Jambor
Founded: 1987
Membership(s): Stock Exchange of German Booksellers.
Subjects: Mysteries, Science Fiction, Fantasy
ISBN Prefix(es): 3-927071

Fachbuchverlag Leipzig GmbH
Zschochersche Str 48 B, 04229 Leipzig
Tel: (0341) 4 90 34-0 *Fax:* (0341) 4 80 62 20
E-mail: voigt@hanser.de
Key Personnel
Editorial: Christine Fritzsch *E-mail:* fritzsch@hanser.de; Yochen Horn; Erika Hotho
 E-mail: hotho@hanser.de
Founded: 1949
Parent Company: Carl Hanser Verlag

Fachbuchverlag Pfanneberg & Co
Duesselbergerstr 23, 42781 Haan-Gruiten
Mailing Address: Postfach 4204 64, 42404 Haan-Gruiten
Tel: (02104) 6916-0 *Fax:* (02104) 6916-27
E-mail: gero.pfanneberg@giessen.netsurf.de
Web Site: www.pfanneberg.de
Key Personnel
Man Dir, Rights & Permissions: Dr Guenther Pfanneberg
Production: Gerhard Duske
Founded: 1949
Subjects: Business, Career Development, Cookery, Health, Nutrition
ISBN Prefix(es): 3-8057

Fachmedien Verlag Winfried Ruf (FMV)+
Parsevalstr 20, 86415 Mering
Mailing Address: Postfach 1248, 86407 Mering
Tel: (08233) 4924 *Fax:* (08233) 4789
Key Personnel
Contact: Winfried Ruf
Founded: 1990
ISBN Prefix(es): 3-928752

Fachverlag fur das graphische Gewerbe GmbH
Friedrichstr 22, 80801 Munich
Mailing Address: Postfach 401929, 80719 Munich
Tel: (089) 33036131 *Fax:* (089) 33036100
Key Personnel
Man Dir & International Rights: Dr Klaus Beichel
Founded: 1955
Subjects: Business
ISBN Prefix(es): 3-87218
Imprints: Mitteilungsblatt der Verbandes deds bayerischen Druckincleestrie eV

Fachverlag Schiele & Schoen GmbH+
Markgrafenstr 11, 10969 Berlin
Mailing Address: Postfach 610280, Berlin 10924
Tel: (030) 253 75 20 *Fax:* (030) 251 72 48
E-mail: service@schiele-schoen.de
Web Site: www.schiele-schoen.de
Key Personnel
Man Dir, Rights & Permissions: Peter Schoen
 Fax: (030) 25 37 52 37 *E-mail:* peter.schoen@schiele-schoen.de
Sales: Ingrid Bade
Production: Lutz Stehr
Founded: 1946
Publishers of technical & scientific publications.
Subjects: Biological Sciences, Communications, Crafts, Games, Hobbies, Engineering (General), Medicine, Nursing, Dentistry, Technology
ISBN Prefix(es): 3-7949
Foreign Rep(s): Norwin A Merens Ltd (North America)

Fackeltrager-Verlag GmbH+
Wurzburgerstr 14, 26121 Oldenburg
Mailing Address: Postfach 3407, 26024 Oldenburg
Tel: (0441) 980 66-0 *Fax:* (0441) 980 66-34
E-mail: info@lappan.de
Web Site: www.lappan.de
Key Personnel
Editorial Dir: Peter Baumann; Dieter Schwalm
Marketing: Michael Bohme *E-mail:* vertrieb@lappan.de; Heike Kroner
International Rights: Heidtun Viampl
Publicity: Elke Horstmann
Rights: Nicola Heinrichs
Advertising: Andrea Groteluschen
 E-mail: presse@lappan.de
Founded: 1949
Subjects: Art, History, Humor
ISBN Prefix(es): 3-89082; 3-8303
Parent Company: Lappan Verlag GmbH

Fahrner & Fahrner
Bergerstr 278, 60385 Frankfurt am Main
Tel: (069) 584777 *Fax:* (069) 584777
E-mail: mfahrner@t-online.de
Web Site: www.themodernword.com/tlon/index.html
Key Personnel
Proprietor: Barbara Fahrner
International Rights: Markus Fahrner
Founded: 1982
Specialize in unique books & small editions.
Subjects: Art, Fiction, Literature, Literary Criticism, Essays
Branch Office(s)
28 Fendyke Rd, Belvedere, Kent DA 175 DP, United Kingdom, Contact: Markus M Fahrner

Christa Falk-Verlag+
Ischl 11, 83370 Seeon
Tel: (08667) 14 13 *Fax:* (08667) 14 17
E-mail: email@chfalk-verlag.de
Web Site: www.chfalk-verlag.de
Key Personnel
Publisher: Christa Falk
Founded: 1982
Specialize in esoteric books.

ISBN Prefix(es): 3-924161; 3-89568
Number of titles published annually: 10 Print; 2 CD-ROM; 1 Audio
Total Titles: 240 Print; 196 Online; 16 Audio
Foreign Rep(s): AS Hoeller (Austria)

Falk Verlag AG, see Mairs Geographischer Verlag Kurt Mair GmbH & Co

Falken-Verlag GmbH+
Schoene Aussicht 21, 65527 Niedernhausen
Mailing Address: Postfach 1120, 65521 Niedernhausen
Tel: (06127) 702-0 *Fax:* (06127) 702-133
E-mail: vertrieb.verlagsgruppe@bertelsmann.de
Web Site: www.randomhouse.de/falken
Key Personnel
Man Dir: Frank Sicker
Publishing Manager: Manfred Abrahamsberg
Production: Josef Jung
Publicity: Stefan Becht *Tel:* (06127) 702-190
 Fax: (06127) 702-248 *E-mail:* presse@falken.de
Foreign Rights: Silke Bruenink *Tel:* (06127) 702-178 *Fax:* (06127) 702-277
Founded: 1923
Subjects: Cookery, Crafts, Games, Hobbies, Education, Gardening, Plants, Health, Nutrition, History, How-to, Humor, Photography, Sports, Athletics
ISBN Prefix(es): 3-8068
Associate Companies: Moeller Verlag
Subsidiaries: Falken Taschenbuch Verlag; Friedrich Bassermann'sche Verlagsbuchhandlung
Orders to: KNO, Schockenriedstr 39, 70565 Stuttgart 80

Ekkehard Faude Verlag
Postfach 100524, 78405 Konstanz
Tel: (041 71) 6883555 *Fax:* (041 71) 6883565

Favorit-Verlag Huntemann und Markus & Co GmbH+
Stettinerstr 16, 76437 Rastatt
Tel: (07222) 2 22 54 *Fax:* (07222) 2 98 38
E-mail: info@favorit-verlag.de
Web Site: www.favorit-verlag.de
Telex: 786630 *Cable:* FAVORITVERLAG
Key Personnel
Man Dir: Trudel Huntemann; Ilse Markus; Michael Markus
Founded: 1965
ISBN Prefix(es): 3-921102; 3-8227

Feinschmecker, *imprint of* Graefe und Unzer Verlag GmbH

Dr Karl Feistle, see Dustri-Verlag Dr Karl Feistle

Feltron-Elektronik Zeissler & Co GmbH
Auf dem Schellerod 22, 53842 Troisdorf
Mailing Address: Postfach 1263, 53822 Troisdorf
Tel: (02241) 48670 *Fax:* (02241) 404241
Key Personnel
Owner: M Zeissler
Founded: 1947
Subjects: Communications, Computer Science, Electronics, Electrical Engineering, Microcomputers
ISBN Prefix(es): 3-88050

Ferd Dummler's Verlag+
Fuggerstr 7, 51149 Cologne
Tel: (02203) 3029-0 *Fax:* (02203) 3029-40
Key Personnel
Man Dir: Helmut Lehmann
Founded: 1808

Membership(s): VGS - Verlagsgesellschaft mbH & Co KG.
Subjects: Chemistry, Chemical Engineering, Civil Engineering, Computer Science, Crafts, Games, Hobbies, Earth Sciences, Government, Political Science, History, Language Arts, Linguistics, Mathematics, Mechanical Engineering, Physical Sciences, Physics, Sports, Athletics
ISBN Prefix(es): 3-427

Ferdinand Enke Verlag+
Oswalt-Hesse-Str 50, 70469 Stuttgart
Tel: (0711) 8931-0 *Fax:* (0711) 8931-706
Web Site: www.enke.de
Telex: 07252275 *Cable:* ENKEBUCH STUTTGART
Key Personnel
Man Dir: Fr Marlis Kuhlmann, PhD; Albrecht Hauff
Sales Dir, Rights & Permissions: Martin Spencker
Publicity: Marcus Boeggemann
Founded: 1837
Subjects: Art, Geography, Geology, Medicine, Nursing, Dentistry, Psychology, Psychiatry, Science (General), Social Sciences, Sociology, Veterinary Science
ISBN Prefix(es): 3-432
Associate Companies: Georg Thieme Verlag KG
Subsidiaries: Deutscher Verlag fur Grundstoffindustrie

Franz Ferzak World & Space Publications+
Am Bachl 1, 93336 Altmannstein
Tel: (09446) 1403
Key Personnel
Owner: Franz Ferzak *Tel:* (089) 82089393
Founded: 1987
Subjects: Astronomy, Electronics, Electrical Engineering, Energy, Engineering (General), Physical Sciences, Physics, Science (General), Technology
ISBN Prefix(es): 3-9801465; 3-9805835
Number of titles published annually: 2 Print
Total Titles: 11 Print
Orders to: Michaels Verlag, 86971 Peiting *Tel:* (08861) 59018 *Fax:* (08861) 67091 *E-mail:* mvv@michaelsverlag.de

Festland Verlag GmbH
Basteistr 88, 53173 Bonn
Mailing Address: Postfach 200561, 53135 Bonn
Tel: (0228) 36 20 21-23 *Fax:* (0228) 35 17 71
E-mail: verlag@festland-verlag.de
Web Site: www.oeckl.de
Key Personnel
International Rights: Heinz H Hey
Founded: 1950
Subjects: Communications, Economics, Education, Government, Political Science, Social Sciences, Sociology
ISBN Prefix(es): 3-87224
Number of titles published annually: 2 Print; 2 CD-ROM; 1 Online
Parent Company: C W Niemeyer GmbH & Co KG, 31784 Hameln

Festo Didactic GmbH & Co KG
Rechbergstr 3, 73770 Denkendorf
Tel: (0711) 3467-0 *Toll Free Tel:* 800 5600967 (orders) *Fax:* (0711) 34754-88500 *Toll Free Fax:* 800 5600843 (orders)
E-mail: did@festo.com
Web Site: www.festo.com/didactic
Key Personnel
Man Dir: Dr Theodor Niehaus; Dr Wilfried Stoll
Founded: 1980
Membership(s): Association of German Publishing Companies.
Subjects: Career Development, Education, Electronics, Electrical Engineering, Engineering (General)
ISBN Prefix(es): 3-8127
U.S. Office(s): Festo Corporation, 395 Moreland Rd, Hauppauge, NY 11788, United States *Tel:* 516-435-0800 *Fax:* 516-435-8026

Fibre Verlag
Martinistr 37, 49080 Osnabrueck
Tel: (0541) 431838 *Fax:* (0541) 432786
E-mail: info@fibre-verlag.de
Web Site: www.fibre-verlag.de
ISBN Prefix(es): 3-929759

Wolfgang Fietkau Verlag+
Ernst-Thaelmannstr 152, 14532 Kleinmachnow
Tel: (033203) 71 105 *Fax:* (033203) 71 109
E-mail: fietkau@fietkau.de
Web Site: www.fietkau.de
Key Personnel
Publisher, Rights & Permissions: Wolfgang Fietkau
Founded: 1959
Acts as booktrader on German Stockmarket.
Subjects: Poetry
ISBN Prefix(es): 3-87352

Barbara Fietz, see Abakus Musik Barbara Fietz

Filmfaust Verlag - Internationale Filmzeitschrift
Schumannstr 64, 60325 Frankfurt
Tel: (069) 748305 *Fax:* (069) 564321
E-mail: info@filmfaust.de
Web Site: www.filmfaust.de
Key Personnel
Man Dir: Bion Steinborn
Rights & Permissions: Dr Christine V Eichel-Streiber
Founded: 1976
Divisions: Redaktion in Berlin; Filmfaust Redaktion

Emil Fink Verlag
Siemensstr 52, 70469 Stuttgart
Tel: (0711) 814646 *Fax:* (0711) 8106070
E-mail: info@fink-verlag.de
Web Site: www.fink-verlag.de
Key Personnel
Publisher, Rights & Permissions: Stefan Scheibel
Founded: 1919
Specialize in calendars, greeting cards & postcards.
Subjects: Art
ISBN Prefix(es): 3-7717
Foreign Rep(s): Arcaldion (Austria, Netherlands, France, Switzerland); Art Bula; Calandars-Cards; Edition Classic Art; Verlagsauslieferung R & B

Verlagsgruppe J Fink GmbH & Co KG+
Siemensstr 52, 70469 Stuttgart
Tel: (0711) 81 4646 *Fax:* (0711) 81 06070
E-mail: info@fink-verlag.de
Web Site: www.fink-verlag.de
Telex: 723737 fkf d *Cable:* Buch-Fink
Key Personnel
Man Dir: Bodo Neiss; Wolfgang Titze
Man Dir, Rights & Permissions: Sigmund Zipperle
Rights & Permissions: Beatrice Weber
Public Relations: Helmut Braun
Founded: 1935
Firm has developed from an association between the German company J Fink (founded 1894) & the Swiss cartographic company Kuemmerly und Frey (founded 1852). The latter firm also continues as an independent company in Switzerland.
Subjects: Health, Nutrition, Nonfiction (General), Outdoor Recreation, Sports, Athletics
ISBN Prefix(es): 3-7718; 3-350; 3-89142; 3-9801113
Parent Company: Kummerly und Frey Verlag, Bern, Switzerland

Wilhelm Fink GmbH & Co Verlags-KG+
Juehenplatz 1-3, 33098 Paderborn
Tel: (05251) 127-5; (05251) 127-842 *Fax:* (05251) 127-860
E-mail: kontakt@fink.de
Web Site: www.fink.de *Cable:* FINK MUNCHEN
Key Personnel
Publisher: Ferdinand Schoeningh *Tel:* (05251) 127-777 *Fax:* (05252) 127-670 *E-mail:* info@schoeningh.de
Editor & Man Dir: Dr Raimar Zons
Founded: 1962
Subjects: Archaeology, Art, History, Language Arts, Linguistics, Literature, Literary Criticism, Essays, Music, Dance, Philosophy, Psychology, Psychiatry, Social Sciences, Sociology
ISBN Prefix(es): 3-7705
Imprints: Poetik und Hermeneutik; Bild und Text
Orders to: Ferdinand Schoeningh Verlag, Juehenplatz 1-3, 33098 Paderborn *Tel:* (05251) 1 27-777 *Fax:* (05251) 1 27-670 *E-mail:* info@schoeningh.de

Finken Junior, *imprint of* Finken Verlag GmbH

Finken-Verlag, see Finken Verlag GmbH

Finken Verlag GmbH+
Zimmersmuhlenweg 40, 61440 Oberursel
Mailing Address: Postfach 1546, 61405 Oberursel
Tel: (06171) 6388-0 *Fax:* (06171) 6388-44
E-mail: info@finken.de
Web Site: www.finken.de *Cable:* NEUER FINKENVERLAG OBERURSEL
Key Personnel
Dir: Manfred Krick
Foreign Rights: Karoline Jockel *E-mail:* karoline.jockel@finken.de
Founded: 1985
Specialize in learning & teaching material for children from 3 to 12 years-old at school & at home, LOGICO™-the new learning system with selfchecking; also reading skills & early learning.
Membership(s): Deutscher Didacta Verband-Germany, Worlddidac Association, Boersenverein des deutschen Buchhandels Germany.
Subjects: Education, English as a Second Language, Mathematics, Natural History
ISBN Prefix(es): 3-8084
Imprints: Finken Junior

Harald Fischer Verlag GmbH+
Theaterplatz 31, 91054 Erlangen
Mailing Address: Postfach 1565, 91005 Erlangen
Tel: (09131) 205620 *Fax:* (09131) 206028
E-mail: info@haraldfischerverlag.de
Web Site: www.haraldfischerverlag.de
Key Personnel
Contact: Dr Claudia Schorcht
Founded: 1984
Microfiche Editions.
Membership(s): Boersenverein des dt Buchhandels.
Subjects: Disability, Special Needs, Engineering (General), History, Language Arts, Linguistics, Library & Information Sciences, Medicine, Nursing, Dentistry, Philosophy, Publishing & Book Trade Reference, Religion - Jewish, Science (General), Women's Studies
ISBN Prefix(es): 3-89131
Total Titles: 350 Print; 2 CD-ROM

Verkehrs-Verlag J Fischer GmbH & Co KG
Paulusstr 1, 40237 Duesseldorf

PUBLISHERS GERMANY

Mailing Address: Postfach 140265, 40072 Duesseldorf
Tel: (0211) 99193-0 *Fax:* (0211) 6801544; (0211) 9919327
E-mail: vvf@verkehrsverlag-fischer.de
Web Site: www.verkehrsverlag-fischer.de
Key Personnel
Publisher: Paul Urban *Tel:* (0211) 9919311
  E-mail: paul.urban@verkehrsverlag-fischer.de
Founded: 1904
Subjects: Transportation
ISBN Prefix(es): 3-87841

Karin Fischer Verlag GmbH+
Wallstr 50, 52064 Aachen
Mailing Address: Postfach 10 21 32, 52021 Aachen
Tel: (0241) 960 90 90 *Fax:* (0241) 960 90 99
Web Site: www.karin-fischer-verlag.de
Key Personnel
President & Editor: Karin Fischer
Reader: Dr Manfred S Fischer
Founded: 1989
Subjects: Fiction, Literature, Literary Criticism, Essays, Nonfiction (General), Philosophy, Poetry, Social Sciences, Sociology
ISBN Prefix(es): 3-927854; 3-89514

Verlag Reinhard Fischer
Weltistr 34, 81477 Munich
Tel: (089) 791 88 92 *Fax:* (089) 791 83 10
E-mail: verlagfischer@compuserve.de
Web Site: www.verlag-reinhard-fischer.de
Key Personnel
Owner: Reinhard Fischer
Founded: 1982
Subjects: Communications, Journalism, Marketing, Radio, TV
ISBN Prefix(es): 3-88927

Rita G Fischer Verlag+
Orberstr 30, 60386 Frankfurt
Tel: (069) 941942-0 *Fax:* (069) 941942-99; (069) 941942-98
E-mail: r.g.fischer.verlag@t-online.de
Web Site: www.buchhandel.de/r.g.fischer/
Key Personnel
Man Dir: Rita G Fischer *E-mail:* r.g.fisher.verlag@t-online.de
Founded: 1977
Subjects: Engineering (General), Fiction, Government, Political Science, How-to, Medicine, Nursing, Dentistry, Poetry, Psychology, Psychiatry, Social Sciences, Sociology
ISBN Prefix(es): 3-88323; 3-89406; 3-89501; 3-8301

S Fischer Verlag GmbH+
Hedderichstr 114, 60596 Frankfurt am Main
Mailing Address: Postfach 700355, 60553 Frankfurt am Main
Tel: (069) 6062-0 *Fax:* (069) 6062-319
Web Site: www.fischerverlage.de *Cable:* BUCHFISCHER
Key Personnel
Man Dir: Dr Joerg Bong; Lothar Kleiner; Peter Lohmann; Monika Schoeller
Founded: 1886
Subjects: Fiction, Literature, Literary Criticism, Essays, Nonfiction (General)
ISBN Prefix(es): 3-10
Subsidiaries: Wolfgang Krueger Verlag; Fischer Taschenbuch Verlag

Fischer Taschenbuch Verlag GmbH+
Subsidiary of S Fischer Verlag GmbH
Hedderichstr 114, 60596 Frankfurt am Main
Tel: (069) 60620 *Fax:* (069) 6062352
Web Site: www.s-fischer.de
Key Personnel
Man Dir: Monika Schoeller; Dr Hubertus Schenkel

Man Dir, Rights & Permissions: Wolfgang Mertz
Sales: Ralf Alkenbrecher
Publicity: Margarete Schwind
Production: Wilfried Meiner
Editorial: Martin Bauer; Dr Ursula Koehler
Founded: 1952
Subjects: Biography, History, Literature, Literary Criticism, Essays, Nonfiction (General), Psychology, Psychiatry, Women's Studies
ISBN Prefix(es): 3-596

Fit fuers Leben Verlag, *imprint of* NaturaViva Verlags GmbH

Flaschenpost, *imprint of* Keysersche Verlagsbuchhandlung GmbH

Flechsig Buchvertrieb
Imprint of Verlagshaus Wurzburg
Beethovenstr 5, 97070 Wurzburg
Tel: (0931) 385235 *Fax:* (0931) 385305
E-mail: info@verlagshaus.com
Web Site: www.verlagshaus.com
Key Personnel
Publishing Dir: Dieter Krause
Dir, Production: Juergen Roth
Sales Dir: Johannes Glesius
Subjects: Travel

Erich Fleischer Verlag
Postfach 1264, 28818 Achim
Tel: (04202) 517-0 *Fax:* (04202) 517-41
E-mail: info@efv-online.de
Web Site: www.efv-online.de
Key Personnel
Contact: Gerhard Schroeter *Tel:* (04202) 51729
  E-mail: schroeter@efv-online.de
Founded: 1954
Subjects: Law
ISBN Prefix(es): 3-8168
Number of titles published annually: 10 Print; 2 CD-ROM
Total Titles: 50 Print; 9 CD-ROM

Fleischhauer & Spohn GmbH & Co
Mundelsheimerstr 3, 74321 Bietigsheim-Bissingen
Mailing Address: Postfach 1764, 74307 Bietigsheim-Bissingen
Tel: (07142) 596161 *Fax:* (07142) 596280
E-mail: info@verlag-fleischhauer.de
Web Site: www.verlag-fleischhauer.de
Telex: 724237 umco d
Key Personnel
Marketing: Dieter Keilbach
Man Dir: Dr Max Bez; Thomas Bez; Martin Roth; Simone Roth
Founded: 1830
Subjects: History, Regional Interests, Travel
ISBN Prefix(es): 3-87230
Associate Companies: Barsortiment G Umbreit GmbH & Co (book wholesaler)

Flensburger Hefte Verlag GmbH+
Holm 64, 24937 Flensburg
Tel: (0461) 2 63 63; (0461) 2 14 72 *Fax:* (0461) 2 69 12
E-mail: flensburgerhefte@t-online.de
Web Site: www.flensburgerhefte.de
Key Personnel
Man Dir: Wolfgang Weirauch
Founded: 1987
Subjects: Education, Health, Nutrition, History, Human Relations, Philosophy, Religion - Other, Social Sciences, Sociology
ISBN Prefix(es): 3-926841; 3-935679
Warehouse: Helemenallee 4, 24937 Flensburg

Flugzeug Publikations GmbH+
Thomas Mannstr 3, 89257 Illertissen
Mailing Address: Postfach 3055, 89253 Illertissen
Tel: (07303) 964220 *Fax:* (07303) 964141

E-mail: flugzeug@charter.net
Web Site: webpages.charter.net/flugzeug
Key Personnel
Sales: Manfred Franzke; Werner Richter
Founded: 1985
Subjects: Aeronautics, Aviation, History
ISBN Prefix(es): 3-927132
Total Titles: 4 Print

FN-Verlag der Deutschen Reiterlichen Vereinigung GmbH+
Freiherr-von-Langenstr 8a, 48231 Warendorf
Tel: (02581) 63 62-115 *Fax:* (02581) 63 31 46
E-mail: fnverlag@fn-dokr.de
Web Site: www.fnverlag.de
Telex: 258113 FENGER
Key Personnel
Manager: Siegmund Friedrich; Rainer Reisloh
  Tel: (02581) 63 62-205
Marketing: Heike Ourajini *Tel:* (02581) 63 62-221
  E-mail: hourajini@fn-dokr.de
Sales: Tamara Erkelenz *Tel:* (02581) 63 62-154
  E-mail: terkelenz@fn-dokr.de; Tanja Kneupper
  Tel: (02851) 63 62-254 *E-mail:* tkneupper@fn-dokr.de
Founded: 1977
Subjects: Film, Video
ISBN Prefix(es): 3-88542

Focus-Verlag Gesellschaft mbH+
Unterer Hardthof 29, 35398 Giessen
Tel: (0641) 76031; (0641) 68225 (orders)
  Fax: (0641) 76031; (0641) 68331 (orders)
E-mail: info@focus-verlag.de
Web Site: www.focus-verlag.de
Key Personnel
Man Dir, Sales, Rights & Permissions: Mr Schmid
Publicity, Advertising Dir: Mr Neuhofer
Founded: 1970
Subjects: Environmental Studies, History, Psychology, Psychiatry, Social Sciences, Sociology
ISBN Prefix(es): 3-920352; 3-88349

Forum, *imprint of* Wissenschaftliche Buchgesellschaft

Forum Verlag GmbH & Co
Schrempfstr 8, 70597 Stuttgart
Tel: (0711) 76727-0 *Fax:* (0711) 76727-28
E-mail: info@forumverlag.de
Web Site: www.forumverlag.de
Founded: 1964
Our journal *Deutsches Architektenblatt* is sent to every architect who is a member of the German Architektenkammer, approximately 110,000 monthly.
Subjects: Architecture & Interior Design
ISBN Prefix(es): 3-8091

Forum Verlag Leipzig Buch-Gesellschaft mbH+
Gottschedstr 30, 04109 Leipzig
Tel: (0341) 9 80 50 08 *Fax:* (0341) 9 80 50 07
E-mail: info@forumverlagleipzig.de
Web Site: www.forumverlagleipzig.de
Key Personnel
Manager: Helen Jannsen
Founded: 1989
Membership(s): Leipzig Topsellers; Specialize in GDR History.
Subjects: Government, Political Science, History, Humor, Nonfiction (General), Regional Interests
ISBN Prefix(es): 3-931801
Total Titles: 1 Audio
Orders to: L K G mbH, Poetzschauer Weg, 04579 Espenhain *Fax:* (0342) 0665110

Forum Wissenschaft Studien, *imprint of* Bund demokratischer Wissenschaftlerinnen und Wissenschafler eV (BdWi)

GERMANY

Fouque-Literaturverlag, *imprint of* Frankfurter Literaturverlag GmbH

Fouque-Publishers Inc, *imprint of* Frankfurter Literaturverlag GmbH

Verlag der Francke Buchhandlung GmbH+
Am Schwanhof 19, 35037 Marburg
Mailing Address: Postfach 200640, 35018 Marburg
Tel: (06421) 17 25-0 *Fax:* (06421) 17 25-30
E-mail: info@francke-buch.de
Web Site: www.francke-buch.de
Key Personnel
Man Dir, Editorial & Publicity: Uwe Schmidt
Sales: Margot Agel
Founded: 1934
Firm is contributor to the Telos series of evangelical paperbacks.
Subjects: Theology
ISBN Prefix(es): 3-88224; 3-86122
Bookshop(s): Gunzenhausen; Velbert; Lemfoerde; Oberursel; Elbingerode; Neustadt

Franckh-Kosmos Verlags-GmbH & Co+
Pfizerstr 5-7, 70184 Stuttgart
Mailing Address: Postfach 10 60 11, 70049 Stuttgart
Tel: (0711) 2191-0 *Fax:* (0711) 2191-422
E-mail: info@kosmos.de
Web Site: www.kosmos.de
Telex: 721669 Kosm d *Cable:* KOSMOS VERLAG STUTTGART
Key Personnel
President: Axel Meffert *Tel:* (0711) 2191341
Publicity Dir: Bettina Schaub *Tel:* (0711) 2191341 *Fax:* (0711) 2191141 *E-mail:* b.schaub@kosmos.de
Production Dir: Juergen Bischoff *Tel:* (0711) 2191221 *Fax:* (0711) 2191121 *E-mail:* j.bischoff@kosmos.de
Foreign Rights Dir: Andrea D Ahlers *Tel:* (0711) 2191254 *Fax:* (0711) 2191154 *E-mail:* a.ahlers@kosmos.de
Marketing Dir: Manfred Haarer *Tel:* (0711) 2191401 *Fax:* (0711) 2191101 *E-mail:* m.haarer@kosmos.de; Heiko Windfelder *Tel:* (0711) 2191322 *Fax:* (0711) 2191122; Birgit Carlsen *Tel:* (0711) 21911205 *Fax:* (0711) 21911205 *E-mail:* b.carlsen@kosmos.de
Founded: 1822
Specialize in fishing & hunting.
Subjects: Animals, Pets, Astronomy, Biological Sciences, Chemistry, Chemical Engineering, Crafts, Games, Hobbies, Electronics, Electrical Engineering, Engineering (General), Environmental Studies, Fiction, Gardening, Plants, Geography, Geology, House & Home, Natural History, Nonfiction (General), Outdoor Recreation, Physics, Science (General), Technology
ISBN Prefix(es): 3-440
Number of titles published annually: 120 Print
Total Titles: 600 Print
Parent Company: Buchverlage Langen Mueller Herbig
Associate Companies: F A Herbig (Munich); Klee-Spiele GmbH (Fuerth)
Warehouse: VVA, An der Autobahn, 33310 Guetersloh

Verlag Frankfurter Buecher, *imprint of* Societaets-Verlag

Frankfurter Literaturverlag GmbH (Frankfurt Publishing Group)+
Formerly Dr Haensel-Hohenhausen AG
Hanauer Landstr 338, 60314 Frankfurt am Main
Tel: (069) 40894-0 *Fax:* (069) 40894-194
E-mail: info@haensel-hohenhausen.de
Web Site: www.cgl-verlag.de
Founded: 1987
Membership(s): AAP; ABA; World Union of Publishers.
ISBN Prefix(es): 3-8267; 3-89349
Number of titles published annually: 250 Print
Total Titles: 2,000 Print
Imprints: Deutsche Bibliothek der Wissenschaften/German Library of Sciences; Deutsche Hochschulschriften/German University Studies; Fouque-Literaturverlag; Fouque-Publishers Inc; Cornelia Goethe Literaturverlag
Foreign Rep(s): Fouque London Publishers

Frankfurter Societaets-Druckerei GmbH, see Societaets-Verlag

FVA-Frankfurter Verlagsanstalt GmbH+
Danneckerstr 39A, 60594 Frankfurt am Main
Tel: (069) 96220610 *Fax:* (069) 96220630
E-mail: info@frankfurter-verlagsanstalt.de
Web Site: www.frankfurter-verlagsanstalt.de
Key Personnel
Publisher: Dr Joachim Unseld
Manager: Dagmar Fretter *E-mail:* fretter@frankfurter-verlagsanstalt.de
Foreign Rights: Ricarda von Bergen *Tel:* (069) 962206 15
Founded: 1986
Subjects: Biography
ISBN Prefix(es): 3-627
Parent Company: Unseld
Associate Companies: Sophienbuchhandlung
Orders to: Libri Distribution, August-Schanz-Str 33, 60433 Frankfurt am Main

Franz-Sales-Verlag+
Rosental 1, 85072 Eichstaett
Tel: (08421) 9 34 89-31 *Fax:* (08421) 9 34 89-35
E-mail: info@franz-sales-verlag.de
Web Site: www.franz-sales-verlag.de
Key Personnel
President & Editor: P Herbert Winklehner *E-mail:* herbert.winklehner@franz-sales-verlag.de
Founded: 1931
Disseminate the work of St Francis de Soles (1567-1622) into the modern world.
Membership(s): VKB, AKB, Borsenverein Des Deutschen Buchhandels & Verband Bayrischer Verleger Und Buchhandler.
Subjects: Art, Biography, Religion - Catholic, Theology
ISBN Prefix(es): 3-7721
Total Titles: 100 Print

Verlag Franz Vahlen GmbH+
Wilhelmstr 9, 80801 Munich
Tel: (089) 38189-381 *Fax:* (089) 38189-402
E-mail: info@vahlen.de
Web Site: www.vahlen.de
Key Personnel
Manager: Dr Hans D Beck
Founded: 1870
Subjects: Economics, Finance, Law, Management, Marketing
ISBN Prefix(es): 3-8006
Associate Companies: Verlag C H Beck (OHG)

Franzis-Verlag GmbH+
Gruberstr 46a, 85586 Poing
Tel: (08121) 95 0 *Fax:* (08121) 95 16 96
E-mail: info@franzis.de
Web Site: www.franzis.de
Key Personnel
Man Dir: Dr Ruediger Hennings; Werner Muetzel
Founded: 1924
Subjects: Communications, Computer Science, Electronics, Electrical Engineering
ISBN Prefix(es): 3-7723
Parent Company: WEKA Firmengruppe GmbH & Co KG

Frauenoffensive Verlagsgesellschaft MbH+
Metzstr 14C, 81667 Munich
Tel: (089) 489500-48 *Fax:* (089) 489500-49
Key Personnel
Dir, Rights & Permissions: Gerlinde Kowitzke
Editorial: H Schlaeger
Sales: S Kohlstadt
Founded: 1974
Subjects: Women's Studies
ISBN Prefix(es): 3-88104

Fraunhofer IRB Verlag Fraunhofer Informationszentrum Raum und Bau+
Division of Fraunhofer-Gesellschaft
Nobelstr 12, 70569 Stuttgart
Mailing Address: Postfach 800469, 70504 Stuttgart
Tel: (0711) 9 70-25 00 *Fax:* (0711) 9 70-25 07
E-mail: irb@irb.fhg.de
Web Site: www.irbdirekt.de
Key Personnel
Man Dir: Dr Wilhelm Wissmann
Sales Manager: Barbara Scherer
Founded: 1947
Specialize in literature on building construction, building damages & regional planning.
Subjects: Architecture & Interior Design, Civil Engineering, Earth Sciences, Environmental Studies, House & Home, Outdoor Recreation, Regional Interests
ISBN Prefix(es): 3-8167
Number of titles published annually: 100 Print; 6 CD-ROM
Total Titles: 20 Print; 6 CD-ROM

frechverlag GmbH+
Turbinenstr 7, 70499 Stuttgart
Tel: (0711) 83086-11 *Fax:* (0711) 83086-86
E-mail: kundenservice@frechverlag.de
Web Site: www.frech.de
Key Personnel
Man Dir: Marion Milkau; Werner Muetzel
Business Manager & Sales: Berud Leuz
Founded: 1955
Specialize in Hobby & Leisure Activities.
Subjects: Crafts, Games, Hobbies, Electronics, Electrical Engineering
ISBN Prefix(es): 3-7724

Fredebeul und Koenen GmbH
Ruhrtalstr 52-60, 45239 Essen
Mailing Address: Postfach 164180, 45221 Essen
Tel: (0201) 49821 *Fax:* (0201) 8492415
Key Personnel
Man Dir: Dr Albert E Fischer
ISBN Prefix(es): 3-87236

Frederking & Thaler Verlag GmbH+
Infanteriestr 19, Haus 2, 80797 Munich
Tel: (089) 4372-0 *Fax:* (089) 4372-2854
Key Personnel
Owner, Publisher & International Rights: Monika Thaler *Tel:* (089) 12113 11 *E-mail:* monikathaler@frederking-thaler.de
Founded: 1988 (as independent publisher, 1998-2001 Bertelsmann/Random House Publishing Group, in 2002 independent publisher)
Specialize in high quality illustrated books in the realm of wonders of nature, foreign cultures & their spiritual worlds. Also nonfiction narrative reports (culture, nature & travel).
Subjects: Archaeology, Art, Foreign Countries, Photography, Travel, World Religions
ISBN Prefix(es): 3-89405
Number of titles published annually: 30 Print
Total Titles: 120 Print; 120 E-Book
Imprints: Villa Arceno; Sierra
Warehouse: VVA Bertelsmann Distribution, 33310 Guetersloh

Erika G Freese Verlag+
Potsdamerstr 16, 12205 Berlin
Tel: (030) 8333077 *Fax:* (030) 8333077

E-mail: eg.freese@t-online.de
Key Personnel
Man Dir, Rights & Permissions: Erika Freese
Founded: 1982
Membership(s): the Stock Market of German Booksellers.
ISBN Prefix(es): 3-88942
Orders to: Buchvertrieb Grimmstrasse, Grimmstrasse 27, 12305 Berlin 16

Verlag Freies Geistesleben+
Division of Verlag Freies Geistesleben & Urachhaus GmbH
Postfach 131122, 70069 Stuttgart
Tel: (0711) 28532 00 *Fax:* (0711) 28532 10
E-mail: info@geistesleben.com
Web Site: www.geistesleben.com
Key Personnel
Publishing Dir: Jean-Claude Lin *Tel:* (0711) 2853221 *E-mail:* lin@geistesleben.com; Andreas Neider *E-mail:* a.neider@geistesleben.com
Sales: Reinhardt Stiehle *Tel:* (0711) 2853232 *E-mail:* r.steihle@geistesleben.com
Founded: 1947
Membership(s): Community of Youth Book Publishers.
Subjects: Art, Biography, Education, History, How-to, Medicine, Nursing, Dentistry, Music, Dance, Philosophy, Psychology, Psychiatry, Religion - Other, Science (General), Social Sciences, Sociology, Picture books
ISBN Prefix(es): 3-7725
Number of titles published annually: 60 Print
Total Titles: 800 Print
Imprints: Aethera
Orders to: Koch, Neff & Oetinger, Schockenriedstr 39, Postfach 800620, Stuttgart *Tel:* (0711) 78992140 *Fax:* (0711) 78991010

Freiherr von Stein Gedaechtnisausgabe, *imprint of* Wissenschaftliche Buchgesellschaft

Freimund-Verlag der Gesellschaft fur Innere und Aeussere Mission im Sinne der Lutherischen Kirche eV
Ringstr 15, 91564 Neuendettelsau
Mailing Address: Postfach 48, 91561 Neuendettelsau
Tel: (09874) 6 89 39 80 *Fax:* (09874) 6 89 39 99
E-mail: info@freimund-verlag.de
Web Site: www.freimund-buchhandlung.de/verlag
Key Personnel
Man Dir: Dr Martin Kobler; Hildegard Wickert
Founded: 1933
Subjects: Religion - Other
ISBN Prefix(es): 3-7726
Bookshop(s): Freimund-Buchhandlung, Hauptstr 2, 91564 Neuendettelsau

Margarethe Freudenberger - selbstverlag fur jedermann+
Gartenstr 22, 97906 Faulbach
Tel: (09392) 8449
Founded: 1979
Subjects: Art, Fiction, How-to, Human Relations, Humor, Poetry
ISBN Prefix(es): 3-924711

Verlag Walter Frey+
Postfach 30 36 26, 10727 Berlin
Tel: (030) 883 25 61 *Fax:* (030) 883 25 61
E-mail: tranvia@aol.com
Key Personnel
Man Dir: Walter Frey
Founded: 1985
Publish literature of & about Spain, Portugal & Latin America.
Subjects: Regional Interests, Spain, Portugal, Latin America

ISBN Prefix(es): 3-925867
Number of titles published annually: 10 Print

FRICK Verlag-GmbH+
Postfach 447, 75104, Pforzheim
Tel: (07231) 102842 *Fax:* (07231) 357744
E-mail: info@frickverlag.de
Web Site: www.frickverlag.de
Key Personnel
Man Dir: Beate D Frick
Founded: 1970
Specialize in Religion, Metaphysics, Esoteric.
Membership(s): Deutschief Bosenverlise.
ISBN Prefix(es): 3-920780
Number of titles published annually: 3 Print
Total Titles: 3 Print
Branch Office(s)
Haupt, Str 279, Rosrath, Contact: Thele Jung *Tel:* (02205) 3308 *Fax:* (02205) 53308
Witere Weinberg, Str 11-1, Eisengen, Contact: Peter D'Orazio *Tel:* (07232) 383083 *Fax:* (07232) 383084

Erhard Friedrich Verlag
Im Brande 17, 30926 Seelze
Mailing Address: Postfach 10 01 50, 30917 Seelze
Tel: (0511) 400040 *Fax:* (0511) 40004-119
E-mail: info@friedrich-verlag.de
Web Site: www.friedrich-verlagsgruppe.de
Telex: 0922923 *Cable:* FRIEDRICH
Key Personnel
International Rights: Uwe Brinkmann
Publisher: Erhard Friedrich
Founded: 1960
Subjects: Art, Drama, Theater, Education
ISBN Prefix(es): 3-617

Friedrich Kiehl Verlag GmbH+
Postfach 140108, 67021 Ludwigshafen
Tel: (0621) 6 35 02-0 *Fax:* (0621) 6 35 02-22
E-mail: info@kiehl.de
Web Site: www.kiehl.de
Telex: 464810 Kiehl d
Key Personnel
Dir: Ernst-Otto Kleyboldt; Dr Karl-Friedrich Peter
Sales Manager: Klaus Bissinger
Rights & Permissions, International Rights: Adolf Schmidt
Founded: 1932
Subjects: Advertising, Business, Career Development, Computer Science, Economics, Education, Finance, Law, Marketing, Medicine, Nursing, Dentistry
ISBN Prefix(es): 3-470
Parent Company: Verlag Neue Wirtschafts-Briefe GmbH
Distributed by Linde-Verlag
Distributor for Linde-Verlag Ostereicli
Warehouse: Schuechtermannstr 180, 44628 Herne

Frieling & Partner GmbH
Huenefeldzeile 18, 12247 Berlin-Steglitz
Tel: (030) 7 66 99 90 *Fax:* (030) 7 74 41 03
Web Site: www.frieling.de *Cable:* FRIELING BERLIN
Key Personnel
Publisher: Wilhelm Ruprecht Frieling
Man Dir: Dr Johann-Friedrich Huffmann *E-mail:* gf@frieling.de
Editor: Peter Hehr *E-mail:* redaktion@frieling.de
Founded: 1871
ISBN Prefix(es): 3-89009

Verlag A Fromm im Druck- u Verlagshaus Fromm GmbH & Co KG+
Breiter Gang 10-16, 49074 Osnabrueck
Mailing Address: Postfach 1948, 49009 Osnabrueck
Tel: (0541) 3100 *Fax:* (0541) 310315; (0541) 310440

Telex: 94916 fromm d
Key Personnel
Publisher: Leo V Fromm
Chief Executive Officer & International Rights: Annette Harms-Hunold
Sales Manager: Annegret Busch
Public Relations: Ursula Malzahn
Founded: 1868 (Parent Company)
Subjects: Economics, Education, Environmental Studies, Ethnicity, Government, Political Science, History, Science (General), Social Sciences, Sociology
ISBN Prefix(es): 3-7729
Parent Company: Druck- und Verlagshaus Fromm GmbH & Co KG
Associate Companies: Fromm International Publishing Corp, 560 Lexington Ave, New York, NY 10022, United States
Imprints: Osnabrueck
Branch Office(s)
Edition Interfrom AG, Postfach 5005, Zurich, Switzerland *Tel:* (0041) 1 202 0900

Friedrich Frommann Verlag+
Koenig-Karlstr 27, 70372 Stuttgart
Tel: (0711) 955969-0 *Fax:* (0711) 955969-1
E-mail: info@frommann-holzboog.de
Web Site: www.frommann-holzboog.de
Key Personnel
Man Dir: Eckhart Holzboog *E-mail:* eckhart.holzboog@frommann-holzboog.de
Editor: Tina Koch *E-mail:* lekorat@frommann-holzboog.de
Press & Promotion Manager: Sybille Wittmann *E-mail:* werbung-presse@frommann-holzboog.de
Production Manager: Karl-Heinz Paczkowski *E-mail:* herstellung@frommann-holzboog.de
Rights & Permissions: Kerstin Hamm
Marketing Assistant: Ulrike Doerr
Founded: 1727
Specialize in fine editions & textbooks. Independent publisher of arts & humanities. Titles with a focus in philosophy, psychoanalysis & theology.
Subjects: History, Language Arts, Linguistics, Law, Literature, Literary Criticism, Essays, Mathematics, Philosophy, Psychology, Psychiatry, Religion - Protestant, Social Sciences, Sociology, Theology
ISBN Prefix(es): 3-7728
Number of titles published annually: 40 Print
Total Titles: 1,300 Print

Fuldaer Verlagsanstalt GmbH
Rangstr 3-7, 36037 Fulda
Tel: (0661) 295-0 *Fax:* (0661) 295-71
E-mail: info@fva.de
Web Site: www.fva.de
Telex: 49739-FVAD
Key Personnel
Contact: Reinhold Hartwich
Subsidiaries: Vito von Eichborn GmbH & Co, Verlag KG

FVA, see FVA-Frankfurter Verlagsanstalt GmbH

G Braun (vormals G Braun'sche Hofbuchdruckerei und Verlag) Gmbh+
Karl-Friedrich-Str 14-18, 76133 Karlsruhe
Tel: (0721) 1607320 *Fax:* (0721) 1607321
E-mail: kohler.buchverlag@gbraun.de
Web Site: www.gbraun.de
Telex: 7826904
Key Personnel
Publisher: Klaus Kapp
Dir: Georg van Griesheim; Peter Scheuble
Founded: 1813
Subjects: Art, History, Regional Interests, Travel
ISBN Prefix(es): 3-7650

Gabal-Verlag GmbH+
Schumannstr 163, 63069 Offenbach

GERMANY

Mailing Address: Postfach 200252, 63077 Offenbach
Tel: (069) 84 000 66-0 *Fax:* (069) 84 000 66-66
E-mail: support@gabal-verlag.de
Web Site: www.gabal-verlag.de
Key Personnel
Man Editor: Helmut Juergen
Founded: 1979 (Vorlaufer)
Subjects: How-to, Literature, Literary Criticism, Essays, Management
ISBN Prefix(es): 3-923984; 3-89749; 3-930799
Parent Company: Juergen Verlag GmbH
Associate Companies: PLS Sprachen, 176 Solothurn, Switzerland
Subsidiaries: Rot Gelb Grain Verlag
Divisions: Verlag

Verlagsbuchhandlung Megapress, Franz-J Gaber+
Gartenstr 12, 63218 Dietzenbach
Tel: (0610) 225951; (0610) 2327044 *Fax:* (0610) 231018
Key Personnel
Publisher: F J Gaber
Founded: 1977
Subjects: Government, Political Science
ISBN Prefix(es): 3-87979

Betriebswirtschaftlicher Verlag Dr Th Gabler+
Unit of GWV Fachverlage GMBH
Abraham-Lincoln-Str 46, 65189 Wiesbaden
Mailing Address: Postfach 1546, 65173 Wiesbaden
Tel: (0611) 7878470 *Fax:* (0611) 787878400
Web Site: www.gwv-fachverlage.de
Key Personnel
General Manager: Dr Hans-Dieter Haenel
  E-mail: hans-dieter.haenel@gwv-fachverlage.de
Man Dir: Dr Heinz Weinheimer
Editorial: Claudia Splittgerber; Ulrike Vetter
Sales & Marketing Manager: Rolf-Guenther Hobbeling
Rights & Permissions: Angelika Bolisega
  Tel: (0611) 7878361 *Fax:* 0611 7878470
  E-mail: angelike.bolisega@gwv-fachverlage.de
Editorial: Maria Akhavan
Founded: 1929
Professional information for managers, personal assistants; textbooks for students, encyclopedias.
Subjects: Accounting, Business, Economics, Finance, Management, Marketing
ISBN Prefix(es): 3-409
Total Titles: 1,500 Print
Parent Company: Springer Science & Business Media
Distribution Center: VVA Bertelsmann Distribution, Postfach 7777, D-33310 Guetersloh

Gabriel Verlag, *imprint of* Thienemann Verlag GmbH

Galerie Der Spiegel-Dr E Stunke Nachfolge GmbH
Richartzstr 10, 50667 Cologne
Tel: (0221) 25 55 52 *Fax:* (0221) 25 55 53
E-mail: der-spiegel@galerie.de
Web Site: www.galerie.de/der-spiegel
Founded: 1945
Specialize in international art editions & book catalogue portfolios.
Membership(s): Bundesverband Deutscher Galerie & Boisenvereln Des Deutschen Buchhandels.
Subjects: Art
ISBN Prefix(es): 3-87285

Galrev Druck-und Verlagsgesellschaft Hesse & Partner OHG+
Lychenerstr 73, 10437 Berlin
Tel: (030) 44 65 01 83 *Fax:* (030) 44 65 01 84
E-mail: galrev@galrev.com
Web Site: www.galrev.com
Key Personnel
Manager: Egmont Hesse; Rainer Schedlinski
Founded: 1989
Subjects: Poetry
ISBN Prefix(es): 3-910161; 3-933149

Gatzanis Verlags GmbH
Alte Weinsteige 28, 70180 Stuttgart
Tel: (0711) 9640570 *Fax:* (0711) 9640572
E-mail: info@gatzanis.de
Web Site: www.gatzanis.de
Key Personnel
Owner: Jolanta Gatzanis
Founded: 1995
Subjects: Art, Biography, Child Care & Development, Gay & Lesbian, Human Relations, Humor, Self-Help
ISBN Prefix(es): 3-932855; 3-9803897
Number of titles published annually: 2 Print
Total Titles: 13 Print

Gebrueder Borntraeger Science Publishers+
Affiliate of E Schweizerbart'sche Verlagsbuchhandlung
Johannesstr 3 A, 70176 Stuttgart
Tel: (0711) 3514560 *Fax:* (0711) 35145699
E-mail: mail@schweizerbart.de
Web Site: www.schweizerbart.de
Key Personnel
Man Dir, Sales: Dr Walter Obermiller
Man Dir, Production: Dr Erhard Naegele
Exhibition Manager: Martina Ihringer
Founded: 1790
Subjects: Biological Sciences, Earth Sciences, Geography, Geology, Maritime
ISBN Prefix(es): 3-443
Imprints: Borntraeger Verlagsbuchhandlung

Konkursbuch Verlag Claudia Gehrke+
Hechingerstr 203, im Sudhaus, 72072 Tuebingen
Tel: (07071) 78779 *Fax:* (07071) 763780
E-mail: office@konkursbuch.com
Web Site: www.konkursbuch.com
Key Personnel
International Rights: Claudia Gehrke
Founded: 1978
Subjects: Literature, Literary Criticism, Essays, Travel, Women's Studies
ISBN Prefix(es): 3-88769

Verlag Junge Gemeinde E Schwinghammer GmbH & Co KG+
Max-Eyth-Str 13, 70771 Leinfelden-Echterdingen
Mailing Address: Postfach 100355, 70747 Leinfelden-Echterdingen
Tel: (0711) 99078-0 *Fax:* (0711) 99078-25 *Cable:* JUNGEGEMEINDEVERLAG
Key Personnel
Manager: Siegfried Krumrey
Founded: 1928
Specialize in books for Sunday school.
Subjects: Education, Religion - Protestant
ISBN Prefix(es): 3-7797

Genius Verlag (Genius Publishing House)+
Aach 34, 87534 Oberstaufen
Tel: (08386) 960401 *Fax:* (08386) 960402
E-mail: contact@genius-verlag.de
Web Site: www.genius-verlag.de
Key Personnel
Contact: Dagmar Neubronner
Founded: 1997
Publish spiritual books.
Subjects: Biblical Studies, Biography, Career Development, Human Relations, Music, Dance, Philosophy, Science (General), Self-Help, Theology
ISBN Prefix(es): 3-9806106; 3-934719
Number of titles published annually: 3 Print
Total Titles: 12 Print

Alfons W Gentner Verlag GmbH & Co KG+
Forststr 131, 70193 Stuttgart
Tel: (0711) 63672-0 *Fax:* (0711) 63672747
E-mail: gentner@gentnerverlag.de
Web Site: www.gentnerverlag.de
Key Personnel
Publisher: E F Reisch
Founded: 1927
Subjects: Automotive, Business, Career Development, Engineering (General), Environmental Studies, Medicine, Nursing, Dentistry
ISBN Prefix(es): 3-87247
Subsidiaries: B & V Kiado Kft; CNTL spool sra; EUROMEDIA; GEMA Strucna Naklada; Instalator Polski zoo; Magyar Mediprint Szakkiado Kft; Technischer Fachverlag GmbH; Verbatim Publishers (Pvt) Ltd

GeoCenter Touristik Medienservice GmbH
Schockenriedstr 44, 70565 Stuttgart
Mailing Address: Postfach 800830, 70508 Stuttgart
Tel: (0711) 781946 10 *Fax:* (0711) 7824375
E-mail: geocenterilh@t-online.de; vertrieb@geocenter.de
Web Site: www.geokatalog.de
Key Personnel
Man Dir: Dr Klaus Hohne *Tel:* (0711) 78 946 41; Hans Jurgen Pfister *Tel:* (0711) 78 946 41
Founded: 1971
Wholesaler in all kinds of maps, guides & geoscientific publications. Publisher of: Geokatalog; Touristic & Geokatalog; Geosciences.
Subjects: Geography, Geology
ISBN Prefix(es): 3-920137
Associate Companies: Touristik & Medien, Beimerstetten

Georgi GmbH+
Theaterstr 77, 52062 Aachen
Key Personnel
Man Dir: Manfred Georgi; Werner Georgi
Rights & Permissions: Adriane Georgi
Sales: Josef Brauers
Founded: 1928
Subjects: History, How-to, Music, Dance, Science (General)
ISBN Prefix(es): 3-87248; 3-8292
Subsidiaries: Georgi Publishers

Carl Gerber Verlag, see Schwaneberger Verlag GmbH

Gerhard Wolf Janus-Press GmbH+
Amalienpark 7, 13187 Berlin
Tel: (030) 47535220 *Fax:* (030) 47533790
Founded: 1990
ISBN Prefix(es): 3-928942

Germanisches Nationalmuseum
Kartausergasse 1, 90402 Nuernberg
Tel: (0911) 13310 *Fax:* (0911) 1331 200
E-mail: info@gnm.de
Web Site: www.gnm.de
Key Personnel
Chief, Publishing Dept: Dr Hermann Maue
Founded: 1853
Books & catalogues about artistic & cultural history from German speaking regions from prehistoric times to present, related to the museum's collections.
Subjects: Archaeology, Art, History, Science (General), Musical Instruments
ISBN Prefix(es): 3-926982; 3-936688
Number of titles published annually: 10 Print
Total Titles: 180 Print; 2 CD-ROM

Gerstenberg Verlag+
Rathausstr 18-20, 31134 Hildesheim
Mailing Address: Postfach 100555, 31105 Hildesheim

Tel: (05121) 1060 *Fax:* (05121) 106498
E-mail: verlag@gerstenberg-verlag.de
Web Site: www.gerstenberg-verlag.de
Telex: 927108 gberg d
Key Personnel
Man Dir: Dr Edmund Jacoby *Tel:* (05121) 106451 *E-mail:* dr.edmund.jacoby@gerstenberg-verlag.de
Editorial: Petra Albers *Tel:* (05121) 106460 *E-mail:* petra.albers@gerstenberg-verlag.de
Manager, Sales & Advertising: Wolfgang J Dietrich *Tel:* (05121) 106470 *E-mail:* wolfgang.dietrich@gerstenberg-verlag.de
Production: Friedrich Weskott *Tel:* (05121) 106465 *E-mail:* friedrich.weskott@gerstenberg-verlag.de
Rights & Permissions: Ina Feist *Tel:* (05121) 106454 *E-mail:* ina.feist@gerstenberg-verlag.de
Publicity: Andrea Deyerling-Baier *Tel:* (05121) 106456 *E-mail:* andrea.deyerlingbaier@gerstenberg-verlag.de
Founded: 1792
Subjects: Architecture & Interior Design, Gardening, Plants, Nonfiction (General)
ISBN Prefix(es): 3-8067

Klaus Gerth Musikverlag+
Dillerberg 2, 35614 Asslar
Mailing Address: Postfach 1148, 35607 Asslar
Tel: (06443) 68-0 *Fax:* (06443) 68-34
E-mail: info@gerth.de
Web Site: www.gerth.de
Key Personnel
Man Dir & International Rights: Klaus Gerth *Tel:* (06443) 6811 *Fax:* (06443) 6813 *E-mail:* gerth@gerth.de
Man Dir: Dieter Spahn
Founded: 1949
Subjects: Music, Dance, Religion - Other, Theology
ISBN Prefix(es): 3-89615; 3-922283
Distributor for Ganzteam Music

Gerth Medien GmbH+
Formerly Verlag Schulte und Gerth GmbH & Co KG
Dillerberg 2, 35614 Asslar
Mailing Address: Postfach 1148, 35607 Asslar-Berghausen
Tel: (06443) 68-0 *Fax:* (06443) 68-34
Web Site: www.gerth.de
Key Personnel
Man Dir: Klaus Gerth
Sales Dir: Rolf Fischer
Marketing Dir: Stefanie Goemmer; Hannes Boehm
Founded: 1949
Subjects: Biography, Fiction, Nonfiction (General), Religion - Other, Self-Help
ISBN Prefix(es): 3-89437
Number of titles published annually: 90 Print; 5 Audio
Total Titles: 500 Print; 25 Audio

Verlag fuer Geschichte der Naturwissenschaften und der Technik+
Schlossstr 1, 49356 Diepholz
Tel: (05441) 92 71 29 *Fax:* (05441) 92 71 27
E-mail: info@gnt-verlag.de
Web Site: www.gnt-verlag.de
Key Personnel
Publisher: Reinald Schroeder
Founded: 1990
Specialize in Scientific Publications.
Subjects: History, History of Science & Technology
ISBN Prefix(es): 3-928186
Shipping Address: LKG, Bestellannahme, Potzschauer Weg, 04579 Espenhain
Warehouse: LKG, Bestellannahme, Potzschauer Weg, 04579 Espenhain
Orders to: LKG Bestellannahme, Poetzschauer Weg, 04579 Espenhain

Gesellschaft fuer Organisationswissenschaft e V+
Haus No 18 A, 95490 Mistelgau-Truppach
Tel: (09206) 480 *Fax:* (09206) 628
Key Personnel
Chairman: Ruediger W Monz
Vice Chairman: Theodor Koenig
Founded: 1956
Spreading of Organization Science according to (& authorized by) the late Dr.techn. Kurt von Wieser, Vienna, by instruction & books. Sell rights of non-English translations.
Subjects: Social Sciences, Sociology
ISBN Prefix(es): 3-926980
Total Titles: 24 Print

Gesundheits-Dialog Verlag GmbH+
Gaenslerweg 1, 82041 Oberhaching
Mailing Address: Postfach 1453, 82033 Oberhaching
Tel: (089) 6 13 40 24 *Fax:* (089) 6 13 37 87
E-mail: dialog.top@t-online.de
Web Site: www.gesundheits-dialog.de
Key Personnel
Publisher: Franz Woellzenmueller
Subjects: Child Care & Development, Health, Nutrition, Medicine, Nursing, Dentistry, Sports, Athletics
ISBN Prefix(es): 3-929732

Gieck-Verlag GmbH+
Nimrodstr 26, 82110 Germering
Tel: (089) 8415906 *Fax:* (089) 8403310
Key Personnel
Contact: R Gieck
Founded: 1931
Subjects: Engineering (General), Mechanical Engineering
ISBN Prefix(es): 3-920379
Orders to: Alfaomega Grupo Editor, SA, Pitagoras 1139, Col Del Valle 03100, Mexico
Brockhaus Commission, Postfach 1220, 70806 Kornwestheim
Delta Press, Endseweg 3 NL, 3959 AT Amerongen, Overberg, Netherlands
Dunod, 5, rue Laromiguiere, 75241 Paris Cedex 05, France
McGraw Hill Inc, 1221 Avenue of the Americas, New York, NY 10020, United States

Verlag Ernst und Werner Gieseking GmbH
Deckertstr 30, 33617 Bielefeld
Mailing Address: Postfach 13 01 20, 33617 Bielefeld
Tel: (0521) 1 46 74 *Fax:* (0521) 14 37 15
E-mail: gieseking-verlag@t-online.de
Web Site: www.gieseking-verlag.de
Key Personnel
Man Dir & Publisher: Dr Klaus Schleicher
Founded: 1937
Subjects: Law, Music, Dance
ISBN Prefix(es): 3-7694
Orders to: VVA

H Gietl Verlag & Publikationsservice GmbH+
Pfaelzerstr 11, 93128 Regenstauf
Mailing Address: Postfach 166, 93122 Regenstauf
Tel: (09402) 93 37-0 *Fax:* (09402) 93 37-24
Web Site: www.gietl-verlag.de
Key Personnel
Man Dir: Heinrich Gietl *Tel:* (09402) 93 37-15 *E-mail:* heinrich.gietl@gietl-verlag.de; Josef Roidl *Tel:* (09402) 93 37-13 *E-mail:* josef.roidl@gietl-verlag.de
Advertising Manager: Kurt Fischer *Tel:* (09402) 93 37-14 *E-mail:* kurt.fischer@gietl-verlag.de
Special publishing house for numismatic literature.
Subjects: Crafts, Games, Hobbies, History

Gildefachverlag GmbH & Co KG+
Foehrster Str 8, 31061 Alfeld
Mailing Address: Postfach 1351, 31043 Alfeld
Tel: (05181) 8004-0 *Fax:* (05181) 8004-90
Key Personnel
Man Dir: Wilhelm Schlame
Founded: 1949
Specialize in Gastronomy & Crafts.
Subjects: Cookery, Crafts, Games, Hobbies, Health, Nutrition
ISBN Prefix(es): 3-7734
Imprints: IWT Magazine Publishing House GmbH
Subsidiaries: Gildebuchverlag

Gilles und Francke Verlag+
Blumenstr 67-69, 47057 Duisburg
Tel: (0203) 362787 *Fax:* (0203) 355520
E-mail: verlag@gilles-francke.de
Web Site: www.gilles-francke.de
Key Personnel
Publisher & Proprietor: Werner Francke
Sales: Barbara Francke
Founded: 1900
Subjects: Fiction, Literature, Literary Criticism, Essays, Poetry
ISBN Prefix(es): 3-921104; 3-925348
Number of titles published annually: 4 Print
Total Titles: 3 Print
Bookshop(s): G & F Buch und Zeitschriftenhandlung *E-mail:* buchversand@gilles-francke.de
Web Site: www.gilles-francke.de

GLB Parkland Verlags-und Vertriebs GmbH+
Schanzenstr 33, 51063 Cologne
Mailing Address: Postfach 800160, 51001 Cologne
Tel: (0221) 96493-0 *Fax:* (0221) 964933
Telex: 721907
Key Personnel
Man Dir: Gerd Fiegweil; Heiner Taubert
Founded: 1974
Subjects: Antiques, Architecture & Interior Design, Art, Gardening, Plants, Poetry, Travel
ISBN Prefix(es): 3-88059; 3-89340
Warehouse: VSB Verlagsservice Braunschweig GmbH, Georg-Westermann-Allee 66, 38104 Braunschweig, Postfach 4738, 38037 Braunschweig
Orders to: VSB Verlagsservice Braunschweig GmbH, Georg-Westermann-Allee 66, 38104 Braunschweig

Gloatz, Hille GmbH & Co KG fur Mehrfarben und Zellglasdruck
Poleigrund 14-20, 12307 Berlin
Mailing Address: Postfach 490108, 12281 Berlin
Tel: (030) 721 99 12; (030) 723 254 93 *Fax:* (030) 721 95 65
E-mail: gloatz.hille.gmbh@gmx.de; info@gloatz-hille.de
Web Site: www.gloatz-hille.de *Cable:* GEHACO D
Key Personnel
Manager: Hans-Peter Gloatz
Founded: 1936
Subjects: Engineering (General), Geography, Geology, Medicine, Nursing, Dentistry
ISBN Prefix(es): 3-920956

Verlag Glueckauf GmbH+
Montebruchstr 2, 45219 Essen
Mailing Address: Postfach 185620, 45206 Essen
Tel: (02054) 924120 *Fax:* (02054) 924129
E-mail: info@vge.de; vertrieb@vge.de
Web Site: www.vge.de
Key Personnel
Man Dir, Editorial, Rights & Permissions: Bernd Litke
Founded: 1918

Membership(s): German Society for Geotechnical Engineering (DGGT) & Austrian Society for Geomechanics (OEGG).
Subjects: Earth Sciences, Energy, Environmental Studies
ISBN Prefix(es): 3-7739

Gmelin Verlag GmbH+
Erlinger Hohe 9, 82346 Andechs
Tel: (08152) 6671 *Fax:* (08152) 5120
E-mail: gerd.gmelin@gmelin-verlag.de
Web Site: www.gmelin-verlag.de
Key Personnel
Owner, Rights & Permissions: Gerd E Gmelin
Founded: 1949
Subjects: Fiction, Health, Nutrition, Literature, Literary Criticism, Essays, Medicine, Nursing, Dentistry, Nonfiction (General), Philosophy, Physical Sciences, Science (General)
ISBN Prefix(es): 3-926253

Bruno Gmuender Verlag GmbH+
Leuschnerdamm 31, 10999 Berlin
Tel: (030) 615003-0 *Fax:* (030) 6159007
E-mail: info@brunogmuender.com
Web Site: www.brunogmuender.com
Key Personnel
Man Dir: B Gmuender
Founded: 1981
Subjects: Gay & Lesbian
ISBN Prefix(es): 3-86187; 3-924163; 3-9800578
Imprints: Albino Verlag
Bookshop(s): Bruno's in Berlin, Nuernbergerstr 53, 10789 Berlin; Bruno's in Cologne, Friesenwall 24, 50672 Cologne
Distribution Center: Abt Vertrieb, Wrangelstr 100, 10997 Berlin *Tel:* (030) 61001-100 *Fax:* (030) 6159008 *E-mail:* vertrieb@brunogmuender.com

GNT-Verlag, see Verlag fuer Geschichte der Naturwissenschaften und der Technik

Cornelia Goethe Literaturverlag, *imprint of* Frankfurter Literaturverlag GmbH

Cornelia Goethe Literaturverlag (Cornelia Goethe Publishers)+
Hanauer Landstr 338, 60314 Frankfurt am Main
Tel: (069) 40894-0 *Fax:* (069) 40894-169
E-mail: literatur@fouque-verlag.de
Web Site: www.cornelia-goethe.de; www.fouque-verlag.de
Founded: 1987
Publisher for new authors.
ISBN Prefix(es): 3-8267
Number of titles published annually: 200 Print
Total Titles: 1,000 Print
Branch Office(s)
70 Fortune Green Rd, London NW6 1DS, United Kingdom

Wilhelm Goldmann Verlag GmbH
Neumarkterstr 28, 81673 Munich
Mailing Address: Postfach 800709, 81607 Munich
Tel: (089) 4136-0; (01805) 990505 (hot line) *Fax:* (089) 43722812
E-mail: vertrieb.verlagsgruppe@bertelsmann.de
Telex: 529965 wgvmn d
Key Personnel
Man Dir: Klaus Eck
Editorial: Dr Georg Reuchlein-Diehl
Publicity: Brigitte Nunner
Founded: 1922
Subjects: Art, Astrology, Occult, Biography, Criminology, Education, Fiction, Film, Video, History, How-to, Law, Medicine, Nursing, Dentistry, Psychology, Psychiatry, Science (General), Science Fiction, Fantasy, Social Sciences, Sociology

ISBN Prefix(es): 3-442
Parent Company: Verlagsgruppe Bertelsmann GmbH
U.S. Office(s): Bettina Schrewe Literary Scouting, 101 Fifth Ave, Suite 11B, NY 10003, United States (US Scout)
Foreign Rep(s): Angelika Straus-Fischer

Goldschneck Verlag+
Burghaldenstr 57, 71384 Weinstadt
Mailing Address: Postfach 1265, 71399 Korb
Tel: (07151) 66 01 19 *Fax:* (07151) 66 07 78
Web Site: www.goldschneck.de
Key Personnel
Owner: Werner Weidert
Founded: 1983
Specialize in Paleontology.
Subjects: Geography, Geology
ISBN Prefix(es): 3-926129
Number of titles published annually: 2 Print
Total Titles: 1 Print

Goll Bruno Verlag fur Aussergewoehnliche Perspektiven (VAP)+
Postfach 1180, 32352 Preussisch Oldendorf
Tel: (05742) 93 04 44 *Fax:* (05742) 93 04 55
Web Site: www.vap-buch.de
Founded: 1972
Subjects: Government, Political Science
ISBN Prefix(es): 3-922367
Divisions: Edition ScienTerra; Edition Freie Energie; Edition Life Energie
Shipping Address: VAP-Verlagsauslieferung, Postfach 1180, 32352 PreuBisch Oldendorf & Mindenerstr 34, PreuBisch Oldendorf

Gondrom Verlag GmbH & Co KG+
Buehlstr 4, 95463 Bindlach
Mailing Address: Postfach 1, 95463 Bindlach
Tel: (09208) 51-0 *Fax:* (09208) 51-21
E-mail: service@gondrom.de
Web Site: www.gondrom.de
Telex: 920882
Key Personnel
President: Volker Gondrom
Man Dir: Jens Brase
Editorial, Rights & Permissions: Reinhard Fabian
Founded: 1974
Subjects: Art, History, Literature, Literary Criticism, Essays, Nonfiction (General)
ISBN Prefix(es): 3-8112
Associate Companies: Loewe Verlag, Buehlstr 4, 95461 Bindlach

Govi-Verlag Pharmazeutischer Verlag GmbH+
Carl-Mannich-Str 26, 65760 Eschborn
Mailing Address: Postfach 5360, 65728 Eschborn
Tel: (06196) 9 28-2 28; (06196) 9 28-2 29 *Fax:* (06196) 9 28-2 33
E-mail: service@govi.de
Web Site: www.govi.de
Key Personnel
Man Dir: Peter J Egenolf *Tel:* (06196) 928 201 *Fax:* (06196) 928 203
Founded: 1949
Subjects: Specialized in Pharmaceuticals & Medicine
ISBN Prefix(es): 3-7741
Total Titles: 140 Print; 20 CD-ROM
Parent Company: Bundesvereinigung Deutscher Apothekerverbaende, Ginnheimer Str 26, 65760 Echborn Tannus
Associate Companies: Werbe-und Vertriebsgesellschaft Deutscher Apotheker mbH; Zentrallaboratorium Deutscher Apotheker; Marketing-Gesellschaft Deutscher Apotheker mbH
Distributor for WHO World-Health-Organization
Bookshop(s): Versandbuchhandlung, 65760 Eschborn Taunus *E-mail:* service@govi.de
Warehouse: Industriestr 1, Eschborn
Returns: Industriestr 1, 65760 Eschborn

Grabert-Verlag+
Am Apfelberg 18, 72076 Tuebingen
Mailing Address: Postfach 1629, 72006 Tuebingen
Tel: (07071) 40700 *Fax:* (07071) 407026 *Cable:* GRABERT-TUBINGEN
Key Personnel
Man Dir & Owner: Wigbert Grabert
Founded: 1953
Subjects: Art, Biography, History
ISBN Prefix(es): 3-87847
Number of titles published annually: 10 Print
Total Titles: 200 Print
Book Club(s): Deutscher Buchkreis

Graefe und Unzer Verlag GmbH+
Grillparzerstr 12, 81675 Munich
Tel: (089) 4 19 81-0 *Fax:* (089) 4 19 81-113
E-mail: leserservice@graefe-und-unzer.de
Web Site: www.graefe-und-unzer.de
Key Personnel
Publisher & Man Dir: Georg Kessler *Tel:* (089) 41981404 *E-mail:* kessler@graefe-und-unzer.de
Man Dir, Distribution & Sales: Guenter Kopietz *Tel:* (089) 41981307 *E-mail:* kopietz@graefe-und-unzer.de
Man Dir, Finances: Urban Meister *Tel:* (089) 41981300 *E-mail:* meister@graefe-und-unzer.de
Rights Dir: Annette Beetz *Tel:* (089) 41981150 *E-mail:* beetz@graefe-und-unzer.de
Foreign Rights Manager (US, UK, Latin America, Spain & Portugal): Manuela Kerkhoff *Tel:* (089) 41981153 *E-mail:* kerkhoff@graefe-und-unzer.de
Foreign Rights Manager (France, Italy, Eastern EU, Asia): Gabriella Hoffman *Tel:* (089) 41981419 *E-mail:* hoffmann@graefe-und-unzer.de
Foreign Rights Manager (Germany & Northern Europe): Ingrid Puchner *Tel:* (089) 41981412 *E-mail:* puchner@graefe-und-unzer.de
Man Editor GU: Doris Birk *Tel:* (089) 41981409 *E-mail:* birk@graefe-und-unzer.de
Editorial Dir, Cookery: Birgit Rademacker *Tel:* (089) 41981401 *E-mail:* rademacker@graefe-und-unzer.de
Editorial Dir, Gardening: Anne Hahnstein *Tel:* (089) 41981319 *E-mail:* hahnstein@graefe-und-unzer.de
Editorial Dir, Pets: Anita Zellner *Tel:* (089) 41981215 *E-mail:* zellner@graefe-und-unzer.de
Editorial Dir, Health: Ulrich Ehrlenspiel *Tel:* (089) 41981118 *E-mail:* ehrlenspiel@graefe-und-unzer.de
Editorial Dir, Travel: Veronica Reisenegger *Tel:* (089) 41981426 *E-mail:* reisenegger@graefe-und-unzer.de
Editorial Dir, Business: Steffen Haselbach *Tel:* (089) 41981486 *E-mail:* haselbach@graefe-und-unzer.de
Distribution & Sales, Trade: Jan Wiesemann *Tel:* (089) 41981305 *E-mail:* wiesemann@graefe-und-unzer.de
Distribution & Sales, Non-Trade: Erik Vogel *Tel:* (089) 41981302 *E-mail:* vogel@graefe-und-unzer.de
Marketing Dir: Kerstin Moskon *Tel:* (089) 41981205 *E-mail:* moskon@graefe-und-unzer.de
Production Manager: Thomas Narr *Tel:* (089) 41981402 *E-mail:* narr@graefe-und-unzer.de
Founded: 1722
Subjects: Animals, Pets, Business, Cookery, Gardening, Plants, Health, Nutrition, Natural History, Self-Help, Travel
ISBN Prefix(es): 3-7742
Number of titles published annually: 120 Print
Total Titles: 1,050 Print
Imprints: Feinschmecker (Gourmet Cookery); Hallwag (Wine); Merian (Travel Guide Series); Teubner Edition (Cookery)
Warehouse: Verlegerdienst Munchen, Gutenbergstr 1, 82205 Gilching

PUBLISHERS — GERMANY

Graf Editions
Elisabethstr 29, 80796 Munich
Tel: (089) 27 159 57 *Fax:* (089) 27 159 97
Web Site: www.graf-editions.de
Key Personnel
Contact: Dieter Graf
Founded: 1993
Subjects: Language Arts, Linguistics, Travel, Hiking
ISBN Prefix(es): 3-9803130
Total Titles: 4 Print
Distributed by Baseline Book Co (UK); Ennsthaler Verlagsauslieferung (Austria); Fotofolio (USA); Geo Center (Germany); Map Link (USA); Museum of Contemporary Art (Australia); Schweizer Buchzentrum (Switzerland); Willems Adventure (Netherlands)
Foreign Rep(s): Baseline Book Company (UK); Cordee Distributors (UK); Fotofolio (USA); Hellenic Distribution Agency (Greece); MapLink (USA); Willems Adventure (Netherlands)
Bookshop(s): Museum of Contemporary Art Bookstore, 250 S Grand Ave, Los Angeles, CA 90012, United States

Grafit Verlag GmbH+
Chemnitzer Str 31, 44139 Dortmund
Tel: (0231) 7214650 *Fax:* (0231) 7214677
E-mail: info@grafit.de
Web Site: www.grafit.de
Key Personnel
Man Dir: Dr Rutger Booss
Founded: 1989
Membership(s): Boersenverein des deutschen Buchhandels.
Subjects: Fiction, Mysteries, Modern detective stories, crime fiction
ISBN Prefix(es): 3-89425
Number of titles published annually: 20 Print
Total Titles: 150 Print
Orders to: CVK Cornelsen, Postfach 100271, 33502 Bielefeld

Verlag der Stiftung Gralsbotschaft GmbH+
Lenzhalde 15, 70192 Stuttgart
Tel: (0711) 294355 *Fax:* (07156) 18663
E-mail: info@gral.de
Web Site: www.gral.de
Key Personnel
Man Dir & Editor: Juergen Sprick
Founded: 1928
Subjects: Health, Nutrition, Human Relations, Nonfiction (General), Parapsychology, Philosophy, Religion - Other, Self-Help
ISBN Prefix(es): 3-87860
U.S. Office(s): Grail Foundation Press, PO Box 45, Gambier, OH 43022, United States

Grass-Verlag
Bleerstr 107, 40789 Monheim
Mailing Address: Postfach 100219, 40766 Monheim
Tel: (02173) 51305 *Fax:* (02224) 770515
Key Personnel
Publisher: Aloys Grass
Founded: 1984
Subjects: Religion - Protestant
ISBN Prefix(es): 3-924974

Greuthof Verlag und Vertrieb GmbH+
Herrenweg 2, 79261 Gutach im Breisgau
Tel: (07681) 6025 *Fax:* (07681) 6027
ISBN Prefix(es): 3-923662

Greven Verlag Koeln GmbH+
Neue Weyerstr 1-3, 50676 Cologne
Mailing Address: Postfach 101644, 50478 Cologne
Tel: (0221) 20 33-161 *Fax:* (0221) 20 33-162
E-mail: greven.verlag@greven.de
Web Site: www.greven-verlag.de
Telex: 8882249 grev d *Cable:* GREVENVERLAG KOLN
Key Personnel
Man Dir, Rights & Permissions: Irene Greven
Publishing Managers: Dr Diethelm Schmidt; Manfred vom Stein
Founded: 1827
Subjects: Art, Regional Interests
ISBN Prefix(es): 3-7743

Griese Ingolf Wipe Griese+
Franz-Hitzestr 15, 44263 Dortmund
Mailing Address: Postfach 300247, 44232 Dortmund
Tel: (0231) 417412 *Fax:* (0231) 418461; (0231) 417418
Key Personnel
President & Publisher: Ingo Griese Privat-Dozent
Subjects: Economics, Sports, Athletics
ISBN Prefix(es): 3-9801985; 3-928594

Grote'sche Verlagsbuchhandlung GmbH & Co KG
Max-Planckstr 12, 50858 Cologne
Mailing Address: Postfach 400263, 50832 Cologne
Tel: (02234) 1060 *Fax:* (02234) 106284
Cable: GROTEVERLAG
Key Personnel
Publisher: Dr Juergen Gutbrod
Founded: 1661
Subjects: History
ISBN Prefix(es): 3-7745
Parent Company: W Kohlhammer GmbH, Hessbruehlstr 69, 70565 Stuttgart
Warehouse: Verlagsvertrieb Stuttgart GmbH, 70549 Stuttgart
Orders to: W Kohlhammer GmbH, 70549 Stuttgart

Verlag Grundlagen und Praxis GmbH & Co+
Bergmannstr 20, 26789 Leer
Tel: (0491) 6 18 86 *Fax:* (0491) 36 34
E-mail: grundlagen-praxis@t-online.de
Web Site: www.grundlagen-praxis.de
Key Personnel
Man Dir, Rights & Permissions: Axel Camici
Founded: 1972
Subjects: Language Arts, Linguistics, Medicine, Nursing, Dentistry
ISBN Prefix(es): 3-921229

Gruner + Jahr AG & Co
Am Baumwall 11, 20459 Hamburg
Tel: (040) 37030 *Fax:* (040) 37036000
E-mail: oeffentlichkeiharbeit@guj.de
Web Site: www.guj.de
Key Personnel
Chief Executive Officer: Gerd Schulte-Hillen
Subjects: Human Relations, Photography
ISBN Prefix(es): 3-570

Gruppe 21 GmbH+
Landsberger Str 101, 45219 Essen
Tel: (02054) 10489-0 *Fax:* (02054) 10489-29
E-mail: redaktion@info21.de
Web Site: www.gruppe21.de
Key Personnel
Manager: Gerhard Klaes
Founded: 1986
Specialize in Database & Electronic Publishing Services.
ISBN Prefix(es): 3-928930
Parent Company: Advanstar Communications GmbH & Co KG
Orders to: Siehe Zeile 010

Verlag Gruppenpaedagogischer Literatur+
Rudolf-Diesel-Str 8, 61273 Wehrheim
Mailing Address: Postfach 1252, 61269 Wehrheim
Tel: (06081) 5 67 40 *Fax:* (06081) 5 74 38
E-mail: info@vglw.de
Web Site: www.vglw.de
Founded: 1976
Membership(s): Boersenverein des deutschen Buchhandels.
Subjects: Career Development, Child Care & Development, Crafts, Games, Hobbies, Education, Music, Dance, Outdoor Recreation, Sports, Athletics
ISBN Prefix(es): 3-921496; 3-89544

Walter de Gruyter GmbH & Co KG+
Genthinerstr 13, 10785 Berlin
Tel: (030) 260 05-0 *Fax:* (030) 260 05-251
E-mail: wdg-info@degruyter.de
Web Site: www.degruyter.de *Cable:* WISSENSCHAFT BERLIN 0184027
Key Personnel
Man Dir: Reinhold Tokar
Marketing Dir: Dorothea Kern *E-mail:* kern@degruyter.de
Marketing: Paul Osborn
Advertising: Dietlind Makswitat *E-mail:* ad@degruyter.de
Public Relations: Ulrike Lippe *E-mail:* ulrike.lippe@degruyter.com
Sales: Harald Hoffmann
Founded: 1919
Subjects: Archaeology, Biological Sciences, History, Language Arts, Linguistics, Law, Literature, Literary Criticism, Essays, Management, Marketing, Mathematics, Medicine, Nursing, Dentistry, Philosophy, Physical Sciences, Physics, Science (General), Social Sciences, Sociology, Theology
ISBN Prefix(es): 0-202; 3-11
Total Titles: 8,500 Print
Subsidiaries: Aldine de Gruyter; Mouton de Gruyter
U.S. Office(s): Walter de Gruyter, Inc, 200 Saw Mill River Rd, Hawthorne, NY 10532, United States *Tel:* 914-747-0110 *Fax:* 914-747-1326

Arthur L Sellier & Co KG-Walter de Gruyter GmbH & Co KG, see Dr Arthur L Sellier & Co KG-Walter de Gruyter GmbH & Co KG OHG

GTB Guetersloher Taschenbuecher (pocketbooks), *imprint of* Guetersloher Verlagshaus

Gunter Olzog Verlag GmbH+
Fuerstenriederstr 250, 81377 Munich
Tel: (089) 71 04 66 60 *Fax:* (089) 71 04 66 61
E-mail: olzog.verlag@t-online.de
Web Site: www.olzog.de
Key Personnel
Publisher: Dr Reinhard Moestl *Tel:* (089) 71 04 66 64 *E-mail:* moestl@olzog.de
Man Dir, Rights & Permissions: Dr Dirk F Passmann
Sales: Stefan Keim *Tel:* (089) 71 04 66 65 *E-mail:* keim@olzog.de
Rights & Permissions: Gerlinde Stanglmeier
Advertising: Martina Gesierich
Publicity: Claudia Franz *E-mail:* franz@olzog.de
Founded: 1949
Membership(s): TR- Verlagsunion GmbH.
Subjects: Economics, Film, Video, Foreign Countries, Government, Political Science, History, Journalism, Management, Marketing, Publishing & Book Trade Reference, Social Sciences, Sociology
ISBN Prefix(es): 3-7892
Parent Company: Verlag Moderne Industrie AG

Guenther Butkus+
Stapenhorststr 15, 33615 Bielefeld

Tel: (0521) 69689 *Fax:* (0521) 174470
E-mail: pendragon.verlag@t-online.de
Web Site: www.pendragon.de
Key Personnel
Publisher: Gunther Butkus
Founded: 1981
Subjects: Art, Fiction, Poetry, Novels, poems & music
ISBN Prefix(es): 3-929096; 3-934872
Total Titles: 250 Print; 20 Audio
Distributed by Prolit

Guetersloher Verlagshaus+
Formerly Guetersloher Verlagshaus Gerd Mohn
Carl-Miele-Str 214, 33311 Guetersloh
Mailing Address: Postfach 450, 33311 Guetersloh
Tel: (05241) 74050 *Fax:* (05241) 740548
E-mail: info@gtvh.de
Web Site: www.guetersloher-vh.de
Telex: 933868 bert d *Cable:* BERTELSMANN GUTERSLOH
Key Personnel
Manager: Ralf Markmeier *E-mail:* ralf.markmeier@gtvh.de
International Rights Contact: Heike Daut-Ruenger *E-mail:* heike.daut-ruenger@gtvh.de
Sales: Hans-Joerg Unger *E-mail:* hans-joerg.unger@gtvh.de
Founded: 1835 (1959)
Subjects: Anthropology, Biblical Studies, Biography, Government, Political Science, Philosophy, Religion - Protestant, Religion - Other, Theology
ISBN Prefix(es): 3-579
Parent Company: Verlagsgruppe Bertelsmann International GmbH
Imprints: GTB Guetersloher Taschenbuecher (pocketbooks); K T Kaiser Taschenbuecher (pocketbooks)
Subsidiaries: Kaiser Christian/Guetersloher Verlaghaus
Shipping Address: VVA Bertelsmann Distribution, Postfach 7777, Guetersloh
Warehouse: VVA Bertelsmann Distribution, Postfach 7777, Guetersloh
Orders to: VVA Bertelsmann Distribution, Postfach 7777, Guetersloh

Guetersloher Verlagshaus Gerd Mohn, see Guetersloher Verlagshaus

Verlag Klaus Guhl
Akazienallee 27A, 14050 Berlin
Mailing Address: Postfach 191532, 14005 Berlin
Tel: (030) 3213062 *Fax:* (030) 30823868
Key Personnel
Man Dir: Dr Klaus-Dieter Guhl
Editorial: Fabian Carlos Guhl
Sales: Florian Robert Guhl
Production: Hans Paul Guhl
Publicity: Dr Kurt Kreiler
Rights & Permissions: Dr Thomas Bark
Founded: 1974
Subjects: Art, Government, Political Science, Literature, Literary Criticism, Essays
ISBN Prefix(es): 3-88220
Subsidiaries: Fanel GmbH; Buchladen Bunter Baer GmbH
Bookshop(s): Bunter Baer-Guhl, Knobelsdorffstr 8, 14059 Berlin

Verlag des Gustav-Adolf-Werks
Pistorisstr 6, 04229 Leipzig
Mailing Address: Postfach 310763, 04211 Leipzig
Tel: (0341) 490 62 0 *Fax:* (0341) 4770505
E-mail: gaw-verlag@t-online.de
Key Personnel
Publishing Manager: Evelin Hoehne
Founded: 1968
Subjects: Developing Countries, Religion - Protestant, Theology
ISBN Prefix(es): 3-87593

Gutenberg-Gesellschaft eV (Gutenberg Society)
Liebfrauenplatz 5, 55116 Mainz
Tel: (06131) 22 64 20 *Fax:* (06131) 23 35 30
E-mail: gutenberg-gesellschaft@freenet.de
Web Site: www.gutenberg-gesellschaft.uni-mainz.de
Key Personnel
President: Jens Beutel
Vice President: Hannetraud Schultheiss
Editor-in-Chief: Dr Stephan Fuessel
Secretary General: Dr Cornelia Fischer
Founded: 1900
International association for past & present history of the art of printing & of the book.
Subjects: Publishing & Book Trade Reference
ISBN Prefix(es): 3-7755
Number of titles published annually: 1 Print
Distributed by Otto Harrassowitz (Yearbook only)

Gutersloher Verlaghaus GmbH /Chr Kaiser/Kiefel/Quell+
Carl-Miele-Str 214, 33311 Guetersloh
Mailing Address: Postfach 450, 33311 Guetersloh
Tel: (05241) 74050 *Fax:* (05241) 740548
E-mail: info@gtvh.de
Web Site: www.gtvh.de
Telex: 933868 bert d
Key Personnel
Man Dir, Rights & Permissions: Hans Juergen Meurer
International Rights Contact: Heike Daut-Ruenger
Founded: 1845
Subjects: Religion - Other, Theology
ISBN Prefix(es): 3-579; 3-7811

H B Verlags und Vertriebs-Gesellschaft mbH
Marco-Polo-Str 1, 73760 Ostfildern
Tel: (040) 4151-04 *Fax:* (040) 41513231
Key Personnel
Dir: Kurt Bortz; Dr Joachim Dreyer; Eike Schmidt
Founded: 1979
ISBN Prefix(es): 3-616; 3-922822

H L Schlapp Buch- und Antiquariatshandlung GmbH und Co KG Abt Verlag
Ludwigsplatz 3, 64283 Darmstadt
Tel: (06151) 17 90-0 *Fax:* (06151) 17 90 40
E-mail: darmstadt@schlapp.de
Web Site: www.schlapp.de
Key Personnel
Owner: Karl-Eugen Schlapp; Eckart Schlapp
Founded: 1836
Subjects: Regional Interests
ISBN Prefix(es): 3-87704

Verlag H M Hauschild GmbH
Hans-Bredow-Str 7, 28307 Bremen
Mailing Address: Postfach 45 02 35, 28296 Bremen
Tel: (0421) 1785-0 *Fax:* (0421) 1785-285
E-mail: info@hauschild.werbedruck.de
Web Site: www.hauschild.werbedruck.de
Key Personnel
Man Dir: Hartmut Schneider; Ingo Steinmeyer
Rights & Permissions: Ernst-August Echtermann
Founded: 1854
Subjects: Art, Regional Interests
ISBN Prefix(es): 3-920699; 3-926598; 3-929902; 3-89757; 3-931785
Parent Company: Werbedruck Bremen Grafischer Betrieb GmbH

Haack, *imprint of* Justus Perthes Verlag Gotha GmbH

Haag und Herchen Verlag GmbH+
Fichardstr 30, 60322 Frankfurt am Main
Tel: (069) 550911-13 *Fax:* (069) 552601; (069) 554922
E-mail: verlag@haagundherchen.de

Web Site: www.haagundherchen.de
Key Personnel
Man Dir, Rights & Permissions: Hans-Alfred Herchen
Founded: 1975
Subjects: Engineering (General), Government, Political Science, How-to, Medicine, Nursing, Dentistry, Psychology, Psychiatry, Science (General), Social Sciences, Sociology
ISBN Prefix(es): 3-88129; 3-86137; 3-89228; 3-89846

C W Haarfeld GmbH & Co
Annastr 32-36, 45130 Essen
Mailing Address: Postfach 101562, 45015 Essen
Tel: (0201) 720950 *Fax:* (0201) 7209533
Key Personnel
Man Dir: Wolfgang Otto
Founded: 1867
ISBN Prefix(es): 3-7747
Parent Company: Wolters Kluwer NV, Netherlands

Wolfgang G Haas - Musikverlag Koeln ek+
Rheinbergstr 92, 51143 Cologne
Tel: (02203) 98 88 3-0 *Fax:* (02203) 98 88 3-50
E-mail: info@haas-koeln.de
Web Site: www.haas-koeln.de
Key Personnel
Contact: Wolfgang G Haas
Founded: 1985
Membership(s): International Trumpet Guild & German Society of Music Publishers.
Subjects: Music, Dance
ISBN Prefix(es): 3-928453

Dr Rudolf Habelt GmbH
Am Buchenhang 1, 53113 Bonn
Mailing Address: Postfach 150104, 53040 Bonn
Tel: (0228) 9 23 83-22 *Fax:* (0228) 9 23 83-23
E-mail: info@habelt.de *Web Site:* www.habelt.de
Tel: (0228) 9 23 83-0 *Fax:* (0228) 9 23 83-6
E-mail: info@habelt.de
Web Site: www.habelt.de
Key Personnel
Man Dir: Wolfgang Habelt
Editorial, Production: Dr Susanne Biegert
Founded: 1954
Subjects: Archaeology, History, Regional Interests
ISBN Prefix(es): 3-7749
Number of titles published annually: 30 Print
Bookshop(s): Antiquarian Bookshop, Am Buchenhang 1, 53115 Bonn, Contact: Wolfgang Habelt *Tel:* (0228) 9 23 83-33 *Fax:* (0228) 9 23 83-6

Hachmeister Verlag+
Klosterstr 12, 48143 Munster
Tel: (0251) 51210 *Fax:* (0251) 57217
E-mail: hachmeister.galerie@t-online.de
Web Site: www.hachmeister-galerie.de
Key Personnel
Dir: Dr Heiner Hachmeister
Founded: 1979
Catalogues & books.
Subjects: Art
ISBN Prefix(es): 3-88829
Number of titles published annually: 2 Print
Total Titles: 35 Print
Parent Company: Hachmeister Galerie

Walter Haedecke Verlag+
Lukas-Moser-Weg 2, 71263 Weil der Stadt
Mailing Address: Postfach 1203, 71256 Weil der Stadt
Tel: (07033) 529830 *Fax:* (07033) 529831
E-mail: haedecke_vlg@t-online.de
Key Personnel
Owner & Publisher: Joachim Graff
Founded: 1919

Subjects: Cookery, Health, Nutrition, Self-Help, Wine & Spirits
ISBN Prefix(es): 3-7750
Number of titles published annually: 16 Print
Total Titles: 112 Print
Distributor for NaturaViva Verlags GmbH

Dr Curt Haefner-Verlag GmbH+
Bachstr 14-16, 69121 Heidelberg
Mailing Address: Postfach 106060, 69050 Heidelberg
Tel: (06221) 6446-0 *Fax:* (06221) 6446-40
E-mail: info@haefner-verlag.de
Web Site: www.haefner-verlag.de
Key Personnel
President: Dieter Neumann
Founded: 1956
Medicine, Nursing & Social Sciences.
Subjects: Business, Child Care & Development, Education, Health, Nutrition, Human Relations, Medicine, Nursing, Dentistry, Public Administration, Science (General), Social Sciences, Sociology, Safety on Work & Occupational Health
ISBN Prefix(es): 3-87284
Total Titles: 22 Print
Subsidiaries: Werkschriften Verlag GmbH

Dr Haensel-Hohenhausen AG, see Frankfurter Literaturverlag GmbH

Haenssler Verlag GmbH+
Langasse 25, 96142 Hollfeld
Tel: (09274) 95051 *Fax:* (09274) 95053
E-mail: info@haenssler.de
Web Site: www.haenssler.de
Key Personnel
Publisher: Joachim Beyer
Founded: 1919
Membership(s): the Telos Group.
Publishes all publications of the American Institute of Musicology.
Subjects: Art, Film, Video, Literature, Literary Criticism, Essays, Music, Dance, Religion - Other
ISBN Prefix(es): 3-7751
Bookshop(s): Hanssler Verlag-Buchhandlung

Heinz-Jurgen Hausser+
Frankfurterstr 64, 64293 Darmstadt
Tel: (06151) 22824 *Fax:* (06151) 26854
Founded: 1989
Subjects: Architecture & Interior Design, Art, Literature, Literary Criticism, Essays
ISBN Prefix(es): 3-927902; 3-89552
Orders to: Lamuv, Nikolaikirchhof 7, 37073 Goettingen

Lehrmittelverlag Wilhelm Hagemann GmbH+
Karlstr 20, 40210 Duesseldorf
Mailing Address: Postfach 103545, 40026 Duesseldorf
Tel: (0211) 17 92 70-0 *Fax:* (0211) 17 92 70-70
E-mail: aktuell@hagemann.de
Web Site: www.hagemann.de *Cable:* HAGEMANNVERLAG DUSSELDORF
Key Personnel
General Manager: Maria Schuette-Hagemann
Sales: Walter Kils-Huetten
Founded: 1929
Membership(s): VGS (Verlagsgesellschaft mbH & Co KG); Association of School Book Publishers; German Didactic Associations; Worlddidac.
Subjects: Biological Sciences, Environmental Studies, Health, Nutrition, Physical Sciences
ISBN Prefix(es): 3-544
Subsidiaries: Hagemann & Partner; Bildungsmedien Verlagsges mbH
Warehouse: Karlstr 16, 40210 Duesseldorf

Hahner Verlagsgesellschaft mbH+
Heidchenberg 11, 52076 Aachen-Hahn
Tel: (02408) 55 05 *Fax:* (02408) 58081
E-mail: office@hvg.de
Key Personnel
Manager: Peter Brand
Founded: 1986
Subjects: Science (General)
ISBN Prefix(es): 3-89294
Parent Company: IZOP-Institut zur Objektivierung von Lern-und Pruefungsverfahren GmbH

Mary Hahn's Kochbuchverlag+
Subsidiary of Buchverlage Langen-Mueller/Herbig
Thomas-Wimmer-Ring 11, 80539 Munich
Tel: (089) 2 90 88-0
E-mail: l.eggs@herbig.net
Web Site: www.herbig.net
Key Personnel
Sales, Publicity Manager: Eva Ohser *E-mail:* e.ohser@herbig.net
Subjects: Cookery, House & Home
ISBN Prefix(es): 3-87287
Orders to: VVA, An der Autobahn, 33310 Guetersloh

Hahnsche Buchhandlung+
Leinstr 32, 30159 Hannover
Mailing Address: Postfach 2460, 30024 Hannover
Tel: (0511) 80 71 80 40 *Fax:* (0511) 36 36 98
E-mail: verlag@hahnsche-buchhandlung.de
Web Site: www.hahnsche-buchhandlung.de
Key Personnel
Manager, Rights & Permissions: Dr Horst Zimmerhackl
Founded: 1792
Specialize in German History.
Membership(s): Stock Exchange of German Booksellers; Association of German Magazine Publishers.
Subjects: Education, History, Regional Interests
ISBN Prefix(es): 3-7752
Bookshop(s): Abt Verlag

Herbert von Halem Verlag
Lindenstr 19, 50674 Cologne
Tel: (0221) 92 58 29 0 *Fax:* (0221) 92 58 29 29
E-mail: info@halem-verlag.de
Web Site: www.halem-verlag.de; www.inpunkto.de
Key Personnel
Contact: Herbert von Halem
Subjects: Communications, Journalism, Library & Information Sciences, Philosophy, Radio, TV, Social Sciences, Sociology, Cultural Studies, Political Science
ISBN Prefix(es): 3-931606
Number of titles published annually: 25 Print
Total Titles: 54 Print

Hallwag, *imprint of* Graefe und Unzer Verlag GmbH

Hamburger Lesehefte Verlag Iselt & Co Nfl mbH+
Subsidiary of Husum Druck- und Verlagsgesellschaft mbH & Co KG
Nordbahnhofstr 2, 25813 Husum
Mailing Address: Postfach 1480, 25804 Husum
Tel: (04841) 8352-0 *Fax:* (04841) 8352-10
E-mail: verlagsgruppe.husum@t-online.de
Web Site: www.verlagsgruppe.de
Key Personnel
Man Dir, Editorial, Rights & Permissions: Ingwert Paulsen
Founded: 1953
ISBN Prefix(es): 3-87291
Associate Companies: Hansa Verlag Ingwert Paulsen Jr; Matthiesen Verlag Ingwert Paulsen Jr; Verlag der Nation

Liselotte Hamecher
Goethestr 18, 34119 Kassel
Tel: (0561) 16611 *Fax:* (0561) 775262
Key Personnel
Owner: Liselotte Hamecher
Founded: 1947
Subjects: History, Maritime, Military Science
ISBN Prefix(es): 3-920307
Shipping Address: Goethestr 74, 34119 Kassel
Warehouse: Goethestr 74, 34119 Kassel

Alfred Hammer+
EJARM Publishing House, Curtigasse 4, 64823 Gross-Umstadt
Tel: (06078) 71622 *Fax:* (06078) 71655
Key Personnel
Man Dir: Freddy Hammer
Founded: 1996
Subjects: Aeronautics, Aviation, Law, Management, European Joint Aviation Requirements
ISBN Prefix(es): 3-9805586

Peter Hammer Verlag GmbH+
Foehrenstr 33-35, 42283 Wuppertal
Mailing Address: Postfach 200963, 42209 Wuppertal
Tel: (0202) 505066; (0202) 505067 *Fax:* (0202) 509252
E-mail: info@peter-hammer-verlag.de
Web Site: www.peter-hammer-verlag.de
Key Personnel
Dir: Hermann Schulz
International Rights: Monika Bilstein
Advertising, Press: Dr Claudia Putz
Founded: 1966
Subjects: Developing Countries, Foreign Countries, Literature, Literary Criticism, Essays
ISBN Prefix(es): 3-87294
Associate Companies: Jugenddienst Verlag, Foehrenstr 33-35, 42283 Wuppertal
Distributed by Prolit Verlagsauslieferung GmbH

Hammonia-Verlag GmbH Fachverlag der Wohnungswirtschaft+
Tangstedter Landstr 83, 22415 Hamburg
Mailing Address: Postfach 620228, 22402 Hamburg
Tel: (040) 520103-0 *Fax:* (040) 520103-30
E-mail: info@hammonia.de
Web Site: www.hvh.de
Key Personnel
Man Dir, Publisher & International Rights: Guenther Hegemann
Sales Manager: Rolf Roemer *Tel:* (040) 520103-35 *E-mail:* rolf.roemer@hammonia.de
Founded: 1946
Subjects: House & Home
ISBN Prefix(es): 3-87292

Verlag Handwerk und Technik GmbH+
Lademannbogen 135, 22339 Hamburg
Mailing Address: Postfach 630500, 22331 Hamburg
Tel: (040) 5 38 08-0 *Fax:* (040) 5 38 08-101
Web Site: www.handwerk-technik-shop.de
Key Personnel
Dir, Rights & Permissions: Johann Carl Buechner
Dir: Oskar Kummer
Founded: 1949
Subjects: Career Development, Education, Labor, Industrial Relations
ISBN Prefix(es): 3-582
Subsidiaries: Holland & Josenhans Gmbh & Co
Showroom(s): Informationsbuero Leipzig mit Verlagsausstellung, August- Bebel-Str 65, 04275 Leipzig; Informationsbuero Stuttgart mit Verlagsausstellung, Feuerseeplatz 2, 70176 Stuttgart
Orders to: Techn Fachbuch - Vertrieb AG M Studer, Spitalstr 12, Postfach 119, 2501 Biel, Switzerland *Tel:* (032) 322 61 41 *Fax:* (032) 322 61 30 *E-mail:* info@tfv.ch (Switzerland)

Veritas - Verlags und Handelsgessellschaft mbH & Co OHG, Hafenstra 1-3, 4010 Linz, Austria
Tel: (0732) 776451-280 *Fax:* (0732) 776451-239 *E-mail:* veritas@veritas.at *Web Site:* www.veritas.at (Austria)

Hanfstaengl-Verlag, *imprint of* Daco Verlag Guenter Blase oHG

Edition Hannemann, *imprint of* Verlag Stephanie Naglschmid

Hannibal-Verlag+
Lochhamerstr 9, 82152 Planegg
Tel: (089) 24 245 415 *Fax:* (089) 24 245 294
E-mail: info@hannibal-verlag.de
Web Site: www.hannibal-verlag.de
Key Personnel
Man Dir & Publisher: Francoise Degrave
  E-mail: francoise.degrave@kochbooks.com
Founded: 1986
Subjects: Literature, Literary Criticism, Essays, Musical Biographies
ISBN Prefix(es): 3-85445
Number of titles published annually: 12 Print
Total Titles: 240 Print
Parent Company: Verlagsgruppe Koch, Gewerbegebiet, 6600 Hoefen/Tirol, Austria
Warehouse: b & i buch und information ag, Centralweg 16, 8910 Affoltern, Switzerland
Prolit Verlagsauslieferung, Siemensstr 16, 35463 Fernwald-Annerod

Hansa Verlag Ingwert Paulsen Jr
Nordbahnhofstr 2, 25813 Husum
Mailing Address: Postfach 1480, 25804 Husum
Tel: (04841) 8352-0 *Fax:* (04841) 8352-10
E-mail: verlagsgruppe.husum@t-online.de
Web Site: www.verlagsgruppe.de
Key Personnel
International Rights: J Paulsen
Founded: 1954
Subjects: Literature, Literary Criticism, Essays
ISBN Prefix(es): 3-920421
Parent Company: Husum Druck-und Verlagsgesellschaft
Associate Companies: Hamburger Lesehefte Verlag Iselt & Co Nfl mbH; Husum Druck- und Verlagsgesellschaft mbH & Co KG; Matthiesen Verlag Ingwert Paulsen Jr; Verlag der Nation

Carl Hanser Verlag+
Kolbergerstr 22, 81679 Munich
Tel: (089) 9 98 30 0 *Fax:* (089) 98 48 09
E-mail: info@hanser.de
Web Site: www.hanser.de/verlag
Key Personnel
Man Dir & Publisher, Fiction & Non-Fiction: Michael Krueger *E-mail:* krueger@hanser.de
Man Dir & Publisher, Technical & Science: Wolfgang Beisler *E-mail:* beisler@hanser.de
Publishing Dir, Professional Books: Dr Hermann Riedel *E-mail:* riedel@hanser.de
Publishing Dir, Professional Magazines: Michael Himmelstoss *E-mail:* himmelstoss@hanser.de
Man Dir, Financial: Stephan D Joss
  E-mail: joss@hanser.de
Sales Dir, Fiction & Nonfiction: Felicitas Feilhauer *E-mail:* feilhauer@hanser.de
Sales Dir, Technical & Science: Barbara Kothe *E-mail:* kothe@hanser.de
Advertising Dir, Technical & Science: Guenter Scheffel *E-mail:* scheffel@hanser.de
Publicity, Fiction & Nonfiction: Christina Knecht *E-mail:* knecht@hanser.de
Foreign Rights, Fiction & Nonfiction: Susanne Bauknecht *E-mail:* bauknecht@hanser.de
Foreign Rights, Technical & Science: Evelyn Waizenegger
Founded: 1928

Subjects: Computer Science, Economics, Electronics, Electrical Engineering, Engineering (General), Environmental Studies, Fiction, Management, Mathematics, Mechanical Engineering, Microcomputers, Nonfiction (General), Philosophy, Physics, Poetry, Plastics
ISBN Prefix(es): 3-446
Imprints: Zsolnay
U.S. Office(s): Hanser Publishers, 6915 Valley Ave, Cincinnati, OH 45244, United States
Hanser/Gardner Publishers Inc, 6915 Valley Ave, Cincinnati, OH 45244, United States

Happy Mental Buch- und Musik Verlag
Am Hoehenberg 21, 82327 Tutzing
Tel: (08158) 993303 *Fax:* (08158) 993305
Subjects: Health, Nutrition, Music, Dance, Religion - Buddhist, Religion - Hindu
ISBN Prefix(es): 3-9805692
Book Club(s): Bertelsmann; Weltbild

Hardt und Worner Marketing fur das Buch+
Saalburgstr 20, 61381 Friedrichsdorf
Tel: (06172) 7005 *Fax:* (01672) 71547
E-mail: hardt.woerner@t-online.de
Founded: 1993
Subjects: Publishing & Book Trade Reference
ISBN Prefix(es): 3-930120
Total Titles: 12 Print
Distributor for Blueprint (Germany)
Distribution Center: LKG, Potsahower Weg, 04579 Espenhain *Tel:* (0206) 165-121
  Fax: (0206) 65-110
Orders to: LKG, Potsahower Weg, 04579 Espenhain

Harenberg Kommunikation Verlags- und Medien-GmbH & Co KG+
Koenigswall 21, 44137 Dortmund
Tel: (0231) 9056-0 *Fax:* (0231) 9056-110
E-mail: post@harenberg.de
Web Site: www.harenberg.de
Key Personnel
Man Dir: Bodo Harenberg; Sven Merten
Founded: 1973
Subjects: Architecture & Interior Design, Art, History, Music, Dance, Travel
ISBN Prefix(es): 3-88379; 3-611; 3-921846

Siegfried Haring Literatten-Verlag Ulm+
Weichselstr 21, 89231 Neu-Ulm
Tel: (0731) 9806040 *Fax:* (0731) 9806042
E-mail: ratart.edition@t-online.de
Key Personnel
Man Dir: Siegfried Haering
Founded: 1986
Subjects: Drama, Theater
ISBN Prefix(es): 3-926217

Harmonie Verlag (Harmony Publications)
Gunterstalstr 12, 79100 Freiburg
Tel: (0761) 709667 *Fax:* (0761) 709662
E-mail: harmonieverlag@aol.com
Key Personnel
Dir: Regina Gaus
Subjects: Religion - Other
ISBN Prefix(es): 3-929474

Harrassowitz Verlag+
Taunusstr 14, 65183 Wiesbaden
Tel: (0611) 530-0 *Fax:* (0611) 530-560 (orders)
E-mail: service@harrassowitz.de
Web Site: www.harrassowitz.de *Cable:* HARRASSOWITZ VERLAG WIESBADEN
Key Personnel
Man Dir & International Rights: Dr Knut Dorn
Man Dir: Ruth Becker-Scheicher; Friedmann Weigel
Founded: 1872
Specialize in Slavic Studies & Eastern European Research.

Subjects: Asian Studies, Language Arts, Linguistics, Library & Information Sciences, Dictionaries, Linguistics, Eastern European Research & Civic Studies
ISBN Prefix(es): 3-447
Total Titles: 2,600 Print

Harth Musik Verlag-Pro musica Verlag GmbH
Frankenforsterstr 40, 51427 Bergisch Gladbach
Tel: (02204) 2003-0 *Fax:* (02204) 2003-33 *Cable:* Musica Leipzig
Key Personnel
Manager: Rita Preiss
Founded: 1946
Subjects: Music, Dance
ISBN Prefix(es): 3-7334

Litteraturverlag Karlheinz Hartmann
Rodheimerstr 17, 61381 Friedrichsdorf
Tel: (06007) 7622; (069) 96206013 (Frankfurt)
  Fax: (06007) 614606
Key Personnel
Man Dir: M A Karlheinz Hartmann
Founded: 1976
Subjects: Film, Video, Literature, Literary Criticism, Essays, Poetry
ISBN Prefix(es): 3-87293
Branch Office(s)
Schneckenhofstr 17, 60596 Frankfurt am Main
Tel: (069) 6032191

Haschemi Edition Cologne Kunstverlag fuer Fotografie+
Mechterstr 44, 50823 Cologne
Tel: (0221) 561007; (0221) 561008 *Fax:* (0221) 529282
E-mail: info@haschemi.de
Web Site: www.haschemi.de
Key Personnel
International Rights: Baback Haschemi
Founded: 1983
Subjects: Photography, Travel
ISBN Prefix(es): 3-924169; 3-931282; 3-936222
Subsidiaries: Haschemi Edition Virginia

von Hase & Koehler Verlag KG+
Bahnhofstr 4-6, 55116 Mainz
Mailing Address: Postfach 2269, 55012 Mainz
Tel: (06131) 232334 *Fax:* (06131) 227952
Key Personnel
Publisher, Rights & Permissions: Volker Hansen
Founded: 1964
Subjects: Biography, Communications, Education, Finance, Literature, Literary Criticism, Essays, Poetry, Radio, TV
ISBN Prefix(es): 3-7758
Subsidiaries: Niederlassung Munchen

Hatje Cantz Verlag (Hatje Cantz Publishers)+
Senefelderstr 12, 73760 Ostfildern
Mailing Address: PO Box 4259, 73745 Ostfildern
Tel: (0711) 44 05-0 *Fax:* (0711) 44 05-220
E-mail: contact@hatjecantz.de
Web Site: www.hatjecantz.de
Key Personnel
Senior Publisher: Gerd Hatje *Tel:* (0711) 44 05-200
Man Dir & Publisher: Annette Kulenkampff
  Tel: (0711) 44 05-200
International Sales Dir & Foreign Rights: Markus Hartmann *Tel:* (0711) 44 05-203 *E-mail:* m.hartmann@hatjecantz.de
International Sales Manager & Foreign Rights: Evelin Georgi *Tel:* (0711) 44 05-218 *E-mail:* e.georgi@hatjecantz.de
Promotion: Stefanie Gommel *Tel:* (0711) 44 05-208 *E-mail:* s.gommel@hatjecantz.de; Martina Reitz *Tel:* (0711) 44 05-213 *E-mail:* m.reitz@hatjecantz.de
Press: Meike Gatermann *Tel:* (0711) 6 57 32 95 *Fax:* (0711) 65 02 12 *E-mail:* presse@hatjecantz.de
Founded: 1945

Publisher of art books, books on architecture, design & photography, exhibition catalogues.
Subjects: Architecture & Interior Design, Art, Photography
ISBN Prefix(es): 3-7757
Number of titles published annually: 150 Print
Total Titles: 1,000 Print
Parent Company: Dr Cantz'sche Druckerei
Associate Companies: belser kunst quartal *Tel:* (0711) 4405226; (0711) 4405227 *Fax:* (0711) 4405228 *E-mail:* belser@hatjecantz.de
Warehouse: Koch, Neff & Oetinger
Orders to: Koch, Neff & Oetinger, Schockenriedstr 39, 70565 Stuttgart *Tel:* (0711) 78992031 *Fax:* (0711) 78991010
Returns: Koch, Neff & Oetinger

Haude und Spenersche Verlagsbuchhandlung+
Gneisenaustr 33, 10961 Berlin
Mailing Address: Postfach 610494, 10928 Berlin
Tel: (030) 6917073 *Fax:* (030) 6914067
Cable: HAUDE
Key Personnel
Owner, Manager, Rights & Permissions: Volker Spiess
Founded: 1614
Subjects: History, Nonfiction (General), Regional Interests, Religion - Jewish, Travel
ISBN Prefix(es): 3-7759
Associate Companies: Wissenschaftsverlag Volker Spiess GmbH; Arani-Verlag GmbH
Orders to: VAH-Jager Verlagsauslieferungen, Miraustr 54, 13509 Berlin

Haufe Mediengruppe
Hindenburgstr 64, 79102 Freiburg
Mailing Address: Postfach 740, 79007 Freiburg
Tel: (0761) 3683-0 *Fax:* (0761) 3683-195
E-mail: online-werburg@haufe.de
Web Site: www.haufe.de
Key Personnel
Executive Board: Helmuth Hopfner; Martin Laqua
Chairman: Uwe Renald Mueller
Founded: 1934 (by Rudolf Haufe in Berlin)
Subjects: Business, Education, Law, Information Management, Taxation
Number of titles published annually: 150 Print
Associate Companies: Haufe Akademie, Freiburg; Haufe + Kisling Verlag AG, Zurich, Switzerland; Haufe Publishing, Planegg; Rudolf Haufe Verlag, Freiburg; Haufe Service Center, Freiburg; Intuit Inc (US); LEGIOS, Frankfurt; Lexware, Freiburg; Memento Verlag AG, Freiburg; Mobilecom AG; Openshop AG, Munich; Max Schimmel Verlag, Wuerzburg; SoftUse, Freiburg; WRS Verlag, Planegg

Rudolf Haufe Verlag GmbH & Co KG+
Hindenburgstr 64, 79102 Freiburg
Mailing Address: Postfach 740, 79007 Freiburg
Tel: (0761) 3683-0 *Fax:* (0761) 3683-195
E-mail: online@haufe.de
Web Site: www.haufe.de *Cable:* HAUFEVERLAG
Key Personnel
Man Dir: Helmuth Hopfner; Martin Laqua; Uwe Renald Mueller
Founded: 1934
Subjects: Accounting, Business, Computer Science, Economics, Finance, Law, Management, Marketing, Real Estate
ISBN Prefix(es): 3-448
Subsidiaries: Lexware Gesellschaft fur Softwareentwicklung der rechts- und steuerberatenden Berufe mbH; WRS Verlag Wirtschaft, Recht und Steuern GmbH & Co
Branch Office(s)
Haufe Berlin, Albrechtstr 146, 10117 Berlin

Haug, *imprint of* Georg Thieme Verlag KG

Karl F Haug Verlag GmbH & Co+
Oswalt-Hesse-Str 50, 70469 Stuttgart
Tel: (00711) 8931-0 *Fax:* (0711) 8931-706
Web Site: www.haug-verlag.de/ *Cable:* HAUGVERLAG
Key Personnel
Man Dir: Florian Fischer; Jens Steinle
Advertising: Gisela Werner
Production: Dietmar Sieber
Sales: Alfred Fuchs
Publicity: Lucie Trauner
International Rights: Rolf Lenzen
Founded: 1903
Subjects: Health, Nutrition, Medicine, Nursing, Dentistry
ISBN Prefix(es): 3-7760
Parent Company: Huethig Verlag, Im Weiher 10, 69121 Heidelberg
Associate Companies: Arkana Verlag; Verlag fuer Medizin Dr Ewald Fischer GmbH
Subsidiaries: Editions Haug International

Dr Ernst Hauswedell & Co+
Haldenstr 30, 70376 Stuttgart
Mailing Address: Postfach 140155, 70071 Stuttgart
Tel: (0711) 54 99 71-0; (0711) 54 99 71-11 *Fax:* (0711) 54 99 71-21
Key Personnel
President: Charles Gerd Hiersemann *E-mail:* hiersemann.hauswedell.verlage@t-online.de
Founded: 1927
Subjects: Antiques, Art, Library & Information Sciences, Publishing & Book Trade Reference, Science (General), Literature, Typography
ISBN Prefix(es): 3-7762
Number of titles published annually: 10 Print
Total Titles: 200 Print; 8 CD-ROM
Associate Companies: Anton Hiersemann KG - Verlag, Haldenstr 30, 70376 Stuttgart *Web Site:* www.hiersenmann.de
Distributor for Staats-und Universitaets-Bibliothek Hamburg
Book Club(s): Maximilian Gesellschaft Hamburg

Hayit Reisefuhrer in der Rutsker Verlag GmbH+
c/o Mundo Media GmbH, Schreberstr 2, 51105 Cologne
Tel: (0221) 921635-0 *Fax:* (0221) 921635-24
E-mail: kontakt@hayit.com
Web Site: www.hayit.com
Key Personnel
Man Dir, Publicity, Rights & Permissions & Sales: Ertay Hayit *E-mail:* ertay.hayit@hayit.com
Editorial: Cornelia Auschra *Tel:* (0221) 921635-13 *E-mail:* cornelia.auschra@hayit.com; Mike Gahn *E-mail:* mike@hayit.com; Ute Hayit *Tel:* (0221) 921635-11 *E-mail:* ute.hayit@hayit.com
Founded: 1988
Subjects: Travel
ISBN Prefix(es): 3-89607; 3-88676; 3-89210; 3-922145; 3-925727
Associate Companies: Adl Hayit, Amsterdam, Netherlands
U.S. Office(s): County Route 9, PO Box 357, Chatham, NY 12037, United States *Tel:* 518-392-4526 *Fax:* 518-392-4557
Hayit Publishing USA Inc, c/o Pratley International, 30 East 81 St, New York, NY 10028, United States *Tel:* 212-772-2267 *Fax:* 212-772-3692 (Telex: 277258)

Heckners Verlag
Harzstr 22/23, 38300 Wolfenbuettel
Mailing Address: Postfach 1559, 38285 Wolfenbuettel
Tel: (05331) 8008-0 *Fax:* (05331) 8008-58

Key Personnel
Dir, Rights & Permissions: Siegfried Mathea
Founded: 1895
Subjects: Career Development, Economics
ISBN Prefix(es): 3-449
Parent Company: Kieser Verlag GmbH, Neusaess
Distributed by Orell Fuessli (Switzerland)

Heel Verlag GmbH+
Gut Pottscheidt, 53639 Koenigswinter
Tel: (02223) 9230-0 *Fax:* (02223) 9230-13; (02223) 9230-26
E-mail: service@heel-verlag.de
Web Site: www.heel-verlag.de
Key Personnel
Man Dir & International Rights: Franz-Christoph Heel
Foreign Rights Manager: Karin Michelberger *Tel:* (02223) 923046 *E-mail:* k.michelberger@heel-verlag.de
Founded: 1980
Subjects: Aeronautics, Aviation, Automotive, Cookery, Crafts, Games, Hobbies, Film, Video, Gardening, Plants, Humor, Maritime, Music, Dance, Nonfiction (General), Outdoor Recreation, Photography, Science Fiction, Fantasy, Sports, Athletics, Transportation, Travel
ISBN Prefix(es): 3-922858; 3-89365
Number of titles published annually: 120 Print
Total Titles: 600 Print
Distributor for Highlights Verlag; Johansens; Editions J R Piccard
Shipping Address: VSB Lager/Wareneingang, Helmstedter Str 99, 38126 Braunschweig
Warehouse: VSB Verlagsservice, Georg-Westermann-Allee 66, 38104 Braunschweig, Contact: Herr Wandert *Tel:* (0531) 708650 *Fax:* (0531) 708608

Joh Heider Verlag GmbH
Paffratherstr 102-116, 51465 Bergisch Gladbach
Tel: (02202) 95 40-35 *Fax:* (02202) 2 15 31
E-mail: anzeigen@marburger-bund.de
Web Site: www.heider-verlag.de/mb/mediadaten/
Key Personnel
Man Dir: Hans Heider
Publisher: Dr Dieter Boeck; Dr Dieter Mitrenga
Editorial: Anna von Borstell; Barbara Huennighausen; Dr Lutz Retzlaff; Angelika Steimer-Schmid
Founded: 1889
Subjects: Economics, Law, Social Sciences, Sociology
ISBN Prefix(es): 3-87314
Sales Office(s): Burgstr 122, 51427 Bergisch Gladbach, Contact: Christine Kaffka *Tel:* (02204) 96 18 18 *Fax:* (02204) 96 29 50

Heigl Verlag, Horst Edition+
Oberhaslach 6, 88633 Heiligenberg
Tel: (07554) 283 *Fax:* (07552) 938756
E-mail: info@heigl-verlag.de
Web Site: www.heigl-verlag.de
Key Personnel
Manager: Horst Heigl
Author: Horst Lozynski
Founded: 1987
Subjects: Art, Astrology, Occult, Physical Sciences, Religion - Other
ISBN Prefix(es): 3-89316

Verlag Otto Heinevetter Lehrmittel GmbH
Papenstr 41, 22089 Hamburg
Tel: (040) 25 90 19 *Fax:* (040) 251 2128
E-mail: info@heinevetter-verlag.de
Web Site: www.heinevetter-verlag.de
Key Personnel
Manager: Werner Klopfer
Founded: 1947
ISBN Prefix(es): 3-87474

Wolfgang Heinold, see Eulenhof-Verlag Wolfgang Ehrhardt Heinold

GERMANY

Heinrichshofen's Verlag GmbH & Co KG+
Liebigstr 16, 26389 Wilhelmshaven
Tel: (04421) 9267-0 *Fax:* (04421) 9267-99
E-mail: info@heinrichshofen.de
Web Site: www.heinrichshofen.de
Key Personnel
President: Juergen Etzoldt
Production, Printing: Peter Hensel *Tel:* (04421) 9267-11
Marketing: Michael Etzoldt
Founded: 1797
Also publish music, printing shop & bindery.
Subjects: Music
Number of titles published annually: 25 Print; 15 CD-ROM
Total Titles: 3,500 Print; 40 CD-ROM
Associate Companies: Otto Heinrich Noetzel Verlag; C F Peters Corporation, 70-30 80 St, Glendale, NY 11385, United States
U.S. Office(s): Heinrichshofen Edition New York, United States
Distributed by CPEA; C F Peters Corporation (New York); Peters Edition (London)

Heinz-Theo Gremme Verlag+
Tobiaspark 2, 44534 Lunen
Tel: (02592) 984200
E-mail: theo.gremme@epost.de
Web Site: www.gremme-verlag.de
Founded: 1991
Subjects: Fiction, Human Relations, Poetry, Science Fiction, Fantasy, Self-Help
ISBN Prefix(es): 3-9802679

Heinze GmbH
Bremer Weg 184, 29223 Celle
Tel: (01805) 339833 *Fax:* (01805) 119877
E-mail: info@heinze.de; kundenservice@heinze.de
Web Site: www.heinze.de/; www.heinzebauoffice.de
Telex: 925202
Key Personnel
President: Michael Hoelker
Founded: 1964
Subjects: Advertising
ISBN Prefix(es): 3-921724
Parent Company: Bertelsmann Fachinformationen Munich

Edition Heitere Poetik, *imprint of* Verlag Beruf und Schule Belz KG

Heitz Librarie, *imprint of* Verlag Valentin Koerner GmbH

HelfRecht Verlag und Druck
Markgrafenstr 32, 95680 Bad Alexandersbad
Tel: (09232) 6010 *Fax:* (09232) 601280
E-mail: info@helfrecht.de
Web Site: www.helfrecht.de
Key Personnel
Man Dir: Manfred Helfrecht; Gottfried Haberkorn; Werner Bayer
Public Relations & International Rights: Christoph Beck
Public Relations Assistant: Theresa Kraupner
Founded: 1975
Subjects: Career Development, Economics
ISBN Prefix(es): 3-920400
Parent Company: Firmengruppe HelfRecht GmbH & Co-Holding KG
Branch Office(s):
Rittet-von-Eitzeuberger-Str 25, 95448 Bayreuth
Tel: (0921) 9088 *Fax:* (0921) 9088

Heliopolis-Verlag+
Schellingstr 41, 72072 Tuebingen
Mailing Address: PO Box 1827, 72008 Tuebingen
Tel: (07473) 5427 *Fax:* (07473) 5427

Key Personnel
Manager: Dr Volker Katzmann
Founded: 1949
ISBN Prefix(es): 3-87324
Associate Companies: Katzmann-Verlag KG, Schellingstr 41, 72072 Tuebingen

Hellerau-Verlag Dresden GmbH
Koenigstr 12, 01097 Dresden
Tel: (0351) 803 5293 *Fax:* (0351) 826 0130
E-mail: info@hellerau-verlag.de
Web Site: www.hellerau-verlag.de/
Key Personnel
Publisher: Lothar Dunsch
Founded: 1990
Subjects: Fiction, History, Regional Interests
ISBN Prefix(es): 3-910184

G Henle Verlag
Forstenrieder Allee 122, 81476 Munich
Tel: (089) 759820 *Fax:* (089) 7598240
E-mail: info@henle.de
Web Site: www.henle.de
Key Personnel
Chief Executive Officer & President: Dr Wolf-Dieter Seiffert *Tel:* (089) 75982-21
  E-mail: seiffert@henle.de
Editor-in-Chief: Dr Norbert Gertsch
  E-mail: gertsch@henle.de
Head of Manufacturing: Gerhard Fischl
  E-mail: fischl@henle.de
Head of Sales & Marketing: Ulrike Lucht-Lorenz
  E-mail: lucht-lorenz@henle.de
Founded: 1948
Subjects: Music, Dance, Complete Editions (Brahms, Haydn & Beethoven), Music Books & Catalogs, Urtext Editions of Classical Music
ISBN Prefix(es): 3-87328
Total Titles: 50 Print
Subsidiaries: G Henle USA Inc

Henschel Verlag, *imprint of* Verlagsgruppe Dornier GmbH

Edition Hentrich Druck & Verlag Gebr Hentrich und Tank GmbH & Co KG+
Hindenburgdamm 78, 12203 Berlin
Tel: (030) 84410001 *Fax:* (030) 84410002
Key Personnel
Publisher & Manager: Werner Buchwald
Founded: 1982
Subjects: Art, Biography, Drama, Theater, Government, Political Science, History, Nonfiction (General), Religion - Jewish, Social Sciences, Sociology
ISBN Prefix(es): 3-89468; 3-926175

Herausgeber, *imprint of* Johann Wolfgang Goethe Universitat

F A Herbig Verlagsbuchhandlung GmbH+
Subsidiary of Buchverlage Langen-Mueller/Herbig
Thomas-Wimmer-Ring 11, 80539 Munich
Tel: (089) 2 90 88-0
E-mail: l.eggs@herbig.net
Web Site: www.herbig.net *Cable:* LANGENMULLER
Key Personnel
Man Dir & Publisher: Dr Herbert Fleissner
Man Dir: Dr Brigitte Sinhuber
Sales: Eva Ohser *E-mail:* e.ohser@herbig.net
Rights & Permissions: Dorothea Estermann; Frauke Hoppen *Tel:* (089) 2 90 88-156 *Fax:* (089) 2 90 88-178 *E-mail:* f.hoppen@herbig.net
Editorial: Dr Bernhard Struckmeyer
Founded: 1821
Subjects: Art, Astronomy, Biography, Cookery, Health, Nutrition, History, Nonfiction (General), Physical Sciences, Travel

ISBN Prefix(es): 3-7766
Orders to: VVA, An der Autobahn, 33310 Guetersloh

Hans-Alfred Herchen & Co Verlag KG
Fichardstr 30, 60322 Frankfurt am Main
Tel: (069) 550911-13 *Fax:* (069) 552601; (069) 554922
Key Personnel
Contact: Hans-Alfred Herchen
Founded: 1984
Subjects: Government, Political Science, Social Sciences, Sociology
ISBN Prefix(es): 3-89184

Verlag Herder GmbH & Co KG+
Hermann-Herder-Str 4, 79104 Freiburg
Tel: (0761) 2717440 *Fax:* (0761) 2717360
E-mail: kundenservice@herder.de
Web Site: www.herder.de/ *Cable:* HERDER FREIBURGBREISGAU
Key Personnel
Man Dir: Dr Hermann Herder; Manuel-Gregor Herder; Ulrich Peters; Dr Klaus-Christoph Scheffels
Rights & Permissions: Franziska Komm
Sales Dir: Rainer Lege
Export: Peter Pagendarm
Founded: 1801
Subjects: Biblical Studies, Education, Government, Political Science, History, Nonfiction (General), Religion - Buddhist, Religion - Catholic, Religion - Islamic, Religion - Other, Self-Help, Theology
ISBN Prefix(es): 3-451
Associate Companies: Herder Editrice e Libreria, Italy; Editorial Herder SA, Spain; Herder Ag, Switzerland
Imprints: Herderbuecherei; Herder/Spektrum; Uerle Verlag; Verlag Ploetz
Subsidiaries: Verlag Karl Alber GmbH; Christophorus-Verlag GmbH
Divisions: Kerle-Verlag; Ploetz
Bookshop(s): Carolus Buchrandlung Herder, Frankfurt am Main
Book Club(s): Herder Buchgemeinde
Shipping Address: Koch, Neff & Oetinger, Schockenriedstr 39, 70565 Stuttgart
Warehouse: Koch, Neff & Oetinger, Schockenriedstr 39, 70565 Stuttgart

Herder/Spektrum, *imprint of* Verlag Herder GmbH & Co KG

Herderbuecherei, *imprint of* Verlag Herder GmbH & Co KG

Hermetische Truhe Buchhandlung fuer Esoterische Literatur Barbara Dethlefsen
Gaertnerplatz 1, 80469 Munich
Tel: (089) 2710650 *Fax:* (089) 2724627
Key Personnel
Owner: Barbara Dethlefsen
Founded: 1983
ISBN Prefix(es): 3-927183

Herold Verlag Dr Wetzel+
Kirchbachweg 16, 81479 Munich
Tel: (089) 7915774
E-mail: wetzel@herold-verlag.de
Web Site: www.herold-verlag.de
Key Personnel
Man Dir & Publisher: Hans Meisinger
Rights & Publicity: Christiane Schneider
Founded: 1871
ISBN Prefix(es): 3-7767
Orders to: MVS Meisinger Verlagsservice GmbH, Am Steinfeld 4, 94065 Waldkirchen
Tel: (08581) 9605-0 *Fax:* (08581) 754

PUBLISHERS — GERMANY

Axel Hertenstein, Hertenstein-Presse
Mathystr 36, 75173 Pforzheim
Tel: (07231) 2 70 84 *Fax:* (07231) 2 70 84
Key Personnel
Publicity Manager: Ulrike Hertenstein
Founded: 1967
Specialize in library books & maps.
Subjects: Poetry

Hertenstein-Presse, see Axel Hertenstein, Hertenstein-Presse

Hessisches Ministerium fuer Umwelt, Landwirtschaft und Forsten
Mainzerstr 80, 65189 Wiesbaden
Tel: (0611) 8150 *Fax:* (0611) 8151941
E-mail: poststelle@hmulu.hessen.de
Web Site: www.mulf.hessen.de
Telex: 4182011 HMUE D
Key Personnel
Contact: Manuela Scharfenberg
Specialize in ecology.
Subjects: Agriculture, Energy, Environmental Studies, Ecology
Total Titles: 120 Print; 3 CD-ROM

Hestra-Verlag Hernichel & Dr Strauss GmbH & Co KG+
Holzhofallee 33, 64295 Darmstadt
Mailing Address: Postfach 100751, 64207 Darmstadt
Tel: (06151) 39070 *Fax:* (06151) 390777
Key Personnel
Man Dir & International Rights: Holger Musset
Tel: (06151) 390731 *E-mail:* musset@hestra.de
Founded: 1948
Subjects: Civil Engineering, Engineering (General), Law, Transportation
ISBN Prefix(es): 3-7771

Hexaglot Holding GmbH+
Sportallee 41, 22335 Hamburg
Tel: (040) 514560 *Fax:* (040) 51456991
E-mail: info@hexaglot.de
Web Site: www.hexaglot.de/ *Cable:* HEXAGER
Key Personnel
Manager: Dr Hans-Werner Scholz
Founded: 1989
ISBN Prefix(es): 3-928824
Parent Company: Langenscheidt KG
Subsidiaries: Sita Daten-und Kommunikations GmbH

Friedrich W Heye Verlag GmbH+
Oberweg 8, 82008 Unterhaching
Tel: (089) 6653201 *Fax:* (089) 66532210
E-mail: verlag@heye.de
Web Site: www.heye-verlag.de
Key Personnel
Man Dir: Peter Keil; Claudia Knauss; Juergen Knauss
Founded: 1962
ISBN Prefix(es): 3-88141; 3-89400
Associate Companies: Heye Top Present GmbH
Warehouse: Kapellenstr 13, 85622 Feldkirchen

Carl Heymanns Verlag KG+
Luxemburgerstr 449, 50939 Cologne
Tel: (0221) 94373-0 *Fax:* (0221) 94373-901
E-mail: marketing@heymanns.com
Web Site: www.heymanns.com
Key Personnel
Man Dir, Rights & Permissions: Andreas Gallus
Tel: (0221) 94373-101 *Fax:* (0221) 94373-105
E-mail: a.gallus@heymanns.com
Editorial: K Endlich *Tel:* (089) 224811
E-mail: endlich@heymanns.com; P Halter *Tel:* (0221) 94373-160 *E-mail:* halter@heymanns.com; H Kruppa *Tel:* (0221) 94373-134 *E-mail:* kruppa@heymanns.com; K Pompe *Tel:* (0221) 94373-600 *E-mail:* pompe@heymanns.com; M Sauerwald *Tel:* (0221) 94373-138 *E-mail:* sauerwald@heymanns.com
Production: M Voges *Tel:* (0221) 94373-200 *E-mail:* voges@heymanns.com
Editorial: K-L Steinhaeuser *Tel:* (0221) 94373-132 *E-mail:* steinhaeuser@heymanns.com
Marketing Manager: Gerd Welb *Tel:* (0221) 94373-300 *Fax:* (0221) 94373-310 *E-mail:* welb@heymanns.com
Founded: 1815
Subjects: Economics, Engineering (General), Government, Political Science, Law, Management, Public Administration
ISBN Prefix(es): 3-452
Total Titles: 2,000 Print; 70 CD-ROM
Subsidiaries: Euroliber Verlags- und Vertriebs-GmbH; Gallus Druckerei KG; Albert Nauck & Co
Branch Office(s)
Gutenbergstr 3-4, Berlin *Tel:* (030) 3914081 *Fax:* (030) 3912861
Steinsdorfstr 10, Postfach 26, 80538 Munich *Tel:* (089) 224811

Wilhelm Heyne Verlag+
Neumarkterstr 28, 81673 Munich
Mailing Address: Postfach 200143, 80001 Munich
Tel: (089) 41 36 0 *Fax:* (089) 51 48 2229
E-mail: heyne-suedwest@randomhouse.de
Web Site: www.heyne.de *Cable:* HEYNEVERLAG MUNCHEN
Key Personnel
Publisher: Rolf Heyne
Editorial Dir: Lothar Menne
Editorial: Ulrich Genzler; Wolfgang Jeschke; Dr Theda Krohm-Linke; Ria Lottermoser; Bernhard Matt; Ingeborg Meier
Sales Dir: Christian Tesch
Advertising Manager: David Hauptmann
Rights & Permissions: Traudel Eckardt
Founded: 1934
Subjects: Astrology, Occult, Biography, Cookery, Fiction, Film, Video, History, How-to, Humor, Mysteries, Psychology, Psychiatry, Romance, Science Fiction, Fantasy
ISBN Prefix(es): 3-453
Subsidiaries: Collection Rolf Heyne, Diana Verlag; Zabert Sandmann
U.S. Office(s): Franklin & Siegal Associates Inc, 1350 Broadway, Suite 2015, New York, NY 10018, United States
Orders to: Schleissheimerstr 106, 85748 Garching-Hochbrueck

Max Hieber KG+
Liebfrauenstr 1, 80331 Munich
Mailing Address: Postfach 330429, 80064 Munich
Tel: (089) 29008023 *Fax:* (089) 229782
E-mail: info@eminent-orgeln.de
Web Site: www.eminent-orgeln.de/kontakte.htm
Key Personnel
Contact: Daniel Stieb
Founded: 1884
Subjects: Music, Dance
ISBN Prefix(es): 3-920456
Branch Office(s)
Max Hieber Musikverlag, Verlagsauslieferung Einkauf, Musikalien-Versand Loewengrube 10, 80331 Munich
Distributed by Musikverlag Preissler

Anton Hiersemann, Verlag+
Haldenstr 30, 70376 Stuttgart
Mailing Address: Postfach 14 01 55, 70071 Stuttgart
Tel: (0711) 5499710; (0711) 5499711 *Fax:* (0711) 54997121
E-mail: info@hiersemann.de
Web Site: www.hiersemann.de *Cable:* HIERSEMANN
Key Personnel
President & Dir, Rights & Permissions: Gerd Hiersemann
Founded: 1884
Also specialize in monographs, publishing & book trade reference.
Subjects: Art, Astronomy, Biography, Drama, Theater, Genealogy, History, Library & Information Sciences, Literature, Literary Criticism, Essays, Religion - Buddhist, Religion - Catholic, Religion - Hindu, Religion - Islamic, Religion - Jewish, Religion - Protestant, Religion - Other, Science (General), Theology, Bookmaking
ISBN Prefix(es): 3-7772
Number of titles published annually: 45 Print
Total Titles: 1,200 Print; 7 CD-ROM
Associate Companies: Dr Ernst Hauswedell & Co
Imprints: Maximilian Gesellschaft eV
Subsidiaries: Karl W Hiersemann
Book Club(s): Geschaeftsstelle von: Literarischer Verein in Stuttgart eV

AIG I Hilbinger Verlag GmbH+
Frauensteiner Str 70, 65199 Wiesbaden
Tel: (0611) 4190088 *Fax:* (0611) 4190088
Key Personnel
Man Dir, Rights & Permissions: Immo A Hilbinger
Founded: 1989
Subjects: Astrology, Occult, Parapsychology, Self-Help
ISBN Prefix(es): 3-927110
Associate Companies: Agentur fuer Informationsgestaltung, Zum Dornhachtal, 65321 Heidenrod

Himmelsturmer Verlag+
Kirchenweg 12, 20099 Hamburg
Tel: (040) 48061717 *Fax:* (040) 48061799
E-mail: himmelstuermer@gmx.de
Founded: 1998
Specialize in gay novels & documentaries.
Subjects: Gay & Lesbian
ISBN Prefix(es): 3-934825; 3-9806249
Number of titles published annually: 6 Print
Total Titles: 25 Print

Verlag Hinder und Deelmann+
Postfach 1206, 35068 Gladenbach
Tel: (06462) 1301 *Fax:* (06462) 3307
Web Site: www.hinderunddeelmann.de/
Key Personnel
Publisher: Johannes Deelmann; Dr Rolf Hinder
Founded: 1953
Subjects: History, Philosophy, Religion - Other, Social Sciences, Sociology
ISBN Prefix(es): 3-87348
Distributor for Pondicherry (India); Sabda (India)

Hinstorff Verlag GmbH+
Lagerstr 7, 18055 Rostock
Tel: (0381) 49 69-0 *Fax:* (0381) 49 69-103
E-mail: sekretariat@hinstorff.de
Web Site: www.hinstorff.de
Key Personnel
Manager: Birgit Heinze
Contact: Birgit Kruggel
Founded: 1831
Subjects: Literature, Literary Criticism, Essays
ISBN Prefix(es): 3-356
Parent Company: Heinz Heise Verlag GmbH & Co KG, Hannover
Warehouse: VSB Verlagsservice Braunschweig GmbH, Helmstedterstr 99, 38126 Braunschweig
Orders to: VSB Verlagsservice Braunschweig GmbH, Postfach 4738, 38037 Braunschweig
Georg Westermann Allee 66, 38104 Braunschweig

Hippokrates, *imprint of* Georg Thieme Verlag KG

Hippokrates-Verlag GmbH+
Oswalt-Hesse Str 50, 70469 Stuttgart
Tel: (0711) 8931-0 *Fax:* (0711) 8931-706
Web Site: www.hippokrates.de
Telex: 7252275 gtvd
   Cable: HIPPOKRATESVERLAG
Key Personnel
Man Dir: A Charo
Publicity: Hans-Guenter Zimnik
Sales: Sabine Zenecker
Rights & Permissions (Thieme Verlag KG): Merit Schuett
Founded: 1925
Subjects: Medicine, Nursing, Dentistry
ISBN Prefix(es): 3-7773
Parent Company: Georg Thieme Verlag KG
Subsidiaries: Sonntag Verlag
Shipping Address: c/o Koch, Neff, Oetinger & Co, Postfach 210, 7000 Stuttgart
Warehouse: c/o Koch, Neff, Oetinger & Co, Postfach 210, 7000 Stuttgart
Orders to: c/o Koch, Neff, Oetinger & Co, Postfach 210, 7000 Stuttgart

Hirmer Verlag GmbH+
Member of Weltkunst Verlagsgruppe
Nymphenburgerstr 84, 80636 Munich
Mailing Address: Postfach 190454, 80604 Munich
Tel: (089) 1215160 *Fax:* (089) 12151610; (089) 12151616 (distribution)
E-mail: vertrieb@hirmerverlag.de
Web Site: www.hirmerverlag.de; www.weltkunstverlag.de
Key Personnel
Man Dir & Editorial: Albert Hirmer
Man Dir: Juergen Kleidt
Editorial: Dr Veronika Birbaumer; Margret Haase
Founded: 1948
Subjects: Archaeology, Art
ISBN Prefix(es): 3-7774

Harro V Hirschheydt
Neue Wiesen 6, 30900 Wedemark-Elze
Tel: (05130) 36758 *Fax:* (05130) 36799
E-mail: kontakt@hirschheydt-online.de
Key Personnel
Owner, Rights & Permissions: Harro V Hirschheydt
Founded: 1950
Subjects: Regional Interests
ISBN Prefix(es): 3-7777

F Hirthammer Verlag GmbH+
Raiffeisenallee 10, 82041 Oberhaching
Tel: (089) 3233360 *Fax:* (089) 3241728
E-mail: info@hirthammerverlag.de
Web Site: www.hirthammerverlag.de
Key Personnel
Manager: Franz Hirthammer
Founded: 1965
Subjects: Animals, Pets, Astrology, Occult, Environmental Studies, Health, Nutrition, Medicine, Nursing, Dentistry, Parapsychology, Philosophy, Religion - Buddhist, Religion - Hindu, Religion - Other, Theosophy
ISBN Prefix(es): 3-88721; 3-921288
Number of titles published annually: 15 Print
Total Titles: 200 Print

S Hirzel Verlag GmbH und Co+
Birkenwaldstr 44, 70191 Stuttgart
Mailing Address: Postfach 101061, 70009 Stuttgart
Tel: (0711) 25820 *Fax:* (0711) 2582290
E-mail: service@hirzel.de
Web Site: www.hirzel.de *Cable:*
   HIRZELVERLAG, STUTTGART
Key Personnel
Man Dir: Dr Klaus Brauer; Andre Caro; Dr Christian Rotta; Dr Thomas Schaber
Rights: Sabine Koerner
Sales: Siegmar Bauer *E-mail:* sbauer@hirzel.de
Founded: 1853
Subjects: Chemistry, Chemical Engineering, Engineering (General), Language Arts, Linguistics, Natural History, Philosophy, Psychology, Psychiatry, Regional Interests, Science (General)
ISBN Prefix(es): 3-7776
Parent Company: Deutscher Apotheker Verlag, Postfach 101061, 70009 Stuttgart
Associate Companies: Medpharm Scientific Publishers; Franz Steiner Verlag Wiesbaden GmbH; Wissenschaftliche Verlagagsellschaft mbH

Verlag Wolfgang Hoelker+
Hafenweg 30, 48155 Muenster
Mailing Address: Postfach 3820, 48021 Muenster
Tel: (0251) 414110 *Fax:* (0251) 4141140
E-mail: info@coppenrath.de
Web Site: www.coppenrath.de
Key Personnel
Man Dir: Wolfgang Hoelker
Sales: Hubert Bergmoser
Production: Wolfgang Foerster
Publicity: Tomas Rensiny
International Rights: Christiane Leesker
Founded: 1973
Subjects: Cookery
ISBN Prefix(es): 3-88117; 3-9800058
Subsidiaries: Coppenrath Verlag
Warehouse: Coppenrath-Hoelker Distribution, Textilstrasse, 48612 Horstmar *Tel:* (02558) 98818 *Fax:* (02558) 98819

Verlag Peter Hoell+
Darmstaedterstr 14 b, 64397 Modautal
Tel: (06167) 912220 *Fax:* (06167) 912221
E-mail: hoell.verlag@t-online.de
Founded: 1987
Subjects: Anthropology, Astrology, Occult, Human Relations, Literature, Literary Criticism, Essays
ISBN Prefix(es): 3-9801439; 3-928564
Total Titles: 5 Print

Hofbauer, Christoph und Trojanow Ilia, Akademischer Verlag Muenchen+
Paul-Heysestr 3la, 80336 Munich
Tel: (089) 51616151 *Fax:* (089) 51616199
E-mail: avm@druckmedien.de
Key Personnel
Contact: Christoph Hofbauer; Ilija Trojanow
Founded: 1991
Subjects: Anthropology, Business, Economics, Literature, Literary Criticism, Essays, Physical Sciences
ISBN Prefix(es): 3-929115; 3-932965
Associate Companies: Marino Verlag, c/o Frederking & Thaler, Neumarkter Str 18, Munich
Distributor for GBI-Verlag; Faktum

Edgar Hoff Verlag, see Reise Know-How

Edition Hoffmann & Co
Roemerstr 47, Goerbelheimer Muehle, 61169 Friedberg
Tel: (06031) 2443 *Fax:* (06031) 62965
Founded: 1967
Subjects: Architecture & Interior Design, Art
ISBN Prefix(es): 3-926026

Dieter Hoffmann Verlag
Senefelderstr 75, 55129 Mainz
Tel: (06136) 95100 *Fax:* (06136) 951037
Key Personnel
Man Dir, Rights & Permissions: Dieter Hoffman
Founded: 1960
Subjects: History, Outdoor Recreation
ISBN Prefix(es): 3-87341

H Hoffmann GmbH
An der Stammbahn 53, 14532 Kleinmachnow
Tel: (033203) 305810 *Fax:* (033203) 305820
E-mail: hhvberlin@t-online.de
ISBN Prefix(es): 3-87344

Hoffmann und Campe Verlag GmbH+
Harvestehuder Weg 42, 20149 Hamburg
Tel: (040) 441880 *Fax:* (040) 44188202
E-mail: email@hoca.de
Web Site: www.hoca.de
Telex: 0214259 HoCa
Key Personnel
Man Dir: Thomas Hackenberg; Uwe Marsen; Dr Rainer Moritz; Manfred Bissinger; Thomas Ganske; Dr Kai Laakmann
Editorial: Hubertus Rabe; Tania Schlie
Marketing Dir: Margrit Osterwold
Production: Roland Kraft
Publicity Dir: Dr Joachim Koehler
Rights & Permissions: Sibylle Chory; Ingeborg Rose
Rights: Nadja Kossack
Founded: 1781
Subjects: Art, Biography, Fiction, History, Music, Dance, Nonfiction (General), Philosophy, Poetry, Psychology, Psychiatry, Science (General), Social Sciences, Sociology
ISBN Prefix(es): 3-455
Foreign Rep(s): Dagmar Bhend (Switzerland); Herbert Pamminger (Austria); Helga Riegler (Austria)

Verlag Karl Hofmann GmbH & Co+
Steinwasenstr 6-8, 73614 Schorndorf
Mailing Address: Postfach 1360, 73603 Schorndorf
Tel: (07181) 4020 *Fax:* (07181) 402111
E-mail: info@hofmann-verlag.de
Web Site: www.hofmann-verlag.de
Key Personnel
Man Dir, Rights & Permissions: Ottmar Hecht
Man Dir, Sales: Thomas Hecht
Founded: 1904
Subjects: Sports, Athletics
ISBN Prefix(es): 3-7780

Friedrich Hofmeister Musikverlag+
Buettnerstr 10, 04103 Leipzig
Tel: (0341) 9 60 07 50 *Fax:* (0341) 9 60 30 55
E-mail: info@hofmeister-musikverlag.com
Web Site: www.friedrich-hofmeister.de; www.hofmeister-musikverlag.com
Key Personnel
Manager: Karl Heinz Schwarze
Founded: 1807
Subjects: Music, Dance
ISBN Prefix(es): 3-7331; 3-87350

Hogrefe Verlag GmbH & Co Kg+
Rohnsweg 25, 37085 Goettingen
Tel: (0551) 496090 *Fax:* (0551) 4960988
E-mail: verlag@hogrefe.de
Web Site: www.hogrefe.de/
Key Personnel
Proprietor: Dr Dr G-Juergen Hogrefe
   E-mail: hogrefe@hogrefe.de
Man Dir: Dr Michael Vogtmeier *Tel:* (0551) 4960921 *E-mail:* vogtmeier@hogrefe.de
Sales Dir: Reinhard Dornieden
Production: B Otto
Promotion: S Otto
Founded: 1949
Subjects: Medicine, Nursing, Dentistry, Psychology, Psychiatry
ISBN Prefix(es): 3-8017
Subsidiaries: Verlag fur Angewandte Psychologie
U.S. Office(s): Hogrefe & Huber Publishing, Seattle Regional Headquarters, PO Box 2487, Kirkland, WA 98083-2487, United States
Bookshop(s): Oettinger & Hogrefe GmbH, Buchhandlung fuer Medizin und Psychologie, Robert-Bosch-Breite 25, 37079 Goettingen

Warehouse: Robert-Bosch-Breite 25, 37079 Goettingen
Orders to: Brockhaus Commission, Kreidlerstr 9, 70806 Kornwestheim

Hohenrain-Verlag GmbH+
Am Apfelberg 18, 72076 Tuebingen
Mailing Address: Postfach 1611, 72006 Tuebingen
Tel: (07071) 40700 *Fax:* (07071) 407026
Key Personnel
Man Dir: Wigbert Grabert
Founded: 1985
Subjects: Art, Biography, Fiction, Government, Political Science, History
ISBN Prefix(es): 3-89180
Number of titles published annually: 3 Print
Total Titles: 70 Print

Matth Hohner AG Verlag
Andreas-Kochstr 9, 78647 Trossingen
Tel: (07425) 200 *Fax:* (07425) 249
E-mail: info@hohner.de
Web Site: www.hohner.de
Telex: 760727 hohnd
Key Personnel
Manager: Dr Ing Horst Braeuning
Founded: 1857
ISBN Prefix(es): 3-920468
Warehouse: Hohnerstr 8, 78647 Trossingen

Holland & Josenhans GmbH & Co+
Subsidiary of Verlag Handwerk und Technik GmbH
Feuerseeplatz 2, 70176 Stuttgart
Mailing Address: Postfach 1023 52, 70019 Stuttgart
Tel: (0711) 6143920 *Fax:* (0711) 6143922
E-mail: verlag@huj.03.net
Web Site: www.holland-josenhans.de/
Key Personnel
Marketing: Heidi Scheurle *Tel:* (0711) 6143925 *Fax:* (0711) 6143955 *E-mail:* marketing@huj.03.net
Founded: 1861
Subjects: Education
ISBN Prefix(es): 3-7782
Foreign Rep(s): Technischer Fachbuchvertrieb AG (Switzerland)

Holos Verlag+
Ermekeilstr 15, 53113 Bonn
Tel: (0228) 263020; (0228) 262332 *Fax:* (0228) 212435
Founded: 1987
Specialize in humanities.
Subjects: Anthropology, Archaeology, Fiction, Gay & Lesbian, Geography, Geology, History, Language Arts, Linguistics, Philosophy, Psychology, Psychiatry, Social Sciences, Sociology
ISBN Prefix(es): 3-926216; 3-86097

Verlagsgruppe Georg von Holtzbrinck GmbH
Gaensheidestr 26, 70184 Stuttgart
Mailing Address: Postfach 105039, 70044 Stuttgart
Tel: (0711) 2150-0 *Fax:* (0711) 2150-269
E-mail: info@holtzbrinck.com
Web Site: www.holtzbrinck.com
Founded: 1971
Subjects: Education, Fiction, Nonfiction (General), Science (General), Newspapers

Guenther Holzboog, see Friedrich Frommann Verlag

Hans Holzmann Verlag GmbH und Co KG
Gewerbestr 2, 86825 Bad Woerishofen
Mailing Address: Postfach 1342, 86816 Bad Woerishofen
Tel: (08247) 35401 *Fax:* (08247) 354170
E-mail: info@holzmannverlag.de
Web Site: www.holzmannverlag.de/
Telex: 539331 *Cable:* HOLZMANN VERLAG
Key Personnel
Man Dir: Alexander Holzmann *E-mail:* alexander.holzmann@holzmannverlag.de
Production Dir: Helmut Mauritz
Publishing Dir: Harald Bos *E-mail:* harald.bos@holzmannverlag.de
Finances: Arthur Fostmaier
Founded: 1936
Subjects: Business, Education, Law, Marketing
ISBN Prefix(es): 3-7783; 3-920416
Subsidiaries: Druck und Werbung Holzmann GmbH
Divisions: Abt Buchverlag; Abt Fach-Zeitschriften; Abt Anzeigen

Homo Oeconomicus, *imprint of* Accedo Verlagsgesellschaft mbH

Hoppenstedt GmbH & Co KG
Havelstr 9, 64295 Darmstadt
Mailing Address: Postfach 100139, 64201 Darmstadt
Tel: (06151) 380-0 *Fax:* (06151) 380-360
E-mail: info@hoppenstedt.de
Web Site: www.hoppenstedt.de
Key Personnel
Man Dir: Werner Reiber; Roland Repp
Contact: Silke Braun *Tel:* (06151) 380-261
Founded: 1926
Subjects: Finance, Marketing, Securities
ISBN Prefix(es): 3-8203
Associate Companies: Druckhaus Darmstadt GmbH, Darmstadt *Tel:* (06151) 80550 *Fax:* (06151) 8055200; Hoppenstedt Bonnier Information GmbH, Darmstadt *Tel:* (06151) 380367 *Fax:* (06151) 380488 *E-mail:* info@catalogic.de; ComHouse AG, Wuerzburg *Tel:* (0931) 3561-0 *Fax:* (0931) 3561-140 *E-mail:* mail@comhouse.net; Belgisch ABC voor Handel en Industrie Bv, Asse, Belgium *Tel:* (021) 4630213 *Fax:* (021) 4630885 *E-mail:* info@abc-de.be; HBI sro, Prague, Czech Republic *Tel:* (02) 6316624 *Fax:* (02) 6516616 *E-mail:* hoppenstedt@televom.cz; Hoppenstedt Bonnier & Tarsa Informacios Kft, Budapest, Hungary *Tel:* (01) 2761333 *Fax:* (01) 2760933 *E-mail:* mail@hoppbonn.hu; HBI SpA Bassano del Grappa, Bassano del Grappa, Italy *Tel:* (0424) 529088 *Fax:* (0424) 529191 *E-mail:* info@hbiitaly.it; ABC voor Handel en Industrie CV, Haarlem, Netherlands *Tel:* (023) 5533533 *Fax:* (023) 5327033 *E-mail:* info@abc-de.nl; Hoppenstedt Bonnier Information Polska Sp zoo, ul Kwiatka 12, 09-400 Plock, Poland *Tel:* (024) 366 33 10 *Fax:* (024) 366 33 33 *E-mail:* hbi@hbi.pl *Web Site:* www.hbi.pl
Subsidiaries: Seibt Verlag GmbH; Verlag Hoppenstedt & Co Wirtschajtsverlag Ges mbH; Hoppenstedt France SNC Compiegne; Hoppenstedt Nederland BV; Hoppenstedt AG Kilchberg

Horlemann Verlag+
Postfach 1307, 53583 Bad Honnef
Tel: (02224) 5589 *Fax:* (02224) 5429
E-mail: horlemann@aol.com
Web Site: www.horlemann-verlag.de/
Key Personnel
Owner & International Rights: Beate Horlemann
Founded: 1990
Membership(s): The Stock Exchange of German Booksellers.
Subjects: Asian Studies, Developing Countries, Education, Environmental Studies, Fiction, Foreign Countries, Government, Political Science, Literature, Literary Criticism, Essays, Nonfiction (General), Philosophy, Poetry, Religion - Islamic, Social Sciences, Sociology
ISBN Prefix(es): 3-927905; 3-89502

Hans Huber+
Laenggass-Str 76, 3000 Bern 9
Tel: (031) 3004500 *Fax:* (031) 3004590
E-mail: verlag@hanshuber.com
Web Site: www.hanshuber.com *Cable:* HUBERVERLAG BERN
Key Personnel
Man Dir: Dr G-Juergen Hogrefe
Editorial Dir: Juerg Flury
Marketing: Christian Liengme
Advertising: Anina Burkhalter
Founded: 1927
Subjects: Education, Medicine, Nursing, Dentistry, Psychology, Psychiatry
ISBN Prefix(es): 3-456
Subsidiaries: Hogrefe & Huber Publishers Inc, Seattle/Toronto; Psychodiagnostika, Brno/Czechia & Bratislava/Slovakia; Testzentrale der Schweizer Psychologen AG
U.S. Office(s): Hogrefe & Huber Publishers Inc, PO Box 2487, Kirkland, WA 98083-2487, United States *Tel:* 425-820-1500 *Fax:* 425-823-8324
Bookshop(s): Schanzenstr 1, 3000 Bern 9, Switzerland *Tel:* (031) 3004646 *Fax:* (031) 3004656 *E-mail:* contactbern@huberlang.com; Zeltweg 6, 8032 Zurich, Switzerland *Tel:* (01) 2683939 *Fax:* (01) 2683920 *E-mail:* contactzurich@huberlang.com

Volker Huber Edition & Galerie+
Berlinerstr 218, 63067 Offenbach
Mailing Address: Postfach 101153, 63011 Offenbach
Tel: (069) 814523 *Fax:* (069) 880155
E-mail: edition-huber@t-online.de
Web Site: www.volkerhuber.de
Key Personnel
Owner: Volker Huber
Founded: 1965
Subjects: Art
ISBN Prefix(es): 3-921785

Max Hueber Verlag GmbH & Co KG+
Max-Hueber Str 4, 85737 Ismaning
Mailing Address: Postfach 1142, 85729 Ismaning
Tel: (089) 9602-0 *Fax:* (089) 9602-358
E-mail: kundenservice@hueber.de
Web Site: www.hueber.de
Telex: 523613 hueb d
Key Personnel
Dir: Wolf Dieter Eggert; Michaela Hueber
Rights: Claudia Harbauer
Founded: 1921
Subjects: Education, Language Arts, Linguistics, Adult Education in Foreign Languages, German as a Foreign Language
ISBN Prefix(es): 3-19
U.S. Office(s): Alder's Foreign Books Inc, 915 Foster St, Evanston, IL, United States
Continental Book Company Inc, 625E 70 Ave, Suite 5, Denver, CO 80229, United States
German Book Center, NA Inc, PO Box 99, Mountaindale, NY 12763-0099, United States
International Book Import Service Inc, 161 Main St, Lynchburg, TN 37352-8188, United States
Schoenhof's Foreign Books, Inc, 76A Mount Auburn St, Cambridge, MA 02138-5051, United States
Distributed by Editorial Idiomas (Spain); Hueber-Hellas (Greece)

Felicitas Huebner Verlag+
Warolderstr 1, 34513 Waldeck
Tel: (05695) 1028 *Fax:* (05695) 1027
Key Personnel
Publisher: Felicitas Huebner
Founded: 1981
Subjects: Film, Video, Health, Nutrition, Sports, Athletics
ISBN Prefix(es): 3-927359
Orders to: Bugrim Verlagsauslieferung Dr Laube & Partner, Saalburgstr 3, 12099 Berlin

Verlag Uta Huelsey
Hansaring 52, 46483 Wesel
Mailing Address: Postfach 101034, 46470 Wesel
Tel: (0281) 27227 *Fax:* (0281) 24682
E-mail: uta.hulsey@t-online.de
ISBN Prefix(es): 3-923185

Heinrich Hugendubel Verlag GmbH+
Holzstr 28, 80469 Munich
Tel: (089) 235586-0 *Fax:* (089) 235586-111
Web Site: www.hugendubel.de
Key Personnel
Managing Partner: Heinrich Hugendubel; Dr Monika Roell
Publishing Dir: Stephanie Ehrenschwendner
Rights & Permissions: Susanna Schoeni
Subjects: Astrology, Occult, Government, Political Science, Health, Nutrition, Human Relations, Management, Nonfiction (General), Psychology, Psychiatry, Religion - Other, Self-Help
ISBN Prefix(es): 3-7205; 3-7162; 3-8267; 3-88034; 3-424
Total Titles: 100 Print
Imprints: Ariston; Diederichs; Irisiana; Kailash
Orders to: VVA-Vereinigte Verlagsanslieferung, An der Antobahn, Postfach 1111, 33310 Guetersloh *Fax:* (05241) 460367

Edition Humanistische Psychologie (EHP)+
Johannesstr 22, 51465 Bergisch Gladbach
Mailing Address: PO Box 200 222, 51432 Bergisch Gladbach
Tel: (02202) 981236 *Fax:* (02202) 981237
E-mail: info@ehp-koeln.com
Web Site: www.ehp-koeln.com; www.ehp.biz
Key Personnel
Vice President & Manager: Michels Kohlhage *Tel:* (0221) 5303817 *E-mail:* mmk@ehp-koeln.com
Editor: Andreas Kohlhage *E-mail:* andrea.kohlhage@ehp-koeln.com
Founded: 1986
Subjects: Human Relations, Literature, Literary Criticism, Essays, Management, Nonfiction (General), Psychology, Psychiatry, Science (General), Social Sciences, Sociology
ISBN Prefix(es): 3-926176; 3-9804784; 3-89797
Number of titles published annually: 5 Print
Total Titles: 60 Print
Orders to: Brockhaus Commission, Kreidlerstr 9, 70806 Kornwestheim, Contract: Mrs Schlayh *Tel:* (07154) 13270 *Fax:* (07154) 132713 *E-mail:* bestell@brocom.de
Hans Huber AG, Langgasstr 76, 3012 Bern, Switzerland, Contract: Mrs Keller *Tel:* (031) 3004-500 *Fax:* (031) 3004-590 *E-mail:* verlag@huberag.com

Humanistischer Verband Deutschlands, Landesverband Berlin eV
Wallstr 61-65, 10179 Berlin
Tel: (030) 6139040 *Fax:* (030) 61390450
E-mail: hvd@humanismus.de
Web Site: www.humanismus.de
Key Personnel
Manager: Wolfgang Hecht
ISBN Prefix(es): 3-924041
Number of titles published annually: 4 Print
Total Titles: 55 Print

Humboldt-Taschenbuch Verlag Jacobi KG+
Member of The Langenscheidt Group
Neusserstr 3, 80807 Munich
Mailing Address: Postfach 401120, 80711 Munich
Tel: (089) 360960 *Fax:* (089) 36096-222 (general); (089) 36096-258 (orders)
E-mail: redaktion@humboldt.de
Key Personnel
Man Dir: Karl Ernst Tielebier-Langenscheidt *E-mail:* redaktion@humboldt.de; Andreas Langenscheidt
Publishing Dir: Rolf Muller
Chief Editor: Claus-Ulrich Schmidt
Sales Dir: Dr Matti Schusseler
Advertising: Brigitte Pasch
Founded: 1953
Sales & promotion through Langenscheidt KG.
Subjects: Nonfiction (General), Travel
ISBN Prefix(es): 3-581
Orders to: Langenscheidt KG, Neusser Str 3, 80807 Munich

Edition Hundertmark
Bruesselerstr 29, 50674 Cologne
Tel: (0221) 237944 *Fax:* (0221) 249146
E-mail: info@hundertmark-gallery.com
Web Site: www.hundertmark-gallery.com
Key Personnel
Man Dir: Armin Hundertmark
Founded: 1970
Subjects: Art, Literature, Literary Criticism, Essays
Showroom(s): Galerie und Edition Hundermark, Brusseler Str 29, 50674 Cologne

Huss-Medien GmbH
Am Friedrichshain 22, 10407 Berlin
Tel: (030) 421510 *Fax:* (030) 42151332
E-mail: huss.medien@hussberlin.de
Web Site: huss-medien.de *Cable:* TECHNIKVERLAG BERLIN
Key Personnel
Dir: Guenther Schwarz *Tel:* (030) 42151203 *E-mail:* guenther.schwarz@hussberlin.de
Secretary: Monika Ebert *Tel:* (030) 42151302 *E-mail:* monika.ebert@hussberlin.de
Founded: 1946
Subjects: Career Development, Electronics, Electrical Engineering, Mechanical Engineering, Radio, TV, Technology
ISBN Prefix(es): 3-341
Parent Company: Huss-Verlag GmbH, Munich
Orders to: LKG-Leipziger Kommissions-und Grossbuchhandel mbH, Poetzschauer Weg, 04579 Espenhain
Zeitschriftenvertrieb, Am Friedrichshain 22, 10400 Berlin

Huss-Verlag GmbH+
Joseph-Dollinger-Bogen 5, 80807 Munich
Mailing Address: Postfach 460480, 80192 Munich
Tel: (089) 323910 *Fax:* (089) 32391416
E-mail: management@huss-verlag.de
Web Site: www.huss-verlag.de/
Key Personnel
President: Wolfgang Huss
Public Relations: Monica-Ines Oppel
Founded: 1975
Subjects: Automotive, Business, Electronics, Electrical Engineering, Engineering (General), Transportation
ISBN Prefix(es): 3-921455
Associate Companies: Huss GmbH, Friedrichshain 22, 10407 Berlin
Subsidiaries: Verlag Technik GmbH; Verlag Die Wirtschaft GmbH; Verlag fuer Bauwesen GmbH
Orders to: Huss-GmbH, Am Friedrichshain 22, 10407 Berlin

Husum Druck- und Verlagsgesellschaft mbH Co KG+
Nordbahnhofstr 2, 25813 Husum
Mailing Address: Postfach 1480, 25804 Husum
Tel: (04841) 83520 *Fax:* (04841) 835210
E-mail: verlagsgruppe.husum@t-online.de
Web Site: www.verlagsgruppe.de/
Key Personnel
Man Dir, Editorial, Production, Rights & Permissions: Ingwert Paulsen
Founded: 1973
Subjects: Regional Interests
ISBN Prefix(es): 3-88042; 3-89876
Associate Companies: Hansa Verlag Ingwert Paulsen Jr; Matthiesen Verlag Ingwert Paulsen Jr; Verlag der Nation
Subsidiaries: Hamburger Lesehefte Verlag Iselt & Co Nfl mbH

Huthig GmbH & Co KG+
Im Weiher 10, 69121 Heidelberg
Mailing Address: Postfach 102869, 69121 Heidelberg
Tel: (06221) 4890 *Fax:* (06221) 489279
E-mail: info@huethig.de
Web Site: www.huethig.de
Key Personnel
Man Dir: Hans-Joern Hoffmann; Huethig Holger; Bernhard Kessler; Clemens Koehler
Marketing: Joseph Weisbrod
Founded: 1925
Subjects: Architecture & Interior Design, Business, Chemistry, Chemical Engineering, Civil Engineering, Communications, Computer Science, Criminology, Earth Sciences, Electronics, Electrical Engineering, Energy, Film, Video, Health, Nutrition, Law, Medicine, Nursing, Dentistry, Science (General), Technology
ISBN Prefix(es): 3-929471
Subsidiaries: Barth Verlag; C F Mue Verlag; Rv Decker's Verlag, G Schenck; dpunkt Verlag; Economica Verlag; Forkel Verlag; Haug Verlagstuppe; Heidelberg, Wichmann Verlag; tuer digitale Technologie
U.S. Office(s): Hennig Wriedt, 29 MacIntosh Dr, Oxford, CT 06478, United States *Tel:* 203-881-2467 *Fax:* 203-881-2795
Warehouse: Verlagsservice Suedwest, Boschstr 2, 68753 Waghaeusel, Kirrlach
Orders to: Heidelberger Verlagsservice GmbH, Im Weiher 10, 69121 Heidelberg

Hyperion - Verlag (Hyperion Publishing House)
Gutenbergstr 25, 85748 Garching
Tel: (089) 32954165 *Fax:* (089) 32954175
E-mail: mail@hyperion-verlag.de
Web Site: www.hyperion-verlag.de
Key Personnel
President & International Rights: Martin Wartelsteiner
Founded: 1906
Subjects: Erotica, Fiction, Literature, Literary Criticism, Essays, Philosophy
ISBN Prefix(es): 3-89914
Number of titles published annually: 8 Print
Total Titles: 1 Print
Associate Companies: Miniaturbuchverlag Leipzig

Edition ID-Archiv/ID-Verlag+
Gneisenaustr 2a, 10961 Berlin
Tel: (030) 6947703 *Fax:* (030) 6947808
E-mail: id-verlag@mail.nadir.org
Web Site: www.txt.de/id-verlag/
Key Personnel
Contact: Andreas Fanizadeh; Wolfgang Tawereit
Founded: 1988
Subjects: Communications, Developing Countries, Government, Political Science, History, Literature, Literary Criticism, Essays, Publishing & Book Trade Reference
ISBN Prefix(es): 3-89408
Foreign Rep(s): Sebastian Count (Switzerland); Seth Meyer Bruhns (Austria)
Orders to: Sova, Friesstr 20-24, 60388 Frankfurt am Main

Idea Verlag GmbH+
Ringstr 40, 82223 Eichenau
Mailing Address: Postfach 1361, 82169 Puchheim
Tel: (08141) 80939 *Fax:* (08141) 80939
E-mail: info@idea-verlag.de
Web Site: www.idea-verlag.de
Key Personnel
Man Dir & Rights: Hariet Paschke
Founded: 1980

Subjects: Crafts, Games, Hobbies, Literature, Literary Criticism, Essays, Science (General), Sports, Athletics, Technology
ISBN Prefix(es): 3-88793; 3-9800371

IDW-Verlag GmbH+
Tersteegenstr 14, 40474 Duesseldorf
Mailing Address: Postfach 320580, 40420 Duesseldorf
Tel: (0211) 45610 *Fax:* (0211) 4541206
E-mail: post@idw-verlag.de
Web Site: www.idw-verlag.de *Cable:* IDEWEVERLAG
Key Personnel
Man Dir: Rainer von Buechau
Founded: 1950
Subjects: Accounting, Business, Finance
ISBN Prefix(es): 3-8021
Subsidiaries: WPA- Wirtschaftsakademie

Igel Verlag Literatur Michael Matthias Schardt
Uhlhornsweg 99A, 26129 Oldenburg
Tel: (0441) 6640262 *Fax:* (0441) 6640263
Key Personnel
Contact: Michael Schardt
ISBN Prefix(es): 3-89621; 3-927104

Ikarus - Buchverlag+
Schuhgasse 6, 36142 Tann Rhoen
Tel: (06682) 919383 *Fax:* (06682) 919385
E-mail: ikarus-verlag@t-online.de
Web Site: www.ikarus-verlag.de
Key Personnel
Man Dir: Dr Wolfgang Hautumm
Founded: 1982
Subjects: Archaeology, History, Literature, Literary Criticism, Essays, Travel
ISBN Prefix(es): 3-9802064; 3-9800471
Number of titles published annually: 2 Print
Total Titles: 25 Print

IKO Verlag fur Interkulturelle Kommunikation+
Postfach 900, 421, 60444 Frankfurt/Main
Tel: (069) 784808 *Fax:* (069) 7896575
E-mail: info@iko-verlag.de
Web Site: www.iko-verlag.de
Key Personnel
Man Dir: Walter Suelberg
Founded: 1982
Subjects: Alternative, Anthropology, Asian Studies, Business, Developing Countries, Education, Environmental Studies, Ethnicity, Labor, Industrial Relations, Science (General), Women's Studies
ISBN Prefix(es): 3-88939
Associate Companies: Holger Ehluig Publishers at Tho-Verlag fur Tutor-Kultaelle Kouierikohou, 4T Leroy House, 436 Essex Rd, London N1 3QP, United Kingdom *Tel:* (020) 7688 1688 *Fax:* (020) 7688 1699

ILS, see Institut fuer Landes- und Stadtentwicklungsforschung des Landes Nordrhein-Westfalen

Impuls-Theater-Verlag+
Postfach 1147, 82141 Planegg
Tel: (089) 8597577 *Fax:* (089) 8593044
E-mail: info@buschfunk.de
Web Site: www.buschfunk.de
Key Personnel
Contact: Florian Laber
Founded: 1932
Specialize in theatre: plays & books.
Subjects: Drama, Theater, Film, Video, Music, Dance
ISBN Prefix(es): 3-7660
Distributed by Teaterverlag elgg (Switzerland)
Distributor for Stutz-Velag (Germany & Austria)

IMSF, see Institut fuer Marxistische Studien und Forschungen eV (IMSF)

Industria-Verlagsbuchhandlung GmbH
Eschstr 22, 44629 Herne
Mailing Address: Postfach 101849, 44621 Herne
Tel: (02323) 1410 *Fax:* (02323) 141123
Telex: 8229870
Key Personnel
Manager: Ernst-Otto Kleyboldt
Subjects: Accounting, Law
ISBN Prefix(es): 3-87373

Industrie- und Handelsverlag GmbH & Co KG
Goettinger Chaussee 76, 30453 Hannover
Tel: (0511) 98489957 *Fax:* (0511) 98489952
E-mail: info@fhb-online.de
Web Site: www.fhb-online.de/
Key Personnel
Man Dir: Heiko Dorn
Procurer: Angelika Lindeberg-Geers
Founded: 1923
Membership(s): The Stock Exchange of German Booksellers.
ISBN Prefix(es): 3-7788
Associate Companies: Verlagsbetriebe Walter Dorn GmbH & Co KG
Branch Office(s)
Berlin
Bremen
Duesseldorf
Filderstadt
Frankfurt
Leipzig
Munich

Industrieschau Verlagsgesellschaft mbH
Berliner Allee 8, 64295 Darmstadt
Mailing Address: Postfach 100264, 64202 Darmstadt
Tel: (06151) 38920 *Fax:* (06151) 389280
E-mail: info@abconline.de
Web Site: www.abconline.de
Key Personnel
Man Dir: Margit Selka
Reference & product directories about German industrial groups.
ISBN Prefix(es): 3-7790
Parent Company: ABC der Deutschen Wirtschaft Verlagsgesellschaft mbH
Branch Office(s)
PO Box 75, 1095 Vienna, Austria *Tel:* (0222) 4053327
U.S. Office(s): Western Hemisphere Publishing Corp, PO Box 847, Hillsboro, OR 97123-0847, United States *Tel:* 503-640-3736 *Fax:* 503-640-2748

Mediteg-Gesellschaft fuer Informatik Technik und Systeme Verlag+
Limesstr 5, 61273 Wehrheim
Tel: (06081) 5171 *Fax:* (06081) 56017
Key Personnel
Manager: Rudolf Putz
Founded: 1984
Subjects: Medicine, Nursing, Dentistry
ISBN Prefix(es): 3-924373

Informationsstelle Suedliches Afrika eV (ISSA) (Information Centre on Southern Africa)
Koenigswinterer Str 116, 53227 Bonn
Tel: (0228) 464369 *Fax:* (0228) 468177
E-mail: issa@comlink.org
Web Site: www.issa-bonn.org
Key Personnel
Man Dir: Hein Moellers
Founded: 1971
Subjects: Developing Countries, Literature, Literary Criticism, Essays
ISBN Prefix(es): 3-921614

Infostelle Industrieverband Deutscher Schmieden e V
Goldene Pforte 1, 58093 Hagen
Tel: (02331) 958828 *Fax:* (02331) 958728
E-mail: orders@metalform.de
Web Site: www.metalform.de
Key Personnel
Marketing: Heinrich Benneker *Tel:* (02331) 958821
Management: Dr Theodore L Tutmann *Tel:* (02331) 958812

Inno Vatio Verlags AG
Kurt Schumacherstr 2, 53113 Bonn
Tel: (0228) 93-444-31 *Fax:* (0228) 93-444-93
E-mail: medien-tenor@innovatio.de
Web Site: www.innovatio.de; www.medien-tenor.de
Founded: 1985
Subjects: Business, History, Specialize in monthly & quarterly newsletters on media content analysis
Total Titles: 25 Print

Insel Verlag+
Lindenstr 29-35, 60325 Frankfurt am Main
Mailing Address: Postfach 101945, 60019 Frankfurt am Main
Tel: (069) 75601-0 *Fax:* (069) 75601-522
Web Site: www.suhrkamp.de *Cable:* INSELVERLAG
Key Personnel
Publisher: Ulla Unseld-Berkewicz
Man Dir: Philip Roeder *Tel:* (069) 75601-500 *E-mail:* roeder@suhrkamp.de
Editorial Director: Dr Rainer Weiss
Sales & Marketing Dir: Dr Georg Rieppel
Rights & Permissions: Dr Petra Hardt
Founded: 1899
Subjects: Art, Ethnicity, Literature, Literary Criticism, Essays
ISBN Prefix(es): 3-458
Associate Companies: Deutscher Klassiker Verlag; Suhrkamp Verlag; Suhrkamp Verlag AG, Switzerland
Branch Office(s)
Liviastr 2, 04105 Leipzig *Tel:* (0341) 988980 *Fax:* (0341) 9889820
Foreign Rep(s): Claudia Brandes (Netherlands, Europe, Scandinavia); Ulrich Breth (Asia, Greece, Turkey); Michael Griesinger (Latin America, Portugal, Spain); Petra Hardt (Australia, China, France, Israel, Italy, Middle East, Taiwan, USA)
Foreign Rights: Agenzia (Italy); Balla & Co Literary Agents (Hungary); Bardon Chinese Media Agency (Taiwan); Hercules Business (China); Internationaal Literatuur Bureau (Netherlands); International Editors (Brazil, Latin America, Spain); Leonhardt & Hoier Literary (Scandinavia); Sakai Agency (Japan)

Institut fuer Baustoffe, Massivbau und Brandschutz/Bibliothek (Institute for Building Materials, Reinforced Concrete Construction & Fire Protection Library)
Beethovenstr 52, 38106 Braunschweig
Tel: (0531) 391 5400 *Fax:* (0531) 391 5900
E-mail: ibmb@tu-bs.de
Web Site: www.ibmb.tu-bs.de
Key Personnel
Librarian: Oliver Dienelt *E-mail:* o.dienelt@tu-bs.de
Founded: 1963
Subjects: Civil Engineering, Proceedings, Reports, Theses
ISBN Prefix(es): 3-89288
Number of titles published annually: 8 Print
Total Titles: 180 Print

GERMANY BOOK

Interconnections Reisen und Arbeiten Georg Beckmann+
Schilerstr 44, 79102 Freiburg
Tel: (0761) 700650 *Fax:* (0761) 700688
Key Personnel
Owner: Georg Beckmann
Founded: 1985
Subjects: Travel
ISBN Prefix(es): 3-924586; 3-86040
Orders to: Internationaler Land Kartenhaus, Schockenreidstr 44a, 705655 Stuttgart

International Thomson Publishing (ITP)+
Koenigswintererstr 418, 53227 Bonn
Tel: (0228) 970240 *Fax:* (0228) 441342
E-mail: mitp@mitp.de
Web Site: www.mitp.de
Key Personnel
President: Hartmut Gante
International Rights: H J Beese
Sales Dir: Markus Kanderer
Founded: 1992
Subjects: Computer Science
ISBN Prefix(es): 3-8266
Subsidiaries: Datacom; ITP - IWT; Wolframs
Warehouse: VVA Bertelsmann, Postfach 7777, 33310 Guetersloh

Verlag fuer Internationale Politik GmbH+
Bachstr 32, 53115 Bonn
Mailing Address: Postfach 1529, 53005 Bonn
Tel: (0228) 7290010 *Fax:* (0228) 7290013
Key Personnel
Partner: Otto Wolff von Amerongen; Alfred Frhr von Oppenheim
Man Dir: Gerhard Eickhorn
Man Dir Assistant: Ulrike Rothe
Sales: Rainer Mertens
Founded: 1971
Subjects: Government, Political Science
ISBN Prefix(es): 3-921011
Parent Company: Europa Union Verlag GmbH

Internationale Studien zen Fatigkeititleone, *imprint of* Bund demokratischer Wissenschaftlerinnen und Wissenschafler eV (BdWi)

Internationale Vereinigung fuer Geschichte und Gegenwart der Druckkunst eV, see Gutenberg-Gesellschaft eV

Intertrans-Verlag GmbH+
Neckarstr 37, 63071 Offenbach
Tel: (069) 871500 *Fax:* (069) 852894
Key Personnel
Manager & International Rights: Bernhard Mueller
Founded: 1982
Subjects: Language Arts, Linguistics
ISBN Prefix(es): 3-8223; 3-922718
Distributor for Edition-Disque Omnivox
Orders to: Kurfuenstenstr 7, 67061 Ludwigshafen

Irisiana, *imprint of* Heinrich Hugendubel Verlag GmbH

Klaus Isele+
Heidelstr 9, 79805 Eggingen
Tel: (07746) 91116 *Fax:* (07746) 91117
E-mail: klaus.isele@t-online.de
Key Personnel
Owner: Klaus Isele
Editorial Dir: Eva Taubert
Founded: 1984
Subjects: Art, Fiction, Literature, Literary Criticism, Essays, Poetry, Religion - Buddhist, Travel
ISBN Prefix(es): 3-925016; 3-86142
Number of titles published annually: 18 Print; 6 Audio

Total Titles: 200 Print; 20 Audio
Orders to: Kock, Neff & Oetinger & Co Verlagsauslieferung GmbH, Schockenriedstr 59, 70565 Stuttgart *Tel:* (0711) 78990

Iselt und Co Nfl mbH, see Hamburger Lesehefte Verlag Iselt & Co Nfl mbH

Verlag der Islam+
Genfer Str 11, 60437 Frankfurt
Tel: (069) 50688-651 *Fax:* (069) 50688-655
Telex: 416187 Islam d *Cable:* ISLAM FRANKFURT MAIN
Key Personnel
Editor: Hadayatullah Huebsch *Tel:* (069) 314596
Founded: 1949
Subjects: Nonfiction (General), Religion - Islamic
ISBN Prefix(es): 3-921458; 3-932244
Total Titles: 110 Print
U.S. Office(s): The Ahmadiyya Movement in Islam Inc, Masjid Bait-ur-Rehman, 15000 Good Hope Rd, Silver Spring, MD, United States *Tel:* (301) 879-0110 *Fax:* (301) 879-0115
Warehouse: Hanauer Landstr 50, 60314 Frankfurt, Contact: Mr Munir *Tel:* (069) 43059519

ISSA, see Informationsstelle Suedliches Afrika eV (ISSA)

ITP, see International Thomson Publishing (ITP)

ITpress Verlag+
Mozartweg 24, 76646 Bruchsal
Mailing Address: Postfach 1744, 76607 Bruchsal
Tel: (07251) 300575 *Fax:* (07251) 14823
E-mail: itpress@acm.org
Web Site: www.itpress.com
Key Personnel
Prof: Dr Reiner Hartenstein *Tel:* (0631) 2052606
Founded: 1994
Subjects: Computer Science, Electronics, Electrical Engineering, Microcomputers, Nonfiction (General), Public Administration
ISBN Prefix(es): 3-929814
Number of titles published annually: 10 Print
Total Titles: 10 Print
Subsidiaries: ITpressHartenstein

Iudicium Verlag GmbH+
Hans-Graessel-weg 13, 81375 Munich
Mailing Address: Postfach 701067, 81375 Munich
Tel: (089) 718747 *Fax:* (089) 7140039
E-mail: info@iudicium.de
Web Site: www.geist.de
Key Personnel
Publisher: Gunter Narr
Manufacturing: Horst Schmid
Publicity Dir: Ingo Neubert
Founded: 1969
Subjects: Communications, Drama, Theater, Language Arts, Linguistics, Literature, Literary Criticism, Essays, Mysteries, Psychology, Psychiatry, Social Sciences, Sociology, Classical Philology, Cultural Science
ISBN Prefix(es): 3-87808; 3-8233
Associate Companies: A Francke Verlag

Iudicium Verlag GmbH+
Hans-Graessel-Weg 13, 81375 Munich
Mailing Address: Postfach 701067, 81310 Munich
Tel: (089) 718747 *Fax:* (089) 7142039
E-mail: info@iudicium.de
Web Site: www.iudicium.de
Key Personnel
Man Dir: Dr Phil Habil
Manager: Dr Peter Kapitza
Contact: Dominique Colmont-Freisinger; Kiyoko Kapitza; Elisabeth Schaidhammer; Dr Lucia Schwellinger

Founded: 1983
Subjects: Anthropology, Art, Asian Studies, Biography, Communications, Drama, Theater, Education, Fiction, Foreign Countries, History, Language Arts, Linguistics, Library & Information Sciences, Literature, Literary Criticism, Essays, Music, Dance, Philosophy, Poetry, Religion - Catholic, Social Sciences, Sociology, Theology, Women's Studies
ISBN Prefix(es): 3-89129

Reisebuchverlag Iwanowski GmbH
Salm-Reifferscheidt-Allee 37, 41540 Dormagen
Tel: (02133) 26030 *Fax:* (02133) 260333
E-mail: info@iwanowski.de
Web Site: www.iwanowski.de
Founded: 1984
Subjects: Travel
ISBN Prefix(es): 3-933041; 3-923975
Number of titles published annually: 5 Print
Total Titles: 70 Print

IWT Magazine Publishing House GmbH, *imprint of* Gildefachverlag GmbH & Co KG

J Ch Mellinger Verlag GmbH+
Burgholzstr 25, 70376 Stuttgart
Tel: (0711) 543787 *Fax:* (0711) 556889
E-mail: mellinger@sambo.de
Key Personnel
Manager: Wolfgang Militz; Tobias Sambo; Gudrun Emmert
Founded: 1926
Subjects: Biography, Education, Fiction
ISBN Prefix(es): 3-88069

Verlag J P Peter, Gebr Holstein GmbH & Co KG
Erlbacher Str 104, 91541 Rothenburg
Tel: (09861) 4 00-3 81 *Fax:* (09861) 4 00-70
E-mail: peter-verlag@rotabene.de
Web Site: www.peter-verlag.de
Key Personnel
Man Dir: Dr Gerhard Prinz; Wolfgang Schneider
Publisher: Dekan Christoph Schmerl
Founded: 1884
Subjects: Poetry, Religion - Other
ISBN Prefix(es): 3-87625; 3-87311
Bookshop(s): Evangel Bucherdrenst Rothenburg

Jaeger & Waldmann, see Telex-Verlag Jaeger & Waldmann GmbH

Jahreszeiten-Verlag GmbH+
Possmoorweg 5, 22301 Hamburg
Tel: (040) 2717-0 *Fax:* (040) 2717-2056
E-mail: press@jalag.de
Web Site: www.jalag.de *Cable:* JALAG
Key Personnel
Publisher: Thomas Ganske
Man Dir: Juergen Knop; Klaus Teichmann; Herrmann Schmidt
Founded: 1948
Subjects: Architecture & Interior Design, Automotive, Cookery, Crafts, Games, Hobbies, Fashion, Foreign Countries, Gardening, Plants, Health, Nutrition, House & Home, How-to, Journalism, Travel, Wine & Spirits, Women's Studies
ISBN Prefix(es): 3-87383
Parent Company: Verlagsgruppe Ganske
Associate Companies: Hoffmann & Campe; Prinz Kommunikations GmbH; DLS GmbH; Graefe & Onzer; Die Woche
U.S. Office(s): Publicitas Globe Media, 261 Madison Ave, 19th floor, New York, NY 10016, United States, Contact: John Moncure *Tel:* 212-599-5057 *Fax:* 212-599-8298

Bookshop(s): Buchhaus Campe, Karolinenstr 13, 90402 Nuremberg; Medienhaus Prinz, T11-3, 68161 Mannheim; Schrobsdorff sche Buchhandlung, Koenigsallee 22, 40212 Dusseldorf

Jan Thorbecke Verlag GmbH & Co+
Senefelderstr 12, 73760 Ostfildern
Mailing Address: Postfach 4201, 73745 Ostfildern
Tel: (0711) 44 06-0 *Fax:* (0711) 44 06-199
E-mail: info@thorbecke.de
Web Site: www.thorbecke.de *Cable:*
  THORBECKE
Key Personnel
Manager: Bardo Jensch; Ulrich Peters
Publisher: Dr Joern Laakmann *Tel:* (0711) 44 06-191 *E-mail:* joern.laakmann@thorbecke.de
Marketing: Matthias Reimann *Tel:* (0711) 44 06-195 *E-mail:* matthias.reimann@thorbecke.de
Founded: 1946
Subjects: Archaeology, Art, Foreign Countries, History, Literature, Literary Criticism, Essays, Regional Interests, Theology, Travel
ISBN Prefix(es): 3-7995
Associate Companies: Bergstadtverlag Wilhelm Gottlieb Korn GmbH, Wuerzburg; Bergstadtverlag Wilhelm Gottlieb Korn GmbH, Karlstr 10, Postfach 546, 75488 Sigmaringen (correspondence & distribution)
Distribution Center: Brockhaus / Commission, Kreidlerstr 9, 70806 Kornwestheim *Tel:* (07154) 13 27-54 *Fax:* (07154) 13 27-13 *E-mail:* info@brocom.de *Web Site:* www.brocom.de
Buch- und Medienvertriebs AG, Hochstr 357, 8200 Schaffhausen, Switzerland *Tel:* (052) 6 43 54 30 *Fax:* (052) 6 43 54 35 *E-mail:* order@buch-medien.ch (Switzerland)

Janus Verlagsgesellschaft, Dr Norbert Meder & Co+
Am Rottmannshof 6, 33619 Bielefeld
Tel: (0521) 1369236 *Fax:* (0521) 1369237
Founded: 1980
Subjects: History, Language Arts, Linguistics, Science (General), Social Sciences, Sociology
ISBN Prefix(es): 3-922607; 3-922977
Orders to: Prolit Buchvertrieb GmbH, Siemensstr 16, 35463 Fernwald

Verlag Winfried Jenior
Lassallestr 15, 34119 Kassel
Tel: (0561) 7391621 *Fax:* (0561) 774148
E-mail: jenior@aol.com
Web Site: www.jenior.de
Publish book series of Kassel University, travel books on Spain, Spanish cookery books, yearbook & books on Kassel & region.
Subjects: Cookery, Regional Interests, Travel
ISBN Prefix(es): 3-9801438; 3-928172; 3-934377
Distributor for Moll Verlag

JKL Publikationen GmbH+
Klausenpas 14, 12107 Berlin
Tel: (030) 74104624 *Fax:* (030) 74104626
E-mail: info@zeitgut.com
Web Site: www.zeitgut.com
Key Personnel
Contact: Juergen Kleindienst *E-mail:* j.kleindienst@zeitgut.com
Membership(s): Boersenverlin des Deutschen Buchhandels.
Subjects: Biography, History
ISBN Prefix(es): 3-933336

Wolfgang Joerg und Ingrid Joerg, see Berliner Handpresse Wolfgang Joerg und Erich Schonig

Johann Wolfgang Goethe Universitat
Senckenberganlage 31-33, 60054 Frankfurt am Main

Tel: (069) 798-22608; (069) 798-23590 *Fax:* (069) 798-28313
E-mail: hrz-verwaltung@rz.uni-frankfurt.de
Web Site: www.rz.uni-frankfurt.de
Key Personnel
President: Prof Werner MeiBhes, PhD
Contact: Ulrike Jaspers
Founded: 1983
Subjects: Science (General)
Imprints: Anzeigenverwaltung & Herstellung; Bezugsbedingungen; Herausgeber; Redaktion & Gestaltung

Johannes Berchmans Verlagsbuchhandlung GmbH
Kaulbachstr 33, 80539 Munich
Tel: (089) 38185-244
Key Personnel
Manager: Manfred Hanke
ISBN Prefix(es): 3-87056

Johannes Verlag Einsiedeln, Freiburg+
Lindenmattenstr 29, 79117 Freiburg
Tel: (0761) 640168 *Fax:* (0761) 640169
E-mail: johverlag@aol.com
Key Personnel
Contact: Susanne Greiner; Cornelia Capol
Founded: 1947
Subjects: Philosophy, Religion - Catholic, Theology
ISBN Prefix(es): 3-89411
Number of titles published annually: 10 Print
Total Titles: 340 Print

Johannis+
Heiligenstr 24, 77933 Lahr
Tel: (07821) 5810 *Fax:* (07821) 581-26
E-mail: johannis-druck@t-online.de
Web Site: www.johannis-verlag.de
Key Personnel
Owner: Reinhold Fels
Publisher: Karlheinz Kern
Founded: 1896
Also publish gift books, booklets, stationery & greeting cards.
Subjects: Biblical Studies, Photography, Religion - Protestant, Theology
ISBN Prefix(es): 3-501
Total Titles: 1,100 Print

Edition Jonas, *imprint of* Dr Wolfgang Baur Verlag Kunst & Alltag

Jonas Verlag fuer Kunst und Literatur GmbH
Weidenhaeuser Str 88, 35037 Marburg
Tel: (06421) 25132 *Fax:* (06421) 210572
E-mail: jonas@jonas-verlag.de
Web Site: www.jonas-verlag.de
Key Personnel
Manager: Dieter Mayer-Guerr
Founded: 1978
Subjects: Art, History
ISBN Prefix(es): 3-89445
Orders to: Prolit *Fax:* (0641) 9439389

Dr Werner Jopp Verlag+
Leibnizstr 26, 65191 Wiesbaden
Tel: (0611) 547116 *Fax:* (0611) 542762
Key Personnel
Publisher: Dr Werner Jopp
Founded: 1987
Specialize in health advice.
Subjects: Health, Nutrition
ISBN Prefix(es): 3-926955; 3-89698

Jovis Verlag GmbH+
Kurfuerstenstr 15/16, 10785 Berlin
Tel: (030) 2636720 *Fax:* (030) 26367272
E-mail: jovis@jovis.de
Web Site: www.jovis.de

Key Personnel
Publisher: Jochen Visscher *E-mail:* visscher@jovis.de
Sales & Marketing Manager: Jutta Bornholdt-Cassetti *E-mail:* bornholdt@jovis.de
Founded: 1994
Subjects: Art, Film, Video, History, Nonfiction (General), Photography, Architecture, History of Art
ISBN Prefix(es): 3-931321; 9-936314
Number of titles published annually: 18 Print
Total Titles: 91 Print
Distribution Center: LKG, Poetzschauer Weg, 04579 Espenhain *Tel:* (034206) 65106 *Fax:* (034206) 65130 *E-mail:* kobarski@lkg-service.de
Orders to: Distributed Art Publishers (DAP), 155 Sixth Ave, New York, NY 10013-1507, United States *Tel:* 212-627-1999 *Fax:* 212-627-9484 *E-mail:* dwingate@dapinc.com

Jowi-Verlag+
Muehlbacher Str 5, 97753 Karlstadt-Laudenbach
Tel: (09353) 2921
Founded: 1991
ISBN Prefix(es): 3-9802897

Joy Verlag GmbH+
Am Fichtelholz 5, 87477 Sulzberg
Tel: (08376) 97383 *Fax:* (08376) 8845
E-mail: joy_verlag@compuserve.com
Key Personnel
Manager: Thomas Kettenring
Founded: 1989
Subjects: Health, Nutrition, Religion - Buddhist, Self-Help
ISBN Prefix(es): 3-928554; 3-9801624

Juedischer Verlag GmbH+
Lindenstr 29-35, 60325 Frankfurt am Main
Mailing Address: Postfach 101945, 60019 Frankfurt am Main
Tel: (069) 75601-0 *Fax:* (069) 75601-522
Web Site: www.suhrkamp.de
Key Personnel
Publisher: Ulla Unseld-Berkewicz
Man Dir: Philip Roeder *Tel:* (069) 75601-500 *E-mail:* roeder@suhrkamp.de
Rights & Permissions: Dr Petra Hardt
Founded: 1902
Subjects: Religion - Jewish
ISBN Prefix(es): 3-633
Parent Company: Suhrkamp Verlag

Jugenddienst-Verlag, see Peter Hammer Verlag GmbH

Julius Klinkhardt Verlagsbuchhandlung+
Ramsauer Weg 5, 83670 Bad Heilbrunn
Tel: (08046) 9304 *Fax:* (08046) 9306
E-mail: info@klinkhardt.de
Web Site: www.klinkhardt.de
Key Personnel
Contact: Andreas Klinkhardt; Rudiger Hartmann
Founded: 1834
Membership(s): The Stock Exchange of German Booksellers & Association of School Book Publishers.
Subjects: Education, Psychology, Psychiatry
ISBN Prefix(es): 3-7815

Junfermann-Verlag+
Imadstr 40, 33102 Paderborn
Mailing Address: Postfach 1840, 33048 Paderborn
Tel: (05251) 1 34 40 *Fax:* (05251) 13 44 44
E-mail: infoteam@junfermann.de
Web Site: www.junfermann.de
Key Personnel
Contact: Heike Carstensen *Tel:* (05251) 13 44 18 *E-mail:* carstensen@junfermann.de

Founded: 1659
Specialize in psychology & psychotherapy.
Subjects: Management, Psychology, Psychiatry, Self-Help
ISBN Prefix(es): 3-87387
Number of titles published annually: 30 Print
Total Titles: 250 Print

Junius Verlag GmbH+
Stresemannstr 375, 22761 Hamburg
Mailing Address: Postfach 500727, 22707 Hamburg
Tel: (040) 892599 *Fax:* (040) 891224
E-mail: info@junius-verlag.de
Web Site: www.junius-verlag.de
Key Personnel
Man Dir: Karl Olaf Petters *E-mail:* petters@junius-verlag.de
Founded: 1979
Subjects: Architecture & Interior Design, Government, Political Science, Philosophy, Social Sciences, Sociology
ISBN Prefix(es): 3-88506
Number of titles published annually: 30 Print
Total Titles: 200 Print
Distributed by AVA Book 2000 (Switzerland)
Foreign Rep(s): Idea Books, Amsterdam (Worldwide)
Orders to: LKG, Poetzschauer Weg, 04529 Esperhain *Tel:* (034206) 65720 *Fax:* (034206) 65770

Justus-Liebig-Universitat Giessen
Ludwigstr 23, 35390 Giessen
Tel: (0641) 99-0 *Fax:* (0641) 99-12289
E-mail: michael.kost@admin.uni-giessen.de
Web Site: www.uni-giessen.de
Key Personnel
President: Dr Stefan Hormuth *Tel:* (0641) 99-12000 *Fax:* (0641) 99-12009
Research institution (international economic & social development & environment).
Subjects: Agriculture, Environmental Studies
ISBN Prefix(es): 3-924840

Jutta Pohl Verlag+
Im Buckeberg 11a, 76307 Karlsbad
Tel: (07202) 2239 *Fax:* (07202) 3879
E-mail: jutta@pohlverlag.de
Web Site: www.pohl-verlag.de *Cable:* POHL, CELLE
Key Personnel
Dir: Udo Meyer *Tel:* (05141) 9889-15
Subjects: Health, Nutrition, Music, Dance, Outdoor Recreation, Sports, Athletics
ISBN Prefix(es): 3-7911
Total Titles: 60 Print; 2 Audio
Parent Company: Cellesche Zeitung Schweiger & Pick Verlag, Pfingsten GmbH & Co KG
Foreign Rep(s): As Bartsch-Holler Gmbh (Austria); Schweizer Buchzentruun (Switzerland); Uitgeverij de Vraseborch (Netherlands)

Juventa Verlag GmbH+
Ehretstr 3, 69469 Weinheim
Tel: (06201) 9020-0 *Fax:* (06201) 9020-13
E-mail: juventa@juventa.de
Web Site: www.juventa.de
Key Personnel
Man Dir: Lothar Schweim *Tel:* (06201) 9020-10 *E-mail:* schweim@juventa.de
Advertising: Andrea Biernatzki *Tel:* (06201) 9020-15 *E-mail:* biernatzki@juventa.de
Founded: 1953
Subjects: Criminology, Education, Health, Nutrition, History, Psychology, Psychiatry, Social Sciences, Sociology
ISBN Prefix(es): 3-7799
Number of titles published annually: 70 Print
Total Titles: 800 Print

Warehouse: Justus-von-Liebigstr 1, 86899 Landsberg/Lech *Tel:* (08191) 125 243 *Fax:* (08191) 125 198
Orders to: WMi Verlags Service *Tel:* (08191) 125 243 *Fax:* (08191) 125 198

K + G Verlagsgesellschaft, see Karto + Grafik Verlagsgesellschaft (K & G Verlagsgesellschaft)

K T Kaiser Taschenbuecher (pocketbooks), *imprint of* Guetersloher Verlagshaus

Kabel Verlag, *imprint of* Piper Verlag GmbH

Kailash, *imprint of* Heinrich Hugendubel Verlag GmbH

KaJo Verlag+
Imprint of Verlagshaus Wurzburg
Beethovenstr 5, 97070 Wurzburg
Tel: (0931) 385235 *Fax:* (0931) 385305
E-mail: info@verlagshaus.com
Web Site: www.verlagshaus.com
Key Personnel
Publishing Dir: Dieter Krause
Dir, Production: Juergen Roth
Sales Dir: Johannes Glesius
Founded: 1985
Subjects: Travel
ISBN Prefix(es): 3-925544

Kallmeyer'sche Verlagsbuchhandlung GmbH+
Im Brande 19, 30926 Seelze
Tel: (0511) 4 00 04-1 75 *Fax:* (0511) 4 00 04-1 76
E-mail: leserservice@kallmeyer.de
Web Site: www.kallmeyer.de
Key Personnel
Man Dir: Uwe Brinkman
Founded: 1986
Specialize in elementary drawings, rhythm & teaching goods.
Subjects: Career Development, Crafts, Games, Hobbies, Education, Engineering (General), Environmental Studies, Music, Dance, Nonfiction (General), Sports, Athletics
ISBN Prefix(es): 3-7800

J Kamphausen Verlag & Distribution GmbH+
Buddestr 15, 33602 Bielefeld
Mailing Address: Postfach 101849, 33518 Bielefeld
Tel: (0521) 172875 *Fax:* (0521) 68771
Key Personnel
Contact: Joachim Kamphausen
Founded: 1989
Subjects: Health, Nutrition, Medicine, Nursing, Dentistry
ISBN Prefix(es): 3-928430; 3-89901; 3-933496
Orders to: Jollenbeckerstr 29, 33613 Bielefeld

S Karger GmbH Verlag fuer Medizin und Naturwissenschaften+
Loerracher Str 16A, 79115 Freiburg
Tel: (0761) 45 20 70 *Fax:* (0761) 45 20 714
E-mail: information@karger.de
Web Site: www.karger.com; www.karger.de *Cable:* KARGERMEDBOOKS
Key Personnel
Man Dir, International Rights: S Karger
Founded: 1890
Subjects: Medicine, Nursing, Dentistry, Psychology, Psychiatry, Science (General)
ISBN Prefix(es): 3-8055
Parent Company: S Karger AG, Allschwilerstr 10, 4009 Basel, Switzerland
U.S. Office(s): S Karger Publishers Inc, 26 W Avon Rd, PO Box 529, Farmington, CT 06085, United States

Bookshop(s): Karger-Buchhandlung Ausstellung und Vertrieb internationaler medizinischer Fachliteratur, Loerracher Str 16a, 79115 Freiburg

Verlag Karl Baedeker GmbH
Member of The Mair Group
Marco-Polo-Zentrum, 73760 Ostfildern
Mailing Address: Postfach 3162, 73751 Ostfildern
Tel: (0711) 4502262 *Fax:* (0711) 4502343
E-mail: baedeker@mairs.de
Key Personnel
Man Dir: Dr Volkmar Mair
Chief Editor: Ranier Eisenschmid
Founded: 1827
Subjects: Travel
ISBN Prefix(es): 3-87504; 3-89525; 3-8297

Karl-May-Verlag Lothar Schmid GmbH+
Schuetzenstr 30, 96047 Bamberg
Tel: (0951) 98 20 60 *Fax:* (0951) 2 43 67
E-mail: info@karl-may.de
Web Site: www.karl-may.de
Key Personnel
Man Dir, Publicity, Rights & Permissions: Lothar Schmid
Man Dir & Publicity: Bernhard Schmid
Founded: 1913
Subjects: Fiction, Western Fiction
ISBN Prefix(es): 3-7802
Number of titles published annually: 7 Print
Total Titles: 200 Print
Imprints: Edition Ustad
Subsidiaries: Karl May Verwaltungs-und Vertriebs-GmbH

Karto + Grafik Verlagsgesellschaft (K & G Verlagsgesellschaft)+
Schoenberger Weg 15, 60488 Frankfurt
Tel: (069) 76 20 31 *Fax:* (069) 76 91 06
E-mail: kugverlag@aol.com
Web Site: www.hildebrands.de
Key Personnel
Publisher: Volker Hildebrand
Man Dir: Hr Stefan Beyer
Founded: 1980
Subjects: Travel
ISBN Prefix(es): 3-88989
Total Titles: 100 Print
Distributed by Map Link; Librairie Ulysse Inc; ITMB Publishing Ltd; World Leisure Marketing

Kartographischer Verlag Reinhard Ryborsch+
Laubenstr 3, 63179 Obertshausen
Mailing Address: Postfach 2105, 63170 Obertshausen
Tel: (06104) 79039 *Fax:* (06104) 75356
Key Personnel
Dir: Reinhard Ryborsch
Founded: 1987
Membership(s): Boersenverein des Deutschen Buchhandels; Deutsche Gesellschaft fuer Kartographie.
Subjects: Aeronautics, Aviation, Geography, Geology, Travel
ISBN Prefix(es): 3-920339; 3-927549

Kastell Verlag GmbH+
Giselastr 15, 80802 Munich
Mailing Address: Postfach 440312, 80752 Munich
Tel: (089) 33 21 75; (089) 399742 *Fax:* (089) 340 11 78
E-mail: kastell-verlag@t-online.de
Key Personnel
Man Dir, Rights & Permissions: Christoph Burgauner
Founded: 1984
Subjects: History, Music, Dance
ISBN Prefix(es): 3-924592

Verlag Katholisches Bibelwerk GmbH+
Silberburgstr 121, 70176 Stuttgart
Tel: (0711) 619200 *Fax:* (0711) 6192044
E-mail: verlag@bibelwerk.de
Web Site: www.bibelwerk.de
Key Personnel
Editor, Rights & Permissions: Herbert Wilfart *Tel:* (0711) 6192027 *E-mail:* wilfart@bibelwerk.de
Man Dir: Juergen M Schymura MA *Tel:* (0711) 6192020-21 *E-mail:* schymura@bibelwerk.de
Editor: Dr Winfried Bader *Tel:* (0711) 6192036 *E-mail:* bader@bibelwerk.de
Founded: 1937
Membership(s): KMV.
Subjects: Biblical Studies, Religion - Catholic
ISBN Prefix(es): 3-460

Katzmann Verlag KG+
Schellingstr 41, 72072 Tuebingen
Mailing Address: Postfach 1827, 72008 Tuebingen
Tel: (07473) 5427 *Fax:* (07473) 5427 *Cable:* KATZMANN VERLAG
Key Personnel
Man Dir, Production, Publicity, Rights & Permissions: Dr Volker Katzmann
Sales Dir: Sibylle Katzmann
Founded: 1945
Specialize in scientific literature.
Subjects: Art, Education, Religion - Other, Social Sciences, Sociology, Theology
ISBN Prefix(es): 3-7805
Associate Companies: Heliopolis-Verlag Ewald Katzmann

Verlag Ernst Kaufmann GmbH+
Alleestr 2, 77933 Lahr
Tel: (07821) 93 90-0 *Fax:* (07821) 9390-11
E-mail: info@kaufman-verlag.de
Web Site: www.kaufmann-verlag.de
Key Personnel
Man Dir: Michael Jacob
Chief Editor: Renate Schupp
Founded: 1816
Membership(s): Verlagsring Religionsunterricht (VRU), ATV & AVJ.
Subjects: Religion - Protestant, Religion - Other
ISBN Prefix(es): 3-7806

KBV Verlags-und Medien - GmbH+
Augustinerstr 1, 54576 Hillesheim
Tel: (06593) 998668 *Fax:* (06593) 998701
E-mail: info@kbv-verlag.de
Web Site: www.kbv-verlag.de
Key Personnel
Man Dir: Herbert Klein
Founded: 1989
Subjects: Fiction, Gay & Lesbian, Government, Political Science, Mysteries, Nonfiction (General), Adventure, Anthologies, Historical, Short Stories, Thriller
ISBN Prefix(es): 3-927658
Warehouse: LKG Leipziges Komissions- und Grosbuchhandels Gesellschaft mbH, Plotzschauer Wey, 04579 Espenhain
Orders to: LKG Leipziges Kommissions- und Grossbuchhandels Gesellschaft mbH, Plotzschauer Wey, 04579 Espenhain

Keip GmbH+
Bayernstr 9, 63773 Goldbach
Tel: (06021) 59 05 0 *Fax:* (06021) 59 05 42
E-mail: info@keip.net
Web Site: www.keip.net
Key Personnel
Manager: Ulrich Keip *Fax:* (06021) 59 05 32 *E-mail:* ulrich@keip.net
Manager & Publisher: Dr Michael Simon *Fax:* (06021) 59 05 24 *E-mail:* simon@keip.net
Founded: 1967
Also antiquarian bookseller.
Membership(s): ILAB.
Subjects: Economics, History, Law, Social Sciences, Sociology
ISBN Prefix(es): 3-8051

SachBuchVerlag Kellner (Kellner Publishing House)+
St-Pauli-Deich 3, 28199 Bremen
Tel: (0421) 77866 *Fax:* (0421) 704058
E-mail: kellner-verlag@t-online.de
Web Site: kellner-verlag.de
Key Personnel
Editor: Klaus Kellner
Founded: 1988
Also acts as shipping house.
Subjects: Government, Political Science, Labor, Industrial Relations, Law, Nonfiction (General), Outdoor Recreation, Public Administration, Travel
ISBN Prefix(es): 3-927155
Number of titles published annually: 6 Print

Martin Kelter Verlag GmbH u Co
Postfach 70 10 09, 22010 Hamburg
Tel: (040) 68 28 95-0 *Fax:* (040) 68 28 95 50
Web Site: www.kelter.de
Telex: 213126
Key Personnel
Man Dir: Gerhard Melchert
Founded: 1938
ISBN Prefix(es): 3-88832
Associate Companies: Mero-Druck Otto Melchert GmbH & Co KG

P Keppler Verlag GmbH & Co KG
Industriestr 2, 63150 Heusenstamm
Mailing Address: Postfach 1353, 63151 Heusenstamm
Tel: (06104) 606 0 *Fax:* (06104) 606 121
E-mail: info@kepplermediengruppe.de
Web Site: www.kepplermediengruppe.de
Key Personnel
Man Dir: Heinz Egon Schmitt
ISBN Prefix(es): 3-87398

Kerber Verlag
Windelsbleicherstr 166-170, 33659 Bielefeld
Tel: (0521) 95008-10 *Fax:* (0521) 95008-88
E-mail: info@kerber-verlag.de
Web Site: www.kerber-verlag.de
Key Personnel
Publisher: Christof Kerber *Tel:* (0521) 95008-11 *Fax:* (0521) 95008-18
Editor: Tanja Kemmer *Tel:* (0521) 96768-30 *Fax:* (0521) 96768-32
Production: Wolfgang Gros *Tel:* (0521) 95008-20
Marketing: Grit Schewe
Specialize in Paintings & Art.
Subjects: Architecture & Interior Design, Art, History
ISBN Prefix(es): 3-924639; 3-933040
Foreign Rep(s): DAP

Verlag Kerle im Verlag Herder+
Hermann Herder Str 4, 79104 Freiburg
Tel: (0761) 2717-0 *Fax:* (0761) 2717-350
E-mail: info@kerle.de
Web Site: www.kerle.de
Key Personnel
Man Dir: Dr Klaus-Christoph Scheffel
Editorial: C Soltau; B Wurster
Sales: W Reisterer
Press, Rights: Helga Theile
Founded: 1886
ISBN Prefix(es): 3-210; 3-85303
Associate Companies: Verlag Herder GmbH & Co KG; Verlag A G Ploetz GmbH & Co KG; Herder Editrice e Libreria, Italy; Editorial Herder SA, Spain; Libraria Herder, Spain; Herder AG
Bookshop(s): Herder Verlag

Keysersche Verlagsbuchhandlung GmbH+
Geibelstr 6, 81679 Munich
Tel: (089) 455540 *Fax:* (089) 45554111
Key Personnel
Publisher, Rights & Permissions: Hermann Farnung
Publisher: Klaus Rudloff
Advertising: Michaela Beck
Sales: Gudrun Shutzenberger
Founded: 1777
Subjects: Science (General)
ISBN Prefix(es): 3-87405
Parent Company: Frankfurter Allgemeine Zeitung GmbH
Associate Companies: BVU Buchverlage Union GmbH; Koehler & Amelang Verlagsgesellschaft mbH
Imprints: Flaschenpost

Kidemus Verlag GmbH+
Ruenderotherstr 15, 51109 Cologne
Mailing Address: Postfach 940225, 51090 Cologne
Tel: (0221) 84 20 97 *Fax:* (0221) 84 20 98
E-mail: info@kidemus.de
Web Site: www.kidemus.de
Key Personnel
Man Dir: Reinhold Schulze
Founded: 1995
ISBN Prefix(es): 3-9804821; 3-9806910
Number of titles published annually: 3 Print
Total Titles: 17 Print

Verlag Kiepenheuer & Witsch+
Rondorfer Str 5, 50968 Cologne
Tel: (0221) 376 85-0 *Fax:* (0221) 38 85 95
E-mail: verlag@kiwi-koeln.de
Web Site: www.kiwi-koeln.de *Cable:* KIEPENBUCHER COLOGNE
Key Personnel
Man Dir: Helge Malchow
Foreign Rights & Permissions: Traudel Jansen *Tel:* (0221) 376 85 22 *E-mail:* tjansen@kiwi-koeln.de
Commercial Man Dir: Peter Roik
Advertising: Ulla Bruemmer *Tel:* (0221) 376 85 26 *Fax:* (0221) 376 85 70 *E-mail:* ubruemmer@kiwi-koeln.de
Founded: 1949
Subjects: Biography, Fiction, History, Nonfiction (General), Social Sciences, Sociology
ISBN Prefix(es): 3-462
Imprints: Kiwi-Reihe
U.S. Office(s): 171 W 79 St, New York, NY 10024, United States, Scout: Alison M Bond
Joan Daves Agency, 21 W 26 St, New York, NY 10010, United States, Agent: Jennifer Lyons

Gustav Kiepenheuer Verlag GmbH+
Gerichtsweg 28, 04103 Leipzig
Mailing Address: Postfach 101563, 04015 Leipzig
Tel: (0341) 9954600 *Fax:* (0341) 9954620
E-mail: info@aufbau-verlag.de
Web Site: www.aufbau-verlag.de
Key Personnel
Program Manager: Peter Birgit
Foreign Rights & Permissions: Astrid Poppenhusen *E-mail:* poppenhusen@aufbau-verlag.de
German Rights & Permissions: Martin Lorento *Tel:* (030) 28394-118 *E-mail:* lorentz@aufbau-verlag.de
Founded: 1909
Subjects: Biography, Nonfiction (General), Regional Interests
ISBN Prefix(es): 3-378
Parent Company: Leipziger Verlags- und Vertriebsgesellschaft mbH
Associate Companies: Sammlung Dieterich Verlagsgesellschaft mbH, Leipzig
Shipping Address: Mohr-Morava Buchvertrieb Gesellschaft mbH, Postfach 260, 1101 Vienna, Austria; Pegasus-Stichting, Uitgeverij-

GERMANY

en-Boekhandel, Rhijuvis Feithstr 28, PO Box 59687, 1054 PZ Amsterdam, Netherlands; Verlagsauslieferung Balmer, Boesch 41, Huenenberg
Orders to: Hans Heinrich Petersen GmbH, Bredowstr 20, 22113 Hamburg

Kierdorf Ute Verlag+
Gut Dohrgaul, 51688 Wipperfuerth
Tel: (02267) 2888 *Fax:* (02267) 4458
E-mail: Kierdorfverlag@t-online.de
Web Site: www.kierdorfverlag.de
Key Personnel
Owner: Ute Kierdorf
International Rights: Wolfgang Kierdorf
Founded: 1978
Subjects: Equestrian & Fung Shui
ISBN Prefix(es): 3-89118
Orders to: Grossohaus Wehling, Friedr Hajewann-Str 5560, 33719 Bielefeld

Kilda Verlag+
Muensterstr 71, 48268 Greven
Tel: (02571) 52115 *Fax:* (02571) 953269
E-mail: info@kildaverlag.de
Web Site: www.kildaverlag.com
Key Personnel
Man Dir: Fritz Poelking
Founded: 1969
Subjects: Photography, Nature
ISBN Prefix(es): 3-921427; 3-88949
Total Titles: 41 Print
Orders to: KSS, Zur Landwehr 2, 33824 Werther *Tel:* (05203) 9189-0 *Fax:* (05203) 9189-25 *E-mail:* info@ks-fotoliteratur.de *Web Site:* www.ks-fotoliteratur.de

Verlag im Kilian GmbH+
Schuhmarkt 4, 35037 Marburg
Tel: (06421) 2 93 30 *Fax:* (06421) 16 38 94
E-mail: verlag@kilian.de
Web Site: www.kilian-verlag.de
Telex: 482381
Key Personnel
Man Dir: Barbara von Stackelberg
Founded: 1994
Specialize in health information & advice to professionals & the general public.
Subjects: Child Care & Development, Health, Nutrition, Medicine, Nursing, Dentistry
ISBN Prefix(es): 3-932091
Parent Company: Deutsches Gruenes Kreuz

Edition Kima, *imprint of* Drei Eichen Verlag Manuel Kissener

Kinderbuchverlag
Formerly Union-Verlag GmbH
Werderstr 10, 69469 Weinheim
Tel: (06201) 6007-0 *Fax:* (06201) 6007-310
Key Personnel
Man Dir: Joachim Radmer
Publicity: Ulrich Stoeriko-Blume
Rights: Charlotte Larat; Kerstin Michaelis
Founded: 1880
Subjects: Nonfiction (General)
ISBN Prefix(es): 3-358
Parent Company: Verlagsgruppe Beltz

Kindler Verlag, *imprint of* Rowohlt Verlag GmbH

Th Kirchbaum, K, *imprint of* Eironeia-Verlag

Peter Kirchheim Verlag+
Postfach 14 04 32, 80454 Munich
Tel: (089) 267474 *Fax:* (089) 2605528
E-mail: info@kirchheimverlag.de
Web Site: www.kirchheimverlag.de
Key Personnel
Owner: Peter Kirchheim
Founded: 1977
Subjects: Literature, Literary Criticism, Essays, Poetry, Regional Interests, Self-Help
ISBN Prefix(es): 3-87410
Warehouse: LKG Leipziger Kommissions - und Grossbuchhandels GmbH, Poetzschauer Weg, 04579 Espenhain (Leipzig)

Kirschbaum Verlag GmbH+
Siegfriedstr 28, 53179 Bonn
Mailing Address: Postfach 210209, 53157 Bonn
Tel: (0228) 9 54 53-0 *Fax:* (0228) 9 54 53-27
E-mail: info@kirschbaum.de
Web Site: www.kirschbaum.de
Key Personnel
Man Dir: Bernhard Kirschbaum *E-mail:* b.kirschbaum@kirschbaum.de
Founded: 1949
Subjects: Automotive, Civil Engineering, Geography, Geology, Law, Transportation
ISBN Prefix(es): 3-7812
Total Titles: 195 Print

Kiwi-Reihe, *imprint of* Verlag Kiepenheuer & Witsch

Klages-Verlag
Eckermannstr 8, 30625 Hannover
Tel: (0511) 5358936 *Fax:* (0511) 5358928
E-mail: kv@lsz.de
Key Personnel
Contact: August-Wilhelm Klages
Founded: 1917
Membership(s): German Electronic Book Committee.
Subjects: Economics, Law, Public Administration
ISBN Prefix(es): 3-7813

Klartext Verlagsgesellschaft mbH+
Hesslerstr 37, 45329 Essen
Tel: (0201) 86 206-0 *Fax:* (0201) 86 206-22
E-mail: info@klartext-verlag.de
Web Site: www.klartext-verlag.de
Key Personnel
Man Dir, Rights & Permissions & Editorial: Dr Ludger Classen *Tel:* (0201) 86206-59 *E-mail:* classen@klartext-verlag.de
Sales: Ariane Rump *Tel:* (0201) 86206-33 *E-mail:* rump@klartext-verlag.de
Advertising: Melanie Brockes *Tel:* (0201) 86206-29 *E-mail:* brockes@klartext-verlag.de
Production: Frank Muenschke *Tel:* (0201) 96206-60 *E-mail:* muenschke@klartext-verlag.de
Founded: 1982
Subjects: Government, Political Science, History, Nonfiction (General), Regional Interests, Self-Help, Social Sciences, Sociology, Sports, Athletics
ISBN Prefix(es): 3-88474; 3-89861
Distributed by Prolit Verlagsauslieferung GmbH (Germany & Austria); Schweizer Buchzentrum (Switzerland)
Foreign Rep(s): Jutta Leitner (Austria)
Warehouse: Postfach 9, 6301 Fernwald (Annerod) *Tel:* (0641) 43071 *Fax:* (0641) 42773
Orders to: Prolit Buchvertrieb, Siemensstr 16

Ingrid Klein Verlag GmbH+
Georgenstr 4, 80799 Munich
Tel: (089) 3818010 *Fax:* (089) 338704
E-mail: info@piper.de
Web Site: www.piper.de
Key Personnel
Man Dirs, Editorial: Joachim Jessen; Ingrid Klein
Man Dir: Detlef Lerch
Sales: Heike Latendorf-Janzen
Founded: 1993
Subjects: How-to, Psychology, Psychiatry, Self-Help, Body, Mind & Spirit, Esoterics, New Age

BOOK

ISBN Prefix(es): 3-89521
Orders to: VVA Bertelsmann Distribution A: Klein Verlag, Postfach 7777, 33310 Guetersloh

Kleine Reike, *imprint of* Beerenverlag

Verlag Kleine Schritte Ursula Dahm & Co (Little Steps Publisher)+
Medardstr 105, 54294 Trier
Tel: (0651) 300 698 *Fax:* (0651) 300 699
E-mail: mail@kleine-schritte.de
Web Site: www.kleine-schritte.de
Key Personnel
Man Dir: Ursula Dahm
Founded: 1980
Subjects: Astrology, Occult, Biography, Fiction, Gay & Lesbian, Human Relations, Nonfiction (General), Poetry, Psychology, Psychiatry, Self-Help, Women's Studies
ISBN Prefix(es): 3-923261

Kleiner Bachmann Verlag fur Kinder und Umwelt+
Hauptstr 279, 51503 Rosrath
Tel: (02205) 904-79 51 *Fax:* (02205) 910 855
E-mail: buch@kleinerbachmann.de
Web Site: www.kleinerbachmann.de
Key Personnel
Editor: Helmut Bachmann
Publishing Editor: Felicitas Jung
Founded: 1997
Specialize in picture books, Scandinavian authors, travel books for children, young authors under 18 years of age. The picture books try to awake sensitivity for environmental issues in a playful & uncomplicated manner.
Membership(s): AVJ (Arbeitsgemeinschaft von Jugendbuchverlagen).
Subjects: Environmental Studies, Fiction, Human Relations, Travel
ISBN Prefix(es): 3-933160
Number of titles published annually: 6 Print
Total Titles: 10 Print; 2 Audio
Distribution Center: Umbreit GmbH & Co KG Verlagsauslieferung, Mundelsheimer Str 3, 74321 Bietigheim-Bissingen, Contact: Ms Haberlandt *Tel:* (07142) 596-385 *Fax:* (07142) 596-387 *E-mail:* umbreit-verlagsauslieferung@t-online.de

Unterwegs Verlag, Manfred Klemann+
Dr Andlerstr 28, 78224 Singen
Tel: (07731) 63544 *Fax:* (07731) 62401
E-mail: uv@reisefuehrer.com
Web Site: www.reisefuehrer.com
Key Personnel
President & Rights: Manfred Klemann
Founded: 1983
ISBN Prefix(es): 3-924334; 3-86112
Subsidiaries: Hohentwiel-Verlag GmbH
Warehouse: VVA-Bertelsmann Distribution GmbH, An der Autonbahn, 33310 Guetersloh

Klens Verlag GmbH+
Carl-Mosterts-Platz 1, 40477 Duesseldorf
Mailing Address: Postfach 320620, 40421 Duesseldorf
Tel: (0211) 944794-0 *Fax:* (0211) 944794-30
E-mail: info@klensverlag.de
Key Personnel
Publisher: Doris Henseler
Founded: 1916
Subjects: Education, Religion - Other
ISBN Prefix(es): 3-87309
Bookshop(s): Buecher & Kunst KlensVerlag

Verlag Klett-Cotta+
Rotebuehlstr 77, 70178 Stuttgart
Tel: (0711) 6672-1256 *Fax:* (0711) 6672-2031
E-mail: info@klett-cotta.de
Web Site: www.klett-cotta.de
Telex: 722225 klet d

PUBLISHERS — GERMANY

Key Personnel
Publisher: Michael Klett
Man Dir: Rainer Just *E-mail:* r.just@klett-cotta.de
Sales & Advertising: Hans-Werner Serwe
 E-mail: h.serwe@klett-cotta.de
Sales Promotion: Horst Flinspach *Tel:* (0711) 6672-1533 *E-mail:* h.flinspach@klett-cotta.de
Advertising: Kirsten Brueckmann *Tel:* (0711) 6672-1429 *E-mail:* k.brueckmann@klett-cotta.de; Axel Loesdau *Tel:* (0711) 6672-1905 *E-mail:* a.loesdau@klett-cotta.de
Sales: Gaby Schuska *Tel:* (0711) 6672-1519 *E-mail:* g.schuska@klett-cotta.de
Public Relations: Ilona Jakobs *Tel:* (0711) 6672-1716 *Fax:* (0711) 6672-2032 *E-mail:* i.jakobs@klett-cotta.de; Katharina Wilts *Tel:* (0711) 6672-1258 *Fax:* (0711) 6672-2032 *E-mail:* k.wilts@klett-cotta.de
Rights & Permissions: Jasmin Fallahi *Tel:* (0711) 6672-1938 *E-mail:* j.fallahi@klett-cotta.de; Susanne Habermann *Tel:* (9711) 6672-1344 *E-mail:* s.habermann@klett-cotta.de; Roland Knappe *Tel:* (0711) 6672-1257 *Fax:* (0711) 6672-2033 *E-mail:* r.knappe@klett-cotta.de
Founded: 1659
Foreign Rep(s): Heinz-Andrea Spychiger & Heinz Marti (Switzerland); Eleonore Littasy (Austria); OBV - Klett-Cotta Verlagsgesellschaft mbH (Austria)
Distribution Center: BDK Buecherdienst Koeln, Koelner Str 248, 51149 Cologne *Tel:* (02203) 1002-0 *Fax:* (02203) 1002-146
Buchauslieferungsgesellschaft mbH & Co KG, Postfach 133, 2355 Wiener Neudorf, Austria *Tel:* (02236) 63535-244 *Fax:* (02236) 63535-243
Buecher Balmer, Boesch 41, 6331 Huenenberg, Switzerland *Tel:* (041) 7807100 *Fax:* (041) 7811520

Ernst Klett Verlag GmbH+
Rotebuehlstr 77, 70178 Stuttgart
Mailing Address: Postfach 106016, 70049 Stuttgart
Tel: (0711) 66 720 *Fax:* (0711) 66 72-20 00
E-mail: klett-kundenservice@klett-mail.de
Web Site: www.klett-verlag.de
Telex: 722232 kletd
Key Personnel
Publisher: Michael Klett
Rights & Export Sales, Klett International: Derrick Jenkins
Founded: 1897
Subjects: Education, Geography, Geology, Educational software
ISBN Prefix(es): 3-12
Associate Companies: Klett International GmbH

Kley, Werner, Beteiligungs GmbH+
Werlerstr 304, 59069 Hamm
Tel: (02381) 95040-0 *Fax:* (02381) 9504019
Key Personnel
Publisher, Rights & Permissions: Kley Werner
Author: Wilhelm Sohlote
ISBN Prefix(es): 3-924607

Erika Klopp Verlag GmbH+
Member of Oetinger Group
Poppenbuetteler Chaussee 53, 22397 Hamburg
Tel: (040) 60790907 *Fax:* (040) 60790959
E-mail: klopp@vsg-hamburg.de
Web Site: www.erika-klopp.de; www.klopp.biz
Key Personnel
Publisher, Rights & Permissions: Jan Weitendorf
Founded: 1925
ISBN Prefix(es): 3-7817
Total Titles: 150 Print
Parent Company: VSG Verlags-Service Gesselschaft mbH
Warehouse: Runge Verlagsauslieferung/Steinhagen *Tel:* (05204) 9181-0 *Fax:* (05204) 9181-93

Klosterhaus-Verlagsbuchhandlung Dr Grimm KG
Klosterhaus, 37194 Wahlsburg
Tel: (05572) 7310 *Fax:* (05572) 999823
Key Personnel
President: Dr Holle Grimm
Founded: 1951
Subjects: History
ISBN Prefix(es): 3-87418

Vittorio Klostermann GmbH+
Frauenlobstr 22, 60487 Frankfurt am Main
Mailing Address: Postfach 90 06 01, 60446 Frankfurt am Main
Tel: (069) 97 08 16-0 *Fax:* (069) 70 80 38
E-mail: verlag@klostermann.de
Web Site: www.klostermann.de
Key Personnel
Man Dir & Publisher: Vittorio E Klostermann
International Rights: Anastasia Urban *Tel:* (069) 97 08 16-17
Marketing: Martin Warny *Tel:* (069) 97 08 16-12 *E-mail:* m.warny@klostermann.de
Publicity: Ms Friedrike Haertling *Tel:* (069) 97 08 16-11 *E-mail:* f.haertling@klostermann.de
Founded: 1930
Subjects: Genealogy, History, Law, Library & Information Sciences, Literature, Literary Criticism, Essays, Philosophy, Publishing & Book Trade Reference, Science (General)
ISBN Prefix(es): 3-465

Verlag Fritz Knapp GmbH+
Aschaffenburger Str 19, 60599 Frankfurt am Main
Mailing Address: Postfach 11 11 51, 60046 Frankfurt
Tel: (069) 97 08 33-0 *Fax:* (069) 7 07 84 00
E-mail: info@kreditwesen.de
Web Site: www.kreditwesen.de
Telex: 411397 Knapp d *Cable:* SCHAUINSLAND
Key Personnel
Man Dir: Klaus-Friedrich Otto
Marketing, Sales & Publicity: Werner Scholz
Production, Rights & Permissions: Claus Wonneberger
Founded: 1949
Subjects: Economics, Finance
ISBN Prefix(es): 3-7819; 3-8314
Associate Companies: Verlag Helmut Richardi GmbH, Theodor-Heuss-Allee 106, 60486 Frankfurt am Main
Subsidiaries: Kreditwesen Service GmbH
Orders to: Koch, Neff & Oetinger, Schockenriedstr 37, 70565 Stuttgart

Albrecht Knaus Verlag GmbH+
Neumarkterstr 28, 81673 Munich
Mailing Address: Postfach 800360, 81603 Munich
Tel: (089) 9984010 *Fax:* (089) 99840144
Telex: 529965
Key Personnel
Publisher: Klaus Eck
Production: Peter Sturm
Publicity: Margit Schoenberger
Founded: 1978
Subjects: Art, Biography, Fiction, History, Nonfiction (General)
ISBN Prefix(es): 3-8135
Parent Company: Verlagsgruppe Bertelsmann GmbH
Orders to: VVA Bertelsmann Distribution, Postfach 7777, 33310 Guetersloh

Knesebeck Verlag+
Holzstr 26, 80469 Munich
Mailing Address: Postfach 140560, 80455 Munich
Tel: (089) 264059 *Fax:* (089) 269258
E-mail: sekretariat@knesebeck-verlag.de
Web Site: www.knesebeck-verlag.de

Key Personnel
Publisher & International Rights: Dr Rosemarie von dem Knesebeck *E-mail:* rknesebeck@knesebeck-verlag.de
Publisher: Herneid von dem Knesebeck
Founded: 1987
Subjects: Architecture & Interior Design, Biography, Photography
ISBN Prefix(es): 3-926901; 3-89660
Number of titles published annually: 20 Print
Total Titles: 70 Print

Doris Knop-Verlag+
Herbststr 13, 28215 Bremen
Tel: (0421) 9885030 *Fax:* (0421) 3509628
Founded: 1985
Specialize in guidebooks.
Subjects: Travel
ISBN Prefix(es): 3-9801077; 3-928760

Knowledge Media International+
Division of Bertelsmann Arvato AG
Weihenstephaner Str 7, 81673 Munich
Tel: (089) 4136-8433 *Fax:* (089) 4136-8411
Web Site: www.k-m-i.com
Key Personnel
International Rights Dir: Vanessa Nowak *E-mail:* vanessa.nowak@bertelsmann.de
International Rights Manager: Ines Killat *E-mail:* ines.killat@bertelsmann.de
Licensing of books & multimedia products to international publishers; IT services & solutions.
Subjects: Animals, Pets, Architecture & Interior Design, Child Care & Development, English as a Second Language, Foreign Countries, Gardening, Plants, Geography, Geology, Health, Nutrition, History, Mysteries, Natural History, Nonfiction (General), Sports, Athletics, Travel

Verlag Knut Reim, Jugendpresseverlag
Dammtorstr 30, 20354 Hamburg
Mailing Address: Postfach 302824, 20310 Hamburg
Tel: (040) 34 26 41 *Fax:* (040) 34 46 87
Key Personnel
General Manager: Jens Christians; Knut Reim
Founded: 1958
Subjects: Economics, Fiction, Law
ISBN Prefix(es): 3-87950
Parent Company: Jugend-Presse-Verlag, Dammtorstr 30, 20354 Hamburg

Verlagsanstalt Alexander Koch GmbH+
Fasanenweg 18, 70771 Leinfelden-Echterdingen
Mailing Address: Postfach 100256, 70746 Leinfelden-Echterdingen
Tel: (0711) 7591-0 *Fax:* (0711) 7591-380
Web Site: www.koch-verlag.de
Key Personnel
Man Dir: Karl-Heinz Weinbrenner; Liselotte Drabarczyk
Founded: 1890
Subjects: Architecture & Interior Design
ISBN Prefix(es): 3-87422
Associate Companies: DRW-Verlag Weinbrenner GmbH & Co; Bit-Verlag Weinbrenner GmbH & Co KG

Kochbuch Verlag Olga Leeb+
Landsbergerstr 238, 80687 Munich
Mailing Address: Postfach 210628, Munich 80679
Tel: (089) 58998303; (089) 583094 *Fax:* (089) 560208; (089) 58995303
Telex: 5212486
Key Personnel
Man Dir: Olli Leeb
Founded: 1976
Subjects: Cookery
ISBN Prefix(es): 3-921799

GERMANY

Koehler & Amelang Verlagsgesellschaft+
c/o Deutsche Verlags-Anstalt GmbH, Koeniginstr 9, 80539 Munich
Tel: (089) 455 54-0 *Fax:* (089) 455 54-100
E-mail: buch@dva.de
Web Site: www.dva.de
Key Personnel
Publisher: Juergen Horbach *Tel:* (089) 455 54-200 *Fax:* (089) 455 54-106 *E-mail:* juergen.horbach@dva.de
Marketing Manager: Susanne Lange *Tel:* (089) 455 54-400 *E-mail:* susanne.lange@dva.de
Sales: Bernhard Fetsch *Tel:* (089) 455 54-406 *E-mail:* bernhard.fetsch@dva.de
Advertising: Ulrike Bachmann *Tel:* (089) 455 54-405 *E-mail:* ulrike.bachmann@dva.de
Public Relations: Markus Desaga *Tel:* (089) 455 54-300 *Fax:* (089) 455 54-115 *E-mail:* markus.desaga@dva.de
Rights: Susanne Seggewiss *Tel:* (089) 455 54-310 *Fax:* (089) 455 54-113 *E-mail:* susanne.seggewiss@dva.de
Founded: 1925
Subjects: Architecture & Interior Design, Art, Biography, History, Regional Interests
ISBN Prefix(es): 3-7338

K F Koehler Verlag GmbH
Am Wallgraben 110, 70565 Stuttgart
Mailing Address: Postfach 800569, 70553 Stuttgart
Tel: (0711) 7892 130; (0711) 7892 149 *Fax:* (0711) 7892 132
E-mail: info@kfk.de; sabine.haegele@kfk.de
Web Site: www.buchkatalog.de
Telex: ueber 7255344 kno d
Key Personnel
Man Dir: Joachim Herkert
Founded: 1789
Subjects: Biography, Geography, Geology, Government, Political Science, History, Law, Publishing & Book Trade Reference, Social Sciences, Sociology
ISBN Prefix(es): 3-87425

Verlagsgruppe Koehler/Mittler+
Striepenweg 31, 21147 Hamburg
Tel: (040) 7971303 *Fax:* (040) 79713324
E-mail: vertrieb@koehler-mittler.de
Web Site: www.koehler-mittler.de
Key Personnel
Publisher: Peter Tamm; Wolf O Storck
Production: Hans-Peter Herfs-George
Manager: Thomas Bantle
Sales & Publicity: Hans-Focko Koehler
Founded: 1789
Group Members: Verlag E S Mittler und Sohn GmbH, Koehlers Verlagsgesellschaft mbH, Verlag Offene Worte, Verlag Europaeische Wehrkunde.
Subjects: Aeronautics, Aviation, Film, Video, History, Law, Maritime, Military Science, Philosophy, Public Administration, Social Sciences, Sociology
ISBN Prefix(es): 3-8132; 3-7822
Branch Office(s)
Godesberger Allee 91, 53175 Bonn *Tel:* (0228) 30789-0 *Fax:* (0228) 30789-15 (for all members of group)

Koehlers Verlagsgesellschaft mbH+
Member of Verlagsgruppe Koehler/Mittler
Striepenweg 31, 21147 Hamburg
Tel: (040) 79713-03 *Fax:* (040) 79713324
E-mail: vertrieb@koehler-mittler.de
Web Site: www.koehler-mittler.de *Cable:* KOEHLERS VLG D-21447 HAMBURG
Key Personnel
Publisher: Wolf O Storck; Peter Tamm
Manager: Thomas Bantle
Sales: Hans-Focko Koehler
Subjects: Fiction, Maritime, Nonfiction (General)

ISBN Prefix(es): 3-7822
Associate Companies: Maximilian-Verlag; E S Mittler und Sohn GmbH; Verlag Offene Worte Verlag Europaeische Wehrkunde
Branch Office(s)
Godesberger Allee 91, 53175 Bonn *Tel:* (0228) 307890 *Fax:* (0228) 3078915

Koelner Universitaets-Verlag GmbH+
Subsidiary of Deutscher Instituts-Verlag
Gustav-Heinemann-Ufer 84-88, 50968 Cologne
Tel: (0221) 48 81-1 *Fax:* (0221) 49 81-533
E-mail: welcome@iwkoeln.de
Web Site: www.iwkoeln.de
Telex: 8882071
Key Personnel
Man Dir & International Rights: Dr Gerhard Fels
Founded: 1953
Subjects: Business, Economics, Education, Government, Political Science, Social Sciences, Sociology
ISBN Prefix(es): 3-87427
Parent Company: Aktiv-informedia verlag GmbH

Koenemann Verlagesellschaft mbH+
Bonnerstr 126, 50968 Cologne
Tel: (0221) 3799-0 *Fax:* (0221) 3799-88
Key Personnel
Publisher: Ludwig Koenemann
Sales Dir: Lutz Billstein
Founded: 1993
Subjects: Architecture & Interior Design, Art, Cookery, History, Literature, Literary Criticism, Essays, Music, Dance, Photography, Transportation
ISBN Prefix(es): 3-89508; 3-8290
Total Titles: 1,200 Print
U.S. Office(s): Koenemann Inc, 137 W 19 St, New York, NY 10011, United States, Chief Executive Officer: Ralf Daab *Tel:* 212-367-8855 *Fax:* 212-367-8866 *E-mail:* rdaab@konemann.com

R Koenig GmbH
Floessergasse 7, 81369 Munich
Tel: (089) 724970 *Fax:* (089) 7238813
E-mail: info@koenig-specials.com
Web Site: www.koenig-specials.com
Key Personnel
Manager: Rosy Koenig
Founded: 1986
ISBN Prefix(es): 3-8126

Koenigs Erlaeuterungen, *imprint of* C Bange GmbH & Co KG

Koenigs Lektueren, *imprint of* C Bange GmbH & Co KG

Koenigsfurt Verlag, Evelin Buerger et Johannes Fiebig+
Koenigsfurt 6, Klein Koenigsfoerde am Nord-Ostsee-Kanal, 24796 Krummwisch
Tel: (04334) 18 99 02; (04334) 18 22 010 *Fax:* (04334) 18 22 011
E-mail: info@koenigsfurt.com
Web Site: www.koenigsfurt.com
Key Personnel
Contact: Evelin Buerger
Founded: 1989
Also German market leader for Tarot & Co nonbooks.
Subjects: Astrology, Occult, Nonfiction (General), Psychology, Psychiatry, Self-Help
ISBN Prefix(es): 3-927808; 3-933939; 3-89875
Number of titles published annually: 100 Print
Total Titles: 500 Print
Imprints: Bewusster Leben

Verlag Koenigshausen und Neumann GmbH+
Theodor Koernerstr 3a, 97072 Wuerzburg

Tel: (0931) 78 40-7 00
E-mail: info@koenigshausen-neumann.de
Web Site: www.koenigshausen-neumann.de/
Key Personnel
Man Dir: Dr Johannes Koenigshausen; Dr Thomas Neumann
Founded: 1979
Subjects: Archaeology, Economics, Education, Ethnicity, Law, Literature, Literary Criticism, Essays, Philosophy, Psychology, Psychiatry, Social Sciences, Sociology
ISBN Prefix(es): 3-88479; 3-8260

Lucy Koerner Verlag+
Bahnhofstr 49, 70734 Fellbach
Mailing Address: Postfach 1106, 70701 Fellbach
Tel: (0711) 588472 *Fax:* (0711) 5789634
Key Personnel
Man Dir: Lucy Koerner
Subjects: Fiction
ISBN Prefix(es): 3-922028

Verlag Valentin Koerner GmbH
Postfach 100164, 76482 Baden-Baden
Tel: (07221) 22423 *Fax:* (07221) 38697
E-mail: info@koernerverlag.de
Web Site: www.koernerverlag.de/ *Cable:* KOERNERVERLAG
Key Personnel
Publisher: Tobias Koerner
Founded: 1954
Subjects: Art, History, Music, Dance, Theology
ISBN Prefix(es): 3-87320
Number of titles published annually: 20 Print
Total Titles: 500 Print
Imprints: Heitz Librarie

Koesel-Verlag GmbH & Co+
Fluegenstr 2, 80639 Munich
Tel: (089) 17801-0 *Fax:* (089) 17801-111
E-mail: leserservice@koesel.de
Web Site: www.koesel.de/ *Cable:* KOESELVERLAG MUNICH
Key Personnel
Man Dir: Juergen Horbach; Winfried Nonhoff
Production: Armin Koehler
Sales: Kathrin Doering
Rights & Permissions: Ingrid Fink
Advertising: Marion Riedl
Founded: 1593
Membership(s): TR-Verlagsunion GmbH; Gesellschafter of Deutscher Taschenbuch Verlag (dtv).
Subjects: Education, Philosophy, Psychology, Psychiatry, Religion - Other
ISBN Prefix(es): 3-466
Distributed by Verlagsauslieferung Balmer (Switzerland); WMI Verlagsservice GmbH & Co KG (Germany)
Bookshop(s): Koeselsche Buchhandlung, Roncalliplatz 2, 50667 Cologne
Orders to: Moderne Industrie Verlagsservice, Landsberg

Koesler Verlag GmbH+
Brandenburger Str 19, 51766 Engelskirchen
Mailing Address: Postfach 2263, 51759 Engelskirchen
Tel: (02263) 951650 *Fax:* (02263) 951691 *Cable:* KOSLER VERLAG
Key Personnel
Man Dir, Rights & Permissions: Wolfgang Koesler
Founded: 1970
Subjects: Nonfiction (General), Sports, Athletics
ISBN Prefix(es): 3-924208

W Kohlhammer GmbH+
Hessbruehlstr 69, 70565 Stuttgart
Tel: (0711) 7863-0 *Fax:* (0711) 7863-8204
E-mail: redaktion@kohlhammer.de

Web Site: www.kohlhammer.de *Cable:* KOHLHAMMER STUTTGART
Key Personnel
Man Dir: Dr Juergen Gutbrod; Hans-Joachim Nagel
Sales Dir: Joerg Neumann
Editorial Dir, Rights & Permissions: Dr Alexander Schweickert
Contact: Gerda Schmid
Founded: 1866
Subjects: Architecture & Interior Design, Business, Economics, Education, Engineering (General), Government, Political Science, History, Language Arts, Linguistics, Law, Management, Marketing, Medicine, Nursing, Dentistry, Philosophy, Psychology, Psychiatry, Public Administration, Religion - Catholic, Religion - Islamic, Religion - Jewish, Religion - Protestant, Religion - Other, Social Sciences, Sociology, Theology
ISBN Prefix(es): 3-17
Total Titles: 3,400 Print
Subsidiaries: Deutscher Gemeindeverlag GmbH; Grote'sche Verlagsbuchhandlung GmbH & Co KG; Kohlhammer und Wallishauser GmbH; W Kohlhammer Druckerei GmbH & Co; W Kohlhammer Communication GmbH; Bruellmann GmbH & Co Repro-und Systemtechnik; Data Images Audiovisuelle Kommunikation; Verlagsvertrieb Stuttgart GmbH; Dienst am Buch GmbH
Divisions: W Kohlhammer Intermedia GmbH
Branch Office(s)
Ernst-Reuter-Haus, Strasse des 17, Juni 110-114, 10623 Berlin
Cologne
Rudolf-Leonhard-Str 28, 01097 Dresden *Tel:* (0351) 8022685 *Fax:* (0351) 8020664
Gustav-Freytag-Str 59, 99096 Erfurt *Tel:* (0361) 3735379 *Fax:* (0361) 3460537
Alexanderstr 3, 30159 Hannover *Tel:* (0511) 327029 *Fax:* (0511) 320143
Jagersberg 17, 24103 Kiel *Tel:* (0431) 554857 *Fax:* (0431) 554944
Schleinufer 14, 39104 Magdeburg *Tel:* (0391) 597080 *Fax:* (0391) 5970813
Alexander-Diehl-Str 10, 55130 Mainz *Tel:* (06131) 891540 *Fax:* (06131) 891624
Werkstr 209, 19061 Schwerin *Tel:* (0385) 616105 *Fax:* (0385) 616146
Warehouse: Verlagsvertrieb Stuttgart GmbH, Hessbruhlstr 69, 70565 Stuttgart

Kolibri-Verlag GmbH+
Wielandstr 37, 22089 Hamburg
Tel: (040) 2202243 *Fax:* (040) 2276368
E-mail: infos@kolibriverlag.de
Key Personnel
International Rights: Mr Foen Tjoeng Lie
Founded: 1990
Subjects: Asian Studies, Health, Nutrition, Nonfiction (General), Philosophy, Religion - Buddhist, Sports, Athletics
ISBN Prefix(es): 3-928288
Number of titles published annually: 5 Print
Total Titles: 50 Print
Subsidiaries: Kolibri Seminare

Kommentator, *imprint of* Hermann Luchterhand Verlag GmbH

Kon & Bundig, *imprint of* C Bange GmbH & Co KG

Konkordia Verlag GmbH
Eisenbahnstr 31, 77815 Buehl
Tel: (07223) 98 89-0 *Fax:* (07223) 98 89-45
E-mail: verlag@konkordia.de
Web Site: www.konkordia.de
Founded: 1881

Subjects: Education, Mathematics, Regional Interests
ISBN Prefix(es): 3-7826; 3-934873

Konkret Literatur Verlag+
Hoheluftchaussee 74, 20253 Hamburg
Tel: (040) 47 52 34 *Fax:* (040) 47 84 15
E-mail: info@konkret-literatur-verlag.de
Web Site: www.konkret-verlage.de
Key Personnel
Man Dir, Rights & Permissions: Dr Dorothee Gremliza
Founded: 1978
Subjects: Developing Countries, Government, Political Science, Health, Nutrition, History, Medicine, Nursing, Dentistry, Nonfiction (General), Poetry, Social Sciences, Sociology, Women's Studies
ISBN Prefix(es): 3-922144; 3-89458
Distributed by B&I (Switzerland); Herder & Co (Austria)
Shipping Address: Bertelsmann Distribution/VVA, Postfach 7777, 33310 Guetersloh *Tel:* (05241) 801499 *Fax:* (05241) 809352
Warehouse: Bertelsmann Distribution/VVA, Postfach 7777, 33310 Guetersloh *Tel:* (05241) 801499 *Fax:* (05241) 809352
Orders to: Bertelsmann Distribution/VVA, Postfach 7777, 33310 Guetersloh *Tel:* (05241) 801499 *Fax:* (05241) 809352

Anton H Konrad Verlag
Schulstr 5, 89264 Weissenhorn
Mailing Address: Postfach 1206, 89259 Weissenhorn
Tel: (07309) 26 57 *Fax:* (07309) 60 69
E-mail: info@konrad-verlag.de
Web Site: www.konrad-verlag.de/
Key Personnel
Man Dir, Rights & Permissions: Anton H Konrad
Founded: 1961
Subjects: Art, Biography, Geography, Geology, History, Philosophy, Regional Interests
ISBN Prefix(es): 3-87437

Konradin-Verlagsgruppe+
Ernst-Mey-Str 8, 70771 Leinfelden-Echterdingen
Tel: (0711) 7594-0 *Fax:* (0711) 7594-390
E-mail: info@konradin.de
Web Site: www.konradin.de
Key Personnel
Manager: Katja Kohlhammer
Founded: 1929
Subjects: Architecture & Interior Design, Chemistry, Chemical Engineering, Computer Science, Electronics, Electrical Engineering, Engineering (General), Technology
ISBN Prefix(es): 3-920560
U.S. Office(s): Trade Media International Corp, 421 Seventh Ave, Suite 607, New York, NY 10001-2002, United States *Tel:* 212-564-3380 *E-mail:* cdgtmicor@cs.com
Shipping Address: PVS, Sonnengasse 2, 74172 Neckarsulm

KONTEXTverlag+
Lindenhoekweg 2, 10409 Berlin
Tel: (030) 94415444 *Fax:* (030) 94415445
E-mail: service@kontextverlag.de
Web Site: www.kontextverlag.de
Key Personnel
Owner: Torsten Metelka *E-mail:* metelka@kontextverlag.de
Founded: 1990
Subjects: Art, Government, Political Science, Literature, Literary Criticism, Essays, Philosophy
ISBN Prefix(es): 3-86161; 3-931337

Kontur, *imprint of* Bonifatius GmbH Druck-Buch-Verlag

kopaed verlagsgmbh
Pfaelzer-Wald-Str 64, 81539 Munich
Tel: (089) 68890098 *Fax:* (089) 6891912
E-mail: info@kopaed.de
Web Site: www.kopaed.de
Key Personnel
Contact: Dr Ludwig Schlump
Subjects: Communications, Education, Film, Video, Nonfiction (General), Radio, TV
ISBN Prefix(es): 3-935686; 3-929061; 3-934079
Number of titles published annually: 25 Print
Total Titles: 180 Print

Koptisch-Orthodoxes Zentrum
St Antonius-Kloster, Pater Michael Hauptstr 10, 35647 Waldsolms-Kroeffelbach
Tel: (06085) 23 17 *Fax:* (06085) 26 66
E-mail: jugend@kopten.de
Web Site: www.kopten.de
Key Personnel
Contact: St Antonius Kloster
Subjects: Nonfiction (General), Religion - Other

Kosmos-Verlag, see Franckh-Kosmos Verlags-GmbH & Co

Dr Anton Kovac Slavica Verlag+
Elizabethstr 22, 80796 Munich
Tel: (089) 2725612 *Fax:* (089) 2716594
E-mail: 101566.2450@compuserve.com
Key Personnel
Owner: Anton Kovac
Founded: 1987
Subjects: Anthropology, Ethnicity, Fiction, Foreign Countries, Government, Political Science, History, Language Arts, Linguistics, Literature, Literary Criticism, Essays, Philosophy, Poetry, Religion - Other
ISBN Prefix(es): 3-927077

Roman Kovar Verlag+
Hauptstr 13, 86492 Egling an der Paar
Tel: (08206) 961977 *Fax:* (08206) 961978
E-mail: romankovar@gmx.net
Web Site: www.kovar-verlag.com
Key Personnel
Publisher: Roman Kovar
Founded: 1986
Subjects: Art, Library & Information Sciences, Literature, Literary Criticism, Essays, Religion - Jewish
ISBN Prefix(es): 3-925845

Karl Kraemer Verlag GmbH und Co+
Schulze-Delitzsch-Str 15, 70565 Stuttgart
Mailing Address: Postfach 80 06 50, 70506 Stuttgart
Tel: (0711) 7 84 96-0 *Fax:* (0711) 7 84 96-20
E-mail: info@kraemerverlag.com
Web Site: www.kraemerverlag.com
Key Personnel
President: Karl H Kraemer *E-mail:* karl.kraemer@kraemerverlag.com
Dir: Gudrun Kraemer *E-mail:* gudrun.kraemer@kraemerverlag.com; Lutz Kraemer *E-mail:* lutz.kraemer@kraemerverlag.com
Founded: 1930
Subjects: Architecture & Interior Design
ISBN Prefix(es): 3-7828
Total Titles: 118 Print
Associate Companies: Verlag Karl Kraemer & Co, Postfach 1209, 8034, Switzerland
Bookshop(s): Fachbuchhandlung Karl Kraemer, Rotebuehlstr 40, Postfach 102842, 701784 Stuttgart *Tel:* (0711) 669930 *Fax:* (0711) 628955 *Web Site:* www.karl.kraemer.de
Orders to: Koch, Neff, Oetinger & Co, Postfach 800620, 70506 Stuttgart

Reinhold Kraemer Verlag+
Rothenbaumchaussee 103F, 20148 Hamburg

Mailing Address: Postfach 13 05 84, 20105 Hamburg
Tel: (040) 4101429 *Fax:* (040) 455770
E-mail: info@kraemer-verlag.de
Web Site: www.kraemer-verlag.de
Key Personnel
Man Dir: Dr Reinhold Kraemer
Founded: 1987
Subjects: Science (General)
ISBN Prefix(es): 3-926952

Adam Kraft Verlag+
Imprint of Verlagshaus Wurzburg
Beethovenstr 5, 97070 Wurzburg
Tel: (0931) 385235 *Fax:* (0931) 385305
E-mail: info@verlagshaus.com
Web Site: www.verlagshaus.com
Key Personnel
Publishing Dir: Dieter Krause
Dir of Production: Juergen Roth
Sales Dir: Johannes Glesius
Founded: 1927
Subjects: Foreign Countries, Regional Interests, Travel
ISBN Prefix(es): 3-8083

Krafthand Verlag Walter Schultz GmbH
Walter-Schulz Str 1, 86825 Bad Woerishofen
Mailing Address: Postfach 1462, 86817 Bad Worishofen
Tel: (08247) 30070 *Fax:* (08247) 300770
E-mail: info@krafthand.de
Web Site: www.krafthand.de
Key Personnel
President, Man Dir & Public Relations: Gottfried Karpstein
Man Dir & Editorial Chief: Walter G Schweizer
Founded: 1927
Subjects: Civil Engineering
ISBN Prefix(es): 3-87441

Verlag Edition Kraftpunkt Anton Fedrigotti+
Steinerne Furt 78, 86167 Augsburg
Tel: (0821) 705011 *Fax:* (0821) 705008
Key Personnel
Owner: Toni Fedrigotti
Founded: 1982
ISBN Prefix(es): 3-925557; 3-928086; 3-89647
U.S. Office(s): Dr Eldon Taylor, 816 W Big Bear Blvd, Big Bear City, CA 92314, United States
Tel: (909) 585-6065 *Fax:* (909) 585-6365

Karin Kramer Verlag+
Postfach 440417, 12004 Berlin
Tel: (030) 6845055; (030) 6842598 *Fax:* (030) 6858577
E-mail: kramer@virtualitas.com
Web Site: www.anares.org/kramer/
Key Personnel
Editorial & Publicity: Bernd Kramer
Founded: 1970
Subjects: Alternative, Art, Biography, Government, Political Science, History, Literature, Literary Criticism, Essays, Nonfiction (General), Philosophy, Poetry, Science Fiction, Fantasy, Social Sciences, Sociology
ISBN Prefix(es): 3-87956

Verlag Waldemar Kramer+
Orberstr 38, 60386 Frankfurt am Main
Mailing Address: Berlinerstr 8a, 61440 Oberursel
Tel: (069) 449045 *Fax:* (069) 449064
E-mail: info@frankfurtbuecher.de
Web Site: www.frankfurtbuecher.de
Key Personnel
Publisher: Dr Henriette Kramer
Founded: 1939
Subjects: Art, Biological Sciences, Education, Environmental Studies, Geography, Geology, History, Natural History, Science (General)

ISBN Prefix(es): 3-7829
Total Titles: 200 Print

Krankenpflegeforschung, *imprint of* Bibliomed - Medizinische Verlagsgesellschaft mbH

Nara Verlag Josef Krauthaeuser+
Akazienring 6a, 85391 Allershausen
Mailing Address: Postfach 1241, 85388 Allershausen
Tel: (08166) 8530; (08166) 8531 *Fax:* (08166) 8530
E-mail: info@nara-verlag.de
Web Site: www.nara-international.de; www.nara-verlag.de
Key Personnel
Manager, Rights & Permissions: Josef Krauthaeuser
Founded: 1982
Subjects: Aeronautics, Aviation
ISBN Prefix(es): 3-925671

Hubert Kretschmar Leipziger Verlagsgesellschaft+
Gerichtsweg 28, 04103 Leipzig
Tel: (0341) 2210229 *Fax:* (0341) 2210226
Key Personnel
Proprietor, Rights & Permissions: Hubert Kretschmar
Founded: 1990
Specialize in high quality catalogs & art books.
Subjects: Art, History, Literature, Literary Criticism, Essays, Regional Interests
ISBN Prefix(es): 3-910143

Verlag Hubert Kretschmer+
Nymphenburgerstr 34, 80335 Munich
Mailing Address: Postfach 260117, 80058 Munich
Tel: (089) 1234530 *Fax:* (089) 1238638
E-mail: hubert.kretschmer@t-online.de
Web Site: www.verlag-hubert-kretschmer.de
Founded: 1980
Specialize in artist's books, catalogs, new & abstract photography.
Subjects: Art, Photography
ISBN Prefix(es): 3-923205
Total Titles: 40 Print
Distributor for ICON

Kriebel Verlag GmbH
Auf der Hoehe 14, 86923 Finning
Tel: (08806) 93 60 *Fax:* (08806) 93 61
E-mail: info@kriebelverlag.de
Web Site: www.kriebel-sat.de; www.kriebelverlag.de
Key Personnel
Manager: Henning Kriebel
Founded: 1986
Subjects: Communications
ISBN Prefix(es): 3-927617
Divisions: Media Service

Krimi-Reihe, *imprint of* Alibaba Verlag GmbH

Alfred Kroner Verlag+
Reinsburgstr 56, 70178 Stuttgart
Mailing Address: Postfach 102862, 70024 Stuttgart
Tel: (0711) 6155363 *Fax:* (0711) 61553646
E-mail: kontak@kroener-verlag.de
Web Site: www.kroener-verlag.de
Key Personnel
Man Dir: Arno Klemm; Dr Imma Klemm; Walter Kohrs
Founded: 1904
Subjects: Art, Drama, Theater, History, Language Arts, Linguistics, Literature, Literary Criticism, Essays, Music, Dance, Philosophy, Religion - Other
ISBN Prefix(es): 3-520

Total Titles: 180 Print
Orders to: VA/KNO Stuttgart

Krueger Verlag GmbH+
Hedderichstr 114, 60596 Frankfurt am Main
Tel: (069) 6062-0 *Fax:* (069) 6062-352
Web Site: www.krueger-verlag.de
Key Personnel
Man Dir: Monika Schoeller; Dr Hubertus Schenkel
Man Dir, Rights & Permissions: Wolfgang Mertz
Sales: Joerg Alkenbrecher
Publicity: Margarete Schwind
Production: Wilfried Meiner
Editorial: Peter Wilfert
Subjects: Fiction, Humor, Nonfiction (General)
ISBN Prefix(es): 3-8105
Parent Company: S Fischer Verlag GmbH

Krug & Schadenberg+
Arndtstr 34, 10965 Berlin
Tel: (030) 61625752 *Fax:* (030) 61625751
E-mail: info@krugschadenberg.de
Web Site: www.krugschadenberg.de
Key Personnel
International Rights: Andrea Krug
Founded: 1993
Membership(s): Women in Publishing.
Subjects: Fiction, Gay & Lesbian, Human Relations, Literature, Literary Criticism, Essays, Self-Help, Women's Studies
ISBN Prefix(es): 3-930041
Number of titles published annually: 6 Print
Total Titles: 30 Print

Verlag Ernst Kuhn+
Mendelssohnstr 7, 10405 Berlin
Mailing Address: PO Box 080147, 10001 Berlin
Tel: (030) 44342230 *Fax:* (030) 4424732
E-mail: ernst-kuhn-verlag@t-online.de
Web Site: www.vek.de
Key Personnel
Publisher: Ernst Kuhn *E-mail:* kuhn@vek.de
Man Dir: Baerbel Bruder *E-mail:* bruder@vek.de
Founded: 1991
Specialize in books on Russian music; also online-bookshop (books on music, sheet music, scores).
Subjects: Biography, History, Music, Dance
ISBN Prefix(es): 3-928864; 3-936637
Orders to: LKG mbH, Potzschauer Weg, 04579 Espenhain bei Leipzig

Kulturbuch-Verlag GmbH
Sprosserweg 3, 12351 Berlin
Mailing Address: Postfach 470449, 12313 Berlin
Tel: (030) 6618484 *Fax:* (030) 6617828
E-mail: kbvinfo@kulturbuch-verlag.de
Web Site: www.kulturbuch-verlag.de
Key Personnel
Manager: Lothar Seikrit
Founded: 1949
Subjects: Environmental Studies, Law, Regional Interests
ISBN Prefix(es): 3-88961

Kulturstiftung der deutschen Vertriebenen
Kaiserstr 113, 53113 Bonn
Tel: (0228) 915120 *Fax:* (0228) 218397
E-mail: kulturstiftung@t-online.de
Web Site: www.kulturstiftung-der-deutschen-vertriebenen.de
Key Personnel
Chairperson: Dr Reinold Schleifenbaum
Man Dir: Dr Hans-Jakob Tebarth
Founded: 1974
Subjects: Art, Government, Political Science, History, Law, Literature, Literary Criticism, Essays
ISBN Prefix(es): 3-88557
Number of titles published annually: 12 Print
Total Titles: 200 Print

PUBLISHERS	GERMANY

Verlag der Kunst/G+B Fine Arts Verlag GmbH+
Rosa-Menzerstr 12, 01309 Dresden
Mailing Address: Postfach 190154, 01281 Dresden
Tel: (0351) 3360742; (0351) 3100052 *Fax:* (0351) 3105245
E-mail: verlag-der-kunst@t-online.de
Web Site: www.verlag-der-kunst.de
Key Personnel
Editor: Martina Buder
Marketing Manager: Dr Barbara Schmidt
Founded: 1952
Specialize in architecture.
Subjects: Architecture & Interior Design, Art, Photography, Regional Interests
ISBN Prefix(es): 3-364; 90-5705
Total Titles: 120 Print
Associate Companies: G+B Arts International
Distributed by IPD
Warehouse: SOVA, Friesstr 20-24, 60388 Frankfurt
Distribution Center: SOVA, Friesstr 20-24, 60388 Frankfurt

Kunst und Wohnen Verlag GmbH, see Dr Wolfgang Schwarze Verlag

Verlag Antje Kunstmann GmbH+
Georgenstr 123, 80743 Munich
Mailing Address: Postfach 431351, Munich 80743
Tel: (089) 1211930 *Fax:* (089) 12119320
E-mail: info@kunstmann.de
Web Site: www.kunstmann.de
Key Personnel
Man Dir, Editorial: Antje Kunstmann
Sales: Ulrich Deurer
Founded: 1970
Subjects: Drama, Theater, Education, Fiction, Government, Political Science, Humor, Literature, Literary Criticism, Essays, Nonfiction (General)
ISBN Prefix(es): 3-921040; 3-88897
Orders to: LKG, Potzschaues Weg, 04579 Espenhain
B & I, Obfelderstr 35, 8910 Affoltern a A, Switzerland
Mohr-Morawa, Sulzengasse 2, 1230 Vienna, Austria

Kunstverlag Maria Laach
56653 Maria Laach
Tel: (02652) 59360 *Fax:* (02652) 59383
E-mail: kunstverlag@maria-laach.de
Web Site: www.maria-laach.de
Key Personnel
Dir: P Cremer

Kunstverlag Weingarten GmbH+
Laegelerstr 31, 88250 Weingarten
Tel: (0751) 561290 *Fax:* (0751) 5612920
E-mail: kunstverlag@weingarten-verlag.de
Web Site: www.kv-weingarten.de
Key Personnel
President: Rainer Berger
Publisher & International Rights: Hero Schiefer
Tel: (0751) 5612940 *E-mail:* hschiefer@weingarten-verlag.de
Founded: 1976
Publishers of art & photo calendars.
Subjects: Animals, Pets, Antiques, Architecture & Interior Design, Art, Cookery, Health, Nutrition, Literature, Literary Criticism, Essays, Music, Dance, Photography
ISBN Prefix(es): 3-8170; 3-921617
Total Titles: 180 Print

Kupfergraben Verlagsgesellschaft mbH+
Luetzowstr 105, 10785 Berlin
Tel: (030) 2622097 *Fax:* (030) 2621990
Key Personnel
Man Dir: Wolfgang Stapp
Founded: 1984
Subjects: Art, Literature, Literary Criticism, Essays
ISBN Prefix(es): 3-89181

Kutz und praktisch, *imprint of* Verlag Hermann Bauer Gmbh & Co KG

Kynos Verlag Dr Dieter Fleig GmbH+
Am Remelsbach 30, 54570 Muerlenbach/Eifel
Tel: (06594) 653 *Fax:* (06594) 452
E-mail: info@kynos-verlag.de
Web Site: www.kynos-verlag.de
Key Personnel
Dir: Herbert Wolter
Foreign Rights: Gisela Ran
Founded: 1980
Subjects: Animals, Pets
ISBN Prefix(es): 3-929545; 3-924008; 3-933228
Total Titles: 210 Print

Laaber-Verlag+
Regensburgerstr 19, 93164 Laaber
Tel: (09498) 2307 *Fax:* (09498) 2543
E-mail: info@laaber-verlag.de
Web Site: www.laaber-verlag.de
Key Personnel
Man Dir: Dr Henning Mueller-Buscher
Editor: Susanne Boehm
Founded: 1977
Subjects: Music, Dance
ISBN Prefix(es): 3-89007; 90-6027
Total Titles: 1,000 Print

Labyrinth Verlag Gisela Ottmer
Yorckstr 3, 38102 Braunschweig
Tel: (0531) 64259 *Fax:* (0531) 681358
E-mail: labyrinthbraunschweig@t-online.de
Web Site: www.frauenart.de/labyrinthbraunschweig
ISBN Prefix(es): 3-9801010; 3-9806542; 3-9807707

Ambro Lacus, Buch- und Bildverlag Walter A Kremnitz
Frieding-Hurtenstr 25, 82346 Andechs
Tel: (08152) 1332 *Fax:* (08152) 40186 *Cable:* KREMNITZ-FRIEDING
Key Personnel
Man Dir, Rights & Permissions: Walter Kremnitz
Bookkeeping: P Kremnitz
Founded: 1974
Subjects: Earth Sciences, Gardening, Plants, Law, Nonfiction (General), Science (General), Travel
ISBN Prefix(es): 3-921445
Number of titles published annually: 2 Print

Lahn-Verlag GmbH+
Hoogeweg 71, 47623 Kevelaer
Tel: (02832) 929-130 *Fax:* (02832) 929-139
E-mail: service@lahn-verlag.de
Web Site: www.lahn-verlag.de *Cable:* LAHN-VERLAG
Key Personnel
Publisher: Dr Gerhard Hartmann *E-mail:* gerhard.hartmann@lahn-verlag.de; Engelbert Tauscher
Editorial: Dr Stefan Ohnesorge; Anne Voorhoeve
Sales: Helmut Kaiser *E-mail:* helmut.kaiser@lahn-verlag.de
Founded: 1900
Subjects: Poetry, Religion - Catholic, Theology
ISBN Prefix(es): 3-7840
Total Titles: 200 Print; 50 Audio
Orders to: Butzon & Bercker GmbH, Hoogeweg 71, 47623 Kevelaer *Tel:* (02832) 9290 *Fax:* (02832) 929 211 *E-mail:* service@butzonbercker.de

Johannis Lahr, see Verlag der Sankt-Johannis-Druckerei C Schweickhardt

Lambda Edition GmbH+
Clemens-Schultzstr 77, 20359 Hamburg
Mailing Address: Postfach 304171, 20324 Hamburg
Tel: (040) 312836 *Fax:* (040) 3192096
Key Personnel
Publisher: Michael P Hartleben
Founded: 1980
Membership(s): the Stock Exchange of German Booksellers.
Subjects: Fiction
ISBN Prefix(es): 3-925495

Lambertus Verlag GmbH+
Mitscherlichstr 8, 79108 Freiburg
Mailing Address: Postfach 1026, 79010 Freiburg
Tel: (0761) 368250 *Fax:* (0761) 3682533
E-mail: info@lambertus.de
Web Site: www.lambertus.de
Key Personnel
Man Dir: Fritz Boll; Gerhild Neugart
Founded: 1898
ISBN Prefix(es): 3-7841
Subsidiaries: Freiburge Buchediemst (verlagsbuchhandlung)
Bookshop(s): Freiburger Buecherdienst, Wolfinstr 4, 79104 Freiburg

Lamuv Verlag GmbH+
Gromerstr 20, 37073 Goettingen
Mailing Address: Postfach 2605, 37016 Goettingen
Tel: (0551) 44024 *Fax:* (0551) 41392
E-mail: info@lamuv.de
Web Site: www.lamuv.de
Key Personnel
Man Dir, Editorial: Karl-Klaus Rabe
Sales: Leonore Frester
Founded: 1976
Subjects: Developing Countries, Government, Political Science, Literature, Literary Criticism, Essays, Regional Interests
ISBN Prefix(es): 3-921521; 3-88977

Landbuch-Verlagsgesellschaft mbH
(Countrybook-Publishing House)+
Kabelkamp 6, 30179 Hannover
Mailing Address: Postfach 160, 30001 Hannover
Tel: (0511) 27046-153 *Fax:* (0511) 27046-150
E-mail: info@landbuch.de
Web Site: www.landbuch.de *Cable:* LANDBUCH HANOVER
Key Personnel
Man Dir: Bernd Kuhrmeier
Sales: Elvira Frede
Sales & Marketing: Rene Busse
Production, Rights & Permissions: Dieter Brodbeck
Public Relations: Ulrike Clever
Founded: 1945
Subjects: Agriculture, Animals, Pets, Cookery, Crafts, Games, Hobbies, House & Home, Humor, Nonfiction (General), Outdoor Recreation, Regional Interests, Travel, Country Cooking, Country Life, Guides for Northern Germany
ISBN Prefix(es): 3-7842

Institut fuer Landes- und Stadtentwicklungsforschung des Landes Nordrhein-Westfalen (Research Institute for Regional & Urban Development of the Federal State of North Rhine-Westphalia)+
Deutsche Str 5, 44339 Dortmund
Tel: (0231) 90 51-0 *Fax:* (0231) 90 51-1 55
E-mail: webmaster@ils.nrw.de
Web Site: www.ils.nrw.de
Key Personnel
Dir: Sierau Ullrich
Founded: 1971

Subjects: Architecture & Interior Design, Energy, Environmental Studies, Law, Outdoor Recreation, Physical Sciences, Public Administration, Regional Interests, Social Sciences, Sociology, Technology, Transportation, Women's Studies
ISBN Prefix(es): 3-8176
Distributed by WAZ-Vertrieb Bitte streichen

Peter Lang GmbH Europaeischer Verlag der Wissenschaften+
Eschborner Landstr 42-50, 60489 Frankfurt am Main
Mailing Address: Postfach 940225, 60460 Frankfurt am Main
Tel: (069) 7807050 *Fax:* (069) 780705-50
E-mail: zentrale.frankfurt@peterlang.com
Web Site: www.peterlang.de
Key Personnel
Man Dir: Ruprecht Sickel; Juergen-Matthias Springer
Licenses: Ruediger Brunsch *Tel:* (069) 78070520 *E-mail:* r.brunsch@peterlang.com
Founded: 1971
Subjects: Education, Government, Political Science, History, Language Arts, Linguistics, Law, Literature, Literary Criticism, Essays, Philosophy, Science (General), Theology
ISBN Prefix(es): 3-631; 3-8204
Parent Company: Verlag Peter Lang AG, Switzerland
Associate Companies: Peter Lang Publishing Inc, 275 Seventh Ave, 28th floor, New York, NY 10001-6708, United States *Tel:* 212-647-7706 *Fax:* 212-647-7707 *E-mail:* customerservice@plang.com *Web Site:* www.peterlang.com
Orders to: Peter Lang AG, Moosstr 1, 2542 Pieterlen, Switzerland *Tel:* (032) 376 17 17 *Fax:* (032) 376 17 27 *E-mail:* customerservice@peterlang.com *Web Site:* www.peterlang.ch

Langenscheidt Fachverlag GmbH+
Mies-van-der-Rohestr 1, 80807 Munich
Tel: (089) 36096-0 *Fax:* (089) 36096-222
E-mail: kundenservice@langenscheidt.de
Web Site: www.langenscheidt.de
Key Personnel
Manager: Marie-Jeanne Derouin *Tel:* (089) 36096 475 *E-mail:* marie-jeanne.derouin@langenscheidt.de
Founded: 1991
Subjects: Specialized bilingual & multilingual print & electronic versions
ISBN Prefix(es): 3-86117
Parent Company: Langenscheidt KG
Warehouse: TVA Gotha, Langenscheidtstr 70, 99867 Gotha
Orders to: Langenscheidt Fachverlag, Postfach 401120, 80711 Munich

The Langenscheidt Group+
Mies-van-der-Rohestr 1, 80807 Munich
Mailing Address: Postfach 401120, 80711 Munich
Tel: (089) 36096-0; (089) 36096-258 (orders) *Fax:* (089) 36096-222; 36096-258
E-mail: kundenservice@langenscheidt.de
Web Site: www.langenscheidt.de
Key Personnel
General Partner: Andreas Langenscheidt; Nare Ernst Tidebier-Langenscheidt
Publishing Dir: Rolf Mueller
Sales Dir & Marketing: Dr Matt Schuesseler
Financial Dir: Dr Eugene Saller
Founded: 1856
The Group consists of: Bibliographisches Institut und F A Brockhaus AG; Axel Juncker Verlag; Langenscheidt KG; Langenscheidt-Hachette GmbH; Langenscheidt-Longman GmbH; Mentor-Verlag; Polyglott Verlag GmbH; Langenscheidt Fachverlag GmbH (all in Germany); Langenscheidt-Verlag GmbH, Austria; Apa Publications; GmbH & Co Verlag KG; Langenscheidt AG, Switzerland; Langenscheidt Publishers, Inc; Creative Sales Corp; American Map Corp; ADC; Trakker Maps Inc Nationwide; Arrow Map Inc; Hagstrom Map Co Inc; The Map Store Inc; Ha ADC Map & Travel Center; Berlitz Publishing; Hammond: Blay Folder SAS France; Langenscheidt Polska; Geo Center International UK.
ISBN Prefix(es): 3-468; 3-86117; 3-595; 3-526; 3-493

Langenscheidt-Hachette+
Mies-van-der-Rohestr 1, 80807 Munich
Mailing Address: Postfach 401120, 80711 Munich
Tel: (089) 360960 *Fax:* (089) 36096-222; (089) 36096-472 (general); (089) 36096-258 (orders)
E-mail: kundenservice@langenscheidt.de
Web Site: www.langenscheidt.de
Key Personnel
Man Dir: Karl Ernst Tielebier-Langenscheidt; Marc Moingeon
Editorial: Dr Herbert Bornebusch
Founded: 1977
Sales & Promotion through Langenscheidt KG.
Membership(s): the Langenscheidt Group.
Subjects: Education, Language Arts, Linguistics
ISBN Prefix(es): 3-595

Langenscheidt KG+
Member of The Langenscheidt Group
Mies-van-der-Roehstr 1, 80807 Munich
Mailing Address: Postfach 401120, 80711 Munich
Tel: (089) 36096-0; (089) 36096-258 (orders) *Fax:* (089) 36096-222
E-mail: kundenservice@langenscheidt.de
Web Site: www.langenscheidt.de
Telex: Munich 5215379 lkgmd *Cable:* LANGENSCHEIDT MUNICH
Key Personnel
Man Dir: Karl Ernst Tielebier-Langenscheidt; Andreas Langenscheidt
Program Manager: Dr Wolfgang Wieter
Chief Editor, English language: Wolfgang Kaul
Chief Editor, Slavonic languages: Dr Paul Ruehl
Chief Editor, German as a Foreign language: Dr Herbert Bornebusch
Chief Editor, Roman languages: Dieter Meier
Production: Helmut Wahl
Sales Dir: Michael Staehler
Advertising: Brigitte Pasch
Publicity: Margrit Philipp
Export: Alan Francis Roberts
Electronic Publishing: Dr Hans Werner Scholz
Rights & Permissions: Walburga Hallet-Wolters
Legal Dept: Dr Martin Wagner
Founded: 1856
Membership(s): TR- Verlagsunion GmbH.
ISBN Prefix(es): 3-526
Subsidiaries: Langenscheidt-Longman GmbH; Langenscheidt-Hachette GmbH; Polyglott-Verlag Dr Bolte KG; Humboldt-Taschenbuchverlag Jacobi KG; Mentor Verlag Dr Ramdohu KG; Karl Baedeker GmbH; Bibliographisches Institut und F L Brockhaus AG; Verlag Enzyklopaedie; Langenscheidt-Verlag GmbH; Langenscheidt AG; Trakker Maps Inc; Arrow Map Inc; Creative Sales Corp; Langenscheidt Publishers Inc; American Map Corp; Hagstrom Map Co; ADC; Apa Publications (HK) Ltd

Verlag Langewiesche-Brandt KG+
Lechnerstr 27, 82067 Ebenhausen (Schaeftlarn)
Tel: (08178) 4857 *Fax:* (08178) 7388
E-mail: textura@langewiesche-brandt.de
Web Site: www.langewiesche-brandt.de
Key Personnel
Man Dir: Kristof Wachinger *E-mail:* wachinger@langewiesche-brandt.de
Founded: 1906
Subjects: Poetry
ISBN Prefix(es): 3-7846
Number of titles published annually: 4 Print
Total Titles: 60 Print
Imprints: Ebenhausen bei Muenchen

Karl Robert Langewiesche Nachfolger Hans Koester KG+
Gruener Weg 6, 61462 Koenigstein
Tel: (06174) 7333 *Fax:* (06174) 933-039
E-mail: info@langewiesche-verlag.de
Web Site: www.langewiesche-verlag.de *Cable:* LANGEWIESCHE KOENIGSTEINTAUNUS
Key Personnel
Publisher & Man Dir, Production: Hans-Curt Koester *E-mail:* koester@langewiesche-verlag.de
Editorial: Gabriele Klempert
Founded: 1902
Specialize in books, journals & calendars.
Membership(s): Motovun Group Association, Lucerne.
Subjects: Antiques, Archaeology, Architecture & Interior Design, Art, History, How-to, Photography
ISBN Prefix(es): 3-7845
Number of titles published annually: 5 Print
Total Titles: 120 Print
Imprints: Die Blauen Buecher (The Blue Book)
Distributed by Abaris Books (USA); Penfield Books (USA)

Ingrid Langner
Buchentwiete 24 A, 25355 Barmstedt
Mailing Address: Postfach 1125, 25349 Barmstedt
Tel: (04123) 7780 *Fax:* (04123) 7885
Key Personnel
Owner: Manfred Langner
Founded: 1985
Subjects: Fiction, Language Arts, Linguistics, Literature, Literary Criticism, Essays
ISBN Prefix(es): 3-9801131

Lappan Verlag GmbH+
Wuerzburger Str 14, 26121 Oldenburg
Mailing Address: Postfach 3407, 26024 Oldenburg
Tel: (0441) 980660 *Fax:* (0441) 9806622; (0441) 9806624; (0441) 9806634
E-mail: info@lappan.de
Web Site: www.lappan.de
Key Personnel
Man Dir: Dieter Schwalm
Editorial Dir: Peter Baumann
Sales: Michael Boehme
International Rights: Heidrun Kaempf
Founded: 1983
Publisher of books for children & humor gift books for adults.
Subjects: Cartoon Books of Uli Stein, Humor
ISBN Prefix(es): 3-89082; 3-8303
Number of titles published annually: 80 Print
Total Titles: 470 Print
Associate Companies: Achterbahn Verlag GmbH
Distributor of Edition C (Switzerland)
Distribution Center: LKG, Poetzschauer Weg, 04579 Espenhain

Michael Lassleben Verlag und Druckerei
(Michael Lassleben Publishing House & Printing Office)
Lange Gasse 19, 93183 Kallmuenz
Mailing Address: Postfach 20, 93183 Kallmunz
Tel: (09473) 205 *Fax:* (09473) 8357
E-mail: druckerei@oberpfalzverlag-lassleben.de
Web Site: www.oberpfalzverlag-lassleben.de
Key Personnel
Owner: Erich Lassleben, Sr
Founded: 1907
Subjects: Archaeology, Geography, Geology, History, Literature, Literary Criticism, Essays

ISBN Prefix(es): 3-7847
Number of titles published annually: 20 Print

J Latka Verlag GmbH+
Heilsbachstr 32, 53123 Bonn
Tel: (0228) 919320 *Fax:* (0228) 9193217
E-mail: info@latka.de
Web Site: www.latka.de
Key Personnel
President, Rights & Permissions: Joachim Latka
 E-mail: jlatka@latka.de
Founded: 1984
Subjects: History, Travel
ISBN Prefix(es): 3-925068
Total Titles: 30 Print
U.S. Office(s): Cosmedia Inc, 560 Sutter St, Suite 300, San Francisco, CA 94102, United States, Contact: Ms E A Olesen *Tel:* 415-677-9700 *Fax:* 415-677-9300 *E-mail:* cosmedia@sirius.com
Foreign Rep(s): Elizabeth A Olesen (North America)
Orders to: Herold, Kolpingring 4, 82041 Oberhaching, Contact: Ms Stanglmeier *Tel:* (089) 6138710 *Fax:* (089) 61387120

H Lauppsche Buchhandlung, *imprint of* Mohr Siebeck

LBO-Dienst, *imprint of* Bauverlag GmbH

Lebenshilfe-Verlag Marburg, Verlag der Bundesvereinigung Lebenshilfe fuer Menschen mit geistiger Behinderung eV+
Raiffeisenstr 18, 35043 Marburg
Tel: (06421) 4 91-0 *Fax:* (06421) 4 91-1 67
E-mail: bundesvereinigung@lebenshilfe.de
Web Site: www.lebenshilfe.de
Key Personnel
Publishing Dir: Dr Bernhard Conrads
Founded: 1958
Subjects: Disability, Special Needs, Health, Nutrition, Law, Medicine, Nursing, Dentistry, Nonfiction (General), Self-Help, Social Sciences, Sociology
ISBN Prefix(es): 3-88617

Lebensstrom eV
Graefestr 71, 10967 Berlin
Mailing Address: Postfach 12 03 07, 10593 Berlin
Tel: (030) 3131247 *Fax:* (030) 3121098
E-mail: info@lebensstrom.com
Web Site: www.lebensstrom.com
Parent Company: Living Stream Ministry

Verlag fuer Lehrmittel Poessneck GmbH+
Neustaedterstr 63, 07381 Poessneck
Mailing Address: Postfach 1465, 07374 Poessneck
Tel: (03647) 425018 *Fax:* (03647) 425020
Key Personnel
Manager: Lothar Stein
Founded: 1947
ISBN Prefix(es): 3-7493

Leibniz Verlag+
Auf dem Haehnchen 34, 56329 St Goar
Tel: (06741) 1720 *Fax:* (06741) 1749
E-mail: reichl-verlag@telda.net
Key Personnel
Man Dir: Matthias Draeger
Founded: 1994
Subjects: Human Relations, Language Arts, Linguistics, Philosophy, Science (General)
ISBN Prefix(es): 3-931155

Leibniz-Buecherwarte+
Robert-Koch-Str 12, 31848 Bad Muender
Mailing Address: Postfach 1214, 31842 Bad Muender
Tel: (05042) 15 28 *Fax:* (05042) 15 28
E-mail: leibniz-buecherwarte@t-online.de
Web Site: www.leibniz-buecherwarte.com
Key Personnel
Contact: Gabrielle Spaeth
Founded: 1985
Specialize in philosophy with children.
Subjects: Literature, Literary Criticism, Essays, Philosophy, Religion - Other
ISBN Prefix(es): 3-925237

Edition Leipzig, *imprint of* Verlagsgruppe Dornier GmbH

Leipziger Universitaetsverlag GmbH+
Oststr 41, 04317 Leipzig
Tel: (0341) 9900440 *Fax:* (0341) 9900440
E-mail: info@univerlag-leipzig.de
Web Site: www.univerlag-leipzig.de
Key Personnel
International Rights: Dr Gerald Diesener
Founded: 1992
Subjects: Communications, History, Law, Medicine, Nursing, Dentistry, Philosophy, Science (General), Women's Studies
ISBN Prefix(es): 3-929031; 3-931922

Leitfadenverlag Verlag Dieter Sudholt+
Oberlandstr 26a, 82335 Berg
Tel: (08151) 51045 *Fax:* (08151) 50357
Key Personnel
Publisher: Dipl Kfm Volker Sudholt
Founded: 1957
Subjects: Business, Economics, Law
ISBN Prefix(es): 3-543
Associate Companies: Leitfadenverlag Gesellschaft mbH, Innsbruck, Austria

Anton G Leitner Verlag (AGLV)+
Buchenweg 3 b, 82234 Wessling
Tel: (08153) 9525-22 *Fax:* (08153) 9525-24
E-mail: info@aglv.com
Web Site: www.dasgedicht.de
Key Personnel
Author: Anton G Leitner
Founded: 1992
Subjects: Education, Literature, Literary Criticism, Essays, Mathematics, Poetry
ISBN Prefix(es): 3-929433
Distributor for Initiative Junger Autoren eV
Foreign Rep(s): Manford Chobot (Austria); Dr Margit Ohuhumma; Markus Hedigo; Jean Portank

Verlag Otto Lembeck+
Gaertnerweg 16, 60322 Frankfurt am Main
Tel: (069) 5970988 *Fax:* (069) 5975742
E-mail: verlag@lembeck.de
Web Site: www.lembeck.de *Cable:* LEMBECKDRUCK FRANKFURTMAIN
Key Personnel
Contact: Dr Wolfgang Neumann
Founded: 1945
Subjects: Religion - Protestant, Religion - Other
ISBN Prefix(es): 3-87476
Warehouse: Stuttgarter Verlagskontor, Expedition Westrampe, Fritz-Klett-Str 61-65, 71404 Korb
Orders to: Stuttgarter Verlagskontor, Rotebuehlstr 77, 70178 Stuttgart, Contact: Ingelborg Hoepner *Tel:* (0711) 66721604 *Fax:* (0711) 66724974 *E-mail:* Ihoepner@svk.de

Lentz Verlag+
Subsidiary of Buchverlage Langen-Mueller/Herbig
Thomas-Wimmer-Ring 11, 80539 Munich
Tel: (089) 290880 *Fax:* (089) 29088-144
E-mail: l.eggs@herbig.net
Web Site: www.herbig.net
Key Personnel
Man Dir & Publisher: Brigitte Fleissner-Mikorey
Rights & Permissions: Frauke Hoppen *Fax:* (089) 29088178
Founded: 1953
Subjects: Fiction, Nonfiction (General)
ISBN Prefix(es): 3-88010
Total Titles: 10 Print
Distributed by Mohr Morawa Buchvertrieb; Schweizer Buchzentrum
Warehouse: VVA-Bertelsmann Distribution GmbH, Warenannahme 100, An der Autobahn, 33310 Guetersloh
Orders to: VVA-Vereinigte, Postfach 7600, 33310 Guetersloh, Contact: Mr Borgartz *Tel:* (05241) 805403 *Fax:* (05241) 806643

Dr Gisela Lermann+
Am Heiligenhaus 18, 55122 Mainz
Tel: (06131) 31149 *Fax:* (06131) 387945
Web Site: www.lermann-verlag.de
Key Personnel
Owner & Dir: Dr Gisela Lermann *E-mail:* dr-gisela-lermann@lermann-verlag.de
Founded: 1988
Subjects: Biography, Fiction, Government, Political Science, Human Relations, Literature, Literary Criticism, Essays, Mysteries, Nonfiction (General), Philosophy, Poetry, Psychology, Psychiatry, Romance, Women's Studies
ISBN Prefix(es): 3-927223
Shipping Address: Herold Verlagsauslieferung, Kolpringring 4, 82041 Oberhaching *Tel:* (089) 6138710 *Fax:* (089) 61387120 *E-mail:* herold-oberhaching@t-online.de
Warehouse: Herold Verlagsauslieferung, Kolpringring 4, 82041 Oberhaching *Tel:* (089) 6138710 *Fax:* (089) 61387120 *E-mail:* herold-oberhaching@t-online.de
Orders to: Herold Verlagsauslieferung, Kolpringring 4, 82041 Oberhaching *Tel:* (089) 6138710 *Fax:* (089) 61387120 *E-mail:* herold-oberhaching@t-online.de

Lettre International Kulturzeitung+
Elisabethhof, Portal 3B, Erkelenzdamm 59/61, 10999 Berlin
Tel: (030) 30870440; (030) 30870462 *Fax:* (030) 2833128
E-mail: lettre@lettre.de
Web Site: www.lettre.de
Key Personnel
Editor-in-Chief: Frank Berberich
Founded: 1988
Subjects: Ethnicity, Government, Political Science, Literature, Literary Criticism, Essays
Branch Office(s)
c/o Kalina Garelova, Metropolis, blvd V Levski 87, 1000 Sofia, Bulgaria *Tel:* (02) 988 86 32 *Fax:* (02) 988 86 62 *E-mail:* letera@hotmail.com
Kozarska ulica 16, 10 000 Zagreb, Croatia *Tel:* (01) 42 43 41 *Fax:* (01) 42 04 12
La Nouvelle Lettre Internationale, 41, rue Bobillot, 75013 Paris, France *Tel:* (01) 45 65 26 29 *Fax:* (01) 45 65 90 01 *E-mail:* lettre_internationale@hotmail.com
Magyar Lettre Internationale, Karolyl Mihaly u 16, Budapest 1053, Hungary *Tel:* (01) 30 30 384 *Fax:* (01) 30 30 384 *E-mail:* letter@c3.hu
c/o Lelio Basso Foundation, Via della Dogana Vecchia 5, 00186 Rome, Italy *Tel:* (06) 68 30 06 44 *Fax:* (06) 687 61 63 *E-mail:* lettera.int@tiscalinet.it *Web Site:* www.letterainternazionale.it
ul 11 Oktomvri 2/6-2, 91000 Skopje, The Former Yugoslav Republic of Macedonia *E-mail:* jvladova@soros.org.mk
Fundatia Culturala Romana, Aleea Alexandru 38, sector 1, Bucharest, Romania *Tel:* (01) 230 13 73 *Fax:* (01) 230 75 59 *E-mail:* lettre-internationale@yahoo.com *Web Site:* www.fcr.ro

GERMANY

Lettre Internationale - Wsemirnoe Slowo, ulica Spalernaja 18, St Petersburg 191187, Russian Federation *Tel:* (0812) 274 54 62 *Fax:* (0812) 274 54 62 *E-mail:* vsslovo@8m.com
Claka Liubina1/V, 11000 Belgrade, Serbia and Montenegro
Letra Internacional, Editorial Pablo Iglesias, Monte Esquinza 30, 2º dcha, 28010 Madrid, Spain *Tel:* (01) 310 46 96 *Fax:* (01) 319 45 85 *E-mail:* fpl@infornet.es *Web Site:* www.arce.es/indicesarce.htm#5

LEU-VERLAG Wolfgang Leupelt+
Herweg 34, 51429 Bergisch Gladbach
Tel: (02204) 981141 *Fax:* (02204) 981143
E-mail: info@leu-verlag.net
Web Site: www.leu-verlag.net
Key Personnel
Publisher: Wolfgang Leupelt
Founded: 1990
Specialize in music play along books with CD.
Subjects: Education, Music, Dance, Sheet Music, Music Education Books with CD
ISBN Prefix(es): 3-928825; 3-89775
Number of titles published annually: 10 Print; 5 Audio
Total Titles: 100 Print; 20 Audio

Leuchter-Verlag EG+
Industriestr 6-8, 64390 Erzhausen
Mailing Address: Postfach 1161, 64386 Erzhausen
Tel: (06150) 97360 *Fax:* (06150) 9736-36
Key Personnel
Man Dir, Sales, Rights & Permissions: Karl-Heinz Neumann
Founded: 1946
Subjects: Religion - Other
ISBN Prefix(es): 3-87482

Verlag Gerald Leue+
Kanzlerweg 24, 12101 Berlin
Tel: (030) 7865020 *Fax:* (030) 78913876
E-mail: vertrieb@leue-verlag.de
Web Site: www.leue-verlag.de
Key Personnel
Publisher: Gerald Leue
Founded: 1982
Subjects: How-to, Humor
ISBN Prefix(es): 3-923421

Libertas- Europaeisches Institut GmbH+
Vaihinger Str 24, 71063 Sindelfingen
Mailing Address: Postfach 5 67, 71047 Sindelfingen
Tel: (07031) 6186-80 *Fax:* (07031) 6186-86
E-mail: info@libertas-institut.com
Web Site: www.libertas-institut.com
Key Personnel
President: Hans-Juergen Zahorka *E-mail:* hj.zahorka@libertas-institut.com
Man Dir: Ute Hirschburger *E-mail:* ute.hirschburger@libertas-institut.com
Founded: 1976
Think-tank on European & international economy & politics with publication division.
Subjects: Business, Developing Countries, Economics, Environmental Studies, Fiction, Finance, Government, Political Science, History, Law, Management, Nonfiction (General), Philosophy, Regional Interests, Social Sciences, Sociology, Transportation
ISBN Prefix(es): 3-921929
Number of titles published annually: 20 Print; 5 CD-ROM; 5 Audio
Total Titles: 50 Print; 2 CD-ROM

Edition Libri Illustri GmbH
Neissestr 31, 71638 Ludwigsburg
Tel: (07141) 84720 *Fax:* (07141) 875117
E-mail: info@libri-illustri.de
Web Site: www.edition-libri-illustri.de
Key Personnel
Publisher: Peter Teicher
Founded: 1987
Subjects: History, Religion - Other, Nuremberg Chronicle, Aesopus, Apocalypsis
ISBN Prefix(es): 3-927506
Number of titles published annually: 1 Print
Total Titles: 8 Print; 1 Audio
U.S. Office(s): Peter KeLehnert, 510 W Forest Dr, Houston, TX 77079-6914, United States

Edition Lidiarte
Knesebeckstr 13/14, 10623 Berlin
Tel: (030) 3137420 *Fax:* (030) 3127117
E-mail: edition@lidiarte.de
Web Site: www.lidiarte.de
Key Personnel
President: Dieter Marx
Founded: 1980
Specialize in architectural posters & postcards.
Subjects: Architecture & Interior Design
ISBN Prefix(es): 3-9801862
Number of titles published annually: 10 Print
Total Titles: 220 Print

Hildegard Liebaug-Dartmann+
J Sebastian Bach Weg 15, 53340 Meckenheim
Tel: (02225) 909343 *Fax:* (02225) 909345
E-mail: liebaug-dartmann@t-online.de
Web Site: www.liebaug-dartmann.de
Key Personnel
Owner: Hildegard Liebaug-Dartmann
Founded: 1982
Membership(s): Boersenveriene des Deutschen Buchhandels.
Subjects: Physics, German as a Foreign Language
ISBN Prefix(es): 3-922989
Distributed by KNO; KV

Liebenzeller Mission, GmbH, Abt. Verlag+
Liobastr 8, 75378 Bad Liebenzell
Tel: (07052) 17-163 *Fax:* (07052) 17-170
E-mail: buch@liebenzell.org
Web Site: www.liebenzell.org/blm/index.htm
Key Personnel
Publishing Dir: Arthur Klenk
Founded: 1906
Membership(s): the Telos paperback series publishing group; also produce Games & Radio Games for Children.
Subjects: Biography, Fiction, Theology
ISBN Prefix(es): 3-88002; 3-921113
Orders to: Ausl Edition VLM, Postfach 5, 7630 Lahr, Johannis Lahr *Tel:* (07821) 581-32 *Fax:* (07821) 581-26

Robert Lienau GmbH & Co KG
Strubbergstr 80, 60489 Frankfurt am Main
Tel: (069) 9782866 *Fax:* (069) 97828689
E-mail: info@lienau-frankfurt.de
Web Site: www.lienau-frankfurt.de
Key Personnel
Manager: Cornelia Grossmann; Michael Voily
Founded: 1810
Music publisher.
Subjects: Drama, Theater, Music, Dance
ISBN Prefix(es): 3-87484

Lienhard Pallast Verlag
Stoeckerfeld 7, 53773 Hennef
Tel: (02244) 5863 *Fax:* (02244) 5863
E-mail: lienhard@pallast-publisher.com
Web Site: www.pallast-publisher.com
Subjects: Literature, Literary Criticism, Essays, Poetry

Limpert Verlag+
Industriepark 3, 56291 Wiebelsheim
Mailing Address: Postfach 1004, 56291 Wiebelsheim
Tel: (06766) 903160 *Fax:* (06766) 903320
E-mail: vertrieb@limpert.de
Telex: 0418135 limp
Key Personnel
Man Dir, Rights & Permissions: Dr Irmgard Meissl *Tel:* (06766) 903242 *Fax:* (06766) 903360 *E-mail:* meissl@aula-verlag.de
Founded: 1921
Subjects: Sports, Athletics
ISBN Prefix(es): 3-7853
Bookshop(s): Humanitas Buchversand

J Lindauer Verlag+
Kaufingerstr 16, 80331 Munich
Mailing Address: Postfach 330 626, 80066 Munich
Tel: (089) 223041 *Fax:* (089) 224315
Web Site: www.lindauer-verlag.de
Key Personnel
Owner, Rights & Permissions: Renate Schaefer
ISBN Prefix(es): 3-87488

H Lindemanns Buchhandlung
Nadlerstr 4, 70173 Stuttgart
Tel: (0711) 248999-0 *Fax:* (0711) 233320
E-mail: lindemannsbuch@t-online.de
Web Site: www.lindemanns-buchhandlung.de
Key Personnel
Contact: Friederike Goetze *E-mail:* friederike-goetze@lindemanns-buchhandlung.de

Linden-Verlag+
Kasseler Str 25, 04155 Leipzig
Tel: (0341) 5902024 *Fax:* (0341) 5904436
E-mail: verlag@linden-buch.de
Web Site: www.linden-buch.de
Key Personnel
International Rights: Thomas Loest
Founded: 1989
Specialize in books by Buecher von Erich Loest.
ISBN Prefix(es): 3-9802139; 3-86152

Martha Lindner Verlags-GmbH+
Jahnstr 22, 76133 Karlsruhe
Tel: (0721) 843965 *Fax:* (0721) 8303716
Key Personnel
Manager: Martha Lindner
Founded: 1975
Subjects: Music, Dance, Science (General), Theology
ISBN Prefix(es): 3-921653

Christoph Links Verlag - LinksDruck GmbH+
Schoenhauser Allee 36 - Haus S, 10435 Berlin
Tel: (030) 440232-0 *Fax:* (030) 44023229
E-mail: mail@linksverlag.de
Web Site: www.linksverlag.de
Key Personnel
Publisher: Christoph Links *E-mail:* links@linksverlag.de
Founded: 1990
Subjects: Biography, Government, Political Science, History
ISBN Prefix(es): 3-86153
Number of titles published annually: 30 Print
Total Titles: 330 Print
Orders to: Prolit Verlagsauslieferung, Siemensstr 16, 35463 Fernwald, Contact: Gaby Boehnen *Tel:* (0641) 94393-21 *Fax:* (0641) 94393-29 *E-mail:* g.boehnen@prolit.de

Siegbert Linnemann Verlag+
Ohlbrocksweg 61, 33330 Guetersloh
Tel: (05241) 14061 *Fax:* (05241) 26439
E-mail: info@linnemann-verlag.com
Web Site: www.linnemann-verlag.com
Key Personnel
Man Dir: Siegbert Linnemann
Founded: 1986
Specialize in travel picture wall calendars.
Subjects: Geography, Geology, Travel
ISBN Prefix(es): 3-926466; 3-89523

Number of titles published annually: 90 Print
U.S. Office(s): Sormani Calendars, Box 6059, Chelsea, MA 02150, United States
Tel: 617-889-9300 *Fax:* 617-889-9306
E-mail: sormani@mindspring.com *Web Site:* www.sormanicalendars.com

LIT Verlag+
Grevenerstr 179, 48159 Muenster
Tel: (0251) 235091 *Fax:* (0251) 231972
E-mail: lit@lit-verlag.de
Web Site: www.lit-verlag.de
Key Personnel
Man Dir & International Rights: Dr Wilhelm Hopf
Founded: 1981
Subjects: Art, Asian Studies, Economics, Ethnicity, Fashion, Public Administration, Science (General), Social Sciences, Sociology
ISBN Prefix(es): 3-88660; 3-89473; 3-8258
Subsidiaries: LII Verlag Muenster-Hamburg
U.S. Office(s): c/o J Bach, 610 W 115 St, No 53B, New York, NY 10025, United States
Tel: 212-666-7674 *Fax:* 212-666-7674

Henry Litolff's Verlag, *imprint of* C F Peters Musikverlag GmbH & Co KG

Rainer Loessl Verlag
Johann-Fichtestr 11, 80805 Munich
Tel: (089) 362646
ISBN Prefix(es): 3-9800376

Antiquariat Oskar Loewe
Subsidiary of Latvijas Nacionala Biblioteka, LV-Riga
Sauerbruchstr 8d, 45661 Recklinghausen-Sued
Tel: (02361) 960813 *Fax:* (02361) 960815
E-mail: loewe.bochum@t-online.de
Web Site: www.antiquariat.net/loewe
Key Personnel
Owner: Oskar Loewe
Founded: 1876
Subjects: Antiquarian (News, Old Books)
Distributed by Zentralverzeichnis Antiquarischer Buecher (ZVAB)

Loewe Verlag GmbH+
Buehlstr 4, 95463 Bindlach
Mailing Address: Postfach 1, 95461 Bindlach
Tel: (09208) 51-0 *Fax:* (09208) 51-309
E-mail: presse@loewe-verlag.de
Web Site: www.loewe-verlag.de
Telex: 920882
Key Personnel
Publisher & Man Dir: Volker Gondrom
Editorial: Alexandra Borisch; Christiane Duering
Publicity, Sales Dir: Hajo Schwabe
Foreign Rights Manager: Jeannette Hammerschmidt *Tel:* (09208) 51202 *E-mail:* lizenzen@loewe-verlag.de
Founded: 1863
ISBN Prefix(es): 3-7855

Logophon Verlag und Bildungsreisen GmbH+
Affiliate of Euro-Schulen-Organisation
Alte Gaertnerei 2, 55128 Mainz
Tel: (06131) 71645 *Fax:* (06131) 72596
E-mail: verlag@logophon.de
Web Site: www.logophon.de
Key Personnel
Man Dir: Jean-Pierre Jouteux; Pierre Semidei
Founded: 1979
Subjects: Business, English as a Second Language, Human Relations, Language Arts, Linguistics
ISBN Prefix(es): 3-922514
Number of titles published annually: 8 Print
Total Titles: 80 Print; 2 CD-ROM

Logos Verlag GmbH+
Ehlenbrucherstr 96, 32791 Lage
Tel: (05232) 960120; (05232) 960124
 Fax: (05232) 960121
Key Personnel
Manager: Johannes Reimer
Purchasing, Sales Manager: Andreas Bergen
Founded: 1989
Christian books in German & Russian.
Subjects: History, Religion - Protestant, Theology, Autobiography, Memoirs, Letters, Bibliography
ISBN Prefix(es): 3-927767; 3-933828

Logos-Verlag Literatur & Layout GmbH+
Auf der Adt 14 Villa Fledermaus, 66130 Saarbruecken
Tel: (06893) 986096 *Fax:* (06893) 986095
Key Personnel
Publisher: Friedhelm Schneidecrond
Founded: 1983
Subjects: Biological Sciences, Fiction, Geography, Geology, Literature, Literary Criticism, Essays, Mysteries, Nonfiction (General), Poetry, Regional Interests, Science Fiction, Fantasy, Social Sciences, Sociology
ISBN Prefix(es): 3-928598; 3-9801790

Lokrundschau Verlag GmbH
Postfach 80 01 07, 21001 Hamburg
Tel: (04151) 896913 *Fax:* (04151) 82889
E-mail: verlag@lokrundschau.de
Web Site: www.lokrundschau.de
Key Personnel
Man Dir: Jan Borchers
Founded: 1995
Specialize in books about German railway & journals.
ISBN Prefix(es): 3-931647

Stefan Loose Verlag+
Zossenerstr 55/2, 10961 Berlin
Tel: (030) 6 91 37 89 *Fax:* (030) 6 93 01 71
E-mail: info@loose-verlag.de
Web Site: www.loose-verlag.de
Key Personnel
President: Renate Ramb
Publisher: Stefan Loose
Founded: 1978
Subjects: Travel
ISBN Prefix(es): 3-922025

Lorber-Verlag & Turm-Verlag Otto Zluhan
Hindenburgstr 5, 74321 Bietigheim Bissingen
Tel: (07142) 940843 *Fax:* (07142) 940844
E-mail: info@lorber-verlag.de; bestellen@lorber-verlag.de
Web Site: www.lorber-verlag.de *Cable:* LORBER, BIETIGHEIM
Key Personnel
Man Dir, Publisher, Rights & Permissions: Friedrich Zluhan
Founded: 1854
Subjects: Parapsychology, Religion - Other
ISBN Prefix(es): 3-87495

Johannes Loriz Verlag der Kooperative Duernau
Im Winkel 11, 88422 Duernau
Tel: (07582) 93000 *Fax:* (07582) 930020
Web Site: www.kooperative.de
Key Personnel
Owner: Johannes Loriz
Subjects: Natural History
ISBN Prefix(es): 3-88861

Verlag an der Lottbek+
Susterfedlstr 83, 52072 Aachen
Tel: (0241) 873434 *Fax:* (0241) 875577
Key Personnel
Editor: Peter Jensen
Founded: 1988

Membership(s): the Stock Exchange of German Booksellers.
Subjects: Science (General)
ISBN Prefix(es): 3-926987; 3-86130
Subsidiaries: Edition Hathor
Divisions: Belletriotik
Showroom(s): Bundes Str 74, 2000 Hamburg 13
Warehouse: Bundes Str 74, 2000 Hamburg 13

Hermann Luchterhand Verlag GmbH
Heddesdorfer Str 31, 56564 Neuwied
Mailing Address: Postfach 2352, 56513 Neuwied
Tel: (02631) 8010 *Fax:* (02631) 801210
E-mail: info@luchterhand.de
Web Site: www.luchterhand.de
Key Personnel
Man Dir: Juergen M Luczak *Tel:* (02631) 801-330 *Fax:* (02631) 801-225 *E-mail:* juergen.luczak@luchterhand.de
Publication Manager: Elke Richter-Weiland *Tel:* (02631) 801-264 *Fax:* (02631) 801-353 *E-mail:* elke.richter-weiland@luchterhand.de; Stefan Wiemuth *Tel:* (06192) 408-229 *Fax:* (06192) 408-248 *E-mail:* 100537.357@compuserve.com; Rainer Joede *Tel:* (06192) 408-200 *Fax:* (06192) 408-248 *E-mail:* rainer.joede@dwd-verlag.de; Rainer Winkler *Tel:* (02631) 801-232 *Fax:* (02631) 801-204; Walter Kastor *Tel:* (02631) 801-239 *Fax:* (02631) 801-415 *E-mail:* walter.kastor@luchterhand.de
Sales Manager: Erminold Malzbender *Tel:* (02631) 801-318 *Fax:* (02631) 801-381
Contact: Evelin Gerlach *Tel:* (02631) 801 275 *Fax:* (02631) 801 225 *E-mail:* evelin.gerlach@luchterhand.de
Founded: 1924
Subjects: Business, Education, Law, Management
ISBN Prefix(es): 3-472
Parent Company: Wolters Kluwer Deutschland GmbH
Ultimate Parent Company: Wolters Kluwer NV, Netherlands
Imprints: Kommentator; Alfred Metzner
Subsidiaries: Werner Verlag GmbH & Co KG
Divisions: Fachverlag Deutscher Wirtschaftsdienst GmbH, Koeln
Branch Office(s)
Pestalozzistr 5-8 13187, Berlin *Tel:* (030) 48839011 *Fax:* (030) 48839020
Gutenbergstr 8, Kriftel *Tel:* (06192) 4080 *Fax:* (06192) 408248

Luchterhand Literaturverlag GmbH/Verlag Volk & Welt GmbH+
Neumarkterstr 28, 81673 Munich
Tel: (089) 4136-0; (01805) 990505 *Fax:* (089) 21215250
E-mail: vertrieb.verlagsgruppe@randomhouse.de
Web Site: www.randomhouse.de/luchterhand
Key Personnel
Owner: Dietrich von Boetticher
Publisher: Gerald J Trageiser
Founded: 1924
Subjects: Fiction, Literature, Literary Criticism, Essays, Nonfiction (General)
ISBN Prefix(es): 3-630
Number of titles published annually: 50 Print
Total Titles: 500 Print
Parent Company: Verlagsgruppe Random House GmbH
Ultimate Parent Company: Bertelsmann AG
Distributor for Gerhard Wolf Janus Press
Orders to: Vereinigte Verlagsauslieferung, An der Autobahn, 33310 Guetersloh

Lucius & Lucius Verlagsgesellschaft mbH+
Gerokstr 51, 70184 Stuttgart
Tel: (0711) 242060 *Fax:* (0711) 242088
E-mail: lucius@luciusverlag.com
Web Site: www.luciusverlag.com

Key Personnel
Publisher: Dr Wulf D von Lucius
Founded: 1996
Specialize in academic books & journals in economics, social sciences & sociology; research monographs & proceedings
Privately owned.
Membership(s): Borsenverein & STM.
Subjects: Economics, Social Sciences, Sociology
ISBN Prefix(es): 3-8282
Number of titles published annually: 35 Print
Total Titles: 420 Print
Warehouse: Brockhaus/Commission, Kreidlerstr 9, 70803 Kornwestheim, Contact: Mrs Rother
Tel: (07154) 132737 *Fax:* (07154) 132713
E-mail: bro@brockhaus-commission.de (Orders)

Luebbe Audio, *imprint of* Verlagsgruppe Luebbe GmbH & Co KG

Gustav Luebbe Verlag, *imprint of* Verlagsgruppe Luebbe GmbH & Co KG

Gustav Luebbe Verlag+
Imprint of Verlagsgruppe Luebbe GmbH & Co KG
Scheidtbachstr 23-31, 51469 Bergisch Gladbach
Mailing Address: Postfach 200180, 51431 Bergisch Gladbach
Tel: (02202) 121-330 *Fax:* (02202) 121-920
E-mail: glv@luebbe.de
Web Site: www.luebbe.de
Key Personnel
Man Dir: Peter Molden; Karlheinz Jungbeck
Founded: 1963
Subjects: Archaeology, Biography, Fiction, History, How-to, Nonfiction (General)
ISBN Prefix(es): 3-404; 3-7857; 3-89185
Associate Companies: Bastei Verlag

Verlagsgruppe Luebbe GmbH & Co KG+
Scheidtbachstr 23-31, 51469 Bergisch Gladbach
Mailing Address: Postfach 200180, 51431 Bergisch Gladbach
Tel: (02202) 121-0 *Fax:* (02202) 121-920
E-mail: info@luebbe.de
Web Site: www.luebbe.de
Key Personnel
Man Dir: Karlheinz Jungbeck; Peter Molden
Founded: 1953
Subjects: Biography, Fiction, Nonfiction (General), Romance
ISBN Prefix(es): 3-404; 3-431; 3-7857; 3-89185
Imprints: Bastei Luebbe Taschenbuecher; Bastei Verlag; BLT; editionLuebbe; Ehrenwirth Verlag; Luebbe Audio; Gustav Luebbe Verlag

Alf Luechow Verlag, *imprint of* Verlagsgruppe Dornier GmbH

Lukas Verlag fur Kunst- und Geistesgeschichte
Kollwitzstr 57, 10405 Berlin
Tel: (030) 44049220 *Fax:* (030) 4428177
E-mail: lukas.verlag@t-online.de
Web Site: www.lukasverlag.com
Key Personnel
Contact: Dr Frank Bottcher
Founded: 1995
Specialize in art history, cistercians, medieval art & GDR.
Subjects: Archaeology, History, Philosophy, Social Sciences, Sociology
ISBN Prefix(es): 3-931836
Total Titles: 30 Print

Lusatia Verlag-Dr Stuebner & Co KG+
Toepferstr 35, 02625 Bautzen
Tel: (03591) 532400; (03591) 532401
Fax: (03591) 532400
E-mail: lusatiaverlag@t-online.de

Founded: 1992
Membership(s): Association of German Booksellers.
Subjects: Art, Fiction, Regional Interests, Travel
ISBN Prefix(es): 3-929091; 3-936758
Number of titles published annually: 10 Print
Total Titles: 115 Print
Distributed by Domowina-Verlag
Distributor for Domowina-Verlag

Luther-Verlag GmbH+
Cansteinstr 1, 33647 Bielefeld
Tel: (0521) 94 40-137 *Fax:* (0521) 94 40-136
E-mail: vertrieb@luther-verlag.de
Web Site: www.ekvw.de/pressehaus/lv/
Telex: 937325 epdgi
Key Personnel
Man Dir, Rights & Permissions: Wolfgang Riewe
Founded: 1911
Subjects: Religion - Protestant
ISBN Prefix(es): 3-7858

Lutherische Verlagsgesellschaft mbH
Gartenstr 20, 24103 Kiel
Mailing Address: Postfach 3169, 24030 Kiel
Tel: (0431) 55779-285 *Fax:* (0431) 55779-292
Key Personnel
Manager: Rainer Thun
Founded: 1956
Subjects: Regional Interests, Theology
ISBN Prefix(es): 3-87503
Parent Company: Evangelischer Presseverband Nord ev, Postfach 3466, 24033 Kiel

Lutherisches Verlagshaus GmbH+
Knochenhauerstr 38-40, 30159 Hannover
Mailing Address: Postfach 3849, 30038 Hannover
Tel: (0511) 1241-716 *Fax:* (0511) 1241-705
E-mail: lvh@lvh.de
Web Site: www.lvh.de
Telex: 922686
Key Personnel
Man Dir, Rights & Permissions: Klaus Woehleke
General Manager: Werner Sass
Management: Dr Hasko von Bassi *Tel:* (0511) 1241720 *Fax:* (0511) 3681098
Marketing: Ralf Mueller *Tel:* (0511) 1241-726 *Fax:* (0511) 3681098; (0511) 3 68 10 98
Sales: Andrea Roecher *Fax:* (0511) 3681098
Advertising: Hannelore Splitt *Tel:* (0511) 1241 710 *Fax:* (0511) 3681098
Founded: 1948
Subjects: Religion - Other, Theology
ISBN Prefix(es): 3-7859
Distributed by CVK Cornelsen Verlagskontor Gmbh & Co KG (Germany); Felix A Gaugler (Switzerland)
Orders to: Cornelsen Verlagskontor, Kammeratsheide 66, 4800 Bielefeld 1

Verlag Waldemar Lutz
Baslerstr 130, 79540 Loerrach
Tel: (07621) 88812 *Fax:* (07621) 12599
E-mail: wlutz@lutz-die-buchhandlung.de
Web Site: www.verlag-lutz.de
Key Personnel
Man Dir, Rights & Permissions: Waldemar Lutz
Founded: 1978
Subjects: Literature, Literary Criticism, Essays, Regional Interests
ISBN Prefix(es): 3-922107
Bookshop(s): Lutz-Die Buchhandlung, Tumringerstr 179, D-79540 Loerrach

Karin Mader
Mittelsmoorerstr 80, 28879 Grasberg
Tel: (04208) 556 *Fax:* (04208) 3429
E-mail: info@mader-verlag.de
Web Site: www.mader-verlag.de
Founded: 1978
Subjects: Travel

ISBN Prefix(es): 3-921957
Distributed by VAH Jager Verlagsauslieferung
Orders to: VAH Jager Verlagsauslieferung, Postfach 3248, 10729 Berlin

Maeander Verlag GmbH+
Diepoltsberg 2, 84326 Falkenberg
Tel: (08727) 1657 *Fax:* (08727) 1569
Key Personnel
Man Dir, Rights & Permissions: Dr Renate Piel
Founded: 1977
Specialize in monographs & art history in general.
Subjects: Archaeology, Art, Philosophy
ISBN Prefix(es): 3-88219
Total Titles: 78 Print
Orders to: Koch, Neff und Oetinger & Co GmbH, Schockenriedstr 39, 80807 Stuttgart

Annemarie Maeger+
Ebertallee 6, 22607 Hamburg
Tel: (040) 8992480 *Fax:* (040) 8904475
E-mail: re@a-maeger-verlag.de
Web Site: www.a-maeger-verlag.de
Key Personnel
Contact: A Maeger
Founded: 1993
Subjects: Drama, Theater, History, Mathematics, Philosophy, Science (General), Theology, Women's Studies
ISBN Prefix(es): 3-929805

Magdalenen-Verlag GmbH
Gewerbering 14a, 83607 Holzkirchen
Tel: (08024) 5051 *Fax:* (08024) 7064
E-mail: info@magdalenen-verlag.de
Web Site: www.magdalenen-verlag.de
Key Personnel
Manager: Clemens Kopp
ISBN Prefix(es): 3-930350; 3-9800186

Magnus Verlag+
Im Teelbruch 60-62, 45219 Essen
Mailing Address: Postfach 185528, 45205 Essen
Tel: (02054) 5080; (02054) 5094; (02327) 292 0 *Fax:* (02054) 83762
Key Personnel
Man Dir: Walter Stender
Rights & Permissions: Michael Salzwedel
ISBN Prefix(es): 3-88400; 3-920617

Karl Mahnke, Dierk Mahnke+
Grossestr 108, 27283 Verden-Aller
Tel: (04231) 3011-0 *Fax:* (04231) 3011-11
E-mail: info@mahnke-verlag.de
Web Site: www.mahnke-verlag.de
Key Personnel
Owner: Dierk Mahnke
Editor: Dieter Jorschik
Founded: 1841
Specialize in Amateur Theater Publishing.
ISBN Prefix(es): 3-920613

Otto Maier Verlag, see Ravensburger Buchverlag Otto Maier GmbH

Mairs Geographischer Verlag+
Marco-Polo-Zentrum, 73760 Ostfildern
Tel: (0711) 45020 *Fax:* (0711) 4502340
E-mail: info@mairs.de
Web Site: www.mairs.de
Telex: 721796 *Cable:* MAIRVERLAG
Key Personnel
Man Dir: Dr Volkmar Mair
Sales Dir: Claus Benath
Founded: 1948
Subjects: Regional Interests, Travel
ISBN Prefix(es): 3-87504
Imprints: Baedeker; Marco Polo
Distributed by Fleischmann (Austria); Hallwag AG (Switzerland)
Distributor for ADAC Verlag

Mairs Geographischer Verlag Kurt Mair GmbH & Co
Formerly Falk Verlag AG
Marco Polo Zentrum, 73760 Ostfildern
Tel: (0711) 4502-0 *Fax:* (0711) 4502-340
Key Personnel
Chief Executive Officer: Hans J Moock
Editorial: Dr Helge Lintzhoeft
Technical: Christoph Riess
Sales & Marketing: Michael Staehler
Founded: 1945
Specialize in, cartography (city maps & atlases, road maps & road atlases).
ISBN Prefix(es): 3-88445; 3-8279; 3-920317
Subsidiaries: GeoData, GmbH & Co KG
Branch Office(s)
Berlin
Hamburg
Lepzig
Stuttgart
Distributor for Berlitz; DCC; Gruner & Jahr; Iwanowski; Ravenstein

Malik Verlag, *imprint of* Piper Verlag GmbH

Manholt Verlag+
Fedelhoeren 88, 28203 Bremen
Tel: (0421) 32 35 94 *Fax:* (0421) 3 36 54 63
E-mail: manholtverlag@t-online.de
Web Site: www.manholt.de
Key Personnel
Editor, Rights & Permissions: Dr Dirk Hemjeoltmanns
Founded: 1985
Publishes French Literature in German.
ISBN Prefix(es): 3-924903

Gebr Mann Verlag GmbH & Co+
Zimmerstr 26-27, 10969 Berlin
Tel: (030) 25913589 *Fax:* (030) 25913537
E-mail: vertrieb-kunstverlage@reimer-verlag.de
Key Personnel
Man Dir, Rights & Permissions: Holger Beer
Publishing Dir: Andreas A Catsch
Founded: 1917
Subjects: Archaeology, Architecture & Interior Design, Art, Crafts, Games, Hobbies, History
ISBN Prefix(es): 3-496; 3-7861
Associate Companies: Deutscher Verlag fuer Kunstwissenschaft
Orders to: Koch, Neff & Oetinger & Co Verlagsauslieferung GmbH, Schockenriedstr 39, Postfach 800620, 70565 Stuttgart

Mannerschwarm Skript Verlag GmbH+
Lange Reihe 102, 20099 Hamburg
Tel: (040) 4302650 *Fax:* (040) 4302932
E-mail: verlag@maennerschwarm.de
Web Site: www.maennerschwarm.de
Key Personnel
Publisher: Joachim Bartholomae; Detlef Grumbach
Founded: 1992
Subjects: Gay & Lesbian
ISBN Prefix(es): 3-928983; 3-935596
Number of titles published annually: 15 Print
Total Titles: 150 Print
Imprints: Schwul Lesbische Studien Universitat Bremen; Edition Waldschloesschen; Bibliothek rosa Winkel
Shipping Address: So Va, Friesstr 20-24, 60388 Frankfurt *Tel:* (069) 410 211 *Fax:* (069) 410 280
Warehouse: So Va, Friesstr 20-24, 60388 Frankfurt
Orders to: So Va, Friesstr 20-24, 60388 Frankfurt

Manutius Verlag+
Eselspfad 2, 69117 Heidelberg
Tel: (06221) 163290 *Fax:* (06221) 167143
E-mail: order@manutius-verlag.de
Web Site: www.manutius-verlag.de
Key Personnel
Publisher: Frank Wuerker
Founded: 1985
Subjects: Art, History, Literature, Literary Criticism, Essays, Music, Dance, Philosophy, Humanist, Jurisprudence, Political Science
ISBN Prefix(es): 3-925678; 3-934877
Total Titles: 80 Print

Manz G J Verlag und Druckerei+
Hermannstr 16, 70178 Stuttgart
Tel: (0711) 6151790 *Fax:* (0711) 6151791
Key Personnel
Dir, Publisher & Editorial: Lydia Franzelius
Founded: 1830
Subjects: Education
ISBN Prefix(es): 3-7863
Parent Company: Ernst Klett Verlag GmbH, Rotebuehlstr 77, 70178 Stuttgart
Subsidiaries: Verlag J Pfeiffer; Erich Wewel Verlag
Orders to: Verlagsgruppe MANZ, AG, Anzingerstr 15, 81671 Munich

Marco Polo, *imprint of* Mairs Geographischer Verlag

Margraf Verlag
Kanalstr 21, 97990 Weikersheim
Tel: (07934) 3071
E-mail: info@margraf-verlag.de
Web Site: www.margraf-verlag.de
Key Personnel
Contact: Dirk Hangstein *E-mail:* hangstein@margraf-verlag.de
Founded: 1985
Subjects: Agriculture, Biological Sciences, Developing Countries, Environmental Studies, Geography, Geology
ISBN Prefix(es): 3-8236; 3-924333
Associate Companies: Backhuys Publishers, PO Box 321, 2300 AH Leiden, Holland, Netherlands, Contact: Mike Ruijsenaars *Web Site:* www.backhuys.com
Distributed by DA Books & Journals

Edition Marhold
Postfach 610494, 10928 Berlin
Tel: (030) 6917073 *Fax:* (030) 6914067
Key Personnel
Contact: Volker Spiess
Subjects: Disability, Special Needs
ISBN Prefix(es): 3-89166
Associate Companies: arani-verlag GmbH; Haude und Spenersche Verlagsbuchhandlung; Wissenschaftsverlag Volker Spiess GmbH

Edition Mariannepresse
Riesbulldeich 2, 25889 Witzort
Tel: (04864) 660
E-mail: quehilie@onlinehome.de

Edition Maritim GmbH+
Raboisen 8, 20095 Hamburg
Tel: (040) 3396670 *Fax:* (040) 33966777
E-mail: mail@edition-maritim.de
Key Personnel
Dir: Konrad Delius *Tel:* (0521) 559-210 *Fax:* (0521) 559-116 *E-mail:* info@delius-klasing.de
Dir, Rights & Permissions: Frank Grube
Founded: 1978
Subjects: Crafts, Games, Hobbies, Fiction, Maritime, Sports, Athletics, Transportation, Travel
ISBN Prefix(es): 3-922117; 3-89225
Parent Company: Delius Klasing Verlag, Siekerwall 21, 33602 Bielefeld

Marketing & Wirtschaft Verlagsges, Flade & Partner mbH+
Elisabethstr 34, 80796 Munich
Tel: (089) 27813417 *Fax:* (089) 2710156
Key Personnel
Publisher: Frido Flade
Chief Editor: Fabian Flade
Founded: 1979
Subjects: Economics, Energy
ISBN Prefix(es): 3-922804
Subsidiaries: Edition Wissen & Literatur
Warehouse: Revilak Verlags-Service, Gutenbergstr 5, 822056 Gilching

Markt & Technik, see Pearson Education Deutschland GmbH

Maro Verlag und Druck, Benno Kasmayr+
Zirbelstrasse 57a, 86154 Augsburg
Tel: (0821) 416034 *Fax:* (0821) 416036
E-mail: info@maroverlag.de
Web Site: www.maroverlag.de
Key Personnel
Proprietor: Benno Kaesmayr
Founded: 1969
Subjects: Fiction, Poetry
ISBN Prefix(es): 3-87512
Number of titles published annually: 10 Print
Total Titles: 120 Print

Institut fuer Marxistische Studien und Forschungen eV (IMSF)
Postfach 500936, 60397 Frankfurt
Tel: (069) 7392934
Key Personnel
Honorary President: Juergen Reusch
Founded: 1968
ISBN Prefix(es): 3-88807

Mattes Verlag GmbH
Steigerweg 69, 69115 Heidelberg
Mailing Address: Postfach 103866, 69028 Heidelberg
Tel: (06221) 45930 *Fax:* (06221) 459322
E-mail: mattes@mattes.de
Web Site: www.mattes.de
Key Personnel
Publisher: Kurt Mattes *E-mail:* info@mattes.de
Founded: 1990
Subjects: Literature, Literary Criticism, Essays, Medicine, Nursing, Dentistry, Psychology, Psychiatry
ISBN Prefix(es): 3-9802440; 3-930978

Matthaes Verlag GmbH
Olgastr 87, 70180 Stuttgart
Mailing Address: Postfach 103144, 70027 Stuttgart
Tel: (0711) 21 33-329 *Fax:* (0711) 21 33-320
E-mail: info@matthaes.de
Web Site: www.matthaes.de *Cable:* MATTHAESVERLAG
Key Personnel
Sales: Albert Pfeffer *Tel:* (0711) 2133 3 02 *E-mail:* a.pfeffer@matthaes.de; Karl-Heinz Suelzle *Tel:* (0711) 2133 3 24 *E-mail:* k.h.suelzle@matthaes.de
Customer Service: Bernd Decker *Tel:* (0711) 2133 2 83 *E-mail:* b.decker@matthaes.de; Rudolf Freudenberg *Tel:* (0711) 2133 2 93 *E-mail:* r.freudenberg@matthaes.de; Herbert Gollhofer *Tel:* (0711) 2133 3 01 *E-mail:* h.gollhofer@matthaes.de
Founded: 1905
Subjects: Cookery
Branch Office(s)
Frankfurt
Hamburg
Munich

Matthes und Seitz Verlag GmbH+
Huebnerstr 11, 80637 Munich
Mailing Address: Postfach 190624, 80606 Munich
Tel: (089) 1232510 *Fax:* (089) 187534
Key Personnel
Man Dir, Rights & Permissions: Axel Matthes
Founded: 1977
Subjects: Art, Fiction, History, Literature, Literary Criticism, Essays, Music, Dance, Philosophy, Poetry, Theology, autobiography, memoirs, letters
ISBN Prefix(es): 3-88221
Orders to: Koch, Neff & Oetinger, Postfach 800620, 70506 Stuttgart

Matthias-Gruenewald-Verlag GmbH
Member of Verlagsgruppe Engagement
Max Hufschmidtstr 4a, 55130 Mainz
Mailing Address: Postfach 3080, 55020 Mainz
Tel: (06131) 92860 *Fax:* (06131) 928626
E-mail: mail@gruenewaldverlag.de
Web Site: members.aol.com/matthgruen
Key Personnel
Publisher: Josef Wagner
Publisher Editorial: Hiltraud Laubach
Man Dir: Josef Wagner
Sales Dir: Jeanine Glaesser
Production: Ellen Schneider
Publicity: Silvia Schumacher
Founded: 1918
Subjects: Biography, Psychology, Psychiatry, Religion - Other, Theology
ISBN Prefix(es): 3-7867
Number of titles published annually: 60 Print; 3 Audio
Total Titles: 840 Print; 40 Audio

Matthiesen Verlag Ingwert Paulsen Jr+
Nordbahnhofstr 2, 25813 Husum
Mailing Address: Postfach 1480, 25804 Husum
Tel: (04841) 83520 *Fax:* (04841) 835210
E-mail: info@verlagsgruppe.de
Web Site: www.verlagsgruppe.de
Key Personnel
Man Dir, Editorial, Rights & Permissions: Ingwert Paulsen
Founded: 1892
Subjects: Science (General)
ISBN Prefix(es): 3-7868
Associate Companies: Hamburger Lesehefte Verlag Iselt & Co Nfl mbH; Hansa Verlag Ingwert Paulsen Jr; Husum Druck- und Verlagsgesellschaft mbH & Co KG; Verlag der Nation

Hans K Matussek Buchhandlung & Antiquariat+
Marktstr 13, 41334 Nettetal
Tel: (02153) 91 64 30 *Fax:* (02153) 1 33 63
Web Site: www.buchkatalog.de/matussek
Key Personnel
Contact: Hans K Matussek; Fabian Matussek *E-mail:* fabian.matussek@t-online.de
Founded: 1961
ISBN Prefix(es): 3-920743

Matzker Verlag DiA
Osternburger Str 30, 28237 Bremen
Mailing Address: Postfach 130193, 13601 Berlin
Tel: (0421) 6207934
Key Personnel
Contact: Dr Reiner Matzker
Founded: 1985
Subjects: Art, Education, Fiction, Poetry
ISBN Prefix(es): 3-925789

Max Schimmel Verlag
Im Kreuz 9, 97076 Wuerzburg
Mailing Address: Postfach 94 44, 97094 Wuerzburg
Tel: (0931) 27 91 400 *Fax:* (0931) 27 91 444
E-mail: info@schimmelverlag.de
Web Site: www.schimmelverlag.de
Key Personnel
Man Dir: Helmuth Hopfner; Ingo Schloo
Subjects: Marketing
ISBN Prefix(es): 3-920834

Maximilian Gesellschaft eV, *imprint of* Anton Hiersemann, Verlag

J A Mayersche Buchhandlung GmbH & Co KG Abt Verlag
Matthiasshofstr 28-30, 52064 Aachen
Tel: (0241) 4777 499 *Fax:* (0241) 4777 467
E-mail: vertrieb@mayersche.de
Web Site: www.mayersche.de *Cable:* MAYER AACHEN
Key Personnel
Man Dir, Publicity: Helmut Falter
Membership(s): AWS-JASV.
Subjects: Regional Interests
ISBN Prefix(es): 3-87519
Branch Office(s)
Anlage, 5100 Aachen
Bookshop(s): Ursulinerstr 17-19, 52062 Aachen *Tel:* (0241) 4777 0 *Fax:* (0241) 4777 167 *E-mail:* aachenurs@mayersche.de; Neumarkt 1B, 50667 Cologne; Hohe Str 68-82, 50667 Cologne; Kuhstr 33, 47051 Duisburg; Hindenburgstr 75, 41061 Moenchengladbach 1; Stresemannstr 43, 41236 Moenchengladbach 2; Bahnhofstr 55-65, 45879 Gelsenkirchen; Pontstr 131, 52062 Aachen *Tel:* (0241) 47494 0 *Fax:* (0241) 47494 1 *E-mail:* aachenth@mayersche.de

Mayr Miesbach Druckerei und Verlag GmbH
Am Windfeld 15, 83714 Miesbach
Tel: (08025) 294-0 *Fax:* (08025) 294-235
E-mail: info@mayrmiesbach.de
Web Site: www.mayrmiesbach.de
Key Personnel
Man Dir, Sales & International Rights: Dieter Bergemann
Man Dir: Wilhelm Friedrich Mayr
Sales & International Rights: Oskar Amann
Parent Company: Schattauer GmbH - Verlag fuer Medizin und Naturwissenschaften, Hoelderlinstr 3, 70174 Stuttgart
Subsidiaries: Verlag Freizeit & Wassersport GmbH

Dr Norbert Meder & Co, see Janus Verlagsgesellschaft, Dr Norbert Meder & Co

Mediapress GmbH+
Hubertusstr 68, 47798 Krefeld
Tel: (02151) 79553334
Telex: 781217
Key Personnel
Man Dir, Rights & Permissions: Dieter Brinzer
Founded: 1982

Medico International eV
Obermainanlage 7, 60314 Frankfurt/Main
Tel: (069) 94438-0 *Fax:* (069) 436002
E-mail: info@medico.de
Web Site: www.medico.de
Telex: 416153 merco d
Key Personnel
Publishing: Gudrun Kortas
Founded: 1968
Subjects: Developing Countries, Health, Nutrition
ISBN Prefix(es): 3-923363

Medien-Verlag Bernhard Gregor GmbH
Rosengasse 7, 36272 Niederaula
Tel: (06625) 5011; (0171) 7723972 *Fax:* (06625) 919743
E-mail: gregor-medien@t-online.de; mail@gregor-medien.de
Web Site: www.gregor-medien.de
Key Personnel
Man Dir: Bernhard Gregor
Founded: 1982
Subjects: Biography, Religion - Catholic, Theology
ISBN Prefix(es): 3-89150; 3-87391; 3-922770
Number of titles published annually: 3 Print
Total Titles: 60 Print
Distributed by Christiana (Switzerland)

Medium-Buchmarkt+
Rosenstr 5-6, D-48143 Munster
Tel: (0251) 46 000 *Fax:* (0251) 46 745
E-mail: info@mediumbooks.com
Web Site: www.mediumbooks.com
Key Personnel
International Rights: Friedrich W Bitzhenner
Editorial: Carsten Schulte
Specialize in books on pop music.
Subjects: Music, Dance
ISBN Prefix(es): 3-933642

Medizinisch-Literarische Verlagsgesellschaft mbH+
Postfach 1151/1152, 29501 Uelzen
Tel: (0581) 808-151 *Fax:* (0581) 808-158
E-mail: mlverlag@mlverlag.de
Web Site: www.mlverlag.de *Cable:* ML-VERLAG 29525 UELZEN
Key Personnel
Chief: Dr D Ippen
Publisher: Helmut Block
Founded: 1957
Subjects: Alternative, Cookery, Health, Nutrition, Medicine, Nursing, Dentistry, Sports, Athletics
ISBN Prefix(es): 3-88136; 3-87522
Parent Company: C Beckers Buchdruckerei, 29525 Uelzen

Medpharm Scientific Publishers+
Birkenwaldstr 44, 70191 Stuttgart
Mailing Address: Postfach 101061, 70009 Stuttgart
Tel: (0711) 2582-0 *Fax:* (0711) 2582-290
E-mail: service@medpharm.de
Web Site: www.medpharm.de
Key Personnel
Man Dir: Dr Klaus Brauer; Andre Caro; Dr Christian Rotta
Contact: Siegmar Bauer
Founded: 1981
Subjects: Medicine, Nursing, Dentistry, Pharmacy
ISBN Prefix(es): 3-88763
Parent Company: Deutscher Apotheker Verlag
Subsidiaries: S Hirzel Verlag GmbH & Co; Franz Steiner Verlag Wiesbaden GmbH; Wissenschaftliche Verlagsgesellschaft mbH
Foreign Rights: Sabine Koerner

Felix Meiner Verlag GmbH+
Richardstr 47, 22081 Hamburg
Mailing Address: Postfach 760742, 22057 Hamburg
Tel: (040) 298756-20 *Fax:* (040) 299361-4
E-mail: info@meiner.de
Web Site: www.meiner.de
Key Personnel
Man Dir: Manfred Meiner *E-mail:* meiner@meiner.de
Rights, Marketing: Johannes Kambylis *Tel:* (040) 298756-23 *E-mail:* kambylis@meiner.de
Founded: 1911
Membership(s): the German Book Trade Association.
Subjects: Philosophy
ISBN Prefix(es): 3-7873
Subsidiaries: Helmut Buske Verlag GmbH

Meisenbach Verlag GmbH
Franz-Ludwigstr 7a, 96047 Bamberg
Tel: (0951) 861-0 *Fax:* (0951) 861-158

Web Site: www.meisenbach.de
Key Personnel
Man Dir: Hans Limmer *E-mail:* geschltg@meisenbach.de
Founded: 1922
Subjects: Technology
ISBN Prefix(es): 3-87525

Otto Meissner Verlag+
Bingerstr 29, 14197 Berlin
Tel: (030) 8249558 *Fax:* (030) 8233338
Key Personnel
Dir, Rights & Permissions: Dieter Beuermann
Founded: 1848
Subjects: Crafts, Games, Hobbies, Human Relations, Nonfiction (General)
ISBN Prefix(es): 3-87527

Melsunger Medizinische Mitteilungen, *imprint of* Bibliomed - Medizinische Verlagsgesellschaft mbH

Idime Verlag Inge Melzer
Kienestr 37/1, 88045 Friedrichshafen
Tel: (07541) 55220 *Fax:* (07541) 55201
E-mail: idime@t-online.de
Web Site: www.idime.de
Key Personnel
Man Dir: Inge Melzer
Founded: 1983
Subjects: Anthropology, Foreign Countries
ISBN Prefix(es): 3-924026; 3-933937

Edition Axel Menges
Esslingerstr 24, 70736 Fellbach
Tel: (0711) 574759 *Fax:* (0711) 574784
Key Personnel
International Rights: Axel Menges *Tel:* (0711) 574753 *E-mail:* axelmenges@aol.com; Dorothea Dune *Tel:* (0711) 514753 *E-mail:* ddune@aol.com
Founded: 1994
Subjects: Architecture & Interior Design, Art, Film, Video, Photography, Travel
ISBN Prefix(es): 3-930698; 3-932565
Number of titles published annually: 20 Print
Total Titles: 10 Print
Associate Companies: Michal Robinson, 125 Stamford Court, Goldhawk Rd, London W6 0XE, United Kingdom *Tel:* (020) 8995 8340 *Fax:* (020) 8995 0113 *E-mail:* mrrobinson@compuserve.com
Distribution Center: National Book Network, 4720 Boston Way, Lanham, MD, United States, Contact: Marianne Bohr *Tel:* 301-459-3366 *Fax:* 301-459-2118 *E-mail:* mbohr@nbnbooks.com (also US representative)

MenSana, *imprint of* Verlagsgruppe Droemer Knaur GmbH & Co KG

Menschenkinder Verlag und Vertrieb GmbH+
An der Kleimannbruecke 97, 48157 Muenster
Tel: (0251) 932520 *Fax:* (0251) 9325290
E-mail: info@menschenkinder.de
Web Site: www.menschenkinder.de
Key Personnel
Man Dir: Detlev Joecker
Subjects: Music, Dance
ISBN Prefix(es): 3-927497; 3-89516; 3-9801811

mentis Verlag GmbH+
Schulze-Delitzschstr 19, 33100 Paderborn
Tel: (05251) 687902; (05251) 687904
Fax: (05251) 687905
E-mail: info@mentis.de
Web Site: www.mentis.de
Founded: 1998
Subjects: Language Arts, Linguistics, Literature, Literary Criticism, Essays, Philosophy
ISBN Prefix(es): 3-89785

Number of titles published annually: 35 Print
Total Titles: 260 Print; 2 CD-ROM
Distribution Center: VSB Verlagsservice Braunschweig
Orders to: VSB Verlagsservice Braunschweig
Returns: VSB Verlagsservice Braunschweig

Mentor-Verlag Dr Ramdohr KG+
Member of The Langenscheidt Group
Mies-van-der-Rohe-Str 1, 80807 Munich
Mailing Address: Postfach 401120, 80711 Munich
Tel: (089) 360960 *Fax:* (089) 36096-222 (general); (089) 36096-258 (orders)
E-mail: mentor@langenscheidt.de
Key Personnel
Man Dirs: Karl Ernst Tielebier-Langenscheidt; Andreas Langenscheidt
Chief Editor: Dr Brigitte Abel
Sales Dir: Dr Matti Schusseler
Advertising: Brigitte Pasch
Founded: 1904
Sales & Promotion through Langenscheidt KG.
ISBN Prefix(es): 3-580

Mercator-Verlag, *imprint of* Verlagshaus Wohlfarth

Mergus Verlag GmbH Hans A Baensch+
Im Wiele 27, 49328 Melle
Tel: (05422) 3636 *Fax:* (05422) 1404
E-mail: info@mergus.de
Web Site: www.mergus.com *Cable:* MERGUS MELLE
Key Personnel
Man Dir, Rights & Permissions: Hans A Baensch
Founded: 1977
Subjects: Animals, Pets, Natural History
ISBN Prefix(es): 3-88244
Distributed by Rolf C Hagen Inc (Canada); Rolf C Hagen (UK) Ltd; ICA SA (Canary Islands, Spain); IMAZO OFF (Sweden); Microcosm Ltd (USA); Tetra Sales (Warner Lamber Co) (USA); Pet Pacific Pty Ltd (Australia); Primaris, Edizioni d'Accuariofilia (Italy); SAVAC Sa; Taikong Trading Corp (Taiwan)

Merian, *imprint of* Graefe und Unzer Verlag GmbH

Merit, *imprint of* Xenos Verlagsgesellschaft mbH

Merlin Verlag Andreas Meyer Verlags GmbH und Co KG+
Gifkendorf Nr 38, 21397 Gifkendorf
Tel: (04137) 7207 *Fax:* (04137) 7948
E-mail: info@merlin-verlag.de
Web Site: www.merlin-verlag.de
Key Personnel
Publisher: Andreas J Meyer
Sales Manager: Ilse K Meyer
Manager, Theater Dept: Lilli Nitsche
Junior Publisher, License & Press: Dr Katharina E Meyer
Founded: 1957
Subjects: Anthropology, Art, Biography, Drama, Theater, Fiction, Gay & Lesbian, Government, Political Science, Literature, Literary Criticism, Essays, Parapsychology, Philosophy, Poetry
ISBN Prefix(es): 3-87536; 3-926112
Number of titles published annually: 12 Print
Total Titles: 200 Print; 3 Audio
Associate Companies: Little Tiger Verlag GmbH, Poppenbuetteler Chausee 53, 22397 Hamburg

Verlag Merseburger Berlin GmbH+
Motzstr 9, 34117 Kassel
Mailing Address: Postfach 103880, 34038 Kassel
Tel: (0561) 789809-0 *Fax:* (0561) 789809-16
E-mail: info@merseburger.de; order@merseburger.de

Web Site: www.merseburger.de
Key Personnel
Contact: Corinne Votteler *Tel:* (0561) 78980311 *E-mail:* corinne.votteler@merseburger.de
Founded: 1849
Specialize in sheet music & books.
Subjects: Music
ISBN Prefix(es): 3-87537

Merve Verlag
Crellestr 22, 10827 Berlin
Tel: (030) 784 8433 *Fax:* (030) 788 1074
E-mail: merve@merve.de
Web Site: www.merve.de
Key Personnel
Man Dir, Rights & Permissions: Hans-Peter Gente; Heidi Paris
Founded: 1970
ISBN Prefix(es): 3-88396; 3-920986

Merz & Solitude - Akademie Schloss Solitude
Solitude 3, 70197 Stuttgart
Tel: (0711) 99 619-471 *Fax:* (0711) 99 619-50
E-mail: mr@akademie-solitude.de
Web Site: www.akademie-solitude.de
Key Personnel
Academy Dir: Jean-Baptiste Joly
Founded: 1989
Publish literary books, artists' books & catalogs by the Akademie Schloss Solitude fellows only.
Subjects: Architecture & Interior Design, Art, Drama, Theater, Fiction, Music, Dance, Photography
ISBN Prefix(es): 3-929085
Number of titles published annually: 12 Print
Total Titles: 110 Print
Distribution Center: GVA, Goettingen

Gustav Mesmer Stiftung, *imprint of* Silberburg-Verlag Titus Haeussermann GmbH

Verlag fuer Messepublikationen, see Verlag fuer Messepubliktionen Thomas Neureuter KG

Metropolis- Verlag fur Okonomie, Gesellschaft und Politik GmbH
Bahnhofstr 16a, 35037 Marburg
Tel: (06421) 67377 *Fax:* (06471) 681918
E-mail: info@metropolis-verlag.de
Web Site: www.metropolis-verlag.de
Key Personnel
Man Dir: Hubert Hoffmann *E-mail:* hoffman@metropolis-verlag.de
Founded: 1987
Subjects: Business, Economics, Environmental Studies, Government, Political Science, Philosophy, Social Sciences, Sociology
ISBN Prefix(es): 3-89518; 3-926570

Metropolitan Verlag+
Haus an der Eisemen Bruecke, 93042 Regensburg
Tel: (0941) 56840 *Fax:* (0941) 5684111
E-mail: walhalla@walhalla.de
Web Site: www.metropolitan.de
Key Personnel
Publisher: Eva-Maria Steckenleiter *E-mail:* walhalla@walhalla.de
Founded: 1995
Also specializing in rights.
Subjects: Economics
ISBN Prefix(es): 3-8029; 3-89623
Total Titles: 180 Print; 1 CD-ROM; 1 Online; 1 E-Book; 1 Audio

Karl-Heinz Metz
Josef-Hollerbachstr 14, 76571 Gaggenau
Tel: (07225) 74098 *Fax:* (07225) 74098
E-mail: metzverlag@aol.com
Web Site: www.metz-verlag.de
Key Personnel
Owner: Karl-Heinz Metz

Subjects: Animals, Pets, History, Mysteries, Social Sciences, Sociology, Adventure, Social Situations, Horror & Ghost, Love & Sexuality
ISBN Prefix(es): 3-927655

J B Metzlersche Verlagsbuchhandlung+
Werastr 21-23, 70182 Stuttgart
Mailing Address: Postfach 103241, 70028 Stuttgart
Tel: (0711) 2194-0 *Fax:* (0711) 2194-249
E-mail: info@metzelverlag.de
Web Site: www.metzlerverlag.de *Cable:* METZLERVERLAG STUTTGART
Key Personnel
Man Dir: Michael Justus *E-mail:* justus@metzlerverlag.de; Dr Bernd Lutz *Tel:* (0711) 2194-220 *E-mail:* lutz@metzlerverlag.de
Marketing & Sales Dir: Michael Schmid *E-mail:* schmid@metzlerverlag.de
Advertising: Sabine Zobeley *E-mail:* zobeley@metzlerverlag.de
Licensing & Rights: Andrea Rupp *Tel:* (0711) 2194 225 *E-mail:* rupp@metzlerverlag.de
Press: Joachim Bader *E-mail:* bader@metzlerverlag.de
Founded: 1682
Membership(s): T R- Verlagsunion GmbH.
Subjects: Antiques, Art, Film, Video, History, Language Arts, Linguistics, Literature, Literary Criticism, Essays, Music, Dance, Philosophy
ISBN Prefix(es): 3-476
Number of titles published annually: 80 Print; 2 CD-ROM
Parent Company: Georg von Holtzbrinck GmbH & Co
Distributor for SFG - Servicecenter Fachverlage GmbH

Alfred Metzner, imprint of Hermann Luchterhand Verlag GmbH

Preubmpassling Verlag Gisela Meussling+
Dixstr 29, 53225 Bonn
Tel: (0228) 466347 *Fax:* (0228) 466347
Key Personnel
Man Dir, Rights & Permissions: Gisela Meussling
Founded: 1978
Subjects: Anthropology, History, Philosophy, Physical Sciences, Women's Studies, Esoterics/New Age, Ethnology
ISBN Prefix(es): 3-922129
Warehouse: Stiftsstr 39, 53225 Bonn

Meyer & Meyer Verlag+
Von-Coels Str 390, 52080 Aachen
Tel: (0241) 95810-0 *Fax:* (0241) 95810-10
E-mail: verlag@m-m-sports.com
Web Site: www.m-m-sports.com
Key Personnel
Man Dir: Hans Juergen Meyer *E-mail:* hjm@m-m-sports.com; Irmgard Meyer-Purpar *E-mail:* i.meyer-purpar@m-m-sports.com
Founded: 1984
Also acts as President of WSA (World Sportpublisher Association).
Subjects: Disability, Special Needs, Drama, Theater, Health, Nutrition, Music, Dance, Nonfiction (General), Sports, Athletics, Travel
ISBN Prefix(es): 3-89124; 3-89899
Number of titles published annually: 120 Print
Total Titles: 960 Print
Divisions: Aachener Buch Service
U.S. Office(s): Lewis International, 2201 NW 102 Pl, No 1, PO Box 5076, Miami, FL 33172, United States
Foreign Rep(s): Continental Sales (USA)
Warehouse: Aachener Buch Service, Tempelhoferstr 21, 52068 Aachen
Distribution Center: Bookwide Asia Pte Ltd, 29 Tampines St, 92, Singapore 528779, Singapore (Southeast Asia)

Bookwise International, PO Box 8892, Symonds Post Office, Auckland, New Zealand *Tel:* (09) 6 23 23 48 *Fax:* (09) 6 23 21 40 (New Zealand)
Bookwise International (Pty) Ltd, 174 Cormack Rd, Winfield, SA 5013, Australia *Tel:* (08268) 82 22 *Fax:* (08268) 87 04 *E-mail:* orders@bookwise.com.au (Australia)
Buchzentrum AG, Postfach, 4601 Olten, Switzerland *Tel:* (062) 2 09 27 05 *Fax:* (062) 2 09 27 88 *Web Site:* www.buchzentrum.de
Commerce Logistic Center, Am Steinfeld 4, 94065 Waldkirchen *Tel:* (085) 81-96 05-0 *Fax:* (085) 81-7 54
Fair Play Sport Bt, Hungary, Contact: Nora Bendiner *Tel:* (01) 4 71 4 325 *E-mail:* nora.bendiner@helka.iif.hu (Hungary)
AS Hoeller GmbH, Schaldorferstr 16, 8641 Saint Marein im Muerztal, Austria *Tel:* (038) 64-67 77 *Fax:* (038) 64-38 88 (Austria/South Tyrol)
Megaform-Sport- & Freetime Equipment, Rue Haute, 177, 4700 Eupen, Belgium *Tel:* (087) 32 17 17 *Fax:* (087) 31 29 99 *E-mail:* info@megaform.be *Web Site:* www.megaform.be (Beglium)
Windsor Books International, 11 The Boundary, Wheatley Rd, Garsington, Oxford OX44 9EJ, United Kingdom *Tel:* (01865) 36 11 22 *Fax:* (01865) 36 11 33 *E-mail:* sales@windsorbooks.co.uk (Great Britain, France, Greece, Ireland, Italy, The Netherlands, Portugal, Scandinavia, Spain, South Africa)

Peter Meyer Verlag (pmv)+
Schopenhauerstr 11, 60316 Frankfurt am Main
Tel: (069) 49 44 49 *Fax:* (069) 44 51 35
E-mail: info@PeterMeyerVerlag.de
Web Site: www.petermeyerverlag.de
Key Personnel
International Rights & Man Dir: Peter Meyer
Man Dir: Annette Sievers
Founded: 1976
Subjects: Language Arts, Linguistics, Regional Interests, Travel
ISBN Prefix(es): 3-922057; 3-89859
Number of titles published annually: 16 Print
Total Titles: 50 Print
Orders to: Prolit Verlagsauslieferung GmbH, Postfach 9, 35461 Fernwald *Tel:* (0641) 943 93-0 *Fax:* (0641) 943 93-93 *E-mail:* service@prolit.de *Web Site:* www.prolit.de

Ursala Meyer und Dr Manfred Duker Ein-Fach-Verlag+
Monheimsallee 21, 52062 Aachen
Tel: (0241) 405501 *Fax:* (0241) 400 96 67
E-mail: einfachverlag@gmx.de
Founded: 1989
Membership(s): Boersenverein.
Subjects: Language Arts, Linguistics, Philosophy, Religion - Hindu, Science (General), Women's Studies, Feminist Philosophy
ISBN Prefix(es): 3-928089
Total Titles: 26 Print
Orders to: GVA - Gemeinsame Verlagsauslieferung, Postfach 20 21, 37010 Gottingen *Tel:* (0551) 487177 *Fax:* (0551) 41392 *E-mail:* rabe@gva-verlage.de

Edition Meyster, imprint of nymphenburger

MICHEL/Schwaneberger Verlag, see Schwaneberger Verlag GmbH

Gertraud Middelhauve Verlag GmbH & Co KG+
Lucile-Grahn Str 39, 81675 Munich
Tel: (089) 41 94 02-0 *Fax:* (089) 47 01 08-1
Key Personnel
Man Dir: Hans Meisinger
Founded: 1947

ISBN Prefix(es): 3-7876
Parent Company: Meisinger Verlagsgruppe
Orders to: MVS Meisinger Verlagsservice GmbH, Am Steinfeld 4, 94065 Waldkirchen *Tel:* (08581) 9605-0 *Fax:* (08581) 754

Midena Verlag+
Hilbestr 54, 80636 Munich
Tel: (089) 9271-0 *Fax:* (089) 9271-168
Web Site: www.droemer-knaur.de
Key Personnel
Editorial Dir: Erhard Held
Rights & Permissions: Silke Breitlaender
Founded: 1981
Subjects: Child Care & Development, Cookery, Education, Health, Nutrition, Human Relations, Medicine, Nursing, Dentistry, Psychology, Psychiatry, Self-Help
Parent Company: Verlagsgruppe Droemer Weltbild GmbH & Co KG

Militzke Verlag+
Huttenstr 5, 04249 Leipzig
Tel: (0341) 42643-0 *Fax:* (0341) 42643-99
E-mail: info@militzke.de
Web Site: www.militzke.de
Key Personnel
Editorial: Dr Siegfried Kaetzel *E-mail:* lektorat@militzke.de
Public Relations, Press & Licensing: Christiane Voelkel *Tel:* (0341) 42643-20 *Fax:* (0341) 42643-26 *E-mail:* presse@militzke.de
Contact for Orders: Melitta Siebert *Tel:* (0341) 42643-12
Founded: 1990 (First privately founded publisher on former GDR territory since 1989)
National & international rights bought & sold, publication of textbooks & special interest hardcovers.
Membership(s): German Publishers & Booksellers Association & Association of Publishers & Bookshops.
Subjects: Biography, Government, Political Science, Special Interest Hardcover, Authentic Criminal Cases, Historical & Political Popular Science & Detective Novels
ISBN Prefix(es): 3-86189
Number of titles published annually: 50 Print
Total Titles: 637 Print; 1 Audio

Minerva Edition Wissen Medizinischer und Naturwissenschaftlicher Verlag und Vertieb+
Kirchheimer Str 60, 67269 Gruenstadt-Pfalz
Tel: (0700) 96 389 352 *Fax:* (0700) 96 389 353
E-mail: info@woetzel.de
Web Site: www.woetzel.de
Key Personnel
President: Martin M Preuss *Tel:* (06351) 41000
Founded: 1987
STM - Books, health, psychology.
ISBN Prefix(es): 3-936611
Total Titles: 32 Print; 1 CD-ROM; 3 Audio
Bookshop(s): Akademische Buchhandlung Woetzel *Tel:* (06359) 924726 *Fax:* (06359) 924723

Miranda-Verlag Stefan Ehlert+
Humboldtstr 145, 28203 Bremen
Mailing Address: PO Box 101021, 28010 Bremen
Tel: (0421) 7943226 *Fax:* (0421) 7943226
E-mail: miranda-verlag@t-online.de
Web Site: www.miranda-verlag.de
Founded: 1997
Subjects: Biography, Literature, Literary Criticism, Essays
ISBN Prefix(es): 3-934790
Number of titles published annually: 2 Print
Total Titles: 6 Print

Missio eV+
Goethestr 43, 52064 Aachen
Mailing Address: Postfach 101253, Aachen 52012

Tel: (0241) 75 07-00 *Fax:* (0241) 75 07-336
E-mail: info@missio-aachen.de
Web Site: www.missio-aachen.de
Telex: 832719 mira d
Subjects: Developing Countries, Religion - Catholic, Religion - Other
ISBN Prefix(es): 3-930556
Bookshop(s): Missio am Dom, Muensterplatz, 52064 Aachen
Warehouse: missio eV, Industriestr 12, 52146 Wuerselen

Missionshandlung
Harmsstr 2, 29320 Hermannsburg
Mailing Address: Postfach 1109, 29314 Hermannsburg
Tel: (05052) 69400 *Fax:* (05052) 3082
E-mail: m-druckerei@t-online.de
Key Personnel
Contact: Hans Peter Schiebe; Wilfried Schulte
Founded: 1856
Subjects: Regional Interests
ISBN Prefix(es): 3-87546
Parent Company: Ev luth Missionswerk in Niedersachsen (ELM)

Mitteilungsblatt der Verbandes deds bayerischen Druckincleestrie eV, *imprint of* Fachverlag fur das graphische Gewerbe GmbH

Mitteldeutscher Verlag GmbH+
Am Steintor 23, 06112 Halle
Tel: (0345) 23322-0 *Fax:* (0345) 23322-66
E-mail: mitteldeutscher.verlag@t-online.de
Web Site: www.buecherkisten.de
Key Personnel
Man Dir: Veronika Schneides
Founded: 1946
Subjects: Art, Fiction, History, Literature, Literary Criticism, Essays, Nonfiction (General), Photography, Poetry, Regional Interests, Travel
ISBN Prefix(es): 3-354; 3-932776

E S Mittler und Sohn GmbH+
Member of Verlagsgruppe Koehler/Mittler
Striepenweg 31, 21147 Hamburg
Mailing Address: Postfach 920463, 21134 Hamburg
Tel: (040) 7 97 13-03 *Fax:* (040) 79713324 *Cable:* MITTLER & SOHN, HERFORD/WESTF
Key Personnel
Publisher: Wolf O Storck; Peter Tamm
Sales: Hans-Focko Koehler
Manager: Thomas Bantle
Founded: 1789
Subjects: Aeronautics, Aviation, Government, Political Science, Maritime, Military Science
ISBN Prefix(es): 3-87547; 3-8132
Associate Companies: Verlag Europaeische Wehrkunde; Koehlers Verlagsgesellschaft; Maximilian-Verlag; Verlag Offene Worte
Branch Office(s)
Godesberger Allee 91, 53175 Bonn *Tel:* (0228) 307890 *Fax:* (0228) 3078915

MM-Verlagsgesellschaft mbH+
Zabergaeustr 3, 73765 Neuhausen
Tel: (07158) 940 800 *Fax:* (07158) 940 802
E-mail: mm@ebb.de
Key Personnel
Manager: Matthias Mueller
License & Press Service.
ISBN Prefix(es): 3-88590

MMV Medizin Verlag GmbH Munich, see Urban & Vogel Medien und Medizin Verlagsgesellschaft mbH & Co KG

Moby Dick Verlag+
Kaistr 33, Eckmann-Speicher, 24103 Kiel
Mailing Address: Postfach 3369, 24032 Kiel
Tel: (0431) 640110 *Fax:* (0431) 6401112
E-mail: mobybook@aol.com
Key Personnel
Publisher: Konrad Delius
Editor: Klaus Bartelt
Subjects: Automotive, Crafts, Games, Hobbies, Mysteries, Outdoor Recreation, Sports, Athletics, Technology, Transportation, Travel
ISBN Prefix(es): 3-922843; 3-930392; 3-89595
Total Titles: 20 Print
Parent Company: Delius Klasing Verlag

mode information Heinz Kramer GmbH
Pilgerstr 20, 51491 Overath
Tel: (02206) 60070 *Fax:* (02206) 600717
E-mail: info@modeinfo.com
Web Site: www.modeinfo.com
Subjects: Architecture & Interior Design, Fashion, Management, Marketing
ISBN Prefix(es): 3-00
Foreign Rights: Eastgate House (UK); Inter Fashion Express (Greece); H Kramer GmbH (Germany); Masolo Representacoes SA (Portugal); Mode Gallery BAJ Oy (Finland); Pej Gruppen Aps (Denmark)

Modellsport Verlag GmbH+
Schulstr 12, 76532 Baden-Baden
Tel: (07221) 95 21-0 *Fax:* (07221) 95 21-45
E-mail: modellsport@modellsport.de
Web Site: www.modellsport.de
Key Personnel
Manager: Heinz Ongsieck
Founded: 1977
ISBN Prefix(es): 3-923142

Moderne Buchkunst und Graphie Wolfgang Tiessen
Meisenstr 9, 63263 Neu-Isenburg
Mailing Address: Postfach 2179, 63243 Neu-Isenburg
Tel: (06102) 53335 *Fax:* (06102) 53335
Founded: 1977
Specialize in limited editions finely printed with illustrations in original graphic.
ISBN Prefix(es): 3-920947; 3-928395

modo verlag GmbH
Runzstr 62, 79102 Freiburg
Tel: (0761) 2022875 *Fax:* (0761) 2022876
E-mail: info@modoverlag.de
Web Site: www.modoverlag.de
Subjects: Architecture & Interior Design, Art, Contemporary Art, Late 20th Century Art
ISBN Prefix(es): 3-922675
Number of titles published annually: 8 Print
Total Titles: 45 Print

Moeck Verlag und Musikinstrumentenwerk, Inhaber Dr Hermann Moeck
Lueckenweg 4, 29227 Celle
Mailing Address: Postfach 3131, 29231 Celle
Tel: (05141) 88 53-0 *Fax:* (05141) 88 53-42
E-mail: info@moeck-music.de
Web Site: www.moeck-music.de
Key Personnel
Owner: Dr Hermann Moeck
ISBN Prefix(es): 3-87549

Karl Heinrich Moeseler Verlag+
Hoffmann-von-Fallerslebenstr 8, 38304 Wolfenbuettel
Tel: (05331) 95970 *Fax:* (05331) 9597-20
Key Personnel
President & International Rights: Dietrich Moeseler
Founded: 1949
Subjects: Music, Dance
ISBN Prefix(es): 3-7877

Moewig, *imprint of* Pabel-Moewig Verlag KG

Mohr Siebeck+
Wilhelmstr 18, 72074 Tuebingen
Mailing Address: Postfach 2040, 72010 Tuebingen
Tel: (07071) 923-0 *Fax:* (07071) 5 11 04
E-mail: info@mohr.de
Web Site: www.mohr.de *Cable:* SIEBECK TUBINGEN
Key Personnel
Owner & Publisher: Georg Siebeck *Tel:* (07071) 923 32 *Fax:* (07071) 923 67 *E-mail:* siebeck@mohr.de
Sales & Marketing Dir: Sabine Stehle
  Tel: (07071) 923 56 *E-mail:* sabine.stehle@mohr.de
Production: Matthias Spitzner *Tel:* (07071) 923 43 *E-mail:* matthias.spitzner@mohr.de
Rights & Permissions: Jill Sopper *Tel:* (07071) 923 61 *E-mail:* jill.sopper@mohr.de
Editorial Dir Law: Dr Franz-Peter Gillig
  Tel: (07071) 923 50 *Fax:* (07071) 923 67
  E-mail: franz-peter.gillig@mohr.de
Editorial Dir Theology: Dr Henning Ziebritzki
  Tel: (07071) 923 59 *Fax:* (07071) 511 04
  E-mail: henning.ziebritzki@mohr.de
Founded: 1801
Academic Books & Journals. Encyclopedias, Historical-critical Editions & Monographs.
Subjects: Economics, History, Law, Philosophy, Religion - Protestant, Religion - Other, Social Sciences, Sociology, Theology, Judaism
ISBN Prefix(es): 3-16
Number of titles published annually: 180 Print
Total Titles: 3,210 Print
Imprints: H Lauppsche Buchhandlung
Warehouse: Christophstr 32, 72072 Tuebingen

Monastica, *imprint of* Verein der Benediktiner zu Beuron- Beuroner Kunstverlag

Monia Verlag+
Strobelallee 62, 66953 Pirmasens
Mailing Address: Postfach 2120, 66929 Pirmasens
Tel: (06331) 41425 *Fax:* (06331) 41425
Key Personnel
Contact: Elisabeth Dillenburger
Founded: 1971
Novels & bilingual poetry for adults.
Subjects: Biography, Fiction, Literature, Literary Criticism, Essays, Poetry
ISBN Prefix(es): 3-926753; 3-9800383

Moritz Verlag+
Kantstr 12, 60316 Frankfurt am Main
Tel: (069) 4305084 *Fax:* (069) 4305083
E-mail: MoritzVerlag@t-online.de
Key Personnel
Contact: Markus Weber
Founded: 1994
ISBN Prefix(es): 3-89565
Parent Company: l'ecole des loisirs, Paris, France
Warehouse: Koch, Neff & Oetinger, 70551 Stuttgart
Orders to: Koch, Neff & Oetinger, 70551 Stuttgart *Tel:* (0711) 78 99 10 10
  E-mail: order@kno-va.de

Morsak Verlag+
Wittelsbacherstr 2-8, 94481 Grafenau
Mailing Address: Postfach 1262, 94476 Grafenau
Tel: (08552) 4200 *Fax:* (08552) 42050
E-mail: info@morsak.de
Web Site: www.morsak.de
Key Personnel
Man Dir, Production: Erich Stecher
Sales: Rosa Zarham
Founded: 1884
Subjects: Regional Interests
ISBN Prefix(es): 3-87553

Morus-Verlag GmbH
Gotzstr 65, 12099 Berlin
Tel: (030) 89 79 37-0 *Fax:* (030) 75 70 81 12
E-mail: mail@morusverlag.de
Web Site: www.morusverlag.de
Key Personnel
Dir: Olaf Lezinsky
Founded: 1945
Subjects: Religion - Other
ISBN Prefix(es): 3-87554

Mosaik Verlag GmbH
Neumarkterstr 28, 81673 Munich
Mailing Address: Postfach 800360, 81673 Munich
Tel: (089) 4372-0; (089) 4136-0; (01805) 990505 (hot line) *Fax:* (089) 4372-2812
E-mail: vertrieb.verlagsgruppe@randomhouse.de
Web Site: www.randomhouse.de/mosaik
Telex: 523259 vbmue d
Key Personnel
Man Dir: Georg Kessler; Lothar Beyer
Publicity: Helga Mahmoud-Treimer
Rights & Permissions: Angelika Straus-Fischer
Subjects: Animals, Pets, Antiques, Architecture & Interior Design, Career Development, Child Care & Development, Cookery, Crafts, Games, Hobbies, Economics, Film, Video, Finance, Gardening, Plants, Health, Nutrition, House & Home, Human Relations, Self-Help, Sports, Athletics, Wine & Spirits, Women's Studies
ISBN Prefix(es): 3-576
Parent Company: Verlagsgruppe Bertelsmann GmbH
U.S. Office(s): Bettina Schrewe Literary Scouting, 101 Fifth Ave, Suite 11B, New York, NY 10003, United States (US Scout)

Motorbuch-Verlag+
Division of Paul Pietsch Verlage GmbH & Co
Olgastr 86, 70180 Stuttgart
Tel: (0711) 210 80 65 *Fax:* (0711) 210 80 70
E-mail: versand@motorbuch.de
Web Site: www.motorbuch-versand.de *Cable:* PICO D
Key Personnel
Man Dir: Paul Pietsch; Dr Patricia Scholten
Sales, Publicity: Thomas Guenther
Rights & Permissions: Patricia Hofmann
Editorial: Martin Benz; Claus-Guergen Jacobson; Joachim Kuch; Oliver Schwarz
Marketing: Jarg Ebert
Founded: 1962
Subjects: Aeronautics, Aviation, Automotive, History, Military Science, Nonfiction (General)
ISBN Prefix(es): 3-87943
Orders to: Koch, Neff, Oetinger & Co Verlagsauslieferung GmbH, Postfach 800620, 70506 Stuttgart

Mueller & Schindler Verlag ek
Sonnenbergstr 55, 70184 Stuttgart
Tel: (0711) 233204 *Fax:* (0711) 2369977
Key Personnel
Owner: Rolf Mueller
Founded: 1965
Subjects: Art, History, Religion - Other
ISBN Prefix(es): 3-87560

C F Mueller Verlag, Huethig Gmb H & Co+
Im Weiher 10, 69121 Heidelberg
Mailing Address: Postfach 10 28 69, 69121 Heidelberg
Tel: (06221) 489 395 *Fax:* (06221) 489623
E-mail: cfmueller@huethig.de
Web Site: www.huethig.de
Founded: 1797
Subjects: Architecture & Interior Design, Energy, Engineering (General), Technology, Technical books
ISBN Prefix(es): 3-7880
Number of titles publishied annually: 16 Print
Parent Company: Huethig GmbH & Co KG

Verlag Karl Mueller GmbH+
Nattermann Allee 1, 50829 Cologne
Tel: (0221) 130 65-0 *Fax:* (0221) 130 65-299
E-mail: info@karl-mueller-verlag.de
Web Site: www.karl-mueller-verlag.de
Key Personnel
Man Dir: Guido Zanolli
Founded: 1980
ISBN Prefix(es): 3-86070

Verlag Norbert Mueller AG & Co KG+
Emmy-Noetherstr 2, 80992 Munich
Tel: (089) 5485201 *Fax:* (089) 54852192
E-mail: info@vnm.de
Web Site: www.vnm.de
Key Personnel
Publications Manager: Traude Wuest *Tel:* (089) 35093213 *E-mail:* t.west@vnm.de
Advertising Manager: Gabriele David *Tel:* (089) 35093204 *E-mail:* g.david@vnm.de
Rights Director, Foreign Affairs: Maria Pinto-Peuckmann *Tel:* (089) 548 52-84 26 *Fax:* (089) 548 52-84 21
Contact: Christian Luetgenau
Founded: 1968
Publisher of newsletters.
Subjects: Finance, Management, Marketing, Real Estate
ISBN Prefix(es): 3-920663; 3-89486
Parent Company: Verlag Moderne Industrie, Justus-Von-Liebig Str 1, 86899 Landsberg am Lech
U.S. Office(s): Verlag Norbert Mueller, 15775 Hillcrest, Suite 508, Dallas, TX 75248-4106, United States
Shipping Address: Verlag Moderne Industrie, Justus-Von-Liebig Str 1, 86899 Landsberg am Lech
Warehouse: Verlag Moderne Industrie, Justus-Von-Liebig Str 1, 86899 Landsberg am Lech

Mueller und Steinicke Verlag
Aidenbachstr 78, 81379 Munich
Tel: (089) 74 99 156 *Fax:* (089) 74 99 157
E-mail: info@mueller-und-steinicke.de
Web Site: www.mueller-und-steinicke.de
Key Personnel
Manager: Werner Gissler
Founded: 1903
Subjects: Medicine, Nursing, Dentistry
ISBN Prefix(es): 3-87569

Muensterschwarzacher Kleinschriften, *imprint of* Vier Tuerme GmbH Verlag Klosterbetriebe

Muensterschwarzacher Studien, *imprint of* Vier Tuerme GmbH Verlag Klosterbetriebe

Multi Media Kunst Verlag Dresden+
Sarrasanistr 13, 01097 Dresden
Tel: (0351) 8041291 *Fax:* (0351) 8041291
Key Personnel
Author, Publisher: Hans Kromer
Founded: 1990
Subjects: Art, Literature, Literary Criticism, Essays
ISBN Prefix(es): 3-9700002

Mundo Verlag GmbH
Schreberstr 2, 51105 Cologne
Tel: (0180) 9216350 *Fax:* (0180) 921635-24
E-mail: info@mundo-media.de
Web Site: www.mundo-text.de
Key Personnel
Man Dir: Ertay Hayit *E-mail:* ertay.hayit@mundo-media.de
Editorial: Cornelia Auschra *Tel:* (0221) 921635-13 *E-mail:* auschra@mundo-media.de; Mike Gahn *E-mail:* gahn@mundo-media.de; Ute Hayit *Tel:* (0221) 921635-11 *E-mail:* ute.hayit@mundo-media.de
Founded: 1982
Subjects: Travel
ISBN Prefix(es): 3-89607; 3-87322

Munich, Edition, Verlag, Handels-und Dienstleistungskontar GmbH
Angererstr 12, 80796 Munich
Mailing Address: Postfach 400128, 80701 Munich
Tel: (089) 349830 *Fax:* (089) 349834
E-mail: bzit99e@benezit.de
Key Personnel
Manager: Harry Blattel
Founded: 1990
Subjects: Art, Wine & Spirits
ISBN Prefix(es): 3-928263

Munzinger-Archiv GmbH Archiv fuer publizistische Arbeit+
Albersfelderstr 34, 88213 Ravensburg
Tel: (0751) 76931-0 *Fax:* (0751) 65 24 24
E-mail: box@munzinger.de
Web Site: www.munzinger.de
Key Personnel
Manager: Ernst Munzinger
Founded: 1913
Subjects: Biography, Economics, Foreign Countries, Government, Political Science, History, Music, Dance, Sports, Athletics

Musikantiquariat und Dr Hans Schneider Verlag GmbH+
Mozartstr 6, 82323 Tutzing
Tel: (08158) 3050; (08158) 6967 *Fax:* (08158) 7636
E-mail: musikbuch@aol.com; musikantiquar@aol.com *Cable:* MUSIKANTIQUAR
Key Personnel
Manager: Dr Hans Schneider
Founded: 1949
Subjects: Antiques, Biography, History, Music, Dance, Science (General)
ISBN Prefix(es): 3-7952

Musikverlag Zimmermann+
Strubbergstr 80, 60489 Frankfurt am Main
Tel: (069) 978286-6 *Fax:* (069) 978286-89
E-mail: info@zimmermann-frankfurt.de; lektorat@zimmermann-frankfurt.de
Web Site: www.zimmermann-frankfurt.de
Key Personnel
Man Dir: Cornelia Grossmann *Tel:* (069) 978 286-79 *E-mail:* grossmann@zimmermann-frankfurt.de; Michael Kary *Fax:* (069) 978 286-79 *E-mail:* kary@zimmermann-frankfurt.de
International Rights: Saskia Herchenroeder
Sales & Distribution: Aynalem Gebremedhim *Tel:* (069) 978 286-86 *E-mail:* info@zimmermann-frankfurt.de; Michael Henne *Tel:* (069) 978 826-86 *E-mail:* henne@zimmermann-frankfurt.de
Rights & Licensing: Saskia Bieber *Tel:* (069) 978 286-72 *Fax:* (069) 978 286-79 *E-mail:* bieber@zimmermann-frankfurt.de
Advertising, Public Relations: Ulrike Osterhage *Tel:* (069) 978 286-75 *Fax:* (069) 978 286-79 *E-mail:* osterhage@zimmermann-frankfurt.de
Editorial & Production: Friedhelm Neubert *Tel:* (069) 978 286-79 *E-mail:* neubert@zimmermann-frankfurt.de; Judith Picard *Tel:* (069) 978 286-76 *Fax:* (069) 978 286-79 *E-mail:* picard@lienau-frankfurt.de; Peter Ruecker *Tel:* (069) 978 286-73 *Fax:* (069) 978 286-79 *E-mail:* ruecker@zimmermann-frankfurt.de
Subjects: Music, Dance
ISBN Prefix(es): 3-921729
Associate Companies: Robert Lienau Musikverlag, Frankfurt

PUBLISHERS — GERMANY

Muster-Schmidt Verlag+
Schuhstr, 37154 Sudheim
Tel: (05551) 908420 *Fax:* (05551) 9084229
E-mail: info@muster-schmidt.de
Web Site: www.muster-schmidt.de *Cable:* MUSTERSCHMIDT
Key Personnel
Dir: Eva Maria Gerhardy-Loecken
  E-mail: muster-schmidt@t-online.de
Founded: 1905
Subjects: Biography, History, Color
ISBN Prefix(es): 3-7881
Branch Office(s)
Nansenstr 1, 8050 Zurich, Switzerland *Tel:* (01) 251 75 71 *Fax:* (01) 252 44 68 *E-mail:* info@muster-schmidt.de

MUT Verlag+
Bahnhofstr 1, 27330 Asendorf
Mailing Address: Postfach 1, 27328 Asendorf
Tel: (04253) 566; (04253) 672 *Fax:* (04253) 1603
Key Personnel
Man Dir, Rights & Permissions: Bernhard C Wintzek
Founded: 1972
Subjects: Government, Political Science, History, Culture
ISBN Prefix(es): 3-89182

MVB Marketing- und Verlagsservice des Buchhandels GmbH
Formerly Buchhaendler-Vereinigung GmbH
Grosser Hirschgraben 17/21, 60311 Frankfurt
Mailing Address: Postfach 10 04 42, 60004 Frankfurt
Tel: (069) 1306-0; (069) 1306-339 (Boersenblatt); (069) 1306-340 (Boersenblatt) *Fax:* (069) 1306-201
E-mail: info@mvb-online.de
Web Site: www.mvb-online.de
Key Personnel
Management: Dr Michael Schoen *Tel:* (069) 1306-225 *Fax:* (069) 1306-545
Advertising Manager: Lilli Fleck *Tel:* (069) 1306-217 *E-mail:* l.fleck@mvb-online.de
Founded: 1947
Subjects: Publishing & Book Trade Reference
ISBN Prefix(es): 3-7657
Total Titles: 200 Print; 15 CD-ROM
Parent Company: Boersenverein des Deutschen Buchhandels ev

Nadif, *imprint of* Daco Verlag Guenter Blase oHG

Verlag Stephanie Naglschmid+
Senefelderstr 10, 70178 Stuttgart
Tel: (0711) 62 68 78 *Fax:* (0711) 61 23 23
E-mail: naglschmid.vsn@t-online.de
Web Site: www.naglschmid.de
Key Personnel
Contact: Dr Friedrich Naglschmid; Stephanie Naglschmid
Founded: 1984
Also acts as book dealer for Diving Literature.
Subjects: Biological Sciences, Environmental Studies, Film, Video, Natural History, Outdoor Recreation, Photography, Physical Sciences, Sports, Athletics, Travel
ISBN Prefix(es): 3-927913; 3-89594; 3-925342
Associate Companies: JLVA Internationale Lizenzvewertungs-Agentur; MTI (Medien - und Touristik Informations Services); Divemaster (Touchmagatin)
Imprints: Edition Hannemann; Edition Schwab

Verlag Natur & Wissenschaft Harro Hieronimus & Dr Jurgen Schmidt (Nature & Science Publishing)+
Dompfaffweg 53, 42659 Solingen
Mailing Address: Postfach 170209, 42624 Solingen
Tel: (0212) 819878 *Fax:* (0212) 816216
E-mail: info@verlagnw.de
Key Personnel
Contact: Harro Hieronimus
Founded: 1989
Membership(s): the Stock Exchange of German Booksellers.
Subjects: Animals, Pets, Biological Sciences, Earth Sciences, Environmental Studies, Gardening, Plants, Geography, Geology, Natural History
ISBN Prefix(es): 3-927889; 3-936616
Imprints: Bibliothek Natur & Wissenschaft
Distributor for ACS-Verlag

NaturaViva Verlags GmbH+
Lukas-Moser-Weg 4, 71263 Weil der Stadt
Mailing Address: Postfach 1203, 71256 Weil der Stadt
Tel: (07033) 529830 *Fax:* (07033) 529831
E-mail: naturaviva@t-online.de
Key Personnel
Man Dir: Simone Graff
Founded: 1999
Membership(s): Borsenverein des Deutschen Buchhandels eV.
Subjects: Health, Nutrition
ISBN Prefix(es): 3-89881; 3-935407
Number of titles published annually: 6 Print
Total Titles: 80 Print
Imprints: Fit fuers Leben Verlag; Waldthausen Verlag
Distributed by Walter Haedecke Verlag

Naumann & Goebel Verlagsgesellschaft mbH
Emil-Hoffmann Str 1, 50996 Cologne
Mailing Address: Postfach 501863, 50978 Cologne
Tel: (02236) 39990 *Fax:* (02236) 399997
E-mail: einstieg@aol.com; fdvemag@netcologne.de
Telex: 8886642
Key Personnel
Manager: Guenter Goebel; Juergen Naumann; Juergen Krause
Subjects: Animals, Pets, Art, Biblical Studies, Computer Science, Cookery, Crafts, Games, Hobbies, Education, Fashion, Fiction, Gardening, Plants, Health, Nutrition, History, House & Home, How-to, Mathematics, Medicine, Nursing, Dentistry, Science (General), Travel, Family & Relationships, Foreign Language Study, Nature
ISBN Prefix(es): 3-625; 3-632; 3-8247; 3-88703; 3-923723
Associate Companies: Delphin AG; Delphin Verlag GmbH; Tigris Verlag GmbH; Naturalis Verlags- u Vertriebsges mbH; Daumueller Werbeges mbH; Reichenbach Verlag GmbH; Verlag Das persoenliche Geburtstagsbuch GmbH; V & M Verlags & Mediengesellschaft Koeln mbH; Neuer Pawlak Verlag GmbH; MZ Medien Zentrum GmbH

Edition Nautilus Verlag+
Alte Hostenstr 22, 21031 Hamburg
Tel: (040) 7213536 *Fax:* (040) 7218399
E-mail: edition-nautilus@t-online.de
Web Site: www.edition-nautilus.de
Key Personnel
Owner: Lutz Schulenburg
Rights & Permissions: Hanna Mittelstaedt
Editiorial & Press: Katharina Leunig
Production: Klaus Voss
Founded: 1974
Subjects: Art, Biography, Government, Political Science, Literature, Literary Criticism, Essays
ISBN Prefix(es): 3-89401; 3-921523
Distributed by Mohr/Morawa (Austria); Scheidegger & Co AG (Switzerland); SoVa Gmbh

NDV Neue Darmstadter Verlagsanstalt
Hauptstr 74, 53619 Rheinbreitbach
Mailing Address: Postfach 1560, 53585 Bad Honnef
Tel: (02224) 3232 *Fax:* (02224) 78639
E-mail: ndv@ndv.info
Web Site: www.ndv-verlag.de
Key Personnel
Publisher, Rights & Permissions: Klaus J Holzapfel; Andreas Holzapfel
Editor: Susanne Dirkwinkel
Sales: Sylke Beyer
Marketing, Sales: Markus Fleischer
Founded: 1949
Subjects: Government, Political Science
ISBN Prefix(es): 3-87576
Branch Office(s)
Wittestr 30 K, 13509 Berlin *Tel:* (030) 8557511 *Fax:* (030) 85605332

Nebel Verlag GmbH
Bahnhofsplatz 4, 86919 Utting
Mailing Address: Postfach 1153, 86917 Utting
Tel: (08806) 9215-0 *Fax:* (08806) 9215-22
Key Personnel
Contact: Pirmin Nebel
Founded: 1989
Subjects: Cookery, Gardening, Plants, History, Literature, Literary Criticism, Essays, Romance, Travel
ISBN Prefix(es): 3-89555

Neckar Verlag GmbH+
Klosterring 1, 78008 Villingen-Schwenningen
Mailing Address: Postfach 1820, 78008 Villingen-Schwenningen
Tel: (07721) 89 87-0 *Fax:* (07721) 89 87-50
E-mail: service@neckar-verlag.de
Web Site: www.neckar-verlag.de
Key Personnel
Man Dir: Inge Holtzhauer; Dr Heinz Loercher
Marketing: Peter Walter *Tel:* (07721) 87 87-45
  E-mail: walter@neckar-verlag.de
Founded: 1945
Subjects: Aeronautics, Aviation, Literature, Literary Criticism, Essays, Literature & Plans for RC-Model Aircraft & RC-Model Ship
ISBN Prefix(es): 3-7883

Neff, *imprint of* Pabel-Moewig Verlag KG

Nelles Verlag GmbH+
Schleissheimerstr 371b, 80935 Munich
Tel: (089) 357 19 40 *Fax:* (089) 357 19 430
E-mail: info@nelles-verlag.de
Web Site: www.nelles-verlag.de
Key Personnel
Man Dir, Rights & Permissions: Guenter Nelles
Man Dir: Martin Nelles
Founded: 1975
Subjects: Travel
ISBN Prefix(es): 3-88618; 3-920397; 3-922539
Orders to: Geocenter/ILH, Postfach 800830, 70508 Stuttgart

Net World Vision GmbH+
Thomas-Wimmer-Ring 11, 80539 Munich
Tel: (089) 290 88 0 *Fax:* (089) 290 88 160
Key Personnel
Publisher: Helmar Hipp *Tel:* (089) 3473-0
  E-mail: helmar.hipp@systhema.de
Founded: 1988
Specialize in film, literature, languages & encyclopedia.
Subjects: Art, Computer Science, History, Language Arts, Linguistics, Natural History, Multimedia
ISBN Prefix(es): 3-89390; 3-634
Total Titles: 180 CD-ROM
Parent Company: United Soft Media GmbH
Bookshop(s): HMH, Sportallee 41, 22335 Hamburg *Tel:* (040) 51456-0

Shipping Address: HMH, Sportallee 41, 22335 Hamburg *Fax:* (040) 51456-990
Warehouse: HMH, Sportallee 41, 22335 Hamburg
Orders to: NVG Neue Verlagsges, Am Ziegelplatz 12, 77746 Schutlerwald *Tel:* (0781) 6396894 *Fax:* (0781) 846145

Neue Darmstadter Verlagsanstalt, see NDV Neue Darmstadter Verlagsanstalt

Neue Dimension Buch und Musikverlag+
In der Lohe 13-15, 90765 Fuerth
Founded: 1987
Subjects: Health, Nutrition, Music, Dance, Religion - Other
ISBN Prefix(es): 3-9802129; 3-928091; 3-89690
Divisions: Hans Peter Neuber
Orders to: Silenzio GmbH, Hainbrunnenstr 8, 91391 Forchheim

Neue Erde Verlags GmbH+
Cecilienstr 29, 66111 Saarbruecken
Tel: (0681) 372313 *Fax:* (0681) 3904102
E-mail: info@neueerde.de
Key Personnel
Publisher: Andreas Lentz
Founded: 1984
Subjects: Environmental Studies, Parapsychology, Self-Help
ISBN Prefix(es): 3-89060
Imprints: Ryvellus

Verlag Neue Kritik KG+
Kettenhofweg 53, 60325 Frankfurt
Tel: (069) 727576 *Fax:* (069) 726585
E-mail: neuekritik@compuserve.com
Key Personnel
Man Dir: Dorothea Rein
Founded: 1965
Subjects: Art, Fiction, Philosophy, Poetry, Women's Studies, Judaica
ISBN Prefix(es): 3-8015
Orders to: Sozialistische Verlagsauslieferung GmbH, Franziusstr 44, 60314 Frankfurt am Main

Verlag Neue Musik GmbH
Grabbeallee 15, 13156 Berlin
Tel: (030) 616981-0 *Fax:* (030) 616981-21
E-mail: vnm@verlag-neue-musik.de
Web Site: www.verlag-neue-musik.de
Key Personnel
Dir: Detlef Kessler
Manager: Axel Muetze-Kern
Founded: 1957
Subjects: Music, Dance
ISBN Prefix(es): 3-7333
Subsidiaries: Edition Margaux

Verlag Neue Musikzeitung GmbH
Brunnstr 23, 93053 Regensburg
Tel: (0941) 94 59 30 *Fax:* (0941) 94 59 350
E-mail: nmz@nmz.de
Web Site: www.nmz.de
Key Personnel
Publisher & Chief Editor: Theo Geissler
Editor-in-Chief: Gerhard Rohde
Editorial Manager: Andreas Kolb
Founded: 1993
Subjects: Art, Ethnicity, Music, Dance
Parent Company: Con Brio Verlagsgesellschaft mbH, Postfach 100245, Brunnstr 23, 93053 Regensburg

Verlag Neue Stadt GmbH+
Mangfallstr 29, 81547 Munich
Tel: (08093) 2091 *Fax:* (08093) 2096 *Cable:* NEUE STADT
Key Personnel
Man Dir: Wolfgang Bader
Sales, Publicity & Advertising: Gabriele Hartl
Rights: Stefan Liesenfeld
Founded: 1961
Subjects: Biblical Studies, Biography, Fiction, How-to, Music, Dance, Religion - Other, Theology, Autobiography, Family & Relationships
ISBN Prefix(es): 3-87996
Parent Company: Citta Nuova Editrice, Italy
Branch Office(s)
Trostr 116, 1100 Vienna, Austria
Seestr 426, Postfach 435, 8038 Zurich, Switzerland

Verlag Neue Wirtschafts-Briefe GmbH & Co+
Eschstr 22, 44629 Herne
Tel: (02323) 141-900 *Fax:* (02323) 141-123
E-mail: info@nwb.de
Web Site: www.nwb.de *Cable:* STEUERBRIEFE HERNE
Key Personnel
Publisher: Dr Karl-Friedrich Peter
Man Dir: E O Kleyboldt
Sales & Advertising Dir: J Mueller-Grote
Founded: 1947
Subjects: Accounting, Business, Career Development, Law
ISBN Prefix(es): 3-482
Associate Companies: Verlag fuer die Rechts- und Anwaltspraxis GmbH & Co KG
Subsidiaries: Friedrich Kiehl Verlag GmbH
Shipping Address: Schuechtermannstr 180, 44628 Herne
Warehouse: Schuechtermannstr 180, 44628 Herne
Orders to: Postfach 101849, 44621 Herne

Neuer Honos Verlag GmbH+
Emil-Hoffmann- Str 1, 50996 Cologne
Tel: (0221) 3 36 20-0 *Fax:* (0221) 3 36 20-99
E-mail: nhonos@netcologne.de
Key Personnel
Chief Executive Officer: Stefan Sommer
Tel: (0221) 336200
Founded: 1998
Subjects: Animals, Pets, Biblical Studies, Computer Science, Cookery, Fiction, Health, Nutrition, How-to, Language Arts, Linguistics, Nonfiction (General), Travel, Health & Fitness, Foreign Language Study, Nature
ISBN Prefix(es): 3-8299
Warehouse: GVA, Gesellschaft fur Verlagsauslieferung & Logistik mbH, Heideweg 8a, 36160 Bad-Bwischenahn *Tel:* (0441) 969412 *Fax:* (0441) 969415

Neuer ISP Verlag GmbH
Marienstr 15, 76137 Karlsruhe
Tel: (0721) 31 183 *Fax:* (0721) 31 250
E-mail: alive@sterneck.net
Web Site: www.sterneck.net/alive/isp
Key Personnel
Manager, Rights & Permissions: Wolfgang Feikert
Subjects: Economics, Government, Political Science, History, Philosophy, Social Sciences, Sociology
ISBN Prefix(es): 3-88332; 3-929008
Orders to: Buro Frankfurt Im, Kassler Str 1 a, 60486 Frankfurt

Neuer Jugendschriften-Verlag, see A Weichert Verlag GmbH & Co KG

Verlag Neuer Weg+
Alte Bottroper Str 42, 45356 Essen
Tel: (0201) 2 59 15 *Fax:* (0201) 61 444 62
E-mail: neuerweg@neuerweg.de
Web Site: www.neuerweg.de
Key Personnel
Rights & Permissions: Gert Bierikoven
Dir: Christoph Klug
Founded: 1971
Subjects: Developing Countries, Education, Environmental Studies, Government, Political Science, Health, Nutrition, History, Physical Sciences, Women's Studies
ISBN Prefix(es): 3-88021
Bookshop(s): Buchladen NeuerWeg, Reuterstr 15, 12053 Berlin; Ernst-Thaelmann-Buchhandlung, Hauptstaetter Str 39, 70173 Stuttgart

Verlag Neues Leben GmbH+
Max-Beerstr 13, 10119 Berlin
Mailing Address: Postfach 35, 10121 Berlin
Tel: (030) 2827148; (020) 2827020 *Fax:* (030) 28388075 *Cable:* NEUESLEBEN BERLIN
Key Personnel
Man Dir, Rights & Permissions: Rudolf Chowanetz
Production: Hannelore Lange
Sales: Walter Toelg
Founded: 1946
Subjects: Biography, Cookery, Fiction, Gay & Lesbian, History, Human Relations, Nonfiction (General), Religion - Jewish
ISBN Prefix(es): 3-355
Warehouse: Moor Morawa Buchvertriebsges mbH, Sulzengasse 2, 1232 Vienna, Austria
Schweizer Bucherzentrum, Postfach, 4601 Olten, Switzerland
Orders to: LKG-Verlagsauslieferung, Poetzschauer Weg, 04579 Espenhain

Neues Literaturkontor+
Goldstr 15, 48147 Muenster
Tel: (0251) 45343 *Fax:* (0251) 40565
E-mail: neues-literaturkontor@t-online.de
Web Site: www.neues-literaturkontor.de
Key Personnel
Contact: Dr Hans D Mummendey
International Rights: Dorothea Potthoff
Founded: 1990
Specialize in novels & short stories.
Subjects: Poetry
ISBN Prefix(es): 3-920591
Number of titles published annually: 5 Print
Total Titles: 60 Print

Neuland-Verlagsgesellschaft mbH+
Markt 24-26, 21502 Geesthacht
Mailing Address: Postfach 1422, 21496 Geesthacht
Tel: (04152) 8 13 42 *Fax:* (04152) 8 13 43
E-mail: vertrieb@neuland.com
Web Site: www.neuland.com
Key Personnel
Manager: Jens Burmester *E-mail:* gf@neuland.com
Founded: 1889
Specialize in the area of addictions.
Subjects: Health, Nutrition, Medicine, Nursing, Dentistry, Psychology, Psychiatry, Self-Help, Social Sciences, Sociology
ISBN Prefix(es): 3-87581

Verlag J Neumann-Neudamm GmbH & Co KG+
Schwalbenweg 1, 34212 Melsungen
Tel: (05661) 52222 *Fax:* (05661) 6008
E-mail: info@neumann-neudamm.de
Web Site: www.neumann-neudamm.de
Key Personnel
Dir: Walter Schwartz
Foreign Rights: Rolf Roosen
Founded: 1872
Subjects: Outdoor Recreation, Science (General), Sports, Athletics
ISBN Prefix(es): 3-7888
Subsidiaries: JANA (Gesellschaft fur Jagd und Natur GmbH)

Neumann Verlag+
Wollgrasweg 41, 70599 Stuttgart
Tel: (0711) 4507-0 *Fax:* (0711) 4507-240
Founded: 1990

Subjects: Animals, Pets, Biological Sciences, Environmental Studies, Gardening, Plants, House & Home, Natural History, Science (General), Travel
ISBN Prefix(es): 3-7402
Orders to: Eugen Ulmer Verlag Stuttgart *Tel:* (0711) 4507-124 *Fax:* (0711) 4507-120 *E-mail:* vertrieb@ulmer.de *Web Site:* www.ulmer.de

Verlag fuer Messepublikationen Thomas Neureuter KG
Sueskindstr 4, 81929 Munich
Tel: (089) 99 30 91-0 *Fax:* (089) 93 78 96
E-mail: info@neureuter.de
Web Site: www.neureuter.de
Telex: 522918 mesu d
Key Personnel
Publisher: Thomas Neureuter
Founded: 1948
ISBN Prefix(es): 3-921362
Branch Office(s)
Leipziger Messe Verlag und Vertriebsgesellschaft mbH, Messe-Allee 1, 04358 Leipzig *Tel:* (0341) 67 877-0 *Fax:* (0341) 67 877-12 *E-mail:* info@leipziger-messeverlag.de *Web Site:* www.leipziger-messeverlag.de
Chuang's Enterprises Bldg, Room 1003, 10/F, 382 Lockhart Rd, Wanchai, Hong Kong *Tel:* 2519 3581 *Fax:* 2519 6941 *E-mail:* info@neureuter.com.hk *Web Site:* www.neureuter.com.hk
Binterimstr 13, Duesseldorf *Tel:* (0211) 34 20 26 *Fax:* (0211) 33 34 85

Neuthor - Verlag+
Obere Pfarrgasse 31, 64720 Michelstadt
Tel: (06061) 40 79 *Fax:* (06061) 26 46
Web Site: www.neuthor-verlag.de
Key Personnel
Publisher: Peter-Jochen Bosse *E-mail:* bosse@neuthor-verlag.de
Founded: 1980
Subjects: Architecture & Interior Design, Biography, Fiction, Foreign Countries, History, Mysteries, Travel
ISBN Prefix(es): 3-88758

New Era Publications Deutschland GmbH
Hittfelder Kirchweg 5a, 21220 Seevetal-Maschen
Tel: (04105) 68330 *Fax:* (04150) 683322
E-mail: buch@newerapublications.de
Web Site: www.newerapublications.com
Key Personnel
Manager: Thomas Goeldenitz
Founded: 1985
Subjects: Religion - Other, Science Fiction, Fantasy, Self-Help
ISBN Prefix(es): 3-929284
Parent Company: New Era Publications Int Aps, Stove Kangensgade 55, 1264 Copenhagen, Denmark

Nicolaische Verlagsbuchhandlung Beuermann GmbH+
Neuenburger Str 17, 10969 Berlin
Tel: (030) 253738-0 *Fax:* (030) 253738-39
E-mail: info@nicolai-verlag.de
Web Site: www.nicolai-verlag.de
Key Personnel
Publisher: Dr Hans von Trotha
Marketing: Susanne Boger *Tel:* (030) 253738-12 *Fax:* (030) 253738-40 *E-mail:* susanne.boger@nicolai-verlag.de
Rights & Licenses: Irene von Trotha *Tel:* (030) 253738-33 *Fax:* (030) 253738-39 *E-mail:* irene.trotha@nicolai-verlag.de
Subjects: Architecture & Interior Design, Art, Biography, Photography, Regional Interests

ISBN Prefix(es): 3-87584; 3-89479; 3-9803217
Orders to: S Fischer Velope, 60591 Frankfurt/Main *Tel:* (069) 6062-0 *Fax:* (069) 6062-21X

Nie/Nie/Sagen-Verlag+
Silvanerweg 17, 78464 Konstanz
Tel: (07531) 53570 *Fax:* (07531) 64496
E-mail: haberkern-imz@t-online.de
Web Site: www.nie-nie-sagen-verlag.de
Key Personnel
Publisher: Atina Haberkern
Founded: 1977
Subjects: Literature, Literary Criticism, Essays, Poetry, Religion - Buddhist, Religion - Other, Self-Help
ISBN Prefix(es): 3-921778

Niederland-Verlag Helmut Michel
Winnendestr 20, 71522 Backnang
Mailing Address: Postfach 1480, 71504 Backnang
Tel: (07191) 3277-200 *Fax:* (07191) 3277-15
E-mail: micheldruck@t-online.de
Key Personnel
Owner: Helmut Michel
Subjects: History, Regional Interests
ISBN Prefix(es): 3-923947

Nielsen Frederic W, see Toleranz Verlag, Nielsen Frederic W

C W Niemeyer Buchverlage GmbH+
Osterstr 19, 31785 Hameln
Tel: (05151) 200-312 *Fax:* (05151) 200-319
E-mail: info@niemeyer-buch.de
Web Site: www.niemeyer-buch.de
Key Personnel
Publisher: Hans Freiwald
Founded: 1797
Membership(s): Borsenverein des Deutschen Buchhandels.
Subjects: Architecture & Interior Design, Art, Fiction, History, Humor, Library & Information Sciences, Literature, Literary Criticism, Essays, Mysteries
ISBN Prefix(es): 3-8271
Subsidiaries: Adolf Sponholtz Verlag
Orders to: VSB - Verlagsservice Braunschweig GmbH, Postfach 4738, 38037 Braunschweig *Tel:* (0531) 708650 *Fax:* (0531) 708608

Max Niemeyer Verlag GmbH+
Pfrondorferstr 6, 72074 Tuebingen
Mailing Address: Postfach 2140, 72011 Tuebingen
Tel: (07071) 98 94 0 *Fax:* (07071) 98 94 50
E-mail: max@niemeyer.de; info@niemeyer.de
Web Site: www.niemeyer.de *Cable:* NIEMEYER TUBINGEN
Key Personnel
Man Dir: Robert Harsch-Niemeyer; Nikolaus Steinberg
Publicity & Marketing: Karin Wenzel *Tel:* (07071) 989413 *E-mail:* wenzel@niemeyer.de
Editorial Dir: Birgitta Zeller *E-mail:* zeller@niemeyer.de
International Rights: Marlene Kirton *Tel:* (07071) 989427 *E-mail:* kirton@niemeyer.de
Marketing: Barbara Opel *E-mail:* opel@niemeyer.de
Sales: Nikolaus Steinberg
Founded: 1870
Subjects: History, Language Arts, Linguistics, Literature, Literary Criticism, Essays, Philosophy
ISBN Prefix(es): 3-484
Number of titles published annually: 160 Print

Nieswand-Verlag GmbH+
Werftbahnstr 8, 24143 Kiel
Tel: (0431) 7028 200 *Fax:* (0431) 7028 228

E-mail: vertrieb@nieswandverlag.de
Web Site: www.nieswandverlag.de
Manager: Jens Nieswand
Co-Editor: Ingo Wulff
Marketing: Ines Heinrich
Rights & Permissions: Melanie Voss
Sales: Carola Dreller *Tel:* (0431) 7028 218
Founded: 1986
Membership(s): the Stock Exchange of German Booksellers.
Subjects: Art, Music, Dance, Photography
ISBN Prefix(es): 3-926048; 3-89567
Orders to: Coen Sligting Bookimport, Paulus Potterstraat 20, 1071 DA Amsterdam, Netherlands (International Distributor)
PNV Vertriebsservice GmbH, Werftbahnstr 8, 24143 Kiel
DAP Distributed Art Publishers, 155 Avenue of the Americas, 2nd floor, New York, NY 10013-1507, United States *Tel:* 212-627-1999

Hans-Nietsch-Verlag+
Poststr 3, 79098 Freiburg
Mailing Address: PO Box 228, 79002 Freiburg
Tel: (0761) 2966930 *Fax:* (0761) 2966960
E-mail: mail@nietsch.de
Web Site: www.nietsch.de
Key Personnel
Contact: Hans Nietsch
Subjects: Religion - Other, Health, Occult
ISBN Prefix(es): 3-934647; 3-929475
Number of titles published annually: 10 Print
Total Titles: 100 Print
Imprints: Edition Sternenprinz
Distributor for Verlag Hans-Juergen Maurer; Edition Synthese
Distribution Center: Val Silberschnur, Steinstr 1, 56593 Guellesheim

Rainar Nitzsche Verlag+
Gasstr 34, 67655 Kaiserslautern
Tel: (0631) 61305 *Fax:* (0631) 61305
E-mail: rainar.nitzscheverlag@t-online.de
Web Site: home.t-online.de/home/Rainar.NitzscheVerlag/nitzscheb.htm
Key Personnel
Contact: Dr Rainar Nitzsche
Founded: 1989
Subjects: Behavioral Sciences, Biological Sciences, Science Fiction, Fantasy
ISBN Prefix(es): 3-9802102; 3-930304

Nobel-Verlag GmbH Vertrieb Neue Medien+
Kronprinzenstr 13, 45128 Essen
Tel: (0201) 81300 *Fax:* (0201) 8130108
E-mail: mplatzkoester@beleke.de
Web Site: www.gewusst-wo.de; www.nobel.de
Key Personnel
Contact: Dr Michael Platzkoester
ISBN Prefix(es): 3-922785

Florian Noetzel Verlag+
Holtermannstr 32, 26384 Wilhelmshaven
Mailing Address: Postfach 1443, 26353 Wilhelmshaven
Tel: (04421) 4 30 03 *Fax:* (04421) 4 29 85
E-mail: florian.noetzel@t-online.de
Key Personnel
Contact: Florian Noetzel
Founded: 1986
Subjects: Music, Dance
ISBN Prefix(es): 3-7959

Nomos Verlagsgesellschaft mbH und Co KG
Waldseestr 3-5, 76530 Baden-Baden
Tel: (07221) 2104-0 *Fax:* (07221) 210427
E-mail: nomos@nomos.de
Web Site: www.nomos.de
Key Personnel
Man Dir: Dr Alfred Hoffmann
Publicity: Christian Kamradt
Founded: 1936

GERMANY

Subjects: Business, Economics, Government, Political Science, Law, Social Sciences, Sociology
ISBN Prefix(es): 3-7890; 3-8329

Nusser Verlag+
Kaufbeurerstr 3, 80997 Munich
Mailing Address: Postfach 701265, 80312 Munich
Tel: (089) 146788 *Fax:* (089) 1493206
Web Site: www.nusserverlag.de
Key Personnel
Man Dir: Dr Horst Nusser *E-mail:* dr.nusser@nusserverlag.de
Sales: Sibylle Nusser-Festner *Tel:* (089) 1406750 *E-mail:* sibylle_nusser@web.de
Founded: 1972
Print books & publishing on demand.
Subjects: Agriculture, Art, Asian Studies, Biological Sciences, Developing Countries, Economics, Education, Environmental Studies, Foreign Countries, Geography, Geology, Government, Political Science, History, Labor, Industrial Relations, Medicine, Nursing, Dentistry, Military Science, Religion - Buddhist, Religion - Catholic, Religion - Hindu, Religion - Islamic, Religion - Jewish, Religion - Protestant, Science (General)
ISBN Prefix(es): 3-88091; 3-86120
Number of titles published annually: 20 Print
Total Titles: 1,000 Print
Subsidiaries: Nusser Verlag; International Picture- & Press-agency

nymphenburger+
Subsidiary of Buchverlage Langen-Mueller/Herbig
Thomas-Wimmer-Ring 11, 80539 Munich
Tel: (089) 2 90 88-0 *Fax:* (089) 2 90 88-1 44
E-mail: nymphenburger@herbig.net
Web Site: www.herbig.net
Key Personnel
Man Dir & Publisher: Brigitte Fleissner-Mikorey
Rights & Permissions: Frauke Hoppen *Fax:* (089) 2 90 88-1 78 *E-mail:* fhoppen@herbig.net
Founded: 1946
Subjects: Art, Biography, Child Care & Development, Crafts, Games, Hobbies, Fiction, Health, Nutrition, Nonfiction (General), Outdoor Recreation, Philosophy, Photography, Religion - Buddhist, Self-Help, Sports, Athletics, True life stories
ISBN Prefix(es): 3-485
Total Titles: 25 Print
Parent Company: F A Herbig Verlagsbuchhandlung GmbH (Germany)
Associate Companies: Langen Mueller Herbig, Thomas-Wimmer-Ring 11, 80539 Munich, Contact: Lydia Eggs *Tel:* (089) 290880 *Fax:* (089) 29088155
Imprints: Edition Meyster
Distributed by Mohr Morawa Buchvertrieb; Schweizer Buchzentrum
Warehouse: VVA-Bertelsmann Distribution GmbH, Warenannahme 100, An der Autobahn, 33310 Gutersloh
Orders to: VVA-Vereinigte Verlagsauslieferung, Postfach 7600, 33310 Gutersloh, Contact: Renate Fechtelhoff *Tel:* (05209) 805403 *Fax:* (05209) 806643

Oberbaum Verlag GmbH+
Friedelstr 6, 12047 Berlin
Tel: (030) 624 69 21 *Fax:* (030) 624 69 21
Key Personnel
Man Dir: Siegfried Heinrichs
Founded: 1966
Subjects: Government, Political Science, History, Literature, Literary Criticism, Essays, Regional Interests
ISBN Prefix(es): 3-926409; 3-928254; 3-933314

Edition Octopus & Okeanos Presse+
Ennigerstr 16, 59320 Ennigerloh
Tel: (02524) 2502
Key Personnel
Man Dir: H G Kestel
Founded: 1987
Subjects: Art, Astrology, Occult, Drama, Theater, Literature, Literary Criticism, Essays, Photography, Poetry, Religion - Other
ISBN Prefix(es): 3-926850

Oeko-Test Verlag GmbH & Co KG Betriebsgesellschaft
Kasslerstr 1A, 60486 Frankfurt am Main
Mailing Address: Postfach 90 07 66, 60447 Frankfurt am Main
Tel: (069) 9 77 77-0 *Fax:* (069) 9 77 77-139
E-mail: oet.verlag@oekotest.de
Web Site: www.oekotest.de
Key Personnel
Man Dir: Bernd Waeltz; Albrecht Martin
Editor: Juergen Stellpflug
Publicity & Marketing: Anette Elnain *Tel:* (069) 9 77 77-133 *E-mail:* anette.elnain@oekotest.de; Friederike Elnain *Tel:* (069) 9 77 77-138 *E-mail:* friederike.elnain@oekotest.de
Founded: 1985
Subjects: Environmental Studies, Health, Nutrition
ISBN Prefix(es): 3-929530

Oekobuch Verlag & Versand GmbH+
Gewerbestr 15a, 79219 Staufen
Mailing Address: Postfach 1126, 79216 Staufen
Tel: (07633) 50613 *Fax:* (07633) 50870
E-mail: oekobuch@t-online.de
Web Site: www.oekobuch.de
Key Personnel
Man Dir: Claudia Ladener
Contact: Heinz Ladener
Founded: 1979
Subjects: Architecture & Interior Design, Civil Engineering, Crafts, Games, Hobbies, Energy, Environmental Studies, House & Home
ISBN Prefix(es): 3-922964
Total Titles: 42 Print

Oekotopia Verlag, Wolfgang Hoffman GmbH & Co KG+
Hafenweg 26a, 48155 Muenster
Tel: (0251) 48198-0 *Fax:* (0251) 48198-29
E-mail: info@oekotopia-verlag.de
Web Site: www.oekotopia-verlag.de
Key Personnel
Man Dir: Wolfgang Hoffmann; Stefan Scholz *E-mail:* scholz@oekotopia-verlag.de
Founded: 1983
Specialize in Environmental/Education.
Subjects: Drama, Theater, Education, Environmental Studies, Fiction, History, Human Relations, Humor, Music, Dance, Nonfiction (General), Outdoor Recreation, Psychology, Psychiatry
ISBN Prefix(es): 3-925169; 3-931902; 3-936286
Foreign Rights: Hercules Business & Culture Development GmbH (Republic of China, Taiwan); Living (Italy); Ute Korner Literary Agent, SL (Brazil, Latin America, Portugal, Spain)

Oekumenischer Verlag Dr R-F Edel
Rathmecker Weg 13, 58513 Luedenscheid
Tel: (02351) 51547 *Fax:* (02351) 568908
Key Personnel
Manager: Klaus Busenius
Founded: 1976
Subjects: Art, Biblical Studies, Ethnicity, History, Language Arts, Linguistics, Philosophy, Religion - Other, Theology
ISBN Prefix(es): 3-87598
Orders to: Verlagsauslieferung Klaus Busenius, Rathmecker Weg 13, 58513 Lundenscheid

Oertel & Sporer GmbH & Co+
Burgstr 1-7, 72764 Reutlingen
Mailing Address: PO Box 1642, D-72706 Reutlingen
Tel: (07121) 302 555; (07121) 302 552 *Fax:* (07121) 302 558
Telex: 729634
Key Personnel
Member of General Management: Mr Ermo Lehari *Tel:* (07121) 302 122 *Fax:* (07121) 302 123 *E-mail:* lehari@compuserve.com
Founded: 1888
Publishing & printing company
Books & Periodicals.
Subjects: Animals, Pets, Cookery, Crafts, Games, Hobbies, Nonfiction (General)
ISBN Prefix(es): 3-921017; 3-88627
Total Titles: 140 Print

Paul Oestergaard GmbH, see Columbus Verlag Paul Oestergaard GmbH

Verlag Friedrich Oetinger GmbH+
Poppenbuetteler Chaussee 53, 22397 Hamburg
Mailing Address: Postfach 658220, 22374 Hamburg
Tel: (040) 607909-02 *Fax:* (040) 6072326
E-mail: oetinger@vsg-hamburg.de
Web Site: www.oetinger.de
Key Personnel
Man Dir & Editorial: Silke Weitendorf
Man Dir & Sales: Thomas Huggle
Editorial: Marleus Niesen
Publicity: Judith Richter *Tel:* (040) 607909-65 *E-mail:* richter@vsg-hamburg.de; Frauke Wedler *Tel:* (040) 607909-23 *E-mail:* wedler@vsg-hamburg.de
Rights & Licensing: Renate Reichstein *Tel:* (040) 607909-13 *Fax:* (040) 607909-51 *E-mail:* lizenzen@vsg-hamburg.de
Sales & Marketing: Dr Juergen Huebner *Tel:* (040) 607909-55 *Fax:* (040) 607909-50 *E-mail:* marketing@vsg-hamburg.de
Marketing: Susanne Weiss *Tel:* (040) 607909-777 *Fax:* (040) 607909-50 *E-mail:* vertrieb@vsg-hamburg.de
Founded: 1946
Subjects: Fiction
ISBN Prefix(es): 3-7891
Subsidiaries: Cecilie Dressler Verlag GmbH

Dr Oetker Verlag KG+
Lutterstr 14, 33617 Bielefeld
Tel: (0521) 521 155-0 *Fax:* (0521) 521 155-2995
E-mail: presse@oetker.de
Web Site: www.oetker-gruppe.de
Key Personnel
Man Dir: Annelore Strullkoetter *Tel:* (0521) 520643 *E-mail:* strullkoetter@oetker-verlag.de
Founded: 1951
Subjects: Cookery
ISBN Prefix(es): 3-7670
Parent Company: August Oetker, Bielefeld

Verlag Offene Worte+
Striepenweg 31, 21147 Hamburg
Tel: (040) 79713-03 *Fax:* (040) 79713-324
E-mail: vertrieb@koehler-mittler.de
Web Site: www.koehler-mittler.de *Cable:* VLG OFFENE WORTE, HAMBURG/W
Key Personnel
Publisher: Wolf O Storck; Peter Tamm
Manager: Thomas Bantle
Sales: Hans-Focko Koehler
Subjects: Government, Political Science, Military Science
ISBN Prefix(es): 3-87599
Associate Companies: Koehlers Verlagsgesellschaft
Branch Office(s)
Godesberger Allee 91, 53175 Bonn *Tel:* (0228) 307890 *Fax:* (0228) 3078915

Oktagon Verlagsgesellschaft mbH+
Albertusstr 1, 50667 Cologne
Tel: (0221) 2059653-54 *Fax:* (0221) 2059660
E-mail: oktagon@buchhandlung-walterkoenig.de
Key Personnel
Manager: Paul Johannes Mueller
Founded: 1989
Subjects: Architecture & Interior Design, Art
ISBN Prefix(es): 3-927789; 3-89611
Bookshop(s): Ehrenstr 4, 50672 Cologne
 Tel: (0221) 20 59 6-0 *Fax:* (0221) 20 59 6-40
 E-mail: order@buchhandlung-walther-koenig.de

R Oldenbourg Verlag GmbH+
Rosenheimerstr 145, 81671 Munich
Mailing Address: Postfach 801360, 81613 Munich
Tel: (089) 45 05 10; (089) 45 05 12 04
Fax: (089) 45051333 (Zeitschriften); (089) 4505200 (Schulbuch); (089) 4505333 (Fachbuch)
Key Personnel
Dir: Dr Thomas von Cornides; Wolfgang Dick; Dr Dieter Hohm; Johannes Oldenbourg
Founded: 1858
Membership(s): TR-Verlagsunion GmbH.
Subjects: Education, Electronics, Electrical Engineering, Engineering (General), History, Psychology, Psychiatry, Science (General), Social Sciences, Sociology, Technology
ISBN Prefix(es): 3-486
Subsidiaries: Verlag Oldenbourg; Michael Proegel Verlag; Vulkan Verlag Essen
Showroom(s): Oldenbourg Verlag Informationszentrum, Kaufingerstr 29, 80331 Munich
Orders to: Verlegerdienst Muenchen, Auslieferung R Oldenbourg Verlag, Gutenbergstr 1, Postfach 1280, 82205 Gilching *Tel:* (08105) 3880 *Fax:* (08105) 388100

Georg Olms Verlag AG+
Hagentorwall 7, 31134 Hildesheim
Tel: (05121) 15010 *Fax:* (05121) 150150; (05121) 32007
E-mail: info@olms.de
Web Site: www.olms.de *Cable:* HILDESHEIM
Key Personnel
Publisher: Dietrich Olms *E-mail:* dietrich.olms@olms.de
Editorial: Dr Peter Guyot *E-mail:* guyot@olms.de; Doris Wendt *E-mail:* wendt@olms.de
Production: Andreas Maybaum
Rights & Permissions: Christiane Busch
Marketing, Editorial (Equestrian Titles): Danielle Schons *E-mail:* marketing@olms.de
Founded: 1945
Subjects: Antiques, Biography, Drama, Theater, Economics, Education, Gardening, Plants, Geography, Geology, Government, Political Science, History, Language Arts, Linguistics, Law, Library & Information Sciences, Literature, Literary Criticism, Essays, Music, Dance, Philosophy, Religion - Islamic, Religion - Jewish, Religion - Protestant, Romance, Science (General), Social Sciences, Sociology, Theology, Travel, Classical Studies, History of Art
ISBN Prefix(es): 3-487
Number of titles published annually: 250 Print; 3 CD-ROM
Total Titles: 5,000 Print
Parent Company: Georg Olms AG, Zurich, Switzerland
Associate Companies: Weidmannsche Verlagsbuchhandlung
Imprints: Olms New Media; Olms Presse
Subsidiaries: Edition Olms AG
U.S. Office(s): Georg Olms Verlag, Empire State Bldg, 350 Fifth Ave, Suite 3304, New York, NY 10118-0069, United States
Warehouse: VVA, Bertelsmann Distribution, 33399 Verl, Contact: Monika Hermesmeier *Tel:* (05241) 803844 *Fax:* (05241) 8060220

Olms New Media, *imprint of* Georg Olms Verlag AG

Olms Presse, *imprint of* Georg Olms Verlag AG

Oncken Verlag KG+
Bodenborn 43, 58452 Witten
Tel: (02302) 930 93 800 *Fax:* (02302) 930 93 801
E-mail: info@brockhaus-verlag.de
Web Site: www.brockhaus-verlag.de
Key Personnel
Chief Executive Officer & Publisher: Erhard Diehl
Editor & Publicity Manager: Hans-Werner Durau
International Rights: Christina Schneider
Founded: 1828
Membership(s): Stiftung Christliche Medien.
Subjects: Fiction, Religion - Other
ISBN Prefix(es): 3-7893
Associate Companies: R Brockhaus Verlag
Distributed by BMU (Austria); Brunnen (Switzerland)

Orbis Verlag fur Publizistik GmbH+
Neumarkter Str 18, 81673 Munich
Mailing Address: Postfach 800360, 81603 Munich
Tel: (089) 4372-0 *Fax:* (089) 4372-2674
Key Personnel
Man Dirs: Ortner Werner; Wolfgang Kunth
Rights & Permissions: Ms Strauss-Fischer
Founded: 1987
Subjects: Animals, Pets, Archaeology, Cookery, English as a Second Language, Gardening, Plants, Health, Nutrition, History, Language Arts, Linguistics
ISBN Prefix(es): 3-572
Parent Company: Verlagsgruppe Bertelsmann GmbH

Oreos Verlag GmbH+
Krottenthal 9, 83666 Waakirchen
Tel: (08021) 86 68 *Fax:* (08021) 17 50
Web Site: www.oreos.de
Key Personnel
Publisher: Walter Lachenmann
 E-mail: lachenmann@oreos.de
Founded: 1982
Subjects: Biography, Music, Dance, Regional Interests
ISBN Prefix(es): 3-923657

Orlanda Frauenverlag+
Zossenerstr 55-58, 10961 Berlin
Tel: (030) 216-3566; (030) 216-2960 *Fax:* (030) 2153958
E-mail: post@orlanda.de
Web Site: www.orlanda.de
Key Personnel
Manager, Rights & Permissions: Prof Dagmar Schultz, PhD
Contact: Ekpenyong Aui
Founded: 1974
Subjects: Developing Countries, Ethnicity, Gay & Lesbian, Health, Nutrition, Literature, Literary Criticism, Essays, Psychology, Psychiatry, Self-Help, Social Sciences, Sociology
ISBN Prefix(es): 3-922166; 3-929823; 3-936937

Oros Verlag+
Borghorster Str 6, 48341 Altenberge
Mailing Address: Postfach 11 45, 48337 Altenberge
Tel: (02505) 947191 *Fax:* (02505) 3534
Key Personnel
Manager: Prof Adel Th Khoury, PhD
Founded: 1988
Subjects: Literature, Literary Criticism, Essays, Philosophy, Theology
ISBN Prefix(es): 3-89375

Osho Verlag GmbH
Gilbachstr 29A, 50672 Cologne
Tel: (0221) 278 04-0 *Fax:* (0221) 278 04-66
E-mail: info@oshoverlag.de
Web Site: www.oshoverlag.de
Key Personnel
Manager: Dr Hansjoerg Sieberer; Joachim Spoh
Founded: 1988
Subjects: Behavioral Sciences, Human Relations, Philosophy, Psychology, Psychiatry, Religion - Buddhist, Religion - Catholic, Religion - Hindu, Religion - Islamic, Religion - Jewish, Religion - Protestant, Religion - Other, Self-Help
ISBN Prefix(es): 3-925205; 3-933556; 3-9800883
Divisions: Osho Times International, Deutsche Ausgabe

Osnabrueck, *imprint of* Verlag A Fromm im Druck- u Verlagshaus Fromm GmbH & Co KG

Ostfalia-Verlag Jurgen Schierer+
Kornbergweg 13, 31224 Peine
Tel: (05171) 41763 *Fax:* (05171) 41769
E-mail: juergen.schierer@t-online.de
Web Site: www.ostfalia-verlag.de
Key Personnel
Manager: Juergen Schierer
Founded: 1980
Subjects: Fiction, Poetry, Regional Interests
ISBN Prefix(es): 3-926560
Number of titles published annually: 2 Print
Total Titles: 32 Print

Ostrecht, *imprint of* Berliner Wissenschafts-Verlag GmbH (BWV)

Erzabtei Sankt Ottilien, see EOS Verlag der Benefiktiner der Erzabtei St. Ottilien

Otto-Friedrich Universitat Bamberg
Kapuzinerstr 20, Room 221-223, 96045 Bamberg
Tel: (0951) 863-1021 *Fax:* (0951) 863-4021
E-mail: presse@uni-bamberg.de
Web Site: www.uni-bamberg.de/zuv/presse/mitarbeiter

Pabel-Moewig Verlag KG+
Postfach 2352, 76413 Rastatt
Tel: (07222) 13 0 *Fax:* (07222) 13 218
E-mail: kontakt@moewig.de
Web Site: www.vpm-online.de
Key Personnel
Book Manager: Eckhard Schwettmann
 E-mail: esch@pobox.com
ISBN Prefix(es): 3-8118
Number of titles published annually: 120 Print
Total Titles: 350 Print
Parent Company: Heinrich Bauer Verlag
Imprints: Moewig; Neff
Subsidiaries: Hestia Verlag; Paul Neff Verlag

Pahl-Rugenstein Verlag Nachfolger-GmbH+
Breitestr 47, 53111 Bonn
Tel: (0228) 632306 *Fax:* (0228) 634968
E-mail: prv@che-chandler.com
Key Personnel
Manager & International Rights: Arnold Bruns
Founded: 1990
Subjects: Biography, Developing Countries, Government, Political Science, History, Philosophy, Religion - Protestant, Social Sciences, Sociology, Theology
ISBN Prefix(es): 3-89144; 3-88142; 3-87682; 3-7609

Pal Verlagsgesellschaft mbH+
Am Oberen Luisenpark 33, 68165 Mannheim
Tel: (0621) 415741 *Fax:* (0621) 415101
E-mail: info@palverlag.de

Web Site: www.pal-verlag.de
Key Personnel
Manager: Dr Rolf Merkle
Founded: 1986
Subjects: Biography, Psychology, Psychiatry
ISBN Prefix(es): 3-923614

Pala-Verlag GmbH+
Rheinstr 37, 64283 Darmstadt
Tel: (06151) 23028 *Fax:* (06151) 292713
E-mail: info@pala-verlag.de
Web Site: www.pala-verlag.de
Key Personnel
Man Dir: Wolfgang Hertling *E-mail:* w.hertling@pala-verlag.de
Editorial: Barbara Reis *E-mail:* b.reis@pala-verlag.de
Sales: Katrin Kolb *E-mail:* k.kolb@pala-verlag.de
Founded: 1980
Subjects: Cookery, Environmental Studies, Gardening, Plants, Health, Nutrition, Medicine, Nursing, Dentistry, Sports, Athletics
ISBN Prefix(es): 3-923176; 3-89566

Palazzi Verlag GmbH+
Ostertorsteinweg 36, 28195 Bremen
Mailing Address: Postfach 102627, 28026 Bremen
Tel: (0421) 321100 *Fax:* (0421) 321300
Key Personnel
Manager: Voller Hedwig
Founded: 1989
Subjects: Aeronautics, Aviation, Earth Sciences, Environmental Studies, Foreign Countries, Geography, Geology, Natural History, Physical Sciences, Travel
ISBN Prefix(es): 3-927956; 3-936421

Palmyra Verlag+
Haupstr 64, 69117 Heidelberg
Tel: (06221) 165409 *Fax:* (06221) 167310
E-mail: palmyra-verlag@t-online.de
Web Site: www.palmyra-verlag.de
Key Personnel
President: Georg Stein
Founded: 1989
Subjects: Anthropology, Foreign Countries, Government, Political Science, Music, Dance, Nonfiction (General)
ISBN Prefix(es): 3-9802298; 3-930378

Pandion-Verlag, Ulrike Schmoll+
Gartenstr 10, 55469 Simmern
Tel: (06761) 7142 *Fax:* (06761) 77172
E-mail: pandion@t-online.de; info@pandion-verlag.de
Web Site: www.pandion-verlag.de
Founded: 1954
Subjects: Art, Fiction, Poetry, Regional Interests, Religion - Other
ISBN Prefix(es): 3-922929

PapyRossa Verlags GmbH & Co Kommanditgesellschaft KG+
Luxemburger Str 202, 50937 Cologne
Tel: (0221) 44 85 45 *Fax:* (0221) 44 43 05
E-mail: mail@papyrossa.de
Web Site: www.papyrossa.de
Key Personnel
Manager: Dr Jurgen Harrer
Founded: 1990
Subjects: Developing Countries, Government, Political Science, History, Human Relations, Social Sciences, Sociology, Women's Studies
ISBN Prefix(es): 3-89438
Orders to: SOVA, Friesstr 20-24, 60388 Frankfurt

Edition Parabolis
Schliemannstr 23, 10437 Berlin
Tel: (030) 44 65 10 65 *Fax:* (030) 444 10 85
E-mail: info@emz-berlin.de

Web Site: www.emz-berlin.de
Publishing section of the Berlin Institute for Comparative Social Research (BIVS).
Membership(s): European Migration Centre.
Subjects: Anthropology, Ethnicity, Nonfiction (General), Social Sciences, Sociology, Migration
ISBN Prefix(es): 3-88402
Number of titles published annually: 20 Print

Paranus Verlag - Bruecke Neumuenster GmbH
Ehndorfer Str 13-17, 24537 Neumuenster
Mailing Address: Postfach 1264, 24502 Neumuenster
Tel: (04321) 2004-500 *Fax:* (04321) 2004-411
E-mail: verlag@paranus.de
Web Site: www.paranus.de
Key Personnel
International Rights: Fritz Bremer
Founded: 1989
Publishing project which involves mentally ill persons in the editing, producing, printing & distribution of books & periodicals.
Subjects: Art, Literature, Literary Criticism, Essays, Psychology, Psychiatry
ISBN Prefix(es): 3-926200

Parey, *imprint of* Georg Thieme Verlag KG

Parey Buchverlag, *imprint of* Blackwell Wissenschafts-Verlag GmbH

Verlag Parzeller GmbH & Co KG+
Frankfurterstr 8, 36043 Fulda
Tel: (0661) 280-663 *Fax:* (0661) 280-285
E-mail: verlag@parzeller.de
Web Site: www.buchkatalog.de/parzeller
Telex: 49838
Key Personnel
Contact: Rainer Klitsch *Tel:* (0661) 280361 *E-mail:* rainer.klitsch@parzeller.de
Founded: 1874
Subjects: Regional Interests, Religion - Catholic, Religion - Protestant, Religion - Other
ISBN Prefix(es): 3-7900
Subsidiaries: Druckerei Parzeller GmbH & Co KG

Passavia Druckerei GmbH, Verlag
Medienstr 5b, 94036 Passau
Tel: (0851) 802670 *Fax:* (0851) 802680
E-mail: contact@just-print-it.com
Web Site: www.passavia.de; www.just-print-it.com
Key Personnel
Man Dir: Erwin Neudecker
Publishing Dir, Rights & Permissions: Peter Oeller
Founded: 1888
Subjects: Fiction, House & Home, Humor, Travel
ISBN Prefix(es): 3-87616
Subsidiaries: Passavia Universitaetsverlag und-Druck GmbH

Passavia Universitaetsverlag und -Druck GmbH
St Englmarstr 11, 94034 Passau
Tel: (0851) 700226 *Fax:* (0851) 700277
Key Personnel
Publishing Dir, Rights & Permissions: Bernd Kammerer
Subjects: Science (General)
ISBN Prefix(es): 3-922016; 3-86036
Parent Company: Passavia Druckerei GmbH

Patio, Galerie und Druckwerkstatt+
Laubestr 24H, 60594 Frankfurt
Tel: (06150) 84566
Key Personnel
Man Dir: Klaus Muenchschwander
Editorial: David Ward
Sales: Regine Behrends; Franz Gaber

Production: Volker Mueller; Walter Zimbrich
Publicity: Yves Daniel Zimbrich
Rights & Permissions: Manfred Linke; Renate Kafitz-Pfeuffer
Founded: 1963

Patmos Verlag GmbH & Co KG+
Am Wehrhahn 100, 40211 Duesseldorf
Tel: (0211) 16795-0 *Fax:* (0211) 16795-75
E-mail: info@patmos.de
Web Site: www.patmos.de *Cable:* PATMOS VERLAG
Key Personnel
Dir: Dr Tullio Aurelio *Tel:* (0211) 1679569 *E-mail:* fauth@patmos.de
Publicity: Ralf Pollmann
Founded: 1910
Subjects: Antiques, Art, History, Literature, Literary Criticism, Essays, Religion - Other, Theology
ISBN Prefix(es): 3-491
Subsidiaries: Walter Verlag AG; Artemis & Winkler Verlag AG; Benziger Verlag AG

Pattloch Verlag GmbH & Co KG+
Hilblestr 54, 80636 Munich
Tel: (089) 9271-0 *Fax:* (089) 9271-168
E-mail: vertrieb@droemer-knaur.de
Web Site: www.droemer-weltbild.de
Founded: 1965
Subjects: Nonfiction (General)
ISBN Prefix(es): 3-629
Parent Company: Verlagsgruppe Droemer Weltbild GmbH & Co KG
Orders to: VVA Bertelsmann Distribution, Postfach 7600, 33310 Guetersloh, Jennifer Strebinger *Tel:* (05241) 801754 *Fax:* (05241) 8060260 *E-mail:* jennifer.strebinger@bertelsmann.de

Paulinus Verlag GmbH+
Maximineracht 11c, 54295 Trier
Tel: (0651) 4608-112 *Fax:* (0651) 4608-221
E-mail: verlag@paulinus.de
Web Site: www.paulinus.de
Key Personnel
Publisher: Siegfried Faeth
Man Dir: Thomas Juncker
Rights & Permissions: Dr Harald Baulig
Founded: 1875
Subjects: Religion - Other, Theology
ISBN Prefix(es): 3-7902; 3-87760
Parent Company: Paulinus Druckerei GmbH, Fleichstr 62-65, 54290 Trier
Associate Companies: Spee Buchverlag GmbH

Ingwert Paulsen Jr, see Hansa Verlag Ingwert Paulsen Jr

Pawel Panpresse+
Zum Seemenbach Nr 1, 63654 Budingen
Tel: (06041) 5822
Key Personnel
Man Dir, Production, Rights: Sascha Juritz
Founded: 1972
Subjects: Art, Literature, Literary Criticism, Essays, Poetry
ISBN Prefix(es): 3-921454
Associate Companies: Edition Druckhuette No 2
Orders to: Siehe Pawel Panpresse

Pearson Education Deutschland GmbH+
Martin-Kollar-Str 10-12, 81829 Munich
Mailing Address: Postfach 820461, 81804 Munich
Tel: (089) 46003-0 *Fax:* (089) 46003-120
E-mail: firstinitiallastname@pearson.de; info@pearson.de
Web Site: www.pearsoned.de
Key Personnel
President: Axel Nehen *Tel:* (089) 46003 401 *Fax:* (089) 46003 410

Vice President, Finance & Operations: Rudolf Nertinger *Tel:* (089) 46003 123
Foreign Rights: Ines Killat *Tel:* (089) 46003 124
Assistant to the President: Britta Tiedtke-Heimers *Tel:* (089) 46003 405
Editorial Dir, M & T: Catherine Magdolen *Tel:* (089) 46003 336 *Fax:* (089) 46003 330
Editorial Dir, Addison Wesley: Christian Rauscher *Tel:* (089) 46003 331 *Fax:* (089) 46003 330
Human Resources Manager: Uschi Jacob *Tel:* (089) 46003 122
Founded: 1993
Subjects: Computer Science
ISBN Prefix(es): 3-89090; 3-87791; 3-922120; 3-8273; 3-8272; 3-89319; 3-925118
Imprints: Que; SAMS; Prentice Hall; X-Games
Distributor for Macmillan Computer Publishing USA; Prentice Hall
Warehouse: Adelmannstr 5, 81827 Munich

Pelikan Vertriebsgesellschaft mbH & Co KG+
Werftstr 9, 30163 Hannover
Tel: (0511) 6969-0 *Fax:* (0511) 6969-212
Web Site: www.pelikan.de
Telex: 175118481 Pelikan
Key Personnel
Man Dir & Marketing Manager: Terry Edwards
Marketing: Michael Fey *E-mail:* m.fey@pelikan.de
Founded: 1978
Subjects: Fiction
ISBN Prefix(es): 3-8144
Parent Company: Pelikan Holding, Switzerland
Associate Companies: Franz-Buttner, AG/Pelikan-Vertrieb, Wollerau, Switzerland
Distributor for Diverse

Pendragon Verlag+
Stapenhorststr 15, 33615 Bielefeld
Tel: (0521) 69689 *Fax:* (0521) 174470
E-mail: pendragon.verlag@t-online.de
Web Site: www.pendragon.de
Key Personnel
Man Dir, Sales, Rights & Permissions: Guenther Butkus
Production & Publicity: Michael Baltus
Founded: 1981
Subjects: Art, Criminology, Fiction, History, Literature, Literary Criticism, Essays, Poetry
ISBN Prefix(es): 3-923306; 3-929096; 3-934872
Imprints: Edition Bielefelden Kunstverein

Perryman, see Babel Verlag Kevin Perryman

Verlag Sigrid Persen
Postfach 260, 21637 Horneburg
Tel: (04163) 81400 *Fax:* (04163) 814050
E-mail: info@persen.de
Web Site: www.persen.de
Key Personnel
Man Dir: Franz-Josef Buechler
Founded: 1976
Subjects: English as a Second Language, Language Arts, Linguistics, Mathematics, Music, Dance
ISBN Prefix(es): 3-921809; 2-89358

Justus Perthes Verlag Gotha GmbH+
Justus-Perthes-Str 1-5, 99867 Gotha
Mailing Address: Postfach 274, 99854 Gotha
Tel: (03621) 385-0 *Fax:* (03621) 385-102
E-mail: perthes@klett-mail.de
Web Site: www.klett-verlag.de/klett-perthes *Cable:* PERTHES GOTHA
Key Personnel
Dir: Volker Streibel
Founded: 1785
Subjects: Geography, Geology, History, Cartography
ISBN Prefix(es): 3-7301; 3-623

Parent Company: Ernst Klett Verlag GmbH, Stuttgart
Imprints: Haack; Schreiber-Naturtafeln

Klett Perthes, see Justus Perthes Verlag Gotha GmbH

C F Peters Musikverlag GmbH & Co KG
Kennedyallee 101, 60596 Frankfurt am Main
Mailing Address: Postfach 700851, 60558 Frankfurt am Main
Tel: (069) 6300990 *Fax:* (069) 635401
E-mail: vertrieb@musia.de; info@musia.de
Web Site: www.musia.de *Cable:* PETERSEDIT
Key Personnel
Partner: Dr Johannes Petschull; Roland Schied
Founded: 1800
Subjects: Music, Dance
ISBN Prefix(es): 3-87626; 3-920735
Associate Companies: C F Peters Corp, NY, United States; Hinrichsen Edition Ltd, London, United Kingdom
Imprints: M P Belaieff; Henry Litolff's Verlag; Edition Peters; Edition Schwann

Edition Peters, *imprint of* C F Peters Musikverlag GmbH & Co KG

Jens Peters Publikationen+
Gotenstr 65, 10829 Berlin
Tel: (030) 7847265 *Fax:* (030) 7883127
E-mail: jens.peters@usa.net
Web Site: www.jenspeters.de
Key Personnel
President, Rights & Permissions: Jens Peters
Founded: 1977
Subjects: Travel
ISBN Prefix(es): 3-923821; 3-9800154
Orders to: Osterholzer Dorfstr 45, 28307 Bremen *Tel:* (0421) 451743 *Fax:* (0421) 455406

Pfaffenweiler Presse+
MittlereStr 23, 79292 Pfaffenweiler
Tel: (07664) 8999 *Fax:* (07664) 8999
E-mail: info@pfaffenweiler-presse.de
Web Site: www.pfaffenweiler-presse.de
Key Personnel
Owner: Herta Flicker
Founded: 1974
ISBN Prefix(es): 3-921365; 3-927702

Pfalzische Verlagsanstalt GmbH
Industriestr 15, 76829 Landau
Mailing Address: Postfach 1950, 76809 Landau
Tel: (06341) 142-0 *Fax:* (06341) 142-265
Key Personnel
Publisher: Herr Karl-Friedrich Geissler
Manager: Rolf Schaefer; Horst K Neubauer
Founded: 1892
Subjects: Art, Biography, Fiction, Foreign Countries, Wine & Spirits
ISBN Prefix(es): 3-87629
Orders to: VSB-Braunschweig, Postfach 4738, 3300 Braunschweig

Pfeiffer bei Klett-Cotta, *imprint of* J G Cotta'sche Buchhandlung Nachfolger GmbH

J Pfeiffer Verlag+
Anzingerstr 15, 81671 Munich
Tel: (089) 4130010
Key Personnel
Publisher & Editorial: Lydia Franzelius
Editor: Dr Christine Treml
Production: Siegbert Seitz
Founded: 1882
Subjects: Psychology, Psychiatry, Religion - Other
ISBN Prefix(es): 3-7904
Parent Company: Manz Verlag

Shipping Address: mi-Verlags Service GmbH, Justus-von-Liebig-Str 1, 8689 Landsberg-Lech
Warehouse: mi-Verlags Service GmbH, Justus-von-Liebig-Str 1, 86898 Landsberg-Lech
Orders to: Verlagsgruppe Manz

Verlag Dr Friedrich Pfeil
Wolfratshauser Str 27, 81379 Munich
Tel: (089) 7428270 *Fax:* (089) 7242772
E-mail: info@pfeil-verlag.de
Web Site: www.pfeil-verlag.de
Key Personnel
Editor: Dr Friedrich Pfeil
Founded: 1981
Subjects: Biological Sciences, Philosophy
ISBN Prefix(es): 3-923871; 3-931516; 3-89937
Branch Office(s)
Falkweg 37, 81243 Munich

Richard Pflaum Verlag GmbH & Co KG+
Lazarettstr 4, 80636 Munich
Mailing Address: Postfach 190737, 80607 Munich
Tel: (089) 12607-0 *Fax:* (089) 12607-333
E-mail: info@pflaum.de
Web Site: www.pflaum.de
Key Personnel
Manager: Beda Bohinger
Head Book Dept: Helmut Brackebusch
Founded: 1919
Subjects: Communications, Electronics, Electrical Engineering, Medicine, Nursing, Dentistry
ISBN Prefix(es): 3-7905
Subsidiaries: Gastgewerbe Verlag GmbH & Co KG; Huethig und Pflaum Verlag GmbH & Co KG Laenderdienst Verlag GmbH
Branch Office(s)
Bad Kissingen
Berlin
Dusseldorf
Heidelberg

Helker Pflug, see Verlag Wissenschaft und Politik

Philipp Reclam Jun Verlag GmbH+
Siemensstr 32, 71254 Ditzingen
Mailing Address: Postfach 1349, 71252 Ditzingen
Tel: (07156) 163 0 *Fax:* (07156) 163 197
E-mail: info@reclam.de
Web Site: www.reclam.de *Cable:* RECLAM DITZINGEN
Key Personnel
Publisher: Dr Frank R Max
Publicity Dir: Dr Karl-Heinz Fallbacher
Sales Manager: Juergen Bernardi; Anja Krauss
Rights & Permissions: Dr Stephan Koranyi
Founded: 1828
Subjects: Art, Fiction, Film, Video, History, Music, Dance, Philosophy, Poetry, Religion - Other, Jazz
ISBN Prefix(es): 3-15
Parent Company: Philipp Reclam jun GmbH & Co, Stuttgart
Distributor for Reclam Verlag Leipzig

Philippka-Sportverlag+
Rektoratsweg 36, 48159 Muenster
Mailing Address: Postfach 150105, 48061 Muenster
Tel: (0251) 23005-0 *Fax:* (0251) 23005-79
E-mail: info@philippka.de
Web Site: www.philippka.de
Key Personnel
Publisher: Konrad Honig *Tel:* (0251) 23005-25
Publicity: Peter Moellers *Tel:* (0251) 23005-28 *E-mail:* moellers@philippka.de
Founded: 1978
Subjects: Sports, Athletics
ISBN Prefix(es): 3-922067
Number of titles published annually: 3 Print; 1 CD-ROM
Total Titles: 50 Print; 2 CD-ROM

Associate Companies: Success in Soccer, Albuquerque, NM, United States
Foreign Rep(s): Manni Klar (USA)
Warehouse: Albuquerque, NM, United States

Philipps-Universitaet Marburg
Biegenstr 10, 35032 Marburg
Tel: (06421) 28-20 *Fax:* (06421) 28-22500
E-mail: verwaltung@ub.uni-marburg.de
Web Site: www.uni-marburg.de
Telex: 482-372
Key Personnel
President: Prof Dr Kern
Public Relations: Klaus Walter
Librarian: Heino Krueger
Subjects: Anthropology, Archaeology, History, Library & Information Sciences, Psychology, Psychiatry, Science (General)
ISBN Prefix(es): 3-8185

Philosophia Verlag GmbH+
Gundelindenstr 4, 80805 Munich
Mailing Address: Postfach 221362, 80503 Munich
Tel: (089) 299975 *Fax:* (089) 299975
E-mail: info@philosophiaverlag.com
Web Site: www.philosophiaverlag.com
Key Personnel
Man Dir & Publisher: Ulrich Staudinger
Editorial Board: Hans Burkhardt; Barry Smith; Ignacio Angelelli; Christian Thiel
Sales & Marketing: Frank Kiesebrink
Founded: 1966
Publishers for philosophy & economics.
Membership(s): Stock Exchange of German Booksellers; Association of Bavarian Publishers & Booksellers
Subjects: Economics, Philosophy
ISBN Prefix(es): 3-88405
Number of titles published annually: 3 Print
Total Titles: 70 Print
Divisions: Medienbuero Muenchen
Distributed by Vrin (France)
Orders to: Herold Verlagsauslieferung, Kolpingring 4, 82041 Oberhaching/Munich, Contact: A Stanglmeier *Tel:* (089) 613871-0 *Fax:* (089) 61387120 *E-mail:* herold-oberhaching@t-online.de *Web Site:* www.herold-va.de

Physica, *imprint of* Springer Science+Business Media GmbH & Co KG

Physica-Verlag+
Imprint of Springer-Verlag
Tiergartenstr 17, 69121 Heidelberg
Mailing Address: PO Box 105280, 69042 Heidelberg
Tel: (06221) 487-0 *Fax:* (06221) 4878-177
E-mail: physica@springer.de
Web Site: www.springer.de
Key Personnel
Man Dir: Dr Dietrich Goetze *Tel:* (06221) 4878-345
Dir, Division Sales/Marketing & Corporate Development: Arnoud de Kemp *Tel:* (06221) 487-397 *Fax:* (06221) 487-288 *E-mail:* dekemp@springer.de
Journals/LINK Dir: Gertraud Griepke *Tel:* (06221) 487-457 *Fax:* (06221) 487-288 *E-mail:* griepke@springer.de
Territory Manager (Middle East, Africa, Greece, Turkey): Franziska Sachsse *Tel:* (06221) 487-628 *Fax:* (06221) 487-620 *E-mail:* sachsse@springer.de
Marketing Communications Dir: Michael Lechler *Tel:* (06221) 487-515 *Fax:* (06221) 487-156 *E-mail:* lechler@springer.de
Sales & Marketing Manager, Client Presses: Sandra Cortes-Hemmerich *Tel:* (06221) 487-289 *Fax:* (06221) 487-620 *E-mail:* cortes@springer.de

Territory Manager (Scandinavia): Bettina Schies *Tel:* (06221) 487-309 *Fax:* (06221) 487-620 *E-mail:* schies@springer.de
Territory Manager (Belgium, The Netherlands): Marc Puma *Tel:* (01) 53 93 37 79 *Fax:* (01) 53 93 36 83 *E-mail:* puma@springer-paris.fr
Specialize in Statistics & Information Systems.
Subjects: Business, Economics, Finance, Regional Interests, Science (General), Econometrics, Information Systems
ISBN Prefix(es): 3-7908
Number of titles published annually: 100 Print
Total Titles: 500 Print
Branch Office(s)
Springer-Verlag Wien New York, Sachsenplatz 4-6, 1201 Vienna, Austria *Tel:* (01) 330 24 15 *Fax:* (01) 330 24 26
Foreign Rep(s): Academic Marketing Services (Pty) Ltd (South Africa); Eastern Book Service Inc (Japan); Michael Lechler (Austria, Germany, Luxembourg, Switzerland); Behruz Neirami (Iran); Springer-Verlag (Australia, Africa, Baltic States, Bangladesh, Eastern Europe, Egypt, India, Israel, Middle East, New Zealand, Nepal, Pakistan, Russia & CIS, Sri Lanka, Turkey); Springer-Verlag France (France, Morocco, Tunisia, Algeria); Springer-Verlag Hong Kong Ltd (China, Hong Kong, Indonesia, Malaysia, Myanmar, Philippines, South Korea, Singapore, Thailand, Vietnam, Macao); Springer-Verlag Iberica SAI (Portugal, Spain); Springer-Verlag Italia Srl (Greece, Italy); Springer-Verlag Liaison Office (Bangladesh, India, Nepal, Pakistan, Sri Lanka); Springer-Verlag London Ltd (Belgium, UK, Netherlands, Ireland, Scandinavia); Springer-Verlag New York Inc (North America, South America); Springer-Verlag Singapore Pte Ltd (Malaysia, SE Asia, Singapore, Thailand); Springer-Verlag Taipei (Taiwan)
Shipping Address: Springer Shipping Centre, Hatschekstr 8, 69126 Heidelberg
Orders to: Customer Service, Haberstr 7, 69126 Heidelberg *Tel:* (06221) 345221 *Fax:* (06221) 345229

PIAG, see PIAG Presse Informations AG

Heinz Pier+
Carl-Schurz-Str 98, 50374 Erftstadt
Mailing Address: Postfach 2462, Erftstadt 50358
Tel: (02235) 3998 *Fax:* (02235) 41654
Key Personnel
Owner: Heinz Pier *Tel:* (02235) 44808
Founded: 1922
ISBN Prefix(es): 3-924576
Branch Office(s)
Bonnerstr 26, Lechenich, 50374 Erftstadt, Contact: Hedwig Pier *Tel:* (02235) 71959 *Fax:* (02235) 953753

Paul Pietsch Verlage GmbH & Co+
Olgastr 86, 70180 Stuttgart
Mailing Address: Postfach 103743, 70032 Stuttgart
Tel: (0711) 2 10 80-0 *Fax:* (0711) 2 10 80-82; (0711) 2 36 04-15
E-mail: ppv@motorbuch.de
Web Site: www.motorbuch.de
Key Personnel
Man Dir: Paul Pietsch
Man Dir & Editorial: Dr Patricia Scholten
Rights & Permissions: Patricia Hofmann
Founded: 1962
Subjects: Aeronautics, Aviation, Automotive, How-to, Maritime, Military Science, Travel
ISBN Prefix(es): 3-87943; 3-613; 3-344
Associate Companies: Verlag Mueller-Rueschlikon
Divisions: Motorbuch-Verlag; Pietsch-Verlag; Schrader-Verlag; Transpress

Distributed by Bucheli-Verlag (Switzerland); Mueller-Rueschlikon (Switzerland)
Warehouse: Koch, Neff & Oetinger & Co, Schockenriedstr 39, 70565 Stuttgart

Piper Verlag GmbH+
Georgenstr 4, 80799 Munich
Tel: (089) 381801-0 *Fax:* (089) 338704
E-mail: info@piper.de
Web Site: www.piper.de
Key Personnel
Publisher: Viktor Niemann
Man Dir: Hartmut Jedicke
Editorial: Ulrike Buergel-Goodwin; Bettina Feldweg; Tanja Graf; Thomas Tebbe; Dr Klaus Stadler; Ulrich Wank
Foreign Rights: Ingrid Fuehrer
Contracts & Rights: Annette Sabelus
Sales Manager: Christa Beiling
Press Manager: Eva Brenndorfer
Advertising Manager: Ingrid Ullrich
Founded: 1904
Specialize in music.
Subjects: Biography, Fiction, History, Music, Dance, Philosophy, Psychology, Psychiatry, Science (General), Theology
ISBN Prefix(es): 3-8225; 3-89521; 3-89029; 3-492; 3-921909
Number of titles published annually: 300 Print
Parent Company: Bonnier Media Holding GmbH
Imprints: Kabel Verlag; Malik Verlag
Orders to: Koch, Neff, Oetinger & Co, Schockenriedstr 39, 70551 Stuttgart

Pixel Transfer Design Studio, *imprint of* Extent Verlag und Service Wolfgang M Flamm

Verlag Ploetz, *imprint of* Verlag Herder GmbH & Co KG

pmi Verlag+
Oberfeldstr 29, 60439 Frankfurt am Main
Tel: (069) 54 80 00-0 *Fax:* (069) 54 80 00 66
E-mail: pmiverlag@aol.com
Web Site: www.pmi-verlag.de
Key Personnel
Editor & Director: Peter Hoffmann
Manager & International Rights: Karin Hoffmann
Founded: 1975
Subjects: Biological Sciences, Finance, Health, Nutrition, Law, Medicine, Nursing, Dentistry
ISBN Prefix(es): 3-89119; 3-89143; 3-921721; 3-922357; 3-926681; 3-9802599; 3-86007; 3-932765; 3-9804734; 3-89786
Subsidiaries: Universimed; Universimed AG
Warehouse: Koch, Neff & Oettinger & Co, Schockenriedstr 3, 70565 Stuttgart *Fax:* (0711) 78991010 (books only)

pmv, see Peter Meyer Verlag (pmv)

Verlag Walter Podszun Burobedarf-Bucher Abt+
Bahnhofstr 9, 59929 Brilon
Tel: (02961) 2507 *Fax:* (02961) 2508
E-mail: verlag.podszun@t-online.de
Key Personnel
Editor: Walter Podszun
International Rights: Brigitte Podszun
Founded: 1969
Subjects: Automotive, Engineering (General), Humor, Transportation
ISBN Prefix(es): 3-86133; 3-923448
Bookshop(s): Buchhandlung Podszun

Podzun-Pallas Verlag GmbH+
Kohlhaeuserstr 8, 61200 Woelfersheim
Tel: (06036) 9436 *Fax:* (06036) 6270
Web Site: www.podzun-pallas.de
Key Personnel
Man Dir, Rights & Permissions: Beate Danker

Editorial & Sales: Mrs Karin Kuenzel
Founded: 1979
Subjects: Military Science
ISBN Prefix(es): 3-7909

Poetik und Hermeneutik, *imprint of* Wilhelm Fink GmbH & Co Verlags-KG

Politik und Spiritualitaet, *imprint of* Drei Eichen Verlag Manuel Kissener

Galerie Eva Poll
Luetzowplatz 7, 10785 Berlin
Tel: (030) 261 70 91 *Fax:* (030) 261 70 92
E-mail: galerie@poll-berlin.de
Web Site: www.germangalleries.com/poll
Key Personnel
International Rights: Lothar C Poll
Founded: 1968
Subjects: Art

POLLeditionen Verlag, see Galerie Eva Poll

Pollner Verlag+
Rotdornstr 7, 85764 Oberschleissheim
Tel: (089) 3151890 *Fax:* (089) 3151890
E-mail: info@pollner-verlag.de
Web Site: www.pollner-verlag.de
Key Personnel
Contact: Max Pollner
Schwerpunkt Kanuliteratur Outdoor Sports.
Subjects: Environmental Studies, Humor, Outdoor Recreation, Travel, Sport, Kanu, Kajak
ISBN Prefix(es): 3-925660

Polyband Gesellschaft fur Bild Tontraeger mbH & Co Betriebs KG
Am Moosfeld 37, 81829 Munich
Tel: (089) 420 03-0 *Fax:* (089) 420 03-42
E-mail: contact@polyband.de
Web Site: www.polyband.de
Telex: 522636 pdy d
Key Personnel
Man Dir: Swetlana Winkel
Marketing: Marco Koesling *E-mail:* marco.koesling@polyband.de
Publicity: Elza Kronthaler *E-mail:* elza.kronthaler@polyband.de
Founded: 1963
Subjects: Film, Video
ISBN Prefix(es): 3-89276

Polyglott-Verlag+
Member of The Langenscheidt Group
Mies-van-der-Rohe-Str 1, 80807 Munich
Mailing Address: Postfach 401120, 80711 Munich
Tel: (089) 360960 *Fax:* (089) 36096-222 (general); (089) 36096-258 (orders)
Key Personnel
Man Dir: Karl Ernst Tielebier-Langenscheidt *E-mail:* redaktion@polyglott.de; Andreas Langenscheidt
Publishing Dir: Rolf Muller
Advertising: Brigitte Pasch
Editorial: Barbara Lennartz
Founded: 1902
Sales & promotion through Langenscheidt KG.
Subjects: Travel
ISBN Prefix(es): 3-493
Orders to: Langenscheidt KG, Neusserstr 3, 80807 Munich

Polygraph Verlag GmbH+
Eckendorfer Str 91, 33609 Bielefeld
Mailing Address: Postfach 101726, 33517 Bielefeld
Tel: (0521) 97044-0 *Fax:* (0521) 97044-33 *Cable:* POLYGRAPHVERLAG FRANKFURT MAIN

Key Personnel
Man Dir, Rights & Permissions: Mrs Ulrike Schulz
Sales Dir & International Rights: Kristian Senn
Production: Dieter Borniger
Editorial-Staff Dir: Walter Mikolasch
Founded: 1947
Subjects: Career Development, Publishing & Book Trade Reference, Technology
ISBN Prefix(es): 3-87641
U.S. Office(s): Fred E Noemer, 50 Sherwood Rd, Norwood, NJ 07648-2320, United States *Tel:* 201-784-1666 *Fax:* 201-784-2666

Portikus
Schoene Aussicht 2, 60311 Frankfurt am Main
Tel: (069) 219 987-60; (069) 219 987-59 *Fax:* (069) 219 987-61
E-mail: portikus@pop.stadt-frankfurt.de
Web Site: www.portikus.de
Key Personnel
Dir: Dr Daniel Birnbaum
Curator: Jochen Volz
Founded: 1987
Specialize in exhibition catalogues.
Subjects: Art
ISBN Prefix(es): 3-928071
Number of titles published annually: 8 Print
Total Titles: 90 Print
Parent Company: Staedelschule

Possev-Verlag GmbH+
Flurscheideweg 15, 65936 Frankfurt
Tel: (069) 34-12-65 *Fax:* (069) 34-38-41
E-mail: possev-ffm@t-online.de
Key Personnel
Manager: Leonid Mueller
Founded: 1945
Also runs a translation agency.
ISBN Prefix(es): 3-7912
Branch Office(s)
Redaktion Possev, Postfach 325, 117602 Moscow, Russian Federation *Tel:* (095) 2831090

W Poth GbR, see Verlagsbuchhandlung Megapress, Franz-J Gaber

Prasenz Verlag der Jesus Bruderschaft eV+
Gnadenthal, 65597 Huenfelden
Tel: (06438) 81281 *Fax:* (06438) 81282
Web Site: www.uni-giessen.de
Key Personnel
Dir: Jens Oertel
Founded: 1962
Subjects: Art, Poetry, Religion - Jewish
ISBN Prefix(es): 3-87630

Premop Verlag GmbH+
Kuechelstr 5, 81375 Munich
Tel: (089) 562257 *Fax:* (089) 5803214
E-mail: premop@mnet-online.de
Key Personnel
Manager: Bernard Schenkel
Founded: 1988
Subjects: Music, Dance
ISBN Prefix(es): 3-927724
Subsidiaries: Edition Premop

Prentice Hall, *imprint of* Pearson Education Deutschland GmbH

PIAG Presse Informations AG+
Landstr 67a, 76547 Sinzheim Baden
Tel: (07221) 301 7560 *Fax:* (07221) 301 7570
E-mail: office@piag.de
Web Site: www.piag.de
Key Personnel
Publisher & Man Dir: Dieter Brinzer
Marketing: Jens Hoeppner *Tel:* (0721) 301 7568 *E-mail:* jhoeppner@piag.de

Sales & Advertising Dir: Sven Kadow *Tel:* (07721) 301 7563 *E-mail:* s.kadow@piag.de
Editor: Dr Stefan Hartmann *Tel:* (07221) 301 7564 *E-mail:* s.hartmann@piag.de
Administration: Christiane Kist *Tel:* (07221) 301 7562 *E-mail:* office@piag.de
Founded: 1963
Publisher of specialized books & magazines for the trade of published photography.
Subjects: Law, Photo law & photo prices in Europe
ISBN Prefix(es): 3-921864; 3-922725

Presse Verlagsgesellschaft mbH+
Ludwigstr 33-37, 60327 Frankfurt am Main
Tel: (069) 97460-0 *Fax:* (069) 97460-400
E-mail: journal@mmg.de
Web Site: www.journal-frankfurt.de
Key Personnel
Man Dir, International Rights: Dr Carsten Brandt *Tel:* (01) 61886 *E-mail:* grundlagen-praxis@t-online.de; Carsten Lienemann
Founded: 1980
Subjects: Regional Interests, Homeopathy
ISBN Prefix(es): 3-928789
Number of titles published annually: 2 Print
Total Titles: 7 Print
Parent Company: MMG - Medieu Marketing Gruppe
Subsidiaries: K/C/E Marketing GmbH

Guido Pressler Verlag+
Auf dem Strifft 19, 52393 Huertgenwald
Tel: (02429) 1385; (02408) 929692 *Fax:* (02408) 955931
E-mail: info@pressler-verlag.com
Web Site: www.pressler-verlag.com
Founded: 1957
Subjects: Art, History, Literature, Literary Criticism, Essays, Philosophy, Psychology, Psychiatry
ISBN Prefix(es): 3-87646

Prestel Verlag+
Koeniginstr 9, 80539 Munich
Tel: (089) 38 17 09 0 *Fax:* (089) 33 51 75
E-mail: info@prestel.de
Web Site: www.prestel.de *Cable:* PRESTELVERLAG
Key Personnel
Publisher: Juergen Tesch
Sales Dir: Juergen Krieger *Tel:* (089) 38 17 09 48
Publicity Dir: Pia Werner *Tel:* (089) 38 17 09 55 *E-mail:* werner@prestel.de
Financial Dir: Rolf Alkenbredner
Founded: 1924
Subjects: Architecture & Interior Design, Art, Photography
ISBN Prefix(es): 3-7913
Branch Office(s)
Prestel Publishing Ltd, 4 Bloomsbury Place, London WC1A 2QA, United Kingdom, Contact: Andrew Hansen *Tel:* (020) 7323 5004 *Fax:* (020) 7636 8004 *E-mail:* sales@prestel-uk.co.uk
U.S. Office(s): Prestel Publishing, 175 Fifth Ave, Suite 402, New York, NY 10010, United States, Contact: Stephen Hulburt *Tel:* 212-995-2720 *Fax:* 212-995-2733 *E-mail:* sales@prestel-usa.com

Preussische Koepfe, *imprint of* Stapp Verlag Wolfgang Stapp

Helmut Preussler Verlag+
Dagmarstr 8, 90482 Nuernberg
Tel: (0911) 95478 0 *Fax:* (0911) 542486
E-mail: preussler_verlag@t_online.de *Cable:* PREUSSLER-VERLAG

GERMANY

Key Personnel
Man Dir, Editorial, Production & Rights & Permissions: Achin Raak
Sales, Publicity: Annemarie Seeberger
Founded: 1973
ISBN Prefix(es): 3-921332; 3-925362; 3-934679
Associate Companies: Preussler Druck & Versand GmbH
Subsidiaries: Versandbuchhandlung Gebhart; Polizei Verlag Heinz Krause
Bookshop(s): Ernst Gebhard, Dagmarstr 8, 90482 Nuremberg

Pro Natur Verlag GmbH+
Ziegelhuettenweg 43A, 60598 Frankfurt am Main
Tel: (069) 9688610 *Fax:* (069) 96886124
Key Personnel
Manager: Rudolf L Schreiber
Founded: 1979
Subjects: Environmental Studies
ISBN Prefix(es): 3-88582
Parent Company: Pro Natur Gesellschaft zur Foerderung des Umweltschutzes mbH

Projektion J Buch- und Musikverlag GmbH+
Dillerberg 2, 35614 Asslar
Tel: (06443) 68-0 *Fax:* (06443) 68-34
E-mail: info@gerth.de
Web Site: www.gerth.de
Key Personnel
International Rights: Christian Goelker
Founded: 1989
Subjects: Fiction, How-to, Human Relations, Management, Music, Dance, Nonfiction (General), Religion - Other, Self-Help, Theology, Western Fiction, study aids
ISBN Prefix(es): 3-89490; 3-925352; 3-9800258
Showroom(s): Rheingaustr 85A, 65203 Wiesbaden
Bookshop(s): Rheingaustr 85A, 65203 Wiesbaden
Shipping Address: Rheingaustr 85A, 65203 Wiesbaden
Warehouse: Rheingaustr 85A, 65203 Wiesbaden
Orders to: Rheingaustr 85A, 65203 Wiesbaden

Propylaeen Verlag, Zweigniederlassung Berlin der Ullstein Buchverlage GmbH+
Charlottenstr 13, 10969 Berlin
Tel: (0302) 5913500 *Fax:* (030) 25913533 *Cable:* ULLSTEINBUCH BERLIN
Key Personnel
Man Dir: Dr Wolfram Goebel
Sales Dir: Karl-Heinz Reimann
Chief Editor (Hardcover): Dr Uwe Heldt
Chief Editor (Paperbacks): Dr Juergen Mueller
Rights: Heidi Walitza
Founded: 1903
Subjects: Architecture & Interior Design, Art, Biography, Education, Ethnicity, Fiction, Film, Video, Geography, Geology, Government, Political Science, Health, Nutrition, History, How-to, Humor, Literature, Literary Criticism, Essays, Maritime, Military Science, Music, Dance, Mysteries, Nonfiction (General), Poetry, Romance, Science (General), Social Sciences, Sociology, Travel
ISBN Prefix(es): 3-549; 3-550; 3-548; 3-333
Parent Company: Ullstein Buchverlage GmbH & Co KG
Associate Companies: SVB Sportverlag Berlin
Subsidiaries: Propylaeen Verlag; Ullstein Taschenbuchverlag; Verlag Gesundheit
U.S. Office(s): 439 Ninth St, No 2, New York, NY 10009, United States, Contact: Liz Fried *Tel:* 212-533-2296
Warehouse: VVA Bertelsmann Distribution GmbH, An der Autobahn, 33310 Gutersloh

Psychiatrie-Verlag GmbH+
Thomas-Mannstr 49a, 53111 Bonn
Tel: (0228) 725340 *Fax:* (0228) 7253420
E-mail: verlag@psychiatrie.de
Web Site: www.psychiatrie.de/verlag
Key Personnel
Publishing Manager: York Bieger
 E-mail: bieger@psychiatrie.de; Ute Hueper
Founded: 1978
Subjects: Health, Nutrition, Psychology, Psychiatry
ISBN Prefix(es): 3-88414
Orders to: VVA, Fr Bienne, Postfach 7777, 33310 Gutersloh

Psychologie Verlags Union GmbH+
Werderstr 10, 69469 Weinheim
Tel: (06201) 60070
E-mail: info@beltz.de
Web Site: www.beltz.de
Key Personnel
Man Dir: Dr Manfred Beltz Ruebelmann
Publishing Manager: Dr Heike Berger
 Tel: (06201) 6007370 *Fax:* (06201) 6007395
 E-mail: h.berger@beltz.de
Contact: Michaela Frommherz *E-mail:* m.frommherz@beltz.de
Founded: 1986
Subjects: Behavioral Sciences, Biological Sciences, Business, Child Care & Development, Communications, Education, Environmental Studies, Psychology, Psychiatry, Social Sciences, Sociology
ISBN Prefix(es): 3-621
Parent Company: Beltz Verlag, Werderstr 10, 69469 Weinheim

Psychosozial-Verlag+
Goethestr 29, 35390 Giessen
Tel: (0641) 77819 *Fax:* (0641) 77742
E-mail: info@psychosozial-verlag.de; bestellung@psychosozial-verlag.de
Web Site: www.psychosozial-verlag.de
Key Personnel
Publisher: Dr Hans-Jurgen Wirth
Founded: 1991
Specialize in psychoanalysis.
Subjects: History, Psychology, Psychiatry, Social Sciences, Sociology
ISBN Prefix(es): 3-932133; 3-930096; 3-89806
Total Titles: 210 Print

Publik-Forum-Verlagsgesellschaft mbH
Krebsmuehle, 61440 Oberursel
Mailing Address: Postfach 2010, 61410 Oberursel
Tel: (06171) 70030 *Fax:* (06171) 700340
Key Personnel
Manager: Dieter Grohmann
ISBN Prefix(es): 3-88095; 3-921807

Pulp Master Frank Nowatzki Verlag+
Imprint of Maas Verlag
Samariterstr 6, 10247 Berlin
Tel: (030) 6868292 *Fax:* (030) 6868292
E-mail: master@txt.de
Web Site: www.maasmedia.de
Key Personnel
Man Dir, Rights & Permissions: Frank Nowatzki
Founded: 1989
Subjects: Fiction, Mysteries
ISBN Prefix(es): 3-927734
Orders to: Bugrim, Saalburgstr 3, 12099 Berlin

Verlag Friedrich Pustet GmbH & Co Kg+
Gutenbergstr 8, 93051 Regensburg
Mailing Address: Postfach 100862, 93008 Regensburg
Tel: (0941) 94 24 105 *Fax:* (0941) 94 24 100
E-mail: buecher@pustet.de
Web Site: www.pustet.de *Cable:* PUSTET
Key Personnel
Man Dir: Elisabeth Pustet
Editorial: Fritz Pustet
Founded: 1826
Subjects: Archaeology, Art, Biography, History, Religion - Catholic, Theology

BOOK

ISBN Prefix(es): 3-7917
Bookshop(s): Buchhandlung Friedrich Pustet, Gesandtenstr 6, Regensburg; Kleiner Exerzierplatz 4, Passau; Karolinenstr 12, Augsburg, Theresieuplatz 41, Straubing; Altstadt 28, Landshut, Residentstr 2-6, 91522 Ausbach

edition q Berlin Edition in der Quintessenz Verlags-GmbH+
Division of Quintessenz Verlags GmbH
Ifenpfad 2-4, 12107 Berlin
Mailing Address: Postfach 42 04 52, 12064 Berlin
Tel: (030) 761 80-5 *Fax:* (030) 761 80-680
E-mail: editionq@quintessenz.de; info@quintessenz.de
Web Site: www.quintessenz.de
Telex: 500/183815
Key Personnel
Publisher: Horst-Wolfgang Haase *Tel:* (030) 761 80-622 *Fax:* (030) 761 80-691
Publishing Director: Johannes W Wolters
 Tel: (030) 761 80-670 *Fax:* (030) 761 80-692
Editor Berlin Edition: Bernhard Thieme
 Tel: (030) 761 80-640
Online Editor: Joachim Liebers *Tel:* (030) 761 80-604 *Fax:* (030) 761 80-693
International Rights: Bernd Burkart *Tel:* (030) 761 80-608 *Fax:* (030) 761 80-693
Sales Manager: Cornelia Gross *Tel:* (030) 761 80-635 *Fax:* (030) 761 80-692
Marketing: Uwe Janssen *Tel:* (030) 761 80-614
Commercial Manager: Thomas Fritz *Tel:* (030) 761 80-658 *Fax:* (030) 761 80-692
Manager Electronic Publishing: Andreas Mueller
 E-mail: mueller@quintessenz.de
Advertising: Gudrun Matthes *Tel:* (030) 761 80-629 *Fax:* (030) 761 80-691 *E-mail:* anzeigen@quintessenz.de
Product Manager Offline-Media: Martin Hecklinger *Tel:* (030) 761 80-677
 E-mail: hecklinger@quintessenz.de
Assistant Manager: Christian Haase *Tel:* (030) 761 80-605
Subscriptions: Angela Koethe *E-mail:* abo@quintessenz.de
Book Orders: Leo Korff *E-mail:* buch@quintessenz.de
Graphics: Ines Bluemel *Tel:* (030) 761 80-608
Founded: 1990
Membership(s): Boersenverein des Deutschen Buchhandels eV.
Subjects: Art, History, Literature, Literary Criticism, Essays, Arts & Culture, Contemporary History, Japanese Literature
ISBN Prefix(es): 3-86124; 3-928024; 3-8148
Total Titles: 200 Print
U.S. Office(s): Quintessence Publishing Co Inc/Edition q Inc, 551 N Kimberly Dr, Carol Stream, IL 60188-1881, United States *Tel:* 630-682-3223 *Fax:* 630-682-3288
 E-mail: quintpub@aol.com *Web Site:* www.quintpub.com
Foreign Rep(s): Edition q Inc (USA); Quintessence Publishing Co Inc (USA)
Foreign Rights: Quintessence Publishing Co Ltd (UK)
Shipping Address: Prolit Verlagsaulieferin GmbH, Siemensstr 16, 35463 Fernwald-Annerod, Contact: Gabriele Boehnen *Tel:* (0641) 94393 21 *Fax:* (0641) 94393 29
Warehouse: Prolit Verlagsaulieferin GmbH, Siemensstr 16, 35463 Fernwald-Annerod, Contact: Gabriele Boehnen *Tel:* (0641) 94393 21 *Fax:* (0641) 94393 29
Orders to: Edition Guides, Quintessenz Verlags GmbH, Berlin, Contact: Helga Schebera *Tel:* (030) 761 80-635 *Fax:* (030) 761 80-692

Que, *imprint of* Pearson Education Deutschland GmbH

PUBLISHERS — GERMANY

Quell Verlag+
Augustenstr 124, 70197 Stuttgart
Tel: (0711) 601000 *Fax:* (0711) 6010076
Key Personnel
Dir, Editorial, Publicity, Rights & Permissions: Walter Waldbauer
Founded: 1830
Subjects: Biography, Fiction, History, Philosophy, Religion - Other
ISBN Prefix(es): 3-7918
Parent Company: Evangelische Gesellschaft, Postfach 103852, 70033 Stuttgart
Subsidiaries: Evangelische Gemeindepresse GmbH; Wartburg Verlag GmbH iG
Bookshop(s): Buchhandlung der Evangelischen Gesellschaft in Heidenheim, Heilbronn Ludwigsburg, Schaebisch Hall, Stuttgart

Quelle und Meyer Verlag GmbH & Co+
Industriepark 3, 56291 Wiebelsheim
Tel: (06766) 903200 *Fax:* (06766) 903320
E-mail: vertrieb@quelle-meyer.de
Web Site: www.quelle-meyer.de
Key Personnel
Man Dir: Gerhard Stahl
Sales: Ralf Simolka
Rights & Permissions: Dr Jrmgard Meissl
Founded: 1906
Subjects: Biological Sciences, Education, History, Language Arts, Linguistics, Literature, Literary Criticism, Essays, Philosophy, Psychology, Psychiatry, Religion - Other, Social Sciences, Sociology
ISBN Prefix(es): 3-494
Associate Companies: AULA-Verlag GmbH, Industrie Park 3, Wiebelsheim 56291 *Tel:* (06766) 903141 *Fax:* (06766) 903320 *E-mail:* vertrieb@aula-verlag.de; Limpert Verlag GmbH, Industrie Park 3, 56291 Wiebelsheim *Tel:* (06766) 903160 *Fax:* (06766) 903360 *E-mail:* vertrieb@limpert.de

Querverlag GmbH
Akazienstr 25, 10823 Berlin
Tel: (030) 78 70 23 39; (030) 78702340
Fax: (030) 788 49 50
E-mail: mail@querverlag.de
Web Site: www.querverlag.de
Key Personnel
Publisher: Jim Baker *E-mail:* jim@querverlag.de; Ilona Bubeck *Tel:* (030) 78702339 *E-mail:* ilona@querverlag.de
Founded: 1995
Germany's first & only gay & lesbian book publisher.
Membership(s): Borsenverein des Deutschen Buchhandels.
Subjects: Fiction, Gay & Lesbian, Nonfiction (General), Homosexuality, Queer Studies, Gay & Lesbian Fiction & Nonfiction
ISBN Prefix(es): 3-89656
Shipping Address: SOVA, Friesstr 20-24, 60388 Frankfurt *Tel:* (069) 410211 *Fax:* (069) 410280

Quintessenz Verlags-GmbH+
Ifenpfad 2-4, 12107 Berlin
Mailing Address: Postfach 420452, 12064 Berlin
Tel: (030) 761805 *Fax:* (030) 76180680
E-mail: info@quintessenz.de
Web Site: www.quintessenz.de
Telex: 183815 quint d
Key Personnel
Publisher: H W Haase
International Rights: Gerda Steinmeyer
E-mail: steinmeyer@quintessenz.de
Founded: 1949
Subjects: Biography, Career Development, Communications, Fiction, Film, Video, Health, Nutrition, Literature, Literary Criticism, Essays, Management, Medicine, Nursing, Dentistry, Mysteries
ISBN Prefix(es): 3-86124; 3-928024; 3-8148; 3-87652; 3-9801163
Subsidiaries: Edition Q
U.S. Office(s): Quintessence Publishing Co Inc, 551 N Kimberly Dr, Carol Stream, IL 60188, United States

Dr Josef Raabe-Verlags GmbH
Kaiser-Friedrich Str 90, 10585 Berlin
Tel: (030) 2129870 *Fax:* (030) 21298730
E-mail: w.heuse@raabe.de
Web Site: www.raabe.de
Key Personnel
Man Dir: Dr Reinhard Sander; Wolfgang Schulz
Founded: 1985
Specialize in loose leaf editions, universities, school management.
Subjects: Education, Environmental Studies, Management, Public Administration, Science (General)
ISBN Prefix(es): 3-88649; 3-8183
Parent Company: Ernst Klett Information GmbH, Rotebuehlstr 77, 70178 Stuttgart
Ultimate Parent Company: Ernst Klett AG
Subsidiaries: RAABE Bulgarien; Dr Josef Raabe Spolka Wydawnicza; Nakladatelstvi RAABE; RAABE Fachverlag fur Bildungsmanagement; RAABE Fachverlag fur Oeffentliche Verwaltung Duesseldorf; RAABE Fachverlag fur Wissenschaftsinformation; RAABE Fachverlag fur die Schule; RAABE Koenyvkiado
Warehouse: BDK Buecherdienst Koeln, Koelner Str 248, 51149 Koeln
Orders to: Dr Josef Raabe Verlags-GmbH, Kundenservice, Postfach 103922, 70034 Stuttgart *Tel:* (0711) 62900-0 *Fax:* (0711) 62900-10 *E-mail:* info@raabe.de

Raben Verlag von Wittern KG+
Frohschammerstr 14, 80807 Munich
Tel: (089) 3594879 *Fax:* (089) 3596622
Key Personnel
Contact: York von Wittern
Founded: 1980
ISBN Prefix(es): 3-922696

Radius-Verlag GmbH+
Olgastr 114, 70180 Stuttgart
Tel: (0711) 6076666; (0172) 7126573 *Fax:* (0711) 6075555
E-mail: radiusverlag@freenet.de
Web Site: www.radius.skileon.de
Key Personnel
Man Dir: Wolfgang Erk
Founded: 1962
Subjects: Fiction, Philosophy, Psychology, Psychiatry, Religion - Other
ISBN Prefix(es): 3-87173

Raethgloben Verlagsgesellschaft mbH
Fraunhoferstr 8, 04430 Boehlitz-Ehrenberg
Tel: (0341) 4511212 *Fax:* (0341) 4427537
E-mail: raethgloben1917@gmx.de *Cable:* RAETHGLOBUS
Key Personnel
Manager: Heinz Goeschel; Hans Joachim Niemeyer
Founded: 1917
Subjects: Education, Geography, Geology, Science (General)
ISBN Prefix(es): 3-7491

Rake Verlag GmbH+
Koenigsweg 20, 24103 Kiel
Tel: (0431) 6611515 *Fax:* (0431) 6611517
E-mail: info@rake.de
Web Site: www.rake.de
Key Personnel
Publisher: Micha Rau *E-mail:* rau@rake.de
Sales: Peter Keune *E-mail:* keune@rake.de
Public Relations: Annette Borchers *E-mail:* borchers@rake.de
Founded: 1994
Subjects: Fiction, Humor, Self-Help, Specialize in contemporary German authors
ISBN Prefix(es): 3-931476
Number of titles published annually: 20 Print
Total Titles: 35 Print; 1 Audio
Branch Office(s)
MediaPartner, Hofackerstr 13, 8032 Zurich, Switzerland *Tel:* (01) 385 55 10 *Fax:* (01) 385 55 19 *E-mail:* mediapartner@access.ch
Distributed by PNV Vertriebs Service

Dr Mohan Krischke Ramaswamy Edition RE+
RE Wolfgang-Doringstr 4, 37077 Goettingen
Tel: (0171) 8026882 *Fax:* (0171) 5311065
E-mail: edition.re@epost.de
Key Personnel
Owner: Dr Mohan Krischke Ramaswamy
E-mail: ramaswamy@epost.de
Founded: 1979
Subjects: Ethnicity, Music, Dance, Social Sciences, Sociology
ISBN Prefix(es): 3-927636

Dr Ramdohr KG, see Mentor-Verlag Dr Ramdohr KG

Rationalisierungs-Kuratorium der Deutschen Wirtschaft eV (RKW)
Sohnstr 70, 40237 Duesseldorf
Tel: (0211) 680010 *Fax:* (0211) 68001 68; (0211) 68001 69
E-mail: info@rkw-nrw.de
Web Site: www.rkwnrw.de
Telex: 4072755 rkw d *Cable:* ERKAWE
Key Personnel
Manager: Dr Gerhard Schrick; Dr H Mueller
Publicity Manager: H Degenhard
Publications, Rights: Dr Natascha Breme
Founded: 1921
Registered Society of the German Industrial Rationalization Board.
Subjects: Business, Economics, Engineering (General), Labor, Industrial Relations, Management, Technology
ISBN Prefix(es): 3-926984; 3-921451; 3-929796; 3-89644

Walter Rau Verlag GmbH & Co KG+
Benderstr 164a, 40625 Duesseldorf
Tel: (0211) 92 80 40 *Fax:* (0211) 28 38 27
Web Site: www.rau.de
Telex: 08586682
Key Personnel
Man Dir: Gisela W Rau; Beatrix Rau-Siegert
Founded: 1930
Subjects: Cookery, Sports, Athletics
ISBN Prefix(es): 3-7919; 3-933886
Associate Companies: Verlag Heim und Werk; Asper Verlag; Walter Rau Versandbuchhandlung (Schach)
Showroom(s): Manfred Maedler, Lilienthalstr 52, 40474 Dusseldorf

Werner Rau Verlag+
Feldbergstr 54 D, 70569 Stuttgart
Tel: (0711) 687 21 43 *Fax:* (0711) 68 22 47
E-mail: info@rau_verlag.de
Web Site: www.rau-verlag.de
Founded: 1986
Subjects: Travel
ISBN Prefix(es): 3-926145
Orders to: Bertelsmann Distribution GmbH, Postfach 7777, 33310 Gutersloh 100

Gerhard Rautenberg Druckerei und Verlag GmbH & Co KG
Imprint of Verlagshaus Wurzburg
Beethovenstr 5, 97070 Wurzburg

Tel: (0931) 385235 *Fax:* (0931) 385305
E-mail: info@verlagshaus.com
Web Site: www.verlagshaus.com
Key Personnel
Publishing Dir: Dieter Krause
Dir of Production: Juergen Roth
Sales Dir: Johannes Glesius
Founded: 1825
Subjects: Drama, Theater, Fiction, Humor, Regional Interests
ISBN Prefix(es): 3-7921
Bookshop(s): Rautenbergsche Buchhandlung, Blinke 8, 26767 Leer

Ravensburger Buchverlag Otto Maier GmbH+
Postfach 1860, 88188 Ravensburg
Tel: (0751) 86 1717 *Fax:* (0751) 861818
E-mail: info@ravensburger.de
Web Site: www.ravensburger.de *Cable:* MAIERVERLAG
Key Personnel
President: Otto Julius Maier; Dorothee Hess-Maier
Man Dir: Claus Runge
Editorial: Michael Kohlhammer; Cornelius Retting; Valeska Schneider-Finke
Production: Max Weishaupt
International Sales: Michael Bartl
Marketing: Michael Pfleiderer
Publicity: Anja Fahs
Rights & Permissions: Michael Ramm; Florence Roux
Founded: 1883
Subjects: Art, Crafts, Games, Hobbies, Education, Fiction, Nonfiction (General)
ISBN Prefix(es): 3-473
Parent Company: Ravensburger AG
Associate Companies: Ravensburger Verlag GmbH; Ravensburger GmbH, Vienna, Austria; Editions Ravensburger SA, Attenschwiller, France; Ravensburger SpA, Milan, Italy; Ravensburger BV, Amersfoort, Netherlands; Carlit und Ravensburger AG, Wueenlos, Switzerland; Ravensburger Ltd, Bicester, United Kingdom
Divisions: Ravensburger SpieleVerlag GmbH; Ravensburger Interactive Media GmbH; Ravensburger Freizeit & Promotion Service GmbH; Ravensburger Film & TV GmbH

Ravenstein Verlag GmbH+
Auf der Krautweide 24, 65812 Bad Soden
Tel: (06196) 609630 *Fax:* (06196) 63619
E-mail: g.koenig@ravenstein-verlag.de
Telex: 4072538 haco d *Cable:* RAVENSTEINVERLAG
Key Personnel
Man Dir: Ruediger Bosse
Founded: 1830
ISBN Prefix(es): 3-87660
U.S. Office(s): Seven Hills Book Div, 49 Central Ave, Cincinnati, OH 45202, United States

Reader's Digest Deutschland Verlag Das Beste GmbH
Augustenstr 1, 70178 Stuttgart
Mailing Address: Postfach 106020, 70049 Stuttgart
Tel: (0711) 66020 *Fax:* (0711) 6602547
E-mail: verlag@readersdigest.de
Web Site: www.readersdigest.de *Cable:* READIGEST STUTTGART
Key Personnel
Man Dir: Werner Neunzig
Founded: 1948
Also publish music & video editions.
ISBN Prefix(es): 3-87070
Parent Company: The Reader's Digest Association Inc, Reader's Digest Rd, Pleasantville, NY 10570-7000, United States
Subsidiaries: Optimail Direktwerbeservice GmbH; Pegasus Buch- und Zeischriften-Vertriebs-GmbH

Verlag Recht und Wirtschaft GmbH+
Haeusserstr 14, 69115 Heidelberg
Mailing Address: Postfach 10 59 60, 69049 Heidelberg
Tel: (06221) 9060 *Fax:* (06221) 906259
E-mail: verlag@ruw.de
Web Site: www.ruw-ruw.de *Cable:* RECHTWIRTSCHAFT HEIDELBERG
Key Personnel
Man Dir: Michael Giesecke
Publisher: Angelika Sauer
Contact: Norbert Konda
Founded: 1946
Subjects: Economics, Law, Social Sciences, Sociology
ISBN Prefix(es): 3-8005
Subsidiaries: I H Sauer Verlag GmbH

Reclam Verlag Leipzig+
Inselstr 26, 04103 Leipzig
Tel: (0341) 997170 *Fax:* (0341) 9971730
E-mail: info@reclam-leipzig.de
Web Site: www.reclam.de *Cable:* RECLAM LEIPZIG
Key Personnel
Man Dir: Dr Frank Rainer Max; Franz Schaefer
International Rights: Dr Stephan Koranyi
Founded: 1828
Subjects: Biography, History, Literature, Literary Criticism, Essays, Philosophy
ISBN Prefix(es): 3-379
Parent Company: Philipp Reclam jun GmbH & Co, Stuttgart
Orders to: Philipp Reclam Jun, 71252 Ditzingen

Redaktion & Gestaltung, *imprint of* Johann Wolfgang Goethe Universitat

Reed Elsevier Deutschland GmbH+
Hans-Cornelius-Str 4, 82166 Grafelfing, Munich
Tel: (089) 898170 *Fax:* (089) 85817-102
Key Personnel
Man Dir: Burkhard Bierschenck
Editor: Wolfram Haase
Founded: 1938
Subjects: Environmental Studies, Medicine, Nursing, Dentistry
ISBN Prefix(es): 3-8040
Parent Company: Reed Elsevier, Netherlands
Subsidiaries: ipc magazin verlag GmbH

REGENSBERG Druck & Verlag GmbH & Co
Harkortstr 25, 48163 Muenster
Mailing Address: Postfach 6667, 48035 Muenster
Tel: (0251) 749800 *Fax:* (0251) 7498040
Key Personnel
Manager: Bernhard Lucas
Founded: 1591
Subjects: Regional Interests
ISBN Prefix(es): 3-7923

Verlag fur Regionalgeschichte+
Windelsbleicher Str 13, 33335 Gutersloh
Mailing Address: Postfach 120423, 33653 Bielefeld
Tel: (05209) 6714; (05209) 980266 *Fax:* (05209) 6519; (05209) 980277
E-mail: regionalgeschichte@t-online.de
Web Site: www.regionalgeschichte.de
Key Personnel
Publisher: Olaf Eimer
Assistant Publisher: Gunda Gaus
Founded: 1987
Subjects: Art, History, Regional Interests, Social Sciences, Sociology
ISBN Prefix(es): 3-927085; 3-89534
Number of titles published annually: 40 Print
Total Titles: 350 Print

Regura Verlag
Kettenhofweg 133, 60325 Frankfurt am Main
Tel: (0711) 2269835 *Fax:* (0711) 2238829
Key Personnel
Contact: Mr Weipert
Founded: 1997
Digital publications, internet solutions & services for publishers
International cultural exchange, priority: Orient, Persia & Germany.
Subjects: Art, Cookery, Fiction
ISBN Prefix(es): 3-932814

Konrad Reich Verlag GmbH+
Kaeppen-Pott-Weg 6, 18055 Rostock Brinckmansdorf
Tel: (0381) 693020 *Fax:* (0381) 693021
Key Personnel
Man Dir, Rights & Permissions: Konrad Reich
Founded: 1990
Subjects: Art, Ethnicity, Fiction, Geography, Geology, Travel
ISBN Prefix(es): 3-86167

Dr Ludwig Reichert Verlag+
Tauernstr 11, 65199 Wiesbaden
Tel: (0611) 461851 *Fax:* (0611) 468613
E-mail: info@reichert-verlag.de
Web Site: www.reichert-verlag.de
Key Personnel
Publisher: Ursula Reichert
Founded: 1970
Worldwide distribution.
Subjects: Archaeology, Art, Asian Studies, Geography, Geology, History, Language Arts, Linguistics, Library & Information Sciences, Music, Dance, Religion - Jewish, Science (General)
ISBN Prefix(es): 3-920153; 3-88226; 3-89500
Warehouse: Brockhaus Commission, Kreidlerstr 9, 70806 Kornwestheim, Contact: Mrs Wunderlich *Tel:* (07154) 132726 *Fax:* (07154) 132713 *E mail:* reichert@brocom.de
Orders to: Brockhaus Commission, Kreidlerstr 9, 70806 Kornwestheim, Contact: Mrs Wunderlich *Tel:* (07154) 132726 *Fax:* (07154) 132713 *E-mail:* reichert@brocom.de

Reichl Verlag Der Leuchter+
Auf dem Haehnchen 34, 56329 St Goar
Tel: (06741) 1720 *Fax:* (06741) 1749
E-mail: reichl-verlag@telda.net
Web Site: www.reichl-verlag.de
Key Personnel
Man Dir: Matthias Draeger
Founded: 1909
Subjects: Astrology, Occult, Medicine, Nursing, Dentistry, Parapsychology, Religion - Other, Self-Help
ISBN Prefix(es): 3-87667
Subsidiaries: Leibniz Verlag
Divisions: Edition Asklepios

Dietrich Reimer Verlag GmbH+
Zimmerstr 26-27, 10969 Berlin
Tel: (030) 25 91 15 70 *Fax:* (030) 25 91 15 77
E-mail: vertrieb-kunstverlage@reimer-verlag.de
Web Site: www.reimer-verlag.de
Key Personnel
Publisher, Rights & Permissions: Dr Friedrich Kaufmann
Editorial & International Rights: Beate Behrens
Sales & Publicity: Gabriele Dornemann
Production: Dieter Eckert; Nicola Willam
Secretary: Brigitte Struck
Founded: 1845
Subjects: Anthropology, Art, Ethnicity, Cartography, Customs & Traditions, Dance, Television, Theatre
ISBN Prefix(es): 3-496; 3-7861
Bookshop(s): Nautische Buchhandlung Dietrich Reimer, Unter den Eichen 57, 12203 Berlin, Contact: Fr Haberey *Tel:* (030) 8312341

Fax: (030) 8313873; Dietrich Reimer Wissenschaftliche Fachbuchhandlung, 12203 Berlin, Contact: Mrs Carina Ebert *Tel:* (030) 8314082 *Fax:* (030) 8313873
Orders to: Koch, Neff, Oetinger & Co Verlagsauslieferung GmbH, Schockenriedstr 39, 70506 Stuttgart

Ernst Reinhardt Verlag GmbH & Co KG+
Kemnatenstr 46, 80639 Munich
Mailing Address: Postfach 380280, 80615 Munich
Tel: (089) 17 80 16 0 *Fax:* (089) 17 80 16 30
E-mail: webmaster@reinhardt-verlag.de
Web Site: www.reinhardt-verlag.de
Key Personnel
Man Dir: Hildegard Wehler *E-mail:* wehler@reinhardt-verlag.de
Production: Dorothea Roll *Tel:* (089) 17 80 16 20 *E-mail:* roll@reinhardt-verlag.de
Finance: Peter Dietz *Tel:* (089) 17 80 16 17 *E-mail:* dietz@reinhardt-verlag.de
Sales: Daniela Postleb *Tel:* (089) 17 80 16 22 *E-mail:* postleb@reinhardt-verlag.de
Founded: 1899
Subjects: Child Care & Development, Education, Management, Medicine, Nursing, Dentistry, Music, Dance, Philosophy, Psychology, Psychiatry, Religion - Other, Science (General), Social Sciences, Sociology, Medicine, Nursing
ISBN Prefix(es): 3-497
Distributed by Buch und Medienvertriebs AG (Switzerland); Koch, Neff & Oetinger & Co (Germany); Mohr Morawa Wien (Australia)
Orders to: Koch, Neff, Oetinger & Co Verlagsauslieferung GmbH, Schockenriedstr 39, 70565 Stuttgart

E Reinhold Verlag (E Reinhold Publishing)
Hillgasse 15, 04600 Altenburg
Tel: (03447) 311889 *Fax:* (03447) 375611
E-mail: erv@querstand.de
Web Site: www.querstand.de
Key Personnel
Publisher: Klaus-Juergen Kamprad
Founded: 1990
Subjects: Biography, History, Photography, Regional Interests, Travel, Regional Interests of East Germany
ISBN Prefix(es): 3-910166; 3-937940
Number of titles published annually: 10 Print
Total Titles: 100 Print

Reise Know-How, *imprint of* Reise Know-How Verlag Peter Rump GmbH

Reise Know-How+
Zwalbacherstr 3, 66709 Rappweiler
Tel: (06872) 91737 *Fax:* (06872) 91738
E-mail: hoff-verlag@reise-know-how.com
Web Site: www.reise-know-how.com
Key Personnel
Man Dir: Edgar P Hoff *E-mail:* edgarhoff@aol.com
Founded: 1981
Publisher of travel guides.
Subjects: Travel, Travel Guides
ISBN Prefix(es): 3-923716
Total Titles: 13 Print
Subsidiaries: Backpacker Information Service

Reise Know-How Verlag-Daerr GmbH+
Osnabruecker Str 79, 33649 Bielefeld
Tel: (0521) 946490 *Fax:* (0521) 441047
E-mail: info@reise-know-how.de
Web Site: www.reise-know-how.de
Key Personnel
Man Dir: Erika Daerr
Founded: 1987
Subjects: Travel
ISBN Prefix(es): 3-921497; 3-89662

Associate Companies: Reise-Know-How, Rump-Verlag, Haupt Str 198, 33647 Bielefeld *Tel:* (0521) 440835; Reise-Know-How Verlag Tondok, Nadistr 18, 808009 Munich; Reise-Know-Verlag, Dr HR Grundmann, Heinrich-Schwarz-Weg 36, 27777 Ganderkesee *Tel:* (04222) 8799; Reise-Know-How-Verlag Hermann, Untere Muehle, 71706 Markgroeningen *Tel:* (07145) 8278
Shipping Address: Prolit, Postfach 9, 35461 Fernwald *Tel:* (0641) 43071 *Fax:* (0641) 42773
Warehouse: Prolit, Postfach 9, 35461 Fernwald *Tel:* (0641) 43071 *Fax:* (0641) 42773
Orders to: Prolit, Postfach 9, 35461 Fernwald *Tel:* (0641) 43071 *Fax:* (0641) 42773

Reise Know-How Verlag Dr Hans-R Grundmann GmbH
Member of Verlagsgruppe Reise Know-How
Am Hamjebusch 29, 26655 Westerstede
Tel: (04488) 761994 *Fax:* (04488) 761030
E-mail: reisebuch@aol.com
Founded: 1988
Specialize in North America travel publications.
ISBN Prefix(es): 3-927554; 3-9800151

Reise Know-How Verlag Helmut Hermann
Member of Verlagsgruppe Reise Know-How
Untere Muhle, 71706 Markgroningen
Tel: (07145) 8278 *Fax:* (07145) 26736
E-mail: rkhhermann@aol.com
Key Personnel
Contact: H Hermann
Founded: 1986
Subjects: Photography, Travel
ISBN Prefix(es): 3-929920; 3-9800975; 3-9803296
Orders to: Prolit, Postfach 9, 35463 Fernwald

Reise Know-How Verlag Peter Rump GmbH+
Member of Verlagsgruppe Reise Know-How
Osnabrucker Str 79, 33649 Bielefeld
Tel: (0521) 94649-0 *Fax:* (0521) 441047
E-mail: info@reise-know-how.de
Web Site: www.reise-know-how.de
Key Personnel
Man Dir: Peter Rump
Founded: 1981
Subjects: Foreign Countries, Geography, Geology, Language Arts, Linguistics, Travel
ISBN Prefix(es): 3-922376; 3-89416
Imprints: Reise Know-How
U.S. Office(s): SCB Distributors, PO Box 5446, Carson, CA 90749-5446, United States
Orders to: Prolit GmbH, Siemensstr 16, Postfach 9, 35463 Fernwald (Annerod)

Reise Know-How Verlag Tondok
Member of Verlagsgruppe Reise Know-How
Nadistr 18, 80809 Munich
Tel: (089) 3514857 *Fax:* (089) 3518485
E-mail: rhk@tondok-verlag.de
Web Site: www.tondok-verlag.de
Key Personnel
Contact: Wil Tondok
Subjects: Travel
ISBN Prefix(es): 3-921838

Verlagsgruppe Reise Know-How+
Osnabruecker str 79, 33649 Bielefeld
Tel: (0521) 946490 *Fax:* (0521) 441047
E-mail: info@reise-know-how.de
Web Site: www.reise-know-how.de
Key Personnel
Rights & Permissions: Peter Rump
Founded: 1981
Subjects: Language Arts, Linguistics, Travel
ISBN Prefix(es): 3-922376; 3-89416; 3-8317
Associate Companies: Reise Know-How Verlag Peter Rump Gmbh, Osnabrucker Str 79, 33649 Bielefeld *Tel:* (0521) 94649-0

Fax: (0521) 44104-7 *E-mail:* info@reise-know-how.de; Reise Know-How Verlag Helmut Hermann, Untere Muhle, 71706 Markgroningen *Tel:* (07145) 8278 *Fax:* (07145) 26736 *E-mail:* rkhhermann@aol.com; Reise Know-How Verlag Tondok, Nadistr 18, 80809 Munich *Tel:* (089) 3514857 *Fax:* (089) 3518485 *E-mail:* rkh@tondok-verlag.de; Reise Know-How Verlag/Hans Grundmann GmbH, Am Hamjebusch 29, 26655 Westerstede *Tel:* (04488) 761994 *Fax:* (04488) 761030 *E-mail:* reisebuch@aol.com
Orders to: Prolit Verlagsauslieferung, Siemensstr 16, 35463 Fernwald (Annerod)

R V Reise- und Verkehrsverlag GmbH+
Neumarkterstr 43, 81673 Munich
Mailing Address: Postfach 800360, 81603 Munich
Tel: (089) 431890; (030) 254098-0 (Berlin) *Fax:* (089) 43189458; (030) 2629115 (Berlin)
Telex: 523259
Key Personnel
Dir: Wolfgang Kunth; Klaus Juergens
Editorial Dir: Dieter Meinhardt
Sales Manager: Michael Maap
Foreign Rights: Konrad Weinstock-Adorno
ISBN Prefix(es): 3-920317
Parent Company: Verlagsgruppe Bertelsmann GmbH, 81664 Munich
Subsidiaries: Guetersloh; Potsdam/Werder
Orders to: Geo Center Verlagsvertrieb GmbH, Neumarkterstr 18, 81603 Munich

Verlag Norman Rentrop+
Ruengsdorferstr 2e, 53173 Bonn
Tel: (0228) 36 88 40 *Fax:* (0228) 36 58 75
E-mail: tt@rentrop.com
Web Site: www.normanrentrop.de
Key Personnel
Man Dir: Norman Rentrop *E-mail:* nr@rentrop.com
Editorial, Publicity: Michael Jansen
Production: Monika Graf
Rights & Permissions: Helmut Graf
Founded: 1975
Specialize in looseleaf services.
Subjects: Business, Finance, Public Administration, Real Estate
Branch Office(s)
Arenbergstr 33, 5020 Salzburg, Austria
Sagestr 14, 5600 Lenzburg/Zurich, Switzerland
One Place du Lycee, 68005 Colmar, France
27A Old Gloucester St, London WC1N 3XX, United Kingdom
U.S. Office(s): Georgetown Publishing House, 1101 30 St NW, Washington, DC 20007, United States *Tel:* 202-337-5960 *Fax:* 202-337-1512
117 W Harrison, Suite R-246, Chicago, IL 60605, United States
Orders to: Buchhandel Deutschland an Buecherdienst Cologne, 51169 Cologne

Respublica Verlag
Kaiserstr 99-101, 53721 Siegburg
Mailing Address: Postfach 1831, 53708 Siegburg
Tel: (02241) 62925; (02241) 64039 *Fax:* (02241) 53891
Key Personnel
President, International Rights: Franz Schmitt
Founded: 1932
Subjects: Music, Dance, Regional Interests
ISBN Prefix(es): 3-87710

Verlagsgruppe Rhein Main GmbH & Co KG
Erich Dombrowskistr 2, 55127 Mainz-Marienborn
Tel: (06131) 48-46-94
Web Site: www.main-rheiner.de
Key Personnel
Manager: Holger Albaum *Tel:* (06131) 48 41 80

Fax: (06131) 48 41 73 *E-mail:* halbaum@vrm.de
ISBN Prefix(es): 3-920615

Verlag Rheinischer Merkur GmbH
Godesberger Allee 91, 53175 Bonn
Mailing Address: Postfach 201164, 53141 Bonn
Tel: (0228) 884-0 *Fax:* (0228) 88 41 70 (sales); (0228) 88 41 99 (editorial); (0228) 88 42 99 (advertising)
E-mail: abo@merkur.de
Web Site: www.merkur.de
Key Personnel
Man Dir: Bert G Wegener
ISBN Prefix(es): 3-9801913

RVBG Rheinland-Verlag-und Betriebsgesellschaft des Landschaftsverbandes Rheinland mbH+
Abtei Brauweiler, 50259 Pulheim
Mailing Address: Postfach 2140, 50250 Pulheim
Tel: (02234) 9854265 *Fax:* (02234) 82503
Telex: uber 8873335 Lvrkd
Key Personnel
Man Dir: Christian Buepel
Founded: 1958
Subjects: Archaeology, History, Regional Interests
ISBN Prefix(es): 3-7927
Subsidiaries: Rhein Eifel Mosel Verlag
Bookshop(s): Versandbuchhandlung, Abtei Brauweiler, 50259 Pulheim
Shipping Address: Dr Rudolf Habelt Verlag, Am Buchenhang 2, 53315 Bonn

Richardi Helmut Verlag GmbH+
Aschaffenburger Str 19, 60599 Frankfurt am Main
Mailing Address: Postfach 11151, 60046 Frankfurt am Main
Tel: (069) 9708330 *Fax:* (069) 7078400
E-mail: kreditwesen@t-online.de
Key Personnel
Owner: Klaus-Friedrich Otto
Publisher: Claus Wonneberger; Werner Scholz
Founded: 1955
Subjects: Finance, Real Estate
ISBN Prefix(es): 3-921722
Associate Companies: Friz Knapp Verlag

Edition Riesenrad, *imprint of* Xenos Verlagsgesellschaft mbH

Rigodon-Verlag Norbert Wehr+
Nieberdingstr 18, 45147 Essen
Tel: (0201) 77 81 11; (0221) 360 21 92
Fax: (0201) 77 51 74; (0221) 360 21 92
E-mail: Schreibheft@NetCologne.de
Web Site: www.schreibheft.de
Key Personnel
Manager: Norbert Wehr
Founded: 1977
Subjects: Literature, Literary Criticism, Essays
ISBN Prefix(es): 3-924071

Rimbaud Verlagsgesellschaft mbH+
Oppenhoffalle 20, 52066 Aachen
Mailing Address: Postfach 10 01 44, 52001 Aachen
Tel: (0241) 54 25 32; (0241) 9019583
Fax: (0241) 514117
E-mail: info@rimbaud.de
Web Site: www.rimbaud.de
Key Personnel
Man Dir, Sales, Publicity: Walter Hoerner
Editorial: Dr Reinhard Kiefer
International Rights: Dr Bernard Albers
Founded: 1983
Subjects: Literature, Literary Criticism, Essays, Music, Dance, Photography, Poetry

ISBN Prefix(es): 3-89086
Distributed by Pegasus Verlagsauslieferung (Switzerland); Hora-Verlag (Austria)

Ritterbach Verlag GmbH
Rudolf-Dieselstr 5-7, 50226 Frechen
Mailing Address: Postfach 1820, 50208 Frechen
Tel: (02234) 18 66 0 *Fax:* (02234) 18 66 90
E-mail: service@ritterbach.de; coeln.ml@ritterbach.de
Web Site: www.ritterbach.de
Founded: 1987
Subjects: Architecture & Interior Design, Art, Career Development, Crafts, Games, Hobbies, Education
ISBN Prefix(es): 3-89314

Ritzau KG Verlag Zeit und Eisenbahn+
Landsbergerstr 24, 86932 Puergen
Tel: (08196) 252 *Fax:* (08196) 1240
E-mail: mail@ritzau.kg.de
Web Site: www.ritzau-kg.de
Founded: 1968
Subjects: History, Transportation
ISBN Prefix(es): 3-921304; 3-935101

RKW, see Rationalisierungs-Kuratorium der Deutschen Wirtschaft eV (RKW)

Roehrig Universitaets Verlag Gmbh
Eichendorffstr 37, 66386 Sankt Ingbert
Tel: (06894) 8 79 57 *Fax:* (06894) 87 03 30
E-mail: info@roehrig-verlag.de
Web Site: www.roehrig-verlag.de
Key Personnel
Publisher: Werner J Roehrig
Founded: 1984
Membership(s): Provincial Federation of Booksellers & Publishers; National Federation of Booksellers & Publishers; Boersenverein des Deutschen Buchhandels.
Subjects: Government, Political Science, History, Language Arts, Linguistics, Literature, Literary Criticism, Essays, Science (General)
ISBN Prefix(es): 3-924555; 3-86110
Number of titles published annually: 40 Print
Total Titles: 400 Print

Erich Roeth-Verlag+
Kastanienweg 4, 39343 Rottmersleben
Tel: (039206) 90103 *Fax:* (039206) 90103 *Cable:* ROTHVERLAG
Key Personnel
Man Dir, Rights & Permissions: Manfred Kaiser
Founded: 1921
Specialize in fairytales.
Subjects: Art, Music, Dance
ISBN Prefix(es): 3-87680
Number of titles published annually: 3 Print; 1 CD-ROM; 1 Audio

Heidi Rogner+
Zum Bosselbach 18, 52393 Huertgenwald
Tel: (02429) 2561
Key Personnel
Contact: Heidi Rogner
Founded: 1995
Subjects: Animals, Pets
ISBN Prefix(es): 3-9804403

Rogner und Bernhard GmbH & Co Verlags KG+
Fettstr 6, 20357 Hamburg
Mailing Address: Postfach 306 243, 20328 Hamburg
Tel: (040) 4302110 *Fax:* (040) 4302716
E-mail: service@on-line.de
Web Site: www.zweitausendeins.de
Key Personnel
Manager: Jarchow Klaas *E-mail:* jarchow@rogner-bernhard.de; Antje Landshoff *E-mail:* jarchow@rogner-bernhard.de
Assistant to the Editor: Marlies Hebler
Founded: 1968
Specialize in popular culture.
Subjects: Art, Fiction, Photography
ISBN Prefix(es): 3-8077; 3-920802
Total Titles: 100 Print
Orders to: Zweitausendeins Versand
Tel: (069) 4208000 *Fax:* (069) 420800198
E-mail: service@zweitausendeins.de

Verlag und Buchversand Wolfgang Roller
Goethestr 15, 63225 Langen
Tel: (06103) 71886 *Fax:* (06103) 929501
E-mail: greif@12move.de
Web Site: www.verlag-roller.de
ISBN Prefix(es): 3-923620

Rombach GmbH Druck und Verlagshaus & Co+
Unterwerkstr 5, 79115 Freiburg
Tel: (0761) 4500 0 *Fax:* (0761) 4500 2125
E-mail: info@buchverlag.rombach.de
Web Site: www.rombach.de
Key Personnel
Man Dirs: Dr Christian H Hodeige
Management: Andreas Hodeige
Dir: Willi Mandery
International Rights: Dr Edelgard Spaude
E-mail: spaude@buchverlag.rombach.de
Sales: Melanie Panzer *Tel:* (0761) 4500-2135
E-mail: panzer@buchverlag.rombach.de
Founded: 1936
Subjects: Art, Government, Political Science, History, Literature, Literary Criticism, Essays, Regional Interests, Social Sciences, Sociology
ISBN Prefix(es): 3-7930
Associate Companies: Rombach Druckhaus KG, Bertoldstr 10, 79098 Freiburg; Rombach Handelshaus KG, Bertoldstr 10, 79098 Freiburg; Rombach Medienhaus KG, Bertoldstr 10, 79098 Freiburg
Bookshop(s): Rombach Buchhandlung, Bertoldstr 10, 79098 Freiburg
Orders to: Waltesverlagsauslieferung, Blochmattastr 11, 7843 Herkesheim

Romiosini Verlag+
Venloerstr 30, 50672 Cologne
Tel: (0221) 5101288 *Fax:* (0221) 5101288
E-mail: romiosini@unisolo.de
Web Site: www.unisolo.de/pls/romiosini/griechische_literatur
Key Personnel
Publisher: Niki Eideneier
Founded: 1982
Specialize in Greek literature in German translation.
Subjects: Cookery, Fiction, History, Literature, Literary Criticism, Essays, Music, Dance, Poetry, Travel
ISBN Prefix(es): 3-923728; 3-929889
Distributed by PHOIBOS Verlag (Austria); MAM (Cypress); Athener Bookshop AG (Greece); Greek Books Elyki (Switzerland)
Orders to: Unisolo/Despina Kazantzidou, Nordohr 11, 38106 Braunschweig *Tel:* (0531) 336050 *Fax:* (0531) 336049 *E-mail:* despina.kazantzidou@unisolo.de *Web Site:* www.unisolo.de/romiosini.htm

Rosenheimer Verlagshaus GmbH & Co KG+
Am Stockel 12, 83022 Rosenheim
Tel: (08031) 2838 0 *Fax:* (08031) 2838 44
E-mail: info@rosenheimer.com
Web Site: www.rosenheimer.com *Cable:* ROSENHEIMER VERLAGSHAUS ROSENHEIM
Key Personnel
Man Dir: Klaus G Foerg
Chief Editor: Dagmar Becker-Goethel

Sales, Rights, Permissions & Publicity: Bernhard Edlmann
Marketing Manager: Uta Lamp *Tel:* (08031) 2838 60
Sales: Angelika Krichbaumer *Tel:* (08031) 2838 61; Regina Rogger *Tel:* (08031) 2838 61
Founded: 1949
Subjects: Crafts, Games, Hobbies, Fiction, History, Regional Interests
ISBN Prefix(es): 3-475
Total Titles: 200 Print; 30 Audio

Rossipaul Kommunikation GmbH+
Menzingerstr 37, 80638 Munich
Mailing Address: Postfach 38 0164, 80614 Munich
Tel: (089) 17 91 06 0 *Fax:* (089) 17 91 06 22
E-mail: info@rossipaul.de
Web Site: www.rossipaul.de
Key Personnel
Man Dir, Rights & Permissions: Rainer Rossipaul
Publicity: Ingo Neubert
Founded: 1952
Subjects: Advertising, Career Development, Computer Science, Finance, Health, Nutrition, Language Arts, Linguistics, Law, Management, Nonfiction (General), Outdoor Recreation
ISBN Prefix(es): 3-87686

Rowohlt Berlin Verlag GmbH, *imprint of* Rowohlt Verlag GmbH

Rowohlt Berlin Verlag GmbH+
Imprint of Rowohlt Verlag GmbH
Kreuzberger Str 30, 10965 Berlin
Tel: (030) 2853840 *Fax:* (040) 28538422
E-mail: info@rowohlt.de
Web Site: www.rowohlt.de
Key Personnel
Man Dir: Dr Helmut Daehne; Alexander Fest; Lutz Kettmann
Editorial Dir: Gunnar Schmidt *E-mail:* gunnar.schmidt@rowohlt.de
Rights & Permissions: Kristina Krombholz
Founded: 1990
Specialize in fiction from East & Central Europe; political nonfiction.
Subjects: Fiction, Nonfiction (General)
ISBN Prefix(es): 3-87134
Number of titles published annually: 30 Print
Total Titles: 160 Print

Rowohlt Taschenbuch Verlag, *imprint of* Rowohlt Verlag GmbH

Rowohlt Verlag GmbH+
Hamburgerstr 17, 21465 Reinbek
Tel: (040) 72720 *Fax:* (040) 7272319
E-mail: info@rowohlt.de
Web Site: www.rowohlt.de
Key Personnel
Man Dir: Dr Helmut Daehne; Alexander Fest
Rights & Permissions: Kristina Krombholz
Contact: Eckhard Kloos *Tel:* (040) 7272214 *E-mail:* eckhard.kloos@rowohlt.de
Man Dir: Lutz Kettmann
Founded: 1908
Subjects: Fiction, Nonfiction (General)
ISBN Prefix(es): 3-498; 3-499; 3-8052
Imprints: Kindler Verlag; Rowohlt Berlin Verlag GmbH; Rowohlt Taschenbuch Verlag; Wunderlich Verlag
U.S. Office(s): Greenburger New York, 55 Fifth Ave, New York, NY 10003, United States

Rudi der Bar ist las, *imprint of* Beerenverlag

Ruetten & Loening Berlin GmbH+
Neue Promenade 6, 10178 Berlin
Mailing Address: Postfach 193, 10105 Berlin
Tel: (030) 283 94 0 *Fax:* (030) 283 94 100
E-mail: info@aufbau-verlag.de
Web Site: www.aufbau-verlag.de
Key Personnel
Program Manager: Rene Strien
Manager: Peter Dempewolf
International Rights: Astrid Poppenhusen *Tel:* (030) 283 94 212 *E-mail:* poppenhusen@aufbau-verlag.de
Contact: Barbara Stang
Rights & Permissions: Kathrin Schulz
Founded: 1844
Subjects: Fiction, Government, Political Science, History, Literature, Literary Criticism, Essays, Mysteries, Poetry, Romance
ISBN Prefix(es): 3-352
Number of titles published annually: 30 Print
Total Titles: 100 Print
Shipping Address: Mohr Morawa, Buchvertrieb Gesellschaft mbH, Postfach 260, A-1101 Vienna, Austria; Buecher Balmer, Verlagsauslieferung, Neugasse 12, 6301 Zurich, Switzerland
Warehouse: Libri-Distributions GmbH, August-Schanzstr 33, 60433 Frankfurt
Orders to: Libri-Distributions GmbH, August-Schanzstr 33, 60433 Frankfurt

Winfried Ruf, see Fachmedien Verlag Winfried Ruf (FMV)

Dieter Ruggeberg Verlagsbuchhandlung+
Wuppermannstr 28, 42275 Wuppertal
Mailing Address: Postfach 13 08 44, 42035 Wuppertal
Tel: (0202) 592811 *Fax:* (0202) 592811
E-mail: vrggeberg@aol.com
Web Site: www.vbdr.de
Key Personnel
Man Dir, Rights & Permissions: Dieter Rueggeberg *E-mail:* vrggeberg@aol.com
Founded: 1968
Subjects: Astrology, Occult, Government, Political Science, Religion - Other
ISBN Prefix(es): 3-921338

Ruhland Verlag Gimblt
Hermann-Steinhaeuserstr 2, 63065 Offenbach Am Main
Tel: (069) 811768 *Fax:* (069) 811769
Key Personnel
Man Dir, Publicity, Rights & Permissions: Margitta Kieltsch-weidl
Founded: 1968
Subjects: Business, Management
ISBN Prefix(es): 3-88509; 3-920793

Verlag an der Ruhr GmbH+
Alexanderstr 54, 45472 Muelheim an der Ruhr
Mailing Address: Postfach 102251, 45422 Muelheim
Tel: (0208) 4395454 *Fax:* (0208) 4395439
E-mail: info@verlagruhr.de
Web Site: www.verlagruhr.de
Key Personnel
Man Dir & Publisher: Wilfried Stascheit
Man Dir: Annelie Loeber-Stascheit
Founded: 1981
Books & worksheets for pedagogical & educational work in school & extracurricular work. Unconventional methods, innovative contents & topical themes.
Membership(s): German Booksellers Association.
Subjects: Art, Communications, Developing Countries, Education, English as a Second Language, Environmental Studies, Geography, Geology, History, Human Relations, Literature, Literary Criticism, Essays, Mathematics, Philosophy, Physical Sciences, Religion - Other
ISBN Prefix(es): 3-86072; 3-927279; 3-924884
Total Titles: 500 Print

Distributed by Schulverlag blmv AG; Veritas
Orders to: Paedexpress GmbH & Co KG
Tel: (0208) 495040 *Fax:* (0208) 4950495
E-mail: info@paedexpress.de

RV, see R V Reise- und Verkehrsverlag GmbH

RVBG, see RVBG Rheinland-Verlag-und Betriebsgesellschaft des Landschaftsverbandes Rheinland mbH

Reinhard Ryborsch, see Kartographischer Verlag Reinhard Ryborsch

Ryvellus, *imprint of* Neue Erde Verlags GmbH

Ryvellus Medienagentur Dopfer+
Cecilienstr 29, 66111 Saarbruecken
Tel: (0681) 372313 *Fax:* (0681) 3904102
Key Personnel
Manager: Manfred Dopfer
Founded: 1989
Subjects: Environmental Studies, Health, Nutrition, Nonfiction (General), Psychology, Psychiatry, Body, Mind & Spirit, Esoterics/New Age, Popular, Non-Fiction
ISBN Prefix(es): 3-89453

Saarbrucker Druckerei und Verlag GmbH (SDV)
Halbergstr 3, 66121 Saarbruecken
Mailing Address: Postfach 102745, 66027 Saarbruecken
Tel: (0681) 66501-0 *Fax:* (0681) 66501-10
Web Site: www.sdv-saar.de
Key Personnel
Man Dir & Editorial: Olanfred Wagner
Sales Manager: Corinne Wuest *E-mail:* cwuest@sdv-saar.de
Founded: 1922
Subjects: Antiques, Archaeology, Art, History, Language Arts, Linguistics, Literature
ISBN Prefix(es): 3-921646; 3-925036; 3-930843

Saatkorn-Verlag GmbH
Luener Rennbahn 16, 21339 Lueneburg
Tel: (04131) 98 35-02 *Fax:* (04131) 98 35 505
E-mail: info@saatkornverlag.de
Web Site: wwww.saatkorn-verlag.de
Key Personnel
Man Dir: Eckhard Boettge
Editorial, Rights & Permissions Secretary: Eli Diez
Sales: Erhard Knirr
Printing Works: Peter Streit
Founded: 1895
Subjects: Health, Nutrition, Theology
ISBN Prefix(es): 3-8150; 3-87689
Subsidiaries: Grindeldruck GmbH
Warehouse: Auf dem Salzstock 11, 21217 Seevetal-Meckelfeld

Verlag Werner Sachon GmbH & Co
Schloss Mindelburg, 87714 Mindelheim
Tel: (08261) 999-0 *Fax:* (08261) 999 391
E-mail: info@sachon.de
Web Site: www.sachon.de
Telex: 539624
Key Personnel
Contact: Wolfgang Burkart; Werner Sachon
Subjects: Engineering (General), Health, Nutrition, Management, Marketing, Mechanical Engineering, Wine & Spirits
ISBN Prefix(es): 3-920819; 3-929032; 3-929032

Sachsenbuch Verlagsgesellschaft Mbh
Bruehl 76, 04109 Leipzig
Mailing Address: Postfach 461, 04004 Leipzig
Tel: (0341) 9784259; (0341) 9784261 *Fax:* (0341) 9784259
Key Personnel
Manager: Wolf-Diethelm Zastrutzki

GERMANY

Editor: Klaus Hoerhold
Public Relations: W U Schuette
Founded: 1990
Membership(s): the Stock Exchange of German Booksellers.
Subjects: Art, Regional Interests
ISBN Prefix(es): 3-910148; 3-89664
Branch Office(s)
Neuer Sachsenverlag Leipzig, Coppistr 36, 04157 Leipzig
Bookshop(s): Buchhandlung, Neue Leipzigerstr 16, 04205 Leipzig; Buchhandlung, Schwarzackerstr, 04229 Leipzig
Shipping Address: Buchhandlung Sachsenbuch, Bruhl 76, Postfach 461, 04109 Leipzig

Verlag Otto Sagner
Subsidiary of Kubon & Sagner Buchexport-Import GmbH
Hessstr 39/41, 80798 Munich
Tel: (089) 54 218-0 *Fax:* (089) 54 218-218
E-mail: postmaster@kubon-sagner.de
Web Site: www.kubon-sagner.de
Key Personnel
Man Dir: Petrols Sagner; Sabine Sagner-Weigl
 E-mail: sabine.sagnerweigl@kubon-sagner.de
Publisher: Otto Sagner
Editorial: Prof Peter Rehder, PhD
Founded: 1947
Book export import publishing company.
Subjects: Language Arts, Linguistics, Literature, Literary Criticism, Essays
ISBN Prefix(es): 3-87690

Eugen Salzer-Verlag GmbH & Co KG+
Titotstr 5, 74072 Heilbronn
Tel: (07131) 68294 *Fax:* (07131) 171331
Key Personnel
Man Dir: Sibylle Salzer
Procurer, Sales Dir, Rights & Permissions: Monika Nissen
Founded: 1891
Subjects: Biography, Fiction, How-to
ISBN Prefix(es): 3-7936

Sammlung, imprint of Bund demokratischer Wissenschaftlerinnen und Wissenschafler eV (BdWi)

SAMS, imprint of Pearson Education Deutschland GmbH

Verlag der Sankt-Johannis-Druckerei C Schweickhardt+
Heiligenstr 24, 77933 Lahr
Tel: (07821) 5810 *Fax:* (07821) 58126
E-mail: johannis-druck@t-online.de
Web Site: www.johannis-verlag.de *Cable:* VERITAS LAHR SCHWARZWALD
Key Personnel
Man Dir: Walter Guthmann
Editorial, Publicity, Rights & Permissions: Dr Thomas Baumann
Sales: Karl Heinz Kern
Production: Helmut Schlegel
Founded: 1896
Membership(s): the Telos Group Publishing Evangelical Paperbacks.
Subjects: Art, Biography, Fiction, Religion - Protestant
ISBN Prefix(es): 3-501
Associate Companies: Edition VLM; SKV-Edition
Distributed by BMK Verlagsauslieferung (Austria); Brunnen Verlag (Switzerland)

Sassafras Verlag
Dreikoenigenstr 146, 47798 Krefeld
Tel: (02151) 787770 *Fax:* (02151) 771302
Key Personnel
Man Dir, International Rights: Klaus Ulrich Duesselberg
Founded: 1975
Subjects: Literature, Literary Criticism, Essays, Poetry
ISBN Prefix(es): 3-922690

Sattva Kunst Verlag+
Rechenau 1, 83730 Fischbachau
Tel: (08028) 90 68-0 *Fax:* (08028) 90 68-10; (08028) 90 68-20
Key Personnel
Contact: Sonja Wiesbeck
Subjects: Music, Dance
ISBN Prefix(es): 3-925035
Divisions: Sattva Music & Sattva Art Design

I H Sauer Verlag GmbH+
Hausserstr 14, 69115 Heidelberg
Mailing Address: Postfach 10 59 60, 69049 Heidelberg
Tel: (06221) 9060 *Fax:* (06221) 906259
E-mail: sauer-verlag@ruw.de
Web Site: www.ruw-ruw.de
Telex: 461665rewhihd
Key Personnel
Man Dir: Michael Giesecke
Publisher: Angelika Sauer
Contact: Norbert Konda
Founded: 1964
Subjects: Career Development, Communications, Economics, Labor, Industrial Relations, Management, Marketing, Psychology, Psychiatry
ISBN Prefix(es): 3-7938
Associate Companies: Verlag Recht und Wirtschaft GmbH

Verlag Sauerlaender GmbH+
Waechtersbacherstr 89, 60386 Frankfurt
Mailing Address: Postfach 630247, 60352 Frankfurt
Tel: (069) 942118-0 *Fax:* (069) 412099
Key Personnel
Publisher: Hans C Sauerlaender
Founded: 1807
Subjects: Fiction, Science (General)
ISBN Prefix(es): 3-7941
Parent Company: Sauerlaender AG, 5001 Aarau, Switzerland
Associate Companies: Verlag Sauerlaender, Muenzgasse 1, A-5020 Salzburg, Austria
Showroom(s): Infortiationsstelle Schlilbuch, Laurentenvorstadt 85, 5001 Arau
Orders to: Sauerlander AG, Laurentenvorstadt 89, 5001 Karan, Switzerland *Tel:* (062) 836 8686 *Fax:* (062) 836 8620

J D Sauerlaender's Verlag+
Finkenhofstr 21, 60322 Frankfurt
Tel: (069) 555217 *Fax:* (069) 5964344
E-mail: j.d.sauerlaenders.verlag@t-online.de
Web Site: www.sauerlaender-verlag.com
Key Personnel
Publisher: Stephanie Aulbach
Founded: 1816
Specialize in forest genetics.
Subjects: Agriculture, Language Arts, Linguistics
ISBN Prefix(es): 3-7939
Number of titles published annually: 6 Print

K G Saur Verlag GmbH, A Gale/Thomson Learning Company+
Unit of Thomson Learning
Ortlerstr 8, 81373 Munich
Mailing Address: Postfach 70 16 20, 81316 Munich
Tel: (089) 76902-0 *Fax:* (089) 76902-150
E-mail: saur.info@thomson.com
Web Site: www.saur.de
Key Personnel
Man Dir: Prof Dr h c mult Klaus G Saur
 E-mail: K.Saur@saur.de
Sales Dir: Paul Fertl *E-mail:* P.Fertl@saur.de
Promotion & Press Service: Petra Huetter
 E-mail: P.Huetter@saur.de
Production Dir: Manfred Link *E-mail:* M.Link@saur.de
Publishing Dir: Clara Waldrich *E-mail:* C.Waldrich@saur.de
Commercial Dir: Christoph Hahne *E-mail:* C.Hahne@saur.de
Rights & Permissions: Christina Hofmann
 E-mail: C.Hofmann@saur.de
Editorial Dir: Barbara Fischer *E-mail:* b.fischer@saur.de
Founded: 1949
Subjects: Art, Biography, Communications, History, Library & Information Sciences, Literature, Literary Criticism, Essays, Music, Dance, Philosophy, Publishing & Book Trade Reference, Social Sciences, Sociology
ISBN Prefix(es): 3-598; 3-7940; 3-907820; 3-908255; 2-86294
Total Titles: 2,500 Print; 100 CD-ROM; 6 E-Book
Parent Company: Gale
Ultimate Parent Company: The Thomson Corporation

Sax-Verlag Beucha
An der Halde 12, 04824 Beucha
Tel: (034292) 75210 *Fax:* (034292) 75220
E-mail: info@sax-verlag.de
Web Site: www.sax-verlag.de
Key Personnel
Contact: Erika Heydick
Founded: 1992
Subjects: Biography, Education, History, Non-fiction (General), Regional Interests, Science (General), Social Sciences, Sociology
ISBN Prefix(es): 3-930076; 3-934544; 3-9802997
Number of titles published annually: 15 Print
Total Titles: 100 Print

scaneg Verlag
Heiglhofstr 24, 81377 Munich
Mailing Address: Postfach 701606, 81316 Munich
Tel: (089) 759 33 36 *Fax:* (089) 759 39 14
E-mail: verlag@scaneg.de
Web Site: www.scaneg.de
Founded: 1983
Subjects: Art, History, Literature, Literary Criticism, Essays, Poetry, Art History
ISBN Prefix(es): 3-89235; 3-9800671

Verlag Th Schaefer im Vicentz Verlag KG
Stockholmer Allee 5, 30539 Hannover
Mailing Address: Postfach 721306, 30533 Hannover
Tel: (0511) 87575-075 *Fax:* (0511) 87575-079
Key Personnel
Publisher: Werner Geisselbrecht
Founded: 1980
Specialize in reprints of professional books.
Subjects: Architecture & Interior Design, Art, Crafts, Games, Hobbies, House & Home
ISBN Prefix(es): 3-88746
Parent Company: Th Schaefer Verlag im Vincentz Verlag KG
Orders to: Vincentz Verlag KG, Postfach 6247, 30062 Hannover *Tel:* (0511) 9910-012 *Fax:* (0511) 9910-013 *Web Site:* www.libri_rari.de

Verlag Anke Schaefer
Ortsstr 43, 56379 Charlottenberg bei Holzappel, Rhein-Lahn-K
Tel: (06439) 7870
Key Personnel
Owner: Anke Schaefer
Founded: 1978
Subjects: Gay & Lesbian, Women's Studies
ISBN Prefix(es): 3-922229

PUBLISHERS — GERMANY

Divisions: Feministischer Buchverlag
Bookshop(s): Frauenbuchversand, Luxemburgstr 2, 65185 Wiesbaden

Schaeffer-Poeschel Verlag fuer Wirtschaft Steuern Recht+
Werastr 21-23, 70182 Stuttgart
Mailing Address: Postfach 10 32 41, 70028 Stuttgart
Tel: (0711) 2194-0 *Fax:* (0711) 2194-119
E-mail: info@schaeffer-poeschel.de
Web Site: www.schaeffer-poeschel.de
Key Personnel
Man Dir: Michael Justus *E-mail:* justus@schaeffer-poeschel.de
General Manager: Volker Dabelstein; Marita Rollnik Mollenhauer
Sales Dir: Michael Schmid
Marketing Manager: Michael Schmid
Rights Manager: Andrea Rupp
Advertising: Sabine Zobeley
Press: Joachim Bader
Electronic Publishing: Ursula Chwalisz
Founded: 1902
Subjects: Accounting, Business, Economics, Finance, Management, Marketing
ISBN Prefix(es): 3-7910; 3-8202; 3-7992
Number of titles published annually: 200 Print
Total Titles: 800 Print
Parent Company: Verlagsgruppe Handelsblatt
Ultimate Parent Company: Verlagsgruppe Georg Von Holtzbrinck

Schangrila Verlags und Vertriebs GmbH+
Lindenstr 45, 87648 Aitrang
Tel: (08343) 581 *Fax:* (08343) 657
E-mail: info@schangrila.com
Web Site: www.schangrila.com
Founded: 1984
Subjects: Cookery, Medicine, Nursing, Dentistry, Philosophy
ISBN Prefix(es): 3-924624

Schapen Edition, H W Louis+
Gartenweg 6b, 38104 Braunschweig
Tel: (0531) 360921 *Fax:* (0531) 363190
E-mail: schapen.edition@t-online.de
Key Personnel
International Rights: Dr Hans Walter Louis
Founded: 1990
Subjects: Environmental Studies, Law
ISBN Prefix(es): 3-927942

M & H Schaper GmbH & Co KG+
Borsigstr 5, 31061 Alfeld-Leine
Mailing Address: Postfach 1642, 31046 Alfeld-Leine
Tel: (05181) 8009-0 *Fax:* (05181) 8009-33
E-mail: info@schaper-verlag.de
Web Site: www.schaper-verlag.de
Key Personnel
International Rights: Wolfgang Habeck
Marketing Manager: Dieter Meyer *Tel:* (05181) 8009-40 *E-mail:* d.meyer@schaper-verlag.de; Rainer Paland *Tel:* (05181) 8009-14 *E-mail:* info@schaper-verlag.de
Sales Manager: Carsten Sadlau *Tel:* (05181) 8009-16 *E-mail:* c.sadlau@schaper-verlag.de
Founded: 1897
Subjects: Animals, Pets, Crafts, Games, Hobbies, Veterinary Science
ISBN Prefix(es): 3-7944

Schattauer GmbH Verlag fuer Medizin und Naturwissenschaften+
Hoelderlinstr 3, 70174 Stuttgart
Tel: (0711) 2 29 87-0 *Fax:* (0711) 2 29 87-50
E-mail: info@schattauer.de
Web Site: www.schattauer.de
Key Personnel
Man Dir: Dieter Bergemann
Founded: 1949
Publishing house for medicine & natural sciences.
Subjects: Medicine, Nursing, Dentistry, Science (General)
ISBN Prefix(es): 3-7945
Shipping Address: Koch, Neff & Oetinger & Co Verlagsauslieferungen, Schockenriedstr 39, 70565 Stuttgart *Tel:* (0711) 78603365
Warehouse: Koch, Neff & Oetinger & Co Verlagsauslieferungen, Schockenriedstr 39, 70565 Stuttgart *Tel:* (0711) 78603365
Orders to: D A Book Depot Pty Ltd, 648 Whitehorse Rd, Mitcham, Victoria 3132, Australia *Tel:* (03) 873 4411 *Fax:* (03) 873 5679
Mohr-Morawa Gesellschaft mbH, Sulzengasse 2, 1232 Vienna, Austria *Tel:* (0222) 684614 *Fax:* (0222) 687130
Allied Publishers Pvt Ltd, 13/14 Asaf Ali Rd, PO Box 155, New Delhi 110002, India *Tel:* 2750001
Verlag Hans Huber AG, Langgassstr 76, 3000 Bern 9, Switzerland *Tel:* (031) 262533 *Fax:* (031) 43380
John Wiley & Sons Inc, Wiley-Liss Division, 111 River St, Hoboken, NJ 07030, United States *Tel:* 201-748-6000 *Fax:* 201-748-6088

Verlag Heinrich Scheffler, *imprint of* Societaets-Verlag

Scheffler-Verlag+
Goethestr 26, 58313 Herdecke
Mailing Address: Postfach 1449, 58304 Herdecke
Tel: (02330) 1743 *Fax:* (02330) 2281
Key Personnel
President: Lothor Scheffler
Vice President: Barbel Scheffler
Founded: 1989
ISBN Prefix(es): 3-89704; 3-9802922; 3-9803249; 3-929885
Total Titles: 15 Print

Schelzky & Jeep, Verlag fuer Reisen und Wissen+
Fidicinstr 29, 10965 Berlin
Tel: (030) 6939495 *Fax:* (030) 6914697
Founded: 1981
Subjects: Architecture & Interior Design, Regional Interests, Social Sciences, Sociology, Travel
ISBN Prefix(es): 3-89541; 3-923024

Renate Schenk Verlag+
Heinkstr 10, 04347 Leipzig
Tel: (0341) 2300825 *Fax:* (0341) 2300826
E-mail: schenk-verlag@t-online.de
Web Site: www.schenk-verlag.de
Founded: 1984
Membership(s): Australian Book Publishers Association (ABPA). Specialize in books about Australia, Australian Books, Antiquariat Aboriginal Art.
Subjects: Anthropology, Earth Sciences, Natural History, Travel
Divisions: Winjeel Shop Alice Springs Australia
Distributor for Magabala (Lansdown); Reader's Digest (Australia); Reed Books (Australia)
Bookshop(s): Koala Trade
Orders to: Geo Center Touristik Medien Service GmbH, Schockenriedstr 44, 70565 Stuttgart, Cornelia Braun *Tel:* (0711) 781946-41143 *Fax:* (0711) 781946-56

Richard Scherpe Verlag GmbH
Glockenspitz 140, 47800 Krefeld
Mailing Address: Postfach 2630, 47726 Krefeld
Tel: (02151) 539-0 *Fax:* (02151) 505390
Key Personnel
Owner: Richard Scherpe
International Rights: Mrs Wendt
Subjects: Education, Fiction, Government, Political Science
ISBN Prefix(es): 3-7948

Ulrich Schiefer bahn Verlag+
Fuerstenriederstr 44, 80686 Munich
Mailing Address: Postfach 210620, 80676 Munich
Tel: (089) 89020999 *Fax:* (089) 89020087
Key Personnel
Owner: Ulrich Schiefer
Founded: 1985
Subjects: Crafts, Games, Hobbies, Film, Video, Transportation
ISBN Prefix(es): 3-924969

Schiffahrts-Verlag
Striepenweg 31, 21147 Hamburg
Tel: (040) 79713-02 *Fax:* (040) 79713-324; (040) 79713-208; (040) 79713-214
E-mail: r_spieckermann@hansa-online.de
Specialize in Shipbuilding & Ship Technology, Shipping.
ISBN Prefix(es): 3-87700
Number of titles published annually: 2 Print
Total Titles: 20 Print

Schild-Verlag GmbH+
Henschelstr 7, 81249 Munich
Tel: (089) 8 64 1189 *Fax:* (089) 8 63 2310
Key Personnel
Man Dir: Gunther Damerau
Founded: 1951
Subjects: Antiques, History, Literature, Literary Criticism, Essays, Military Science
ISBN Prefix(es): 3-88014
Total Titles: 35 Print

Verlag der Schillerbuchhandlung Hans Banger OHG
Guldenbachstr 1, 50935 Cologne
Tel: (0221) 46014-0 *Fax:* (0221) 46014-25; (0221) 46014-26
E-mail: banger@banger.de
Web Site: www.banger.de
Key Personnel
Man Dir: Ruth Jepsen; Elisabeth Mueller
Founded: 1950
ISBN Prefix(es): 3-87856

Schillinger Verlag GmbH+
Wallstr 14, 79098 Freiburg
Mailing Address: Postfach 1502, 79015 Freiburg
Tel: (0761) 33233 *Fax:* (0762) 39055
E-mail: schillingerverlag@t-online.de
Web Site: schillingerverlag.de
Key Personnel
Man Dir: Helga Schillinger; Wolfgang Schillinger
Founded: 1984
Membership(s): the Stock Exchange of German Booksellers.
Subjects: Art, Asian Studies, Environmental Studies, Fiction, Foreign Countries, History, Regional Interests, Travel
ISBN Prefix(es): 3-89155
Number of titles published annually: 15 Print
Total Titles: 214 Print

Schirmer/Mosel Verlag GmbH+
Widenmayerstr 16, 80538 Munich
Mailing Address: Postfach 221641, 80506 Munich
Tel: (089) 2126700 *Fax:* (089) 338695
E-mail: mail@schirmer-mosel.com
Web Site: www.schirmer-mosel.com
Key Personnel
Executive Dir: Lothar Schirmer
Production: Roland Hepp
International Rights: Dr Franz Ringel
Founded: 1975
Specialize in Collector's Editions.
Subjects: Art, Photography

ISBN Prefix(es): 3-88814; 3-8296; 3-921375
U.S. Office(s): PO Box 457, New York, NY 10012, United States, US Representative: Phillip Galgiani

Schirner Verlag+
Zerninstr 7, 64297 Darmstadt
Tel: (06151) 29 39 59 *Fax:* (06151) 29 39 87
E-mail: verlag@schirner.com
Web Site: www.schirner.com
Key Personnel
Man Dir: Kirsten Glueck *Tel:* (06151) 29 39 52; Markus Schirner
Bookkeeper: Erika Furbush *Tel:* (06151) 29 33 69
Contact: Gabriele Olschok; Uta Wagner
Founded: 1994
Subjects: Buddhist, Ethno-dictionaries, Mandala Painting Books, Practical Workbooks & Spiritual Self-Help
ISBN Prefix(es): 3-930944; 3-89767
Total Titles: 300 Print; 35 Audio
Foreign Rep(s): Dessauer (Switzerland); Hartmut Gindler Verlagsvertretur (Germany); Verlagsvertretung Klaus-Dieter Guhl (Germany); Verlagsvertretur Mareile & Peter Handrich (Germany); AS Hoeller Gmbh (Austria); Verlagsvertretung Martina & Detief Jessen (Germany); Verlagsagentur Reinhard Lieber (Germany); Handelsvertretung Hannelore Lindemann (Germany); Verlagsvertretung Herbert Pamminger (Austria); Walter Stolte Verlagsvertretung mH Herz (Germany)
Foreign Rights: Daniel Doglioli (Italy); Peter Schmidt Media Service International (France, Spain)

Agora Verlag Manfred Schlosser+
Grunewaldstr 53, 10825 Berlin
Tel: (030) 8545372; (030) 8545915 *Fax:* (030) 8545372
E-mail: agora2@gmx.net *Cable:* AGORA BERLIN
Key Personnel
Man Dir, Production: Manfred Schloesser
Sales & Publicity: Monika Schloesser-Fischer
Founded: 1960
Subjects: Fiction, Literature, Literary Criticism, Essays, Music, Dance, Poetry, Religion - Jewish
ISBN Prefix(es): 3-87008
Total Titles: 140 Print
Subsidiaries: Erato-Presse
Orders to: Bugrim Saalburgstr 3, 712099 Berlin

Schmetterling Verlag Jorg Hunger und Paul Sander+
Lindenspuerstr 38B, 70176 Stuttgart
Tel: (0711) 62 67 79 *Fax:* (0711) 62 69 92
E-mail: info@schmetterling-verlag.de
Web Site: www.schmetterling-verlag.de
Key Personnel
Production: Paul Sander
Public Speaker: Joerg Hunger
Contact: Joerg Exner
Subjects: Culture, Politics
ISBN Prefix(es): 3-926369; 3-89657

Schmid Verlag GmbH
Hedwigstr 13b, 93049 Regensburg
Tel: (0941) 21519 *Fax:* (0941) 28766
E-mail: info@schmid-verlag.de
Web Site: www.schmid-verlag.de
Key Personnel
Owner: Irmigard Schmid
Founded: 1947
Subjects: Travel
ISBN Prefix(es): 3-930572; 3-921657
Branch Office(s)
Karl-Wurmbstr 3, 5020 Salzburg, Austria

Schmidmusic, *imprint of* Silberburg-Verlag Titus Haeussermann GmbH

Verlag Dr Otto Schmidt KG+
Unter den Ulmen 96-98, 50968 Cologne (Marienburg)
Tel: (0221) 9 37 38-01 *Fax:* (0221) 9 37 38 931
E-mail: info@ottoschmidt.de; verlag@ottoschmidt.de
Web Site: www.otto-schmidt.de
Telex: 8883381 osvd *Cable:* SCHMIDTVERLAG
Key Personnel
Man Dir: K P Winters
Editorial: Dr Katherine Knauth
Sales, Publicity & Advertising: Michael Rieck
Organization, Financial: Arno Harms
Founded: 1905
Subjects: Business, Finance, Law
ISBN Prefix(es): 3-504
Associate Companies: Centrale fur GmbH Dr Otto Schmidt
Subsidiaries: Anwalt-Suchservice GmbH; Centrale fur Verbaende und Vereine Verlag Dr Otto Schmidt GmbH
Branch Office(s)
Haus Bayenthalguertel, Bayenthalguertel 13, 50968 Cologne (Marienburg)
Buerocenter Bonnerstr 484-486, 50968 Cologne (Marienburg)
Bookshop(s): Friedrich-Verlegerstr 7, 33602 Bielefeld; Am Yustizzentrum 3, 50939 Cologne 47; Buchhandlung Hermann Sack, Klosterstr 22, 40211 Duesseldorf; Buchhandlung Hermann Sack, Guenthersburgallee 1, 60316 Frankfurt am Main; Harkortstr 7, 04107 Leipzig; Struppe u Winckler, Postfach 10 24 91, 33527 Bielefeld
Distribution Center: Kirschbaumweg 18a, 50966 Cologne (Rodenkirchen)

Erich Schmidt Verlag GmbH & Co
Genthiner Str 30 G, 10785 Berlin
Mailing Address: Postfach 304240, 10724 Berlin
Tel: (030) 25 00 85-0 *Fax:* (030) 25 00 85-305
E-mail: esv@esvmedien.de
Web Site: www.erich-schmidt-verlag.de
Key Personnel
Man Dir: Claus-Michael Rast *E-mail:* c.rast@esvmedien.de; Dr Joachim Schmidt *E-mail:* j.schmidt@esvmedien.de
Sales Manager: Sibylle Boehler *E-mail:* s.boehler@esvmedian.de
Founded: 1924
Subjects: Accounting, Business, Finance, Law, Philological Topics
ISBN Prefix(es): 3-503; 3-89161
Number of titles published annually: 220 Print

Verlag Hermann Schmidt Universitatsdruckerei GmbH & Co+
Robert Kochstr 8, 55129 Mainz-Hechtsheim (Gewerbegebiet)
Tel: (06131) 506030 *Fax:* (06131) 506080
E-mail: info@typografie.de
Web Site: www.typografie.de
Key Personnel
International Rights: Karin Schmidt-Friderichs
Founded: 1950
Specialize in typography & design.
Subjects: Art
ISBN Prefix(es): 3-87439
Orders to: Verlag Hermann Schmidt Mainz, Luisenstr 6, 55124 Mainz

Schmidt Periodicals GmbH
Dettendorf Romerring 12, 83075 Bad Feilnbach
Tel: (08064) 221 *Fax:* (08064) 557
E-mail: schmidt@periodicals.com
Web Site: www.periodicals.com
Key Personnel
Dir: Gerhard Schmidt
Sales & Marketing: Victoria Smith *Tel:* (0034) 921 412194 *Fax:* (0034) 921 412625 *E-mail:* vsmith@periodicals.com
Founded: 1962
Specialize in back sets, volumes & issues of periodicals, serials & reference works in all subjects & languages.
Subjects: Science (General), Medical, Technical
Total Titles: 9,999 Print
U.S. Office(s): Periodicals Service Company, 11 Main St, Germantown, NY 12526, United States, Contact: James Curran *Tel:* 518-537-4700 *Fax:* 518-537-5899 *E-mail:* psc@periodicals.com

Max Schmidt-Roemhild Verlag+
Mengstr 16, 23552 Luebeck
Tel: (0451) 70 31-01 *Fax:* (0451) 70 31-253
E-mail: msr-luebeck@t-online.de
Web Site: www.schmidt-roemhild.de
Key Personnel
Publisher: Norbert Beleke
Man Dir, Rights & Permissions: Hans-Juergen Sperling
Editorship: Dr Edwin Kube *Tel:* (0228) 28044-40 *Fax:* (0228) 28044-41 *E-mail:* kube@forum-kriminalpraevention.de
Layout: Peter Koesling *Tel:* (0201) 8130-200 *Fax:* (0201) 8130-196
Contact: Dr M Platzkoester
Founded: 1579
Subjects: Criminology, History, Law, Medicine, Nursing, Dentistry, Regional Interests, Social Sciences, Sociology, Sports, Athletics
ISBN Prefix(es): 3-7950; 3-8016
Associate Companies: Schmidt-Roemhild Verlagsgesellschaft mbH Brandenburg, August-Bebelstr 23-27, 14470 Brandenburg *Tel:* (03381) 3693-0
Subsidiaries: Hansisches Verlags Kontor
Branch Office(s)
Schmidt-Roemhild Verlagsgesellschaft mbH Leipzig, Coppistr 2, 04129 Leipzig *Tel:* (0341) 90 48 50
Schmidt-Roemhild Verlagsgesellschaft mbH Rostock, Platz der Freundschaft 1, 18059 Rostock *Tel:* (0381) 44 84 55
Schmidt-Roemhild Verlagsgesellschaft mbH Schwerin, Graf-Schack-Allee 6, 19053 Schwerin *Tel:* (0385) 5 91 88-0
Verlag fur Polizeiliches Fachschrifttum Georg Schmidt- Roemhild, Mengstr 16, 23552 Luebeck

Wilhelm Schmitz Verlag+
Am Weidacker 12, 35435 Wettenberg-Launsbach
Tel: (0641) 877 3939
Web Site: www.wilhelm-schmitz-verlag.de
Key Personnel
Man Dir, Rights & Permissions: Siegfried Schmitz
Founded: 1847
Subjects: Art, Ethnicity, Foreign Countries, Language Arts, Linguistics, Literature, Literary Criticism, Essays, Medicine, Nursing, Dentistry
ISBN Prefix(es): 3-87711

Schneekluth Verlag+
Hilblestr 54, 80636 Munich
Tel: (089) 92710 *Fax:* (089) 9271168
Web Site: www.schneekluth.de
Key Personnel
Man Dir: Ralf Mueller; Christian Tesch; Dr Hans-Peter Uebleis
Founded: 1949
ISBN Prefix(es): 3-7951
Number of titles published annually: 30 Print
Parent Company: Verlagsgruppe Droemer Weltbild

Rudolf Schneider Verlag+
Luitpoldstr 16, 91781 Weissenburg
Tel: (089) 8113466 *Fax:* (089) 8110619
Key Personnel
Publisher & Man Dir: Karl-Heinz Biebl

Founded: 1926
Divisions: Edition Hohenstaufen

Verlag Schnell und Steiner GmbH+
Leibnizstr 13, 93055 Regensburg
Mailing Address: Postfach 200429, 93063 Regensburg
Tel: (0941) 787850 *Fax:* (0941) 7878516
E-mail: susvertrieb@t-online.de *Cable:* SCHNELLSTEINER REGENSBURG
Key Personnel
Publisher: Conrad Lienhardt
Sales & Marketing: Rainer Boos; Christian Pflug
Founded: 1934
Subjects: Archaeology, Art, Biblical Studies, Biography, History, Music, Dance, Religion - Catholic, Religion - Protestant, Theology, Travel
ISBN Prefix(es): 3-7954
Number of titles published annually: 45 Print
Total Titles: 3,500 Print
Imprints: Zodiaque
Distributed by Rex Verlag (Switzerland)

Schnitzer GmbH & Co KG+
Feldbergstr 11, 78112 St Georgen
Tel: (07724) 9432-0 *Fax:* (07724) 9432-20
Founded: 1966
Subjects: Health, Nutrition
ISBN Prefix(es): 3-922894; 3-921123

Schoeffling & Co+
Kaiserstr 79, 60329 Frankfurt am Main
Tel: (069) 92 07 87-0 *Fax:* (069) 92 07 87-20
E-mail: info@schoeffling.de
Web Site: www.schoeffling.de
Key Personnel
Publisher: Klaus Schoeffling
Publicity, Editorial: Ida Schoeffling
Rights & Permissions, International Rights: Kathrin Scheel
Founded: 1993
Subjects: Biography, Fiction, Literature, Literary Criticism, Essays, Travel
ISBN Prefix(es): 3-89561
Number of titles published annually: 30 Print

Verlag Hans Schoener GmbH+
Walther-Rathenaustr 13, 75203 Koenigsbach-Stein
Mailing Address: Postfach 69, 75197 Koenigsbach-Stein
Tel: (07232) 4007-0 *Fax:* (07232) 4007-99
E-mail: info@verlag-schoener.de
Web Site: www.verlag-schoener.de
Key Personnel
Man Dir: Elke Schoener *Tel:* (07232) 40 07-20 *E-mail:* es@verlag-schoener.de; Jourg Schoener *Tel:* (07232) 40 07-11 *E-mail:* js@verlag-schoener.de
Editorial: Michael Franz *Tel:* (07232) 40 07-22 *E-mail:* wimo@verlag-schoener.de; Wilfried Morlock *Tel:* (07232) 40 07-23 *E-mail:* mic@verlag-schoener.de
Founded: 1971
Subjects: Fashion, Music, Dance, Photography
ISBN Prefix(es): 3-923765

Ferdinand Schoeningh Verlag GmbH+
Am Juhenplatz 1-3, 33098 Paderborn
Mailing Address: Postfach 2540, 33055 Paderborn
Tel: (05251) 1275 *Fax:* (05251) 127860; (05251) 127670
E-mail: info@schoeningh.de
Web Site: www.schoeningh.de
Key Personnel
Man Dir: Ferdinand Schoeningh
Press: Hansgeorg Enzian
Production: Friedhelm Meyer
Editor, Scholarly Books: Dr Hans Jacobs; Dr Diatlund Sawicki; Michael Werner
Founded: 1847
Specialize in scholarly books.
Subjects: Biography, Government, Political Science, History, Language Arts, Linguistics, Literature, Literary Criticism, Essays, Philosophy, Religion - Catholic, Theology
ISBN Prefix(es): 3-506
Number of titles published annually: 100 Print
Total Titles: 1,500 Print
Warehouse: F Schoeningh GmbH, Otto-Stadler-Str 6, 33100 Paderborn

Schott Musik International GmbH & Co KG+
Weihergarten 5, 55116 Mainz
Tel: (06131) 246-0 *Fax:* (06131) 246-211
Web Site: www.schott-online.com *Cable:* SCOTSON
Key Personnel
Man Dir: Dr Peter Hansen-Strecker; Rolf Reisinger; Dr Christian Sprang
Editorial: Dr Rainer Mohrs
Production & Printing: Herwig Suess
Sales: Helmut Fischer
Rights & Permissions: Volker Landtag
Founded: 1770
Subjects: Biography, Education, Music, Dance
ISBN Prefix(es): 3-7957
Associate Companies: Wiener Urtext Edition-Musikverlag GmbH & Co KG, Australia (jointly owned with Universal Edition AG, Austria)
Subsidiaries: Ars-Viva-Verlag GmbH; Atlantis Musikbuch-Verlag AG; Cranz GmbH; Ernst Eulenburg & Co GmbH; Eulenburg AG; Fuerstner Musikverlag GmbH; Arnold Schoenberg Gesamtausgabe GmbH; Music Factory GmbH; Musikverlag Kompositor International GmbH; Panton International GmbH; Schotta Wergo Music Media GmbH; SMD Schott Music Distribution GmbH; Wega Verlag GmbH
Branch Office(s)
Espanola de Ediciones Musicales Schott SL, Alcala 70, 28009 Madrid, Spain
Schott & Co Ltd, 48 Great Marlborough St, London W1V 2BN, United Kingdom
Schott Japan Co Ltd, Toyko, Japan
Schott Paris SARL, 40 rue Blomet, 75015 Paris, France
U.S. Office(s): European American Music Distributors Corp, Valley Forge, PA, United States
Bookshop(s): Mainzer Musikalienzentrum, Weihergarten 9, Mainz
Orders to: SMD Schott Music Distribution GmbH, Postfach 3640, 55026 Mainz *Tel:* (06131) 5050 *Fax:* (06131) 505115

Schrader Verlag Paul Pietsch Verlage GmbH & Co KG
Olgastr 86, 70180 Stuttgart
Tel: (0711) 210 80 12 *Fax:* (0711) 236 04 15
Web Site: www.paul-pietsch-verlag.de

Schreiber-Naturtafeln, *imprint of* Justus Perthes Verlag Gotha GmbH

Verlag Silke Schreiber+
Agnesstr 12, 80798 Munich
Mailing Address: Postfach 431161, 80741 Munich
Tel: (089) 2710180 *Fax:* (089) 2716957
E-mail: metzel@verlag-Silke-schreiber.de
Web Site: www.verlag-silke-schreiber.de
Key Personnel
Manager, Rights & Permissions: Dr Luise Metzel *E-mail:* metzel@t.online.de
Founded: 1982
Subjects: Art, Modern Art
ISBN Prefix(es): 3-88960

U.S. Office(s): Chris Pichler, Fulfillment Services, 1355 West Grand Rd, Suite 230, Tucson, AZ 85745, United States
Orders to: Vice Versa, Waldemarstr 81, 10997 Berlin, Contact: Gabriela Wachter *Tel:* (030) 61609237 *Fax:* (030) 61609238

Schriften zur Kontemplation, *imprint of* Vier Tuerme GmbH Verlag Klosterbetriebe

Schriftenfeibe Wissenschaft und Frieden, *imprint of* Bund demokratischer Wissenschaftlerinnen und Wissenschafler eV (BdWi)

Verlag und Schriftenmission der Evangelischen Gesellschaft Wuppertal+
Kaiserstr 78, 42329 Wuppertal
Mailing Address: Postfach 110533, 42305 Wuppertal
Tel: (0202) 278500 *Fax:* (0202) 2785040
Key Personnel
Man Dir: Hans Mohr
Sales, Production: Herbert Becker
Founded: 1954
Membership(s): the Telos group publishing evangelical paperbacks. Publishing House & Scriptural Mission of the German Evangelical Society.
Subjects: Literature, Literary Criticism, Essays, Religion - Other
ISBN Prefix(es): 3-87857

Schroedel Schulbuchverlag GmbH
Hildesheimerstr 202-206, 30519 Hannover
Tel: (0511) 83880 *Fax:* (0511) 8388425
E-mail: sco@schroedel.de
Web Site: www.schroedel.de
Key Personnel
Manager: Hans Dieter Moeller
ISBN Prefix(es): 3-285

Ferdinand Schroll, see Titania-Verlag Ferdinand Schroll

Carl Ed Schuenemann KG
Zweite Schlachtpforte 7, 28195 Bremen
Mailing Address: Postfach 10 60 67, 28060 Bremen
Tel: (0421) 369030 *Fax:* (0421) 3690339
E-mail: kontakt@kunstverlag.de
Web Site: www2.schuenemann-verlag.de
Key Personnel
Man Dir, Sales & Publicity: Klaus Kirchner
Founded: 1810
Subjects: Art, Regional Interests
ISBN Prefix(es): 3-7961

Schueren Verlag GmbH+
Universitaetsstr 55, 35037 Marburg
Tel: (06421) 6 30 84; (06421) 6 30 85 *Fax:* (06421) 68 11 90
E-mail: info@schueren-verlag.de
Web Site: www.schueren-verlag.de
Key Personnel
Manager: Dr Annette Schueren
Founded: 1985
Subjects: Biography, Communications, Economics, Film, Video, Government, Political Science, Labor, Industrial Relations, Nonfiction (General), Radio, TV, Regional Interests, Science (General), Self-Help, Social Sciences, Sociology
ISBN Prefix(es): 3-89472
Number of titles published annually: 20 Print
Total Titles: 150 Print

Verlag Karl Waldemar Schuetz+
Postfach 1433, 96404 Coburg
Tel: (09561) 80780 *Fax:* (09561) 807820

Key Personnel
Man Dir, Rights & Permissions: Peter Dehoust
Editorial: Karl Richter
Founded: 1948
Subjects: History, Military Science
ISBN Prefix(es): 3-87725
Parent Company: Nation Europa Verlags GmbH, Bahnhofstr 25, 96450 Coburg

Verlag Schulte und Gerth GmbH & Co KG, see Gerth Medien GmbH

Schulz-Kirchner Verlag GmbH+
Mollweg 2, 65510 Idstein
Mailing Address: Postfach 1275, 65502 Idstein
Tel: (06126) 93200 *Fax:* (06126) 9320-50
E-mail: info@schulz-kirchner.de
Web Site: www.schulz-kirchner.de
Key Personnel
Manager: Berit Felgentreff
Founded: 1984
Subjects: Business, Economics, Energy, Finance, Health, Nutrition, History, Labor, Industrial Relations, Language Arts, Linguistics, Marketing, Medicine, Nursing, Dentistry, Philosophy, Science (General), Social Sciences, Sociology
ISBN Prefix(es): 3-8248; 3-925196

Verlag R S Schulz GmbH+
Enzianstr 4a, 82319 Starnberg
Mailing Address: Postfach 1780, 82317 Starnberg
Tel: (089) 36007-0 *Fax:* (089) 36007-3310
E-mail: rss@rss.de
Web Site: www.rss.de
Key Personnel
Man Dir: Dr Wilhelm Warth
Subjects: Architecture & Interior Design, Fiction, Health, Nutrition, Law, Social Sciences, Sociology, Veterinary Science
ISBN Prefix(es): 3-7962

H O Schulze KG
Laurenzistr 2, 96215 Lichtenfels
Tel: (09571) 78010 *Fax:* (09571) 78055
E-mail: verkauf@schulze-kg.de
Web Site: www.schulze-kg.de
Key Personnel
Publisher: Heinrich Schulze
Founded: 1865
Subjects: Art, Fiction, Geography, Geology, History, Nonfiction (General), Travel
ISBN Prefix(es): 3-87735
Distributed by Colloquium Historicum Wirsbergense; Verlag des Historischen Vereins Bamberg

Theodor Schuster
Muehlenstr 15/17, 26789 Leer
Mailing Address: Postfach 1944, 26769 Leer
Tel: (0491) 925900 *Fax:* (0491) 9259059
E-mail: buchhandlung-Schuster@t-online.de
Key Personnel
Contact: Theo Schuster
Subjects: Fiction, Humor, Nonfiction (General), Poetry
ISBN Prefix(es): 3-7963
Number of titles published annually: 5 Print; 1 CD-ROM; 2 Audio

Edition Schwab, *imprint of* Verlag Stephanie Naglschmid

Heinrich Schwab Verlag KG+
Eglofstal 42, 88260 Argenbuehl
Mailing Address: Gschwend 77, 6932 Langen bei Bregenz, Austria
Tel: (05575) 20101 *Fax:* (05575) 4745
E-mail: heinrichschwabverlag@aon.at
Web Site: www.heinrichschwabverlag.de
Key Personnel
Manager: Verena Brocksieper

Founded: 1926
Subjects: Parapsychology, Philosophy, Psychology, Psychiatry, Religion - Other, Alternative Medicine, Biological Horticulture, Breathe Therapies, Border Sciences, Esoteric Works & Meditation, Life Assistance, Life-Wise, Medicine, Mental Healing, Naturopathy, Positive Thinking, Religion Science, Spirituality, Yoga
ISBN Prefix(es): 3-7964
Total Titles: 130 Print; 5 CD-ROM; 10 Audio

Schwabenverlag Aktiengesellschaft+
Senefelderstr 12, 73760 Ostfildern
Tel: (0711) 4406-0 *Fax:* (0711) 4406-177
E-mail: info@schwabenverlag.de
Web Site: www.schwabenverlag.de
Key Personnel
President: Ulrich Peters
International Rights: Gertrud Widmann
Founded: 1848
Subjects: Art, Regional Interests, Religion - Catholic, Religion - Other, Theology
ISBN Prefix(es): 3-7966
Subsidiaries: Rottenburger Druckerei; Sueddeutsche Verlagsgesellschaft mbH Ulm
Distributed by Auslieferung (Austria & Germany); Auslieferung Schweiz Herder; Brockhaus/Commission; Osterreichisches Katholisches Bibelwerk
Bookshop(s): Schwabenverlag Buchhandlung, Bahnhofstr 20, 89073 Ulm; Schwabenverlag Buchhandlung, Spitalstr 19, 73479 Ellwangen; TheoBuch Rottenburg, Karmeliterstr 2, 72108 Rottenburg

Schwaneberger Verlag GmbH
Muthmannstr 4, 80939 Munich
Tel: (089) 3239302 *Fax:* (089) 3232402
E-mail: webmaster@michel.de
Web Site: www.michel.de
Key Personnel
Man Dir, Rights & Permissions: Hans Hohenester
Editorial: Jochen Stenzke
Sales: Joachim Stolz
Publicity: Werner Maier
Founded: 1910
Subjects: Crafts, Games, Hobbies
ISBN Prefix(es): 3-87858
Associate Companies: Carl Gerber Verlag GmbH

Edition Schwann, *imprint of* C F Peters Musikverlag GmbH & Co KG

Otto Schwartz Fachbochhandlung GmbH+
Annastr 7, 37075 Goettingen
Tel: (0551) 31051 *Fax:* (0551) 372812
E-mail: schwartz.stadt@t-online.de
Key Personnel
Man Dir: Dr Herbert Weisser
Man Dir, Rights & Permissions: Konrad Weisser
Rights & Permissions: Ernst Leopold
Branch Manager: Marlis Potthast *Tel:* (0551) 5085978
Sales: Mrs Barke *Tel:* (0551) 5085978; Mrs Beuermann *Tel:* (0551) 5085978; Ms Willgerodt *Tel:* (0551) 5085978
Founded: 1871
Subjects: Ethnicity, Law, Public Administration, Social Sciences, Sociology
ISBN Prefix(es): 3-509
Bookshop(s): Fachbuchhandlung Otto Schwartz & Co

Dr Wolfgang Schwarze Verlag+
Richard Strauss Allee 35, 42289 Wuppertal
Mailing Address: Postfach 201744, 42217 Wuppertal
Tel: (0202) 622005; (0202) 622006 *Fax:* (0202) 63631

Key Personnel
Man Dir, Rights & Permissions: Dr Wolfgang Schwarze
Sales, Office Chief: Ursula Schwarze
Founded: 1968
Subjects: Antiques, Architecture & Interior Design, Art, House & Home
ISBN Prefix(es): 3-87741

Verlag Schweers + Wall GmbH+
Rudolfstr 65-67, 52070 Aachen
Mailing Address: Postfach 1586, 52016 Aachen
Tel: (0241) 87 22 51 *Fax:* (0241) 8 52 06
E-mail: schweers.wall@t-online.de
Founded: 1986
Subjects: Transportation, Travel
ISBN Prefix(es): 3-921679; 3-89494

E Schweizerbart'sche Verlagsbuchhandlung (Naegele und Obermiller)+
Affiliate of Gebrueder Borntraeger Verlagsbuchhandlung
Johannesstr 3A, 70176 Stuttgart
Tel: (0711) 3514560 *Fax:* (0711) 351456-99
E-mail: mail@schweizerbart.de
Web Site: www.schweizerbart.de
Key Personnel
Man Dir, Production: Dr Erhard Naegele
Man Dir, Sales: Dr Walter Obermiller
Exhibition Manager: Martina Ihringer
Founded: 1826
Subjects: Anthropology, Archaeology, Biological Sciences, Earth Sciences, Environmental Studies, Geography, Geology, Maritime, Science (General)
ISBN Prefix(es): 3-510 (Schweizerbart); 3-443 (Borntraeger)
U.S. Office(s): Balogh International Inc, 1911 N Duncan Rd, Champaign, IL 61822, United States, Contact: Pamela Burns-Balogh *Tel:* 217-355-9331 *Fax:* 217-355-9413 *E-mail:* balogh@balogh.com *Web Site:* www.balogh.com
Distributor for Bundesanstalt fuer Geowissenschaften und Rohstoffe; Senckenbergische Naturforschende Gesellschaft

Schwul Lesbische Studien Universitat Bremen, *imprint of* Mannerschwarm Skript Verlag GmbH

Scientia Verlag und Antiquariat Schilling OHG
Adlerstr 65, 73434 Wurtt
Mailing Address: Postfach 1660, 73406 Wurtt
Tel: (07361) 41700 *Fax:* (07361) 45620
Cable: SCIENTIA AALENWUERTT
Key Personnel
Man Dir: Guenter Schilling
Founded: 1953
Subjects: Archaeology, Economics, Education, History, Law, Philosophy, Religion - Other, Social Sciences, Sociology, Theology
ISBN Prefix(es): 3-511

SDV, see Saarbrucker Druckerei und Verlag GmbH (SDV)

EA Seemann Verlag, *imprint of* Verlagsgruppe Dornier GmbH

Seibt Verlag GmbH
Havelstr 9, 64295 Darmstadt
Tel: (06151) 380-140 *Fax:* (06151) 380-141
E-mail: info@seibt.com
Web Site: www.seibt.de
Key Personnel
Man Dir: Alfred Augustine; Werner Reiber; Roland Repp
Advertising Dir: Brita Graef
Founded: 1921
Membership(s): VDAV (Verband Deutscher Adressbuchveleger) & EADP (European Association of Directory Publishers).

Subjects: Environmental Studies, Mechanical Engineering, Medicine, Nursing, Dentistry
ISBN Prefix(es): 3-922948; 3-931336
Parent Company: Hoppenstedt GmbH & Co

Dr Arthur L Sellier & Co KG-Walter de Gruyter GmbH & Co KG OHG+
Genthinerstr 13, 10785 Berlin
Mailing Address: PO Box 303421, 10728 Berlin
Tel: (030) 26005-0 *Fax:* (030) 260 05-251
E-mail: wdq-info@degruyter.de
Web Site: www.degruyter.de
Telex: 184027 *Cable:* WISSENSCHAFT BERLIN
Key Personnel
Contact: Georg Broeckelmann
Founded: 1990
Subjects: Law, Commentary to the German Civil Code
ISBN Prefix(es): 3-8059
U.S. Office(s): 200 Saw Mill River Rd, Hawthorne, NY 10532, United States *Tel:* 914-747-0110 *Fax:* 914-747-1326

Siebeck, see Mohr Siebeck

Siebenberg-Verlag+
Warolder Str 1, 34513 Waldeck-Dehringhausen
Tel: (05695) 1028 *Fax:* (05695) 1027
E-mail: fh@huebner-books.de
Web Site: www.huebner-books.de
Key Personnel
Publisher: Felicitas Huebner
Founded: 1936
Subjects: Art, Asian Studies, Poetry
ISBN Prefix(es): 3-87747
Orders to: Bugrim Verlagsauslieferung
Dr Laube & Partner, Saalburgstr 3, 12099 Berlin

Siebert Verlag GmbH+
Werderstr 10, 69469 Weinheim
Tel: (06201) 6007-0 *Fax:* (06201) 6007-310
Key Personnel
Man Dir & Publisher: Hans Meisinger
Rights & Publicity: Christiane Schneider
Founded: 1967
Subjects: Crafts, Games, Hobbies
ISBN Prefix(es): 3-8089; 3-920215; 3-89050
Parent Company: Verlagsgruppe Beltz
Orders to: MVS Meisinger Verlagsservice GmbH, Am Steinfeld 4, 94065 Waldkirchen *Tel:* (08581) 9605-0 *Fax:* (08581) 754

Siedler Verlag+
Griefswalder Str 207, 10405 Berlin
Tel: (030) 44 38 45-0
E-mail: bettine.vonborries@bertelsmann.de
Web Site: www.randomhouse.de/siedler
Key Personnel
Foreign Rights: Sabine Oswald *Tel:* (030) 44 38 45-15 *Fax:* (030) 44 38 45-46 *E-mail:* sabine.oswald@bertelsmann.de
Press: Gisela Maria Nicklaus *Tel:* (030) 44 38 45-28 *Fax:* (030) 44 38 45-55 *E-mail:* giselamaria.nicklaus@bertelsmann.de
Founded: 1982
Subjects: Biography, Government, Political Science, History, Journalism, Nonfiction (General)
ISBN Prefix(es): 3-88680; 3-8275
Parent Company: Bertelsmann Verlagsgruppe GmbH, Postfach 800360, 81603 Munich
Orders to: Siedler Verlag Vertiel, Neumarkterstr 18, 81673 Munich

Siegler & Co Verlag fuer Zeitarchive GmbH+
Einsteinstr 10, 53757 St Augustin
Mailing Address: Postfach 1455, 53732 St Augustin
Tel: (02241) 3164-0
Key Personnel
Manager & International Rights: Dr Werner Hippe

Publishing Dir: Gerd Meiser
Founded: 1931
Subjects: Government, Political Science, History
ISBN Prefix(es): 3-87748
Parent Company: Asgard Verlag Dr Werner Hippe KG

Georg Siemens Verlagsbuchhandlung
Boothstr 11, 12207 Berlin
Mailing Address: Postfach 450169, 12171 Berlin
Tel: (030) 769904-0 *Fax:* (030) 769904-18
E-mail: gsiemensv@t-online.de
Key Personnel
Contact: Hans Klessinger *Tel:* (030) 76990412
Founded: 1891
Subjects: Specializes in Railway transportation & Craft Sanitary facilities & heating
ISBN Prefix(es): 3-87749

Sierra, *imprint of* Frederking & Thaler Verlag GmbH

Sigloch Edition Helmut Sigloch GmbH & Co KG+
Am Buchberg 8, 74572 Blaufelden
Mailing Address: Postfach 1201, Blaufelden 74568
Tel: (07953) 883-0 *Fax:* (07953) 883-320
E-mail: info@sigloch.de
Web Site: www.sigloch.de
Telex: 74 161
Key Personnel
President: Helmut Sigloch
Production Manager: Michael Sanny
Founded: 1972
Subjects: Cookery, Technology
ISBN Prefix(es): 3-89393
Warehouse: Sigloch Distribution GmbH

Edition Sigma e.Kfm+
Karl-Marxstr 17, 12043 Berlin
Tel: (030) 623 23 63 *Fax:* (030) 623 93 93
E-mail: verlag@edition-sigma.de
Web Site: www.edition-sigma.de
Key Personnel
Contact: Mr R Bohn
Founded: 1984
Subjects: Social Sciences, Sociology
ISBN Prefix(es): 3-924859; 3-89404

Silberburg-Verlag Titus Haeussermann GmbH+
Schoenbuchstr 48, 72074 Tuebingen-Bebenhausen
Tel: (07071) 6885-0 *Fax:* (07071) 6885-20
E-mail: info@silberburg.de
Web Site: www.silberburg.com
Key Personnel
Editor-in-Chief: Titus Haeussermann
Sales & Advertising: Christel Werner
Founded: 1985
Membership(s): Stock Exchange of German Booksellers & Association of Publishers & Booksellers in Baden-Wuerttemberg.
Subjects: Regional Interests
ISBN Prefix(es): 3-925344; 3-87407
Number of titles published annually: 50 Print; 20 Audio
Total Titles: 300 Print; 50 Audio
Imprints: Gustav Mesmer Stiftung; Schmidmusic Distributed by Maule & Gosch Tontragervertrieb
Distributor for JS Film-Produktion GmbH; Maeule & Gosch Tontragervertrieb; Musekater Musikverlag; Schwoissfuass GmbH
Warehouse: Silberburg-Verlag, c/o Koch, Neff & Oetinger & Co, Verlagsauslieferung GmbH, Schockenriedstr 39, 70565 Stuttgart-Vaihingen *Tel:* (0711) 78600

Die Silberschnur Verlag GmbH+
Steinstr 1, 56593 Guellesheim
Tel: (02687) 929068 *Fax:* (02687) 929524

E-mail: info@silberschnur.de
Web Site: www.silberschnur.de
Key Personnel
Man Dir: Tom Hockemeyer; Manfred Huber
Publisher's Reader: N Kugberg *Tel:* (02687) 929089
Founded: 1982
Subjects: Alternative, Astrology, Occult, Parapsychology, Alternative healing, Esoteric Teachings & Life After Death
ISBN Prefix(es): 3-923781; 3-931652; 3-89845
Number of titles published annually: 20 Print
Total Titles: 300 Print
Distributor for Adwaita; Arun; Corona; Coudris; Devas Edition; Dude; EVT; Genius; Grasmuck; Heindel; Hubner; ICH; Kopp; l zu l; Larimar; Lichtring; Medicum Keg; Naam; Nietsch; NLS; Omega; Ostergaard; PAN; Quadropol; Riechel; Rocke; Sequoyah; Silberschnur; Simeunovic; Sternentor; Subtilis; Weltenhuter

Buchkonzept Simon KG+
Kaiserstr 33, 80801 Munich
Mailing Address: Postfach 431062, 80740 Munich
Tel: (089) 21939012 *Fax:* (089) 21939014
Key Personnel
Man Dir: Claudia Magiera; Gerd Simon
Founded: 1979
Subjects: Asian Studies, Fiction, Foreign Countries, Travel
ISBN Prefix(es): 3-88676
Subsidiaries: Tutto Mondo

Rudolf G Smend+
Mainzerstr 31, 50678 Cologne
Tel: (0221) 312047 *Fax:* (0221) 9 32 07 18
E-mail: smend@smend.de
Key Personnel
Contact: Rudolf G Smend
Founded: 1973
Art gallery & publisher of catalogues.
Subjects: Art, Asian Studies, Indonesian art, textile art
ISBN Prefix(es): 3-926779
Number of titles published annually: 1 Print
Total Titles: 10 Print
Orders to: Mainzerstr 33, Cologne *Fax:* (0221) 325134

Societaets-Verlag+
Frankenallee 71-81, 60327 Frankfurt am Main
Tel: (069) 75 01-0 *Fax:* (069) 75 01-48 77
Web Site: www.societaets-verlag.de
Telex: 0411655 *Cable:* Zeitung Frankfurtmain
Key Personnel
Publisher: Dr Juergen Kron *Tel:* (069) 75 01-45 11 *E-mail:* juergen.kron@fsd.de
Sales: Henrike Brueck *Tel:* (069) 75 01-42 97 *Fax:* (069) 75 01-45 11 *E-mail:* henrike.brueck@fsd.de
Production: Cordula Tippkoetter *Tel:* (069) 75 01-42 98 *Fax:* (069) 75 01-45 11 *E-mail:* cordula.tippkoetter@fsd.de
Publicity: Silvie Horch *Tel:* (069) 75 01-45 71 *Fax:* (069) 75 01-45 11 *E-mail:* silvie.horch@fsd.de
Founded: 1921
Subjects: Art, Business, Economics, History, Literature, Literary Criticism, Essays
ISBN Prefix(es): 3-7973
Imprints: Verlag Frankfurter Buecher; Verlag Heinrich Scheffler

Soldi-Verlag im Drockzentrum Harburg
Steinbeckerstr 97, 21244 Buchholz id Nordheide
Tel: (04181) 29 16 22 *Fax:* (04181) 29 16 23
E-mail: kontakt@karismaverlag.de
Web Site: www.karismaverlag.de
Key Personnel
Man Dir: Horst Ernst
Founded: 1977
ISBN Prefix(es): 3-928028; 3-923744; 3-931877

GERMANY

Sonnentanz-Verlag Roland Kron+
Waterloostr 25, 86165 Augsburg
Tel: (0821) 311070 *Fax:* (0821) 158979
E-mail: sonnentanz@t-online.de
Key Personnel
Contact: Roland Kron
Founded: 1988
Specialize in rock literature & rock biographies.
Subjects: Biography, Music, Dance
ISBN Prefix(es): 3-926794

Sonntag, *imprint of* Georg Thieme Verlag KG

Johannes Sonntag Verlagsbuchhandlung GmbH+
Oswalt-Hesse-Str 50, 70469 Stuttgart
Tel: (0711) 8931-0 *Fax:* (0711) 8931-706
Web Site: www.sonntag-verlag.com
Key Personnel
President: Andre Caro *Tel:* (0711) 18931-700
Founded: 1927
Specialize in books, magazines, medicine, complementary medicine.
ISBN Prefix(es): 3-87758
Number of titles published annually: 25 Print
Total Titles: 150 Print
Parent Company: Hippokrates Verlag

Spee Buchverlag GmbH+
Maximineracht 11C, 54295 Trier
Mailing Address: Postfach 3040, 54220 Trier
Tel: (0651) 4608121 *Fax:* (0651) 4608220
Key Personnel
Publisher: Dr Harold Boulig; Siegfried Faeth
Founded: 1967
Subjects: Art, History
ISBN Prefix(es): 3-7902; 3-87760
Parent Company: Paulinus GmbH Verlag
Associate Companies: Paulinus Verlag

Spektrum der Wissenschaft Verlagsgesellschaft mbH
Slevogtstr 3-5, 69126 Heidelberg
Mailing Address: PO Box 10 48 40, 69038 Heidelberg
Tel: (06221) 9126600 *Fax:* (06221) 9126751
E-mail: marketing@spektrum.com
Web Site: www.spektrum.de
Key Personnel
Man Dir: Markus Bossle
Publicity: Barbara Kuhn
Founded: 1978
Subjects: Science (General), Technology
Parent Company: Scientific American Inc, 415 Madison Ave, New York, NY 10017, United States

Spiegel-Verlag Rudolf Augstein GmbH & Co KG+
Brandstwiete 19, 20457 Hamburg
Mailing Address: Postfach 110413, 20404 Hamburg
Tel: (040) 3007-0 *Fax:* (040) 3007-2247
E-mail: spiegel@spiegel.de
Telex: 2161221
Key Personnel
Man Dir: Karl-Dietrich Seikel
International Rights: Dietrich Krause
Founded: 1946
ISBN Prefix(es): 3-87763
Subsidiaries: A&I Art & Information GmbH & Co KG; Manager Magazine; Spiegel TV GmbH
Orders to: Postfach 105840, 20039 Hamburg

Spiess Volker Wissenschaftsverlag GmbH+
Gneisenaustr 33, 10961 Berlin
Mailing Address: Postfach 610494, 10928 Berlin
Tel: (030) 6917073-74 *Fax:* (030) 6914067
Cable: SPIESSVERLAG
Key Personnel
Publisher: Volker Spiess
Founded: 1967
Subjects: Communications, Film, Video, History, Journalism, Language Arts, Linguistics, Social Sciences, Sociology
ISBN Prefix(es): 3-89166; 3-89776
Associate Companies: Haude und Spenersche VerlagsBuchhandlung, Postfach 303046, 10928 Berlin *Tel:* (030) 2165061 *Fax:* (030) 2165064
Subsidiaries: Edition Marhold; Edition colloquium

Spieth-Verlag Verlag fuer Symbolforschung+
Postfach 31 13 08, 10643 Berlin
Tel: (0331) 2705199 *Fax:* (0331) 2010849
Key Personnel
Owner: Rudolf Arnold Spieth
Founded: 1969
Subjects: Anthropology, Astrology, Occult, Parapsychology, Philosophy, Psychology, Psychiatry, Religion - Other, Self-Help
ISBN Prefix(es): 3-88093
Subsidiaries: Bund der Runenforscher Deutschlands (BRD)/Internationaler Zentralverband Germanischer Runenforscher (IZGR)

Spiridon-Verlags GmbH+
Dorfstr 18A, 40699 Erkrath
Tel: (02104) 47260 *Fax:* (0211) 786823
Key Personnel
Publisher: Manfred Steffny
Founded: 1974
Subjects: Health, Nutrition, Sports, Athletics
ISBN Prefix(es): 3-922011
Bookshop(s): Steffnys Laufladen, Linienstr 12, 40227 Dusseldorf

Adolf Sponholtz Verlag+
Subsidiary of C W Niemeyer Buchverlage GmbH
Osterstr 19, 31785 Hameln
Mailing Address: Postfach 100752, 31763 Hameln
Tel: (05151) 200312 *Fax:* (05151) 200319
Web Site: www.niemeyer-buch.de
Key Personnel
Dir: Hans Freiwald
Founded: 1894
Subjects: Animals, Pets, Energy, Environmental Studies, Fiction, History, Literature, Literary Criticism, Essays, Nonfiction (General), Outdoor Recreation
ISBN Prefix(es): 3-87766
Orders to: VSB Verlagsservice Braunschweig GmbH, Westerman- Allee 66, 38104 Braunschweig *Tel:* (0531) 708650 *Fax:* (0531) 708608

Sportverlag Berlin GmbH SVB+
Hohenzollerndamm 56, 14199 Berlin
Tel: (030) 8973666 *Fax:* (030) 2591-3516
E-mail: marketing@sportverlag-berlin.de
Web Site: www.sportverlag-berlin.de *Cable:* UND SPORTVERLAG BERLIN
Key Personnel
Man Dir: Dr Wolfram Goeibel
Sales, Rights & Permissions: Brigitte Kummer
Marketing Manager: Helmut Krueger
Editor-in-Chief: Raymund Stolze
Founded: 1947
Subjects: How-to, Sports, Athletics
ISBN Prefix(es): 3-328; 3-333
Warehouse: VVA, A64 DFB/F An der Autobahn, 33370 Gutersloh

Axel Springer Verlag AG
Axel-Springer-Platz 1, Hamburg 20350
Tel: (040) 347-00 *Fax:* (040) 345811
E-mail: info@asv.de
Web Site: www.asv.de
Telex: 2170010; 402255
Key Personnel
Contact: Edda Fels
ISBN Prefix(es): 3-921305; 3-926949

Springer Science+Business Media GmbH & Co KG+
Tiergartenstr 17, 69121 Heidelberg
Mailing Address: Postfach 105280, 69042 Heidelberg
Tel: (06221) 487-0 *Fax:* (06221) 487-8366
E-mail: orders@springer.de
Web Site: www.springer.de
Key Personnel
Chairman, Supervisory Board of the Springer Group: Derk Haank
Man Dir: Rudiger Gebauer; Peter Hendriks; Martin Mos; Dr Ulrich Vest
Founded: 1991
Membership(s): TR- Verlagsunion GmbH.
Subjects: Agriculture, Architecture & Interior Design, Art, Astronomy, Behavioral Sciences, Biography, Biological Sciences, Business, Chemistry, Chemical Engineering, Child Care & Development, Civil Engineering, Computer Science, Cookery, Criminology, Earth Sciences, Economics, Electronics, Electrical Engineering, Energy, Engineering (General), Environmental Studies, Finance, Geography, Geology, Government, Political Science, Health, Nutrition, History, Law, Management, Marketing, Mathematics, Mechanical Engineering, Medicine, Nursing, Dentistry, Nonfiction (General), Philosophy, Physical Sciences, Physics, Psychology, Psychiatry, Science (General), Social Sciences, Sociology, Technology
ISBN Prefix(es): 0-8194; 0-387; 3-7643; 3-7985; 2-287; 3-540; 3-211; 4-431; 3-7908; 84-07; 1-85233; 3-18; 88-470; 3-88537; 0-8716; 0-907259; 981-3083
Parent Company: Springer Science+Business Media GmbH & Co KG, Berlin
Associate Companies: Springer-Verlag New York LLC, 175 Fifth Ave, New York, NY 10010, United States *Tel:* 212-460-1500 *Fax:* 212-473-6272; Springer-Verlag London Ltd, Sweetapple House, Cateshall Rd, Surrey, Godalming GU7 3DJ, United Kingdom *Tel:* (01483) 418822 *Fax:* (01483) 415151; Springer-Verlag France, One rue Paul Cezanne, 75375 Paris, France *Tel:* (01) 5393-3644 *Fax:* (01) 5393-3683; Springer-Verlag Tokyo Inc, 3-13, Hougo 3-chome, Bunkyo-ku, Tokyo, Japan *Tel:* (03) 38120337 *Fax:* (03) 38187454; Eastern Book Service Inc, 3-13, Hongo 3-chome, Bunkyo-ku, Tokyo 113, Japan *Tel:* (03) 38180861 *Fax:* (03) 38180864; Springer-Verlag Hong Kong Ltd, Unit 1702 Tower I, Enterprise Square, 9 Sheung Yuet Rd, Kowloon Bay, Hong Kong *Tel:* 27239698 *Fax:* 27242366; Springer-Verlag Iberica SA, Corcega 505, entlo 3, 08025 Barcelona, Spain; Springer-VDI-Verlag GmbH & Co KG, Heinrichstr, 40239 Duesseldorf *Tel:* (0211) 6103-222 *Fax:* (0211) 6103-113; Springer-Verlag Wien, Sachsenpl 4-6, 1201 Vienna, Austria *Tel:* (01) 3302415 *Fax:* (01) 3302426; Springer Italia, Via Podgora 14, 20122 Mailand, Italy *Tel:* (02) 54259721 *Fax:* (02) 55193360; Springer-Verlag GmbH & Co KG, Indian Liaison Office, 906-907, Akash Deep Bldg, Barakhamba Rd, 110001 New Delhi, India *Tel:* (011) 3358590 *Fax:* (011) 3358716; Urban und Vogel Medien und Medizin Verlagsgesellschaft GmbH, Neumarkter Str 43, 81673 Munich; Springer PWN Ltd, Warsaw, Poland
Imprints: Copernicus; Physica; TELOS
Distributor for AIP Press (American Institute of Physics)
Bookshop(s): Minerva Wissenschaftliche Buchhandlung GmbH, Sachsenplatz 4-6, 7207 Vienna, Austria *Tel:* (01) 330 2433 *Fax:* (01) 330 2439

Warehouse: Springer GmbH & Co Auslieferungs-Gesellschaft, Haberstr 7, 69126 Heidelberg *Tel:* (06221) 345-112 *Fax:* (06221) 345-182 *E-mail:* orders@springer.de

Springer Science+Business Media GmbH & Co KG, Berlin+
Formerly BertelsmannSpringer Science & Business Media GmbH
Heidelberger Platz 3, 14197 Berlin
Mailing Address: Postfach 140201, 14302 Berlin
Tel: (030) 82787-0; (030) 82787 5282 (press & public relations) *Fax:* (030) 8214091; (030) 82787 5707 (press & public relations)
E-mail: press@springer-sbm.com
Web Site: www.springer-sbm.de
Key Personnel
Chief Executive Officer: Derk Haank
Chief Operating Officer: Martin Mos
Chief Financial Officer: Dr Ulrich Vest
Founded: 1842
Publisher of scientific & specialist literature. In addition to scientific literature provides competent information service for the B-to-B (business to business) market.
Subjects: Architecture & Interior Design, Economics, Engineering (General), Medicine, Nursing, Dentistry, Science (General), Transportation, Construction
ISBN Prefix(es): 0-306 (Kluwer Academic Publishers); 1-56898 (Princeton Architectural Press); 0-387 (Springer-Verlag New York); 3-519 (Teubner); 3-409 (Gabler); 3-7643 (Birkhaeuser); 3-528 (Vieweg); 3-540 (Spring-Verlag Berlin/Heidelberg); 3-7908 (Physica); 1-4020 (Kluwer Academic Publishers)
Number of titles published annually: 5,000 Print
Total Titles: 40,000 Print
Branch Office(s)
ArchiPoint, Draaiboomstraat 6, B-2160 Wommelgem, Belgium *Tel:* (03) 3555010 *Fax:* (03) 3555020
ARZTE WOCHE Zeitungsverlagsgesellschaft mbH, Wiesingerstr 1, A-1010 Vienna, Austria, Contact: Rodolf Siegle *Tel:* (01) 3302415 *Fax:* (01) 3302426 *E-mail:* siegle@springer.at
Artze Zeitung Verlagsgesellschaft mbH, Am Forsthaus Gravenbruch 5, D-63263 Neu-Isenburg, Austria, Contact: Gerald Kosaris *Tel:* (0049) 6102/506-150 *Fax:* (0049) 6102/506-100 *E-mail:* gerald.kosaris@aerztezeitung.de
Auto Business Verlag GmbH & Co KG, Robert-Bosch-Str 7, D-85521 Ottobrunn, Contact: Dr Carsten Thies *Tel:* (089) 4372 1130 *Fax:* (089) 4372 1275 *E-mail:* carsten.thies@springer-sbm.de
Bau-Data Osterreich GmbH, Langgasse 182, A-5140 Hallein-Vigaun, Austria, Contact: Bernhard Bogensperger *Tel:* (062) 45 797 18 *Fax:* (062) 45 797 90 *E-mail:* bernhard.bogensperger@bau-data.co.at
BauDatenbank GmbH, Bremer Weg 184, D-29219 Celle, Contact: Michael Hoelker *Tel:* 5141 50 370; 5141 50 233 *Fax:* 5141 50 374 *E-mail:* michael.hoelker@heinze.de
BauNetz Online-Dienst GmbH & Co KG, Schluterstr 42, D-10707 Berlin, Contact: Jurgen Paul *Tel:* (030) 887 26 301 *Fax:* (030) 887 26 303 *E-mail:* paul@baunetz.de
Bauverlag GmbH, Avenwedder Str 55, D-33311 Gutersloh, Contact: Stefan Ruehling *Tel:* 5241 80 24 76 *Fax:* 5241 80 95 82 *E-mail:* stefan.ruehling@bauverlag.der
Business Solutions Medicine (BSMO), Johannisberger Str 74, D-14197 Berlin, France, Contact: Dr Joerg Zorn *Tel:* (030) 884 293 18 *Fax:* (030) 884 293 41 *E-mail:* joerg.zorn@bsmo.de
Birkhauser Verlag AG, Viadukstr 42, CH-4051 Basel, Switzerland, Contact: Sven Fund *Tel:* (061) 20 50 710 *Fax:* (061) 20 50 790 *E-mail:* fund@birkhauser.ch
Birkhauser Verlag GmbH form, Am Forsthaus Gravenbrunch 5, 63263 Neu-Isenburg, Contact: Anja Beyersdorff *Tel:* 6102 59980 10 *Fax:* 6102 59980 99 *E-mail:* anja.beyersdorff@form.de
CoboSystems NV, Draaiboomstr 6, B-2160 Wommelgem, Belgium *Tel:* (03) 3555010 *Fax:* (03) 3555020
Codes Rosseau SAS, 135 rue de Plesses, BP93, F-85103 Les Sables d'Olonne Cedex, France, Contact: Michel Goepp *Tel:* 251 231 117 *Fax:* 251 220 525 *E-mail:* michel.goepp@code-rousseau.fr
Deutscher Universitats-Verlag GmbH, Abraham-Lincoln Str 46, D65189 Wiesbaden, Contact: Dr Hans-Dieter Haenel *Tel:* 611 78 78 102 *Fax:* 611 78 78 104 *E-mail:* hans-dieter.haenel@gwv-fachverlage.de
ETRASA Editorial Trafico Vial SA, C/Puerto de Navacerrada 128, Pol Ind Las Nieves, E-28935 Mostoles Madrid, Spain, Contact: Efa Rimoldi *Tel:* (091) 665 80 01 *Fax:* (091) 665 80 03 *E-mail:* efa@estrasa.com
Eurosoft, C/Puerto de Navacerrada 128, Pol Ind Las Nieves, E-28935 Mostoles Madrid, Spain, Contact: Efa Rimoldi *Tel:* (091) 665 80 01 *Fax:* (091) 665 80 03 *E-mail:* efa@etrasa.com
FachMediaCom AG, Rutistra 2, CH-8952 Schlieren, Switzerland, Contact: Heike Findeis *Tel:* (01) 7385 252 *Fax:* (01) 7385 128 *E-mail:* heike.findeis@fachmediacom.ch
Fachmedien Verlag GmbH, Inkustra 16, A-3403 Klosterneuburg, Austria, Contact: Ferenc Papp *Tel:* 2243 30111 235 *Fax:* 2243 30111 222 *E-mail:* papp@technopress.at
Dr Hans Fuchs GmbH Verlag FUCHSBRIEFE, Albrechtstr 22, D-10117 Berlin, Contact: Ralf Vielhaber *Tel:* (030) 28 88 17 0 *Fax:* (030) 28 04 55 76 *E-mail:* ralf.vielhaber@fuchsbriefe.de
Betriebswirtschaftlicher Verlag Dr Th Gabler, Abraham-Lincoln Str 46, D-65189 Wiesbaden, Contact: Hans-Dieter Haenel *Tel:* (0611) 78 78 102 *Fax:* (0611) 78 78 104 *E-mail:* hans-dieter.haenel@gwv-fachverlage.de
GOF Verlag, Inkustra 16, A-3403 Klosterneuburg, Austria, Contact: Ferenc Papp *Tel:* 2243 30111 235 *Fax:* 2243 30111 222 *E-mail:* papp@technopress.at
Grupa Image Sp zoo, ul Witkiewicza 14, PL-03-305 Warsaw, Poland, Contact: Witold Wisniewski *Tel:* (022) 811 01 99 *Fax:* (022) 811 19 93 *E-mail:* witold@grupaimage.com.pl
GWV Fachverlage GmbH, Abraham-Lincoln Str 46, D-65189 Wiesbaden, Contact: Dr Hans-Dieter Haenel *Tel:* (0611) 78 78 102 *Fax:* (0611) 78 78 104 *E-mail:* hans-dieter.haenel@gwv-fachverlage.de
Heinrich Vogel Verlag Schweiz, Rutistra 22, CH-8952 Schlieren, Switzerland, Contact: Heike Findeis *Tel:* (01) 73 85 252 *Fax:* (01) 73 85 128 *E-mail:* heike.findeis@fachmediacom.ch
Heinze GmbH, Bremer Weg 184, D-29219 Celle, Contact: Michael Hoelker *Tel:* 5141 50 370 *Fax:* 5141 50 374 *E-mail:* michael.hoelker@heinze.de
ibau Informationsdienst fur den Baumarkt GmbH, Anton-Bruchausen Str, Munster D-48147, Contact: Dr Roland Ehrenfels *Tel:* 251 78 05 116 *Fax:* 251 78 05 244 *E-mail:* r.ehrenfels@ibau.de
ICW Publications Ltd, The Chapter House, Hinderton Hall Estate, Neston South Wirral CH 64 7UX, United Kingdom, Contact: Simon Mahoney *Tel:* (0151) 353 35 11 *Fax:* (0151) 353 35 02 *E-mail:* simon.mahoney@abibuildingdata.com
IMS Investitions Media Service Werbe- & Public Relations GmbH, Inkustra 16, A-3403 Klosterneuburg, Austria, Contact: Ferenc Papp *Tel:* (022) 43 301 11 235 *Fax:* (022) 43 301 11 222 *E-mail:* papp@technopress.at
INFO-BUILD NV, Groeningestr 39 Bus 21, B-8500 Kortrijk, Belgium *Tel:* 56 24 37 30 *Fax:* 56 24 37 31
InfoChem Gesellschaft fur chemische Information mbH, Landsberger Str 408, D-81241 Munich, Contact: Dr Peter Low *Tel:* (089) 58 93 91 14 *Fax:* (089) 58 93 91 30 *E-mail:* infochem@t-online.de
Kluwer Academic Publishers (KAP), Van Godewijckstr 30, NL-3311 GX Dordrecht, Netherlands, Contact: Peter Hendriks *Tel:* 786576283 *Fax:* 786576322 *E-mail:* peter.hendriks@wkap.nl
Kompetenz Interkon doo, MB 3876608, Bosutska 9, HR-10000 Zagreb, Croatia, Contact: Nenad Zunec *Tel:* (01) 6311 800 *Fax:* (01) 6311 810 *E-mail:* direktor@kompetenz-interkon.hr
Kompetenz-Verlag, Prenterweg 9, A-8045 Weinitzen, Austria, Contact: Wolfgang Hasenhuetl *Tel:* 3132 4660 33 *Fax:* 3132 4660 32 *E-mail:* hasenhuetl@kompetenz.at
Media-Daten Ag, Kanzleistra 80, CH-8026 Zurich, Switzerland, Contact: Heike Findeis *Tel:* (01) 29 69 798 *Fax:* (01) 29 69 702 *E-mail:* heike.findeis@fachmediacom.ch
Media-Daten Verlag, Abraham-Lincoln Str 46, D-65189 Wiesbaden, Contact: Jan Peter Kruse *Tel:* (0611) 78 78 *Fax:* (0611) 78 78 *E-mail:* jan-peter.kruse@gwv-fachverlage.de
Mediacom Springer-Verlag Italia, Via Decembrio 28, I-20137 Milano, Italy, Contact: Dr Madeleine Hofmann *Tel:* (02) 54209741 *Fax:* (02) 55193360 *E-mail:* m.hofmann@springer.it
MED.Komm Gesellschaft fur medizinische Kommunikation mbH, Neumarkter Str 43, D-81673 Munich, Contact: Dr Georg Ralle *Tel:* (089) 43 72 13 72 *Fax:* (089) 43 72 13 70 *E-mail:* ralle@urban-vogel.de
MMV Medien & Medizin Verlag AG, Viadukstr 42, CH-4051 Basel, Switzerland, Contact: Eleonore E Droux *Tel:* (061) 205 01 73 *Fax:* (061) 205 01 75 *E-mail:* droux@medien-medizin.ch
Physica-Verlag, Tiergartenstr 17, D-69121 Heidelberg, Contact: Dr Werner A Mueller *Tel:* (06221) 487 83 45 *Fax:* (06221) 487 81 77 *E-mail:* w.a.mueller@springer.de
Scientific Publishing Services (SPS), 195 Double Rd, Indira nagar, Bangalore 560038, India, Contact: Sharad Wasani *Tel:* 8025259595 *Fax:* 8025259961 *E-mail:* sharad.wasani@sps.sify.net
Springer Science+Business Media Benelux NV, Draaiboomstr 6, B-2160 Wommelgen *Tel:* (03) 3555010 *Fax:* (03) 3555020
Springer Science+Business Media Czech Republic sro, Nadrazni 32, CZ-15000 Prague, Czech Republic, Contact: Tomas Tkacik *Tel:* (02) 25351 111 *Fax:* (02) 25351 151 *E-mail:* tkacik@springermedia.cz
Springer Science+Business Media Magyarorszag Kft, Neumann Janos u 1, H-2040 Budaors, Contact: Janos Adam *Tel:* 23 422 455 *Fax:* 23 422 383 *E-mail:* janos.adam@springermedia.hu
Springer Science+Business Media Schweiz AG, Rutistra 22, CH-8952 Schkieren, Switzerland, Contact: Heike Findeis *Tel:* (01) 73 85 252 *Fax:* (01) 73 85 128 *E-mail:* heike.findeis@fachmediacom.ch
Springer-Verlag Berlin/Heidelberg, Heidelberger Platz 3, D-14197 Berlin, Contact: Derk Haank *Tel:* (030) 827 87 0 *Fax:* (030) 8214091 *E-mail:* derk.haank@springer-sbm.com
Springer-Verlag France S A R L, One rue Paul Cezanne, F-75375 Paris Cedex 08, France, Contact: Dr Rolf Lange *Tel:* 6221 487 8145 *Fax:* 6221 487 8572 *E-mail:* lange@springer.de
Springer-Verlag Hong Kong Ltd, Unit 1702 Tower l, Enterprise Square, 9 Sheung Yuet Rd, Kowloon Bay, Kowloon, Hong Kong, Contact: Maurice Kwong *Tel:* 27 2 3 96 98 *Fax:* 27 24 23 66 *E-mail:* mauricek@springer.com.hk
Springer-Verlag GmbH & Co KG Indian Liaison Office, 906-907 Akash Deep Bldg, Barakhamba Rd, New Delhi 110 001, India, Contact: Sanjiv

Goswami *Tel:* (011) 335 85 90 *Fax:* (011) 335 87 16 *E-mail:* sanjiv.goswami@springer.firm.in

Springer-Verlag Italia Srl, Via Decembrio 28, I-20137 Milan, Italy, Contact: Dr Madeleine Hofmann *Tel:* (02) 54 25 97 21 *Fax:* (02) 55 19 33 60 *E-mail:* m.hofmann@springer.it

Springer-Verlag London Ltd, Sweetapple House, Catteshall Rd, Godalming GU7 3DJ, United Kingdom, Contact: John Watson *Tel:* (014) 83 52 70 51 *Fax:* (014) 83 41 51 44 *E-mail:* john@svl.co.uk

Springer-Verlag KG Wein New York, Sachsenplatz 4-6, A-1201 Wein, Austria, Contact: Rudolf Siegle *Tel:* (01) 330 24 15 *Fax:* (01) 330 24 26 *E-mail:* siegle@springer.at

Springer-Verlag Tokyo Inc, 3-13 Hongo 3-chome, Bunkyo-ku, Toyko 113-0033, Japan, Contact: Terumasa Hirano *Tel:* (03) 38 12 03 31 *Fax:* (03) 38 18 74 54 *E-mail:* t-hirano@svt-ebs.co.jp

Springer-VDI-Verlag GmbH & Co KG, Heinrichstr 24, D-40239 Dusseldorf, Contact: Christian W Scheyko *Tel:* (0211) 61 03 222 *Fax:* (0211) 61 03 113 *E-mail:* scheyko@technikwissen.de

Steinkopff-Verlag, Poststr 9, D-64293 Darmstadt, Contact: Dr Thomas Thiekoetter *Tel:* 6151 828 99 0 *Fax:* 6151 828 99 30 *E-mail:* thiekoetter.steinkopff@springer.de

technopress Fachzeitschriftenverlags-Ges m b H, Inkustr 16, A-3403 Klosterneuburg, Austria, Contact: Ferenc Papp *Tel:* 2243 30111 235 *Fax:* 2243 30111 222 *E-mail:* papp@technopress.at

B G Teubner GmbH, Abraham-Lincoln Str 46, D-65189 Wiesbaden, Contact: Dr Hans-Dieter Haenel *Tel:* (0611) 78 78 102 *Fax:* (0611) 78 78 104 *E-mail:* hans-dieter.haenel@gwv-fachverlage.de

Universitatsdruckerei H Sturz AG, Beethovenstr 5, D-97080 Wurzburg, Contact: Dr Konrad Hartmann *Tel:* (0931) 385 255 359 *Fax:* (0931) 385 359 *E-mail:* drkhartmann@stuertz.de

Urban & Vogel Medien und Medizin Verlagsgesellschaft mbH, Neumarkter Str 43, D-81673 Munich, Contact: Dr Georg Ralle *Tel:* (089) 43 72 13 72 *Fax:* (089) 43 72 13 70 *E-mail:* ralle@urban-vogel.de

Verlag Aktuelle Information GmbH DER PLATOW BRIEF, Stuttgarter Str 25-29, D-60329 Frankfurt am Main, Contact: Albrecht Schirmacher *Tel:* (069) 24 26 39 15 *Fax:* (069) 23 69 09 *E-mail:* albrecht.schirmacher@platow.de

Verlag Dieter Zimpel, Lucile-Grahn Str 37, D-81675 Munich, Contact: Dr Hans-Dieter Haenel *Tel:* (089) 306385 21 *Fax:* (089) 306385 77 *E-mail:* hans-dieter.haenel@gwv-fachverlage.de

Verlag Heinrich Vogel GmbH Fachverlag, Neumarkter Str 18, D-81664 Munich, Contact: Andreas Koesters *Tel:* (089) 43 72 28 77 *Fax:* (089) 43 72 28 79 *E-mail:* andreas.koesters@bertelsmann.de

Friedr Vieweg & Sohn Verlagsgesellschaft, Abraham-Lincoln Str 46, D-65189 Wiesbaden, Contact: Hans-Dieter Haenel *Tel:* (0611) 78 78 102 *Fax:* (0611) 78 78 104 *E-mail:* hans-dieter.haenel@gwv-fachverlage.de

VS Verlag fur Sozialwissenschaften, Abraham-Lincoln Str 46, D-65189 Wiesbaden, Contact: Hans-Dieter Haenel *Tel:* (0611) 78 78 102 *Fax:* (0611) 78 78 104 *E-mail:* hans-dieter.haenel@gwv-fachverlage.de

Wendel-Verlag GmbH, Giebergstr 41-45, D-34117 Kassel, Contact: Gaby Kraus-Nitsch *Tel:* (0561) 860 02 *Fax:* (0561) 860 03 *E-mail:* gaby.kraus-nitsch@bertelsmann.de

U.S. Office(s): Birkhauser Verlag Boston, 675 Massachusetts Ave, Cambridge, MA 02139-3309, United States, Contact: Rudiger Gebauer *Tel:* 617-876-2333 *Fax:* 617-876-1272 *E-mail:* rgebauer@springer-ny.com

Key Curriculum Press, 1150 65 St, Emeryville, CA 94608, United States *Tel:* 510-595-7000 *Fax:* 510-595-7040 *E-mail:* srasmussen@keypress.com

Princeton Architectural Press, 37 E Seventh St, New York, NY 10011, United States, Contact: Kevin Lippert *Tel:* 212-995-9620 *Fax:* 212-995-9454 *E-mail:* lippert@papress.com

Springer-Verlag New York Inc, 175 Fifth Ave, New York, NY 10010, United States, Contact: Rudiger Gebauer *Tel:* 212-460-1501 *Fax:* 212-505-6528 *E-mail:* rgebauer@springer-ny.com

L Staackmann Verlag KG+
Lochenerstr 6, 83623 Dietramszell-Linden
Tel: (08027) 337; (089) 342248 *Fax:* (08027) 816
Key Personnel
Man Dir: Dr Friedrich Vogel
Founded: 1869
Second Address: Verlagsbuero Dr Vogel, Lochener Str 6, 83623 Linden/Obb.
Subjects: Fiction
ISBN Prefix(es): 3-920897; 3-88675

Staatliche Museen Kassel
Schloss Wilhelmshoehe, 34131 Kassel
Mailing Address: Postfach 410420, 34066 Kassel
Tel: (0561) 93 77-7 *Fax:* (0561) 93 77-6 66
E-mail: info@museum-kassel.de
Web Site: www.museum-kassel.de
Key Personnel
Contact: S Naumer *E-mail:* bibliothek@museum-kussel.de
Subjects: Antiques, Architecture & Interior Design, Art, History
ISBN Prefix(es): 3-931787
Divisions: Museums Bibliothek

Staatsbibliothek zu Berlin - Preussischer Kulturbesitz (Berlin State Library - Prussian Cultural Foundation)
Unter den Linden 8, 10117 Berlin
Mailing Address: Potsdamer Str 33, 10785 Berlin
Tel: (030) 266-0
E-mail: webserveradmin@sbb.spk-berlin.de
Web Site: www.sbb.spk-berlin.de; www.staatsbibliothek-berlin.de
Telex: 183160 staab d
Key Personnel
General Dir: Dipl Ing Barbara Schneider-Kempf *E-mail:* barbara.schneider-kempf@sbb.spk-berlin.de
Founded: 1661
Subjects: Library & Information Sciences
ISBN Prefix(es): 3-88053; 3-7361

Stadler Verlagsgesellschaft mbH+
Max-Stromeyerstr 172, 78462 Konstanz
Tel: (07531) 898-0 *Fax:* (07531) 898-101
E-mail: info@verlag-stadler.de
Web Site: www.verlag-stadler.de
Founded: 1815
Membership(s): Berscuvevcin des Deutschen Buchhandels ev.
Subjects: Art, Geography, Geology, History, Maritime, Music, Dance, Nonfiction (General), Outdoor Recreation, Regional Interests
ISBN Prefix(es): 3-7977

Stadt Duisburg - Amt Fuer Statistik, Stadtforschung und Europaangelegenheiten
Bismarckstr 150-158, 47049 Duisburg
Tel: (0203) 283 4502 *Fax:* (0203) 288 4404
E-mail: amt12@stadt-duisburg.de
Key Personnel
Dir: German Bensch
Administrator: Anita Rauser *E-mail:* a.rauser@stadt-duisburg.de
Specialize in public administration-abstracting, statistics & bibliographies.
Periodicals & irregulars.
Subjects: Public Administration

ISBN Prefix(es): 3-89279
Total Titles: 15 Print

Staedte-Verlag, E v Wagner und J Mitterhuber GmbH+
Steinbeisstr 9, 70736 Fellbach b Stuttgart
Mailing Address: Postfach 2080, 70710 Fellbach b Stuttgart
Tel: (0711) 576201 *Fax:* (0711) 5762199
E-mail: info@staedte-verlag.de
Web Site: www.staedte-verlag.de *Cable:* STAEDTEVERLAG
Key Personnel
Man Dir: Meinhard Mitterhuber; Michael Mitterhuber; Manfred von Wagner
Publicity Dir: Rolf Mueller
Rights Dir: Ulrich Groh
Founded: 1951
Subjects: Geography, Geology, Outdoor Recreation
ISBN Prefix(es): 3-8164; 3-920900
Number of titles published annually: 500 Print
Subsidiaries: NovoPrint Verlags GmbH

Verlag Stahleisen GmbH+
Sohnstr 65, 40237 Duesseldorf
Mailing Address: Postfach 105164, 40042 Duesseldorf
Tel: (0211) 6707-0 *Fax:* (0211) 6707-117
E-mail: stahleisen@stahleisen.de
Web Site: www.stahleisen.de *Cable:* STAHLEISEN DUSSELDORF
Key Personnel
Man Dir, Rights Permissions: Dipl Ing Adrian Schommers *E-mail:* adrian.schommers@stahleisen.de
Founded: 1908
Specialize in Steel, Casting-Practice.
Subjects: Chemistry, Chemical Engineering, Civil Engineering, Engineering (General), Mechanical Engineering, Technology
ISBN Prefix(es): 3-514
Associate Companies: Giesserei-Verlag GmbH, Postfach 102532, 40016 Duesseldorf *E-mail:* giesserei@stahleisen.de
Subsidiaries: Montan- und Wirtschaftsverlag GmbH

Verlag H Stam GmbH+
Fuggerstr 7, 51149 Cologne
Tel: (02203) 30290 *Fax:* (02203) 302940
Telex: 887708
Founded: 1959
Subjects: Economics, Technology
ISBN Prefix(es): 3-8018; 3-8181; 3-87183; 3-87772; 3-8237
Branch Office(s)
Lindenstr 54a, 10969 Berlin
Karl-Liebknecht Str 143, 04227 Leipzig
Frauenstr 32, 80469 Munich

Verlag fuer Standesamtswesen GmbH
Hanauer Landstr 197, 60314 Frankfurt am Main
Tel: (069) 40 58 94 0 *Fax:* (069) 40 58 94 99
E-mail: info@vfst.de
Web Site: www.vfst.de
Key Personnel
Manager: Klaudia Metzner
Founded: 1929
Subjects: Law
ISBN Prefix(es): 3-8019

Stapp Verlag Wolfgang Stapp+
Luetzowstr 106, 10785 Berlin
Tel: (030) 2622097 *Fax:* (030) 2621990
Key Personnel
Owner, Rights & Permissions: Wolfgang Stapp
Founded: 1953
Subjects: Biography, Geography, Geology, History, Literature, Literary Criticism, Essays, Music, Dance, Natural History, Nonfiction (Gen-

eral), Outdoor Recreation, Regional Interests, Travel
ISBN Prefix(es): 3-87776
Associate Companies: Kupfergraben Verlags Gesellschaft mbH, Lutzowstr 105, 10785 Berlin *Tel:* (030) 2621990 *Fax:* (030) 2621990
Imprints: Preussische Koepfe
Distributed by Neue Buecher (Switzerland)
Distributor for Kupfergraben Verlag

C A Starke Verlag+
Zeppelinstr 2, 65549 Limburg
Tel: (06431) 96 15-0 *Fax:* (06431) 96 15 15
E-mail: starkeverlag@t-online.de
Web Site: www.starkeverlag.de
Key Personnel
Manager Dipl Kfm: Rasched Salem
Founded: 1847
Subjects: Biography, Genealogy, History, Nonfiction (General), Heraldry, Family
ISBN Prefix(es): 3-7980

Stattbuch Verlag GmbH+
Gneisenaustr 2a, 10961 Berlin
Tel: (030) 6913094; (030) 6913095 *Fax:* (030) 6943354
Founded: 1978
Subjects: Literature, Literary Criticism, Essays, Travel
ISBN Prefix(es): 3-922778
Orders to: Rotation, Mehringdamm 51, 10961 Berlin

Stauffenburg Verlag Brigitte Narr GmbH+
Stauffenbergstr 42, 72074 Tuebingen
Mailing Address: Julius Groos Verlag, Postfach 2525, 72015 Tuebingen
Tel: (07071) 9730-0 *Fax:* (07071) 973030
E-mail: info@stauffenburg.de
Web Site: www.stauffenburg.de
Key Personnel
Man Dir & Publisher: Brigitte Narr *Tel:* (07071) 973097 *E-mail:* narr@stauffenburg.de
Founded: 1982
Subjects: Communications, English as a Second Language, Language Arts, Linguistics, Literature, Literary Criticism, Essays, Women's Studies
ISBN Prefix(es): 3-923721; 3-86057
Number of titles published annually: 70 Print
Total Titles: 800 Print
Associate Companies: Julius Groos Verlag, Postfach 2525, 72015 Tuebingen

Steidl Verlag+
Duestere Str 4, 37073 Goettingen
Tel: (0551) 49 60 60 *Fax:* (0551) 49 60 649
E-mail: mail@steidl.de
Web Site: www.steidl.de
Key Personnel
Marketing & International Rights: Jan Menkens *Tel:* (0551) 49 60 618 *Fax:* (0551) 49 60 617 *E-mail:* jmenkens@steidl.de
Public Relations: Claudia Glenewinkel *Tel:* (0551) 49 60 650 *Fax:* (0551) 49 60 644 *E-mail:* cglenewinkel@steidl.de
Sales: Friederike Sprenger *Tel:* (0551) 49 60 616 *E-mail:* fsprenger@steidl.de
Founded: 1968
Hauseigene Druckerei
Specializes in marketing.
Subjects: Art, Biography, Fiction, History, Literature, Literary Criticism, Essays, Marketing, Nonfiction (General), Philosophy, Photography, Poetry, Psychology, Psychiatry
ISBN Prefix(es): 3-88243
Distributed by DAP Book Distribution Center (USA); Gemeinsame Verlagsauslieferung Goettingen (GVA) (Germany, Switzerland & Austria); Thames & Hudson Ltd; VILO DIFFUSION (France)

Steiger Verlag+
Hilblestr 54, 80636 Munich
Mailing Address: Postfach 80632, Munich
Tel: (089) 9271-0 *Fax:* (089) 9271-68
Key Personnel
Man Dir: Dr Petra Altmann
Editor: Frank Heins
Rights & Permissions: Silke Breitlaender
Founded: 1979
Subjects: Astronomy, Earth Sciences, Foreign Countries, Geography, Geology, Outdoor Recreation, Regional Interests, Sports, Athletics, Travel
ISBN Prefix(es): 3-8043; 3-89441; 3-89440; 3-89652
Parent Company: Weltbild Verlag GmbH
Book Club(s): Weltbild-Versandhandel

Conrad Stein Verlag GmbH+
Dorfstr 3a, 59514 Welver
Mailing Address: Postfach 1233, 59512 Welver
Tel: (02384) 963912 *Fax:* (02384) 963913
E-mail: outdoor@tng.de
Web Site: outdoor.tng.de
Key Personnel
Rights & Permissions: Conrad Stein
Founded: 1980
Subjects: Outdoor Recreation, Travel
ISBN Prefix(es): 3-922965; 3-89392
Total Titles: 150 Print

Franz Steiner Verlag Wiesbaden GmbH+
Birkenwaldstr 44, 70191 Stuttgart
Mailing Address: Postfach 101061, 70009 Stuttgart
Tel: (0711) 2582 0 *Fax:* (0711) 2582 290
E-mail: service@steiner-verlag.de
Web Site: www.steiner-verlag.de
Key Personnel
Publishing Dir: Dr Thomas Schaber
Man Dir: Dr Klaus Brauer *Tel:* (0711) 2582 226 *Fax:* (0711) 2582 296 *E-mail:* Service@ Deutscher-Apotheker-Verlag.de; Andre Caro *Tel:* (0711) 2582 364 *Fax:* (0711) 2582 296 *E-mail:* Service@Deutscher-Apotheker-Verlag.de; Dr Christian Rotta *Tel:* (0711) 2582 225 *E-mail:* Service@Wissenschaftliche-Verlagsgesellschaft.de
Publicity: Susanne Szoradi *Tel:* (0711) 2582 321 *E-mail:* sszoradi@steiner-verlag.de
Distribution: Siegmar Bauer *Tel:* (0711) 2582 219 *E-mail:* Service@Deutscher-Apotheker-Verlag.de
Production: Gregor Hoppen *Tel:* (0711) 2582 305 *E-mail:* ghoppen@steiner-verlag.de
Founded: 1949
Membership(s): Borsenverein des Deutschen Buchhandels.
Subjects: African American Studies, Archaeology, Art, Asian Studies, Developing Countries, Earth Sciences, Education, Foreign Countries, Geography, Geology, History, Language Arts, Linguistics, Law, Music, Dance, Philosophy, Religion - Buddhist, Religion - Hindu, Religion - Islamic, Classical Studies, History of Science
ISBN Prefix(es): 3-515
Number of titles published annually: 180 Print
Total Titles: 4,800 Print
Parent Company: Deutscher Apotheker Verlag
Associate Companies: S Hirzel Verlag GmbH & Co *E-mail:* service@hirzel.de; Wissenschaftliche Verlagsgesellschaft mbH *E-mail:* service@wissenschaftliche-Verlagegesellschaft.de
Subsidiaries: Medpharm Scientific Publishers
Warehouse: Brockhaus/Commission, Kornwestheim *Tel:* (07154) 1327-0 *Fax:* (07154) 132713 *E-mail:* bestell@brocom.de

J F Steinkopf Verlag GmbH+
Uhlandstr 24, 70182 Stuttgart

Key Personnel
Man Dir: Rainer Thun
International Rights: Johannes Keussen
Founded: 1792
Subjects: Art, Biblical Studies, History, How-to, Literature, Literary Criticism, Essays, Religion - Other, Social Sciences, Sociology
ISBN Prefix(es): 3-7984

Dr Dietrich Steinkopff Verlag GmbH & Co+
Poststr 9, 64293 Darmstadt
Mailing Address: Postfach 100462, 64204 Darmstadt
Tel: (06151) 82899-0 (bestellungen) *Fax:* (06151) 82899-40
E-mail: info.steinkopff@springer.de
Web Site: www.steinkopff.springer.de *Cable:* STEINKOPFF
Key Personnel
Chief Executive Officer: Dr Thomas Thiekoetter *E-mail:* thiekoetter.steinkopff@springer.de
Marketing & Product Manager: Sabine Scheffler *E-mail:* scheffler.steinkopff@springer.de
Founded: 1908
Advertising through Springer-Verlag.
Subjects: Health, Nutrition, Medicine, Nursing, Dentistry, Psychology, Psychiatry
ISBN Prefix(es): 3-7985
Total Titles: 850 Print; 2 CD-ROM
Parent Company: Springer-Verlag GmbH & Co KG, Tiesgastenstr 17, Heidelberg 69121
U.S. Office(s): Springer Verlag New York Inc, 175 Fifth Avenue, New York, NY 10010, United States *Tel:* 212-493-6272
Distributed by Springer-Verlag
Warehouse: Springer GmbH & Co, Auslieferungs-Gesellschaft, Haberstr 7, 69126 Heidelberg *Tel:* (06221) 345-0 *E-mail:* orders@springer.de

Steintor Verlag GmbH
Grapengiesserstr 30, 23556 Luebeck
Tel: (0451) 8798849 *Fax:* (0451) 8798837
E-mail: info@steintor-verlag.de
Web Site: www.steintor-verlag.de
Key Personnel
Owner: Rudolf Juedes
Founded: 1969
Subjects: Art
ISBN Prefix(es): 3-9801506
Bookshop(s): Gallerie Meiborssen, 37647 Meiborssen *Tel:* (05535) 8851

Steinweg-Verlag, Jurgen vomHoff+
Fasanenstr 6, 38102 Braunschweig
Tel: (0531) 2339197 *Fax:* (0531) 2336649
Key Personnel
Contact: Juergen Vom Hoff
Founded: 1986
Subjects: Art, History, Photography, Regional Interests, Social Sciences, Sociology
ISBN Prefix(es): 3-925151

Verlag Stendel+
Untere Sackgasse 9, 71332 Waiblingen
Mailing Address: Postfach 1713, 71307 Waiblingen
Tel: (07151) 956603 *Fax:* (07151) 956605
E-mail: info@stendel-verlag.de; verlag.stendel@t-online.de
Web Site: www.verlag-stendel.de
Key Personnel
Manager: Dagmar Kuebler
Editor: Roland Kuebler
Founded: 1987
Subjects: Fiction, Literature, Literary Criticism, Essays, Psychology, Psychiatry, Science Fiction, Fantasy
ISBN Prefix(es): 3-926789

Stephanus Edition Verlags GmbH+
Gebhardsweiler 10, 88690 Uhldingen-Muehlofen

Mailing Address: Postfach 1260, 88683 Uhldingen-Muehlofen
Tel: (07556) 8331 *Fax:* (07556) 8373
E-mail: 0755692110@tonline.de
Key Personnel
Man Dir: Sabastian Braun
Editorial: Hans Braun
Founded: 1978
Subjects: Religion - Other
ISBN Prefix(es): 3-921213; 3-922816; 3-932880

Annemarie Stern, *see* Asso Verlag

Stern-Verlag Janssen & Co+
Friedrichstr 24-26, 40001 Duesseldorf
Mailing Address: Postfach 101053, 40217 Duesseldorf
Tel: (0211) 3881-0 *Fax:* (0211) 3881-280
E-mail: webmaster@buchhaus-sternverlag.de
Web Site: www.buchsv.de
Key Personnel
Man Partner: Horst Janssen; Klaus Janssen
Founded: 1900
Subjects: Biography, History, Language Arts, Linguistics, Nonfiction (General), Philosophy
ISBN Prefix(es): 3-87784
Associate Companies: Artibus et Literis
Bookshop(s): Universitaetsbuchhandlung, Universitaetstr 1, 40225 Duesseldorf

Sternberg-Verlag bei Ernst Franz+
Industriestr 8, 72585 Riederich
Tel: (07123) 938922 *Fax:* (07123) 938920
Key Personnel
Manager: Gerhard Heinzelmann
Founded: 1950
Subjects: Biblical Studies, Biography, History, Religion - Protestant, Theology
ISBN Prefix(es): 3-87785
Parent Company: Ernst Franz Verlag
Distributed by Haenssler; KNO; K&V; Libri; Umbreit (D)

Edition Sternenprinz, *imprint of* Hans-Nietsch-Verlag

Steyler Verlag+
Postfach 2460, 41311 Nettetal
Tel: (02157) 120220 *Fax:* (02157) 120260
E-mail: verlag@steyler.de
Web Site: www.steyler.de
Key Personnel
Man Dir: Andreas Heider; Paul Langer
Founded: 1927
Subjects: Anthropology, Biography, Developing Countries, Language Arts, Linguistics, Religion - Catholic, Science (General)
ISBN Prefix(es): 3-87787; 3-8050
Parent Company: Steyler Verlagsbuchhandlung GmbH, Bahnofstr 9, 41334 Nettetal

Stiebner Verlag GmbH+
Nymphenburger Str 86, 80636 Munich
Tel: (089) 1257378 *Fax:* (089) 12162282
Founded: 1998
Specialize in reproductions.
Subjects: Art, Sports, Athletics
ISBN Prefix(es): 3-7679; 3-8307

Stiefel Eurocart GmbH+
Felix-Wankel-Ring 13a, 85101 Lenting
Tel: (08456) 924100 *Fax:* (08456) 924134
E-mail: stiefel.gmbH@stiefel-online.de
Web Site: www.stiefel-online.com
Key Personnel
Manager: Heinrich Stiefel
International Rights: Franz Hofherr
Founded: 1982
Membership(s): World Didac Borsezvenez.
Subjects: Biological Sciences, English as a Second Language, Environmental Studies, Geography, Geology, History, Language Arts, Linguistics, Mathematics, Religion - Other, French
ISBN Prefix(es): 3-929627
Subsidiaries: Stiefel Digitalprint GmbH (Austria); Stiefel Digitalprint GmbH (Germany); Stiefel Eurocart Kft; Stiefel Eurocart KG/SAS; Stiefel Eurocart Spzoo; Stiefel Eurocart srl; Stiefel Eurocart sro (Czech Republic); Stiefel Eurocart sro (Slovakia); Stiefel Verlag; Steinberger Verlag GmbH

Stiftung Buchkunst (Book Art Foundation)
Adickesallee 1, 60322 Frankfurt am Main
Tel: (069) 1525-1800 *Fax:* (069) 1525-1805
E-mail: buchkunst@dbf.ddb.de
Web Site: www.stiftung-buchkunst.de
Key Personnel
Man Dir: Uta Schneider
Founded: 1966
Branch Office(s)
Buero Leipzig, Gerichtsweg 26, Leipzig
Tel: (0341) 9954-210 *Fax:* (0341) 9954-211

Edition Gunter Stoberlein
Niethammerstr 15, 80997 Munich
Tel: (089) 8115289
Key Personnel
Owner: Gunter Stoberlein
Founded: 1972
Membership(s): Boirsenverein Des Deutschen Buchhandels.
Subjects: Art, Literature, Literary Criticism, Essays, Poetry
ISBN Prefix(es): 3-88045; 3-921430

Stoeppel Verlag-Buchvertrieb KG+
Mandichostr 18, 86504 Merching
Tel: (08233) 381-186 *Fax:* (08233) 381-246
E-mail: service@stoeppel.de
Web Site: www.stoeppel.de
Key Personnel
Man Dir: Norbert Bretsch; Ronald Herkert
Founded: 1981
Subjects: Outdoor Recreation, Travel
ISBN Prefix(es): 3-924012; 3-89306
Orders to: GeoLenter, Neumarkterstr 18, 81673 Munich

Stollfuss Verlag Bonn GmbH & Co KG+
Dechenstr 7, 53115 Bonn
Mailing Address: Postfach 2428, 53014 Bonn
Tel: (0228) 7 24-0 *Fax:* (0228) 7 24-9 11 81
E-mail: info@stollfuss.de
Web Site: www.stollfuss.de *Cable:* STOLLFUSSVERLAG
Key Personnel
Man Dir: Michael Stollfuss; Wolfgang Stollfuss
Editorial: Hans-Josef Metz
Rights & Permissions, Production: Reinhard Just
Founded: 1913
Specialize in Tax & Fiscal Law.
Subjects: Accounting, Economics, Finance, Law, Public Administration
ISBN Prefix(es): 3-08
Distributor for Schriften des BMF und BMA
Warehouse: Justus-von Liebig Str 6, 53121 Bonn

Straelener Manuskripte Verlag GmbH+
Venloerstr 45, 47638 Straelen
Mailing Address: Postfach 1324, 47630 Straelen
Tel: (02834) 6588 *Fax:* (02834) 6588
Web Site: www.straelener-manuskripte.de
Key Personnel
Manager: Renate Birkenhauer, PhD *E-mail:* r.birkenhauer@straelener-manuskripte.de
Founded: 1983
Subjects: Literature, Literary Criticism, Essays, Poetry
ISBN Prefix(es): 3-89107
Number of titles published annually: 2 Print
Total Titles: 33 Print

Stroemfeld/Nexus, *imprint of* Stroemfeld Verlag

Stroemfeld/Roter Stern, *imprint of* Stroemfeld Verlag

Stroemfeld Verlag+
Holzhausenstr 4, 60322 Frankfurt
Tel: (069) 955 226-0 *Fax:* (069) 955 226-22
E-mail: info@stroemfeld.de
Web Site: www.stroemfeld.de
Key Personnel
Publisher: Karl D Wolff
International Rights: Doris Kern
Founded: 1981 (Nexus)
Subjects: Literature, Literary Criticism, Essays, Psychology, Psychiatry
ISBN Prefix(es): 3-87877; 3-86109
Parent Company: Stroemfeld Verlag AG, Basel, Switzerland
Imprints: Stroemfeld/Roter Stern; Stroemfeld/Nexus
Branch Office(s)
Basel, Switzerland
Orders to: SOVA, Friesstr 20-24, 60388 Frankfurt

STS Standard Tabellen und Software Verlag GmbH
Subsidiary of Rudolf Haufe Verlag GmbH & Co KG
Fraunhoferstr 5, 82152 Planegg
Mailing Address: Postfach 1363, 82142 Planegg
Tel: (089) 89517-0 *Fax:* (089) 89517290
Key Personnel
Dir: Helmuth Hopfner; Martin Lagua; Uwe Renald Muller
Founded: 1939
ISBN Prefix(es): 3-86027

Sturtz Verlag GmbH
Imprint of Verlagshaus Wurzburg
Beethovenstr 5, 97070 Wurzburg
Tel: (0931) 385235 *Fax:* (0931) 385305
E-mail: info@verlagshaus.com
Web Site: www.verlagshaus.com
Key Personnel
Publishing Dir: Dieter Krause
Dir, Production: Juergen Roth
Sales Dir: Johannes Glesius
Founded: 1830
Subjects: Travel
ISBN Prefix(es): 3-8003

Sueddeutsche Verlagsgesellschaft mbH+
Sendlingerstr 8, 80331 Munich
Tel: (089) 2183-0 *Fax:* (089) 2183-787
E-mail: verlag@sueddeutsche.de; redaktion@sueddeutsche.de
Web Site: www.sueddeutsche.de
Key Personnel
Man Dir, Rights & Permissions: Udo Vogt
Contact: Reinhard Keller
Founded: 1898
Subjects: Art, History, Nonfiction (General), Regional Interests, Religion - Catholic
ISBN Prefix(es): 3-88294; 3-920921
Parent Company: Schwabenverlag AG, Senefelderstr 12, Ostfildern
Branch Office(s)
Schwabenverlag AG, Abt Buchhandlung, Bahnhofstr 21, Aalen
Bookshop(s): Sueddeutsche Verlagsges mbH, Sedelhofgasse, 89073 Ulm/Donau; Schwabenverlag AG, Abt Buchhandlung, Spital Str 19, 73479 Ellwangen

Suedverlag GmbH+
Schuetzenstr 24, 78462 Konstanz
Mailing Address: Postfach 10 20 51, 78420 Konstanz
Tel: (07531) 9053-0 *Fax:* (07531) 9053-98
E-mail: willkommen@uvk.de

Web Site: www.suedverlag.de
Key Personnel
Publishing Manager: Walter Engstle *Tel:* (07531) 905312 *E-mail:* walter.engstle@uvk.de
Founded: 1945
Subjects: Biography, Humor, Regional Interests
ISBN Prefix(es): 3-87800
Associate Companies: UVK Verlagsgesellschaft mbH
Orders to: Brockhaus Commission Verlagsauslieferung, Kreidlerstr 9, 70806 Kornwestheim

Suedwest Verlag GmbH & Co KG+
Bayerstr 71-73, 80335 Munich
Tel: (089) 4136-0; (01805) 990505 (hotline) *Fax:* (089) 5148-2229
E-mail: heyne-suedwest@randomhouse.de
Web Site: www.suedwest-verlag.de
Key Personnel
Man Partner: Christian Strasser
Publicity & Co-production: Bettina Breitling
Founded: 1945
Subjects: Cookery, Health, Nutrition, Nonfiction (General), Travel
Associate Companies: Paul List Verlag GmbH; W Ludwig Verlag GmbH; C J Bucher Verlag GmbH

Suhrkamp Verlag+
Lindenstr 29-35, 60325 Frankfurt am Main
Mailing Address: Postfach 101945, 60019 Frankfurt am Main
Tel: (069) 75601-0 *Fax:* (069) 75601-522; (069) 75601-314
Web Site: www.suhrkamp.de *Cable:* SUHRKAMPVERLAG
Key Personnel
Publisher: Ulla Unseld-Berkewicz
Man Dir: Philip Roeder *Tel:* (069) 75601-500 *E-mail:* roeder@suhrkamp.de
Editorial Dir: Dr Raines Weiss
Sales & Marketing Dir: Georg Rieppel
Rights & Permissions: Dr Petra Hardt
Founded: 1950
Subjects: Biography, Fiction, Philosophy, Poetry, Psychology, Psychiatry, Science (General)
ISBN Prefix(es): 3-518
Associate Companies: Deutscher Klassiker Verlag; Insel Verlag; Juedischer Verlag; Suhrkamp Verlag AG, Switzerland
Foreign Rep(s): Agenzia Letteraria Internazionale (Italy); Balla & Co Literary Agents (Hungary); Bardon Chinese Media Agency (Taiwan); Claudia Brandes (Netherlands, Eastern Europe, Scandinavia); Ulrich Breth (Asia, Greece, Turkey); Michael Griesinger (Africa, Latin America, Portugal, South America, Spain); Petra Christina Hardt (Australia, British Commonwealth & UK, China, France, Israel, Italy, Middle East, USA); Hercules Business (China); International Editors (Latin America, Portugal, Spain); International Literature Bureau (Netherlands); Leohardt & Hoier Literary Agency (Scandinavia); Sakai Agency (Japan)

Suin Buch-Verlag
Kappstr 29, 64678 Lindenfels
Tel: (06255) 2657 *Fax:* (06255) 9596875
Key Personnel
Owner: Dr Bernhard Suin de Boutemard
Founded: 1975
Subjects: Alternative, Anthropology, Civil Engineering, Education, History, Human Relations, Philosophy, Religion - Catholic, Religion - Protestant, Religion - Other, Self-Help, Social Sciences, Sociology, Theology
ISBN Prefix(es): 3-921559

Sulamith Wulfing Edition, *imprint of* Aquamarin Verlag

Sulamith Wulfing Verlag, *imprint of* Aquamarin Verlag

Svato Zapletal+
Missundestr 18, 22769 Hamburg
Tel: (040) 4390004 *Fax:* (040) 4390004
Key Personnel
Contact: Svato Zapletal
Founded: 1976
Subjects: Art, Fiction, Poetry
ISBN Prefix(es): 3-924283

Sybex Verlag GmbH+
Postfach 501253, 50972 Cologne
Tel: (02236) 399920-0 *Fax:* (02236) 399922-9
E-mail: sybex@sybex.de
Web Site: www.sybex.de
Key Personnel
Manager: Gerhard Prollius
Founded: 1981
Subjects: Computer Science
ISBN Prefix(es): 3-88745; 3-8155
Associate Companies: Sybex Uitgeverij BV, Birkstr 95, 3768 HD Soest, Netherlands *Tel:* (031) 3560 27625 *Fax:* (031) 3560 26556 *E-mail:* sybex@sybex.nl; Sybex SARL, 76 Ave Pierre Brossolette, 92247 Malakoff Paris Cedex 14, France *Tel:* (01) 55 58 4000 *Fax:* (01) 49 65 0410 *Web Site:* www.sybex.fr
U.S. Office(s): Sybex Inc, 1151 Marine Village Parkway, Alameda, CA 94501, United States *Tel:* 510-523-8233 *Fax:* 510-523-2373 *E-mail:* info@sybex.com
Orders to: VVA, Postfach 7777, 33310 Gutersloh *Tel:* (05) 2410805906 *Fax:* (05) 2410460130

Synthesis Verlag+
Postfach 14 32 06, 45262 Essen
Tel: (0201) 51 01 88 *Fax:* (0201) 51 10 49
E-mail: synthesis@synthesis-verlag.com
Web Site: www.synthesis-verlag.com
Founded: 1979
Subjects: Health, Nutrition, Science (General)
ISBN Prefix(es): 3-922026
Orders to: VSB-Verlagsservice Braunschweig GmbH, Georg-Westermann-Allee 66, 38104 Braunschweig *Tel:* (0531) 7080708277 *Fax:* (0531) 708 619

Tangens Systemverlag GmbH+
Donnerstr 5-7, 22763 Hamburg
Tel: (040) 3985860 *Fax:* (040) 395118
Key Personnel
Contact: Thomas E Panzer
Founded: 1987 (under the name Verlagsgnindung)
Subjects: Computer Science, Fiction, Marketing, Nonfiction (General), Poetry
ISBN Prefix(es): 3-926622

Taoasis Verlag, Birgit Meyer+
Bismarckstr 23, 32657 Lemgo
Tel: (05261) 2321 *Fax:* (05261) 9383-21
E-mail: info@taoasis.de
Web Site: www.taoasis.de
Key Personnel
Contact: Axel Luye

TASCHEN GmbH
Hohenzollernring 53, 50672 Cologne
Tel: (0221) 201 80 0 *Fax:* (0221) 25 49 19
E-mail: contact@taschen.com
Web Site: www.taschen.com
Key Personnel
Dir: Benedikt Taschen
Chief Editor: Dr Angelika Taschen
Founded: 1980
Subjects: Architecture & Interior Design, Art, Erotica, Photography
ISBN Prefix(es): 3-8228

Subsidiaries: TASCHEN America; TASCHEN Deutschland; TASCHEN Espana; TASCHEN France; TASCHEN Japan; TASCHEN UK
Bookshop(s): 2 rue de Buci, 75006 Paris, France *Tel:* (01) 40 51 79 22 *E-mail:* store@taschen-france.com; Hohenzollernring 28, 50672 Cologne *Tel:* (0221) 2573304 *Fax:* (0221) 254968 *E-mail:* store@taschen.com; 354 N Beverly Hills Dr, Beverly Hills, CA 90210, United States *Tel:* 310-274-4300 *Fax:* 310-274-4040 *E-mail:* store-la@taschen.com

Te-Wi Verlag Unternehmensbereich Buch der Ziff Verlag GmbH+
Riesstr 25, Haus D, 80992 Munich 50
Tel: (089) 14312470 *Fax:* (089) 14312469
Key Personnel
Man Dir: Gunther Frank
Founded: 1977
Subjects: Computer Science
ISBN Prefix(es): 3-89362
Parent Company: Ziff Verlag GmbH, Riesstr 25, Haus D, 80992 Munich
U.S. Office(s): Ziff Davis Press, 5903 Christie Ave, Emeryville, CA, United States *Tel:* 510-601-2005
Orders to: Revilak Verlagsservice, Gutenbergstr 5, 8031 Gilching, Munich *Tel:* (08105) 5051 *Fax:* (08105) 5408

Verlag fuer Technik und Wirtschaft GmbH & Co KG, *see* Vereinigte Fachverlage GmbH

Hochschule fur Technik Wirtschaft und Kultur Leipzig (FH)
Karl Liebknechtstr 132, 04277 Leipzig
Mailing Address: Postfach 30 11 66, 04251 Leipzig
Tel: (0341) 3076-0 *Fax:* (0341) 3076-6456
E-mail: ebert@r.htwk.leipzig.de
Web Site: www.htwk-leipzig.de
Key Personnel
Contact: Prof Torsten Seela
Founded: 1992

Otto Teich+
Hilpertstr 9, 64295 Darmstadt
Mailing Address: Postfach 200144, 64300 Darmstadt
Tel: (06151) 824120 *Fax:* (06151) 895656
Key Personnel
Man Dir & International Rights: Christine Otto
Founded: 1889
Specialize in humorous performances.
Subjects: Drama, Theater, Humor
ISBN Prefix(es): 3-8069
Associate Companies: Eduard Bloch Verlag, Hilpertstr 9, 64295 Darmstadt; Bergwald Verlag, Hilpertstr 9, 64295 Darmstadt
Imprints: Baerenreiter-Spieltexte

Telex-Verlag Jaeger & Waldmann GmbH
Birkenweg 8-10, 64295 Darmstadt
Mailing Address: Postfach 111454, 64229 Darmstadt
Tel: (06151) 33 02-0 *Fax:* (06151) 33 02-50
E-mail: jwemail@aol.com; jwdir@aol.com
Telex: 419389 jwtlx d
Key Personnel
General Manager: Wolfgang Lich *Tel:* (06151) 33 02-12 *Fax:* (06151) 33 02-70
Contact: D Ashimolowo *Tel:* (06151) 33 02-22
Founded: 1953
Telecommunication company with representation worldwide.
Subjects: Business, Communications
ISBN Prefix(es): 3-87810

Alf Teloeken Verlag KG, *see* Alba Fachverlag GmbH & Co KG

TELOS, *imprint of* Springer Science+Business Media GmbH & Co KG

Edition Temmen+
Hohenlohestr 21, 28209 Bremen
Tel: (0421) 34843-0 *Fax:* (0421) 348094
E-mail: info@edition-temmen.de
Web Site: www.edition-temmen.de
Key Personnel
Owner: Horst Temmen
Founded: 1983
Subjects: Government, Political Science, History, Literature, Literary Criticism, Essays, Maritime, Military Science, Nonfiction (General), Social Sciences, Sociology, Travel
ISBN Prefix(es): 3-926958; 3-86108

teNeues Verlag GmbH & Co KG+
Am Selder 37, 47906 Kempen
Tel: (02152) 916-0 *Fax:* (02152) 916-111
E-mail: verlag@teneues.de
Web Site: www.teneues.com
Key Personnel
Publisher & Man Dir: Hendrik te Neues
  Tel: (02152) 916210 *E-mail:* hteneues@aol.com
Man Dir, Marketing: Hartmut Rau *Tel:* (02152) 916126 *E-mail:* hrau@teneues.de
Man Dir, International Division: Marcus Herfort *Tel:* (02152) 916117 *E-mail:* mherfort@teneues.de
Dir, Sales & Marketing Book Trade: Ralf Daab *Tel:* (02152) 916120
Man Dir, Product Development: Sebastian te Neues
Dir, Editorial Dept: Kristina Kruger; Sabine Wurfel *Tel:* (02152) 916245
Man Dir, Chief Financial Officer/Administration: Dieter Schepers
Founded: 1950
International publishing group with offices in Kempen, New York & London, world wide distribution in over 60 countries
Calendars, art merchandise & internet reference guides.
Subjects: Architecture & Interior Design, Art, Fashion, Photography, Travel
ISBN Prefix(es): 3-8238; 3-87580
Total Titles: 20 E-Book
Parent Company: teNeues Publishing Co, c/o Macmillan Canada, 29 Birch Ave, Toronto, ON M4V 1E2, Canada
Associate Companies: teNeues Publishing UK, Aldwych House, 71-91 Aldwych, London WC2B 4HN, United Kingdom *Tel:* (020) 8283 6426 *Fax:* (020) 8283 6426; teNeues France, 140 rue de la Croix Nivert, 75015 Paris, France *Tel:* (01) 55-766205 *Fax:* (01) 55-766419 *E-mail:* teneuesfrance@wanadoo.fr
Divisions: teNeues Publishing Canada
U.S. Office(s): teNeues Publishing Company, 16 W 22 St, New York, NY 10010, United States, Dir, Sales & Marketing: Stephen Hulburt *Tel:* 212-627-9090 *Fax:* 212-627-9534
Orders to: teNeus Publishing Co New York, 16 W 22 St, New York, NY 10010, United States *Tel:* 212-627-9090 *Fax:* 212-627-9511 *E-mail:* tnp@teneues-usa.com (USA orders)

Terra-Verlag GmbH
Neuhauserstr 21, 78464 Konstanz
Mailing Address: Postfach 102144, 78421 Konstanz
Tel: (07531) 81220 *Fax:* (07531) 812299
E-mail: info@terra-verlag.de
Web Site: www.terra-verlag.de
Key Personnel
Publisher: Eberhard Heizmann
Founded: 1946
ISBN Prefix(es): 3-920942
Total Titles: 10 Print
Subsidiaries: Terra Media Kft

Tessloff Verlag Ragnar Tessloff GmbH & Co KG
Burgschmietstr 2-4, 90419 Nuernberg
Tel: (0911) 39906-0 *Fax:* (0911) 39906-39
E-mail: tessloff@osn.de
Web Site: www.tessloff.com
Key Personnel
General Manager: Dr Thomas Seng
ISBN Prefix(es): 3-7886

Tetra Verlag Gmbh+
Berliner Str 8, 16727 Berlin-Velten
Tel: (03304) 20 22-0 *Fax:* (03304) 20 22-20
E-mail: info@tetra-verlag.de
Web Site: www.tetra-verlag.de
Key Personnel
Publisher: Dr Hans-Joachim Herrmann
  E-mail: hermann@tetra-verlag.de
Founded: 1972
Publish calendars
Member of Boersenverein des Deutsche Buchhandels.
Subjects: Animals, Pets, Maritime, Popular Scientific & Lobbyist Literature
ISBN Prefix(es): 3-89745
Number of titles published annually: 8 Print
Total Titles: 93 Print

Tetzlaff Verlag
Nordkanalstr 36, 20097 Hamburg
Mailing Address: Postfach 101607, 20010 Hamburg
Tel: (040) 237 14-03 *Fax:* (040) 237 14-233
Web Site: www.eurailpress.com
Key Personnel
Man Dir: Detlev K Suchanek *Tel:* (040) 237 14-228 *Fax:* (040) 237 14-236 *E-mail:* suchanek@etp.net
Editor: Christoph Mueller *Tel:* (040) 237 14-152 *Fax:* (040) 237 14-205 *E-mail:* mueller@eurailpress.com
Sales: Riccardo di Stefano *Tel:* (040) 237 14-101 *Fax:* (040) 237 14-233 *E-mail:* belsen@eurailpress.com; Sophie Elfendahl *Tel:* (040) 237 14-220 *Fax:* (040) 237 14-236 *E-mail:* elfendahl@eurailpress.com
Founded: 1900
Subjects: Transportation
ISBN Prefix(es): 3-87814

B G Teubner Verlag+
Unit of GWV Fachverlage Gmbh
Abraham-Lincoln-Str 46, 65189 Wiesbaden
Tel: (0611) 78780 *Fax:* (0611) 7878470
Web Site: www.teubner.de; www.gwv-fachverlage.de
Key Personnel
Man Dir: Dr Heinz Weinheimer
Rights & Permissions Manager: Mrs Angelika Bolisega *E-mail:* angelika.bolisega@gwv-fachverlage.de
General Manager: Hans-Dieter Haenel
Editorial: Ulrike Schmickler-Hirzebruch; Ewald Schmitt
Founded: 1811
Subjects: Chemistry, Chemical Engineering, Civil Engineering, Computer Science, Electronics, Electrical Engineering, Mathematics, Mechanical Engineering, Physics, Technology
ISBN Prefix(es): 3-519; 3-8154
Total Titles: 1,500 Print; 14 Online
Parent Company: Springer Science & Business Media
Orders to: VVA Bertelsmann Distribution, Postfach 7777, 33310 Guetersloh

Teubner Edition, *imprint of* Graefe und Unzer Verlag GmbH

edition Text & Kritik im Richard Boorberg Verlag GmbH & Co+
Levelingstr 6a, 81673 Munich
Mailing Address: Postfach 800529, 81605 Munich
Tel: (089) 43600012 *Fax:* (089) 43600019
E-mail: info@etk-muenchen.de
Web Site: www.etk-muenchen.de
Key Personnel
Man Dir: Dr Berndt Oesterhelt
International Rights: Dr Monika Bopp *E-mail:* m.bopp-edition-text+kritik@boorberg.de
Founded: 1975
Subjects: Film, Video, Literature, Literary Criticism, Essays, Music, Dance
ISBN Prefix(es): 3-921402; 3-88377
Divisions: Auslieferung von Verlag der Autoren

Thalacker Medien GmbH Co KG+
Member of Horti Media Europe (HME)
Postfach 83 64, 38133 Braunschweig
Tel: (0531) 38004 0 *Fax:* (0531) 38004 25
E-mail: info@thalackermedien.de
Web Site: www.thalackermedien.de
Key Personnel
Contact: Brigitte Mayr *Tel:* (0531) 3800447 *Fax:* (0531) 38004830 *E-mail:* b.mayr@thalackermedien.de
Founded: 1867
Specialize in technical literature of gardening & floral design, newspapers, magazines, technical books & reference books.
Membership(s): Boersenverein des Deutschen Buchandels & Verband Deutscher Zeitschriften Verleger.
Subjects: Agriculture, Gardening, Plants
ISBN Prefix(es): 3-87815
Number of titles published annually: 10 Print
Total Titles: 80 Print

Thauros Verlag GmbH
Jakob-Huberstr 9, 88171 Weiler-Simmerberg
Mailing Address: Postfach 1141, 88168 Weiler im Allgaeu
Tel: (08387) 2510 *Fax:* (08387) 3731
E-mail: thaurosverlag@t-online.de
Key Personnel
Editor: Christian Schneider
Founded: 1978
Subjects: Astrology, Occult, Biblical Studies, Biography, Religion - Jewish, Religion - Other
ISBN Prefix(es): 3-88411

Konrad Theiss Verlag GmbH+
Moenchhaldenstr 28, 70191 Stuttgart
Tel: (0711) 255 27-0 *Fax:* (0711) 255 27-17
E-mail: service@theiss.de
Web Site: www.theiss.de *Cable:* THEISSVERLAG STUTTGART
Key Personnel
Man Dir: Christian Rieker *Tel:* (0711) 255 27-12
Sales: Ruth Kessler *E-mail:* kessler@theiss.de
Production: Karin Dechow *Tel:* (0711) 255 27-18 *E-mail:* dechow@theiss.de
Program Manager: Jurgen Beckedorf *Tel:* (0711) 255 27-16 *E-mail:* beckedorf@theiss.de
Founded: 1997
Subjects: Archaeology, Art, History, Nonfiction (General)
ISBN Prefix(es): 3-8062
Total Titles: 2 CD-ROM
Distributed by Wissenschiftliche Buchgesellschaft

Druck-und Verlagshans Thiele & Schwarz GmbH+
Werner-Heisenbergstr 7, 34123 Kassel
Tel: (0561) 9 59 25-0 *Fax:* (0561) 9 59 25-68
E-mail: info@thiele-schwarz.de
Web Site: www.thiele-schwarz.de *Cable:* THIELE & SCHWARZ KASSEL-WALDAU
Key Personnel
Proprietor: Rolf Schwarz
Founded: 1879
ISBN Prefix(es): 3-87816

Associate Companies: Verlag Schule und Elternhaus
Bookshop(s): Buch und Musik Center Wilhelmshoehe, Wilhelmshoeheer Allee 256, 34119 Kassel; Buchhandlung Am Markt, Markstr 10, 99310 Armkstadt

Georg Thieme Verlag KG+
Ruedigerstr 14, 70469 Stuttgart
Mailing Address: Postfach 301120, 70451 Stuttgart
Tel: (0711) 8931-0 *Fax:* (0711) 8931-298
E-mail: kunden.service@thieme.de
Web Site: www.thieme.de *Cable:* THIEMEBUCH
Key Personnel
Publisher: Albrecht Hauff
Man Dir: Dr Wolfgang Knueppe
Press: Anne-Katrin Doebler
Division Head, Marketing & Sales: Dr Harald Steiner
International Rights Manager: Barbara Pfeifer
  Tel: (0711) 8931-184 *Fax:* (0711) 8931-143
  E-mail: barbara.pfeifer@thieme.de
Dir, International Marketing & Sales: Malik Lechelt *E-mail:* malik.lechelt@thieme.de
Founded: 1886
Subjects: Biological Sciences, Chemistry, Chemical Engineering, Health, Nutrition, Medicine, Nursing, Dentistry, Psychology, Psychiatry, Physiotherapy
ISBN Prefix(es): 3-13; 3-8304; 1-58890
Number of titles published annually: 600 Print; 20 CD-ROM; 10 Audio
Total Titles: 5,100 Print; 100 CD-ROM; 50 Audio
Associate Companies: MVS Medizinverlage Stuttgart GmbH & Co KG, Oswald-Hesse-Str 50, 70469 Stuttgart, Foreign Rights: Susanne Seeger *Tel:* (0711) 8931-147 *Fax:* (0711) 8931-143
Imprints: Enke; Haug; Hippokrates; Parey; Sonntag; TRIAS
U.S. Office(s): Thieme Medical Publishers, 333 Seventh Ave, 5th Floor, New York, NY 10001, United States
Distributed by Academi-text (US); Baker & Taylor (US); Miguel Concha SA (Chile); Coutts Library Services (US); Distribuna Libreria Medica Digital (Colombia); Editorial Cientifica Interamericana (Argentina); Elsevier Australia; Hwa Eng Trading Co (Taiwan - books only); Jaypee Brothers Medical Publishers (P) Ltd (India - medicine & dentistry only); Liberia Internacional SA de CV (Mexico); Lidel Edicoes Tecnicas LDA (Portugal, Angola, Mozambique, Guine-Bissau, Cabo-Verde, Sao Tome - books & journals); Login Brothers Canada (Canada); J A Majors Co (US); Matthews Medical Books (US); Medical Books in Print (US); Midwest Library Services (US); Nobel Tip Kitabevleri (Turkey); PF Book Importer (Indonesia - books only); Promociones Editorales (Mexico); Redwing Book Co (US); Ernesto Reichmann Distribuidora de Livros Ltda (Brazil); Rittenhouse Book Distributors (US); Sandi SA Bookstore (Mexico); Seoul Medical Scientific Books Co (South Korea - books only); Wexford Hall (US); Yankee Book Pedler Inc (US)
Distributor for AANS
Foreign Rep(s): Academic Marketing Services (Pty) Ltd (Botswana, Namibia, South Africa); Amin Al-Abini (North Africa, Middle East exc Iran); Jamshid Fattahi (Iran); Michael Goh (Brunei, Burma, Cambodia, China, Indonesia, Korea, Laos, Philippines, Singapore & Malaysia, Taiwan, Thailand, Vietnam); Laszlo Horvath (Eastern Europe, Russia); Akio Hosoya (Japan); Anwer Igbal (Pakistan); Momenta Publishing Ltd (Belgium, Netherlands, UK & Ireland); David Towle International (Scandinavia); Trinidad Lopez Gonzalez (Spain); Katia Zevelekakis (Greece)

Bookshop(s): Frohberg Buchhandlung fuer Medizin, Tempelhofer Weg 11-12, 10829 Berlin
Tel: (030) 8390030
Warehouse: Koch, Neff & Oetinger & Co, Verlagsauslieferung, Schockenriedstr 39, Postfach 800620, 70506 Stuttgart

Thien, Hans-Gunter, u Hanns Wienold
Verlag Westfalisches Dampfboot, Hafenweg 26a, 48145 Muenster
Tel: (0251) 3900480 *Fax:* (0251) 39004850
E-mail: info@dampfboot-verlag.de
Web Site: www.dampfboot-verlag.de
Key Personnel
Man Dir: Dr Hans-Guenther Thien; Dr Hanns Wienold
Founded: 1984
ISBN Prefix(es): 3-89691
Number of titles published annually: 40 Print
Distributor for Prolit Verlagaushiferung

Thienemann Verlag GmbH+
Blumenstr 36, 70182 Stuttgart
Tel: (0711) 210 55-0 *Fax:* (0711) 210 55 39
E-mail: info@thienemann.de
Web Site: www.thienemann.de
Key Personnel
Man Dir: Klaus Willberg
Editor-in-Chief: Stefan Wendel
Foreign & Domestic Rights: Doris Keller-Riehm
Founded: 1849
Subjects: Fiction
ISBN Prefix(es): 3-522
Number of titles published annually: 100 Print
Total Titles: 800 Print
Imprints: Gabriel Verlag (religious children's books)
Distribution Center: Koch, Neff & Oetinger & Co GmbH, Stuttgart

Verlag Theodor Thoben
Langestr 77-79, 49610 Quakenbrueck
Tel: (05431) 3486 *Fax:* (05431) 3584
E-mail: info@buecher-thoben.de
Web Site: www.buecher-thoben.de
Key Personnel
Publisher: Theodor Thoben
Founded: 1903
Subjects: Regional Interests
ISBN Prefix(es): 3-921176
Bookshop(s): Buecher-Thoben, Lange Str 77-79, 49610 Quakenbrueck

Hans Thoma Verlag GmbH Kunst und Buchverlag
Vorholzstr 7, 76137 Karlsruhe
Mailing Address: Postfach 6345, 76043 Karlsruhe
Tel: (0721) 932750 *Fax:* (0721) 9327520
Key Personnel
Manager: Herwig Schelling
Subjects: Art
ISBN Prefix(es): 3-87297
Parent Company: Evangelischer Presseverband

Tipp Creative, *imprint of* Xenos Verlagsgesellschaft mbH

Tipress Deutschland, *imprint of* Tipress Dienstleistungen fur das Verlagswesen GmbH

Tipress Dienstleistungen fur das Verlagswesen GmbH+
Johannes-Fechtstr 2, 79295 Sulzburg
Tel: (07634) 591193 *Fax:* (07634) 591192
E-mail: tipress@tipress.com
Web Site: www.tipress.com
Key Personnel
President: Roberto Toso
Literary agency & services for publishers in four languages; projects of series of books, realization of books & consultants.

Subjects: Cookery, Crafts, Games, Hobbies, Health, Nutrition
Imprints: Tipress Deutschland
Branch Office(s)
Via Cernaia 34, I-10122 Torino, Italy, Contact: Claudia Robert *Tel:* (011) 533487 *Fax:* (011) 535283 *E-mail:* tipress@fileita.it

Titania-Verlag Ferdinand Schroll+
Forststr 104B, 70193 Stuttgart
Mailing Address: Postfach 104832, 70042 Stuttgart
Tel: (0711) 63 81 25 *Fax:* (0711) 63 69 872
  Cable: TITANIAVERLAG STUTTGART
Key Personnel
Publisher, International Rights: Wolfgang Schroll
Publisher: Gerdi Schroll
Founded: 1949
Subjects: Fiction
ISBN Prefix(es): 3-7996

S Toeche-Mittler Verlag GmbH
Hindenburgstr 33, 64295 Darmstadt
Tel: (06151) 33665 *Fax:* (06151) 314048
E-mail: info@net-library.de
Web Site: www.net-library.de
Key Personnel
Sales Manager: Albrecht Lueft
Founded: 1789
Subjects: Economics, Law, Nonfiction (General), Sports, Athletics
ISBN Prefix(es): 3-87820
Divisions: TRIOPS, Tropical Scientific Books

Toleranz Verlag, Nielsen Frederic W
Sundgauallee 19, 79114 Freiburg im Breisgau
Mailing Address: Postfach 6009, 79114 Freiburg im Breisgau
Tel: (0761) 81415
E-mail: irenenielsen@web.de
Founded: 1971
Subjects: Biography, Government, Political Science, History, Poetry
ISBN Prefix(es): 3-925745; 3-9800069

Tomus Verlag GmbH+
Am Steinfeld 4, 94065 Waldkirchen Niederbay
Tel: (08581) 910666 *Fax:* (08581) 910668
E-mail: info@tomus.de
Web Site: www.tomus.de
Key Personnel
Publisher: Dr Gerhard Braunsperger
Dir: Oliver A Frank
Founded: 1962
Membership(s): Stockmarket Association.
Subjects: Animals, Pets, Cookery, Crafts, Games, Hobbies, Humor, Science (General), Travel
ISBN Prefix(es): 3-8231
Associate Companies: Telelit Verlag AG/Fakt Verlag AG
Branch Office(s)
Dr Wernerstr 5, 82194 Groebenzell
Warehouse: VVA, An der Autobahn, 33310 Gutersloh

P J Tonger Musikverlag GmbH & Co
Auf dem Brand 10, 50996 Cologne
Tel: (0221) 935564-0 *Fax:* (0221) 935564-11
E-mail: musikverlag@tonger.de
Web Site: www.tonger.de
Key Personnel
Man Dir & Publicity: Peter Tonger
Founded: 1822
Subjects: Sheet Music books
ISBN Prefix(es): 3-920950
Subsidiaries: Carl Engels Musikverlag; Musikverlage Gerhard Rabe; Fritz Spies GmbH

TR - Verlagsunion GmbH+
Thierschstr 11/III Stock, 80538 Munich

Mailing Address: Postfach 260202, 80059 Munich
Tel: (089) 2121 390 *Fax:* (089) 296129; (089) 296357
E-mail: vertrieb@tr-verlag.de
Web Site: www.tr-verlag.de
Key Personnel
Man Dir, Rights & Permissions: Andreas Keiser
  E-mail: andreaskeiser@tr-verlag.de
Editorial: Gabriele Rieth-Winterherbst
  Tel: (089) 212139-13 *E-mail:* rieth@tr-verlag.de; Inga Dopatka *Tel:* (089) 212139-29
  E-mail: dopatka@tr-verlag.de
Publicity: Cornelia Wiedemann *Tel:* (089) 212139-18 *E-mail:* wiedemann@tr-verlag.de; Elke Funke *Tel:* (089) 212139-25
Sales: Imogen Fries *Tel:* (089) 212139-17 *E-mail:* fries@tr-verlag.de; Elisabeth Kroier *Tel:* (089) 212139-20 *E-mail:* kroier@tr.verlag.de
Founded: 1968
The Union publishes & distributes books, audio & videocassette, software, sets of lessons etc to link up with TV & radio programs.
The TR (Television & Radio) Publishing Union comprises two broadcasting companies (Bayerischer Rundfunk & Suedwest und Funk) & the following publishing companies: Ludwig Auer GmbH; BLV Verlagsgesellschaft mbH; Verlag C H Beck; C Bertelsmann Verlag GmbH; Verlag Bruckmann Muenchen; Ernst Klett Verlag; Koesel-Verlag GmbH & Co; Langenscheidt KG; Suddeutscher Verlag, Buchverlag GmbH; JB Metzler Poeschel; R Oldenbourg Verlag GmbH; Guenter Olzog Verlag; K G Saur Verlag; Springer Verlag.
Subjects: Architecture & Interior Design, Education, English as a Second Language, Film, Video, Health, Nutrition, Radio, TV, Religion - Other, Travel
ISBN Prefix(es): 3-8058
Total Titles: 150 Print; 5 CD-ROM; 50 Audio
Branch Office(s)
TR-Verlagsunion Buero Potsdam, August-Bebel-Str 16, Potsdam, Contact: Harald Smeja
  Tel: (0331) 7312815 *Fax:* (0331) 7312815
Orders to: Moderne Industrie Verlagsservice, Justus-von-Liebig-Str 1, 86899 Landsberg

Traditionell Bogenschiessen Verlag Angelika Hornig
Siebenpfeifferstr 16, 67071 Ludwigshafen
Tel: (0621) 68 94 41 *Fax:* (0621) 68 94 42
E-mail: info@bogenschiessen.de
Web Site: www.bogenschiessen.de
Key Personnel
Editor: Angelika Hoernig *E-mail:* ah@bogenschiessen.de
Subjects: Archaeology, History, How-to, Outdoor Recreation, Sports, Athletics

Trans Tech Publications+
Freibergerstr 1, 38678 Clausthal-Zellerfeld
Tel: (05323) 96970 *Fax:* (05323) 969796
E-mail: ttp@transtech-online.com
Web Site: www.transtech-online.com
Key Personnel
Publisher: Reiner Grochowski
Founded: 1972
International journals for the powder & bulk industry.
Subjects: Chemistry, Chemical Engineering, Civil Engineering, Earth Sciences, Mechanical Engineering
ISBN Prefix(es): 0-87849

Transpress Verlagsgesellschaft mbH+
Olgastr 86, 70180 Stuttgart
Tel: (0711) 210 80 65 *Fax:* (0711) 210 80 70
E-mail: versand@motorbuch.de
Web Site: www.motorbuch-versand.de *Cable:* TRANSPRESS STUTTGART
Key Personnel
Man Dir: Paul Pietsch; Dr Patricia Schotten
Founded: 1990
Subjects: Automotive, Transportation
ISBN Prefix(es): 3-344
Parent Company: Paul Pietsch Verlage GmbH & Co
Bookshop(s): Transpress Buchhandlung, Hauptbahnhof, Mittelbau-Ladenstr, 04103 Leipzig
Shipping Address: Koch, Neff & Oetinger & Co, Postfach 800620, 70506 Stuttgart
Warehouse: Koch, Neff & Oetinger & Co, Postfach 800620, 70506 Stuttgart

Trautvetter & Fischer Nachf
Gladenbacher Way 57, 35037 Marburg
Tel: (06421) 33309 *Fax:* (06421) 34959
E-mail: bestell@trautvetterfischerverlag.de
Web Site: www.trautvetterfischerverlag.de
Key Personnel
Publisher: Dr Wilhelm A Eckhardt
  E-mail: eckhardt@trautvetterfischerverlag.de
Founded: 1941
Specialize in history of Hessen.
Membership(s): Borsenverein Des Deutschen Buchhandels.
Subjects: History, Regional Interests
ISBN Prefix(es): 3-87822
Number of titles published annually: 2 Print
Total Titles: 50 Print

Trees Wolfgang Triangel Verlag+
Fuchserde 44, 52066 Aachen, Permony
Tel: (0241) 6 99 00 *Fax:* (0241) 6 99 15
E-mail: info@triangelverlag.de
Web Site: www.triangel-verlag.de
Key Personnel
Owner: Wolfgang Trees
Founded: 1981
Membership(s): Borsenverein de deutschen Buchhandels.
Subjects: History, Military Science, Regional Interests, Travel, Books about the history & tourism in Euregio Meuse-Rhine, ie Aachen (D), Maastricht (NL) & Liege (B). Especially WWII 1933-1945, Rhineland, Huertpen Forest & smugglings 1545-1953
ISBN Prefix(es): 3-922974
Number of titles published annually: 2 Print
Total Titles: 12 Print

Trescher Verlag GmbH
Reinhardtstr 9, 10117 Berlin
Tel: (030) 2 83 24 96 *Fax:* (030) 2 81 59 94
E-mail: post@trescherverlag.de
Web Site: www.trescherverlag.de
Key Personnel
Sales: Bernd Schwenkros
Production: Tom Schuelke
Founded: 1993
Subjects: Film, Video, Nonfiction (General), Outdoor Recreation, Travel
ISBN Prefix(es): 3-928409; 3-89794

Treves Editions Verein Zur Foerderung der Kuenstlerischen Taetigkeiten (Club for the Promotion of Artistic Work)+
Medardstr 105, 54294 Trier
Mailing Address: Postfach 1550, 54205 Trier
Tel: (0651) 309 010 *Fax:* (0651) 300 699
E-mail: mail@treves.de
Web Site: www.treves.de
Key Personnel
Man Dir: Rainer Breuer
Man Dir, Rights & Permissions: Ursula Dahm
Founded: 1974
Subjects: Art, Erotica, Fiction, Health, Nutrition, History, Literature, Literary Criticism, Essays, Music, Dance, Mysteries, Nonfiction (General), Poetry, Travel
ISBN Prefix(es): 3-88081

TRIAS, *imprint of* Georg Thieme Verlag KG

Trias Verlag in MVS Medizinverlage Stuttgart GmbH & Co KG+
Subsidiary of Georg Thieme Verlag KG
Oswald-Hesse-Str 50, 70469 Stuttgart
Tel: (0711) 8931-0 *Fax:* (0711) 8931-298
E-mail: kunden.service@thieme.de
Web Site: www.thieme.de; www.medizinverlage.de
Key Personnel
Man Dir: Dr Thomas Scherb
Foreign Rights: Susanne Seeger *Tel:* (0711) 8931-147 *Fax:* (0711) 8931-143 *E-mail:* susanne.seeger@thieme.de
Founded: 1989
Subjects: Health, Nutrition, Nonfiction (General), Psychology, Psychiatry
ISBN Prefix(es): 3-8304
Associate Companies: Enke Verlag; Karl F Haug Verlag; Hippokrates Verlag; Parey Verlag; Sonntag Verlag

Trotzdem-Verlags Genossenschaft eG+
Postfach 1159, 71117 Grafenau
Tel: (07033) 44273 *Fax:* (07033) 45264
E-mail: trotzdemusf@t-online.e
Web Site: www.trotzdem-verlag.de; www.txt.de/trotzdem
Key Personnel
Contact: Wolfgang Haug *E-mail:* wolfganghaug@aol.com
Founded: 1978
Publishing of books & magazines from a libertarian viewpoint.
Subjects: Alternative, Biography, Drama, Theater, Education, Government, Political Science, History, Photography, Social Sciences, Sociology
ISBN Prefix(es): 3-922209; 3-931786
Divisions: Redaktion Schwarzer Faden
Distributor for Anares; Anarchijtische Buchhandlung

Mario Truant Verlag+
Frauenlobstr 95, 55118 Mainz
Tel: (06131) 961660
E-mail: viva@truant.com
Web Site: www.truant.com
Key Personnel
Publisher: Mario Truant
Founded: 1990
Subjects: Crafts, Games, Hobbies, Fiction, Parapsychology, Science Fiction, Fantasy
ISBN Prefix(es): 3-926801

Tuduv Verlagsgesellschaft mbH+
Zieblandstr 7, 80799 Munich
Mailing Address: Postfach 340163, 80098 Munich
Tel: (089) 280 90 95 *Fax:* (089) 280 95 28
E-mail: info@tuduv.de
Web Site: www.tuduv.de
Key Personnel
Manager: Sonya Rosnovsky
Founded: 1974
Subjects: Art, Biography, Communications, Ethnicity, Government, Political Science, History, Language Arts, Linguistics, Literature, Literary Criticism, Essays, Medicine, Nursing, Dentistry, Social Sciences, Sociology, Technology
ISBN Prefix(es): 3-88073
Associate Companies: Verlag V Florentz GmbH (WF)

Tuebinger Vereinigung fur Volkskunde eV (TVV)
Ludwig-Uhland-Institut, Schloss Hohentuebingen, 72070 Tuebingen
Tel: (07071) 295449; (07071) 2972374 (orders) *Fax:* (07071) 295330
E-mail: info@tvv-verlag.de
Web Site: www.tvv-verlag.de

Key Personnel
Man Dir, Editorial, Production & Sales: Bernd Juergen Warneken
Editorial, Production & Sales: Utz Jeggle; Hermann Bausinger; Ute Bechdolf; Gottfried Korff
Founded: 1963
Subjects: Ethnicity, Film, Video, History, Language Arts, Linguistics, Regional Interests, Social Sciences, Sociology, Women's Studies
ISBN Prefix(es): 3-925340; 3-932512

TUeV-Verlag GmbH
Am Grauen Stein, 51105 Cologne
Tel: (0221) 806-3535 *Fax:* (0221) 806-3510
E-mail: tuev-verlag@de.tuv.com
Web Site: www.tuev-verlag.de; www.qm-aktuell.de; www.mt-medizintechnik.de
Key Personnel
Manager: Dr Anton Reiter
Founded: 1971
Subjects: Energy, Environmental Studies, Regional Interests, Technology, Transportation
ISBN Prefix(es): 3-8249; 3-88585; 3-921059
Parent Company: TUeV Rheinland Holding AG

Turkischer Schulbuchverlag Onel Cengiz+
Silchesto 13, 50827 Cologne
Tel: (0221) 5879084; (0221) 5879085 *Fax:* (0221) 488093; (0221) 5879004
Key Personnel
Vice President: Ibrahim Ilbasi
Publisher: C Hayati Oenel
Founded: 1981
Subjects: Travel
ISBN Prefix(es): 3-924542; 3-929490; 3-933348

Edition U, *imprint of* Dr Wolfgang Baur Verlag Kunst & Alltag

Wirtschaftsverlag Carl Ueberreuter+
Lurgialle 6-8, 60439 Frankfurt am Main
Tel: (069) 580905-80 *Fax:* (069) 580905-10
E-mail: info@redline-wirtschaft.de
Web Site: www.redline-wirtschaft.de
Key Personnel
Manager: Hans-Joachim Hartmann
Publisher: Juergen Diessl
Rights Director, Foreign Affairs: Maria Pinto-Peuckmann *Tel:* (089) 548 52-84 26 *Fax:* (089) 548 52-84 21
Founded: 1988
Subjects: Accounting, Business, Law, Management
ISBN Prefix(es): 3-220

Uerle Verlag, *imprint of* Verlag Herder GmbH & Co KG

Verlag Dr Alfons Uhl+
Mittlere Gerbergasse 1, 86720 Noerdlingen
Tel: (09081) 87248 *Fax:* (09081) 23710
Key Personnel
Dir, Rights & Permissions: Dr Alfons Uhl
Subjects: Architecture & Interior Design, Art, Geography, Geology
ISBN Prefix(es): 3-921503

Ullstein Heyne List GmbH & Co KG+
Bayerstr 71-73, 80335 Munich
Tel: (089) 51 48 0 *Fax:* (089) 51 48 2229
Web Site: www.ullstein.de
Key Personnel
Managing Partner: Hubertus Meyer-Burckhardt; Christian Strasser
Publicity: Claus Martin Carlsberg
Founded: 1894
Membership(s): TR-Verlagsunion GmbH.
Subjects: Art, Biography, Fiction, History, Literature, Literary Criticism, Essays, Philosophy, Psychology, Psychiatry, Religion - Other, Science (General), Social Sciences, Sociology

ISBN Prefix(es): 3-471
Associate Companies: Bucher Verlag GmbH; W Ludwig Verlag GmbH; Suedwest Verlag

Guenter Albert Ulmer Verlag
Hauptstr 16, 78609 Tuningen
Tel: (07464) 98740 *Fax:* (07464) 3054
E-mail: info@ulmertuningen.de
Web Site: www.ulmertuningen.de
Key Personnel
Man Dir: Guenter Albert Ulmer
Founded: 1983
Subjects: Earth Sciences, Environmental Studies, Gardening, Plants, Health, Nutrition, Human Relations, Natural History, Nonfiction (General), Poetry, Regional Interests, Religion - Protestant, Theology, Meditation
ISBN Prefix(es): 3-924191; 3-932346

Verlag Eugen Ulmer GmbH & Co (Eugen Ulmer Publishers)+
Wollgrasweg 41, 70599 Stuttgart, BRD
Tel: (0711) 4507-0 *Fax:* (0711) 4507-120
E-mail: info@ulmer.de
Web Site: www.ulmer.de
Telex: 723634
Key Personnel
Man Dir: Roland Ulmer
Deputy Dir: Matthias Ulmer *E-mail:* mulmer@ulmer.de
Production: Dieter Kleinschrot
Reader: Dr Nadja Kneissler *E-mail:* lektorat@ulmer.de
Sales Dir: Michael Kurzer
Rights & Permissions Man: Sigrun Wagner *E-mail:* wagner@ulmer.de
Founded: 1868
Membership(s): VGS - Verlagsgesellschaft mbH & Co KG.
Subjects: Agriculture, Animals, Pets, Environmental Studies, Gardening, Plants, How-to, Science (General), Veterinary Science
ISBN Prefix(es): 3-8001
Total Titles: 900 Print
Subsidiaries: Editions Eugen Ulmer; Neumann Verlag, Radebeul

Ulrike Helmer Verlag+
Altkoenigstr 6a, 61462 Koenigstein
Tel: (06174) 936060 *Fax:* (06174) 936065
E-mail: info@ulrike-helmer-verlag.de
Web Site: www.ulrike-helmer-verlag.de
Key Personnel
Man Dir: Ulrike Helmer
Founded: 1988
Subjects: Fiction, Gay & Lesbian, History, Literature, Literary Criticism, Essays, Philosophy, Social Sciences, Sociology, Women's Studies
ISBN Prefix(es): 3-927164; 3-89741
Warehouse: SOVA, Friesstr 20-24, 60388 Frankfurt/M

Neuer Umschau Buchverlag+
Maximilianstr 35, 67433 Neustadt/Weinstr
Mailing Address: Postfach 110262, 60037 Frankfurt am Main
Tel: (06321) 877850 *Fax:* (06321) 877859
E-mail: info@umschau-buchverlag.de
Web Site: www.umschau-buchverlag.de
Key Personnel
Man Dir, Publisher: Katharina Toebben
Sales: Cornelia Pendt
Founded: 1850
Also acts as Distributor.
Membership(s): Boersenverein.
Subjects: Cookery, Health, Nutrition, Nonfiction (General), Science (General)
ISBN Prefix(es): 3-524
Parent Company: Unternehmensgruppe Niederberger

Uni-Taschenbuecher UTB Fuer Wissenchaft CmbH, see UTB fuer Wissenchaft Uni Taschenbuecher GmbH

Union-Verlag GmbH, see Kinderbuchverlag

Universitaetsverlag Winter GmbH Heidelberg GmbH+
Dassenheimer Landstra 13, 69121 Heidelberg
Mailing Address: Postfach 10 61 40, 69051 Heidelberg
Tel: (06221) 7702-60 *Fax:* (06221) 7702-69
E-mail: info@winter-verlag-hd.de
Web Site: www.winter-verlag-hd.de
Key Personnel
President & Editor: Dr Andreas Barth *Tel:* (06221) 7702-63 *E-mail:* a.barth@winter-verlag-hd.de
Production: Ralf Stemper *Tel:* (06221) 7702-67 *E-mail:* r.stemper@winter-verlag-hd.de
Sales Manager: Klaus Philipp Mertens *Tel:* (06221) 7702-65 *E-mail:* kp.mertens@winter-verlag-hd.de
Customer Service: Rotraud Hohlbein *E-mail:* r.hohlbein@winter-verlag-hd.de
Founded: 1993
Subjects: Language Arts, Linguistics, Literature, Literary Criticism, Essays
ISBN Prefix(es): 3-8253
Total Titles: 2,600 Print
Associate Companies: Heidelberger Verlagsanstalt (HVA) & Edition S
Distribution Center: Engros-Buchhandlung Dessauer, Raffelstr 32, 8036 Zurich, Switzerland *Tel:* (01) 4 66 96 66 *Fax:* (01) 4 66 96 69 (Switzerland)

Universitatsverlag Ulm GmbH
Bahnhofstr 20, 89073 Ulm
Tel: (0731) 15 28 60 *Fax:* (0731) 15 28 62
E-mail: info@uni-verlag-ulm.de
Web Site: www.uni-verlag-ulm.de
Key Personnel
Manager: Alexander Schraut
Founded: 1988
Specialize in neurology, psychiatry & brain research.
Subjects: Medicine, Nursing, Dentistry, Physical Sciences
ISBN Prefix(es): 3-927402; 3-89559
Parent Company: Schwaebischer Verlag KG, 7970 Leutkirch
Shipping Address: Dalnheph 20, 89073 Ulm

UNO-Verlag GmbH
Am Hofgarten 10, 53113 Bonn
Tel: (0228) 94 90 2-0 *Fax:* (0228) 94 90 2-22
E-mail: info@uno-verlag.de
Web Site: www.uno-verlag.de
Key Personnel
Man Dir: Wolfgang Fischer
Founded: 1982
Subjects: Aeronautics, Aviation, Agriculture, Developing Countries, Economics, Education, Energy, Environmental Studies, Finance, Government, Political Science, Health, Nutrition, Labor, Industrial Relations, Social Sciences, Sociology
ISBN Prefix(es): 3-923904
Distributor for Asian Development Bank; Council of Europe; FAO; Inter-American Development Bank; International Atomic Energy Agency; International Civil Aviation Organization; International Monetary Fund (IMF); Nordic Council of Ministers Publications; OECD; UNDP; UNESCO; UNIDO; United Nations Publications; WHO; Worldbank; World Intellectual Property Organization; World Tourism Organization; World Trade Organization

Unrast Verlag e V+
Postfach 8020, 48043 Munster

Tel: (0251) 666293 *Fax:* (0251) 666120
E-mail: kontakt@unrast-verlag.de
Web Site: www.unrast-verlag.de
Key Personnel
International Rights: Martin Schuering
Founded: 1989
Subjects: Developing Countries, Fiction, Government, Political Science, Women's Studies
ISBN Prefix(es): 3-89771; 3-928300

Urania Verlag mit Ravensburger Ratgebern+
Dircksenstr 48, 10178 Berlin
Tel: (030) 28447-112; (030) 28447-113
 Fax: (030) 28447-123
E-mail: urania.ravensburger@dornier-verlage.de
Web Site: www.urania-ravensburger.de *Cable:* URANIA LEIPZIG
Key Personnel
Manager: Dr Juergen A Bach
Publishing Manager: Bernd Scheiba
Publicity: Ulrike Baak *Tel:* (030) 28447-137 *E-mail:* baak@dornier-verlage.de
Sales Manager: Yvonne de Andres *Tel:* (030) 28447-111 *E-mail:* deandres@dornier-verlage.de
Founded: 1924
Subjects: Biological Sciences, Nonfiction (General)
ISBN Prefix(es): 3-332
Parent Company: Dornier Medienholding
Shipping Address: Leipziger Kommissions- und Grosbuchhandelsgesellschaft mbH, Polzschauer Weg, 04579 Espenhain
Orders to: Leipziger Kommissions- und Grosbuchhandelsgesellschaft mbH, Polzchauer Weg, 04579 Espenhain

Urban & Vogel Medien und Medizin Verlagsgesellschaft mbH & Co KG
Neumarkterstr 43, 81673 Munich
Tel: (089) 4372-0 *Fax:* (089) 4372-2633
E-mail: verlag@urban-vogel.de
Web Site: www.urban-vogel.de
Telex: 524631 vervo d
Key Personnel
Manager: Dr George Ralle
Sales & Marketing: Frank Niemann
Founded: 1972
Subjects: Medicine, Nursing, Dentistry
ISBN Prefix(es): 3-8208
Parent Company: Verlagsgruppe Bertelsmann International GmbH
Distributed by Vleweg Verlag (Germany)

Edition Ustad, *imprint of* Karl-May-Verlag Lothar Schmid GmbH

UTAS-Verlag fur Moderne Lernmethoden Uta Stechl+
Kellerstr 15, 84577 Tussling
Mailing Address: Postfach 62, 84577 Tussling
Tel: (08633) 1450 *Fax:* (08633) 7805
Key Personnel
Owner: Uta Stechl
Founded: 1981
ISBN Prefix(es): 3-925220

UTB fuer Wissenschaft Uni Taschenbuecher GmbH
Breitwiesenstr 9, 70565 Stuttgart
Tel: (0711) 7 82 95 55-0 *Fax:* (0711) 7 80 13 76
E-mail: utb@utb-stuttgart.de
Web Site: www.utb.de
Key Personnel
Man Dir: Volker Huehn
Manager: Ferdinand Schoeningh; Dr Michael Schoeningh
Founded: 1970
The company represents a group of 13 publishers (shareholders) producing paperbacks of a general academic/technical/scientific nature.

Subjects: Agriculture, Biological Sciences, Business, Chemistry, Chemical Engineering, Computer Science, Economics, Electronics, Electrical Engineering, Engineering (General), Government, Political Science, Health, Nutrition, History, Language Arts, Linguistics, Library & Information Sciences, Literature, Literary Criticism, Essays, Medicine, Nursing, Dentistry, Philosophy, Physics, Psychology, Psychiatry, Religion - Other, Social Sciences, Sociology, Veterinary Science
ISBN Prefix(es): 3-8252; 3-920971
Distributed by Mohr Morawa (Austria); Reinhardt Media-Service (Switzerland)
Warehouse: Brockhaus Commission, Kreidlerstr 9, Postfach 1220, 708016 Kornwestheim

UVK Universitatsverlag Konstanz GmbH+
Schuetzenstr 24, 78462 Konstanz
Mailing Address: PO Box 10 20 51, 78420 Konstanz
Tel: (07531) 90530 *Fax:* (07531) 905398
E-mail: willkommen@uvk.de
Web Site: www.uvk.de
Key Personnel
Publishing Manager & International Rights Contact: Walter Engstle *Tel:* (07531) 905312 *E-mail:* walter.engstle@uvk.de
Founded: 1963
Subjects: Archaeology, History, Literature, Literary Criticism, Essays, Philosophy, Science (General)
ISBN Prefix(es): 3-87940
Number of titles published annually: 10 Print
Total Titles: 700 Print
Associate Companies: Suedverlag GmbH/uvk Verlagsgesellschaft mbH
Orders to: Brockhaus Commission Verlagsauslieferung, Kreidlerstr 9, 70806 Kornwestheim

UVK Verlagsgesellschaft mbH+
Schutzenstr 24, 78462 Konstanz
Mailing Address: PO Box 10 20 51, 78420 Konstanz
Tel: (07531) 90530 *Fax:* (07531) 905398
E-mail: willkommen@uvk.de
Web Site: www.uvk.de
Key Personnel
Publishing Manager & International Rights: Walter Engstle *Tel:* (07531) 905312 *E-mail:* walter.engstle@uvk.de
Founded: 1995
Subjects: Communications, Film, Video, History, Journalism, Radio, TV, Social Sciences, Sociology
ISBN Prefix(es): 3-89669
Number of titles published annually: 80 Print
Total Titles: 650 Print
Associate Companies: UVK Universitaetsverlag Konstanz GmbH (University Press)
Orders to: Brockhaus Commission Verlagsauslieferung, Kreidlerstr 9, 70806 Kornwestheim bei Stuttgart

Dorothea van der Koelen
Hinter der Kapelle 54, 55128 Mainz
Tel: (06131) 346 64 *Fax:* (06131) 36 90 76
E-mail: dvanderkoelen@xterna-net.de
Key Personnel
Contact: Dorothea van der Koelen
Founded: 1986
Art publisher & art gallery.
Subjects: Art, Science (General), Art History
ISBN Prefix(es): 3-926663
Parent Company: Vander Koelen Verlag
Distribution Center: Austria
France
Switzerland

Vandenhoeck & Ruprecht+
Robert Bosch-Breite 6, 37070 Gottingen
Tel: (0551) 5084-40 *Fax:* (0551) 5084-422

E-mail: info@v-r.de
Web Site: www.v-r.de
Key Personnel
Man Dir: Dr Dietrich Ruprecht
Man Dir, Editorial Theology & Religion: Jorg Persch
Man Dir, International Rights & Permissions: Reinhilde Ruprecht
Man Dir, Rights & Permissions: Dr Arndt Ruprecht
Marketing Dir: Carola Mueller *Tel:* (0551) 5084-470 *E-mail:* c.mueller@v-r.de
Sales: Ingo Halscheidt
Publicity: Regina Lange
Editorial German Literature, Classics/Antiquity, Philosophy: Dr Ulrike Giessmann
Editorial History & Economics: Martin Rethmeier
Editorial Psychology: Dr Bernd Rachel
Founded: 1735
Subjects: Education, History, Language Arts, Linguistics, Philosophy, Psychology, Psychiatry, Religion - Other, Theology
ISBN Prefix(es): 3-525
Associate Companies: Buchhandlung Deuerlich
Subsidiaries: Druckerei Hubert & Company; V&R Unipress GmbH
Distributor for V&R Unipress GmbH; Wallstein Verlag; Weidle Verlag

VAP-Verlag, see Goll Bruno Verlag fur Aussergewoehnliche Perspektiven (VAP)

VAS-Verlag fuer Akademische Schriften+
Wielandstr 10, 60318 Frankfurt am Main
Tel: (069) 77 93 66 *Fax:* (069) 7073967
E-mail: info@vas-verlag.de
Web Site: www.vas-verlag.de
Key Personnel
International Rights: Karl-Heinz Balon
Founded: 1982
Subjects: Education, Environmental Studies, Government, Political Science, History, Human Relations, Language Arts, Linguistics, Psychology, Psychiatry, Social Sciences, Sociology, Women's Studies
ISBN Prefix(es): 3-88864

VDE-Verlag GmbH+
Bismarckstr 33, 10625 Berlin
Mailing Address: PO Box 120143, 10591 Berlin
Tel: (030) 34 80 01 0 *Fax:* (030) 341 70 93
E-mail: voss@vde-verlag.de
Web Site: www.vde-verlag.de
Telex: 181683 vde d
Key Personnel
Manager: Dr Ing A Gruetz
Founded: 1929
Subjects: Communications, Electronics, Electrical Engineering
ISBN Prefix(es): 3-8007
U.S. Office(s): Hallenbook, County Route 9, PO Box 357, Chatham, NY 12037, United States

VDI Verlag GmbH+
Heinrichstr 24, 40239 Duesseldorf
Tel: (0211) 61 88-0 *Fax:* (0211) 61 88-306
E-mail: info@vdi-nachrichten.com
Web Site: www.vdi-nachrichten.com *Cable:* INGENIEURVERLAG DUSSELDORF
Key Personnel
Man Dir: Raymond Johnson-Ohla
 E-mail: geschaeftsfuehrung@vdi-nachrichten.com
Founded: 1923
Subjects: Engineering (General), Science (General), Technology
ISBN Prefix(es): 3-18

Verein der Benediktiner zu Beuron- Beuroner Kunstverlag+
Abteistr 2, 88631 Beuron
Tel: (07466) 17-0 *Fax:* (07466) 17-107
E-mail: kunstverlag@erzabtei-beuron.de

Web Site: www.erzabtei-beuron.de *Cable:* BEURONER KUNSTVERLAG
Key Personnel
Dir: Gabriel Gawletta
Publicity Manager: Siegfried Studer
Founded: 1898
Subjects: Art, Biblical Studies, Humor, Religion - Catholic, Religion - Protestant, Religion - Other
ISBN Prefix(es): 3-87071
Imprints: Monastica

Vereinigte Fachverlage GmbH
Lise-Meitner-Str 2, 55129 Mainz
Mailing Address: Postfach 100465, 55135 Mainz
Tel: (06131) 992-0 *Fax:* (06131) 992-100
Key Personnel
Manager: Manfred Grunenberg
Founded: 1937
ISBN Prefix(es): 3-7830
Subsidiaries: VF Verlagsgesellschaft GmbH

Vereinte Evangelische Mission, Abt Verlag (United Evangelical Mission)
Rudolfstr 137, 42285 Wuppertal
Mailing Address: Postfach 20 19 63, 42219 Wuppertal
Tel: (0202) 89004 0 *Fax:* (0202) 89004 79
E-mail: info@vemission.org
Web Site: www.vemission.org
Key Personnel
Editor-in-chief: Thomas Sandner
Founded: 1828
Communion of churches in 3 continents.
Subjects: Theology
ISBN Prefix(es): 3-87855; 3-921900
Total Titles: 2 Print

Verkehrs-Verlag J Fischer, see Verkehrs-Verlag J Fischer GmbH & Co KG

Verlag Beltz & Gelberg+
Werderstr 10, 69469 Weinheim
Tel: (06201) 60070
E-mail: info@beltz.de
Web Site: www.beltz.de
Key Personnel
Man Dir: Joachim Radmer
Publishing Dir: Ulrich Stoeriko-Blume
Rights: Charlotte Larat; Kerstin Michaelis
ISBN Prefix(es): 3-407
Parent Company: Beltz Publishing Group

Verlag fuer die Frau GmbH
Haus des Buches, Gerichtsweg 28, 04103 Leipzig
Mailing Address: Postfach 100348, 04003 Leipzig
Tel: (0341) 99540 *Fax:* (0341) 9954367
E-mail: kuratorium.hdb@t-online.de
Telex: 311419
Key Personnel
Manager: Brunhilde Laumann; Adolf Silbermann
Founded: 1946
Subjects: Fashion, Science (General)
ISBN Prefix(es): 3-7304
Parent Company: Gong Verlagsgruppe

Verlag fur die Rechts- und Anwaltspraxis GmbH & Co+
Beisingerweg 1a, 45657 Recklinghausen
Mailing Address: Postfach 101953, 45619 Recklinghausen
Tel: (02361) 9142-0 *Fax:* (02361) 9142-35
E-mail: hotline@zap-verlag.de
Web Site: www.zap-verlag.de
Key Personnel
Publisher: Dr Karl-Friedrich Peter
Man Dir: Hermann Boger
Founded: 1989
Subjects: Law
ISBN Prefix(es): 3-927935; 3-89655

Shipping Address: Schuechtermannstr 180, 44628 Herne
Warehouse: Schuechtermannstr 180, 44628 Herne
Orders to: Postfach 101849, 44621 Herne

Verlag fur Schweissen und Verwandte Verfahren (Publishing House for Welding)+
Subsidiary of Deutscher Verband fur Schweissen und verwandte Verfahren eV
Aachenerstr 172, 40223 Duesseldorf
Mailing Address: Postfach 101965, 40010 Duesseldorf
Tel: (0211) 15910 *Fax:* (0211) 1591150
E-mail: verlag@dvs-hg.de
Web Site: www.dvs-verlag.de
Key Personnel
Manager: M Stumpf; Dr Ing D von Hofe
Founded: 1955
Subjects: Engineering (General), Mechanical Engineering, Technology, Welding & Allied Processes
ISBN Prefix(es): 3-87155
Number of titles published annually: 15 Print; 3 CD-ROM
Total Titles: 419 Print; 10 CD-ROM
Parent Company: German Welding Society

Verlag Moderne Industrie AG & Co KG+
Emmy-Noetherstr 2, 80992 Munich
Tel: (089) 5484202 *Fax:* (089) 548428428
E-mail: info@mi-verlag.de
Web Site: www.mi-verlag.de
Telex: 527114 moin d
Key Personnel
President: Klaus Hengster *Fax:* (08191) 125-542
Publisher: Evelyn Boos *E-mail:* e.boos@mvg-verlag.de
Rights Dir, Foreign Affairs: Maria Pinto-Peuckmann *Tel:* (089) 548 52-84 26 *Fax:* (089) 548 52-84 21 *E-mail:* m.pinto-p@redline-wirtschaft.de
Marketing & Sales: Martin Brueninghaus *E-mail:* m.brueninghaus@mvg-verlag.de
Founded: 1952
Also publishes loose-leaf editions.
Membership(s): EBP-Network.
Subjects: Advertising, Business, Career Development, Communications, Computer Science, Economics, Management, Marketing, Technology, Investment, Money, Success Stories
ISBN Prefix(es): 3-478; 3-87957; 3-920716; 3-87959
Associate Companies: mvg Verlag *Fax:* (089) 548 52-84 21 *E-mail:* info@mvg-verlag.de (career development, communications, motivation & self-help; ISBN 3-478); Verlag Moderne Industrie Buch AG & Co KG, Koenigswintererstr 418, 53227 Bonn *Tel:* (0228) 97024 41 *Fax:* (0228) 97024 21 *E-mail:* info@vmi-buch.de

Verlag Puppen & Spielzeug, *imprint of* Verlagshaus Wohlfarth

Verlag und Druckkontor Kamp GmbH
Kurfuerstenstr 4a, 44791 Bochum
Tel: (0234) 51617-0 *Fax:* (0234) 51617-18
E-mail: verlag@kamp-verlag.de
Web Site: www.kamp-verlag.de
Key Personnel
Owner: Dr Ferdinand Kamp
Founded: 1996
Subjects: Education
ISBN Prefix(es): 3-89709

Verlag und Studio fuer Hoerbuchproduktionen+
Bahnhofstr 24, 35037 Marburg/Lahn
Tel: (06421) 889-110 *Fax:* (06421) 889-1111
E-mail: verlag@hoerbuch.de; info@hoerbuch.de
Web Site: www.hoerbuch.de; www.hoerbuch.com

Key Personnel
Publisher: Hans Eckardt; Heidemarie Eckardt
Founded: 1987
Subjects: Biblical Studies, Career Development, Management, Marketing, Mysteries, Poetry
ISBN Prefix(es): 3-89614
Total Titles: 200 Audio
Distribution Center: Koch, Neff & Oettinger

Verlag Volk & Welt GmbH, see Luchterhand Literaturverlag GmbH/Verlag Volk & Welt GmbH

Verlagsbereich Bau, *imprint of* Verlagshaus Wohlfarth

Verlagsgruppe Jehle-Rehm GmbH
Emmy-Noetherstr 2, 80992 Munich
Mailing Address: Postfach 500699, 80976 Munich
Tel: (089) 54 8 52-06 *Fax:* (089) 54 8 52-82 30
E-mail: info@HJR-verlag.de
Web Site: www.jehle-rehm.de
Key Personnel
Manager: Wolfgang Quadflieg
Publisher: Peter Habit
Founded: 1988
Subjects: Business, Economics, Law
ISBN Prefix(es): 3-8073; 3-7825; 3-87253
Parent Company: Sueddeutscher Verlag, Munich
Divisions: Fachbuchhandlung Kova
Branch Office(s)
Friedrichstr 130a, 10117 Berlin *Tel:* (030) 283098-0 *Fax:* (030) 283098-10 *E-mail:* verlagsgruppe@jehle-rehm.de
Bookshop(s): Kova & Rau, Einsteinstr 172, 81675 Munich

Vervuert Verlagsgesellschaft
Wielandstr 40, 60318 Frankfurt
Tel: (069) 597 4617 *Fax:* (069) 5978743
E-mail: info@iberoamericanalibros.com
Web Site: www.ibero-americana.net
Key Personnel
Manager: Klaus Dieter Vervuert
Founded: 1988
Also bookshop & library supplier.
Subjects: Developing Countries, Drama, Theater, Ethnicity, Foreign Countries, Language Arts, Linguistics, Literature, Literary Criticism, Essays, Social Sciences, Sociology
ISBN Prefix(es): 3-89354; 3-921600; 3-86527; 84-8489; 84-95107
Distributor for Iberoamericana (Madrid, Spain); Latin American Bookstore (USA)

Vice Versa Verlag+
Leuschnerdamm 5, 10999 Berlin
Tel: (030) 61609237 *Fax:* (030) 61609238
E-mail: viceversa@comp.de
Key Personnel
Publisher: Gabriela Wachter
Founded: 1992
Subjects: Architecture & Interior Design, Art
ISBN Prefix(es): 3-9803212; 3-932809
Associate Companies: Vice Versa Vertrieb; Vice Versa Vertretung

Vier Tuerme GmbH Verlag Klosterbetriebe+
Schweinfurterstr 40, 97359 Muensterschwarzach Abtei
Tel: (09324) 20292 *Fax:* (09324) 20495
E-mail: info@vier-tuerme.de
Web Site: www.vier-tuerme.de
Key Personnel
Publisher: Dr Mauritius Wilde
Man Dir: Christoph Gerhard
Founded: 1955
Subjects: How-to, Religion - Catholic, Theology
ISBN Prefix(es): 3-87868
Number of titles published annually: 15 Print; 10 Audio

Total Titles: 35 Audio
Imprints: Muensterschwarzacher Kleinschriften; Muensterschwarzacher Studien; Schriften zur Kontemplation

Friedr Vieweg & Sohn Verlag+
Unit of GWV Fachverlage GMBH
Abraham-Lincolnstr 46, 65189 Wiesbaden
Mailing Address: Postfach 1546, 65173 Wiesbaden
Tel: (0611) 7878-0 *Fax:* (0611) 7878-470
E-mail: vieweg.service@bertelsmann.de
Web Site: www.vieweg.de; www.gwv-fachverlage.de
Key Personnel
General Manager: Dr Hans-Dieter Haenel
 E-mail: hans-dieter.haenel@gwv-fachverlage.de
Man Dir: Dr Heinz Weinheimer
Editorial: Dr Reinald Klockenbusch; Ulrike Schmickler-Hirzebruch; Ewald Schmitt
Sales Marketing Manager: Rolf-Guenther Hobbeling
Rights & Permissions: Angelika Bolisega
 Fax: (0611) 7878361 *E-mail:* angelika.bolisega@gwv-fachverlage.de
Founded: 1786
Professional information for engineers & technicians; textbooks for students in technology & mathematics.
Subjects: Civil Engineering, Computer Science, Electronics, Electrical Engineering, Mathematics, Mechanical Engineering, Technology
ISBN Prefix(es): 3-528
Number of titles published annually: 5 CD-ROM
Total Titles: 1,500 Print; 25 CD-ROM
Parent Company: Springer Science+Business Media
Orders to: VVA Bertelsmann Distribution, Postfach 7777, D-33310 Guetersloh

Villa Arceno, *imprint of* Frederking & Thaler Verlag GmbH

Edition Vincent Klink
Alte Weinsteige 71, 70597 Stuttgart
Tel: (0711) 62007211 *Fax:* (0711) 6409408
E-mail: edition@vincent-klink.de
Founded: 1988
Subjects: Fiction, Music, Dance, Poetry, Religion - Buddhist
ISBN Prefix(es): 3-927350; 3-00

Curt R Vincentz Verlag+
Schiffgraben 43, 30175 Hannover
Mailing Address: Postfach 6247, 30062 Hannover
Tel: (0511) 9910000 *Fax:* (0511) 9910099
E-mail: info@vincentz.de
Web Site: www.vincentz.de *Cable:* VINHA
Key Personnel
Man Dir, Rights & Permissions: Dr Lothar Vincentz
Commercial Dir: Helmut Fitting
Sales: Ina Baatz
Founded: 1893
Subjects: Chemistry, Chemical Engineering, Medicine, Nursing, Dentistry
ISBN Prefix(es): 3-87870
Warehouse: Emil-Meyer-Str 22, 30165 Hannover

Edition Curt Visel+
Weberstr 36, 87700 Memmingen
Tel: (08331) 2853 *Fax:* (08331) 490364
E-mail: info@edition-curt-visel.de
Web Site: www.edition-curt-visel.de
Key Personnel
Man Dir, Editorial, Production, Publicity, Rights & Permissions: Curt Visel
Sales: Jurgen Schweitzer
Founded: 1963
Subjects: Art, Biography

ISBN Prefix(es): 3-922406
Parent Company: Maximilian Dietrich Verlag

Vista Point Verlag GmbH+
Haendelstr 25-29, 50674 Cologne
Mailing Address: Postfach 270572, 50511 Cologne
Tel: (0221) 921613-0 *Fax:* (0221) 921613-14
E-mail: info@vistapoint.de
Web Site: www.vistapoint.de
Key Personnel
Manager: Dr Horst Schmidt-Bruemmer *E-mail:* h.schmidt-bruemmer@vistapoint.de; Andreas Schulz
Founded: 1977
Subjects: Travel
ISBN Prefix(es): 3-88973

VJK Verlag Josef Knecht Carolusdruckerei GmbH+
Liebfrauenberg 37, 60313 Frankfurt
Tel: (069) 281767; (069) 281768 *Fax:* (069) 296653
Key Personnel
Man Dir: Dr Hermann Herder; Dr Marianne Regnier
Rights & Permissions: Dieter Naveau
Founded: 1946
Specialize in religion, philosphy, social problems, human sciences. Special interest: the situation of mankind in post modern times.
Subjects: Philosophy, Regional Interests, Religion - Other, Social Sciences, Sociology, Theology, Travel, Cultural History
ISBN Prefix(es): 3-7820

VNW, see Verlag Neuer Weg

Vogel Medien GmbH & Co KG+
Max-Planckstr 7/9, 97082 Wuerzburg
Tel: (0931) 418-2028 *Fax:* (0931) 418-2860
E-mail: info@vogel-medien.de
Web Site: www.vogel.de *Cable:* VOGELVERLAG WURZBURG
Key Personnel
Man Dir: Dietmar Salein; Claus Wuestenhagen
Founded: 1891
Subjects: Automotive, Chemistry, Chemical Engineering, Civil Engineering, Communications, Computer Science, Electronics, Electrical Engineering, Environmental Studies, Management, Mechanical Engineering
ISBN Prefix(es): 3-8023
U.S. Office(s): Vogel Europublishing, 632 Sunflower Court, San Ramon, CA 94583, United States, Contact: Mark Hauser *Tel:* 510-648-1170 *Fax:* 510-648-1171

Voggenreiter-Verlag+
Viktoriastr 25, 53173 Bonn-Bad Godesberg
Tel: (0228) 93 575-0 *Fax:* (0228) 35 50 53
E-mail: info@voggenreiter.de
Web Site: www.voggenreiter.de
Key Personnel
Proprietor: Charles Voggenreiter; Ralph Voggenreiter
Founded: 1919
Music publisher of Rock & Pop
Also specialize in full tutorials, reference books, sheet music & videos.
Membership(s): NAMM, RPMDA, DMV.
Subjects: Music, Dance
ISBN Prefix(es): 3-8024
Total Titles: 200 Print; 5 CD-ROM; 15 Audio
U.S. Office(s): MTC, 495 Lorimer St, Brooklyn, NY 11211, United States, Contact: Marcus Demuth *Tel:* 718-963-2777 *Fax:* 718-302-4890 *E-mail:* mtc@inditec.com
Distribution Center: Voggenreiter Logistikeentuim, Wittfelder Stich 1, 53343 Wachtberg-Villip *Tel:* (0228) 34 10 43 *Fax:* (0228) 95 16 334

Ellen Vogt Garbe Verlag+
Kinkelstr 15, 90482 Nuernberg
Tel: (0911) 5430983 *Fax:* (0911) 5430983
Key Personnel
Contact: Ellen Vogt
Founded: 1994
Subjects: Environmental Studies, Humor, Philosophy, Poetry
ISBN Prefix(es): 3-930143

Verlag Volk & Welt GmbH+
Neumarkterstr 18, 81673 Munich
Tel: (089) 4372 2769 *Fax:* (089) 4372 2743
Cable: VOLKWELT BERLIN
Key Personnel
Dir: Dierich von Boetticher; Dietrich Simon
Sales Dir: Monika Mueller
Founded: 1947
Membership(s): Stock Exchange of German Booksellers.
Subjects: Fiction, History, Nonfiction (General)
ISBN Prefix(es): 3-353
Distributor for Janus Press
Shipping Address: VSB Verlagsservice Braunschweig, Georg-Westermann-Allee 66, 38104 Braunschweig
Warehouse: VSB Verlagsservice Braunschweig, Georg-Westermann-Allee 66, 38104 Braunschweig
Orders to: VSB Verlagsservice Braunschweig, Georg-Westermann-Allee 66, 38104 Braunschweig

Volk und Wissen Verlag GmbH & Co+
Axel-Springerstr 54b, 10117 Berlin
Mailing Address: Postfach 270, 10107 Berlin
Tel: (030) 201 83-502 *Fax:* (030) 2041846
E-mail: mail@vwv.de
Web Site: www.vwv.de
Telex: 112181 vowiv dd *Cable:* VOLKWISSEN BERLIN
Key Personnel
Man Dir: Walter Funken
Program Dir: Dr Jochen Becher
Business Manager: Dr Roland Tischer
Rights & Permissions: Ortrud Liebau
Sales: Michael Lochner
Editor: Marjus Bente; Dr Sigfrid Motschmann; Dr Gerhild Schenk
Founded: 1945
Subjects: Biological Sciences, Chemistry, Chemical Engineering, Education, Geography, Geology, Mathematics, Physical Sciences, Physics
ISBN Prefix(es): 3-06
Parent Company: Franz-Cornelsen-Stiftung, Berlin
Subsidiaries: Paedagogischer Zeitschriftenverlag GmbH & Co

Verlag Deutsches Volksheimstaettenwerk GmbH+
Neefestr 2a, 53115 Bonn
Tel: (0228) 7259930 *Fax:* (0228) 7259919
E-mail: ibn@bonn.ihk.de
Web Site: www.ibn.ihk-bonn.de
Key Personnel
Contact: I Hilderbrand
Founded: 1982
Subjects: House & Home, Law
ISBN Prefix(es): 3-87941

Dokument und Analyse Verlag Bogislaw von Randow
Barer Str 43, 80799 Munich
Tel: (089) 2720100 *Fax:* (089) 2720311
Key Personnel
Publisher: Bogislaw von Randow
Founded: 1972
Subjects: Economics, Government, Political Science, Law, Science (General), Social Sciences, Sociology

PUBLISHERS — GERMANY

Votum Verlag GmbH+
Grevenerstr 89-91, 48159 Muenster
Tel: (0251) 26514-0 *Fax:* (0251) 26514-20
E-mail: info@votum-verlag.de
Web Site: www.votum-verlag.de
Key Personnel
Man Dir: Dr Klaus Muenstermann
Founded: 1986
Subjects: Law, Psychology, Psychiatry, Social Sciences, Sociology, Women's Studies
ISBN Prefix(es): 3-926549; 3-930405; 3-933158; 3-935984

VS Verlag fur Sozialwissenschaften+
Unit of GWV Fachverlage GMBH
Abraham-Lincoln-Str 46, 65189 Wiesbaden
Tel: (0611) 78780 *Fax:* (0611) 7878-470
Web Site: www.vs-verlag.de; www.gwv-fachverlage.de
Key Personnel
General Manager: Dr Hans-Dieter Haenel
  E-mail: hans-dieter.haenel@gwv-fachverlage.de
Editorial: Annette Kirsch *Tel:* (0611) 7878-368 *Fax:* (0611) 7878-368 *E-mail:* annette.kirsch@gwv-fachverlage.de
Rights & Permissions: Angelika Bolisega *Fax:* (0611) 7878-470 *E-mail:* angelika.bolisega@gwv-fachverlage.de
Founded: 1947
Books & periodicals which cover all important topics in the social sciences.
Subjects: Communications, Social Sciences, Sociology
ISBN Prefix(es): 3-8100; 3-531
Total Titles: 2,000 Print
Parent Company: Springer Science+Business Media
Orders to: VVA Bertelsmann Distribution, Postfach 7777, D-33311 Guetersloh

VUA (agricultural titles), *imprint of* BLV Verlagsgesellschaft mbH

Vulkan-Verlag GmbH+
Huyssenalle 52-56, 45128 Essen
Mailing Address: Postfach 10 39 62, 45039 Essen
Tel: (0201) 82002-0 *Fax:* (0201) 82002-40
Web Site: www.oldenbourg.de/vulkan-verlag
Key Personnel
Man Dir: Dr Dieter Hohm *E-mail:* d.hohm@vulkan-verlag.de
Marketing Manager: Thomas Steinbach *E-mail:* t.steinbach@vulkan-verlag.de
Sales: Silvia Spies *E-mail:* s.spies@vulkan-verlag.de
Founded: 1928
Subjects: Chemistry, Chemical Engineering, Energy, Engineering (General), Environmental Studies, Mechanical Engineering
ISBN Prefix(es): 3-8027
Parent Company: R Oldenbourg Verlag, Rosenheimerstr 145, 81671 Munich

VVF Verlag V Florentz GmbH+
Furstenstr 15, 80333 Munich
Mailing Address: Postfach 34 01 63, 80098 Munich
Tel: (089) 2809095 *Fax:* (089) 2809528
Key Personnel
Manager: Franz Frank
Rights & Permissions: Hans Frank
Founded: 1975
Subjects: Government, Political Science, Labor, Industrial Relations, Law, Regional Interests
ISBN Prefix(es): 3-88259; 3-89481; 3-921491
Associate Companies: Tuduv Verlagsgesellschaft mbH

VWB-Verlag fur Wissenschaft & Bildung, Amand Aglaster
Zossenerstr 55, 10833 Berlin
Mailing Address: PO Box 11 03 68, 10833 Berlin
Tel: (030) 251 04 15 *Fax:* (030) 251 11 36
E-mail: 100615.1565@compuserve.com
Web Site: www.vwb-verlag.com
Key Personnel
Owner: Amand Aglaster
Founded: 1988
Subjects: Anthropology, Art, Biological Sciences, Education, Ethnicity, Geography, Geology, Medicine, Nursing, Dentistry, Music, Dance, Psychology, Psychiatry, Science (General), Social Sciences, Sociology, Women's Studies
ISBN Prefix(es): 3-927408; 3-86135

W Ludwig Verlag GmbH+
Bayerstr 71-73, 80335 Munich
Tel: (089) 41360; (01805) 990505 (hotline)
E-mail: heyne-suedwest@randomhouse.de
Web Site: www.ludwig-verlag.de
Telex: 151329
Key Personnel
Managing Partner: Bettina Breitling; Christian Strasser
Founded: 1945
Subjects: Art, Fiction, History, Nonfiction (General), Travel
ISBN Prefix(es): 3-7787
Associate Companies: C J Bucher Verlag GmbH; Paul List Verlag GmbH; Suedwest Verlag GmbH & Co KG

Wachholtz Verlag GmbH
Rungestr 4, 24537 Neumuenster
Tel: (04321) 250-930 *Fax:* (04321) 906-275
E-mail: info@wachholtz.de
Web Site: www.wachholtz.de
Key Personnel
Man Dir & Permissions: Gabriele Wachholtz; Dr Gisela Wachholtz
Production: Renate Braus; Henner Wachholtz
Founded: 1871
Subjects: Archaeology, Art, History, Language Arts, Linguistics, Social Sciences, Sociology
ISBN Prefix(es): 3-529

Verlag Klaus Wagenbach (Klaus Wagenbach Publishers)+
Emser Str 40/41, 10719 Berlin
Tel: (030) 23 51 51-0 *Fax:* (030) 2 11 61 40
E-mail: mail@wagenbach.de
Web Site: www.wagenbach.de
Key Personnel
Man Dir, Editorial: Dr Susanne Schuessler
Sales Dir: Nina Wagenbach
Rights Dir: Petra Biesenkamp *Tel:* (030) 23 51 51 21
Public Relations: Annette Wassermann *Tel:* (030) 23 51 51 11 *E-mail:* presse@wagenbach.de
Publicity: Julie August *Tel:* (030) 23 51 51 31 *E-mail:* werbung@wagenbach.de
Distribution: Katrin Haas *E-mail:* vertrieb@wagenbach.de
Founded: 1964
Subjects: Art, Fiction, Government, Political Science, History, Literature, Literary Criticism, Essays, Nonfiction (General), Poetry, Social Sciences, Sociology
ISBN Prefix(es): 3-8031
Number of titles published annually: 60 Print; 4 Audio
Orders to: Koch, Neff & Oetinger, Postfach 800220, 70506 Stuttgart

Friedenauer Presse Katharina Wagenbach-Wolff+
Carmerstr 10, 10623 Berlin
Tel: (030) 312 99 23 *Fax:* (030) 312 99 02
Web Site: www.friedenauer-press.de
Key Personnel
Man Dir & International Rights: Katharina Wagenbach-Wolff
Founded: 1963
Subjects: Literature, Literary Criticism, Essays
ISBN Prefix(es): 3-921592; 3-932109

Edition Waldschloesschen, *imprint of* Mannerschwarm Skript Verlag GmbH

Waldthausen Verlag, *imprint of* NaturaViva Verlags GmbH

Walhalla Fachverlag GmbH & Co KG Praetoria+
Haus an der Eisernen Bruecke, 93042 Regensburg
Mailing Address: Postfach 10 10 53, 93010 Regensburg
Tel: (0941) 5684-0 *Fax:* (0941) 5684-111
E-mail: walhalla@walhalla.de
Web Site: www.walhalla.de
Key Personnel
Manager: Bernhard Roloff
Founded: 1949
Subjects: Business, Career Development, Law, Public Administration
ISBN Prefix(es): 3-8029

Uwe Warnke Verlag+
Sonntagstr 22, 10245 Berlin
Tel: (030) 29049903
E-mail: warnke@snafu.de
Key Personnel
Publisher/Author: Uwe Warnke *E-mail:* warnke@snafu.de
Founded: 1982
Subjects: Art, Literature, Literary Criticism, Essays, Photography, Poetry
ISBN Prefix(es): 3-910165
Total Titles: 100 Print; 1 CD-ROM

Wartburg Verlag GmbH+
Lisztstr 2 A, 99423 Weimar
Tel: (03643) 24 61-44 *Fax:* (03643) 24 61-18
E-mail: buch@wartburgverlag.de
Web Site: www.wartburgverlag.de
Key Personnel
Man Dir: Torsten Bolduan; Barbara Harnisch
Founded: 1990
Subjects: Art, Literature, Literary Criticism, Essays, Regional Interests, Religion - Protestant
ISBN Prefix(es): 3-86160
Number of titles published annually: 12 Print
Total Titles: 90 Print

Ernst Wasmuth Verlag GmbH & Co+
Fuerstr 133, 72072 Tuebingen
Mailing Address: Postfach 27 28, 72017 Tuebingen
Tel: (07071) 97 55 00 *Fax:* (07071) 97 55 013
E-mail: info@wasmuth-verlag.de
Web Site: www.wasmuth-verlag.de
Key Personnel
Man Dir: Ernst-Juergen Wasmuth
Sales: Annerose Fischer
Rights & Permissions: Dorah Schneider
Editorial Dir: Dr Sigrid Hauser
Production: Rosa Wagner
Founded: 1872
Subjects: Archaeology, Architecture & Interior Design, Art
ISBN Prefix(es): 3-8030
Number of titles published annually: 20 Print
Total Titles: 250 Print
Distributor for L'Arcaedizioni
Bookshop(s): Wasmuth Buchhandlung & Antiquariat GmbH & Co, Pfalzburgerstr 43-44, 10707 Berlin *Tel:* (030) 8 63 09 90 *Fax:* (030) 86 30 99 99 *E-mail:* info@wasmuth.de *Web Site:* www.wasmuth.de

Waxmann Verlag GmbH+
Steinfurterstr 555, 48046 Muenster
Mailing Address: Postfach 8603, 48046 Muenster
Tel: (0251) 265040 *Fax:* (0251) 2650426
E-mail: info@waxmann.com

Web Site: www.waxmann.com
Key Personnel
Man Dir: Dr Ursula Heckel *E-mail:* heckel@waxmann.com
Contact: Beate Plugge *E-mail:* plugge@waxmann.com
Founded: 1987
Subjects: Education, Ethnicity, History, Literature, Literary Criticism, Essays, Psychology, Psychiatry, Science (General), Social Sciences, Sociology, Theology, Women's Studies
ISBN Prefix(es): 3-89325; 3-8309
Number of titles published annually: 120 Print
Total Titles: 1,200 Print
Branch Office(s)
Torstr 195, 10115 Berlin *Tel:* (030) 283900-49 *Fax:* (030) 283900-59 *E-mail:* berlin@waxmann.com
U.S. Office(s): Waxmann Publishing Co, PO Box 1318, New York, NY 10028, United States

WDV Wirtschaftsdienst Gesellschaft fur Medien & Kommunikation mbH & Co OHG+
Siemensstr 6, 61352 Bad Homburg
Mailing Address: Postfach 2551, 61295 Bad Homburg
Tel: (06172) 670-0 *Fax:* (01672) 670144
E-mail: info@wdv.de
Web Site: www.wdv.de
Telex: 414452 widi d
Key Personnel
Managers: Bernhard Frisch; Diether Kuhn; Rolf M Laufer
Founded: 1948
Subjects: Health, Nutrition, Travel
ISBN Prefix(es): 3-926181
Parent Company: Zeitschriften VVG Verlags- und Verwaltungsgesellschaft mbH & Co KG
Subsidiaries: Analyse & Concept Kommunikationsberatung GmbH; Montan-Wirtschaftsverlag GmbH
U.S. Office(s): Conover Brown, International Media, 21 E 40 St, Suite 901, New York, NY 10016, United States
Warehouse: Hertzweg 4, 63071 Offenbach am Main

Weber Zucht & Co+
Steinbruchweg 14a, 34123 Kassel
Tel: (0561) 519194; (0561) 515953 *Fax:* (0561) 5102514
E-mail: wezuco@t-online.de
Key Personnel
International Rights: Helga Weber
Contact: Wolfgang Zucht
Founded: 1980
Subjects: Alternative, Biography, Education, Environmental Studies, Government, Political Science, History, Military Science, Nonfiction (General), Philosophy, Science (General), Self-Help, Social Sciences, Sociology
ISBN Prefix(es): 3-88713

Wege der Forschung, *imprint of* Wissenschaftliche Buchgesellschaft

Wehr & Wissen Verlagsgesellschaft mbH+
Heilsbachstr 26, 5300 Bonn 1
Mailing Address: PO Box 1, 5300 Bonn 1
Tel: (0228) 64830 *Fax:* (0228) 6483109
E-mail: 101336.245@compuserve.com; advert@moench-group.com
Key Personnel
Man Dir: Manfred Sadlowski
Man Dir, Publicity: Joachim Knoche
Marketing, Intern: Juergen Hensel
Marketing, National: Hans Werner Steinhoff
Subjects: History, How-to
ISBN Prefix(es): 3-921528

A Weichert Verlag GmbH & Co KG+
Waechtersbacher Str 89, 60386 Frankfurt
Mailing Address: Postfach 630248, 60352 Frankfurt
Tel: (069) 942118-22 *Fax:* (069) 942118-17
Key Personnel
Man Dir: Alfred Trippo
Sales: Hans H Droste
Rights & Permissions: Renate Gruetzemacher
Founded: 1872
Subjects: Fiction
ISBN Prefix(es): 3-483; 3-8034
Associate Companies: Neuer Jugendschriften-Verlag, Tiestestr 14, 30171 Hannover

Weidler Buchverlag Berlin+
Luebecker Str 8, 10559 Berlin
Mailing Address: Postfach 21 03 15, 10503 Berlin
Tel: (030) 394 86 68 *Fax:* (030) 394 86 98
E-mail: weidler_verlag@yahoo.de
Web Site: www.weidler-verlag.de
Key Personnel
Man Dir: Joachim Weidler
Founded: 1985
Membership(s): Boersenverein des Deutschen Buchhandels.
Subjects: Drama, Theater, Earth Sciences, Education, Fiction, Geography, Geology, Language Arts, Linguistics, Literature, Literary Criticism, Essays, Management, Marketing, Nonfiction (General), Philosophy, Poetry, Psychology, Psychiatry, Regional Interests, Science (General), Social Sciences, Sociology
ISBN Prefix(es): 3-925191; 3-89693
Number of titles published annually: 30 Print
Total Titles: 215 Print
Imprints: Edition Belletriste

Weidlich Verlag+
Imprint of Verlagshaus Wurzburg
Beethovenstr 5, 97070 Wurzburg
Tel: (0931) 385235 *Fax:* (0931) 385305
E-mail: info@verlagshaus.com
Web Site: www.verlagshaus.com
Key Personnel
Publishing Dir: Dieter Krause
Dir, Production: Juergen Roth
Sales Dir: Johannes Glesius
Subjects: Foreign Countries, Travel
ISBN Prefix(es): 3-8035

Weidmannsche Verlagsbuchhandlung GmbH+
Hagentorwall 7, 31134 Hildesheim
Tel: (05121) 15010 *Fax:* (05121) 150150
E-mail: info@olms.de
Web Site: www.olms.de
Key Personnel
Publisher: Dr W Georg Olms
Publishing Dir: Dietrich Olms
Founded: 1680
Subjects: Antiques, History, Language Arts, Linguistics, Philosophy, Romance, Classical Studies, Medieval Studies
ISBN Prefix(es): 3-615; 3-296
Number of titles published annually: 20 Print
Total Titles: 450 Print
U.S. Office(s): Empire State Bldg, 350 Fifth Ave, Suite 3304, New York, NY 10118-0069, United States
Warehouse: VVA, PO Box 1254, 33399 Verl, Contact: Herr Stronz *Tel:* (05241) 803844 *Fax:* (05241) 8060220

Verlag W Weinmann+
Beckerstr 7, 12157 Berlin
Tel: (030) 855 48 95 *Fax:* (030) 8 55 94 64
E-mail: info@weinmann-verlag.de
Web Site: www.weinmann-verlag.de
Key Personnel
Man Dir: Dr Weinmann
Founded: 1961

Membership(s): Boersenverein.
Subjects: Humor, Sports, Athletics, Martial Arts
ISBN Prefix(es): 3-87892
Total Titles: 70 Print
Foreign Rep(s): Dessauer CH; Ennsthaler A

Weisser Ring, Gemeinnutzige Verlagsgesellschaft mbH
Bundesgeschaeftsstelle, Weberstr 16, 55130 Mainz
Tel: (06131) 83 03 01 *Fax:* (06131) 83 03 45
E-mail: info@weisser-ring.de
Web Site: www.weisser-ring.de
Key Personnel
Editor: Dieter Eppenstein
Founded: 1989
Specializing in the production of books (Mainzer Schriften) relating to issues concerning victims of crime.
Total Titles: 20 Print
Parent Company: Weisser Ring eV

WEKA Firmengruppe GmbH & Co KG+
Roemerstr 4, 86438 Kissing
Mailing Address: Postfach 1209, 86425 Kissing
Tel: (08233) 23-0 *Fax:* (08233) 23-7500
E-mail: service@weka.de
Web Site: www.weka.de; www.weka-group.de; www.weka-group.com
Telex: 533287
Key Personnel
Chairman: Werner Muetzel; Rainer B Wozny
Man Dir: Robert Boss; Wolfgang Materna; Taap Mulder; Gerhard Schierbling
Founded: 1973
Subjects: Architecture & Interior Design, Behavioral Sciences, Business, Career Development, Civil Engineering, Communications, Electronics, Electrical Engineering, Energy, Engineering (General), Environmental Studies, How-to, Law, Management, Mechanical Engineering, Medicine, Nursing, Dentistry, Outdoor Recreation, Real Estate, Technology
ISBN Prefix(es): 3-8111
Subsidiaries: Demeter Verlag GmbH & Co KG, Batinger; DMV Daten-und Medien-Verlag GmbH & Co KG; ECPA; Editions WEKA SA; Editions WEKA SARL; Edizioni WEKA SpA; Franzis-Verlag GmbH & Co KG; Interest-Verlag GmbH; Nidderau und Busborn; Spitta Verlag GmbH; Turnus GmbH; Uitgeverij BV; Verlag Recht & Praxis GmbH; Verwaltungs-Verlag GmbH; WAGO-Curadata Steuerberatungs-Systeme GmbH; WEKA Baufach-Software GmbH; WEKA Baufachverlage GmbH; WEKA Fachverlag fuer Behoerden und Institutionen; WEKA Fachverlag fur technische Fuhrungskrafte GmbH; WEKA Handels-GmbH; WEKA Informationsschriften- und Werbefachverlage GmbH; WEKA Management Fachverlag GmbH; WEKA Publishing Inc; WEKA-Verlag AG; WEKA Verlag Ges mbH; WEKA Verlagsgesellschaft fuer aktuelle Publikationen mbH; WEKA Verlagsservice GmbH
U.S. Office(s): WEKA Publishing Inc, Huntington Point, 1077 Bridgeport Ave, Sheldon, CT 06484, United States *Tel:* 203-925-1711

Verlagsgruppe Weltbild GmbH (Publishing Group Weltbild GmbH)+
Steinerne Furt, 86167 Augsburg
Tel: (0821) 70 04-70 00 *Fax:* (0821) 70 04-17 90
E-mail: info@weltbild.com
Web Site: www.weltbild.com
Key Personnel
President: Carel Halff
Man Dir: Dr Klaus Driever; Werner Ortner; Herbert Zoch
Founded: 1949
Subjects: Animals, Pets, Art, Cookery, Crafts, Games, Hobbies, Environmental Studies, Ethnicity, Fashion, Fiction, Gardening, Plants,

Health, Nutrition, History, Nonfiction (General), Philosophy
ISBN Prefix(es): 3-86047; 3-8289; 3-89350; 3-89604; 3-927117
Associate Companies: Verlagsgruppe Droemer Weltbild GmbH & Co KG, Hilblestr 54, 80636 Munich *Tel:* (0821) 92 71-0 *Fax:* (0821) 92 71-168 *E-mail:* info@droemer-weltbild.org *Web Site:* www.droemer-weltbild.de; Bechtermuenz Verlag; Weltbild Verlag
Subsidiaries: Andreas & Dr Mueller Verlagsbuchhandel GmbH; Bauer-Weltbild Media Spzoo, SpK; Booxtra GmbH & Co Kg; DMC Direkt Marketing Consulting GmbH; Olzog Verlag GmbH; Publica-Data-Service GmbH; Sailer Verlag GmbH & Co KG; Weltbildplus Medienvertriebs GmbH & Co KG; Weltbild Verlag Schweiz GmbH
Shipping Address: VVA-Bertelsmann Distribution GmbH, Postfach 7600, 33310 Guetersloh
Warehouse: VVA-Bertelsmann Distribution GmbH, Postfach 7600, 33310 Guetersloh

Weltforum Verlag GmbH+
Subsidiary of Deutscher Wirtschaftsdienst John von Freyend GmbH
Hohenzollernplatz 3, 53173 Bonn
Tel: (0228) 3682436 *Fax:* (0228) 3682436
E-mail: wfv@internationsafrikaforum.de
Key Personnel
Dir, Sales, Rights & Permissions: Peter John von Freyend
Publicity: Deonika Langer
Founded: 1963
Subjects: Developing Countries
ISBN Prefix(es): 3-8039

Weltkunst Verlag GmbH+
Nymphenburgerstr 84, 80636 Munich
Tel: (089) 1269900 *Fax:* (089) 12699011
E-mail: info@weltkunstverlag.de
Web Site: www.weltkunstverlag.de
Key Personnel
Contact: Felix Frohn-Bernau
Founded: 1930
Subjects: Art
ISBN Prefix(es): 3-921669
Parent Company: Time Beteiligungs AG, Starnberg
Subsidiaries: Antiquitaeten-Zeitung Verlag; Hirmer Verlag GmbH; W B Verlag
U.S. Office(s): Axel Springer Group Inc, 500 Fifth Ave, Suite 2800, New York, NY 10110, United States *Tel:* 212-972-1720 *Fax:* 212-972-1724 *E-mail:* asg-usa@msn.com

Wer liefert was? GmbH (Who Supplies What?)
Normannenweg, 16-20, 20537 Hamburg
Mailing Address: Postfach 100549, 20004 Hamburg
Tel: (040) 25440-0 *Fax:* (040) 25440-100
E-mail: info@wlw.de
Web Site: www.wlw.de
Key Personnel
Man Dir: Andrew Pylyp; Peter Schulze
Founded: 1948
Membership(s): Informationsgemeinschaft zur Feststel ung der Verbreitung von Wer bertraegern eV; Verband Deutscher Andressbuchverleger eV; Europaeischen Andressbuchverleger-Verband; Verband Deutscher Wirtschaftsnachschlagewerke eV.
Subjects: Business, Marketing
ISBN Prefix(es): 3-923878
Total Titles: 1 Print; 5 CD-ROM; 1 Online; 1 E-Book
Parent Company: Eniro AB, Stockholm, Sweden
Branch Office(s)
Wer liefert was? Ges mbH, Inkustr 1-7/6/1 OG, 3400 Klosterneuburg, Austria *Tel:* (02243) 33765 *Fax:* (02243) 33765-88 *E-mail:* info@wlw.at *Web Site:* www.wlw.at
Wer liefert was? GmbH, succ belge, Louizalaan 65/11, 1050 Brussels, Belgium *Tel:* (02) 2452228 *Fax:* (02) 2456213 *E-mail:* info@wlw.be *Web Site:* www.wlw.be
Wer liefert was? spol s r o, Sokolska 52, 120 00 Prague-2, Czech Republic *Tel:* (02) 96330-200 *Fax:* (02) 96330-201 *E-mail:* info@wlw.cz *Web Site:* www.wlw.cz
Wer liefert was? doo, Fallerovo setaliste 22, 10000 Zagreb, Croatia *Tel:* (01) 3030500 *Fax:* (01) 3030501 *E-mail:* info@wlw.hr *Web Site:* www.wlw.hr
Wer liefert was? Nederlandse Vestiging, Hoogorddreef 9, 1101 BA Amsterdam, Netherlands *Tel:* (020) 6960706 *Fax:* (020) 6968866 *E-mail:* info@wlw.nl *Web Site:* www.wlw.nl
Wer liefert was? Doo, Gregorciceva ulica 7, 3000 Celje, Slovenia *Tel:* (03) 42508 00 *Fax:* (03) 42508 01 *E-mail:* info@wlw.si *Web Site:* www.wlw.si
Wer liefert was AG, Blegistr 15, 6340 Baar-Walterswil, Switzerland *Tel:* (041) 7603438 *Fax:* (041) 7603430 *E-mail:* info@wlw.ch *Web Site:* www.wlw.ch

Werner Verlag GmbH & Co KG+
Karl-Rudolf-Str 172, 40215 Duesseldorf
Mailing Address: Postfach 10 53 54, 40044 Duesseldorf
Tel: (0211) 3 87 98-0 *Fax:* (0211) 3 87 98-11
E-mail: info@werner-verlag.de
Key Personnel
Publishing Dir: Klaus-Juergen Schneider
Founded: 1945
Subjects: Economics, Engineering (General), Law
ISBN Prefix(es): 3-8041
Parent Company: Wolters Kluwer

Georg Westermann Verlag GmbH+
Georg-Westermann-Allee 66, 38104 Braunschweig
Tel: (0531) 708-244 *Fax:* (0531) 708-248
E-mail: westermann@plus.at *Cable:* GEWEBUCH
Key Personnel
Man Dir: Hans-Dieter Moeller
Founded: 1838
Subjects: Nonfiction (General)
ISBN Prefix(es): 3-07
Parent Company: Georg Westermann Verlag, Druckerei und Kartographische Anstalt GmbH & Co, Brunswick (printing & publishing management company)
Orders to: VSB Verlagsservice Braunschweig GmbH, Postfach 3320, 38104 Braunschweig *Tel:* (0531) 708-0

Westermann Schulbuchverlag GmbH
Georg-Westermann-Allee 66, 38104 Braunschweig
Tel: (0531) 7 08-0 *Fax:* (0531) 70 82 09
E-mail: schulservice@westermann.de
Web Site: www.westermann.de
Telex: 0952841 wbuch d *Cable:* GEWEBUCH
Key Personnel
Editorial, Production: Juergen Grimm
Sales, Publicity: Hartmut Becker
Subjects: Education, History
ISBN Prefix(es): 3-14; 3-8045
Parent Company: Georg Westermann Verlag, Druckerei und Kartographische Anstalt GmbH & Co, (Printing & Publishing Management Co), Brunswick

Verlag Westfaelisches Dampfboot+
Hafenweg 26a, 48145 Muenster
Tel: (0251) 3900480 *Fax:* (0251) 39004850
E-mail: info@dampfboot-verlag.de
Web Site: www.dampfboot-verlag.de
Key Personnel
Editor: Prof H G Thien, PhD; Prof H Wienold, PhD
Founded: 1984
Subjects: Labor, Industrial Relations, Law, Social Sciences, Sociology, Women's Studies
ISBN Prefix(es): 3-924550; 3-929586; 3-89691
Orders to: Prolit Verlagsauslieferung, Siemensstr 13, 35463 Fernwald *Tel:* (0641) 9439333 *Fax:* (0641) 9439339 *Web Site:* www.prolit.de

Westholsteinische Verlagsanstalt und Verlagsdruckerei Boyens & Co+
Wulf-Isebrand-Platz, 25746 Heide
Tel: (0481) 6886-151; (0481) 6886-152
Fax: (0481) 688467
E-mail: buchhandlung@sh-nordsee.de
Web Site: www.sh-nordsee.de
Telex: 28833 boyens d
Key Personnel
Dir: Dipl Kfm Boyens Uwe
Man Dir: Bernd Rachuth
Sales Dir: Reinhard Lipinski
Technical Dir: Heinz Fuhrberg
Founded: 1869
Subjects: Cookery, Literature, Literary Criticism, Essays, Regional Interests
ISBN Prefix(es): 3-8042
Subsidiaries: Brunsbuetteler Zeitung GmbH
Branch Office(s)
Albersdorf
Busum
Marne
Meldorf Wesselburen
St Michaelisdorn

Erich Wewel Verlag GmbH+
Heilig-Kreuz-Str 16, 86609 Donauwoerth
Tel: (0906) 73-0 *Fax:* (0906) 73-1 77
Web Site: www.klett.de/geschaeftsbereiche/grundschule.html
Key Personnel
Dir & Editorial: Lydia Franzelius
Founded: 1936
Subjects: Philosophy, Religion - Other, Theology
ISBN Prefix(es): 3-403; 3-87904
Parent Company: Klett Gruppe

Wichern Verlag GmbH+
Georgenkirchstr 69-70, 10249 Berlin
Tel: (030) 28 87 48 10 *Fax:* (030) 28 87 48 12
E-mail: info@wichern.de
Web Site: www.wichern.de
Key Personnel
Contact: Dr Elke Rutzenhofer
Founded: 1880
Specialize in Christian Literature.
Membership(s): the Stock Exchange of German Booksellers & the Association of Publishers & Bookstores in Berlin-Brandenburg.
Subjects: Biography, History, Religion - Other, Theology
ISBN Prefix(es): 3-88981; 3-7674
Distributed by BMK Buchauslieferung (Austria); Evangelische Verlagsauslieferung

Wichern-Verlag GmbH+
Georgenkirchstr 69-70, 10249 Berlin
Mailing Address: Postfach 350954, 10218 Berlin
Tel: (030) 288748-0 *Fax:* (030) 28874812
E-mail: 101711.1207@compuserve.com
Key Personnel
Publisher: Wolfgang Fietkau
Founded: 1982
Membership(s): the Stock Exchange of German Booksellers & the Association of Publishers & Bookstores in Berlin-Brandenburg.
Subjects: History, Religion - Other
ISBN Prefix(es): 3-88981; 3-7674
Divisions: CZV-Verlag
Distributed by BMK Buchauslieferung (Austria); Evangelische Verlagsauslieferung (Switzerland)
Warehouse: Mehringdamm 32-34, 10961 Berlin

Herbert Wichmann Verlag+
Im Weiher 10, 69121 Heidelberg

Mailing Address: Postfach 102869, 69018 Heidelberg
Tel: (06221) 4890 *Fax:* (06221) 489279
E-mail: wichmann@huethig.de
Web Site: www.huethig.de
Founded: 1889
Subjects: Aeronautics, Aviation, Communications, Earth Sciences, Geography, Geology
ISBN Prefix(es): 3-87907
Number of titles published annually: 11 Print
Parent Company: Huethig GmbH & Co KG

Wiechmann-Verlag Betriebs GmbH
Deggenhauser Str 8, 88693 Deggenhausertal
Tel: (0700) 08000035 *Fax:* (0700) 08000036
Key Personnel
Manager: Carsta Korhammer; Heidi Wiechmann
Founded: 1893
ISBN Prefix(es): 3-87908

Wiley-VCH Verlag GmbH+
Boschstr 12, 69469 Weinheim
Mailing Address: Postfach 101161, 69451 Weinham
Tel: (06201) 606 0 *Fax:* (06201) 606 328
E-mail: info@wiley-vch.de
Web Site: www.wiley-vch.de
Telex: 467-155-vchwh d
Key Personnel
Publishing Dir: Dr Eva E Wille *Tel:* (030) 6201-606272 *Fax:* (030) 6201-606205
E-mail: ewille@wiley-vch.de
Human Resources Dir: Sven Kroeger *Tel:* (030) 6201-606159 *Fax:* (030) 6201-606192
E-mail: skroeger@wiley-vch.de
Marketing & Sales Dir: Juergen Boos *E-mail:* j-boos@wiley-vch.de
Finance & Administration Dir: Bijan Ghawami
Information Technology: Petra Wyrwa
Editorial Dir Business: Bettina Querfurth
Founded: 1921
Subjects: Biological Sciences, Chemistry, Chemical Engineering, Law, Physical Sciences, Physics, Science (General)
ISBN Prefix(es): 3-527
Total Titles: 1,580 Print
Parent Company: John Wiley & Sons Inc, 111 River St, Hoboken, NJ 07030, United States
Subsidiaries: Wilhelm Ernst & Sohn Verlag fuer Architekur und technische Wissenschaft; Chemical Concepts; Verlagsservice Suedwest; Verlag Helvetica Chimica Actc AG

Windmuehle GmbH Verlag und Vertrieb von Medien+
Gosslerstr 22/24, 22587 Hamburg
Mailing Address: Postfach 551080, 22570 Hamburg
Tel: (040) 86 83 07 *Fax:* (040) 866 31 23
E-mail: info@windmuehle-verlag.de
Web Site: www.windmuehle-verlag.de
Key Personnel
Manager: Rita Bolte
Founded: 1981
Further Education in Organization & Management.
Subjects: Education, Management
ISBN Prefix(es): 3-922789
Warehouse: Metzler-Poeschel, Hermann Leins Auslieferungsdienst, Postfach 7, 7408 Kusterdingen *Tel:* (07071) 93530 *Fax:* (07071) 93530

Windpferd Verlagsgesellschaft mbH+
Friesenriederstr 45, 87648 Aitrang
Mailing Address: Postfach 87648, Aitrang
Tel: (08343) 1404 *Fax:* (08343) 1403
E-mail: info@windpferd.de
Web Site: www.windpferd.de
Key Personnel
Manager: Monika Junemann
Founded: 1987

Subjects: Psychology, Psychiatry
ISBN Prefix(es): 3-89385

Bibliothek rosa Winkel, *imprint of* Mannerschwarm Skript Verlag GmbH

Rosa Winkel Verlag GmbH+
Kufsteinerstr 12, 10825 Berlin
Mailing Address: Postfach 302949, 10777 Berlin
Tel: (030) 85729295 *Fax:* (030) 85729296
E-mail: rosawinkel@t-online.de
Key Personnel
Publisher: Egmont Fassbinder
Subjects: Gay & Lesbian, Nonfiction (General)
ISBN Prefix(es): 3-921495; 3-86149

Dr Dieter Winkler+
Katharinastr 37, 44793 Bochum
Mailing Address: Postfach 102665, 44726 Bochum
Tel: (0234) 9650200 *Fax:* (0234) 9650201
E-mail: winkler-verlag.bochum@tonline.de
Web Site: www.winklerverlag.de
Key Personnel
Owner: Dr Dieter Winkler
Founded: 1984
Membership(s): Boersenverein des Dt Buchhandels.
Subjects: Education, History, Nonfiction (General), Regional Interests, Science (General), Social Sciences, Sociology
ISBN Prefix(es): 3-924517; 3-930083; 3-89911
Number of titles published annually: 10 Print
Total Titles: 115 Print

Winklers Verlag Gebrueder Grimm
Alsfelderstr 7, 64289 Darmstadt
Mailing Address: Postfach 111552, 64230 Darmstadt
Tel: (06151) 87 68-0 *Fax:* (06151) 87 68-61
E-mail: service@winklers.de
Web Site: www.winklers.de
Key Personnel
Manager: Ulrike Jurgens; Thomas Michael
Manager, Rights & Permissions: Michael Wolf
Founded: 1902
Subjects: Career Development
ISBN Prefix(es): 3-8045
Shipping Address: Elisabethenstr 34, 64283 Darmstadt

Verlag fuer Wirtschaft & Verwaltung Hubert Wingen GmbH & Co KG+
Alfredistr 32, 45127 Essen
Mailing Address: Postfach 103824, 45038 Essen
Tel: (0201) 22 25 41; (0201) 22 25 42; (0201) 221451-52 *Fax:* (0201) 229660
Key Personnel
Manager: Martha Wingen; Rainer Wingen
Founded: 1958
Subjects: Architecture & Interior Design, Civil Engineering, Law, Public Administration, Real Estate, Religion - Catholic
ISBN Prefix(es): 3-8028
Subsidiaries: Lugerus Verlag GmbH & Co KG

Wirtschaft, Recht & Steuern, see WRS Verlag Wirtschaft, Recht und Steuern GmbH & Co KG

Wison Verlag GmbH
Weyertal 59, 50937 Cologne 41
Mailing Address: Postfach 410948, 50869 Cologne
Tel: (0221) 4722-0 *Fax:* (0221) 448911
Telex: 2214310
Key Personnel
Publicity: Michael Wienand
Founded: 1976
Subjects: Economics, Engineering (General)
ISBN Prefix(es): 3-87951

Verlag fuer Wissenschaft & Bildung, see VWB-Verlag fur Wissenschaft & Bildung, Amand Aglaster

Verlag Wissenschaft und Politik
Markt 13, 06785 Oranienbaum
Mailing Address: PO Box 1107, 06782 Oranienbaum
Tel: (034904) 32946 *Fax:* (034904) 32946
E-mail: helker.pflug@t-online.de
Key Personnel
Owner & Man Dir: Helker Pflug
Founded: 1961
Specialize in books on Central & Eastern Europe.
Subjects: Ethnicity, Genealogy, Government, Political Science, History, Language Arts, Linguistics, Law, Religion - Jewish, Science (General), Social Sciences, Sociology
ISBN Prefix(es): 3-8046
Number of titles published annually: 8 Print
Total Titles: 120 Print

Wissenschaftliche Buchgesellschaft+
Hindenburgstr 40, 64295 Darmstadt
Tel: (06151) 33 08-0 *Fax:* (06151) 31 41 28
E-mail: service@wbg-darmstadt.de
Web Site: www.wbg-darmstadt.de
Key Personnel
Acting Dir: Andreas Auth
Chief Reader: Martin Bredol
Rights & Permissions: Friedericke Ludolph
Press: Barbara Gese *Tel:* (06151) 3308-161
E-mail: gese@wbg-darmstadt.de
Founded: 1949
Subjects: Archaeology, Art, Economics, Education, History, Language Arts, Linguistics, Law, Literature, Literary Criticism, Essays, Mathematics, Medicine, Nursing, Dentistry, Music, Dance, Philosophy, Psychology, Psychiatry, Religion - Other, Science (General), Social Sciences, Sociology
ISBN Prefix(es): 3-534
Imprints: Bibliothek Klassischer Texte; Einfuehrungen; Ertraege der Forschung zur Forschung-; Forum; Freiherr von Stein Gedaechtnisausgabe; Wege der Forschung
Distributor for AVA B&I (Switzerland); Dr Franz Hain Verlagsauslieferung (Austria)
Book Club(s): Wissenschaftliche Buchgesellschaft

Wissenschaftliche Verlagsgesellschaft mbH+
Birkenwaldstr 44, 70191 Stuttgart
Mailing Address: Postfach 101061, 70009 Stuttgart
Tel: (0711) 2582-0 *Fax:* (0711) 2582-290
E-mail: service@wissenschaftliche-verlagsgesellschaft.de
Web Site: www.dav-buchhandlung.de
Key Personnel
Man Dir: Dr Klaus Brauer; R Hack; Dr Christian Rotta
Contact: Siegmar Bauer
Founded: 1921
Subjects: Biological Sciences, Medicine, Nursing, Dentistry, Science (General), Pharmacy
ISBN Prefix(es): 3-8047
Parent Company: Deutscher Apotheker Verlag
Subsidiaries: S Hirzel Verlag GmbH & Co; Medpharm Scientific Publishers; Franz Steiner Verlag Wiesbaden GmbH

Wissenschaftlicher Autoren Verlag KG, see Verlag Grundlagen und Praxis GmbH & Co

Wissenschaftsrat
Brohlerstr 11, 50968 Cologne
Tel: (0221) 3776-0 *Fax:* (0221) 38 84 40
E-mail: post@wissenschaftsrat.de
Web Site: www.wissenschaftsrat.de
Founded: 1957
ISBN Prefix(es): 3-923203; 3-935353

Verlag Claus Wittal
Fliednerstr 27, 65195 Wiesbaden-Bierstadt
Tel: (0611) 502907 *Fax:* (0611) 503021
E-mail: cw@exlibrisart.com
Web Site: www.exlibrisart.com
Founded: 1979
Subjects: Art, Exlibris/bookplates
ISBN Prefix(es): 3-922835

Friedrich Wittig Verlag GmbH+
Gartenstr 20, 24103 Kiel
Mailing Address: Postfach 3169, 24030 Kiel
Tel: (0431) 55779 206 *Fax:* (0431) 55779 292
  Cable: WITTIGVERLAG
Key Personnel
Man Dir: Rainer Thun
Sales: Wolfgang Steinmeier
International Rights: Johannes Keussen
Founded: 1946
Subjects: Art, Biblical Studies, History, Religion - Other
ISBN Prefix(es): 3-8048
Associate Companies: J F Steinkopf Verlag GmbH

Verlag Konrad Wittwer GmbH+
Postfach 105343, 70046 Stuttgart
Tel: (0711) 25 07 0 *Fax:* (0711) 25 07 145
E-mail: info@wittwer.de
Web Site: www.wittwer.de
Key Personnel
Man Dir: Christian Wittwer; Dr Konrad M Wittwer; Konrad P Wittwer; Michael Wittwer
Founded: 1867
Subjects: Earth Sciences, Mathematics, Nonfiction (General), Science (General)
ISBN Prefix(es): 3-87919
Bookshop(s): Koenigstr 30, 70173 Stuttgart

WLW, see Wer liefert was? GmbH

Wochenschau, *imprint of* Wochenschau Verlag, Dr Kurt Debus GmbH

Wochenschau Verlag, Dr Kurt Debus GmbH+
Adolf-Damaschkestr 10, 65824 Schwalbach-Taunus
Tel: (06196) 8 60 65 *Fax:* (06196) 8 60 60
E-mail: info@wochenschau-verlag.de
Web Site: www.wochenschau-verlag.de
Key Personnel
Publishing Dir: Bernward Debus
Manager & Editor-in-Chief: Ursula Buch
Founded: 1949
Subjects: Education, Geography, Geology, Government, Political Science, History
ISBN Prefix(es): 3-87920
Imprints: Wochenschau

Verlagshaus Wohlfarth+
Stresemannstr 20-22, 47051 Duisburg
Tel: (0203) 3 05 27-0 *Fax:* (0203) 3 05 27-820
E-mail: info@wohlfarth.de
Web Site: www.wohlfarth.de
Key Personnel
Man Dir, Publishing: Frank Wohlfarth
Man Dir, Editorial: Uwe Hennig
Book Sales Manager: Lothar Koopmann
  E-mail: l.koopmann@wohlfarth.de
Contact: Stephen Hasselbach *E-mail:* s.hasselbach@wohlfarth.de
Founded: 1953
Membership(s): Borsenverein des Deutschen Buchhandels.
Subjects: Architecture & Interior Design, Crafts, Games, Hobbies, House & Home, Regional Interests
ISBN Prefix(es): 3-87463
Total Titles: 5 Print
Imprints: Mercator-Verlag; Verlag Puppen & Spielzeug; Verlagsbereich Bau

Wolf's-Verlag Berlin+
Bergedorferstr 180, 12623 Berlin
Tel: (030) 5675190
Key Personnel
Publishing Manager: Evelyn Wolf
Founded: 1990
Subjects: Fiction, Literature, Literary Criticism, Essays, Travel
ISBN Prefix(es): 3-86164

Wolgang Fietkau
Ernst-Thaelmann Str 152, 14532 Kleinmachnow
Tel: (0203) 71 105 *Fax:* (0203) 71 109
E-mail: fietkau@fietkau.de
Web Site: www.fietkau.de
Key Personnel
Publisher: Wolfgang Fietkau
Founded: 1959
Subjects: Literature, Literary Criticism, Essays, Poetry, Theology
ISBN Prefix(es): 3-87352

Wolke Verlags GmbH+
Niederholfheimerstr 45 a-c, 65719 Hofheim
Tel: (06192) 7243 *Fax:* (06192) 952939
E-mail: wolke-verlag@t-online.de
Web Site: www.wolke-verlag.de
Key Personnel
Man Dir: Peter Mischung
Subjects: Music, Dance
ISBN Prefix(es): 3-923997; 3-936000

The World of Books Literaturverlag+
Friedrich-Ebertstr 80, Worms 67549
Tel: (06241) 205352 *Fax:* (06241) 205352
E-mail: info@twobl-online.de
Web Site: www.twobl-online.de
Key Personnel
Contact: Reinhard Becker
Founded: 1981
ISBN Prefix(es): 3-88325

The World Society of Victimology eV+
Richard-Wagner Str 101, 41065 Moenchengladbach
Tel: (02161) 186 609 *Fax:* (02161) 186 633
Web Site: www.world-society-victimology.de/
Key Personnel
Professor: Dr Gerd Ferdinand Kirchhoff
  Fax: (02161) 186633 *E-mail:* kirchhoff@bigfoot.com
Founded: 1992
ISBN Prefix(es): 3-929441
Number of titles published annually: 1 Print; 4 Audio

Verlag DAS WORT GmbH
Max-Braunstr 2, 97828 Martheidenfeld-Altfeld
Tel: (09391) 504135 *Fax:* (09391) 504133
E-mail: info@das-wort.com
Web Site: www.das-wort.com; www.universal-spirit.cc
Key Personnel
General Manager: Christine Schulte *Tel:* (09391) 504132
Membership(s): Borsenverein.
Subjects: Health, Nutrition, Human Relations, Philosophy, Religion - Other, Self-Help
ISBN Prefix(es): 3-89201
Total Titles: 68 Print
Branch Office(s)
Universal Life, The Inner Religion, PO Box 651, Gilford, CT 06437, United States *Fax:* 203-457-9693 *Web Site:* www.universal-life.com

WRS Verlag Wirtschaft, Recht und Steuern GmbH & Co KG
Subsidiary of Rudolf Haufe Verlag GmbH & Co KG
Fraunhoferstr 5, 82152 Planegg
Mailing Address: Postfach 1363, 82142 Planegg
Tel: (089) 89 517-0 *Fax:* (089) 89 517-250
E-mail: info@wrs.de
Web Site: www.wrs.de *Cable:* WRS VERLAG
Key Personnel
Dir: Martin Laqua; Helmuth Hopfner; Mueller Uwe Renald
Founded: 1973
Subjects: Accounting, Advertising, Business, Computer Science, Economics, House & Home, Law, Management, Marketing, Nonfiction (General)
ISBN Prefix(es): 3-8092
Subsidiaries: STS Standard Tabellen-und Software Verlag

Das Wunderhorn Verlag GmbH
Bergstr 21, 69120 Heidelberg
Tel: (06221) 402428 *Fax:* (06221) 402483
E-mail: info@wunderhorn.de
Web Site: www.wunderhorn.de
Key Personnel
Publisher: Manfred Metzner *E-mail:* metzner@wunderhorn.de
Founded: 1978
Subjects: Art, Biography, Fiction, Film, Video, History, Literature, Literary Criticism, Essays, Poetry, Science (General), Women's Studies
ISBN Prefix(es): 3-88423
Number of titles published annually: 16 Print
Total Titles: 230 Print
Distributed by Rudi Deuble; Leitner Verlagsvertretungen (Austria); Prolit Buchvertrieb GmbH (Austria & Germany); Scheidegger & Co AG

Wunderlich Verlag, *imprint of* Rowohlt Verlag GmbH

Wunderlich Verlag+
Hamburgerstr 17, 21453 Reinbek
Tel: (040) 72 72 0 *Fax:* (040) 72 72 319
E-mail: info@rowohlt.de
Web Site: www.rowohlt.de
Key Personnel
Man Dir: Helmut Daehne; Alexander Fest; Lutz Kettmann
Contact: Eckhard Kloos
Rights & Permissions: Kristina Krombholz
Subjects: Biography, Fiction, History, Nonfiction (General)
Parent Company: Rowohlt Verlag GmbH

Fachbuchverlag Armin W Wuth+
Ahornstr 26a, 44534 Luenen
Tel: (02306) 205247 *Fax:* (02306) 55686
Key Personnel
President, Rights & Permissions: Armin W Wuth
Vice President: Susanne L Schenk-Wuth
Founded: 1982
Specializes in Stock Exchange.
Subjects: Business, Computer Science, Economics, Medicine, Nursing, Dentistry
ISBN Prefix(es): 3-924018; 3-87082
Parent Company: Wuth-Verlag, Luenen
Subsidiaries: Wuth-Publishing

X-Games, *imprint of* Pearson Education Deutschland GmbH

Xenos Verlagsgesellschaft mbH (Xenos Publishing)+
Affiliate of Lies & Spiel Publishing Co
Am Hehsel 40, 22339 Hamburg
Tel: (040) 538093-0 *Fax:* (040) 5386000
E-mail: xenos.verlag@t-online.de
Web Site: www.xenosverlag.de
Key Personnel
Man Dir: Bjoern Heimberger *Tel:* (040) 53809329; Erwin Heimberger *Tel:* (040) 53809320
Sales, Germany: Wolfgang Steigner

Sales Manager, Germany: Oliver Draeger
   Tel: (040) 53809344
Production: Meino Dorbandt *Tel:* (040) 53809340
   Fax: (040) 5387863
Founded: 1975
Children's Book Publishers. Specialize in wall charts, colony & activity books, atlases.
Also acts as book packager.
Membership(s): Borsenverein Chamber of Commerce.
Subjects: Nonfiction (General)
ISBN Prefix(es): 3-8212; 3-933697; 3-935746
Number of titles published annually: 180 Print
Parent Company: Frankfurter Allgemeine Zeitung, Hellerhofstr 2-4, Frankfurt am Main
Imprints: Edition Riesenrad; Merit; Tipp Creative
Subsidiaries: Lies & Spiel Hausparty GmbH
Shipping Address: Spedition Rapid, Wilhelm-Iwan-Ring 5, 21035 Hamburg *Tel:* (040) 734130
Warehouse: PVS Fulfillment Service, Werner-Hassstr 5, 74172 Neckarsulm, Contact: Mr Jurgens *Tel:* (07132) 9690 *Fax:* (07132) 969170
Distribution Center: PVS Fulfillment, Werner-Haas-Str 5, 74172 Neckarsulm *Tel:* (07132) 969166 *Fax:* (07132) 969170

Verlag Philipp von Zabern
Philipp-von-Zabern Platz 1-3, 55116 Mainz
Tel: (06131) 28747-0 *Fax:* (06131) 28747-44
E-mail: zabern@zabern.de
Web Site: www.zabern.de
Key Personnel
Man Dir: Dr Annette Nuennerich Asmus
Management: Felix Frohn-Bernau
Sales: Christine Vorhoelzer *Tel:* (089) 121516-61; (089) 121516-26 *Fax:* (089) 12151616 *E-mail:* vertrieb@verlagvonzabern.de
Advertising: Ms Manuela Dressen *Tel:* (06131) 28747 11 *E-mail:* m.dressen@zabern.de
Founded: 1802
Subjects: Archaeology, Art, History, Regional Interests
ISBN Prefix(es): 3-8053
Number of titles published annually: 100 Print
Orders to: PO Box 190930, 80689 Munich, Sales: Christine Vorhoelzer *Tel:* (089) 121516-61; (089) 121516-26 *Fax:* (089) 121516-16 *E-mail:* vertrieb@verlagvonzabern.de

Zambon Verlag+
Leipziger Str 24, 60487 Frankfurt am Main
Tel: (069) 779223 *Fax:* (069) 773054
E-mail: zambon@online.de
Web Site: www.zambonverlag.de
Key Personnel
Publisher: Dr Giuseppe Zambon
Founded: 1974
Subjects: Cookery, Developing Countries, Government, Political Science, History, Poetry, Regional Interests, Travel
ISBN Prefix(es): 3-88975
Bookshop(s): Internationale Buchhandlung, Kaiserstr 55, 60329 Frankfurt *Fax:* (069) 23 02 77

Zebulon Verlag GmbH & Co KG+
Wormserstr 37, 50677 Cologne
Mailing Address: Postfach 250 369, 50519 Cologne
Tel: (0221) 3405620 *Fax:* (0221) 3405622
E-mail: zebulon-koeln@t-online.de
Key Personnel
Man Dir & Publishing Dir: Hajo Leib
Founded: 1992
Subjects: Criminology, Environmental Studies, Government, Political Science, Health, Nutrition, Nonfiction (General), Women's Studies
ISBN Prefix(es): 3-928679
Warehouse: Prolit Verlagsauslifrung GmbH, Siemensstr 16, 35463 Fernwald (Annerod)

Zeitgeist Media GmbH+
Duesseldorfer Str 60, 40545 Duesseldorf
Tel: (0211) 55 62 55 *Fax:* (0211) 57 51 67
E-mail: info@zeitgeistmedia.de
Web Site: www.zeitgeistverlag.de
Key Personnel
Man Dir, Rights & Permissions: Hubert Buecken *E-mail:* hb@zeitgeistmedia.de
Founded: 1989
Subjects: Human Relations, Humor, Outdoor Recreation, Travel
ISBN Prefix(es): 3-926224; 3-934046

Verlag Zeitschrift fur Naturforschung
Uhlandstr 11, 72072 Tuebingen
Mailing Address: Postfach 2645, 72016 Tuebingen
Tel: (07071) 31555 *Fax:* (07071) 360571
E-mail: mail@znaturforsch.com
Web Site: www.znaturforsch.com
Key Personnel
Man Dir: Tamina Greifeld *Tel:* (089) 3541485 *E-mail:* greifeld@znaturforsch.com
Founded: 1946
Publish scientific periodicals.
Subjects: Biological Sciences, Chemistry, Chemical Engineering, Physical Sciences
Total Titles: 3 Print; 3 Online
Branch Office(s)
Beuthenerstr 17, 55131 Mainz *Tel:* (06131) 573276 *Fax:* (06131) 571061

Verlag Clemens Zerling+
Goethestr 9, 83435 Bad Reichenhall
Tel: (08651) 602295 *Fax:* (08651) 602295
Key Personnel
Man Dir, Editorial: Clemens Zerling
Sales: Daniela Moeser
Founded: 1979
Subjects: Anthropology, Astrology, Occult, Biography, History, Religion - Other
ISBN Prefix(es): 3-88468
Associate Companies: Edition Weber, Berlin

Zettner Verlag GmbH & Co KG+
Hofweg 12, 97209 Veitshoechheim
Tel: (0931) 91970 *Fax:* (0931) 960 097
E-mail: info@zettnerverlag.com
Web Site: www.zettnerverlag.com
Founded: 1955
Subjects: Art, Erotica, Fiction, Science (General)
ISBN Prefix(es): 3-87931
Number of titles published annually: 30 Print
Total Titles: 500 Print

ZfKf-Zentrum fur Kulturforschung, see ARCult Media

Verlag im Ziegelhaus Ulrich Gohl+
Pflasteraeckerstr 20, 70186 Stuttgart
Tel: (0711) 46 63 63 *Fax:* (0711) 46 13 41
E-mail: gohl@n.zgs.de
Key Personnel
Owner: Ulrich Gohl
Founded: 1984
Subjects: History
ISBN Prefix(es): 3-925440
Number of titles published annually: 3 Print

Ziethen-Panorama Verlag GmbH+
Flurweg 15, 53902 Bad Muensterzfel
Tel: (02253) 6047 *Fax:* (02253) 6756
E-mail: annette@ziethen-panoramaverlag.de
Web Site: www.ziethen-panoramaverlag.de
Key Personnel
Owner: Horst Ziethen
Bookkeeping: Karin Gallmann *Tel:* (02236) 3989-15 *Fax:* (02236)3989-39
Founded: 1992
Subjects: Foreign Countries, Regional Interests, Travel
ISBN Prefix(es): 3-921268; 3-929932; 3-934328
Parent Company: Ziethen Farbdruckmedien GmbH
Warehouse: Ziethen-Panorama Verlag GmbH, Unter Buschweg 17, 50999 Cologne

Zodiaque, *imprint of* Verlag Schnell und Steiner GmbH

ZS Verlag Zabert Sandmann GmbH+
Barerstr 9, 80333 Munich
Tel: (089) 548 25 '15-0 *Fax:* (089) 550 18 19
E-mail: contact@zsverlag.de
Web Site: www.zsverlag.de
Telex: 114 Jekret
Key Personnel
Man Dir: Friedrich-Karl Sandmann
Licensing Manager: Dr Katrin Bernhard
Editorial Manager: Kathrin Ullerich
Press: Claudia Limmer
Production: Karin Mayer
Founded: 1983
Subjects: Cookery, Health, Nutrition, Wine & Spirits
ISBN Prefix(es): 3-924678; 3-932023; 3-89883
Associate Companies: Verlag Elisabeth Sandmann
Warehouse: Schleissheimerstr 106, 85748 Garching-Hochbrueck
Orders to: Schleissheimerstr 106, 85748 Garching-Hochbrueck

Zsolnay, *imprint of* Carl Hanser Verlag

Zweipunkt Verlag K Kaiser KG+
Gestuet Rossbacher Hof, 64711 Erbach
Tel: (06062) 61108 *Fax:* (06062) 63422
Key Personnel
Partner, Rights & Permissions: Kurt Kaiser
Subjects: Crafts, Games, Hobbies
ISBN Prefix(es): 3-88168

Ghana

General Information

Capital: Accra
Language: English
Religion: About 42% Christian, remainder follow traditional beliefs
Population: 16.2 million
Bank Hours: 0830-1400 Monday-Thursday; 0830-1500 Friday
Shop Hours: 0830-1230, 1330-1730 Monday, Tuesday, Thursday, Friday; 0830-1330 Wednesday & Saturday
Currency: 100 pesawas = 1 new cedi
Export/Import Information: No tariffs on books; advertising matter over 1 kg gross weight 50%. Import license required, but single copies of books under Open General License. Levy charged on import lecenses required. Credit terms not permitted.
Copyright: UCC, Berne, Florence (see Copyright Conventions, pg xi)

Adaex Educational Publications Ltd+
2R MacCarthy Hill, Accra
Tel: (024) 367145
E-mail: epublication@yahoo.com
Key Personnel
Publisher: Asare Konadu Yamoah *E-mail:* asareyamoah@onebox.com
Founded: 1995
Membership(s): Ghana Book Publishers Association
Also acts as printer, book & literary agent.
Subjects: Cookery, Fiction, Health, Nutrition, History, How-to
ISBN Prefix(es): 9988-573

Number of titles published annually: 5 Print
Total Titles: 37 Print

The Advent Press+
PO Box 0102, Osu, Accra
Tel: (021) 777861; (021) 775327 *Fax:* (021) 774338; (021) 2119
Telex: 2119 *Cable:* ADVENT GH
Key Personnel
General Manager: E C Tetteh
Founded: 1937
Subjects: Religion - Other
ISBN Prefix(es): 9964-962

Adwinsa Publications (Ghana) Ltd+
PO Box M 18, Accra
Tel: (021) 221654; (021) 21577
Key Personnel
Man Dir, Rights & Permissions: Kwabena Amponsah
General Manager & Production: Kofi Kyere-Amponsah
Accountant & Sales: Kwadwo Oppong-Kyeremeh
Editorial & Personnel: Grace Amponsah
Founded: 1977
Membership(s): Ghana Book Publishers Association.
ISBN Prefix(es): 9964-955; 9964-975
Branch Office(s)
Adwinsa Bookstand (Eredec Hotel), PO Box 845, Koforidua
Bookshop(s): Adwinsa Distribution Agency Ltd, Adwinsa House (North Legon), PO Box 92, Legon
Orders to: Adwinsa Distribution Agency Ltd, PO Box M18, Accra

Afram Publications, *imprint of* Afram Publications (Ghana) Ltd

Afram Publications (Ghana) Ltd+
C 184/22 Midway Lane, Abofu, Achimota, Accra
Mailing Address: PO Box M18, Accra
Tel: (021) 412561; (021) 406060
E-mail: aframpub@punchgh.com *Cable:* AFRAMBOOKS
Key Personnel
Man Dir, Rights & Permissions: Eric Ofei
  E-mail: ericofei@yahoo.co.uk
Editorial Manager: Mr E C Tetteh
Founded: 1974
Membership(s): Ghana Book Publishers Association; Afro-Asian Book Council.
Subjects: Fiction, Nonfiction (General)
ISBN Prefix(es): 9964-70
Imprints: Afram Publications
Distributed by African Books Collective

Africa Christian Press+
PO Box 30, Achimota
Tel: (021) 244147; (021) 244148 *Fax:* (021) 220271; (021) 668115
E-mail: acpbooks@ghana.com
Key Personnel
General Manager: Richard Crabbe
Deputy General Manager: Mork Eiwuley
Founded: 1964
Specialize in Christian literature & children's books.
Membership(s): Ghana Publishers Association.
Subjects: Biography, Fiction, Nonfiction (General), Religion - Other
ISBN Prefix(es): 9964-87
Number of titles published annually: 12 Print
Total Titles: 110 Print
Imprints: Children's Activity Series; Student's Series
Branch Office(s)
50 Loxwood Ave, Worthing, Sussex BN14 7RA, United Kingdom
U.S. Office(s): 130 N Bloomingdale Rd, Suite 101, Bloomingdale, IL 60108, United States

Anowuo Educational Publications+
PO Box 3918, Accra
Tel: (021) 669961 *Cable:* ANOWUO PUBS, ACCRA
Key Personnel
Publisher: S A Konadu
Sales Manager: Yamoah Konadu
Founded: 1966
Also acts as copyright broker.
Membership(s): Ghana Publishers Association.
Subjects: Fiction, History, How-to, Poetry, Regional Interests, Science (General)
ISBN Prefix(es): 9964-79
Branch Office(s)
PO Box 1, Asamang Ashanti Region
Showroom(s): 2R McCarthy Hill, PO Box 3918, Accra

Asempa Publishers+
PO Box 919, Accra
Tel: (021) 221706
E-mail: asempa@ghana.com
Key Personnel
General Manager: Rev Emmanuel Borlabi Bortey
Production: Sarah Apronti
Finance: Stephen K Darku
International Rights: E B Bortey; S Apronti
Founded: 1970
Membership(s): Ghana Book Publishers Association.
Subjects: Biblical Studies, Biography, Fiction, Music, Dance, Nonfiction (General), Poetry, Religion - Protestant, Religion - Other, Social Sciences, Sociology, Theology
ISBN Prefix(es): 9964-78; 9964-91
Number of titles published annually: 20 Print
Total Titles: 112 Print
Parent Company: Christian Council of Ghana
Imprints: IBRA (Ghana)

Beginners Publishers+
Box CT 785, Cantonments, Accra
Tel: (021) 503040 *Fax:* (051) 772642 Attn: Beginners Publishers
Telex: 3047 Attn: Beginners Publishers
Key Personnel
President & Editor: Nana Opoku Ankama-Fofie
Publisher & Author: Akosua Gyamfuaa-Fofie
Vice President: Kwabena Owusu-Peprah
Founded: 1988
Subjects: English as a Second Language, Fiction, Language Arts, Linguistics, Mathematics, Romance
ISBN Prefix(es): 9964-90; 9964-995
Associate Companies: Hope & Faith Agencies, Box C 1096, Cantonments, Accra
Branch Office(s)
Cape Coast
Sunyani
Tamale
Tema
Distributed by Makna Publications
Distributor for Makna Publications; Speedy Variety Publications
Showroom(s): House No 020, North Suntresu, Kumasi; House No Wab-34 TI; New Ashaley Botwe, Madina, Accra
Bookshop(s): Adwen Pa, Madina, Winners & Nsempii-Kumasi; Afram, Box N18, Accra; Catholic Bookshop, Kumasi; Dorilad Bookshop, Abeka, Accra; Gyawu Bookshop, Tamale; Legon Bookshop, Box 1, Legon, Accra; Makna, Box 9820 Airport, Accra; Methodist Bookshops, Accra, Kumasi, Cape-Coast; Obrapa Bookshop, Tema; Omari Bookshop, Labone, Accra; Presbyterian Bookshops, Accra, Kumasi, Cape-Coast, Swedru; Speedy Variety Agencies Ltd, Box 5337, Accra; Topman Book Center, Accra
Warehouse: Box BP 313, Bohyen-Kumasi

Black Mask Ltd+
PO Box 252, Fante New Town, Kumasi
Tel: (021) 500178 *Fax:* (021) 667701
E-mail: balme@ug.gn.apc.org *Cable:* BML
Key Personnel
Man Dir: Yaw Owusu Asante
Publicity: Kwasi Asante
Rights & Permissions: Opia-Mensah Kumah
Founded: 1979
Subjects: Cookery, Drama, Theater, Economics, Education, Social Sciences, Sociology
ISBN Prefix(es): 9964-960

BP, see Beginners Publishers

BRRI, see Building & Road Research Institute (BRRI)

Building & Road Research Institute (BRRI)
University of Science & Technology, PO Box 40, Kumasi
Tel: (051) 60064; (051) 60065 *Fax:* (051) 60080
E-mail: brri@ghana.com
Web Site: www.csir.org.gh/brri.html
Key Personnel
Dir: Dr K Amoah-Mensah
Founded: 1952
Subjects: Architecture & Interior Design, Civil Engineering, Computer Science, Earth Sciences, Real Estate, Technology, Transportation
ISBN Prefix(es): 9964-86; 9964-977
Parent Company: Council for Scientific & Industrial Research (CSIR)

Bureau of Ghana Languages
PO Box 1851, Accra
Tel: (021) 665461; (021) 65194
Key Personnel
Dir, Rights & Permissions: J N Nanor
Sales Manager: J C Abbey
Founded: 1951
Also acts as a translation agency/association.
Subjects: Biography, Drama, Theater, Fiction, Poetry, Science (General)
ISBN Prefix(es): 9964-2
Branch Office(s)
PO Box 177, Tamale, Northern Region

Children's Activity Series, *imprint of* Africa Christian Press

Educational Press & Manufacturers Ltd+
PO Box 4434, Kumasi
Tel: (051) 5003; (051) 5845 *Fax:* (051) 227572
Web Site: www.diana.com.mx
Telex: 2236 gh
Key Personnel
International Rights: George Koduah
Founded: 1979
Subjects: Fiction
ISBN Prefix(es): 9964-89
Subsidiaries: Knowledge Publishing & Trading Ltd
Branch Office(s)
PO Box 5381, Accra-North

Educational Publishers Ltd
PO Box 9184, Accra-Airport
Tel: (021) 220395 *Fax:* (021) 227572
Telex: 2236GH *Cable:* EDU PRESS
ISBN Prefix(es): 9964-953
Parent Company: Halko Book & Educational Assories Ltd

Ekab Business Ltd+
PO Box 6262, Accra-North
Tel: (021) 225318 *Cable:* Emmapus Accra
Key Personnel
Dir: Emmanuel K Nsiah
Founded: 1978

Company has reprint arrangements in Ghana for Oxford University Press publications.
Subjects: Education
ISBN Prefix(es): 9964-91; 9964-73
Bookshop(s): Mayan Book Centre, PO Box 6173, Accra

EPP Books Services+
PMB TUC Post Office, La Education Centre Bldg, Behind Ghana Trade Fair Centre, La, Accra
Mailing Address: PO Box TF 490, Accra
Tel: (021) 778853; (021) 778347 Fax: (021) 779099
E-mail: info@eppbooks.com
Web Site: www.eppbooks.com
Key Personnel
Executive Dir: Gibrine Adam
Founded: 1991
Also acts as bookseller & stationery distributor.
Subjects: Accounting, Mathematics, Social Sciences, Sociology
ISBN Prefix(es): 9964-997
Associate Companies: Excellent Publishing & Printing; Staples Systems Ghana Ltd
Foreign Rep(s): Epp Books Services (Nigeria)
Foreign Rights: Sterling Publishers Pvt (India)
Bookshop(s): EPP Bookshop, Accra-Nsawam Rd, Achimota-Accra, Mutawakilu Adam Tel: (021) 408885 Fax: (021) 779099 E-mail: epp@africaonline.com.gh Web Site: www.eppbooks.com; EPP Bookshop, PO Box TF 490, La, Accra, Koforidua Tel: (021) 779099 E-mail: epp@africaonline.com.gh Web Site: www.eppbooks.com; EPP Bookshop, Behind Kumasi Polytechnic, Amakom-Kumasi, Kumasi, Constance Nuamah Tel: (051) 23367 Fax: (021) 779099 E-mail: epp@africaonline.com.gh Web Site: www.eppbooks.com

Frank Publishing Ltd+
PO Box M414, Ministry Branch Post Office, Accra
Tel: (021) 240711 Cable: KNOWLEDGE
Key Personnel
Man Dir, Editorial, Production: Francis K Dzokoto
Sales, Public Relations: Moses K Dzokoto
Founded: 1976
Specialize in school textbooks & typesetting for other publishing houses.
Membership(s): Ghana Publishers Association; Ghana Association of Book Editors.
Subjects: Economics, English as a Second Language, Government, Political Science, Religion - Catholic, Religion - Protestant, Religion - Other
ISBN Prefix(es): 9964-959

Ghana Academy of Arts & Sciences+
PO Box M32, Accra
Tel: (021) 777651
E-mail: gaas@ghastinet.gn.apc.org
Key Personnel
President: D A Bekoe
Founded: 1959
Subjects: Art, Literature, Literary Criticism, Essays, Music, Dance, Science (General)
ISBN Prefix(es): 9964-90; 9964-969; 9964-950

Ghana Institute of Linguistics Literacy & Bible Translation (GILLBT)
PO Box 7271, Accra North
Tel: (021) 777525
Founded: 1962
Subjects: Anthropology, Biblical Studies, English as a Second Language, Environmental Studies, Health, Nutrition, Language Arts, Linguistics, Religion - Protestant, Women's Studies
ISBN Prefix(es): 9964-92; 9988-7525

Ghana Publishing Corporation
PO Box 124, Accra
Tel: (021) 664338 Fax: (021) 664330
E-mail: asspcom@africaonline.com.gh
Web Site: www.africaonline.com.gh/assembly
Telex: Publishing Tema
Key Personnel
Man Dir: F K Nyarko
General Manager (Publishing Division): K B Arkorful
Editor-in-Chief: J K Fuachie-Sobreh
Rights & Permissions: Miss O Agbenyega
Sales Manager: W D Opare
Production: Fred Odametey
Publicity: Fidelis D Adzakey
Founded: 1965
Subjects: Biography, Ethnicity, Fiction, History, Language Arts, Linguistics, Nonfiction (General), Poetry, Science (General), Social Sciences, Sociology, Technology
ISBN Prefix(es): 9964-1
Parent Company: Ghana Publishing Corporation, Head Office, PO Box 4348, Accra
Branch Office(s)
Accra
Bolgatanga
Cape Coast
Ho
Hohoe
Koforidua
Sunyani
Swedru
Tamale
Wa
Sales Office(s): PO Box 3632, Accra
Distribution Center: PO Box 3632, Accura

Ghana Standards Board, see GSB (Ghana Standards Board)

Ghana Universities Press (GUP)+
PO Box GP 2419, Accra
Tel: (021) 22532
Telex: Univpress Accra
Key Personnel
Dir: K M Ganu Tel: (020) 8178075 E-mail: balme@libr.ug.edu.gh
Senior Business Manger: J K Bosomtwe
Founded: 1962
Membership(s): Ghana Book Publishers Association, International Association of Scholarly Publishers, African Books Collective
Subjects: Agriculture, Biological Sciences, Communications, Government, Political Science, History, Language Arts, Linguistics, Medicine, Nursing, Dentistry, Social Sciences, Sociology
ISBN Prefix(es): 9964-3
Associate Companies: African Books Collective Ltd, Oxford

GILLBT, see Ghana Institute of Linguistics Literacy & Bible Translation (GILLBT)

Goodbooks Publishing Co+
PO Box 10416, Accra North
Tel: (021) 665629 Fax: (021) 302993
E-mail: allgoodbooks@hotmail.com
Key Personnel
Contact: Alberta Asirifi; Mary Asirifi
Founded: 1992
ISBN Prefix(es): 9964-88
Bookshop(s): D803/4 Granville Ave, Okaishie, Accra

GSB (Ghana Standards Board)
PO Box MB 245, Accra
Tel: (021) 662942; (021) 665461
Telex: 2545 MINCOM Attn GSB
ISBN Prefix(es): 9964-990

IBRA (Ghana), imprint of Asempa Publishers

Kwamfori Publishing Enterprise+
Dansoman-Estates, Accra
Mailing Address: PO Box 1325, Accra
Key Personnel
Proprietor: Ofori Akuamoah
Founded: 1991
Subjects: Economics, English as a Second Language, Humor
ISBN Prefix(es): 9964-987

Manhill Publication+
PO Box 548, Madina, Accra
Tel: (021) 508251 Fax: (021) 669078
Key Personnel
President & Author: Paul N Maanoh
Vice President: Hilda Maanoh
Editor & Author: Asuma Karikari
Author: Ferkah Ahenkorah; George Amable; Chris Darkwaa
Founded: 1986
Also distributes wares for Ghana Bible Society. Dealers in printing materials.
Membership(s): Ghana Bible Society.
Subjects: English as a Second Language, Fiction, Literature, Literary Criticism, Essays
ISBN Prefix(es): 9964-999
Associate Companies: Manhill Enterprise
Branch Office(s)
Kumasi
Sunyani
Distributed by Gospel Tracts Information (USA)
Orders to: Manhill Publications, PO Box 1075, Madina-Accra

Moxon Paperbacks
PO Box M 160, Osu, Accra
Tel: (021) 665397
Key Personnel
Man Dir: James Moxon
Founded: 1967
Subjects: Ethnicity, Fiction, History, Nonfiction (General), Poetry, Travel
ISBN Prefix(es): 9964-954
Branch Office(s)
28 Corve St, Dudlow, Shropshire SY8 IDA, United Kingdom
Bookshop(s): The Atlas Bookshop

Osimpam Educational Books
PO Box 1851, Accra
Key Personnel
Man Editor: Armah Asiedu
Founded: 1991
ISBN Prefix(es): 9964-994

Quick Service Books Ltd+
PO Box 15403, Accra North
Tel: (021) 224236
Key Personnel
Man Dir: Isaac Mensah Dankyi
Editor: D A Addo
Marketing Manager: Kwasi Saka-Dankyi
Founded: 1986
Subjects: Education
ISBN Prefix(es): 9964-90; 9964-970; 9964-985

Sam Woode Ltd+
House No 1, Adole Abla Link, Sahara-Dansoman
Mailing Address: PO Box 12719, Accra North
Tel: (021) 305287 Fax: (021) 310482
E-mail: samwoode@ghana.com Cable: SAM WOODE ACCRA
Key Personnel
Executive Chairman: Kwesi Sam-Woode
Publishing Manager: Pamela Woode
Marketing Manager: Luke Dery
Founded: 1986
Membership(s): Ghana Book Publishers Association.

Subjects: Agriculture, Career Development, English as a Second Language, Mathematics, Physical Sciences, Science (General)
ISBN Prefix(es): 9964-979
Imprints: SWL Books
Distributed by West African Book Publishers Ltd (Nigeria)

Sedco, *imprint of* Sedco Publishing Ltd

Sedco Publishing Ltd+
Sedco House, Labon St, Off Ring Rd Central North Ridge, Accra
Mailing Address: PO Box 2051, Accra
Tel: (021) 221332 *Fax:* (021) 220107
E-mail: sedco@africaonline.com.gh
Telex: 2456
Key Personnel
Man Dir: Courage Kwami Segbawu
Marketing Dir: Frank Segbawu
Founded: 1975
Educational materials for all levels.
Subjects: Agriculture, Biological Sciences, Chemistry, Chemical Engineering, Education, English as a Second Language, Fiction, History, Law, Mathematics, Physics, Science (General)
ISBN Prefix(es): 9964-72
Number of titles published annually: 5 Print
Total Titles: 145 Print
Parent Company: Pearson Plc
Imprints: Sedco

Student's Series, *imprint of* Africa Christian Press

Sub-Saharan Publishers+
PO Box 358, Legon-Accra
Tel: (021) 228398
E-mail: sub-saharan@ighmail.com
Key Personnel
Man Dir: Akoss Ofori-Mensah
Founded: 1992
Membership(s): Ghana Publishers Association.
Subjects: Education, Environmental Studies, African Literature
ISBN Prefix(es): 9988-550
Total Titles: 30 Print
Distributed by African Books Collective
Orders to: Sub-Saharan Publishers, PO Box 1176, Cantonments, Accra

SWL Books, *imprint of* Sam Woode Ltd

Unimax Macmillan Ltd
42 Ring Rd South, Industrial Area, Accra North
Mailing Address: PO Box 10722, Accra North
Tel: (021) 227 443; (021) 223 709 *Fax:* (021) 225 215
E-mail: info@unimacmillan.com
Web Site: www.macmillan-africa.com; www.unimacmillan.com
Key Personnel
Man Dir: Edward Addo
Marketing Manager: Abubakari Wumbei
Founded: 1985
International education division of Macmillan Publishers Ltd.
Subjects: Agriculture, Environmental Studies, Mathematics, Science (General)
ISBN Prefix(es): 9988-553
Parent Company: Macmillan Publishers Ltd
Branch Office(s)
Unicorn House, Prempah 11 St, PO Box KS, 1169 Kumasi, Manager: Edward Udzu *Tel:* (051) 39284; (051) 39286 *Fax:* (051) 39285
Showroom(s): Unicorn House, Prempah 11 St, PO Box KS, 1169 Kumasi, Manager: Edward Udzu *Tel:* (051) 39284; (051) 39286 *Fax:* (051) 39285
Warehouse: Unicorn House, Prempah 11 St, PO Box KS, 1169 Kumasi, Manager: Edward Udzu *Tel:* (051) 39284; (051) 39286 *Fax:* (051) 39285

Waterville Publishing House+
Thorpe Rd, Accra
Mailing Address: PO Box 195, Accra
Tel: (01) 3254591; (01) 3314403 *Fax:* (01) 3314403 *Cable:* BOOKS ACCRA
Key Personnel
Man Dir: H W O Okai
Founded: 1963
Subjects: Biography, Ethnicity, Fiction, History, Nonfiction (General), Poetry, Religion - Other, Science (General), Social Sciences, Sociology
ISBN Prefix(es): 9964-5
Parent Company: Presbyterian Book Depot Ltd
Divisions: Presbyterian Press

Woeli Publishing Services
PO Box K601, Accra-New Town
Tel: (021) 227182; (021) 229294 *Fax:* (021) 777098; (021) 229294
E-mail: woeli@libr.ug.edu.gh; asempa@ghana.com
Key Personnel
Publisher: Mr Woeli Dekutsey
Founded: 1984
Membership(s): the Ghana Book Publishers Association.
Subjects: Drama, Theater, Fiction, Poetry, Women's Studies
ISBN Prefix(es): 9964-90; 9964-970; 9964-978
Total Titles: 6 Print
Orders to: African Books Collective, 27 Park End St, Oxford OX1 1HU, United Kingdom

World Literature Project
PO Box 290, Legon, Accra
Tel: (022) 2119 *Fax:* (022) 2119
Key Personnel
Publisher: Friedolin Ankrama-Afarie
Founded: 1991
Specialize in dissemination of vital information on better health, welfare, new books, literature, etc.
Subjects: Advertising, Biblical Studies, Child Care & Development, Cookery, Developing Countries, Film, Video, Health, Nutrition, How-to, Human Relations, Humor, Marketing, Medicine, Nursing, Dentistry, Mysteries, Outdoor Recreation, Psychology, Psychiatry, Publishing & Book Trade Reference, Religion - Other, Securities, Self-Help, Women's Studies
ISBN Prefix(es): 9964-986

Greece

General Information

Capital: Athens
Language: Greek (official), English, French
Religion: Predominately Greek Orthodox
Population: 10.6 million
Bank Hours: 0800-1400 Monday-Friday
Shop Hours: Vary. Generally 0800-1500 Monday, Wednesday, Saturday; 0800-1400, 1730-2030 Tuesday, Thursday, Friday
Currency: 100 Eurocents = 1 Euro; 340.750 Greek drachmas = 1 Euro
Export/Import Information: Member of the European Economic Community. No tariff on non-Greek books except children's picture books (free from EEC). Foreign-language advertising catalogues & other advertising matter free from EEC. Children's picture books & advertising matter subject to stamp duty, and books & advertising subject to small additional taxes, University Tax & Bank Fee, Contribution for Farmer's Social Assistance. Only books printed in Greek need import license; all advertising matter other than price lists require license. No special exchange controls. 4% VAT on books.
Copyright: UCC, Berne, Florence (see Copyright Conventions, pg xi)

AE Expaideftikon Vivlion Kai Diskon
19 Antinoros, 11634 Athens
Tel: (010) 7239474 *Fax:* (010) 7239483
Key Personnel
President & Man Dir: John Drossos
Founded: 1963
ISBN Prefix(es): 960-7351; 960-7972
Parent Company: Educational Books & Records SA

Akritas+
24 Efesou, 17121 N Smyrni, Athens
Tel: (0210) 9314968; (0210) 9334554 *Fax:* (0210) 9311436
Key Personnel
Contact: Maria Kokkinou
Founded: 1979
Subjects: Art, Child Care & Development, Cookery, History, Human Relations, Psychology, Psychiatry, Religion - Other, Theology
ISBN Prefix(es): 960-7006; 960-328

Alamo Hellas+
6, Sarantaporou St, 111 44 Athens
Tel: (01) 2280027 *Fax:* (01) 2280027
Key Personnel
President: Dr Ath I Delikastopoulos
Subjects: Biblical Studies, Cookery, English as a Second Language, Gardening, Plants, Law, Philosophy, Religion - Catholic, Religion - Islamic, Religion - Jewish, Religion - Protestant, Theology, Travel
Associate Companies: Alpha Delta

Vefa Alexiadou Editions+
4 Leonidou Str, 144 52 Metmorphos, Athens
Tel: (0210) 2848 086 *Fax:* (0210) 2849 689
E-mail: vefaeditions@ath.forthnet.gr
Web Site: www.addgr.com/comp/vefa/index.htm
Key Personnel
Marketing & Sales Dir: Alexia Alexiadou
Founded: 1979
Membership(s): IACP.
Subjects: Cookery
ISBN Prefix(es): 960-85018; 960-8125; 960-90137; 960-91230
Associate Companies: Vefa's House, Alba Editions
Branch Office(s)
16, Nevrokopiou Str, 55226 Thessaloniui
Distributed by Howell Press (USA & Canada); Tower Books (Australia)
Distributor for Sterling Editions (USA)
Bookshop(s): One Kresnas St, 14123 Ly Kovrisi, Athens

Anemonylos, *imprint of* Ilias Kambanas Publishing Organization, SA

Anixis Publications+
23 Viltanioti Str, Kifisia, 145 64 Athens
Tel: (01) 6205436 *Fax:* (01) 8079357
Key Personnel
International Rights: Mr Aristotelis Papadimitriou
E-mail: apapa@hol.gr
Founded: 1993
Subjects: Child Care & Development, Geography, Geology, History
Total Titles: 105 Print

Apostoliki Diakonia tis Ekklisias tis Hellados
One Iassiou St, 115 21 Athens

Tel: (010) 7239417; (010) 7248681-9 *Fax:* (010) 7238149
E-mail: apostoliki-diakonia@ath.forthnet.gr
Web Site: www.apostoliki-diakonia.gr
Key Personnel
Chief Executive: Archim Agathaggelos Charamantidis
Editorial Manager, Rights & Permissions: Evangelos Lekkos
Production: Socrates Mavrogonatos
Founded: 1936
Subjects: Biblical Studies, Film, Video, History, Music, Dance, Religion - Other, Social Sciences, Sociology, Theology
ISBN Prefix(es): 960-315
Bookshop(s): 2 Dragatsaniou St, 10559 Athens *Tel:* (010) 3228637; (010) 3310977 *Fax:* (010) 3228637; 9-A Ethnikis Aminis & Tsimiski Str, 54621 Thessaloniki *Tel:* (0310) 275126 *Fax:* (0310) 278559; 143 Riga Ferreou Str, Filopimenos, Patra *Tel:* (0610) 223 110 *Fax:* (0610) 223 110

Aquarius Ekdotiki Etaireia
39 Valtetsiou, 10681 Athens
Tel: (01) 3842354 *Fax:* (01) 8826060
ISBN Prefix(es): 960-7002

D I Arsenidis Publications
57, Akademias Str, 10679 Athens
Tel: (01) 36-29-538; (01) 36-33923 *Fax:* (01) 36-18-707
Web Site: www.arsenidis.gr
Key Personnel
Man Dir: John Arsenides
Subjects: Biography, History, Philosophy, Social Sciences, Sociology
ISBN Prefix(es): 960-253

Athina, Mary Mavrogiannis+
37 Arachovis, 10681 Athens
Tel: (010) 3821308 *Fax:* (010) 3838228
Key Personnel
Contact: Mary G Mavrogianni
Founded: 1982
Subjects: Biological Sciences, Education, Mathematics, Poetry
ISBN Prefix(es): 960-7319; 960-514; 960-7819
Total Titles: 100 Print
Orders to: Mesologiou 5, 106 81 Athens

Editions Athina-Mavrogianni+
Formerly Mavrogianni Publications
37 Arachovis, 10681 Athens
Tel: (01) 3304628; (01) 3821308 *Fax:* (01) 3838228
Key Personnel
Contact: G Mavrogiannis
Subjects: Education, Language Arts, Linguistics, Mathematics, Physics
ISBN Prefix(es): 960-514; 960-7819
Total Titles: 150 Print

Atlantis M Pechlivanides & Co SA+
23 Leontiou Str & 37 Fr Smit, Neos Kosmos, 117 45 Athens
Tel: (010) 9220071; (010) 9220073 *Fax:* (01) 9025773
Founded: 1927
Subjects: Art, Education, Fiction, Nonfiction (General)
ISBN Prefix(es): 960-07
Bookshop(s): Korai 8, 105 64 Athens *Tel:* (01) 323-1624

Atlas
Tzavella 96, Nafpactos, TK 30 300
Tel: (01) 3627342 *Fax:* (01) 3300257
E-mail: c_poulos@hotmail.com

Axiotelis G+
18 Char Trikaupi, Akadimias, 10679 Athens
Tel: (010) 3610091; (010) 3636264; (010) 3634264 *Fax:* (010) 3610887
Key Personnel
Contact: George Axiotelis
Founded: 1974
Membership(s): European Educational Publishers Group.
Subjects: Education, Government, Political Science
ISBN Prefix(es): 960-7053; 960-7807

Bell Best-Seller, *imprint of* Harlenic Hellas Publishing SA

Bell Literature, *imprint of* Harlenic Hellas Publishing SA

Bergadis
Mavromichali 4, 106 79 Athens
Tel: (01) 3614263
Subjects: History, Social Sciences, Sociology
Branch Office(s)
Doryleou 22, Athens *Tel:* (01) 3614263

Beta Medical Publishers+
3 Adrianiou St, Athens 115 25
Tel: (010) 6714340; (010) 6714371 *Fax:* (010) 6715015
E-mail: betamedarts@hol.gr
Web Site: www.betamedarts.gr
Key Personnel
General Manager: Anastasia Vassilakou
Founded: 1976
Subjects: Medicine, Nursing, Dentistry, Veterinary Science
ISBN Prefix(es): 960-7308; 960-8071
Total Titles: 106 Print

Blaze, *imprint of* Harlenic Hellas Publishing SA

Boukoumanis' Editions+
One Mavromichalistr, 10679 Athens
Tel: (01) 3618502; (01) 3637436 *Fax:* (01) 3630669
E-mail: info@boukoumanis.gr
Web Site: www.boukoumanis.gr *Cable:* 214422 RC GR
Key Personnel
Man Dir: Elias Boukoumanis
Rights & Permissions: Mrs Trisevgeni Vourgarides
Founded: 1968
Subjects: Education, Environmental Studies, Government, Political Science, History, Philosophy, Psychology, Psychiatry, Social Sciences, Sociology
ISBN Prefix(es): 960-7458

Chrysi Penna - Golden Pen Books+
16, Zoodohou Pigis Str, 10681 Athens
Tel: (01) 03805672 *Fax:* (01) 03825205
E-mail: xpenna@acci.gr; info@chrissipenna.com
Web Site: www.chrissipenna.com
Key Personnel
Man Dir: Anne Hood; K Papachrysanthou
Founded: 1964
Specializes in cookbooks & paperback books.
Subjects: Animals, Pets, Astrology, Occult, Child Care & Development, Cookery, Education, Fiction, Health, Nutrition, Nonfiction (General), Technology
ISBN Prefix(es): 960-245
Number of titles published annually: 18 Print
Total Titles: 120 Print
Warehouse: H Trikoupi Str 157, 11472 Athens

Chryssos Typos AE Ekodeis
7 Z Pigis St, 10678 Athens

Tel: (01) 3637945 *Fax:* (01) 3824417
Subjects: Art, History, Medicine, Nursing, Dentistry, Photography, Science (General)

Diachronikes Ekdoseis+
77 Vas Sofias, 11521 Athens
Tel: (01) 7213225 *Fax:* (01) 7246180
Key Personnel
President: Costas Sioras
ISBN Prefix(es): 960-85630
Parent Company: ASCENT Ltd - Public Relations-Publications, Athens

Diavlos+
10 Valtetsiou St, 106 80 Athens
Tel: (0210) 3631169 *Fax:* (0210) 3617473
E-mail: info@diavlos-books.gr
Web Site: www.diavlos-books.gr
Key Personnel
Man Dir: Emmanuel Deligiannakis
Founded: 1988
Subjects: Astronomy, Computer Science, How-to, Humor, Mathematics, Nonfiction (General), Physical Sciences, Physics, Science (General), Science Fiction, Fantasy
ISBN Prefix(es): 960-7140; 960-531
Bookshop(s): 5 Pezmazoglou St, Athens 10564, Contact: Mr D Gongos *Tel:* (01) 3312413

Difros Publications
57 Akadimias St, 10679 Athens
Tel: (01) 3610811
Subjects: Literature, Literary Criticism, Essays
ISBN Prefix(es): 960-314

Dioptra Publishing
9 Zalongou str, 10678 Athens
Tel: (01) 33 02 828 *Fax:* (01) 3302882
E-mail: info@dioptra.gov
Web Site: www.dioptra.gr
Key Personnel
Manager: George Papadopoulos *E-mail:* george@dioptra.gr
Rights Manager: Costas Papadopoulos *E-mail:* costas@dioptra.gr
Sales Manager: Helen Papadopoulos *E-mail:* helen@dioptra.gr
Founded: 1985
Specialize in alternative therapies, metaphysics & esotericism.
Subjects: Literature, Literary Criticism, Essays, Psychology, Psychiatry
ISBN Prefix(es): 960-364
Total Titles: 100 Print
Distribution Center: 27 Zoodochou Str, 10681 Athens *Tel:* (01) 38 05 228 *Fax:* (01) 33 00 439 *E-mail:* sales@dioptra.gr

Dodoni Publications
Asklipiou 3, 106 79 Athens
Tel: (01) 36 37 067 *Fax:* (01) 36 30 312
Subjects: Fiction, History, Nonfiction (General)
ISBN Prefix(es): 960-248

Ekdoseis Domi AE+
Ippokratous 67, Arachovis, 10680 Athens
Tel: (01) 3637389; (01) 3672056 *Fax:* (01) 3601782
Key Personnel
President: Elias Maniateas
Marketing Manager: George Dimitropoulos
International Rights: Aris Petropoulos
Subjects: Cookery, Geography, Geology
ISBN Prefix(es): 960-8177

Dorikos Publishing House+
9 Charalampi Sotiriou, 11472 Athens
Tel: (010) 6854726 *Fax:* (01) 3301866
Key Personnel
Man Dir, Rights & Permissions: Aristides Klados
Editor: Roussos Vranas
Founded: 1958

Subjects: Biography, Crafts, Games, Hobbies, Drama, Theater, Fiction, Government, Political Science, History, Literature, Literary Criticism, Essays, Philosophy, Poetry, Psychology, Psychiatry
ISBN Prefix(es): 960-279
Associate Companies: Aposperitis Editions, Eressou 9, 106 80 Athens *Tel:* (01) 3604161

Ecole francaise d'Athenes+
Didotou 6, 10680 Athens
Tel: (010) 36 79 900 *Fax:* (010) 36 32 101
E-mail: efa@efa.gr
Web Site: www.efa.gr *Cable:* ECOFRANCE
Key Personnel
Man Dir, Editorial: Dominique Mulliez
Publications: Gilles Touchais *Tel:* (01) 36 79 921
 E-mail: gilles.touchais@efa.gr
Founded: 1846
Subjects: Archaeology, Architecture & Interior Design, Art, History, Social Sciences, Sociology, Ancient History, Ancient Religions, Greek Archaeology & History, Mythology, Sculpture, Town Planning
ISBN Prefix(es): 2-86958
Number of titles published annually: 6 Print
Total Titles: 200 Print; 2 CD-ROM
Distributed by De Boccard Edition-Diffusion
Orders to: Diffusion de Boccard, 11 rue de Medicis, 75006 Paris, France, Contact: Mr J B Chaulet *Tel:* (01) 43260037 *Fax:* (01) 43548583 *E-mail:* deboccard@deboccard.com
Web Site: www.deboccard.com

Ekdoseis Kazantzaki (Kazantzakis Publications)+
116 Charilaou Trikoupi, 11472 Athens
Tel: (01) 3642829 *Fax:* (01) 3642829
Key Personnel
Owner & Editor: Mr Patroklos Stavrou
Publish only works by Nickos Kazantzakis & his wife Helen.
Subjects: Drama, Theater, Fiction, Literature, Literary Criticism, Essays, Philosophy, Poetry, Travel
ISBN Prefix(es): 960-7948

Ekdoseis Thetili
Formerly Thetili Publications
6 Emm Benaki, 10564 Athens
Tel: (010) 3215229; (010) 7212226
Founded: 1983
Subjects: History, Psychology, Psychiatry, Women's Studies, Drugs
ISBN Prefix(es): 960-85198

Ekdotike Athenon SA+
34 Akadimias, 10672 Athens
Tel: (010) 360-8911 *Fax:* (010) 3606157
Key Personnel
President: George A Christopoulos
Man Dir: John C Bastias
Founded: 1961
Specialize in books on Greek history & culture.
Subjects: Archaeology, Art, History, Travel
ISBN Prefix(es): 960-213
Associate Companies: Ekdotike Hellados SA, Philadelphias 8, Athens (Printer)

Ekdotikos Oikos Adelfon Kyriakidi A E+
5K Melenikou, 54635 Thessaloniki
Tel: (02310) 208540 *Fax:* (02310) 245541
E-mail: johnkyr@the.forthnet.gr
Key Personnel
President: Dimitrios Kyriakidis
Vice President: Anastasios Kyriakidis
Founded: 1970
Subjects: Accounting, Chemistry, Chemical Engineering, Economics, History, Mathematics, Theology
ISBN Prefix(es): 960-343

Eleftheroudakis, GCSA International Bookstore
37 Panepistimiou, 10563 Athens
Tel: (010) 3229388 *Fax:* (01) 325 48 89
E-mail: elebooks@netor.gr
Key Personnel
Man Dir: Virginia Eleftheroudakis-Gregos
Founded: 1915
Subjects: Fiction
ISBN Prefix(es): 960-200

Elliniki Leschi Tou Vivliou
3, A Tsocha St, 115 21 Athens
Tel: (01) 6463888 *Fax:* (01) 6463263
E-mail: elli@gezmanosnet.gz
Subjects: Fiction, History, Human Relations, Nonfiction (General), Philosophy, Poetry, Romance, Science Fiction, Fantasy

Epikerotita+
60 Mavromihali Str, 10680 Athens
Tel: (01) 3636083
Key Personnel
Contact: Michalis Mpakirtzis
Founded: 1980
Subjects: Computer Science
ISBN Prefix(es): 960-205

Etaireia Spoudon Neoellinikou Politismou Kai Genikis Paideias (The Moraitis Foundation for Literary & Cultural Studies)+
A Papanastasiou & A Dimitriou St, 15452 Athens
Tel: (01) 06795 000 *Fax:* (01) 06795 090
E-mail: admin@moraitis.edu.gr
Web Site: www.moraitis.edu.gr
Key Personnel
President: Prof N Hourmouziadis
Founded: 1972
Subjects: Drama, Theater, Education, History, Literature, Literary Criticism, Essays, Poetry, Social Sciences, Sociology
ISBN Prefix(es): 960-259

Eurotyp, *imprint of* Stochastis

Evrodiastasi
49 Kallifrona St, 11364 Athens
Tel: (01) 8611303
Founded: 1992
Folios with collection of engravings & texts. Ideal for libraries, museums, universities, schools & collections.
Subjects: Archaeology, Art, History, Travel
ISBN Prefix(es): 960-85724; 960-86262

Exandas Publishers
Didotou, 57, 10681 Athens
Tel: (01) 3822064; (01) 3084885 *Fax:* (01) 3813065
E-mail: exandas@otenet.gr
Web Site: www.exandasbooks.gr
Key Personnel
President: Magda N Kotzia
Vice President: Lena Philippou
Editor: Manuela Berki; Alexander Panoussis
Founded: 1975
Subjects: Art, Cookery, Economics, Environmental Studies, Erotica, Fiction, Government, Political Science, History, Literature, Literary Criticism, Essays, Mysteries, Psychology, Psychiatry, Public Administration, Romance, Science Fiction, Fantasy, Social Sciences, Sociology, Fairy Tales, Horror
ISBN Prefix(es): 960-256

F & D Stephanides OE, see Sigma

Ekdoseis Filon (Friends' Publications)
10 Panepistimiou St, 10671 Athens
Tel: (01) 3618705 *Fax:* (01) 3618705
Key Personnel
Publisher: Antonios Tsakiris; Kostas Tsiropoulos
Founded: 1961
Subjects: Literature, Literary Criticism, Essays, Philosophy, Poetry
ISBN Prefix(es): 960-289 (Filon); 960-8150 (Eythini Publications)
Number of titles published annually: 20 Print
Total Titles: 915 Print
Parent Company: Eythini

Forma Edkotiki E P E+
One Klimenis, L Ionias, 10445 Athens
Tel: (01) 8327008 *Fax:* (01) 8325650
Key Personnel
President: Peter Cottis
Vice President: Themis Sfaellos
Editor: Aristidis Liakouras; Zaphiria Cotti MSc
Founded: 1980
Membership(s): Cooperative of Greek Publishers.
Subjects: Architecture & Interior Design, Economics, History, Literature, Literary Criticism, Essays, Poetry
ISBN Prefix(es): 960-271

Gartaganis D
3 Kon Melenikou, 54006 Thessaloniki
Tel: (02310) 209680
Founded: 1934
Subjects: Agriculture, Veterinary Science, Food Technology
ISBN Prefix(es): 960-7013

Giourdas Moschos+
4 Sergiou Patriarchou St, 114 72 Athens
Tel: (01) 3624947
E-mail: mgiurdas@acci.gr
Web Site: www.mgiurdas.gr
Key Personnel
Foreign Rights & Sales Manager: Panagiotis Assonitis *E-mail:* notisass@hotmail.com
Founded: 1967
Translations from USA & German titles
Self ruling publishing company.
Subjects: Architecture & Interior Design, Computer Science, Engineering (General)
ISBN Prefix(es): 960-512
Total Titles: 500 Print; 18 Online; 25 E-Book

Giovanis Publications, Pangosmios Ekdotikos Organismos
Zoodohou Pigis 7, 10678 Athens
Tel: (01) 3825798; (01) 3301511 *Fax:* (01) 3824417
E-mail: giovani1@otenet.gr
Web Site: www.geocities.com/giovanis_pub/en_main1.htm
Subjects: Geography, Geology, History, Medicine, Nursing, Dentistry, Photography, Religion - Other, Science (General)

Govostis Publishing SA+
21 Zoodohou Pigis, 106 81 Athens
Tel: (010) 3816661
Key Personnel
President: Costas Govostis *E-mail:* cotsos@gorostis.gr
Founded: 1926
Subjects: Art, Astrology, Occult, Biography, Child Care & Development, Computer Science, Drama, Theater, Fiction, Government, Political Science, History, Nonfiction (General), Physics, Poetry
ISBN Prefix(es): 960-270
Warehouse: 58-60 Laskareos, 114 72 Athens

Gutenberg Dardanos, see Gutenberg Publications

Gutenberg Publications+
37 Didotou, 10680 Athens

Tel: (01) 3642003; (01) 3641979; (01) 3641996
Fax: (01) 3642030; (01) 3611384
E-mail: gut_ub@otenet.gr
Key Personnel
Man Dir, Editorial & Sales in Bookshops: George Dardanos
Production: Christos Stavropoulos
Retail Sales: Karakatsanis Haralambos
Founded: 1963
Specialize in books for education at all degrees.
Membership(s): POEV, SEVA, PFPB.
Subjects: Art, Economics, Education, Government, Political Science, History, Literature, Literary Criticism, Essays, Philosophy, Psychology, Psychiatry, Social Sciences, Sociology
ISBN Prefix(es): 960-01
Associate Companies: Spoudi; Typothito
Distributor for Litera
Bookshop(s): Solonos 103, 106 79 Athens

Harlenic Hellas Publishing SA+
57 Ippokratous St, 10680 Athens
Tel: (01) 3609438 *Fax:* (01) 3614846
E-mail: harlenic@otenet.gr
Web Site: www.harlenic.gr
Key Personnel
Man Dir: Constantine N Ordolis *Tel:* (010) 3610 218 *E-mail:* c.n.ordolis@harlenic.gr
Financial Manager: Eleftheria Chrissicopoulou
Marketing Manager: Evily Sakkalis
Sales Manager: Costas Apostolakis
Editorial Manager: Marina Kouloumoundra
Production Manager: Charalambos Rigas
Founded: 1979
Subjects: Fiction, Literature, Literary Criticism, Essays, Romance
ISBN Prefix(es): 960-450
Number of titles published annually: 450 Print
Parent Company: Harlequin Enterprises Ltd, 225 Duncan Mill Rd, Don Mills, ON M3B 3K9, Canada
Associate Companies: Cora Verlag, Germany; Forlaget Harlequin AB, Sweden; Harlequin SA, France; Harlequin Iberica SA, Spain; Harlequin Holland, Netherlands; Harlequin Japan, Japan; Harlequin Mills & Boon (London); Harlequin Mondadori
Imprints: Bell Best-Seller; Bell Literature; Mira; Harlequin; Red Dress Ink; Blaze

Harlequin, *imprint of* Harlenic Hellas Publishing SA

Harmi-Press Publications, Haroula D Papadimitriou G P+
85 Kifisou Ave, 12241 Athens
Tel: (01) 3456734 *Fax:* (01) 3474732
Telex: 210804 aste gr
Key Personnel
Man Dir: Haroula Papadimitriou
Editorial Dir: Anastasia Papadimitriou
Founded: 1980
Parent Company: D A Papadimitrion S A, Agyra Publishing House

Denise Harvey
Katounia, 340 05 Limni, Evia
Tel: (02270) 31154 *Fax:* (02270) 31154
Key Personnel
Man Dir: Denise Harvey *E-mail:* denise@teledomenet.gr
Founded: 1972
Subjects: Biography, Ethnicity, Literature, Literary Criticism, Essays, Nonfiction (General), Philosophy, Poetry, Theology
ISBN Prefix(es): 960-7120
Number of titles published annually: 3 Print
Total Titles: 50 Print
Imprints: Romiosyni (series)
Distributed by Cosmos Publishing Co Inc (United States); Orthodox Christian Books Ltd (UK & Europe)

Hestia-I D Hestia-Kollaros & Co Corporation+
Odos Solonos 60, 10672 Athens
Tel: (01) 3635970; (01) 36-15-077; (01) 360574 *Fax:* (01) 3606758; (01) 3606759
Web Site: www.ianos.gr
Key Personnel
Publicity Manager: Eva Karaitidi
President: Marina Karaitidi
Founded: 1885
Subjects: Animals, Pets, Anthropology, Archaeology, Architecture & Interior Design, Art, Astrology, Occult, Behavioral Sciences, Biblical Studies, Biography, Business, Career Development, Child Care & Development, Communications, Drama, Theater, Education, Energy, Fiction, Geography, Geology, History, Human Relations, Journalism, Language Arts, Linguistics, Law, Library & Information Sciences, Literature, Literary Criticism, Essays, Management, Music, Dance, Mysteries, Natural History, Philosophy, Photography, Poetry, Psychology, Psychiatry, Public Administration, Romance, Science Fiction, Fantasy, Social Sciences, Sociology, Travel, Veterinary Science, Women's Studies
ISBN Prefix(es): 960-05
Divisions: Hestia
Bookshop(s): Hestia Bookstore, 60 Solonas St, 106 72 Athens
Warehouse: 85, Evripidou Str, Athens

Hiotellis P+
17, Ippokratous St, 106 79 Athens
Tel: (01) 3638066; (01) 3611159 *Fax:* (01) 2113112
E-mail: panos-x@otenet.gr
Founded: 1949
Bookshop & publishing.
Subjects: Electronics, Electrical Engineering, History, Literature, Literary Criticism, Essays, Poetry
Total Titles: 150 Print

I Prooptiki, Ekdoseis+
152 G Septemvriou, 11251 Athens
Tel: (01) 8226254 *Fax:* (01) 8226254
E-mail: info@prooptikibooks.gr
Web Site: wwws.prooptikibooks.gr
Key Personnel
Contact: Polychronis Papacristou
Founded: 1991
Specialize in educational books & editions.
Subjects: Education
ISBN Prefix(es): 960-7331
Total Titles: 8 Print

Ianos+
Aristotelous 7, 546 24 Thessaloniki
Tel: (02301) 284833 *Fax:* (02310) 284832
E-mail: internet@ianos.gr
Web Site: www.ianos.gr
Key Personnel
Contact: N Karatzas
Founded: 1984
Membership(s): Thessaloniki's Booksellers Association.
Subjects: Biography, Ethnicity, History, Literature, Literary Criticism, Essays, Philosophy
ISBN Prefix(es): 960-7771; 960-7827
Parent Company: Bookstore Ianos AE
Subsidiaries: Gallery Ianos
Branch Office(s)
Metamorphoseos 24 Kalamaria, 551 31 Thessaloniki *Tel:* (031) 426-780 *Fax:* (031) 426-780
Filippoupoleos 57 Ambelokipi, 561 23 Thessaloniki *Tel:* (031) 727-075 *Fax:* (031) 727-075

Idmon Publications+
106 Ag Glykerias, 13231 Athens
Mailing Address: PO Box 48030, 132 31 Petroupoli, Athens
Tel: (01) 5015550 *Fax:* (01) 5015550
E-mail: idmon@in.gr
Key Personnel
Editor: Nikos Deligiannis
Subjects: History, Literature, Literary Criticism, Essays, Poetry
ISBN Prefix(es): 960-85270; 960-7547

Idryma Meleton Chersonisou tou Aimou
(Institute for Balkan Studies)
Meg Alexandrou 31A, 54641 Thessaloniki
Mailing Address: PO Box 50932, 54014 Thessaloniki
Tel: (0310) 832143 *Fax:* (0310) 831429
E-mail: imxa@imxa.gr
Founded: 1953
Subjects: Art, Economics, Education, Ethnicity, History, Social Sciences, Sociology, Balkan Area from Ancient Times to Present Day
ISBN Prefix(es): 960-7387
Number of titles published annually: 6 Print
Total Titles: 276 Print
Distribution Center: Pournaras Panagiotis, Kastritsiou 12, 54623 Thessaloniki *Fax:* (0310) 270941 *E-mail:* pournarasbooks@theforthnet.gr

Ikaros Ekdotiki
4 Voulis St, 10562 Athens
Tel: (01) 3225152 *Fax:* (01) 3235262
Founded: 1943
Subjects: Literature, Literary Criticism, Essays
ISBN Prefix(es): 960-7233

Institute of Neohellenic Studies, Manolis Triantaphyllidis Foundation+
Aristotelcio Parepistimio Thessalonikis, 54006 Thessaloniki
Tel: (02310) 997128 *Fax:* (02310) 997122
E-mail: ins@phil.auth.gr
Telex: 418562
Key Personnel
Contact: K Prokovas
Founded: 1959
Subjects: Education, Language Arts, Linguistics
ISBN Prefix(es): 960-231
Orders to: S Patakis, Valtesiou 14, 10680 Athens *Fax:* (01) 3628950

Irini Publishing House - Vassilis G Katsikeas SA+
130 Solonos str, 106 81 Athens
Tel: (01) 38-39-259; (01) 38-10-465 *Fax:* (01) 38-00-651; (01) 38-05-113
E-mail: katsikgr@hol.gr
Web Site: www.infomedacoop.gr
Telex: 223639 Kats gr *Cable:* CATGROUP ATHENS
Key Personnel
President, Rights & Permissions: Vassilis G Katsikeas
Editorial, Production, Publicity: Vicky Pantazopoulou
Sales: Georges V Katsikeas; Konstantin V Katsikeas
Subjects: Biography, Economics, Fiction, Government, Political Science, History, Poetry, Social Sciences, Sociology
Associate Companies: K and K Ltd *Tel:* (01) 3609489 *Fax:* (01) 3606669
Subsidiaries: Ekdotiki Irini Ltd; Irini Foundation
Branch Office(s)
Aristotelous 7, 54624 Salonika *Tel:* (031) 261069

Kalentis & Sia+
Mavromichali 11, 10679 Athens
Tel: (0210) 36-01-551 *Fax:* (0210) 36-23-553
E-mail: kalendis@ath.forthnet.gr
Key Personnel
Contact: Alexandros Kalentis; Marianna Kalentis; Nikos Kalentis; Emily Stamou
Founded: 1983

Subjects: Biological Sciences, Child Care & Development, Cookery, Erotica, Fiction, Health, Nutrition, History, Medicine, Nursing, Dentistry, Philosophy, Poetry
ISBN Prefix(es): 960-219
Number of titles published annually: 40 Print; 10 CD-ROM; 10 Online
Total Titles: 822 Print; 32 CD-ROM; 32 Online
Distributor for Delithanasis Publications; Ereynites Publications; Kirki Publicatitons; Malliaris Publications
Showroom(s): CR Smirnis A Korai, 162 32 Biron
Bookshop(s): Parametros No I, 62 Metonos Str, 15561 Holargos *Tel:* 6523145; Parametros No II, 56 Perikleous Str, 15561 Holargos *Tel:* 6528176
Warehouse: A Kalendis-A Stamou, 62 Metonos Str, 15561 Holargos
Orders to: A Kalendis-A Stamou, 62 Metonos Str, 15561 Holargos

Ilias Kambanas Publishing Organization, SA+
66 Paparrigopoulou St, 121 33 Peristeri-Athens
Tel: (0210) 5762791 *Fax:* (0210) 5743988
E-mail: kambanas@internet.gr
Key Personnel
President: Thalia Kambana
Vice President & Man Dir: Sophia Charokopou
Marketing Manager: Kirsten Janz
Founded: 1969
Specialize in textbooks for elementary schools, atlases, dictionaries, educational materials, novelty books, picture books, cut-out models.
Membership(s): Panhellenic Federation of Publishers & Booksellers.
Subjects: Crafts, Games, Hobbies
ISBN Prefix(es): 960-257
Imprints: Anemonylos; Superkids
Bookshop(s): 49 Char Trikoupi St, 106 81 Athens *Tel:* (01) 3647600 *Fax:* (01) 5743988
Warehouse: 65 Paparrigopoulou St, 121 33 Peristeri-Athens

Dionysuis P Karavias Ekdoseis
35 Asklipiou, 10680 Athens
Tel: (01) 3620465 *Fax:* (01) 3620465
Subjects: History
ISBN Prefix(es): 960-258

Kardamitsa A+
Hippokratous 8, 10679 Athens
Tel: (01) 36 15 156 *Fax:* (01) 36 31 100
E-mail: info@kardamitsa.gr
Web Site: kardamitsa.gr
Key Personnel
Contact: Mina Kardamitsa-Psychoyos; Basil Psychoyos
Founded: 1970
Subjects: Archaeology, History, Literature, Literary Criticism, Essays, Philosophy
ISBN Prefix(es): 960-7262; 960-354
Number of titles published annually: 10 Print
Total Titles: 270 Print
Parent Company: Institut du Livre, A Kardamitsa, 10679 Athens

Kastaniotis Editions SA+
11 Zalogou St, 10678 Athens
Tel: (01) 3301208; (01) 3301327 *Fax:* (01) 3822530
E-mail: info@kastaniotis.com
Web Site: www.kastaniotis.com
Key Personnel
Man Dir, Editorial: Athanasios Kastaniotis
Editorial: Anna Stamatopoulou
Sales: Stelios Kanakis
Production: Voula Vrachati
Publicity, Rights & Permissions: Sophie Catris
Founded: 1968
Membership(s): Association of Publishers & Booksellers of Athens.
Subjects: Anthropology, Architecture & Interior Design, Art, Astrology, Occult, Biography, Business, Child Care & Development, Computer Science, Cookery, Crafts, Games, Hobbies, Drama, Theater, Economics, Education, Fiction, Film, Video, Government, Political Science, Health, Nutrition, History, Humor, Literature, Literary Criticism, Essays, Philosophy, Poetry, Psychology, Psychiatry, Astrology, Beauty, Cartoons & Comics, Esoterics & New Age
ISBN Prefix(es): 960-03
Associate Companies: Ath Kastaniotis & Co General Partnership
Subsidiaries: Ath A Kastaniotis & Co Ltd Partnership

Katoptro Publications+
8, Korizi Str, 11743 Athens
Tel: (0210) 9244827; (0210) 9244852 *Fax:* (0210) 9244756
E-mail: info@katoptro.gr
Web Site: www.katoptro.gr
Founded: 1986
Specialize in sciences.
Subjects: Mathematics, Nonfiction (General), Philosophy, Science (General)
ISBN Prefix(es): 960-7023; 960-7778
Bookshop(s): 5, Pesmazogloustr, 10564 Athens *Tel:* (01) 3247785

Kedros Publishers+
3, G Gennadiou Str, 10678 Athens
Tel: (0210) 3089712 *Fax:* (0210) 3302655
E-mail: books@kedros.gr
Web Site: www.kedros.gr
Key Personnel
Man Dir: Evangelos Papathanassopoulos
Foreign Rights: Laura McDowell
Founded: 1954
Subjects: Biography, Child Care & Development, Drama, Theater, Fiction, History, Humor, Literature, Literary Criticism, Essays, Philosophy, Poetry, Psychology, Psychiatry, Romance, Science (General), Self-Help, Social Sciences, Sociology, Travel
ISBN Prefix(es): 960-04
Distributed by Cosmos Publishing Co (USA)

Kentro Byzantinon Erevnon
12 Kastritsiou Str, 546 23 Thessaloniki
Tel: (031) 270941 *Fax:* (031) 228922

Kleidarithmos, Ekdoseis+
27V Stournari, 10682 Athens
Tel: (01) 3832044
Key Personnel
Man Dir: Giannis Faldamis
Founded: 1985
Subjects: Architecture & Interior Design, Automotive, Civil Engineering, Computer Science, Electronics, Electrical Engineering, Management, Marketing, Mechanical Engineering, Microcomputers
ISBN Prefix(es): 960-209
Bookshop(s): Stournari 37, 10682 Athens *Tel:* (01) 3829629

Knossos Publications
8 Soultani, 10683 Athens
Tel: (01) 3810108; (01) 3804681 *Fax:* (01) 3804681
Founded: 1972
Subjects: Biography, History, Literature, Literary Criticism, Essays, Poetry, Travel
ISBN Prefix(es): 960-207
Parent Company: Stelios Chalkiadakis
Bookshop(s): 29, Evans Str, Iraklion Kreta 71201

Kritiki Publishing+
1-3 Tsamadou Str, 10683 Athens
Tel: (0210) 3803730 *Fax:* (01) 3803740
E-mail: biblia@kritiki.gr
Web Site: www.kritiki.gr
Key Personnel
Directing Manager: Yannis Zirinis
Founded: 1987
Specialize in social sciences.
Subjects: Anthropology, Business, Economics, Fiction, Finance, Government, Political Science, History, Literature, Literary Criticism, Essays, Management, Marketing, Nonfiction (General), Philosophy, Self-Help, Social Sciences, Sociology
ISBN Prefix(es): 960-218
Number of titles published annually: 60 Print
Total Titles: 300 Print

Kyriakidis Vasileios
96 Solonos, 10680 Athens
Tel: (01) 3607725
E-mail: bkyriakid@otenet.gr
Key Personnel
Publisher: Sotiris Nikolopoulos
Founded: 1994
Publish books for Greek language as a foreign language.
Membership(s): Book Publishers Association.
Subjects: History, Literature, Literary Criticism, Essays, Psychology, Psychiatry, Social Sciences, Sociology, Grammar, Vocabulary, Orthography, Ancient Greek History, Byzantine, European, Global, Ancient Greek Literature
ISBN Prefix(es): 960-7634
Total Titles: 100 Print

Leon, *imprint of* Vivliofilia K Ch Spanos

A G Leventis Foundation
9 Fragoklissias St, 15 125 Maroussi
Tel: (0210) 6165232 *Fax:* (0210) 6165235
E-mail: leventcy@zenon.logos.cy.net; eleni.mariolea@leventis.net
Web Site: www.leventisfoundation.org
Founded: 1979
Subjects: Archaeology, Art, History
ISBN Prefix(es): 9963-560
Branch Office(s)
40 Gladstonos St, PO Box 2543, 1095 Nicosia, Cyprus *Tel:* (022) 667706; (022) 674018 *Fax:* (022) 675002

Libro Ltd
10-12 Glykonos, 10675 Athens
Tel: (010) 7247116; (010) 7228647 *Fax:* (010) 7226648
E-mail: libro@hol.gr
ISBN Prefix(es): 960-7009

Livani Publishing Organization SA, see Nea Synora Publications

Logos+
Em Benaki 28, 10678 Athens
Tel: (01) 03823495 *Fax:* (01) 4834000
E-mail: amglogos@otenet.gc
Founded: 1950
Specialize in evangelical books & magazines.
Subjects: Religion - Protestant
Parent Company: AMG International
Branch Office(s)
Egnatia 61, 54631 Thessalonoki *Tel:* (031) 232210
U.S. Office(s): 6815 Shallowford Rd, Chattanooga, TN 37421, United States *Tel:* 423-894-6060 *Fax:* 423-894-6863

Longman, *imprint of* Pearson Education Hellas SA

Lycabettus Press
Afaias 54, P Psychiko, 15452 Athens
Tel: (210) 6741 788 *Fax:* (210) 6710 666

Web Site: lycabettus.com
Key Personnel
Editor: John Chapple *E-mail:* j.chapple@lycabettus.com
Founded: 1968

Macmillan Heinemann ELT
80 Kousidi St, 157-72 Zografou, Athens
Tel: (01) 748 2828 *Fax:* (01) 748 8735
E-mail: mhelt@ath.forthnet.gr
Web Site: www.mhelt.com
Key Personnel
Market Manager: Francis Baker *E-mail:* f.baker@athens.mhelt.com
Subjects: English as a Second Language
Parent Company: Macmillan Publishers Ltd

Mamuth Comix EPE+
130 Solonos, 10681 Athens
Tel: (010) 3625054 *Fax:* (010) 3625055
E-mail: themask@athena.gr
Key Personnel
International Rights: Irene Tzourou
Founded: 1982
Subjects: Humor
ISBN Prefix(es): 960-321
Distributed by Ehapa Verlag Germany

Mavrogianni Publications, see Editions Athina-Mavrogianni

Medusa/Selas Publishers+
Didotou 26, 10680 Athens
Tel: (01) 36483234 *Fax:* (01) 3648321
E-mail: medusa@otenet.gr
Web Site: www.medusaselas.gr
Key Personnel
Contact: Yannis Perdikogiannis
Founded: 1994
Subjects: Art, Fiction, Film, Video, Health, Nutrition, Music, Dance, Nonfiction (General), Science Fiction, Fantasy, Comics & Cartoons, Humor
ISBN Prefix(es): 960-7246; 960-85004
Associate Companies: Topos, Lithi
Imprints: Topos, Lithi
Bookshop(s): Synergasia Andrea Metaxa 4, Athens
Warehouse: 63 Eressou Str, 10683 Athens

Melissa Publishing House+
58 Skoufa St, 10680 Athens 10680
Tel: (010) 3611692 *Fax:* (010) 3600865
E-mail: sales@melissabooks.com
Web Site: www.melissabooks.com
Key Personnel
Man Dir: George Ragias
Sales Dir: Chrys Ragias
Contact: Annie Ragia *E-mail:* annieragia@melissabooks.com
Founded: 1954
Book publishers.
Subjects: Architecture & Interior Design, Art, History, Maritime, Greek Civilization
ISBN Prefix(es): 960-204
Subsidiaries:
Divisions: Dictionary of Greek Artists
Distributed by Harry N Abrams Inc

Minoas SA+
One Poseidonos St, Athens-Irakleio 14121
Tel: (0210) 2711222 *Fax:* (0210) 2711056
E-mail: info@minoas.gr
Web Site: www.minoas.gr
Key Personnel
Man Dir: Yannis Konstantaropoulos
Executive Manager: Andreas Konstantaropoulos
Sales Manager: Christos Hatzipantelides
Founded: 1958
Publications.

Subjects: Art, Biography, Fiction, History, Music, Dance, Nonfiction (General)
ISBN Prefix(es): 960-240; 960-542; 960-699
Number of titles published annually: 80 Print
Total Titles: 800 Print
Bookshop(s): Patission 126, Athens 11257
Tel: (01) 8215664 *Fax:* (01) 8215664

Mira, *imprint of* Harlenic Hellas Publishing SA

Editions Moressopoulos+
2 Chairefonts, 10310 Athens
Tel: (01) 3234217 *Fax:* (01) 3232082
E-mail: hcp@photography.gr
Telex: 216465 masgr
Key Personnel
Man Dir: Stavros Moressopoulos
Rights & Permissions: Voula Moressopoulos
Founded: 1977
Membership(s): Union of Book Publishers (Athens), Association of Photo Biennials (Paris, France), Union of Journalists, Owners of Periodical Press (Athens)
Subjects: Animals, Pets, Crafts, Games, Hobbies, How-to, Music, Dance, Photography, Sports, Athletics, Travel, Wine & Spirits
ISBN Prefix(es): 960-366
Parent Company: Moressopoulos SA
Associate Companies: Hellenic Centre of Photography (nonprofit making) European School of Photography, Iperidou 19, 105 58 Athens
Subsidiaries: Photografia Magazine

Morfotiki Estia AE+
50 Veranzerou, 10438 Athens
Tel: (01) 5227830 *Fax:* (01) 5200534
Key Personnel
Contact: Makas
Founded: 1975
ISBN Prefix(es): 960-215
Bookshop(s): 49 Har Tricoupi St, Athens 10681
Warehouse: 13 Haralambous St, Athens

Morfotiko Idryma Ethnikis Trapezas (National Bank Cultural Foundation)+
13 Thoukydidou, 10558 Athens
Tel: (01) 3230841; (01) 3221335 *Fax:* (01) 3245089; (01) 3227057
Founded: 1966
Subjects: Archaeology, History, Language Arts, Linguistics, Literature, Literary Criticism, Essays, Nonfiction (General), Philosophy, Science (General)
ISBN Prefix(es): 960-250

Mouseio Benaki
One Koumpari, 10674 Athens
Tel: (01) 3611617; (01) 3612694 *Fax:* (01) 3622547
ISBN Prefix(es): 960-7671; 960-85160

Nakas Music House+
147 Skiathou Skokou, 11255 Athens
Tel: (01) 364-711; (01) 364-716 *Fax:* (01) 2112303
E-mail: bookw@nakas.gr
Telex: 8018NAKAGR
Key Personnel
Contact: George Nakas
Founded: 1937
Subjects: Music, Dance
ISBN Prefix(es): 960-290
Distributor for Boosey & Hawkes; Henley Verlag; Ricordi

Ed Nea Acropolis+
29 Ag Meletiou, 11361 Athens
Tel: (01) 8231301 *Fax:* (01) 8810830
Key Personnel
President: Panagiotis Goumas
Vice President: Peter Kostinis

Editor: Costula Giannopulu
Founded: 1981
Subjects: Anthropology, Archaeology, Drama, Theater, History, Music, Dance, Mysteries, Parapsychology, Philosophy
ISBN Prefix(es): 960-8407
Branch Office(s)
Hania
Heraklion
Ioannina
Kallithea
Kavala
Patras
Rethymno
Salonica
Volos

Nea Synora Publications+
98 Solonos St, 106 80 Athens
Tel: (01) 3610589; (01) 3600398 *Fax:* (01) 3617791
E-mail: neasynora@otenet.gr
Web Site: www.nea-synora.gr
Telex: 21812269spa
Key Personnel
President: Giota Livani; Ilias Livani
Editor: Tonia Chourchouli
Founded: 1972
ISBN Prefix(es): 960-236; 960-237; 960-238; 960-14
Parent Company: Livani Publishing Organization SA
Associate Companies: Mythos, Klydi
Subsidiaries: Multimedia Electronic Publishing SA
Warehouse: 135 Platonos St, 17673 Athens

Nea Thesis - Evrotas+
Hippokratoys St 65, 10680 Athens
Tel: (01) 3643932 *Fax:* (01) 3617592
Key Personnel
Contact: John Schinas
Subjects: Archaeology, Ethnicity, Government, Political Science, History, Philosophy
ISBN Prefix(es): 960-7076

Nikas
Solonos 102, 10680 Athens
Tel: (010) 3634686; (010) 3633754
ISBN Prefix(es): 960-297

Nomiki Bibliothiki+
51 Mavromichali St, 10680 Athens
Tel: (01) 3600968 *Fax:* (01) 3636422
E-mail: legalinn@otenet.gr
Key Personnel
Man Dir & International Rights Contract: Adonis Karatzas *Tel:* (01) 3678856 *E-mail:* adonik@nb.org
Founded: 1977
Internet & legal services, professional training courses & seminars.
Subjects: Economics, Labor, Industrial Relations, Law, Publishing & Book Trade Reference
ISBN Prefix(es): 960-272

Notos
Omirou 15, 10672 Athens
Tel: (01) 3636577; (01) 3629746 *Fax:* (01) 3636737
Telex: 515418
ISBN Prefix(es): 960-8491

Oceanida+
38 Dervenion St, 10681 Athens
Tel: (0210) 3806137 *Fax:* (0210) 3805531
E-mail: oceanida@internet.gr
Key Personnel
Publisher: Louisa Zaoussi
Founded: 1986

Subjects: Art, History, Literature, Literary Criticism, Essays
ISBN Prefix(es): 960-7213; 960-410
Number of titles published annually: 30 Print
Total Titles: 250 Print
Distributor for Erevnites
Distribution Center: 25 Solomon St, 10682 Athens *Tel:* (0210) 3827341

Odysseas Publications Ltd+
3 Moraitou, 11471 Athens
Tel: (01) 3624326; (01) 3625575 *Fax:* (01) 3648030
Key Personnel
Contact: Titos Mylonopoulos
Founded: 1973
Subjects: Biography, Child Care & Development, History, Human Relations, Philosophy, Psychology, Psychiatry, Romance, Women's Studies
ISBN Prefix(es): 960-210

Opera
23 Koletti, 10677 Athens
Tel: (0210) 3304546 *Fax:* (0210) 3303634
E-mail: opera@acci.gr
Key Personnel
Contact & Opera Editions: George Miressiotis
Founded: 1989 (Private book publishing house)
Literary Books & Translations
Specialize in European & Latin American authors.
ISBN Prefix(es): 960-7073
Total Titles: 90 Print

Orfanidis Publications+
8 Lontou St, 10681 Athens
Tel: (01) 3836925 *Fax:* (01) 3845623
Founded: 1940
Subjects: Astrology, Occult, Automotive, Cookery, Gardening, Plants, Geography, Geology, Mysteries, Philosophy

Pagoulatos Bros+
56 Panepistimiou St, 10678 Athens
Tel: (01) 03818780; (01) 03801485 *Fax:* (01) 03838028
E-mail: pagoulatos_publ@ath.forthnet.gr
Founded: 1965
Subjects: Biography, English as a Second Language, Mathematics
ISBN Prefix(es): 960-7208

Pagoulatos G-G P Publications
50 Sina, 10672 Athens
Tel: (0210) 3604895; (0210) 3600720 *Fax:* (0210) 3604897
Key Personnel
Editor: Gerasimos Pagoulatos
Subjects: English as a Second Language
ISBN Prefix(es): 960-294

Panepistimio Ioanninon
PO Box 1186, 45110 Ioannina
Tel: (026510) 97122 *Fax:* (026510) 97015
E-mail: intlrel@uoi.gr
Web Site: www.uoi.gr
Key Personnel
Publications Office: Mrs E Gouma
Subjects: Anthropology, Archaeology, Chemistry, Chemical Engineering, Education, History, Physics, Psychology, Psychiatry, Social Sciences, Sociology
ISBN Prefix(es): 960-233

D Papadimas+
8 Ippokratous, 10679 Athens
Tel: (01) 3627318 *Fax:* (0210) 3610271
Subjects: Antiques, Archaeology, Geography, Geology, History, Regional Interests, Theology
ISBN Prefix(es): 960-206

Haroula D Papadimitriou G P, see Harmi-Press Publications, Haroula D Papadimitriou G P

Kyr I Papadopoulos E E+
9, Kapodistriou St, 14452 Athens
Tel: (0210) 2816134; (0210) 2846074; (0210) 2846075 *Fax:* (0210) 2817127
E-mail: info@picturebooks.gr
Web Site: www.picturebooks.gr
Telex: 225176 Book Gr
Key Personnel
Man Dir: Kyr Papadopoulos
Sales: P Hatjibodojis
Production: George Papadopoulos
Rights & Permissions: Yiannis Papadopoulos
Founded: 1953
Subjects: Animals, Pets, Fiction, History, Literature, Literary Criticism, Essays, Nonfiction (General), Adventure, Classics, Social Situations
ISBN Prefix(es): 960-261; 960-412
Number of titles published annually: 100 Print
Total Titles: 600 Print

Papazissis Publishers SA
2 Nikitara, 10678 Athens
Tel: (0210) 3838020; (0210) 3822496 *Fax:* (0210) 3809150
Telex: 219807 Itec
Key Personnel
Man Dir: Victor Papazissis
Sales, Advertising: Thalia Papazissis
Rights & Permissions: Stefanos Vlachos
Founded: 1929
Subjects: Economics, Education, Environmental Studies, Government, Political Science, History, Law, Regional Interests, Social Sciences, Sociology
ISBN Prefix(es): 960-02
Parent Company: Corais Ltd

Patakis Publishers+
16 Emm Benaki, 10678 Athens
Tel: (0210) 3831078; (0210) 3811850; (0210) 3650000 *Fax:* (0210) 3628950
E-mail: info@patakis.gr
Web Site: www.patakis.gr
Key Personnel
President: Stefanos Patakis
Production: Alexander Patakis
Sales: Peter Lazaridis
Publicity: Hara Mavrogonatou
Rights & Permissions: Yiannis Ntzoufras
Editorial: Nikitas Stellas
Foreign Rights Assistant: Vicky Stamatopoulou
Tel: (01) 3615356 *E-mail:* vstamat@patakis.gr
Founded: 1974
Subjects: Anthropology, Art, Biography, Business, Child Care & Development, Cookery, Drama, Theater, Education, Fiction, Health, Nutrition, History, Language Arts, Linguistics, Literature, Literary Criticism, Essays, Management, Nonfiction (General), Philosophy, Poetry, Psychology, Psychiatry, Social Sciences, Sociology, Travel
ISBN Prefix(es): 960-293; 960-360; 960-600; 960-378; 960-16
Number of titles published annually: 500 Print
Total Titles: 3,000 Print
Branch Office(s)
N Monastiriou 122, Thessaloniki *Tel:* (031) 706354 *Fax:* (031) 706355
Distributor for Conceptum (CD-ROM); Goulandri-Horn Institute; Iolkos Publications; Triantafyllidis Institute
Bookshop(s): Akadimias 65, 10678 Athens *Tel:* (01) 3811740 *Fax:* (01) 3811850
Warehouse: These Tzaverdela, Aspropyrgos 19300
Distribution Center: Em Benaki 16, Athens *Tel:* (01) 3831078 (Also showroom)

Pearson Education Hellas SA
229 Syngrou Ave, Nea Smyrni, 17121 Athens
Tel: (01) 937 3170 *Fax:* (01) 937 3194
Web Site: www.pearsoneduc.com
Key Personnel
Man Dir: Themis Zoulias
Sales Manager: Liz Hammon
Publisher: Loukas Ioannou
Founded: 1985
ELT supplementary titles.
ISBN Prefix(es): 0-582
Number of titles published annually: 10 Print
Total Titles: 20 Print
Parent Company: Pearson Plc
Imprints: Longman
Branch Office(s)
12 Mackenzie King St, 54622 Thessaloniki *Tel:* (031) 271163 *Fax:* (031) 241056
Foreign Rights: Loukas Ioannou

Pergamini, *imprint of* Vivliofilia K Ch Spanos

Galousis P Petros
48 Solomou, 10682 Athens
Tel: (01) 360 5004

Pontiki Publications SA+
10 Massalias, 10680 Athens
Tel: (0210) 3609531; (0210) 3609533 *Fax:* (0210) 3645406
Key Personnel
Publisher: Kostas Papayoannou
Man Dir: Kostas Yabanis
Editorial Dir: Roussos Vranas
Founded: 1979
Subjects: Government, Political Science, History
ISBN Prefix(es): 960-8402

Proskinio Spyros Ch Marinis
76 Solonos, 10681 Athens
Tel: (0210) 3648170 *Fax:* (0210) 3648033
Key Personnel
President: A Sideratos
Founded: 1990
Subjects: Government, Political Science, History
ISBN Prefix(es): 960-7107; 960-8342

M Psaropoulos & Co EE+
3 Kriezotou, 10671 Athens
Tel: (01) 3606808 *Fax:* (01) 3609645
Key Personnel
Man Dir: Tassos Psaropoulos
Editorial: Thalia Iacovidis
Sales: John Psaropoulos
Production: D Mavromatis
Publicity: P Pissanos
Rights & Permissions: M Psaropoulos
Founded: 1962
Subjects: Fiction, Medicine, Nursing, Dentistry
ISBN Prefix(es): 960-7147
Parent Company: Althayia SA
Subsidiaries: Finedawn Publishers

Psichogios Publications SA+
Mavromichali 1, 10679 Athens
Mailing Address: Zaimi 8, 10683 Athens
Tel: (0210) 3302535; (0210) 3302234 *Fax:* (0210) 3640683; (0210) 3302098
E-mail: psicho@otenet.gr
Telex: 225874 Mps Gr
Key Personnel
Man Dir: Athanassios Psichogios
E-mail: thanospsicho@otenet.gr
Editorial, Rights & Permission: Elly Solomon
Founded: 1978
Subjects: Fiction, Philosophy, Human Science
ISBN Prefix(es): 960-7020; 960-274; 960-7021
Number of titles published annually: 100 Print
Total Titles: 800 Print

Branch Office(s)
Vassileos Irakliou 32, 54624 Thessaloniki
Bookshop(s): Pesmazoglou 5, 10564 Athens
Warehouse: Edessis 29, 11855 Votanikos

Red Dress Ink, *imprint of* Harlenic Hellas Publishing SA

Romiosyni (series), *imprint of* Denise Harvey

Rossi, E Kdoseis Eleni Rossi-Petsiou+
5 Kiafas, 10676 Athens
Tel: (0210) 3304440; (0210) 3301854 *Fax:* (0210) 3304410
Founded: 1895
Subjects: Education, Student's Aid
ISBN Prefix(es): 960-225

Sakkoulas Publications SA+
23, Ippokratous Str, 106 79 Athens
Tel: (0210) 33 87 500 *Fax:* (0210) 33 90 075
E-mail: info@sakkoulas.gr
Web Site: www.sakkoulas.gr
Key Personnel
Man Dir: Panagiotis I Sakkoulas
Founded: 1958
Subjects: Business, Economics, Labor, Industrial Relations, Law, Management, Maritime, Public Administration, Social Sciences, Sociology
ISBN Prefix(es): 960-301
Branch Office(s)
42, Ethnikis Amyis Str, 546 21 Thessaloniki
Tel: (02310) 244 228; (02310) 244 229 *Fax:* (02310) 244 230
Distributor for Nomos Verlagsgesellschaft; Verlag Recht und Wirtschaft mbH
Bookshop(s): 42, Ethnikis Amyis Str, 546 21 Thessaloniki *Tel:* (02310) 244 228; (02310) 244 229 *Fax:* (02310) 244 230; One Fragon Str, 546 26 Thessaloniki *Tel:* (02310) 535 381 *Fax:* (02310) 546 812

Scripta Theofilus Palevratzis-Ashover+
25 3is Septemvriou, 10432 Athens
Tel: (0210) 5230382 *Fax:* (0210) 5233574
Key Personnel
Contact: Theophilos Palevratzis-Ashover
Founded: 1980
Subjects: English as a Second Language
ISBN Prefix(es): 960-7166; 960-8341

Siamantas VA A Ouvas
60 Lpeirou & 1-3 Akakiou, 10439 Athens
Tel: (0210) 8824960 *Fax:* (0210) 8824960
Subjects: Fiction, History, Nonfiction (General)
ISBN Prefix(es): 960-87184

J Sideris OE Ekdoseis
115 Alexandreias, 10441 Athens, Akadimia Platonos
Tel: (0210) 3833434; (0210) 5140627 *Fax:* (0210) 3832294
Key Personnel
Contact: Andreas Sideris
Subjects: Language Arts, Linguistics, Literature, Literary Criticism, Essays, Science (General)
ISBN Prefix(es): 960-08

Michalis Sideris
Andr Metaxa 28 & Themistokleous, 10681 Athens
Tel: (0210) 3301165; (0210) 03301161 (bookstore) *Fax:* (0210) 3301164
Founded: 1978
Subjects: Earth Sciences, Education, Energy, English as a Second Language, Mathematics, Physics
ISBN Prefix(es): 960-7012

Sigma+
20, Mavromihali St, 10680 Athens
Tel: (0210) 3638941; (0210) 3607667 *Fax:* (0210) 3638941
E-mail: sigma@sigmabooks.gr
Web Site: www.sigmabooks.gr
Key Personnel
Contact: Dimitris Stephanides
Founded: 1973
Subjects: Art, Fiction, Mythology, Folk Tales
ISBN Prefix(es): 960-425
Total Titles: 95 Print
Distributed by Cosmos Publishing Co Inc (US); Hellidon Press (UK)
Foreign Rep(s): Cosmos Publishing Co Inc (Canada, USA)
Foreign Rights: Shin Won Agency Co (China, Japan, Korea)

Alex Siokis & Co+
54 Alex Svolou, 50041 Thessaloniki
Tel: (02310) 230257; (02310) 287016 *Fax:* (02310) 281014
E-mail: siokis@spark.net.gr
Key Personnel
Medical Publisher: Niki Sioki
Founded: 1960
Subjects: Medicine, Nursing, Dentistry
ISBN Prefix(es): 960-7461

Society for Macedonian Studies
4 Ethnikis Amynis Ave, 546 21 Thessaloniki
Tel: (031) 268710 *Fax:* (031) 971501
E-mail: ems@hyper.gr
Founded: 1939
Promotes the research in the topics of history, archaeology, linguistics & folklore concerning the region of Macedonia.
Subjects: Anthropology, Archaeology, History, Philosophy, Humanities
Total Titles: 4 Print
Foreign Rights: Ebsco; Faxon; Wasmuth; Dawson; Raabe; Readmore; Dokomente-Verlag; Sweis

Vivliofilia K Ch Spanos
7 Mavromichali, 10679 Athens
Tel: (0210) 3623917; (0210) 3614332 *Fax:* (0210) 8953076
E-mail: biblioph@otenet.gr *Cable:* Bibliospan
Key Personnel
Man Dir, Editorial: C Spanos
Sales: John Papadakis
Publicity: Sophia Tjimoianni
Subjects: Regional Interests
ISBN Prefix(es): 960-262
Imprints: Leon; Pergamini

Spyropoulos A+
74, Ag Georgiou, 15451 Neo Psychico
Tel: (0210) 671 2991 *Fax:* (0210) 671 9622
Founded: 1972
Specialize in ELT material.
ISBN Prefix(es): 960-7302

Stochastis+
39 Mavromichali, 10680 Athens
Tel: (0210) 3601956; (0210) 3610445 *Fax:* (0210) 3610445
Key Personnel
President: Loukas Axelos
Founded: 1969
Subjects: Ethnicity, History, Literature, Literary Criticism, Essays, Philosophy, Social Sciences, Sociology, Travel
ISBN Prefix(es): 960-303
Associate Companies: Koinopraktiki (Union of Greek Publishers)
Imprints: Eurotyp
Book Club(s): Cosmos Book Club; Mos Book Club; The Friends of Book Book Club

Superkids, *imprint of* Ilias Kambanas Publishing Organization, SA

Technical Chamber of Greece
4 Karageorgi Servias Str, 10248 Athens
Tel: (0210) 3254591; (0210) 3314403 *Fax:* (0210) 3314403
E-mail: registry@central.tee.gr
Telex: 218374 Teegr
Key Personnel
General Dir: V Torolopoulos
Founded: 1923
The Technical Chamber of Greece (TEE) is a corporate body, under public law, supervised by the Ministry of Public Works.
Subjects: Science (General), Technology
ISBN Prefix(es): 960-7018

Tekmirio
17 Z Pigis, 10681 Athens
Tel: (01) 3637912; (01) 2287548

Thetili Publications, see Ekdoseis Thetili

Thymari Publications+
24 Har Trikoupi Str, 10679 Athens
Tel: (0210) 3634901; (0210) 3643015 *Fax:* (0210) 3636591
E-mail: thymari@thymari.gr
Web Site: thymari.gr
Key Personnel
Dir & Editor-in-Chief: T H Grammenou
Psychologist, Marketing: I Grammenou
Key Author: G Pinteris PhD
Editorial Advisor: A Grammenou
Psychologist, Translator: M Koulentianou
Founded: 1978
Subjects: Human Relations, Psychology, Psychiatry, Social Sciences, Sociology
ISBN Prefix(es): 960-7161; 960-349
Warehouse: Sarantaporou 98, 15561 Holargos
Tel: (01) 6512216; (01) 6540811 *Fax:* (01) 6549207

To Rodakio+
Apollonos 35, 10556 Athens
Tel: (0210) 3221700; (0210) 3221742 *Fax:* (0210) 3221700
E-mail: rodakio@otenet.gz
Key Personnel
International Rights: Julia Tsiakiris
Founded: 1992
Subjects: Art, Drama, Theater, Fiction, Literature, Literary Criticism, Essays, Poetry
ISBN Prefix(es): 960-7360; 960-8372
Number of titles published annually: 10 Print
Total Titles: 110 Print
Foreign Rights: Kleoniki Douqe (France)

Topos, Lithi, *imprint of* Medusa/Selas Publishers

Toubis M
519 Vouliagmenis Ave, 163 41 Athens
Tel: (01) 9923876; (01) 9923806 *Fax:* (01) 9923 867
E-mail: toubis@otenet.gr
Key Personnel
Secretary: Katerina Koumarianou
Founded: 1965
Development, production & distribution of high quality tourist publication.

Tropos Zois+
One Solomou St, 15232 Athens, Chalandri
Tel: (0210) 6840156; (0210) 6858852 *Fax:* (0210) 6858851
Subjects: Alternative medicine, natural eating & living, nutrition, yoga, reflexology
ISBN Prefix(es): 960-7118

Number of titles published annually: 6 Print; 1 CD-ROM
Total Titles: 10 Print; 2 CD-ROM; 50 Audio

Typos
3-5 Gravias, 10678 Athens
Tel: (01) 3819083; (01) 3819085; (01) 3619083 *Fax:* (01) 3825012
ISBN Prefix(es): 960-246

D & J Vardikos Vivliotechnica Hellas
2 A Metaxa, 10681 Athens
Tel: (0210) 3631148 *Fax:* (0210) 9564354
Key Personnel
Man Dir: Dimitrios Vardikos
Founded: 1978
Subjects: Aeronautics, Aviation
ISBN Prefix(es): 960-7810
Branch Office(s)
Davaki 34, Kallithea, Athens
Bookshop(s): Inter-Attica, Davaki 34, Kallithea, Athens

J Vassiliou Bibliopolein+
15e Ippokratous St, 10679 Athens
Tel: (01) 3623382; (01) 3623480 *Fax:* (01) 3623580
Key Personnel
President: J Vassiliou
Founded: 1913
Membership(s): Association of Publishers & Booksellers of Athens.
Subjects: Fiction, History, Philosophy

Vivliothiki Eftychia Galeou+
39 Chalandriou, 15125 Maroussi, Athens
Tel: (0210) 6841191 *Fax:* (0210) 6825862
Key Personnel
Contact: N S Galeos
Subjects: Advertising, Business, Finance, Management, Marketing
ISBN Prefix(es): 960-7126
Bookshop(s): 19 Kolokotroni St, Athens *Tel:* (01) 3227840

Vlassis+
2-4 Lontou, 10681 Athens
Tel: (0210) 3812900; (0210) 3827557 *Fax:* (0210) 3827557
E-mail: amvlassi@otenet.gr
Key Personnel
General Manager: Nickos Vlassis
Publisher, Marketing Manager & International Rights Contact: Anna-Maria Vlassis *Tel:* (01) 3833013 *E-mail:* amvlassi@otenet.gr
Founded: 1964
Hard cover & paper back.
Subjects: Biography, Fiction, Literature, Literary Criticism, Essays
ISBN Prefix(es): 960-302
Total Titles: 600 Print

S J Zacharopoulos SA Publishing Co+
Parodos Leof Kryoneriou, Agio Stefanos, 14565 Athens
Tel: (0210) 3231525; (0210) 3225011; (0210) 8142611 *Fax:* (0210) 3243814
Key Personnel
President, Publicity, Rights & Permissions: Stavros Zacharopoulos
Production: Loucas Zacharopoulos
Editorial: Stefanos Zacharopoulos
Sales: George Zacharopoulos
Founded: 1959
Subjects: Drama, Theater, History, Poetry, Science (General)
ISBN Prefix(es): 960-208
Bookshop(s): Praxitelous 141, GR-18535 Piraeus

Zacharopoulos Z & G
22-24 Atlantos k patisia, 11254 Athens
Tel: (0210) 211 1895-7 *Fax:* (0210) 211 1897
E-mail: zachapub@otenet.gr
ISBN Prefix(es): 960-281

ZOI
Subsidiary of "Zoe", Brotherhood of Theologians
14 Karytsi, 10561 Athens
Tel: (01) 3223560 *Fax:* (01) 3221283
Key Personnel
Man Dir: P Anastopoulos
Founded: 1907
Subjects: Religion - Other
Bookshop(s): St Sophia 41, Salonika *Tel:* (031) 54623 (also in three other Greek cities)

Har Zolindakis
65 Panepistimiou, 10564 Athens
Tel: (01) 3216504
Subjects: History

Zyrichidi Bros
30 Aristotelous, 54623 Thessaloniki
Tel: (031) 227915; (031) 266036 *Fax:* (031) 266036
Key Personnel
Contact: Zyrichidi Bros *Tel:* (031) 285 856
Founded: 1959
Publisher of books, selling all other book publishing companies
General Partnership.
Subjects: Literature, Literary Criticism, Essays
Total Titles: 15 Print
Branch Office(s)
Zsimiski 115 *Tel:* (031) 285856 *Fax:* (031) 266036
Bookshop(s): Zsimiski 115 *Tel:* (031) 266036 *Fax:* (031) 266036

Guadeloupe

General Information

Capital: Basse-Terre
Language: French, Creole patois
Religion: Roman Catholic
Population: 400,000
Bank Hours: 0800-1200, 1400-1600 Monday-Friday
Shop Hours: 0900-1300, 1500-1800 Monday-Friday
Currency: 100 centimes = 1 French franc

JASOR
46 rue Schoelcher, 97110 Pointe-a-Pitre
Tel: (0590) 911848 *Fax:* (0590) 210701
Telex: 919-2333
Subjects: Language Arts, Linguistics, Literature, Literary Criticism, Essays
ISBN Prefix(es): 2-912594

Guatemala

General Information

Capital: Guatemala City
Language: Spanish
Religion: Roman Catholic
Population: 10 million
Bank Hours: 0900-1500 Monday-Friday
Shop Hours: 0900-1300, 1500-1900 Monday-Friday; 0900-1300 Saturday
Currency: 100 centavos = 1 quetzal

Export/Import Information: Member of the Central American Common Market. Duty on catalogues is Q 0.03 per gross kilo. No import licenses, no exchange control.
Copyright: UCC, Buenos Aires, Florence (see Copyright Conventions, pg xi)

Cultura de La Universidad, *imprint of* Grupo Editorial RIN-78

Editorial Cultura
O Calle 16-40, Zona 15, Guatemala
Tel: (02) 692080 *Fax:* (02) 346135
Telex: 5805 *Cable:* CAN EXO

Fundacion para la Cultura y el Desarrollo
9 calle 2-75, zona 1, 01001 Guatemala
SAN: 003-1429
Tel: (02) 500216 *Fax:* (02) 325508
Key Personnel
General Manager: Carlos I Castaneda Acuna
  E-mail: ccast@intelnet.net.gt
Founded: 1986
Subjects: History
ISBN Prefix(es): 84-88622
Parent Company: Asociacion de Amigos del Pais

Grupo Editorial RIN-78+
O Calle 16-40, Zona 15, Guatemala 692080
Tel: (02) 692080 *Fax:* (02) 601834
Key Personnel
Contact: Juan F Cifuentes
Founded: 1984
Subjects: Archaeology, Fiction, History, Literature, Literary Criticism, Essays, Military Science, Philosophy, Poetry, Science Fiction, Fantasy, Social Sciences, Sociology
Associate Companies: Servicios Editoriales "Palabra Tras Palabra"
Imprints: Cultura de La Universidad; Pedernal; Ymoescuento
Subsidiaries: Editorial "Palo de Hormigo"
Divisions: Centro de Documentacion de Estudios Literarios
U.S. Office(s): Roberto Quezada, 3442 N Delta Ave, Rosemead, CA 91770, United States
  Fax: 818-572-0964
Distributed by Oscar de Leon Castillo
Distributor for Artemis y Edimter

Editorial del Ministerio de Educacion
15 Ave 3-22, Zona 1, Guatemala

Pedernal, *imprint of* Grupo Editorial RIN-78

Editorial Piedra Santa
5 Calle, Zona 1, 7-55 Guatemala
SAN: 002-6204
Tel: (02) 29053
E-mail: piedrasanta.sal@salnet.net
Key Personnel
President: Irene Piedra Santa
  E-mail: irene_piedra_santa@hotmail.com
Founded: 1947
ISBN Prefix(es): 84-8377; 99922-1; 99922-58
Subsidiaries: Editorial y Libreria Piedra Santa SA de CV
Bookshop(s): 11 Calle 6-50, Zona 1

Ymoescuento, *imprint of* Grupo Editorial RIN-78

Guinea-Bissau

General Information

Capital: Bissau
Language: Portuguese (official), Criolo, Tribal Languages

Religion: Indigenous Beliefs (65%), Muslim (30%), Christian (5%)
Population: 1 million
Currency: Peso (12,068 = $1 US)
Copyright: Berne (see Copyright Conventions, pg xi)

Instituto Nacional de Estudos e Pesquisa (INEP)
PO Box 112, Bairro Cobornel, Bissau
Tel: 21 17 15; 21 44 97; 21 13 01 *Fax:* 25 11 25
Web Site: www.inep.gov.br
Key Personnel
Dir: Mamadu Jao *E-mail:* mama_jao@hotmail.com
Founded: 1984
Subjects: Agriculture, Anthropology, Developing Countries, Environmental Studies, Health, Nutrition, History, Social Sciences, Sociology, Technology

Guyana

General Information

Capital: Georgetown
Language: English & Amerindian dialects
Religion: Christian, Hindu, Islamic
Population: 739,000
Shop Hours: 0800-1130, 1300-1600 Monday-Friday; 0800-1130 Saturday
Currency: 100 cents = 1 Guyana dollar
Export/Import Information: No tariff on books. Only advertising of commercial value, subject to duty. There are numerous businesses that import books. Import license required. Nominal exchange controls.
Copyright: Berne (see Copyright Conventions, pg xi)

Amerindian Research Unit
University of Guyana, PO Box 101110, Georgetown
Tel: (02) 4930 *Fax:* (02) 54885
Web Site: www.wisard.org

Caribbean Community Secretariat
Bank of Guyana Bldg, Ave of the Republic, PO Box 10827, Georgetown
Tel: (02) 26-9280; (02) 26-9281; (02) 26-9282; (02) 26-9283; (02) 26-9284; (02) 26-9285; (02) 26-9286; (02) 26-9287; (02) 26-9288; (02) 26-9289 *Fax:* (02) 26-7816; (02) 25-7341; (02) 25-8031
E-mail: carisec1@caricom.org; carisec2@caricom.org; carisec3@caricom.org
Web Site: www.caricom.org *Cable:* CARIBSEC GUYANA
Key Personnel
Senior Project Officer (Documentation Center): Maureen Newton
Founded: 1973
Regional integration movement whose ultimate goal is the improvement of the standard of living of all peoples in the Community. At present the Community has 14 member states. The Secretariat is the administrative arm of the Community.
ISBN Prefix(es): 976-600
Total Titles: 24 Print; 1 CD-ROM

Guyana Community Based Rehabilitation Progeamme
c/o European Union, 72 High St, Georgetown
Tel: (022) 64004 *Fax:* (022) 62615
Founded: 1986
Subjects: Child Care & Development, Developing Countries, Disability, Special Needs, Education
ISBN Prefix(es): 976-8107

The Hamburgh Register+
c/o Walter Roth Museum of Anthropology, 61 Main St, Georgetown
Mailing Address: PO Box 10187, Georgetown
Tel: (02) 258486 *Fax:* (02) 258511
E-mail: wrma@sdup.org.gy
Key Personnel
Contact: Jennifer Wishart
Founded: 1996
Subjects: Anthropology, Archaeology
ISBN Prefix(es): 976-8152

New Guyana Co Ltd
Lot 8, Industrial Site, Ruimveldt, Georgetown
Mailing Address: PO Box 101088
Tel: (02) 262471 *Cable:* NEWCO GEORGETOWN GUYANA
Printers of Mirror Newspaper.
ISBN Prefix(es): 976-8000

Roraima Publishers Ltd
76 Robb St, Lacytown, Georgetown
Mailing Address: PO Box 10322, Georgetown
Tel: (02) 2-73551; (02) 2-2363; (02) 2-5057
Fax: (02) 62319; (02) 58844
E-mail: roraima-distributors@solutions2000.net
Key Personnel
Man Dir: David Yhann
Founded: 1994
Subjects: Fiction, Nonfiction (General), Guyanese Works
ISBN Prefix(es): 976-8147
Associate Companies: Roraima Distributors

Haiti

General Information

Capital: Port-au-Prince
Language: French and Creole
Religion: Predominantly Roman Catholic (about 75%)
Population: 6.4 million
Bank Hours: 0900-1300 Monday-Friday
Currency: 100 centimes = 1 gourde. US currency is widely used
Export/Import Information: Books charged ad valorem, children's picture books per kilo net. Advertising matter under 1 kilo gross weight duty-free. No import licenses or exchange controls, other than occasional exchange rationing, leading to delays.
Copyright: UCC (see Copyright Conventions, pg xi)

Editions Caraibes SA
Lalue, Port-au-Prince
Mailing Address: PO Box 2013, Port-au-Prince
Tel: 23179
Telex: ITT 2030198
Key Personnel
Contact: Pierre J Elie
Founded: 1973
Subjects: Agriculture, Business, English as a Second Language, History, Marketing, Physics
Distributor for L'Ecole SA; Hatier International; LeRobert; LaRousse

Deschamps Imprimerie
Rue Jean Gilles Varneux, Port-au-Prince
Mailing Address: PO Box 164, Port-au-Prince
Tel: 2461 905; 2501 474; 56-3853; 56-2253
Fax: 2491 225
E-mail: henrid@acn2.net
Key Personnel
Man Dir: Jacques Deschamps
Editorial Dir: Henri R Deschamps; Mael Fouchard
Production Dir: Claude Deschamps; Wilhelm Frisch, Jr
Financial Dir: Jacques Deschamps, Jr
Sales Dir: Peter J Frisch
Read extensively in English & French.
Subjects: Education, Fiction, Literature, Literary Criticism, Essays, Religion - Other
ISBN Prefix(es): 99935-0
Divisions: Imprimerie Henri Deschamps

Editions du Soleil
Rue du Centre, Port-au-Prince
Mailing Address: PO Box 2471, Port-au-Prince
Tel: (01) 23147
Telex: Ppbooth 2030001 attn Lisocial *Cable:* LISOCIAL
Key Personnel
Contact: Edouard A Tardieu
Founded: 1952
Subjects: Education

Theodor (Imprimerie)
rue Dantes Destouches, Port-au-Prince
Subjects: Fiction, History, Literature, Literary Criticism, Essays

Holy See (Vatican City State)

General Information

Language: Italian and Latin
Religion: Roman Catholic
Population: 802
Currency: Vatican lira = Italian lira. Italian currency is used
Copyright: UCC, Berne (see Copyright Conventions, pg xi)

Biblioteca Apostolica Vaticana (Vatican Apostolic Library)
Cortile del Belvedere, 00120 Citta del Vaticano
Tel: (06) 6987 9402 *Fax:* (06) 6988 4795
E-mail: bav@vatlib.it
Telex: 2024 Dirgental VA
Key Personnel
Dir & Chief Executive: Don Raffaele Farina
Subjects: Art, History, Language Arts, Linguistics, Law, Philosophy, Theology
ISBN Prefix(es): 88-210

Archivio Segreto Vaticano
Cortile del Belvedre, 00120 Citta del Vaticano
Tel: (06) 69883314 *Fax:* (06) 69885574
ISBN Prefix(es): 88-85042

LEV, *imprint of* Libreria Editrice Vaticana

Pontificia Academia Scientiarum (The Pontifical Academy of Sciences)
Casina Pio IV, V-00120 Vatican City S
Tel: 0669883195 *Fax:* 0669885218
E-mail: academy.sciences@acdscience.va
Web Site: www.vatican.va/roman_curia/pontifical_academies/index_it.htm
Telex: 2024
Key Personnel
President: Prof Nicola Cabibbo
Founded: 1936

"To promote the progress of the mathematical, physical & natural sciences & the study of epistemological problems relating thereto".
Subjects: Biological Sciences, Chemistry, Chemical Engineering, Earth Sciences, Environmental Studies, Mathematics, Medicine, Nursing, Dentistry, Physics, Science (General)
ISBN Prefix(es): 88-7761
Number of titles published annually: 3 Print
Total Titles: 100 Print

Scuola Vaticana Paleografia - Scuola Vaticana di Paleografia Diplomatica e Archivistica
Cortile del Belvedere, 00120 Citt a del Vaticano
Tel: (06) 69883595 *Fax:* (06) 69881377
E-mail: pagano@librs6k.vatlib.it
Key Personnel
Dir: Rev Sergio B Pagano *E-mail:* pagano@librs6k.vatlib.it
Founded: 1884
Subjects: Human Relations, Language Arts, Linguistics, Library & Information Sciences
ISBN Prefix(es): 88-85054

Libreria Editrice Vaticana+
Via Della Tipografia, 00120 Vatican City
Tel: (06) 698-85003 *Fax:* (06) 698-84716
Telex: 5042024 Dirgentel Va
Key Personnel
Dir: Don Nicolo Suffi
Founded: 1926
Subjects: Art, History, Literature, Literary Criticism, Essays, Philosophy, Religion - Other, Theology
ISBN Prefix(es): 88-209
Imprints: LEV

Honduras

General Information

Capital: Tegucigalpa
Language: Spanish (English on northern coast)
Religion: Predominantly Roman Catholic
Population: 5.0 million
Bank Hours: 0900-1200, 1400-1630 Monday-Friday
Shop Hours: Tegucigalpa: 0800-1800, 1330-1800 Monday-Friday; 0800-1200 Saturday; San Pedro Sula: 0700-1200, 1400-1900 Monday-Friday; 0800-1200 Saturday
Currency: 100 centavos = 1 lempira
Export/Import Information: Member of the Central American Common Market but has applied tariffs to imports from other CACM countries since December 1970. No tariff on books. Duty on catalogues is per kilo. No import licenses. No exchange controls.
Copyright: Berne, Buenos Aires (see Copyright Conventions, pg xi)

Editorial Guaymuras+
Calle Adolfo Zuniga, Bo La Ronda, PO Box 1843, Tegucigalpa
Mailing Address: Apdo Postal 1843, Tegucigalpa
Tel: 237 54 33 *Fax:* 238 45 78
E-mail: editorial@sigmanet.hn
Key Personnel
Dir: Isolda Arita Melzer
Manager: Rosendo Antunez *Tel:* 2375433
Founded: 1980
Also acts as printer, bookseller & distributor.
Membership(s): the Library Group of America.
Subjects: Anthropology, Education, Environmental Studies, Ethnicity, Government, Political Science, History, Language Arts, Linguistics, Social Sciences, Sociology
ISBN Prefix(es): 99926-15
Number of titles published annually: 54 Print

Total Titles: 320 Print
Distributed by Abya-Yala de Ecuador; Arco Iris de El Salvador; Libros sin Fronteras (USA); Piedra Santa de Guatemala
Distributor for Centro Editorial; ENLACE y Nuevos Libros de Nicaragua; Libreria de la UNAH; Roxsil; UCA de El Salvador
Bookshop(s): Libreria Guaymuras, Ave Cervantes No 1055, Tegucigalpa *Tel:* 2224140

Editorial Nuevo Continente
Ave Cervantes, Tegucigalpa
Tel: 22-5073
Key Personnel
Dir: Leticia Oyuela

Editorial Universitaria
c/o Universidad de Honduras, Tegucigalpa
Mailing Address: PO Box 3560, Tegucigalpa
Tel: 312110
Telex: 1289

Hong Kong

General Information

Language: English and Chinese (Cantonese Chinese community)
Religion: Predominately Buddhist, also some Confucianism, Islamic, Hinduism & Daoism
Population: 5.8 million
Bank Hours: 0900-1640 Monday-Friday; 0900-1200 Saturday
Shop Hours: 1000-2000 Monday-Saturday
Currency: 100 cents = 1 Hong Kong dollar
Export/Import Information: No tariffs on books and advertising. No import licenses required. No exchange controls.
Copyright: Berne, UCC (see Copyright Conventions, pg xi)

Adsale Publishing Co Ltd
Units 1101-1106, 11/F, Island Place Tower, 510 King's Rd, North Point, Hong Kong
Tel: 2811 8897 *Fax:* 2516 5024
E-mail: publicity@adsale.com.hk
Web Site: www.adsale.com.hk
Key Personnel
Contact: Annie Chu; Ms P Y Ho
Publish Chinese & English industrial trade magazines to foster trade links between foreign companies & China.
Subjects: Automotive, Technology (packaging, plastics, rubber, textile)
ISBN Prefix(es): 962-7036
Number of titles published annually: 26 Print; 4 Online
Total Titles: 624 Print; 8 Online
U.S. Office(s): 21070 Homestead Rd, Suite 100, Cupertino, CA 95014, United States, Contact: Monica Kan *Tel:* 408-737-2820 *Fax:* 408-737-2369 *E-mail:* info@us.adsale.com.hk

Asia Pacific Communications Ltd
Fook Lee Community Centre, Suite 2803, 33 Lockhart Rd, Wanchai
Tel: 2861 0102 *Fax:* 2529 6816
E-mail: asiapac@attglobal.net
Key Personnel
Editor & Publisher: Kathleen Ng
Founded: 1991
Subjects: Finance, Asian Private Equity, Venture Capital
ISBN Prefix(es): 962-85096
Subsidiaries: Institute of Asian Private Equity Investment

Asia 2000 Ltd+
Tung Yiu Commercial Bldg, 5th floor, 31A Wyndham St Central, Hong Kong
Tel: 2530 1409 *Fax:* 2526 1107
E-mail: info@asia2000.com.hk; editor@asia2000.com.hk
Web Site: www.asia2000.com.hk
Key Personnel
Publisher: Michael Morrow *E-mail:* mmorrow@asia2000.com.hk
Marketing, Distribution Manager: Edowan Bersma
Founded: 1980
Independent publisher of English language books
Distributor for overseas publishers
Subjects: Art, Asian Studies, Fiction, Government, Political Science, Photography, Regional Interests
ISBN Prefix(es): 962-7160; 962-8783
Parent Company: Asia 2000 Group
Associate Companies: Manager Media, China
Subsidiaries: Asia Inc
Distributor for St Martens Press; World Bank; World Trade Press

B & I Publication Co Ltd, see Business & Industrial Publication Co Ltd

Benefit Publishing Co+
PO Box 92310, Tsim Sha Tsui Post Office, Kowloon
Founded: 1994
Subjects: Art, Film, Video, Music, Dance, Publishing & Book Trade Reference
ISBN Prefix(es): 962-598
Book Club(s): Hong Kong Book & Magazine Trade Association Ltd

Book Marketing Ltd+
North Point Industrial Bldg, Flat A, 17F, 499 King's Rd, North Point, Hong Kong
Tel: (02) 5620121 *Fax:* (02) 5650187
Key Personnel
Man Dir: Bernard King Sum Chiu
Founded: 1973
Wholesaler.
Subjects: English as a Second Language, Self-Help
ISBN Prefix(es): 962-211
Associate Companies: Leo Publications Ltd, 499 King's Rd, 17F, Flat A, Hong Kong

Breakthrough Ltd - Breakthrough Publishers+
Breakthrough Village, 11th floor, 33A Kung Kok Shan Rd, New Territories
Tel: 2632 0257 *Fax:* 2632 0288
Web Site: www.teachlikethis.com
Key Personnel
Contact: Karen Chan
Founded: 1973
Membership(s): Hong Kong Book & Magazine Trade Association Ltd, Hong Kong Article Numbering Association.
Subjects: Fiction, How-to, Human Relations, Humor, Literature, Literary Criticism, Essays, Poetry
ISBN Prefix(es): 962-264; 962-8791
Warehouse: Flats A, S-V, 14/F, Haribest Industrial Bldg, Shatin Town Lot 173, Fo Tan, Shatin

Business & Industrial Publication Co Ltd+
China Overseas Bldg, Rm B-C 5/F, 139 Hennessy Rd, Wan Chai, Hong Kong
Tel: 25273377 *Fax:* 28667732
Key Personnel
Dir: Alan Kwok
Founded: 1974
Subjects: Mechanical Engineering, Technology
ISBN Prefix(es): 962-7701
Associate Companies: Business & Industrial Trade Fairs Ltd

HONG KONG

Butterworths Hong Kong
12/F, Hennessey Centre, 500 Hennessey Rd, Causeway Bay
Tel: 2965-1400 *Fax:* 2976-0840
E-mail: customer.care@butterworths-hk.com
Web Site: www.butterworths-hk.com
Key Personnel
Commissioning Editor: Anisha Sakhrani
Senior Editor (Hong Kong Cases): Victoria Lai
Advertising Sales Manager: Simon King
General Manager, Customer Service: Wong Wai Cheng
Subjects: Law
Parent Company: Reed Elsevier
Associate Companies: Butterworths India, 14th floor, Vijaya Bldg, 17, Barakhamba Rd, New Delhi 110001, India, Publishing Manager: Ambika Nair *Tel:* (011) 373 9614 *Fax:* (011) 332 6456 *Web Site:* www.butterworths-india.com; Malayan Law Journal Sdn Bhd, Unit A-5-1, 5th floor, Wisman HB, Megan Phileo Ave, 12 Jalan Yap Kwan Seng, 50450 Kuala Lumpur, Malaysia, Managing Editor, New Product Development: Julie Anne Thomas *Tel:* (03) 2162-2882 *Fax:* (03) 2162-3811 *Web Site:* www.mlj.com.my; Butterworths Singapore, No 1 Temasek Ave, 17-01 Millenia Tower, Singapore 039192, Singapore, Regional Publishing Dir: Conita Leung *Tel:* 336 9661 *Fax:* 336 9662 *Web Site:* www.butterworths.com.sg

Celeluck Co Ltd+
Rm 603, Opulent Bldg, 402 Hennessy Rd, Wan Chai
Tel: 2893 9197; 2893 9147 *Fax:* 2891 5591
E-mail: open@open.com.hk
Web Site: www.open.com.hk
Key Personnel
Chief Editor: Jin Zhong
Subjects: Asian Studies, Government, Political Science, History, Journalism, Specializes in China affairs
ISBN Prefix(es): 962-7934

CFW Publications Ltd+
130 Connaught Rd Central, Hong Kong
Tel: 2554 3004 *Fax:* 2543 8007
Founded: 1979
Subjects: Cookery, Travel
ISBN Prefix(es): 962-7031

China Express Media Ltd
Flat/Room 07-10, 26F, North Point MLC Millennia Plaza, 663 King's Rd, Hong Kong
Tel: 2575 7288 *Fax:* 2575 7088
E-mail: kcchan@ossima.com
ISBN Prefix(es): 962-86560

Chinese Christian Literature Council Ltd+
Flat A, 4/F, 138 Nathan Rd, Kowloon
Tel: 2367 8031
Key Personnel
Contact: Mr Sau-Chung Fung
Administration Secretary: Ms Yvonne Mak
E-mail: yvonne@cclc.biz.com.hk
An interdenominational publishing house-mainly in the Chinese Language & also a nonprofit making organization.
Membership(s): WACC; UK.
Subjects: Literature, Literary Criticism, Essays, Music, Dance, Religion - Protestant, Theology
ISBN Prefix(es): 962-294
Bookshop(s): 10 Tung Fong St G/F, Kowloon
Warehouse: 77 Wong Chuk Yeung St, Room 702, Yan Hing Centre, Fo Tan, Shatin

The Chinese University Press+
The Chinese University of Hong Kong, Sha Tin, New Territories
Tel: 2609 6508 *Fax:* 2603 6692; 2603 7355
E-mail: cup@cuhk.edu.hk
Web Site: www.cuhk.edu.hk/cupress.w1.htm; www.chineseupress.com
Telex: 50301 cuhk hx *Cable:* SINOVERSITY
Key Personnel
Dir: Steven K Luk *Tel:* 2609 6460
E-mail: stevenkluk@cuhk.edu.hk
Sales, Rights & Permissions & Business Manager: Angelina Wong *Tel:* 2609 6500
E-mail: laifunwong@cuhk.edu.hk
Production: Kingsley Ma *Tel:* 2609 6467
E-mail: kwaihungma@cuhk.edu.hk
Editorial Manager: Y K Fung *Tel:* 2609 6543
E-mail: yatkongfung@cuhk.edu.hk
Accountant: Yvonne Tam *Tel:* 2609 6507
E-mail: yvonnetam@cuhk.edu.hk
Founded: 1977
Membership(s): Association of American University Press; Association for Asian Studies; International Association of Scholarly Publishers; Society of Scholarly Publishing.
Subjects: Art, Asian Studies, Business, Child Care & Development, Education, Geography, Geology, Government, Political Science, History, Journalism, Language Arts, Linguistics, Law, Literature, Literary Criticism, Essays, Philosophy, Psychology, Psychiatry, Science (General), Social Sciences, Sociology
ISBN Prefix(es): 962-201; 962-996
Total Titles: 500 Print; 4 CD-ROM; 2 Audio
Distributed by Columbia University Press (North America); The Eurospan Group (UK, Europe, Middle East, Africa & Central Asia)
Foreign Rep(s): Columbia University Press (North America); The Eurospan Group (Africa, Europe, Middle East, Central Asia)

Chopsticks Publications Ltd+
8A Soares Ave, Ground floor, Kowloon
Tel: 2336-8433 *Fax:* 2338-1462
E-mail: chopsticks1971@netvigator.com
Key Personnel
Manager: Caroline Au-Yeung
Founder & Dir, Rights & Permissions: Cecilia Jennie Au-Yang *E-mail:* cauyeung@netvigator.com
Sales, Production & Publicity: Chiu Mei Au-Yeung
Founded: 1971
Train caterers in the art of Chinese cooking. Offers classes that last one, four, eight & 13 weeks as well as a 17-week teacher training course.
Membership(s): International Association of Culinary Professionals, USA; Specialize in Oriental cuisine.
Subjects: Cookery, Oriental Cuisine, Dim Sum, Health Cookery
ISBN Prefix(es): 962-7018
Associate Companies: Cherrytree Press Ltd
Distributed by Gazelle Book Services Ltd (UK)

Christian Communications Ltd
3/F, 128 Castle Peak Rd, Kowloon
Tel: 2725-8558 *Fax:* 2386-1804
Web Site: www.ccfellow.org
Key Personnel
General Secretary: Thomas Tang
Founded: 1971
Also acts as bookseller & printing service.
Subjects: Biblical Studies, Religion - Protestant
ISBN Prefix(es): 962-202; 962-8740; 962-8810
U.S. Office(s): 1711 Branham Lane, Suite A-4A, San Jose, CA 95118, United States
Bookshop(s): 1/F 46 Morrison Hill Rd, Wan Chai; 2/F Hing Pong Commercial Bldg, 749A Nathan Rd, Kowloon; 1/F Kolok Bldg, 722 Nathan Rd, Kowloon; 1/F Hong Lok House, 475 Nathan Rd, Kowloon
Shipping Address: Tsuen Tung Factory Bldg, Block D 18/F, 38-40 Chai Wai Kok St, Tsuen Wan NT
Warehouse: Block D 18/F Tsuen Tung Factory Bldg, 38-40 Chai Wai Kok St, Tsuen Wan
Orders to: Tsuen Tung Factory Bldg, Block D 18/F, 38-40 Chai Wai Kok St, Tsuen Wan NT

Chung Hwa Book Co (HK) Ltd+
Unit 1, 2F Fu Hang Bldg, One Hok Yuen St E, Hung Hom, Kowloon
Tel: 2715 0176 *Fax:* 2713 8202; 2713 4675
E-mail: info@chunghwabook.com.hk; pub-dept@chunghwabook.com.hk
Web Site: www.chunghwabook.com.hk *Cable:* 5494
Key Personnel
Man Dir & Editor-in-Chief: Kwok-fai Chan
Publishing Manager: Shirley Cheung
Sales Manager: Belgrid Wong
Founded: 1927
Membership(s): the Hong Kong Publishing Professionals Society Ltd; Hong Kong Publishing Federation Ltd (permanent member).
Subjects: Antiques, Art, Asian Studies, Business, Career Development, Computer Science, English as a Second Language, History, Language Arts, Linguistics, Literature, Literary Criticism, Essays, Management, Marketing, Philosophy, Religion - Buddhist, Self-Help, Social Sciences, Sociology
ISBN Prefix(es): 962-231; 962-8820
Parent Company: Sino United Publishing (Holdings) Ltd
Divisions: Publishing, Marketing & Sales, Retail
Distributor for Longman Asia Ltd; Open Learning Univeristy of Hong Kong (Macau & Hong Kong); Oxford University Press (Hong Kong); Publications (Holding) Ltd; University of H K Press
Bookshop(s): 5B Ma Hang Chung Rd, 2nd floor, Tokwawan, Kowloon; Reader's Service Centre, 450-452 Nathan Rd, Kowloon; Mongkok Branch, 740A Nathan Rd, Kowloon; 88 Fu Yan St, Kwun Tong, Kowloon; Tsuen Wan Branch, 245 Sha Tsui Rd, Tsuen Wan

Commercial Press (Hong Kong) Ltd+
8/F, Eastern Central Plaza, 3 Yiu Hing Rd, Shau Kei Wan
Tel: 25651371 *Fax:* 25651113; 25654277
E-mail: info@commercialpress.com.hk
Web Site: www.commercialpress.com.hk
Telex: 86564 Cmprs HX *Cable:* COMPRESS
Key Personnel
Man Dir & Chief Editor: Chan Man Hung
Deputy General Manager: Chan Kwok Fai
Assistant General Manager: Leung Chung Ho; Tseng Kwok Tai
Marketing Manager & Copyright Controller: Charlemagne Choi
Production Manager: Yam Kin Wah
Founded: 1897
Subjects: Art, Education, Ethnicity, How-to, Language Arts, Linguistics, Medicine, Nursing, Dentistry
ISBN Prefix(es): 962-07
Subsidiaries: Hong Kong Educational Publishing Co
Branch Office(s)
KL Commercial Book Malaysia Sdn. Bhd Co, Malaysia
Commercial Press Ltd, Republic of Singapore, Singapore
Bookshop(s): Book Centre, 9-15 Yee Wo St, Causeway Bay, China *Tel:* (05) 8908028 *Fax:* (05) 8951027; Central Branch & Stamp Centre, 28 Wellington St, Central, China *Tel:* (05) 5250315 *Fax:* (05) 8450035; Shatin Book Plaza, 165 Level 1 & 266-270 Level 2, Phase 1, Shatin, China; North Point Branch, 395 King's Rd, North Point *Tel:* (05) 5620266 *Fax:* (05) 5656763; Mongkok Branch, 608 Nathan Rd, Kowloon, China *Tel:* (05) 3848228 *Fax:* (05) 7703861; Tuen Mun Branch, G/F, Yaohan Stores, Tuen Mun Town Plaza, NT,

PUBLISHERS HONG KONG

Tuen Mun, NT, China *Tel:* (05) 4589332 *Fax:* (05) 4591925; Kornhill Branch, 3/F, Jusco Stores, Quarry Bay, China *Tel:* (05) 5600238 *Fax:* (05) 5679801; Tai Po Branch, 212-215, 1/F Tai Wo Shopping Mall, Tai Po, NT, China *Tel:* (05) 6502628; New Town Plaza, Shatin, China *Tel:* (05) 6931933 *Fax:* (05) 6912064
Orders to: 2/F, Heng Ngai Jewelry Centre, 4 Hok Yuen St E, Hunghom, Kowloon

Courseguides International Ltd
1505, Seaview Centre, 139-141 Hoi Bun Rd, Kwun Tong, Kowloon
Tel: 2737 3322 *Fax:* 2793 1188
Key Personnel
Publisher: T P C Street
Founded: 1982
Subjects: Sports, Athletics
Subsidiaries: Courseguides International (UK) Ltd

Design Human Resources Training & Development+
10C, Mountain View Ct, Discovery Bay, Lantau Island, Hong Kong
Tel: 29877018 *Fax:* 29877018
Key Personnel
Author & International Rights: Robert Wright
E-mail: wright@hkusua.hku.hk
Subjects: Management, Self-Help
ISBN Prefix(es): 962-85036
Distributor for Asia 2000
Orders to: Robert Wright School of Business, University of Hong Kong, 7/F Men Wah Complex, Pokfulam Rd, Hong Kong

The Dharmasthiti Buddist Institute Ltd+
Block A, 2nd floor, Cambridge Court, 84 Waterloo Rd, Kowloon
Tel: 2760 8878 *Fax:* 2760 1223
Key Personnel
Contact: Ms Lai Jill; Cho Karen
Founded: 1982
A registered nonprofit, religious & cultural organization; also participates in cultural education.
Subjects: Education, Ethnicity, Philosophy, Regional Interests, Religion - Buddhist, Academic, Chinese Culture, Life Growth
ISBN Prefix(es): 962-7541

Easy Finder Ltd
10 Tseung Kwan O Industrial Estate W, 8 Chun Ying St, Tseung Kwan O
Tel: 2990 7100 *Fax:* 2623 9315
E-mail: easybook@nextmedia.com.hk
Web Site: www.nextmedia.com.hk
ISBN Prefix(es): 962-85324; 962-85533; 962-8751

Economy and Press
A1, 5/F, Lo Yong Court Commercial Bldg, 220 Lockhart Road, Room 210, Wanchai
Tel: 28917556
ISBN Prefix(es): 962-7277

The Educational Publishing House Ltd
16/F Tsuen Wan Industrial Centre, 220-248 Texaco Rd, Tsuen Wan, Hong Kong
Tel: 24088801 *Fax:* 2810 4201
Telex: 35330 eph hx
ISBN Prefix(es): 962-12
Associate Companies: Fook Hing Offset Printing Co Ltd; The World Publishing Co; Kam Pui Enterprises Ltd; The Seashore Publishing Co; Harris Book Co Ltd; Hong Kong Housing Projects Corp Ltd; Pan-Lloyds (HK) Ltd

Electronic Technology Publishing Co Ltd+
9/F, Room 1, 15 Shing Yip St, Kwun Tong, Kowloon
Tel: 2342 8298; 2342 8299; 2342 9845 *Fax:* 2341 4247
E-mail: info@electronictechnology.com
Web Site: www.electronictechnology.com
Key Personnel
General Manager: Peter Luk
Founded: 1969
Branch offices located in China & Taiwan, Province of China.
Subjects: Communications, Computer Science, Electronics, Electrical Engineering, How-to, Marketing, Radio, TV, Technology
ISBN Prefix(es): 962-7007
Subsidiaries: Modern Electronic & Computing Publishing Co Ltd

Federal Publications Ltd, see Times Publishing (Hong Kong) Ltd

FormAsia Books Ltd+
706 Yu Yuet Lai Bldg, 45 Wyndham St, Central Hong Kong
Tel: (02) 2525 8572 *Fax:* (02) 2522 4234
E-mail: formasia@hkstar.com
Web Site: www.formasiabooks.com
Key Personnel
Dir: Frank Fischbeck
Founded: 1985
Essentially Hong Kong.
Subjects: Art, History, Specialize in Chinese colonial arts, culture & history
ISBN Prefix(es): 962-7283
Distributed by Weatherhill

Friends of the Earth (Charity) Ltd
53-55 Lockhart Road, 2/F, Wan Chai
Tel: 2528 5588 *Fax:* 2529 2777
E-mail: foehk@hk.super.net
Subjects: Agriculture, Energy, Environmental Studies, Government, Political Science, Health, Nutrition
ISBN Prefix(es): 962-8119

Geocarto International Centre
Wah Ming Centre, 2nd floor, Rooms 16 & 17, 421 Queen's Rd W, Hong Kong
Tel: 2546-4262 *Fax:* 2559-3419
E-mail: geocarto@geocarto.com
Web Site: www.geocarto.com
Key Personnel
Contact: K N Au
Subjects: Earth Sciences, Geography, Geology
ISBN Prefix(es): 962-8226

Good Earth Publishing Co Ltd
Flat A 10/F Chiap King Industrial Bldg, 714 Prince Edward Rd, San Po Kong, Kowloon
Tel: 2338 6103 *Fax:* 2338 3610
Key Personnel
General Manager: Yu Chen Fan
ISBN Prefix(es): 962-7878

Hong Kong China Tourism Press
24/F Westlands Centre, 20 Westlands Rd, Quarry Bay
Tel: 2561 8001 *Fax:* 2561 8196
E-mail: edit-e@hkctp.com.hk
Web Site: www.hkctp.com.hk
Key Personnel
Editor-in-Chief: Wang Miao
Vice General Manager & International Rights: Catherine Lee
Founded: 1980
Subjects: Travel
ISBN Prefix(es): 962-7799; 962-7166; 962-8746
Subsidiaries: HK China Tourism Company Ltd

Hong Kong Publishing Co Ltd
307 Yue Yuet Lai Bldg, 43-45 Wyndham St, Central Hong Kong
Tel: 25259053
Telex: 78018 stkhx hx *Cable:* Hkpublish
Key Personnel
Man Dir: Dean Barrett
Editor: Julia Birch
Founded: 1975
Subjects: Asian Studies, Fiction, Travel
ISBN Prefix(es): 962-7035

Hong Kong University Press+
14/F Hing Wai Centre, 7 Tin Wan Praya Rd, Aberdeen
Tel: 2550 2703 *Fax:* 2875 0734
E-mail: upweb@hkucc.hku.hk
Web Site: www.hkupress.org *Cable:* University, Hong Kong
Key Personnel
Publisher, Rights & Permissions: Colin Day
Editor: Dennis Cheung
Marketing: Winnie Chau *E-mail:* hkupress@hkucc.hku.hk
Founded: 1956
Specialize in academic Publishing in Chinese & English.
Subjects: Anthropology, Art, Asian Studies, Behavioral Sciences, Biography, Biological Sciences, Child Care & Development, Communications, Criminology, Disability, Special Needs, Education, English as a Second Language, Environmental Studies, Film, Video, Geography, Geology, Government, Political Science, History, Labor, Industrial Relations, Language Arts, Linguistics, Law, Library & Information Sciences, Medicine, Nursing, Dentistry, Natural History, Philosophy, Public Administration, Real Estate, Religion - Buddhist, Social Sciences, Sociology, Women's Studies
ISBN Prefix(es): 962-209
Total Titles: 250 Print
Distributed by Apac Publishers Services Pte Ltd (Singapore); Eleanor Brasch Enterprises (Australia & New Zealand); The Eurospan Group (Europe); University of Washington Press (USA)
Distributor for Centre of Asian Studies at the University of Hong Kong (Hong Kong, Macau, UK); Comparative Education Research Centre (at the University of Hong Kong); Department of Comparative Literature at the University of Hong Kong (at the University of Hong Kong); Department of Social Work & Social Administration at the University of Hong Kong (at the University of Hong Kong); INSTEP Faculty of Education (at the University of Hong Kong); Oriental Ceramic Society of Hong Kong (Worldwide); University Museum & Art Gallery at the University of Hong Kong (Worldwide); Zed Books Ltd (UK, Hong Kong & Macau)

Island Press+
3/F, Flat A, 33 Hill Rd, Hong Kong
Tel: 28588176 *Fax:* 2482 9889
Key Personnel
Man Dir: Ho Leung-mau
Founded: 1983 (originally founded under the names Li Weijia, Lee Chik-Yuet, Ho Leung-mau)
Subjects: Education, Environmental Studies, Journalism, Literature, Literary Criticism, Essays, Publishing & Book Trade Reference, Travel
ISBN Prefix(es): 962-431

Joint Publishing (HK) Co Ltd
10/F, 9 Queen Victoria St, Central Hong Kong
Mailing Address: 10/F, Tsuen Wan Industrial, Bldg, 220-248 Texaco Rd, Tsuen Wan, NT
Tel: 2523 0105 *Fax:* 2525 8355
E-mail: jpchk@hk.super.net
Web Site: www.jointpublishing.com *Cable:* JOINT PCO
Key Personnel
Man Dir: Mr Zhao Bin
Deputy General Manager: Mr Au Kang Lam

Assistant General Manager: Mr Li Chi Kin; Mr Ho Pui Tong
Dir & Deputy Chief Editor: Mr Li Xin
Rights & Permissions: Judith Luk
Bookshop Manager: Mr Wong Ming Pang
Founded: 1948
Overseas Office: Guangzhou, China.
Subjects: Architecture & Interior Design, Art, Asian Studies, Business, Environmental Studies, Film, Video, Finance, Health, Nutrition, History, Language Arts, Linguistics, Law, Literature, Literary Criticism, Essays, Management, Marketing, Medicine, Nursing, Dentistry
ISBN Prefix(es): 962-04
Parent Company: Sino United Publishing (Holdings) Ltd
Subsidiaries: JPC Collection Ltd (Flags & Gifts); JPC Data Chu Ltd
Bookshop(s): BC & Sino United Publishing (Toronto) Ltd; Eastwind Books & Arts Inc, San Francisco, CA, United States; Foshan H, China; Foshan United Book Co Ltd, China; Guangzhou, China; Joint Publishing Co, Beijing; JPC Bookstore & SUP Bookstore, China; Kwai Chung; Kwai-Fong Branch; Lam Tin Branch, Kowloon; Oriental Culture Enterprise, New York, NY, United States; Readers Service Centre, 9/F Chung Sheung Bldg, 9 Queen Victoria St, Central; Sino United (Canada) Ltd; Sino United Publishing (LA) Ltd, Monterey Park, CA, United States; Whampoa Branch; Tsuen Wan Cultural Plaza, Tsuen Wan

Lands Department, Survey & Mapping Office
Murray Bldg, 14/F, Garden Rd, Central Hong Kong
Tel: 2848 2182 *Fax:* 2521 8726
Subjects: Air photo
ISBN Prefix(es): 962-567

Lea Publications Ltd+
499 King's Rd, 17/F, Flat A, North Point, Hong Kong
Tel: 25-620121 *Fax:* 2565 0187
Key Personnel
Chairman: Bernard K S Chiu
Founded: 1976
Subjects: English as a Second Language, Fiction
ISBN Prefix(es): 962-213
Associate Companies: Book Marketing Ltd
Distributed by Book Marketing Ltd (Hong Kong)

Ling Kee Publishing Group+
Top floor, Zung Fu Industrial Bldg, 1067 King's Rd, Quarry Bay, Hong Kong
Tel: 25616151 *Fax:* 2811 1980
Web Site: www.lingkee.com *Cable:* BOOKLAND
Key Personnel
Founder-owner, Chairman & Chief Executive: Bak Ling Au
Man Dir: Albert Au
Founded: 1945
Membership(s): Hong Kong Educational Publishers Association.
Subjects: Antiques, Education, English as a Second Language, History, How-to, Nonfiction (General)
ISBN Prefix(es): 962-605; 962-608; 962-609; 962-610
Parent Company: Ling Kee Group Ltd
Subsidiaries: Ling Kee Publishing Co Ltd; Ling Kee Book Store Ltd; Unicorn Books Ltd; Unicorn Book (S) Ltd; Ling Lee Publishing Co (S) Ltd; Ling Kee (UK) Ltd; Ward Lock Educational Co Ltd; BLA Publishing Ltd; Thames Head Publishers; Unicorn Publications Inc; Ling Kee Publishing Co Inc
Distributor for Encyclopedia of China Publishing House (Beijing, China)
Showroom(s): 755 Nathan Rd, Kowloon
Bookshop(s): Ling Kee Bookstore Ltd, 127-131 Des Voeux Rd, Central Hong Kong *Tel:* 2545 1540 *Fax:* 2541 1383; Ling Kee Bookstore Ltd, 755 Nathan Rd, Mongkok *Tel:* 2394 1800 *Fax:* 2393 3288

Steve Lu Publishing Ltd
Rm 1203, Man Yee Bldg, 60-68 Des Voeux Rd Central, Hong Kong
Tel: 25210681 *Fax:* 28450492
E-mail: ltlahk@netvigator.com
Key Personnel
Dir: Steve Lu
Subjects: Art, Natural History, Photography, Travel
ISBN Prefix(es): 962-85043

Macmillan Publishers (China) Ltd
Unit 1812, 18/F Paul Y Centre, 51 Hung To Rd, Kwun Tong, Kowloon
Tel: 2811 8781 *Fax:* 2811 0743
Web Site: www.macmillan.com.hk
Key Personnel
Man Dir: Yiu Hei Kan *E-mail:* yhk@macmillan.com.hk
Founded: 1969
Subjects: Foreign Countries
ISBN Prefix(es): 962-03
Parent Company: Macmillan Publishers Ltd, United Kingdom

Med Info Publishing Co
401 Man Yee Bldg, 60 Des Voeux Rd, C, Hong Kong
Tel: 2522 2713
Key Personnel
Sales Manager: Stella Ng
ISBN Prefix(es): 962-363

Ming Pao Publications Ltd+
Subsidiary of Ming Pao Enterprise Corp Ltd
Ming Pao Industrial Centre, 15/F, Block A, 18 Ka Yip St, Hong Kong
Tel: 2595 3084 *Fax:* 2898 2646
E-mail: geocomm@mingpao.com
Web Site: security.mingpao.com/books
Key Personnel
General Man & Chief Editor: Mr Poon Yiu Ming *Tel:* 2595 3318
Dir: Tiong Kiew Chiong
Founded: 1986
Subjects: Biography, Business, Child Care & Development, Cookery, Economics, Fiction, Health, Nutrition, Management, Nonfiction (General), Philosophy, Psychology, Psychiatry, Regional Interests, Comics, Investment
ISBN Prefix(es): 962-357; 962-973
Associate Companies: Ming Pao Magazines Ltd, Mr Lung King Cheong *Tel:* 2515 5111 *Fax:* 2505 7841 *Web Site:* www.mpweekly.com; Ming Pao Newspapers Ltd, Mr Cheung Kin Bor *Fax:* 2898 3282 *Web Site:* www.mingpao.com; Yazhou Zhoukan Ltd, Mr Yau Lop Poon *Fax:* 2505 9662 *Web Site:* www.yzzk.com
Book Club(s): Ming Pao Book Club, Mr Poon Yiu Ming

Modern Electronic & Computing Publishing Co Ltd+
Blk 1, 9/F, 15 Shing Yip St, Kwun Tong, Kowloon
Tel: 2342 8299 *Fax:* 2341 4247
E-mail: info@computertoday.com.hk
Web Site: www.computertoday.com.hk
Key Personnel
General Manager: Peter Luk *Tel:* 2342 9844
Founded: 1989
Subjects: Communications, Computer Science, Education, How-to, Microcomputers, Technology
ISBN Prefix(es): 962-7007
Parent Company: Electronic Technology Publication Co
Branch Office(s)
China
Taiwan, Province of China

Next Magazine Publishing Ltd
8 Chun Ying St, TKO Industial Estate West, Tseung Kwan O
Tel: 2744 2733 *Fax:* 2790 7240
E-mail: editorial@nextmedia.com.hk
Web Site: www.nextmedia.com.hk

Peace Book Co Ltd+
Rm 1502 Wing On House, 71 Des Voeuk Rd C, Central Hong Kong
Tel: 2804-6687 *Fax:* 2804-6409 *Cable:* PEACEBOOK
Key Personnel
Dir: Qian Wangsi
Founded: 1979
Subjects: Asian Studies, Health, Nutrition
ISBN Prefix(es): 962-7176

Pearson Education China Ltd
18/F Cornwall House, Taikoo Place, 979 King's Rd, Quarry Bay
Tel: (852) 3181-0000 *Fax:* (852) 2565-7440
E-mail: info@ilongman.com
Web Site: www.pearsoned.com.hk
Key Personnel
President, North Asia: T C Goh
Finance Dir, North Asia: Marion Cameron
Marketing & Sales Dir: KP Tse
Publishing Dir: Cynthia Lam; Kenneth Ma
Dir, Bilingual Dictionaries & Home Edueation: T C Wong
Dir, Asia ELT: Farrah Ching

Philopsychy Press+
PO Box 1224, 2A Tower 1 22 Sui ho Rd, Shatin, New Territories
Tel: 2604 4403 *Fax:* 2604 4403
E-mail: ppp@hkbu.edu.hk
Web Site: www.hkbu.edu.hk
Key Personnel
International Rights: Dr Stephen R Palmquist *E-mail:* StevePq@hkbu.edu.hk
Founded: 1993
Philopsychy means soul-loving. The society is a global, internet-based community of writers & those interested in supporting the society's principles.
Subjects: Biblical Studies, Philosophy, Psychology, Psychiatry, Religion - Protestant, Self-Help, Theology
ISBN Prefix(es): 962-7770

Photoart Ltd+
Flat D, 8/F, 51 Paterson St, Causeway Bay, Hong Kong
Tel: 2117 1198 *Fax:* 2507 2878
E-mail: info@photoart.com.hk
Web Site: www.photoart.com.hk
Key Personnel
Man Dir: Mr Lee Georming
Founded: 1960
Subjects: Photography, Publishing & Book Trade Reference
ISBN Prefix(es): 962-8165

Press Mark Media Ltd+
Flat D, 1/F, Prospect Mansion, 66-72 Paterson St, Causeway Bay
Tel: 28822230 *Fax:* 2882 3949; 2882 2471
E-mail: magazine@todayliving.com
Founded: 1987
Publishing & advertising.
Subjects: Architecture & Interior Design, Art, House & Home, Publishing & Book Trade Ref-

erence, Regional Interests, Sports, Athletics, Travel, Wine & Spirits
ISBN Prefix(es): 962-7608

Research Centre for Translation+
Institute of Chinese Studies, Chinese University of Hong Kong, Shatin, New Territories
Tel: 2609 7399; 2609 7407 *Fax:* 2603 5110; 2603 5195
E-mail: rct@cuhk.edu.hk
Web Site: www.cuhk.edu.hk/rct/home.html
Telex: 50301 CUHK HX *Cable:* SINOVERSITY
Key Personnel
Dir & Editor: Eva Hung *Tel:* 2609 7385
  E-mail: evahung@cuhk.edu.hk
Man Editor: David E Pollard *E-mail:* pollard-david@cuhk.edu.hk
Production Assistant: Cecilia Ip *E-mail:* ceci@cuhk.edu.hk
Founded: 1971
Specialize in English translations of Chinese literature.
Subjects: Asian Studies, Fiction, Literature, Literary Criticism, Essays, Poetry
ISBN Prefix(es): 962-7255
Distributed by China Books (Australia); Chinese University Press (Worldwide)

SCMP Book Publishing Ltd+
No 1 Leighton Rd, Causeway Bay, Hong Kong
Tel: 2836 6088 *Fax:* 2838 4061
Key Personnel
Publishing Manager: Leung Ka Kei
Editor: Ms Tse Yin Fong
Marketing Manager: Mr Fung Ka Wai
Founded: 1980
Subjects: Accounting, Advertising, Animals, Pets, Antiques, Astrology, Occult, Business, Career Development, Child Care & Development, Cookery, Crafts, Games, Hobbies, Fiction, Finance, Gardening, Plants, Health, Nutrition, How-to, Management, Marketing, Mysteries, Nonfiction (General), Psychology, Psychiatry, Travel
ISBN Prefix(es): 962-17
Parent Company: TVE International Ltd
Associate Companies: CV Idaysu; TV Week Ltd; Retail Corp Ltd; Audio-Visual Travel Ltd; Highlight Tours Ltd

Sesame Publication Co+
Room 505, 4/F, Winner House, 310 King's Rd, North Point, Hong Kong
Tel: 2508 9920; 2508 9311 *Fax:* 2508 9603
E-mail: sesame01@hkstar.hk
Key Personnel
Man Dir: Dick Paul Wong
Founded: 1987
Specialize in children's books & printing services.
Subjects: Animals, Pets, Child Care & Development, English as a Second Language, Fiction
ISBN Prefix(es): 962-347; 962-8795; 962-983; 962-8811; 962-8818
Warehouse: Blk B, 23/F, Jing Ho Ind Bldg, 78-84 Wang Lung St, Tsuen Wan *Tel:* 2408 7685 *Fax:* 2407 2565

Shanghai Book Co Ltd
5th floor, Block A, 345 Des Voeux Rd, West, Hong Kong
Tel: 2548 6160
Key Personnel
Man Dir: Lap Shan Wong
Founded: 1946
Subjects: Music, Dance
ISBN Prefix(es): 962-239
Associate Companies: Shanghai Book Co (Pte) Ltd, Singapore; Shanghai Book Co, (KL) Sdn Bhd, Malaysia; China Cultural Corporation
Imprints: The Won Yit Book Co
Distributor for People's Music Publishing House

Sin Min Chu Publishing Co
Hunghom Commercial Centre, Room 1015, Hunghom, 39 Ma Tau Wai Rd, Tower A, Kowloon
Tel: (02) 2334 9327 *Fax:* (02) 76 58 471
ISBN Prefix(es): 962-336

South China Morning Post Ltd+
22 Dai Fat St, Tai Po
Tel: 2680 8888
Web Site: www.scmp.com
Telex: hx 86008 *Cable:* Postscript Hong Kong
Key Personnel
Editor: Adrian Oosthuizen
Publisher: Christopher Axberg
Marketing Manager: Sharon Galistan
Founded: 1976
Subjects: Asian Studies, Radio, TV
ISBN Prefix(es): 962-10
Bookshop(s): SCM Post Family Bookshops in Star Ferry, Furama Hotel, Ocean Centre

Springer-Verlag Hong Kong Ltd
Room 701, Mirror Tower, 61 Mody Rd, Tsim Sha Tsui, Kowloon Bay, Kowloon
Tel: 27 23 96 98 *Fax:* 27 24 23 66
Founded: 1986
ISBN Prefix(es): 962-430
Parent Company: Springer-Verlag GmbH & Co KG, Heidelberger Platz 3, 14197 Berlin, Germany

Summerson Eastern Publishers Ltd+
4/F, Block B, 434 Queen's Rd W, Hong Kong
Tel: 25408123 *Fax:* 2559 7869
Key Personnel
Man Dir: Mr M K Woo
Executive Dir: Ms M M Chong
Senior Manager: Bill M P Lo
Founded: 1976
Membership(s): Hong Kong Educational Publishers Association Ltd.
ISBN Prefix(es): 962-221

Sun Mui Press
PO Box 366, Shatin, NT
Tel: 2694 8525 *Fax:* 2610 1202
E-mail: auly@chevalier.net
Key Personnel
Contact: Au Loong-Yu
Subjects: Economics, Government, Political Science, History
ISBN Prefix(es): 962-7529

Sun Ya Publications (HK) Ltd+
Rm 1306, Eastern Centre, 1065 King's Rd, Hong Kong
Tel: 2562 0161 *Fax:* 2565 9951
E-mail: info@sunya.com.hk
Web Site: www.sunya.com.hk
Telex: 85849 Clwso Hx *Cable:* 6386
Key Personnel
Man Dir, Editorial, Rights & Permissions: Irene Yim
Man Dir: Yim Ng Seen Ha
Sales: Chan Chung-Chiu
Production: Miss Tsang Suet-Ying
Publicity: Wai Kim-Hung
Founded: 1961
Subjects: Fiction, Nonfiction (General)
ISBN Prefix(es): 962-08
Parent Company: Sino United Publishing (Holdings) Ltd
Subsidiaries: Sunbeam Publications (HK) Ltd
Bookshop(s): 111 N Atlantic Blvd, Suite 228, Monterey Park, CA 91754, United States

Ta Kung Pao (HK) Ltd
6/F 342 Hennessy Rd, Hong Kong
Tel: 25737213; 25757181 *Fax:* 257463316

Key Personnel
Marketing Manager, Circulation & Marketing Executive: Summy Ho
Subjects: China
ISBN Prefix(es): 962-582

Tai Yip Co+
1/F Capitol Plaza, 2-10 Lyndhurst Terrace, Central Hong Kong
Tel: 2524-5963 *Fax:* 2845-3296
E-mail: tybook@taiyipart.com.hk
Web Site: www.taiyipart.com.hk
Key Personnel
Dir: Ying-Lau Cheung
Subjects: Art
ISBN Prefix(es): 962-7239
Bookshop(s): Tai Yip Art Book Centre, 1/F, Hong Kong Museum of Art, 10 Salisbury Rd, Tsim Sha Tsui, Kowloon *Tel:* 2732-2088 *Fax:* 2312-1208

Technology Exchange Ltd+
Fo Tan Industrial Centre, 26-28 Au Pui Wan St, Suite 1102, Fotan Sha Tin, New Territories, Hong Kong
Tel: 2602 6300 *Fax:* 2609 1687
Key Personnel
General Manager: Francis K F Ng
  E-mail: publication@tech-ex.com
Founded: 1987
Specialize also in medical devices, instrumentation of automation & cable tv.
Subjects: Communications, Electronics, Electrical Engineering, Radio, TV
ISBN Prefix(es): 962-452
Total Titles: 6 Print

Thomson Corporation
17/F Lyndhurst Tower, One Lyndhurst Terrace, Central Hong Kong
Tel: 2533 5416 *Fax:* 2530 3588
Web Site: www.tfibcm.com
Key Personnel
Editor-in-Chief: Tony Shale
General Manager & International Rights: Geoff Defreitas
Subjects: Finance

Times Publishing (Hong Kong) Ltd+
Formerly Federal Publications Ltd
9-10/F, Block C, Seaview Est, 2-8 Watson Rd, North Point, Hong Kong
Tel: 23342421 *Fax:* 27645095; 23657834
E-mail: admin@federalbooks.com
Key Personnel
Man Dir: Tom Y L Ng
Founded: 1959
Membership(s): Hong Kong Educational P A, Educational Booksellers Association.
Subjects: Biblical Studies, Biological Sciences, Computer Science, Geography, Geology, Health, Nutrition, Mathematics, Religion - Protestant, Science (General)
ISBN Prefix(es): 962-302; 962-8781
Parent Company: Times Publishing Ltd, Singapore
Associate Companies: Federal Publications Sdn Bhd, Malaysia; Federal Publications (S) Pte Ltd; Times Books International
Bookshop(s): The Times Book Centre, Centre, Shops C & E, Mitlon Mansion, 96 Nathan Rd, Kowloon; The Times Book Centre, Shop G31, Hutchison House, Central District; Howard Book Store, G/F 74 Argyle St, Kowloon
Warehouse: Federal Publications Ltd, 2D Freder Centre, 68 Sung Wong Toi Rd, Kowloon

Times Ringier Ltd
11-13 Dai Kwai St, Tai Po, Industrial Estate, Tai Po, New Territories
Tel: 2854 4266 *Fax:* 2854 4009
E-mail: contact@ringierpacific.com
Web Site: www.ringierpacific.com

Key Personnel
Manager: Peter Siau
Founded: 1998
Publishes trade journals which help to satisfy the need for specialized business information in China.
Parent Company: TPL & Ringier AG

Unicorn Books Ltd+
14/F Zung Fu Industrial Bldg, 1067 King's Rd, Hong Kong
Tel: 2561 6151 *Fax:* 2811 1980
Key Personnel
Chief Operating Officer: Albert K W Au
Membership(s): The Ling Kee Group, Hong Kong.
Subjects: Antiques, Child Care & Development, Crafts, Games, Hobbies, Gardening, Plants, How-to, Self-Help, Chinese Language, Encyclopedia, Hong Kong History
ISBN Prefix(es): 962-232
Parent Company: Ling Kee Publishing Group
Distributed by Encyclopeida Publishing House of China (Beijing, China)

Union Press Ltd
3/F, Hong Lok Mansion, 74 Argyle St, Kowloon
Tel: 2567 3762 *Fax:* 2394 5084
ISBN Prefix(es): 962-207

The University of Hong Kong, Department of Philosophy
Pokfulam Rd, Hong Kong
Tel: 28592797 *Fax:* 2559 8452
E-mail: fctmoore@hkuxa.hku.hk
Key Personnel
Contact: Prof Laurence Goldstein
Subjects: Computer Science, Philosophy
ISBN Prefix(es): 962-375

Vision Pub Co Ltd+
Flat 33, 5/F, Tower B, Cambridge Plaza, 510 King's Rd, North Point, New Territories
Tel: 23147627; 92676502 *Fax:* 29078838
E-mail: pcgameos@pcgame.com.hk
Web Site: www.pcgame.com.hk
Key Personnel
Manager: Kai-man Pang
Founded: 1987
Membership(s): HK Educational Publishers Association Ltd.
Subjects: Mathematics, Technology
ISBN Prefix(es): 962-407

Vista Productions Ltd
Room A 7/F, Melbourne Industrial Bldg, 16 Westlands Rd, Hong Kong
Tel: 25632492 *Fax:* 25655803
Telex: 63321 Timbk Hx
Subjects: Education
ISBN Prefix(es): 962-05
Associate Companies: Times Educational Co Sdn Bhd, Malaysia

Wellday Ltd
Rm 1901, Kai Tak Commercial Bldg, 317-321 Des Voeux Rd Central, Hong Kong
Tel: 23628489 *Fax:* 23628564
Key Personnel
General Manager: Ms Shen Miao
Subjects: Advertising, Business
ISBN Prefix(es): 962-85051
Distributor for Miller Freeman Publishers Ltd

Witman Publishing Co (HK) Ltd+
9-11 Tsat Tse Mui Rd, North Point, Hong Kong
Tel: 2562 6279 *Fax:* 2565 5482
E-mail: witmanp@hk.star.com
Key Personnel
Dir: Yau Suk Ching
Founded: 1978

Specialize in English language books, cassettes, videos & diskettes.
Membership(s): ACTPO.
Subjects: Fiction, History, Language Arts, Linguistics, Mathematics
ISBN Prefix(es): 962-7044; 962-304

The Won Yit Book Co, *imprint of* Shanghai Book Co Ltd

Yazhou Zhoukan Ltd
15/F, Blk A, Ming Pao Industrial Centre, 18 Ka Yip St, Chai Wan
Tel: 2515 5483 *Fax:* 2595 0497
E-mail: yzad@mingpao.com
Web Site: www.yzzk.com
Key Personnel
Contact: Tracy Cheung; Patrick Lo; Ruby Lo; Ivy Sze
Founded: 1987
Subjects: Asian Studies, Business, Economics, Finance, Regional Interests
ISBN Prefix(es): 962-85434
Parent Company: Ming Pao Grou

Zie Yongder Co Ltd
14/F, Aik San Bldg, 14 Westlands Road, Quarry Bay, Hong Kong
Tel: 29630111
ISBN Prefix(es): 962-7359

ZYC Holding Ltd
Aik San Factory Bldg 14 Westlands Rd, Quarry Bay, Hong Kong
Tel: 2963 0111

Hungary

General Information

Capital: Budapest
Language: Hungarian (German widely known)
Religion: Predominantly Roman Catholic, also Hungarian Reformed, Lutheran & Hungarian Orthodox
Population: 10.3 million
Bank Hours: 0800-1630 Monday-Friday
Shop Hours: 1000-1800 Monday-Friday; 1000-1500 Saturday
Currency: 100 filler = 1 forint
Export/Import Information: Any companies should be registered at the Registry Court. 12% VAT on books. Book importing & exporting is through Kultura - Hungarian Foreign Trading Co, H-1389 Budapest 62, Postfi0k 149; atlases through Cartographica, H-1443 Budapest, Postafiok 132. Magyar Hirdeto, Budapest, is a full service advertising agency.
Copyright: UCC, Berne (see Copyright Conventions, pg xi)

Advent Kiado+
Borsfa u 55, 1171 Budapest
Tel: (01) 256-5205 *Fax:* (01) 2565205
E-mail: advent12@matavnet.hu
Key Personnel
Publishing Dir: Laszlo Erdelyi
Founded: 1988
Subjects: Astrology, Occult, Biblical Studies, Cookery, Education, Health, Nutrition, Medicine, Nursing, Dentistry, Poetry, Religion - Protestant
ISBN Prefix(es): 963-7817; 963-9122

Agape Ferences Nyomda es Konyvkiado Kft
Matyas ter 26, 6725 Szeged

Tel: (062) 444-002; (062) 323-002 *Fax:* (062) 442-592
E-mail: agape@tiszanet.hu
Key Personnel
Dir: Karoly Harmath
Founded: 1991
Subjects: Religion - Catholic
ISBN Prefix(es): 963-458; 963-8112
Parent Company: Agape, Cara Dusana 4, Novi Sad, Serbia and Montenegro

Agrargazdsagi Kutato es Informatikai Intezet
Zsil u 3/5, 1093 Budapest
Mailing Address: Postfach 5, 1355 Budapest
Tel: (01) 2171011 *Fax:* (01) 1177037
Telex: 22-6923
ISBN Prefix(es): 963-491

Akademiai Kiado+
Prielle Korneila u 19, 1117 Budapest
Mailing Address: PO Box 245, 1519 Budapest
Tel: (01) 4648220; (01) 4648282; (01) 4648221; (01) 4648231
Key Personnel
President & Man Dir: Zsolt Bucsi Szabo
Sales, Promotion, Home & International: Rita Nemeth
Editorial Dir: Peter Bajor; Gyongyi Pomazi
Founded: 1828
Publishing House of the Hungarian Academy of Sciences.
Subjects: Archaeology, Art, Biological Sciences, Earth Sciences, Economics, Engineering (General), History, Language Arts, Linguistics, Law, Literature, Literary Criticism, Essays, Medicine, Nursing, Dentistry, Music, Dance, Philosophy, Science (General), Social Sciences, Sociology, Veterinary Science
ISBN Prefix(es): 963-05
U.S. Office(s): ISBS (International Specialized Book Service Inc), 5804 NE Hassolo St, Portland, OR 97213-3644, United States

Aranyhal Konyvkiado Goldfish Publishing+
Dolmany u 5-7, 1131 Budapest
Tel: (01) 239-6721 *Fax:* (01) 239-6730
E-mail: sprinter@com.kibernet.hu
Key Personnel
Owner & Manager: Gandor Radvan
Marketing Manager: Zulton Takacs
Artistic & Design Manager: Xenia Radvan
International Rights Contact: S Emege David
Founded: 1993
Specialize in children's books, mainly board books & activity books.
Membership(s): MKKE (Association of Hungarian Book Publishers & Distributors).
Subjects: Animals, Pets, Child Care & Development, Cookery, Crafts, Games, Hobbies, Education, Humor, Language Arts, Linguistics, Literature, Literary Criticism, Essays, Nonfiction (General), Outdoor Recreation, Physics
ISBN Prefix(es): 963-348; 963-8366; 963-9196; 963-9268; 963-9394
Number of titles published annually: 70 Print; 2 CD-ROM
Total Titles: 35 Print
Ultimate Parent Company: MKKE (Association of Hungarian Book Publishers & Distributors)
Subsidiaries: Sprinter Prest Romania SRL
Distributed by Sprinter Rft
Foreign Rep(s): Sprinter Prest Romania SRL (Romania)
Distribution Center: SICC Nagykereskede's

Atlantisz Kiado+
Gerloczy u 4, 1052 Budapest
Tel: (01) 4065645 *Fax:* (01) 4065645
E-mail: atlantis@budapest.hu
Key Personnel
Publisher: Dr Tamas Miklos
Founded: 1990
Also International Bookshop.

Subjects: History, Philosophy, Religion - Other, Social Sciences, Sociology, Theology
ISBN Prefix(es): 963-7978; 963-9165

Balassi Kiado Kft+
Muranyi u 61, 1078 Budapest
Tel: (01) 3518075; (01) 3518343
E-mail: balassi@mail.datanet.hu
Key Personnel
Dir: Peter Koeszeghy
International Rights: Judit Borus
Founded: 1990
Membership(s): The Association of Hungarian Bookpublishers & Booksellers.
Subjects: Art, History, Language Arts, Linguistics, Literature, Literary Criticism, Essays, Nonfiction (General), Philosophy, Social Sciences, Sociology
ISBN Prefix(es): 963-506; 963-7873
Total Titles: 533 Print; 1 CD-ROM
Distributed by Harrassowitz; Polis (Romania)
Distributor for Cambridge UP; Kaligram (Romania, Slovakia); Polis (Romania)
Bookshop(s): Margit u 1, Budapest 1023, Contact: Hannus Zsuzaa *Tel:* (01) 212-0214 *Fax:* (01) 212-0214
Book Club(s): Balassi-Klub, Margit u 1, Budapest 1023 *Tel:* (01) 335-2885 *Fax:* (01) 335-2885

Budapesti Muszaki es Gazdasagtudomanyi Egyetem
Formerly Orszagos Mueszaki Informacios Kozpont es Konyvtar
Muegyetem rkp 3, 1111 Budapest
Mailing Address: Postfach 91, 1521 Budapest
Tel: (01) 4632441; (01) 4632440
Telex: 224944 omikk h
Key Personnel
Dir General: Dr Peter Horvath
Dir: Lajos Janszky
ISBN Prefix(es): 963-420; 963-421

Cartographia Ltd+
Bosnyak Ter 5, 1149 Budapest
Mailing Address: PO Box 80, 1590 Budapest
Tel: (01) 222-6727 *Fax:* (01) 222-6728
E-mail: mail@cartographia.hu
Web Site: www.cartographia.hu *Cable:* CARTOGRAPHIA
Key Personnel
Man Dir: Dr Arpad Papp-Vary *Tel:* (01) 252-8507 *Fax:* (01) 363-3649 *E-mail:* apappvary@cartographia.hu
Sales, Publicity, Rights & Permissions: Ms Zsuzsa Nemenyi
Founded: 1954
ISBN Prefix(es): 963-350; 963-350; 963-351; 963-353
Bookshop(s): Bajcsy-Zsilinszky u 37, Budapest 1067

Central European University Press+
Szent Istvan ter 11b, 2nd floor, 1051 Budapest
Mailing Address: Postfach 519/2, 1397 Budapest
Tel: (01) 327 3000 *Fax:* (01) 327 3183
E-mail: ceupress@ceupress.com
Web Site: www.ceupress.com
Key Personnel
Dir: Istvan Bart *Tel:* (01) 327 3270 *E-mail:* barti@ceu.hu
Executive Manager: Peter Inkei *Tel:* (01) 327 3181 *E-mail:* inkeip@ceu.hu
Founded: 1994
Dedicated to broadening the range of literature available in English or topics concerning the past & present history & culture of people living in the countries of central & eastern Europe.
Subjects: Economics, Government, Political Science, History, Literature, Literary Criticism, Essays, Social Sciences, Sociology, Cultural studies & medieval history
ISBN Prefix(es): 1-85866; 963-9116; 963-9241
Total Titles: 98 Print; 1 Online
U.S. Office(s): 400 W 59 St, New York, NY 10019, United States, Contact: Martin Greenwald *Tel:* 212-547-6932 *Fax:* 646-557-2416 *E-mail:* mgreenwald@sorosny.org (USA & Canada)
Orders to: Books International, PO Box 605, Herndon, VA 20172, United States *Tel:* 703-661-1500 *Fax:* 703-661-1501 (Orders for USA & Canada)
Plymbridge Distributors Ltd, Estover Rd, Plymbridge, United Kingdom *Tel:* (01752) 202301 *Fax:* (01752) 202333 (Orders for UK & Western Europe)

Corvina Books Ltd+
Rakoczi ut 16, 1072 Budapest
Mailing Address: PO Box 108, 1364 Budapest 4
Tel: (01) 1184347 *Fax:* (01) 1184410
E-mail: corvina@axelero.hu *Cable:* CORVINA BUDAPEST
Key Personnel
General Manager: Laszlo Kunos
Founded: 1955
Subjects: Art, Cookery, History, Language Arts, Linguistics, Social Sciences, Sociology
ISBN Prefix(es): 963-13

Europa Konyvkiado+
Kossuth Lajos ter 13-15, 1055 Budapest
Mailing Address: Postfach 65, 1363 Budapest
Tel: (01) 331-2700 *Fax:* (01) 331-4162
E-mail: info@europakiado.hu
Web Site: www.europakiado.hu
Telex: 225645 *Cable:* EUROLIBER
Key Personnel
Publisher: Levente Osztovits
Executive Dir: Dr P Roman
Production: T Nevery
Sales: M Kertesz
Publicity: G Joo
Founded: 1945
Subjects: Biography, Fiction, Philosophy, Poetry
ISBN Prefix(es): 963-07

Foldmuvelesugyi Miniszterium Muszaki Intezet
Tessedik S u 4, 2101 Godollo
Tel: (028) 320-644 *Fax:* (028) 320-960
E-mail: dekani@eng.gau.hu
Telex: 022-5816 *Cable:* FMMI GODOLLO
Key Personnel
Dir: Dr Fozsef Hajdu
Founded: 1954
Subjects: Agriculture, Electronics, Electrical Engineering, Energy, Engineering (General), Environmental Studies, Mechanical Engineering, Science (General), Technology
ISBN Prefix(es): 963-611
Imprints: Mezogazdasagi; Technika
Orders to: FMMI, Postfach 103, 2101 Godollo

Gondolat Kiado
Brody S u16, 1088 Budapest
Mailing Address: Postfach 225, 1368 Budapest
Tel: (01) 38-3358 *Fax:* (01) 138-4540
Key Personnel
Editor-in-Chief: Miklos Hernadi, PhD
Dir: Gyorgy Feher
Subjects: Nonfiction (General)
ISBN Prefix(es): 963-280; 963-281; 963-282

Greger-Delacroix
Amfiteatrum u3, Budapest 1031
Tel: (01) 608936
E-mail: gregerdelacroix@compuserve.com; greger@elender.hu
Key Personnel
President & Dir: Andras J Kereszty
E-mail: biograph@greger.hu
Bureau Chief: Erika Kormendy *Tel:* (01) 302-5149 *E-mail:* delacroix@greger.hu
Founded: 1990
Reliable books.
ISBN Prefix(es): 963-85811; 963-86144

Hatagu Sip Alapitvany
Vaci ut 100, Budapest 1133
Tel: (01) 1403728
ISBN Prefix(es): 963-7615

Hatter Lap- es Konyvkiado Kft+
Vaci ut 19, 1134 Budapest
Mailing Address: Postfach 97, 1525 Budapest
Tel: (01) 3208230; (01) 3297293 *Fax:* (01) 3208230; (01) 3297293
E-mail: hatterkiado@matavnet.hu
Telex: 1311343
Key Personnel
Dir: Kalman Lantos
Founded: 1985
Subjects: Science (General), Transportation
ISBN Prefix(es): 963-7403; 963-7455; 963-8128; 963-9365

Helikon Kiado+
Bajcsy-Zsilinsky ut 37, 1065 Budapest
Tel: (01) 428-9450; (01) 428-9429 *Fax:* (01) 428-9481
E-mail: helikon@helikon.hu
Web Site: www.helikon.hu
Key Personnel
Man Dir: Janos Szilagyi
Founded: 1982
Subjects: Art, History
ISBN Prefix(es): 963-207; 963-208
Bookshop(s): Helikon Bookshop, Suetoe u 2, 1052 Budapest; Litea Bookshop & Teagarden, Hess A ter 4, 1014 Budapest

Holnap Kiado Vallalat
Zenta u 5, 1111 Budapest
Tel: (01) 666928 *Fax:* (01) 656624
Key Personnel
Dir: Dr Eszter Milkovich
ISBN Prefix(es): 963-345; 963-346

Idegenforgalmi Propaganda es Kiado Vallalat+
Angol u 22, 1149 Budapest
Mailing Address: Postfach 164, 1440 Budapest
Tel: (01) 633652; (01) 633653 *Fax:* (01) 1837320
Telex: 225309 *Cable:* 1PV-BUDAPEST
Key Personnel
General Dir: Istvan Fazekas
Assistant Dir: Tamas Moldovan; Andras Vaczi
Founded: 1971
32 different services in sport & Congressional events.
Membership(s): WTO.
Subjects: Science (General), Travel
ISBN Prefix(es): 963-316
Imprints: IPV Herausgeben
Branch Office(s)
Brussels, Belgium
Milan, Italy
Warehouse: IPV Buecherlager, 1135 Budapest

Ifjusagi Lap-eskonyvkiado Vallalat (Youth Publishing House)+
Revay u 16, 1065 Budapest
Mailing Address: Postfach 601, 1373 Budapest
Tel: (01) 1116660 *Fax:* (01) 1530959
Telex: 226183
Key Personnel
Dir: Bela Koncz
Assistant Dir: Jozsef Gebler
Founded: 1957
Subjects: Crafts, Games, Hobbies, Fiction, House & Home, Mysteries, Romance, Science Fiction, Fantasy
ISBN Prefix(es): 963-422; 963-423

Ikon Publishing Ltd
Toeroekvesz ut 46/d, 1025 Budapest
Tel: (01) 1761404 *Fax:* (01) 1158089
Key Personnel
Man Dir: Dr Andras Renyi
ISBN Prefix(es): 963-7948

IPV Herausgeben, *imprint of* Idegenforgalmi Propaganda es Kiado Vallalat

Janus Pannonius Tudomanyegyetem
Postfach 9, 7601 Pecs
Tel: (072) 411 433 *Fax:* (072) 15738
Key Personnel
President of Publishing Committee: Lovasz Gyoergy
Founded: 1991
Subjects: Earth Sciences, History, Law, Management, Marketing, Philosophy, Physical Sciences, Social Sciences, Sociology
ISBN Prefix(es): 963-641

Jelenkor Verlag+
Munkacsy Mihaly u 30/A, 7621 Pecs
Tel: (072) 314-782; (072) 335-767 *Fax:* (072) 532-047
E-mail: jelenkor@mail.datanet.hu
Web Site: www.jelenkor.com
Key Personnel
Dir: Dr Gabor Csordas *E-mail:* jk.csg@freemail.hu
Founded: 1993
Promote contemporary Hungarian poetry, fiction & philosophy.
Subjects: Art, Drama, Theater, Fiction, Film, Video, History, Literature, Literary Criticism, Essays, Philosophy, Poetry
ISBN Prefix(es): 963-676; 963-7770
Branch Office(s)
Rakoczi ut 59 II/9, 1081 Budapest *Tel:* (01) 3133804 *Fax:* (01) 3230376

Joszoveg Muhely Kiado+
Kecskemeti u 6, 1053 Budapest
Tel: (01) 266 0393; (01) 317 3536 *Fax:* (01) 266 0393
E-mail: joszoveg@euroweb.hu
Key Personnel
Publications Manager: Dr Peter Foti
Distribution Manager: Eva Fay
Founded: 1997
Specialize in bilingual books & ethnography.
Subjects: Government, Political Science, Philosophy, Psychology, Psychiatry, Social Sciences, Sociology, Ethnography
ISBN Prefix(es): 963-9134
Total Titles: 5 Print

Kepzoemueveszeti Kiado+
Rozsa u 4-6, 1077 Budapest
Tel: (01) 3517585; (01) 3423323
Telex: 22405
Key Personnel
Manager: Kemenczey Zolt an
Founded: 1954
Fine arts publishing house.
ISBN Prefix(es): 963-336
Bookshop(s): Poszterhaz, V, Bajcsy-Zsilinszky ut 62; Kepesbolt, Budapest V; 1, Deak Ferenc ter 6
Orders to: Kerepesi ut 62, 1148 Budapest

Vince Kiado Kft+
Margit korut 64/B, 1027 Budapest
Tel: (01) 375-7288 *Fax:* (01) 202-7145
E-mail: hl2618vin@ella.hu
Key Personnel
Publisher & General Manager: Gabor Vince
Publishing Dir: Magda Molnar
Founded: 1991
Membership(s): Museum Store Association.
Subjects: Art, Health, Nutrition, How-to, Physical Sciences
ISBN Prefix(es): 963-7826; 963-9069; 963-9192; 963-9323
Distributor for Bonechi; Konemann; Taschen International
Showroom(s): Muecsarnox, Konyvesbolt, Dozsa Cyoergy ut37, 1146 Budapest; Budacyongye Bevagarouozpont, 1026 Budapest
Bookshop(s): Kulturtrade Konyvesbolt, Krisztina Urt 34, 1013 Budapest
Warehouse: Bakfark Balint u 1-3, 1027 Budapest

Kiiarat Konyvdiado
Verder u 20, 1035 Budapest
Tel: (01) 388-6312 *Fax:* (01) 388-6312
Key Personnel
Manager: Gyorgy Palinkas
Founded: 1995
Three book series: Hungarian architecture, philosophical essays & youngest generation of Hungarian literature.
Limited Partnership.
Membership(s): MKKE-Budapest.
Subjects: Architecture & Interior Design, Literature, Literary Criticism, Essays, Philosophy
ISBN Prefix(es): 963-85415; 963-85696; 963-9136
Total Titles: 69 Print
Foreign Rights: Agency Balla & Co (Hungary)
Showroom(s): Mucsarnok Kunsthalle, Dozsa gyu-37, 1146 Budapest, Contact: Gabriella Nagy *Tel:* (01) 3437401 *Fax:* (01) 3435205
Bookshop(s): Irok Boltja, Andrassy ut 45, 1061 Budapest, Contact: Bernadette Nagy *Tel:* (01) 3221645
Warehouse: Helikon Bookhouse, Bajosy-zs. u 37, 1065 Budapest, Contact: Ipdiko Hortobagyi *Tel:* (01) 3312329

Kijarat, *see* Kiiarat Konyvdiado

KJK-Kerszov+
Prielle Kornelia u 21-35, 1117 Budapest
Mailing Address: Postfach 101, 1518 Budapest
Tel: (01) 464-5656 *Fax:* (01) 464-5657
E-mail: complex@kjk-kerszov.hu
Web Site: www.kerszov.hu
Key Personnel
Man Dir: David G Young
Editorial: Judit Fogarasi
Contact: Bucsi Szabo Zsolt
Founded: 1955
Rights & Permissions/Distribution: Artisjus, Budapest Bookstore for Specialists.
Subjects: Business, Economics, Education, Government, Political Science, Journalism, Law, Marketing, Psychology, Psychiatry, Social Sciences, Sociology
ISBN Prefix(es): 963-222; 963-220; 963-221; 963-224
Total Titles: 500 Print; 10 CD-ROM; 5 Online; 5 E-Book
Bookshop(s): Economy & Law, Nador utca 8, 1051 Budapest; Szechenyi Istvan Bookstore, Szent Istvan ter 4, 1064 Budapest V
Warehouse: 1106 Jaszberenyi ut 29, Budapest

Koenyveshaz Kft+
Vaci ut 19, 1134 Budapest
Tel: (01) 1311566 *Fax:* (01) 1311566
Key Personnel
President: Mr Jozsef Ronga
Also a distribution house.

Magyar Tudomanyos Akademia Koezponti Fizikai Kutato Intezet Koenyvtara
Konkoly Thege M ut 29-33, 1121 Budapest
Mailing Address: Postfach 49, 1525 Budapest
Tel: (01) 1382344 (ext 44) *Fax:* (01) 1316954
E-mail: kolcs@sunserv.kfki.hu *Cable:* MTA KFKI KOENYVTAR
Key Personnel
Head of Library: Erika Eory
Systems Librarian: Zsolt Banhegyi
E-mail: zsolt@vax.mtak.hu
Founded: 1950
Subjects: Chemistry, Chemical Engineering, Computer Science, Electronics, Electrical Engineering, Mathematics, Microcomputers, Physical Sciences, Physics
ISBN Prefix(es): 84-7248; 84-9768
Orders to: KFKI Konyvtara, Spain

Kossuth Kiado RT (Kossuth Publishing)+
Csanyi Laszlo utca 34, 1043 Budapest
Mailing Address: PO Box 55, 1327 Budapest
Tel: (01) 3700607 *Fax:* (01) 3700602
E-mail: rt@kossuted.hu
Web Site: www.kossuth.hu
Key Personnel
Man Dir: Mr Andras Sandor Kocsis *Tel:* (01) 3700600 *E-mail:* andrass@kossuted.hu
Book Publishing Dir: Mrs Jolanta Szabone Szuba *Tel:* (01) 3700603 *E-mail:* jolanta@kossuted.hu
Multimedia Manager: Mr Laszlo Foldes *Tel:* (01) 3700608 *E-mail:* hobo@kossuted.hu
International Relations Manager: Mr Balint Ordogh *E-mail:* balinto@kossuted.hu
Rights Manager: Eszter Gyorfi *E-mail:* rightskossuth@axelero.hu
Subjects: Business, Child Care & Development, Communications, Education, Finance, Geography, Geology, Health, Nutrition, Management, Natural History, Philosophy, Psychology, Psychiatry, Religion - Catholic, Travel, Wine & Spirits
Number of titles published annually: 80 Print; 12 CD-ROM
Total Titles: 80 Print; 45 CD-ROM
Showroom(s): Andrassy Ut 13, 1061 Budapest *Tel:* (01) 266-3514 *Fax:* (01) 266-3515

Lang Kiado+
Balassi Balint u 7, 1055 Budapest
Tel: (01) 301-3888 *Fax:* (01) 301-3833
E-mail: holding@lang.hu
Web Site: www.lang.hu *Cable:* 1055 BUDAPEST, BALASSI BALINT U 7
Key Personnel
President: Dr Erdoes Akos
Vice President: Zsuzsanna Vadas
Founded: 1988
Subjects: Business, Literature, Literary Criticism, Essays, Public Administration
ISBN Prefix(es): 963-8054; 963-7840
Subsidiaries: Kner Printing House; Victoria Kft; Sorger-Kolon Kft: B & W Kft; Wien- Budapest Kft; Publicitas Kft; Cash Flow Kft; Europrospekt Kft; Indikator Kft; Magyar Installateur Kft; CompAlmanach CSFR; Televital Kft; Repro Express Kft
Bookshop(s): Pozsonyi ut 5 Ungarn, 1134 Budapest

Magveto Koenyvkiado+
Szervita ter 5, 1052 Budapest
Mailing Address: Postfach 123, 1806 Budapest
Tel: (01) 302 2798; (01) 302 2799 *Fax:* (01) 302 2800
E-mail: magveto@mail.datanet.hu
Telex: 22-3502-Magve H
Key Personnel
Man Dir: Geza Morcsanyi
Chief Dir: Zsuzsa Koermendy
Sales & Publicity: Rozalia Janos
Founded: 1955
Rights & Permissions: Artisjus (under Literary Agents).
Membership(s): MKKE.
Subjects: Art, Fiction, History, Music, Dance, Philosophy, Poetry
ISBN Prefix(es): 963-14; 963-270; 963-271

Bookshop(s): Magvetoe Koenyvesbolt, Szent Istvan Koerut 26, 1137 Budapest
Warehouse: Vaci ut 19, 1134 Budapest

Magyar Kemikusok Egyesulete (Hungarian Chemical Society)
Fo utca 68, 1027 Budapest
Mailing Address: Postfach 451, 1372 Budapest
Tel: (01) 2016883 *Fax:* (01) 343 25 41
E-mail: webinfo@mtesz.hu
Web Site: www.mtesz.hu
Telex: 224343 MTESZ H
Key Personnel
President: Dr Alajos Kalman
Vice President: Dr Laszlo Pallos
Secretary General: Dr Gyula Koertvelyessy
Subjects: Travel
ISBN Prefix(es): 963-8191

Magyar Koenyvkiadok es Koenyvterjesztoek Egyesuelese Vereinigung der Ungarischen Buchverlage & Vertriebsunternehmen
(Association of Hungarian Publishers & Booksellers)
Kertesz u 41 I/4, 1073 Budapest
Mailing Address: Postfach 130, 1367 Budapest
Tel: (01) 343-25-40 *Fax:* (01) 343 25 41
E-mail: mkke@mkke.hu
Web Site: www.mkke.hu
Key Personnel
President: Peter Laszlo *E-mail:* zpl@mkke.hu
ISBN Prefix(es): 963-7002; 963-7409

Marton Aron Kiado Publishing House
Division of The Hungarian Pastoral Institute
Korhaz u 37, 1035 Budapest
Tel: (01) 3689527; (01) 3678415 *Fax:* (01) 1689869
E-mail: oli@hcbc.hu
Key Personnel
Dir: Miklos Blanckenstein
Founded: 1992
Subjects: Education, Human Relations, Religion - Catholic, Theology
ISBN Prefix(es): 963-7947; 963-9011; 963-9439

Medicina Koenyvkiado+
Zoltan utca 8, 1054 Budapest
Mailing Address: Postfach 1012, 1245 Budapest
Tel: (01) 312-2650 *Fax:* (01) 312-2450
Cable: MEDICINA H-1054 BUDAPEST, BELOISNNISZ 8
Key Personnel
Man Dir: Prof Istvan Arky, PhD
Editor: Dr Bulcsu Buda; Bela Ortutay
Production: Marton Orlai
Founded: 1957
Publishing house of medical literature.
Membership(s): MKKE-HPBA(Hungarian Publishers & Booksellers Association).
Subjects: Medicine, Nursing, Dentistry, Sports, Athletics, Travel
ISBN Prefix(es): 963-240; 963-242; 963-241

Mezogazda Kiado (Farmer Publishing House)
Koronafurt u 44, 1165 Budapest
Tel: (01) 4071018 *Fax:* (01) 4071787
E-mail: mezogazda@matavnet.hu
Key Personnel
Dir: Dr Lajos Lelkes
Founded: 1992
Subjects: Agriculture, Animals, Pets, Environmental Studies, Gardening, Plants, Science (General), Veterinary Science, Wine & Spirits
ISBN Prefix(es): 963-7362; 963-8160; 963-8439; 963-9121; 963-9239; 963-9358
Number of titles published annually: 50 Print
Total Titles: 150 Print

Mezogazdasagi, *imprint of* Foldmuvelesugyi Miniszterium Muszaki Intezet

Mezogazdasagi Kiado Vallalat, see Pro Natura

Mora Ferenc Ifjusagi Koenyvkiado Rt+
Vaci ut 19, 1134 Budapest
Tel: (01) 320 4740 *Fax:* (01) 320 5328
E-mail: mora.kiado@elender.hu
Telex: 227027
Key Personnel
Contact: Dr Janos Cs Toth
Founded: 1950
Intellectual workshop of the Hungarian literature for children & the young by bringing out quality new books.
Subjects: Science Fiction, Fantasy
ISBN Prefix(es): 963-11
Bookshop(s): Bobita Koenyvesbolt, Bajcsy-Zsilinszky ut 27, 1065 Budapest; Mora Ferenc Koenyvesbolt, Szabadsag ter 3/A, 6000 Kecskemet
Book Club(s): Mora Koenyvklub (Mora Bucklub)-Kinderbuecher

Mueszaki Koenyvkiado Ltd+
Szentharomsag ter 1, 1014 Budapest
Mailing Address: Postfach 385, 1536 Budapest
Tel: (01) 1557122
E-mail: berczis@muzakikiado.hu
Telex: 226490
Key Personnel
Man Dir: Sandor Berczi *E-mail:* berczis@muszakikiado.hu
BCI, Textbooks: Maria Kekes
BC2, Vocational Textbooks: Norbert Baranyi
Rights & BC3, Professional: Zoltan Lakatos
Founded: 1955
Subjects: Architecture & Interior Design, Career Development, Chemistry, Chemical Engineering, Computer Science, Electronics, Electrical Engineering, Management, Mathematics, Physics, Science (General), Technology
ISBN Prefix(es): 963-10; 963-16

Mult es Jovo Kiado+
Keleti Karoly u 27, 1024 Budapest
Tel: (01) 316-70-19; (01) 438-38-06; (01) 438-38-07 *Fax:* (01) 316-70-19
E-mail: mandj@multesjovo.hu
Web Site: www.multesjovo.hu
Key Personnel
Dir & Chief Editor: Janos Kobanyai
Founded: 1989
Subjects: History, Literature, Literary Criticism, Essays, Social Sciences, Sociology, Jewish Literature, History & Culture
ISBN Prefix(es): 963-85295; 963-85697; 963-85817; 963-9171
Foreign Rep(s): Liepman AG Literary Agency

Nemzeti Tankoenyvkiado+
Szobranc u 6-8, 1143 Budapest
Mailing Address: Postfach 620, 1439 Budapest
Tel: (01) 460-1800 *Fax:* (01) 460-1862
E-mail: public@ntk.hu
Web Site: www.ntk.hu
Key Personnel
Man Dir: Dr Abraham Istvan
Editorial: Mr Rethy Endre
Sales: Dr Danka Attila
Production: Mrs Etclka Babies Vasvan
International Rights Contact: Mrs Fudit Farago *Tel:* (01) 460-1868
Founded: 1949
Textbook Publishing House.
Subjects: Biological Sciences, Education, Geography, Geology, History, Language Arts, Linguistics, Law, Literature, Literary Criticism, Essays, Marketing, Mathematics, Mechanical Engineering, Music, Dance, Philosophy, Physics, Psychology, Psychiatry
ISBN Prefix(es): 963-17; 963-18; 963-19
Shipping Address: Pontus Book Shop & Delivery Service, Gat u 25, 1095 Budapest

Nemzetkozi Szinhazi Intezet Magyar Kozpontja
Krisztina krt 57, 1013 Budapest
Tel: (01) 1752372 *Fax:* (01) 1751184
Key Personnel
President: Gyoergy Lengyel
Dir: Erzsebet Bereczky
Subjects: Drama, Theater, Literature, Literary Criticism, Essays
ISBN Prefix(es): 963-691

Novorg International Szervezo es Kiado kft+
Csanadi u 7, 1132 Budapest
Mailing Address: Postfach 52, 1553 Budapest
Tel: (01) 603790; (01) 603596; (01) 602300 *Fax:* (01) 495581
E-mail: info@hu.inter.net
Key Personnel
Manager: P Boris
Founded: 1986
Subjects: Business, Cookery, Economics, Finance, How-to, Law, Management, Marketing, Public Administration, Real Estate
ISBN Prefix(es): 963-485
Parent Company: Wolters Kluwer
Associate Companies: Koezgazdasagi Es Jogi Koenyvkiado
Showroom(s): W K Koenyvkereskedelmi Koezpont, Szentendrei ut 89-93, 1033 Budapest
Warehouse: W K Koenyvkereskedelmi Koezpont, Szentendrei ut 89-93, 1033 Budapest

Officina Nova, Koenyv-es Lapkiado/Bertelsmann Media Kft, see Officina Nova Konyvek

Officina Nova Konyvek+
Formerly Officina Nova, Koenyv-es Lapkiado/Bertelsmann Media Kft
Marvany u 17, 1012 Budapest
Tel: (01) 557282 *Fax:* (01) 1686674
Key Personnel
Dir: Katalin Balogh
Editor-in-Chief: Andras Szekely
Founded: 1987
Subjects: Antiques, Art, Cookery, Gardening, Plants, Health, Nutrition, History, Humor, Travel
ISBN Prefix(es): 963-7835; 963-7836; 963-8185; 963-477
Parent Company: Bertelsmann Verlagsgruppe GmbH, Munich,, Germany
Associate Companies: Bertelsmann Professional Information
Divisions: Media Nova

OKKER Kiado
Formerly OKKER Oktatasi Iroda
Csengery u 68, 1067 Budapest
Tel: (01) 3324587
Key Personnel
Dir: Susanna Nouakne Gal
ISBN Prefix(es): 963-7315; 963-85136; 963-85351; 963-85206; 963-9228

OKKER Oktatasi Iroda, see OKKER Kiado

Orszagos Mueszaki Informacios Kozpont es Konyvtar, see Budapesti Muszaki es Gazdasagtudomanyi Egyetem

Osiris Kiado (Osiris Publishing)+
Egyeten Ter 5, 2/10a, 1053 Budapest
Tel: (01) 266-6560 *Fax:* (01) 267-0935
E-mail: kiado@osirismail.hu
Web Site: www.osiriskiado.hu
Key Personnel
Dir: Janos Gyurgyak *Tel:* (01) 266-6560, Ext 106
Founded: 1993

HUNGARY

Subjects: Anthropology, Communications, Economics, Film, Video, Government, Political Science, History, Language Arts, Linguistics, Law, Library & Information Sciences, Literature, Literary Criticism, Essays, Philosophy, Psychology, Psychiatry, Religion - Catholic, Religion - Protestant, Social Sciences, Sociology, Theology
Number of titles published annually: 200 Print
Distribution Center: Vaci ut 100, 1133 Budapest

Panem+
Ov u 146, 1147 Budapest
Mailing Address: Postafiok 809, 1385 Budapest
Tel: (01) 460-0273 *Fax:* (01) 460-0274
E-mail: panem@mail.datanet.hu
Web Site: www.panem.hu
Key Personnel
Dir: Ms Zsuzsa Tarr
Founded: 1990
Subjects: Computer Science, Economics, Engineering (General), Science (General)
ISBN Prefix(es): 963-545; 963-7628

Park Konyvkiado Kft (Park Publisher)+
Keleti K u 29, 1024 Budapest
Tel: (01) 2125534; (01) 2125535; (01) 2124363
E-mail: park@mail.matav.hu
Key Personnel
Manager: Andras Rochlitz
Marketing: Mr Aniko Zambo
Founded: 1989
Subjects: Art, Child Care & Development, Gardening, Plants, History, House & Home, Management, Nonfiction (General), Self-Help
ISBN Prefix(es): 963-7737; 963-7970; 963-8227
Total Titles: 110 Print

Planetas Kiadoi es Kereskedelmi Kft
Koronafurt u 44, 1165 Budapest
Tel: (01) 4071018 *Fax:* (01) 4071787
Key Personnel
Dir: Dr Lajos Lelkes
Founded: 1990
Specialist art publications.
Subjects: Art, Music, Dance, Folk art
ISBN Prefix(es): 963-7931; 963-9014; 963-9414

Polgar Kiado Kft+
Attila ut 20, 1013 Budapest
Tel: (01) 1752854 *Fax:* (01) 1568358
Key Personnel
Editor-in-Chief: Tamas Bekes
Founded: 1994
Provides values & guidance for the slowly developing Hungarian middle classes.
Subjects: Literature, Literary Criticism, Essays, Science (General)
ISBN Prefix(es): 963-9002
Subsidiaries: Polgar Video Ltd

Pro Natura+
Formerly Mezogazdasagi Kiado Vallalat
Bathori u 10, 1054 Budapest
Tel: (01) 1317330 *Fax:* (01) 1117270
Telex: 61 20 2536
Key Personnel
Manager: Dr Csaba Gallyas
Founded: 1950
Agricultural publishing house.
Subjects: Agriculture, Science (General)
ISBN Prefix(es): 963-7518
Subsidiaries: Natura
Bookshop(s): Agricultural Bookshop, Vecsei u 5, Budapest

Saldo Penzugyi Tanacsado es Informatikai Rt+
Bartok B ut 120, 1113 Budapest
Mailing Address: Postfach 64, 1364 Budapest
Tel: (01) 203 8213 *Fax:* (01) 203 8217
E-mail: kiado@saldo.datanet.hu

Telex: 226387
Key Personnel
General Dir: Dr Andras Mohos
Marketing Manager: Dr Jozsef Racz
Founded: 1959
Subjects: Accounting, Economics, Finance, Law, Public Administration
ISBN Prefix(es): 963-621; 963-638

Springer Hungarica Kiado Kft
Csanyi Laszlo utca 36, 1043 Budapest
Mailing Address: Postfach 94, 1327 Budapest
Tel: (01) 3700599 *Fax:* (01) 3709075
Telex: 2515973
Founded: 1990
Subjects: Earth Sciences, Engineering (General), Medicine, Nursing, Dentistry
ISBN Prefix(es): 963-7775

Statiqum Kiado es Nyomda Kft+
Kaszasdulo u 2, 1033 Budapest
Mailing Address: Postfach 99, 1300 Budapest
Tel: (01) 1803311 *Fax:* (01) 1688635
Telex: 226699 Skv h
Key Personnel
Man Dir: Benedek Belecz
Sales Dir: Gyoergy Szehr
Founded: 1991 (predecessor 1954)
Legal successor of Statistical Publishing House.
Subjects: Computer Science, Economics, Mathematics, Social Sciences, Sociology
ISBN Prefix(es): 963-340
Parent Company: State Property Agency, Vigado u 6, 1051 Budapest
Bookshop(s): Statistical & Computing Bookshop, Keleti Karoly u 10, Budapest *Tel:* (01) 1158018
Orders to: KULTURA Aussenhandelsunternehmen fur Bucher und Zeintschriften, PO Box 149, 1389 Budapest

Szabad Ter Kiado+
Postfach 95, 1525 Budapest
Tel: (01) 3561565; (01) 3755922 *Fax:* (01) 1560998
Telex: 223553
Key Personnel
Dir: Gabor Koltay
Deputy Dir, Productions Dir: Jozsef Lovasi
Founded: 1988
Cultural Service Guidance, Expense Sheet.
Subjects: Fashion, Government, Political Science, Literature, Literary Criticism, Essays, Mysteries
ISBN Prefix(es): 963-7810; 963-9201

Szabvanykiado+
Ulloi u 25, 1091 Budapest
Mailing Address: Postfach 24, 1450 Budapest
Tel: (01) 1183011; (01) 1183442 *Fax:* (01) 1185125
Telex: 225723 norm h
Founded: 1972
Subjects: Nonfiction (General)
ISBN Prefix(es): 963-402

Szarvas Andras Cartographic Agency+
Repassy jeno u, 2, 1149 Budapest
Tel: (01) 363 0672; (01) 221 68 30 *Fax:* (01) 363 0672; (01) 221 68 30
E-mail: szarvas.andras@mail.datanet.hu
Key Personnel
Owner: Szarvas Andras E-mail: szarvas.andras@mail.datanet.hu
Founded: 1991
Map publishing & distribution.
Subjects: Earth Sciences, Geography, Geology, Regional Interests, Transportation, Travel
ISBN Prefix(es): 963-9251
Number of titles published annually: 20 Print
Total Titles: 40 Print

Szazadveg
U Benczur u 33, 1068 Budapest
Mailing Address: Menesi ut 12, 1118 Budapest
Tel: (01) 4795280 *Fax:* (01) 479 5290
E-mail: szazadveg@szazadveg.hu
Web Site: www.szazadveg.hu
Key Personnel
Dir: GyurgyaK Janos
Marketing Manager: Pesti Zsuzsa
Founded: 1990
Nonpartisan, nonprofit organization financed by the contributions of its supporters & the sale of its publications & services.
ISBN Prefix(es): 963-379; 963-7911; 963-8384

Szepirodalmi Koenyvkiado Kiado
Gyongyvirag u 41, 1038 Budapest
Mailing Address: Postfach 58, 1428 Budapest
Tel: (01) 3117293
Key Personnel
Man Dir: Marton Tarnoc
Founded: 1950
Subjects: Education, Fiction, Poetry
ISBN Prefix(es): 963-15; 963-86184

Magyar Eszperanto Szoevetseg
Kenyermezw u 6, 1081 Budapest
Mailing Address: Postfach 193, 1368 Budapest
Tel: (01) 1334343; (01) 1563659 *Cable:* ESPERANTOCENTRO, BUDAPEST
Key Personnel
Dir: Mr Oszkar Princz
ISBN Prefix(es): 963-571

Tajak Korok Muzeumok Egyesuelet
Konyves K krt 40, 1087 Budapest
Mailing Address: Postfach 54, 1476 Budapest
Tel: (01) 303 4069 *Fax:* (01) 303 4069
E-mail: tkmets@elender.hu
Key Personnel
Publisher: Istvan Eri
Founded: 1977
Organizes the movements which play a significant role in popularizing Hungary's natural resources, monuments & exhibitions.
Subjects: Archaeology, Architecture & Interior Design, Art, History, Natural History
ISBN Prefix(es): 963-554; 963-555

Taltos Kiadasszervezesi Ltd
Bajza u 1, 1071 Budapest
Tel: (01) 1213515; (01) 1420676
ISBN Prefix(es): 963-7825

Technika, *imprint of* Foldmuvelesugyi Miniszterium Muszaki Intezet

Tevan Kiado Vallalat+
Luther u 12, Bekescsaba 5600
Tel: 66441181
Key Personnel
Dir: Dr Janos Cs Toth
Deputy Dir: Kantor Zsolt
Founded: 1989
Subjects: Fiction, Poetry
ISBN Prefix(es): 963-7900; 963-7278

Typotex Kft Elektronikus Kiado+
Retek u 33-35, 1024 Budapest
Tel: (01) 316-2473; (01) 316-3759 *Fax:* (01) 316-3759
E-mail: info@typotex.hu
Web Site: www.typotex.hu
Key Personnel
Man Dir: Zsuzsa Votisky E-mail: votis@typotex.hu
Editor-in-Chief: Kinga Nemeth E-mail: kinga@typotex.hu
Sales Manager: Zsolt Nemeth E-mail: nezsolt@typotex.hu
Marketing: Borbala Pinter E-mail: bori@typotex.hu

Founded: 1989
Subjects: Mathematics, Philosophy, Physics
ISBN Prefix(es): 963-7546; 963-9132; 963-9326
Total Titles: 100 Print
Subsidiaries: Index Buchladen

Magyar Tudomanyos Akademia VilagGazdasagi Kutato Intezet
Kallo esp u 15, 1124 Budapest
Mailing Address: PO Box 936, 1535 Budapest
Tel: (01) 1668433 *Fax:* (01) 1620661
Telex: 227713 *Cable:* BUWORLDINST
Key Personnel
Dir: Prof Andras Inotai
ISBN Prefix(es): 963-301

Zenemukiado Vallalat+
Voeroesmarty ter 1, 1051 Budapest
Mailing Address: PO Box 322, 1370 Budapest
Tel: (01) 1176222
E-mail: musicpubl@emb.hu
Telex: 225500 *Cable:* EDITIOMUSICA
Key Personnel
Man Dir: Istvan Homolya
International Rights: Antal Boronkay
Founded: 1950
Subjects: Biography, Music, Dance
ISBN Prefix(es): 963-330
Bookshop(s): Andrassy ut h5, 1061 Budapest
Tel: (01) 322-4091 *Fax:* (01) 322-4091

Zrinyi Kiado
Kerepesi u 29/b, 1087 Budapest
Tel: (01) 4595371; (01) 3339113
Key Personnel
Manager: Mate Eszes
Publishing House of the Hungarian Army.
Subjects: Military Science, Science (General)
ISBN Prefix(es): 963-327; 963-326

Iceland

General Information

Capital: Reykjavik
Language: Icelandic (widespread knowledge of English
Religion: Lutheran
Population: 259,000
Bank Hours: 0915-1600 Monday-Friday (winter); 0800-1600 (summer); some open 1700-1800 Thursday
Shop Hours: 0900-1800 Monday-Thursday; 0900-1700/1900 Friday; most open 0900-1600 Saturday (winter)
Currency: 100 aurar = 1 krona
Export/Import Information: Member of the European Economic Area. 14% VAT on books. Sales Tax. No import licenses required. No exchange controls for books but they may not be imported on credit.
Copyright: UCC, Berne, Florence (see Copyright Conventions, pg xi)

AEskan
Eiriksgata 5, 101 Reykjavik
Mailing Address: Postholf 523, 121 Reykjavik
Tel: 551-0248
Key Personnel
Editor: Karl Helgason
Founded: 1930
ISBN Prefix(es): 9979-808; 9979-9395; 9979-9411; 9979-9416

Almenna Bokafelagid
Nybylavegur 16, 200 Kopavogur
Tel: 564-3170 *Fax:* 564-3190

Key Personnel
Man Dir: Fridriksson Fridrik
Editor: Bjarni Thorsteinsson *E-mail:* bjarni.thorsteinsson@edda.is
Editorial: Eirikur Hreinn Finnbogason
Sales Dir: Andri Thor Gudmundsson
Rights & Permissions: Stefania Petursdottir
Founded: 1955
Subjects: Biography, Fiction, History, Nonfiction (General), Poetry
ISBN Prefix(es): 9979-4
Book Club(s): The AB Book Club (BAB); The MAT Cookery Book Club; TAB (Music Club)

Arnamagnaean Institute in Iceland, see Stofnun Arna Magnussonar a Islandi

Hjalmar R Bardarson
Hrauntunga vio Alftanesveg, 210 Garoabaer
Mailing Address: Postholf 998, 121 Reykjavik
Tel: 555-0729
Key Personnel
Editor: Hjalmar R Bardarson
ISBN Prefix(es): 9979-818
Warehouse: Sidumuli 21, PO Box 8181, IS-128 Reykjavik
Orders to: Islensk Bokadrefin HF

Bokaforlag Birtingur+
Laugavegur 66, 101 Reykjavik
Tel: 562-7700 *Fax:* 562-7710
Founded: 1988
Subjects: Astrology, Occult, Health, Nutrition, Mysteries, Parapsychology, Philosophy, Psychology, Psychiatry, Religion - Other
ISBN Prefix(es): 9979-815; 9979-9002

Bokautgafan Orn og Orlygur ehf+
Dvergshoefoi 27, 112 Reykjavik
Tel: 568-4866 *Fax:* 5671240
Telex: 2197
Key Personnel
Man Dir: Pall Bragi Kristjonsson *E-mail:* pbk@centrum.is
Founded: 1966
Subjects: Biography, Cookery, Gardening, Plants, Health, Nutrition, How-to
ISBN Prefix(es): 9979-55

Bokaverslun Sigfusar Eymundssonar
Austurstr 18, 101 Reykjavik
Tel: 13135 *Fax:* 15078
Subjects: Education

Draupnisutgafan, Loegberg, *imprint of* Idunn

Filadelfia forlag
Hatuni 2, 105 Reykjavik
Mailing Address: Postholf 5135, 125 Reykjavik
Tel: 552-5155; 552-0735 *Fax:* 562-0735
E-mail: filadelfia-forlag@gospel.is
Telex: 3000 simtexisforlag
Key Personnel
Man Dir: Hronn Svansdottir
ISBN Prefix(es): 9979-803

Fjolvi
Njoervasundi 15 A, 104 Reykjavik
Tel: 5688433 *Fax:* 5588142
E-mail: fjolvi@fjolvi.is
Web Site: www.fjolvi.is
Telex: 2159 Rethor
Key Personnel
Man Dir: Sturla Eiriksson
Dir: Ingunn Thorarensen; Thorsteinn Thorarensen
Founded: 1966
Subjects: Fiction, Nonfiction (General)
ISBN Prefix(es): 9979-58
Book Club(s): Bokaklubbur Fjolva; Particip 'Verold'

Forlagid+
Sudurlandsbraut 12, 108 Reykjavik
Tel: 522 2000 *Fax:* 522 2022
E-mail: edda@edda.is
Key Personnel
Publishing Dir: Kristjan B Jonasson
Founded: 1984
Subjects: Photography, Travel
ISBN Prefix(es): 9979-53
Parent Company: Edda Publishing

Frjals fjolmiolun hf-Urvalsbaekur
bverholt 11, 105 Reykjavik
Mailing Address: Postholf 5380, 125 Reykjavik
Tel: 550-500; 550-5999 *Fax:* 550-5022
Key Personnel
Editor: Sig Hreidar Hreidarsson
Founded: 1981 (an amalgamation of firms from 1910)
Subjects: Fiction, Mysteries, Romance
ISBN Prefix(es): 9979-9006; 9979-9023; 9979-840; 9979-9493

Godord
Njardargata 39, 101 Reykjavik
Tel: 551-6998
Key Personnel
Editor: Brynjar Viborg
Founded: 1989
Subjects: Poetry
ISBN Prefix(es): 9979-9017

Haskolautgafan - University of Iceland Press
Haskoli Islands, Adalbygging v/Sudurgoetu, 107 Reykjavik
Tel: 5254003 *Fax:* 525-5255
Web Site: www.haskolautgafan.hi.is
Key Personnel
Dir: Joerundur Godmundsson *E-mail:* jorig@hi.is
Contact: Bryndis Erla Hjalmarsdottir *E-mail:* bryndihj@hi.is
Founded: 1988
Subjects: History, Philosophy, English & Icelandic titles on Norse studies
ISBN Prefix(es): 9979-54

Hid Islenzka Bokmenntafelag (Icelandic Literary Society)+
Sidumula 21, 128 Reykjavik
Mailing Address: PO Box 8935, 128 Reykjavik
Tel: 5889060 *Fax:* 5889095
Key Personnel
President: Sigurdur Lindal
Dir: Sverrir Kristinsson
Man Dir: Gunnar H Ingimundarson
Founded: 1816
Subjects: Art, Government, Political Science, History, Language Arts, Linguistics, Literature, Literary Criticism, Essays, Natural History, Psychology, Psychiatry, Social Sciences, Sociology, Icelandic art, literature, philosophy & saga
ISBN Prefix(es): 9979-804; 9979-66

Iceland Review+
Borgartuni 23, 105 Reykjavik
Tel: 512-7575 *Fax:* 561-8646
E-mail: icelandreview@icelandreview.com
Web Site: www.icelandreview.com
Telex: 2121
Key Personnel
Chairman of the Board: Haraldur J Hamar
Founded: 1963
Subjects: Art, Literature, Literary Criticism, Essays, Regional Interests
ISBN Prefix(es): 9979-51

Idunn+
Seljavegi 2, IS-101 Reykjavik
Mailing Address: PO Box 294, IS-121 Reykjavik
Tel: 5155500 *Fax:* 5155579

ICELAND

E-mail: idunn@idunn.is
Web Site: www.idunn.is
Telex: 2308 *Cable:* REYKJAVIK PUBLISHERS
Key Personnel
Dir: Jon Karlsson *E-mail:* jk@idunn.is
Editor: Thorgunnur Skuladottir
 E-mail: thorgunnur@idunn.is
Founded: 1945
Subjects: Biography, Fiction, History, Nonfiction (General), Poetry
ISBN Prefix(es): 9979-1
Imprints: Draupnisutgafan, Loegberg
Subsidiaries: Islenski bokaklubburinn
Book Club(s): Draupnisutgafan

Independent Media Inc, see Frjals fjolmiolun hf-Urvalsbaekur

Isafoldarprentsmidja hf+
Tverholti 9, 105 Reykjavik
Tel: 550-5990 *Fax:* 550-5994
E-mail: isafold@isafold.is
Web Site: www.isafold.is
Key Personnel
Contact: Ragnar Ragnarsson *E-mail:* ragnar@isafold.is
Founded: 1877
Subjects: Education, Fiction
ISBN Prefix(es): 9979-809

Katholska kirkjan a Islandi - Landakot Publishers Thorlakssjodur
Landakoti, 101 Reykjavik
Tel: 555-0188
Key Personnel
Contact: Torfi Olafsson
Founded: 1987
Subjects: Religion - Catholic
ISBN Prefix(es): 9979-9261

Landakot Publishers Thorlakssjodur, see Katholska kirkjan a Islandi - Landakot Publishers Thorlakssjodur

Mal og menning+
Imprint of Edda Publishing
Sudurlandsbraut 12, 108 Reykjavik
Tel: 522 2500 *Fax:* 522 2505
E-mail: edda@edda.is
Web Site: www.edda.is
Key Personnel
Man Dir: Pall Bragi Kristjonsson *E-mail:* pall.bragi@edda.is
Editorial Dir: Sigurdur Svavarsson
 E-mail: sigurdur.svavarsson@edda.is
Founded: 1937
Subjects: Education, Fiction, Literature, Literary Criticism, Essays, Nonfiction (General), Poetry, Travel
ISBN Prefix(es): 9979-3
Associate Companies: Vaka-Helgafell, Sudurlandsbraut 12, 108 Reykjavik *Tel:* 522 2000 *Fax:* 522 2022
Imprints: Uglan Paperback Bookclub
Subsidiaries: Heimskringla
Book Club(s): Mal og menning; Uglan

Namsgagnastofnun
Laugavegi 166, 105 Reykjavik
Tel: 5528088 *Fax:* 5624137
E-mail: upplysingar@nams.is
Web Site: www.namsgagnastofnun.is
Telex: 3000 Simtext Is-Edice *Cable:* EDICE
Key Personnel
Dir: Ingibjoerg Asgeirsdottir *E-mail:* ingibjorg@nams.is; Asgeir Gudmundsson
Editor: Bogi Indridason *E-mail:* bogi@nams.is
Rights & Permissions: Eirikur Grimsson
Publicity, Sales: Hoerour Ragnarsson
Editor: Tryggvi Jakobsson *E-mail:* tryggvij@nams.is

Founded: 1937
National Centre for Educational Materials is a nonprofit publishing housen run by the Icelandic government.
Membership(s): ICEM - International Council for Educational Media.
Subjects: Disability, Special Needs, Education
ISBN Prefix(es): 9979-0

Ormstunga+
Ranargotu 20, 101 Reykjavik
Tel: 561 0055 *Fax:* 552 4650
E-mail: books@ormstunga.is
Web Site: www.ormstunga.is
Key Personnel
Man Dir: Gisli Mar Gislason
Founded: 1992
ISBN Prefix(es): 9979-63; 9979-9048

Prentsmidjan Oddi
Hofdabakka 3-7, 110 Reykjavik
Tel: 5155000 *Fax:* 5155001
E-mail: oddi@oddi.is
Web Site: www.oddi.is
Key Personnel
Dir: Thorgeir Baldursson *E-mail:* thorgeir@oddi.is
Vice President: Hilmar Baldursson
Founded: 1943
U.S. Office(s): PO Box 415, Lincroft, NJ 07738, United States

Setberg
Freyjugoetu 14, IS-101 Reykjavik
Mailing Address: Postholf 619, 121 Reykjavik
Tel: 5517667; 552-9150 *Fax:* 5526640
Telex: 3000 Simtex ls *Cable:* Setbergpublish
Key Personnel
Dir: Arnbjoern Kristinsson
Subjects: Cookery, Education, Fiction, Nonfiction (General)
ISBN Prefix(es): 9979-52

Skjaldborg Ltd+
Grensasvegur 14, 108 Reykjavik
Tel: 5882400 *Fax:* 5888994
E-mail: skjaldborg@skjaldborg.is
Key Personnel
Dir: Bjorn Eiriksson *E-mail:* bjorn@skjaldborg.is
Editorial Manager: Helgi Magnusson
Subjects: Animals, Pets, Astrology, Occult, Biography, Crafts, Games, Hobbies, Fiction, Gardening, Plants, How-to, Humor, Nonfiction (General)
ISBN Prefix(es): 9979-57
Associate Companies: Heima er bezt
Subsidiaries: Childrens Educational Bookclub
Book Club(s): Educational Book Club for Children

Skuggsja bokaforlag
Strandgata 31, 220 Hafnarfjoerour
Mailing Address: Postholf 202, 222 Hafnarfjoeour
Tel: 555-0045
Subjects: Fiction
ISBN Prefix(es): 9979-829

Stofnun Arna Magnussonar a Islandi (Arni Magnusson Manuscript Institute)
Unit of University of Iceland
Arnagaroi v/Suourgoetu, 101 Reykjavik
Tel: 525-4010 *Fax:* 525-4035
E-mail: rosat@hi.is
Web Site: www.am.hi.is
Key Personnel
Dir: Vesteinn Olason *E-mail:* vesteinn@hi.is
Founded: 1972
Specialize in research & publication of Icelandic manuscripts & folklore.
Membership(s): FIDEM.

BOOK

Subjects: History, Language Arts, Linguistics, Literature, Literary Criticism, Essays, Music, Dance, Poetry, Regional Interests
ISBN Prefix(es): 9979-819
Number of titles published annually: 4 Print
Total Titles: 70 Print; 7 CD-ROM
Distributed by University of Iceland Press

Thjodsagao ehf
Dvergshofda 27, IS-112 Reykjavik
Tel: 567-1777 *Fax:* 567-1240
E-mail: pbk@centrum.is

Uglan Paperback Bookclub, *imprint of* Mal og menning

Vaka-Helgafell
Sueurlandsbraut 12, 108 Reykjavik
Tel: 522 2000 *Fax:* 522 2022
E-mail: vaka@edda.is
Web Site: www.vaka.is
Telex: 3190 vakice
Key Personnel
International Rights: Petur Mar Olafsson
Marketing Dir: Edda Bjorgvinsdottir
Chairman of the Board: Olafur Ragnarsson
Founded: 1981
Preserves, promotes & enriches the Icelandic language & the cultural heritage of the Icelandic people.
ISBN Prefix(es): 9979-2

India

General Information

Capital: New Delhi
Language: Hindi & English are used for official purposes. Seventeen regional languages are accorded recognition by the constitution. Generally each administrative state includes speakers of a particular major language. In all, over 1500 languages & dialects are spoken
Religion: Predominantly Hindu, some Muslims (about 11%)
Population: 886.4 million
Bank Hours: 1000-1400 (1100-1500 Mumbai) Monday-Friday; 1000-1200 (1100-1300 Mumbai) Saturday
Shop Hours: Delhi: 0930-1930; Kolkata & Mumbai: 1000-1830; Chennai: 0900-1930. All effective Monday-Saturday, some open Sunday. Many close 2 hours for lunch
Currency: 100 paise = 1 Indian rupee
Export/Import Information: No tariff on books but advertising matter is dutied. Import Licenses required. Educational books may be imported by booksellers under open general license. Exchange transactions restricted.
Copyright: UCC, Berne, Buenos Aires (see Copyright Conventions, pg xi)

Aarti Books, *imprint of* Spectrum Publications

ABC, see Allied Book Centre

Abhinav Publications+
E-37 Hauz Khas, New Delhi 110016
Tel: (011) 26566387; (011) 26524658 *Fax:* (011) 26857009
Web Site: www.abhinavexports.com
Key Personnel
Dir: Shakti Malik *E-mail:* shakti@nde.vsnl.net.in
Founded: 1972
Subjects: Archaeology, Architecture & Interior Design, Art, Criminology, Drama, Theater, Ethnicity, Government, Political Science, History, Human Relations, Literature, Literary Criti-

cism, Essays, Music, Dance, Philosophy, Religion - Other, Social Sciences, Sociology
ISBN Prefix(es): 81-7017
Number of titles published annually: 18 Print
Distributed by South Asia Books (USA)

Abhishek Publications
SCO 57-59 Sector 17-C, Chandigarh 160 017
Mailing Address: PO Box 34, Chandigarh 160017
Tel: (0172) 707562 *Fax:* (0172) 704668
Key Personnel
Chief Executive, Production, Publicity: SLM Prachand
Editorial: Mrs Geeta Mehndiratta
Sales, Rights & Permissions: Bharat Bhushan
Founded: 1977
Subjects: Government, Political Science, History, Philosophy
ISBN Prefix(es): 81-85733
Associate Companies: Nirjhar Prakashan, 3625 Sector 23-D, Chandigarh 160023

Academic Book Corporation+
C-1491, Rajaji Puram, Lucknow 22 6017
Tel: (0522) 418421; (0522) 416584 *Fax:* (0522) 22061; (0522) 210376 *Cable:* ACADEMIC
Founded: 1982
Subjects: Law, Management
ISBN Prefix(es): 81-238

The Academic Press+
Old Subzi Mandi, Gurgaon, Haryana 122 001
Tel: (0124) 6322779; (0124) 6322005 *Fax:* (0124) 6324782
E-mail: indoc@indiatimes.com
Key Personnel
Dir: Pankaj Jain *E-mail:* pancoj@indiatimes.com
Editorial: Satya Prakash
Sales: Kapil Jain
Production, Rights & Permissions: Sanjeev Jain Satyaprakash
Founded: 1968
Subjects: History, Human Relations, Philosophy, Religion - Other, Social Sciences, Sociology
ISBN Prefix(es): 81-85260

Academic Publishers
12/1A Bankim Chatterjee St, Kolkata 700073
Mailing Address: PO Box 12341, Kolkata 700073
Tel: (033) 241-4857 *Fax:* (033) 241-3702
E-mail: acabooks@cal.vsnl.net.in *Cable:* ACABOOKS
Key Personnel
Man Dir: Bimal Kumar Dhur
Sales Dir: B L Dutta
Founded: 1958
Subjects: Accounting, Business, Management, Medicine, Nursing, Dentistry
ISBN Prefix(es): 81-86358; 81-85086; 81-87504
Distributed by UBS Publishers Distributors Ltd (outside Kolkata)

Addison Wesley, *imprint of* Addison-Wesley Pte Ltd

Addison-Wesley Pte Ltd+
India Branch, 482 FIE Patparganj, Delhi 110 092
Tel: (011) 214 6067 *Fax:* (011) 214 6071
E-mail: info@pearsoned.co.in
Web Site: www.pearsonedindia.com
Key Personnel
General Manager: Subroto Mozumdar
  E-mail: subroto.mozumdar@pearsonedindia.com
Finance: Dipankar Rose
Founded: 1997
One of the world's largest educational publishers. It has played a very important role in publishing both higher education/academic titles as well as school products. The India Office is a liaison office, headquartered in Singapore. Since its inception in 1997, Addison Wesley Longman India has reprinted classic higher academic & professional titles & recently dictionaries & ELT products to make them available to students in India at affordable prices.
Subjects: Biological Sciences, Business, Chemistry, Chemical Engineering, Civil Engineering, Computer Science, Economics, Electronics, Electrical Engineering, English as a Second Language, Management, Mathematics, Physics, Science (General), Social Sciences, Sociology
Number of titles published annually: 200 Print
Total Titles: 303 Print
Parent Company: Pearson Plc
Imprints: Addison Wesley; Scott Foresman; Peachpit Press; Benjamin Cummings; Prentice Hall; Allyn & Bacon; Globe Fearon; Silver Burdett Ginn; Longman; Prentice Hall; Benjamin Cummings; SAMS; PTR; QUE; New Riders; Penguin Longman Publishing; Pitman; Financial Times PH; Merrill Education

Advaita Ashrama+
5 Dehi Entally Rd, Kolkata 700 014
Tel: (033) 22440898; (033) 22452383; (033) 22164000 *Fax:* (033) 22450050
E-mail: advaita@vsnl.com
Web Site: www.advaitaonline.com
Key Personnel
Manager: Swami Bodhasarananda
Founded: 1899
Publication department of Ramakrishina Mission.
Subjects: Art, Religion - Hindu
ISBN Prefix(es): 81-85301; 81-7505
Number of titles published annually: 150 Print
Total Titles: 400 Print; 2 CD-ROM; 2 Online
Ultimate Parent Company: Ramakrishna Math
Distributed by Ramakrishna Vedanta Centre (UK); Vedanta Society of Southern California (USA); Vivekananda Vedanta Society (USA)

Affiliated East West Press Pvt Ltd+
105 Nirmal Tower, 26 Barakhamba Rd, New Delhi 110001
Tel: (011) 23315398; (011) 23279113; (011) 23264180 *Fax:* (011) 23260538
E-mail: aewp.newdel@axcess.net.in; affiliat@vsnl.com
Key Personnel
Man Dir: Sunny Malik
Dir: Kamil Malik
Founded: 1962
Membership(s): Delhi State Booksellers' & Publishers Association; Federation of Publishers & Booksellers Associations of India; Federation of Indian Publishers
Subjects: Aeronautics, Aviation, Agriculture, Anthropology, Biological Sciences, Chemistry, Chemical Engineering, Civil Engineering, Computer Science, Economics, Electronics, Electrical Engineering, Environmental Studies, Geography, Geology, Management, Mathematics, Mechanical Engineering, Microcomputers, Physical Sciences, Physics, Poetry, Psychology, Psychiatry, Science (General), Veterinary Science, Women's Studies
ISBN Prefix(es): 81-85095; 81-85336; 81-85938; 81-7671
Imprints: EWP
Distributor for Academic Press; American Association of Petroleum Geologists; American Ceramic Society; American Society for Quality; American Water Works Association; William Andrew; ASM International; Blackwell Science; Convenor Equipment Manufacturers Association; CRC Press; Elsevier Science; FAO (Food & Agriculture Organization); Geological Society Publishing House; HarperCollins Publishers; Horwood Publishing; Humana Press; IEEE; Institute of Petroleum; Lippincott Williams Wolkins; MIT Press; Palgrave; Pira; Portland; Prentice-Hall; RAPRA Technology; Routledge; W B Saunders; Society for Mining, Metallurgy & Exploration; Society of Manufacturing Engineers; TAPPI Press; Thomson Learning; John Wiley
Orders to: G-1/16 Ansari Rd, Darya Ganj, New Delhi 110 002

Agam Kala Prakashan
34, Central Market, Ashok Vihar, New Delhi 110 005
Tel: (011) 713395 *Fax:* (011) 7401485
Key Personnel
Editorial, Sales, Publicity, Rights & Permissions: Agam Prasad
Founded: 1977
Membership(s): Capexal & Intach.
Subjects: Anthropology, Antiques, Archaeology, Art, Asian Studies, Earth Sciences, History, Language Arts, Linguistics
ISBN Prefix(es): 81-85415; 81-7186; 81-7320
Associate Companies: Agam Prakashan; Rahul Publishing House; Swati Publication
Distributed by M/S, Munshiram Manoharlal (P) Ltd; M/S, UBS Publishers & Distributors Ltd
Distributor for Rahul Publishing House; Swati Publications

Agricole Publishing Academy+
208, Shopping Complex, Defence Colony Flyover, New Delhi 110024
Tel: (011) 692703 *Cable:* AGRIPUBLIS
Key Personnel
Dir: Lalita Jain
Chief Executive: T C Jain
Founded: 1978
Subjects: Agriculture, Behavioral Sciences, Biological Sciences, Economics, Education, Energy, Engineering (General), Environmental Studies, Health, Nutrition, Labor, Industrial Relations, Real Estate, Social Sciences, Sociology, Technology
ISBN Prefix(es): 81-85005
Associate Companies: Yatan Publications; Agricole Reprints Corp

Ajanta Publications (India)+
One UB Jawahar Nagar, Bangalow Rd, New Delhi 110 007
Mailing Address: 1743 Outram Lane, SGTB Nagar, Delhi 110 009
Tel: (011) 2917375; (011) 2926182 *Fax:* (011) 741 5016; (011) 713 2908; (011) 7213076
Key Personnel
Chief Executive: Atwal Amit
Founded: 1975
Also acts as Academic/General/Literary Agent & Printer.
Membership(s): FIP.
Subjects: Anthropology, Archaeology, Art, Ethnicity, Government, Political Science, Language Arts, Linguistics, Literature, Literary Criticism, Essays, Management, Philosophy, Public Administration, Religion - Other, Social Sciences, Sociology
ISBN Prefix(es): 81-202
Parent Company: Ajanta Books International

Akshat Publications+
B-250, Ashok Vihar, Phase I, Delhi 110052
Tel: (011) 7247234; (011) 7114425; (011) 7240483 *Fax:* (011) 7254734; (011) 7218836
Cable: SAYONARA
Key Personnel
Contact: Dr Roopa Vohra; Mr K L Jain
Founded: 1985
ISBN Prefix(es): 81-85069
Parent Company: Sayonara Group

AL Publishers+
44 Bhimangar, Opp Indira Park, Hyderabad 500380
Tel: (040) 7611600

Key Personnel
President: Mrs K Rama Dev
Author: Prof K M Lakshmana Rao
Founded: 1987
Subjects: Medicine, Nursing, Dentistry
ISBN Prefix(es): 81-900416

Allied Book Centre+
9/5 Rajpur Rd, 1st floor, Dehra Dun, Uttarranchal 248001
Tel: (0135) 656526; (0135) 650949; (0135) 9837066875 *Fax:* (0135) 656554
E-mail: abc_book@rediffmail.com
Key Personnel
Proprietor: Mohit Gahlot *E-mail:* gahlotmohit@rediffmail.com
Founded: 1995
Also acts as printer & distributor.
Membership(s): Association of Indian Publishers & Booksellers.
Subjects: Agriculture, Animals, Pets, Biological Sciences, Computer Science, Earth Sciences, Energy, Environmental Studies, Gardening, Plants, Geography, Geology, Natural History, Science (General), Technology, Veterinary Science, Botany, Forestry, Hydrology, Remote Sensing, Wildlife, Zoology
ISBN Prefix(es): 81-7089
Number of titles published annually: 10 Print
Total Titles: 20 Print

Allied Publishers Pvt Ltd+
1-13/14 Asaf Ali Rd, New Delhi 110 002
Mailing Address: PO Box 7203, New Delhi 110 002
Tel: (011) 3239001; (011) 3233002; (011) 5402792 *Fax:* (011) 3235967
E-mail: allied.delhi@vsnl.com; delhi.allied@excess.net.in
Web Site: www.alliedpublishers.com
Telex: 315153
Key Personnel
Man Dir: S M Sachdev
Editorial, Rights & Permissions: Sunil Sachdev
Manager: R N Purwar
Production: Ravi Sachdev
Publicity: S Banerjee
Founded: 1934
Subjects: Agriculture, Economics, Education, Energy, Government, Political Science, Management
ISBN Prefix(es): 81-7023; 81-7764
Associate Companies: Allied Publishers Subscription Agency
Branch Office(s)
15, J N Heredia Marg, Ballard Estate, Mumbai 400038 *Tel:* (022) 2617926; (022) 2617927 *Fax:* (022) 2617928 *E-mail:* allredpl@vsnl.com
17 Chittaranjan Ave, Kolkata 700072 *Tel:* (033) 2257023; (033) 2252514 *Fax:* (033) 261158 *E-mail:* alliedcal@vsnl.com
3-5-1129 Kachiguda Cross Rd, Hyderabad 500027 *Tel:* (040) 4619079; (040) 4619081 *Fax:* (040) 4619079; (040) 4619081
Patiala House, 16-A, Ashok Marg, Lucknow 226 001 (UP) *Tel:* (0522) 214253; (0522) 280358 *Fax:* (0522) 214253
Prarthana Flats, Opposite Thakor Baug, Navrangpura, Ahmedabad 380009 *Tel:* (079) 6465916; (079) 6630079 *Fax:* (079) 6465916 *E-mail:* alliedad@ad1.vsnl.net.in
81 Hill Rd, Ramnagar, Nagpur 440010 *Tel:* (0712) 52122; (0712) 542625 *Fax:* (0712) 542625

Allyn & Bacon, *imprint of* Addison-Wesley Pte Ltd

Amar Prakashan+
A-1/139-B Lawrence Rd, New Delhi 110035
Tel: (011) 713182 *Cable:* AMARPRA

Key Personnel
Chief Executive: M S Juneja
Editorial: Ganesh Rao
Sales: Maheep Singh
Publicity: Priya Chibbar
Production: Harbajan Singh
Founded: 1977
Membership(s): FPBAI.
Subjects: Economics, Ethnicity, Government, Political Science, History, Management, Social Sciences, Sociology
ISBN Prefix(es): 81-85061; 81-85420
Divisions: Ideal Publications, Eternal Books
Branch Office(s)
UBS Publishers Dist, 5 Ansari Rd, Darya Ganj, Delhi 110002

Ambar Prakashan+
88, East Park Rd, Karol Bagh, New Delhi 110 005
Tel: (011) 2362 5528 *Fax:* (011) 2574 3569
E-mail: pitambar@bol.net.in
Key Personnel
Partner: Ved Bhushan *Tel:* (011) 23535406 *Fax:* (011) 23676058
Founded: 1977
Subjects: Education, English as a Second Language, Mathematics, Science (General)
ISBN Prefix(es): 81-7289
Total Titles: 100 Print
Parent Company: Pitambar Publishing Co Pvt Ltd
Distributed by Pitambar Publishing Co Pvt Ltd

Anand Paperbacks, *imprint of* Orient Paperbacks

Ananda Publishers Pvt Ltd+
45 Beniatola Lane, Kolkata 700 009
Tel: (033) 2241 4352; (033) 2241 3417 *Fax:* (033) 2253240; (033) 2253241
E-mail: ananda@cal3.vsnl.net.in
Web Site: www.anandapub.com
Key Personnel
Manager: Dwijendranath Basu
Subjects: Anthropology, Art, Biography, Cookery, Drama, Theater, Economics, Fiction, Finance, Gardening, Plants, History, Music, Dance, Mysteries, Philosophy, Photography, Poetry, Psychology, Psychiatry, Science (General), Science Fiction, Fantasy, Social Sciences, Sociology, Sports, Athletics
ISBN Prefix(es): 81-7215; 81-7066; 81-7756

Ankur Publishing Co
C/1, Anandvan, Anandpark, Thane (West), Maharashtra, Mumbai 400 601
Tel: (022) 543 2817; (022) 536 9907 *Fax:* (022) 543 2817
E-mail: ankur@bom3.vsnl.net.in
Web Site: www.satyamplastics.com/ankurpublishing/
Key Personnel
Man Dir: Mrs Seema Mukherjee
Founded: 1976
Subjects: Government, Political Science, Literature, Literary Criticism, Essays, Science (General)
ISBN Prefix(es): 81-85043
Associate Companies: Sanjay Composers & Printers, Uphar Cinema Bldg, Green Park Extension, New Delhi 110016

Anmol Publications Pvt Ltd+
4374/4B, Ansari Rd, Daryaganj, New Dehli 110 002
Tel: (011) 3255577; (011) 3261597; (011) 3278000 *Fax:* (011) 3280289
E-mail: anmol@nde.vsnl.net.in
Founded: 1985
Subjects: Education, Environmental Studies, Geography, Geology, Library & Information Sciences, Management, Science (General), Social Sciences, Sociology, Women's Studies
ISBN Prefix(es): 81-7041; 81-7488; 81-261

APH Publishing Corp+
5 Ansari Rd, Darya Ganj, New Delhi 110026
Tel: (011) 5100581; (011) 5410924; (011) 3285807 *Fax:* (011) 3274050
E-mail: aph@mantrasonline.com
Key Personnel
Editorial & International Rights: S B Nangia
Sales: Gopal Sharma
Founded: 1974
Also acts as distributor.
Membership(s): Federation of Indian Publishers.
Subjects: Accounting, Agriculture, Archaeology, Architecture & Interior Design, Biography, Chemistry, Chemical Engineering, Criminology, Economics, Education, Energy, Environmental Studies, Ethnicity, Fiction, Geography, Geology, Government, Political Science, Health, Nutrition, History, Labor, Industrial Relations, Law, Library & Information Sciences, Management, Marketing, Natural History, Philosophy, Public Administration, Religion - Hindu, Religion - Islamic, Religion - Other, Science (General), Social Sciences, Sociology, Travel, Women's Studies
ISBN Prefix(es): 81-7024; 81-7648
Number of titles published annually: 100 Print
Total Titles: 1,200 Print
Branch Office(s)
8/81, Punjabi Bagh, New Delhi 110026
Distributed by UBS Publishers & Distributors Ltd

Arihant Publishers+
Opp Rajasthan University, Jawahar Lal Nehru Marg, Jaipur 302004
Tel: (0141) 515192
Key Personnel
Contact: Sumer Jain
Also acts as distributor.
Membership(s): The Federation of Publishers & Booksellers Associations in India.
Subjects: Biological Sciences, Human Relations, Social Sciences, Sociology
ISBN Prefix(es): 81-7230
Parent Company: Bookmen Associates, 9 Opp Rajasthab University, JLN Marg, Jaipur 302004

Arya Medi Publishing House
c/o Arya Book Depot, 4805/24 Bharat Ram Rd, Darya Ganj, New Delhi 110002
Tel: (011) 5717012 *Fax:* (011) 5715850
Key Personnel
Man Dir: Naveen Gupta
Founded: 1980
Subjects: Science (General), Social Sciences, Sociology
ISBN Prefix(es): 81-7063; 81-7064; 81-86809

Asia Pacific Business Press Inc+
c/o National Institute of Industrial Research, 106-E, Kamla Nagar, New Delhi 110 007
Mailing Address: PO Box No 2162, New Delhi 110 007
Tel: (011) 23845886; (011) 23845654; (011) 23843955; (011) 23844729 *Fax:* (011) 23841561
E-mail: niir@vsnl.com
Web Site: www.niir.org
Key Personnel
Chief Executive Officer & President: Mr Ajay Kr Gupta
Senior Vice President: Mr P K Tripathi
Senior Project Consultant: Mr P K Chattopadhyay
Founded: 2000
Subjects: Business, Chemistry, Chemical Engineering, Science (General), Technology
ISBN Prefix(es): 81-7833
Number of titles published annually: 50 Print
Distributed by National Institute of Industrial Research

PUBLISHERS

INDIA

Asian Educational Services+
C-2/15, SDA, New Delhi 110016
Mailing Address: PO Box 4534, New Delhi 110016
Tel: (011) 661493 *Fax:* (011) 6852805; (011) 6855499
E-mail: asianeds@nda.vsnl.net.in *Cable:* ASIABOOKS NEW DELHI
Key Personnel
Publisher: Jagdish Jetley
Chief Executive: Gaurav Jetley
Publicity, Rights & Permissions: Mrs Saroj Jetley; Gautam Jetley
Founded: 1972
Subjects: Anthropology, Archaeology, Asian Studies, Astrology, Occult, Biography, Ethnicity, History, Language Arts, Linguistics, Military Science, Music, Dance, Natural History, Philosophy, Religion - Buddhist, Religion - Hindu, Religion - Islamic, Religion - Other, Social Sciences, Sociology, Theology, Travel
ISBN Prefix(es): 81-206
Subsidiaries: Antiquarian Publication and Reprographic Services Pvt Ltd
Branch Office(s)
31 Hauzkhas Village, New Delhi 110016
Tel: (011) 668594
PO Box 4534, 5 Scripuram First St, Chennai
Tel: (044) 8265040 *Fax:* (044) 8211291
Distributed by Alexandra & Leigh Copeland; Bay Foreign Language Books; Editions Kailash; French & European Publications; Hippocrene Books, Inc; Jeremy Tenniswood; Kalaimahal Book Depot; Lake House Bookshop; La Librairie Du Trefle; Laurier Books Ltd; Libri Dall'Asia; Messages of Gods Love Multi; Sarasavi Book Shop (Pvt) Ltd; Schoenhof's Foreign Books; Selous Books Ltd; South Asia Books; Vijitha Yapa Book Shop; West Port Books; Wuest GmbH & Co Kg
Warehouse: 17 Shahpur Jat, New Delhi 110 017

Asian Trading Corporation+
58, Second Cross, Da Costa Layout, St Mary's Town, Bangalore 560 084
Mailing Address: PO Box 8444, Bangalore 560 084
Tel: (080) 5487444; (080) 5490444 *Fax:* (080) 5479444
E-mail: mail@atcbooks.net; sales@atcbooks.net
Web Site: www.atcbooks.net *Cable:* PASPIN
Key Personnel
Partner: C C Pais *Tel:* (080) 216846 *Fax:* (080) 216944; Nigel Fernandes
Founded: 1946
Also exporters, importers & booksellers.
Subjects: Communications, Philosophy, Religion - Catholic, Religion - Other, Social Sciences, Sociology, Theology
ISBN Prefix(es): 81-7086
Total Titles: 125 Print
Imprints: Nil
Branch Office(s)
Mallikatte, Mangalore *Tel:* (0824) 216846 *Fax:* (0824) 216944

Associated Publishing House+
New Market, Karol Bagh, New Delhi 110005
Tel: (011) 2429392
Key Personnel
Man Dir, Sales: Ravinder K Paul
Editorial, Production Dir: Ashok K Paul
Publicity Dir, Rights & Permissions: Sharda Paul
Founded: 1966
Subjects: Art, Business, Economics, History, Philosophy, Poetry, Public Administration, Religion - Other, Social Sciences, Sociology, Travel
ISBN Prefix(es): 81-7045
Imprints: Associated Travel Series

Associated Travel Series, *imprint of* Associated Publishing House

Atma Ram & Sons
1376 Kashmere Gate, Delhi 110006
Mailing Address: PO Box 1429, Delhi 110006
Tel: (011) 223092
E-mail: yogesh2@ndf.vsnl.net.in *Cable:* BOOKS
Key Personnel
Man Dir, Publicity, Rights & Permissions: Sushil Kumar Puri
Sales: Ashutosh Pury
Founded: 1909
Subjects: Art, Education, Engineering (General), History, How-to, Medicine, Nursing, Dentistry, Philosophy, Science (General), Social Sciences, Sociology, Technology
ISBN Prefix(es): 81-7043
Branch Office(s)
17 Ashok Marg, Lucknow

Authorspress
E-35, Jawahar Park, Laxmi Nagar, Delhi 110092
Tel: (011) 22436299; (011) 22460145 *Fax:* (011) 22460145
E-mail: authorspress@yahoo.com
Key Personnel
Contact: Mr H S Negi
Publishers of Scholarly Books.
Subjects: Asian Studies, Computer Science, Economics, Education, Finance, History, Journalism, Library & Information Sciences, Philosophy, Religion - Islamic, Social Sciences, Sociology, Technology, Women's Studies
ISBN Prefix(es): 81-7273
Total Titles: 84 Print

Avinash Reference Publications+
W-70, MIDC, Shirali, Kolhapur 416122
Tel: (0231) 21024 *Fax:* (0231) 27262
Telex: 195272 IN
Key Personnel
Chief Editor: Dr J A Naik
Manager: Rajesh Naik
Founded: 1978
Subjects: Agriculture, Economics, Social Sciences, Sociology
ISBN Prefix(es): 81-85175
Associate Companies: Dr Naik & Co, W-70, MIDC, Shirali, Kolhapur 416122

B I Churchill Livingstone, *imprint of* B I Publications Pvt Ltd

B I Publications Pvt Ltd+
54 Janpath, New Delhi 110 001
Tel: (011) 3274443; (011) 3259352; (011) 3255118 *Fax:* (011) 3261290
E-mail: bigroup@del3.vsnl.net.in
Telex: 31-63352
Key Personnel
Chairman: R D Bhagat
Chief Executive: K S Mani
Publishing Dir: Y R Chadha *E-mail:* yrchadha@bipgroup.com
Founded: 1959
Subjects: Biological Sciences, Chemistry, Chemical Engineering, Electronics, Electrical Engineering, Engineering (General), Health, Nutrition, Mechanical Engineering, Medicine, Nursing, Dentistry, Physics
ISBN Prefix(es): 81-7225; 81-7042; 81-7431
Associate Companies: British Institute of Eng Technology (India) Pvt Ltd, 359, D N Rd, Mumbai 400 023
Imprints: B I Churchill Livingstone; B I Waverly
Subsidiaries: B I Churchill Livingstone Pvt Ltd (BICL); B I Waverly Pvt Ltd (BIW)
Branch Office(s)
One Aishwarya Apts 9/B, Kumkum Society Stadium Rd, Ahmedabad 380014 *Tel:* (079) 459847
147, Infantry Rd, Bangalore 560 001 *Tel:* (080) 2204652 *Fax:* (080) 2205696

35 Mount Rd, Chennai 600 002 *Tel:* (044) 8521851 *Fax:* (044) 8525361
13-1A, Govt Pl East, Kolkata 700001 *Tel:* (033) 2488742 *Fax:* (033) 2488743
18 Landsdowne Rd, Mumbai 400 039 *Tel:* (020) 2021766 *Fax:* (020) 2046778
13 Daryaganj, New Delhi 110 002 *Tel:* (011) 3274443 *Fax:* (011) 3261290
Dharhara House, Nayatola (Police Chowki), Patna 800 004 *Tel:* (0612) 657814 *Fax:* (0612) 663794
Distributor for Edward Arnold; ASM International; Elsevier Science; Lippincott-Williams & Wilkins; Macmillan Group; Routledge Chapman & Hall; Roskill

B I Waverly, *imprint of* B I Publications Pvt Ltd

K P Bagchi & Co+
286 BB, Ganguli St, Kolkata 700012
Tel: (033) 267474; (033) 269496 *Fax:* (033) 2482973 *Cable:* KHPIBEE
Key Personnel
Chief Executive, Publicity, Rights & Permissions: P K Bagchi
Editorial, Sales, Production: K K Bagchi
Founded: 1972
Subjects: Anthropology, Economics, Government, Political Science, History, Language Arts, Linguistics, Literature, Literary Criticism, Essays, Social Sciences, Sociology
ISBN Prefix(es): 81-7074
Associate Companies: Kusum Book Agency, Kalyan Nagar, PO Pansila 743180, Dist North 24, Parganas, Bengla

Baha'i Publishing Trust of India+
F-3/6 Okhla Industrial Area, Phase-I, New Delhi 110 020
Tel: (011) 26819391; (011) 26818990 *Fax:* (011) 26812703
E-mail: publisher@bahaindia.org; bptindia@del3.vsnl.net.in; nsaindia@bahaindia.org
Web Site: www.bahaindia.org
Telex: 0314881 Nsa In *Cable:* BAHAIFAITH
Key Personnel
General Manager: Mr Jiten Mishra
Founded: 1954
Subjects: Education, Religion - Other, Social Sciences, Sociology
ISBN Prefix(es): 81-85091; 81-7896; 81-86953
Parent Company: National Spiritual Assembly of the Baha'is of India, 6-Shrimant Madhavrao Scindia Marg, New Delhi 110 001
U.S. Office(s): Baha'i Publishing Trust, 415 Linden Ave, Wilmette, IL 60091, United States

The Bangalore Printing & Publishing Co Ltd+
88 Mysore Rd, Bangalore 560018
Tel: (080) 6709638; (080) 6709027 *Fax:* (080) 6704053
E-mail: marketing@bangalorepress.com
Web Site: www.bangalorepress.com *Cable:* MUDRASALA
Key Personnel
Man Dir: H R Ananth
General Marketing Manager: C A Krishnaswamy
Founded: 1916
Membership(s): Federation of Indian Publishers.
Subjects: Agriculture, Biography, Fiction, Health, Nutrition, Philosophy, Psychology, Psychiatry, Religion - Other, Social Sciences, Sociology
ISBN Prefix(es): 81-87145
Branch Office(s)
The Bangalore Press, Statue Sq, Mysore *Tel:* 570-001
Distributed by U B S Publishers' Distributors Ltd (India)

Bani Mandir, Book-Sellers, Publishers & Educational Suppliers+
Ranibari, Panbazar, Guwahati 781 001

Tel: (0361) 520241; (0361) 513886
E-mail: utpal@gwl.vsnl.net.in
Web Site: www.banimandir.cjb.net
Telex: 235-2455 NEWS IN *Cable:* LABANYA GUWAHATI
Key Personnel
Chief Executive: Chandra Kanta Hazarika
Editorial, Rights & Permissions: Surjya Kanta Hazarika
Sales: Ujjal Kumar Hazarika
Publicity: Utpal Kumar Hazarika
Founded: 1949
Membership(s): Federation of Indian Publishers; Federations of Indian Booksellers & Publishers Association.
Subjects: Anthropology, Biological Sciences, Chemistry, Chemical Engineering, Cookery, Economics, Education, Environmental Studies, Ethnicity
ISBN Prefix(es): 81-7206
Subsidiaries: Chandra Kanta Press Pvt Ltd

Benjamin Cummings, *imprint of*
Addison-Wesley Pte Ltd

Bharat Law House Pvt Ltd+
T-1/95 Mangolpuri Industrial Area, New Delhi 110 083
Tel: (011) 791 0001; (011) 791 0002; (011) 791 0003 *Fax:* (011) 791 0004
E-mail: blh@nda.vsnl.net.in
Key Personnel
Chairman, Man Dir, Rights & Permissions: D C Puliani
Sales: Ashok Puliani
Editorial: Ravi Puliani
Publicity, Production: Mahesh Puliani
Founded: 1957
Subjects: Law
ISBN Prefix(es): 81-85397; 81-7737
Branch Office(s)
Shop 6, 1st floor, Amar Towers 1, First Cross, Gandhinagar, Bangalore 560009 *Tel:* (080) 2263434
Showroom(s): 4779/23 Ansari Rd, Daryaganj, New Delhi *Tel:* (011) 3275884; (011) 3278282

Bharat Publishing House+
Flat No 123, Durga Chambers, Desh Bandhu Gupta Rd, Karol Bagh, New Delhi 110005
Tel: (011) 25757081; (011) 23670067 *Fax:* (011) 23676058
E-mail: pitambar@bol.net.in
Key Personnel
Contact: Manish Aggarwal
Founded: 1990
Membership(s): Federation of Indian Publishers, New Delhi (India).
Subjects: Geography, Geology, Language Arts, Linguistics, Mathematics, Physics, Science (General)
ISBN Prefix(es): 81-86378
Parent Company: Pitambar Publishing Co (P) Ltd, 888 E Park Rd, Karol Bagh, New Delhi 11005
Associate Companies: Ambar Parkashan
Distributed by Pitambar Publishing Co (P) Ltd
Foreign Rep(s): S Rattan (Middle East)

Bharatiya Vidya Bhavan
Munshi Sadan Marg Kulapathikm, Mumbai 400 007
Tel: (022) 3631261; (022) 8118261; (022) 8118262 *Fax:* (022) 3630058 *Cable:* BHAVIDYA BOMBAY GIRGAON
Key Personnel
Executive Secretary, Editorial, Rights & Permissions: S Ramakrishnan
Founded: 1938
Subjects: Art, Biography, Ethnicity, Fiction, History, Literature, Literary Criticism, Essays, Philosophy, Religion - Other, Social Sciences, Sociology
ISBN Prefix(es): 81-7276
Branch Office(s)
Ahmedabad
Bangalore
Baroda
Belgaum
Bharuch
Bharwari
Bhatpara
Bhimavaram
Bhopal
Bhubaneswar
Calicut
Cannanore
Chandigarh
Chennai
Coimbatore
Dakor
Delhi
Ernakulam
Guntur
Hyderabad
Jaipur
Jammu
Jamnagar
Jodhpur
Kakinada
Kannyakumari
Kanpur
Kodaikanal
Kolkata
Kurkunta
Lucknow
Mangalore
Mukundgarth
Nagpur
New Delhi
Palghat
Patna
Pune
Ramachandrapuram
Ratangarh
Renukoot
Rourkela
Serampore
Tadapalligudam
Trichur
Trivandrum
Varanasi
Visakhapatnam
4-A Castle Town Rd, London W14 9HQ, United Kingdom *Tel:* (020) 83813086
U.S. Office(s): 79 Milk St, Boston, MA, United States *Tel:* (617) 426-4525
65-09 Queens Blvd, Woodside, NY 11377, United States

Bhawan Book Service, Publishers & Distributors+
13/2 Pant Nagar, New Delhi 110014
Tel: 2258836; 271559; 612-67-2506 *Fax:* 265315; 612-67-0010
E-mail: bbpdpat@glascl01.vsnl.net.in
Key Personnel
Contact: Sanjay Bose
Founded: 1942
Membership(s): Federation of Indian Publishers; Federation of Educational Publishers.
Subjects: Agriculture, Chemistry, Chemical Engineering, Computer Science, Earth Sciences, Economics, Education, English as a Second Language, Geography, Geology
ISBN Prefix(es): 81-87090
Branch Office(s)
Darbhanga
Kolkata
Muzaffarpur
New Delhi
Ranchi

Biblia Impex Pvt Ltd
2/18 Ansari Rd, New Delhi 110002
Tel: (011) 23278034; (011) 23262515 *Fax:* (011) 2328-2047
E-mail: info@bibliaimpex.com
Web Site: www.bibliaimpex.com *Cable:* ELYSIUM
Key Personnel
Man Dir: P K Goel
Founded: 1980
Also export Indian publications.
ISBN Prefix(es): 81-85012

Big Database Publishing Pvt Ltd
36-C Connaught Pl, New Delhi 110001
Key Personnel
Man Dir, Publicity: Sudhir Malhorta
Editorial: Arun Coyal
Sales: S Khanna
Production: K D Sharma
Founded: 1984
Subjects: Economics
ISBN Prefix(es): 81-85166
Associate Companies: Orient Paperbacks; Vision Books Pvt Ltd

Bihar Hindi Granth Akademi
One Premchand Marg, Rajender Nagar, Patna 800016
Tel: (0612) 50390
Key Personnel
Chairman: Lokesh Nath Jha
Dir, Rights & Permissions: Dr B N Thakur
Editorial: Yoganand Jha
Sales, Production & Publicity: Ramchandra Singh
Founded: 1970
Subjects: Human Relations, Science (General)
ISBN Prefix(es): 81-7351

Book Circle
Subsidiary of Disha Prakashan
109, Daryaganj, New Delhi 110002
Tel: (011) 23266258; (011) 23288283; (011) 23257798 *Fax:* (011) 23263050
E-mail: info@meditechbooks.com
Web Site: www.meditechbooks.com
Key Personnel
Proprietor: Himanshu Chawla
Specialize in medical & technical books.
Subjects: Agriculture, Architecture & Interior Design, Asian Studies, Criminology, Engineering (General), Mathematics, Mechanical Engineering, Medicine, Nursing, Dentistry, Philosophy, Religion - Buddhist, Social Sciences, Sociology, Veterinary Science, Women's Studies
Ultimate Parent Company: Heritage Publishers

Book Faith India+
Flat No 416, Express Tower, Azadpur Commercial Complex, Delhi 110033
Tel: (011) 713-2459 *Fax:* (011) 724-9674
E-mail: pilgrim@del2.vsml.net.in
Key Personnel
Publisher: Rawa Tiwari
Man Editor: Praveen Sareen *Tel:* (011) 7462427
Executive Editor: John Snyder Jr
Founded: 1990
Membership(s): New Delhi Association of Publishers.
Subjects: Asian Studies, Religion - Buddhist, Religion - Hindu
ISBN Prefix(es): 81-7303
Associate Companies: Pilgrim Book House, B-27/98 A-8 Durgakund, Habasganj, Varanasi *E-mail:* Pilgrim@RW1.vsnl.net.in
U.S. Office(s): Pilgrims Book Distributors, PO Box 72, Lake City, MI 49651-0072, United States
Distributed by Moving Books; Pilgrims Book House (Nepal)
Orders to: PO Box 3872, Kathmandu, Nepal

Book Field Centre, *imprint of* Era Books

PUBLISHERS   INDIA

Bookionics
Member of The Book Syndicate
3-5 1114/7, Opp Hotel Traveller Kachiguda X Rd, Hyderabad 500 027
Tel: (040) 593654 *Fax:* (040) 595678
E-mail: bookionics@yahoo.com
Key Personnel
Owner: Chandrakant P Shah
Founded: 1985
Subjects: Computer Science, Engineering (General), Management

Booklinks Corporation
3-4-423/5 & 6 Narayanguda, Hyderabad 500029
Tel: (0842) 65021; (0842) 62282; (0842) 65550
Cable: BOOKLINKS
Key Personnel
Chief Executive, Editorial: K B Satyanarayana
Sales, Production, Publicity: K Ramakrishna
Founded: 1965
Subjects: Social Sciences, Sociology, Humanities
ISBN Prefix(es): 81-85194

Books & Books+
C4A/20A, Janakpuri, New Delhi 110058
Tel: (011) 551252
Key Personnel
Contact: Indramohan Sharma; Aniruddha Bhaskar
Founded: 1980
Membership(s): Federation of Indian Publishers; Specializes in Archaeology & Art.
Subjects: Anthropology, Archaeology, Architecture & Interior Design, Art, History, Philosophy, Religion - Buddhist, Religion - Hindu, Religion - Islamic
ISBN Prefix(es): 81-85016

BPB Publications+
20 Munish Plaza, 20 Ansari Rd, Darya Ganj, New Delhi 110002
Tel: (011) 3281723; (011) 3254990; (011) 3254991 *Fax:* (011) 3266427
E-mail: admin@bpbonline.com
Web Site: www.bpbonline.com
Telex: 31 66971qyanin *Cable:* Radiocraft
Key Personnel
President: Manish Jain
Founded: 1958
Subjects: Computer Science, Electronics, Electrical Engineering
ISBN Prefix(es): 81-7029; 81-7656
Branch Office(s)
8/1 Ritchie St, Mount Rd, Chennai 600002
4-3-269 Giriraj Lane, Bank St, Hyderabad 500001
Bookshop(s): Radio & Craft Publications, 4794 Bharat Ram Rd, 23 Daryaganj, New Delhi 110002

BR Publishing Corporation+
A-6, Nimri Commercial Centrem, Ashok Vihar Phase IV, Shastri Nagar, Delhi 110052
Tel: (011) 7430113; (011) 7143353
Telex: 31-66778 DK IN *Cable:* INDLIT
Key Personnel
Chief Executive, Editorial, Production & Publicity: Praveen Mittal
Founded: 1974
Subjects: Agriculture, Anthropology, Archaeology, Art, Economics, Government, Political Science, Health, Nutrition, History, Literature, Literary Criticism, Essays, Social Sciences, Sociology
ISBN Prefix(es): 81-7018
Parent Company: BRPC (India) Ltd
Associate Companies: Books for All; Low Price Publications
U.S. Office(s): South Asia Books, PO Box 502, Columbia, MO, United States
Showroom(s): One Ansari Rd, Daryaganj, New Delhi 110002
Orders to: D K Publisher's Distributors Pvt Ltd, One Ansari Rd, New Delhi 2

Brijbasi Printers Pvt Ltd+
E-46/11 Okhia Industrial Area, Phase II, New Delhi 110020
Tel: (011) 6914115; (011) 6841897 *Fax:* (011) 6837835
Key Personnel
Dir: Saurabh Garg; M L Garg
Founded: 1980
Subjects: Art, Cookery, Natural History, Religion - Hindu, Travel
ISBN Prefix(es): 81-7107
Associate Companies: S S Brijbasl & Sons

BS Publications+
Member of The Book Syndicate
Sultan Bazaar, Girraj Lane, 4-4-309, 2nd floor, 500 095 Hyderabad
Tel: (040) 23445600; (040) 23445601 *Fax:* (040) 23445611
E-mail: contactus@bspublications.net
Key Personnel
Owner: Nikhil Nandan C Shah
Founded: 1999
Subjects: Biological Sciences, Chemistry, Chemical Engineering, Communications, Computer Science, Earth Sciences, Electronics, Electrical Engineering, Energy, Engineering (General), Environmental Studies, Geography, Geology, Management, Mechanical Engineering, Medicine, Nursing, Dentistry, Microcomputers, Physical Sciences, Physics, Transportation
ISBN Prefix(es): 81-7800
Total Titles: 25 Print

BSMPS - M/s Bishen Singh Mahendra Pal Singh+
23A Connaught Pl, Dehra Dun 248 001
Mailing Address: PO Box 137, Dehra Dun 248 001
Tel: (0135) 655748 *Fax:* (0135) 650107
E-mail: info@bishensinghbooks.com
Web Site: www.bishensinghbooks.com
Key Personnel
Man Dir, Sales: Gajendra Singh Gahlot
Editorial, Publicity, Rights & Permissions: R G S Gahlot
Production: Srimati Jaswanti Devi
Founded: 1957
Subjects: Agriculture, Biological Sciences, Earth Sciences, Environmental Studies, Geography, Geology, Natural History
ISBN Prefix(es): 81-211
Distributed by Koeltz Scientific Books (Germany)

Business Information Group, see Big Database Publishing Pvt Ltd

Central Tibetan Secretariat
c/o Library of Tibetan Works & Archives, Gangchen Kyishong, Dharamsala 176215
Tel: (01892) 22467 *Fax:* (01892) 23723
E-mail: ltwa@ndf.vsnl.net.in
Key Personnel
General Secretary: Sonam Topgyal
Sales Manager: Pasang Tsering
Production, Publicity, Rights & Permissions: Lodi G Gyari
Founded: 1961
Subjects: Ethnicity, Journalism, Religion - Other
Subsidiaries: Sheja Press, McLeod Ganj, Dharamsala Cantt, Himachal Pradesh; Tibetan Bulletin, c/o Library of Tibetan Works & Archives; Tibetan Freedom Press, Toon Soong, Tenzin Norgay Rd, Darjeeling, Bengla

Chanakya Publications+
F 10/14, Model Town, Delhi 110009
Tel: (011) 711976 *Cable:* CHANAKYA
Key Personnel
Proprieter: Akhileshwar Jha
Sales: R P Maurya
Production: Chakradhar
Editorial, Publicity, Rights & Permissions: S K Jha
Founded: 1980
Subjects: Ethnicity, Fiction, Human Relations, Poetry, Social Sciences, Sociology
ISBN Prefix(es): 81-7001
Subsidiaries: Prism India Paperbacks

S Chand & Co Ltd+
Ram Nagar, Hotel Tourist Complex, New Delhi 110 055
Mailing Address: PO Box 5733, Ram Nagar, New Delhi 110 055
Tel: (011) 3672080; (011) 3672081; (011) 3672082 *Fax:* (011) 3677446
E-mail: schand@vsnl.com
Telex: 31-61310 *Cable:* ESCHAND, NEW DELHI
Key Personnel
Man Dir, Editorial & Publishing Dir, Rights & Permissions: Rajendra Kumar Gupta
General Administration & Export: B N Chatterjee
Sales & Marketing: R K Sahni
Founded: 1917
Subjects: Art, Business, Economics, Government, Political Science, Medicine, Nursing, Dentistry, Philosophy, Science (General), Social Sciences, Sociology, Technology
ISBN Prefix(es): 81-219
Associate Companies: Rajendra Ravindra Printers Pvt Ltd, New Delhi; Shyamlal Charitable Trust, New Delhi (Publications)
Subsidiaries: Eurasia Publishing House Pvt Ltd
Divisions: S Chand Education Worldwide (direct sales for Encyclopeadia Britannica products)
Branch Office(s)
No 6, Ahuja Chambers, 1st Cross, Kumara Krupa Rd, Bangalore 560001, Contact: Mr P Rajalingam *Fax:* (080) 2268048 *E-mail:* schandpublish@vsnl.net
SCO 6, 7 & 8, Sector 9D, Chandigarh 160016, Contact: B L Ghai *Tel:* (0712) 692680
152, Anna Salai, Chennai 600002, Contact: A M Arunachalam *Fax:* (044) 8460026 *E-mail:* mdschand@del6.vsnl.net.in
613-7, M G Rd, Ernakulam, Kochi, Contact: Mr Mohan Das Menon *Tel:* (0484) 381740 *E-mail:* schandco@md4.vsnl.net.in
Dilip Commercial, 1st floor, M N Rd, Pan Bazaar, Guwahati 780001, Contact: S K Bagal *Fax:* (0361) 522155 *E-mail:* guschand@gw1.vsnl.net.in
Sultan Bazaar, Hyderabad 500195, Contact: Mr I J Talwar *Tel:* (040) 4744815 *Fax:* (040) 4651135 *E-mail:* schand@hd2.dot.net.in
Mai Hiran Gate, Jalandhar 144008, Contact: M P J Singh *Tel:* (0181) 401630 *E-mail:* jaschand@vsnl.com
285/j Bipin Bihari, Ganguly St, Kolkata 700012, Contact: Mrs R M Nath *Tel:* (033) 2367459 *Fax:* (033) 2373914 *E-mail:* clschnd@del6.vsnl.net.in
Mahavir Market, 25-Gwynne Rd, Aminabad, Lucknow 226801, Contact: Mr Vipin Kr Gupta *Tel:* (0522) 284815 *Fax:* (0522) 226801 *E-mail:* schand_luk@ayadh.net
Blackie House, 103/5 Walchand Hirachand Marg, Opp GPO, Mumbai 400001, Contact: Mr D R Parab *Tel:* (022) 2690881 *Fax:* (022) 2610885 *E-mail:* schand@del6.vsnl.net.in
Gandhi Sagar E, Nagpur 440002, Contact: Mr B Kaushik *Tel:* (0712) 723901 *E-mail:* naschand@nagpur.dot.net.in
104 CitiCentre Ashok, Govind Mitra Rd, Patna 800004, Contact: Mr R C Bhatt *Tel:* (0612) 671366 *E-mail:* paschand@dte.vsnl.net.in
Distributor for Britannica (India)
Orders to: Nirja Construction & Development Co (P) Ltd, Publishers, Ram Nagar, New Delhi 110055

Charotar Publishing House
Opp Amul Dairy, Civil Court Rd, PO Box 65, Anand Gujarat 388001
Tel: (02692) 256237 *Fax:* (02692) 240089
E-mail: charotar@icenet.net; charotar@cphbooks.com
Web Site: www.cphbooks.com
Key Personnel
Chief Executive, Publicity, Right & Permissions: Ramanbhai C Patel
Sales: Bhavin R Patel; Pradeep R Patel
Founded: 1944
Subjects: Civil Engineering, Engineering (General)
ISBN Prefix(es): 81-85594
Total Titles: 50 Print
Parent Company: Charotar Associate, Charotar Books Distributors
Subsidiaries: Charotar Book Distributors
Bookshop(s): Charotar Book Stall, nr Post Office, Vallabh Vidyanagar, Via Anand Gujarat 388120

Chetana Private Ltd Publishers & International Booksellers
K Dubash Marg, Kala Ghoda, Mumbai 400023
Tel: (022) 228 81159; (022) 282 4983 *Fax:* (022) 262 4316
E-mail: orders@chetana.com; chetana1946@chetana.com
Web Site: www.chetana.com *Cable:* Indology
Key Personnel
Man Dir: Sudhakar S Dikshit
Publicity: K T Vaidya
Founded: 1946
Subjects: Philosophy, Religion - Other
ISBN Prefix(es): 81-85300

Children's Book Trust+
Nehru House, 4 Bahadur Shah Zafar Marg, New Delhi 110 002
Tel: (011) 23316974; (011) 23316970 *Fax:* (011) 23721090
E-mail: cbtnd@vsnl.com
Web Site: www.childrensbooktrust.com *Cable:* CHILDTRUST
Key Personnel
Chief Executive: Yamuna Shankar
General Manager, Rights & Permissions: Ravi Shankar
Sales Manager & Publicity: H R Khurana
Founded: 1957
ISBN Prefix(es): 81-7011
Branch Office(s)
18-C, Rayala Towers, Anna Salai, Chennai 600002, Contact: V Badrinarynan *Tel:* (044) 28521850
G-14, Kamalalaya Centre, 156-A, Lenin Sarani, Kolkata 700013, Contact: Bimal Datta *Tel:* (033) 22155094

Chowkhamba Sanskrit Series Office
K-37/99 Gopal Mandir Lane, Varanasi 221 001
Mailing Address: PO Box 1008, Varanasi 221 001
Tel: (0542) 2333458 *Fax:* (0542) 2333458
E-mail: cssoffice@satyam.net.in
Web Site: www.chowkhambaseries.com *Cable:* CHOWKHAMBA SERIES VARANASI
Key Personnel
Man Dir, Publicity: Brajmohan Das Gupta
  Tel: (0542) 2335020
Sales, Production: Kamalesh Kumar Gupta
  Tel: (0542) 2334032
Founded: 1892
Printing & selling Ayurvedic books & books on Indology.
Subjects: Anthropology, Archaeology, Architecture & Interior Design, Art, Asian Studies, Astrology, Occult, Astronomy, Biography, Economics, Geography, Geology, Health, Nutrition, History, Music, Dance, Philosophy, Physical Sciences, Poetry, Religion - Other

ISBN Prefix(es): 81-7080
Number of titles published annually: 20 Print
Total Titles: 450 Print
Associate Companies: Chowkhamba Krishnadas Academy, K-37/118 Gopal Mandir Lane, PO Box 1118, Varanasi 221001 *Tel:* (0542) 2335020 *E-mail:* cssoffice@satyam.net.in

The Christian Literature Society+
No 68, Evening Bazaar Rd, Park Town, Chennai 600 003
Mailing Address: PO Box No 501, Park Town, Tamil Nadu 600 003
Tel: (044) 25354296; (044) 25354297 *Fax:* (044) 25354297 *Cable:* Vedic
Key Personnel
Contact: Joshua J Singh
Founded: 1858
Subjects: Asian Studies, Biblical Studies, Biography, Philosophy, Religion - Protestant, Technology, Women's Studies
ISBN Prefix(es): 81-85884
Distributed by ISPCK
Bookshop(s): CLS Bookshop, The Estate, Ground floor, Rear Block, 121, Dickenson Rd, Bangalore 560 042 *Tel:* (080) 25582729; CLS Bookshop, PO Box 501, Park Town, Chennai 600 003; CLS Bookshop, M G Rd, Cochin 682 011 *Tel:* (0484) 2381677; CLS Bookshop, 775, Avanashi Rd, Coimbatore 641 018 *Tel:* (0422) 2301609; CLS Bookshop, Nampally Station Rd, Hyderabad 500 001 *Tel:* (040) 23202046; CLS Bookshop, 15-D, W Veli St, Madurai 625 001 *Tel:* (0452) 2342405; CLS Bookshop, M G Rd, Pulimood, Trivandrum 695 001 *Tel:* (0471) 478115

Chugh Publications
2, Strachey Rd, Civil Lines, Allahabad 211001
Tel: (0532) 623561
Key Personnel
Chief Executive, Production, Publicity, Rights & Permissions: Ramesh Chugh
Sales: Suman Chugh
Founded: 1973
Subjects: Human Relations, Social Sciences, Sociology
ISBN Prefix(es): 81-85076; 81-85613
Associate Companies: R S Publishing House, 20 Mahatma Gandhi Marg, Allahabad
Bookshop(s): Universal Book Shop

CICC Book House, Leading Publishers & Booksellers
Press Club Rd, Cochin, Kerala 682011
Tel: (0484) 353557; (0484) 355658
Key Personnel
Contact: T Jayachandran
Founded: 1962
Subjects: Drama, Theater, Fiction, Literature, Literary Criticism, Essays
ISBN Prefix(es): 81-7174
Book Club(s): Crime Book Club

Clarion, *imprint of* Hind Pocket Books Private Ltd

Clarion Books, *imprint of* Full Circle Publishing

Clarion Books, see Full Circle Publishing

Classical Publishing Co
c/o Indological Publishers & Booksellers, 28 Shopping Centre, Karampura, New Delhi 110015
Tel: (011) 563689
Key Personnel
Man Dir, Editorial: Bal Krishan Taneja
Marketing: Miss Suman Sharma
Production: Nirmal Rani
Publicity: R P Singh

Founded: 1976
Subjects: Social Sciences, Sociology
ISBN Prefix(es): 81-7054

Comdex Computer Publishing, *imprint of* Pustak Mahal

Concept Publishing Co+
A/15-16, Commercial Block, Mohan Garden, New Delhi 110059
Mailing Address: PO Box 6274, New Delhi 11015
Tel: (011) 5648039 *Fax:* (011) 5648053
E-mail: publishing@conceptpub.com
Web Site: www.conceptpub.com *Cable:* CONPUBCO, New Delhi-59
Key Personnel
Proprietor & Chief Executive: Ashok Kumar Mittal
Editorial, Sales, Publicity: Nitin Mittal
Founded: 1974
Subjects: Alternative, Anthropology, Asian Studies, Behavioral Sciences, Communications, Earth Sciences, Economics, Education, Energy, Environmental Studies, Ethnicity, Geography, Geology, History, Journalism, Library & Information Sciences, Management, Philosophy, Psychology, Psychiatry, Public Administration, Self-Help, Social Sciences, Sociology, Women's Studies
ISBN Prefix(es): 81-7022; 81-8069
Number of titles published annually: 50 Print
Total Titles: 1,400 Print
Parent Company: D K Agencies (P) Ltd
Subsidiaries: Logos Press
Showroom(s): 23 Ansari Rd, New Delhi 110002 *Tel:* (011) 3272187
Bookshop(s): 23 Ansari Rd, New Delhi 110002 *Tel:* (011) 3272187

Cosmo Publications+
24-B Ansari Rd, Daryaganj, New Delhi 110002
Mailing Address: PO Box 7206, New Delhi 110002
Tel: (011) 3278779; (011) 3280455 *Fax:* (011) 3274597
E-mail: genesis.cosmo@axcess.net.in; genesis@ndb.vsnl.net.in
Key Personnel
Chairman & Man Dir: Rani Kapoor
Chief Editor & Sales Dir: Subodh Kapoor
Dir Foreign Sales, Rights & Permissions: Sunil Kapoor
Founded: 1972
Membership(s): Federation of Indian Publishers; Federation of Publishers & Booksellers Association in India; Chemicals & Allied Export Promotions Council.
Subjects: Agriculture, Anthropology, Archaeology, Art, Asian Studies, Developing Countries, Drama, Theater, Economics, Education, Ethnicity, Government, Political Science, History, Language Arts, Linguistics, Library & Information Sciences, Literature, Literary Criticism, Essays, Music, Dance, Natural History, Nonfiction (General), Philosophy, Religion - Buddhist, Religion - Hindu, Religion - Islamic, Social Sciences, Sociology, Veterinary Science
ISBN Prefix(es): 81-7020; 81-7755
Total Titles: 1,225 Print
Parent Company: Genesis Publishing Pvt Ltd
Imprints: Siddhi Books
Subsidiaries: Cosmopolitan Book House
Divisions: Cosmo Dictionaries; Falcon Books
Warehouse: 4/16 West Patel Nagar, New Delhi 110 008

Current Books
D C Bookshop Poorna Complex, Thrissur 680001
Tel: (0487) 2444322
E-mail: info@dcbooks.com
Web Site: www.dcbooks.com/currentbooks.htm
  Cable: Current Books

Key Personnel
Chief Executive: D C Kizhakemuri
Editorial: M S Chandrasekhara Warrier
Sales: Kiliroor Radhakrishnan
Production, Publicity: Vadayar Vijayakumar
Rights & Permissions: Ponnamma Deecee
Founded: 1952
Subjects: Fiction, Nonfiction (General)
ISBN Prefix(es): 81-226
Associate Companies: D C Books; Kairali Children's Book Trust; Kairali Mudralayam
Branch Office(s)
Alappuzha *Tel:* (0477) 2261197
Aluva *Tel:* (0484) 2626006
Ernakulam *Tel:* (0484) 2351590
Irinjalakuda *Tel:* (0480) 2820667
Kalpetta *Tel:* (0493) 6203766
Kollam *Tel:* (0474) 2749055
Kottayam *Tel:* (0481) 2560342
Kozhikode *Tel:* (0495) 2727299
Palakkad *Tel:* (0491) 2535314
Pathanamthitta *Tel:* (0468) 2321268
Thalassery *Tel:* (0490) 2320668
Thiruvanathapuram *Tel:* (0471) 2477693
Thodupuzha *Tel:* (0486) 2223915
Vadakara *Tel:* (0496) 2523810
Book Club(s): VIP Book Club

D C Press, *imprint of* Kairali Children's Book Trust

Dastane Ramchandra & Co+
830, Sadashiv Peth, Chitrashala Chowk, Pune, Maharashtra 411 030
Tel: (020) 447 8193; (020) 448 5950; (020) 551 1964 *Fax:* (020) 4478193
Key Personnel
Man Dir, Editorial, Production: Vishwas Dastane
Sales, Publicity, Rights & Permissions: Mrs Bharati Dastane
Founded: 1960
Membership(s): Marathi Publishers' Association; Specialize in Social Sciences, Career Development & Help-books.
Subjects: Career Development, Economics, History, Library & Information Sciences, Literature, Literary Criticism, Essays, Science (General), Science Fiction, Fantasy, Self-Help, Social Sciences, Sociology, Sports, Athletics, Women's Studies
ISBN Prefix(es): 81-85080
Associate Companies: Abhang Stores, Printers & Stationers, 830 Sadashiv Peth, Chitrashala Chowk, Pune 411030; Sports Publications, 830 Sadashiv Peth, Chitrashala Chowk, Pune 411030; Anuja Prakashan Publishers, 13A, Abhang Poona-Bombay Rd, Pune
Bookshop(s): 456 Raviwar Peth, Pune 411002

Daya Publishing House+
4762-63/23, Ansari Rd, Darya Ganj, New Delhi 110 002
Tel: (011) 23245578; (011) 23244987 *Fax:* (011) 23244987
E-mail: dayabooks@vsnl.com
Web Site: www.dayabooks.com
Key Personnel
Contact: Anil Mittal
Founded: 1986
Subjects: Agriculture, Biological Sciences, Earth Sciences, Environmental Studies, Geography, Geology, Natural History, Veterinary Science
ISBN Prefix(es): 81-7035
Number of titles published annually: 25 Print

DC Books+
Good Shepherd St, Kottayam, Kerala 686001
Mailing Address: PO Box 214, Kottayam, Kerala 686001
Tel: (0481) 2563114; (0481) 2301614
Web Site: www.dcbooks.com *Cable:* Deecibooks

Key Personnel
Chief Executive, Rights & Permissions: D C Kizhakemuri
Editorial: M S Chandrasekhara Warrier
Sales: T K Murukesan
Production, Publicity: D Sreekumar
Founded: 1974
Subjects: Fiction, Literature, Literary Criticism, Essays, Poetry
ISBN Prefix(es): 81-7130; 81-264
Associate Companies: Current Books; Kairali Children's Book Trust; Kairali Mudralayam
Book Club(s): Classics Club; D C Book Club

Diamond Comics (P) Ltd+
A-22, Sector-63, Gobird Villa, Phase-3, Noida-201 301, Uttar Pradesh
Tel: 9810003062 (Mobile) *Fax:* (0120) 2401093; (0120) 2401094; (0120) 2401095; (0120) 2401073
E-mail: comicsdiamond@mantraonline.com
Web Site: www.comicsdiamond.com
Key Personnel
Man Dir: Narender Kumar
Editorial: Gulshan Rai
International Rights: Mr Marrish Verma
Founded: 1948
Subjects: Cookery, Crafts, Games, Hobbies, Criminology, Fiction, Health, Nutrition, How-to, Religion - Hindu
ISBN Prefix(es): 81-7184
Associate Companies: Diamond Books International, X-30, Okhala Industrial Estate Phase II, New Delhi 110020; Diamond Pocket (P) Ltd Books, X-30, Okhala Industrial Estate Phase II, New Delhi 110020; Punjabi Pustak Bhandar
Subsidiaries: Diamond Magazines
Book Club(s): Diamond Book Club

Disha Prakashan
138/16 Onkar Nagar-B, Tri Nagar, Delhi 110035
Tel: 7108832
Key Personnel
Man Dir, Publicity: B R Chawla
Founded: 1973
Subjects: Biography, Economics, History, Language Arts, Linguistics, Literature, Literary Criticism, Essays, Philosophy, Religion - Other, Social Sciences, Sociology
ISBN Prefix(es): 81-85045; 81-88081
Parent Company: Heritage Publishers
Associate Companies: Intellectuals' Rendezvous, Aggarwal Bhawa, 4C Ansari Rd, New Delhi 110002; Pankaj Publications International
Subsidiaries: Book Circle

DK Printworld (P) Ltd+
Srikunj, F-52 Bali Nagar, New Delhi 110015
Tel: (011) 25453975; (011) 25466019 *Fax:* (011) 25465926
E-mail: dkprintworld@vsnl.net
Key Personnel
Dir: Mr Susheel K Mittal
Founded: 1992
Specialize in books on Indology.
Subjects: Archaeology, Art, Asian Studies, Astrology, Occult, Drama, Theater, History, Music, Dance, Philosophy, Religion - Buddhist, Religion - Hindu, Religion - Islamic
ISBN Prefix(es): 81-246
Total Titles: 300 Print

Doaba Publications
4497/14 Guru Nanak Market, Nai Sarak, New Delhi 110 006
Tel: (011) 3274669; (011) 3259753
Key Personnel
Chief Executive, Editorial, Sales, Rights & Permissions: S N Malhotra
Production, Publicity: Rajiv Malhotra; A C Seth
Founded: 1924

Subjects: Education, English as a Second Language, Literature, Literary Criticism, Essays
ISBN Prefix(es): 81-85173; 81-87764

Dolphin Publications+
203-5 Shiv Darshan M G Rd, Opp Station Santacruz (West), Mumbai 400054
Tel: (022) 6490184 *Fax:* (022) 6233674
Key Personnel
Editor: Mrs Renu Nauriyal
Founded: 1986
Membership(s): Federation of Indian Publishers & Export Promotion Council; Specialize in children's books, general & nonfiction books.
Subjects: Animals, Pets, Biblical Studies, Crafts, Games, Hobbies, History, Mathematics, Natural History, Nonfiction (General)
ISBN Prefix(es): 81-85523
Associate Companies: India Book House, 203-5 Shiv Darshan M G Rd, Opp Station Santacruz (West), Mumbai 400054
Subsidiaries: J Moolur & Co

Dreamland Publications+
J-128, Kirti Nagar, New Delhi 110015
Tel: (011) 25106050; (011) 25435657 *Fax:* (011) 25428283
E-mail: dreamland@vsnl.com
Web Site: www.dreamlandpublications.com
Key Personnel
Contact: Ved Chawla
Founded: 1986
ISBN Prefix(es): 81-7301
Parent Company: Indian Book Depot

Dutta Baruah Publishing Co Pvt Ltd, see Dutta Publishing Co Ltd

Dutta Publishing Co Ltd+
Formerly Dutta Baruah Publishing Co Pvt Ltd
College Hostel Rd, Panbazar, Guwahati-1, Assam 781 001
Tel: (0361) 543995
Key Personnel
Man Dir: J N Dutta Baruah
Founded: 1938
Also act as distributors.
Membership(s): Federation of Indian Publishers.
Subjects: Art, Cookery, Language Arts, Linguistics, Literature, Literary Criticism, Essays, Poetry, Religion - Hindu, Religion - Other, Sports, Athletics
ISBN Prefix(es): 81-7373
Subsidiaries: M/S Parbati Prakashan

Eastern Book Centre+
Publishers Distributors & Library Suppliers, F-26, Shankar Market Connaught Circus, New Delhi 110001
Tel: (011) 3314191
Key Personnel
Contact: Subir Ghosh
Founded: 1989
Membership(s): Federation of Indian Publishers.
Subjects: Social Sciences, Sociology
ISBN Prefix(es): 81-85186

Eastern Book Co+
34 Lalbagh, Lucknow 226 001
Tel: (0522) 2223171; (0522) 2226517 *Fax:* (0522) 2224328
E-mail: sales@ebc-india.com
Web Site: www.ebc-india.com *Cable:* LAWBOOK; LUCKNOW
Key Personnel
Chief Executive: P L Malik
Editorial: Surendra Malik
Production, Publicity & Exports: Vijay Malik
Founded: 1947
Specialize in law books & law reports in print media & electronic media (CD-ROM).

Membership(s): Federation of Publishers & Booksellers Association of India, New Delhi; Avadh Chamber of Commerce & Industry; Lucknow Management Association; Indian Industries Association; Lalbagh Vyapar Mandal; Chemicals & Allied Products Export Promotion Council.
Subjects: Law
ISBN Prefix(es): 81-7012
Number of titles published annually: 100 Print; 2 CD-ROM
Total Titles: 1,200 Print; 8 CD-ROM
Associate Companies: Eastern Book Co, 5-B, Atma Ram House, 1, Tolstoy Marg, Connaught Pl, Delhi 110054, Contact: Vijay Malik *Tel:* (011) 23752321 *Fax:* (011) 23752320; Eastern Book Company Pvt Ltd, Contact: Sumain Malik *E-mail:* sales@scconline.com *Web Site:* www.scconline.com; EBC Publishing Pvt Ltd; Manav Law House, 8-10, MG Marg, Opp Bishop Johnson School, Allahabad 211001 *Tel:* (0532) 2623551; (0532) 2560710 *Fax:* (0532) 2623584
Distributed by Anupam Gyan Bhandar (Bangladesh); Blackwell's (Periodicals Division) (UK); Gurley & Associates (Trinidad & Tobago); Kokusai Shobo Ltd (Japan); Law Book Traders (Malaysia); Mabrochi International Co Ltd (Nigeria); Pakistan Law House (Pakistan); State Mutual Book & Periodical Services Ltd (US)

Eastern Law House Pvt Ltd+
54 Ganesh Chunder Ave, Kolkata 700 013
Tel: (033) 237 4989; (033) 237 2301 *Fax:* (033) 215 0491
E-mail: elh@cal.vsnl.net.in
Web Site: easternlawhouse.com
Key Personnel
Director: Asok De
Founded: 1918
Subjects: Accounting, Government, Political Science, Law, Social Sciences, Sociology
ISBN Prefix(es): 81-7177
Number of titles published annually: 20 Print
Total Titles: 1,000 Print
Bookshop(s): 36 Netaji Subhash Marg, Daryaganj, New Delhi 11002
Orders to: 36 Netaji Subhash Marg, Daryaganj, New Delhi 110002 *Tel:* (011) 327 9982 *Fax:* (011) 325 3844

Enkay Publishers Pvt Ltd
Enkay House, 3-4 Malcha Marg, Shopping Centre, Diplomatic Enclave, New Delhi 110021
Tel: (011) 301-6994; (011) 301-2314 *Fax:* (011) 301-2314
Telex: 031-6312nkayin *Cable:* ENTRAVEL
Key Personnel
Contact: S Narinder Singh Kohli
Membership(s): Federation of Indian Publishers.
Subjects: Biography, History, Religion - Other, Social Sciences, Sociology
ISBN Prefix(es): 81-85148
Subsidiaries: Enkay International Pvt Ltd

Era Books
52/47 Ramjas Rd, Karol Bagh, New Delhi 110005
Tel: (011) 473993; (022) 5741764 *Cable:* Goldenhill
Key Personnel
Chief Executive, Rights & Permissions: Eranna R Jinde
Editorial: C V Bhimasankaram
Sales: V R Jinde
Production: B Ramakumar
Publicity: J E Rao
Founded: 1979
Subjects: Education, Mathematics
ISBN Prefix(es): 81-900270
Imprints: Book Field Centre

Subsidiaries: Book Field Centre
Branch Office(s)
2-30 Khariboudi St, Adoni 518301

Ess Ess Publications+
CA 100929, Allahabad Bank, Darya Ganj Branch, Ansari Rd, New Delhi 110 002
Tel: (011) 3260807 *Fax:* (011) 3274173
E-mail: sumitsethi@vsnl.com
Web Site: www.essess.8m.com *Cable:* ESS ESS PUBLICATIONS
Key Personnel
Man Dir, Publicity, Rights & Permissions: Mrs Sheel Sethi
Editorial, Sales, Production: Sumit Sethi
E-mail: sumitsethi@vsnl.com
Founded: 1974
Specialize in all Indian books on library & information science.
Subjects: Economics, History, Human Relations, Library & Information Sciences, Management, Philosophy, Religion - Hindu, Social Sciences, Sociology
ISBN Prefix(es): 81-7000
Parent Company: Ess Ess Publishers' Distributors, KD-6A Ashok Vihar, Delhi 110052
Subsidiaries: Sumit Publications
Orders to: Ess Ess Publishers' Distributors, KD-6A Ashok Vihar, Delhi 110052 *Tel:* (011) 7437308

Eurasia Publishing House Private Ltd
PO Box 5733, New Delhi 110 055
Tel: (011) 7779891 *Fax:* (011) 7777446
E-mail: schandco@giasdl01.vsnl.net.in
Telex: 3161310 Sccl In *Cable:* escahand
Key Personnel
Man Dir, Sales Dir, Rights & Permissions: Rajendra Kumar Gupta
Founded: 1960
Subjects: Education, Engineering (General), Psychology, Psychiatry, Science (General), Social Sciences, Sociology
ISBN Prefix(es): 81-219
Parent Company: S Chand & Co Ltd, Ram Nagar, New Delhi 110055
Shipping Address: S Chand & Co Ltd, Ram Nagar, New Delhi 110055
Warehouse: S Chand & Co Ltd, Ram Nagar, New Delhi 110055
Orders to: S Chand & Co Ltd, Ram Nagar, New Delhi 110055

EWP, *imprint of* Affiliated East West Press Pvt Ltd

Financial Times PH, *imprint of* Addison-Wesley Pte Ltd

Firewall Media, *imprint of* Laxmi Publications Pvt Ltd

Firma KLM Privatee Ltd, Publishers & International Booksellers+
257-B BB Ganguly St, Kolkata 700012
Tel: (033) 274391; (033) 4681209 *Fax:* (033) 276544
Key Personnel
Man Dir, Rights & Permissions: R N Mukherti
Editorial, Production: K Roy
Founded: 1950
Subjects: Alternative, Human Relations, Social Sciences, Sociology, Humanities, Indology
ISBN Prefix(es): 81-7102
Associate Companies: Firma Mukhopadhyay, 2/1 Dr Aksay Pal Rd, Kolkata 700034
Distributed by Blue Dove Press (USA); Malshow Co Ltd (Japan); South Asia Books (USA)
Distributor for Asiatic Society Calcutta Publications; Burdwan University; Sanskrit College (Kolkata)

Focus, *imprint of* Popular Prakashan Pvt Ltd

Frank Brothers & Co Publishers Ltd+
4675-A Ansari Rd, 21 Darya Ganj, New Delhi 110002
Tel: (011) 263393; (011) 279936; (011) 278150; (011) 260796 *Fax:* (011) 3269032
E-mail: fbros@ndb.vsnl.net.in
Telex: 0313265 Fran In
Key Personnel
Chairman: R C Govil
Dir: Neeraj Govil
Founded: 1930
Subjects: Accounting, Art, Biological Sciences, Business, Computer Science, Cookery, Economics, Education, English as a Second Language, Environmental Studies, Fiction, Geography, Geology, Government, Political Science, Health, Nutrition, History, Management, Mathematics, Nonfiction (General), Physics, Science (General)
ISBN Prefix(es): 81-7170
Number of titles published annually: 50 Print
Total Titles: 1,000 Print
Bookshop(s): IV/85 Chandni Chowk, Delhi 110006 *Tel:* (011) 3276791

Full Circle Publishing+
Formerly Clarion Books
J-40 Jorbagh Lane, New Delhi 110003
Tel: (011) 55654197 *Fax:* (011) 24645795
E-mail: gbp@del2.vsnl.com; fullcircle@vsnl.com
Web Site: www.atfullcircle.com
Key Personnel
Chairman: D N Malhotra
Founded: 1970
Membership(s): Federation of Indian Publishers.
Subjects: Archaeology, Asian Studies, Astrology, Occult, Child Care & Development, Cookery, Economics, Gardening, Plants, Health, Nutrition, How-to, Humor, Language Arts, Linguistics, Law, Management, Marketing, Nonfiction (General), Poetry, Religion - Other, Self-Help, Arts of India, Indology, Mind/Body/Spirit
ISBN Prefix(es): 81-85120
Parent Company: Hind Pocket Books (P) Ltd
Imprints: Clarion Books; Mainstreet Books
Distributor for Embassy Books; Manjul Publications; Pentagon Press; Wilco

Galgotia Publications Pvt Ltd+
5 Ansari Rd, Daryaganj, New Delhi 110002
Mailing Address: PO Box 7221, New Delhi 110002
Tel: (011) 589334 *Fax:* (011) 3281909; (011) 321909
E-mail: gppl.galgtia@axcess.net.in
Telex: 03171161 Star In
Key Personnel
Chief Executive, Editorial: Suneel Galgotia
Sales: Vinod Behl
Founded: 1972
Subjects: Computer Science, Engineering (General), Management, Medicine, Nursing, Dentistry
ISBN Prefix(es): 81-7515; 81-85623; 81-86011; 81-86340
Branch Office(s)
Galgotia Towers, G-64, Manserovar Business Complex Sector 18, Noida
Showroom(s): 17B Conn Pl, New Delhi 110001
Bookshop(s): E D Galgotia & Sons

Ganesh & Co+
38 Thanikachalam Rd T Nagar, Chennai 600017
Tel: (044) 4344519 *Fax:* (044) 4342009
E-mail: ksm@md2.vsnl.net.in; service@kkbooks.com
Key Personnel
Dir: K Srinivasamurthy
Founded: 1910
Subjects: Philosophy, Religion - Other

ISBN Prefix(es): 81-85988
Parent Company: Productivity & Quality Publishing Pvt Ltd

Geeta Prakashan
Hindi Book Centre, 4-5-769, 1st floor, Badichowdi 500027
Tel: (0821) 33589
Key Personnel
General Manager: Gopala Krishna
Sales Manager: Gururaja Rao
Rights & Permissions: Sathyanarayana Rao
Founded: 1958
Subjects: Biography, History, Literature, Literary Criticism, Essays, Philosophy, Poetry, Religion - Other, Science (General), Social Sciences, Sociology
ISBN Prefix(es): 81-900754

General Book Depot+
1691, Nai Sarak, Delhi 110006
Mailing Address: PO Box 1220, Delhi 110006
Tel: (011) 2326 3695; (011) 2325 0635
 Fax: (011) 2394 0861
E-mail: contact@goyalbookshop.com
Web Site: www.goyalbookshop.com
Key Personnel
Contact: Kaushal Goyal
Founded: 1936
Specialize in English & German language reprints & French language books.
Subjects: Business, Career Development, English as a Second Language, How-to, Language Arts, Linguistics, Nonfiction (General), Self-Help, Travel
ISBN Prefix(es): 81-85288
Imprints: GOYL Saab Publishers & Distributors
Distributor for Oscar Brandstetter Verlag (Indian Sub-continent)

General Printers & Publishers+
263/F Raja Rammohan Roy Rd, Girgaon, Mumbai 400 004
Tel: (022) 2387 3113; (022) 2382 6854
 Fax: (022) 2382 7197
Key Personnel
Executive Dir: Vijay P Thakker *E-mail:* thakker@bom3.vsnl.net.in
Founded: 1952
Membership(s): Federation of Indian Publishers, Federation of Educational Publishers in India.
Subjects: Education, Workbooks, Testpapers
ISBN Prefix(es): 81-85619
Number of titles published annually: 20 Print
Total Titles: 100 Print

Gitanjali Publishing House
2/12 Vikram Vihar, Lajpat Nagar-IV, New Delhi 110024
Tel: (011) 621991; (011) 6237555
Founded: 1962
Subjects: Economics, Government, Political Science, History, Human Relations, Social Sciences, Sociology
ISBN Prefix(es): 81-85060
Bookshop(s): Indian Book Service, 2/12 Vikram Vihar, Lajpat Nagar-IV, New Delhi 110024

Globe Fearon, *imprint of* Addison-Wesley Pte Ltd

Goel Prakashen
359, Alam Geri Ganj, Bareilly, UP 250 002
Tel: (0121) 642946; (0121) 644766 *Fax:* (0121) 645855
Key Personnel
Man Dir, Editorial: B D Rastogi
Sales: Atul Krishna
Production: K Krishna
Publicity & Advertising Dir: Kamalni Rastogi
Founded: 1948
Subjects: Art, Chemistry, Chemical Engineering, Economics, Government, Political Science, History, Mathematics
ISBN Prefix(es): 81-85932
Subsidiaries: Krishna Prakashan Mandir
Bookshop(s): Goel Publishing, Krishna Prakashan Mandir, Subhash Bazar, Meerut 250002 UP

Golden Bells, *imprint of* Laxmi Publications Pvt Ltd

GOYL Saab, Publishers and Distributors, *see* General Book Depot

GOYL Saab Publishers & Distributors, *imprint of* General Book Depot

Gyan Bharati, *imprint of* National Publishing House

Gyan Books (P) Ltd, *see* Gyan Publishing House

Gyan Publishing House+
5 Ansari Rd, Daryaganj, New Delhi 110002
Tel: (011) 23261060; (011) 23282060 *Fax:* (011) 23285914
E-mail: gyanbook@del2.vsnl.net.in
Web Site: www.gyanbooks.com
Key Personnel
Chief Executive: B P Garg
Dir, Publications & International Rights: Amit Garg
Founded: 1984
Specialize in humanities & social science books.
Membership(s): Federation of Indian Publishers, Federation of Indian Publishers & Booksellers Association, Delhi State Booksellers & Publishers Association.
Subjects: Agriculture, Anthropology, Archaeology, Art, Asian Studies, Astrology, Occult, Astronomy, Biography, Career Development, Child Care & Development, Communications, Cookery, Crafts, Games, Hobbies, Developing Countries, Drama, Theater, Earth Sciences, Economics, Education, Environmental Studies, Geography, Geology, Government, Political Science, History, Human Relations, Journalism, Language Arts, Linguistics, Law, Library & Information Sciences, Management, Music, Dance, Natural History, Philosophy, Psychology, Psychiatry, Public Administration, Religion - Buddhist, Religion - Hindu, Religion - Islamic, Self-Help, Social Sciences, Sociology, Sports, Athletics, Travel, Women's Studies
ISBN Prefix(es): 81-212
Number of titles published annually: 150 Print
Total Titles: 2,000 Print
Associate Companies: Gyan Books (P) Ltd; Gyan Exports
Warehouse: 30-C, Satyawati Colony, Ashok Vihar, Phase III, New Delhi 110052
E-mail: gyanbook@vsnl.com

Hans Prakashan
18 Nyaya Marg, Allahabad, Uttar Pradesh 211001
Mailing Address: PO Box 103, Allahabad 211001
Tel: (0532) 623077
E-mail: ar@nde.vsnl.net.in
Key Personnel
Chief Executive: Mahendra Pal Jha
Production: Amrit Rai
Founded: 1950
Subjects: Fiction
ISBN Prefix(es): 81-85954

HarperCollins Publishers India Pty Ltd+
7/61 Ansari Rd (Makhanial St), Daryaganj, New Delhi 110 002
Tel: (011) 3278586; (011) 3268185 *Fax:* (011) 3277294
E-mail: harper@ndf.vsnl.net.in
Telex: 21-66641 Rupa In
Key Personnel
Man Dir: R K Mehra
Founded: 1991
Subjects: Biography, Education, Fiction, Poetry
ISBN Prefix(es): 81-7223
Parent Company: HarperCollinsPublishers
Associate Companies: East-West Press Pvt Ltd
Imprints: Indus Books; Peacock Books

Health-Harmony, *imprint of* B Jain Publishers Overseas

Arnold Heinman Publishers (India) Pvt Ltd
AB/9, 1st floor Safdaoung Enclave, New Delhi 110029
Tel: (011) 6383422; (011) 60780; (011) 664256
 Fax: (011) 6877571
Telex: 31-72370ahpiin *Cable:* Heinemann
Key Personnel
Man Dir: G A Vazirani
Editorial, Rights & Permissions: Ms Rashmi Bhushan
Production: Mukesh Vazirani
Publicity: Ms Rani Roy
Sales: R K Rana
Founded: 1969
Subjects: Art, Engineering (General), Fiction, Government, Political Science, Literature, Literary Criticism, Essays, Medicine, Nursing, Dentistry, Philosophy, Poetry, Religion - Other, Social Sciences, Sociology
ISBN Prefix(es): 81-7031
Associate Companies: Edward Arnold (Publishers) Ltd, United Kingdom
Imprints: Mayfair Paperbacks; Sanskriti; Zebra Books for Children

Heritage Publishers+
32 Prakash Apt, 5, Ansari Rd, Darya Ganj, Delhi 110002
Tel: (011) 23266258 *Fax:* (011) 23263050
E-mail: heritage@nda.vsnl.net.in; info@meditechbooks.com *Cable:* HERIPUB
Key Personnel
Proprietor: B R Chawla
Founded: 1973
Subjects: Aeronautics, Aviation, Agriculture, Architecture & Interior Design, Art, Astronomy, Automotive, Biography, Chemistry, Chemical Engineering, Civil Engineering, Computer Science, Crafts, Games, Hobbies, Disability, Special Needs, Economics, Education, Electronics, Electrical Engineering, Engineering (General), Health, Nutrition, History, Language Arts, Linguistics, Literature, Literary Criticism, Essays, Medicine, Nursing, Dentistry, Military Science, Philosophy, Physics, Religion - Other, Social Sciences, Sociology, Medical & Technical Books
ISBN Prefix(es): 81-7026
Associate Companies: Heritage Impex Worldwide
Subsidiaries: Book Circle; Intellectuals' Rendezvous, K-3/5
Distributor for Blackwell; CRC Press; Routledge; Taylor & Francis; Thames & Hudson

Himalaya Publishing House
Pooja Apartment, 4B Murarilai S, Ansari Rd, Daryaganj, New Delhi 110002
Tel: (011) 3270392; (011) 652225 *Fax:* (022) 3956286
Key Personnel
Chief Executive, Editorial, Publicity: D P Pandey
Production: Anuj Pandey
Rights & Permissions: Mrs Meena Pandey
Sales: Sudhir Joshi; K N Pandey
Founded: 1976
Subjects: Art, Business, Law, Management, Psychology, Psychiatry, Science (General), Social Sciences, Sociology
ISBN Prefix(es): 81-7040

Parent Company: Randoot, Kelewadi, Girgaon, Mumbai 400004
Associate Companies: Geetanjali Press Pvt Ltd, Kundanlal Chandak Industrial Estate, Ghat Rd, Nagpur *Tel:* (0712) 24747
Branch Office(s)
Kudanlal Chandak Industrial Estate, Ghat Rd, Nagpur *Tel:* (0712) 24747
Bookshop(s): Randoot, Kelewadi, Girgaon, Mumbai 400004
Shipping Address: Randoot, Kelewadi, Girgaon, Mumbai 400004 *Tel:* (022) 360170 (022) 355798 (022) 363863
Warehouse: Randoot, Kelewadi, Girgaon, Mumbai 400004 *Tel:* (022) 360170 (022) 355798 (022) 363863
Orders to: Randoot, Kelewadi, Girgaon, Mumbai 400004

Himalayan Books+
17-L, Connaught Circus, New Delhi 110 001
Tel: (011) 352126; (011) 351731 *Fax:* (011) 332-1731
E-mail: ebs@vsnl.com *Cable:* HIMALAYAN BOOKS
Key Personnel
Chief Executive Officer, Man Dir, Editorial: Ms Pawan Chowdhri
Sales, Production, Publicity, Rights & Permissions: Ms P Chowdhri
Founded: 1986
Specializes in aviation, Indian art & culture, travel, religion & philosophy.
Subjects: Aeronautics, Aviation, Architecture & Interior Design, Military Science, Philosophy, Regional Interests, Religion - Other, Travel
ISBN Prefix(es): 81-7002
Number of titles published annually: 12 Print
Total Titles: 200 Print
Associate Companies: English Book Store

Hind Pocket Books Private Ltd+
18/19 Dilshad Garden, G T Rd, Shahdar, Delhi 110095
Tel: (011) 202046; (011) 202332; (011) 202467 *Fax:* (011) 2282332 *Cable:* POCKETBOOK DELHI
Key Personnel
Man Dir: Dina N Malhotra
Marketing, Rights & Permissions: Shekhar Malhotra
Founded: 1957
Membership(s): Federation of Indian Publishers.
Subjects: Biography, Fiction, How-to, Nonfiction (General), Self-Help
ISBN Prefix(es): 81-216
Associate Companies: Clarion Books; Global Business Press; Indian Book Company; Sarswati
Imprints: Clarion
Book Club(s): Clarion Book Club; Gharelu Library Yojna

Hindi Pracharak Sansthan+
C/21/30 Pisachmochan, Varanasi 220010
Mailing Address: PO Box 1106, Varanasi
Tel: (0542) 54470; (0542) 52425; (0542) 52670; (0542) 355168; (0542) 56850; (0542) 361452
Key Personnel
Editorial: K C Beri; V P Beri; R P Beri; A K Beri
Sales: Vivek Beri
Subjects: Fiction
ISBN Prefix(es): 81-7337
Parent Company: Hindi Pracharak Sansthan
Associate Companies: Sahitya Bharati Publications Pvt Ltd; H P S Publications Pvt Ltd; Hindi Pracharak Publications Pvt Ltd
Subsidiaries: Kashi Offset Printers Pvt Ltd
Branch Office(s)
Pishach Mochan, Varanass (UP)
Cal Sahitya Bharati Publications Pvt Ltd, 211/1, Bidhan Sarin

IBD, see International Book Distributors

IBD Publisher & Distributors+
S-5, 3rd floor, Akarshanbhawan, 23, Ansari Rd, Daryaganj, New Delhi 110002
Tel: (011) 3251094 *Fax:* (011) 3259102
E-mail: piyush_gahlot@rediffmail.com
Founded: 2001
Also distributor.
Membership(s): Delhi State Booksellers & Publisher Association (DSBPA).
Subjects: Agriculture, Biological Sciences, Environmental Studies, Science (General), Technology
ISBN Prefix(es): 81-7089
Number of titles published annually: 15 Print
Associate Companies: Allied Book Centre; International Book Distributors
Distributed by DAYA; DK Publishers; Koeltz Scientific; Kramer; UBS Publishers
Distributor for CAB International; Koeltz Scientific
Showroom(s): Dehra Dun, New Delhi
Warehouse: Dehra Dun, New Delhi

IBH, see India Book House Pvt Ltd

ICSSR, see Indian Council of Social Science Research (ICSSR)

Idara Ishaat-E-Diniyat Ltd
168/2 Jha House, Hazrat Nizamuddin, New Delhi 110 013
Tel: (011) 26926832; (011) 26926833 (office); (011) 461676; (011) 4631786 (showroom) *Fax:* (011) 26932787; (011) 4632786
E-mail: sales@idara.com; idara@yahoo.com
Web Site: www.idara.com *Cable:* DINIYAT
Key Personnel
Man Dir: Mohammad Anas
Dir, Exports: Mohammad Yunus
Dir: Mohammad Yusuf
Founded: 1950
Specialize in Holy Qur'an & Islamic Religious Books. Cover Urdu, Arabic, English, French, Hindi & Gujrati Languages.
ISBN Prefix(es): 81-7101
Warehouse: D 80-81, Near Masjid Bilal, Abul Fazal Enclave Phase-I, Jamia Nagar, New Delhi 110 025

India Book House Pvt Ltd+
Mahalaxmi Chambers, 5th floor, 22 Bhulabhai Desai Rd, Mumbai 400026
Tel: (022) 2840165 *Fax:* (022) 2835099
E-mail: padmini@ibhindia.com
Key Personnel
Man Dir: Deepak Mirchandani
Editorial & Publishing Dir: Padmini Mirchandani
Founded: 1952
Distripress.
Subjects: Architecture & Interior Design, Art
ISBN Prefix(es): 81-7508; 81-85028
Parent Company: Mirchandani & Co Pvt Ltd
Associate Companies: IBH Magazine Services, Jesia House, 137 Modi St, Fort, Mumbai 400 001, Lata Vasvani *Tel:* (022) 2840165 *Fax:* (022) 2633067 *E-mail:* subscriptions@ibhworld.com; IBH Subscription Agency, Fleet Fasteners Bldg, MV Rd, Marol Naka, Andheri (East), Mumbai 400 059, Moti Wadhwani *Tel:* (022) 8501999 *Fax:* (022) 8500645 *E-mail:* journals@ibhworld.com; Rishi Exports, Arch 29, Below Mahalaxmi Bridge, Mahalaxmi, Mumbai 400 034, Mohan Shahani *Tel:* (022) 4927463 *Fax:* (022) 4950392
Distributed by Antique Collectors' Club (UK)
Distributor for Harper Collins (United States); Hodder & Stoughton Ltd (United Kingdom); Little Hampton Publishers (United Kingdom); Random House Inc (United States); Simon Schuster (United States & United Kingdom); Transworld Publishers Ltd (United Kingdom)

The Indian Anthropological Society, see Indian Museum

Indian Book Depot+
J-128, Kirti Nagar, New Delhi 110015
Tel: (011) 3673927; (011) 3523635 *Fax:* (011) 3552096
E-mail: ibdmaps@ndb.vsnl.net.in; indiabo@indiabookfair.net
Key Personnel
Proprietor: Harish Chawla
Subjects: Mathematics, Travel
ISBN Prefix(es): 81-87172
Total Titles: 464 Print
Warehouse: 2937 Bahadur Garh Rd, New Delhi 110006
Orders to: 2937 Bahadur Garth Rd, New Delhi 110006

Indian Council for Cultural Relations
Azad Bhavan, Indraprastha Estate, New Delhi 110002
Tel: (011) 3370732; (011) 3378647 *Fax:* (011) 3712639
E-mail: iccr@vsnl.com
Web Site: education.vsnl.com/iccr
Telex: 3161860; 3166004 *Cable:* Culture
Founded: 1950
Subjects: Art, Drama, Theater, Ethnicity, Literature, Literary Criticism, Essays
ISBN Prefix(es): 81-85434
Branch Office(s)
Bangalore
Chandigarth
Chennai
Kolkata
Mumbai
Varanasi

Indian Council of Agricultural Research
Krishi Anusandhan Bhavan Dr, New Delhi 110001
Tel: (011) 388991 (ext 496); (011) 23382306 *Fax:* (011) 387293
E-mail: jssamra@icar.delhi.nic.in
Web Site: www.icar.org.in
Telex: 03162249 Icar In *Cable:* Agrisec
Key Personnel
Dir: Sh A Chatravarty *Tel:* 257-16010 *E-mail:* dirdipa@kab.delhi.nic.in
Business, Advertising: S K Joshi *Tel:* 257-13657 *E-mail:* bmicar@kab.delhi.nic.in
Publicity & Public Relations: S K Sharma *Tel:* 258-54649 *E-mail:* kuldeep@kab.delhi.nic.in
Subjects: Agriculture, Animals, Pets
ISBN Prefix(es): 81-7164

Indian Council of Social Science Research (ICSSR)
35, Ferozeshah Rd, New Delhi 110 001
Mailing Address: PO Box 10528, Aruna Asfa Ali Marg, New Delhi 110 067
Tel: (011) 23385959; (011) 26717066 *Fax:* (011) 26179836
E-mail: info@icssr.org
Web Site: www.icssr.org *Cable:* ICSORES
Key Personnel
Chief Executive, Editorial, Production, Rights & Permissions & Chairman: Prof V R Panchmukhi
Director, NASSDOC: Dr P R Goswami *E-mail:* prgoswami@icssr.org
Founded: 1969
Promote, sponsor & support social science research & social science information activities in India by providing financial assistance in the form of fellowship, sponsorship, study grants

& grants-in-aid to individuals as well as institutions.
Subjects: Anthropology, Business, Criminology, Economics, Education, Geography, Geology, History, Law, Management, Psychology, Psychiatry, Public Administration, Social Sciences, Sociology
ISBN Prefix(es): 81-85008
Total Titles: 500 Print
Branch Office(s)
Dr Baba Sahib Ambedkar National Institute of Social Sciences, Dongargaon AB Rd, Mhow Cantonment, Mhow 453441, Contact: Prof Nandu Ram *Tel:* (07324) 272830; (07324) 274377; (07324) 272534 *Fax:* (07324) 273645 *E-mail:* solanki_baniss@rediff.com
AN Sinha Institute of Social Studies, Patna 800 001, Contact: Dr B B Srivastava *Tel:* (0612) 221395; (0612) 223320; (0612) 227856 *Fax:* (0612) 226226; (0612) 226227
Centre for Development Studies, Ulloor, Thiruvananthapuram 695 011, Contact: Dr K P Kannan *Tel:* (0471) 2448881 *Fax:* (0471) 2447137 *E-mail:* cdsedp@vsnl.com
Centre for Economic & Social Studies, Nizamia Observatory Campus, Begumpet, Hyderabad 500 016, Contact: Prof S Mahendra Dev *Tel:* (040) 23402789; (040) 23416780 *Fax:* (040) 23406808 *E-mail:* cesshyd@hd1.vsnl.net.in
Centre for Policy Research, Dharma Marg, Chanakyapuri, New Delhi 110 021, Contact: Dr Charan Wadhwa *Tel:* (011) 26114797; (011) 26115273 *Fax:* (011) 26872746; (011) 26886902 *E-mail:* president_cpr@vsnl.com
Centre for Research in Rural & Industrial Development, 21, Sector, 19-A, Madhya Marg, Chandigarh 160 019, Contact: Rashpal Malhotra *Tel:* (0172) 549450 *Fax:* (0172) 725215 *E-mail:* sscrrid@ren.nic.in
Centre for Social Studies, South Gujarat University Campus, Udhna-Magdalla Rd, Surat 395 007, Acting Dir: Prof Biswaroop Das *Tel:* (0261) 2227173; (0261) 2227174; (0261) 3210503 *Fax:* (0261) 2223851 *E-mail:* css_surat@satyam.net.in
Centre for Studies in Social Sciences, R1, Baishnabghata, Patuli Township, Kolkata 700 094, Contact: Prof Partha Chatterjee *Tel:* (033) 24627252; (033) 24625794 *Fax:* (033) 24626183 *E-mail:* cssscal@vsnl.net
Centre for the Study of Developing Societies, 29, Rajpur Rd, Delhi 110 054, Contact: Dr R K Shrivastava *Tel:* (011) 23951190; (011) 23942199 *Fax:* (011) 23943450 *E-mail:* csds@del2.vsnl.net.in
Council for Social Development-Southern Regional Office, Plot No 230, Shiva Nagar Colony, Hydderguda Village, Rajendranagar Rd, Bahadurpura Post Office, Hyderabad 500 064, Contact: Prof K S Bhat *Tel:* (040) 24016395 *Fax:* (040) 24001958 *E-mail:* csdhyd@hotmail.com
Giri Institute of Development Studies, Sector 'O', Aliganj Housing Scheme, Lucknow 226024, Contact: Dr G P Mishra *Tel:* (0522) 2373640; (0522) 2325021 *Fax:* (0522) 2373640 *E-mail:* gids@sancharnet.in
Gujarat Institute of Development Research, Sarkhej, Gandhinagar Highway, Gota Char Rasta, PO High Court, Gota, Ahmedabad 380 060, Contact: Prof Sudarshan Iyengar *Tel:* (079) 3742366 *Fax:* (079) 3742365 *E-mail:* gidrad1@sancharnet.in
ICSSR Eastern Regional Centre, R1, Baishnabghata, Patuli Township, Kolkata 700 094, Contact: Prof Partha Chatterjee *Tel:* (033) 24512482; (033) 24625795; (033) 24627252 *Fax:* (033) 24626183 *E-mail:* cssscal@vsnl.net
ICSSR North Eastern Regional Centre, Upper Nongthymmai, Shillong 793014, Contact: Prof David Reid Syiemlieh *Tel:* (0364) 2231173 *Fax:* (0364) 2231631 *E-mail:* icssrnerc@sancharnet.in

ICSSR Northern Regional Centre, JNU, Central Library Bldg, New Campus, NW Mehrauli Rd, New Delhi 110067, Contact: Prof M H Qureshi *Tel:* (011) 26167557; (011) 26107676 (ext 2536) *Fax:* (011) 26165886 *E-mail:* ssnrc@rec.nic.in
ICSSR North-Western Regional Centre, Punjab University Library Bldg, Chandigarh 160 014, Acting Dir: P K Saini *Tel:* (0172) 2541015; (0172) 2541491 *Fax:* (0172) 2541022 *E-mail:* icssr@pu.ac.in
ICSSR Southern Regional Centre, Osmania University Library, Hyderabad 500007, Acting Dir: Dr Masood Ali Khan *Tel:* (040) 27098756; (040) 27098951 (ext 306) *Fax:* (040) 27098754 *E-mail:* src@icssr.cmc.net.in
ICSSR Western Regional Centre, J P Nayak Bhavan, Vidyanagari, Vidyanagari Marg, Mumbai 400098, Acting Dir: M R Prabhu *Tel:* (022) 26526050; (022) 26113091 (ext 375) *Fax:* (022) 26528712 *E-mail:* wrcicssr@vsnl.in
Indian Institute of Education, 128/2, J P Naik Rd, Kothrud, Pune 411 029, Contact: Dr S R Kakade *Tel:* (020) 5436980; (020) 5424580 *Fax:* (020) 5435239 *E-mail:* iiepune@giaspn01.vsnl.net.in
Institute of Development Studies, 8-B, Jhalana Institutional Area, Jaipur 302 004, Contact: Prof S S Acharya *Tel:* (0141) 2705726 *Fax:* (0141) 2705348 *E-mail:* ids@sancharnet.in
Institute of Economic Growth, University Enclave, Delhi 110 007, Contact: Prof B B Bhattacharya *Tel:* (011) 27667288 *Fax:* (011) 27667401 *E-mail:* bbb@ieg.ernet.in
Institute of Public Enterprise, Osmania University Campus, Hyderabad 500 007, Contact: Dr K Harigopal *Tel:* (040) 27097445 *Fax:* (040) 27095478 *E-mail:* ipeouc@vsnl.in
Institute of Social & Economic Change, Nagarbhabhavi, Bangalore 560072, Contact: Prof Gopal Kadekodi *Tel:* (080) 3215519; (080) 3215468 *Fax:* (080) 3217008; (080) 3211798 *E-mail:* registrar@isec.ac.in
Institute of Studies in Industrial Development, PO Box 7151, Narendra Niketan, Indraprastha Estate, New Delhi 110 002, Contact: Prof S K Goyal *Tel:* (011) 23702449 *Fax:* (011) 23702448 *E-mail:* info@vidur.delhi.nic.in
Madhya Pradesh Institute of Social Science Research, 19-20, Mahasweta Nagar, Ujjain 456010, Contact: Dr D C Sah *Tel:* (0734) 2510978 *Fax:* (0734) 2512450 *E-mail:* mpissr@epatra.com
Madras Institute of Development Studies, 79, Second Main Rd, PO Box 948, Gandhinagar, Adyar, Chennai 600 020, Contact: Prof V K Natraj *Tel:* (044) 24412589 *Fax:* (044) 24910872 *E-mail:* director@mids.tn.nic.in
NKC Centre for Development Studies, Plot No A, Chandrasekharpur, Bhubaneswar 751 013, Contact: Prof G C Kar *Tel:* (0674) 2300471; (0674) 2301094 *Fax:* (0674) 2300471 *E-mail:* ncdsvc@sancharnet.in
OKD Institute of Social Change & Development, K K Bhatta Rd, Chenikuthi, Guwahati 781 003, Contact: Dr Abu Nasar Saied Ahmed *Tel:* (0361) 2667493; (0361) 2665903; (0361) 2668321 *Fax:* (0361) 2663589 *E-mail:* dkdscd@hotmail.com
G B Pant Social Science Institute, 3 No Yamuna Enclave, Jhusi, Sangam Nagar, Allahabad 221 019, Contact: Prof R C Tripathi *Tel:* (0532) 2667206 *Fax:* (0532) 2667207 *E-mail:* rctripathi@rediffmail.com
Sardar Patel Institute of Economic & Social Research, Thaltej Rd, Ahmedabad 380 054, Acting Dir: R G Nambiar *Tel:* (079) 6850598 *Fax:* (079) 6851714; (079) 6850714 *E-mail:* arpu@x400nicgw.nic.in
Bookshop(s): Centre for Multi-Disciplinary Development Research, D B Rodda Rd, Jubilee Circle, Dharwad 580001, Contact: Prof P R Panchamukhi *Tel:* (0836) 2745273; (0836) 2447639 *Fax:* (0836) 2447627 *E-mail:* cmdr@sancharnet.in; Centre for Women's Development Studies, 25, Bhai Vir Singh Marg, New Delhi 110 001, Contact: N K Banerjee *Tel:* (011) 23345530; (011) 23365541; (011) 23366930 *Fax:* (011) 23346044 *E-mail:* cwds@ndb.vsnl.net.in

Indian Defence Review, *imprint of* Lancer Publisher's & Distributors

Indian Documentation Service+
2 Ansari Rd, Panna Bhawan Daryaganj, New Delhi 110 002
Mailing Address: PO Box 13, Nai Subzi Mandi, Gurgaon 122 001
Tel: (0124) 6322005; (0124) 6322779 *Fax:* (0124) 6324782
E-mail: indoc@indiatimes.com
Key Personnel
Dir: Pankaj Jain
Editorial, Production, Rights & Permissions: Mr Satyaprakash
Sales, Publicity: Pankaj Kumar
Founded: 1970
Membership(s): Federation of Indian Publishers & Booksellers.
ISBN Prefix(es): 81-85258

Indian Institute of Advanced Study
Rashtrapati Nivas, Shimla, Himachal Pradesh 171005
Tel: (0177) 72303; (0177) 75139 *Fax:* (0177) 75139
E-mail: info@iias.org
Web Site: www.iias.org *Cable:* INSTITUTE
Key Personnel
Dir: Prof V C Srivastava
Sales: A K Sharma
Founded: 1965
Subjects: Social Sciences, Sociology
ISBN Prefix(es): 81-85952; 81-7986

Indian Institute of World Culture+
6 B P Wadia Rd, Basavangudi, Bangalore 560 004
Tel: (080) 6678581
Web Site: www.ultindia.org/culture.htm
Key Personnel
Vice President: Prof V K Doraswamy
Honorary Secretary: Y M Balakrishna
Founded: 1945
Subjects: Ethnicity

Indian Museum
27 Jawaharlal Nehru Rd, Kolkata 700016
Tel: (033) 249 9902; (033) 249 9979; (033) 249 8948; (033) 249 8931 *Fax:* (033) 249 5699
E-mail: imbot@cal2.vsnl.net.in
Web Site: www.indianmuseum-calcutta.org
Telex: 0021-4472IMIN *Cable:* Imbot
Key Personnel
Dir: Dr Sakti Kali Basu
Founded: 1814
Subjects: Anthropology, Archaeology, Art, Geography, Geology, Science (General)
ISBN Prefix(es): 81-85525

Indian Society for Promoting Christian Knowledge (ISPCK)+
PO Box 1585, 1654, Madarsa Rd, Kashmere Gate, Delhi 110 006
Tel: (011) 23866323 *Fax:* (011) 23865490
E-mail: ispck@nde.vsnl.net.in
Web Site: ispck.org.in *Cable:* LITHOUSE DELHI
Key Personnel
Dir: Rev Ashish Amos
Financial & Administrative Secretary: Rev Dr J D M Stuart
Marketing & Distribution Manager: Mr Sundeep Chowdhry
Founded: 1957 (as autonomous body 1958)

Subjects: Biblical Studies, Biography, Government, Political Science, Religion - Other, Social Sciences, Sociology, Theology
ISBN Prefix(es): 81-7214
Subsidiaries: Navdin Prakashan Kendra
Branch Office(s)
Andrhra Christian Theological College, Lower Tank Bund Rd, Gandhi Nagar (PO), Hyderabad, Andhra Pradesh 500080 *Tel:* (033) 22421804 *E-mail:* sales@ispck.org.in
Christian Book Depot, Diocese of Eastern Himilaya CNI, Diocesan Centre, Gandhi Rd, Darjeeling, Bengla *Tel:* 0354256389 *Fax:* 91113865490 *E-mail:* ispck@nde.vsnl.net.in
The Church of South India, CSI Center, No 5, White Rd, Royapettah, Chennai, Tamilnadu 600014
Leonard Theological College, Post Box 36, Civil Lines, Jabalpur, Madhya Pradesh 482001
Bookshop(s): 51, Chowringhee Rd, Kolkata, Bengla 700071 *Tel:* (033) 22821804 *E-mail:* sales@ispck.org.in; Opp Liberty Cinema, Residency Rd, Sadar, Nagpur, Maharastra 440001 *Tel:* (0712) 2543425 *E-mail:* sales@ispck.org.in; Chotanagpur Diocesan Bookshop, PO Church Rd, Ranchi, Bihar 834001; Jabalpur Diocesan Bookshop, Mission Boys Hostel, Jarbhata, Bilashpur, Madhya Pradesh 495001

Indus Books, *imprint of* HarperCollins Publishers India Pty Ltd

Indus Publishing Co+
FS-5 Tagore Garden, New Delhi 110027
Tel: (011) 25935289; (011) 25151333 *Fax:* (011) 25922102
E-mail: indus@indusbooks.com
Web Site: www.indusbooks.com
Key Personnel
Man Dir: M L Gidwani
Dir Sales & Product Development: Lokesh Gidwani *E-mail:* lgidwani@indusbooks.com
Founded: 1987
Publishers, booksellers & exporters. Specialize in Himalayan Studies, Forestry, Environment, Mountaineering & Trekking.
Membership(s): Delhi State Booksellers' & Publishers' Association.
Subjects: Agriculture, Archaeology, Environmental Studies, History, Natural History, Religion - Buddhist, Religion - Hindu, Social Sciences, Sociology, Travel, Botany, Himalayan Studies, Horticulture
ISBN Prefix(es): 81-85182; 81-7387
Number of titles published annually: 25 Print
Total Titles: 250 Print
Associate Companies: Indus International, 5-A (MIG), Rajouri Garden, New Delhi 110027, Contact: Lokesh Gidwani *Tel:* (011) 5151333 *Fax:* (011) 5449682 *E-mail:* mail@indus-intl.com *Web Site:* www.indus-intl.com (exporters of Indian books & journals; worldwide delivery)
Book Club(s): Indus Club (special discount for members)

Institute of Book Publishing, *imprint of* Sterling Publishers Pvt Ltd

Intellectual Publishing House+
23 Darya Ganj, Pratap Gali, New Delhi 110002
Tel: (011) 3275860
Key Personnel
International Rights: D R Chopra
Founded: 1974
Subjects: Archaeology, Art, Government, Political Science, History, Literature, Literary Criticism, Essays, Philosophy, Religion - Other, Social Sciences, Sociology

ISBN Prefix(es): 81-7076
Parent Company: Intellectual Book Corner Pvt Ltd

Inter-India Publications+
D-17 Raja Garden, New Delhi 110015
Tel: (011) 5441120; (011) 5467082
Key Personnel
Chief Executive, Editorial, Rights & Permissions: M C Mittal
Sales: Praveen Mittal
Founded: 1975
Membership(s): Federation of Indian Publishers, New Delhi; specialize in tribes, women & forests.
Subjects: Agriculture, Anthropology, Archaeology, Art, Asian Studies, Crafts, Games, Hobbies, Economics, Ethnicity, Geography, Geology, Government, Political Science, History, Philosophy, Religion - Other, Social Sciences, Sociology, Transportation, Women's Studies
ISBN Prefix(es): 81-210
Parent Company: DK Publishers' Distributors Pvt Ltd

International Book Distributors+
9/3 Rajpur Rd, 1st floor, Dehra Dun, Uttaranchal 248001
Tel: (0135) 2656526; (0135) 2657497; (0135) 2650949 *Fax:* (0135) 2656554
E-mail: ibdbooks@sancharnet.in
Web Site: ibdbooks.com
Key Personnel
Proprietor: R P Singh *E-mail:* rpsinghgahlot@yahoo.co.in
Founded: 1976
Specialize in printing, scanning & planning.
Also distributor & publisher of scientific & technical books & journals.
Membership(s): All India Federation of Booksellers & Publishers, New Delhi.
Subjects: Agriculture, Animals, Pets, Biological Sciences, Crafts, Games, Hobbies, Environmental Studies, Gardening, Plants, Natural History, Science (General), Technology, Veterinary Science, Botany, Forestry, Wildlife
ISBN Prefix(es): 81-7089
Number of titles published annually: 50 Print
Total Titles: 500 Print
Associate Companies: IBD Publisher & Distributors, 23 Ansari Rd, Daryaganj, New Delhi 110002 *Tel:* (011) 23251094 *Fax:* (011) 23259102 *E-mail:* piyush_gahlot@rediffmail.com; Valley Offset Printers & Publishers, 15/2 B, Rajpur Rd, Dehra Dun, Uttranchal 248001, Contact: Mr Prashant Gahlot *Tel:* (0135) 2653998; (0135) 2656172 *Fax:* (0135) 2656554 *E-mail:* ibdbooks2003@yahoo.co.in
Bookshop(s): Allied Book Centre, 9/5 Rajpur Rd, Dehra Dun, Uttranchal 248001

Interprint, *imprint of* Mehta Publishers

Intertrade Publications Pvt Ltd+
55 Gariahat Rd, Ballygunge, Kolkata 700019
Mailing Address: PO Box 10210, Kolkata 700 019
Tel: (033) 474872; (033) 475069 *Cable:* HELBELL
Key Personnel
Man Dir, Rights & Permissions: Dr K K Roy
Sales Dir: S Paul
Publicity Dir: Renu Kochhar
Advertising Dir: Pradip Raj
Founded: 1954
Subjects: Biography, History, Medicine, Nursing, Dentistry, Philosophy, Poetry, Religion - Other
Subsidiaries: Intertrade Publications (India) Pvt Ltd

Islamic Publishing House+
Islamic Service Trust Bldgs, 10-529 Maideen Pali Rd Calicut, Kerala 673 001
Tel: (0495) 720092; (0495) 724618 *Fax:* (0495) 724524
E-mail: iphcalicut@eth.net
Key Personnel
International Rights: Sheikh Mohamed
Manager: A P Moosa-Koya
Founded: 1945
Subjects: Biography, Government, Political Science, Health, Nutrition, History, Human Relations, Law, Philosophy, Religion - Islamic, Travel
ISBN Prefix(es): 81-7204
Number of titles published annually: 150 Print
Parent Company: Islamic Service Trust, Kerala
Distributed by Current Books Kottayam
Distributor for Markazi Maktaba Islami (India)

ISPCK, *see* Indian Society for Promoting Christian Knowledge (ISPCK)

Jaico Publishing House
127 Mahatma Gandhi Rd, Mumbai 400 023
Tel: (022) 2676702; (022) 2676802; (022) 2674501 *Fax:* (022) 2656412
E-mail: jaicowbd@vsnl.com
Web Site: www.jaicobooks.com
Telex: 113369 Jai In *Cable:* JAICOBOOKS
Key Personnel
Man Dir: Ashwin J Shah
Executive Dir: S C Sethi
Editor: R H Sharma
Founded: 1946
Subjects: Astrology, Occult, Behavioral Sciences, Biography, Cookery, Criminology, Economics, Engineering (General), Ethnicity, Government, Political Science, Health, Nutrition, History, Humor, Language Arts, Linguistics, Law, Management, Philosophy, Psychology, Psychiatry, Religion - Other, Self-Help
ISBN Prefix(es): 81-7224
Subsidiaries: Jaico Press Pvt Ltd
Branch Office(s)
Jaico Book Agency, No 57, Dr Giri Rd, T Nagr, Chennai 600 017 *Tel:* (044) 2826 2874 *E-mail:* jaicoche@md3.vsnl.net.in
Jaico Book Distributors, 194, Patpur Ganj Indl Area, Delhi *Tel:* (011) 2214 4204; (011) 2214 4205 *Fax:* (011) 224 4206 *E-mail:* jaicobook@vsnl.net
Jaico Book Distributors, G-2, 16 Ansari Rd, Daryaganj, New Delhi 110 002 *Tel:* (011) 2326 0651 *Fax:* (011) 2327 8469 *E-mail:* sethidel@del6.vsnl.net.in
Jaico Book Enterprises, 302 Acharya Prafulla Chandra Roy Rd, Park Circus, Kolkata 700 009 *Tel:* (033) 2360 0542; (033) 2360 0543 *E-mail:* jaicocal@cal2.vsnl.net.in
Jaico Book House, 14-1 1st Main Rd, 6th Cross, Gandhi Nagar, Bangalore 560 009 *Tel:* (080) 226 7016; (080) 225 7083 *Fax:* (080) 228 5492 *E-mail:* jaicobgr@blr.vsnl.net.in
Jaico Book House, 3-4-494/1/2, Barkatpura, Hyderabad 500 027 *Tel:* (040) 2755 1992 *E-mail:* hyd1_jaicohyd@sancharnet.in
Jaicos' Wholesale Book Distributors, ELGI House, 2 Mill Officers' Colony, Opp Times of India, Ashram Rd, Ahmedabad 380 009 *Tel:* (079) 657 9865; (079) 657 5262 *E-mail:* jaicoahm@vsnl.com
Bookshop(s): Jaicos

B Jain Publishers Overseas+
Subsidiary of B Jain Publishers (P) Ltd
1921 Street No 10, Chuna Mandi, Paharganj, New Delhi 110055
Tel: (011) 2358 0800; (011) 5169 8991; (011) 2358 3100 *Fax:* (011) 2358 0471; (011) 5169 8993
E-mail: bjain@vsnl.com

PUBLISHERS   INDIA

Web Site: www.bjainbooks.com *Cable:* BOOKCENTRE
Key Personnel
CEO: Kuldeep Jain
Dir & Editorial, Rights & Permissions: Ashok Jain
Dir Sales & Publicity: Nishant Jain
  E-mail: nishant@bjainbooks.com
Founded: 1972
Subjects: Alternative, Health, Nutrition, Medicine, Nursing, Dentistry, Self-Help
ISBN Prefix(es): 81-7021; 81-8056
Number of titles published annually: 80 Print
Total Titles: 1,250 Print
Imprints: Health-Harmony

B Jain Publishers (P) Ltd+
1921 Street No 10, Chuna Mandi Paharganj, New Delhi 110055
Tel: (011) 23580800; (011) 23581100; (011) 23583100 *Fax:* (011) 23580471
E-mail: bjain@vsnl.com
Web Site: www.bjainbooks.com *Cable:* Bookcentre
Key Personnel
Chief Executive Officer: Sh Kuldeep Jain
Man Dir: Dr Premnath Jain *Tel:* (011) 2169633
Dir & Editorial, Rights & Permissions: Ashok Jain
Founded: 1967
Subjects: Health, Nutrition, Medicine, Nursing, Dentistry, Religion - Buddhist, Religion - Hindu
ISBN Prefix(es): 81-7021
Number of titles published annually: 40 Print
Total Titles: 1,330 Print
Associate Companies: B Jain Exports India
Subsidiaries: B Jain Publishers Overseas
Distribution Center: New Leaf Distributors, 401 Thoronton Rd, Atlanta, GA 30122-1557, United States (USA)

Jaipur Publishing House
5, Lalji Sand Ka Rasta, Chaura Rasta, Jaipur 302 004
Tel: (0141) 319198; (0141) 319094
E-mail: jph@indiaresult.com
Key Personnel
Manager: Rajesh Agarwal
Production: R C Agarwal
Sales: Dhoop Chand Jain
Founded: 1960
ISBN Prefix(es): 81-8047

Jaypee Brothers Medical Publishers Pvt Ltd+
B-3 EMCA House, 23/23B Ansari Rd, Daryaganj, New Delhi 110002
Mailing Address: PO Box 7193, New Delhi 110 002
Tel: (011) 3272143; (011) 3282021; (011) 3272703 *Fax:* (011) 3276490
E-mail: jpmedpub@del2.vsnl.net.in
Web Site: www.jpbros.20m.com
Key Personnel
Editorial: Jitendar Vij
Sales: Pawaninder Vij
Subjects: Medicine, Nursing, Dentistry
ISBN Prefix(es): 81-7179; 81-8061
Associate Companies: BMJ; F A Davis Co; Mosby Year Book
Branch Office(s)
202 Batavia Chambers, 8 Kumara Kruppa Rd, Kumara Park East, Bangalore 560 001 *Tel:* (080) 2281761 *Fax:* (080) 2382956 *E-mail:* jaypeebc@bgl.vsnl.net.in
282, 3rd floor, Khaleel Shirazi Estate, Fountain Plaza, Pantheon Rd, Chennai 600 008 *Tel:* (044) 8262665 *Fax:* (044) 8262331 *E-mail:* jpmedpub@md3.vsnl.net.in
One-A Indian Mirror St, Wellington Sq, PO Box 8880, Kolkata 700 013 *Tel:* (033) 2451926 *Fax:* (033) 2456075 *E-mail:* jpbcal@cal.vsnl.net.in
106 Amit Industrial Estate, 61 Dr SS Rao Rd, Near MGM Hospital, Parel, Mumbai 400 012 *Tel:* (022) 4124863 *Fax:* (022) 4160828; (022) 4104532 *E-mail:* jpmedpub@bom7.vsnl.net.in

Kairali Children's Book Trust
PO Box 624- Railway Station Rd, Current Books Bldg, Kottayam, Kerala 686 001
Tel: (0481) 563226; (0481) 560918 *Fax:* (0481) 564758
Web Site: www.dcbooks.com/kcbt.htm
Key Personnel
Chief Executive, Rights & Permissions: D C Kizhakemuri
Editorial: Dr K Velayudhan Nair
Production: V P Sreedharan Nayanar
Publicity: G Sreekumar
Founded: 1980
Subjects: Biography, Fiction, Foreign Countries
ISBN Prefix(es): 81-7152
Associate Companies: Current Books; DC Books; Kairali Mudralaya
Imprints: D C Press
Book Club(s): Kairali Club
Orders to: Current Books, VIII/493 Railway Station Rd, Kottayam 686001

Kairalee Mudralayam
D C Books Complex, Good Shepherd St, Kottayam 686001
Tel: (0481) 2563114; (0481) 2301614 *Fax:* (0481) 2564758
E-mail: info@dcbooks.com
Web Site: www.dcbooks.com/kairali.htm
Key Personnel
Manager: D C Kizhakemuri
Editorial: M S Chandrasekhara Warrier
Sales: D C Ponnamma
Production, Publicity, Rights & Permissions: Mary John
Founded: 1978
Subjects: Biography, Fiction, Humor
ISBN Prefix(es): 81-85226
Associate Companies: Current Books; D C Books; Kairali Children's Book Trust

Kali For Women+
K-92, Hauz Khas Enclave, 1st floor, New Delhi 10016
Tel: (011) 6864497; (011) 6852530 *Fax:* (011) 6864497
E-mail: kaliw@del2.vsnl.net.in
Web Site: www.kalibooks.com
Key Personnel
Contact: Ritu Menon; Urvashi Butalia
Editor: Preeti Gill
Founded: 1984
Subjects: Art, Biography, Drama, Theater, Environmental Studies, Fiction, Health, Nutrition, History, Law, Nonfiction (General), Social Sciences, Sociology, Women's Studies
ISBN Prefix(es): 81-85107; 81-86706

Kalyani Publishers+
4863-2B Bharat Ram Rd, 24 Daryaganj, New Delhi 110002
Tel: (011) 3274393; (011) 3271469
Key Personnel
Man Dir: Raj Kumar
Subjects: Science (General), Humanities
ISBN Prefix(es): 81-272; 81-7663
Bookshop(s): Lyall Book Depot, Chaura Bazar, Ludhiana *Tel:* (0161) 2760031; (0161) 2745872

Kerala University, Department of Publications
Thiruvananthapuram, Kerala 695 034
Tel: (0471) 306422; (0471) 305931 *Fax:* (0471) 307158
E-mail: unikereg@md4.vsnl.net.in
Web Site: www.collegeskerala.com
Key Personnel
Chief Executive: Dr A Razaludeen
Production: Dr P Balachandran
Sales: Dr M A Karim
Founded: 1939
ISBN Prefix(es): 81-86397

Khanna Publishers+
2-B Nath Market, Nai Sarak, New Delhi 110 006
Tel: (011) 2912380; (011) 7224179
Key Personnel
Dir: R C Khanna; Vineet Khanna
Founded: 1959
Subjects: Civil Engineering, Communications, Computer Science, Electronics, Electrical Engineering, Energy, Engineering (General), Environmental Studies, Management, Mathematics, Mechanical Engineering, Technology
ISBN Prefix(es): 81-7409
Branch Office(s)
11 Community Centre, Ashok Vihar, Phase II, Delhi 110052 *Tel:* (011) 7224179

Kitab Ghar
24/4855 Ansari Rd, Darya Ganj, New Delhi 110 002
Tel: (011) 213206
Key Personnel
Chief Executive, Rights & Permissions: Satya Brat Sharma
Editorial, Production: Jagat Ram Sharma
Sales, Publicity: Dev Datt
Founded: 1970
Subjects: Biography, Drama, Theater, Fiction, Poetry, Science (General), Social Sciences, Sociology
ISBN Prefix(es): 81-7016; 81-7891

Konark Publishers Pvt Ltd+
A-149, Main Vikas Marg, Shakarpur, Delhi 110092
Tel: (011) 22504101; (011) 22455731; (011) 22507103 *Fax:* (011) 22507103
E-mail: kppl23@eth.net; konarkpublishers@hotmail.com *Cable:* THE KONARK DELHI
Key Personnel
Man Dir: KPR Nair *E-mail:* kprn07@hotmail.com
Founded: 1986
Membership(s): Federation of Publishers & Booksellers Association in India.
Subjects: Government, Political Science, Human Relations, Labor, Industrial Relations, Social Sciences, Sociology
ISBN Prefix(es): 81-220
Number of titles published annually: 40 Print
Total Titles: 750 Print

Kosi Books, *imprint of* Vidyarthi Mithram Press

Krishna Prakashan Media (P) Ltd, see Goel Prakashen

Lalit Kala Akademi
Rabindar Bhavan, 35 Ferozshah Rd, New Delhi 110001
Tel: (011) 23387241; (011) 23387243; (011) 23387242 *Fax:* (011) 23782485
E-mail: lka@lalitkala.org.in
Web Site: www.lalitkala.org.in *Cable:* Artakademi
Key Personnel
Chairman: Prof Sankho Chaudhuri
Acting Secretary: M Rajaram
Sales: Kewal Krishan
Founded: 1954
Subjects: Art, Ethnicity
ISBN Prefix(es): 81-87507

Lancer International, *imprint of* Lancer Publisher's & Distributors

Lancer Paperbacks, *imprint of* Lancer Publisher's & Distributors

Lancer Publishers, *imprint of* Lancer Publisher's & Distributors

Lancer Publisher's & Distributors+
56 Gautam Nagar, New Delhi 110049
Tel: (011) 6867339; (011) 6854691 *Fax:* (011) 6862077
Web Site: www.geocites.com/TheTropics/3328/lancer.htm
Key Personnel
Man Dir & International Rights: Capt Bharat Verma
Founded: 1983
Also acts as printer & manufacturer for foreign publishers, importers, exporters & distributors.
Subjects: Asian Studies, Military Science, Self-Help
ISBN Prefix(es): 81-7062; 81-85096
Associate Companies: Spantech & Lancer, Spantech House Lagham Rd, South Godstone, Surrey RH9 8HB, United Kingdom *Tel:* (01342) 893239 *Fax:* (01342) 892584; Spantech & Lancer, 3986 Ernst Rd, Hartford, WI 53027, United States *Tel:* 414-673-9064 *Fax:* 414-673-9064
Imprints: Lancer Paperbacks; Lancer International; Lancer Publishers; Indian Defence Review
Divisions: Indian Defence Review
Distributor for Raweltte Books (UK); Greenhill Books (UK)
Orders to: Spantech & Lancer, Spantech House, Lagham Rd, South Godstone, Surrey RH9 8H8, United Kingdom
Spantech & Lancer, 3986 Ernst Rd, Hartford, WI 53027, United States

Law Publishers+
Sardar Patel Marg, Civil Lines, Allahabad 211 001
Mailing Address: PO Box 1077, Allahabad 211 001
Tel: (0532) 2622758; (0532) 2420974 *Fax:* (0532) 2622781; (0532) 2609943
E-mail: lawpub@vsnl.com; lawpub@sancharnet.in
Web Site: www.law-publishers.com *Cable:* PUBLISHERS
Key Personnel
Chief Executive: Naresh Sagar
Manager: Shekhar Srivastava
Founded: 1961
Export of law & non-law journals & subscription service on back sets.
Subjects: Agriculture, Business, Criminology, Economics, Engineering (General), Environmental Studies, Government, Political Science, History, Law, Library & Information Sciences, Management, Mechanical Engineering, Physical Sciences, Psychology, Psychiatry, Religion - Buddhist, Religion - Hindu, Religion - Islamic, Science (General), Technology, Women's Studies
ISBN Prefix(es): 81-7111

Laxmi Publications Pvt Ltd+
22, Prakashdeep Bldg, Daryaganj, New Delhi 110 002
Tel: (011) 23262368; (011) 23262370 *Fax:* (011) 23262279
E-mail: colaxmi@hotmail.com
Web Site: www.laxmipublications.com
Key Personnel
Chairman: Mr R K Gupta
Man Dir: Mr Saurabh Gupta *E-mail:* guptas@global.t-bird.edu
Founded: 1974
Specialize in computer books, engineering, college & school textbooks.
Membership(s): Federation of Indian Publishers.

Subjects: Civil Engineering, Computer Science, Electronics, Electrical Engineering, Mathematics, Mechanical Engineering
ISBN Prefix(es): 81-7008
Number of titles published annually: 50 Print
Total Titles: 900 Print
Imprints: Firewall Media; Golden Bells; New Age International

Learners Press Private Ltd+
A-59, Okhla Industrial Area Phase II, New Delhi 110020
Tel: (011) 26387070; (011) 26386209 *Fax:* (011) 26383788
E-mail: info@sterlingpublishers.com
Web Site: www.sterlingpublishers.com *Cable:* PAPERBACKS
Key Personnel
Rights & Permissions: Vikas Ghai
Editorial: Marry Joseph
Production: Shammi Kapoor
Founded: 1990
Membership(s): Federation of Indian Publishers.
ISBN Prefix(es): 81-7181

LexisNexis Butterworths (India), see LexisNexis India

LexisNexis India
Formerly LexisNexis Butterworths (India)
14th floor, Vijaya Bldg, 17, Barakhamba Rd, New Delhi 110001
Tel: (011) 373 9614; (011) 373 9615; (011) 373 9616; (011) 332 6454 customer service; (011) 332 6455 customer service *Fax:* (011) 332 6456
E-mail: info@lexisnexis.co.in; customer.care@lexisnexis.co.in
Web Site: www.lexisnexis.co.in
Key Personnel
Publishing Manager: Ambika Nair
  E-mail: ambika.nair@lexisnexis.co.in
Editorial Manager: Sandeep Joshi
  E-mail: sandeep.joshi@lexisnexis.co.in
Commissioning Editor: Vidyaranya Chakravarthy
  E-mail: vidyaranya.chakravathy@lexisnexus.co.in
General Manager: Sudarshan Sharma
  E-mail: sudarshan.sharma@lexisnexis.co.in
Assistant Manager, Customer Service: Ruchika Malik *E-mail:* ruchika.malik@lexisnexis.co.in
Assistant Manager, Sales: Vikas Saddar
  E-mail: vikas.saddar@lexisnexis.co.in
Publishers: law, taxation, business.
Parent Company: Reed Elsevier
Associate Companies: LexisNexis Hong Kong, 12/F, Hennessey Centre, 500 Hennessey Rd, Causeway Bay, Hong Kong, Commissioning Editor: Anisha Sakhrani *Tel:* 2965 1400 *Fax:* 2976 0840 *Web Site:* www.lexisnexis.com.uk; Malayan Law Journal Sdn Bhd, Unit A-5-1, 5th floor, Wisma HB, Megan Phileo Ave, 12 Jalan Yap Kwan Seng, 50450 Kuala Lumpur, Malaysia, Managing Editor, New Product Development: Julie Ann Thomas *Tel:* (03) 2166-7558 *Fax:* (03) 2166-7550 *Web Site:* www.mlj.com.my; LexisNexis Singapore, 3 Killiney Rd, 08-08, Winsland House 1, Singapore 239519, Singapore, Regional Publishing Dir: Conita Leung *Tel:* 6733 1380 *Fax:* 6733 1175 *Web Site:* www.lexisnexis.com.sg; LexisNexis Butterworths Australia, Tower 2, 475-495 Victoria Ave, Chatswood, NSW 2067, Australia *Tel:* (02) 9422-2222 *Fax:* (02) 9422-2444; LexisNexis China, LexisNexis China Representative Office, Rm 1808, 18/F, Tower E3, Oriental Plaza No.1, East Chang An Ave, Dong Cheng District, Beijing, China *Tel:* (010) 8518 5801 *Fax:* (010) 8518 9287; LexisNexis Japan, Toranomon 19, Mori Bldg 9F 1-2-20, 105-0001 Minato-ku, Tokyo *Tel:* (03) 3509-1844 *Fax:* (03) 3509-1845; LexisNexis Korea, 1119 Punglim Bldg, Gongduck-Dong, Mapo Gu, Seoul 121-718, Republic of Korea *Tel:* (02) 713 8605 *Fax:* (02) 713 8602; LexisNexis Malaysia, Unit A-5-1, 5th fl, Wisma HB, Megan Phileo Ave, 12 Jalan Yap Kwan Seng, 50450 Kuala Lumpur, Malaysia *Tel:* (03) 2166 7558 *Fax:* (03) 2166 7550; LexisNexis Butterworths New Zealand, 205-207 Victoria St, PO Box 472, Wellington, New Zealand *Tel:* (04) 385 1479 *Fax:* (04) 385 1598 *E-mail:* customer.service@lexisnexis.co.nz *Web Site:* www.lexisnexis.com.au/nz; LexisNexis Taiwan, 17 F/B, No 167 Tun Hwa N Rd, Hung Kuo Bldg, 105, Taipei, Taiwan, Province of China *Tel:* (02) 2717 1999 ext 1111 *Fax:* (02) 2717 2886

Lokvangmaya Griha Pvt Ltd
Bhupesh Gupta Bhavan, 85, Sayan Rd, Prabhadevi, Mumbai 400025
Tel: (022) 4362474 *Fax:* (022) 4313220
E-mail: lokvang@bol.net.in
Key Personnel
General Manager: Sukumar Damle
Founded: 1973
Subjects: Human Relations, Social Sciences, Sociology
ISBN Prefix(es): 81-86995
Bookshop(s): 5-22-32 Tilak Path, Aurangabad 431001; People's Book House, IS Cawasji Patel St, Fort Bombay 400001; Red Flag Bldg, Bindu Chowk, Kolhapur 416002; 562 Sadashiv Peth, Chirtashala Prakalp, Pune 411030

Longman, *imprint of* Addison-Wesley Pte Ltd

Lotus, *imprint of* Roli Books Pvt Ltd

Lustre Press, *imprint of* Roli Books Pvt Ltd

Lustre Press Pvt Ltd, see Roli Books Pvt Ltd

M/S Family Books Pvt Ltd, *imprint of* Pustak Mahal

M/S Motilal Banarsidass Publishing (P) Ltd
41-UA Bungalow Rd, Jawahar Nagar, New Delhi 110 007
Tel: (011) 23851985; (011) 23858335; (011) 23854826; (011) 23852747 *Fax:* (011) 23850689; (011) 25797221
E-mail: mail@mlbd.com
Web Site: www.mlbd.com
Key Personnel
Chairperson: Leela Jain
Founded: 1903
ISBN Prefix(es): 81-208

Mahajan Publishers Pvt Ltd+
Super Market Basement, Near Natraj Cinema, Ashram Rd, Ahmedabad 380009
Tel: 78547 *Fax:* (079) 6589101
E-mail: mahajan2000@hotmail.com *Cable:* PERIODICAL
Key Personnel
Man Dir: Mr Dinker Mahajan
  E-mail: mahajan2000@hotmail.com
Founded: 1953
Specializes in textiles.
ISBN Prefix(es): 81-85401
Associate Companies: Mahajan Book Distributors

Mainstreet Books, *imprint of* Full Circle Publishing

Manohar Publishers & Distributors+
4753/23 Ansari Rd, Daryaganj, New Delhi 110 002

Tel: (011) 23284848; (011) 23289100; (011) 23262796; (011) 23260774 *Fax:* (011) 23265162
E-mail: manbooks@vsnl.com; sales@manoharbooks.com
Web Site: www.manoharbooks.com
Key Personnel
Man Dir, Rights & Permissions, Publicity: Ajay Jain
Editorial: B N Varma
Publicity: Siddharth Chowdhury
Founded: 1969
Subjects: Anthropology, Architecture & Interior Design, Art, Economics, Education, Ethnicity, Government, Political Science, History, Literature, Literary Criticism, Essays, Philosophy, Religion - Other, Science (General), Social Sciences, Sociology, Politics
ISBN Prefix(es): 81-85054; 81-85425; 81-7304
Number of titles published annually: 50 Print
Associate Companies: Manohar Book Service, 2/6 Ansari Rd, Daryaganj, New Delhi 110 002
Distributed by South Asia Books

Manosabdam Books, *imprint of* Vidyarthi Mithram Press

Mapin Publishing Pvt Ltd+
31 Somnath Rd, Usmanpura, Ahmedabad, Gujarat 380013
Tel: (079) 2755-1793; (079) 2755-1833 *Fax:* (079) 2755-0955
E-mail: info@mapinpub.com
Web Site: www.mapinpub.com
Key Personnel
Man Dir: Mallika Sarabhai
International Rights: Bipin Shah
Founded: 1985
Specialize in books on art, crafts, architecture, culture of India, heritage & archaeology.
Membership(s): Federation of Indian Publishers.
Subjects: Archaeology, Architecture & Interior Design, Art, Asian Studies, Crafts, Games, Hobbies, Photography, Religion - Hindu, Religion - Islamic
ISBN Prefix(es): 81-85822; 81-7380; 81-88204
Number of titles published annually: 15 Print; 2 CD-ROM
Total Titles: 70 Print; 2 CD-ROM
Associate Companies: Grantha Corp, 77 Daniele Drive, Ocean, NJ 07712, United States *Tel:* (732) 493-3466 *Fax:* (309) 409-6399 *E-mail:* mapinpub@aol.com
Orders to: Antique Collector's Club Ltd, 91 Market St Industrial Park, Wappingers' Falls, NY 12590, United States *Fax:* (845) 297-0068 *E-mail:* info@antiquecc.com *Web Site:* www.antiquecc.com (North America)
Art Books International, Unit 007, The Chandlery, 50 Westminster Bridge Rd, London SE1 7QY, United Kingdom *Tel:* (020) 7953 8290 *Fax:* (020) 7953 8290 *E-mail:* sales@art-bks.com *Web Site:* www.art-bks.com (UK & Europe)
MapinLit, 31 Somnath Rd, Usmanpura, Ahmedabad 380013 *Tel:* (079) 2755-1793 *Fax:* (079) 2755-0955 *E-mail:* mapin@icenet.net

Marg Publications
Army & Navy Bldg, 3rd floor, 148 Mahatma Gandhi Rd, Mumbai 400001
Tel: (022) 2821151; (022) 2045947-8; (022) 842520 *Fax:* (022) 047102
E-mail: margpub@tata.com
Web Site: www.tata.com/marg
Telex: 118-2618, 118-2731 TATA IN
Key Personnel
Publisher: J J Bhabha
Editorial: Ms Chandiramani Savita
Sales, Publicity: Baptist Sequeira
Design: Miss Naju Hirani
Contact: Radhika Sabavala
Business Development Manager: Baptist Sequeira
Founded: 1946
Marg meaning pathway leads the reader through the cultural heritage of India & its neighboring countries.
Publisher of books & magazines.
Subjects: Architecture & Interior Design, Art, Music, Dance, Indian Art, Paintings, Sculpture
ISBN Prefix(es): 81-85026
Parent Company: National Centre for the Performing Arts, Nariman Point, Mumbai 400021
Branch Office(s)
Tata Services Ltd, Jeevan Bharati Tower No 1, 10th floor, 124 Connaught Circus, New Delhi, Contact: Mr R K Gupta *Tel:* (011) 3327072-76 *Fax:* (011) 3226265
Distributed by Art Media Resources Ltd/Paragon Book Gallery

Sri Ramakrishna Math
31 Ramakrishna Math Rd, Mylapore, Chennai 600 004
Tel: (044) 24621110 *Fax:* (044) 24934589
E-mail: srkmath@vsnl.com
Web Site: www.sriramakrishnamath.org
Key Personnel
President: Sri Ramakrishna Math
Founded: 1897
Subjects: Biography, Philosophy, Religion - Hindu
ISBN Prefix(es): 81-7120; 81-7823
Distributor for Advaita Ashrama (Kolkata)
Showroom(s): 99, Pondy Baza, T Nagar, Chennai 600 017; Chennai Central Railway Station, Chennai 600 004
Bookshop(s): 16 Ramakrishna Math Rd, Mylapore, Chennai 600 004; No 26, S Mada St, Mylapore, Chennai 600 004

Maya Publishers Pvt Ltd+
303/4 Kawshalya Park, New Delhi 110 016
Tel: (011) 6494878; (011) 6494850; (011) 649 0451; (011) 649 0959 *Fax:* (011) 6491039; (011) 686 4614
E-mail: surit@del2.vsnl.net.in
Key Personnel
Contact: Surit Mitra
ISBN Prefix(es): 81-86268
Associate Companies: Gulmohur Press Pvt Ltd

Mayfair Paperbacks, *imprint of* Arnold Heinman Publishers (India) Pvt Ltd

Mayoor Paperbacks, *imprint of* National Publishing House

Mehta Publishers+
1216, Sadashiv Peth, Pune 411030
Tel: (011) 4476924 *Fax:* (011) 4475462
E-mail: mopl@vsnl.com
Key Personnel
Man Dir, Production, Rights & Permissions: Gautam Mehta
Publicity & Marketing Manager: G P S Bawa
Founded: 1971
Subjects: Agriculture, Asian Studies, Computer Science, Education, Medicine, Nursing, Dentistry, Orientalia
ISBN Prefix(es): 81-7161; 81-7766
Number of titles published annually: 200 Print
Total Titles: 2,000 Print
Parent Company: Mehta Offset Pvt Ltd
Imprints: Interprint
Subsidiaries: Mehta Book Sellers
Book Club(s): T Book Club

Merrill Education, *imprint of* Addison-Wesley Pte Ltd

Minerva Associates (Publications) Pvt Ltd+
7-B Lake Pl, Kolkata 700 029
Tel: (033) 2466 3783
Key Personnel
Chairman, Publicity, Rights & Permissions: Sushil Mukherjea
Editorial Dir: O K Ghosh
Sales: T K Mukherjee
Founded: 1973
Publication of serious studies.
Subjects: Agriculture, Anthropology, Asian Studies, Economics, Education, Ethnicity, Government, Political Science, History, Journalism, Labor, Industrial Relations, Literature, Literary Criticism, Essays, Natural History, Philosophy, Psychology, Psychiatry, Public Administration, Religion - Buddhist, Religion - Hindu, Social Sciences, Sociology
ISBN Prefix(es): 81-7715
Number of titles published annually: 7 Print
Total Titles: 175 Print

Ministry of Information & Broadcasting
Publications Division, Patiala House, Tilak Marg, New Delhi 110 001
Tel: (011) 3387983; (011) 3386879; (011) 3387069; (011) 3386452 *Fax:* (011) 3387341
E-mail: indiapub@nda.vsnl.net.in; dpd@sb.nic.in
Web Site: mib.nic.in *Cable:* EXINFOR
Key Personnel
Dir: Shri S Jaipal Reddy
Subjects: Art, Biography, Environmental Studies, Ethnicity, History, Science (General), Social Sciences, Sociology
ISBN Prefix(es): 81-230
Branch Office(s)
Government Press, Press Rd, Thiruvananthapuram
LL Auditorium, Anna Salai, Chennai
State Archaeological Museum Bldg, Public Garden, Hyderabad
8 Esplanade East, Kolkata
Commerce House, Currimbhoy Rd, Ballard Pier, Mumbai
Super Bazar, 2nd floor, Connaught Circus, New Delhi
Bihar State Co-operative Bank Bldg, Ashoka Rajpath, Patna

Mittal Publications
B-2/19-B Lawrence Rd, Delhi 110035
Tel: (011) 5163610; (011) 5648028; (011) 3250398 *Fax:* (011) 5648725
E-mail: mittalp@ndf.vsnl.net.in
Key Personnel
Contact: K M Mittal
Founded: 1979
Membership(s): India Federation of Publishers' & Booksellers' Association.
Subjects: Social Sciences, Sociology
ISBN Prefix(es): 81-7099
Orders to: A-110 Mohan Garden, New Delhi 110059

Motilal Banarsidass Publishers Pvt Ltd+
41 U A Bungalow Rd, Jawahar, Nagar, Delhi 110007
Tel: (011) 23911985; (011) 23918335; (011) 23974826 *Fax:* (011) 23930689; (011) 25797221
E-mail: mlbd@vsnl.com
Web Site: www.mlbd.com
Telex: 03166053 Enky In; 03165367 Kkrc In
Cable: GLORYINDIA
Key Personnel
Dir, Editorial, Rights & Permissions & Publishing: N P Jain
Home Sales: J P Jain
Finance: Ravi P Jain
Publishing: Anurag Jain
Founded: 1903
Subjects: History, Language Arts, Linguistics, Literature, Literary Criticism, Essays, Medicine, Nursing, Dentistry, Philosophy, Religion - Other
ISBN Prefix(es): 81-208

Branch Office(s)
16, St Mark's Rd, Bangalore, Karnataka 560001
PO Box 75, Chowk, Varanasi 221 001 *Tel:* (0542) 62898
Ashok Raipath, opposite Patna College, Patna, Bihar 800 004 *Tel:* (0612) 51442
120 Royapettah High Rd, Mylapore, Chennai 600004
Warehouse: 45 A, Naraina Industrial Area phase-I, New Delhi 28

Mudgala Trust+
Kaveri 12, Fourth Cross St, Ramakrishna Nagar, Chennai 600028
Tel: (044) 837257
Key Personnel
Founder: S R Balasubrahmanyam
Secretary, Treasurer: B Natarajan
President: Meenakshi Natarajan
Joint Secretary,Treasurer: Dr B Venkataraman
Member: Leela Venkataraman; Dr B Ramachandran; Asha Ramachandran
Founded: 1965
Subjects: Architecture & Interior Design, Art, Drama, Theater, Ethnicity, Music, Dance, Philosophy, Religion - Other
ISBN Prefix(es): 81-86392
U.S. Office(s): Mohan Venkataraman, 361 Bancroft Court, No 2, Rockford, IL 61107, United States *Tel:* 815-227-4553

Mudrak Publishers & Distributors+
W-152 Greater Kailash-1, New Delhi 110 048
Tel: (011) 3730818; (011) 3738319; (011) 6416317
Key Personnel
Prop: S P Kumria
Books of academic interest on subjects of humanities.
ISBN Prefix(es): 81-87161
Total Titles: 5 Print

A Mukherjee & Co Pvt Ltd
2, Bankim Chatterjee St, Kolkata 700 073
Tel: (033) 2417406; (033) 2418199 *Fax:* (033) 440-8641
Key Personnel
Dir: Rajeev Neogi
Founded: 1940
Subjects: Education, Government, Political Science, Nonfiction (General), Religion - Other, Travel
ISBN Prefix(es): 81-86043

Multitech Publishing Co+
15 Yogesh Hingwala Lane, Ghatkopar East, Mumbai 400077
Tel: (022) 5118820; (022) 5154206 *Fax:* (022) 5115904
Key Personnel
Contact: Sevantilal Shah
Founded: 1978
Membership(s): Federation of India Publishers.
Subjects: Chemistry, Chemical Engineering, Engineering (General), Management, Mechanical Engineering, Technology
Branch Office(s)
Ahmedabad Book Centre, D/122, Mahavir Chamber, Near Relief Cinema, Salapose Rd, Ahmedabad 380 001

Munshiram Manoharlal Publishers Pvt Ltd+
54 Rani Jhansi Rd, New Delhi 110055
Mailing Address: PO Box 5715, New Delhi 110055
Tel: (011) 3671668; (011) 3673650 *Fax:* (011) 3612745
E-mail: mrml@mantraonline.com
Web Site: www.mrmlbooks.com
Key Personnel
Chief Executive, Man Dir: Devendra Jain
Production, Publicity: Pankaj D Jain
E-mail: pankaj.mrml@mantraonline.com
Sales Dir: Ashok Jain
Founded: 1952
Also major book dealer.
Subjects: Anthropology, Archaeology, Architecture & Interior Design, Art, Asian Studies, Astrology, Occult, Drama, Theater, History, Language Arts, Linguistics, Music, Dance, Philosophy, Religion - Buddhist, Religion - Hindu, Religion - Islamic, Religion - Other
ISBN Prefix(es): 81-215
Number of titles published annually: 80 Print
Total Titles: 1,200 Print
Bookshop(s): 4416 Nai Sarak, Delhi 110006 (Amir Chand Marg)

M/S Gulshan Nanda Publications+
7-Sheesh Mahal 5-A Pali Hill, Bandra, Mumbai 50
Tel: (022) 6406994 *Fax:* (022) 4303696
Key Personnel
President: Himanshu Nanda
Vice President: Rahul Nanda
Founded: 1984
Membership(s): Federation of Indian Publishers' Association.
Subjects: Fiction
ISBN Prefix(es): 81-7241
Associate Companies: Sonex Marketing & Publishing, United Kingdom *Tel:* (081) 4225172

Naresh Publishers+
111 Shankar Rd Market, New Rajendra Nagar, New Delhi 110016
Tel: (011) 572-3235; (011) 575-4442 *Fax:* (011) 574-6485
Key Personnel
Contact: Mohinder Kumar Chowdhry
Founded: 1972
Membership(s): Federation of Educational Publishers in India, Federation of Indian Publishers, & Federation of Publishers & Booksellers in India.
ISBN Prefix(es): 81-7005
Associate Companies: Paramount Sales (India) Pvt Ltd, 484 Double Storey, PO Box 2860, New Rajinder Nagar, New Delhi 110060 *Tel:* (011) 5723235 *Fax:* (011) 5746485

Narosa Publishing House+
22, Daryaganj, Delhi Medical Association Rd, Delhi 110002
Tel: (011) 23243224; (011) 23243415; (011) 23243416 *Fax:* (011) 23243225; (011) 23258934
E-mail: narosa@ndc.vsnl.net.in/narosadl@nda.vsnl.net.in
Web Site: www.narosa.com *Cable:* Narosa New Delhi
Key Personnel
Man Dir: N K Mehra
Marketing Manager: S Mehra
Senior Executive: P.K. Chopra
Founded: 1977
Subjects: Biological Sciences, Chemistry, Chemical Engineering, Computer Science, Engineering (General), Environmental Studies, Mathematics, Medicine, Nursing, Dentistry, Philosophy, Physics, Psychology, Psychiatry, Religion - Other
ISBN Prefix(es): 81-85015; 81-85198; 81-7319
Associate Companies: Narosa Book Distributors Pvt Ltd, 22, Daryaganj, Delhi Medical Association Rd, Delhi 110002
Branch Office(s)
35-36 Greams Rd, Thousand Lights, Chennai 600006 *Tel:* (044) 28295362 *Fax:* (044) 28290377 *E-mail:* narosamds@vsnl.net
2F-2G Shivam Chambers, 53 Syed Amir Ali Ave, Kolkata 700019 *Tel:* (033) 22814809 *Fax:* (033) 22814778
306 Shiv Centre, D B C Sector 17 PO KU Bazar, New Bombay 400705 *Tel:* (022) 27890977 *Fax:* (022) 27891930

National Academy of Art, see Lalit Kala Akademi

National Academy of Letters, India, see Sahitya Akademi

National Book Organization+
A-5 Green Park, New Delhi 110016
Tel: (011) 6518378 *Fax:* (011) 6851795
E-mail: nbtindia@ndb.vsnl.net.in
Web Site: www.nbtindia.com
Telex: 031 73034nbt-in
Founded: 1984
Acts also as distributor.
Subjects: Agriculture, Anthropology, Archaeology, Architecture & Interior Design, Behavioral Sciences, Child Care & Development, Developing Countries, Economics, Education, Environmental Studies, Geography, Geology, Government, Political Science, History, Human Relations, Labor, Industrial Relations, Law, Management, Military Science, Religion - Other, Social Sciences, Sociology, Women's Studies
ISBN Prefix(es): 81-85135; 81-237; 81-87521
Branch Office(s)
Delhi
Distributed by UBS Publishers & Distributors Ltd
Bookshop(s): Municipal Flat No 18, Bungalos Rd, Delhi 110007

National Book Trust, see National Book Organization

National Book Trust India
A5 Green Park, New Delhi 110016
Tel: (011) 6518378; (011) 23379868 *Fax:* (011) 6851795
E-mail: nbtindia@ndb.vsnl.net.in
Web Site: www.nbtindia.com
Telex: 031-73034 *Cable:* Nabotrust
Key Personnel
Chairman: Anand Sarub
Dir: Arvind Kumar
Joint Dir, Administration & Finance: S N Madan
Deputy Dir, Arts: Jyotish Datta Gupta
Deputy Dir, Exhibitions: Talewar Giri
Deputy Dir, Subsidies: R Gupta
Deputy Dir, Information & Publicity: D Das Gupta
Deputy Dir, Production: Dhruv Bhargava
Founded: 1957
Subjects: Foreign Countries, Human Relations
ISBN Prefix(es): 81-85135; 81-237; 81-87521
Bookshop(s): Jayanagar Shopping Complex, Bangalore; S A Bhabari, Dutt Lane, Kolkata; A-4 Green Park, New Delhi; CIDCO Bldg, Sector 1, 2nd floor, Vashi, Mumbai

National Council of Applied Economic Research, Publications Division
Parisila Bhawan, 11, Indraprastha Estate, New Delhi 110 002
Tel: (011) 23379861; (011) 23379862; (011) 23379863; (011) 23379865; (011) 23379866; (011) 23379868 *Fax:* (011) 23370164
E-mail: infor@ncaer.org
Web Site: www.ncaer.org
Key Personnel
Dir-General: Mr Suman Bery
Founded: 1956
Subjects: Agriculture, Business, Economics
ISBN Prefix(es): 81-85877

PUBLISHERS   INDIA

National Council of Educational Research & Training, Publication Department
Sri Aurobindo Marg, New Delhi 110016
Tel: (011) 6851070; (011) 662708 *Fax:* (011) 6868419
E-mail: crc@giasdlo1.vsnl.net.in
Web Site: ncert.nic.in
Telex: 31-73024 NCRT-IN *Cable:* EDUPRINT, NEW DELHI
Key Personnel
Dir: Dr K Gopalan
Founded: 1962
Membership(s): Afro-Asian Book Council. Specializes in school textbooks, research monographs, supplementary readers.
Subjects: Education
ISBN Prefix(es): 81-7450

National Institute of Industrial Research (NIIR)
Affiliate of NIIR Project Exports India (P) Ltd
106-E Kamla Nagar, Delhi 110 007
Mailing Address: PB No 2162, Delhi 110 007
Tel: (011) 3923955; (011) 3935654; (011) 3945886 *Fax:* (011) 3941561
E-mail: niir@usnl.com
Web Site: www.niir.org
Key Personnel
President & Chief Executive Officer: Mr Ajay Kumar Gupta *E-mail:* akgupta@niir.org
Senior Vice President: Mr P K Tripathi *E-mail:* pktripathi@niir.org
Senior Project Consultant: Mr P K Chattopadhyay *E-mail:* chattopadhyay@niir.org
Founded: 1994
Publishers of process technology books, Business & Industrial Directory, Worldwide Importers Directory & Industrial Monthly Magazine.
Subjects: Business, Chemistry, Chemical Engineering, Science (General), Technology
ISBN Prefix(es): 81-86623
Number of titles published annually: 20 Print
Total Titles: 70 Print
Distributor for M/S Small Industry Research Institute

National Museum
Janpath, New Delhi 110 011
Tel: (011) 3018415; (011) 3019272; (011) 3019237
E-mail: rdchoudh@ndf.vsnl.net.in
Web Site: www.nationalmuseumindia.org
Key Personnel
Public Relations: Mr U Das
Subjects: Art, Ethnicity
ISBN Prefix(es): 81-85832

National Publishing House
23, Daryaganj, New Delhi 110002
Tel: (011) 3274161; (011) 3275267
Key Personnel
Man Dir: K L Malik
Editorial, Production, Rights & Permissions: S K Malik
Sales: M K Malik
Founded: 1950
A-95 Sector 5, Noida 201301 (UP) Tel: 3683/4507.
Subjects: Ethnicity, Human Relations, Social Sciences, Sociology
ISBN Prefix(es): 81-214
Parent Company: K L Malik & Sons Pvt Ltd, 23 Daryaganj, New Delhi 110 002
Imprints: Mayoor Paperbacks; Gyan Bharati
Branch Office(s)
K L Malik & Sons Pvt Ltd, 34 Netaji Subhash Marg, Allahabad 3
Malik & Co, Chaura Rasta, Jaipur 302003
Bookshop(s): 23 Daryaganj, New Delhi 110002

Natraj Prakashan, Publishers & Exporters+
A-98, Ashok Vihar, Phase 1, Delhi 110052
Telex: 316 5503 FXRS IN
Key Personnel
Owner: Mrs Kusum Goyanka
Founded: 1987
Subjects: Biography, Fiction, Literature, Literary Criticism, Essays, Poetry, Religion - Hindu
ISBN Prefix(es): 81-85979

Navajivan Trust+
Post Navajivan, Ahmedabad, Gujarat 380 014
Tel: (079) 27541329; (079) 27542634; (079) 27540635 *Fax:* (079) 27541329
Web Site: www.navajivantrust.org
Key Personnel
Chairman: Biharibhai P Shah
Managing Trustee: Jitendar T Desai *E-mail:* jdesai@navajivantrust.org
Manager, Sales & Permissions: Kapil Rawal
Founded: 1919
Printing, publishing & distribution of Gandhian literature.
Subjects: Biography, History, Philosophy, Religion - Other
ISBN Prefix(es): 81-7229
Branch Office(s)
130 Princess St, Mumbai 400 002

Navrang Booksellers & Publishers+
RB-7 Inderpuri, New Delhi 110 012
Tel: (011) 5835914; (011) 5836197 *Fax:* (011) 5836113; (011) 5836761
E-mail: navrang@del2.vsn.net.in
Key Personnel
Proprietor: Mrs Nirmal Singal
Founded: 1968
Subjects: Archaeology, Art, Developing Countries, Education, Ethnicity, History, Philosophy, Religion - Buddhist, Religion - Hindu
ISBN Prefix(es): 81-7013

Navyug Publishers
K-24 Hauz Khas, New Delhi 110 016
Tel: (011) 278370
Key Personnel
Editorial: Pritam Singh
Sales: Gurbachan Singh
Founded: 1949
Subjects: Ethnicity
ISBN Prefix(es): 81-7599; 81-85267; 81-86216

Naya Prokash+
206 Bidhan Sarani, Kolkata 700 006
Tel: 349566 *Fax:* (033) 5523366; (033) 5524053
Cable: Napkas
Key Personnel
Production, Rights & Permissions, Editorial: Barin Mitra
Partner, Sales, Publicity: D Roy
Founded: 1962
Subjects: Agriculture, Environmental Studies, Gardening, Plants, Government, Political Science, History, Language Arts, Linguistics, Management, Military Science, Science (General), Social Sciences, Sociology
ISBN Prefix(es): 81-85109; 81-85421
Parent Company: Darbari Offset Pvt Ltd
Associate Companies: Mitrata Offset Print; Prokash Pvt Ltd
Subsidiaries: NP Sales Pvt Ltd

Neeta Prakashan+
A-4 Ring Rd, South Extension Part-1, New Delhi 110 049
Mailing Address: PO Box 3853, New Delhi 110049
Tel: (011) 692013 *Fax:* (011) 4636011
E-mail: neeta@giasdl01.vsnl.net.in *Cable:* Loveneeta
Key Personnel
Man Proprietor: Shanti Devi
Sales, Production, Publicity, Rights & Permissions Executive: Rakesh Gupta
Founded: 1960
Subjects: Education
ISBN Prefix(es): 81-7202

Neha Mini Katha, *imprint of* Spectrum Publications

Nem Chand & Brothers+
Civil Lines, Roorkee 247667 U P
Tel: (01332) 72258; (01332) 72752; (01332) 74343 *Fax:* (01332) 73258 *Cable:* ENGINJOUR
Key Personnel
Man Dir, Rights & Permissions: N C Jain
Editorial Dir: Dr Ashok K Jain
Sales Dir: Anil Jain
Production Dir: Shanil Jain
Publicity, Advertising Dir: Mrs Shashi Jain
Founded: 1951
Membership(s): Chemical & Allied Products Export Promotion Council (Books Division); Also book packager.
Subjects: Agriculture, Architecture & Interior Design, Career Development, Earth Sciences, Fashion, Gardening, Plants, House & Home, Women's Studies
ISBN Prefix(es): 81-85240
Subsidiaries: Roorkee Press
Warehouse: Opposite Old Dy S P Office, Roorkee 247667

New Age International, *imprint of* Laxmi Publications Pvt Ltd

New Light Publishers+
B-8 Rattan Jyoti, 18 Rajendra Pl, New Delhi 110008
Tel: (011) 5712137 *Fax:* (011) 5812385
E-mail: newlight@vsnl.net *Cable:* ENELPEE
Key Personnel
Man Partner: Vikas Chowdhary
Editorial: Prof R P Chopra
Publicity, Advertising: R K Chowdhry
Founded: 1963
Subjects: Language Arts, Linguistics, Self-Help
ISBN Prefix(es): 81-85018; 81-86332

New Riders, *imprint of* Addison-Wesley Pte Ltd

Newspread International+
E 2 Greater Kailish II, New Delhi 110048
Tel: (011) 2331402 *Fax:* (011) 2607252
Telex: 22143 Bureau *Cable:* NEWSPREAD
Key Personnel
Executive Editor: Kul Bhushan
Production Manager: Benedict Mutisya Nzomo
Founded: 1971
ISBN Prefix(es): 81-86858
Showroom(s): Leader House, Moi Ave, Kenya

Nil, *imprint of* Asian Trading Corporation

Niyo Software
Unit 1B, Devgiri Ind Estate, S No 17/1B Plot No14 Kothrud, Pune 411029
Tel: (020) 546 7296; (020) 400 1603 *Fax:* (020) 400 1603
E-mail: info@niyoindia.com
Web Site: www.niyoindia.com
Key Personnel
President: Milind Chudgar
Founded: 1995
Document conversion & e-enabling services, animation & graphic generation. Various formats including LIT, Adobe PDF, Palm Devices (PDB), XML, OEB & all possible ebook formats.
ISBN Prefix(es): 81-88303

Omsons Publications+
Publishers & Distributors, T-7, Rajouri Garden, New Delhi 110027
Tel: (011) 5412452 *Fax:* (011) 3289353
E-mail: omsons@satyam.net.in
Key Personnel
Contact: Ramesh Kumar Virmani
Founded: 1983
Subjects: Agriculture, Anthropology, Behavioral Sciences, Biography, Business, Career Development, Drama, Theater, Economics, Education, Environmental Studies, Fiction, Foreign Countries, Geography, Geology, Government, Political Science, History, Humor, Library & Information Sciences, Literature, Literary Criticism, Essays, Management, Marketing, Philosophy, Psychology, Psychiatry, Social Sciences, Sociology, Travel, Veterinary Science, Women's Studies
ISBN Prefix(es): 81-7117
Parent Company: Western Book Depot, Panbazar, Guwahati 781001
Branch Office(s)
Jasomanta Rd, Panbazar, Guwahati 781001
Bookshop(s): Western Book Depot, Panbazar, Guwahati 781001
Orders to: Omsons, Prakash House, 4379/4B Ansari Rd, New Delhi 110002

Orient Paperbacks+
Imprint of Vision Books Pvt Ltd
1590 Madarsa Rd, Kashmere Gate, Delhi 110006
Tel: (011) 2386-2267; (011) 2386-2201
Fax: (011) 2386-2935
E-mail: orientpbk@vsnl.com
Web Site: www.orientpaperbacks.com *Cable:* VISIONBOOK, DELHI 110006
Key Personnel
Man Dir: Vishwa Nath
Editorial, Production: Kapil Malhotra
Sales, Publicity, Rights & Permissions: Sudhir Malhotra *E-mail:* smalhotra@orientpaperbacks.com
Exports, Mideast & Asia: Sidharth Malhotra
Founded: 1977
Specialize in fitness.
Subjects: Astrology, Occult, Business, Career Development, Cookery, Crafts, Games, Hobbies, Drama, Theater, Fiction, Health, Nutrition, How-to, Humor, Nonfiction (General), Poetry, Self-Help, Sports, Athletics, Fitness
ISBN Prefix(es): 81-222
Number of titles published annually: 50 Print
Total Titles: 650 Print
Associate Companies: Rajpal & Sons; Ravindra Printing Press; Shiksha Bharati; Shiksha Bharati Press, G T Rd, Shadara, Delhi 110 032
Imprints: Anand Paperbacks
Branch Office(s)
3-6-280/A/5 Himayatnagar, Hyderabad, K M Govindan *Tel:* (040) 2322-3252
Vasant, Ground floor, 3-B Pedder Rd, Mumbai 400026 *Tel:* (022) 2351-0343 *Fax:* (022) 2351-0229
24 Feroze Gandhi Marg, Lajpat Nagar, New Delhi 110024 *Tel:* (011) 2983-6470; (011) 2983-6480 *Fax:* (011) 2983-6490
Book Club(s): Orient Book Club

Oxford & IBH Publishing Co Pvt Ltd+
66 Janpath, 2nd floor, New Delhi 110001
Tel: (011) 2332 45 78; (011) 2332 05 18 *Fax:* (011) 2371 0090
E-mail: oxford@vsnl.com
Key Personnel
Dir: Mohan Primlani; Raju Primlani; Vijay Primlani
Founded: 1962
Subjects: Agriculture, Asian Studies, Biological Sciences, Civil Engineering, Earth Sciences, Engineering (General), Mechanical Engineering, Natural History, Psychology, Psychiatry, Science (General)
ISBN Prefix(es): 81-204; 81-205; 81-7087
Subsidiaries: Science Publishers Inc
Branch Office(s)
22 Park Mansion, Park St, Kolkata 700016

Oxford University Press+
YMCA Library Bldg, 1st floor, One Jai Singh Rd, New Delhi 110 001
Tel: (011) 2021029; (011) 2021198; (011) 2021396 *Fax:* (011) 3732312; (011) 3360897
E-mail: admin.in@oup.com
Telex: OXORIENT
Key Personnel
Man Dir: Manzar Khan
Finance Dir: Vivek Dayal
Educational & Higher Educational Publishing Dir: Ranjan Kaul
Educational Marketing Dir: K.M. Thomas
Academic Publishing Dir: Nitasha Devasar
Dir HR & Administration: Sanjay Gaur
Academic Marketing Dir: Yogesh Saxena
Regional Sales Dir, North: Shammi Manik
Regional Sales Dir, West: Vimal Kohli
Regional Manager, East: Anindya Sengupta
Regional Manager, South: Venugopal Bhaskaran
Publicity Manager: Rowena Kapparath
Founded: 1912
Subjects: Biography, Business, Developing Countries, Economics, History, Literature, Literary Criticism, Essays, Natural History, Philosophy, Religion - Hindu, Politics, Sociology, Culture Studies, Gender Studies. Ecology, Science, Medicine
ISBN Prefix(es): 81-7025; 0-19-56
Parent Company: Oxford University Press, United Kingdom
Branch Office(s)
Oxford House, 289 Anna Salai, Chennai 600006 *Tel:* (044) 28110832; (044) 28111861; (044) 28112107 *Fax:* (044) 28110962
2/11 Ansari Rd, Daryaganj, New Delhi 110002 *Tel:* (011) 23273841; (011) 23273842; (011) 23253647 *Fax:* (011) 23277812
Plot No A1-5, Block GP, Sector V, Salt Lake Electronics Complex, Kolkata 700091 *Tel:* (033) 23573739; (033) 23573740; (033) 23573741 *Fax:* (033) 23573738
167, Vidyanagari Marg, Kalina, Santacruz (East), Mumbai 400098 *Tel:* (022) 26521034; (022) 26521035; (022) 56973891; (022) 56973892 *Fax:* (022) 26521133
U.S. Office(s): US University Press, 198 Madison Ave, New York, NY 11016, United States
Showroom(s): 94 Industrial Area, 4th B Cross, Fifth Block, Koramangala, Bangalore 560095 *Tel:* (080) 5534786 *Fax:* (080) 5538736; SCO 45 & 46, First fl, Sector 8C, Madhya Marg, Chandigarh 160009 *Tel:* (0172) 2545794; Danish Rd, Panbazar, Guwahati 781001 *Tel:* (0361) 2524050 *Fax:* (0361) 2513310; 8-2-577, First fl, Rd No 7, Banjara Hills, Hyderabad 500029 *Tel:* (040) 23356425 *Fax:* (040) 23356424; A-19, Main Sahakar Path, Jaipur 302001 *Tel:* (0141) 5179892; (0141) 2743816; B-7/18, Sector K, Aliganj, Lucknow 226024 *Tel:* (0522) 2364215; (0522) 762472; H/o Mr M.K. Sinha, 178/B, S.K. Puri, Patna 800001; Gayatri Sadan, 2060 Sadashiv Peth, V N Colony, Pune 411030 *Tel:* (020) 4334537 *Fax:* (020) 4337262; Kesava Bldgs, First fl, TC No 25/1437 (2), Thampanoor, Thiruvananthapuram 695001 *Tel:* (0471) 2330995

Oxonian Press (P) Ltd+
N-66 Connaught Circus, New Delhi 110001
Tel: (011) 44957; (011) 3313584 *Fax:* (011) 3322639
E-mail: oxford.publ@axcess.net.in *Cable:* INDAMER
Key Personnel
Dir, Rights & Permissions: Gulab Primlani
Sales Dir: Dr A M Primlani
Publicity Manager: Ms Chandra Naharwar
Subjects: Engineering (General), Music, Dance, Science (General)
ISBN Prefix(es): 81-7087
Parent Company: Oxford & IBH Publishing Co Pvt Ltd
Associate Companies: Amerind Publishing Co P Ltd
Branch Office(s)
17 Park St, Kolkata 700016
29 Wodehouse Rd, Mumbai
165 Golf Links, New Delhi 110003
Showroom(s): Oxford Book & Stationery Co, Scindia House, New Delhi 110 001
Warehouse: Plot No 6, Sector 27A, Industrial Area, Faridabad

Paico Publishing House+
M G Rd, Cochin, Kerala 682035
Mailing Address: PO Box 2560, Ernakulam, Cochin 682035
Tel: (0484) 355835
Web Site: www.paicoindia.com *Cable:* PAICO
Key Personnel
Man Dir: Kanchana V Pai
Founded: 1955
Subjects: Fiction, History, Science (General)
Associate Companies: Broadway; Ernakulam; Pai & Co
Branch Office(s)
New Rd, Mattancherry, Cochin 682002
Paico Buildings, Press Rd, Trivandrum 1
Bookshop(s): 181 Mount Rd, Chennai 600002; Paico Books & Arts, Cochin; Kallai Rd, Calicut 673002; K K Rd, Kottayam 686002

Panchasheel Prakashan
Film Colony, Chaura Rasta, Jaipur 302 003
Tel: (0141) 65072 *Fax:* (0141) 326554
Key Personnel
Editorial: M C Gupta
Sales: O P Agarwal
Founded: 1968
Subjects: Fiction
ISBN Prefix(es): 81-7056

Panjab University Publication Bureau
Chandigarh 160 014
Tel: (0172) 541782; (0172) 534373
Key Personnel
Manager: H R Grover
Founded: 1948
Membership(s): Federation of Indian Publishers.
Subjects: Biography, History, Philosophy, Poetry, Religion - Other, Social Sciences, Sociology
ISBN Prefix(es): 81-85822

Pankaj Publications+
3 Regal Bldg, Sansad Marg, New Delhi 110001
Tel: (011) 3363395; (011) 3348805 *Fax:* (011) 5163525; (01) 5511684
E-mail: pankajbooks@hotmail.com
Key Personnel
Manager: Vikas Bajaj *E-mail:* bajajvikas@hotmail.com
Subjects: Crafts, Games, Hobbies, Ethnicity, Music, Dance
ISBN Prefix(es): 81-87155
Number of titles published annually: 20 Print
Total Titles: 150 Print
Bookshop(s): Cambridge Book Depot, 3 Regal Bldg, Connaught Circus, New Delhi 110001, Mr Ranjana Bajaj *E-mail:* cambridgebooks@hotmail.com

Paramount Sales (India) Pvt Ltd+
484, Double Storey, New Rajinder Nagar, New Delhi 110060
Tel: (011) 7776821; (011) 5746485 *Fax:* (011) 5746485
Key Personnel
Dir: Naresh Kumar Chowdhry
Founded: 1986

PUBLISHERS — INDIA

Subjects: Art, Language Arts, Linguistics
ISBN Prefix(es): 81-7103
Associate Companies: Naresh Publishers, 111 Shankar Rd Market, New Rajinder Nagar, New Delhi 110060 *Tel:* (011) 5723235 *Fax:* (011) 5746485

Parimal Prakashan+
Parimal Bldg, Khadkeshwar, Maharashtra, Aurangabad 431001
Tel: (0240) 4556
Key Personnel
Man Dir, Production: A B Dashrathe
Sales: S B Padalkar
Founded: 1974
Subjects: Archaeology, Astrology, Occult, Career Development, Education, Ethnicity, Human Relations, Literature, Literary Criticism, Essays, Medicine, Nursing, Dentistry, Social Sciences, Sociology
ISBN Prefix(es): 81-7088
Branch Office(s)
159/2 Shaniwar Peth Pune, Kennedy Bridge, Mumbai
Bookshop(s): Marathwada Book Distributors, Parimal Bldg, Khadkeshwar, Maharashtra, Aurangabad 431001

Peachpit Press, *imprint of* Addison-Wesley Pte Ltd

Peacock Books, *imprint of* HarperCollins Publishers India Pty Ltd

Penguin Longman Publishing, *imprint of* Addison-Wesley Pte Ltd

People's Publishing House (P) Ltd
5-E Rani Jhansi Rd, New Delhi 110 055
Tel: (011) 529365 *Cable:* QUAMIKITAB
Key Personnel
Chairman: T Madhavan
General Manager: P P C Joshi
Founded: 1948
Subjects: Biography, Engineering (General), History, Philosophy, Poetry, Social Sciences, Sociology
ISBN Prefix(es): 81-7007
Bookshop(s): 2 Marina Arcade, Connaught Pl, New Delhi 110001 *Tel:* (011) 344064

Pitambar Publishing Co (P) Ltd+
888 E Park Rd, Karol Bagh, New Delhi 110 005
Tel: (011) 776058; (011) 776067 *Fax:* (011) 2367 6058
E-mail: pitambar@bol.net.in *Cable:* PITAMBAR NEW DELHI
Key Personnel
Man Dir, Production, Rights & Permissions: Ved Bhushan
Man Dir, Publicity: Anand Bhushan
Sales: Manish Aggarwal; V P Jugaan
Production: Jaideep Aggarwal
Founded: 1947
Membership(s): Federation of Indian Publishers, New Delhi, Akhil Bhartia Hindi Prakashak Sangh, New Delhi.
Subjects: Accounting, Chemistry, Chemical Engineering, Computer Science, Economics, Electronics, Electrical Engineering, Fiction, History, Mathematics, Microcomputers, Religion - Buddhist, Religion - Hindu
ISBN Prefix(es): 81-209
Total Titles: 800 Print
Associate Companies: Ambar Prakashan, 888 E Park Rd, New Delhi 110 005, Contact: Ved Bhushan; Bharat Publishing House, 123 Durga Chambers, Desh Bandhu Gupta Rd, New Delhi 110005, Contact: Karol Bagh; Computel Systems & Services, 10 Community Centre, Mayapuri, Phase I, New Delhi, Contact: Dr V B Aggarwal *Tel:* (011) 25136652 *Fax:* (011) 25133088; Piyush Printers Publishers Pvt Ltd, G-12 Udyog Nagar, Rohtak Road Industrial Area, New Delhi 110041, Contact: Jaideep Aggarwal; Reliant Microsystems Pvt Ltd, 10 Community Centre, Mayapuri, Phase-I, New Delhi 64, Contact: Prof V B Aggarwal
Branch Office(s)
H No 6/2, III Main Rd, SK Garden, Bensen Town Post, Bangalore 560046 *Tel:* (080) 3534673
1-1-230/6 (407) Vivek Nagar, Chikkadapally, Hyderabad 500020 *Tel:* (04) 7645614
Warehouse: 415-1-3, Mundika, New Delhi 110041

Pitman, *imprint of* Addison-Wesley Pte Ltd

Pointer Publishers+
807, Vyas Bldg, SMS Highway, Jaipur 302 003
Tel: (0141) 2568159 *Fax:* (0141) 2568159
E-mail: info@pointerpublishers.com; pointerpub@hotmail.com
Web Site: www.pointerpublishers.com
Key Personnel
Manager: Vipin Jain
Founded: 1986
Publish reference & general books in agriculture, humanities arts, science & commerce.
Subjects: Accounting, Agriculture, Biological Sciences, Child Care & Development, Economics, Education, Environmental Studies, Geography, Geology, Government, Political Science, History, Library & Information Sciences, Literature, Literary Criticism, Essays, Management, Social Sciences, Sociology, Women's Studies
ISBN Prefix(es): 81-7132
Total Titles: 200 Print

Popular Prakashan Pvt Ltd+
35C Pandit Madan Mohan, Malviya Marg, Popular Press Bldg, Tardeo, Mumbai 400 034
Tel: (022) 494 1656 *Fax:* (022) 24945294
E-mail: info@popularprakashan.com
Web Site: www.popularprakashan.com *Cable:* NANDIBOOK
Key Personnel
Chairman: Sadanand Ganesh Bhatkal
Man Dir: Ramdas Ganesh Bhatkal
Dir: Harsha Ramdas Bhatkal
Founded: 1926
Subjects: Anthropology, Biography, Computer Science, Cookery, Economics, Government, Political Science, Health, Nutrition, History, Management, Medicine, Nursing, Dentistry, Music, Dance, Social Sciences, Sociology, Women's Studies
ISBN Prefix(es): 81-7154
Parent Company: Popular Book Depot
Associate Companies: Bhatkal & Sen; Indiancookery.com Pvt Ltd, 501, Damini, Plot No 889, Juhu Tara Rd, Juhu, Mumbai 400049 *Tel:* (022) 26171070 *Fax:* (022) 26132416
Imprints: Focus
Branch Office(s)
16 Southern Ave, Kolkata 700026 *Tel:* (033) 761413
4648-1 Ansari Rd, 21 Daryaganj, New Delhi 110002 *Tel:* (011) 3265245

Prabhat Prakashan+
4-19 Asaf Ali Rd, New Delhi 110002
Tel: (011) 3264676; (011) 3289555; (011) 3289666 *Fax:* (011) 3253233
E-mail: prabhat@indianabooks.com; prabhat1@vsnl.com
Web Site: www.indianabooks.com
Key Personnel
Chief Executive: Shyam Sunder
Executive: Pawan Agrawal
Editorial: Shyam Bahadur Verma
Sales: Raghuvir Verma
Production: Dharam Vir
Founded: 1958
Subjects: Art, Biography, Cookery, Fiction, Humor, Library & Information Sciences, Nonfiction (General), Poetry
ISBN Prefix(es): 81-7315
Branch Office(s)
Mathura
Bookshop(s): 4-19 Asaf Ali Rd, New Delhi 110002

Pratibha Pratishthan+
1685 Dakhnirai St, Netaji Subhash Marg, New Delhi 110 002
Tel: (011) 3289666 *Toll Free Tel:* (011) 3253233
Key Personnel
President: Prabhat Kumar
Vice President: Piyush Agrawal
Sales Executive: Ajay Kumar; D S Negi
Founded: 1981
Subjects: Art, Biography, Cookery, Fiction, Humor, Library & Information Sciences, Nonfiction (General), Poetry
ISBN Prefix(es): 81-85827; 81-88266

Prentice Hall, *imprint of* Addison-Wesley Pte Ltd

Prima Communications Inc, *imprint of* Rajendra Publishing House Pvt Ltd

Promilla & Publishers
Sonali, C-127 Sarvodaya Enclave, New Delhi 110017
Tel: (011) 668720 *Fax:* (011) 6448947
Key Personnel
President & Editor: Prof D H Butani
Production, Rights & Permissions Dir: Ashok Butani
General Manager: M M Khanna
Sales Manager: Sutikshan Naithani
Chief Executive: Nirmala Butani
Founded: 1970
Subjects: Art, Biography, Economics, Government, Political Science, History, Religion - Other, Social Sciences, Sociology, Women's Studies
ISBN Prefix(es): 81-85002

PTR, *imprint of* Addison-Wesley Pte Ltd

Publications & Information Directorate, CSIR+
Hillside Rd, New Delhi 110012
Tel: (011) 5785359; (011) 5786301 (ext 288) *Fax:* (011) 5787062
Telex: 031-77271pidin *Cable:* PUBLIFORM
Key Personnel
Editorial: G P Phondka
Sales: A K Srivastava
Founded: 1942
Subjects: Biological Sciences, Chemistry, Chemical Engineering, Physics, Science (General), Technology
ISBN Prefix(es): 81-7236; 81-85038
Parent Company: Council of Scientific & Industrial Research, New Delhi

Pustak Mahal+
F2/16, Anasari Rd, Darya Ganj, New Delhi 110 002
Tel: (011) 23276539; (011) 23272783; (011) 23272784 *Fax:* (011) 3260518
E-mail: pustakmahal@vsnl.net.in
Web Site: www.pustakmahal.com
Telex: 031-78090 SBP IN
Key Personnel
Chairman: T R Gupta
Man Dir: Ram Avtar Gupta
Marketing & Publishing Dir: Vikas Gupta
Dir, Sales: Ramesh Kumar Gupta
Dir, Marketing: Dr Ashok Kumar Gupta
Production Dir: Venod Gupta

Founded: 1974
Specialize in supplementary educational literature for children & informative books of mass appeal. Publishes in twelve languages.
Membership(s): Federation of Indian Publishers; Federation of Publishers; Booksellers Association; Federation of Educational Publishers of India; Akhil Bharatiye Hindi Prakashak Sangh; Delhi State Booksellers Association; Chemical & Allied Products Export Promotion Council; Association of Booksellers; Publishers of South India.
Subjects: Architecture & Interior Design, Astrology, Occult, Biography, Computer Science, Cookery, Crafts, Games, Hobbies, Health, Nutrition, History, House & Home, Language Arts, Linguistics, Medicine, Nursing, Dentistry, Music, Dance, Parapsychology, Romance, Science (General)
ISBN Prefix(es): 81-223
Imprints: M/S Family Books Pvt Ltd; Comdex Computer Publishing
Subsidiaries: M/S Hind Pustak Bhandar
Divisions: Industrial Books Division
Branch Office(s)
22/2, Mission Rd, Bangalore *Tel:* (080) 2234025 *Fax:* (080) 2240209 (Shama Rao's Compound)
23-25 Zaoba Wadi, Thakurdwar, Mumbai 400 002 *Tel:* (022) 2010941 *Fax:* (022) 2053387 *E-mail:* rapidex@bom5.net.in
Khemka House, Ashok Rajpath, Patna 4 *Tel:* (0612) 653644 *Fax:* (0612) 653644
Book Club(s): Comdex Book Club

QUE, *imprint of* Addison-Wesley Pte Ltd

Radiant Publishers+
E-155, State Bank of India Bldg, Kalkaji, New Delhi 110019
Tel: (011) 6435477; (011) 6482861 *Fax:* (011) 6479870
E-mail: rpbooksind@yahoo.com
Key Personnel
Man Dir, Sales, Production, Publicity & Editorial, Rights & Permissions: Sunita Jain
Founded: 1973
Subjects: Economics, Education, Environmental Studies, Government, Political Science, Religion - Other, Social Sciences, Sociology, Women's Studies
ISBN Prefix(es): 81-7027
Number of titles published annually: 10 Print
Total Titles: 200 Print

Rahul Publishing House
3348, Naisadak, Shastri Nagar, Meerut 250005
Tel: (0121) 2774518
Key Personnel
Editorial & Production: Rahul Singhal
Founded: 1993
Subjects: Anthropology, Antiques, Archaeology, Art, Asian Studies, Earth Sciences, History, Language Arts, Linguistics, Regional Interests
ISBN Prefix(es): 81-7388
Associate Companies: Agam Kala Prakashan; Agam Prakashan; Swati Publication

Rajasthan Hindi Granth Academy+
A-26/2, Vidya laya Marg, Tilak Nagar, Jaipur 302 004
Tel: (0141) 61410; (0141) 511129
Key Personnel
Dir: Dr Ved Prakash *Tel:* (0141) 510341
Sales, Publicity: K N Agrawal
Production: Mahesh Jain
Founded: 1969
Subjects: Agriculture, Art, Chemistry, Chemical Engineering, Economics, Education, Human Relations, Language Arts, Linguistics, Law, Library & Information Sciences, Medicine, Nursing, Dentistry, Philosophy, Physics, Science (General), Social Sciences, Sociology
ISBN Prefix(es): 81-7137

Rajendra Publishing House Pvt Ltd+
202 Patel Estate, B-40, New Link Rd, Andheri (W), Mumbai Worii 400053
Tel: (022) 6300741; (022) 6300742; (022) 6301930 *Fax:* (022) 6301940; (022) 6322146
E-mail: books@rajendrabooks.com
Web Site: www.rajendrabooks.com
Key Personnel
Chairman: Mr R K Tandon
Man Dir: Ms Swarn Tandon
Executive Dir: Ms Bindu Swaminathan Tandon; Mr Vivek Tandon *Tel:* (022) 8755935 *Fax:* (022) 8738551
Founded: 1989
Specialize in direct mail sale of high quality books.
Subjects: Astronomy, Geography, Geology, Health, Nutrition, History, How-to, Management, Science (General), Self-Help, Social Sciences, Sociology
ISBN Prefix(es): 81-900085; 81-86406; 81-900279
Total Titles: 10 Print
Imprints: Prima Communications Inc
Distributed by Gazelle Book Services Ltd
Distributor for Conari Press; Dorling Kindersley; Elements Books Ltd; Rodale Press Inc

Rajesh Publications+
One Ansari Rd, Daryaganj, New Delhi 110002
Tel: (011) 274550
Key Personnel
Man Dir: Mohan Lal *Tel:* 981111605 (mobile)
Contact: Sanjay Gupta
Founded: 1970
Subjects: Economics, Education, Geography, Geology, History, Management, Philosophy, Religion - Other
ISBN Prefix(es): 81-85891
Distributed by Janki Prakashan
Distributor for Seema Publications

Rajkamal Prakashan Pvt Ltd
One-B, Netaji Subhash Marg, Darya Ganj, New Delhi 110002
Tel: (011) 3288769; (011) 3274463 *Fax:* (011) 3278144
Subjects: Education
ISBN Prefix(es): 81-7178
Branch Office(s)
M/D Ravkamal Prakashan Pvt Ltd

Rajpal & Sons+
1590 Madarasa Rd, Kashmere Gate, Delhi 110006
Tel: 223904; 229174 *Fax:* (0141) 2967791 *Cable:* RAJPALSONS DELHI
Key Personnel
Man Dir: Vishwa Nath
Sales: Satish Kumar
Editorial: Meera Johri
Publicity, Rights & Permissions: Kapil Malhotra
Founded: 1947
Specialize in dictionaries.
Subjects: Fiction, Human Relations, Literature, Literary Criticism, Essays, Science (General)
ISBN Prefix(es): 81-7028
Associate Companies: Orient Paperbacks; Shiksha Bharati; Vision Books Pvt Ltd
Branch Office(s)
3-6-280/A5, Himayat Nagar, Hyderabad 500 029
3B Peddar Rd, Mumbai 400026 *Tel:* (022) 4929343
Bookshop(s): Lothian Rd, Kashmere Gate, Delhi 110006 *Tel:* (011) 2516602

Rastogi Publications+
Gangotri Shivaji Rd, Meerut 250 002
Tel: 24142; 24688
E-mail: vrastogi@vsnl.com; info@indianbookmart.com
Telex: 0549-209 *Cable:* RASTOGICO
Key Personnel
Editorial, Production, Rights & Permissions: R K Rastogi
Sales, Publicity: H K Rastogi
Sales, Publicitiy: Vivek Rastogi
Founded: 1966
Subjects: Agriculture, Animals, Pets, Biological Sciences, Earth Sciences, Education, Government, Political Science, Science (General)
ISBN Prefix(es): 81-7133; 81-85711
Subsidiaries: Pioneer Printers

Rebel Publishing House Pvt Ltd
50 Koregaon Park, Pune 411001
Tel: (0212) 628562 *Fax:* (0212) 624181
Key Personnel
Contact: Narain Das; Anando Ma Deva; Yoga Amit Swami
Founded: 1988
Subjects: Philosophy, Religion - Other, Theology
ISBN Prefix(es): 81-7261
Orders to: Sadhana Foundation, 17 Koreganon Park, Pune 411001

Regency Publications+
20/36-G Old Market, West Patel Nagar, New Delhi 110008
Tel: (011) 5712539; (011) 5740038 *Fax:* (011) 5783571
E-mail: regency@satyam.net.in
Key Personnel
Owner: Arun Verma
Founded: 1993
Membership(s): Delhi State Publishers & Booksellers Association.
Subjects: Agriculture, Anthropology, Archaeology, Art, Biological Sciences, Education, Environmental Studies, Ethnicity, Fiction, Geography, Geology, Government, Political Science, History, Language Arts, Linguistics, Law, Philosophy, Regional Interests, Religion - Other, Social Sciences, Sociology, Sports, Athletics, Women's Studies
ISBN Prefix(es): 81-86030; 81-87498
Number of titles published annually: 20 Print
Total Titles: 150 Print
Distributed by DK Agencies; D K Publishers/Distributors; UBS Publishers' Distributors

Rekha Prakashan+
16 Daryaganj, New Delhi 110 002
Tel: (011) 23279907; (011) 23279904 *Fax:* (011) 2321783
E-mail: rprakashan@satyam.net.in
Web Site: www.museumoffolkandtribalart.org
Key Personnel
Chief Executive, Rights & Permissions: K C Aryan
Editorial: S Aryan
Sales: B N Aryan
Publicity Dir: G D Aryan
Founded: 1973
Membership(s): Delhi State Booksellers' & Publishers' Association.
Subjects: Art, Regional Interests, History of Art (India); Indian Folk & Tribal Art
ISBN Prefix(es): 81-900002; 81-900003
Number of titles published annually: 3 Print
Total Titles: 27 Print

Reliance Publishing House+
3026/7-H, Ranjit Nagar, New Delhi 110008
Tel: (011) 5852605; (011) 5772768; (011) 5737377 *Fax:* (011) 5786769
Fax on Demand: (011) 5852605
E-mail: reliance@indiatimes.com
Key Personnel
Man Dir, Rights & Permissions: Dr S K Bhatia

Sales: M K Bhatia
Publicity: Geeta Saxena *Tel:* (011) 5786769
Editorial: Bhatia Durgesh *Tel:* (011) 5737377
Founded: 1985
Publishers of reference books on the Indian book industry, humanities & social sciences.
Subjects: Accounting, Advertising, Agriculture, Anthropology, Archaeology, Architecture & Interior Design, Art, Asian Studies, Astrology, Occult, Astronomy, Behavioral Sciences, Biography, Biological Sciences, Business, Career Development, Child Care & Development, Communications, Criminology, Developing Countries, Disability, Special Needs, Drama, Theater, Earth Sciences, Economics, Education, Energy, Environmental Studies, Ethnicity, Fiction, Finance, Geography, Geology, Government, Political Science, History, Human Relations, Humor, Journalism, Labor, Industrial Relations, Library & Information Sciences, Literature, Literary Criticism, Essays, Management, Marketing, Medicine, Nursing, Dentistry, Military Science, Music, Dance, Mysteries, Mythology, Nonfiction (General), Philosophy, Poetry, Psychology, Psychiatry, Public Administration, Publishing & Book Trade Reference, Regional Interests, Religion - Buddhist, Religion - Hindu, Science Fiction, Fantasy, Social Sciences, Sociology, Sports, Athletics, Technology, Travel, Women's Studies
ISBN Prefix(es): 81-85047; 81-85972; 81-7510
Total Titles: 525 Print; 4 Online; 4 E-Book
Associate Companies: Geeta Graphics, J436, Baljit Nagar, New Delhi 110008, Contact: Manish K Bhatia *Tel:* (011) 25845330 *Fax:* (011) 25842605; (011) 25846769; Geeta Enterprises, J436, Baljit Nagar, New Delhi 110008 *Tel:* (011) 5772748; (011) 5875330 *Fax:* (011) 5786769
Distributed by DK Publishers' Distributors; UBS Publishers Distributors Ltd
Warehouse: J-436, Baljit Nagar, New Delhi 110008 *Tel:* (011) 25845330 *Fax:* (011) 25846769; (011) 25842748 *E-mail:* reliance@indiatimes.com
Distribution Center: 3026/7H, Shiv Chowk, S Patel Nagar, New Delhi 110008 *Tel:* (011) 5852605 *Fax:* (011) 5786769

Research Signpost
37/661(2), Fort, PO, Thiruvananthapuram, Kerala 695023
Tel: (0471) 2460384 *Fax:* (0471) 2573051
E-mail: ggcom@vsnl.com
Web Site: www.researchsignpost.com
Key Personnel
Man Editor: Shankar Pandalai
Publications Manager: Anandavalli Gayathri
Publishers of scientific, technical, medical & agricultural books & journals. Also produces CD-ROMs.
Subjects: Agriculture, Medicine, Nursing, Dentistry, Science (General)
ISBN Prefix(es): 81-86481
Number of titles published annually: 150 Print

Researchco Reprints+
25-B/2, New Rohtak Rd, Near Liberty Cinema, New Dehli 110005
Tel: (011) 28712565; (011) 55150446; (011) 28714057 *Fax:* (011) 28716134
Telex: 31-79055 *Cable:* SEARCHBOOK
Key Personnel
Dir: Anil Jain *E-mail:* akjain@de12.vsnl.net.in; Arvind Jain
Founded: 1969
Specialize in stocking & supplying of books & back volume journals.
Subjects: Science (General), Technology
Warehouse: 1865 Trinagar, Delhi 110035

Response, *imprint of* SAGE Publications India Pvt Ltd

Roli Books Pvt Ltd+
M-75 Greater Kailash-II (Mkt), New Delhi 110 048
Tel: (011) 6462782; (011) 6442271; (011) 6460886 *Fax:* (011) 6467185
E-mail: roli@vsnl.
Web Site: rolibooks.com
Key Personnel
Publishing Manager & Managing Editor: Renuka Chaudmury *Tel:* (011) 6420516
Contact: Kiran Kapoor *Tel:* (011) 29215924; Pramod Kapoor *Tel:* (011) 29212271
Founded: 1978
Publishing house & distributor for foreign publishers. Sells titles to other houses under their logo. Specializes in plain text & coffee table books, destinations & monuments & politics.
Subjects: Art, Business, Cookery, Erotica, Fiction, Government, Political Science, History, Management, Music, Dance, Religion - Buddhist, Religion - Hindu, Religion - Islamic, Religion - Jewish, Travel
ISBN Prefix(es): 81-7437
Total Titles: 122 Print; 122 Online; 4 Audio
Parent Company: Roli Books
Imprints: Lotus; Lustre Press

Roorkee Press, see Nem Chand & Brothers

Rupa & Co+
15 Bankim Chatterjee St, College Sq, Kolkata 700 073
Mailing Address: PO Box 7071, New Delhi 110002
Tel: (011) 344821; (011) 346305 *Fax:* (011) 327 7294
E-mail: rupa@ndb.vsnl.net.in; del.rupaco@axcess.net.in *Cable:* RUPANCO
Key Personnel
Man Dir: D Mehra
Sales: R N Barman
Productions & International Rights: R K Mehra
Accounts: S K Mehra
Publicity: C K Mehra
Founded: 1936
Subjects: Art, Crafts, Games, Hobbies, Education, Fiction, History, Literature, Literary Criticism, Essays, Philosophy, Religion - Other, Sports, Athletics
ISBN Prefix(es): 81-7167
Associate Companies: HarperCollins Publishers India
Imprints: Rupa Paperbacks
Branch Office(s)
94 South Malaka, Allahabad *Tel:* (0532) 53936
G1 & 2 Ghaswalla Tower, P G Solanki Path, Mumbai 400007
7/16 Makhanlal St, Ansari Rd, Daryaganj, New Delhi 2
Distributor for Affiliated East-West (India); Elbs titles (UK); Faber & Faber (UK); Hamlyn (UK); Ladybird (UK); Macmillan (UK); McGraw-Hill Kogakusha (Singapore); Penguin (UK); Prentice-Hall (India); Tata McGraw-Hill (India); Unwin Hyman (UK); Wiley Eastern (India)

Rupa Paperbacks, *imprint of* Rupa & Co

SABDA+
Unit of Sri Aurobindo Ashram Trust
No 123, S V Patel Salai, Pondicherry 605 002
Tel: (0413) 2334980; (0413) 2223328 *Fax:* (0413) 2223328
E-mail: sabda@sriaurobindoashram.org
Web Site: sabda.sriaurobindoashram.org
Telex: 0469221 Sas In *Cable:* SABDA
Key Personnel
Manager: Mira Gupta; Jay Raichura
International Rights & Permissions: Manoj Das Gupta
Founded: 1952
Specialize in works by or on the philosopher Sri Aurobindo & his spiritual collaborator known as "the Mother".
Membership(s): Federation of Indian Publishers; Akhil Bharatiya Hindi Prakashak Sangh; CAPEXIL (Export Promotion Council).
Subjects: Asian Studies, Education, Government, Political Science, Literature, Literary Criticism, Essays, Philosophy, Poetry, Psychology, Psychiatry, Religion - Hindu, Religion - Other, Social Sciences, Sociology, The spriutal teachings & system of "Integral Yoga" of Sri Aurobindo
ISBN Prefix(es): 81-7058; 81-7060; 81-86413
Total Titles: 1,700 Print
Branch Office(s)
Sri Aurobindo Bhavan, 8 Shakespeare Sarani, Kolkata 700071 *Tel:* (033) 22829261 *E-mail:* sabdacalcutta@vsnl.net
Distributed by Auromere (USA only); East-West Cultural Center (USA only); Lotus Press (USA only); Matagiri (USA only)
Distributor for Sri Aurobindo Ashram; Sri Aurobindo Society; Sri Mira Trust
Showroom(s): 13 Marine St, Pondicherry *Tel:* (0413) 2334072 *Fax:* (0413) 2223328 *E-mail:* sabda@sriaurobindoashram.org
Bookshop(s): Sri Aurobindo Society, 11 Sahakar, B Rd, Churchgate, Mumbai 400 020 *Tel:* (022) 22043076; Sri Aurobindo Marg, New Delhi 110 016 *Tel:* (011) 26524810 *Fax:* (011) 26857449 *E-mail:* aurobindo@vsnl.com

Ratna Sagar Pvt Ltd+
A-8 Mukherjee Nagar, Commercial Complex, Delhi 110009
Tel: (011) 7654095; (011) 7654099 *Fax:* (011) 7250787
E-mail: rsagar@giasdlo1.vsnl.net.in; rsagar@nda.vsnl.net.in
Telex: 61604 AEROIN *Cable:* RATNABOOKS
Key Personnel
Contact: Dhanesh Jain
Founded: 1982
ISBN Prefix(es): 81-7070

SAGE Publications India Pvt Ltd+
B-42 Panchsheel Enclave, New Delhi 110 017
Mailing Address: PO Box 4109, New Delhi 110 017
Tel: (011) 2649 1290 *Fax:* (011) 2649 2117
E-mail: sage@vsnl.com; marketing@indiasage.com; editors@indiasage.com
Web Site: www.indiasage.com *Cable:* SAGEPUB NEW DELHI 110048
Key Personnel
Man Dir & Sales: Tejeshwar Singh
Editorial: Omita Goyal
Marketing: Sunanda Ghosh
Founded: 1981
Subjects: Anthropology, Asian Studies, Behavioral Sciences, Business, Communications, Developing Countries, Economics, Environmental Studies, Government, Political Science, Management, Psychology, Psychiatry, Public Administration, Social Sciences, Sociology, Women's Studies
ISBN Prefix(es): 81-7036; 81-7829
Total Titles: 900 Print
Associate Companies: Sage Publications Inc, 2455 Teller Rd, Thousand Oaks, CA 91320, United States *E-mail:* info@sagepub.com *Web Site:* www.sagepub.com; Sage Publications Ltd, One Oliver's Yard, 55 City Rd, London EC1Y 1SP, United Kingdom *Tel:* (020) 7324 8500 *Fax:* (020) 7324 8600 *E-mail:* info@sagepub.co.uk *Web Site:* www.sagepub.co.uk
Imprints: Response; Vistaar
Branch Office(s)
11 Sararana St, T Nagar, Chennai 600 017 *Tel:* (044) 2434 5822 *E-mail:* sage.chennai@vsnl.net *Web Site:* www.indiasage.com

31, LB Stadium, Post Box 131, Hyderabad 500 001 *Tel:* (040) 2323 1447 *E-mail:* sage.hyderabad@vsnl.net *Web Site:* www.indiasage.com

59-5 Prince Baktiar Shah Rd, Ground floor, Tollygunge, Kolkata 700 033 *Tel:* (033) 2417 2642 *E-mail:* sage.kolkata@vsnl.net *Web Site:* www.indiasage.com

1187/37 Ameya, Shivajinagar, Off Ghole Rd, Pune 411 005 *Tel:* (020) 2551 3407 *E-mail:* sagepune@vsnl.net

Sahasrara Publications+
1143, Sector 37, Arun Vihar, Noida 201303
Tel: (011) 2432617
E-mail: sahasrarapublications@yahoo.co.in
Key Personnel
Contact: Opender Nath Karir
Founded: 1996
Encyclopedia Bharatam Series: *The A's of India, The B's of India, The C's of India, The D's of India, The E's, F's, G's of India; Treasury of Indian Quotations & Extracts; Democracy is Demon-o-cracy, Selectocracy is Heaven.*
Membership(s): Federation of Publishers & Booksellers Association of India.
Subjects: Regional Interests
ISBN Prefix(es): 81-86568
Number of titles published annually: 2 Print
Total Titles: 7 Print; 2 E-Book
Parent Company: Sahasrara Publications
Branch Office(s)
De-Addiction Centre, Brahmani Rd, Bagun Nagar, Jamshedpur, Bihar 831017, Contact: Mrs Daya Mukherjee *Tel:* (0657) 845226 *E-mail:* daya_js-r@satyam.net.in
48 Ripon St, Kolkata, Contact: Mrs Daya Mukherjee
Distributed by DK Publishers Distributors; Manohar Book Service (New Delhi); UBS Publishers' Distribution (New Delhi)

Sahitya Akademi (National Academy of Letters)
Rabindra Bhawan, 35, Ferozeshah Rd, New Delhi 110001
Tel: (011) 3386626; (011) 3735297; (011) 3364207 (sales); (011) 3386629 *Fax:* (011) 3382428; (011) 3364207
E-mail: sesy@ndl.vsnl.net.in *Cable:* SAHITYAKAR
Founded: 1955
Subjects: Literature, Literary Criticism, Essays
ISBN Prefix(es): 81-7201; 81-260

Sahitya Pravarthaka Co-operative Society Ltd
PO Box 94, Kottayam, Kerala 686001
Tel: (0481) 4111; (0481) 4112 *Cable:* Sahithyam
Key Personnel
Secretary: P Gopinadh
Sales: N C Rayi
Production: Yalath Mopasang
Founded: 1945
Subjects: Literature, Literary Criticism, Essays
ISBN Prefix(es): 81-213
Bookshop(s): National Book Stall, PO Box 40, Kottayam 686001 (with branches throughout Kerala)
Orders to: National Book Stall, c/o Sales Manager, Kottayam

Sai Early Learners (P) Ltd, *imprint of* Sterling Publishers Pvt Ltd

Samkaleen Prakashan
2762, Rajguru Marg, Paharganj, New Delhi 110055
Tel: (011) 3523520; (011) 3518197
Key Personnel
Editor: Krishan Khullar
Founded: 1976
Specialize in Indology.

Subjects: Art, Language Arts, Linguistics, Law, Poetry, Religion - Other, Technology, Indology
ISBN Prefix(es): 81-7083
Total Titles: 180 Print

SAMS, *imprint of* Addison-Wesley Pte Ltd

Samya, *imprint of* Stree

Sanskriti, *imprint of* Arnold Heinman Publishers (India) Pvt Ltd

Saraswati Publishers & Distributors+
434, Avadh Bihari Ki Gali, Govind Rao Ji Ka Rasta, Jaipur 302001
Key Personnel
Contact: Onkar Nath Tripathi
Founded: 1986
ISBN Prefix(es): 81-85808

M C Sarkar & Sons (P) Ltd+
14 Bankim Chatterjee St, Kolkata 700 012
Tel: (033) 2417490
Founded: 1910
Subjects: Fiction, Nonfiction (General)
ISBN Prefix(es): 81-7157

Sasta Sahitya Mandal+
N-77 Connaught Circus, New Delhi 110 001
Tel: (011) 3310505 *Cable:* SATSAHITYA
Key Personnel
President: Dharam Vira
Secretary: Yashpal Jain
Founded: 1925
Subjects: Agriculture, Animals, Pets, Biography, Economics, Education, Ethnicity, History, Literature, Literary Criticism, Essays, Philosophy, Religion - Hindu, Politics
ISBN Prefix(es): 81-7309
Branch Office(s)
Zero Rd, Allahabad *Tel:* (0532) 50034

Sat Sahitya Prakashan+
205-B, Chawri Bazar, Delhi 110006
Tel: (011) 3276316
Key Personnel
Chief Executive: S Sunder
Editorial: Nabab Singh Chauhan
Sales: P N Tiwari
Production: Rajan Chaudhary; P Kumar
Founded: 1970
Subjects: Art, Biography, Cookery, Fiction, Humor, Library & Information Sciences, Nonfiction (General), Poetry
ISBN Prefix(es): 81-7721; 81-85830

Sri Satguru Publications+
40/5 Shakti Nagar, 1st floor, Delhi 110007
Tel: (011) 716497; (011) 7434930 *Fax:* (011) 7227336
E-mail: ibcindia@vsnl.com
Web Site: www.indianbookscentre.com
Key Personnel
Man Dir, Rights & Permissions: Anil Gupta
Export, Sales: Naresh Gupta
Publicity: Virender Gupta
Founded: 1980
Subjects: Art, History, Language Arts, Linguistics, Literature, Literary Criticism, Essays, Medicine, Nursing, Dentistry, Music, Dance, Philosophy, Religion - Buddhist, Religion - Other, Indology, Ayurveda
ISBN Prefix(es): 81-7030
Parent Company: Indian Books Centre
Associate Companies: Bibliotheca Indo-Buddhica Series; Sri Garib Dass Oriental Series

Satprakashan Sanchar Kendra+
Division of Divine Word Society
Bhanwarkna Chowraha, Indore M P 452 001

Mailing Address: PO Box 507, Indore 452001
Tel: (0731) 475744; (0731) 475637 *Fax:* (0731) 47573
E-mail: sskin@sancharnet.in
Key Personnel
Dir: Sony Sebastian
Founded: 1980
Subjects: Biblical Studies, Communications, Religion - Catholic
ISBN Prefix(es): 81-85357; 81-85428
Number of titles published annually: 10 Print
Total Titles: 108 Print; 48 Audio

Sawan Kirpal Publications
H-11 Vi'jay Nagar, New Delhi 110009
Tel: (011) 7110722; (011) 7222244 *Fax:* (011) 7210720
Key Personnel
Man Dir: Sant Rajinder Singh
Editorial: Dr Vinod Sena
Sales Dir: Rajesh Seth
Production: Jay Linksman
Publicity: Gary Moed
Founded: 1977
Subjects: Religion - Other
ISBN Prefix(es): 81-85380
Parent Company: Sawan Kirpal Publications Spiritual Society
U.S. Office(s): SK Publications, 4S 175 Naperville Rd, Naperville, IL 60563, United States
PO Box 24, Bowling Green, VA 22427-0024, United States

SBW Publishers+
7/9A Makhab Lal St, Ansari Rd, Daryaganj, New Delhi 110002
Tel: (011) 3279603
Key Personnel
Contact: K L Sabharwal
Founded: 1980
Subjects: Philosophy, Regional Interests, Religion - Other, Social Sciences, Sociology
ISBN Prefix(es): 81-85708
Parent Company: Sabharwal Book Wholesalers

Scientific Book Agency+
56-D Mirza Ghalib St, Kolkata 700016
Tel: (033) 292915; (033) 4642206
E-mail: debmalya@giase101.vsnl.net.in
Key Personnel
Man Dir: J Sinha
Editorial: P Sinha
Science Editor, Publicity & Advertising: Dr Snehamoy Sinha
Market Development Manager, Rights & Permissions: Swapan Mitra
Sales Dir: S P Sinha
Production: S Sinha
Publicity, Advertising & Chief Domestic Sales & Exports: Rajasi Sinha
Founded: 1954
Membership(s): Federation of Publishers & Booksellers in India.
Subjects: Accounting, Agriculture, Anthropology, Archaeology, Architecture & Interior Design, Astronomy, Behavioral Sciences, Biological Sciences, Business, Chemistry, Chemical Engineering, Civil Engineering, Communications, Computer Science, Cookery, Developing Countries, Earth Sciences, Economics, Education, Electronics, Electrical Engineering, Energy, Engineering (General), Environmental Studies, Fiction, Finance, Foreign Countries, Geography, Geology, Government, Political Science, Health, Nutrition, History, Human Relations, Humor, Journalism, Labor, Industrial Relations, Law, Management, Marketing, Mathematics, Mechanical Engineering, Medicine, Nursing, Dentistry, Microcomputers, Military Science, Mysteries, Natural History, Parapsychology, Philosophy, Physical Sciences, Physics, Psychology, Psychiatry, Public Administration,

PUBLISHERS   INDIA

Science (General), Social Sciences, Sociology, Technology, Veterinary Science
Total Titles: 8 Print
Parent Company: J Sinha & Co
Associate Companies: Industries Alliance, 49/13 Hindusthan Park, Kolkata 700029, Contact: Mrs Prakriti Sinha *Tel:* (033) 464-2206
Bookshop(s): 79/2 Mahatma Gandhi Rd, PO Box 239, Kolkata
Warehouse: 49/13 Hindusthan Park, Kolkata 700029
Orders to: 49/13 Hindusthan Park, Kolkata 700029

Scientific Publishers India+
Maan Bhawan, Ratanda Rd, Jodhpur 342001
Mailing Address: PO Box 91, Jodhpur 342001
Tel: (0291) 512712; (0291) 433323 *Fax:* (0291) 512580
E-mail: scienti@sancharnet.in *Cable:* SCIENTIFIC-JODHPUR 342001
Key Personnel
Man Dir, Editorial: Pawan Kumar
Sales: Dawal Gawr
Founded: 1978
Also acts as booksellers & subscriptiion agents.
Subjects: Agriculture, Biological Sciences, Engineering (General), Natural History, Social Sciences, Sociology
ISBN Prefix(es): 81-85046; 81-7233; 81-85519
Total Titles: 350 Print
Parent Company: United Book Traders, 5A, New Pali Rd, Jodhpur 342001
Divisions: Publications & Export

Scott Foresman, *imprint of* Addison-Wesley Pte Ltd

Selina Publishers
4725/21A Dayanand Marg, Daryaganj, New Delhi 110002
Tel: (011) 3280711 *Fax:* (011) 3277230
Key Personnel
Man Dir, Publicity, Rights & Permissions: H L Gupta
Editorial: Preeti Mehra
Production: Subhash Arora
Sales: D M D'Bras
Founded: 1975
Subjects: Education
ISBN Prefix(es): 81-85612
Associate Companies: Granth Bharati (printing press)
Subsidiaries: Mudra Prakashan
Branch Office(s)
48 Daryaganj, New Delhi 110002
Book Club(s): Sanket Library Yojna

Shaibya Prakashan Bibhag+
86/1, Mahatma Gandhi Rd, Kolkata 700009
Tel: (033) 388268; (033) 2411748
Founded: 1984
Subjects: Biography, Computer Science, Electronics, Electrical Engineering, English as a Second Language, Publishing & Book Trade Reference, Religion - Hindu, Science (General), Science Fiction, Fantasy
ISBN Prefix(es): 81-87051

Sharda Prakashan
33/1, Bhul Bhullaian Rd, Mehrauli, New Delhi 110030
Tel: (011) 653982
Key Personnel
Chief Executive, Production, Rights & Permissions: Vijay Dev Jhari
Editorial, Publicity: Ravinder Jhari
Sales: R D Jhari
Founded: 1971
Subjects: Biography, Drama, Theater, Fiction, Literature, Literary Criticism, Essays

ISBN Prefix(es): 81-85023
Associate Companies: Itihas Shodh Sansthan, 33/1 Mehrauli, New Delhi 110030; Jharison, Bhullehullian Rd, Mehrauli, New Delhi 110030
Subsidiaries: Nalanda Prakashan
Bookshop(s): 16-F3 Ansari Rd, Daryaganj, New Delhi 110002 *Tel:* (011) 279853

R R Sheth & Co+
110-112 Princess St, Keshav Baug, Mumbai 400 002
Tel: (022) 2013441 *Fax:* (079) 5321732
E-mail: chintan@rrsheth.com
Web Site: www.rrsheth.com
Key Personnel
Proprietor: Bhagatbhai Bhuralal Sheth *Tel:* (022) 6183182
Founded: 1926
Publisher, bookseller & exporter. Specialize in Gujarati language.
Subjects: Fiction, Literature, Literary Criticism, Essays
Total Titles: 100 Print
Associate Companies: Lokpriya Prakashan, 110, Princess St, Mumbai 400 002 *Tel:* (022) 2058293
Branch Office(s)
Opp Phuvara, Gandhi Rd, Ahmedabad *Tel:* (079) 5356573 *E-mail:* rrsheth_co@hotmail.com

Shiksha Bharati+
Kashmere Gate, Delhi 110006
Tel: (011) 386-7791 *Fax on Demand:* (011) 386-7791
Key Personnel
Man Dir, Rights & Permissions: Sudhir Malhotra
Editorial: Meera Johri
Founded: 1959
Subjects: Education
ISBN Prefix(es): 81-7483
Associate Companies: Orient Paperbacks; Rajpal & Sons; Vision Books Pvt Ltd
Subsidiaries: Shiksha Bharati Press
Bookshop(s): Lothian Rd, Kashmere Gate, Delhi 110006 *Tel:* (011) 2516602

Siddhi Books, *imprint of* Cosmo Publications

Silver Burdett Ginn, *imprint of* Addison-Wesley Pte Ltd

SIRI, see Small Industry Research Institute (SIRI)

Sita Books & Periodicals Pvt Ltd+
308, Arjun Centre, Govandi Station Rd, Govandi (E), Govandi, Mumbai 400 088
Mailing Address: PO Box TF B-8, Govandi, Mumbai 400 088
Tel: (022) 5555589; (022) 5973281; (022) 5973282; (022) 5973283 *Fax:* (022) 5561622
E-mail: ssrao@bom5.vsnl.net.in; sitabook@bom7.vsnl.net.in
Web Site: www.sitabooks.com
Telex: SITAJAB
Key Personnel
Contact: S S Rao
Founded: 1987
Also acts as International Publishers Agent.
Subjects: Accounting, Advertising, Aeronautics, Aviation, Agriculture, Architecture & Interior Design, Automotive, Biological Sciences, Business, Chemistry, Chemical Engineering, Child Care & Development, Civil Engineering, Computer Science, Economics, Education, Electronics, Electrical Engineering, Energy, Engineering (General), Environmental Studies, Fashion, Finance, Labor, Industrial Relations, Library & Information Sciences, Literature, Literary Criticism, Essays, Management, Maritime, Marketing, Mathematics, Mechanical Engineering,

Microcomputers, Physics, Psychology, Psychiatry, Publishing & Book Trade Reference, Technology
ISBN Prefix(es): 81-86052
Parent Company: Sita Books
Associate Companies: Sita Books & Periodicals Pvt Ltd, 308, Arjun Centre, Govandi(E), Mumbai 400 088 *Tel:* (022) 5561622 *Fax:* (022) 5561622
Branch Office(s)
Sita Books & Periodicals, 'Sita Villa', Chakrapani Rd, Mangalore 575 001 *Tel:* (0824) 426968 (behind K M C Hospital)
Bookshop(s): Herikripa,, 3 Krishna, Govandi(E), Mumbai 400 088

Small Industry Research Institute (SIRI)+
Gali No 6, 4/43, Roop Nagar, New Delhi 110007
Tel: (011) 23841893; (011) 2916804 *Fax:* (011) 2910805
E-mail: siri@ndf.vsnl.net.in; siricon@vsnl.com
Key Personnel
Dir: D C Gupta
Founded: 1972
Industrial consultancy, publishing & exporting of industrial process technology books, directories, project reports, etc.
Membership(s): Capexil; FIP; DSBPA; JBC (FICCI); ITA (London) Niesbud; BIS (Lib); Indo German Chamber of Commerce & Industry; Indo Italian Chamber of Commerce.
Subjects: Technology
ISBN Prefix(es): 81-85480
Number of titles published annually: 15 Print
Total Titles: 120 Print
Subsidiaries: SIRI Consultants & Engineers
Showroom(s): Small Industry Research Institute, 4/43, Roop Nagar, Delhi 110007

Somaiya Publications Pvt Ltd+
Fazalbhoy Bldg, 45/47 M G Rd, Fort Mumbai 400 001
Tel: (022) 2048272 *Fax:* (022) 2047297
Web Site: www.somaiya.com
Telex: 0118-4588 SOC IN *Cable:* MANIKAKA
Key Personnel
Chairman: Dr S K Somaiya *E-mail:* mridughar@bol.net.in
Mumbai Executive: K S Hattangadi
Delhi Executive: T V Kunni Krishnan
Ordering Contact: Mr N S Narayanan
Founded: 1967
Membership(s): Federation of Indian Publishers.
Subjects: Agriculture, Anthropology, Archaeology, Asian Studies, Astrology, Occult, Behavioral Sciences, Business, Communications, Disability, Special Needs, Economics, Education, Engineering (General), English as a Second Language, Fiction, Government, Political Science, History, Journalism, Labor, Industrial Relations, Language Arts, Linguistics, Management, Marketing, Mechanical Engineering, Music, Dance, Nonfiction (General), Parapsychology, Philosophy, Psychology, Psychiatry, Religion - Buddhist, Religion - Hindu, Social Sciences, Sociology, Technology, Women's Studies
ISBN Prefix(es): 81-7039
Total Titles: 300 Print
Parent Company: The Godavari Sugar Mills Ltd
Associate Companies: The Book Centre Ltd, Ranade Rd, Dadar, Mumbai 400028 (Book Sales Division); The Book Centre Ltd, Plot No 103, Sixth Rd, Sion, Mumbai, Contact: S S Sathe *Tel:* (022) 4076812; (022) 4077416 (Printing Press Division)
Branch Office(s)
Bank of Baroda Bldg, 6th floor, Parliament St, New Delhi 110 001 *Tel:* (011) 3324929; (011) 3324939; (011) 3325134 *Fax:* (011) 3723351

South Asia Publications+
29, Central Market, Ashok Vihar, Delhi 110052

Tel: (011) 7241869; (011) 7235539
Key Personnel
Contact: S P Garg
Founded: 1986
Subjects: Advertising, Agriculture, Anthropology, Art, Business, Economics, Finance, History, Management, Religion - Other
ISBN Prefix(es): 81-7433
Associate Companies: SanPark Press Pvt Ltd

South Asian Publishers Pvt Ltd+
36, Netaji Subhash Marg, Darya Ganj, New Delhi 110002
Tel: (011) 276292; (011) 276740
E-mail: vchigs@giasdla.vsnl.net.in
Key Personnel
Chief Executive, Editorial, Rights & Permissions: Vinod Kumar
Production, Publicity: K A Rastogi
Founded: 1980
Specialize in International Relations.
Subjects: Anthropology, Asian Studies, Biological Sciences, Chemistry, Chemical Engineering, Civil Engineering, Developing Countries, Electronics, Electrical Engineering, Engineering (General), Environmental Studies, Government, Political Science, Labor, Industrial Relations, Mathematics, Physics, Religion - Buddhist, Religion - Hindu, Science (General), Social Sciences, Sociology, Technology
ISBN Prefix(es): 81-7003
Warehouse: Sector IX, H 65, UP India

Spectrum Publications+
Hembarua Rd, Pan Bazar, Guwahati, Assam 781001
Mailing Address: PO Box 45, Guwahati, Assam 781001
Tel: (0361) 26381; (0361) 24791 *Fax:* (0361) 544791 *Cable:* UNIPUB GUWAHATI
Key Personnel
Publisher: Krishan Kumar
Editorial: Ms Aarti Kumar
Sales: Ms Anita Kumar
Publicity: Ms Neha Kumar
Founded: 1976
Membership(s): Federation of Indian Publishers.
Subjects: Anthropology, Asian Studies, Social Sciences, Sociology, Travel
ISBN Prefix(es): 81-85319; 81-87502; 81-900396; 81-900750
Imprints: Aarti Books; Neha Mini Katha; Sunny Classics
Branch Office(s)
298 Tagore Park, Model Town 1, Delhi 110009
Tel: (011) 7122641
GS Rd, Shilcong 793001 *Tel:* (0364) 223476
Distributor for Abilac; DIPR Arunachal Pradesh; Law Research Institute; Nehu Publications
Showroom(s): 4754-57 Daryaganj, 23 Ansari Rd, New Delhi 110002
Bookshop(s): The Modern Book Depot, Panbazar, Main Rd, Guwahati 781 001; United Publishers
Orders to: United Publishers, Panbazar, PO Box 82, Guwahati 781001

Sree Rama Publishers
15-1-513 Siddiamber Bazar, Hyderabad 50012
Tel: (040) 2522609
E-mail: thehindu@usnl.com
Web Site: www.hinduonnet.com *Cable:* BOOKS SECUNDERABAD
Key Personnel
Man Dir: Shiva Ramaiah Pabba
Editorial: Sreenivas Prabhu Pabba
Sales: Subash Chandra Sekhar Pabba
Production, Publicity, Rights & Permissions: Shivarajaiah Pabba
Contact: P Bhaskar Rao
Founded: 1916
Subjects: Theology
ISBN Prefix(es): 81-7275

Parent Company: Sree Rama Book Depot, Market St, Secunderabad
Associate Companies: Popular Book House; Secunderabad; Sree Sita Rama Book Depot
Bookshop(s): Sree Rama Book Depot, Gunfoundry, Hyderabad 500001; Sree Rama Book Depot, Siddiamber Bazar, Hyderabad
Orders to: 113 Sarojinin Devi Rd, Secunderabad 500003

Sri Satguru Publications+
40/5 Shakti Nagar, 1st floor, Delhi 110 007
Tel: (011) 27126497; (011) 27434930 *Fax:* (011) 27227336
E-mail: ibcindia@giasdlo1.vsnl.net.in or ibcindia@ibcindia.com
Key Personnel
Man Dir, Rights & Permissions: Naresh Gupta
Export Dir: Sunil Gupta
Sales: Anil Gupta
Publicity: Virender Gupta
Founded: 1976
Subjects: Asian Studies, Music, Dance, Regional Interests, Religion - Buddhist
ISBN Prefix(es): 81-7030
Associate Companies: Bibliotheca Indo-Buddhica Series, 40/5 Shakti Nagar, Delhi 110 007; Sri Garib Dass Oriental Series, 40/5 Shakti Nagar, Delhi 110 007

Star Publications (P) Ltd+
4/5 B Asaf Ali Rd, New Delhi 110002
Tel: (011) 23268651; (011) 23286757; (011) 23258993; (011) 23261696 *Fax:* (011) 23273335; (011) 26481565
Web Site: www.starpublic.com
Key Personnel
Chairman & Man Dir: Amar N Varma
Chief Executive: Anil K Varma *Tel:* (011) 3258993
Production, Publicity: Sanjay Varma *Tel:* (011) 3274874
Dir: Sunil Varma *Tel:* (011) 6468427
Founded: 1957
Publisher & distributor of English & Indian language books.
Subjects: English as a Second Language, History, Language Arts, Linguistics, Literature, Literary Criticism, Essays, Religion - Hindu, Politics, Religion-Islam, Religion-Jain, Religion-Sikh
ISBN Prefix(es): 81-85243
Total Titles: 600 Print; 50 Audio
Associate Companies: Star Book Centre, 4/5B Asaf Ali Rd, New Delhi 110002
Subsidiaries: Publications India; Hindi Book Centre; Star Publishers Distributors
Showroom(s): Hindi Book Centre, Star Publications (P) Ltd
Bookshop(s): Hindi Book Centre
Shipping Address: D-92/3 Okhla Industrial Area I, New Delhi 110020

Sterling Information Technologies+
L-11, Green Park Extension, New Delhi 110 016
Tel: (011) 669560 *Fax:* (011) 26383788
Cable: PAPERBACKS
Key Personnel
Rights & Permission: Vikas Ghai
Editorial: Malhotra Vandana
Founded: 1993
Subjects: Computer Science, Management, Marketing, Microcomputers, Technology
Distributed by Goodwill Book Store (Philippines); S S Mubaruks Bros Pte Ltd (Singapore); Vanguard Books Ltd (Pakistan)

Sterling Press (P) Ltd, *imprint of* Sterling Publishers Pvt Ltd

Sterling Publishers Pvt Ltd+
A-59 Okhla Industrial Area, Phase II, New Delhi 110020

Tel: (011) 26387070; (011) 26386209; (011) 26386165; (011) 26385677 *Fax:* (011) 26383788
E-mail: info@sterlingpublishers.com
Web Site: www.sterlingpublishers.com *Cable:* PAPERBACKS
Key Personnel
Chairman & Man Dir: S K Ghai *E-mail:* ghai@nde.vsnl.net.in
Rights & Permissions: Shuchita Ghai
Editorial: Marry Joseph
Sales: Vikas Ghai
Production: Shreeh Kumar
Publicity: Mr Mohammed Khan
Export: Kusum Malik
Founded: 1965
Specialize in humanities & social science.
Membership(s): Federation of Indian Publishers; Asian Association of Scholarly Publishers; Afro Asian Book Council.
Subjects: Agriculture, Art, Asian Studies, Astrology, Occult, Biography, Communications, Developing Countries, Economics, Education, English as a Second Language, Fiction, Gardening, Plants, Government, Political Science, History, Journalism, Library & Information Sciences, Literature, Literary Criticism, Essays, Management, Medicine, Nursing, Dentistry, Philosophy, Public Administration, Religion - Hindu, Religion - Islamic, Religion - Other, Science (General), Social Sciences, Sociology, Technology, Women's Studies, Humanities
Associate Companies: Learners Press (P) Ltd, Sterling House, New Delhi
Imprints: Institute of Book Publishing; Sai Early Learners (P) Ltd; Sterling Press (P) Ltd

Stree+
Imprint of Bhatkal & Sen
16 Southern Ave, Kolkata 700 026
Tel: (033) 2466 0812 *Fax:* (033) 2464 4614; (033) 2466 6677
E-mail: stree@vsnl.com
Web Site: www.streebooks.com
Key Personnel
Dir: Mandira Sen *E-mail:* stree@cal2.vsnl.net.it
Founded: 1990
Publish women's studies in English & Bengali, also culture & dissent (under Samya imprint). Jointly founded by popular Prakashan, Mumbii & Mandira, Kolkata, who formed Bhatkal & Sen.
Subjects: Asian Studies, Women's Studies
ISBN Prefix(es): 81-85604
Total Titles: 30 Print
Imprints: Samya
Branch Office(s)
Popular Prakashan, 46481 Ansari Rd, 21 Daryaganj, Delhi 110002, Contact: C Kothari *Tel:* (011) 23265245 *E-mail:* populardel@mantraonline.com *Web Site:* www.samyabooks.com
Popular Prakashan, 35C Pandit MM Malariya Marq, Popular Press Bldg, Tardeo, Mumbai 400034, Contact: Harsha Bhatkal *Tel:* (022) 24941556 *E-mail:* harshab@hotmail.com
Distributed by Gazelle Book Services (UK, Europe & USA)

Sultan Chand & Sons Pvt Ltd
4859/24 Darya Ganj, New Delhi 110002
Tel: (011) 3266105; (011) 3277843; (011) 3281876 *Fax:* (011) 3266357
E-mail: nbcnd@ndb.vsnl.net.in
Key Personnel
Man Dir: Satish Agarwal *Tel:* 3278018
Founded: 1950
Membership(s): Federation of Publishers & Booksellers Associations of India.
Subjects: Accounting, Behavioral Sciences, Biological Sciences, Business, Career Development, Chemistry, Chemical Engineering, Computer Science, Economics, Education, Electronics, Electrical Engineering, Engineering (Gen-

eral), English as a Second Language, Finance, Geography, Geology, Government, Political Science, Health, Nutrition, History, How-to, Human Relations, Labor, Industrial Relations, Law, Management, Marketing, Mathematics, Physics, Public Administration, Self-Help, Social Sciences, Sociology, Technology
Distributed by Prakash Sons

Suman Prakashan Pvt Ltd+
24B/9, Desh Bandhu Gupta Rd, Dev Nagar, New Delhi 110 005
Tel: (011) 5842253; (011) 5721750 *Fax:* (011) 5754739
E-mail: info@sumanprakashan.com
Web Site: www.sumanprakashan.com
Key Personnel
Dir: R N Malhotra
Founded: 1970
Specialize in children's textbooks.
Membership(s): PHDCCI; FICCI.
Subjects: Art, History, Mathematics, Science (General)
ISBN Prefix(es): 81-85869; 81-7795
Associate Companies: Pearl (India) Publishing House (P) Ltd
Branch Office(s)
108, Lingapur Bldg, Amrutha Estate, Himayat Naggar, Hyderabad 500029 *Tel:* (040) 3224078
2, Bankim Chatterjee St, 2nd floor, Kolkata 700073 *Tel:* (033) 2190463
1st floor, Shiv Vindhaya Complex, Sector-22, mrapali Bazaar, Indira Nagar, Lucknow 226016
10 Kitab Bhavan Rd, North Shri Krishnapura, Patna 800013 *Tel:* (0612) 261093

Sunny Classics, *imprint of* Spectrum Publications

Surjeet Publications+
7-K Kolhapur Rd, Kamla Nagar, Delhi 110 007
Mailing Address: PO Box 2157, Kamla Nagar, Delhi 110 007
Tel: (011) 3914746; (011) 3914174 *Fax:* (011) 3918475
E-mail: surpub@del3.vsnl.net.in
Telex: 31-78101asiain
Key Personnel
Managing Partner: Harnam Singh
Founded: 1976
Also acts as bookseller, distributor & remainder dealer.
Subjects: Literature, Literary Criticism, Essays, Social Sciences, Sociology
ISBN Prefix(es): 81-229

Tara Publishing+
38/GA, Shoreham, Fifth Ave, Besant Nagar, Chennai 600090
Tel: (044) 24401696; (044) 24912846 *Fax:* (044) 24453658
E-mail: mail@tarabooks.com
Web Site: www.tarabooks.com
Key Personnel
Publisher: Gita Wolf *E-mail:* gita.wolf@tarabooks.com
Editorial Dir: V Geetha *E-mail:* v.geetha@tarabooks.com
Editorial Dir & Rights Manager: Sirish Rao *E-mail:* sirish.rao@tarabooks.com
Founded: 1994
Independent publishing house.
Subjects: Art, Asian Studies, Crafts, Games, Hobbies, Education, Fiction, History, How-to, Religion - Buddhist, Religion - Hindu
ISBN Prefix(es): 81-86211
Number of titles published annually: 15 Print
Total Titles: 50 Print
Foreign Rights: The English Agency (Japan); Alice Gruenfelder (Germany); Motovun (Japan); Sea of Stories (France & Spain); Servizi Editoriali (Italy); Sigma (Korea)

Shipping Address: Consortium Book Sales & Distribution, 1045 Westgate Drive, Saint Paul, MN 55114, United States, Contact: John Baynes *E-mail:* jbaynes@cbsd.com
Warehouse: Consortium Book Sales & Distribution, 1045 Westgate Drive, Saint Paul, MN 55114, United States, Contact: John Baynes *E-mail:* jbaynes@cbsd.com
Distribution Center: Consortium Book Sales & Distribution, 1045 Westgate Drive, Saint Paul, MN 55114, United States
Orders to: Consortium Book Sales & Distribution, 1045 Westgate Drive, Saint Paul, MN 55114, United States *Fax:* 651-221-0124 *E-mail:* nliberty@cbsd.com
Returns: Consortium Book Sales & Distribution, 1045 Westgate Drive, Saint Paul, MN 55114, United States, Contact: John Baynes *E-mail:* jbaynes@cbsd.com

DB Taraporevala Sons & Co Pvt Ltd
210 Dr D Naoroji Rd, Fort, Mumbai 400001
Tel: 2041433; 2041434 *Cable:* BOOKSHOP BOMBAY
Key Personnel
Chief Executive: Prof Russi J Taraporevala
Dir: Mrs Manekbai J Taraporevala; Miss Sooni J Taraporevala
Founded: 1864
Subjects: Art, Ethnicity, History, Social Sciences, Sociology

Tata McGraw-Hill Publishing Co Ltd+
Subsidiary of The McGraw-Hill Companies Inc
7, West Patel Nagar, New Delhi 110 008
Tel: (011) 2588 2743; (011) 2588 2746; (011) 2588 9304; (011) 2588 9307
E-mail: info_india@mcgraw-hill.com
Web Site: www.tatamcgrawhill.com
Key Personnel
Chairman: Dr F.A. Mehta
Founded: 1970
40% owned by McGraw-Hill Book Co, 1221 Ave of the Americas, New York, NY 10020, USA.
Subjects: Business, Engineering (General), Management, Science (General), Social Sciences, Sociology
ISBN Prefix(es): 0-07

Theosophical Publishing House
Division of Theosophical Society (Worldwide)
Adyar, Chennai 600020
Tel: (044) 412904 *Fax:* (044) 4901399; (044) 4902706
E-mail: intl-hq@ts-adyar.org
Web Site: ts-adyar.org *Cable:* THEOTHECA
Key Personnel
Manager: D K Govindaraj *E-mail:* theos.soc@gems.vsnl.net.in
Publications Officer: T Albert Echikwa *E-mail:* theos.soc@gems.vsnl.net.in
Founded: 1913
Provide books on Theosophy & Allied subjects at easily affordable prices. Do not buy rights but permit the use of excerpts conditionally.
Subjects: Biography, History, Human Relations, Mysteries, Parapsychology, Philosophy, Religion - Other, Science (General), Theology
ISBN Prefix(es): 81-7059
Total Titles: 291 Print
Associate Companies: TPH Manila, Iba St, Quezon City, Metro, Manila, Philippines *Tel:* (02) 741-5740 *Fax:* (02) 740-3751 *E-mail:* tspeace@mnl.sequel.net; Theosophical Publishing House, 306 W Geneva Rd, PO Box 270, Wheaton, IL 60189, United States *Tel:* (630) 665-0130 *Fax:* (630) 665-8791 *E-mail:* olcott@theosophia.org
Bookshop(s): Adelaide, Australia; Brisbane, Australia; Perth, Australia; Sydney, Australia; Victoria, Australia; Accra, Ghana; Amsterdam, Netherlands; Manila, Philippines; Quezon City, Philippines; Stockholm, Sweden; London, United Kingdom; CA, United States

Today & Tomorrow's Printers & Publishers+
24-b/5 Desh Bandhu, Gupta Marg, Karol Bagh, New Delhi 110005
Tel: (011) 5721928; (011) 5727770
Key Personnel
Man Dir, Editorial, Rights & Permissions: R K Jain
Sales, Publicity, Production: S K Jain
Founded: 1960
Membership(s): The Federation of Publishers & Booksellers Association of India; Chemical & Allied Product Export Promotion Council.
Subjects: Agriculture, Natural History, Science (General)
ISBN Prefix(es): 81-7019
U.S. Office(s): Scholarly Publications, 2825 Wilcrest, Suite 255, Houston, TX 77042, United States *Tel:* (713) 781-0070 *Fax:* (713) 781-2112
Distributed by Scholarly Pub (USA)

Transworld Research Network
37/661(2), Fort PO, Thiruvananthapuram, Kerala 695023
Tel: (0471) 2460384 *Fax:* (0491) 2573051
E-mail: ggcom@vsnl.com
Web Site: www.transworldresearch.com
Key Personnel
Man Editor: Shankar Pandalai
Publications Manager: Anandavalli Gayathri
Founded: 1996
Publishes review books in all areas of science, agriculture, medicine, pure science & technology. Also does CD-ROM production & software development.
Subjects: Agriculture, Medicine, Nursing, Dentistry, Science (General)
ISBN Prefix(es): 81-86846; 81-7895

N M Tripathi Pvt Ltd Publishers & Booksellers
164 Shamaldas Gandhi Marg, Mumbai 400002
Tel: (022) 22013651 *Fax:* (022) 22050048
Key Personnel
Man Dir & Executive Manager: K R Tripathi
Founded: 1888
Gujrati language & literature, poetry & novels.
Subjects: Business, Ethnicity, Religion - Hindu
ISBN Prefix(es): 81-7118
Total Titles: 50 Print
Parent Company: Bombay Booksellers & Publishers' Association, Mumbai
Ultimate Parent Company: Federation of Publishers' & Booksellers' Associations, Delhi

UBS Publishers Distributors Ltd
5 Ansari Rd, Darya Ganj, New Delhi 110 002
Tel: (011) 273601; (011) 3266646 *Fax:* (011) 3276593; (011) 3274261
E-mail: ubspd@ubspd.com
Web Site: www.ubspd.com *Cable:* ALLBOOKS
Key Personnel
Man Dir: C M Chawla
Exec Dir: Sukumar Das
Gen Mgr: Vivek Ahuja
Publish political, current affairs, cookery, religion, biography, fiction, self-improvement, management & general books. Distribute all types of books.
Subjects: Biography, Cookery, Fiction, Government, Political Science, Management, Religion - Other, Current Affairs, Self Improvement
ISBN Prefix(es): 81-7476; 81-85273; 81-85674; 81-85944; 81-86112
Branch Office(s)
6 First Main Rd, PO Box 9713, Ghandi-Nagar Bangalore 560 009 *Tel:* (0172) 2263901; (0172) 2263902; (0172) 2253903 *Fax:* (0172) 2263904

6 Sivaganga Rd, Nugambakkam, Chennai 700 016 *Tel:* (044) 8276355; (044) 8270189 *Fax:* (044) 8278920
8/1-B Chowringhee Lane, Kolkata 700-016 *Tel:* (033) 2441821; (033) 2442910; (033) 244973 *Fax:* (033) 2450027 *E-mail:* ubspdcal@cal.vsnl.net.in
80 Noronha Rd, Cantonment Kanpur 208 004 *Tel:* (0512) 369124; (0512) 362665; (0512) 352665, 357488 *Fax:* (0512) 315122
5 A Rajendra Nagar, Patna 800 016 *Tel:* (0612) 672856; (0612) 673973; (0612) 656170 *Fax:* (0612) 656169

UBSPD, see UBS Publishers Distributors Ltd

Vakils Feffer & Simons Ltd+
Hague Bldg, 9 Sprott Rd, Ballard Estate, Maharashtra, Mumbai 400001
Tel: (022) 2611221; (022) 2619121 *Fax:* (022) 2614924; (022) 2610432
Telex: oil83668vkilin *Cable:* FLEETBOOKS
Key Personnel
Dir: Mr Arun K Mehta
Founded: 1960
Subjects: Art, Cookery, Gardening, Plants, Management, Religion - Hindu, Religion - Islamic, Religion - Other, Travel
ISBN Prefix(es): 81-87111
Showroom(s): Vakil & Sons Ltd, Vakils House, 18 Ballard Estate, Mumbai 400001
Bookshop(s): Vakil & Sons Ltd, Vakils House, 18 Ballard Estate, Mumbia 400001

Vani Prakashan+
4697/5, 21-A Daryaganj, Ansari Rd, New Delhi 110002
Tel: (011) 23273167 *Fax:* (011) 23275710
E-mail: vani-prakashan@yahoo.com
Key Personnel
Chief Executive, Editorial, Production, Publicity & Sales: Arun Kumar Maheshwari
Founded: 1968
Subjects: Ethnicity, Fiction, History, Literature, Literary Criticism, Essays, Poetry, Hindi (with various subjects)
ISBN Prefix(es): 81-7055; 81-8143
Associate Companies: Navodaya Sales, 35, A, DDA Flat, Mansarovar Park, Shadhara, Delhi 32; Swarn Jyanti, 1/5971, Kabool Nagar, Shadhara, Delhi 32
Branch Office(s)
Book Corner, Sri Ram Center, Safdar Hashni Marg, New Delhi
Book Club(s): Jan Sulakh Pathak Manch

Vastu Gyan Publication
9/1, Institutional Area, Aruna Asat All Rd (opp Jnu East Gate), New Delhi 110067
Tel: (011) 3318730
Key Personnel
Author: Mr BB Puri
Subjects: Architecture & Interior Design
ISBN Prefix(es): 81-900614

Vidhi
Vibhagiya Prakashan Bikri Kendra, Vikas Bhawan, Secretariate, Patna 800015
Tel: (011) 389001 *Cable:* PATRIKA
Key Personnel
Sales Manager: C B Deogam
Assistant Manager: Ram Labhaya
Founded: 1975
Specialize in publications of the Acts in diglot form.
Subjects: Law
ISBN Prefix(es): 81-85956
Divisions: Vidhi Sahitya Prakashan

Vidhi Sahitya Prakashan, see Vidhi

Vidya Puri+
Balu Bazar, Cuttack 753002
Tel: (0671) 620637; (0671) 617260 *Cable:* VIDYAPURI
Key Personnel
Man Partner, Edit: Pitamber Mishra
Partner: Ramananda Mishra; Rupananda Mishra; Bhabananda Mishra; Jivananda Mishra
Sales: S K Sarangi
Founded: 1961
Subjects: Accounting, Animals, Pets, Biography, Biological Sciences, Business, Chemistry, Chemical Engineering, Computer Science, Literature, Literary Criticism, Essays
ISBN Prefix(es): 81-7411
Associate Companies: Goswami Press, Alamchand Bazar, Cuttack 753002; Graftek Pvt Ltd, Bhubaneswar 751002; Rainbow Offset (P) Ltd, Bhubaneswar 751002
Divisions: Vidyashre DTP Centre

Vidyarthi Mithram Press+
Market Rd, Kochi 11
Tel: (0481) 354003; (0481) 563282; (0481) 564713; (0481) 562616 (after office hours) *Fax:* (0481) 562616 *Cable:* VIDYARTHI
Key Personnel
Man Dir: Koshy P John
Founded: 1928
Subjects: Biography, Biological Sciences, Chemistry, Chemical Engineering, Child Care & Development, Computer Science, Cookery, Drama, Theater, Economics
Associate Companies: Auroville Publishers, Kottayam
Imprints: Kosi Books; Manosabdam Books
Branch Office(s)
Ernakulam
Kollam
Kozhikode
Palakkad
Thiruvalla
Thiruvananthapuram
Thrissur
Bookshop(s): Vidyarthi Mithram Book Depot, Baker Rd, Kottayam
Book Club(s): Vidyarthi Mithram Novel Club

Vikas Higher Education Books/Madhuban Educational Books, *imprint of* Vikas Publishing House Pvt Ltd

Vikas Publishing House Pvt Ltd+
576, Masjid Rd, Jangpura, New Delhi 110 014
Tel: (011) 24315313; (011) 24315570; (011) 24317857 *Fax:* (011) 24310879
E-mail: helpline@vikaspublishing.com
Key Personnel
Dir: Piyush Chawla; Sajili Shirodkar
Man Dir: C M Chawla
Founded: 1969
Vikas focuses on textbooks & professional books on management, computers, engineering & technology. Madhuban, the children's book imprint, offers a high quality range from preschool upwards.
Subjects: Chemistry, Chemical Engineering, Computer Science, Economics, Education, Engineering (General), Management, Mathematics, Physics, Science (General), Technology
ISBN Prefix(es): 81-259
Number of titles published annually: 100 Print
Total Titles: 1,200 Print
Imprints: Vikas Higher Education Books/Madhuban Educational Books
Distributor for Thomson Learning (Routledge)

Vision Books Pvt Ltd+
24 Feroze Gandhi Rd, Lajpat Nagar-III, New Delhi 110024
Tel: (011) 2386-2267; (011) 2386-2201 *Fax:* (011) 2386-2935

E-mail: mail@orientpaperbacks.com *Cable:* VISIONBOOK DELHI
Key Personnel
Chairman: Vishwa Nath
Man Dir, Rights & Permissions, Sales: Sudhir Malhotra
Publishing Dir: Kapil Malhotra
Publicity, Exports: Sidharth Malhotra
Editor: Dr O P Jaggi
Founded: 1975
Membership(s): Federation of Indian Publishers, Delhi State Booksellers & Publishers Association.
Subjects: Anthropology, Cookery, Education, Fiction, Health, Nutrition, History, How-to, Humor, Management, Medicine, Nursing, Dentistry, Military Science, Nonfiction (General), Religion - Other, Science (General), Travel, Career Guides, Fitness, Puzzle Books
ISBN Prefix(es): 81-7094
Total Titles: 700 Print
Associate Companies: Rajpal & Sons; Ravindra Printing Press; Shiksha Bharati; Vision Enterprises
Subsidiaries: Anand Paperbacks; Orient Paperbacks
Branch Office(s)
3-B Peddar Rd, Vasant Ground floor, Mumbai *Tel:* (022) 492 9343 *Fax:* (022) 496 0229
24 Firoze Gandhi Rd, Lajpat, Nagar *Tel:* (011) 2983-6470-80 *Fax:* (011) 2983-6490
3-6-280/A/5 Himayatnagar, Hyderabad *Tel:* (040) 2322-3252
Book Club(s): Anand Book Club; Orient Book Club

Vistaar, *imprint of* SAGE Publications India Pvt Ltd

S Viswanathan (Printers & Publishers) Pvt Ltd+
38, McNichols Rd, Chetput, Chennai 600 031
Tel: (044) 826 5623; (044) 826 5633 *Fax:* (044) 825 6002
E-mail: svprint@md2.vsnl.net.in
Key Personnel
Contact: Mr V Subramanian
Founded: 1971
Subjects: Biological Sciences, Chemistry, Chemical Engineering, Computer Science, English as a Second Language, History, Mathematics, Medicine, Nursing, Dentistry, Physics, Religion - Hindu, Science (General)
ISBN Prefix(es): 81-87156
Associate Companies: Beta Photo-Comps Pvt Ltd
Bookshop(s): Ananda Book Depot, 38, McNichols Rd, Chetput, Chennai 600 031

Viva Books Pvt Ltd+
4262/3 Ansari Rd, Daryaganj, New Delhi 110 002
Tel: (011) 3258325; (011) 3283121 *Fax:* (011) 3267224
E-mail: viva@mantraonline.com
Web Site: www.vivagroupindia.com
Key Personnel
Man Dir: Vinod Vasishtha
Subjects: Business, Career Development, Chemistry, Chemical Engineering, Child Care & Development, Civil Engineering, Communications, Earth Sciences, Economics, Education, Electronics, Electrical Engineering, Energy, Engineering (General), English as a Second Language, Environmental Studies, Management, Marketing, Mechanical Engineering, Military Science, Psychology, Psychiatry, Public Administration, Science (General), Social Sciences, Sociology, Technology, Travel
ISBN Prefix(es): 81-7649; 81-85617
Number of titles published annually: 100 Print
Total Titles: 500 Print

Vivek Prakashan
7-UA Jawahar Nagar, Delhi 110007
Tel: (011) 2529649; (011) 2944014 *Fax:* (011) 6827347
Key Personnel
Contact: Asha Rani
Founded: 1980
Subjects: Economics, Fiction, Literature, Literary Criticism, Essays, Social Sciences, Sociology
ISBN Prefix(es): 81-7004

A H Wheeler & Co Ltd+
23 Lal Bahadur Shastri Marg, Allahabad 211 001
Tel: (011) 3312629; (011) 3318537 *Fax:* (011) 3357798
E-mail: wheelerpub@mantraonline.com
Key Personnel
Contact: Arunjeet Banerjee
Founded: 1879
Membership(s): Federation of Indian Publishers.
Subjects: Accounting, Advertising, Behavioral Sciences, Business, Career Development, Civil Engineering, Communications, Computer Science
ISBN Prefix(es): 81-7544; 81-85614; 81-85814
Associate Companies: Wheeler Leather Corporation Ltd
Subsidiaries: Symonds & Co
Divisions: Wheeler Exports; Wheeler Offset Press; Wheeler Publishing
Branch Office(s)
Bangalore
Chennai
Delhi
Kolkata
Mumbai

Zebra Books for Children, *imprint of* Arnold Heinman Publishers (India) Pvt Ltd

Indonesia

General Information
Capital: Jakarta
Language: Bahasa Indonesia (a form of Malay) is official language. English is common second language. About 25 local languages & over 250 dialects are spoken
Religion: About 87% Islamic, 10% Christian & some Hindu & Buddhist
Population: 195 million
Bank Hours: Generally 0800-1400 Monday-Thursday; 0800-1500 Friday; 0800-1300 Saturday
Currency: Rupiah
Export/Import Information: Books subject to import tax & VAT tax. No exchange control. Books & printed matter using Indonesian languages prohibited. Importers require no license but are categorized into four groups for credit arrangement controls.
Copyright: No copyright conventions signed but Indonesia has recently enacted tougher domestic copyright laws

Mandira Jaya Abadi+
Jl Letjen, Mt Haryono 501, Semarang, Jawa Tengah 50241
Tel: (024) 3519547; (024) 3519548 *Fax:* (024) 3542189
Founded: 1984
ISBN Prefix(es): 979-490

Advent Indonesia Publishing
Jalan Raya Cimindi No 72, Yogyakarta
Tel: (022) 630392; (022) 642006 *Fax:* (022) 630588 *Cable:* Indopub
Key Personnel
Manager: Djinan Sinaga
Chief Editor: Jahotner F Manullang
Treasurer: Agus Ricky
Founded: 1954
Subjects: Child Care & Development, Health, Nutrition, Human Relations, Religion - Protestant, Religion - Other
ISBN Prefix(es): 979-504

Akadoma CV
Jl Kalasan No 1, Jakarta Pusat
Tel: (021) 3904323
Key Personnel
Man Dir: Adam Saleh

Al-Bayan, *imprint of* Mizan

Alma'Arif PT
Jl Tamblong No 48-50, Bandung 40112
Tel: (022) 4207177; (022) 4203708 *Fax:* (022) 439194
Key Personnel
Man Dir: H M Barthah
ISBN Prefix(es): 979-400

Alumni PT
Jl Dr Djundjunan, Bandung 40197
Tel: (022) 2501251; (022) 2503039; (022) 2503038 *Fax:* (022) 2503044
Telex: 28640
Key Personnel
Man Dir, Rights & Permissions: Eddy Damian
Editorial: Yayat Ruchiyat
Sales: Punomo
Production Manager: Philips
Founded: 1966
Subjects: Economics, Law, Medicine, Nursing, Dentistry, Psychology, Psychiatry, Social Sciences, Sociology
ISBN Prefix(es): 979-414
Branch Office(s)
Jl Jend A Yani 206E, Banjarmasin
Wisma Sawah Besar, 8th floor, Jl Sukarjo Wiryopranoto 30, Jakarta *Tel:* (021) 372730 (Telex: 46810 Alumni Ia)
Putri Hijaubaru 37, Medan *Tel:* (061) 510615
Jl Kartini 22B, Tanjungkarang *Tel:* (0721) 53135
Bookshop(s): H Juanda St 54, Bandung *Tel:* (022) 58290

Andi Offset+
Jln Beo No 38-40, Yogyakarta 55281
Tel: (0274) 561881 *Fax:* (0274) 588282
E-mail: andi_pub@indo.net.id
Key Personnel
Dir: J H Gondowijoyo
Founded: 1980
Membership(s): Indonesian Publishers Association.
Subjects: Accounting, Chemistry, Chemical Engineering, Computer Science, Electronics, Electrical Engineering, Management, Marketing, Science (General), Technology
ISBN Prefix(es): 979-533
Distributor for Prenhallindo

Angkasa CV+
Jl Merdeka, No 6, Bandung 40111
Mailing Address: PO Box 354/Ed, Bandung
Tel: (022) 4208955; (022) 4204795 *Fax:* (022) 439183
Telex: 28276 Panghegar Bandung
Key Personnel
Chief Executive: Dr Fachri Said
Editorial Manager, Rights & Permissions: R Djajoesman
Sales Manager: Kofindar
Production Manager: Tom Gunadi
Founded: 1966
Subjects: Fiction, Nonfiction (General), Religion - Other
ISBN Prefix(es): 979-404; 979-547; 979-665
Associate Companies: PT Mutiara Sumber Widya
Bookshop(s): Balai Buku Angkasa, Jl Merdeka, No 6, Jawa Barat, Bandung

PT Pustaka Antara Publishing & Printing+
Taman Kebon Sirih III/13, 10250 Jakarta Pusat
Tel: (021) 3156994; (021) 3156995 *Fax:* (021) 322745
E-mail: nacelod@indo.net.id
Key Personnel
Dir: Aida Joesoef Ahmad
Founded: 1952
Membership(s): Board of IKAPI (Indonesian Publishers Association)
Also acts as Director of Research, Training & International Relations.
Subjects: Religion - Islamic
ISBN Prefix(es): 979-8013
Associate Companies: CV Idayus *Tel:* (06221) 322745
Warehouse: P T Demina, Jl Rempoa Mulya, No 12, Bintaro, Jakarta Selatan *Tel:* (021) 7370966; (021) 7370967

Aries Lima, see New Aqua Press

Aurora+
Jln Bambu Betung VII No 8, Bojong Indah, Jakarta 11740
Tel: (021) 5810413
Key Personnel
International Rights: Ms Nanik Hardjono
Subjects: Asian Studies, Biblical Studies, Education, Religion - Catholic, Religion - Protestant
ISBN Prefix(es): 979-564

Badan Penerbit Kristen Gunung Mulia
(Gunung Mulia Christian Publishing House Ltd Co)+
Jalan Kwitang 22-23, Jakarta 10420
Tel: (021) 3901208 *Fax:* (021) 3901633
E-mail: corp.off@bpkgm.com
Web Site: www.bpkgm.com
Key Personnel
President: Ichsan Gunawan *E-mail:* ichsan@bpkgm.com
Dir: Viveka Nanda Leimena
Founded: 1951
Membership(s): CBA.
Subjects: Christian, Theological General Literature
ISBN Prefix(es): 979-415; 979-9290
Number of titles published annually: 100 Print
Total Titles: 900 Print

Balai Pustaka+
Jl Gunung Sahari Raya No 4, Jakarta Pusat 10710
Tel: (021) 3447003; (021) 3447006 *Fax:* (021) 3446555
E-mail: mail@balaiperaga.com
Web Site: www.balaiperaga.com
Telex: 45905 Pnbp Jkt *Cable:* PERUM BALAI PUSTAKA
Key Personnel
President, Dir: Dr Zakaria Idris
Editorial, Production Dir: Kuntjono Sastrodarmodjo
Sales, Publicity Dir: Dr Chasan Mintara
Rights & Permissions Dir: Ismu Amran
Founded: 1917
Subjects: Education, Ethnicity
ISBN Prefix(es): 979-651
Branch Office(s)
Jl Pulogadung Kav Jl5, Pulogadung, Jakarta Timur
Jl Rawagate 17, Pulogadung, Jakarta Timur
Book Club(s): KPI (Klub Perpustakaan Indonesia)

Bhratara Karya Aksara+
Jl Rawabal, Kawawan Industri Pulogadung, Jakarta, Timur 13340
Tel: 021 81858
Telex: 48292 Bhranmia
Key Personnel
President: Ahmad Jayusman
Dir: Adit Jayusman; Robinson Rusdi
Founded: 1958
Membership(s): IKAPI. Sales agent of UNU, UNESCO, ICPE, Journal IMMA, IDRC Pubs. Also printer & book importer/exporter.
Subjects: Agriculture, Economics, Education, Health, Nutrition, History, Language Arts, Linguistics, Science (General), Social Sciences, Sociology, Technology
ISBN Prefix(es): 979-410
Subsidiaries: P T Bhratara Tekno Komputer
Divisions: P T Karya Upaya Arta
Branch Office(s)
Jogja
Malang
Medan
Padang
Surabaya Ujung Pandang
Distributed by Indonesian Book Sellers
Distributor for ICPE; IDRC; Journal Muslim Minority Affairs; UNESCO
Showroom(s): Bhratara Bookshop, Jl Otista III/29, Jakarta, India *Tel:* (021) 8191858
Bookshop(s): Bhratara Bookshop, Jl Otista III/29, Jakarta, Timur, India *Tel:* 021 8191858
Shipping Address: Bhratara Bookshop, Jl Otista III/29, Jakarta, Timur *Tel:* (021) 8191858
Warehouse: Bhratara Bookshop, Jl Otista III/29, Jakarta, Timur *Tel:* (021) 8191858
Orders to: Bhratara Bookshop, Jl Otista III/29, Jakarta, Timur *Tel:* (021) 8191858

Bina Aksara Parta+
Jln Raya Ubud, 80571 Bali
Tel: (361) 95240
Key Personnel
Contact: Silvio Santosa
Founded: 1983
Subjects: Fiction, Music, Dance, Religion - Hindu, Travel
ISBN Prefix(es): 979-8042
Associate Companies: Orti Co, Jl Sandat 22, Ubud, Bali 80571
Orders to: Orti Co, PO Box 20, Ubud, Bali 80571

Bina Cipta PT
Jl Ganesha No 4, Bandung
Tel: (022) 2504319 *Fax:* (022) 2504319
Key Personnel
Dir: O Bardin
ISBN Prefix(es): 979-8928

Bina Ilmu
Jl Tunjungan No 53 E-F, Surabaya 60275
Tel: (031) 5323214; (031) 5340076 *Fax:* (031) 5315421
Key Personnel
Man Dir: H Mc Ariefin Noor
ISBN Prefix(es): 979-422

Bina Rena Pariwara
Jl Pejaten Raya No 5-E, Pasar Minggu, Jakarta Selatan 12510
Tel: (021) 7901938 *Fax:* (021) 7901939
Key Personnel
President & Dir: Yullia Himawati
Founded: 1988
Membership(s): Indonesian Publishers Association (IKAPI).
Subjects: Communications, Economics, Education, Finance, Government, Political Science, Nonfiction (General), Religion - Islamic, Travel
ISBN Prefix(es): 979-8175; 979-9056

Parent Company: Yayasan Bina Pembangunan (Development Foundation)
Associate Companies: Center for Fiscal & Monetary Studies-CFMS
Divisions: BRP Consultant Division
Distributor for Pt Penakencana Nusadwipa
Bookshop(s): Most Big Book Stores in the Capital Cities of All Provinces in Indonesia
Book Club(s): Indonesian Publishers Association (IKAPI)
Warehouse: Depok Bogor

Biro Pusat Statistik (Bureau of Statistical Information System)
Jl dr Sutomo No 8, Kotak Pos 1003, Jakarta 10010
Tel: (021) 3507057 *Fax:* (021) 3857046
E-mail: bpsha@bps.go.id
Web Site: www.bps.go.id
Telex: 45159 *Cable:* KBPS
Key Personnel
Chief of Bureau: Yuwono Hadipramono

PT Bulan Bintang+
Jl Kramat Kitang I/8, Jakarta Pusat 10420
Tel: (021) 3901651; (021) 3901652 *Fax:* (021) 3107027 *Cable:* BULANBINTANG
Key Personnel
President: Amran Zamzami
Vice President, Editor-in-Chief: Fauzi Amelz
Founded: 1954
Subjects: Art, Business, Economics, Education, Engineering (General), Fiction, Finance, Government, Political Science, History, Law, Literature, Literary Criticism, Essays, Nonfiction (General), Philosophy, Psychology, Psychiatry, Religion - Islamic, Science (General), Social Sciences, Sociology, Sports, Athletics, Technology
ISBN Prefix(es): 979-418

Bumi Aksara PT+
Jl Sawo Raya No 18, Rawamangun, Jakarta Timur 13220
Tel: (021) 4717049; (021) 4700988 *Fax:* (021) 4700989
Key Personnel
Dir: H Amir Hamzah
Founded: 1990
Membership(s): Indonesian Book Association.
Subjects: Accounting, Agriculture, Business, Economics, Law, Management, Marketing, Religion - Islamic
ISBN Prefix(es): 979-526

Institut Dagang Muchtar
Jl Embong Wungu 8, Surabaya
Tel: (031) 42973
ISBN Prefix(es): 979-417

PT Dian Rakyat+
Kawasan Industri Pulogadung, Jl Rawa Gelam I No 4, Jakarta Timur
Tel: (021) 460-4444
Telex: 62338 Fega Ia *Cable:* DIAN RAKYAT
Key Personnel
Dir: H Mohammad Ais
Publishing Division Man: Mlle Harmiel M Soekardjo
Founded: 1963
Subjects: Cookery, Economics, Literature, Literary Criticism, Essays, Medicine, Nursing, Dentistry
ISBN Prefix(es): 979-523

Dinastindo+
Jl Senopati No 54, Kebayoran Baru, Jakarta 12110
Tel: (021) 7250002; (021) 72799307 *Fax:* (021) 7262145
E-mail: dinastindo@yahoo.com

Key Personnel
Contact: Rijanto Tosin
Founded: 1984
Membership(s): ASP: IKAPI; Apkomindo.
Subjects: Business, Career Development, Computer Science, Management, Self-Help
ISBN Prefix(es): 979-552
Branch Office(s)
Surabaya & Bandung
Distributor for Abdi Tandu Publisher; Der Die Das; Pisi 2 Ribu Software; Solid Pro Publisher

Dioma, Kanisius, Obor, *imprint of* Nusa Indah

Diponegoro CV+
Jl Mohammad Toha 44-46, Bandung 40252
Tel: (022) 5201215 *Fax:* (022) 5201215 *Cable:* C V DIPONEGORO BANDUNG
Key Personnel
Man Dir: H A Dahlan
Editorial, Sales, Production, Publicity: Dr Anwaruddin
Founded: 1963
Membership(s): Indonesian Publishers Association.
Subjects: Religion - Other
ISBN Prefix(es): 979-8155; 979-9405

Djambatan PT
Jl Kramat Raya, Jakarta 10430
Tel: (021) 7203199 *Fax:* (021) 7208562
Key Personnel
Manager: Roswitha Pamoentjak
Founded: 1958
Subjects: Art, Literature, Literary Criticism, Essays, Philosophy, Religion - Other, Social Sciences, Sociology
ISBN Prefix(es): 979-428

Dunia Pustaka Jaya PT
Jl Kramat Raya 5-K, Jakarta Pusat 10450
Tel: (021) 3909322; (021) 3909284 *Fax:* (021) 3909320 *Cable:* Depeje
Key Personnel
Dir: Ahad Rifai
Editor: S W Rukasah; Sugiarta Sriwibawa
Founded: 1971
Subjects: Art, Drama, Theater, Ethnicity, Fiction, Literature, Literary Criticism, Essays, Philosophy, Poetry
ISBN Prefix(es): 979-419

Duta Wacana University Press+
Jl Dr Wahidin 5-19, Yogyakarta 55224
Tel: (0274) 563929 *Fax:* (0274) 513235
E-mail: humas@ukdw.ac.id
Web Site: www.ukdw.ac.id
Telex: 25486 UKDW IA
Key Personnel
Dir: S H Hadi Purnomo
Founded: 1989
ISBN Prefix(es): 979-8139

Eresco PT
Jl Megger Girang No 98, Bandung 40254
Tel: (022) 5205985 *Fax:* (022) 5205984 *Cable:* Erescopete Bandung
Key Personnel
Man Dir: Dr Arfan Razali
Editorial: Dr H Rochmat Soemitro
Sales: Mr Amun; Mr Harsono
Founded: 1956
Subjects: Economics, Law, Philosophy, Psychology, Psychiatry
ISBN Prefix(es): 979-8020
Bookshop(s): Jl Perapatan 22 Pav, Jakarta *Tel:* (021) 368000
Book Club(s): Himpunan Masyarakat Pencinta Buku (HMPB)

Penerbit Erlangga
Jl H Baping Raya No 100, Ciracas, Jakarta 13740

Tel: (021) 8717006 *Fax:* (021) 8717011
E-mail: erlprom@rad.net.id
Web Site: www.erlangga.com
Key Personnel
Dir: Gunawan Hutauruk
ISBN Prefix(es): 979-411

Fortunajaya+
Jl Diponegoro 11, Klaten
Tel: (0272) 22030 *Fax:* (0272) 22543
Founded: 1985
ISBN Prefix(es): 979-557
Showroom(s): Jln Pemuda, Selatan 44 B, Klaten

Gaya Favorit Press+
Jl HR Rasuna Said, Kav B 32-33, Jakarta Selatan 12910
Mailing Address: Kuningan
Tel: (021) 513816 *Fax:* (021) 5209366; (021) 4609115
E-mail: ptgfp1@rad.net.id
Telex: 62338 Fega IA
Key Personnel
Man Dir: Mirta Kartohadiprodjo
Editorial: Wied Harry Apriadji
Sales: Irwan SLT
Editorial, Publicity, Rights & Permissions: R H Yus Kayam
Founded: 1972
Subjects: Crafts, Games, Hobbies, Fiction, Nonfiction (General)
ISBN Prefix(es): 979-515
Parent Company: PT Gaya Favorit Press, Jln HR Rasuna Said blok B, Kav 32-33, Jakarta 12910

Gramedia+
Jl Palmerah Selatan 22-28, Jakarta Pusat 10270
Tel: (021) 5483008; (021) 5490666 *Fax:* (021) 5300545
Web Site: www.gramedia.co.id
Telex: Kompas Jkt 46327 *Cable:* KOMPAS JAKARTA
Key Personnel
President: Jakob Detama
Group Director: Teddy Surianto
Executive Manager: Al Adhi Mardhiyond
Production: Slamet M Jaeni
Rights & Permissions: Puspita Dewi
Publicity: Y Suliantoro
Founded: 1985
Publisher, software house, multimedia.
Specialize in educational software & comics.
Subjects: Accounting, Animals, Pets, Antiques, Child Care & Development, Computer Science, Cookery, Crafts, Games, Hobbies, Electronics, Electrical Engineering, Fiction, Gardening, Plants, How-to, Management, Microcomputers, Mysteries, Technology
ISBN Prefix(es): 979-511; 979-605; 979-655; 979-686
Parent Company: Kompas-Gramedia Group

PT BPK Gunung Mulia (Gunung Mulia Christian Publishing House Limited Company)+
Jl Kwitang 22-23, Jakarta Pusat 10420
Tel: (021) 3901208 *Fax:* (021) 3901633
E-mail: corp.off@bpkgm.com
Web Site: www.bpkgm.com
Key Personnel
Dir: Budi Arlianto
Founded: 1950
Subjects: Religion - Other
ISBN Prefix(es): 979-415; 979-9290
Bookshop(s): Toko Buku PT BPK Gunung Mulia

Harris+
Jln Veteran GOR 6, Medan
Tel: (061) 22272
Key Personnel
Man Dir: Ny Maswari

Founded: 1952
Membership(s): Indonesian Publishers Association.

ILMU-ILMU Islam, *imprint of* Mizan

PT Indira+
Jl Borobudur No 20, Jakarta, Pusat 10320
Tel: (021) 3904290; (021) 3148868 *Fax:* (021) 3929373
E-mail: indirawb@mweb.co.id
Key Personnel
Man Dir: Dr Bambang P Wahyudi
Founded: 1950
Subjects: Automotive, Business, Career Development, Computer Science, Crafts, Games, Hobbies, Energy, English as a Second Language, Film, Video
ISBN Prefix(es): 979-8063
Parent Company: Grolier Inc, United States
Associate Companies: PT Widyadara
Subsidiaries: PT Radio Prambors-Commercial Radio Broadcasting

Indrajaya CV
Jl Jatibaru No 20, Jakarta Pusat
Tel: (021) 3457039; (021) 3457041 *Fax:* (021) 3457039

Institut Teknologi Bandung+
Jl Tamansari 64, Bandung 40116
Tel: (022) 2550935 *Fax:* (022) 2550935
E-mail: info-center@itb.ac.id
Web Site: www.itb.ac.id
Key Personnel
Editor-in-Chief: Sofia Niksolihin
Founded: 1959
Subjects: Chemistry, Chemical Engineering, Education, Electronics, Electrical Engineering, Engineering (General), Health, Nutrition, Mathematics, Science (General), Technology
ISBN Prefix(es): 979-8001; 979-8591; 979-9299

Islamiyah
Jln Sutomo 329, Kotakpos 11, Medan
Tel: (061) 25421

Karunia CV
Jln Peneleh 18, Surabaya
Tel: (031) 5344120 *Fax:* (031) 5343409
ISBN Prefix(es): 979-9039

Karya Anda, CV+
Jl Praban No 55, Surabaya 60001
Tel: (031) 5344215; (031) 522580; (031) 5315402 *Fax:* (031) 5310594
Key Personnel
Man Dir: Moechlis
Subjects: Agriculture, Anthropology, Automotive, Behavioral Sciences, Education, Environmental Studies, Fiction, Humor
ISBN Prefix(es): 979-8002

Katalis PT Bina Mitra Plaosan
Jl Pratama 111/18 Pulo Mas, Jakarta, Timur 13220
Tel: (021) 7510477
Key Personnel
Publisher, Rights & Permissions: Elisabeth Soeprapto-Hastrich
Senior Editor: Ms Rasfiati Iskarno
Marketing Supervisor: Gertrud Moeljono
Business Manager, Production: Kisbandi Soeprapto
Editorial Assistant, Publicity: Gabriella Martiyah
Founded: 1986
Subjects: Career Development, How-to, Literature, Literary Criticism, Essays, Nonfiction (General), Science (General)

ISBN Prefix(es): 979-8060
Imprints: Siemens-Penuntun Berencana

Kesaint Blanc+
Jl Lentong No 9, Narogong Raya Km 17116
Tel: (021) 4204847; (021) 4204851 *Fax:* (021) 4216792
Web Site: www.kesaintblanc.com
Key Personnel
Dir: Antonius Bangun
Founded: 1979
ISBN Prefix(es): 979-8295; 979-593
Associate Companies: Kesaint Krakatau; Kesaint Sibayak; Mitra Utama
Imprints: Megapoin; Oriental; Renaisans; Tamtan Gabara; Visipro
Branch Office(s)
Bandar Lampung
Bandung
Medan
Surabaya
Yogyakarta
Warehouse: Jl Mekar Sari, Cimanggis, Bogor

Kinta CV
Jl Tengku Cikditiro 54A, Jakarta 10310
Tel: (021) 5494751
Key Personnel
Man Dir: Dr Mohammad Saleh
ISBN Prefix(es): 979-8004

Kurnia Esanata
Jl Jenderal Sudirman Kav 36A, Jakarta Pusat 10420
Tel: (021) 361974; (021) 3104948
Telex: 44328
Key Personnel
Man Dir: Taufik H Das
ISBN Prefix(es): 979-446

Lembaga Demografi Fakultas Ekonomi Universitas Indonesia
Jl Salemba Raya 4, Jakarta Pusat, 10430
Tel: (021) 3900703; (021) 336434; (021) 336539 *Fax:* (021) 3102457
E-mail: demofeui@indo.net.id *Cable:* FEKODEM
Key Personnel
Dir: Dr Haidy A Pasay
Founded: 1964
Subjects: Child Care & Development, Developing Countries, Economics, Education, Environmental Studies, Ethnicity, Health, Nutrition, Labor, Industrial Relations, Library & Information Sciences, Social Sciences, Sociology, Women's Studies
ISBN Prefix(es): 979-525
Parent Company: Faculty of Economics University of Indonesia

Madju FA
Jl Sisingamangaraja 25, Medan 20215
Tel: (061) 711990; (061) 710430 *Fax:* (061) 717753
ISBN Prefix(es): 979-8005

Marfiah, CV
Jln Kalibutuh No 131, Surabaya
Tel: (031) 46023
Key Personnel
Man Dir: Ellyati Wahyuni

Megapoin, *imprint of* Kesaint Blanc

Mizan+
Jl Yodkali 16, Bekamin Suci, Bandung 40124
Tel: (022) 7200931
E-mail: info@mizan.com
Web Site: www.mizan.com
Key Personnel
President & Dir: Haidar Bagir

Man Dir: Putut Widjanarko *E-mail:* pututw@mizan.com
Founded: 1983
Membership(s): the Association of Indonesian Publishers (IKAPI).
Subjects: Asian Studies, Religion - Islamic
ISBN Prefix(es): 979-433
Imprints: Al-Bayan; ILMU-ILMU Islam; Mizan: Khazanah; Mizan Pustaka: Kronik Indonesia Baru; Mizan Sobat Bocah Muslim; Mizan Sahabat Remaja Muslim
Branch Office(s)
Jl Duren Tiga Selatan WII 8A, Jakarta
Bookshop(s): (Many throughout Indonesia, Singapore, Malaysia & Brunei)

Mizan: Khazanah, *imprint of* Mizan

Mizan Pustaka: Kronik Indonesia Baru, *imprint of* Mizan

Mizan Sahabat Remaja Muslim, *imprint of* Mizan

Mizan Sobat Bocah Muslim, *imprint of* Mizan

Mutiara Sumber Widya PT+
Gedurg Maya Indah, Jakarta Pusat 10440
Tel: (021) 3909864; (021) 3909261; (021) 3909247 *Fax:* (021) 3160313
Telex: 46709 Mutiara Ia
Key Personnel
Chief Executive: H Firdaus Oemar
Dir: Fahmi Umar
Subjects: Economics, Education, Mathematics, Music, Dance, Physics, Religion - Other
ISBN Prefix(es): 979-8011; 979-9331
Associate Companies: CV Angkasa (Publishers)
Subsidiaries: CV Mutiara Bhakti; Mutiara Permata Widya

New Aqua Press
Kawasan Indrustri Pulo Gadung, Jl Rawagela II/4, Jakarta Timur 13012
Tel: (021) 4897566
ISBN Prefix(es): 979-441

Nusa Indah+
Jl El Tari, Ende Flores-NTT 86318
Tel: (0381) 21502 *Fax:* (0381) 21645; (0381) 22373 *Cable:* NUSAINDAHENDE
Key Personnel
Dir: Henri Daros *Tel:* (0381) 21081
Vice Dir & Sales Manager: Frans Ndoi
Man Editor: Lucas Lege
Production, Design: Eman Diaz
Library & Documents: Rofinus Jamin
Founded: 1970
Membership(s): Ikapi, Seksama, Kokosia, SVD Publishers, PLKI.
Subjects: Biblical Studies, Human Relations, Language Arts, Linguistics, Literature, Literary Criticism, Essays, Poetry, Religion - Catholic, Theology
ISBN Prefix(es): 979-429
Total Titles: 350 Print
Parent Company: PT ANI
Imprints: Dioma, Kanisius, Obor (East Indonesia)
Branch Office(s)
Gudang Buku Nusa Indah, Jln Polisi Istimewa 9, Surabaya 60265 *Tel:* (031) 5617746 *Fax:* (031) 5684307
Perwakilan Nusa Indah, Jln Matraman Raya 125, Jakarta *Tel:* (021) 8582403 *Fax:* (021) 8502403
Distributed by Dioma (East Java); Gramedia (all Gramedia bookshops in Jakarta, Surabaya, Kalimantan, Timor Timur, etc.); Kanisius (Central Java); Obor (Jakarta)
Showroom(s): Jln Matraman Raya 125, Jakarta 13012; Jln Polisi Istimewa 9, Surabaya 60265
Book Club(s): Kanisius Reading Community

Oriental, *imprint of* Kesaint Blanc

PATCO
Jln Sawahan Sarimulyo 14, Surabaya
Tel: (031) 310021
Key Personnel
Man Dir: Adolf Pattyranie
Founded: 1972
Subjects: Regional Interests
Bookshop(s): TB Puncak Agung, Pasar Tambahrejo Blok A 21A, Jl Kapas Krampung, Surabaya

Pelita Masa PT
Jl Lodaya No 25, Bandung 40262
Tel: (022) 50823
Key Personnel
Man Dir: Rochdi Partamatmadja

Pembimbing Masa PT
Pusat Perdagangan Senen, Blok 1, Lantai IV No 2, Jakarta, Pusat
Mailing Address: PO Box 3281, Jakarta Pusat
Tel: (021) 367645; (021) 366042
Key Personnel
Man Dir: Setia Dharma Majiid
ISBN Prefix(es): 979-8023
Bookshop(s): Pembimbing Masa PT

PT Bhakti Baru
Jln Jend Akhmad Yani 15, Ujung Pandang
Tel: (0411) 5192 *Fax:* (0411) 7156
Telex: 7156 Hakalla UP *Cable:* Bhakti Baru
Key Personnel
Man Dir: Dr H M Jusuf Kalla
Publicity Manager: Alwi Hamu
Founded: 1972
Subjects: Religion - Other
Branch Office(s)
Jl Lembang 9, Jakarta, India *Tel:* (021) 336364

PT Pradnya Paramita
Jl Bunga No 8-8A, Jakarta 13140
Tel: (021) 8583369 *Fax:* (021) 8504944
Cable: PRADNYA JKT
Key Personnel
President & Dir: Soenarto Sindoepranoto
Production Dir: Dr Mimien Saleh
Sales Executive: J Josojuwono
Editorial: A F Julianto
Founded: 1973
ISBN Prefix(es): 979-408
Bookshop(s): (See under Major Booksellers)

PT Pustaka LP3ES Indonesia
Jl Letjen S Parman 81, Slipi, Jakarta Barat 11420
Tel: (021) 5674211; (021) 5667139; (021) 56967920 *Fax:* (021) 5683785
Web Site: www.lp3es.or.id
Key Personnel
Dir: Imam Ahmad
Man Dir: Sudar Dwi Atmanto
Founded: 1971
Membership(s): The Institute for Economics & Social Research, Education & Information.
Subjects: Science (General)
ISBN Prefix(es): 979-8015
Parent Company: LP3ES

Pusat Penelitian Perkebunan Sumbawa+
Palembang, 30001 Sumsel
Mailing Address: PO Box 1127, Palembang 30001
Tel: (0711) 312182; (0711) 361793 *Fax:* (0711) 361793
Key Personnel
Contact: Mr Anwar Chairil
ISBN Prefix(es): 979-529

Pustaka Utama Grafiti, PT+
Utan Kayu Utara, Jl Utan Kayu No 68, E, F, G, Jakarta Timur 13120
Tel: (021) 8567502 *Fax:* (021) 8582430
Telex: 62797 TEMPO IA
Key Personnel
Man Dir: Zulkifly Lubis
Production Manager: A Rahman Tolleng
Commercial Manager: Yusril Djalinus
Founded: 1986
Membership(s): IKAPI.
Subjects: Anthropology, Art, Biography, Business, Economics, Government, Political Science, History, Humor, Literature, Literary Criticism, Essays, Philosophy, Religion - Other, Social Sciences, Sociology
ISBN Prefix(es): 979-444
Parent Company: Grafiti Pers
Bookshop(s): Ancol, Pasar Seni, Jakarta Utara; Slipi Jaya Plaza, Basement, Jl S Parman Kav 17-18, Jakarta 11410; Pertokoan Italiano, Jl Margonda Raya No 166, Depok; J1 Sumatera 31 Block G-H, Surabaya
Warehouse: Jl Cipinang Kebembem I No 3 A, Jakarta Timur

Remaja Rosdakarya CV
Jl Ciateul 34-36, Bandung
Tel: (022) 5200287
ISBN Prefix(es): 979-514; 979-425; 979-692

Renaisans, *imprint of* Kesaint Blanc

Rosda Jaya Putra
Jl Kramat Raya 5J, Jakarta Pusat 10450
Tel: (021) 3904984; (021) 3901692; (021) 3904985 *Fax:* (021) 3901703
Key Personnel
Man Dir: H Rozali Usman
ISBN Prefix(es): 979-426

Sastra Hudaya PT
Jl Proklamasi 61, Jakarta Pusat
Tel: (021) 3904223
Key Personnel
Man Dir: Doddy Yudhista
ISBN Prefix(es): 979-8016

Universitas Sebelas Maret
Jl Ir Sutami No 36A, Surakarta
Tel: (0271) 646994; (0271) 646761; (0271) 646624 *Fax:* (0271) 46655
E-mail: due-uns@slo.mega.net.id; pptk-uns@slo.mega.net.id
Web Site: www.uns.ac.id
ISBN Prefix(es): 979-498
Bookshop(s): Toko Buku, Jln Ir Sutami 36A, Solo 57126

Siemens-Penuntun Berencana, *imprint of* Katalis PT Bina Mitra Plaosan

Sumatera Utara University Press
Jl Universitas 21A, Medan, Sumatera Utera 20155
Mailing Address: Sumatera Utara
Tel: (061) 811045 *Fax:* (061) 816264
Telex: 51753
Key Personnel
Chairman: Mukmin Saraan
ISBN Prefix(es): 979-458

Tamtan Gabara, *imprint of* Kesaint Blanc

Tintamas Indonesia PT+
Jl Kramat Raya No 60, Jakarta Pusat 10420
Tel: (021) 3107148; (021) 7393701 *Fax:* (021) 3911459; (021) 3107148
Key Personnel
Dir: Marhamah Djambek

Founded: 1947
Membership(s): IKAPI (Indonesian Publishers Association).
Subjects: Biography, History, Law, Philosophy, Religion - Other
ISBN Prefix(es): 979-590

Usaha Baru CV
Jln Apel Kedjoran 11/5, Surabaya
Tel: (031) 22128
Key Personnel
Man Dir: Imron Siregar

Visipro, *imprint of* Kesaint Blanc

Widjaya Penerbit
Jl Pecenongan No 48-C, Jakarta Pusat
Tel: (021) 3813446
Branch Office(s)
Jl Dalem Kaum 86, Bandung

CV Yasaguna
Jl Minangkabau, 44, Jakarta Selatan
Tel: (021) 8290422
Key Personnel
Manager: Hilman Madewa
Subjects: Agriculture
ISBN Prefix(es): 979-443

Yayasan Jaya Baya
Jln Penghela 2, Surabaya
Mailing Address: Kotakpos 250, Surabaya
Tel: (031) 41169

Yayasan Kawanku
Jln Setiabudi Raya, Gg Sumbangsih 11/3A, Jakarta
Tel: (021) 583100

Yayasan Lontar (Lontar Foundation)+
Jl Danau Laut Tawar No 53, Pejombongan, Jakarta 10210
Tel: (021) 574-6880 *Fax:* (021) 572-0353
E-mail: lontar@attglobal.net
Web Site: www.lontar.org
Key Personnel
Chairperson: Adila Suwarmo
Vice Chairperson: Indra Harbani
Secretary: Miriam Widodo
Treasurer: Fikri Jufri
Editor-in-Chief: John H McGlynn
Founded: 1987
Subjects: Art, Ethnicity, Literature, Literary Criticism, Essays
ISBN Prefix(es): 979-8083

Yayasan Obor Indonesia+
Jl Plaju, No 10, Jakarta Pusat 10230
Tel: (021) 3920114; (021) 31926978 *Fax:* (021) 31924488
E-mail: obor@ub.net.id
Web Site: www.obor.or.id
Key Personnel
Chairman & International Rights: Mochtar Lubis
General Manager: Kartini Nurdin
Founded: 1978
Subjects: Advertising, Asian Studies, Business, Child Care & Development, Developing Countries, Earth Sciences, Economics, Education, Environmental Studies, Government, Political Science, History, Literature, Literary Criticism, Essays, Military Science, Natural History, Nonfiction (General), Philosophy, Publishing & Book Trade Reference, Science (General), Social Sciences, Sociology, Technology, Global Issues, Human Rights
ISBN Prefix(es): 979-461
U.S. Office(s): Obor Inc, 501 Cherry St, Philadelphia, PA 19102, United States

Islamic Republic of Iran

General Information

Capital: Tehran
Language: Persian (Farsi), Turkish and Armenian in Northwest, Arabic in Southwest, Kurdish in Kurdistan (English or French also)
Religion: Islamic (Shi'a sect and some Sunni sect)
Population: 61.2 million
Bank Hours: Generally Winter: 0800-1300 Saturday-Thursday; 1600-1800 Saturday-Wednesday; Summer: 0730-1300, 1700-1900 Saturday-Wednesday, 0730-1130 Thursday
Shop Hours: Generally Winter: 0800-2000 Saturday-Thursday; 0800-1200 Friday; Summer: 0800-1300, 1700-2100 Saturday-Thursday, 0800-1200 Friday
Currency: 100 dinars = 1 Iranian rial
Export/Import Information: No tariff on books and advertising subject to VAT. Import licenses required. Publications offending public order, official religion or morality prohibited. Exchange controls, with new regulations issued each March.
Copyright: No copyright conventions signed

Amir Kabir Book Publishing & Distribution Co
PO Box 1136-54191, Tehran
Tel: (021) 3933996; (021) 3933997; (021) 3900751-2; (021) 3112118 *Fax:* (021) 3903747
Telex: 212421 NJR IR
Key Personnel
Dir: H Anwary
Production: Masdjed-Jamee
Publicity: A Poormomtaz
Sales: Emany
Founded: 1948
ISBN Prefix(es): 964-00
Parent Company: Sasman-e Tablighat-e Eslami
Subsidiaries: Shokufeh Books

Scientific and Cultural Publications
Ministry of Culture & Higher Education, 64 St, Sayyed Jamal-E-Din Asad Abadi Ave, Tehran
Tel: (021) 685475; (021) 686278
Founded: 1953
Subjects: History, Philosophy, Religion - Other, Science (General)
Bookshop(s): Enghelab St, Tehran

University of Tehran Publications & Printing Organization
Univ of Tehran, Control Administration, Enghelab Ave & 16 Azar St, Tehran
Tel: (021) 6462699; (021) 6419831; (021) 6405047 *Fax:* (021) 6409348
Web Site: www.ut.ac.ir
Key Personnel
Man Dir: Dr A Rastgou
Sales & Publicity: Mr R Farahani
Rights & Permissions: J Qajarieh
Founded: 1944
Bookshop(s): Enqelab Ave, Tehran

Iraq

General Information

Capital: Baghdad
Language: Arabic (official), and some Kurdish (English is the principal foreign language in Baghdad)
Religion: Islamic (predominantly the Shiite sect)
Population: 18.4 million
Bank Hours: Winter: 0900-1300 Saturday-Wednesday; 0900-1200 Thursday; Summer: 0800-1200 Saturday-Wednesday, 0800-1100 Thursday
Shop Hours: Winter: 0830-1430, 1700-1900 Saturday-Wednesday, 0830-1330 Thursday; Summer: 0800-1400, 1700-1900 Saturday-Wednesday, 0800-1300 Thursday
Currency: 1,000 fils = 20 dirhams = 1 Iraqi dinar
Export/Import Information: No tariffs on books & advertising. Import licenses required. Exchange control, influenced by annual foreign exchange budget. Importation by state trading company or established importer. The state trading company is the National House for Publishing, Distributing & Advertising, Aljamhuria St, 624, Baghdad.
Copyright: No copyright conventions signed

National House for Publishing, Distributing & Advertising
Rashid St, Baghdad
Mailing Address: PO Box 624, Baghdad
Tel: (01) 4251846
Telex: 2392 *Cable:* Donta
Founded: 1972
Firm is attached to the Ministry of Information & is the sole importer & distributor of newspapers, magazines, periodicals & books.
Subjects: Agriculture, Business, Economics, Education, Government, Political Science, Science (General), Social Sciences, Sociology

Ireland

General Information

Capital: Dublin
Language: English & Irish (Gaelic)
Religion: Predominately Roman Catholic, some Church of Ireland
Population: 3.8 million
Bank Hours: 1000-1230, 1330-1500 Monday-Friday. Open until 1700 one night a week
Shop Hours: 0900 or 0930-1730 Monday-Saturday
Currency: 100 Eurocents = 1 Euro; 0.787564 Irish pounds = 1 Euro
Export/Import Information: Member of the European Community. BH & VMcK No tariff on books except on prayer & similar books from non-UK & children's picture books from non-EC. Pamphlets dutied from non-EEC. VAT is charged. No import licenses. Exchange controls.
Copyright: UCC, Berne (see Copyright Conventions, pg xi)

A & A Farmar+
Beech House, 78 Ranelagh Village, Dublin 6
Tel: (01) 4963625 *Fax:* (01) 4970107
E-mail: afarmar@iol.ie
Web Site: www.farmarbooks.com
Key Personnel
International Rights & Dir: Anna Farmar
Founded: 1992

Specializes in general literature, food & wine, business & social history.
Subjects: Business, Child Care & Development, Cookery, Literature, Literary Criticism, Essays, Wine & Spirits
ISBN Prefix(es): 1-899047
Number of titles published annually: 12 Print
Total Titles: 50 Print
U.S. Office(s): Irish Books & Media Inc, 1433 Franklin Ave East, Minneapolis, MN 55404-2135, United States
Orders to: Columba Mercier Distribution Ltd, 55A Spruce Ave, Stillorgan Industrial Park, Blackrock, Dublin

AIS
7 Merrion Sq, Dublin 2
Tel: (01) 6616522 *Fax:* (01) 6612378
Also acts as distributor for all Irish language publications.
ISBN Prefix(es): 0-946339
Parent Company: Bord Na Gaeilge

An Gum+
44 Sraid Ui Chonaill Uacht, Baile Atha Cliath, Dublin 1
Tel: (01) 8734700 *Fax:* (01) 8731104
E-mail: gum@educ.irlgov.ie
Telex: 31136
Key Personnel
Editorial: Maire Nic Mhaolain
Production: John Dixon
Publicity: Seosamh O'Murchu
Founded: 1926
Subjects: Art, Cookery, Education, Geography, Geology, Mathematics, Science (General)
ISBN Prefix(es): 1-85791
Parent Company: The Department of Education, Dublin 1
Imprints: Oifig an tSolathair
Bookshop(s): Oifig Dhiolta Foilseachain Rialtais, Sr Theach Laighean, Dublin 2
Warehouse: Bishop S, Dublin 8
Orders to: An Ais, 31 Sr na bhFinini, Dublin 2

Atrium, *imprint of* Cork University Press

Attic Press, *imprint of* Cork University Press

Attic Press Ltd+
Imprint of Cork University Press (CUP)
c/o Cork University Press, Crawford Buiness Park, Crosses Green, Cork
Tel: (021) 4321 725 *Fax:* (021) 315 329
E-mail: corkunip@ucc.ie
Web Site: www.corkuniversitypress.com
Key Personnel
Publisher: Mike Collins *E-mail:* mike.collins@ucc.ie
Founded: 1984
Subjects: Biography, Cookery, Government, Political Science, Health, Nutrition, History, Humor, Literature, Literary Criticism, Essays, Social Sciences, Sociology, Women's Studies
ISBN Prefix(es): 0-946211; 1-85594
Orders to: Dufour Editions Inc, Buyers Rd, PO Box 7, Chester Springs, PA 19425-0007, United States *Tel:* 610-458-5005 *Fax:* 610-458-7103 *Web Site:* www.dufoureditions.com
Gill & Macmillan, Goldenbridge Hume Ave, Park West, Dublin 12
Marston Book Services Ltd, PO Box 269, Abingdon OX14 4YN, United Kingdom *Tel:* (01235) 465500 *Fax:* (01235) 465555 *E-mail:* trade.orders@marston.co.uk

Avoca Publications+
Lonsdale Avoca Ave, Blackrock, Dublin
Tel: (01) 889218
Founded: 1983

Subjects: Aeronautics, Aviation
ISBN Prefix(es): 0-9509206

Ballinakella Paperbacks, *imprint of* Ballinakella Press

Ballinakella Press+
Whitegate, Clare
Tel: (061) 927030 *Fax:* (061) 927418
E-mail: info@ballinakella.com
Key Personnel
President: Dr Hugh W L Weir
Vice President: Mrs Hugh W L Weir
Founded: 1984
Specialize in Irish historical, topographical, genealogical & biographical books.
Subjects: Architecture & Interior Design, Biography, Genealogy, Geography, Geology, History, Regional Interests, Travel
ISBN Prefix(es): 0-946538
Number of titles published annually: 2 Print
Total Titles: 32 Print
Parent Company: Weir Publishing
Imprints: Ballinakella Paperbacks; Bell'acards; Weir's Guides
Subsidiaries: Bell'acards

Beehive Books, *imprint of* Veritas Co Ltd

Bell'acards, *imprint of* Ballinakella Press

Blackwater Press, *imprint of* Folens Publishers

Blue Flag, *imprint of* The O'Brien Press Ltd

Brandon, *imprint of* Mount Eagle Publications Ltd

Brandon Book Publishers Ltd+
Cooleen, Dingle, Co Kerry
Tel: (066) 9151463 *Fax:* (066) 9151234
Web Site: www.brandonbooks.com
Key Personnel
Man Dir, Editorial: Steve MacDonogh
Founded: 1982
Subjects: Biography, Fiction, Literature, Literary Criticism, Essays, Nonfiction (General)
ISBN Prefix(es): 0-86322
Parent Company: Mount Eagle Publications Ltd
Orders to: Gill & Macmillan Distribution, Goldenbridge, Inchicore, Dublin 8

Edmund Burke Publisher+
Division of De Burca Rare Books
27 Priory Dr, Blackrock, County Dublin
Mailing Address: 51 A Dawson St, Dublin 2
Tel: (01) 2882159; (01) 6719777 *Fax:* (01) 2834080
E-mail: deburca@indigo.ie
Web Site: www.deburcararebooks.com
Key Personnel
Contact: Eamonn de Burca; Regina McAuley
Founded: 1980
Historical, topographical & genealogical works on Ireland.
Subjects: Biography, History, Academic, Bibliography
ISBN Prefix(es): 0-946130

Campus, *imprint of* Campus Publishing Ltd

Campus Publishing Ltd+
26 Tirellan Heights, Galway City
Tel: (091) 524662; (091) 767408 *Fax:* (091) 527505
Key Personnel
Publisher: Kevin T Brophy
Founded: 1990

Subjects: Drama, Theater, Education, Literature, Literary Criticism, Essays, Religion - Catholic, Religion - Protestant, Religion - Other, Self-Help, Social Sciences, Sociology, Playscripts
ISBN Prefix(es): 1-873223
Imprints: Campus; Playscripts

Careers & Educational Publishers Ltd+
Lower James St, Claremorris, County Mayo
Tel: (094) 71093
Key Personnel
Man Dir, Editorial, Publicity, Rights & Permissions: Eamonn Patrick O'Boyle
Sales: Christina O'Boyle
Production: William J O'Keeffe
Founded: 1976
Subjects: Career Development, Cookery, Crafts, Games, Hobbies, Education
ISBN Prefix(es): 0-906121
Imprints: Heritage Books
Bookshop(s): Eamonn P O'Boyle's Book Sales, Lower James St, Claremorris, County Mayo; Kilcolman Press Bookshop, Convent Rd, Claremorris, County Mayo

Cathedral Books Ltd
4 Sackville Pl, Dublin 1
Tel: (01) 8787372 *Fax:* (01) 8787704
E-mail: cathedra@indigo.ie
Subjects: Biblical Studies, Philosophy, Psychology, Psychiatry, Religion - Catholic, Self-Help, Theology, Women's Studies
ISBN Prefix(es): 0-9517132; 1-871337

Children's Poolbeg, *imprint of* Poolbeg Press Ltd

The Children's Press+
45 Palmerston Rd, Dublin 6
Tel: (01) 497-3628 *Fax:* (01) 496-8263
E-mail: cle@iol.ie
Web Site: www.irelandseye.com *Cable:* CHILDREN'S PRESS DUBLIN
Key Personnel
Publisher: John Murphy
Founded: 1981
Subjects: Biography, Fiction, History
ISBN Prefix(es): 0-900068; 0-947962; 1-901737
Parent Company: Anvil Books Lts

Clo Iar-Chonnachta Teo+
Indreabhan, Conamara, Galway, County Galway
Tel: (091) 593 307 *Fax:* (091) 593 362
E-mail: cic@iol.ie
Web Site: www.cic.ie
Key Personnel
Man Dir: Michael O'Conghaile
General Manager: Deirdre Thuathail
Marketing Executive: Caitriona Bhaoill
Founded: 1985
Most publications are in the Irish language.
Subjects: Drama, Theater, Fiction, History, Music, Dance, Poetry, Regional Interests
ISBN Prefix(es): 1-874700; 1-900693; 1-902420
Number of titles published annually: 15 Print; 2 Audio
Total Titles: 300 Print; 20 Audio
Distributed by Dufour Editions
Foreign Rep(s): Dufour Editions (Canada, USA)
Foreign Rights: AIS (Iceland); Maggie Doyle (France); Harry Smith (USA); Hansevik Tonnheiu (Sweden)

Clodhanna Teoranta
Chonradh na Gaeilge, 6 Sraid Fhearchair, Dublin 2
Key Personnel
Publicity Manager: Donnchadh O Laodha
ISBN Prefix(es): 0-905027; 0-9501264

The Collins Press+
West Link Park, Doughcloyne, Wilton, Cork

Tel: (021) 4347717 Fax: (021) 4347720
E-mail: enquiries@collinspress.le
Web Site: www.collinspress.com
Key Personnel
Contact: Con Collins
Founded: 1990
Independent Book Publisher.
Membership(s): Irish Publishers Association (CLE).
Subjects: Archaeology, Biography, History, Human Relations, Natural History, Photography, Drama, Mind, Body & Spirit
ISBN Prefix(es): 0-9516036; 1-895256; 1-903464
Number of titles published annually: 17 Print
Total Titles: 91 Print
Distributed by Columbia Mercier Distribution (Ireland & Northern Ireland); Drake International Services (Britain, Common Wealth & Europe); Dufour Editions (US); Irish Books & Media (US)
Foreign Rep(s): Brookside Publishing Services (Ireland, Northern Ireland)
Foreign Rights: AMV Agencia Literaria SL; Gundhild Lenz-Mulligan

The Columba Book Service+
Stillorgan Industrial Park, 55A Spruce Ave, Blackrock, Dublin
Tel: (01) 2942556 Fax: (01) 2942564
E-mail: info@columba.ie
Web Site: www.columba.ie
Key Personnel
Sales Dir: Cecilia West E-mail: west@columba.ie
Man Dir: Sean O Boyle
Founded: 1985
Membership(s): CLE (Irish PA); Booksellers Association of Great Britain & Ireland.
Subjects: Religion - Catholic, Religion - Protestant, Religion - Other, Self-Help, Theology
Associate Companies: The Columba Press
Distributor for Australian Theological Forum (ATF) (Australia); Canterbury Press (Ireland); Continuum (Ireland); Cowley Publications (USA); Eagle (Ireland); Michael Glazier (USA); The Liturgical Press (USA); Loyola Press (USA); Novalis (Canada); Paulist Press (USA); Pueblo Publishing (USA); Resource Publications (USA); St Mary's Press (USA); SCM Press (Ireland); Twenty-Third Publications (USA)

The Columba Press+
55A Spruce Ave, Stillorgan Industrial Park, Blackrock, Dublin
Tel: (01) 2942556 Fax: (01) 2942564
E-mail: info@columba.ie
Web Site: www.columba.ie
Key Personnel
Chief Executive & Editorial: Sean O'Boyle E-mail: sean@columba.ie
Sales Dir & International Rights: Cecilia West E-mail: west@columba.ie
Marketing & Publicity: Brian Lynch E-mail: brian@columba.ie
Founded: 1985
Membership(s): Cle-The Irish Book Publisher's Association.
Subjects: Art, History, Religion - Catholic, Religion - Protestant, Self-Help, Theology
ISBN Prefix(es): 0-948183; 1-85607
Total Titles: 250 Print
Imprints: Currach Press; Gartan, Preas Cholmcille
Subsidiaries: Columba Bookservice

Cork University Press+
Crawford Business Park, Crosses Green, Cork
Tel: (021) 4902980 Fax: (021) 4315329
E-mail: corkunip@ucc.ie
Web Site: www.corkuniversitypress.com
Key Personnel
Editorial Manager: Tom Dunne E-mail: t.dunne@ucc.ie

Sales & Marketing: Mike Collins E-mail: mike.collins@ucc.ie
Founded: 1925
Specialize in Irish studies, history, literature, cultural studies & politics.
Membership(s): CLE (Irish Publishers' Association).
Subjects: Archaeology, Geography, Geology, History, Social Sciences, Sociology, Women's Studies
ISBN Prefix(es): 0-902561; 1-85918; 0-9502440
Number of titles published annually: 10 Print
Total Titles: 150 Print
Imprints: Atrium; Attic Press
U.S. Office(s): Stylus Publishing LLC, 22883 Quicksilver Drive, Sterling, VA 20166-2012, United States, Contact: John von Knorring Fax: 703-661-1501 E-mail: stylusmail@presswarehouse.com Web Site: www.styluspub.com
Foreign Rep(s): Peter Prout (Spain & Portugal); Stylus (USA)

Currach Press, *imprint of* The Columba Press

Dee-Jay Publications+
3 Meadows Lane, Arklow, County Wicklow
Tel: (0402) 39125 Fax: (0402) 39064
Key Personnel
Contact: Jim Rees E-mail: jrees@eircom.net
Founded: 1992
Subjects: Biography, Genealogy, History, Maritime, Nonfiction (General), Travel
ISBN Prefix(es): 0-9519239
U.S. Office(s): Irish Books & Media Inc, 1433-E Franklin Ave, Minneapolis, MN 55404-2135, United States
Distributor for Arklow Enterprise Centre

Dominican Publications
42 Parnell Sq, Dublin 1
Tel: (01) 872-1611; (01) 873-1355 Fax: (01) 873-1760
E-mail: sales@dominicanpublications.com
Web Site: www.dominicanpublications.com
Key Personnel
Chief Executive, Editorial, Sales: Austin Flannery
Advertising, Production: Bernard Treacy
Founded: 1897
Subjects: Biography, History, Religion - Catholic, Theology, Books & periodicals on theology
ISBN Prefix(es): 0-9504797; 0-907271; 1-871552
Total Titles: 20 Print; 2 CD-ROM
Distributed by Columba
Book Club(s): Doctrine & Life Book Club; Religious Life Review Book Club; Scripture in Church Book Club

Dublin Institute for Advanced Studies
10 Burlington Rd, Dublin 4
Tel: (01) 6140100 Fax: (01) 6680561
Web Site: www.dias.ie
Telex: 31687 Dias Ei
Key Personnel
Registrar: John Duggan
Founded: 1940
Specialize in research & advanced study in Celtic studies & physics.
Subjects: Ethnicity, Physics
ISBN Prefix(es): 0-901282; 1-85500

Eason & Son Ltd
66 Middle Abbey St, Dublin 1
Tel: (01) 873 3811 Fax: (01) 873 3545
E-mail: info@eason.ie
Web Site: www.eason.ie
Telex: 32566
Key Personnel
Man Dir: Gordon Bolton
Editorial, Sales, Production, Publicity, Rights & Permissions: Tom Owens

Founded: 1886
Subjects: Regional Interests
ISBN Prefix(es): 0-900346; 1-873430
Imprints: Irish Heritage Series
Subsidiaries: Eason & Son (NI) Ltd; Eason Advertising
Warehouse: Brickfield Dr, Crumlin, Dublin 12

The Economic & Social Research Institute
4 Burlington Rd, Dublin 4
Tel: (01) 6671525 Fax: (01) 6686231
E-mail: admin@esri.ie
Web Site: www.esri.ie
Key Personnel
Dir: Prof Brendan J Whelan E-mail: brendan.whelan@esri.ie
Assistant Dir, Secretary, Sales & Publicity: Gillian Davidson E-mail: admin@esri.ie
Founded: 1960
Subjects: Economics, Education, Environmental Studies, Finance, Health, Nutrition, Social Sciences, Sociology
ISBN Prefix(es): 0-7070; 0-901809
Total Titles: 300 Print

The Educational Company of Ireland
Ballymount Rd, Walkinstown, Dublin 12
Tel: (01) 4500611 Fax: (01) 4500993
E-mail: info@edco.ie
Web Site: www.edco.ie
Key Personnel
Chief Executive: Frank Maguire
Executive Dir Sales & Marketing: Mr Oisin Mulcahy
Executive Dir: R McLoughlin
Founded: 1910
Firm is a trading unit of Smurfit Ireland Ltd.
Subjects: Business, Career Development, Computer Science, Ethnicity, Geography, Geology, History, Mathematics, Religion - Other, Science (General)
ISBN Prefix(es): 0-901802; 0-904916; 0-86167
Branch Office(s)
20-1 Talbot St, Dublin 1

Emerald Publications+
The Studio, 22 Summerstown Grove, Wilton Cork
Tel: (021) 962853 Fax: (021) 310983
E-mail: alongk@iol.ie
Key Personnel
Contact: Denis Linehan
Founded: 1980
Also acts as legal consultant.
Subjects: Criminology, Government, Political Science, Health, Nutrition, Law, Theology
ISBN Prefix(es): 0-9525813

Environmental Research Unit
St Martin's House, Waterloo Rd, Dublin 4
Tel: (01) 660 25 11 Fax: (01) 668 00 09
Telex: 30846 Cable: Foras Dublin
Key Personnel
Chief Executive Officer: L M McCumiskey
Information & Training: S Smyth
Founded: 1964
National Institute for Physical Planning & Construction Research.
Subjects: Environmental Studies
ISBN Prefix(es): 0-906120; 0-9500200; 0-9501356; 1-85053; 0-900115

Estragon Press Ltd+
Durrus, County Cork 7
Tel: (027) 61186 Fax: (027) 61186
E-mail: estragon@iol.ie
Key Personnel
Dir, Publisher, Author: John McKenna; Sally McKenna
Founded: 1991
Subjects: Cookery, Travel, Wine & Spirits
ISBN Prefix(es): 1-874076

European Foundation for the Improvement of Living & Working Conditions
Wyattville Rd, Loughlinstown, Dublin
Tel: (01) 2043100 *Fax:* (01) 2826456
E-mail: postmaster@eurofound.eu.int
Web Site: www.eurofound.ie
Key Personnel
Press Officer: Mans Martensson
Founded: 1975
Subjects: EU Social Policy
ISBN Prefix(es): 92-897

European Healthcare Management Association
Vergemount Hall, Clonskeagh, Dublin 6
Tel: (01) 283 9299 *Fax:* (01) 283 8653
E-mail: office@ehma.org
Web Site: www.ehma.org
ISBN Prefix(es): 0-907727

Fact Pack Ireland Guides, *imprint of* Morrigan Book Co

C J Fallon
Lucan Rd, Palmerston, Dublin 20
Key Personnel
Man Dir: H McNicholas
Editorial: N White
Secretary: P Tolan
Founded: 1927
ISBN Prefix(es): 0-7144

Fitzwilliam Publishing Co Ltd+
1488 Assumpta Villas, Kildare
Tel: (01) 614575 *Fax:* (01) 614575
Key Personnel
Man Dir: Kevin McCaffrey
Marketing: Tom Madden
Subjects: Education, Ethnicity
ISBN Prefix(es): 1-871423

Flyers, *imprint of* The O'Brien Press Ltd

Flyleaf Press+
4 Spencer Villas, Glenageary, County Dublin
Tel: (01) 2845906 *Fax:* (01) 2831693
E-mail: flyleaf@indigo.ie
Web Site: www.flyleaf.ie
Key Personnel
Man Editor: James Ryan *E-mail:* jim.ryan@circa.ie
Founded: 1982
Membership(s): Cle - Irish Book Publishers Association.
Subjects: Genealogy, Natural History, Family History
ISBN Prefix(es): 0-9508466; 0-9539974
Number of titles published annually: 2 Print
Total Titles: 16 Print
Distributed by Irish Books & Media (USA)

Folens Publishers+
Hibernian Industrial Estate, Greenhills Rd, Tallaght, Dublin 24
Tel: (01) 4137200 *Fax:* (01) 4137280
E-mail: info@folens.ie
Web Site: www.folens.ie
Key Personnel
Man Dir: John O'Connor *E-mail:* john.o'connor@folens.ie
Financial Controller: Aoife Geraghty
Primary Publisher: Deirdre Whelan
Secondary Publisher: Anna O'Donovan
Founded: 1957
Subjects: Education
ISBN Prefix(es): 0-86121; 0-902592; 1-84131
Associate Companies: Folens Limited, United Kingdom; JUKA-91 Spzoo, Poland
Imprints: Blackwater Press

Four Courts Press Ltd+
7 Malpas St, Dublin 8
Tel: (01) 453-4668 *Fax:* (01) 453-4672
E-mail: info@four-courts-press.ie
Web Site: www.four-courts-press.ie
Key Personnel
Man Dir: Michael Adams
Dir: Martin Healy *E-mail:* martin.healy@four-courts-press.ie
Founded: 1970
Subjects: Art, History, Law, Literature, Literary Criticism, Essays, Philosophy, Religion - Catholic, Theology, Celtic & Medieval Studies
ISBN Prefix(es): 0-906127; 1-85182
Number of titles published annually: 50 Print
Total Titles: 400 Print
Imprints: Open Air
Warehouse: Gill & Macmillan Book Distributors, Hume Ave, Park West, Dublin 12
Distribution Center: ISBS, 920 NE 58th Ave, Suite 300, Portland, OR 97213, United States (North America)
Orders to: Gill & Macmillan Book Distributors, Hume Ave, Park West, Dublin 12

The Gallery Press
Loughcrew, Oldcastle, Co Meath
Tel: (049) 8541779 *Fax:* (049) 8541779
E-mail: gallery@indigo.ie
Web Site: www.gallerypress.com
Key Personnel
Chief Executive, Editorial: Peter Fallon
Administration: Jean Barry
Administrator: Suella Wynne
Sales: Anne Duggan
Founded: 1970
Specialize in contemporary Irish literature by Irish authors only.
Subjects: Drama, Theater, Poetry
ISBN Prefix(es): 0-902996; 0-904011; 1-85235
Distributed by Dufour Editions Inc (USA)

Gandon Editions+
Oysterhaven, Kinsale, County Cork
Tel: (021) 770830 *Fax:* (021) 770755
Key Personnel
Editor & International Rights: John O'Regan
Founded: 1983
Specialize in art & architecture books.
Subjects: Archaeology, Architecture & Interior Design, Art, Environmental Studies, History, Nonfiction (General)
ISBN Prefix(es): 0-946641; 0-946846; 0-948037

Gartan, Preas Cholmcille, *imprint of* The Columba Press

Gateway, *imprint of* Gill & Macmillan Ltd

Gill & Macmillan Ltd+
10 Hume Ave, Park West, Dublin 12
Tel: (01) 500 9500 *Fax:* (01) 500 9599
E-mail: sales@gillmacmillan.ie
Web Site: www.gillmacmillan.ie
Key Personnel
Man Dir: Michael Gill *E-mail:* mhgill@gillmacmillan.ie
Publishing Dir, Educational Books: H J Mahony *E-mail:* hmahony@gillmacmillan.ie
Marketing & Sales Dir: P A Thew *E-mail:* pthew@gillmacmillan.ie
Finance Dir: M D O'Dwyer *E-mail:* dodwyer@gillmacmillan.ie
Production Dir: M O O'Keeffe *E-mail:* mokeefe@gillmacmillan.ie
Distribution Dir: J Manning *E-mail:* jmanning@gillmacmillan.ie
Publishing Dir, General Books: F M Tobin *E-mail:* ftobin@gillmacmillan.ie
Founded: 1968 (formerly Gill & Son)
Representation Overseas

Australia (Education titles): Macmillan Education Australia, Level 4 & 5, 627 Chapel St, Locked Bag 1400, South Yarra, Victoria 3141, Australia
Australia (General, Newleaf & Gateway titles): Banyan Tree Book Distributors, 13 College Rd, Kent Town, Adelaide, SA 5067, Australia
Canada (General, Newleaf & Gateway titles): Hushion House Publishing, 36 Northline Rd, Toronto, ON M4B 3E2, Canada
Europe (Switzerland, Germany, Austria, Belgium, Netherlands, France & Luxembourg): Michael Geoghegan, 14 Frognal Gardens, London NW3 6UX, UK
Scandinavia: Hanne Rotovnik, PO Box 5, Strandvejen 685B, 2930 Klampenbourg, Denmark
India, Pakistan, Sri Lanka (Newleaf & Gateway): Rajdeep Mukherjee, Pan Macmillan India, 5A/12 Ansari Rd, Daryaganj, New Delhi 110002, India
New Zealand: New Holland Publishers, Unit 1A, 218 Lake Rd, Northcote, Auckland, New Zealand
Singapore, Indonesia, Brunei & Malaysia: Pansing Distribution Sdn Bhd, 7 Tai Seng Dr, No 05-00, Nicosia Warehouse, Singapore 535217, Singapore
South Africa (Education Titles): Macmillan Boleswa, 2nd Floor, Old Trafford No 4, Isle of Houghton, Corner of Boundary & Carsed Gowrie Rds, Houghton, Johannesburg 2017, South Africa
South Africa (General, Newleaf & Gateway titles): Pan Macmillan South Africa, 2nd Floor, North Block, Hyde Park Corner, Corner Jan Smuts & First Rd, 2196 Hyde Park, Johannesburg, South Africa
UK (General, Newleaf & Gateway titles): Bounce Marketing, Islington Business Centre, 3-5 Islington High St, London N1 9LQ, UK
USA (General & Irish Interest titles): Irish Books & Media Inc, 1433 Franklin Ave East, Minneapolis, MN 55404-2102, USA
USA (Newleaf & Gateway titles): Hushion House Publishing, 36 Northline Rd, Toronto, ON M4B 3E2, Canada
West Indies: Macmillan Caribbean, Between Towns Rd, Oxford OX4 3PP, UK.
Subjects: Biography, Business, Child Care & Development, Cookery, Economics, Education, Fiction, Government, Political Science, Health, Nutrition, History, Law, Literature, Literary Criticism, Essays, Psychology, Psychiatry, Regional Interests, Self-Help, Travel
ISBN Prefix(es): 0-7171
Total Titles: 800 Print
Associate Companies: Macmillan Publishers Ltd, United Kingdom
Imprints: Gateway; Newleaf; Tivoli; Ri Ra
Foreign Rep(s): Hagenbach & Bender GmbH Literary and Media Agency

The Goldsmith Press Ltd+
Newbridge, Co Kildare
Tel: (045) 433613 *Fax:* (045) 434648
E-mail: de@iol.ie
Key Personnel
Publicity Manager: Peter Mulreid
Business Manager: V M Abbott
Company Secretary: Patricia McGuane
Founded: 1972
Publisher of Irish poetry & books of Irish interest.
Subjects: Art, Cookery, Fiction, History, Literature, Literary Criticism, Essays, Poetry, Regional Interests
ISBN Prefix(es): 0-904984; 1-870491
Number of titles published annually: 6 Print
Total Titles: 100 Print

Government Publications Ireland
Division of Government Supplies Agency
51 St Stephens Green, Dublin 2

Tel: (01) 6476000 *Fax:* (01) 6610747
E-mail: info@opw.ie
Web Site: www.opw.ie *Cable:* ENACTMENTS
Key Personnel
Contact: Fintan Butler *E-mail:* finton.butler@opw.ie
Founded: 1922
Heritage books, Irish language books, government reports, daily & senate debates.
Subjects: Government, Political Science
ISBN Prefix(es): 0-7076; 0-7557
Ultimate Parent Company: Office of Public Works
Bookshop(s): Government Publications Sale Office, Sun Alliance House, Molesworth St, Dublin 2
Warehouse: Mount Shannon Rd, Rialto Dublin 8

The Hannon Press+
5 Carriff Bridge, Ballivor, County Meath
Tel: (0405) 46089 *Fax:* (0405) 46089
Key Personnel
International Rights: Patricia Oliver
 E-mail: poliver@indigo.ie
Founded: 1995
Subjects: Biography, Business, How-to
ISBN Prefix(es): 0-9516472

Harbinger House, *imprint of* Roberts Rinehart Publishers

Heritage Books, *imprint of* Careers & Educational Publishers Ltd

Heritage Maps & Guides, *imprint of* Morrigan Book Co

Herodotus Press+
PO Box 4674, Dublin 8
Tel: (01) 4540120 *Fax:* (01) 4541134
Founded: 1995
Subjects: Archaeology, Genealogy, History, Maritime
ISBN Prefix(es): 0-9525414

History House Publishing+
5 Bindon St, Ennis, County Clare
Mailing Address: PO Box 50, Ennis, County Clare
Tel: (065) 24066 *Fax:* (065) 20388
Key Personnel
Man Dir: James Williams
Founded: 1983
Specialize in genealogy.
Subjects: Genealogy, History
ISBN Prefix(es): 0-86366

IAP, *imprint of* Irish Academic Press

Institute of Public Administration
Vergemount Hall, Clonskeagh, Dublin 6
Tel: (01) 240 3600 *Fax:* (01) 2698644
E-mail: information@ipa.ie
Web Site: www.ipa.ie
Telex: 90533 INPA EI *Cable:* ADMIN DUBLIN
Key Personnel
Publication Dir: Declan McDonagh
Production: Hannah Ryan
Sales: Eileen Kelly
Founded: 1957
Subjects: Economics, Education, Government, Political Science, Health, Nutrition, History, Law, Public Administration, Social Sciences, Sociology, International Affairs, Public Affairs
ISBN Prefix(es): 0-902173; 0-906980; 1-872002; 1-902448

Irish Academic Press+
44 Northumberland Rd, Ballsbridge, Dublin
Tel: (01) 668 8244 *Fax:* (01) 660 1610
E-mail: sales@iap.ie
Web Site: www.iap.ie
Key Personnel
Managing Editor: Linda Longmore
Founded: 1974
Subjects: Art, History, Literature, Literary Criticism, Essays, Military Science
ISBN Prefix(es): 0-7165
Imprints: IAP; Irish University Press
U.S. Office(s): ISBS, 5804 NE Hassalo St, Portland, OR 97213, United States *Tel:* (503) 287-3093 *Fax:* (503) 280-8832
Orders to: Gill & Macmillan Book Distributors, Goldenbridge, Inchicore, Dublin 8

Irish Heritage Series, *imprint of* Eason & Son Ltd

Irish Management Institute+
Sandyford Rd, Dublin 16
Tel: (01) 2078400 *Fax:* (01) 2955150
E-mail: 3025reception@imi.ie
Web Site: www.imi.ie
Telex: 30325
Key Personnel
Dir of Human Resources: Martin Farelly
Founded: 1952
The Institute is concerned with management, education, training & development. Publishing & bookselling are complementary activities.
Membership(s): Cle, The Irish Book Publishers Association.
Subjects: Accounting, Business, Communications, Economics, Finance, Labor, Industrial Relations, Management
ISBN Prefix(es): 0-903352; 0-9500327; 1-902664

Irish Texts Society (Cumann Na Scribeann nGaedhilge)
31 Fenian St, Dublin 2
Tel: (01) 6616522 *Fax:* (01) 6612378
E-mail: shuttonseanfile@aol.com
Key Personnel
President: Prof Padraig ORiain
Honorary Treasurer: Michael J Burns
Founded: 1898
Specialize in educational charity publishing Irish language texts with translations, & a subsidiary series of supporting commentaries, studies, indexes, etc; organization of annual seminar in conjunction with the combined departments of Irish, University College, Cork, Ireland; publication of catalogue & newsletter.
Subjects: Anthropology, History, Poetry
ISBN Prefix(es): 1-870166
Orders to: Michael J Burns, Tibradden Rd, Rockbrook, Dublin 16 *E-mail:* burnsfam@iol.ie

Irish Times Ltd+
11-15 D'Olier St, Dublin 2
Tel: (01) 6758000 *Fax:* (01) 6773282
Web Site: www.ireland.com
Telex: 25167
Key Personnel
Prize Administrator: Gerard Cavanagh
Founded: 1859
Membership(s): the Committee of Irish Book Publishers Association; Council Member Dublin City Center Business Association.
Subjects: Fiction, Genealogy, Literature, Literary Criticism, Essays
ISBN Prefix(es): 0-907011; 0-9503418
Branch Office(s)
Farum House, 10 Great Victoria St, Belfast BT27BE *Tel:* (01232) 04890-323324 *Fax:* (01232) 04890-231469
76 Shoe Lane, London EC4A 3JB, United Kingdom *Tel:* (0207) 353 8981 *Fax:* (0207) 353 8809
U.S. Office(s): Irish Trade Board, 880 Third Ave, 8th floor, New York, NY 10020, United States
Showroom(s): 16 D'Olier St, Dublin 2

Irish University Press, *imprint of* Irish Academic Press

Irish YouthWork Press
National Youth Federation, 20 Lower Dominick St, Dublin 1
Tel: (010) 8729933 *Fax:* (010) 8724183
E-mail: info@nyf.ie
Web Site: www.nyf.ie
Key Personnel
Services Executive: Mr Fran Bissett
Specialize in Youth Work Publications.
Subjects: Child Care & Development, Education, Social Sciences, Sociology
ISBN Prefix(es): 0-9522207; 1-900416
Total Titles: 17 Print

Kells Publishing Company Ltd
John St, Kells, Co Meath
Tel: (046) 40117; (046) 40255 *Fax:* (046) 41522
ISBN Prefix(es): 1-872490

Albertine Kennedy Publishing
5 Henrietta St, Dublin 1
Tel: (01) 6607090 *Fax:* (01) 6607090
Key Personnel
Man Dir: Tom Kennedy
ISBN Prefix(es): 0-906002

Kerryman Ltd
Clash, Tralee, Co Kerry
Tel: (066) 21666 *Fax:* (066) 21608
E-mail: info@kerryman.ie
Web Site: www.unison.ie/kerryman
Telex: 28100
Key Personnel
Man Dir: Bryan G Cunningham
Editorial: Gerard Colleran
Sales, Production: Brendan Doran
Founded: 1970
Subjects: History, Religion - Other
ISBN Prefix(es): 0-946277
Parent Company: Independent Newspapers Ltd, Middle Abbey St, Dublin 1

Libra House Ltd
PO Box 1127, Dublin 8
Tel: (01) 4542717
Key Personnel
Contact: Cathal Tyrrell
Founded: 1972
Subjects: Labor, Industrial Relations, Transportation, Travel
ISBN Prefix(es): 0-904169

The Lilliput Press Ltd+
62-63 Sitric Rd, Arbour Hill, Dublin 7
Tel: (01) 6711647 *Fax:* (01) 6711233
E-mail: info@lilliputpress.ie
Web Site: www.lilliputpress.ie
Key Personnel
Publisher: Antony Farrell
Founded: 1984
Membership(s): Irish Book Publishers' Association (Cle).
Subjects: Architecture & Interior Design, Biography, Fiction, History, Literature, Literary Criticism, Essays, Natural History, Poetry, Regional Interests
ISBN Prefix(es): 0-946640; 1-874675; 1-901866; 1-84351

Lindisfarne, *imprint of* Veritas Co Ltd

Little Rhino Books, *imprint of* Roberts Rinehart Publishers

Marino Books, *imprint of* Mercier Press Ltd

Mentor Publications+
Sandyford Industrial Estate, 43 Furze Rd, Dublin 18
Tel: (01) 2952112 *Fax:* (01) 2952114
E-mail: admin@mentorbooks.ie
Web Site: www.mentorbooks.ie
Total Titles: 200 Print

Mercier, *imprint of* Mercier Press Ltd

Mercier Press Ltd+
Douglas Village, Cork
Tel: (021) 489 9858 *Fax:* (021) 489 9887
E-mail: books@mercierpress.ie
Web Site: www.mercierpress.ie
Key Personnel
Man Dir: John F Spillane
Founded: 1944
Subjects: Biography, Fiction, History, Humor, Nonfiction (General), Regional Interests, Religion - Catholic
ISBN Prefix(es): 0-85342; 1-85635; 1-86023
Number of titles published annually: 30 Print
Total Titles: 380 Print
Imprints: Marino Books; Mercier
Branch Office(s)
Mercier/Marino, Douglas Village, Cork
 Tel: (021) 489 9858 *Fax:* (021) 489 9887
 E-mail: books@mercierpress.ie
Distributed by Irish Books & Media (USA); Tower Books (Australia)
Foreign Rights: Amer-Asia (Asia); Lora Fountain (France); Natoli Stefan Oliva (Italy); Kristin Olson (Czech Republic); P&P Fritz (Germany); Rosenstone/Wender (USA); Margit Schaleck (Denmark, Norway); Julio F Yanez (Latin America, Spain)
Warehouse: CMD (Columba Mercier Distribution), 55a Spruce Ave, Stillorgan Industrial Park, Blackrock, Co Dublin *Tel:* (01) 2942560 *Fax:* (01) 2942564 *E-mail:* cmd@columbia.ie

Messenger Publications
37 Lower Leeson St, Dublin 2
Tel: (01) 6767 491; (01) 6767 492 *Fax:* (01) 661 16 06
E-mail: sales@messenger.ie
Web Site: www.messenger.ie
Key Personnel
Editor: Brendan Murray SJ
Assistant Editor: Anne Duff
Founded: 1888
ISBN Prefix(es): 0-901335; 1-872245

Mizen Books, *imprint of* Roberts Rinehart Publishers

Morrigan Book Co+
Gore St, Killala, Ballina, County Mayo
Tel: (096) 32555 *Fax:* (096) 32555
E-mail: admin@atlanticisland.ie
Key Personnel
Publisher: Gerald Conan Kennedy *E-mail:* gerry.kennedy@online.ie
Founded: 1982
Subjects: Archaeology, Folklore, Mythology & General Irish Interest
ISBN Prefix(es): 0-907677
Parent Company: Morigna Mediaco Teoranta
Imprints: Fact Pack Ireland Guides; Heritage Maps & Guides

Mount Eagle Publications Ltd+
Cooleen, Dingle, Co Kerry
Mailing Address: PO Box 32, Dingle, Co Kerry
Tel: (066) 9151463 *Fax:* (066) 9151234
Web Site: www.brandonbooks.com
Key Personnel
Publisher: Steve MacDonogh
Founded: 1997

Subjects: Biography, Fiction, History, Literature, Literary Criticism, Essays, Nonfiction (General)
ISBN Prefix(es): 0-86322; 1-902011
Imprints: Brandon
Subsidiaries: Brandon Book Publishers

National Library of Ireland
Kildare St, Dublin 2
Tel: (01) 603 02 00 *Fax:* (01) 6766690
E-mail: info@nli.ie
Web Site: www.nli.ie
Key Personnel
Acting Dir: Aongus O hAonghusa
Founded: 1877
Subjects: Regional Interests
ISBN Prefix(es): 0-907328

New Books/Connolly Books
43 E Essex St, Temple Bar, Dublin 2
Tel: (01) 6711943 *Fax:* (01) 6711943
Subjects: Economics, Government, Political Science, History, Philosophy
ISBN Prefix(es): 0-902912

New Writers' Press
61 Clarence Mangan Rd, Dublin 8
Key Personnel
Man Dir: Michael Smith
Founded: 1967
Subjects: Literature, Literary Criticism, Essays, Poetry
ISBN Prefix(es): 0-905582

Newleaf, *imprint of* Gill & Macmillan Ltd

Oak Tree Press+
19 Rutland St, Cork
Tel: (021) 431 3855 *Fax:* (021) 431 3496
E-mail: info@oaktreepress.com
Web Site: www.oaktreepress.com
Key Personnel
Man Dir: Brian O'Kane *E-mail:* brian.okane@oaktreepress.com
Founded: 1991
Business book publishers & developers of enterprise training & support materials.
Subjects: Accounting, Business, Career Development, Finance, Labor, Industrial Relations, Law, Management, Marketing
ISBN Prefix(es): 1-872853; 1-86076; 1-904887
Number of titles published annually: 15 Print
Total Titles: 170 Print
Parent Company: Cork Publishing

O'Brien Educational
20 Victoria Rd, Rathgar, Dublin 6
Tel: (01) 4923333 *Fax:* (01) 4922777
E-mail: books@obrien.ie
Web Site: www.obrien.ie
Key Personnel
Editorial, Rights & Permissions, Sales, Production: Michael O'Brien
Founded: 1974
Publishers to the Curriculum Development Unit, Trinity College, Dublin 2, & to other educational institutions in Ireland & the EEC.
Subjects: Art, Business, Career Development, Environmental Studies, History, Science (General)
ISBN Prefix(es): 0-905140; 0-86278; 0-9502046
Associate Companies: The O'Brien Press
Orders to: Gill & Macmillan Ltd, Goldenbridge Industrial Estate, Dublin 8 *Tel:* (01) 531005 *Fax:* (01) 541688
Central Books, 99 Wallis Rd, London E9 5LN, United Kingdom *Tel:* (020) 8986 4854 *Fax:* (020) 8533 5821
Michael Geoghegan, 15A Tower Terrace, Wood Green, London N22 6SX, United Kingdom *Tel:* (020) 8889 7094

Keith Ainworth (Pty), 66A Abel St, Suite 4, Penrith, NSW 2750, Australia *Tel:* (047) 323411 *Fax:* (047) 218259
Riverwood Publishers Ltd, 6 Donlands Ave, PO Box 70, Sharon, ON L0G 1V0, Canada *Tel:* 416-478-8396 *Fax:* 416-478-8380
Irish Books & Media, 1433 Franklin Ave E, Minneapolis, MN 55404-2135, United States *Tel:* 612-871-3505 *Fax:* 612-871-3358

The O'Brien Press Ltd+
20 Victoria Rd, Rathgar, Dublin 6
Tel: (01) 4923333 *Fax:* (01) 4922777
E-mail: books@obrien.ie
Web Site: www.obrien.ie
Key Personnel
Man Dir, Rights & Permissions: Michael O'Brien
Editorial: Ide ni Laoghaire
Sales Dir: Ivan O'Brien
Founded: 1974
Subjects: Architecture & Interior Design, Biography, Business, Cookery, Criminology, Fiction, History, Humor, Music, Dance, Nonfiction (General), Self-Help, Sports, Athletics, Travel, Wine & Spirits, Women's Studies
ISBN Prefix(es): 0-905140; 0-86278; 0-9502046
Associate Companies: O'Brien Educational
Imprints: Blue Flag; Flyers; Pandas; Red Flag; Solos
Foreign Rights: Agenzia Letteraria Internazionale SRL (Italy); Akcali Ltd (Turkey); Big Apple Tuttle-Mori (Republic of China); Valerie Hoskins & Associates (UK); Ilustrata SL (Portugal, Spain); Japan Foreign-Rights (Japan); Liepman AG (Germany); Lora Fountain (France, Russia); Kristin Olson Literary Agency (Czech Republic); Silkroad Agency (Thailand)
Distribution Center: Compass Independent Book Sales, 6 Waldeck Rd, Strand on the Green, Chiswick, London W4 3NP *Tel:* (0181) 995 6324 *Fax:* (0131) 558 1500 (Britain)
David Forrester Books NZ, Private Bag 102907, MSMC, Auckland *Tel:* (09) 4152080 *Fax:* (09) 4152083 (New Zealand)
Gill & MacMillan Distribution, Hume Ave, Park West, Dublin *Tel:* (01) 500 9500 *Fax:* (01) 500 9599 (Ireland & World excluding other territories listed)
Independent Publishers Group (IPG), 814 N Franklin St, Chicago, IL 60610, United States *Tel:* 312-337-0747 *Fax:* 312-337-5985 *Web Site:* www.ipgbook.com (USA/Canada)
Irish Books & Media, 1433 Franklin Ave E, Minneapolis, MN 55404-2135, United States *Tel:* 612-871-3505 *Fax:* 612-871-3358 *E-mail:* irishbook@aol.com (Irish gift shops, North America)
Tower Books, Unit 9/19 Rodborough Rd, Frenchs forest, NSW 2086, Australia *Tel:* (02) 99755566 *Fax:* (02) 9975599
Orders to: Gill & Macmillan Ltd, Hume Ave, Park West, Dublin 12 *Tel:* (01) 500 9500 *Fax:* (01) 500 9599
Irish Books & Media, 1433 Franklin Ave E, Minneapolis, MN 55404-2135, United States *Tel:* 612-871-3505 *Fax:* 612-871-3358

Oifig an tSolathair, *imprint of* An Gum

The On Stream Local History Collection, *imprint of* On Stream Publications Ltd

On Stream Publications Ltd+
Currabaha, Cloghroe, Blarney, County Cork
Tel: (021) 4385798 *Fax:* (021) 4385798
E-mail: info@onstream.ie
Web Site: www.onstream.ie
Key Personnel
Man Dir: Roz Crowley
Founded: 1992
Specialize in quality publications.

Subjects: Agriculture, Behavioral Sciences, Biography, Cookery, Developing Countries, Health, Nutrition, History, How-to, Medicine, Nursing, Dentistry, Nonfiction (General), Travel, Wine & Spirits
ISBN Prefix(es): 1-897685
Number of titles published annually: 3 Print
Total Titles: 13 Print
Imprints: The On Stream Local History Collection; Tackling Series of Practical Books

Open Air, *imprint of* Four Courts Press Ltd

Ossian Publications+
40 MacCurtain St, Cork, County Cork
Mailing Address: PO Box 84, Cork, County Cork
Tel: (021) 4502040 *Fax:* (021) 4502025
E-mail: ossian@iol.ie
Web Site: www.ossian.ie
Key Personnel
Dir: John Loesberg
Founded: 1989
Irish music publisher & distributor.
Subjects: Ethnicity, How-to, Music, Dance, Irish Music
ISBN Prefix(es): 0-946005; 1-900428
Associate Companies: Bookmark
U.S. Office(s): Ossian USA, 118 Beck Rd, Loudon, NH 03301, United States *E-mail:* ossianusa@attbi.com
Distributed by Dufour Editions; Music Exhange; Music Sales Corp; Soar Valley Music
Distributor for Halshaw; Dave Malinson Publications; Music Sales Corp; Waltons

Pandas, *imprint of* The O'Brien Press Ltd

Playscripts, *imprint of* Campus Publishing Ltd

Poolbeg Press Ltd+
Imprint of Auburn House
Poolbeg Group Services, 123 Baldoyle Industrial Estate, Baldoyle, Dublin 13
Tel: (01) 832 1477 *Fax:* (01) 832 1430
E-mail: info@poolbeg.com
Web Site: www.poolbeg.com
Key Personnel
Man Dir: Philip MacDermott
Finance Dir: Kieran Devlin
Editorial Dir: Kate Cruise O'Brien
Marketing Manager: Michael McLoughlin
Founded: 1976
Subjects: Fiction, History, Nonfiction (General)
ISBN Prefix(es): 1-85371; 0-905169; 1-84223
Imprints: Salmon; Torc; Children's Poolbeg
Subsidiaries: Torc Books Ltd; Salmon Publishing Ltd

PSAI Press
Political Studies Association of Ireland, c/o Dublin City University Business School, Glasnevin, Dublin 9
Tel: (01) 6081651
E-mail: nconnol4@tcd.ie
Web Site: www.politics.tcd.ie/psai
Key Personnel
Contact: Dr Gary Murphy *Tel:* (01) 7005664 *E-mail:* gary.murphy@dcu.ie
Founded: 1982
Specializes in: Political Science
Publications include: Journals & Irish Political Books.
ISBN Prefix(es): 0-9519748
Ultimate Parent Company: Political Studies Association of Ireland

Publishers Group South West (Ireland)+
Allihies, Bantry, Co Cork
Tel: (027) 73025 *Fax:* (027) 73131
E-mail: 73551.655@compuserve.com

Key Personnel
President: Tony Lowes
Vice President: Peter Haston
Secretary: Guy Cotten
Founded: 1984
Membership(s): An Taise, The National Trust; Specialize in promotional T-shirts, buttons & balloons.
Subjects: Fiction, Philosophy, Poetry
ISBN Prefix(es): 1-870618; 0-9511629
Imprints: Christa-Jo Utley
Divisions: Cod's Head Preservation Society; Friends of Allihies Artists

Real Ireland Design
27 Beechwood Close, Boghall Rd, Bray
Tel: (01) 2860799 *Fax:* (01) 2829962
E-mail: info@realireland.ie
Web Site: www.realireland.ie
Key Personnel
Man Dir: Leonard Desmond
Founded: 1981
Subjects: Photography, Travel
ISBN Prefix(es): 0-946887

Red Flag, *imprint of* The O'Brien Press Ltd

Relay Books+
Tyone, Nenagh Co Tipperary
Tel: (067) 31734 *Fax:* (067) 31734
E-mail: relaybooks@eiscom.net
Key Personnel
Dir & Editor: Donal A Murphy
Founded: 1982
Membership(s): Cle, Book Publishers Association of Ireland.
Subjects: History, Literature, Literary Criticism, Essays, Regional Interests
ISBN Prefix(es): 0-946327
Distributed by Irish Books & Media (USA)

Rhino Books, *imprint of* Roberts Rinehart Publishers

Ri Ra, *imprint of* Gill & Macmillan Ltd

Roberts Rinehart Publishers+
Trinity House, Charlestown Rd, Ranelagh, Dublin 6
Tel: (01) 497-6860 *Fax:* (01) 497-6861
E-mail: books@townhouse.ie
Key Personnel
President: Rick Rinehart
Vice President: Jack van Zandt
Rights Dir: Mary Hegarty
Founded: 1983
Subjects: Anthropology, Art, Biography, Environmental Studies, Ethnicity, Fiction, History, Natural History, Photography, Regional Interests, Travel
ISBN Prefix(es): 0-911797; 1-879373; 1-57098
Parent Company: 6309 Monarch Park Place, Nivot, CO 80503, United States
Imprints: Rhino Books; Little Rhino Books; Mizen Books; Harbinger House
U.S. Office(s): 5309 Monarch Park Pl, Niwot, CO 80503, United States *Tel:* 303-652 2685 *Fax:* 303-652 2689 *E-mail:* books@robertrinehart.com

Sean Ros Press
Millquarter, Foulkesmill, Co Wexford
Tel: (051) 28666
Key Personnel
Contact: Bernard Browne
Founded: 1993
Subjects: Genealogy, History, Natural History
ISBN Prefix(es): 0-9525771; 1-903922
Total Titles: 9 Print

Round Hall Sweet & Maxwell+
43 Fitzwilliam Pl, Dublin 2
Tel: (01) 662 5301
E-mail: info@roundhall.ie
Web Site: www.roundhall.ie
Key Personnel
Dir: Catherine Dolan
Marketing Manager: Maura Smyth
Founded: 1982
Subjects: Criminology, Finance, Labor, Industrial Relations, Law
ISBN Prefix(es): 0-947686; 1-899738; 0-9508725; 0-85800
Total Titles: 200 Print
Parent Company: The Thomson Corporation
Orders to: Gill & Macmillan Distribution, Goldenbridge, Inchicore, Dublin 8, Contacts: Karen/ Karen Gallagher/ Donoghue *Tel:* (01) 4531005 *Fax:* (01) 4541688

Royal Dublin Society
Ballsbridge, Dublin 4
Tel: (01) 6680866 *Fax:* (01) 6604014
E-mail: info@rds.ie
Web Site: www.rds.ie *Cable:* SOCIETY DUBLIN
Key Personnel
Science Development Executive: Annette McDonnell *E-mail:* amcdonnell@rds.ie
Founded: 1731
Subjects: Biological Sciences, Science (General)
ISBN Prefix(es): 0-86027

Royal Irish Academy+
19 Dawson St, Dublin 2
Tel: (01) 6762570 *Fax:* (01) 6762346
E-mail: admin@ria.ie
Web Site: www.ria.ie
Key Personnel
Executive Secretary, Rights & Permissions: Patrick Buckley
Editor, Productions: Rachel McNicholl
Publications Officer: Hugh Shiels *Tel:* (01) 6380911 *E-mail:* h.shiels@ria.ie
Founded: 1785
Subjects: Archaeology, Biological Sciences, Earth Sciences, Environmental Studies, Ethnicity, Geography, Geology, Government, Political Science, History, Mathematics, Physical Sciences
ISBN Prefix(es): 0-901714; 1-874045; 0-9543855
Number of titles published annually: 6 Print
Distributor for Environmental Institute; University College Dublin

Runa Press
2 Belgrave Terrace, Monkstown, Co Dublin
Tel: (01) 2801869
Subjects: Philosophy, Poetry
ISBN Prefix(es): 0-903543

Salmon, *imprint of* Poolbeg Press Ltd

Salmon Publishing+
Cliffs of Moher, Co Clare
Tel: (065) 7081941 *Fax:* (065) 7081941
E-mail: info@salmonpoetry.com
Web Site: www.salmonpoetry.com
Founded: 1980
Subjects: Poetry
ISBN Prefix(es): 1-897648; 0-948339; 1-903392

Solos, *imprint of* The O'Brien Press Ltd

Tackling Series of Practical Books, *imprint of* On Stream Publications Ltd

Tir Eolas (Knowledge of the Land)
Newtownlynch, Doorus, Kinvara, Co Galway
Tel: (091) 637452 *Fax:* (091) 637452
E-mail: info@tireolas.com
Web Site: www.tireolas.com
Key Personnel
Dir: Anne Korff

Founded: 1987
Membership(s): CIe.
Subjects: Anthropology, Archaeology, Biography, Environmental Studies, History, Natural History, Outdoor Recreation
ISBN Prefix(es): 1-873821
Total Titles: 10 Print
Distributed by Eason & Son (Ireland); Irish Books & Media (USA); Colin Smythe Publisher (England)
Orders to: Colin Smythe Publishers, PO Box 6, Gerrands Cross, Bucks SL9 8XA, United Kingdom
Eason & Sons, Furry Park Industrial Esate, Santry, Dublin 9
Irish Books & Media, 1433 Franklin Ave E, Minneapolis, MN 55404-2123, United States

Tivenan Publications+
Dually, New Castle West, Co Limerick
Tel: (069) 62596 *Fax:* (069) 62933
E-mail: wellwoman@wellwoman.info
Web Site: www.wellwoman.info
Key Personnel
Publisher: Nancy Murphy
Founded: 1993
Specialize in health, pregnancy & women's health.
Subjects: Child Care & Development, Health, Nutrition, Self-Help, Childbirth & Pregnancy
ISBN Prefix(es): 0-9522578
Number of titles published annually: 1,000 Print
Total Titles: 1 E-Book
Parent Company: SIA
Distributed by Easons Dublin (Ireland)
Bookshop(s): Easons Wholesalers, Furry Park Industrial Estate, Santry, Dublin 9 (Books)

Tivoli, *imprint of* Gill & Macmillan Ltd

Tomar Publishing Ltd+
Bloom House, 78 Eccles St, Dublin 7
Fax: (01) 744697
Key Personnel
Publisher: Mr Tom Breen
Founded: 1982
Subjects: History
ISBN Prefix(es): 1-871793

Topaz Publications+
10 Haddington Lawn, Glenageary, Co Dublin
Tel: (01) 2800460 *Fax:* (01) 2800460
Key Personnel
Man Partner: Mrs Davida Murdoch
Founded: 1988
Subjects: Law
ISBN Prefix(es): 0-9514032
Distributed by LexisNexis Export Team

Torc, *imprint of* Poolbeg Press Ltd

Town House & Country House
Trinity House, Charleston Rd, Ranelagh, Dublin 6
Tel: (01) 4972399 *Fax:* (01) 4970927
E-mail: books@townhouse.ie
Web Site: www.irelandseye.com/cle/publish/townhouse.html
Key Personnel
Man Dir, Rights & Permissions: Treasa Coady
Editorial: Siobhan Parkinson
Production: John McCurrie
Sales & Marketing: Brud Ni Chuilinn
Founded: 1984
Also acts as Publisher to Trinity College Dublin.
Subjects: Archaeology, Art, Biography, Fiction, Romance
Associate Companies: Town House Publications Ltd
Imprints: Trinity College Dublin Press
Distributed by Roberts Rinehart Publishers (Canada & USA)
Distributor for Roberts Rinehart Publishers (USA)
Book Club(s): BCA
Warehouse: Gill & Macmillan, Goldenbridge Industrial Estate, Ichicore, Dublin
Orders to: Gill & Macmillan, Goldenbridge Industrial Estate, Inchicore, Dublin 8

Trinity College Dublin Press, *imprint of* Town House & Country House

Christa-Jo Utley, *imprint of* Publishers Group South West (Ireland)

Veritas Co Ltd+
Veritas House, 7-8 Lower Abbey St, Dublin 1
Tel: (01) 878 8177 *Fax:* (01) 8786507
E-mail: publications@veritas.ie
Web Site: www.veritas.ie
Key Personnel
Dir: Maura Hyland
Editorial, Rights & Permissions: Helen Carr
Retail: Maureen Sanders
Marketing, Publicity: Amanda Conlon-McKenna
Founded: 1969
Veritas Publications is the publishing division of the Catholic Communications Institute of Ireland Inc.
Subjects: Biblical Studies, Biography, Child Care & Development, Developing Countries, Disability, Special Needs, Education, Environmental Studies, Nonfiction (General), Philosophy, Religion - Catholic, Religion - Protestant, Religion - Other, Theology, Catechetical
ISBN Prefix(es): 0-905092; 0-86217; 0-901810; 1-85390
Number of titles published annually: 40 Print; 1 CD-ROM
Parent Company: The Catholic Communications Institute of Ireland
Imprints: Beehive Books; Lindisfarne; Veritas Publications
Branch Office(s)
Cork
Dublin
Ennis
Letterkenny
Sligo
Leamington Spa, United Kingdom
Warehouse: 8 Hanover Quay, Dublin 2

Veritas Publications, *imprint of* Veritas Co Ltd

Weir's Guides, *imprint of* Ballinakella Press

Wolfhound Press Ltd+
Imprint of Merlin Publishing
16 Upper Pembroke St, Dublin 2
Tel: (01) 6764373 *Fax:* (01) 6764373
E-mail: websales@wolfhound.ie
Key Personnel
Publisher: Seamus Cashman
Sales, Marketing & Rights: Seamus O'Reilly
Founded: 1974
Subjects: Biography, Fiction, Photography
ISBN Prefix(es): 0-9503454; 0-905473; 0-86327
Total Titles: 300 Print
Orders to: Gill & Macmillan Ltd, Goldenbridge Industrial Estate, Inchicore, Dublin 8 *Tel:* (01) 4531005 *Fax:* (01) 4541688

Israel

General Information

Capital: Jerusalem
Language: Hebrew and Arabic (English and German widely known)
Religion: Predominantly Jewish (about 82%) and Muslim (about 14%)
Population: 4.7 million
Bank Hours: 0830-1230 Sunday-Thursday; also 1600-1700 Sunday-Tuesday & Thursday
Shop Hours: Usually Sunday 0900-1300, 1600-1800; weekdays 0900-1300, 1600-1900; many close Friday afternoon
Currency: 100 agorot = 1 new sheqel
Export/Import Information: Books (except for children's picture books) and advertising duty-free. 17% VAT on books. No import license required for books but must apply for importing number; exchange granted automatically. Import restrictions on Hebrew books.
Copyright: UCC, Berne, Florence (see Copyright Conventions, pg xi)

Academon Publishing House
Hebrew University, 91000 Jerusalem
Mailing Address: PO Box 24130, Jerusalem
Tel: (02) 5882163 *Fax:* (02) 5815558
Founded: 1952
ISBN Prefix(es): 965-350
Bookshop(s): Academon, at the four Hebrew University campuses, Jerusalem & Rehovot

Academy of the Hebrew Language
Givat Ram, Jerusalem 91034
Mailing Address: PO Box 3449, Jerusalem 91034
Tel: (02) 6493555 *Fax:* (02) 5617065
E-mail: acad2u@vms.huji.ac.il
Web Site: hebrew-academy.huji.ac.il
Key Personnel
President: Prof Moshe Bar-Asher
Man Dir: Dr Nathan Efrati
Founded: 1953
Specialize in research & development of the Hebrew language.
Subjects: Hebrew Language & Linguistics
ISBN Prefix(es): 965-481
Number of titles published annually: 12 Print

Ach Publishing House+
PO Box 170, Kiriat Bialik 27000
Tel: (04) 8727227 *Fax:* (04) 8417839
Fax on Demand: (03) 9342850
Founded: 1967
Subjects: Behavioral Sciences, Education
ISBN Prefix(es): 965-267

Achiasaf Publishing House Ltd
1A Zorn St, S Industrial Zone, Netanya
Mailing Address: PO Box 8414, 42504 Netanya
Tel: (09) 8851390 *Fax:* (09) 8851391
E-mail: info@achiasaf.co.il
Web Site: www.achiasaf.co.il
Key Personnel
Man Dir: Matan Achiasaf; Shachna Achiasaf
Founded: 1933
Subjects: Fiction, Nonfiction (General), Science (General)

Achiever
22 Hahistadrut St, Jerusalem 94230
Tel: (02) 6253627 *Fax:* (02) 6255740
Key Personnel
Manager: D Kessler
Man Dir: Ayala Atzmon; Sara Atzmon

Agudat Sabah+
PO Box 2415, Natanya 42123
Tel: (09) 8620544 *Fax:* (09) 8620546
Key Personnel
Author & Editor: Sidney Pimienta
Founded: 1978
Subjects: Anthropology, Genealogy, History, Language Arts, Linguistics, Management, Regional Interests, Religion - Jewish
ISBN Prefix(es): 965-453

Subsidiaries: SIIAC (Societe Internationale d'Intervention et d'Action Commerciale)
Branch Office(s)
SIIAC-Pimienta

Am Oved Publishers Ltd
22 Mazeh St, 65213 Tel Aviv
Mailing Address: PO Box 470, 61003 Tel Aviv
Tel: (03) 6291526 *Fax:* (03) 6298911
E-mail: info@am-oved.co.il
Web Site: www.am-oved.co.il
Telex: 1568 *Cable:* AMOVED TELAVIV
Key Personnel
Man Dir: Yaron Sadan
Founded: 1942
Subjects: Biography, Fiction, History, Philosophy, Poetry, Psychology, Psychiatry, Social Sciences, Sociology
ISBN Prefix(es): 965-13
Orders to: Distributor's Centre for Israeli Books Ltd, 22 Nachmani St, PO Box 2811, Tel Aviv

Amichai Publishing House Ltd
19 Yad Harotzim St, PO Box 8448, Netanyah 42505
Tel: (09) 8859099 *Fax:* (09) 8853464
Key Personnel
Man Dir: Dr Itzhak Oron *E-mail:* oron@idc.ac.ii
Founded: 1948
Subjects: Fiction, Language Arts, Linguistics, Science (General)

Ariel Publishing House
28 Nayqdot St, Pisgat Zeev, 91033 Jerusalem
Tel: (02) 6434540 *Fax:* (02) 6436164
Key Personnel
Chief Executive: Ely Schiller *E-mail:* elysch@netvision.net.il
Founded: 1976
Subjects: Geography, Geology, History, Regional Interests, Religion - Other
ISBN Prefix(es): 965-439

Arsan Publishing House Ltd, see Kivunim-Arsan Publishing House

Astrolog Publishing House+
PO Box 1123, 45111 Hod Hasharon
Tel: (09) 7412044 *Fax:* (09) 7442044
Key Personnel
Man Dir: Sara Ben-Mordechai *E-mail:* sarabm@netvision.net.il
Editor-In-Chief: Elisha Ben-Mordechai
Founded: 1994
A general publisher in the Hebrew language, New Age & alternative medicine in English & other languages. Also specializing in mysticism, prediction of the future, awareness & various religions.
Membership(s): Israel Publishers' Association.
Subjects: Astrology, Occult, Nonfiction (General), Religion - Other, Alternative Medicine, New Age
ISBN Prefix(es): 965-494
Total Titles: 600 Print
Distributed by Independent Publishers Group (IPG) (United States)

Aurora Semanario Israeli de Actualidad+
PO Box 18066, Tel Aviv 61180
Tel: (03) 5462785; (03) 5463297 *Fax:* (03) 5625082
E-mail: aurorail@netvision.net.il
Founded: 1963
ISBN Prefix(es): 965-333
Parent Company: Aurora
Associate Companies: Aurora Em Poreuquce
Subsidiaries: Isnet
Divisions: Internet
Branch Office(s)
Buenos-Aires

Aviv Publishers Ltd, *imprint of* Bitan Publishers Ltd

Bar Ilan University Press
Bar Ilan University, 52900 Ramat Gan
Tel: (03) 5318111 *Fax:* (03) 5353446
E-mail: press@mail.biu.ac.il
Web Site: www.biu.ac.il/Press
Key Personnel
General Manager: Margalit Avisar
Chairman, Book Committee: Prof Yehuda Friedlander
Founded: 1978
Membership(s): Israel Association of Publishers.
Subjects: Archaeology, Behavioral Sciences, Biblical Studies, Economics, Education, Geography, Geology, History, Language Arts, Linguistics, Law, Literature, Literary Criticism, Essays, Philosophy, Psychology, Psychiatry, Religion - Jewish, Social Sciences, Sociology
ISBN Prefix(es): 965-226
Number of titles published annually: 25 Print

Ben-Zvi Institute+
12 Abarbanel St, 91076 Jerusalem
Mailing Address: PO Box 7660, 91076 Jerusalem
Tel: (02) 5398844; (02) 5398848; (02) 5639202; (02) 5639203; (02) 5639204 *Fax:* (02) 5612329
E-mail: mahonzvi@h2.hum.huji.ac.il
Web Site: www.ybz.org.il
Key Personnel
Dir: Menahem Ben-Sasson
Academic Secretary: Michael Glatzer
Founded: 1948
Specialize in Sephardi & Eastern Jewry.
Subjects: Ethnicity, Foreign Countries, History, Language Arts, Linguistics, Literature, Literary Criticism, Essays, Regional Interests, Religion - Jewish
ISBN Prefix(es): 965-235
Total Titles: 100 Print
Parent Company: Yad Izhak Ben-Zvi & the Hebrew University of Jerusalem

Bezalel Academy of Arts & Design
Mt Scopus, PO Box 24046, 91240 Jerusalem
Tel: (02) 589 3333 *Fax:* (02) 582 3094
E-mail: mail@bezalel.ac.il
Web Site: www.bezalel.ac.il
Subjects: Architecture & Interior Design, Art, Photography
ISBN Prefix(es): 965-324

The Bialik Institute+
PO Box 92, 91000 Jerusalem
Tel: (02) 6783554; (02) 6797942 *Fax:* (02) 6783706
E-mail: bialik@actcom.co.il
Web Site: www.bialik-publishing.com
Key Personnel
Man Dir: Yitzchak Taub
Founded: 1935
Subjects: Archaeology, Art, Biblical Studies, History, Literature, Literary Criticism, Essays, Philosophy, Poetry, Religion - Jewish
ISBN Prefix(es): 965-342
Number of titles published annually: 46 Print
Distributor for Ben Gurion University of the Neger Press; Moreshet (Holocaust publications); The Zionist Library

Bitan Publishers Ltd+
50 Yeshayahu St, 62494 Tel Aviv
Mailing Address: PO Box 3068, 47130 Ramat Hasharon
Tel: (03) 6040089; (054) 664575 *Fax:* (03) 5404792
Key Personnel
Man Dir: Asher Bitan
Founded: 1965
Also acts as director of the Israeli Publisher Association & Optimum Educational Software (1993) Ltd.
Subjects: Aeronautics, Aviation, Biography, Child Care & Development, Fiction, How-to, Human Relations, Literature, Literary Criticism, Essays, Mysteries, Nonfiction (General), Outdoor Recreation, Poetry, Self-Help, Travel, Women's Studies
Parent Company: ABM Publishers Ltd
Imprints: Orbach Editions Ltd; Aviv Publishers Ltd
Subsidiaries: Bitan United Multimedia Ltd
Divisions: Multimedia
Orders to: 14 Valenberg St, 69719 Tel Aviv

The Book Publishers Association of Israel
29 Carlebach St, 67132 Tel Aviv
Mailing Address: PO Box 20123, 61201 Tel Aviv
Tel: (03) 5614121 *Fax:* (03) 5611996
E-mail: info@tbpai.co.il
Web Site: www.tbpai.co.il
Key Personnel
Man Dir: Amnon Ben-Shmuel
Founded: 1939

Books in the Attic Publishers Ltd+
PO Box 23146, Tel Aviv 61231
Tel: (03) 248324 *Fax:* (03) 623630
Key Personnel
President: Dr Yehuda Melzer
Founded: 1989
Subjects: Health, Nutrition, Medicine, Nursing, Dentistry
ISBN Prefix(es): 965-419

Boostan Publishing House
36 Meskek, Ben-Shemen Moshav 73115
Tel: (03) 9221821 *Fax:* (03) 9221299 *Cable:* Boostanmod Telaviv
Key Personnel
Man Dir: Mordechai Boostan
Sales Dir: Roni Birkenfield
Publicity Dir: Riva Almagor
Advertising Dir: Sara Wohlfeiler
Rights & Permissions: Dalia Sheingarten
Founded: 1969
Subjects: Biography, Education, Fiction, History, How-to, Medicine, Nursing, Dentistry, Poetry, Psychology, Psychiatry
ISBN Prefix(es): 965-275
Subsidiaries: Distributors' Centre for Israeli Books Ltd

Breslov Research Institute+
PO Box 5370, Jerusalem 91053
Tel: (02) 5824641 *Fax:* (02) 5825542
E-mail: info@breslov.org
Web Site: www.breslov.org/catalog.html
Key Personnel
Executive Dir: Rabbi Chaim Kramer
Founded: 1979
Subjects: Biblical Studies, Biography, Education, Health, Nutrition, History, Literature, Literary Criticism, Essays, Nonfiction (General), Philosophy, Psychology, Psychiatry, Religion - Jewish, Self-Help, Theology, Specialize in writings in English, French, Spanish, Russian & in Hebrew
ISBN Prefix(es): 965-290
Number of titles published annually: 5 Print
Total Titles: 70 Print; 70 Online; 70 E-Book
Imprints: Tsohar Publications
U.S. Office(s): PO Box 587, Monsey, NY 10952-0587, United States *Tel:* 914-425-4258 *Fax:* 914- 425-3018
Distributed by Jewish Lights

Carta, The Israel Map & Publishing Co Ltd+
18 Ha'uman St, Jerusalem 91024
Mailing Address: PO Box 2500, Jerusalem 91024
Tel: (02) 678 3355 *Fax:* (02) 678 2373

E-mail: carta@carta.co.il
Web Site: www.holyland-jerusalem.com
Key Personnel
Chairman: Emanuel Hausman
President, Chief Executive Officer: Shay Hausman
Editorial: Lorraine Kessel; Pirchia Cohen; Barbara Ball
Art Dir: Eli Kellerman
Founded: 1958
Cartographic & foreign language publisher - English, German & Russian, Hebrew.
Subjects: Archaeology, Education, Health, Nutrition, History
ISBN Prefix(es): 965-220
Number of titles published annually: 30 Print; 1 CD-ROM
Total Titles: 300 Print; 3 CD-ROM
Imprints: Nitzanim
Subsidiaries: Cana Publishing House; W Van Leer Publishing Ltd
Warehouse: Lonnie Kahn Ltd, 20, Eliahu Eitan, Rishon Le Zion 58851, Aaron Segal *Tel:* (03) 9520158/9518408 *Fax:* (03) 9520251/9518415/9518416

Center for Research & Study of Sephardi & Oriental Jewish History, see Misgav Yerushalayim

Centre for Educational Technology
PO Box 39513, 61394 Tel Aviv
Tel: (03) 6460183 *Fax:* (03) 6460821
Key Personnel
Publishing Dir: Dani Dolev
ISBN Prefix(es): 965-354

Classikaletet+
22 Derekh Hashalom St, 67892 Tel Aviv
Tel: (03) 5616996 *Fax:* (03) 5615526
E-mail: kimbooks@netvision.net.it
Key Personnel
Man Dir: Yoram Ros
Founded: 1980
Subjects: Child Care & Development, Cookery, House & Home, How-to, Humor, Music, Dance, Nonfiction (General), Psychology, Psychiatry, Travel
ISBN Prefix(es): 965-286; 965-509

Cordinata Ltd (Holy Land 2000)
27 Sutin St, 64684 Tel Aviv
Tel: (03) 5226885 *Fax:* (03) 5276661
E-mail: cordinata@isdn.net.il
Key Personnel
General Manager: Eliezer Sacks
Marketing Manager: Yaron Goldfisher
Founded: 1995
Specialize in books, mainly albums on the Holy Land. Also produce old & new maps, CD-ROM, videos & calendars - all about the Holy Land.
ISBN Prefix(es): 965-7143
Number of titles published annually: 10 Print; 5 CD-ROM; 5 Online; 15 E-Book; 5 Audio
Total Titles: 10 Print; 5 CD-ROM; 5 Online; 15 E-Book; 5 Audio
U.S. Office(s): Argecy Co, 27280 Haggerty, Farmington Hills, MI 48331, United States, General Manager: Mr Coby Gutkovitch *Tel:* 248-324-1800 (ext 124) *Fax:* 248-324-1900 *E-mail:* argecy@msn.com
Distributed by Riverside Distributors

Dalia Peled Publishers, Division of Modan+
36 Moshav, Ben-Shemen 73115
Tel: (08) 4221821 *Fax:* (08) 4221299
Key Personnel
Man Dir, Publicity, Rights & Permissions: Dahlia Peled
Editorial: Israel Peled
Sales: Raanan Rogel
Production: Ruti Bar-Lev
Founded: 1980
Subjects: Computer Science, Humor
ISBN Prefix(es): 965-269
Subsidiaries: People and Computers

DAT Publications+
PO Box 27019, Jaffa 61270
Tel: (03) 5071239 *Fax:* (03) 5070458
E-mail: dat@y-dat.co.il
Web Site: www.y-dat.co.il
Key Personnel
General Dir & Rights Contact: Yigal Miller *Tel:* (03) 5071239
Dir: Benci Sharon *Tel:* (03) 5072683
Public Relations: Gilah Bonen *Tel:* (03) 6095460 *Fax:* (03) 6035460
Founded: 1969
Publishers of original fiction & nonfiction in Hebrew & English. Occasionally, we publish some gift & audio titles.
Publisher & international Agent of Shlomo Kalo's works (Sold in 15 countries). Privately owned.
Subjects: Biblical Studies, Fiction, History, Humor, Literature, Literary Criticism, Essays, Nonfiction (General), Philosophy, Religion - Other, Self-Help, Theology
ISBN Prefix(es): 965-7028
Total Titles: 60 Print; 4 Audio
U.S. Office(s): Forevermore Bible Discovery Books, PO Box 92613, South Lake, TX 76092, United States, Contact: Moshe Haber *Tel:* 817-605-3688 *Fax:* 817-605-3684 *E-mail:* ForEvrMor1@aol.com
Foreign Rep(s): Forevermore (USA)
Showroom(s): 22 Dov Mimezeritz, Jaffa, Contact: Nizah Miller *Tel:* (03) 6580221
Warehouse: 22 Dov Mimezeritz, Jaffa, Contact: Nizah Miller *Tel:* (03) 5072149

Dekel Academic Press, *imprint of* Dekel Publishing House

Dekel Publishing House+
62 Arlozorov St, 61450 Tel Aviv
Mailing Address: PO Box 45094, 61450 Tel Aviv
Tel: (03) 5230063 *Fax:* (03) 5273011
E-mail: dekelpbl@netvision.net.il
Web Site: www.dekelpublishing.com
Key Personnel
Man Dir: Mr Zu Morik
Founded: 1975
Membership(s): PMA.
Subjects: Cookery, Crafts, Games, Hobbies, How-to, Language Arts, Linguistics, Mathematics, Military Science, Securities, Self-Help, Sports, Athletics, Self-defense; Krav Maga
ISBN Prefix(es): 965-7178
Imprints: Dekel Academic Press; Duvdevan; Tamai Books
Distributed by Frog Co Ltd; North Atlantic Books

Devora Publishing Co, *imprint of* Pitspopany Press

Doko Video Ltd
33 Hayetzira St, 52521 Ramat Gan
Tel: (03) 5753555 *Fax:* (03) 5753189
E-mail: dokoa@ibm.net
Key Personnel
Sales & Marketing Manager: Sharon Moss
Founded: 1981
Subjects: Music, Dance, Religion - Other
ISBN Prefix(es): 965-478

Domino, *imprint of* Keter Publishing House Ltd

Duvdevan, *imprint of* Dekel Publishing House

Dvir Publishing Ltd+
11 Lev Pesach, 71293 N Industrial Area Lod
Mailing Address: PO Box 149, 61001 Tel Aviv
Tel: (08) 9246565 *Fax:* (08) 9251770
E-mail: info@zmora.co.il
Key Personnel
Man Dir & Editorial: Ohad Zmora
Sales: Eran Zmora
Founded: 1924
Subjects: Literature, Literary Criticism, Essays, Poetry, Religion - Jewish
ISBN Prefix(es): 965-01
Total Titles: 1,500 Print
Parent Company: Zmora-Bitan Publishers Ltd
Subsidiaries: Dvir Distribution; Karni Publishers Ltd; Megiddo Publishing Co Ltd

Dyonon/Papyrus Publishing House of the Tel-Aviv+
Tel Aviv University, PO Box 39287, 61392 Tel Aviv
Tel: (03) 6427545 (head office) *Fax:* (03) 6423149
Key Personnel
General Manager: Eitan Zinger
Import Manager: Rachel Hamo
Editor-in-Chief: Raya Itzkovich
Founded: 1977
Membership(s): National Association of College Stores, USA.
Subjects: Behavioral Sciences, Business, Chemistry, Chemical Engineering, Child Care & Development, Criminology, Economics, Education, Finance, Genealogy, History, Medicine, Nursing, Dentistry, Nonfiction (General), Philosophy, Social Sciences, Sociology
ISBN Prefix(es): 965-306
Imprints: Papyrus
Branch Office(s)
Ben Gurion (Beer Sheva) University Campus
Bookshop(s): Bar-Ilan University; Ben-Guryon University; Tel Aviv University

Edanim Publishers Ltd+
Division of Yedlot Aharonot Books
5 Mikunis St, 61376 Tel Aviv
Mailing Address: PO Box 37744, 61376 Tel Aviv
Tel: (03) 688-8466 *Fax:* (03) 537-7820
Telex: 33847
Key Personnel
Publisher: Asher Weill
Founded: 1975
Subjects: Biography, History, Regional Interests
ISBN Prefix(es): 965-248

Encyclopedia Judaica, *imprint of* Keter Publishing House Ltd

Encyclopedia Judaica+
Industrial Zone, Givat Shaul B, 91071 Jerusalem
Mailing Address: PO Box 7145, 91071 Jerusalem
Tel: (02) 6557822 *Fax:* (02) 6528962
E-mail: info@keter-books.co.il
Web Site: www.keter-books.co.il
Key Personnel
Man Dir: Yiftach Dekel
ISBN Prefix(es): 965-07
Parent Company: Keter Publishing House Ltd, Jerusalem

Eretz Hemdah Institute for Advanced Jewish Studies
5 HaMem Gimmel St, 94428 Jerusalem
Mailing Address: PO Box 36236, 91360 Jerusalem
Tel: (02) 537-1485 *Fax:* (02) 537-9626
E-mail: eretzhem@netvision.net.il
Web Site: www.eretzhemdah.org
Key Personnel
President: Harav Shaul Israeli
Founded: 1987

PUBLISHERS
ISRAEL

Subjects: Law, Religion - Jewish
ISBN Prefix(es): 965-436
Distributor for Rubin Mass Ltd (Israel)

ESH (English for Speakers of Hebrew), *imprint of* University Publishing Projects Ltd

Eshkol Books Publishers & Printing Ltd
24 Avodat Israel St, Jerusalem 95155
Tel: (02) 5370451; (02) 5370179 *Fax:* (02) 5372732
Key Personnel
Manager: S Weinfeld
Subjects: Religion - Jewish

Feldheim Publishers Ltd
PO Box 35002, 91350 Jerusalem
Tel: (02) 6513947 *Fax:* (02) 6536061
E-mail: sales@feldheim.com
Web Site: www.feldheim.com
Key Personnel
Man Dir: Yaakov Feldheim
Sales Dir: Chaim Vomberg
Founded: 1939
Subjects: Biography, Cookery, Health, Nutrition, History, Philosophy, Religion - Jewish
ISBN Prefix(es): 0-87306; 1-58350
U.S. Office(s): 200 Airport Executive Park, Nanuet, NY 10954, United States *Tel:* 845-356-2282 *Fax:* 845-425-1908

The Arnold & Leona Finkler Institute of Holocaust Research
Bar-Ilan University, 52900 Ramat-Gan
Tel: (03) 5340333 *Fax:* (03) 5351233
E-mail: michmad@mail.biu.ac.il
Web Site: www.biu.ac.il
Key Personnel
Prof & Chair: Dan Michman
Founded: 1979
Subjects: History, Religion - Jewish, Holocaust, 20th Century Jewish History
Total Titles: 40 Print
Parent Company: Bar-Ilan University

Rodney Franklin Agency
53 Mazeh St, Tel Aviv 61376
Mailing Address: PO Box 37727, Tel Aviv 61376
Tel: (03) 5600724 *Fax:* (03) 5600479
E-mail: rodneyf@netvision.net.il
Founded: 1974
Publishers representatives, book & journal conference exhibitions.

Freund Publishing House Ltd+
PO Box 35010, 61350 Tel Aviv
Tel: (03) 5662925 *Fax:* (03) 5605335
Key Personnel
Chief Executive Officer: Edmund Freund
Founded: 1968
Also translation agency.
Subjects: Aeronautics, Aviation, Behavioral Sciences, Biography, Chemistry, Chemical Engineering, Engineering (General), Environmental Studies, Mathematics, Mechanical Engineering, Medicine, Nursing, Dentistry, Science (General), Social Sciences, Sociology
ISBN Prefix(es): 965-294
Branch Office(s)
Suite 500, Chesham House, 150 Regent St, London W1R 5FA, United Kingdom

S Friedman Publishing House Ltd
27 Gruzenberg St, Tel Aviv 61292
Mailing Address: PO Box 29350, 65152 Tel Aviv
Tel: (03) 5176091 *Fax:* (03) 5179756
Key Personnel
General Manager: Shmuel Friedman
Man Dir: Dov Friedman; Malka Friedman Shapir

Gefen, *imprint of* Gefen Publishing House Ltd

Gefen Publishing House Ltd+
7 Ariel St, 91060 Jerusalem
Mailing Address: PO Box 36004, 91060 Jerusalem
Tel: (02) 5380247 *Fax:* (02) 5388423
E-mail: info@gefenpublishing.com
Web Site: www.israelbooks.com
Key Personnel
Chief Executive, Publicity: Murray S Greenfield
Publisher: Dror Greenfield; Ilan Greenfield
Founded: 1981
Subjects: Archaeology, Art, Biblical Studies, Biography, Cookery, English as a Second Language, Fiction, Government, Political Science, Health, Nutrition, History, How-to, Language Arts, Linguistics, Law, Medicine, Nursing, Dentistry, Military Science, Nonfiction (General), Photography, Poetry, Psychology, Psychiatry, Religion - Jewish, Theology, Travel, Wine & Spirits
ISBN Prefix(es): 965-229
Imprints: Gefen
Subsidiaries: Israbook Purchasing Service
U.S. Office(s): Gefen Books, 12 New St, Hewlett, NY 11557, United States, Contact: Maury J Storch *Tel:* 516-295-2805 *Fax:* 516-295-2739 *E-mail:* gefenbooks@compuserve.com
Distributor for Magnes Press Ltd; MOD Publishing Ltd; Yad Uashem
Shipping Address: Gefen Books, 12 New St, Hewlett, NY 11557, United States, Contact: Maury J Storch *Tel:* 516-295-2805 *Fax:* 516-295-2739 *E-mail:* gefenbooks@compuserve.com
Warehouse: Gefen Books, 12 New St, Hewlett, NY 11557, United States, Contact: Maury J Storch *Tel:* 516-295-2805 *Fax:* 516-295-2739 *E-mail:* gefenbooks@compuserve.com
Orders to: Gefen Books, 12 New St, Hewlett, NY 11557, United States, Contact: Maury J Storch *Tel:* 516-295-2805 *Fax:* 516-295-2739 *E-mail:* gefenbooks@compuserve.com

Gvanim Publishing House+
29 Bar Kochba St, Tel Aviv 61111
Mailing Address: PO Box 11138, 61111 Tel Aviv
Tel: (03) 5281044; (03) 5283648 *Fax:* (03) 5283648
E-mail: traklinm@zahav.net.il
Key Personnel
Man Dir: Maritza Rosman
Founded: 1959
Subjects: Fiction, Poetry
Number of titles published annually: 100 Print
Total Titles: 6,000 Print
Parent Company: Traklin Ltd, Halonot
Associate Companies: Traklin Ltd, Gvanim
Foreign Rights: Pikarsky

Habermann Institute for Literary Research+
20 King David Blvd, 71103 Lod
Mailing Address: PO Box 383, 71103 Lod
Tel: (08) 9244569; (08) 9241160 *Fax:* (08) 9249466
E-mail: zmalachi@post.tau.ac.il
Key Personnel
Dir: Dr Michal Saraf
Founded: 1982
Subjects: Ethnicity, Literature, Literary Criticism, Essays, Poetry, Religion - Jewish
ISBN Prefix(es): 965-351
Number of titles published annually: 15 Print
Total Titles: 75 Print
Subsidiaries: MAHUT- Journal For Jewish Culture

Hadar Publishing House Ltd
32 Schocken St, 66556 Tel Aviv
Tel: (03) 6812244 *Fax:* (03) 6826138
E-mail: info@zmora.co.il

Key Personnel
Manager: Uzi Shavit
Man Dir: Zvi Zmora
Founded: 1950
Subjects: History, Literature, Literary Criticism, Essays
ISBN Prefix(es): 965-211

Haifa University Press
Mount Carmel, Haifa 31905
Tel: (04) 8240111 *Fax:* (04) 8342245
Web Site: www.haifa.ac.il
Key Personnel
Chairman: Prof Manfred Lahnstein
Subjects: Archaeology, Biblical Studies, Education, History, Language Arts, Linguistics, Literature, Literary Criticism, Essays, Philosophy, Public Administration
ISBN Prefix(es): 965-311
Distributed by University Press of New England (Outside of Israel)

Hakibbutz Hameuchad Publishing House Ltd
Hayarkon 23, Bnei Brak 51114
Tel: (03) 5785810 *Fax:* (03) 5785811
Key Personnel
Man Dir: Uzi Shavit
Sales Manager: Nahman Gil
Founded: 1940
Subjects: Agriculture, Archaeology, Art, Biblical Studies, Biography, Biological Sciences, Drama, Theater, Economics, Education, Fiction, Foreign Countries, Geography, Geology, Government, Political Science, Health, Nutrition, History, Human Relations, Literature, Literary Criticism, Essays, Music, Dance, Natural History, Nonfiction (General), Philosophy, Poetry, Psychology, Psychiatry, Regional Interests, Religion - Jewish, Social Sciences, Sociology, Theology, Travel, Women's Studies
ISBN Prefix(es): 965-02

Otzar Hamore
c/o Israel Teachers' Union, 8 Ben Saruk St, Tel Aviv 62969
Tel: (03) 6922983 *Fax:* (03) 6922903
Key Personnel
Manager: Avigdor Biton
Man Dir: Joseph Salomon
Founded: 1951
Subjects: Education, Mathematics, Psychology, Psychiatry

Hanitzotz A-Sharara Publishing House
PO Box 41199, 61411 Jaffa
Tel: (03) 6839145 *Fax:* (03) 6839148
E-mail: oda@netvision.net.il
Web Site: www.odaction.org; www.hanitzotz.com/challenge
Key Personnel
Publisher: Shimon Tzabar
Editor-in-Chief: Ms Roni Ben Efrat
Editor: Liz Leyh Levac
Language Editor: Stephen Langfur
Founded: 1985
Publishes a bimonthly magazine on the Israeli-Palestinian Conflict, *Challenge*.
Subjects: Developing Countries, Economics, Education, Film, Video, Foreign Countries, Labor, Industrial Relations, Social Sciences, Sociology, Politics; Israelai Palestinian Conflict

Beth Hatefutsoth
Tel Aviv University Campus, Klausner St, 61392 Ramat Aviv
Mailing Address: PO Box 39359, 61392 Tel Aviv
Tel: (03) 640 8000 *Fax:* (03) 640 5727
E-mail: bhwebmas@post.tau.ac.il
Web Site: www.bh.org.il

Key Personnel
Contact: Yossi Avner *E-mail:* bhyavner@post.tau.ac.il
ISBN Prefix(es): 965-425

Hod-Ami, Computer Books Ltd+
3 Bilu St, 46426 Herzliya
Mailing Address: PO Box 6108, 46160 Herzliya
Tel: (09) 9541207 *Fax:* (09) 9571582
E-mail: info@hod-ami.co.il
Web Site: www.hod-ami.co.il
Key Personnel
Chief Executive Officer: Itzhak Amihud
Founded: 1968
Subjects: Computer Science
ISBN Prefix(es): 965-361
Total Titles: 180 Print

IMI, see Israel Music Institute (IMI)

Inbal Publishers+
24 Amal St, 48092 Park Afek-Rosh Haayin
Mailing Address: PO Box 11415, 48092 Park Afek-Rosh Haayin
Tel: (03) 9030111 *Fax:* (03) 9030888
E-mail: inbalpub@internet-zahav.net
Key Personnel
Man Dir: Shahrokh Sabzerov
Founded: 1980
Specialize in children's board books.
ISBN Prefix(es): 965-332
Distributor for Pestalozzi Verlan (Germany)

Inbal Travel Information+
18 Hayet Zira St, 52521 Ramat Gan
Tel: (03) 5753032 *Fax:* (03) 5753130
Key Personnel
President: Michael Shichor
Founded: 1983
Subjects: Travel
ISBN Prefix(es): 965-288
Imprints: Michael's Guides

The Institute for Israeli Arabs Studies
PO Box 810, Ra'anana 43107
Tel: (09) 7486738 *Fax:* (09) 7486341
Founded: 1995
Subjects: Anthropology, Economics, Ethnicity, Government, Political Science, Labor, Industrial Relations, Regional Interests, Religion - Islamic, Social Sciences, Sociology, Women's Studies
ISBN Prefix(es): 965-454

The Institute for the Translation of Hebrew Literature+
23 Baruch Hirsch St, Bnei Brak
Mailing Address: PO Box 1005 1, 52001 Ramat Gan
Tel: (03) 5796830 *Fax:* (03) 5796832
E-mail: hamachon@inter.net.il; litscene@ithl.org.il
Web Site: www.ithl.org.il
Key Personnel
Man Dir: Mrs Nilli Cohen
Office Manager: Debbie Dagan
Founded: 1962
Subjects: Literature, Literary Criticism, Essays, Poetry
ISBN Prefix(es): 965-255

Intermedia Audio, Video Book Publishing Ltd+
20 Ha-hashmal St, Tel Aviv 61367
Tel: (03) 5608501 *Fax:* (03) 5608513
E-mail: freed@inter.net.il
Key Personnel
Man Dir: Arie Fried
Founded: 1993
Subjects: Business, Education, English as a Second Language, Health, Nutrition, Journalism, Mathematics, Medicine, Nursing, Dentistry, Philosophy, Self-Help, Specialize in Alternative Medicine
ISBN Prefix(es): 965-7079
Total Titles: 25 Print; 6 Audio

The Israel Academy of Sciences & Humanities+
43 Jabotinsky Rd, 91040 Jerusalem
Mailing Address: PO Box 4040, 91040 Jerusalem
Tel: (02) 5636211 *Fax:* (02) 5666059
E-mail: isracado@vms.huji.ac.il
Key Personnel
Man Dir: Dr Meir Zadok
Publications Dept: Tami Korman
Founded: 1959
Subjects: Biological Sciences, Environmental Studies, Geography, Geology, History, Philosophy, Religion - Jewish
ISBN Prefix(es): 965-208

Israel Antiquities Authority
Rockefeller Museum Bldg, PO Box 586, Jerusalem 91004
Tel: (02) 5638421 *Fax:* (02) 6289066
Web Site: www.israntique.org.il
Key Personnel
Editor-in-Chief: Tsvika Gal *Tel:* (02) 5638424 *Fax:* (02) 5630526 *E-mail:* tsvika@israntique.org.il
Dir: Shuka Dorfman *Tel:* (02) 6204600/1/8 *Fax:* (02) 6288391 *E-mail:* oshrat@israntique.org.il
Secretary: Harriet Menahem *Tel:* (02) 6204622 *E-mail:* harriet@israntique.org.il
Founded: 1990 (Formerly a Department of the Israel Ministry of Education)
Designated by the government of Israel to administer the Law of Antiquities, responsible for all archeological matters, custodianship of all archeological sites, conducts excavations & surveys, issues excavation permits, curatorship, documentation & storage of all finds. Also, lends finds to museums, conservation & restoration of antiquities sites & antiquities, documentation, publication & education. Publications include excavation reports, surveys, bibliographies, monographs, guide books & video cassettes.
Subjects: Archaeology, Archaeology of Israel (the Holy Land)
ISBN Prefix(es): 965-406
Total Titles: 74 Print
Orders to: Eisenbrauns (USA)

Israel Book and Printing Centre
Industry House, 29 Hamered St, Tel Aviv 68125
Tel: (03) 5142895
Web Site: www.expot.gov.il
Key Personnel
Executive: Ronit Adler *Tel:* (03) 5142916 *Fax:* (03) 5142881 *E-mail:* adler@export.gov.il

Israel Exploration Society+
5 Avidah St, 91070 Jerusalem
Mailing Address: PO Box 7041, 91070 Jerusalem
Tel: (02) 6257991 *Fax:* (02) 6247772
E-mail: ies@vms.huji.ac.il
Web Site: www.hum.huji.ac.il/ies
Key Personnel
Man Dir: J Aviram
Founded: 1913
Subjects: Archaeology, Biblical Studies, Geography, Geology, History
ISBN Prefix(es): 965-221

The Israel Institute for Occupational Safety & Hygiene
22 Maze St, Tel Aviv
Mailing Address: PO Box 1122, 61010 Tel Aviv
Tel: (03) 6875037 *Fax:* (03) 6875038
Web Site: www.osh.org.il
Key Personnel
Dir: Menachem Schwartz *Tel:* (03) 5266444 *E-mail:* menachem@osh.org.il
Deputy Dir: Chaim Eliyahu *Tel:* (03) 5266432
Head of Publishing: Andrei Matias *Tel:* (03) 5266476 *Fax:* (03) 6208232
Distribution Manager: Hizkiya Israel *Tel:* (03) 6575147 *Fax:* (03) 6575148
Subjects: Specialize in books about safety & hygiene in the work place
ISBN Prefix(es): 965-490

Israel Museum Products Ltd
PO Box 71117, Jerusalem 91710
Tel: (02) 6708883 *Fax:* (02) 6631833
Web Site: www.imj.org.il
Key Personnel
Dir: Rita Gans
Founded: 1965
ISBN Prefix(es): 965-278

Israel Music Institute (IMI)
55 Menachem Begin Rd, 67138 Tel Aviv
Mailing Address: PO Box 51197, 67138 Tel Aviv
Tel: (03) 624 70 95 *Fax:* (03) 561 28 26
E-mail: musicinst@bezeqint.net
Web Site: www.imi-org.il
Key Personnel
Dir: Paul Landau
Founded: 1962
Membership(s): IAMIC, International Federation Serious Music Publishers.
Subjects: Music, Dance
Associate Companies: Music in Israel (MII) (production of CDs)
Distributed by AB Nordiska Musikfoerlaget (Sweden); Albersen & Co BV (Holland); Cesky Hudebni Fond (Czech Republic, Hungary & Slovak Republik); Editions Musicales Europeennes (EME) (France, Belgium, Luxembourg, Spain & Portugal); Engstrom & Sodring Musikforlag AS (Denmark); Harald & Lyche & Co AS (Norway); Peer Musikverlag GmbH (Germany, Austria & Switzerland); Ricordi Americana SAEC (Argentina); Theodore Presser Co (USA, Canada & Mexico); Editions Musicales Europeennes (EME)
Distributor for Alkor-Baerenreiter

Israel Program for Scientific Translations, see Keter Publishing House Ltd

Israel Universities Press+
Givat Shaul B, Jerusalem 91071
Mailing Address: PO Box 7145, Jerusalem 91071
Tel: (02) 6557822 *Fax:* (02) 6528962
Key Personnel
Man Dir: Yiftach Dekel
Founded: 1969
Subjects: Government, Political Science, Regional Interests, Social Sciences, Sociology
ISBN Prefix(es): 965-07
Parent Company: Keter Publishing House Ltd

Israeli Music Publications Ltd
25 Keren Hayesod St, 94188 Jerusalem
Mailing Address: PO Box 7681, 94188 Jerusalem
Tel: (02) 6241377; (02) 6241378 *Fax:* (02) 62413708
E-mail: khanukaev@pop.isracom.net.il
Key Personnel
Dir: Sergei Khanukaev
Founded: 1949
Subjects: Music, Dance
ISBN Prefix(es): 965-259
Distributed by Theodore Presser Co (USA)

Jabotinsky Institute in Israel
38 King George St, Tel Aviv
Mailing Address: PO Box 23110, 61230 Tel Aviv
Tel: (03) 6210611; (03) 5287320 *Fax:* (03) 5285587

E-mail: jabo@actcom.co.il
Web Site: www.jabotinsky.org
Key Personnel
Chairman: Peleg Tamir
Founded: 1937
Subjects: Government, Political Science, History
ISBN Prefix(es): 965-416

(JDC) Brookdale Institute of Gerontology & Adult Human Development in Israel
JDC Hill, Jerusalem 91130
Mailing Address: PO Box 13087, Jerusalem 91130
Tel: (02) 6557445 *Fax:* (02) 5635851
E-mail: brook@jdc.org.il
Web Site: www.jdc.org.il/brookdale/
Key Personnel
Dir, Human Resources & Administration: Rebecca Caspi
Founded: 1974
Subjects: Health, Nutrition, Social Sciences, Sociology
ISBN Prefix(es): 965-353

Jerusalem Center for Public Affairs
c/o Beit Milken, 13 Tel Hai St, 92107 Jerusalem
Tel: (02) 5619281 *Fax:* (02) 5619112
E-mail: jcenter@jcpa.org
Web Site: www.jcpa.org
Key Personnel
President: Dr Dore Gold
Publications Coordinator: Mark Ami-El
Founded: 1976
Specialize in Israel, Jewish communities, Jewish political tradition & federalism.
ISBN Prefix(es): 965-218
Total Titles: 60 Print

The Jerusalem Publishing House Ltd+
39 Tchernichovsky St, Jerusalem 91071
Mailing Address: PO Box 7147, Jerusalem 91071
Tel: (02) 5617744 *Fax:* (02) 5634266
E-mail: jphgagi@netvision.net.il
Key Personnel
Man Dir: Shlomo S Gafni *Fax:* (02) 54346016
Man Editor: Rachel Gilon
Founded: 1966
Israel Export Institute.
Subjects: Archaeology, History, Religion - Jewish

Biblioteca Judaica, see L B Publishing Co

K Dictionaries Ltd+
Formerly Password Publishers Ltd
10 Nahum St, Tel Aviv 63503
Tel: (03) 5468102 *Fax:* (03) 5468103
E-mail: kd@kdictionaries.com
Web Site: kdictionaries.com
Key Personnel
Man Dir: Ilan Kernerman *E-mail:* ilan@kdictionaries.com
Founded: 1993
Specialize in the development & global marketing of English learner's dictionaries for different levels & all electronic applications, multilingual dictionaries & general bilingual (non-English) dictionaries. Localized language versions appear by local publishers worldwide.
Subjects: English as a Second Language, Language Arts, Linguistics
ISBN Prefix(es): 965-90207
Imprints: Kernerman Semi-Bilingual Dictionaries
Distributed by Alma Littera (Lithuania); Aschehoug (Norway); Andrew Betsis, ELT (Greece); Bookman Books (Taiwan); Colibri (Bulgaria); DZS (Slovenia); EDDA (Iceland); ELI (Italy); Festart (Estonia); Fragment (Czech Republic); Inkilap (Turkey); Kernerman Publishing (Israel); Kesaint Blanc (Indonesia); Kielikone (Finland); Martins Fontes Editora (Brazil); Mlada Leta (Slovak Republic); Mlada Fronta (Czech Republic); Modulo Editeur (Canada); Nemzeti Tankonivkiado (NTK) (Hungary); Niculescu (Romania); The Popular Group (USA); PWN (Poland); Rokus (Slovenia); Shanghai Lexicographical Publishing House (China); Skolska Knjiga (Croatia); Ediciones SM (Spain); Student Literature (Sweden); System Publishing House (Malaysia); TEA (Estonia); Thai Watana Panich (Thailand); WSOY (Finland); Russky Yazyk (Russia); YBM Si-sa-yong-o-sa (Korea); Zanichelli Editore (Italy); Zvaigzne ABC Publishers (Latvia)

Karni Publishers Ltd
32 Schocken St, 66556 Tel Aviv
Tel: (03) 812244 *Fax:* (03) 826138
E-mail: info@zmora.co.il
Key Personnel
Man Dir: Ohad Zmora
Founded: 1951
Subjects: Biography, Fiction, How-to, Poetry
ISBN Prefix(es): 965-254
Parent Company: Dvir Publishing House
Subsidiaries: Megiddo Publishing Co Ltd

The Harry Karren Institute for the Analysis of Propaganda, Yad Labanim
Yad Labanim, Wolfson Str, 46489 Herzliya
Tel: (09) 9573736 *Fax:* (09) 9546896
Key Personnel
Contact: Elisa Mermelstein
Subjects: Film, Video, Journalism
ISBN Prefix(es): 965-414

Kernerman Semi-Bilingual Dictionaries, *imprint of* Kernerman Publishing Ltd

Kernerman/Password, see K Dictionaries Ltd

Kernerman Publishing Ltd+
Affiliate of K Dictionaries Ltd
10 Nahum St, 63503 Tel Aviv
Tel: (03) 5468102 *Fax:* (03) 5468103
E-mail: kd@kdictionaries.com
Web Site: www.kdictionaries.com
Key Personnel
Chief Executive: Ari Kernerman
Production Manager: Nili Sadeh
Founded: 1969
Specialize in English learner's dictionaries for non-native speakers & general English-Hebrew dictionaries.
Subjects: Education, English as a Second Language
ISBN Prefix(es): 965-307
Associate Companies: Password Publishers Ltd
Imprints: Password; Kernerman Semi-Bilingual Dictionaries
Distributor for Chambers-Harrap; Oxford University Press (Israel); Simon & Schuster Education
Orders to: Lonnie Kahn Ltd, 20 Eliahu Eitan St, 75703 Rishon L'Tsion *Tel:* (03) 9518418 *Fax:* (03) 9518415 *E-mail:* kpu@internet-zahav.net

Kernerman Semi-Bilingual Dictionaries, *imprint of* K Dictionaries Ltd

Keter, *imprint of* Keter Publishing House Ltd

Keter Publishing House Ltd+
16th Beit Hadfus, Givat Sahul B, 91071 Jerusalem
Mailing Address: PO Box 7145, 91071 Jerusalem
Tel: (02) 6557822 *Fax:* (02) 6528962
E-mail: info@keter-books.co.il
Web Site: www.keter-books.co.il
Key Personnel
Man Dir: Yiftach Dekel
Publisher & Editor: Zvika Meir
Founded: 1959
Subjects: Art, Fiction, How-to, Philosophy, Psychology, Psychiatry, Social Sciences, Sociology
ISBN Prefix(es): 965-07
Imprints: Domino; Encyclopedia Judaica; Keter
Subsidiaries: Domino Press; Encyclopaedia Judaica; Israel Program for Scientific Translations

Kiryat Sefer
66 Allenby St, Tel Aviv 65812
Tel: (03) 5178922 *Fax:* (03) 5100227
Key Personnel
Man Dir: Avi Sivan
Founded: 1933
Subjects: Fiction, Poetry, Religion - Other
ISBN Prefix(es): 965-17

Kivunim-Arsan Publishing House+
21 Hgalgal St, Industrial Area, Rehovot 76488
Tel: (08) 9470791 *Fax:* (08) 9469740
Key Personnel
Man Dir: Arieh Sandler
Founded: 1980
Subjects: Humor, Management
ISBN Prefix(es): 965-276
Showroom(s): Elhad Haam 20, Rehovot 76260
Bookshop(s): Elhad Haam 20, Rehovot 76260

Koren Publishers Jerusalem Ltd
33 Herzog St, 42622 Jerusalem
Mailing Address: PO Box 4044, 91040 Jerusalem
Tel: (02) 5660188 *Fax:* (02) 5666658
Web Site: www.koren-publishers.co.il
Key Personnel
Dir: Eli Koren
Man Dir: Eli Kahn
Founded: 1962
Subjects: Biblical Studies, Religion - Jewish
ISBN Prefix(es): 965-301
Parent Company: Maron Publishing Co Ltd
Distributed by Feldheim Publishers
Distributor for Maron Publishing Co Ltd

L B Publishing, *imprint of* L B Publishing Co

L B Publishing Co+
Imprint of Editorial D A Let C A
PO Box 32056, Jerusalem 91000
Tel: (02) 5664637 *Fax:* (02) 5290774
E-mail: editorial_lb@yahoo.com
Key Personnel
President: Lili Breziner
Editor-in-Chief: Salomon Lewinsky
Founded: 1993
Also acts as mediator & publisher for third parties; Specialize in Judaica.
Membership(s): Publishers Association (Israel).
Subjects: Regional Interests, Religion - Jewish, Israel Dispora, Jewish History
ISBN Prefix(es): 965-484
Number of titles published annually: 5 Print
Total Titles: 35 Print
Parent Company: Reencuentro L B Publishing Co
Associate Companies: Reencuentro L B Editorial C A, Calle Santa Clara, Edif Bertolini, Piso 3, Boleita Norte, Caracas, Venezuela *Tel:* 2345554 *Fax:* 2345555
Imprints: L B Publishing
Subsidiaries: Biblioteca Judaica
Distributed by Galerna (Buenos Aires); Nuevas Estructuras (Madrid)
Distributor for Anaya; Planeta; Universidad de Salamanca
Foreign Rep(s): Galerna (Argentina); Gandhi (Mexico); Nuevas Estructuras (Spain)

Le'Dory Publishing House+
10 Trumpeldor St, 75657 Tel Aviv
Mailing Address: PO Box 26507, 75150 Tel Aviv
Tel: (03) 5178555

Key Personnel
Manager: Gil Gefner
ISBN Prefix(es): 965-402

Maaliyot-Institute for Research Publications
Mitzpeh Nevo, 90610 Maaleh Adumim
Mailing Address: PO Box 113, 90610 Maaleh Adumim
Tel: (02) 5353655 Fax: (02) 5353947
E-mail: ybm@virtual.co.il
Subjects: Religion - Jewish
ISBN Prefix(es): 965-417

Ma'alot Publishing Company Ltd
29 Carlebach St, 67132 Tel Aviv
Mailing Address: PO Box 20123, 61201 Tel Aviv
Tel: (03) 5614121 Fax: (03) 5611996
E-mail: maalot@tbpai.co.il
Web Site: www.tbpai.co.il
Key Personnel
Man Dir: Amnon Ben-Shmuel
Founded: 1969
Established by the Book Publishers' Association of Israel as a jointly-owned publishing house in which most of the members of the Association are shareholders.
Parent Company: Book Publishers Association of Israel

Maarachot, imprint of Ministry of Defence Publishing House

Ma'ariv Book Guild (Sifriat Ma'ariv)
3A Yoni Netanyahu St, 60376 Or Yehuda
Tel: (03) 5333333 Fax: (03) 5333619
Telex: 033735 Cable: Ma'ariv Telaviv
Key Personnel
Publisher & Editor-in-Chief: Aryeh Nir
Man Dir: Yitzhak Kfir
Founded: 1954
Subjects: Biography, Education, Fiction, Geography, Geology, Government, Political Science, History, Religion - Other, Science (General), Travel
ISBN Prefix(es): 965-239
Book Club(s): Ma'ariv Book Club

Machbarot Lesifrut
11 Lev Pesach St, North Industrial Area, Lod 71293
Mailing Address: PO Box 4020, Lod 71110
Tel: (08) 9246565 Fax: (08) 9251770
E-mail: info@zmora.co.il
Key Personnel
Man Dir: Zvi Zmora
Subjects: Fiction, Government, Political Science, History, Language Arts, Linguistics, Literature, Literary Criticism, Essays
Number of titles published annually: 20 Print
Total Titles: 250 Print
Associate Companies: Zmora Bitan-Publishing House

The Magnes Press+
The Hebrew University, PO Box 39099, 91390 Jerusalem
Tel: (02) 6586656 Fax: (02) 5633370
E-mail: magnes@vms.huji.ac.il
Web Site: www.huji.ac.il
Key Personnel
Man Dir: Dan Benovici
Founded: 1929
Subjects: Archaeology, Art, Biography, History, Law, Music, Dance, Philosophy, Psychology, Psychiatry, Science (General)
ISBN Prefix(es): 965-223; 965-493
Parent Company: The Hebrew University, Jerusalem
Imprints: Mount Scopus Press

MAP-Mapping & Publishing Ltd+
17 Tchernichovsky St, 61560 Tel Aviv
Mailing Address: PO Box 56024, 61560 Tel Aviv
Tel: (03) 6210500 Fax: (03) 5257725
E-mail: info@mapa.co.il
Web Site: www.mapa.co.il
Key Personnel
Man Dir: Dani Tracz
Editor-in-Chief: Mulli Meltzer
Founded: 1985
Subjects: History, Nonfiction (General), Travel
ISBN Prefix(es): 965-7009
Number of titles published annually: 35 Print
Total Titles: 200 Print
Imprints: Tel Aviv Books
Book Club(s): The Map Children Book Club

Massada Press Ltd+
PO Box 1232, 91000 Jerusalem
Tel: (02) 6719441 Fax: (02) 6719442 Cable: ENCYCLOMAS
Key Personnel
Board Chairman, Chief Executive, Rights & Permissions: Alexander Peli
Man Dir: Nathan Regev
Founded: 1932
Subjects: Art, Biography, Cookery, Education, History, How-to, Music, Dance, Philosophy, Psychology, Psychiatry, Religion - Jewish, Religion - Other, Science (General), Social Sciences, Sociology
ISBN Prefix(es): 965-257
Associate Companies: Yeda Lakol Publishing Co Ltd

Massada Publishers Ltd
9 Bialik St, 53447 Givatayim
Mailing Address: PO Box 187, 53101 Givatayim
Tel: (03) 5716659; (03) 5712702 Fax: (03) 5716639
Telex: 361211 Mape Il Cable: PELIPRINT
Key Personnel
Man Dir: Yoav Barash
Founded: 1932
Subjects: Art, Cookery, Fiction, History, How-to
ISBN Prefix(es): 965-10
Associate Companies: Peli Printing Works Ltd; Reprocolor Ltd

Matar Publishing House
43 Brodetsky St, 69052 Tel Aviv
Tel: (03) 7441199 Fax: (03) 7441314
E-mail: mtriwaks@netvision.net.il
Key Personnel
Man Dir: Moshe Triwacks
Subsidiaries: Triwaks Books Ltd

Medcom Ltd
PO Box 751, 49107 Petach-Tikva
Tel: (03) 9343853 Fax: (03) 9343850
Founded: 1981
Subjects: Chemistry, Chemical Engineering, Medicine, Nursing, Dentistry
ISBN Prefix(es): 965-272

Megiddo Publishing Co Ltd, see Karni Publishers Ltd

Michael's Guides, imprint of Inbal Travel Information

Midrashiat Naom, Pardess Hanna
3 Achuzat Bayit St, Tel Aviv 65143
Tel: (09) 5172637 Fax: (09) 5100594
ISBN Prefix(es): 965-469

Ministry of Defence Publishing House+
27 David Elazar St, 67673 Hakiryah
Mailing Address: PO Box 7103, 67673 Tel Aviv
Tel: (03) 6917940 Fax: (03) 6375509

Key Personnel
Dir: Joseph Perlovitch
Deputy Dir & Chief Editor: Yishai Cordova
Tel: (03) 5655956
Founded: 1939
Subjects: Foreign Countries, History, Military Science, History of the Land of Israel & Geography; Holocaust; Albums, Picture Books
ISBN Prefix(es): 965-05
Total Titles: 1,500 Print
Imprints: MOD: Broadcast University; Maarachot; To Live (Holocaust)

Mirkam Publishers+
PO Box 10209, Nof-Kingreth, Post Office Rosh Pina 12000
Tel: (06) 6900967 Fax: (06) 6900967
Key Personnel
Owner, Chief Editor & General Manager: Yafa Shoham
Founded: 1993
Mostly translations of material to acquaint the Israeli reader with current metaphysical understanding & information
Privately owned enterprise.
Subjects: Spiritual Growth & Channeling
Total Titles: 15 Print
Distributed by Lior Sharf Marketing & Distribution

Misgav Yerushalayim
Unit of Faculty of Humanities
Faculty of Humanities, The Hebrew University of Jerusalem, Mount Scopus, 91905 Jerusalem
Mailing Address: PO Box 4035, 91040 Jerusalem
Tel: (02) 5883962 Fax: (02) 5815460
E-mail: misgav@h2.hum.huji.ac.il
Web Site: www.hum.huji.ac.il/misgav
Key Personnel
Dir: Prof Zeev W Harvey
Deputy Dir: Ms Nitza Genuth
Founded: 1972
University Research Center specializing in academic teaching & research on Shephardi & Oriental Jewry (multi-disciplinary).
Subjects: Art, Ethnicity, History, Language Arts, Linguistics, Literature, Literary Criticism, Essays, Philosophy, Religion - Jewish
ISBN Prefix(es): 965-296; 965-493
Total Titles: 1 Print
Ultimate Parent Company: The Hebrew University, Jerusalem

Miskal Publishing Ltd+
20 Magshimim St, Petah-Tikwa 49348
Tel: (03) 9246980 Fax: (03) 9246985
Key Personnel
President: Dov Eichenwald
Man Dir: Haim Eichenwald
Founded: 1984
Parent Company: Yedioth Ahronot
Warehouse: 19 Merkava St, Holon

M Mizrahi Publishers
67 Levinsky St, Tel Aviv 66855
Tel: (03) 6870936 Fax: (03) 5475399 Cable: MIZEDITION TELAVIV
Key Personnel
Man Dir: Meir Mizrahi; Israel Mizrahi
Founded: 1960
Subjects: Fiction, History, Medicine, Nursing, Dentistry, Science (General)
Branch Office(s)
33 Hagivea St, Savyon Tel: 344661

MOD: Broadcast University, imprint of Ministry of Defence Publishing House

Modan Publishers Ltd
8 Meshek 33, 73115 Moshav Ben-Shemen
Tel: (08) 9221821 Fax: (08) 9221299

E-mail: modan@modan.co.il
Web Site: www.modan.co.il
Key Personnel
Man Dir: Oded Modan
Dir: A Friedman
Subjects: Cookery, Religion - Jewish, Classics
ISBN Prefix(es): 965-341; 965-7141

The Moshe Dayan Center for Middle Eastern & African Studies
Tel Aviv University, Ramat Aviv, Tel Aviv 69978
Tel: (03) 640-9646 *Fax:* (03) 641-5802
E-mail: dayancen@post.tau.ac.il
Web Site: www.dayan.org *Cable:* 342171 vesy il
Key Personnel
Head of Center: Dr Martin Kramer
Founded: 1959
Subjects: History, Modern Middle East
ISBN Prefix(es): 965-224
Distributed by Frank Cass; Oxford University Press; Syracuse University Press; Westview Press

Mossad Harav Kook, see Rav Kook Institute

Mount Scopus Press, *imprint of* The Magnes Press

Nehora Press
3 Kiryat Sara, Har Canaan, Safed 13410
Mailing Address: PO Box 2586, Safed 13410
Tel: (04) 6970255 *Fax:* (04) 6970255
E-mail: nehora@canaan.co.il
Web Site: www.nehorapress.com
Key Personnel
Publisher: Amanda Goodman-Cohen
Founded: 2002
Publish authentic translations of Kabbalah from Hebrew into English.
Membership(s): Publishers Marketing Association.
Subjects: Philosophy, Religion - Jewish
ISBN Prefix(es): 965-7222
Number of titles published annually: 3 Print
Shipping Address: 8153 Hansen Rd NE, Bainbridge Island, WA 98110, United States, Contact: D Steinecher *Tel:* 206-780-0124
Returns: 8153 Hansen Rd NE, Bainbridge Island, WA 98110, United States, Contact: D Steinecher

Nitzanim, *imprint of* Carta, The Israel Map & Publishing Co Ltd

Open University of Israel+
16 Klausner St, Ramat Aviv, Tel Aviv 61392
Mailing Address: PO Box 39328, Tel Aviv 61392
Tel: (03) 6460460 *Fax:* (03) 6419279
E-mail: englishsite@openu.ac.il
Web Site: www.openu.ac.il
Key Personnel
President: Prof Eliahu Nissim
Founded: 1974
Occasionally engages in joint publications with Yale University Press & Boston University
Specialize in Academic Publications & Textbooks in Hebrew.
Subjects: Accounting, Biblical Studies, Biological Sciences, Chemistry, Chemical Engineering, Computer Science, Economics, Education, Government, Political Science, History, Journalism, Literature, Literary Criticism, Essays, Management, Mathematics, Physics, Psychology, Psychiatry, Religion - Jewish, Social Sciences, Sociology
ISBN Prefix(es): 965-302; 965-06
U.S. Office(s): American Friends of the Open Univerity of Israel, 180 W 80 St, New York, NY 10024, United States *Tel:* 212-712-1800 *Fax:* 212-496-3296

Or-Teva, *imprint of* Or'am Publishers

Or'am Publishers+
28 Itzhak Sade St, Tel Aviv 67212
Tel: (03) 5372277 *Fax:* (03) 5372281
E-mail: orampub@netvision.net.il
Web Site: www.oram.co.il
Key Personnel
Man Dir: Or'am Shatz; Shoshana Shatz
Founded: 1974
ISBN Prefix(es): 965-230
Total Titles: 1,700 Print; 10 Audio
Imprints: Or-Teva

Orbach Editions Ltd, *imprint of* Bitan Publishers Ltd

Papyrus, *imprint of* Dyonon/Papyrus Publishing House of the Tel-Aviv

Password, *imprint of* Kernerman Publishing Ltd

Password Publishers Ltd, see K Dictionaries Ltd

Pitspopany Press+
c/o Simcha Publishing Co, PO Box 4636, Jerusalem 91044
Tel: (02) 6233507 *Fax:* (02) 6233510
E-mail: pitspop@netvision.net.il
Web Site: www.pitspopany.com
Key Personnel
President: Yaacov Peterseil
Administrator: Wendy Tohar
Founded: 1993
Subjects: Cookery, Fiction, Health, Nutrition, Humor, Mysteries, Religion - Jewish, Science Fiction, Fantasy, Self-Help, Adult Fiction & Non-Fiction
ISBN Prefix(es): 965-483; 1-930143; 0-943706
Number of titles published annually: 15 Print
Total Titles: 100 Print
Imprints: Devora Publishing Co; Simcha Pub
U.S. Office(s): 40 E 78 St, Suite 16D, New York, NY 10021, United States *Tel:* 212-472-4959 *Fax:* 212-472-6253
Shipping Address: 7253 Grayson Rd, Harrisburg, PA 17111, United States *Tel:* 712-564-2111
Distribution Center: Stackpole Distribution

Prolog Publishing House
PO Box 300, 48101 Rosh Ha'ayin
Tel: (03) 9022904 *Fax:* (03) 9022906
E-mail: info@prolog.co.il
Web Site: www.prolog.co.il
Key Personnel
Man Dir: Ben Naim Raanan
Founded: 1988
Specialize in language teaching audio-video cassette courses, how-to books.
Subjects: How-to, Language Arts, Linguistics

Rav Kook Institute+
Maimon St, Jerusalem 91006
Mailing Address: PO Box 642, Jerusalem 91006
Tel: (02) 6526231 *Fax:* (02) 6526968
Key Personnel
Dir General: Rabbi Joseph Mowshovitz
Founded: 1937
A non-profit-making public corporation supported by the Jewish Agency, Ministry of Education & Culture & Ministry of Religious Affairs. Also provides financial support for works in above subjects.
Subjects: Biography, Philosophy, Religion - Jewish, Religion - Other, Theology
Number of titles published annually: 10 Print
Total Titles: 3,000 Print

Rolnik Publishers+
PO Box 17075, 61170 Tel Aviv
Tel: (03) 6496663 *Fax:* (03) 6478661
E-mail: rolnik@attglobal.net
Web Site: www.rolnik.com; www.bible2000.com
Key Personnel
Publisher: Amos Rolnik
Founded: 1970
Subjects: Art, Biblical Studies, Film, Video, Israel, Hebrew Studies
ISBN Prefix(es): 965-326

Rubin Mass Ltd+
PO Box 990, Jerusalem 91009
Tel: (02) 627-7863 *Fax:* (02) 627-7864
E-mail: rmass@barak.net.il
Web Site: www.rubin-mass.com
Key Personnel
Man Dir: Mr Oren Mass
Founded: 1927
Also acts as exporters of Israeli publications & periodicals.
Subjects: Biblical Studies, Biography, Education, Government, Political Science, Medicine, Nursing, Dentistry, Philosophy, Psychology, Psychiatry, Publishing & Book Trade Reference, Religion - Jewish, Religion - Other
ISBN Prefix(es): 965-09
Total Titles: 1,600 Print; 3 CD-ROM
Distributor for Carta; Yad Vashm

Saar Publishing House
39 Basel St, Tel Aviv 62744
Mailing Address: POB 26243, Tel Aviv 62744
Tel: (03) 5445292 *Fax:* (03) 5445293
Key Personnel
Man Dir: Saar Hanoch
Founded: 1979
Specialize in the publication of original & translated poetry.
Subjects: Fiction, Humor, Travel

Sadan Publishing Ltd+
One David Hamelech St, Tel Aviv 64953
Mailing Address: PO Box 16096, Tel Aviv 64953
Tel: (03) 6954402 *Fax:* (03) 6953122
Key Personnel
President: David Sadan
Founded: 1962
Firm is also an international co-publisher & packager.
Subjects: Archaeology, Biblical Studies, Law
ISBN Prefix(es): 965-234
Subsidiaries: Sadan Publication International Inc

Schlesinger Institute
Shaare Zedek Medical Center, PO Box 3235, Jerusalem 91031
Tel: (02) 655-5266 *Fax:* (02) 655-5266
E-mail: medhal@szmc.org.il
Web Site: www.szmc.org.il
Key Personnel
Dir: Dr Mordechai Halperin
Subjects: Law, Medicine, Nursing, Dentistry, Religion - Jewish

Schocken Publishing House for Children, *imprint of* Schocken Publishing House Ltd

Schocken Publishing House Ltd+
24 Nathan Yelin Mor St, Tel Aviv 67015
Mailing Address: POB 2316, Tel Aviv 61022
Tel: (03) 5610130 *Fax:* (03) 5622668
E-mail: find@schocken.co.il *Cable:* SCHOCKENIS
Key Personnel
Man Dir: Racheli Edelman *E-mail:* racheli@haaretz.co.il
Production: Dita Eliaz
Rights & Permissions: Ms Shira Asher
Founded: 1938

Membership(s): Israeli Book Publishers Association.
Subjects: Anthropology, Behavioral Sciences, Child Care & Development, Criminology, Drama, Theater, Economics, Education, Fiction, Health, Nutrition, History, Law, Literature, Literary Criticism, Essays, Nonfiction (General), Philosophy, Poetry, Psychology, Psychiatry, Religion - Jewish, Travel, Women's Studies
ISBN Prefix(es): 965-19
Imprints: Schocken Publishing House for Children; Shin, Shin, Shin
Divisions: Schocken Publishing House
Warehouse: Schocken Publishing House, 19 Lilienblum St, Tel Aviv

Shalem Press
22A Hatzfira St, 93102 Jerusalem
Tel: (02) 566-0601 *Fax:* (02) 566-0590
E-mail: shalem@shalem.org.il
Web Site: www.shalem.org.il
Key Personnel
Contact: Anat Altman *E-mail:* anata@shalem.org.il; Shmnel Reisman *E-mail:* shmuelr@shalem.org.il
Founded: 1994
Publish original books in Hebrew & English. Translate books into Hebrew.
Subjects: Economics, Government, Political Science, History, Philosophy, Cultural Issues
ISBN Prefix(es): 965-7052
Total Titles: 3 Print
Parent Company: The Shalem Center
U.S. Office(s): The Shalem Center, 1140 Connecticut Ave NW, Suite 801, Washington, DC 20036, United States *Tel:* 202-887-1270 *Fax:* 202-887-1277
Distributed by Armony Ltd

Shin, Shin, Shin, *imprint of* Schocken Publishing House Ltd

Sifri, *imprint of* Steimatzky Group Ltd

Sifri Ltd
PO Box 526, Tel Aviv 61004
Tel: (03) 5784679
Key Personnel
Dir: Yehoshua Matzliah; Eri M Steimatzky

Sifriat Poalim Ltd
24 Kibbutz Galuyot St, Merkazim Buil Gate 3, Tel Aviv 68166
Mailing Address: PO Box 37068, Tel Aviv 61369
Tel: (03) 5183143 *Fax:* (03) 5183191
E-mail: akantor@inter.net.il
Key Personnel
Man Dir: Avram Kantor
Management: Shlomo Zur
Encyclopedias: Amram Gordon
Production: Yaakov Shaia
Rights & Permissions: Yona Herzberg
Founded: 1939
Subjects: Art, Fiction, History, Labor, Industrial Relations, Philosophy, Social Sciences, Sociology
ISBN Prefix(es): 965-04

Simcha Pub, *imprint of* Pitspopany Press

Samuel Simson Ltd
5 Tel Giborim St, Teper House, Tel Aviv 68105
Tel: (03) 5181604 *Fax:* (03) 5181544
E-mail: sefer-lakol@mixam.co.il
Key Personnel
Man Dir: Rahamim Zalof
Founded: 1954

Sinai Publishing Co
72 Allenby St, 65812 Tel Aviv
Tel: (03) 5163672 *Fax:* (03) 5163672
Key Personnel
Man Dir: Moshe Schlesinger
Founded: 1853
Subjects: Religion - Jewish
ISBN Prefix(es): 965-7055
Subsidiaries: Sinai Export Co Ltd
Bookshop(s): Sinai Bookstore

R Sirkis Publishers Ltd+
13 Bialik St, 52523 Ramat-Gan
Mailing Address: POB 22027, 61220 Tel Aviv
Tel: (03) 7510792 *Fax:* (03) 7513750
E-mail: sirkispb@inter.net.il
Key Personnel
Man Dir: Rafael Sirkis
President & Chief Editor: Ruth Sirkis
Founded: 1983
Subjects: Archaeology, Art, Child Care & Development, Cookery, Crafts, Games, Hobbies, Fashion, Gardening, Plants, Health, Nutrition, How-to, Psychology, Psychiatry, Self-Help, Travel
ISBN Prefix(es): 965-387

Y Sreberk+
16 Balfour St, Tel Aviv 65211
Tel: (03) 6293343 *Fax:* (03) 6299297
Key Personnel
Man Dir: Zeev Namir
Production Manager: Y Namir
Founded: 1951
Subjects: Literature, Literary Criticism, Essays, Music, Dance, Classics

Steimatzky, *imprint of* Steimatzky Group Ltd

Steimatzky Group Ltd+
11 Hakishon St, Bnei-Brak 51114
Mailing Address: PO Box 1444, Bnei-Brak 51114
Tel: (03) 5775777 *Fax:* (03) 5794567
E-mail: info@steimatzky.co.il
Web Site: www.steimatzky.com
Key Personnel
Chief Executive Officer: Eri M Steimatzky
Man Dir: Yehoshua Matzliah
Founded: 1925
130 bookshops around the country. Also wholesaler, distributor, publisher, book club & mail order.
Subjects: Art, Biography, Cookery, Fiction, Religion - Jewish, Travel
ISBN Prefix(es): 965-236
Associate Companies: SIFRI Ltd
Imprints: Sifri; Steimatzky

Steinhart-Katzir Publishers+
PO Box 16540, 61164 Tel Aviv
Tel: (03) 6960995 *Toll Free Tel:* 800-22-5854 *Fax:* (09) 8854771
E-mail: webmaster@haolam.co.il
Web Site: www.haolam.co.il
Key Personnel
Man Dir: Ohad Sharav
Founded: 1991
Subjects: Travel
ISBN Prefix(es): 965-420
Number of titles published annually: 20 Print
Total Titles: 100 Print
Distributor for Berndtson & Berndtson; Freytag & Berndt; ITM; Karto Alatier; National Geographic

Talmudic Encyclopedia Publications
One Hapisga St, 91160 Jerusalem
Mailing Address: PO Box 16066, 91160 Jerusalem
Tel: (02) 6423242 *Fax:* (02) 6423919
Key Personnel
Man Dir: Rabbi Yehoshua Hutner
Founded: 1949
Subjects: Religion - Jewish
ISBN Prefix(es): 965-445

Tamai Books, *imprint of* Dekel Publishing House

Tcherikover Publishers Ltd
12 Hasharon St, Tel Aviv 66185
Tel: (03) 6870621; (03) 6396099
Toll Free Tel: 800-828-080 *Fax:* (03) 6874729
E-mail: barkay@inter.net.il
Key Personnel
Man Dir: Moshe Barkay *E-mail:* barkay@inter.net.il
Manager, Editorial: S Tcherikover
Subjects: Art, Criminology, Economics, Education, Geography, Geology, History, Language Arts, Linguistics, Literature, Literary Criticism, Essays, Management, Nonfiction (General), Psychology, Psychiatry
ISBN Prefix(es): 965-16

Tel Aviv Books, *imprint of* MAP-Mapping & Publishing Ltd

Tel Aviv Books Ltd
Imprint of MAP - Mapping & Publishing
17 Tchernikhovsky St, Tel Aviv 61560
Tel: (03) 6210500 *Fax:* (03) 5257725

Tel Aviv University+
The Jaffee Center for Strategic Studies, The Yariv Wing, Gilman Bldg, 69978 Tel Aviv
Mailing Address: PO Box 39040, 69978 Tel Aviv
Tel: (03) 6408111; (03) 6424571; (03) 6409200; (03) 6426682 *Fax:* (03) 6422404; (03) 6408355
E-mail: tauinfo@post.tau.ac.il
Web Site: www.tau.ac.il
Key Personnel
Prof: Zeev Maoz
Founded: 1977
Subjects: Foreign Countries, Government, Political Science, History, Military Science, Regional Interests, Social Sciences, Sociology
ISBN Prefix(es): 965-459
U.S. Office(s): Westview Press, Boulder, CO, United States
Distributed by Jerusalem Post (Israel); Westview Press

Terra Sancta Arts+
PO Box 10009, Tel Aviv 61100
Tel: (03) 6499520; (03) 6499525 *Fax:* (03) 6490532
Key Personnel
Man Dir: Gil Ran; Nachman Ran
Founded: 1972
Subjects: Biblical Studies, Religion - Other
ISBN Prefix(es): 965-260
Shipping Address: 31 Ehud Str, Tel Aviv 69936

Tirosh Communication Ltd
PO Box 6428, Tel Aviv 61063
Tel: (03) 6044959 *Fax:* (03) 6053840
E-mail: hgeffen@netvision.net.il
Key Personnel
International Rights: Amos Geffen
Founded: 1969
ISBN Prefix(es): 965-330

To Live (Holocaust), *imprint of* Ministry of Defence Publishing House

Harry S Truman Research Institute for the Advancement for Jerusalem+
Hebrew University of Jerusalem, Mount Scopus, Jerusalem 91905
Tel: (02) 58823000; (02) 58823001; (02) 5882315 *Fax:* (02) 5828076
E-mail: mstruman@pluto.mscc.huji.ac.il
Web Site: atar.mscc.huji.ac.il/~truman
Telex: SCOPUS JERUSALEM

Key Personnel
Chairman: Ambassador William A Brown
Dir: Prof Amnon Cohen *E-mail:* mstruman@mscc.huji.ac.il
Executive Dir: Dr Edy Kaufman *E-mail:* msek@mscc.huji.ac.il
Founded: 1966
ISBN Prefix(es): 965-222

Tsohar Publications, *imprint of* Breslov Research Institute

University of Haifa Library
Mount Carmel, 31905 Haifa
Tel: (04) 257753 *Fax:* (04) 342104
E-mail: webmaster@lib.haifa.ac.il
Web Site: lib.haifa.ac.il
Key Personnel
Dir: Baruch Kipnis *E-mail:* baruch@univ.haifa.ac.il
Head of Administration: Ms Humi Rekem
Subjects: Library & Information Sciences

University Publishing Projects Ltd+
10 Zarhin St, 43104 Raanana
Mailing Address: PO Box 393, 43104 Raanana
Tel: (09) 745-9955 *Fax:* (09) 745-9977
E-mail: upp@upp.co.il
Web Site: www.upp.co.il
Key Personnel
Dir: Nathan Eden
Founded: 1970
Subjects: English as a Second Language, Religion - Jewish, English as a Foreign Language (EFL)
ISBN Prefix(es): 965-372
Number of titles published annually: 25 Print
Total Titles: 348 Print
Imprints: ESH (English for Speakers of Hebrew)

Urim Publications+
9 Hauman St, 2nd floor, 91521 Jerusalem
Mailing Address: PO Box 52287, 91521 Jerusalem
Tel: (02) 679-7633 *Fax:* (02) 679-7634
E-mail: publisher@urimpublications.com
Web Site: www.urimpublications.com
Key Personnel
Publisher: Tzvi Mauer
Children's Book Editor: Shari Dash Greenspan *E-mail:* children@urimpublications.com
Founded: 1997
Also worldwide distributor of new & classic books with Jewish content.
Subjects: Biblical Studies, Biography, Ethnicity, Fiction, Human Relations, Literature, Literary Criticism, Essays, Religion - Jewish, Women's Studies
ISBN Prefix(es): 965-7108
Number of titles published annually: 8 Print
Total Titles: 22 Print; 1 CD-ROM
U.S. Office(s): Lambda Publishers, 3709 13 Ave, Brooklyn, NY 11218, United States *Tel:* 718-972-5449 *Fax:* 718-972-6307
Distributed by Ingram (North America)
Distributor for Lambda Publishers, Inc (Jewish bookstores in North America)
Distribution Center: Lambda Publishers, 3709 13 Ave, Brooklyn, NY 11218, United States *Tel:* 718-972-5449 *Fax:* 718-972-6307

The Van Leer Jerusalem Institute
43 Jabotinsky St, 91040 Jerusalem
Mailing Address: PO Box 4070, 91040 Jerusalem
Tel: (02) 5605222 *Fax:* (02) 5619293
E-mail: values@vanleer.org.il
Web Site: www.vanleer.org.il
Key Personnel
Executive Editor: Esther Shashar
Founded: 1959

Subjects: Foreign Countries, Government, Political Science, Psychology, Psychiatry, Science (General), Social Sciences, Sociology
ISBN Prefix(es): 965-271

Yachdav, United Publishers Co Ltd
29 Carlebach St, 67132 Tel Aviv
Mailing Address: POB 20123, 61201 Tel Aviv
Tel: (03) 5614121 *Fax:* (03) 5611996
E-mail: maalot@tbpai.co.il
Web Site: www.tbpai.co.il
Key Personnel
Man Dir: Amnon Ben-Shmuel
Founded: 1960
Established by the Book Publishers' Association of Israel as a jointly-owned publishing house in which most of the members of the Association are shareholders.
Subjects: Philosophy, Psychology, Psychiatry, Public Administration, Social Sciences, Sociology
Parent Company: Book Publishers Association of Israel

Yad Eliahu Kitov
PO Box 894, 91008 Jerusalem
Tel: (02) 6248868 *Fax:* (02) 6248838
E-mail: benarza@netvision.net.il
Key Personnel
Man Dir: Chanoch Ben Arza *E-mail:* benarza@netvision.net.il
Subjects: Religion - Jewish
ISBN Prefix(es): 965-252

Yad Izhak Ben-Zvi Press+
Ben-Zvi Institute, 12 Abrabanel St, Gan Hakuzari, 91076 Jerusalem
Mailing Address: PO Box 7660, 91076 Jerusalem
Tel: (02) 5398887; (02) 5398888 *Fax:* (02) 5638310
E-mail: ybz@ybz.org.il
Web Site: ybz.org.il
Key Personnel
Dir: Dr Zvi Zameret
Chairman, Public Governing Council: Dr Shimshon Shoshani
English Publications Coordinator: Yohai Goell *Tel:* (02) 5398825
Founded: 1966
Specialize in the history of Palestine/Israel & the Oriental Jewish Communities.
Subjects: Geography, Geology, History, Regional Interests, Religion - Jewish
ISBN Prefix(es): 965-235; 965-217
Total Titles: 320 Print

Yad Tabenkin
52960 Ramat Efal
Tel: (03) 5346268 *Fax:* (03) 5346376
E-mail: yadtab@inter.net.il
Web Site: www.ic.org
Founded: 1976 (Research Institute)
ISBN Prefix(es): 965-282
Number of titles published annually: 4 Print

Yad Vashem - The Holocaust Martyrs' & Heroes' Remembrance Authority+
PO Box 3477, Jerusalem 91034
Tel: (02) 6443400 *Fax:* (02) 6443443
E-mail: general.information@yadvashem.org.il
Web Site: www.yad-vashem.org.il *Cable:* YADVASHEM JERUSALEM
Key Personnel
Chairman: Avner Shalev
Vice Chairman: Johanan Bein
Editorial: Prof Israel Gutman
Yad Vashem Studies: David Silberklang
Secretary-General: Ishai Amrami
Administrative Dir: Vashem Yad
Publications: Esther Aran
Founded: 1953

Subjects: Biography, Education, History, Nonfiction (General), Holocaust Research
ISBN Prefix(es): 965-308
Branch Office(s)
Heychal Wolyn, 10 Korazin St, PO Box 803, Givatayim
U.S. Office(s): American Society for Yad Vashem, 500 Fifth Ave, No 1600, New York, NY 10110, United States
Distributed by Rubin Mass Ltd, Publishers & Booksellers
Bookshop(s): Yad Vashem Distribution, PO Box 3477, Jerusalem 91034

Yaron Golan Publishers
3 Burla St, Tel Aviv 69364
Tel: (03) 6992867 *Fax:* (03) 6952664
Specializes in Hebrew books of prose & poetry.
ISBN Prefix(es): 965-395
Total Titles: 10 Print

Yavneh Publishing House Ltd+
4 Mazeh St, 65213 Tel Aviv
Tel: (03) 6297856 *Fax:* (03) 6293638
Web Site: www.dbook.co.il
Key Personnel
Man Dir: Eliav Cohen
Founded: 1932
Subjects: Fiction, Music, Dance, Religion - Jewish, Religion - Other, Science (General)

Yedioth Ahronoth Books+
10 Kehilat Venezia St, 61534 Tel Aviv
Mailing Address: PO Box 53494, 61534 Tel Aviv
Tel: (03) 768-3333 *Fax:* (03) 768-3300
E-mail: info@yedbooks.co.il
Web Site: www.ybook.co.il
Telex: 33847
Key Personnel
Man Dir: Mr Dov Eichenwald
Editor-in-Chief: Aliza Ziegler
Founded: 1952
Subjects: Fiction, Health, Nutrition, How-to, Music, Dance, Nonfiction (General), Religion - Jewish
ISBN Prefix(es): 965-482
Number of titles published annually: 120 Print
Parent Company: Yedioth Ahronoth (The Evening Newspaper of Israel)
Associate Companies: Books in the Attaic, Amdan 5, Tel Aviv, Editor-in-Chief: Yehuda Melzer *Tel:* (03) 602-9010 *E-mail:* ilai@actcom.co.il
Subsidiaries: Miskal
Warehouse: 19 Hamerkava St, Holon

Y L Peretz Publishing Co
14 Brenner St, Tel Aviv 63826
Tel: (03) 5281751 *Fax:* (03) 5257983
Key Personnel
Man Dir: Israel Stein
Founded: 1956
Subjects: Art, History, Literature, Literary Criticism, Essays, Philosophy, Poetry, Religion - Jewish, Social Sciences, Sociology
ISBN Prefix(es): 965-7012

Zakheim Publishing House+
3 Bar Kochva St, 51263 Bney-Brak
Mailing Address: PO Box 2238, 52111 Bney-Brak
Tel: (03) 5708840 *Fax:* (03) 5708850
E-mail: zakheim@netvision.net.il
Key Personnel
General Manager: Eli Zakheim
Founded: 1967
Publishing house, wholesaler & distributor of educational materials & electronic kits of educational subjects. Specializes in children's books, educational equipment, encyclopedias & dictionaries for youths & children.
Total Titles: 4 Print

ISRAEL

The Zalman Shazar Center+
2 Betar, 91041 Jerusalem
Mailing Address: PO Box 4179, 91041 Jerusalem
Tel: (02) 5650444; (02) 5650445 *Fax:* (02) 6712388
E-mail: shazar@shazar.org.il
Web Site: www.shazar.org.il
Key Personnel
Chairman & Editorial, Hebrew: Prof Richard I Cohen
Executive Dir & Dir, Rights & Permissions: Zvi Yekutiel
Editorial Board Secretary: Maayan Avineri-Rebhun *E-mail:* maayan@shazar.org.il
Founded: 1973
Specialize in Jewish history.
Membership(s): The Historical Society of Israel.
Subjects: History, Religion - Jewish, Collected Essays, Historical Novels for Youth, Monographs, Pictorial Albums, Textbooks
ISBN Prefix(es): 965-227
Total Titles: 250 Print

Zmora-Bitan, Publishers Ltd
11 Lev Pesach, 71293 N Industrial Area Lod
Tel: (08) 9246565 *Fax:* (08) 9251770
E-mail: info@zmora.co.il
Key Personnel
Man Dir: Ohad Zmora
Publisher & Publicity: Asher Bitan
Sales: Eran Zmora
Production: Maya Dvash
Founded: 1973
Subjects: Anthropology, Biography, Cookery, Economics, Fiction, Government, Political Science, History, Nonfiction (General), Self-Help
ISBN Prefix(es): 965-03
Associate Companies: Bitan; Machbarot Lesifrut
Subsidiaries: Alpha Publishing House; Dvir Publishing House; Erez Books; Metziuth Books; Marganit Books

Italy

General Information

Capital: Rome
Language: Italian. Various others according to region
Religion: Predominantly Roman Catholic
Population: 57.6 million
Bank Hours: 0830-1330, 1500-1600 Monday-Friday
Shop Hours: 0830 or 0900-1300, 1500 or 1600-1930 or 2000 Monday-Saturday; many close Monday morning
Currency: 100 Eurocents = 1 Euro; 1936.27 Italian lira = 1 Euro
Export/Import Information: Member of the European Economic Community. 4% VAT on books; advertising matter other than single copies is dutied. No import license required.
Copyright: UCC, Berne, Florence (see Copyright Conventions, pg xi)

A & A+
Via Montenapoleone, 18, 20121 Milan
Tel: (02) 876 999 *Fax:* (02) 877 928
Founded: 1988
Also photojournalist agent.
Subjects: Photography
ISBN Prefix(es): 88-85279

Gruppo Abele+
Corso Trapani, 95, 10141 Turin
Tel: (011) 3841066
E-mail: segreteria@gruppoabele.it
Web Site: www.gruppoabele.it
Key Personnel
Man Dir & Editorial: Carla Martino
Sales: Doretta Graneris
Production: Pierangelo Bassignana
Publicity, Rights & Permissions: Silvia Mazza
Founded: 1983
Subjects: Child Care & Development, Communications, Education, Environmental Studies, Ethnicity, Health, Nutrition, Human Relations, Military Science
ISBN Prefix(es): 88-7670
Warehouse: Via Bologne 164, Turin

Edizioni Abete+
Via Prenestina 685, 00155 Rome
Tel: (06) 225821 *Fax:* (06) 2282960
Telex: 620370 ABETE I
Key Personnel
Chief Executive: Dr Luigi Abete
Editorial: Dr Giancarlo Abete
Sales: Dr Francesco Matassi; Franco Morbiducci
Founded: 1946
Subjects: Drama, Theater, Economics, Environmental Studies, Literature, Literary Criticism, Essays, Philosophy
ISBN Prefix(es): 88-7047
Parent Company: ABeTE SpA - Azienda Beneventana Tipografica Editoriale

Editrice Abitare Segesta
Via Ventura, 5, 20134 Milan
Tel: (02) 210581 *Fax:* (02) 21058316
Web Site: www.abitare.it
Telex: 315302 ABIT I
Key Personnel
Publisher: Renato Minetto
Founded: 1976
ISBN Prefix(es): 88-86116

Accademia (Milano)
Via Columella 36, Milan 20128
Tel: (02) 2552593
Founded: 1967
Subjects: Literature, Literary Criticism, Essays

Mario Adda Editore SNC
Via Tanzi 59, 70121 Bari
Tel: (080) 5539502 *Fax:* (080) 5539502
E-mail: info@addaeditore.it
Web Site: www.addaeditore.it
Key Personnel
Man Dir: Mario Adda
Founded: 1963
Subjects: Archaeology, Architecture & Interior Design, Art, Crafts, Games, Hobbies, History, Literature, Literary Criticism, Essays, Music, Dance, Philosophy, Photography, Poetry, Regional Interests, Social Sciences, Sociology
ISBN Prefix(es): 88-8082

Adea Books, *imprint of* Adea Edizioni

Adea Edizioni+
Via Lago Gerundo 31, 26100 Cremona
Tel: (0372) 430402 *Fax:* (0372) 43363
E-mail: info@adea.it
Web Site: www.adea.it/edizioni.html
Key Personnel
Editor: Mauro Maggio
Founded: 1992
Subjects: Astrology, Occult, Biography, Human Relations, Literature, Literary Criticism, Essays, Philosophy, Physical Sciences, Religion - Buddhist, Theology
ISBN Prefix(es): 88-86274
Imprints: Adea Books
Subsidiaries: Adea Education; Adea Incense; Adea Music; Adea SRL

Adelphi Edizioni SpA+
Via San Giovanni sul Muro 14, 20121 Milan

BOOK

Tel: (02) 725731 *Fax:* (02) 89010337
E-mail: info@adelphi.it
Web Site: www.adelphi.it
Key Personnel
Man Dir, Editorial Dir & Chairman: Roberto Calasso
Publicity: Matteo Codignola
Foreign Rights Manager: Simonetta Mazza
E-mail: rightsdept@adelphi.it
Founded: 1962
Subjects: Anthropology, Biography, Fiction, History, Literature, Literary Criticism, Essays, Mathematics, Mysteries, Philosophy, Physics, Poetry, Religion - Buddhist, Religion - Hindu, Science (General)
ISBN Prefix(es): 88-459
Foreign Rights: Ute Koerner Literary Agency (Spain); Nouvelle Agence (France)
Bookshop(s): Via Brentano 2, 20121 Milano
Warehouse: Via Mecenate 87/4, 20138 Milan
Orders to: Servizio Vendita Libri c/o RCS Libri & Grandi Opere SpA, Via Mecenate 91, 20138 Milan *Tel:* (02) 50951

AdP, *imprint of* Segretariato Nazionale Apostolato della Preghiera

Adriana Gallina Editore, *imprint of* Adriano Gallina Editore sas

Aesthetica
Via Giusti 25, 90144 Palermo
Tel: (091) 308290 *Fax:* (091) 308290
E-mail: aesthetica@unipa.it
Key Personnel
President: Lucia Pizzo
Editorial Dir: Luigi Russo
Founded: 1985
Subjects: Art, Philosophy
ISBN Prefix(es): 88-7726

Edizioni della Fondazione Giovanni Agnelli (Giovanni Agnelli Foundation Publishing)+
Via Giacosa 38, 10125 Turin
Tel: (011) 6500500 *Fax:* (011) 6502777
E-mail: staff@fga.it
Web Site: www.fondazione-agnelli.it
Key Personnel
President: Marco Demarie
Sales Mgr: Franco Picollo
Subjects: Economics, Geography, Geology, Government, Political Science, Social Sciences, Sociology
Number of titles published annually: 8 Print

De Agostini Scolastica
Via Montefeltro 6/A, 20156 Milan
Tel: (02) 380861 *Fax:* (02) 38086448
Web Site: www.scuola.com
Subjects: Education, Geography, Geology, History, Science (General)
ISBN Prefix(es): 88-423; 88-402; 88-415

AIB Associazione Italiana Bibliotheche (Italian Library Association)+
Viale del Castro Pretorio 105, 00185 Rome
Tel: (06) 4463532 *Fax:* (06) 4441139
E-mail: aib@aib.it
Web Site: www.aib.it
Key Personnel
President: Miriam Scarabo *E-mail:* presidenza@aib.it
Vice President: Maria Cristina Di Martino
Secretary: Marco Cupellaro *E-mail:* cupellaro@aib.it
Founded: 1930
The Italian association of professional librarians & information specialists.
Membership(s): IFLA; EBLIDA; IASL.
Subjects: Library & Information Sciences
ISBN Prefix(es): 88-7812

Number of titles published annually: 13 Print; 1 CD-ROM; 2 Online
Total Titles: 148 Print; 1 CD-ROM; 2 Online

L'Airone Editrice+
Imprint of Gremese Editore
Via Virginia Agnelli, 88, 00151 Rome
Tel: (06) 6570758 *Fax:* (06) 65740509
E-mail: gremese@gremese.com
Web Site: www.gremese.com
Key Personnel
Publisher & Executive Manager: Alberto Gremese *Tel:* (06) 65740507 *E-mail:* alberto@gremese.com
Founded: 1992
Subjects: Astrology, Occult, Crafts, Games, Hobbies, Humor, Mysteries, Nonfiction (General), Parapsychology, Photography, Sports, Athletics, Travel
ISBN Prefix(es): 88-7944

Alba
Corso Porta Po 82/A, 44100 Ferrara
Tel: (0532) 249854 *Fax:* (0532) 249854
E-mail: alba_editrice@virgilio.it
Key Personnel
Head of Company: Flavio Puviani
Founded: 1971
Subjects: Art, Literature, Literary Criticism, Essays, Poetry

Ermanno Albertelli Editore+
CP 395, 43100 Parma
Tel: (0521) 290387 *Fax:* (0521) 290387
E-mail: info@tuttostoria.it
Web Site: www.tuttostoria.it *Cable:*
ALBERTELLI PARMA
Key Personnel
Chief Executive, Production: Ermanno Albertelli
Sales: Viviana de Luca
Founded: 1968
Subjects: Military Science, Transportation
ISBN Prefix(es): 88-85909; 88-87372
Subsidiaries: Tuttostoria (Azienda di distribuzione)

Alberti Libraio Editore
Corso Garibaldi 74, 28921 Verbania
Tel: (0323) 402534 *Fax:* (0323) 401074
E-mail: info@albertilibraio.it
Web Site: www.albertilibraio.it
Founded: 1954
Subjects: History, Natural History, Regional Interests
ISBN Prefix(es): 88-7245; 88-85004
Number of titles published annually: 5 Print; 1 CD-ROM
Total Titles: 200 Print; 1 CD-ROM

Aleph, see Enna

Alessandro Tesauro Editore, *imprint of* Edizioni Ripostes

Libreria Alfani Editrice SRL
Via Alfani 84/86R, 50121 Florence
Tel: (055) 2398800 *Fax:* (055) 218251
E-mail: info@librerialfani.it
Web Site: www.librerialfani.it
Key Personnel
Chief Executive: Umberto Panerai
Founded: 1968
ISBN Prefix(es): 88-88288
Total Titles: 40 Print
Bookshop(s): Libreria Alfani, Via degli Alfani 84-86 R, 1-50121 Florence

Edizioni Alice
Viale Col di Lana, 4, 20136 Milan
Tel: (02) 83 61 347
E-mail: info@hod.it
Web Site: www.hod.it

Alinari Fratelli SpA Istituto di Edizioni Artistiche
Largo Fratelli Alinari, 15, 50123 Florence
Tel: (055) 23951 *Fax:* (055) 2382857
E-mail: info@alinari.it
Web Site: www.alinari.com
Telex: 572123 Alidea
Key Personnel
Man Dir: Claudio de Polo Saibanti
Founded: 1852
Subjects: Art, Education, Photography
ISBN Prefix(es): 88-7292
Bookshop(s): Fratelli Alinari, Via Vigna Nuova 48r, Florence; Fratelli Alinari, Via Alibert 16, Rome

Alinea+
Via Pl da Palestrina 17/19R, 50144 Florence
Tel: (055) 333428 *Fax:* (055) 331013
E-mail: ordini@alinea.it; info@alinea.it
Web Site: www.alinea.it
Founded: 1980
Specialize in architecture, art & engineering.
Subjects: Architecture & Interior Design, Art, Engineering (General)
ISBN Prefix(es): 88-8125
Distributed by Kappa-Clean
Book Club(s): Internazionale

All'Insegna del Giglio
Via Piccinni 32, 50141 Florence
Tel: (055) 451593 *Fax:* (055) 450030
Founded: 1976
Subjects: Archaeology, History
ISBN Prefix(es): 88-7814

Umberto Allemandi & C SRL+
Via Mancini 8, 10131 Turin
Tel: (011) 8199111 *Fax:* (011) 8193090
E-mail: info@allemandi.com
Web Site: www.allemandi.com
Key Personnel
Contact: Dr Christiano Casassa Mont
Founded: 1982
Subjects: Antiques, Archaeology, Architecture & Interior Design, Art, House & Home, Photography, Science (General)
ISBN Prefix(es): 88-422
Associate Companies: Umberto Allemandi & Co Publishing Srl

Editrice Ancora+
Via G B Niccolini 8, 20154 Milan
Tel: (02) 3456081 *Fax:* (02) 34560866
E-mail: editrice@ancora-libri.it
Web Site: www.ancora-libri.it
Key Personnel
Man Dir: Gilberto Zini
Foreign Rights Manager: Gloria Mari
Founded: 1934
Subjects: Religion - Other, Social Sciences, Sociology
ISBN Prefix(es): 88-7610; 88-514
Bookshop(s): Brescia *E-mail:* libreria.brescia@ancora-libri.it; Milan *E-mail:* libreria.hp@ancora-libri.it; Rome *E-mail:* libreria.zoma@ancora-libri.it; Trento *E-mail:* libreria.trento@ancora-libri.it

Franco Angeli SRL+
Viale Monza 106, 20127 Milan
Tel: (02) 28 37 141 *Fax:* (02) 26 14 47 93
E-mail: redazioni@francoangeli.it
Web Site: www.francoangeli.it
Key Personnel
Man Dir: Dr Franco Angeli
Sales: Dr Stefano Angeli *Fax:* (02) 2613268
Founded: 1955
Subjects: Anthropology, Business, Economics, History, How-to, Management, Marketing, Psychology, Psychiatry, Social Sciences, Sociology
ISBN Prefix(es): 88-204; 88-464
Number of titles published annually: 600 Print
Total Titles: 9,000 Print

Editrice Antroposofica SRL
Via Sangallo 34, 20133 Milan
Tel: (02) 7491197 *Fax:* (02) 70103173
Key Personnel
Man Dir: Dr Iberto Bavastro
Founded: 1959
Subjects: Religion - Other
ISBN Prefix(es): 88-7787
Parent Company: Rudolf Steiner Verlag, Switzerland

APE, *imprint of* Organizzazione Didattica Editoriale Ape

Apimondia+
Corso Vittorio Emanuele II 101, 00186 Rome
Tel: (06) 6852286 *Fax:* (06) 6852287
E-mail: apimondia@mclink.it
Web Site: www.apimondia.org
Key Personnel
President: A S Jorgensen *Tel:* (045) 57561777 *Fax:* (045) 57561703 *E-mail:* asj@krl.dk
General Secretary: R Jannoni-Sebastianini
Founded: 1949
Subjects: Agriculture, Biological Sciences, Economics, Marketing, Technology, Veterinary Science
ISBN Prefix(es): 88-7643

Apogeo srl - Editrice di Informatica
Via Battaglia, 12, 20127 Milan
Tel: (02) 289981 *Fax:* (02) 26116334
E-mail: apogeo@apogeonline.com
Web Site: www.apogeonline.com
Key Personnel
Contact: Ivo Quartiroli
ISBN Prefix(es): 88-85146; 88-7303; 88-503

Apostolato della Preghiera+
Segretariato Nazionale Apostolato della Preghiera, Via Degli Astalli, 16, 00186 Rome
Tel: (06) 697 607 1 *Fax:* (06) 67 81 063
E-mail: adp@adp.it
Web Site: www.adp.it
Key Personnel
Dir: Massimo Taggi *E-mail:* mt@adp.it
Contact: Roberto Izzi *Tel:* (06) 697607205
Founded: 1844 (in France, 1861 in Italy)
Bibles, books & leaflets.
Subjects: Psychology, Psychiatry, Religion - Other, Bibles, spirituality, pastoral activities, & prayer
ISBN Prefix(es): 88-7357
Total Titles: 198 Print; 198 Online
Parent Company: ADP International
Distributed by Messaggero Distribution SRL
Bookshop(s): Via Degli Astalli, 17, 00186 Rome *Tel:* (06) 697 607 201

Arcadia Edizioni Srl+
Via Caselline, 121, 41058 Vignola MO
Tel: (059) 76 60 34 *Fax:* (059) 77 92 79
E-mail: edizioni@arcadiabooks.com
Web Site: www.arcadiabooks.com
Key Personnel
Contact: Antony Shugaar
Subjects: Architecture & Interior Design, Art, Environmental Studies, Sports, Athletics, Travel
ISBN Prefix(es): 88-85684

Arcanta Aries Gruppo Editoriale
Via Makelle 97/1, 35138 Padova
Tel: (049) 8712477 *Fax:* (049) 8713851
Key Personnel
Chief Executive: Dr Franco Muzzio

Production: Sergio Fardin
Publicity: Stella Longato Muzzio
Founded: 1956
Subjects: Astrology, Occult, Health, Nutrition, Psychology, Psychiatry, Sports, Athletics
ISBN Prefix(es): 88-87564
Associate Companies: Franco Muzzio & C Editore SpA

Archimede Edizioni™, *imprint of* Paravia Bruno Mondadori Editori

Archimede Edizioni
Imprint of Paravia Bruno Mondadori Editori
Via Archimede 23, 20129 Milan
Tel: (02) 748231 *Fax:* (02) 74823278
Key Personnel
Man Dir: Roberto Gulli
Editorial Dirs & International Rights: Paola Rosci
Sales Dir: Dario Ramilli
Editorial Dirs & International Rights: Emilio Zanette
Founded: 1990
Educational publisher.
Subjects: Biological Sciences, Earth Sciences, Education, English as a Second Language, Fiction, History, Mathematics
ISBN Prefix(es): 88-7952

Rosellina Archinto Editore+
Via Santa Valeria 3, 20123 Milan
Tel: (02) 86460237 *Fax:* (02) 86451955
E-mail: info@archinto.it
Web Site: www.archinto.it
Key Personnel
President: Rosellina Archinto
Founded: 1986
Subjects: Biography, Literature, Literary Criticism, Essays, Nonfiction (General), Poetry
ISBN Prefix(es): 88-7768
Number of titles published annually: 20 Print
Shipping Address: Vivalibri, Via Isonzo, 25, 00198 Rome, Contact: Pietro D'Amore
Tel: (06) 84242153 *Fax:* (06) 84085679
E-mail: vivalibri@tin.it
Distribution Center: Messaggerie Libri, Via Tevere, 8, Assago-Milano 20090, Contact: Carlo Cherichi *Tel:* (02) 45774200, 45774210 *Fax:* (02) 45774230, 45774240
Orders to: Messaggerie Libri, Via Verdi, 8, Assago-Milano 20090 *Tel:* (02) 45774200, 45774210 *Fax:* (02) 45774230, 45774240

Archivio Guido Izzi Edizioni
Via Lazzarini 19, 00136 Rome
Tel: (06) 39735580 *Fax:* (06) 39734433
Founded: 1984
Subjects: Art, History, Literature, Literary Criticism, Essays
ISBN Prefix(es): 88-85760

L'Archivolto+
Via Marsala 3, 20121 Milan
Tel: (02) 29010444; (02) 29010424 *Fax:* (02) 29001942
E-mail: info@archivolto.com
Web Site: www.archivolto.com
Founded: 1986
Specialize in architecture & interior design.
Subjects: Architecture & Interior Design, Art, Gardening, Plants, Photography
ISBN Prefix(es): 88-7685
Subsidiaries: Edizioni L'Archivolto

Arcipelago Edizioni di Chiani Marisa+
Formerly Cooperativa Libraria IULM SCRL
Via Carlo d'Adda, 21, 20143 Milan
Tel: (02) 36525177 *Fax:* (02) 36553002
E-mail: arcipelago@arcipelagoedizioni.fastwebnet.it
Web Site: www.arcipelagoedizioni.com

Key Personnel
Owner: Marisa Chiani
Founded: 1971
Subjects: Advertising, English as a Second Language, Film, Video, Language Arts, Linguistics, Literature, Literary Criticism, Essays, Management, Marketing, Social Sciences, Sociology, Italian as a Second Language
ISBN Prefix(es): 88-7695
Number of titles published annually: 30 Print; 1 CD-ROM; 1 Audio
Total Titles: 1 CD-ROM; 1 Audio

Edizioni ARES+
Via Stradivari 7, 20131 Milan
Tel: (02) 29514202; (02) 29526156 *Fax:* (02) 29520163
E-mail: aresed@tin.it; info@ares.mi.it
Web Site: www.ares.mi.it
Key Personnel
Dir: Dr Cesare Cavalleri *E-mail:* cesare.cavalleri@ares.mi.it
Assistant Dir: Andrea Beolchi *E-mail:* andrea.beolchi@ares.mi.it
Founded: 1957
Subjects: Architecture & Interior Design, Philosophy, Psychology, Psychiatry, Theology
ISBN Prefix(es): 88-8155

Argalia Editore delle Arti Grafiche Editoriali SRL
Via S Donato 148/c, 61029 Urbino PS Pesaro
Tel: (0722) 328756 *Fax:* (0722) 328756
Web Site: www.culturitalia.uibk.ac.at
Founded: 1942
Also book packager.
Subjects: Drama, Theater, Economics, Education, Fiction, History, Literature, Literary Criticism, Essays, Philosophy, Poetry, Science (General)

Aries, see Arcanta Aries Gruppo Editoriale

Edizioni Arka SRL+
Via Sanzio, 7, 20149 Milan
Tel: (02) 4818230 *Fax:* (02) 4816752
E-mail: arka.edizioni@tin.it
Key Personnel
Man Dir: Ginevra Viscardi
Founded: 1984
Subjects: Animals, Pets, Art
ISBN Prefix(es): 88-8072; 88-85762
Number of titles published annually: 20 Print

Arktos
Via Valobra, 128, 10022 Carmagnola TO
Tel: (011) 9773941 *Fax:* (011) 9715340
Founded: 1976
Subjects: Astrology, Occult, Philosophy, Religion - Islamic
ISBN Prefix(es): 88-7049

Editore Armando Armando SRL+
Viale Trastevere, 236, 00153 Rome
Tel: (06) 5894525 *Fax:* (06) 5818564
E-mail: info@armandoeditore.com
Web Site: www.armando.it
Key Personnel
President: Enrico Iacometti
Founded: 1963
Subjects: Anthropology, Behavioral Sciences, Child Care & Development, Communications, Disability, Special Needs, Education, Health, Nutrition, Journalism, Language Arts, Linguistics, Medicine, Nursing, Dentistry, Philosophy, Psychology, Psychiatry, Radio, TV, Self-Help, Social Sciences, Sociology
ISBN Prefix(es): 88-7144
Number of titles published annually: 150 Print; 4 CD-ROM
Total Titles: 4 CD-ROM

Parent Company: Sovera Multimedia SRL, Via V Brunacci 55
Associate Companies: Sovera Multimedia, via Brunacci 55/55A, Rome, Caludia Iacometti *Tel:* (06) 5562429 *Fax:* (06) 5580723
Bookshop(s): Via Vincenzo Brunacci, 53, 00146 Rome *Tel:* (06) 5587850 *Fax:* (06) 5580723
Warehouse: Sovera Multimedia SRL, Via V Brunacci, 55, 00146 Rome

Gruppo Editoriale Armenia SpA+
Via Valtellina 63, 20159 Milan
Tel: (02) 683911 *Fax:* (02) 6684884
E-mail: armenia@armenia.it
Web Site: www.armenia.it
Key Personnel
Chief Executive: Dr Giovanni Armenia
Rights & Permissions: Fabiola Marchet *E-mail:* editoriale@armenia.it
International Rights: Simona Lari
Founded: 1972
Specialize in New Age, positive thinking & fantasy.
Subjects: Animals, Pets, Astrology, Occult, Crafts, Games, Hobbies, Fiction, Health, Nutrition, How-to, Humor, Nonfiction (General), Parapsychology, Science Fiction, Fantasy, Self-Help, New Age
ISBN Prefix(es): 88-344; 88-7216
Number of titles published annually: 80 Print
Total Titles: 500 Print; 2 CD-ROM
Warehouse: Via Vialba 71, 20026 Novate Milanese, Milano *Tel:* (02) 38200208 *Fax:* (02) 38200208
Distribution Center: Massaggerie Libri SA, Via Giuseppe Verdi 8, Assago, Milano *Tel:* (02) 457741 *Fax:* (02) 45701032

Arnaud Editore SRL+
Via Nardi 27, 50132 Florence
Tel: (055) 216485 *Fax:* (055) 260466
Key Personnel
Chief Executive: Alfredo Meletti
Founded: 1944
Subjects: Art, Government, Political Science, History
ISBN Prefix(es): 88-8015
Associate Companies: Nuova Expolibro Toscana SRL, Via Ricasoli 7, I-50122 Florence
Warehouse: Via De' Pucci 2, 50122 Florence

Arsenale Editrice SRL+
Via Monte Comun, 40, 37057 Verona
Tel: (04) 5545166 *Fax:* (04) 5545057
Telex: 480481 Apiver I sub 128
Key Personnel
Man Dir, Rights & Permissions & Production: Andrea Grandese
Editorial: Cinzia Boscolo
Sales: Giorgio Tamaro
Production: Andrea Grandese
Founded: 1984
Subjects: Architecture & Interior Design, Art
ISBN Prefix(es): 88-7743
Parent Company: Editoriale Bortolazzi - Stei SRL
U.S. Office(s): Moseley Assoc, 19 West 44 St, Suite 1200, New York, NY 10036, United States, Contact: Bert Paolucci
Bookshop(s): San Croce 29, 30135 Venice

Artema
Via Borgone 57, 10139 Turin
Tel: (011) 3853656 *Fax:* (011) 3853244
E-mail: cse@estorinese.inet.it
Key Personnel
President: Francesco Martiny
International Rights: Valentina Kalk
Founded: 1992
Subjects: Art
ISBN Prefix(es): 88-8052

Edi.Artes srl+
Viale Enrico Forlanini 65, 20134 Milan

Tel: (02) 70209917 *Fax:* (02) 70209919
Key Personnel
Man Dir: Raffaele Grandi
Founded: 1985
Subjects: Art
ISBN Prefix(es): 88-7724
Associate Companies: Edi.Ermes srl, Viale Enrico Forlanini 65, 20134 Milan

Artioli Editore
Via Emilia Ovest 669, 41100 Modena
Tel: (059) 827181 *Fax:* (059) 826819
E-mail: artiolip@pianeta.it
Founded: 1899
Subjects: Antiques, Architecture & Interior Design, Art, Drama, Theater, Photography, Regional Interests
ISBN Prefix(es): 88-7792

Associazione Carmelo Teresiano Italiano, OCD
Carmelitani Scalzi, Via Anagnina, 662 b, 00040 Morena (Rome)
Tel: (06) 7989081 *Fax:* (06) 79890840
Key Personnel
Dir: Rodolfo Girardello *Tel:* (06) 79890821; Arnaldo Pigna *Tel:* (06) 79890834
Officer: Fiorenzo Bugin *Tel:* (06) 79890836; Massimo Angelelli *Tel:* (06) 79890830
Administration: Luigia Paolitti *Tel:* (06) 79890822; Teresa Alpini *Tel:* (06) 79890823; Onelia Paoletti *Tel:* (06) 79890824
ISBN Prefix(es): 88-7229
Branch Office(s)
Edizioni Cattoliche

Associazione Internazionale di Archeologia Classica
Formerly Istituto Nazionale di Archeologia e Storia dell'Arte
Piazza San Marco, 49, 00186 Rome
Tel: (06) 6798798 *Fax:* (06) 69789119
E-mail: info@aiac.org; segreteria@aiac.org
Web Site: www.aiac.org
Key Personnel
President: Prof Paolo Liverani
Vice President: Dr Elizabeth Fentress
Founded: 1922
Membership(s): International Association of Research Institutes in the History of Art (RIHA); the International Union of the Institutes of Archeology, History & History of Art in Rome; The International Association of Classical Archeology; The National Institute of Studies of the Renaissance; Associated with the National Committee of Research & The Jean Berard Centre in Naples.
Subjects: Archaeology, Art
ISBN Prefix(es): 88-7275

Casa Editrice Astrolabio-Ubaldini Editore+
Via Guido D'Arezzo 16, 00198 Rome
Tel: (06) 855 21 31 *Fax:* (06) 855 27 56
Key Personnel
Chief Executive: Francesco Gana *E-mail:* f.gana@astrolabio-ubaldini.com
Editorial: Francesco Cardelli
Sales, Production: Fiorenzo Bertillo
Founded: 1946
Subjects: Philosophy, Psychology, Psychiatry, Social Sciences, Sociology, Oriental studies
ISBN Prefix(es): 88-340
Number of titles published annually: 35 Print
Total Titles: 1,050 Print

Editrice Atanor SRL+
Via Avezzano, 16, 00182 Rome
Tel: (06) 7024595 *Fax:* (06) 7014422
Key Personnel
Man Dir: Anna Maria Papini
Editorial: Francesco Albanese
Founded: 1912
Subjects: Asian Studies, Astrology, Occult, Science (General)
ISBN Prefix(es): 88-7169

Edizioni Dell'Ateneo Sr, see Instituti Editoriali E Poligrafici Internazionali SRL

Athesia Verlag Bozen+
Portici 41, 39100 Bolzano
Tel: (0471) 92 72 03 *Fax:* (0471) 92 72 07
E-mail: buchverlag@athesia.it *Cable:* ATHESIA VERLAG, BOZEN
Key Personnel
Man Dir, Production: Dr Peter Silbernagl
Sales Manager: Richard Fieg
Publicity Manager: Aron Mairhofer
Founded: 1907
Subjects: Art, Cookery, Geography, Geology, History, How-to, Humor, Law, Military Science, Outdoor Recreation, Poetry, Religion - Catholic, Travel
ISBN Prefix(es): 88-7014; 88-8266
Subsidiaries: Athesiadruck GmbH
Bookshop(s): Bozen; Brixen; Bruneck; Meran; Schlanders; Sterzing

Atlantica Editrice SARL
Casella Postale 34, 71100 Foggia
Founded: 1974
Subjects: Language Arts, Linguistics, Regional Interests, Science (General)
ISBN Prefix(es): 88-7085
Branch Office(s)
Casella Postale 38, 71043 Manfredonia

Automobilia srl+
Via Mario 16, 20149 Milan
Tel: (02) 4802 1671 *Fax:* (02) 4819 4968
E-mail: automobilia@tin.it
Key Personnel
President: Bruno Alfieri
Editorial: Ippolito Alfieri
Sales: Luisa Alfieri
Production: Verde Alfieri
Founded: 1979
Subjects: Architecture & Interior Design, Art, Automotive, Maritime, Transportation
ISBN Prefix(es): 88-85058; 88-85880; 88-7960

Baha'i
Via F Turati 9, 00040 Ariccia, Rome
Tel: (06) 9334334 *Fax:* (06) 9334335
E-mail: ceb@bahai.it
Web Site: www.bahai.it
Founded: 1969
Subjects: Biography, Economics, Education, Religion - Other, Social Sciences, Sociology
ISBN Prefix(es): 88-7214

Bancaria Editrice SpA
Subsidiary of ABI Italian Banking Association
via della Cordonata, 7, 00187 Rome
Tel: (06) 6767222; (06) 6767475 *Fax:* (06) 6767250
Web Site: www.bancariaeditrice.it
Key Personnel
Dir: Nicola Forti
Subjects: Business, Economics, Finance, Law, Management, Marketing
ISBN Prefix(es): 88-449

Bardi Editore srl
Via Piave 7, 00817 Rome
Tel: (06) 4817656 *Fax:* (06) 48912574
E-mail: bardied@tin.it
Web Site: www.bardieditore.com
Key Personnel
Man Dir: Garcia Y Garcia Laurent
Founded: 1921
Specialize in Oriental studies, scientific books, subscription & mail order books.
Subjects: Antiques, Archaeology, Architecture & Interior Design, History, Music, Dance
ISBN Prefix(es): 88-85699
Total Titles: 300 Print

Bastogi
Via Zara, 47, 71100 Foggia FG
Tel: (0881) 725070 *Fax:* (0881) 728119
E-mail: bastogi@tiscali.it
Web Site: www.bastogi.it
Founded: 1979
Subjects: History, Literature, Literary Criticism, Essays, Religion - Other
ISBN Prefix(es): 88-86452; 88-8185

Casa Editrice Luigi Battei
Str Cavour 5/C, 43100 Parma
Tel: (0521) 233733 *Fax:* (0521) 231291
Key Personnel
Chief Executive: Antonio Battei
Founded: 1872
Subjects: Architecture & Interior Design, Literature, Literary Criticism, Essays, Regional Interests
Showroom(s): La Pillotta
Bookshop(s): La Pillotta
Warehouse: Borgo Serena 3, 43100 Parma
Tel: (0521) 234747

Battelloavapore, *imprint of* Edizioni Piemme SpA

BC News, *imprint of* Edizioni del Centro Camuno di Studi Preistorici

BCSP, *imprint of* Edizioni del Centro Camuno di Studi Preistorici

BEL srl, *imprint of* Belforte Editore Libraio srl

Belforte Editore Libraio srl+
Via dei Cavalieri, 8, 57123 Livorno
Tel: (0586) 210919 *Fax:* (0586) 210349
E-mail: belforte@librinformatica.it
Web Site: www.librinformatica.it
Key Personnel
International Rights: Dr Riccardo Tagliati
Founded: 1834
Subjects: Antiques, Art, Behavioral Sciences, Biography, Child Care & Development, Education, Fiction, Human Relations, Library & Information Sciences, Literature, Literary Criticism, Essays, Nonfiction (General), Philosophy, Poetry, Psychology, Psychiatry, Regional Interests, Religion - Jewish, Wine & Spirits, Women's Studies
ISBN Prefix(es): 88-7997
Imprints: BEL srl
Subsidiaries: Librinformatica SRL

BeMa
Via Teocrito 50, 20128 Milan
Tel: (02) 252071 *Fax:* (02) 27000692
E-mail: segreteria@bema.it
Web Site: www.bema.it
Founded: 1975
Subjects: Antiques, Architecture & Interior Design, Earth Sciences, Engineering (General), English as a Second Language, Geography, Geology, Technology
ISBN Prefix(es): 88-7143
Imprints: Visual Itineraries

Bertello Edizioni
Via Bassigiano 46, 12100 Cuneo
Tel: (0171) 699002 *Fax:* (0171) 697729
ISBN Prefix(es): 88-8067

Bianco
Via Messina, 31, 00198 Rome

Tel: (06) 8554962 *Fax:* (06) 8844703 *Cable:* DEL BIANCO UDINE
Founded: 1933
Subjects: Art, Engineering (General), History, Science (General)

Editrice Bibliografica SpA
Via Bergonzoli, 1/5, 20127 Milan
Tel: (02) 28315996 *Fax:* (02) 28315906
E-mail: bibliografica@bibliografica.it
Web Site: www.bibliografica.it
Key Personnel
Administrator: Michele Costa
Editor: Giuliano Vigini
Founded: 1974
Membership(s): Associazione Italiana Editori; Associazione Italiana per la difesa della reprografia delle opere; gestisce l'agenzia Italiana dell'ISBN.
Subjects: Library & Information Sciences
ISBN Prefix(es): 88-7075
Number of titles published annually: 40 Print
Total Titles: 300 Print; 1 CD-ROM
Associate Companies: Informazioni Editoriali-IE SRL, Via Bergonzoli 1/5, 20127 Milan, Contact: Mauro Zerbini *Tel:* (02) 283151 *Fax:* (02) 28315900

Bibliopolis - Edizioni di Filosofia e Scienze Srl
Via Arangio Ruiz 83, 80122 Naples
Tel: (081) 664606 *Fax:* (081) 7616273
E-mail: info@bibliopolis.it
Web Site: www.bibliopolis.it
Key Personnel
Man Dir: Dr Francesco del Franco
Contact: Emilia del Franco
 E-mail: emiadelfranco@fiscolinet.it
Founded: 1976
Subjects: Archaeology, Literature, Literary Criticism, Essays, Mathematics, Philosophy, Physical Sciences, Physics, Science (General)
ISBN Prefix(es): 88-7088
Total Titles: 374 Print

Biblioteca Elle, *imprint of* Mondolibro Editore SNC

Biblioteca World, *imprint of* Mondolibro Editore SNC

Bibliotheca, see Bookservice

Biblos srl+
Via delle Pezze 33, 35013 Cittadella, Padova
Tel: (049) 5975236 *Fax:* (049) 9409875
Subjects: Architecture & Interior Design, Art
ISBN Prefix(es): 88-86214; 88-88064
Showroom(s): Buchmesse Frankfurt

Editoriale Bios+
Via Sicilia, 5, 87100 Cosenza CS
Tel: (0984) 398300 *Fax:* (0984) 398300
Key Personnel
Contact: Irene Olivieri
Founded: 1981
Subjects: Engineering (General), Medicine, Nursing, Dentistry
ISBN Prefix(es): 88-7740

Edizioni Blues Brothers, *imprint of* Kaos Edizioni SRL

BMG Ricordi SpA+
Via Liguria, 4, 20098 San Giuliano Milan
Tel: (02) 988131 *Fax:* (02) 88812212
E-mail: bmgricordi@bmg.com
Web Site: www.bmgricordi.it
Telex: 310177 Ricor I
Key Personnel
President: Adrian Berwick

Vice President: Gianni Babini
Founded: 1808
Subjects: Art, Drama, Theater, Music, Dance
ISBN Prefix(es): 88-7592; 88-8192; 88-492; 88-87018
Associate Companies: Ricordi Americana SAEC, Argentina; Ricordi Brasileira S/A, Rua Conselheiro Nebias 1136, 012036 Sao Paulo SP, Brazil; Ricordi Canada, Canada; Ricordi Londra, United Kingdom; G Ricordi & Co, Paseo de la Reforma 481-A, 06500 Mexico, DF, Mexico; Ricordi Monaco, Monaco; Ricordi Parigi, France
Subsidiaries: Arti Grafiche Ricordi SpA; Dischi Ricordi SpA; Gruppo Editoriale Musica Leggera Ricordi
Warehouse: via Salomone 77, 20138 Milano

Bollati Boringhieri Editore+
Corso Vittorio Emanuele II 86, 10121 Turin
Tel: (011) 55 91 711 *Fax:* (011) 54 30 24
E-mail: info@bollatiboringhieri.it
Web Site: www.bollatiboringhieri.it *Cable:* EDIBOR
Key Personnel
Man Dir, Editorial: Romilda Bollati
Foreign Rights: Christa Pardatscher
Founded: 1957
Subjects: Economics, History, Literature, Literary Criticism, Essays, Philosophy, Science (General), Social Sciences, Sociology
ISBN Prefix(es): 88-339

Bompiani-RCS Libri+
Via Mecenate 91, 20138 Milan
Tel: (02) 50951 *Fax:* (02) 5065361
Web Site: www.rcslibri.it; www.bompiani.rcslibri.it
Telex: 311321 Fabbri I *Cable:* LIBRIFABBRI MILANO
Key Personnel
Dir: Mario Andreose
Editor-in-Chief: Elisabetta Sgarbi
 Tel: (02) 50952666 *Fax:* (02) 50952788
 E-mail: elisabetta.sgarb@res.it
Founded: 1929
Membership(s): Gruppo Editoriale Fabbri, Bompiani, Sonzogno, Etas SpA.
Subjects: Art, Drama, Theater, Fiction, Nonfiction (General), Science (General)
ISBN Prefix(es): 88-451; 88-452

Bonacci editore+
Via Mercuri 8, 00193 Rome
Tel: (06) 68300004 *Fax:* (06) 68806382
E-mail: info@bonacci.it
Web Site: www.bonacci.it
Key Personnel
Man Dir: Alessandra Bonacci
Founded: 1942
Specialize in the production of material for the teaching of Italian as a foreign language.
Subjects: Education, Italian as a Foreign Language
ISBN Prefix(es): 88-7573
Total Titles: 4 Print; 1 Audio
Foreign Rep(s): Attica (France); Grivas (Greece); Intext Book (Australia); Klett Verlag (Germany); SGEL (Spain)
Warehouse: Via Pietro Cavallini 24/B *Tel:* (06) 321 57 08 *Fax:* (06) 321 57 08

Giuseppe Bonanno Editore+
Via Vittorio Emanuele, 194, 95024 Acireale, Catania
Tel: (095) 601984 *Fax:* (095) 604380
Web Site: www.bonannoedizioni.it
Key Personnel
Editorial: Giuseppe Bonanno
Dir: Dr Mauro Bonanno *E-mail:* bonannomauro@tiscalinet.it
Founded: 1966

Subjects: Architecture & Interior Design, Art, Behavioral Sciences, Cookery, Economics, Fiction, Foreign Countries, Government, Political Science, History, Law, Literature, Literary Criticism, Essays
ISBN Prefix(es): 88-7796
Number of titles published annually: 30 Print
Total Titles: 250 Print
Divisions: AEB Editrice
Branch Office(s)
Bonanno Editore Roita, Via Torino 150, Rome
 Tel: (064) 740467
Bookshop(s): Libreria Bonanno
Warehouse: Via Cozzale, 36 95024 Acireale, Catania

Casa Editrice Bonechi+
Via dei Cairoli 18B, 50131 Florence
Tel: (055) 576841 *Fax:* (055) 5000766
E-mail: redazione@bonechi.it; informazioni@bonechi.it
Web Site: www.bonechi.it
Telex: 571323 CEB
Key Personnel
Man Dir: Giampaolo Bonechi
Editorial: Marco Banti; Giovanna Magi
Sales Dir: Claudio Magnani
Founded: 1973
Subjects: Art, Cookery, Travel
ISBN Prefix(es): 88-7009; 88-8029; 88-476
Imprints: CEB

Bonechi-Edizioni Il Turismo Srl
Via G Di Vittorio 31, 50145 Florence
Tel: (055) 375739; (055) 3424527 *Fax:* (055) 374701
E-mail: info@bonechionline.com
Web Site: www.bonechionline.com
Key Personnel
Editorial Dir: Barbara Bonechi *E-mail:* barbara@bonechionline.com
Contact: Piero Bonechi *E-mail:* bbonechi@dada.it
Founded: 1954
Subjects: Archaeology, Art, Travel
ISBN Prefix(es): 88-7204

Bonsignori Editore SRL+
Viale dei Quattro Venti 47, Rome 00152
Tel: (06) 5881496 *Fax:* (06) 5882839
E-mail: redazione@bonsignori.it
Key Personnel
Chief Executive: Mario Bonsignori; Simona Bonsignori
Founded: 1992
Subjects: Archaeology, Architecture & Interior Design, Art, History, Specializes in archeology, architecture & history of art
ISBN Prefix(es): 88-7597
Number of titles published annually: 20 Print

Book Editore
Via della Chiesa 49/b, 40013 Castel Maggiore, Bologna
Tel: (051) 71 47 20 *Fax:* (051) 71 12 16
E-mail: bookeditore@libero.it
Web Site: web.tiscali.it/bookeditore
Key Personnel
Dir: Massimo Scrignoli
Founded: 1987
Subjects: Language Arts, Linguistics, Literature, Literary Criticism, Essays, Philosophy, Poetry
ISBN Prefix(es): 88-7232
Bookshop(s): Diest, Via Cavalcanti, 11, 10132 Torino *Tel:* (011) 89 81 164 *Fax:* (011) 89 81 164

Bookservice+
Formerly Bibliotheca
Via Maresca, 66b, 04024 Gaeta Latina
Tel: (0771) 744350 *Fax:* (0771) 744350
Key Personnel
Man Dir: Gabriele Chiusano

Founded: 1992
Subjects: History, Literature, Literary Criticism, Essays, Philosophy, Poetry, Social Sciences, Sociology
ISBN Prefix(es): 88-87106

Edizioni Bora SNC di E Brandani & C
Via Jacopo di Paolo 42, 40128 Bologna
Tel: (051) 356133 *Fax:* (051) 4159651
E-mail: daniele.brandani@mailbox.dsnet.it
Founded: 1971
Subjects: Art, Biography
ISBN Prefix(es): 88-85638; 88-85345; 88-88600
Total Titles: 4 Print

Edizioni Borla SRL+
Via delle Fornaci 50, 00165 Rome
Tel: (06) 39376728 *Fax:* (06) 39376620
E-mail: borla@edizioni-borla.it
Web Site: www.edizioni-borla.it
Key Personnel
Man Dir: Dr Vincenzo D'Agostino
Founded: 1863
Subjects: Anthropology, Education, Government, Political Science, History, Philosophy, Psychology, Psychiatry, Religion - Other, Social Sciences, Sociology
ISBN Prefix(es): 88-263

Bovolenta
Via della Ginestra, 227, 44100 Ferrara
Tel: (0532) 259386 *Fax:* (0532) 259387
Founded: 1975
Subjects: History, Literature, Literary Criticism, Essays, Philosophy
ISBN Prefix(es): 88-369

Edizioni Brenner+
Via Monte S Michele, 13A, 87100 Cosenza
Tel: (0984) 74537 *Fax:* (0984) 74537
Key Personnel
Man Dir, Editorial: Walter Brenner
Sales: Maria Gerbasi
Founded: 1956
Subjects: Ethnicity, History, Medicine, Nursing, Dentistry, Regional Interests

Editore Giorgio Bretschneider
Via Crescenzio 43, 00193 Rome
Mailing Address: CP 30011, Roma 47, 00193 Rome
Tel: (06) 6879361 *Fax:* (06) 6864543
E-mail: info@bretschneider.it
Web Site: www.bretschneider.it *Cable:* GIOBREROM
Key Personnel
Man Dir: Boris Bretschneider *E-mail:* bb@bretschneider.it
Founded: 1974
Subjects: Archaeology, History, Ancient History, Greek & Roman Antiquities, Greek & Roman Archaeology
ISBN Prefix(es): 88-85007; 88-7689
Number of titles published annually: 20 Print
Total Titles: 400 Print
Distributor for Italiana Di Atene; Scuola Archaeologica; Universita di Messina; Universita di Macerata

Edizioni Bucalo SNC
Casella Postale 51, 04100 Latina
Tel: (0773) 410036 *Fax:* (0773) 410036
E-mail: info@bucalo.it
Web Site: www.bucalo.it
Key Personnel
Chief Executive: Andrea Bucalo
Founded: 1965
Subjects: Law
ISBN Prefix(es): 88-7456
Parent Company: C Sopra

Buffetti
Via del Fosso di Santa Maura snc, 00169 Rome
Tel: (06) 231951 *Fax:* (06) 2389796
Web Site: www.buffetti.it
Founded: 1973
Subjects: Economics, Law, Management
ISBN Prefix(es): 88-19

Bulzoni Editore SRL (Le Edizioni Universitarie d'Italia)+
via dei Liburni, 14, 00185 Rome
Tel: (06) 4455207 *Fax:* (06) 4450355
E-mail: bulzoni@bulzoni.it
Web Site: www.bulzoni.it
Key Personnel
Man Dir, Editorial: Anna Bulzoni
Sales: Ivana Capitani
Production: Paola Bulzoni
Publicity: Anna Catarinozzi
Founded: 1969
Subjects: Art, Drama, Theater, Engineering (General), Fiction, Film, Video, Language Arts, Linguistics, Law, Literature, Literary Criticism, Essays, Philosophy, Science (General), Social Sciences, Sociology
ISBN Prefix(es): 88-7119; 88-8319
Bookshop(s): Libreria Ricerche, Via Liburni 10/12, I-00185 Rome *Tel:* (06) 491851

Cacucci Editore+
Via Nicolai 39, 70122 Bari
Tel: (080) 521 42 20 *Fax:* (080) 523 47 77
E-mail: info@cacucci.it
Web Site: www.cacucci.it
Key Personnel
Man Dir: Dr Nicola Cacucci
Contact: Nicholas Abbatangelo
Founded: 1929
Subjects: Economics, Law, Mathematics, Public Administration
ISBN Prefix(es): 88-8422
Showroom(s): Salone del Libro Torino; Expolibro Bari
Bookshop(s): Via Cairoli 140, Bari; Via S Matarrese 2/D, Bari

Edizioni Cadmo SRL+
Via Benedetto da Maiano 3, 50014 Fiesole (Florence)
Tel: (055) 50 18 1 *Fax:* (055) 50 18 201
E-mail: info@casalini.it
Web Site: www.casalini.it
Key Personnel
Man Dir: Mario Casalini
Founded: 1975
Subjects: Art, History, Language Arts, Linguistics, Music, Dance, Philosophy, Social Sciences, Sociology
ISBN Prefix(es): 88-86101; 88-7923

CADSR, *imprint of* Centro Ambrosiano di Documentazione e Studi Religiosi

Calosci+
Loc Vallone 35L, 52042 Camucia-Cortona (Arezzo)
Tel: (0575) 678282 *Fax:* (0575) 678282
E-mail: info@calosci.com
Web Site: www.calosci.com
Founded: 1964
Subjects: Archaeology, Architecture & Interior Design, Art, History, Literature, Literary Criticism, Essays, Medicine, Nursing, Dentistry, Music, Dance, Regional Interests, Transportation
ISBN Prefix(es): 88-7785
Distributed by The Courier srl

Camera dei Deputati Ufficio Pubblicazioni Informazione Parlamentare+
Palazzo Montecitorio-Piazza Montecitorio, 00186 Rome
Tel: (06) 67601 *Fax:* (06) 67603522; (06) 6783082
Web Site: www.camera.it
Telex: 612523
Key Personnel
Chief Executive: Dr Stefano Rizzo *Fax:* (06) 67602449 *E-mail:* rizzo_s@camera.it
Sales: Monica Fier *Tel:* (06) 67609909 *E-mail:* fier_m@camera.it
Founded: 1848
Specialize in bibliographies, books, pamphlets, proceedings, reference works.
Subjects: Economics, History, Law
Number of titles published annually: 20 Print
Total Titles: 250 Print
Bookshop(s): Libreria della Camera dei Deputati, Via Uffici del Vicario 17, Rome *Tel:* (06) 67603715 *E-mail:* sg-pi_libreria@camera.it

Campanotto+
Via Marano 46, 33037 Pasian di Prato (UD)
Tel: (0432) 699390; (0432) 690155 *Fax:* (0432) 644728
E-mail: edizioni@campanottoeditore.it
Web Site: www.campanottoeditore.it
Key Personnel
President: Frank Campanotto
Publishing Dir: Carlo Marcello Conti
Contact: Inga Conti
Founded: 1976
Subjects: Archaeology, Art, Fiction, History, Literature, Literary Criticism, Essays, Music, Dance, Philosophy, Photography, Poetry, Radio, TV, Religion - Catholic, Religion - Other
ISBN Prefix(es): 88-456
Subsidiaries: Grafiche Piratello

Canova SRL
Libreria Canova, Via Calmaggiore 31, 31100 Treviso
Tel: (0422) 262397 *Fax:* (0422) 433673
E-mail: info@canovaedizioni.it
Web Site: www.canovaedizioni.it
Key Personnel
Man Dir: Danilo Gasparini
Sales: Luigi Facchini
Founded: 1945
Subjects: Art, History
ISBN Prefix(es): 88-85066; 88-86177; 88-8409
Bookshop(s): Libreria Canova, Via Cavour 6/b, 31015 Conegliano

Edizioni Cantagalli+
Str Massetana Romana, 12, 53100 Siena
Tel: (0577) 42102 *Fax:* (0577) 45363
E-mail: cantagalli@edizionicantagalli.com
Web Site: www.edizionicantagalli.com
Key Personnel
Chief Executive: Pietro Cantagalli *E-mail:* david@edizionicantagalli.com
Founded: 1927
Subjects: Biblical Studies, Disability, Special Needs, History, Music, Dance, Nonfiction (General), Philosophy, Regional Interests, Religion - Catholic, Science (General), Theology
ISBN Prefix(es): 88-8272

Franco Cantini Editore, see OCTAVO Produzioni Editoriali Associale

Capone Editore SRL+
Sp Lecce-Cavallino, Km 1, 250, 73100 Lecce
Tel: (0832) 612618 *Fax:* (0832) 611877
Key Personnel
Editorial: Lorenzo Capone
Founded: 1980

Subjects: Art, Communications, Ethnicity, History, Literature, Literary Criticism, Essays, Philosophy, Regional Interests
ISBN Prefix(es): 88-8349

Cappelli Editore+
Via Farini 14, 40124 Bologna
Tel: (051) 239060 *Fax:* (051) 239286
E-mail: info@cappellieditore.com
Web Site: www.cappellieditore.com *Cable:* CAPPELLI EDITORE BOLOGNA
Key Personnel
Man Dir: Mario Musso
Editorial: Massimo Manzoni
Founded: 1851
Subjects: Art, Biography, Drama, Theater, Fiction, Film, Video, Government, Political Science, History, Medicine, Nursing, Dentistry, Music, Dance, Philosophy, Poetry, Psychology, Psychiatry, Religion - Other, Science (General), Social Sciences, Sociology
ISBN Prefix(es): 88-379
Associate Companies: Nicola Milano Editore

Edizioni Del Capricorno, *imprint of* Centro Scientifico Torinese

Edizioni del Capricorno
Via Borgone, 37, 10139 Turin
Tel: (011) 386500 *Fax:* (011) 3853244
E-mail: cse@estorinese.inet.it
Key Personnel
Editor: Dr Walter Martiny
Foreign Rights Manager: Valentine Kalk
Subjects: Photography
ISBN Prefix(es): 88-7707
Parent Company: Centro Scientific Torinese SrL

Edizioni Carmelitane
Via Sforza Pallavicini, 10, 00193 Rome
Tel: (06) 68100886 *Fax:* (06) 68100887
E-mail: edizioni@ocarm.org
Web Site: www.carmelites.info/edizioni
Key Personnel
Dir: E Evaldo Xavier Gomes
Founded: 1954
Publishing house of the Carmelite Order.
Subjects: Biblical Studies, History, Religion - Catholic, Theology
ISBN Prefix(es): 88-7229; 88-7288
Number of titles published annually: 5 Print
Total Titles: 1,000 Print

Edizioni Carroccio
Via Alfieri, 1, 35010 Vigodarzere (Padova)
Tel: (049) 700568 *Fax:* (049) 700568
Key Personnel
Man Dir: Luciano Lincetto
Founded: 1947
Subjects: Religion - Catholic, Religion - Other

Edizioni Cartedit SRL+
Via Industriale 7, 26010 Monte Cremasco (Cremona)
Tel: (0373) 277410 *Fax:* (0373) 277405
Key Personnel
Editor: Sig Pigon Lavinio
Founded: 1992
ISBN Prefix(es): 88-86170; 88-8070

Edizioni Cartografiche Milanesi+
Via Reali 3/5, 20037 Padermo Dugnano (MI)
Tel: (02) 9101649 *Fax:* (02) 9101118
E-mail: info@ortelio-ecm.it
Web Site: www.ortelio-ecm.it
Subjects: Geography, Geology
ISBN Prefix(es): 88-8151
Number of titles published annually: 40 Print
Total Titles: 70 Print
Imprints: Ortelio

Cartoonseries, *imprint of* Stampa Alternativa - Nuovi Equilibri

Casa Editrice Dr A Milani, see CEDAM (Casa Editrice Dr A Milani)

Casa Editrice Felice Le Monnier, see Edumond Le Monnier

Casa Editrice Giuseppe Principato Spa+
Via Fauche 10, 20154 Milan
Tel: (02) 312025; (02) 3315309 *Fax:* (02) 33104295
E-mail: info@principato.it
Web Site: www.principato.it
Key Personnel
Publishing Dir: Franco Menin
Founded: 1887
Subjects: Biological Sciences, Chemistry, Chemical Engineering, Earth Sciences, English as a Second Language, Geography, Geology, History, Literature, Literary Criticism, Essays, Mathematics, Philosophy, Physics
ISBN Prefix(es): 88-416
Number of titles published annually: 30 Print
Total Titles: 500 Print

Casa Editrice Libraria Ulrico Hoepli SpA+
Via U Hoepli 5, 20121 Milan
Tel: (02) 864871 *Fax:* (02) 864322
E-mail: hoepli@hoepli.it
Web Site: www.hoepli.it *Cable:* HOEPLI MILAN
Key Personnel
Man Dir: Gianni Hoepli; Dr Ulrico Carlo Hoepli
Rights & Permissions: Dr Susanna Schwarz Bellotti
Contact: Daniela Grazi
Founded: 1870
Subjects: Art, Engineering (General), How-to, Law, Social Sciences, Sociology, Technology
ISBN Prefix(es): 88-203
Bookshop(s): Hoepli Ulrico Libreria Internazionale
Shipping Address: Via Mameli 13, 20129 Milan

Casa Editrice Lint Srl
Via di Romagna 30, 34134 Trieste
Tel: (040) 360396 *Fax:* (040) 361354
Key Personnel
President: Prof Riccardo Maetzke
Advisor: Maria Rosa Casagrande Maetzke
Founded: 1962
Subjects: Art, Science (General)
ISBN Prefix(es): 88-86179; 88-85083; 88-8190

Casa Musicale Edizioni Carrara SRL
Via Calepio 2/4, 24125 Bergamo
Tel: (035) 243618 *Fax:* (035) 270398
E-mail: info@edizionicarrara.it
Web Site: www.edizionicarrara.it *Cable:* CARRARA MUSICA BERGAMO
Key Personnel
Editorial, Production: Vinicio Carrara
Sales, Publicity: Vittorio Carrara
Founded: 1912
Subjects: Music, Dance, Religion - Catholic

Casa Musicale G Zanibon SRL+
Via Berchet, 2, 20121 Milan
Tel: (02) 88811 *Fax:* (02) 88814317
Telex: 88814317 *Cable:* IDROCIR MILANO
Key Personnel
Contact: Cristiano Giovannini
Founded: 1908
Subjects: Education, Music, Dance
ISBN Prefix(es): 88-86642
Imprints: GZ; ZAN
Subsidiaries: Edizioni Drago; Edizioni Orfeo

Casalini Libri
Via Benedetto da Maiano, 3, 50014 Florence
Tel: (055) 5018 1 *Fax:* (055) 5018 201
E-mail: info@casalini.it
Web Site: www.casalini.it *Cable:* CASALINI FIESOLE
Key Personnel
President: Gerda von Grebmer
Man Dir: Barbara Casalini *E-mail:* barbara@casalini.it; Michele Casalini *E-mail:* michele@casalini.it
Founded: 1958
Firm's main functions are book exporter, bibliographic agent & library supplier.
ISBN Prefix(es): 88-85297
Associate Companies: CADMO

Casa Editrice Castalia (Castalia Books Limited)+
Via Peyron 38, 10143 Turin
Tel: (011) 4374176 *Fax:* (011) 4374176
Key Personnel
Chairperson: Dr Mario Miglietti
Dir: Silvia Camodeca
Founded: 1984
Publisher of children's books.
Subjects: Fiction
ISBN Prefix(es): 88-7701
Number of titles published annually: 10 Print
Total Titles: 98 Print
Imprints: Mario Miglietti

Il Castello srl+
Via Scarlatti, 12, 20090 Trezzano sul Naviglio, Milan
Tel: (02) 48401629 *Fax:* (02) 4453617
E-mail: il_castello@tin.it
Key Personnel
Chief Executive: Luca Belloni
Editorial: Mose Menotti
Founded: 1955
Subjects: Art, Astronomy, Cookery, Crafts, Games, Hobbies, Outdoor Recreation, Photography, Fitness
ISBN Prefix(es): 88-8039; 88-88112
Number of titles published annually: 60 Print
Total Titles: 300 Print

Editrice Il Castoro+
Viale Abruzzi 72, 20131 Milan
Tel: (02) 29513529 *Fax:* (02) 29529896
E-mail: editrice.castoro@iol.it
Web Site: www.castoro-on-line.it
Key Personnel
Administrator & Editor: Renata Gorgani
Rights: Marta Spinelli
Editorial: Silvia Pareti
Founded: 1993
Subjects: Biography, Fiction, Film, Video
ISBN Prefix(es): 88-8033

CCSP, *imprint of* Edizioni del Centro Camuno di Studi Preistorici

CEB, *imprint of* Casa Editrice Bonechi

CEDAM (Casa Editrice Dr A Milani)
Via Jappelli 5/6, 35121 Padova
Tel: (049) 8239111 *Fax:* (049) 8752900
E-mail: info@cedam.com
Web Site: www.cedam.com
Key Personnel
President: Dott Antonio Milani
Administrator: Francesco Giordano; Carlo Porta
Founded: 1903
Subjects: Biological Sciences, Criminology, Economics, Finance, Government, Political Science, Law, Management, Marketing, Mathematics, Medicine, Nursing, Dentistry, Philosophy, Psychology, Psychiatry, Public Administration, Social Sciences, Sociology

ISBN Prefix(es): 88-13
Warehouse: Via Uruguay n 14, 35127 Camin PD

Edizioni CELI, *imprint of* Gruppo Editoriale Faenza Editrice SpA

CELID
Via Enrico Cialdini 26, 10138 Turin
Tel: (011) 447 47 74 *Fax:* (011) 447 47 59
E-mail: edizioni@celid.it
Web Site: www.celid.it
Key Personnel
Contact: Antonio Catalano; Vanda Cremona
Founded: 1974
Subjects: Architecture & Interior Design, Engineering (General), History
ISBN Prefix(es): 88-7661
Branch Office(s)
V Mattioli 39, 10125 Turin
Corso Duca Degli Abruzzi 24, 10129 Turin
Bookshop(s): Via S Ottavio 20, 10124 Turin

Celuc Libri
Via Santa Valeria 5, 20123 Milan
Tel: (02) 86 45 07 76 *Fax:* (02) 86 45 14 24
Key Personnel
Man Dir: Rita Barbatiello
Founded: 1969 (as CELUC), 1974 (as Celuc Libri SRL)
Subjects: Economics, Government, Political Science, History, Law, Literature, Literary Criticism, Essays, Mathematics, Philosophy, Religion - Other, Science (General), Social Sciences, Sociology
Bookshop(s): Libreria Celuc Libri, Via Santa Valeria 5, 20123 Milan

CEM, see Casa Editrice Maccari (CEM)

Istituto Centrale per il Catalogo Unico delle Biblioteche Italiane e per le Informazioni Bibliografiche (Central Institute of the Union Catalog of Italian Libraries & Bibliographical Information)
Viale del Castro Pretorio 105, 00185 Rome
Tel: (06) 4989484 *Fax:* (06) 4959302
Web Site: www.iccu.sbn.it
Key Personnel
Dir: Dr Luciano Scala
Subjects: Library & Information Sciences
ISBN Prefix(es): 88-7107

Centro Ambrosiano di Documentazione e Studi Religiosi
Corso di Porta Ticenese 33, 20123 Milan
Tel: (02) 83.75.476 *Fax:* (02) 58.10.09.49
E-mail: cadr@cadr.it
Web Site: www.cadr.it
Founded: 1972
Subjects: History, Religion - Other
ISBN Prefix(es): 88-7098
Imprints: CADSR

Centro Biblico
Via Masseria Vecchia 112, 80014 Giugliano, Naples
Tel: (081) 8048933 *Fax:* (081) 8048933
Key Personnel
Dir: David Freitag
Founded: 1952
Subjects: Biblical Studies, Religion - Protestant, Theology
ISBN Prefix(es): 88-7054

Centro Di
Lungarno Serristori, 35, 50125 Florence
Tel: (055) 2342668 *Fax:* (055) 2342667
Cable: Centrodi Florence
Key Personnel
Man Dir: Alessandra Marchi
Founded: 1968
Subjects: Art
ISBN Prefix(es): 88-7038

Centro Documentazione Alpina
Via Invorio 24a, 10146 Turin
Tel: (011) 7720444 *Fax:* (011) 7732170
Web Site: www.cda.it
Key Personnel
Editorial: Pietro Giglio; Mario Frasciome
Founded: 1970
Subjects: Geography, Geology
ISBN Prefix(es): 88-85504

Centro Editoriale Valtortiano SRL+
Viale Piscicelli 91, 03036 Isola del Liri FR
Tel: (0776) 807032 *Fax:* (0776) 809789
E-mail: cev@mariavaltorta.com
Web Site: www.mariavaltorta.com
Key Personnel
Editor: Emilio Pisani
Author: Maria Valtorta
Founded: 1985
Subjects: Religion - Catholic, Theology
ISBN Prefix(es): 88-7987
Number of titles published annually: 6 Print
Total Titles: 94 Print

Centro Italiano di Studi Sull'Alto Medioevo, see CISAM

Centro Italiano Studi Alto Medioevo
Piazza della Liberta 12, 06049 Spoleto (Perugia)
Tel: (0743) 225630 *Fax:* (0743) 49902
E-mail: cisam@cisam.org
Web Site: www.cisam.org
Key Personnel
President: Prof Enrico Menesto
Founded: 1952
To promote meetings & scientific publications on the high Middle Ages.
Subjects: Art, History, Literature, Literary Criticism, Essays, Philosophy
ISBN Prefix(es): 88-7988
Number of titles published annually: 24 Print
Total Titles: 500 Print
Imprints: CISAM

Centro Programmazione Editoriale (CPE)
Via Canaletto, 20 b, 41030 San Prospero MO
Tel: (059) 908065 *Fax:* (059) 908271
Founded: 1973
Subjects: Education, Mathematics, Psychology, Psychiatry
ISBN Prefix(es): 88-7378

Centro Scientifico Editore, *imprint of* Centro Scientifico Torinese

Centro Scientifico Torinese+
Via Borgone 57, 10139 Turin
Tel: (011) 3853656 *Fax:* (011) 3853244
E-mail: cse@estorinese.inet.it
Key Personnel
President: Francesco Martiny
Editor: Dr Walter Martiny
Administrator: Pier Luigi Massaza
Founded: 1973
Subjects: Health, Nutrition, Human Relations, Medicine, Nursing, Dentistry, Psychology, Psychiatry
ISBN Prefix(es): 88-7640
Associate Companies: Artema Srl; Centro Scientifico Internazionale
Imprints: Edizioni Del Capricorno; Centro Scientifico Editore; Soleverde

Edizioni Centro Studi Erickson+
Loc Spini di Gardolo, 38014 Gardolo, Trento
Tel: (0461) 950690 *Fax:* (0461) 950698
E-mail: info@erickson.it
Web Site: www.erickson.it
Key Personnel
Dir: Dario Ianes; Fabio Folgheraiter
Editor: Carmen Calovi *E-mail:* calovi@erickson.it; Francesca Cretti *E-mail:* cretti@erickson.it; Riccardo Mazzeo *E-mail:* ric@erickson.it
Founded: 1984
Subjects: Behavioral Sciences, Child Care & Development, Education, Nonfiction (General), Psychology, Psychiatry, Self-Help, Social Sciences, Sociology
ISBN Prefix(es): 88-7946; 88-85857
Number of titles published annually: 30 Print; 8 CD-ROM
Total Titles: 250 Print; 8 CD-ROM

Centro Studi Terzo Mondo (Study Center for the Third World)+
Via GB Morgagni 39, 20129 Milan
Tel: (02) 29409041 *Fax:* (02) 29409041
E-mail: cstm@libero.it
Key Personnel
Chief Executive: Prof Umberto Melotti
Tel: (0330) 687866 *E-mail:* melotti@uniroma1.it
Editorial, Rights & Permissions: Elena Sala
Founded: 1964
Books & journals on social sciences & on the problems of the Third World.
Subjects: Anthropology, Economics, Ethnicity, Geography, Geology, Government, Political Science, History, Literature, Literary Criticism, Essays, Poetry, Social Sciences, Sociology
Number of titles published annually: 12 Print
Total Titles: 120 Print
Imprints: CSTM; Ed La Cultura Sociologica

il Cerchio Iniziative Editoriali+
via Dell' Allodola n 8, 47900 Rimini
Tel: (0541) 21158; (0541) 708190 *Fax:* (0541) 799173
E-mail: info@ilcerchio.it
Web Site: www.ilcerchio.it
Key Personnel
Man Dir, Production, Rights & Permissions: Dr Adolfo Morganti
Editorial: Dr Maurizio Mecozzi
Sales: Gloria Rubinato
Publicity: Dr Sergio de Vita
Desktop Publishing: Davide Peggi
Founded: 1978
Subjects: Anthropology, Art, Economics, Government, Political Science, History, Literature, Literary Criticism, Essays, Mythology, Nonfiction (General), Philosophy, Religion - Islamic, Religion - Other, Science (General), Social Sciences, Sociology
ISBN Prefix(es): 88-86583
Parent Company: Cooperativa Culturale Il Cerchio, Via Gambalunga, 91, 47037 Rimini
Bookshop(s): Libreria Cooperativa Il Cerchio, Via Gambalunga, 91, 47900 Rimini

CG Ediz Medico-Scientifiche+
Via Viberti 7, 10141 Turin
Tel: (011) 338507 *Fax:* (011) 3852750
Web Site: www.cgems.it
Key Personnel
Contact: Pier Paola Pratis Palazzo
Founded: 1958
Specialize in medical books.
Subjects: Biological Sciences, Medicine, Nursing, Dentistry, Veterinary Science
ISBN Prefix(es): 88-7110

CIC Edizioni Internazionali+
Corso Trieste, 42, 00198 Rome
Tel: (06) 8412673 *Fax:* (06) 8412688; (06) 8412687
E-mail: info@gruppocic.it
Web Site: www.gruppocic.it
Telex: 622099 CICI

Key Personnel
President: Prof Andrea Salvati *E-mail:* a.salvati@gruppocic.it
Dir General: Dr Raffaele Salvati *E-mail:* r.salvati@gruppocic.it
Advertising Dept: Patrizia Arcangioli
 E-mail: arcangioli@gruppocic.it
Foreign Rights Dept: Marilena Cefa
 E-mail: cefa@gruppocic.it
Sales & Subscriptions Dept: Amelia Assi
 E-mail: assi@gruppocic.it
Founded: 1970
Membership(s): ANES; USPI.
Subjects: Health, Nutrition, Medicine, Nursing, Dentistry, Psychology, Psychiatry
ISBN Prefix(es): 88-7141
Number of titles published annually: 150 Print; 10 CD-ROM; 15 Audio
Total Titles: 600 Print; 10 CD-ROM; 30 Audio
Subsidiaries: Centro Italiano Congressi; Kairos; Librerie CIC Edizioni Internazionali
Branch Office(s)
Centro Italiano Congress, CIC SUD, via le Escriva Nº 28, 70124 Bari, Contact: Olimpia Cassano *Tel:* (080) 5043737 *Fax:* (080) 5043736
Viale E Caldara, 35/A, 20122 Milan, Contact: Antonietta Garzonio *Tel:* (02) 55187057 *Fax:* (02) 55187061
Distributor for George Thieme Verlag (Italian territory)
Warehouse: Circonvallazione Nomentana, 482, 00162 Rome

Cideb Editrice SRL+
Via Venezia 93, 16035 Rapallo (Genova)
Tel: (0185) 60241 *Fax:* (0185) 230100
E-mail: info@cideb.com
Web Site: www.cideb.it
Key Personnel
Manager: Ornella Caffo
Founded: 1992
Subjects: Literature, Literary Criticism, Essays
ISBN Prefix(es): 88-7754; 88-530
Orders to: Cideb SRL, Via Torre Civica 8, 16035 Rapallo (Genova)

Il Cigno Galileo Galilei-Edizioni di Arte e Scienza
Piazza San Salvatore Lauro 15, 00186 Rome
Tel: (06) 6865493; (06) 6873842 *Fax:* (06) 6892109
E-mail: info@ilcigno.org
Key Personnel
Contact: Delfina Bergamaslhi
Founded: 1968
Also specialize in printing graphic works & publish catalogues & art volumes.
Subjects: Art, Law, Mathematics, Science (General)
ISBN Prefix(es): 88-7831
Number of titles published annually: 40 Print; 4 CD-ROM
Total Titles: 385 Print; 4 CD-ROM
Showroom(s): Archivi Greco, Museo Mastroianni & Il Cigno Galileo Galilei La Stamperia
Distribution Center: Gaetano Amodio, Via Francesco Battiato 24, 95039 Catania *Tel:* (03095) 321328 (South Italy)
Pecorini Sas, Foro Buonaparte 48, 20121 Milano *Tel:* (02) 86460660 *Fax:* (02) 72001462 (North Italy)

Ciranna e Ferrara
Via Solferino, 163, 20038 Seregno (Milan)
Tel: (0362) 230849 *Fax:* (0362) 326213
Founded: 1976
ISBN Prefix(es): 88-8144

Ciranna - Roma
Via Besio 127, 143, 90145 Palermo
Tel: (091) 224499 *Fax:* (091) 311064
E-mail: info@ciranna.it
Web Site: www.ciranna.it
Key Personnel
Chief Executive, Rights & Permissions: Dr Lidia Fabiano
Founded: 1953
Subjects: Art, Business, Education, Geography, Geology, History, Language Arts, Linguistics, Law, Literature, Literary Criticism, Essays, Mathematics, Philosophy, Psychology, Psychiatry, Public Administration, Science (General), Technology
ISBN Prefix(es): 88-8322
Orders to: Via Capograssa 1115

Cisalpino, *imprint of* Monduzzi Editore SpA

Cisalpino
Via Eustachi, 12, 20129 Milan
Tel: (02) 2040 4031 *Fax:* (02) 2040 4044
Web Site: www.monduzzi.com/cisalpino
Founded: 1946
Subjects: Economics, History, Language Arts, Linguistics, Law, Literature, Literary Criticism, Essays, Management
ISBN Prefix(es): 88-205; 88-323
Parent Company: Monduzzi Editore SpA, Via Ferrarese 119/2, 40128 Bologna

CISAM, *imprint of* Centro Italiano Studi Alto Medioevo

CISAM
Palazzo Ancaiani, Piazza della Liberta 12, 06049 Spoleto, Perugia
Tel: (0743) 225630 *Fax:* (0743) 49902
E-mail: cisam@cisam.org
Web Site: www.cisam.org
Key Personnel
Chairman: Enrico Menesio
Dir: Stefano Brufani
ISBN Prefix(es): 88-7988
Branch Office(s)
Palazzo Ancaiani, 06049 Spoleto, Perugia
Orders to: Indirizzo Sopra

Citta Nuova Editrice+
Via degli Scipioni 265, 00192 Rome
Tel: (06) 3216212 *Fax:* (06) 3207185
E-mail: segr.rivista@cittanuova.it
Web Site: www.cittanuova.it
Key Personnel
Man Dir: Dr Vittorio Fasciotti; Dr Giovanni Battista Dadda
Founded: 1959
Subjects: Biblical Studies, Education, Philosophy, Psychology, Psychiatry, Religion - Other, Social Sciences, Sociology, Theology
ISBN Prefix(es): 88-311
Subsidiaries: Ciudad Nueva (Argentina); Unistad Verspreiding RV (Belgium); Cidade Nova Editora (Brazil); Ciudad Nueva (Colombia); Nouvelle Cite (France); Verlag Neue Stadt GmbH (Germany); Nieuwe Stad (Netherlands); New City (Philippines); Cidade Nova (Portugal); Editorial Ciutat Nova (Spain); Verlag Neue Stadt (Switzerland); New City (United Kingdom); New City Press (United States)
Shipping Address: Via V Ussani 88, 00151 Rome
Warehouse: Via V Ussani 88, 00151 Rome

Cittadella Editrice+
Imprint of Pro Civitate Christiana
Via Ancajani 3, 06081 Assisi (Perugia)
Tel: (075) 813595 *Fax:* (075) 813719
E-mail: amministrazione@cittadellaeditrice.com
Web Site: www.cittadellaeditrice.com *Cable:* CITTADELLA EDITRICE
Key Personnel
Trans Off: Gabriella Persico *E-mail:* redazione@cittadellaeditrice.com
Editorial Manager: Giuseppina Pompei
 E-mail: gpompei@cittadellaeditrice.com
Foreign Rights: Franco Ferrari *E-mail:* fferrari@cittadellaeditrice.com
Press Office Manager: Franco Ferrari *Tel:* (075) 813231
Founded: 1939
Subjects: Biblical Studies, Biography, Psychology, Psychiatry, Religion - Catholic, Religion - Other, Social Sciences, Sociology, Theology
ISBN Prefix(es): 88-308
Number of titles published annually: 21 Print
Total Titles: 501 Print
Bookshop(s): Libreria Cittadella

Claudiana Editrice+
Via Principe Tommaso 1, 10125 Turin
Tel: (011) 6689804 *Fax:* (011) 6504394
E-mail: info@claudiana.it
Web Site: www.claudiana.it
Key Personnel
Dir: Manuel Kromer
Founded: 1855
Membership(s): AIE.
Subjects: Biblical Studies, History, Religion - Protestant, Theology
ISBN Prefix(es): 88-7016
Distributor for Edizioni GBU (Rome)
Bookshop(s): Libreria Claudiana, Via Francesco Sforza 12A, 20122 Milan; Libreria Claudiana, Piazza Liberta, 10066 Torre Pellice (Turin); Via Pr Tommaso 1, 10125 Turin; Libreria di Cultura Religiosa, Piazza Cavour 32, 00193 Rome

CLEUP - Cooperative Libraria Editrice dell 'Universita di Padova+
Via Prati 19, 35122 Padova
Tel: (049) 8753496 *Fax:* (049) 650261
E-mail: redazione@cleup.it
Key Personnel
President: Fulvio Ursini
Vice President: Sergio Relai
Founded: 1962
Also book packager.
Subjects: Engineering (General), Government, Political Science, Language Arts, Linguistics, Mathematics, Medicine, Nursing, Dentistry, Psychology, Psychiatry, Science (General)
ISBN Prefix(es): 88-7178
Bookshop(s): Libreria CLEUP, Via San Francesco 64, 35100 Padua *Tel:* 049-39557

CLUEB (Cooperativa Libraria Universitaria Editrice Bologna)+
Via Marsala 31, 40126 Bologna
Tel: (051) 220736 *Fax:* (051) 237758
E-mail: clueb@clueb.com; info@clueb.com
Web Site: www.clueb.com
Key Personnel
Man Dir: Luigi Guardigli *E-mail:* gua@clueb.com
Editorial Man: Giulio Forconi *E-mail:* g.forconi@clueb.com
Founded: 1959
Specialize also in theatre, detective stories & criticism of D.S.
Subjects: Accounting, Agriculture, Architecture & Interior Design, Art, Business, Economics, Education, History, Human Relations, Language Arts, Linguistics, Literature, Literary Criticism, Essays, Music, Dance, Philosophy, Psychology, Psychiatry, Science (General)
ISBN Prefix(es): 88-8091; 88-491
Number of titles published annually: 150 Print; 3 CD-ROM
Total Titles: 15 Print; 1 CD-ROM
Subsidiaries: Clueb DPE
U.S. Office(s): Paul & Company Publishers Consortium, PO Box 442, Concord, MA 01742, United States
Distributor for Universita' di Trento
Bookshop(s): Libreria Clueb, Bologna

CLUT Editrice+
Corso Duca degli Abruzzi 24, 10129 Turin
Tel: (011) 5647980 *Fax:* (011) 542192
E-mail: informazioni@clut.it
Web Site: www.clut.it
Key Personnel
Man Dir: Michele Ruffino
Editorial: Toscano Donatella
Founded: 1960
Subjects: Human Relations, Science (General), Technology
ISBN Prefix(es): 88-7992
Parent Company: Cooperativa Libraria Universitaria Torinese Scrl, Corso Duca degli Abruzzi 24, 10129 Turin

La Coccinella Editrice SRL
Via Crispi, 77/79, 21100 Varese
Tel: (0332) 224690 *Fax:* (0332) 222025
Telex: 326169 per La Coccinella
Key Personnel
Editorial Dir: Domenico Caputo
Sales, Rights & Permissions: Giuliana Crespi
Production Dir: Valerio Morelli
Founded: 1977
Subjects: Crafts, Games, Hobbies, Education
ISBN Prefix(es): 88-7703
Subsidiaries: RCS Rizzoli Libri
Warehouse: RCS Rizzoli, Via Angelo Rizzoli 4, Milan

Collana, *imprint of* Mondolibro Editore SNC

Colonnese Editore+
Via San Pietro a Majella, 7, 80138 Naples
Tel: (081) 293900 *Fax:* (081) 455420
E-mail: info@colonnese.it
Web Site: www.colonnese.it
Key Personnel
Dir, Publishing & Sales: Gaetano Colonnese
Rights & Permissions: Edgar Colonnese
  E-mail: edgar@colonnese.it
Founded: 1965
Subjects: Archaeology, Drama, Theater, Fiction, History, Humor, Language Arts, Linguistics, Literature, Literary Criticism, Essays, Photography, Poetry, Women's Studies
ISBN Prefix(es): 88-87501
Number of titles published annually: 12 Print
Total Titles: 400 Print
Distributed by Zambon Verlag & Vertrieb (Germany)
Foreign Rights: Guido Lagomarsino (Italy)
Bookshop(s): Libreria Colonnese SAS, Via San Pietro a Majella 32/33, 80138 Naples *Tel:* (081) 459858
Distribution Center: PDE SRL, Via Tevere 54, 50019 Osmannoro, Carlo Cherici
Orders to: Colonnese, Via S Pa Majella 32-33, 80138 Naples *Tel:* (081) 459858

Le Comete, *imprint of* Passigli Editori

Edizioni di Comunita SpA+
Division of Mondadori
Via Biancamano 2, 10121 Turin
Tel: (011) 5656363 *Fax:* (011) 5656351
E-mail: novarese@amemail.mondadori.it
Web Site: www.comunita.einaudi.it
Key Personnel
Res Administrator: R Veglia *Tel:* (011) 5656205
  E-mail: veglia@amemail.mondadori.it
Founded: 1946
Subjects: Architecture & Interior Design, Art, Computer Science, Economics, Government, Political Science, History, Law, Science (General), Social Sciences, Sociology
ISBN Prefix(es): 88-245
Total Titles: 70 Print
Ultimate Parent Company: Einaudi

Associate Companies: Arnoldo Mondadori Editore SpA
Distributed by A Mondadori

Consiglio Nazionale delle Ricerche Rep Pubblicazioni e Informazioni Scientifiche
(National Research Council)
P le Aldo Moro, 7, 00185 Rome
Tel: (06) 49932019 *Fax:* (06) 49933077
E-mail: pgiugni@dcire.cnr.it
Web Site: www.urp.cnr.it

Continental SRL Editrice
Via Suardi 7, 24100 Bergamo
Tel: (035) 237088 *Fax:* (035) 237039
Key Personnel
Man Dir, Rights & Permissions: Luigi Maria Facheris
Editorial: Ornella Crispiatico
Sales, Publicity: Paola Sala
Production: Roberto Poli
Founded: 1974
Subjects: Education

Convivio (Nardini Editore), *imprint of* Nardini Editore srl

Cooperativa Libraria Editrice dell' Universita, see CLEUP - Cooperative Libraria Editrice dell 'Universita di Padova

Cooperativa Libraria IULM SCRL, see Arcipelago Edizioni di Chiani Marisa

Cooperativa Libraria Universitaria Editrice Bologna, see CLUEB (Cooperativa Libraria Universitaria Editrice Bologna)

Cooperativa Libraria Universitaria Torinese, see CLUT Editrice

Edizioni Cooperative Scarl
Via Stelvio, 1, 00141 Rome
Tel: (06) 844391 *Fax:* (06) 84439406
Key Personnel
President: Giuliano Poletti
ISBN Prefix(es): 88-7361

Casa Editrice Corbaccio srl+
Cso Italia 13, 20122 Milan
Tel: (02) 80206338 *Fax:* (02) 804067
E-mail: info@corbaccio.it
Web Site: www.corbaccio.it
Key Personnel
President: Mario Spagnol
Man Dir: Stefano Mauri
Editorial: Cecilia Perucci
Sales: Giuseppe Somenzi
Production: Alfredo Bonfiglio
Publicity: Valentina Fortichiari
Rights & Permissions: Cristina Foschini
Founded: 1992
ISBN Prefix(es): 88-7972
Parent Company: Longanesi & C
Associate Companies: Finarte, GdP
U.S. Office(s): Nina Collins Association, 584 Broadway, Suite 607, New York, NY 10012, United States
Warehouse: Messaggerie Italiane Spa, Maggazzino Editoriale Via Bereguardina, Casarile 20080
Orders to: Pro Libro, Corso Italia 13, 20122 Milan

Libreria Cortina Editrice SRL+
Via Alberto Mario 10, 37121 Verona
Tel: (045) 594177 *Fax:* (045) 597551
E-mail: info@libreriacortina.it; cortinab@tin.it
Web Site: www.libreriacortina.it

Key Personnel
Chief Executive, Editorial: Cunego Pierpiorgio
Founded: 1971
Also book packager.
Subjects: Medicine, Nursing, Dentistry, Science (General)
ISBN Prefix(es): 88-85037; 88-7749
Bookshop(s): Palazzetto d'Ingresso, Policlinico Borgo Roma, Via delle Menegone, 1-37134 Verona *Tel:* (065) 505270 *Fax:* (065) 584594
E-mail: cortinab@tin.it

Costa e Nolan SpA+
Via Boscovich, 44, 20124 Milan
Tel: (022) 9402156 *Fax:* (022) 047922
Key Personnel
Man Dir, Rights & Permissions: Carla Costa
Editorial: Eugenio Buonaccorsi
Sales, Publicity: Stefano Tettamanti
Founded: 1982
Subjects: Art, Drama, Theater, Economics, Fiction, Literature, Literary Criticism, Essays
ISBN Prefix(es): 88-7648

CPE, see Centro Programmazione Editoriale (CPE)

Edizioni Cremonese SRL+
Borgo S Croce 17, 50122 Florence
Tel: (055) 2476371 *Fax:* (055) 2476372
E-mail: cremonese@ed-cremonese.it
Web Site: www.ed-cremonese.it *Cable:* EDIZIONI CREMONESE
Key Personnel
Man Dir: Alberto Stianti *E-mail:* cremonese@ed-cremonese.it
Founded: 1930
Subjects: Aeronautics, Aviation, Civil Engineering, Electronics, Electrical Engineering, Engineering (General), Mathematics, Mechanical Engineering, Science (General), Technology
ISBN Prefix(es): 88-7083

Crisalide+
Via Campodivivo 43, 04020 Spigno Saturnia (Latina)
Tel: (0771) 64463 *Fax:* (0771) 639121
E-mail: crisalide@crisalide.com
Web Site: www.crisalide.com
Key Personnel
President & Owner: Raffaele Iandolo *Tel:* (0771) 639121
Founded: 1988
Subjects: Astrology, Occult, Parapsychology, Psychology, Psychiatry, Religion - Buddhist
ISBN Prefix(es): 88-7183
Number of titles published annually: 20 Print
Total Titles: 150 Print
Distributed by C D A

CSTM, *imprint of* Centro Studi Terzo Mondo

Edizioni Cultura della Pace+
Via Venezia, 18b, 50121 Florence
Tel: (055) 576149 *Fax:* (055) 5088003
Key Personnel
President: Enrico Palmerini
Founded: 1986
Subjects: Anthropology, Biography, Communications, Developing Countries, Education, Environmental Studies, Ethnicity, Foreign Countries, Government, Political Science, History, Human Relations, Philosophy, Religion - Buddhist, Religion - Catholic, Religion - Hindu, Religion - Islamic, Religion - Jewish, Religion - Protestant, Religion - Other, Social Sciences, Sociology, Theology, Women's Studies
ISBN Prefix(es): 88-09; 88-87183
Imprints: ECP
Orders to: Edizioni Cultura della Pace, Via Brunetto Latini 49, 50131 Florence

Ed La Cultura Sociologica, *imprint of* Centro Studi Terzo Mondo

La Cultura Sociologica+
Via GB Morgagni 39, 20129 Milan
Tel: (02) 29409041 *Fax:* (02) 29409041
Key Personnel
Chief Executive: Prof Umberto Melotti
 Tel: (0330) 687866 *E-mail:* melotti@uniroma1.it
Editorial, Rights & Permissions: Elena Sala
Founded: 1964
Books on social sciences.
Subjects: Biological Sciences, Economics, Ethnicity, Government, Political Science, History, Philosophy, Social Sciences, Sociology
Number of titles published annually: 8 Print
Total Titles: 100 Print
Associate Companies: Centro Studi Terzo Mondo

Edizioni Curci SRL+
Galleria del Corso 4, 20122 Milan
Tel: (02) 760361 *Fax:* (02) 76014504
E-mail: info@edizionicurci.it
Web Site: www.edizionicurci.it
Key Personnel
President & General Manager: Giuseppe Gramitto Ricci
Man Dir: Michele Delvecchio
Classical Dept: Laura Moro
Founded: 1860
Subjects: Music, Dance
ISBN Prefix(es): 88-485
Associate Companies: Edizioni Accordo SRL
Warehouse: Via Ripamonti, 129, 20141 Milan, Lina Manfra *Tel:* (02) 57410561 *Fax:* (02) 5390043

Damanhur Edizioni
Via Pramarzo, 3, 10080 Baldissero Canavese (Turin)
Tel: (0124) 512213 *Fax:* (0124) 512213
E-mail: dhbooks@damanhurbooks.com
Web Site: www.damanhurbooks.com
Founded: 1978
Membership(s): Casa Edittice Della Comunita Di Damanhur.
Subjects: Astrology, Occult, Earth Sciences, Mysteries, Social Sciences, Sociology
ISBN Prefix(es): 88-7012

Dami Editore SRL+
Via Gesu 10, 20121 Milan
Tel: (02) 76006533 *Fax:* (02) 784010
E-mail: damieditore@damieditore.it
Web Site: www.damieditore.it
Founded: 1972
Subjects: Animals, Pets, Fiction
ISBN Prefix(es): 88-09

D'Anna+
Via Dante da Castiglione, 8, 50125 Florence
Tel: (055) 2335513 *Fax:* (055) 225932
E-mail: gdanna@tin.it; gdanna@mbox.vol.it
Cable: D'ANNA FLORENCE
Key Personnel
Man Dir, Sales, & Rights & Permissions: Albertina D'Anna
Editorial & Production: Gabriele D'Anna; Guido D'Anna
Founded: 1926
Subjects: Art, Chemistry, Chemical Engineering, Education, History, Literature, Literary Criticism, Essays
ISBN Prefix(es): 88-8104; 88-8321
Imprints: Editoriale Paradigma; G D'Anna-Sintesi
Warehouse: Loescher Editore, via Vajont 93, Cascine Vica Rivoli, Torino
Orders to: Loescher Editore, Via V Amedeo II, 18-1021 Torino

G D'Anna-Sintesi, *imprint of* D'Anna

Datanews+
Via di S Erasmo, 22, 00184 Rome
Tel: (06) 70450318/9 *Fax:* (06) 70450320
E-mail: info@datanews.it
Web Site: www.datanews.it
Key Personnel
President: Corrado Perna
Man Dir: Francisco Florentano
Founded: 1985
Subjects: Economics, Environmental Studies, Ethnicity, Government, Political Science, History
ISBN Prefix(es): 88-7981

M d'Auria Editore SAS+
Palazzo Pignatelli, Calata Trinita Maggiore 52-53, 80134 Naples
Tel: (081) 5518963 *Fax:* (081) 5493827; (081) 5518963
E-mail: info@dauria.it
Web Site: www.dauria.it
Key Personnel
Dir: Gianni Macchiavelli
Publicity: Paola Raeli
Founded: 1837
Also acts as sales agent.
Subjects: Antiques, Archaeology, History, Literature, Literary Criticism, Essays, Religion - Other
ISBN Prefix(es): 88-7092
Number of titles published annually: 20 Print
Total Titles: 45 Print
Distributor for Edizioni Di Storia E Letteratura SRL; Instituto Universitario Orientale
Bookshop(s): Libreria Internazionale-International Book Center M d'Auria, Calata Trinita Maggiore 52/53, 80134 Naples

G De Bono Editore+
Via Masaccio, 220, 50132 Florence
Tel: (055) 576022 *Fax:* (055) 5001665
Key Personnel
Chief Executive: Giuseppe De Bono
Editorial: Prof Aldo De Bono
Founded: 1958
Subjects: Education, Fiction, Philosophy

Giovanni De Vecchi Editore SpA+
Via Pisani, 16, 20124 Milan
Tel: (02) 66984851 *Fax:* (02) 6701548
Founded: 1973
Subjects: Agriculture, Animals, Pets, Antiques, Astrology, Occult, Business, Career Development, Crafts, Games, Hobbies, Gardening, Plants, Health, Nutrition, How-to, Humor, Law, Medicine, Nursing, Dentistry, Outdoor Recreation, Sports, Athletics
ISBN Prefix(es): 88-412

DEA, see DEA Diffusione Edizioni Anglo-Americane

DEA Diffusione Edizioni Anglo-Americane
Via Lima 28, 00198 Rome
Tel: (06) 8551441 *Fax:* (06) 8543228
E-mail: info@deanet.it
Web Site: www.deanet.com
ISBN Prefix(es): 88-86188
Branch Office(s)
Massimo D'Azeglio 27, 40123 Bologna *Tel:* (051) 236100 *Fax:* (051) 220882
Via Pascoli 56, 20133 Milan *Tel:* (02) 2364306 *Fax:* (02) 2362738
Via Domenico Cimarosa 91/c, 80127 Naples *Tel:* (081) 5787576 *Fax:* (081) 5780739
Via G D Cassini 75/8, 10129 Torino *Tel:* (011) 503202 *Fax:* (011) 595559
Via Diaz 19/1, 34124 Trieste *Tel:* (040) 301257 *Fax:* (040) 310993

Edizioni Dedalo SRL+
Viale Luigi Jacobini 5, 70123 Bari
Mailing Address: CP BA/19, 70123 Bari
Tel: (080) 5311413; (080) 5311400; (080) 5311401 *Fax:* (080) 5311414
E-mail: info@edizionidedalo.it
Web Site: www.edizionidedalo.it
Key Personnel
Man Dir: Raimondo Coga
Editorial Manager: Claudia Coga
 E-mail: claudiacoga@edizionidedalo.it
Founded: 1965
Also acts as printing house.
Subjects: Anthropology, Architecture & Interior Design, Art, Film, Video, Government, Political Science, History, Philosophy, Physical Sciences, Physics, Psychology, Psychiatry, Science (General), Social Sciences, Sociology
ISBN Prefix(es): 88-220
Number of titles published annually: 30 Print
Total Titles: 1,000 Print
Parent Company: Dedalo Litostampa Srl

Edizioni Dehoniane Bologna (EDB)+
Via Nosadella, 6, 40123 Bologna
Tel: (051) 4290011 *Fax:* (051) 4290099
E-mail: webmaster@dehoniane.it
Web Site: www.dehoniane.it
Key Personnel
Man Dir: Alfio Filippi
Sales Dir, Rights & Permissions: Cesano Giacomo
Publicity Dir: Gabriella Zucchi
Contact: Vanda Persiani
Founded: 1965
Subjects: Biblical Studies, Education, Religion - Catholic, Religion - Other, Theology
ISBN Prefix(es): 88-10
Associate Companies: Data Service Center
Imprints: EDB
Distributed by Dehoniana Libri SpA
Bookshop(s): Dehoniana Libri, Via Nosadella, 6, 40123 Bologna
Shipping Address: Via Dal Ferro 4, 40138 Bologna

Edizioni Dehoniane+
Via Casale S Pio, 20, 00165 Rome
Tel: (06) 624996 *Fax:* (06) 6628326
E-mail: webmaster@dehoniane.it
Web Site: www.dehoniane.it *Cable:* EDIZIONI DEHONIANE ROME
Key Personnel
Chief Executive: Vitantonio Giampietro
Editorial: Luigi Cortese
Sales, Publicity: Antonio Bozza
Production: Umberto Chiarello
Founded: 1956
Subjects: Education, Philosophy, Psychology, Psychiatry, Religion - Other, Social Sciences, Sociology, Theology
ISBN Prefix(es): 88-396
Parent Company: Provincia Meridonale Italiana della Congregazi one dei Sacerdoti del S Cuore di Gesu', via Marechiaro, 46 Naples
Bookshop(s): Libreria Dehoniana, Via Depretis 60, 80133 Naples

DEI Tipographia del Genio Civile
Via Nomentana 16/20, 00161 Rome
Tel: (06) 44163792 *Fax:* (06) 4403307
E-mail: dei@build.it
Web Site: www.build.it
Key Personnel
Man Dir, Production: Maria Cecilia Bartoli
Editorial, Publicity, Sales: Giuseppe Rufo
Founded: 1869
Subjects: Architecture & Interior Design, Civil Engineering, Electronics, Electrical Engineering, Law, Technology
ISBN Prefix(es): 88-7722; 88-496
Warehouse: Via Mesula 12, 00161 Rome

PUBLISHERS

ITALY

Casa Editrice Istituto della Santa
Via dei Caccia 5, Novara 28100
Tel: (0321) 22371 *Cable:* Dellasanta Novara
Founded: 1956
Subjects: Business

Edizioni Della Torre di Salvatore Fozzi & C SAS+
Via Contivecchi 8/2, 09122 Cagliari
Tel: (070) 270507 *Fax:* (070) 270507
Key Personnel
Chief Executive: Salvatore Fozzi *Tel:* (070) 271411 *Fax:* (070) 272542
Founded: 1974
Subjects: Archaeology, Art, Geography, Geology, History, Language Arts, Linguistics, Natural History, Poetry, Regional Interests
ISBN Prefix(es): 88-7343
Total Titles: 225 Print
Associate Companies: Scuola Domani, via Toscana 82, 09124 Cagliari
Subsidiaries: Agenzia Libraria Fozzi
Bookshop(s): Libreria Fozzi, Via Dante 72, 09100 Cagliari

Edizioni dell'Orso+
Via Rattazzi 47, 15100 Alessandria
Tel: (0131) 252349 *Fax:* (0131) 257567
E-mail: direzione.commerciale@ediorso.it
Web Site: www.ediorso.it
Key Personnel
Man Dir: Gian Paolo Calligaris
Editorial: Lorenzo Massobrio
Founded: 1979
Subjects: History, Language Arts, Linguistics, Poetry, Regional Interests
ISBN Prefix(es): 88-7694

Demetra SRL+
Via Stra 167, 37030 Colognola al Colli (Verona)
Tel: (045) 6159711 *Fax:* (045) 6159700
Key Personnel
Man Dir: Silvano Pizzighella
Founded: 1983
Subjects: Agriculture, Biological Sciences, Health, Nutrition, Literature, Literary Criticism, Essays
ISBN Prefix(es): 88-7122; 88-440

Di Baio Editore SpA+
Via Settembrini, 11, 20124 Milan
Tel: (02) 6692254 *Fax:* (02) 6709257
Key Personnel
President: Giuseppe Maria Jonghi Lavarini
Man Dir: Fabio Alberti
Founded: 1973
Subjects: Architecture & Interior Design, Cookery, Crafts, Games, Hobbies, Gardening, Plants, House & Home, Technology
ISBN Prefix(es): 88-7080

Organizzazione Didattica Editoriale Ape+
Via degli Artisti, 8b, 50132 Florence
Tel: (055) 572584 *Fax:* (055) 578243 *Cable:* APE MURRI 565 BOLOGNA
Key Personnel
Chief Executive, Editorial, Production, Rights & Permissions: Gina Cesari
Sales: Giorgio Ognibene
Founded: 1964
Subjects: Fiction, Regional Interests
ISBN Prefix(es): 88-86515
Imprints: APE
Bookshop(s): Gottardi Concession, via Zanardi 60, IV Bologna

Dimensione Umana, *imprint of* Le Stelle Scuola

Directorate of Archives, see Direzione Generale Archivi

Direzione Generale Archivi
Via Gaeta 8a, 00185 Rome
Tel: (06) 4742177 *Fax:* (06) 4742177
E-mail: studi@archivi.beniculturali.it
Web Site: www.archivi.beniculturali.it
Telex: (06) 623278
Key Personnel
Dir: Antonio Dentoni-Litta
Publishing branch of the Italian State Archives Administration.
Subjects: History, Law, Library & Information Sciences, Public Administration
ISBN Prefix(es): 88-7125
Number of titles published annually: 20 Print
Total Titles: 450 Print
Parent Company: Ministero Beni e Attivita Culturali
Orders to: Istituto poligrafico e Zecca dello stato, Via Marciana Marina, No A, 00199 Rome *Tel:* (06) 85 081 *Fax:* (06) 85 084117
Direzione editoriale, Via Marciana Marina, No A, 00199 Rome *Tel:* (06) 85 081 *Fax:* (06) 85 084117
Libreria dello Stato, Via Marciana Marina, No A, 00199 Rome *Tel:* (06) 85 081 *Fax:* (06) 85 084117

Domus Academy
via Savona 97, 20144 Milan
Tel: (02) 42414001 *Fax:* (02) 4222525
E-mail: info@domusacademy.it
Web Site: www.domusacademy.com
ISBN Prefix(es): 88-7184; 88-85187

Editoriale Domus SpA+
Via Gianni Mazzocchi 1/3, 20089 Rozzano, Milan
Tel: (02) 82472 1
E-mail: editorialedomus@edidomus.it
Web Site: www.edidomus.it
Key Personnel
Publicity: Gabriele Vigano
Founded: 1929
Subjects: Aeronautics, Aviation, Architecture & Interior Design, Art, Automotive, Cookery, Transportation, Travel
ISBN Prefix(es): 88-7212

Dunod, *imprint of* Masson SpA

Edizioni E - Elle SRL
via S Cilino 16, 34126 Trieste
Tel: (040) 566821 *Fax:* (040) 566819
Telex: (040) 637969
Key Personnel
Man Dir: Giancarlo Stavro Santarosa
Editorial: Orietta Fatucci
Rights & Permissions: Sandra Goruppi
Founded: 1984
ISBN Prefix(es): 88-85326

Edizioni E/O+
Via Camozzi, 1, 00195 Rome
Tel: (06) 3722829 *Fax:* (06) 37351096
E-mail: info@edizionieo.it
Web Site: www.edizioni-eo.it
Key Personnel
Man Dir, Rights & Permissions: Sandro Ferri
Editorial: Sandra Ozzola
Sales: Tom Joannucci
Production: Alfredo Lavarini
Publicity: Sergio Vezzali
Founded: 1979
Subjects: Fiction
ISBN Prefix(es): 88-7641

Edizioni EBE
Via dei Magazzini 22, 01016 Tarquinia (Viterbo)
Tel: (0766) 858878 *Fax:* (0766) 858877
Key Personnel
Chief Executive: Giovanni Di Capua
Sales: Norma Merli
Founded: 1973
Subjects: Government, Political Science, History
ISBN Prefix(es): 88-7977
Orders to: Via FS Nitti 12, 00191 Rome *Tel:* (06) 3272972

EBF, *imprint of* Biblioteca Francescana

ECIG+
Via Brignole de Ferrari 9, 16125 Genoa
Tel: (010) 2512399 *Fax:* (010) 2512398
Key Personnel
Man Dir: Dr Gian Luigi Blengino
Founded: 1971
Specialize in Sapiential essays.
Subjects: Literature, Literary Criticism, Essays, Philosophy, Psychology, Psychiatry
ISBN Prefix(es): 88-7545
Showroom(s): Salone Del Libro Torino, Largo Regio Parco, 9-10152 Torino; Frankfurt Buchmesse, Frankfurt, Germany
Bookshop(s): Piazza Santa Sabina 2 sc A/2, Genoa *Tel:* (010) 203788; Salita Inf della Noce 8 rosso 16131, Genoa *Tel:* (010) 510355; Via S Gallo 21R, Florence *Tel:* (055) 261693; Viale Morgagni 31, Florence *Tel:* (055) 4361722; Via Ormea 90, Torino *Tel:* (011) 683527; Via Santa maria 7, Pisa *Tel:* (050) 501426; Via dei Mille 32, Pisa *Tel:* 050 35310; Via De Amicis 60, Naples *Tel:* (081) 5469304
Orders to: CLU - Salita Inferiore, Della NOCE 10 R, IDEM, 16143 Genoa

Ecole Francaise de Rome+
Piazza Farnese, 67, 00186 Rome
Tel: (06) 68 60 11 *Fax:* (06) 687 48 34
E-mail: publ@ecole-francaise.it
Web Site: www.ecole-francaise.it
Key Personnel
Publisher: Francois-Charles Uginet *Tel:* (06) 68885305
Founded: 1881
Subjects: Archaeology, Art, History, Law
ISBN Prefix(es): 2-7283
Number of titles published annually: 30 Print
Total Titles: 400 Print

ECP, *imprint of* Edizioni Cultura della Pace

Edagricole - Edizioni Agricole+
Via Goito, 13, 40126 Bologna
Tel: (051) 65751 *Fax:* (051) 6575800
E-mail: sede@gce.it
Web Site: www.edagricole.it
Key Personnel
Man Dir & Editorial: Alberto Perdisa
Sales: Luigi Perdisa, Jr *Tel:* (051) 6226849 *Fax:* (051) 540000
Publicity: Franco Metri *Tel:* (051) 6226818 *E-mail:* stampa@calderini.agriline.it
Founded: 1935
Subjects: Agriculture, Animals, Pets, Biological Sciences, Gardening, Plants, Health, Nutrition, Science (General), Veterinary Science
ISBN Prefix(es): 88-206
Total Titles: 2,000 Print
Parent Company: Calderini SRL, Via Emilia Levante N 31/2, 40139 Bologna
Associate Companies: Edizioni Calderini; Calderini Industrie Grafiche ed Editoriali SRL; Edagricole Periodici SpA
Bookshop(s): Via Zamboni 18, Bologna; Via Bronzino 14, Milan; Via Boncompagni 73, Rome

EDAS
Via Bosco, 17, 98122 Messina
Tel: (090) 675653 *Fax:* (090) 675653
E-mail: info@edas.it
Web Site: www.edas.it
Founded: 1975

Subjects: History, Science (General)
ISBN Prefix(es): 88-7820
Number of titles published annually: 10 Print
Total Titles: 100 Print

EDB, *imprint of* Edizioni Dehoniane Bologna (EDB)

EDB, see Edizioni Dehoniane Bologna (EDB)

Ediart Editrice
Imprint of Livro Grai
Loc Montelupino, 82/13, 06059 Todi (PG)
Tel: (075) 8943594 *Fax:* (075) 8942411
E-mail: ediart@ediart.it
Web Site: www.ediart.it
Key Personnel
Editor: Leonilde Dominici
Founded: 1983
Specialize in the history of art & architecture.
Subjects: Architecture & Interior Design, Art
ISBN Prefix(es): 88-85311
Number of titles published annually: 4 Print
Total Titles: 70 Print

Edicart
Via Jucker, 28, 20025 Legnano, Milan
Tel: (0331) 74291 *Fax:* (0331) 74292
E-mail: info@edicart.it
Web Site: www.edicart.it
Founded: 1986
ISBN Prefix(es): 88-474; 88-7774

Ediciclo Editore SRL+
Via Cesar Beccaria, 13/15, 30026 Portogruaro (Venezia)
Tel: (0421) 74475 *Fax:* (0421) 282070
E-mail: posta@ediciclo.it
Web Site: www.ediciclo.it
Key Personnel
Administrative Dir: Vittorio Anastasia
Founded: 1992
Subjects: Economics, Environmental Studies, History, Outdoor Recreation, Science (General), Social Sciences, Sociology, Sports, Athletics, Travel
ISBN Prefix(es): 88-85327; 88-85318; 88-88829
Imprints: Nuova Dimensione

EDIFIR SRL+
Edizioni Firenze, Via Fiume, 8, 50123 Florence
Tel: (055) 289506 *Fax:* (055) 289478
Key Personnel
President: Wanda Miletti Ferragamo
Administrator: Dr Pierfrancesco Pacini
International Rights: Dr Fabio Tongiorgi
Founded: 1985
Subjects: Architecture & Interior Design, History
ISBN Prefix(es): 88-7970

Edipuglia+
Via Dalmazia 22/b, 70050 S Spirito (Bari)
Tel: (080) 5333056 *Fax:* (080) 5333057
E-mail: edipuglia@tin.it
Web Site: www.edipuglia.it
Key Personnel
Administrator: Ceglie Oronzo
Founded: 1979
Subjects: Antiques, Archaeology, History
ISBN Prefix(es): 88-7228
Number of titles published annually: 10 Print
Total Titles: 150 Print

Editrice Edisco+
Via Pastrengo 28, 10128 Turin
Tel: (011) 54 78 80 *Fax:* (011) 51 75 396
E-mail: info@edisco.it
Web Site: www.edisco.it
Key Personnel
General Manager: Corrado Jaria

Founded: 1952
Subjects: Chemistry, Chemical Engineering, Education, Electronics, Electrical Engineering, English as a Second Language, Literature, Literary Criticism, Essays, Mechanical Engineering, Physics, Science (General)
ISBN Prefix(es): 88-441
Number of titles published annually: 25 Print
Total Titles: 300 Print
Shipping Address: Via Barletta 124, 10136 Turin
Warehouse: Via Barletta 124, 10136 Turin

Edisport Editoriale SpA
Via Gradisca 11, 20151 Milan
Tel: (02) 380851 *Fax:* (02) 38010393
E-mail: edisport@edisport.it
Web Site: www.edisport.it
Telex: 353629 EDISP I
Key Personnel
Marketing: Donatella Tardini

Edistudio+
Via Bruno, 6/8, 56125 Pisa
Tel: (050) 48670; (050) 2208745 *Fax:* (050) 500585
E-mail: edistudio@edistudio.it *Cable:* Edistudio CP 213 Pisa
Key Personnel
Chief Executive: Brunetto Casini
Founded: 1977
Also specialize in local culture & local magazines.
Subjects: Drama, Theater, Education, Fiction, Geography, Geology, Language Arts, Linguistics, Literature, Literary Criticism, Essays, Music, Dance, Poetry, Science (General), Sports, Athletics
ISBN Prefix(es): 88-7036
Total Titles: 70 Print
Subsidiaries: Composit (Fotocomposizione elaborazione grafica)

Editalia (Edizioni d'Italia)
Via Marine Marciana 28, 00138 Rome
Tel: (06) 85081 *Toll Free Tel:* 800 01 4858 *Fax:* (06) 85085165
Web Site: www.editalia.it
Key Personnel
Man Dir: Lidio Bozzini
Rights & Permissions: Arrigo Pecchioli
Founded: 1952
Subjects: Art, Ethnicity, History
ISBN Prefix(es): 88-7060

Editori Laterza+
Via di Villa Sacchetti, 17, 00197 Rome
Tel: (06) 3218393 *Fax:* (06) 3223853
E-mail: laterza@laterza.it
Web Site: www.laterza.it
Key Personnel
President: Dr Giuseppe Laterza
Founded: 1901
Subjects: Anthropology, Archaeology, Communications, History, Law, Philosophy, Religion - Other
Number of titles published annually: 120 Print
Foreign Rep(s): Alice Chambers; Eulama Literary Agency

Edizioni Associate/Editrice Internazionale Srl+
Viale Ippocrate 156, 00161 Rome
Tel: (06) 44704513 *Fax:* (06) 44704513
E-mail: easso@tin.it
Key Personnel
President: Livio Fabjan
Administrative Delegate & Editorial Dir: Rean Mazzone
Founded: 1992
Subjects: Government, Political Science, Literature, Literary Criticism, Essays
ISBN Prefix(es): 88-267

Associate Companies: Editrice Ila Palma, Tea Nova Srl
Showroom(s): Torino e Francoforte
Bookshop(s): Distribuzione Libraria PDE
Warehouse: c/o Tea Nova Srl, Via Isidoro la Lumia 5/7, 90139 Palermo
Orders to: c/o Sede V Le, Via Casini 8, 00153 Rome

Edizioni d'Arte Antica e Moderna EDAM+
Via di Monte Oliveto, 2, 50124 Florence
Tel: (055) 2298578 *Fax:* (055) 220837
Founded: 1962
Subjects: Antiques, Architecture & Interior Design, Art
ISBN Prefix(es): 88-7244

Edizioni del Centro Camuno di Studi Preistorici+
Division of Centro Camuno di Studi Preistoric
Via Marconi, 7, 25044 Capo di Ponte (Brescia)
Tel: (0364) 42091 *Fax:* (0364) 42572
E-mail: ccspreist@tin.it
Web Site: www.rockart-ccsp.com *Cable:* CENTROSTUDI CAPODIPONTE
Key Personnel
Chief Executive: Prof Emmanuel Anati
Production: Ariela Fradkin
Founded: 1964
Publishing division of a research institution.
Subjects: Anthropology, Antiques, Archaeology, Art, Biblical Studies, Ethnicity, History, Religion - Other
ISBN Prefix(es): 88-86621
Number of titles published annually: 3 Print
Total Titles: 90 Print
Associate Companies: Arts & Crafts International; IDAPEE (Institut des Arts Prehistoriques et Ethnologique), Paris, France
Imprints: BCSP; BC News; CCSP
Subsidiaries: WARA: World Archives of Rock Art

Edizioni del Delfino, *imprint of* Adriano Gallina Editore sas

Edizioni di Storia e Letteratura
Via delle Fornaci, 24, 00165 Rome
Tel: (06) 39670307 *Fax:* (06) 39671250
E-mail: info@storialetteratura.it
Web Site: www.storialetterature.it
Key Personnel
Chief Executive: Lodovico Steide
Founded: 1943
Subjects: History, Literature, Literary Criticism, Essays, Philosophy
ISBN Prefix(es): 88-900138; 88-87114; 88-8498
Number of titles published annually: 120 Print; 10 Online
Total Titles: 1,000 Print; 10 Online

Edizioni di Torino, see EDT Edizioni di Torino

Edizioni Giuridiche Economiche Aziendali, see EGEA (Edizioni Giuridiche Economiche Aziendali)

Edizioni Gruppo Abele, see Gruppo Abele

Edizioni Il Punto d'Incontro SAS
Via Zamenhof 685, 36100 Vicenza
Tel: (0444) 239189 *Fax:* (0444) 239266
E-mail: ordini@edizionilpuntocontro.it
Web Site: www.edizionilpuntodincontro.it
Subjects: Astrology, Occult, Ethnicity, Health, Nutrition, Philosophy, Religion - Buddhist, Religion - Catholic, Religion - Hindu, Religion - Islamic, Religion - Other
ISBN Prefix(es): 88-8093

PUBLISHERS — ITALY

Edizioni la Scala
Abbazia Madonna Della Scala, Zona B 58, 70015 Noci (Bari)
Tel: (080) 4975838 *Fax:* (080) 4975839
E-mail: lascala@abbazialascala.com
Web Site: www.abbazialascala.com *Cable:* BENEDETTINI NOCI
Key Personnel
Chief Executive, Editorial: Padre Giuseppe Quirino Poggi
Founded: 1947
Subjects: Biography, Music, Dance, Philosophy, Religion - Catholic

Edizioni l'Arciere SRL+
Viale Sarrea, 7, 12025 Dronero, Cuneo
Tel: (0171) 905566 *Fax:* (0171) 905730
Cable: ARCIERE EDIZIONI CUNEO
Key Personnel
Chief Executive, Sales, Rights & Permissions: Aldo Sacchetti
Editorial, Production & Publicity: Mario Donadei
Founded: 1973
Subjects: Art, Biography, Fiction, Geography, Geology, History, Literature, Literary Criticism, Essays, Military Science, Poetry, Regional Interests, Travel
ISBN Prefix(es): 88-86398

Edizioni L'Eta Dell'Acqua Rio, *imprint of* Lindau

Edizioni Qiqajon+
Comunita monastica di Bose, 13887 Magnano (Biella)
Tel: (015) 679115 *Fax:* (015) 6794949
E-mail: acquisti@qiqajon.it
Web Site: www.qiqajon.it
Key Personnel
President: Enzo Bianchi
International Rights: Guido Dotti *E-mail:* guido.dotti@qiqajon.it
Founded: 1983
Subjects: Religion - Catholic, Religion - Jewish, Religion - Protestant, Theology
ISBN Prefix(es): 88-85227; 88-8227
Number of titles published annually: 20 Print
Total Titles: 220 Print

Edizioni Realizzazioni Grafiche - Artigiana, *see* ERGA SNC di Carla Ottino Merli & C (Edizioni Realizzazioni Grafiche - Artigiana)

Edizioni Studio Domenicano (ESD)+
Via Dell' Osservanza 72, 40136 Bologna
Tel: (051) 582034 *Fax:* (051) 331583
E-mail: esd@alinet.it
Web Site: www.esd-domenicani.it
Key Personnel
Dir: Benetollo Ottorino *E-mail:* esd.benetollo@tiscalinet.it
Founded: 1985
Subjects: Philosophy, Religion - Catholic, Social Sciences, Sociology, Theology, Works of St Thomas Aquinas (Latin & Italian)
ISBN Prefix(es): 88-7094
Number of titles published annually: 60 Print
Total Titles: 500 Print

Edizioni Universitarie di Lettere Economia Diritto, *see* LED - Edizioni Universitarie di Lettere Economia Diritto

EDT Edizioni di Torino+
Via Alfieri, 19, 10121 Turin
Tel: (011) 5591816 *Fax:* (011) 2307034
E-mail: edt@edt.it
Web Site: www.edt.it
Key Personnel
Chief Executive: Enzo Peruccio
Founded: 1976
Subjects: Music, Dance, Travel
ISBN Prefix(es): 88-7063
Distributor for Instituto di Studi Verdiani; Lonely Planet Inc

EE, *imprint of* Edi.Ermes srl

EE, *imprint of* Editrice Eraclea

Effata Editrice+
Via Tre Denti 1, Cantalupa, Turin
Tel: (0121) 353452 *Fax:* (0121) 353839
E-mail: info@effata.it
Web Site: www.effata.it
Key Personnel
Dir: Paolo Pellegrino
Founded: 1994
A publishing house that is engaged to spread significant words to answer the deepest questions of the human soul.
Subjects: Drama, Theater, Education, Fiction, Human Relations, Psychology, Psychiatry, Religion - Catholic, Self-Help, Words for helping & giving joy
ISBN Prefix(es): 88-86617; 88-7402
Number of titles published annually: 20 Print
Total Titles: 80 Print
Orders to: Mescat, Viale Bacchiglione 20/A, 20139 Milan, Contact: Francesco Crespi
Tel: (02) 55210800 *Fax:* (02) 55211315

EFR, *imprint of* EFR-Editrici Francescane

EFR-Editrici Francescane
Via Orto Botanico, 11, 35123 Padova
Tel: (049) 8225702 *Fax:* (049) 8225713
E-mail: info@bibliotecafrancescana.it
Web Site: www.biblia.it
Key Personnel
President & International Rights: Aristide Cabassi
Tel: (02) 29002736
Founded: 1995
Subjects: Religion - Catholic
ISBN Prefix(es): 88-8135
Associate Companies: Edizioni Bibliotea Francescana Milano, Piazza S Angelo, 2, 20121 Milan; Edizioni Messaggero Padova, Via Orto Botanico, 11, 35123 Padova; Edizioni Porziuncola Assisi, Piazza Porziuncola, 1, 06088 Santa Maria Degli Angeli (PG); Libreria Internazionale Edizioni Francescane, Borgo S Lucia 38/40, 36100 Vicenza
Imprints: EFR
Distributor for Messaggero Distribuzione

EGEA (Edizioni Giuridiche Economiche Aziendali)+
Via Sarfatti, 25, 20136 Milan
Mailing Address: Via Calatafimi, 10, 20122 Milan
Tel: (02) 58365751 *Fax:* (02) 58365753
E-mail: egea.edizioni@egea.uni-bocconi.it
Key Personnel
President: Prof Alberto Bertoni
Editor: Adriana Macchi
Founded: 1988
Subjects: Advertising, Career Development, Economics, Finance, History, Law, Management, Marketing, Philosophy, Public Administration
ISBN Prefix(es): 88-238
Associate Companies: Giuffre Editore SpA, Via Busto Arsizio 40, 20151 Milan
Bookshop(s): EGEA SpA, Via Sarfatti 25, 20136 Milan
Orders to: Messaggerie Libri SpA, Via G Carcano 32, 20141 Milan

EGGM, *imprint of* EuroGeoGrafiche Mencattini

International EILES, *see* Edizioni Internazionali di Letteratura e Scienze

Giulio Einaudi Editore SpA+
Via Biancamano, 2, 10121 Turin
Tel: (011) 56561 *Fax:* (011) 542903
Key Personnel
President: Giulio Einaudi
Vice President: Leonardo Mondadori
Editor: Vittorio Bo
Founded: 1933
Subjects: Art, Fiction, History, Music, Dance, Philosophy, Poetry, Psychology, Psychiatry, Social Sciences, Sociology
ISBN Prefix(es): 88-06
Parent Company: A Mondadori Editore SpA
Associate Companies: Elemond SpA/ Edizioni E Elle SpA
Bookshop(s): Libreria Einaudi, Via Manzoni 40, 20121 Milano
Warehouse: Arnoldo Mondadori, Via Montelun, 37131 Verona
Orders to: Ufficio Commerciale, Via Biancamano 2, 10121 Turin

EL, *imprint of* Editrice Liguria SNC di Norberto Sabatelli & C

EL, *imprint of* Edizioni Lavoro SRL

Electa
Via Trentacoste, 7, 20134 Milan
Tel: (02) 215631 *Fax:* (02) 26413121
Telex: 350523 Eleper I
Key Personnel
Dir: Giorgio Fantoni; Massimo Vitta Zelman
Editorial: Carlo Pirovano
Rights & Permissions: Marisa Inzaghi; Mirella Tenderini
Founded: 1948
Subjects: Architecture & Interior Design, Art, Photography
ISBN Prefix(es): 88-435; 88-370
Subsidiaries: Alfieri Edizioni d'Arte; Giulio Einaudi Editore SpA; Electa Firenze; Electa Editori Umbri Associati; Electa Napoli; Fantonigrafica; Electa Moniteu

Edizioni dell'Elefante+
Piazza dei Caprettari, 70, 00186 Rome
Tel: (06) 68803710 *Fax:* (06) 6832526
Key Personnel
Chief Executive: Dr Enzo Crea
Editorial: Benedetta Origo Crea
Founded: 1964
Subjects: Art
ISBN Prefix(es): 88-7176

Eliseo, *imprint of* Loescher Editore SRL

Elle Di Ci - Libreria Dottrina Cristiana
C So Francia, 214, 10090 Cascine Vica-Rivoli Turin
Tel: (011) 9552111 *Fax:* (011) 9574048
E-mail: editoriale@elledici.org
Web Site: www.elledici.org
Founded: 1941
Subjects: Biblical Studies, Child Care & Development, Education, Music, Dance, Religion - Catholic, Theology
ISBN Prefix(es): 88-01
Branch Office(s)
Corso C Alberto 77, 60127 Ancona *Tel:* (071) 2810306 *Fax:* (071) 2810306
Via Martiri d'Otranto, 69, 70123 Bari *Tel:* (080) 5740059 *Fax:* (080) 5797054
Via G Matteotti, 23/D, 40129 Bologna *Tel:* (051) 355242 *Fax:* (051) 355242
Viale M Rapisardi, 95124 Catania *Tel:* (095) 441379 *Fax:* (095) 441379
Via S Giovanni Bosco, 98122 Messina *Tel:* (090) 718874 *Fax:* (090) 718874

ITALY

Via M Gioia, 62, 20124 Milan *Tel:* (02) 67072085 *Fax:* (02) 67071776
Via Donnaregina, 7, 80138 Napoli *Tel:* (081) 449167 *Fax:* (081) 291862
Via G Jappelli, 6, 35121 Padova *Tel:* (049) 875138 *Fax:* (049) 875138
Corso Francia, 214, 10090 Rivoli *Tel:* (011) 9552333
Via Marsala, 40, 00185 Rome *Tel:* (06) 491400 *Fax:* (06) 4450370
Via Conciliazione, 26/28, 00193 Rome *Tel:* (06) 68806735 *Fax:* (06) 6874559
Via C Rolando, 63/r, 16151 GE Sampierdarena *Tel:* (010) 6459306 *Fax:* (010) 6459306
Via M Ausiliatrice, 10152 Turin *Tel:* (011) 5211925 *Fax:* (011) 5211925

Ellissi, *imprint of* Esselibri

Elmedi™, *imprint of* Paravia Bruno Mondadori Editori

ELS, *imprint of* Edizioni Librarie Siciliane

EMI, see Editrice Missionaria Italiana (EMI)

EMP, see Messaggero di San Antonio

Enna
Formerly Aleph
Via S Agata 90, 94100 Enna
Tel: (0935) 500368 *Fax:* (0935) 500568
ISBN Prefix(es): 88-7154

Enne+
Via Monforte, 7, 86100 Campobasso
Tel: (0874) 412357 *Fax:* (0874) 412357
Founded: 1965
ISBN Prefix(es): 88-7213

EQ, *imprint of* Edizioni Quasar di Severino Tognon SRL

ER, *imprint of* Editori Riuniti

Editrice Eraclea
Imprint of Compagnia Delle Cinque Vie SRL
Via del Bollo 8, 20123 Milan
Tel: (02) 8693635 *Fax:* (02) 86453613
E-mail: cinquevie@libero.it
Key Personnel
Man Dir: Mario Calori
Founded: 1974
Number of titles published annually: 10 Print
Total Titles: 85 Print
Imprints: EE

ERGA SNC di Carla Ottino Merli & C (Edizioni Realizzazioni Grafiche - Artigiana)+
Via Biga 52r, 16144 Genoa
Tel: (010) 8328441 *Fax:* (010) 8328799
Key Personnel
Chief Executive: Marcello Merli
Editorial: Marco Merli
Founded: 1964
Subjects: Art, Cookery, Ethnicity, History, Law, Literature, Literary Criticism, Essays, Music, Dance, Poetry, Regional Interests, Religion - Other, Romance, Science (General), Self-Help, Sports, Athletics
ISBN Prefix(es): 88-8163

L'Erma di Bretschneider SRL+
Via Cassiodoro 19, 00193 Rome
Tel: (06) 6874127 *Fax:* (06) 6874129
E-mail: edizioni@lerma.it
Web Site: www.lerma.it

Key Personnel
Chief Executive & Editorial: Dr Roberto Marcucci *E-mail:* roberto.marcucci@lerma.it
Founded: 1946
Subjects: Archaeology, Architecture & Interior Design, Art, History, Language Arts, Linguistics, Religion - Other
ISBN Prefix(es): 88-7062; 88-8265
Number of titles published annually: 65 Print
Total Titles: 2,000 Print
Bookshop(s): Libreria L'Erma

Edi.Ermes srl+
Viale Enrico Forlanini 65, 20134 Milan
Tel: (02) 7021121 *Fax:* (02) 70211283
E-mail: eeinfo@eenet.it
Key Personnel
Chief Executive: Raffaele Grandi
Founded: 1973
Also book packager.
Subjects: Art, Biological Sciences, Economics, Medicine, Nursing, Dentistry, Sports, Athletics, Veterinary Science
ISBN Prefix(es): 88-85019; 88-7051
Associate Companies: Edi.Artes srl, Viale Enrico Forlanini 65, 20134 Milan
Imprints: EE

ES, *imprint of* Editoriale Scienza

ESI SpA, see Edizioni Scientifiche Italiane

Essegi+
Via Faentina 362, 48010 Ravenna RA
Tel: (0544) 499203 *Fax:* (0544) 499076
E-mail: essegi_libri@libero.it
Key Personnel
President: Dal Re Patrizia
Editorial Dir: Rieel Matteo
Founded: 1982
Specialize in contemporary art.
Subjects: Anthropology, Antiques, Archaeology, Architecture & Interior Design, Art, Astronomy, Drama, Theater, Fashion, History, Language Arts, Linguistics, Literature, Literary Criticism, Essays, Photography
ISBN Prefix(es): 88-7189
Divisions: Spazio Espositivo Essegi
Showroom(s): Spazio Espositivo Essegi

Esselibri+
Via Russo, 33, 80123 Naples
Tel: (081) 5757255 *Fax:* (081) 5757944
E-mail: info@simone.it
Web Site: www.simone.it
Founded: 1989
Publish academic, technical & professional books.
Subjects: Architecture & Interior Design, Business, Communications, Computer Science, Economics, Government, Political Science, Labor, Industrial Relations, Law, Psychology, Psychiatry, Public Administration, Securities, Technology
ISBN Prefix(es): 88-244
Number of titles published annually: 450 Print
Imprints: Ellissi; Finanze & Lavoro; Nissolino; Sigma; Edizioni Giuridiche Simone; Simone per la Scuola; Sistemi Editoriali

l'Eta dell'Acquario+
Via Galliari, 15b, 10125 Turin
Tel: (011) 6693910 *Fax:* (011) 6693929
Key Personnel
Dir: Count Bernardino del Boca Di Villaregia
International Rights: Isabella Bresci
Founded: 1971
Membership(s): New York Academy of Science.
Subjects: Nonfiction (General), Parapsychology, Religion - Other
ISBN Prefix(es): 88-7136

Imprints: Edizioni L' Eta dell'Acquario
Showroom(s): c/o Lingotto, Salone del Libro Di Torino, Turin

Etas Libri+
Division of RCS Libri Spa
Via Mecenate, 91, 20138 Milan
Tel: (02) 50951 *Fax:* (02) 50952309
E-mail: etaslab@rcs.it
Web Site: www.etaslab.it
Key Personnel
Contact: Lorena Ferrari *E-mail:* lorena.ferrari@rcs.it
Professor: Dr Direttore Divisione
Founded: 1963
Subjects: Business, Economics, Engineering (General), Management, Mathematics
ISBN Prefix(es): 88-453
Orders to: RCS Libri Spa *Tel:* (050) 952333 *Fax:* (050 952300

ETR (Editrice Trasporti su Rotaie) (Rail Transport Publishing)+
Member of FerPress
Piazza Vittorio Emanuele 42, 25087 Salo (BS)
Tel: (03) 6541092 *Fax:* (03) 6541092
E-mail: etr@itreni.com
Web Site: www.itreni.com
Key Personnel
President: Hans Juergen Rosenberger
Founded: 1980
Publish the monthly illustrative magazine *TRENI*.
Subjects: Crafts, Games, Hobbies, Transportation, Travel
ISBN Prefix(es): 88-85068
Number of titles published annually: 2 Print

EUR, *imprint of* Edizioni Universitarie Romane

Eura Press, *imprint of* Todariana Editrice

EuroGeoGrafiche Mencattini+
Via Po, 45, 52100 Arezzo
Tel: (0575) 900010 *Fax:* (0575) 911161
E-mail: eurogeo@egm.it
Web Site: www.egm.it
Key Personnel
President: Dr Silvano Mencattini
Vice President: Daniel Mencattini
Founded: 1974
Specialize in tourist guides & cartography.
Membership(s): USPI; AIE; AIPE.
Subjects: Geography, Geology, Travel
ISBN Prefix(es): 88-86263
Imprints: EGGM

Edizioni Europa
Via G Martini, 6, 00198 Rome
Tel: (06) 8419124
Founded: 1944
Subjects: Art, Economics, Government, Political Science, History, Music, Dance
Subsidiaries: Le Edigioni del Lavors

Editoriale Europress (Nardini Press), *imprint of* Nardini Editore srl

Fanucci
Via delle Fornaci, 66, 00165 Rome
Tel: (06) 639366384 *Fax:* (06) 6382998
E-mail: info@fanucci.it
Web Site: www.fanucci.it
Key Personnel
Editor: Sergio Fanucci
Founded: 1972
Subjects: Science Fiction, Fantasy
ISBN Prefix(es): 88-347
Imprints: FE

Fatatrac+
Via Ricorboli 28, 50126 Florence
Tel: (055) 6810124 *Fax:* (055) 6810260

PUBLISHERS — ITALY

E-mail: info@fatatrac.com
Web Site: www.fatatrac.com/
Key Personnel
Publisher: Nicoletta Codignola *E-mail:* n.codignola@fatatrac.com
Founded: 1978
Subjects: Animals, Pets, Art, Child Care & Development, Developing Countries, Education, Literature, Literary Criticism, Essays, Photography, Science Fiction, Fantasy
ISBN Prefix(es): 88-85089; 88-86228; 88-8222
Number of titles published annually: 18 Print
Foreign Rep(s): Nicoletta Codignola

FE, *imprint of* Fanucci

Federico Motta Editore SpA+
Via Branda Castiglioni, 7, 20156 Milan
Tel: (02) 300761; (02) 30076231 *Fax:* (02) 38010046; (02) 33403275
E-mail: info@mottaeditore.it
Web Site: www.mottaeditore.it
Telex: 350397 Motta I
Key Personnel
Chief Executive Officer & Publisher: Federico Motta
Dir, Financial & Administration: Massimo Fumagalli
Sales, Encyclopaedia Dept: Patrizia Ruffo
Press & Advertising Relations: Natalina Costra
Dir, Sales, Book Dept: Lorena Vazzola
Founded: 1929
Subjects: Architecture & Interior Design, Art, Photography
ISBN Prefix(es): 88-7179

Feguagiskia' Studios+
Via Crosa di Vergagni, 3 r, 16124 Genoa
Tel: (010) 2757544 *Fax:* (010) 2510838
Key Personnel
Publisher: Gualtiero Schiaffino
Founded: 1982
Subjects: Child Care & Development, Literature, Literary Criticism, Essays

Giangiacomo Feltrinelli SpA
Via Andegari, 6, 20121 Milan
Tel: (02) 725721 *Fax:* (02) 72572500 *Cable:* Fedit Milan
Founded: 1954
Subjects: Art, Fiction, History, Philosophy, Poetry, Science (General)
ISBN Prefix(es): 88-07

Fenice 2000+
Via della Maggiolina, 24, 20125 Milan
Tel: (02) 66984638; (02) 67075155 *Fax:* (02) 67074283
Key Personnel
President: Dr Enzo Angelucci
Man Dir: Dr Pierluigi Bozzia
Founded: 1986
Subjects: Aeronautics, Aviation, Animals, Pets, Art, Cookery, Crafts, Games, Hobbies, Gardening, Plants, Photography
ISBN Prefix(es): 88-8017

Festina Lente Edizioni+
via della Croce, 11, 50023 Impruneta, Florence
Tel: (055) 292612 *Fax:* (055) 292612
Key Personnel
Contact: Paolo Gori Savellini; Andrea del Sere
Founded: 1989
Subjects: Architecture & Interior Design, Art, History, Literature, Literary Criticism, Essays, Medicine, Nursing, Dentistry, Psychology, Psychiatry
ISBN Prefix(es): 88-85171

Fiabesca, *imprint of* Stampa Alternativa - Nuovi Equilibri

Finanze & Lavoro, *imprint of* Esselibri

Flaccovio Dario+
Via E Oliveri Mandala 35, 90146 Palermo
Tel: (091) 202533 *Fax:* (091) 227702
E-mail: press@darioflaccovio.com
Web Site: www.darioflaccovio.com
Key Personnel
Contact: Marisa Flaccovio
Founded: 1980
ISBN Prefix(es): 88-7758
Bookshop(s): Via Ausonia, 70-90144 Palermo

Flaccovio Editore
Via Ruggiero Settimo, 37, 90139 Palermo
Tel: (091) 589442 *Fax:* (091) 331992
E-mail: info@flaccovio.com
Web Site: www.flaccovio.com
Founded: 1939
Membership(s): AIE.
Subjects: Archaeology, Architecture & Interior Design, Art, History, Regional Interests, Science (General)
ISBN Prefix(es): 88-7804
Parent Company: S F Flaccovio sas
Bookshop(s): Libreria SF Flaccovio, Via Ruggiero Settimo, 34, 90139 Palermo

FMR, see Franco Maria Ricci Editore (FMR)

Fogola Editore in Torino+
Piazza Carlo Felice, 19, 10123 Turin
Tel: (011) 535897 *Fax:* (011) 530305
Web Site: www.culturitalia.uibk.ac.at
Founded: 1965
Subjects: Fiction, History, Literature, Literary Criticism, Essays
Total Titles: 115 Print
Showroom(s): Paztecipozione al Salone Del Libro Ditorino
Bookshop(s): Libreria Dante Alighieri, Piazza Carlo Felice 19, 10123 Turin

Editoriale Fernando Folini, *imprint of* Editoriale Fernando Folini

Editoriale Fernando Folini+
Il Battaglino, 15052 Casalnoceto, Alessandria
Tel: (0131) 807001 *Fax:* (0131) 807001
E-mail: edifolini@edifolini.com
Web Site: www.edifolini.com
Key Personnel
President: Dr Fernando Folini *E-mail:* folinif@edifolini.com
Founded: 1986
Membership(s): Associazione Italiana Editori.
Subjects: Biological Sciences, Cookery, Environmental Studies, Health, Nutrition, Medicine, Nursing, Dentistry, Self-Help
ISBN Prefix(es): 88-7266
Imprints: Editoriale Fernando Folini

Arnaldo Forni Editore SRL
Via Gramsci 164, 40010 Sala Bolognese (Bologna)
Tel: (051) 6814142; (051) 6814198 *Fax:* (051) 6814672
E-mail: info@fornieditore.com
Web Site: www.fornieditore.com
Key Personnel
Man Dir: Aurelia Forni
Founded: 1973
Subjects: Antiques, Archaeology, Architecture & Interior Design, Art, Astrology, Occult, Astronomy, Biography, Cookery, Drama, Theater, Earth Sciences, Economics, Gardening, Plants, Genealogy, Geography, Geology, History, Language Arts, Linguistics, Law, Literature, Literary Criticism, Essays, Mathematics, Medicine, Nursing, Dentistry, Music, Dance, Philosophy, Psychology, Psychiatry, Regional Interests, Religion - Catholic, Religion - Other
ISBN Prefix(es): 88-271
Number of titles published annually: 20 Print
Total Titles: 3,200 Print
Bookshop(s): Via Galliera 15, 40121 Bologna
Tel: (051) 221417 *Fax:* (051) 6814672
E-mail: rarebooks@fornieditore.com

Biblioteca Francescana+
Piazza S Angelo, 2, 20121 Milan
Tel: (02) 29002736 *Fax:* (02) 29002736
E-mail: info@bibliotecafrancescana.it
Web Site: www.bibliotecafrancescana.it
Key Personnel
International Rights: Cabassi Aristide
Founded: 1977
Specialize in Francescanesimo.
Subjects: History, Religion - Catholic, Theology
ISBN Prefix(es): 88-7962
Imprints: EBF
Distributor for Messaggero Distribuzione (Italy)

Edizioni Frassinelli SRL+
Via Durazzo 4, 20134 Milan
Tel: (02) 217211 *Fax:* (02) 21721277
Key Personnel
President & Publisher: Valerio Anna Patrizia
Editorial Dir: Carla Tanzi
Marketing Dir: Giuseppe Baroffio
Rights & Permissions: Laura Casonato
Scout: Linda Clark
Contracts: Marica Fioroni
Founded: 1932
Subjects: Art, Biography, Fiction, Nonfiction (General)
ISBN Prefix(es): 88-7684; 88-7824; 88-8274; 88-88320
Parent Company: Sperling e Kupfer Editori SpA
U.S. Office(s): 225 Lafayette St, Suite 602, New York, NY 10012, United States (Scout Office)

Fratelli Conte Editori SRL+
Via Andrea D'Isernia, 59, 80122 Naples
Tel: (081) 7611858 *Fax:* (081) 7613667
Web Site: www.clio.it/sr/ce/conte/conte_ed.html
Key Personnel
Man Dir: Ferdinando Conte; Mario Conte
Founded: 1967
Subjects: Fiction

Frati Editori di Quaracchi
Via Vecchia per Marino 28-30, 00046 Grottaferrata (Rome)
Tel: (06) 94551259 *Fax:* (06) 94551267
E-mail: quaracchi@ofm.org
Web Site: www.quaracchi.ofm.org
Founded: 1877
Subjects: History, Religion - Other, Theology
ISBN Prefix(es): 88-7013
Parent Company: Fondazione Collegio San Bonaventura Grottaferrata

Edizioni Futuro SRL
Via Cesiolo, 10, 37126 Verona
Tel: (045) 915622 *Fax:* (045) 8300261
Telex: 480833
Key Personnel
Chief Executive: Vinicio de Lorentiis
Editorial: Francesca Pomini
Sales: Marta de Lorentiis
Rights & Permissions: Elena Zoccatelli
Founded: 1979
Subjects: Art, Biography, Environmental Studies, How-to
ISBN Prefix(es): 88-7650
Subsidiaries: Edizioni Vinicio de Lorentiis; Moderna International

Adriano Gallina Editore sas+
Salita Tarsia, 143, 80135 Naples

Tel: (081) 5496730 *Fax:* (081) 5448747
Key Personnel
Man Dir: Rossana Gallina
Editorial: Maria Gallina
Sales: Giuseppe Gallina
Founded: 1968
Subjects: Archaeology, Art, Cookery, Ethnicity, Music, Dance, Poetry, Regional Interests, Travel
ISBN Prefix(es): 88-87350
Imprints: Adriana Gallina Editore; Edizioni del Delfino
Divisions: Edizioni del Delfino

Galzerano Editore+
84040 Casalvelino Scalo, Salerno
Tel: (0974) 62028 *Fax:* (0974) 62028 *Cable:* GALZERANO CASALVELINO SCALO (SA)
Key Personnel
Chief Executive: Giuseppe Galzerano
Founded: 1975
Subjects: Biography, Ethnicity, Fiction, Government, Political Science, History, Poetry
Number of titles published annually: 10 Print

Gamberetti Editrice SRL+
Via Faa di Bruno 28, 00195 Rome
Tel: (06) 3728394 *Fax:* (06) 3728394
E-mail: gamberetti@gamberetti.it
Web Site: www.gamberetti.it
Key Personnel
Contact: Stefano Chiarini
Founded: 1992
Specializes in the conflicts of the "New World Order", Middle East, Former Yugoslavia, Ireland, Italy, Latin America, Armenia, Polisario, & North-South relationship.
Subjects: Fiction, Literature, Literary Criticism, Essays
ISBN Prefix(es): 88-7990
Total Titles: 32 Print
Distributed by PDE Distribuzione (Firenze)

Gammalibri-Rock Books, *imprint of* Kaos Edizioni SRL

Gangemi Editore spa+
Piazza S Pantaleo 4, 00186 Rome
Tel: (06) 6872774; (06) 68806189 (orders) *Fax:* (06) 68806189
E-mail: info@gangemieditore.it
Web Site: www.gangemieditore.it
Key Personnel
Chief Executive: Giuseppe Gangemi
Marketing Executive Manager: Emilia Gangemi
Publishing Editor Manager: Fabio Gangemi
Founded: 1962
Subjects: Agriculture, Anthropology, Archaeology, Architecture & Interior Design, Art, Disability, Special Needs, History, Literature, Literary Criticism, Essays, Medicine, Nursing, Dentistry, Philosophy, Romance, Social Sciences, Sociology
ISBN Prefix(es): 88-492; 88-7448
Number of titles published annually: 100 Print
Total Titles: 2,500 Print
Distributed by Accorn Aviante; Arobaleno; CDM; Licosa; Messaggerie Libri; Plymbridge
Distributor for Iter Mundi
Bookshop(s): Corso Garibaldi, 168, 89100 Reggio Calabria *Tel:* (0965) 894844 *Fax:* (0965) 894845; Via Cavour, 255, 00184 Rome *Tel:* (06) 4821661

Editrice Garigliano SRL+
Via Aligerno, 91/93, 03043 Cassino (Frosinone)
Tel: (0776) 21869 *Fax:* (0776) 21869 *Cable:* Editrice Garigliano Cassino
Key Personnel
Chief Executive: Marisa Canzano; Stefano Vitale
Editorial: Rodolfo Vitale

Sales: Brunella Martucci
Production: Antonio Violo
Publicity: Giovanni Violo
Rights & Permissions: Elena Vettese
Founded: 1968
Subjects: Education, Literature, Literary Criticism, Essays, Philosophy, Psychology, Psychiatry
ISBN Prefix(es): 88-7103
Bookshop(s): Libreria Universitaria

Garolla
Via Guido d'Arezzo 4, 20145 Milan
Tel: (02) 48005574 *Fax:* (02) 48003915
Key Personnel
Contact: Federico Garolla
Subjects: Archaeology, Art
ISBN Prefix(es): 88-7682

Garzanti Libri+
Via Gasparotto 1, 20124 Milan
Tel: (02) 674171 *Fax:* (02) 67417323
Telex: 325218 Gared *Cable:* Garzantieditore
Key Personnel
Publisher: Dr Livio Garzanti
Editorial: Dr Giananarea Piccioli
Sales Manager: Francesco Rampini
Rights & Permissions: Marie Louise Zarmanian
Founded: 1861
Subjects: Art, Biography, Fiction, Government, Political Science, History, Literature, Literary Criticism, Essays, Poetry
ISBN Prefix(es): 88-11
Associate Companies: A Vallardi, Via Newton, 18A, 20148 Milan
Bookshop(s): Libreria Garzanti, Galleria Vittorio Emanuele 66-68, 20121 Milan; Libreria Garzanti, Palazzo Dell' Universita, Pavia; Libreria della Spiga, Via della Spiga 30, 20121 Milan

Edizioni GB+
Via Callegari, 33, 35133 Padova
Tel: (049) 8647834 *Fax:* (049) 8647834
Founded: 1985
Membership(s): WWF.
Subjects: Alternative, Anthropology, Architecture & Interior Design, Biological Sciences, Environmental Studies, Government, Political Science, Library & Information Sciences, Medicine, Nursing, Dentistry, Philosophy, Physical Sciences, Science (General), Social Sciences, Sociology, Sports, Athletics, Travel
ISBN Prefix(es): 88-86272
Subsidiaries: Edizioni GB - Brasile

Istituto Geografico de Agostini SpA
Via Giovanni da Verrazzano 15, 28100 Novara
Tel: (0321) 4241 *Fax:* (0321) 471286
E-mail: info@deagostini.it
Web Site: www.deagostini.it
Telex: 200290 Edidea I *Cable:* GEOGRAFICO NOVARA
Key Personnel
Contact: Chiara Boroli
Founded: 1901
Subjects: Art, Gardening, Plants, Geography, Geology, History, Literature, Literary Criticism, Essays, Regional Interests, Religion - Other
ISBN Prefix(es): 88-402; 88-415; 88-410; 88-418; 88-406
Branch Office(s)
Uffici di Milano, Via Montefeltro 6/A, 20156 Milan *Tel:* (02) 380861 *Fax:* (02) 38086324

Gereria Cortina Editrice SRL, see Libreria Cortina Editrice SRL

Bruno Ghigi Editore+
Via Pleiadi, 6, 47900 Rimini
Tel: (0541) 791727 *Fax:* (0541) 791727

Key Personnel
All offices: Bruno Ghigi
Founded: 1955
Subjects: Geography, Geology, History
ISBN Prefix(es): 88-85640

Ghisetti e Corvi Editori
Corso Concordia 7, 20129 Milan
Tel: (02) 76006232 *Fax:* (02) 76009468
E-mail: sedes.spa@gpa.it
Web Site: www.ghisetticorvi.it
Founded: 1937
ISBN Prefix(es): 88-8013

Giancarlo Politi Editore
Via Carlo Farini 68, 20159 Milan
Tel: (02) 6887341 *Fax:* (02) 66801290
E-mail: politi@interbusiness.it
Web Site: politi.undo.net
Key Personnel
Publisher: Giancarlo Politi
Editor: Helena Kontova
Subjects: Art
ISBN Prefix(es): 88-7816
U.S. Office(s): 799 Broadway, Room 226, New York, NY 10003, United States

G Giappichelli Editore SRL+
Via Po, 21, 10124 Turin
Tel: (011) 8153111 *Fax:* (011) 8125100
E-mail: spedizioni@giappichelli.com
Web Site: www.giappichelli.it
Founded: 1921
Subjects: Economics, Government, Political Science, Law, Philosophy, Social Sciences, Sociology
ISBN Prefix(es): 88-348
Bookshop(s): Libreria Editrice Scientifica di G Giappichelli, Via Vasco 2, 1-10124 Turin

Giovanni Tranchida Editore, *imprint of* Giovanni Tranchida Editore

Edizioni del Girasole srl
Via P Costa, 10, 48100 Ravenna
Tel: (0544) 212830 *Fax:* (0544) 38432
E-mail: info@europart.it
Key Personnel
President: Lapucci Egle
Publishing Dir: Ivan Simonini
Founded: 1965
Subjects: Archaeology, Art, History, Photography, Poetry, Romance
ISBN Prefix(es): 88-7567

A Giuffre Editore SpA+
Via Busto Arsizio, 40, 20151 Milan
Tel: (02) 380891 *Fax:* (02) 38009582
E-mail: giuffre@giuffre.it
Web Site: www.giuffre.it
Key Personnel
Man Dir: Giuseppe Giuffre
Chief Editor: Gaetano Giuffre
Founded: 1931
Subjects: Economics, Government, Political Science, History, Law, Social Sciences, Sociology
ISBN Prefix(es): 88-14
Branch Office(s)
Via V Colonna 40, I-00193 Rome *Tel:* (06) 659938; (06) 6569792
Bookshop(s): Giuffre Libreria, Pza S Stefano, 5, 20122 Milan

Giunti Gruppo Editoriale (Giunti Publishing Group)+
Via Bolognese 165, 50139 Florence
Tel: (055) 5062376 *Fax:* (055) 5062397
E-mail: informazioni@giunti.it
Web Site: www.giunti.it
Telex: 571438 Giunti *Cable:* MARZOLIB FLORENCE

Key Personnel
Dir: Dr Sergio Giunti
Rights & Permissions: Roberto Borrani
Founded: 1840
Group comprises: Giunti Marzocco, ME/DI Sviluppo, OS (Organizzazioni Speciali SRL), Lisciani e Giunti Editori, Edizioni Primavera.
Subjects: Art, Chemistry, Chemical Engineering, Education, Fiction, History, How-to, Language Arts, Linguistics, Literature, Literary Criticism, Essays, Mathematics, Psychology, Psychiatry, Science (General)
ISBN Prefix(es): 88-09
Imprints: Giunti Marzocco
Subsidiaries: Lisciani & Giunti; ME/DI Sviluppo; Edizioni Primavera; OS Org Speciali; Giunti Industrie Grafiche; Giunti Multimedia
Branch Office(s)
Ancona
Bari
Cagliari
Catania
Genoa
Lamezia Terme
Milan
Naples
Padua
Palermo
Rome

Editrice la Giuntina
Via Ricasoli 26, 50122 Florence
Tel: (055) 268684 *Fax:* (055) 219718
E-mail: giuntina@fol.it
Web Site: www.giuntina.it
Key Personnel
Contact: Daniel Vogelmann
Founded: 1980
Specialize in Jewish subjects.
Subjects: Religion - Jewish
ISBN Prefix(es): 88-85943; 88-8057
Total Titles: 240 Print

Edizioni Giuridico Scientifiche (SRL)+
Via Donizetti, 37, 20122 Milan
Tel: (02) 55192219 *Fax:* (02) 76009444
Key Personnel
Editor: Ennio Alessio Mizzau
ISBN Prefix(es): 88-85874

Gius Laterza e Figli SpA+
Piazza Umberto I, 54, 70121 Bari
Tel: (080) 5281211 *Fax:* (080) 5243461
E-mail: laterza@laterza.it
Web Site: www.laterza.it
Telex: 623168
Key Personnel
Man Dir, Rome: Vito Laterza
Editorial Dir, Rome: Alessandro Laterza; Giuseppe Laterza
Production: Claudio Lodoli
Press, Publicity & Advertising (Rome): Karina Laterza
Rights & Permissions: Antonia Sollecito
Sales Dir, Bari: Caterina D'Ambrosio
Founded: 1885
Subjects: Archaeology, Architecture & Interior Design, Art, Biography, Economics, History, Philosophy, Psychology, Psychiatry, Religion - Other, Science (General), Social Sciences, Sociology
ISBN Prefix(es): 88-420
Bookshop(s): Libreria Internazionale Laterza, Via Sparano 134, 1-70121 Bari
Shipping Address: Via F Zippitelli 3, Zona Industriale, 70123 Bari

Giuseppe Laterza Editore+
Via Suppa 16, 70122 Bari
Tel: (080) 5237936 *Fax:* (080) 5237360
Key Personnel
Editor: Giuseppe Laterza
Founded: 1980
Subjects: Computer Science, Electronics, Electrical Engineering, Government, Political Science, Law, Literature, Literary Criticism, Essays, Poetry, Psychology, Psychiatry, Veterinary Science
ISBN Prefix(es): 88-86243; 88-8231
Imprints: Edizioni Fratelli Laterza
Subsidiaries: Laterza Litostampa; Libreria Fratelli Laterza; Cartoleria Fratelli Laterza

Glossa+
Piazza Paolovi, 6, 20121 Milan
Tel: (02) 877609 *Fax:* (02) 72003162
E-mail: informazioni@glossaeditrice.it
Web Site: www.glossaeditrice.it
Founded: 1987
Subjects: Theology
ISBN Prefix(es): 88-7105
Number of titles published annually: 12 Print
Total Titles: 165 Print
Distribution Center: Dehoniana Libri Spa, Via Scipione dal Ferro 4, Bologna

GM, *imprint of* Giorgio Mondadori & Associati

Gozzini, see Libreria Gozzini di Pietro e Francesco Chellini (SNC)

Grafica e Arte srl+
Via Francesco Coghetti 108, 24128 Bergamo
Tel: (035) 255014 *Fax:* (035) 250164
E-mail: info@graficaearte.it
Web Site: www.graficaearte.it
Key Personnel
Man Dir: Emilio Agazzi
Founded: 1975
Subjects: Art, Ethnicity, History, Photography
Number of titles published annually: 10 Print
Total Titles: 250 Print
Distributed by Dehoniana Libri Sp
Showroom(s): Via Francesco Coghetti, 90, 24128 Bergamo

Marchesi Grafiche Editoriali SpA
Via Bomarzo 32, 00191 Rome
Tel: (06) 331359 *Fax:* (06) 3336505
Founded: 1927
Specialize in publishing & printing for other firms.
ISBN Prefix(es): 88-86248

Grafo
Via Maiera 27, 25123 Brescia
Tel: (030) 393221 *Fax:* (030) 3701411
Key Personnel
Chief Executive: Matteo Montagnoli
Sales: Franco Agnelli
Founded: 1973
Subjects: Anthropology, Archaeology, Art, Ethnicity, History, Regional Interests
ISBN Prefix(es): 88-7385

Libreria Editrice Gregoriana
Via Roma 82, 35122 Padova
Tel: (049) 657493 *Fax:* (049) 659777
Key Personnel
Man Dir: Don Giancarlo Minozzi
Contact: Claudio Zanetto
Founded: 1922
Subjects: Philosophy, Psychology, Psychiatry, Religion - Other, Social Sciences, Sociology
ISBN Prefix(es): 88-7706
Parent Company: Euganea Editoriale Comunicazion SRL, Via Roma 82, 35122 Padova
Bookshop(s): Via Roma 37, Padova; Via Vescovado 33, Padova; Piazza Duomo 5, Padova

Ernesto Gremese Editore srl+
Via Virginia Agnelli 88, V Le Dei Colli Portuensi 537, 00151 Rome
Tel: (06) 65740507 *Fax:* (06) 65740509
E-mail: gremese@gremese.com
Web Site: www.gremese.com
Key Personnel
Chief Executive: Alberto Gremese
E-mail: alberto@gremese.com
Founded: 1954
Subjects: Art, Astrology, Occult, Cookery, Crafts, Games, Hobbies, Drama, Theater, Erotica, Fashion, Fiction, Film, Video, Health, Nutrition, House & Home, How-to, Literature, Literary Criticism, Essays, Music, Dance, Radio, TV, Sports, Athletics, Travel, Wine & Spirits
ISBN Prefix(es): 88-7605; 88-7742; 88-8440
Number of titles published annually: 80 Print
Total Titles: 700 Print
Imprints: L'Airone Editrice
Bookshop(s): Libreria Internazionale Ernesto Gremese SNC, Via Cola di Rienzo 136, 00192 Rome *Tel:* (06) 3235367 *Fax:* (06) 3235374 *E-mail:* info@liberia.gremese.it *Web Site:* www.liberiagremese.it

Gremese International srl+
Via Virginia Agnelli, 88, 00151 Rome
Tel: (06) 65740507 *Fax:* (06) 65740509
E-mail: gremese@gremese.com
Web Site: www.gremese.com
Key Personnel
Chief Executive: Alberto Gremese
Founded: 1991
Subjects: Art, Astrology, Occult, Cookery, Crafts, Games, Hobbies, Film, Video, History, Music, Dance, Nonfiction (General), Photography, Travel
ISBN Prefix(es): 88-7301
Parent Company: Ernest Gremese Editore rrl
Subsidiaries: Gremese Editore
Distribution Center: National Book Network, 4720 Boston Way, Lanham, MD 20706, United States

Piero Gribaudi Editore+
Via C Baroni, 190, 20141 Milan
Tel: (02) 89302244 *Fax:* (02) 89302376
E-mail: info@gribaudi.it
Web Site: www.gribaudi.it
Key Personnel
Publisher: Cesare Crespi; Maurizio Sola
Foreign Rights: Sandra Zerilli *E-mail:* szerilli@gribaudi.it
Founded: 1966
Subjects: Behavioral Sciences, Biblical Studies, Biography, Education, Human Relations, Humor, Religion - Catholic, Religion - Jewish, Self-Help, Theology
ISBN Prefix(es): 88-7152
Number of titles published annually: 50 Print
Total Titles: 750 Print
Imprints: PGE

Gruppo Editoriale Faenza Editrice SpA+
Via pier de Crescenzi, 44, 48018 Faenza (Ravenna)
Tel: (0546) 670411 *Fax:* (0546) 660440
E-mail: info@faenza.com
Web Site: www.faenza.com
Key Personnel
Man Dir: Franco Rossi
Sales: Luisa Teston *E-mail:* lteston@faenza.com
Founded: 1965
Subjects: Architecture & Interior Design, Art, Engineering (General), Medicine, Nursing, Dentistry, Science (General)
ISBN Prefix(es): 88-8138
Number of titles published annually: 98 Print
Imprints: Edizioni CELI

Gruppo Editoriale Internazionale SRL (GEI),
see Instituti Editoriali E Poligrafici Internazionali SRL

Ugo Guanda Editore+
Corso Italia 13, 20122 Milan
Tel: (02) 80206322 *Fax:* (02) 72000306
E-mail: info@guanda.it
Web Site: www.guanda.it
Telex: 353273 LONG I
Key Personnel
President: Mario Spagnol
Man Dir: Stefano Mauri
Editorial: Luigi Brioschi
Sales: Giuseppe Somenzi
Production: Alfredo Bonfiglio
Publicity: Valentina Fortichiari
Rights & Permissions: Cristina Foschini
Founded: 1932
Subjects: Art, Poetry
ISBN Prefix(es): 88-7746; 88-235; 88-8246
Parent Company: Longanesi & C
Subsidiaries: Gdp
U.S. Office(s): Nina Collins Association, 584 Broadway, Suite 607, New York, NY 10012, United States
Warehouse: Messaggerie Italiane Spa, Magazzino Editoriale, Via Bereguardina, 20080 Casarile (Mi)
Orders to: Pro Libro, Strada della Repubblica 56, 43100 Parma

Edizioni Guerini e Associati SpA+
Viale Filippetti 28, 20122 Milan
Tel: (02) 582980 *Fax:* (02) 58298030
E-mail: info@guerini.it
Web Site: www.guerini.it
Key Personnel
President: Angelo Guerini
Printing Office: Federico Gagliardo *Tel:* (02) 58298017
Foreign Rights Manager: Claudia Premoli *Tel:* (02) 58298016
Founded: 1987
Essays, Books & Reviews.
Subjects: Anthropology, Management, Philosophy, Psychology, Psychiatry, Social Sciences, Sociology, Literary Criticism, Architecture & Gardens, Media Studies & Geopolitics
ISBN Prefix(es): 88-7802; 88-8107 (Guerini scientifica); 88-8335; 88-8195 (contiere italia)
Total Titles: 1,000 Print
Bookshop(s): Libreria Guerini, Piazza Soldini 5, 21053 Castellanza *Tel:* (0331) 508918 *Fax:* (0331) 508972 *E-mail:* libreria@liuc.it
Shipping Address: Pea Italia, Via Spallanzani 16, 20129 Milan

Guerra Edizioni GURU srl
Via A Manna, 25/27, 06132 Perugia
Tel: (075) 5289090 *Fax:* (075) 5288244
E-mail: geinfo@guerra-edizioni.com
Web Site: www.guerra-edizioni.com
Telex: Cuper I Rux
Key Personnel
Publicity Manager: Chellini Gastone
Founded: 1883
Subjects: Education, Language Arts, Linguistics
ISBN Prefix(es): 88-7715
Orders to: RUX edel, Via E Fermi 26, 06100 Perugia *Tel:* (075) 751324

Guide del Cuore, *imprint of* Passigli Editori

Guide del Sole, *imprint of* Passigli Editori

GZ, *imprint of* Casa Musicale G Zanibon SRL

Herbita Editrice di Leonardo Palermo+
Via Errante, 44, 90127 Palermo
Tel: (091) 6167732 *Fax:* (091) 6167716
Cable: HERBITA PALERMO
Key Personnel
Chief Executive: Leonardo Palermo
Founded: 1973

Subjects: Archaeology, Art, Computer Science, Economics, Geography, Geology, Government, Political Science, Law, Literature, Literary Criticism, Essays, Mathematics, Philosophy, Religion - Catholic
ISBN Prefix(es): 88-7994

Herder Editrice e Libreria
Piazza Montecitorio, 120, 00186 Rome
Tel: (06) 679 53 04; (06) 679 46 28 *Fax:* (06) 678 47 51
E-mail: distr@herder.it
Web Site: www.herder.it
Key Personnel
Man Dir: Oriol Schaedel
Founded: 1925
Subjects: Archaeology, Asian Studies, History, Language Arts, Linguistics, Philosophy, Religion - Other, Theology, Classical Philology, Languages & Oriental studies
ISBN Prefix(es): 88-85876
Associate Companies: Verlag Herder & Co, Austria; Verlag Herder GmbH & Co KG, Germany; Herder and Herder GmbH, Germany; Verlag A G Ploetz GmbH & Co KG, Germany; Editorial Herder SA, Spain; Herder AG, Switzerland
Distributor for Academia Latinitati Fovendae (Rome); Academy Cardinalis Bessarionis (Rome); Center Studies "Girolamo Baruffaldi" (Hundreds); Center Studies Varroniani (Rieti); Church Abbaziale di Montecassino (Cassino); Department of Linguistica, University (Florence); Editions Universitaires Fribourg (Switzerland) (Italy); European Comunity (Rome); Faculty of Mastery University (Messina); Institute for East "C to Nallino" (Rome); Institute for the Ecclesiastical History Padovana (Padova); Institute of Indologia University (Turin); Instituto Espanol de Historia Eclesiastica (Rome); Institutum Historicum Polonicum (Rome); Italian Institute for the Mean & Far East (IsMEO) (Rome); Italian Institute of Germanic Studies (Rome); OECD, Paris (Rome); Properziana Academy of the Subasio (Assisi); Sargon Publishing limited liability company (Padova); University Institute Orients Them (Naples); University of the Studies of Rome "the Wisdom"; World Bank (Rome)

Hermes Edizioni SRL+
Subsidiary of Edizioni Mediterranee SRL
Via Flaminia 109, 00196 Rome
Tel: (06) 3235433 *Fax:* (06) 3236277
E-mail: info@ediz-mediterranee.com
Web Site: www.ediz-mediterranee.com
Key Personnel
General Manager: Giovanni Canonico
Editorial: Paola Maria Canonico
Sales: Maria Satulli
Rights & Permissions: Canonico Assia
Contact: Eleasa Canonico
Founded: 1979
Subjects: Anthropology, Health, Nutrition, How-to, Medicine, Nursing, Dentistry, Parapsychology, Psychology, Psychiatry, Religion - Buddhist, Religion - Hindu, Religion - Other, Sports, Athletics
ISBN Prefix(es): 88-7938
Total Titles: 300 Print

Institutum Historicum Societatis Iesu (Jesuit Historical Institute)
Via dei Penitenzieri, 20, 00193 Rome
Tel: (06) 689 77673 *Fax:* (06) 686 1342; (06) 689 77663
E-mail: ihsiroma@tin.it
Web Site: space.tin.it/scuola/mmorales/ihsi.html
Key Personnel
Dir: Rev Martin M Morales
Editor: Rev Thomas M McCoog

Founded: 1932
Subjects: History
Total Titles: 50 Print

Hopeful Monster Editore
Via Santa Chiara, 30, 10122 Turin
Tel: (011) 4367197; (011) 4358519 *Fax:* (011) 4369025
E-mail: info@hopefulmonster.net
Web Site: www.hopefulmonster.net
Key Personnel
Publisher: Beatrice Merz *E-mail:* beatricemerz@hopefulmonster.net
Founded: 1986
Specialize in art books & catalogues concerning contemporary art.
Subjects: Art, History, Philosophy, Photography, Science (General), Travel
ISBN Prefix(es): 88-7757
Number of titles published annually: 15 Print
Distributed by Albolibro (Italy); Angelo Vecchi & C (Italy); Art Books International (UK & Eire); Campania Libri; Centro Di (Europe, Giappone & USA); Centro Distribuzione Editoriale (CDE) (Italy); Distribook (Italy); Distributed Art Publishers (DAP) (USA, Canada, South America & Asia); Erre Libri (Italy); Italia Libri SRL (Italy); Joker Art Diffusion (France & Belgium); L'Aquilone (Italy); Licosa (Europe (except UK, Eire)); Serena Libri (Italy)

Hora+
Milano 2, Res Tre Fili, 421, 20090 Segrate Milan
Tel: (02) 26412203 *Fax:* (02) 26412203
Key Personnel
Contact: Rosella Hoffer; Mariangela Ragazzi
Founded: 1989
Subjects: English as a Second Language
ISBN Prefix(es): 88-85144

Ibis+
Via Crispi 8, 22100 Como
Tel: (031) 3371367; (031) 306836 *Fax:* (031) 306829
E-mail: info@ibisedizioni.it
Web Site: www.ibisedizioni.it
Key Personnel
President: Giulio Veronesi
Editorial Dir: Paolo M Veronesi
Founded: 1989
Subjects: Anthropology, Biological Sciences, Fiction, History, Literature, Literary Criticism, Essays, Philosophy, Social Sciences, Sociology, Travel
ISBN Prefix(es): 88-7164
Number of titles published annually: 15 Print
Total Titles: 130 Print

Idea Books+
Via Regia, 53, 55049 Viareggio LU
Tel: (0584) 425410 *Fax:* (0178) 609 8685
E-mail: ideab@tiscali.it *Cable:* IDEABOOKS MILANO
Key Personnel
Dir: Filippo Passigli
Founded: 1979
Subjects: Architecture & Interior Design, Art, Fashion, Photography
ISBN Prefix(es): 88-7017; 88-88033
Number of titles published annually: 8 Print

Casa Editrice Libraria Idelson di G Gnocchi+
Via Michele Pietravalle, 85, 80131 Naples
Tel: (081) 5453443 *Fax:* (081) 5464991
E-mail: info@idelson-gnocchi.com
Web Site: www.idelson-gnocchi.com *Cable:* IDELSON NAPLES
Key Personnel
Chief Executive: Guido Gnocchi
Founded: 1908
Subjects: Biological Sciences, Medicine, Nursing, Dentistry
ISBN Prefix(es): 88-7069

PUBLISHERS

ITALY

Idelson-Gnocchi Edizioni Scientifiche
Via Michele Pietravalle, 85, 80131 Naples
Tel: (081) 5453443 *Fax:* (081) 5464991
E-mail: ordini@idelson-gnocchi.com
Web Site: www.idelson-gnocchi.com
Key Personnel
Contact: Guido Gnocchi
Founded: 1993
Subjects: Medicine, Nursing, Dentistry
ISBN Prefix(es): 88-7947
U.S. Office(s): Idelson Gnocchi Scientific Publications, 12255 NW Highway 225A, Reddick, FL 32686, United States *Tel:* 352-591-1136 *Fax:* 352-591-1189

Istituto Idrografico della Marina
Passo dell'Osservatorio 4, 16134 Genoa
Tel: (010) 24431 *Fax:* (010) 261400
E-mail: iim.sre@marina.difesa.it
Web Site: www.marina.difesa.it
Telex: 270435; 275521 Maridr I *Cable:* MARIDROGRAFICO
Key Personnel
Dir: Corrado Fiori
Vice Dir: Giuseppe Borsa
Production: Antonio Sfregola
Public Relations: Antonio Cairo
Map Division: Raffaele Gargiulo
Founded: 1872
Subjects: Maritime

IHT Gruppo Editoriale SRL
Via Monte Napoleone 9, 20121 Milan
Tel: (02) 794181 *Fax:* (02) 784021
E-mail: info@iht.it
Web Site: www.iht.it
Key Personnel
Founder, President & Publisher: Lisa Massimiliano
Founded: 1985
Subjects: Art, Film, Video, Microcomputers, Military Science, Science (General), Technology
ISBN Prefix(es): 88-7803
Imprints: IHT Video
Distributed by Messaggerie Periodic
Orders to: IHT Publishing Group, Via Monte Napoleone 9, 20121 Milan

IHT Video, *imprint of* IHT Gruppo Editoriale SRL

Ila - Palma, Tea Nova+
Via La Lumia 5/7, 90139 Palermo
Tel: (091) 332051 *Fax:* (091) 6259260
Key Personnel
Editor: Rean Mazzone
Founded: 1960
Subjects: Archaeology, Art, Economics, History, Literature, Literary Criticism, Essays, Management, Philosophy
ISBN Prefix(es): 88-7704
Subsidiaries: Nef; Tea; Tea Nova
Orders to: Via Benedetto Castiglia 6, 90141 Palermo

In Dialogo+
Via S Antonio 5, 20122 Milan
Tel: (02) 58391342 *Fax:* (02) 58391345
E-mail: indial@tin.it
Founded: 1980
Subjects: Biblical Studies, Child Care & Development, Communications, Education, Government, Political Science, Human Relations, Religion - Catholic, Theology
ISBN Prefix(es): 88-8123; 88-85985
Shipping Address: Via Andolfato 3, 20126 Milan
Warehouse: Via Andolfato 3, 20126 Milan
Orders to: Dehoniana Libri SRL

Iniziative Culturali SRL, see Servitium

Editrice Innocenti SNC+
Via Zara 36, 38100 Trento
Tel: (0461) 236521 *Fax:* (0461) 230115
Cable: EDITRICE INNOCENTI TRENTO
Key Personnel
Chief Executive: Luciano Innocenti
Publicity: Silvia Nones
Founded: 1972
Subjects: Language Arts, Linguistics
Associate Companies: Casa Editrice Bulgarini, Via Petrolin, 8-50137 Firenze; Casa Editrice Principato, Via Fauche, Milan

Instituti Editoriali E Poligrafici Internazionali SRL+
Via Giosue Carducci, 60, 56010 Ghezzano (Pisa)
Tel: (050) 878066 *Fax:* (050) 878732
E-mail: iepi@iepi.it
Web Site: www.iepi.it
Key Personnel
Man Dir: Lucia Carmignani
Founded: 1995
Specialize in philosophy, archaeology, history, sociology, anthropology & Italian.
Subjects: Anthropology, Archaeology, History, Language Arts, Linguistics, Philosophy, Social Sciences, Sociology, Transportation
ISBN Prefix(es): 88-8147
Shipping Address: The Courier srl, viel A DeBasis 25, 50165 Firenze *Tel:* (055) 300443 *Fax:* (055) 300036
Warehouse: The Courier srl, viel A DeBasis 25, 50165 Firenze *Tel:* (055) 300443 *Fax:* (055) 300036
Orders to: The Courier srl, Viel A DeBasis 25, 50165 Firenze *Tel:* (055) 300443 *Fax:* (055) 300036

International Ediemme
Via Innocenzo XI, 41, 00165 Rome
Tel: (06) 39378788 *Fax:* (06) 6380839
E-mail: iscd@colosseum.it
Key Personnel
Editor-in-Chief: Pierfrancesco Morganti
ISBN Prefix(es): 88-7821

International Federation of Beekeepers' Associations, see Apimondia

International University Press Srl+
Via Monte della Gioie 22, 00199 Rome
Tel: (06) 8380067 *Fax:* (06) 8380064
Key Personnel
President: Felice Alivernini
Founded: 1987
Membership(s): USPI.
Subjects: Medicine, Nursing, Dentistry
ISBN Prefix(es): 88-85314
U.S. Office(s): Little, Brown & Company, 24 Beacon St, Boston, MA 02108, United States

Edizioni Internazionali di Letteratura e Scienze+
Via Casal Selce, 264, 00166 Rome
Tel: (06) 61905463 *Fax:* (06) 3016728
Founded: 1972
Also specialize in historical experimentation of dynamic physiology comparison.
Subjects: History, Language Arts, Linguistics, Literature, Literary Criticism, Essays, Romance, Science Fiction, Fantasy, Social Sciences, Sociology
ISBN Prefix(es): 88-7130

Iperborea
Via Palestro 22, 20121 Milan
Tel: (02) 781458 *Fax:* (02) 798919
E-mail: iperborea@iol.it
Key Personnel
President & Editorial Dir: Emilia Lodigiani
Founded: 1987
Subjects: Literature, Literary Criticism, Essays
ISBN Prefix(es): 88-7091

ISAL (Istituto Storia dell'Arte Lombarda)
Via Garibaldi, 20, 20031 Milan
Tel: (03) 62528118 *Fax:* (03) 62659417
E-mail: isalbibl@tin.it
Key Personnel
Editor: Maria Luisa Gatti Perer
Founded: 1955
Subjects: Archaeology, Art
ISBN Prefix(es): 88-85153

ISMEO, see Istituto Italiano Per Il Medio Ed Estremo Oriente (ISMEO)

Isper SRL+
Corso Dante 122, 10126 Turin
Tel: (011) 66 47 803 *Fax:* (011) 66 70 829
E-mail: isper@isper.org
Web Site: www.isper.org
Key Personnel
Chief Executive: Dr Carlo Actis Grosso
Contact: Paola Riccardi
Founded: 1965
Subjects: Business, Management
Branch Office(s)
Via Lambro 4, 20129 Milan
Via N Porpora 12, 00198 Rome
Corso del Popolo 46, 30172 Venice
Book Club(s): Isper Club

Ist Patristico Augustinianum
Via Paolo VI 25, 00193 Rome
Tel: (06) 680 069 *Fax:* (06) 680 06 298
E-mail: segr_ipa@aug.org
Key Personnel
President: Angelo Di Berardino
Founded: 1969
Subjects: Antiques, Literature, Literary Criticism, Essays, Religion - Catholic
ISBN Prefix(es): 88-7961
Imprints: SEA

Istituto della Enciclopedia Italiana+
Piazza Paganica, 4, 00186 Rome
Tel: (06) 68981 *Fax:* (06) 68982294
Web Site: www.treccani.it *Cable:* ENCICLOPEDIA
Key Personnel
Dir: Francesco Schino
Editorial Dir: Bray Massimo
Founded: 1925
Subjects: Art
ISBN Prefix(es): 88-12

Istituto Storia dell'Arte Lombarda, see ISAL (Istituto Storia dell'Arte Lombarda)

Itaca+
Piazza De Angeli, 1, 20146 Milan
Tel: (02) 48009484 *Fax:* (02) 48009493
Key Personnel
Communications: Barbara Crepaldi
Administrator: Girolamo Frisina
Founded: 1985
Specialize in total quality management.
Subjects: Business, Communications, Management, Marketing
ISBN Prefix(es): 88-7206

Edizioni Italiane, *imprint of* Todariana Editrice

Istituto Italiano Edizioni Atlas+
Via Crescenzi 88, 24123 Bergamo
Tel: (035) 249711 *Fax:* (035) 216047
E-mail: edizioniatlas@edatlas.it
Web Site: www.edatlas.it

ITALY

Key Personnel
Contact: Dr Marco Carreri
ISBN Prefix(es): 88-268

Istituto Italiano Per Il Medio Ed Estremo Oriente (ISMEO)
Via Merulana 248, 00185 Rome
Tel: (06) 732741; (06) 732742; (06) 732743
E-mail: iias@let.leidenuniv.nl
Web Site: www.iias.nl
Telex: 624163
Founded: 1933

Editoriale Jaca Book SpA+
Via Gioberti, 7, 20123 Milan
Tel: (02) 48561520-29 *Fax:* (02) 48193361
E-mail: jacabook@jacabook.it
Web Site: www.jacabook.it
Key Personnel
President & Publisher: Sante Bagnoli
Editorial Dir: Maretta Campi
Administrative Dir: Guido Orsi *E-mail:* admin@jacabook.it
Academic Dep: Massimo Guidetti
Co-editions: Silvia Vassena *E-mail:* coeditions@jacabook.it
Rights: Ida Bonali *E-mail:* produzione@jacabook.it
Founded: 1978
Subjects: Anthropology, Archaeology, Architecture & Interior Design, Art, Asian Studies, Earth Sciences, Economics, Fiction, Geography, Geology, Government, Political Science, History, Human Relations, Literature, Literary Criticism, Essays, Music, Dance, Native American Studies, Natural History, Nonfiction (General), Philosophy, Photography, Physics, Poetry, Religion - Catholic, Religion - Other, Science (General), Social Sciences, Sociology, Theology
ISBN Prefix(es): 88-16
Total Titles: 130 Print
Subsidiaries: Jaca/Edizioni Universitarie

Gruppo Editoriale Jackson SpA
Via XXV Aprile, 39, 20091 Bresso (Milan)
Tel: (02) 665261 *Fax:* (02) 66526222
E-mail: ordini@futura-ge.com
Telex: 316213
Key Personnel
Man Dir, President: Paolo Reina
Marketing Manager: Filippo Canavese
Dir, Periodicals: Pierantonio Palerma
Dir, Book Shops: Roberto Pancaldi
Administrative Dir: Luigi Gadola
Dir, Production & Aquisitions: Luigi Beccaria
International: Stefania Scroglieri
Founded: 1975
ISBN Prefix(es): 88-7056; 88-256
Subsidiaries: Jackson Hispania SA; GEJ Publishing Group Inc
Warehouse: Piazza Amendola 45, Paderno Dugnano, Milano

Jandi-Sapi Editori
Via Crescenzio 62, 00193 Rome
Tel: (06) 68805515; (06) 6876054 *Fax:* (06) 68218203
E-mail: info@jandisapi.com
Web Site: www.jandisapi.com
Founded: 1941
Subjects: Art, Law
ISBN Prefix(es): 88-7142
Imprints: JSE
Divisions: Archivi Arte Antica

Editrice Janus SpA+
Via dei Capoferro 12, 24121 Bergamo
Tel: (035) 24 71 80 *Fax:* (035) 24 70 92
Key Personnel
Sales, Production: Marcello Riva

Founded: 1956
Subjects: Literature, Literary Criticism, Essays

L Japadre Editore+
Corso Federico 11, 49, 67100 l'Aquila
Tel: (0862) 26025 *Fax:* (0862) 25587
Key Personnel
Man Dir: Leandro Ugo Japadre
Founded: 1966
Subjects: Art, Economics, Ethnicity, Fiction, History, Language Arts, Linguistics, Literature, Literary Criticism, Essays, Philosophy, Poetry, Psychology, Psychiatry, Religion - Other, Science (General), Social Sciences, Sociology, Technology
ISBN Prefix(es): 88-7006
Branch Office(s)
Via G Boni 20, 00162 Rome *Tel:* (06) 44291182
Distributor for DASP (Deputazione Abruzzese Di Storia Patria)
Warehouse: Contrada Cappelli
Pal Prosperini

Jazz People, *imprint of* Stampa Alternativa - Nuovi Equilibri

Jouvence+
Via Monte Zebio 24, 00195 Rome
Tel: (06) 3211500 *Fax:* (06) 3202897
E-mail: jouvence@flashnet.it
Web Site: www.jouvence-ed.com
Key Personnel
Editorial Dir: Alessandro Gallo
Administrator: Claudia Pozzessere
Founded: 1979
Subjects: Archaeology, Asian Studies, History, Literature, Literary Criticism, Essays, Philosophy, Religion - Islamic
ISBN Prefix(es): 88-7801
Warehouse: Via Cassia, 1081-00189 Rome

Casa Editrice Dott Eugenio Jovene SpA
Via Mezzocannone, 109, 80134 Naples
Tel: (081) 5521019; (081) 5521274; (081) 5523471 *Fax:* (081) 5520687
E-mail: info@jovene.it
Web Site: www.jovene.it *Cable:* JOVENE
Key Personnel
Man Dir: Dr Alessandro Rossi
Founded: 1854
Subjects: Economics, Law
ISBN Prefix(es): 88-243

JSE, *imprint of* Jandi-Sapi Editori

Kaos Edizioni SRL+
Via Catone, 3, 20158 Milan
Tel: (02) 39310296 *Fax:* (02) 39325749
E-mail: kaosedizioni@kaosedizioni.com
Web Site: www.kaosedizioni.com
Key Personnel
Man Dir: Lorenzo Ruggiero
Founded: 1985
Subjects: Biography, Drama, Theater, Film, Video, Government, Political Science, History, Music, Dance, Nonfiction (General), Social Sciences, Sociology
ISBN Prefix(es): 88-7953
Imprints: Gammalibri-Rock Books; Edizioni Blues Brothers

Kompass Fleischmann
Localita Ghiaie 166/d, 38014 Gardolo (Trento)
Tel: (0461) 961240 *Fax:* (0461) 961203
Key Personnel
Dir: Mario Cont
Administrator: Dr Petra Fleischmann
Founded: 1973
Subjects: Animals, Pets, Geography, Geology, Natural History, Travel
ISBN Prefix(es): 88-431

L'Airone Editrice, *imprint of* Ernesto Gremese Editore srl

Edizioni L' Eta dell'Acquario, *imprint of* l'Eta dell'Acquario

LAC - Litografia Artistica Cartografica Srl
Via del Romito 11/13 R, 50134 Florence
Tel: (055) 483 557 *Fax:* (055) 483 690
E-mail: info@lac-cartografia.it
Web Site: www.lac-cartografia.it
Key Personnel
President: Maria G Garbarino
Contact: Mrs Cinzia Cassai
Founded: 1949
Subjects: Geography, Geology, Travel
ISBN Prefix(es): 88-7914

Lalli Editore SRL+
Via Fiume, 60, 53036 Poggibonsi (Siena)
Tel: (0577) 933305 *Fax:* (0577) 983308
E-mail: lalli@lallieditore.it
Web Site: www.lallieditore.it *Cable:* LALLIEDIT POGGIBONSI
Key Personnel
Chief Executive: Antonio Lalli
Editorial: Fioranna Casamenti
Founded: 1966
Subjects: Art, Biography, Drama, Theater, Education, Ethnicity, Fiction, Film, Video, Government, Political Science, Humor, Philosophy, Poetry, Regional Interests, Religion - Other, Science (General), Social Sciences, Sociology
Warehouse: Via Modena 12, 53036 Poggibonsi SI

Lanfranchi
Via Madonnina 10, 20121 Milan
Tel: (02) 86465210 *Fax:* (02) 8056083
E-mail: info@lanfranchieditore.it
Web Site: www.lanfranchieditore.com
ISBN Prefix(es): 88-363

Lang Edizioni™, *imprint of* Paravia Bruno Mondadori Editori

Laruffa Editore SRL+
Via dei Tre Mulini, 14, 89124 Reggio, Calabria
Tel: (0965) 814948 *Fax:* (0965) 814954
E-mail: laruffa@laruffaeditore.com
Web Site: www.laruffaeditore.com
Founded: 1980
Subjects: Agriculture, Archaeology, Architecture & Interior Design, Education, History, Religion - Catholic, Social Sciences, Sociology, Travel
ISBN Prefix(es): 88-7221

Editrice LAS+
Piazza dell'Ateneo Salesiano 1, 00139 Rome
Tel: (06) 87290626
E-mail: las@ups.urbe.it
Web Site: www.las.ups.urbe.it
Founded: 1974
Subjects: Biblical Studies, Education, Philosophy, Psychology, Psychiatry, Religion - Catholic, Social Sciences, Sociology, Theology
ISBN Prefix(es): 88-213
Number of titles published annually: 20 Print
Total Titles: 300 Print; 2 CD-ROM

Edizioni Fratelli Laterza, *imprint of* Giuseppe Laterza Editore

Edizioni Lavoro SRL+
Via Lancisi 25, 00161 Rome
Tel: (06) 44251174 *Fax:* (06) 44251177
E-mail: info@edizionilavoro.it
Web Site: www.edizionilavoro.it
Key Personnel
President: Peter Gelardi

Editorial: Alessandra Belardelli
Founded: 1982
Subjects: Economics, Government, Political Science, History, Labor, Industrial Relations, Philosophy, Religion - Islamic, Romance, Social Sciences, Sociology
ISBN Prefix(es): 88-7910; 88-7313
Number of titles published annually: 40 Print
Imprints: EL
Foreign Rights: Eulama Literary Agency (Worldwide)

Il Lavoro Editoriale+
Division of Progetti Editoriale SRL
Via de Bosis 8, 60100 Ancona
Mailing Address: CP 297, 60100 Ancona
Tel: (071) 2072210 *Fax:* (071) 2083058
E-mail: ilepro@tin.it
Web Site: www.illavoroeditoriale.com
Key Personnel
Editorial Board Chief: Giorgio Mangani
Founded: 1980
Subjects: Art, History, Human Relations, Literature, Literary Criticism, Essays, Marche Region, Italy
ISBN Prefix(es): 88-7663
Number of titles published annually: 15 Print

LED - Edizioni Universitarie di Lettere Economia Diritto (LED - University Press)+
Via Cervignano 4, 20137 Milan
Tel: (02) 59902055 *Fax:* (02) 55193636
E-mail: led@lededizioni.it
Web Site: www.lededizioni.it
Key Personnel
Man Dir: Maria Grazia Gelo
International Rights: Valeria Passerini
Founded: 1991
Subjects: Economics, History, Law, Literature, Literary Criticism, Essays, Philosophy, Psychology, Psychiatry, Social Sciences, Sociology
ISBN Prefix(es): 88-7916
Number of titles published annually: 20 Print; 7 Online; 4 E-Book
Total Titles: 240 Print; 16 Online; 9 E-Book

L'Editrice Scientifica, see Nagard

LEF, *imprint of* Libreria Editrice Fiorentina

LER, see Libreria Editrice Rogate (LER)

L'eta D'oro Dell Illustrazione, *imprint of* Stampa Alternativa - Nuovi Equilibri

Casa Editrice Le Lettere SRL
Costa S Giorgio 28, 50125 Florence
Tel: (055) 2342710 *Fax:* (055) 2346010
Key Personnel
Chief Executive: Dr Giovanni Gentile
Publishing Dir: Nicoletta Pescarolo
Sales, Administration: Carlo De Simone
Founded: 1956
Subjects: History, Language Arts, Linguistics, Literature, Literary Criticism, Essays, Philosophy
ISBN Prefix(es): 88-7166
Associate Companies: Progedi Srl, Viale Gramsci, 18, 50132 Florence
Shipping Address: Licosa Spa, Via Duca Di Calabria 1/1, 50125 Florence
Warehouse: Via Francesco Gioli 5-11, 50018 Scandicci

Levante Editori+
Via Napoli 35, 70123 Bari
Tel: (080) 5213778 *Fax:* (080) 5213778
E-mail: levanted@tin.it
Web Site: www.levantebari.com
Key Personnel
Contact: Sara Cavalli
Founded: 1967
Subjects: Criminology, Drama, Theater, Mysteries, Philosophy, Psychology, Psychiatry, Travel
ISBN Prefix(es): 88-7949
Number of titles published annually: 20 Print

Levrotto e Bella Libreria Editrice Universitaria SAS+
Corso Vittorio Emanuele 26f, 10123 Turin
Tel: (011) 8121205 *Fax:* (011) 8124025
E-mail: levrotto@ipsnet.it
Key Personnel
Sales: Carmela Bueti; Giampiero Garnero
Founded: 1942
Also book packager.
Subjects: Science (General), Technology
ISBN Prefix(es): 88-8218
Bookshop(s): Libreria del Politecnico, Corso Einaudi 57, 10129 Turin

Libreria Editrice Fiorentina+
Via Giambologna, 5, 50132 Florence
Tel: (055) 579921 *Fax:* (055) 579921
Key Personnel
Editorial: Vittorio Zani
Founded: 1902
Subjects: Education, Regional Interests, Religion - Other, Social Sciences, Sociology
Imprints: LEF

Librex
Via Bellezza 15, 20136 Milan
Tel: (02) 58302006
Telex: 320208 *Cable:* Librex Milan
Key Personnel
General Manager: Antonio Mancia
Export: M Luisa Franceschini
Production: Luciano Baroni
Founded: 1966

Liguori Editore SRL+
Via Posillipo 394, 80123 Naples
Tel: (081) 7206111; (081) 7206202 (orders)
Fax: (081) 7206244
E-mail: liguori@liguori.it
Web Site: www.liguori.it *Cable:* LIGUORI NAPOLI
Key Personnel
Man Dir, Editorial, Rights & Permissions: Guido Liguori
Sales: Franco Liguori
Publicity: Maria Liguori
Founded: 1949
Subjects: Anthropology, Economics, History, Language Arts, Linguistics, Law, Literature, Literary Criticism, Essays, Mathematics, Medicine, Nursing, Dentistry, Philosophy, Science (General), Social Sciences, Sociology, Theology
ISBN Prefix(es): 88-207
Number of titles published annually: 150 Print; 3 E-Book
Total Titles: 3,500 Print; 10 CD-ROM
Bookshop(s): Librerie Commissionarie Liguori SRL, Via Mezzocannone 21-23, 80134 Naples *Tel:* (081) 5527702; Via Cinthia 36/B, 80126 Naples *Tel:* (081) 7675228
Warehouse: Via Ciccarelli 16G, 80167 Naples

Editrice Liguria SNC di Norberto Sabatelli & C
Via De Mari 4r, 17100 Savona
Tel: (019) 829917 *Fax:* (019) 8387798
Key Personnel
Chief Executive: Norberto Sabatelli
Founded: 1934
Subjects: Art, Drama, Theater, Fiction, History, Literature, Literary Criticism, Essays, Poetry, Technology, Travel
ISBN Prefix(es): 88-8055
Imprints: EL

LIM, *imprint of* LIM Editrice SRL

LIM Editrice SRL+
Via di Arsina 296f, 55100 Lucca
Mailing Address: PO Box 198, 55100 Lucca
Tel: (0583) 394464 *Fax:* (0583) 394469
E-mail: lim@lim.it
Web Site: www.lim.it
Key Personnel
Contact: Paola Borriero *E-mail:* p.borriero@lim.it
Founded: 1988
Membership(s): AIE.
Subjects: Music, Dance
ISBN Prefix(es): 88-7096
Associate Companies: Akademos, LIM Antiquaria, Una Cosa Rara
Imprints: LIM
Distributor for Adeva; Alamire; Broude Brothers; Garland; Fondazione Locatelli; Pendragon Press; Fondazione Rossini
Orders to: PO Box 198, 55100 Lucca

L'immaginazion, *imprint of* Piero Manni srl

Lindau, *imprint of* Lindau

Lindau+
Via Galliari, 15b, 10125 Turin
Tel: (011) 6693910; (011) 6693924 *Fax:* (011) 6693929
E-mail: info@lindau.it
Web Site: www.lindau.it
Key Personnel
Executive & Editorial Dir: Ezio Quarantelli
E-mail: quarantelli@lindau.it
Founded: 1989
Subjects: Fiction, Film, Video
ISBN Prefix(es): 88-7180
Number of titles published annually: 80 Print
Total Titles: 450 Print
Imprints: Lindau; Edizioni L'Eta Dell'Acqua Rio

Linea d'Ombra Libri (Linea D'Ombra Books)
Via della Madonna, 9, 31015 Conegliano (TV)
Tel: (0438) 412647 *Fax:* (0438) 412690
E-mail: info@lineadombra.it
Web Site: www.lineadombra.it
Founded: 1996
Publisher of art books & exhibition catalogues.
Subjects: Art, Photography, Poetry
ISBN Prefix(es): 88-09
Number of titles published annually: 20 Print
Parent Company: Linea D'Ombra

Linea Verde, *imprint of* Le Stelle Scuola

Lisciani e Giunti Editori, see Giunti Gruppo Editoriale

Litografia Artistica Cartografia Srl - LAC, see LAC - Litografia Artistica Cartografica Srl

Vincenzo Lo Faro Editore
Via S Giovanni Laterano 276, 00184 Rome
Tel: (06) 70451187 *Fax:* (06) 70451641
Web Site: culturitalia.uibk.ac.at
Key Personnel
Chief Executive: Vincenzo Lo Faro
Editorial: Letizia Carile
Founded: 1967
Subjects: Art, Drama, Theater, Education, Environmental Studies, Fiction, Law, Medicine, Nursing, Dentistry, Philosophy, Poetry, Religion - Other, Social Sciences, Sociology
ISBN Prefix(es): 88-87428

Editrice la Locusta
Via del Castello 20, 36100 Vicenza
Tel: (0444) 324051
E-mail: la_locusta@yahoo.com

Web Site: space.tin.it/io/pibeltra/lalocust.htm
Key Personnel
Chief Executive & Publishing Dir: Rienzo Colla
Founded: 1954
Subjects: History, Literature, Literary Criticism, Essays, Poetry

Loescher Editore SRL+
Via Vittorio Amedeo II 18, 10121 Turin
Tel: (011) 5654111 *Fax:* (011) 56 25822
E-mail: mail@loescher.it
Web Site: www.loescher.it
Key Personnel
President: Lorenzo Enriques
Vice President: Federico Enriques
Dir General: Riccardo Botrini
Editorial Head: Aron Buttarelli
Commerical Dir: Giorgio Sacco
Founded: 1867
Subjects: Chemistry, Chemical Engineering, English as a Second Language, Geography, Geology, History, Language Arts, Linguistics, Literature, Literary Criticism, Essays, Philosophy
ISBN Prefix(es): 88-201; 88-7608; 88-8094; 88-7159
Parent Company: Zanichelli Editore SpA
Imprints: The Ma; Eliseo
Distributed by Cambridge (Italy); Klett Edition Deutsch (Italy)

Loffredo Editore Napoli SpA®
Via Consalvo 99 h, Parco S Luigi isolato D, 80126 Naples
Tel: (081) 5937073 *Fax:* (081) 5936953
E-mail: info@loffredo.it
Web Site: www.loffredo.it
Key Personnel
Chief Executive: Mario Loffredo
Editorial, Sales, Rights & Permissions: Alfredo Loffredo
Production: Alfredo Loffredo, Jr
Publicity: Enzo Loffredo
Founded: 1880
Subjects: History, Language Arts, Linguistics, Literature, Literary Criticism, Essays, Philosophy, Religion - Other, Science (General)
ISBN Prefix(es): 88-8096
Bookshop(s): Libreria Luigi Loffredo, Via Kerbaker 19/21, 1-80129 Naples

Longanesi & C+
Corso Italia 13, 20122 Milan
Tel: (02) 80206310 *Fax:* (02) 72000306
E-mail: info@longanesi.it
Web Site: www.longanesi.it
Key Personnel
President: Stefano Passigli
Sales: Giuseppe Somenzi
Production: Alfredo Bonfiglio
Publicity: Valentina Fortichiari
Rights & Permissions: Cristina Foschini
  E-mail: christina.foschini@longanesi.it
Editorial Dir: Luigi Brioschi
Founded: 1946
Subjects: Art, Biography, Fiction, History, How-to, Medicine, Nursing, Dentistry, Music, Dance, Philosophy, Psychology, Psychiatry, Religion - Other, Science (General), Social Sciences, Sociology
ISBN Prefix(es): 88-304
Number of titles published annually: 100 Print
Total Titles: 5 Print
Parent Company: Messaggerie Italiane
Associate Companies: Guanda, Cristina Foschini; Corbaccio, Cristina Foschini; Neri Pozza, Cristina Foschini; Ponte alle Grazie, Cristina Foschini
Subsidiaries: Finarte
Orders to: Pro Libro, Corso Italia 13, 20122 Milan

Longman Italia srl
Via G Fara, 28, 20124 Milan
Tel: (02) 6739761 *Fax:* (02) 673976501
E-mail: longman-italia@pearsoned-ema.com
Web Site: www.longman-elt.com
Key Personnel
Man Dir, ELT: David Evans
Finance Manager, ELT: Lucia Donatellis
Publishing Manager, ELT: Barbara Cunsolo
Sales & Marketing Manager, ELT: Alan Osman
ISBN Prefix(es): 88-8339

Angelo Longo Editore+
Via Paolo Costa 33, 48100 Ravenna
Tel: (0544) 217026 *Fax:* (0544) 217554
E-mail: longo-ra@linknet.it
Web Site: www.longo-editore.it
Key Personnel
General Manager: Alfio Longo
Founded: 1965
Subjects: Archaeology, Art, Drama, Theater, Fiction, Film, Video, History, Language Arts, Linguistics, Literature, Literary Criticism, Essays, Music, Dance, Philosophy, Photography, Poetry, Women's Studies
ISBN Prefix(es): 88-8063
Number of titles published annually: 60 Print; 30 Online
Total Titles: 1,180 Print; 68 Online
Bookshop(s): Libreria Dante di A M Longo, Via Diaz 39, 48100 Ravenna, Contact: Roberta Plazzi *Tel:* (0544) 33500

Carlo Lorenzini Editore+
Via Cavour 9, 33037 Pasiandi Prato (Ud)
Tel: (0432) 691412 *Fax:* (0432) 691412
Founded: 1981
ISBN Prefix(es): 88-7093

Lorenzo Editore+
Via Monza, 6, 10152 Turin
Tel: (011) 2485387 *Fax:* (011) 2485387
Cable: ITALSCAMBI CP 23 TURIN
Key Personnel
Chief Executive: Lorenzo Masetta
Founded: 1975
Specialize in poetry.
Subjects: Fiction, Literature, Literary Criticism, Essays, Poetry
ISBN Prefix(es): 88-85199; 88-87362
Subsidiaries: 'Talento' (current events periodical)

LPE, *imprint of* Luigi Pellegrini Editore

Lubrina+
Via Cesare Correnti, N 50, 24124 Bergamo
Tel: (035) 3470139396 *Fax:* (035) 241547
E-mail: editorelubrina@lubrina.it
Web Site: www.lubrina.it
Key Personnel
Man Dir: Ornella Bramani Mastropietro
  E-mail: obramas@lubrina.it
Founded: 1995
Membership(s): EQ Consorzio di Editor di Qualita.
Subjects: Biblical Studies, Biography, Literature, Literary Criticism, Essays, Philosophy, Psychology, Psychiatry
ISBN Prefix(es): 88-7766

Edizioni de Luca SRL
Via Visconti, 11, 00193 Rome
Tel: (06) 32650712 *Fax:* (06) 32650715
Web Site: culturitalia.uibk.ac.at
Founded: 1935
Subjects: Archaeology, Art, History
ISBN Prefix(es): 88-8016

La Luna+
Via DiGiovanni, 14, 90144 Palermo
Tel: (091) 345799 *Fax:* (091) 301650
E-mail: laluna@arcidonna.it
Key Personnel
President: Valeria Ajovalasit
Vice President: Roberta Messina
Founded: 1986
Membership(s): Arcidonna.
Subjects: Anthropology, Art, Fiction, Journalism, Literature, Literary Criticism, Essays, Nonfiction (General), Romance, Women's Studies
ISBN Prefix(es): 88-7823
Distributed by PDE

Luni
Via Procaccini, 11, 20154 Milan
Tel: (02) 89693000 *Fax:* (02) 89693011
Key Personnel
Prof: Matteo Luteriani; Laura Niccolini
Founded: 1992
Subjects: Literature, Literary Criticism, Essays, Philosophy, Religion - Buddhist, Religion - Islamic, Religion - Other, Sports, Athletics
ISBN Prefix(es): 88-7984

Lusva Editrice
Via Roncaglia, 27, 20146 Milan
Tel: (02) 4985386
Key Personnel
Chief Executive: Luca Maria Vizzotto
Founded: 1977
Subjects: Education, Fiction, Poetry

Lybra Immagine+
Via Vincenzo Monti 6, 20123 Milan
Tel: (02) 48000818 *Fax:* (02) 48012748
E-mail: lybra@lybra.it
Web Site: www.lybra.it
Key Personnel
Editor: Mario Mastropietro
Founded: 1984
Subjects: Architecture & Interior Design, Fashion, Marketing, Photography
ISBN Prefix(es): 88-8223

Lyra Libri
Via Polidoro daCaravaggio, 37, 20156 Milan
Tel: (02) 30 241 311 *Fax:* (02) 30 241 333
Key Personnel
Chief Executive, Editorial: Maurizio Rosenberg Colorni
Founded: 1986
Subjects: Health, Nutrition, Psychology, Psychiatry, Self-Help, Women's Studies
ISBN Prefix(es): 88-7733

The Ma, *imprint of* Loescher Editore SRL

Casa Editrice Maccari (CEM)+
Via Palermo, 44, 43100 Parma
Tel: (0521) 771268 *Fax:* (0521) 771268
Cable: CEMPARMA
Key Personnel
Man Dir: Cesare Maccari, Jr
Production: Camilla Albera
Founded: 1946
Subjects: Biological Sciences, Literature, Literary Criticism, Essays, Medicine, Nursing, Dentistry
ISBN Prefix(es): 88-7532
Number of titles published annually: 12 Print
Total Titles: 4 Print
Subsidiaries: Editrice La Pilotta

Macmillan Heinemann ELT
Via di Campigliano (ang Via Meucci), 50015 Grassina (FI)
Tel: (055) 649 1289 *Fax:* (055) 649 1501
E-mail: mheltinfo@dada.it
Web Site: www.mhelt.com
Key Personnel
Marketing Manager: Nick Broom *E-mail:* n.broom@dada.it
Subjects: English as a Second Language, Language Arts, Linguistics

Parent Company: Macmillan Publishers Ltd
Associate Companies: Casa Editrice Felice Le Monnier spa, Via Antonio Meucci, 2, 50015 Grassina (FI)

Macro Edizioni+
Via Savona 66, 47023 Diegaro di Cesena
Tel: (0547) 346290; (0547) 346317 *Fax:* (0547) 345091; (0547) 345141
E-mail: ordini@macroedizioni.it
Web Site: www.macroedizioni.it
Key Personnel
President & Editor: Giorgio Gustavo Rosso
 E-mail: dizezione@macroedizione.it
Founded: 1987
Membership(s): AIE (Association Itaugna Editori).
Subjects: Alternative, Archaeology, Biblical Studies, Cookery, Education, Environmental Studies, Health, Nutrition, House & Home, How-to, Philosophy, Psychology, Psychiatry, Religion - Other, Science (General)
ISBN Prefix(es): 88-7507
Total Titles: 300 Print
Associate Companies: Macro/Post
Distributor for Edizioni Essere Felici
Showroom(s): Salone Del Libro, Torino
Book Club(s): Il Giardino Dei Libri; Macro Librarsi, Via Savona 66-Diagaro, 47023 Cesena (Forli)
Orders to: Macro/Post, Via San Mauro 55, 47041 Bellaria *Tel:* (0541) 344820 *Fax:* (0541) 344824

Magnus Edizioni SpA+
Via dei Fabrizio, 57, 33034 Fagagna (Udine)
Tel: (0432) 800081 *Fax:* (0432) 810071
E-mail: info@magnusedizioni.it
Web Site: www.magnusedizioni.it
Key Personnel
Chief Executive & Editorial: Rene Leonarduzzi
Sales & Publicity: Antonio Stella
Founded: 1977
Subjects: Architecture & Interior Design, Art, Photography
ISBN Prefix(es): 88-7057
Subsidiaries: Grafiche Lema SpA

Giuseppe Maimone Editore+
Via A di Sangiuliano, 278, 95124 Catania
Tel: (095) 310315 *Fax:* (095) 310315
E-mail: maimone@maimone.it
Web Site: www.maimone.it
Key Personnel
Administrator: Guiseppe Maimone
Founded: 1985
Subjects: Architecture & Interior Design, Art, Biography, Film, Video, History, Literature, Literary Criticism, Essays, Regional Interests
ISBN Prefix(es): 88-7751
Subsidiaries: Maimone & Associati; SAS di Maimone Giuseppe
Showroom(s): Salone Del Libro Torino, 19-24 Maggio, c/o Palazzo Lingotto, 10152 Torino; Mostra Parole Nel Tempo, 25-26 Settembre, c/o Castello Di Belgioioso, via Garibaldi 1, Belgioioso (Pavia); Il Libro, Salone Della Editoria Siciliana, 24 27 Marzo, c/o Ente Autonomo Fiera Di Messina Campionaria Internazionale, Viale Della Liberta, 98121 Messina

Manfrini Editori
SS del Brennero, 2, 38060 Calliano (TN)
Tel: (0464) 839111 *Fax:* (0464) 835086
Telex: 400581 Manfri I·*Cable:* Grafiche Manfrini
Key Personnel
Man Dir: Edoardo Manfrini
Founded: 1919
Subjects: Art, History, Literature, Literary Criticism, Essays, Nonfiction (General), Science (General), Travel
ISBN Prefix(es): 88-7024

Parent Company: R Manfrini SpA Vallagarina Arti Grafiche, SS del Brennero, 2, 38060 Calliano (Trento)
Branch Office(s)
Via Virgilio 6, 39100 Bolzano

Manif, see Manifestolibri

Manifestolibri+
Via Tomacelli, 146, 00186 Rome
Tel: (06) 588 1496 *Fax:* (06) 588 2839
E-mail: redazione@manifestolibri.it; book@manifestolibri.it
Web Site: www.manifestolibri.it
Key Personnel
Chief Editor: Marco Bascetta
General Manager: Simona Bonsignori
 E-mail: bons@bonsignori.it
Founded: 1990
Publishing house in the group of "il Manifesto" daily newspaper. Member of il Manifesto & carries books, online services, audio & CD-ROMs.
Subjects: Government, Political Science, Philosophy, Social Sciences, Sociology, Socio economic issues & affairs
ISBN Prefix(es): 88-7285
Total Titles: 400 Print; 2 CD-ROM; 10 Audio
Parent Company: Il Manifesto Daily Newspaper
Branch Office(s)
Manifestolibri, Viale Dei 4, Venti 47, 00152 Rome, Contact: Simona Bonsignori

Manni/Lupetti, *imprint of* Piero Manni srl

Marchese Grafiche Editoriali SpA, see Marchesi Grafiche Editoriali SpA

Casa Editrice Marietti SpA+
Via Pisani 31, 20124 Milan
Tel: (02) 67101053 *Fax:* (02) 67389081
E-mail: marietti1820@split.it
Key Personnel
President: Flavio Repetto
Editor: Carla Villata
Foreign Rights: Carla Palazzesi
Founded: 1820
Subjects: Biblical Studies, History, Literature, Literary Criticism, Essays, Philosophy, Religion - Catholic, Religion - Islamic, Religion - Jewish, Theology
ISBN Prefix(es): 88-211
Number of titles published annually: 30 Print
Total Titles: 550 Print

Aldo Marino Editore
Via Caronda, 136, 95128 Catania
Tel: (095) 438064 *Fax:* (095) 438064
Founded: 1977
Subjects: Literature, Literary Criticism, Essays, Science (General)

Tommaso Marotta Editore Srl+
Via dei Mille 78/82, Naples
Tel: (081) 5758060 *Fax:* (081) 418411
Key Personnel
Man Dir: Thomas F Marianos
Editorial: Teresa Nuzzo
Founded: 1979
Subjects: Art, Biography, Fiction, History, Music, Dance, Poetry, Regional Interests

Marsilio Editori SpA+
Marittima Fabbricato 205, 30135 Venice
Tel: (041) 2406511 *Fax:* (041) 5238352
E-mail: info@marsilioeditori.it
Web Site: www.marsilioeditori.it
Key Personnel
President & Sales Dir: Prof Cesare De Michelis
Editorial Dir: Emanuela Bassetti

Rights & Permissions & Acquisitions: Rita Vivian
Founded: 1961
Subjects: Art, Computer Science, Fiction, Film, Video, Literature, Literary Criticism, Essays, Nonfiction (General), Psychology, Psychiatry, Social Sciences, Sociology
ISBN Prefix(es): 88-317; 88-7693
U.S. Office(s): Marsilio Publishers, 853 Broadway, Suite 1509, New York, NY 10003, United States *Tel:* 212-473-5300 *Fax:* 212-473-7865
Distributor for Giovanni Tranchida Editore

Giunti Marzocco, *imprint of* Giunti Gruppo Editoriale

Marzorati Editore SRL+
Via Tirso, 26, 00198 Rome
Tel: (06) 8546146 *Fax:* (06) 8411225
Key Personnel
Man Dir & Editorial: Antonio Marzorati
Sales: Carlo Marzorati
Production: Franco Faglioni
Publicity: Patrizia Fatigati
Rights & Permissions: Francesca Marzorati
Founded: 1942
Subjects: Geography, Geology, History, Literature, Literary Criticism, Essays, Philosophy
ISBN Prefix(es): 88-280
Warehouse: Via Galilei 1/5, 20010 Cornaredo

Editrice Massimo SAS di Crespi Cesare e C+
Viale Bacchiglione 20A, 20139 Milan
Tel: (02) 55 21 08 00 *Fax:* (02) 55 21 13 15
Key Personnel
Man Dir: Dr Cesare Crespi
Founded: 1951
Subjects: Astronomy, Biblical Studies, Biography, Drama, Theater, Fiction, History, Literature, Literary Criticism, Essays, Philosophy, Psychology, Psychiatry, Religion - Catholic, Religion - Other, Romance, Science (General), Social Sciences, Sociology, Theology
ISBN Prefix(es): 88-7030
Total Titles: 400 Print
Bookshop(s): Agenzia Mescat, Milan

Masson, *imprint of* Masson SpA

Masson SpA+
Via Attendolo, 7/9, 20141 Milan
Tel: (02) 574952315 *Fax:* (02) 574952-371
E-mail: info@masson.it
Web Site: www.masson.it
Key Personnel
Man Dir: Jean-Paul Baudouin
Publicity: Gianluigi Cervi
Rights & Permissions: Lidia Lupi
Founded: 1976
Subjects: Chemistry, Chemical Engineering, Medicine, Nursing, Dentistry, Physics, Science (General), Technology
ISBN Prefix(es): 88-214
Parent Company: Masson, France
Imprints: Dunod; Masson; Massonscoula

Massonscoula, *imprint of* Masson SpA

Edizioni Gabriele Mazzotta SRL+
Foro Buonaparte Hole, 52, 20121 Milan
Tel: (02) 8055803 *Fax:* (02) 8693046
E-mail: mazzotta@milanoweb.com
Key Personnel
Rights & Permissions & Man Dir: Gabriele Mazzotta
Sales Dir: Antonio Vitagliano
Publicity Dir: Alessandra Pozzi
Founded: 1966
Subjects: Architecture & Interior Design, Art, Film, Video, Photography
ISBN Prefix(es): 88-202

ITALY

McGraw-Hill Libri Italia SRL
Via Ripamonti 89, 20139 Milan
Tel: (02) 5357181 *Fax:* (02) 5398775
E-mail: editor@mcgraw-hill.it
Key Personnel
International Rights Contact: Italo Raimondi
ISBN Prefix(es): 88-386; 88-7700
Parent Company: The McGraw-Hill Companies, 1221 Avenue of the Americas, New York, NY 10020, United States
Associate Companies: McGraw-Hill Book Co Europe
Warehouse: McGraw-Hill Magazzine Editoriale, Via Milano 6/2, 20068 Peschiera Borroreo, Milan

McRae Books+
Via dei Rustici 5, Florence 50122
Tel: (055) 264384 *Fax:* (055) 212573
Key Personnel
Publisher: Anne McRae *E-mail:* mcrae@tin.it
Packagers of children's & adults illustrated nonfiction books for the international co-edition market.
Subjects: Art, Cookery, Geography, Geology, History, Nonfiction (General), Religion - Other, Science (General)
ISBN Prefix(es): 88-88166; 88-900126; 88-900466

Edizioni Medicea SRL
via della Villa Lorenzi, 8, 50139 Florence
Tel: (055) 416048 *Fax:* (055) 416048
E-mail: edizionimedicea@tiscalinet.it
Web Site: www.edizionimedicea.it
Founded: 1975
Subjects: Architecture & Interior Design, Government, Political Science, Radio, TV, Science (General), Social Sciences, Sociology
ISBN Prefix(es): 88-900171

Mediserve SRL+
Via G Quagliariello 35/E, 80131 Naples
Tel: (081) 5452717 *Fax:* (081) 5462026
E-mail: contact@mediserve.it
Web Site: www.mediserve.it
Key Personnel
Man Dir, Editorial: Luigi Martinucci
Sales: Giuseppe Cerasuolo
Rights & Permissions: Ivonne Carbonaro
Founded: 1978
Subjects: Medicine, Nursing, Dentistry, Science (General)
ISBN Prefix(es): 88-8204
Bookshop(s): Libreria Scienze Mediche Martinucci, Via T de Amicis 60, 80145 Naples

Edizioni Mediterranee SRL+
Via Flaminia 109, 00196 Rome
Tel: (06) 3235433 *Fax:* (06) 3236277
E-mail: info@ediz-mediterranee.com
Web Site: www.ediz-mediterranee.com *Cable:* 0039-6
Key Personnel
General Manager: Giovanni Canonico *Tel:* (06) 3222797
Editorial: Paola Maria Canonico
Sales: Maria Satulli
Rights & Permissions: Assia Canonico; Eleasa Canonico
Founded: 1953
Subjects: Alternative, Archaeology, Art, Astrology, Occult, Biography, Gardening, Plants, Health, Nutrition, How-to, Medicine, Nursing, Dentistry, Military Science, Parapsychology, Philosophy, Psychology, Psychiatry, Religion - Other, Sports, Athletics, Alchemy, Esotherism, Magic, Martial Arts, Meditation, New Age, UFO, Yoga
ISBN Prefix(es): 88-272

Total Titles: 1,500 Print
Subsidiaries: Hermes Edizioni SRL; Edizioni Studio Tesi

Memorie Domenicane
Piazza San Domenico 1, 51100 Pistoia
Tel: (0573) 22056; (0573) 28158 *Fax:* (0573) 975808
E-mail: centroriviste@tiscalinet.it
Key Personnel
Editorial: Eugenio Marino; Armando F Verde
E-mail: armando.verde@tin.it
Founded: 1884
Subjects: History, Theology
Parent Company: Centro Riviste della Provincia Romana dei Frati Predicatori
Shipping Address: Centro Riviste della Provincia Romana dei Frati Predicatori
Warehouse: Centro Riviste della Provincia Romana dei Frati Predicatori
Orders to: Centro Riviste della Provincia Romana dei Frati Predicatori

Casa Editrice Menna di Sinisgalli Menna Giuseppina+
Via Scandone 16, 83100 Avellino
Tel: (0825) 24080 *Fax:* (0825) 24080
Key Personnel
Chief Executive: Nunzio Menna
Founded: 1976
Subjects: Drama, Theater, History, Law, Literature, Literary Criticism, Essays, Poetry
Imprints: Verso il Futuro
Warehouse: CE MENNA, CP 80 Avellino

Meravigli, Libreria Milanese
Via Plezzo 36, 20132 Milan
Tel: (02) 2157240 *Fax:* (02) 2157833
ISBN Prefix(es): 88-7954; 88-7955

Messaggero di San Antonio+
Via Orto Botanico 11, 35123 Padova
Tel: (049) 8225000 *Fax:* (049) 8225688
E-mail: info@mess-s-antonio.it
Web Site: www.mess-s-antonio.it
Telex: 430855 Msa I *Cable:* Messaggero Padova
Key Personnel
Chief Executive: P Luciano Marini
Editorial: P Giacomo Panteghini
Sales, Production, Publicity, Rights & Permissions: P Agostino Varotto
Subjects: Biography, History, Journalism, Religion - Other
ISBN Prefix(es): 88-7026; 88-250
Bookshop(s): Libreria Messaggero, Piazza del Santo 17, 35123 Padova

Mario Miglietti, *imprint of* Casa Editrice Castalia

Milano Libri
Via Mecenate, 91, 20138 Milan
Tel: (02) 50951 *Fax:* (02) 5065361
Subjects: Fiction, Literature, Literary Criticism, Essays
ISBN Prefix(es): 88-318; 88-7811; 88-17
Associate Companies: RCS Rizzoli Libri SpA

Nicola Milano Editore+
Via Farini 14, 40124 Bologna
Tel: (051) 239060 *Fax:* (051) 239286
E-mail: scuola@nicolamilano.com
Web Site: www.nicolamilano.com
Key Personnel
Chief Executive: Mario Musso
Founded: 1969
ISBN Prefix(es): 88-419

Milella di Lecce Spazio Vivo srl+
Via Palmieri 30, 73100 Lecce
Tel: (0832) 241131 *Fax:* (0832) 303057

E-mail: leccespaziovivo@tiscalinet.it
Key Personnel
President: Antonio Pati
Professor: Gaetano Quarta
Founded: 1945
Subjects: Disability, Special Needs, Education, English as a Second Language, History, Human Relations, Literature, Literary Criticism, Essays, Philosophy, Psychology, Psychiatry, Social Sciences, Sociology
ISBN Prefix(es): 88-7048
Bookshop(s): Via M DePietro, Via Palmieri 30, 73100 Lecce; Via G Palmieri, Viale dell'UniVersite, 1, 30-73100 Lecce *Tel:* (0832) 308885 *Fax:* (0832) 308885
Warehouse: Via M DePietro, Via Palmieri, 30, 9-73100 Leece *Tel:* (0832) 308885
Orders to: Via M DePietro, Viale dell'UniVersite, 1, 9-73100 Lecce *Tel:* (0832) 308885

Minerva Italica SpA
Via Durazzo 4, 20134 Milan
Tel: (02) 21213643 *Fax:* (02) 21213698
E-mail: info@minervaitalica.it
Web Site: www.minervaitalica.it
Key Personnel
Man Dir: Arnoldi Gianni
Founded: 1951
Subjects: Art, Education, Fiction
ISBN Prefix(es): 88-298
Branch Office(s)
Via Lattanzio 90-94, 70126 Bari
Via Alfani 68, 50121 Florence
Via S Sebastiano is 247a, 98100 Messina
Via Petrella 6, 20124 Milan
Via A Emo 162-168, 00136 Rome

Il Minotauro+
Via Quirino Majorana 221, 00152 Rome
Tel: (06) 5591864 *Fax:* (06) 5592337
E-mail: ilminotauro@tin.it
Web Site: www.ilminotauroeditore.it
Key Personnel
Contact: Dr Giorgio Ferrari
Founded: 1993
Subjects: Fiction, Government, Political Science, Literature, Literary Criticism, Essays, Philosophy, Travel
ISBN Prefix(es): 88-8073
Distributed by PDE Milano

Editrice Missionaria Italiana (EMI)+
Via di Corticella 181, 40128 Bologna
Tel: (051) 326027 *Fax:* (051) 327552
E-mail: sermis@emi.it
Web Site: www.emi.it
Key Personnel
Man Dir, Editorial, Production: Francesco Grasselli
Sales: Father Noe Cereda
Administrator: Father Giuseppe Mariani
Founded: 1977
Subjects: Anthropology, Religion - Other, Social Sciences, Sociology
ISBN Prefix(es): 88-307
Bookshop(s): Libreria Comboniana, Galleria Mazzini, 37121 Verona

mnemes - Alfieri & Ranieri Publishing+
Via F Bentivegna, 38, 90139 Palermo
Tel: (091) 588813 *Fax:* (091) 588813
E-mail: info@mnemes.com
Web Site: www.mnemes.com
Founded: 1995
Subjects: Music, Dance
ISBN Prefix(es): 88-8161

Arnoldo Mondadori Editore SpA+
Via Mondadori, 1, 20090 Segrate (Milan)
Tel: (02) 75421 *Fax:* (02) 75422302
Web Site: www.mondadori.it
Telex: 320457 Mondmi I *Cable:* MONDADORI SEGRATE (MI)

Key Personnel
Vice President & Deputy Chairman: Luca Formenton
Chief Executive Officer: Maurizio Costa
Corporate Communications & Advertising Dir: Andrea Zagami
Press Relations Officer: Angelo Allegri *Tel:* (02) 75422729 *E-mail:* aallegri@mondadori.it
Founded: 1907
Legal Headquarters: Via Bianca di Savoia 12, 20122 Milan
Representative Office: Via Sicilia, 136, 00187 Rome
Foreign Offices: Artes Graficas Toledo SA (officine grafiche): Carretera Toledo Ocono km 8, Poligono Industriale SIN/N, Toledo, and Calle Principe De Vergara, 13, 28016 Madrid (both Spain); Mondadori UK Ltd, 43-45 Charlotte St, London W1P 1HA, UK; A Mondadori Deutschland GmbH, Tal 21, 80331 Munich, Germany; A Mondadori Editore, c/o Mondgraph, 9/11 Ave F Roosevelt, 75008 Paris, France; AME Publishing Ltd, 740 Broadway, New York, NY 10003, USA; Random House Mondori, Arago, 385, 08013 Barcelona.
Subjects: Art, Biography, Education, Fiction, History, How-to, Medicine, Nursing, Dentistry, Music, Dance, Mysteries, Philosophy, Poetry, Psychology, Psychiatry, Religion - Other, Romance, Science (General)
ISBN Prefix(es): 88-04
Parent Company: Fininvest
Associate Companies: Agenzia Lombarda Distribuzione, Via Stamira d'Ancona 30, 20127 Milan *Tel:* (02) 26113470 *Fax:* (02) 26113351; Gruner & Jahr Mondadori SpA, Corso Monforte 54, 20122 Milan *Tel:* (02) 762101 *Fax:* (02) 76013439; Harlequin Mondadori SpA, Corso Concordia, 7, 20129 Milan *Tel:* (02) 760381 *Fax:* (02) 780397; Mach 2 Libri SpA, Via B Quaranta, 40, 20139 Milan *Tel:* (02) 55210585 *Fax:* (02) 5396931; SIES Società Italiana Editrice Stampatrice SpA *Fax:* (02) 66724360; Società Europea di Edizioni SpA, Via Negri 4, 20123 Milan *Tel:* (02) 85661 *Fax:* (02) 73023880
Subsidiaries: Cemit Direct Media SpA; Club delgi Editori Sp; Edizioni di Comunita Srl; Edizioni Frassinelli Srl; Elemond Srl; Ellemme Srl; Giulio Einaudi Editore SpA; Random House Mondadori S A; Leonardo Arte Srl; Mondadori Franchising SpA; Mondadori Informatica SpA; Mondadori Pubblicita SpA; Riccardo Ricciardi Editore SpA; Sperling & Kupfer Editori SpA
Branch Office(s)
Corso Europa 5/7, 20122 Milan *Tel:* (02) 77941 *Fax:* (02) 7794359
Via Sicilia 136, 00187 Rome *Tel:* (06) 474971 *Fax:* (06) 47497336
Via Virgilio 8, 00195 Rome *Tel:* (06) 6838899 *Fax:* (06) 6874107
Via Mondadori 15, 37131 Verona *Tel:* (045) 934111 *Fax:* (045) 934697
Foreign Rights: AME Publishing Ltd (USA); Continental Printing Ltd (UK); E-M Livres (France); Mondadori (Spain); Arnoldo Mondadori Deutschland GmbH (Germany); Mondgraph (France); Tuttle Mori Agency Inc (Japan)
Bookshop(s): Largo Corsia de Servi 11, 20122 Milan *Tel:* (02) 76005832 *Fax:* (02) 76014902; Piazza Cola Di Rienzo 81/83, 00192 Rome *Tel:* (06) 3220188 *Fax:* (06) 3210323; Via Appia Vuova 51, 00183 Rome *Tel:* (06) 7003690 *Fax:* (06) 7003450; Via XX Settembre 210/R, 16121 Genova *Tel:* (010) 585743 *Fax:* (010) 5704810; Via Vittorio Emanuele 36, 22100 Como *Tel:* (031) 273424 *Fax:* (031) 273314

Bruno Mondadori™, *imprint of* Paravia Bruno Mondadori Editori

Edizioni Scolastiche Bruno Mondadori™, *imprint of* Paravia Bruno Mondadori Editori

Giorgio Mondadori & Associati+
Corso Magenta 55, 20123 Milan
Tel: (02) 433 131 *Fax:* (02) 89125880
E-mail: edgmonai@tin.it
Telex: GIOMON 1 314369
Key Personnel
President: Giorgio Mondadori
Dir General, Administration & Finance: Vito Leovino
Founded: 1978
Subjects: Antiques, Architecture & Interior Design, Art, Foreign Countries, Gardening, Plants, House & Home
ISBN Prefix(es): 88-374
Imprints: GM
Subsidiaries: Gardenia srl; Giorgio Mondadori Periodici/Airone di Giorgio Mondadori & Associati; Editoriale Giorgio Mondadori; Giorgio Mondadori Editore; Giorgio Mondadori srl

Edizioni del Mondo Giudiziario
Viale Angelico 90, 00195 Rome
Tel: (06) 3721071 *Fax:* (06) 35350961
E-mail: info@mguidiziario.it
Web Site: www.mguidiziario.it
Key Personnel
Man Dir: Augusto Brusca
Editorial, Sales: Anna Tabili Brusca; Federico Carlo Brusca
Founded: 1946
Subjects: Law

Mondolibro Editore SNC+
Via Sillano 11a, 50022 Greve in Chianti (FI)
Tel: (055) 2658269 *Fax:* (055) 2679522
E-mail: info@mondolibroeditore.com
Web Site: www.mondolibroeditore.com
Key Personnel
Contact: Dr Ettore de Parentela
 E-mail: eparentela@yahoo.it
Founded: 1987
Bookshops located in major cities throughout Italy, as well as New York, Los Angeles, London, Paris, Frankfurt & Tokyo.
Subjects: Art, Drama, Theater, Fiction, Film, Video, Literature, Literary Criticism, Essays, Nonfiction (General), Travel
ISBN Prefix(es): 88-85143
Imprints: Collana; Biblioteca Elle; Biblioteca World
Subsidiaries: Coloristi
Distributed by Albolibro SrL; Casalini Libri SpA; Cosma Libraria snc; DEM Libri SrL; L'Acquilone; Medialibri SrL; Midilibri SrL; Rossano Libri SrL

Monduzzi Editore SpA
Via Ferrarese 119/2, 40128 Bologna
Tel: (051) 4151123 *Fax:* (051) 4151125
Web Site: www.monduzzi.com
Telex: 512654 Mondbo I
Key Personnel
President: Dr Gianni Monduzzi
Man Dir: Dr Mauro Bettocchi
Founded: 1978
Subjects: Biological Sciences, Chemistry, Chemical Engineering, Economics, Engineering (General), Law, Literature, Literary Criticism, Essays, Medicine, Nursing, Dentistry, Physics, Psychology, Psychiatry, Social Sciences, Sociology
ISBN Prefix(es): 88-323
Imprints: Cisalpino
Divisions: International Proceedings Division

Le Monnier, *imprint of* Edumond Le Monnier

Edumond Le Monnier+
Formerly Casa Editrice Felice Le Monnier
Via Bianca di Savoia 12, 20122 Milan
Tel: (055) 64910 *Fax:* (055) 6491200
E-mail: monnier@tin.it
Key Personnel
President: Giuseppe De Rita
Vice President: Dr Enrico Paoletti
Publishing Dir: Dr Guglielmo Paoletti
Man Dir: Dr Vanni Paoletti
Office Prints: Dr Simone Paoletti
Founded: 1836
Subjects: Biography, Education, History, Language Arts, Linguistics, Philosophy, Religion - Catholic
ISBN Prefix(es): 88-00
Imprints: Le Monnier

Editrice Morcelliana SpA+
Via Gabriele Rosa 71, 25121 Brescia
Tel: (030) 46451 *Fax:* (030) 2400605
E-mail: redazione@morcelliana.it
Web Site: www.morcelliana.it
Key Personnel
Man Dir: Stefano Minelli
Founded: 1925
Subjects: History, Philosophy, Religion - Other, Social Sciences, Sociology
ISBN Prefix(es): 88-372
Associate Companies: Editrice La Scuola SpA

Moretti & Vitali Editori srl+
Via Segantini 6a, 24128 Bergamo
Tel: (035) 251300 *Fax:* (035) 4329409
E-mail: info@morettievitali.it
Web Site: www.morettievitali.it
Key Personnel
President & Publishing Dir: Enrico Moretti
 E-mail: direzione@morettievitali.it
Administration: Fanny Honegger
 E-mail: administrazione@morettievitali.it
Editor-in-Chief: Salvatore Zingale
 E-mail: redozione@morettievitali.it
Founded: 1989
Subjects: Architecture & Interior Design, Art, Biography, Human Relations, Literature, Literary Criticism, Essays, Psychology, Psychiatry
ISBN Prefix(es): 88-7186

Federico Motta Editore
Via Branda Castiglioni, 7, 20156 Milan
Tel: (02) 300761; (02) 30076231 *Fax:* (02) 38010046; (02) 33403275
E-mail: info@mottaeditore.it
Web Site: www.mottaeditore.it
ISBN Prefix(es): 88-7179

Motta Junior Srl
Via Branda Castiglioni, 7, 20156 Milan
Tel: (02) 300761; (02) 30076231 *Fax:* (02) 38010046; (02) 33403275
E-mail: info@mottaeditore.it
Web Site: www.mottaeditore.it
Key Personnel
Dir, Sales Books Department: Lorena Vazzola
Pres: Massimo Fumagalli
Edit Dir: Madeleine Thoby
ISBN Prefix(es): 88-8279

Mucchi Editore SRL
Via Emilia Est 1527, 41100 Modena
Tel: (059) 374094 *Fax:* (059) 282628
E-mail: info@mucchieditore.it
Web Site: www.mucchieditore.it
Founded: 1646
Subjects: Crafts, Games, Hobbies, Education, History, Language Arts, Linguistics, Law, Literature, Literary Criticism, Essays, Philosophy, Science (General)
ISBN Prefix(es): 88-7000

Societa Editrice Il Mulino+
Str Maggiore 37, 40125 Bologna
Tel: (051) 256011 *Fax:* (051) 256034
E-mail: info@mulino.it

Web Site: www.mulino.it
Key Personnel
Man Dir: Giuliano Bassani
Sales Dir: Maria Selleri
Publicity Dir: Ida Meneghello
Rights & Permissions: Paola Pecchioli
  E-mail: paola.pecchioli@mulino.it
Editorial Dir: Giovanni Evangelisti
Founded: 1954
Subjects: Economics, Government, Political Science, History, Language Arts, Linguistics, Law, Philosophy, Psychology, Psychiatry, Social Sciences, Sociology
ISBN Prefix(es): 88-15

Ass Italiana Sclerosi Multipla
Vico Chiuso Paggi, 3, 16128 Genova
Tel: (010) 27131 *Fax:* (010) 2470226
ISBN Prefix(es): 88-7148

Mundici - Zanetti
Via dei Lapidari, 10, 40129 Bologna
Tel: (051) 325347 *Fax:* (051) 326109
Founded: 1977
Subjects: Astrology, Occult, Cookery, House & Home, Humor
ISBN Prefix(es): 88-7410

Gruppo Ugo Mursia Editore SpA+
Via Melchiorre Gioia 45, 20124 Milan
Tel: (02) 67378500 *Fax:* (02) 67378605
E-mail: info@mursia.it
Web Site: www.mursia.com
Key Personnel
President & Publisher: Fiorenza Mursia
Publicity: Lorenza Sala
Rights & Permissions: Milena Molinari
Founded: 1922
Subjects: Art, Biography, Education, Fiction, History, Maritime, Philosophy, Poetry, Religion - Other, Science (General), Social Sciences, Sociology, Sports, Athletics
ISBN Prefix(es): 88-425
Warehouse: Via Cassanese antica, 20060 Vignate, Milano

Museo storico in Trento+
Via Torre d'Augusto, 41, 38100 Trento
Tel: (0461) 230482 *Fax:* (0461) 237418
E-mail: info@museostorico.tn.it
Web Site: www.museostorico.tn.it/editoria_ricerca
Key Personnel
Editorial Coordinator: Rodolfo Taiani *Tel:* (0461) 264660 *E-mail:* rtaiani@museostorico.tn.it
Founded: 1923
Subjects: History, Literature, Literary Criticism, Essays, Social Sciences, Sociology
ISBN Prefix(es): 88-7197
Number of titles published annually: 5 Print
Total Titles: 110 Print

Musumeci SpA+
Localita Amerique 99, 11020 Quart (Acosta)
Tel: (0165) 761216 *Fax:* (0165) 761296
Key Personnel
Dir: Piero Minuzzo
ISBN Prefix(es): 88-7032

Franco Muzzio Editore+
Via Riccardo Grazioli Lante, 5, 00195 Rome
Tel: (06) 3725748 *Fax:* (06) 6868696
E-mail: franco@muzzioeditore.it
Web Site: www.muzzioeditore.it
Telex: 432005 Muzzio
Key Personnel
Chief Executive & Publicity: Franco Muzzio
Editorial: Riccardo Degli Innocenti
Sales: Ennio Pengo
Production: Massi Miliano Muzzio
Rights & Permissions & Editorial: Stella Longato
Founded: 1973

Subjects: Computer Science, Electronics, Electrical Engineering, Energy, Music, Dance, Nonfiction (General), Science (General)
ISBN Prefix(es): 88-7021; 88-7413
Associate Companies: Arcana Editrice SRL, Viale Sondrio 7, 20124 Milan; Casa Editice MEB SRL
Warehouse: Via Makalle 73, 35138 Padua

N, *imprint of* Pizzicato Edizioni Musicali

Giorgio Nada Editore SRL+
Via Treves 15/17, 20090 Vimodrone MI
Mailing Address: Via Claudio Treves 15/17, 20090 Vimodrone MI
Tel: (02) 27301126 *Fax:* (02) 27301454
E-mail: info@giorgionadaeditore.it
Web Site: www.giorgionadaeditore.it
Key Personnel
Chairman: Giorgio Nada *E-mail:* giorgio.nada@giorgioeditore.it
Founded: 1988
Specialize in books on history of Italian cars & motorcycle makes (Ferrari, Ducati, etc).
Subjects: Automotive, History, Transportation
ISBN Prefix(es): 88-7911
Number of titles published annually: 15 Print
Total Titles: 200 Print
Subsidiaries: Libreria dell'Automobile
Distributed by Haynes Publishing-Sparkford Yeovil (England); MBI Publishing Company (US)
Book Club(s): Corso Venezia, 43, 20121 Milan

Nagard
Via Larga 9, 20122 Milan
Tel: (02) 58371400 *Fax:* (02) 58304790
Founded: 1977
Subjects: Chemistry, Chemical Engineering, Education
ISBN Prefix(es): 88-85010

Casa Editrice Roberto Napoleone
Via Antonio Chinotto, 16, 00195 Rome
Tel: (06) 3729096 *Fax:* (06) 3729103
Key Personnel
Chief Executive: Roberto Napoleone
Founded: 1974
ISBN Prefix(es): 88-7124

Nardini Editore srl+
Piazza della Signoria 4/A, 50122 Florence
Tel: (055) 238551 *Fax:* (055) 2385529
E-mail: info@nardinieditore.it
Web Site: www.nardinieditore.it
Key Personnel
Manager: Ruth Mueller Nardini
Dir General: Fabio Nardini
Editorial Dir: Claudio Nardini
Founded: 1970
Subjects: Art, Biography, Economics, Education, Literature, Literary Criticism, Essays, Medicine, Nursing, Dentistry, Philosophy, Poetry, Religion - Other
ISBN Prefix(es): 88-404
Imprints: Convivio (Nardini Editore); Editoriale Europress (Nardini Press)

Accademia Naz dei Lincei
Via della Lungara 10, 00165 Rome
Tel: (06) 680271 *Fax:* (06) 6893616
E-mail: pugwash@iol.it
Founded: 1847
Subjects: Archaeology, Art, Biological Sciences, Economics, History, Management, Mathematics
ISBN Prefix(es): 88-218; 88-7052

Istituto Nazionale di Archeologia e Storia dell'Arte, *see* Associazione Internazionale di Archeologia Classica

Istituto Nazionale di Studi Romani
Piazza dei Cavalieri di Malta, 2, 00153 Rome
Tel: (06) 5743442; (06) 5743445 *Fax:* (06) 5743447
E-mail: studiromani@studiromani.it
Web Site: www.studiromani.it
Key Personnel
President: Prof Mario Mazza
Vice President: Prof Letizia Ermini Pani
Dir: Dr Fernanda Roscetti
Founded: 1925
Subjects: Architecture & Interior Design, Art, History, Literature, Literary Criticism, Essays
ISBN Prefix(es): 88-7311
Number of titles published annually: 7 Print
Total Titles: 848 Print

New Magazine Edizioni+
Via dei Mille 69, 38100 Trento
Tel: (0461) 925007 *Fax:* (0461) 925007
E-mail: newmagazine@tin.it
Web Site: www.newmagazine.it; www.rivistamedica.it
Key Personnel
International Rights: Bruno Zanotti
Founded: 1982
Specialize in medicine.
Subjects: Civil Engineering, Literature, Literary Criticism, Essays, Medicine, Nursing, Dentistry
ISBN Prefix(es): 88-8041
Distributed by Del Porto SpA (Worldwide)

Newton & Compton Editori
Via Portuense 1415, 00050 Rome
Tel: (06) 65002553 *Fax:* (06) 65002892
E-mail: info@newtoncompton.com
Web Site: www.newtoncompton.com
Founded: 1969
Subjects: Anthropology, Archaeology, Fiction, Government, Political Science, History, How-to, Mathematics, Philosophy, Poetry, Psychology, Psychiatry, Science (General), Social Sciences, Sociology
ISBN Prefix(es): 88-7983; 88-8183; 88-8289

NIE, *imprint of* La Nuova Italia Editrice SpA

Nissolino, *imprint of* Esselibri

Nistri - Lischi Editori+
Via XXIV Maggio 28, 56123 Pisa
Tel: (050) 563371 *Fax:* (050) 562726
Web Site: www.nistri-lischi.it *Cable:* LISCHI PISA
Key Personnel
Man Dir: Luciano Lischi
Sales: Lucia Lischi
Founded: 1780
Subjects: Literature, Literary Criticism, Essays
Warehouse: Via Carducci, La Fontina, Pisa

NodoLibri+
Via Volta, 38, 22100 Como
Tel: (031) 243113 *Fax:* (031) 3306370
Founded: 1989
Subjects: Art, History, Photography, Regional Interests
ISBN Prefix(es): 88-7185

Nord, *imprint of* Casa Editrice Nord SRL

Casa Editrice Nord SRL
Via Rubens, 25, 20148 Milan
Tel: (02) 405708 *Fax:* (02) 4042207
E-mail: nord@fantascienza.it
Web Site: www.nord.fantascienza.it
Key Personnel
President: Gianfranco Viviani
Vice President: Marco Viviani
Editorial: Alex Voglino; Piergiorgio Nicolazzini

Founded: 1964
Subjects: Science Fiction, Fantasy
ISBN Prefix(es): 88-429
Imprints: Nord

Novecento Editrice Srl+
Via Siracusa, 16, 90141 Palermo
Tel: (091) 587417 *Fax:* (091) 585702
E-mail: novedi@mbox.vol.it
Key Personnel
Administrator: Alessi Maria Caterina Domitilla
Founded: 1980
Subjects: Art, Literature, Literary Criticism, Essays, Photography
ISBN Prefix(es): 88-373
Bookshop(s): Libreria Novelento, via Siracusa 7/A, 90141 Palermo *Tel:* (091) 6256814
Warehouse: Via Agrigento 15, 90141 Palermo

Nugae, Interli Nee, Libri Di Bron, Cuccioli, *imprint of* Pagano Editore

Nuova Alfa Editoriale+
Via Trentacoste, 7, 20134 Milan
Tel: (02) 215631 *Fax:* (02) 26413121
Key Personnel
Man Dir, Production: Maurizio Armaroli
Editorial, Publicity: Emanuela Spinsanti
Sales: Piera Raimondi
Founded: 1954
Subjects: Art, Literature, Literary Criticism, Essays
ISBN Prefix(es): 88-7779

Nuova Coletti Editore Roma
Via Clitunno 24/f, 00198 Rome
Tel: (06) 8557981 *Fax:* (06) 8557981
E-mail: materiale.web@futura-ge.com
Founded: 1987
Subjects: Biblical Studies, Education, History, Literature, Literary Criticism, Essays, Philosophy, Religion - Catholic, Theology
ISBN Prefix(es): 88-7826
Warehouse: Borgo Pio 105, 00193 Rome

Nuova Dimensione, *imprint of* Ediciclo Editore SRL

Nuova Ipsa Editore srl
Via G Crispi 50, 90145 Palermo
Tel: (091) 6819025 *Fax:* (091) 6816399
E-mail: info@nuovaipsa.it
Web Site: www.nuovaipsa.it
Key Personnel
Editorial Dir: Claudio Mazza
Founded: 1982
ISBN Prefix(es): 88-7676

La Nuova Italia Editrice SpA
Via Mecenate, 91, 20138 Milan
Tel: (02) 50951 *Fax:* (02) 50952309
Key Personnel
Man Dir: Federico Codignola; Sergio Colleoni; Mario Ermini; Carmelo Sambugar
Founded: 1926
Subjects: Art, Biography, History, Philosophy, Psychology, Psychiatry, Social Sciences, Sociology
ISBN Prefix(es): 88-221
Imprints: NIE
Branch Office(s)
Via Sacco Vantetti 8, 60131 Ancona
Via E Bernardi 14, 40133 Bologna
Via Del Fangario 25, 09122 Cagliari
Via Degli Stan 28, 87100 Cosenza
Via B Lupi 1, 50129 Florence
Via di Serretto 41/2, 16131 Genoa
Via Negroli 12, 20133 Milan
Ste St Le 98 Km 79,400 (Complesso Big Center), 70026 Modugno-Bari
Via S Alfonso Maria de'Liguori 3, 80141 Naples

Via Altichiero da Zevio 3, 35100 Padua
Via Olanda 15, 90146 Palermo
Viale Carso 46, 00195 Rome
Via Bassano 16, 10136 Turin
Arbizzano- Negrar, Via L da Vinci, 37020 Verona

Editrice Nuovi Autori
Via Gaudenzio Ferrari 14, 20123 Milan
Tel: (02) 89409338 *Fax:* (02) 58107048
E-mail: faglier@tin.it
Web Site: www.paginegialle.it/ednuoviaut
Key Personnel
Man Dir: Fulvio Aglieri
Editorial & Publicity: Alessandra Aglieri
Sales: Graziella Mosconi
Founded: 1980
Also acts as book packager.
Subjects: Biography, History, Literature, Literary Criticism, Essays, Poetry
ISBN Prefix(es): 88-7230

Nuovi Sentieri Editore
Via Ripa 2, 32100 Belluno
Tel: (0437) 590308
Key Personnel
Man Dir: Bepi Pellegrinon
Editorial: Loris Santomaso
Sales: Antonio Zullo
Founded: 1971
Subjects: Art, History, Literature, Literary Criticism, Essays, Photography, Poetry, Regional Interests
ISBN Prefix(es): 88-85510

Il Nuovo Melangolo+
Via di Porta Soprana 3/1, 16123 Genoa
Tel: (010) 2514002 *Fax:* (010) 2514037
E-mail: info@ilmelangolo.com
Web Site: www.ilmelangolo.com
Founded: 1976
Subjects: Fiction, Literature, Literary Criticism, Essays, Philosophy, Poetry, Religion - Buddhist, Religion - Catholic, Religion - Jewish, Religion - Other, Theology
ISBN Prefix(es): 88-7018

OCTAVO Produzioni Editoriali Associale+
Borgo Santa Croce 8, 50122 Florence
Tel: (055) 2346022 *Fax:* (055) 2346109
Key Personnel
Man Dir: Franco Cantini
Founded: 1993
Specialize in art.
Subjects: Antiques, Archaeology, Architecture & Interior Design, Art, Education, Fiction, History, Photography
ISBN Prefix(es): 88-8030

OEMF, see OEMF srl International

OEMF srl International+
Via Muzio Attendolo detto Sforza 7/9, 20141 Milan
Tel: (02) 5749521 *Fax:* (02) 33210200
E-mail: info@mason.it
Web Site: www.oemf.it
Key Personnel
Dir: Carlo Marini
Founded: 1940
Subjects: Medicine, Nursing, Dentistry, Veterinary Science
ISBN Prefix(es): 88-7076

Officina Edizioni di Aldo Quinti+
Via Nicola Ricciotti 11, 00195 Rome
Tel: (06) 316336 *Fax:* (06) 65740514
E-mail: officinaedizioni@yahoo.com
Key Personnel
Chief Executive: Aldo Quinti
Publicity: Jolanda Ridolfi
Founded: 1966

Subjects: Architecture & Interior Design, Art, Drama, Theater, Ethnicity, Film, Video, Language Arts, Linguistics, Social Sciences, Sociology
Warehouse: Via Virginia Agnelli, 52, 00151 Rome

Editoriale Olimpia SpA+
Via E Ferni, 24, 50019 Fiorentino, Florence
Tel: (055) 30321 *Fax:* (055) 3032280
E-mail: editore@edolimpia.it; moie@edolimpia.it
Web Site: www.edolimpia.it
Telex: 573084 Edol I
Key Personnel
Man Dir, Editorial, Rights & Permissions: Renato Cacciaputi
Founded: 1939
Specialize in publications on hunting, fishing, dogs, scuba diving, weapons, handgliding-paragliding, tourism, digital photography, etc.
Subjects: Aeronautics, Aviation, Animals, Pets, Biological Sciences, Outdoor Recreation, Sports, Athletics, Technology
ISBN Prefix(es): 88-253
Number of titles published annually: 220 Print
Subsidiaries: Editoriale Olimpia

Edizioni Olivares
Via Pietro Mascagni, 7, 20122 Milan
Tel: (02) 76001753 *Fax:* (02) 76002579
E-mail: olivares@edizioniolivares.com
Web Site: www.edizioniolivares.com
Founded: 1986
Membership(s): AIPE (Associazione Italiano Piccoli Editori) & AIE.
Subjects: Business, Management, Women's Studies
ISBN Prefix(es): 88-85982
Parent Company: Redifin SpA, Via P Mascagni, 7, 20122 Milan
Showroom(s): Parole In Tasca-Salone del libro tascabile, c/o Castello di Belgioso, Via Garibaldi 1, 27011 Belgioso (Paira)
Warehouse: M ED Via dei Mille 20, Carugate (MI)

Leo S Olschki
Viuzzo del Pozzetto, 8, 50126 Florence
Tel: (055) 6530684 *Fax:* (055) 6530214
E-mail: celso@olschki.it
Web Site: www.olschki.it
Founded: 1886
Subjects: Anthropology, Archaeology, Architecture & Interior Design, Art, Astronomy, Biblical Studies, Geography, Geology, Government, Political Science, History, Language Arts, Linguistics, Library & Information Sciences, Literature, Literary Criticism, Essays, Music, Dance, Natural History, Philosophy, Physical Sciences, Religion - Catholic, Religion - Jewish, Science (General), Social Sciences, Sociology, Theology
ISBN Prefix(es): 88-222
Number of titles published annually: 150 Print
Total Titles: 3,000 Print

Organizzazioni Speciali SRL, see OS (Organizzazioni Speciali SRL)

Ortelio, *imprint of* Edizioni Cartografiche Milanesi

OS (Organizzazioni Speciali SRL)+
Via Sarpi, 7a, 50136 Florence
Tel: (055) 6236501 *Fax:* (055) 669446
Telex: 571438
Founded: 1950
Membership(s): Giunti Publishing Group.
Subjects: Psychology, Psychiatry
ISBN Prefix(es): 88-09
Associate Companies: O S Consulting

Branch Office(s)
Milano
Ripa Porta Ticinese
Showroom(s): Via Campo nell'Elba, 27 Rome

Osanna Venosa+
Via Appia 3 a, 85029 Venosa, Potenza
Tel: (0972) 35952 *Fax:* (0972) 35723
Key Personnel
Editorial Dir: Antonio Vaccaro
Subjects: Archaeology, History, Literature, Literary Criticism, Essays
ISBN Prefix(es): 88-8167

Maria Pacini Fazzi Editore
Via dell'Angelo Custode, 33, 55100 Lucca
Mailing Address: CP 394, 55100 Lucca
Tel: (0583) 440188 *Fax:* (0583) 464656
E-mail: mpf@pacinifazzi.it
Web Site: www.pacinifazzi.it
Key Personnel
President: Maria Pacini Fazzi
Vice President: Giovan Pio Moretti
Editorial Dir: Francesca Fazzi
Founded: 1966
Subjects: Art, Cookery, Drama, Theater, History, Literature, Literary Criticism, Essays, Philosophy, Social Sciences, Sociology
ISBN Prefix(es): 88-7246

Pagano Editore+
Piazza San Domenico Maggiore 9, 80134 Naples
Tel: (081) 5642968 *Fax:* (081) 5646694
E-mail: redazione@paganoeditore.com
Key Personnel
Man Dir: Flavio Pagano
Founded: 1985
Subjects: History, Literature, Literary Criticism, Essays, Music, Dance
ISBN Prefix(es): 88-85228
Parent Company: Edipica
Imprints: Nugae, Interli Nee, Libri Di Bron, Cuccioli
Subsidiaries: Vox Neapolis
Divisions: Scompaginate

Paideia Editrice+
Via A Manzoni 20, 25020 Flero (Brescia)
Tel: (030) 3582434 *Fax:* (030) 3582691
E-mail: paideiaeditrice@tin.it
Key Personnel
Man Dir: Prof Giuseppe Scarpat, PhD
Editorial: Dr Marco Scarpat
Founded: 1945
Subjects: Art, Asian Studies, Biblical Studies, Music, Dance, Philosophy, Poetry, Religion - Catholic, Religion - Jewish, Religion - Protestant, Religion - Other
ISBN Prefix(es): 88-394

Palatina Editrice
Borgo Tommasini 9/A, 43100 Parma
Tel: (0521) 282388 *Fax:* (0521) 282388
Web Site: culturitalia.uibk.ac.at
Key Personnel
Chief Executive: Carlotta Capacchi
Editorial: Guglielmo Capacchi
Founded: 1965
Subjects: Art, Genealogy, History, Language Arts, Linguistics, Literature, Literary Criticism, Essays, Music, Dance, Regional Interests, Religion - Other, Travel
Number of titles published annually: 9 Print
Total Titles: 37 Print
Bookshop(s): Libreria Palatina Editrice, Borgo Tommasini 9/A, Parma 43100 *Tel:* (0521) 282388 *Fax:* (0521) 282388

Fratelli Palombi SRL
Via dei Gracchi 181-185, 00192 Rome
Tel: (06) 3214150 *Fax:* (06) 3214752
E-mail: flli.palombi@mail.stm.it
Key Personnel
Man Dir: Dr Mario Palombi
Founded: 1914
Subjects: Art, History, Regional Interests
ISBN Prefix(es): 88-7621
Subsidiaries: Organizzazione Rab (sales)

G B Palumbo & C Editore SpA+
Via Ricasoli 59, 90139 Palermo
Tel: (091) 588850 *Fax:* (091) 6111848
E-mail: redazione@palumboeditore.it
Web Site: www.palumboeditore.it
Key Personnel
President: Giorgio Palumbo
Founded: 1939
Subjects: Language Arts, Linguistics, Literature, Literary Criticism, Essays
ISBN Prefix(es): 88-8020
Warehouse: Via Maggiore G Galliano 17, Palermo

Franco Cosimo Panini Editore
Viale Corassori, 24, 41100 Modena
Tel: (059) 343572 *Fax:* (059)344274
E-mail: info@fcp.it
Web Site: www.fcp.it
Telex: 510260 Matex I *Cable:* MALIPIERO
Key Personnel
Chairman: Franco Panini
Man Dir: Dr Enrico Berardi
Editorial Dir: Dr Ermanno Mammarella
Founded: 1969
Subjects: Crafts, Games, Hobbies, Education
ISBN Prefix(es): 88-7686; 88-248; 88-8290
Parent Company: Gruppo Editoriale Franco Panini SPA
Subsidiaries: Franco Panini Editore
Branch Office(s)
Malipiero France SA Editeur, S rue du Faubourg St, Honore, Paris, France

Franco Cosimo Panini Editore SpA+
Viale Corassori 24, 41100 Modena
Tel: (059) 343572 *Fax:* (059) 344274
E-mail: info@fcp.it
Web Site: www.fcp.it; www.francopanini.com
Founded: 1990
Subjects: Archaeology, Architecture & Interior Design, Art, Literature, Literary Criticism, Essays, Poetry
ISBN Prefix(es): 88-7686; 88-248; 88-8290

Edizioni Franco Cosimo Panini+
Viale Corassori, 24, 41100 Modena
Tel: (059) 343572 *Fax:* (059) 344274
E-mail: info@fcp.it
Web Site: www.fcp.it
Telex: 510650 *Cable:* EDIPAN MODENA ITALIA
Key Personnel
Publisher: Franco Panini
Founded: 1963
Subjects: Education, Sports, Athletics
ISBN Prefix(es): 88-7686; 88-248; 88-8290

Editoriale Paradigma, *imprint of* D'Anna

Paramond™, *imprint of* Paravia Bruno Mondadori Editori

Paravia™, *imprint of* Paravia Bruno Mondadori Editori

Paravia Bruno Mondadori Editori+
Subsidiary of Edizioni Bruno Mondadori
Via Archimede 10/23/27/51, Corso Trapani 16
10139 Torino, 20129 Milan
Tel: (02) 748231 *Fax:* (02) 74823362
Web Site: www.paravia.it; www.paramond.it; langedizoni.it; edizioniscolastichebrunomondadori.it
Key Personnel
Chairman: Marco Galateri
General Manager: Agostino Cattaneo
Man Dir: Roberto Gulli; T U Paravia
Editorial Dir: R Formento; A Fresco; M Garena; Paola Rosci; Emilio Zanette
Founded: 1998
Membership(s): AIE member Publisher Educational.
Subjects: Biological Sciences, Earth Sciences, Education, English as a Second Language, Geography, Geology, History, Literature, Literary Criticism, Essays, Mathematics, Philosophy
ISBN Prefix(es): 88-424
Total Titles: 200 Print
Associate Companies: Edizioni Electa-Bruno Mondadori
Imprints: Archimede Edizioni™; Elmedi™; Lang Edizioni™; Bruno Mondadori™; Edizioni Scolastiche Bruno Mondadori™; Paramond™; Paravia™
Distributor for Edizioni Electa-Bruno Mondadori

G B Paravia & C SpA
Corso Trapani 16, 10139 Turin
Tel: (011) 7502111 *Fax:* (011) 75021510
E-mail: master@paravia.it
Web Site: www.paravia.it
Telex: 221652 Edito I
Key Personnel
Editorial: Dr Guido Gay
Founded: 1700
ISBN Prefix(es): 88-395

Passigli Editori+
Via Chiantigiana, 62, 50011 Antella (Florence)
Tel: (055) 640265 *Fax:* (055) 644627
E-mail: info@passiglieditori.it
Web Site: www.passiglieditori.it
Key Personnel
Man Dir: Prof Stefano Passigli
Editorial: Dr Fabrizio Dall'Aglio; Dr Luca Merlini
Sales: Dr Alvise Passigli
Rights: Domitilla Baldeschi
Founded: 1981
Subjects: Biography, History, Literature, Literary Criticism, Essays, Music, Dance, Poetry, Travel
ISBN Prefix(es): 88-368; 88-86161
Imprints: Guide del Sole; Guide del Cuore; Le Comete
Subsidiaries: Scala, Instituto Fotografico Editoriale

Patron Editore SrL+
Via Badini 12, 40050 Quarto Inferiore (Bologna)
Tel: (051) 767003 *Fax:* (051) 768252
Key Personnel
General Dir: Riccardo Patron
Founded: 1925
Subjects: Agriculture, Art, Engineering (General), History, Language Arts, Linguistics, Law, Literature, Literary Criticism, Essays, Medicine, Nursing, Dentistry, Philosophy, Psychology, Psychiatry, Social Sciences, Sociology
ISBN Prefix(es): 88-555
Bookshop(s): Libreria Internazionale Patron, Via Zamboni 26, 40121 Bologna

PE, *imprint of* Pizzicato Edizioni Musicali

Editoriale PEG
Via Vittoria Colonna 4, 20149 Milan
Tel: (02) 4859181 *Fax:* (02) 485918220
E-mail: info@millerfreeman.it
Telex: 323088
Key Personnel
President: Solly Cohen

Administrator: Giancarlo Meani
Founded: 1950
ISBN Prefix(es): 88-7067

Luigi Pellegrini Editore+
Via de Rada, 67, 87100 Cosenza
Tel: (0984) 795065 *Fax:* (0984) 792672
E-mail: info@pellegrinieditore.it
Web Site: www.pellegrinieditore.it *Cable:* PELLEGRINI EDITORE COSENZA
Key Personnel
Chief Executive, Rights & Permissions: Luigi Pellegrini
Editorial, Sales: Walter Pellegrini
Publicity: Erminia Petramala
Founded: 1952
Subjects: Drama, Theater, Fiction, History, Literature, Literary Criticism, Essays, Poetry
ISBN Prefix(es): 88-8101
Imprints: LPE
Branch Office(s)
Via Rendano, 25, 87040 Castrolibero

Il Pensiero Scientifico Editore SRL+
Via Bradano, 3/C, 00199 Rome
Tel: (06) 862821 *Fax:* (06) 86282250
E-mail: pensiero@pensiero.it
Web Site: www.pensiero.it
Key Personnel
President: Annamaria De Feo
General Manager: Francesco De Fiore
Publicity Manager: Luciano De Fiore
Marketing & Sales Manager: Luca De Fiore
Foreign Rights: Andres De Fiore; Silvana Guida
Founded: 1946
The publishing mission is the statement of the human values as the basis of medical research & the development of all evidence based clinical practice.
Subjects: Education, Health, Nutrition, Psychology, Psychiatry, Medicine, Nursing & Oncology
ISBN Prefix(es): 88-7002
Number of titles published annually: 50 Print

PGE, *imprint of* Piero Gribaudi Editore

Pheljna Edizioni d'Arte e Suggestione
Stradale Torino 11, 10018 Pavone Canavese (Turin)
Tel: (0125) 234114 *Fax:* (0125) 230085
Key Personnel
Editor: Ljdia Priuli
Founded: 1982
Subjects: Art, Cookery, Photography

PIAC, *imprint of* Pontificio Istituto di Archeologia Cristiana

Daniela Piazza Editore+
Via Sanfront 13, 10138 Turin
Tel: (011) 434 27 06 *Fax:* (011) 434 24 71
E-mail: daniela.piazza@tiscalinet.it
Web Site: www.danielapiazzaeditore.com
Key Personnel
Publisher: Daniela Piazza
Founded: 1972
Subjects: Art, Biography, Cookery, History, Poetry, Regional Interests, Travel
ISBN Prefix(es): 88-7889

Piccin Nuova Libraria SpA+
Via Altinate 107, 35121 Padua
Tel: (049) 655566 *Fax:* (049) 8750693
E-mail: info@piccinonline.com
Web Site: www.piccinonline.com
Key Personnel
Man Dir, Production: Dr Massimo Piccin
Editorial & Sales: Dr Antonella Noventa
   E-mail: a.noventa@piccinonline.com
Founded: 1980
Subjects: Biological Sciences, Law, Literature, Literary Criticism, Essays, Medicine, Nursing, Dentistry, Science (General)
ISBN Prefix(es): 88-299
Foreign Rep(s): Scholium International Inc (Canada, Mexico, USA)

Piemme Junior, *imprint of* Edizioni Piemme SpA

Edizioni Piemme SpA+
Via del Carmine 5, 15033 Casale Monferrato (AL)
Tel: (0142) 3361 *Fax:* (0142) 74223
Web Site: www.edizpiemme.it
Key Personnel
Man Dir: Pietro Marietti
Piemme Editorial: Francesca Cristoffanini
Rights & Permissions: valeria Casonato
Press Officer: Valerie Caprioglio
Piemme Junior Editorial: Elisabetta Dami
Founded: 1982
Subjects: Biblical Studies, Cookery, Fiction, Gardening, Plants, Nonfiction (General), Religion - Catholic, Romance, Self-Help, Theology
ISBN Prefix(es): 88-384
Imprints: Battelloavapore; Piemme Junior

Piero Lacaita Editore+
Vico degli Albanesi, 4, 74024 Manduria (Taranto)
Tel: (099) 9711124 *Fax:* (099) 9711124
Key Personnel
Editorial Dir: Piero Lacaita
Founded: 1987
Subjects: History, Literature, Literary Criticism, Essays
ISBN Prefix(es): 88-87280; 88-88546

Piero Manni srl+
Via Bixio, 11b, 73100 Lecce
Tel: (0832) 387057 *Fax:* (0832) 387057
E-mail: pieromannisrl@clio.it
Key Personnel
Contact: Grazia Manni; Piero Manni; Anna Grazia D'Oria
Founded: 1983
Subjects: Human Relations, Literature, Literary Criticism, Essays, Poetry, Social Sciences, Sociology
ISBN Prefix(es): 88-8176
Imprints: Manni/Lupetti; L'immaginazion

Libreria Gozzini di Pietro e Francesco Chellini (SNC)
V Ricasoli 49, 50122 Florence
Tel: (055) 212433 *Fax:* (055) 211105
E-mail: gozzini@gozzini.it; info@gozzini.com
Web Site: www.gozzini.com
Founded: 1850
Membership(s): Socio ALAI-LILA.
Total Titles: 200 E-Book

La Pilotta Editrice Coop RL+
Str Universtia, 11, Via Palermo, 44, 43100 Parma
Tel: (0521) 771268 *Fax:* (0521) 771268
Key Personnel
President: Maria Pia Luchini
Editorial: Cesare Maccari
Founded: 1978
Subjects: Fiction, Literature, Literary Criticism, Essays, Poetry
Parent Company: Cemcasa Editrice Maccari

Francesco Pirella Editore+
Via Casaregis 51, 16129 Genoa
Tel: (010) 363628 *Fax:* (010) 1782281081
Web Site: www.pirella.net
Key Personnel
Man Dir: Francesco Pirella
Founded: 1972
ISBN Prefix(es): 88-85514
Orders to: Serena Libri, Via Monte Zovetto 23 R, 16145 Genoa

Pitagora Editrice SRL+
Via del Legatore 3, 40138 Bologna
Tel: (051) 530003 *Fax:* (051) 535301
E-mail: pited@pitagoragroup.it
Web Site: www.pitagoragroup.it
Key Personnel
Chief Executive: Franco Stignani
Editorial: Mauro Bovini
Sales: Adolfo Francioni
Publicity: Antonella Valzania
Founded: 1958
Subjects: Engineering (General), Environmental Studies, Geography, Geology, Language Arts, Linguistics, Mathematics, Technology
ISBN Prefix(es): 88-371
Number of titles published annually: 60 Print
Total Titles: 900 Print
Associate Companies: Tecnoprint S N C, Via del Legatore 3, 40138 Bologna *Tel:* (051) 531159 *Fax:* (051) 535301
Bookshop(s): Via Saragozza 112, 40136 Bologna; Via Zamboni 57, 40126 Bologna

Amilcare Pizzi SpA+
Via Pizzi, 14, 20092 Cinisello Balsamo, Milan
Tel: (02) 618361 *Fax:* (02) 61836283
Key Personnel
Chief Executive: Massimo Pizzi *E-mail:* massimo.pizzi@amilcarepizzi.it
Founded: 1914
Subjects: Art
Associate Companies: American Pizzi Offset Co, 370 Lexington Ave, Suite 505, New York, NY 10017, United States
Subsidiaries: Silvana Editoriale SpA

Pizzicato Edizioni Musicali
Via Monte Ortigara 10, 33100 Udine
Tel: (0432) 45288 *Fax:* (0432) 45288
Web Site: www.pizzicato.it
Key Personnel
President: Anna Maria Fasano
Editor: Bruno Rossi
Founded: 1985
Subjects: Biography, Ethnicity, Music, Dance
ISBN Prefix(es): 88-7736
Imprints: N; PE; PVH

Plurigraf SPA
Via Cairoli, 18a, 50131 Florence
Tel: (05) 5576841 *Fax:* (05) 55000766
E-mail: plurigraf@tiscalinet.it
Key Personnel
President: Mr Mario Previsani
Founded: 1972
Subjects: Travel
ISBN Prefix(es): 88-7280

Il Polifilo
Via Borgonuovo, 2, 20121 Milan
Tel: (02) 6551549 *Fax:* (02) 6598045
ISBN Prefix(es): 88-7050

Istituto Poligrafico e Zecca dello Stato+
Piazza Verdi, 10, 00198 Rome
Tel: (06) 85081 *Toll Free Tel:* 800-864035
   Fax: (06) 85082517
E-mail: infoipzs@ipzs.it
Web Site: www.ipzs.it
Telex: 611008 IPZSRO
Key Personnel
Dir: Salvatore Ficaio
Founded: 1928
State Publishing House & Italian State Stationery Office.
Subjects: Art, Government, Political Science, Language Arts, Linguistics, Law, Literature, Literary Criticism, Essays

ISBN Prefix(es): 88-240
Subsidiaries: Editalia SpA

Il Poligrafo
Via Cassan, 34, 35121 Padova
Tel: (04) 98360887 *Fax:* (04) 98360864
Key Personnel
Contact: Chiara Finesso
Founded: 1987
Subjects: History, Literature, Literary Criticism, Essays, Philosophy, Psychology, Psychiatry, Regional Interests, Science (General)
ISBN Prefix(es): 88-7115

Il Pomerio
Via Della Costa N, 4, 26900 Lodi
Tel: (0371) 420381 *Fax:* (0371) 422080
Key Personnel
Contact: Andrea Schiavi
Founded: 1994
Subjects: Architecture & Interior Design, Art, History
ISBN Prefix(es): 88-7121

Pontificio Istituto di Archeologia Cristiana
Via Napoleone III 1, 00185 Rome
Tel: (06) 4465574; (06) 4453169 *Fax:* (06) 4469197
E-mail: piac@piac.it
Web Site: www.piac.it
Key Personnel
Rector: Prof Philippe Pergola
Library Dir: Dr Giorgio Nestori
Founded: 1925
Subjects: Archaeology, History, Religion - Other, Christianity-last Roman painting, sculpture, mosaics; epigraphy
ISBN Prefix(es): 88-85991
Imprints: PIAC

Pontifico Istituto Orientale
Piazza Santa Maria Maggiore 7, 00185 Rome
Tel: (06) 447417177; (06) 4474170 *Fax:* (06) 4465576
E-mail: informatica@pitagoragroup.it
Web Site: www.pio.urbe.it
Key Personnel
General Dir: Jaroslaw Dziewicki
  E-mail: jdziewi@tin.it
Founded: 1923
Subjects: Antiques, Archaeology, Asian Studies, Biblical Studies, Religion - Catholic, Religion - Other
ISBN Prefix(es): 88-7210

Neri Pozza Editore+
Contra Oratorio dei Servi, 21, 36100 Vicenza
Tel: (0444) 320787; (0444) 323036 *Fax:* (0444) 324613
Web Site: www.neripozza.it
Key Personnel
President: Silvio Fortune
Man Dir: Alexander Zelger
Founded: 1946
Subjects: Art, History, Literature, Literary Criticism, Essays
ISBN Prefix(es): 88-7305
Parent Company: Longanesi & C
Subsidiaries: Athesis, Longanesi, GdP

Edizioni Luigi Pozzi SRL+
Via Panama, 68, 00198 Rome
Tel: (06) 8553548 *Fax:* (06) 8554105
Key Personnel
Chief Executive: Luigi Pozzi
Editorial: Maurizio Pozzi
Founded: 1893
Subjects: Medicine, Nursing, Dentistry
ISBN Prefix(es): 88-7025
Number of titles published annually: 15 Print

Pratiche Editrice+
Via Melzo, 9, 20129 Milan
Tel: (02) 29403460 *Fax:* (02) 29513061
Key Personnel
Chief Executive: Vittorio Bo
Editorial, Production, Publicity, Rights & Permissions: Susanna Boschi
Founded: 1976
Subjects: Drama, Theater, History, Philosophy
ISBN Prefix(es): 88-7380

Primavera, see Giunti Gruppo Editoriale

Edizioni Primavera SRL+
Via Bolognese, 165, 50139 Florence
Tel: (055) 50621 *Fax:* (055) 5062298
E-mail: d.bascialfarei@giunti.it
Key Personnel
President: Bruno Piazzesi
Editor: Roberto Cappello
Founded: 1981
Subjects: Travel
ISBN Prefix(es): 88-09
Imprints: Edizioni Quadrifoglio
Orders to: Giunti Marzocco, Via V Gioberti 34, 50121 Florence

Principato+
Via Fauche 10, 20154 Milan
Tel: (02) 312025 *Fax:* (02) 33104295
E-mail: princi.red@comm2000.it
Key Personnel
Advisory Delegate: G Potesta
Publishing & Editorial Dir: Franco Menin
Founded: 1926
Subjects: Chemistry, Chemical Engineering, Earth Sciences, English as a Second Language, Geography, Geology, History, Literature, Literary Criticism, Essays, Mathematics, Physics
ISBN Prefix(es): 88-416

Prismi - Editrice Politecnica
Via Caracciolo, 13, 80122 Naples
Tel: (081) 7612884 *Fax:* (081) 668339
ISBN Prefix(es): 88-7065

Priuli e Verlucca, Editori+
Stradale Torino, 11, 10018 Pavone Canavese (Turin)
Tel: (0125) 23 99 29 *Fax:* (0125) 23 00 85
E-mail: info@priulieverlucca.it
Web Site: www.priulieverlucca.it
Key Personnel
Chairman: Gherardo Priuli
Founded: 1971
Subjects: Anthropology, Antiques, Art, Cookery, Environmental Studies, Ethnicity, Photography, Regional Interests, Travel
ISBN Prefix(es): 88-8068

Psicologica Editrice+
Viale delle Medaglie, d'Oro, 428, 00136 Rome
Tel: (06) 35453558 *Fax:* (06) 35341466
E-mail: ontonet@tin.it
Subjects: Art, Economics, Education, Philosophy, Psychology, Psychiatry, Science (General), Women's Studies, Ontopsychology
ISBN Prefix(es): 88-86766
Number of titles published annually: 5 Print
Total Titles: 60 Print

Il Punto D Incontro+
Via Zamenhof, 685, 36100 Vicenza
Tel: (0444) 239189 *Fax:* (0444) 239266
E-mail: ordini@edizionilpuntodincontro.it
Web Site: www.edizionilpuntodincontro.it
Key Personnel
International Rights: Christina Levi; Patrizia Saterini
Contact: Sergio Peterlini

Specialize in books intended to sustain life's deepest foundations.
Subjects: Alternative, Astrology, Occult, Health, Nutrition, Philosophy, Religion - Buddhist, Religion - Hindu, Self-Help
ISBN Prefix(es): 88-8093

PVH, *imprint of* Pizzicato Edizioni Musicali

Il Quadrante SRL
Via Morgioni, 48, 80077 Ischia (Na)
Tel: (081) 991433 *Fax:* (081) 981672
E-mail: info@ilquadrante.com
Web Site: www.ilquadrante.com
Key Personnel
Man Dir: Franco Di Costanzo
  E-mail: fdicostanzo@ilquadrante.com; Michele Lacono *E-mail:* miacono@ilquadrante.com
Sales: Grazia Angelini
Publicity: Marcella Longo
Rights & Permissions: Simonetta Violi
Founded: 1980
Subjects: Art, Biography, Fiction, Literature, Literary Criticism, Essays
ISBN Prefix(es): 88-381
Associate Companies: Edizioni Studio Tesi SRL
Subsidiaries: Mostre e Musei SRL

Edizioni Quadrifoglio, *imprint of* Edizioni Primavera SRL

Edizioni Quasar di Severino Tognon SRL+
Via Ajaccio 43, 00198 Rome
Tel: (06) 84241993; (06) 85358444 *Fax:* (06) 85833591
E-mail: qn@edizioniquasar.it
Web Site: www.edizioniquasar.it
Key Personnel
Contact: Stesso Indirizzo
Founded: 1972
Subjects: Archaeology, Art, History, Poetry, Travel
ISBN Prefix(es): 88-7097; 88-7140; 88-85086
Imprints: EQ
Bookshop(s): Libreria Archeologica Srl, Via Palermo 23, 00184 Rome *Tel:* (06) 4828504

Edizioni Quattroventi SNC+
Via Dini 16, 61029 Urbino PS
Tel: (0722) 2588 *Fax:* (0722) 320998
Key Personnel
Man Dir, Editorial: Anna Veronesi
Sales, Production: Giorgio Balestrieri
Founded: 1981
Subjects: Archaeology, Art, History, Literature, Literary Criticism, Essays, Philosophy, Sports, Athletics
ISBN Prefix(es): 88-392
Bookshop(s): Libreria La Goliardica, Piazza Rinascimento 7, 61029 Urbino PS

Editrice Queriniana+
Via Ferri, 75, 25123 Brescia
Tel: (030) 2306925 *Fax:* (030) 2306932
E-mail: direzione@queriniana.it; redazione@queriniana.it
Web Site: www.queriniana.it
Key Personnel
Man Dir: Rosino Gibellini
Sales & Advertising: Mario de Risio
Rights & Permissions: Giordana Maranesi
Founded: 1965
Subjects: Biblical Studies, Philosophy, Religion - Catholic, Religion - Other, Theology
ISBN Prefix(es): 88-399

Quesire SRL
Via Ovidio 20, 00192 Rome
Tel: (06) 68136068 *Fax:* (06) 68134167
E-mail: ristucciad@quesire.it
Web Site: www.ristucciaadvisors.com

Key Personnel
President: Sergio Ristuccia
ISBN Prefix(es): 88-391

Queste Istituzioni Ricerche, see Quesire SRL

Aldo Quinti, see Officina Edizioni di Aldo Quinti

Edition Raetia Srl-GmbH
23 Via Grappoli, 39100 Bolzano
Tel: (0471) 976904 *Fax:* (0471) 976908
E-mail: info@raetia.com
Subjects: Art, Government, Political Science, History, Humor, Photography, Regional Interests
ISBN Prefix(es): 88-7283

RAI-ERI+
Viale Mazzini 14, 00195 Rome
Tel: (06) 36864418 *Fax:* (06) 36822071
E-mail: rai-eri@rai.it
Web Site: www.eri.rai.it *Cable:* EDRAD TURIN 06/37513749
Key Personnel
Dir General: Dr Guiseppe Marchetti Tricamo *Fax:* (06) 36822072
Founded: 1949
Membership(s): AIE-FEIG.
Subjects: Art, Communications, Fiction, Film, Video, Journalism, Nonfiction (General), Radio, TV, Social Sciences, Sociology
ISBN Prefix(es): 88-397
Parent Company: RAI Radiotelevisione Italiana
Associate Companies: Raitrade, Via U Novaro 18, 00195 Rome; Sipra, Via Bertola 34, Turin; Telespazio, Via Alberto Bergamini 50, Rome

Edizioni RAI Radiotelevisione Italiano SpA, see RAI-ERI

Rara Istituto Editoriale di Bibliofilia e Reprints
Via Monti, 8, 20123 Milan
Tel: (02) 4983264 *Fax:* (02) 4814676
Founded: 1990
Subjects: Cookery, History, Literature, Literary Criticism, Essays, Medicine, Nursing, Dentistry, Technology
ISBN Prefix(es): 88-7270

RCS Libri SpA+
Via Mecenate 91, 20138 Milan
Tel: (02) 50951 *Fax:* (02) 5065361
Telex: 311321 Fabbri I *Cable:* LIBRIFABBRI MILAN
Key Personnel
Man Dir: Gianni Vallardi
International Dir of Coeditions: Massimo Rondinelli *Tel:* (02) 50952420 *Fax:* (02) 50952311 *E-mail:* massimo.rondinelli@rcs.it
Rights: Giovanna Canton *Tel:* (02) 50952288 *Fax:* (02) 50952288 *E-mail:* giovanna.canton@zcs.it
Founded: 1945
Other members of the group are Rizzoli, Bompiani, Fabbri, Sonzogno.
Subjects: Art, Business, Crafts, Games, Hobbies, History, Medicine, Nursing, Dentistry, Music, Dance, Outdoor Recreation, Science (General)
ISBN Prefix(es): 88-17; 88-451; 88-452; 88-318; 88-7811; 88-486
Parent Company: RCS Editori

RCS Rizzoli Libri SpA
Via Mecenate 91, 20138 Milan
Tel: (02) 50951 *Fax:* (02) 5065361
Telex: Rizzoli 333543 *Cable:* RCS EDITORI SPA, MILAN
Key Personnel
Chairman: Dr Giorgio Fattori
Dir General: Giovanni Ungarelli
Editorial: Rosaria Carpinelli; Evaldo Violo
Marketing: Bruno Appelius
Founded: 1909
Also literary agent.
Subjects: Art, Biography, Crafts, Games, Hobbies, Economics, Fiction, History, Medicine, Nursing, Dentistry, Music, Dance, Religion - Other, Social Sciences, Sociology
ISBN Prefix(es): 88-17; 88-451; 88-452; 88-318; 88-7811; 88-486
Associate Companies: Milano Libri; Sansoni Editore Nuova
Subsidiaries: Rizzoli International Publications
Bookshop(s): Libreria Rizzoli, Bologna, Milan, Rome, Torino

RE, *imprint of* Rugginenti Editore

Red Ezizioni, *imprint of* Red/Studio Redazionale

Red/Studio Redazionale+
Via Polidoro daCaravaggio, 37, 20156 Milan
Tel: (02) 30 241 311 *Fax:* (02) 30 241 333
Key Personnel
Chief Executive, Editorial: Maurizio Rosenberg Colorni
Manager Foreign Rights: Mrs Meriem Peillet
Founded: 1977
Subjects: Agriculture, Child Care & Development, Earth Sciences, Environmental Studies, Health, Nutrition, Medicine, Nursing, Dentistry, Psychology, Psychiatry, Technology
ISBN Prefix(es): 88-7031
Imprints: Red Ezizioni

Reverdito Edizioni+
Via G Catoni, 49, Mattarello, Trento TN 38060
Tel: (0461) 942285 *Fax:* (0461) 946563
E-mail: reverditoedizioni@virgilio.it
Web Site: www.culturitalia.uibk.ac.at
Key Personnel
Contact: Luigi Reverdito
Founded: 1990
Subjects: Cookery, Health, Nutrition, History, Literature, Literary Criticism, Essays, Parapsychology, Poetry, Religion - Catholic
ISBN Prefix(es): 88-7978
Number of titles published annually: 4 Print
Total Titles: 130 Print

Franco Maria Ricci Editore (FMR)
Via Montecuccoli 32, 20147 Milan
Tel: (02) 414101 *Fax:* (02) 48301473
E-mail: ricci@fmrmagazine.it
Web Site: www.fmrspa.it
Key Personnel
Publisher: Franco Maria Ricci
Contact: Pietro Ruffini *Tel:* (02) 41410354 *E-mail:* ruffini@frmmagazine.it
Founded: 1965
Subjects: Art
ISBN Prefix(es): 88-216
Number of titles published annually: 30 Print
Bookshop(s): Librerie Ricci
Book Club(s): Club dei Bibliofili; Collectors Club of Franco Maria Ricci

Riccardo Ricciardi Editore SpA
Via Biancamano, 2, 10121 Turin
Tel: (01) 156561
Key Personnel
President: Prof Gian Arturo Ferrari
Founded: 1907
Subjects: History, Language Arts, Linguistics, Literature, Literary Criticism, Essays, Philosophy, Poetry
ISBN Prefix(es): 88-7817
Parent Company: Arnoldo Mondadori Editore SpA
Distributed by Arnoldo Mondadori Editore SpA

Edizioni del Riccio SAS di G Bernardi+
Via Lungagnana 30, 50025 Montespertoli (Florence)
Tel: (0571) 609338 *Fax:* (055) 716362
Key Personnel
Chief Executive: Giuliano Bernardi
Founded: 1977
Subjects: Cookery, Medicine, Nursing, Dentistry, Psychology, Psychiatry, Travel
ISBN Prefix(es): 88-7099
Number of titles published annually: 8 Print

Edizioni Ripostes+
Via Lungomare Colombo, 225, 84129 Salerno
Tel: (089) 336049 *Fax:* (089) 336049
Key Personnel
Man Dir, Sales: Alessandro Tesauro
Editorial: Marco Amendolara; Serafina Bartoli; Elvira Spena
Founded: 1981
Subjects: Architecture & Interior Design, Art, History, Literature, Literary Criticism, Essays, Philosophy, Photography, Poetry, Psychology, Psychiatry
ISBN Prefix(es): 88-86819
Imprints: Alessandro Tesauro Editore
Branch Office(s)
Viale delle Tamerici 4, 84100 Salerno
Warehouse: Viale delle Tamerici, 4-89100 Salerno

RIREA, *imprint of* Rirea Casa Editrice della Rivista Italiana di Ragioneria e di Economia Aziendale

Rirea Casa Editrice della Rivista Italiana di Ragioneria e di Economia Aziendale+
Via delle Isole 30, 00198 Rome
Tel: (06) 8417690 *Fax:* (06) 8845732
E-mail: rirea_@infinito.it
Key Personnel
Dir: Dr Giovanna Nobile
Founded: 1901
Subjects: Accounting, Economics, Management
ISBN Prefix(es): 88-85333
Number of titles published annually: 20 Print
Imprints: RIREA

Editori Riuniti+
Via Alberico II, 33, 00193 Rome
Tel: (06) 6889951 *Fax:* (06) 6868696
Web Site: www.editoririuniti.it
Key Personnel
Man Dir: Motarianni Michelangelo
Sales Dir, Publicity: Claudio Capotosti
Rights & Permissions: Ombretta Borgia
Founded: 1953
Subjects: Art, Economics, Education, Fiction, Government, Political Science, History, Language Arts, Linguistics, Law, Literature, Literary Criticism, Essays, Philosophy, Psychology, Psychiatry, Science (General), Social Sciences, Sociology
ISBN Prefix(es): 88-359
Imprints: ER

Laurus Robuffo Edizioni
Via della Macchiarella 146, 00119 Rome
Tel: (06) 5651492 *Fax:* (06) 5651233
Key Personnel
Chief Executive: Mario Robuffo
Founded: 1973
Subjects: Law
ISBN Prefix(es): 88-8087
Associate Companies: Edizioni FAG Srl, Via Garibaldi 5, 20090 Assago MI; NDM SRL, Via E Toti, 69/be, 70125 Bari; Epidromo SRL, Via Selva di Pescarola 6/6, 40131 Bologna; Giampaolo Fornasiero, Via Guido Rossa 2, 60020 Candia AN; Tecnolibri srl, Via Pratesi 217, 50145 Florence; Libraria Ligure, Via Luigi Conepa, 11, 1, 16165 Geneva; Alfe snc, Via

Stefano Breda 24/26, 35010 Limena PD; DLC snc, Via Nazionale Delle Puglie 200/a 105, 80026 Napoli Arpino Casoria; Libraria Distribuzioni snc, Via Olbia 33, 08100 Nuoro; M M Distribuzione Libraria Di C Marinaci & C snc, 90145 Palermo; Distributrice; Libraria Laziales srl, Via di Tor Florence, 27 00199 Roma
Bookshop(s): Libreria Laurus Robuffo, Via S Martino delle Battaglia 35, 00185 Rome

Libreria Editrice Rogate (LER)+
Via dei Rogazionisti 8, 00182 Rome
Tel: (06) 7023430 *Fax:* (06) 7020767 *Cable:* ROGATE ROGAZIONISTI ROME
Key Personnel
Editorial: Vito Magno
Publicity: Nunzio Spinelli
Founded: 1976
Subjects: Religion - Other, Theology
ISBN Prefix(es): 88-8075

Edizioni Universitarie Romane
Via Michelangelo Poggioli 3, 00161 Rome
Tel: (06) 491503; (06) 4940658 *Fax:* (06) 4453438
E-mail: eur@eurom.it
Web Site: www.eurom.it
Key Personnel
Contact: Gian Vittorio Pallai
Founded: 1974
Subjects: Biological Sciences, Business, Chemistry, Chemical Engineering, Human Relations, Mathematics, Medicine, Nursing, Dentistry, Psychology, Psychiatry, Science (General), Social Sciences, Sociology
ISBN Prefix(es): 88-7730
Imprints: EUR

Rosenberg e Sellier Editori in Torino
Via Doria 14, 10123 Turin
Tel: (011) 8127820 *Fax:* (011) 8127808 *Cable:* ROSENBERG SELLIER
Key Personnel
Man Dir: Katie Roggero
Sales, Marketing: Teresa Silletti
Production: Ada Lanteri
Founded: 1883
Subjects: Language Arts, Linguistics, Philosophy, Social Sciences, Sociology, Women's Studies
ISBN Prefix(es): 88-7011
Associate Companies: Rosenberg e Sellier Libreria Pera Documentazione Scientifica

Rossato+
Via Bella Venezia, 13/C, 36074 Novale di Valdagno (Vicenza)
Tel: (0455) 411000 *Fax:* (0455) 411550
E-mail: grossato@didanet.it
Key Personnel
Contact: Gino Rossato; Vania Rossato
Membership(s): AIE.
Subjects: History, Military Science, Travel
ISBN Prefix(es): 88-8130

Rubbettino Editore+
Viale Rosario Rubbettino, 8, 88049 Soveria Mannelli (CZ)
Tel: (0968) 662034 *Fax:* (0968) 662035
E-mail: info@rubbettino.it
Web Site: www.rubbettino.it *Cable:* RUBBETTINO SOVERIA MANNELLI
Key Personnel
President: Florindo Rubbettino
Editorial Dir: Giacinto Marra
Editorial: Angela Cimino; Gabriella Grandinetti
Sales: Antonio Colosino
Founded: 1972
Subjects: Anthropology, Art, Drama, Theater, Economics, Government, Political Science, History, Law, Literature, Literary Criticism, Essays, Philosophy, Poetry, Public Administration, Religion - Other, Romance, Social Sciences, Sociology, Theology, Women's Studies
ISBN Prefix(es): 88-7284; 88-498
Parent Company: Rubbettino SRL
Associate Companies: Calabria Letteraria Editrice
E-mail: cle@rubbettino.it

Rugginenti Editore+
Via Dei Fontanili 3, 20141 Milan
Tel: (02) 89501283 *Fax:* (02) 89531273
E-mail: info@rugginenti.com
Web Site: www.rugginenti.com
Key Personnel
Editor: Gianni Rugginenti
Founded: 1968
Subjects: Music, Dance
ISBN Prefix(es): 88-7665
Total Titles: 40 Audio
Imprints: RE

Rusconi Libri Srl+
via del Progresso, 21, 47822 Santarcangelo di Romagna
Tel: (05) 41326306 *Fax:* (05) 41392344
E-mail: relazioniesterne@rusconi.it
Telex: 312233 *Cable:* RUSCONI EDITORE MILANO
Key Personnel
Editorial Dir: Alberto Conforti
Chief Editor: Pieranna Pagan
Sales: Marco Mattio
Foreign Rights: Olivia Olivieri
Founded: 1968
Subjects: Biography, History, Literature, Literary Criticism, Essays, Music, Dance, Nonfiction (General), Philosophy, Psychology, Psychiatry, Religion - Other
ISBN Prefix(es): 88-18
Parent Company: Rusconi Editore
Associate Companies: Eurolibri
U.S. Office(s): Rusconi Inc, 375 Park Ave, Suite 3307, New York, NY 10152, United States
Warehouse: Via Pacinotti, 16-20092 Cinisello Balsamo
Orders to: Eurolibri

Norberto Sabatelli & C, see Editrice Liguria SNC di Norberto Sabatelli & C

SAGEP Libri & Comunicazione Srl
Galleria Mazzini 1/8, 16121 Genoa
Tel: (010) 593355 *Fax:* (010) 581713
E-mail: info@sagep.it
Web Site: www.sagep.it
Telex: 281343 SAGEP I
Key Personnel
Publisher: Eugenio de Andreis
Sales Manager: Carla Bisacchi
Founded: 1965
Subjects: Architecture & Interior Design, Art, Economics, Ethnicity, History, Science (General), Travel
ISBN Prefix(es): 88-7058

Il Saggiatore+
Via Melzo 9, 20129 Milan
Tel: (02) 202301 *Fax:* (02) 29513061
E-mail: stampa@saggiatore.it
Web Site: www.saggiatore.it
Key Personnel
President: Luca Formenton
Editorial Dir: Marco Tropea
Founded: 1958
Subjects: Anthropology, Art, Asian Studies, Fiction, History, Literature, Literary Criticism, Essays, Music, Dance, Nonfiction (General), Philosophy, Poetry, Romance, Science (General), Social Sciences, Sociology
ISBN Prefix(es): 88-428; 88-515
Associate Companies: Marco Tropea Editore; Nuova Practiche Editrice

SAIE Editrice SRL
Subsidiary of Edizioni San Paolo SRL
Corso Regina Margherita 2, 10153 Turin
Tel: (011) 871022 *Fax:* (011) 830826
Web Site: www.culturitalia.uibk.ac.at
Key Personnel
Publicity: Fedele Molino
Founded: 1954
Subjects: Art, Earth Sciences, Economics, Education, Film, Video, Language Arts, Linguistics, Literature, Literary Criticism, Essays, Medicine, Nursing, Dentistry, Philosophy, Radio, TV, Religion - Other
Associate Companies: Edizioni Paoline SRL

Adriano Salani Editore srl+
Corso Italia, 13, 20122 Milan
Tel: (028) 0206624 *Fax:* (027) 2018806
E-mail: info@salani.it
Telex: 353273 LONG I
Key Personnel
President: Mario Spagnol
Man Dir: Luigi Spagnol
General Manager: Stefano Maure
Editorial: Maria Grazia Mazzitelli
Sales: Giuseppe Somenzi
Production: Alfredo Bonfiglio
Publicity: Allessandra Gnecchi
Rights & Permissions: Cristina Foschini
Founded: 1862
Subjects: Fiction
ISBN Prefix(es): 88-7782; 88-8451
Parent Company: Longanesi & C
Subsidiaries: Messaggerie Italiane
U.S. Office(s): Nina Collins Association, 584 Broadway, Suite 607, New York 10012, United States
Warehouse: Messaggerie Italiane, Magazzino Editoriale, Via Bereguardina, 20080 Casarile (Mi)
Orders to: Pro Libro, Florence

Salerno Editrice SRL+
Via Valadier 52, 00193 Rome
Tel: (06) 3608201 *Fax:* (06) 3223132
E-mail: info@salernoeditrice.it
Web Site: www.salernoeditrice.it
Key Personnel
Chief Executive: Prof Enrico Malato
Founded: 1972
Subjects: Biography, Fiction, History, Language Arts, Linguistics, Literature, Literary Criticism, Essays, Social Sciences, Sociology, Italian Literature & Historic Studies
ISBN Prefix(es): 88-85026; 88-8402
Number of titles published annually: 40 Print
Warehouse: Viale dei Colli Portuensi, 591, Rome 00151 *Tel:* (06) 55266684

Samaya SRL
Localita Lu Cupuneddu, 07028 Teresa di Gallura (Sassari)
Tel: (0789) 750039 *Fax:* (0789) 750081
E-mail: info@benesseresardegna.com
Key Personnel
President: Milvia Pagan
Founded: 1980
Subjects: Child Care & Development, Health, Nutrition
ISBN Prefix(es): 88-85302

Editoriale San Giusto SRL Edizioni Parnaso
Via Coroneo 5, 34133 Trieste
Tel: (040) 370200 *Fax:* (040) 3728970
E-mail: info@edizioniparnaso.it
Web Site: www.edizioniparnaso.it
Subjects: Literature, Literary Criticism, Essays, Philosophy
ISBN Prefix(es): 88-86474
Number of titles published annually: 10 Print
Total Titles: 90 Print

Edizioni San Lorenzo
Via Gandhi 24, 42100 Reggio Emilia
Tel: (0522) 323140 *Fax:* (0522) 323140
E-mail: redazione@edizioni-sanlorenzo.it
Web Site: www.edizioni-sanlorenzo.it
Founded: 1985
ISBN Prefix(es): 88-8071

Editrice San Marco SRL+
Via Abbadia 13, 24069 Trescore Balneario (Bergamo)
Tel: (035) 940178 *Fax:* (035) 944385
E-mail: info@editricesanmarco.it
Web Site: www.editricesanmarco.it
Key Personnel
Man Dir: Giulio Belotti
Founded: 1955
Subjects: Agriculture, Biological Sciences, Education, Energy, Government, Political Science, Labor, Industrial Relations, Marketing, Technology
ISBN Prefix(es): 88-86285

Edizioni San Paolo SRL+
Piazza Soncino 5, 20092 Cinisello Balsamo (Milan)
Tel: (02) 660751 *Fax:* (02) 66075211
E-mail: sanpaoloedizioni@stpauls.it
Key Personnel
Man Dir: Emilio Bettati
General Manager: Vincenzo Santarcangelo
Editorial: Elio Sala
Production: Angelo Zenzalari
Founded: 1914
Subjects: Art, Biography, Fiction, History, How-to, Medicine, Nursing, Dentistry, Music, Dance, Philosophy, Psychology, Psychiatry, Religion - Other
ISBN Prefix(es): 88-215
Parent Company: Societa San Paolo, Rome
Subsidiaries: DISP SRL; Multimedia San Paolo SRL; Periodici San Paolo SRL; SAIE Editrice SRL
Warehouse: DISP SRL, Piazza San Paolo 14, I-12051 Alba *Tel:* (0173) 361040 (Cuneo)

Sansoni-RCS Libri+
Division of RCS Libri Spa
Via Mecenate, 91, 20138 Milan
Tel: (02) 50951 *Fax:* (02) 5065361
E-mail: sansoni@rcs.it
Founded: 1873
Subjects: Fiction
ISBN Prefix(es): 88-383
Associate Companies: RCS Rizzoli Libri SpA
Warehouse: RCS Libri Spa, Via Mecanate 91, 20138 Milan

Sapere 2000 SRL
Piazza Fanti 42, 00185 Rome
Tel: (06) 4465363 *Fax:* (06) 4465363
E-mail: sapere2000@flshnet.it
Key Personnel
Man Dir: Angelo Ruggieri
Founded: 1976
Subjects: Architecture & Interior Design, Ethnicity, Government, Political Science, Religion - Other, Social Sciences, Sociology
ISBN Prefix(es): 88-7673

Sardini Editrice+
Via della Pace 37, 25046 Bornato in Franciacorta (BS)
Tel: (030) 7750430 *Fax:* (030) 7254348
E-mail: sardini@intelligenza.it
Web Site: www.sardini.it *Cable:* Fausto Sardini-Editore-Bornato
Key Personnel
Chief Executive: Fausto Sardini
Editorial: Davide Sardini
Founded: 1969

Subjects: Art, Fiction, History, Poetry, Regional Interests, Religion - Catholic, Science (General), Theology
ISBN Prefix(es): 88-7506
Subsidiaries: Intelligenza e Informatica SRL
Divisions: Informatica

Scala Group spa
Via Chiantigiana 62, 50011 Antella, Florence
Tel: (055) 623311 *Fax:* (055) 6233280
E-mail: info@scalagroup.com
Web Site: scalagroup.it
Key Personnel
President: Dr Alberto Milla
Vice President & Chief Executive Officer: Alvise Passigli *E-mail:* a.passigli@scalagroup.com
Man Dir: Gianni Mancassola
Founded: 1953
Also book packager & broadband files.
Subjects: Archaeology, Art, Education, Film, Video, Photography, Travel, Museums & Art Guides
ISBN Prefix(es): 88-8117; 88-87090
Number of titles published annually: 10 Print; 20 CD-ROM; 5 Online
Total Titles: 100 Print; 200 CD-ROM
Subsidiaries: E-ducation.it
Distributed by Hazan (Francophone countries); Riverside (US & Canada); Slovo (Russia)

Lo Scarabeo Srl+
Via Varese 15C, 10152 Turin
Tel: (011) 283793; (011) 283978 *Fax:* (011) 280756
E-mail: info@loscarabeo.com
Web Site: www.loscarabeo.com
Key Personnel
President: Pietro Alligo
Founded: 1987
Subjects: Art
ISBN Prefix(es): 88-86131

Schena Editore+
Viale Stazione 177, 72015 Fasano (Brindisi)
Tel: (080) 4414681 *Fax:* (080) 4426690
E-mail: info@schenaeditore.com
Web Site: www.schenaeditore.it
Key Personnel
Editor: Nunzio Schena
Founded: 1972
Subjects: Archaeology, Architecture & Interior Design, Art, Language Arts, Linguistics, Literature, Literary Criticism, Essays
ISBN Prefix(es): 88-7514; 88-8229

Salvatore Sciascia Editore
Corso Umberto I°, 111, 93100 Caltanissetta
Tel: (0934) 551509 *Fax:* (0934) 551366
Cable: SCIASCIA EDITORE
Key Personnel
Man Dir: Quiseppe Sciascia
Editor: Salvatore Sciascia
Founded: 1946
Subjects: Art, History, Literature, Literary Criticism, Essays, Poetry
ISBN Prefix(es): 88-8241
Warehouse: Via Pietro Leone SN, 93100 Caltanissetta

Libreria Scientifica Cortina, see Libreria Cortina Editrice SRL

Edizioni Scientifiche Italiane+
Via Chiatamone 7, 80121 Naples
Tel: (081) 7645443 *Fax:* (081) 7646477
E-mail: info@esispa.com
Key Personnel
President: Pietro Perlingieri
Administration: Francesco De Simone
Editorial Dir: Giovanna Delfino
Founded: 1945

Subjects: Architecture & Interior Design, Art, Cookery, Drama, Theater, Economics, Geography, Geology, History, Law, Literature, Literary Criticism, Essays, Medicine, Nursing, Dentistry, Music, Dance, Philosophy, Psychology, Psychiatry, Science (General), Social Sciences, Sociology, Technology
ISBN Prefix(es): 88-7104; 88-8114; 88-495
Branch Office(s)
Via Porta Rettori, 19, 82100 Benevento *Tel:* (0824) 43752 *Fax:* (0824) 43666
Via F lli Bronzetti, 11, 20129 Milan *Tel:* (02) 730846 *Fax:* (02) 730849
Via dei Taurini, 27, 00185 Rome *Tel:* (06) 4462664 *Fax:* (06) 4461308

Editoriale Scienza (Science Publishing)+
Via Romagna 30, 34134 Trieste
Tel: (040) 364810 *Fax:* (040) 364909
E-mail: info@editscienza.it
Web Site: www.editscienza.it
Founded: 1990
Specialize in science books for children.
Membership(s): Associazione Aie.
Subjects: Animals, Pets, Astronomy, Biological Sciences, Computer Science, Crafts, Games, Hobbies, Earth Sciences, Geography, Geology, Health, Nutrition, Mathematics, Nonfiction (General), Physical Sciences, Science (General), Science Fiction, Fantasy, Technology
ISBN Prefix(es): 88-7307
Number of titles published annually: 20 Print
Imprints: ES
Distributed by Messaggerie Libri

Casa Editrice Marietti Scuola SpA
Str del Portone 179, 10095 Grugliasco, Turin
Tel: (011) 2098741; (011) 2098720 *Fax:* (011) 2098765
E-mail: redazione@mariettiscuola.it
Web Site: www.mariettiscuola.it
Key Personnel
Man Dir: Dr Federico Franchi
ISBN Prefix(es): 88-393

Editrice la Scuola SpA+
Via L Cadorna, 11, 25186 Brescia
Tel: (030) 29931 *Fax:* (030) 2993299
Web Site: www.lascuola.it *Cable:* SCUOLA BRESCIA
Key Personnel
President: Dr Ing Luciano Silveri
Man Dir: Dr Ing Adolfo Lombardi
General Manager: Giuseppe Covone
Founded: 1904
Subjects: Education, Philosophy, Psychology, Psychiatry, Religion - Other
ISBN Prefix(es): 88-350
Associate Companies: Editrice Morcelliana SpA
Branch Office(s)
Bari
Bologna
Milan
Naples
Padua
Pescara
Rome

SEA, *imprint of* Ist Patristico Augustinianum

Edizioni Segno SRL+
Via E Fermi, 80, 33010 Tavagnacco Udine
Tel: (0432) 575179 *Fax:* (0432) 575589
E-mail: info@edizionisegno.it
Web Site: www.edizionisegno.it
Key Personnel
Dir: Pietro Mantero *E-mail:* collaboratori@edizionisegno.it
Founded: 1988
Subjects: Biblical Studies, Fiction, Mysteries, Nonfiction (General), Poetry, Religion - Catholic, Theology, Private Revelations, Signs

of the Times Based on a Catholic Background, Supernatural
ISBN Prefix(es): 88-7282
Number of titles published annually: 70 Print; 1 Audio
Total Titles: 400 Print; 1 Audio

Segretariato Nazionale Apostolato della Preghiera+
Via degli Astalli 16, 00186 Rome
Tel: (06) 6976071 *Fax:* (06) 6781063
E-mail: adp@adp.it
Web Site: www.adp.it
Key Personnel
Administrative Dir: Massimo Taggi *Tel:* (06) 697607 Ext 202 *E-mail:* mt@adp.it
Founded: 1844
Subjects: Religion - Catholic
ISBN Prefix(es): 88-7357
Imprints: AdP

SEI - Societa Editrice Internazionale, see Societa Editrice Internazionale - SEI

Sellerio Editore
Via Siracusa, 50/2, 90141 Palermo
Tel: (091) 6259475 *Fax:* (091) 6258802
Founded: 1969
Subjects: Anthropology, Archaeology, Art, History, Literature, Literary Criticism, Essays, Photography, Social Sciences, Sociology
ISBN Prefix(es): 88-7681

SEMAR Publishers SRL+
Via Arco Di Parma, 18, 00186 Rome
Tel: (06) 6876523; (06) 6879333 *Fax:* (06) 68308601
E-mail: info@semarweb.com
Web Site: www.semarweb.com *Cable:* SEMAR
Key Personnel
President: Luciano Sahlan Momo
  E-mail: momo@semarweb.com
Founded: 1986
Specialize in editions with conservation criteria.
Subjects: Anthropology, Archaeology, Art, Asian Studies, Drama, Theater, Environmental Studies, Literature, Literary Criticism, Essays, Music, Dance, Philosophy, Photography, Poetry, Religion - Islamic, Theology
ISBN Prefix(es): 88-7778
Number of titles published annually: 15 Print; 2 CD-ROM; 5 E-Book; 5 Audio
Total Titles: 194 Print; 8 CD-ROM; 194 Online; 13 Audio
Imprints: SPANDA
Branch Office(s)
Nachtegaallaan, 1, 2566 JJ The Hague, Netherlands *Tel:* (070) 345 90 38; (070) 356 04 03 *Fax:* (070) 360 24 71
Distributed by Diest
Distribution Center: Nachtegaallaan, 1, 2566 JJ The Hague, Netherlands
Orders to: Nachtegaallaan, 1, 2566 JJ The Hague, Netherlands

Servitium
Priorato S Egidio, 24039 Sotto il Monte (Bergamo)
Tel: (035) 4398011 *Fax:* (035) 792030
E-mail: servitium@spm.it
Subjects: Anthropology, Religion - Catholic, Romance, Theology, Spiritual
ISBN Prefix(es): 88-8166
Distributed by Dehoniana Libri SpA (Italy only)

Servizio Italiano Pubblicazioni Internazionali Srl, see SIPI (Servizio Italiano Pubblicazioni Internazionali) Srl

Edizioni Dr Antonino Sfameni, see EDAS

Sicania+
Via Catania 62, 98124 Messina
Tel: (090) 2936373 *Fax:* (090) 2932461
Key Personnel
Publisher: Ugo Magno
Editorial Dir: Gianvito Resta
Editor: Giovanni Molonia
Public Relations: Caterina Pastura
Founded: 1986
Subjects: Art, Drama, Theater, History, Language Arts, Linguistics, Literature, Literary Criticism, Essays, Philosophy, Photography, Regional Interests
ISBN Prefix(es): 88-7268
Subsidiaries: Edizioni GBM

Edizioni Librarie Siciliane+
Via da Portella Rebuttone, 90030 Santa Cristina Gela, Palermo
Tel: (091) 8570221 *Fax:* (091) 342670
Key Personnel
Dir General: Gaetano Mantovani
Founded: 1978
Subjects: Anthropology, Antiques, Archaeology, Architecture & Interior Design, Art, History, Human Relations, Natural History, Philosophy
Imprints: ELS

Sigma, *imprint of* Esselibri

Silva
Via Nazionale, 23, 43044 Collecchio (Parma)
Tel: (0521) 804106 *Fax:* (0521) 804406
ISBN Prefix(es): 88-7765

Silvana Editoriale SpA+
Via Margherita de Vizzi 86, 20092 Cinisello Balsamo Milan
Tel: (02) 618361 *Fax:* (02) 6172464
E-mail: international@silvanaeditoriale.it
Web Site: www.silvanaeditoriale.it
Telex: 330006 Ampiz I
Key Personnel
Chief Executive: Massimo Pizzi
Founded: 1953
Subjects: Architecture & Interior Design, Art, Photography
ISBN Prefix(es): 88-366; 88-8215
Parent Company: Amilcare Pizzi SpA
Associate Companies: American Pizzi Offset Co, 141 E 44 St, New York, NY 10017, United States

Edizioni Giuridiche Simone, *imprint of* Esselibri

Simone per la Scuola, *imprint of* Esselibri

SIPI, *imprint of* SIPI (Servizio Italiano Pubblicazioni Internazionali) Srl

SIPI (Servizio Italiano Pubblicazioni Internazionali) Srl
Viale Pasteur 6, 00144 Rome
Tel: (06) 5920509 *Fax:* (06) 5924819
Founded: 1951
Subjects: Economics, Government, Political Science, Labor, Industrial Relations, Regional Interests
ISBN Prefix(es): 88-7153
Imprints: SIPI

Sistemi Editorali, *imprint of* Esselibri

Societa Editrice Internazionale - SEI+
Corso Regina Margherita 176, 10152 Turin
Tel: (011) 52271 *Fax:* (011) 5211320
Telex: 216216 SEI TO I *Cable:* SEI TORINO
Key Personnel
President: Alessandro Braja
Man Dir & General Manger: Gian Nicola Pivano
Dir, Editorial Management, Marketing & Public Relations: Alessandro Rangaioli
Founded: 1908
Subjects: Education, Geography, Geology, History, Literature, Literary Criticism, Essays, Mathematics, Philosophy, Physics, Psychology, Psychiatry, Religion - Catholic
ISBN Prefix(es): 88-05

Societa Editrice la Goliardica Pavese SRL+
Viale Golgi, 6, 27100 Pavia
Tel: (0382) 529570 *Fax:* (0382) 423140
Key Personnel
Chief Executive: Dario De Bona
Founded: 1977
Subjects: Biological Sciences, Chemistry, Chemical Engineering, Medicine, Nursing, Dentistry, Physical Sciences, Physics, Science (General)
ISBN Prefix(es): 88-7830
Branch Office(s)
Via Lombroso 21, Pavia *Tel:* (0382) 525709
Bookshop(s): Via Lombroso u 21, 27100 Pavia

Societa Napoletana Storia Patria Napoli
Via Marina 33, 80133 Naples
Tel: (081) 2536340 *Fax:* (081) 2536509
E-mail: snsp@unina.it
Web Site: www.storia.unina.it
Key Personnel
Dir: Prof Giovanni Muto
Subjects: History, Monographies, diplomatics & history of art
ISBN Prefix(es): 88-8044

Societa Stampa Sportiva+
Via Guinizelli 56, 00152 Rome
Tel: (06) 5817311 *Fax:* (06) 5806526
E-mail: segreteria@stampasportiva.com
Web Site: www.stampasportiva.com
Key Personnel
President: Francesco Paolo Palumbo
Founded: 1967
Subjects: Physical Sciences, Sports, Athletics
ISBN Prefix(es): 88-8313
Number of titles published annually: 20 Print
Total Titles: 532 Print
Warehouse: Via Di Villa Pamphili 33/F, 00152 Rome

Societa Storica Catanese
Via Etnea 248, 95131 Catania
Tel: (095) 434782
Key Personnel
Man Dir: Dr Michele D'Agata
Editorial: Giuseppe Trovato Pennisi
Sales: Francesco Romeo Giuzzetta
Production: Giovanni Assaro
Publicity: Dr Davide D'Agata
Rights & Permissions: Prof Rita Siciliano
Founded: 1955
Subjects: History, Law, Literature, Literary Criticism, Essays, Poetry, Regional Interests, Social Sciences, Sociology
Imprints: SSC

Edizioni Rosminiane Sodalitas
Corso Umberto I, 15, 28838 Stresa (Verbania)
Tel: (0323) 30091 *Fax:* (0323) 31623
E-mail: edizioni@rosmini.it
Web Site: www.rosmini.it/EdRosminiane.htm
Key Personnel
Publicity: Muratore Umberto
Founded: 1906
Subjects: Philosophy, Theology

Il Sole 24 Ore Libri
Via Lomazzo 51, 20154 Milan
Tel: (02) 30223944 *Fax:* (02) 3022405
E-mail: servizioclienti.libri@ilsole24ore.com
Web Site: www.ilsole24ore.com

Telex: 331325 I 24 Ore
Key Personnel
Dir General: Gianni Rizzoni
Editorial: Francesco Bogliari
Founded: 1983
Subjects: Economics, Law, Management
ISBN Prefix(es): 88-7187; 88-8363

Il Sole 24 Ore Pirola
Via Castellanza, 11, 20151 Milan
Tel: (02) 30226651 *Fax:* (02) 38011205
E-mail: servizio.abbonamenti@ilsole24ore.com
Web Site: www.ilsole24ore.com
Founded: 1781
Subjects: Architecture & Interior Design, Business, Economics, Engineering (General), Law, Management, Social Sciences, Sociology
ISBN Prefix(es): 88-324

Soleverde, *imprint of* Centro Scientifico Torinese

Edizioni Sonda+
Corso Indipendenza, 63, 15033 Casale Monferrato (Al)
Tel: (0142) 461516 *Fax:* (0142) 461523
E-mail: sonda@sonda.it
Web Site: www.sonda.it
Key Personnel
Contact: Antonio Monaco
Founded: 1988
ISBN Prefix(es): 88-7106
Associate Companies: Consorzio "Leonardo"; Consorzio "Omniatech"; Il Tappeto Volante srl

Sonzogno
Via Mecenate 91, 20138 Milan
Tel: (02) 50951 *Fax:* (02) 5065361
Telex: 311321 Fabbri I *Cable:* Librifabbri Milan
Key Personnel
Dir: Mario Andreose
Rights & Permissions: Carla Tanzi
Founded: 1818
Membership(s): Gruppo Editoriale Fabbri, Bompiani, Sonzogno, Etas SpA.
Subjects: Fiction, Mysteries, Nonfiction (General)
ISBN Prefix(es): 88-451; 88-452; 88-454

Sorbona+
Via Pietravalle, 85, 80131 Naples
Tel: (08) 15453443 *Fax:* (08) 15464991
Key Personnel
Contact: Dr F Bonadei
Founded: 1981
Subjects: Chemistry, Chemical Engineering, Medicine, Nursing, Dentistry, Physics, Science (General)
ISBN Prefix(es): 88-7150

SPANDA, *imprint of* SEMAR Publishers SRL

Sperling e Kupfer Editori SpA+
Via Durazzo, 4, 20134 Milan
Tel: (02) 217211 *Fax:* (02) 21721277
Web Site: www.sperling.it
Key Personnel
Chief Executive Officer: Roberto Avanzo
President: Valerio Anna Patrizia
Editorial Dir: Carla Tanzi
Rights & Permissions & Contract: Stefania Klein De Pasquale *E-mail:* sdepas@mondadori.it
Scout (US): Linda Clark
Scout (France): Zeline Guena
Scout (UK): Ros Ramsay
Founded: 1899
Subjects: Biography, Economics, Fiction, Health, Nutrition, How-to, Management, Nonfiction (General), Science (General), Sports, Athletics, Travel
ISBN Prefix(es): 88-200; 88-86845; 88-87592; 88-7339
Parent Company: Mondadori

Subsidiaries: Edizioni Frassinelli SRL
U.S. Office(s): 28 E 57 St, 7th Floor, New York, NY 10022, United States (scout office)

Spirali Edizioni+
Via Fratelli Gabba 3, 20121 Milan
Tel: (02) 8054417; (02) 8053602 *Fax:* (02) 8692631
E-mail: redazione@spirali.com
Web Site: www.spirali.it; www.spirali.com
Key Personnel
President: Armando Verdiglione
Man Dir: Cristina Frua De Angeli
Editorial: Annalisa Scallo
Founded: 1978
Subjects: Art, Law, Literature, Literary Criticism, Essays, Music, Dance, Philosophy, Poetry, Psychology, Psychiatry
ISBN Prefix(es): 88-7770
Number of titles published annually: 10 Print

SSC, *imprint of* Societa Storica Catanese

Stampa Alternativa - Nuovi Equilibri+
Strada Tuscanese Km 4, 800, 01100 Viterbo
Tel: (0761) 352277; (0761) 353485 *Fax:* (0761) 352751
E-mail: nuovi.equilibri@agora.it
Web Site: www.stampalternativa.it
Key Personnel
Man Dir, Editorial: Marcello Baraghini
Sales: Angelo Leone
Founded: 1971
Subjects: Art, Health, Nutrition, Literature, Literary Criticism, Essays, Medicine, Nursing, Dentistry, Music, Dance
ISBN Prefix(es): 88-7226
Imprints: Cartoonseries; Fiabesca; Jazz People; L'eta D'oro Dell Illustrazione
Orders to: Nuovi Equilibri, PO Box 97, 01100 Viterbo *Tel:* (0761) 352277 *Fax:* (0761) 352751

Edizoni Le Stelle, *imprint of* Le Stelle Scuola

Le Stelle Scuola
Via Vasari 15, 20135 Milan
Tel: (02) 55181460 *Fax:* (02) 5400017
Founded: 1954
Subjects: Education, Fiction, Geography, Geology, History, Music, Dance, Religion - Other, Science (General)
Imprints: Dimensione Umana; Linea Verde; Edizoni Le Stelle

Istituto Storico Italiano per l'Eta Moderna e Contemporanea
Via Caetani 32, 00186 Rome
Tel: (06) 68806922 *Fax:* (06) 6875127
E-mail: iststor@libero.it
Key Personnel
Man Dir: Prof Luigi Lotti
Editorial: Dr Marina Maura
Founded: 1934
Subjects: History

Studio Bibliografico Adelmo Polla+
Via Prato 2, 67044 Cerchio
Tel: (0863) 78522 *Fax:* (0863) 78522
Key Personnel
Man Dir: Adelmo Polla
Editorial: Maria G Romanelli
Founded: 1974
Subjects: Archaeology, History, Language Arts, Linguistics, Literature, Literary Criticism, Essays, Travel

Studio Editoriale Programma
Via S Eufemia, 5, 35121 Padova
Tel: (049) 8753110 *Fax:* (049) 8755870
Founded: 1981

Subjects: Art, History, Literature, Literary Criticism, Essays, Travel
ISBN Prefix(es): 88-7123

Edizioni Studio Tesi SRL
Subsidiary of Edizioni Mediterranee SRL
Via Flaminia, 109, 00196 Rome
Tel: (06) 3235433 *Fax:* (06) 3236277
E-mail: info@ediz-mediterranee.com
Web Site: www.ediz-mediterranee.com *Cable:* EST
Key Personnel
Chief Executive & Editorial: Giovanni Canonico
Founded: 1977
Subjects: Economics, Fiction, History, Literature, Literary Criticism, Essays, Music, Dance, Science (General)
ISBN Prefix(es): 88-7692
Subsidiaries: Edizioni dello Zibaldone

Edizioni Studium SRL+
Via Cassiodoro 14, 00193 Rome
Tel: (06) 68 65 846 *Fax:* (06) 68 75 456
E-mail: edizionistudium@libero.it *Cable:* STUDIUM ROME
Founded: 1927
Periodicals.
Subjects: History, Literature, Literary Criticism, Essays, Philosophy, Religion - Other, Science (General), Social Sciences, Sociology
ISBN Prefix(es): 88-382
Number of titles published annually: 30 Print
Total Titles: 600 Print
Associate Companies: Editrice La Scuola SpA
Distributed by Editrice Le Seulo - Buscie

Sugarco Edizioni SRL
Via Gnocchi 4, 20148 Milan
Tel: (02) 4078370 *Fax:* (02) 4078493
Key Personnel
Man Dir: Dr Oliviero Cigada
Founded: 1956
Subjects: Biography, Fiction, History, How-to, Philosophy
ISBN Prefix(es): 88-7198

ME/DI Sviluppo, see Giunti Gruppo Editoriale

Tappeiner
Zona Industriale, 6, 39011 Lana d'Adige (Bolzano)
Tel: (0473) 563666 *Fax:* (0473) 563689
E-mail: tappeiner@pass.dnet.it
Subjects: Archaeology, Architecture & Interior Design, Art, Cookery, Geography, Geology, History, Outdoor Recreation
ISBN Prefix(es): 88-7073

La Tartaruga Edizioni SAS
Via Crocefisso 21, 20122 Milan
Tel: (02) 584501 *Fax:* (02) 58307512
Founded: 1975
Subjects: Cookery, Drama, Theater, Literature, Literary Criticism, Essays, Women's Studies
ISBN Prefix(es): 88-7738; 88-85678

Tassotti Editore
Via San F Lazzaro 103, 36061 Bassano del Grappa (Vicenza)
Tel: (0424) 566105 *Fax:* (0424) 566205
E-mail: info@tassotti.it
Web Site: www.tassotti.it
Founded: 1984
Subjects: Art, History, Travel
ISBN Prefix(es): 88-7691
Divisions: Grafiche Tassotti SRL

TEA Tascabili degli Editori Associati SpA+
Corso Italia 13, 20122 Milan
Tel: (02) 80206625 *Fax:* (02) 8900844
Web Site: www.tealibri.it

Key Personnel
President: Stefano Mauri
Man Dir: Marco Taro
Editorial Dir: Stefano Res *E-mail:* stefano.res@tealibri.it
Sales: Giuseppe Somenzi
Production: Alfredo Bonfiglio
Publicity: Elena Cristiano; Valentina Fortichiari
Rights & Permissions: Sabine Schultz
Founded: 1987
Subjects: Art, Cookery, Fiction, Health, Nutrition, History, How-to, Humor, Nonfiction (General), Philosophy, Poetry, Psychology, Psychiatry, Science Fiction, Fantasy, Self-Help
ISBN Prefix(es): 88-7818; 88-502; 88-7819
Number of titles published annually: 180 Print
Total Titles: 1,500 Print
Subsidiaries: Longanesi

Tecniche Nuove SpA+
Via Eritrea, 21, 20157 Milan
Tel: (02) 390901 *Fax:* (02) 7610351
E-mail: info@tecnichenuove.com; vendite-libri@tecnichenuove.com
Web Site: www.tecnichenuove.com
Key Personnel
Man Dir: Giuseppe Nardella
Editorial: E Guaglione
Publicity: S Savona
Founded: 1960
Subjects: Business, Computer Science, Electronics, Electrical Engineering, Energy, Health, Nutrition, Technology
ISBN Prefix(es): 88-7081; 88-85009; 88-481
Number of titles published annually: 150 Print; 15 CD-ROM; 20 E-Book
Total Titles: 700 Print; 30 CD-ROM; 30 E-Book
Subsidiaries: Grafica Quadrifoglio
U.S. Office(s): Tecniche Nuove USA, 844 Gage Drive, San Diego, CA 92106, United States
Warehouse: Via Castel Morrone 15

Tema Celeste
10 Piazza Borromeo, 20123 Milan
Tel: (02) 8065171; (02) 80651732 (subscriptions) *Fax:* (02) 80651743
E-mail: editorial@temaceleste.com; subscriptions@temaceleste.com
Web Site: www.gabrius.com/default_tc.htm
Key Personnel
Publisher: Alberico Cetti Serbelloni
Editor: Simona Vendrame *E-mail:* vendrame@temaceleste.com
Man Editor: Daniele Perra *E-mail:* perra@temaceleste.com
Advertising: Roberta Pollio *E-mail:* ad@temaceleste.com
Founded: 1983
Subjects: Art
ISBN Prefix(es): 88-85265; 88-7304

Edizioni del Teresianum
Piazza San Pancrazio 5/A, 00152 Rome
Tel: (06) 585401 *Fax:* (06) 58540300
Key Personnel
Chief Executive: Cumer Dario
Sales, Publicity: Piergiorgio Mantovani
Founded: 1966
Subjects: Biblical Studies, Biography, History, Religion - Catholic, Theology
ISBN Prefix(es): 88-85317
Parent Company: Edizioni dei Padri Carmelitani Scalzi, Corso d'Italia 38, 00198 Rome

Nicola Teti e C Editore SRL
Via Rezia, 4, 20135 Milan
Tel: (02) 55015584 *Fax:* (02) 55015595
E-mail: teti@teti.it
Web Site: www.teti.it
Key Personnel
Man Dir: Nicola Teti
Editorial: Piero Lavatelli

Sales: Vincenzo Fracchiolla
Rights & Permissions & Production: Rita Vaccari
Production: Vanna Guzzi
Publicity: Nino Oppo
Founded: 1971
Subjects: Education, Government, Political Science, History, Natural History, Social Sciences, Sociology
ISBN Prefix(es): 88-7039

Edizioni Thyrus SRL+
Via della Rinascita 12, 05031 Arrone (Terni)
Tel: (0744) 389496 *Fax:* (0744) 388700
   Cable: UFFICIO POSTALE ARRONE
Key Personnel
Man Dir, Production, Rights & Permissions: Dr Osvaldo Panfili
Editorial: Prof Lido Pirro
Sales: Nobili Nevia
Founded: 1956
Subjects: Education, Fiction, History, Literature, Literary Criticism, Essays, Psychology, Psychiatry, Regional Interests, Social Sciences, Sociology, Theology
ISBN Prefix(es): 88-87675
Book Club(s): Circolo Astrolabio

Tilgher-Genova sas
Via Assarotti 31/15, 16122 Genoa
Tel: (010) 839 11 40 *Fax:* (010) 870653
E-mail: tilgher@tilgher.it
Web Site: www.tilgher.it
Key Personnel
Chief Executive: Lucio Bozzi
Founded: 1971
Subjects: Biological Sciences, Literature, Literary Criticism, Essays, Philosophy

Editrice Tirrenia Stampatori SAS
Via Ferrari 5, 10124 Turin
Tel: (011) 877010 *Fax:* (011) 8177010
Key Personnel
Editorial & Publicity: Anna Maria Bertolina
Founded: 1977
Specialize in University publishing.
Subjects: Geography, Geology, History, Language Arts, Linguistics, Literature, Literary Criticism, Essays, Mathematics, Philosophy, Psychology, Psychiatry, Social Sciences, Sociology
ISBN Prefix(es): 88-7763
Orders to: The Courier SRL, Distibozione Libr, VLA Debosis, 25-27, 80145 Firenze

Todariana Editrice+
Via Gardone, 29, 20139 Milan
Tel: (02) 56812953 *Fax:* (02) 55213405
E-mail: toeurs@tin.it
Key Personnel
Chief Executive: Teodoro Giuttari
Founded: 1967
Subjects: Fiction, Language Arts, Linguistics, Literature, Literary Criticism, Essays, Poetry, Psychology, Psychiatry, Science Fiction, Fantasy, Social Sciences, Sociology, Travel
ISBN Prefix(es): 88-7015
Number of titles published annually: 12 Print
Imprints: Eura Press; Edizioni Italiane

Tomo Edizioni srl+
Via Pienza, 255, 00138 Rome
Tel: (081) 00920 *Fax:* (081) 00920
Founded: 1989
Subjects: Art, Photography
ISBN Prefix(es): 88-7151

Trainer International Editore-I Libri del Bargello+
Corso Italia 29, 50123 Florence
Tel: (055) 288162 *Fax:* (055) 218951
Telex: 571136

Key Personnel
Editorial Dir: Enrico Bosi
Coordinator: Enrica Fuligni Nannelli
Founded: 1990
Subjects: Art, History, Travel, Wine & Spirits
ISBN Prefix(es): 88-85271
Warehouse: V Baldanzese, 118-50041 Calenzano Firenze

Giovanni Tranchida Editore+
Via Giuseppe Frua 18, 20146 Milan
Tel: (02) 66802270 *Fax:* (02) 69003425
E-mail: tranchida@infinito.it
Web Site: www.tranchida.it
Key Personnel
Man Dir: Giovanni Tranchida
Founded: 1983
Membership(s): AIE.
Subjects: Architecture & Interior Design, Fiction, Literature, Literary Criticism, Essays, Philosophy, Psychology, Psychiatry
ISBN Prefix(es): 88-8003; 88-85685
Imprints: Giovanni Tranchida Editore
Distributor for Nessaggerie Libri Spa

Transeuropa+
Via Boscovich 44, 20124 Milan
Tel: (02) 29 402156 *Fax:* (02) 20 47922
Key Personnel
Man Dir: Massimo Canalini
Founded: 1988
Subjects: Architecture & Interior Design, Biological Sciences, Fiction, Film, Video, History, Literature, Literary Criticism, Essays, Medicine, Nursing, Dentistry, Philosophy, Women's Studies
ISBN Prefix(es): 88-7828
Orders to: PO Box 118, Ancona

Editrice Trasporti su Rotaie, see ETR (Editrice Trasporti su Rotaie)

Casa Editrice Luigi Trevisini
Via Livio 10/12, 20137 Milan
Tel: (02) 5450704 *Fax:* (02) 55195782 *Cable:* TREVISINI-MILANO
Key Personnel
Chief Executive: Luigi Trevisini
Editorial: Dr Giusi Trevisini
Founded: 1849
ISBN Prefix(es): 88-292

Marco Tropea Editore+
Via Melzo 9, 20129 Milan
Tel: (02) 202301 *Fax:* (02) 29513061
E-mail: stampa@saggiatore.it
Web Site: www.saggiatore.it
Key Personnel
President: Luca Formenton
Editor: Marco Tropea
Founded: 1995
Subjects: Fiction, Nonfiction (General)
ISBN Prefix(es): 88-438
Associate Companies: Il Saggiatore SpA e Nuova Pratiche Editrice

Turris+
Corso Garibaldi, 215, 26100 Cremona
Tel: (0372) 23845 *Fax:* (0372) 23845
Founded: 1981
Subjects: Art, Music, Dance
ISBN Prefix(es): 88-85635; 88-7929

Edizioni Ubulibri SAS+
Via Ramazzini 8, 20129 Milan
Tel: (02) 20241604 *Fax:* (02) 29510265
E-mail: edizioni@ubulibri.it
Key Personnel
Man Dir, Editorial: Franco Quadri
General Manager & Publicity: Tania Rainini
Founded: 1979

Subjects: Drama, Theater, Film, Video, Music, Dance
ISBN Prefix(es): 88-7748
Number of titles published annually: 12 Print
Total Titles: 160 Print
Warehouse: Messaggerie Libri SPA, Via Verdi 8, 20090 Assago *Tel:* (02) 457741

Editoriale Umbra SAS di Carnevali e
Via Pignattara, 34, 06034 Foligno (Perugia)
Tel: (0742) 357541 *Fax:* (0742) 351156
E-mail: editumbra@libero.it
Web Site: www.italand.com/eu *Cable:* EDITORIALE UMBRA FOLIGNO
Key Personnel
Man Dir, Editorial, Rights & Permissions, Sales: Giovanni Carnevali
Publicity: M Lise Burget
Founded: 1982
Subjects: Art, History, Literature, Literary Criticism, Essays, Regional Interests
ISBN Prefix(es): 88-85659

Edizioni Unicopli SpA+
Via Rosalba Carriera, 11, 20146 Milan
Tel: (02) 42299666 *Fax:* (02) 76021612
E-mail: info@edizioniunicopli.it
Web Site: www.edizioniunicopli.it
Key Personnel
Chief Executive: Michele Salvatore
Chief Editor: Marzio Zanantoni
Editorial, Psychology, Psychiatry: Stefano Nutini
Publicity: Roselle Savari
Founded: 1985
Subjects: Literature, Literary Criticism, Essays
ISBN Prefix(es): 88-7061; 88-400; 88-7090

Unipress+
Via Battisti, 231, 35121 Padova
Tel: (049) 8752542 *Fax:* (049) 8752542
Key Personnel
Editorial Dir: Gian Luigi Borgato
Founded: 1987
Subjects: Agriculture, Biological Sciences, Chemistry, Chemical Engineering, Language Arts, Linguistics, Literature, Literary Criticism, Essays, Philosophy, Psychology, Psychiatry
ISBN Prefix(es): 88-8098

Editrice Uomini Nuovi
Via Mazzini 73, 21030 Marchirolo (Varese)
Tel: (0332) 723007 *Fax:* (0332) 723264
E-mail: libreria@eun.ch; eunitaly@eun.ch
Web Site: www.eun.ch
Key Personnel
Chief Executive, Editorial: Dr Giuseppe E Laiso
Sales: Ruth Laiso
Publicity: Anna Rossinelli
Founded: 1964
Subjects: Biblical Studies, Biography, Human Relations, Psychology, Psychiatry, Religion - Other, Self-Help
ISBN Prefix(es): 88-8077
Subsidiaries: Radio Uomini Nuovi (Radio Cristiana Internazionale)
Bookshop(s): EUN

Urbaniana University Press+
Division of Pontificia Universitas Urbaniana
Via Urbano VIII, 16, 00120 Citta del Vaticano
Tel: (06) 6988 2182 *Fax:* (06) 6988 2182
E-mail: uupamm@urbaniana.edu
Web Site: www.urbaniana.edu/uup
Key Personnel
Dir: Gaspare Mura, PhD *Tel:* (06) 6988 9651
 E-mail: uupdir@urbaniana.edu
Administration: Giuseppe de Summa
 E-mail: uupamm@tiscali.it
Editorial: Sandro Scalabrin *Tel:* (06) 6988 1745
 E-mail: uupamm@urbaniana.it
Founded: 1968

Specialize in periodicals & essays.
Subjects: Anthropology, Biblical Studies, Law, Philosophy, Psychology, Psychiatry, Religion - Catholic, Theology, Missiology
ISBN Prefix(es): 88-401
Number of titles published annually: 14 Print
Total Titles: 500 Print
Imprints: UUP
Distributed by Dehoniana Libri
Showroom(s): Franfurt Book Messe
Bookshop(s): Libreria Bookshop, Pontificia Universita Urbaniana, 00120 Citta Del Vaticano; Libreria Vaticana
Orders to: Dehoniana Libri, Via Delle Fornaci, 47-51, 00165 Rome *Tel:* (06) 6382607 *Fax:* (06) 6390402

UT Orpheus Edizioni Srl+
Piazza di Porta Ravegnana, 1, 40126 Bologna
Tel: (051) 226468 *Fax:* (051) 263720
E-mail: mail@utorpheus.com
Web Site: www.utorpheus.com
Key Personnel
Contact: Roberto De Caro; Dr Antonello Lombardi
Sales Manager: Prof Valeria Tarsetti
 E-mail: vtarsetti@utorpheus.com
Founded: 1994
Italian publisher specializing in the publication of books on different music subjects, classical music.
Subjects: Music, Dance, Classical Music Editions
ISBN Prefix(es): 88-8109
Number of titles published annually: 100 Print
Total Titles: 820 Print
Distributor for Forni (Facsimiles); Spes (Facsimiles)
Foreign Rep(s): MKT (Italy)
Bookshop(s): Ut Orpheus Libreria Musicale, Via Marsala 31/E, 40126 Bologna *Fax:* (051) 239295
Warehouse: Via Aldina 26/A Calderara Di Reno, Elisabetta Pistolozzi *Tel:* (051) 726138
Distribution Center: MKT Musikit, Via Sardegna 7, 25124 Brescia *Fax:* (030) 222067
Orders to: Ut Orpheus Libreria Musicale, Via Marsala 31/E, 40126 Bologna *Fax:* (051) 239295

UTET Periodici Scientifici
Viale Tunisia, 37, 20124 Milan
Tel: (02) 6241171 *Fax:* (02) 62411720
E-mail: utet@utet.it
Web Site: www.utetperiodici.it
Key Personnel
General Manager: Corrado Trevisan
International Rights: Grazia Raccolli
Founded: 1987
Subjects: Medicine, Nursing, Dentistry
ISBN Prefix(es): 88-7933; 88-85647
Parent Company: UTET SpA

UTET (Unione Tipografico-Editrice Torinese)
Corso Raffaello 28, 10125 Turin
Tel: (011) 2099111 *Fax:* (011) 2099394
E-mail: utet@utet.it
Web Site: www.utet.it *Cable:* UTET Turin
Founded: 1791
Subjects: Architecture & Interior Design, Art, History, Law, Music, Dance, Philosophy, Psychology, Psychiatry, Religion - Other, Science (General), Social Sciences, Sociology, Veterinary Science
ISBN Prefix(es): 88-02

UUP, *imprint of* Urbaniana University Press

Vaccari SRL
Via M Buonarroti 46, 41058 Vignola Modena
Tel: (059) 764106; (059) 771251 *Fax:* (059) 760157

E-mail: info@vaccari.it
Web Site: www.vaccari.it
Key Personnel
Book Manager: Valeria Vaccari
Founded: 1989
Subjects: Crafts, Games, Hobbies, Collecting, Philately, Postal History
ISBN Prefix(es): 88-85335
Number of titles published annually: 10 Print; 10 Online
Total Titles: 80 Print; 80 Online

Valdonega SRL
Division of Stamperia Valdomega
Via Genova 17, 37020 Arbizzano, Verona
Tel: (045) 6020444 *Fax:* (045) 6020334
E-mail: valdonega@valdonega.it
Specialize in books on books, limited art editions & quality productions.
ISBN Prefix(es): 88-85033
Number of titles published annually: 3 Print
Total Titles: 15 Print

Vallardi & Assoc
Via Galilei 6, 20124 Milan
Tel: (02) 6555545 *Fax:* (02) 6555640
Telex: 330326 GECVAL I
ISBN Prefix(es): 88-85202

Vallardi Industrie Grafiche+
Via Trieste 20, 20020 Lainate, Milan
Tel: (02) 9370284 *Fax:* (02) 93570442
Key Personnel
Publisher: Giuseppe Vallardi
Editorial: Emanuela Vallardi
Founded: 1969
ISBN Prefix(es): 88-7696

Valmartina Editore SRL+
Stra del Portone 179, 10095 Grugliasco, Turin
Tel: (011) 2098741; (011) 2098720 *Fax:* (011) 2098765
E-mail: redazione@valmartina.it
Web Site: www.valmartina.it
Key Personnel
President: Luigi Vecchia
Editorial: Carlo Pasquinelli
Production: Giorgio Raccis
Rights & Permissions: Michela Melchiori
Founded: 1951
Subjects: Language Arts, Linguistics, Travel
ISBN Prefix(es): 88-494
Orders to: Via L Dottesio 1, 35138 Padua *Tel:* (049) 8710099

Societa Editrice Vannini
Via Mandolossa, 117/A, 25064 Gussago
Tel: (030) 313374 *Fax:* (030) 314078
E-mail: info@vanninieditrice.it
Web Site: www.vanninieditrice.it *Cable:* VANNINI BRESCIA
Founded: 1950
ISBN Prefix(es): 88-86430; 88-7436

Libreria Editrice Vaticana
Via della Tipografia, 00120 Citta del Vaticano
Tel: (06) 69885003 *Fax:* (06) 69884716
E-mail: lev@publish.va
Web Site: www.libreriaeditricevaticana.com
ISBN Prefix(es): 88-209

Giovanni De Vecchi Editore SpA, see Giovanni De Vecchi Editore SpA

Verso il Futuro, *imprint of* Casa Editrice Menna di Sinisgalli Menna Giuseppina

Vianello Libri+
Via Postioma 85, 31050 Ponzano (Treviso)
Tel: (0422) 440666 *Fax:* (0422) 440645
E-mail: info@vianellolibri.it
Web Site: www.vianellolibri.it

ITALY

Key Personnel
Contact: Giancarlo Buscaini; Andrea Montagnani; Livio Scibilia
Subjects: Architecture & Interior Design, Photography
ISBN Prefix(es): 88-7200
Orders to: Grafiche Vianello

Vinciana Editrice sas+
Via V Foppa, 14, 20144 Milan
Tel: (02) 4982306 *Fax:* (02) 48003275
E-mail: info@vinciana.com
Web Site: www.vinciana.com
Founded: 1976
Specialize in fine art.
Subjects: Art, Crafts, Games, Hobbies, How-to, Veterinary Science
ISBN Prefix(es): 88-86256
Total Titles: 42 Print

Vision Srl
Via Livorno, 20, 00161 Rome
Tel: (06) 44292688 *Fax:* (06) 44292688
E-mail: info@visionpubl.com
Web Site: www.visionpubl.com
Founded: 1959

Visual Itineraries, *imprint of* BeMa

Vita e Pensiero+
L go A Gemelli, 1, 20123 Milan
Tel: (02) 72342335; (02) 72342259 *Fax:* (02) 72342260
E-mail: editvep@mi.unicatt.it
Web Site: www.vitaepensiero.it
Telex: 321033 Ucatmi I
Key Personnel
President: Prof Sergio Zaninelli
Editorial Dir: Dr Aurelio Mottola *Fax:* (02) 72342660 *E-mail:* aurelio.mottola@unicatt.it
Founded: 1918
Membership(s): Associazione Italiana Editori, Unione Editori Cattolici Italiani, Unione Stampa Periodica Italiana, Associazione Librai Italiani.
Subjects: History, Literature, Literary Criticism, Essays, Mathematics, Medicine, Nursing, Dentistry, Philosophy, Psychology, Psychiatry, Religion - Other
ISBN Prefix(es): 88-343
Number of titles published annually: 100 Print
Bookshop(s): Libreria Vita e Pensiero, L go A Gemelli, 1, 20123 Milan *E-mail:* eibreria.vp@mi.umicatt.it

Edizioni La Vita Felice
Via Tadino 52, 20129 Milan
Tel: (02) 29 52 46 00 *Fax:* (02) 29 40 18 96
E-mail: lavitafelice@iol.it
Web Site: www.lavitafelice.it
Key Personnel
Publishing Dir: Gerardo Mastrullo
Public Relations: Chicca Gagliardo Marina Mauri
Editorial Dir: Cesare Salami
Editor: Paola Gerevini
Founded: 1993
Subjects: Fiction, Literature, Literary Criticism, Essays, Poetry
ISBN Prefix(es): 88-86314; 88-7799
Number of titles published annually: 24 Print
Total Titles: 80 Print

Vivalda Editori SRL+
Via Invorio 24 a, 10146 Turin
Tel: (011) 7720444 *Fax:* (011) 7732170
Web Site: www.cdavivalda.it
Key Personnel
President: Dr Giorgio Vivalda
General Dir & Administrative Representative: Mario Dalmaviva
Founded: 1972

Subjects: Sports, Athletics
ISBN Prefix(es): 88-7808
Divisions: CDA

Vivere In SRL
Contrada Piangevio, 224a, 70043 Bari
Tel: (08) 06907030 *Fax:* (08) 06907026
E-mail: edizioniviverein@tint.it
Web Site: www.viverein.it
Subjects: Biblical Studies, Biography, Philosophy, Poetry, Regional Interests, Religion - Catholic, Social Sciences, Sociology, Theology, Essays
ISBN Prefix(es): 88-7263
Number of titles published annually: 15 Print
Total Titles: 350 Print
Distributed by Agenzia Libraria GALL SRL; Agenzia Libraria S Fozzi; Citta Nuova Centro; DEM Libri SRL; Distrimedia SRL; Ditta Restivo SRL; L'Editoriale SRL; Ferrari Libri SRL

Viviani Editore srl+
Piazza della Maddalena 6, 00186 Rome
Tel: (06) 6872855 *Fax:* (06) 6872856
Key Personnel
Contact: Lia Viviani
Founded: 1992
Membership(s): AIE.
Subjects: Art, Biography, Drama, Theater, Literature, Literary Criticism, Essays
ISBN Prefix(es): 88-7993

Voce della Bibbia
Via Cavallotti 14, 41043 Formigine (Modena)
Tel: (059) 55 63 03; (059) 55 79 10 *Fax:* (059) 57 31 05
E-mail: bbitaly@tin.it
Web Site: www.vocedellabibbia.org
Key Personnel
General Dir: Ettore Calanchi
Founded: 1961
Subjects: Biblical Studies, Health, Nutrition, Music, Dance
Parent Company: Back to the Bible Broadcast, Box 82808, Lincoln, NE 68501, United States

Who's Who In Italy srl
Via E De Amicis 2, 20091 Bresso Milan
Tel: (02) 66503753; (02) 6101627 *Fax:* (02) 6105587
E-mail: whoswhogc@attglobal.net
Web Site: www.whoswho-sutter.com
Key Personnel
Man Dir: Giancarlo Colombo
Founded: 1977
Specialize in reference books, International publishers of Who's Who titles in 6 different nations in the English language & of particular interest to the world of business, politics, culture, art, science, education, etc, with cross-references between biographies & profiles of companies & institutions.
Membership(s): Associazione Italiana Editori (Italian Publishers' Association).
Subjects: Biography, Business, Management
ISBN Prefix(es): 88-85246
Number of titles published annually: 3 Print; 3 Online
Parent Company: Who's Who Sutters International Red Series Verlag AG, Seestr 357, 8038 Zurich, Switzerland
Subsidiaries: Who's Who in Spain; Who's Who Strategic Area
Distributed by The Eurospan Group (England); Independent Publishers Group (USA & Canada); United Publishers Services Ltd (Japan)

Silvio Zamorani editore
Saint Course Maurizio 25, 10124 Turin
Tel: (011) 8125700 *Fax:* (011) 8126144

BOOK

E-mail: szamora@tin.it
Web Site: www.zamorani.com
Founded: 1984
ISBN Prefix(es): 88-7158

ZAN, *imprint of* Casa Musicale G Zanibon SRL

Zanfi-Logos+
Via Curtatona 5/2, 41100 Modena
Mailing Address: PO Box 70, 41100 Modena
Tel: (059) 418810 *Fax:* (059) 418747
Telex: 522272
Key Personnel
Contact: Celestino Zanfi
Founded: 1979
Membership(s): Distripress.
Subjects: Cookery, Fashion, Gardening, Plants, Health, Nutrition, Outdoor Recreation, Religion - Buddhist, Travel
ISBN Prefix(es): 88-85168; 88-86169; 88-8169

Zanichelli Editore SpA+
Via Irnerio 34, 40126 Bologna
Tel: (051) 293111; (051) 245024 *Fax:* (051) 249782
E-mail: zanichelli@zanichelli.it
Web Site: www.zanichelli.it
Key Personnel
Chairman: Lorenzo Enriques
Dir General & Vice President: Federico Enriques
Founded: 1859
Subjects: Anthropology, Architecture & Interior Design, Biological Sciences, Chemistry, Chemical Engineering, Computer Science, Earth Sciences, Economics, Education, Electronics, Electrical Engineering, Engineering (General), English as a Second Language, Geography, Geology, History, Language Arts, Linguistics, Law, Literature, Literary Criticism, Essays, Mechanical Engineering, Medicine, Nursing, Dentistry, Philosophy, Photography, Physics, Psychology, Psychiatry, Science (General), Social Sciences, Sociology
ISBN Prefix(es): 88-08
Subsidiaries: CEA Casa Editrice Ambrosiana srl; ESAC Edizioni Scientifiche A Cremonese srl; Loescher Editore srl
Distributor for Bovolenta; Decibel; Lucisano; Signorelli
Warehouse: Via Del Lavoro 15, 40050 Quarto Inferiore (BO)

Edizioni Zara
Via Portilia 6, 43100 Parma
Tel: (0521) 489956 *Fax:* (0521) 241750
Key Personnel
Chief Executive: Isabella Marchesi
Editorial: Giancarlo Zarattini
Founded: 1979
Also acts as distributor for Edizioni Artegrafica Silva, Parma.
Subjects: Drama, Theater, Environmental Studies, Geography, Geology, Language Arts, Linguistics, Literature, Literary Criticism, Essays, Natural History, Philosophy, Religion - Catholic
Distributor for Parita; Silva Editore

Jamaica

General Information

Capital: Kingston
Language: English
Religion: Predominantly Protestant
Population: 2.5 million
Bank Hours: 0900-1400 Monday-Thursday; 0900-1200, 1430-1700 Friday
Shop Hours: Downtown Kingston: 0900-1600 Monday and Tuesday, Thursday-Saturday;

0900-1200 Wednesday. Other areas: 0900-1700, with early closing Thursday
Currency: 100 cents = 1 Jamaican dollar
Export/Import Information: No tariff on books, but advertising matter dutied. No import license required for books; no obscene literature permitted. No exchange restrictions.
Copyright: Berne (see Copyright Conventions, pg xi)

American Chamber of Commerce of Jamaica+
81 Knutsford Blvd, Kingston 5
Tel: 876-929-7866 *Fax:* 876-929-8597
E-mail: info@amchamjamaica.org
Web Site: www.amchamjamaica.org
Key Personnel
Chief Executive Officer: Dr Ofe S Dudley
Editor: Becky Stockhausen
Membership(s): Chamber of Commerce of The USA.
Subjects: Environmental Studies, Management, Marketing
ISBN Prefix(es): 976-8113
Parent Company: Chamber of Commerce of The USA (COCUSA)
Divisions: Association of American Chamber of Commerce of Latin America (AACCLA)

Association of Development Agencies
14 South Ave, Kingston 10
Tel: 876-960-2319; 876-968-3605 *Fax:* 876-929-8773
Founded: 1985
Forum for collective analysis, discussion, planning & collaboration.
Subjects: Communications, Developing Countries, House & Home, Regional Interests, Self-Help, Women's Studies
ISBN Prefix(es): 976-8112

Canoe Press, *imprint of* University of the West Indies Press

Canoe Press+
Imprint of The University of the West Indies Press
One A Aqueduct Flats, Mona, Kingston 7
Tel: 876-935-8432; 876-935-8470; 876-977-2659 *Fax:* 876-977-2660
E-mail: uwipress_marketing@cwjamaica.com; cuserv@cwjamaica.com (customer service & orders)
Web Site: www.uwipress.com
Key Personnel
General Manager: Linda Speth *E-mail:* lspeth@cwjamaica.com
Founded: 1992
Primarily publishes scholarly discourse such as conference papers & textbooks.
ISBN Prefix(es): 976-640
Distributor for UWI Publications

Carib Publishing Ltd+
Formerly West Indies Publishing Ltd
78 Slipe Rd, Kingston 5
Tel: 876-960-2602 *Fax:* 876-960-2602
E-mail: carib@toj.com
Key Personnel
Chairman: Patrick H O Rousseau
Man Dir: D Andrew Rousseau
Publishing Manager: Diane Browne
Production & Communications Manager: Gina Harrison
Founded: 1976
Subjects: Cookery, Education, Fiction, Geography, Geology, History, Mathematics, Science (General)
ISBN Prefix(es): 976-605
Subsidiaries: The Book Shop Ltd; Book Traders (Caribbean) Ltd
Distributor for Heinemann UK (Northern Caribbean)
Bookshop(s): The Springs, 15-17 Constant Spring Rd, Kingston 10; LOJ Shopping Centre, Shop No 12, 28-48 Barbados Ave, Kingston 5; LOJ Shopping Centre, Shop No 17, 28-48 Barbados Ave, Kingston 5; Lane Plaza, 36 Manchester Rd, Mandeville, Manchester; 17 Burke Rd, Spanish Town; Montego Bay Shopping Centre, Shops 12 & 13, Howard Cooke Blvd, Montego Bay, St James
Orders to: Book Traders (Caribbean) Ltd, Kingston

Caribbean Authors Publishing
12 Brentford Rd, Kingston 5
Tel: 876-926-6163 *Fax:* 876-929-1226
Key Personnel
Dir: Peter D Clarke
ISBN Prefix(es): 976-8037
Associate Companies: Multi Sector Consultants Ltd

Caribbean Food & Nutrition Institute
University of the West Indies, Mona, Kingston 7
Mailing Address: Jamaica Centre, PO Box 140, Kingston 7
Tel: 876-927-3829; 876-927-1927 *Fax:* 876-927-2657
E-mail: e-mail@cfni.paho.org
Telex: 3705 *Cable:* CAJANUS
ISBN Prefix(es): 976-626

Carlong Publishers (Caribbean) Ltd+
33 Second St, Newport West, Kingston 10
Mailing Address: PO Box 489, Kingston 10
Tel: (876) 923-7008 *Fax:* (876) 923-7003
E-mail: sales@carlpub.com *Cable:* CARLONG KINGSTON
Key Personnel
Publisher: Jenni Anderson *E-mail:* janderson@carlongpublishers.com
Publishing Manager, Rights & Permissions: Dorothy Noel *E-mail:* dnoel@carlongpublishers.com
Man Dir: Shirley Carby
Sales & Distribution: Lorna Allen
Editor: Benedicta Nakawuki *E-mail:* bnakawuki@carlongpublishers.com; Stacy Ramanand-Howard *E-mail:* showard@carlongpublishers.com; Sasha Robins *E-mail:* srobins@carlongpublishers.com
Founded: 1990
Subjects: Business, Drama, Theater, Foreign Countries, Geography, Geology, History, Human Relations, Language Arts, Linguistics, Literature, Literary Criticism, Essays, Mathematics, Science (General), Social Sciences, Sociology
ISBN Prefix(es): 976-8010; 976-638
Total Titles: 92 Print
Distributor for Pearson Education (Restrictions: Publishing); Penguin Books Ltd (N B Now own the right to publish some titles formerly belonging to Carib Publishing Limited)
Foreign Rights: Lloyd Austin (Guyana); Louis Forde (Barbados); Ken Jaikaransingh (Trinidad & Tobago); Franklyn Laws (Saint Kitts-Nevis); Henry Nathaniel (Saint Lucia)
Showroom(s): 17 Ruthven Rd, Bldg 3, Kingston 10, Contact: Mrs Dorothy Noel
Tel: (876) 960 9364-6 *Fax:* (876) 968 1353
E-mail: commissioning@carlpub.com (Publishing)

CFM Publications+
University of the West Indies, Mona Campus, Kingston 7
Tel: 876-927-1660; 876-927-1669 *Fax:* 876-927-0997
E-mail: helpdesk@uwimona.edu.jm
Web Site: www.uwimona.edu.jm
Key Personnel
International Rights: Margaret Mendes
Founded: 1987
Specialize in Caribbean accounting texts.
Subjects: Accounting, Management
ISBN Prefix(es): 976-8053
Distributed by The Press; University of the West Indies

Eureka Press Ltd
5 1/2 Caledonia Rd, Mandeville
Mailing Address: PO Box 628, Mandeville
Tel: 876-962-3947 *Fax:* 876-961-5383
E-mail: eurekapr@cwjamaica.com
Subjects: Biography, Education, Religion - Other, Theology
ISBN Prefix(es): 976-8029

Gleaner Co Ltd
7 North St, Kingston
Mailing Address: PO Box 40, Kingston
Tel: 876-922-2340 *Fax:* 876-922-2319; 876-922-6297; 876-922-6223
Telex: 2319
ISBN Prefix(es): 976-612

Green Island Press, *imprint of* Ian Randle Publishers Ltd

Institute of Jamaica Publications+
2A Suthermere Rd, Kingston 10
Tel: 876-929-4785; 876-929-4786 *Fax:* 876-926-8817
Key Personnel
Man Dir: Patricia V Stevens
Founded: 1967
Subjects: Ethnicity, Fiction, History, Natural History, Nonfiction (General), Science (General), Social Sciences, Sociology
ISBN Prefix(es): 976-8017

The Jamaica Bauxite Institute
PO Box 355, Kingston 6
Tel: (876) 927-2073; (876) 927-2079 *Fax:* (876) 927-1159
E-mail: info@jbi.org.jm
Telex: 2309 *Cable:* JAMBAUX JA
Key Personnel
Chairman: Carlton E Davis
General Manager: Mr Parris A Lyew-Ayee
Public Relations Officer: Hilary Coulton
Founded: 1975
Subjects: Earth Sciences, Economics
ISBN Prefix(es): 976-8072

Jamaica Bureau of Standards
6 Winchester Rd, Kingston 10
Mailing Address: PO Box 113, Kingston 10
Tel: (876) 926-3140; (876) 926-3145 *Fax:* (876) 929-4736
E-mail: info@jbs.org.jm
Web Site: www.jbs.org.jm/
Telex: 2291 Stanbur Ja *Cable:* STANBUREAU
Key Personnel
Executive Dir: Omer S Lloyd Thomas
Librarian: Andrea Robins
Founded: 1968
Formulate, promote & implement standards for products, processes & practices.
Membership(s): the International Organization for Standardization.
ISBN Prefix(es): 976-604

Jamaica Information Service
58A Half Way Tree Rd, Kingston 10
Tel: (876) 926-3740; (876) 926-3749 *Fax:* (876) 926-6715
E-mail: jis@jis.gov.jm; research@jis.gov.jm
Web Site: www.jis.gov.jm
ISBN Prefix(es): 976-633
Ultimate Parent Company: Office of the Prime Minister

JAMAICA

U.S. Office(s): 1520 New Hampshire Ave NW, Washington, DC 20036, United States *Tel:* 202-452-0660 *Fax:* 202-986-0184
Jamaica Consulate General, 842 Ingraham Bldg, 25 SE Second Ave, Miami, FL 33131, United States *Tel:* 305-374-8385 *Fax:* 305-374-9674 *E-mail:* jismiami@bellsouth.net
767 Third Ave, 3rd floor, New York, NY 10017, United States *Tel:* 212-935-9000 *Fax:* 212-935-7507 (ext 7) *E-mail:* jis_nyc@yahoo.com

Jamaica Printing Services
77 1/2 Duke St, Kingston
Tel: 876-967-2250; 876-967-2253; 876-967-2279; 876-967-2280; 876-922-3957 *Fax:* 876-967-2225
E-mail: info@jps1992.com; sales@jps1992.com
Web Site: www.jps1992.com/
Subjects: Law

Jamaica Publishing House Ltd+
97 Church St, Kingston
Tel: (876) 922-1385; (876) 967-3866 *Fax:* (876) 922-5412
E-mail: jph@jol.com.jm *Cable:* JAPUB
Key Personnel
Chairman: Woodburn Miller
Manager: Elaine R Stennett
Founded: 1969
Subjects: Biography, Education, Geography, Geology, History, House & Home, Language Arts, Linguistics, Literature, Literary Criticism, Essays, Mathematics, Psychology, Psychiatry, Social Sciences, Sociology
ISBN Prefix(es): 976-606
Parent Company: Jamaica Teachers' Association
Distributor for A & C Black; Schofield & Sims

Jamrite Publications+
Suite 22, Spanish Court, One Lucia Ave, Kingston 5
Tel: (876) 926-1180; (876) 926-1181 *Fax:* (876) 968-4519
E-mail: blackolive@cwjamaica.com
Key Personnel
Contact: Christopher Issa *Tel:* (876) 968 9939
Founded: 1981
Subjects: Books on Jamaican Culture
Parent Company: Richard James & Associates Ltd

LMH Publishing Ltd
LOJ Industrial Complex, 7 Norman Rd, Suite 10, Kingston CSO
Mailing Address: PO Box 8296, Kingston CSO
Tel: (876) 938-0005 *Fax:* (876) 759-8752
E-mail: lmhbookpublishing@cwjamaica.com
Web Site: www.lmhpublishingjamaica.com
Telex: Fitzgram 2293 *Cable:* KINGBOOKS
Key Personnel
Chairman & Publisher: Mike Henry
Managing/Marketing Dir, Overseas: Dawn Chambers-Henry
Editor: Kevin Harris; Charles Moore
Subjects: Cookery, Fiction, Music, Dance, Nonfiction (General), Romance, Travel
Foreign Rep(s): Turnaround Publisher Services Ltd (UK & Europe)
Shipping Address: Caribtrans Inc, 12600 NW 107th Ave, Miami, FL 33178, United States *Tel:* 305-696-1200 *Fax:* 305-691-3786
E-mail: miaterminal@caribtrans.com

Packer-Evans & Associates Ltd+
13 Stevenson Ave, Kingston 8
Mailing Address: PO Box 525, Kingston 8
Tel: 876-929-0531 *Fax:* 876-926-3487
Key Personnel
Chairman, Rights & Permissions & Sales: Omri I Evans
Man Dir & Sales: Dr Claude Packer

Sales & Publicity: Norma Evans
Production: Gloria Foresythe; Carol Anglin
Publicity: Lisa Packer
Founded: 1984
Subjects: Mathematics
ISBN Prefix(es): 976-8022

The Press, *imprint of* University of the West Indies Press

The Press+
Imprint of University of the West Indies
One A Aqueduct Flats, Mona, Kingston 7
Tel: (876) 977-2659 *Fax:* (876) 977-2660
E-mail: uwipress_marketing@cwjamaica.com; cuserv@cwjamaica.com (customer service & orders)
Web Site: www.uwipress.com
Key Personnel
General Manager: Linda Speth *E-mail:* lspeth@cwjamaica.com
Marketing & Sales Manager: Donna Muirhead
Founded: 1992
Also acts as marketer & distributor for departments of the University of the West Indies.
Membership(s): Book Industry Association of Jamaica.
Subjects: Ethnicity, Government, Political Science, History
ISBN Prefix(es): 976-640

Ian Randle Publishers Ltd+
11 Cunningham Ave, Kingston 6
Mailing Address: PO Box 686, Kingston 6
Tel: (876) 978-0739; (876) 978-0745
 Toll Free *Tel:* 866-330-5469 (orders) *Fax:* (876) 978-1156
E-mail: info@ianrandlepublishers.com
Web Site: www.ianrandlepublishers.com
Key Personnel
Chairman & Publisher: Ian Randle *E-mail:* ianr@colis.com
Man Dir: Christine Randle *E-mail:* clp@ianrandlepublishers.com
Business Manager: Carlene Randle
Founded: 1992
Specialize in Caribbean Studies as well as trade & general books.
Also acts as publishers agent.
Subjects: Art, Biography, Cookery, History, Law, Literature, Literary Criticism, Essays, Music, Dance, Poetry, Sports, Athletics, Women & Gender Studies
ISBN Prefix(es): 976-8100; 976-8123; 976-8167
Number of titles published annually: 50 Print
Total Titles: 200 Print
Imprints: Green Island Press
Distributor for Houghton Mifflin
Foreign Rep(s): Global Book Marketing (UK/Europe)

Scientific Research Council
Hope Gardens, Kingston 6
Mailing Address: PO Box 350, Kingston 6
Tel: 876-927-1771; 876-927-1774 *Fax:* 876-927-1990
E-mail: prinfo@src-jamaica.org
Web Site: www.src-jamaica.org
Telex: 3631 SRCSTIN *Cable:* SCIENTIST
Founded: 1960
The National center for the transformation, acquisition, conversion & application of knowledge to run the engine of growth & development.
ISBN Prefix(es): 976-8126
Subsidiaries: Marketech Ltd

Twin Guinep Ltd+
Seymour Park, Suite 21, 2 Seymour Ave, Kingston 10
Tel: 876-927-5390; 876-944-4324 *Fax:* 876-944-4324

E-mail: info@twinguinep.com; sales@twinguinep.com
Web Site: www.twinguinep.com
Key Personnel
International Rights: Dennis Ranston
 E-mail: ranston@kasnet.com; Jacqueline Ranston
Founded: 1974
ISBN Prefix(es): 976-8007

University of the West Indies Press+
One A Aqueduct Flats, Mona, Kingston 7
Tel: (876) 977-2659 *Fax:* (876) 977-2660
E-mail: cuserv@cwjamaica.com (customer service & orders); uwipress_marketing@cwjamaica.com
Web Site: www.uwipress.com
Key Personnel
General Manager: Linda E Speth *E-mail:* lspeth@cwjamaica.com
Finance Manager: Nadine Buckland
 E-mail: nbuckland@cwjamaica.com
Administrative Officer: Dionne Williams
 E-mail: d_wills@cwjamaica.com@cwjamaica.com
Marketing & Sales Manager: Donna Muirhead
Man Editor: Shivaum Hearne *E-mail:* hearnes@cwjamaica.com
Sales & Distribution Coordinator: Karen Smith
Founded: 1992
Academic book publisher.
Subjects: Anthropology, Environmental Studies, Ethnicity, History, Literature, Literary Criticism, Essays, Natural History, Social Sciences, Sociology, Women's Studies
ISBN Prefix(es): 976-8125; 976-640; 976-41
Number of titles published annually: 25 Print
Total Titles: 160 Print
Imprints: Canoe Press; The Press
Distributed by University of Oklahoma Press
Distributor for The Mill Press; Sir Arthur Lewis Institute
Foreign Rep(s): Eurospan (Middle East, UK & the continent); EWEB (Australia, Asia, New Zealand, Pacific); Lexicon (Trinidad West Indies); University of Oklahoma Press (Canada, North America)
Distribution Center: The University of Oklahoma Press, 4100 28 Ave NW, Norman, OK 73069, United States
Eurospan, 3 Henrietta St, Covent Garden, London WC2E 8LU, United Kingdom *Tel:* (020) 7240-0856 *Fax:* (020) 7379-0609

UWI Publishers' Association
University of West Indies, Mona Campus, Kingston 7
Mailing Address: PO Box 42, Kingston
Tel: 876-927-1660; 876-927-1669 *Fax:* 876-977-2660
E-mail: helpdesk@uwimona.edu.jm
Key Personnel
Publication Officer: Annie Paul
Subjects: Literature, Literary Criticism, Essays
ISBN Prefix(es): 976-43

West Indies Publishing Ltd, see Carib Publishing Ltd

Japan

General Information

Capital: Tokyo
Language: Japanese
Religion: Shinto and Buddhism
Population: 125 million

PUBLISHERS

Bank Hours: 0900-1500 Monday-Friday; 0900-1200 Saturday
Shop Hours: Same as bank hours
Currency: 100 yen = 1 dollar
Export/Import Information: 3% consumption; tax on books.
Copyright: UCC, Berne, Florence, Rome (see Copyright Conventions, pg xi)

ACCJ, *imprint of* The American Chamber of Commerce in Japan

ADA Edita Tokyo Co Ltd
12-14 Sendagaya chome, Shibuya-ku, Tokyo 151-0051
Tel: (03) 3403-1581 *Fax:* (03) 3497-0649
E-mail: info@ga-ada.co.jp
Web Site: www.ga-ada.co.jp
Key Personnel
Dir: Yukio Futagawa
Sales Manager: Tatsuo Futagawa
Founded: 1972
Subjects: Architecture & Interior Design
ISBN Prefix(es): 4-87140
U.S. Office(s): G A International/Co Ltd, 180 Varick St, 4th Floor, New York, NY 10014, United States *Tel:* 212-741-6329 *Fax:* 212-741-6283

Aiki News
14-17-103 Matsugae-cho, Sagamihara-shi, Kanagawa 228-0813
Tel: (042) 748-1240 *Fax:* (042) 748-2421
Key Personnel
Editor-in-Chief: Stanley A Pranin
English Editor: Diane Skoss
Founded: 1988
Membership(s): COSMEP.
Subjects: Sports, Athletics
ISBN Prefix(es): 4-900586

Akita Shoten Publishing Co Ltd
2-10-8 Iidabashi, Chioyoda-ku, Tokyo 102-8101
Tel: (03) 3264-7248 *Fax:* (03) 3265-9076
Key Personnel
President: Sadami Akita
Editorial: Nobumichi Akutsu; Taizo Kabemura
Sales: Toshimichi Okubo
Foreign Rights: Noriyoshi Oda
Foreign Rights & Trade: Hirokazu Takahashi
Founded: 1948
Subjects: Fiction, History, Literature, Literary Criticism, Essays, Social Sciences, Sociology
ISBN Prefix(es): 4-253

Alice-Kan+
14-13 Mejirodai 2 chome, Bunkyo-ku, Tokyo 112-0015
Tel: (03) 5976-7013 *Fax:* (03) 3943-8396
Key Personnel
President: Yu Kobayashi
Founded: 1981
Subjects: Child Care & Development
ISBN Prefix(es): 4-7520
Parent Company: Rodojunposh

The American Chamber of Commerce in Japan+
Mesonick 39 MT Bldg 10f, 2-4-5 Azabudai, Minato-ku, Tokyo 106-0041
Tel: (03) 3433-5381 *Fax:* (03) 3433-8454
E-mail: info@accj.or.jp
Web Site: www.accj.or.jp
Key Personnel
Dir, Publications: Jeanmarie Todd
Founded: 1948
Specialize in helping US business expand in Japan.
Subjects: Business, Foreign Countries, Marketing, Travel
ISBN Prefix(es): 4-915682
Imprints: ACCJ

U.S. Office(s): ACCJ, c/o US Chamber of Commerce, International Division, 1615 "H" St NW, Washington, DC 20062, United States
Tel: 202-463-5460 *Fax:* 202-463-3114
Distributed by Charles E Tuttle Co (Japan & USA)

Aoki Shoten Co Ltd
60, Kanda-Jimbocho 1 chome, Chiyoda-ku, Tokyo 101-0051
Tel: (03) 32192341 *Fax:* (03) 32192585
Key Personnel
President, Foreign Rights & Trade: Masato Aoki
Founded: 1948
Subjects: Economics, Education, History, Philosophy, Social Sciences, Sociology
ISBN Prefix(es): 4-250

Asahiya Shuppan
Seisen-Ichigaya Bldg, 4 Ichigaya-Sadowara-cho-3 chome, Tokyo 162-8402
Tel: (03) 3267-0865 *Fax:* (03) 3267-0875
Web Site: www.amgakuin.com
Key Personnel
President: Takeshi Hayashima
ISBN Prefix(es): 4-7511

Asakura Publishing Co Ltd+
6-29 Shin-Ogawa machi, Shinjuku-ku, Tokyo 162-8707
Tel: (03) 32600141 *Fax:* (03) 32600180
Key Personnel
President: Kunizo Asakura
Foreign Trade: Hideo Shirahara
Foreign Rights: Haruo Obata
Founded: 1929
ISBN Prefix(es): 4-254

Atelier Publishing Co Ltd
Shinichi Bldg, 8 Yotsuya 2 chome, Shinjuku-ku, Tokyo 160-0004
Tel: (03) 3357-2741 *Fax:* (03) 3357-2194
Key Personnel
President: Taisuke Hirabayashi
ISBN Prefix(es): 4-7518

AVACO - Christian Mass Communications Center
2-3-18 W Waseda, Shinjuku-ku, Tokyo 169-0051
Tel: (03) 3203-4121 *Fax:* (03) 3203-4186
E-mail: avaco@ppp.fastnet.ne.jp
Web Site: www.fastnet.ne.jp
Key Personnel
Executive Dir: Ohta Futoshi
Subjects: Education, Religion - Protestant

Baberu Inc+
3-1 Ariake, TFT Bldg, Koutou-ju, Tokyo 135-8071
Tel: (03) 5530-2205 *Fax:* (03) 5530-2204
E-mail: buc@babel.co.jp
Web Site: www.babel.co.jp
Key Personnel
President: Miyoko Yuasa
Dir, Planning & Editing Dept: Mr Maruhama Tetsuro
Founded: 1974
ISBN Prefix(es): 4-931049; 4-89449
U.S. Office(s): San Francisco, CA, United States

Baifukan Co Ltd
4-3-12 Kudan-Minami, Chyoda-ku, Tokyo 102-0074
Tel: (03) 3262-5270 *Fax:* (03) 3262-5276
E-mail: bfkeigyo@mx7.mesh.ne.jp
Web Site: www.baifukan.co.jp/
Key Personnel
Chairman: Kenji Yamamoto
President & Foreign Rights & Trade: Itaru Yamamoto

Editorial: Masayuki Gotou; Kazunori Matsumoto; Takashi Murayama
Production: Fumio Shigematu
Editorial, Rights & Permissions: Tsuyoshi Nohara
Founded: 1924
Subjects: Biological Sciences, Chemistry, Chemical Engineering, Computer Science, Engineering (General), Mathematics, Physics, Psychology, Psychiatry, Social Sciences, Sociology
ISBN Prefix(es): 4-563

Baseball Magazine-Sha Co Ltd+
10-10 Misakicho 3 chome, Chiyoda-ku, Toyko 101-8381
Tel: (03) 3238-0285 *Fax:* (03) 3238-0084
Web Site: www.bbm-japan.com
Key Personnel
President: Tetsuo Ikeda
Founded: 1946
Subjects: History, Psychology, Psychiatry, Sports, Athletics, Travel
ISBN Prefix(es): 4-583
Subsidiaries: Kobunsha Co Ltd
Branch Office(s)
Doujma TSS Bldg, 6F 2-5-3 Sonezaki-Shinchi, Kita-ku, Osaka-shi, Osaka 530-0002 *Tel:* (06) 3418825

Bijutsu Shuppan-Sha, Ltd
Inaokakudan Bldg, 2-38 Kanda Jinbo-cho, Chiyoda-ku, Tokyo 101-8417
Tel: (03) 32342159 *Fax:* (03) 32349451
Web Site: www.bijutsu.co.jp *Cable:* FINEART BOOK TOKYO
Key Personnel
Chairman: Atsushi Oshita
President: Kentaro Oshita
Sales Manager: Hiroshi Mizukoshi
Founded: 1905
Subjects: Architecture & Interior Design, Art, Crafts, Games, Hobbies, How-to
ISBN Prefix(es): 4-568

Bun-ichi Sogo Shuppan
Kawakami Bldg, 2-5 Nishi-Gokencho, Shinjuku-ku, Tokyo 162-0812
Tel: (03) 3235-7341 *Fax:* (03) 3269-1402
E-mail: bunichi@bun-ichi.co.jp
Web Site: www.bun-ichi.co.jp/
Key Personnel
President: Hiroshi Saito
Founded: 1959
Subjects: Biological Sciences, Electronics, Electrical Engineering, Engineering (General), Environmental Studies, Natural History, Photography, Science (General), Bird watching
ISBN Prefix(es): 4-8299

Bunkasha Publishing Co Ltd+
29-6, Ichibancho, Chiyoda-ku, Tokyo 102-8405
Tel: (03) 3222-5111 *Fax:* (03) 3222-3672
E-mail: fukai@bunkasha.co.jp
Web Site: www.bunkasha.co.jp
Key Personnel
President: Kenichi Kai
Founded: 1948
Membership(s): Japan Book Publishers Association; Japan Publishers Club; Japan Magazine Publishers Association; Japan Magazine Fair Trade Council for Promotion of Book Reading; Publishers Association for Cultural Exchange; National Council to Promote Ethic of Massmedia.
Subjects: Fashion, Fiction, Film, Video, History, Humor, Literature, Literary Criticism, Essays, Social Sciences, Sociology, Sports, Athletics

Bunkashobo-Hakubun-Sha
9-9 Mejirodai 1 chome, Bunkyo-ku, Tokyo 112-0015
Tel: (03) 3947-2034 *Fax:* (03) 3947-4976
Key Personnel
President: Sadayoshi Suzuki

Foreign Rights & Trade: Yoshio Amano
Founded: 1957
Subjects: Education, History, Literature, Literary Criticism, Essays, Social Sciences, Sociology
ISBN Prefix(es): 4-8301

Business Center for Academic Societies Japan
C-21 Gakkai Center, 5-16-9 Honkomagome, Bunkyo-ku, Tokyo 113-8622
Tel: (03) 5814-5800 *Fax:* (03) 5814-5823
E-mail: nuehara@bcasj.or.jp; haraki@bcasj.or.jp
Web Site: www.bcasj.or.jp
Key Personnel
Dir General: Mitsuoka Tomotari, PhD
Man Dir, Rights & Permissions: Konno Shozo
Production: B Todoroki
Founded: 1971
Subjects: Science (General)
ISBN Prefix(es): 4-930813; 4-89114
Associate Companies: Japan Scientific Societies Press, 2-10 Hongo 6-chome, Bunkyo-ku, Tokyo 113; Center for Academic Publications Japan, 4-16, Yayoi 2-chome, Bunkyo-ku, Tokyo 113

Chijin Shokan Co Ltd+
15, Naka-machi, Shinjuku-ku, Tokyo 162-0835
Tel: (03) 3235-4422 *Fax:* (03) 3235-8984
E-mail: chijinshokan@nifty.com
Web Site: www.chijinshokan.co.jp
Key Personnel
President: Osamu Kamijo
Editorial Manager: Akira Tsuda
Man Dir: Tomoaki Ogawa
Founded: 1930
Membership(s): Japan Book Publishers Association.
Subjects: Engineering (General), Medicine, Nursing, Dentistry, Physical Sciences, Science (General), Technology
ISBN Prefix(es): 4-8052
Total Titles: 450 Print
Foreign Rep(s): Asano Agency (Worldwide); English Agency (Japan); Japan Uni Agency (Japan); Orion Press (Worldwide); Tuttle-Mori Agency (Japan)

Chikuma Shobo Publishing Co Ltd+
5-3 Kuramae, Komuro Bldg, 2 Chome, Taito-ku, Tokyo 111-8755
Tel: (03) 5687-2671 *Fax:* (03) 5687-1585
Web Site: www.chikumashobo.co.jp
Key Personnel
President: Akio Kikuchi *E-mail:* kikuchia@chikumashobo.co.jp
Editorial, Rights & Permissions: Tetsuo Matsuda
Sales, Publicity: Tatsuji Tanaka
Production: Isao Miyazono
Founded: 1940
Subjects: Biography, Communications, Economics, Education, Fiction, History, Human Relations, Nonfiction (General), Philosophy, Religion - Buddhist, Social Sciences, Sociology, Women's Studies
ISBN Prefix(es): 4-480

Chikyu-sha Co Ltd
3-5 Akasaka 4 chome, Minato-ku, Tokyo 107-0052
Tel: (03) 3585-0087 *Fax:* (03) 3589-2902
Key Personnel
President: Minoru Toda
Foreign Rights & Trade: Yutaka Toda
Founded: 1946
Subjects: Agriculture, Civil Engineering, Education, Forestry; Home economics
ISBN Prefix(es): 4-8049

Child Honsha Co Ltd+
24-21 Koishikawa 5 chome, Bunkyo-ku, Tokyo 112-8512
Tel: (03) 3813-3781 *Fax:* (03) 3818-3778

Key Personnel
President: Yoshiaki Shimazaki
Foreign Rights & Trade: Kazuhisa Uemura
Sales, Publicity & Foreign Trade: Katsuharu Mibu
Production: Shunzi Asaka
Rights & Permissions: Kotaro Ohashi
Founded: 1930
Subjects: Education
ISBN Prefix(es): 4-8054
Associate Companies: Kyodo Printing Co Ltd
Subsidiaries: Basic Inc; Hisakata Child Co Ltd

Chuo-Tosho Co Ltd+
Aburakoji-dori, Motoseiganji-sagaru, Kamigyo-ku, Kyoto 602-0952
Tel: (075) 441-2174 *Fax:* (075) 441-3300
Key Personnel
President: Toshihiko Hirokou
Editorial, Publicity, Rights & Permissions: Takanori Ikeda
Sales: Tetsuo Hattori
Production: Tsuneo Takeuchi
Founded: 1950
Subjects: Education
ISBN Prefix(es): 4-482

Chuokoron-Shinsha Inc
2-8-7 Kyobashi, Yomiuri-Chuko Bldg, Chuo-ku, Tokyo 104-8320
Tel: (03) 3563-1431 *Fax:* (03) 3561-5922
E-mail: honyaku-irie@chuko.co.jp
Web Site: www.chuko.co.jp
Telex: J32505 Chuokor *Cable:* Chuokoron Tokyo
Key Personnel
President: Jin Nakamura
Foreign Rights & Trade: Norio Irie
Founded: 1886
Subjects: Art, Economics, Government, Political Science, History, Literature, Literary Criticism, Essays, Philosophy, Religion - Other, Science (General), Social Sciences, Sociology
ISBN Prefix(es): 4-12

CMC Publishing Co Ltd+
5-4 Uchi-Kanda 1 chome, Miyako Bldg, Chiyoda-ku, Tokyo 101-0047
Tel: (03) 3293-2065 *Fax:* (03) 3293-2069
E-mail: info@cmcbooks.co.jp
Web Site: www.cmcbooks.co.jp
Key Personnel
President: Kentaro Shima
Foreign Rights & Trade: Takashi Fukuda
Founded: 1961
Subjects: Biological Sciences, Business, Electronics, Electrical Engineering, Science (General), Technology
ISBN Prefix(es): 4-88231
Branch Office(s)
Osaka

Contex Corporation+
Suzuki Bldg 1-13-14, Akebono-cho, Tachikawa, Tokyo 190-0012
Tel: (03) 42-522-0051 *Fax:* (03) 42-526-2345; (03) 42-548-2400
E-mail: contex@jade.dt.ne.jp
Web Site: contex.co.jp/
Key Personnel
President: Shigeru Tsukakoshi
Contact: Yuko Tsukakoshi
Founded: 1982
Restaurant menu guide consisting of ten language interpretations. English, Chinese, Korean, Japanese, French, Spanish, German, Italian & Portuguese cookery books & travel guides. Chinese, Korean & Japanese foods.
Subjects: Cookery, Travel
ISBN Prefix(es): 4-907653
Total Titles: 1 Print
Foreign Rep(s): Value Supply Inc

Corona Publishing Co Ltd
46-10 Sengoku 4 chome, Bunkyo-ku, Tokyo 112-0011
Tel: (03) 3941-3131 *Fax:* (03) 3941-3137
E-mail: info@coronasha.co.jp
Web Site: www.coronasha.co.jp
Key Personnel
President: Tatsumi Gorai
Editorial Dir: Sumio Hatano; Hiroshi Nakamata
Foreign Rights & Trade: Masaya Gorai
Founded: 1927
Subjects: Civil Engineering, Computer Science, Electronics, Electrical Engineering, Mechanical Engineering, Science (General), Technology, Metallurgy
ISBN Prefix(es): 4-339

Daiichi Shuppan Co Ltd
39, Kanda-Jimbocho, Chiyoda-ku, Tokyo 101-0051
Tel: (03) 3291-4576 *Fax:* (03) 3291-4579
Web Site: www.daiichi-shuppan.co.jp
Key Personnel
President & Foreign Rights & Trade: Hideji Ishikawa *E-mail:* ishikawa@japan.email.ne.jp
Founded: 1944
Subjects: Economics, Health, Nutrition, House & Home, Medicine, Nursing, Dentistry
ISBN Prefix(es): 4-8041
Number of titles published annually: 10 Print; 1 CD-ROM
Total Titles: 150 Print; 5 CD-ROM

Dainippon Tosho Publishing Co, Ltd+
9-10 Ginza 1 chome, Chuo-ku, Tokyo 104-0061
Tel: (03) 3561-8672 *Fax:* (03) 3563-5596
Web Site: www.dainippon-tosho.co.jp
Key Personnel
President: Kentaro Kaneko
Founded: 1890
Subjects: Chemistry, Chemical Engineering, Education, Fiction, Psychology, Psychiatry, Science (General)
ISBN Prefix(es): 4-477

Diamond Inc+
6-12-17 Jingumae, Shibuya-ku, Tokyo 150-8409
Tel: (03) 5778-7232 *Fax:* (03) 5778-6612
Web Site: www.diamond.co.jp
Key Personnel
President: Norio Tamura
Foreign Rights & Trade: Eiji Mitachi
Founded: 1913
Subjects: Business, Career Development, Economics, Environmental Studies, Management, Marketing, Nonfiction (General), Psychology, Psychiatry, Science (General), Self-Help, Forecasting, Industrial, Research & Development
ISBN Prefix(es): 4-478
Subsidiaries: Diamond Agency; Diamond Big; Diamond Fund; Diamond Graphics; Diamond Service
Branch Office(s)
Osaka, India

Dobunshoin Publishers Co
24-3 Koishikawa 5 chome, Bunkyo-ku, Tokyo 112-0002
Tel: (03) 3812-7777 *Fax:* (03) 3812-7792
Key Personnel
President: Fumihiro Uno
Foreign Rights & Trade: Sawako Shimaya
Founded: 1928
Subjects: Business, Computer Science, How-to, Medicine, Nursing, Dentistry, Microcomputers, Nonfiction (General), Science (General), Social Sciences, Sociology, Sports, Athletics
ISBN Prefix(es): 4-8103

Dogakusha Inc
10-7 Suido 1 chome, Bunkyo-ku, Tokyo 112-0005

Tel: (03) 3816-7011 *Fax:* (03) 3816-7044
E-mail: eigyoubu@dogakusha.co.jp
Web Site: www.dogakusha.co.jp
Key Personnel
President: Kusuji Kondo
Founded: 1950
All publications in German.
ISBN Prefix(es): 4-8102

Dohosha Publishing Co Ltd+
Tas Bldg, 2-5-2 Nishi-Kanda, Chiyoda-ku, Tokyo 101-0065
Tel: (03) 5276 0831 *Fax:* (03) 5276 0840
Key Personnel
President: Satoru Imada
Foreign Rights: Takuya Kosaka
Founded: 1918
Subjects: Architecture & Interior Design, Art, Asian Studies, Cookery, History, How-to, Medicine, Nursing, Dentistry, Religion - Buddhist
ISBN Prefix(es): 4-8104
Associate Companies: DDP Digital Publishing Inc; Ochanomizu Management Laboratory; OML Information Service Center
Subsidiaries:
Warehouse: 34-1, Shironokoshi-cho, Shimotoba, Fushimi-ku, Kyoto 612

Eichosha Company Ltd
Kusaka Bldg, 28 Kanda Jimbocho 2 chome, Chiyoda-ku, Tokyo 101-0051
Tel: (03) 3263-1641 *Fax:* (03) 3263-6174
E-mail: info@eichosha.co.jp
Web Site: www.eichosha.co.jp
Key Personnel
President: Shozo Doki
Subjects: English as a Second Language, Language Arts, Linguistics, Literature, Literary Criticism, Essays
ISBN Prefix(es): 4-268

The Eihosha Ltd
21 Sanaicho, Ichigaya, Shinjuku-ku, Tokyo 162-0846
Tel: (03) 5206-6020 *Fax:* (03) 5206-6022
Key Personnel
President: Hajime Sasaki
Contact: Masao Uji
Founded: 1949
Subjects: Literature, Literary Criticism, Essays
ISBN Prefix(es): 4-269

Elsevier Science
9-15 Higashi-Azabu 1-chome, Minato-ku, Tokyo 106-0044
Tel: (03) 5561-5033 *Toll Free Tel:* (0120) 383-608 (within Japan) *Fax:* (03) 5561-5047
E-mail: info@elsevier.co.jp
Web Site: www.elsevier.co.jp
Key Personnel
Man Dir: Ryoji Fukada
Sales & editorial services office of Elsevier Science BV, Netherlands.
ISBN Prefix(es): 4-86034
Parent Company: Elsevier Science BV, Netherlands

Froebel - kan Co Ltd+
14-9 Honkomagome 6 chome, Bunkyo-ku, Tokyo 113-8611
Tel: (03) 5395-6600 *Fax:* (03) 5395-6627
E-mail: info-e@froebel-kan.co.jp
Web Site: www.froebel-kan.co.jp
Telex: J24907
Key Personnel
President: Kennosuke Arai *E-mail:* arai-k@froebel.kan.co.jp
Dir: Mitsuhiro Tada *E-mail:* tada-m@froebel-kan.co.jp
Founded: 1907

Subjects: Animals, Pets, Education, Anpanman
ISBN Prefix(es): 4-577
Number of titles published annually: 120 Print
Total Titles: 1,000 Print; 1 CD-ROM
Parent Company: Toppan Printing Co Ltd

Fuji Keizai Company Ltd
FK Bldg, 2-5 Nihombashi Kodemma-cho, Chou-ku, Tokyo 103-0001
Tel: (03) 3644-5811 *Fax:* (03) 3661-0165
Web Site: www.fuji-keizai.co.jp
Key Personnel
President: Hideo Abe
Founded: 1962
Subjects: Electronics, Electrical Engineering
ISBN Prefix(es): 4-89225; 4-8349
Subsidiaries: Fuji Khimera Institute
U.S. Office(s): Fuji Keizai, 141 E 55 St, Suite 3F, New York, NY, United States

Fukuinkan Shoten Publishers Inc+
6-6-3, Honkomagome, Bunkyo-ku, Tokyo 113-8686
Tel: (03) 39420032 *Fax:* (03) 39421401
Web Site: www.fukuinkan.co.jp *Cable:* FUKUINKANSHOTEN TOKYO
Key Personnel
Chairman: Katsumi Sato
President: Shiro Tokita
Sales Dir: Noboru Ogura
Dir (International Dept): Mariko Ogawa
Founded: 1952
Specialize in children's books, including illustrated books.
Subjects: Fiction, Literature, Literary Criticism, Essays, Nonfiction (General), Science (General), Science Fiction, Fantasy
ISBN Prefix(es): 4-8340
Number of titles published annually: 150 Print
Total Titles: 1,000 Print

Fukumura Shuppan Inc
2-30-7 Hongo, Bunkyo-ku, Tokyo 113-0033
Tel: (03) 3813-3981 *Fax:* (03) 3818-2786
Web Site: www.fukumura.co.jp
Key Personnel
President: Junichi Fukumura
Founded: 1939
Subjects: Education, History, Philosophy, Psychology, Psychiatry, Social Sciences, Sociology
ISBN Prefix(es): 4-571

Fumaido Publishing Company Ltd+
14-9 Otsuka 2 chome, Bunkyo-ku, Tokyo 112-0012
Tel: (03) 3946-2345 *Fax:* (03) 3947-0110
E-mail: fumaido@tkd.att.ne.jp
Key Personnel
President: Michio Miyawaki
Founded: 1960
Subjects: Education, Health, Nutrition, Sports, Athletics, Physical education, recreation
ISBN Prefix(es): 4-8293

Fuzambo Publishing Co+
1-3, Kanda-Jimbocho, Chiyoda-ku, Toyko 101-0051
Tel: (03) 3291-2171 *Fax:* (03) 3291-2179
Key Personnel
President: Kiichi Sakamoto
Founded: 1886
Subjects: Art, Geography, Geology, History, Language Arts, Linguistics, Law, Literature, Literary Criticism, Essays, Philosophy, Religion - Other, Social Sciences, Sociology
ISBN Prefix(es): 4-572

Gakken Co Ltd+
4-40-5 Kamiikedai, Ota-ku, Tokyo 145-8502
Tel: (03) 3726-8440 *Fax:* (03) 3726-8858

Key Personnel
President: Yoichiro Endo
Foreign Rights & Trade: Takeshi Kubodera
Founded: 1946
Subjects: Art, Astrology, Occult, Automotive, Business, Child Care & Development, Computer Science, Education, Electronics, Electrical Engineering, Environmental Studies, Gardening, Plants, House & Home, Nonfiction (General), Outdoor Recreation, Radio, TV, Comic Books
ISBN Prefix(es): 4-05

GakuseiSha Publishing Co Ltd
2-2-4 Kudan-minami, Chiyoda-ku, Tokyo 102-0074
Tel: (03) 3857-3031 *Fax:* (03) 3857-3037
E-mail: info@gakusei.co.jp
Web Site: www.gakusei.co.jp
Key Personnel
President: Ichiro Tsuruoka
Foreign Rights Executive: Shigeru Ohas
Founded: 1952
Subjects: Archaeology, Business, Geography, Geology, History, Language Arts, Linguistics, Law, Literature, Literary Criticism, Essays, Philosophy, Religion - Other, Social Sciences, Sociology
ISBN Prefix(es): 4-311

Genko-Sha
1-5 Iidabashi 4 chome, Chiyoda-ku, Tokyo 102-8716
Tel: (03) 3263-3515 *Fax:* (03) 3239-5886
E-mail: gks@genkosha.co.jp
Web Site: www.genkosha.co.jp
Key Personnel
President: Morio Kitahara *Tel:* (03) 3263 3511 *Fax:* (03) 3263 3830
Dir: Chuichi Kaneko *E-mail:* kaneko@genkosha.co.jp
Founded: 1931
Membership(s): JBPA.
Subjects: Art, Film, Video, How-to, Photography
ISBN Prefix(es): 4-7683
Subsidiaries: Salon Agency Co Ltd (advertising agency)
Warehouse: Ono Poking Co Ltd, Inari Souka City *Tel:* (0489) 32 2911 *Fax:* (0489) 36 5333
Orders to: Nippan IPS Co Ltd, 11-6, 3 Cho-Me, Iidabashi, Chiyoda-Ku, Toyko 102 *Tel:* (03) 3238 0700 *Fax:* (03) 3238 0707 *E-mail:* ips05@nippan-ips.co.jp

Gyosei Corporation
30-16, Ogikubo 4 chome, Suginami-ku, Tokyo 167-8088
Tel: (03) 5349-6666 *Fax:* (03) 5349-6655
E-mail: eigyo1@gyosei.co.jp
Web Site: www.gyosei.co.jp
ISBN Prefix(es): 4-324

Hakubunkan-Shinsha Publishers Ltd
14-6, Koishikawa, 2 Chome, Bunkyo-ku, Tokyo 112-0002
Tel: (03) 3811-4721; (03) 3811-6693 *Fax:* (03) 3818-1431
Web Site: www.hakubunkan.co.jp
Key Personnel
President: Kazuhiro Ohashi
ISBN Prefix(es): 4-89177
Parent Company: Hakuyusha Publishing Co Ltd

Hakusui-Sha Co Ltd
3-24, Kanda-Ogawa-cho, Chiyoda-ku, Tokyo 101-0052
Tel: (03) 3291-7811 *Fax:* (03) 3291-8448
E-mail: hpmaster@hakusuisha.co.jp
Web Site: www.hakusuisha.co.jp *Cable:* Hakusuisha Tokyo

Key Personnel
President: Masayuki Kawamura
Foreign Rights & Trade: Motofumi Ibuki
Founded: 1915
Subjects: Art, Drama, Theater, Fiction, History, Language Arts, Linguistics, Literature, Literary Criticism, Essays, Music, Dance, Nonfiction (General), Philosophy
ISBN Prefix(es): 4-560

Hakutei-Sha+
65-1, Ikebukuro 2 chome, Toshima-ku, Tokyo 171-0014
Tel: (03) 3986-3271 *Fax:* (03) 3986-3272
E-mail: LDX00227@nifty.ne.jp
Key Personnel
President: Yasuo Sato
Foreign Rights & Trade: Takako Sato
Founded: 1977
Subjects: Health, Nutrition, Language Arts, Linguistics, Literature, Literary Criticism, Essays, Religion - Buddhist, Sports, Athletics
ISBN Prefix(es): 4-89174

Hakuyo-Sha
3F Hakuyo Dai 2 Bldg, 7-7 Kandasurugadai, One Chome, Chiyoda-ku, Tokyo 101-0062
Tel: (03) 5281-9772 *Fax:* (03) 5281-9886
E-mail: hakuyo@mars.dti.ne.jp
Web Site: www.hakuyo-sha.co.jp
Key Personnel
President: Hiroshi Nakamura
Founded: 1920
Subjects: Animals, Pets, Nonfiction (General), Psychology, Psychiatry, Science (General)
ISBN Prefix(es): 4-8269

Hakuyu-Sha
2-27, Agebacho, Shinjuku-ku, Tokyo 162-0824
Tel: (03) 3268-8271 *Fax:* (03) 3268-8273
Web Site: www.hakubunkan.co.jp
Key Personnel
President: Kazuhiro Ohashi
Foreign Trade Executive: Montaro Ono
Publicity & Advertising: Kazuya Baba
Foreign Rights: Eiji Takamori
Founded: 1948
Subjects: Agriculture, Labor, Industrial Relations, Science (General), Haiku
ISBN Prefix(es): 4-8268

Hayakawa Publishing Inc
2 Kanda-Tacho 2 chome, Chiyoda-ku, Tokyo 101-0046
Tel: (03) 3252-3111 *Fax:* (03) 3254-1550
Telex: 02222331 Books J *Cable:* Hayakawa Tokyo
Key Personnel
President: Hiroshi Hayakawa
Founded: 1945
Subjects: Art, Biography, Business, Drama, Theater, Fiction, Government, Political Science, History, Literature, Literary Criticism, Essays, Management, Mysteries, Nonfiction (General), Philosophy, Religion - Other, Science (General), Science Fiction, Fantasy, Social Sciences, Sociology
ISBN Prefix(es): 4-15

Heibonsha Ltd, Publishers+
2-29-4 Hakusan, Izumi Hakusan Bldg, Bunkyo Ku, Tokyo 112-0001
Tel: (03) 3818-0873; (03) 3818-0874 (sales) *Fax:* (03) 3818-0857
E-mail: shop@heibonsha.co.jp
Web Site: www.heibonsha.co.jp *Cable:* BOOKSHEIBONSHA
Key Personnel
President: Naoto Shimonaka
Foreign Rights & Trade: Hidenori Sekiguchi
Founded: 1914
Subjects: Art, Education, History, Nonfiction (General), Philosophy, Science (General), Social Sciences, Sociology
ISBN Prefix(es): 4-582; 4-256

Hikarinokuni Ltd
3-2-14 Uehonmachi, Tennoji-ku, Osaka 543-0001
Tel: (06) 6768-1151 *Fax:* (06) 6768-6795
E-mail: hikari@skyblue.ocn.ne.jp
Web Site: www.hikarinokuni.co.jp
Key Personnel
President: Takeshi Okamoto
Man Dir: Yotaro Matsumoto
Editorial & Export Dir: Masaaki Tsuchiya
Founded: 1945
Subjects: Economics, Education, House & Home
ISBN Prefix(es): 4-564

Hinoki Publishing Co Ltd
One Kanda-Ogawa-machi, 2 Chome, Chiyoda-ku, Tokyo 101-0052
Tel: (03) 32912488 *Fax:* (03) 32953554
E-mail: info@hinoki-shoten.co.jp
Web Site: www.hinoki-shoten.co.jp
Key Personnel
Chairman: Hisako Suginomori
President: Tsunemasa Hinoki
Founded: 1659
Publisher of Noh & Kyogen Books.
ISBN Prefix(es): 4-8279

Hirokawa Publishing Co+
3-27-14 Hongo, Bunkyo-ku, Tokyo 113-0033
Tel: (03) 38153651 *Fax:* (03) 38153650
Cable: HIGESEHI TOKYO
Key Personnel
President: Setsuo Hirokawa
Vice President: Hideo Hirokawa
Dir: Haruo Hirokawa
Founded: 1926
Subjects: Biological Sciences, Chemistry, Chemical Engineering, Medicine, Nursing, Dentistry, Science (General)
ISBN Prefix(es): 4-567
Total Titles: 50 Print

Hoikusha Publishing Co Ltd
1-6-12 Kawamata, Higashi-Osaka City, Osaka 577-0063
Tel: (06) 6788-4470 *Fax:* (06) 6788-4970
Web Site: www.hoikusha.co.jp *Cable:* Hoikusha
Key Personnel
President: Yuki Imai
Man Dir: Osamu Yoshino
Editorial: Hiroshi Murakami
Founded: 1947
Subjects: Art, Biography, Crafts, Games, Hobbies, Geography, Geology, History, How-to, Music, Dance, Natural History, Poetry, Science (General)
ISBN Prefix(es): 4-586
Branch Office(s)
1-1 Minami-Otsuka, Toshima-ku, Tokyo 170

Hokkaido University Press
Kito-9-Jo, Nishi 8-chome, Kita-Kujo Sapporo-shi, Hokkaido 060-0809
Tel: (011) 747-2308 *Fax:* (011) 736-8605
Key Personnel
President: Tomio Kanno
Vice President: Mutsuo Nakamura
Foreign Rights & Trade: Hideki Kudanami
Founded: 1970
Subjects: Science (General), Social Sciences, Sociology, Technology, Humanities, natural science
ISBN Prefix(es): 4-8329

Hokuryukan Co Ltd+
8-14, Takanawa 3 chome, Minato-ku, Tokyo 108-0074
Tel: (03) 5449-4591 *Fax:* (03) 5449-4950
E-mail: hk-ns@mk1.mqcnet.or.jp
Key Personnel
President: Hisako Fukuda
Foreign Rights & Trade: Masako Kamase
Founded: 1891
Subjects: Agriculture, Biological Sciences, Education, Medicine, Nursing, Dentistry, Science (General)
ISBN Prefix(es): 4-8326
Subsidiaries: New Science Publishing Co

The Hokuseido Press
32-4 Honkomagome, 3 Chome, Bunkyo-ku, Tokyo 113-0021
Tel: (03) 38270511 *Fax:* (03) 38270567
E-mail: info@hokuseido.com *Cable:* HOKSEDPRES TOKYO
Key Personnel
Dir: Masazo Yamamoto
Sales, Advertising, Rights & Permissions: Keisuke Yamamoto
Founded: 1914
Subjects: Biography, Philosophy, Poetry, Religion - Other
ISBN Prefix(es): 4-590
Orders to: Book East, PO Box 13352, Portland, OR 97213, United States *Tel:* 503-287-0974 *Fax:* 503-281-3693 *E-mail:* kwakiyama@aol.com

Holp Book Co Ltd
Shinhana Bldg, 19-7 Shinjuku 1 chome, Shinjuku-ku, Tokyo 160
Tel: (03) 5285-5011 *Fax:* (03) 3225-1663
E-mail: holp@holp.co.jp
Web Site: www.holp.co.jp
Key Personnel
President: Mr Seiji Ohyabu
Founded: 1964
Subjects: Art, Education, Geography, Geology, Literature, Literary Criticism, Essays, Mathematics, Science (General)
ISBN Prefix(es): 4-89427
Subsidiaries: Holp Shuppan Publishers

Horitsu Bunka-Sha
71, Iwagakakiuchicho, Kamigamo, Kita-ku, Kyoto 603-8053
Tel: (075) 791-7131 *Fax:* (075) 721-8400
E-mail: eigy@hou-bun.co.jp
Web Site: web.kyoto-inet.or.jp/org/houritu
Key Personnel
President: Tsutomu Okamura
Founded: 1947
Subjects: Economics, Law, Philosophy, Public Administration, Social Sciences, Sociology, Politics
ISBN Prefix(es): 4-589

Hyoronsha Publishing Co Ltd
2-21 TsukudoHachimancho, Shinjuku-ku, Tokyo 162-0815
Tel: (03) 3260-9401 *Fax:* (03) 3260-9408
Key Personnel
President: Harunobu Takeshita
Chief Editor: Kunio Hitomi
Sales Manager: Zenzo Uchida
Founded: 1948
Subjects: Education, History, Language Arts, Linguistics, Law, Philosophy, Religion - Buddhist, Religion - Other, Social Sciences, Sociology
ISBN Prefix(es): 4-566

Ichiryu-Sha
5-18 Yanaka 2 chome, Taito-ku, Tokyo 110-0001
Tel: (03) 3822-0585 *Fax:* (03) 3821-3964
Key Personnel
President: Tsuguo Hikosaka
Founded: 1951
Subjects: Law, Social Sciences, Sociology
ISBN Prefix(es): 4-7527

PUBLISHERS — JAPAN

Ie-No-Hikari Association+
11 Ichigaya-Funagawaracho, Shinjuku-ku, Tokyo 162-8448
Tel: (03) 3266-9029 *Fax:* (03) 3266-9053
E-mail: hikari@mxd.meshnet.or.jp
Web Site: www.ienohikari.or.jp
Key Personnel
President: Masahiko Takada
Man Dir: Masaya Kakunaka
Executive Dir: Katsuro Kawaguchi; Kazuyuki Morishita
Book Publication: Kenji Yokoyama
Foreign Rights & Trade: Satoshi Sekiguchi
Founded: 1925
Subjects: Agriculture, Economics, House & Home, Social Sciences, Sociology, Cooperatives
ISBN Prefix(es): 4-259

Igaku-Shoin Ltd+
24-3 Hongo, 5 Chome, Bunkyo-ku, Tokyo 113-8719
Tel: (03) 38175600 *Fax:* (03) 38157791
E-mail: info@igaku-shoin.co.jp
Web Site: www.igaku-shoin.co.jp
Key Personnel
President: Yu Kanehara
Vice President, Medical Publications: Hideho Nakamura
Vice President, Sales: Kensaku Kobayashi
Senior Manager, Foreign Books & Journals: Kazuo Kuwabara *Tel:* (03) 3817 5676
 E-mail: k-kuwabara@igaku-shoin.co.jp
Founded: 1944
Subjects: Medicine, Nursing, Dentistry
ISBN Prefix(es): 4-260
Subsidiaries: Medical Sciences International Ltd; LWW Igaku-Shoin Ltd; Igaku-Shoin Medical Publishers Inc

Institute for Financial Affairs Inc-KINZAI
Kinyu-Zaisei-Kaikan, 19 Minami-motomachi, Shinjuku-ku, Tokyo 160-8520
Tel: (03) 3358-0052 *Fax:* (03) 3358-2069
Key Personnel
President: Mr Hiromi Tokuda
General Manager: Mr Akifumi Kohno
Founded: 1950
Subjects: Accounting, Finance
ISBN Prefix(es): 4-322
Subsidiaries: KINZAI Corporation
Branch Office(s)
Osaka, Nagoya & Fukuoka
U.S. Office(s): 600 Third Ave, 23rd floor, New York, NY 10016, United States *Tel:* 212-687-8316 *Fax:* 212-687-8317

International Society for Educational Information (ISEI)
Affiliate of Ministry of Foreign Affairs, Japan
Shinko Ofisomu 502, 20-3 San'ei-cho, Shinjuku-ku, Tokyo 160-0008
Tel: (03) 33581138 *Fax:* (03) 33597188
E-mail: kaya@isei.or.jp
Web Site: www.isei.or.jp
Key Personnel
Chair, Board of Directors: Michiko Kaya
 E-mail: kaya@isei.or.jp
Founded: 1958
Specialize in publications about Japan.
Subjects: Art, Crafts, Games, Hobbies, Economics, Geography, Geology, History, Culture, Japan
Number of titles published annually: 10 Print
Total Titles: 48 Print

Ishihara Publishing Co Ltd
13-2, Nishi-Sengokucho, Kagoshima City, Kagoshima 892-0847
Tel: (0992) 391200 *Fax:* (0992) 391202
Key Personnel
President: Kanichiro Ishihara
Foreign Rights/Trade: Tetsu Nakahata
Founded: 1990
ISBN Prefix(es): 4-900611
Imprints: Ishihara's Decade Diary
Distributed by Japan Publication & Selling Co Ltd; Mail Order House Catalog House Co Ltd; Tokyo Book Seller's Co Ltd

Ishihara's Decade Diary, *imprint of* Ishihara Publishing Co Ltd

Ishiyaku Publishers Inc
1-7-10, Honkomagome, Bunkyo-ku, Tokyo 113-8612
Tel: (03) 5395-7600 *Fax:* (03) 5395-7603
E-mail: dev-mdp@nna.so-net.ne.jp
Telex: 2723298 Mdp J *Cable:* MEPHARMA TOKYO
Key Personnel
President: Katsuji Fujita
Publisher, Dental Books: Yukuhide Yonekawa
Publisher, Medical: Akio Fukushima
Publisher, Dental Journals: Takao Suda
Marketing Dir: Akira Iwase; Tai Watanabe
Foreign Rights/Trade: Ms Shoko Ishimura
Founded: 1921
Subjects: Health, Nutrition, Medicine, Nursing, Dentistry, Veterinary Science, Natural Science
ISBN Prefix(es): 4-263; 4-281
Branch Office(s)
c/o Manden Bldg, 11-23 Nishi-Tenma 4-Chome, Kita-ku, Osaka-shi
Orders to: Tokyo Mail Service Co Ltd, 1-30-6 Sugamo, Toshimaku, Tokyo 170

Itaria Shobo Ltd
2-23, Kanda-Jimbocho, Chiyoda-ku, Tokyo 101-0051
Tel: (03) 3262-1656 *Fax:* (03) 3234-6469
E-mail: HQM01271@nifty.ne.jp *Cable:* ITALIASHOBO
Key Personnel
President: Motomichi Ito
Foreign Rights/Trade: Doichi Ito
Founded: 1958
Specialize in Italian, Spanish & Portuguese imported books.
ISBN Prefix(es): 4-900143

Iwanami Shoten, Publishers+
2-5-5, Hitotsubashi, Chiyoda-ku, Tokyo 101-0003
Tel: (03) 5210-4115 *Fax:* (03) 3239-9619
Web Site: www.iwanami.co.jp
Key Personnel
President: Nobukazu Otsuka
Editorial Dir: Suzuki Minoru
Foreign Rights Manager: Sachiko Kagaya
Foreign Rights: Rika Ito *E-mail:* rika-ito@iwanami.co.jp; Noa Shimizu
Founded: 1913
Subjects: Art, Biography, Economics, Electronics, Electrical Engineering, History, Literature, Literary Criticism, Essays, Philosophy, Photography, Psychology, Psychiatry, Science (General), Social Sciences, Sociology
ISBN Prefix(es): 4-00
Number of titles published annually: 700 Print; 10 CD-ROM
Total Titles: 5,000 Print; 30 CD-ROM; 10 Audio
Orders to: Japan Publications Trading Co, Ltd, 1-2-1 Sarugakucho, Chiyoda-ku, Tokyo *Tel:* (03) 32923751 *Fax:* (03) 32920410

Iwasaki Shoten Publishing Co Ltd
1-9-2 Suido, Bunkyo-ku, Tokyo 112-0005
Tel: (03) 3812-9131 *Fax:* (03) 3816-6033
E-mail: ask@iwasakishoten.co.jp
Web Site: www.iwasakishoten.co.jp
Key Personnel
President: Hiro Iwasaki
Sales Manager: Tutomu Yasuda
Editorial: Toshio Iino
Founded: 1934
Membership(s): Japan Children's Books Association.
Subjects: Art
ISBN Prefix(es): 4-265
Associate Companies: Iwasaki Gakujitsu Publishing Co
Subsidiaries: Iwasaki Art Publishing Co

Japan Bible Society
4-5-1 Ginza, Chuo-ku, Tokyo 104-0061
Mailing Address: PO Box 6, Kyobashi
Tel: (03) 3567-1990; (03) 3567-1987 (distribution) *Fax:* (03) 3567-4436 (administration)
E-mail: info@bible.or.jp
Web Site: www.bible.or.jp
Key Personnel
President: Hiroshi Omiya
Foreign Rights/Trade: Rev Makoto Watabe
 E-mail: makoto-w@bible.or.jp
Founded: 1875
Membership(s): United Bible Societies.
ISBN Prefix(es): 4-8202

Japan Broadcast Publishing Co Ltd+
41-1, Udagawacho, Shibuya-ku, Tokyo 150-8081
Tel: (03) 3780-3356 *Fax:* (03) 3780-3348
E-mail: webmaster@npb.nhk-grp.co.jp
Key Personnel
President: Takeshi Matsuo
Contact: Chieako Ishizuka
Foreign Rights/Trade: Masahiro Kizaki
Founded: 1931
Subjects: Art, Crafts, Games, Hobbies, Education, Fiction, Geography, Geology, History, How-to, Language Arts, Linguistics, Literature, Literary Criticism, Essays, Nonfiction (General), Science (General), Social Sciences, Sociology
ISBN Prefix(es): 4-14
Parent Company: NHK (Japan Broadcasting Corporation)

Japan Educational Publishing Co Ltd, see Nihon-Bunkyo Shuppan (Japan Educational Publishing Co Ltd)

Japan Industrial Publishing Co Ltd+
Suzuki Bldg, 10-1 Azabu-10-Ban 3 chome, Minato-ku, Tokyo 106-0045
Tel: (03) 3456-1827 *Fax:* (03) 3944-6826
E-mail: info@nikko-pb.co.jp; yktech@mx.nikko-pb.co.jp
Web Site: www.nikko-pb.co.jp
Key Personnel
President: Sakutarou Kobayashi
Founded: 1953
Subjects: Construction Machinery & Equipment, Hydraulics & Pneumatics
ISBN Prefix(es): 4-88045
Subsidiaries: Nikkoh Techno Research Co Ltd

Japan Publications Inc+
5F Nichibo Bldg, 1-2-2 Sarugaku-cho, Chiyoda-ku, Tokyo 101-0064
Tel: (03) 32958411 *Fax:* (03) 32958416
Telex: J27161 *Cable:* NICHIBOSHUPPAN TOKYO
Key Personnel
President: Toshihiro Kuwahara
Vice President: Yoshiro Fujiwara
Editor-in-Chief: Yukishige Takahashi
Rights & Permissions: Masatoshi Sato
Founded: 1942
Subjects: Agriculture, Asian Studies, Child Care & Development, Cookery, Crafts, Games, Hobbies, Health, Nutrition
ISBN Prefix(es): 4-8170
Parent Company: Japan Publications Trading Co Ltd (Import & Export)
Orders to: Oxford University Press, 198 Madison Ave, New York, NY 10016, United States

Japan Scientific Societies Press, see Business Center for Academic Societies Japan

The Japan Times Ltd
4-5-4 Shibaura, Minato-ku, Tokyo 108-0023
Tel: (03) 3453-2013 *Fax:* (03) 3453-8023
E-mail: books@japantimes.co.jp
Web Site: bookclub.japantimes.co.jp
Key Personnel
President: Toshiaki Ogasawara
Foreign Rights/Trade: Junichi Saito
Founded: 1897
Subjects: Asian Studies, Nonfiction (General)
ISBN Prefix(es): 4-7890

Japan Travel Bureau Inc
JTB 6F-7F, 2-3-11, Higashi, Shinagwa-ku, Tokyo 140-8603
Tel: (03) 5796-5525 *Fax:* (03) 5796-5529
Web Site: www.jtb.co.jp
Telex: 2228020 Jtb Bok J *Cable:* Jtbbook Tokyo
Key Personnel
Vice President, Publishing: Mitsumasa Iwada
Man Dir: Reiji Aoki
Editor-in-Chief, Books in English: Teruo Saito
Foreign Rights/Trade: Hiroshi Miyazaki
Founded: 1947
Subjects: Geography, Geology, History, Language Arts, Linguistics, Travel, Fine Arts
ISBN Prefix(es): 4-533
Subsidiaries: Densan Process Co; Kotsu Print Co; Kotsu Seihon Co; Toyo Books Co
Branch Office(s)
The Royal Exchange Bldg, 56 Pitt St, Sydney, Australia
5 Rue Chantepoulet, Geneva, Switzerland
20 rue Quentin Bauchart, Paris 75008, France
50-51 Russell Sq, London WC1B 4JQ, United Kingdom
c/o Guam Hilton Hotel, Ipao Beach, Guam
Hotel Miramar, Rm 2123, Nathan Rd, Kowloon, Hong Kong
Via Emilia 47, Rome, Italy
U.S. Office(s): 624 S Grand Ave, Suite 1410, Los Angeles, CA 90014, United States
402 Qantas Bldg, Union Sq, 360 Post St, San Francisco, CA 94018, United States
Waikiki Business Plaza, 2270 Kalakaua Ave, Honolulu, HI 96815, United States
The International Bldg, 45 Rockfeller Plaza, New York, NY 10020, United States

Jiho
Formerly Yakugyo Jiho Sha Co Ltd
Hitotsbashi Bldg, 2-6-3 Hitotsubashi, Chiyoda-ku, Tokyo 101-8421
Tel: (03) 3265-7755 *Fax:* (03) 3265-8855
Key Personnel
President: Shozo Takeda
Specialize in pharmaceutical industry & regulation, & pharmaceutical sciences.
ISBN Prefix(es): 4-8407

Journey Editions, *imprint of* Charles E Tuttle Publishing Co Inc

JUSE Press Ltd, see Nikkagiren Shuppan-Sha (JUSE Press Ltd)

Kadokawa Shoten Publishing Co Ltd
2-13-3 Fujimi, Chiyoda-ku, Tokyo 102-8177
Tel: (03) 32388431 *Fax:* (03) 32627733
E-mail: K-master@kadokawa.co.jp
Web Site: www.kadokawa.co.jp
Key Personnel
Man Dir: Ohora Kunimitsu
Editorial: Kichinosuke Sato
President, Sales: Tsuguuhiko Kadokawa
Production: Yukio Hashimoto
Publicity: Masatoshi Tojo
Rights & Permissions: Hiroshi Tagami
Founded: 1945
Subjects: Art, Fiction, History, Literature, Literary Criticism, Essays, Religion - Other
ISBN Prefix(es): 4-04

Kaibundo Publishing Co Ltd, see Kaibundo Shuppan

Kaibundo Shuppan
Formerly Kaibundo Publishing Co Ltd
5-4 Suido 2 chome, Bunkyo-ku, Tokyo 112-0005
Tel: (03) 3815-3291 *Fax:* (03) 3815-3953
E-mail: LED04737@nifty.ne.jp
Key Personnel
President: Yoshihiro Okada
Editorial Dir & Foreign Rights/Trade: Yuhji Tamura
Founded: 1914
Subjects: Business, Engineering (General), Maritime, Microcomputers, Technology, Navigation, Ship-building
ISBN Prefix(es): 4-303

Kaisei-Sha Publishing Co Ltd+
3-5 Ichigaya Sadohara-cho, Shinjuku-ku, Tokyo 162-8450
Tel: (03) 32603229 *Fax:* (03) 32603540
E-mail: foreign@kaiseisha.co.jp
Web Site: www.kaiseisha.co.jp
Key Personnel
President: Masaki Imamura
Editorial Dir: Kimiko Matsukura
Editor, Foreign Rights: Hiroshi Konno
Founded: 1936
Subjects: Animals, Pets, Art, Biography, Crafts, Games, Hobbies, Disability, Special Needs, Environmental Studies, Foreign Countries, History
ISBN Prefix(es): 4-03
Number of titles published annually: 150 Print
Total Titles: 4,000 Print

Kaitakusha+
2-5-4, Kanda-Jinbocho, Chiyoda-ku, Tokyo 101-0051
Tel: (03) 5842-8900 *Fax:* (03) 5842-5560
E-mail: webmaster@kaitakusha.co.jp
Web Site: www.kaitakusha.co.jp
Key Personnel
President: Yoshiko Naganuma
Foreign Trade: Kenichi Naganuma
Foreign Rights: Yasuhiko Yamamoto
Founded: 1927
Subjects: Education, English as a Second Language, Language Arts, Linguistics, Literature, Literary Criticism, Essays
ISBN Prefix(es): 4-7589
Number of titles published annually: 30 Print; 3 CD-ROM; 3 Audio
Total Titles: 300 Print; 10 CD-ROM; 50 Audio

Kajima Institute Publishing Co Ltd
6-5-13 Akasaka, Minato-ku, Tokyo 107-8345
Tel: (03) 5561-2550 *Fax:* (03) 5561 2560
E-mail: info@kajima-publishing.co.jp
Web Site: www.kajima-publishing.co.jp
Telex: 02422467 Kajima J attn Kajima Inst Pub Co
Key Personnel
President: Takaaki Ida
Foreign Rights/Trade: Humio Odagiri
Founded: 1963
Subjects: Architecture & Interior Design, Civil Engineering, Engineering (General), Social Sciences, Sociology, Fine Arts, Urban Problems
ISBN Prefix(es): 4-306
Bookshop(s): Kasumigaseki Bookstore, 3-2-5 Kasumigaseki, Chiyoda-ku, Tokyo; Shinjuku Mitsui Building Bookstore, 2-1 Nishishinjuku, Shinjuku-ku, Tokyo; Shibuya Tohoseimei Building Bookstore, 2-15 Shibuya, Shibuya-ku, Tokyo

Kanehara & Co Ltd
2-31-14 Yushima, Bunkyo-ku, Tokyo 113-8687
Tel: (03) 3811-7185; (03) 3811-7184 (sales)
Fax: (03) 3813-0288
Web Site: www.kanehara-shuppan.co.jp *Cable:* Kaneharaco Tokyo
Key Personnel
President: Hiromitsu Kawai
Founded: 1875
Subjects: Medicine, Nursing, Dentistry
ISBN Prefix(es): 4-307

Kansai University Press
3-3-35, Yamatecho, Suita-Shi, Osaka 564-8680
Tel: (06) 6368-1171 *Fax:* (06) 6389-5162
Web Site: www.kansai-u.ac.jp/index.html
Key Personnel
Chairman, Board of Trustees: Heian Hazama
Founded: 1947
Subjects: Social Sciences, Sociology, Natural Science
ISBN Prefix(es): 4-87354

Kawade Shobo Shinsha Publishers
2-32-2 Sendagaya, Shibuya-ku, Tokyo 151-0051
Tel: (03) 3404-1201 *Fax:* (03) 3404-6386
E-mail: info@kawade.co.jp
Web Site: www.kawade.co.jp
Key Personnel
President: Shigeo Wakamori
Founded: 1886
Subjects: Art, Fiction, History, Nonfiction (General), Philosophy, Science (General), Social Sciences, Sociology
ISBN Prefix(es): 4-309

Kazamashobo Co Ltd+
1-34 Kanda Jimbocho, Chiyoda-ku, Tokyo 101-0051
Tel: (03) 3291-5729 *Fax:* (03) 3291-5757
E-mail: kazama@wd6.so-net.ne.jp
Web Site: www.kazamashobo.co.jp
Key Personnel
President: Tsutomu Kazama
Founded: 1933
Membership(s): Japan Book Publishers Association.
Subjects: Education, History, Literature, Literary Criticism, Essays, Philosophy, Psychology, Psychiatry, Social Sciences, Sociology
ISBN Prefix(es): 4-7599

Keigaku Publishing Co Ltd+
1-46 Kanda-Jimbo-cho 1 chome, Chiyoda-ku, Tokyo 101-0051
Tel: (03) 3233-3733 *Fax:* (03) 3233-3730
Key Personnel
Publisher: Kazumi Mitsui
Editorial Dir, Foreign Rights Manager: Kiyoshi Yoshizaki
Sales Manager: Yoshiaki Tokunaga
Production Manager: Isoyoshi Yamamoto
Foreign Rights Associate: Naoko Sakaki
Founded: 1969
Subjects: Computer Science, Electronics, Electrical Engineering, Science (General)
ISBN Prefix(es): 4-7665
Associate Companies: Yugaku-sha Ltd

Keisuisha Publishing Company Ltd
1-4 Komachi, Naka-ku, Hiroshima 733-0041
Tel: (082) 2467909 *Fax:* (082) 2467876
E-mail: info@keisui.co.jp
Web Site: www.keisui.co.jp
Key Personnel
President: Itsushi Kimura *E-mail:* kimura@keisui.co.jp
Founded: 1975
Subjects: Asian Studies, Economics, Education, History, Language Arts, Linguistics, Literature,

Literary Criticism, Essays, Philosophy, Social Sciences, Sociology
ISBN Prefix(es): 4-87440
Number of titles published annually: 40 Print
Total Titles: 710 Print

Kenkyusha Ltd
2-11-3, Fujimi, Chiyoda-ku, Tokyo 102-0071
Tel: (03) 3288-7777; (03) 3288-7856 *Fax:* (03) 3288-7799
Web Site: www.kenkyusha.co.jp
Key Personnel
President: Kunikatsu Araki
Foreign Trade Executive: Hiroji Yamazaki
Foreign Rights Executive: Josuke Okada
Founded: 1907
Subjects: Language Arts, Linguistics
ISBN Prefix(es): 4-327

Kin-No-Hoshi Sha Co Ltd
4-3 Kojima 1 chome, Taito-ku, Tokyo 111-0056
Tel: (03) 3861-1861 *Fax:* (03) 3861-1507
E-mail: gonta@kinnohoshi.co.jp
Web Site: www.kinnohoshi.co.jp
Key Personnel
President: Masakazu Saito
Vice President: Matsuo Ishibashi
Editor: Masao Okohira
Foreign Rights: Yuko Saito
Founded: 1919
Subjects: Education
ISBN Prefix(es): 4-323
Warehouse: 1997-1 Hizaore 3-chome, Asaka-City, Saitama

Kindai Kagaku Sha Co Ltd+
Kindai Kagaku-Sha Bldg, 2-7-15 Ichigaya-Tamachi, Shinjuku City, Tokyo 162-0843
Tel: (03) 3260-6160 *Fax:* (03) 3269-6060
Key Personnel
Chief Executive Officer: Ryohji Sakurai
Founded: 1959
Membership(s): Kohgakusho Kyokai (Association of Engineering Book Publishers); Shokyoh (Japan Book Publishers Association.
Subjects: Computer Science, Electronics, Electrical Engineering, Mathematics, Physics
ISBN Prefix(es): 4-7649

Kinokuniya Co Ltd (Publishing Department)+
3-13-11 Higashi, Shibuya-ku, Tokyo 150-0011
Tel: (03) 5469-5919 *Fax:* (03) 5469-5958
E-mail: publish@kinokuniya.co.jp; info@kinokuniya.co.jp
Web Site: www.kinokuniya.co.jp *Cable:* KINOKUNI
Key Personnel
General Manager: Shinjiro Kuroda
Sales: Yoshichika Ogasawara
Founded: 1926
Subjects: Art, Biography, History, Literature, Literary Criticism, Essays, Philosophy, Psychology, Psychiatry, Science (General), Social Sciences, Sociology
ISBN Prefix(es): 4-314
Associate Companies: Kinokuniya Bookstores of America Co Ltd, 1581 Webster St, San Francisco, CA 94115, United States; Kinokuniya Publications Service of New York Co Ltd, 10 W 49 St, New York, NY 10020, United States; Kinokuniya Publications Service of London Co Ltd, Radnor House, 93-97 Regent St, London W1R 7TG, United Kingdom

Kinpodo
34, Nishi-Teramaecho, Shishigatani, Sakyo-ku, Kyoto 606-8425
Tel: (075) 751-1111 *Fax:* (075) 751-6858
E-mail: kkinpodo@kb3.so-net.ne.jp
Key Personnel
President: Katsusuke Shibata
Foreign Rights/Trade: Terukazu Ichii
Founded: 1948
Subjects: Medicine, Nursing, Dentistry
ISBN Prefix(es): 4-7653

KINZAI Corporation+
19, Minami-Motomachi, Shinjuku-ku, Tokyo 160-8520
Tel: (03) 33580011 *Fax:* (03) 33580036
Web Site: www.kinzai.or.jp
Key Personnel
President: Akira Kanai
General Manager: Shigeru Abe *E-mail:* s.abe@kinzai.or.jp
Founded: 1971
Subjects: Finance, Banking, Security Business
ISBN Prefix(es): 4-322
Parent Company: Institute for Financial Affairs Inc
Branch Office(s)
Fukuoka Cities
Nagoya
Osaka

Kodansha International Ltd+
Subsidiary of Kodansha Ltd
1-17-14 Otowa, Bunkyo-ku, Tokyo 112-8652
Tel: (03) 39446491 *Fax:* (03) 39446394
E-mail: sales@kodansha-intl.co.jp
Web Site: www.thejapanpage.com; www.kodansha-intl.co.jp
Key Personnel
President: Fumio Hatano
Editorial Vice President: Kazuichi Ohmura
Sales Vice President: Kazuhide Sainowaki
Editorial Dir: Stephen Shaw *Tel:* (03) 3944-6493 *E-mail:* shaw@kodansha-intl.co.jp
International Rights: Ayako Akaogi
Founded: 1963
Specialize in Japan & Asia.
Subjects: Art, Cookery, Crafts, Games, Hobbies, Fiction, History, How-to, Language Arts, Linguistics, Philosophy, Sports, Athletics, Martial arts
ISBN Prefix(es): 4-7700
Branch Office(s)
Kodansha Europe, 95 Aldwych, London WC2B 4JF, United Kingdom *Tel:* (020) 7304 4095 *Fax:* (020) 7304 4096
U.S. Office(s): Kodansha America, 575 Lexington Ave, New York, NY 10022, United States *Tel:* (917) 322-6200 *Fax:* (212) 935-6929

Kodansha Ltd+
2-12-21 Otowa, Bunkyo-ku, Tokyo 112-8001
Tel: (03) 5395-3420 (foreign rights dept) *Fax:* (03) 3942-8017 (foreign rights dept)
Web Site: www.kodansha.co.jp
Telex: J34509 Kodansha *Cable:* KODANSHAPUBLISH TOKYO
Key Personnel
President: Sawako Noma
Editorial: Akira Higashiura
Sales: Hironobu Hamada
Rights & Permissions: Takashi Kasahara *E-mail:* t-kasahara@kodansha.co.jp
Founded: 1909
Subjects: Art, Economics, Education, Fiction, Geography, Geology, History, House & Home, Humor, Language Arts, Linguistics, Literature, Literary Criticism, Essays, Medicine, Nursing, Dentistry, Nonfiction (General), Philosophy, Religion - Other, Social Sciences, Sociology
ISBN Prefix(es): 4-06
Subsidiaries: Kodansha Europe Ltd (London, UK); Kodansha International Ltd (Tokyo, Japan)
Branch Office(s)
Osaka
U.S. Office(s): Kodansha America, 575 Lexington Ave, New York, NY 10022, United States *Tel:* (917) 322-6200 *Fax:* (212) 935-6929
Book Club(s): Kodansha Disney Children's Book Club

Kodansha Scientific Ltd
2-12-21 Otowa, Bunko-ku 112-8001
Tel: (03) 5395 3420 *Fax:* (03) 3942 8017
Key Personnel
President: Sawako Noma
General Manager: Katsuhiro Ohbori
Founded: 1970
Subjects: Science (General)
ISBN Prefix(es): 4-06
Parent Company: Kodansha Ltd

Kogyo Chosakai Publishing Co Ltd
2-14-7, Hongo, Bunkyo-ku, Tokyo 113-8466
Tel: (03) 3817-4701 *Fax:* (03) 3817-4748
E-mail: m-order@po.iijnet.or.jp; rtb87919@mtd.biglobe.ne.jp
Web Site: www.iijnet.or.jp/kocho
Key Personnel
President: Yukio Shimura
Foreign Rights/Trade: Shigeki Shintani
Founded: 1954
Subjects: Architecture & Interior Design, Engineering (General), Science (General), Technology

Kokudo-Sha Co Ltd
1-17-6, Mejirodai, Bunkyo-ku, Tokyo 112-0015
Tel: (03) 3943-3721 *Fax:* (03) 3943-3740
Web Site: www.koutoku.co.jp/kokudosha
Key Personnel
President: Michiaki Suzuki
Founded: 1948
Subjects: Biography, Child Care & Development, Education, Literature, Literary Criticism, Essays, Psychology, Psychiatry, Social Sciences, Sociology
ISBN Prefix(es): 4-337

Kokushokankokai Co Ltd
2-10-5, Shimura, Itabashi-ku, Tokyo 174-0056
Tel: (03) 5970-7421 *Fax:* (03) 5970-7427
E-mail: info@kokusho.co.jp
Web Site: www.kokusho.co.jp
Key Personnel
President: Kesao Sato
Chief Editor: Junichi Isozaki
Editor: Reiko Iwamoto
Founded: 1971
Subjects: Asian Studies, Education, Fiction, History, Language Arts, Linguistics, Literature, Literary Criticism, Essays, Military Science, Religion - Buddhist, Western Fiction
ISBN Prefix(es): 4-336
Warehouse: 3-11-26 Vchiya, Vrawa-sh, Saitama Prefecture 336

Komine Shoten Co Ltd
4-11, Ichigaya-Daimachi, Shinjuku-ku, Tokyo 162-0066
Tel: (03) 3357-3521 *Fax:* (03) 3357-1027
E-mail: info@komineshoten.co.jp
Web Site: www.komineshoten.co.jp
Key Personnel
President: Norio Komine
Foreign Rights/Trade: Noriko Kojima
Founded: 1947
Subjects: Education, Science (General)
ISBN Prefix(es): 4-338

Kosei Publishing Co Ltd+
Affiliate of Rissho Kosei-kai
7-1 Wada, 2 Chome, Suginami-ku, Tokyo 166-8535
Tel: (03) 5385-2319 *Fax:* (03) 5385-2331
Web Site: www.kosei-shuppan.co.jp/english/

Key Personnel
President: Yukio Yokota
Foreign Trade, Foreign Rights Executive: Toru Nakagawa
Dir, International Publishing Section: Koichiro Yoshida E-mail: yoshida@kosei-shuppan.co.jp
Founded: 1966
Membership(s): Japan Book Publishers Association.
Subjects: Art, Child Care & Development, Education, History, Human Relations, Literature, Literary Criticism, Essays, Music, Dance, Nonfiction (General), Philosophy, Psychology, Psychiatry, Religion - Buddhist, Self-Help, Travel
ISBN Prefix(es): 4-333
Number of titles published annually: 59 Print
Total Titles: 1,024 Print; 2 Audio
Distributed by Charles E Tuttle Co Inc

Koseisha-Koseikaku Co Ltd
8, San'eicho, Shinjuku-ku, Tokyo 160-0008
Tel: (03) 3359-7371 *Fax:* (03) 3359-7375
E-mail: koseisha@po.iijnet.or.jp
Web Site: www.vinet.or.jp/~koseisha; www.kouseisha.com
Key Personnel
President: Hisao Satake
Editorial: Fukase Simao
Publishing: Hajime Torizuka
Founded: 1922
Subjects: Astrology, Occult, Astronomy, Education, Labor, Industrial Relations, Philosophy, Science (General), Social Sciences, Sociology, Technology, Fishery
ISBN Prefix(es): 4-7699

Koyo Shobo+
7 Kita-Yakakecho, Saiin, Ukyo-ku, Kyoto 615-0026
Tel: (075) 312-0788 *Fax:* (075) 312-7447
Key Personnel
President: Yoshiki Ueda
Foreign Rights/Trade: Tatsuo Murata
Founded: 1960
Subjects: Archaeology, Art, Business, Developing Countries, Drama, Theater, Economics, Education, Environmental Studies, Ethnicity, Government, Political Science, History, Law, Management, Marketing, Philosophy, Psychology, Psychiatry, Social Sciences, Sociology
ISBN Prefix(es): 4-7710

Kyodo-Isho Shuppan Co Ltd+
3-21-10 Hongo, Bunkyo-ku, Tokyo 113-0033
Tel: (03) 3818-2361 *Fax:* (03) 3818-2368
E-mail: kyodo-ed@fd5.so-net.ne.jp
Web Site: www.kyodo-isho.co.jp
Key Personnel
President & Foreign Rights/Trade: Setsu Kinoshita
Founded: 1947
Subjects: Medicine, Nursing, Dentistry
ISBN Prefix(es): 4-7639

Kyoritsu Shuppan Co Ltd
4-6-19, Kohinata, Bunkyo-ku, Tokyo 112-8700
Tel: (03) 3947-2511 *Fax:* (03) 3944-8182
E-mail: general@kyoritsu-pub.co.jp
Web Site: www.kyoritsu-pub.co.jp
Key Personnel
President, Editorial Dir & Foreign Rights/Trade: Mitsuaki Nanjo
Sales Dir: Hiroshi Todoroki
Founded: 1926
Subjects: Biological Sciences, Chemistry, Chemical Engineering, Computer Science, Engineering (General), Mathematics, Medicine, Nursing, Dentistry, Natural History, Physics, Technology, Information Science, Natural Science
ISBN Prefix(es): 4-320

La Verve, *imprint of* Yohan Shuppan

Library & Information Science, *imprint of* Riso-Sha

Lotus, *imprint of* Yohan Shuppan

Maruzen Co Ltd
2-3-10, Nihombashi, Chuo-ku, Tokyo 103-8245
Mailing Address: PO Box 5050, Tokyo International 100-3191
Tel: (03) 3272-0514 *Fax:* (03) 3272-0527
E-mail: webmaster@maruzen.co.jp
Web Site: www.maruzen.co.jp; www.maruzen.co.jp/home-eng/index.html
Telex: J26516; J26517 *Cable:* MARUYA TOKYO
Key Personnel
Chairman: Kumao Ebihara
President: Nobuo Suzuki
Executive Dir: Ryozo Fujiwara
Man Dir: Isamu Tanahashi; Hiroshi Muko
Senior General Manager: Tsuneo Miyama
Founded: 1869
Subjects: Architecture & Interior Design, Biological Sciences, Chemistry, Chemical Engineering, Civil Engineering, Computer Science, Electronics, Electrical Engineering, Mechanical Engineering, Physics, Science (General)
ISBN Prefix(es): 4-621
Associate Companies: Maruzen Planet Co Lt, Tokyo
Subsidiaries: Maruzen Asia (Pte) Ltd; Maruzen International Co Ltd
Branch Office(s)
Fukuoka
Hiroshima
Kanazawa
Kobe
Kyoto
Nagoya
Okayama
Osaka
Sendai
Tsukuba
Yokohama
Warehouse: 5-7-1, Heiwajima, Ohta-ku, Tokyo 143

Medical Sciences International Ltd+
1-28-36 Hongo, Bunkyo-ku, Tokyo 113-0033
Tel: (03) 5804-6050 *Fax:* (03) 5804-6055
E-mail: info@medsi.co.jp
Web Site: www.medsi.co.jp *Cable:* MEDSIJAPAN TOKYO
Key Personnel
President: Hiroshi Wakamatsu
Founded: 1979
Subjects: Medicine, Nursing, Dentistry
ISBN Prefix(es): 4-89592; 4-943921
Imprints: MEDSI

MEDSI, *imprint of* Medical Sciences International Ltd

Meiji Shoin Co Ltd
1-1-7 Okubo, Shinjuku-ku, Tokyo 169-0072
Tel: (03) 5292-0117 *Fax:* (03) 5292-6182
E-mail: nihongo1@oak.ocn.ne.jp
Web Site: www.meijishoin.co.jp
Key Personnel
President: Yuzuru Miki
Editorial: Kunio Kawami
Sales: Harunori Saito
Foreign Rights/Trade: Kazuo Kitsuuchi
Founded: 1896
Subjects: History, Literature, Literary Criticism, Essays, Philosophy, Poetry, Chinese Philosophy & Literature, Haiku & Tanka Poetry, Japanese & Chinese Classic Literature, Japanese & Kanji Dictionaries, Japanese Textbooks
ISBN Prefix(es): 4-625
Branch Office(s)
Fukuoka
Osaka

Mejikaru Furendo-sha (Medical Friend)+
2-4 Kudan Kita 3 Chome, Chiyoda-ku, Tokyo 102-0073
Tel: (03) 32646611 *Fax:* (03) 32616602 (distribution); (03) 32640704 (editorial affairs)
E-mail: mfhensyu@mb.infoweb.ne.jp; mfeigyou@mb.infoweb.ne.jp; mfsoumu@mb.infoweb.ne.jp
Key Personnel
President, Rights & Permissions: Yoshihiro Ogura
Foreign Rights: Hiromi Ikoma
Founded: 1947
Subjects: Art, Health, Nutrition, Medicine, Nursing, Dentistry
ISBN Prefix(es): 4-8392
Associate Companies: The International Nursing Foundation of Japan (INFJ)
Warehouse: 36-1 Hiraoka-cho, Hachioji, Tokyo 192

Minerva Shobo Co Ltd+
One Tsutsumidani-cho, Hinooka, Yamashina-ku, Kyoto 607-8494
Tel: (075) 581-5191 *Fax:* (075) 581-0589
E-mail: info@minervashobo.co.jp
Web Site: www.minervashoboco.jp
Key Personnel
President: Nobuo Sugita *Tel:* (071) 581 5191 93
Foreign Trade: Keizo Sugita
Editorial Dir: Kiyoshi Igarashi
Foreign Rights: Hiroshi Inui
Founded: 1948
Membership(s): Japan Book Publishers Association.
Subjects: Child Care & Development, Disability, Special Needs, Economics, Education, Government, Political Science, History, Medicine, Nursing, Dentistry, Philosophy, Psychology, Psychiatry, Social Sciences, Sociology
ISBN Prefix(es): 4-623
Total Titles: 4,000 Print
Imprints: Tohan-Nippan
Branch Office(s)
3-6 Nishiki-cho, Kanda, Chiyoda-Ku, Tokyo 101-0034 *Tel:* (03) 8296-1615 *Fax:* (03) 3396-1620
Distributed by Nihon Shuppan Hanbai Co
Foreign Rights: The Asano Agency Inc

Mirai-Sha
3-7-2, Koishikawa, Bunkyo-ku, Tokyo 112-0002
Tel: (03) 3814-5521 *Fax:* (03) 3814-8600
Key Personnel
President & Foreign Rights/Trade: Yoshihide Nishitani E-mail: nishitani@sjk.mag.ne.jp
Founded: 1951
Subjects: History, Human Relations, Literature, Literary Criticism, Essays, Philosophy, Religion - Other, Social Sciences, Sociology, Politics, Theatre
ISBN Prefix(es): 4-624

Misuzu Shobo Ltd+
5-32-21 Hongo, Bunkyo-ku, Tokyo 113-0033
Tel: (03) 3815-9181 *Fax:* (03) 3818-8497
E-mail: nakagawa@msz.co.jp
Web Site: www.msz.co.jp
Key Personnel
President: Takashi Arai
Editorial Dir: Shogo Morita
Foreign Rights: Ms Misako Nakagawa
Founded: 1946
Subjects: Art, Human Relations, Literature, Literary Criticism, Essays, Psychology, Psychiatry, Science (General), Social Sciences, Sociology
ISBN Prefix(es): 4-622

Mita Press, Mita Industrial Co Ltd+
Ochanomizu Center Bldg, 2-12 Hongo 3 chome, Bunkyo-ku, Tokyo 113
Tel: (03) 3817-7200 *Fax:* (03) 3817-7207

Key Personnel
President: Yoshihiro Mita
Man Dir: Akio Etori
International Relations Manager: Atsushi Mifune
Founded: 1988 (originally founded 1934 as Mita Industrial Co, Ltd)
Subjects: Astronomy, Biological Sciences, Medicine, Nursing, Dentistry, Nonfiction (General), Physical Sciences, Physics, Psychology, Psychiatry, Science (General), Technology
ISBN Prefix(es): 4-89583

Morikita Shuppan Co Ltd
1-4-11, Fujimi, Chiyoda-ku, Tokyo 102-0071
Tel: (03) 3265-8341 *Fax:* (03) 3264-8709
E-mail: hiro@morikita.co.jp
Web Site: www.morikita.co.jp
Key Personnel
President: Hajime Morikita
Foreign Trade Executive: Kazuo Mori
Foreign Rights: Hiroshi Morikita
Founded: 1950
Subjects: Earth Sciences, Geography, Geology, Mathematics, Physics, Science (General), Technology, Botany, Natural Science
ISBN Prefix(es): 4-627

Myrtos Inc+
Kudan-Sakura Bldg, 1-10-5, Kudan-Kita, Chiyoda-ku, Tokyo 102-0073
Tel: (03) 3288-2200 *Fax:* (03) 3288-2225
E-mail: pub@myrtos.co.jp
Web Site: www.myrtos.co.jp
Key Personnel
President: Kazumitsu Kawai
Founded: 1985
Subjects: Archaeology, Education, History, Literature, Literary Criticism, Essays, Philosophy, Religion - Jewish, Religion - Protestant
ISBN Prefix(es): 4-89586
Branch Office(s)
Jerusalem, Israel

Nagai Shoten Co Ltd
21-15, Fukushima, 8 Chome, Fukushima-ku, Osaka 553-0003
Tel: (06) 6452-1881 *Fax:* (06) 6452-1882
E-mail: nagai05@gold.ocn.ne.jp
Key Personnel
President: Tadao Nagai
Founded: 1946
Subjects: Medicine, Nursing, Dentistry
ISBN Prefix(es): 4-8159

Nagaoka Shoten Co Ltd+
1-7-14, Toyotama-Kami, Nerima-ku, Tokyo 176-8515
Tel: (03) 3992-5155 *Fax:* (03) 3948-3021
E-mail: info@nagaokashoten.co.jp
Key Personnel
President: Shuichi Nagaoka
Foreign Rights/Trade: Yoji Tamaki
Founded: 1963
Subjects: Animals, Pets, Cookery, Crafts, Games, Hobbies, Gardening, Plants, Health, Nutrition, House & Home, How-to, Law, Sports, Athletics, Travel
ISBN Prefix(es): 4-522
Subsidiaries: Cosumo Shuppan Company Ltd; Lesson Company Ltd; Okaichi Company Ltd

Nakayama Shoten Co Ltd+
1-25-14 Hakusan, Bunkyo-ku, Tokyo 113-8666
Tel: (03) 3813-1100 *Fax:* (03) 3816-1015
Web Site: www.nakayamashoten.co.jp
Key Personnel
President: Kurohiko Nakayama
Founded: 1948
Membership(s): Japan Book Publishers Association; Japan Medical Publishers Association.
Subjects: Biological Sciences, Medicine, Nursing, Dentistry, Science (General)
ISBN Prefix(es): 4-521
Number of titles published annually: 70 Print; 5 CD-ROM
Total Titles: 3,850 Print; 5 CD-ROM
Distributor for American Heart Association

Nankodo Co Ltd+
42-6, Hongo 3-Chrome, Bunkyo-ku, Tokyo 113-8410
Tel: (03) 3811-7239 *Fax:* (03) 3811-7230
E-mail: info@nankodo.co.jp
Web Site: www.nankodo.co.jp
Telex: 2722203 Nankod J *Cable:* Booknankodo
Key Personnel
President: Nobuhiko Hongo
Dir, Publications: Makoto Ueda
Foreign Rights/Trade: Masao Takahashi
Sales Dir: Makoto Sagwara
Manager, Planning, Publicity: Shun Takahashi
Manager, Imports: Iwao Tojo
Founded: 1879
Subjects: Language Arts, Linguistics, Medicine, Nursing, Dentistry, Science (General), Technology, Pharmacology
ISBN Prefix(es): 4-524
Branch Office(s)
Oike-minami Teramachi dori, Nakakyo-ku, Kyoto 604

Nan'un-Do Co Ltd+
361, Yamabukicho, Shinjuku-ku, Tokyo 162-0801
Tel: (03) 3268-2362 *Fax:* (03) 3268-2650
Key Personnel
President: Kazunori Nagumo
Foreign Rights/Trade: Goro Saso
Founded: 1950
Membership(s): J P A
Subjects: Education, Language Arts, Linguistics, Literature, Literary Criticism, Essays
ISBN Prefix(es): 4-523
Subsidiaries: Nan'un-Do Phoenix Co Ltd

Nanzando Co Ltd
1-11 Yushima 4 chome, Bunkyo-ku, Tokyo 113-0034
Tel: (03) 56897868 *Fax:* (03) 56897857
E-mail: info@nanzando.com
Web Site: www.nanzando.com
Key Personnel
Man Dir: Hajime Suzuki
Founded: 1901
Subjects: Medicine, Nursing, Dentistry, Pharmaceutical
ISBN Prefix(es): 4-525

Nensho-Sha
3-5, Kitayamacho, Tennoji-ku, Osaka 543-0035
Tel: (06) 6771-9223 *Fax:* (06) 6771-9424
Key Personnel
President: Masaru Fujinami
Founded: 1934
Subjects: History, Science (General), Technology, Secretarial Science
ISBN Prefix(es): 4-88978

NHK Publishing, *imprint of* Nippon Hoso Shuppan Kyokai (NHK Publishing)

Nigensha Publishing Co Ltd+
2-2, Kanda-Jimbocho, Chiyoda-ku, Tokyo 101-8419
Tel: (03) 5210-4703 *Fax:* (03) 5210-4704
E-mail: sales@nigensha.co.jp
Web Site: www.nigensha.co.jp
Key Personnel
President: Mr Takao Watanabe
Marketing Manager, Overseas: Yuji Nagai
Foreign Rights/Trade: Yukiko Kurosu
Founded: 1955
Membership(s): Japan Book Publishers Association; Azusakai Publishers Association.
Subjects: Art, Automotive, History, Art Reproduction, Calligraphy
ISBN Prefix(es): 4-544

Nihon Bunka Kagakusha Co Ltd
6-15-17 Honkomagome, 6 Chome, Bunkyo-ku, Tokyo 113-0021
Tel: (03) 39463137 *Fax:* (03) 39450908
Cable: Nihonbunkamm Tokyo
Key Personnel
President: Hideyuki Motegi
Foreign Trade Executive: Yoshihiro Hoshi
E-mail: y_hoshi@nichibun.co.jp
Founded: 1948
Subjects: Education, Medicine, Nursing, Dentistry, Social Sciences, Sociology
ISBN Prefix(es): 4-8210

Nihon-Bunkyo Shuppan (Japan Educational Publishing Co Ltd)
7-5, Minami-Sumiyoshi 4 chome, Sumiyoshi-ku, Osaka 558-0041
Tel: (06) 6692-1261 *Fax:* (06) 6606-5172; (06) 6692-8927
E-mail: webadmin@nichibun-g.co.jp
Web Site: www.nichibun-g.co.jp
Key Personnel
President: Rituro Shimono
Founded: 1951
Subjects: Art, Education, English as a Second Language, Social Sciences, Sociology, Sports, Athletics
ISBN Prefix(es): 4-536
Subsidiaries: Kiroku Eigasha Production Co Ltd; Shugakusha Co Ltd

Nihon Hoso Shuppan Kyokai, see Japan Broadcast Publishing Co Ltd

Nihon Keizai Shimbun Inc Publications Bureau
1-9-5, Otemachi, Chiyoda-ku, Tokyo 100-8066
Tel: (03) 3270-0251 *Fax:* (03) 5201-7505
Web Site: www.nikkei.co.jp/pub
Key Personnel
President: Toyohiko Kobayashi
General Manager: Takeshi Higuchi
Foreign Rights/Trade: Katsuharu Uchida
Founded: 1946
Subjects: Business, Economics, Science (General), Social Sciences, Sociology, Fine Arts
ISBN Prefix(es): 4-532
Associate Companies: Nikkei Science Inc
Subsidiaries: Nikkei Publications Services Inc

Nihon Rodo Kenkyu Kiko
4-8-23 Kami Shakujii, Nerima-Ku, Tokyo 177-8502
Tel: (03) 5903-6111 *Fax:* (03) 3594-1113
E-mail: jil@jil.go.jp
Web Site: www.jil.go.jp
Key Personnel
Dir, Publishing Dept: Ms Atsuko Hojo
Subjects: Labor, Industrial Relations
ISBN Prefix(es): 4-538
Divisions: Research Institute

Nihon Tosho Center Co Ltd
3-8-2 Otsuka, Bunkyo-ku, Tokyo 112-0012
Tel: (03) 3945-6448 *Fax:* (02) 3945-4515
E-mail: info@nihontosho.co.jp
Web Site: www.nihontosho.co.jp
Key Personnel
President: Yoshio Takano
Editorial Dir: Yochisada Kyuma
Sales Dir: Minami Nonaka
Founded: 1975
Subjects: Education, History, Literature, Literary Criticism, Essays, Social Sciences, Sociology, Autobiography, Social Welfare

ISBN Prefix(es): 4-8205
Branch Office(s)
Osaka

Nihon Vogue Co Ltd+
3-23 Ichigaya-Honmuracho, Shinjuku-ku, Tokyo 162-8705
Tel: (03) 5261-5081 *Fax:* (03) 3269-8760
E-mail: nvsales@giganet.net
Web Site: www.tezukuritown.com
Key Personnel
President: Nobuaki Seto *Tel:* (03) 5261 5089 *Fax:* (03) 3269 7874 *E-mail:* seto@tezukuritown.com
Manager, Overseas Department: Takuya Wada
Founded: 1954
Specialize in publication of handicrafts books.
Subjects: Cookery, Crafts, Games, Hobbies, Gardening, Plants, Health, Nutrition, Sports, Athletics
ISBN Prefix(es): 4-529
Subsidiaries: NV Planing Co Ltd

Nikkagiren Shuppan-Sha (JUSE Press Ltd)
Nikka-Giren-3-Gokan, 5-4-2, Sendagaya, Shibuya-ku, Tokyo 151-0051
Tel: (03) 5379-1238 *Fax:* (03) 3356-3419
E-mail: sales@juse-p.co.jp
Web Site: www.juse-p.co.jp
Key Personnel
President: Teruhide Haga
Foreign Rights/Trade: Goro Fukushima
Founded: 1955
Subjects: Business, Computer Science, Education, Finance, Human Relations, Library & Information Sciences, Management, Mathematics, Science (General), Self-Help, Technology
ISBN Prefix(es): 4-8171

The Nikkan Kogyo Shimbun Ltd
1-8-10, Kudan-Kita, Chiyoda-ku, Tokyo 102-8181
Tel: (03) 3222-7131 *Fax:* (03) 3234-8504
Web Site: www.nikkan.co.jp
Telex: NIKKANKO J29687 *Cable:* DAILYKOGYO TOKYO
Key Personnel
President: Taihei Kanno
President, Osaka: Kiyosi Muramoto
President, Tohoku: Tatsuo Uchida
Bureau Chief, New York: Joji Ito
Bureau Chief, Los Angeles: Etsuji Nakamura
Bureau Chief, London: Hidemasa Naka
Bureau Chief, SE Asia: Yasushi Abe
Editor, Chu-Shikoku: Keijyu Moriwaki
Editor, Osaka: Toshiyuki Takakura
Editor, Nagoya: Koichi Ota
Editor, Seibu: Tsutomu Sasaki
Editor, Tohoku: Susuma Suzuki
Foreign Rights/Trade: Toru Suzuki
Founded: 1945
Subjects: Business, Engineering (General), Technology, Information Management
ISBN Prefix(es): 4-526
Branch Office(s)
1-17-18 Uesugi, Aoba-ku, Sendai
2-16 Kitahama-higashi, Chuo-ku, Osaka
2-21-28 Izumi, Higashi-ku, Nagoya, 1-1 Furumonndo-Cho, Hakata-ku, Fukuoka
10 Anson Rd, No 27-04, International Plaza, Singapore 0207, Singapore
No 44 Ludgate House, 107/111 Fleet St, London EC4, United Kingdom
U.S. Office(s): 611 W Sixth St, No 3201, Los Angeles, CA 90017, United States
60 E 42 St, No 1411, New York, NY 10165, United States

Nippon Hoso Shuppan Kyokai (NHK Publishing)+
41-1, Udagawacho, Shibuya-ku, Tokyo 150-8081
Tel: (03) 3780-3356 *Fax:* (03) 3780-3348
E-mail: webmaster@npb.nhk-grp.co.jp
Web Site: www.nhk-grp.co.jp *Cable:* NHPUBLISHCO TOKYO
Key Personnel
President: Takeshi Matsuo
Man Dir: Fumihiko Inatsugu
Project Development Editor & Foreign Rights/Trade: Masahiro Kizaki
Founded: 1931
Subjects: Art, Astronomy, Biological Sciences, Business, Chemistry, Chemical Engineering, Communications, Cookery, Crafts, Games, Hobbies, Drama, Theater, Earth Sciences, Economics, Education, Electronics, Electrical Engineering, English as a Second Language, Environmental Studies, Fashion, Fiction, Foreign Countries, Gardening, Plants, Geography, Geology, Government, Political Science, Health, Nutrition, History, Language Arts, Linguistics, Law, Literature, Literary Criticism, Essays, Management, Mathematics, Mechanical Engineering, Music, Dance, Mysteries, Nonfiction (General), Regional Interests, Religion - Buddhist, Religion - Catholic, Religion - Hindu, Religion - Islamic, Religion - Jewish, Religion - Protestant, Religion - Other, Science (General), Social Sciences, Sociology, Sports, Athletics, Technology, Travel, Western Fiction
ISBN Prefix(es): 4-14
Parent Company: NHK (Japan Broadcasting Corporation)
Imprints: NHK Publishing
Subsidiaries: Hoso-Shuppan Circulation Center; Hoso-Shuppan Production; Niiza-Biso
Branch Office(s)
Fukuoka
Hiroshima
Matsuyama
Nagoya
Osaka
Sapporo
Sendai
Distributed by Weatherhill Inc
Warehouse: Hoso-Shuppan Circulation Center, 1-7-7 Hatanaka, Niiza-City, Saitama 352
Orders to: Japan Broadcast Publishing Co, Ltd, Shibuya-ku, Tokyo

Nippon Jitsugyo Publishing Co Ltd+
3-2-12, Hongo, Bunkyo-ku, Tokyo 113-0033
Tel: (03) 3814-5161 *Fax:* (03) 3818-1881
E-mail: int@njg.co.jp
Web Site: www.njg.co.jp
Key Personnel
Chairman: Yoichiro Nakamura
Founded: 1950
Subjects: Accounting, Business, Computer Science, Economics, Management, Marketing, Psychology, Psychiatry, Science (General)
ISBN Prefix(es): 4-534
Associate Companies: Four U (Publishing) Co Ltd

Nishimura Co Ltd+
1-754-39, Asahi-cho-dori, Asahimachi-dori, Niigata 951-8122
Tel: (025) 223-2388 *Fax:* (025) 224-7165
Key Personnel
President: Masanori Nishimura
General Dir: Masanobu Nishiyama
Sales Manager: Masaru Gotoh; Kenji Sakai
Production & Publicity Manager: Tsutomu Maeda; Keiichi Ninomiya
Foreign Rights/Trade: Azumi Nishimura
Founded: 1916
Subjects: Art, Medicine, Nursing, Dentistry, Veterinary Science
ISBN Prefix(es): 4-89013
Associate Companies: West Village Co Ltd *Fax:* (025) 2235750
Branch Office(s)
Akita
Toyko
Bookshop(s): 68-2 Aza-Hasunuma, Hiroomote, Akita-shi 010; 1-754-39, Asahi-cho-dori, Asahimachi-dori, Niigata 951-8122

Nobunkyo (Rural Village Culture Association), see Nosangyoson Bunka Kyokai

Nosangyoson Bunka Kyokai
Formerly Nobunkyo (Rural Village Culture Association)
7-6-1 Akasaka, Minato-ku, Tokyo 107-0052
Tel: (03) 35851141 *Fax:* (03) 35891387
E-mail: mbk@mail.ruralnet.or.jp
Key Personnel
Chief Dir: Takashi Sakamoto
Founded: 1940
Subjects: Agriculture, Education, Environmental Studies, Health, Nutrition, Medicine, Nursing, Dentistry
ISBN Prefix(es): 4-540
Bookshop(s): Nobunkyo Otemachi Branch, JA Bldg, Basement floor, 1-8-3 Otemachi, Chiyoda-ku, Tokyo 100

Obunsha Co Ltd
78, Yaraicho, Shinjuku-ku, Tokyo 162-8680
Tel: (03) 3266-6487; (03) 3266-6000 *Fax:* (03) 3266-6478
Web Site: www.obunsha.co.jp *Cable:* OBUNSHA TOKYO
Key Personnel
Chief Executive Officer: Fumio Akao
Advertising Manager: Masaru Wakabayashi
Foreign Rights/Trade: Hong Sung Keun
Founded: 1931
Subjects: Computer Science, Education, History, Language Arts, Linguistics, Science (General), Sports, Athletics
ISBN Prefix(es): 4-01
Associate Companies: The Asahi National Broadcasting Co Ltd, 1-1-1 Roppong, Minato-ku, Toyko 106; English Educational Foundation of Japan, 55 Yokodera-cho, Shinjuku-ku, Toyko 162; Japan LL Education Center, Tokyo; Nippon Cultural Broadcasting Inc, 1-5 Wakabacho, Shinjuku-ku, Toyko 160; The Society for Testing English Proficiency, 1 Yarai-cho, Shinjuku-ku, Tokyo 162
Branch Office(s)
Fukuoka
Hiroshima
Nagoya
Osaka
Sapporo
Sendai

Ohmsha Ltd+
3-1 Kanda-Nishiki-cho, Chiyoda-ku, Tokyo 101-8460
Tel: (03) 3233-0641 *Fax:* (03) 3233-2426
E-mail: kaigaika@ohmsha.co.jp
Web Site: www.ohmsha.co.jp
Key Personnel
President: Seiji Sato
Dir, Foreign Rights & International Business: Osami Takeo *Tel:* (03) 3233-2425 *E-mail:* takeo@ohmsha.co.jp
Founded: 1914
Subjects: Engineering (General), Science (General)
ISBN Prefix(es): 4-274
Number of titles published annually: 300 Print
Total Titles: 3,000 Print
Distributed by IOS Press
Distributor for IOS Press

Ondorisha Publishers Ltd
4 Tsukiji-machi, Shinjuku-ku, Tokyo 162-8708
Tel: (03) 3268-3108 *Fax:* (03) 3235-8695

Key Personnel
President: Hideaki Takeuchi
Editor: Hideaki Sanada
Sales: Yoshihiro Ikuta
Foreign Rights/Trade: Hiroshi Morozumi
Founded: 1945
Subjects: Crafts, Games, Hobbies, Crochet, Embroidery, Knitting, Lacework
ISBN Prefix(es): 4-277

Ongaku No Tomo Sha Corporation+
6-30, Kagurazaka, Shinjuku-ku, Tokyo 162-8716
Tel: (03) 3235-2091 *Fax:* (03) 3235-2148
E-mail: home@ongakunotomo.co.jp
Web Site: www.ongakunotomo.co.jp
Key Personnel
President: Hiroshi Okabe
Copyright Dept: Kazuyuki Nabeshima
Foreign Rights/Trade: Tetsuo Morita
Founded: 1941
Subjects: Education, Music, Dance
ISBN Prefix(es): 4-276
Subsidiaries: Musica Nova Co (at above main address); Suiseisha Music Publishers; T O A Music International Co; Tomo Music Enterprise Co (at above main address)
Branch Office(s)
Osaka
Distributed by Theodore Presser Co
Distributor for Theodore Presser Co

The Oriental Economist, see Toyo Keizai Shinpo-Sha

Otsuki Shoten Publishers+
2-11-9, Hongo, Bunkyo-ku, Tokyo 113-0033
Tel: (03) 3813-4651 *Fax:* (03) 3813-4656
E-mail: otsuki@meibun.or.jp
Key Personnel
President, Production & Foreign Rights/Trade: Sadamu Nakagawa
Editorial: Kunio Shuto
Sales: Atsuo Harada
Founded: 1946
Subjects: Economics, History, Literature, Literary Criticism, Essays, Philosophy, Social Sciences, Sociology, Politics
ISBN Prefix(es): 4-272

Oxford University Press KK
Edomizaka Mori Bldg 6F, 4-1-10-6F Toranomon, Minato-ku 171-0043
Tel: (03) 3459 6489 *Fax:* (03) 3459 8661
Web Site: www.oupjapan.co.jp
Key Personnel
Man Dir: Sumio Takiguchi
General Manager, Academic & General Books Dept: Fumiha Ito
General Manager, English Language Teaching Dept: Paul Riley
ISBN Prefix(es): 4-7552
Parent Company: Oxford University Press, United Kingdom

Pacifica Ltd, see Seibu Time Co Ltd

Pearson Education Japan+
Nishi-Shinjuku KF Bldg 101, 8-14-24 Nishi Shinjuku, Shinjuku-ku, Tokyo 160-0023
Tel: (03) 3365 9001 *Fax:* (03) 3365 9009
E-mail: firstname.lastname@pearsoned.co.jp; elt@pearsoned.co.jp
Web Site: www.pearsoned.co.jp
Key Personnel
Man Dir: Naoto Ono
Business Development Dir: Katsuhiro Kawahara
General Manager, Local Publishing: Yukio Miwa
General Manager, ELT: Mieko Otaka
Founded: 1978
Subjects: Business, Computer Science, Economics, English as a Second Language, Medicine, Nursing, Dentistry, Microcomputers
ISBN Prefix(es): 4-938712; 4-88735; 4-87471; 4-89471; 4-931356
Number of titles published annually: 100 Print
Total Titles: 400 Print
Parent Company: Pearson Education, One Lake St, Upper Saddle River, NJ 07458, United States
Branch Office(s)
1-13-19 Sekiguchi, Bunkyo-ku, Tokyo 112-0014 *Tel:* (03) 3266 0404 *Fax:* (03) 3266 0326
Distributed by Hachette (France); SGEL (Spain)
Distributor for Chambers Harrap (UK); Hachette (France); SGEL (Spain)
Foreign Rights: Fumi Nishijima

Periplus Editions, *imprint of* Charles E Tuttle Publishing Co Inc

PHP Institute Inc
3-10 Sanban-cho, Chiyoda-ku, Tokyo 102-8331
Tel: (03) 3239-6233 *Fax:* (03) 3239-6263
Telex: J5422 402 PHPJ
Key Personnel
President: Masaharu Matsushita
Man Dir: Katsuhiko Eguchi
Founded: 1946
Subjects: Business, Social Sciences, Sociology
ISBN Prefix(es): 4-569
Subsidiaries: PHP Editors Group Inc; PHP Institute of America Inc; PHP International (Singapore) Pte Ltd
Branch Office(s)
Kizu
Kyushu
Nagoya
Tokyo

Poplar Publishing Co Ltd+
5, Sugacho, Shinjuku-ku, Tokyo 160-8565
Tel: (03) 3357-2211 *Fax:* (03) 3359-2359
E-mail: henshu@poplar.co.jp
Web Site: www.poplar.co.jp *Cable:* POPLARPUB
Key Personnel
President: Hiroyuki Sakai
Foreign Rights/Trade: Kiyoshi Fukushima
Foreign Rights: Mari Sasaki
Founded: 1948
Subjects: Biography, Fiction, Geography, Geology, History, Science (General)
ISBN Prefix(es): 4-591

President Inc+
Bridge Stone Hirakawa-cho Bldg, 13-12 Hirakawa-cho, 2 Chome, Chiyoda-ku, Tokyo 102-0093
Tel: (03) 32373734 *Fax:* (03) 32373746
E-mail: matu-pre@po.iijnet.or.jp
Web Site: www.president.co.jp; www.president.co.jp/pre/english.html
Key Personnel
President: Yoshio Watabiki
International Rights: Keijiro Amano
Founded: 1963
Subjects: Business, Cookery, Economics, Finance, Government, Political Science, Management, Marketing, Philosophy
ISBN Prefix(es): 4-8334
Parent Company: Time Warner Publishing BV
Branch Office(s)
2-3-18 Nakanoshima, Kita-ku, Osaka

Reimei-Shobo Co Ltd+
EBS-Bldg, 3-6-27 Marunouchi, Naka-ku, Nagoya 460-0002
Tel: (052) 9623045 *Fax:* (052) 9519065
E-mail: reimei@mui.biglobe.ne.jp
Web Site: wwwl.biz.biglobe.ne.jp/~reimei/
Key Personnel
President: Kunihiro Buma
International Rights: Masako Yoshikawa
Founded: 1947
Membership(s): Japan Book Publishers Association.
Subjects: Child Care & Development, Disability, Special Needs, Education, Psychology, Psychiatry
ISBN Prefix(es): 4-654
Number of titles published annually: 50 Print
Total Titles: 1,700 Print
Warehouse: 374 Sangen-cho, Kita-ku, Nagoya 462-0004

Rinsen Book Co Ltd+
No 8, Tanaka-Shimoyanagi-Cho, Sakyo-Ku, Kyoto 606-8204
Tel: (075) 721-7111 *Fax:* (075) 781-6168
E-mail: kyoto@rinsen.com
Web Site: www.rinsen.com *Cable:* RINSEN KYOTO
Key Personnel
President: Eizo Kataoka
Foreign Rights/Trade: Satoko Matsumura
Founded: 1932
Publisher & Antiquarian Bookseller.
Membership(s): International League of Antiquarian Booksellers; Antiquarian Booksellers' Association of Japan.
Subjects: Archaeology, Asian Studies, History, Literature, Literary Criticism, Essays, Religion - Buddhist, Fine Arts, Japanology, Orientalism
ISBN Prefix(es): 4-653
Branch Office(s)
Saikachizaka Bldg, 2-11-16 Kanda-Surugadai, Chiyoda-Ku, Tokyo 101-0062 *Tel:* (03) 3293-5021 *Fax:* (03) 3293-5023 *E-mail:* tokyo@rinsen.com

Riso-Sha
614-17, Minoridai, Matsudo City, Chiba 270-2231
Tel: (047) 366-8003 *Fax:* (047) 360-7301
Key Personnel
President: Sumio Miyamoto
Founded: 1927
Subjects: Education, Library & Information Sciences, Philosophy, Psychology, Psychiatry, Religion - Buddhist, Religion - Catholic, Social Sciences, Sociology
ISBN Prefix(es): 4-650
Parent Company: Iwao-Syobou
Imprints: Library & Information Science

Ryosho-Fukyu-Kai Co Ltd
8-2 Kasuga 1 chome, Bunkyo-ku, Tokyo 112-0003
Tel: (03) 3813-1251 *Fax:* (03) 3811-6490
E-mail: ryosho@po.iijnet.or.jp
Key Personnel
President: Ichigaku Kawanaka
Foreign Trade Executive: Isao Hiramatsu
Foreign Rights Executive: Fumio Kimura
Man Dir: Kiyoshi Funakoshi
Founded: 1914
Subjects: Economics, Government, Political Science, Law, Public Administration, Social Sciences, Sociology, Local administration & politics
ISBN Prefix(es): 4-656

Saela Shobo (Librairie Ca et La)+
3-1, Ichigaya-Sadowaracho, Shinjuku-ku, Tokyo 162-0842
Tel: (03) 3268-4261 *Fax:* (03) 3268-4264
E-mail: info@saela.co.jp
Web Site: www.saela.co.jp
Key Personnel
President: Toshiichi Uraki *E-mail:* uraki@saela.co.jp
Founded: 1948

Subjects: Education, Fiction, Language Arts, Linguistics, Mathematics, Science (General), Technology
ISBN Prefix(es): 4-378
Number of titles published annually: 24 Print
Total Titles: 450 Print
Imprints: Toshiichi Uraki

Sagano Shoin
39 Ushigase-Minami-No-Kuchi-Cho, Nishikyo-ku Kyoto-shi, Kyoto 615-8045
Tel: (075) 391-7686 *Fax:* (075) 391-7321
E-mail: sagano@mbox.kyoto-inet.or.jp
Web Site: www.saganoshoin.co.jp
Key Personnel
President: Tadayoshi Nakamura
Contact: Takayo Shito
Founded: 1968
Subjects: Business, Computer Science, Economics, Education, Ethnicity, Law, Literature, Literary Criticism, Essays, Marketing, Sports, Athletics, Women's Studies
ISBN Prefix(es): 4-7823

Saiensu-Sha Co Ltd
1-3-25 Sendagaya, Shibuya-ku, Tokyo 151-0051
Tel: (03) 5474-8500 *Fax:* (03) 5474-8900
E-mail: rikei@saiensu.co.jp
Key Personnel
President: Yuzo Morihira
Contact: Nobuhiko Tajima
Founded: 1969
ISBN Prefix(es): 4-7819
Subsidiaries: Shinsei-sha Co Ltd; Suurikougakusha Co Ltd

The Sailor Publishing Co, Ltd
OCM Bldg, 10-18 Mouri 2 chome, Koutou-ku, Tokyo 135-0001
Tel: (03) 3846-2955 *Fax:* (03) 3846-0452
Key Personnel
President & Foreign Rights & Trade: Etsu Ogawa
Founded: 1985
ISBN Prefix(es): 4-88330; 4-915632
Parent Company: The Sailor Fountain Pen Co Ltd

Salesian Press/Don Bosco Sha+
9-7 Yotsuya 1 Chome, Shinjuku-ku, Tokyo 160
Tel: (03) 3351-7041 *Fax:* (03) 3351-5430
Key Personnel
President: Aldo Cipriani
Founded: 1930
Subjects: Religion - Catholic
ISBN Prefix(es): 4-88626
Warehouse: 1-22-12 Wakaba Cho, Shinjuku-ku, Tokyo

Sangyo-Tosho Publishing Co Ltd
11-3, Iidabashi 2 chome, Chiyoda-ku, Tokyo 102-0072
Tel: (03) 3261-7821 *Fax:* (03) 3239-2178
E-mail: info@san-to.co.jp
Web Site: www.san-to.co.jp
Key Personnel
President & Foreign Rights & Trade: Takehiko Ezura
Sales: Koji Nara
Founded: 1925
Subjects: Biological Sciences, Chemistry, Chemical Engineering, Computer Science, Electronics, Electrical Engineering, Engineering (General), Mathematics, Mechanical Engineering, Philosophy, Physical Sciences, Physics, Psychology, Psychiatry, Religion - Other, Science (General), Technology, Natural science, industry
ISBN Prefix(es): 4-7828
Total Titles: 500 Print

Sankyo Publishing Company Ltd
2, Kanda-Jimbocho 3 chome, Chiyoda-ku, Tokyo 101-0051
Tel: (03) 3264-5711 *Fax:* (03) 3264-5713
Key Personnel
President: Sachiko Hagiwara
Founded: 1948
Subjects: Chemistry, Chemical Engineering, Economics, House & Home, Physics, Science (General)
ISBN Prefix(es): 4-7827

Sanseido Co Ltd
22-14, Misakicho 2 chome, Chiyoda-ku, Tokyo 101-8371
Tel: (03) 3230-9404 *Fax:* (03) 3230-9569
Web Site: www.sanseido-publ.co.jp/
Key Personnel
Chairman: Hisanori Ueno
President: Toshio Gomi
Man Dir: Masaaki Moriya
Editorial, Publicity: Eiichi Tsunoda
Production: Akihiko Ejima
Foreign Rights & Trade: Yasuaki Horiuchi
Founded: 1881
Subjects: Earth Sciences, Education, History, Language Arts, Linguistics, Law, Literature, Literary Criticism, Essays, Science (General), Social Sciences, Sociology
ISBN Prefix(es): 4-385

Sanshusha Publishing Co, Ltd+
5-34, Shitaya 1 chome, Taito-ku, Tokyo 110-0004
Tel: (03) 3842-1711 *Fax:* (03) 3845-3965
E-mail: info@sanshusha.co.jp
Web Site: www.sanshusha.co.jp
Telex: Oisco J33380
Key Personnel
President: Kanji Maeda *E-mail:* maeda-k@sanshusha.co.jp
Foreign Rights & Trade: Toshihide Maeda
Founded: 1938
Membership(s): MEBIC (Multimedia & Electronic Book International Committee), JBPA (Japan Book Publishers Association), APPA (Asian Pacific Publishers Association)
Specialize in Electronic Publishing.
Subjects: Education, English as a Second Language, Language Arts, Linguistics, Literature, Literary Criticism, Essays, Philosophy, Religion - Buddhist, Science (General), Social Sciences, Sociology, Travel
ISBN Prefix(es): 4-384

Sanyo Shuppan Boeki Co Inc+
No 2 Taiko Bldg, 3F 3-11-16 Nishi-Shinjuku, Shiniuku-ku, Tokyo 160-0023
Tel: (03) 5351-3021 *Fax:* (03) 5351-3028
Telex: 2524435 Sanyob *Cable:* Sanyobook Tokyo
Key Personnel
President: Hisatoshi Hattori
Foreign Trade: Koichi Ohnishi
Founded: 1956
Also importers & booksellers.
Subjects: Chemistry, Chemical Engineering, Cookery, Science (General)
ISBN Prefix(es): 4-87930
Associate Companies: ITO-Sanyo SA
Branch Office(s)
Niihama
Osaka

Seibido+
22, Kanda-Ogawamachi 3 chome, Chiyoda-ku, Tokyo 101-0052
Tel: (03) 3291-2261 *Fax:* (03) 3293-5490
E-mail: seibido@mua.biglobe.ne.jp
Web Site: www.seibido.co.jp
Key Personnel
President: Yoshimitsu Sano
Foreign Rights & Trade: Eiichiro Sano
Editor: Toshiko Kobayashi; Mark Brown
Founded: 1955
Publisher of ESL textbooks for the university market.
Subjects: English as a Second Language, Language Arts, Linguistics, Literature, Literary Criticism, Essays
ISBN Prefix(es): 4-7919

Seibido Shuppan Company Ltd
8-2 Suido 1 chome, Bunkyo-ku, Tokyo 112-8533
Tel: (03) 3814-4351 *Fax:* (03) 3814-4355
Web Site: www.seibidoshuppan.co.jp
Key Personnel
President & Man Dir: Etsuji Fukami
Founded: 1966
Subjects: Agriculture, Animals, Pets, Astrology, Occult, Automotive, Business, Career Development, Child Care & Development, Computer Science, Cookery, Crafts, Games, Hobbies, Gardening, Plants, Health, Nutrition, House & Home, How-to, Medicine, Nursing, Dentistry, Music, Dance, Outdoor Recreation, Photography, Sports, Athletics, Travel
ISBN Prefix(es): 4-415
Number of titles published annually: 300 Print; 5 CD-ROM
Total Titles: 1,200 Print; 10 CD-ROM

Seibu Time Co Ltd
SSC, Kinzan Bldg, 3-18-3 Kanda-nishiki-cho, Chiyoda-ku, Tokyo 101-8467
Tel: (03) 5283-0270 *Fax:* (03) 5283-0234
Key Personnel
Publisher: Sueaki Takaoka
Editor-in-Chief: Masatoshi Takeuchi
Founded: 1983
Subjects: Fiction, Nonfiction (General)
ISBN Prefix(es): 4-8275
Parent Company: S S Communications

Seibundo
514, Waseda-Tsurumakicho, Shinjuku-ku, Tokyo 162-0041
Tel: (03) 3203-9201 *Fax:* (03) 3203-9206
E-mail: eigyobu@seibundoh.co.jp
Web Site: www.seibundoh.co.jp
Key Personnel
President: Koichi Abe
Founded: 1947
Subjects: Business, Economics, Law, Social Sciences, Sociology, Politics
ISBN Prefix(es): 4-7923

Seibundo Shinkosha Publishing Co Ltd
IPB Ochanomizu Bldg, 3-3-1, Honogo, Bunkyo-ku, Tokyo 113-0033
Tel: (03) 5800-5780 *Fax:* (03) 5800-5781
Web Site: www.seibundo.net
Key Personnel
President: Yuichi Ogawa
Editorial: Hajime Hishikawa
Foreign Rights & Trade: Kiyoshi Motoki
Founded: 1912
Subjects: Business, Crafts, Games, Hobbies, Electronics, Electrical Engineering, Gardening, Plants, Management, Science (General), Technology, Graphic design
ISBN Prefix(es): 4-416

Seibundo Shuppan+
2-8-5, Shimonouchi, Chuo-ku, Osaka 542-0082
Tel: (06) 6211-6265 *Fax:* (06) 6211-6492
Key Personnel
President: Shigeo Maeda
Foreign Rights & Trade: Hiroo Maeda
Founded: 1963
Subjects: History, Language Arts, Linguistics, Literature, Literary Criticism, Essays, Regional Interests
ISBN Prefix(es): 4-7924
Distributed by Japan Publication Trading Co Ltd
Distributor for Tohan Co LTD

PUBLISHERS — JAPAN

Seishin Shobo
20-6, Otsuka 3 chome, Bunkyo-ku, Tokyo 112-0012
Tel: (03) 3946-5666 *Fax:* (03) 3945-8880
Key Personnel
President: Shukuko Shibata
Founded: 1955
Subjects: Psychology, Psychiatry, Social Sciences, Sociology, Psychoanalysis, social work & welfare, Zen
ISBN Prefix(es): 4-414

Seiun-Sha+
Formerly The Zion Press
3-21-10 Otsuka, Bunkyo-ku, Toyko 112 0012
Tel: (03) 3947-1021 *Fax:* (03) 3947-1617
E-mail: greatobe@yo.rim.ur.jp
Key Personnel
President: Keiko Moritani
Foreign Rights & Trade: Mineo Moritani
Founded: 1982
Publicize Christian Truth.
Membership(s): Japan Book Publishers Association.
Subjects: All fields of learning helpful to Christian purpose
ISBN Prefix(es): 4-7952; 4-434
Total Titles: 1,000 Print
Parent Company: The Zion Press Corporation

Seiwa Shoten Co Ltd
2-5 Kamitakaido, 1-chome, Suginami-ku, Tokyo 168-0074
Tel: (03) 3329-0033 *Fax:* (03) 5374-7186
E-mail: sales@seiwa-pb.co.jp
Web Site: www.seiwa-pb.co.jp *Cable:* Seiwapublishers
Key Personnel
President: Youji Ishizawa
Editor-in-Chief: Yoshinori Asanuma
Sales Manager: Masaharu Fujiwara
System Manager: Yukio Shimura
Foreign Books Manager: Yumi Matsuzawa
Founded: 1976
Subjects: Language Arts, Linguistics, Medicine, Nursing, Dentistry, Psychology, Psychiatry
ISBN Prefix(es): 4-7911
Bookshop(s): 1-11 Kamitakaido, 1-chome, Suginamiku, Tokyo 168
Book Club(s): Bookclub Psyche

Seizando-Shoten Publishing Co Ltd
Seizando Bldg, 4-51, Minami-Motomachi, Shinjuku-ku, Tokyo 160-0012
Tel: (03) 3357-5861 *Fax:* (03) 3357-5867
Key Personnel
President: Minoru Ogawa
Foreign Rights & Trade: Yoshihiro Munekata
Sales: Yoshio Kimura
Production: Yuhei Shibuya
Publicity: Masayuki Toyama
Rights & Permissions: Kokichi Shioji
Founded: 1954
Subjects: Economics, Law, Maritime, Technology, Transportation, Aviation, Fishery
ISBN Prefix(es): 4-425

Sekai Bunka-Sha
2-29, Kudan-Kita 4 chome, Chiyoda-ku, Tokyo 102-8187
Tel: (03) 3262-5111 *Fax:* (03) 3237-8446
Web Site: www.sekaibunka.com *Cable:* Sebunpub
Key Personnel
President: Tsutomu Suzuki
Foreign Rights & Trade: Kosei Kobayashi
Founded: 1946
Subjects: Art, Education, Geography, Geology, History
ISBN Prefix(es): 4-418
U.S. Office(s): 501 Fifth Ave, Suite 2102, New York, NY 10017, United States

Shakai Hoken Shuppan-Sha
Hikida Bldg, 9 Kanda-Surugadai 2 chome, Chiyoda-ku, Tokyo 101-0062
Tel: (03) 3291-9841 *Fax:* (03) 3291-9847
Key Personnel
President: Hidefumi Sano
ISBN Prefix(es): 4-7846

Shakai Shiso-Sha
25-13, Hongo 3 chome, Bunkyo-ku, Tokyo 113-0033
Tel: (03) 3813-8101 *Fax:* (03) 3813-9061
Key Personnel
President: Yasuo Miyakawa
Sales: Tadashi Kamatsuka
Founded: 1947
Subjects: Architecture & Interior Design, Art, Drama, Theater, Fiction, History, Music, Dance, Poetry, Social Sciences, Sociology, Travel
ISBN Prefix(es): 4-390

Shibun-Do
4-2, Nishi Goken-machi, Shinjuku-ku, Tokyo 162-0812
Tel: (03) 3268-2441 *Fax:* (03) 3268-3550
Key Personnel
President: Jun Kawakami
Foreign Rights & Trade: Mitsuharu Ouchi
Founded: 1915
Subjects: Art, Asian Studies, History, Literature, Literary Criticism, Essays, Philosophy, Regional Interests
ISBN Prefix(es): 4-7843

Shiko-Sha Co Ltd
10-12 Hiroo 2 chome, Shibuya-ku, Tokyo 150-0012
Tel: (03) 3400-7151 *Fax:* (03) 3400-7294
Telex: J24903 *Cable:* Lmdecw Tokyo
Key Personnel
Man Dir: Yasoo Takeichi
Founded: 1950
Subjects: Religion - Catholic, Religion - Protestant
ISBN Prefix(es): 4-7834

Shimizu-Shoin
1-11, Higashi-Gokencho, Shinjuku-ku, Tokyo 162-0813
Tel: (03) 3260-5261 *Fax:* (03) 3260-5270
Key Personnel
President: Kyuya Nomura
Founded: 1946
Subjects: Biography, History, Nonfiction (General), Philosophy, School aids
ISBN Prefix(es): 4-389

Shincho-Sha Co Ltd+
71 Yaraicho, Shinjuku-ku, Tokyo 162-0805
Tel: (03) 3266 5138 *Fax:* (03) 3266 5377
Telex: G27433 Shincho *Cable:* SHINCHOSHA
Key Personnel
President: Takanobu Sato
Sales: Tadahiko Arai
Publishing Dept: Masaya Kurihara
Foreign Rights: Hisashi Miyabe
Founded: 1896
Subjects: Biography, Business, Fiction, Film, Video, Literature, Literary Criticism, Essays, Mysteries, Nonfiction (General), Photography, Romance, Science (General), Science Fiction, Fantasy
ISBN Prefix(es): 4-10

Shingakusha Co Ltd+
11-39 Higashino-Naka-Inove-cho, Yamashina-ku Kyoto-shi, Kyoto 607-8501
Tel: (075) 581-6111 *Fax:* (075) 501-0514
E-mail: info@sing.co.jp
Web Site: www.sing.co.jp

Key Personnel
President: Miki Iwasaki
Executive Dir: Toshihiro Ueda; Takeshi Yoshikawa
Foreign Rights & Trade: Mikio Yamamoto
Founded: 1957
Subjects: Education
ISBN Prefix(es): 4-7868
Branch Office(s)
Fukuoka
Sapporo
Tokushima
Tokyo

Shinkenchiku-Sha Co Ltd+
31-2, Yushima 2 chome, Bunkyo-ku, Tokyo 113-8501
Tel: (03) 38117101 *Fax:* (03) 38128229
Cable: JAPANARCH TOKYO
Key Personnel
President: Yoshio Yoshida
Man Dir: Nobuyuki Yoshida
General Manager, Foreign Rights Executive: Ryugo Maru
Founded: 1925
Subjects: Architecture & Interior Design
ISBN Prefix(es): 4-7869
Associate Companies: A&U Publishing Co, Ltd

Akane Shobo Co Ltd+
2-1, Nishi-Kanda 3 chome, Chiyoda-ku, Tokyo 101-0065
Tel: (03) 3263-0641 *Fax:* (03) 3263-5440
E-mail: mail@akaneshobo.co.jp
Web Site: www.akaneshobo.co.jp/
Key Personnel
President: Masaharu Okamoto
Foreign Rights & Trade: Tadao Sudo *Tel:* (03) 3263-0644 *Fax:* (03) 3263-2094
Founded: 1949
Subjects: Fiction, Literature, Literary Criticism, Essays, Nonfiction (General), Science (General)
ISBN Prefix(es): 4-251

Hara Shobo
2-3 Kanda Jimbocho, Chiyoda-ku, Tokyo 101-0051
Tel: (03) 5212-7801 *Fax:* (03) 3230-1158
E-mail: toshi@harashobo.com
Web Site: www.harashobo.com
Key Personnel
President: Kyo Naruse
Handle wide variety of ukiyo-e prints, paintings, illustrated books from 17th century to 20th century, & shin-hanga (modern prints) as well as reproductions, catalogues & reference books.
Membership(s): Ukiyo-e Dealers Association of Japan, board member of International Ukiyo-e Society, founding member of Japan Print of Art Auction (JPAA).
ISBN Prefix(es): 4-562

Shobunsha Publications Inc+
3-1, Kojimachi, Chiyoda-ku, Tokyo 102-8238
Tel: (03) 3556-8154 *Fax:* (03) 3556-5973
E-mail: LEH05353@niftyserve.or.jp
Web Site: www.mapple.co.jp
Key Personnel
President: Eiji Aoyagi
Foreign Rights & Trade: Kesayuki Tsunoda
Founded: 1960
Membership(s): Japan Book Publishers Association, Mapping Enterprises Association of Japan & Japan Digital Road Map Association.
Subjects: Travel
ISBN Prefix(es): 4-398
Total Titles: 300 Print
Subsidiaries: Shobunsha Map Research Center

Shogakukan Inc+
2-3-1 Hitotsubashi, Chiyoda-ku, Tokyo 101-8001
Tel: (03) 3230-5211 *Fax:* (03) 3234-5660

E-mail: info@shogakukan.co.jp
Web Site: skygarden.shogakukan.co.jp
Key Personnel
President: Masahiro Ohga
Dir: Tetsuo Takaishi
Senior Manager, Foreign Rights: Toshiki Ishii
Founded: 1922
Subjects: Art, Earth Sciences, Economics, Education, Geography, Geology, History, Comics, Japanese Manga, Magazines
ISBN Prefix(es): 4-09

Mitsumura Suiko Shoin+
Higashi-iru, Kitayama-dori, Kita-ku, Kyoto-shi 603-8115
Tel: (075) 493-8244 *Fax:* (075) 493-6011
E-mail: mitsumur@mbox.kyoto-inet.or.jp
Web Site: www.mitsumura-suiko.co.jp
Key Personnel
President: Kozo Nagasawa
Editor: Ueda Keiichiro
Founded: 1958
Subjects: Architecture & Interior Design, Art, Philosophy, Religion - Buddhist
ISBN Prefix(es): 4-8381

Shokabo Publishing Co Ltd
8-1, Yombancho, Chiyoda-ku, Tokyo 102-0081
Tel: (03) 3262-9166 *Fax:* (03) 3262-9130
E-mail: shkb-01@cb3.so-net.ne.jp
Web Site: www.shokabo.co.jp/
Key Personnel
President: Tatsuji Yoshino
Foreign Rights & Trade: Saneatsu Makiya
Founded: 1716
Subjects: Mathematics, Science (General), Technology
ISBN Prefix(es): 4-7853

Shokokusha Publishing Co Ltd
25, Sakamachi, Shinjuku-ku, Tokyo 160-0002
Tel: (03) 3359-3231 *Fax:* (03) 3357-3961
Key Personnel
President: Takeshi Goto
Sales Dir: Mineharu Matsuba
Founded: 1932
Subjects: Architecture & Interior Design, Art, Education, Engineering (General), Science (General), Technical
ISBN Prefix(es): 4-395

Shorin-Sha Co ltd+
Kasuga-syougaku Bldg, 3-23 Koishikawa 2 chome, Bunkyo-ku, Tokyo 112-0002
Tel: (03) 5689-7377 *Fax:* (03) 5689-7577
Founded: 1985
Subjects: Medicine, Nursing, Dentistry
ISBN Prefix(es): 4-7965

Shueisha Inc
5-10 Hitotsubashi 2 chome, Chiyoda-ku, Tokyo 101-8050
Tel: (03) 3230-6393 *Fax:* (03) 3230-2547
Key Personnel
President & Chief Executive Officer: Tamio Kojima
Editorial: Toshio Kawaguchi
Sales & Foreign Trade: Katsunori Kawaziri
Foreign Rights: Norifumi Sunou; Takaaki Ike
Foreign Rights & Trade: Takaaki Nanao
Founded: 1926
Specialize in comics, magazines & smaller-sized paperbacks.
Subjects: Art, Fiction, Language Arts, Linguistics, Literature, Literary Criticism, Essays, Nonfiction (General)
ISBN Prefix(es): 4-08
Associate Companies: Shogakukan Inc

Shufu-to-Seikatsu Sha Ltd
3-5-7, Kyobashi, Chuo-ku, Tokyo 104-8357
Tel: (03) 3563-5124 *Fax:* (03) 3563-5005
Key Personnel
President: Hideo Kikuchi
Editor-in-Chief: Miss Miyako Kiyohara
Publishing Dept, Foreign Rights: Shujiro Murakawa
Founded: 1935
Subjects: Art, Cookery, Crafts, Games, Hobbies, Economics, Fashion, Fiction, History, House & Home, Literature, Literary Criticism, Essays, Medicine, Nursing, Dentistry, Philosophy, Religion - Other, Technology, Comics, Fishing, Interior, Recreation
ISBN Prefix(es): 4-391

Shufunotomo Co Ltd+
9, Kanda-Surugadai 2 chome, Chiyoda-ku, Tokyo 101-8911
Tel: (03) 5280-7539 *Fax:* (03) 5280-7587
E-mail: international@shufunotomo.co.jp
Web Site: www.shufunotomo.co.jp
Key Personnel
President: Kunihiko Muramatsu
Foreign Rights & Trade: Shunichi Kamiya
Founded: 1916
Subjects: Architecture & Interior Design, Career Development, Child Care & Development, Cookery, Crafts, Games, Hobbies, Education, Fashion, Fiction, Gardening, Plants, Health, Nutrition, House & Home, How-to, Medicine, Nursing, Dentistry, Nonfiction (General), Photography, Religion - Buddhist, Travel
ISBN Prefix(es): 4-07
Total Titles: 1,200 Print; 10 CD-ROM; 3 E-Book

Shunjusha
18-6, Soto-Kanda 2 chome, Chiyoda-ku, Tokyo 101-0021
Tel: (03) 3255-9611 *Fax:* (03) 3253-1384
Key Personnel
President: Akira Kanda
Founded: 1918
Subjects: Economics, History, Literature, Literary Criticism, Essays, Music, Dance, Psychology, Psychiatry, Religion - Other, Social Sciences, Sociology
ISBN Prefix(es): 4-393

Shuppan News Co Ltd
40-7 Kanda-Jimbo-cho 2 chome, Chiyoda-ku, Tokyo 101-0051
Tel: (03) 3262-2076 *Fax:* (03) 3261-6817
Key Personnel
Editorial: Takeo Yoshizawa
Sales: Keiji Kinoshita
Rights & Permissions: Tetsuzo Suzuki
Founded: 1949
ISBN Prefix(es): 4-7852

Oru Shuppan+
2-4 Kudan-Kita 3 chome, Chiyoda-ku, Tokyo 102-0073
Tel: (03) 3234-0971 *Fax:* (03) 3261-6602
Key Personnel
Contact: Mika Hirano
ISBN Prefix(es): 4-279

The Simul Press Inc
13-9 Araki-cho, Shinjuku-ku, Tokyo 160-0007
Tel: (03) 3226-2861 *Fax:* (03) 3226-2860
Key Personnel
President: Katsuo Tamura
Senior Man Dir: Eiko Ikuta
Dir, Overseas Affairs: Masumi Muramatsu
Senior Editor: Daitaro Suwabe
Founded: 1967
Subjects: Business, Economics, Education, History, Language Arts, Linguistics, Literature, Literary Criticism, Essays, Philosophy, Regional Interests, Religion - Other, Social Sciences, Sociology
ISBN Prefix(es): 4-377
Associate Companies: Simul International Inc

Sobun-Sha
6-7, Kojimachi 2 chome, Chiyoda-ku, Tokyo 102-0083
Tel: (03) 3263-7101 *Fax:* (03) 3263-6789
E-mail: info@sobunsha.co.jp
Web Site: www.sobunsha.co.jp
Key Personnel
President: Hirotoshi Kuboi
Vice President: Masaaki Kuboi
Founded: 1951
Academic Publishers.
Subjects: Asian Studies, Biblical Studies, Business, Developing Countries, Economics, Education, Ethnicity, Finance, Foreign Countries, History, Law, Philosophy, Religion - Other, Humanities
ISBN Prefix(es): 4-423

Sogensha Publishing Co Ltd+
3-6 Awaji-machi 4 chome, Chuo-ku Osaka-shi Osaka 541-0047
Tel: (06) 62319011 *Fax:* (06) 62333112
E-mail: sgse@email.msn.com
Web Site: www.sogensha.co.jp
Key Personnel
President: Keiichi Yabe
Founded: 1925
Subjects: Art, Education, History, Medicine, Nursing, Dentistry, Philosophy, Psychology, Psychiatry, Religion - Other
ISBN Prefix(es): 4-422
Associate Companies: Tokyo Sogensha Co Ltd

Sony Magazines Inc+
5-1, Gobancho, Chiyoda-ku, Tokyo 102-8679
Tel: (03) 3234-5811 *Fax:* (03) 3234-8042
Key Personnel
President: Iwao Kono
Foreign Rights & Trade: Kenichi Shigematsu
Founded: 1979
Subjects: Literature, Literary Criticism, Essays, Music, Dance
ISBN Prefix(es): 4-7897
Parent Company: Sony Music Entertainment Inc

Soryusha
5 Koji-machi 3 chome, Chiyoda-ku, Tokyo 102
Tel: (03) 32631471 *Fax:* (03) 32632943
Key Personnel
President & Manager: Kotaro Tanaka
Subjects: How-to, Mathematics
ISBN Prefix(es): 4-88176
Parent Company: Tokyo Hyoujun
Associate Companies: Kougakusha; Tokyo Souken
Book Club(s): Japan Book Publishers Association

Soshisha Co Ltd+
2-33-8, Sendagaya, Shibuya-ku, Tokyo 151-0051
Tel: (03) 3476-6565 *Fax:* (03) 3470-2640
E-mail: soshisha@magical-egg.or.jp
Key Personnel
President: Masao Kase
Editor-in-Chief: Haruo Kitani
Sales Manager: Tomio Kobayashi
Founded: 1966
Subjects: Literature, Literary Criticism, Essays, Nonfiction (General), Science (General)
ISBN Prefix(es): 4-7942

Springer-Verlag Tokyo+
3-3-13 Hongo, Bunkyo-ku, Tokyo 113-0033
Tel: (03) 3812-0757 *Fax:* (03) 3812-0719
Web Site: www.springer-tokyo.co.jp/
Founded: 1983
Subjects: Economics, Mathematics, Medicine, Nursing, Dentistry, Science (General)
ISBN Prefix(es): 4-431

Total Titles: 300 Print; 15 CD-ROM
Parent Company: Springer-Verlag GmbH & Co KG, Heidelberger Platz 3, 14197 Berlin, Germany

Surugadai-Shuppan Sha
Surugadai Bldg, 7, Kanda-Surugadai 3 chome, Chiyoda-ku, Tokyo 101-0062
Tel: (03) 3291-1676 *Fax:* (03) 3291-1675
E-mail: edit@surugadai.com
Web Site: www.e-surugadai.com
Key Personnel
President: Yoji Ida
Founded: 1954
Subjects: Economics, Law, Literature, Literary Criticism, Essays, Philosophy
ISBN Prefix(es): 4-411

Taimeido Publishing Co Ltd
3-22, Kanda-Ogawamachi, Chiyoda-ku, Tokyo 101-0052
Tel: (03) 3291-2374 *Fax:* (03) 3291-2376
E-mail: taimei1@ibm.net
Key Personnel
President: Yuzo Kanbe
Founded: 1918
Subjects: Agriculture, Economics, Geography, Geology, History, Philosophy, Religion - Other, Population
ISBN Prefix(es): 4-470

Takahashi Shoten Co Ltd
22-13, Otowa 1 chome, Bunkyo-ku, Tokyo 112-0013
Tel: (03) 3943-4525 *Fax:* (03) 3943-4288
Web Site: www.takahashishoten.co.jp
Key Personnel
President: Hideo Takahashi
Foreign Rights & Trade: Takashi Okubo
Founded: 1952 (as Kowado Co Ltd)
Guidebooks, juvenile, picture books.
Subjects: Education, Language Arts, Linguistics, Law, Medicine, Nursing, Dentistry, Technology
ISBN Prefix(es): 4-471

Tamagawa University Press+
1-1, Tamagawa-Gakuen 6 chome, Machida-shi, Tokyo 194-8610
Tel: (042) 739-8935 *Fax:* (042) 739-8940
E-mail: tup@tamagawa.ac.jp
Web Site: www.tamagawa.ac.jp/sisetu/up
Key Personnel
President: Yoshiaki Obara
Dir & Editor: Mikio Shionoya
Foreign Rights & Trade: Takamasa Narita
Founded: 1929
Membership(s): The Association of Japanese University Press (AJUP); International Association of Scholarly Publishers (IASP).
Subjects: Art, Education, Philosophy, Regional Interests, Religion - Other, Social Sciences, Sociology
ISBN Prefix(es): 4-472

Tankosha Publishing Co Ltd
19-1, Murasakino miya-Nishi-machi, Kita-ku, Kyoto-shi 603-8158
Tel: (075) 432 5151 *Fax:* (075) 432 0275
E-mail: info@tankosha.co.jp
Web Site: tankosha.topica.ne.jp
Key Personnel
President: Yoshito Naya
Founded: 1949
Subjects: Antiques, Architecture & Interior Design, Art, Cookery, Crafts, Games, Hobbies, Ethnicity, Gardening, Plants, History, Philosophy, Photography, Religion - Other
ISBN Prefix(es): 4-473
Total Titles: 4,000 Print
Branch Office(s)
Sugaya Bldg, 39-1 Ichigaya Yanagi-cho, Shinjuku-ku, Tokyo 162-0061

TBS-Britannica Co Ltd
Itochu Nenryo Bldg, 24-12, Meguro 1 chome, Meguro-ku, Tokyo 153-8940
Tel: (03) 5436-5721 *Fax:* (03) 5436-5759
Key Personnel
President: Shinichi Hamanaka
Foreign Rights & Trade: Hiroshi Ishikawa
Founded: 1969
Subjects: Art, Literature, Literary Criticism, Essays, Social Sciences, Sociology
ISBN Prefix(es): 4-484

Teikoku-Shoin Co Ltd
29 Kanda Jimbo-cho 3 chome, Chiyoda-ku, Tokyo 101-0051
Tel: (03) 32620834 *Fax:* (03) 32627770
E-mail: kenkyu@teikokushoin.co.jp
Web Site: www.teikokushoin.co.jp
Key Personnel
President: Misao Moriya
Manager, Research Section: Jun Hirayama
Founded: 1926
Subjects: Geography, Geology, Government, Political Science, History
ISBN Prefix(es): 4-8071

Thomson Learning Japan+
3F Hirakawacho Kyowa Bldg, 2-1 Hirakawa-cho 2 chome, Chiyoda-ku, Tokyo 102
Tel: (03) 3221-1385 *Fax:* (03) 3237-1459
E-mail: elt@tlj.co.jp
Web Site: www.tlj.co.jp
Key Personnel
General Manager: Yuko Matsuoka
 E-mail: yuko@tlj.co.jp
Founded: 1989
Publisher for ELT & academic texts
Also acts as importing agent for Thompson affiliated companies.
Subjects: Communications, English as a Second Language, Language Arts, Linguistics
ISBN Prefix(es): 4-900718; 4-931321
Parent Company: The Thomson Corporation
Distributor for Boyd & Fraser; Brooks/Coe; Chapman & Hall/Blackie & Son Academic; Course Technology Inc; Delmar; Gale Research/St James; Heinle & Heinle/Newbury House; Little, Brown/Legal (Japan); MacMillan (ELT only-USA); Thomas Nelson & Sons Ltd (UK); Onword; PWS-Kent; South-Western; Van Nostrand Reinhold; Wadsworth

3A Corporation
6-3, Sarugaku-cho 2 chome, Chiyoda-ku, Tokyo 101
Tel: (03) 32925751 *Fax:* (03) 32925754
E-mail: 3ac@mail.at-m.or.jp
Web Site: www.at-m.or.jpl~3ac
Key Personnel
President: Michihiro Takai
Founded: 1973
Subjects: Language Arts, Linguistics, Management
Distributed by Chapman & Hall, London (except USA & Japan); Quality Resources, New York (USA)

Tohan-Nippan, *imprint of* Minerva Shobo Co Ltd

Toho Book Store+
1-9-4F Kanda-Jinbo-cho, Chiyoda-ku, Tokyo 101-0051
Tel: (03) 32331001 *Fax:* (03) 32950800
Key Personnel
President: Masakazu Fukushima
Founded: 1951
Specialize in China.
Membership(s): Japan Book Publisher's Association.
Subjects: Archaeology, Art, Asian Studies, Crafts, Games, Hobbies, Economics, Geography, Geology, History, Language Arts, Linguistics, Literature, Literary Criticism, Essays, Medicine, Nursing, Dentistry, Nonfiction (General), Philosophy, Regional Interests, Religion - Other
ISBN Prefix(es): 4-497
Branch Office(s)
Osaka
Bookshop(s): 1-10-2 Takashimadaira, Itabashi-Ku, Tokyo 175
Warehouse: 1-10-2 Takashimadaira, Itabashi-Ku, Tokyo 175
Orders to: 1-10-2 Takashimadaira, Itabashi-ku, Tokyo 175

Toho Shuppan+
Yasuda Seimei Tennouji Bldg, 1-8-15, Oomichi, Tennoji-ku, Osaka 543-0052
Tel: (03) 6779-9571 *Fax:* (06) 6779-9573
Web Site: www.tohoshuppan.co.jp
Key Personnel
President: Shigeto Imahigashi
Founded: 1978
Subjects: Art, Asian Studies, Crafts, Games, Hobbies, History, Philosophy, Photography, Religion - Buddhist
ISBN Prefix(es): 4-88591

Tokai University Press
Tokai University Alumni Hall, 3-10-35 Miramiyana, Hadano-shi, Kanagawa 257-0003
Tel: (0463) 79-3921 (Sales); (0463) 79-3921 (Editorial) *Fax:* (0463) 69-5087
E-mail: webmaster@press.tokai.ac.jp
Web Site: www.press.tokai.ac.jp
Key Personnel
President: Tatsuro Matsumae
Dir: Sumio Semizu
Editor-in-Chief, Foreign Rights & Trade: Yoshihiro Miura
Founded: 1962
Subjects: Art, Biological Sciences, Earth Sciences, History, Language Arts, Linguistics, Literature, Literary Criticism, Essays, Philosophy, Religion - Other, Social Sciences, Sociology, Technology
ISBN Prefix(es): 4-486

Tokuma Shoten Publishing Co Ltd+
2-2-1 Shiba-daimon, Minato-ku, Tokyo 105-8055
Tel: (03) 5403-4300 *Fax:* (03) 3573-8771
E-mail: iwabuchi@shoten.tokuma.com
Web Site: www.tokuma.jp
Key Personnel
President: Takeyoshi Matsushita
Foreign Rights & Trade: Kyoko Aoyama
Founded: 1954
Specialize in classics.
Subjects: Art, Crafts, Games, Hobbies, Economics, Fiction, History, House & Home, How-to, Literature, Literary Criticism, Essays, Nonfiction (General), Social Sciences, Sociology, Sports, Athletics
ISBN Prefix(es): 4-19
U.S. Office(s): 150 Skyline Tower, 10900 NE Fourth, Bellevue, WA 98004, United States

Tokyo Kagaku Dojin Co Ltd+
36-7, Sengoku 3 chome, Bunkyo-ku, Tokyo 112-0011
Tel: (03) 3946-5311 *Fax:* (03) 3946-5316
E-mail: tokyokagakudozin@a.email.ne.jp
Key Personnel
President: Minako Ozawa
Foreign Rights & Trade: Mutsure Sumita
Founded: 1961
Subjects: Biological Sciences, Chemistry, Chemical Engineering, Engineering (General), Medicine, Nursing, Dentistry, Science (General)
ISBN Prefix(es): 4-8079

Tokyo Shoseki Co Ltd+
17-1 Horifune 2 chome, Kita-ku, Tokyo 114-0004
Tel: (03) 5390-7531 *Fax:* (03) 5390-7409
E-mail: home@tokyo-shoseki.co.jp
Web Site: www.tokyo-shoseki.co.jp
Key Personnel
President & Chief Executive Officer: Yoshikatsu Kawauchi
Foreign Rights & Trade: Shigeki Oyama
 E-mail: shoseki@tokyo-shoseki.co.jp
Founded: 1909
Associated with Toppan International Group.
Subjects: Art, Disability, Special Needs, Education, English as a Second Language, Fiction, History, Mathematics, Religion - Buddhist, Science (General), Travel
ISBN Prefix(es): 4-487
Total Titles: 1,000 Print; 100 CD-ROM
Subsidiaries: Astro Publishing Co Ltd (Domestic Only); Froebel-Kan Co Ltd
Branch Office(s)
Chubu (domestic only)
Chugoku (domestic only)
Hokkaido (domestic only)
Kansai (domestic only)
Kyushu (domestic only)
Tohoku (domestic only)

Tokyo Sogensha Co Ltd
1-5, Shin-Ogawamachi, Shinjuku-ku, Tokyo 162-0814
Tel: (03) 3268-8201 *Fax:* (03) 3268-8230
Key Personnel
Chairman: Takao Akiyama
President: Yasunobu Togawa
Sales: Haruo Hashimoto
Foreign Rights & Trade: Mari Igaki
Founded: 1954
Subjects: Art, Criminology, History, Literature, Literary Criticism, Essays, Music, Dance, Mysteries, Philosophy, Science Fiction, Fantasy, Social Sciences, Sociology
ISBN Prefix(es): 4-488
Associate Companies: Sogensha Publishing Co Ltd

Tokyo Tosho Co Ltd
5-22, Suido 2 chome, Bunkyo-ku, Tokyo 112-0005
Tel: (03) 3816-2563 *Fax:* (03) 3815-7330
Key Personnel
President: Hiroyasu Katayama
Foreign Rights & Trade: Shizuo Sudo
Founded: 1954
Subjects: Biography, Mathematics, Physics, Science (General), Technical
ISBN Prefix(es): 4-489

Toppan Co Ltd+
c/o Toppan Shibaura Bldg, 3-19-26 Shibaura, Minato-ku, Tokyo 108-0023
Tel: (03) 5418-2535 *Fax:* (03) 5418-2529
E-mail: kouhou@toppan.co.jp
Web Site: www.toppan.co.jp
Key Personnel
Chief Executive: Hiroshi Yuri *Tel:* (03) 5418-253
 E-mail: yuri@top.co.jp
Man Dir: Naomi Yoshikawa
Founded: 1963
Membership(s): Japan Book Association of International Publications.
Subjects: Biological Sciences, Computer Science, Environmental Studies, Library & Information Sciences
ISBN Prefix(es): 4-8101
Total Titles: 350 Print
Parent Company: Toppan Printing Co Ltd
Associate Companies: Tokyo Shoseki Co Ltd
Distributor for Prentice Hall Japan Ltd (Japan)

Tosui Shobo Publishers
Touho Gakki Honkan, 4-1, Nishi-Kanda 2 chome, Chiyoda-ku, Tokyo 101-0065
Tel: (03) 3261-6190 *Fax:* (03) 3261-2234
Key Personnel
President: Michiya Kuwabara
Foreign Rights & Trade: Fumie Nakamura
Founded: 1978
Subjects: Anthropology, Archaeology, History, Comparative study of civilizations, folklore
ISBN Prefix(es): 4-88708

Toyo Keizai Shinpo-Sha+
2-1, Nihombashi-Hongokucho 1 chome, Chuo-ku, Tokyo 103-8345
Tel: (03) 3246-5467 *Fax:* (03) 3270-4127
E-mail: tk@toyokeizai.co.jp
Web Site: www.toyokeizai.co.jp/
Key Personnel
President: Junji Asano
Rights Manager: Kurono Yukiharu
Foreign Rights & Trade: Mahito Fujii
Founded: 1895
Subjects: Business, Economics, Finance, Labor, Industrial Relations, Nonfiction (General), Social Sciences, Sociology
ISBN Prefix(es): 4-492
U.S. Office(s): Toyo Keizai America Inc, 380 Lexington Ave, Room 4505, New York, NY 10168, United States *Tel:* 212-949-6737

Tsukiji Shokan Publishing Co
7-4-4-201, Tsukiji, Chuo-ku, Tokyo 104-0045
Tel: (03) 3542-3731 *Fax:* (03) 3541-5799
Key Personnel
President & Foreign Rights & Trade: Jiro Doi
 E-mail: JDHO7647@niftyserve.or.jp
Founded: 1953
Subjects: Anthropology, Archaeology, Biological Sciences, Child Care & Development, Earth Sciences, Environmental Studies, Social Sciences, Sociology, Sports, Athletics
ISBN Prefix(es): 4-8067

Tutbooks, *imprint of* Charles E Tuttle Publishing Co Inc

Charles E Tuttle Publishing Co Inc+
RK Bldg, 2nd floor, 2-12-10 Shimo-Meguro, Meguro-ku, Tokyo 153
Tel: (03) 5437-0171 *Fax:* (03) 5437-0755
E-mail: info@tuttlepublishing.com
Web Site: www.tuttlepublishing.com
Key Personnel
President, Singapore: Eric Oey
Man Dir, Tokyo Office: John Moore
Rights & Permissions & International Right, Boston Office: Penny Probst
Founded: 1948
Subjects: Art, Asian Studies, Cookery, Crafts, Games, Hobbies, Fiction, Language Arts, Linguistics, Literature, Literary Criticism, Essays, Poetry, Public Administration, Social Sciences, Sociology, Sports, Athletics, Travel
ISBN Prefix(es): 4-8053
Imprints: Journey Editions; Periplus Editions; Tutbooks; Yenbooks
Subsidiaries: Periplus Editions (HK) Ltd
Divisions: Berkeley Books Pte Ltd
U.S. Office(s): Charles E Tuttle Publishing Co Inc, 153 Milk St, Boston, MA 02109-4809, United States *Tel:* 617-951-4080 *Fax:* 617-951-4045
Airport Industrial Park, 364 Innovation Dr, North Clarendon, VT 05759-9436, United States *Tel:* 802-773-8930 *Fax:* 802-773-6993

United Nations University Press+
53-70, Jingumae 5-chome, Shibuya-ku, Tokyo 150-8925
Tel: (03) 3499-2811 *Fax:* (03) 3406-7345
E-mail: mbox@hq.unu.edu
Web Site: www.unu.edu/unupress
Telex: 25442 unat unix *Cable:* UNATUNIV TOKYO
Key Personnel
Marketing Manager: Marc Benger
Publications Officer: Scott McQuade
Founded: 1975
Specialize in books in the social sciences, humanities & pure & applied natural sciences related to the University's research into the pressing global problems of human survival, development & welfare.
Subjects: Asian Studies, Developing Countries, Economics, Environmental Studies, Ethnicity, Geography, Geology, Health, Nutrition, Social Sciences, Sociology
ISBN Prefix(es): 92-808
Number of titles published annually: 17 Print; 17 Online
Total Titles: 300 Print; 150 Online
Online services available through ebrary, netLibrary.
Imprints: UNU/WIDER Publications; UNU-INTECH Publications
Branch Office(s)
UNU Office in North America, 2 UN Plaza, DC2-2062, New York, NY 10017, United States
Foreign Rep(s): Brookings Institution Press (UK, USA)
Warehouse: Brookings Institution Press, c/o Tasco, 9 Jay Gould Court, Waldorf, MA 20601, United States

Universal Academy Press, Inc+
BR-Hongo-5 Bldg, 6-16-2, Hongo, Bunkyo-ku, Tokyo 113-0033
Tel: (03) 3813-7232 *Fax:* (03) 3813-5932
E-mail: general@uap.co.jp
Web Site: www.uap.co.jp
Key Personnel
President: Masahito Sakui
Founded: 1986
Specialize in publishing Japanese research in English.
Subjects: Engineering (General), Medicine, Nursing, Dentistry, Science (General), Technology
ISBN Prefix(es): 4-946443
Orders to: CPO, Box 235, Tokyo 100-8691

The University of Nagoya Press
Furo-cho, Chikusa-ku, Nagoya 464-8601
Tel: (052) 789-3678; (052) 789-3683 (inter-library loan); (052) 789-3680 (reference) *Fax:* (052) 789-3694
E-mail: info@unp.nagoya-u.ac.jp
Web Site: www.nul.nagoya-u.ac.jp
Key Personnel
President: Shin-ichi Hirano
Orders to: Japan Publications Trading Co Ltd, 1-2-1 Sarugaku-cho 1 chome, PO Box 5030, Chiyoda-ku, Tokyo 101-0064 *Tel:* (03) 3292-3751 *Fax:* (03) 3292-0410

University of Tokyo Press+
7-3-1 Hongo, Bunkyo-ku, Tokyo 113-8756
Tel: (03) 3815-7789 *Fax:* (03) 3812-6958
Web Site: www.u-tokyo.ac.jp *Cable:* UNIVERSITYPRESS
Key Personnel
Man Dir: Tadashi Yamashita
Associate Dir: Isao Watanabe
Manager, International Publications: Etsuko Hamao
Founded: 1951
Membership(s): AAUP, STM, AJUP.
Subjects: Engineering (General), History, Medicine, Nursing, Dentistry, Philosophy, Psychology, Psychiatry, Religion - Other, Science (General), Social Sciences, Sociology

ISBN Prefix(es): 4-13
U.S. Office(s): Columbia University Press, 136 S Broadway, Irvington, NY 10533, United States

UNU-INTECH Publications, *imprint of* United Nations University Press

UNU/WIDER Publications, *imprint of* United Nations University Press

Toshiichi Uraki, *imprint of* Saela Shobo (Librairie Ca et La)

Waseda University Press
1-104-25 Totsukamachi, Shinjuku-ku, Tokyo 169-0071
Tel: (03) 32031551; (03) 32031570 *Fax:* (03) 32070406; (03) 32031570
E-mail: info@waseda-up.co.jp
Web Site: www.waseda-up.co.jp
Key Personnel
President: Shigenor Watabe
Foreign Rights & Trade: Koji Terayama
Founded: 1886
Subjects: Anthropology, Archaeology, Economics, Education, Film, Video, Finance, Government, Political Science, History, Law, Literature, Literary Criticism, Essays, Philosophy, Psychology, Psychiatry, Social Sciences, Sociology, Sports, Athletics
ISBN Prefix(es): 4-657
Number of titles published annually: 35 Print
Total Titles: 550 Print

Yakugyo Jiho Sha Co Ltd, see Jiho

Yakuji Nippo Ltd
One Kanda-Izumicho, Chiyoda-ku, Tokyo 101-8648
Tel: (03) 3862-2141 *Fax:* (03) 3866-8495
E-mail: shuppan@yakuji.co.jp
Web Site: www.yakuji.co.jp/
Key Personnel
President: Osamu Tanemura
Foreign Rights & Trade: Terue Hasshu
Founded: 1948
Subjects: Medicine, Nursing, Dentistry, Pharmacy
ISBN Prefix(es): 4-8408

Yama-Kei Publishers Co Ltd+
1-1-33 Shiba-Daimon, Minato-ku, Tokyo 105-8503
Tel: (03) 3436-4055 *Fax:* (03) 34334057
E-mail: info@yamakei.co.jp
Key Personnel
General Manager, International Division: Tony S Endo
President: Yoshimitsu Kawasaki
Founded: 1930
Subjects: Earth Sciences, Geography, Geology, Sports, Athletics, Travel
ISBN Prefix(es): 4-635
Branch Office(s)
1-12-12 Esaka-cho, Fukita-Shi, Osaka

Yamaguchi Shoten+
72, Ichijoji-Tsukudacho, Sakyo-ku, Kyoto 606-8175
Tel: (075) 781-6121 *Fax:* (075) 705-2003
Key Personnel
President: Kanya Yamaguchi
Founded: 1949
Subjects: Education, English as a Second Language, Language Arts, Linguistics, Literature, Literary Criticism, Essays
ISBN Prefix(es): 4-8411
Branch Office(s)
Fukuoka
Hiroshima
Nagoya
Tokyo

Yenbooks, *imprint of* Charles E Tuttle Publishing Co Inc

Yohan Shuppan+
3F Sanpo Ikebukuro Bldg, 4-32-8- Ikebukuro, Toshmia-ku, Tokyo 117-0014
Tel: (03) 3984-0221 *Fax:* (03) 3984-0223
E-mail: shinsuke@yohan-pub.co.jp
Telex: 2324818 Yohan J *Cable:* BOOKYOHAN
Key Personnel
President: Masanori Watanabe
Senior Man Dir: Shinsuke Suzuki
Editor-in-Chief: Yoshio Kida
Founded: 1963
Subjects: Art, Asian Studies, English as a Second Language, Language Arts, Linguistics
ISBN Prefix(es): 4-89684
Parent Company: Yohan (Western Publications Distribution Agency)
Imprints: Lotus; La Verve
Distributed by Weatherhill (North/South America)

Yokendo Ltd
30-15, Hongo 5 chome, Bunkyo-ku, Tokyo 113-0033
Tel: (03) 3814-0911 *Fax:* (03) 3812-2615
E-mail: yokendo@gol.com
Key Personnel
President: Kiyoshi Oikawa
Foreign Rights: Akira Suzuki
Founded: 1914
Subjects: Agriculture, Engineering (General), Physical Sciences, Science (General)
ISBN Prefix(es): 4-8425

Yoshioka Shoten
87, Tanaka-Monzencho, Sakyo-ku, Kyoto 606-8225
Tel: (075) 781-4747 *Fax:* (075) 701-9075
Key Personnel
President: Makoto Yoshioka
Foreign Rights & Trade: Masaji Kamikawa
Founded: 1964
Subjects: Science (General), Technical
ISBN Prefix(es): 4-8427

Yugaku-sha Ltd+
46 Kanda Jinbo-cho 1 chome, Chiyoda-ku, Tokyo 101-0051
Tel: (03) 32333731 *Fax:* (03) 32333730
Key Personnel
Publisher: Kazumi Mitsui
Editorial, Sales Manager: Yoshiaki Tokunaga
Production Manager: Isoyoshi Yamamoto
Foreign Rights Associate: Naoko Sakaki
Founded: 1969
ISBN Prefix(es): 4-8416
Associate Companies: Keigaku Publishing Co Ltd

Yuhikaku Publishing Co Ltd
2-17, Kanda Jimbocho, Chiyoda-ku, Tokyo 101-0051
Tel: (03) 3264-1319 *Fax:* (03) 3264-5030
E-mail: soumu@yuhikaku.co.jp *Cable:* Yuhikakubook
Key Personnel
Chairman: Shiro Egusa
President: Tadataka Egusa
Foreign Trade & Rights: Osamu Nomura
Foreign Rights & Trade: Susumu Ito
Founded: 1877
Subjects: Economics, Education, History, Law, Management, Psychology, Psychiatry, Social Sciences, Sociology
ISBN Prefix(es): 4-641

Yuki Shobo
39-12, Sekiguchi 1 chome, Bunkyo-ku, Tokyo 112-0014
Tel: (03) 3203-0151 *Fax:* (03) 3203-0157
Key Personnel
President: Kazuo Take
Foreign Rights & Trade: Hideo Oku
Founded: 1957
Subjects: Social Sciences, Sociology, Sports, Athletics, Home economics; recreation
ISBN Prefix(es): 4-638

Yushodo Shuppan+
29, San-ei-cho, Shinjuku-ku, Tokyo 160-0008
Tel: (03) 3943-5791 *Fax:* (03) 3351-5855; (03) 3943-6024
E-mail: intl@yushodo.co.jp
Web Site: www.yushodo.co.jp
Key Personnel
Chief Executive Officer: Mitsuo Nitta
President: Tamio Kawashima
Contact: R Carpenter
Founded: 1932
Specialize in antiquarian books, periodicals, new books & microforms. Also wholesaler & book dealer.
Subjects: Asian Studies, Economics, Regional Interests
ISBN Prefix(es): 4-8419
Associate Companies: JCC-Culture Japan; Newfield Building Co Ltd
Subsidiaries: Yushodo Fantas Corp; Yushodo Press Co Ltd
Branch Office(s)
Kansai
Kyoto
Ohtsuka
Warehouse: Yushodo Operation Center, 1542 Nakagawa, Isawa-cho, Higashiyatsushiro-gun, Yamanashi-Ken 406

Zeikei insatsu, *imprint of* Zeimukeiri-Kyokai

Zeimukeiri-Kyokai+
5-13 Simo-Ochiai 2 chome, Shinjuku-ku, Toyko 161-0033
Tel: (03) 3953 3325 *Fax:* (03) 3565 3391
E-mail: katsu@zeikei.co.jp
Web Site: www.zeikei.co.jp
Key Personnel
President: Yoshiharu Otsubo
Founded: 1945
Subjects: Accounting, Behavioral Sciences, Business, Economics, Human Relations, Law, Management, Marketing
ISBN Prefix(es): 4-419
Number of titles published annually: 100 Print
Total Titles: 1,700 Print
Imprints: Zeikei insatsu
Subsidiaries: Senbundo (Japan)

Zenkoku Kyodo Shuppan
10-32, Wakaba 1 chome, Shinjuku-ku, Tokyo 160-0011
Tel: (03) 3359-4811 *Fax:* (03) 3358-6174
Key Personnel
President: Takao Onaka
Founded: 1946
Subjects: Agriculture, Economics, Law, Management, Social Sciences, Sociology, Co-operatives
ISBN Prefix(es): 4-7934

The Zion Press, see Seiun-Sha

Zoshindo JukenKenkyusha
2-19-15, Shinmachi, Nishi-ku, Osaka 550-0013
Tel: (06) 6532-1581 *Fax:* (06) 6532-1588
E-mail: jzoshindo@ybb.ne.jp
Web Site: www.zoshindo.co.jp
Key Personnel
President: Akitaka Okamoto

Foreign Rights & Trade: Masataka Sakamoto
Founded: 1890
Subjects: Education, Bookkeeping
ISBN Prefix(es): 4-424

Jordan

General Information

Capital: Amman
Language: Arabic. English widely used by business people
Religion: Predominantly Sunni Muslim
Population: 3.6 million
Bank Hours: 0830-1230 Saturday-Thursday
Shop Hours: 0900-1300, 1500-1900 Saturday-Thursday
Currency: 1000 fils = 1 dinar; 10 fils is known as a piastre
Export/Import Information: No tariffs on books and advertising matter, but tax applies. Import licenses required but granted freely. Air freight must be by Jordanian national airline. Transportation insurance must be arranged in Jordan.
Copyright: No copyright conventions signed

Al-Tanwir Al Ilmi (Scientific Enlightenment Publishing House)+
PO Box 4237, al-Mahatta, Amman 11131
Tel: (026) 4899619 *Fax:* (026) 4899619
Key Personnel
Owner: Dr Taisir Subhi Mahmoud
  E-mail: taisir@yahoo.com
Founded: 1990
Subjects: Education, Electronics, Electrical Engineering, Philosophy, Science (General), Social Sciences, Sociology
Total Titles: 55 Print

JBC, *imprint of* Jordan Book Centre Co Ltd

Jordan Book Centre Co Ltd+
PO Box 301, Amman 11941
Tel: (06) 5151-882; (06) 5156-882; (06) 5155-882; (06) 606-882; (06) 676-882 *Fax:* (06) 5152016
E-mail: jbc@go.com.jo
Telex: 21153 *Cable:* JORDAN BOOK CENTRE/AMMAN
Key Personnel
Chief Executive: I Sharbain
Founded: 1982
Subjects: Business, Computer Science, Economics, Engineering (General), Fiction, Medicine, Nursing, Dentistry, Nonfiction (General)
Imprints: JBC
Showroom(s): University St, Amman

Jordan Distribution Agency Co Ltd
PO Box 375, Amman 11118
Tel: (06) 30191; (06) 4630192 *Fax:* (06) 635152
E-mail: jda@go.com.jo
Telex: 22083 Distag Jo *Cable:* JODISTAG AMMAN
Key Personnel
Chairman & General Manager: Raja Elissa
Deputy Chairman, Dir: Nadia Elissa
Founded: 1951
Subjects: History

Jordan House for Publication
Basman St, Amman
Mailing Address: PO Box 1121, Amman
Tel: (06) 24224 *Fax:* (06) 51062
Telex: 22056 bestours jo

Key Personnel
Man Dir: Mursi El-Ashkar
Editorial: Dr Mohamad Takrouri
Founded: 1952
Subjects: Medicine, Nursing, Dentistry
Bookshop(s): 2 Basman St; Jabal Amman St, Amman

Kazakstan

General Information

Capital: Almaty
Language: Kazakh
Religion: Islamic (mostly Sunni Muslim)
Population: 17.1 million
Bank Hours: Generally open for short hours between 0930-1230 Monday-Friday
Shop Hours: Generally 0900-1800 Monday-Friday; often open weekends
Currency: 100 kopeks = 1 rubl
Export/Import Information: According to Ukrainian quotas and customs duties, companies engaged in trade should register with the Ukraine Ministry of Foreign Relations. Licenses for export and import are also required for trade with Russia.
Copyright: UCC (see Copyright Conventions, pg xi)

Gylym, Izd-Vo
Ul Puskina 111/113, 480100 Almaty
Tel: (03272) 618005; (03272) 618845
  Fax: (03272) 618845; (03272) 618005
Telex: 251232 PTB Su
Key Personnel
Contact: Sagin-Girey Baimenov
Founded: 1946
Subjects: Biological Sciences, Chemistry, Chemical Engineering, Earth Sciences, Economics, Engineering (General), Mathematics, Physical Sciences, Science (General), Social Sciences, Sociology
ISBN Prefix(es): 5-628

Al-Farabi Kazakh National University+
Al-Farabi Ave 71, Almaty 480078
Tel: (03272) 471691 *Fax:* (03272) 472609
E-mail: anurmag@kazsu.kz
Web Site: www.kazsu.kz
Founded: 1934
Subjects: Archaeology, Asian Studies, Biological Sciences, Business, Chemistry, Chemical Engineering, Computer Science, Criminology, Economics, Environmental Studies, Foreign Countries, Geography, Geology, Government, Political Science, History, Journalism, Law, Management, Mathematics, Mechanical Engineering, Philosophy, Physics, Psychology, Psychiatry, Social Sciences, Sociology

Kazakhstan, Izd-Vo
Prospect Abaja 143, Dom Izdatel'stv, Almaty 480009
Tel: (03272) 422929; (03272) 428562
  Fax: (03272) 422929
Key Personnel
Dir: E H Syzdykov
Editor-in-Chief: M A Rashev; M D Sit'ko
Founded: 1920
Subjects: Economics, Government, Political Science, Medicine, Nursing, Dentistry, Science (General), Social Sciences, Sociology
ISBN Prefix(es): 5-615

Kramds-reklama Publishing & Advertising+
Ul Mira 115, Almaty 480091
Tel: (03272) 453968 *Fax:* (03272) 696753

Telex: 251233 RPAMS SU *Cable:* 251103 Y CNEX
Key Personnel
Dir: Lubov Shabykina
Chief Editor & Producer: Olga Tolanova
Chief Designer: Hasan Baimuratov
Manager: Tatyana Shah
Journalist: Rakip Nasyrow
Photographer: Oleg Belyalov; Vladimir Morozov
Founded: 1990
Subjects: Photography
ISBN Prefix(es): 5-86636
Parent Company: Kramds Corporation

Respublikanskij izdatei skij Kabinet
Ul Dzambula 25, Almaty 48000
Tel: (03272) 910703; (03272) 910333
  Fax: (03272) 631207
ISBN Prefix(es): 5-8380

Zazusy, Izd-Vo+
Prospect Abaya 143, Almaty 480009
Tel: (03272) 422849
Key Personnel
Dir: D I Isabekov
Editor-in-Chief: A T Saraev
Founded: 1934
Subjects: Literature, Literary Criticism, Essays, Poetry
ISBN Prefix(es): 5-605

Kenya

General Information

Capital: Nairobi
Language: Kiswahili (officially); English, Kikuyu & Luo also spoken
Religion: Most follow traditional beliefs; some Christian and Muslim also
Population: 26.2 million
Bank Hours: 0900-1400 Monday-Friday; 0900-1100 first and last Saturday of each month (except on coast, where banks open and close half an hour earlier)
Shop Hours: 0830-1230, 1400-1630 Monday-Friday; 0830-1200 or 1230 Saturday
Currency: 100 cents = 1 Kenya shilling
Export/Import Information: No tariff on books or advertising matter. Import licenses and exchange controls.
Copyright: UCC, Berne (see Copyright Conventions, pg xi)

AALAE, see African Association for Literacy & Adult Education (AALAE)

Academy Science Publishers+
Miotoni Rd, Off Miotoni Lane, Karen, Nairobi
Mailing Address: PO Box 24916-00502, Nairobi
Tel: (020) 884401; (020) 884405 *Fax:* (020) 884406
E-mail: aas@africaonline.co.ke; asp@africaonline.co.ke
Web Site: www.aasciences.org
Key Personnel
Founder: Prof Thomas R Odhiambo
Editor-in-Chief: Prof Keno E Mshigani
Publishing Manager: Prof Samuel O Okatch
Founded: 1989
Membership(s): African Book Collectives Ltd London; APNET; KPA; African Academy of Sciences; Third World Academy of Sciences.
Subjects: Developing Countries, Environmental Studies, Science (General), Technology
ISBN Prefix(es): 9966-831
Number of titles published annually: 4 Print

PUBLISHERS   KENYA

Total Titles: 23 Print
Parent Company: The African Academy of Sciences
Subsidiaries: Third World Academy of Sciences
Showroom(s): African Books Collective, The Jam Factory, 27 Park End St, Oxford OX1 1KU, United Kingdom
Bookshop(s): Prestige Bookshop, Nairobi; Textbook Centre Nairobi

Action Publishers+
PO Box 74419, Nairobi
Tel: (020) 608-810 *Fax:* (020) 753-227
E-mail: actonpublishersinfo@acton.co.ke
Web Site: www.acton.co.ke
Key Personnel
Man Dir & Publisher: Dr J N K Mugambi
Founded: 1992
Subjects: Career Development, Developing Countries, Education, How-to, Music, Dance, Philosophy, Religion - Other, Self-Help, Theology
ISBN Prefix(es): 9966-888

ACTS, see African Centre for Technology Studies (ACTS)

AFER (African Ecclesial Review), *imprint of* Gaba Publications Amecea, Pastoral Institute

Africa Book Services (EA) Ltd+
Rattansi Educational Trust Bldg, Koinange St, Nairobi
Mailing Address: PO Box 45245, Nairobi
Tel: (020) 223641 *Fax:* (020) 330272
E-mail: abs@mref.co.ke
Key Personnel
Dir: Talat Lone
Founded: 1955
Membership(s): Kenya Publishers Association & Kenya Book Sellers Association.
Subjects: Accounting, Library & Information Sciences, Nonfiction (General)
ISBN Prefix(es): 9966-914
U.S. Office(s): Dars, 919 Blair Ave, Neenah, WI 54956-2000, United States
Distributor for IMF; UNESCO; World Bank

African Association for Literacy & Adult Education (AALAE)
PO Box 50768, Nairobi
Tel: (02) 222-391; (02) 331-512 *Fax:* (02) 340-849
Telex: 22096
ISBN Prefix(es): 9966-9901

African Centre for Technology Studies (ACTS)+
PO Box 45917, Nairobi
Tel: (02) 524700; (02) 524000 *Fax:* (02) 524701; (02) 524001
E-mail: acts@cgiar.org
Web Site: www.acts.or.ke
Key Personnel
Communications & Publications Officer: Harrison Maganga
Founded: 1988
Specialize in academic books, also conduct research; offer training in editing, DTP & technical publishing.
Subjects: Agriculture, Biological Sciences, Developing Countries, Earth Sciences, Education, Environmental Studies, Health, Nutrition, Law, Science (General), Social Sciences, Sociology, Technology
ISBN Prefix(es): 9966-41
Divisions: Acts Press, Outreach, Training
Distributed by Zed Books (UK)

African Council for Communication Education
PO Box 47495, Nairobi
Tel: (020) 215270-33424 (ext 2068, 2328); (020) 227043 *Fax:* (020) 216135; (020) 750329; (020) 229168
E-mail: acceb@arcc.or.ke; acceb@form-net.com
Key Personnel
President: Francis Wete
Documentalist: Lydiah Gachung
Founded: 1976
ISBN Prefix(es): 9966-45

Book Sales (K) Ltd
PO Box 20377, Nairobi
Key Personnel
Chief Executive: Adrian Louis
Founded: 1976
Also bookseller.
ISBN Prefix(es): 9966-840
Subsidiaries: Kesho Book Centre

Bookman Consultants Ltd+
PO Box 31191, Nairobi
Tel: (02) 336771 *Fax:* (02) 217267
Key Personnel
Man Dir: Stanley Irura
Founded: 1988
Organizers of the Nairobi Book Fair.
Membership(s): Kenya Publishers Association, Afro-Asian Book Council; also acts as Publishing Consultant & Publisher of the Kenya Bookseller.
Subjects: Publishing & Book Trade Reference
ISBN Prefix(es): 9966-867

British Institute in Eastern Africa
Nairobi
Mailing Address: PO Box 30710, Nairobi
Tel: (02) 4343190; (02) 4343330 *Fax:* (02) 43365
E-mail: britinst@insightkenya.com
Web Site: www.britac.ac.uk/institutes/eafrica
Key Personnel
Dir: Dr Paul Lane
Secretary: Elizabeth Kiarie
Founded: 1962
Subjects: Archaeology, Ethnicity, History, Language Arts, Linguistics
Number of titles published annually: 1 Print
Branch Office(s)
10 Carlton House Terrace, London SW1Y5AH, United Kingdom *Tel:* (020) 7969 5201 *Fax:* (020) 7969-5401 *E-mail:* biea@britac.ac.uk
Distributed by Oxbow Books (UK); Oxbow Books (USA)

Camerapix Publishers International Ltd+
3rd Floor, ABC Place, Waiyaki Way, Nairobi
Mailing Address: PO Box 45048, Nairobi
Tel: (02) 4448923; (02) 4448924; (02) 4448925 *Fax:* (02) 4448818
E-mail: info@camerapix.com; camerapix@iconnect.co.ke
Web Site: www.camerapix.com
Telex: 22576 *Cable:* MOVIETONE NAIROBI
Key Personnel
Chief Executive Officer, Operations & Business Development Dir: Salim Amin
Man Dir: Rukhsana Haq; Rand Pearson
Founded: 1960
Subjects: Art, Regional Interests, Travel
ISBN Prefix(es): 1-874041
Imprints: CPI
Subsidiaries: Camerapix Daares Salaam; Camerapix Karachi
Branch Office(s)
Camerapix London, 8 Ruston Mews, London W11 1RB, United Kingdom *Tel:* (020) 7221 0077 *Fax:* (020) 7792 8105 *E-mail:* camerapixuk@btinternet.com
Distributor for Hunter & Struik

Cosmopolitan Publishers Ltd+
PO Box 18470, Nairobi

Tel: (020) 333448 *Fax:* (020) 333448
Telex: 22143
Key Personnel
Chairman: Dr Afrifa K Gitonga
Dir: Mr Murithi K Micheu
Marketing & Operations Dir: Boniface Wangaine
Founded: 1991
Subjects: Government, Political Science, Management, Mathematics, Psychology, Psychiatry
ISBN Prefix(es): 9966-881

CPI, *imprint of* Camerapix Publishers International Ltd

Danmar Publishers+
PO Box 75493, Nairobi
Tel: (020) 504818
Key Personnel
President: Daniel Irungu
Vice President & Author: Mary Irungu
Editor: Robert Irungu
Founded: 1990
Specialize in reading & spelling guides for beginners.
Subjects: English as a Second Language
ISBN Prefix(es): 9966-863
Parent Company: Danmar Publishers Printers & Stationer
Showroom(s): Chania Bookshop, PO Box 32413, Nairobi; Savanis Book Centre, PO Box 42157, Nairobi
Bookshop(s): Chania Bookshop, PO Box 32413, Nairobi; Savanis Book Centre, PO Box 42157, Nairobi

Dhillon Publishers Ltd+
PO Box 32197, Nairobi
Tel: (020) 505393
Founded: 1992
Subjects: English as a Second Language
ISBN Prefix(es): 9966-890

Egerton University
PO Box 536, Njoro
Tel: (051) 62265; (051) 622491; (051) 62271; (051) 62280 *Fax:* (051) 62527; (051) 62442; (051) 62389
E-mail: eujdlib@africaonline.co.ke
Telex: 33075
ISBN Prefix(es): 9966-838

Evangel Publishing House+
Lumumba Drive, Roysambu, Off Thika Rd, Nairobi
Mailing Address: Private Bag 28963, Nairobi 00200
Tel: (020) 860839; (020) 802033 *Fax:* (020) 802034
E-mail: evanglit@maf.or.ke; evanglit@panafricachristian.cominsightkenya.com
Cable: EVANGELIT NAIROBI
Key Personnel
Man Editor, Rights & Permissions: Paul Kimani
Man Dir: Barine A Kirimi *E-mail:* kirimi.barine@juno.com
Founded: 1952
Christian Publishing.
Subjects: Religion - Protestant, Religion - Other, Theology
ISBN Prefix(es): 9966-850; 9966-20
Number of titles published annually: 12 Print
Total Titles: 265 Print

Focus Publications Ltd+
PO Box 28176, Nairobi
Tel: (020) 600737
E-mail: focus@africaonline.co.ke
Key Personnel
Man Dir: Serah T K Mwangi
Founded: 1991

Subjects: Accounting, Business, Education, English as a Second Language, Fiction, Finance, Law, Religion - Catholic
ISBN Prefix(es): 9966-882
Distributor for Scepter Ltd (UK); Sinag-Tala (Philippines)
Bookshop(s): Focus Books, PO Box 48328, Nairobi

Foundation Books Ltd
PO Box 73435, Nairobi
Tel: (020) 765485
Key Personnel
Man Dir: F O Okwanya
Editorial: C O Ojienda
Sales Promotion: Moses Gondi
Production: Sophia Wanjiku Ojienda
Founded: 1974
Sub-regional Co-ordinator, Regional Centre for Book Promotion in Africa; Co-publishing program Eastern Africa Region.
Subjects: Biography, Poetry
ISBN Prefix(es): 9966-849

Gaba Publications Amecea, Pastoral Institute+
PO Box 4002, 30100 Eldoret
Tel: (0321) 61218; (0321) 62153 *Fax:* (0321) 62570
E-mail: gabapubs@africaonline.co.ke
Web Site: www.amecea.org
Key Personnel
Dir & Editor: Fr Eugene Ngoma
Assistant Dir & Editor: Sr Justin Nabushawo
Founded: 1959
Subjects: Anthropology, Biblical Studies, Religion - Catholic, Religion - Other, Theology
ISBN Prefix(es): 9966-836
Imprints: AFER (African Ecclesial Review); Spearhead

Government Press
PO Box 30128, Nairobi
Tel: 334075

Guru Publishers Ltd+
PO Box 32542, Nairobi
Tel: (020) 764146
Key Personnel
Man Dir, Proprietor & International Rights: Krishan Kumar Prabhakar
Founded: 1989
Specialize in secondary math & mathematical tables.
Membership(s): Kenya Publishers Association.
Subjects: Mathematics
ISBN Prefix(es): 9966-9878
Distributed by Book Distributors Ltd-NBI (Kenya)

Heinemann Kenya Ltd (EAEP)+
PO Box 45314, Nairobi
Mailing Address: PO Box 45314, Nairobi
Tel: (020) 222057; (020) 222144; (020) 228949 *Fax:* (020) 448753; (020) 226286 *Cable:* EDPUBS NAIROBI
Key Personnel
Man Dir, Chief Executive & Rights & Permissions: Henry Chakava
Publishing Dir: Jimmi Makotsi
Sales & Marketing Dir: Winston Mutua Nzioki
Finance Dir: Fabian Murugu
Warehouse Dir: Charles Oduor Munjal
Publicity Manager: James Ogola
Publishing Manager, English Language Teaching: B O Muluka
Editor, Kiswahili: G Lilian Dhahabu
Editorial, Secondary: Anne Mithamo
Off Manager: Onyango Ogutu
Accountant: Mark Abonyo
Founded: 1965
Membership(s): Kenya Publishers Association; Co-publishers with James Currey Africa Books Collective Publishers (UK), Ohio University Press (USA), African Publishing Network (APNET) (Zimbabwe).
Subjects: Accounting, Agriculture, Art, Automotive, Biological Sciences, Business, Cookery, Drama, Theater, Economics, Education, Fashion, Fiction, Finance, Geography, Geology, Government, Political Science, History, Literature, Literary Criticism, Essays, Management, Music, Dance, Nonfiction (General), Philosophy, Physical Sciences, Physics, Poetry, Public Administration, Religion - Other, Social Sciences, Sociology, Theology
ISBN Prefix(es): 9966-46
Associate Companies: East African Educational Publishers (Uganda Branch) Ltd, Pioneer House, Suite 9, Plot 28, Jinja Rd, PO Box 11542, Kampala, Uganda
Imprints: Spear Books, EAEP Kenya Writers Series; Wandishi wa Kiafricka
Subsidiaries: Kenway Publications
Distributor for James Currey Publishers (UK); Heinemann International (UK)
Warehouse: East African Book Distributors Ltd, PO Box 10324, Nairobi *Tel:* (02) 220520 *Fax:* (02) 226286 (EABD)
Orders to: East African Book Distributors Ltd (EABD), PO Box 10324, Nairobi *Tel:* (02) 220520 *Fax:* (02) 226286

Horizon Books, *imprint of* Space Sellers Ltd

ICRAF, see International Centre for Research in Agroforestry (ICRAF)

International Centre for Research in Agroforestry (ICRAF)
United Nations Ave, Gigiri, Nairobi
Mailing Address: PO Box 30677, Nairobi
Tel: (02) 524000 *Fax:* (02) 524001
E-mail: icraf@cgiar.org
Web Site: www.worldagroforestrycentre.org
Key Personnel
Dir General: Dr Dennis P Garrity
Assistant Dir General: Bruce Scott
Founded: 1977
International not-for-profit organization.
Subjects: Agriculture, Environmental Studies
ISBN Prefix(es): 92-9059

Jacaranda Designs Ltd+
PO Box 76691, Nairobi
Tel: 569736; (02) 568353 *Fax:* 740524
Key Personnel
Man Dir & International Rights: Susan Scull Carvalho
Marketing Manager: Brown Onduso
Man Editor: Bridget King
Founded: 1991
Membership(s): Multi-Cultural Publishers Exchange Association, Kenya Publishers Association & Association of International Schools in Africa (AISA).
Subjects: Fiction, Nonfiction (General)
ISBN Prefix(es): 9966-884
U.S. Office(s): Jacaranda Designs Ltd USA, PO Box 7936, Boulder, CO 80306, United States
Distributed by Southern Book Publishers (South Africa)

JKF, *imprint of* The Jomo Kenyatta Foundation

KEMRI, see Kenya Medical Research Institute (KEMRI)

Kenway Publications Ltd+
Woodvale Grove, Westlands, Brick Court, Nairobi
Mailing Address: PO Box 45314-00100 GPO, Nairobi
Tel: (02) 444700; (02) 445260; (02) 445261 *Fax:* (02) 448753
E-mail: eaep@africaonline.co.ke
Web Site: www.eastafricanpublishers.com
Telex: EDPUBS
Key Personnel
Chairman & Chief Executive Officer: Henry Chakava
Man Dir: Barrack O Muluka
Sales & Marketing Dir: Winston Mutua Nzioki
Tel: (02) 544295
Publicity Manager: Rebecca Wabwoba
Founded: 1981
Specialize in tourism books, city maps.
Membership(s): African Publishing Network; Kenya Publishers Association.
Subjects: Animals, Pets, Anthropology, Biography, Cookery, Government, Political Science, History, Humor, Language Arts, Linguistics, Music, Dance, Natural History, Nonfiction (General), Regional Interests, Sports, Athletics, Travel
ISBN Prefix(es): 9966-46; 9966-848; 9966-25
Number of titles published annually: 4 Print
Total Titles: 56 Print
Parent Company: East African Educational Publishers Ltd, Nairobi, Man Dir: Barrack Muluka
Associate Companies: Transmedia Uganda, Plot 51/53, Nkrumah Rd, PO Box 28104, Kampala, Uganda, Ignatius Tumwesigye *Tel:* (041) 235860 *Fax:* (041) 347235 *E-mail:* transmed@swiftuganda.com *Web Site:* www.eastafricanpublishers.com
Distributed by African Books Collective (UK)
Foreign Rep(s): African Books Collective (UK/Europe)
Shipping Address: East African Book Distributors Ltd, PO Box 10324, Nairobi
Warehouse: East African Book Distributors Ltd, PO Box 10324, Nairobi, Warehouse Manager: Charles Munjal *Tel:* (02) 544321, (02) 545903, (02) 534020 *Fax:* (02) 532095 *E-mail:* eaep@nbnet.co.ke *Web Site:* www.eastafricanpublishers.com
Orders to: East African Book Distributors Ltd, PO Box 10324, Nairobi, Warehouse Manager: Charles O Munjal *Tel:* (02) 534020, (020) 544321, (020) 545903 *Fax:* (02) 532095 *E-mail:* eaep@nbnet.co.ke *Web Site:* www.eastafricanpublishers.com

Kenya Energy & Environment Organisation, Kengo
PO Box 48197, Nairobi
Tel: (020) 749747; (020) 748281 *Fax:* (020) 749382
Telex: 25222 *Cable:* KENGO KE
Key Personnel
Executive Dir: Mr Achoka Awori
Assistant Marketing Officer: Julie Kariuki
Founded: 1981
Subjects: Agriculture, Energy, Environmental Studies
ISBN Prefix(es): 9966-841

Kenya Literature Bureau
Bellevue Area, Off Mombasa Rd, Nairobi
Mailing Address: PO Box 30022, Nairobi
Tel: (02) 608305; (02) 608806; (02) 605595; (02) 351196; (02) 351197; (02) 506158 *Fax:* (02) 605600 Fax on Demand: 601474
E-mail: klb@onlinekenya.com *Cable:* Literature Nairobi
Key Personnel
Man Dir: M A Karauri
Publishes, prints & distributes affordable books & other reading materials. Also encourages Kenyan authors through financial incentives, advice on how to write, etc.
Subjects: Agriculture, Animals, Pets, Education, Health, Nutrition, Law, Mathematics, Medicine, Nursing, Dentistry, Science (General), Science Fiction, Fantasy, Veterinary Science

ISBN Prefix(es): 9966-44
Total Titles: 700 Print

Kenya Medical Research Institute (KEMRI)
PO Box 54840, Nairobi
Tel: (02) 722541; (02) 722672; (02) 722532 *Fax:* (02) 720030
E-mail: kemrilib@ken.healthnet.org
Web Site: www.kemri.org
Key Personnel
Dir: Dr Davy Koech
Subjects: Biological Sciences, Environmental Studies, Health, Nutrition, Medicine, Nursing, Dentistry
ISBN Prefix(es): 9966-869

Kenya Meteorological Department
PO Box 30259, Nairobi
Tel: (02) 567880 *Fax:* (02) 576955
E-mail: director@lion.meteo.go.ke; imtr@lion.meteo.go.ke
Web Site: www.meteo.go.ke
Telex: 22208 Weather *Cable:* WEATHER NAIROBI
Key Personnel
Dir: Dr Joseph Romanus Mukabana
Subjects: Electronics, Electrical Engineering, Environmental Studies
ISBN Prefix(es): 9966-830

Kenya Quality & Productivity Institute+
PO Box 57225, Nairobi
Key Personnel
Contact: Silas Gachanja Maina
Founded: 1992
Subjects: Developing Countries, Economics, Management, Mathematics, Self-Help
ISBN Prefix(es): 9966-894

The Jomo Kenyatta Foundation+
Industrial Area, Enterprise Rd, Nairobi
Mailing Address: PO Box 30533, Nairobi
Tel: (02) 557222; (02) 531965 *Fax:* (02) 531966
E-mail: publish@jomokenyattaf.com
Web Site: www.kenyaweb.com/education/klb.html
Cable: Foundation
Founded: 1966
Membership(s): Kenya Publishers Association.
ISBN Prefix(es): 9966-22
Parent Company: Ministry of Education, PO Box 30040, Nairobi
Imprints: JKF
Warehouse: Kijabe St, PO Box 30533, Nairobi
Orders to: c/o Sales & Marketing Manager, Industrial Area, Enterprise Rd, PO Box 30533, Nairobi

Lake Publishers & Enterprises Ltd+
PO Box 1743, Kisumu
Tel: (057) 42750
Key Personnel
President: James C Odaga
Dir: Mrs Asenath Bole Odaga
Editor: Aol Ohito
Founded: 1982
Membership(s): Kenya Publishers Association; Kenya Booksellers Association; African Publishing Network (APNET), Harare, Zimbabwe.
Subjects: Biological Sciences, Drama, Theater, Education, Fiction, Government, Political Science, Labor, Industrial Relations, Literature, Literary Criticism, Essays, Mathematics, Music, Dance, Poetry, Religion - Protestant
ISBN Prefix(es): 9966-847
Associate Companies: Thu Tinda Book Distribution Ltd; Thu Tinda Bookshop
Subsidiaries: Innervision Communication
Distributor for ABC (outside Africa)
Showroom(s): Kenya Industrial Estate, Airport Rd, Kisumu

Life Challenge AFRICA
PO Box 50770, Nairobi
Tel: (02) 561121; (02) 722314 *Fax:* (02) 564030
E-mail: lca@umsg.org
Key Personnel
Contact: Eric Walter
Subjects: Religion - Islamic, Religion - Other
ISBN Prefix(es): 9966-895
U.S. Office(s): SIM Int, Box 7900, Charlotte, NC 28241, United States

Macmillan Kenya Publishers Ltd+
Kijabe St, Nairobi
Mailing Address: PO Box 30797, Nairobi
Tel: (02) 220 012; (02) 224 485 *Fax:* (02) 212 179
Web Site: www.macmillan-africa.com
Key Personnel
Man Dir: David Muita *E-mail:* dmuita@macken.co.ke
Founded: 1970
ISBN Prefix(es): 9966-885
Parent Company: Macmillan Publishers Ltd, United Kingdom

Midi Teki Publishers+
PO Box 52906, Nairobi
Tel: (02) 506993
Founded: 1977
Subjects: Accounting, Business, Developing Countries, Government, Political Science, Public Administration, Social Sciences, Sociology
ISBN Prefix(es): 9966-861
Bookshop(s): Mihuti Bookshop, Box 31, Kangema, Muringo *Tel:* 0157-22164

Nairobi University Press+
Jomo Kenyatta Memorial Library Bldg, PO Box 30197, Nairobi
Tel: (02) 334244 (ext 28581) *Fax:* (02) 336885
E-mail: nup@uonbi.ac.ke
Web Site: www.uonbi.ac.ke
Telex: 22095 Varsity KE
Key Personnel
Secretary: Omari E Gichobi *Tel:* (02) 334244, ext 222235 *E-mail:* gichobi@uonbi.ac.ke
Founded: 1984
Subjects: Accounting, African American Studies, Behavioral Sciences, Developing Countries, Geography, Geology, Government, Political Science, History, Law, Mathematics, Philosophy, Physical Sciences, Physics, Real Estate, Religion - Protestant, Social Sciences, Sociology, Veterinary Science
ISBN Prefix(es): 9966-846
Parent Company: University of Nairobi (Company fully-owned by University of Nairobi)
Distributed by African Books Collective (Europe, USA)

Paulines Publications-Africa+
PO Box 49026, Nairobi
Tel: (020) 4447202; (020) 4447203 *Fax:* (020) 4442097
E-mail: publications@paulinesafrica.org
Web Site: www.paulinesafrica.org
Key Personnel
President: Sr Samuela Gironi
Dir: Sr Teresa Marcazzan
Editor: Silvano Borruso; Peter Onyango-Ajus
Founded: 1985
Subjects: Biblical Studies, Biography, Child Care & Development, Communications, Education, History, Nonfiction (General), Psychology, Psychiatry, Religion - Catholic, Religion - Other, Theology, Women's Studies
ISBN Prefix(es): 9966-21
Number of titles published annually: 70 Print
Total Titles: 800 Print
Parent Company: Paulines Publications, Ring Rd Riverside, Nairobi 00100 GPO
Ultimate Parent Company: Daughters of St. Paul, 6 Amore Str off Toyin Str, IKEJA, PMB 21243, Lagos, Nigeria
Branch Office(s)
Catholic Book Centre, PO Box 2454, Addis Ababa, Ethiopia
Catholic Book Centre, PO Box CY738, Causway, Harare, Zimbabwe
Livraria Edicoes Paulistas, CP 3659, Maputo, Mozambique *Tel:* (01) 303397 *Fax:* (01) 304257 *E-mail:* paulines@virconn.com
Paulines Book & Media Centre, PMP 21243, Lagos State, Nigeria *Tel:* (01) 7741636 *Fax:* (01) 4932128 *E-mail:* paulines@infoweb.com.ng
San Paolo Multimedia, Via del Mascherino 94, 00193 Rome, Italy *Tel:* (06) 6872354 *Fax:* (06) 68308093 *E-mail:* pmultimedia@pcn.net
Bookshop(s): Cathedral Bookshop, PO Box 2381, Dar Es Salaam, United Republic of Tanzania, Contact: Sister Carmel *Tel:* (022) 2113204 *Fax:* (022) 2113204 *E-mail:* cathbshop@cats-net.com; Catholic Bookshop, PO Box 30249, Nairobi *Tel:* (020) 3338514 *Fax:* (020) 4442144 *E-mail:* cbsn@bidii.com; Paulines Book & Media Centre, PO Box 4392, Kampala, Kampala, Uganda *Tel:* (041) 256346 *Fax:* (041) 349135 *E-mail:* paulines@africaonline.co.ug; Paulines Catholic Bookshop, PO Box 36291, Lusaka, Zambia *Tel:* (01) 220264 *Fax:* (01) 250134 *E-mail:* paulines@zamnet.zm; Paulines Multimedia Centre, PO Box 641, Bruma, Johannesburg 2026, South Africa *Tel:* (011) 6220488; (011) 6220489 *Fax:* (011) 6220490 *E-mail:* paulines@iafrica.com

Phoenix Publishers Ltd+
PO Box 18650, Nairobi 00500
Tel: (020) 223262; (020) 222309 *Fax:* (020) 339875
E-mail: phoenix@insightkenya.com
Web Site: www.phoenixpublishers.co.ke
Key Personnel
Secretary: Ann Wanjiru
Contact: G Woruingi
Founded: 1988
Membership(s): Kenya Publishers' Association.
Subjects: Education, Environmental Studies, Geography, Geology, History, Mathematics, Physical Sciences, Poetry, Social Sciences, Sociology, Women's Studies
ISBN Prefix(es): 9966-47
Distributed by MK Publishers (Uganda); Taasisi ya Uchunguzi wa Kiswahili (TUKI) (Tanzania)
Distributor for MK Publishers (Uganda); Taasisi ya Uchunguzi wa Kiswahili (TUKI) (Tanzania)
Foreign Rep(s): MK Publishers (Uganda)
Foreign Rights: Taasisi ya Uchunguzi wa Kiswahili (TUKI) (Tanzania)
Distribution Center: Kijabe St, Nairobi

Sasa Sema Publications Ltd+
South Gate Centre, Suite 6, South B, Nairobi
Mailing Address: PO Box 13956, Nairobi 00800
Tel: (020) 550400; 722-200544; 734-600887
E-mail: sasasema@wananchi.com
Web Site: www.sasasema.com
Key Personnel
Man Dir: Lila Luce *E-mail:* lucelila@yahoo.fr
Publishing Manager: Silas Okutoyi
Marketing Manager: Simon Mwangi
Founded: 1996
Publisher of Kenyan children's books, especially comic books (graphic novels; bandes dessinees) in Swahili & English; children's biographies of great African women & men in English; short literature in English & Swahili. Also publish editorial cartoons, study guides & pre-school activity books.
Membership(s): Kenya Publishers Association.
Subjects: African American Studies, Biography, Developing Countries, Fiction, Foreign Countries, History, Humor, Poetry, Religion - Is-

lamic, Religion - Protestant, Science Fiction, Fantasy
ISBN Prefix(es): 9966-9609; 9966-951
Number of titles published annually: 6 Print
Total Titles: 35 Print
Distributed by Peppercorn Books & Press (Canada & USA)
Distributor for Readit Books (Kenya, Uganda, USA & Canada)
Orders to: Peppercorn Books & Press, PO Box 693, Snow Camp, NC 27349, United States, Contact: Andrew Pates E-mail: post@peppercornbooks.com

Shirikon Publishers+
PO Box 46154, Nairobi
Key Personnel
Dir: Sylvester J Ouma
Subjects: Accounting, Anthropology, Biblical Studies, Business, Developing Countries, Economics, Education, History, Literature, Literary Criticism, Essays, Management, Philosophy, Religion - Catholic, Religion - Protestant, Social Sciences, Sociology, Theology, Women's Studies
ISBN Prefix(es): 9966-870; 9966-9842

Space Sellers Ltd+
PO Box 47186, Nairobi
Tel: (02) 555811; (02) 557517; (02) 557863 *Fax:* (02) 557815; (02) 558847
E-mail: sstms@africaonline.co.ke *Cable:* salespower
Key Personnel
Contact: Sylvia King *Tel:* (02) 530598
Founded: 1975
Membership(s): NPA.
Subjects: Automotive, Business, Career Development, Gardening, Plants, How-to, Self-Help, Travel
ISBN Prefix(es): 9968-68
Number of titles published annually: 6 Print
Total Titles: 23 Print
Associate Companies: Target Mail Services, PO Box 30759, Nairobi, Contact: Ann Thieth *Tel:* (02) 556916 *Fax:* (02) 558847 *E-mail:* sstms@africaonline.co.ke
Imprints: Horizon Books

Spear Books, EAEP Kenya Writers Series, *imprint of* Heinemann Kenya Ltd (EAEP)

Spearhead, *imprint of* Gaba Publications Amecea, Pastoral Institute

Sudan Literature Centre
Lenana Rd, PO Box 44838, Nairobi 00100 GPO
Tel: (020) 565641 *Fax:* (020) 564141
E-mail: across@across-sudan.org
Web Site: www.across-sudan.org
Key Personnel
Coordinator: Rev Anthony Poggo
Founded: 1988
Producer of church books for Sudan.
Subjects: Health, Nutrition, Religion - Protestant
ISBN Prefix(es): 9966-876
Number of titles published annually: 20 Print
Total Titles: 20,000 Print
Parent Company: Across

Transafrica Press
PO Box 48239, Nairobi
Tel: (020) 244724
Key Personnel
Man Dir: John Nottingham
Founded: 1976
Subjects: Biography, Education, Fiction, History, How-to, Nonfiction (General), Poetry, Regional Interests, Religion - Other, Social Sciences, Sociology

Tree Shade Technical Services
PO Box 71222, Nairobi
Tel: (02) 225798; (02) 220712
Key Personnel
Dir: Timothy Gathirimu
Founded: 1992
Subjects: Environmental Studies
ISBN Prefix(es): 9966-892

Uzima, *imprint of* Uzima Press Ltd

Uzima Press Ltd+
PO Box 48127, Nairobi
Tel: (020) 21239
E-mail: uzima@nbnet.co.ke
Key Personnel
Gen Mgr: Kiraka James
Founded: 1974
Membership(s): KPA (Kenya Publishers Association) & CBA (Christian Booksellers Association).
Subjects: Fiction, Nonfiction (General), Religion - Protestant, Religion - Other, Social Sciences, Sociology, Theology
ISBN Prefix(es): 9966-855
Imprints: Uzima

Vipopremo Agencies
PO Box 47717, Nairobi
Tel: (02) 227189; (02) 333882
Subjects: Education, How-to
ISBN Prefix(es): 9966-845

Wandishi wa Kiafricka, *imprint of* Heinemann Kenya Ltd (EAEP)

Gideon S Were Press+
PO Box 10622, Nairobi
Tel: (020) 331135
E-mail: gswere@nbnet.co.ke
Founded: 1983
Home science; Christian religious education.
Subjects: Anthropology, Government, Political Science, History, Social Sciences, Sociology, Women's Studies
ISBN Prefix(es): 9966-852
Total Titles: 68 Print
Associate Companies: Star Academy

Democratic People's Republic of Korea

General Information

Capital: Pyongyang
Language: Korean
Religion: Buddhism, Christian & Chundo Kyo
Population: 22.2 million
Currency: 100 chon = 1 won
Export/Import Information: No tariff information; all importation and exportation must go through Korea Publications Export & Import Corporation, Pyongyang.

Academy of Sciences Publishing House
Nammundung, Dir Choe Kwan Sik, Pyongyang
Tel: (02) 51956
Founded: 1953
Subjects: Biological Sciences, Chemistry, Chemical Engineering, Economics, Education, Geography, Geology, History, Philosophy, Physics, Science (General)

Educational Books Publishing House
Pyongyang
Subjects: Education

The Foreign Language Press Group
Pyongyang Publishing Trade Association, Sochon-dong, Sosong District, Pyongyang
Tel: (02) 841342 *Fax:* (02) 812100
Telex: 37021 PP KP
Key Personnel
President: Sun Myong Hwang
Subjects: Archaeology, Art, Biography, Child Care & Development, Cookery, Education, History, Philosophy

Foreign Languages Publishing House
Sosong District, Pyongyang
Tel: (02) 51-863
Key Personnel
Dir: Hwang Sun Myong
Subjects: Asian Studies

Grand People's Study House
PO Box 200, Pyongyang
Tel: (02) 84 40 66 *Fax:* (08502) 381-4427; (08502) 381-2100
Subjects: Alternative, Asian Studies, Biblical Studies, Biography, Child Care & Development, Communications, Education, Electronics, Electrical Engineering

Industrial Publishing House
Botonggang District, Pyongyang
Key Personnel
Dir: Kim Tong Su
Subjects: Business

Korea Science and Encyclopedia Publishing House (Guahak Baikkwa Sajon Chulpansa)+
Jangyongdong, Sosong District, Pyongyang
Mailing Address: PO Box 73, Pyongyang
Tel: (02) 381 8091 (Call between 18 & 21 hours Pyongyang local time, Mon, Wed & Fri only) *Fax:* (02) 381 4550 (24 hours)
Key Personnel
President & Dir General: Kim Yong Il
Contact: Mr Jean Bahng
Founded: 1953
Editing & publishing; Dictionaries, Encyclopedias, various books & periodicals (magazines).
Subjects: Agriculture, Animals, Pets, Architecture & Interior Design, Art, Biological Sciences, Chemistry, Chemical Engineering, Civil Engineering, Communications, Economics, Education, Electronics, Electrical Engineering, Engineering (General), Geography, Geology, Government, Political Science, History, Law, Literature, Literary Criticism, Essays, Mathematics, Mechanical Engineering, Medicine, Nursing, Dentistry, Natural History, Philosophy, Physical Sciences, Physics, Science (General), Social Sciences, Sociology, Technology, Veterinary Science

Literature and Art Publishing House
Pyongyang
Key Personnel
President: Jong So Chon
Subjects: Art, Fiction

Transportation Publishing House
Namgyo-dong, Hyongjaesan District, Pyongyang
Key Personnel
Editor: Paek Jong Han
Subjects: Travel

Working People's Organization Publishing House
Pyongyang
Key Personnel
Dir: Pak Se Hyok
Subjects: Fiction, Government, Political Science

Republic of Korea

General Information

Capital: Seoul
Language: Korean (English also spoken in business)
Religion: Predominantly Mahayana Buddhist and Christian
Population: 44.1 million
Bank Hours: 0930-1600 Monday-Friday; 0930-1300 Saturday
Shop Hours: 1000-1900 Monday-Saturday
Currency: 100 chun = 10 hwan = 1 won
Export/Import Information: No tariffs on books and advertising matter. Authorizations for import of books and publications are reviewed annually by the Korean government. Import licenses are required. Exchange controls; prior deposits required at present.
Copyright: UCC (see Copyright Conventions, pg xi)

Ahn Graphics+
260-88 Songbuk 2-dong Seongbug, Songbuk-gu, Seoul 136-823
Tel: (02) 743 8065; (02) 743 8066; (02) 743 4154; (02) 743 3353 *Fax:* (02) 743 3352
E-mail: ask@ag.co.kr
Web Site: www.ag.co.kr
Key Personnel
President: Ok-Chul Kim
Founded: 1985
Specialize in art books.
Membership(s): Korean Publishers Association.
Subjects: Art, Computer Science
ISBN Prefix(es): 89-7059

Anam Publishing Co+
386-125, Sindang2-dong, Jung-gu, Seoul 100-452
Tel: (02) 22380491 *Fax:* (02) 22524334
Key Personnel
President: Lee Chang-Sik
Founded: 1978
Subjects: Career Development
ISBN Prefix(es): 89-7235

Ario Company Ltd+
5-36 Hyochang-dong, Yongsan-gu, Seoul 140-120
Tel: (02) 7122001; (02) 7122003 *Fax:* (02) 7023156
Key Personnel
Publisher: Yoong-Yeoup Lee
Founded: 1970
Subjects: Career Development
ISBN Prefix(es): 89-86063
Associate Companies: ARIO JSC Ltd, 5-36 Hyoch'ang-dong, Yongsan-gu, Seoul 140-120

B & B+
4F Yureka Bldg, 15-12, Nonhyeon-dong, Gangnam-gu, Seoul 135-811
Tel: (02) 540-4425 *Fax:* (02) 517-8793
E-mail: bbpress-98@hanmail.net
Key Personnel
Planning Dir: Jae-Woo Lee
Founded: 1996
Subjects: Computer Science
ISBN Prefix(es): 89-86929

Ba-reunsa Publishing Co
355-8, Misa-dong, Hanam-si Gyeonggi-do 465-140
Tel: (031) 792-0185
Key Personnel
International Rights: Joung-Ouk Park
Founded: 1987
Subjects: History, Poetry, Science (General)
ISBN Prefix(es): 89-7109

Bakyoung Publishing Co
Jungam Bldg, 13-31 Pyeong-Dong, Jongroo-gu Seoul 110-102
Tel: (02) 7336771 *Fax:* (02) 7364818
E-mail: psy@pakyoungsa.co.kr
Key Personnel
President: Jong-man Ahn
Founded: 1952
Subjects: Language Arts, Linguistics, Literature, Literary Criticism, Essays, Philosophy, Science (General), Social Sciences, Sociology
ISBN Prefix(es): 89-10

Bal-eon+
2F, 238-66 Yongdu-dong, Dongdaemun-gu, Seoul 130-070
Tel: (02) 293546; (02) 293547 *Fax:* (02) 293548
Subjects: Architecture & Interior Design, Art
ISBN Prefix(es): 89-7763

BCM Media Inc+
10 F Dongil Bldg, 1305-7 Seocho-dong, Seocho-gu, Seoul 137-070
Tel: (02) 567-0644; (02) 533-0089 *Fax:* (02) 552-9169
E-mail: bcmpub@nuri.net
Web Site: www.bcm.co.kr
Key Personnel
Chairman: Dr Byoung-Chul Min
Also distributes language educational materials.
Subjects: Education, Language Arts, Linguistics, English, Japanese & Chinese educational publications
ISBN Prefix(es): 89-7512
Distributor for Child's Play; Houghton Mifflin; Steck-Vaughn
Shipping Address: 752-27 Yuksam-Dong, B1 Jeil Bldg, Gangnam-gu, Seoul 135-080
Warehouse: 752-27 Yuksam-Dong, B1 Jeil Bldg, Gangnam-gu, Seoul 135-080
Returns: 752-27 Yuksam-Dong, B1 Jeil Bldg, Gangnam-gu, Seoul 135-080

Bi-bong Publishing Co
3F Milinae Bldg, 480-10, Seogyo-dong, Mapa-gu, Seoul 121-842
Tel: (02) 3142-6555 *Fax:* (02) 3142-6556
E-mail: beebook@hitel.net
Key Personnel
Publisher: Kie-Bong Park
Founded: 1980
Subjects: Business, Economics, Management
ISBN Prefix(es): 89-376

Big Tree Publishing+
215 Hongjae-Dong, Seodaemun-Ku, Seoul 120-090
Tel: (02) 7369653 *Fax:* (02) 7328694
E-mail: kennamu@unitel.co.kr
Key Personnel
Contact: Ik-Su Han
Founded: 1993
Subjects: Fiction, Nonfiction (General), Romance

BIR Publishing Co, *imprint of* Min-eumsa Publishing Co Ltd

Biryongso Publishing Co+
5F Kangnam Publishing Culture Center, 506 Shinsa-dong, Kangnam-Gu, Seoul 135-120
Tel: (02) 3443-4318; (02) 3443-4319 *Fax:* (02) 3442-4661
Web Site: www.bir.co.kr
Key Personnel
President: Park Sang Hee *Tel:* (02) 515 2003
Foreign Rights Manager: Michelle Nam
 E-mail: michellenam@minumsa.com
Founded: 1996
Picture & story books for young children.
ISBN Prefix(es): 89-491
Total Titles: 100 Print
Parent Company: Minumsa Publishing Co Ltd

Bo-jinjae Printing Co Ltd
8, Dangsandong 5-ga, Yeongdeungpo-gu, Seoul 150-045
Tel: (02) 6792351; (02) 6792355 *Fax:* (02) 6762821
Key Personnel
President: Dai-Hoon Lee
Founded: 1912
ISBN Prefix(es): 89-7197

Bo Moon Dang+
448-6 Sinsoo-Dong, Mapo-Ku, Seoul 121-110
Tel: (02) 7047025 *Fax:* (02) 7042324
Key Personnel
President: Byung-Gye Kim
Subjects: Architecture & Interior Design, Chemistry, Chemical Engineering, Civil Engineering, Computer Science, Electronics, Electrical Engineering, Engineering (General), Mechanical Engineering, Science (General)

Bo Ri Publishing Co Ltd+
480-26 Seogyo-dong, Mapo-gu Seoul 121-842
Tel: (02) 3233676 *Fax:* (02) 3240285
Key Personnel
Contact: Kwang-Ju Cha
International Rights: Ri Bo
Founded: 1991
Specialize in books for children.
Subjects: Child Care & Development, Education, Labor, Industrial Relations, Literature, Literary Criticism, Essays
ISBN Prefix(es): 89-85494
Associate Companies: Dotori Publishing Co; Jakenchak Publishing Co

Borim Publishing Co+
Geumsan Bldg, 4th floor, 364-22 Seogyo-Dong, Mapo-gu, Seoul 121-210
Tel: (02) 3141-2222 *Fax:* (02) 3141-8474
E-mail: namu@borimplc.co.kr
Web Site: www.borimplc.co.kr
Key Personnel
President: Kwon Jong-Taek
Executive Dir: Park Sang-Yong
Founded: 1976
Subjects: Animals, Pets, Fiction, History, Nonfiction (General), Science (General), Picture Book
ISBN Prefix(es): 89-433
Distribution Center: Network International Inc, PO Box 1081, Northbrook, IL 60065-1081, United States (exclusive distribution for US & Canada)

Bum-Woo Publishing Co
21-1 Gusu-dong, Mapo-gu, Seoul 121-130
Tel: (02) 7172121; (02) 7172122 *Fax:* (02) 7170429
E-mail: yhd@bumwoos.co.kr
Key Personnel
Chief Executive: Hyung-Doo Yoon
Founded: 1966
Subjects: Communications, Drama, Theater, Fiction, History, Literature, Literary Criticism, Essays, Philosophy, Publishing & Book Trade Reference, Social Sciences, Sociology
ISBN Prefix(es): 89-08
Associate Companies: Yoon Communications

Cham Kae, *imprint of* O Neul Publishing Co

Chang-josa Publishing Co
20-1, Shinmunro 2-ga, Jongro-gu, Seoul 110-062
Tel: (02) 7380393
Key Personnel
President: Duk-kyo Choi
Founded: 1963
Subjects: History, Language Arts, Linguistics, Literature, Literary Criticism, Essays
ISBN Prefix(es): 89-85139

Cheong-mun-gag Publishing Co+
Cheongmun Bldg, 486-9 Gileum 3-Dong, Seongbug-gu, Seoul 136-113
Tel: (02) 9851451; (02) 9897423; (02) 9897421 *Fax:* (02) 9828679
E-mail: CMGbook@hitel.kol.co.kr
Key Personnel
Chief Executive: Hong-Seok Kim
International Rights: Han-Seung Kim
Founded: 1975
Subjects: Science (General), Technology
ISBN Prefix(es): 89-7088
Subsidiaries: Ham Seung Publishing Co
Divisions: Trade Books

Chong No Books Publishing Co Ltd
45-1 Gwancheol-Dong, Jongro-gu, Seoul 110-111
Tel: (02) 7325381 *Fax:* (02) 7326202
Key Personnel
Chief Executive: Ha-Gu Chang
Founded: 1954
Subjects: History, Language Arts, Linguistics, Literature, Literary Criticism, Essays, Philosophy, Religion - Other
ISBN Prefix(es): 89-305

The Chosun Ilbo Co, Ltd
61 Taepyongro 1-ga, Jung-gu, Seoul 100-756
Tel: (02) 7245114 *Fax:* (02) 7246199
Key Personnel
Contact: Sang-Hoon Bang

The Christian Literature Society of Korea
169-1 Samsung-Dong, Gangnam-gu, Seoul 135-090
Tel: (02) 553-0870 *Fax:* (02) 555-7721
Key Personnel
President: So Young Kim
Founded: 1890
ISBN Prefix(es): 89-511
Bookshop(s): CLS Bookstore, 136-46, Yonjidong, Chongro-ku, Seoul

Chung Rim Publishing Co Ltd
Member of Chung Rim Interactive Co Ltd
Young Bldg 63, Nonhyn-Dong, Gangnam-gu, Seoul 135-010
Tel: (02) 544-4341 *Fax:* (02) 5468053
Key Personnel
Contact: Koh Young-Soo *Tel:* (02) 5464341
Founded: 1971
Also acts as Director of Korea Publication Association.
Subjects: Accounting, Advertising, Art, Behavioral Sciences, Biography, Business, Career Development, Child Care & Development, Communications, Computer Science, Crafts, Games, Hobbies, Economics, Education, Electronics, Electrical Engineering, English as a Second Language, Fiction, Finance, History, How-to, Human Relations, Humor, Journalism, Labor, Industrial Relations, Law, Literature, Literary Criticism, Essays, Management, Marketing, Music, Dance, Nonfiction (General), Philosophy, Psychology, Psychiatry, Real Estate, Religion - Protestant, Romance, Science (General), Science Fiction, Fantasy, Social Sciences, Sociology, Technology, Travel, Women's Studies

ISBN Prefix(es): 89-352
Number of titles published annually: 80 Print; 3 CD-ROM; 6 Online; 6 E-Book
Total Titles: 1,300 Print; 3 CD-ROM; 6 Online; 6 E-Book
Associate Companies: Pan Rae Wolbo SA; Woo Jin Publishing Co; Kolis Co Ltd

Dae Won Sa Co Ltd+
358-17 Huam-Dong, Yongsan-gu, Seoul 140-190
Tel: (02) 7576717 *Fax:* (02) 7758043
Key Personnel
Vice President: S W Chang
Contact: Min-Do Cha
Founded: 1986
Subjects: Antiques, Architecture & Interior Design, Art, Crafts, Games, Hobbies, Environmental Studies, Philosophy, Science (General), Travel
ISBN Prefix(es): 89-369

Daehan Printing & Publishing Co Ltd
344-12, Sangdaewon 1-dong, Jungwon-gu, Seongnam-si, Gyeonggi-do, Seoul
Tel: (031) 730-3850 *Fax:* (031) 735-8104
E-mail: mschung@daehane.com; james@daehane.com; sabrachili@daehane.com
Web Site: www.daehane.com
Key Personnel
President: Lee Hae-Dong
Subjects: Advertising, Agriculture, Antiques, Architecture & Interior Design, Art
ISBN Prefix(es): 89-378
U.S. Office(s): 3271 Sawtelle Blvd, No 104, Los Angeles, CA 90066, United States *Tel:* 310-737-0058 *Fax:* 310-737-9213

Daeyoung Munhwasa+
200 Jeil Bldg, 178-2 Cheongpa-Dong 1-Ga, Yongsan-Gu, Seoul 140-131
Tel: (02) 716-3883 *Fax:* (02) 703-3839
E-mail: spotto29@hotmail.com
Key Personnel
Contact: Choon-Hwan Rim
Subjects: Public Administration, Philosophy of Administration
ISBN Prefix(es): 89-7644
Book Club(s): Korean Publish Association

Dai Hak Publishing Co
420-5 Ahyon 1- Dong, Mapo-ku, Seoul 121-011
Tel: (02) 364-9788 *Fax:* (02) 393-9045
Key Personnel
President: Jin Young Yoon
Subjects: Technology

DanKook University Press
San 8 Hannam-dong, Yongsan-ku, Seoul 140-714
Tel: (02) 793-5034 *Fax:* (02) 709-5814
E-mail: omslit@dankook.ac.kr; pencil58@yahoo.com
Web Site: www.dankook.ac.kr
Key Personnel
President: Seung-Kook Kim
Subjects: History, Literature, Literary Criticism, Essays
ISBN Prefix(es): 89-7092

Dong-A Publishing & Printing Co Ltd
20F Dusan Tower Bldg, 18-12, Euljiro 6-ga, Jung-gu, Seoul 100-730
Tel: (02) 3398-8800 *Fax:* (02) 3398-2660
Key Personnel
Chief Executive: Hyun-Shik Kim
Founded: 1980
ISBN Prefix(es): 89-00

Dong Hwa Publishing Co
130-4 Weonhyoro 1-ga, Yongsan-gu, Seoul 140-111

Tel: (02) 7135411; (02) 7135415 *Fax:* (02) 7017041
Key Personnel
President: In-Kyu Lim
Editorial Dir: Kyoung-Sik Roh
Sales Dir: Byong-Don Ann
Production Dir: Chong-Choon Seo
Publicity Dir: Kun-Han Park
Founded: 1968
Subjects: Art, History, Literature, Literary Criticism, Essays, Philosophy
ISBN Prefix(es): 89-431

Eulyu Publishing Co Ltd+
46-1 Susong-Dong, Jongro-Ju, Seoul 110-603
Tel: (02) 7338151; (02) 7338152; (02) 7338153 *Fax:* (02) 7329154 *Cable:* EULYOO SEOUL
Key Personnel
President: Chin Sook Chung
Man Dir: Pil Young Choung
Editorial & Production: Ko Jung Gi
Sales: Sam Taek Huh
Founded: 1945
Subjects: History, Language Arts, Linguistics, Literature, Literary Criticism, Essays, Philosophy
ISBN Prefix(es): 89-324
Distributor for UN Publications

Ewha Womans University Press
11-1 Daehyun-Dong, Seodaemun-gu, Seoul 120-170
Tel: (02) 3277-2114 *Fax:* (02) 393-5903
Web Site: www.ewha.ac.kr/
Key Personnel
President: Li Sook Cheung
Dir: Young-Il Kim
Founded: 1949
Subjects: Art, Education, Human Relations, Language Arts, Linguistics, Music, Dance, Philosophy, Religion - Other, Science (General), Social Sciences, Sociology
ISBN Prefix(es): 89-7300

Gim-Yeong Co+
170-4 Gahoe-dong, Jongro-gu, Seoul 110260
Tel: (02) 7454823; (02) 7454825 *Fax:* (02) 7454826
Key Personnel
President: Jung Sup Gimm
International Rights Contact: Mee Sung Kim
Founded: 1976
Subjects: Business, Environmental Studies, Fiction, How-to, Management, Marketing, Mysteries, Philosophy, Religion - Other, Science (General), Self-Help
ISBN Prefix(es): 89-349

Golden Bough Publishing Co, *imprint of* Min-eumsa Publishing Co Ltd

Gomdori, *imprint of* Woongjin Media Corporation

Gyeom-jisa
375-13 Seokyo-Dong, Mapo-gu Seoul 121-210
Tel: (02) 3351985 *Fax:* (02) 3351986
Key Personnel
Publisher: Chung Hae-Sang
Founded: 1964
Subjects: Science (General)
ISBN Prefix(es): 89-7169
Distributed by Min Jung Book Distribution Co

Haedong+
15-4 Namyeong-dong, Yongsan-gu, Seoul 140-160
Tel: (02) 953707 *Fax:* (02) 953707
Key Personnel
President & Author: B Ryong Chung
Founded: 1993
Subjects: Poetry

ISBN Prefix(es): 89-86861
Distributed by Bomoon-Dang; Han-yang Distributor

Hainaim Publishing Co Ltd
5-6F Hainaim Bldg, 368-4 Seokyo-dong, Mapo-gu, Seoul 121-210
Tel: (02) 326-1600 *Fax:* (02) 326-1625
Web Site: www.hainaim.com
Key Personnel
President: Young-Seok Song
Rights Dir: Duran Kim *E-mail:* durankim@hainaim.com
Rights Manager: Karen Lee *E-mail:* karenlee@hainaim.com
Founded: 1982
Subjects: Education, Fiction, History, Nonfiction (General), Science (General), Comics
ISBN Prefix(es): 89-7337

Hak Won Publishing Co
25-36, Chungsin-Dong, Jongro-gu, Seoul 110-490
Tel: (02) 741-4621; (02) 741-4623 *Fax:* (02) 765-1877
E-mail: ccnstar@hanmail.net
Key Personnel
President: Young-Su Kim
Founded: 1945
Subjects: Art, Child Care & Development, Cookery, Literature, Literary Criticism, Essays, Social Sciences, Sociology
ISBN Prefix(es): 89-16

Hakgojae Publishing Inc+
77 Sogyeog-Dong, Jongro-gu, Seoul 110-200
Tel: (02) 7361713 *Fax:* (02) 7398592
E-mail: hkjass@hitel.kol.co.kr
Key Personnel
Contact: Chan-Kyu Woo
International Rights: Hyun-ki Park
Founded: 1991
Subjects: Archaeology, Architecture & Interior Design, Art, Asian Studies, Foreign Countries, History, Literature, Literary Criticism, Essays, Photography, Korean Studies
ISBN Prefix(es): 89-85846
Book Club(s): Kyobo Book Club

Hakmunsa Publishing Co+
6F Sahaghoegwan, 7-2, Sajik-dong, Jongro-gu Seoul 110-054
Tel: (02) 738-5118 *Fax:* (02) 733-8998
E-mail: hakmun@hakmun.co.kr
Web Site: www.hakmun.co.kr
Key Personnel
President: Young Chul Kim
Internal Dept: Ki-Hyoung Kim
Founded: 1963
Subjects: Business, Child Care & Development, Computer Science, Education, Engineering (General), English as a Second Language, Science (General), Social Sciences, Sociology
ISBN Prefix(es): 89-467; 89-87510
Branch Office(s)
Pusan *Tel:* (051) 502-8104
Taegu *Tel:* (053) 422-5000

Hanjin Publishing Co
4f, 40-21, Munbae-dong, Yongsan-gu, Seoul 140-100
Tel: (02) 7137453 *Fax:* (02) 7135510
Key Personnel
President: Gab Han Jin
Subjects: Art, Literature, Literary Criticism, Essays, Religion - Other
ISBN Prefix(es): 89-86412

Hangil Art Vision
401 Gangnamculpanmunhwa Senter, 506, Sinsa-dong, Gangnam-gu, Seoul 135-120
Tel: (02) 5154811; (02) 5154813 *Fax:* (02) 5154816
Key Personnel
Chief Executive: Euon-Ho Kim
Founded: 1976
Subjects: History, Literature, Literary Criticism, Essays, Philosophy, Social Sciences, Sociology
ISBN Prefix(es): 89-436; 89-437

Hanul Publishing Co+
501 Hyuam Bldg, 503-24 Changcheon-dong, Seodaemun-gu, Seoul 120-180
Tel: (02) 3260095; (02) 3366183 *Fax:* (02) 3337543
E-mail: newhanul@nuri.net
Key Personnel
Publisher: Kim Chong-Soo
Dir: Ms Lim Hee-Kun *Tel:* (02) 336-6183
Founded: 1980
Subjects: Asian Studies, Economics, Geography, Geology, Health, Nutrition, History, Journalism, Law, Literature, Literary Criticism, Essays, Medicine, Nursing, Dentistry, Philosophy, Social Sciences, Sociology, Theology, Women's Studies
ISBN Prefix(es): 89-460; 89-7058
Number of titles published annually: 150 Print
Total Titles: 1,200 Print
Associate Companies: Seoul Media Co; Siinsa Publishing Co

Haseo Publishing Co+
370-27, Shindang-Dong, Jung-gu, Seoul 100-454
Tel: (02) 2378161; (02) 2378165 *Fax:* (02) 2376575
E-mail: haseo@haseo.co.kr
Web Site: www.haseo.co.kr
Key Personnel
Chief Executive: Sang-Wook Kim
Founded: 1964
Subjects: Art, Literature, Literary Criticism, Essays, Social Sciences, Sociology
ISBN Prefix(es): 89-7330
Subsidiaries: Jigyung Publishing Co

Hollym Corporation; Publishers
13-13 Gwancheol-dong, Jongno-gu, Seoul 110-111
Tel: (02) 735-7551-4 *Fax:* (02) 730-5149; (02) 730-8192
E-mail: hollym@chollian.net; info@hollym.co.kr
Web Site: www.hollym.co.kr
Key Personnel
President: Kiman Ham
Sales Dir: Ki Lee
Founded: 1963
Subjects: Art, Cookery, Economics, Fiction, History, Poetry, Travel
ISBN Prefix(es): 0-930878; 1-56591; 89-7094
U.S. Office(s): Hollym International Corp, 18 Donald Pl, Elizabeth, NJ 07208, United States
Tel: (908) 353-1655 *Fax:* (908) 353-0255

Hongik Media Plus Ltd+
1515 Hanseo River Park Bldg, 11-11, Yeoyido-dong, Youngdeungpo-gu, Seoul 120-010
Tel: (02) 786-1016 *Fax:* (02) 786-1709
E-mail: hongikcb@soback.kornet.nm.kr
Subjects: Biography, Career Development, Computer Science, Education, English as a Second Language
Subsidiaries: Hongik Media CNC Ltd

Hw Moon Publishing Co
30 Kyunji-dong, Chongno-ku, Seoul 110
Tel: (02) 724897
Key Personnel
Man Dir: Myong Hui Yi
Founded: 1961
Subjects: Biography, Fiction, History, Philosophy, Poetry, Religion - Other

Hyangmunsa Publishing Co
201 Jiseong Bldg, 645-20, Yeogsam-Dong, Gangnam-gu, Seoul 135-080
Tel: (02) 5385671; (02) 5385672 *Fax:* (02) 5385673
Key Personnel
President: Joong Ryol Nah
Founded: 1957
Subjects: Agriculture, Economics, Engineering (General), History, Science (General)
ISBN Prefix(es): 89-7187

Hyein Publishing House
Usin Bldg, Suite 202, 11-2 Gusan-Dong, Eunpyeoung-Gu, Seoul 122-060
Tel: (02) 3836928 *Fax:* (02) 3836929
E-mail: vvh103@chollian
Web Site: www.hyeinbooks.co.kr
Key Personnel
Contact: Choon-Won Cho
Founded: 1993
Subjects: Education, Health, Nutrition, Science (General), Travel
ISBN Prefix(es): 89-7853

Hyun Am Publishing Co
1660-15, 7-dong Bongceon, Gwanag, gu, Seoul 151-057
Tel: (02) 877-2565 *Fax:* (02) 877-2566
Key Personnel
Man Dir: Keun-Tae Cho
Publicity: Sang-Won Cho
Founded: 1951
Subjects: Literature, Literary Criticism, Essays, Philosophy, Religion - Other
ISBN Prefix(es): 89-87969

Iljisa Publishing House
46-1 Junghag-Dong, Jongro-gu, Seoul 110-150
Tel: (02) 7329320 *Fax:* (02) 7222807
Key Personnel
Man Dir: Sung-Jae Kim
Publicity Dir: Byungki Yoo; Donhong Cho
Founded: 1956
Subjects: Archaeology, Fiction, History, Language Arts, Linguistics, Philosophy, Poetry, Social Sciences, Sociology
ISBN Prefix(es): 89-312

Iljo-gag Publishers+
9 Gongpyeuung-Dong, Jongro-gu, Seoul 110-160
Mailing Address: KPO Box 279, Seoul 110-160
Tel: (02) 7335430; (02) 7335431 *Fax:* (02) 7385857
E-mail: ilchokak@hitel.kol.co.kr; ilchokak@chollian.dacom.co.kr *Cable:* ICHOPUBLICO SEOUL
Key Personnel
President: Man-Nyun Han
Sales Dir: J Y Chot
Publicity Dir: J Y Choi
Founded: 1953
Subjects: Anthropology, Education, Engineering (General), History, Law, Medicine, Nursing, Dentistry, Psychology, Psychiatry, Science (General), Social Sciences, Sociology
ISBN Prefix(es): 89-337

Jeong-eum Munhwasa
203, 182-22, Nonhyeon-dong, Gangnam-gu, Seoul 135-010
Tel: (02) 5680070 *Fax:* (02) 5650352 *Cable:* Jeongeumsa
Key Personnel
President: Tong-Seek Chair
Sales Dir: Choong-tae Kim
Publicity & Advertising: Joo Park
Founded: 1928
Subjects: Fiction, Philosophy, Social Sciences, Sociology
ISBN Prefix(es): 89-7158

REPUBLIC OF KOREA

Jigyungsa Ltd+
790-14, Yeoksam-Dong, Kangnam, Seoul 135-080
Tel: (02) 557-6351 *Fax:* (02) 557-6352
E-mail: jigyung@uriel.net
Web Site: www.jigyung.co.kr
Key Personnel
President: Byung-Joon Kim
Dir, International & Planning Dept: Hyosik Kim
Dir, Marketing: Seong-Ho Lee
Dir, Production: Byung-Sik Kim
Founded: 1978
Subjects: Fiction, Nonfiction (General)
Subsidiaries: Miraejungbosa
Divisions: Walt Disney Books & Magazines

Jung-ang Media, see Jung-ang Munhwa Sa

Jung-ang Munhwa Sa
172-11 Yeomri-dong, Mapo-gu, Seoul 121-090
Tel: (02) 717-2114 *Fax:* (02) 716-1369
Key Personnel
Chief Executive: Duck-Ke Kim
Founded: 1972
ISBN Prefix(es): 89-7511

Ke Mong Sa Publishing Co Ltd+
772 Yoksam-dong, Kangnam-gu, Seoul 135-080
Tel: (02) 531-5535 *Fax:* (02) 531-5550
Key Personnel
President: Choon-sik Kim
Man Dir: Jong-uk Lee
Assistant Manager, Foreign Rights: Park Yeon
Founded: 1947
Specialize in children's books.
Subjects: Biography, English as a Second Language, Fiction, Geography, Geology, Nonfiction (General), Science (General)
ISBN Prefix(es): 89-06
Subsidiaries: Young Printing Co, Ltd; Kemong Enterprise Co Ltd; EMI - Kemongsa Co Ltd

Ki Moon Dang
286-20 Haengdang-dong, Sungdong-gu, Seoul 133-070
Tel: (02) 2295-6171 *Fax:* (02) 296-8188
E-mail: kimoon2@chollian.net
Key Personnel
Chief Executive: Hae-Jak Kang
Founded: 1976
Subjects: Art, Engineering (General)

Korea Britannica Corp
701 Jeilsangho B/D 7th Floor, 117 Jangchung-dong 1-ga, Jung-gu Seoul 100-391
Tel: (02) 2272-9731; (02) 2264-0924 (sales) *Fax:* (02) 2278-9983
E-mail: corporate@britannica.co.kr
Web Site: www.britannica.co.kr
Key Personnel
President: Hosang Jang
Founded: 1968
Subjects: Education
ISBN Prefix(es): 89-7544
Parent Company: Encyclopaedia Britannica Inc, Britannica Centre, 310 South Michigan Ave, Chicago, IL 60604, United States

Korea Local Authorities Foundation for International Relations
Royal Bldg 720, 5 Dangju-dong, Jongro-gu, Seoul 110-721
Tel: (02) 730 2711; (02) 2170-6098 *Fax:* (02) 737 8970; (02) 737-7903
E-mail: others@klafir.or.kr
Web Site: www.klafir.or.kr/
Subjects: Public Administration
ISBN Prefix(es): 89-86815

Korea Psychological Testing Institute+
501 Sambohojeong Bldg, 14-24, Yeoyidodong Yeongdeunpogu, Seoul 150-010
Tel: (02) 784-0990 *Fax:* (02) 784-0993
E-mail: KPIT@unitel.co.kr
Web Site: www.kpti.com
Key Personnel
Contact: Myung-Joon Kim
Founded: 1972
Subjects: Psychology, Psychiatry
Associate Companies: Consulting Psychologists Press

Korea Textbook Co, see Kwangmyong Publishing Co

Korea Textbook Co Ltd
3F, 299-2, Seongsu 2-ga 3-dong, Seongdong-gu, Seoul 133-833
Tel: (02) 465-1341 *Fax:* (02) 464-1318
E-mail: kpp0114@hanmail.net
Key Personnel
President: Keun-Woo Lee
Subjects: Art, Education, Government, Political Science
ISBN Prefix(es): 89-85182
Parent Company: Kwangmyong Printing & Publishing Co Ltd

Korea University Press
1-2 Anam-dong 5-ga, Seongbug-gu, Seoul 136-701
Tel: (02) 3290 4231 *Fax:* (02) 923 6311
Key Personnel
President: Sung Gi Jon
Founded: 1956
Subjects: Agriculture, Earth Sciences, Education, Engineering (General), History, Language Arts, Linguistics, Literature, Literary Criticism, Essays, Philosophy, Psychology, Psychiatry, Social Sciences, Sociology
ISBN Prefix(es): 89-7641

Korean Publishers Association+
105-2 Sagan-Dong, Chongno-Gu, Seoul 110-190
Tel: (02) 735-2701; (02) 735-2704 *Fax:* (02) 738-5414
E-mail: kpa@kpa21.or.kr
Web Site: www.kpa21.or.kr
Key Personnel
President: Jung Il Lee
Secretary General: Jong Jin Jung
Founded: 1947
Subjects: Publishing & Book Trade Reference
ISBN Prefix(es): 89-85231

Koreaone Press Inc+
9F Gyeongun Bldg, 70 Gyeongun-dong, Jongho-gu, Seoul 100-310
Tel: (02) 739-1156 *Fax:* (02) 734-3512
Key Personnel
Chief Executive: Nark-Cheon Kim
Man Dir: Cho Il-Kwan
Founded: 1978
Subjects: Biography, Business, Career Development, Economics, Education, English as a Second Language, Environmental Studies, Fiction, Language Arts, Linguistics, Literature, Literary Criticism, Essays, Management, Mysteries, Nonfiction (General), Philosophy, Religion - Buddhist, Romance, Science (General), Science Fiction, Fantasy, Social Sciences, Sociology, Western Fiction
ISBN Prefix(es): 89-12
Associate Companies: Koreaone Media Inc; Koreaone Chest Inc
Divisions: Foreign Rights Department
U.S. Office(s): Koreaone International, 520 W Eighth St, Los Angeles, CA 90005, United States

Kukmin Doseo Publishing Co Ltd+
822, Guro-dong, Guro-gu, Seoul 152-050
Tel: (02) 858-2461; (02) 858-2463 *Fax:* (02) 858-2464
E-mail: younhlee@chollian.net
Key Personnel
President: Young-Hoon Lee
Founded: 1978
Specializes in religious books.
Subjects: Religion - Protestant, Theology
ISBN Prefix(es): 89-401
Associate Companies: Kookmin Daily News Press
Subsidiaries: Yae-In Publishing Co
Distributor for Koonmin Daily News Press

Kukminseokwan Publishing Co Ltd
257-3 Gongdeog-dong Bldg, Mapo-gu, Seoul 121-804
Tel: (02) 7107722; (02) 7107724 *Fax:* (02) 7155771
Key Personnel
Chief Executive: Yoo-Kwang Lee
Founded: 1961
Subjects: Social Sciences, Sociology
ISBN Prefix(es): 89-11

Kumsung Publishing Co Ltd+
242-63 Gongdeok-Dong, Mapo-gu, Seoul 121-803
Tel: (02) 713-9651 *Fax:* (02) 704-1979; (02) 718-4362
E-mail: webmaster@kumsungpub.co.kr
Web Site: www.kumsungpub.com
Key Personnel
Chairman: Moo-Sang Kim
Editorial Dir: Sung-Chul Kang
Man Dir: Lee Jeong-Sam
Manager: Dae-Shik Kim
Assistant Manager: Chae-Hyung Lee; Gwang-So Lee
Founded: 1965
Subjects: Fiction, Nonfiction (General)
ISBN Prefix(es): 89-07
Associate Companies: Shin Won Editorial Center, 250-4 Towha-dong, Mapo-ku, Seoul; Shinwon Agency Co, 372-6 Seogyo-dong, Mapo-gu, Seoul 121-022
Subsidiaries: Kumsung Textbook Co Ltd; Kumsung Artcom
Branch Office(s)
Kaiserstr 42, 60329 Frankfurt am Main, Germany

Kwangmyong Publishing Co
5F Gyeongbok Bldg, 40, Euljiro 6-ga, Jung-gu, Seoul 100-196
Tel: (02) 2274-1552 *Fax:* (02) 2264-3309
E-mail: kwangmgl@hanmail.net
Telex: K27229 Kortuna *Cable:* Kwangmyong, Seoul
Key Personnel
President: Keun-Woo Lee
Dir: Yun Bai Yoon
Founded: 1951
Subjects: Art, Regional Interests
ISBN Prefix(es): 89-90022; 89-952319
Subsidiaries: Korea Textbook Co; Kwangmyong Toppan Moore Printing Co

Kyobo Book Centre Co Ltd
Gyobosaengmyeong Bldg, 1, Jongnol-ga, Jongro-gu, Seoul 110-714
Mailing Address: PO Box 1685, Kwangwhamun, Seoul 110-121
Tel: (02) 3973508; (02) 3973509 *Fax:* (02) 7350030
E-mail: eslee@kyobobook.co.kr
Web Site: www.kyobobook.co.kr
Subjects: Government, Political Science, Law, Literature, Literary Criticism, Essays
ISBN Prefix(es): 89-7085

Kyohaksa Publishing Co Ltd+
150-67 Gongdeok-Dong, Mapo-Ku, Seoul 152-020
Tel: (02) 7174561; (02) 8592017 *Fax:* (02) 7183976

Key Personnel
President: Cheol-Woo Yang
Subjects: Business, Nonfiction (General)

Kyungnam University Press
449 Wolyong-dong, Masan, Kyungnam 631-701
Tel: (055) 245-5000 *Fax:* (055) 246-6184
Web Site: www.kyungnam.ac.kr
Key Personnel
President: Soon Bok Lee
Subjects: Philosophy, Social Sciences, Sociology

Literature Academy Publishing
133 Iwha-Dong, Jongro-Gu, Seoul 110-500
Tel: (02) 7645057 *Fax:* (02) 7458516
E-mail: webmaster@munhakac.co.kr
Web Site: www.munhakac.co.kr
Key Personnel
Contact: Je-Chun Park
Founded: 1988
Subjects: Art, Language Arts, Linguistics, Literature, Literary Criticism, Essays, Poetry
ISBN Prefix(es): 89-400
Total Titles: 280 Print

Maeil Gyeongje
51-9, Phil-Dong 1-ga, Jung-gu, Seoul 100-728
Tel: (02) 276-0210; (02) 2760211; (02) 2760212; (02) 2760213; (02) 2760214; (02) 2760215 *Fax:* (02) 271-0463
E-mail: mpd@unitel.co.kv
Key Personnel
President & Publisher: Dae-Whan Chang, PhD
Subjects: Business, Economics

Min-eumsa Publishing Co Ltd+
5F Kangnam Publishing Culture Center, 506 Sinsa-Dong, Gangnam-gu, Seoul 135-120
Tel: (02) 515-2000; (02) 515-2005; (02) 515-9108 *Fax:* (02) 515-2007; (02) 3444-5185
Web Site: www.minumsa.com
Key Personnel
President: Park Maeng-ho
Vice President: Park Geun-sup
Editorial: Park Sang Soon
Sales: Jung Dae Yong
Foreign Rights Manager: Michelle Nam *Tel:* (02) 515-2003, ext 206 *E-mail:* michellenam@minumsa.com
Founded: 1966
Publishes a literary magazine, *World Literature*.
Subjects: Fiction, History, Literature, Literary Criticism, Essays, Nonfiction (General), Philosophy, Science (General), Social Sciences, Sociology
ISBN Prefix(es): 89-374
Total Titles: 200 Print
Imprints: BIR Publishing Co; Golden Bough Publishing Co; Science Books Ltd
Subsidiaries: BIR Publishing Co Ltd; Golden-Bough Publishing Co Ltd

Min Jung Seo Rim Publishing Co
161-7 Yeomni Dong, 4F Hancheong-Sireob Bldg, Mapo-gu, Seoul 121-090
Tel: (02) 7036541; (02) 7036547 *Fax:* (02) 7036549
E-mail: editmin@minjungdic.co.kr
Web Site: www.minjungdic.co.kr
Key Personnel
President: Chul Hwan Kim
Editorial: Cha Hyun Yun
Founded: 1979
ISBN Prefix(es): 89-387
Parent Company: Beupmun Sa Publishing Co

Minjisa Publishing Co+
673-3 Mia-Dong, Gangbug-gu, Seoul 132-105
Tel: (02) 9806382 *Fax:* (02) 9861531
E-mail: minjisa@nownuri.net
Web Site: www.minjisa.co.kr

Key Personnel
President: Tai-Seung Ri *Tel:* (02) 9434385; (02) 9858035 *E-mail:* tsri201@yahoo.co.kr
Founded: 1982
Subjects: Child Care & Development, Education, Health, Nutrition, History, Literature, Literary Criticism, Essays, Psychology, Psychiatry
ISBN Prefix(es): 89-7362
Number of titles published annually: 8 Print
Total Titles: 136 Print

Mirinae+
1011 Singeong Sangaa, 192-30, Inhyeondong 2 ga, Junggu, Seol 100-282
Tel: (02) 2279-2669 *Fax:* (02) 2279-2665
E-mail: mrn@lycos.co.kr
Key Personnel
Publisher: Kim Jin-Shik
Subjects: Literature, Literary Criticism, Essays, Poetry
ISBN Prefix(es): 89-7082

The Monthly Magazine for Ceramics Co, Ltd
130-27, Nonhyeon-dong, Gangnam-gu, Seoul 135-010
Tel: (02) 583-2747 *Fax:* (02) 597-8639
Founded: 1988
ISBN Prefix(es): 89-86742
Parent Company: Daeho Yeoop Co Ltd

Moon Jin Media Co Ltd
6F, Seojeong Bldg, 1308-14 Seocho-4dong, Seocho-ku, Seoul 137-074
Tel: (02) 3453-9800 *Fax:* (02) 3453-4001
E-mail: mjmedia@hitel.kol.co.kr
Key Personnel
President: Sang Chuu Lee
International Rights: Jong Yeon Park
Subjects: English as a Second Language
Bookshop(s): Kim & Johnson, 4F, Seojeong Bl 1308-14, Seocho-4-dong, Seocho-ku, Seoul 137-074

Mun Un Dang
45-3 Myeongryundong 1-ga, Jongro-gu, Seoul 110-521
Tel: (02) 7433504; (02) 7433505 *Fax:* (02) 7450265
Key Personnel
President: Seoung-Beum Lee
Founded: 1962
Subjects: Engineering (General), Science (General)
ISBN Prefix(es): 89-7393

Munhag-gwan
34-22, Sinsu-dong, Mapo-gu, Seoul 121-130
Tel: (02) 7186810 *Fax:* (02) 7062225
Key Personnel
Chief Executive: Byong-Ik Kim
Founded: 1975
Subjects: Art, History, Literature, Literary Criticism, Essays, Philosophy, Social Sciences, Sociology
ISBN Prefix(es): 89-7077

Munye Publishing Co+
32-11 Chungjeongro 3-ga, Seodaemun-gu, Seoul 120-013
Tel: (02) 3935681; (02) 3935684 *Fax:* (02) 3935685
Key Personnel
Chief Executive: Byung-Suk Chun
Founded: 1966
Subjects: Art, Fiction, History, Literature, Literary Criticism, Essays, Nonfiction (General), Philosophy, Social Sciences, Sociology, Women's Studies
ISBN Prefix(es): 89-310

Nanam Publications Co+
501 Jihun Bldg, 1364-39 Seocho-dong, Seocho-gu, Seoul 137-070
Tel: (02) 552-8535; (02) 552-8537 *Fax:* (02) 552-0711
E-mail: nanamcom@soback.kornet21.net; edit@nanamcom.co.kr; post@nanamcom.co.kr
Web Site: www.nanamcom.co.kr
Key Personnel
Chief Executive: Sang-Ho Cho
Founded: 1979
Subjects: Advertising, Art, Communications, Journalism, Literature, Literary Criticism, Essays, Poetry, Social Sciences, Sociology
ISBN Prefix(es): 89-300
Parent Company: Korea Society Review

O Neul Publishing Co+
458 Yonggang-dong, Mapo-gu, Seoul 121-070
Tel: (02) 716-2811 *Fax:* (02) 712-7392
Key Personnel
Editor: Yoon-Seon Park
Contact: Jong-Chun Lee
Founded: 1980
Subjects: Child Care & Development, Fiction, History, House & Home, Mysteries, Nonfiction (General), Poetry, Women's Studies
ISBN Prefix(es): 89-355
Imprints: Cham Kae

Ohmsa+
Sekee Bldg, 17 Kalweol-Dong, Yongsan-Ku, Seoul
Tel: (02) 776-4868-9 *Fax:* (02) 779-6757
E-mail: ohm@ohm.co.kr
Web Site: www.ohm.co.kr
Key Personnel
Contact: Jong-Hak Kwak
Founded: 1975
Subjects: Computer Science, Microcomputers, Telecommunication
Subsidiaries: Robot & Computer Company (R&C Sha)

Omun Gak
Madang Bldg, 3rd Floor, Yeoksam-Dong, Kangnam-Ku, Seoul 135-080
Tel: (02) 3453-8278 *Fax:* (02) 508-5210
Key Personnel
President: Sun-Ki Jeon
Editorial: Kyun Hee Kim
Publicity: Jai Yung You
Sales: Jai Yong Kim
Production: In Soo Kim
Rights & Permissions: Kae Choong Chang
Founded: 1959
Subjects: Literature, Literary Criticism, Essays, Social Sciences, Sociology
Associate Companies: Yueil Publishing and Marketing Cooperation, Room 509, Jungeun Bldg, 22-5 Chungmu-ro Fifth Avenue, Chung-ku, Seoul 100

The Organizing Committee of the 11th International Zeolite Conference
Hwahaggonghaggwa KAIST, 373-1 Guseong-dong, Yuseong-gu, Daejeon 305-701
Tel: (042) 69-8161 *Fax:* (042) 69-8170
E-mail: skihm@sorak.kaist.ac.kr
Key Personnel
International Rights: Prof Son-Ki Ihm
ISBN Prefix(es): 89-950030

Oriental Books
375-5 Seogyo-Dong, Mapo-gu, Seoul 121-210
Tel: (02) 334-9404 *Fax:* (02) 334-6624
Key Personnel
Contact: Tae-Woong Kim
Founded: 1993
ISBN Prefix(es): 89-8300; 89-85705

REPUBLIC OF KOREA

Oruem Publishing House+
1420-6, 1-dong Seoco, Seoco-gu, Seoul 137-070
Tel: (02) 5859122; (02) 5859123 *Fax:* (02) 5847952
Key Personnel
President: Seong-Ok Boo
Founded: 1993
Subjects: Asian Studies, Business, Communications, Economics, Education, Government, Political Science, Public Administration, Social Sciences, Sociology
ISBN Prefix(es): 89-7778

Pan Korea Book Corporation
1-222, 2-Ga, Shinmun-Ro, Chongno-Ku, Seoul 110-601
Tel: (02) 733-2011; (02) 733-2018 *Fax:* (02) 736-8696
E-mail: info@bumhanbook.co.kr
Web Site: www.bumhanbook.co.kr
Telex: Pkbook K24149 *Cable:* Pankorbooks Seoul
Key Personnel
President: Mr Yoon-Sun Kim
Founded: 1956
Also book importer & distributor.
Subjects: Language Arts, Linguistics, Literature, Literary Criticism, Essays, Technology
ISBN Prefix(es): 89-7129

Panmun Book Co Ltd+
No 41-34 Anam-Dong 4Ka, 136-074 Sungbuk-ku, Seoul
Mailing Address: CPO Box 1016, 136-074 Sungbuk-ku, Seoul
Tel: (02) 953-2451 (ext 5) *Fax:* (02) 953-2456 (ext 7)
E-mail: pmbtrd2@chollian.net; pmbimp@unitel.co.kr
Telex: K27546 Panmuse *Cable:* PANMUSE SEOUL
Key Personnel
Chairman & Chief Executive Officer: S K Liu
Man Dir: I H Liu
Sales Dir: S H Kim
Founded: 1955
Subjects: Medicine, Nursing, Dentistry, Science (General), Social Sciences, Sociology
Associate Companies: International Publications Service Inc
Subsidiaries: The STM Books & Journals Inc
Branch Office(s)
Kwangju
Pusan
Taegu
Taejon
Bookshop(s): 16 Kwangbok-dong 1-ka, Pusan; 40 Chongno 1-ga, Chongno-gu, Seoul
Warehouse: 15-7 Anam-dong 4-Ka, Sungbuk-ku, Seoul

Pearson Education Korea Ltd+
No 402 Sin La 2 Bldg, 137-5 Yeonhee-Dong, Seodaemun-ku, Seoul 120-111
Tel: (02) 353 0422 *Fax:* (02) 335 0092
E-mail: elt@pearsoned.co.kr
Key Personnel
General Manager: Yong-Jin Oh *E-mail:* yongjin.oh@pearsoned.co.kr
Senior Sales Manager, HE: Pock-Man Hur
 Tel: (02) 335 7987 *Fax:* (02) 335 7988
 E-mail: pockman.hur@pearsoned.co.kr
Finance/Administration Manager: Eun-Ja Lee
 Tel: (02) 335 0267 *Fax:* (02) 335 7988
 E-mail: eunja.lee@pearsoned.co.kr
Sales Manager: Bong- Jo Choi *Tel:* (02) 335 7987 *Fax:* (02) 335 7988 *E-mail:* bongjo.choi@pearsoned.co.kr; Chong-Dae Chung *E-mail:* chongdae.chung@pearsoned.co.kr
Rights/Publishing Manager: Yeon-Jung Lee
 Tel: (02) 3142 5776 *Fax:* (02) 335 7988
 E-mail: yeonjung.lee@pearsoned.co.kr
Founded: 1997
Subjects: Computer Science, Engineering (General)
ISBN Prefix(es): 89-450
Number of titles published annually: 30 Print
Total Titles: 500 Print
Parent Company: Pearson Education, One Lake Street, Upper Saddle River, NJ 01867, United States
Ultimate Parent Company: Pearson Plc
Holding Company: Pearson Education Korea
Branch Office(s)
PEK Daegu Office, 1160-12 Jisan-Dong, Susung-Ku, 3rd Floor, Daegu 706-090

PoChinChai Printing Co Ltd
11-1, PaJoo Book City, San-Nam-Ri, Kyotta-Eub, PaJoo-Si, Kyungki-Do 413-834
Tel: (031) 955-1150; (031) 955-1151 *Fax:* (031) 943-3234
Web Site: www.pochinchai.com
Telex: Pochcha K33448
Key Personnel
Chairman: Kim Joon-Ki
President: Kim Jung-Sun
Chief Executive: Dal-Hoon Lee
Editorial: Kang Hurh
Founded: 1912
Subjects: Art, History, Social Sciences, Sociology, Technology

Prompter Publications+
PO Box 167, Chongnyangni, Tongdaemoon-gu, Seoul 130-650
SAN: 297-4584
Tel: (02) 82 2214 1794
Key Personnel
President & International Rights: Myungkark Park
Founded: 1989
US publisher.
Subjects: Chemistry, Chemical Engineering, Computer Science, Crafts, Games, Hobbies, Library & Information Sciences, Mathematics, Philosophy, Physics, Science (General)
ISBN Prefix(es): 1-877974
Number of titles published annually: 5 Print
Total Titles: 35 Print

Pyeong-hwa Chulpansa+
150 Palpan-Dong, Jongro-gu, Seoul 110-220
Mailing Address: CPO Box 5066, Seoul 121-110
Tel: (02) 7343341; (02) 7343343 *Fax:* (02) 7392129
Key Personnel
Publisher: Chang-Sung Huh
Founded: 1963
Subjects: Crafts, Games, Hobbies, English as a Second Language, Gardening, Plants, How-to, Literature, Literary Criticism, Essays, Outdoor Recreation, Sports, Athletics, Travel
ISBN Prefix(es): 89-367
Subsidiaries: Jinsun Publishers
Distributed by Seoul Publication Distribution Co Ltd

St Pauls+
103-36 Mia 9-Dong, Kangbug-gu, Seoul 142-109
Tel: (02) 9861361; (02) 9861364 *Fax:* (02) 984-4622
E-mail: miari@paolo.net; felix@paolo.net; stpaul@paolo.net
Web Site: www.paolo.net
Key Personnel
General & Editiorial Dir: Chang-Ouk Lee
 Tel: (02) 986-1361-4 *Fax:* (02) 986-1365
 E-mail: felix@paolo.net
Founded: 1991
Publication of literary, children's books, theology & philosophy books, religious books. Publishes *My Friends,* monthly comic magazine.
Subjects: Biblical Studies, Fiction, Human Relations, Philosophy, Poetry, Religion - Catholic, Theology
Total Titles: 150 Print; 30 Audio
Book Club(s): St Pauls Book Club *Tel:* (02) 986-1361; 986-1365 *E-mail:* bookclub@paolo.net

Samho Music Publishing Co Ltd
718-8, Banpo 1-Dong, Seocho-gu, Seoul 137-041
Tel: (02) 512-3578 *Fax:* (02) 512-3594
E-mail: webmaster@samhomusic.com
Web Site: www.samhomusic.com
Key Personnel
President: Jung-Tae Kim
International Rights: Sang-min Lee
Founded: 1977
Subjects: Art, Crafts, Games, Hobbies, Music, Dance, Outdoor Recreation, Publishing & Book Trade Reference, Sports, Athletics
ISBN Prefix(es): 89-326
Subsidiaries: Samho Media Co

Samhwa Publishing Co Ltd
15, 2-ga Euljiro, Jung-gu, Seoul 110-192
Tel: (02) 7766687 *Fax:* (02) 7732993
Key Personnel
President: Kon Su Yu
Founded: 1962
Subjects: Art, Language Arts, Linguistics, Social Sciences, Sociology
ISBN Prefix(es): 89-87846

Samkwang Publishing Co
499-39 Seokyo-Dong, Mapo-Ku, Seoul
Tel: (02) 3237275 *Fax:* (02) 3251153
Key Personnel
Contact: Myung-Woo Lee
Founded: 1978
Subjects: Social Sciences, Sociology

Samseong Publishing Co Ltd+
1516-2, Seocodong, Seoco-gu, Seoul 137-070
Tel: (02) 3470-6852 *Fax:* (02) 3452-2907
Key Personnel
President: Bong-Kyu Kim
Planning & Coordination Dir: Seok Hyun Cho
Founded: 1952
Subjects: Art, Business, History, Literature, Literary Criticism, Essays, Women's Studies
ISBN Prefix(es): 89-15
Orders to: 60-32 Garibong-dong, Guro-gu, Seoul

Science Books Ltd, *imprint of* Min-eumsa Publishing Co Ltd

Se-Kwang Music Publishing Co+
232-32 Seogye-Dong, Yongsan-gu, Seoul 140-140
Tel: (02) 714-0046 *Fax:* (02) 719-2191
Key Personnel
President & Chairman: Shin-Joon Park
Sales Dir: Moon-Suk Kang
Publicity & Publication Manager: Nam-Jae Kang
Copyright Manager: Kichul Han
Founded: 1953
Subjects: Music, Dance
ISBN Prefix(es): 89-03
U.S. Office(s): Park Soon Tai, 3170 W Olympic Blvd, No E, Los Angeles, CA 90006, United States

Sejong Daewang Kinyom Saophoe
1-57 Chongryangli-dong, San, Iongno-ku, Seoul
Key Personnel
President: Gwan Ku Yi
Subjects: History, Religion - Other

Seogwangsa+
119-46 Yongdu 2-Dong, Dongdaemun-gu, Seoul 130-072
Tel: (02) 9246161; (02) 9246165 *Fax:* (02) 9224993
Key Personnel
President: Shin-Hyeok Kim
Editor: Min-Sook Bae

Founded: 1974
Subjects: Anthropology, Asian Studies, Education, Philosophy, Religion - Buddhist, Religion - Catholic, Religion - Hindu, Religion - Other
ISBN Prefix(es): 89-306

Seoul International Publishing House
94-60 Hwayang-dong, Seongdong-gu, Seoul 133-130
Tel: (02) 4698326; (02) 4698327
Key Personnel
President: Chung-Gil Shim
Founded: 1977
Subjects: Art, Cookery, History, Language Arts, Linguistics, Photography, Regional Interests, Travel
ISBN Prefix(es): 89-85113
Orders to: European Book Service, Flevolaan 36-38, Postbus 124, 1380 AC Weesp, Netherlands
Charles E Tuttle Co Inc, PO Box 410, Rutland, VT 05701, United States

Seoul National University Press
San 56-1, Sinrim-dong, Kwanak-gu, Seoul 151-742
Tel: (02) 880-5114 *Fax:* (02) 885-5272
Web Site: www.snu.ac.kr
Key Personnel
President: Un-Chan Chung
Dir: Prof Soon Jong Lee *Tel:* (02) 880-5217 *Fax:* (02) 881-4148
Founded: 1961
Subjects: Art, Earth Sciences, History, Language Arts, Linguistics, Literature, Literary Criticism, Essays, Medicine, Nursing, Dentistry, Philosophy, Science (General), Social Sciences, Sociology
ISBN Prefix(es): 89-7096

Shinkwang Publishing Co
278-1 Bomun-Dong 6-ka, Sungbuk-ku, Seoul 136-086
Tel: (02) 9255051; (02) 9255053 *Fax:* (02) 9255054
Key Personnel
Chief Executive: Yong-Ha Lee
Founded: 1972
Subjects: Cookery, Medicine, Nursing, Dentistry, Science (General)

Sogang University Press
CPO Box 1142, Seoul 100-611
Tel: (02) 705-8213 *Fax:* (02) 705-0797
E-mail: chisook@ccs.sogang.ac.kr
Web Site: www.sogang.ac.kr
Key Personnel
Contact: Ku Jae Sung
Founded: 1978
Subjects: History, Language Arts, Linguistics, Literature, Literary Criticism, Essays, Science (General), Social Sciences, Sociology
ISBN Prefix(es): 89-7273

Sohaksa+
10-1 Namyeong-dong, Yongsan-gu, Seoul 140-160
Tel: (02) 7967600 *Fax:* (02) 7968700
Key Personnel
Contact: Young-Whan Suhl
Founded: 1988
Subjects: Anthropology, Archaeology, English as a Second Language, History, Management, Philosophy, Psychology, Psychiatry, Social Sciences, Sociology

Suhagsa
1586-4 Seocho 3-Dong, Seocho-Ku, Seoul 137-073
Tel: (02) 584-4642 *Fax:* (02) 521-1458
Key Personnel
President: Young-Ho Lee *Tel:* (02) 584-4642

Founded: 1953
Subjects: Fashion, Health, Nutrition, House & Home
ISBN Prefix(es): 89-7140
Total Titles: 143 Print
Book Club(s): KPA

Twenty-First Century Publishers, Inc+
5 FIil Bldg, 315-3, 1 dong, Ganseog, Namdong-gu, Inceon 405-231
Tel: (032) 429-9411 *Fax:* (032) 4299418
Key Personnel
President: Mr Y D Ahn
Editor: Ms Youngmi Kwon
Founded: 1988
Subjects: Business, Economics, Management
ISBN Prefix(es): 89-89457

Universal Publications Agency Press
54, Gyeonji-dong, Jongro-gu, Seoul 110-170
Tel: (02) 32-8175 *Fax:* (02) 32-8176
E-mail: upa@upa.co.kr
Web Site: www.upa.co.kr
Telex: K28504 Unipub *Cable:* CHANGHOSHIN SEOUL
Key Personnel
Manager: Il Chung Ha
ISBN Prefix(es): 89-7613

Woongjin Media Corporation+
Ungjinmedia Bldg, 343-7, Gasandong, Geumceongu, Seoul 153-023
Tel: 3281-6471 *Fax:* 3281-6473
E-mail: wjmhky@woongjin.co.kr
Web Site: www.woongjin.com
Key Personnel
Chairman: Suck-keum Yoon
President: Hwan-kee Ryu
Man Dir: Heungsung Lee
Founded: 1987
Specialize in multi-media packages, educational & home videos, CAI-software, compact discs.
Subjects: Business, Fiction, History, Nonfiction (General), Science (General)
ISBN Prefix(es): 89-02
Parent Company: Woongjin Publishing Co Ltd
Imprints: Gomdori
Subsidiaries: Woongjin (USA) Inc

Woongjin.com Co Ltd+
112-2 Inyi-dong, Jongno-gu, Seoul 110-717
Tel: (02) 3670-1064 *Fax:* (02) 3670-1474
E-mail: wjmap@chollian.dacom.co.kr
Key Personnel
Foreign Rights Manager: Seang-Ju Hong
Founded: 1980
Subjects: Business, Education, English as a Second Language, How-to, Literature, Literary Criticism, Essays, Mysteries, Nonfiction (General), Romance, Travel
ISBN Prefix(es): 89-01; 89-345
Subsidiaries: Woong Nin Media Co Ltd

Word of Life Press+
Division of TEAM Mission Korea
32-43 Songwol Dong, Jongro-ku, Seoul 110-101
Mailing Address: PO Box 680, Kwanghwamoon, Seoul 110-062
Tel: (02) 738 6555 *Fax:* (02) 739 3824
Key Personnel
President & International Rights: Jay-Kwon Kim *E-mail:* jaykkim@chollian.net
Founded: 1953
Specialize in Christian book publishing.
Subjects: Religion - Protestant, Missionary Work
ISBN Prefix(es): 89-04
Number of titles published annually: 510 Print
Total Titles: 2,000 Print
Divisions: World of Life Books in USA
U.S. Office(s): Los Angeles, CA, United States

Washington, DC, United States
Chicago, IL, United States

YBM/Si-sa+
YBM Bldg, Editorial Dept, 10th floor, 55-1 Chongno 2-ga, Chongno-gu, Seoul 110-122
Tel: (02) 2000-0501; (02) 2000-0330 (orders) *Fax:* (02) 2265-7573
E-mail: suite@ybmsisa.co.kr
Web Site: www.ybm.co.kr; www.ybmsisa.co.kr
Key Personnel
Chairman: Young-Bin Min
President: Sun-Shik Min
Editorial Dir: Hye-Ryoung Kim *E-mail:* hrkim@ybmsisa.com
Sales Dir: Jong-Chul Kim
Founded: 1961
Book & Magazine Publishing, Language Schools, Testing Activities, Music Company, IT Business, ELT Materials, Multi-media Publications, On-line Publishing, English Language Study Materials, TOETL & TOEIC Prep Books.
Membership(s): IPA; FIPP; ABC.
Subjects: Economics, English as a Second Language, Literature, Literary Criticism, Essays, Photography, Travel
ISBN Prefix(es): 89-17
Number of titles published annually: 1,000 Print; 24 CD-ROM; 48 Online; 100 E-Book; 600 Audio
Total Titles: 13,000 Print; 50 CD-ROM; 89 Online; 199 E-Book; 6,500 Audio
Branch Office(s)
Beijing City Chaoyang District Waisi Language Training Center, America School of English, China Merchants Onward Center, 4th floor, No 118, Chaoyang District Jianguo Rd, Beijing 100022, China *Tel:* (010) 6566 0786
YBM/ELS Language Centers, 549 Howe St, 6th floor, Vancouver, BC V6C 2C2, Canada, Dir: Mike Walkey *Tel:* 604-684-9577 *Fax:* 604-684-9588 *E-mail:* info@elscanada.com *Web Site:* www.elscanada.com
YBM/ELS Language Centers, 36 Victoria St, Toronto, ON M5C 1H3, Canada, Dir: Zbigniew Andrzejcuk *Tel:* 416-203-6466 *Fax:* 416-203-6766 *E-mail:* info@elscanada.com *Web Site:* www.elscanada.com
U.S. Office(s): Young & Son Global, 3250 Wilshire Blvd, Suite 2007, Los Angeles, CA 90010, United States *E-mail:* hylee58@ybmsisa.com
Distributor for Barron's; ETS/Chauncey; McGraw Hill; McMillan; National Geographic Society; Newsweek International; Pearson; Peterson's; Reader's Digest; Simon & Schuster

Yearimdang Publishing Co
Yearim Bldg, 153-3, Samseong-dong, Gangnam-gu, Seoul 135-878
Tel: (02) 5661004 *Fax:* (02) 5679660
E-mail: webmaster@yearim.co.kr
Web Site: www.yearim.co.kr
Key Personnel
Chief Executive: Choon Na
Founded: 1973
Subjects: Cookery, Education, Fiction, Nonfiction (General)
ISBN Prefix(es): 89-507; 89-302; 89-87941

Yeha Publishing Co+
736-37, Yeogsam-dong, Gangnam-gu, Seoul 135-080
Tel: (02) 5535933; (02) 5535936 *Fax:* (02) 5525149
Key Personnel
Contact: Khil-Boo Park
Founded: 1987
Membership(s): Korean Publishers Association.
Subjects: Business, Literature, Literary Criticism, Essays, Music, Dance
ISBN Prefix(es): 89-7359

REPUBLIC OF KOREA

Yonsei University Press
134 Sinchon-dong, Seodaemun-gu, Seoul 120-749
Tel: (02) 3926201 *Fax:* (02) 3931421
E-mail: ysup@bubble.yonsei.ac.kr
Web Site: www.yonsei.ac.kr
Key Personnel
President: Byung-Soo Kim
Dir: Suk-Hyun Kim
Business Manager: Ho-Sun Choi
Founded: 1955
Subjects: Art, History, Medicine, Nursing, Dentistry, Philosophy, Religion - Other, Science (General), Social Sciences, Sociology, Technology
ISBN Prefix(es): 89-7141

Youlhwadang Publisher+
520-10, Paju Book City, Munbal-Ri, Gyoha-Eup, Paju-Si, Gyeonggi-Do
Tel: (031) 955-7000-5; (02) 5153143; (02) 5153142 *Fax:* (031) 955-7010
E-mail: yhdp@hitel.net; horang2@unitel.co.kr; webmaster@youlhwadang.co.kr
Web Site: www.youlhwadang.co.kr
Key Personnel
President: Ki-Ung Yi
Editor & Foreign Rights: Ji-Hong Park
Founded: 1971
Specialize in Korean traditional art.
Subjects: Antiques, Architecture & Interior Design, Art, Crafts, Games, Hobbies, Film, Video, Music, Dance, Photography, Korean Art
ISBN Prefix(es): 89-301
Number of titles published annually: 20 Print
Total Titles: 500 Print

Kuwait

General Information

Capital: Kuwait
Language: Arabic. English also used commercially
Religion: Muslim
Population: 1.58 million
Bank Hours: 0800-1200 (0830-1230 during Ramadan) Saturday-Thursday
Shop Hours: 0800-1200 or 1230, 1530 or 16-2030 Saturday-Thursday; 0800-1200 Friday (markets and shopping centers also open 1530-2030); during Ramadan: 0830 or 0900-1230, 1930-1030 or 0200 Saturday-Thursday. Some shopping centers open 1600-2100 Friday
Currency: 1000 fils = approximately 3 US dollars
Export/Import Information: No tariffs on books or advertising in reasonable quantity; all immoral and seditious publications prohibited. Import license required. No exchange permit required.
Copyright: No copyright conventions signed

Kuwait Publishing House
PO Box 5209, 13053 Safat, Kuwait City
Tel: 2414697
Key Personnel
Dir: Amin Hamadeh

Ministry of Information
Ministry of Communication, Bldg 2, Shuwaikh, 13008 Safat, Kuwait City
Mailing Address: PO Box 748, 13008 Safat, Kuwait City
Tel: 245-1566 *Fax:* 245-9530
E-mail: admin@media.gov.kw
Web Site: www.moinfo.gov.kw
Telex: Mi 22030 Kt, Mi 46151 Kt *Cable:* ALIRSHAD

Subjects: Art, Education, Geography, Geology, History, Language Arts, Linguistics, Literature, Literary Criticism, Essays, Mathematics, Physics, Social Sciences, Sociology

Press Agency+
PO Box 1019, 13011 Safat
Tel: 432269 *Fax:* 411495
Telex: Matboat 46046 Kt; Matboat 46246 Kt
Cable: MATBOAT
Key Personnel
Man Dir: Abdullah M N Harami
Editorial: K A Harami; Ibrahim M Hadi
Founded: 1954
Bookshop(s): in Kuwait & Salmaiy

Laos People's Democratic Republic

General Information

Capital: Vientiane
Language: Lao (official), French, English and Tribal dialects
Religion: Theravada Buddhist
Population: 4.47 million
Bank Hours: 0800-1700 Monday-Friday
Shop Hours: 0800-2200 Monday-Friday, seven days a week for Vietnamese Morning Market
Export/Import Information: Import license required. Exchange controls.
Copyright: UCC (see Copyright Conventions, pg xi)

Lao-phanit
Vientiane Ministere de l'Education nationale, Bureau des manuels, scolaires, Vientiane
Subjects: Art, Cookery, Economics, Education, Fiction, Geography, Geology, History, Music, Dance, Physics, Social Sciences, Sociology

Pakpassak Kanphin
9-11 quai Fa-Hguun, Vientiane

Latvia

General Information

Capital: Riga
Language: Latvian (Lettish)
Religion: Predominantly Christian (mostly Lutheran)
Population: 2.7 million
Bank Hours: Generally open for short hours between 0930-1230 Monday-Friday
Shop Hours: Generally 0900-1800 Monday-Friday; often open weekends
Currency: 100 kopeks = 1 rubl
Copyright: Berne (see Copyright Conventions, pg xi)

Alberts XII+
Katolu 22, Riga 1003
Tel: (02) 7205286 *Fax:* (02) 7205284
E-mail: alberts@internet.lv
Key Personnel
Man Dir: Karlis Skruzis
Membership(s): Latvian Book Publishers Association.
Subjects: Astrology, Occult, Cookery, Crafts, Games, Hobbies, Health, Nutrition, Nonfiction (General), Romance, Science Fiction, Fantasy
ISBN Prefix(es): 9984-557; 9984-645

Artava Ltd+
Bezdeligu 12, 1007 Riga
Tel: (02) 7222472 *Fax:* (02) 7830254
E-mail: arta@com.latnet.lv
Key Personnel
Dir: Vladis Spare
Foreign Rights: Elfrida Melbarzde
Founded: 1991
Membership(s): Latvia Book Publishers Association.
Subjects: Biography, Fiction, How-to, Poetry, Romance, Science Fiction, Fantasy, Self-Help
ISBN Prefix(es): 9984-12; 9984-529

Avots+
Puskina 1a, Riga LV-1050
Tel: (02) 7211394 *Fax:* (02) 7225824
E-mail: avots@apollo.lv
Web Site: www.vardnicas.lv
Key Personnel
Man Dir: Janis Leja
Contact: Dzintra Kalnina
Founded: 1980
Membership(s): Book Publishers Association.
Subjects: English as a Second Language, Gardening, Plants, House & Home, How-to, Language Arts, Linguistics, Nonfiction (General)
ISBN Prefix(es): 9984-757

Bibliography Institute of the National Library of Latvia
K Barona 14, Riga LV-1423
Tel: (02) 7289874 *Fax:* (02) 7280851
E-mail: lnb@com.latnet.lv; lnb@lbi.lnb.lv
Web Site: www.lnb.lv
Key Personnel
Deputy Dir, NLL: Anita Goldberga
 E-mail: anitag@lnb.lv
Founded: 1940
Statistical information & analysis of publishing activities & national bibliography.
Membership(s): The Latvian Publishers Association.
Subjects: Publishing & Book Trade Reference, Publishing/reference library & information sciences
ISBN Prefix(es): 9984-607; 9984-9006; 9984-9007
Total Titles: 3 Print; 2 Online
Parent Company: The National Library of Latvia

Egmont Latvia SIA+
Balasta dambis 3, LV-1081 Riga
Mailing Address: PO Box 30, LV-1081 Riga
Tel: (07) 244066; (07) 467931; (07) 468671
 Fax: (07) 860049
E-mail: egmont@egmont.lv
Web Site: www.egmont.lv
Key Personnel
Man Dir: Roman Filippov
General Manager: Janis Blums *E-mail:* janis@egmont.lv
Editor-in-Chief: Antra Chigure
Founded: 1991
Subjects: Advertising, Fiction, Film, Video, Nonfiction (General), Sports, Athletics, Western Fiction, Comics & Cartoons
Parent Company: International Egmont Holding A/S

Finland-Lestvian, *imprint of* S/A Tiesiskas informacijas cerfus

Hermess Ltd+
Maskavas iela 150, Riga 1058
Tel: (02) 7112743 *Fax:* (02) 7313130

E-mail: hermess@binet.lv
Key Personnel
Executive Dir: Juris Zablovskis
Dir: Natalija Sazenova
Founded: 1993
Subjects: Science Fiction, Fantasy
ISBN Prefix(es): 9984-580; 9984-9036

Lielvards Ltd+
Skolas Iela 5, 5070 Lielvarde Ogresraj
Tel: (050) 71860 *Fax:* (050) 71861
E-mail: lielvards@lielvards.lv
Web Site: www.lielvards.lv *Cable:* 030
Founded: 1992
Membership(s): Latvian Book Publishers Association.
Subjects: Biological Sciences, Chemistry, Chemical Engineering, Computer Science, Geography, Geology, Health, Nutrition, History, Physics, Social Sciences, Sociology
ISBN Prefix(es): 9984-11; 9984-513
Showroom(s): Araisu iela 37, Riga LV-1039, Riga

Madonas Poligrafistr Ltd, *imprint of* S/A Tiesiskas informacijas cerfus

Madris+
Tallinas iela 36a, Riga LV-1001
Tel: 7374000; 7374700 *Fax:* 7374000
E-mail: madris@latnet.lv
Key Personnel
General Manager: Skaidrite Naumova
Founded: 1996
Subjects: Fiction, Poetry, Science (General), Travel
Number of titles published annually: 20 Print

Nordik/Tapals Publishers Ltd+
Daugavgrivas 36-9, Riga LV-1007
Tel: (02) 7602672; (02) 7602816 *Fax:* (02) 7602818
E-mail: nordik@nordik.lv
Web Site: www.nordik.lv
Key Personnel
Dir: Janis Juska *E-mail:* janis@tapals.lv
Editor-in-Chief: Ieva Janaite
Founded: 1991
Membership(s): Latvian Publishers Association.
Subjects: Animals, Pets, Astrology, Occult, Biography, Communications, Crafts, Games, Hobbies, Criminology, Earth Sciences, Environmental Studies, Fiction, History, Human Relations, Law, Nonfiction (General), Poetry
ISBN Prefix(es): 9984-510
Number of titles published annually: 85 Print
Warehouse: Elijas 17, 1st floor, Riga LV-1007
Tel: (02) 7225667

Patmos, izdevnieciba
Baznicas iela 12a, Riga 1050
Tel: (02) 7289674 *Fax:* (02) 7820437
E-mail: bauc@mail.bkc.lv
Key Personnel
Publishing Dir: Zigurds Laudurgs
Editor: Dace Morica
Subjects: Biblical Studies, Health, Nutrition, Religion - Protestant, Theology

Preses Nams+
Division of Preses Nams Corp
3, Balasta Dambis, Riga LV-1081
Tel: (02) 7062270 *Fax:* (02) 7062344
E-mail: presesnams@presesnams.lv
Web Site: www.presesnams.lv
Key Personnel
Dir, Publishing House: Mara Caune
Founded: 1990
Publisher of books, calendars, etc.
Membership(s): Latvian Association of Book Publishers.

Subjects: Agriculture, Animals, Pets, Art, Astrology, Occult, Behavioral Sciences, Biography, Biological Sciences, Business, Child Care & Development, Civil Engineering, Crafts, Games, Hobbies, Disability, Special Needs, Drama, Theater, Education, Environmental Studies, Fiction, Film, Video, Gardening, Plants, Health, Nutrition, History, House & Home, Human Relations, Humor, Literature, Literary Criticism, Essays, Music, Dance, Philosophy, Photography, Poetry, Psychology, Psychiatry, Sports, Athletics, Travel, Women's Studies
ISBN Prefix(es): 9980-0
Total Titles: 600 Print
Ultimate Parent Company: AS Ventspils Nafta

S/A Tiesiskas informacijas cerfus
Baznicas icla 27/29, Riga 1010
Tel: (02) 7220422 *Fax:* (02) 7213854
E-mail: mariss@date.lv
Key Personnel
Dir: Signe Terihova
Founded: 1991
Subjects: Law
Parent Company: a/s SWHIS Kemerccentas
Imprints: Madonas Poligrafistr Ltd; Finland-Lestvian
Subsidiaries: LR Tieslictuministrijas A/S Dati
Book Club(s): Association of Latvian Book's publishers

Spriditis Publishers+
Kaleju iela 51, Riga 1050
Tel: (02) 7286516 *Fax:* (02) 7286818
Founded: 1990
Subjects: Biblical Studies, Fiction, History, Religion - Catholic, Religion - Protestant, Travel
ISBN Prefix(es): 5-7960
Bookshop(s): Kaleju St 51, Riga LV-1050

Vaidelote, SIA+
Kekava 17-19, Kekavas Pag, 2123 Rigas Rajons
Tel: 937943; 9552391 *Fax:* 7570828
Founded: 1993
Subjects: Animals, Pets, Fiction
ISBN Prefix(es): 9984-507

Vieda, SIA+
Lubanas 6-4, Riga 1019
Tel: 7249728 *Fax:* (02) 7140680
Key Personnel
Dir General: Aivars Gardo
Founded: 1989
Subjects: Astrology, Occult, History, Parapsychology, Philosophy
ISBN Prefix(es): 5-85745

Zvaigzne ABC Publishers Ltd+
K Valdemara 6, Riga 1010
Tel: (0371) 7508799 *Fax:* (0371) 7508798
E-mail: foreign.rights@zvaigzne.lv
Web Site: www.zvaigzne.lv
Key Personnel
President: Vija Kilbloka
Editorial Dir: Ilze Brige *Tel:* (02) 7372112
Foreign Rights & Sales Manager: Ruta Keisa *Tel:* (02) 7372358
Foreign Rights & Sales Executive: Vija Birnbauma *Tel:* (02) 7372358
Founded: 1965
Specialize in educational literature for the needs of Latvia.
Subjects: Animals, Pets, Astrology, Occult, Child Care & Development, Education, English as a Second Language, Fiction, Literature, Literary Criticism, Essays, Nonfiction (General), Psychology, Psychiatry, Romance, Science Fiction, Fantasy, Travel, Adventure, Astrology, Classics, Estoerics/New Age, Fairy Tales

ISBN Prefix(es): 5-405; 9984-04; 9984-17; 9984-560
Total Titles: 1,700 Print
Foreign Rights: Zvaigzne ABC Publishers

Lebanon

General Information

Capital: Beirut
Language: Arabic (French widely used)
Religion: 43% Christian (mostly Roman Catholic, predominantly Maronite), 57% Muslim (mostly Sunni & Shiite)
Population: 3.4 million
Bank Hours: 0830-1230 Monday-Friday; 0830-1200 Saturday
Shop Hours: Vary. Generally 0900-1900 in winter, 0800-1500 in summer
Currency: 100 piastres = 1 Lebanese pound
Copyright: UCC, Berne (see Copyright Conventions, pg xi)

Arab Institute for Research & Publishing
Sakiyat Al Janzeer, Carlton Tower Bldg, Beirut
Mailing Address: PO Box 11, 5460 Beirut
Fax: (01) 751438; (01) 752308
E-mail: mkayyali@jonet.com
Telex: 40067; (01) 807900 *Cable:* MOUKAYALI
Key Personnel
Dir: Maher Kayyali *Tel:* (079) 5521004 (mobile for Amman, Jordan) *E-mail:* mkayyali@jonet.com
Subjects: Animals, Pets, Architecture & Interior Design, Art, Business, Computer Science, Cookery, Economics, Health, Nutrition, Language Arts, Linguistics, Law, Medicine, Nursing, Dentistry, Military Science, Philosophy, Psychology, Psychiatry
Divisions: AlFaris Publishing & Distribution Co Ltd
Warehouse: Al-Faris Publishing & Distribution Co Ltd, PO Box 9157, Amman, 11191 Jordan *Fax:* (06) 685501
Orders to: Al-Faris Publishing & Distribution Co, Amman Office, Shemsiani Petra Bldg, PO Box 9157, Amman 11191, Jordan *Tel:* 5605432 *Fax:* 5685501

Arab Scientific Publishers BP+
Ayn Al-Tenah Reem Bldg, POB 13-5574, Beirut
Tel: (01) 785107; (01) 785108; (01) 786607
Fax: (01) 786230; (01) 860138
E-mail: asp@asp.com.lb
Web Site: www.asp.com.lb
Key Personnel
President: Bassam Chebaro *E-mail:* bchebaro@asp.com.lb
Founded: 1986
Subjects: Automotive, Biological Sciences, Computer Science, Cookery, Travel
ISBN Prefix(es): 2-84409; 9953-29
Number of titles published annually: 300 Print; 10 CD-ROM; 15 E-Book
Associate Companies: Abjad Graphics; Mediterranean Press, Arabization & Software Center
Bookshop(s): Book Maze, Marriott Square

Editions Arabes, *imprint of* Naufal Group Sarl

Dar Al-Kitab Al-Loubnani
BP13-5352, Beirut
Mailing Address: PO Box 11, 8330 Beirut
Tel: 861563; (01) 735732 *Fax:* (01) 351433
E-mail: info@daralkitab-online.com
Telex: 22865 Ktl *Cable:* DAKALBAN-BEIRUT-LEBANON

LEBANON

Key Personnel
Man Dir: Dr Hasan El-Zein
Founded: 1929
Specialize in educational publications & textbooks for many countries worldwide.
Associate Companies: Dar Al-Kitab Al-Masri, 33 Kasr El Nil St, PO Box 156, Cairo 11511, Egypt (Arab Republic of Egypt) *Tel:* (02) 3922168; (02) 3924614 *Fax:* (02) 3924657
Branch Office(s)
Paris, France
Casablanca, Morocco
Madrid, Spain
Geneva, Switzerland

Dar Al-Maaref-Liban Sarl
BP 11-232, Beirut
Tel: (01) 931243 *Cable:* Damaref Beirut
Key Personnel
Man Dir: Dr Fouad Ibrahim
General Manager: Joseph Nachou
Sales: Joseph Ibrahim
Founded: 1959
Parent Company: Dar Al-Maaref, Egypt (Arab Republic of Egypt)

Dar Al-raed Al-Llubnani
Kamel Al Assad Bldgs, Hazmieh St, Beirut
Mailing Address: BP 93, Beirut
Tel: (01) 450757; (01) 451581
Telex: 43499 Raed *Cable:* Kassammoury
Key Personnel
Chief Executive: Raed Sammouri
Editorial: Fadia Khoury
Sales: Ola Ramadan
Production: George Jabro
Publicity: Rima Khoury
Rights & Permissions: Hussein Ibrahim
Founded: 1971
Branch Office(s)
Dar Al Raed Al Rabi, Rawchi Blvd, Al Istiklal

Dar An-Nahar Sal
36, rue Andraos Achrafieh, Beirut
Mailing Address: PO Box 11-226, Beirut
Tel: (01) 561 687 *Fax:* (01) 561 693
Key Personnel
President: Mohamed Ali Hamade
Founded: 1967
ISBN Prefix(es): 2-84289

Dar El Ilm Lilmalayin
Center Metco, 2nd Floor, Mar Elias St, Beirut 2045-8402
Mailing Address: PO Box 1085, 1085 Beirut
Tel: (09611) 306666 *Fax:* (09611) 701657
E-mail: info@malayin.com
Web Site: www.malayin.com
Subjects: Business, Cookery, Education, Literature, Literary Criticism, Essays, Science (General)

EDIFRAMO, see Edition Francaise pour le Monde Arabe (EDIFRAMO)

Editions de la Revue d'Etudes Palestiniennes, see Institute for Palestine Studies, Publishing & Research Organization (IPS)

Dar-El-Machreq Sarl+
Rue de l'Universite Saint-Joseph, Beirut 1100 2150
Mailing Address: BP 166778, Achrafie, Beirut 1100 2150
Tel: (01) 202423; (01) 202424 *Fax:* (01) 329348
E-mail: machreq@cyberia.net.lb
Web Site: www.darelmachreq.com
Key Personnel
Man Dir, Rights & Permissions: Camille Hechaime
Founded: 1853

Subjects: Biblical Studies, History, Language Arts, Linguistics, Literature, Literary Criticism, Essays, Philosophy, Religion - Catholic, Religion - Islamic, Theology
ISBN Prefix(es): 2-7214
Number of titles published annually: 25 Print
Total Titles: 600 Print
Orders to: Librairie Orientale, PO Box 1986, Beirut, Contact: M Maroun Nehme *Tel:* (01) 485793; (01) 492112 *Fax:* (01) 485793; (01) 485794; (01) 485795 *E-mail:* libor@cyberia.net.lb

Edition Francaise pour le Monde Arabe (EDIFRAMO)
Immeuble Elissar, Rue Bliss, Beirut
Mailing Address: BP 113, 6140 Beirut
Tel: (01) 862437; (01) 341650; (01) 441614
Telex: 42530 LE
Key Personnel
Manager: Tahseen S Khayat
Branch Office(s)
Julie Hse, 3 Themistocles Dervis St, PO Box 1612, Nicosia, Cyprus
22 blvd Poissonnieer, 75009 Paris, France

GEOprojects Sarl
PO Box 8375, Beirut
Tel: (01) 350721; (01) 344236 *Fax:* (01) 353000
Telex: 22661 Eltoup le
Key Personnel
Man Dir: Tahseen Khayat
Founded: 1978
Subjects: Regional Interests, Travel
Branch Office(s)
GEOprojects Ltd, Newtown Rd, Henley-on-Thomas, Oxon R69 1HG, United Kingdom *Tel:* (049) 122175

Institute for Palestine Studies, Publishing & Research Organization (IPS)
Anis Nsouli St Verdun, PO Box 11-7164, 1107 2230 Beirut
Tel: (01) 814175; (01) 804959 *Fax:* (01) 814193; (01) 868387
E-mail: ipsbrt@palestine-studies.org
Web Site: www.palestine-studies.org
Telex: Madaf 23317 le *Cable:* DIRASAT
Key Personnel
Dir: Mr Mahmoud Soueid
Chairperson: Dr Hisham Nashabe
Executive Secretary: Prof Walid Khalidi
Founded: 1963
Independent nonprofit research & publication center, not affiliated with any political organization or government.
Subjects: Government, Political Science, Social Sciences, Sociology
ISBN Prefix(es): 2-905448
Branch Office(s)
c/o Les Editions de Minuit, 7 Rue Bernard - Palissy, 75006 Paris, France *Tel:* (01) 44393920 *Fax:* (01) 45448236 *E-mail:* ipsfr@palestine-studies.org
13 Hera St, PO Box 5658, Nicosia, Cyprus, Greece *Tel:* (02) 456165 *Fax:* (02) 456324
Institute of Jerusalem Studies, Sheikh Jarah, Nablus St 1, PO Box 54769, Jerusalem, Israel *Tel:* (02) 5826366 *Fax:* (02) 5828901 *E-mail:* ipsquds@palestine-studies.org
London, United Kingdom
U.S. Office(s): 3501 "M" Street NW, Washington, DC 20007, United States *Tel:* 202-342-3990 *Fax:* 202-342-3927 *E-mail:* ipsdc@palestine-studies.org
Orders to: IPS Marketing Dept, 3501 "M" St NW, Washington, DC 20007, United States *Tel:* 202-342-3990

The International Documentary Centre of Arab Manuscripts
Immeuble Hanna, Beirut

Mailing Address: PO Box 2668
Key Personnel
Proprietor: Zouhair Baalbaki
Founded: 1965

Khayat Book and Publishing Co Sarl
90-94 rue Bliss, Beirut
Key Personnel
Man Dir: Paul Khayat
Subjects: Art, Crafts, Games, Hobbies, Education, Fiction, History, Medicine, Nursing, Dentistry, Religion - Other, Social Sciences, Sociology, Sports, Athletics

Librairie du Liban Publishers (Sal)+
Sayegh Bldg, Zouk Mosbeh, Kesrouan
Mailing Address: PO Box 11-9232, Beirut
Tel: (09) 217 944; (09) 217945; (09) 217 946; (09) 217 735 *Fax:* (09) 217734; (09) 217 434
E-mail: info@ldlp.com
Web Site: www.ldlp.com
Telex: 21037-45297 libsayle *Cable:* LIBRARIE DU LIBAN, BEIRUT
Key Personnel
Man Dir, Rights & Permissions: Khalil Sayegh
Man Dir, Publicity: George S Trad
Editorial: Ahmad Khatib; George Abdel Massih
Sales: Suheil Berjawi
Production: Wafic Mizhir
Founded: 1944
Subjects: Animals, Pets, Astronomy, Child Care & Development, Computer Science, Cookery, Education, Fiction, Health, Nutrition, Language Arts, Linguistics, Literature, Literary Criticism, Essays, Mysteries, Physics, Science (General), Science Fiction, Fantasy, Technology, Travel, Adventure, Nature, Thriller
Showroom(s): Longman Arab World Centres, PO Box 11-945, Beirut; Amir Mohamed St, Al Houjairi Bldg, PO Box 6587, Amman *Tel:* (06) 637871; (06) 624216; 15 St, Central Khartoum, PO Box 1391, Sudan *Tel:* 80344
Bookshop(s): Lebanon Bookshop; Sayegh Bookshop, Diab Bldg, Al Salhieh, in Front of the Parliament, PO Box 784, Damascus, Syrian Arab Republic *Tel:* (011) 218456
Distribution Center: Sayegh Bldg, Zokak el Blat, PO Box 11-945, Beirut *Tel:* (01) 376 821; (01) 376 822; (01) 376 823 *Fax:* (01) 376 818
E-mail: sberjaoui@ldlp.com

Librairie Orientale sal+
Sin el-Fil, Jisr el-Wati, Immeuble Librairie, Orientale, Beirut
Mailing Address: PO Box 55-206, Orientale, Beirut
Tel: (01) 485793; (01) 485794; (01) 485795 *Fax:* (01) 485796; (01) 216021
E-mail: libor@cyberia.net.lb
Key Personnel
Chief Executive Officer: M Maroun Nehme
Founded: 1948
Specialize in dictionaries, research, philosophy, literature, children books & text books in Arabic, French & English.
Subjects: Accounting, Animals, Pets, Archaeology, Child Care & Development, Cookery, Education, English as a Second Language, History, How-to, Language Arts, Linguistics, Literature, Literary Criticism, Essays, Nonfiction (General), Philosophy, Regional Interests, Religion - Catholic, Theology
Number of titles published annually: 200 Print
Total Titles: 1,000 Print
Branch Office(s)
Ashrafieh-Park Bldg, Beirut, Contact: Mrs Achou *Tel:* (01) 200875; (01) 216364 *Fax:* (01) 216021
Distributor for Dar el-Majani; Dar el-Mashreq
Foreign Rep(s): Aladdin Books UK (Middle East, North Africa); DTV Germany (Middle East, North Africa); Edicart-Italy (Middle East, North Africa)

Macdonald, *imprint of* Naufal Group Sarl

Naufal, *imprint of* Naufal Group Sarl

Naufal Group Sarl+
99, Sourati St, Beirut
Mailing Address: BP 11-2161, Beirut
Tel: 354394 *Fax:* 354898
Key Personnel
Man Dir, Editorial & Rights & Permissions: Tony P Naufal
Editorial: Kamal Khauli
Sales, Production: Khaled Shamaa
General Manager (Paris): Sami Naufal
Founded: 1970
Subjects: Fiction, History, Law, Literature, Literary Criticism, Essays
ISBN Prefix(es): 2-906958
Imprints: Editions Arabes; Macdonald; Naufal
Subsidiaries: Les Editions Arabes SA; Macdonald Middle East Sarl
Bookshop(s): Librairies Antoine, Hamra, PO Box 656, Beirut (five shops)

Publitec Publications+
BP 166142, Jisr Bacha, Beirut
Tel: (01) 495401; (01) 495403 *Fax:* (01) 493330
Telex: 44828
Key Personnel
President: Charles Gedeon
Manager: B Calfa
Assistant Manager: Ms M Sarkissian
Founded: 1953
ISBN Prefix(es): 2-903188
Subsidiaries: Publitec Publications
Distributed by Gale Research Inc (USA)

Rihani Printing & Publishing House
Abdallah Mashnouk St, Beirut
Mailing Address: PO Box 13-5378, Beirut
Tel: 868384 *Fax:* 868384
Key Personnel
Proprietor: Albert Rihani
Manager: Daoud Stephan
Founded: 1963

World Book Publishing+
Sanayeh, 282 Emile Edee St, Beirut
Mailing Address: PO Box 11-3176, Beirut
Tel: (01) 349370; (01) 743357; (01) 743358
Fax: (01) 351226
E-mail: info@wbpbooks.com
Web Site: www.arabook.com *Cable:* KITALIBAN
Key Personnel
Director-General: El Zein Said-Mohamed
 E-mail: editor@wbpbooks.com
Vice President: Toufic El Zein *E-mail:* toufic@wbpbooks.com
Vice President & Man Dir: Rafic El Zein
 E-mail: rafic@wbpbooks.com
Founded: 1929
Subjects: Education, Literature, Literary Criticism, Essays, Philosophy, Poetry, Religion - Islamic
ISBN Prefix(es): 1-55206
Total Titles: 3,000 Print; 1,000 Online
Associate Companies: Editions Africaines/Dar Al Kitab Al-Alami
Subsidiaries: Librairie De L'ecole
Divisions: Livre Scolaire
Showroom(s): Hawd Al-Wilaga, Basta, Beirut
Bookshop(s): Librairie de l'Ecole, Rue Emile Edde, Beirut

Lesotho
General Information
Capital: Maseru
Language: English, Sesotho (a Bantu language)
Religion: Roman Catholic, Lesotho, Evangelical and Anglican
Population: 1.8 million
Bank Hours: 0830-1300 Monday-Friday; 0830-1100 Saturday
Shop Hours: Winter: 0830-1630 Monday-Friday; 0830-1300 Saturday; Summer: 0800-1630 Monday-Friday; 0800-1300 Saturday. Usually closed weekdays 1300-1400
Currency: 100 lisente = 1 loti South African currency is also legal tender
Export/Import Information: No tariffs on books or advertising matter. No import license required; no obscene literature permitted. Exchange controls being relaxed.
Copyright: Berne (see Copyright Conventions, pg xi)

Government Printer
PO Box 527, Maseru 100
Tel: 313023
ISBN Prefix(es): 99911-10

Mazenod Book Centre
PO Box 39, Mazenod 160
Tel: 35 0224 *Fax:* 35 0010
Telex: 427KO
Key Personnel
Manager: Fr B Mohlalisi
Founded: 1933
Subjects: History, Literature, Literary Criticism, Essays, Regional Interests, Religion - Other
ISBN Prefix(es): 99911-24

Saint Michael's Mission Social Centre
PO Box 25, Roma
Key Personnel
Man Dir: Rev Fr M Ferrange
Production: Peter Ntsaoana
Founded: 1968
Subjects: Anthropology, Biography, History, Regional Interests, Religion - Other, Social Sciences, Sociology

Libyan Arab Jamahiriya
General Information
Capital: Tripoli
Language: Arabic (official), also English and Italian
Religion: Muslim
Population: 4.5 million
Bank Hours: Generally Winter: 0830-1230; Summer: 0800-1200 Saturday-Thursday
Shop Hours: Vary greatly. Friday is weekly holiday but some Christian shops closed Sunday. Many are open 0830-1230, 1500-1730 Saturday-Thursday (slightly earlier hours in summer months)
Currency: 1,000 dirhams = 1 Libyan dinar
Export/Import Information: No tariff on books; advertising dutied. Charity Tax and Municipal Tax levied on dutiable goods. Open General License for books. Exchange permit, liberally granted, is required. Import and export of books is handled by the General Company for Publishing, Advertising and Distribution, Tripoli.
Copyright: Berne (see Copyright Conventions, pg xi)

Al-Fatah University, General Administration of Libraries, Printing & Publications
PO Box 13543, Tripoli
Tel: (02133) 621988
Telex: 20629 TP Univ Ly
Founded: 1955
Bookshop(s): University Bookshop, PO Box 13113, Tripoli

Liechtenstein
General Information
Capital: Vaduz
Language: German
Religion: Predominantly Roman Catholic
Population: 28,642
Bank Hours: 0800-1200, 1330-1630 Monday-Friday
Shop Hours: 0800-1200, 1330-1830 Monday-Friday; 0800-1600 Saturday
Currency: 100 rapen = 1 francen (swiss franc)
Export/Import Information: 2% VAT on books. Most books exempt from Turnover Tax. Advertising matter usually dutiable, some exempt from Turnover Tax. No import licenses required. No exchange controls. Swiss regulations to a Customs Treaty.
Copyright: UCC, Berne, Florence (see Copyright Conventions, pg xi)

Bonafides Verlags-Anstalt
Austr 50, 9490 Vaduz
Tel: (075) 82510
Founded: 1991
Subjects: Accounting, Finance, Government, Political Science, Nonfiction (General)
ISBN Prefix(es): 3-905193

Botanisch-Zoologische Gesellschaft
Liechtenstein-Sargans-Werdenberg, Heiligkreuz 52, 9490 Vaduz
Tel: (00423) 2324819 *Fax:* (00423) 2332819
E-mail: renat@pingnet.li
Key Personnel
Contact: Georg Willi
Founded: 1970
Subjects: Animals, Pets, Earth Sciences, Gardening, Plants, Physical Sciences
ISBN Prefix(es): 3-905195

Buchervertriebsanstalt
Postfach 461, 9490 Vaduz
ISBN Prefix(es): 3-905238

A R Gantner Verlag KG
Industriestr 105A, 9491 Ruggell
Mailing Address: Postfach 131, 9491 Ruggell
Tel: 377 1808 *Fax:* 377 1802
E-mail: bgc@adon.li
Web Site: www.gantner-verlag.com *Cable:* GANTR FL
Key Personnel
Manager: Mrs Bruni Gantner-Caplan
ISBN Prefix(es): 3-7182
Associate Companies: Litag Anstalt

Verlag HP Gassner AG
Austr 7, 9494 Vaduz
Tel: (075) 2327253 *Fax:* (075) 2323720

LIECHTENSTEIN

Key Personnel
Publisher: Hans Peter Gassner; Traugott Schneidtinger
Founded: 1979
Subjects: Art, History, Literature, Literary Criticism, Essays
ISBN Prefix(es): 3-906250

Historischer Verein fur das Furstentum Liechtenstein (Historical Society for the Principality of Liechtenstein)
Messinastr 5, 9495 Triesen
Mailing Address: Postfach 626, 9495 Triesen
Tel: 392 17 47 *Fax:* 392 17 05
E-mail: info@hvfl.li
Web Site: www.hvfl.li
Key Personnel
Man Dir: Klaus Biedermann *E-mail:* kgb@adon.li
Founded: 1901
Historical research.
Subjects: Archaeology, History
ISBN Prefix(es): 3-906393
Number of titles published annually: 1 Print

Kliemand Verlag
Sonnblickstr 6, 9490 Vaduz
Tel: 2321048
Subjects: Art, Poetry
ISBN Prefix(es): 3-906603

Kunstmuseum Liechtenstein Vaduz
Staedtle 32, 9490 Vaduz
Mailing Address: Postfach 370, 9490 Vaduz
Tel: 235 03 00 *Fax:* 235 03 29
E-mail: mail@kunstmuseum.li
Web Site: www.kunstmuseum.li
Specialize in 19th Century to Contemporary Art.
Number of titles published annually: 5 Print
Total Titles: 40 Print

Liechtenstein Verlag AG+
Herrengasse 21, 9490 Vaduz
Mailing Address: PO Box 339, 9490 Vaduz
Tel: 2396010 *Fax:* 2396019
E-mail: flbooks@verlag-ag.lol.li
Web Site: www.lol.li/verlag_ag
Key Personnel
Man Dir: Albart Piet Schiks
Founded: 1945
Also acts as Literary Agent.
Subjects: Finance, Government, Political Science, History, Law
ISBN Prefix(es): 3-85789

Verlag der Liechtensteinischen Akademischen Gesellschaft
Bahnhofstr 15a, 9494 Schaan
Mailing Address: Postfach 829, 9494 Schaan
Tel: 232 30 28 *Fax:* 233 14 49
Key Personnel
Dir: Norbert Jansen *E-mail:* jansen@mediateam.li
Founded: 1972
Subjects: Economics, Government, Political Science, Law
ISBN Prefix(es): 3-7211
Number of titles published annually: 3 Print

Litag Anstalt- Literarische, Medien und Kuenstler Agentur
Industriestr 105A, 9491 Ruggell
Mailing Address: Postfach 131, 9491 Ruggell
Tel: (0423) 3771809 *Fax:* (0423) 3771802
Key Personnel
Dir: Mrs B Gantner-Caplan
Founded: 1956
ISBN Prefix(es): 3-7211
Parent Company: Verlag der Liechtensteinischen Akademischeen Gesellschaft, Am Schragenluegz, 9490 Vaduz

Megatrade AG+
Aeulestrasse 45, 9490 Vaduz, Fuerstentum
Tel: 237 5252 *Fax:* 237 5253
E-mail: info@wanger.net
Web Site: www.wanger.net *Cable:* JURT FL
Key Personnel
Managing Partner: Markus Wille
Senior Partner: Dr Markus Wanger
Subjects: Art, Business, Economics, Law
ISBN Prefix(es): 3-9520331
Parent Company: Wanger Group

Rheintal Handelsgesellschaft Anstalt
Industriestr Postfach 444, 9495 Triesen
Tel: (075) 3921882; (01) 8442786 *Fax:* (075) 3923646; (01) 8442806
E-mail: vetsch.p@bluewin.ch
Key Personnel
International Rights: Nick U Schweinfurth
Founded: 1889
Subjects: Career Development, Education, Interactive Audio Courses on CD-ROM
ISBN Prefix(es): 3-9520574
Orders to: Rheintal Hondelsgesellschaft Niederlassung ZH/Huttikon, Birkenweg 3, 8115 Huttikon, Switzerland

Saendig Reprint Verlag, Hans-Rainer Wohlwend
Am Schraegen Weg 12, 9490 Vaduz
Tel: 232 36 27 *Fax:* 232 36 49
E-mail: saendig@adon.li
Web Site: www.saendig.com
Key Personnel
Manager: Christian Wohlwend
Founded: 1981
Subjects: Art, History, Language Arts, Linguistics, Mathematics, Music, Dance, Physical Sciences, Religion - Other, Science (General)
ISBN Prefix(es): 3-253

Topos Verlag AG
Industriestr 105A, 9491 Ruggell
Mailing Address: Postfach 551, 9491 Ruggell
Tel: 3771111 *Fax:* 3771119
E-mail: topos@supra.net
Web Site: www.topos.li *Cable:* TOPOS
Key Personnel
Man Dir: Graham A P Smith
Founded: 1977
Subjects: Economics, Education, Law, Social Sciences, Sociology
ISBN Prefix(es): 3-289

Frank P van Eck Publishers+
Haldenweg 9, 9495 Triesen
Mailing Address: Postfach 565, 9495 Triesen
Tel: (075) 3923000 *Fax:* (075) 3922277
E-mail: vaneck@datacomm.ch
Telex: 77030
Key Personnel
Manager: Elisabeth van Eck-Schaedler
Editor: Frank P van Eck
Founded: 1982
Subjects: Art, Sports, Athletics
ISBN Prefix(es): 3-905501
Associate Companies: Saentis Verlag
Subsidiaries: Edition Fuchs & Hase
Shipping Address: Schweizer Buchzertrum, Industrie Ost, 4614 Magendorf
Warehouse: Schweizer Buchzertrum, Industrie Ost, 4614 Magendorf
Orders to: Schweizer Buchzertrum, Industrie Ost, 4614 Magendorf

Lithuania

General Information

Capital: Vilnius
Language: Lithuanian
Religion: Predominantly Roman Catholic
Population: 3.8 million
Bank Hours: 0900-1200/1300 Monday-Friday
Shop Hours: 0900-1300 and 1400-1800 Monday-Friday
Currency: 100 cents = 1 litas
Export/Import Information: There are no customs duties and very few export restrictions.
Copyright: Berne (see Copyright Conventions, pg xi)

Academia
A Gostauto 12, 2600 Vilnius
Tel: (02) 626851 *Fax:* (02) 226351
Key Personnel
Dir: A Garliauskas *Tel:* (02) 626861
Founded: 1990
Subjects: Agriculture, Art, Biological Sciences, Chemistry, Chemical Engineering, Energy, Geography, Geology, Language Arts, Linguistics, Medicine, Nursing, Dentistry, Philosophy, Social Sciences, Sociology

Algarve+
Rinktines 3/11, 2600 Vilnius
Tel: (02) 725910; (02) 721635 *Fax:* (02) 721462
Key Personnel
Publisher: Algimantas Matulevicius
Founded: 1995
Joint stock company.
Subjects: Advertising, Fiction, Health, Nutrition, Science (General), esoteric, applied health education literature
ISBN Prefix(es): 9986-856
Total Titles: 40 Print

Alma Littera+
A Juozapavieiaus g 6/2, 2005 Vilnius
Tel: (05) 272 82 46; (05) 272 56 85 *Fax:* (05) 272 80 26
E-mail: post@almali.lt
Web Site: www.almali.lt
Key Personnel
Dir: Arvydas Andrijauskas
Founded: 1990
Membership(s): EEPG.
Subjects: English as a Second Language, Fiction
Number of titles published annually: 2 CD-ROM
Total Titles: 600 Print; 8 Audio

Andrena Publishers+
Pasilaiciu 8-13, 2022 Vilnius
Tel: (02) 703834; (02) 627015
E-mail: andrena@takas.lt
Key Personnel
Contact: Nijole Petrosiene
Founded: 1995
Subjects: Poetry, Psychology, Psychiatry, Religion - Catholic, Romance
ISBN Prefix(es): 9986-37
Total Titles: 27 Print

AS Narbuto Leidykla (AS Narbutas' Publishers)+
Klevu 9, 5400 Siauliai
Tel: (075) 420868 *Fax:* (075) 429335
Key Personnel
Contact: Amalijus S Narbutas *E-mail:* amalijus@siauliai.aiva.lt
Founded: 1990
Subjects: Art, Astrology, Occult, Humor, Language Arts, Linguistics, Literature, Literary Criticism, Essays, Medicine, Nursing, Dentistry, Parapsychology

PUBLISHERS — LITHUANIA

Baltos Lankos+
Laisves pr 115a-54, 2022 Vilnius
Tel: (05) 240 86 73; (05) 240 79 06 *Fax:* (05) 240 74 46
E-mail: leidykla@baltoslankos.lt
Web Site: www.baltoslankos.lt
Key Personnel
Dir: Saulius Zukas
Foreign Rights: Daiva Cibutaviciene
Founded: 1992
A humanities & social sciences publisher.
Subjects: Art, Biography, Cookery, Education, Fiction, History, Language Arts, Linguistics, Literature, Literary Criticism, Essays, Mysteries, Nonfiction (General), Philosophy, Photography, Poetry, Romance, Social Sciences, Sociology, Classics
U.S. Office(s): 2016 W Huron, No 2F, Chicago, IL, United States, Contact: Jura Avizienis
Tel: 312-243-0799

Centre of Legal Information
Gedimino pr 30/1, 2695 Vilnius
Tel: (02) 61 75 29; (02) 62 36 50 *Fax:* (02) 62 15 23
E-mail: webadm@utic.tm.lt
Subjects: Law
ISBN Prefix(es): 9986-452

Dargenis Publishers+
PO Box 2090, 44 009 Kaunas
Tel: (037) 205241 *Fax:* (037) 205241
E-mail: dargenis@kaunas.omnitel.net
Key Personnel
Dir: Dalia Celiesiute
Founded: 1997
Subjects: Child Care & Development, English as a Second Language, Human Relations, Psychology, Psychiatry, Self-Help
ISBN Prefix(es): 9986-9196; 9955-403

Egmont Lietuva+
Algirdo 51A, 2006 Vilnius
Tel: (02) 231265; (02) 231266; (02) 231267
Fax: (02) 231269
E-mail: egmont@egmont.com
Web Site: www.egmont.com
Key Personnel
Dir: Irina Glagoleva
Founded: 1993
Subjects: Fiction, Nonfiction (General), Comics & Cartoons
ISBN Prefix(es): 9986-22
Parent Company: Egmont International Holding A/S

Eugrimas+
Silutes 42A, 2042 Vilnius
Tel: 52 733 955; 52 754 754 *Fax:* 52 733 955
E-mail: info@eugrimas.lt
Web Site: www.eugrimas.lt
Key Personnel
Dir: Eugenija Petruliene
Founded: 1995
Subjects: Criminology, Economics, Education, Government, Political Science, History, Law, Philosophy
ISBN Prefix(es): 9986-752

Klaipedos Universiteto Leidykla+
H Manto 84, 92294 Klaipeda
Tel: (06) 398890 *Fax:* (06) 398999
E-mail: leidykla@ku.lt
Web Site: www.ku.lt
Key Personnel
Manager: Lolita Zemliene *Tel:* (06) 398891
E-mail: lolita.zemliene@ku.lt
Founded: 1992
Subjects: Agriculture, Archaeology, Art, Biological Sciences, Chemistry, Chemical Engineering, Computer Science, Drama, Theater, Economics, Education, Geography, Geology, History, Library & Information Sciences, Literature, Literary Criticism, Essays, Management, Maritime, Marketing, Mathematics, Mechanical Engineering, Music, Dance, Philosophy, Physical Sciences, Poetry, Psychology, Psychiatry, Public Administration, Religion - Catholic, Religion - Protestant, Science (General), Social Sciences, Sociology, Technology, Theology
Number of titles published annually: 100 Print
Total Titles: 800 Print
Parent Company: Klaipeda University

Lietus Ltd+
A Jakto 8/10, 2600 Vilnius
Tel: (02) 312298; (02) 8299 35423; (02) 745720
Fax: (02) 312298
Key Personnel
President: Liudas Pilius
International Rights: Agne Kudirkaite
Founded: 1991
Membership(s): Lithuanian Publisher's Association.
Subjects: Education, Fiction, Nonfiction (General)
ISBN Prefix(es): 9986-431
Total Titles: 70 Print
Warehouse: Musu Knyga Ltd, Vilkpedes 20, Vilnius *Tel:* (02) 632921

Lietuvos Rasytoju Sajungos Leidykla
(Lithuanian Writers' Union Publishers)+
K Sirvydo 6, LT-01101 Vilnius
Tel: (05) 2628945; (05) 2628643 *Fax:* (05) 2628945
E-mail: info@rsleidykla.lt
Web Site: www.rsleidykla.lt
Key Personnel
Dir: Giedre Soriene
Editor-in-Chief: Valentinas Sventickas
Editor: Saulius Repecka *Tel:* (02) 628643
Founded: 1990
Membership(s): Lithuanian Publishers Association.
Subjects: Fiction, Literature, Literary Criticism, Essays, Poetry
ISBN Prefix(es): 9-986
Number of titles published annually: 45 Print
Bookshop(s): Atzalynas, Antakalnio g 97, 2040 Vilnius; Fabijoniskiy, Stanevicouis g 24, 2029 Vilnius

Lithuanian National Museum Publishing House
Division of National Museum of Lithuania
Arsenalo g 1, 01100 Vilnius
Tel: (05) 262 77 74 *Fax:* (05) 261 10 23
E-mail: info@lnm.lt; muziejus@lnm.lt
Web Site: www.lnm.lt
Key Personnel
Dir: Birute Kulnyte
Subjects: Archaeology, History, Photography, Ethnography, Iconography, Numismatics
ISBN Prefix(es): 9955-415
Number of titles published annually: 10 Print
Total Titles: 105 Print

Lithuanian Publishers' Association
Z Sierakausko 15, 2600 Vilnius
Tel: (02) 332943 *Fax:* (02) 330519
Key Personnel
Dir: Aleksandras Krasnovas
Founded: 1990
Membership(s): International Publishers Association.

Martynas Mazvydas National Library of Lithuania (Lietuvos Nacionaline Martyno Mazvydo Biblioteka)+
Gedimino pr 51, 01504 Vilnius
Tel: 52398687 *Fax:* 52639111
E-mail: leidyba@lnb.lt
Web Site: www.lnb.lt
Key Personnel
Acting Dir: Vytautas Gudaitis *Tel:* 52497023
Fax: 52496129 *E-mail:* gudaitis@lnb.lt
Founded: 1919
Subjects: Library & Information Sciences
ISBN Prefix(es): 9986-530

Mokslo ir enciklopediju leidybos institutas
(Science & Encyclopedia Publishing Institute)+
L Asanaciutes g 23, 2050 Vilnius
Tel: (02) 45 85 26; (02) 457980; (02) 458528
Fax: (02) 45 85 37
E-mail: meli@meli.lt
Web Site: www.meli.lt
Key Personnel
Dir: Rimantas Kareckas *Tel:* 02 458525
Chief Editor: Jonas Varnauskas
Founded: 1992
Membership(s): the Lithuanian Publishers' Association.
Subjects: Agriculture, Biological Sciences, History, Language Arts, Linguistics, Literature, Literary Criticism, Essays, Mathematics, Medicine, Nursing, Dentistry, Physics, Science (General)
Imprints: Vilnius

Margi Rastai Publishers+
Laisves pr 60, 2056 Vilnius
Tel: (02) 429526; (02) 427909; (02) 429527; (02) 426705 *Fax:* (02) 426705
E-mail: margirastai@takas.lt
Subjects: Agriculture, Economics, Fiction, History, Sports, Athletics
ISBN Prefix(es): 9986-09

Scena+
Tuskulenu 13-14, 2051 Vilnius
Tel: (02) 751 828; (02) 614 145 *Fax:* (02) 610 814
Key Personnel
Dir: Rasa Andrasiunaite
Founded: 1992
Specialize in books about theater.
Subjects: Art, Drama, Theater

Sviesa Publishers+
Vytauto Ave 25, 3000 Kaunas
Tel: (0837) 409126 *Fax:* (0837) 342032
E-mail: mail@sviesa.lt
Web Site: www.sviesa.lt
Key Personnel
Dir: Vaidotas Gadliauskas *Tel:* (0837) 341834
E-mail: v.gadliauskas@sviesa.lt
Founded: 1945
Subjects: Career Development, Child Care & Development, Crafts, Games, Hobbies, Education, English as a Second Language, House & Home, Sports, Athletics, Travel
ISBN Prefix(es): 5-430

Svietimo ir mokslo ministerijos Leidybos centras+
Gelezinio vilko 12, 2600 Vilnius
Tel: (02) 617480, (02) 611060; (02) 616081
Fax: (02) 617480
E-mail: office@smmlc.elnet.lt
Key Personnel
Dir: Kareckas Rimantas
Founded: 1991
Membership(s): Publishers Association of Lithuania.
Subjects: Education, English as a Second Language, History, Mathematics, Music, Dance, Religion - Protestant
Associate Companies: Enterprise of Printing Service, Strazdelio 1, Vilnius 2600
Subsidiaries: Book-Collecting Department
Distributor for Langenscheidt (Germany); Longman Group (UK)

Bookshop(s): Latako 6, 2600 Vilnius; Pilies 22, 2600 Vilnius
Warehouse: Vilkpedes 20, 2637 Vilnius

Teisines Informacijos Centras, see Centre of Legal Information

TEV Leidykla+
Akademijos 4, 2021 Vilnius
Tel: (02) 729318; (02) 729803 *Fax:* (02) 729804
E-mail: tev@tev.lt
Web Site: www.tev.lt
Key Personnel
Contact: Elmundas Zalys
Founded: 1991
Subjects: Computer Science, Education, Engineering (General), Mathematics, Physics, Science (General)
ISBN Prefix(es): 9986-546
Distributed by VSP International Publications; Zeist
Distributor for VSP International Publications; Zeist

Tyto Alba Publishers+
J Jasinskio 10, 2600 Vilnius
Tel: (02) 498 602; (02) 497 453; (02) 497 597 *Fax:* (02) 498 602
E-mail: tytoalba@taide.lt
Web Site: www.tytoalba.lt
Key Personnel
Dir: Lolita Varanaviciene
Rights Manager: Ausra Viliuniene
Founded: 1993 (joint-stock company)
Subjects: Art, Biography, Business, Education, Fiction, How-to, Human Relations, Nonfiction (General), Philosophy, Self-Help
ISBN Prefix(es): 9986-16
Number of titles published annually: 50 Print
Total Titles: 300 Print

Vaga Ltd+
Gedimino str 50, 2600 Vilnius
Tel: (02) 49 81 21 *Fax:* (02) 49 81 22
E-mail: info@vaga.lt
Web Site: www.vaga.lt
Key Personnel
Dir: Arturas Mickevicius
Dir General: Kornelijus Platelis
Founded: 1945
Subjects: Art, Biography, Ethnicity, Fiction, Government, Political Science, Literature, Literary Criticism, Essays, Nonfiction (General), Philosophy, Photography, Poetry, Religion - Catholic, Religion - Jewish, Self-Help, Social Sciences, Sociology, Theology
ISBN Prefix(es): 5-415
Associate Companies: Vaga Trading Ltd; Vaga Publishers Ltd
Bookshop(s): M K Ciurlionio St 75, Druskininkai *Tel:* (0233) 5 15 25; Gedimino St 25/2, Kaisedorys *Tel:* (0256) 6 03 91; Smilgos St 2, Kedainiai *Tel:* (0257) 5 26 61; Aitvaras, Taikos pr 39, Klaipeda *Tel:* (026) 41 06 64; Centras, Turgaus aikste 2, Klaipeda *Tel:* (026) 41 15 90; Taikos pr 97, Klaipeda *Tel:* (026) 34 59 69; H Manto St, Klaipeda *Tel:* (026) 41 15 93; Lyros St 13, Siauliai *Tel:* (021) 55 26 05; Tauragnu St 2, Utena *Tel:* (0239) 5 96 79; Draugyste, Gedimino pr 2, Vilnius *Tel:* (02) 61 18 23; Versme, Didzioji St 27, Vilnius *Tel:* (02) 62 64 10; Ateities St 20, Vilnius *Tel:* (02) 71 46 88; Darbininku St 16, Vilnius *Tel:* (02) 26 49 48; Gedvydziu St 17, Vilnius *Tel:* (02) 47 86 56; Pergales St 13/2, Vilnius *Tel:* (02) 67 49 03; Ukmerges St 25, Vilnius, Luxembourg

Victoria Publishers+
Sviesos 4-6, Grigskes, 4058 Traku rajonas
Tel: (02) 221915; (02) 632632; (02) 221914 *Fax:* (02) 630797

Key Personnel
Contact: Natalija Stagiene
Founded: 1991
Subjects: Animals, Pets, Child Care & Development, Crafts, Games, Hobbies, Geography, Geology, Romance, Women's Studies

Vilnius, *imprint of* Mokslo ir enciklopediju leidybos institutas

Vilnius Art Academy Publishing House
The Old House, 3rd floor, Maironio St 6, 2600 Vilnius
Tel: (02) 22 30 63 *Fax:* (02) 61 99 66
E-mail: muziejus@vda.lt
Web Site: vdamuziejus.mch.mii.lt
Key Personnel
Chief Curator: Valentas Cibulskas

Vyturys Vyturio leidykla, UAB
J Tumo, Vaiganto 2, 2600 Vilnius
Tel: (02122) 027404; (02122) 622542 *Fax:* (02122) 629407
E-mail: vyturys@vyturys.lt
Web Site: www.vyturys.lt
Founded: 1985
Subjects: Education, Fiction, Literature, Literary Criticism, Essays, Poetry, Romance, Comics & Cartoons
ISBN Prefix(es): 5-7900

Magazyn Wilenski
Laisves pr 60, 2056 Vilnius
Tel: (05) 242 77 18
E-mail: magazyn@magwil.lt
Web Site: www.magwil.lt
Key Personnel
Editor: Michal Mackiewicz *Tel:* (05) 242 60 76 *Fax:* (05) 242 90 65
ISBN Prefix(es): 9986-542

Luxembourg

General Information

Capital: Luxembourg
Language: Luxembourgian, German, French, English
Religion: Predominantly Roman Catholic (about 97%)
Population: 437,389
Bank Hours: Vary. Generally 0830-1200, 1330-1630 Monday-Friday
Shop Hours: 0830-1200, 1330-1800 Monday-Saturday. Most close Monday morning. Some have late night shopping until 2000
Currency: 100 Eurocents = 1 Euro; 40.3399 Luxembourg francs = 1 Euro
Export/Import Information: Member of the European Union. In economic and monetary union with Belgium and Netherlands. No Tariff on books except children's picture books from non-EU; advertising other than single copied dutied. VAT on books and advertising. No import license required. No exchange controls.
Copyright: UCC, Berne, Florence (see Copyright Conventions, pg xi)

Editions APESS ASBL
17, rue Muller-Fromes, Diekirch, 9261 Luxembourg
Tel: 80 8358 *Fax:* 80 2813
E-mail: apess@ci.edu.lu
Web Site: www.restena.lu/apess
Key Personnel
Contact: Carlo Felten
Founded: 1982

Subjects: Art, Education, History, Literature, Literary Criticism, Essays, Philosophy, Poetry, Science (General)
ISBN Prefix(es): 2-87979
Total Titles: 35 Print

ARA International
58, Domaine Mehlstrachen, 6942 Niederanven
Tel: 34 85 91 *Fax:* 34 85 91
E-mail: amisrelart@pt.lu
Web Site: www.ara-international.lu
Key Personnel
International President: Emile van der Vekene
  E-mail: evekene@pt.lu
Founded: 1996
Associate Companies: ARA-Belgique, Ave de Messidor 184, bte 1, 1180 Brussels, Belgium, Contact: Marianne Delvaulx *Tel:* (02) 346 10 02 *Fax:* (02) 346 10 02 *E-mail:* marianne.delvaulx@belgacom.net; ARA-Canada, 1275, chemin Sainte-Foy, Quebec, PQ G1S 4W8, Canada, President: Jonathan Tremblay *Tel:* 416-843-2238 *E-mail:* ara-canada@oricom.ca *Web Site:* www.aracanada.org; ARA-Catalunya, Carrer Camprodon, 17 baixos, 08021 Barcelona, Spain, President: Germana Cavalcanti *Tel:* (093) 200 18 68 *E-mail:* germanacavalcanti@yahoo.com; ARA-France, 122, blvd Murat, 75016 Paris, France, President: Annick Terrasson *E-mail:* fc.terrasson@wanadoo.fr; ARA-Grece, 19 rue Didotou, 106 80 Athens, Greece, President: Sotirios K Koutsiaftis *Tel:* (010) 802 03 16 *Fax:* (010) 362 01 88 *E-mail:* sotkoutsiaftis@yahoo.gr; ARA-Italia, Fondazione Querini Stampalia, Castello 5252, 30122 Venice, Italy, President: Gabriele Giannini *Tel:* (041) 522 52 35 *Fax:* (041) 522 49 54 *E-mail:* info.ara@libero.it *Web Site:* www.amicirilegaturadarte.com; ARA-Suisse, 31 Beausejour, 1762 Givisiez, Switzerland, President: Gian-Andri Barblan *E-mail:* g-a.barblan@bluemail.ch *Web Site:* www.arasuisse.com
Foreign Rep(s): Pedro de Azevedo (Portugal); Joel Benarrous (Israel); Marisa Garcia de Souza (Brazil); Paula Maria Gourley (USA); Fred Kroon (Netherlands); Sabine Pierard (Australia); Ivan Piskov (Russia); Emile van der Vekene (Luxembourg); Reuko Yamanue (Japan)

Guy Binsfeld & Co Sarl+
14, pl du Parc, 2313 Luxembourg
Tel: 49 68 68-1 *Fax:* 40 76 09; 48 87 70
E-mail: editions@binsfeld.lu
Web Site: www.editionsguybinsfeld.lu
Key Personnel
Man Dir, Production, Publicity, Rights & Permissions: Guy Binsfeld *E-mail:* gbinsfeld@binsfeld.lu
Founded: 1979
Subjects: Biography, Cookery, Fiction, Gardening, Plants, How-to, Law, Nonfiction (General), Photography
ISBN Prefix(es): 3-88957; 2-87954
Total Titles: 204 Print
Divisions: Binsfeld-Conseils Communications Agency
Distributed by Altera Diffusion (Belgium); Fausto Gardini (US); Gollenstein Verlag (Germany, Austria & Switzerland); Lanaguages de Luxe (Great Britain); Messageries du Livre (Luxembourg & other countries); Editions Serpenoise (France); Willems Adventure (Netherlands)

Editions Emile Borschette
21 Fielserstrooss, 7640 Christnach
Tel: 87177 *Fax:* 879599
Founded: 1987
Subjects: Accounting, Career Development, Cookery, Drama, Theater, Education, Gardening, Plants, History, How-to, Humor, Language Arts, Linguistics, Literature, Literary Criticism,

Essays, Mathematics, Music, Dance, Photography, Poetry, Regional Interests
ISBN Prefix(es): 2-87982
Subsidiaries: Atelier de Reliures

Cahiers Luxembourgeois
67, rue Roger Barthel, 7212 Bereldingen
Tel: 338885 *Fax:* 336513
Key Personnel
Publisher: Nic Weber
Founded: 1993
Subjects: Biography, History, Literature, Literary Criticism, Essays, Poetry, Regional Interests
ISBN Prefix(es): 2-919976
Divisions: Edition Raymon Mehlen

Centre Culturel De Differdange
69, rue Prinzenberg, 4650 Niederkorn
Tel: 587045 *Fax:* 580295
Key Personnel
President & Editor: Cornel Meder *E-mail:* cornel.meder@ci.culture.lu
Founded: 1982
Subjects: Ethnicity, Literature, Literary Criticism, Essays
ISBN Prefix(es): 2-87991

Chambre des Employes Prives
13, rue de Bragance, 1255 Luxembourg
Tel: 44 40 91-1 *Fax:* 44 40 91-250
E-mail: info@cepl.lu
Web Site: www.cepl.lu
Key Personnel
President: Jos Kratochwil
Dir: Theo Wiltgen

Editpress
44, rue du Canal, 4050 Esch/Alzette
Tel: 547131 *Fax:* 547130
E-mail: tageblatt@tageblatt.lu

Eiffes Romain
293, Avenue de Luxembourg, L-4940 Bascharage
Tel: (023) 65 10 52
E-mail: rend@pt.lu
Key Personnel
Contact: Mr Romain Eiffes
Founded: 1995
Membership(s): SACEM/Paris (Societe des Auteurs Compositeurs et Editeurs de Musique Paris).
Subjects: English as a Second Language, Music, Dance, Poetry
ISBN Prefix(es): 2-9599899

Essay und Zeitgeist Verlag
c/o Patrick Kontz BP 2116, 1021 Luxembourg
Fax: 425227
Founded: 1994
Subjects: Literature, Literary Criticism, Essays, Philosophy, Social Sciences, Sociology
ISBN Prefix(es): 2-9599981
Orders to: BP 2767, L-1207 Luxembourg

Galerie Editions Kutter
BP 319, 2013 Luxembourg
Tel: 22 35 71 *Fax:* 47 18 84
E-mail: kuttered@pt.lu
Web Site: www.kutter.lu
Founded: 1960
Subjects: Art, Photography, Regional Interests
ISBN Prefix(es): 2-87952

Grande Loge de Luxembourg
5, rue de la Loge, 2018 Luxembourg
Mailing Address: BP 851, 2018 Luxembourg
Tel: 463-566 *Fax:* 463566
ISBN Prefix(es): 2-9599875

Hubsch
24, rue des Genets, 3482 Dudelange
E-mail: 101755.3213@compuserve.com
Subjects: Humor, Romance, Science Fiction, Fantasy
ISBN Prefix(es): 2-9599996

Keyware sarl+
11, rue de la Montagne, 5460 Trintange
Tel: 358660
E-mail: texthaus@webcom.com
Founded: 1996
Subjects: Education
ISBN Prefix(es): 2-919891

Ministere de la Culture
20 Montee de la Pe'trusse, 2327 Luxembourg
Tel: 478-1 *Fax:* 40-24-27
ISBN Prefix(es): 2-87984

Edition Objectif Lune+
One rue de Schoenfels, 8151 Bridel
Tel: 335230 *Fax:* 335230
E-mail: objectif.lune@cmdnet.lu
Key Personnel
President: Jean-Paul Kieffer
Specialize in photographic stills.
Subjects: Drama, Theater, Film, Video, Photography
ISBN Prefix(es): 2-9599934

Office des Publications Officielles des Communautes Europeennes (Office for Official Publications of the European Communities)
2 rue Mercier, 2985 Luxembourg
Tel: 292942001 *Fax:* 292942700
Founded: 1969
U.S. Office(s): Bernan Associates, 4611-F Assembly Drive, Lanham, MD 20706-4391, United States *E-mail:* query@bernan.com *Web Site:* www.bernan.com

Op der Lay+
19, rue d'Eschdorf, 9650 Esch-sur-Sure
Tel: 83 97 42 *Fax:* 89 93 50
E-mail: opderlay@pt.lu
Web Site: webplaza.pt.lu/public/opderlay; www.phi.lu
Key Personnel
Contact: Robert Gollo Steffen; Renee Weber
Founded: 1987
Specialize in compact disc & music cassettes, literature & music from Luxembourg. Also music publisher.
Subjects: Music, Dance, Poetry, Travel
ISBN Prefix(es): 2-87967
Total Titles: 7 Audio

Passerelle Editions, *imprint of* Editions Promoculture

Editions Phi+
PO Box 321, 4004 Esch, Alzette
Tel: 541382-220 *Fax:* 541387
E-mail: editions.phi@editpress.lu; phi@phi.lu
Web Site: www.phi.lu
Key Personnel
Dir: Angelika Thome
Editorial: Jean Portante
Founded: 1980
Subjects: Art, Drama, Theater, Literature, Literary Criticism, Essays
ISBN Prefix(es): 3-88865; 2-87962

Editions Promoculture+
14 rue Duchscher, 1424 Luxembourg
Mailing Address: BP 1142, 1011 Luxembourg
Tel: 480691 *Fax:* 400950
E-mail: promocul@pt.lu

Web Site: www.promoculture.lu
Key Personnel
Dir: Albert Daming *E-mail:* daming@pt.lu
Founded: 1989
Law & fiscal publisher.
Also major book dealer.
Subjects: Accounting, Economics, Finance, Law
ISBN Prefix(es): 2-87974
Number of titles published annually: 15 Print; 1 CD-ROM; 2 E-Book
Total Titles: 120 Print; 2 CD-ROM; 2 E-Book
Imprints: Passerelle Editions
Warehouse: One rue Duchscher, 1424 Luxembourg *E-mail:* info@promoculture.lu

Editions Saint-Paul+
5 rue Christophe Plantin, 2988 Luxembourg
Tel: 49931 *Fax:* 485876
Telex: Wortlu 3471; 275256
Key Personnel
Man Dir: Paul Zimmer
Production: Jean Breser
Publicity: Patrick Ludovicy
Publishing Manager: Dirk Sumkoetter *Tel:* 4993256 *E-mail:* dirk.sumkoetter@editions.lu
Founded: 1886
Subjects: History, Literature, Literary Criticism, Essays
ISBN Prefix(es): 2-87963
Parent Company: Group Saint-Paul SA
Bookshop(s): Librarie Beaumont, 24 rue Beaumont, 1249; Librairie Bourbon, rue du Fort Bourbon, 1249; Librairie du Sud, 74 rue de l'Alzette, 4010 Eschalzette; Librairie Daman, 4 rue de Brabant, 9213 Diekirch

Service Central de la Statistique et des Etudes Economiques (STATEC)
Les bureaux du Statec se trouvent au centre de Luxembourg-Ville, Centre Administratif Pierre Werner, 13, rue Erasme, 1468 Luxembourg-Kirchberg
Mailing Address: BP 304, 2013 Luxembourg
Tel: 478-4384 *Fax:* 464289
E-mail: info@statec.etat.lu
Web Site: www.statec.lu; www.statec.public.lu
Key Personnel
Dir: Serge Allegrezza
Principal Inspector & Head of Information: Guy Zacharias *Tel:* 478-4281 *E-mail:* guy.zacharias@statec.etat.lu
Founded: 1962
National Statistical Institute of Luxembourg, under the authority of the Minister of the Economy.
Subjects: Agriculture, Business, Economics, Finance, Labor, Industrial Relations, Library & Information Sciences, Public Administration, Social Sciences, Sociology
ISBN Prefix(es): 2-87988
Number of titles published annually: 100 Print

Service Central des Imprimes et des Fournitures de Bureau de l'Etat
22, rue des Bruyeres, 1274 Howald
Mailing Address: BP 1302, 1013 Howald
Tel: (00352) 4988111 *Fax:* (00352) 400881
E-mail: hotline@scie.etat.lu
Web Site: www.scie.etat.lu
Key Personnel
Contact: Claude Schaber *Tel:* 498811-901 *E-mail:* claude.schaber@scie.etat.lu
Founded: 1969
Specialize in textbooks.
Subjects: Archaeology, Art, Law, Natural History, Public Administration
ISBN Prefix(es): 2-495
Number of titles published annually: 70 Print
Total Titles: 1,023 Print

STATEC, see Service Central de la Statistique et des Etudes Economiques (STATEC)

Thesen Verlag Soc Civile, see Thesen Verlag Vowinckel

Thesen Verlag Vowinckel
Formerly Thesen Verlag Soc Civile
Place de la Gare, 3, 6674 Mertert
Mailing Address: Postfach 3570, 54225 Trier, Germany
Tel: (0352) 748715 *Fax:* (0352) 26740429
Key Personnel
Man Dir: Dr Ilse Schirmer-Vowinckel
  E-mail: schirm.vow@pt.lu
Founded: 1969 (Founded in Germany since 1992 resident in the Grand-Duche of Luxembourg)
Specialize in scholarly books, book review "Kritikon Litterarum" literary criticism.
Membership(s): Borsenverein des Deutschen Buchhandels.
ISBN Prefix(es): 3-7677

Editions Tousch+
8 rue Ernest Koch, 1864 Luxembourg
Tel: 452977 *Fax:* 458743
Subjects: Art, History, Humor, Photography, Poetry
ISBN Prefix(es): 2-919971

Varkki Verghese+
Maison 23A, 9769 Roder
Tel: 923121 *Fax:* 929076
Founded: 1993
Membership(s): GEMA (Music).
Subjects: Alternative, Asian Studies, Economics, Government, Political Science, Music, Dance, Poetry, Theology, Women's Studies
ISBN Prefix(es): 2-9599891
Associate Companies: Whitelion Ltd, United Kingdom
Divisions: Acanthus Records
Distributed by Oyster (India only)

Macau

General Information

Capital: Macau
Language: Portuguese and Chinese (Cantonese dialect) both official. English also widely spoken
Religion: Roman Catholic, Chinese Buddhist, Daoism, & Confuscianism
Population: 373,904
Bank Hours: 0930-1700 Monday-Friday; 0930-1200 Saturday
Shop Hours: 0900-1730 Monday-Saturday
Currency: 100 avos= 1 pataca. Hong Kong currency is also widely used but there is no fixed exchange rate.
Export/Import Information: Macau is a free port.
Copyright: Berne (see Copyright Conventions, pg xi)

Livros Do Oriente+
Edificio Marina Gardens, Av Amizade, 876, 15 E Macau
Tel: 700320; 700421 *Fax:* 700423
E-mail: livros.macau@loriente.com
Web Site: www.loriente.com
Key Personnel
General Manager: Rogerio Beltrao Coelho
Executive Manager: Cecilia Jorge
Founded: 1990
Subjects: Anthropology, Biography, Photography, Romance, Social Sciences, Sociology, Travel
ISBN Prefix(es): 972-9418
Branch Office(s)
Rua da Fonte Santa, 91, 2050-112 Aveiras de Cima, Portugal, Contact: Chacara Lilau
Fax: (0263) 476890 *E-mail:* chacara@mail.telepac.pt

Museu Maritimo (Maritime Museum)
Largo do Pagode da Barra, n 1, Sul da China
Tel: (0853) 595481; (0853) 595483 *Fax:* (0853) 512160
E-mail: museumaritimo@marine.gov.mo
Web Site: www.museumaritimo.gov.mo
Key Personnel
Dir: Wu Chu Pang
Subjects: Asian Studies, History, Maritime, Technology, Transportation
Number of titles published annually: 3 Print
Total Titles: 58 Print

Instituto Portugues Oriente
Rua Pedro Nolasco da Silva, nº 45, 1º andar, Macau
Tel: 530227; 530243 *Fax:* 530277
E-mail: info@ipor.org
Web Site: www.ipor.org
Key Personnel
President: Prof Antonio Vasconcelos de Saldanha
  E-mail: presidente@ipor.org
Founded: 1989
Subjects: Asian Studies, History, Language Arts, Linguistics, Literature, Literary Criticism, Essays
ISBN Prefix(es): 972-8013
Bookshop(s): Livraria Portuguesa, Rua de Sao Domingos, No 16-18, Contact: Manuel Almeida *Tel:* (0853) 566442; (0853) 356235 *Fax:* (0853) 378014 *E-mail:* malmeida.livraria@ipor.org

The Former Yugoslav Republic of Macedonia

General Information

Capital: Skopje
Language: Macedonian
Religion: Predominantly Eastern Orthodox, some Muslim
Population: 2.1 million
Copyright: UCC, Berne (see Copyright Conventions, pg xi)

Detska radost+
Mito Hadzivasilev bb, 91000 Skopje
Tel: (091) 112394; (091) 213059 *Fax:* (091) 225830; (091) 213059
E-mail: detskaradost@yahoo.com
Web Site: www.detskaradost.com
Telex: YUNOVMAK 51154
Key Personnel
International Rights: Kiril Donev
Editor-in-Chief: Aleksandar Cvetkovski
Founded: 1945
Specialize in children's books.
Subjects: Fiction, Literature, Literary Criticism, Essays, Nonfiction (General), Poetry, Science Fiction, Fantasy
Associate Companies: NIP, Nova Makedonija, Skopje

Gjurgja Journalistic & Publishing Firm
11 Oktomvri 2/6-2, 1000 Skopje
Tel: (091) 228076
Key Personnel
Dir: Olga Kosteska
ISBN Prefix(es): 9989-676
Subsidiaries: Literary-Painting Salon

Ktitor+
Engelsova 8/18, 2000 Stip
Tel: (092) 21903; (092) 34746 *Fax:* (092) 34746
Telex: 53618 MAK.YU
Subjects: Drama, Theater, Literature, Literary Criticism, Essays, Music, Dance, Philosophy, Poetry, Religion - Other, Science (General)
ISBN Prefix(es): 9989-608

Macedonia Prima Publishing House+
ul Krste Misirkov 8, 6000 Ohrid
Tel: (096) 37-109 *Fax:* (096) 23-172
Key Personnel
Editor-in-Chief: Pasko Kuzman
Dir: Nikola Bozdoganov
Editor: Slave Banar
Artistic Designer: Slavko Upevce
Founded: 1993
Membership(s): Association of Macedonian Publishers.
Subjects: Archaeology, Art, History, Literature, Literary Criticism, Essays, Photography, Poetry, Science Fiction, Fantasy, Social Sciences, Sociology
ISBN Prefix(es): 9989-619

Makedonska kniga (Knigoizdatelstvo)
11-ti Oktomvri, 1000 Skopje
Tel: (091) 116 473; (091) 3 1610; (091) 235 524 *Fax:* (091) 1212 77
Telex: 51637 *Cable:* MAKEDONSKA KNIGA
Key Personnel
Dir: Ms Nada Miloshevska-Ristovska
Founded: 1947
Subjects: Art, Fiction
ISBN Prefix(es): 9989-46

Medis, Skopje+
M Hadzhivasilev 36/1-2, 91000 Skopje
Tel: (091) 118-104 *Fax:* (091) 272-253
E-mail: medis@informa.mk
Web Site: www.medis.com.mk
Key Personnel
President: Dr Mirko Spiroski
Founded: 1991
Specialize in medicine & computer science.
Subjects: Biological Sciences, Communications, Computer Science, Education, Electronics, Electrical Engineering, Mathematics, Medicine, Nursing, Dentistry, Microcomputers
Total Titles: 10 E-Book

Menora Publishing House
bul Jane Sandanski 36-4/13, 1000 Skopje
Tel: (02) 458447 *Fax:* (02) 418872
E-mail: menora@lotus.mpt.com.mk
Key Personnel
Dir: Jordan Pop-Atanasov
Specialize in literature with scientific & scholarly contents.
Subjects: Science (General)
ISBN Prefix(es): 9989-632
Bookshop(s): Porta Bunjakovec, A-2, Dijadema, Lam I, BR 12-I, 91000 Skopje

Mi-An Knigoizdatelstvo
vl Ivan Agouski 1/I, 91000 Skopje
Tel: (091) 252565
E-mail: mtimes@soros.org.mk
Key Personnel
President: Vanja Tosevski
Vice President: Mishel Pavlovski
Editor-in-Chief: Jovan Pavlovski
Assistant Editor-in-Chief: Boshko Nacevski
Founded: 1991

Subjects: Journalism, Literature, Literary Criticism, Essays, Poetry, Publishing & Book Trade Reference
ISBN Prefix(es): 9989-613
Branch Office(s)
American Information Centre, str, Nikola Vaptsarov 8 *Tel:* 116-623

Murgorski Zoze+
ul Budimpestanska 37B, 1000 Skopje
Tel: (091) 241340
Founded: 1991
Subjects: Education, English as a Second Language, Language Arts, Linguistics
ISBN Prefix(es): 9989-651
Distributed by Kultura (Macedonia)

Narodna i univerzitetska biblioteka, see St Clement of Ohrid National & University Library

Nov svet (New World)+
Briselska 1, 1000 Skopje
Tel: (02) 3078-662
Key Personnel
Academic Poet: Dr Jozo T Boskovski Jon
Founded: 1966
Specialize in translations. The Company "Nov svet" (New World) was an illegal editorial of the Desidents Writers. Now is all regular Publish House - sponsored (on programs) by the Government of Republic of Macedonia.
Also acts as wholesaler & publishing house for books, newspapers & periodicals.
Subjects: Art, Journalism, Literature, Literary Criticism, Essays, Philosophy, Poetry, Science (General)
Total Titles: 2,000 Print
Associate Companies: Cross-Cultural Communications, 239 Wynsum Ave, Merrick, NY, United States

Prosvetno Delo Publishing House
Dimitie Cupovski 15, 1000 Skopje
Tel: (02) 117 255; (02) 2 225 434 *Fax:* (02) 129 402; (02) 225 434
E-mail: prodelo@nic.mpt.com.mk
Web Site: www.prodelo.com.mk
Key Personnel
General Manager: Pavle Petrov
Editor-in-Chief: Jelica Makazlieva
Contact: Nadica Mihajlovska
Founded: 1945
Specialize in school textbooks, pedagogical materials & teaching aids.
Subjects: Education
ISBN Prefix(es): 86-351
Number of titles published annually: 400 Print
Total Titles: 8,000 Print
Bookshop(s): Dame Gruev BB, 91000 Skopje *Tel:* (02) 2 222 621 *Fax:* (02) 2 222 621
Warehouse: Aco Sopov, 6 91000 Skopje

St Clement of Ohrid National & University Library+
Bul Goce Delcev 6, 91000 Skopje
Tel: (02) 3115 177; (02) 3133 418 *Fax:* (02) 3226 846
E-mail: kliment@nubsk.edu.mk
Web Site: www.nubsk.edu.mk
Key Personnel
Dir & Chief Executive: Vera Kalajlievska
Contact: Veljan Ristevski
Founded: 1944
Scholarly & scientific works collections, including monograph titles, periodicals, newspapers & other printed materials (patents, standards, etc). Specialized collections include: old Slavonic manuscripts, printed & rare books & periodicals, oriental manuscripts, archive copies of Macedonia publications (1944 to present), prints & drawings, cartographic items, microfilms, doctoral dissertations, Master's theses, scientific & scholarly research projects. Online catalogue available.
Subjects: Library & Information Sciences
ISBN Prefix(es): 9989-652
Membership(s): International Federation of Library Associations & Institutions (IFLA)

Seizmoloska Opservatorija+
PO Box 422, 91000 Skopje
Tel: (091) 231953 *Fax:* (091) 114042
E-mail: ljupco@iunona.pmf.ukim.edu.mk
Key Personnel
Editor & International Rights: Vera Cejkovska; Dragana Cernih
Membership(s): International Association of Seismology & Physics of the Earth's Interior - IASPEI; International Union of Geodesy & Geophysics - IUGG
Subjects: Computer Science, Earth Sciences, Electronics, Electrical Engineering, Geography, Geology
ISBN Prefix(es): 9989-631

Strk Publishing House+
ul Jurij Gagarin Br 17-2-17, 1000 Skopje
Tel: (091) 20 53 93 *Fax:* (091) 20 53 93
Key Personnel
Dir: Nikola Strkovski
Editor: Snezana Strkovska
Founded: 1992
Also acts as importer/exporter of office supplies & paper; wholesale & retail.
Subjects: Astrology, Occult, Behavioral Sciences, Biography, Economics, History, Literature, Literary Criticism, Essays, Poetry, Romance
ISBN Prefix(es): 9989-662

Zumpres Publishing Firm+
ul Vanjamin Madukovski 6, P fah 363, 1000 Skopje
Tel: (091) 163-539; (091) 425-175 *Fax:* (091) 429-196; (091) 425-175
E-mail: zumpres@yahoo.com
Key Personnel
Dir & Editor-in-Chief: Vinka Sazdova
Founded: 1994
Subjects: Anthropology, Archaeology, Architecture & Interior Design, Art, Astrology, Occult, Astronomy, Behavioral Sciences, Biblical Studies, Biography, Computer Science, Fiction, History, Human Relations, Language Arts, Linguistics, Literature, Literary Criticism, Essays, Mysteries, Parapsychology, Philosophy, Poetry, Psychology, Psychiatry
ISBN Prefix(es): 9989-42

Madagascar

General Information

Capital: Antananarivo
Language: French and Malagasy
Religion: Most follow traditional beliefs, about 43% Christian and some Islamic
Population: 12.6 million
Bank Hours: 0800-1100, 1400-1600 Monday-Friday. Closed afternoon preceding a holiday
Shop Hours: 0800-1200, 1400-1800 Monday-Saturday
Currency: 100 centimes = 1 franc malgache (Malagasy franc)
Export/Import Information: For books and advertising matter, customs and import duties, also unique tax. Import license required.
Copyright: Berne, Florence (see Copyright Conventions, pg xi)

Editions Ambozontany
c/o Librairie St Paul Ambatomena, BP 1170, Fianarantsoa 301
Tel: (07) 50027; (07) 51441
Key Personnel
Man Dir: Justin Bethaz
Editorial: Nicola Giambrone
Sales: Jose Minien
Founded: 1962
Subjects: Ethnicity, History, Religion - Other, Social Sciences, Sociology

Librairie Ambozontany
BP 1170, 301 Fianarantsoa
Tel: (07) 50027; (07) 51441

Maison d'Edition Protestante ANTSO+
19 Lalana Venance Manifatra, Tananrive 101
Mailing Address: BP 660, Imarivolanitra Tananrive 101
Tel: (022) 20886 *Fax:* (022) 26372
E-mail: fjkm@dts.mg *Cable:* FIJEKRIMA ANTSO
Key Personnel
Man Dir: Hans Andriamampianina
Founded: 1966
Subjects: Biblical Studies, Developing Countries, Education, Journalism, Literature, Literary Criticism, Essays, Religion - Protestant
Number of titles published annually: 6 Print
Total Titles: 13 Print
Bookshop(s): Bookshop Antso, Lot IIB 18, Totohabato Ranavalona 1, Tananarive 101 *Tel:* (022) 347 10; Librairie ANTSO, rue Bertho Anjoma, Toamasina 501 *Tel:* 33944

Centre National de Production de Materiel Didactique (CNAPMAD)
BP 665, Ankorondrano, Tananrive 101
Tel: (02) 289-54 *Fax:* (02) 200-53
Key Personnel
Manager: Mr Jersin Manjato Razafimahefa

CNAPMAD, see Centre National de Production de Materiel Didactique (CNAPMAD)

Foibe Filan-Kevitry NY Mpampianatra (FOFIPA)
BP 202, Tananrive 101
Mailing Address: rue Jean Andriamady Faravohitra, BP760, Tananrive
Tel: (02) 27500 *Fax:* (02) 35788
Subjects: Accounting, Agriculture, Cookery, English as a Second Language
Distributed by Les Libraries de Madagascar

Government Printer (Imprimerie Nationale)
BP 38, Ambatomena, Tananrive 101
Tel: (02) 23675

JEAG
120 rue Rainandriamampandry, 101 Tananrive
Tel: (02022) 24141 *Fax:* (02022) 20397
Key Personnel
Director: Harilala Adrianarimanana
ISBN Prefix(es): 2-910885
Parent Company: Jureco SA
Distributor for Foi & Justice

Librarie Mixte
BP 3204, 37, rue 26 Jona 1960 Analakely, Tananrive 101
Tel: (02) 25130 *Fax:* (02) 25130

Madagascar Print & Press Company+
rue Rabesahala - Antsakaviro, Tananrive 101
Mailing Address: BP 953, Tananrive 101
Tel: (02) 22526 *Fax:* (02) 2234534
E-mail: roi@dts.mg

MADAGASCAR

Key Personnel
Man Dir, Editorial: Georges Ranaivosoa
Founded: 1969
Sales, Publicity: Societe CEMOI.
Subjects: History, Literature, Literary Criticism, Essays
Imprints: Editions Revue de l'Ocean Indien
Subsidiaries: Communication et Media - Ocean Indien (Societe CEMOI)
Sales Office(s): Societe CEMOI

MADPRINT, see Madagascar Print & Press Company

Societe Malgache d'Edition+
Route des Hydrocarbures, Ankorondrano, BP 659, Antananarivo/Tananrive 101
Tel: (020) 2222635 *Fax:* (020) 2222254
E-mail: tribune@bow.dts.mg
Telex: 22340 RAMEX MG TANANARIVE
Key Personnel
Man Dir: Rahaga Ramaholimihaso
Founded: 1943
Subjects: Communications, Economics, Education, Finance, Journalism, Law
Imprints: SME

Musee d'Art et d'Archaeologie
Universite de Madagascar, 17 rue Dr Villette, Isoraka, Tananrive 101
Mailing Address: BP 564, Tananrive 101
Tel: (02) 21047 *Fax:* (02) 28218
E-mail: musedar@syfed.refer.mg
Key Personnel
Dir: Dr J A Rakotoarisoa
Subjects: Travel

Editions Revue de l'Ocean Indien, *imprint of* Madagascar Print & Press Company

SME, *imprint of* Societe Malgache d'Edition

Imprimerie Takariva
rue Radley Antanimena, Tananrive 101
Mailing Address: BP 1029, Tananrive
Tel: 02 23856
Key Personnel
Man Dir: Paul Rapatsalahy
Founded: 1933
Subjects: Fiction

Trano Printy Fiangonana Loterana Malagasy (TPFLM)-(Imprimerie Lutherienne)
Imprint of Fiangonana Loterana Malagasy
9 ave Grandidier Isoraka, Tananrive 101
Mailing Address: BP 538, Tananrive 101
Tel: (020) 223340 *Fax:* (020) 262643
E-mail: impluth@dts.mg
Key Personnel
Man Dir: Raymond Randrianatoandro
 Tel: 2224569
Editorial: Pastor Samoela Georges
Founded: 1877
Membership(s): F L M, Union Professionnelle Des Imprimeurs De Madagascar.
Subjects: Fiction, Religion - Other
Number of titles published annually: 100 Print
Associate Companies: Fiangonana Loterana Malagasy, BP 1741, 101 Tananrive, Contact: Raymond Randrianatoandro *Tel:* 022 24569
Bookshop(s): Analakely & Antsahamanitra
Distribution Center: BP 533, Tananrive

Tsileondriaka Edition
Lot II M 79 Andravoahangy, Tananrive 101
Mailing Address: BP 1239, Tananrive 101
Tel: (02) 31033; (02) 30659 *Fax:* (02) 31033

Tsipika Edition
48 rue Ny Havana-Antsahabe, Tananrive 101

Tel: (02) 24595
Key Personnel
Manager: Claude Rabenoro
Founded: 1990
Subjects: Environmental Studies, History
Distributed by Harmattan (France)

Malawi

General Information

Capital: Lilongwe
Language: English and Chichewa
Religion: About 50% Christian (Roman Catholic and Presbyterian), some Islamic and Hindu, remainder traditional beliefs
Population: 9.6 million
Bank Hours: 0800-1300 Monday-Friday; Saturday closed
Shop Hours: 0730 or 0800-1600 or 1700 Monday-Friday (with some closing for lunch); until midday Saturday
Currency: 100 tambala = 1 Malawi kwacha
Export/Import Information: No tariff on books; some advertising matter subject to duty. Import license required on certain category of goods. Exchange controls.
Copyright: UCC, Berne (see Copyright Conventions, pg xi)

Central Africana Ltd+
PO Box 631, Blantyre
Tel: 631509; 243595 *Fax:* 622236
E-mail: africana@sdwp.org.mw
Key Personnel
Chairman & Publisher: Frank M I Johnston
 Tel: 821316
Founded: 1989
Subjects: History, Travel
ISBN Prefix(es): 99908-14
Number of titles published annually: 3 Print
Total Titles: 15 Print
Branch Office(s)
A231 St Martini Gardens, Queen Victoria St, Cape Town 8000, South Africa
 Tel: (021) 4243595 *Fax:* (021) 4243595
 E-mail: africana@iafrica.com
Foreign Rep(s): Struik & Southern Book Publishers (South Africa)

Christian Literature Association in Malawi
PO Box 503, Blantyre
Tel: 620839; 673091
Key Personnel
General Manager: J T Matenje
Sales Manager: E C Mtumbati
Founded: 1968
Subjects: Biography, Fiction, History, Poetry, Regional Interests, Religion - Other
ISBN Prefix(es): 99908-16

Dzuka Publishing Co Ltd (Rise Publishing Co Ltd)
Private Bag 39, Blantyre
Tel: (01) 672548; (01) 670637 *Fax:* (01) 671114; (01) 670021
E-mail: dzuka@malawi.net
Telex: 44112 AFNEWSMI
Key Personnel
General Manager: Iness Malemia
Founded: 1975
Publisher of educational & other materials.
Subjects: Agriculture, Biography, Business, Education, Fiction, Geography, Geology, History, Mathematics
ISBN Prefix(es): 99908-17
Total Titles: 150 Print
Parent Company: Blantyre Printing & Publishing Co Ltd

Government Printer (Imprimerie Nationale)
PO Box 37, Zomba
Tel: (050) 523155 *Fax:* (050) 52230133
Telex: 45162 Geoprint MI
ISBN Prefix(es): 99908-20

Popular Publications+
PO Box 5592, Limbe 651 833
Tel: 651 833 *Fax:* 651 17133
E-mail: mpp@malawi.net
Telex: 44814 Montfort Ml
Key Personnel
General Manager, Publisher, Rights & Permissions: Vales Machila
Editorial: Prince C Shonga
Sales: M Kapelewera
Production: H Chinawa
Founded: 1976
Subjects: Biblical Studies, Fiction
ISBN Prefix(es): 99908-29
Parent Company: Montfort Press, PO Box 5592, Limbe
Bookshop(s): Moni Bookshop, PO Box 5592, Limbe

Malaysia

General Information

Capital: Kuala Lumpur
Language: Bahasa Malaysia (based on Malay) is official language; English widely used; Chinese, Tamil and Iban also spoken
Religion: Islam predomininates, there is a large Buddhist group among the Chinese, Hindu among the Indians
Population: 18.4 million
Bank Hours: West Malaysia (some states observe Muslim weekly holiday): 1000-1500 Monday-Friday; 0930-1130 Saturday. Sabah: 0800-1200, 1400-1500 Monday-Friday; 0900-1100 Saturday. Sarawak: 1000-1500 Monday-Friday; 0930-1130 Saturday
Shop Hours: West Malaysia varies; average 0830-1830 Monday-Saturday. Sabah: 0800-1830 Monday-Saturday. Sarawak: 0900-1800 Monday-Friday; 0900-1300 Saturday
Currency: 100 sen = 1 ringgit or Malaysian dollar
Export/Import Information: No tariff on books. Advertising matter dutied per lb, subject to CIF surtax. No obscene literature allowed. Import licenses required only in Sabah, for books not having the name, printer and publisher on first or last printed page. No exchange controls.
Copyright: Berne (see Copyright Conventions, pg xi)

S Abdul Majeed & Co+
7 Jalan 3/82B, Bangsar Utama, Off Jalan Bangsar, 59000 Kuala Lumpur
Tel: (03) 283-2230 *Fax:* (03) 282-5670
E-mail: peer@pc.jaring.my
Key Personnel
Man Partner: Peer Mohamed Majid
 E-mail: peer@pc.jaring.my
Founded: 1952
Subjects: Asian Studies, Child Care & Development, Cookery, English as a Second Language, Health, Nutrition, Management, Marketing, Religion - Islamic, Travel
ISBN Prefix(es): 983-9629; 983-9550
Imprints: Malaysia Heritage Series
Branch Office(s)
35, Jalan Sekerat Off Tranofer Rd, 10050 Pinang
Showroom(s): 107c, Jalan Rajalaut, 50350 Kuala Lumpur

PUBLISHERS — MALAYSIA

Academia Publications P Ltd
22, Jalan Bukit Bintang, 55100 Kuala Lumpur
Tel: (03) 572455
ISBN Prefix(es): 967-9925

Pustaka Aman Press Sdn Bhd
4200A, Jalan Sultan Yahya Putra, 15700 Kota Bahru, Kelantan
Tel: (09) 7481849 *Fax:* (09) 784058
ISBN Prefix(es): 983-63

Amiza Associate Malaysia Sdn Bhd+
71 Jalan SS 6/12, Kelana Jaya, 47301 Petaling Jaya, Selangor Darul Ehsan
Tel: (03) 7036100 *Fax:* (03) 7034268
Key Personnel
Marketing Manager: Jeremy Thor
Founded: 1982
Membership(s): Malaysian Book Publishers Association.
Subjects: Business, Education
ISBN Prefix(es): 967-966
Parent Company: Johore State Economic Development Corp Johor Bahru, Malaysia

AMK Interaksi Sdn Bhd+
NO7, Jalan 3/82 B Bangsar Utama, Off Jalan Bangsar, 59200 Kuala Lumpur
Tel: (03) 215306 *Fax:* (03) 718067
Telex: MA 30226 MAHIR
Key Personnel
President: Miss Chin Choo Yuen
Founded: 1988
ISBN Prefix(es): 983-9617; 983-99555
Parent Company: Mahir Holdings Sdn Bhd
Shipping Address: Master Agencies Sdn Bhd, 110 Jl 27, Kawasan 16, Sungei Rasa, 41300 Kelang
Warehouse: 28, Jl SS26/13 Taman Mayang Jaya, 47301 Petaling Jaya

Pustaka Antara
399A Jalan Tuanku Abdul Rahman, 50100 Kuala Lumpur
Tel: (03) 292 5823 *Fax:* (03) 291 7997
Telex: MA 28140 *Cable:* Antara
ISBN Prefix(es): 967-937

Associated Educational Distributors (M) Sdn Bhd+
550 Taman Melaka Raya, 75000 Melaka
Tel: (06) 2844786 *Fax:* (06) 2844697
Subjects: Fiction
ISBN Prefix(es): 967-948

Berita Publishing Sdn Bhd
Desa Business Park, Taman Desa, 16-20 Jalan 4/109E, 58100 Kuala Lumpur
Tel: (03) 7620 8111 *Fax:* (03) 7620 8026
Web Site: www.beritapublishing.com.my
Telex: MA 30259
Key Personnel
Senior General Manager: Swaminathan Mv
 E-mail: swami@beritapub.com.my
Editor-in-Chief: Datuk A Kadir Jasin
 E-mail: akadirjasin@beritapub.com.my
Senior Editor: Ibrahim Yahaya *E-mail:* tiger@beritapub.com.my
Senior Manager, Ads & Promotions: Vs Ganesan
 E-mail: ganesan@beritapub.com.my
Senior Manager, Circulation: Mohd Azizi Bin Puteh *E-mail:* azizi@beritapub.com.my
Founded: 1973
Subjects: Business, Cookery, Education, Fiction
ISBN Prefix(es): 967-969
Parent Company: The New Straits Times Press (Malaysia) Berhad Balai Berita, 31 Jalan Riong, Kuala Lumpur 22-03
Subsidiaries: Berita Book Centre Sdn Bhd; Berita Distributors Sdn Bhd (both at above address)

Biro Penyediaan Teks Itm (Biroteks)+
Institut Teknologi Mara, 40450 Shah Alam, Selangor Darul Ehsan
Tel: (03) 59271 ext 495 *Fax:* (03) 500226; (03) 55692733
Key Personnel
Contact: Head of Biroteks
Founded: 1981
ISBN Prefix(es): 967-958

Butterworths, *imprint of* Malayan Law Journal Sdn Bhd

Castle, *imprint of* Glad Sounds Sdn Bhd

Darulfikir+
329-B Jl Abd Rahman Idris off Jl Raja Muda, 50300 Kuala Lumpur
Tel: (03) 2981636; (03) 26913892 *Fax:* (03) 26928757
E-mail: e-mel@darulfikir.com.my
Web Site: www.darulfikir.com.my
Telex: MA 31533 Action
Key Personnel
Man Dir: Mohamad Ahmad
Founded: 1984
Subjects: Education, Language Arts, Linguistics, Religion - Islamic
ISBN Prefix(es): 983-99583; 983-9668
Number of titles published annually: 40 Print
Total Titles: 1,700 Print

Dewan Bahasa dan Pustaka+
Peti Surat 10803, 50926 Kuala Lumpur
Tel: (03) 21481011; (03) 2481820; (03) 21483839 *Fax:* (03) 2482726; (03) 2142005; (03) 21414109; (03) 2148420; (03) 21444460
Web Site: www.dbp.gov.my *Cable:* Bahasa
Key Personnel
Dir General: Dato Haji A Aziz Deraman *Tel:* (03) 2486785; (03) 21485656 *E-mail:* aziz@dbp.gov.my
Dir, Publishing: Dato Anuar Rethwan *Tel:* (03) 2488136; (03) 21482230 *Fax:* (03) 2449614
 E-mail: anuar@dbp.gov.my
Rights & Licensing: Othman Ismail
 E-mail: othman@dbp.gov.my
Founded: 1956
Specialize in Malay language & linguistics, Malay literature & Malay culture.
ISBN Prefix(es): 967-65; 983-62
Number of titles published annually: 300 Print
Branch Office(s)
Dewan Bahasa dan Pustaka Cawangan Sabah, PO Box 149, Teluk Likas, 88999 Kota Kinabalu, Sabah, Contact: Hamzah Hamdani *Tel:* (088) 439217; (088) 439316 *Fax:* (088) 439732; (088) 439314
Dewan Bahasa dan Pustaka Cawangan Sarawak, PO Box 1390, 93728 Kuching, Sarawak, Contact: Zaini Oje *Tel:* (082) 444706; (082) 444711 *Fax:* (082) 444707
Dewan Bahasa dan Pustaka Wilayah Selatan, Larkin Perdana Business Park, No 1-3, Jalan Susur Dewata I, Johor Bharu, Johor, Zubaidi Abas *Tel:* (07) 2361616; (07) 2358686 *Fax:* (07) 2358686
Dewan Bahasa dan Pustaka Wilayah Timur, Jalan Abdul Kadir Adabi, Lot PT 107-109, Kota Bharu, Kelantan, Contact: Sallehuddin Abang Shokeran *Tel:* (09) 7475656 *Fax:* (09) 7475252
Dewan Bahasa dan Pustaka Wilayah Utara, No 31, Lorong PS 2, Bandar Perda, 14000 Bukit Mertajam, Pulau Pinang, Contact: Mohamad Yussop Ishak *Tel:* (04) 6211011 *Fax:* (04) 6211013; (04) 621914

Dewan Pustaka Islam+
10-2-1, Jln 14/22, 46100 Petaling Jaya, Selangor Darul Ehsan
Tel: (03) 755 7225 *Fax:* (03) 755 7871
Key Personnel
Executive Chairman: Mohd Anuar Tahir
Man Dir: Ahmad Azam Abdul Rahman
Founded: 1971
Membership(s): Book Contractor Association of Malaysia.
Subjects: Religion - Islamic
ISBN Prefix(es): 983-66
Associate Companies: Blue-T Sdn Bhd
Subsidiaries: Budaya Ilmu Sdn Bhd; Tradisi Ilmu Sdn Bhd
Distributed by Cekap Edar; Hizbi
Distributor for Institut Kajan Dasar; Institute of Strategic & International Studies (ISIS); Juta & Co (South Africa); Universiti Malaya Publication
Bookshop(s): Tradisi Ilmu Sdn Bhd, 10-2 Right Angle Jln 14/22, 46100 Petaling Jaya Selangor Darul Ehsan
Warehouse: Lot 1032, Jln Cempaka, Kg Sg Kayu Ara, 47400 Damansara Utama

Earlybird, *imprint of* Federal Publications Sdn Bhd

Eastview Malaysiana Library, *imprint of* Eastview Productions Sdn Bhd

Eastview Productions Sdn Bhd
11 Lorong 51A/227C, 46100 Petaling Jaya, Selangor Darul Ehsan
Tel: (03) 7762669; (03) 7762614; (03) 7556639 *Fax:* (03) 7550731
Key Personnel
Man Dir: Johnny Ong
Founded: 1980
ISBN Prefix(es): 967-60
Associate Companies: Anthonian Store Sdn Bhd; Pacific Book Centre, Singapore; Pan Pacific Publications Pte Ltd, Singapore
Imprints: Eastview Malaysiana Library; Eastview Visual Library

Eastview Visual Library, *imprint of* Eastview Productions Sdn Bhd

Fairy Tales, *imprint of* Mecron Sdn Bhd

Federal, *imprint of* Federal Publications Sdn Bhd

Federal Publications Sdn Bhd+
Tingkat 1, Bangunan Times Publishing, Lot 46, Subang Hi-Tech Industrial Park, Batu Tiga, 40000 Shah Alam, Selangor Darul Ehsan
Tel: (03) 7351511 *Fax:* (03) 73 64620
E-mail: kesoon@pc.jaring.my
Key Personnel
Vice President & General Manager: Stephen Lim *Tel:* (03) 7364621
Founded: 1957
Subjects: Astronomy, Career Development, Child Care & Development, Computer Science, Education, English as a Second Language, Gardening, Plants, Mathematics, Science (General), Self-Help, Sports, Athletics
Total Titles: 500 Print
Parent Company: Times Publishing Limited
Associate Companies: Federal Publications (HK) Ltd, Hong Kong; Federal Publications (S) (Pte) Ltd, Singapore
Imprints: Earlybird; Federal; Times
Divisions: Times Trade Direcories
Shipping Address: Federal Publications (HK) Ltd, Hong Kong
Warehouse: Federal Publications (HK) Ltd, Hong Kong
Orders to: Federal Publications (S) (Pte) Ltd, Singapore
Federal Publications (HK) Ltd, Hong Kong

MALAYSIA

FEP International Sdn Bhd
6 Jalan SS 4C/5, 47301 Petaling Jaya, Selangor Darul Ehsan
Mailing Address: PO Box 1091, Petaling Jaya, Selangor Darul Ehsan
Tel: (03) 7036150; (03) 7036152; (03) 7036154
Fax: (03) 7036989 *Cable:* BOOKMARK
Key Personnel
Man Dir: Mok Hai Lim
ISBN Prefix(es): 967-63
Associate Companies: FEP International Private Ltd, Singapore

Forum Publications+
11 Jalan 11-4E, 46200 Petaling Jaya, Selangor Darul Ehsan
Tel: (03) 7554007 *Fax:* (03) 7561879
E-mail: g2jomo@umcsd.um.edu.my
Key Personnel
President: Abdul Karim Hassan
Marketing Dir: Tong-Sin Chong
Founded: 1978
Subjects: Anthropology, Developing Countries, Economics, Government, Political Science, History, Labor, Industrial Relations, Regional Interests, Religion - Islamic
ISBN Prefix(es): 983-876
Parent Company: Institute of Social Analysis (INSAN)
Associate Companies: Malaysian Social Science Association
Subsidiaries: Ikraq

Geetha Publishers Sdn Bhd
13A Jalan Kovil Hilir, 51100 Kuala Lumpur
Tel: (03) 4417073
Key Personnel
Man Dir: Soma Narayanan
Subjects: Education, History, How-to, Publishing & Book Trade Reference
ISBN Prefix(es): 983-9594

Glad Sounds Sdn Bhd+
20 Jalan SS 21/35, Damansara Utama, 47400 Petaling Jaya, Selangor Darul Ehsan
Tel: (03) 7562901; (03) 7556442 *Fax:* (03) 7560528
E-mail: gladsnd@po.jaring.my
Key Personnel
General Manager: Peter Khong
Founded: 1976
Subjects: Management, Religion - Other, Self-Help
ISBN Prefix(es): 983-897
Imprints: Castle
Branch Office(s)
Jaya Shopping Centre
Kota Raya Complex
Yik Foong Complex

Holograms (M) Sdn Bhd+
6, Jorong Bukit Pantai Satu, 59100 Kuala Lumpur
Tel: (03) 2824002 *Fax:* (03) 2822751
Key Personnel
International Rights: Chuah Guat Eng
Founded: 1994
Subjects: Developing Countries, Ethnicity, Fiction
ISBN Prefix(es): 983-9132

IBS Buku Sdn Bhd
24 20/16A-06, PJ Industrial Park, Jalan Kennajuan, 46300 Petaling Jaya, Selangor Darul Ehsan
Tel: (03) 7751763; (03) 775-1566; (03) 7760514
Fax: (03) 79576026; (03) 776-8551
E-mail: ibsbuku@po.jaring.my
Key Personnel
Man Dir, Production, Rights & Permissions: M N Meera
Editorial: Miss Chong
Dir, Sales & Publicity: Mohamed Mustafa

Founded: 1972
Subjects: Career Development
ISBN Prefix(es): 967-950
Subsidiaries: Pelanduk Publications (M) Sdn Bhd

International Book Service, see IBS Buku Sdn Bhd

International Law Book Services+
Lot 4.1, 4th floor, Wisma Shen 149, Jalan Masjid India, 50100 Kuala Lumpur
Mailing Address: PO Box 11664, 50752 Kuala Lumpur
Tel: (03) 7727 4121; (03) 7727 4122; (03) 7727 3890; (03) 7728-3890 *Fax:* (03) 7727 3884
E-mail: gbc@pc.jaring.my
Web Site: bookgold.com
Key Personnel
Sole Proprietor: Syed Ibrahim
Founded: 1981
Publishes the *Malaysian Law Statutes & other general titles pertaining to law.*
Membership(s): Malaysian Book Publishers Association.
Subjects: Law
ISBN Prefix(es): 967-89; 967-9960
Number of titles published annually: 75 Print
Total Titles: 950 Print; 1 CD-ROM

Jabatan Penerbitan Universiti Malaya, see University of Malaya, Department of Publications

K Publishing & Distributors Sdn Bhd+
Stadium Shah Alam, Aras 1, Quadron B, Seksyen 13, 40000 Shah Alam, Selangor
Tel: (03) 5501755; (03) 5501442 *Fax:* (03) 5501826
Telex: MA 30226 MAHIR
Key Personnel
President: En Ahmad Mahir Kamaruddin
Founded: 1985
Subjects: Fiction
ISBN Prefix(es): 967-9906; 983-852
Parent Company: Mahir Holdings Sdn Bhd
Shipping Address: Master Agencies Sdn Bhd, 110 Jl 27, Kawasan 16, Sungei Rasa, 41300 Kelang
Warehouse: 28, Jl SS26/13 Taman Mayang Jaya, 47301 Petaling Jaya

Kharisma Publications Sdn Bhd
22 Jl USJ 9/5P, Subang Business Centre, 47620 Subang Jaya
Tel: (03) 724660 *Fax:* (03) 724602
Parent Company: Kharisma Group of Companies

Lamina Series, *imprint of* Mecron Sdn Bhd

Little Board Books, *imprint of* Mecron Sdn Bhd

Mahir Publications Sdn Bhd+
Stadium Shah Alam 1 Quadran B Seksyen 13, 40000 Shah Alam, Selangor
Tel: (03) 5501826; (03) 5501442; (03) 5501755
Fax: (03) 5501826
Telex: MA30226MAHIR
Key Personnel
Man Dir: Ahmad Mahir Kamaruddin
Publishing Manager: Choo Yuen Chin
Founded: 1990
Specialize in School Titles.
Subjects: Education, English as a Second Language
ISBN Prefix(es): 983-70
Parent Company: Mahir Holdings Sdn Bhd
Subsidiaries: Quill Publishers

Shipping Address: Master Agencies Sdn Bhd, 110 Jalan 27, Kawasan 16, Sungai Rasa, 41300 Kelang
Warehouse: Taman Mayang Jaya, 28 Jalan SS 26/16, 47310 Petaling Jaya

Malaya Books Suppliers Co
272-E Jalan Air Itam, 11400 Pulau Pinang
Tel: (03) 7910420
Key Personnel
Manager: Tony Lau
ISBN Prefix(es): 983-835

Malaya Educational Supplies Sdn Bhd
306, Block C, Glomac Business Centre, 10, JISS 6/1 Kelana Jaya, 47301 Plaling Jaya, Selangor
Tel: (03) 7046628 *Fax:* (03) 7046629
Subjects: Education
ISBN Prefix(es): 967-9923

The Malaya Press Sdn Bhd
6 Jalan TPK 1/4, Taman Perindustrian Kinrara, 58200 Kuala Lumpur
Tel: (03) 5755890; (03) 5757817 *Fax:* (03) 5757194
Key Personnel
Man Dir: Lai Wing Chun
Editorial: Yiu Hong
Sales: Chong Tim Seng
Founded: 1958
Subjects: Education
ISBN Prefix(es): 967-934
Parent Company: Union Cultural Organization Sdn Bhd, 10 Jalan 217, Petaling Jaya
Associate Companies: Hong Kong Cultural Press Ltd, 9 College Rd, Kowloon, Hong Kong; Singapore Press (Pte) Ltd, 303 North Bridge Rd, Singapore 7, Singapore
Bookshop(s): Ipoh Book Co, 75 Market St, Ipoh, Perak; Malaya Book Co, 22-24 Jalan Bukit Bintang, Kuala Lumpur

Malayan Law Journal Sdn Bhd
Unit A-5-1, 5th Floor, Wisma HB, Megan II Ave, 12 Jalan Yap Kwan Seng, 50450 Kuala Lumpur
Tel: (03) 2162 2822 *Fax:* (03) 2162 3811
Web Site: www.mlj.com.my
Key Personnel
Managing Editor, New Product Development: Julie Anne Thomas
Commissioning Editor: Prema Arumugam
Sales Dir: Ronald Tan
Area Sales Manager: Lawrence Tan
Commercial Dir: Pook Li Ping
Fulfillment Manager: Chow Wai Leng
Founded: 1932
Member of the LexisNexis Group.
Subjects: Law
ISBN Prefix(es): 967-962
Parent Company: Butterworth & Co (Publishers) Ltd, United Kingdom
Ultimate Parent Company: Reed Elsevier plc, 25 Victoria St, London SW1H 0EX, United Kingdom
Associate Companies: Butterworths Hong Kong, 12/F, Hennessy Centre, 500 Hennessy Rd, Causeway Bay, Hong Kong, Commissioning Editor: Anisha Sakhrani *Tel:* 2965 1400 *Fax:* 2976 0840 *Web Site:* www.butterworths-hk.com; Butterworths India, Vijaya Bldg, 14th Floor, 17, Barakhamba Rd, New Delhi 110001, India, Publishing Manager: Ambika Nair *Tel:* (011) 373 9614 *Fax:* (011) 332 6456 *Web Site:* www.butterworths-india.com; Butterworths Singapore, No 1 Temasek Ave, 17-01 Millenia Tower, Singapore 039192, Singapore, Regional Publishing Dir: Conita Leung *Tel:* 336 9661 *Fax:* 336 9662 *Web Site:* www.butterworths.com.sg
Imprints: MLJ; Butterworths

Shipping Address: No 3, Jalan PJS 11/20, Bandar Sunway, 46150 Petaling Jaya, Selangor *Tel:* (03) 733 1893 *Fax:* (03) 733 1823
Warehouse: No 4, Lot 752, Jalan Subang 3, Taman Perindustrian Subang, 47610 Subang Jaya, Selangor Darul Ehsan, Warehouse Manager: Patrick Lee *Tel:* (03) 5636 1740
Orders to: No 3, Jalan PJS 11/20, Bandar Sunway, 46150 Petaling Jaya, Selangor *Tel:* (03) 733 1893 *Fax:* (03) 733 1823

Malaysia Heritage Series, *imprint of* S Abdul Majeed & Co

The Malaysian Current Law Journal Sdn Bhd+
Jalan Selaman 1/2, E1-2, 2nd floor, Dataran Palma, 68000 Ampang
Tel: (03) 42705400 *Fax:* (03) 42705402
E-mail: rahim@cljlaw.com
Web Site: www.cljlaw.com
Key Personnel
Chief Editor: Gan Peng Chiang
Man Dir: Abdul Latiff Ibrahim
Founded: 1981
Subjects: Law
ISBN Prefix(es): 983-9680

MDC Publishers Printers Sdn Bhd+
2717 & 2718, Wisma MDC, Jalan Permata Empat, Taman Permata, Ulu Kelang, 53300 Kuala Lumpur
Tel: (03) 41086600 *Fax:* (03) 41081506
E-mail: mdcpp@mdcpp.com.my
Web Site: www.mdcpp.com.my
Key Personnel
Dir: Tajuddin Husain
Marketing Executive: Ameer Hussain; Ahmed Hussain
Founded: 1976
Reprinting & translation of foreign publications & co-publishing with foreign publishers.
Membership(s): Malaysian Book Publishers Association; Malaysian Booksellers Association; Malaysian Book Importers Association.
Subjects: Business, Economics, Law, Management
Number of titles published annually: 300 Print
Branch Office(s)
L3-04, 3rd floor, Shaw Parade, Changkat Thambi Dollah, Kuala Lumpur *Tel:* (03) 2457745
Distributor for International Labour Organization (ILO); Japan External Trade Organization (JETRO); UNESCO; United Nations; World Bank; World Intellectual Property Organization (WIPO); World Trade Organization

Mecron Sdn Bhd+
No B5-3 Binova Ind Center, No 1 Jalan 2/57 B, 51200 Kuala Lumpur
Tel: 16 280 8772 *Fax:* (03) 6251 9869
Web Site: www.mecronbooks.com *Cable:* MECROMAN KUALA LUMPUR
Key Personnel
Chief Executive: Dr Y Mansoor Marican
E-mail: nmansoor@tm.net.my
Dir: Zaliha B Samsudeen
Founded: 1984
Specialize in children's books; also act as packager.
ISBN Prefix(es): 983-9072; 983-9556; 983-9387
Imprints: Fairy Tales; Lamina Series; Little Board Books; See & Read Series; Well Loved Tales
Warehouse: Binova No B5-3, No 1, Jalan 2/57B (Segambut), 51200 Kuala Lumpur

Pustaka Melayu Baru
One Bangunan Wisma Yakin, Jalan Melayu, 50100 Kuala Lumpur
Tel: (03) 2985281 *Fax:* (03) 2414457
ISBN Prefix(es): 967-9931

Minerva Publications
96 Jalan Dato' Bandar, Tunggal, 70000 Seremban, Negeri Sembilan
Tel: (06) 734439 *Fax:* (06) 734439
Key Personnel
Man Dir: Haji Tajuddin MS
Founded: 1964
Subjects: Business, Career Development, English as a Second Language, Religion - Islamic, Self-Help
ISBN Prefix(es): 983-68
Parent Company: News & Periodicals Store, 96 Jalan Dato Bandar Tunggal, Negeri Sembilan Darul Khusus
Divisions:

MLJ, *imprint of* Malayan Law Journal Sdn Bhd

Oscar Book International+
37A Jl 20-16, Paramount Garden, 46300 Petaling Jaya, Selangor Darul Ehsan
Tel: (03) 7753515; (03) 7762797 *Fax:* (03) 7762797
Key Personnel
Proprietor: Windfred Chee Moon Hock
Founded: 1980
Specialize in English & Malay.
Subjects: Language Arts, Linguistics
ISBN Prefix(es): 967-941
Total Titles: 120 Print

Pan Malayan Publishing Co Sdn Bhd
72C, Jalan Sungai Besi, 57100 Kuala Lumpur
Tel: (603) 7910420 *Fax:* (603) 92214333
ISBN Prefix(es): 967-922

Panther Publishing
130-1 Jalan Thamby Abdullah, 50470 Kuala Lumpur
Tel: (03) 2749854
Key Personnel
Chief Executive, Publicity: R Vijesurier
Editorial, Production: Bella Mary Peters
Sales: Mary Rajam
Founded: 1972
Subjects: Travel
ISBN Prefix(es): 983-99627
Branch Office(s)
Block 151, No 650-K, Lorong 4, Toa Payoh, Singapore 1231, Singapore

Parry's Press
60 Jalan Negara, Taman Melawati, 58100 Kuala Lumpur
Tel: (03) 4079179 *Fax:* (03) 4079180
E-mail: haja@pop.3.jaring.my
Telex: Parry's MA 33243 *Cable:* PABOKCENT
ISBN Prefix(es): 983-9342
Subsidiaries: Parry's Book Center Pte Ltd (Singapore)
Orders to: 528-A MacPherson Rd, Singapore 368217, Singapore

Pearson Education Malaysia Sdn Bhd+
Lot 2, Jalan 215, Off Jalan Templer, 46050 Petaling Jaya, Selangor Darul Ehsan
Tel: (03) 7782 0466; (03) 7782 0659; (03) 7782 0702 *Fax:* (03) 7781 8005
E-mail: inquiry@pearsoned.com.my
Web Site: www.pearson.com
Telex: 37600
Key Personnel
General Manager/Dir, School Pub: Wong Mei Mei
General Manager/HE: Edward Teoh Swee Ong
Publishing Manager: Poh Swee Hiang
Finance Dir: Mok Chek Khek
Founded: 1961
Subjects: Literature, Literary Criticism, Essays, Mathematics, Physics, Science (General)
ISBN Prefix(es): 967-976
Number of titles published annually: 300 Print
Total Titles: 2,000 Print
Parent Company: Pearson Education
Holding Company: Addison Wesley

Pelanduk Publications (M) Sdn Bhd+
Subang Jaya Industrial Estate, 12, Jalan SS13/3E, 47500 Subang Jaya, Selangor Darul Ehsan
Mailing Address: PO Box 8265, 46785 Kelana Jaya, Selangor Darul Ehsan
Tel: (03) 56386573; (03) 56386885 *Fax:* (03) 56386577; (03) 56386575
E-mail: pelpub@tm.net.my
Web Site: www.pelanduk.com
Key Personnel
Man Dir, Production: Ng Tieh Chuan
Editorial: Chong Meow Lian
Sales & Publicity: Jackson Tan
Editorial: Woo Kum Wah
Contact: Ms M H Chong
Founded: 1984
Subjects: Biography, Business, Economics, Language Arts, Linguistics, Management, Religion - Islamic, Social Sciences, Sociology
ISBN Prefix(es): 967-978
Distributed by China Books (Australia); IBS Buku Sdn Bhd (Malaysia); National Book Store (Philippines); Peace Book Co Ltd (Hong Kong); Recreaids Pte Ltd (Singapore); Weatherhill Inc (US)
Distribution Center: Asia Books, Bahnhofstr 132, 69151 Neckargemund, Germany *Tel:* (06223) 6849 *Fax:* (06223) 72466 *E-mail:* chris.rieger@t-online.de
Asia Books Co Ltd, 5 Sukhumuit Rd, Soi 61, Bangkok 10110, Thailand *Tel:* (02) 3912680 *Fax:* (02) 3811621 *E-mail:* asiabook@comnet2.ksc.net.th
Australian Book Exports, 9/30 Pitt St, Parramatta, NSW 2150, Australia *Tel:* (02) 9687 8286 *Fax:* (02) 9687 8286 *E-mail:* dsoh@enternet.com.au
Combined Book Services, Units 1/K, Paddock Wood Dist. Centre, Paddock Wood, Tonbridge, Kent TN12 6UU, United Kingdom *Tel:* (01892) 837171 *Fax:* (01892) 837272 *E-mail:* orders@combook.co.uk
Ming Ya Books & Trade Co, PO Box 803, 1000 AV Amsterdam, Netherlands *Tel:* (070) 3651887 *Fax:* (070) 3652146
Pacific Century Distribution, G/F 2-, Lower Kai Yuen Lane, North Point, Hong Kong, Hong Kong *Tel:* 2811 5505 *Fax:* 2565 8624 *E-mail:* pcdltd@hknet.com
PT Gramedia Asri Media, Jl Gajah Mada 109, Jakarta 11140, Indonesia *Tel:* (021) 2601234 *Fax:* (021) 6337268
I J Sangun Enterprises, PO Box 4322, CPO Manila 1099, Philippines *Tel:* (02) 6651946 *Fax:* (02) 6588466
United Publishers Services Ltd, Kenkyu-sha Bldg, 9 Kanda Surugadai 2-chome, Chiyoda-ku Tokyo, Japan *Tel:* (03) 3291-4541 *Fax:* (03) 3292-8610

Pelangi Publishing Pte Ltd, see Penerbitan Pelangi Sdn Bhd (Pelangi Publishing Pte Ltd)

Penerbit Fajar Bakti Sdn Bhd+
4 Jalan U1/15, Seksyen U1, Hicom Glenmarie Industrial Park, 40000 Shah Alam, Selangor
Tel: (03) 7047011 *Fax:* (03) 7047024
Key Personnel
Man Dir: M Sockalingam
Founded: 1969
ISBN Prefix(es): 967-65; 967-933
Parent Company: Oxford University Press, United Kingdom
Subsidiaries: South-East Asian Publishing Unit

Penerbit Jayatinta Sdn Bhd+
No 18 Jalan 51A/223, 46100 Petaling Jaya, Selangor Darul Ehsan
Tel: (03) 7764036
Telex: MA20382 AB Delta
Key Personnel
Man Dir: Mr Lim Swee Sing; Mr Lim Kim Wah
Executive Dir: Ms Lee Yuet Yee
Group General Manager: Mr Phang Sang Choy; Mr Phang Sang Moi
Founded: 1988
Subjects: Economics, English as a Second Language, Environmental Studies, Geography, Geology, History, Philosophy, Religion - Islamic, Science (General)
ISBN Prefix(es): 983-883
Parent Company: Group of Delta Publishing
Subsidiaries: Pustaka Delta Pelajaran Sdn Bhd; Baron Production Sdn Bhd; Delta Distributors Sdn Bhd; Gunung Mutiara Sdn Bhd; Tempo Publishing (M) Sdn Bhd; Gedung Ilmu Sdn Bhd; Delta Publishing Sdn Bhd; Delta Editions Sdn Bh
Branch Office(s)
No 174 Jalan Pasar, 41400 Kelang, Selangor Darul Ehsan (Factory)

Penerbit Prisma Sdn Bhd+
129A Jalan SS 25/2 Taman Mewah, Petaling Jaya, 47301 Selangor Darul Ehsan, Petaling Jaya
Tel: (03) 7034393 *Fax:* (03) 7039367
Key Personnel
Man Dir: Wong Peng Khuen
Founded: 1986
ISBN Prefix(es): 983-9665; 983-99556; 983-823; 983-877

Penerbit Universiti Sains Malaysia+
d/a Perpustakaan Universiti Sains Malaysia, Minden, 11800 Pulau Pinang
Tel: (04) 6533888 *Fax:* (04) 6575714
E-mail: penerbitusm@notes.usm.my or rashidah@usm.my
Web Site: www.lib.usm.my/press
Telex: MA40254 *Cable:* UNISAINS
Key Personnel
Chairman: Prof Jamjan Rajikan
Secretary: Ms Rashidah Begum
Chief Editor: Mr Akhiar Salleh *Tel:* (04) 6534422 *E-mail:* akhiar@notes.usm.my
Founded: 1974
Subjects: Biological Sciences, Chemistry, Chemical Engineering, Computer Science, Education, Electronics, Electrical Engineering, Management, Mathematics, Social Sciences, Sociology
Bookshop(s): Co-operative Bookshop Ltd, Universiti Sains Malaysia, d/a Perpustakaan Universiti Sains Malaysia, 11800 Pulau Pinang

Penerbitan Jaya Bakti+
No 28 & 30 Wisma Jaya Bakti, Jalan Cenderuh 2, Baut 4, Jalan Ipoh, 51200 Kuala Lumpur
Tel: (03) 6219399 *Fax:* (03) 6219585
Key Personnel
Man Dir: Silvaraju A L Kunjupillai
Founded: 1980
Membership(s): Malaysian Book Publishers Association.
ISBN Prefix(es): 967-900
Showroom(s): 30, Wisma Jaya Bakti, Jalan Cenderuh 2, Batu 4, Jalan Ipoh, 51200 Kuala Lumpur

Penerbitan Pelangi Sdn Bhd (Pelangi Publishing Pte Ltd)+
Jalan Pingai, Taman Pelangi, Johor Bahru, 80400 Johor Darul Takzim
E-mail: info@pelangibooks.com; ppsb@po.jaring.my
Web Site: www.pelangibooks.com

Key Personnel
Chief Executive Officer & Man Dir: Mr Sum Kown Cheek
Founded: 1979
Subjects: Art, English as a Second Language, Photography
ISBN Prefix(es): 967-951; 983-50; 983-878
Number of titles published annually: 200 Print
Total Titles: 8,000 Print
Branch Office(s)
Bangi, Selangor

Penerbitan Tinta+
32-B, Jalan Cemur, Off Jalan Tun Razak, 50400 Kuala Lumpur
Tel: (03) 4424163 *Fax:* (03) 4424640
Key Personnel
Dir: Mohd Haneefa
Founded: 1974
Subjects: Business, Education, English as a Second Language, Management, Marketing
ISBN Prefix(es): 983-9588; 983-044
Associate Companies: Fargoes Books Sdn Bhd
Subsidiaries: Penerbitan Fargoes Sdn Bhd

Institut Penyelidikan Minyak Kelapa Sawit Malaysia
PO Box 10620, 50720 Kuala Lumpur
Tel: (03) 8335155; (03) 8259775 *Fax:* (03) 8259446
E-mail: pub@porim.gov.my
Telex: MA 31609
Key Personnel
Dir-General: Dr Yusof bin Basiron
ISBN Prefix(es): 967-961

Perfect Frontier Sdn Bhd
B201, Block B, No 11, Jalan Sepadu, Taman United, Off Jalan Klang Lama, 58200 Kuala Lumpur
Tel: (03) 7832926 *Fax:* (03) 7816448
ISBN Prefix(es): 983-865

Preston Corporation Sdn Bhd
18 Jalan 19/3, 46300 Petaling Jaya, Selangor Darul Ehsan
Tel: (03) 7574222 *Fax:* (03) 7573607
Telex: Prest MA 37433
Subjects: Education
ISBN Prefix(es): 967-917
Associate Companies: Times Educational Co Sdn Bhd; Vista Productions Ltd, A7/F Melbourne Industrial Bldg, 16 Westlands Rd, Quarry Bay, Hong Kong; Preston Corporation (Pte) Ltd, 9 Irving Pl, Singapore 1336, Singapore

Pustaka Cipta Sdn Bhd+
58 C Jalan Kampung Attap, 50460 Kuala Lumpur
Tel: (03) 2744593 *Fax:* (03) 2749588
E-mail: rrapc@pc.jaring.my
Key Personnel
President: Baharuddin Zainal
Publication Dir: Rosihan Juara Baharuddin
Founded: 1985
Membership(s): IKATAN, Malaysian Burriputra Publishers Association.
Subjects: Art, Biography, Communications, Computer Science, Education, English as a Second Language, Fiction, Journalism, Literature, Literary Criticism, Essays, Nonfiction (General), Poetry, Publishing & Book Trade Reference, Religion - Islamic, Science (General), Science Fiction, Fantasy, Technology, Travel, Women's Studies
ISBN Prefix(es): 967-9974; 967-99962; 983-101
Associate Companies: Essential Mark (M) Sdn Bhd; Puncak Indah Sdn Bhd
Subsidiaries: Dasar Buku Sdn Bhd; Dasar Cetak Sdn Bhd; Dasar Padu Sdn Bhd

Pustaka Delta Pelajaran Sdn Bhd+
Lot 18 Jalan 51A/223, Jalan Sultan, 46770 Petaling Jaya, Selangor Darul Ehsan
Mailing Address: PO Box 621
Tel: (03) 7570000 *Fax:* (03) 7576688
Telex: MA20382 AB Delta
Key Personnel
Man Dir: Mr Lim Swee Sing; Mr Lim Kim Wah
Executive Dir: Ms Lee Yuet Yee
Group General Manager: Mr Phang Sang Choy; Mr Phang Sang Moi
Founded: 1979
Subjects: Economics, English as a Second Language, Environmental Studies, Geography, Geology, History, Mathematics, Religion - Islamic, Science (General)
ISBN Prefix(es): 967-67
Parent Company: Group of Delta Publishing
Subsidiaries: Baron Production Sdn Bhd; Delta Distributors Sdn Bhd; Gunung Mutiara Sdn Bhd; Tempo Publishing (M) Sdn Bhd; Gedung Ilum Sdn Bhd; Delta Publishing Sdn Bhd; Delta Editions Sdn Bhd; Penerbit Jayatinta Sdn Bhd
Branch Office(s)
No 174 Jalan Pasar, 41400 Kelang, Selangor Darul Ehsan

Pustaka Sistem Pelajaran Sdn Bhd+
17-22 Jl Satu, Ber Satu Industrial Park, 43200 Balakong, Selangor
Tel: (03) 904-7558; (03) 904-7017; (03) 904-7018 *Fax:* (03) 904-7573
Key Personnel
Man Dir: Michael Ong
Founded: 1973
ISBN Prefix(es): 967-902
Subsidiaries: Pustaka Yakin Pelajar Sdn Bhd; B H S Book Printing Sdn Bhd
Bookshop(s): The Bintang Store, 251 Jl Tun Sambanthan, 50470 Kuala Lumpur

SBT Professional Publications
Menara Summit, 10th floor, 14-20, Jl Hang Lekir, 47600 Persiaran Kewajipan
Tel: (03) 80265811; (03) 80235663 *Fax:* (03) 8023566; (03) 80265999
E-mail: admin@sbtpp.com
Web Site: www.sbtpp.com
Key Personnel
Editor: Vivien Khoo
Manager: Ah Tu Yeoh
Founded: 1985
Membership(s): Malaysian Book Publishers Association.
Subjects: Accounting
ISBN Prefix(es): 967-9924

See & Read Series, *imprint of* Mecron Sdn Bhd

Syarikat Cultural Supplies Sdn Bhd+
306 Block C Glomac Business Centre, 10 Jalan 556/1, Kelana Jaya, 47301 Selangor Darul Ehsan
Tel: (03) 7046628; (03) 7554103; (03) 7915728 *Fax:* (03) 7046629
E-mail: malian@po.jaring.my
Key Personnel
Dir: Kow Ching Chuan
Founded: 1977
Subjects: Education
ISBN Prefix(es): 967-9917

Tempo Publishing (M) Sdn Bhd+
Bilik 118, Wisma Delta 18, Jalan 51A/223, Jalan 51A/223, 46100 Petaling Jaya, Selangor Darul Ehsan
Tel: (03) 7570000 *Fax:* (03) 7576688; (03) 7587001
Telex: MA20382 AB Delta
Key Personnel
Man Dir: Mr Lim Swee Sing; Mr Lim Kim Wah
Executive Dir: Ms Lee Yuet Yee

Group General Manager: Mr Phang Sang Choy; Mr Phang Sang Moi
Founded: 1990
Subjects: Fiction, Literature, Literary Criticism, Essays, Nonfiction (General)
ISBN Prefix(es): 983-888
Parent Company: Group of Delta Publishing
Subsidiaries: Pustaka Delta Pelajaran Sdn Bhd; Baron Production Sdn Bhd; Delta Distributors Sdn Bhd; Gunung Mutiara Sdn Bhd; Penerbit Jayatinta Sdn Bhd; Gedung Ilmu Sdn Bhd; Delta Publishing Sdn Bhd; Delta Editions Sdn Bhd
Branch Office(s)
No 174 Jalan Pasar, 41400 Kelang, Selangor Darul Ehsan

Text Books Malaysia Sdn Bhd
39 Jalan Buluh Kesap, 85007 Segamat, Johore Darul Ta'zim
Mailing Address: PO Box 30, 85007 Segamat, Johore
Tel: (074) 911181 Fax: (074) 911181
E-mail: textbook@tm.net.my
Founded: 1969
ISBN Prefix(es): 967-9929
Bookshop(s): Tai Kuang & Co, 41 Jalan Awang, 85000 Segamat, Johor D Ta'Zim

Time Track (M) Sdn Bhd
69, Medan Gopeng 5, Jalan Lapangan Terbang, 31350 Ipoh, Perak
Tel: (05) 3124329; (05) 3127541 Fax: (05) 2630305
ISBN Prefix(es): 983-069

Times, imprint of Federal Publications Sdn Bhd

Times Educational Co Sdn Bhd
22 Jalan 19/3, Petaling Jaya, Selangor Daral Ehsan, 46300 Selangor
Tel: (03) 7571766 Fax: (03) 7573607
Telex: MA 37433 Cable: Timesbooks
Subjects: Cookery
ISBN Prefix(es): 967-919
Parent Company: Times Educational Co Ltd, Hong Kong
Associate Companies: Preston Corporation Sdn Bhd; Preston-Times Printing & Publishing, Selangor; Preston Corporation (Private) Ltd, Singapore
Orders to: Preston Corporation Sdn Bhd, 18 Jalan 19/3, Petaling Jaya, Selangor

Trix Corporation Sdn Bhd+
Pusat Bandar Damansara, Damansara Heights, Block G, Room 2 level 6, 50490 Kuala Lumpur
Tel: (03) 253 2019 Fax: (03) 255 1068
E-mail: cpd@trix.po.my
Key Personnel
Man Dir: Mr B S Neoh
Subjects: Career Development, Education, Securities
ISBN Prefix(es): 983-9102

Tropical Press Sdn Bhd+
56-1 Jalan Maarof, Bangsar Baru, 59100 Kuala Lumpur
Tel: (03) 22825138; (03) 22825338 Fax: (03) 22823526
E-mail: feedback@tpress.po.my
Key Personnel
Man Dir: Winston Ee
Founded: 1975
Membership(s): the Malaysian Book Publishers Association.
Subjects: Child Care & Development, Mathematics, Natural History, Physical Sciences, Science (General), Technology

ISBN Prefix(es): 967-73
Associate Companies: Art Printing Works Sdn Bhd

Uni-Text Book Co
42B Jl SS 20/10, Damansara Kim, 47400 Petaling Jaya, Selangor Darul Ehsan
Tel: (03) 7185426
Key Personnel
Man Dir: Bob E S Lim
Editorial: E S Lim
Production: E H Lim
Sales: Theresa Chung
Subjects: Education, History, Literature, Literary Criticism, Essays, Regional Interests, Religion - Other
ISBN Prefix(es): 967-935
Associate Companies: Uni-Text Distributors Private Ltd, 42B Jl SS 20/10, Damansara Kim, 47400 Petaling Jaya, Sellangor Darul Ehsan

Unit Penerbitan Akademik Cancelori, Universiti Teknologi Malaysia, see Penerbit Universiti Teknologi Malaysia

Penerbit Universiti Teknologi Malaysia
(Universiti Teknologi Malaysia Press)+
Formerly Unit Penerbitan Akademik Cancelori, Universiti Teknologi Malaysia
34-38 JLN Kebudayaan 1, Taman Universiti, 81300 Skudai, Johor
Tel: (07) 521 8131; (07) 521 8180; (07) 521 8166 Fax: (07) 521 8174
E-mail: penerbit@utm.my
Web Site: www.penerbit.utm.my
Telex: MA60205
Key Personnel
Dir: Dr Ummul Khair Ahmad
Marketing & Sales: Yosman Mohd Bain
Founded: 1986
Subjects: Aeronautics, Aviation, Behavioral Sciences, Chemistry, Chemical Engineering, Civil Engineering, Computer Science, Education, Electronics, Electrical Engineering, Engineering (General), Mathematics, Mechanical Engineering, Physical Sciences, Physics, Regional Interests, Religion - Islamic, Science (General), Social Sciences, Sociology, Technology
ISBN Prefix(es): 983-52
Number of titles published annually: 30 Print
Total Titles: 350 Print
Ultimate Parent Company: Universiti Teknologi Malaysia, Skudai, Johor

University of Malaya, Department of Publications+
Lembah Pantai, 50603 Kuala Lumpur
Tel: (03) 79574361 Fax: (03) 79574473
E-mail: terbit@um.edu.my
Web Site: www.um.edu.my/umpress
Telex: MA 39845 Cable: VARSITIPRESS KUALA LUMPUR
Key Personnel
Head of Dept, Publicity, Rights & Permissions, Editorial: Dr Hamedi Mohd Adnan
E-mail: hamedi@um.edu.my
Founded: 1954
Subjects: Biography, Economics, Fiction, Foreign Countries, Government, Political Science, History, Medicine, Nursing, Dentistry, Poetry, Science (General), Social Sciences, Sociology
ISBN Prefix(es): 967-9940; 983-9705; 983-100
Number of titles published annually: 30 Print
Total Titles: 250 Print

Utusan Publications & Distributors Sdn Bhd+
108 Jalan, Pudu ulu, Cheras, 56100 Kuala Lumpur
Tel: (03) 9287 7777 Fax: (03) 9282 7751
E-mail: shafina@utusan.com.my
Web Site: www.utusangroup.com.my

Key Personnel
Group Editor-in-Chief: Khalid Mohd
E-mail: khalidm@utusan.com.my
Group Manager, Publishing: Roselina Johari
E-mail: rose@utusan.com.my
Subjects: Business, Economics, Education, Management, Religion - Other, Technology
ISBN Prefix(es): 967-61

Vinpress Sdn Bhd+
5 & 7 Lorong Datuk Sulaiman 7, Taman Tun Dr Ismail, 60000 Kuala Lumpur
Tel: (03) 7173333; (03) 7188877 Fax: (03) 7192942
E-mail: vinsoh@pc.jaring.my
Key Personnel
Man Dir: Thomas Soh
Founded: 1985
Membership(s): Malaysian Book Publishers Association.
Subjects: Ethnicity, Health, Nutrition, Philosophy, Regional Interests, Religion - Other
ISBN Prefix(es): 967-81
Associate Companies: Vintrade SDN BHD

Well Loved Tales, imprint of Mecron Sdn Bhd

Maldive Islands

General Information

Capital: Male
Language: Dhivehi (Maldivian)
Religion: Islam is the state religion (most Sunni Muslim)
Population: 226,000
Currency: 100 laari (larees) = 1 rufiyaa (maldivian rupee)

Non-Formal Education Centre
Salahuddeen Bldg, Male 20-03
Tel: 325763 Fax: 322231
Key Personnel
Deputy Dir: Abdul Raheem Hasan
Founded: 1986
Subjects: Agriculture, Child Care & Development, Education, English as a Second Language, Environmental Studies, Health, Nutrition, Religion - Islamic, Science (General), Social Sciences, Sociology, Sports, Athletics
ISBN Prefix(es): 99915-50; 99915-58
Parent Company: Ministry of Education

Novelty Printers & Publishers+
Maafannu, Vaarey Villa, Izzudhdheen Magu, Male 20317
Tel: 318844 Fax: 327039
E-mail: novelty@dhivehinet.net.mv
Key Personnel
Chairman: Ali Hussain
Man Dir: Asad Ali
Founded: 1965
Subjects: Animals, Pets, Foreign Countries, Regional Interests, Travel
ISBN Prefix(es): 99915-3
Subsidiaries: Novelty Bookshop

Mali

General Information

Capital: Bamako
Language: French
Religion: Predominantly Islamic

MALI

Population: 10 million
Currency: 100 centimes = 1 CFA franc
Export/Import Information: Member of the West African Economic Community. No tariff on books but subject to VAT at varying rates. Advertising matter (more than single copy) subject to tariff, import tax and VAT. All goods subject to local tax of percentage of customs value. Import license required. Importation is either by private importers or state enterprises. Exchange controls for non-franc zone.
Copyright: Berne (see Copyright Conventions, pg xi)

EDIM SA+
642 av Mardiagne, Bamako
Mailing Address: BP 2412, Bamako
Tel: 225522 *Fax:* 238503
Key Personnel
Man Dir: Aliou Tomota
Editor: Hr E Alain Kone
Founded: 1972
Subjects: Biography, Fiction, History, Nonfiction (General), Poetry, Religion - Other, Social Sciences, Sociology
ISBN Prefix(es): 2-913213
Subsidiaries: Editions populaires; Imprimerie Kasse Keita; Imprimerie nationale
Bookshop(s): Librairie Papeterie du Sondan, BP 21, Bamako

Malta

General Information

Capital: Valletta
Language: Maltese and English (official), Italian widely spoken
Religion: Predominantly Roman Catholic
Population: 365,000
Bank Hours: 0830-1230 Monday-Thursday; 0830-1230, 1700-1900 Friday; 0830-1200 Saturday
Shop Hours: 0900-1300, 1530-1900 Monday-Saturday
Currency: 1,000 mils = 100 cents = 1 Maltese lira
Export/Import Information: No tariff on books or advertising. No import license required. Exchange control by Central Bank. Trade Association agreement with the European Economic Community all Malta made goods that enter the European Economic Community are duty and quota free. Different rates of duty apply for imports with special preference for European Economic Community countries.
Copyright: Berne, UCC (see Copyright Conventions, pg xi)

Fondazzjoni Patrimonju Malti+
115 Triq it-Teatru l-Qadim, Valletta VLT 09
Tel: 21231515 *Fax:* 21250118
E-mail: patrimonju@keyworld.net
Web Site: www.patrimonju.org.mt
Key Personnel
Administration Executive: Peter Calascione
Tel: 21244777
Founded: 1996
Specialize in catalogues raisonne, collections of essays, art quality of Maltese history & cultural heritage subjects (known collectively as "Melitensia").
Subjects: Antiques, Archaeology, Art, Biography
ISBN Prefix(es): 9932-10
Number of titles published annually: 5 Print
Total Titles: 54 Print

Gaulitana
2, Triq Gedrin, Rabat - Gozo VCT 104
Tel: 2155-4212 *Fax:* 2155-4598
E-mail: joseph.bezzina@um.edu.mt
Founded: 1985
Subjects: History, Religion - Catholic, Travel
ISBN Prefix(es): 99909-57
Number of titles published annually: 6 Print

Gozo Press
Mgarr Rd, Gh'sielem, Gh'sielem, Gozo GSM102
Mailing Address: Str 1 Main Gate St, 1st Floor, Str 2 Victoria, Gozo VCT 103
Tel: 551534; 564395 *Fax:* 560857
E-mail: gozopress@orbit.net.mt
Key Personnel
Dir: Achilles F Cauchi
Manager: Carmel Mizzi
Membership(s): The Periodical & Book Publishers Association.
Subjects: Crafts, Games, Hobbies, History, Literature, Literary Criticism, Essays, Religion - Other
Orders to: Gozo Press Office, Main Gate St, Victoria, Gozo

Media Centre+
Media Centre Complex, National Rd, Blata I-Bajda HMR 02
Tel: 21249005; 21223047; 21244913; 21247460; 25699113; 25699114; 25699115 *Fax:* 21246716
Key Personnel
Man Dir: Jeffrey Calafato
Manager Publications: George Fava
Manager Marketing: Sylvana Magro
Founded: 1981
Subjects: Biblical Studies, Communications, Education, Religion - Catholic, Social Sciences, Sociology
ISBN Prefix(es): 99909-2
Book Club(s): Klaab Qari Nisrani (Maltese Language Publications)

Merlin Library Ltd
Mountbatten Str, Blata 1-Badja
Tel: 221205; 23 44 38 *Fax:* 221135
E-mail: mail@merlinlibrary.com
Web Site: www.merlinlibrary.com
Key Personnel
Dir: Arthur J Gruppetta
Founded: 1964
ISBN Prefix(es): 99909-1

PEG Ltd, see Publishers' Enterprises Group (PEG) Ltd

Progress Press Co Ltd+
Strickland House, 341 St Paul St, Valletta VLT 01
Tel: 21241464; 21241469; 21241411; 21241412 *Fax:* 21241171
Telex: Mw 341 *Cable:* PROGRESS
Key Personnel
Man Dir: Dr Austin Bencini
Publication Manager: Joseph Tortell
E-mail: jtortell@timesofmalta.com
Founded: 1957
Also wholesaler.
Subjects: Literature, Literary Criticism, Essays
ISBN Prefix(es): 99909-3
Number of titles published annually: 10 Print
Total Titles: 63 Print
Parent Company: The Allied Newspapers Ltd, 341 St Paul St, Valletta VLT07, Vincent Buhagiar
Distributed by Bay Foreign Language Books
Distributor for Apple; Brimax; Brown Watson; Carlton; David & Charles; Egmont; Hodder Headline; New Holland; The Octopus Group; Orion; Osprey; Piatkus; Time Warner
Bookshop(s): 4 Castille Pl, Valletta VLT 01

Publishers' Enterprises Group (PEG) Ltd
PEG Bldg, UB7 Industrial Estate, San Gwann SGN09
Tel: 21440083; 21448539; 21490540 *Fax:* 21488908
E-mail: contact@peg.com.mt
Web Site: www.peg.com.mt
Key Personnel
Man Dir, Editorial, Rights & Permissions: Emanuel Debattista
Sales: Victor Mifsud
Production & Publicity: Gaetan Cilia
Founded: 1983
Subjects: Cookery, Crafts, Games, Hobbies, Education, Outdoor Recreation, Travel
ISBN Prefix(es): 99909-0

The University of Malta Publications Section
The University of Malta, Administration Bldg, Msida MSD06
Tel: 21333903-6 *Fax:* 21336450
Web Site: www.um.edu.mt
Telex: Mw 407 Hieduc *Cable:* University Malta
Founded: 1953
Subjects: Ethnicity, Language Arts, Linguistics, Law, Natural History, Regional Interests

Martinique

General Information

Capital: Fort-de-France
Language: French and Creole
Religion: Predominantly Roman Catholic
Population: 359,579
Currency: 100 centimes = 1 French franc
Export/Import Information: Tariff same as France. Overseas tax and reduced VAT on books. Small quantity of advertising free. No import licenses required. Exchange restrictions as in France.
Copyright: Berne (see Copyright Conventions, pg xi)

Editions Gondwana+
Morne Pavillon Tartane, 97220 Trinite
Tel: 580676; 580014 *Fax:* 580014
Key Personnel
Contact: Eric Leroy
Founded: 1987
Subjects: Agriculture, Archaeology, Gardening, Plants
ISBN Prefix(es): 2-908490
Distributed by Distique (France Metropolitan & Europe)

George Lise-Huyghes des Etages
108 rue de la Republique, 97200 Fort-de-France
Tel: 736819
Subjects: Behavioral Sciences, Education, Human Relations, Psychology, Psychiatry
ISBN Prefix(es): 2-909260

Virlogeux Francoise-COMEDIT
Rue de la Reine-Hortense, 97229 Les Trois Ilets
Tel: 683985 *Fax:* 683423
Founded: 1994
ISBN Prefix(es): 2-910746

Mauritania

General Information

Capital: Nouakchott
Language: Arabic (official and national), Poular, Wolof and Solinke (national)
Religion: Islamic
Population: 2.1 million
Bank Hours: 0800-1115, 1430-1630 Monday-Friday
Shop Hours: Vary. Generally 0800-1200, 0730-1500 Saturday-Thursday. Some closed Monday morning, some open Sunday morning
Currency: 5 khoums = 1 ouguiya
Export/Import Information: Member of the West African Economic Community. No tariff on books. Advertising matter (other than single copies) subject to fiscal, customs duty and added tax. Import licenses and exchange controls apply to imports outside of EEC and franc zone.
Copyright: Berne (see Copyright Conventions, pg xi)

Imprimerie Commerciale et Administrative de Mauritanie
BP 164, Nouakchott
Subjects: Education

Mauritius

General Information

Capital: Port Louis
Language: English (official) and Creole
Religion: Hindu, Christian and Muslim
Population: 1.1 million
Bank Hours: 1000-1400 Monday-Friday, 0930-1130 Saturday
Shop Hours: 0800-1600 or later Monday-Saturday
Currency: 100 cents = 1 Mauritian rupee
Export/Import Information: No tariff on books and advertising but there is a special levy. No import license required.
Copyright: UCC, Berne (see Copyright Conventions, pg xi)

African Cultural Centre
Bell Village, Port Louis
Tel: 2124131 *Fax:* 2088620
Founded: 1985
ISBN Prefix(es): 99903-904

Mauritus Bhojpuri Institute
15 Menagerie Rd, Cassis, Port Louis
Tel: 2082956 *Fax:* 4643445
Distributed by ELP; EOI; Mauritius; Mauritius Reading Association; Port Louis; Rose Hill; Vacoas

De l'edition Bukie Banane
5 Lari Edwin Ythier, Rose Hill
Tel: 4542327
E-mail: limem@intnet.mu
Web Site: pages.intnet.mu/develog/
Key Personnel
Man Dir: Dev Virahsawmy
Founded: 1979
Subjects: Drama, Theater, Poetry, Regional Interests
Orders to: Librairie le Cygne, Royal Rd, Rose Hill

Editions Capucines
20 Ave des Capucines, Quatre Bornes
Tel: 4641563 *Fax:* 4641563
E-mail: edcapsee@intnet.mu
Key Personnel
Manager: S Seewoochurn *Tel:* 464 1563
Founded: 1994
Subjects: Asian Studies, Education, History, Religion - Hindu, Religion - Other
Number of titles published annually: 5 Print
Total Titles: 8 Print
Distributed by Editions de l'Ocean Indien; Editions Le Printemps
Distributor for Editions de l'Ocean Indien

EOI Ltd, see Editions de l'Ocean Indien Ltd

Golden Publications
4 Cite Pere Laval St, Port Louis
Tel: 2416640
ISBN Prefix(es): 99903-44

Government Printer (Imprimerie Nationale)
La Tour Koenig, GRNW, Port Louis
Tel: 2345294; 2345295

Hemco Publications
7 Virgil Naz St, Rose Hill
Tel: 4643141
Key Personnel
Editor: Dr H Gyaram
Founded: 1993
Subjects: Education, Medicine, Nursing, Dentistry, Religion - Buddhist, Religion - Catholic, Religion - Hindu, Religion - Islamic, Religion - Other

Imprimerie et Papeterie Commerciale, IPC
23 Menagerie Rd, Cassis
Tel: 2124190; 2127701; 2127702 *Fax:* 2083523
ISBN Prefix(es): 99903-38

Editions de l'Ocean Indien Ltd+
Stanley, Rose Hill
Tel: 4646761 *Fax:* 4643445
E-mail: eoibooks@intnet.mu
Telex: MESYND 4739 IW
Key Personnel
Gen Mgr: A Beeharry Panray
Founded: 1977
Subjects: Accounting, Agriculture, Art, Biography, Business, Career Development, Computer Science, Cookery, Economics, Education, Fiction, Geography, Geology, Health, Nutrition, Literature, Literary Criticism, Essays, Management, Marketing, Philosophy, Poetry, Science (General), Travel
ISBN Prefix(es): 2-7410
Number of titles published annually: 89 Print
Total Titles: 365 Print
Subsidiaries: Mauritius Printing Specialists Ltd
Branch Office(s)
Gound floor, Manhattan, Curepipe *Tel:* 6749065
Vel Plaza, Royal Rd, Goodlands *Tel:* 2838729
1st Floor, NPF Bldg, Jules Koeing St, Port-Louis *Tel:* 2111310
30, Joseph Riviere St, Kung Hing Mall Bldg, Port-Louis *Tel:* 2423738
Student Complex, University of Mauritius, Reduit *Tel:* 4542258
Arcades Rond Point, Rose-Hill *Tel:* 4646391
Virginie Commercial Centre, Centre de Flacq *Tel:* 4132273
Distributed by Librarie L' Harmattan; African Books Collective Ltd (UK)
Distributor for Librarie L' Harmattan

EDITIONS Le Printemps+
4 Club Rd, Vacoas
Tel: 6961017 *Fax:* 6867302
E-mail: elp@intnet.mu
Key Personnel
Man Dir: Ahmud Islam Sulliman
Subjects: Biography
ISBN Prefix(es): 99903-23
Subsidiaries: AIS Marketing
Divisions: Editions Le Printemps Ltd

Vizavi Editions+
29, rue Saint Georges St, Port Louis
Tel: 2112435 *Fax:* 2113047
E-mail: vizavi@intnet.mu
Key Personnel
Dir: Mrs P M Siew
Founded: 1993
Membership(s): Association of Mauritian Publishers.
Subjects: Biography, Cookery, Government, Political Science, History, Literature, Literary Criticism, Essays, Nonfiction (General)
ISBN Prefix(es): 99908-37
Number of titles published annually: 3 Print

Mexico

General Information

Capital: Mexico City
Language: Spanish
Religion: Predominantly Roman Catholic
Population: 92.4 million
Bank Hours: 0900-1330 Monday-Friday
Shop Hours: 1000-1900 Monday, Tuesday, Thursday, Friday; 1100-2000 Wednesday and Saturday
Currency: 100 centavos = 1 Mexican peso
Export/Import Information: Member of the Latin American Free Trade Association. Foreign language books and textbooks generally dutied per kg legal weight, children's picture books ad valorem or per kg, whichever greater, and require import license. Three copies of non-Spanish advertising catalogs free but all others require license and dutied ad valorem. Customs request from Bank of Mexico all necessary information to decide cases of tariff.
Copyright: UCC, Berne, Buenos Aires (see Copyright Conventions, pg xi)

Aconcagua Ediciones y Publicaciones SA
Xochicalco 352, Col Narvarte, 03020 Mexico, DF
Tel: (05) 536-1660 *Fax:* (05) 5432280
Key Personnel
Dir: Julio Sanz Crespo
Subjects: Education, History, How-to, Literature, Literary Criticism, Essays, Religion - Other, Technology
ISBN Prefix(es): 968-6000
Associate Companies: Editorial Timun Mas SA, Spain
Branch Office(s)
Ediciones Ceac SA, Spain

Addison Wesley, *imprint of* Pearson Educacion de Mexico, SA de CV

Adivinar y Multiplicar, SA de CV (Guess & Multiply)+
Av Cuauhtemoc 1129-202, Col Letran-Valle, 03650 Mexico, DF
Tel: (055) 5604-1005; (055) 1304-0802 (mobile) *Fax:* (055) 5604-1583
E-mail: multiplimx@msn.com
Key Personnel
Dir General: Jesus E Rodriguez y Rodriguez
Founded: 1985
Publisher of didactic books for children.
Subjects: Education, Mathematics
ISBN Prefix(es): 968-7458
Number of titles published annually: 1 Print
Total Titles: 1 Print

MEXICO

Editorial AGATA SA de CV+
Pino Suares No 169, Colcentro Hidalgo, 44100 Guadalajara Jalisco
Tel: (033) 614-4902; (03) 614-4909 *Fax:* (033) 6138429
Key Personnel
Editor: Jaime Alvarez G Alvarez del Castillo
Founded: 1986
Membership(s): National Commerce Association; National Art Graphics Association; Publishers Association.
Subjects: Drama, Theater, Journalism, Literature, Literary Criticism, Essays, Poetry, Regional Interests, Travel
ISBN Prefix(es): 968-7310; 970-657

AGT Editor SA
Au Progreso No 202 PA Escandon, Col Escandon, 11800 Mexico, DF
Tel: (05) 273-9228 *Fax:* (05) 2771696
Key Personnel
Contact: Roger Grasa Soler
Founded: 1978
Membership(s): the Mexican National Publishing Industry.
Subjects: Agriculture, Biological Sciences, Veterinary Science
ISBN Prefix(es): 968-463
Imprints: Rustica

Aguilar Altea Taurus Alfaguara SA de CV
Av Universidad 767, Colonia Del Valle, 03100 Mexico, DF
Tel: (05) 688 89 66; (05) 688 82 77; (05) 688 75 66 *Fax:* (05) 6042304; (05) 6886538
E-mail: info@editorialaguilar.com
Web Site: www.alfaguara.com.mx
Key Personnel
Dir: Miguel Angel Cayuela
Subjects: Advertising, Biography, Drama, Theater, Education, Fiction, Language Arts, Linguistics, Literature, Literary Criticism, Essays, Music, Dance, Philosophy, Photography, Poetry, Psychology, Psychiatry, Self-Help, Social Sciences, Sociology
ISBN Prefix(es): 968-19
Parent Company: Grupo Santillana

Alfaomega Grupo Editor SA de CV+
Pitagoras 1139, Colonia Del Valle, 03100 Mexico, DF
Tel: (05) 5755022 (ext 126); (05) 5755022 (ext 222) *Fax:* (052) 5752490
E-mail: universitaria@alfaomega.com.mx
Web Site: www.alfaomega.com.mx
Key Personnel
Dir: Benito Juarez
Dir de Edicione: Ferreyrs C Gonzalo
  E-mail: gferreyrs@spin.com.mx
Founded: 1965
Subjects: Computer Science, Electronics, Electrical Engineering, Engineering (General), Management, Microcomputers, Technology
ISBN Prefix(es): 968-6062; 968-6223
Associate Companies: Publicaciones Marcombo SA

Alianza Editorial Mexicana, SA de CV
Renacimiento No 180, San Juan Tlihuaca, 02400 Mexico, DF
Tel: (05) 5618333; (05) 6704712 *Fax:* (05) 5619797
Key Personnel
Man Dir: Alberto E Diaz
ISBN Prefix(es): 968-6001; 968-6354; 968-6423
Associate Companies: Alianza Editorial SA, Spain

Allyn & Bacon, *imprint of* Pearson Educacion de Mexico, SA de CV

Ediciones Alpe+
Artemio del Valle Arizpe 18-er Piso, Col del Valle, 03100 Mexico, DF
Tel: (05) 5365749; (05) 2033157 *Fax:* (05) 2033157
Founded: 1991
Subjects: Cookery, Fiction, Health, Nutrition, Humor, Poetry, Radio, TV, Religion - Hindu, Romance, Self-Help
ISBN Prefix(es): 968-6426

Arbol Editorial SA de CV+
Ave Cuauhtemoc, No 1430, Col Santa Cruz Atoyac, 03310 Mexico, DF
Tel: (05) 6887677; (05) 6057600
Key Personnel
Man Dir, Production: Gerardo Gally
Rights & Permissions: Gilda Moreno
Founded: 1979
Subjects: Drama, Theater, Environmental Studies, Health, Nutrition, Religion - Other
ISBN Prefix(es): 968-461

Ariel, see Editorial Planeta Mexicana SA

Grupo Editorial Armonia+
Rio Balsas 101, Colonia Cuauhtemoc, 06500 Mexico, DF
Tel: 54 42 96 00
E-mail: corporativo@grupoarmonia.com.mx
Web Site: www.grupoarmonia.com.mx
Key Personnel
Founder: Maria Eugenia Moreno
General Dir: Liliana Moreno
International Development Dir: Ileana Ramirez
Planning & Development Dir: Javier Pina
Founded: 1977
Membership(s): the Mexican Association of Publishers.
Subjects: Cookery, Fashion, Health, Nutrition, House & Home
ISBN Prefix(es): 968-6598

Artes de Mexico y del Mundo SA de CV+
Plaza Rio de Janeiro 52, Colonia Roma, 06700 Mexico, DF
Tel: (05) 208 3684; (05) 525 4036; (05) 525 5905 *Fax:* (05) 525 5925
E-mail: artesmex@internet.com.mx; artesdemexico@artesdemexico.com
Web Site: www.artesdemexico.com
Key Personnel
Contact: Alberto Ruy Sanchez Lacy
Founded: 1953
Subjects: Architecture & Interior Design, Art, Poetry

Editores Asociados Mexicanos SA de CV (EDAMEX)+
Heriberto Frias No 1104, Del Valle, 03100 Mexico, DF
Tel: (05) 5598588 *Fax:* (05) 5757035; (05) 5750555
Web Site: www.edamex.com
Key Personnel
Man Dir: Manuel G Colmenares
Executive President: Octavio V Colmenares
Sales: Irene Fohri
Production: Antonio Escamilla
Founded: 1963
Also acts as Literary Agent for authors.
Subjects: Economics, Government, Political Science, Humor, Literature, Literary Criticism, Essays, Social Sciences, Sociology
ISBN Prefix(es): 968-409; 970-661
Associate Companies: Colmenares Editores SA; Editorial Meridiano SA
Divisions: Noroeste
Bookshop(s): Centro Cultural Edamex, Mexico DF

Editorial Avante SA de Cv
Luis Gonzalez Obregon No 9, Col Centro, 06020 Mexico, DF
Tel: (05) 5214548; (05) 5217563; (05) 5127634; (05) 5127563 *Fax:* (05) 5215245
E-mail: editorialavante@infosel.net.mx
Web Site: www.editorialavante.com.mx
Key Personnel
Man Dir: Mario Alberto Hinojosa Saenz
Production: Ana Luisa Quiros Esteban
Sales, Publicity: Luis Quiros Esteban
Founded: 1950
Subjects: Biography, Drama, Theater, Education, Language Arts, Linguistics, Poetry, Social Sciences, Sociology
ISBN Prefix(es): 968-6006
Imprints: Impresora Galve SA; Impresora Multiple SA; Heidel Impresos SA de CV

Azteca, *imprint of* Fondo de Cultura Economica

Editorial Azteca SA+
Calle de la Luna No 225, Col Guerrero, 06300 Mexico, DF
Tel: (05) 5261157 *Cable:* Edasa
Key Personnel
Man Dir: Alfonso Alemon Jalomo
Sales Dir: Juan Alemon Jalomo
Founded: 1956
Subjects: Literature, Literary Criticism, Essays, Science (General)
ISBN Prefix(es): 968-6008

Editorial Banca y Comercio SA de CV
Insurgentes No 107, 3er Piso, 06600 Mexico, DF
Tel: (05) 2089692; (05) 2081785; (05) 2081705 *Fax:* (05) 2081803
E-mail: edbyc@prodigy.net
Web Site: www.edbyc.com.mx
Key Personnel
Man Dir: Carlos Prieto Sierra
Assistant Manager: Amparo Quintanar
Founded: 1934
Subjects: Business, Law, Mathematics
ISBN Prefix(es): 968-6010

Biblioteca Interamericana Bilingue, *imprint of* Ediciones Euroamericanas

Libreria y Ediciones Botas SA
Sierra No 52, Col Centro, 06020 Mexico, DF
Tel: (05) 5702-4083; (05) 5702-5403 *Fax:* (02) 55101788
E-mail: botas@mail.nextgeninter.net.mx
Key Personnel
Man Dir: Andres Botas Herandez
Sales Dir: Laura Botas Herandez
Founded: 1910
Subjects: Art, Economics, Fiction, History, Law, Medicine, Nursing, Dentistry, Philosophy, Science (General)
ISBN Prefix(es): 970-92521

Ediciones el Caballito SA
Ixpantenco No 20-A, Los Reyes Coyoacan, 04330 Mexico, DF
Tel: (05) 5443284; (05) 5963400
Key Personnel
Rights & Permissions & Man Dir, Editorial: Manuel Lopez Gallo
Sales: Alfonso Garcia Espino
Production & Rights & Permissions: Teresa Dey
Founded: 1967
Subjects: Economics, History, Nonfiction (General), Regional Interests, Social Sciences, Sociology
ISBN Prefix(es): 968-6125
Associate Companies: Impoli SA, Isabel la Catolica 922, Col Postal, 03140 Mexico, DF
Subsidiaries: Presencia Latinoamerica
Bookshop(s): Libreria del Soltano SA, Ave Juarez 64, Satano Centro, Mexico, DF 1

PUBLISHERS

MEXICO

Camion Escolar y Limusa, *imprint of* Editorial Limusa SA de CV

Casa & Gente, *imprint of* Cuernavaca Editorial S A

Editorial la Cebra
Av Revolucion 528-700, Col San Pedro de Los Pinos, 03800 Mexico, DF
Tel: (05) 2779529; (05) 2779797; (05) 2737717; (05) 2737888 *Fax:* (05) 2737866
E-mail: info@adcebra.com
Key Personnel
Dir General & Administrator: Andrzej Rattinger Aranda
Editor: Alejandro Ayala; Selene Monforte; Diana Penagos
Founded: 1992
Publishers of ADCEBRA, Mexico's Marketing & Advertising magazine.

CEMCA, see Centro de Estudios Mexicanos y Centroamericanos

CEMLA, see Centro de Estudios Monetarios Latinoamericanos (CEMLA)

CEMO SA, see Centro Editorial Mexicano Osiris SA

Centro de Estudios Mexicanos y Centroamericanos+
Sierra Leona No 330, Lomas de Chapultepec, 11000 Mexico, DF
Mailing Address: Apdo 41-879, 11000 Mexico, DF
Tel: (05) 5 40 59 21; (05) 5 40 59 22 *Fax:* (05) 2 02 77 94
E-mail: cemca.lib@francia.org.mx
Web Site: www.francia.org.mx/cemca
Key Personnel
Dir: Joelle Gaillac *E-mail:* cemca.pub@francia.org.mx
Head of Publications: Catherine Marielle
Founded: 1982
Edition De Boccard (Europe).
Subjects: Anthropology, Archaeology, Biological Sciences, Earth Sciences, Economics, Environmental Studies, Ethnicity, Foreign Countries, Government, Political Science, History, Music, Dance, Science (General), Social Sciences, Sociology
ISBN Prefix(es): 968-6029
Subsidiaries: Ministere des Affaires Etrangeres
Distributed by INAH

Centro Editorial Mexicano Osiris SA
Sierra Ventana No 545, Col Lomas de Chapultepec, 11000 Mexico, DF
Tel: (05) 5406902; (05) 2027185 *Fax:* (05) 2027185
Key Personnel
Contact: Thania Nicolopulos Joannides
Founded: 1976
Subjects: Astrology, Occult, Cookery, Literature, Literary Criticism, Essays, Parapsychology, Poetry

Editora Cientifica Medica Latinoamerican SA de CV
Fernando Alencastre No 110, Col Lomas Virreyes, 11000 Mexico, DF
Tel: (05) 55206702 *Fax:* (05) 52020926
Founded: 1986
Subjects: Computer Science, Medicine, Nursing, Dentistry
ISBN Prefix(es): 968-6166

El Coleccionista, Centro Historico, *imprint of* Cuernavaca Editorial S A

El Colegio de Mexico AC
Camino al Ajusco No 20, Col Pedregal de Santa Teresa, 10740 Mexico, DF
Mailing Address: Apdo Postal 20671, 01000 Mexico, DF
Tel: (05) 54953080 *Fax:* (05) 54493083
E-mail: fgomez@colmex.mx
Web Site: www.colmex.mx
Telex: 1777585 Colme *Cable:* COLMEX
Key Personnel
Publications Coordinator: Marta Lilia Prieto
Founded: 1940
Subjects: Anthropology, Asian Studies, Business, Economics, Environmental Studies, Government, Political Science, History, Language Arts, Linguistics, Library & Information Sciences, Literature, Literary Criticism, Essays, Nonfiction (General), Philosophy, Science (General), Social Sciences, Sociology, Women's Studies
ISBN Prefix(es): 968-12

Colegio de Postgraduados en Ciencias Agricolas
Km 36.5 Carretera Mex-Texcoco, Montecillo, 56230 Mexico, DF
Tel: (0595) 95 2 02 00; (055) 58 04 59 00
E-mail: seia@colpos.mx
Web Site: www.colpos.mx
Key Personnel
Secretary: Dr Alfonso Larque Saavedra
Founded: 1959
Membership(s): Mexican National Association of Publishers.
Subjects: Agriculture, Biological Sciences, Economics, Education, Mathematics, Science (General), Social Sciences, Sociology, Technology, Veterinary Science
ISBN Prefix(es): 968-839
Bookshop(s): LIC Enrique Moreno Sanchez, Carr, Mexico-Texcoco KM, 35.5 Montecillo, 56230 Chapingo Edo
Orders to: LIC Enrique Moreno

Comision Nacional Forestal
Periferico Pte Int 5º Piso, 45019 Zapopah Jalisco
Tel: (05) 5349707; (05) 5247862
Subjects: Government, Political Science, History, Medicine, Nursing, Dentistry, Social Sciences, Sociology
ISBN Prefix(es): 968-6021

Compania Editorial Continental SA de CV+
Calzada de Tiapan 4620, Col Barrio del Nino Jesus, Mexico, DF 14000
Tel: (05) 5442776; (05) 6890088 *Fax:* (05) 5618155
Key Personnel
President: Carlos Frigolet Lerma
Dir General, Editorial, Production & Sales: Victorico Albores Santiago
Rights & Permissions: Demetrio Garmendia Guerrero
Production: Mario Munoz Rodriguez
Founded: 1954
Subjects: Engineering (General), Management, Mathematics, Science (General), Technology
ISBN Prefix(es): 968-26; 968-7249

Compania General de Ediciones SA de CV, see Selector SA de CV

Ediciones Contables y Administrativas SA
Heriberto Frias 1451-101, Col Del Valle, 03100 Mexico, DF
Tel: (05) 6040140; (05) 6041998; (05) 6040260 *Fax:* (05) 6056730
Key Personnel
Man Dir: Pedro Gasca Rocha
Sales Dir: Gustavo Gasca Breton
Founded: 1967
Subjects: Accounting, Business
ISBN Prefix(es): 968-6014; 968-6317; 970-617
Branch Office(s)
Zaragoza 39-106, Guadalajara, Jalisco

Ediciones Corunda SA de CV+
Oaxaca No 1, Con Periferico, Col Magdalena Contreras, San Jeronimo Aculco, 10000 Mexico, DF
Tel: (05) 6525511; (05) 6525581 *Fax:* (05) 6525211
Key Personnel
Contact: Silvia Molina
Founded: 1988
Subjects: Literature, Literary Criticism, Essays, Science Fiction, Fantasy
ISBN Prefix(es): 968-6044; 968-7444

Publicaciones Cruz O SA
Patriotismo No 875-D, Colonia Mixcoac, Delegacion Benito Juarez, 03910 Mexico, DF
Tel: (055) 56-80-61-22 *Fax:* (055) 56-80-61-22
E-mail: infolibros@libros.com.mx; atencionaclienteslibros@libros.com.mx
Web Site: www.libros.com.mx
Telex: 01776232
Key Personnel
General Dir: Oscar Rene Cruz
Founded: 1977
Cultural divulgation.
Membership(s): National Association of Publishers.
Subjects: Biography, Economics, Law, Philosophy, Psychology, Psychiatry, Religion - Buddhist, Religion - Catholic, Religion - Jewish, Social Sciences, Sociology
ISBN Prefix(es): 968-20
Total Titles: 285 Print
Subsidiaries: Libreria Cruz O SA
Divisions: Publicaciones Cruz O SA de Guatemala CA

Cuernavaca Editorial S A+
Oxford No 23, Col Juarez, 06600 Mexico, DF
Tel: (05) 5113619; (05) 5142529; (05) 2867794 *Fax:* (05) 2117112
Telex: 1771422 PROME
Key Personnel
Editor: Nicolas H Sanchez-Osorio; Elia Cordova; Anne de Sanchez Osorio
Founded: 1985
Membership(s): De Camara Nal Industria Editorial.
Subjects: Art
ISBN Prefix(es): 968-6188
Parent Company: Ediarte SA de CV
Imprints: Casa & Gente; El Coleccionista, Centro Historico

Ediciones Culturales Internacionales SA de CV Edicion Compra y Venta de Libros, Casetes, Videos+
Lago mask No 393, Col Granada, 11520 Mexico, DF
Tel: (05) 2508099 (ext 200) *Fax:* (05) 55311597
Key Personnel
General Dir: Mireya Cuentas Montejo
Editorial Manager: Ma Aurora Aguilar Chavez
Founded: 1983
Subjects: Art, Child Care & Development, Ethnicity
ISBN Prefix(es): 968-418

Ediciones CUPSA, Centro de Comunicacion Cultural CUPSA, AC
Heroes No 83, Guerrero, 06300 Mexico, DF
Tel: (05) 5925252; (05) 5662307; (05) 5462100
Key Personnel
Dir: Moises Valderrama
Founded: 1958

Subjects: Astrology, Occult, Biblical Studies, Poetry, Religion - Protestant, Religion - Other, Theology
ISBN Prefix(es): 968-7011

Ediciones Dabar, SA de CV+
Calzada del Acueducto 165-D, San Lorenzo Huipulco, 14370 Mexico, DF
Tel: (05) 6550396 *Fax:* (05) 6033674
E-mail: dabar@data.net.mx
Key Personnel
Contact: Jose Vaderrey Falagan
Founded: 1991
Also distributors of religious books in Spanish; theological, Bibles, spiritual & catechisms.
Subjects: Religion - Other
ISBN Prefix(es): 968-6768; 968-7506

Maria Esther De Fleischmann
Atlaltunco No 57, Colonia San Miguel Techmacalco, 53970 Mexico
Mailing Address: San Francisco 109, Colonia Rancho San Francisco 01800
Tel: (05) 5852698; (05) 5852698 *Fax:* (05) 5854296
E-mail: fleischmann1@compuserve.com.mx
Key Personnel
Contact: Maria Esther Serafin Garcia
Subjects: Disability, Special Needs
ISBN Prefix(es): 968-499; 970-91523

Del Verbo Emprender SA de CV+
Fuente de Piramides No 20, Planta Baja Local B, Tecamachalco, CP 53950 Mexico
Tel: (05) 294-1160; (05) 294-8633 *Fax:* (05) 294-8633
Key Personnel
Founder & Dir: Salo Grabinsky *E-mail:* gsalo@mail.internet.com.mx
Founded: 1989
Subjects: Child Care & Development, Human Relations, Management, Self-Help
ISBN Prefix(es): 968-6427

Editorial Diana SA de CV+
Arenal No 24, Edif Norte, Ex Hacienda Guadalupe Chimalistac, Delegacion Alvaro Obregon, 01050 Mexico, DF
Tel: (055) 5089-1220 *Fax:* (052) 5089-1230
E-mail: 4sales@diana.com.mx; editors@diana.com.mx
Web Site: www.diana.com.mx *Cable:* EDISA
Key Personnel
President: Jose Luis Ramirez C
Vice President: Jose Luis Ramirez M
Literature Editor: Fausto Rosales
  E-mail: faustoro@diana.com.mx
General Interest Editor: Doris Bravo V
Technical Books Editor: V Manuel Fernandez
  E-mail: manfer@diana.com.mx
Sales: Vincente Perez *E-mail:* vincenteperez@diana.com.mx
Founded: 1946
Membership(s): National Association of the Mexican Publishing Industry.
Subjects: Advertising, Animals, Pets, Archaeology, Astrology, Occult, Biography, Career Development, Child Care & Development, Cookery, Economics, Education, Fiction, Health, Nutrition, History, Human Relations, Journalism, Literature, Literary Criticism, Essays, Management, Nonfiction (General), Parapsychology, Philosophy, Religion - Catholic, Self-Help, Sports, Athletics
ISBN Prefix(es): 968-13
Imprints: Edivision Cia, Editorial, SA de CV
Branch Office(s)
Buenos Aires, Argentina
Santafe de Bogota, Colombia
Barcelona, Spain
Caracas, Venezuela
Shipping Address: Roberto Cayol 1323, Col del Valle, 03100 Mexico, DF

Direccion General de Publicaciones CNCA Coordinacion Juridica
Av Mexico Coyocan 371 col xoco, 03330 Mexico, DF
Tel: (05) 605-85-89 (ext 5127-149) *Fax:* (05) 605-87-31
Key Personnel
Dir General: Felipe Garrido Reyes *Tel:* (05) 601-02-60; (05) 601-02-85 *E-mail:* dpg01@conaculta.gob.mx
Production Dir: Miguel Angel Echegaray Zuniga
ISBN Prefix(es): 968-29; 970-18
Parent Company: Educal, SA de CV, Av Ceylan 450, 02660 Col Euzkadi

Directorio, *imprint of* Medios y Medios, Sa de CV

Ediciones Don Bosco SA de C
Moneda, No 24, Centro, CP 06060 Mexico, DF
Tel: (05) 3963349
Key Personnel
Dir: Argeo Corona Thelian Cortes
Deputy Dir, Rights & Permissions: Milagros Magana del Campo
Sales: Jorge Rangel
Founded: 1958
Subjects: Religion - Other
ISBN Prefix(es): 968-6662; 968-6969
Associate Companies: Central Catequista Salesiana, Madrid Alcala 164, Madrid, Spain; Libreria Dectrina Cristiana, Corzo Francia 214, 10096 Leuman (Turin), Italy
Bookshop(s): 5 de Mayo 23, 06000 Mexico, DF; Ignacio Mariscal 8, Col revolucion, 06030 Mexico, DF

Ediciones Eca SA de CV+
Member of Cachoy Balcarcel, SA
Calle B Manzana 11 No 20, Col Educacion, 04400 Mexico, DF
Tel: (055) 5787325 *Fax:* (055) 6891826
Web Site: www.centroescolareca.edu.mx
Key Personnel
Contact: Gracia Ma Cacho
Founded: 1950
Subjects: Accounting, Business
ISBN Prefix(es): 968-14

Edamex SA de CV+
Heriberto Frias No 1104, Col Del Valle, Del Benito Juarez, 03100 Mexico, DF
Tel: (05) 55598588 *Toll Free Tel:* 800 024 8588 *Fax:* (05) 55750555; (05) 55757035
E-mail: info@edamex.com
Web Site: www.edamex.com
Key Personnel
President: Octavio Colmenares Vargas
Dir General: Monica Colmenares
Foreign Sales: Valeria Bastarrachea
Founded: 1963
Membership(s): Camara Nacional de la Industria Editorial Socio No 40.
Subjects: Architecture & Interior Design, Art, Biography, Journalism, Management, Parapsychology, Public Administration, Self-Help, Social Sciences, Sociology, Sports, Athletics
ISBN Prefix(es): 968-409; 970-409
Number of titles published annually: 120 Print; 120 E-Book
Total Titles: 60 Print; 420 Online; 420 E-Book
Parent Company: Edamex
Foreign Rep(s): Books Information & Services (Puerto Rico); Distribuidora Lewis, SA (Panama); Giron Spanish Books; Internacional Libros; Libreria Alexandria (Costa Rica); Libreria Cientifica (Ecuador); Philobliblia, SA (Dominican Republic); Presa Peyran Editores, CA (Venezuela)

Editorial Edicol SA
esq Actipan No 45, Murcia No 2, Col Mixcoac Insurgentes, 03920 Mexico, DF
Tel: (05) 55637203; (05) 55637900 *Fax:* (05) 5636966
Key Personnel
Man Dir: Jorge Silva Escamilla
Founded: 1970
Subjects: Architecture & Interior Design, Communications, Education, History, Language Arts, Linguistics, Social Sciences, Sociology
ISBN Prefix(es): 968-408

Edivision Cia, Editorial, SA de CV, *imprint of* Editorial Diana SA de CV

Education Pabla, see Direccion General de Publicaciones CNCA Coordinacion Juridica

El Colegio de Michoacan A C
Martinez de Navarete 505, Las Fuentes, Apdo 207, 59699 Zamora, Michoacan CP
Tel: (0351) 515 71 00 *Fax:* (0351) 5157100 (ext 1742)
E-mail: publica@colmich.cmich.udg.mx; publica@colmich.edu.mx
Web Site: www.colmich.edu.mx
Key Personnel
President: Rafael Diego-Fernandez
Publications: Patricia Delgado Gonzalez
  E-mail: pdelgado@colmich.edu.mx
Founded: 1979
Subjects: Americana, Regional, Anthropology, Archaeology, Behavioral Sciences, Developing Countries, Education, Environmental Studies, Government, Political Science, History, Language Arts, Linguistics, Native American Studies, Philosophy, Religion - Catholic, Social Sciences, Sociology, Theology
ISBN Prefix(es): 968-6959; 968-7230
Number of titles published annually: 30 Print

Editorial El Manual Moderno SA de CV+
Av Sonora 206, Hipodromo, 06100 Mexico, DF
Tel: (055) 2651100; (055) 2651124; (055) 2651121 *Fax:* (055) 2651175
E-mail: mmoderno@compuserve.com.ux
Web Site: www.manualmoderno.com.mx
Key Personnel
Chairman: Dr Gustavo Setzer
President: Ing Hugo Setzer
Vice President: C P Hector Morales
Editorial: Iug Felipe Gerua
Marketing & Sales: Jose Pesez
Founded: 1958
Membership(s): The International Association of Scientific, Technical & Medical Publishers; STM.
Subjects: Biological Sciences, Health, Nutrition, Medicine, Nursing, Dentistry, Psychology, Psychiatry, Self-Help, Veterinary Science
ISBN Prefix(es): 968-426
Subsidiaries: Editorial El Manual Moderno (Colombia), Ltda
Distributed by Ediciones Nueva Vision, CA (Venezuela); Ediciones Tecnicas Paraguayas (Paraguay); Ediciones Trecho, SA (Uruguay); Editorial Atlante Argentina, SRL (Argentina); H F Martinez de Murguia, SA (Espana)
Distributor for Appleton & Lange (Mexico); Atlante Argenti (Mexico); Celsus (Mexico); Ediciones Diaz de Santos, Medicina (America Latina); Harcourt Brace/Mosby-Doyma Libros (Mexico); Springer Verlag Iberica (America Latina)

Empresas Editoriales SA
Praga No 56, Planta Baja Col Juarez, 06600 Mexico, DF
Tel: (05) 5288979; (05) 5288417 *Fax:* (05) 5288417
Founded: 1944
Subjects: Fiction
ISBN Prefix(es): 968-7035

Entretenlibro SA de CV
Wahsington No 1127-Altos, 64007 Monterrey, Nuevo Leon
Tel: (09183) 425570
Key Personnel
Contact: Jesus Rendon Contreras
Founded: 1983
Subjects: Education
ISBN Prefix(es): 968-462

Ediciones Era SA de CV+
Calle del Trabajo 31, Col La Fama Del Tlalpan, 14269 Mexico, DF
Tel: (055) 55 28 1221 *Fax:* (055) 56 06 2904
E-mail: erapedidos@laneta.apc.org
Web Site: www.edicionesera.com.mx
Key Personnel
Man Dir: Mrs Nieves Espresate Xirau
Founded: 1960
Subjects: Art, Economics, Fiction, Government, Political Science, History, Literature, Literary Criticism, Essays, Social Sciences, Sociology
ISBN Prefix(es): 968-411
Number of titles published annually: 25 Print
Total Titles: 300 Print

Revista Mensual Escuela, *imprint of* Fernandez Editores SA de CV

Editorial Esfinge SA de CV
Esfuerzo 18-A Fracc Industrial Atoto, Naucalpan, CP 53510 Mexico
Tel: (05) 3591313; (05) 3591111; (05) 3591515 *Fax:* (05) 5761343
E-mail: editorial@esfinge.com.mx
Web Site: www.esfinge.com.mx
Founded: 1957
Membership(s): the National Chamber of the Industrial Editorial; Specialize in textbooks.
Subjects: Accounting, Chemistry, Chemical Engineering, Geography, Geology, History, Law, Literature, Literary Criticism, Essays, Mathematics, Physics
ISBN Prefix(es): 968-412
Parent Company: Grupo Cultural Esfinge SA de CV
Associate Companies: Altadir SA de CV; Inmobiliaria Acribia SA de CV; Distr Imagen Esfinge SA de CV
Distributor for Addison-Wesley Iberoamericana Mexico

Espasa-Calpe Mexicana SA
Insurgentes Sur N 1162, Col Del Valle, CP 03100 Mexico, DF
Tel: (05) 5758585 *Fax:* (05) 5758980
ISBN Prefix(es): 968-413
Branch Office(s)
Editorial Espasa-Calpe SA, Spain

Centro de Estudios Monetarios Latinoamericanos (CEMLA)+
Durango 54, 06700 Mexico, DF
Tel: (05) 533-0300 *Fax:* (05) 525-4432
E-mail: cemlasub@mail.internet.com.mx
Web Site: www.cemla.org
Key Personnel
Man Dir: Lic Sergio Ghigliazza
Editorial, Rights & Permissions & Production: Juan Manuel Rodriguez *Tel:* (05) 5114020 *Fax:* (05) 2077024
Sales: Claudio Antonovich

Founded: 1952
Subjects: Computer Science, Economics, Finance
ISBN Prefix(es): 968-6154

Ediciones Euroamericanas+
Apdo 69-774, 04461 Mexico, DF
Tel: (05) 56 10 01 33 *Fax:* (05) 56 10 01 33
E-mail: thielemedina@prodigy.net.mx
Key Personnel
Man Dir: Klaus Thiele
Founded: 1971
Direct sales only to booksellers worldwide.
Subjects: Anthropology, Archaeology, History, Regional Interests
ISBN Prefix(es): 968-414
Number of titles published annually: 2 Print
Total Titles: 16 Print
Imprints: Biblioteca Interamericana Bilingue; Paginas Mesoamericanas

Ediciones Exclusivas SA+
Monrovia 1105, Apdo 21-148, Mexico, DF
Tel: (05) 815878
Key Personnel
Contact: Jose Figueroa Marti
Founded: 1973
Membership(s): La Camara Nacional de la Industria Editorial.
Subjects: Health, Nutrition, Human Relations, Medicine, Nursing, Dentistry, Psychology, Psychiatry
ISBN Prefix(es): 968-7039
U.S. Office(s): Latin Trading Corp, 539 "H" St, Suite B, Chula Vista, CA 91911, United States
Tel: 619-427-7867

Editorial Extemporaneos SA
Poniente 126-A-400, Col Nueva Vallejo, 07750 Mexico, DF
Tel: (05) 5875424 *Fax:* (05) 5878785 *Cable:* EDIEXTEMPO MEXICO
Key Personnel
Dir-General, Editorial: Lautaro Gondalez Porcel
Sales, Publicity, Production: Romeo Medina
Rights & Permissions: Eva Somlo
Founded: 1975
Subjects: Anthropology, Architecture & Interior Design, Art, Drama, Theater, Economics, Education, Government, Political Science, Humor, Literature, Literary Criticism, Essays, Philosophy, Social Sciences, Sociology
ISBN Prefix(es): 968-415
Bookshop(s): Librerias Extemporaneos SA, Hamburgo 260, Mexico 6, DF
Book Club(s): Club de Lectores Extemporaneos

Editorial Fata Morgana SA de CV+
Virgilio No 7-12, Col Polanco, 11560 Mexico, DF
Mailing Address: Monte Elbruz 164-13, Lomas Chapultepec, 11000 Mexico, DF
Tel: (055) 52 80 08 29 *Fax:* (055) 52 80 81 37
E-mail: editorial@fatamorgana.com.mx
Web Site: www.fatamorgana.com.mx
Key Personnel
Contact: Maria Abac Klemm
Founded: 1990
Subjects: Psychology, Psychiatry
ISBN Prefix(es): 968-6757
Number of titles published annually: 1 Print
Total Titles: 8 Print
Orders to: Virgilio No 7, Dept 12, Col Polanco, 11560 Mexico, DF

Fernandez Editores SA de CV+
Eje 1 Poniente Mexico Coyoacan 321, Col Xoco, 03330 Mexico, DF
Tel: (05) 6056557 *Fax:* (05) 6889173
Web Site: www.fernandezeditores.com.mx
Key Personnel
President: Gonzalez Luis Fernandez

Man Dir: Luis Gerardo Fernandez
Production Manager: Luis Benjamin Fernandez
Commercial Manager: Luis Miguel Fernandez
Founded: 1943
Membership(s): Camara Editorial of Mexico & manufacture of game tables & materials.
Subjects: Animals, Pets, Child Care & Development, Education, Environmental Studies, History, Literature, Literary Criticism, Essays, Mathematics, Nonfiction (General), Physics, Religion - Catholic, Science (General), Science Fiction, Fantasy, Social Sciences, Sociology
ISBN Prefix(es): 970-03; 968-416
Imprints: Revista Mensual Escuela

Fondo de Cultura Economica+
Carretera Picacho-Ajusco 227-1, Heroes de Padierna, 14200 Mexico, DF
Tel: (05) 2274672 *Fax:* (05) 2274640
E-mail: adiezc@fce.com.mx (editorial)
Web Site: www.fondodeculturaeconomica.com
Key Personnel
Man Dir: Miguel de la Madrid
Senior Editor: Adolfo Castanon
Production: Alejandro Ramirez
Sales: David Turner y Barragan
Publicity: Maria Luisa Armendariz
Foreign Rights: Socorro Cano
Founded: 1934
Specialize in editorial materials.
Subjects: Advertising, Agriculture, Anthropology, Archaeology, Architecture & Interior Design, Art, Behavioral Sciences, Biological Sciences, Communications, Developing Countries, Drama, Theater, Earth Sciences, Economics, Education, Energy, Ethnicity, Fiction, Government, Political Science, History, Literature, Literary Criticism, Essays, Nonfiction (General), Philosophy, Photography, Poetry, Psychology, Psychiatry, Public Administration, Science (General), Science Fiction, Fantasy, Social Sciences, Sociology, Women's Studies
ISBN Prefix(es): 968-16
Imprints: Azteca; Galeras; La Gaceta; El Trimestre Economico
Branch Office(s)
Fondo de Cultura Economica de Argentina SA, El Salvador 5665, C1414BQE Capital Federal, Buenos Aires, Argentina, Contact: Alejandro Katz *Tel:* (01) 14-777-1547; (01) 14-777-1934; (01) 14-777-1219 *Fax:* (01) 14-771-8977 (ext 19) *E-mail:* info@fce.com.ar
Fondo de Cultura Economica Brasil Ltda, Rua Bartira 351, Perdizes, Sao Paulo CEP 05009-000, Brazil, Contact: Isac Vinic *Tel:* (011) 3672-3397; (011) 3672-3864; (011) 3672-1496 *Fax:* (011) 3862-1803 *E-mail:* aztecafondo@uol.com.br
Fondo de Cultura Economica Chila SA, Paseo Bulnes 152, Santiago, Chile, Contact: Julio Sau Aguayo *Tel:* (02) 697-2644; (02) 695-4843; (02) 699-0189; (01) 688-1630 *Fax:* (02) 696-2329 *E-mail:* fcechile@ctcinternet.cl
Fondo de Cultura Economica Ltda, Carrera 16 No 80-18, Barrio el Lago, Bogota, Colombia, Contact: Juan Camilo Sierra *Tel:* (01) 531-2288 *Fax:* (01) 531-1322 *E-mail:* fondoc@cable.net.co *Web Site:* www.fce.com.co
Fondo de Cultura Economica de Guatemala SA, 6a Ave 8-65, Zona 9, Guatemala, Contact: Sagrario Castellanos *Tel:* 334-3351; 362-6563; 362-6539; 334-3354 *Fax:* 332-4216 *E-mail:* fceguate@gold.guate.com
Fondo de Cultura Economica del Peru SA, Jiron Berlin No 238, Miraflores, Lima 18, Peru, Contact: German Carnero Roque *Tel:* (01) 242-0559; (01) 242-9448; (01) 447-2848 *Fax:* (01) 447-0760 *E-mail:* fce-peru@terra.com.pe *Web Site:* www.fceperu.com.pe
Fondo de Cultura Economica de Espana SL, C/Fernando El Catolico No 86, Conjunto Residencial Galaxia, Madrid 28015, Spain, Contact: Maria Luisa Capella *Tel:* (091) 543-2904; (091)

543-2960; (091) 549-2884 *Fax:* (091) 549-8652
E-mail: capella@terra.es
Fondo de Cultura Economica EUA Inc, 2293 Verus St, San Diego, CA 92154, United States, Contact: Benjamin Mireles *Tel:* (619) 429-0455 *Fax:* (619) 429-0827 *E-mail:* info@fceusa.com
Web Site: www.fecusa.com
Fondo de Cultura Economica Venezuela SA, Edif Torre Polar, PB Local E, Plaza Venezuela, Caracas, Venezuela, Contact: Pedro Juan Tucat Zunino *Tel:* (02) 574-4753 *Fax:* (02) 574-7442 *E-mail:* salonofc@cantv.net
Bookshop(s): Carret Picacho Ajusco, No 227, Mexico, DF CP 14200
Shipping Address: Jose Maria Joaristi 205, Paraje San Juan, San Lorenzo, Iztapalapa 09830

Fondo Editorial de la Plastica Mexicana+
Cda de Malitzin No 28, 04100 Mexico, DF
Tel: (05) 5549-4291 *Fax:* (05) 5688-1168
Founded: 1961
Subjects: Art, Regional Interests
ISBN Prefix(es): 968-6658
Number of titles published annually: 3 Print
Total Titles: 20 Print

Scott Foresman, *imprint of* Pearson Educacion de Mexico, SA de CV

La Gaceta, *imprint of* Fondo de Cultura Economica

Galeras, *imprint of* Fondo de Cultura Economica

Impresora Galve SA, *imprint of* Editorial Avante SA de Cv

Ediciones Gili SA de CV
Valle de Bravo No 21, Fracc-el Mirador, Naucalpan, 53050 Mexico
Tel: (05) 373-1744; (05) 5606011 *Fax:* (05) 3601453
Telex: 1772918 Gilime *Cable:* GUSTO MEXICO
ISBN Prefix(es): 968-887
Associate Companies: Editorial Gustavo Gili SA, Spain

Gomez Gomez Hermanos Editores S de RL Edicion de Libros y Revistas+
Moneda 19-B, 06060 Mexico, DF
Tel: (05) 55225903; (05) 6123906 *Fax:* (05) 633786
Key Personnel
Contact: Victor J Gomez
ISBN Prefix(es): 968-7030
Subsidiaries: El Mejor Regalo un Libro SRL

Editorial Grijalbo SA de CV+
Calzado San Bartolo, Naucalpan No 282, Argentina Poniente, 11230 Mexico, DF
Tel: (05) 3584355 *Fax:* (05) 3584312
Web Site: www.grijalbo.com.mx
Telex: 1771415 Egsame *Cable:* GRIJALMEX
Key Personnel
Editorial: Rogelio Carvajal Davila; Ariel Rosales Ortiz
Sales: Rodolfo Munguia Calderon; Irma P Chavarria
Publicity: Oscar Davalos; Alicia Velazquez
Founded: 1936
Membership(s): Camara Espanola de Comercio & Mexico y Camara Italiana de Comercio en Mexico.
Subjects: Fiction, Mythology, Nonfiction (General), Poetry, Self-Help
ISBN Prefix(es): 968-419; 970-05
Parent Company: Ediciones Grijalbo SA, Spain
Associate Companies: Arnoldo Mondadori Editore

Branch Office(s)
Guadalajara, Jal
Mexicali, BC
Monterrey, NL

Grupo Editorial Iberoamerica, SA de CV+
Rio Ganges No 64, Col Cuauhtemoc, 06500 Mexico, DF
Tel: (05) 5111267; (05) 5116760
Key Personnel
President: Nicolas Grepe Philp
Founded: 1983
Book publisher & distributor to Latin America.
Subjects: Agriculture, Career Development, Chemistry, Chemical Engineering, Computer Science, Economics, Engineering (General), Environmental Studies, Finance, Management, Mathematics, Mechanical Engineering
ISBN Prefix(es): 968-7270
Branch Office(s)
Grupo Editorial Iberoamerica de Colombia, SA, Carrera 23 No 49-30, Barrio Palermo, Santa Fe de Bogota, Colombia *Tel:* (0571) 3202010 *Fax:* (0571) 3106553

Grupo Editorial Z Zeta SA de CV
Oculistas No 43, Col Sifon, 09400 Mexico, DF
Tel: (05) 6705627; (05) 5817929 *Fax:* (05) 5758280
Key Personnel
Contact: Francisco Campos Fontanet
ISBN Prefix(es): 970-610
Warehouse: Ignacio Manuel Aaltamirano, 212 B Col Hank Gonzalez, 09750 Mexico, DF

Heidel Impresos SA de CV, *imprint of* Editorial Avante SA de Cv

Editorial Hermes SA+
Calz Ermita Iztapalapa No 266, Col Sinatel, 09470 Mexico, DF
Tel: (05) 6741425; (05) 6741894; (05) 6744385 (ext 71) *Fax:* (05) 6743949 *Cable:* EDITERMES
Key Personnel
Man Dir: Sergio Sanchez Davila
Sales: Adolfo de la Becerril
Production, Rights & Permissions: Virginia Garcia Fiesco
Founded: 1944
Subjects: Art, Fiction, History
ISBN Prefix(es): 968-446
Associate Companies: Editorial Albastros SA ci, Buenos Aires, Argentina; Tercer Mundo Distribuidores, Santa Fe de Bogota, Colombia

Editorial Herrero SA
Rio Amazonas No 44, Col Cuauhtemoc, 06500 Mexico, DF
Tel: (05) 5664900 *Fax:* (05) 5664900
Key Personnel
General Dir: Donato Elias Herrero
Manager: Ricardo Arancon L
Founded: 1945
Subjects: Art
ISBN Prefix(es): 968-420

Hoja Casa Editorial SA de CV+
Av Cuauhtemoc No 1430, Col Santa Cruz Atoyac, 03310 Mexico, DF
Tel: (055) 688-4828; (055) 688-6458; (055) 605-7677; (055) 604-0843 *Fax:* (055) 605-7677
E-mail: editorialpax@editorialpax.com
Web Site: www.editorialpax.com
Key Personnel
General Dir: Gerardo Gally
General Manager: Consuelo Saizar
Rights & Permissions: Gilda Moreno
Founded: 1990

Subjects: Astrology, Occult, Fiction, Literature, Literary Criticism, Essays, Self-Help
ISBN Prefix(es): 968-6565

Ibcon SA+
Gutenberg 224, Col Anzures, 11590 Mexico, DF
Tel: (055) 5255 4577 *Fax:* (055) 5255 4577
E-mail: ibcon@ibcon.com.mx; ibcon@infosel.net.mx
Web Site: www.ibcon.com.mx
Key Personnel
Editor: Gabriel Zaid
Founded: 1954
Specialized directories (print, CD, online).
Subjects: Business, Government, Political Science, Health, Nutrition, Law, Library & Information Sciences, Marketing, Microcomputers, Women's Studies
ISBN Prefix(es): 968-6289; 968-5097
Number of titles published annually: 19 Print; 3 CD-ROM; 1 Online
Total Titles: 20 Print; 2 CD-ROM; 1 Online
Online services available through netLibrary.

Instituto Indigenista Interamericano
(Inter-American Indian Institute)
Av de las Fuentes 106, Col Jardines del Pedregal, Delegacion Alvaro, 01900 Mexico, DF
Mailing Address: Apdo 20315, 01001 Mexico, DF
Tel: (05) 5595 8410; (05) 5595 4324 *Fax:* (05) 595 8410
E-mail: ininin@data.net.mx *Cable:* INDIGENI
Key Personnel
Man Dir, Rights & Permissions: Dr Jose Matos Mar
Founded: 1940
Membership(s): OEA; specialize in the development of the Pueblo Indian in America.
Subjects: Anthropology, History
ISBN Prefix(es): 968-6020
Number of titles published annually: 600 Print

INEGI, see Instituto Nacional de Estadistica, Geographia e Informatica

Informatica Cosmos SA de CV+
Calzado del Hueso 122-A12, Col Ex-Hacienda Coapa, 14300 Mexico, DF
Tel: (05) 6774868; (05) 6776043 *Fax:* (05) 6793575
E-mail: online@cosmos.com.mx
Web Site: www.cosmos.com.mx
Key Personnel
Man Dir: Raul Macazaga *E-mail:* macazaga@cosmos.com.mx
Dir, International Sales: Mary Christen *E-mail:* christen@cosmos.com.mx
Founded: 1956
Specialize in industry guides, products, producers, suppliers of industry, chemicals, food & feed, container & packaging, rubber, plastics & resins & equipment.
U.S. Office(s): Schnell Publishing Co Inc, 2 Rector St, 26th Floor, New York, NY 10006-1819, United States, Contact: Stacey Davis *Tel:* 212-791-4251 *Fax:* 212-791-4311 *E-mail:* sdavis@chemepo.com

Editorial Institucional y Desarrollo Humanistico SA de CV Edicion de Libros
(IDH Ediciones)+
Av Juarez No 14-7 Piso, 11560 Mexico, DF
Tel: (05) 5215060; (05) 5215009
Key Personnel
Contacts: Ms Alicia Sosa; Enrique Martinez Cruz
Founded: 1982
ISBN Prefix(es): 968-883
Parent Company: Grupo IDH

PUBLISHERS

Intersistemas SA de CV+
Pennsylvania 109, Colonia Napoles, 03810 Mexico, DF
Tel: (055) 1107-1903 *Fax:* (055) 1107-0196
E-mail: ventas@medikatalogo.com
Web Site: www.medikatalogo.com
Telex: 5403764
Key Personnel
Man Dir: Pedro Vera-Cervera
Editorial: Elvia Espino-Barros
Sales: Miguel Alberto Gonzalez
Founded: 1970
Subjects: Medicine, Nursing, Dentistry
ISBN Prefix(es): 970-655
Associate Companies: Graficas Enar SA, Pedro Muguruza 3-1, Madrid 16, Spain; Intermedica Inc, 322 West Port Ave, Norwalk, CT 06851, United States; Vier Lista Anexa, EMC Columbia Federal Buenos Aires, Buenos Aires, Argentina

El Inversionista Mexicano SA de CV
Felix Cuevas 301-204, Col Del Valle, Deleg Benito Juarez, CP 03100 Mexico, DF
Tel: (05) 5245396; (05) 5349297 *Fax:* (05) 5243794
E-mail: elimmbi@iserve.net.mx
Key Personnel
Contact: Evangelina Astorga Dorantes
Founded: 1969

Editorial Iztaccihuatl SA+
Miguel E Schultz No 21, Col San Rafael, 06470 Mexico, DF
Mailing Address: Apdo 2343, 06470 Mexico DF
Tel: (05) 7050938; (05) 7051063 *Fax:* (05) 5352321 *Cable:* EIZTAMEXA
Key Personnel
President: Orlando Vieyra Legorreta
Founded: 1946
Subjects: Cookery, Literature, Literary Criticism, Essays, Wine & Spirits
ISBN Prefix(es): 968-421

Janibi Editores SA de CV
Matias Romero 1221-3, Col Del Valle, Del Benito Juarez, 03100 Mexico, DF
Tel: (05) 6046160 *Fax:* (05) 6882848
Key Personnel
Contact: Victor Munoz Polit
Founded: 1975
Subjects: Fashion, Music, Dance

Editorial Jilguero, SA de CV
Administracion de Correos 10, 11000 Mexico, DF
Tel: (05) 2590939; (05) 2590814 *Fax:* (05) 5401771
E-mail: mexdesco@compuserve.com.mx
Web Site: www.mexicodesconocido.com.mx
Subjects: Animals, Pets, Anthropology, Antiques, Archaeology, Architecture & Interior Design, Cookery, Crafts, Games, Hobbies, History, Music, Dance, Outdoor Recreation, Travel

Editorial Joaquin Mortiz SA de CV+
Insurgentes Sur No 1162, Col del Valle, 03100 Mexico, DF
Tel: (05) 5598781 *Fax:* (05) 5758980
Telex: 1764458 EDARME
Key Personnel
Man Dir, Production, Rights & Permissions: Joaquin Diez-Canedo
Founded: 1962
Membership(s): the Grupo Editorial Planeta.
Subjects: Fiction, History, Literature, Literary Criticism, Essays, Nonfiction (General), Philosophy, Poetry, Psychology, Psychiatry, Social Sciences, Sociology
ISBN Prefix(es): 968-27
Associate Companies: Editorial Planeta SA, Spain

Warehouse: Ave Gavilan 3, Bodega 1 & 2, Col Guadalupe del Mora, Delegacion Iztapalapa, 09360 Mexico, DF
Orders to: Editorial Planeta Mexicana, Ave Insurgentes Sur No 1162-3, Col Del Valle, 03100 Mexico DF

Editorial Jus SA de CV+
Plaza de Abasolo 14, Col Guerrero, 06300 Mexico, DF
Tel: (05) 5260538; (05) 5260540 *Fax:* (05) 5290951
E-mail: editjus@data.net.mx
Key Personnel
President: Juan Landerreche
Man Dir: Tomas Reynoso
Sales Manager: Jorge Espinosa
Founded: 1941
Subjects: Biblical Studies, Economics, Education, Government, Political Science, History, Law, Literature, Literary Criticism, Essays, Philosophy, Religion - Catholic, Self-Help, Social Sciences, Sociology, Theology
ISBN Prefix(es): 968-423
Subsidiaries: Distribuidora Editorial Jus SA

Ediciones Larousse SA de CV+
Dinamarca No 81 B1, Colonia Juarez, 06600 Mexico, DF
Tel: (05) 52082005; (05) 2085677 *Fax:* (05) 2086225
E-mail: dbertin@larousse.com.mx
Web Site: www.larousse.com.mx
Key Personnel
President: Dominique Bertin
Founded: 1965
Subjects: English as a Second Language
ISBN Prefix(es): 970-607; 968-6042; 968-6147; 968-6347
Parent Company: Havas Publications Edition, France
Warehouse: Acalotenco 94-1, Mexico DF

Lasser Press Mexicana SA de CV
Praga 56 - Piso 4, Col Juarez, 06600 Mexico, DF
Tel: (05) 5112312; (05) 5142705 *Fax:* (05) 5112576
Telex: 1777529 Coseme *Cable:* LASPRESA
Key Personnel
President: Guillermo Menendez Castro
Editorial Dir: Elisa Tovar
Founded: 1972
Subjects: Biography, Literature, Literary Criticism, Essays, Nonfiction (General)
ISBN Prefix(es): 968-458; 968-7063

Phillip Richard Conover Lazo+
c/o The Huautla Press, Galeana No 25, Col San Angel, Del Alvaro Obregon, 01000 Mexico, DF
Tel: (05) 5482663 *Fax:* (05) 5500641
E-mail: mel778@latinmail.com
Key Personnel
Owner, Editor & Writer: Phillip Richard Conover Lazo
Founded: 1990
Author, publisher, editor of Teo Nana Acatl. Searching for distributors & publishers desiring joint publishing ventures.
Membership(s): Camara Nacional de la Industria Editorial Mexicana #2705.
Subjects: Anthropology, History, Literature, Literary Criticism, Essays, Philosophy, Poetry, Religion - Buddhist, Religion - Hindu, Theology, Specialize in English language books
ISBN Prefix(es): 968-6744
Total Titles: 1 Print
Branch Office(s)
Aitken, Stone & Wylie Ltd, 29 Fernshaw Rd, London SW10 0TG, United Kingdom
Tel: (071) 351 7561 *Fax:* (071) 376 3594
E-mail: 100303.1765@compuserve.com

U.S. Office(s): Wylie, Aitken & Stone, 250 W 57 St, Suite 2114, New York, NY 10107, United States *Tel:* 212-246-0069 *E-mail:* 74454-3324@compuserve.com
Distributed by Libra Administraciones y Promociones'
Foreign Rep(s): Wylie, Aitken & Stone
Bookshop(s): Libreria el Juglar, Manuel M Ponce, 233 Col, Guadalupe Inn DF 01020, Facundo Caletti *Tel:* 660 7900
Orders to: Huantha Press, Galeana 25, San Angel DF 01000, Philip Conover *Tel:* (05) 509705

Ediciones Libra, SA de CV
Matias Romero 1221, Loc B, Col Del Valle, CP 03100 Mexico, DF
Tel: (05) 6049926 *Fax:* (05) 6882848
Founded: 1986
Subjects: Crafts, Games, Hobbies, Fashion, Music, Dance

Libra Editorial SA de CV+
Melesio Morales No 16, Colonia Guadalupe Inn, 01000 Mexico, DF
Tel: (05) 6641454; (05) 6514156 *Fax:* (05) 6641454
Key Personnel
President: Georgina Greco y Herrera
Editor: Gabriela Escalante de Figueroa
Founded: 1984
Subjects: Astrology, Occult, Child Care & Development, Cookery, Education, Gay & Lesbian, How-to, Humor, Language Arts, Linguistics, Nonfiction (General), Self-Help, Women's Studies
ISBN Prefix(es): 970-606; 968-6636
Warehouse: Av Centenario 514, Letra A

Libreria Parroquial de Claveria SA Edicion Compra y Venta de Libros+
Floresta No 79, Col Claveria, 02080 Mexico, DF
Tel: (05) 3967027; (05) 3967718 *Fax:* (05) 3991243
Key Personnel
Contact: Padre Basilio Nunez Garcia
Founded: 1964
ISBN Prefix(es): 968-442

Libros y Revistas SA de CV
Mier y Pesado 130, Col del Valle, 03100 Mexico, DF
Tel: (05) 5437295 *Fax:* (05) 5364622
Telex: 01771403 dsayme
Key Personnel
General Dir, Editorial, Rights & Permissions: Marcial Frigolet Lerma
General Manager, Commercial Dir: Joaquin Roca Romero
Production: Miguel Montano
Founded: 1925
Subjects: Crafts, Games, Hobbies, Education, Fashion, Health, Nutrition
ISBN Prefix(es): 968-7066
Parent Company: Publicaciones Sayrols SA de CV
Associate Companies: Metropolitana de Publicaciones SA

Editorial Limusa SA de CV+
Balderas No 95, Col Centro, 06040 Mexico, DF
Tel: (05) 5128503; (05) 5128050 *Fax:* (05) 512 2903
E-mail: limusa@noriega.com.mx
Web Site: www.noriega.com.mx
Key Personnel
Chairman of the Board: Carlos Noriega Milera
Chairman & Chief Executive Officer: Carlos Noriega Arias
Vice President & Editorial Dir: Miguel Noriega Arias
Founded: 1962

MEXICO

Subjects: Accounting, Advertising, Aeronautics, Aviation, Agriculture, Architecture & Interior Design, Art, Astronomy, Automotive, Behavioral Sciences, Biological Sciences, Business, Career Development, Chemistry, Chemical Engineering, Child Care & Development, Civil Engineering, Communications, Computer Science, Cookery, Crafts, Games, Hobbies, Criminology, Drama, Theater, Earth Sciences, Economics, Education, Electronics, Electrical Engineering, Energy, Engineering (General), Finance, Geography, Geology, Government, Political Science, Health, Nutrition, House & Home, Human Relations, Journalism, Labor, Industrial Relations, Law, Management, Marketing, Mathematics, Mechanical Engineering, Medicine, Nursing, Dentistry, Microcomputers, Physical Sciences, Physics, Psychology, Psychiatry, Public Administration, Radio, TV, Real Estate, Religion - Catholic, Science (General), Social Sciences, Sociology, Sports, Athletics, Technology, Transportation, Veterinary Science
ISBN Prefix(es): 968-18
Total Titles: 2,500 Print
Parent Company: Grupo Noriega Editores
Imprints: Camion Escolar y Limusa; Nori; Noriega Editores; Uteha
Subsidiaries: Limex; Alamex; Grupo Noriega Editores de Colombia LTDA
Divisions: Uteha; Nori; Limusa; Noriega Editores; Camion Escolar
Branch Office(s)
E Robles Gil No 437, Col Americana SJ, Guadalajara, Contact: Francisco Haro *Tel:* (03) 269 032 *Fax:* (03) 268 899 *E-mail:* limusa@noriega.com.mx
M M Del Llano 417 Ote, NL Monterrey, Contact: Sra Agustin Medina *Tel:* (08) 345 7505 *Fax:* (08) 345 7505 *E-mail:* limusa@noriega.com.mx
Distributed by Anisa (Puerto Rico); Cuspide CIA (Argentina); Dimaxi (Ecuador); Ediciones Tecnicas Paraguayas (Paraguay); Hispania SRL; Fundacion Del Libro Universitario Libun (Peru)
Distributor for Meditor (America Latina); V Vives (Mexico)
Showroom(s): Ayuntamiento 112, Centro 06040
Bookshop(s): Libreria Bellas Artes, Av Juarez, No 18-D, 6770 Mexico DF *Tel:* (05) 518 2917; Integra Escolar, Felix Berenguer 106, Lomas Virreyes *Tel:* (05) 520 6592
Book Club(s): Librerias de Cristal, Tehuantepec 170, Roma Sur, 06770 Mexico D F *Tel:* (05) 564 4677
Warehouse: Oriente 171 No 108, Col Aragon Inguaran, Contact: Sra Carlos Sanchez *Tel:* (057) 81 61 57 *Fax:* (057) 81 08 74 *E-mail:* limusa@noriega.com.mx

Logos Consorcio Editorial SA+
General Molinos del Capo 64, Col San Miguel Chapultepec, 11850 Mexico, DF
Key Personnel
Man Dir: Enrico Garcia Alonso S
ISBN Prefix(es): 968-425

Longman, *imprint of* Pearson Educacion de Mexico, SA de CV

Macmillan Editores SA de CV
Av Prolongacion San Antonio 170, Col Carola, CP 01180 Mexico, DF
Tel: (05) 482 2200 *Fax:* (05) 482 2203
E-mail: elt@macmillan.com.mx
Web Site: www.macmillan.com.mx/
Key Personnel
Chief Executive: Christopher West
  E-mail: cwest@macmillan.com.mx
Man Dir: Helen Melia *E-mail:* hmelia@macmillan.com.mx
Founded: 1982
Parent Company: Macmillan Publishers Ltd, United Kingdom
Associate Companies: Editorial Macmillan de Mexico SA de CV

Editorial Macmillan de Mexico SA de CV
Av Prolongacion San Antonio 170, Col Carola, 01180 Mexico, DF
Tel: (05) 482 2200 *Fax:* (05) 482 2202
Web Site: www.macmillan.com.mx
Key Personnel
Chief Executive: Christopher West
  E-mail: cwest@macmillan.com.mx
Man Dir: Helen Melia *E-mail:* hmelia@macmillan.com.mx
Founded: 1982
English language teaching publishers.
Parent Company: Macmillan Publishers Ltd, United Kingdom
Associate Companies: Macmillan Editores SA de CV

Mass + Medios, *imprint of* Medios y Medios, Sa de CV

Masson Editores
Dakota No 383, Col Napoles, 03810 Mexico, DF
Tel: (05) 6870933
Telex: 1777604
Key Personnel
President: Dr Jerome Talamon
Man Dir: Bruno Vanneuville
Founded: 1978
ISBN Prefix(es): 968-6099
Parent Company: Masson Editeur, France
Associate Companies: Editora Masson do Brasil Ltda, Brazil; Masson italia editori - ETM, via Pascoli 55, I-20133 Milan, Italy; Masson SA, Spain; Masson Publishing USA Inc, 211 E 43 St, Rm 1306, New York, NY 10017, United States

McGraw-Hill Interamericana Editores, SA de CV+
Atlacomulco 499, San Andres Atoto, Naucalpan, 53500 Mexico, DF
Tel: 576-73-04; 576-90-44 ext 156
E-mail: mcgraw-hill@infosel.net.mx
Web Site: www.mcgraw-hill.com.mx
Telex: 01774284 LMCHME
Key Personnel
Man Dir: Carlos Rios
Controller & Business Manager: Hugo Solis
Production Manager: Miguel Palafox
EDP Manager: Javier Carranza
Human Resources Manager: Rocio Gonzalez
Publisher, Professional Division: David Mejia
Publisher, College Division, BCV: Javier Neyra
Publisher, High School Division, BCV: Enrique Pereda
Publisher, Elementary-Junior High School Division, K-9: Joaquin Esponda
Distributor & Bookstore Sales Manager, Mexico: Rodolfo Munguia
Export Division Manager, Central America, Caribbean & South America: Lynette Kew
Founded: 1966
Sales Manager, Central America: Nathaniel Maxwell; Hotel Republica, Avenida Republica y Azuai, Quito, Ecuador. Tel: (02) 437667 Fax: (02) 436553. Sales Manager-College, Ecuador, Peru & Chile: Gilberto Capellan
Markets served: Mexico, Central America (Guatemala, Honduras, El Salvador, Costa Rica, Nicarauga, Panama), South America (Ecuador, Peru, Bolivia, Chile).
Subjects: Business, Engineering (General), Mathematics, Public Administration, Social Sciences, Sociology
ISBN Prefix(es): 968-25; 968-451; 968-422; 970-10

Parent Company: The McGraw-Hill Companies, 1221 Avenue of the Americas, New York, NY 10020, United States
Sales Office(s): 13 Calle "A" 31-76, Zona 7, Apdo 1477, Colonia Tika III, Guatemala, Guatemala *Tel:* (02) 914793 *Fax:* (02) 519598

McGraw-Hill Mexico/Latin America Group
Division of The McGraw-Hill Companies
Editores, SA de CV, Cedro no 512 Col Atlampa, 06450 Mexico, DF
Tel: (055) 5117-1515 *Fax:* (055) 5117-1516
Web Site: www.mcgraw-hill.com.mx
Key Personnel
Group VP: Francisco Albisua
Regional offices in Mexico, Venezuela, Colombia, Chile, Puerto Rico.

Medios Publicitarios Mexicanos SA de CV
Editora de Directorios de Medios
Av Eugenia No 811, Col Del Valle, Mexico, DF CP 03100
Tel: (05) 523-3346; (05) 523-3342 *Fax:* (05) 523-3379
E-mail: suscrip@mpm.com.mx; editorial@mpm.com.mx
Web Site: www.mpm.com.mx
Key Personnel
Contact: A Fernando Villamil
Founded: 1958
SRDS, LP 1700 Higgins Rd, Des Plaines, IL 60018.
Subjects: Advertising
Associate Companies: SRDS, United States

Medios y Medios, Sa de CV
Av Universidad 783-4, Col Del Valle, Del Benito Juarez, 03100 Mexico, DF
Tel: (05) 56-01-85-11 *Fax:* (05) 56-88-59-85
E-mail: mass+medios@camoapa.com.mx
Key Personnel
Dir: David Ramirez-Solis
Founded: 1993
Subjects: Advertising, Radio, TV
Imprints: Directorio; Mass + Medios

Mercametrica Ediciones SA Edicion de Libros
Av Universidad 1621, piso 3, Col Hacienda de Guadalupe Chimalistac, 01050 Mexico, DF
Tel: (055) 56-61-62-93; (055) 56-61-92-86
Fax: (055) 56-62-33-08
E-mail: mercametrica@mercametrica.com
Web Site: www.mercametrica.com.mx
Key Personnel
President: Ignacio Gomez
Founded: 1976
Subjects: Economics, Management, Marketing
ISBN Prefix(es): 968-7267

Editores Mexicanos Unidos SA
Luis Gonzalez Obregon, No 5, Colonia Centro, 06020 Mexico, DF
Tel: (05) 5218870 al 74 *Fax:* (05) 5218516
E-mail: editmusa@mail.internet.com.mx
Web Site: www.editmusa.com.mx
Key Personnel
Man Dir, Editorial: Fidel Miro Solanes
Dir: Sonia Miro de Laclau
Manager: Roque Laclau Gaona
Founded: 1954
Subjects: Fiction, Nonfiction (General)
ISBN Prefix(es): 968-15
Bookshop(s): Libro-Mex Editores SRL, Argentina 23, Mexico 1 DF

Editorial Minutiae Mexicana SA
Insurgentes Centro No 114-207, Col Revolucion, 06030 Mexico, DF
Tel: (052) 55-5535-9488 *Fax:* (052) 722-232-0662

Key Personnel
Publisher: Virginia V De Barrios
 E-mail: barriosb@prodigy.net.mx
Founded: 1963
Specialize in Books in English only.
Subjects: Anthropology, Archaeology, Biological Sciences, Cookery, Crafts, Games, Hobbies, History, Natural History, Religion - Catholic, Travel
ISBN Prefix(es): 968-7074
U.S. Office(s): MEX/ICS, 124 Cota Ave, San Clemente, CA 92672, United States, Contact: Jean Stenzel *Tel:* 949-492-1257 *Fax:* 949-492-1257

Galeria de Arte Misrachi SA
Genova No 20-A, Col Juarez, 06600 Mexico, DF
Tel: (05) 5334551 *Fax:* (05) 55257187
E-mail: misrachi@acnet.net
Key Personnel
Manager: Enrique Beraha Misrachi
Editorial, Sales, Production, Rights & Permissions, Publicity: Beraha Carlos Cohen
Founded: 1961
Subjects: Art
ISBN Prefix(es): 968-7047
Subsidiaries: Galeria Misrachi SA de CV

Impresora Multiple SA, *imprint of* Editorial Avante SA de Cv

Mundo Medico SA de CV Edicion y Distribucion de Revistas Medicas
Ejercito Nacional No 381, Col Granada, 11520 Mexico, DF
Tel: (05) 5203-8111 *Fax:* (05) 5601-0815
E-mail: info@grupomundomedico.com
Web Site: www.mundomedico.com.mx
Key Personnel
Contact: Julieta Cano Garcia
Founded: 1973
Subjects: Medicine, Nursing, Dentistry
ISBN Prefix(es): 968-7204
U.S. Office(s): Mundo Medico, 600 B Lake St, Ramsey, NJ 07446, United States

Instituto Nacional de Antropologia e Historia (National Institute of Anthropology & History)+
Cordoba 45, Col Roma, Mexico, DF 06700
Mailing Address: Editor Coord Nat Difusion/Alvaro Obregon, No 151-3 Col Roma, CP 06700 Mexico DF
Tel: (055) 5335246; (055) 5332272; (055) 2074559; (055) 2074584 *Fax:* (055) 2074633
E-mail: difusion.cdifus@inah.gob.mx
Web Site: www.inah.gob.mx
Key Personnel
International Rights: Gerardo Jaramillo
Founded: 1822
Governmental Institution devoted to the preservation, research & promotion of Mexican historical heritage.
Subjects: Americana, Regional, Anthropology, Antiques, Archaeology, Art, History, Language Arts, Linguistics, Music, Dance, Native American Studies, Photography, Social Sciences, Sociology
ISBN Prefix(es): 968-6038; 968-6068; 968-6487
Total Titles: 120 Print
Distributed by Educal Libros y Arte
Orders to: Coord Control y Promocion, Calle Frontera, No 53, Col San Angel, Mexico DF CP 01000, Contact: Laura Hernandez *Tel:* (055) 550-9714; (055) 550-9676; (055) 550-8631 *Fax:* (055) 550-3503
E-mail: coordinacion.cncpbs@inah.gob.mx *Web Site:* www.tiendadelmuseo.com.mx

Instituto Nacional de Estadistica, Geographia e Informatica (National Institute of Statistics, Geography & Informatics)
Av Heroe de Nacozari Sur No 2301, Jardines del Parque, 20270 Aguascalientes Ags CP
Tel: 449 910 5300 (ext 5021) *Fax:* 449 918 2232
E-mail: ventas@dgd.inegi.gob.mx
Web Site: www.inegi.gob.mx
Key Personnel
Contact: Daniel de Lira Luna
Subjects: Developing Countries, Earth Sciences, Economics, Geography, Geology, Social Sciences, Sociology
ISBN Prefix(es): 970-13; 968-892

Naves Internacional de Ediciones SA+
Amores No 135, Col Del Valle, Del Benito Juarez, 03100 Mexico, DF
Tel: (05) 6690595; (05) 9180055595 *Fax:* (05) 6823728
E-mail: niesa@mpsnet.com.mx
Key Personnel
Contact: Pablo Llaca
Founded: 1981
Subjects: Advertising, Architecture & Interior Design, Art, Cookery, Photography
Associate Companies: Ramon Llaca y Cia SA
Distributor for Celeste; Folio; Idea Books; Juventud; Naturart; Tursen
Book Club(s): Club de Editores, AC

Nori, *imprint of* Editorial Limusa SA de CV

Noriega Editores, *imprint of* Editorial Limusa SA de CV

Nova Grupo Editorial SA de CV+
Panama 820-3, Portales, 03300 Mexico, DF
Tel: 5320946 *Fax:* (05) 6050879
Key Personnel
Contact: Oscar Pruneda Portilla
Founded: 1987
Subjects: Communications, Education, Health, Nutrition, Language Arts, Linguistics, Mathematics, Nonfiction (General), Science (General), Self-Help
ISBN Prefix(es): 968-6197
Associate Companies: Oscar Edwin Pruneda Alvarez
Distributor for Oscar Edwin Pruneda Alvarez
Orders to: Zacahuitzco 165, Mexico 09440 DF
Tel: 5397678 *Fax:* 5497666

Editorial Nova, SA de CV
Goldsmith 37-401, Col Polanco, CP 11550 Mexico, DF
Tel: (05) 2 80 60 80 *Fax:* (05) 2 80 31 94
E-mail: bolind@viernes.iwm.com.mx
Key Personnel
Dir: Valades Humberto *E-mail:* hvaldes@iwm.com.mx
Subjects: Advertising

Editorial Nuestro Tiempo SA+
Av Copilco 300 Locales 6 y 7, 04360 Mexico, DF
Tel: (05) 5503165; (05) 5503170
Key Personnel
Man Dir: Esperanza Nacif Barquet
Founded: 1966
Subjects: Social Sciences, Sociology
ISBN Prefix(es): 968-427
Branch Office(s)
Agencia Guadalajara, Federalismo 958 Sur, Sol Moderna, 44100 Guadalajara, Jalisco *Tel:* (036) 126037

Editorial Nueva Imagen SA
Blvd Adolfo Lopez Mateos 202 50 Piso, Col San Pedro de los Pinos, 03800 Mexico, DF
Tel: (05) 2711980

Telex: 1771427 Eni Me
Key Personnel
Administrative Dir: Enrique Sealtiel Alatriste L
Editorial Dir: Guillermo J Schavelzon
Founded: 1976
Subjects: Anthropology, Art, Economics, Fiction, Health, Nutrition, History, Humor, Language Arts, Linguistics, Regional Interests, Science (General), Social Sciences, Sociology
ISBN Prefix(es): 968-429

Organizacion Cultural LP SA de CV+
Praga No 56 - 40 Piso, Col Juarez, 06600 Mexico, DF
Tel: (05) 55112312; (05) 147608
E-mail: orgcult@mail.internet.com.mx
Key Personnel
Contact: Joaquin Martin Gamero Castillo
Subjects: Accounting, Astronomy, Biological Sciences, Child Care & Development, Computer Science, Cookery, Management, Sports, Athletics
ISBN Prefix(es): 968-6007; 970-01

Origen Editorial SA
c/o Editorial Diana SA de CV, Arenal No 24-Edif Norte, Ex Hacienda Guadalupe Chimalistac, Delegacion Alvaro Obregon, 01050 Mexico, DF
Tel: (055) 50-89-12-20 *Fax:* (055) 50-89-12-30
ISBN Prefix(es): 968-847

Editorial Orion
Sierra Mojada No 325, Col Lomas de Chapultepec, CP 11000 Mexico 10, DF
Tel: (05) 5200224 *Fax:* (05) 5200224
Key Personnel
Man Dir: Silvia Hernandez Vda de Cardenas
Sales Dir, Rights & Permissions: Laura Hernandez Baltazar
Publicity Dir: Silvia Hernandez Baltazar
Founded: 1942
Subjects: Astrology, Occult, Literature, Literary Criticism, Essays, Parapsychology, Philosophy, Psychology, Psychiatry, Religion - Other
ISBN Prefix(es): 968-6053; 968-6957
Subsidiaries: Edit Cuzamil SA

Paginas Mesoamericanas, *imprint of* Ediciones Euroamericanas

Editorial Paidos Mexicana, SA
Ruben Dario 118, Colonia Moderna, 03510 Mexico, DF
Tel: (05) 5795922; (05) 5795113 *Fax:* (05) 5904361
E-mail: epaidos@paidos.com.mx
Web Site: www.paidos.com
Key Personnel
International Rights: Mauricio M Morlett
Founded: 1945
ISBN Prefix(es): 968-853

Palabra Ediciones S A de C V
Formerly Palabra Ediciones Verlagsgesellschaft mbh
Triunfo de la Libertad No 5-2, Col Tlalpan, 14000 Tlalpan
Tel: (05) 5730985 *Fax:* (05) 5730985
Key Personnel
Contact: Henry C Bergonzi Braconi
Subjects: Religion - Catholic
ISBN Prefix(es): 968-6460; 968-7515
Associate Companies: Cosmos Libros SRL, Moreno, 1369 1 A Buenos Aires, Argentina

Palabra Ediciones Verlagsgesellschaft mbh, see Palabra Ediciones S A de C V

Instituto Panamericano de Geografia e Historia
Ex-Arzobispado 29, Col Observatorio, 11800 Mexico, DF

MEXICO

Tel: (05) 2775888; (05) 5151910; (05) 2775791
Fax: (05) 2716172
E-mail: cvasi@ipgh.spin.com.mx *Cable:* IPAGHIS
Key Personnel
Secretary-General: Carlos Carvallo Yanez
Founded: 1928
Specialized Organization of the OEA.
Subjects: Anthropology, Archaeology, Ethnicity, Geography, Geology, History, Regional Interests
ISBN Prefix(es): 968-6384; 84-8420

Pangea Editores, Sa de CV+
Arenal 2553-4, Santa Ursula Xitla, 14420 Mexico, DF
Tel: (05) 5738684 *Fax:* (05) 5130638
E-mail: pangea@data.net.mx
Founded: 1986
Subjects: Anthropology, Archaeology, Astrology, Occult, Astronomy, Biography, Biological Sciences, Science Fiction, Fantasy, Self-Help
ISBN Prefix(es): 968-6177

Panorama Editorial, SA+
Manuel Maria Contreras, No 45 B, Col San Rafael, 06470 Mexico, DF
Tel: (05) 5359348; (05) 5359074; (05) 5350377
Fax: (05) 5359202; (05) 5351217
E-mail: panorama@iserve.net.mx
Web Site: www.panoramaed.com.mx
Key Personnel
Dir General: Luis Castaneda
Commercial Dir: Pilar Marquez
Founded: 1979
Subjects: Business, Health, Nutrition, History, Human Relations, Humor, Management, Regional Interests, Self-Help, Travel
ISBN Prefix(es): 968-38

Editorial Libreria Parroquial de Claveria SA de CV+
Floresta 79, Col Claveria, 02080 Mexico, DF
Tel: (05) 3991102; (05) 3994975; (05) 3995412; (05) 3995716 *Fax:* (05) 3991243
ISBN Prefix(es): 968-442

Editorial Patria SA de CV+
Av San Lorenzo No 160, Col Esther Zuno de Echeverria-1, 09860 Mexico, DF
Tel: (05) 6704712 *Fax:* (05) 5613218
Telex: 1764172
Key Personnel
Man Dir: Rene Solis
Deputy Manager & Administrator, Rights & Permissions: Isabel Lasa
Sales & Publicity Dir: Rogelio Villarreal
Founded: 1933
Subjects: Biography, History, How-to, Literature, Literary Criticism, Essays, Philosophy
ISBN Prefix(es): 968-6054; 968-39
Divisions: Alianza; Nueva Imagen; Promexa

Editorial Pax Mexico+
Av Cuauhtemoc 1430, Col Santa Cruz Atoyac, 03310 Mexico, DF
Tel: 5688-4828; 5604-0843 *Fax:* 5605-7677
E-mail: editorialpax@editorialpax.com
Web Site: www.editorialpax.com
Key Personnel
Man Dir: Gerardo Gally *E-mail:* gerardogally@editorialpax.com
Founded: 1936
Subjects: Business, Career Development, Education, Health, Nutrition, How-to, Psychology, Psychiatry
ISBN Prefix(es): 968-860
Associate Companies: Hoja Casa Editorial SA
Subsidiaries: Arbol Editorial SA

Pearson Educacion de Mexico, SA de CV+
Atlacomulco No 500, 4to, Piso Industrial Atoto Naucalpah, Estado de Mexico 53370
Toll Free Tel: 01 800 0054276 *Fax:* (05) 387-0700
E-mail: firstname.lastname@pearsoned.com
Web Site: www.pearson.com.mx
Key Personnel
President, Mexico, Central America & Caribbean: Steve Marban
Dir, Finance & Operations: Sven Boes
Dir, ELT & School USP Division: Juan M Abarca
Dir, Edition & Manufacturing: Juan A Rodriguez
Founded: 1984
Subjects: Art, Biological Sciences, Business, Chemistry, Chemical Engineering, Computer Science, Economics, Education, History, Language Arts, Linguistics, Management, Mathematics, Microcomputers, Physics, Psychology, Psychiatry, Science (General), Securities, Sports, Athletics, Technology
ISBN Prefix(es): 968-444; 968-880; 970-17
Total Titles: 76 Print
Parent Company: Pearson Plc
Imprints: Addison Wesley; Allyn & Bacon; Scott Foresman; Longman; Penguin Readers; Prentice Hall Hispanoamericana; Silver Burdette Ginn
Branch Office(s)
Barrio La Guaria Moravia, 75 M Norte del Porton Norte del Club la Guaria, Casa con Reja Blanca, San Jose, Costa Rica, Regional Man: Luis Diego Barrientos *Tel:* 382-3931 *Fax:* 280-6569
El Monte Mall-Suite 21-B, Ave Munoz Rivera, Hato Rey 00918-4621, Puerto Rico, Regional Man: Jose Javier Rivera *Tel:* (787) 751-4830 *Fax:* (787) 751-1677
Warehouse: Calle Negra Modelo No 12 & 12B, Fracc Industrial Alce Blanco, Naucalpan de Juarez, Estado de Mexico 53770 *Tel:* (05) 363 0842 *Fax:* (05) 363 4579

Penguin Readers, *imprint of* Pearson Educacion de Mexico, SA de CV

Publicaciones Piramide, SA de CV+
3ra Cerrada del Lago Silverio, No 30 Col Anahuac, 11320 Mexico, DF
Tel: (05) 5313215 *Fax:* (05) 2725883
Key Personnel
Dir General: Clive Alexander Bayne
Founded: 1983
ISBN Prefix(es): 968-6070

Editorial Planeta Mexicana SA
Insurgentes Sur No 1162, Col Del Valle, Del Benito Juarez, 03100 Mexico, DF
Tel: (05) 5758585; (05) 5758019; (05) 5755320 *Fax:* (05) 5758980
Web Site: www.editorialplaneta.com.mx
Key Personnel
Man Dir, Editorial: Joaquin Diez-Canedo
Production, Rights & Permissions: Francisco Campos
Founded: 1977
Subjects: Fiction, History, Nonfiction (General), Psychology, Psychiatry, Social Sciences, Sociology
ISBN Prefix(es): 968-6640
Parent Company: Grupo Planeta
Branch Office(s)
Editoriales Ariel, Planeta, Seix Barral, Joaquin Planeta

Plaza y Valdes SA de CV+
Cedro No 299, Col Sta Maria La Rivera, 06400 Mexico, DF
Tel: (05) 5359851; (05) 5664055
E-mail: editorial@plazayvaldes.com.mx
Key Personnel
Dir General: Fernando Valdes

Founded: 1987
Membership(s): Mexican Publishing Association.
Subjects: Agriculture, Anthropology, Archaeology, Communications, Public Administration, Religion - Buddhist, Science (General), Science Fiction, Fantasy, Social Sciences, Sociology
ISBN Prefix(es): 968-856
Associate Companies: Libermex SA-de-CV Libreria Bunuel
Branch Office(s)
Libros Sin Fronteras, PO Box 2085, Olympia, WA 98507-2085, United States *Tel:* 206-357-4332 *Fax:* 206-357-4332
Bookshop(s): Insurgentes sur 32 Col Juarez, 06600 Mexico DF

Editorial Porrua SA
Ave Republica, Argentina No 15, Centro, 06020 Mexico, DF
Tel: (05) 7024934; (05) 7024574 *Fax:* (05) 7026529 *Cable:* PORRUAS MEXICO
Key Personnel
Dir General & President: Jose Antonio Perez Porrua
Founded: 1900
Subjects: Literature, Literary Criticism, Essays
ISBN Prefix(es): 968-432; 968-452; 970-07
Orders to: Libreria de Porrua Hnos y Cia SA, Apdo M-7990, Argentina 15

Ediciones Cientificas La Prensa Medica Mexicana SA de CV+
Arquitectura No 29, Col Copilco Universidad, 04360 Mexico, DF
Tel: (05) 5504500 *Fax:* (05) 6589193 *Cable:* LAPREMEMEX
Key Personnel
Man Dir, Rights & Permissions: Carlos A Fournier Amor
Administration & Assistant Manager: Abel Zavaleta
Sales & Promotion: Angelica Ruiz
Founded: 1945
Membership(s): National Chamber of the Mexican Editorial Industry.
Subjects: Biological Sciences, Education, Medicine, Nursing, Dentistry, Social Sciences, Sociology, Veterinary Science
ISBN Prefix(es): 968-435

Prentice Hall Hispanoamericana, *imprint of* Pearson Educacion de Mexico, SA de CV

Editorial Progreso SA de C V
Naranjo 248, Col Santa Maria La Ribera, 06400 Cuauhtemoc
Tel: (05) 5477304 *Fax:* (05) 5415342
E-mail: editprogresosav@infosel.net.mx
Key Personnel
Dir: Joaquin Flores Segura *Fax:* (055) 41 11 89 *E-mail:* progdir@webtelmex.net.mx
Founded: 1952
Subjects: Education, Religion - Catholic
ISBN Prefix(es): 968-436; 970-641
Number of titles published annually: 300 Print
Total Titles: 3,000,000 Print

Ediciones Promesa, SA de CV+
Justo Sierra, 53-A, Circuito Educadores, Ciudad Satelite, Edo de
Mailing Address: Apdo P.97 CP 53140 Boulevares, Edo de Mexico, Mexico
Tel: (05) 5623174; (05) 3938707 *Fax:* (05) 5623174
E-mail: promesa@mati.net.mx; riveraluisa@hotmail.com
Key Personnel
Contact: Fernando B Rivera
Founded: 1979
Subjects: Anthropology, Architecture & Interior Design, Biography, Child Care & Development, Education, Fashion, Fiction, Film, Video, Human Relations, Language Arts, Linguistics,

Music, Dance, Philosophy, Poetry, Psychology, Psychiatry, Religion - Catholic, Theology, Women's Studies
ISBN Prefix(es): 968-7224

Promociones de Mercados Turisticos SA de CV
Gral Juan Cano No 68, Col San Miguel Chapultepec, Del Miguel Hidalgo, 11850 Mexico, DF
Mailing Address: Apartado 6-1007, 06600 Mexico, DF
Tel: (05) 2771480; (05) 5160162; (05) 2714736 *Fax:* (05) 2725942
E-mail: tm@mail.internet.com.mx
Web Site: www.travelguidemexico.com
Key Personnel
Dir: Chris A Luhnow
Specialize in publishing & editing.
Subjects: Travel, Most complete & sold guide book to Mexico
Total Titles: 3 Print

Publicaciones Cultural SA de CV
Renacimiento 180, Col San Juan Tlihuaca, Azcapotzalco, 02400 Mexico, DF
Tel: (05) 55618333; (05) 55619299 *Fax:* (05) 5615231; (05) 55614063
E-mail: info@patriacultural.com.mx
Web Site: www.patriacultural.com.mx
Key Personnel
President: Carlos Frigolet Lerma
General Dir, Editorial, Production & Sales: Victorico Albores Santiago
Rights & Permissions: Ofelia Garcia Martinez
Production: Mario Munoz Rodriguez
Founded: 1965
ISBN Prefix(es): 968-439; 970-16

Publicaciones Importantes SA
Bolivar No 8-601, Apdo 1907, 06000 Mexico 1, DF
Tel: (05) 5101884; (05) 5109489 *Fax:* (05) 5129411
Key Personnel
Contact: Alfredo Farrugia Reed

Editorial Quehacer Politico SA
Manuael Gonzales No 545, Col Atlampa, CP 06450 Mexico, DF
Tel: (05) 5414245 *Fax:* (05) 5384855
Web Site: 148.233.5.66/qp/
Key Personnel
General Dir: Miguel Canton Zetina
Editorial Dir: Jorge Luis Sierra Guzman
ISBN Prefix(es): 968-6553

Red Editorial Iberoamericana Mexico SA de CV+
Lago Mayor No 186, Col Anahuac, 11320 Mexico, DF
Tel: (05) 5456860; (05) 5456861 *Fax:* (05) 5619112
Key Personnel
President: Carlos Frigolet Lerma
Rights & Permissions: Victorico Albores Santiago
Production: Mario Munoz Rodriguez
Founded: 1986
ISBN Prefix(es): 968-456

Ediciones Roca, SA+
Insurgentes Sur 1162, Col Del Valle, 03100 Mexico, DF
Tel: (05) 5758585; (05) 2770946 *Fax:* (05) 5758980
Telex: 1772155
Key Personnel
General Manager: Victor Lemus Dominquez
Founded: 1972
Subjects: Education, Environmental Studies, Fiction, History, Literature, Literary Criticism, Essays, Religion - Other
ISBN Prefix(es): 968-21

Rustica, *imprint of* AGT Editor SA

Salvat Editores de Mexico+
Presidente Mazarik No 101-5 Piso, Col Chapultepec Morales, 11560 Mexico, DF
Tel: (05) 2034813; (05) 2034393 *Fax:* (05) 5318773
E-mail: hachettemex@hachette.ex.com.mx
Key Personnel
President, Editorial, Rights & Permissions: Jean Claude Lhomme
Sales (Encyclopedias): Jacobo Jimenez Parker
Production: Teresa Ponce
Subjects: Cookery, Fiction, Geography, Geology, History, Medicine, Nursing, Dentistry
ISBN Prefix(es): 968-32
Parent Company: Salvat Editores SA, Spain
Subsidiaries: Promotora Editorial SA De C V
Bookshop(s): Libreria de Cd Universitatia, Odontologia 69, Local 9; Libreria Satelite, Plaza Satelite, Local D-155, Cd Satelite; Libreri de Morelia, Ave Francisco I Madero Pte 533, Centro, Mrelia, Mich

Editorial Santillana
Av Universidad No 767, Col Del Valle, 03100 Mexico, DF
Tel: (05) 6887566; (05) 6888227; (05) 6888966 *Fax:* (05) 6042304
E-mail: mexico@santillana.com.mx
Web Site: www.gruposantillana.com
Key Personnel
Dir, Publications: Fernando Garcia Cortes
ISBN Prefix(es): 968-430; 970-642
Parent Company: Grupo Santillana

Grupo Santillana
Av Universidad No 767, Col Del Valle, 03100 Mexico, DF
Tel: (05) 6888966; (05) 6887566; (05) 6888227 *Fax:* (05) 6042304
E-mail: mexico@santillana.com.mx
Web Site: www.gruposantillana.com
Key Personnel
Dir General: Jorge Delkader Teig
Contact: Manuel Sabido Duran
ISBN Prefix(es): 968-430; 970-642
Divisions: Actea; Aguilar; Distribuidora Aguilar; Aguilar Mexicana de Ediciones; Alfaquara SA Dec v; Altea Taurus; Editorial Santillana SA Dec v; Taurus

Sayrols Editorial SA de CV+
Mier y Pesado No 128, Col Del Valle, 03100 Mexico, DF
Tel: (05) 660-3535 *Fax:* (05) 687-4699
E-mail: ventas@sayrols.com.mx
Web Site: www.sayrols.com.mx
Key Personnel
General Dir: Roberto Davo *E-mail:* rodavo@sayrols.com.mx
Corporate Sales Dir: Federico Falkner *E-mail:* ffalkner@sayrols.com.mx
Business & Technology Sales Manager: Beatriz Coria *Tel:* (0525) 536-4115 *E-mail:* beatrizc@sayrols.com.mx
Administrative Dir: Lourdes Noriega *E-mail:* lnoriega@sayrols.com.mx
Finance Manager: Raul Saryols *E-mail:* rauls@saryols.com.mx
Circulation Manager: Luis Sayrols *E-mail:* luiss@sayrols.com.mx
Founded: 1925
Specialize in information technology & business titles.
Provides editorial, printing & distribution services.
Subjects: Astrology, Occult, Automotive, Business, Computer Science, Cookery, Crafts, Games, Hobbies, Education, Fashion, Sports, Athletics, Women's Studies
ISBN Prefix(es): 968-6117

Total Titles: 30 Print
Associate Companies: Mystic Impresiones, SA (Printing); Publicaciones Sayrols, SA
Subsidiaries: Servicios Editoriales Sayrols Sa de W
Distributor for AIE (Italy); Grupo Editorial Ideas, SA (Mexico); Hymsa Edipress (Spain); Ediciones Pleyades (Spain); Servicios de Edicion Mexico, SA (Editorial); Servicios Editoriales Sayrols, SA (Editorial); Servicios Graficos Sayrols, SA (Design & pre press services)

SCRIPTA - Distribucion y Servicios Editoriales, SA de CV+
Copilco 178 Edif 21-501, Col Copilco Universidad, 04340 Mexico, DF
Mailing Address: Apdo Postal 70 649, 140000 Mexico, DF
Tel: (05) 5481716 *Fax:* (05) 6161496
E-mail: dyse@data.net.mx
Key Personnel
Contact: Bertha R Alavez Magana
Founded: 1986
Also acts as Exporter & Distributor.
Subjects: Art, Business, Film, Video, History
ISBN Prefix(es): 968-6269
Branch Office(s)
Scripta, 4011 Creek Rd, Youngstown, NY 14174, United States *Tel:* 716-754-8145 *Fax:* 716-754-2707

Selector SA de CV+
Dr Erazo 120 Colonia Doctores, 06720 Mexico, DF
Tel: (055) 588-7272 *Fax:* (055) 761-5716
E-mail: info@selector.com.mx
Web Site: www.selector.com.mx
Key Personnel
President: Gonzalo Araico Montes de Oca
Sales Dir: Francisco Merino Nieto
Publisher: Ma del Carmen Leal
Editorial Assistant: Rocio Flores
Management Dir: Maricruz Vazquez Ruiz
Production Dir: Victor Becerra Rodriguez
Founded: 1949
Subjects: Child Care & Development, Crafts, Games, Hobbies, English as a Second Language, Health, Nutrition, Human Relations, Humor, Nonfiction (General), Science Fiction, Fantasy, Self-Help
ISBN Prefix(es): 968-403; 970-643
Number of titles published annually: 77 Print
Branch Office(s)
Priscilano Sanchez 579, Col Centr, 44100 Guadalajara, Jalisco
Sucursal Monterrey, Washington 112 B, Altos, Col Centro, Monterrey, NL, Contact: Francisco Mendoza Salazar *Tel:* (08) 340 3260
Distributed by Ediciones Oceano Argentina SA; Editorial Diana Colombia Ltda; Carlos Federspiel y Co SA; Editorial Diana Chilena Ltd; Editorial Oceano Ecuatorian SA; Almacenes Siman SA; Distribuciones Alfaomega SA; Publicaciones Yuquivo; Central De Libros C POR A; Giron Spanish Book; Lectorum Publications Inc; Editorial Oceno Peruana SA; Vendiana Editorial AC; Editorial Oceano De Venezuela SA
Foreign Rep(s): Almacenes Siman (El Salvador); Central de Libros C. Por A. (Dominican Republic); Distribuciones Alfaomega, S.A. (Spain); Ediciones Oceano Argentina, SA (Argentina); Editorial Diana Chilena Ltda (Chile); Editorial Diana Colombiana Ltda (Colombia); Editorial Oceano Ecuatoriana, S.A. (Ecuador); Carlos Federspiel y Co., S.A. (Costa Rica); Giron Spanish Books Dist. Inc (USA); Lectorum Publications Inc (USA); Libreria Lehmann, S.A. (Costa Rica); Publicaciones Yuquiyu (Puerto Rico); Santa Maria Representaciones Editoriales (Central America); Venediana Editorial, A.C. (Venezuela)

MEXICO

Bookshop(s): Lectorum, SA de CV, Calzada Del Hueso 809, Locales 8 y 9, Col Mirador Coapa, Mexico, DF *Tel:* (055) 6030790; Un Paseo Por Libros, Pasaje Zocalo-Pino Suarez, Local 21, Mexico, DF *Tel:* (055) 522 3578; (055) 522 3486

Servicios Especiales Maciel SA de CV+
Dallas 85 201, Col Napoles, 03810 Mexico, DF
Tel: 05 5435533
Key Personnel
General Dir: Maria Luisa Sabau Garcia
Foreign Rights Manager: Jorge Ruiz Esparza
Founded: 1987
Membership(s): the National Association of the Publishing Industry.
Subjects: Architecture & Interior Design, Art, Cookery, Photography
ISBN Prefix(es): 968-6084

Siglo XXI Editores SA de CV+
Av Cerro del Agua, No 248, Col Romero de Terreros, 04310 Mexico, DF
Tel: (05) 6587999; (05) 6587588 *Fax:* (05) 6587599
E-mail: sigloxxi@inetcorp.net.mx
Web Site: www.sigloxxi-editores.com.mx *Cable:* SIGLOEDIT
Key Personnel
Man Dir, Editorial: Arnaldo Orfila; Jaime Labastida
General Manager, Rights & Permissions & Publicity: Guadalupe Ortiz
Sales & Contact: Marta De la Rosa
Production: Maria Oscos
Founded: 1966
Subjects: Anthropology, Architecture & Interior Design, Art, Criminology, Economics, Education, Government, Political Science, Health, Nutrition, History, Language Arts, Linguistics, Law, Literature, Literary Criticism, Essays, Philosophy, Psychology, Psychiatry, Regional Interests, Science (General), Social Sciences, Sociology
ISBN Prefix(es): 968-23

Silver Burdette Ginn, *imprint of* Pearson Educacion de Mexico, SA de CV

Sistemas Tecnicos de Edicion SA de CV+
San Marcos No 102, Col Tlalpan, 14000 Mexico, DF
Tel: (05) 6559144; (05) 6845220 *Fax:* (05) 5739412
Telex: 1771410 *Cable:* SITEME
Key Personnel
President: Jose Ignacio Echeverria
Editor: Marsella Cruz
International Operations: Emma Moreno
Founded: 1985
Subjects: Animals, Pets, Behavioral Sciences, Biological Sciences, Cookery, Earth Sciences, History, Language Arts, Linguistics, Management, Mathematics, Self-Help
ISBN Prefix(es): 968-6579; 970-629

Sistemas Universales, SA+
Insurgentes Centro 123, Col San Rafael, 06470 Mexico, DF
Mailing Address: Apdo Postal 61-178, 06470 Mexico, DF
Tel: (05) 705-4568; (05) 705-5937 *Fax:* (05) 705-3421
E-mail: 73661.405@coms
Key Personnel
Contact: Arturo Delgado
Founded: 1970
Specialize in Post Secondary technical books for distance education.
Subjects: Accounting, Automotive, Electronics, Electrical Engineering, English as a Second Language, Microcomputers

ISBN Prefix(es): 968-6064
Total Titles: 290 Print
Distributed by Hemphill California Corporation

Ediciones Suromex SA+
General Francisco Murguia No 7, Col Hipodromo de la Condesa, 06170 Mexico, DF
Tel: (055) 2770744; (055) 2723570; (055) 2723630; (055) 2734989 *Fax:* (055) 2710470; (055) 2719378
E-mail: suromex@mail.internet.com.mx
Web Site: www.intralector.com/suromex/
Key Personnel
General Manager: Victor Lemus Dominguez
Founded: 1982
Subjects: Animals, Pets, Art, Astrology, Occult, Astronomy, Biography, Cookery, Earth Sciences, Gardening, Plants, House & Home, Religion - Other, Self-Help, Sports, Athletics, House & home
ISBN Prefix(es): 968-855
Number of titles published annually: 70 Print
Total Titles: 350 Print
Parent Company: Susaeta Ediciones SA
Subsidiaries: Susaeta Ediciones SA

Time-Life Internacional de Mexico
Paseo de la Reforma 195-10º, Decimo Piso, Col Cuauhtemoc, 06500 Mexico, DF
Tel: (055) 5469000 *Fax:* (055) 5159764
Web Site: www.timelife.com
Key Personnel
General Manager: Koos H Siewers
Founded: 1962
Subjects: Nonfiction (General)
ISBN Prefix(es): 968-7123

Travelers Guide to Mexico, see Promociones de Mercados Turisticos SA de CV

Editorial Trillas SA de CV+
Av Rio Churubusco 385, Pedro Maria Anaya, 03340 Mexico, DF
Tel: (055) 6330612; (055) 6331112 *Fax:* (055) 6330870; (055) 6342221
E-mail: laviga@trillas.com.mx; Trillasenvios@att.net.mx
Web Site: www.trillas.com.mx
Telex: 1762109 Etrime *Cable:* ETRILLASA
Key Personnel
Man Dir: Francisco Trillas
Editorial: Carlos Trillas
Sales: Jesus Galera
Production: Alfonso Duran
Publicity: Sergio Shinji
Founded: 1953
Subjects: Architecture & Interior Design, Business, Child Care & Development, Crafts, Games, Hobbies, Education, English as a Second Language, House & Home, Law, Mathematics, Medicine, Nursing, Dentistry, Psychology, Psychiatry, Science (General), Social Sciences, Sociology, Veterinary Science
ISBN Prefix(es): 968-24
Associate Companies: Cia Editorial Carmex SA, Venezuela 1962, Buenos Aires, Argentina; Cia Editorial Atlante, Argentina S RL Junin 827; Apdo aereo 15-15, Bogota, Spain; Limex Venezolana CA, Ave Lima Quinta Lourdes, Los Caobos, Caracas, Venezuela; Trillas Colombia, Carreroi 15 No 33-71 Apdo, Aereo 15-151, Santa Fe de Boqota, Colombia, Joslyne Reyno; Biblouex SA, Raigizas 10.28026, Madrid, Spain
Branch Office(s)
Calzada de la Viga 1132, Col Apatlaco, Delegacon Iztapalapa, 09439 Mexico, DF *Tel:* (055) 6579188 *Fax:* (055) 6579235
Showroom(s): Av Cuahutemoc, 12000
Orders to: Calzada de la Viga 1132, Col Apatlaco, Delegacon Iztapalapa, 09439 Mexico, DF *Tel:* (055) 6579188 *Fax:* (055) 6579235

El Trimestre Economico, *imprint of* Fondo de Cultura Economica

Editorial Turner de Mexico
Edificio Condesa, Cda de Matehuala 1-6, Colonia Condesa, 06140 Mexico, DF
Tel: (055) 5553 1183 *Fax:* (055) 5211 2070
Web Site: www.turnerlibros.com
Key Personnel
Rights: Alexandra Garcia *E-mail:* alexgarcia@turnermexico.com
Founded: 2003
General nonfiction in the fields of history, literary criticism, art philosophy, music & bullfighting.
Subjects: Art, Business, Economics, Finance, Literature, Literary Criticism, Essays, Photography, Bullfighting
Number of titles published annually: 120 Print
Total Titles: 400 Print
Parent Company: Turner Publicaciones
Branch Office(s)
Turner Publicaciones SL, C/Rafael Calvo, 42, esc izda, 2a planta, 28010 Madrid, Spain, Contact: Juan Garcia de Oteyza *Tel:* (091) 308 33 36 *Fax:* (091) 319 39 30 *E-mail:* turner@turnerlibros.com
Distributed by Distributed Art Publishers (DAP) (USA); Editorial Oceano, SA DE CV (Latin America)

Universidad Nacional Autonoma de Mexico (National University of Mexico)+
Zona Cultural s/n Edificio B 3er Piso, Col Ciudad Universitaria, 04510 Mexico, DF
Tel: (05) 6226329; (05) 6226330 *Fax:* (05) 6226328
E-mail: libros@bibliounam.unam.mx
Key Personnel
Dir: Mario Mendoza Castaneda
Assistant Dir: Leonardo Duenas Garcia
Founded: 1935
Subjects: Anthropology, Archaeology, Architecture & Interior Design, Chemistry, Chemical Engineering, Drama, Theater, Economics, Education, Engineering (General), Ethnicity, Geography, Geology, History, Journalism, Language Arts, Linguistics, Law, Literature, Literary Criticism, Essays, Mathematics, Medicine, Nursing, Dentistry, Music, Dance, Philosophy, Physics, Psychology, Psychiatry, Science (General), Social Sciences, Sociology, Technology, Veterinary Science
ISBN Prefix(es): 968-36
U.S. Office(s): Hemisfair Plaza, PO Box 830426, San Antonio, TX 78283-0426, United States
Bookshop(s): Libreria Central, Corredor de Zona Comercial, Ciudad Universitaria, 04510 Mexico DF; Libreria del Palacio de Mineria, Tacuba 5, 06000 Mexico DF; Casa Universitaria del Libro, Orizaba y Puebla, Col Roma, 06710 Mexico DF; Libreria Julio Torri, Zona Cultura, Cuidad Universitaria, 04510 Mexico DF

Universidad Veracruzana Direccion General Editorial y de Publicaciones
Lomas del Estadio s/n, Col Centro, 91000 Jalapa, Veracruz
Tel: (029) 71316
E-mail: direditaspeedy@coacade.uv.mx
Web Site: www.uv.mx
Key Personnel
Sales & Subscriptions: Jaime Pasqual Brash
Founded: 1957
Subjects: Anthropology, Art, Drama, Theater, Education, Fiction, History, Music, Dance, Philosophy, Psychology, Psychiatry, Social Sciences, Sociology
ISBN Prefix(es): 968-834
Total Titles: 15 Print

Parent Company: Universidad Veracruzana
Distributed by Direccion Editorial Universidad Veracruzana (Mexico)

Universo Editorial SA de CV Edicion de Libros Revistas y Periodicos+
c/o Arco Iris Editorial, Emelia Carranza No 105, 78290 San Luis Potosi
Tel: (048) 21593
Key Personnel
Contact: Edmundo Llamas
Founded: 1991
Subjects: Biological Sciences, Fiction, Journalism, Literature, Literary Criticism, Essays, Medicine, Nursing, Dentistry, Poetry
ISBN Prefix(es): 968-6504

Editorial Universo SA de CV
Roberto Gayol No 1219, Col Del Valle, 03100 Mexico, DF
Tel: (05) 5750711 ext 30; (05) 5750711 ext 31
Key Personnel
Man Dir, Rights & Permissions: Enrique Ivan H Garcia
Editorial: Fausto Rosales
Sales: Manuel Valdez Islas
Production: Enrique Escamilla
Publicity: Maria del Refugio Salinas
Founded: 1979
Subjects: Fiction, Nonfiction (General)
ISBN Prefix(es): 968-35
Parent Company: Editorial Diana SA
Associate Companies: Editorial Origen SA; Edivision Cia Editorial SA
Branch Office(s)
Buenos Aires, Argentina
Guadalajara
Monterrey
Caracas, Venezuela

Uteha, *imprint of* Editorial Limusa SA de CV

Editorial Varazen SA+
Herodoto No 42, Col Anzures, 11590 Mexico, DF
Tel: (05) 5459230; (05) 5335274 *Fax:* (05) 2555172
Key Personnel
Man Dir: Luis Maria Molachino Agostena
Founded: 1968
Subjects: Education, Ethnicity
ISBN Prefix(es): 968-7128
Associate Companies: Editorial Juventud, SA, Barcelona, Spain

Ventura Ediciones, SA de CV
Rio Ganges No 64, Col Cuauhtemoc, 06500 Mexico, DF
Tel: (05) 2087681; (05) 5530798 *Fax:* (05) 5431173
Key Personnel
General Dir: Nicolas Grepe
Founded: 1988
Subjects: Computer Science, Microcomputers
ISBN Prefix(es): 968-6346; 968-7393

Javier Vergara Editor SA de CV
Av Cuauhtemoc 1100, Col Vertiz Navarte, 03600 Mexico, DF
Tel: (05) 6053374; (05) 6048283
Key Personnel
General Manager: Elsa Marino
Founded: 1978
Subjects: Biography, Business, Fiction, History, Music, Dance, Nonfiction (General), Psychology, Psychiatry, Self-Help
ISBN Prefix(es): 968-497
Parent Company: Javier Vergara Editor Argentina

Editorial Vuelta, SA de CV+
Presidente Carranza No 210, Coyoacan, 04000 Mexico, DF
Tel: (05) 5548810; (05) 5548811 *Fax:* (05) 6580074
Key Personnel
President: Octavio Paz
Manager: Patricia Rodriguez Ochoa
Secretary: Enrique Krauze
ISBN Prefix(es): 968-6229

Martha Zamora Edicion de Libros
Bosque del Castillo 35, La Herradura, Huixquilucan Edo, 53920 Mexico, DF
Tel: (05) 2940231 *Fax:* (05) 2943856
Key Personnel
Contact: Martha Zamora

Zona Ediciones y Publications SA de CV
Beta No 97 Col Romero de Terreros-Coyoacan, 04310 Mexico, DF
Tel: (05) 5547438
Key Personnel
Contact: Francisco Campos Fontanet
ISBN Prefix(es): 968-6174
Warehouse: Ignacio Manuel Altamirano, 212 B Col Hank Gonzalez, 09750 Mexico, DF

Republic of Moldova

General Information

Capital: Kishinev
Language: Romanian
Religion: Predominantly Christian (mostly Eastern Orthodox)
Population: 4.5 million
Bank Hours: Generally open for short hours between 0930-1230 Monday-Friday
Shop Hours: Generally 0900-1800 Monday-Friday; often open weekends
Currency: 100 kopeks = 1 rubl
Export/Import Information: According to Ukrainian quotas & customs duties, companies engaged in trade should register with the Ukraine Ministry of Foreign Economic Relations. Licenses for export & import are also required for trade with Russia.
Copyright: UCC (see Copyright Conventions, pg xi)

Editura Cartea Moldovei
bd Stefan Cel Mare 180, 2004 Chisinau
Tel: (02) 246550 *Fax:* (02) 246411
Key Personnel
Dir: N N Mumzhi
Editor-in-Chief: I A Tsurkanu
Founded: 1927
Subjects: Agriculture, Economics, Fiction, Government, Political Science, Human Relations, Literature, Literary Criticism, Essays, Social Sciences, Sociology, Scientific Research Literature
ISBN Prefix(es): 5-362

Editura Hyperion
Bdl Stefan cel Mare 180, Chisinau 277004
Tel: (02) 244259
Key Personnel
Dir: Valeriu Matei
Founded: 1976
Subjects: Art, Fiction, Literature, Literary Criticism, Essays, Music, Dance
ISBN Prefix(es): 5-368

Editura Lumina
bd Stefan cel Mare, 180, et 5, 505, 2004 Chisinau
Tel: (02) 246397; (02) 246398 *Fax:* (02) 246395
E-mail: lumina@mdl.net
Key Personnel
Manager: Vladimir Chistruga
Editor-in-Chief: Chiril Vaculovschi
Founded: 1966
Specialize in Textbooks, University Presses, Scholarly Books.
Subjects: Biological Sciences, Chemistry, Chemical Engineering, Child Care & Development, Geography, Geology, History, Language Arts, Linguistics, Literature, Literary Criticism, Essays, Mathematics, Medicine, Nursing, Dentistry, Physics, Psychology, Psychiatry, Training Manuals & Literature
ISBN Prefix(es): 5-372; 9975-65

Monaco

General Information

Capital: Monaco
Language: French. Monegasque, Italian and English also spoken
Religion: Roman Catholic
Population: 29,712
Bank Hours: 0830-1730 Monday-Friday
Shop Hours: 0830-1300, 1600-1930 Monday-Friday
Currency: 100 centimes = 1 franc
Copyright: Berne, UCC (see Copyright Conventions, pg xi)

Editions Alphee+
28 rue Comte-Felix-Gastaldi, 98015 Monaco Cedex
Mailing Address: BP 524, 98015 Monaco Cedex
Tel: (093) 30-40-06 *Fax:* (099) 99-67-18
ISBN Prefix(es): 2-907573
Associate Companies: Editions du Rocher
Tel: (099) 99-67-17 *E-mail:* info@editionsdurocher.net

Editions EGC+
9 Av du Prince Hereditair Albert, BP 438, 98011 Monaco Cedex
Tel: (093) 97984006 *Fax:* (093) 92052422
E-mail: multip@webstore.mc
Key Personnel
Administrator: M Gerard Comman
Subjects: Economics, History, Literature, Literary Criticism, Essays
ISBN Prefix(es): 2-911469

Editions Victor Gadoury
57, rue Grimaldi, MC-98000 Monaco
Tel: (093) 251296 *Fax:* (093) 501339
E-mail: contact@gadoury.com
Web Site: www.gadoury.com
Founded: 1967
ISBN Prefix(es): 2-906602

Marsu Productions SAM
9, Ave des Castelans, Monte-Carlo 98000
Tel: (093) 92056111 *Fax:* (093) 92057660
E-mail: info@marsupilami.com; marsuproductions@compuserve.com
Web Site: www.marsupilami.com
ISBN Prefix(es): 2-9502211

Editions de l'Oiseau-Lyre SAM
Les Remparts, MC 98015 Monaco, Cedex
Mailing Address: BP 515, MC 98015 Monaco, Cedex
Tel: (093) 300944 *Fax:* (093) 301915
E-mail: oiseaulyre@monaco377.com

MONACO

Web Site: www.oiseaulyre.com
Key Personnel
Man Dir: Moroney Davitt
Founded: 1932
Subjects: Music, Dance
ISBN Prefix(es): 2-87855

Publications du Palais de Monaco
Archives du Palais Princier, BP 518, MC-98015 Monaco Cedex
Tel: 093 251831
ISBN Prefix(es): 2-903147

Les Editions du Rocher+
28 rue Comte Felix Gastaldi, 98015 Monaco, Cedex
Tel: (093) 40465400 *Fax:* (093) 43293506
E-mail: jpb.droits@wanadoo.fr
Founded: 1943
Subjects: Antiques, Astrology, Occult, Biography, Crafts, Games, Hobbies, Drama, Theater, Fiction, Health, Nutrition, History, How-to, Humor, Literature, Literary Criticism, Essays, Military Science, Mysteries, Philosophy, Psychology, Psychiatry, Religion - Other, Romance, Science Fiction, Fantasy, Self-Help, Sports, Athletics, Western Fiction
ISBN Prefix(es): 2-268
Subsidiaries: Jean-Paul Bertrand Editeur
Shipping Address: 6 Place Saint, Sulpice, F-75279 Paris, France *Tel:* (01) 40465400 *Fax:* (01) 40469136

Rondeau Giannipiero a Monaco+
4 rue Langl e, 98000 Monaco
Tel: (093) 303075 *Fax:* (093) 257047
Key Personnel
President: S Roudeau
International Rights: G Roudeau
Founded: 1993
Subjects: Art, Fiction, History, Humor, Literature, Literary Criticism, Essays
ISBN Prefix(es): 2-910305

Editions Andre Sauret SA
One blvd Suisse, 98000 Monaco
Tel: (093) 506794 *Fax:* (093) 307104
Subjects: Art, Fiction, Library & Information Sciences
ISBN Prefix(es): 2-85051

Mongolia

General Information

Capital: Ulaanbaatar
Language: Mongolian
Religion: Buddhist Lamaism, Islamic, Christian
Population: 2.6 million
Bank Hours: 0900-1200, 1400-1700 Monday-Saturday
Shop Hours: 0900-1900 Monday-Saturday
Currency: 100 mongo = 1 togrog (tughrik)

Mongol Knigotorg
41 Ul Lenina, Ulan-Bator
Also functions as distributor.

State Press
Ulan-Bator
Subjects: Geography, Geology, Government, Political Science, Law

Morocco

General Information

Capital: Rabat
Language: Arabic (official), Berber, French, Spanish (northern regions)
Religion: Islamic
Population: 27 million
Bank Hours: Summer: 0830-1130, 1500-1700 Monday-Friday; rest of year: 0815-1130, 1415-1630 Monday-Friday
Shop Hours: Tangiers: 0900-1200, 1600-2000; rest: 0900-1200, 1500-1800 or 1900
Currency: 100 centimes = 1 Moroccan dirham
Export/Import Information: No tariff on books; most advertising dutiable. Special Tax, and Stamp Duty of percentage of import duty. No import licenses required. Exchange controls but permission liberally granted.
Copyright: UCC, Berne (see Copyright Conventions, pg xi)

Access International Services+
80 Blvd La Resistance, Casablanca
Tel: (02) 316068 *Fax:* (02) 304685
Key Personnel
President: Rachid Bennis
Founded: 1985
Also acts as editor & exporter of Moroccan publications.
Subjects: Advertising, Art, Business, Communications, Economics, How-to, Human Relations, Law, Publishing & Book Trade Reference, Religion - Islamic
ISBN Prefix(es): 9981-9756
Imprints: Le Repere
Branch Office(s)
African Imprint Library Services, 236 Main St, Falmouth, MA 02540, United States

Editions Al-Fourkane+
8, rue Ibn Habbous, Av Yacoub El Mansour, App No 2, Casablanca
Mailing Address: BP 20362, Hay Salam, Casablanca
Tel: (02) 983351 *Fax:* (02) 983351
Key Personnel
Dir: Dr El Otmani Saad-Dine
Subjects: Biography, Government, Political Science, Religion - Islamic, Social Sciences, Sociology
ISBN Prefix(es): 9981-811
Parent Company: Al Fouruane

Annuaine Fax Telex, *imprint of* Office Marocain D'Annonces-OMA

Association de la Recherche Historique et Sociale+
BP 57, Ksar El Kebir 92-150
Tel: 918239
Key Personnel
Contact: Mohamed Akhrif
Subjects: Antiques, Archaeology, Art, Biography, History, Natural History, Poetry
ISBN Prefix(es): 9981-9778
Distributed by Editeurs Particuliers
Distributor for Imprimerie de Tanger SA

Cabinet Conseil CCMLA
44 rue Oued Ziz, Agdal, 10000 Rabat
Tel: (07) 770229; (07) 770264 *Fax:* (07) 770264
Key Personnel
Manager: Michele Malaval
Founded: 1992
Subjects: Accounting, Developing Countries, Economics
ISBN Prefix(es): 9981-9699

Dar El Kitab
Place de la Mosquee, 4018, Habous, Casablanca
Tel: (02) 304581; (02) 305419 *Fax:* (02) 304581
Telex: 26630 Darki
Key Personnel
President: Boutaleb Abdou Abdelhay
Manager: Mrs Soad Kadiri
Publicity Manager: Mounjedine Abdel-Ghani
Production: Ferhat Mohamed
Founded: 1948
Subjects: History, Philosophy, Regional Interests, Science (General), Social Sciences, Sociology
ISBN Prefix(es): 9981-133

Dar Nachr Al Maarifa Pour L'Edition et La Distribution+
Cite Yacoub El-Mansour, Rue Errakha, Quartier Industriel, BP 1213, Rabat
Mailing Address: 10, Ave Fadela, QI CYM Rabat
Tel: (07) 795702; (07) 796914 *Fax:* (07) 790343
Key Personnel
Contact: Mr Zhiri M'Hamed
Founded: 1988
Also acts as distributor.
Membership(s): Moroccan Association of Publishers; International Publishers Association.
Subjects: Economics, Education, History, Law, Literature, Literary Criticism, Essays, Mathematics, Science (General), Social Sciences, Sociology
ISBN Prefix(es): 9981-808
Number of titles published annually: 10 Print
Total Titles: 3 Print
Distributor for APREJ
Bookshop(s): Librairie EL Maarif, SA, Rue Bab Chellah, BP 239, Rabat *Tel:* (07) 726524; 730701

Edition Diffusion de Livre au Maroc+
71 ave des Forces armees royales, 21000 Casablanca
Mailing Address: BP 7537, Casablanca
Tel: (02) 442375; (02) 442376; (02) 445986 *Fax:* (02) 313565
E-mail: info@eddif.net.ma
Telex: 23793M
Key Personnel
Chairman: Abdelkader Retnani
Dir: Fadwa Akkor
Founded: 1979
Membership(s): Moroccan Association of Profession of Books (AMPL).
Subjects: Archaeology, Art, Drama, Theater, Education, Fiction, History, How-to, Humor, Law, Literature, Literary Criticism, Essays, Medicine, Nursing, Dentistry, Music, Dance, Philosophy, Psychology, Psychiatry, Religion - Other, Social Sciences, Sociology, Travel, Women's Studies
ISBN Prefix(es): 2-908801; 9981-09
Total Titles: 300 Print
Associate Companies: Comptoir Marocain du Livre, Angles rues des Landes et Vignemale, Casablanca 20000 *Tel:* (022) 258781
Branch Office(s)
La Croisee Des Chemins
Distributor for Ceres Production (Tunisia)
Bookshop(s): Carrefour Des Arts, Rue Essanaani, Quartier Boorgogne Casablanca 20000 *Tel:* (022) 26 05 01 05 *Fax:* (022) 29 43 64
E-mail: mrctruni@caromail.com; Carrerour Des Livres, Angle rues des landes et Vignemale, Maarif Casablanca 20000 *Tel:* (022) 258781; Librairie 11 Janview, 53 av de madagascar, Rabat *Tel:* (07) 704580

Europages, *imprint of* Office Marocain D'Annonces-OMA

Editions Le Fennec+
193 av Hassan II, 01 Casablanca

Tel: (02) 220519; (02) 268008; (02) 264380
 Fax: (02) 264941
E-mail: fennec@techno.net.ma
Telex: 45468
Key Personnel
President, Editor: Laila Chaouni
Author: Fatima Mernissi
Founded: 1987
Subjects: Drama, Theater, Economics, Fiction, Health, Nutrition, Language Arts, Linguistics, Literature, Literary Criticism, Essays, Mysteries, Poetry, Psychology, Psychiatry, Religion - Islamic, Social Sciences, Sociology, Women's Studies
ISBN Prefix(es): 9981-838
Distributed by Vilo-Diffusion-Paris (Europe & Canada)

Formation Entreprises, *imprint of* Office Marocain D'Annonces-OMA

Le Gourmand, *imprint of* Office Marocain D'Annonces-OMA

Government Printer (Imprimerie Officielle)
Ave Jean Mermoz, Rabat-Chellah
Tel: (077) 65024

Les Editions du Journal L' Unite Maghrebine+
2, Lotissement El Menza H, Bettana, Sale
Tel: 780169 *Fax:* 780169
Telex: 780169
Key Personnel
Founder: Mohamed El Alami
Dir: Buthayma Ebrahim
Founded: 1988
Subjects: Economics, Ethnicity, Government, Political Science, Science (General), Sports, Athletics
Parent Company: Agence Afro-Asiatique de Press et d'Information (API)

Les Editions Maghrebines, EDIMA
Quartier Industriel, Blvd E, N 15, Ain Sebaa, Casablanca 05
Tel: (02) 353230; (02) 353249; (02) 351797
 Fax: (02) 355541
Telex: 26954
ISBN Prefix(es): 9981-24
Bookshop(s): Librairie EDIMA-5, Place de la Mosquee Mohammadi, Habous, Casablanca

Office Marocain D'Annonces-OMA
332 Blvd Brahim Roudani, Casablanca
Tel: (02) 234891; (02) 232342 *Fax:* (02) 234892
Key Personnel
Contact: Assya Djellab
Membership(s): Satellite de l'AEEA & de l'ATC Paris.
Subjects: Career Development
Imprints: Annuaine Fax Telex; Europages; Formation Entreprises; Le Gourmand; Les Pages Jannes Maroc
Distributor for Euredit pour le Maroc

Editions Okad+
4, Av Hassan II, route de Casablanca, Quartier Industriel Vita, Cite Yacoub El-Mansour, Rabat
Tel: (07) 796970; (07) 796971; (07) 796973
 Fax: (07) 798556
E-mail: okad@wanadoo.net.ma
Telex: 32687
Key Personnel
Dir General: El Hadi Lasmer
Founded: 1981
Subjects: Economics, History, Language Arts, Linguistics, Poetry
ISBN Prefix(es): 9981-806

Editions Oum+
25 rue Ibn Battouta, Casablanca 20000
Tel: (02) 274972; (02) 220454 *Fax:* (02) 208882; (02) 950963
Key Personnel
PDG: M Sijelmassi
Founded: 1992
Subjects: Art, How-to, Medicine, Nursing, Dentistry, Photography
Distributor for ACR; Flammarion; Gallimand

Les Pages Jannes Maroc, *imprint of* Office Marocain D'Annonces-OMA

Editions La Porte+
281 Ave Mohammed-V, Rabat
Mailing Address: BP 331, Rabat
Tel: (07) 709958; (07) 706476 *Fax:* (07) 709958; (07) 706478
Key Personnel
Man Dir: Mohamed Rafii Doukkali
Subjects: Economics, Government, Political Science, Language Arts, Linguistics, Law, Religion - Islamic, Religion - Other, Travel
ISBN Prefix(es): 9981-889
Subsidiaries: Librairie aux Belles Images (bookshop)

Le Repere, *imprint of* Access International Services

Editions Services et Informations pour Etudiants+
Cite Al Inara 1, No 155 Ave Dakhla, Casablanca 02
Mailing Address: BP 156691 CASA-PrP, Casablanca 20001
Tel: (02) 210163
Key Personnel
Dir: Mr Aitcaid Mustapma
Subjects: How-to

Societe Ennewrasse Service Librairie et Imprimerie
70 Ave Okba Bnou Nafie, Agdal, 10000 Rabat
Tel: (077) 6413 *Fax:* (077) 6413
Key Personnel
Contact: Mohamed Ali Omar
Subjects: Anthropology, Antiques, Business, Communications, Criminology, History, Human Relations, Law, Literature, Literary Criticism, Essays, Religion - Islamic, Women's Studies
Parent Company: Annawrasse (Sarl)

Mozambique

General Information

Capital: Maputo
Language: Portuguese
Religion: Catholic, Protestant & Islamic
Population: 16.6 million
Bank Hours: 0800-1200 Monday - Friday
Shop Hours: 0800-1230, 1400-1700 Monday-Saturday
Currency: One US dollar = 11,251 meticais
Export/Import Information: Children's picture books dutied per kg net weight, otherwise books and advertising matter duty-free. No additional taxes apply. Import licenses and strict exchange controls; authorities have classified books and advertising as List 3 in priorities.

Associacao dos Escritores Mocambicanos (AEMO)
Av 24 de Julho, 1420 Maputo
Mailing Address: CP 4187, 1420 Maputo
Tel: (01) 420727
Key Personnel
Man Dir: Pedro Chissano

Empresa Moderna Lda
Avda 25 de Setembro, Maputo CP 473
Tel: (01) 424594
Key Personnel
Man Dir: Louis Galloti
Founded: 1937
Subjects: Education, Fiction, History, Regional Interests

Centro De Estudos Africanos+
Universidade Eduardo Mondlane, CP 1993, Maputo
Tel: (01) 490828; (01) 499876 *Fax:* (01) 491896
E-mail: ceadid@zebra.uem.mz
Web Site: www.cea.uem.mz
Telex: 6-740 CEA MO
Key Personnel
Dir: Coronel Sergio Vieira
Founded: 1976
Specializes in Social Science.
Subjects: Economics, Foreign Countries, Government, Political Science, History, Regional Interests

Editora Minerva Central
Rua Consiglieri Pedroso, 66/84, Maputo
Tel: (01) 420198 *Fax:* (01) 423677
E-mail: minerva@sortmoz.com
Telex: 6-561 Miner Mo
Key Personnel
Man Dir: J F Carvalho
Founded: 1908
Subjects: Medicine, Nursing, Dentistry, Science (General)
Subsidiaries: J A Carvalho & Co Ltd

Myanmar

General Information

Capital: Yangon
Language: Burmese (English used for foreign correspondence)
Religion: Buddhism
Population: 42.6 million
Bank Hours: 1000-1400 Monday-Friday; 1000-1200 Saturday
Shop Hours: Generally 0800-1700 Monday-Saturday
Currency: 100 pyas = 1 kyat
Export/Import Information: Myanmar has own complex tariff system, but duties are paid by State Trading Corporation No 9, 550-552 Merchant St, Rangoon, and Printing and Publishing Corporation, 228 Theinbyu St, Rangoon, principally. No tariffs on advertising. Books exempt from sales tax. Import license required. Exchange controls; priorities apply.
Copyright: No copyright conventions signed

Hanthawaddy Book House
157 Bo Aung Gyaw St, Rangoon
Bookshop(s): Hanthawaddy Bookshop

Knowledge Press & Bookhouse
130, Bogyoke Aung San St, Pazundaung Tsp
Tel: (01) 290927
Subjects: Art, Education, Government, Political Science, Religion - Other, Social Sciences, Sociology
Bookshop(s): Knowledge Book House

Kyi-Pwar-Ye Book House
84 St, Letse-gan Mandalay

MYANMAR

Tel: (02) 21003 *Cable:* LUDU
Subjects: Art, Religion - Other, Travel

Sarpay Beikman Public Library
529-531 Merchand St, Rangoon
Tel: (01) 83611 *Cable:* Sarbeikman
Key Personnel
Chairman: Aung Htay
Secretary: Lt-Col Mg MgLay
Sales, Publicity & Advertising: U Tin Gyi
Editorial: Myo Thant
Founded: 1947
Subjects: Agriculture, Biography, Ethnicity, History, Law, Literature, Literary Criticism, Essays, Science (General)
Bookshop(s): Sarpay Beikman Bookshop
Book Club(s): Sarpay Beikman Book Club

Shumawa Publishing House
146 Bogyoke Aung San Market, Rangoon
Subjects: Mechanical Engineering
Bookshop(s): Shumawa Book House

Shwepyidan Printing & Publishing House
12 A Hninban, Yegwaw Quarter, Rangoon
Subjects: Government, Political Science, Law, Religion - Other

Smart & Mookerdum
221 Sule Pagoda Rd, Rangoon
Subjects: Art, Cookery, Science (General)

Thudhammawaddy Press
Moung Khine St, Rangoon
Mailing Address: PO Box 419, 55-56, Rangoon
Subjects: Religion - Other

Universities Administration Office
Prome Rd, University Post Office, Rangoon
Key Personnel
Chief Editor, Translations & Publications Department: U Wun

Namibia

General Information

Capital: Windhoek
Language: English (official), Afrikaans and German widely used
Religion: Predominantly Christian
Population: 1.6 million
Bank Hours: 0900-1530 Monday-Friday
Shop Hours: 0830-1700 Monday-Friday, 0800-1300 Saturday
Currency: 100 cents = 1 Namibian dollar
Export/Import Information: Part of the Southern African Customs Union (SACU). Import licenses required. Payment of hard currency or any other currency for trade transactions strictly against documentation. Strict foreign exchange controls and regulations. No exchange control applicable to non-residents. Gradual easing exchange control of residents.
Copyright: Berne (see Copyright Conventions, pg xi)

Agrivet Publishers+
PO Box 3134, Windhoek
Tel: (061) 228909 *Fax:* (061) 230619
E-mail: agrivet@iafrica.com.na
Founded: 1992
Subjects: Foreign Countries, Travel, Veterinary Science

Bible Society of Namibia
PO Box 13294, Windhoek 9000
Tel: (061) 235090 *Fax:* (061) 228663
E-mail: bsn@nambible.org.na
Web Site: www.biblesociety.org
Founded: 1986
ISBN Prefix(es): 99916-713

Desert Research Foundation of Namibia (DRFN)
7 Rossini St, Windhoek
Mailing Address: PO Box 202 32, Windhoek
Tel: (061) 229855 *Fax:* (061) 228286
E-mail: info@drfn.org.na
Web Site: www.drfn.org.na
Key Personnel
Dir: Mary Seely *Fax:* (061) 230770
  E-mail: mseely@drfn.org.na
Founded: 1963
Subjects: Agriculture, Behavioral Sciences, Biological Sciences, Developing Countries, Earth Sciences, Education, Energy, Environmental Studies, Geography, Geology, Natural History, Physical Sciences, Regional Interests, Science (General), Botany, Zoology, Desertification Issues, Environmental Training, Water Management
ISBN Prefix(es): 99916-709
U.S. Office(s): Friends of Gobabeb, c/o Prof C S Crawford, Dept of Biology, University of New Mexico, Albuquerque, NM, United States

DRFN, see Desert Research Foundation of Namibia (DRFN)

Gamsberg Macmillan Publishers (Pty) Ltd
19 Faraday St, Windhoek
Mailing Address: PO Box 22830, Windhoek
Tel: (061) 232165 *Fax:* (061) 233538
E-mail: gmp@iafrica.com.na
Web Site: www.macmillan-africa.com
Key Personnel
Man Dir, Editorial, Rights & Permissions: Herman van Wyk
Publishing: Peter Reiner *E-mail:* gmpubl@iafrica.com.na
Production: Ingrid van Graan
Sales, Publicity: Kotie van der Merwe
Orders & Prices: Cecelia Blom *Fax:* (061) 234830
Founded: 1977
Subjects: Literature, Literary Criticism, Essays
ISBN Prefix(es): 0-86848; 99916-0
Shipping Address: 19 Faraday S, Windhoek

Kuiseb-Verlag
PO Box 67, Windhoek
Tel: (061) 225372 *Fax:* (061) 226846
E-mail: nwg@iafrica.com.na
Key Personnel
Contact: Ingrid Demasius
Founded: 1925
ISBN Prefix(es): 99916-703

McGregor Publishers
PO Box 9338, Windhoek
Tel: (061) 62155 *Fax:* (061) 63059
E-mail: gmcgregor@unam.na
Key Personnel
Contact: Gordon McGregor
Founded: 1990
Specialize in German occupied South-West Africa.
Subjects: Military Science
ISBN Prefix(es): 99916-700

Media Institute of Southern Africa (MISA)
PMB 13386, Windhoek
Tel: (061) 232975 *Fax:* (061) 248016
E-mail: postmaster@ingrid.misa.org.na

Web Site: www.misanet.org
Key Personnel
Regional Dir: Luckson Chipare *E-mail:* director@misa.org.na

Multi-Disciplinary Research Centre Library
340 Mundume Ndemufayo Ave, Pioneers Park, Windhoek
Mailing Address: PMB 13301, Windhoek
Tel: (061) 206 3909; (061) 206 3051 *Fax:* (061) 206 3050; (061) 206 3684
E-mail: tgases@unam.na
Web Site: www.unam.na
Key Personnel
Head: Dr L Hangula
Contact: Dr Ben Fuller
Coordinator: Selma Nangulah
  E-mail: snangulah@unam.na
Founded: 1989
Subjects: Agriculture, Developing Countries, Economics, Environmental Studies, Geography, Geology, Government, Political Science, Science (General), Social Sciences, Sociology, Gender Issues, Life Sciences
Parent Company: University of Namibia
Divisions: Life Sciences Division; Science & Technology Division; Social Sciences Division
U.S. Office(s): J Diescho, University of Namibia Office, Africa/American Institute, 833 United Nations Plaza, New York, NY 10017, United States

Nepal

General Information

Capital: Kathmandu
Language: Nepali (official), also Maithir & Bhojpuri
Religion: Predominantly Hindu, also some Buddhist and Muslim
Population: 20.1 million
Bank Hours: 1000-1430 Sunday-Thursday; 1000-1230 Friday
Shop Hours: 1000-2000 Sunday-Friday
Currency: 100 paisa = 1 Nepalese rupee
Export/Import Information: No tariff on books and advertising. Import licenses required. Exchange controls.

International Standards Books & Periodicals (P) Ltd+
Kamabakshee Tole, Gha 3-333, Chowk Bhitra, Kathmandu 44601
Mailing Address: PO Box 3000-ISB-NFSLA Kathmandu-3-30-15B, Kathmandu 44601
Tel: (01) 212289; (01) 224005; (01) 223036
  Fax: (01) 223036
Telex: 3000 ISB-ASS-NP *Cable:* ANTERRASHTRIYASTARKOSAPHOOPASA, KATHMANDU
Key Personnel
Chairman: Sugat Dass Tuladhar
Chief Executive Man Dir: Ganesh Lall Chhipa
Chief Man Dir: Suindra Lall Chhipa
Senior Man Dir: Yogendra Lall Chhipa
Junior Man Dir: Bijendra Lall Upasak
Man Dir: Ganesh Dass Chhipa
Company Secretary: Udhdab Lall Chhipa
Editorial Dir: Dharma Ratna Ranjit
Marketing Dir: Chandra Lexmee Ranjit
General Sales Dir: Pawan Ratna Tuladhar
General Order Dir: Bhawanyshowr Ranjit
Production Dir: Bhumaheshwor Ranjit
Promotion Dir: Suneeta Shobha Ranjit
Subscription Dir: Aneeta Shobha Ranjit
Distribution Dir: Miss Nanee Shobha Tuladhar
Customer Dir: Miss Bheem Shobha Tuladhar

Publishing Dir: Mrs Rameeta Shobha Tuladhar
Foreign Rights Dir: Rajendra K Ranjit
Supplies Dir: Shant Shobha Ranjit
Sales Manager: Basant Bahadur Basnet
Business Manager: Bijendra Man Tuladhar
General Trade Dir: Amrit Lall Ranjit
Circulation Dir: Surya Man Ranjit
Reference Dir: Ms Saraswati Shrestha
Acquisition Dir: Mrs Subarna Laxmi Chhipa
Export Dir: Jaya Ram Ranjit
Import Dir: Mrs Saroja Ranjit
Rights & Permission Dir: Shanta Dass Ranjit
Information Dir: Shanta Lall Ranjit
Publicity Manager: Mona Ranjit
Foreign Order Manager: Jambu Ranta Ranjitkar
Subsidiary Rights Manager: Ms Babee Shobha Ranjit
Marketing Manager: Jambu Ranta Ranjit
Founded: 1965
Centre for Central General Selling, Distribution & Wholesales, Order Supplies, Subscription & Publication.
Subjects: Agriculture, Anthropology, Archaeology, Architecture & Interior Design, Art, Business, Career Development, Chemistry, Chemical Engineering, Earth Sciences, Economics, Education, Engineering (General), Gardening, Plants, Geography, Geology, Government, Political Science, History, Human Relations, Language Arts, Linguistics, Law, Literature, Literary Criticism, Essays, Mathematics, Medicine, Nursing, Dentistry, Music, Dance, Natural History, Philosophy, Physics, Psychology, Psychiatry, Social Sciences, Sociology
Branch Office(s)
Arniko Main, Arniko Barhabise - 9, Ariko Rajmarg 87 KM
Ason Kamabakshee Tole, Kathmandu City
Bhotahity Tole, Kathmandu Valley
Showroom(s): Ason Kamabakshee Tole, Cha 1/112, Chowk Bhitra, Kathmandu 3
Bookshop(s): A R N I K O, Barhabise-9, Arniko Rajmarg-87 KM, Bagmati Anchal, Kathmandu 45303; S A A R C Books & Periodicals Shop, 09-53-01 Bhindyo Tole, Purano Bazar, Kathmandu
Shipping Address: Naradevee Tole, Gha 3/460, Nyata Twa, Chowk Bhitra, PO Box 3000-ISB, Kathmandu City 44601-3000
Warehouse: Bhurungkhel Tole, Cha 4/394, Ikhapokhary, Kshetrapaty, PO Box 5000-ISB, Kathmandu City 44601-5000
Orders to: Bhotahity Tole, Cha 1/333, Chowk Bhitra, 5th floor, PO Box 5000-ISB, Kathmandu City 44601-5000
Maroohity Tole, Chha 3/333, Chowk Bhitra, 1st Floor, PO Box 3000-ISB, Kathmandu City 44601-3000

Royal Nepal Academy
Khumaltar, Lalitpur 178 MEMS
Mailing Address: PO Box 3323, Katmandu
Tel: (01) 547714; (01) 547715; (01) 547716; (01) 547717; (01) 547718 Fax: (01) 547713
E-mail: info@ronast.org.np; ronast@mos.com.np
Web Site: www.ronast.org.np
Key Personnel
President: Prof Dayanand Bajracharya
Library Chief: T D Bhandari
Founded: 1957
Subjects: Art, History, Literature, Literary Criticism, Essays, Science (General), Social Sciences, Sociology

Sajha Prakashan, Co-operative Publishing Organization
Pulchowk, Lalitpur, Kathmandu
Tel: (01) 5521118
Key Personnel
Chairman: Deepak Baskota
General Manager: Narayan S Gajurel
Marketing Manager: Ram Krishna Bhandari

Founded: 1966
Subjects: Literature, Literary Criticism, Essays

Worldwide Publishings Systems, see International Standards Books & Periodicals (P) Ltd

Netherlands

General Information

Capital: Amsterdam
Language: Dutch; Frisian in Friesland (though all speakers of Frisian also speak Dutch). English is common second language
Religion: Mainly Roman Catholic and Protestant
Population: 15.9 million
Bank Hours: 0900-1600 Monday-Friday; some open Saturday morning and on late night shopping evenings
Shop Hours: 0900-1730 or 1800 Monday-Saturday. Many close Monday morning
Currency: 100 Eurocents = 1 Euro; 2.20371 Dutch guilders = 1 Euro
Export/Import Information: Member of the European Economic Community. No tariff on books except children's picture books from non-EEC; advertising other than single copies is dutied; 6% VAT on books. Import licenses required for certain countries (not USA or UK).
Copyright: UCC, Berne, Florence (see Copyright Conventions, pg xi)

Academic Publishers Associated, see APA (Academic Publishers Associated)

Agathon, *imprint of* Unieboek BV

Agon, *imprint of* Uitgeverij de Arbeiderspers

Uitgeversmaatschappij Agon B V+
Herengracht 376, 1016 CH Amsterdam
Tel: (020) 521 97 77 Fax: (020) 622 49 37
E-mail: info@boekboek.nl
Web Site: www.boekboek.nl
Key Personnel
Publisher: R J W Dietz
Founded: 1987
Subjects: History, Regional Interests, Travel
ISBN Prefix(es): 90-5157
Parent Company: Weekblad pers groep

Agora, *imprint of* Uitgeverij J H Kok BV

Allert de Lange BV
Damrak 62, 1012 LM Amsterdam
Tel: (020) 6246744 Fax: (020) 6384975
Key Personnel
Man Dir: W J van Loon
Founded: 1880
ISBN Prefix(es): 90-6133; 90-5336
Parent Company: Allert de Lange Beheer BV
Associate Companies: Nilsson & Lamm BV
Bookshop(s): Robert Premsela, Van Baerlestraat 78, 1071 BB Amsterdam; Ala Carte, Utrechtsestraat 110-112, 1017 VS Amsterdam

Altamira-Becht, *imprint of* Gottmer Uitgevers Groep

Uitgeverij Ambo BV+
Keizersgracht 630, 1017 ER Amsterdam
Tel: (020) 5245411 Fax: (020) 4200422
E-mail: info@amboanthos.nl
Web Site: www.amboanthos.nl
Telex: 43272

Key Personnel
Publisher: Ms Eva Cossee
Founded: 1963
Membership(s): Combo Group, Netherlands.
Subjects: Biography, Fiction, History, Literature, Literary Criticism, Essays, Music, Dance, Non-fiction (General), Philosophy, Photography, Psychology, Psychiatry, Religion - Other, Social Sciences, Sociology, Theology
ISBN Prefix(es): 90-263; 90-6074; 90-414
Warehouse: Combo Nijkerk, Gezellestraat 16, 3861 RD Nijkerk
Orders to: Combo, Postbus 1, 3740 AA Baarn

Ankh-Hermes BV+
Smyrnastr 5, 7413 BA Deventer
Mailing Address: Postbus 125, 7400 AC Deventer
Tel: (0570) 678911 Fax: (0570) 624632
E-mail: info@ankh-hermes.nl
Web Site: www.ankh-hermes.com
Key Personnel
Dir: Nicole de Haas
Financial Dir: Mr A L Steenbergen
Founded: 1949
Subjects: Astrology, Occult, Education, Gardening, Plants, Health, Nutrition, Management, Parapsychology, Philosophy, Religion - Buddhist, Religion - Protestant
ISBN Prefix(es): 90-202

Uitgeverij Anthos+
Keizersgracht 630, 1017 ER Amsterdam
Tel: (020) 5245411 Fax: (020) 4200422
E-mail: info@amboanthos.nl
Web Site: www.amboanthos.nl
Key Personnel
Man Dir: Robbert Ammerlaan
Membership(s): the Combo Group.
Subjects: Biography, Fiction, Science (General)
ISBN Prefix(es): 90-6074

AO, *imprint of* Stichting IVIO

APA (Academic Publishers Associated)
Postbus 806, 1000 AV Amsterdam
Tel: (020) 626 5544 Fax: (020) 528 5298
E-mail: info@apa-publishers.com
Web Site: www.apa-publishers.com
Key Personnel
Man Dir: G van Heusden
Founded: 1966
Subjects: Art, Asian Studies, Biblical Studies, History, Human Relations, Language Arts, Linguistics, Law, Library & Information Sciences, Philosophy, Religion - Other, Science (General), Social Sciences, Sociology, Theology
ISBN Prefix(es): 90-6037; 90-6023; 90-302; 90-6039; 90-6022; 90-6024; 90-6025; 90-6042
Subsidiaries: Fontes Pers; Gerard Th van Heusden; Hissink & Co; Holland University Press BV; Oriental Press BV; Philo Press CV

Aramith, *imprint of* Gottmer Uitgevers Groep

Uitgeverij de Arbeiderspers+
Herengracht 370-372, 1016 CH Amsterdam
Tel: (020) 5247500
E-mail: info@arbeiderspers.nl
Web Site: www.ap-archipel.nl
Key Personnel
Man Dir: R J W Dietz
Subjects: Biography, Criminology, Fiction, History, Literature, Literary Criticism, Essays, Nonfiction (General), Philosophy, Poetry, Romance, Travel
ISBN Prefix(es): 90-295
Parent Company: Weekbladpers Group
Imprints: Agon

Uitgeverij Arbor+
Member of The Combo Group
Postbus 1, 3740 AA Baarn

NETHERLANDS

Tel: (035) 5422141 *Fax:* (035) 15433
Key Personnel
Man Dir: Robbert Ammerlaan
Subjects: Religion - Other
ISBN Prefix(es): 90-5158

Architectura & Natura
Leliegracht 22, 1015 DG Amsterdam
Tel: (020) 6236186 *Fax:* (020) 6382303
E-mail: info@architectura.nl
Web Site: www.architectura.nl
Key Personnel
Contact: G Kemme *E-mail:* kemme@architectura.nl
Founded: 1939
Specialize in Architecture & Landscape Architecture.
Subjects: Architecture & Interior Design
ISBN Prefix(es): 90-71570
Number of titles published annually: 6 Print
Total Titles: 96 Print
Imprints: Goose Press
Subsidiaries: Goose Press

Arena, *imprint of* J M Meulenhoff bv

Uitgeverij Arena BV+
Subsidiary of J M Meulenhoff BV
Herengracht 505, 1017 BV Amsterdam
Mailing Address: PO Box 100, 1000 AC Amsterdam
Tel: (020) 55 40 500 *Fax:* (020) 42 16 868
E-mail: info@boekenarena.nl
Web Site: www.meulenhoff.nl; www.boekenarena.nl
Key Personnel
Man Dir: Anne Rube
Publisher: Tanja Hendriks
Editorial: Ingrid Meurs; Maaike Le Noble
Production: Bregitta Kramer
Publicity: Piet van Riele
Founded: 1989
Subjects: Biography, Fiction, Literature, Literary Criticism, Essays, Nonfiction (General), Travel
ISBN Prefix(es): 90-6974
Total Titles: 50 Print
Ultimate Parent Company: PCM Algemene boeken

Uitgevirj Aristos+
Provenierssingel 73a, 3033 EJ Rotterdam
Tel: (010) 243 73 70 *Fax:* (010) 243 76 00
E-mail: aristos@xs4all.nl
Web Site: www.xs4all.nl/~feico/aristos
Key Personnel
Publisher: Gerrit Bussinh
Founded: 1997
Subjects: Fiction, Literature, Literary Criticism, Essays, Management, Nonfiction (General)
ISBN Prefix(es): 90-6935
Total Titles: 27 Print
Warehouse: Centraal Boehh, Erasmusweg 19, 4101 AK Culemberg *Tel:* (0345) 475911
Orders to: Uitgevserij Aristos

Ark Boeken+
Donauweg 4, 1043 AJ Amsterdam
Tel: (020) 6114847 *Fax:* (020) 6114864
E-mail: arkboeken@wxs.nl
Key Personnel
General Dir: J Kor *Tel:* (020) 4802981
Publishing Dir: P Foget
Founded: 1913
Ark Boeken Publishing House combines the activities of Vereniging tot Verspreising der Heilige Schrift (Association for Distribution of the Holy Scripture) & Bijbel Kiosk Vereniging (Bible Kiosk Society).
Subjects: Religion - Protestant
ISBN Prefix(es): 90-338

Total Titles: 500 Print; 1 Audio
Bookshop(s): BKV-Lektuurcentrum, Hoofdstraat 55, 3971 KB Driebergen

Uitgeverij Jan van Arkel+
A Numankd 17, 3572 KP Utrecht
Tel: (030) 2731840 *Fax:* (030) 2733614
E-mail: i-books@antenna.nl
Web Site: www.antenna.bl/i-books
Key Personnel
Chief Executive: Jan van Arkel
Founded: 1974
Specialize in books on the environment & development, in books in the Dutch & English languages.
Subjects: Economics, Environmental Studies, Geography, Geology, Government, Political Science, Social Sciences, Sociology, Women's Studies
ISBN Prefix(es): 90-6224; 90-5727 (International Books)
Total Titles: 150 Print
Imprints: International Books
Distributed by Bushbooks; Jon Carpenter Publishing (UK); International Books (Netherlands); Paul & Company, Publishers Consortium Inc (US)
Shipping Address: Central Books, 99 Wallis Rd, London E9 5LN, United Kingdom *Tel:* (020) 986 4854 *Fax:* (020) 533 5821
Orders to: c/o A Weitsel, 2 Home Farm Cottages, Sandy Lane, St Paul's Cray, Kent BR5 3HZ, United Kingdom *Tel:* (1689) 870437
Independent Publishers Group - IPG, 814 N Franklin St, Chicago, IL 60610, United States *Tel:* 312-337-0747 *Fax:* 312-337-5985
E-mail: frontdesk@ipgbook.com

Ars Scribendi bv Uitgeverij+
Productieweg 5, 3481 MH Harmelen
Mailing Address: PO Box 65, 3480 DB Harmelen
Tel: (0348) 443998 *Fax:* (0348) 444076
E-mail: info@arsscribendi.com
Web Site: www.arsscribendi.com
Key Personnel
President: R E C Richter
Founded: 1988
Membership(s): KVB. Also acts as publishers' agents.
ISBN Prefix(es): 90-72718; 90-5495; 90-74777; 90-5566
Number of titles published annually: 20 Print
Total Titles: 300 Print
Parent Company: Richter's Alg Boek Centrale bv
Associate Companies: Intertext PvbA
Imprints: Corona; Fantom; Flash; Magnum
Subsidiaries: Handelsonderneming Dykhof bv; De Laude Scriptorum bv
Distributed by Agora bvba

Athenaeum-Polak & Van Gennep, *imprint of* Em Querido's Uitgeverij BV

B M Israel BV
Lamoraalweg 73, 1934 CC Egmond aan den Hoef, 1012 WL Amsterdam
Tel: (020) 624 70 40 *Fax:* (020) 507 20 32
E-mail: bmisrael@xs4all.nl
Web Site: www.nvva.nl/israelbm
Key Personnel
General Manager: M Israel
Subjects: Art, Medicine, Nursing, Dentistry, Science (General), Technology, Travel
ISBN Prefix(es): 90-6078
Bookshop(s): B M Israel Boekhandel en Antiquariaat BV

Backhuys Publishers BV+
Warmonderweg 80, 2341 KZ Oegstgeest
Mailing Address: PO Box 321, 2300 AH Leiden
Tel: (071) 5170208 *Fax:* (071) 5171856

E-mail: info@backhuys.com
Web Site: www.backhuys.com
Key Personnel
President: Dr W Backhuys
Editor: Mike Ruijsenaars *E-mail:* mike@backhuys.com
Publisher: Wil R Peters *Tel:* (071) 5170927
E-mail: peters@backhuys.com
Founded: 1989
Publish & distribute scholarly books in the natural sciences (botany, zoology, geology)
Also acts as distributor of Museum Publications, University Presses & sells antiquarian books in the same subjects.
Subjects: Biological Sciences, Earth Sciences, Geography, Geology, Natural History
ISBN Prefix(es): 90-73348; 90-73239; 90-220; 90-327; 90-5103; 2-85653; 90-5782; 2-86515
Number of titles published annually: 40 Print
Total Titles: 400 Print
Subsidiaries: Seashell Treasure Books
U.S. Office(s): Balogh Scientific Books, Champaign, IL 61822, United States, Contact: Pamela Burns *Tel:* 217-355-9331 *Fax:* 217-355-9413
Distributed by Balogh Scientific Books (North America)
Distributor for Editions Boubee (France); Israel Academy of Sciences & Humanities (Zoology & Botany titles only); Museum national d'Histoire naturelle (France); Naturalis (Netherlands); Service du Patrimoine Naturel (France)
Foreign Rep(s): Balogh Scientific Books

Uitgeverij Balans+
Herengracht 370/372, 1016 CH Amsterdam
Mailing Address: Postbus 2877, 1000 CW Amsterdam
Tel: (020) 524 75 80 *Fax:* (020) 524 75 89
E-mail: balans@uitgeverijbalans.nl
Web Site: www.uitgeverijbalans.nl
Key Personnel
Publisher: Jan G Gaarlandt
Rights & Permissions: Francoise Gaarlandt-Kist
Founded: 1986
Subjects: Biography, Fiction, History, Journalism, Literature, Literary Criticism, Essays, Nonfiction (General), Regional Interests, Religion - Other
ISBN Prefix(es): 90-5018
Total Titles: 40 Print
Orders to: Centraal Boekhuis, Postbus 100, 4100 BA Culemborg *Tel:* (0345) 475896

A A Balkema Uitgevers BV+
Member of Taylor & Francis Group
PO Box 825, 2160 SZ Lisse
Tel: (0252) 435111 *Fax:* (0252) 435447
E-mail: orders@swets.nl
Web Site: www.balkema.nl
Key Personnel
Man Dir: Martin Scrivener *Tel:* (0252) 435101
E-mail: scrivy@swets.nl
Rights & Permissions: Rosemarie Daal
Sales Promotion: Ms Deet van Toledo
Founded: 1972
Specialize in Engineering.
Subjects: Archaeology, Biological Sciences, Civil Engineering, Earth Sciences, Engineering (General), Environmental Studies, Geography, Geology, Mechanical Engineering, Natural History, Physics
ISBN Prefix(es): 90-6191 (90-5809); 90-5410
Total Titles: 1,000 Print; 10 CD-ROM
U.S. Office(s): A A Balkema Publishers, 2252 Ridge Rd, Brookfield, VT 05036-9704, United States *Tel:* 802-276-3162 *Fax:* 802-276-3837
E-mail: info@ashgate.com

Benjamin & Partners Art Books, *imprint of* BoekWerk

John Benjamins BV+
Klaprozenweg 105, 1033 NN Amsterdam
Mailing Address: PO Box 36224, 1020 ME Amsterdam
Tel: (020) 6304747 *Fax:* (020) 6739773
E-mail: customer.services@benjamins.nl
Web Site: www.benjamins.com
Key Personnel
Editorial: Isja Conen *E-mail:* isja.conen@benjamins.nl; Bertie Kaal *E-mail:* bertie.kaal@benjamins.nl; Anke de Looper *E-mail:* anke.delooper@benjamins.nl; Kees Vaes *E-mail:* kees.vaes@benjamins.nl
Marketing & Promotion: Karin Plijnaar
Production: Ian Spoelstra *E-mail:* ian.spoelstra@benjamins.nl
Founded: 1964
Subjects: Art, Education, Language Arts, Linguistics, Literature, Literary Criticism, Essays, Philosophy, Psychology, Psychiatry, Social Sciences, Sociology, Applied Linguistics, Pragamatics, Translation Cognition, Historical Linguistics
ISBN Prefix(es): 90-272
Imprints: B R Gruener Publishing Co
Branch Office(s)
John Benjamins North America Inc, 821 Bethlehem Pike, Philadelphia, PA 19038, United States *Tel:* 215-836-1200 *Fax:* 215-836-1204

Bertollucci, *imprint of* J M Meulenhoff bv

Bertollucci, *imprint of* Uitgeverij Vassallucci bv

De Bezige Bij B V Uitgeverij
Van Miereveldstr 1, 1071 DW Amsterdam
Mailing Address: PO Box 75184, 1070 AD Amsterdam
Tel: (020) 3059810 *Fax:* (020) 3059824
E-mail: info@debezigebij.nl
Web Site: www.debezigebij.nl *Cable:* BEEBOOK
Key Personnel
President & Publisher: Robbert Ammerlaau
Founded: 1944
Subjects: Fiction, Literature, Literary Criticism, Essays, Nonfiction (General), Poetry
ISBN Prefix(es): 90-234

Big Balloon BV+
Fonteinlaan 5, 2012 JG Haarlem
Mailing Address: Postbus 701, 2003 RS Haarlem
Tel: (023) 5176620 *Fax:* (023) 5176630
E-mail: info@bigballoon.nl
Web Site: www.bigballoon.nl
Key Personnel
Man Dir: Cees de Groot *E-mail:* degroot@bigballoon.nl
Marketing Manager: Kees Kooijman *E-mail:* kooijman@bigballoon.nl
Marketing: Willemijn Roselaar *E-mail:* roselaar@bigballoon.nl
Licensing: Corinne van Roozendaal *E-mail:* vanroozendaal@bigballoon.nl
Editorial: Annerieke Bijeman *E-mail:* bijeman@bigballoon.nl; Rikky Schrever *E-mail:* schrever@bigballoon.nl
Founded: 1990
ISBN Prefix(es): 90-320; 90-5425

Erven J Bijleveld+
Janskerkhof 7, 3512 BK Utrecht
Tel: (030) 2310800 *Fax:* (030) 2311774
E-mail: info@bijveldbooks.nl
Web Site: www.bijveldbooks.nl
Key Personnel
Man Dir: J B Bommelje, Sr
Founded: 1865
Subjects: Child Care & Development, Computer Science, History, Microcomputers, Philosophy, Psychology, Psychiatry, Religion - Jewish, Religion - Other, Social Sciences, Sociology, Theology
ISBN Prefix(es): 90-72019; 90-5548; 90-6131
Imprints: Bijleveld Press

Bijleveld Press, *imprint of* Erven J Bijleveld

BIS Publishers
Herengracht 370-372, 1016 CH Amsterdam
Mailing Address: Postbox 323, 1000 AH Amsterdam
Tel: (020) 524 75 60 *Fax:* (020) 524 75 57
E-mail: bis@bispublishers.nl
Web Site: www.bispublishers.nl
Key Personnel
Owner & Dir: Rudolf van Wezel
Founded: 1986
Subjects: Architecture & Interior Design, Communications
ISBN Prefix(es): 90-72007
Distributed by Hearst Books International

H W Blok Uitgeverij BV
Vd Sande Bakhuijzenstr 4, 1061 AG Amsterdam
Mailing Address: Postbus 152, 1000 AD Amsterdam
Tel: (020) 5159222 *Fax:* (020) 5159100
ISBN Prefix(es): 90-70008; 90-72763

Boek Promotions BV
Hilversumseweg 16, 1251 EX Laren Nh
Mailing Address: Postbus 88, 1250 AB Laren Nh
Tel: (035) 5310154
Key Personnel
Owner: Peter J Houbolt
Act mainly as packagers for sponsored books.
ISBN Prefix(es): 90-6459

Boekencentrum BV+
Goudstr 50, 2700 AA Zoetermeer
Mailing Address: Postbus 29, 2700 AA Zoetermeer
Tel: (079) 3615481; (079) 3628282 (sales) *Fax:* (079) 3615489
E-mail: info@boekencentrum.nl
Web Site: www.boekencentrum.nl
Key Personnel
General Dir: N A de Waal
Founded: 1948
Subjects: Education, Religion - Protestant, Theology
ISBN Prefix(es): 90-239; 90-211
Imprints: Meinema

De Boekerij BV+
Herengracht 540, 1017 CG Amsterdam
Tel: (020) 535 31 35 *Fax:* (020) 535 31 30
E-mail: info@boekerij.nl
Web Site: www.boekerij.nl
Key Personnel
Editorial Dir: Marijke Bartels
Man Dir & Sales: R C M Hogenes
Editorial, Children's: Dorine Louwerens
Publicity: Marc Van Biezen
Production: Hans Van den Broek
Contracts & Rights: Frederike Leffelaar
Founded: 1986
Subjects: Biography, Child Care & Development, Criminology, Fiction, Health, Nutrition, History, Mysteries, Nonfiction (General), Romance, Science Fiction, Fantasy
ISBN Prefix(es): 90-225
Ultimate Parent Company: PCM Algemene Boeken
Associate Companies: Bruna; T M Meulenhoff; Prometherus/Bert Bakker; Standaard; Unieboek/Van Reemst
Imprints: Forum; Parel Pockets; Piccolo; Van Goor

BoekWerk+
Waldeck Pyrmontstr 2, 9722 GM Groningen
Tel: (050) 5265559 *Fax:* (050) 5268198
Key Personnel
Dir: G M Nuis
Founded: 1988
Subjects: Art, Business, Computer Science, Management, Marketing, Microcomputers
ISBN Prefix(es): 90-5402; 90-71677
Imprints: Benjamin & Partners Art Books

Bohn Scheltema en Holkema, see Uitgeverij Bohn Stafleu Van Loghum BV

Uitgeverij Bohn Stafleu Van Loghum BV
Het Spoor 2, 3994 AK Houten
Mailing Address: Postbus 246, 3990 GA Houten
Tel: (030) 63 83 838 *Fax:* (030) 63 83 839
Web Site: www.bsl.nl
Key Personnel
Man Dir: H J Demoet
Founded: 1752
Part of Wolters Kluwer Business Publishing.
Subjects: Biography, Human Relations, Medicine, Nursing, Dentistry, Social Sciences, Sociology
ISBN Prefix(es): 90-313; 90-368; 90-6016; 90-6065; 90-311; 90-6001; 90-6014; 90-6051; 90-6060; 90-6502

Boom Uitgeverij (Boom Publishers)+
Affiliate of Boom Law Publishers
Prinsengracht 747-751, 1017 JX Amsterdam
Tel: (020) 625 33 27 *Fax:* (020) 625 33 27
E-mail: info@uitgeverijboom.nl
Web Site: www.uitgeverijboom.nl
Key Personnel
President: Dries van Ingen *Tel:* (020) 5200 131 *E-mail:* vaningen@uitgeverijboom.nl
Deputy Manager: Sjef van de Wiel *Tel:* (020) 5200 134 *E-mail:* s.vandewiel@uitgeverijboom.nl
Product Coordinator: Katrien Buising *Tel:* (020) 622 61 07 *E-mail:* kbuising@uitgeverijboom.nl
Publicity: Margreet Flink *Tel:* (020) 5218 145 *E-mail:* m.flink@uitgeverijboom.nl
Marketing Coordinator: Marieke Hoogwout *Tel:* (020) 5200 123 *E-mail:* hoogwout@uitgeverijboom.nl
Founded: 1842
Subjects: Behavioral Sciences, Child Care & Development, Communications, Education, Environmental Studies, Government, Political Science, History, Language Arts, Linguistics, Law, Philosophy, Psychology, Psychiatry, Social Sciences, Sociology, Statistics
ISBN Prefix(es): 90-6009; 90-5352
Parent Company: Royal Boom Publishers, Postbus 1058, 7940 KB Meppel (directie@boom.nl)
Distributor for Institute for Politics; Netherlands Institute for Banking; Royal Institute of the Tropes; TMC Asser Institute
Orders to: Boom Distributiecentrum, Postbus 400, 7940 AK Meppel

Brill Academic Publishers+
Plantijnstr 2, 2321 JC Leiden
Mailing Address: Postbus 9000, 2300 PA Leiden
Tel: (071) 53 53 500 *Fax:* (071) 53 17 532
E-mail: cs@brill.nl
Web Site: www.brill.nl
Telex: 39296 *Cable:* BRILL LEIDEN
Key Personnel
Manager: R J Kasteleijn *E-mail:* kasteleijn@brill.nl
International Sales Manager: L Empringham *E-mail:* empringham@brill.nl
Marketing Manager: Alexander Dek *E-mail:* dek@brill.nl
Founded: 1683
Subjects: Archaeology, Asian Studies, Behavioral Sciences, Biological Sciences, History, Religion - Islamic, Religion - Jewish, Religion - Other,

Science (General), Social Sciences, Sociology, Theology
ISBN Prefix(es): 90-04
Total Titles: 2,700 Print
Imprints: Leiden University Press
Subsidiaries: Brill Academic Publishers Inc
Branch Office(s)
VSP BV, International Science Publishers, Godfried van Seijstlaan 47, 3700 BR Zeist, Marketing Manager: Els van Egmond *Tel:* (060) 693 2081 *Fax:* (060) 692 5790 *E-mail:* vsppub@compuserve.com
U.S. Office(s): Brill Academic Publishers Inc, 112 Water St, Suite 601, Boston, MA 02109, United States, Contact: Patrick Alexander *Tel:* 617-263-2323 *Fax:* 617-263-2324 *E-mail:* cs@brillusa.com
Distribution Center: PO Box 605, Herndon, VA 20172, United States *Tel:* 703-661-1585 *Fax:* 703-661-1501 *E-mail:* cs@brillusa.com (For USA, Canada & Mexico orders, shipping & returns; All other countries order at Brill, NL)

D van Brummen, *imprint of* Buijten en Schipperheijn BV Drukkerij en Uitgeversmaatschappij

A W Bruna Uitgevers BV+
Kobaltweg 23-25, 3504 AA Utrecht
Mailing Address: Postbus 40203, 3504 AA Utrecht
Tel: (030) 2470411 *Fax:* (030) 2410018
E-mail: a.w.bruna@awbruna.nl
Web Site: www.awbruna.nl
Key Personnel
Dir: Joop Boezeman
Aquiring Editor, Fiction & Non-fiction: Steven Maat
Founded: 1868
Subjects: Computer Science, Fiction, History, Mysteries, Nonfiction (General), Philosophy, Psychology, Psychiatry, Science (General), Social Sciences, Sociology, Thrillers, Suspense
ISBN Prefix(es): 90-229; 90-449; 90-5672
Parent Company: PCM Algemene Boeken bv, Utrecht
Imprints: Zwarte Beertjes; A W Bruna Informatica; Signature
Branch Office(s)
Standaard Uitgeverij, Belgium
U.S. Office(s): Mary Anne Thompson Associates, 80 E 11 St, Suite 441, New York, NY, United States

A W Bruna Informatica, *imprint of* A W Bruna Uitgevers BV

BSL, see Uitgeverij Bohn Stafleu Van Loghum BV

Buijten en Schipperheijn BV Drukkerij en Uitgeversmaatschappij+
Paasheuvelweg 44, 1105 BJ Amsterdam
Mailing Address: PO Box 22708, 1011 DE Amsterdam
Tel: (020) 5241010 *Fax:* (020) 5241011
E-mail: info@bijten.nl
Key Personnel
Man Dir: G Sneep
Founded: 1902
Subjects: Biblical Studies, Human Relations, Philosophy, Poetry, Psychology, Psychiatry, Religion - Other, Theology, Travel
ISBN Prefix(es): 90-6064; 90-5881
Imprints: D van Brummen; Buijten en Schipperheijn Motief; Buijten en Schipperheijn Recreatief

Buijten en Schipperheijn Motief, *imprint of* Buijten en Schipperheijn BV Drukkerij en Uitgeversmaatschappij

Buijten en Schipperheijn Recreatief, *imprint of* Buijten en Schipperheijn BV Drukkerij en Uitgeversmaatschappij

Business Contact BV+
Subsidiary of Veen, Bosch & Keuning Uitgevers NV
Herengracht 481, 1017 BT Amsterdam
Mailing Address: Postbus 13, 1000 AA Amsterdam
Tel: (020) 5249800 *Fax:* (020) 6276851
E-mail: info@contact-bv.nl
Web Site: www.boekenwereld.com
Key Personnel
Dir: Marij Bertram
Publisher: Mizzi van der Pluijm
Marketing: Anne Schroen *E-mail:* aschroen@contact-bv.nl
Publicity: Anne Kramer; May Meurs *E-mail:* mmeurs@contact-bv.nl
Sales: Thea Bon; Ingrid Kee; Petra Wildvank
Subjects: Accounting, Business, Career Development, Economics, Finance, How-to, Management, Marketing
ISBN Prefix(es): 90-254
Number of titles published annually: 30 Print
Total Titles: 400 Print

BV Uitgevery NZV (Nederlandse Zondagsschool Vereniging)+
Van Hogendorpplaan 10, 3800 BL Amersfoort
Mailing Address: Postbus 1492, 3800 BL Amersfoort
Tel: (033) 460 60 11 *Fax:* (035) 460 60 20
E-mail: info@nzv.nl
Web Site: www.nzv.nl
Key Personnel
Manager: Sir E K van de Plassche
International Rights & Publisher: Sir J Graafland
Subjects: Crafts, Games, Hobbies, Religion - Other, Affectionate Development, Nature & Environment
ISBN Prefix(es): 90-6986
Parent Company: NZV
Imprints: Kwintessens
Distributor for Ark Boeken; Boekencentrum; Callenbach; Christofoor; Clavis; Groen/Jongbloed; Kok; NBG; Piramide

BZZTOH Publishers+
Laan van Meerdervoort 10, 2517 AJ The Hague
Tel: (070) 3632934 *Fax:* (070) 3631932
E-mail: info@bzztoh.nl
Web Site: www.bzztoh.nl
Key Personnel
Dir: Phil Muysson
Financial Dir: Arend Meijboom
Foreign Rights Manager: Karin Hasselo *E-mail:* karin@bzztoh.nl
Founded: 1970
Subjects: Animals, Pets, Astrology, Occult, Biography, Cookery, Fiction, Finance, Health, Nutrition, Humor, Literature, Literary Criticism, Essays, Music, Dance, Mysteries, Nonfiction (General), Philosophy, Real Estate, Religion - Buddhist, Religion - Hindu, Religion - Jewish, Romance, Self-Help, Sports, Athletics, Travel, Women's Studies
ISBN Prefix(es): 90-6291; 90-5501; 90-453
Number of titles published annually: 130 Print

Cadans, *imprint of* Sjaloom Uitgeverijen

Cadans+
Imprint of Sjaloom Uitgeverij
Postbus 1895, 1000 BW Amsterdam
Tel: (020) 6206263 *Fax:* (020) 4288540
E-mail: post@sjaloom.nl
Web Site: www.sjaloom.com
Founded: 1992
Subjects: Criminology, Erotica, Fiction, History, Literature, Literary Criticism, Essays, Mysteries, Nonfiction (General), Poetry, Regional Interests, Travel
ISBN Prefix(es): 90-5132

Callenbach BV+
Ijsseldijk 31, 8266 AD Kampen
Mailing Address: Postbus 5019, 8260 GA Kampen
Tel: (038) 3392555 *Fax:* (038) 3311776
E-mail: algemeen@kok.nl
Key Personnel
Man Dir: G F Callenbach
Foreign Rights: Lia van Essen
Founded: 1854
Membership(s): Combo Group, Netherlands.
Subjects: Animals, Pets, Biblical Studies, Fiction, History, Mysteries, Poetry, Religion - Protestant, Religion - Other, Theology
ISBN Prefix(es): 90-266

Uitgeverij Cantecleer BV+
Subsidiary of Veen Bosch & Keuning Uitgevers NV
Julianalaan 11, 3743 JG Baarn
Mailing Address: Postbus 309, 3740 AH Baarn
Tel: (035) 5486600 *Fax:* (035) 5486615
E-mail: cancleer@worldonline.nl
Key Personnel
Man Dir & Editor: J Van Beusekom
Editor: J Junge; E Neele; L Uyterlinde
Founded: 1948
Subjects: Art, Crafts, Games, Hobbies, Film, Video, House & Home, Nonfiction (General), Photography, Wine & Spirits
ISBN Prefix(es): 90-246; 90-213
Shipping Address: Magazyn Centraal Boekhuis, Evasmusweg 10, Culemborg

Casterman NV+
Subsidiary of Editions Casterman SA
Fazantendreef 13/1, 8251 JR Dronten
Mailing Address: Postbus 324, 8250 AH Dronten
Tel: (0321) 313553 *Fax:* (0321) 318205
Key Personnel
General Manager: Pierre Rummens
ISBN Prefix(es): 90-303

Castrum Peregrini Presse+
Herengracht 401, 1017 BP Amsterdam
Mailing Address: PO Box 645, 1000 AP Amsterdam
Tel: (020) 235287 *Fax:* (020) 6247096
E-mail: mail@castrumperegrini.nl
Web Site: castrumperegrini.nl
Key Personnel
Man Dir & International Rights: M Defuster
Contact: Andrea Korte *E-mail:* a.korte@castrumperegrini.nl
Founded: 1951
Subjects: Antiques, Biography, Literature, Literary Criticism, Essays, Poetry
ISBN Prefix(es): 90-6034
Total Titles: 100 Print
Orders to: Hermannstr 61, 53225 Bonn, Germany

De Centaur, *imprint of* Omega Boek BV

Uitgeverij Christofoor
Steniaweg 32, 3702 AG Zeist
Mailing Address: Postbus 234, 3700 AE Zeist
Tel: (030) 692 39 74 *Fax:* (030) 691 48 34
E-mail: info@christofoor.nl
Key Personnel
Contact: Dhr E Hezemans
Subjects: Animals, Pets, Biblical Studies, Biography, Child Care & Development, Cookery, Crafts, Games, Hobbies, Education, Fiction,

History, How-to, Philosophy, Psychology, Psychiatry, Science Fiction, Fantasy
ISBN Prefix(es): 90-6238

de Cocon, *imprint of* Unieboek BV

Uitgeverij Conserve+
Tureluur 12, 1873 JW Groet Schoorl
Mailing Address: Postbus 74, 1870 AB Schoorl
Tel: (072) 5093693 *Fax:* (072) 5094370
E-mail: info@conserve.nl
Web Site: www.conserve.nl
Key Personnel
President: Kees De Bakker
Founded: 1983
Subjects: Biography, Fiction, History, Literature, Literary Criticism, Essays, Mysteries, Caribbean, Surinam, World War II
ISBN Prefix(es): 90-71380; 90-5429
Total Titles: 250 Print

Corona, *imprint of* Ars Scribendi bv Uitgeverij

Uitgeverij Coutinho BV (Coutinho Publishing)+
Slochterenlaan 7, 1405 AL Bussum
Mailing Address: Postbus 333, 1400 AH Bussum
Tel: (035) 6949991 *Fax:* (035) 6947165
E-mail: info@coutinho.nl
Web Site: www.coutinho.nl
Key Personnel
Man Dir, Editorial: Dick Coutinho
  E-mail: coutinho@coutinho.ul; Marleen Klein
  E-mail: kleijn@coutinho.nl
Marketing: Carlijn Leijen *E-mail:* leijen@coutinho.nl
Founded: 1976
Specialize in Dutch as a second language.
Membership(s): NUW.
Subjects: Communications, Economics, Education, English as a Second Language, History, Human Relations, Language Arts, Linguistics, Literature, Literary Criticism, Essays, Philosophy
ISBN Prefix(es): 90-6283
Distributed by EPO (Belgium)

Otto Cramwinckel Uitgever
Herengracht 416, 1017 BZ Amsterdam
Tel: (020) 627 66 09 *Fax:* (020) 638 38 17
E-mail: info@cram.nl
Web Site: www.cram.nl
Founded: 1985
Subjects: Communications, Radio, TV
ISBN Prefix(es): 90-71894; 90-75727

Davaco Publishers
Beukenlaan 3, 8085 RK Doornspijk
Tel: (0525) 661823 *Fax:* (0525) 662153
E-mail: main@davaco.nl
Web Site: www.davaco.com
Founded: 1969
Specialize in 16th & 17th century Dutch painting & Flemish art.
Subjects: Art
ISBN Prefix(es): 90-70288

De Brink (adult books), *imprint of* Uitgeverij Ploegsma BV

De Graaf Publishers
Zuideinde 40, 2420 AK Nieuwkoop
Mailing Address: Postbus 6, 2420 AA Nieuwkoop
Tel: (0172) 57 1461 *Fax:* (0172) 57 2231
E-mail: degraaf.books@wxs.nl
Web Site: www.antiqbook.nl/degraafbooks
Key Personnel
Man Dir: Maria Emilie de Graaf
Founded: 1959
Subjects: Religion - Other
ISBN Prefix(es): 90-6004

Total Titles: 350 Print
Subsidiaries: Miland Publishers

De Ruiter, *imprint of* Educatieve Partners Nederland bv

De Toorts, *imprint of* Uitgeverij De Toorts

De Vier Windstreken, *imprint of* Meander Uitgeverij BV

De Walburg Pers
Zaadmarkt 86, 7201 DE Zutphen
Mailing Address: Postbus 4159, 7200 BD Zutphen
Tel: (0575) 510522 *Fax:* (0575) 542289
E-mail: info@walburgpers.nl
Web Site: www.walburgpers.nl
Key Personnel
Man Dir, Publicity, Rights & Permissions: Dr C F Schriks; J Smal; J van't Leven
Founded: 1961
Subjects: Architecture & Interior Design, Drama, Theater, Ethnicity, History
ISBN Prefix(es): 90-6011; 90-5730

Delft University Press+
Prometheusplein 1, 2628 ZC Delft
Mailing Address: PO Box 98, 2600 MG Delft
Tel: (015) 2785706 *Fax:* (015) 2785678
E-mail: info@library.tudelft.nl
Web Site: www.library.tudelft.nl
Key Personnel
Dir: Pam Maas
Dir of Publishing: Lydia M ter Horst-ten Wolde
  Tel: (015) 2781616 *E-mail:* l.m.terhorst@library.tudelft.nl
Dir of Electronic Publications: Dr Nicole Potters
  Tel: (015) 2783254 *E-mail:* n.potters@library.tudelft.nl
Founded: 1972
Subjects: Architecture & Interior Design, Chemistry, Chemical Engineering, Civil Engineering, Electronics, Electrical Engineering, Engineering (General), Mechanical Engineering, Physics, Science (General), Technology
ISBN Prefix(es): 90-6275; 90-407
Parent Company: Delft University of Technolog

van Dishoeck, *imprint of* Unieboek BV

Uitgeversmaatschappij Ad Donker BV+
Kon Emmaplein 1, 3016 AA Rotterdam
Mailing Address: Postbus 23096, 3001 KB Rotterdam
Tel: (010) 4363009 *Fax:* (010) 4362963
E-mail: donker@bart.nl
Web Site: www.uitgeverijdonker.nl
Key Personnel
Dir & Publisher: Willem A Donker
  E-mail: donker@bart.nl
Founded: 1938
Subjects: Biography, Education, Fiction, History, Psychology, Psychiatry, Social Sciences, Sociology
ISBN Prefix(es): 90-6100
Number of titles published annually: 25 Print
Total Titles: 150 Print
Imprints: Wilkerdon

Drempelreeks, *imprint of* Uitgeverij Vrij Geestesleven

De Driehoek BV, Uitgeverij+
Keizersgracht 756, 1017 EZ Amsterdam
Tel: (020) 624 64 26 *Fax:* (020) 638 71 55
E-mail: driehoek.uitgeverij@planet.nl
Key Personnel
Dir: H J Heule; Dr W Heule
Founded: 1933

Subjects: Asian Studies, Health, Nutrition, Medicine, Nursing, Dentistry, Religion - Buddhist
ISBN Prefix(es): 90-6030

Uitgeverij Dwarsstap, *imprint of* Uitgeverij SUN

East-West Publications Fonds BV+
Anna Paulownastr 78, 2518 BJ The Hague
Mailing Address: Postbus 85617, 2508 CH The Hague
Tel: (70) 364 45 90 *Fax:* (70) 361 48 64
E-mail: epublica@packardbell.org
Key Personnel
Chief Executive: L W Carp
Sales: A Neuvel
Founded: 1966
Subjects: Music, Dance, Regional Interests, Religion - Other, Esoteric/spiritual
ISBN Prefix(es): 90-70104; 90-5340
Number of titles published annually: 8 Print
Total Titles: 10 Print
Associate Companies: East-West Publications (UK) Ltd
Orders to: 8 Caledonia St, London N1 9DZ, United Kingdom *Tel:* (20) 7837 5061 *Fax:* (20) 7278 4429

ECI voor Boeken en platen BV+
Laanakkerweg 14-16, 4131 PB Vianen Zh
Mailing Address: Postbus 400, 4130 EK Vianen Zh
Tel: (0347) 379214 *Fax:* (0347) 379380
E-mail: service@eci.nl
Web Site: www.eci.nl
Telex: 47449 ecihk nl
Key Personnel
Man Dir: Mr B M Tromp
Editorial, Nonfiction: Mrs B Eggels
Editorial, Fiction: Mr J Boezeman
Rights & Permissions: Mrs R Swaalf
Founded: 1967
Subjects: Fiction, Nonfiction (General)
ISBN Prefix(es): 90-70038; 90-5108
Parent Company: Bertelsmann AG, Munich, Germany
Book Club(s): ECI voor Boeken en Platen BV

EDECEA & WFE, *imprint of* West-Friesland/Boekproject-ontwikkeling

Educatieve Uitgeverij Edu'Actief BV+
Zomerdijk 9-e, 7942 JR Meppel
Mailing Address: Postbus 1056, 7940 KB Meppel
Tel: (0522) 235235 *Fax:* (0522) 235222
E-mail: info@edu-actief.nl
Web Site: www.edu-actief.nl
Key Personnel
Man Dir: I Buwalda
Founded: 1848
Membership(s): GEU.
Subjects: Communications, Economics, Education, Foreign Countries, Geography, Geology, Management, Marketing, Nonfiction (General)
ISBN Prefix(es): 90-5117; 90-372; 90-5766
Parent Company: Koninklyke Boom Pers BV

Educaboek, *imprint of* Educatieve Partners Nederland bv

Educatieve Partners Nederland bv+
Het Spoor 2, 3994 DB Houten
Mailing Address: Postbus 666, 3990 Dr Houten
Tel: (030) 6383001 *Fax:* (030) 6383004
E-mail: info@epn.nl
Web Site: www.epn.nl
Key Personnel
Man Dir: J H van Vloten
Founded: 1970
Part of Wolters Kluwer Educational Activities.
Subjects: Science (General)

ISBN Prefix(es): 90-11; 90-05; 90-207
Parent Company: Wolters Kluwer NV
Imprints: Stam Techniek; Stenfert Kroese; Schoolpers; De Ruiter; Robyns; Educaboek

Eekhoorn BV Uitgeverij+
Alexander Bellstr 11, 3261 LX Oud-Beijerland
Tel: (036) 610577 *Fax:* (036) 620982
E-mail: info@weton-wesgram.nl
Web Site: www.eekhoorn.com
Key Personnel
President: M G Stenvert
Editor: E H Kolk
Producer: F H A Kanters
Founded: 1920
Membership(s): GAU.
ISBN Prefix(es): 90-6056
Showroom(s): Sutton 10, 7327 AB Apeldoorn, New Zealand
Warehouse: Sutton 10, 7327 AB Apeldoorn, New Zealand

Elektor, *imprint of* Segment BV

Elektuur, *imprint of* Segment BV

Element Uitgevers+
Oude Haven 32, 1411 WB Naarden
Tel: (035) 6941750 *Fax:* (035) 6945824
E-mail: element@wxs.nl
Key Personnel
Publisher: Jan van Willegen
Founded: 1995
ISBN Prefix(es): 90-5689
Total Titles: 50 Print

Elmar BV+
Delftweg 147, 2289 BD Delft
Tel: (015) 215 32 32 *Fax:* (015) 215 32 30
E-mail: elmar@elmar.nl
Web Site: 212.83.197.79
Key Personnel
Man Dir: H Masthoff; M Roodnat
Founded: 1961
Subjects: Biography, Health, Nutrition, History, How-to, Humor, Nonfiction (General), Sports, Athletics, Travel
ISBN Prefix(es): 90-6120; 90-389; 90-5814

Elsevier, *imprint of* Elsevier Science BV

Elsevier Science BV
Sara Burgerhartstr 25, 1055 KV Amsterdam
Tel: (020) 5862560 *Fax:* (020) 4852457
E-mail: nlinfo-f@elsevier.nl
Telex: 10704
Key Personnel
Chairman & Chief Executive Officer: H P Spruijt
Dir: C J Blake; G P Joebsis; R C White; Frans H J Visscher; P Nientker; K J Leeflang; N Farmer; P Shepherd; R Dietz; H Gerbrandy; R Van Charldorp
Founded: 1946
Subjects: Biological Sciences, Chemistry, Chemical Engineering, Computer Science, Earth Sciences, Economics, Engineering (General), Mathematics, Medicine, Nursing, Dentistry, Physics, Science (General), Technology
ISBN Prefix(es): 0-444; 90-444
Parent Company: Reed Elsevier, Van de Sande Bakhuyzenstr 4, Postbus 470, 1000 AL Amsterdam
Associate Companies: Editora Campus, Brazil; Elsevier Science Ireland Ltd, Ireland; Elsevier Science SA, Switzerland; Elsevier Science Ltd, United Kingdom; Elsevier Science Inc
Imprints: Elsevier; Excerpta Medica; North Holland; Pergamon
Subsidiaries: Elsevier Geo Abstracts
Divisions: Secondary Publishing Division; Elsevier Science NL
U.S. Office(s): Elsevier Scientific Inc, 655 Ave of the Americas, New York, NY 10010, United States
Orders to: Elsevier Science BV, PO Box 211, Amsterdam *Tel:* (020) 4853753 *Fax:* (020) 4853705

Uitgeverij Elzenga
Singel 262, 1016 AC Amsterdam
Tel: (020) 55 11 262
Key Personnel
Man Dir: Hans Elzenga
Founded: 1982
Subjects: Fiction, Mysteries
ISBN Prefix(es): 90-6692

Johan Enschede Amsterdam BV
Donauweg 6, 1043 AJ Amsterdam
Mailing Address: Postbus 8023, 1005 AA Amsterdam
Tel: (020) 585 86 00 *Fax:* (020) 585 86 01
E-mail: info@jea.nl
Web Site: www.jea.nl
Telex: 41049
Key Personnel
Manager, Sales & Marketing: Henk Reuter
 E-mail: h.reuter@jea.nl
ISBN Prefix(es): 90-70024

ENTERBOOKS, *imprint of* Uitgeverij De Toorts

Excerpta Medica, *imprint of* Elsevier Science BV

Fantom, *imprint of* Ars Scribendi bv Uitgeverij

Frank Fehmers Productions+
Pr Hendrikkade 161/b, 1011 TB Amsterdam
Tel: (020) 6238766 *Fax:* (020) 6246262
Web Site: www.fbg.nl/34927
Telex: 16740 fepro nl *Cable:* Intpubcon
Key Personnel
Man Dir: Frank Fehmers
International Co-productions: Meghan Ferrill
Subjects: Business, Film, Video, Publishing & Book Trade Reference, Radio, TV
ISBN Prefix(es): 90-6151
Associate Companies: Frank Fehmers Productions Inc, 300 E 59 St, New York, NY 10022, United States; Frank Fehmers Productions Ltda, Estrada do Tombo 401, Bloco N Apt 102, 22450 Rio de Janeiro RJ, Brazil; Frank Fehmers Publishing BV, Groot Davelaarweg 20, Curacao, Netherlands Antilles

Fibula, *imprint of* Unieboek BV

Flash, *imprint of* Ars Scribendi bv Uitgeverij

Uitgeverij De Fontein BV
Subsidiary of Veen, Bosch & Keuning Uitgevers NV
Prinses Marielaan 8, 3743 JA Baarn
Tel: (035) 5486311 *Fax:* (035) 5423855
E-mail: info@defonteinbaarn.nl
Web Site: www.veenboschenkeuning.nl/pages/fontein.htm
Key Personnel
Dir: Toine Akveld
Head of Sales & Marketing: Theo van der Voort *Tel:* (035) 5486337 *E-mail:* tvoort@defonteinbaarn.nl
Promotion & Publicity: Ruth ter Voort *Tel:* (035) 5486335 *E-mail:* rtervoort@defonteinbaarn.nl
Founded: 1946
Membership(s): The Combo Group.
Subjects: Cookery, Fiction, History, Humor, Mysteries, Nonfiction (General), Science (General), Technology, Women's Studies
ISBN Prefix(es): 90-325; 90-261
Associate Companies: De Prom Uitgeverij
Imprints: De Fontein jeugd; De Kern; Piramide; Sesam Junior

De Fontein jeugd, *imprint of* Uitgeverij De Fontein BV

Fontes Pers, *imprint of* Holland University Press BV (APA)

Forum, *imprint of* De Boekerij BV

W Gaade, *imprint of* Unieboek BV

Gaberbocchus Press+
PO Box 3547, 1001 AH Amsterdam
Tel: (020) 6245181 *Fax:* (020) 6230672
E-mail: info@deharmonie.nl
Web Site: www.gaberbocchus.nl
Subjects: Literature, Literary Criticism, Essays
ISBN Prefix(es): 90-6169
Total Titles: 26 Print
Parent Company: De Harmonie Publishers, Spuistraat 272, 1012 VW Amsterdam

Uitgeverij Vrij Geestesleven+
Steniaweg 32, 3702 AG Zeist
Mailing Address: Postbus 851, 3700 AW Zeist
Tel: (030) 6924953 *Fax:* (030) 6932304
Key Personnel
General Manager: Mr M Ockeloen
Founded: 1952
Subjects: Art, Biography, Education, Health, Nutrition, Literature, Literary Criticism, Essays, Psychology, Psychiatry
ISBN Prefix(es): 90-6038
Imprints: Drempelreeks
Bookshop(s): De Nieuwe Boekerij, Steynlaan 55, 3701 EC Zeist

Uitgeverij en boekhandel Van Gennep BV+
Niuwezijds Voorburgwal 330, 1012 RW Amsterdam
Tel: (20) 6247033 *Fax:* (20) 6247035
E-mail: vangennep@wxs.nl
Key Personnel
Man Dir: BIM Kat
Founded: 1969
Subjects: Art, Fiction, Foreign Countries, Government, Political Science, History, Literature, Literary Criticism, Essays, Philosophy, Psychology, Psychiatry, Religion - Buddhist, Religion - Catholic, Religion - Hindu, Religion - Islamic, Religion - Jewish, Religion - Protestant, Religion - Other, Social Sciences, Sociology
ISBN Prefix(es): 90-6012; 90-5515
Imprints: Sara

Uitgeverij De Geus BV+
Oude Vest 9, 4811 HR Breda
Mailing Address: Postbus 1878, 4801 BW Breda
Tel: (076) 522 81 51 *Fax:* (076) 522 25 99
E-mail: email@degeus.nl
Web Site: www.degeus.nl
Key Personnel
President: E Visser
Contact: Marie-Lou Huijts *E-mail:* m.huijts@degeus.nl
Founded: 1983
Subjects: Fiction, Nonfiction (General)
ISBN Prefix(es): 90-5226; 90-6222; 90-70610

BV Uitgeversbedryf Het Goede Boek+
Koningin Wilhelminastr 8, 1271 PH Huizen
Mailing Address: Postbus 122, 1270 AC Huizen
Tel: (35) 525 35 08 *Fax:* (35) 525 40 13
Key Personnel
Dir: F Rikmans
Founded: 1932
Also acts as distributor.

Subjects: Aeronautics, Aviation, Maritime, Sports, Athletics
ISBN Prefix(es): 90-240
Number of titles published annually: 3 Print
Total Titles: 48 Print

Gooi & Sticht, *imprint of* Uitgeverij J H Kok BV

Van Goor BV+
Herengracht 406, 1017 BX Amsterdam
Tel: (020) 5353135 *Fax:* (020) 5353130
E-mail: boekerij@boekery.nl
Web Site: www.van-goor.nl
Key Personnel
Editorial Dir: Mrs Henny Bodenkamp; Mrs Dorine Louwerens
Publicity: Marc Van Biezen
Production: Hans van den Broek
International Rights Contact: Geri Brandjes
Parent Company: De Boekery BV
Ultimate Parent Company: Meulenhoff & Co BV
Associate Companies: Bruna; T M Meulenhoff; Prometheus/Bert Bakker; Standaard; Unieboek/Van Reemst
Imprints: Piccolo
Subsidiaries: De Boekeryij bv

Goose Press, *imprint of* Architectura & Natura

Uitgeverij CJ Goossens BV+
Delftweg 147, 2289 BD Rijswijkzh Zn
Tel: (015) 2123623 *Fax:* (015) 2124295
Founded: 1980
Subjects: Literature, Literary Criticism, Essays
ISBN Prefix(es): 90-6551

Gottmer Uitgevers Groep (Gottmer Publishing Group)+
Wilhelminapark 6, 2012 KA Haarlem
Mailing Address: Postbus 317, 2000 AH Haarlem
Tel: (023) 541 11 90 *Fax:* (023) 527 44 04
E-mail: info@gottmer.nl
Web Site: www.gottmer.nl
Telex: 41856
Key Personnel
Man Dir: Mr Cees van Wijk
Founded: 1937
Subjects: Crafts, Games, Hobbies, Fiction, House & Home, Nonfiction (General), Religion - Other, Science (General), Travel, Body-Mind-Spirit, Lifestyle, Nautical
ISBN Prefix(es): 90-257; 90-230; 90-6834
Imprints: Altamira-Becht; Aramith; Hollandia

Griffioen Paperbacks, *imprint of* Em Querido's Uitgeverij BV

De Groot Goudriaan, *imprint of* Uitgeverij J H Kok BV

B R Gruener Publishing Co, *imprint of* John Benjamins BV

de Haan, *imprint of* Unieboek BV

Hagen & Stam Uitgeverij Ten
Postbus 34, 2501 AG The Hague
Tel: (070) 3045700 *Fax:* (070) 3045800
Membership(s): the Wolters Kluwer Group.
Subjects: Architecture & Interior Design, Biological Sciences, Chemistry, Chemical Engineering, Civil Engineering, Computer Science, Electronics, Electrical Engineering, Energy, Engineering (General), Environmental Studies, Labor, Industrial Relations, Management, Mechanical Engineering, Microcomputers, Real Estate, Science (General), Technology, Transportation

ISBN Prefix(es): 90-70011; 90-71694; 90-76304; 90-76383; 90-440
Parent Company: Wolter Kluwer

De Harmonie Uitgeverij (De Harmonie Publishers)+
Spuistr 272, 1012 VW Amsterdam
Mailing Address: PO Box 3547, 1001 AH Amsterdam
Tel: (020) 6245181 *Fax:* (020) 6230672
E-mail: info@deharmonie.nl
Web Site: www.deharmonie.nl
Key Personnel
Man Dir: Jaco Groot
Rights & Permissions: Elsbeth Louis
Founded: 1972
Subjects: Fiction, Humor, Literature, Literary Criticism, Essays, Poetry
ISBN Prefix(es): 90-6169; 90-803481
Number of titles published annually: 35 Print
Total Titles: 1,200 Print; 6 Audio
Subsidiaries: Gaberbocchus Press

Uitgeverij Ten Have+
Division of Bosch en Keuning NV
Member of Bosch & Keuning Group
Ijsseldijk 31, 8266 AD Kampen
Mailing Address: Postbus 5018, 8260 AG Kampen
Tel: (038) 3392556 *Fax:* (038) 3392518
Key Personnel
Man Dir: C Sbiti
Managing Editor: P de Boer
Founded: 1831
Subjects: Biblical Studies, Philosophy, Religion - Jewish, Religion - Protestant, Religion - Other, Theology
ISBN Prefix(es): 90-259
Total Titles: 300 Print

Hemma Holland BV
Willemsparkweg 94, 1071 HN Amsterdam
Tel: (020) 675 53 26 *Fax:* (020) 679 62 54
ISBN Prefix(es): 90-6804; 90-380; 90-412

HES & De Graaf Publishers BV+
Tuurdijk 16, 3997 MS 'tGoy-Houten, Utrecht
Tel: (030) 6011955 *Fax:* (030) 6011813
E-mail: info@hesdegraaf.nl
Web Site: www.hesdegraaf.com
Key Personnel
Chief Executive, Editorial & Publicity: S S Hesselink *E-mail:* hesselink@forum-hes.nl
Contact: E Kempers
Founded: 1971
Subjects: History, Language Arts, Linguistics, Literature, Literary Criticism, Essays, Philosophy, Theology
ISBN Prefix(es): 90-6194

Heuff Amsterdam Uitgever
Lauriehof 8, 1016 MA Amsterdam
Tel: (020) 620 46 25 *Fax:* (020) 620 46 25
Cable: Heuff/Nieuwkoop
Key Personnel
Man Dir: H Heuff
Founded: 1970
Subjects: Art, Fiction, History, Music, Dance
ISBN Prefix(es): 90-6141

Uitgeverij Heureka
Hooqstr 20, 1381 VS Weesp
Tel: (0294) 480 000 *Fax:* (0294) 415 183
E-mail: heureka@belboek.com
Web Site: www.belboek.com/heureka; www.belboek.com/index.html
Key Personnel
Man Dir: F H B Cladder
Founded: 1976
Subjects: History

ISBN Prefix(es): 90-6262
Bookshop(s): Belboek - Int order Bookshop, Weesp *Tel:* (0294) 80000

Historische Uitgeverij+
Westersingel 37, 9718 CC Groningen
Tel: (050) 3181700; (050) 3135258 *Fax:* (050) 3146383
E-mail: info@histuit.nl
Web Site: www.histuitg.nl
Key Personnel
Publisher: Patrick M Th Everard *E-mail:* p.everard@histuitg.nl
Founded: 1986
Subjects: History, Journalism, Literature, Literary Criticism, Essays, Nonfiction (General), Philosophy, Poetry, Psychology, Psychiatry
ISBN Prefix(es): 90-6554
Number of titles published annually: 20 Print
Total Titles: 150 Print

van Holkema en Waren Holkema en Warendorf, *imprint of* Unieboek BV

Uitgeverij Holland
Spaarne 110, 2011 CM Haarlem
Tel: (023) 5323061 *Fax:* (023) 5342908
E-mail: info@uitgeverijholland.nl
Web Site: www.uitgeverijholland.nl
Key Personnel
Man Dir: Rolf van Ulzen
Sales Dir, Permissions: Ruurt van Ulzen
Founded: 1921
Subjects: Fiction, Poetry, Science (General)
ISBN Prefix(es): 90-251

Holland University Press BV (APA)
Subsidiary of APA (Academic Publishers Associated)
Postbus 806, 1000 AV Amsterdam
Tel: (020) 626 5544 *Fax:* (020) 528 5298
E-mail: info@apa-publishers.com
Web Site: www.apa-publishers.com
Subjects: History, Human Relations, Language Arts, Linguistics, Law, Theology
ISBN Prefix(es): 90-6037; 90-302; 90-6039; 90-6042
Imprints: Fontes Pers

Hollandia, *imprint of* Gottmer Uitgevers Groep

Uitgeverij Hollandia BV+
Professor van Vlotenweg 1-A, 2061 EB Bloemendaal
Mailing Address: Postbus 160, 2060 AD Bloemendaal
Tel: (023) 5257150 *Fax:* (023) 52574404
E-mail: gottmer@x54all.nl
Web Site: www.hiswa.nl
Key Personnel
Man Dir: Tonnis Muntinga
Founded: 1899
Subjects: Fiction, Maritime, Sports, Athletics, Transportation, Travel
ISBN Prefix(es): 90-6410; 90-6045

Uitgeverij Homeovisie BV+
Postbus 9292, 1800 GG Alkamaar
Tel: (072) 566 1133 *Fax:* (072) 566 1295
E-mail: info@vsm.nl
Web Site: www2.vsminfo.nl
Key Personnel
President: Mr F Bech
Editor: Marianne Meijer
Founded: 1976
Specialize in Homeopathy.
Subjects: Health, Nutrition, Medicine, Nursing, Dentistry
ISBN Prefix(es): 90-71669

Hotei Publishing, *imprint of* KIT - Royal Tropical Institute Publishers

Hotei Publishing+
Imprint of KIT Publishers - Royal Tropical Institute
Mauritskade 63, 1092 AD Amsterdam
Mailing Address: PO Box 95001, 1090 HA Amsterdam
Tel: (020) 568 8330 *Fax:* (020) 568 8286
Web Site: www.kit.nl/hotei
Key Personnel
Man Dir: Ron Smit *E-mail:* r.smit@kit.nl
Publisher: Arlette Kouwenhoven *E-mail:* a.kouwenhoven@kit.nl
Manager Marketing & Sales: Erik Rasmussen *E-mail:* e.rasmussen@kit.nl
Finance Dir: Stefan van Goor *E-mail:* s.v.goor@kit.nl
Founded: 1999
Membership(s): Dutch Publishers Association.
Subjects: Art, Asian Studies, Gardening, Plants, History, Photography, Religion - Buddhist, Japan
ISBN Prefix(es): 90-74822
Number of titles published annually: 15 Print
Total Titles: 40 Print; 1 CD-ROM
Foreign Rep(s): Bookwise Asia (Southeast Asia); Bookwise International (Australia & New Zealand); Durnell Marketing (Europe & UK); Premier Book Marketing (UK); Yagi Shoten (Japan); Stylus Publishing, LLC (Canada, USA); Yohan (Japan)

ICG Publications BV+
Dr H P Bremmerstr 20, 2552 MJ The Hague
Tel: (070) 4480203 *Fax:* (070) 4480177
Cable: INTERGRAPH DORDRECHT
Key Personnel
Man Dir: Henk J La Porte
Founded: 1978
Subjects: Language Arts, Linguistics, Medicine, Nursing, Dentistry
ISBN Prefix(es): 90-5569; 90-6765; 90-70176
Parent Company: Holland Academic Graphics
Subsidiaries: I C G Printing BV

International Books, *imprint of* Uitgeverij Jan van Arkel

Uitgevery International Theatre & Film Books+
Nieuwpoortkade 2A, 1055 RX Amsterdam
Tel: (020) 60 60 911 *Fax:* (020) 60 60 914
E-mail: info@itfb.nl
Web Site: www.itfb.nl
Key Personnel
President: Mrs M Oele
Founded: 1975
Specialize in theatre & film books.
Subjects: Drama, Theater, Film, Video, Music, Dance
ISBN Prefix(es): 90-6403
Number of titles published annually: 25 Print
Total Titles: 500 Print

Uitgeverij Intertaal BV
Transistorstr 80, 1322 CH Amsterdam
Mailing Address: PO Box 60081, 1320 AB Almere
Tel: (036) 5471650 *Fax:* (036) 5471582
E-mail: int@intertaal.nl
Web Site: www.intertaal.nl
Founded: 1963
Subjects: Language Arts, Linguistics
ISBN Prefix(es): 90-70885; 90-5451; 90-800002
Showroom(s): Inter L, Schuttershofstraat 43, 2000 Antwerpen
Warehouse: Lemelerbergweg 21-22, 1101 AJ Amsterdam Z O

IOS Press BV+
Nieuwe Hemweg 6B, 1013 BG Amsterdam
Tel: (020) 688 33 55 *Fax:* (020) 620 3419
E-mail: info@iospress.nl
Web Site: www.iospress.nl
Key Personnel
Dir: Dr E H Fredriksson
Founded: 1987
Subjects: Biological Sciences, Chemistry, Chemical Engineering, Computer Science, Electronics, Electrical Engineering, Environmental Studies, Health, Nutrition, Language Arts, Linguistics, Management, Mathematics, Mechanical Engineering, Medicine, Nursing, Dentistry, Physics, Technology
ISBN Prefix(es): 90-5199; 1-58603
Number of titles published annually: 90 Print
Total Titles: 500 Print
Subsidiaries: IOS Press Inc
Branch Office(s)
IOS Press/Lavis Marketing, 73 Lime Walk, Oxford OX3 7AD, United Kingdom *Tel:* (01865) 76 7575 *Fax:* (01865) 75 0079
IOS Press, Akademische Verlagsgesellschaft aka GmbH, Neue Promenade 6, 10178 Berlin, Germany *Tel:* (030) 2472 9840 *Fax:* (030) 2839 4100
Distributor for OHMSHA Ltd (Japan)

JeugdSalamander Paperbacks, *imprint of* Em Querido's Uitgeverij BV

Kartoen
Salland 231, 9405 GL Assen
Tel: (050) 3110505 *Fax:* (050) 3112299
E-mail: mondria@worldonline.nl
Subjects: Humor, Self-Help

Katholieke Bijbelstichting (Catholic Bible Center Netherlands)+
Orthenstr 290, 5211 SX Hertogenbosch
Mailing Address: Postbus 1274, 5200 BH 's-Hertogenbosch
Tel: (073) 6133220 *Fax:* (073) 6910140
Web Site: www.willibrordbijbel.nl/kbs
Key Personnel
Manager: Ph L van Heusden *E-mail:* p.v.heusden@rkbijbel.nl
Founded: 1961
Subjects: Biblical Studies, Religion - Catholic
ISBN Prefix(es): 90-6173
Number of titles published annually: 10 Print; 2 CD-ROM; 1 Online; 1 Audio
Total Titles: 100 Print; 2 CD-ROM; 1 Online; 1 Audio

De Kern, *imprint of* Uitgeverij De Fontein BV

Kimio Uitgeverij bv+
Postbus 1117, 1400 BC Bussum
Tel: (035) 6950760 *Fax:* (035) 6951548
E-mail: info@kimio.nl
Web Site: www.kimio.nl
Key Personnel
Publishing & Man Dir: J van den Boom
Founded: 1985
ISBN Prefix(es): 90-71368

KIT - Royal Tropical Institute Publishers
Mauritskade 63, 1092 AD Amsterdam
Mailing Address: PO Box 95001, 1090 HA Amsterdam
Tel: (020) 5688 272 *Fax:* (020) 5688 286
E-mail: publishers@kit.nl
Web Site: www.kit.nl/publishers
Key Personnel
Man Dir: Ron Smit
Subjects: Agriculture, Anthropology, Art, Developing Countries, Health, Nutrition
ISBN Prefix(es): 90-6832
Imprints: Hotei Publishing
Distributed by Bookwise Asia (Southeast Asia); Bookwise International (Australia & New Zealand); Marston Book Services (UK & Europe (except Holland)); Media Logistics (Netherlands); Stylus Publishing LLC (USA & Canada)
Foreign Rep(s): Bookwise Asia (Southeast Asia); Bookwise International (Australia & New Zealand); Durnell Marketing (UK, Europe); Premier Book Marketing (UK); Stylus Publishing LLC (Canada, USA)

KITLV Press Royal Institute of Linguistics & Anthropology+
Division of Royal Institute of Linguistics & Anthropology
Reuvensplaats 2, 2311 BE Leiden
Mailing Address: PO Box 9515, 2300 RA Leiden
Tel: (071) 5272295 *Fax:* (071) 5272638
E-mail: kitlvpress@kitlv.nl
Web Site: www.iias.leidenuniv.nl/institutes/kitlv
Key Personnel
Dir: Prof W A L Stokhof
Founded: 1851
Subjects: Anthropology, Asian Studies, Economics, Environmental Studies, History, Language Arts, Linguistics, Social Sciences, Sociology, Women's Studies, Caribbean Studies
ISBN Prefix(es): 90-6718
Number of titles published annually: 15 Print
Total Titles: 250 Print
Distributed by The Asian Experts (Australia & the South Pacific); United Publishers Services Ltd (Japan); University of Washington Press
Distributor for Monash Asia Institute; Research School of Pacific & Asian Studies

Uitgeverij Kluitman Alkmaar BV
Jan Ligthartstr 11, 1817 MR Alkmaar
Mailing Address: Postbus 9000, 1800 GR Alkmaar
Tel: (072) 52 75 075 *Fax:* (072) 52 09 400
E-mail: webmaster@kluitman.nl
Web Site: www.kluitman.nl
Key Personnel
Dir: Dr P F A Stanco; Mrs H Stanco-Gerla
Founded: 1864
ISBN Prefix(es): 90-206

Kluwer Academic/Plenum Publishers, *imprint of* Kluwer Academic Publishers

Kluwer Academic Publishers
Van Godewijckstr 30, 3300 AA Dordrecht
Mailing Address: Postbus 17, 3300 AA Dordrecht
Tel: (078) 657 6000 *Fax:* (078) 657 6254
Telex: 29245
Key Personnel
President: Jeffery K Smith
Vice President, Boston: M Stephen Dane
Vice President, New York: Robert W Holland
Vice President, Boston: Zachary Rolnik
Vice President, Dordrecht: Alexander W Schimmelpennick; Caroline F Vogelzang
Dir, Library Relations, Dordrecht: J F Hattink
Sales Dir, Dordrecht: S D Dissel
Sales Manager, Boston: Lawrence D Salas
Subjects: Behavioral Sciences, Law, Medicine, Nursing, Dentistry, Science (General), Social Sciences, Sociology, Technology
ISBN Prefix(es): 0-7923; 90-247; 90-286; 90-277
Parent Company: Wolters Kluwer NV
Imprints: Martinus Nijhoff; Kluwer Academic/Plenum Publishers
U.S. Office(s): Kluwer Academic Publishers, 101 Philip Dr, Norwell, MA 02061, United States *Tel:* 781-871-6600 *Fax:* 781-871-6528
Kluwer Academic Plenum Publisher, 233 Spring St, New York, NY 10013-1578, United States *Tel:* 212-620-8000
Orders to: Distributiecentrum KAP Group, Maxwellstr 4-12, 3316 GP Dordrecht *Tel:* (078) 654 6427 *Fax:* (078) 6546 627

Kluwer Academic Publishers/Kluwer Academic Plenum Publishers, 101 Philip Dr, Norwell, MA 02061, United States *Tel:* 781-871-6600 *Fax:* 781-871-6528

Kluwer Bedrijfswetenschappen
Leeuwenbrug 99-103, 7411 TH Deventer
Mailing Address: PO Box 23, 7400 GA Deventer
Tel: (0570) 647111 *Fax:* (0570) 638040
Telex: 49774
Key Personnel
Publisher: P J A Snakkers
Chief Executive: A Langevoort
Subjects: Business, Economics, Technology
ISBN Prefix(es): 90-267
Parent Company: Wolters Kluwer NV
Warehouse: Intermedia bv, PO Box 4, 2400 MA Alphen 4d Ryn

Kluwer Law International+
PO Box 85889, The Hague 2508 CN
Tel: (070) 308 1500 *Fax:* (070) 308 1515
Key Personnel
Man Dir: Mr A Fillingham
Dir of Sales & Marketing: Ms A Timmers
Marketing Manager: Ms Joyce M Rivers
Founded: 1995
Subjects: Law, Specialize in International Law & International Relations
ISBN Prefix(es): 90-411
Parent Company: Wolters Kluwer NV
U.S. Office(s): Aspen Publishers, 11015 Avenue of the Americas, 37th fl, New York, NY 10036, United States
Warehouse: Extenza Turpin
Orders to: Extenza Turpin, Stratton Business Park, Pegasus Dr, Biggleswade, SG18 8QB Bedfordshire *Tel:* 01767 604853 *Fax:* 01767 604948 *E-mail:* sales@kluwerlaw.com *Web Site:* www.kluwerlaw.com

Kluwer Technische Boeken BV+
Leeuwenbrug 99-103, 7411 TH Deventer
Mailing Address: PO Box 23, 7400 GA Deventer
Tel: (0570) 647111 *Fax:* (0570) 638040
Telex: 49560 KLUTB NL
Key Personnel
Man Dir & Chief Executive: N H L van Herk
Editorial: Benno van Lochem; Rob van Berkel; Jan Schukking
Sales: Hans Ulenberg
Production: Dick Laus
Part of Wolters Kluwer Trade Publishing.
Subjects: Management, Mechanical Engineering, Science (General), Technology
ISBN Prefix(es): 90-267; 90-201; 90-5576; 90-5577
Parent Company: Wolters Kluwer NV
Subsidiaries: Kluwer Technische Boeken Belgie
Warehouse: Intermedia bv, PO Box 4, 2400 MA Alphen 4d Ryn

Koenen, *imprint of* Van Dale Lexicografie BV

Uitgeverij J H Kok BV+
Subsidiary of Veen Bosch & Keuning Uitgevers NV
Ijsseldijk 31, 8266 AD Kampen
Mailing Address: Postbus 5019, 8260 GA Kampen
Tel: (038) 3392555 *Fax:* (038) 3311776
E-mail: algemeen@kok.nl
Web Site: www.kok.nl
Key Personnel
Man Dir: B A Endedijk
Publisher: P de Boer; F J Jonkers; C Verboom
Executive Secretary: Tineke Bouma *Tel:* (038) 3392528 *E-mail:* tbouma@kok.nl
Founded: 1894
Subjects: Fiction, History, Poetry, Religion - Other, Science (General), Social Sciences, Sociology
ISBN Prefix(es): 90-266; 90-242; 90-6140; 90-297; 90-435; 90-205; 90-391; 90-304
Imprints: Agora; Gooi & Sticht; De Groot Goudriaan; VCL (series of novels)/Westfriesland; Voorhoeve
Subsidiaries: Callenbach; Kok; Ten Have

Koninklijke Vermande bv+
Postbus 20025, 2500 EA The Hague
Tel: (070) 3789880 *Fax:* (070) 3789783
E-mail: sdu@sdu.nl
Web Site: www.sdu.nl/uitg/vermande
Key Personnel
President: Dr J Emeis
Founded: 1750
Subjects: Accounting, Criminology, Environmental Studies, Law, Management, Science (General)
ISBN Prefix(es): 90-6040; 90-5458
Divisions: Kugler Publications BV
Orders to: SDU Service Centrum, PO Box 20014, 2500 EA The Hague *Tel:* (070) 3789880

Kugler Publications+
Imprint of SPB Academic Publishing bv
Prinsegracht 59A, 2512 EX The Hague
Mailing Address: PO Box 97747, 2509 GC The Hague
Tel: (070) 33-00253 *Fax:* (070) 33-00254
E-mail: kuglerspb@wxs.nl
Web Site: www.kuglerpublications.com
Key Personnel
President & International Rights: S P Bakker
Founded: 1974
Subjects: Criminology, Medicine, Nursing, Dentistry, Specializes in ophthalmology, otorhinolaryngolgy, neurology & neurosciences
ISBN Prefix(es): 90-6299
Number of titles published annually: 10 Print
Total Titles: 115 Print

Kwintessens, *imprint of* BV Uitgevery NZV (Nederlandse Zondagsschool Vereniging)

LCG Malmberg BV
Leeghwaterlaan 16, 5223 BA Hertogenbosch
Tel: (073) 6288811 *Fax:* (073) 6210512
Web Site: www.malmberg.nl *Cable:* MALMBERG'S-HERTOGENBOSCH
Key Personnel
General Manager: Dr J V Nelthoven
Publisher: Dr J J Mathigssen
Founded: 1885
Firm is a part of Educational Publishing division of VNU BV.
Subjects: Biological Sciences, Chemistry, Chemical Engineering, Education, Physics
ISBN Prefix(es): 90-208; 90-345

Leiden University Press, *imprint of* Brill Academic Publishers

Uitgeverij Lemma BV+
Furkaplateau 15, 3524 ZH Utrecht
Mailing Address: Postbus 3320, 3502 GH Utrecht
Tel: (030) 2545652 *Fax:* (030) 2512496
E-mail: infodesk@lemma.nl
Web Site: www.lemma.nl
Key Personnel
Dir: Ruud K Veen *E-mail:* rveen@lemma.nl
Publisher: Stephanie Harmon *E-mail:* stephanie.harmon@lemma.nl; Karin Vlug *E-mail:* karin.vlug@lemma.nl
Founded: 1988
Independent educational & scientific publishing company.
Subjects: Business, Communications, Economics, Education, Health, Nutrition, Labor, Industrial Relations, Law, Management, Marketing, Physical Sciences, Psychology, Psychiatry, Social Sciences, Sociology, Technology
ISBN Prefix(es): 90-5189
Total Titles: 400 Print

Lemniscaat+
Vyverlaan 48, 3062 HL Rotterdam
Mailing Address: Postbus 4066, 3006 AB Rotterdam
Tel: (010) 2062929 *Fax:* (010) 4141560
E-mail: info@lemniscaat.nl
Web Site: www.lemniscaat.nl *Cable:* LEMNISCAAT ROTTERDAM
Key Personnel
Dir: J C Boele van Hensbroek *Tel:* (010) 2062920 *E-mail:* jcboele@lemniscaat.nl
Editor: Monique Postma *Tel:* (010) 2062925 *E-mail:* monique@lemniscaat.nl
Rights & Permissions: Susanne Padberg *Tel:* (010) 2062924 *E-mail:* susanne@lemniscaat.nl
Contact: F M van den Hoek *Tel:* (010) 2062927
Founded: 1963
Subjects: Psychology, Psychiatry, Social Sciences, Sociology
ISBN Prefix(es): 90-6069; 90-5637
Total Titles: 380 Print

Uitgeverij Leopold BV
Singel 262, 1016 AC Amsterdam
Mailing Address: Postbus 3879, 1001 AR Amsterdam
Tel: (020) 5511250 *Fax:* (020) 4204699
E-mail: verkoop@leopold.nl
Web Site: www.leopold.nl
Key Personnel
Man Dir: Liesbeth ten Houten
Permissions: Jacolien Kingmans
Founded: 1923
Subjects: Fiction, History
ISBN Prefix(es): 90-258
Parent Company: Nijgh en Van Ditmar NV
Associate Companies: BV Uitgeverij de Arbeiderspers

Van Loghum Slaterus, see Uitgeverij Bohn Stafleu Van Loghum BV

Magnum, *imprint of* Ars Scribendi bv Uitgeverij

Meander Uitgeverij BV+
Industrieweg 7, 2254 AE Voorschoten
Tel: (071) 5601040 *Fax:* (071) 5619741
E-mail: info@vierwindstreken.com
Web Site: www.vierwindstreken.com
Key Personnel
Contact: Bob Markus
Founded: 1996
ISBN Prefix(es): 90-5579; 90-5116
Number of titles published annually: 50 Print
Imprints: De Vier Windstreken

Stichting Evangelische Uitgeverij H Medema
Emsterweg 96, 8171 PK Vaassen
Mailing Address: Postbus 113, 8170 AC Vaassen
Tel: (0578) 574995 *Fax:* (0578) 573099
E-mail: info@medema.nl
Web Site: www.medema.nl
Key Personnel
Contact: H P Medema
Founded: 1951
ISBN Prefix(es): 90-6353

Meinema, *imprint of* Boekencentrum BV

Uitgeverij Meinema+
Postbus 29, 2700 AA Zoetermeer
Tel: (079) 3615481 *Fax:* (079) 3615489
E-mail: info@boekencentrum.nl
Web Site: www.boekencentrum.nl

Key Personnel
Editor: C Korenhof *E-mail:* korenhof@boekencentrum.nl
Subjects: Religion - Catholic, Religion - Protestant, Theology
ISBN Prefix(es): 90-211
Number of titles published annually: 40 Print
Total Titles: 220 Print
Parent Company: Boekencentrum, Goudstr 50, 2718 RC Zoetermeer
Distributed by Denis

Mets & Schilt Uitgevers en Distributeurs+
Westeinde 16, 1017 ZP Amsterdam
Tel: (020) 6256087 *Fax:* (020) 6270242
E-mail: info@metsenschilt.com
Web Site: www.metsenschilt.com
Key Personnel
Dir: J Mets; M J Schilt
Founded: 1981
Subjects: Art, Biography, Business, Cookery, Developing Countries, Foreign Countries, History, Journalism, Nonfiction (General), Social Sciences, Sociology, Travel
ISBN Prefix(es): 90-5330
Distributed by Van Halewyck (Belgium); Transaction Publishers (USA) (Africa, Asia, Australia, Ireland, New Zealand, North America, South America, UK)

J M Meulenhoff bv+
Herengracht 505, 1017 BV Amsterdam
Mailing Address: PO Box 100, 1000 AC Amsterdam
Tel: (020) 55 33 500 *Fax:* (020) 62 58 511
E-mail: info@meulenhoff.nl
Web Site: www.meulenhoff.nl
Key Personnel
Man Dir: Anne Rube
Publisher: Annette Portegies
Editorial: Leonoor Broeder; Reinjan Mulder; Pieter Swinkels
Production: Breditta Kramer
Publicity: Piet van Riele
Founded: 1895
Subjects: Biography, Fiction, History, Literature, Literary Criticism, Essays, Nonfiction (General), Poetry, Travel, Also specializing in commercial & Dutch language books
ISBN Prefix(es): 90-290
Total Titles: 1,000 Print
Parent Company: Meulenhoff & Co BV
Ultimate Parent Company: PCM Algemene boeken
Imprints: Arena; Bertollucci; Meulenhoff/Manteau; Vassallucci
Subsidiaries: Meulenhoff International

Meulenhoff/Manteau, *imprint of* J M Meulenhoff bv

Miland Publishers
Zuideinde 40, 2421 AK Nieuwkoop
Mailing Address: Postbus 6, 2420 AA Nieuwkoop
Tel: (0172) 57 1461 *Fax:* (0172) 57 2231
E-mail: degraaf.books@wxs.nl
Web Site: www.antiqbook.nl/degraafbooks
Founded: 1969
ISBN Prefix(es): 90-6003
Parent Company: De Graaf Publishers

Uitgeverij Mingus+
Meidoornalaan 12, 3461 ET Linschoten
Mailing Address: Postbus 242, 3440 AE Woerden
Tel: (0348) 42 55 07 *Fax:* (0348) 42 55 07
E-mail: mingus-vk@planet.nl
Key Personnel
Contact: Teus Verweij
Founded: 1981
Subjects: Fiction, Nonfiction (General)
ISBN Prefix(es): 90-6564

Ministerie van Verkeer en Waterstaat (Information & Documentation Division)
Plesmanweg 1-6, 2597 JG The Hague
Mailing Address: Postbus 20901, 2500 EX The Hague
Tel: (070) 3517086 *Fax:* (070) 3516430
E-mail: venwinfo@postbus51.nl
Web Site: www.minvenw.nl
Telex: 32562 minvwnl
Subjects: Transportation
ISBN Prefix(es): 90-369

Mirananda Publishers BV+
Postbus 85749, 2508 CK The Hague
Tel: (070) 358 59 43 *Fax:* (070) 358 68 43
E-mail: info@mirananda.nl
Web Site: www.mirananda.nl
Key Personnel
Man Dir: Jan-Carel Diecken
Contact: Reinoud Douwes
Founded: 1976
Subjects: Art, Astrology, Occult, Education, Language Arts, Linguistics, Philosophy, Psychology, Psychiatry, Religion - Other, Science (General)
ISBN Prefix(es): 90-6271
Number of titles published annually: 25 Print
Total Titles: 250 Print
Imprints: Moon Press (children's)
Orders to: Centraal Boekhuis, Erasmusweg 10, Culemborg

Mirran+
Oude Trambaan 23, 5085 NH Esbeek
Tel: (013) 5169534 *Fax:* (013) 4684764
E-mail: info@mirran.com
Web Site: www.mirran.com
Key Personnel
Director: Mieke de Jonge
Founded: 1996
Specialize in Danish children's books in Dutch translations.
Membership(s): GAU.
ISBN Prefix(es): 90-75837
Total Titles: 11 Print
Foreign Rep(s): Denis & Co (Belgium)
Shipping Address: Centraal Boekhuirs, PO Box 125, Culemborg

Mondria Publishers+
Westerkade 13a, 9718 AR Groningen
Tel: (050) 3110505 *Fax:* (050) 3112299
E-mail: post@mondria.nl
Key Personnel
Chief Executive, Sales & Publicity: E Vos
Founded: 1980
Subjects: Humor
ISBN Prefix(es): 90-6555; 90-432

Moon Press (children's), *imprint of* Mirananda Publishers BV

De Muiderkring BV+
Hogeweyselaan 227, 1382 JL Weesp
Mailing Address: Postbus 313, 1380 AH Weesp
Tel: (0294) 450460 *Fax:* (0294) 412782
Key Personnel
Man Dir: Van Lidth de Jeude
Sales: B Hofman
Founded: 1929
Subjects: Computer Science, Crafts, Games, Hobbies, Electronics, Electrical Engineering
ISBN Prefix(es): 90-6082

Mulder Holland BV+
Transformatorweg 35, 1014 AJ Amsterdam
Mailing Address: Postbus 8064, 1005 AB Amsterdam
Tel: (020) 442022; (020) 441682; (020) 824805 *Fax:* (020) 465228
Telex: 14627 *Cable:* Emzet Amsterdam
Key Personnel
Publisher: John Winkel
Parent Company: Internatio Mueller

Uitgeverij Maarten Muntinga+
Nieuwezijds Voorburgwal 292, 1012 RT Amsterdam
Mailing Address: Postbus 2465, 1000 CL Amsterdam
Tel: (020) 521 67 67 *Fax:* (020) 626 05 96
E-mail: info@rainbow.nl
Web Site: www.rainbow.nl
Key Personnel
President: Maarten Muntinga
Publisher: Hilbrand Gringhuis
Founded: 1983
Subjects: Biography, Fiction, History, Humor, Literature, Literary Criticism, Essays, Nonfiction (General), Self-Help
ISBN Prefix(es): 90-6766; 90-417
Imprints: Rainbow Crime; Rainbow Pocketboeken

Nai Publishers
Mauritsweg 23, 3012 JR Rotterdam
Tel: (010) 2010133 *Fax:* (010) 2010130
E-mail: info@naipublishers.nl
Web Site: www.naipublishers.nl
Key Personnel
Publisher & Director: Simon Franke
Editor & Production: Caroline Gautier; Barbera van Kooij
Office Manager: Marion Pot
Finance: Peter Pols
Founded: 1994
Publisher of books about architecture, art & urban design.
Subjects: Architecture & Interior Design, Art, Urban Design
Foreign Rep(s): Art Data (UK, Ireland); Coen Sligting Bookimport (Austria, Belgium, Germany, Switzerland); DAP (Central America, North America, South America); Le Funambule (France); Modern Journal (Australia, New Zealand); Penny Padovani (Gibraltar, Greece, Italy, Portugal, Slovenia, Spain); Roger Ward International Book Marketing (Asia)

Narratio Theologische Uitgeverij+
Kwakernaat 10, 4205 PK Gorinchem
Mailing Address: Postbus 1006, 4200 CA Gorinchem
Tel: (0183) 62 81 88 *Fax:* (0183) 64 04 96
E-mail: lvdherik@narratio.nl
Web Site: www.narratio.nl
Key Personnel
International Rights: L van den Herik
Founded: 1989
Subjects: Biblical Studies, History, Religion - Catholic, Religion - Protestant, Theology, Women's Studies
ISBN Prefix(es): 90-5263
Total Titles: 220 Print; 7 Audio

Nederlands Literair Produktie-en Vertalingen Fonds (NLPVF) (Foundation for the Production & Translation of Dutch Literature)
Singel 464, 1017 AW Amsterdam
Tel: (020) 620 62 61 *Fax:* (020) 620 71 79
E-mail: office@nlpvf.nl
Web Site: www.nlpvf.nl
Key Personnel
Man Dir: Henk Propper
Subjects: Fiction, Nonfiction (General), Poetry
ISBN Prefix(es): 90-803223

Uitgeverij H Nelissen BV
Birkstr 95-97, 3768 HD Soest
Mailing Address: Postbus 3167, 3760 DD Soest
Tel: (035) 5412386 *Fax:* (035) 5423877
E-mail: info@nelissen.nl
Web Site: www.nelissen.nl

Key Personnel
Man Dir, Editorial, Permissions: Dick Boer
 E-mail: dickboer@nelissen.nl
Sales & Publicity: Pieter Zwart
Founded: 1922
Subjects: Business, Communications, Economics, Education, Government, Political Science, Labor, Industrial Relations, Management, Philosophy, Psychology, Psychiatry, Religion - Other, Social Sciences, Sociology
ISBN Prefix(es): 90-244

Nieuwe Stad Stichting
Utrechtseweg 171, 3818ED Amersfoort
Tel: (033) 4614615 *Fax:* (033) 4635885
Founded: 1960
ISBN Prefix(es): 90-71734
Parent Company: Citta Nuova Editrice, Italy

Nieuwe Wieken, *imprint of* Omega Boek BV

Nijgh & Van Ditmar Amsterdam+
Singel 262, 1016 AC Amsterdam
Mailing Address: Postbus 3879, 1001 AR Amsterdam
Tel: (020) 55 11 262 *Fax:* (020) 6203509
E-mail: verkoop@querido.nl; info@querido.nl
Web Site: www.querido.nl
Key Personnel
President: Ary Langbroek
Vice President: Vic va de Reijt
Editor: Lidewijde Paris
Founded: 1837
Publisher of Zoetermeer: young/young debut writers' upmarket literary fiction & nonfiction.
Subjects: Fiction, Humor, Literature, Literary Criticism, Essays, Mysteries, Nonfiction (General), Poetry, Social Sciences, Sociology
ISBN Prefix(es): 90-388
Parent Company: Em Querido bv
Imprints: Zoetermeer
Divisions: Dedalus (for Belgium)

Martinus Nijhoff, *imprint of* Kluwer Academic Publishers

NLPVF, see Nederlands Literair Produktie-en Vertalingen Fonds (NLPVF)

North Holland, *imprint of* Elsevier Science BV

Omega Boek BV+
Fregat 35, 1113 EE Diemen
Tel: (020) 690 59 97 *Fax:* (020) 695 74 28
E-mail: info@omegaboek.nl
Founded: 1968
Subjects: Art, Fiction, Management, Military Science, Nonfiction (General)
ISBN Prefix(es): 90-6057; 90-6142
Imprints: De Centaur; Nieuwe Wieken; Omega Jeugdboekerij; Triton Pers
Book Club(s): ECI voor boeken en platen BV
Orders to: Centraal Boekhuis, Erasmusweg 10, Culemborg

Omega Jeugdboekerij, *imprint of* Omega Boek BV

Ooievaar+
Herengracht 507, 1017 BV Amsterdam
Mailing Address: Postbus 1662, 1000 BR Amsterdam
Tel: (020) 624 19 34 *Fax:* (020) 622 54 61
E-mail: pbo@pbo.nl
Web Site: www.pbo.nl
Key Personnel
Man Dir & Publisher: Plien van Albada
Editor: Josje Kraamer; Job Lisman; Bertram Mourits; Maaike le Noble
Foreign Rights: Hedda Sanders *Fax:* (020) 427 93 81 *E-mail:* rights@pbo.nl
Associate Companies: Bert Bakker; Prometheus

Oriental Press BV (APA)
Subsidiary of APA (Academic Publishers Associated)
Postbus 806, 1000 AV Amsterdam
Tel: (020) 626 5544 *Fax:* (020) 528 5298
E-mail: info@apa-publishers.com
Web Site: www.apa-publishers.com
Subjects: Asian Studies, Religion - Islamic
ISBN Prefix(es): 90-6023

Parel Pockets, *imprint of* De Boekerij BV

Partners Training & Innovatie
Dwerggras 30, 3068 PC Rotterdam-Ommoord
Tel: (010) 4071599 *Fax:* (010) 4202227
E-mail: info@ced.nl
Web Site: www.ced-groep.nl
Key Personnel
Publisher: Mr C A van Dongen
Founded: 1992
Subjects: Education
ISBN Prefix(es): 90-5819; 90-75074
Total Titles: 104 Print; 11 Audio
Parent Company: LED

Passage, Uitgeverij+
Camphuysenstr 58, 9721 KH Groningen
Mailing Address: Postbus 216, 9700 AE Groningen
Tel: (050) 5271332
E-mail: info@uitgeverijpassage.nl
Web Site: www.uitgeverijpassage.nl
Key Personnel
Publisher: Anton Scheepstra
Founded: 1991
Specialize in Dutch literature.
Membership(s): KVB; NUV (GAU).
Subjects: Dutch Literature
ISBN Prefix(es): 90-5452
Total Titles: 60 Print
Distributed by Maklu
Foreign Rep(s): Maklu (Belgium)

Pearson Education Netherlands
Concertgebouwplein 25, 1071 LM Amsterdam
Mailing Address: Postbus 75598, 1070 AM, Amsterdam
Tel: (020) 575-5800 *Fax:* (020) 664-5334
E-mail: firstname.lastname@mail.aw.nl; amsterdam@pearsoned-ema.com
Web Site: www.pearsoneducation.nl
Key Personnel
President: Rita Snaddon
Finance & P&O: Hennie Haverkort
Marketing Manager, Professional Education: Sue Young
Publishing Manager: Arianne Strating
Founded: 1942
Subjects: Business, Computer Science, Economics, Education, Management, Technology
ISBN Prefix(es): 0-201
Parent Company: Pearson Plc

Penguin Books Netherlands BV
Herengracht 418-2H, 1017 BZ Amsterdam
Mailing Address: Postbus 3507, 1001 AH Amsterdam
Tel: (020) 6259566 *Fax:* (020) 6258676
ISBN Prefix(es): 90-75320

The Pepin Press+
PO Box 10349, 1001 EH Amsterdam
Tel: (020) 420 20 21 *Fax:* (020) 420 11 52
E-mail: mail@pepinpress.com
Web Site: www.pepinpress.com
Key Personnel
Publisher & International Rights: Mr Pepin Van Roojen
Founded: 1995
Specialize in high quality art publications.
Subjects: Antiques, Archaeology, Architecture & Interior Design, Art, Asian Studies, Fashion, History
ISBN Prefix(es): 90-5496

Pergamon, *imprint of* Elsevier Science BV

Philo Press (APA)
Subsidiary of APA (Academic Publishers Associated) (Netherlands)
Postbus 806, 1000 AV Amsterdam
Tel: (020) 626 5544 *Fax:* (020) 528 5298
E-mail: info@apa-publishers.com
Web Site: www.apa-publishers.com
Founded: 1963
Firm incorporates Gerard Th Van Heusden (APA) & G W Hissink & Co (APA).
Subjects: Art, Asian Studies, Biblical Studies, History, Human Relations, Religion - Islamic, Religion - Jewish, Science (General), Theology
ISBN Prefix(es): 90-6022; 90-6024; 90-6025

Picaron Editions+
Postbus 8024, 6710 AA Ede Gid
Tel: (020) 6201484
Founded: 1987
Subjects: Art, Philosophy
ISBN Prefix(es): 90-71466

Piccolo, *imprint of* De Boekerij BV

Piccolo, *imprint of* Van Goor BV

Piramide, *imprint of* Uitgeverij De Fontein BV

Plateau, *imprint of* Uitgeverij De Vuurbaak BV

Uitgeverij Ploegsma BV+
Singel 262, 1016 AC Amsterdam
Tel: (020) 5511250 *Fax:* (020) 6203504
E-mail: info@ploegsma.nl
Web Site: www.ploegsma.nl
Key Personnel
President: Peter Frohlich
Founded: 1901
Subjects: Child Care & Development, Fiction, How-to, Nonfiction (General), Science (General)
ISBN Prefix(es): 90-216
Imprints: Ploegsma (children's books); De Brink (adult books)

Ploegsma (children's books), *imprint of* Uitgeverij Ploegsma BV

Podium Uitgeverij+
Singel 450, 1017 AV Amsterdam
Tel: (020) 421 38 30 *Fax:* (020) 421 37 76
E-mail: post@uitgeverijpodium.nl
Web Site: www.uitgeverijpodium.nl
Key Personnel
Dir: Joost Nijsen *Fax:* (020) 421 37 76
 E-mail: jn@uitgeverijpodium.nl
Founded: 1997
Specializes in Dutch Literature.
Subjects: Anthropology, Fiction, History, Literature, Literary Criticism, Essays, Nonfiction (General), Social Sciences, Sociology
ISBN Prefix(es): 90-5759
Number of titles published annually: 25 Print
Total Titles: 100 Print

De Prom
Subsidiary of Veen Bosch & Keuning Uitgevers NV
Prinses Marielaan 8, 3743 JA Baarn
Mailing Address: Postbus 1, 3740 AA Baarn
Tel: (035) 5482403 *Fax:* (035) 5418221
E-mail: info.fontein@defonteinbaarn.nl
Key Personnel
Man Dir: U Hazeu
Subjects: Art, Biography, History, Literature, Literary Criticism, Essays, Music, Dance, Photography, Religion - Catholic, Religion - Protestant, Theology
ISBN Prefix(es): 90-6801

Prometheus
Herengracht 507, 1017 BV Amsterdam
Tel: (020) 624 19 34 *Fax:* (020) 622 54 61
E-mail: pbo@pbo.nl
Web Site: www.pbo.nl
Key Personnel
Man Dir & Publisher: Ms Plien van Albada
Editor: Josje Kraamer; Job Lisman; Bertram Mourits; Maaike le Noble
Foreign Rights: Hedda Sanders *Tel:* (020) 427 93 81 *E-mail:* rights@pbo.nl
Founded: 1893
Subjects: Gay & Lesbian, History, Language Arts, Linguistics, Literature, Literary Criticism, Essays, Nonfiction (General), Philosophy, Poetry, Psychology, Psychiatry, Science (General)
ISBN Prefix(es): 90-6019; 90-5333; 90-351
Number of titles published annually: 300 Print
Associate Companies: Ooievaar
Orders to: Ivec, Postbus 154, 1380 AD Weesp

Promotional Publications Int BV
Montalbaendreef 2, 3562 LC Utrecht
Tel: (030) 2650650 *Fax:* (030) 2620850
ISBN Prefix(es): 90-5344
Parent Company: Uitgeverij Het Spectrum BV, Postbus 2073, 3500 GB Utrecht

Publitronic, *imprint of* Segment BV

Em Querido's Uitgeverij BV
Singel 262, 1016 AC Amsterdam
Mailing Address: Postbus 3879, 1001 AG Amsterdam
Tel: (020) 55 11 200 *Fax:* (020) 55 11 256
E-mail: info@querido.nl
Web Site: www.querido.nl
Key Personnel
Editor-in-Chief: Jacques Dohmen *E-mail:* j.dohmen@querido.nl
President: Ary T Langbroek *E-mail:* b.langbroek@querido.nl
Foreign Rights: Lucienne van der Leije *E-mail:* l.van.der.leije@querido.nl
Publisher: Baerbel Dorweiler *E-mail:* b.dorweiler@querido.nl
Founded: 1915
Subjects: Art, Biography, Drama, Theater, Fiction, History, Mathematics, Poetry, Romance
ISBN Prefix(es): 90-214; 90-253
Imprints: Athenaeum-Polak & Van Gennep; Griffioen Paperbacks; JeugdSalamander Paperbacks; Salamander Paperbacks; De Viergang

Rainbow Crime, *imprint of* Uitgeverij Maarten Muntinga

Rainbow Pocketboeken, *imprint of* Uitgeverij Maarten Muntinga

Rebo Productions BV+
1e Poellaan 6, 2161 LB Lisse
Mailing Address: PO Box 314, 2160 AH Lisse
Tel: (0252) 431 556 *Fax:* (0252) 431 557
E-mail: info@rebo-publishers.com
Web Site: www.rebo-publishers.com

Key Personnel
President: Henk Wagner *E-mail:* h.wagner@rebo-publishers.com
Commercial Dir: E P A Veltman
International Rights: J A M Wagner
Founded: 1983
Subjects: Animals, Pets, Crafts, Games, Hobbies, Gardening, Plants
ISBN Prefix(es): 90-366
Associate Companies: Zuid Boekprodukties BV
Subsidiaries: Rebo Productions SRO; Celetna ii

Reed Elsevier Nederland BV+
Van de Sande Bakhuyzenstr 4, 1061 AG Amsterdam
Tel: (020) 515 9111 *Fax:* (020) 618 0325
Web Site: www.elsevier.com
Key Personnel
Chief Executive: Derk Haank
Legal Dir: Erik Ekker
Operating Companies: Argus; Bonaventura; Dagbladunie; Elsevier Opleidingen; Krips Repro; Misset; Pan European Publishing Company
Divisions, Subsidiaries & Branches: Elsevier Training NV, Brussels, International Equipment News Europe NV, Brussels (both Belgium); Editions Elsevier Thomas SA, Boulogne Billancourt, France; Elsevier Thomas Fachverlag GmbH, Mainz, Germany; Audet Tijdschriften, Arnheim, De Dordtenaar BV, Dordrecht, Toeristiek BV, Oostwoud, Dagblad van Rijn en Gouwe BV, Alphen aan den Rijn, Brabants Niewsblad BV, Roosendaal, Rotterdams Dagblad CV, Rotterdam, Nederlands Studiecentrum, Vlaardingen, CBBM BV, Zwijndrecht (all Netherlands); Elsevier Prensa SA, Barcelona, Arte y Cemento Bilbao (Both Spain).
Subjects: Science (General)

La Riviere Creatief
Postbus 309, 3740 AH Baarn
Tel: (035) 5486600 *Fax:* (035) 5486675

Robyns, *imprint of* Educatieve Partners Nederland bv

Rodopi
Tijnmuiden 7, 1046 AK Amsterdam
Tel: (020) 6114821 *Fax:* (020) 4472979
E-mail: info@rodopi.nl
Web Site: www.rodopi.nl
Key Personnel
Dir: Fred van der Zee *E-mail:* f.van.der.zee@rodopi.nl
Founded: 1966
Subjects: Human Relations
ISBN Prefix(es): 90-6203; 90-5183; 90-420
Number of titles published annually: 3 CD-ROM; 50 Online
Total Titles: 4,000 Print; 100 Online
U.S. Office(s): One Rockefeller Plaza, Suite 1420, New York, NY 10020, United States *Tel:* 212-265-6360 *Fax:* 212-265-6402 *E-mail:* info@rodopi.nl *Web Site:* www.rodopi.nl

Rothschild & Bach+
Kleine Garmanplantsoen 21 VII, 1017 RP Amsterdam
Tel: (020) 6389329
ISBN Prefix(es): 90-5371
Associate Companies: International Theatre & Film Books

Salamander Paperbacks, *imprint of* Em Querido's Uitgeverij BV

Samsom BedrijfsInformatie BV
Alphen 22n den Rijn, 2400 MA Amsterdam
Mailing Address: Prinses Margrietlaanz, 2404 HA Alphenaanden Rijn
Tel: 0172 466633 *Fax:* 0172 475933

E-mail: info@kluwer.nl
Web Site: www.kluwer.nl
Key Personnel
Man Dir: C J Steur
Founded: 1882
Part of Wolters Kluwer Business Publishing.
Subjects: Advertising, Business, Finance, Labor, Industrial Relations, Management, Marketing, Public Administration, Social Sciences, Sociology, Technology
ISBN Prefix(es): 90-6500
Parent Company: Wolters Kluwer NV
Divisions: Hofstad Vakpers

Samsom Stafleu, see Uitgeverij Bohn Stafleu Van Loghum BV

Sara, *imprint of* Uitgeverij en boekhandel Van Gennep BV

Schoolpers, *imprint of* Educatieve Partners Nederland bv

Scriptum+
Postbus 293, 3100 AG Schiedam
Tel: (010) 4271022 *Fax:* (010) 4736625
E-mail: info@scriptum.nl
Web Site: www.scriptum.nl
Key Personnel
Publisher: Hans Ritman *E-mail:* ritman@scriptum.nl
Founded: 1985
Subjects: Antiques, Art, Business, Management, Marketing
ISBN Prefix(es): 90-71542; 90-5594
Number of titles published annually: 25 Print
Total Titles: 200 Print
Imprints: Scriptum Art; Scriptum Management; Scriptum Topography

Scriptum Art, *imprint of* Scriptum

Scriptum Management, *imprint of* Scriptum

Scriptum Topography, *imprint of* Scriptum

SDU Juridische & Fiscale Uitgeverij
Christoffel Plantijnstr 2, 2515 TZ The Hague
Mailing Address: Postbus 20024, 2500 EA The Hague
Tel: (070) 3789880; (070) 3789911 *Fax:* (070) 3854321; (070) 3789783; (070) 3458068
E-mail: sdu@sdu.nl
Web Site: www.sdu.nl
Key Personnel
Marketing Manager: Mrs M J Geevers
Founded: 1991
Subjects: Finance, Law
ISBN Prefix(es): 90-5409

Sdu Uitgevers bv
Christoffel Plantijnstr 2, 2515 TZ The Hague
Mailing Address: Postbus 20014, 2500 EA The Hague
Tel: (070) 378 99 11; (070) 378 98 80 *Fax:* (070) 385 43 21; (070) 378 97 83
E-mail: sdu@sdu.nl
Web Site: www.sdu.nl
Telex: 32486
Subjects: Government, Political Science
ISBN Prefix(es): 90-12; 90-399; 90-5332

Segment BV+
Peter Treckpoelstr 2, 6191 VK Beek Lb
Mailing Address: PO Box 75, 6190 AB Beek Lb
Tel: (046) 43894444 *Fax:* (046) 4389401; (046) 4370161
E-mail: secretariant@segment.nl
Web Site: www.segment.nl

Key Personnel
Man Dir: Menno M J Landman
Founded: 1961
Part of Wolters Kluwer Trade Publishing.
Subjects: Electronics, Electrical Engineering, Philosophy, Science (General)
ISBN Prefix(es): 90-5381; 90-70160; 90-73035; 0-905705
Parent Company: Wolters Kluwer NV
Imprints: Elektuur; Elektor; Publitronic
Subsidiaries: Elektor (Germany, France & UK)

Semic Junior Press
Zwarteweg 6c, 1412 GD Naarden
Tel: (035) 6944914 *Fax:* (035) 6944909
Telex: 4473114 cacjp nl
Key Personnel
Man Dir: Guillermo Hierro
Subjects: Astrology, Occult
ISBN Prefix(es): 90-305; 90-72073; 90-6236; 90-940020; 90-940025; 90-940054; 90-940058; 90-940060; 90-940061; 90-940067; 90-940077; 90-940137
Parent Company: Semic International AB, Sweden

Servire BV Uitgevers+
St Jacobstr 125, 3511 Utrecht
Mailing Address: Postbus 14095, 3508 SC Utrecht
Tel: (030) 2349211 *Fax:* (030) 2349247
E-mail: servire@pi.net
Key Personnel
Chief Executive: Felix Erkelens
Founded: 1921
Subjects: Alternative, Astrology, Occult, Health, Nutrition, Human Relations, Psychology, Psychiatry, Religion - Buddhist, Religion - Hindu, Religion - Islamic, Religion - Jewish, Religion - Protestant, Religion - Other, Self-Help, Theology, Women's Studies
ISBN Prefix(es): 90-6077; 90-6325
Associate Companies: Hunter House Inc, Publishers, PO Box 2914, Alameda, CA 94501, United States

Sesam Junior, *imprint of* Uitgeverij De Fontein BV

Signature, *imprint of* A W Bruna Uitgevers BV

Sjaloom Uitgeverijen+
Postbus 1895, 1000 BW Amsterdam
Tel: (020) 6206263 *Fax:* (020) 4288540
E-mail: post@sjaloom.nl
Web Site: www.sjaloom.nl
Founded: 1982
Subjects: Criminology, Erotica, Fiction, Health, Nutrition, History, Literature, Literary Criticism, Essays, Mysteries, Nonfiction (General), Regional Interests
ISBN Prefix(es): 90-6249
Imprints: Cadans

Koninklijke Smeets Offset (Royal Smeets Offset)+
Molenveldstr 90, 6001 HL Weert
Mailing Address: Koninklijke Smeets Offset BV, Postbus 17, 6000 AA Weert
Tel: (0495) 57 09 11 *Fax:* (0495) 54 29 05
E-mail: rswinfo@rotosmeets.com
Telex: 37550
Key Personnel
Manager: V Pokorny
Subjects: Art
ISBN Prefix(es): 90-6220
Associate Companies: VBI/Smeets

Sociaal en Cultureel Planbureau+
Postbus 16164, 2500 BD The Hague
Tel: (070) 3407000 *Fax:* (070) 3407044
E-mail: info@scp.ul
Web Site: www.scp.nl
Key Personnel
Dir: Prof Paul Schnabel
Founded: 1973
Subjects: Child Care & Development, Criminology, Education, Ethnicity, Government, Political Science, Health, Nutrition, Radio, TV, Real Estate, Social Sciences, Sociology, Women's Studies
ISBN Prefix(es): 90-377

Uitgeverij Het Spectrum BV
Postbus 2073, 3500 GB Utrecht
Tel: (030) 2650650 *Fax:* (030) 2620850
E-mail: het@spectrum.nl
Web Site: www.spectrum.nl
Key Personnel
Dir: Joost C Bloemsma
Vice Dir, Sales Publicity: Yvonne Koolen
Editorial: Marjon Aardema; Bart Drubbel; Mechteld Jansen; George Pape; Renee Swaalf; Henk ter Borg
Production: Ludger van Zwetszelaar
Publisher, Multimedia: Ton von Bladel
Rights & Permissions: Jane Baird; Anry van Esch *Tel:* (030) 2650656 *E-mail:* anry@spectrum.nl
Sales: Caroline Clasen *Tel:* (030) 2650683 *Fax:* (030) 2627045 *E-mail:* verkoop@spectrum.nl
Marketing: Aukje van den Berg *Tel:* (030) 2650697 *E-mail:* a.vandenberg@spectrum.nl; Mariska Hoksbergen *Tel:* (030) 2650671 *E-mail:* m.hoksbergen@spectrum.nl; Francoise Parlevliet *Tel:* (030) 2650618 *E-mail:* francoise@spectrum.nl
Founded: 1935
Subjects: Astrology, Occult, Computer Science, Criminology, Environmental Studies, History, Literature, Literary Criticism, Essays, Management, Mysteries, Nonfiction (General), Science Fiction, Fantasy, Travel
ISBN Prefix(es): 90-315; 90-274
Total Titles: 800 Print; 100 CD-ROM

Spunk, *imprint of* Uitgeverij Vassallucci bv

Stam Techniek, *imprint of* Educatieve Partners Nederland bv

Stedelijk Van Abbemuseum
Bilderdijklaan 10, 5600 AE Eindhoven
Mailing Address: Postbus 235, 5600 AE Eindhoven
Tel: (040) 2381000 *Fax:* (040) 2460680
E-mail: info@vanabbemuseum.nl
Web Site: www.vanabbemuseum.nl
Key Personnel
Dir: J Debbaut
Founded: 1936
Subjects: Art, Library & Information Sciences
ISBN Prefix(es): 90-70149

Steltman Editions
Teniersstr 6, Johannes Vermeerstr, 1071 DX Amsterdam
Tel: (020) 622 8683 *Fax:* (020) 620 7588
E-mail: steltman@steltman.com
Web Site: www.steltman.com
Key Personnel
President: Gerrit Steltman
Founded: 1982
Specialize in Art Design, Michael Parkes exclusive.
Subjects: Art
ISBN Prefix(es): 90-71867
U.S. Office(s): Steltman, 41 E 57 St, New York, NY 10022, United States

Stenfert Kroese, *imprint of* Educatieve Partners Nederland bv

Stenvert Systems & Service BV
Postbus 593, 3800 AN Amersfoort
Tel: (033) 457 0199 *Fax:* (033) 457 0198
E-mail: info@stenvert.nl
Web Site: www.stenvert.nl
Key Personnel
President: M G Stenvert
Editor: E H Kolk
Producer: F H A Kanters
Founded: 1925
Membership(s): GEU.
ISBN Prefix(es): 90-281
Showroom(s): Sutton 10, 7327 AB Apeldoorn
Warehouse: Sutton 10, 7327 AB Apeldoorn

Stichting IVIO+
Pascallaan 70c, 8218 NJ Lelystad
Mailing Address: Postbus 37, 8200 AA Lelystad
Tel: (0320) 229900 *Fax:* (0320) 229999
E-mail: info@ivio.nl
Web Site: www.ivio.nl
Key Personnel
Manager: A L Greiner *Tel:* (0320) 229912 *E-mail:* jmoes@ivio.nl
Founded: 1936
Subjects: Education
ISBN Prefix(es): 90-6121
Total Titles: 200 Print
Imprints: AO; Wereldschool

A J G Strengholt's Boeken, Anno 1928, BV+
Hofstede Oud-Bussem, Flevolaan 41, 1411 KC Naarden
Mailing Address: Postbus 338, 1400 AH Bussum
Tel: (035) 695 84 11 *Fax:* (035) 694 61 73
E-mail: boeken@strengholt.nl *Cable:* EDITORAS
Key Personnel
Man Dir: Mrs C I C Bakker
Founded: 1928
Subjects: Biography, Health, Nutrition, History, How-to, Mathematics, Nonfiction (General)
ISBN Prefix(es): 90-6010
Parent Company: Strengholt BV

Uitgeverij SUN
Prinsengracht 747-751, 1017 JX Amsterdam
Tel: (020) 622 61 07 *Fax:* (020) 625 33 27
E-mail: info@uitgeverijboom.nl
Web Site: www.uitgeverijboom.nl
Key Personnel
Publisher: Sjef van de Wiel *Tel:* (020) 5200 134 *E-mail:* s.vandewiel@uitgeverijsun.nl
Editor: Mayke van Dieten *Tel:* (020) 5218 148 *E-mail:* m.vandieten@uitgeverijsun.nl; Henk Hoeks *Tel:* (020) 5200 133 *E-mail:* h.hoeks@uitgeverijsun.nl; Lucy Klaasen *Tel:* (020) 5218 147 *E-mail:* l.klaasen@uitgeverijsun.nl
Founded: 1969
Subjects: Architecture & Interior Design, Ethnicity, History, Philosophy
ISBN Prefix(es): 90-6168
Parent Company: Royal Boom Publishers, PO Box 1058, 7940 KB Meppel
Imprints: Uitgeverij Dwarsstap

Swets & Zeitlinger Publishers+
Member of Taylor & Francis Group plc
Heereweg 347 B, 2161 CA Lisse
Mailing Address: Postbus 800, 2160 SZ Lisse
Tel: (0252) 435111 *Fax:* (0252) 415888
E-mail: info@nl.swets.com
Web Site: www.swets.nl
Telex: 41325 szlis nl *Cable:* SWEZEIT-LISSE
Key Personnel
Chief Executive Officer: Eric van Amerongen
Founded: 1901
Also subscription agent.
Subjects: Education, Engineering (General), Health, Nutrition, Labor, Industrial Relations, Language Arts, Linguistics, Medicine, Nursing,

Dentistry, Music, Dance, Psychology, Psychiatry, Science (General), Technology
ISBN Prefix(es): 90-70430; 90-265
U.S. Office(s): PO Box 582, Downingtown, PA 19335-9998, United States

SWP, BV Uitgeverij+
Plantage Middenlaan 2-H, 1018 DD Amsterdam
Mailing Address: PO Box 257, 1000 AG Amsterdam
Tel: (020) 3307200 *Fax:* (020) 3308040
E-mail: swp@wxs.nl
Web Site: www.swpbook.com
Key Personnel
Publisher: Paul E Roosenstein
Founded: 1982
Specialize in early childhood education, health issues & social welfare.
Subjects: Child Care & Development, Criminology, Management, Psychology, Psychiatry
ISBN Prefix(es): 90-6665
Number of titles published annually: 40 Print; 1 CD-ROM
Total Titles: 300 Print; 2 CD-ROM

Sybex BV+
Birkstr 95, 3768 HD Soest
Mailing Address: PO Box 3177, 3760 DD Soest
Tel: (031) 3560 27625 *Fax:* (031) 3560 26556
E-mail: sybex@sybex.nl
Web Site: www.sybex.nl
Key Personnel
General Manager & Publisher: G Beyering
Founded: 1988
Subjects: Computer Science
ISBN Prefix(es): 90-5160; 90-419
Branch Office(s)
Sybex Inc, 1151 Marina Village Parkway, Alameda, CA 94501, United States *Tel:* 510-523-8233 *Fax:* 510-523-6840 *E-mail:* info@sybex.com *Web Site:* www.sybex.com
Warehouse: Centraal Boekhuis, Culemborg, Holland

Syntax Publishers, *imprint of* Tilburg University Press

Synthese-Miranda, see Mirananda Publishers BV

Telos Boeken+
c/o Buyten en Schipperheijn, PO Box 22708, 1000 Amsterdam
Tel: (020) 5241010 *Fax:* (020) 5241011
E-mail: info@buijten.nl
Web Site: www.buijten.nl
Key Personnel
International Rights: Guido Sneep
Founded: 1902
Subjects: Human Relations, Philosophy, Religion - Protestant, Theology, Travel
ISBN Prefix(es): 90-6064; 90-6353 (Medema); 90-324; 90-5560 (De Vuurbaak); 90-5881

Uitgeverij Terra bv+
Postbus 1080, 7230 AB Warnsveld
Tel: (0575) 58 13 10 *Fax:* (0575) 52 52 42
E-mail: terra@terraboek.nl
Web Site: www.terraboek.nl
Key Personnel
President: H Weesjes
Man Dir: T van Lexmond
Founded: 1971
Subjects: Architecture & Interior Design, Cookery, Crafts, Games, Hobbies, Gardening, Plants, Health, Nutrition
ISBN Prefix(es): 90-6255
Warehouse: Terra Magazijn, Distrimedia NV, Meulenbeeksesteenweg 20, 8700 Tielt

ThiemeMeulenhoff+
Postbus 19240, 3501 DE, Utrecht
Tel: (030) 239 2 111 *Fax:* (030) 239 2 270
E-mail: info.bao@thiememeulenhoff.nl
Web Site: www.thiememeulenhoff.nl
Key Personnel
Man Dir: C J J van Steijn
Publishing Dir: P A Stadhouders
Subjects: Education
ISBN Prefix(es): 90-03; 90-238; 90-06; 90-433
Parent Company: Meulenhoff & Co BV
Subsidiaries: NIB-Software

Thoth Publishers+
Prins Hendriklaan 13, 1405 AK Bussum
Tel: (035) 6944144 *Fax:* (035) 6943266
E-mail: thoth@euronet.nl
Key Personnel
Publisher: Kees van den Hoek
Founded: 1985
Subjects: Architecture & Interior Design, Art, Literature, Literary Criticism, Essays, Nonfiction (General)
ISBN Prefix(es): 90-6868

Uitgeverij de Tijdstroom BV+
Asschatterweg 44, 3831 JW Leusden
Tel: (0342) 450867 *Fax:* (0342) 450365
E-mail: info@tijdstroom.nl
Web Site: www.tijdstroom.nl
Founded: 1924
Subjects: Health, Nutrition, Management, Medicine, Nursing, Dentistry, Physics, Psychology, Psychiatry, Social Sciences, Sociology
ISBN Prefix(es): 90-5898

Tilburg University Press
Warandelaan 2, Bldg L, 5037 AB Tilburg
Mailing Address: PO Box 90153, 5000 LE Tilburg
Tel: (013) 466 2124 *Fax:* (013) 466 2996
E-mail: library@kub.nl
Web Site: www.tilburguniversity.nl
Key Personnel
Librarian: Hans Geleijnse
Subjects: Behavioral Sciences, Biblical Studies, Economics, Language Arts, Linguistics, Library & Information Sciences, Philosophy, Psychology, Psychiatry, Theology
ISBN Prefix(es): 90-361
Imprints: Syntax Publishers

Tirion Uitgevers BV+
Subsidiary of Veen Bosch & Keuning Uitgevers NV
Julianalaan 11, 3743 JG Baarn
Mailing Address: PO Box 309, 3704 AH Baarn
Tel: (035) 5486600 *Fax:* (035) 5486675
E-mail: info@tirionuitgevers.nl
Web Site: www.tirionuitgevers.nl
Key Personnel
Dir: Aernoud Oosterholt
Marketing: Joanneke van Zadelhoff *Tel:* (035) 5486609 *E-mail:* jvzadelhoff@tirionuitgevers.nl
Founded: 1987
Subjects: Animals, Pets, Archaeology, Biography, Child Care & Development, Computer Science, Crafts, Games, Hobbies, Film, Video, Health, Nutrition, History, Humor, Medicine, Nursing, Dentistry, Music, Dance, Philosophy, Photography, Psychology, Psychiatry, Religion - Protestant, Social Sciences, Sociology, Sports, Athletics, Theology, Travel, Veterinary Science
ISBN Prefix(es): 90-5121; 90-5210; 90-439
Distributed by Agora
Distributor for Davidsfonds (Belgium)

Ton Bolland, *imprint of* Uitgeverij De Vuurbaak BV

Uitgeverij De Toorts+
Conradkade 6, 2031 CL Haarlem
Mailing Address: Postbus 9585, 2003 LN Haarlem
Tel: (023) 5532920 *Fax:* (023) 5320635
E-mail: uitgeverij@toorts.nl
Web Site: www.toorts.nl
Key Personnel
Man Dir & Production: J Hesseling
Sales, Editorial, Publicity, Rights & Permissions: Mrs M Klis
Founded: 1936
Subjects: Behavioral Sciences, Child Care & Development, Cookery, Health, Nutrition, Human Relations, Music, Dance, Psychology, Psychiatry, Self-Help, Wine & Spirits
ISBN Prefix(es): 90-6020
Imprints: De Toorts; ENTERBOOKS

Triton Pers, *imprint of* Omega Boek BV

Twente University Press
Unit of University of Twente
Postbus 217, 7500 AE Enschede
Tel: (053) 4899111 *Fax:* (053) 4892000
E-mail: info@utwente.nl
Web Site: www.utwente.nl/tupress
Key Personnel
Coordinator: Henny Leferink
Editing: Hans van Eerden
Founded: 1995
Subjects: Career Development, Computer Science, Education, Environmental Studies, Management, Mechanical Engineering, Medicine, Nursing, Dentistry, Public Administration, Regional Interests, Social Sciences, Sociology, Technology
ISBN Prefix(es): 90-365
Total Titles: 60 Print

Uitgeverij Altamira-Becht BV+
Postbus 317, 2000 AH Haarlem
Tel: (023) 54 11 190 *Fax:* (023) 52 74 404
E-mail: post@gottmer.nl
Web Site: www.altamira-becht.nl
Founded: 1985
Subjects: Literature, Literary Criticism, Essays
ISBN Prefix(es): 90-6963
Parent Company: Gottmer Uitgevers Groep

Uitgeverij Contact (Contact Publishers)
Subsidiary of Veen, Bosch & Keuning Uitgevers NV
Herengracht 481, 1017 BT Amsterdam
Mailing Address: PO Box 13, 1000 AA Amsterdam
Tel: (020) 5249800 *Fax:* (020) 6276851
E-mail: businesscontact@contact-bv.nl
Web Site: www.boekenwereld.com
Key Personnel
Dir: Marij Bertram
Marketing: Anne Schroen *E-mail:* aschroen@contact-bv.nl
Publicity: Anne Kramer; May Meurs *E-mail:* mmeurs@contact-bv.nl
Publisher: Mizzi van der Pluijm
Sales: Thea Bon; Ingrid Kee; Petra Wildvank
ISBN Prefix(es): 90-254

Uitgeversmy Segment BV, see Segment BV

Unieboek BV+
Onderdoor 7, 3995 DB Houten
Mailing Address: Postbus 97, 3990 DB Houten
Tel: (030) 63 77 660 *Fax:* (030) 63 77 600
E-mail: info@unieboek.nl
Web Site: www.unieboek.nl
Telex: 40468 Uboek nl *Cable:* UNIEBOEK
Key Personnel
Man Dir: Wouter van Gils
Editorial Dir: Toine Akveld
Sales Dir: Ramon Dahmen

Publisher: Riet Goes; Frank Noe; Dick Rog; Martine Schaap
Founded: 1891
Subjects: Animals, Pets, Architecture & Interior Design, Child Care & Development, Computer Science, Cookery, Crafts, Games, Hobbies, Fiction, History, How-to, Human Relations, Literature, Literary Criticism, Essays, Mysteries, Nonfiction (General), Photography, Romance, Self-Help, Travel, Women's Studies
ISBN Prefix(es): 90-226; 90-228; 90-269
Parent Company: Meulenhoff & Co BV
Associate Companies: De Boekerij BV; A W Bruna BV; M & P BV; Meulenhoff Nederland BV; Prometheus BV; Standaard Uitgeverij
Imprints: Agathon; de Cocon; van Dishoeck; Fibula; W Gaade; de Haan; van Holkema en Waren Holkema en Warendorf; het Wereldvenster

Uniepers BV+
Heinkuitenstr 26, 1390 AB Abcoude
Mailing Address: Postbus 69, 1390 AB Abcoude
Tel: (0294) 285111 *Fax:* (0294) 283013
E-mail: info@uniepers.nl
Web Site: www.uniepers.nl
Key Personnel
Chief Executive & Sales: Marinus H van Raalte
Dir: Marieke Bemelman
Sales Manager: Ingrid de Jong
Production: Albert van de Klashorst
Founded: 1961
Also book packagers.
Subjects: Anthropology, Antiques, Archaeology, Architecture & Interior Design, Art, Ethnicity, Health, Nutrition, History, Music, Dance, Natural History, Photography, Regional Interests, Culture, Nature
ISBN Prefix(es): 90-6825

V S P International Science Publishers
Subsidiary of Brill Academic Publishers
PO Box 346, 3700 AH Zeist
Tel: (030) 692 5790 *Fax:* (030) 693 2081
E-mail: vsppub@brill.nl
Web Site: www.vsppub.com
Key Personnel
Contact: Ms Els van Egmond
Founded: 1983
Specialize in STM Journal Publishing & STM Book Publishing.
Membership(s): STM.
Subjects: Astronomy, Biological Sciences, Chemistry, Chemical Engineering, Earth Sciences, Mathematics, Medicine, Nursing, Dentistry, Physics, Psychology, Psychiatry, Science (General), Technology, Transportation
ISBN Prefix(es): 90-6764
Orders to: Books International Inc, PO Box 605, Herndon, VA 22070, United States *Tel:* 703-661-1500 *Fax:* 703-661-1501

Van Buuren Uitgeverij BV+
Hallenhof 18, 6006 NC Weert
Mailing Address: Postbus 10356, 6000 GJ Weert
Tel: (023) 5325440 *Fax:* (023) 5327017
Key Personnel
Publisher: Gerrit van Buuren; Jenny van Buuren; Patrick van Buuren
Founded: 1995
Membership(s): Royal Dutch Booktrade Organization.
Subjects: Fiction, History, Mysteries, Nonfiction (General)
ISBN Prefix(es): 90-5695
Total Titles: 50 Print
Distributed by Standaard Uitgeverij NV (Dutch speaking part of Belgium)

De Grote Van Dale, *imprint of* Van Dale Lexicografie BV

Van Dale Grote Woordenboeken voor hedendaags taalgebruik, *imprint of* Van Dale Lexicografie BV

Van Dale Handbibliotheek, *imprint of* Van Dale Lexicografie BV

Van Dale Handwoordenboeken, *imprint of* Van Dale Lexicografie BV

Van Dale Kinderwoordenboeken, *imprint of* Van Dale Lexicografie BV

Van Dale Lexicografie BV
Subsidiary of Veen Bosch & Keuning Uitgevers NV
St Jacobsstr 127, 3511 BP Utrecht
Mailing Address: Postbus 19232, 3501 DE Utrecht
Tel: (031) 232 47 11 *Fax:* (031) 231 68 50
E-mail: info@vandale.nl
Web Site: www.vandale.nl
Key Personnel
Chief Operating Officer: Jan Egas
Man Dir, Export Sales, Rights & Permissions: Bram Wolthoorn
Publisher: Marcel Jansen; Margreet Moerland; Rick Schutz
Sales Dir: Tanja Nijhuis
Production: J Butterfield
Founded: 1976
ISBN Prefix(es): 90-6648
Imprints: De Grote Van Dale; Van Dale Grote Woordenboeken voor hedendaags taalgebruik; Van Dale Handwoordenboeken; Koenen; Van Dale Kinderwoordenboeken; Van Dale Handbibliotheek
Branch Office(s)
Van Dale Lexicografie Belgie, Ternesselei 326, 2160 Wommelgem, Belgium *Tel:* 0032-3-3552830 *Fax:* 0032-3-3552841 (Distributor)
Orders to: PO Box 19232, 3501 DE Utrecht

Van Goor, *imprint of* De Boekerij BV

Van Gorcum & Comp BV+
Industrieweg 38, 9403 AB Assen
Mailing Address: Postbus 43, 9400 AA Assen
Tel: (0592) 37 95 55 *Fax:* (0592) 37 20 64
E-mail: assen@vgorcum.nl
Web Site: www.vangorcum.nl *Cable:* VANGORCUM
Key Personnel
General Dir & Publisher: Louwe Dijkema *Tel:* (0592) 379550 *Fax:* (0592) 379552 *E-mail:* l.dijkema@vangorcum.nl
Publisher, Medical Sciences: Wouter Oude Groothuis *Tel:* (0592) 379564 *Fax:* (0592) 379552 *E-mail:* w.oudegroothuis@vangorcum.nl
Publisher, Theology, History, Philosophy, Language & Literature: Theo Joppe *Tel:* (0592) 376936 *Fax:* (0592) 379552 *E-mail:* t.joppe@vangorcum.nl
Publisher, Social Sciences & Geography: Roelof Meijering *Tel:* (0592) 379566 *Fax:* (0592) 379552 *E-mail:* r.meijering@vangorcum.nl
Editor: Nathan Brinkman *Tel:* (0592) 379568 *Fax:* (0592) 379552 *E-mail:* n.brinkman@vangorcum.nl; Meta Kampen *Tel:* (0592) 379563 *Fax:* (0592) 379552 *E-mail:* m.kampen@vangorcum.nl
Production Leader: Bert Veenstra *Tel:* (0592) 379569 *Fax:* (0592) 379552 *E-mail:* l.veenstra@vangorcum.nl
Marketing: Susanne Gerritsen *Tel:* (0592) 379573 *Fax:* (0592) 379552 *E-mail:* s.gerritsen@vangorcum.nl
Head of Sales: Jan van Veen *Tel:* (0592) 379572 *Fax:* (0592) 379552 *E-mail:* j.van.veen@vangorcum.nl
Production Leader: Berta Oosterloo *Tel:* (0592) 379567 *Fax:* (0592) 372064 *E-mail:* b.oosterloo@vangorcum.nl
Founded: 1800
Subjects: Anthropology, Economics, Education, Geography, Geology, History, Language Arts, Linguistics, Law, Literature, Literary Criticism, Essays, Medicine, Nursing, Dentistry, Philosophy, Psychology, Psychiatry, Religion - Other, Social Sciences, Sociology
ISBN Prefix(es): 90-232; 90-255; 90-5693; 90-72371
Subsidiaries: Styx Publications

Uitgeverij G A van Oorschot bv+
Herengracht 613, 1017 CE Amsterdam
Tel: (020) 623 14 84 *Fax:* (020) 625 40 83
E-mail: verkoop@vanoorschot.nl
Key Personnel
President: W J van Oorschot
Vice President: Mrs G M Nefkens
Founded: 1945
Membership(s): KNUB.
Subjects: Literature, Literary Criticism, Essays, Nonfiction (General), Poetry
ISBN Prefix(es): 90-282

Uitgeverij Van Walraven BV
Ericastr 18, 3742 SG Baarn
Mailing Address: Postbus 122, 3740 AC Baarn
Tel: (035) 5482421 *Fax:* (035) 5421672
Membership(s): the Combo Group.
ISBN Prefix(es): 90-6049

Uitgeverij Van Wijnen+
Froonacker 12, 8801 KD Franeker
Mailing Address: Postbus 172, 8800 AD Franeker
Tel: (0517) 394588 *Fax:* (0517) 397179
E-mail: info@uitgeverijvanwijnen.nl
Web Site: www.uitgeverijvanwijnen.nl
Key Personnel
Dir: D van Wijnen
Founded: 1988
Subjects: Government, Political Science, History, Philosophy, Religion - Other, Theology
ISBN Prefix(es): 90-5194

Vassallucci, *imprint of* J M Meulenhoff bv

Uitgeverij Vassallucci bv+
Subsidiary of J M Meulenhoff bv
Herengracht 505, 1017 BV Amsterdam
Mailing Address: PO Box 100, 1000 AC Amsterdam
Tel: (020) 521 8322 *Fax:* (020) 623 6761
E-mail: info@vassallucci.nl
Web Site: www.vassallucci.nl
Key Personnel
Man Dir: Anne Rube
Dir & Publisher: Oscar van Gelderen
Publicity: Joni Zwart
Founded: 1995
Specialize in literary fiction.
Subjects: Fiction, Literature, Literary Criticism, Essays, Nonfiction (General)
ISBN Prefix(es): 90-5000
Total Titles: 80 Print
Ultimate Parent Company: PCM Algemene boeken
Imprints: Bertollucci; Spunk
Foreign Rep(s): Laura Susijn (London)
Shipping Address: Central Boekhuis, Culemborg

VCL (series of novels)/Westfriesland, *imprint of* Uitgeverij J H Kok BV

Veen Bosch & Keuning Uitgevers NV+
Postbus 8049, 3503 RA Utrecht
Tel: (030) 2349311 *Fax:* (030) 2349208
E-mail: algemeen@veenboschenkeuning.nl
Web Site: www.veenboschenkeuning.nl

Key Personnel
Man Dir: A de Groot *Fax:* (030) 2300145
An independent trade publisher of books, magazines, dictionaries & CD-ROM.
ISBN Prefix(es): 90-246; 90-263; 90-266; 90-213; 90-259; 90-204; 90-245; 90-218; 90-215; 90-254
Number of titles published annually: 500 Print; 30 CD-ROM; 10 E-Book
Total Titles: 4,000 Print; 100 CD-ROM; 1 Online; 20 E-Book
Subsidiaries: Ambo-Anthos bv; Atlas; Augustus; Bekadidact bv; Uitgeverij Cantecleer BV; Contact bv; Uitgeverij Contact bv; Uitgeverij De Fontein BV; HBuitgevers bv; Uitgeverij Houtekiet; J H Kok bv; Kosmos-Z&K Uitgevers; Uitgeverij Luitingh-Sijthoff; Nijgh Versluys bv; Poema Pandora; De Prom; Tirion Uitgevers bv; Van Dale Lexicografie; Veen Algemene Boeken; Veen Magazines; Veen Uitgevers Groep Belgie

Uitgeverij Verloren (Verloren Publishers)+
Torenlaan 25, 1211 JA Hilversum
Mailing Address: PO Box 1741, 1200 BS Hilversum
Tel: (035) 6859856 *Fax:* (035) 6836557
E-mail: info@verloren.nl
Web Site: www.verloren.nl
Key Personnel
President: Mr L M VerLoren van Themaat
Founded: 1979
Subjects: Biography, Genealogy, History
ISBN Prefix(es): 90-6550
Number of titles published annually: 70 Print
Total Titles: 900 Print

De Viergang, *imprint of* Em Querido's Uitgeverij BV

VNU Business Press Group BV+
Ceylonpoort 5-25, 2037 AA Haarlem
Mailing Address: PO Box 1920, 2003 BA Haarlem
Tel: (023) 546 5666 *Fax:* (023) 546 5541
Web Site: www.vnubp.nl
Key Personnel
Man Dir: F X I Koot
Subjects: Business, Career Development, Computer Science, Library & Information Sciences, Marketing
ISBN Prefix(es): 90-72802

VNU Business Publications BV
Ceylonpoort 5-25, 2037 AA Haarlem
Mailing Address: PO Box 1920, 2003 BA Haarlem
Tel: (023) 546 5666 *Fax:* (023) 546 5541
Web Site: www.vnubp.nl
Telex: 41549
ISBN Prefix(es): 90-72802; 90-6434
Parent Company: VNU - Verenigde Nederlandse Uitgeversbedrijven BV
Subsidiaries: Educational Publishing (comprising LCG Malmberg BV qv); Uitgeverij Het Spectrum; Uitgeverij J van In; WNU Business Information Services; VNU Business Press Group BV; VNU Magazine Group; VNU Newspaper Group; VNU Printing Group; VNU Sales Group

Voorhoeve, *imprint of* Uitgeverij J H Kok BV

VU Boekhandel/Uitgeverij BV+
De Boelelaan 1105, 1081 HV Amsterdam
Tel: (020) 64 443 55 *Fax:* (020) 646 27 19
E-mail: info@vuboekhandel.nl
Web Site: www.vuboekhandel.nl
Key Personnel
Man Dir & Editorials: M Rienks; P R Rienks
Production: Karin Sinnema

Sales: M Zitman
Founded: 1980
Subjects: Biological Sciences, Economics, History, Language Arts, Linguistics, Law, Medicine, Nursing, Dentistry, Philosophy, Psychology, Psychiatry, Public Administration, Science (General), Social Sciences, Sociology, Theology
ISBN Prefix(es): 90-6256; 90-5383
Imprints: VU Uitgeverij; VU University Press

VU Uitgeverij, *imprint of* VU Boekhandel/Uitgeverij BV

VU University Press, *imprint of* VU Boekhandel/Uitgeverij BV

Uitgeverij De Vuurbaak BV (The Lighthouse)+
Hermesweg 20, 3771 ND Barneveld
Mailing Address: Postbus 257, 3770 AG Barneveld
Tel: (0342) 411731 *Fax:* (0342) 411731
E-mail: vuurbaak@nd.nl; plateau@nd.nl
Web Site: www.vuurbaak.nl
Key Personnel
President & International Rights: B M van Hulst
Founded: 1965
Subjects: Religion - Protestant, Theology
ISBN Prefix(es): 90-6015; 90-5560; 90-5804
Number of titles published annually: 60 Print; 2 CD-ROM
Total Titles: 300 Print; 4 CD-ROM
Parent Company: Nedag Holding bv
Associate Companies: Telos; Uitgeverij
Imprints: Plateau; Ton Bolland
Divisions: Nedag Beheer

Uitgeverij Waanders BV+
Faradaystr 17, 8013 PH Zwolle
Mailing Address: Postbus 1129, 8001 BC Zwolle
Tel: (038) 4658628 *Fax:* (038) 4655989
E-mail: info@waanders.nl
Web Site: www.waanders.nl
Key Personnel
President: W J G M Waanders
Man Dir: H van de Wal
Deputy Director: M L M Waanders
Founded: 1836
Subjects: Antiques, Art, Ethnicity, History
ISBN Prefix(es): 90-6630; 90-400; 90-70072
Parent Company: Waanders Printers
Bookshop(s): Eiland 9, Zwolle

Wageningen Academic Publishers+
Bldg 304, Dreijenlaan 2, 6703 HA Wageningen
Mailing Address: PO Box 220, 6700 AE Wageningen
Tel: (0317) 47 65 16 *Fax:* (0317) 45 34 17
E-mail: info@wageningenacademic.com
Web Site: www.wageningenacademic.com
Key Personnel
Man Dir: Mike Jacobs *E-mail:* jacobs@wageningenacademic.com
Marketing & Sales: Dineke van den Biezenbos *E-mail:* biezenbos@wageningenacademic.com
Technical Dir: Enrico Kunst *E-mail:* kunst@wageningenacademic.com
Founded: 2002
Publisher of scientific & technical books. Specialize in animal science & agriculture Textbooks, Proceedings & Monographs.
Subjects: Agriculture, Animals, Pets
ISBN Prefix(es): 90-74134
Total Titles: 80 Print

Wegener Falkplan BV
Battesakker 19-21, 5625 TC Eindhoven
Mailing Address: Postbus 9510, 5602 LM Eindhoven
Tel: (040) 2 642 111 *Fax:* (040) 2 410 955
E-mail: info@suurland.nl

Web Site: www.suurland.nl
Telex: 51874 svehv
Key Personnel
Man Dir: D R A Suurland; J A Suurland
Sales: Agnes Roag *Tel:* (040) 2 645 680 *E-mail:* a.roag@falk.nl
ISBN Prefix(es): 90-287
Associate Companies: Suurland Holding BV

Wereldbibliotheek+
Spuistr 283, 1012 VR Amsterdam
Tel: (020) 638 18 99 *Fax:* (020) 638 44 91
E-mail: info@wereldbibliotheek.nl
Web Site: www.wereldbibliotheek.nl
Key Personnel
Man Dir: J B I M Kat
Publisher: Koen van Gulik; Joos Kat
Editor: Gerda Scheltes
Founded: 1905
Subjects: Fiction, History, Nonfiction (General), Philosophy, Public Administration
ISBN Prefix(es): 90-284
Total Titles: 200 Print

Wereldschool, *imprint of* Stichting IVIO

het Wereldvenster, *imprint of* Unieboek BV

West-Friesland/Boekproject-ontwikkeling+
Protonweg 32, 1627 LD Hoorn, Nh
Tel: (0229) 212625 *Fax:* (0229) 216949
Key Personnel
Man Dir, Editorial, Publicity: J W Hondelink
Sales: Maya Schaafsma-Rotte
Rights & Permissions: P Dubois
Founded: 1918
Specialize in packaging & local history.
Subjects: Literature, Literary Criticism, Essays, Nonfiction (General), Regional Interests
ISBN Prefix(es): 90-72420
Parent Company: Drukkery West-Friesland/EDECEA, Protonweg 32, 1627 LD Hoorn, Nh
Imprints: EDECEA & WFE

Uitgeverij Westers
Hammarskjoeldhof 35, 3527 HD Utrecht
Tel: (030) 2931043 *Fax:* (030) 2944586
E-mail: boekhandel@westers-utrecht.nl *Cable:* WESTERS UTRECHT
Key Personnel
Man Dir: R J N M Westers, Sr
Founded: 1967
Subjects: Fiction
ISBN Prefix(es): 90-6107

Wilkerdon, *imprint of* Uitgeversmaatschappij Ad Donker BV

Wolters Kluwer Academic Publishers BV, see Kluwer Academic Publishers

Wolters Kluwer B.V. Juridische Boekenen Tijschriften
Staverenstr 15, 7418 CJ Deventer
Mailing Address: PO Box 23, 7400 GA Deventer
Tel: (0570) 647111 *Fax:* (0570) 636683
Founded: 1972
Subjects: Law
ISBN Prefix(es): 90-271; 90-268
Parent Company: Wolters Kluwer Rechtswetenschappen BV
Ultimate Parent Company: Wolters Kluwer NV

Wolters-Noordhoff B V+
Damsport 157, 9728 PS Groningen
Mailing Address: PO Box 58, 9700 MB Groningen
Tel: (050) 5226922 *Fax:* (050) 5277599
E-mail: info@wolters.nl
Web Site: www.wolters.nl

Key Personnel
Acting Manager: Dr M J van Dalen
Founded: 1836 (1852)
Part of Wolters Kluwer Nederland.
ISBN Prefix(es): 90-01
Parent Company: Wolters-Kluwer
Subsidiaries: Martinus Nijhoff; Wolters-Noordhoff

Uitgeverij 010+
Watertorenweg 180, 3063 HA Rotterdam
Tel: (010) 4333509 *Fax:* (010) 4529825
E-mail: office@010publishers.nl
Web Site: www.010publishers.nl
Key Personnel
Publisher: Hans Oldewarris; Peter de Winter
Founded: 1983
Subjects: Architecture & Interior Design, Art, History, Photography
ISBN Prefix(es): 90-6450

Zoetermeer, *imprint of* Nijgh & Van Ditmar Amsterdam

Zuid Boekprodukties BV+
PO Box 314, 2160 AH Lisse
Tel: (0252) 431565 *Fax:* (0252) 431567
E-mail: info@rebo-publishers.com
Web Site: www.rebo-publishers.com
Key Personnel
Dir: F Voerman
Founded: 1983
Subjects: Animals, Pets, Cookery, Crafts, Games, Hobbies, Gardening, Plants
ISBN Prefix(es): 90-6248
Associate Companies: REBO Productions BV
Imprints: Zuidboek

Zuidboek, *imprint of* Zuid Boekprodukties BV

Zwarte Beertjes, *imprint of* A W Bruna Uitgevers BV

Uitgeverij Zwijsen BV
Gasthuisring 58, 5041 DT Tilburg
Mailing Address: Postbus 805, 5000 AV Tilburg
Tel: (013) 5838800 *Fax:* (013) 5838880
E-mail: klantenservice@zwijsen.nl
Web Site: www.zwijsen.nl
Key Personnel
Man Dir: Robert Francissen
Publisher & Rights Manager: Jan Plooij; Agnes Starmans
Publicity Manager: Miranda de Jong
Founded: 1846
ISBN Prefix(es): 90-276

Netherlands Antilles

General Information

Capital: Willemstad
Language: Dutch and Papiamento. English and Spanish widely spoken
Religion: Roman Catholic and Protestant
Population: 184,000
Bank Hours: 0830-1130, 1400-1600 Monday-Friday. St Maarten: 0800-1300 Monday-Friday (also 1600-1700 on Friday)
Shop Hours: 0800-1200, 1400-1800 Monday-Saturday
Currency: 100 cents = 1 Netherlands Antilles gulden or florin

Export/Import Information: No tariff on books or advertising. No import licenses. No exchange controls.
Copyright: UCC, Berne (see Copyright Conventions, pg xi)

Bredero+
Reigerweg 51, Willemstad, Curacao
Tel: (09) 7376751
Key Personnel
Author: L H Bredero
Specialize in World War II memorabilia.
Subjects: Foreign Countries, History, Maritime, Nonfiction (General), Travel, World War II
ISBN Prefix(es): 90-940021
Orders to: Janus Publishing Co, 76 Titchfield Rd, London W1P 7AF, United Kingdom
Tel: (020) 7580 7664 *Fax:* (020) 7636 5756
E-mail: publisher@januspublishing.co.uk *Web Site:* www.januspublishing.co.uk

De Wit Stores NV
L G Smith Blvd 110, Oranjestad, Aruba
Tel: (0297) 823500 *Fax:* (0297) 821575
E-mail: dewitstores@sctarnet.aw *Cable:* Dewitstores
Key Personnel
Man Dir: R de Zwart
Founded: 1948
Subjects: Gardening, Plants, Health, Nutrition, Regional Interests, Self-Help, Travel, Women's Studies
ISBN Prefix(es): 90-6163; 99904-81
Bookshop(s): De Wit Book & Gift Store, Aruba; Aruba Post, Aruba; Boulevard Book and Drugstore, Aruba

Drukkerij Scherpenheuvel Haseth
Scherpenheuvel 1, Curacao
Tel: (09) 7671134
Key Personnel
Dir: Ronald Yrausquin
Subjects: Law
ISBN Prefix(es): 99904-915

New Caledonia

General Information

Capital: Noumea
Language: French
Religion: Predominantly Roman Catholic and Protestant
Population: 145,368
Currency: 100 centimes = CFP or Pacific franc
Export/Import Information: No tariff on books except luxury bindings and children's picture books. Advertising matter generally dutiable. Special Tax on all. No import licenses required.

Editions du Santal
BP 3072, 98800 Noumea
Tel: (0687) 262533 *Fax:* (0687) 262533
E-mail: santal@offratel.nc
Key Personnel
Director: Paul-Jean Stahl
Subjects: History, Travel
ISBN Prefix(es): 2-9508739

Savannah Editions SARL
49 rue de la Boudeuse magenta Que mo, 98846 Noumea
Tel: (0687) 252919 *Fax:* (0687) 282470
Founded: 1994
Subjects: How-to, Maritime, Outdoor Recreation, Sports, Athletics, Travel
ISBN Prefix(es): 2-9508530
Distributed by Editions Vilo Paris

New Zealand

General Information

Capital: Wellington
Language: English
Religion: Predominantly Christian (mostly Anglican & Roman Catholic)
Population: 3.3 million
Bank Hours: 0930-1600 Monday-Friday
Shop Hours: Vary. Most open 6-7 days a week
Currency: 100 cents = 1 New Zealand dollar
Export/Import Information: No tariffs on books and advertising. No import licenses, but literature which is indecent, advocates violence, lawlessness, disorder or seditiousness is prohibited. No special exchange controls.
Copyright: UCC, Berne, Florence (see Copyright Conventions, pg xi)

ABA Books
2d/6 Brooklyn Rd, Claudelands, Hamilton
Mailing Address: PO Box 11-099, Hamilton
Tel: (07) 8549360 *Fax:* (07) 8549361
Web Site: www.ababooks.co.nz
Key Personnel
Dir: Elizabeth Maree Abbott
Man Dir: Graeme Hamilton Abbott
 E-mail: graeme@ababooks.co.nz
Founded: 1986
Educational book publishers.
Subjects: Chemistry, Chemical Engineering, Cookery, Language Arts, Linguistics, Mathematics, Physical Sciences, Physics, Science (General)
ISBN Prefix(es): 0-908866

Aoraki Press Ltd
PO Box 11-699, Wellington 6034
Tel: (04) 3858528 *Fax:* (03) 3858528
E-mail: aoraki@actrix.gen.nz
Key Personnel
Editor: Dr Maarire Goodall
Founded: 1990
Subjects: Drama, Theater, Foreign Countries, History, Law, Music, Dance, Regional Interests, Social Sciences, Sociology
ISBN Prefix(es): 0-908925
Distributor for Aoraki Productions; Otago Heritage Press
Orders to: PO Box 25-029, Christchurch *Tel:* (03) 3524001 *Fax:* (03) 3524001

Aspect Press
Subsidiary of Association of Handcraft Printers (AHP)
13 Kinross, St Levin
Tel: (06) 368-2887
Key Personnel
Editor & Author: P J Parr
Founded: 1971
Specialize in Private Press Booklets.
Subjects: History, Religion - Buddhist
ISBN Prefix(es): 0-908779
Total Titles: 48 Print
Book Club(s): TSP

Auckland University Press+
University of Auckland, 1-11 Short St, Auckland
Mailing Address: University of Auckland, Private Bag 92019, Auckland
Tel: (09) 373 7528 *Fax:* (09) 373 7465
E-mail: aup@auckland.ac.nz
Web Site: www.auckland.ac.nz/aup/
Key Personnel
Dir: Elizabeth P Caffin *E-mail:* e.caffin@auckland.ac.nz
Office Manager: Annie Irving *E-mail:* a.irving@auckland.ac.nz
Marketing Manager: Christine O'Brien *E-mail:* c.obrien@auckland.ac.nz

NEW ZEALAND

Production Editor: Katrina Duncan *E-mail:* k.duncan@auckland.ac.nz
Founded: 1966
Subjects: Archaeology, Art, Biography, Government, Political Science, History, Literature, Literary Criticism, Essays, Poetry, Social Sciences, Sociology, Women's Studies
ISBN Prefix(es): 1-86940
Distributed by HarperCollins (New Zealand)
Shipping Address: Anzac Ave entrance, 1-11 Short St, Auckland
Warehouse: HarperCollins, 31 View Rd, Glenfield, Auckland
Orders to: Eurospan, 3 Henrietta St, London WC2E 8LU, United Kingdom *Tel:* (020) 7240 0856 *Fax:* (020) 7379 0609 *E-mail:* info@eurospan.co.uk *Web Site:* www.eurospan.co.uk
HarperCollins, PO Box 1, Auckland
Independent Publishers Group (IPG), 814 N Franklin St, Chicago, IL 60610, United States *Tel:* 312-337-0747 *Fax:* 312-337-5985 *E-mail:* frontdesk@ipgbook.com *Web Site:* www.ipgbook.com
Unireps, University of New South Wales, Sydney, NSW 2034, Australia *Tel:* (02) 9664 0999 *Fax:* (02) 9664 5420 *E-mail:* info.press@unsw.edu.au *Web Site:* www.unswpress.com.au

Barkfire Press+
Newton, Auckland 1032
Mailing Address: PO Box 68582, Newton, Auckland 1032
Tel: (09) 3031039 *Fax:* (09) 3031059
E-mail: info@barkfire.com
Web Site: www.barkfire.com
Key Personnel
Man Dir: Ralph Talmont *E-mail:* ralph@barkfire.com
Founded: 1996
Packager, contract publisher, book producer.
Subjects: Americana, Regional, Architecture & Interior Design, Art, Asian Studies, Cookery, Ethnicity, Geography, Geology, Health, Nutrition, House & Home, How-to, Journalism, Music, Dance, Native American Studies, Natural History, Outdoor Recreation, Photography, Religion - Jewish, Travel, Wine & Spirits, Women's Studies, Yachting & Mythology
ISBN Prefix(es): 0-9583668
Parent Company: Mandragora Productions Ltd

David Bateman Ltd+
30 Tarndale Grove, Albany, Auckland
Tel: (09) 415 7664 *Fax:* (09) 415 8892
E-mail: bateman@bateman.co.nz
Web Site: www.bateman.co.nz
Key Personnel
Chairman & Publisher: David L Bateman
Man Dir, Sales & Distribution: Paul C Parkinson *Tel:* (09) 415 5922
Man Dir, Publishing, Rights & Permissions: Paul Bateman
Secretary: Maureen Robinson
Founded: 1979
Membership(s): Booksellers New Zealand & Book Publishers Association of New Zealand.
Also acts as agent for overseas publishers.
Subjects: Art, Business, Cookery, Gardening, Plants, Natural History, Travel
ISBN Prefix(es): 1-86953
Total Titles: 250 Print

Book Data Asia Pacific, see Nielsen BookData

Brick Row Publishing Co Ltd+
37 Margot St, Epsom, Auckland 3
Mailing Address: PO Box 100057, Auckland 10
Tel: (09) 4106993 *Fax:* (09) 4106993
Key Personnel
Man Dir, Editorial: Oswald L Kraus
Sales, Publicity: Ruth Kraus
Founded: 1978
Subjects: Biography, Fiction, Literature, Literary Criticism, Essays, Nonfiction (General), Poetry, Science (General)
ISBN Prefix(es): 0-908595
Total Titles: 30 Print
Imprints: Southern Lights
U.S. Office(s): 1040 E Paseo El Mirador, Palm Springs, CA 92262, United States, Contact: O L Kraus *Tel:* 760-322-4342 *Fax:* 760-322-4342
Distributor for John Calder (UK); Excalibur (USA); Free Spirit (USA)

Brookers Ltd
Level 1, Guardian Trust House, 15 Willeston St, Wellington
Mailing Address: PO Box 43, Wellington
Tel: (04) 4998178 *Fax:* (04) 4998173
E-mail: service@brookers.co.nz
Web Site: www.brookers.co.nz
Key Personnel
Man Dir: Neil Story
GM Publishing & Marketing: Nigel Royfee
GM Market Development: Geoff Adlam
GM Technology & Business Development: Carl Olson
Founded: 1910
Specialize in looseleaf & electronic legal, tax & professional information.
Subjects: Accounting, Business, Law
ISBN Prefix(es): 0-86472
Parent Company: The Thomson Corporation
Distributed by Carswell; Lawbook Co; Sweet & Maxwell; Westlaw
Distributor for Carswell; Lawbook Co; Sweet & Maxwell; Westlaw

Brookfield Press
PO Box 1201, Auckland 5
Tel: (09) 5765438 *Fax:* (09) 5736222
Key Personnel
Man Dir, Editorial: Richard Webster
Sales, Publicity: Don Kaye
Founded: 1971
Subjects: Astrology, Occult, Philosophy
ISBN Prefix(es): 0-86467
Parent Company: Brookings Bookshop 1971 Ltd
Distributed by Peaceful Living Publications (New Zealand)

Bush Press Communications Ltd
4 Bayview Rd, Hauraki Corner, Takapuna, Auckland 1309
Mailing Address: PO Box 33029, Takapuna, Auckland 1309
Tel: (09) 486 2667 *Fax:* (09) 486 2667
E-mail: bush.press@clear.net.nz
Key Personnel
Man Dir: Gordon Ell
Founded: 1979
Also television production & publishing services.
Subjects: Archaeology, Art, Cookery, Crafts, Games, Hobbies, Earth Sciences, Gardening, Plants, Genealogy, Geography, Geology, History, How-to, Natural History, Nonfiction (General), Outdoor Recreation, Photography, Regional Interests
ISBN Prefix(es): 0-908608
Number of titles published annually: 6 Print
Total Titles: 24 Print
Imprints: The Bush Press of New Zealand
Divisions: Bush Films; The Bush Press
Distributor for Geological Society of New Zealand
Warehouse: Forrester Books (NZ) Ltd, 10 Tarndale Dr, Albany, Auckland 1310 *Tel:* (09) 415 2080 *Fax:* (09) 415 2083 *E-mail:* forr@forrester.co.13

The Bush Press of New Zealand, *imprint of* Bush Press Communications Ltd

Business Bureau Christchurch Ltd+
PO Box 8226, Christchurch
Tel: (03) 3585287
Key Personnel
Contact: Geoff McDonnell
Founded: 1981
Subjects: Finance, Gardening, Plants
ISBN Prefix(es): 0-908852

Butterworths New Zealand Ltd
205-207 Victoria St, Wellington 1
Mailing Address: PO Box 472, Wellington 1
Tel: (04) 385 1479 *Fax:* (04) 385 1598
E-mail: Customer.Relations@butterworths.co.nz
Web Site: www.butterworths.co.nz; www.lexisnexis.com/au/nz
Key Personnel
Man Dir: Philip G Kirk
Legal Publishing Dir: Hellen Papadopoulos
National Sales Manager: Lara Stewart *E-mail:* Lara.Stewart@butterworths.co.nz
Founded: 1914
Subjects: Law
ISBN Prefix(es): 0-409; 0-407; 0-408; 0-406
Parent Company: Reed Elsevier plc, 25 Victoria St, London SW1H 0EX, United Kingdom
Associate Companies: Butterworths Australia Ltd, Reed Elsevier Bldg, Tower 2, 475-495 Victoria Ave, Chatswood, NSW 2067, Australia *Tel:* (02) 9422 2222 *Fax:* (02) 9422 2444 *Web Site:* www.butterworths.com.au; Butterworths Canada Ltd, 75 Clegg Rd, Markham, ON L6G 1A1, Canada *Tel:* 905-479-2665 *Fax:* 905-479-2826 *Web Site:* www.butterworths.ca; Butterworths Asia, 3/F Baskerville House, 13 Duddell St, Central, Hong Kong, Hong Kong *Tel:* 537 6662 *Fax:* 537 6672; Butterworth India, C71-A Malviya Nagar, New Delhi 100 017, India *Tel:* (011) 623 6124 *Fax:* (011) 621 3861; Butterworth (Ireland) Ltd, 16 Upper Ormand Quay, Dublin 7, Ireland *Tel:* (031) 731 555 *Fax:* (031) 873 1876; Butterworths, C/- Shin Nichibo Bldg, 2-1 Sarugaku-cho, 1 Chome, Chiyoda-Ku, Tokyo 101, Japan *Tel:* (03) 3291 3970 *Fax:* (03) 3219 5260; Malayan Law Journal Sdn Bhd, No 18, Jalan Tuanku Abdul Rahman, 50100 Kuala Lumpur, Malaysia *Tel:* (03) 291 7273 *Fax:* (03) 291 6440; Butterworth & Co Publishers Ltd, 7 Jahangir St, Islamia Park, Poonch Rd, Lahore, Pakistan *Tel:* (042) 41 5226; Butterworths Asia/Malayan Law Journal, 10 Anson Rd, No 33-01 International Plaza, Singapore 0207, Singapore *Tel:* 220 3684 *Fax:* 225 5026; Butterworth Publishers Pty Ltd, 8 Walter Place, Waterval Park, Mayville, Durban 4001, South Africa *Tel:* (03) 1268 3111 *Fax:* (03) 1268 3108 *Web Site:* www.butterworths.co.za; Butterworth & Co (Publishers) Ltd, Halsbury House, 35 Chancery Lane, London, United Kingdom *Tel:* (020) 7400 2500 *Fax:* (020) 7400 2842 *Web Site:* www.butterworth.co.uk; LEXIS Law Publishing, 701 E Water St, Charlottesville, VA 22906-7587, United States *Tel:* 804-972-7600 *Fax:* 804-972-7666 *Web Site:* www.michie.com

C&S Publications
121 Taupo Rd, Taumarunui
Mailing Address: PO Box 148, Tau Marunui
Tel: (0812) 56807 *Fax:* (0812) 8966583
Key Personnel
Contact: Ron Cooke
Founded: 1980
Subjects: History
ISBN Prefix(es): 0-908724

Canterbury University Press+
University of Canterbury, Private Bag 4800, Christchurch
Tel: (03) 364-2914 *Fax:* (03) 364-2044
E-mail: mail@cup.canterbury.ac.nz
Web Site: www.cup.canterbury.ac.nz

Key Personnel
Dir: Jeff Field
Editor: Richard King
Office Manager: Kaye Godfrey
Founded: 1964
Specialize in botany, marine science, history, Maori & Pacific studies.
Subjects: Biography, Biological Sciences, History, Natural History, Nonfiction (General)
ISBN Prefix(es): 0-900392; 0-908812
Distributed by Book Representation & Distribution Ltd (UK & Europe); HarperCollins (NZ) Ltd (New Zealand); UNIREPS (Australia); University of New South Wales Press

Cape Catley Ltd+
83 Ngataringa Rd, Devonport, Auckland
Mailing Address: PO Box 32-622, Devonport, Auckland
Tel: (09) 445-9668 *Fax:* (09) 445-9668
E-mail: cape.catley@xtra.co.nz
Web Site: www.capecatleybooks.co.nz
Key Personnel
Man Dir: Christine Cole Catley
Founded: 1973
Subjects: Biography, Fiction, History, Literature, Literary Criticism, Essays, Mysteries, Nonfiction (General), Poetry
Number of titles published annually: 5 Print
Total Titles: 100 Print
Distributed by HarperCollins NZ Ltd (New Zealand)

The Caxton Press
113 Victoria St, Christchurch
Tel: (03) 366 8516 *Fax:* (03) 365 7840
E-mail: print.design@caxton.co.nz
Web Site: www.caxton.co.nz
Key Personnel
Man Dir: Bruce Bascand *Tel:* (03) 353 0731
General Manager: Peter Watson *Tel:* (03) 353 0734
Customer Services: Lorene Soli
Founded: 1935
Subjects: Biography, Gardening, Plants, Nonfiction (General)
ISBN Prefix(es): 0-908563

CCEAM, see Commonwealth Council for Educational Administration & Management

CCH New Zealand Ltd
24 The Warehouse Way, Northcote, Auckland
Mailing Address: PO Box 2378, Auckland 1
Tel: (09) 488 2760 *Toll Free Tel:* 800 500224 (New Zealand only) *Fax:* (09) 488 6911
E-mail: nzsales@cch.co.nz
Web Site: www.cch.co.nz
Founded: 1973
Subjects: Accounting, Law
ISBN Prefix(es): 0-86475; 0-86903
Parent Company: Walters Kluwer NV
U.S. Office(s): Walters Kluwer USA, 161 N Clark, 48th floor, Chicago, IL 60601, United States

Church Mouse Press
38 Joseph St, Palmerston North
Tel: (063) 357-2445 *Fax:* (063) 357-2445
Key Personnel
Proprietor: Anne De Roo
Founded: 1989
Direct sales & through bookshops & churches, books for adults & children.
Subjects: Biblical Studies, Fiction, Theology
ISBN Prefix(es): 0-908949
Total Titles: 16 Print

Cicada Press+
PO Box 34509, Birkenhead South, Auckland 10
Tel: (09) 4180890 *Fax:* (09) 4181142
Key Personnel
Man Dir: R K St Cartmail
Founded: 1978
Subjects: Art, Fiction, Poetry, Religion - Other
ISBN Prefix(es): 0-908599

Clerestory Press+
PO Box 21-120, Christchurch 8001
Tel: (03) 3553588 *Fax:* (03) 3553588
E-mail: young.writers@xtra.co.nz
Key Personnel
International Rights: Dr Glyn Strange; Francine Bills
Founded: 1994
Membership(s): BPANZ.
Subjects: Archaeology, Biography, Drama, Theater, Education, Genealogy, History, Law, Literature, Literary Criticism, Essays, Regional Interests, Women's Studies
ISBN Prefix(es): 0-9583706; 0-9582201
Shipping Address: 31 Mersey St, Christchurch

Commonwealth Council for Educational Administration & Management
AUT Technology Park, PO Box 12397, Penrose, Auckland 1135
Tel: (09) 917 9568 *Fax:* (09) 917 9501
Web Site: www.cceam.org
Key Personnel
President: Mrs Jo Howse *E-mail:* jo.howse@cceam.org
Founded: 1970
Publisher of International Studies in Educational Administration.
Subjects: Education, Management
Distributed by The Education Publishing Co Ltd (UK)

Concept Publishing Ltd+
30 Tiri Rd, Milford, Auckland
Tel: (09) 489 1121 *Fax:* (09) 489 5335
Key Personnel
Man Dir: Richard Beckett
Founded: 1997
Specialize in photoframe cards & personalized stationery.
Subjects: Cookery
Total Titles: 32 Print
Foreign Rights: Peter Elek & Associates

Craig Potton Publishing+
98 Vickerman St, Nelson
Mailing Address: PO Box 555, Nelson
Tel: (03) 5489009 *Fax:* (03) 5489009
E-mail: info@cpp.co.nz
Web Site: www.cpp.co.nz
Key Personnel
Man Dir & Publisher: Robbie Burton *E-mail:* robbie@cpp.co.nz
Founded: 1987
Specialize in wilderness photography & writing & high-quality, illustrated nonfiction; also acts as book packagers, produce calendars, posters, postcards.
Subjects: Architecture & Interior Design, Art, Biological Sciences, Crafts, Games, Hobbies, Natural History, Nonfiction (General), Outdoor Recreation, Photography
ISBN Prefix(es): 0-908802

Craig Printing Co Ltd
122 Yarrow St, Invercargill
Mailing Address: PO Box 99, Invercargill
Tel: (03) 211-0393 *Fax:* (03) 214-9930
E-mail: sales@craigsatlas.co.nz
Web Site: www.craigprint.co.nz
Key Personnel
Chief Executive Officer: Rodger Wills
General Manager: Neil Jackson
Founded: 1876
Subjects: Aeronautics, Aviation, History, Nonfiction (General), Regional Interests, Travel
ISBN Prefix(es): 0-9597554
Branch Office(s)
5 Athol St, Queenstown *Tel:* (03) 441 3367 *Fax:* (03) 441 3368 *E-mail:* qtown@craigprintco.nz

Wendy Crane Books
53 Wilford St, Lower Hutt
Tel: (04) 5664228
Key Personnel
Contact: Wendy Crane
Subjects: Biological Sciences, Earth Sciences, Geography, Geology, Physical Sciences
ISBN Prefix(es): 0-908895

Curly Tales, *imprint of* Magari Publishing

Current Pacific Ltd+
7 La Roche Pl, Northcote, Auckland 1309
Mailing Address: PO Box 36-536 Northcote, Auckland 1330
Tel: (09) 480-1388 *Fax:* (09) 480-1387
E-mail: info@cplnz.com
Web Site: www.cplnz.com
Key Personnel
Editor: Amy M Yeung
Founded: 1992
Publisher of *New Zealand Trade Directory*, a business/trade directory containing more than 6000 firms including manufacturers, importers, exporters, distributors, food processors, banks & financial firms, tourism services, trade promotion organizations, government departments, tertiary & secondary education institutions, professional institutions, libraries, etc.
Subjects: Business
Total Titles: 2 Print

David's Marine Books
121 Beaumont St, Westhaven, Auckland
Mailing Address: PO Box 1874, Auckland
Tel: (09) 303 1459 *Toll Free Tel:* 508 242 787; 800 422 427 *Fax:* (09) 307 8170
E-mail: sales@transpacific.co.nz
Web Site: www.transpacific.co.nz
Founded: 1963
Subjects: Crafts, Games, Hobbies, Electronics, Electrical Engineering, Fiction, How-to, Sports, Athletics, Travel, Marine
Parent Company: Trans Pacific Marine
Distributor for Adlard Coles; Fernhurst; Sheridan House; Stationery Office

Doubleday New Zealand Ltd+
One Parkway Dr, Mairangi Bay Industrial Estate, Auckland 10
Mailing Address: Private Bag 102947, North Shore Mail Centre, Auckland 1333
Tel: (09) 4782846; (09) 4792200 (member service hotline)
E-mail: membercare@doubledayclubs.co.nz
Telex: NZ60589
Key Personnel
Contact: Petrus van der Schaaf

Dunmore Press Ltd+
PO Box 5115, Palmerston North
Tel: (06) 3579242 *Fax:* (06) 3579242
E-mail: books@dunmore.co.nz
Web Site: www.dunmore.co.nz
Key Personnel
Dir & Editorial: Murray Gatenby
Dir & Marketing & Editorial, Rights & Permissions: Sharmian Firth *E-mail:* sharmian@dunmore.co.nz
Founded: 1975
Independent publishing house specializing in academic & nonfiction titles.

Subjects: Accounting, Business, Economics, Education, Ethnicity, History, Nonfiction (General)
ISBN Prefix(es): 0-908564; 0-86469
Number of titles published annually: 25 Print
Total Titles: 180 Print
Subsidiaries: Dunmore Printing Company Ltd
Foreign Rep(s): Federation Press (Australia)

Educational Distributors Ltd
1/1 Akatea Rd, Glendene, Auckland 7
Tel: (09) 818 4473 *Fax:* (09) 836 2399
E-mail: ed.nz@xtra.co.nz
Key Personnel
Manager: Ron Simpson
Founded: 1976
Specialize in distribution of educational & library lists within New Zealand.
Membership(s): BPANZ.
Parent Company: School Supplies Ltd

ESA Publications (NZ) Ltd+
Box 9453, Newmarket, Auckland
Tel: (09) 579 3126 *Fax:* (09) 579 4713
E-mail: info@esa.co.nz
Web Site: www.esa.co.nz
Key Personnel
Man Dir: Mark Sayes *E-mail:* mark@esa.co.nz
Founded: 1985
Publisher of educational books.
Subjects: Accounting, Biological Sciences, Chemistry, Chemical Engineering, Computer Science, Economics, English as a Second Language, Geography, Geology, Health, Nutrition, History, Mathematics, Physics, Science (General), Social Sciences, Sociology
ISBN Prefix(es): 0-908756; 0-9597692; 1-877234; 1-877291
Number of titles published annually: 30 Print
Total Titles: 95 Print
Parent Company: Sayes Corp Ltd
Warehouse: 665 Great South Rd, Unit G, Penrose, Auckland
Membership(s): Book Publishers Association of New Zealand

Eton Press (Auckland) Ltd
35 Enterprise St, Unit N, Birkenhead, Auckland 1310
Tel: (09) 4183635 *Fax:* (09) 4806488
E-mail: info@eton.co.nz
Web Site: www.eton.co.nz
Key Personnel
Dir: Anthony Matthews
Founded: 1968
Also acts for Tarquin & Dime Publications, Haese & Harris.
Subjects: Mathematics
Membership(s): Book Publishers Association of New Zealand

Evagean Publishing+
205A Whittaker St, TeAroha
Mailing Address: PO Box 199, TeAroha
Tel: (07) 884-8783 *Fax:* (07) 884-8783
E-mail: alison.honeyfield@clear.net.nz
Web Site: www.evagean.co.nz
Key Personnel
Owner: Andrew Honeyfield; Alison Jane Hunter
Founded: 1990
Specialize in compiling, publishing & marketing family histories & genealogies.
Subjects: Genealogy
Branch Office(s)
18 Waygrove Ave, Earlwood NSW 2206, Australia *Tel:* (02) 9789-4550 *Fax:* (02) 9789-4550
PO Box 1167, South Perth WA 6951, Australia *Tel:* (08) 3676578 *Fax:* (08) 3676578
PO Box 288, Warragul, Victoria 3820, Australia *Tel:* (03) 56236887 *Fax:* (03) 56236882
14 Kaweka St, Havelock Maith *Tel:* (06) 877 1210

Exisle Publishing Ltd+
PO Box 60490, Titirangi, Auckland
Tel: (09) 817 9192 *Fax:* (09) 817 2295
E-mail: admin@exisle.co.nz
Web Site: www.exisle.co.nz
Key Personnel
Publisher: Tim Chamberlain *E-mail:* tc@exisle.co.nz
International Rights: Benny Thomas
Founded: 1993
Membership(s): Book Publishers of New Zealand.
Subjects: Biography, Business, Maritime, Natural History, Nonfiction (General), Outdoor Recreation, Pacific Studies
ISBN Prefix(es): 0-908988
Number of titles published annually: 4 Print
Total Titles: 12 Print
Parent Company: Exisle Holdings Ltd
Branch Office(s)
PO Box 1358, Strawberry Hills BC, Strawberry Hills 2012 NSW, Australia
Distributed by Berkeley Books (Singapore/SE Asia); Celebrity Books Ltd; Kirby Books Ltd
Distribution Center: Pacific Island Books, 2802 E 132 Circle, Thornton, CO 80241, United States, Contact: Kathy Tundermann *Tel:* (303) 457 9795 *E-mail:* pacificbks@aol.com

Flamingo, *imprint of* HarperCollins Publishers (New Zealand) Ltd

Fraser Books
Ranginui, Chamberlain Rd, RD 8, Masterton
Tel: (06) 3771359 *Fax:* (06) 3771359
Key Personnel
Partner: Diane Grant *E-mail:* degrant@xtra.co.nz; Ian F Grant *E-mail:* ifgrant@xtra.co.nz
Founded: 1980
Specialize in book packaging.
Subjects: Agriculture, Biography, Economics, Government, Political Science, History, Regional Interests, Social Sciences, Sociology
ISBN Prefix(es): 0-9582052
Number of titles published annually: 10 Print
Total Titles: 100 Print
Shipping Address: Nationwide Book Distributors, PO Box 4176, Christchurch
Warehouse: Nationwide Book Distributors, PO Box 4176, Christchurch
Distribution Center: Nationwide Book Distributors, PO Box 4176, Christchurch
Orders to: Nationwide Book Distributors, PO Box 4176, Christchurch
Returns: Nationwide Book Distributors, PO Box 4176, Christchurch

Gauntlet Press, *imprint of* Hazard Press Ltd

GCL Publishing (1997) Ltd+
Level 1, 15 Bath St, Parnell, Auckland
Mailing Address: PO Box 37745, Parnell, Auckland
Tel: (09) 3092444 *Fax:* (09) 3092449
E-mail: info@gcl.co.nz
Web Site: www.gcl.co.nz; www.auto.co.nz
Key Personnel
Publisher: Mr Vern Whitehead *E-mail:* vern@gcl.co.nz
Founded: 1972
Publishers for the auto industry including newsletters, manuals, stock lists & pricing guides.
Subjects: Automotive
ISBN Prefix(es): 0-9598007
Number of titles published annually: 2 Print
Total Titles: 6 Print

Gnostic Press Ltd
100 Riverland Rd, Kumeu, Auckland
Mailing Address: RD 2, Kumeu, Auckland
Tel: (09) 4838619 *Fax:* (09) 4190319

E-mail: gnostic.press@ihug.co.nz
Web Site: homepages.ihug.co.nz/~gnosticpress
Key Personnel
Dir: John Searle
Founded: 1978
Created for the dispersment of the works of Abdullah Dougan (Sufi teacher).
Subjects: Philosophy, Religion - Buddhist, Religion - Hindu, Religion - Islamic, Religion - Other, Self-Help
ISBN Prefix(es): 0-473; 0-9597566; 0-477; 0-478; 0-475

Godwit Publishing Ltd+
PO Box 34-683, Birkenhead, Auckland
Tel: (09) 4805410 *Fax:* (09) 4805930
Founded: 1990
Subjects: Art, Gardening, Plants, Genealogy, Natural History, Nonfiction (General)
ISBN Prefix(es): 0-908877; 1-86962
Orders to: Reed Publishing, Birkenhead, Auckland 1310

Gondwanaland Press
24 Glasgow St, Kelburn, Wellington 6005
Tel: (04) 4758092 *Fax:* (04) 4756194
Key Personnel
Manager: Hugh Price *E-mail:* randellprice@xtra.co.nz
Founded: 1992
Small private book publisher.
Subjects: Education, Government, Political Science, History, Public Administration, Chiefly education
ISBN Prefix(es): 0-9597766; 0-9582083
Number of titles published annually: 3 Print
Total Titles: 20 Print

GP Publications, see Legislation Direct

Grantham House Publishing+
6/9 Wilkinson St, Oriental Bay, Wellington
Tel: (04) 3813071 *Fax:* (04) 3813067
E-mail: gstewart@iconz.co.nz
Key Personnel
Chief Executive: Graham Stewart
Founded: 1985
Membership(s): Booksellers New Zealand; Specialize in Railways, Tramways, Aviation, Shipping, Naval, Air Force, New Zealand history.
Subjects: History, Regional Interests, Transportation
ISBN Prefix(es): 1-86934
Total Titles: 40 Print
Parent Company: Bookprint Consultants Ltd
Shipping Address: PO Box 17256, Karosi, Wellington 6005
Warehouse: PO Box 17256, Karosi, Wellington 6005

Graphic Educational Publications
514 Dominion Rd, Auckland 3
Tel: (09) 6300488 *Fax:* (09) 6234196
Key Personnel
President, Editor & International Rights: Tom Newnham *E-mail:* tom@pl.net
Founded: 1963
Subjects: Asian Studies, Biography, Genealogy
ISBN Prefix(es): 0-9597819
Number of titles published annually: 3 Print
Total Titles: 10 Print

Halcyon Publishing Ltd+
PO Box 360, Auckland 1
Tel: (09) 4895337 *Fax:* (09) 4442399
E-mail: info@halcyonpublishing.co.nz
Key Personnel
Man Dir, Sales: Graham Gurr *E-mail:* gurr@halcyonpublishing.co.nz
Editorial Consultant: Antony Entwistle
Founded: 1984
Membership(s): BPANZ & BSNZ.

PUBLISHERS

NEW ZEALAND

Subjects: Cookery, Crafts, Games, Hobbies, Maritime, Outdoor Recreation, Sports, Athletics
ISBN Prefix(es): 0-908685; 0-908689; 1-877256
Imprints: Halcyon Sporting Heritage
Subsidiaries: Halcyon Books; The Halcyon Press; Hole in the Bank Books
Warehouse: Unit 11 Diana Court, 101-111 Diana Dr, Glenfield Auckland

Halcyon Sporting Heritage, *imprint of* Halcyon Publishing Ltd

Harlen Books, *imprint of* R P L Books

HarperCollins Publishers (New Zealand) Ltd+
31 View Rd, Glenfield, Auckland
Tel: (09) 4439400 *Fax:* (09) 4439403
E-mail: editors@harpercollins.co.nz
Web Site: www.harpercollins.co.nz *Cable:* Folio
Key Personnel
Chief Executive Officer: Brian Murray
Man Dir: Tony Fisk
Commissioning & International Rights: Lorain Day *Tel:* (09) 443-9408
Founded: 1888
Subjects: Art, Biography, Cookery, Fiction, Gardening, Plants, History, Humor, Natural History, Regional Interests, Self-Help, Sports, Athletics, Travel
ISBN Prefix(es): 1-86950
Total Titles: 100 Print
Parent Company: HarperCollins Publishers, United States
Ultimate Parent Company: News Corporation
Imprints: HarperCollins New Zealand; Flamingo; Harper Sports
U.S. Office(s): HarperCollins Publishers, 10 E 53 St, New York, NY 10032, United States
Distributor for Auckland University Press; Canterbury University Press; Collinson Brown; Daphne Brasell Publishing; Lion Publishing; Otago University Press; Usborne; Western Publishers

Harper Sports, *imprint of* HarperCollins Publishers (New Zealand) Ltd

HarperCollins New Zealand, *imprint of* HarperCollins Publishers (New Zealand) Ltd

Hazard Press Ltd+
202 Hereford St, Christchurch 8000
Mailing Address: PO Box 2151, Christchurch
Tel: (03) 3770370 *Fax:* (03) 3770390
E-mail: info@hazard.co.nz
Web Site: www.hazardpress.com
Key Personnel
Publisher & Man Dir: Quentin Wilson
 E-mail: quentin@hazard.co.nz
Founded: 1987
Membership(s): Booksellers Association of New Zealand & Book Publishers Association of New Zealand.
Subjects: Art, Biography, Cookery, Drama, Theater, Fiction, Gardening, Plants, Government, Political Science, History, Humor, Literature, Literary Criticism, Essays, Nonfiction (General), Poetry, Travel
ISBN Prefix(es): 0-908790; 1-877161; 1-877270
Number of titles published annually: 30 Print
Total Titles: 320 Print; 2 E-Book
Imprints: Gauntlet Press

Heinemann Education, *imprint of* Reed Publishing (NZ) Ltd

Heritage Press Ltd
9B Pounamu Ave, Greenhithe, Auckland 1450
Tel: (09) 4137503; (09) 4139343 *Fax:* (09) 4137503; (09) 4139343

E-mail: heritagepressltd@xtra.co.nz
Web Site: www.heritagepress.co.nz
Key Personnel
Managing Editor: Alyson B Cresswell
Founded: 1984
Subjects: Biography, Genealogy, History, Regional Interests
ISBN Prefix(es): 0-908708

Hodder Moa Beckett Publishers Ltd+
4 Whetu Pl, Mairangi Bay 1330
Mailing Address: PO Box 100-749, North Shore Mail Centre, Auckland 1330
Tel: (09) 4781000 *Fax:* (09) 4781010
E-mail: admin@hoddermoa.co.nz
Key Personnel
Man Dir: Neil Aston Aston
Publisher: Sarah Beresford
Founded: 1971
Publishes & distributes a broad range of titles in New Zealand.
Subjects: Architecture & Interior Design, Biography, Business, Cookery, Fiction, Humor, Nonfiction (General), Sports, Athletics, Transportation
ISBN Prefix(es): 1-86958; 1-86957; 1-86947; 0-908570; 0-908676; 0-9597562
Parent Company: Hodder Headline Ltd, United Kingdom

Huia Publishers+
39 Pipitea St, Wellington, Aotearoa
Mailing Address: PO Box 17335, Aotearoa, Wellington
Tel: (04) 473-9262 *Fax:* (04) 473-9265
E-mail: customer.services@huia.co.nz
Web Site: www.huia.co.nz
Key Personnel
International Rights: Robyn Bargh
Books Manager: Brian Bargh *E-mail:* brian.b@huia.co.nz
Founded: 1991
Specializes in books about & by Maori; educational resources in Maori language; children's books in English & Maori; histories of colonization in New Zealand.
Subjects: Art, Biography, Drama, Theater, Education, Erotica, Ethnicity, Fiction, History, Bi-cultural, Indigenous Studies, Maori, Maori English Language
ISBN Prefix(es): 0-908975
Number of titles published annually: 30 Print
Total Titles: 100 Print
Parent Company: Huia (NZ) Ltd
Divisions: Huia Communications
Foreign Rep(s): South Pacific Books (USA)
Distribution Center: Reed Publishing (NZ)
South Pacific Books (United States)

IPL Publishing Group+
Transpress House, 8 Chisbury St, Wellington
Mailing Address: PO Box 10-215, Wellington
Tel: (04) 477 3032 *Fax:* (04) 477 3035
E-mail: transpress@paradise.net.nz
Web Site: www.transpressnz.com
Key Personnel
Contact: G Churchman
Founded: 1985
Membership(s): BPANZ.
Subjects: History, Transportation, Technical & Practical
ISBN Prefix(es): 0-908876
Number of titles published annually: 10 Print
Total Titles: 5 Print
Parent Company: Transpress New Zealand
Subsidiaries: IPL Books (Australia) Pty Ltd; IPL Wordprint
Divisions: IPL Books; IPL Video; IPL Publishing Services
Distributed by Gary Allen Pty Ltd (Australia); Pacific Island Books (USA)
Warehouse: 10 Tarndale Grove, Auckland

The Joint Board of Christian Education, see Uniting Education

Junior Publications Ltd
PO Box 56278, Auckland
Tel: (09) 620 5459 *Fax:* (09) 620 5459
Key Personnel
Dir: Jo Noble *E-mail:* jo@quicksilver.net.nz
Specialize in magazines related to children's books.

Kahurangi Cooperative+
Formerly Te Ropu Kahurangi
43 Landscape Rd, Papatoetoe
Tel: (09) 2782731
Key Personnel
Publisher & Editor: Bernard Gadd
Founded: 1983
Non-profit educational project.
Specialize in Learn-to-read books for ages 10 & over, novels & short stories for teenagers.
Subjects: Literature, Literary Criticism, Essays, Regional Interests
ISBN Prefix(es): 0-86477
Subsidiaries: Hallard Press
Showroom(s): Brick Row, 11 Cockayne Crescent, Sunnynook, Auckland 10

Knowing Science, *imprint of* Magari Publishing

Kotuku Media Ltd+
Box 54/234, Plimmerton, Wellington
Tel: (04) 2331842
E-mail: kotuku.media@xtra.co.nz
Key Personnel
Contact: Ross Miller
Founded: 1991
Subjects: Regional Interests
ISBN Prefix(es): 0-908967

Kowhai Publishing Ltd
10 Peacock St, Auckland 5
Mailing Address: PO Box 25-325, St Heliers
Tel: (09) 5759126 *Fax:* (09) 5753178
Key Personnel
Contact: Bruce Campbell
Specialize in photographic books of New Zealand scenery.
Subjects: Travel
ISBN Prefix(es): 0-908598

Landcare Research NZ
Canterbury Agricultural & Science Center, Gerald St, Lincoln 8152
Mailing Address: PO Box 40, Lincoln 8152
Tel: (03) 3256700 *Fax:* (03) 3252127
E-mail: mwpress@landcare.cri.nz
Web Site: www.landcare.cri.nz/mwpress/
Key Personnel
Manager: Greg Comfort
Sales: Catherine Montgomery
Founded: 1992
Specialize in scientific publications.
Subjects: Biological Sciences, Earth Sciences, Natural History, Science (General)
ISBN Prefix(es): 0-477; 0-478
Imprints: Manaaki Whenua Press
U.S. Office(s): Balogh Scientific Books, 1911 N Duncan Rd, Champaign, IL, United States
Distributor for Csiro Publishing (Australia)

Learning Guides (Writers & Publishers Ltd)+
PO Box 48-147, Upper Hut
Tel: (04) 239 9400 *Fax:* (04) 239 9400
E-mail: learning.guides@xtra.co.nz
Key Personnel
Manager: Lynda Litchfield
Founded: 1996
Subjects: Business, Computer Science, How-to, Management, Science (General)

NEW ZEALAND

ISBN Prefix(es): 0-9583643
Parent Company: Ecological Research Associates of New Zealand Inc, Upper Hutt

Learning Media Ltd+
State Services Commission Bldg, 100 Molesworth St, Level 3, Wellington 6001
Mailing Address: Box 3293, Wellington 6001
Tel: (04) 472 5522 *Fax:* (04) 472 6444
E-mail: info@learningmedia.co.nz
Web Site: www.learningmedia.co.nz; www.learningmedia.com
Key Personnel
Chief Executive: Neale Pitches
Founded: 1993
Membership(s): NZ Book Publishers Association.
Subjects: Education
ISBN Prefix(es): 0-478
Total Titles: 2 CD-ROM
U.S. Office(s): Learning Media, 1235 Indiana Court, Suite 108, Redlands, CA 92374, United States
Distributed by Celebration Press (USA); Learning Media (New Zealand); Madeleine Lindley Ltd (UK); Thomas Nelson (UK)
Distributor for ITP Nelson (Canada); Lioncrest Pty Ltd (Australia); Pacific Stores Pty Ltd (Singapore)
Orders to: SSC Bldg, Level 3, Private Bag 3293, Wellington 6015

Legislation Direct+
Division of Blue Star Print Group
PO Box 12-418, Wellington
Tel: (04) 495 2882 *Fax:* (04) 495 2880
E-mail: ldorders@legislationdirect.co.nz
Web Site: gplegislation.co.nz
Key Personnel
General Manager: Chris Eales
Administration Manager: Wendy Gaylor
 E-mail: wendy@legislationdirect.co.nz
Subjects: Career Development, Finance, Government, Political Science, Law, Nonfiction (General)
ISBN Prefix(es): 0-86956
Associate Companies: Bennetts Government London Bookshops, London, United Kingdom; Whitcoulls (retail)
U.S. Office(s): Aubrey Books, 721 Ellsworth Dr, Suite 203A, Silver Spring, MD 20910-4436, United States
Distributor for Business Round Table; Ministry for the Environment; Ministry of Justice; NZ Statistics; Parliamentary Commission for the Environment
Bookshop(s): 47 Stephenson St, Birmingham B2 4DH, United Kingdom

Lincoln College Centre for Resource Management+
Lincoln University, Ellesmere Junction Rd/Springs Rd, Lincoln, Canterbury
Mailing Address: Lincoln University, PO Box 56, Canterbury 8150
Tel: (03) 3252811 *Fax:* (03) 325156
Web Site: www.lincoln.ac.nz
Telex: 4200 NZ
Key Personnel
Dir, Rights & Permissions: Dr John Hayward
Founded: 1960
Subjects: Environmental Studies
ISBN Prefix(es): 0-908584; 1-86931

Lincoln University Press+
8 Glenbervie Terrace, Thorndon, Wellington
Mailing Address: PO Box 12-214, Thorndon, Wellington
Tel: (04) 4710601 *Fax:* (04) 4710489
E-mail: learn@lincoln.ac.nz
Web Site: learn.lincoln.ac.nz

Key Personnel
Man Dir & Publisher: Daphne Brasell
 E-mail: daphne@brasell.co.nz
International Rights: Maureen Marshall
 E-mail: dba@clear.net.nz
Founded: 1987
Membership(s): Book Publishers Association of New Zealand; Booksellers New Zealand.
Subjects: Fiction, Gay & Lesbian, Literature, Literary Criticism, Essays, Women's Studies, Resource Management
ISBN Prefix(es): 0-9597837; 0-908896
Parent Company: Daphne Brasell Associates Ltd & Lincoln University
Ultimate Parent Company: Daphne Brasell Associates Ltd
Imprints: Whitireia Publishing
Subsidiaries: Lincoln University Press; Whitireia Publishing
Branch Office(s)
Orchard Hall, Lincoln University, PO Box 195, Lincoln, Canterbury, Contact: Daphne Brasell *Tel:* (03) 325 3873 *Fax:* (03) 325 3890 *E-mail:* braselld@lincoln.ac.nz
Distributed by Unireps (Australia)
Foreign Rep(s): Hemisphere (East Asia, Pacific); Unireps (Australia)

David Ling Publishing+
67 Hinemoa St, Birkenhead, Auckland 10
Mailing Address: PO Box 34-601, Birkenhead, Auckland 10
Tel: (09) 4182785 *Fax:* (09) 4182785
Key Personnel
Man Dir & International Rights: David Ling
 E-mail: davidling@xtra.co.nz
Founded: 1992
Publisher & packager.
Membership(s): Booksellers NZ & Book Publishers Association of NZ.
Subjects: Aeronautics, Aviation, Art, Biography, Fiction, History, Maritime
ISBN Prefix(es): 0-908990
Number of titles published annually: 10 Print
Total Titles: 80 Print
Distributed by David Bateman Ltd

Longacre Press+
9 Dowling St, Dunedin
Mailing Address: PO Box 5340, Dunedin
Tel: (03) 4772911 *Fax:* (03) 4772911
E-mail: longacre.press@clear.net.nz
Key Personnel
Managing Editor: Barbara Larson
Publicity Manager: Annette Riley
Founded: 1994
Subjects: Biography, Gardening, Plants, Gay & Lesbian, Natural History, Nonfiction (General), Sports, Athletics
ISBN Prefix(es): 0-9583405; 0-9583465; 1-877135
Number of titles published annually: 10 Print
Total Titles: 75 Print
Distributed by Dennis Jones & Associates (Australia); Reed Publishing (NZ) Ltd (New Zealand)

Longman, *imprint of* Pearson Education (PENZ)

Macmillan Publishers New Zealand Ltd+
6 Ride Way, Albany, Auckland
Tel: (09) 414 0350; (09) 414 0356 (customer service); (09) 414 0352 (trade sales) *Fax:* (09) 414 0351
Web Site: www.macmillan.co.nz *Cable:* Macpublish
Key Personnel
Man Dir: David Joel *E-mail:* david@macmillan.co.nz
Trade Sales: Chris Baty *E-mail:* chris@macmillan.co.nz

BOOK

School Sales: Robyn Garvan *E-mail:* robyn@macmillan.co.nz
Academic Sales: Victoria Johnson *E-mail:* vicki@macmillan.co.nz
Customer Service: Lyn O'Connor *E-mail:* lyn@macmillan.co.nz
Founded: 1843
ISBN Prefix(es): 0-908923
Parent Company: Macmillan Publishers Ltd, United Kingdom
Associate Companies: Macmillan Education Australia; Pan Macmillan Australia

Magari Publishing+
Imprint of Natural Expressions Ltd
PO Box 104, Taupo 2730
Tel: (07) 3770169 *Fax:* (07) 3773134
E-mail: frontdesk@magari.co.nz
Web Site: www.magari.co.nz
Key Personnel
Publisher: Margaret Woodhouse
 E-mail: margaret@magari.co.nz
Marketing Dir: Jack Gower
Founded: 1987
Subjects: Education, Humor, Self-Help, Cat books & Fun books
ISBN Prefix(es): 0-908801
Imprints: Curly Tales; Knowing Science
Warehouse: 3/29 Manuka St, Taupo

Mallinson Rendel Publishers Ltd+
15 Courtenay Pl, Level 5, Wellington
Mailing Address: PO Box 9409, Wellington
Tel: (04) 802 5012 *Fax:* (04) 802 5013
E-mail: publisher@mallinsonrendel.co.nz
Web Site: www.mallinsonrendel.co.nz
Key Personnel
Man Dir: E A Mallinson
Account: J D Harper
Publisher: Ann Mallinson *E-mail:* ann@mallinsonrendel.co.nz
Founded: 1980
ISBN Prefix(es): 0-908783; 0-908606
Number of titles published annually: 6 Print
Total Titles: 180 Print

Manaaki Whenua Press, *imprint of* Landcare Research NZ

Maori Publications Unit
PO Box 2061, Koyeopeo, Whakatane
Tel: (07) 3087254 *Fax:* (07) 3085098
Key Personnel
Contact: Dir
Subjects: English as a Second Language
ISBN Prefix(es): 1-877152; 0-908771
Showroom(s): Cor Domain Rd & McAlister St, Whakatane

Mills Group+
PO Box 30818, Lower Hutt
Tel: (04) 5696744 *Fax:* (04) 5697464
Web Site: www.millsonline.com
Key Personnel
Chief Executive: Harry Mills *E-mail:* harry.mills@millsonline.com
Founded: 1982
Subjects: Nonfiction (General)
ISBN Prefix(es): 0-908722

Millwood Press Ltd
291B Tinakori Rd, Wellington
Tel: (04) 4735176 *Fax:* (04) 4735177
Telex: 31255 *Cable:* Siersprod
Key Personnel
Dir: Jim Siers; Judy Siers
Founded: 1972
Subjects: Foreign Countries

Moss Associates Ltd+
7 Dorset Way, Wadestown, Wellington 6001

Tel: (04) 4728226 *Fax:* (04) 4728226
E-mail: moss@xtra.co.nz
Key Personnel
Dir: Geoffrey R Moss
Founded: 1986
Subjects: Business, Career Development, Communications, Human Relations, Management
ISBN Prefix(es): 0-9583538
Distributed by Bagolyvar Publishing House (Hungary); Best Literary & Rights Agency (Korea); CCH (Australia); DPB Publications (India); Dragon's Eye Communications (Korea); Federal Publications (S) Pte Ltd (Singapore); Francolin Publishers (Pty) Ltd (South Africa); Joint Publishing (China); Kogan Page (UK); LDI Training (Indonesia); McGraw-Hill (USA); McGraw-Hill Book Co Australia Pty Ltd (Australia); Moss Associates Ltd (New Zealand); Prommociones Jumerca (Spain); Qingdao Publishing House (China); SE-Education Public Co Ltd (Thailand); Singapore Institute of Management (Singapore & Malaysia); Tech Publications Pty Ltd (Singapore); Times Media Pvt Ltd (Singapore); UBS Publishers' Distributors Ltd (India); Vijay Nicole Imprints (India); Vikas Publishing House Pvt Ltd (India); Yale International Publishing House (Taiwan)

Nagare Press+
PO Box 934, Palmerston North
Tel: (06) 3572531
Key Personnel
Editor & International Rights: Dr Wilhelmina Drummond
Subjects: Child Care & Development, Education, Fiction, Human Relations, Poetry, Wine & Spirits, Adolescence, Human Development
ISBN Prefix(es): 0-908822

Nahanni Publishing Ltd+
PO Box 34-179, Birkenhead, Auckland 10
Tel: (09) 419 0681 *Fax:* (09) 419 0695
E-mail: info@nahanni-publishing.com; sales@nahanni.co.nz (for orders)
Web Site: www.nahanni-publishing.com
Key Personnel
Man Dir: Dr Ian Brooks *E-mail:* brooks@nahanni.co.nz
Founded: 1995
Subjects: Business
ISBN Prefix(es): 0-9583506; 0-9582036

Nelson Price Milburn Ltd+
One Te Puni St, Petone, Wellington
Mailing Address: PO Box 38-945, Wellington Mail Centre, Petone, Wellington
Tel: (04) 5687179 *Fax:* (04) 5682115
Web Site: www.thomsonlearning.com.au/primary
Key Personnel
General & Publishing Manager: Greg Browne
Secretary: John Heffernan
Founded: 1957
Distributor for Thomas Nelson UK & Thomas Nelson Australia.
Subjects: Accounting, Biological Sciences, Business, Chemistry, Chemical Engineering, Child Care & Development, Communications, Computer Science, Drama, Theater, Economics, Education, Electronics, Electrical Engineering, Finance, Geography, Geology, Health, Nutrition, History, Language Arts, Linguistics, Law, Management, Marketing, Mathematics, Outdoor Recreation, Physical Sciences, Physics, Poetry, Science (General), Social Sciences, Sociology, Sports, Athletics, Technology
ISBN Prefix(es): 0-7055; 1-86955; 1-86961
Parent Company: Thomas Nelson Australia, Australia
Ultimate Parent Company: The Thomson Corp, Suite 2706, Toronto Dominion Bank Tower, PO Box 24, Toronto Dominion Centre, Toronto, ON M5K 1A1, Canada
Associate Companies: 102 Dodds St, South Melbourne, Victoria 3205, Australia

Nestegg Books+
46 Owhiro Bay Pde, Wellington 6002
Tel: (04) 3836645
Key Personnel
Author, Editor & Publisher: Sheila Natusch
Founded: 1991
Subjects: Biography, History, Natural History, Regional Interests
ISBN Prefix(es): 0-473; 0-908629; 0-9597965; 0-9583757

New House Publishers Ltd+
31 Castor Bay Rd, Takapuna, Auckland
Mailing Address: PO Box 33376, Takapuna, Auckland
Tel: (09) 4106517 *Fax:* (09) 4106329
E-mail: service@newhouse.co.nz
Web Site: www.newhouse.co.nz
Key Personnel
Dir: David Heap *E-mail:* david@newhouse.co.nz
Founded: 1988
Specialize in educational textbooks & materials.
Subjects: Accounting, Chemistry, Chemical Engineering, Earth Sciences, Economics, English as a Second Language, Geography, Geology, Language Arts, Linguistics, Mathematics, Physics, Science (General), Technology
ISBN Prefix(es): 1-86946
Number of titles published annually: 25 Print
Total Titles: 300 Print

New Women's Press Ltd+
PO Box 47339, Auckland
Tel: (09) 3767150 *Fax:* (09) 3767150
Key Personnel
Man Dir: Wendy Harrex
Founded: 1982
Subjects: Women's Studies
ISBN Prefix(es): 0-908652
Warehouse: HarperCollins Publishers, PO Box 1, Auckland

New Zealand Council for Educational Research+
10th floor, West Block, Education House, 178-182 Willis St, Wellington
Mailing Address: PO Box 3237, Wellington
Tel: (04) 384 7939 *Fax:* (04) 384 7933
Web Site: www.nzcer.org.nz
Key Personnel
Dir: Robyn Baker *E-mail:* robyn.baker@nzcer.org.nz
Publicity Dir, Rights & Permissions: Bev Webber *E-mail:* bev.webber@nzcer.org.nz
Founded: 1934
Subjects: Education
ISBN Prefix(es): 0-908567; 0-908916; 1-877140
Imprints: NZCER
Distributor for ACER; NFER; SCRE
Showroom(s): Education House, 178 Willis St, Wellington
Bookshop(s): Education House, 178 Willis St, Wellington
Shipping Address: Education House, 178 Willis St, Wellington
Warehouse: Education House, 178 Willis St, Wellington
Orders to: Education House, 178-182 Willis St, Wellington 6000 (Distribution Services)

Nielsen BookData
Formerly Book Data Asia Pacific
Division of Nielsen Book Services Ltd
PO Box 46-018, Herne Bay, Auckland 1030
Tel: (09) 360 3294 *Fax:* (09) 360 8853
E-mail: info@nielsenbookdata.co.nz
Web Site: www.nielsenbookdata.co.nz
Key Personnel
Man Dir: Ka Meechan *E-mail:* ka.meechan@nielsenbookdata.co.nz
Founded: 1987
Specialize in a range of computer-based bibliographic information services for the international book trade; bibliographic CD-ROM database & online services.
Ultimate Parent Company: VNU

Northland Historical Publications Society
PO Box 285, Kerikeri, Northland
Tel: (09) 4028244 *Fax:* (09) 4028296
Founded: 1989
Subjects: History
ISBN Prefix(es): 0-9583705; 0-9597926

NZCER, *imprint of* New Zealand Council for Educational Research

Orca Publishing, Certes Press, *imprint of* Orca Publishing Services Ltd

Orca Publishing Services Ltd
202 Hereford St, Christchurch
Mailing Address: PO Box 2151, Christchurch
Tel: (03) 377-0370 *Fax:* (03) 377-0390
E-mail: info@hazard.co.nz
Web Site: www.hazardonline.com
Key Personnel
Man Dir & Publisher: Quentin Wilson *E-mail:* quentin@hazard.co.nz
Editor: Antoinette Wilson *E-mail:* antoinette@orcapublishing.co.nz
Founded: 1986
Membership(s): Book Publishers Association of NZ.
Subjects: Fiction, Nonfiction (General), Poetry
ISBN Prefix(es): 1-877162
Associate Companies: Hazard Press Ltd
Imprints: Orca Publishing, Certes Press
Distributed by Mosaic Press

Otago Heritage Books
PO Box 6318, Dunedin
Tel: (03) 477 1500 *Fax:* (03) 477 1500
E-mail: otagoheritagebooks@clear.net.nz
Key Personnel
Editorial: G J Griffiths
Rights & Permissions: J A Cox
Founded: 1977
Specialize in regional books; also acts as retailer.
Subjects: History, Natural History, Regional Interests
ISBN Prefix(es): 0-908774; 0-9597723
Total Titles: 55 Print

Outrigger Publishers
PO Box 1198, Hamilton
Tel: (07) 856 6981
Key Personnel
Man Dir, Editorial: Norman Simms *E-mail:* nsimms@waikato.ac.nz
Founded: 1973
Publishes small magazines.
Subjects: Anthropology, Archaeology, Biblical Studies, History, Language Arts, Linguistics, Literature, Literary Criticism, Essays, Psychology, Psychiatry, Religion - Jewish
ISBN Prefix(es): 0-908571
Number of titles published annually: 2 Print

Oxford University Press
Wellesley St, Auckland
Mailing Address: GPO Box 2784Y, Melbourne 3001, Australia
Tel: (03) 9934 9123 *Toll Free Tel:* 1300 650 616 (Australia); 0800 442 502 (New Zealand)
Fax: (03) 9934 9100 *Toll Free Fax:* 0800-442-503

NEW ZEALAND

E-mail: cs@oup.com.au
Web Site: www.oup.com.au
Key Personnel
Publisher: Linda Cassells
Subjects: Agriculture, Art, Biography, Economics, History, Law, Literature, Literary Criticism, Essays, Natural History, Poetry
ISBN Prefix(es): 0-19
Parent Company: Oxford University Press, United Kingdom

Paerangi Books
PO Box 13-320, Johnsonville, Wellington 6004
Tel: (04) 4787789
Key Personnel
Contact: Trevor M Cobeldick
Founded: 1979
Subjects: Regional Interests
ISBN Prefix(es): 0-908965

Pearson Education (PENZ)+
46 Hillside Rd, Glenfield, Auckland 10
Mailing Address: Private Bag 102908, North Shore Mail Centre, Auckland 10
Tel: (09) 444 4968 *Fax:* (09) 444 4957
E-mail: firstname.lastname@pearsoned.co.nz
Web Site: www.pearsoned.co.nz
Key Personnel
Man Dir: Rosemary Stagg *E-mail:* rosemary.stagg@pearsoned.co.nz
Publisher, Schools: Ken Harrop
Marketing Manager Schools: Pat Fisk
Publisher, Tertiary: Bronwen Nicholson
Tertiary Sales Manager: Adrian Keane
Trade National Accounts Manager: John Cummerfield
Design/Production Manager: Polly Faulks
Administration Manager: Vera Bainbridge
Operations Manager: Ingeborg Van Elburg
Assistant to Man Dir: Sheila Jenkins
Founded: 1968
All New Zealand curriculum subjects in schools, higher education focus on business, economics & the social sciences.
ISBN Prefix(es): 0-582
Number of titles published annually: 60 Print
Total Titles: 600 Print
Parent Company: Pearson Education
Ultimate Parent Company: Pearson Plc
Imprints: Longman; Prentice Hall
Distributor for Sybex (New Zealand); WW Norton (New Zealand)

Penguin Books (NZ) Ltd
Corner Rosedale & Airborne Rds, Auckland
Mailing Address: PMB 102902, North Shore Mall, Auckland 10
Tel: (09) 415-4700; (09) 415-4702 (orders)
 Fax: (09) 415-4701; (09) 415-4703 (orders)
E-mail: marketing@penguin.co.nz
Web Site: www.penguin.co.nz
Key Personnel
Man Dir: Tony Harkins
Sales Dir: Colin Cox
Publishing Dir: Geoff Walker
Marketing Dir: Karen Ferns
Founded: 1973
ISBN Prefix(es): 0-14
Parent Company: Penguin Publishing Co Ltd, United Kingdom

Polynesian Press+
PO Box 68 446, Newton, Auckland 1
Tel: (09) 3032349 *Fax:* (09) 3779528
Key Personnel
Contact: Robert Holding
Founded: 1976
ISBN Prefix(es): 0-908597
Distributed by University of Hawaii Press
Distributor for University of Hawaii Press

Prentice Hall, *imprint of* Pearson Education (PENZ)

Profile Publishing Ltd
Suite 2.1, 72 Dominion Rd, Mt Eden, Auckland
Mailing Address: PO Box 5544, Auckland
Tel: (09) 6308940; (09) 3585455 *Fax:* (09) 6302307; (09) 6301046; (09) 3585462
E-mail: info@profile.co.nz
Web Site: www.profile.co.nz
Key Personnel
Publisher & Editor: Reg Birchfield
 E-mail: editor@management.co.nz
General Manager: Kevin Lawrence
 E-mail: kevin@profile.co.nz
ISBN Prefix(es): 0-9582045

Publishing Solutions Ltd
86-90 Lambton Quay, 9th floor, Wellington
Tel: (04) 4710582 *Fax:* (04) 4710717
E-mail: gen@pubsol.co.nz
Founded: 1992
Specialize in technical publishing.
Subjects: Maritime, Veterinary Science
ISBN Prefix(es): 0-9582063

Pursuit Publishing+
22 Second Ave, Whangarei
Mailing Address: PO Box 984, Whangarei
Tel: (09) 4385725 *Fax:* (09) 4382543
Web Site: www.pursuit.co.nz
Key Personnel
Author & President: Frank Newman
 E-mail: frank@newman.co.nz
Founded: 1988
Subjects: Business
ISBN Prefix(es): 0-9597904
Distributed by Reed (NZ) Ltd (New Zealand)

R P L Books+
10 Rozella Pl, Murrays Bay, Auckland
Mailing Address: North Shore Mail Center, PO Box 100 243, Auckland 1330
Tel: (09) 4437448 *Fax:* (09) 4430147
E-mail: rplbooks@rplbooks.co.nz
Key Personnel
Man Dir: Duncan Sutherland *E-mail:* duncan@rplbooks.co.nz
Founded: 1970
Subjects: Biography, Sports, Athletics
ISBN Prefix(es): 0-908630; 0-908757; 0-9583371; 0-9597553; 0-9597884
Total Titles: 20 Print; 3 E-Book
Parent Company: Medialine Holdings Ltd
Imprints: Harlen Books; The Sporting Press
Subsidiaries: Harlen Publishing Company Ltd; The Sporting Press Ltd
Distribution Center: Forrester Books NZ Ltd, 10 Tarndale Grove, Auckland, Contact: David Forrester *Tel:* (09) 4152080 *Fax:* (09) 4152083 *E-mail:* forr@forrester.co.nz
Orders to: Forrester Books NZ Ltd, Private Bag 102907, NSMC, Auckland, David Forrester *Tel:* (09) 4152080 *Fax:* (09) 4152083

Reach Publications+
PO Box 10-010, Dominion Rd, Auckland
Tel: (09) 376 3235 *Fax:* (09) 376 3250
E-mail: giftedednz@xtra.co.nz
Key Personnel
Managing Editor: Rory Cathcart
Founded: 1994
Subjects: Child Care & Development, Disability, Special Needs, Education
ISBN Prefix(es): 0-473
Parent Company: George Parkyn Centre for Gifted Education

Reed, *imprint of* Reed Publishing (NZ) Ltd

Reed Children's Books, *imprint of* Reed Publishing (NZ) Ltd

Reed Publishing (NZ) Ltd+
39 Rawene Rd, Birkenhead, Auckland 10
Mailing Address: PO Box 34901, Birkenhead, Auckland 10
Tel: (09) 441 2960 *Fax:* (09) 480 4999
E-mail: info@reed.co.nz (customer service)
Web Site: www.reed.co.nz
Key Personnel
Man Dir: Alan Smith *E-mail:* asmith@reed.co.nz
Publishing Manager: Peter Janssen
 E-mail: pjanssen@reed.co.nz
Founded: 1988 (part of the company founded in 1907)
Subjects: Biography, Cookery, Fiction, History, Natural History, Nonfiction (General), Outdoor Recreation, Regional Interests, Travel
ISBN Prefix(es): 0-589; 0-7900; 0-86863; 1-86948; 0-474; 1-86944
Number of titles published annually: 100 Print
Total Titles: 280 Print; 2 Audio
Parent Company: Reed Education & Professional Publishing, United Kingdom
Ultimate Parent Company: Reed Elsevier plc, 25 Victoria St, London SW1H 0EX, United Kingdom
Associate Companies: Butterworths
Imprints: Reed; Heinemann Education; Reed Children's Books
Divisions: Reed Consumer Books; Heinemann Educational; Book Circle
U.S. Office(s): Heinemann USA, 361 Hanover St, Portsmouth, NH 03801-3912, United States
Distributor for BBC Books; John Murray

Resource Books Ltd+
37 Pembroke Crescent, Glendowie, Auckland 1005
Mailing Address: PO Box 25-598, St Heliers, Auckland 1130
Tel: (09) 5758030 *Fax:* (09) 5758055
E-mail: sales@resourcebooks.co.nz
Web Site: www.resourcebooks.co.nz
Key Personnel
Manager: Peter Biggs *E-mail:* pbiggs@resourcebooks.co.nz
Founded: 1984
Subjects: Art, Education, Medicine, Nursing, Dentistry
ISBN Prefix(es): 0-908618

RIMU Publishing Co Ltd
49 Casey Ave Fairfield, Hamilton
Tel: (07) 8555536 *Fax:* (07) 8555536
Key Personnel
Man Dir: Theola Wyllie
Founded: 1984
Subjects: Nonfiction (General)
ISBN Prefix(es): 0-908703

River Press
41 York St, Picton
Mailing Address: PO Box 10, Picton
Tel: (03) 5738383 *Fax:* (03) 5738383
Key Personnel
Contact: Carol Dawber *E-mail:* carol.dawber@xtra.co.nz
Founded: 1992
Also acts a book packager.
Subjects: History, Maritime, Mysteries, Nonfiction (General), Romance, Travel
ISBN Prefix(es): 0-9598041
Subsidiaries: Best Books

RSVP Publishing Co Ltd+
24 Tiri Rd, Oneroa, Waiheke Island, Auckland
Mailing Address: PO Box 47166, Ponsonby, Auckland
Tel: (09) 3723480 *Fax:* (09) 3728480
E-mail: rsvppub@iconz.co.nz
Web Site: www.rsvp-publishing.co.nz

PUBLISHERS   NEW ZEALAND

Key Personnel
Publisher: Stephen Picard
Editorial Manager: Rosie Parkes
Founded: 1990
Membership(s): BPANZ.
Subjects: Alternative, Astrology, Occult, Environmental Studies, Fiction, Law, Nonfiction (General), Photography, Social Sciences, Sociology, Travel, Also specializes in eclectic & metaphysical books, illustrated books
ISBN Prefix(es): 0-9597948; 0-9582182
Number of titles published annually: 3 Print
Total Titles: 12 Print; 9 Online; 9 E-Book
Distributed by Banyan Tree Book Distributors
Foreign Rep(s): Banyan Tree (Australia)

Saint Publishing+
11 Akepiro St, Mt Eden, Auckland
Mailing Address: PO Box 8157, Symonds St, Auckland
Tel: (09) 623-2510 *Fax:* (09) 623-2890
E-mail: info@saintpublish.co.nz
Key Personnel
Man Dir: Selwyn Jacobson
Editor: Tom Hepburn
Founded: 1979
Specialize in calendars & lifestyle/coffee table books.
Subjects: Art, Humor, Sports, Athletics
ISBN Prefix(es): 1-877186; 1-877247
Number of titles published annually: 2 CD-ROM
Total Titles: 6 Print
Distributor for Avalanche Publishing (New Zealand)

Seagull Press
2/226 Marine Parade, New Brighton, Christchurch
Tel: (03) 3899338
Key Personnel
Author: R B Mehlhopt
Subjects: Poetry
ISBN Prefix(es): 0-908738; 0-9597686; 1-877278

Shearwater Associates Ltd+
108 Mana Esplanade, Paremata, Wellington
Mailing Address: PO Box 54-224, Plimmerton
Tel: (04) 2399024 *Fax:* (04) 2399024
Key Personnel
Contact: Michael Keith
Founded: 1990
Specialize in children's & educational publishing.
Subjects: Education, Fiction, History, Natural History, Nonfiction (General)
ISBN Prefix(es): 0-908864
Imprints: Shearwater Books; Titi Tuhiwai

Shearwater Books, *imprint of* Shearwater Associates Ltd

Shoal Bay Press Ltd+
4 Cliff St, Moncks Bay, Christchurch
Mailing Address: PO Box 17661, Christchurch
Tel: (03) 384 6057 *Fax:* (03) 384 6087
E-mail: ros@shoalbay.co.nz
Key Personnel
Contact: David Elworthy *E-mail:* david@shoalbay.co.nz
Founded: 1984
Subjects: Business, Child Care & Development, Crafts, Games, Hobbies, Finance, Gardening, Plants, History, Management, Marketing, Natural History, Nonfiction (General), Outdoor Recreation, Photography, Sports, Athletics, Travel
ISBN Prefix(es): 0-908704; 1-877251
Warehouse: Macmillan Publishers, 6 Ridge Way, Albany, Auckland
Orders to: Macmillan Publishers, 6 Ridge Way, Albany, Auckland

Shortland Publications Ltd
PO Box 11-904, Auckland 5
Tel: (09) 687128 *Fax:* (09) 6230143
E-mail: heather_peach@mcgraw-hill.com *Cable:* NEWSPRESS
Key Personnel
Man Dir: Avelyn Davidson
Sales Manager: Jenny Boyd
Founded: 1977
Subjects: Sports, Athletics
ISBN Prefix(es): 0-7901; 0-86867
Parent Company: Wilson & Horton Ltd, 46 Albert St, PO Box 32, Auckland

SIR Publishing+
Science House, 11 Turnbull St, Thorndon, Wellington
Mailing Address: PO Box 399, Wellington
Tel: (04) 472 7421 *Fax:* (04) 473 1841
E-mail: sirp@rsnz.govt.nz
Web Site: www.rsnz.govt.nz/publ *Cable:* SIDSIR
Key Personnel
Manager: Robert Lynch
Founded: 1991
Publishers of Scientific Research journals, focusing on New Zealand, Australia, SW Pacific & Antarctica, Scientific Proceedings of Symposia & Workshops; Scientific Treatises; Science Education Resources. Incorporated within The Royal Society of New Zealand.
Subjects: Agriculture, Biological Sciences, Earth Sciences, Environmental Studies, Science (General)
ISBN Prefix(es): 0-477; 0-908654
Parent Company: The Royal Society of New Zealand, 4 Halswell St, Thorndon, PO Box 598, Wellington
Branch Office(s)
Eurospan Ltd, 3 Henrietta St, Covent Garden, London WC2E 8LU, United Kingdom *Tel:* (020) 7240 0856 *Fax:* (020) 7379 0609
U.S. Office(s): Allen Press Inc, PO Box 1897, Lawrence, KS 66044-8897, United States *Tel:* 913-843-1234 *Fax:* 913-843-1274

Southern Lights, *imprint of* Brick Row Publishing Co Ltd

Southern Press Ltd
PO Box 50-134, Porirua
Tel: (04) 233-1899
Key Personnel
Man Dir, Editorial: R H Stott
Publicity: J Stott
Founded: 1971
Subjects: Aeronautics, Aviation, Archaeology, Civil Engineering, Maritime, Mechanical Engineering, Technology, Transportation
ISBN Prefix(es): 0-908616
Distributed by ARHS, NSW Division
Distributor for Australian Railway Historical Society, NSW Division
Shipping Address: High Ridge, Paekakariki Hill Rd, Pauatahanui, R D 1, Porirua Wellington

Spinal Publications New Zealand Ltd+
8 Parata St, Waikanae
Mailing Address: PO Box 93, Waikanae
Tel: (04) 2937020 *Fax:* (04) 2932897
E-mail: enquiries@spinalpublications.co.nz
Web Site: www.spinalpublications.co.nz
Key Personnel
General Manager: Jan McKenzie
Founded: 1980
Membership(s): BPANZ.
Subjects: Health, Nutrition, Self-Help, Diagnosis & Treatment of Lumbar & Cervical Spine
ISBN Prefix(es): 0-9583647; 0-9598049; 0-9597446; 0-9597746
Distributed by Esaki Medical Instrument Co (Japan); Spine Care Products Benelux (Switzerland, Austria); Spinal Publications Italia (Italy)

The Sporting Press, *imprint of* R P L Books

Statistics New Zealand
Aorangi House, 85 Molesworth St, Wellington
Mailing Address: PO Box 2922, Wellington
Tel: (04) 931 4600 *Fax:* (04) 931 4610
E-mail: info@stats.govt.nz
Web Site: www.stats.govt.nz
Subjects: Agriculture, Business, Economics, Education, Finance, Mathematics, Women's Studies
ISBN Prefix(es): 0-478

Sunshine Books International Ltd+
PO Box 74543, Auckland 1130
Tel: (09) 5203049 *Toll Free Fax:* 0800 85 1000
E-mail: orders@my-dictionary.com
Web Site: www.my-dictionary.com
Key Personnel
Co-Dir: Jenny Aston *E-mail:* jenny@my-dictionary.com
ISBN Prefix(es): 0-9597734

Sunshine Multi Media Ltd, Wendy Pye Ltd
413 Great South Rd, Penrose, Auckland 1005
Tel: (09) 525-3575 *Fax:* (09) 525-4205
E-mail: admin@sunshine.co.nz
Web Site: www.sunshine.co.nz
Founded: 1986
ISBN Prefix(es): 1-877190
Branch Office(s)
433 Wellington St, Clifton Hill, Melbourne, Victoria 3068, Australia *Tel:* (0613) 9489-3968 *Fax:* (0613) 9482-2416
Maaholm Publishing House, Almevej 12, 2900 Hellerup, Denmark *Tel:* (0453) 9627 892 *Fax:* (0453) 9627 891
20 Heathbridge, Brooklands Rd, Weybridge, Surrey KT13 OUN, United Kingdom *Tel:* (044-1932) *Fax:* 850062

Tandem Press+
2 Rugby Rd, Birkenhead, Auckland 10
Mailing Address: PO Box 34-272, Birkenhead, Auckland
Tel: (09) 480-1452 *Fax:* (09) 480-1455
E-mail: customers@tandempress.co.nz
Web Site: www.tandempress.co.nz
Key Personnel
Man Dir, Editorial: Robert M Ross *E-mail:* bobross@tandempress.co.nz
Dir Marketing: Helen E Benton *E-mail:* helenb@tandempress.co.nz
Founded: 1990
Subjects: Business, Cookery, Ethnicity, Fiction, Health, Nutrition, Nonfiction (General), Outdoor Recreation, Photography, Psychology, Psychiatry, Self-Help, Travel, Women's Studies
ISBN Prefix(es): 1-877178; 0-908884; 9-781877
Total Titles: 135 Print
Distributed by Forrester Books
Distributor for New Women's Press (NZ)
Distribution Center: Australian Book Group, PO Box 214, Gembrook, Victoria 3783, Australia, Contact: Morgan Blackthorne *Tel:* (03) 5967 7009

Taylor Books+
51 Sixth Ave, Tauranga
Tel: (07) 5786024
Key Personnel
Head: Peter Rotherham
Founded: 1994
Subjects: English as a Second Language, Self-Help

Te Ropu Kahurangi, see Kahurangi Cooperative

Te Waihora Press
PO Box 512, Christchurch
Tel: (03) 348-8675 *Fax:* (03) 348-8675

NEW ZEALAND

Key Personnel
Man Editor: Dr John Wilson
  E-mail: johnwilson56@xtra.co.nz
Founded: 1984
Subjects: Architecture & Interior Design, History
ISBN Prefix(es): 0-908714
Total Titles: 2 Print

Titi Tuhiwai, *imprint of* Shearwater Associates Ltd

Transworld Publishers (NZ) Ltd
3 William Pickering Dr, Albany, Auckland
Tel: (09) 4156210 *Fax:* (09) 4156221
Key Personnel
Contact: Jacqui Dimes
ISBN Prefix(es): 0-908821
Parent Company: Bertelsmann AG, Germany
Associate Companies: Transworld Publishers, Australia; Bantam Doubleday Dell Inc, 1540 Broadway, New York, NY 10036, United States; Transworld Publishers, United Kingdom
Distributor for Avon; Dover (US); Langenscheidt; David Ling Publishing; Lonely Planet Publications; Workman; Trail Blazer; de Roos

Uniting Education
Formerly The Joint Board of Christian Education
75 Taranaki St, Wellington 3000
Mailing Address: PO Box 1245, Collingwood, Victoria 3066, Australia
Tel: (03) 94164262 *Fax:* (03) 94164264
ISBN Prefix(es): 0-85819; 1-86407
Parent Company: Joint Board of Christian Education, 65 Oxford St, PO Box 1245, Collingwood, Victoria 3006, Australia

Universal Business Directories, Australia Pty Ltd
2 Robert St, Ellerslie, Auckland
Mailing Address: PO Box 11-264, Ellerslie, Auckland
Tel: (09) 526-6300 *Toll Free Tel:* 800 823-225 (New Zealand only) *Fax:* (09) 526-6313
Toll Free Fax: 800 329 823 (New Zealand only)
E-mail: sales@ubd.co.nz
Web Site: www.ubd.co.nz
Key Personnel
General Manager: Allan Parker
Founded: 1932
Subjects: Business
ISBN Prefix(es): 0-7261
Parent Company: Wilson & Horton Ltd
Associate Companies: New Zealand Herald
Subsidiaries: Wises Mapping

University of Otago Press+
398 Cumberland St, Level 1, Dunedin
Mailing Address: PO Box 56, Dunedin
Tel: (03) 479 8807 *Fax:* (03) 479 8385
E-mail: university.press@otago.ac.nz
Web Site: www.otago.ac.nz
Key Personnel
Man Editor & International Rights: Wendy Harrex *E-mail:* wendy.harrex@stonebow.otago.ac.nz
Publicist: Amanda Smith *Tel:* (03) 479 9094
  E-mail: amanda.smith@stonebow.otago.ac.nz
Founded: 1958
Membership(s): IASP (International Association of Scholarly Publishers)
Subjects: Anthropology, Art, Biography, Education, Environmental Studies, Ethnicity, Fiction, Government, Political Science, History, Literature, Literary Criticism, Essays, Natural History, Photography, Poetry, Psychology, Psychiatry, Social Sciences, Sociology
ISBN Prefix(es): 0-908569; 1-877133; 1-877276
Number of titles published annually: 24 Print
Total Titles: 130 Print

Branch Office(s)
UniReps, University of New South Wales Press, Randwick (Sydney), NSW 2034, Australia
Tel: (02) 96640999 *Fax:* (02) 96645420
E-mail: info.press@unsw.edu.au
U.S. Office(s): International Specialized Book Services, 920 NE 58th Ave, Suite 300, Portland, OR 97213-3786, United States *Tel:* 503-287-3093 *Fax:* 503-280-8832 (North America)
Distributed by International Specialized Book Services (USA)
Orders to: HarperCollins, 31 View Rd, Glenfield, Auckland 10 *Tel:* (09) 4439400 *Fax:* (09) 4439402
Membership(s): Book Publishers Association of New Zealand

Victoria University Press+
49 Rawhiti Terrace, Kelburn, Wellington 6001
Mailing Address: PO Box 600, Wellington
Tel: (04) 463 6580 *Fax:* (04) 463 6581
E-mail: victoria-press@vuw.ac.nz
Web Site: www.vuw.ac.nz
Key Personnel
Publisher: Fergus Barrowman
Editor: Rachel Lawson *E-mail:* rachel.lawson@vuw.ac.nz
Founded: 1979
Membership(s): Booksellers New Zealand.
Subjects: Anthropology, Architecture & Interior Design, Drama, Theater, Government, Political Science, History, Language Arts, Linguistics, Law, Literature, Literary Criticism, Essays, Poetry, Social Sciences, Sociology
ISBN Prefix(es): 0-86473
Total Titles: 180 Print
Distributed by Random House (New Zealand)
Warehouse: Random House NZ Ltd, 18 Poland Rd, Glenfield, Auckland
Orders to: Archetype Book Agents, PO Box 105, Auckland 200 *Tel:* (09) 3773800 *Fax:* (09) 3773811

Viking Sevenseas Ltd, *imprint of* Viking Sevenseas NZ Ltd

Viking Sevenseas NZ Ltd
23B Ihakara St, Paraparaumu, Wellington
Mailing Address: PO Box 152, Paraparaumu 6150, Wellington
Tel: (04) 902-8240 *Fax:* (04) 902-8240
E-mail: vikings@paradise.net.nz *Cable:* VIKSEVEN
Key Personnel
Man Dir: Murdoch Riley
Founded: 1957
Subjects: Ethnicity, Natural History
ISBN Prefix(es): 0-85467
Imprints: Viking Sevenseas Ltd

Wellington Orchid Society Publications
60 Horokiwi Rd West Newlands, Wellington
Tel: (04) 4783901
Key Personnel
Manager: N D Neilson
Subjects: Culture Guides-Cymbidium, Lycaste/Anguloa, Oncidium, Paphiopedilum, Cattleya
ISBN Prefix(es): 0-908684

Whitireia Publishing, *imprint of* Lincoln University Press

Bridget Williams Books Ltd+
6 Glenbervie TCE, Thorndon, Wellington
Mailing Address: PO Box 5482, Wellington
Tel: (04) 4738317 *Fax:* (04) 4738417
E-mail: bwbooks@ihug.co.nz
Key Personnel
Dir: Bridget Williams
Business Manager: John Schiff
Founded: 1990

An independent publishing company focusing on New Zealand subjects, including Maori history & politics.
Subjects: Biography, Government, Political Science, History, Nonfiction (General), Women's Studies
ISBN Prefix(es): 0-908912; 0-908912
Number of titles published annually: 10 Print
Total Titles: 30 Print
Distributed by Independent Publishing Group (IPG)
Distributor for NIL
Distribution Center: Craig Potton Publishing Ltd, PO Box 555, Nelson

Wilson & Horton Publications Ltd
318 Richmond Rd, Grey Lynn, Auckland 1002
Mailing Address: PO Box 90119, Auckland Mail Centre, Auckland
Tel: (09) 360 3820 *Fax:* (09) 360 3831
E-mail: whpubs@listener.co.nz
Web Site: www.wilsonandhorton.co.nz
Telex: NZ 2325 *Cable:* HERALD
Key Personnel
Man Dir: H M Horton
Sales Manager: B Morgan
ISBN Prefix(es): 0-86864; 0-9583614
Branch Office(s)
NZ1 Bldg, Hamilton
22 Panama St, Wellington

Words Work
31 Robertson St, Rotorua
Mailing Address: PO Box 604, Rotorua 3201
Tel: (07) 3482953 *Fax:* (07) 3482953
E-mail: wordswrk@clear.net.nz
Key Personnel
Dir: Philippa Harrison *E-mail:* philippa@wordswo-k.co.nz; philippa@nzbike.co.nz
Founded: 1996
Prepress, graphic design, editing. Publish New Zealand's only cycling magazine
50% partner in Phoenix Publishing.
Subjects: Child Care & Development, Fiction, How-to, Poetry, Religion - Protestant

Nicaragua

General Information

Capital: Managua
Language: Spanish
Religion: Predominantly Roman Catholic
Population: 3.8 million
Bank Hours: 0830-1500 Monday-Friday; 0830-1130 Saturday
Shop Hours: 0800-1200, 1430-1730 or longer Monday-Saturday
Currency: 100 centavos = 1 new cordoba
Export/Import Information: Catalogues dutied per gross kilo Compensatory tax on advertising. No import licenses or exchange controls.
Copyright: UCC, Buenos Aires, Florence (see Copyright Conventions, pg xi)

Academia Nicaraguense de la Lengua
(Nicaraguan Academy of Letters)
Apdo 2711, Managua
Subjects: Language Arts, Linguistics

ENN, see Editorial Nueva Nicaragua

Editorial Nueva Nicaragua
Paseo Salvador Allende, Km 3 1/2 Carretera Sur, Apdo RP-073, Managua
Tel: (02) 666520
Key Personnel
Dir Gen: Roberto Diaz Castillo

President: Sergio Ramirez Mercado
Production Dir: Irene Menocal Bravo
Financial: Mayra Rivera Juarez
Sales: Maria Jose Bermudez Moreno
Founded: 1981
Also acts as co-productions.
Subjects: Ethnicity, Fiction, Government, Political Science, Literature, Literary Criticism, Essays, Nonfiction (General), Poetry, Religion - Other, Social Sciences, Sociology

Niger

General Information

Capital: Niamey
Language: French (official) and 10 other national languages
Religion: 85% Islamic, most of remainder traditional beliefs
Population: 8.1 million
Bank Hours: 0800-1100, 1600-1700 (cool season 1530-1700) Monday-Friday
Currency: 100 centimes = 1 CFA franc
Export/Import Information: Member of West African Economic Community. No tariff on books; advertising matter subject to fiscal and customs duties (EEC members pay percentage of customs duty). Also statistical tax.
Copyright: UCC, Berne (see Copyright Conventions, pg xi)

Government Printer (Societe De L'Imprimerie Nationale Du Niger)
BP 61, Niamey
Tel: 734798
Telex: 5313

Nigeria

General Information

Capital: Abuja
Language: English (official), also Hausa, Yoruba, Ibo & Fulani
Religion: Islamic (mainly in north), Christian, and traditional beliefs
Population: 88.5 million
Bank Hours: 0800-1500 Monday; 0800-1300 Tuesday-Friday
Shop Hours: Vary locally. 0800-1230, 1400-1630 Monday-Friday; 0800-1230 Saturday
Currency: 100 kobo = 1 naira
Export/Import Information: No tariffs on books or advertising matter. Open general license. Obscene literature prohibited. Exchange controls.
Copyright: UCC, Berne, Florence (see Copyright Conventions, pg xi)

ABIC Books & Equipment Ltd+
18 Kenyatta St, Nsukka Enugu
Mailing Address: PO Box 13740, Nsukka Enugu
Tel: (042) 331827 *Fax:* (042) 334811
Key Personnel
President: C N C Asomugha
Founded: 1987
Membership(s): Nigerian Publishers Assoc. Specializes in Reference Books & Children's Books; also participates in Book Selling & as a Literary Agent.
Subjects: History, Poetry
ISBN Prefix(es): 978-2269
Branch Office(s)
PO Box 71391, Victoria Island, Lagos

Abisega Publishers (Nigeria) Ltd+
Isolak Bldg, 9 Queen Elizabeth Rd, Mokola, Rounabout
Mailing Address: PO Box 14398 UI, Ibadan
Tel: (022) 415802
Key Personnel
Man Dir: Adedeji Muyiwa
Membership(s): Nigerian Publishers Association.
Subjects: Accounting
ISBN Prefix(es): 978-30339
Imprints: Opatoki Press

Adebara Publishers Ltd
PO Box 1970, Ibadan
Telex: 20311
Key Personnel
Man Dir, Editorial: Dele Adebara
Sales, Publicity: Bisi Oke
Production: Layi Bankole
Rights & Permissions: Kayode Ayeni
Founded: 1979
Subjects: Biography, Business, Education, Ethnicity, Fiction, Foreign Countries, Religion - Other
ISBN Prefix(es): 978-147
Imprints: Awoko; Gangan; Kakaki
Book Club(s): Amebo Book Club

African Books Collective Ltd, imprint of Nigerian Institute of International Affairs

African Universities Press+
305 Herbert Macaulay St, Yaba, Lagos
Mailing Address: PO Box 3560, Yaba, Lagos
Tel: (022) 317218
Telex: 20311 Box 078 *Cable:* PILGRIM IBADAN
Key Personnel
Executive Dir: Dr E A M Leigh
Founded: 1963
ISBN Prefix(es): 978-148
Parent Company: Pilgrim Books Ltd
Subsidiaries: Aureol Publishers Ltd (West Africa)
Branch Office(s)
Klm 8 Zaria/Kaduna Rd, Nr Wasasa Junction, PMB 146 Kaduna State
187 Awka Rd, Onitsha, Anambra State

Africana-FEP Publishers Ltd+
13B Oguta Rd, Onitsha Anambra State
Mailing Address: PMB 1639, Onitsha Anambra State
Tel: (046) 210669 *Cable:* AFRIBOOK, ONITSHA, NIGERIA
Key Personnel
Man Dir: Ralph O Ekpeh *Tel:* (080) 33125 705
Founded: 1971
Subjects: How-to, Science (General)
ISBN Prefix(es): 978-175
Branch Office(s)
3 Main St, Gidan Juma
9 Old Lagos Rd, PMB 5632 Ibadan *Tel:* (022) 311383
53 Barracks Rd Uyo, Presbook BP 13 Limbe, Cameroon

Ahmadu Bello University Press Ltd+
PMB 1094, Zaria, Kaduna State
Tel: (069) 550054
E-mail: abupl@abu.edu.ng
Telex: 57241 ZARABU NIG *Cable:* Unibello Press Zaria
Key Personnel
Man Dir, Editorial, Rights & Permissions: Saidu H Adamu
Editorial: George Ibrahim
Production: Oko Sunday
Marketing: Onwuaha I Sunday
Founded: 1974
Publishing & printing.

Subjects: Biography, Education, Environmental Studies, Government, Political Science, History, Law, Literature, Literary Criticism, Essays, Science (General), Social Sciences, Sociology, Sports, Athletics, Technology, Veterinary Science
ISBN Prefix(es): 978-125

Albah Publishers+
136a Ibolo Rd, Bompal-Kano, Kano State
Mailing Address: PO Box 6177, Bompal-Kano, Kano State
Cable: Albah Kano
Key Personnel
Chairman, Editorial: Bashari F Roukbah
Sales & Publicity Manager: Idris A Muhammad
Production: Basiru Ahmad
Founded: 1978
Subjects: Education
ISBN Prefix(es): 978-2380
Parent Company: Elbash Limited
Associate Companies: Brunswick Publishing Co, PO Box 555, Lawrenceville, VA 23868, United States
Subsidiaries: Albah Research Centre
Bookshop(s): Baban Layi, Gyadi-Gyadi, Zariya Rd, Kano

Alliance West African Publishers & Co
Orindingbin Estate, New Aketan Layout, Oyo
Mailing Address: PMB 1039, Oyo
Tel: (085) 230798
Key Personnel
Chairman, Man Dir: Chief M O Ogunmola
Sales: L Oyeniji
Publicity & Permissions: Kehinde Ogunmola
Founded: 1971
Subjects: Biography, Ethnicity, Foreign Countries, History, How-to, Science (General)

Aromolaran Publishing Co Ltd+
Ibadan, Oyo State
Mailing Address: PO Box 1800, Ibadan, Oyo State
Tel: (02) 24392
Telex: 31158NG
Key Personnel
Man Dir: Dr Gabriel Adekunle Aromolaran
Sales: Mrs V M Aromolaran
Founded: 1970
Subjects: Art, Biography, How-to, Poetry, Religion - Other, Science (General)
ISBN Prefix(es): 978-127

Awoko, imprint of Adebara Publishers Ltd

Black Academy Press+
Owerri, Imo State
Mailing Address: PO Box 255, Owerri, Imo State
Tel: (083) 230606; (083) 232606 *Cable:* BAPRESS
Key Personnel
Man Dir: Dr S Okechukwu Mezu
Founded: 1970
Subjects: Biography, History, Nonfiction (General), Poetry
ISBN Prefix(es): 978-150
Parent Company: Mezu International Ltd, 6 Mezu Lane, Owerri, Imo State
Associate Companies: Black Academy Press Inc
Orders to: PO Box 66142, Baltimore, MD 21239, United States

Book Representation & Publishing Co Ltd
Agodi/Loyola College Rd, PMB 5349, Ibadan Oyo State
Tel: (022) 710242
Key Personnel
Executive Chairman, Dir: Chief B A Ajayi
Dirs: Chief M A Ajasin; Chief R F Fasoranti; Chief Funso Afelumo; Chief 'Bola Ige
General Manager: 'Bisi Taiwo

Administrative Manager: A L Salawu
Founded: 1973
Subjects: Education
ISBN Prefix(es): 978-172
Associate Companies: Circle Books Ltd, Ibadan

CEM Publishers Ltd
4 Yemi Ogunniyi St, Ajao Estate, Anthony Village, Lagos
Mailing Address: PO Box 4267, Lagos
ISBN Prefix(es): 978-176

Cross Continent Press Ltd+
PO Box 282, Yaba, Lagos State
Tel: (01) 862437 *Fax:* (01) 685679 *Cable:* Croconpres Yaba, Lagos
Key Personnel
Man Dir: Dr T C Nwosu
Editorial: Prof Theo Vincent
Production: Kess Nwagwu
Publicity: Miss A A Ikeme
Marketing: Miss P N Ikekwem
Sales Coordinator: Dr J O Enwerem
General Consultant: Prof E J Nwosu
Founded: 1974
Subjects: Biography, Fiction, How-to, Nonfiction (General), Poetry
ISBN Prefix(es): 978-134
Parent Company: Tanhigh Holdings Ltd
Associate Companies: Vista Books Ltd
Subsidiaries: Editorial Consultancy & Agency Services
Branch Office(s)
Senator E P Echeruo, Executive Director, PO Box 2273, Owerri, Imo State
Showroom(s): 59 Awolowo Rd, SW Ikoyi, Lagos, Nigeria
Orders to: 59 Awolowo Rd, SW Ikoyi, Lago

CSS Bookshops+
Division of CSS Limited
19 Broad St, Lagos
Mailing Address: PO Box 174, Lagos
Tel: (01) 2633081; (01) 2637009; (01) 2637023; (01) 2633010 *Fax:* (01) 2637089
E-mail: cssbookshops@skannet.com.ng *Cable:* BOOKSHOPS
Key Personnel
Chief Executive: Kola Olaitan
Secretary: Dotun Adegboyega
Subjects: Biography, Ethnicity, Foreign Countries, History, Law, Medicine, Nursing, Dentistry, Nonfiction (General), Religion - Other, Science (General)
ISBN Prefix(es): 978-143; 978-2951; 978-32292

Daily Times of Nigeria Ltd (Publication Division)
3, 5 & 7 Kakawa St, Marina, Lagos
Mailing Address: Lateef Jakande Rd, Agidingbi, PMB, 21340 Ikeja, Lagos
Tel: (01) 4977280 *Fax:* (01) 4977284
Web Site: www.dailytimesofnigeria.com
Telex: 21333 Times Ng *Cable:* Daily Times Lagos
Key Personnel
Chief Executive: Segun Osoba
Editorial: Faruk Mohammed
Sales: Funsho Akindele
Production: J M Teshola
Founded: 1925
Subjects: Foreign Countries
ISBN Prefix(es): 978-144; 978-2171
Subsidiaries: Times Press Ltd; Newsstand Agencies Limited
Book Club(s): Times Book Club

Daystar Press (Publishers)+
Daystar House, Ibadan, Oyo State
Mailing Address: PO Box 1261, Ibadan, Oyo State
Tel: (022) 412670
Telex: 31176
Key Personnel
Man Dir, Editorial, Rights & Permissions & Publicity: Phillip Adelakun Ladokun
Trade: James Akinboye
Marketing: Tunde Felix
Founded: 1962
Subjects: Ethnicity, Health, Nutrition, House & Home, Religion - Other
ISBN Prefix(es): 978-122

Delta Publications (Nigeria) Ltd+
172 Ogui Rd, Enugu, Enugu State
Mailing Address: PO Box 3606, Lagos
Tel: (042) 3606
Key Personnel
Man Dir, Rights & Permissions: C D E Onyeama
Editorial Dir: Mrs E O Onyeama
Sales: Nicholas Ohaekweiro; Ebere Nwadigbo
Production, Publicity: Miss Nwanneka Okwu
Founded: 1982
Subjects: Biography, Fiction
ISBN Prefix(es): 978-2335
Bookshop(s): Enugu Airport Bookshop
Book Club(s): The Delta Book Club

ECWA Productions Ltd
10 Kano Rd, Jos Plateau State
Mailing Address: PMB 2010, Jos Plateau State
Tel: (073) 53897; (073) 52230
Telex: 81120 Ecwap Ng
Key Personnel
Man Dir: Dr Philip S Usman
General Manager, Publications: Jonathan A Babstunde
Challenge Publications is Publishing Division of ECWA Productions Ltd.
Subjects: Education, Religion - Other
ISBN Prefix(es): 978-137
Bookshop(s): Challenge Bookshops

Educational Research & Study Group
Institute of Ed, Univ of Ibadan, c/o Prof. Pai Obanya, Ibadan
Key Personnel
Man Dir: Areoye Oyebola
Founded: 1970
Subjects: Biography, Ethnicity, Foreign Countries, History, How-to, Nonfiction (General), Religion - Other, Science (General), Social Sciences, Sociology
ISBN Prefix(es): 978-30054

Egret Books, *imprint of* Paperback Publishers Ltd

Egret Stars Series, *imprint of* Paperback Publishers Ltd

Ethiope Publishing Corporation+
34 Murtala Mohammed St, Benin City, Edo State
Mailing Address: PMB 1192, Benin City, Edo State
Tel: (052) 253036
Telex: 41110NG *Cable:* Ethiope
Key Personnel
Sole Administrator: Rev P O Ross-Imienwanrin
Founded: 1970
Subjects: Fiction, Foreign Countries, History, Law, Social Sciences, Sociology
ISBN Prefix(es): 978-123
Total Titles: 55 Print

Evans Brothers (Nigeria Publishers) Ltd
Jericho Rd, Ibadan
Mailing Address: PMB 5164, Ibadan
Tel: (022) 417570; (022) 417601; (022) 407626
Telex: 31104 Edbook *Cable:* EDBOOKS IBADAN
Key Personnel
Man Dir: B O Bolodeoku
Sales Dir: S A Oke
General Manager: V A Aladejana
Founded: 1966
Membership(s): Nigerian Publishers Association (NPA).
Subjects: Accounting, Agriculture, Child Care & Development, Civil Engineering, Drama, Theater, Economics, Education, Electronics, Electrical Engineering, Environmental Studies, Fiction, Geography, Geology, Government, Political Science, History, Journalism, Law, Literature, Literary Criticism, Essays, Management, Mathematics, Medicine, Nursing, Dentistry, Philosophy, Romance, Science (General), Self-Help, Social Sciences, Sociology, Sports, Athletics, Technology
ISBN Prefix(es): 978-167; 978-020
Associate Companies: Evans Brothers Ltd, UK, United Kingdom
Branch Office(s)
Kaduna
Lagos
Owerri

Olaiya Fagbamigbe Ltd (Publishers)
Agodi Gate, 11 Methodist Church Rd, Akure
Mailing Address: PO Box 1176, Agodi Gate, Ibadan
Tel: (034) 2075 *Cable:* Fagbamigbe Akure
Key Personnel
Man Dir: Mrs M E Fagbamigbe
Editor: Yemi Fagbamigbe
Publicity: Gbenga Fagbamigbe
Rights & Permissions: Yetunde Fagbamigbe
Founded: 1976
Specialize in children's books, novels & textbooks.
Subjects: Education
ISBN Prefix(es): 978-164
Warehouse: New Ife Rd, PO Box 1176, Agodi Gate, Ibadan

Fountain Series, *imprint of* Paperback Publishers Ltd

Fourth-Dimension Publishers, *imprint of* Fourth Dimension Publishing Co Ltd

Fourth Dimension Publishing Co Ltd+
Fourth Dimension Plaza, 16 Fifth Ave, City Layout, PMB 01164, Enugu 400001
Tel: (042) 459969 *Fax:* (042) 456904
E-mail: info@fdpbooks.com; fdpbook@aol.com
Web Site: www.fdpbooks.com
Key Personnel
Chief Executive & Rights & Permissions: Mrs Oby Nwankwo
General Manager: Jeremiah O Udochu
E-mail: jerryudochu@yahoo.com
Publishing & Editorial: Eva Igwilo
Production: Carolene Okorafor
Founded: 1976
Membership(s): Nigerian Publishers' Association (NPA); African Publishers' Network (APNET); Nigerian Book Foundation (NBF); International Publishers' Association (IPA).
Subjects: Biography, Business, Cookery, Education, Fiction, Government, Political Science, Law, Social Sciences, Sociology
ISBN Prefix(es): 978-156
Number of titles published annually: 100 Print
Total Titles: 1,555 Print
Imprints: Fourth-Dimension Publishers
Foreign Rep(s): African Books Collective Ltd (Europe, USA)
Foreign Rights: African Books Collective Ltd (Europe, USA)
Showroom(s): ABC Ltd, 27 Park End St, Oxford OX1 1HU, United Kingdom, Contact: Justin Cox
Warehouse: ABC Ltd, Unite 3, Off Pytts Lane, Burford, Oxon OX18 4SJ, United Kingdom, Contact: Mary Jay

Distribution Center: World Bank Publishers, Marketing Division (Nigeria)
Orders to: ABC Ltd, 27 Park End St, Oxford OX1 1HU, United Kingdom

Gangan, *imprint of* Adebara Publishers Ltd

Gbabeks Publishers Ltd
L16 Ibadan St, Kaduna
Mailing Address: PO Box 3538, Kaduna, Kaduna State
Tel: (062) 217976
Key Personnel
Man Dir: Tayo Ogunbekun
Founded: 1982
Membership(s): National Publishers Association.
Subjects: Education, Language Arts, Linguistics, Science (General), Social Sciences, Sociology
ISBN Prefix(es): 978-2416

Goldland Business Co Ltd+
85 Saint Finbarrs College Rd, Akoka, Lagos
Mailing Address: PO Box 2541, Yaba, Lagos
Tel: (01) 8023179087; (01) 821203
E-mail: goldland@consultant.com
Key Personnel
Author & International Rights Contact: Dr Jonathan A O Ifechukwu
Founded: 1982
Business consultants, researchers, trainers & publishers
Specialize in publishing books in business & related fields.
Subjects: Business, Finance, Government, Political Science, How-to, Management, Marketing, Technology
ISBN Prefix(es): 978-30035
Number of titles published annually: 1 Print
Total Titles: 8 Print

Heritage Books+
2-8 Calcutta Crescent, Gate 1, 101251 Apapa, Lagos
Mailing Address: PO Box 610, 101251 Apapa, Lagos
Tel: (01) 5871333; (01) 5871333
E-mail: obw@infoweb.abs.net
Key Personnel
Editor: Naiwu Osahon
Senior Editor, Rights & Permissions: Bakin Kunama
Publicity: Edia Apolo
Founded: 1971
Subjects: Ethnicity, Fiction, Nonfiction (General), Poetry, Pan-Africanism
ISBN Prefix(es): 978-2358
Associate Companies: Third World First Publications
Imprints: Heritage Series; Obobo Series; Oyoyo Series
Subsidiaries: Obobo Books
Bookshop(s): Heritage (The Bookshop), PO Box 930, 101251 Apapa, Lagos *Tel:* (01) 5871 333 *E-mail:* obw@infoweb.abs.net

Heritage Series, *imprint of* Heritage Books

Hudanuda Publishing Co Ltd+
PO Box 984, Zaria, Kaduna State
Tel: (069) 5141
Key Personnel
Man Dir: Abdullahi Khalil
Founded: 1981
Membership(s): Nigerian Publishers Association (NPA).
Subjects: Literature, Literary Criticism, Essays
ISBN Prefix(es): 978-2368
Associate Companies: Hodder & Stoughton Publishers, Mill Rd, Dunton Green, Sevenoaks, Kent TN13 2YA, United Kingdom

Branch Office(s)
Islamic Publsihing Co, Kukuru Byepass, Jos
Dal Arabia Publishing Co Ltd, Kano
Showroom(s): Zangon Shanu, Samaru, Zaria
Bookshop(s): No 28 Sobon Gari, Zaria
Warehouse: Zangon Shanu, PO Box 984, Zaria, Kaduna State

Ibadan University Press+
PMB 16, University of Ibadan Post Office, Ibadan
Tel: (022) 400550; (022) 400614 (ext 1244, 1042, 1032, 1093) *Cable:* Univpress Ibadan
Key Personnel
Head of Marketing: Bisi Ogunleye
Founded: 1952
Subjects: Agriculture, Ethnicity, Foreign Countries, History, Law, Medicine, Nursing, Dentistry, Philosophy, Psychology, Psychiatry, Science (General), Social Sciences, Sociology, Technology
ISBN Prefix(es): 978-121

Institute of African Studies, Onyeka, A
University of Nigeria, Nsukka
Tel: (022) 400550; (022) 400614 (ext 12444)
Key Personnel
Dir, Editorial, Rights & Permissions: Prof Bolanle Awe
Editorial, Sales, Production: Dele Layiwola
Founded: 1962
Subjects: Ethnicity
ISBN Prefix(es): 978-2450; 978-31426

International Publishing & Research Company+
PO Box 1210, Festac City, Lagos
Tel: (080) 2317-5915 *Fax:* (080) 4213 2351
Key Personnel
Executive Chairman: Dr M J A Iginla
Founded: 1990
Subjects: Developing Countries, Government, Political Science, Philosophy, Publishing & Book Trade Reference, Social Sciences, Sociology, Women's Studies
ISBN Prefix(es): 978-30855; 978-2438
Parent Company: Ipreco Group of Companies
Subsidiaries: Unity Publishing & Research Co Ltd
Shipping Address: 711 Road B Close, H 33 Festac City, Lagos

JAD Publishers Ltd+
40 Adamson St, Keta, Victoria Island, Lagos
Mailing Address: PO Box 72320, Victoria Island, Lagos
Founded: 1989
Subjects: Behavioral Sciences, Biography, Biological Sciences, Developing Countries, Economics, Environmental Studies, Government, Political Science, History, Law, Mathematics, Social Sciences, Sociology
ISBN Prefix(es): 978-2863

Kakaki, *imprint of* Adebara Publishers Ltd

Kola Sanya Publishing Enterprise
2 Epe Rd, Oke-Owa, Ijebu-Ode
Mailing Address: PMB 2099, Ijebu-Ode
Tel: (037) 432638
Key Personnel
Man Dir: Chief K Osunsanya
Subjects: How-to, Nonfiction (General), Science (General)
ISBN Prefix(es): 978-171

Lantern Books, *imprint of* Literamed Publications Nigeria Ltd

Literamed Publications Nigeria Ltd+
Plot 45, Alausa Bus Stop, Oregun Rd, PMB 1068, Ikeja
Tel: (01) 4962512; (01) 4935258 *Fax:* (01) 4972217
E-mail: information@lanternbooks.com
Web Site: www.lantern-books.com
Key Personnel
Production Mgr: M O Dawodu
Publishing Director: L A Aladesuyi
Finance Director: S O Ayorinde
Founded: 1969
Membership(s): the Nigeria Publishers Association (NPA).
Subjects: Education, Government, Political Science, Social Sciences, Sociology
ISBN Prefix(es): 978-142
Number of titles published annually: 25 Print
Total Titles: 120 Print
Imprints: Lantern Books

Longman Nigeria Plc
52 Oba Akran Ave, PMB 21036, Ikeja, Lagos State
Tel: (01) 497 89259 *Fax:* (01) 496 4370
E-mail: longman@infoweb.abs.net
Telex: 26639 longman ng *Cable:* Longman Ikeja
Key Personnel
Man Dir & Chief Executive: Abiodun Olowoniyi
Executive Dir (Northern Area Operations): Alhaji Musa Halliru
Deputy Chief Executive: Azed Echebiri
Marketing Dir: Dan Obidiegwu
Founded: 1961
Subjects: Biography, Ethnicity, Fiction, History, Nonfiction (General), Poetry, Psychology, Psychiatry, Religion - Other, Science (General), Social Sciences, Sociology, Technology
ISBN Prefix(es): 978-139

Merryland, *imprint of* Joe-Tolalu & Associates

Thomas Nelson (Nigeria) Ltd+
8 Ilupeju Bypass, Ikeja Lagos
Mailing Address: PMB 1303, Ileja Lagos
Tel: (01) 961452
Telex: 26736 *Cable:* NELPITMAN IKEJA
Key Personnel
Executive Chairman Chief: C O Taiwo
General Manager: A Fasemore
Marketing Dir: L Solarin
Editor, Science: M O Omotoye
Editor, Humanities: F O Bada
Founded: 1965
Also acts as publishers for (NERDC) Nigerian Education Research & Development Council & the University of Lagos Press.
Subjects: Fiction, Nonfiction (General), Science (General), Social Sciences, Sociology
ISBN Prefix(es): 978-126
Parent Company: The Thomson Corp, Toronto Dominion Bank Tower, Suite 2706, PO Box 24, Toronto Dominion Centre, Toronto, ON M5K 1A1, Canada
Associate Companies: University Publishing Co
Branch Office(s)
Edo Textile Mills Rd, Benin City, Edo State
120, Orlu Rd, Owerri 3

New Africa Publishing Company Ltd
PO Box 1178, Owerri, Imo State
Tel: (083) 231891
Key Personnel
Chairman & Man Dir: H K Offonry
Dir: S O Igwe; B E Ogbuagu
Founded: 1981
Subjects: Art, Biography, Business, Education, Finance, Human Relations, Humor, Law, Management
ISBN Prefix(es): 978-2357

New Era Publishers+
PO Box 27720, Agodi, Ibadan
Tel: (022) 715706
Key Personnel
Executive Chairman: Prof O Imoagene
Founded: 1991
Also acts as consultants.
Subjects: Fiction, Science (General)
ISBN Prefix(es): 978-2853
Parent Company: New-Era Holdings Ltd
Associate Companies: New-Era Equippers; Petro-Allied Services Ltd
Subsidiaries: New-Era Consultants Ltd
Distributed by Africa Book Centre (UK)

New Horn Press Ltd
Olatunbosun Rd, Sharp Corner, Oke Bola, Ibadan
Mailing Address: PO Box 4138, Ibadan
Tel: (02) 41 29 72
Key Personnel
Chairman: Dr Abiola Irele
Senior Editor, Rights & Permissions: Mrs Bassey Irele
Founded: 1974
Subjects: Fiction, How-to, Nonfiction (General), Poetry
ISBN Prefix(es): 978-2266

Nigerian Environmental Study Team
Oluokun St, Bodija, Ibadan
Mailing Address: University of Ibadan, PO Box 5297, Ibadan
Tel: (02) 8102644; (02) 8105167 *Fax:* (02) 8102644
E-mail: nesting@nest.org.ng
ISBN Prefix(es): 978-31203

Nigerian Institute of Advanced Legal Studies
University of Lagos Campus, Akoka, PMB 12820, Lagos
Tel: (01) 821752; (01) 821711; (01) 821753 *Fax:* (01) 497 6076; (01) 825558; (09) 234 6505
Telex: 27506
Subjects: Law
ISBN Prefix(es): 978-31963

Nigerian Institute of International Affairs
13/15 Kofo Abayomi Rd, Victoria Island, Lagos
Mailing Address: GPO Box 1727, Lagos
Tel: (01) 61 56 06; (01) 61 56 07; (01) 61 56 09; (01) 61 56 10 *Fax:* (01) 61 64 04; (01) 61 63 60
E-mail: niia@ric.nig.com
Telex: 22638 *Cable:* INTERNATIONS LAGOS
Key Personnel
Ag Dir-General Editorial: Prof R A Akindele
Editorial: Dr Bola Akinterinwa; Prof Bassey Ate; Dr Cyril Obi; Dr R O Olaniyan
Marketing & Sales: E A Ude
Founded: 1961 (Established as an independent, nonofficial, nonpolitical & nonprofit making organization. In Aug 1991, the Institute taken over by the Nigerian govern)
Encourage & facilitate the understanding of international affairs; circumstances, conditions & attitudes of foreign countries & their people. Provide & disseminate information upon international questions, as we also promote the study & investigation of such international questions through such fora as conferences, lectures, discussions, to compliment our publications, journals & records.
Subjects: Economics, Law
ISBN Prefix(es): 978-2276
Imprints: African Books Collective Ltd

Nigerian Trade Review
10, Makinde St, Alausa, Ikeja, Lagos State
Mailing Address: PO Box 427, Ikeja, Lagos State
Tel: (01) 961147

Key Personnel
Man Dir: Chief P A Dawodu
Founded: 1958
ISBN Prefix(es): 978-2242

Northern Nigerian Publishing Co Ltd+
Gaskiya Bldg, Zaria, Kaduna State
Mailing Address: PO Box 412, Zaria, Kaduna State
Tel: (069) 32087
Telex: 75243
Key Personnel
Man Dir: Hussain Hayat
Man Editor: Muhammad Abubakar
Marketing Manager: Aliyu Haruna
Sales Manager: Johanna Madaki
Founded: 1966
Membership(s): Nigerian Publishers Association.
Subjects: Nonfiction (General), Poetry, Regional Interests, Religion - Other
ISBN Prefix(es): 978-169
Parent Company: Gaskiya Corp Ltd
Branch Office(s)
Kano, Kaduna & Jos

NPS Educational Publishers Ltd (Nigeria Publishers Services)+
South West Ring Rd, off Akinyemi Way, Ibadan
Mailing Address: PO Box 62, Ibadan
Tel: (02) 2316006; (803) 370-0838
Key Personnel
Chairman & Man Dir: Chief Duro Otesanya
General Manager: Dr Isaac Muyiwa-Ojo
Also distributors.
Membership(s): Nigeria Publishers Association.
Subjects: Mathematics, Science (General)
ISBN Prefix(es): 978-2556
Number of titles published annually: 13 Print
Total Titles: 32 Print
Branch Office(s)
37A Omeagana St, off Modebe Ave, PO Box 4073, Onitsha *Tel:* (046) 413774
BB2 Old Jos Rd, PO Box 722, Zaria *Tel:* (069) 34170

Nwamife Publishers Ltd+
10, Ibiam St, Uwani, Enugu, Anambra State
Tel: (042) 338454 *Cable:* Nwamife Enugu
Key Personnel
Chairman: Dr Felix C Adi
Sales, Production, Publicity: Samuel Umesike
Editorial, Rights & Permissions: Dr Nina Mba
Founded: 1970
Subjects: Biography, Education, Ethnicity, Fiction, History, How-to, Law, Nonfiction (General), Poetry, Science (General)
ISBN Prefix(es): 978-124

Obafemi Awolowo University Press Ltd+
Obafemi Awolowo University, Ile-Ife, Oyo State
Mailing Address: PMB 004, OAU Post Office, Ile-Ife
Tel: (036) 230290-9; (036) 230284
Telex: AVPL *Cable:* PRESS AWOVARSITY
Key Personnel
General Manager: Akin Fatokun
Editorial: Stephen Eyeh
Production: Isola Akinremi
Marketing: T A Kudoro
Founded: 1968
Specializes in professional texts.
Membership(s): International Publishers Association; National Publishers Association.
Subjects: Biography, Education, Ethnicity, History, Law, Medicine, Nursing, Dentistry, Philosophy, Religion - Other, Social Sciences, Sociology
ISBN Prefix(es): 987-136
Number of titles published annually: 6 Print
Total Titles: 100 Print
Foreign Rep(s): ABC London (Europe, USA)

Obobo Books+
2/8 Calcutta Crescent, Gate 4, Apapa, 101251 Lagos
Mailing Address: PO Box 610, Apapa, 101251 Lagos
Tel: (01) 871333; (01) 875389
E-mail: obw@infoweb.abs.net
Key Personnel
Chief Executive: Ms Osahon Obobo
Editorial: Bakin Kunama
Sales, Publicity: Edia Apolo
Production: Edun Osahon
Founded: 1981
Also produce the television program *Obobo Playhouse*.
Subjects: Biography, Fiction, History, Coloring books
ISBN Prefix(es): 978-186
Number of titles published annually: 3 Print
Total Titles: 106 Print
Parent Company: Heritage Books, 2, Culcutta Crescent, Gate 4, PO Box 610 Apapa, 101251 Lagos
Associate Companies: Third World First Publications
Bookshop(s): Heritage, PO Box 930, 2-8 Calcutta Crescent, Gate 1, Apapa, 101251 Lagos

Obobo Series, *imprint of* Heritage Books

Ogunsanya Press, Publishers and Bookstores Ltd
64, Agbeni St, Ibadan
Mailing Address: PO Box 95, Ibadan
Tel: (022) 310924 *Cable:* Pombapress
Key Personnel
Man Dir, Editorial, Rights & Permissions: Chief Lucas Justus Popo-Ola Ogunsanya
Sales & Publicity: E A Faleke
Production: A S Banjo
Founded: 1970
Subjects: Geography, Geology, History, Language Arts, Linguistics, Mathematics, Science (General), Social Sciences, Sociology
ISBN Prefix(es): 978-170
Branch Office(s)
Popo-Ola Jubilee Lodge, Oke Imoru, PO Box 155, Ijebu Ode, Ogun State

Onibon-Oje Publishers
Felele Layout, Molete, Ibadan
Mailing Address: PO Box 3109, Ibadan
Tel: (022) 313956
Telex: 31657 Bonoje NG
Key Personnel
Chairman: Gabriel Onibonoje
Man Dir: J Olu Onibonoje
Founded: 1958
Subjects: Biography, Ethnicity, Fiction, Foreign Countries, History, How-to, Nonfiction (General), Poetry, Religion - Other, Science (General), Social Sciences, Sociology
ISBN Prefix(es): 978-145
Branch Office(s)
Benin City
Jos
Kano
Lagos
Onitsha
Sokoto
Zaria
Ikot Ekpene
Bookshop(s): SW8/77 Oke-Ado, Ibadan
Book Club(s): Onibonoje Book Club

Opatoki Press, *imprint of* Abisega Publishers (Nigeria) Ltd

Oyoyo Series, *imprint of* Heritage Books

PUBLISHERS

NIGERIA

Paperback Publishers Ltd+
Alafin Ave, Plot 7, Block 10, Oluyole Estate, SW, Ring Rd, Ibadan
Mailing Address: UI PO Box 14470, Ibadan
Tel: (022) 317363
Key Personnel
Man Dir: Agbo Areo
Sales Dir: S G Oyetunde
Founded: 1985
Membership(s): the Nigerian Publishers Association.
Subjects: Education, Fiction
ISBN Prefix(es): 978-2432
Imprints: Egret Books; Fountain Series; Egret Stars Series
Branch Office(s)
Dayspring House, 15 Ogunsefunmi Str, Anifowose IKEJA

Riverside Communications+
100C Elelenwo, GRA Phase 1, Port Harcourt, Rivers State
Mailing Address: PO Box 7390, Port Harcourt, Rivers State
Tel: (084) 334042 *Fax:* (084) 334042
E-mail: isoun@aol.com; rvsdcom@aol.com
Key Personnel
President: Prof T T Isoun
Executive Dir: Miriam Isoun
Founded: 1987
Subjects: Anthropology, Biological Sciences, Chemistry, Chemical Engineering, Cookery, Developing Countries, Environmental Studies, History, Language Arts, Linguistics, Mathematics, Medicine, Nursing, Dentistry, Nonfiction (General), Religion - Catholic, Religion - Protestant, Science (General), Veterinary Science
ISBN Prefix(es): 978-31226; 978-30333
Parent Company: Riverside Biotech Nigeria Limited 100
U.S. Office(s): Riverside Communications, 5575 Seminary Rd, No 104, Falls Church, VA 22041, United States, Contact: Miriam Isoun
E-mail: isoun@aol.com

Saros International Publishers
24, Aggrey Rd, Port-Harcourt
Mailing Address: PO Box 193, Port-Harcourt
Tel: (084) 331763 *Fax:* (084) 331763
Key Personnel
Publisher: Ken Saro-Wiwa
Founded: 1985
Subjects: Drama, Theater, Fiction, Literature, Literary Criticism, Essays, Poetry
ISBN Prefix(es): 978-2460
Orders to: African Books Collective Ltd, The Jam Factory, 27 Park End St, Oxford OX1 1KU, United Kingdom

Spectrum Books Ltd+
Ring Rd, Spectrum House, Ibadan
Mailing Address: PO Box 1319, Ibadan
Tel: (02) 2310058; (02) 2311215; (02) 2312705 *Fax:* (02) 2312705; (02) 2318502
E-mail: admin1@spectrumbooksonline.com
Web Site: www.spectrumbooksonline.com
Key Personnel
Chief Executive: Joop Berkhout
Editorial: Tony Igboekwe
Sales & Publicity: Edgman Igbinosun
Founded: 1978
Subjects: Education, Fiction
ISBN Prefix(es): 978-029
Associate Companies: Safari Books (Export) Ltd, 17 Bond St, 1st Floor, St Helier, Jersey, Channel Islands, United Kingdom
Distributed by ABC Oxford

Tabansi Press Ltd+
135 Awka Rd, Onitsha, Anambra State
Mailing Address: PO Box 243, Onitsha, Anambra State
Tel: (046) 211661; 08033243783; 08033418218
Key Personnel
Chief Executive: F N Tabansi
Deputy Chief Executive: P O Tabansi
Editor: Angus Abalum
Author: M O Odiaka
Founded: 1955
Printer & publisher. Specialize in educational book publishing.
Subjects: Government, Political Science, Religion - Other, Science (General), Social Sciences, Sociology
Number of titles published annually: 50,000 Print
Total Titles: 2,500,000 Print

Tana Press Ltd & Flora Nwapa Books Ltd+
2A, Menkiti Lane, Ogui, Enugu
Mailing Address: PO Box 62, Enugu
Tel: (042) 338857
Telex: 51164 Lake NG *Cable:* TANA
Key Personnel
Man Dir, nee Nwapa: Flora Nwakuche
Editorial: Dipl Ing Nina Mba
Production: E N Benyeogo; M A Ubah
Founded: 1979
Rights & Permissions: Tana Press, Ltd, Books Ltd.
Subjects: Fiction
ISBN Prefix(es): 978-2272
Branch Office(s)
PO Box 2, Oguta, Imo State
Warehouse: 22 Mbanugo, St Ogbete, Enugu
Orders to: Nigerian Publishers Services Ltd, Trusthouse, PO Box 62, Ibadan
Three Continents Press, 1346 Connecticut Ave NW, Washington, DC 20036, United States

Joe-Tolalu & Associates+
PO Box 3333, Mapo Post Office, Ibadan, Oyo State
Tel: (01) 4925078
Key Personnel
Man Dir: Tosin Awolalu
Founded: 1983
Also acts as literary agent & publishing consultant.
Subjects: Biography, Humor, Religion - Other, Travel
ISBN Prefix(es): 978-2415
Imprints: Merryland
Subsidiaries: Interprint Services
Divisions: Booktrust
Distributor for Delphi Publications; New Pen Publishing; Pelins Ltd

University of Lagos Press+
PO Box 132, Unilag PO, Akoka, Lagos
Tel: (01) 825048 *Fax:* (01) 825048
Telex: 21210 *Cable:* UNILAG PRESS, LAGOS
Key Personnel
Dir: Mrs B A Awere
Editor: Bukola Olugasa *E-mail:* bukiolu@yahoo.com
Founded: 1980
Europe & UK.
Subjects: Biography, Education, Ethnicity, Foreign Countries, Human Relations, Law, Medicine, Nursing, Dentistry, Social Sciences, Sociology
ISBN Prefix(es): 978-2264; 978-017
Distributed by African Books Collective
Showroom(s): Marketing Unit, Commercial Rd, Unilag Akoka, Yaba, Lagos

University Publishing Co+
11, Central School Rd, Onitsha
Mailing Address: PO Box 386, Onitsha
Tel: (046) 230013 *Cable:* Varsity Box 386 Onitsha
Key Personnel
Dir: F C Ogbalu; W C Ifezue
Editorial: J Oranyeludike
Sales: D O Dandy
Production: I Nweke
Publicity: Christian Ogbalu
Permissions: Cecilia Ogbalu
Founded: 1959
Subjects: Biography, Ethnicity, Foreign Countries, History, Nonfiction (General), Philosophy, Poetry, Religion - Other
ISBN Prefix(es): 978-160
Associate Companies: Cynako International Press, Aba; Thomas Nelson (Nigeria) Ltd; African Literature Bureau, Aba
Branch Office(s)
Azikiwe Rd, Aba
Varsity Bookshop/Press, Oye Agu Junction, Abagana, Njikoka LGA
Afor Igwe, Ogidi
Oye Olisa Ogbunike, Onitsha-Enugu Rd, Awka
Eke-Amawbia, Awka
64 New Market Rd, Onitsha
Bookshop(s): Varsity Bookshop/Press at: Oye-Agu, Abagana, Njikoka LGA; Eke-Amawbia, Amawbia, Awka LGA; Aba; Abiriba, Ohafia LGA
Orders to: Varisty Bookshop, 64 New Market Rd, Onitsha

Vantage Publishers International Ltd+
98A Samonda, Old Airport Area, Ibadan, Oyo State
Mailing Address: PO Box 7669 Secretariat PO, Ibadan
Tel: (022) 415341
Key Personnel
Chairman & Publisher: Mr 'Poju Amori
Executive Dir: Mr Adewale Abiodun Amori
Founded: 1983
Membership(s): International Scholary Publishers; Specialize in scholarly journals for Research Institutes & Faculty of Law & Publishing (editorial & production consulting).
Subjects: Biblical Studies, Biography, Biological Sciences, Business, Drama, Theater, Education, English as a Second Language, Fiction, Government, Political Science, Language Arts, Linguistics, Literature, Literary Criticism, Essays, Nonfiction (General), Poetry, Public Administration, Religion - Protestant, Social Sciences, Sociology
ISBN Prefix(es): 978-2458
Subsidiaries: Vantage Paper & Stationeries
Divisions: Vantage Productions
Bookshop(s): 98A Airport Area, Ibadan, Oyo State

West African Book Publishers Ltd+
One Babalola St, Mushin, Lagos
Mailing Address: Ilupeju Industrial Estate, PO Box 3445, Lagos
Tel: (01) 960760; (01) 960764; (01) 825020; (01) 526616 *Fax:* (01) 619835
Telex: 26144 *Cable:* ACADPRESS
Key Personnel
Chairman: B A Idris Animashaun
Dir: Mrs A O Obadagbonyi
Editor: H O Mazi
Founded: 1967
Subjects: Advertising, Agriculture, Chemistry, Chemical Engineering, Child Care & Development, Economics, Geography, Geology, Government, Political Science, Human Relations, Mathematics, Science (General)
ISBN Prefix(es): 978-153; 978-31973
Associate Companies: Academy Computers LTD; Academy Press PLC; Lithotec LTD; Richware Pottery LTD

John West Publications Co Ltd+
Acme Rd, Lagos
Mailing Address: PO Box 2416, Lagos
Tel: (01) 932011

Telex: 26446 wepal ng *Cable:* JAKPRESS
Founded: 1962
Subjects: Biography, How-to, Nonfiction (General)
ISBN Prefix(es): 978-163

Norway

General Information

Capital: Oslo
Language: Norwegian. There are two distinct forms, Bokmal (sometimes called Riksmal) and Nynorsk (formerly called Landsmal) whose relative importance has changed in recent years. About 90% of Norwegian books are now published in Bokmal and it is the medium of instruction in most schools. Danish and Swedish are usually intelligible to speakers of Norwegian
Religion: Predominantly Evangelical Lutheran
Population: 4.3 million
Bank Hours: 0830-1530 Monday-Friday; 0830-1500 (summer)
Shop Hours: 0830 or 0900-1700 or 1800 Monday-Friday; 0830 or 0900-1400 or 1600 Saturday
Currency: 100 ore = 1 Norwegian krone
Export/Import Information: Member of the European Free Trade Association. No tariff on books except children's picture books. Books exempt from VAT. No duty on advertising. No import license required. Nominal exchange controls.
Copyright: UCC, Berne, Florence (see Copyright Conventions, pg xi)

Altera Forlag A/S
Postboks 2657, St Hanshaugen, 0131 Oslo
Tel: 22569590 *Fax:* 22565088
ISBN Prefix(es): 82-7608; 82-90494; 82-990826

Andresen & Butenschon AS+
Tollbugt 3, 0107 Sentrum, Oslo
Mailing Address: PO Box 1153, 0107 Sentrum, Oslo
Tel: (047) 23139240 *Fax:* (047) 22335805
E-mail: abforlag@abforlag.no
Key Personnel
Man Dir: Sverre Morkhagen
Publisher: Hans B Butenschon *E-mail:* hb@abforlag.no
Founded: 1992
Subjects: Antiques, Architecture & Interior Design, Art, Biography, History, How-to, Cultural Heritage
ISBN Prefix(es): 82-7694; 82-91004
Number of titles published annually: 25 Print
Total Titles: 150 Print
Distribution Center: Sentraldistribusjon ANS, O Aker vei 61, 0581 Oslo

Ansgarboker, *imprint of* Atheneum Forlag A/S

Ariel Lydbokforlag+
Postboks 1546 Vika, 0117 Oslo
Tel: 64943510 *Fax:* 64943510
Key Personnel
Chief Editor: Inger Schjoldager
Founded: 1988
Subjects: Education, Fiction, Poetry
ISBN Prefix(es): 82-7509

Aschehoug Forlag
Sehestedsgate 3, 0102 Oslo
Mailing Address: PO Box 363 Sentrum, 0102 Oslo
Tel: 22400400 *Fax:* 22206395
E-mail: epost@aschehoug.no
Web Site: www.aschehoug.no
Subjects: Antiques, Architecture & Interior Design, Art, Business, Child Care & Development, Economics, Education, Fiction, Gardening, Plants, Health, Nutrition, History, How-to, Language Arts, Linguistics, Law, Mathematics, Philosophy, Poetry, Science (General), Self-Help, Social Sciences, Sociology, Travel
Parent Company: H Aschehoug & Co (W Nygaard) A/S

H Aschehoug & Co (W Nygaard) A/S
Sehestedsgate 3, 0164 Oslo
Mailing Address: PO Box 363, Sentrum, 0102 Oslo
Tel: 22400400 *Fax:* 22206395
E-mail: epost@aschehoug.no
Web Site: www.aschehoug.no *Cable:* ACO OSLO
Key Personnel
Man Dir & Publr: William Nygaard
Dir: Erik Holst
Dir, School Book Dept: Kari-Anne Haugen
Editorial: Marit Notaker; Irja Thorenfeldt
Rights & Permissions: Ivar Havnevik
Founded: 1872
Subjects: Antiques, Architecture & Interior Design, Art, Business, Child Care & Development, Economics, Education, Fiction, Gardening, Plants, Health, Nutrition, How-to, Language Arts, Linguistics, Law, Mathematics, Philosophy, Poetry, Science (General), Science Fiction, Fantasy, Self-Help, Social Sciences, Sociology, Travel
ISBN Prefix(es): 82-03
Subsidiaries: Kunnskapsforlaget I/S (jointly owned with Gyldendal Norsk Forlag); Olaf Norlis Bokhandel A/S (jointly owned with Norake Skog A/S); Tano A/S Forlaget; Kirkelig Kulturverksted A/S; Universitetsforlaget A/S; Yrkesopplaring ANS; Oktober Forlag A/S; Lydbokforlaget A/S
Book Club(s): Den Norske Bokklubben A/S (with three other Norwegian publishers)

Atheneum Forlag A/S+
Mollerveien 4, 0182 Oslo
Tel: 23292072; 23291900 *Fax:* 23291901
Key Personnel
Executive Dir, Publisher, Rights & Permissions: Svenn Otto Brechan
Founded: 1934
Subjects: Art, Biography, Fiction, Poetry, Psychology, Psychiatry, Religion - Other
ISBN Prefix(es): 82-503; 82-7334
Associate Companies: Ansgarboker
Imprints: Ansgarboker
Warehouse: Ansgar/Atheneum, Nesset, 1433 Vinterbro

Bedriftsokonomens Forlag A/S, see Cappelen akademisk forlag

Bladkompaniet A/S+
Apotedergaten 12, 0180 Oslo
Mailing Address: Postboks 6974, St Olavs plass, 0130 Oslo
Tel: 24 14 68 00 *Fax:* 24 14 68 01
E-mail: bladkompaniet@bladkompaniet.no
Web Site: www.bladkompaniet.no
Key Personnel
Man Dir: Tor Erik Solberg
Administration Coordinator: Gro Gundersen
Secretary: Inger Lise Lovasen
Founded: 1915
Subjects: Fiction
ISBN Prefix(es): 82-509

F Bruns Bokhandel og Forlag A/S
Kongensgate 10, 7484 Trondheim
Tel: 73510022; 73509320 *Fax:* 73509320
E-mail: brunslb@online.no
Key Personnel
Dir: Fridthjov Brun
Founded: 1873
Subjects: Science (General), Technology
ISBN Prefix(es): 82-7028

Cappelen akademisk forlag
Formerly Bedriftsokonomens Forlag A/S
Postboks 9047, Groenland, 0133 Oslo
Tel: 22985800 *Fax:* 22985841
Web Site: www.cappelen.no/main/info.asp
Key Personnel
Man Dir: Kai Solheim
Subjects: Economics, Management, Nonfiction (General)
ISBN Prefix(es): 82-7037; 82-456

J W Cappelens Forlag A/S
Mariboesgt 13, 0183 Oslo
Mailing Address: Postboks 350, Sentrum, 0101 Oslo
Tel: (022) 365000 *Fax:* (022) 365040
E-mail: web@cappelen.no
Web Site: www.cappelen.no *Cable:* CAPPELEN
Key Personnel
Chairman: Sigmund Stromme
Man Dir: Sindre Guldvog
Editorial: Per Glad; Aase Gjerdrum; Tove Storsveel; Anders Heger; Ola Haugen
Sales: Kirsti Soegstad
Production: Kjell Nordahl
Rights & Permissions: Kirsten Lier
Editorial: Jan O Bruvik
Founded: 1829
Subjects: Fiction, Nonfiction (General), Religion - Other
ISBN Prefix(es): 82-02
Parent Company: Albert Bonniers Foerlag AB, Sweden
Subsidiaries: Bedriftsoekonomens Forlag A/S; Boksenteret A/S; Aventura Forlag A/S; Chr Grondahls Forlag A/S; Sentraldistribusson ANS
Book Club(s): Den Norske Bokklubben A/S (with three other Norwegian publishers)

Credo, *imprint of* Genesis Forlag

N W Damm og Son A/S
Fridtjof Nansens vei 14, 0055 Oslo
Tel: 24 05 10 00 *Fax:* 24 05 10 99
E-mail: post@egmont.no
Web Site: www.damm.no
Key Personnel
Man Dir: Tom H Jenssen *E-mail:* tom.harald.jenssen@damm.no
Founded: 1845
Subjects: Fiction, Nonfiction (General)
ISBN Prefix(es): 82-517
Parent Company: Egmont Group, Copenhagen, Denmark

Det Norske Samlaget+
JensBjelkes gate 12, 0506 Oslo
Tel: (022) 70 78 00 *Fax:* (022) 68 75 02
E-mail: det.norske@samlaget.no
Web Site: www.samlaget.no
Key Personnel
Man Dir: Audun Heskestad
Editorial, Rights & Permissions: Nina Refseth
Sales: Sjur Mossige
Production: Olav Stokkmo
Founded: 1868
Membership(s): Den norske Forleggerforening.
Subjects: Biography, Cookery, Education, Fiction, History, Humor, Literature, Literary Criticism, Essays, Nonfiction (General), Philosophy, Poetry, Religion - Other
ISBN Prefix(es): 82-521
Number of titles published annually: 200 Print
Associate Companies: Noregs Boklag L/L

PUBLISHERS

NORWAY

J W Eides Forlag A/S+
Postboks 4081, Dreggen 5835 Bergen
Mailing Address: Sandbrugaten 11, Dreggen 5835 Bergen
Tel: (05) 32 90 40 *Fax:* (05) 31 90 18
Web Site: www.eideforlag.no
Key Personnel
Man Dir: Trine Kolderup Flaten
Subjects: Art, Education, Film, Video, History, Music, Dance, Radio, TV
ISBN Prefix(es): 82-514

Elanders Publishing AS
Brobekkvn 80, Sentrum, 0107 Oslo
Mailing Address: Postboks 1156, Sentrum, 0107 Oslo
Tel: 22636400 *Fax:* 22636594
Key Personnel
Publisher: Aina Thorstensen *Tel:* 22636281
E-mail: aina.thorstensen@elanders.no
Founded: 1844 (AS Fabritius)
Subjects: Chemistry, Chemical Engineering, Law, Maritime, Medicine, Nursing, Dentistry, Transportation
ISBN Prefix(es): 82-90545; 82-07; 82-7180
Parent Company: Elanders Norge AS
Ultimate Parent Company: Elanders AB

Ex Libris Forlag A/S+
Tordenskioldsgt 6B, 0055 Oslo
Tel: (022) 47 11 00 *Fax:* (022) 47 11 49
E-mail: nwd@egmont.no
Key Personnel
Publisher: Hagen Oyvind
Editor: Toruun Andersen
Founded: 1982
Subjects: Alternative, Cookery, Health, Nutrition, Human Relations, Humor, Publishing & Book Trade Reference
ISBN Prefix(es): 82-7384; 82-474; 82-90473

Forlaget Fag og Kultur
Biskop Jens Nilssons gate 5A, 0659 Oslo
Mailing Address: Postbox 6633 Etterstad, 0607 Oslo
Tel: (022) 23 30 24 00 *Fax:* (022) 23 30 24 04
E-mail: firmapost@fagogkultur.no
Web Site: www.fagogkultur.no
Key Personnel
Publisher: Mari Ettre Olsen
Founded: 1987
Subjects: Gardening, Plants, Language Arts, Linguistics, Science (General), Technology
ISBN Prefix(es): 82-11

Fonna Forlag L/L
St Olavs Plass 3, 0130 Oslo
Mailing Address: Postboks 6912, St Olavs Plass, 0130 Oslo
Tel: 22201303 *Fax:* 22201201
Founded: 1940
Subjects: Biography, Fiction, Poetry
ISBN Prefix(es): 82-513

Fono Forlag+
Postboks 169, 1361 Billingsted
Tel: 66846490 *Fax:* 66847507
E-mail: mail@fonoforlag.no
Web Site: www.fonoforlag.no
Key Personnel
General Manager: Halvor Haneborg *E-mail:* h.haneborg@fonoforlag.no
Membership: Norsk Forleggerforening.
Subjects: Education, Fiction, Humor, Literature, Literary Criticism, Essays, Mysteries, Nonfiction (General)
ISBN Prefix(es): 82-7844; 82-91171

Genesis Forlag+
Kongens gt 22, 0153 Oslo
Mailing Address: Postboks 1180 Sentrum, 0107 Oslo
Tel: (022) 31 02 40 *Fax:* (022) 31 02 05
E-mail: genesis@genesis.no
Web Site: www.genesis.no
Key Personnel
Publisher: Magne Lero
International Rights: Anne Mant Jordahl
Founded: 1996
Subjects: Biography, Health, Nutrition, Human Relations, Nonfiction (General), Psychology, Psychiatry, Religion - Protestant, Theology
ISBN Prefix(es): 82-476
Parent Company: Vaart Land
Imprints: Credo

Glydendal Akademisk+
Subsidiary of Gyldendal Norsk Forlag
Kristian IVs g 13, 0164 Oslo
Mailing Address: PO Box 6730, St Olavs Pl, 0130 Oslo
Tel: (022) 034300 *Fax:* (022) 034305
E-mail: akademisk@gyldendal.no
Web Site: www.gyldendal.no/akademisk
Key Personnel
Man Dir: Fredrik Nissen *E-mail:* fredrik.nissen@gyldendal.no
Founded: 1988
Subjects: Accounting, Business, Economics, Education, Finance, Government, Political Science, Health, Nutrition, Law, Medicine, Nursing, Dentistry, Philosophy, Psychology, Psychiatry, Social Sciences, Sociology
ISBN Prefix(es): 82-05
Number of titles published annually: 100 Print

John Grieg Forlag AS
Valkendorfs gt 1a, 5012 Bergen
Mailing Address: Postboks 248, 5001 Bergen
Tel: 55213181 *Fax:* 55218180 *Cable:* Bokgrieg
Key Personnel
Man Dir: Hermond J Berg Lindersen
Founded: 1721
Subjects: Fiction, Nonfiction (General), Sports, Athletics
ISBN Prefix(es): 82-533; 82-7129

Gyldendal Norsk Forlag A/S+
Sehestedsgt 4, 0130 Oslo
Mailing Address: Postboks 6860, St Olavs plass, 0130 Oslo
Tel: 22034100 *Fax:* 22034105
E-mail: gnf@gyldendal.no
Web Site: www.gyldendal.no
Telex: 72880 Gyldn n *Cable:* Gyldendal
Key Personnel
Man Dir: Bjorgun Hysing
Dir, Marketing: Jorgen Klafstad
Dir, Educational: Paul Hedlund
Dir, Fiction: Bjarne Buset
Dir, Nonfiction & Children: Unni Fjesme
Dir, Legal: Torger Andersen
Dir, University Press: Fredrik Nissen
Rights & Permissions: Eva Lie-Nielsen
Founded: 1925
Subjects: Art, Biography, Fiction, Government, Political Science, History, How-to, Music, Dance, Philosophy, Poetry, Psychology, Psychiatry, Religion - Other, Science Fiction, Fantasy, Social Sciences, Sociology
ISBN Prefix(es): 82-05
Subsidiaries: Kunnskapsforlaget I/S (jointly owned with H Aschehoug & Co A/S)
Book Club(s): Den Norske Bokklubben A/S (with three other Norwegian publishers)

Hilt & Hansteen A/S+
Fossveien 24b, 0554 Oslo
Mailing Address: Postboks 2062 G, 0505 Oslo
Tel: (022) 38 40 10 *Fax:* (022) 37 40 15
Web Site: hilt-hansteen.no
Telex: 72400 fotex n att: hiltoslo *Cable:* HILTOSLO
Key Personnel
Publisher: Bjorn Hansteen Fossum; Torstein Hilt *E-mail:* torstein.hilt@genrica.no
Founded: 1983
Subjects: Alternative, Health, Nutrition, Human Relations, Mysteries, Parapsychology, Self-Help
ISBN Prefix(es): 82-7413
Book Club(s): Bokklubben Energica A/S
Orders to: Forlagsentralen 1/S, Postboks 1, 1010 Oslo

Hjemmenes Forlag
Postboks 25 Holmenkollen, 0324 Oslo
Tel: 22143151 *Fax:* 22920738
Key Personnel
Publisher: Yngve Woxholth
Subjects: Ethnicity, History
ISBN Prefix(es): 82-7006

Kolibri Forlag A/S
Postboks 33, Bygdoy, 0211 Oslo
Tel: (022) 438778 *Fax:* (022) 447740
E-mail: post@kolibriforlag.no
Web Site: www.kolibriforlag.no
ISBN Prefix(es): 82-7917; 82-90478

Kunnskapsforlaget ANS
Kristian Augustsgate 10, 0130 Oslo
Mailing Address: Postboks 6736 St Olvas plass, N 0130 Oslo
Tel: (022) 03 66 00 *Fax:* (022) 03 66 05
E-mail: kundeservice@kunnskapsforlaget.no
Web Site: www.kunnskapsforlaget.no
Key Personnel
Man Dir: Harald S Stromme
Sales Dir: Tor Hallaraker
Chief Editor: Petter Henricksen
Multimedia Man: Finn Jorgen Solberg
Production: Svein F Heige
Founded: 1975
ISBN Prefix(es): 82-573
Parent Company: H Aschehoug & Co A/S, Gyldendal Norsk Forlag; Gyldendal Norah Forlag ASA

Libretto Forlag+
Eilert Sundts Gate 32, 0259 Oslo
Tel: (022) 443011 *Fax:* (022) 443012
Key Personnel
Publisher: Tom Thorsteinsen *E-mail:* tomthor@online.no
Founded: 1991
ISBN Prefix(es): 82-91091; 82-7886

Lunde Forlag AS+
Sinsenveien 25, 0572 Oslo
Tel: (022) 00 73 50 *Fax:* (022) 00 73 73
E-mail: lunde@nlm.no
Web Site: www.lunde-forlag.no
Key Personnel
President & Publisher: Asbjorn Kvalbein
Production & International Rights: Reidun Lindheim
Editor: Ingeborg Eidsvaag
Founded: 1905
Subjects: Biography, Education, Fiction, Poetry, Religion - Other, Theology
ISBN Prefix(es): 82-520
Number of titles published annually: 90 Print
Total Titles: 250 Print
Book Club(s): Perspektiv, 4604 Kristiansand *Tel:* 38 02 10 06

Luther Forlag A/S
Grensen 15, 0129 Oslo
Mailing Address: Postboks 6640, St Olavs Pl, 0129 Oslo
Tel: (022) 33 06 08 *Fax:* (022) 42 10 00

E-mail: postkasse@lutherforlag.no
Web Site: www.lutherforlag.no
Key Personnel
Man Dir: Kurt Hjemdal; Asle Dingstad
  E-mail: asle.dingstad@lutherforlag.no
Founded: 1868
Subjects: Biography, Fiction, Religion - Protestant, Religion - Other
ISBN Prefix(es): 82-531
Number of titles published annually: 40 Print
Total Titles: 250 Print

Ernst G Mortensens Forlag A/S+
Kr Augustsgt 14, Majorstua, Oslo
Mailing Address: PO Box 5461, 0305 Majorstua
Tel: 22941000 *Fax:* 22113040
Telex: 77626 *Cable:* Pressmort
Key Personnel
Man Dir: Per Stokken
Editorial: Knut Enger; Solveig Hoysaeter
Sales: Egil Storaas
Information: Knut-Jorgen Erichsen
Advertising: R Marthinsen
Rights & Permissions: Per R Mortensen
Founded: 1933
ISBN Prefix(es): 82-527
Subsidiaries: NPS (Norsk Presseservice A/S); Forenede Trykkerier A/S

NKI Forlaget
Hans Burums vei 30, 1357 Bekkestua
Mailing Address: Postboks 111, 1319 Bekkestua
Tel: (067) 58 88 00 *Fax:* (067) 53 05 00
E-mail: post-fj@nki.no
Web Site: www.nki.no
Key Personnel
Publisher: Marit Anmarkrud
Sales & Marketing Manager: Randi Flugstad
Founded: 1967
Subjects: Chemistry, Chemical Engineering, Electronics, Electrical Engineering, English as a Second Language, Environmental Studies, Mathematics, Mechanical Engineering, Physics, Transportation
ISBN Prefix(es): 82-562

Norsk Bokreidingslag L/L
Postboks 684, 5807 Bergen
Tel: 55301899 *Fax:* 55320356
E-mail: post@bodonihus.no
Key Personnel
Manager: Froydis Lehmann *Tel:* 55136942
  E-mail: fr-lehm@online.no
Founded: 1939
Subjects: Fiction, History, Language Arts, Linguistics, Poetry
ISBN Prefix(es): 82-90186; 82-7834
Number of titles published annually: 4 Print

Novus Forlag+
Herman Foss' Gate 19, 0171 Oslo
Tel: 2271 7450 *Fax:* 2271 8107
E-mail: novus@novus.no
Web Site: www.novus.no
Key Personnel
Publisher: Olav Rosset
Founded: 1972
Subjects: Education, Science (General)
ISBN Prefix(es): 82-7099
Total Titles: 300 Print

Forlaget Oktober A/S
Kristian Augusts gate 11, 0130 Oslo
Mailing Address: PO Box 6848, St Olavs plass, 0130 Oslo
Tel: (022) 23 35 46 20 *Fax:* (022) 23 35 46 21
E-mail: oktober@oktober.no
Web Site: www.oktober.no
Key Personnel
Publisher: Geir Berdahl *Tel:* (022) 23 35 46 25
  E-mail: geir.berdahl@oktober.no
ISBN Prefix(es): 82-7094

Omnipax, *imprint of* Pax Forlag A/S

Origo Forlag
Postboks 28, 0905 Grorud, Oslo
Tel: 22160769 *Fax:* 22164837
Key Personnel
President: Leif-Runa R Forsth
Editor: Bodil Nordvik
ISBN Prefix(es): 82-597

Pax Forlag A/S+
Huitfeldtsgt 15, N-0201 Oslo
Mailing Address: Postboks 2336 Solli, N-0201 Oslo
Tel: (023) 136900 *Fax:* (023) 136919
Key Personnel
Man Dir: Bjorn Smith Simonsen
Editorial & Rights & Permissions: Birgit Bjerck
Founded: 1964
Subjects: Fiction, Nonfiction (General), Philosophy, Psychology, Psychiatry, Social Sciences, Sociology, Women's Studies
ISBN Prefix(es): 82-530
Imprints: Omnipax (Children's books)

Sambandet Forlag+
Vestlandskes bokhandel, Vetrisalm, 1, 5014 Bergen
Tel: 55317963 *Fax:* 55310944
E-mail: vestlandskes.bokhandel@c2i.net
Key Personnel
Publishing Dir: Ingar Hjelset
Founded: 1945
Subjects: Religion - Other
ISBN Prefix(es): 82-7752

Erik Sandberg+
Kongensgt 14, 0153 Oslo
Tel: 22335555 *Fax:* 22413562
Telex: 17580
Key Personnel
Chief Executive, Rights & Permissions: Trond Wikborg
Editorial: Arild Ronsen; Per Martinsen
Sales: Tor Nilsen
Production: Iril Kolle
Publicity: Solveig Thime
Founded: 1973
Subjects: Fiction, Nonfiction (General)
ISBN Prefix(es): 82-7316; 82-90160

Sandviks Bokforlag+
Strandsvingen 14, N-4032 Stavanger
Tel: (051) 44 00 00 *Fax:* (051) 44 00 99
Web Site: www.sandviks.com
Key Personnel
Publisher: Sigurd Sandvik
Editor: Eli Aleksandersen Cantillon
Project Manager: Nina Sandvik Bashforth
Production: Tim Houghton *E-mail:* tim@sandviks.com
Publisher, International Log Book: Mark A Bashforth
President, Baby's First Book Club: Mikkel Sandvik
Sales: Jane Seljestad *E-mail:* jane@sandviks.com
International Sales: Tor Petter Johansen
  E-mail: tor@sandviks.com
Founded: 1965
Subjects: Health, Nutrition, Maritime, Medicine, Nursing, Dentistry
ISBN Prefix(es): 82-7106
Subsidiaries: Baby's First Book Club; Go'boken Book Club, Helsingborg, Sweden & Stavanger; The International Log Book, Bath (UK & Stavanger)
U.S. Office(s): Sandvik Publishing Ltd, Folcroft, PA, United States
Warehouse: DFU-huset, Figgjo

Scandinavian University Press, see Universitetsforlaget

Chr Schibsteds Forlag A/S+
Akersgaten 32, 0107 Oslo
Mailing Address: Postboks 1178, 0107 Sentrum, Oslo
Tel: (022) 863000 *Fax:* (022) 864150
E-mail: schibsted.forlag@schibsted.no
Web Site: www.schibsted-forlag.no
Telex: 71230 aft n
Key Personnel
Man Dir, Rights & Permissions: Per G Damsgaard
Sales Dir: Lise Hammergren
Founded: 1839
Subjects: Biography, Earth Sciences, How-to, Nonfiction (General), Travel
ISBN Prefix(es): 82-516
Parent Company: Schibsted ASA
Warehouse: Forlagsentralen, Postboks 1, Furuset, 1001 Oslo 10
Orders to: Forlagsentralen, Postboks 1, Furuset, 1001 Oslo 10

Snofugl Forlag+
Radhusvegen 3, Melhus
Mailing Address: Postboks 95, 7221 Melhus
Tel: 72872411 *Fax:* 72871013
E-mail: snofugl@online.no
Key Personnel
Manager: Asmund Snofugl
Founded: 1972
Membership(s): Den Norske Forleggerforening.
Subjects: Biography, Fiction, Government, Political Science, History, Literature, Literary Criticism, Essays, Nonfiction (General), Poetry
ISBN Prefix(es): 82-7083
Total Titles: 150 Print
Associate Companies: A/S Bygdetrykk, 7084 Melhus
Warehouse: Melhus skysstasjon, 7221 Melhus

Solum Forlag A/S+
Postboks 140 Skoyen, 0212 Oslo
Tel: (022) 50 04 00 *Fax:* (022) 50 14 53
E-mail: solumfor@online.no
Web Site: www.solumforlag.no
Key Personnel
Man Dir: Knut Endre Solum
Founded: 1974
Subjects: Disability, Special Needs, Fiction, Poetry, Science (General), Educational materials, Humanities
ISBN Prefix(es): 82-560
Distributed by International Specialized Book Service (USA)

Stabenfeldt A/S+
NorSea Dusavik, Bygg 19, 4068 Stavanger
Mailing Address: Postboks 8054, 4068 Stavanger
Tel: (051) 84 54 00 *Fax:* (051) 84 54 91
E-mail: int.post@stabenfeldt.no
Web Site: www.stabenfeldt.no *Cable:* BOKORM
Key Personnel
Man Dir: Tor Tjeldflat
Marketing Dir: J O Skara Hansen
Founded: 1920
Subjects: Fiction, Nonfiction (General)
ISBN Prefix(es): 82-532
Parent Company: Bongs AB, Sweden
Divisions: Stabenfeldt AB

Teknologisk Forlag
Tordenskioldsgt 6B, 0055 Oslo
Tel: 22471100 *Fax:* 22471149
Key Personnel
Man Dir, Rights & Permissions: Rudolf Jenssen
Assistant Dir: Tom Harald Jenssen
Editorial Dir: Tore Egeberg
Sales Dir: Karl H Ormen

Founded: 1958
Subjects: Engineering (General), How-to, Philosophy, Science (General)
ISBN Prefix(es): 82-512

Tell Forlag+
Nilsemarka 5c, 1390 Vollen
Mailing Address: Postboks 62, 1390 Vollen
Tel: 66780918 *Fax:* 66900572
E-mail: tell@online.no
Web Site: www.tell.no
Key Personnel
Publisher: Tell-Chr Wagle
Founded: 1987
Subjects: Art, Crafts, Games, Hobbies, Dance, Educational Books, Textbooks, Theatre
ISBN Prefix(es): 82-7522
Number of titles published annually: 25 Print

Tiden Norsk Forlag
Kristian Augusts gt 12, Oslo
Mailing Address: Postboks 6704, St Olavs plass, N-0130 Oslo
Tel: (022) 23 32 76 60 *Fax:* (022) 23 32 76 97
E-mail: tiden@tiden.no
Web Site: www.tiden.no *Cable:* TIDEN
Key Personnel
Dir: Liv Lysaker
Editorial, Rights & Permissions: Per Bangsund; Bjorn Willadssen
Production: Torgeir Aass
Editor-in-Chief: Sindre Hovdenakk *Tel:* 23 32 7674 *E-mail:* sindre.hovdenakk@tiden.no
Founded: 1933
Subjects: Fiction, Literature, Literary Criticism, Essays, Management, Nonfiction (General), Science Fiction, Fantasy
ISBN Prefix(es): 82-10; 82-990075
Book Club(s): Den Norske Bokklubben A/S (with three other Norwegian publishers)

Universitetsforlaget+
Sehesteds gt 3, 0105 Oslo
Mailing Address: Postboks 508, 0105 Oslo
Tel: (022) 24147500 *Fax:* (022) 24147501
E-mail: post@universitetsforlaget.no
Web Site: www.universitetsforlaget.no
Telex: 11896 Ufor N
Cable: UNIVERSITYPRESS, OSLO
Key Personnel
Man Dir: Ms Siri Hatlen *Fax:* (022) 575354 *E-mail:* sha@scup.no
Publishing Dir, Books: Ms Inger M Tellefsen *Tel:* 22575496 *Fax:* 22575352 *E-mail:* ite@scup.no
Publishing Dir, Journals: Mr Arne Henrik Frogh *Tel:* 22575349 *Fax:* 22575454 *E-mail:* afr@scup.no
Personnel Dir: Ms Randi Bauer *Tel:* 22575386 *Fax:* 22575352 *E-mail:* rba@scup.no
Head of Marketing, Books: Ms Anne Borch-Nielson *Tel:* 22575490 *E-mail:* ani@scup.no
Head of Marketing, Journals: Ms Claire Sharp-Sundt *Tel:* 22575414 *Fax:* 22575454 *E-mail:* csu@scup.no
Rights Manager: Mr Lars Allden *Tel:* 22575401 *Fax:* 22575499 *E-mail:* lal@scup.no
Founded: 1950
Publishers for Scandinavian Universities & other institutions of higher learning, Learned Societies of Scandinavia
Member of STM, Norwegian Publishers' Association, European Union Publishers Forum & EEPG.
Subjects: Behavioral Sciences, Biological Sciences, Business, Education, Language Arts, Linguistics, Law, Mathematics, Mechanical Engineering, Medicine, Nursing, Dentistry, Philosophy, Science (General), Health Care & Modern Language
ISBN Prefix(es): 82-00

Total Titles: 2,000 Print; 10 CD-ROM; 35 Online; 20 Audio
Subsidiaries: Scandinavian University Press
Branch Office(s)
Scandinavian University Press United Kingdom, 60 St Aldates, Oxford OX1 1ST, United Kingdom, Mr George Drennan *Tel:* (01865) 791 891 *Fax:* (01865) 791 891
Copenhagen, Denmark
Stockholm, Sweden
U.S. Office(s): Scandinavian University Press North America, 875 Massachusetts Ave, Suite 84, Cambridge, MA 02139, United States, Contact: Charles Germain *Tel:* 617-497-6515 *Fax:* 617-354-6875 *E-mail:* 75201.571@compuserve.com
Membership(s): American Association of University Presses

Verbum Forlag
Underhaugsvn 15, 0306 Oslo
Mailing Address: Postboks 7062 Majorstua, 0306 Oslo
Tel: (022) 93 27 00 *Fax:* (022) 93 27 27
E-mail: verbumforlag@verbumforlag.no
Web Site: www.verbumforlag.no
Key Personnel
Editor: Turid Barth Pettersen *Tel:* (022) 93 27 20 *E-mail:* tbp@verbumforlag.no

Vett & Viten AS+
Vakaas vn 7, Hvalstad, Asker
Mailing Address: Postboks 203, 1379 Nesbru
Tel: 66849040 *Fax:* 66845590
E-mail: vv@vettviten.no
Web Site: www.vettviten.no
Key Personnel
Publisher: Jan Lien *Tel:* 66983984 *E-mail:* jan.lien@vettviten.no
Marketing & Sales: Tormod Tvinnereim *E-mail:* tormod.tvinnereim@vettviten.no
Finance: Jan Kveine *Tel:* 66983982 *E-mail:* jan.kveine@vettviten.no
Founded: 1987
Subjects: Computer Science, Earth Sciences, Electronics, Electrical Engineering, Engineering (General), Environmental Studies, Film, Video, Geography, Geology, Medicine, Nursing, Dentistry, Radio, TV, Technology, Specialize in Dance
ISBN Prefix(es): 82-412
Number of titles published annually: 50 Print; 20 E-Book
Total Titles: 350 Print
Divisions: Norsk Bokdistribusjon (Computer Books)
Branch Office(s)
Vett & Viten Toensberg, Fjordgaten 13, N-3125 Toensberg, Ragnar Kihle *Tel:* 33381900 *Fax:* 33381901 *E-mail:* ragnar.kihl@vettviten.no
Sales Office(s): J A Sisson, 8713 Prudence Dr, Annadale, VA 22003, United States

Oman

General Information

Capital: Muscat
Language: Arabic, English in business
Religion: Predominantly Muslim (mostly Ibadi, some Sunni)
Population: 1.6 million
Currency: 1,000 baiza = 1 rial Omani

Apex Press & Publishing
PO Box 2616, Ruwi 112, Muscat
Tel: 799388 *Fax:* 793316

E-mail: apexoman@gto.net.om
Web Site: www.apexstuff.com
Key Personnel
President: Saleh M Talib
Editor: Anju Visen-Singh
Founded: 1980
Specialize in Oman.
Subjects: Art, Business, Gardening, Plants, History, Outdoor Recreation, Travel

Pakistan

General Information

Capital: Islamabad
Language: Urdu is national language but English is used extensively. Other principal languages are Punjabi, Pushto, Sindhi and Saraiki
Religion: Predominantly Islamic
Population: 121.7 million
Bank Hours: 0900-1300 Saturday-Wednesday; 0900-1100 Thursday
Shop Hours: 0930-1300, 1500-2000 Saturday-Thursday
Currency: 100 paisa = 1 Pakistan rupee
Export/Import Information: No tariff on books, magazines and advertising matter. Import license issued freely if required. Anti-Islamic and obscene literature prohibited. Exchange controls.
Copyright: UCC, Berne, Buenos Aires, Florence (see Copyright Conventions, pg xi)

Academy of Education Planning & Management (AEPAM)
Taleemi chowk, G-8/1, Islamabad 44000
Tel: (051) 926-1096 *Fax:* (051) 926-1353; (051) 926-1359
E-mail: webinfo@aepam.gov.pk
Web Site: www.aepam.gov.pk *Cable:* AEPAM
Key Personnel
Chief Documentation Officer: M H Shabab
Founded: 1982
Subjects: Economics, Education, English as a Second Language, Library & Information Sciences, Management, Microcomputers
ISBN Prefix(es): 969-444
Parent Company: Ministry of Education

Admission Times International, *imprint of* International Educational Services

AEPAM, see Academy of Education Planning & Management (AEPAM)

Aina-e-Adab
Chowk Minar Anarkali, Lahore 1
Tel: (042) 54069
Key Personnel
Proprietor: Sh Abdul Salam
ISBN Prefix(es): 969-430

Sheikh Shaukat Ali & Sons+
MA Jinnah Urdu Bazar, Karachi 74200
Tel: (021) 214585; (021) 212289 *Fax:* (021) 2637877
Key Personnel
Marketing Executive: Mohammad Ali *E-mail:* m_ali_sheikh@hotmail.com
Subjects: Poetry, Religion - Islamic
ISBN Prefix(es): 969-440
Branch Office(s)
Mian Market, Ghazni St, Lahore

Sheikh Muhammad Ashraf Publishers
7 Aibak Rd, New Anarkali, Lahore 7

Tel: (042) 353171; (042) 353489 *Fax:* (042) 353489 *Cable:* ISLAMICLIT LAHORE
Key Personnel
Publisher: Sh Muhammad Ashraf
Man Dir: Sh Shahzad Riaz
Home Sales: Muhammad Hamayun
Export Sales: Muhammad Amin
Literary Adviser: A Hassan
Founded: 1923
Subjects: Biography, Geography, Geology, Government, Political Science, History, Law, Religion - Other
ISBN Prefix(es): 969-432
U.S. Office(s): Halalco Books, 108 E Fairfax St, Falls Churchs, VA 20046, United States
Specialty Promotions Co Inc, 841 S Cregier Ave, Chicago, IL 60649, United States
Bookshop(s): Ghazni St, Urdu Bazar; Kashmiri Bazar
Warehouse: 9 Aibak Rd, New Anarkali, Lahore 7

ASR Publications+
Flat 8, 2nd floor, Sheraz Plaza, Main Market Gulberg II, Lahore
Mailing Address: PO Box 3154, Lahore
Tel: (042) 877613; (042) 877496 *Fax:* (042) 5711575 *Cable:* SOCFEM
Key Personnel
International Rights: Nighat Said Khan
Subjects: Women's Studies
ISBN Prefix(es): 969-8217
Distributed by Mr Books; Saeed Book Bank

The Book House+
8 Malik Jala Trust Bldg, Urdu Bazar, Lahore 2
Mailing Address: PO Box 734, Urdu Bazar, Lahore 54000
Tel: (042) 61212; (042) 232415 *Fax:* (042) 6360955 *Cable:* BOOKHOUSE
Key Personnel
Proprietor: Muhammad Saeed
General Manager: Muhammad Sheikh Saeed
Founded: 1951
Exporters of English & Urdu books & Textbooks.
Subjects: Antiques, Education
ISBN Prefix(es): 969-437

Centre for South Asian Studies
Quaid-i-Azam Campus, University of the Punjab, Lahore 54590
Tel: (042) 864014 *Fax:* (042) 5867206 *Cable:* SASCUP
Key Personnel
Dir: Dr Rafique Ahmed
Dir & Editor: Dr Sarfaraz Hussain Mirza
Publication Officer: Ovais Nizaini
  E-mail: ovaisn@hotmail.com
Founded: 1973
Subjects: Asian Studies, Economics, Ethnicity, Government, Political Science, Social Sciences, Sociology, Foreign Affairs, South Asia
ISBN Prefix(es): 969-471

Classic+
42 The Mall, Lahore 54000
Tel: (042) 323963; (042) 312977 *Fax:* (042) 7238236 *Cable:* CLASSIC LAHORE
Key Personnel
Man Dir, Editorial, Production, Permissions: Agha Amir Hussain
Sales, Publicity: S Rashid Hussain Agha
Founded: 1956
Subjects: Art, Fiction
ISBN Prefix(es): 969-28; 969-8136
Parent Company: Classic Publishers & Booksellers
Associate Companies: Menarva Publications, Lahore
Subsidiaries: Shish Mahal Kitab Ghar; Classic Bookshop

East & West Publishing Co+
22-Corner Chambers, I I Chundrigar Rd, Karachi 74200
Tel: (021) 212036 *Fax:* (021) 7784362 *Cable:* GOODBOOKS
Key Personnel
Publisher: Rafique Akhtar
Man Dir: Dr Nasir Rafique
Founded: 1971
Subjects: Biography, Regional Interests
ISBN Prefix(es): 969-8017

Fazlee Sons (Pvt) Ltd+
Temple Rd, Urdu Bazar, 74200 Karachi
Tel: (021) 214585; (021) 212289 *Fax:* (021) 6640522
E-mail: fazlee@tarique.khi.sdnpk.undp.org
Founded: 1948
Membership(s): Association of Pakistan Printing & Graphic Arts Industry (PAPGAI); Pakistan Booksellers & Publishers Association (PBSPA).
Subjects: Literature, Literary Criticism, Essays, Religion - Other
ISBN Prefix(es): 969-441
Associate Companies: Printing Services (Pvt) Ltd
Subsidiaries: IS Asia
Bookshop(s): Fazlee Book Supermarket, 4 Mama Parsi Bldg, Temple Rd, Urdu Bazar, Karachi 74200
Orders to: 1-K-5/A, Commercial Area, Nazimabad No 1, Karachi *Tel:* 6622212-5

Ferozsons (Pvt) Ltd
60, Shahrah-e-Quaid-e-Azam, Lahore
Tel: (042) 6301196; (042) 6301197; (042) 6301198 *Fax:* (042) 6369204
E-mail: ferozsons@showroom.edunet.sdnpk.undp.org
Telex: 44382 Feroz PK *Cable:* FEROZSONS
Key Personnel
Man Dir & Publicity: A Salam
Editorial & Sales Dir: Mr Zaheer Salam
Founded: 1894
Subjects: Regional Interests, Religion - Islamic
ISBN Prefix(es): 969-0
Branch Office(s)
33/C-6, Karachi 29

Hamdard Foundation Pakistan
Hamdard Centre, No 3, Nazimabad, Karachi 74600
Tel: (021) 6616001; (021) 6616002; (021) 6616003; (021) 6616004; (021) 6620945 *Fax:* (021) 6611755
E-mail: hamdard@khi.paknet.com.pk
Web Site: www.hamdard.com.pk
Key Personnel
President: Mrs Sadia Rashid
Founded: 1953
Also education & philanthropy.
Subjects: Biography, Education, Health, Nutrition, History, Literature, Literary Criticism, Essays, Religion - Islamic
ISBN Prefix(es): 969-412
Parent Company: Hamdard Laboratories (Waqf) Pakistan
Branch Office(s)
Karachi
Lahore
Peshawar
Rawalpindi
Bookshop(s): Hamdard Kitabistan, Seva Kunj Building, Shahrah-e-Liaquat, Karachi *Tel:* (021) 3371

HMR Publishing Co+
725, Shadman House, Main Bullavard Shadmad Colony, Lahore
Tel: (042) 7588972; (042) 7588967 *Fax:* (042) 7581212

Key Personnel
Man Dir: M Akhter *E-mail:* makhter@1hr.comsats.net.lk
Founded: 1986
Subjects: Biological Sciences, Health, Nutrition, Medicine, Nursing, Dentistry, Religion - Islamic, Science (General)
ISBN Prefix(es): 969-8019

Idara-e-Tehqiqat-e-Islami
Shah Faisal Masjid, Islamabad
Mailing Address: PO Box 1035, Islamabad
Tel: (051) 850751-5; (051) 850755
Telex: 54068 IIU Pak *Cable:* ISLAMSERCH
Key Personnel
Contact: Mr Zafar Ishaque Ansary
ISBN Prefix(es): 969-408

Idara Siqafat-e-Islamia
Club Rd, Lahore 3
Tel: (042) 53908
ISBN Prefix(es): 969-429

Institute of Islamic Culture
2 Club Rd, Lahore
Tel: (042) 6305920; (042) 6363127 *Cable:* ICULT
Key Personnel
Chairman of the Board: Sayyid Wajid Ali Shah
Founded: 1951
Subjects: Religion - Islamic
ISBN Prefix(es): 969-469

International Educational Services+
617 Husain Centre, Shahrah-e-Iraq, Saddar, Karachi 74400
Mailing Address: PO Box 10505, Saddar, Karachi
Tel: (021) 732-6602 *Fax:* (021) 813-1919
Key Personnel
Dir: Mohammad S Mirza
Founded: 1980
Subjects: Advertising, Business, Education, English as a Second Language, Language Arts, Linguistics, Management, Marketing, Publishing & Book Trade Reference
ISBN Prefix(es): 969-33
Imprints: Admission Times International

International Institute of Islamic Thought+
28, Main Double Rd, F-10/2, Islamabad
Mailing Address: PO Box 1959, Islamabad
Tel: (051) 229-3734 *Fax:* (051) 228-0489
E-mail: ziansari@iiitpak.sdnpk.undp.org
Web Site: www.iiit.org
Key Personnel
Man Dir, Editorial, Publicity, Rights & Permissions: Muhammad Jamil
Production: Zeb Alam
Founded: 1981
Subjects: Ethnicity, Religion - Islamic
ISBN Prefix(es): 969-462

Islamabad, *imprint of* Pakistan Institute of Development Economics (PIDE)

Islamic Book Centre+
25B Masson Rd, Lahore 54000
Mailing Address: PO Box 1625, Lahore 54000
Tel: (042) 6316803 *Fax:* (042) 6360955 *Cable:* ISLAMIBOOK
Key Personnel
Man & Publicity Dir: Muhammad Sajid Saeed
Sales, Advertising Dir & Proprietor: Muhammad Hamid Saeed
Founded: 1961
Subjects: Religion - Other
ISBN Prefix(es): 969-436
Subsidiaries: Book House
Branch Office(s)
26 Paisa Akhbar (Anarkali), Lahore 2 *Tel:* (042) 61212
Malik, Jal-al Bldg, Urdu Bazar, Lahore 54000

Islamic Publications (Pvt) Ltd
13-E Shah Alam Market, Lahore 54000
Tel: (042) 325243; (042) 3664504 *Fax:* (042) 7248676 *Cable:* ALILM
Key Personnel
Man Dir: Prof Muhammad Aminv Javed
General Manager: Muhammad Munir Afzal
 Tel: (042) 7669546
Finance Manager: Abdul Ghaffar
Founded: 1960
Specialize in literature on Islam.
Membership(s): Lahore Chamber of Commerce & Industry; Pakistan Publishers & Booksellers Association.
Subjects: Religion - Islamic
ISBN Prefix(es): 969-423
Number of titles published annually: 20 Print
Total Titles: 700 Print
Parent Company: Corporate Law Authority (Pakistan)
Showroom(s): Islamic Publications, 10-Chaterjee Rd, Urdu Bazar, Lahore
Bookshop(s): Islamic Publications, 10-Chaterjee Rd, Urdu Bazar, Lahore

Islamic Research Institute
International Islamic University, Faisal Masjid, PO Box 1035, Islamabad
Tel: (051) 850751; (051) 850755 *Fax:* (051) 853360
E-mail: dg-iri@iri-iiu.sdnpd.undp.org
Telex: 54068 IIU Pak *Cable:* Islamserch
Key Personnel
Dir-General: Dr Zafar Ishaque Ansari
Sales: Mumtaz Liaqat
Founded: 1960
The Institute is a Faculty of the International Islamic University, Islamabad.
Subjects: History, Law, Religion - Other
ISBN Prefix(es): 969-462

H I Jaffari & Co Publishers+
Tahir Plaza 37/B, Blue Area, Islamabad 440000
Tel: (051) 811153 *Cable:* AMBOOKCO
Key Personnel
President: Hasan I Jaffri
Vice President: Raza I Jaffri
Contact: Muneer Hussain
Founded: 1959
Membership(s): Pakistan Publishers & Booksellers Association (Federal Zone) Islamabad.
Subjects: History, Poetry, Religion - Islamic, Sports, Athletics
ISBN Prefix(es): 969-467
Subsidiaries: American Book Co

Jang Publishers+
13-Sir Aga Khan Rd, Lahore
Tel: (042) 6367480-83 *Fax:* (042) 6361026; (042) 6362316
E-mail: thenewslhr@jang.group.com
Web Site: www.jang-group.com
Telex: 44103 JANG PK *Cable:* Daily JANG
Key Personnel
Chief Editor: Shakeel ur Rehman *Tel:* (042) 6367480-3
Editor-in-Charge: Muzaffar Muhammad Ali
 Tel: (042) 630780-3,4; 7847219
Founded: 1985
Printing, marketing
Specializes in Political Autobiography, Pakistani Politics & National Current History.
Subjects: Cookery, Government, Political Science, History, Humor, Literature, Literary Criticism, Essays, Mysteries, Nonfiction (General), Poetry, Regional Interests, Religion - Islamic, Sports, Athletics, Travel
ISBN Prefix(es): 969-36
Total Titles: 325 Print
Parent Company: Jang Group of Newspapers
Ultimate Parent Company: Jang Enterprises Ltd

Associate Companies: Daily AWAM; Daily AWAZ; Daily Jang (URDU); Daily The News International; Daily News; Weekly Akhbar-e-Jehan; Weekly Mag
Subsidiaries: Jang Publishers Press
Distributed by Welcome Book Port
Book Club(s): Jang Book Club, 13-Sir Aga Khan Rd, Lahore, Contact: Syed Mohammad Anis *Tel:* (042) 6367480-83

Kazi Publications
121-Zulqarnain Chambers, Ganpat Rd, Lahore
Tel: (042) 7311359; (042) 7350805 *Fax:* (042) 7117606; (042) 7324003
E-mail: kazip@brain.net.pk; kazipublications@hotmail.com
Web Site: www.brain.net.pk/~kazip
Key Personnel
Proprietor: Muhammad Ikram Siddiqi
Founded: 1978
Subjects: Islam

Library Promotion Bureau+
Karachi University Campus, Dastagir Society, Federal B Area, Karachi 75270
Mailing Address: PO Box 8421, Karachi 75270
Tel: (021) 632-1959 *Fax:* (021) 632-1959
Key Personnel
President: Dr Ghaniul Akram Sabzwari
 E-mail: gsabzwari@hotmail.com
Secretary General: Nasim Fatima
Man Editor: R A Samdani
Founded: 1966
Subjects: Library & Information Sciences
ISBN Prefix(es): 969-459
Distributed by M S Royal Book Co

Maktaba-i-Danial, *imprint of* Pakistan Publishing House

Malik Sirajuddin & Sons+
Kashmiri Bazar, Lahore 8
Tel: (042) 7657527 *Fax:* (042) 7657490
E-mail: sirajco@brain.net.pk
Telex: 44942 CTOLH PK *Cable:* TAJIRKUTUB; LAHORE
Key Personnel
Man Dir: A R Malik *Tel:* (042) 7225809
Editorial, Publicity: S A Malik *Tel:* (042) 5867839 *Fax:* (042) 5861620
Sales: A A Malik *Tel:* (042) 7225812 *Fax:* (042) 7224586
Founded: 1934
Subjects: Biography, Fiction, How-to, Psychology, Psychiatry, Religion - Islamic
ISBN Prefix(es): 969-29
Associate Companies: Gul I Khandan, Urdu Monthly, Kashmiri Baza, Lahore 8; Islamic Juntri, Kashmiri Baza, Lahore 8
Subsidiaries: Siraj Mohammadi Press; Ayaz Book Binding Works
Branch Office(s)
Chowk Urdu Bazar, Lahore *Tel:* (042) 7666226, (042) 7669062 *Fax:* (042) 7224586
 E-mail: sirajco@brain.net.pk
18-19 M J Hospital (WAQF), O/S Mori Gate, Circular Rd, Lahore
Shipping Address: 48C Lower Mall Rd, PO Box 2250, Lahore, Ayaz Ahmad Malik *Tel:* (042) 7225809, (042) 7225812 *Fax:* (042) 7225809, (042) 7225812 *Fax:* (042) 7225809, (042) 7225812 *Fax:* (042) 7225886
 E-mail: sirajco@brain.net.pk

Maqbool Academy+
199 Circular Rd, Chowk Anarkali, Lahore 2
Tel: (042) 7233165 *Fax:* (042) 7324164
Key Personnel
Proprietor: Maqbool Ahmed Malik *Tel:* (042) 7324164 *Fax:* (042) 7324164
Chief Executive: Dr Zafar Maqbool
 E-mail: zmaqbool@yahoo.com
Founded: 1954

Membership(s): Lahore Chamber of Commerce & Industries.
Subjects: Asian Studies, Cookery, Drama, Theater, Education, Fashion, Fiction, Gardening, Plants, Government, Political Science, History, Humor, Literature, Literary Criticism, Essays, Poetry, Religion - Islamic, Religion - Other, Romance, Science (General)
ISBN Prefix(es): 969-442; 969-510
Total Titles: 100 Print
Associate Companies: Maqbool Academy, Abuzar Lentre Modeltown Link Rd, Lahore *Tel:* (042) 5169923; (042) 5169924
Subsidiaries: Bustan-E-Adab
Branch Office(s)
Good Books, 3 Iqra Center, Ghazni St, Urdu Bazar, Lahore 2 *Tel:* (042) 7121966
Distributed by Book Centre
Showroom(s): Maqbool Academy, 10 Dayalsingh Mansion, The Mall, Lahore *Tel:* (042) 7357058/7238241 *Fax:* (042) 7238241
Bookshop(s): Igraa Centre, Ghazni St, Urdu Bazar, Lahore *Tel:* (042) 7121966

Nafees Academy
Tirath Das Rd, Karachi
Mailing Address: PO Box 91, Urdu Bazaar
Key Personnel
Proprietor: Tariq Iqbal Gahandri
Subjects: Education, History
ISBN Prefix(es): 969-421

Nashiran-e-Quran Pvt Ltd+
38-Urdu Bazar, Lahore
Tel: (042) 58581; (042) 58581
Key Personnel
Chairman: Abdul Hamid Khan
Man Dir: Adbul Rashid Khan
Dir: Khan Abdul Khaliq
Founded: 1967
Subjects: Literature, Literary Criticism, Essays, Religion - Islamic
ISBN Prefix(es): 969-431
Parent Company: Kitabistan Publishing Co 38-Urdu Bazar, Lahore
Warehouse: 4C Mela Ram Darbar Market, Lahore

National Book Foundation+
6-Mauve Area, G-8/4, PO Box 1169, Taleemi Chowk, Islamabad
Tel: (051) 9261533; (051) 9261534 *Fax:* (051) 2264283; (051) 2264283
E-mail: nbf@paknet2.ptc.pk
Web Site: nbf.org.pk *Cable:* BOOKFOUND ISLAMABAD PAKISTAN
Key Personnel
Man Dir: Dr Ahmad Faraz *Tel:* (051) 2255572
Secretary: Muhammad Aslam Rao
Deputy Dir Sales: Abdul Hafeez Tauqir *Tel:* (051) 9261535
Assistant Dir, Production: Maqbool Ahmad
 Tel: (051) 9261036
Founded: 1972
Specialize in publishing & provision of books at low prices, book development & promotion, promotion of reading habit.
Membership(s): Asia/Pacific Publishers Association.
Subjects: Accounting, Agriculture, Behavioral Sciences, Biological Sciences, Business, Career Development, Chemistry, Chemical Engineering, Civil Engineering, Religion - Islamic
ISBN Prefix(es): 969-37
Number of titles published annually: 135 Print
Total Titles: 320 Print
Branch Office(s)
First floor, Public Library, Jalal Baba Auditorium, Abbottabad *Tel:* (0992) 9310291
Quaid-i-Azam Medical College, Near Library, Bahawalpur
Shop No 10, Cantt Market, Railway Rd, Bannu, Mr Muhammad Barik Khan *Tel:* (0928) 621991

PAKISTAN

D I Khan
Agriculture University, Faisalabad
GOR Colony, Latifabad No 1, Hyderabad, Mr Lutuf Ali Narejo *Tel:* (0221) 783859 *Fax:* (0221) 783859
11-Aabpara, Islamabad, Mr Khizar Hayat *Tel:* (051) 9213458
Shop No 14, Liaquat University of Medical & Health Sciences, Jamshoro
Liaquat Memorial Library Premises, Ground Floor, Stadium Rd, Karachi, Mr Muhammad Yaqub *Tel:* (021) 9231806 *Fax:* (021) 9231806
56-57 Tufail Market, Shadman Colony, Lahore, Mr Muhammad Nasim *Tel:* (042) 7587735; (042) 7530329; (042) 755061 *Fax:* (042) 7587735
Chandka Medical College, Main Gate, Larkana, Mr Lutuf Ali Narejo *Tel:* (0741) 458215 *Fax:* (0741) 458215
Shop No 43, Cantonment Plaza, Mardan Cantt
1-A, Gulgasht Colony, Bosan Rd, Near UBL College Chowk, Multan, Mr Ghulam Murtaza *Tel:* (061) 9210119 *Fax:* (061) 9210119
Pupil's Medical Girls College, Nawabshah
48/D, F-6, Jamrud Rd, University Town, Peshawar, Mr Nazir Ahmad Yousufzai *Tel:* (091) 9216303 *Fax:* (091) 9216904
3-7/5, Faiz Muhammad Rd, Quetta, Mr Muhammad Idrees *Tel:* (081) 9201570 *Fax:* (081) 9201869
178-B Sarwar Rd, Rawalpindi, Kanwar Tariq Mahmood *Tel:* (051) 5568242 *Fax:* (051) 5568242
Public Library, Sukkur, Mr Jahan Khan Jamro *Tel:* (071) 25103

National Institute of Historical & Cultural Research
102 Rauf Centre, Fazlul Haq Rd, Blue Area, Islamabad
Tel: (051) 218535
Key Personnel
Dir: Dr S M Zaman
Founded: 1973
Specialize in history & culture of South Asia with special emphasis on Pakistan.
Subjects: Biography, Ethnicity, History, Regional Interests
ISBN Prefix(es): 969-415

Pak American Commercial (Pvt) Ltd
53/2 Kashmir Rd, Rawalpindi
Mailing Address: PO Box 294, Rawalpindi
Tel: (051) 563709 *Fax:* (051) 565190 *Cable:* PAKACINC KARACHI
Key Personnel
Dir: Agha M Jaffri
Editorial, Production: M Younus Shaikh
Sales, Publicity: Ahsan Jaffri
Rights & Permissions: Abbas Jaffri
Founded: 1949
Subjects: Government, Political Science, History
ISBN Prefix(es): 969-8152
Branch Office(s)
1st floor, Pak Chambers, 5 Temple Rd, Lahore

Pakistan Institute of Development Economics (PIDE)
Quaid-e-Azam University Campus, Islamabad
Mailing Address: PO Box 1091, Islamabad
Tel: (051) 9206610-27 *Fax:* (051) 9210886
E-mail: pide@apollo.net.pk
Web Site: www.pide.org.pk *Cable:* PIDE
Key Personnel
Dir: Dr A R Kemal
Literary Editor & Chief, Publications Division: Prof Aurangzeb A Hashmi
Founded: 1957
Focal Points of the following organizations: World Bank; International Labor Organization; Asian Development Bank; International Development Research Centre; South Asia Network of Economic Research Institutes.
Subjects: Agriculture, Anthropology, Developing Countries, Economics, Environmental Studies, Labor, Industrial Relations, Library & Information Sciences, Religion - Islamic, Social Sciences, Sociology, Women's Studies, Demography, Economics
ISBN Prefix(es): 969-461
Total Titles: 50 Print
Parent Company: Government of Pakistan Planning & Development Division
Imprints: PIDE; Islamabad

Pakistan Publishing House+
Victoria Chambers, Abdullah Haroon Rd, Saddar Karachi 74400
Tel: (021) 5681457
Telex: 23259 HONEY Pk Attn Noorani *Cable:* PRILECT
Key Personnel
Dir: Ms Hoori Noorani
Sales Manager: Aamir Hussain
Production Manager: Mohammad Yusuf
Rights & Permissions: Mohammad Iqbal
Founded: 1966
Subjects: History, Law, Literature, Literary Criticism, Essays
ISBN Prefix(es): 969-419
Associate Companies: Pakistan Law House, Pakistan Chowk, PO Box 90, Karachi 1
Imprints: PPH; Maktaba-i-Danial

PIDE, *imprint of* Pakistan Institute of Development Economics (PIDE)

PPH, *imprint of* Pakistan Publishing House

Publishers United Pvt Ltd+
176, Anarkali, Lahore 54000
Tel: (042) 7352238 *Fax:* (042) 6316015
E-mail: smalipub2@hotmail.com; smalipub@wol.net.pk *Cable:* PUBUN
Key Personnel
Man Dir: Ahmad Ali Sheikh
Founded: 1942
Subjects: Accounting, Agriculture, Anthropology, Antiques, Archaeology, Art, Asian Studies, Biography, Biological Sciences, Chemistry, Chemical Engineering, Economics, Geography, Geology, History, Library & Information Sciences, Mathematics, Philosophy, Physics, Psychology, Psychiatry, Religion - Islamic, Theology
ISBN Prefix(es): 969-433
Book Club(s): National Book Foundation of Pakistan
Warehouse: 9 Rattigan Rd, Lahore *Tel:* (042) 353423

Quaid-i-Azam University Department of Biological Sciences
Quaid-i-Azam University, Islamabad
Tel: (051) 2482513 *Fax:* (051) 2482513
E-mail: qau@gmx.net; daud@gmx.net
Web Site: members.tripod.com/qau *Cable:* Quaid-i-Azam University Islamabad
Key Personnel
Manager: Rashid Ahmed Khan
Founded: 1973
Subjects: Chemistry, Chemical Engineering, Social Sciences, Sociology
ISBN Prefix(es): 969-8329

Research Society of Pakistan
University of the Punjab, Old Campus, Lahore 3
Tel: (042) 322542
ISBN Prefix(es): 969-425

BOOK

Royal Book Co+
232 Saddar Co-operative Market, Abdullah Haroon Rd, Karachi 74400
Mailing Address: PO Box 7737, Karachi 74400
Tel: (021) 5684244 *Fax:* (021) 5683706
Key Personnel
Proprietor: Jamshed Mirza
Founded: 1963
Subjects: Economics, Finance, Government, Political Science, History
ISBN Prefix(es): 969-407
Showroom(s): 402 Rehman Centre, Zaibunisa St, Karachi 74400
Warehouse: 402 Rehman Centre, Zaibunisa St, Karachi 74400

Sang-e-Meel Publications+
Chowk Urdu Bazar, Lahore
Tel: (042) 7220100; (042) 7228143; (042) 7667970 *Fax:* (042) 7245101
E-mail: smp@sang-e-meel.com
Web Site: www.sang-e-meel.com
Key Personnel
Chief Executive: Niaz Ahmad *E-mail:* nahmad@sang-e-meel.com
Production Dir: Afzaal Ahmad *E-mail:* aahmad@sang-e-meel.com
Founded: 1964
Membership(s): Pakistan Publishers & Booksellers Association & Lahore Chamber of Commerce & Industry.
Subjects: Agriculture, Anthropology, Art, Asian Studies, Criminology, Drama, Theater, Fiction, Health, Nutrition, History, Journalism, Literature, Literary Criticism, Essays, Poetry, Travel
Showroom(s): 25-Lower Mall, Lahore

Sh Ghulam Ali & Sons (Pvt) Ltd+
Ashrafia Park, Ferozepur Rd, Lahore
Tel: (042) 7588979; (042) 7501664 *Fax:* (042) 7583611
Key Personnel
Dir: Sh Bashir Ahmad; Sh Niaz Ahmed; Mr Arshad Niaz
Subjects: Education, Religion - Islamic
ISBN Prefix(es): 969-31
Divisions: Printing & Packaging Division; Food Processing Division; Satellite Equipment
Branch Office(s)
Chotki Ghitti, Hyderabad *Tel:* (0221) 24431
M A Jinnah Rd, Karachi *Tel:* (0221) 722254
Yadkar Line, Chotki Ghitti, Hyderabad *Tel:* (0221) 24431

Shibil Publications (Pvt) Ltd
2nd Floor, Uzma Arcade, Main Clifton Rd, Karachi 75600
Tel: (021) 533414; (021) 539570; (021) 571488 *Cable:* SHAMAILS KARACHI
Key Personnel
Author: Jawaid A Siddiqi
Founded: 1985
Membership(s): Pakistan Publishers & Booksellers Association.
Subjects: Government, Political Science
ISBN Prefix(es): 969-451
Parent Company: Messrs Shamail Traders (Pvt) Ltd
Imprints: Urdu

Urdu, *imprint of* Shibil Publications (Pvt) Ltd

Urdu Academy Sind+
16-Bahadur Shah Market, M A Jinah Rd, Karachi 2
Tel: (021) 2631485 *Cable:* LITERATURE
Key Personnel
Dir & International Rights: Aziz Khalid
Also acts as printer.
Membership(s): Pakistan Publishers & Booksellers Association.

Subjects: Education, Literature, Literary Criticism, Essays, Science (General)
ISBN Prefix(es): 969-30
Associate Companies: Falak Publishers, Karachi
Subsidiaries: Kitab Agency
Branch Office(s)
Urdu Markaz, Ganpat Rd, Lahore
Showroom(s): Rahmat Bldg, M A Jinnah Rd
Bookshop(s): Rahmat Bldg, M A Jinnah Rd
Shipping Address: Westwharf, Karachi

Vanguard Books Ltd+
45 The Mall, Lahore
Tel: (042) 7243779; (042) 7120776; (042) 7120781; (042) 7243783; (042) 7235767
  Fax: (042) 7245097; (042) 73551978
Web Site: www.vanguardbooks.com
Key Personnel
Chief Executive Officer & International Rights: Najam Sethi *E-mail:* nasethi@lhr.comsats.net.pk
Chief Accountant: Aleem Ansari
Founded: 1978
Membership(s): Pakistan Publishers & Booksellers Association.
Subjects: Asian Studies, Economics, Regional Interests, Religion - Islamic
ISBN Prefix(es): 969-402
Number of titles published annually: 30 Print
Total Titles: 325 Print
Branch Office(s)
Vanguard Books, Mashriq Centre, Shah Suleman Rd, Gulshan Iqbal, Karachi
Vanguard Books, 3 Commercial St, Karachi
Vanguard Books, Jinnah Super Market, Islamabad
Vanguard Books, 5-L Commercial, Lahore
Vanguard Books, Mussee Road, Rawalpindi
Distributor for Blackwell; Macmillan Press; Penguin Books (UK); Pluto Press; Routledge; I B Tauris; Zed Press
Foreign Rep(s): Curzon Press (UK); Zed Press (UK)
Bookshop(s): Vanguard Books, Ejaz Center, Main Blvd, Gulberg, Lahore; Vanguard Books, Lok Virsa Bldg, Super Market, Islamabad; Vanguard Books, Mashriq Center, Gulshan Iqbal, Karachi

West-Pakistan Publishing Co (Pvt) Ltd
17 Urdu Bazar, Lahore
Mailing Address: GPO Box No 374, Lahore
Tel: (042) 52427 *Cable:* WESPUBLISH LAHORE
Key Personnel
Chief Executive: Syed Mahmud Shah
Founded: 1932
Also government printers.
Subjects: Religion - Islamic
ISBN Prefix(es): 969-434

Panama

General Information

Capital: Panama
Language: Spanish (English widely used)
Religion: Roman Catholic
Population: 2.7 million
Bank Hours: 0800-1600 Monday-Friday; 0900-1200 Saturday
Shop Hours: 9000-1800 Monday-Saturday
Currency: 100 centismos = 1 balboa. US currency also used
Export/Import Information: No tariffs on books and advertising matter. No import licenses or exhange controls.
Copyright: UCC, Buenos Aires (see Copyright Conventions, pg xi)

Focus Publications International SA
Ave Justo Arosemena y Calle 42, Apdo Aereo 6-3287, Bella Vista
Tel: 225 6638 *Fax:* 225 0466
E-mail: focusint@sinfo.net
Web Site: focuspublicationsint.com
Key Personnel
Publisher: Kenneth Jones *Tel:* 2256638
  Fax: 2250466
Founded: 1970
Subjects: Marketing, Travel
ISBN Prefix(es): 958-95276

Fondo Educativo Interamericano
Edificio Eastern 6, Avda Federico Boyd y Calle 51, Apdo 6-3099, Panama
Tel: 2691511; 2230210
Telex: 2481
Key Personnel
Dir: Alicia Chavarria
President: Juan J Fernandez
Vice President: J Rose
Marketing Manager: C Merodio
Founded: 1985

Editorial Universitaria
Urb El Cangrejo Calle Jose, Apdo Aereo Estafeta Universitaria, Panama 4
Tel: 264-2087 *Fax:* 269-2684 *Cable:* Cuidad Universitaria
Key Personnel
Man Dir, Editorial: Dr Carlos M Gasteazoro
Sales: Eduvigis Vergara
Production: Prof Carlos N Ho
Publicity: Mary R de Natera
Founded: 1969
Subjects: Architecture & Interior Design, Art, Education, Geography, Geology, History, Law, Literature, Literary Criticism, Essays, Philosophy, Science (General), Social Sciences, Sociology
Bookshop(s): University Bookshop

Papua New Guinea

General Information

Capital: Port Moresby
Language: Pidgin, English and Motu (all official) as well as approximately 742 native languages
Religion: Predominantly Christian
Population: 4 million
Bank Hours: 0900-1400 Monday-Thursday; 0900-1700 Friday
Shop Hours: 0900-1800 Monday-Friday; 0900-1200 Saturday
Currency: 100 teoa = 1 kina
Export/Import Information: No tariff on books and advertising but import tax on non-educational books. No import license for books, but no obscene literature permitted.
Copyright: No copyright law

Assemblies of God Mission
PO Box 34, Maprik, East Sepik Province
Tel: 881256
Subjects: Religion - Other
ISBN Prefix(es): 9980-85
Parent Company: Assemblies Publications
Orders to: PO Box 254, Mitcham, Victoria 3132, Australia

The Christian Book Centre
PO Box 712, Madang
Tel: 852 2043 *Fax:* 852 3376

Key Personnel
Manager: Rex Bangs
Subjects: Literature, Literary Criticism, Essays, Religion - Other
ISBN Prefix(es): 9980-74; 0-85804
Parent Company: Kristen Press

Coffee Industry Corporation
PO Box 137, Goroka, Eastern Highlands Province 441
Tel: 732 1266; 732 2466 *Fax:* 732 1431
E-mail: cicgka@daltron.com.pg
Web Site: www.coffeecorp.org.pg
Telex: NE 72647 COFFEE
ISBN Prefix(es): 9980-85

IMPS Research Ltd
PO Box 986, Port Moresby, National Capital District 121
Tel: 3213283 *Fax:* 3217360
E-mail: imps@online.net.pg
Key Personnel
Man Dir: Steve Landon
Founded: 1989
Information services.
Subjects: Economics, Government, Political Science, Mining/Petroleum
ISBN Prefix(es): 9980-916; 9980-920
Number of titles published annually: 3 Print
Distributor for Focus Economics; Insights PNL

KPI, *imprint of* Kristen Press

Kristen Press+
PO Box 712, Madang 511
Tel: 8522988 *Fax:* 823313
Key Personnel
Executive Dir: Dennis T Brown
Publishing Manager & International Rights: Rev Kasek Kautil
Founded: 1969
Also act as printers & stationers.
Subjects: Agriculture, Biblical Studies, Biography, Business, Education, Fiction, Health, Nutrition, Religion - Protestant, Theology, Women's Studies
ISBN Prefix(es): 9980-74; 0-85804
Imprints: KPI; Yangpela Didiman
Bookshop(s): Christian Book Centre, PO Box 3098, Lae; Christian Book Centre, PO Box 712, Madang Province

Melanesian Institute
PO Box 571, Goroko, Eastern Highlands Province
Tel: 732 1777 *Fax:* 732 1214
Subjects: Anthropology, Religion - Catholic, Religion - Protestant, Religion - Other, Social Sciences, Sociology, Theology
ISBN Prefix(es): 9980-65

National Research Institute of Papua New Guinea
PO Box 5854, Boroko, NCD
Tel: 326 0061; 326 0079; 326 0083 *Fax:* 326 0213
E-mail: nri@global.net.pg
Web Site: www.nri.org.pg
Key Personnel
Assistant Dir: Dr Richard Guy
Publishing Manager: James Robins
Founded: 1975
Applied research & policy making.
Subjects: Anthropology, Criminology, Developing Countries, Economics, Education, Environmental Studies, Government, Political Science, Social Sciences, Sociology
ISBN Prefix(es): 9980-75

Nazarene Publications, see Victory Books

PAPUA NEW GUINEA

Office of Libraries & Archives, Papua New Guinea
131, National Capital District, PO Box 734, Waigani
Tel: 325 6200 *Fax:* 325 1331
E-mail: ola@datec.com.pg
Key Personnel
Dir General: Daniel Paraide
Founded: 1975
Also acts as country's ISBN Agency.
ISBN Prefix(es): 9980-69

Papua New Guinea Institute of Medical Research
PO Box 60, Goroko, Eastern Highlands Province
Tel: 732-2800 *Fax:* 732-1998
E-mail: general@pngimr.org.pg
Web Site: www.pngimr.org.pg
Key Personnel
Dir: Prof John Reeder *Tel:* 732-1469
   E-mail: jreeder@pngimr.org.pg
Produces *PNG Bibliography on Medicine.*
Subjects: Anthropology, Medicine, Nursing, Dentistry, Social Sciences, Sociology
ISBN Prefix(es): 0-909531; 9980-71
Number of titles published annually: 1 Print

Summer Institute of Linguistics+
PO Box 413, Ukarumpa vie Lae, Eastern Highlands Province
Tel: 7373544 *Fax:* 7374111
E-mail: png@sil.org
Founded: 1957
Subjects: Anthropology, Language Arts, Linguistics, Papua New Guinea Studies
ISBN Prefix(es): 9980-0; 0-909456; 0-7263
Total Titles: 24,000 Print

University of Goroka
PO Box 1078, Goroka, Eastern Highlands Province
Tel: 731 1700 *Fax:* 732 2620
E-mail: infouog@uoginfo.ac.pg
Web Site: www.uog.ac.pg
Key Personnel
Librarian: N Amarasinghe
ISBN Prefix(es): 0-9599993; 9980-915

University of Papua New Guinea Press
PO Box 320 University Post Office, Boroko
Tel: 3267654 *Fax:* 3260127
Key Personnel
Development Manager: John Evans *Tel:* 3267260
   Fax: 367187 *E-mail:* john.evans@upng.ac.pg
Founded: 1995
Books on & about Papua New Guinea in any subject area.
ISBN Prefix(es): 9980-84
Total Titles: 30 Print
Parent Company: National Capital District

Victory Books
Formerly Nazarene Publications
PO Box 376, Mount Hagen, Western Highlands Province
Tel: 5421081 *Fax:* 5423030
E-mail: bcbes@datec.com.pg
Key Personnel
Publications Dir: Brian Bett
Subjects: Religion - Protestant, Theology
ISBN Prefix(es): 9980-67
Number of titles published annually: 7 Print
Bookshop(s): Nazarene Book Store, PO Box 456, Mount Hagen, Western Highlands Province

Yangpela Didiman, *imprint of* Kristen Press

Paraguay

General Information

Capital: Asuncion
Language: Spanish & Guarani (both official)
Religion: Predominantly Roman Catholic
Population: 4.9 million
Bank Hours: 0930-1145 Monday-Friday
Shop Hours: 0900-2000 Monday-Saturday
Currency: $1.00 US = 2000 Guarani
Export/Import Information: Member of Latin American Free Trade Association; MERCOSUR; ALADI; GATT & WTO. Children's picture books and atlases are dutied, plus added tax and compensatory tax. Advertising catalogs subject to added tax compensatory tax. Additional taxes on all goods; also Consular fee. No import licenses required. Exchange controls; foreign exchange surcharge.
Copyright: UCC, Berne, Buenos Aires (see Copyright Conventions, pg xi)

Instituto de Ciencias de la Computacion (NCR)+
EE UU 961 c/ Tte Farina, 4 to piso, Asuncion
Tel: (021) 490076 *Fax:* (021) 497849
Key Personnel
Dir: Javier Cosp *E-mail:* jcosp@ecsalink.com.py
Founded: 1969
Entrenamiento en Computacioi.
Subjects: Computer Science, Microcomputers, Technology, Computation
Branch Office(s)
Mcal Estigarribia 134, Fernando de la Mora
Distributed by Rafael Peroni Editor

Intercontinental Editora+
Caballero 270, Asuncion
Tel: (021) 496991; (021) 449738 *Fax:* (021) 448721
Web Site: www.libreriaintercontinental.com.py
Key Personnel
Dir: Alejandro Gatti *E-mail:* agatti@pla.net.py
Subjects: Computer Science, Government, Political Science, History, Law, Literature, Literary Criticism, Essays, Parapsychology, Poetry, Self-Help, Economy, Languages, Software

NCR, see Instituto de Ciencias de la Computacion (NCR)

Peru

General Information

Capital: Lima
Language: Spanish, Quechua & Aymara (all official)
Religion: Predominantly Roman Catholic
Population: 22.8 million
Bank Hours: January-December 0900-1500 Monday-Friday
Shop Hours: 1000-1500 Monday- Friday
Currency: 100 centisimos = 1 new sol
Export/Import Information: Member of Andean Group within the Latin American Free Trade Association. Children's picture books and advertising matter dutied per kg plus VAT, sales tax applies on advertising matter. No freight tax on books, but there is a wholesaler's tax. No import licenses required. No exhange controls.
Copyright: UCC, Berne, Buenos Aires (see Copyright Conventions, pg xi)

Librerias ABC SA
Avda Paseo de la Republica 3440, Local B-32, Lima
Tel: (054) 422900; (054) 422902 *Fax:* (054) 422901
Key Personnel
Man Dir: Herbert H Moll
Founded: 1956
Subjects: Archaeology, Art, History

American Bookstore Center SA, see Librerias ABC SA

Biblioteca Nacional
Av Abancay 4ta cuadra, Lima
Tel: (01) 4287690; (01) 4287696 *Fax:* (01) 4277331
E-mail: dn@binape.gob.pe
Web Site: www.binape.gob.pe
ISBN Prefix(es): 9972-601

Ediciones Brown SA+
Av Arequipa No 4455, Miraflores, 18 Lima
Tel: (01) 4462753 *Fax:* (01) 4462753
Key Personnel
Dir: Brown P Fortunato
Founded: 1985
Subjects: Communications, English as a Second Language, How-to, Language Arts, Linguistics, Nonfiction (General)
ISBN Prefix(es): 9972-9030

Asociacion Editorial Bruno+
Av Arica 751, Brena
Mailing Address: Apdo 1759, Lima 5
Tel: (01) 4244134; (01) 4251248 *Fax:* (01) 4251248
Key Personnel
Dir: Maximo Segredo
Manager: Federico Diaz Pineo
Founded: 1950
Subjects: Education, Religion - Catholic
ISBN Prefix(es): 9972-1

Bulletin de l'Institut Francais d'Etudes Andines, *imprint of* Instituto Frances de Estudios Andinos, IFEA

Carvajal SA
Av Jorge Basadre 990 San Isidro, Lima 27
Tel: (01) 440 9685; (01) 440 9618 *Fax:* (01) 440 5871
E-mail: carvajal@correo.dnet.com.pe
Web Site: www.carvajal.com.co
Telex: 055555; 055650 *Cable:* Carvajales Cali
ISBN Prefix(es): 9972-745
Subsidiaries: Editorial Norma SA

Catalogo, *imprint of* Ediciones Peisa (Promocion Editorial Inca SA)

Centro de la Mujer Peruana Flora Tristan
(Peruvian Women's Centre Flora Tristan)
Division of Comunicaciones
Parque Hernan Velarde 42, Lima 1
Tel: (01) 433-2765; (01) 433-1457; (01) 433-9060
   Fax: (01) 433-9500
E-mail: postmast@flora.org.pe
Web Site: www.flora.org.pe
Key Personnel
Executive Dir: Blanca Fernandez
Editor: Gaby Cevasco *E-mail:* gaby@flora.org.pe
Founded: 1979
NGO & Feminist
Specialize in issues on communication, development, feminism, gender, health, library, research, tell-stories, violence, women's rights, history, literature & poetry.
Subjects: Government, Political Science, Health, Nutrition, History, Literature, Literary Criti-

cism, Essays, Poetry, Science (General), Social Sciences, Sociology
ISBN Prefix(es): 9972-610
Number of titles published annually: 10 Print; 5 Online
Total Titles: 50 Print

Editorial Desarrollo SA+
Ica 242, OF 106, Apdo 3824, Lima 1
Tel: (01) 428-5380 *Fax:* (01) 428-6628
Key Personnel
Man Dir: Luis Sosa Nunez
Assistant Manager: Bertha de Berrospi
Founded: 1965
Subjects: Accounting, Business

Instituto de Estudios Peruanos+
Horacio Urteaga 694, Jesus Maria, Lima
Tel: (01) 332-6194; (01) 332-2156; (01) 332-6173; (01) 431-3167 *Fax:* (01) 432-4981
E-mail: libreria@iep.org.pe
Web Site: iep.perucultural.org.pe *Cable:* IEPERU
Key Personnel
Dir: Carolina Trivelli
Publications Dir: Carlos Contreras
Founded: 1964
Subjects: Anthropology, Archaeology, Developing Countries, Economics, Education, Ethnicity, Government, Political Science, Health, Nutrition, History, Social Sciences, Sociology, Technology, Women's Studies
ISBN Prefix(es): 9972-51

Fondo Editorial de la Pontificia Universidad Catolica del Peru
Avda Universitaria cdra 18, San Miguel, Apdo 1761, Lima 100
Tel: (01) 4602870 *Fax:* (01) 4626390
Web Site: www.pucp.edu.pe
Key Personnel
Executive Dir: Agueero Gonzalex
Man Dir: Jose Enrique
Subjects: Anthropology, Archaeology, Computer Science, Economics, Education, Ethnicity, History, Language Arts, Linguistics, Law, Literature, Literary Criticism, Essays, Philosophy, Physical Sciences, Psychology, Psychiatry, Science (General), Social Sciences, Sociology, Theology
ISBN Prefix(es): 84-8390; 84-89309; 9972-42; 84-89292

Instituto Frances de Estudios Andinos, IFEA
Av Arequipa 4595-2º piso, Miraflores, Lima 18
Tel: (01) 447-6070 *Fax:* (01) 445-7650
E-mail: postmaster@ifea.org.pe
Web Site: www.ifeanet.org
Key Personnel
Dir: Henri Godard
Founded: 1948
Research institution.
Subjects: Agriculture, Anthropology, Archaeology, Earth Sciences, Geography, Geology, History, Language Arts, Linguistics, Social Sciences, Sociology
ISBN Prefix(es): 84-89302; 9972-623
Number of titles published annually: 7 Print
Imprints: Bulletin de l'Institut Francais d'Etudes Andines; Travaux de l'Institut Francais d'Etudes Andines

Editorial Horizonte
Av Nicolas de Pierola 995, Lima 1
Tel: (01) 427-9364 *Fax:* (01) 427-4341
Key Personnel
Manager: Humberto Damonte
Production Manager: Eduardo Collazos
Sales Manager: Fernando Damonte
Founded: 1968
Subjects: Anthropology, Art, Economics, Education, History, Language Arts, Linguistics, Literature, Literary Criticism, Essays, Philosophy, Social Sciences, Sociology
ISBN Prefix(es): 84-89307
Associate Companies: Codice Ediciones, Casilla 2118, Lima 100

Editorial Lima 2000 SA
Av Arquipa 2625, Lince, Lima 14
Tel: (01) 440-3486 *Fax:* (01) 440-3480
E-mail: informes@lima2000.com.pe
Web Site: www.lima2000.com.pe
Key Personnel
Dir: Doris C Lopez
Subjects: Cartography
ISBN Prefix(es): 9972-654

Lluvia Editores Srl+
Av Inca Garcilaso de la Vega 1976, Lima 1
Tel: (01) 3326641 *Fax:* (01) 4320732
E-mail: lluviaeditores2002@yahoo.com
Key Personnel
Contact: Esteban Quiroz Cisneros
Founded: 1978
Subjects: Literature, Literary Criticism, Essays
ISBN Prefix(es): 9972-627

Ediciones Peisa (Promocion Editorial Inca SA)
Av Dos de Mayo 1285, San Isidro, Lima 27
Tel: (01) 4404603; (01) 4410473 *Fax:* (01) 4425906
E-mail: peisa@terro.com.pe
Key Personnel
Man Dir: German Coronado Vallenas
Editor: Martha Munoz de Coronado
Founded: 1969
Subjects: Foreign Countries
ISBN Prefix(es): 9972-40
Imprints: Catalogo
Distributor for Aranco (Spain); Concorcio Natuzart (Spain); Folio (Spain); Tres Torres (Spain)

Libreria Studium SA+
Pl Francia 1164, Lima 1
Tel: (01) 326278; (01) 275960; (01) 325528 *Fax:* (01) 4325354
Key Personnel
Manager: Enrique Remy V
Purchasing & Exporting Manager: Sergio Costa B
Founded: 1936
Subjects: Ethnicity

Sur Casa de Estudios del Socialismo
Av Brasil 1329-201, Lima 11
Tel: (01) 4235431 *Fax:* (01) 4235431
E-mail: casasur@terra.com.pe
Web Site: www.casasur.org
Key Personnel
Dir: Cecilia Rivera Orams
Founded: 1986
Membership(s): The Camara Peruana del Libro.
Subjects: Anthropology, Developing Countries, Economics, History, Literature, Literary Criticism, Essays, Philosophy, Social Sciences, Sociology
ISBN Prefix(es): 9972-619

Tarea Asociacion de Publicaciones Educativas+
Parque Oseres 161, Pueblo Libre, Lima 21
Tel: (01) 424-0997 *Fax:* (01) 332-7404
E-mail: postmaster@tarea.org.pe
Web Site: www.tarea.org.pe
Key Personnel
President: Luisa Pinto
Dir: Julio del Valle Ramos
Founded: 1974
Subjects: Education
ISBN Prefix(es): 84-89296; 9972-618

Tassorello, SA
Ave Flora Trstan 574, Magdalena del Mar, Lima 17
Tel: (01) 460-2040; (01) 460-0255 *Fax:* (01) 461-5714
E-mail: tassorello@terra.com.pe
Key Personnel
Contact: Andres Carbone
Founded: 1992
Subjects: Accounting, Education, Human Relations
ISBN Prefix(es): 9972-609

Travaux de l'Institut Francais d'Etudes Andines, *imprint of* Instituto Frances de Estudios Andinos, IFEA

Universidad de Lima-Fondo de Desarollo Editorial+
Av Manuel Olguin 125, Urb Los Granados, Surco, Lima 33
Tel: (01) 437-6767 *Fax:* (01) 437-8066; (01) 435-3396
E-mail: fondo_ed@lima.edu.pe
Web Site: www.ulima.edu.pe
Key Personnel
Executive Dir: Jose Valdizan Ayala
Founded: 1962
Subjects: Communications, Computer Science, Economics, Engineering (General), Film, Video, Finance, Journalism, Law, Management, Marketing, Photography, Psychology, Psychiatry, Radio, TV, Science (General)
ISBN Prefix(es): 84-89358; 9972-45
Number of titles published annually: 40 Print
Total Titles: 500 Print

Universidad Nacional Mayor de San Marcos
Ciudad Universitaria, Av German Amezaga, Lima
Tel: (01) 428-9272; (01) 433-5922 *Fax:* (01) 428-5210
Web Site: www.unmsm.edu.pe
Key Personnel
Man Dir: Dr Wilson Reateggui Chavez; Rector de la Universidad
Founded: 1952
Subjects: Engineering (General), Law, Literature, Literary Criticism, Essays, Medicine, Nursing, Dentistry, Science (General)
Bookshop(s): Av Nicolas de Pierola 1222, Lima 1

Editorial Universo SA
Ave Nicolas Arriola 2285, Urb Apolo, La Victoria, Apdo 241, Lima 30
Tel: (014) 241639; (014) 233190
Key Personnel
Man Dir: Jose Antonio Aquino Benavides
Executive Manager: Salvador Lau Barraza
Founded: 1967
Subjects: Social Sciences, Sociology

Philippines

General Information

Capital: Quezon City
Language: Filipino (based on Tagalog) is the native national language. English widely used. Nine other major languages of the Malayo-Polynesian group, and about 60 other languages, are also spoken
Religion: Predominantly Roman Catholic and some Islamic
Population: 67.1 million
Bank Hours: 0900-1600 Monday-Friday

PHILIPPINES

Shop Hours: Vary. Many open 0900-1200, 1400-1930 Monday-Saturday (some close 1730; some open Sunday)

Currency: 100 centavos = 1 Philippine peso

Export/Import Information: Duty on books except those which are philosophical, historical, economic, scientific, technical or vocational, approved by Department of Education for use of certain institutions (not exceeding 10 copies for an institution, or two for an individual) or for encouragement of sciences or fine arts; no tariffs on Bibles and similar religious books. No duty on advertising matter. No import licenses, but no obscene or immoral literature permitted. Release certificate issued on behalf of Central Bank required to clear goods. Imports subject to sales tax. No formal exchange controls but most imports need Letter of Credit (over $100 in any month, for example).

Copyright: UCC (see Copyright Conventions, pg xi)

Abiva Publishing House Inc+
851-881 Gregorio Araneta Ave, 1113 Quezon City
Tel: (02) 7120245 *Fax:* (02) 7320308
E-mail: info@abiva.com.ph
Web Site: www.abiva.com.ph
Key Personnel
President: Luis Q Abiva Jr
Executive Vice President: Nena A Garcia
Vice President, International Rights: Jorge Abiva Garcia
Founded: 1936
Subjects: Education, History, Religion - Other, Science (General)
ISBN Prefix(es): 971-553
Total Titles: 1 CD-ROM; 1 Audio
Associate Companies: ACG Asian Tradelinks Inc
Subsidiaries: Hiyas Press; ACG Asian Tradelinks Inc
Branch Office(s)
2/F, Cebu Holdings Cente, Cebu Business Park, Cebu City
Matina Highway, Davao City

Anvil Publishing Inc+
Team Pacific Bldg, 2nd Floor, Jose Cruz St, Bo Ugong, Pasig City
Tel: (02) 671888 *Fax:* (02) 6719235
E-mail: anvil@fc.emc.com.ph; pubdept@anvil.com.ph
Key Personnel
General Manager: Cecilia R Licauco
Publishing Manager: Karina A Bolasco
Marketing Consultant: Gwenn Jessica A Galvez
Founded: 1990
Also acts as wholesaler & distributor of paperbacks & tradebooks from the US & UK.
Subjects: Cookery, Crafts, Games, Hobbies, Fiction, Gardening, Plants, Health, Nutrition, How-to, Humor, Language Arts, Linguistics, Literature, Literary Criticism, Essays, Mysteries, Religion - Catholic, Romance, Science Fiction, Fantasy, Western Fiction, Women's Studies
ISBN Prefix(es): 971-27
Number of titles published annually: 150 Print
Total Titles: 600 Print
Parent Company: National Bookstore, 125 Pioneer St, Mandaluyong City, Metro Manila
Associate Companies: Megastrat Inc
Shipping Address: 8007-B Pioneer St, Brgy, Kapitolyo, 1600 Pasig City *Tel:* (02) 637-5692; (02) 637-3621 *Fax:* (02) 637-6084 *E-mail:* anvilsales@eudoramail.com
Warehouse: 8007-B Pioneer St, Brgy, Kapitolyo, 1600 Pasig City *Tel:* (02) 637-5692; (02) 637-3621 *Fax:* (02) 637-6084 *E-mail:* anvilsales@eudoramail.com

Ateneo de Manila University Press+
Katipunan Rd, Loyola Heights, Quezon City 1108
Tel: (02) 4265984; (02) 4261238 *Fax:* (02) 4265909
E-mail: unipress@pusit.admu.edu.ph (business/operations)
Web Site: www.admu.edu.ph
Key Personnel
Dir: Esther M Pacheco *E-mail:* empachec@pusit.admu.edu.ph
Founded: 1972
Membership(s): the International Association of Scholarly Publishers & Book Development Association of the Philippines.
Subjects: Anthropology, Architecture & Interior Design, Asian Studies, Behavioral Sciences, Drama, Theater, Economics, Education, Environmental Studies, Fiction, Government, Political Science, History, Literature, Literary Criticism, Essays, Poetry, Psychology, Psychiatry, Religion - Catholic, Social Sciences, Sociology, Theology, Women's Studies, Social Sciences
ISBN Prefix(es): 971-550
Number of titles published annually: 25 Print
Total Titles: 150 Print
Parent Company: Ateneo de Manila University
Distributed by University of Hawaii Press

BFP Super Romance, *imprint of* Books for Pleasure Inc

Bookman Printing & Publishing House Inc+
2/F Bookman Bldg, 373 Quezon Ave, 1114 Quezon City
Tel: (02) 712-4813; (02) 712-4818; (02) 712-4843; (02) 740-8108; (02) 740-8107; (02) 712-3587 *Fax:* (02) 712-4843
E-mail: bookman@info.com.ph *Cable:* BOOKMAN
Key Personnel
President: Lina P Enriquez
Vice President: Marietta P Martinez
Editorial Dir: Ursula G Picache
Founded: 1945
Subjects: Education, English as a Second Language, Mathematics, Nonfiction (General), Science (General)
ISBN Prefix(es): 971-712

Bookmark Inc+
264-A Pablo Ocampo Sr Ave, Makati City
Tel: (02) 8958061; (02) 8958062; (02) 8958063; (02) 8958064; (02) 8958065 *Fax:* (02) 8970824; (02) 8994248
E-mail: bookmark@info.com.ph; bookmktg@info.com.ph
Web Site: www.bookmark.com.ph
Telex: Bookmark Manila
Key Personnel
President: Amb Bienvenido A Tan, Jr
Vice President: Florencia D Reyes
General Manager: Jose Maria Lorenzo Tan
Founded: 1945
Membership(s): Association of Philippine Booksellers.
Subjects: Child Care & Development, Cookery, Gardening, Plants, History, Religion - Other, Travel
ISBN Prefix(es): 971-569
Branch Office(s)
Taft Ave, Makati, Metro Manila
Delta Arcade Bldg, Makati, Metro Manila
Showroom(s): 357 T Pinpin Escolta, Manila; Delta Arcade Bldg, Makati, Metro Manila
Bookshop(s): Delta Arcade Bldg, Makati, Metro Manila; 357 T Pinpin Escolta, Manila

Books for Pleasure Inc+
Room 302, Forc Bldg, N Domingo Cor F Roman St, 1500 San Juan, Metro Manila
Tel: (02) 771807 *Fax:* (02) 7275240
E-mail: vromance@compass.com.ph
Key Personnel
Vice President: Ramon A Fabella

Founded: 1976
Subjects: Cookery, Mysteries, Romance
ISBN Prefix(es): 971-502
Imprints: BFP Super Romance; Hiwaga Mystery Novels; Valentine Romance; Young Love

Bright Concepts Printing House+
Sto Nino, San Fernando, 2000 Pampanga
Tel: (045) 9612865
E-mail: dawnphilatelics@yahoo.com
Key Personnel
Author, Publisher: Jorge H Cuyugan *Tel:* (0918) 2318248
Founded: 1992
Subjects: Business, Crafts, Games, Hobbies
ISBN Prefix(es): 971-607
Subsidiaries: Dawn Philatelic
Orders to: Booklore Publishing Corp, Blk 2, Lot 13, Ridgemont Village, Cainta, Rizal *Tel:* 252-4280, 251-0771 *Fax:* 563-7629

Cacho Publishing House, Inc+
Pines Cor Union St, 1501 Mandaluyong City, Metro Manila
Tel: (02) 783011-13 *Fax:* (02) 6315244
E-mail: cacho@s.com.ph
Key Personnel
President: Herbert T Veloso
General Manager: Ramon C Sunico
Founded: 1880
ISBN Prefix(es): 971-19
Parent Company: National Bookstore Inc
Associate Companies: Anvil Publishing Inc; Cacho Hermanos Inc *Tel:* (02) 6318361 *Fax:* (02) 6315244 *E-mail:* cacho@mozcom.com
Distributed by Impex (Japan)

Capitol Publishing House Inc
Pacific Bldg, 13 Jose C Cruz Cor Francisco Legaspi Sts, Bo Ugong, 1604 Pasig
Tel: (02) 6712662 *Fax:* (02) 6712663
E-mail: capitolpublishing@e-yellowpages.ph
Key Personnel
General Manager: Manuel Atienza *Tel:* (02) 6712662
Subjects: Binding, Camera Works, Embossing, Folding, Four Color Sheetfed Printing, Negative Stripping, Rewinding, Sheeting, Slitting, Stamping, Typesetting with Laser Printing, Web Printing,

Claretian Communications Inc+
UPPO Box 4, 1101 Diliman, Quezon City
Tel: (02) 9213984 *Fax:* (02) 9217429
E-mail: cci@claret.org; claret@info.com.ph
Web Site: www.bible.claret.org
Key Personnel
Executive Dir, Rights & Permissions: Fr Alberto Rossa *Fax:* 02 921 9429
Founded: 1983
Subjects: Biblical Studies, Environmental Studies, Law, Theology, Women's Studies
ISBN Prefix(es): 971-501
Bookshop(s): Claretian Publications (CP) Bookstore, Fr Alberto Rossa

Communication Foundation for Asia Media Group (CFAMG)
4427 Second Old Sta Mesa, SM434 Manila
Mailing Address: PO Box SM 434
Tel: (02) 607411; (02) 607412; (02) 607413; (02) 607414; (02) 607415; (02) 607416; (02) 7132981 *Fax:* (02) 612504; (02) 7132974
E-mail: cfa@mozcom.com
Telex: 27854 Cfa Ph *Cable:* SOCOMTER MANILA
Key Personnel
Moderator: Filoteo C Pelingon
Founded: 1965
Membership(s): The People in Communication Network (BOARD); The Association of Foundations; Philippine Partnership for the Devel-

opment of Human Resources in Rural Areas (PHILDHRRA); OCICUNDA.
Subjects: Agriculture, Biblical Studies, Biography, Communications, Environmental Studies, Film, Video, Philosophy, Religion - Other, Theology, AV Productions, Communication Training, Communication Research & Planning, Development Communication, Print Media & Publications
ISBN Prefix(es): 971-577
Publication(s): *Barkada Magazine*; *Catholic Digest*; *Gospel Komiks*; *Pambata Magazine*
Branch Office(s)
Dr John Tondowidjojo, Communication Training Center (Sanggar Bina Tama), Suddirman no 3, Surayaba 60136, Indonesia

De La Salle University+
DBB-B Dasmarinas, De La Salle University, Cavite 4115
Tel: (02) 741-9271; (046) 416-0338; (046) 416-3878 *Fax:* (02) 5264237
E-mail: mcovatg@dlsu.edu.ph
Web Site: www.dasma.dlsu.edu.ph
Key Personnel
Contact: Mr Anthon Garcia
Founded: 1983
Membership(s): International Association of Scholarly Publishers.
Subjects: Asian Studies, Business, Education, Fiction, Literature, Literary Criticism, Essays, Philosophy, Poetry, Religion - Catholic
ISBN Prefix(es): 971-92082

Estrella Publishing+
66 Niog St, Bacoor, 4102 Cavite
Key Personnel
Author & Publisher: Ervie Nangca-Antonio
Founded: 1993
Pocket book form.
Subjects: Fiction, Romance
ISBN Prefix(es): 971-645
Book Club(s): Kapisanan Ng Mga Manunulat Ng Nobelang Popular

Galleon Publications+
National Federation of Womens Club Bldg, 962 Josefa Escoda St, 1000 Emrita, Manila
Tel: (02) 592-519; (02) 523-1825 *Fax:* (02) 525-6129
Key Personnel
President & Publisher: Alfonso J Aluit
Founded: 1968
Publish guidebooks to Philippine destinations & works on topical Philippine history.
Subjects: Biography, History, Travel
ISBN Prefix(es): 971-8521
Total Titles: 30 Print
Distributed by Bookmark Inc
Membership(s): SATW

Garotech
903 Quezon Ave, 4332 Quezon City, Metro Manila
Tel: (02) 993286 *Cable:* Romgar Manila
Key Personnel
Man Dir, Sales, Publicity: Rolando M Garcia
Editorial: Maridel Garcia
Founded: 1951
Subjects: Business, Education, Ethnicity, Foreign Countries, Government, Political Science, History
ISBN Prefix(es): 971-8711
Parent Company: Garcia Publishing House Inc
Orders to: PO Box 1860, Manila

Heritage Publishing House
33 4th Ave, Corner Main Avenue, Cubao, Quezon City
Tel: (02) 7248114 *Fax:* (02) 6471393
E-mail: heritage@iconn.com.ph
Web Site: www.iconn.com.ph/heritage
Key Personnel
President: Mario R Alcantara
Man Dir: Ricardo S Sanchez
Previously MCS Enterprises Inc.
Subjects: Anthropology, Art, Government, Political Science, History
Orders to: Heritage Publishing House, PO Box 3667, Manila

Hiwaga Mystery Novels, *imprint of* Books for Pleasure Inc

International Rice Research Institute (IRRI)
Los Banos, Laguna
Mailing Address: PO Box 7777, Metro Manila
Tel: (02) 845-0563; (02) 845-0569 *Fax:* (02) 845-0606
E-mail: irri@cgiar.org
Web Site: www.irri.org
Telex: (IIT) 45365 RICE INST PM
Key Personnel
Dir General: Ronald P Cantrell
Founded: 1960
A nonprofit agricultural research & training established to improve the well-being of present & generations of rice farmers & consumers, particularly with low incomes.
Membership(s): Consultative Group on International Agricultural Research.
Subjects: Agriculture
ISBN Prefix(es): 971-22
Parent Company: CGIAR: Consultative Group on International Research
Imprints: IRRI
Bookshop(s): Agribookstore IADS Inc, 1611 North Kent St, Arlington, VA 22209, United States; American Overseas Company, 550 Walnut St, Norwood, NJ 07648, United States; Harvest Farm Magazine, 14 Wenchow St, Taipei, Taiwan, Province of China; Haryana Scientific Corporation, Gandhi Chowk, Hisar, Haryana 125001, India; Oxford Book & Stationery Co, Scindia House, New Delhi 11001, India; S Toeche-Mittler Verlag, Hindenburgstr 33, 6100 Darmstadt, Germany

IRRI, *imprint of* International Rice Research Institute (IRRI)

J C Palabay Enterprises+
67 Gen Ordonez St, Marikina Heights, 1800 Marikina City
Tel: (02) 9424512 *Fax:* (02) 9424513
Telex: 29001 PXO PH; 23322 PXO PH
Key Personnel
President: Jescie L Palabay
Vice President: Jemellie P Gonzales
Author: Concepcion Javier; Servillano Marquez, Jr
Editor: Lourdes Arellano; Erlinda Valientes
Founded: 1974
Also importer of science laboratory equipment & globes.
Subjects: History
ISBN Prefix(es): 971-13
Parent Company: J C Palabay Enterprises Inc
Associate Companies: Four J Arts; Instructional Material Council, Meralco Ave, Pasig City; Mhelle L Publications

Kadena Press+
2 Mayumi St, Up Village, Dilman, 1101 Quezon City, Metro Manila
Tel: (02) 9217429; (02) 9213984
Key Personnel
Executive Dir: Fr Alberto Rossa
Founded: 1991
Subjects: Fiction
ISBN Prefix(es): 971-32
Parent Company: Claretian Communications Inc

Logos (Divine Word) Publications Inc+
1916 Oroquieta St, Sta Cruz Manila
Tel: (02) 7111323 *Fax:* (02) 7322736
E-mail: dwpsvd@rp1.net
Key Personnel
Dir: Fr Gerry del Pinado SVD
Founded: 1987
Subjects: Business, Communications, Education, Religion - Other
ISBN Prefix(es): 971-510
Total Titles: 5 Audio
Parent Company: Society of the Divine Word

Marren Publishing House, Inc
851 Oroquieta St, 1003 Santa Cruz, Manila
Tel: (02) 7115829 *Fax:* (02) 7115830
Key Personnel
Sales & Marketing Manager: Joan Elena B Cellona
Subjects: Cookery, Fiction
ISBN Prefix(es): 971-649
Subsidiaries: MRE Trading Inc

Sonny A Mendoza+
Unit 31, Parian Commercial Center, Commonwealth Ave, Dilman, 1100 Quezon City, Metro Manila
Tel: (02) 8691111
Key Personnel
Publisher: Sonny Mendoza
Marketing Manager: Ramon N Orbeta
Production Manager: Armando S Peralta
Founded: 1991
Specialize in Filipino/Tagalog crosswords puzzles; also acts as distributor of Tagalog romance novels.
Subjects: Crafts, Games, Hobbies, Humor, Romance
ISBN Prefix(es): 971-599
Orders to: Apt 2, No 59 Paseo de Roxas, Urbaneta Village, Makati, Metro Manila

Mindanao State University - Mamitua Saber Research Center
Andres Bonifacio Ave, 9200 Iligan City
Tel: (063) 2214050; (063) 3516151; (063) 3516152; (063) 3516172; (063) 3516174; (063) 3516153; (063) 3516154; (063) 3516155; (063) 3516156 *Fax:* (063) 221405
ISBN Prefix(es): 971-8708

Mutual Book Inc+
425 Shaw Blvd, Mandaluyong City
Tel: (02) 796050 *Cable:* MUBINC
Key Personnel
President: Alfredo S Nicdao, Jr
Founded: 1959
Subjects: Accounting, Business, Computer Science, Economics, Management, Mathematics
ISBN Prefix(es): 971-587
Associate Companies: Alfredo S Nicdao Jnr Inc
Shipping Address: PO Box 245, Greenhills, San Juan, 1502 Metro Manila

National Book Store Inc
Quad Alpha Centrum, 125 Pioneer St, 1550 Mandaluyong City
Tel: (02) 6318061; (02) 6318062; (02) 6318063; (02) 6318064; (02) 6318065; (02) 6318066 *Fax:* (02) 6318079
E-mail: info@nationalbookstore.com.ph
Web Site: www.nationalbookstore.com.ph
Telex: 27890 NBS-PH; 41144 NBS-PM
Cable: Nabost Manila
Key Personnel
Man Dir: Mr Benjamin C Ramos
Sales Dir: Mitto Licauco
Publicity, Advertising: Mrs Socorro C Ramos
Rights & Permissions: Mr Alfredo C Ramos
Founded: 1945
Firm reprints over 300 titles annually for foreign publishers.

Subjects: Art, Fiction, How-to, Music, Dance, Nonfiction (General)
ISBN Prefix(es): 971-08

National Historical Institute
Affiliate of National Commission on Culture & the Arts
TM Kalaw St, 4th floor, Ermita, Manila
Tel: (02) 590646; (02) 572644 *Fax:* (02) 5250144
Key Personnel
Curator: Teresita L Pagulayan
ISBN Prefix(es): 971-538

National Museum of the Philippines
P Burgos St, 1000 Manila
Tel: (02) 5271215 *Fax:* (02) 5270306
E-mail: nmuseum@i-next.net
Web Site: members.tripod.com/philmuseum/index; nmuseum.tripod.com/index.htm
Key Personnel
Dir & Proprietor: Gabriel S Casal
Curator: Rosario B Tantoco
Founded: 1901
The National Museum collects, identifies, preserves & exhibits the country's rich cultural heritage.
Subjects: Anthropology, Archaeology, Art, Biological Sciences, Geography, Geology, Natural History, Botanical, Ethnological, Zoological collections
ISBN Prefix(es): 971-567
Total Titles: 50 Print; 4 CD-ROM; 1 Online; 1 E-Book
Bookshop(s): National Museum Souvenir Shop, P Burgos St, Manila, Contact: Elenita D V Alba *Tel:* (02) 5270278 *Fax:* (02) 5270306 *E-mail:* nmuseum@i-next.net *Web Site:* nmuseumi-next.net

New Day Publishers+
11 Lands St, VASRA, 1100 Quezon City
Mailing Address: PO Box 1167, 1100 Quezon City
Tel: (02) 9988046; (02) 9275982 *Fax:* (02) 9246544
E-mail: newday@pworld.net.ph; newdayorders@edsamail.com.ph
Key Personnel
Executive Dir, Rights/Permissions & Manuscript Submissions: Ms Bezalie Bautista Uc-Kung *Tel:* (02) 9268049
Publicity, Marketing & Promotions: Mr Jesus Bacolores
Founded: 1969
Membership(s): World Association for Christian Communication; Book Development Association of the Philippines; National Book Development Board.
Subjects: Anthropology, Asian Studies, Behavioral Sciences, Biblical Studies, Biography, Business, Career Development, Communications, Cookery, Economics, Education, Ethnicity, Fiction, History, How-to, Human Relations, Humor, Labor, Industrial Relations, Literature, Literary Criticism, Essays, Management, Marketing, Nonfiction (General), Philosophy, Poetry, Religion - Catholic, Religion - Protestant, Romance, Science Fiction, Fantasy, Self-Help, Theology
ISBN Prefix(es): 971-10
Number of titles published annually: 20 Print
Total Titles: 500 Print

Newark International Enterprises+
Room 507, FUBC Bldg, Escolta, Manila
Tel: (02) 2432077 *Fax:* (02) 2414893
Key Personnel
General Manager & Publisher: Mabini D Castillo
ISBN Prefix(es): 971-9071
Distributed by Goodwill Bookstore/Goodwill Trading Co Inc; Merriam & Webster Inc

Our Lady of Manaoag Publisher+
3078-B Reposo Ext, Sta Mesa, Manila
Tel: (02) 610214; (02) 610219 *Fax:* (06) 610219
Key Personnel
President: Dr Tomas Q D Andres
Marketing Dir: Pilar Corazon I Andres
Circulation Manager: Pilar Philamer I Andres; Thomas Philamer Andres
Founded: 1980
Also acts as a training centre that conducts Philippine based managment in Filipino language.
Subjects: Anthropology, Art, Asian Studies, Behavioral Sciences, Biblical Studies, Business, Career Development, Child Care & Development, Communications, Developing Countries, Education, Ethnicity, Film, Video, History, Humor, Management, Philosophy, Religion - Catholic
ISBN Prefix(es): 971-26; 971-91093
Parent Company: Values & Technologies Management Centre
Subsidiaries: Management Business Achievers Inc
Divisions: Philippine Institute of Management
Warehouse: 2004 C Arellano St, Sta Mesa, Manila

Pearson Education Asia
2/F J-L Bldg, 23 Matalino St, Bgy. Central, Dillman, 11011 Quezon City
Tel: (02) 434 5501 *Fax:* (02) 433466
E-mail: custserv@pearsoned.com.ph
Web Site: www.pearsoned.com
Key Personnel
Marketing Executive: Mary Antonette Tucit *E-mail:* dovie@pearsoned.com.ph; Ariel Pagdanganan *E-mail:* arielp@pearson.com.ph; Mary Ann Gonzalez *E-mail:* gonzalez@pearson.com.ph
Sales Manager: Dennis Elmer Lazo *E-mail:* denlazo@pearsoned.com.ph
Number of titles published annually: 30 Print
Total Titles: 60 Print
Parent Company: Pearson Education

Philippine Baptist Mission SBC FMB Church Growth International
2444 Taft Av, Malate, Metro Manila
Tel: (02) 526-0264; (02) 526-0265; (02) 526-0266; (02) 526-0267; (02) 599256; (02) 599257 *Fax:* (02) 522-4639
E-mail: csm@i-manila.com.ph
Web Site: www.fsbc.org.ph
Key Personnel
Mission Administrative Officer: J Allen Hill *E-mail:* pbml-maoffice@netasia.net
Dir, Business Services: David "Chip" Clary *E-mail:* pbml-bservices@netasia.net
Dir, Field Services: Phillip Brewster *E-mail:* brewster@skyinet.net
Subjects: Biblical Studies, History, Religion - Protestant, Theology
ISBN Prefix(es): 971-512
Shipping Address: Church Strengthening Ministry, 4796 Mercado St, Makati, Metro Manila
Orders to: Church Strengthening Ministry, 4796 Mercado St, Makati, Metro Manila

Philippine Education Co Inc
140 Amorsolo St, Metro Manila
Tel: (02) 487215; (02) 487317
E-mail: publications@pidsnet.pids.gov.ph
Web Site: www.pids.gov.ph
Telex: 7222321 *Cable:* Pecoi Manila
Key Personnel
General Manager: Antero L Soriano
Subjects: Art, Education, Fiction, Social Sciences, Sociology
ISBN Prefix(es): 971-09

Rex Bookstores & Publishers+
84 P Florentino St, Sta Mesa Heights, 1008 Quezon City, Metro Manila
Tel: (02) 7437688; (02) 4143512; (02) 4146774 *Fax:* (02) 7437687
E-mail: rex@usinc.net
Key Personnel
President: Dominador D Buhain
International Sales & Foreign Rights Coordinator: Sonia A Santiago *E-mail:* sasantiago@rexpublishing.com.ph
Founded: 1950
Membership(s): Asia/Pacific Publishers Association; International Publishers Association.
Subjects: Accounting, Agriculture, Anthropology, Archaeology, Behavioral Sciences, Biological Sciences, Business, Child Care & Development, Cookery, Criminology, Economics, Education, Environmental Studies, Finance, History, Human Relations, Labor, Industrial Relations, Law, Maritime, Marketing, Mathematics, Parapsychology, Physics, Psychology, Psychiatry, Science (General), Social Sciences, Sociology, Theology, Travel
ISBN Prefix(es): 971-23
Number of titles published annually: 100 Print
Ultimate Parent Company: Rex Group of Companies
Branch Office(s)
1906 Cecile Bldg, Mac-Arthur H-way, Balibago, Angeles City, Acting Officer In Charge: Almira Manaloto *Tel:* (045) 892-17-21
Ateneo Professional School, 1st floor, Rockwell Center, Bel-Air Makati, Helen Riosa *Tel:* 729-20-75
Duran Bldg, del Pilar Ext (crossing) Sangitan E, Cabanatuan, Officer In Charge: Gigi Yatco *Fax:* (044) 600-56-84
Cor J Serina St, Valmenta Blvd, Carmen, Cagayan de Oro, Officer In Charge: Lourdes Dicipulo *Tel:* (088) 858-67-75
11 Sanciangko St, Cebu City, Officer In Charge: Mabel Quijano *Tel:* (032) 254-67-73; (032) 254-67-74 *Fax:* (032) 254-64-66
Rustan's Superstore Bldg, Unit 4-A, Cubao, Officer In Charge: Luisa Lagat *Fax:* 911-10-70
156 CM Recto St, Davao City, Officer In Charge: Lourdes Dicipulo *Tel:* (082) 225-31-67; (082) 221-78-40 *Fax:* (088) 221-02-72
Aparente St, Dadiangas Heights, General Santos City, Officer In Charge: Hilda Malayao *Tel:* (083) 554-71-02
75 Brgy San Isidro Lopez-Jaena Jaro, Iloilo, Officer In Charge: Mabel Quijano *Tel:* (033) 329-03-32 *Fax:* (033) 329-03-36
Magallanes cor Alonzo St, Legaspi City, Officer In Charge: Ben Pring *Tel:* (052) 820-22-70
Star Centrum Bldg, Unit UG-2, Sen Gil Puyat Ave, Makati, Officer In Charge: Helen Riosa *Tel:* 893-37-44, 818-53-63
Facilities Center Bldg, 548 Shaw Blvd, Mandaluyong, Officer In Charge: Tina de la Cruz *Tel:* 531-13-06 *Fax:* 531-13-39
Zone 6 Pinmaludpod Urdaneta, Pangasinan, Officer In Charge: Che che Agcamaran *Fax:* (075) 568-39-75
856 Nicanor Reyes St, Samp, Manila, Officer In Charge: Fatima Yumiaco *Tel:* 736-05-67 *Fax:* 736-41-91
1977 CM Recto Ave, Sampaloc, Manila, Officer In Charge: Teodora Anastacio *Tel:* 735-55-27 *Fax:* 735-55-34
Lot 6, Blk 5 Cityview IV Brgy Tanauan, Tanza Cavity, Officer In Charge: Easter Rapada
Book Club(s): Phil Educational Publishers Association, Contact: Dominador D Buhain
Warehouse: 84 P Florentino Av, 1008 Quezon City *Tel:* (02) 712 4101 (ext 128) *Fax:* (02) 740 2702 *E-mail:* sasantiago@rexpublishing.com.ph

Saint Mary's Publishing Corp+
3/F VCC Bldg, 1308 P Guevarra St, Sta Cruz, Manila

PUBLISHERS

Tel: (02) 7119730; (02) 7119743 *Fax:* (02) 7350955
Key Personnel
Contact: Jerry Vicente S Catabijan
Founded: 1995
Membership(s): PEPA; BDAP; CLAPI.
Subjects: Economics, Education, English as a Second Language, Geography, Geology, History, Language Arts, Linguistics, Mathematics, Science (General), Social Sciences, Sociology
ISBN Prefix(es): 971-509

Salesiana Publishers Inc+
Pasay Rd cor Pasong Tamo, Makati City, Manila
Tel: (02) 8161506; (02) 889234 *Fax:* (02) 8922154 *Cable:* SALESIANA PUBLISHERS MANILA
Key Personnel
Rector, Editor-in-Chief & all other offices: Fr Demetrio M Carmona
Founded: 1979
Subjects: Communications, Computer Science, Earth Sciences, Human Relations, Language Arts, Linguistics, Literature, Literary Criticism, Essays, Mathematics, Physics, Religion - Catholic, Science (General), Social Sciences, Sociology, Technology
ISBN Prefix(es): 971-8532; 971-522
Branch Office(s)
Salesiana-Bacolod, c/o RU Commercial Center, North Drive, Bacolod City (in front of Riverside Hospital)
Salesiana-Baguio, UB Commercial Complex, Gen Luuna St, Baguio City
Book Club(s): Philippine Bookfair Association

San Carlos Publications
University of San Carlos, 6000 Cebu City
Mailing Address: P Del Rosario St, 6000 Cebu City
Tel: (032) 253-1000 *Fax:* (032) 255-4341
E-mail: uscjournals@lycos.com
Key Personnel
Editor: Harold Olofson
Founded: 1973
Membership(s): International Association of Scholarly Publishers & Council of Editors of Learned Journals.
Subjects: Anthropology, Archaeology, Biological Sciences, History, Social Sciences, Sociology
ISBN Prefix(es): 971-539

SIBS Publishing House Inc
8/F Globe Telecom Plaza II, Pioneer Highlands, Pioneer Corner Madison Streets, 1552 Mandaluyong City
Tel: 687-6164 *Fax:* 687-1716
E-mail: sibsbook@info.com.ph; sibs@eyp.ph
Web Site: www.sibs.com.ph
Key Personnel
President: Carmen Mimette M Sibal
Vice President, Operations: Anita S Mangalindan
Head, Research & Development: Dr Juanita S Guerrero
Editor-in-Chief: Rogelio Mangahas
Managing Editor: Mamel Teh
Art Dir: Antonio M Concepcion
Head, Promotions Department: Cora A Sapo
Project Coordinator: Agnes S Apostol *Tel:* (062) 372-7313
Founded: 1996
Membership(s): International Publishers Association; Philippine Educational Publishers Association.
Subjects: Art, Biological Sciences, Economics, Education, English as a Second Language, Environmental Studies, History, Journalism, Language Arts, Linguistics, Literature, Literary Criticism, Essays, Mathematics, Nonfiction (General), Religion - Other, Science (General), Social Sciences, Sociology, Christian Living Education, Civics & Culture, English, Filipino,

Preschool books - reading, language, math & art, Values Education
ISBN Prefix(es): 971-791
Branch Office(s)
Mayor Maximo V Patalinghug Ave, Barangay Pajo, 6015 Lapu-Lapu City, Cebu
Tel: (032) 340-6809 *Fax:* (032) 340-6808
E-mail: vismin@sibs.com.ph

Silsilah Publication
Edificio Ciudad, San Jose Rd, Zamboanga City
Tel: (02) 5663
ISBN Prefix(es): 971-31

Sinag-Tala Publishers Inc+
4th floor, Regina Bldg, cor Trasierra St, Legaspi Village, Makati City, Manila
Tel: (02) 8192681 *Fax:* (02) 8192563
Key Personnel
Man Dir, Rights & Permissions: L A Uson
Marketing Dir: V A Tur
Founded: 1969
Subjects: Business, Economics, Religion - Catholic
ISBN Prefix(es): 971-554

Solidaridad Publishing House
531 Padre Faura, Ermita, Manila
Tel: (02) 586581; (02) 591241 *Fax:* (02) 525-5038 *Cable:* SOLDAD MANILA
Key Personnel
General Manager: F Sionil Jose
Founded: 1965
Subjects: Biography, Fiction, History
ISBN Prefix(es): 971-8845

University of the Philippines Press+
Unit of University of the Philippines System
E de los Santos St, Diliman, 1101 Quezon City
Tel: (02) 9205301; (02) 9205302; (02) 9205303; (02) 9205304; (02) 9205305; (02) 9266642; (02) 9253243; (02) 9253244 *Fax:* (02) 9282558
E-mail: press@nicole.upd.edu.ph; uppress@uppress.org
Web Site: www.upd.edu.ph
Key Personnel
Dir, Rights & Permissions: Cristina Pantoja Hidalgo
Sales, Publicity: Mabi David Balangue
Production: Conrado Calma
Editorial: Gerardo Los Banos
Founded: 1965
Subjects: Art, Business, Education, Fiction, Government, Political Science, How-to, Law, Medicine, Nursing, Dentistry, Music, Dance, Philosophy, Psychology, Psychiatry, Religion - Other, Science (General), Social Sciences, Sociology, Technology
ISBN Prefix(es): 971-542
Number of titles published annually: 40 Print
Total Titles: 300 Print

UST Publishing House+
Beato Angelico Bldg, Espana St, Sampaloc, 1008 Manila
Tel: (02) 7313101 *Fax:* (02) 7811473
E-mail: qui_test@ust.edu.ph
Web Site: www.ust.edu.ph
Key Personnel
Contact: Joselito B Zulueta
Founded: 1593
Subjects: Architecture & Interior Design, Asian Studies, Biblical Studies, Biological Sciences, Business, Chemistry, Chemical Engineering, Economics, Education, English as a Second Language, Health, Nutrition, History, Literature, Literary Criticism, Essays, Medicine, Nursing, Dentistry, Philosophy, Poetry, Religion - Catholic, Social Sciences, Sociology, Theology
ISBN Prefix(es): 971-506

POLAND

Parent Company: University of Santo Tomas
Distributor for Bookmark; Heritage; Rarebook; Solidaridad
Book Club(s): Book Development Association of the Phillipines; Asian Catholic Publishers

Valentine Romance, *imprint of* Books for Pleasure Inc

Vera-Reyes Inc+
4th floor, Mariwasa Bldg, 77 Aurora Blvd, Quezon City 1112
Tel: (02) 7218792 *Fax:* (02) 7218782
Telex: 63740 Vri pn *Cable:* Verareyes Manila
Key Personnel
Man Dir: L O Reyes
Publishing Dir: Gerardo P Legaspi
Dir, Medical Books: Gia Reyes
Founded: 1964
Subjects: Art, History, Medicine, Nursing, Dentistry, Philosophy, Religion - Other
ISBN Prefix(es): 971-575
Subsidiaries: International Typesetting Services; Vera-Reyes Medical Books
Bookshop(s): Vera-Reyes Medical Books

Vibal Publishing House Inc (VPHI)
1253 G Araneta Ave, Quezon City
Tel: (02) 712-9156; (02) 712-2722; (02) 712-9157; (02) 712-9158; (02) 712-9159 *Fax:* (02) 711-8852
E-mail: sales@vibalpublishing.com
Web Site: www.vibalpublishing.com
Telex: ITT 40404 *Cable:* VIBAL INC, MANILA
Key Personnel
Chief Executive: Esther A Vibal
Editorial: Rhodora S Yatco
Sales: Dina C Tapang
Production: Rolando S Mata
Publicity, Rights & Permissions: Carian M Espino
Founded: 1955
Subjects: Ethnicity, Foreign Countries, Language Arts, Linguistics, Mathematics, Religion - Other, Science (General), Social Sciences, Sociology
ISBN Prefix(es): 971-07
Parent Company: Nasionale Boekhandel Ltd
Subsidiaries: ASN Graphics; SD Publications
Branch Office(s)
VPHI Cebu Branch, 0290 Nivel Hills, Lahug, Cebu City *Tel:* (032) 2330173; (032) 2330176; (032) 2332568 *Fax:* (032) 2332983
E-mail: vpcebu@vibalpublishing.com
Kalamansi St, Juna Subdivision, First St, Matina, Davao City *Tel:* (082) 2975226 *Fax:* (082) 2978550 *E-mail:* vpdavao@vibalpublishing.com

VPHI, *see* Vibal Publishing House Inc (VPHI)

Young Love, *imprint of* Books for Pleasure Inc

Poland

General Information

Capital: Warsaw
Language: Polish and some German. English also used, especially among young people
Religion: Predominantly Roman Catholic
Population: 38.4 million
Bank Hours: 0800-1900 Monday-Friday, 0800-1600 Saturday
Shop Hours: 1100-1900 Monday-Friday; 0900-1300 Saturday
Currency: 100 groszy = 1 zloty
Export/Import Information: Import of books and newspapers, duty free, no tax. Individual private importers allowed to act. Advertising may

POLAND

be placed through AGPOL Foreign Trade Advertising agency, ul Kierbedzia 4, 7, 00-957 Warsaw. No import licenses as such required. All overseas trade is conducted in foreign currency. Small quantities of advertising materials duty free.
Copyright: UCC, Berne (see Copyright Conventions, pg xi)

Albatros
Kazury 2/12, 02-795 Warsaw
Tel: (022) 842-9867 *Fax:* (022) 842-9867
Key Personnel
Owner & Editor-in-Chief: Andrzej Kurylowicz
  E-mail: akurylowicz@wp.pl
Subjects: Fiction, Nonfiction (General)
Number of titles published annually: 80 Print
Total Titles: 110 Print

Alfa, *imprint of* Wydawnictwa Normalizacyjne Alfa-Wero

Aritbus et Historiae, Rivista Internationale di arti visive ecinema, Institut IRSA - Verlagsanstatt+
61 Szczepanska 9, 31-011 Krakow
Tel: (012) 421 90 30; (012) 421 91 55 *Fax:* (012) 421 48 07
E-mail: irsa@irsa.com.pl
Web Site: www.irsa.com.pl
Key Personnel
Publisher: Dr Jozef Grabski
Founded: 1979
Specialize in History of Art.
Subjects: Architecture & Interior Design, Art, History
ISBN Prefix(es): 3-900731

Wydawnictwo Arkady+
ul Dobra 28, skrytka pocztowa 137, 00-344 Warsaw
Tel: (022) 8268980; (022) 8267079; (022) 8269316; (022) 635 83 44 *Fax:* (022) 827 41 94
E-mail: arkady@arkady.com.pl
Web Site: arkady.com.pl
Key Personnel
President & Dir: Janina Krysiak *Tel:* (022) 826 93 16
Editor-in-Chief: Elzbieta Leszczynska *Tel:* (022) 826 22 57
Production Dir: Wieslaw Pyszka *Tel:* (022) 828 38 17; (022) 826 75 80
International Rights: Jadwiga Marek *Tel:* (022) 826 75 80
Founded: 1957
Subjects: Antiques, Architecture & Interior Design, Art, Crafts, Games, Hobbies, Environmental Studies, Photography
ISBN Prefix(es): 83-213

Arlekin-Wydawnictwo Harlequin Enterprises sp zoo
Ul Rakowiecka 4, 00-975 Warsaw
Mailing Address: PO Box 11, 02-600 Warsaw 13
Tel: (022) 8499557; (022) 8499498; (022) 8498630 *Fax:* (022) 8499557
Key Personnel
Man Dir: Barbara Jozwiak
Founded: 1991
Subjects: Romance
ISBN Prefix(es): 83-7149; 83-7070

Wydawnictwa Artystyczne i Filmowe
ul Pulawska 61, 02-595 Warsaw
Tel: (022) 8455301; (022) 8455584; (022) 8455465; (022) 8453936 *Fax:* (022) 8455584; (022) 8455465; (022) 8453936
Key Personnel
Man Dir: Janusz Fogler
Editorial: Edward Rylukowski

Editorial, Publicity: Andrzej Dulewicz
Founded: 1959
Subjects: Art, Drama, Theater, Film, Video, Photography
ISBN Prefix(es): 83-221

Atena
Ul Warszawska 13, 85-959 Bydgoszcz
Tel: (061) 228685 *Fax:* (061) 524082
E-mail: atena@poz1.commet.pl
ISBN Prefix(es): 83-902443

Wydawnictwo Baturo (Baturo Publishers)+
ul Drobniewicza 26, 43-309 Bielsko-Biala
Tel: (033) 81 25 086; (033) 81 40 955; (033) 81 62 703 *Fax:* (033) 81 40 955
  Fax on Demand: (033) 8140955
E-mail: baturo@baturo.com.pl
Web Site: www.baturo.com.pl
Key Personnel
Contact: Andrzej Baturo; Inez Baturo
Founded: 1991
Membership(s): PTWK; PIK; Polish Book Chamber; Polish Association of Book Publishers.
Subjects: Animals, Pets, Architecture & Interior Design, Gardening, Plants, How-to, Photography
ISBN Prefix(es): 83-900564; 83-905021
Number of titles published annually: 5 Print

Beta Books, *imprint of* Wydawnictwa Normalizacyjne Alfa-Wero

Beta Comics, *imprint of* Wydawnictwa Normalizacyjne Alfa-Wero

Biblioteka Narodowa
ul Niepodleglosci 213, 02-086 Warsaw
Tel: (022) 608-2999; (022) 452-2999 *Fax:* (022) 825-7751
E-mail: biblnar@bn.org.pl
Web Site: www.bn.org.pl
Telex: 816761
Key Personnel
Head, Conservation Division: Ms Maria A Wozniak
Founded: 1928
Membership(s): IFLA; FID; IAM; AIB; ASLIB.
Subjects: Library & Information Sciences
ISBN Prefix(es): 83-7009

BOSZ scp+
Olszania 311, 38-722 Olszanica
Tel: (013) 469 90 00 *Fax:* (013) 469 61 88
E-mail: biuro@ks.onet.pl
Web Site: www.bosz.com.pl
Subjects: Architecture & Interior Design, Art, Photography, Travel

Spoldzielnia Wydawnicza 'Czytelnik'+
ul Wiejska 12a, 00-490 Warsaw
Tel: (022) 6281441 *Fax:* (022) 6283178
E-mail: sekretariat@czytelnik.pl
Web Site: www.czytelnik.pl *Cable:* CZYTELNIK WARSAW
Key Personnel
Man Dir, Chairman: Zakowski Marek
Foreign Rights: Anna Mencwel *Tel:* (022) 6289508 *E-mail:* am@czytelnik.pl
Founded: 1944
Subjects: Biography, Fiction, Journalism, Poetry, Social Sciences, Sociology
ISBN Prefix(es): 83-07
Number of titles published annually: 90 Print

Wydawnictwo DiG (DiG Publishing)+
Aleja Wojska Polskiego 4, 01-524 Warsaw
Tel: (022) 839 0838 *Fax:* (022) 828-00-96
E-mail: biuro@dig.com.pl
Web Site: www.dig.com.pl

Key Personnel
Managing Dir: Slawomir Gorzynski
Dir: Krzysztof Dabrowski *E-mail:* kjd@dig.com.pl
Founded: 1991
Independent publishing company specializing in history & humanities.
Membership(s): Polska Izba Ksiazki (Polish Book Chamber).
Subjects: Antiques, Archaeology, Art, Biography, Genealogy, History, Language Arts, Linguistics, Library & Information Sciences, Literature, Literary Criticism, Essays
ISBN Prefix(es): 83-7181; 83-85490
Number of titles published annually: 80 Print; 2 CD-ROM; 2 Online; 2 E-Book
Total Titles: 250 Print
Distributed by Polnische Buchhandlung; Orbis Book Ltd
Bookshop(s): Al Niepodleglosci 213, 02-086 Warsaw

Wydawnictwo Dolnoslaskie+
ul Straznicza 1-3, 50-206 Warsaw
Tel: (071) 328 89 54; (071) 328 89 52; (071) 328 89 51 *Fax:* (071) 328 89 54
E-mail: sekretariat@wd.wroc.pl
Web Site: ksiegarnia.bellona.pl
Key Personnel
President: Andrzej Adamus
Vice President & Editorial Manager: Jan Stolarczyk
Executive Secretary: Barbara Kocowska
  Tel: (071) 3288951 *E-mail:* kocowska@wd.wvoc.pl
Production: Jacek Sajdak
Founded: 1986
Membership(s): the Polish Book Chamber.
Subjects: Art, Fiction, History, Literature, Literary Criticism, Essays, Mysteries, Poetry
ISBN Prefix(es): 83-7023
Number of titles published annually: 70 Print
Orders to: Ars Polona SAV, Krakowskie Przedmiescie 7, 00-950 Warsaw

Dom Wydawniczy Bellona
ul Grzybowska 77, 00-844 Warsaw
Tel: (022) 6202044 *Fax:* (022) 6522695
E-mail: biuro@bellona.pl
Web Site: ksiegarnia.bellona.pl
Key Personnel
Dir: Jozef Skrzypiec

Drukarnia I Ksiegarnia Swietego Wojciecha, Dziat Wydawniczy
pl Wolnosci 1, 61-738 Poznan
Tel: (061) 8529186 *Fax:* (061) 8523746
E-mail: wydawnictwo.ksw@archpoznan.org.pl
Telex: 0414220 Kmp *Cable:* Albertinum Poznan
Key Personnel
Man Dir: Bogdan Reformat
Founded: 1895
Subjects: Biblical Studies, Religion - Catholic, Theology
ISBN Prefix(es): 83-7015
Branch Office(s)
ul Freta 48, 00-227 Warsaw
ul Krolewska 15, 20-109 Lubin
Bookshop(s): St Adalbert's Bookshop, pl Wolnosci 1, 61-738 Poznan

Polskie Wydawnictwo Ekonomiczne PWE SA+
ul Canaletta 4, Warsaw 00-099
Tel: (022) 827 80 01 *Fax:* (022) 827 55 67
E-mail: pwe@pwe.com.pl
Web Site: www.pwe.com.pl
Key Personnel
President & Editor-in-Chief: Alicja Rutkowska
  Tel: (022) 826 41 82 *E-mail:* arutko@pwe.com.pl
Dir: Blandyna Chmiel *Tel:* (022) 827 74 87
  E-mail: chmiel@pwe.com.pl; Mariola Rozmus

Tel: (022) 826 41 82 *E-mail:* mrozmus@pwe.com.pl
Founded: 1949
Polish economics publishers.
Membership(s): Polish Chamber of Books.
Subjects: Accounting, Advertising, Business, Economics, Environmental Studies, Finance, Management, Marketing
ISBN Prefix(es): 83-208
Number of titles published annually: 70 Print
Total Titles: 5,000 Print

Energeia sp zoo Wydawnictwo
ul Szturmowa 1, 02-678 Warsaw
Mailing Address: Skr Poczt 43, 00-976 Warsaw
Tel: (022) 847 00 53 *Fax:* (022) 847-00-53
Key Personnel
Man Dir: Jan E Okuniewski
Founded: 1991
Subjects: Drama, Theater, English as a Second Language, Language Arts, Linguistics, Literature, Literary Criticism, Essays
ISBN Prefix(es): 83-85118; 83-88236
Distributor for Julius Groos Verlag Heidelberg (Germany)

Gdanskie Wydawnictwo Psychologiczne SC
 (Gdansk Psychology Publishing Company)+
ul Bema 4/1a, 81-753 Sopot
Tel: (058) 551-61-04; (058) 550-16-04; (058) 551-11-01 *Fax:* (058) 551-61-04; (058) 550-16-04
Web Site: www.gwp.pl
Key Personnel
General Manager: Magdalena Zylicz
 E-mail: magdaz@gwp.gda.pl
Founded: 1991
Publishes exclusively psychology books: academic textbooks, counselling books for psychotherapists & practical psychology for the general market.
Subjects: Psychology, Psychiatry, Self-Help
ISBN Prefix(es): 83-85416; 83-87957; 93-89120
Number of titles published annually: 20 Print
Total Titles: 100 Print

Wydawnictwa Geologiczne
ul Rakowiecka 4, 02-517 Warsaw
Tel: (022) 495351 (ext 518)
Key Personnel
Dir: Dr Marian Soldan
Founded: 1953
Subjects: Geography, Geology, Mathematics
ISBN Prefix(es): 83-220

Instytut Historii Nauki PAN+
Unit of Polish Academy of Sciences
ul Nowy Swiat 72, Pok 9, 00-330 Warsaw
Tel: (022) 826 87 54; (022) 65 72 746 *Fax:* (022) 826 61 37
E-mail: ihn@ihnpan.waw.pl
Web Site: www.ihnpan.waw.pl
Key Personnel
Editorial Manager: Anna Zawadzka
International Rights: Prof Andrzej Srodka
Subjects: Astronomy, Biography, Biological Sciences, Chemistry, Chemical Engineering, Earth Sciences, Education, Geography, Geology, History
ISBN Prefix(es): 83-900065; 83-900482; 83-900891; 83-86062
Total Titles: 10 Print

Wydawnictwo Harcerskie 'Horyzonty', see
 Spotdzielna Anagram

Impuls+
31-559 Krakow ul, Grzegorzecka, 69-107 Krakow
Tel: (012) 422-41-80 *Fax:* (012) 422-59-47
E-mail: impuls@impulsoficyna.com.pl
Web Site: www.impulsoficyna.com.pl

Key Personnel
Dir: Wojciech Sliwerski
Editor-in-Chief: Piotr Niwinski
Founded: 1989
Membership(s): Polish Book Chamber.
Subjects: Education, Environmental Studies, Literature, Literary Criticism, Essays, Philosophy, Religion - Catholic, Social Sciences, Sociology
ISBN Prefix(es): 83-86994; 83-85543; 83-88030

Instytut Meteorologii i Gospodarki Wodnej
 (Institute of Meteorology & Water Management)
ul Podlesna 61, 01-673 Warsaw
Tel: (022) 56-94-100 *Fax:* (022) 834-54-66
E-mail: sekretariat@imgw.pl
Web Site: www.imgw.pl
Key Personnel
Dir: Prof Jan Zielinski
Founded: 1945
Subjects: Earth Sciences, Environmental Studies, Foreign Countries, Geography, Geology, Library & Information Sciences, Physical Sciences, Meteorology, Hydrology, Oceanology, Water Management, Water Engineering, Water Quality
ISBN Prefix(es): 83-88887
Number of titles published annually: 20 Print
Parent Company: Ministry of Environment
Branch Office(s)
Gdynia
Katowice
Krakow
Poznan
Wroclaw

Instytut Wydawniczy Pax, Inco-Veritas+
Wybrzeze Kosciuszkowskie 21a, 00390 Warsaw
Tel: (022) 625 23 01 *Fax:* (022) 625 68 86
E-mail: iwpax@com.pl
Web Site: www.iwpax.com.pl
Key Personnel
Chief Editor: Amelia Szafranska
Founded: 1949
Subjects: Biblical Studies, Education, History, Literature, Literary Criticism, Essays, Philosophy, Poetry, Religion - Catholic, Theology
ISBN Prefix(es): 83-211
Bookshop(s): Piekna 16b, 00-449 Warsaw
Warehouse: Biuro Sprzedazy IW Pax, Wybrzeze Kosciuszkowskie 21a, 00390 Warsaw
Orders to: Biuro Handlu Zagranicznego Inco-Veritas, ul Wspolna 25, 00-159 Warsaw
 Tel: (022) 293216 *Fax:* (022) 295202

Interpress+
ul Bagatela 12, 00-585 Warsaw
Tel: (022) 6214876; (022) 6289331; (022) 6289202; (022) 6282818; (022) 6291060; (022) 6282225 *Fax:* (022) 6289331; (022) 6289202; (022) 6226850
E-mail: paiwydaw@pol.pl
Telex: 816336 pai pL *Cable:* INTERPRESS WARSZAWA
Key Personnel
Editor-in-Chief, Publicity: Bohdan Gawronski
Publicity, Rights & Permissions: Zofia Lewandowska
Production, Sales: Jawusz Malinowski
Founded: 1967
Subjects: History, Regional Interests, Science (General)
ISBN Prefix(es): 83-223
Branch Office(s)
Buero der Polnischen Informationen Agentur (PAI), Vinohradska 1616, Praha 2, Czech Republic *Tel:* 236117
Orders to: Dzial Handlowy, Wydawnictwo Interpress, ul Bagatela 12, 00-585 Warsaw

Iskry - Publishing House Ltd spotka zoo+
ul Smolna 11, 00-375 Warsaw

Tel: (022) 827 94 15 *Fax:* (022) 827 94 15
E-mail: iskry@iskry.com.pl
Web Site: www.iskry.com.pl
Key Personnel
President: Wieslaw Uchanski
Dir: Krzysztof Oblucki *Tel:* (022) 827 94 24; Marek Rosiecki *Tel:* (022) 827 87 79
Founded: 1952
Subjects: Aeronautics, Aviation, Biography, Cookery, History, Literature, Literary Criticism, Essays, Maritime, Mysteries, Parapsychology, Philosophy, Regional Interests, Science Fiction, Fantasy, Self-Help, Travel
ISBN Prefix(es): 83-207

ITB, *imprint of* Instytut Techniki Budowlanej, Dzial Wydawniczo- Poligraficzny

Katolicki Uniwersytet Wydawniczo -Redakcja+
ul Konstantynow 1, 20-708 Lublin
Tel: (081) 5257151 *Fax:* (081) 541246
E-mail: sekret@kul.lublin.pl
Key Personnel
Dir: Edward Pudelko *E-mail:* pudelko@kul.lublin.pl
Founded: 1957
Subjects: Biblical Studies, History, Law, Philosophy, Psychology, Psychiatry, Religion - Catholic, Social Sciences, Sociology, Theology
ISBN Prefix(es): 83-228
Imprints: RW-KUL
Divisions: Redakcja Wydawnictw KUL; Zaklad Malej Poligrafii KUL
Orders to: Kolportaz Dzialu Wydawniczo-Poligraficznego KUL, ul Konstantynow 1, 20-708 Lublin *Tel:* (081) 5257166 *Fax:* (081) 5241246 *E-mail:* kolprw@kul.lublin.pl

KAW Krajowa Agencja Wydawnicza
ul Smolna 12, 00-375 Warsaw
Tel: (022) 6578886 *Fax:* (022) 6578887
E-mail: kaw@univcomp.waw.pl
Web Site: www.polska2000.pl
Telex: 813487 Kaw Pl
Key Personnel
Man Dir & Editor-in-Chief: Dobroslaw Kobielski
Editorial: Jedrzej Bednarowicz
Deputy Editor: Tadeusz Kaczmarek; Zbigniew Zlotnicki
Production: Wladyslaw Szeszko
Sales: Jozef Maka
Founded: 1974
Membership(s): RSW.
Subjects: Education, Ethnicity, Government, Political Science, Science (General), Travel
ISBN Prefix(es): 83-03; 83-88072
Branch Office(s)
ul Podedwornego 12a, 15-269 Bialystok
ul sw Ducha 111/113, 80-801 Gdansk
ul 3 Maja 36, 40-097 Katowice
ul Florianska 33, 31-019 Krakow
ul Sienkiewicza 3/5, 90-113 Lodz
ul Buczka 28, 20-076 Lublin
ul Slowackiego 22, 60-823 Poznan
ul Komunistow 10, 35-030 Rzeszow
ul Orla Bialego 5, 70-562 Szczecin
pl Solny 14, 50-062 Wroclaw

Komputerowa Oficyna Wydawnicza Help+
Dworcowa 8, 05-816 Michalowice
Tel: (022) 723 89 21 *Fax:* (022) 723 87 64
E-mail: kowhelp@pol.pl
Web Site: www.besthelp.pl
Key Personnel
Man Dir: Piotr Gomolinski *E-mail:* piotr@besthelp.pl
Founded: 1989
Specialize in computer books.
Subjects: Computer Science
ISBN Prefix(es): 83-87211
Number of titles published annually: 15 Print
Total Titles: 200 Print

POLAND

Wydawnictwa Komunikacji i Lacznosci Co Ltd+
ul Kazimierzowska 52, 02-546 Warsaw 12
Tel: (022) 849 27 51 *Fax:* (022) 849 23 22
E-mail: wkl@wkl.com.pl
Web Site: www.wkl.com.pl
Key Personnel
Dir: Jerzy Kozlowski
Editor-in-Chief: Bogumil Zielinski
Sales & Marketing Dir: Ewa Berus
Founded: 1949
Transport & Communications Publishers.
Subjects: Aeronautics, Aviation, Communications, Electronics, Electrical Engineering, Mechanical Engineering, Radio, TV, Transportation
ISBN Prefix(es): 83-206
Bookshop(s): ul Kazimierzowska 52, 02-546 Warsaw 12 *Tel:* (022) 8492032
Warehouse: ul Kazimierzowska 52, 02-546 Warsaw 12 *Tel:* (022) 8492304

Krajowa Agencja Wydawnicza, see KAW
Krajowa Agencja Wydawnicza

'Ksiazka i Wiedza' Spotdzielnia Wydawniczo-Handlowa+
ul Smolna 13, 00-375 Warsaw
Tel: (022) 8275401; (022) 8279416 *Fax:* (022) 8279416; (022) 8279423
E-mail: publisher@kiw.com.pl
Web Site: www.kiw.com.pl
Telex: 817630 Kiw Pl *Cable:* KIW WARSZAWA
Key Personnel
Dir & Editor-in-Chief: Stanistan Soltus; Marta Stuhr
Editor: Jaroslaw Ladosz; Tadeusz Tarnogrodzki
Production: Andrzej Gierkowski
Founded: 1918
Membership(s): RSW.
Subjects: Animals, Pets, Biography, Government, Political Science, History, Philosophy, Social Sciences, Sociology, Travel
ISBN Prefix(es): 83-05

Ksiaznica Publishing Ltd+
ul Powstancow 30/401, 40-039 Katowice
Tel: (032) 257 22 16 *Fax:* (032) 257 22 17
E-mail: ksiaznica@domnet.com.pl
Key Personnel
President: Mariusz Morga
Vice President: Bozena Sek
International Rights: Joanna Ociepka
Specialize in encyclopedic thematic dictionaries.
Membership(s): Polish Chamber of Books.
Subjects: Fiction, Health, Nutrition, Nonfiction (General), Romance
ISBN Prefix(es): 83-85348; 83-7132

Laumann-Polska+
ul Zymierskiego 53A/4, 58-573 Piechowice
Tel: (075) 7617182 *Fax:* (075) 7617192
Key Personnel
President: Maria Iburg
Subjects: Regional Interests, Travel
ISBN Prefix(es): 83-85716
Book Club(s): Polska Izba Ksiazki

Wydawnictwo Literackie+
ul Dluga 1, 31-147 Krakow
Tel: (012) 4225423; (012) 4232254; (012) 4231251 *Fax:* (012) 4225423
E-mail: redakcja@wl.interkom.pl; handel@wl.net.pl; promocja@wl.net.pl
Web Site: www.wl.net.pl
Key Personnel
Dir: Janusz Adamczyk
Finance Dir: Halina Ofiarska
Editorial Staff: Krzysztof Lisowski
Sales & Marketing: Barbara Leszczynska
Publicity: Boguslawa Stanowska-Cichon
Founded: 1953
Subjects: Art, Biography, Drama, Theater, Film, Video, History, Literature, Literary Criticism, Essays
ISBN Prefix(es): 83-08

Wydawnictwo Lodzkie+
ul Piotrkowska 171, Skr Poczt 372, 90-447 Lodz
Tel: (042) 6360331; (042) 6366189 *Fax:* (042) 6368524
Key Personnel
Editorial Dir: Jacek Zaorski
Sales & Publicity: Janina Sobczak
Production: Grazyna Bis-Stepniak
Rights & Permissions: Alfreda Gorzkiewicz
Founded: 1957
Subjects: Biography, Human Relations
ISBN Prefix(es): 83-218

Wydawnictwo Lubelskie
ul Droga Meczennikow Majdanka 67, 20-325 Lublin
Tel: (081) 7442667
Key Personnel
Dir & Editor-in-Chief: Ireneusz Caban
Deputy Editor: Ludwik Zabielski
Founded: 1957
Subjects: Government, Political Science, Human Relations, Poetry, Science (General), Social Sciences, Sociology
ISBN Prefix(es): 83-87399

Ludowa Spoldzielnia Wydawnicza+
ul Grzybowska 4, 00-131 Warsaw
Tel: (022) 6205718; (022) 6205719 *Fax:* (022) 6207277 *Cable:* LSW, WARSZAWA
Key Personnel
Chairman & Editor-in-Chief: Rajewski Krzysztof
Editorial: Jerzy Dobrzanski
Founded: 1946
People's publishing cooperative.
Subjects: Agriculture, Biography, History, Literature, Literary Criticism, Essays, Poetry
ISBN Prefix(es): 83-205

Magnum Publishing House Ltd+
ul Narbutta 25A, 02-536 Warsaw
Tel: (022) 6460085; (022) 8485505 *Fax:* (022) 8485505
E-mail: magnum@it.com.pl
Key Personnel
President: Jolanta Woloszanska
Vice President: Marcin Jarek
Founded: 1994
Membership(s): Polish Chamber of Books.
Subjects: Biography, Government, Political Science, History
ISBN Prefix(es): 83-85852

Wydawnictwo Medyczne Urban & Partner+
ul M Sklodowskiej-Curie 55/61, 50-950 Wroclaw
Tel: (071) 328 54 87; (071) 328 30 68 *Fax:* (071) 328 43 91
E-mail: info@urbanpartner.pl
Web Site: www.urbanpartner.pl
Key Personnel
President: Wieslawa Hombek
President & International Rights: Miroslaw Gornicki
Founded: 1992
Subjects: Medicine, Nursing, Dentistry
ISBN Prefix(es): 83-85842; 83-87944
Parent Company: Urban & Schwarzenberg, Munich, Germany

Muza SA+
ul Marszalkowska 8 IIp, 00-590 Warsaw
Tel: (022) 621-17-75; (022) 621-50-58; (022) 629-50-83 *Fax:* (022) 629-23-49
E-mail: muza@muza.com.pl
Web Site: www.muza.com.pl
Key Personnel
President: Marcin Garlinski
International Rights: Agata Radkiewicz *E-mail:* a.radkiewicz@muza.com.pl
Founded: 1991
Subjects: Art, Cookery, Education, Fiction, House & Home, Nonfiction (General), Social Sciences, Sociology, Travel
ISBN Prefix(es): 83-7079; 83-7200; 83-85325; 83-7319
Imprints: Sport I Turystyka; Warszawskie Wydawnictwo Literackie
Book Club(s): Klub Czytelnikow Muza SA
Warehouse: ul Cybernetyki 9, 00-677 Warsaw

Polskie Wydawnictwo Muzyczne+
ul Krasijskiego 11a, 31-111 Krakow
Tel: (012) 4227171; (012) 4227044 *Fax:* (012) 4227171
E-mail: pwm@pwm.com.pl
Web Site: www.pwm.com.pl
Telex: 813370 *Cable:* PWM
Key Personnel
Editor-in-Chief: Andrzej Kosowski
Head, Copyright: Janina Warzecha
Editorial: Ewa Nyozek
Production: Grazyna Adamczyk
Founded: 1945
Polish music publishers.
Subjects: Music, Dance
ISBN Prefix(es): 83-224
Imprints: Poligrafia PWM
Subsidiaries: Centralnaa Biblioteka Muzyczna-Nutowa (PWM Hire Department)
U.S. Office(s): Theodore Presser, One Presser Place, Bryn Mawr, PA 19010-3490, United States *Fax:* 610-527-7841
Distributed by Kalmvs (Great Britain Commonwealth & Australia); Leduc (France); Schott (Germany & Switzerland); Universal (Austria)

Wydawnictwo Nasza Ksiegarnia Sp zoo (Nasza Ksiegarnia Publishing House)+
ul Sarabandy 24c, 02-868 Warsaw
Tel: (022) 643 93 89 *Fax:* (022) 643 70 28
Cable: NASZA KSIEGARNIA
Key Personnel
President: Agnieszka Tokarczyk
Editor-in-Chief: Jolanta Sztuczynska
Founded: 1921
Subjects: Education, Fiction, Science (General)
ISBN Prefix(es): 83-10

Wydawnictwo Naukowe PWN, see Polish Scientific Publishers PWN

Wydawnictwa Naukowo-Techniczne+
ul Mazowiecka 2/4, 00-048 Warsaw
Tel: (022) 826-72-71 *Fax:* (022) 826-86-20
E-mail: wnt@pol.pl
Web Site: www.wnt.com.pl *Cable:* ENTE WARSZAWA
Key Personnel
General Manager: Dr Aniela Topulos
Rights & Permissions: Agnieszka Koztowska *Tel:* (022) 8272833
Founded: 1949
Subjects: Chemistry, Chemical Engineering, Computer Science, Electronics, Electrical Engineering, Mathematics, Mechanical Engineering, Microcomputers, Physics, Technology
ISBN Prefix(es): 83-204
Imprints: WNT

Norbertinum+
ul Ksiezycowa 15, 20-060 Lublin
Tel: (081) 5333895 *Fax:* (081) 5341243
E-mail: norbertinum@norbertinum.com.pl
Web Site: www.norbertinum.com.pl
Key Personnel
President & International Rights: Norbert Wojciechowski
Founded: 1989

Subjects: Biography, Fiction, History, Literature, Literary Criticism, Essays, Poetry, Religion - Catholic, Science (General), Social Sciences, Sociology, Theology
ISBN Prefix(es): 83-85131; 83-86837; 83-7222

Wydawnictwa Normalizacyjne, see Wydawnictwa Normalizacyjne Alfa-Wero

Wydawnictwa Normalizacyjne Alfa-Wero+
Ul Nowogrodzka 22, 00-511 Warsaw
Tel: (02) 6218750 *Fax:* (02) 6218750
Telex: 812374 Wuen Pl
Key Personnel
Editor-in-Chief: Jerzy Wysokinski
Production Dir: Zdzislaw Adamski
Sales Manager: Malgorzata Lukaszczuk
Foreign Rights Manager: Wiktor Bukato
Founded: 1956
Subjects: Crafts, Games, Hobbies, Fiction, Science (General), Science Fiction, Fantasy
ISBN Prefix(es): 83-7001; 83-7179
Imprints: Alfa; Beta Books; Beta Comics
Bookshop(s): ul Sienna 63, Warsaw

Ossolineum Zaklad Narodowy im Ossolinskich - Wydawnictwo+
pl Solny 14a, 50-062 Wroclaw
Tel: (071) 3436961 *Fax:* (071) 3448103
E-mail: wydawnictwo@ossolineum.pl
Telex: 0712771
Key Personnel
Man Dir: Wojciech Karwacki
Editor-in-Chief: Stanislaw Roscicki
Founded: 1817
Subjects: Archaeology, Architecture & Interior Design, Art, Biography, Biological Sciences, Environmental Studies, History, Language Arts, Linguistics, Literature, Literary Criticism, Essays, Medicine, Nursing, Dentistry, Philosophy, Poetry, Science (General), Social Sciences, Sociology
ISBN Prefix(es): 83-04
Bookshop(s): Sw Marka 12, 31-018 Krakow; ul Marcinkowskiego 30, 61-745 Poznam; Jaworzynska 4, 00-634 Warsaw; Rynek 6, 50-106 Wroclaw
Orders to: Export Dept c/o Ossolineum, Plac Solny 14a, 50-062 Wroclaw

P P H Penta
ul Bogumila ZUGA 27/1, 01-806 Warsaw
Tel: (022) 834 08 43 *Fax:* (022) 8641854; (022) 8340843
E-mail: penta@pol.pl
Web Site: www.penta.pl
Founded: 1988
Membership(s): Polish Book Charitex.
ISBN Prefix(es): 83-85440; 83-900031

Pallottinum Wydawnictwo Stowarzyszenia Apostolstwa Katolickiego+
al Przybyszewskiego 30 skr poczt 23, 60-959 Poznan
Tel: (061) 867-52-33 *Fax:* (061) 867-52-38
E-mail: pallottinum@pallottinum.pl
Web Site: www.pallottinum.pl
Key Personnel
Dir: Stefan Dusza *Tel:* (061) 8672118
 E-mail: dusza@pallottinum.pl
Deputy Dir: Stanislaw Gawrylo
Editorial: Kazimierz Jacaszek
Founded: 1948
Publishers of the Catholic Apostolate Association.
Subjects: Biblical Studies, Philosophy, Religion - Catholic, Theology
ISBN Prefix(es): 83-7014

Panstwowe Przedsiebiorstwo Wydawnictw Kartograficznych
ul Solec 18, 00-410 Warsaw
Tel: (022) 6283251; (022) 6214850 *Fax:* (022) 6280236; (022) 6214850
E-mail: ppwk@pdsox.com *Cable:* PEPEWUKA WARSZAWA
Key Personnel
Dir: Alina Meljon
Founded: 1951
ISBN Prefix(es): 83-7000

Panstwowe Wydawnictwo Rolnicze i Lesne+
Al Jerozolimskie 28, poczt 374, 00-950 Warsaw
Tel: (022) 8276338 *Fax:* (022) 8276338
Telex: 817509 Pl Pwril *Cable:* Pewril Warszawa
Key Personnel
Dir & Chief Editor: Mr Marian Bajorek
Deputy Editor: Halina Gutowski
Deputy Editor, Periodicals: Jan Czajka
Production: Danuta Kozlowska
Founded: 1947
State Agricultural & Forestry Publishers.
Subjects: Agriculture, Environmental Studies, Health, Nutrition, Veterinary Science
ISBN Prefix(es): 83-09
Branch Office(s)
ul Ratajczaka 33, 61-816 Poznan

Panstwowy Instytut Wydawniczy (PIW)
(National Publishing Institute)+
ul Foksal 17, 00-372 Warsaw
Mailing Address: skr poczt 377, 00-372 Warsaw
Tel: (022) 8260201; (022) 8260202; (022) 8260203; (022) 8260204; (022) 826-02-05
 Fax: (022) 826-15-36
E-mail: piw@piw.pl
Web Site: www.piw.pl
Telex: 8261536 *Cable:* PIW
Key Personnel
Dir: Radoslaw J Utnik *Tel:* (022) 8264879
 E-mail: dyrektor@piw.pl
Sales: Malgorzata Stawida
Production: Irena Rzepkowska
Rights: Stanislawa Lewicka
Founded: 1946
State Publishing Institute.
Subjects: Biography, Drama, Theater, Ethnicity, Fiction, History, Literature, Literary Criticism, Essays, Poetry, Science (General)
ISBN Prefix(es): 83-06
Number of titles published annually: 60 Print

Pearson Education Polska Sp z oo
ul Jana Olbrachta 94, 01-102 Warsaw
Tel: (022) 533 1533 *Toll Free Tel:* 0800 1200 76
 Fax: (022) 533 1534
E-mail: office@longman.com.pl
Web Site: www.longman.com.pl
Key Personnel
Man Dir: Ms Danuta A Lapkiewicz *Tel:* (022) 533 1555 *Fax:* (022) 533 1556
Finance & Operations Dir: Marcin Rudnik *Tel:* (022) 533 1551 *Fax:* (022) 533 1556
Commercial Dir: Rajmund Sawka *Tel:* (022) 553 1565
Marketing Manager: Anna Dadej *Tel:* (022) 533 1571
PA Marketing Dir: Katarzyna Glowinska *Tel:* (022) 533 1557 *Fax:* (022) 533 1556
Founded: 1991
ISBN Prefix(es): 83-88291

PIW, see Panstwowy Instytut Wydawniczy (PIW)

Wydawnictwo Podsiedlik-Raniowski i Spolka+
ul Zmigrodzka 41/49, 60-171 Poznan
Tel: (061) 867 95 46 *Fax:* (061) 867 68 50
E-mail: office@priska.com.pl
Key Personnel
Dir: Michal Stecki *E-mail:* michals@priska.com.pl
Founded: 1990
Specialize also in read-alongs & popular-scientific.
Subjects: Crafts, Games, Hobbies, Education, History, How-to, Poetry
ISBN Prefix(es): 83-85165; 83-7083

Poligrafia PWM, *imprint of* Polskie Wydawnictwo Muzyczne

Polish Scientific Publishers PWN+
ul Miodowa 10, 00-251 Warsaw
Tel: (022) 6954321; (022) 6954181
 Fax: (022) 8267163; (022) 6954288
 Fax on Demand: 080020145
E-mail: pwn@pwn.com.pl
Web Site: www.pwn.pl *Cable:* PEWUEN WARSZAWA
Key Personnel
Manager International Dept Rights & Contracts: Anna Raiter-Rosinska *E-mail:* anna.rosinska@pwn.com.pl
President: Richard Knauff *E-mail:* richard.knauff@pwn.com.pl
Editorial Dir: Anna Szemberg
Founded: 1951
Reference & academic publisher. Cooperates with foreign publishers
Member of STM-Scientific, Technical & Medical Publishers Association.
Subjects: Agriculture, Art, Behavioral Sciences, Biological Sciences, Business, Chemistry, Chemical Engineering, Civil Engineering, Computer Science, Earth Sciences, Economics, Education, Electronics, Electrical Engineering, Engineering (General), English as a Second Language, Environmental Studies, Finance, Geography, Geology, History, Language Arts, Linguistics, Management, Marketing, Mathematics, Mechanical Engineering, Philosophy, Physical Sciences, Physics, Psychology, Psychiatry, Science (General), Social Sciences, Sociology, Technology
ISBN Prefix(es): 83-01
Subsidiaries: All-Poland Distribution System-AZYMUT; School Publishers PWN; Wydawnictwo Lekarskie PZWL (medical & health)
Bookshop(s): Ksiegarnia PWN, ul Miodowa 10, 00-251 Warsaw; ul SW Tomasza 30, 31-027 Krakow; ul Wieckowskiego 13, 90-721 Lodz; ul Kuznicza 56, 50-138 Wroclaw
Book Club(s): Biblioteka PWN

Oficyna Wydawnicza Politechniki Wroclawskiej
Wybrzeze Wyspianskiego 27, 50-370 Wroclaw
Tel: (071) 320 29 94; (071) 320 38 23; (071) 328 29 40 *Fax:* (071) 328 29 40
E-mail: oficwyd@pwr.wroc.pl
Web Site: wsww.pwr.wroc.pl
Telex: 712254
Key Personnel
Dir: Halina Dudek
Founded: 1968
Subjects: Architecture & Interior Design, Engineering (General), Environmental Studies, Microcomputers, Physical Sciences, Physics, Science (General), Technology
ISBN Prefix(es): 83-7085
Bookshop(s): Pl Grunwaldzki 13, PL 50-370 Wroclaw

Wydawnictwo Polskiego Towarzystwa Wydawcow Ksiazek
Mazowiecka 2/4, 00048 Warsaw
Tel: (022) 826 72 71, Ext 345; (022) 826 07 35
 Fax: (022) 826 07 35
Key Personnel
President: Janusz Fogler
Contact: Jacek Gdaniec
Founded: 1921
ISBN Prefix(es): 83-7029; 83-85000

POMORZE-Pomorskie Wydawnictwo Prasowe
ul Paderewskiego 26, 85-075 Bydgoszcz
Tel: (052) 220237; (052) 211396; (052) 210452
Membership(s): RSW.
ISBN Prefix(es): 83-7003

Pomorze Wydawnictwo Spoldzielnia Pracy
ul Paderewskiego 26, 85-075 Bydgoszcz
Tel: (052) 220237; (052) 211396; (052) 210452
Telex: 0562845
Key Personnel
Chief Executive: Zbigniew Cieslinski
Editorial: Dr Ryszard Zietek
Sales, Production, Publicity, Rights & Permissions: Ewa Grinberg
Founded: 1982
ISBN Prefix(es): 83-7003
Bookshop(s): Ksiegarnia Domu Ksiazki, ul Marii Konopnickiej 30, 85-124 Bydgoszcz

Wydawnictwo Prawnicze Co
ul gen K Sosnkowskiego 1, 02-495 Warsaw
Tel: (022) 5729500; (022) 5729507 *Fax:* (022) 5729509
E-mail: biuro@lexisnexis.pl
Web Site: sklep.lexpolonica.pl
Key Personnel
President, Dir & Editor-in-Chief: Dr Jerzy Kowalski
Founded: 1952
Subjects: Criminology, Law, Marketing, Public Administration, Securities
ISBN Prefix(es): 83-219; 83-7334
Shipping Address: ul Sosnkowskiego 1, 02-495 Warsaw-Ursus
Warehouse: ul Sosnkowskiego 1, 02-495 Warsaw-Ursus

Przedsiebiorstwo Wydawniczo-Handlowe Wydawnictwo Siedmiorog+
ul Swiatnicka 7, 52-018 Wroclaw
Tel: (071) 341 68 71 *Fax:* (071) 341 68 87
E-mail: siedmiorog@siedmiorog.com.pl
Web Site: www.siedmiorog.pl
Key Personnel
Man Dir: Tomasz Michalowski
Subjects: Philosophy, Science Fiction, Fantasy
ISBN Prefix(es): 83-7162
Number of titles published annually: 100 Print
Total Titles: 570 Print
Showroom(s): ul Swiatniche 7, Wroclaw
Bookshop(s): ul Ch Toohue 39, Warsaw

Wydawnictwa Przemyslowe WEMA+
ul Danilowiczowska 18, 00-950 Warsaw
Tel: (022) 8275456; (022) 8272117 *Fax:* (022) 6355779
Telex: 814548
Key Personnel
Chief Executive: Andrzej Januszewicz
Founded: 1967
Also specialize in printing.
Subjects: Electronics, Electrical Engineering, Mechanical Engineering
ISBN Prefix(es): 83-85250

PWE, see Polskie Wydawnictwo Ekonomiczne PWE SA

PZWL Wydawnictwo Lekarskie Ltd+
Unit of PWN Publishers Group
ul Miodowa 10, 00-251 Warsaw
Mailing Address: Skr poczt 379, 00-950 Warsaw
Tel: (022) 6954033; (022) 6954497 *Fax:* (022) 6954032; (022) 6954497
E-mail: promocja@pzwl.pl
Web Site: www.pzwl.pl *Cable:* WYDLEK WARSZAWA
Key Personnel
President: Krystyna Regulska
Foreign Rights Manager: Anna Czyzewska
Tel: (022) 8314345 *Fax:* (022) 8314345
E-mail: anna.czyzewska@pzwl.pl
Founded: 1945
Medical Publishers Company Ltd.
Subjects: Biological Sciences, Chemistry, Chemical Engineering, Child Care & Development, Health, Nutrition, Medicine, Nursing, Dentistry, Psychology, Psychiatry, Veterinary Science
ISBN Prefix(es): 83-200
Total Titles: 400 Print; 2 CD-ROM
Parent Company: Scientific Publishers
Distributed by Scientific Publishers PWN
Distributor for Harcourt Brace & Co Ltd
Warehouse: ul Rolnicza 11, 05-092 Dziekanow Polski *Tel:* (022) 7511334 *Fax:* (022) 7511334

Wydawnictwa Radia i Telewizji
ul Chelmska 9, 00-724 Warsaw
Tel: (022) 412264
Key Personnel
Dir & Editor-in-Chief: Teresa Bartoszek
Production: Maciej Pcion
Founded: 1968
Subjects: Education, Fiction, Radio, TV, Science (General)
ISBN Prefix(es): 83-212

Oficyna Wydawnicza Read Me (Read Me Publishing House)+
Skr Poczt 144, 00-987 Warsaw 4
Tel: (022) 8706024 (ext 130) *Fax:* (022) 6771425
E-mail: readme@rm.com.pl
Web Site: www.rm.com.pl
Key Personnel
Man Dir: Wlodzimierz Binczyk
Licensing Coordinator & International Rights: Joanna Kopanczyk *E-mail:* joanna@rm.com.pl
Contact: Janusz Fajfer; Tomasz Zajbt
Founded: 1991
Subjects: Computer Science, Economics, Education, Health, Nutrition, Microcomputers, Outdoor Recreation, Self-Help, Travel
ISBN Prefix(es): 83-85769; 83-7147; 83-87216; 83-900451
Number of titles published annually: 100 Print
Associate Companies: Wydawnictwo Eremis; Wydawnictwo RM

Res Polona+
ul Gdanska 80, 90-613 Lodz
Tel: (042) 6363634; (042) 6374587; (042) 6374607 *Fax:* (042) 6373010
E-mail: info@res-polona.com.pl
Web Site: www.res-polona.com.pl
Key Personnel
President: Jozef Fraszczynski
Founded: 1989
Subjects: Education
ISBN Prefix(es): 83-85063; 83-7071
Subsidiaries: Res Polona

Rosikon Press+
Aleja Debow 4, 05-080 Izabelin Warsaw
Tel: (022) 7226101; (022) 7226102; (022) 7226666 *Fax:* (022) 7226667
E-mail: biuro@rosikonpress.com; office@rosikompress.com
Web Site: www.rosikonpress.com
Key Personnel
Man Dir: Grazyna Kasprzycka-Rosikon *Tel:* (022) 7226666 *E-mail:* g.kasprzycka@rosikonpress.com
Founded: 1990
Membership(s): Polish Chamber of Books.
Subjects: Art, History, Photography, Religion - Catholic
ISBN Prefix(es): 83-900695
Number of titles published annually: 5 Print
Total Titles: 3 Print
Distributed by Azymut (Poland)

Wydawnictwo RTW+
ul Broniewskiego 9a, 01-780 Warsaw
Tel: (022) 633 70 10; (022) 663 74 74 *Fax:* (022) 633 70 10; (022) 39120123
E-mail: rtw@wydawrtw.media.pl
Key Personnel
Rights Manager: Anna Wisniewska
Foreign Relations Assistant: Dorota Trusiak
Founded: 1992
Independent, Individual Company.
Subjects: Animals, Pets, Education, Geography, Geology, History, Science (General), Atlases
ISBN Prefix(es): 83-86822; 83-7294; 83-85493; 83-87974
Number of titles published annually: 50 Print; 20 Audio
Total Titles: 80 Print; 25 Audio
Warehouse: ul Koleyowa 19/21, Warsaw, Contact: Dorota Trusiak

RW-KUL, *imprint of* Katolicki Uniwersytet Wydawniczo-Redakcja

Wydawnictwo SIC+
ul Chelmska 27/23, 00-724 Warsaw
Tel: (022) 8400753 *Fax:* (022) 8400753
E-mail: sic@sic.ksiazka.pl
Key Personnel
Man Dir: Elzbieta Czerwirlska
Editor-in-Chief: Ranata Lis
Founded: 1993
Subjects: Human Relations, Self-Help
ISBN Prefix(es): 83-86056; 83-88807
Total Titles: 50 Print
Orders to: Hydawnictwo Siel, ul Tucka 2/4/6 m 21, 00-845 Warsaw, Contact: Katarzyna Jaskiewicz *Fax:* (022) 6546784 *E-mail:* sic@sic.ksiazka.pl

'Slask' Ltd+
Al W Korfantego 51, 40-161 Katowice
Tel: (032) 258 07 56; (032) 2581812; (032) 2583222; (032) 2581910 *Fax:* (032) 2583229
E-mail: biuro@slaskwn.com.pl
Web Site: www.slaskwn.com.pl
Key Personnel
President: Tadeusz Sierny
Manager: Grzegorz Bociek; Bogumila Cyron
Founded: 1954
Membership(s): The Polish Chamber of the Book.
Subjects: Advertising, English as a Second Language, History, Literature, Literary Criticism, Essays, Nonfiction (General), Poetry, Regional Interests, Science (General)
ISBN Prefix(es): 83-900705; 83-900814; 83-85831; 83-7164

Spoleczny Instytut Wydawniczy Znak+
ul Kosciuszki 37, 30-105 Krakow
Tel: (012) 4291469; (012) 4219776 *Fax:* (012) 4219814
E-mail: rucinska@znak.com.pl
Web Site: www.znak.com.pl *Cable:* KOSCIUSZKI 37
Key Personnel
Contact: Jolanta Wlodarczyk
Founded: 1959
Subjects: History, Philosophy, Religion - Other
ISBN Prefix(es): 83-7006
Bookshop(s): ul Slawkowska 1, 31-007 Krakow

Sport I Turystyka, *imprint of* Muza SA

Spotdzielnia Anagram
al 3 Maja 2 Pok, 4, 00-391 Warsaw
Tel: (022) 6229324; (022) 6229326
Key Personnel
Agency Editor-in-Chief: Zygmunt Konopka
Editorial: Andrzej Murawski
Sales: Halina Popiolek
Production: Wieslaw Felczak
Founded: 1974

Youth Publishing Agency & Publishing Co-operative.
This organization replaces the former Wydawnictwo Harcerskie 'Horyzonty'. It is also a Workers' Publishing Co-operative, allied to RSW. Mlodziezowa acts as both agency & publisher for Polish youth.
Subjects: Ethnicity, Government, Political Science, Science (General), Social Sciences, Sociology
ISBN Prefix(es): 83-203; 83-86086

Wydawnictwa Szkolne i Pedagogiczne (Polish Educational Publishers)+
Al Jerozolimskie, 136, 02-305 Warsaw
Mailing Address: skr poczt 480, 00-959 Warsaw
Tel: (022) 8265451; (022) 8265452; (022) 8265453; (022) 8265454; (022) 8265455; (022) 5762500; (022) 5762501 *Toll Free Tel:* 800-220555 *Fax:* (022) 8279280
E-mail: wsip@wsip.com.pl
Web Site: www.wsip.com.pl
Telex: 816132 *Cable:* WUESIPE WARSZAWA
Key Personnel
Man Dir: Andrzej Chrzanowski
Rights & Permissions: Maciej Lipko
Advertising: Wojciech Krasuski
Contact: Maria Bogobowicz
Founded: 1945
Membership(s): EEPG, Polish Chamber of the Book.
Subjects: Education, Psychology, Psychiatry
ISBN Prefix(es): 83-02
Branch Office(s)
Delegatura WSiP, Basztowa 15, 31-143 Cracow
Orders to: Ars Polona, PO Box 1001, 00-068 Warsaw

Oficyna Wydawnicza Szkoly Glownej Handlowej w Warszawie Oficyna Wydawnicza SGH+
ul Rakowiecka 24, Budynek "A" 6, 13, 14 & 17, 02-554 Warsaw
Tel: (022) 337 92 13; (022) 337 92 17; (022) 337 97 61; (022) 337 97 69 *Fax:* (022) 646 61 03
E-mail: dwz@sgh.waw.pl
Web Site: www.sgh.waw.pl
Telex: 816031sgh
Key Personnel
Dir: Dr Bogdan Radomski *E-mail:* bradomski@sgh.waw.pl
Deputy Dir: Elzbieta Fonberg-Stokluska *E-mail:* estokl@sgh.waw.pl
Founded: 1917
Subjects: Economics, English as a Second Language, Finance, History, Law, Mathematics, Philosophy, Public Administration, Social Sciences, Sociology
ISBN Prefix(es): 83-86689; 83-7225; 83-7378

Instytut Techniki Budowlanej, Dzial Wydawniczo- Poligraficzny
ul Ksawerow 21, 02-656 Warsaw
Tel: (022) 8431471 *Fax:* (022) 8432931
E-mail: wydawnictwa_itb@pro.onet.pl
Web Site: www.itb.pl
Key Personnel
Man Dir: Stanislaw Wierzbicki
Founded: 1945
Subjects: Civil Engineering
ISBN Prefix(es): 83-7130; 83-7226; 83-7290; 83-7321; 83-7370
Imprints: ITB
Bookshop(s): ul Filtrowa 1, 00-611 Warsaw
Tel: (022) 825 52 29 *Fax:* (022) 57 96 295

Towarzystwo Naukowe w Toruniu
ul Wysoka 16, 87-100 Torun
Tel: (056) 6223941 (ext 8)
Key Personnel
Editorial Manager: Bozena Soltys
Founded: 1875
Specialize in humanities.
Subjects: Archaeology, Art, Biological Sciences, Geography, Geology, History, Language Arts, Linguistics, Law, Medicine, Nursing, Dentistry, Physical Sciences, Regional Interests
ISBN Prefix(es): 83-85196; 83-87639

Wydawnictwo TPPR Wspolpraca+
ul Marszalkowska 115, 00-932 Warsaw
Tel: (022) 200301 (ext 227)
Key Personnel
Chief Executive: Ryszard Pogonowski
Production: Kazimierz Andruk
Founded: 1984
Subjects: Government, Political Science, Literature, Literary Criticism, Essays
ISBN Prefix(es): 83-7018

Wydawnictwa Uniwersytetu Warszawskiego+
Imprint of Wydawnictwa Uniwersytetu Warszawskiego
ul Nowy Swiat 4, 00-497 Warsaw
Tel: (022) 5531318 *Fax:* (022) 5531318
E-mail: wuw@uw.edu.pl
Key Personnel
Dir: Michal Szewielow
Rights & Permissions: Ryszard Burek
Assistant Marketing Manager: Monika Glowacz
Founded: 1956
A predominant share in our offer is taken by the publications of the Polish Faculty (theory & history of literature, linguistics) & books on culture written from the point of view of various humanistic disciplines.
Subjects: African American Studies, Agriculture, Americana, Regional, Anthropology, Archaeology, Asian Studies, Behavioral Sciences, Biography, Biological Sciences, Chemistry, Chemical Engineering, Economics, Education, English as a Second Language, Environmental Studies, Ethnicity, Genealogy, Geography, Geology, Government, Political Science, History, Social Sciences, Sociology
ISBN Prefix(es): 83-230; 83-235
Number of titles published annually: 38 Print
Total Titles: 2,319 Print
Orders to: Centrala Handlu Zagranicznego, Ars Polona SA, ul Obroncow 25, 00-933 Warsaw *Tel:* (022) 5098638 *Fax:* (022) 5098637
E-mail: arspolona@arspolona.com.pl

Wydawnictwo Uniwersytetu Wroclawskiego SP ZOO
pl Uniwersytecki 9/13, 50-137 Wroclaw
Tel: (071) 3752809 *Fax:* (071) 3752735
E-mail: marketing@wuwr.com.pl
Web Site: www.wuwr.com.pl
Key Personnel
President: Marek Gorny
Founded: 1996
Scientific handbooks for students of Wroclawskiego University.
ISBN Prefix(es): 83-229

Verbinum Wydawnictwo Ksiezy Werbistow+
ul Ostrobramska 98, 04-118 Warsaw
Tel: (022) 6107878; (022) 8703286 *Fax:* (022) 6107775
Key Personnel
Editor: P Antoni Koszorz
Founded: 1983
Subjects: Developing Countries, Religion - Other
ISBN Prefix(es): 83-85009; 83-85762; 83-7192
Parent Company: Verbinum
Subsidiaries: Verbinum, Dzial Kolportazu

Videograf II Sp z o o Zaklad Poracy Chronionej
al W Korfantego 191, 40-153 Katowice
Tel: (03) 2036558; (03) 2036559; (03) 2036560 *Fax:* (03) 2036558; (03) 2036559; (03) 2036560
E-mail: videograf@videograf.dnd.com.pl
Key Personnel
Editor-in-Chief & International Rights: Jacek Illg
Man Dir: Franciszek Leki
Founded: 1996
Subjects: Biography, Education, Fiction, Film, Video, Gardening, Plants, Mysteries, Photography
ISBN Prefix(es): 83-7183; 83-86831

Vocatio Publishing House+
Skr Poczt 41, Polnej Rozy 1, PL-02792 Warsaw 78
Tel: (022) 648-5450 *Fax:* (022) 648-6382
E-mail: vocatio@vocatio.com.pl
Web Site: www.vocatio.com.pl
Key Personnel
President & Chief Executive Officer: Piotr Waclawik *E-mail:* wydawca@vocatio.com.pl
Founded: 1991
Membership(s): ECPA, ICCC.
Subjects: Biblical Studies, Religion - Catholic, Religion - Protestant, Theology, Bible reference books; children's books, video books, music
ISBN Prefix(es): 83-85435; 83-7146

Wydawnictwo WAB (WAB Publishers)+
Lowicka 31 Str, 02-502 Warsaw
Tel: (022) 646 05 10; (022) 646 05 11; (022) 646 01 74; (022) 646 01 75 *Fax:* (022) 646 05 10; (022) 646 05 11; (022) 646 01 74; (022) 646 01 75
E-mail: wab@wab.com.pl
Web Site: www.wab.com.pl
Key Personnel
Editor: Beata Stasinska
Founded: 1991
Specialize in promoting & publishing Polish contemporary literary fiction, as well as translations.
Subjects: Fiction, Health, Nutrition, Human Relations, Nonfiction (General)
ISBN Prefix(es): 83-87021; 83-88221; 83-85554
Number of titles published annually: 40 Print
Total Titles: 450 Print

Warszawskie Wydawnictwo Literackie, *imprint of* Muza SA

'Wiedza Powszechna' Panstwowe Wydawnictwo+
ul Jasna 26, 00-054 Warsaw
Tel: (022) 8277651 *Fax:* (022) 8269592; (022) 8268594
Key Personnel
Dir: Teresa Korsak
Deputy: Tadeusz Mazurek
Founded: 1952
Subjects: Language Arts, Linguistics, Science (General)
ISBN Prefix(es): 83-214

Wydawnictwo Wilga sp zoo (Wilga Publishing Ltd)+
ul Smulikowskiego 1/3, 00-389 Warsaw
Tel: (022) 826-08-82; (022) 827-90-11 (ext 282) *Fax:* (022) 826-06-43
E-mail: wilga@wilga.com.pl
Key Personnel
President & Foreign Rights: Jan Wojnilko
Vice President: Anna Sikorska-Michalak
Editor-in-Chief: Olga Wojnilko
Founded: 1993
Subjects: Education, Fiction
ISBN Prefix(es): 83-7156; 83-86664; 83-901029; 83-903028
Number of titles published annually: 300 Print
Total Titles: 1,200 Print
Subsidiaries: Wilga Marketing
Warehouse: Panstwowe Magazyny Ustugowe, Przejazdowa 25, 05-800 Pruszkow

WNT, *imprint of* Wydawnictwa Naukowo-Techniczne

WOSI "Wspolna Sprawa" Warsaw, *imprint of* Wydawn Na Sprawa' Wydawniczo-Oswiatowa Spotdzielnia Inwalidow

WUW, see Wydawnictwa Uniwersytetu Warszawskiego

Wydawn Na Sprawa' Wydawniczo-Oswiatowa Spotdzielnia Inwalidow+
ul Zelazna 40, 00-832 Warsaw
Tel: (022) 6209071 (ext 26) *Fax:* (022) 6209197
Key Personnel
President: Zdzislaw Kozanecki
Vice President, Publishing Manager: Marianna Malejko
Founded: 1956
Educational Publishing Co-operative of the Disabled.
Subjects: Crafts, Games, Hobbies
ISBN Prefix(es): 83-85048
Imprints: WOSI "Wspolna Sprawa" Warsaw
Showroom(s): Al Solidarnosci, 82

Zaklad Wydawnictw Statystycznych
al Niepodleglosci 208, 00-925 Warsaw
Tel: (022) 6083223; (022) 608-32-10 (orders); (022) 608-38-10 (orders) *Fax:* (022) 625-9078; (022) 608-38-67 (orders)
Telex: 814581a *Cable:* GUS 12WS
Key Personnel
Man Dir: Andrzej Stasiun
Marketing: Christo Cwetkow
Founded: 1966
Statistical Publications Board of the Central Statistical Office.
Subjects: Economics, Mathematics, Social Sciences, Sociology
ISBN Prefix(es): 83-7027
Divisions: Zaklad Wydawnictwo

Instytut Wydawniczy Zwiazkow Zawodowych
ul Jaracza 5, 00-378 Warsaw
Tel: 6250765
Key Personnel
Dir: Andrzej Wacowski
Founded: 1950
Publishing house of trade unions.
Subjects: Labor, Industrial Relations
ISBN Prefix(es): 83-202
Bookshop(s): Ksiegarnia Skladowa, Marienszat 8, 00-302 Warsaw

Portugal

General Information

Capital: Libson
Language: Portuguese
Religion: Predominately Roman Catholic, some Protestant
Population: 10 million
Bank Hours: 0830-1500 Monday-Friday
Shop Hours: 0900-1300, 1500-1900 Monday-Friday (some do not close midday); 0900-1300 Saturday. Generally closed Monday morning October-November
Currency: 100 Eurocents = 1 Euro; 200.482 Portuguese escudos = 1 Euro
Export/Import Information: Member of European Economic Community. Foreign language books from most countries dutied per kg (free from UK and reduced from EEC); atlases and children's picture books have higher tariff rate and children's picture books have an import surcharge. 5% VAT on books. Small quantity of advertising duty-free. No import license required for goods not exceeding a certain value, otherwise license including permission to transfer foreign exchange required.
Copyright: UCC, Berne (see Copyright Conventions, pg xi)

Academia das Ciencias de Lisboa
R Academia das Ciencias 19-1, 1200 Lisbon
Tel: (021) 346-3866 *Fax:* (021) 342-0395
Key Personnel
President: Prof J M Toscano Rico
ISBN Prefix(es): 972-623

Africa Literatura Arte Cultura - ALAC
Av D Pedro V 11-2° D, 2795 Linda-A-Velha
Tel: (021) 4192274
ISBN Prefix(es): 972-9041

Edicoes Afrontamento+
Rua Costa Cabral 859, 4200-225 Porto
Tel: (02) 507 42 20 *Fax:* (02) 507 42 29
E-mail: afrontamento@mail.telepac.pt
Key Personnel
Man Dir, Editorial, Production: Jose Sousa Ribeiro
Sales, Publicity, Rights & Permissions: Andrea Peniche
Founded: 1963
Subjects: Film, Video, Government, Political Science, Literature, Literary Criticism, Essays, Social Sciences, Sociology
ISBN Prefix(es): 972-36
Number of titles published annually: 40 Print
Total Titles: 900 Print

ALAC, see Africa Literatura Arte Cultura - ALAC

Publicacoes Alfa SA+
Rua Luis Pastor de Macedo, 1-B, 1700 Lisbon
Tel: (021) 7587320
Key Personnel
Administrator: Francisco Lyon de Castro
Founded: 1973
Subjects: History
ISBN Prefix(es): 972-626
Parent Company: Publicacoes Europa-America
Branch Office(s)
Commercial & Editorial Departments, Estrada Lisboa-Sintra, Km 14, Edificio CETOP, 2725-377 Mem Martins
Bookshop(s): Livraria Alfa, Avenida Antonio Augusto de Aguiar 150-A, 1050 Lisbon; Livraria Alfa, Rua Luis Pastor de Macedo, 1-B, 1750 Lisbon

Livraria Almedina
Arco de Almedina 15, 3000 509 Coimbra
Tel: 239 851 903
E-mail: editora@almedina.net
Web Site: www.almedina.net
Telex: 52207 acic p
Key Personnel
Man Dir: Joaquim Machado
Founded: 1955
Subjects: Education, Law
ISBN Prefix(es): 972-40
Associate Companies: Edicoes Globo Ltda, Rua S Filipe Nery 37A, 1250; Porto Ltda, Rua de Ceuta 79, 4050 Oporto
Bookshop(s): Arco de Almedina 15, Rua Ferreira Borges 121, 3049 Coimbra, Codex

Armenio Amado Editora de Simoes, Beirao & Ca Lda+
Rua Estrela 2-2°, 3000 Coimbra
Tel: (039) 92150 *Fax:* (039) 851901
Key Personnel
Man Dir: Joaquim Machado
Founded: 1929
Subjects: Architecture & Interior Design, Government, Political Science, History, Language Arts, Linguistics, Law, Philosophy, Psychology, Psychiatry, Religion - Other, Social Sciences, Sociology
ISBN Prefix(es): 972-628

Edicoes Antigona
Rua Jorge Barradas, 212-4° D, 1500 Lisbon
Tel: (021) 749483 *Fax:* (021) 749483
Key Personnel
Editorial, Sales: Manuel Luis de Oliveira
Founded: 1979
Subjects: Fiction, Government, Political Science, History, Literature, Literary Criticism, Essays, Social Sciences, Sociology
ISBN Prefix(es): 972-608

Apaginastantas - Cooperativa de Servicos Culturais
Apdo 4254, 1507 Lisbon Codex
Tel: (021) 668987
Key Personnel
Man Dir: Anabela Mendes
Editorial: Joao Barrento
Founded: 1982
Subjects: Literature, Literary Criticism, Essays, Social Sciences, Sociology
ISBN Prefix(es): 972-607

Apostolado da Oracao Secretariado Nacional
Largo das Teresinhas 5, 4719-504 Braga Codex
Tel: (053) 22485 *Fax:* (053) 201221
Key Personnel
Man Dir, Editorial: Manuel Morujao; Americo Nunes
Founded: 1874
Subjects: Biography, Poetry, Religion - Other, Theology
ISBN Prefix(es): 972-39

Livraria Arnado Lda
Rua Joao Machado 9-11, 3007 Coimbra Codex
Tel: (0239) 27573 *Fax:* (0239) 22598
Key Personnel
Man Dir: Vasco Antunes Domingos
Founded: 1966
Subjects: Law, Literature, Literary Criticism, Essays, Mathematics
ISBN Prefix(es): 972-701
Parent Company: Porto Editora Lda
Associate Companies: Empresa Literaria Fluminense, Lda

Arquivo Universidade de Coimbra
Rua S Pedro 11-2, 3000 Coimbra
Tel: (0239) 25422 *Fax:* (0239) 25841
Web Site: www.uc.pt
Telex: 52273
Key Personnel
Contact: Manuel Augusto Rodrigues
ISBN Prefix(es): 972-594

Arvore Coop de Actividades Artisticas, CRL
Pr Azevedo Albuquerque 1, 4000 Porto
Tel: (02) 383867 *Fax:* (02) 2002684
Key Personnel
President: Jose Rodrigues
Founded: 1963
Subjects: Architecture & Interior Design, Art
ISBN Prefix(es): 972-9089

Assirio & Alvim
R Passos Manuel 67B, 1100 Lisbon
Tel: (021) 555580 *Fax:* (021) 3152935
Key Personnel
Editor: Herminio Monteiro
Subjects: Art, History, Literature, Literary Criticism, Essays, Photography
ISBN Prefix(es): 972-37

PUBLISHERS
PORTUGAL

Atica, SA Editores e Livreiros
Rua Alvaro Coutinho, 2-3º D, 1100 Lisbon
Tel: (021) 8153220 *Fax:* (021) 8153219
Key Personnel
Man Dir: Vasco Silva; Jose Rodrigues
Editorial, Rights & Permissions: Vasco Silva
Founded: 1935
Subjects: Drama, Theater, Literature, Literary Criticism, Essays, Poetry, Social Sciences, Sociology
ISBN Prefix(es): 972-617

Basica Editora
Rua de Entrecampos 36 - r/c E, 1700 Lisbon
Tel: (021) 779273
Key Personnel
Man Dir, Rights & Permissions: Francisco Prata Ginja
Editorial: Rui Ferreira Lopes da Costa
Production, Publicity: Maria Jorge Lopes da Costa
Founded: 1974
Subjects: Education
ISBN Prefix(es): 972-631
Imprints: BE
Sales Office(s): Platano Editora SARL
Bookshop(s): Livraria Basica, Ave Elias Garcia 49-B, 1000 Lisbon

BE, *imprint of* Basica Editora

Bertrand Editora Lda+
Rua Anchieta 29 1ro, 1200 Lisbon
Tel: (021) 320084 *Fax:* (021) 3468286
Telex: 42748
Key Personnel
Man Dir: Joao Carlos Alvim
Sales, Rights & Permissions: Teresa Mendonca
Production: Mario Correia
Publicity: Laura Pinheiro
Founded: 1727
Subjects: Art, Literature, Literary Criticism, Essays, Social Sciences, Sociology
ISBN Prefix(es): 972-25
Bookshop(s): Sociedades Livreiras Bertrand

Bezerr-Editorae e Distribuidora de Abel Antonio Bezerra
Bairro Duarte Pacheco, Rua do Rosmaninho 110, 4703 Braga Codex
Mailing Address: Apdo 313, Braga Codex
Tel: (0253) 22604 *Fax:* (0253) 617105
Key Personnel
Man Dir: Abel Antonio Bezerra
Founded: 1996
Subjects: Drama, Theater, Education, Ethnicity, Fiction, History, Poetry, Travel
ISBN Prefix(es): 972-97378

Biblioteca Geral da Universidade de Coimbra
Division of Universidade de Coimbra
Largo da Porta Ferrea, 3000-447 Coimbra
Tel: (0239) 859800; (0239) 859900 *Fax:* (0239) 827135
E-mail: bguc@ci.uc.pt
Web Site: www.uc.pt
Key Personnel
Dir: Prof Carlos Fiolhais
Contact: Paula Fernandes Martins
Subjects: Education, History, Library & Information Sciences, Literature, Literary Criticism, Essays, Music, Dance, Religion - Catholic, Religion - Other
ISBN Prefix(es): 972-616
Parent Company: Universidade de Coimbra

Biblioteca Publica Municipal do Porto
Rua D Joao IV, 4049 017 Porto
Tel: (022) 5193480 *Fax:* (022) 5193488
E-mail: bpmp@em-porto.pt
Founded: 1833
ISBN Prefix(es): 972-634

Brasilia Editora (J Carvalho Branco)+
Rua Jose Falcao 173, 4000 Porto
Tel: (02) 315854 *Fax:* (02) 2055854 *Cable:* BRASILIAEDITORA
Key Personnel
Man Dir: J Carvalho Branco *Tel:* 02 2001896 *Fax:* 02 2001904
Editorial, Rights & Permissions: Dr Zulmira C Branco
Sales, Publicity: Dr Isabel C Branco
Production: Joana Carvalho Branco
Founded: 1961
Subjects: Astrology, Occult, Biography, Fiction, Government, Political Science, Health, Nutrition, How-to, Philosophy, Poetry, Psychology, Psychiatry, Religion - Other, Social Sciences, Sociology
ISBN Prefix(es): 972-557
Parent Company: Livraria Leitura - Fernandes e Branco Lda, Rua de Ceuta 88, 4050
Associate Companies: Livraria Leitura - Fernandes e Branco Lda, Rua de Ceuta 88, 4050 Porto
Subsidiaries: Livraria Brasilia Editora
Bookshop(s): Livraria Brasilia Editora, Ave Almirante Reis 256B, 1000 Lisbon

Broteria Associacao Cultural e Cientifica
Rua Maestro Antonio Taborda, 14, 1293 Lisbon Codex
Tel: (021) 3961660 *Fax:* (021) 3956629
ISBN Prefix(es): 972-9076

Camara Municipal de Castelo
R Candido Reis-Viana Castelo, 4901-887 Viana do Castelo
Tel: (058) 809300 *Fax:* (058) 809347
Telex: 32582
Subjects: Antiques, Archaeology, Architecture & Interior Design, Art, History, Poetry
ISBN Prefix(es): 972-588
Associate Companies: Biblioteca Municipal, Museo Municipal
Subsidiaries: Livraria Municipal

Editorial Caminho SARL+
Al Santo Antonio dos Capuchos, 6 B, 1100 Lisbon
Tel: (021) 3152683 *Fax:* (021) 534346
E-mail: caminho@mail.telepac.pt
Telex: 65792
Key Personnel
Man Dir: Zeferino Antas de Coelho
Founded: 1977
Subjects: Fiction, Government, Political Science
ISBN Prefix(es): 972-21

CAPU
Av Almirante Gago Coutinho, 158, 1700 Lisbon
Tel: (021) 8429190 *Fax:* (021) 8409361
E-mail: capu@capu.pt
Web Site: www.capu.pt
Key Personnel
President: Torcato Lopes
ISBN Prefix(es): 972-580

Editora Caravela+
Rua General Morais Sarmento 9 c/v, 1500 Lisbon
Tel: (01) 7155848 *Fax:* (021) 155848
Key Personnel
Man Dir & International Rights: Jose Chaves Ferreira
Founded: 1986
ISBN Prefix(es): 972-639

Casa Publicadora da Convencao das Assembleias de Deus em Portugall, *see* CAPU

Celta Editora, Lda
Rua Vera Cruz 2B, 2780-305 Oeiras
Tel: (021) 4417433 *Fax:* (021) 4467304
E-mail: mail@celtaeditora.pt; celtaeditora@mail.telepac.pt
Web Site: www.celtaeditora.pt
Key Personnel
Editorial: Carla Pinheiro
ISBN Prefix(es): 972-8027; 972-774

Centro Estudos Geograficos
Faculdade de Letras Cidade Universitaria, 1699 Lisbon Codex
Tel: (021) 778883 *Fax:* (021) 7938690
E-mail: ceg@mail.telepac.pt
Key Personnel
President: Dr Diogo de Abreu
Founded: 1944
Subjects: Geography, Geology, Social Sciences, Sociology
ISBN Prefix(es): 972-636

Centro Psicologia Clinica+
Via Lucania 42, 65121 Pescara
Tel: (085) 4211986 *Fax:* (085) 4211986
E-mail: cdibera@tin.it
Web Site: www.centro-psicologia.it
Key Personnel
President: Dr Carlo Di Berardino
ISBN Prefix(es): 972-725

Edicoes Cetop+
PO Box 7, 2726 Mem Martins Codex
Tel: (021) 926 3222 *Fax:* (021) 921 7940
Telex: 42255 pea p
Key Personnel
Man Dir: Tito Lyon de Castro
Editorial Dir, Rights & Production: Jose Antonio Rosa *E-mail:* jose.rosa@oninet.pt
Founded: 1965
Membership(s): Euro-Business Publishing Network.
Subjects: Advertising, Business, Career Development, Computer Science, Finance, Management, Microcomputers, Technology, Travel
ISBN Prefix(es): 972-641
Subsidiaries: Lyon Multimedia Edicoes
Orders to: Publicacoes Europa America, Apdo 8, 2726 Mem Martins Codex

Cidade Nova Editora
Rua Dr Camilo Dionisio Alvares, 233, 2775 Parede
Tel: (01) 2478734 *Fax:* (01) 2476369
Web Site: perola.net-rubi.com.br
ISBN Prefix(es): 972-9159

Publicacoes Ciencia e Vida Lda+
Rua Victor Cordon 24-1º D, 1200 Lisbon
Tel: (021) 3427989 *Fax:* (021) 3460224
Key Personnel
Man Dir, Editorial: Jeronimo Simoes
Founded: 1979
Subjects: Agriculture, Animals, Pets, Environmental Studies, Medicine, Nursing, Dentistry
ISBN Prefix(es): 972-590

Livraria Civilizacao (Americo Fraga Lamares & Ca Lda)+
R Dr Alberto Aires de Gouveia, 27, 4000 Porto
Tel: (022) 20002286 *Fax:* (022) 312382
Cable: Alamares
Key Personnel
Man Dir: Arquitecto Moura Bessa
Rights & Permissions: Maria Alice Moura Bessa
Founded: 1921
Subjects: Art, Economics, Fiction, Government, Political Science, History, Social Sciences, Sociology

ISBN Prefix(es): 972-26
Branch Office(s)
Ave Almirante Reis 102 r/c-Dto, Lisbon 1
Tel: (021) 823389 *Fax:* (021) 823389

Editora Classica+
R da Gloria, 10 - R/C, 1298 Lisbon Codex
Tel: (021) 372386 *Fax:* (021) 3474729
Telex: 18570 escoli p.
Key Personnel
Editorial: Francisco Paulo
Subjects: Behavioral Sciences, Business, Communications, Drama, Theater, Fiction, History, Management, Science Fiction, Fantasy, Social Sciences, Sociology, Wine & Spirits
ISBN Prefix(es): 972-561
Bookshop(s): Cascais Shopping, Loja 12B, 2675 Cascais; Shopping dos Clerigos, 4000 Porto
Orders to: Distribuidora Internacional de Livros Lda, Rua Vale Formoso 37, 1900 Lisbon
Tel: (021) 8681183 *Fax:* (021) 8581257

Coimbra Editora Lda+
Rua do Arnado, 3001-951 Coimbra
Mailing Address: Apdo 101, 3001-951 Coimbra
Tel: (0239) 85 2650 *Fax:* (0239) 85 2651
E-mail: sede@mail.coimbraeditora.pt; revistas@mail.coimbraeditora.pt
Web Site: www.coimbraeditora.pt
Key Personnel
Man Dir: Antonio Frederico Araujo Serpa
Founded: 1920 (5)
Subjects: Education, Language Arts, Linguistics, Law, Literature, Literary Criticism, Essays, Psychology, Psychiatry
ISBN Prefix(es): 972-32; 972-96761
Bookshop(s): Faculdade de Direito da Universidade do Porto, Praca Coronel Pacheco 15, 4050-453 Porto *Tel:* (022) 339 0587 *Fax:* (022) 339 0588 *E-mail:* liv_FDP@mail.coimbraeditora.pt; Livraria AAC, Rua Padre Antonio Vieira, Edificio AAC, 3000-315 Coimbra *Tel:* (0239) 83 4123 *Fax:* (0239) 85 2651 *E-mail:* liv_AAC@mail.coimbraeditora.pt; Livraria Chiado, Rua Nova do Almada, 90, 1200-290 Lisbon *Tel:* (021) 342 4917 *Fax:* (021) 347 1464 *E-mail:* liv_chiado@mail.coimbraeditora.pt; Livraria FDL, Faculdade de Direito da Universidade de Lisboa, 1649-014 Lisbon *Tel:* (021) 796 3122 *Fax:* (021) 780 0763 *E-mail:* liv_FDL@mail.coimbraeditora.pt; Livraria Ferreira Borges, Rua Ferreira Borges 77-79, 3000-180 Coimbra *Tel:* (0239) 85 2650 *Fax:* (0239) 85 2651 *E-mail:* liv_fborges@mail.coimbraeditora.pt; Livraria Juridica - Centro Comercial Arco-Iris, Av Julio Dinis, 6 A-Lj 30, 36, 37 & 38, 1069-215 Lisbon *Tel:* (021) 780 0468 *Fax:* (021) 780 0469 *E-mail:* liv_jurarcoiris@mail.coimbraeditora.pt

Edicoes Colibri+
Apdo 42 001, Telheiras, 1601-801 Lisbon Codex
Tel: (021) 7964038 *Fax:* (021) 7964038
E-mail: colibri@edi-colibri.pt
Web Site: www.edi-colibri.pt
Key Personnel
Man Dir: Fernando Mao de Ferro
Founded: 1991
Membership(s): Associacao Portuguesa de Editores e Livreiros (APEL).
Subjects: Archaeology, Environmental Studies, Geography, Geology, History, Literature, Literary Criticism, Essays, Philosophy, Social Sciences, Sociology, Political science
ISBN Prefix(es): 972-772; 972-8047; 972-8288
Number of titles published annually: 50 Print
Total Titles: 400 Print; 400 Online
Distributed by Dinapress; Sodilivros (Only in Portugal); Sodiexpor
Bookshop(s): Livraria Colibri-Faculdade de Ciencias Sociais e Humanas da Universidade Nova de Lisboa, Av de Berna, 26-C, 1069-061 Lisbon

Comissao para a Igualdade e Direitos das Mulheres+
Av Republica 32-1 E, 1050-193 Lisbon
Tel: (021) 7983000 *Fax:* (021) 7983099
E-mail: cidm@mail.telepac.pt
Key Personnel
President: Maria Amelia Paiva
Editor: Madalena Barbosa
Founded: 1977
Subjects: Women's Studies
ISBN Prefix(es): 972-597

Editorial Confluencia Lda+
Calcada do Combro 99, 1116 Lisbon Codex
Tel: (021) 663853 *Fax:* (021) 326921
E-mail: livroshorizonte@mail.telepac.pt
Key Personnel
Man Dir & Editorial: Rogerio Mendes de Moura; Eduardo Loureiro de Moura
Sales, Rights & Permissions: Manuela Duarte
Production: Paulo Caracas
Publicity: M Conceicao Silva
Founded: 1945
ISBN Prefix(es): 972-9014

Constancia Editores, SA
Estrada da Outurela, 118, 2794-084 Carnaxide
Tel: (021) 4246901; (021) 4246902
E-mail: info@constancia-editores.pt; prosa@santillana.pt
Web Site: www.constancia-editores.pt; www.santillana.pt
Founded: 1989
Subjects: Art, Astronomy, Biological Sciences, Chemistry, Chemical Engineering, Earth Sciences, Economics, Education, Energy, English as a Second Language, Geography, Geology, History, Language Arts, Linguistics, Mathematics, Music, Dance, Natural History, Philosophy, Physical Sciences, Social Sciences, Sociology, Technology
ISBN Prefix(es): 972-761; 972-8150; 972-9444
Branch Office(s)
Rua da Venezuela, 177, 4150-744 Porto
Tel: (022) 6099195 *Fax:* (022) 6007277

Contexto Editora+
Rua Rosa 105-2° Dto, 1200 Lisbon
Tel: (021) 347 97 69 *Fax:* (021) 347 97 70
E-mail: context-editora@clix.pt
Key Personnel
Dir: Manuel de Brito
Founded: 1979
Subjects: Fiction, Poetry
ISBN Prefix(es): 972-575

Edicoes Cosmos+
Rua Emenda, 111-1°, 1200 Lisbon
Tel: (021) 3468201 *Fax:* (021) 799 99 79
E-mail: cosmos@liv-arcoiris.pt *Cable:* COSMOS LISBOA
Key Personnel
Man Dir: Mario de Couceicas dos Reis
Founded: 1938
Subjects: Anthropology, Economics, Geography, Geology, History, Language Arts, Linguistics, Law, Literature, Literary Criticism, Essays, Music, Dance, Philosophy, Public Administration, Social Sciences, Sociology
ISBN Prefix(es): 972-762

Didactica Editora
Av Ilha da Madeira, 26-A, 1400 Lisbon
Tel: (021) 301 17 31 *Fax:* (021) 273 04 23
E-mail: didacticaeditora@mail.telepac.pt; info@didactica.pt
Web Site: viriato.viatecla.pt/didactica
Key Personnel
President: Francisco Prata Ginja
Founded: 1944
Membership(s): APEL (Portuguese Association of Publishers & Booksellers).
Subjects: Mathematics, Physical Sciences, Science (General)
ISBN Prefix(es): 972-650
Bookshop(s): Av da Ilha da Madeira, 22-A, 1400 Lisbon

DIFEL - Difusao Editorial SA+
Rua D Estefania, 46B, 1000 Lisbon
Tel: (021) 537677 *Fax:* (021) 545886
E-mail: difel.as@mail.telepac.pt
Telex: 64030
Key Personnel
Man Dir & Editorial: Rita Fezas Vital
General Dir: Francisco Vicente
Founded: 1983
Subjects: Fiction, Nonfiction (General)
ISBN Prefix(es): 972-29

Difusao Cultural+
Rua Luis Freitas Branco, 3A/B, 1000 Lisbon
Tel: (021) 7599364 *Fax:* (021) 7594418
Telex: 60380
Key Personnel
General Manager: Dr Eduardo Martins Soares
Editorial Dir: Paulo Ramos
Founded: 1989
Subjects: Art, Behavioral Sciences, Child Care & Development, Cookery, Economics, Environmental Studies, Fiction, Management
ISBN Prefix(es): 972-709
Number of titles published annually: 40 Audio
Total Titles: 180 Print

Dinalivro+
Travessa Convento de Jesus, 15-r/c, 1200 Lisbon
Tel: (021) 670 348 *Fax:* (021) 60 84 89
E-mail: dinalivro@ip.pt
Key Personnel
President: Silverio Amaro
Founded: 1969
Subjects: Accounting, Aeronautics, Aviation, Architecture & Interior Design, Art, Astronomy, Biological Sciences, Computer Science, Education, Electronics, Electrical Engineering, Engineering (General), Gardening, Plants, Health, Nutrition, History, Literature, Literary Criticism, Essays, Medicine, Nursing, Dentistry, Photography, Physics, Psychology, Psychiatry, Science (General), Social Sciences, Sociology
ISBN Prefix(es): 972-576
Subsidiaries: Dinapress
Bookshop(s): Centro Cultural Brasileiro, Largo Dr Antonio de Sousa de Macedo, 5, 1200 Lisbon; Nova Fronteira-Shopping Center Brasilia, 5 Piso-Loja 505-A, 4000 Porto
Shipping Address: Travessa do Convento de Jesus, 14, 1200 Lisbon
Warehouse: Travessa do Convento de Jesus, 14, 1200 Lisbon

Direccao Geral Familia
Praca Londres 2-5°, 1091 Lisbon Codex
Tel: (021) 8470430 *Fax:* (021) 8491516
Subjects: Child Care & Development, Social Sciences, Sociology
ISBN Prefix(es): 972-718

Distri Cultural Lda
R Vasco da Gamma, 4-4 A, 2685 Sacavem
Tel: (021) 942 53 94 *Fax:* (021) 941 98 93; (021) 942 52 14
Telex: 15094
Key Personnel
Man Dir: Karl-Heinz Petzler
Sales Dir: Carlos Alberto
Editorial: Jose Maria Rogagels
Founded: 1980
Subjects: Architecture & Interior Design, Art, Nonfiction (General), Travel
ISBN Prefix(es): 972-9472; 972-655

PUBLISHERS   PORTUGAL

Parent Company: Grupo Distri
Bookshop(s): Internation Book Centre, Cenrto Comercial de Amoreiras, P-1000 Lisbon

Elo, imprint of Perspectivas e Realidades, Artes Graficas, Lda

Edicoes ELO+
Rua Almirante Gago Coutinho, 2640 Mafra
Tel: (061) 812 143; (061) 812 344 *Fax:* (061) 81 28 20
E-mail: eloag@elografica.pt
Web Site: www.elografica.pt
Key Personnel
Man Dir: Joao Osorio de Castro
Founded: 1962
Subjects: Art, Education, History, House & Home, Travel
ISBN Prefix(es): 972-9181

Editorial Estampa, Lda+
Rua da Escola do Exercito, 9 R/C, Dto, 1150 Lisbon
Tel: (021) 355 56 63 *Fax:* (021) 314 19 11
E-mail: estampa@mail.telepac.pt
Web Site: www.browser.pt/estampa
Telex: 66012 estampp
Key Personnel
Contact: Antonio Carlos Pinheiro
Founded: 1960
Subjects: Anthropology, Antiques, Architecture & Interior Design, Art, Astrology, Occult, Cookery, Drama, Theater, Economics, Education, Fiction, Geography, Geology, Health, Nutrition, History, Law, Literature, Literary Criticism, Essays, Medicine, Nursing, Dentistry, Nonfiction (General), Parapsychology, Philosophy, Psychology, Psychiatry, Religion - Other, Romance, Social Sciences, Sociology, Sports, Athletics
ISBN Prefix(es): 972-33
Warehouse: Travessa da Escola Araujo, 34 C, 1150 Lisbon

Publicacoes Europa-America Lda
Estr Lisbon-Sintra Km 14, 2725 Mem Martins
Tel: (01) 9211461; (01) 9211462 *Fax:* (01) 9217846
Telex: 42255 peap *Cable:* EUROPAMERICA
Key Personnel
Man Dir: Francisco Lyon de Castro
Sales Dir: Eduardo Lyon de Castro
Manager: Tito Lyon de Castro
Founded: 1945
Subjects: Art, Biography, Education, Engineering (General), Fiction, History, How-to, Medicine, Nursing, Dentistry, Music, Dance, Philosophy, Poetry, Psychology, Psychiatry, Science (General), Social Sciences, Sociology, Technology
ISBN Prefix(es): 972-1
Subsidiaries: Editorial Inquerito Lda; Grafica Europam Lda; Publicacoes Forum Lda; Publicacoes Trevo Lda; Edicoes Cetop
Branch Office(s)
Delegacao de Lisboa, Rua das Flores, 45 - 2 Lisbon
Delegacao do Porto, Rua 31 de Janeiro, 221 Oporto
Bookshop(s): Lojas Europa-America, Ave Marques de Tomar 1-B; Ave 28 de Maio 61, Castelo Branco; Pr Ferreira de Almeida 21-22, Faro; Ave 25 de Abril 48, Almada; Rua Jose Relvas, 15 B-C Parede; Arcadas do Parque, Estoril; 225 Estrada Nacional 6-25, Cascais (Centro Comercial Pao de Acucar, Lojas 6, 7); Ave dos Bons Amigos 27-A, Cacem; Ave Antonio Enes 14-B; Ave Elias Garcia 104-B, Queluz

Europress Editores e Distribuidores de Publicacoes Lda+
Praceta da Republica, Loja A Iote A-1, 2675 Povoa de Santo Adriao

Tel: (01) 9387180; (01) 9387190; (01) 9387317; (01) 9877560; (01) 9381450 *Fax:* (01) 9381452; (01) 9877560
E-mail: europress@mail.telepac.pt
Key Personnel
Publisher, Man Dir, Editorial: Antonio Bento Vintem
Editor: Dulia Maia Rebocho
Sales: Carlos Vladimiro Ricardo Vintem
Production: Victor M Pinto Pedro
Publicity: Ana Christina Amaro
Founded: 1982
Also acts as national & international distributor, exporter & printer.
Membership(s): APEL; APIGT.
Subjects: Chemistry, Chemical Engineering, Drama, Theater, Fiction, Health, Nutrition, History, Humor, Law, Literature, Literary Criticism, Essays, Medicine, Nursing, Dentistry, Nonfiction (General), Poetry, Religion - Other, Romance, Science (General), Sports, Athletics, Western Fiction
ISBN Prefix(es): 972-559
Associate Companies: Pentaedro-Publicidade e Artes Graficas Lda, Praceta da Republica, Lote A-1, Loja B, Povoa Sto Adriao, 2675 Odivelas; Revista de Biotecnologia e Bioquimica Aplicada, Rua D Luisa de Gusmao 6 - 1 Esq, 1600 Lisbon
Subsidiaries: Heuris; Lua Viajante, Ed Com de Livros e Material Audiovisual, Lda
Branch Office(s)
Maputo, Mozambique
Cidade Da Praia, Cabo Verde
Distributor for Ed-Maputo (Mozambique); Livraria LEIA; Sintra Editora
Bookshop(s): Bolsonoite I-Livraria Bar Lda, Avenida Rainha D Leonor 25-A, 1600 Lisbon; Bolsonoite II, Rua Augusto Gil 6-A, 2675 Odivelas
Warehouse: Rua Augusto Gil 6-A, 2675 Odivelas
Tel: 9347366; 9347367 *Fax:* 9347368

Everest Editora
Parque Industrial - Edificio Meramar II - Armazem 1 - Cabra Figa, 2635 047 Rio de Mouro
Tel: (021) 9152483; (021) 9152510 *Fax:* (021) 9152525
E-mail: everesteditora@mail.telepac.pt
Web Site: www.everest.pt
Key Personnel
Publisher: Carla Pires
Founded: 1994
Subjects: Cookery, Travel
ISBN Prefix(es): 972-750

FCA Editora de Informatica
Rua D Estefania 183, 1º E-Lisbon, 1096 Lisbon Codex
Tel: (021) 3151218 *Fax:* (021) 577827
Telex: 15432
Founded: 1991
Subjects: Computer Science
ISBN Prefix(es): 972-722

Fenda Edicoes+
Affiliate of APEL
Apdo 21334, 1131 Lisbon, Codex
Tel: (021) 8823650 *Fax:* (021) 8823659
E-mail: info@fenda.pt
Key Personnel
Editor: Mr Vasco Santos *E-mail:* vasco.santos@fenda.pt
Public Relations: Elsa Sertorio *E-mail:* elsa.sertorio@fenda.pt
Founded: 1979
Specialize in edition of books.
Subjects: Literature, Literary Criticism, Essays, Poetry, Psychology, Psychiatry
ISBN Prefix(es): 972-9184
Total Titles: 93 Print

Distributed by Sodilivros
Foreign Rights: Capra Press (USA); Carmen Balcells (Europe); Gallimard (France); Rowohlt (Denmark)

Chaves Ferreira Publicacoes SA
Rua D Carlos Mascarenhas, 16A Porta-A, 1000 Lisbon
Tel: (021) 3871373 *Fax:* (021) 7161396
E-mail: chavesferreira@mail.telepac.pt
Key Personnel
Man Dir: Fernando Duval Chaves Ferreira
Founded: 1989
Subjects: Art, History, Technology
ISBN Prefix(es): 972-9402

Livraria Editora Figueirinhas Lda
Praca Liberdade, 68, 4000 Porto
Tel: (022) 324985 *Fax:* (022) 3325907
E-mail: correio@liv-figueirinhas.pt
Key Personnel
Editorial, Rights & Permissions: Francisco Pimenta
Founded: 1944
Subjects: Literature, Literary Criticism, Essays
ISBN Prefix(es): 972-661

Empresa Literaria Fluminense, Lda
Rua S Joao Nepomuceno, 8A, 1200 Lisbon
Tel: (021) 601138 *Fax:* (021) 3963371
Key Personnel
Man Dir: Antonio Nobre
Founded: 1905
ISBN Prefix(es): 972-555
Parent Company: Porto Editora Lda
Associate Companies: Livraria Arnado Lda

Editorial Franciscana+
Areal de Cima - Montariol, 4710 Braga Codex
Mailing Address: Apdo 1217, 4711-856 Braga Codex
Tel: (0253) 22490 *Fax:* (0253) 619735
Key Personnel
Man Dir: Antonio Pedro da Anunciacao
Founded: 1922
Membership(s): Filiada na APEL - Lisbon.
Subjects: Art, Biography, History, Music, Dance, Philosophy, Religion - Other, Theology
ISBN Prefix(es): 972-9190; 972-784
Subsidiaries: Delegacao da Editorial Franciscana
Bookshop(s): Livraria Editorial Franciscana, Rua de Cedofeita 350, Oporto

Editorial Futura+
Rua Gen Morais Sarmento, 9 C/V, 1600 Lisbon
Tel: (021) 7155848 *Fax:* (021) 155848
Key Personnel
Man Dir: Jose Chaves Ferreira
Founded: 1970
Subjects: Humor, Literature, Literary Criticism, Essays
ISBN Prefix(es): 972-587

Gabinete de Especializcao e Cooperacao Tecnica Internacional, see GECTI (Gabinete de Especializacao e Cooperacao Tecnica Internacional L)

GECTI (Gabinete de Especializacao e Cooperacao Tecnica Internacional L)+
Ave Republica 47-6 Dt, 1050 Lisbon
Tel: (021) 7968877; (021) 7971940; (021) 7972154 *Fax:* (021) 7963465
E-mail: gecti@mail.telepac.pt
Web Site: www.inedita.com/gecti
Key Personnel
Man Dir, Editorial: A Almeida Teixeira
Founded: 1963
Subjects: Business, Marketing, Public Administration
ISBN Prefix(es): 972-9012

PORTUGAL

Girassol Edicoes, LDA+
Affiliate of Susaeta Ediciones
Rua Actriz Adelina Fernandes, 19-A, 2795 Linda a Velha
Tel: (021) 41 43942 *Fax:* (021) 41 43518
E-mail: girassol@mail.telepac.pt
Key Personnel
General Manager: Fernando Sarmento
Founded: 1994
ISBN Prefix(es): 972-756
Number of titles published annually: 120 Print
Total Titles: 775,000 Print
Imprints: Multinova; Susaeta Ediciones
Branch Office(s)
Banco Espirito Santo *Tel:* (021) 4185367
Banco Santander *Tel:* (021) 4588390

Gradiva-Publicacnoes Lda+
Rua Almeida & Sousa 21, R/C Esq, 1399-041 Lisbon
Tel: (021) 397 40 67; (021) 397 40 68; (021) 397 13 57 *Fax:* (021) 395 34 71
E-mail: geral@ip.pt
Web Site: www.gradiva.pt
Key Personnel
Man Dir: Deolinda Valente
Editor: Guilherme de Carvalho Negrnao Valente
Foreign Rights Department: Joana Gongalves
Vice Dir, Sales & Rights & Permissions: Rodolfo Miguel D S B Begonha
Production: Fernando Guerreiro
Sales Manager: Carlos Rosa
Founded: 1981
Specialize in science books.
Subjects: Anthropology, Asian Studies, Astronomy, Behavioral Sciences, Biological Sciences, Communications, Computer Science, Crafts, Games, Hobbies, Earth Sciences, Economics, Education, Engineering (General), Environmental Studies, Fiction, Geography, Geology, Government, Political Science, History, Human Relations, Humor, Journalism, Literature, Literary Criticism, Essays, Management, Mathematics, Natural History, Nonfiction (General), Philosophy, Physics, Psychology, Psychiatry, Romance, Science (General), Science Fiction, Fantasy, Self-Help, Social Sciences, Sociology
ISBN Prefix(es): 972-662
Number of titles published annually: 80 Print
Total Titles: 700 Print
Distributor for Sinais de Fogo

Guimaraes Editores, Lda+
Rua da Misericordia, 68-70, 1200-273 Lisbon
Tel: (021) 324 3120 *Fax:* (021) 324 3129
E-mail: guimaraes.ed@mail.telepac.pt
Web Site: www.guimaraes-ed.pt
Telex: 16337
Key Personnel
Man Dir: Isabel Leao
Man Dir, Editorial: Francisco da Cunha Leao
Founded: 1899
Subjects: Drama, Theater, Fiction, History, Philosophy, Poetry, Social Sciences, Sociology
ISBN Prefix(es): 972-665
Bookshop(s): Livraria Guimaraes, Rua da Misericordia 68, 1200-273 Lisbon
Shipping Address: Rua Conceiccao da Gloria 75, 1250-080 Lisbon
Warehouse: Rua Conceiccao da Gloria 75, Lisbon
Orders to: Rua Conceiccao da Gloria 75, 1250-080 Lisbon

Impala
Rua Cristino da Silva, 1 B, Monte Abraao, 2745 Queluz
Tel: (021) 4364401 *Fax:* (021) 4366572
Telex: 16088 cendi p
Founded: 1983
Membership(s): APCT; AIND.
Subjects: Astronomy, Biography, Career Development, Child Care & Development, Economics, Education, Fashion, Gardening, Plants, Geography, Geology, How-to, Humor, Literature, Literary Criticism, Essays, Microcomputers, Music, Dance, Photography, Radio, TV, Sports, Athletics, Women's Studies
ISBN Prefix(es): 972-574; 972-766
Imprints: Lisgrafica
Book Club(s): AIND

Imprensa Nacional-Casa da Moeda
Av Antonio Jose de Almeida, 1000 042 Lisbon
Tel: (021) 781 07 00 *Fax:* (021) 781 07 54
Web Site: www.incm.pt
Telex: 15328 incmp *Cable:* INCM
Key Personnel
President: Antonio Braz Teixeira
Editorial Dir: Dr Margarida Santos
  E-mail: margarida.santos@incm.pt
Founded: 1768
Subjects: Anthropology, Archaeology, Art, Biography, Economics, Ethnicity, Government, Political Science, History, Language Arts, Linguistics, Law, Literature, Literary Criticism, Essays, Medicine, Nursing, Dentistry, Philosophy, Poetry, Public Administration, Social Sciences, Sociology
ISBN Prefix(es): 972-27
Branch Office(s)
Coimbra
Lisbon
Porto
Bookshop(s): Rua de D Francisco Manuel de Melo, 5, 1070 002 Lisbon *Tel:* (021) 383 58 00 *Fax:* (021) 383 58 34 *E-mail:* livraria.m.melo@incm.pt; Rua do Marques de Sa da Bandeira, 16-A e 16-B, Lisbon 1050 148 *Tel:* (021) 330 17 00 *Fax:* (021) 330 17 07 *E-mail:* livraria.s.bandeira@incm.pt; Rua da Escola Politecnica, Lisbon 1250 100 *Tel:* (021) 394 57 00 *Fax:* (021) 394 57 33 *E-mail:* livraria.r.escola@incm.pt; Ave de Fernao de Magalhaes, 486, 3000 173 Coimbra *Tel:* (023) 985 64 00 *Fax:* (023) 985 64 16 *E-mail:* livraria.coimbra@incm.pt; Praca de Guilherme Gomes Fernandes, 84, 4050 294 Porto *Tel:* (022) 339 58 20 *Fax:* (022) 339 58 23 *E-mail:* livraria.porto@incm.pt; Livraria Camoes, Rua Bittencourt da Silva nº 12 Loja C, Rio de Janeiro RJ, Brazil *Tel:* (021) 2624776 *E-mail:* livraria.camoes@incm.com.br; Rua des Portas de Santo Antao nº 2-2A, (Palacio da Independencia), 1150 320 Lisbon *Tel:* (021) 324 04 07 *Fax:* (021) 324 04 09 *E-mail:* livraria.s.antao@incm.pt; Rua D Filipa de Vilhena 12, 12A, 1000 136 Lisbon *Fax:* (021) 781 07 95 *E-mail:* livraria.f.vilhena@incm.pt; Av Roma, 1000 260 Lisbon *Tel:* (021) 840 10 23 *Fax:* (021) 840 09 61 *E-mail:* livraria.roma@incm.pt

INCM, see Imprensa Nacional-Casa da Moeda

Editorial Inquerito Lda+
Apdo 8, 2726 Mem Martins Codex
Tel: (021) 9211 460 *Fax:* (021) 9217 940
E-mail: publicidade@iol.pt
Telex: 42255
Key Personnel
Man Dir: Francisco Lyon de Castro
Founded: 1938
Subjects: Economics, History, Law, Philosophy, Social Sciences, Sociology
ISBN Prefix(es): 972-670
Parent Company: Publicacoes Europa-America Lda
Associate Companies: Publicacoes Europa-America
Distributed by Publicacoes Europe-America
Distribution Center: Publicacoes Europe-America
Orders to: Publicacoes Europa-America Lda, Estrada Lisboa-Sintra, Km 14, Apartado 8, 2726-901 Mem Martins

Instituto Tecnico de Alimentacao Humana, see Edicoes ITAU (Instituto Tecnico de Alimentacao Humana) Lda

Instituto de Investigacao Cientifica Tropical
  (Tropical Sciences Research Institute)
Rua da Junqueira, nº 86-1º, 1300-344 Lisbon
Tel: (021) 361 63 40 *Fax:* (021) 363 14 60
E-mail: iict@iict.pt
Web Site: www.iict.pt
Telex: IICT 66932
Key Personnel
Contact: Maria Virginia Aires Magrio
Founded: 1883
Specialize in tropical areas.
Subjects: Agriculture, Anthropology, Archaeology, Biological Sciences, Earth Sciences, Environmental Studies, Ethnicity, Geography, Geology, History, Social Sciences, Sociology, Veterinary Science
ISBN Prefix(es): 972-672
Number of titles published annually: 23 Print
Bookshop(s): Imprensa Nacional-Casa da Moeda, Rua D Francisco Manuel de Melo, 5-D, 1000 Lisbon; Livraria Portugal, Rua do Carmo, 70, 1200-094 Lisbon *Tel:* (021) 347 49 82 *Fax:* (021) 347 02 64 *E-mail:* liv.portugal@mail.telepac.pt; Sodilivros, Sociedade Distribuidora de Livros e Publicacoes, SA, Rua de Campolide, Nº 783-B, 1070-029 Lisbon *Tel:* (021) 381 56 00 *Fax:* (021) 387 62 81 *E-mail:* sodilivros@mail.telepac.pt
Warehouse: Travessa Paulo Martins, Nº 31-A, 1300 Lisbon *Tel:* (021) 363 59 38 *Fax:* (021) 363 59 38
Orders to: Centro de Documentacao e Informacao, IICT, Rua General Joao de Almeida, Palacio do Conde da Calheta, 1300-266 Lisbon *Tel:* (021) 361 97 30 *Fax:* (021) 362 82 18 *E-mail:* cdi@iict.pt

Edicoes ITAU (Instituto Tecnico de Alimentacao Humana) Lda
Rua Dr Oliveira Salazar 2, 2665 Malveira
Tel: (01) 9661603 *Fax:* (01) 9661227
Key Personnel
Man Dir: Julio Roberto
Editorial, Sales, Production, Publicity: Jose Maria Paula
Founded: 1969
Subjects: Education, Health, Nutrition, Literature, Literary Criticism, Essays, Poetry, Social Sciences, Sociology
ISBN Prefix(es): 972-9055
Parent Company: Instituto Tecnico de Alimentacao Humana Lda
Orders to: Ave Elias Garcia 87-A, Lisbon 1

Americo Fraga Lamares & Ca Lda, see Livraria Civilizacao (Americo Fraga Lamares & Ca Lda)

Latina Livraria Editora
Rua de Santa Catarina 2-10, 4000-441 Porto
Tel: (02) 2001294 *Fax:* (02) 2086053
Key Personnel
President: Henrique Fonseca Perdigao
Vice President: Maria Luisa Fonseca Perdigao
Founded: 1941
Subjects: Aeronautics, Aviation, Architecture & Interior Design, Art, History, House & Home, Literature, Literary Criticism, Essays, Music, Dance, Photography, Romance, Travel, Wine & Spirits
ISBN Prefix(es): 972-95647; 972-95657

Edicoes Manuel Lencastre+
Vale de Vigueria, 22, 2300, Tomar
Tel: 4688328
Founded: 1988
Subjects: Asian Studies, Astrology, Occult, Health, Nutrition, Philosophy, Religion - Bud-

dhist, Religion - Catholic, Religion - Hindu, Religion - Islamic, Religion - Other
ISBN Prefix(es): 972-9054

Lidel Edicoes Tecnicas, Lda+
Rua D Estefania 183 r/c Dto, 1096 Lisbon Codex
Tel: (021) 571288 *Fax:* (021) 577827
Telex: 15432
Key Personnel
Man Dir: Engo Frederico Annes
Editorial Dir: Jose Jomem de Mello
Founded: 1963
Membership(s): Publishers & Booksellers Portuguese Association.
Subjects: Computer Science, Labor, Industrial Relations, Language Arts, Linguistics
ISBN Prefix(es): 972-9018

Lisgrafica, *imprint of* Impala

Livraria Apostolado da Imprensa+
Largo das Teresinhas, 5, 4719 Braga Codex
Tel: (0253) 22485 *Fax:* (0253) 201221
Key Personnel
Man Dir, Editorial: Manuel Morujao; Americo Nunes
Founded: 1922
Subjects: Biography, Philosophy
ISBN Prefix(es): 972-571
Branch Office(s)
Rua da Lapa 111, 1200 Lisbon

Livraria Luzo-Espanhola Lda
Rua Nova do Almada 86, 1200 Lisbon
Tel: (021) 3424917 *Cable:* LIVRALUSO
Key Personnel
Man Dir: Inocencio Casimiro Araujo; Joao Pinto Soares
Founded: 1941
Subjects: Economics, Medicine, Nursing, Dentistry
ISBN Prefix(es): 972-9465
Bookshop(s): Livraria Luzo-Espanhola e Brasileira Lda, Ave 13 Maio 23 - 4, Rio de Janerio, Brazil; Livraria Luzo-Espanhola Lda, Rua da Sofia 121 - 1, Coimbra; Livraria Cientifico Medico do Porto, Rua do Carmo 14, Oporto

Livraria Minerva+
Rua dos Gatos 10, 3000 Coimbra
Tel: (0239) 26259 *Fax:* (0239) 717267
E-mail: livrariaminerva@mail.telepac.pt
Key Personnel
Manager: Isabel Garcia; Jose Alberto Garcia
Founded: 1985
Subjects: Computer Science, Drama, Theater, Finance, Literature, Literary Criticism, Essays, Medicine, Nursing, Dentistry, Philosophy, Poetry, Romance
ISBN Prefix(es): 972-9316; 972-9318
Distributed by Faculdade de Letras da Universidade de Coimbra
Showroom(s): Rua Carlos Seixas, 74-P, 3000 Coimbra
Bookshop(s): Rua de Macau, 52, 3030 Coimbra

Editora Livros do Brasil Sarl
Rua Caetanos, 22, 1200 Lisbon
Tel: (021) 3426113 *Fax:* (021) 342 84 87
E-mail: livbrasil@clix.pt *Cable:* Librasil
Key Personnel
Man Dir, Rights & Permissions: Antonio de Souza-Pinto
Editorial, Publicity: Joao Palma-Ferreira
Sales: Jose Manuel Lopes Filipe
Founded: 1944
Subjects: Biography, Government, Political Science, History, Philosophy, Science (General), Science Fiction, Fantasy
ISBN Prefix(es): 972-38

Associate Companies: Editores Associados Lda
Branch Office(s)
Rua de Ceuta 80, Oporto

Livros Horizonte Lda+
Rua Chagas 17-1º D, 1200 Lisbon
Tel: (021) 346 69 17 *Fax:* (021) 326921
E-mail: livroshorizonte@mail.telepac.pt *Cable:* LIVROSHORIZONTE
Key Personnel
Man Dir & Editorial: Rogerio de Mendes Moura; Eduardo de Loureiro Moura
Sales, Rights & Permissions: Manuela Duarte
Production: Paulo Caracas
Publicity: M Conceicao Silva
Founded: 1953
Subjects: Art, Education, History, Psychology, Psychiatry, Social Sciences, Sociology
ISBN Prefix(es): 972-24

Livraria Lopes Da Silva-Editora de M Moreira Soares Rocha Lda
Rua Cha 101-103, 4000 Porto
Tel: (02) 21678 *Fax:* (02) 2006017
Key Personnel
Man Dir: Adelino Silva
Founded: 1870
Subjects: Medicine, Nursing, Dentistry, Science (General), Technology
ISBN Prefix(es): 972-682

Lua Viajante-Edicao e Distribuicao de Livros e Material Audiovisual, Lda
Praceta Republica Ioja A, 2675 Povoa de Santo Adriao
Tel: (01) 9376180 *Fax:* (01) 9381452; (01) 9377560
E-mail: europress@mail.telepac.pt
Key Personnel
Publisher & Man Dir, Editorial: Antonio Bento Vintem
Editor: Dulia Maria Rebocho
Sales: Carlos Vladimiro Ricardo Vintem
Production: Victor M Pinto Pedro
Publicity: Ana Christina Amaro
Founded: 1992
Subjects: Computer Science
ISBN Prefix(es): 972-8038
Associate Companies: Europress-Editores & Distribuidores de Publicacoes Lda, Praceta Republca Ioja A, 2675 Povoa de Santo Adriao; Pentaedro-Publicidade e Artes Graficas Lda, Praceta Republica Loja A, 2675 Povoa de Santo Adriao
Distributed by Europress Editores & Distribuidores
Warehouse: Rua Augusto Gil 6-A, Odivelas
Tel: (01) 9347366; (01) 9347367 *Fax:* (01) 9347368

Mafra, *imprint of* Perspectivas e Realidades, Artes Graficas, Lda

Livraria Tavares Martins+
Rua Clerigos, 14, 4000 Porto
Tel: (022) 23459
Key Personnel
Man Dir: Jorge de Amorim
Founded: 1911
Subjects: Art, Biography, Drama, Theater, History, Law, Philosophy, Poetry, Religion - Other
ISBN Prefix(es): 972-694

Editora McGraw-Hill de Portugal Lda
Rua Barata Salgueiro, Ed Castilho 5 r/chao fraccao "A", Lisbon
Tel: (021) 355 3180 *Fax:* (021) 355 3189
E-mail: servico-clientes@mcgraw-hill.com
Web Site: www.mcgraw-hill.pt
Telex: 14724

Key Personnel
General Manager: Francisco Paes Mamede
Business Manager: Jose Temes
Sales Manager: Joao Esquivel
Editor: Hugo Xavier
Founded: 1977
Subjects: Agriculture, Architecture & Interior Design, Biological Sciences, Business, Chemistry, Chemical Engineering, Civil Engineering, Computer Science, Economics, Education, Electronics, Electrical Engineering, Engineering (General), Environmental Studies, Government, Political Science, Health, Nutrition, Human Relations, Law, Management, Marketing, Mathematics, Mechanical Engineering, Medicine, Nursing, Dentistry, Physics, Psychology, Psychiatry, Science (General), Social Sciences, Sociology
ISBN Prefix(es): 972-9241; 972-773; 972-8298
Parent Company: The McGraw-Hill Campanies, 1221 Avenue of the Americas, New York, NY 10020, United States
Associate Companies: Distribuidora Cuspide, Suipacha 764, 1008 Buenos Aires, Argentina, President: Joaquin Gil Paricio *Tel:* (01) 3228366 *Fax:* (01) 3223456; (01) 3223465; Makron Books do Brazil Editora Ltda, Rua Tabapua 1105, Itaim Bibi, CP 20689, 04533 Sao Paulo, Brazil, President: Milton Mira de Assumpcao, Filho *Tel:* (011) 8206622; (011)8208528; (011) 8296251 *Fax:* (011) 8294970

Melhoramentos de Portugal Editora, Lda+
Rua Embaixador Teixeira Sampaio, 4, 1300 Lisbon
Tel: (021) 3963225 *Fax:* (021) 678254
Telex: 42802 SAGRIL P
Key Personnel
Man Dir: Carolina Andrade
Founded: 1990
Subjects: Literature, Literary Criticism, Essays
ISBN Prefix(es): 972-713
Associate Companies: Companhia Melhoramentos de Sao Paulo, Brazil

Meriberica/Liber+
Av Duque d'Avila, 69-r/c E, 1000 Lisbon
Tel: (021) 8583849 *Fax:* (021) 8581536
E-mail: geral@meriberica.pt; bd@meriberica.pt; encomendar@meriberica.pt (orders)
Web Site: www.meriberica.pt
Telex: 14598 merlib p
Key Personnel
Partner: Bruno Protasio; Daniel Protasio; Marlos Protasio
Partner & Manager: Patricia Protasio
Manager: J Ribeiro Teles
Founded: 1974
Membership(s): Apel Portuguesa de Editores e Livreiros Associagao.
Subjects: Cookery, Humor, Comics
ISBN Prefix(es): 972-45
Number of titles published annually: 40 Print
Total Titles: 650 Print
Distributor for Casterman; Dargaud; Delcourt; Hachette; La Martiniere; Albin Michel; NORMA

Editorial Minerva+
R Luz Soriano 33, 1200-246 Lisbon
Tel: (021) 3220540 *Fax:* (021) 3220549
Key Personnel
Dir: Joao Fernandes Domingues
Founded: 1927
Subjects: Fiction
ISBN Prefix(es): 972-591

Monitor-Projectos e Edicoes, LDA+
R Abade Faria, 6, 2º-D-Lisbon, 1900 006 Lisbon
Tel: (021) 849-48-93 *Fax:* (021) 793-45-51
E-mail: monitor@esoterica.pt

Key Personnel
Prof: Victor Roldao *Tel:* (021) 7973656
Subjects: Career Development, Engineering (General), Human Relations, Management, Self-Help
ISBN Prefix(es): 972-9413; 972-95278
Total Titles: 65 Print
Branch Office(s)
Av Igreja, 66,3º-E-Lisbon, 1700 240 Lisbon *Tel:* (021) 7973656 *Fax:* (021) 7934551

Mosaico Editores, LDA
Calcada Mestres-1-6º D, 1000 Lisbon
Tel: (021) 681902 *Fax:* (021) 387-10-81
E-mail: mosaico@mail.telepac.pt
ISBN Prefix(es): 972-95663

Multinova, *imprint of* Girassol Edicoes, LDA

Multinova+
Av Santa Joana Princesa, 12-C/E, 1700 357 Lisbon
Tel: (021) 8481820 *Fax:* (021) 8483436
E-mail: geral@multinova.pt
Web Site: www.multinova.pt
Key Personnel
Contact: Carlos Santos
Founded: 1970
Also specialize in directing commercials.
ISBN Prefix(es): 972-9035

Musicoteca Lda
Rua Joao Pereira da Rosa, 8, 1200 Lisbon
Tel: (021) 3462653 *Fax:* (021) 3476637
E-mail: musicoteca@mail.telepac.pt
Founded: 1990
Subjects: Music, Dance
ISBN Prefix(es): 972-9449

Editorial Noticias+
Rua Padre Luis Aparicio, n 10, 1º, 1150-248 Lisbon
Tel: (021) 3552130 *Fax:* (021) 3552168; (021) 3552169
E-mail: geral@editorialnoticias.pt
Web Site: www.editorialnoticias.pt
Telex: 64381
Key Personnel
Executive Editor: Marta Ramires *E-mail:* marta.ramires@editorialnoticias.pt
Contact: Alexandra Manuel
Founded: 1985
Also acts as editor, distributor & bookseller.
Subjects: Cookery, Fiction, History, Journalism, Law, Religion - Other, Self-Help
ISBN Prefix(es): 972-46
Total Titles: 90 Print
Ultimate Parent Company: Lusomundo
Associate Companies: Oficina Do Livro
Subsidiaries: Oficina Do Livro
Bookshop(s): Aveiro Forum, Rua Homem Cristo Filho, Centro Comercial Forum Loja 1, 01, 3810 Aveiro; Aveiro Glicinias, Centro Comercial Glicinias, Loja 41, 3810 Aveiro; Livraria Noticias, Centro Comercial Eborim, R do Eborim, 18, 7000-659 Evora; Livraria Noticias, Rua de Sao Francisco, nº 8 A, 9000-050 Funchal; R da Olivenca 9, 2800 Almada; Rossio, 11, 1100 Lisbon *Tel:* (021) 342 17 77 *Fax:* (021) 322 57 33; Rossio, 13, 1100-199 Lisbon; Avenida da Libserdade, 266-1250, 1250 Lisbon *Tel:* (021) 318 78 43

Internationale Nouvelle Acropole (New Acropolis International)+
Rua Maria, 48-3º, 1100 Lisbon
Tel: (021) 827097
Web Site: www.acropolis.org
Key Personnel
Contact: Paulo Loucao
Founded: 1979

Specialize in human sciences & esoterism.
Subjects: Anthropology, Archaeology, Astrology, Occult, History, Philosophy
ISBN Prefix(es): 972-9026
Branch Office(s)
4710 Braga
R Prof Machado Nilela, 285-3d90

Nova Arrancada Sociedade Editora SA+
Rua Vitor Cordon, 41-47, 1200 Lisbon
Tel: (021) 3468837 *Fax:* (021) 3475122
E-mail: novaarrancada@mail.telepac.pt
Key Personnel
Executive Dir: Jose Luis Henriques
Founded: 1995
Subjects: Drama, Theater, Economics, Government, Political Science, History, Literature, Literary Criticism, Essays, Religion - Catholic, Social Sciences, Sociology
ISBN Prefix(es): 972-8369
Number of titles published annually: 30 Print

Editorial O Livro Lda
R Maj Neutel Abreu 16-A/B/C, 1500 Lisbon
Tel: (021) 7783577 *Fax:* (021) 7783536
E-mail: prof@editorialolivro.pt
Web Site: www.editorialolivro.pt
Key Personnel
Man Dir: Carlos de Moura
ISBN Prefix(es): 972-552

Observatorio Astronomico de Lisboa
Tapada da Ajuda, 1349-018 Lisbon
Tel: (021) 361 6739; (021) 361 6730 *Fax:* (021) 362 1722
E-mail: info@oal.ul.pt
Web Site: www.oal.ul.pt
ISBN Prefix(es): 972-573

Edicoes Ora & Labora
Mosteiro de Singeverga, 4780 Santo Tirso
Tel: (0252) 94 11 76 *Fax:* (0252) 87 29 47
E-mail: msingeverga@net.sapo.pt
Founded: 1950
Membership(s): Society of Portuguese Publishers & Booksellers.
Subjects: Anthropology, Biography, Religion - Catholic, Theology
ISBN Prefix(es): 972-9278

Palas Editores Lda+
Rua Quirino da Fonseca, 4-c/v D, 1000 Lisbon
Tel: (021) 574903 *Fax:* (021) 795-4019
Key Personnel
Editor: Maria De Fatima De Sa Ressoa
Founded: 1973
Membership(s): APEL.
Subjects: Education, History
ISBN Prefix(es): 972-9000

Paulinas+
Rua Alexandre Rey Colaco, 1700 Lisbon
Tel: (021) 848 43 55 *Fax:* (021) 847 41 51
E-mail: paulinas@mail.telepac.pt
Founded: 1950
Subjects: Biblical Studies, Biography, Human Relations, Literature, Literary Criticism, Essays, Religion - Catholic, Romance, Science Fiction, Fantasy, Securities
ISBN Prefix(es): 972-751
Bookshop(s): Paulinas Multimedia, Rua Morais Soares, 56 A-1900 Lisbon *Tel:* (021) 813 90 38 *Fax:* (021) 847 41 51; Paulinas Multimedia, Rua de Cedofeita, 355-4050 Porto *Tel:* (02) 31 49 56 *Fax:* (02) 32 08 31; Paulinas Multimedia, Rua Dr Fernao de Ornelas, 379050 Funchal-Maderia *Tel:* (091) 23 56 99 *Fax:* (091) 23 36 17; Paulinas Multimedia, Rua do Municipio, 12-8000 Faro *Tel:* (089) 82 30 27 *Fax:* (089) 80 56 79; Paulinas Multimedia, Praca Teofilo Braga, 12-13, 2900 Setubal *Tel:* (065) 53 42 14 (Centro Social S Francisco Xavier)

Paz-Editora de Multimedia, LDA+
Rua da Bela Vista a Graca, 27-A, 1170 Lisbon
Tel: (021) 8101282 *Fax:* (021) 8101287
E-mail: paz@esoterica.pt
Key Personnel
Partner: Helfried Bauer
Jr Partner: Peter C Wiesenthal
Founded: 1996
Membership(s): APEL.
Subjects: Health, Nutrition, Well being & reference
ISBN Prefix(es): 972-8416
Associate Companies: Felecidade-Editora de Multimidia Ltda, Rio de Janeiro, Brazil

Editora Pergaminho Lda
Rua Tierno Galvan, torre 3, sala 607, 1200 Lisbon
Tel: (021) 652441 *Fax:* (021) 687543
E-mail: pergaminho@mail.telepac.pt
Key Personnel
Contact: Mario Mendes Moura
Founded: 1990
Subjects: Art, Music, Dance, Radio, TV
ISBN Prefix(es): 972-711

Perspectivas e Realidades, Artes Graficas, Lda
Rua Ruben A Leitao 4,2º Esq, 1200-392 Lisbon
Tel: (021) 3471371 *Fax:* (021) 3471372
Telex: 42458 Perspe P
Key Personnel
Man Dir: Dr Joao Soares
Executive Dir: Dr Carlos Capelas
Publicity: Rui Perdigao
Founded: 1975
Subjects: Government, Political Science, Literature, Literary Criticism, Essays, Poetry
ISBN Prefix(es): 972-620
Associate Companies: Diglivro Lda
Imprints: Elo; Mafra

Petrony Livraria
Rua Assuncao nº 90, 1100 Lisbon
Tel: (021) 3423911 *Fax:* (021) 3431602
Founded: 1955
Subjects: Law
ISBN Prefix(es): 972-685

Planeta Editora, LDA+
Trav do Noronha 21-1 F, 1200 Lisbon
Tel: (021) 397-87-56 *Fax:* (021) 395-10-26
Key Personnel
International Rights: Gloria Ribeiro
Subjects: Astrology, Occult, Astronomy, Biblical Studies, Earth Sciences, Fiction, Mysteries, Science Fiction, Fantasy
ISBN Prefix(es): 972-731

Platano Editora SA+
Av de Berna, 31-2º Esq, 1069 Lisbon Codex
Tel: (021) 7979278 *Fax:* (021) 7954019
E-mail: geral@platanoeditora.pt
Web Site: www.plantanoeditora.pt
Key Personnel
President: Francisco Prata Ginja
Founded: 1972
Membership(s): the Portuguese Association of Book Publishers.
Subjects: Drama, Theater, Poetry
ISBN Prefix(es): 972-621; 972-707; 972-770
Subsidiaries: Alicerce Editora Lda; Paralelo Editora Lda; Didactica Editora Lda; Platano Edicoes Tecnicas Lda; Editora de Ensino a Distancia Lda
Branch Office(s)
Platano Editora SA, Coimbra
Bookshop(s): Alicerce Editora Lda, Rua Guerra Junqueiro 456, 4100 Porto

Warehouse: Rua Joao Ortigao Ramos 29-B, 1500 Lisbon
Servicor Ceutrais de Preducco e Armazens Quinta dos Lagoas, Almada 2800

Porto Editora Lda+
Rua da Restauracao, 365, 4099 023 Porto
Tel: (02) 2005813 *Fax:* (02) 313072
E-mail: pe@portoeditora.pt
Web Site: www.portoeditora.pt
Telex: 27205 ported p
Key Personnel
Man Dir: Graciete Teixeira; Jose A Teixeira; Rosalia G Teixeira; Vasco F Teixeira
Founded: 1944
Subjects: Education, Language Arts, Linguistics, Nonfiction (General)
ISBN Prefix(es): 972-0
Associate Companies: Empresa Literaria Fluminense Lda, Av Almirante Gago Coutinho 57 A, 1700 Lisbon *Tel:* (021) 8430900 *Fax:* (021) 8430901
Subsidiaries: Livraria Arnado Lda
Bookshop(s): Rua da Fabrica 90, Oporto *Tel:* (02) 2087669 *Fax:* (02) 2087669; Praca D Filipa de Lencastre 42, Oporto *Tel:* (02) 2087681 *Fax:* (02) 2087681

Portugalmundo+
Rua Graca, 28, 1100 Lisbon
Tel: (021) 877611 *Fax:* (021) 8144746
Key Personnel
Dir: Maria Jose Palmela Pinto
Founded: 1976
Membership(s): APEL.
Subjects: Law
ISBN Prefix(es): 972-9288

Editorial Presenca+
Estrada das Palmeiras, 59, Queluz de Baixo, 2745-578 Barcarena
Tel: (021) 4347000 *Fax:* (021) 4346502
E-mail: info@editpresenca.pt
Web Site: www.editpresenca.pt
Telex: 62596 *Cable:* PRESENCA LISBOA
Key Personnel
President: Francisco Espadinha
Executive Dir: Manuel Aquino
Production: Maria Eugenia Queiroz
Rights & Permissions: Manuela Cardoso
Administration: Joao Espadinha
Finance Executive: Hugo Moura
Founded: 1960
Subjects: Animals, Pets, Architecture & Interior Design, Art, Astrology, Occult, Biography, Business, Child Care & Development, Computer Science, Cookery, Crafts, Games, Hobbies, Education, Fiction, Gardening, Plants, Government, Political Science, Health, Nutrition, History, How-to, Human Relations, Language Arts, Linguistics, Management, Marketing, Mysteries, Nonfiction (General), Philosophy, Poetry, Psychology, Psychiatry, Religion - Buddhist, Science (General), Self-Help, Social Sciences, Sociology, Sports, Athletics, Travel, Travel Guides, Art Techniques, Esoterics, Lesiure Books
ISBN Prefix(es): 972-23
Divisions: Marketing Department
Warehouse: Estrada das Palmeiras, 59, 2745-663 Barcarena *Tel:* (021) 4357544 *Fax:* (021) 4357540

Publicacoes Dom Quixote Lda+
Rua Luciano Cordeiro 116-2, 1098 Lisbon
Tel: (021) 538079 *Fax:* (021) 574595
Telex: 14331 quixot p *Cable:* QUIXOTE
Key Personnel
Man Dir: Nelson de Matos; Isabel Dionisio
Production: Gina Martins
Publicity: Cecilia Andrade
Rights & Permissions: Cecilia Andrade
Founded: 1965
Subjects: Education, Fiction, History, Philosophy, Poetry, Science (General), Social Sciences, Sociology
ISBN Prefix(es): 972-20

Puma Editora Lda
Rua Vasco da Gama, 4-4 A, 2685 Sacavem
Tel: (021) 9425394 *Fax:* (021) 9425214
Key Personnel
Man Dir: Karl-Heinz Petzler
Editorial, Rights & Permissions: Adriano Lopes
Founded: 1990
Subjects: Fiction, Nonfiction (General)
ISBN Prefix(es): 972-9469
Parent Company: Grupo Distri
Sales Office(s): Distri Cultural

Quatro Elementos Editores+
Rua Arneiros, 54-lote F-2º F, 1500 Lisbon
Tel: (021) 703695
Founded: 1978
Subjects: Art, Fiction, Literature, Literary Criticism, Essays, Photography, Poetry
ISBN Prefix(es): 972-9296

Quetzal Editores+
Affiliate of Livrania Bertrand, SGPS
Rua da Rosa 105, 2º Esq, 1200 Lisbon
Tel: (021) 3426172 *Fax:* (021) 3426173
E-mail: quetzal@ip.pt
Telex: 65732 pegest p
Key Personnel
Chairman: Maria Da Piedade Ferreira
Subjects: Art, Literature, Literary Criticism, Essays, Poetry, Romance, Travel
ISBN Prefix(es): 972-564
Shipping Address: Distribuidorz de Livnos Bertrand, Rua Terras do Vale, Amadora, Contact: Eduardo Morais *Tel:* (01) 4958787 *Fax:* (01) 4960255

Quid Juris - Sociedade Editora+
A Marques da Fronteira, 92-1º Dtº, 1000 Lisbon
Tel: (021) 651946 *Fax:* (021) 3875538
E-mail: quidjuris@mail.telepac.pt
Key Personnel
Contact: Rua Sarmento Beires
Founded: 1988
Subjects: Criminology, Economics, Journalism, Law, Social Sciences, Sociology
ISBN Prefix(es): 972-724

Quimera Editores Lda+
R Actor Isidoro, 17-R/C Esq, 1900-015 Lisbon
Tel: (021) 845 59 50 *Fax:* (021) 845 59 51
E-mail: quimera@quimera-editores.com
Web Site: www.quimera-editores.com
Key Personnel
Contact: Jose Alfaro
Founded: 1987
Subjects: Art, Biography, Drama, Theater, Fiction, History
ISBN Prefix(es): 972-589

Realizacoes Artis
Apdo 8, 2726 Mem Martins
Tel: (01) 363796 *Fax:* (01) 9170130
Key Personnel
Man Dir: Rogerio de Freitas; Ermelinda Penedo
Founded: 1950
Subjects: Art, Biography, Poetry
ISBN Prefix(es): 972-9298

Editora Replicacao Lda+
Ave Infante Santo 343, r/c Esq, 1300 Lisbon
Tel: (021) 677058 *Fax:* (021) 396 9808
E-mail: replic@mail.telepac.pt
Key Personnel
Dir: J C Anaia Cristo; Luisa Galhardo
Founded: 1982
La Spiga Language representative.
Subjects: Astrology, Occult, Biological Sciences, English as a Second Language, Health, Nutrition, Humor, Mathematics, Science (General), Sports, Athletics, Study of Foreign Languages
ISBN Prefix(es): 972-570
Associate Companies: Leianaia-Livreiros, Editores e Importadores Anaia, Idc

Revista Penteado
Rua Bacalhoeiros 99, 2º E, 1100 Lisbon
Tel: (021) 862963 *Fax:* (021) 870972
E-mail: rromano@mail.telepac.pt
Telex: 64904
Key Personnel
International Rights: Leonor Veiga De Macedo
Parent Company: Rui Romano Lda

M Moreira Soares Rocha Lda, see Livraria Lopes Da Silva-Editora de M Moreira Soares Rocha Lda

Edicoes Rolim Lda
Rua Fialho de Almeida, 38-2º D, 1000 Lisbon
Tel: (021) 526375
Key Personnel
Man Dir: Maria Rolim Ramos
Founded: 1976
Subjects: Government, Political Science, History, Language Arts, Linguistics, Literature, Literary Criticism, Essays, Social Sciences, Sociology
ISBN Prefix(es): 972-687

Edicioes Joao Sa da Costa Lda+
Av Brasil, 118-3 3/4 E, 1700 Lisbon
Mailing Address: Av 5 Outubro, 10-7 3/4 /4, 1000 Lisbon
Tel: (021) 8400428; (021) 571118; (021) 563603 *Fax:* (021) 534194
Telex: 43534 fundis p
Key Personnel
Man Dir: Joao Sa da Costa
Executive Dir: Idalina Sa da Costa
Founded: 1984
ISBN Prefix(es): 972-9230

Sa da Costa Livraria
Praca Luis de Camoes, 22-4º, 1200 Lisbon
Tel: (021) 346 07 21; (021) 346 07 23; (021) 346 07 24; (021) 346 07 25 *Fax:* (021) 346 07 22
Telex: Sacost 15574 P *Cable:* Livrosacosta
Founded: 1913
Subjects: History, Literature, Literary Criticism, Essays, Philosophy
ISBN Prefix(es): 972-562
Bookshop(s): Livraria Sa da Costa

Edicoes Salesianas
Rua Dr Alves da Veiga 124, 4022 Porto Codex
Tel: (022) 565750 *Fax:* (022) 536 58 00
E-mail: edisal@clix.pt
Key Personnel
Man Dir: Jose Santos
Editorial, Production & Publicity: Jose Pedrosa Ferreira
Founded: 1947
Subjects: Biography, Education, Humor, Psychology, Psychiatry, Religion - Other
ISBN Prefix(es): 972-690
Branch Office(s)
Rua Saraiva de Carvalho 275, Lisbon *Tel:* (021) 3964142
Bookshop(s): Livraria Salesiana, Largo Luis de Camoes 7-9, 7000 Evora *Tel:* (066) 24570; Rua Saraiva de Carvalho 275, 1300 Lisbon *Tel:* (021) 609065

Edicoes 70 Lda+
Rua Luciano, Cordeiro, 123-2 Esq, 1069-157 Lisbon
Tel: (021) 319 02 40 *Fax:* (021) 319 02 49

E-mail: edi.70@mail.telepac.pt
Web Site: www.edicoes70.pt
Founded: 1970
Subjects: Animals, Pets, Anthropology, Architecture & Interior Design, Art, Astrology, Occult, Education, History, Language Arts, Linguistics, Literature, Literary Criticism, Essays, Music, Dance, Nonfiction (General), Parapsychology, Philosophy, Photography, Social Sciences, Sociology
ISBN Prefix(es): 972-44
Number of titles published annually: 24 Print
Total Titles: 1,000 Print

Edicoes Silabo+
Rua Passos Manuel, 99-5º E, 1100 Lisbon
Tel: (021) 525880 *Fax:* (021) 314 58 80
E-mail: silabo@mail.telepac.pt
Key Personnel
Marketing Dir: Manuel Robalo
 E-mail: manuelrobalo@silabo.pt
Founded: 1983
Membership(s): APEL.
Subjects: Computer Science, Economics, Management, Mathematics, Philosophy, Physics, Science (General)
ISBN Prefix(es): 972-618

SocTip SA
Estrada Nacional 10, Km 10813 Porto Alto, 2135-114 Samora Correia
Tel: (021) 263 00 99 00 *Fax:* (021) 263 00 99 99
E-mail: soctip@soctip.pt
Web Site: www.soctip.pt
Telex: 65517 SOCTIP P
Key Personnel
Dir: Cristina Ferreira *E-mail:* cristinaferreira@soctip.pt
Founded: 1936
Subjects: Art
ISBN Prefix(es): 972-9435

Solivros+
Alto do Castelo, Villa de Trofa, 4780 Santo Tirso
Tel: (0252) 42385
Key Personnel
President & Editor: David Jorge Pereira
Founded: 1974
Specialize in publications of art works.
Subjects: Art, English as a Second Language, Literature, Literary Criticism, Essays, Poetry, Regional Interests, Religion - Catholic
ISBN Prefix(es): 972-693

Sousa & Almeida Livraria
Rua da Fabrica 42, 4050 245 Porto
Tel: (022) 2050073 *Fax:* (022) 2050073
E-mail: sousaealmeida@net.sapo.pt; geral@sousaealmeida.com
Web Site: www.sousaealmeida.com
Key Personnel
Contact: Sousa Almeida
ISBN Prefix(es): 972-9329

Susaeta Ediciones, *imprint of* Girassol Edicoes, LDA

Edicoes Talento+
Av Gomes Pereira, 41-1º E, 1500 Lisbon
Tel: (021) 7154281 *Fax:* (021) 7154257
Key Personnel
Dir: Francisco Santos
Financial Dir: Francisco Neves Ferro
Editorial Manager: Patricia Samos
Founded: 1988
Subjects: Biography, Music, Dance, Sports, Athletics
ISBN Prefix(es): 972-8065

Branch Office(s)
Edipromo-Edicoes e Promocoes Ltda, 143 Vila Mariana, 0415 San Paulo SP, Brazil
Book Club(s): Club Mania Show

Almerinda Teixeira
Av 25 de Abril, 5-16 E, 2800 Almada
Tel: (021) 2762352 *Cable:* Classica
Key Personnel
Editorial, Rights & Permissions: Francisco Paulo
Production, Publicity: Jose Ramos
Founded: 1903
Subjects: Agriculture, Economics, Electronics, Electrical Engineering, Fiction, History, Language Arts, Linguistics, Management, Poetry, Psychology, Psychiatry, Religion - Other, Science (General), Social Sciences, Sociology
ISBN Prefix(es): 972-95393

Teorema+
Rua Padre Luis Aparicio 9-1º F, 1100 Lisbon
Tel: (021) 529988 *Fax:* (021) 352 14 80
E-mail: editorial.teorema@netc.pt
Key Personnel
President: Dr Carlos Da Veiga Ferreira
Founded: 1973
Subjects: Anthropology, Economics, Fiction, History, Literature, Literary Criticism, Essays, Nonfiction (General), Philosophy, Psychology, Psychiatry, Romance, Science (General), Social Sciences, Sociology
ISBN Prefix(es): 972-695

Texto Editora+
Estrada de Paco de Arcos, 66, 66-A, 2735-336 Cacem
Tel: (021) 427 22 00 *Fax:* (021) 427 22 01
E-mail: info@te.pt
Web Site: www.textoeditora.pt; www.te.pt
Key Personnel
Man Dir: Manuel Jose Ferrao; Luis Carlos Veloso; Carlos Santiago
Founded: 1977
Subjects: Cookery, Education, Fiction, Health, Nutrition, Management
ISBN Prefix(es): 972-47
Associate Companies: Publilivro - Editora e Distribuidora de Publicacoes Lda, Alto da Bela Vista, Casal Vale de Mourao, Apdo 237, 2735 Cacem
Branch Office(s)
Beco Veloso Salgado, 31, 4450-808 Ceca da Palmeira
Bookshop(s): Livraria Texto Editora, Rua Joaquim Paco D'Arcos, 13, 1500-365 Lisbon; Rua Damiao De Gois, 45, 4050-225 Porto

Sociedade Tipografica SA, see SocTip SA

Publicacoes Trevo Lda
Apdo 50, 2726 Mem Martins Codex
Tel: (021) 9211461 *Fax:* (021) 9217940
Telex: 42255 pea p
Key Personnel
Man Dir, Editorial: Tito de Lyon Castro
Sales: Eduardo de Lyon Castro
Founded: 1976
ISBN Prefix(es): 972-696
Parent Company: Publicacoes Europa-America Lda

Turinta-Turismo Internacional
Rua Marques de Pombal, 347, Murches, 2755 247 Alcabideche Cascais
Tel: (021) 487 9420 *Fax:* (021) 487 2099
E-mail: info@turinta.pt
Web Site: www.turinta.pt
Key Personnel
General Dir: Hilario Sanches
International Rights: Eva Sanches
Founded: 1975

Membership(s): IMTA.
ISBN Prefix(es): 972-8134; 989-556
Distributed by Map Link (USA)

Editora Ulisseia Lda+
Av August Antonio de Aguiar, 148, 1069-019 Lisbon
Tel: (021) 380 1100 *Fax:* (021) 386 5397
Web Site: www.editorialverbo.pt
Telex: 15177 Verbo P
Key Personnel
Man Dir: Fernando Guedes
Editorial, Production: Martins de Oliveira
Sales: Jose Luis Fonseca
Publicity: Carlos Castro
Founded: 1950
Subjects: Literature, Literary Criticism, Essays
ISBN Prefix(es): 972-568
Parent Company: Editorial Verbo SA
Warehouse: Alto da Bela Vista, Calem 2735
Orders to: Rua Carlos Testa 1 - 2, 1000 Lisbon

Usus Editora+
Rua Viana do Castelo, 8 c/v Esq, 2775 Carcavelos
Tel: (021) 4535000 *Fax:* (021) 4426482
Key Personnel
Contact: Josi Caselas
Subjects: Law, Literature, Literary Criticism, Essays, Philosophy, Poetry, Theology
ISBN Prefix(es): 972-8070

Vega-Publicacao e Distribuicao de Livros e Revistas, Lda+
Alto dos Moinhos, 6A, 1500 Lisbon
Tel: (021) 789414 *Fax:* (021) 786395
Key Personnel
Contact: Dr Assirio Bacelar
Founded: 1975
Subjects: Anthropology, Architecture & Interior Design, Art, Astrology, Occult, Behavioral Sciences, Biography, Child Care & Development, Communications, Computer Science, Cookery, Drama, Theater, Economics, Education, Fashion, Fiction, Gay & Lesbian, History, Humor, Law, Literature, Literary Criticism, Essays, Philosophy, Photography, Poetry, Religion - Buddhist, Religion - Other, Romance, Science Fiction, Fantasy, Social Sciences, Sociology
ISBN Prefix(es): 972-699

Editorial Verbo SA+
Av Antonio Augusto de Aguiar, 148-6º, 1069-019 Lisbon
Tel: (021) 380 21 31; (021) 380 11 00 *Fax:* (021) 386 11 22; (021) 386 53 97
Web Site: www.editorialverbo.pt
Telex: 15177 Verbo P *Cable:* VERBO
Key Personnel
Man Dir: Fernando Guedes
Dir, Commercial: Dr Jose Luis Fonseca
Founded: 1959
Door-to-door sales by EDC-Empresa de Divulgacao Cultural Sarl, Ave Duque de Avila 193, Lisbon; direct mail sales by Verbo Postal.
Subjects: Education, History, Science (General)
ISBN Prefix(es): 972-22
Subsidiaries: Editora Verbo, S Paulo; Editora Ulisseia Lda; Verbo Publicacoes Periodicas; Litecnica, Luanda

Livraria Verdade e Vida Editora
Rua Santa Isabel, 16, 2495 Fatima
Tel: (0249) 531417 *Fax:* (0249) 531417
Founded: 1945
Subjects: Biography, Education, Fiction, History, Philosophy, Psychology, Psychiatry, Religion - Other, Theology
ISBN Prefix(es): 972-96166

Puerto Rico

General Information

Capital: San Juan
Language: Spanish and English
Religion: Predominantly Roman Catholic
Population: 3.6 million
Bank Hours: 0900-1430 Monday-Friday
Shop Hours: 0900-1730 or 1800 Monday-Saturday
Currency: US currency: 100 cents = 1 US dollar
Export/Import Information: No tariff on books and advertising matter. No import licenses required.
Copyright: UCC (see Copyright Conventions, pg xi)

Editorial Antillana, *imprint of* Editorial Cultural Inc

Editorial Cordillera Inc
Calle Mexico 17, Oficina 1-A, Hato Rey 00917
Mailing Address: PO Box 192363, San Juan 00919-2363
Tel: 787-767-6188 *Fax:* 787-767-8646
E-mail: info@editorialcordillera.com
Web Site: www.editorialcordillera.com
Key Personnel
President & Editorial: Hector E Serrano
Sales & Publicity: Isaac Serrano
Founded: 1962
Subjects: Literature, Literary Criticism, Essays, Social Sciences, Sociology
ISBN Prefix(es): 0-88495

Instituto de Cultura Puertorriquena (Institute of Puerto Rican Culture)
Apdo 9024184, San Juan 00902-4184
Tel: 787-724-0700 *Fax:* 787-724-8393
E-mail: www@icp.gobierno.pr
Web Site: www.icp.gobierno.pr
Telex: 3859686
Key Personnel
Dir: Carmelo Degardo Cintron
Editorial Dir: Marta Aponte Alsina
Sales: Ileana Colon de Barreto
Founded: 1955
Subjects: Anthropology, History, Literature, Literary Criticism, Essays, Music, Dance, Poetry
ISBN Prefix(es): 0-86581
Bookshop(s): Libreria del Instituto de Cultura Puertorriquena, San Francisco 305, San Juan 00901
Orders to: San Francisco 305, San Juan 00901

Editorial Cultural Inc
Calle El Roble No 51, Rio Piedras 00925
Mailing Address: Apdo 21056, Rio Piedras 00928
Tel: 787-765-9767 *Fax:* 787-765-9767
E-mail: cultural@coqui.net
Web Site: www.editorialcultural.com
Key Personnel
Man Dir: Francisco M Vazquez
  E-mail: francesco@editorialcultural.com
Administrator: Thin Sonia
Founded: 1949
Subjects: Biography, History, Literature, Literary Criticism, Essays
ISBN Prefix(es): 1-56758; 84-399
Imprints: Editorial Antillana
Bookshop(s): Libreria Cultural

EDUPR, see University of Puerto Rico Press (EDUPR)

Libros-Ediciones Homines+
PO Box 190374, Hato Rey, San Juan 00919
Tel: (787) 250-1912 (ext 2347)

Key Personnel
International Rights: Dr Aline Frambes-Buxeda
  E-mail: a.frambes@inter.edu
Founded: 1977
Subjects: Behavioral Sciences, Government, Political Science, Regional Interests, Social Sciences, Sociology, Women's Studies
ISBN Prefix(es): 0-9623590
Number of titles published annually: 2 CD-ROM
Total Titles: 45 Print; 7 CD-ROM
Ultimate Parent Company: Universidad Interamericana de Puerto Rico

Ediciones Huracan Inc+
Avenida Gonzalez 1002, Rio Piedras 00925
Tel: (787) 763-7407 *Fax:* (787) 763-7407
Key Personnel
Dir: Carmen Rivera-Izcoa
Founded: 1975
Subjects: History, Literature, Literary Criticism, Essays, Social Sciences, Sociology
ISBN Prefix(es): 0-940238; 0-929157

McGraw-Hill Intermericana del Caribe, Inc
1121 Ave Munoz Rivera, Rio Piedras 00925
Tel: (787) 751-2451; (787) 751-3451 *Fax:* (787) 764-1890
Web Site: www.mhschool.com/contactus/international.html
Key Personnel
Regional Manager: Carlos Davila
  E-mail: carlos_davila@mcgrawhill.com
Subjects: Architecture & Interior Design, Business, Education, Engineering (General), English as a Second Language, Medicine, Nursing, Dentistry, Nonfiction (General), Technology

Modern Guides Company+
804 Calle Marti, San Juan 00907-3324
Mailing Address: PO Box 9021340, San Juan 00902-1340
Tel: (787) 723-9105 *Fax:* (787) 723-4380
E-mail: avc1941@attglobal.net
Key Personnel
President: Cristina Banac
Founded: 1985
Also provides marketing support & distribution.
Subjects: Fiction, Travel
ISBN Prefix(es): 0-940788
Number of titles published annually: 2 Print; 2 Online
Total Titles: 3 Print; 2 Online
Distributed by Spanish Periodicals (USA)

Piedras Press, Inc
Carr 173, Km 4 6, Int Bo Hato Nuevo, Guaynabo 00931
Mailing Address: PO Box 21735, San Juan 00931-1735
Tel: (809) 731-9215
Key Personnel
President: Marc Schnitzer *Tel:* (787) 789-8928
Vice President & Treasurer: Emily Krasinski
Subjects: How-to, Language Arts, Linguistics, Self-Help
ISBN Prefix(es): 0-9630685
Number of titles published annually: 1 Print
Total Titles: 2 Print

Publishing Resources Inc
373 San Jorge St, 2nd floor, Santurce 00912
Mailing Address: PO Box 41307, Santurce 00940
Tel: (787) 268-8080 *Fax:* 787-774-5781
E-mail: publishingresources@att.net
Key Personnel
Owner & President: Ronald J Chevako
Owner & Editor-in-Chief: Anne W Chevako
Retail Manager: Terry C Burns
Publishes magazines including *San Juan, Puerto Rico's City Magazine*; *Bienestar* (environmental) & *Dimension* (engineering).

Subjects: Ethnicity, Regional Interests, Science (General), Travel
ISBN Prefix(es): 0-89825

Ediciones Puerto+
Edif Olimpic Mills, Guaynabo
Mailing Address: PO Box 3309, Old San Juan Station, San Juan 00902
Tel: 787-721-0844 *Fax:* 787-725-0861
E-mail: feriapr@caribe.net
Key Personnel
President: Jose Carvajal
Founded: 1971
Subjects: Poetry, Social Sciences, Sociology
ISBN Prefix(es): 0-942347

University of Puerto Rico Press (EDUPR)+
University of Puerto Rico Sta, Rio Piedras 00931-3322
Mailing Address: PO Box 23322
Tel: (787) 758-6932; (787) 758-8345 (sales)
  Fax: (787) 753-9116
Telex: 9573 *Cable:* EDUPR
Key Personnel
Dir: Marta Aponte-Alsina
Manager: Dalidia Colon-Pieretti
Production Manager: Juan Abascal
Editor-in-Chief: Gloria Madrazo-Vicens
Editor: Ana Garcia San Inocencio; Jesus Tome
Founded: 1932
Subjects: Art, Education, History, Nonfiction (General), Philosophy, Poetry, Psychology, Psychiatry, Social Sciences, Sociology
ISBN Prefix(es): 0-8477
Branch Office(s)
Edificio Vick Center-D Ave, Munoz Rivera No 867, Ofic 304, Rio Piedras 00925
Warehouse: Planta Piloto de Ron, Rd No 1 to Caguas, Rio Piedras

Publicaciones Voz de Gracia
PO Box 50581, Levittown 00950
Tel: 809-784-4366 *Fax:* 809-261-5401
E-mail: vozdegra@caribe.net
Web Site: www.cristo.org
Founded: 1994
Subjects: Biblical Studies, Music, Dance
ISBN Prefix(es): 0-9633439
Divisions: Ministerios Alabanza y Adoracion

Reunion

General Information

Capital: Saint-Denis
Language: French
Religion: Predominantly Roman Catholic
Population: 626,000
Bank Hours: 0800-1500
Currency: 100 centimes = 1 French franc
Export/Import Information: No tariff on books and advertising. Books have reduced VAT. No import license. Nominal exchange control over certain value.
Copyright: Berne (see Copyright Conventions, pg xi)

ADER, see Association des Ecrivains Reunionnais (ADER)

Association des Ecrivains Reunionnais (ADER)
36, rue de Gaulle, 97400 Saint-Denis de La Reunion
Tel: (0262) 213317 *Fax:* (0262) 431601
Key Personnel
President: Alain Gili *E-mail:* agili@guetali.fr
Founded: 1975
Books, little review.
ISBN Prefix(es): 2-9507282

Number of titles published annually: 3 Print
Total Titles: 7 Audio

Editions Ocean
305, rue de la Communaute, 97440 Saint Andre
Tel: 588400 *Fax:* 588410
E-mail: ocean@guetali.fr
Key Personnel
Contact: Jean-Pierre Boyer
Founded: 1987
Subjects: Crafts, Games, Hobbies, History, Social Sciences, Sociology
ISBN Prefix(es): 2-907064
Distributor for ARS-Terres Creoles; CNH; CRI

Romania

General Information

Capital: Bucharest
Language: Romanian
Religion: Predominantly Romanian Orthodox
Population: 23.2 million
Bank Hours: 0900-1200, 1300-1500 Monday-Friday; 0900-1200 Saturday
Shop Hours: 0900-1900 Monday-Friday; early closing Saturday
Currency: 100 bani = 1 leu
Export/Import Information: Book import and export coordinated by Centrala Editoriala, Piata Sciinteii 1, R-79715 Bucharest. The commercial operations are carried out by Artexim-Foreign Trade Co, 33-16, R-70055 Bucharest. Import licenses required. Exchange controls: terms of payment established in the sales contract.
Copyright: Berne (see Copyright Conventions, pg xi)

Editura Academiei Romane (Publishing House of the Romanian Academy)
Str 13 Septembrie, nr 13, Bucuresti, sector 5, 791717 Bucharest
Tel: (0410) 411 90 08; (0410) 410 32 00 *Fax:* (0410) 410 39 83
E-mail: edacad@ear.ro
Web Site: www.ear.ro *Cable:* EDACAD
Key Personnel
General Manager: Prof Gheorghe Mihaila
Executive Manager: Dr Ing Ioan Ganea
Executive Manager Technical Dept: Elena Popescu
Executive Manager Economic, Commercial Dept: Liliana Ionescu
Founded: 1948
Publishing House of the Academy of Romania.
Subjects: Anthropology, Archaeology, Art, Astronomy, Biological Sciences, Chemistry, Chemical Engineering, Computer Science, Earth Sciences, Electronics, Electrical Engineering, Energy, Foreign Countries, History, Language Arts, Linguistics, Law, Mathematics, Medicine, Nursing, Dentistry, Philosophy, Physical Sciences, Physics, Psychology, Psychiatry, Social Sciences, Sociology
ISBN Prefix(es): 973-27
Orders to: Orion Srl, Press International, Sos Oltenitei 35-37, Sect 4, PO Box 61-170, Bucharest *Tel:* (01) 534 63 45 *Fax:* (01) 312 51 09

Aion Verlag+
Str Cantacuzino No 8F, bl PB 18, et 1, ap 7, Oradea
Tel: (059) 147595
Key Personnel
President & Editor: Nicolae Olteanu
Founded: 1994
Subjects: Anthropology, Communications, How-to, Human Relations, Journalism, Philosophy, Psychology, Psychiatry, Religion - Other, Social Sciences, Sociology
ISBN Prefix(es): 973-97662
Parent Company: S C Varsatorul Impex SRL
Bookshop(s): Varsatorul Company

Editura Aius+
Str Nicolae Titulescu, bl 46, et 1, ap 7, Craiova 1100
Tel: (051) 196136 *Fax:* (051) 196135
E-mail: aius@euroweb.ro
Key Personnel
Executive Manager: George Sorin Singer
Founded: 1991
Subjects: Economics, History, Literature, Literary Criticism, Essays, Medicine, Nursing, Dentistry
ISBN Prefix(es): 973-9251; 973-95229; 973-96340; 973-96913; 973-97385
Total Titles: 3 Print

Editura Albatros
Piata Presei Libere 1, 79718 Bucharest
Tel: (01) 2228493 *Fax:* (01) 2228493
Key Personnel
Man Dir: Dan Petrescu
Chief Publisher: Georgetta Dimisianu
Founded: 1969
Subjects: History, Literature, Literary Criticism, Essays, Religion - Other
ISBN Prefix(es): 973-24

Alcor-Edimpex (Verlag) Ltd+
Bd 1 Mihalache 45, bl 16B+C, SC D, ap 116, sector 1, Bucurest
Tel: (01) 665-34-40 *Fax:* (01) 665 34 40
E-mail: ed_alcor@yahoo.com
Web Site: www.rotravel.com/alcor
Key Personnel
General Manager: Corina Firuta
Founded: 1994
Subjects: Art, Crafts, Games, Hobbies, History, Religion - Other, Travel
ISBN Prefix(es): 973-96752; 973-97200; 973-97901; 973-98341; 973-95673; 973-96304; 973-98935; 973-8160
Number of titles published annually: 10 Print
Imprints: Arta Grafica Printing House, ao; Editura CNI Coresi

Editora All+
B-dul Timisoara 58, 76548 Bucharest
Tel: (01) 402 26 00 *Fax:* (01) 402 26 10
E-mail: info@all.ro
Web Site: www.all.ro
Key Personnel
President: Mihail Penescu
Rights Manager: Carmen Penescu
Founded: 1992
Subjects: Computer Science, Education, Fiction, History, Medicine, Nursing, Dentistry, Nonfiction (General), Science (General)
ISBN Prefix(es): 973-96090; 973-9156; 973-571; 973-684; 973-8171
Number of titles published annually: 300 Print
Total Titles: 1,800 Print
Parent Company: Bic All

Alternative Editura+
Casa Presei Corp A, Et 6, Piata Presei Libere, 1, 71341 Bucharest 1
Tel: (01) 2234966; (01) 2229468 *Fax:* (01) 6756074; (01) 2234971
Key Personnel
Contact: Nicolae Lotreanu

Ararat -Tiped, Editura+
Formerly Ararat Verlag und Druckerei
Bdul Carlo I nr 45, Sector 2, Bucharest
Tel: (01) 3111425; (01) 6134050 *Fax:* (01) 3111420
Key Personnel
General Manager: Sirun Terzian
Dir: Stefan Agopian
Founded: 1994
Also book manufacturer.
Subjects: History, Literature, Literary Criticism, Essays, Philosophy, Social Sciences, Sociology
ISBN Prefix(es): 973-9310; 973-97869; 973-97127; 973-96682
Distributed by Humanitas (Romania)

Ararat Verlag und Druckerei, see Ararat -Tiped, Editura

Ars Longa Publishing House+
Str Elena Doamna 2, 700398 Iasi
Tel: (0232) 215078 *Fax:* (0232) 215078
E-mail: arslonga@mail.dntis.ro
Key Personnel
President: Christian Tamas
International Rights: Mrs Brandusa Tamas
Founded: 1994
Subjects: Fiction, History, Language Arts, Linguistics, Literature, Literary Criticism, Essays, Philosophy, Poetry, Religion - Catholic, Theology
ISBN Prefix(es): 973-96681; 973-97252; 973-9325
Number of titles published annually: 55 Print
Total Titles: 260 Print

Arta Grafica Printing House, ao, *imprint of* Alcor-Edimpex (Verlag) Ltd

Artemis Verlag
Piata Presei Libere nr 1, sector 1, Bucharest 71341
Tel: (01) 2226661
Key Personnel
Contact: Mirella Acsente
Founded: 1991
Subjects: Art, Biography, History, Nonfiction (General), Religion - Other
ISBN Prefix(es): 973-566

Editura Cartea Romaneasca
Calea Victoriei nr 115, Sector 1, 79721 Bucharest
Tel: (01) 3123733; (01) 6148802 *Fax:* (01) 3110025
Key Personnel
Dir: George Balaita
Founded: 1969
Subjects: Drama, Theater, Fiction, Literature, Literary Criticism, Essays, Poetry
ISBN Prefix(es): 973-23

Casa Editoriala Independenta Europa+
Str Brazda lui Novac, Bl nr 6/III/7, Craiova
Tel: (051) 153487; (051) 425801 *Fax:* (051) 153487
Key Personnel
Dir: Ion Deaconescu
Founded: 1990
Subjects: Art, History, Literature, Literary Criticism, Essays, Science (General)
ISBN Prefix(es): 973-9013; 973-95780; 973-99118
Associate Companies: Editura Libertatea, Serbia and Montenegro; Editura Hyperion, Republica Moldova
Subsidiaries: Brasov
Branch Office(s)
Brasov
Bucharest
Showroom(s): rue A I Cuza nr 10, Craiova
Warehouse: Calea Bucuresti, bl M5, Craiova

PUBLISHERS

The Center for Romanian Studies+
Oficiul Postal 1, Casuta Postala 108, Str Poligon nr 11a, 6600 Iasi
Tel: (032) 219000 *Fax:* (032) 219010
Key Personnel
Dir: Dr Kurt W Treptow
Office Manager: Petronela Postolache
Editor-in-Chief: Viorica Rusu
Founded: 1996
Membership(s): Romanian Publishers Association.
Subjects: Biography, Foreign Countries, History, Language Arts, Linguistics, Literature, Literary Criticism, Essays, Poetry, Sports, Athletics
ISBN Prefix(es): 973-9432; 973-98391; 973-98091; 973-9155
Number of titles published annually: 12 Print
Total Titles: 60 Print; 2 CD-ROM
Imprints: Iasi; Oxford; Portland
Branch Office(s)
40 Drake International Services, Market Moose, Market Place, Deddington 0X15 OSE, United Kingdom, Contact: Norman Drake *Tel:* (01869) 338240 *Fax:* (01869) 338310 *E-mail:* romcen@drakeint.co.uk
U.S. Office(s): c/o ISBS, 5804 NE Hassalo St, Portland, OR 97213-3644, United States, Contact: Tamma Greenfield *Tel:* 503-287-3093 *Fax:* 503-280-8832 *E-mail:* tamma@isbs.com
Distributed by International Specialized Book Services (North America)

Editura Ceres
Piata Presei Libere nr 1, 79722 Bucharest
Tel: (01) 2224836
Key Personnel
Man Dir: Ecaterina Mosu
Founded: 1953
Subjects: Agriculture, Animals, Pets, Environmental Studies, Veterinary Science
ISBN Prefix(es): 973-40

Editura Clusium+
Piata Unirii nr 1, 3400 Cluj
Tel: (064) 196940 *Fax:* (064) 196940
E-mail: clusium@codec.ro
Key Personnel
Man Dir: Valentin Tascu
Chief Editor: Corina Tascu
Copyright/Foreign Rights: Nicolae Mocanu
Founded: 1990
Subjects: Art, Biography, Computer Science, Engineering (General), Fiction, History, Humor, Literature, Literary Criticism, Essays, Medicine, Nursing, Dentistry, Nonfiction (General), Philosophy, Poetry, Religion - Other, Science (General), Social Sciences, Sociology, Technology
ISBN Prefix(es): 973-555

Editura CNI Coresi, *imprint of* Alcor-Edimpex (Verlag) Ltd

Coresi SRL+
Str Dem I. Dobrescu 4-6, Sector 1, Bucharest 78302
Tel: (01) 6386045; (01) 6386158; (01) 6386164; (00) 3127115; (00) 6154781 *Fax:* (01) 2230177
Key Personnel
Executive Manager: Michiela Gaga
General Manager: Vasile Poenaru
Founded: 1989
Specialize in children's literature & educational publications.
Subjects: Career Development, English as a Second Language, Language Arts, Linguistics
ISBN Prefix(es): 973-608
Number of titles published annually: 50 Print
Total Titles: 300 Print

Corint Publishing Group+
54A Mihal Eminescu St, Bucharest 010517
Tel: (0212) 11 97 66 *Fax:* (0212) 10 70 86
E-mail: corint@dnt.ro
Key Personnel
President: Cristian Gresanu
Vice President: Daniel Penescu
International Rights: Andreea Riess
Foreign Rights: Raluca Popescu
Founded: 1994
Specialize in scholarly books.
Subjects: Education, Fiction, Geography, Geology, History, Mathematics, Outdoor Recreation, Physics, Social Sciences, Sociology, Travel
ISBN Prefix(es): 973-6536; 973-7785; 973-7786; 973-7789; 973-86877; 973-86878; 973-86879; 973-86887
Number of titles published annually: 250 Print
Total Titles: 1,200 Print
Book Club(s): Corint

Editure Ion Creanga
P-ta Presei Libere 1, 79725 Bucharest
Tel: (01) 2231112
Key Personnel
Deputy Dir: Daniela Crasnaru
Editor-in-Chief: Gheorghe Zarafu
Founded: 1969
Subjects: Art, Biography, Fiction, History, Literature, Literary Criticism, Essays, Music, Dance, Poetry
ISBN Prefix(es): 973-25

Editura Cronos SRL
Str Progresului bl 39, ap 6, 70700 Baicoi
Tel: (044) 262245; (044) 7690952 *Fax:* (01) 2231025
E-mail: cronos@dial.kappa.ro
Key Personnel
Manager: Florin Chita
Founded: 1990
Cronos Publishing House by Cronos Foreign Service offers at request encyclopedic materials, informations & statistical data regarding Romania, also provides illustrations & maps of Romania, & proofs or actualizes different materials concerning Romania for foreign publishing houses, including encyclopedic articles.
Subjects: Advertising, Business, Travel
ISBN Prefix(es): 973-9000
Orders to: Str Progresului 39, Ap 6, 2064 BAICOI Prahova

Editura Dacia
Str Dorobantilor nr 3, Ap 13, 3400 Judetul Cluj
Tel: (0264) 452178 *Fax:* (0264) 452178
E-mail: office@edituradacia.ro
Web Site: www.edituradacia.ro; www.cjnet.ro
Telex: 31347
Key Personnel
Dir General: Ion Vadan
Founded: 1969
Subjects: Astrology, Occult, Biological Sciences, Chemistry, Chemical Engineering, Electronics, Electrical Engineering, Fiction, Finance, Geography, Geology
ISBN Prefix(es): 973-35

Editura Didactica si Pedagogica+
12 Spiru Haret St, 70738 Bucharest
Tel: (01) 3150043 *Fax:* (01) 3122885
E-mail: edpdirector@mail.codecnet.ro
Key Personnel
General Manager: Adrian-Paul Iliescu
Founded: 1951
ISBN Prefix(es): 973-30
Number of titles published annually: 300 Print

Editura DOINA SRL
Plaiul Unirii nr 39, Bl m12, sc B35, Bucharest
Tel: (01) 3228107 *Fax:* (01) 3227541
Key Personnel
Dir: Jenica Panaitescu
Founded: 1992
Subjects: Biography, Literature, Literary Criticism, Essays
ISBN Prefix(es): 973-95318; 973-95859; 973-96301; 973-9193

Editura Eminescu
One, Piata Presei Libere, Bucharest 1
Tel: (01) 2228540
Key Personnel
Man Dir: Valerin Rapeanu
Subjects: History, Poetry
ISBN Prefix(es): 973-22

Editura Enciclopedia RAO, *imprint of* Grupul Editorial RAO

Enzyklopadie Verlag+
Piata Presei Libere nr 1, Bucharest 79737
Tel: (01) 2243667; (01) 2244014 *Fax:* (01) 2243667
Key Personnel
Dir: Marcel Popa
International Rights: Irina Popa
Founded: 1968
Subjects: Antiques, Archaeology, Biography, Biological Sciences, Economics, History, Religion - Other
ISBN Prefix(es): 973-45
Total Titles: 24 Print

Euro Print Verlag
Str Sibiu 5, bl E3, ap 24, sector 6, Bucharest 77314
Tel: (01) 745-20-11 *Fax:* (01) 312-42-25
Key Personnel
Contact: Neculai Bratu
Founded: 1994
Editing & distribution. Specializes in stories, fairy tales, coloring & painting books for children.
Limited company.

Editura Excelsior Art (Excelsior Verlag - Publishing House)+
Affiliate of The Association of the Romanian Publishers
Cam 24A, Nr 5, Proclamatia de la Timisoara, 300054 Timisoara
Mailing Address: CP 262, OP 1, 1900 Timisoara
Tel: (0256) 201078 *Fax:* (0256) 201078
E-mail: edituraelcelsior@rdslink.ro
Key Personnel
Dir: Corina Victoria Badulescu
Founded: 1990
Membership(s): Writers Union of Romenien.
Subjects: Anthropology, Archaeology, Biblical Studies, Biography, Business, Communications, Cookery, Crafts, Games, Hobbies, Drama, Theater, Economics, Education, Ethnicity, Fiction, Health, Nutrition, History, Human Relations, Humor, Journalism, Language Arts, Linguistics, Library & Information Sciences, Literature, Literary Criticism, Essays, Mechanical Engineering, Medicine, Nursing, Dentistry, Mysteries, Nonfiction (General), Parapsychology, Philosophy, Poetry, Psychology, Psychiatry, Publishing & Book Trade Reference, Regional Interests, Religion - Other, Science (General), Science Fiction, Fantasy, Social Sciences, Sociology, Technology, Western Fiction, Science & fiction
ISBN Prefix(es): 973-9015; 973-592
Number of titles published annually: 50 Print
Total Titles: 680 Print
Distributor for Aletheia-Bistrita; Compact-Brasov; Dacia Traina-Sibiu; Libraria Eminescu; Librarii-TG Mures; Libris-Galati; Novus-Craiova; Prolibris-Ramnicu Valcea; Sedcomlibris-Iasi; Sedcomlibris-Suceava; Timlibris Timisoara

Editura Fahrenheit, *imprint of* Grupul Editorial RAO

ROMANIA

FF Press
Calea Mosilor 209, sc A et 7, ap 26, Sector 2, Bucharest
Tel: (01) 6191544 *Fax:* (01) 3129694
Key Personnel
President: Serban Florea
Editor: Ion Covaci
Contact: Dr Florea Doina
Founded: 1992
Subjects: Finance, History, Literature, Literary Criticism, Essays, Poetry, Science (General)
ISBN Prefix(es): 973-96089; 973-96745; 973-96837

Casa de editura Globus+
Piata Presei Libere 1, et 8, cam 853, Sector 1, Bucharest 78202
Tel: (01) 2231510; (01) 2231530 *Fax:* (01) 6664265
Key Personnel
President: Tudor Stoica
Publisher: Petre Barbulescu
Author: Mihai Ungheanu
Founded: 1990
Subjects: Economics, Government, Political Science, History
ISBN Prefix(es): 973-49

Editura Gryphon+
Division of Gryphon Ltd
Str IL Caragiale, No 6, 500413 Brasov
Tel: (0268) 313 642; (0268) 312 888 *Fax:* (0268) 312 888
E-mail: gryphon@gryphon.ro
Web Site: www.gryphon.ro
Key Personnel
President & General Manager: Eugen Ioan Popa *Tel:* (0722) 609 253
Founded: 1990
Specialize in importing books, provider for libraries & universities publishing house.
Subjects: Art, Civil Engineering, Earth Sciences, Health, Nutrition, Medicine, Nursing, Dentistry, Science (General), Technology, Veterinary Science
ISBN Prefix(es): 973-604
Number of titles published annually: 6 Print
Total Titles: 17 Print
Distributor for Grolier Inc USA

Gryphon Publishing Ltd, see Editura Gryphon

Hasefer
Bd I C Bratianu 35, et 2, ap 9, sector 3, 970478 Bucharest
Tel: (021) 312 22 84 *Fax:* (021) 312 22 84
E-mail: hasefer@fx.ro
Key Personnel
Dir: Sandu Singer
Subjects: Biblical Studies, Education, History, Literature, Literary Criticism, Essays, Religion - Other
ISBN Prefix(es): 973-8056
Number of titles published annually: 30 Print
Parent Company: Romanian Federation of Jewish Communities

Humanitas Publishing House+
One Piata Presei Libere, 79734 Bucharest
Tel: (01) 223-1501; (01) 222-8546 *Fax:* (01) 224-3632
E-mail: editors@agora.humanitas.ro
Web Site: www.humanitas.ro
Key Personnel
General Dir: Gabriel Liiceanu
Editorial Dir: Adriana Irimia
Foreign Rights Executive: Livia Stoia *Tel:* (01) 2243638 *E-mail:* lstoia@agora.humanitas.ro
Founded: 1990
Specialize in humanities & fiction.
Subjects: Biography, Fiction, Government, Political Science, History, Literature, Literary Criticism, Essays, Philosophy, Psychology, Psychiatry, Religion - Buddhist, Religion - Catholic, Religion - Hindu, Religion - Islamic, Religion - Jewish, Science (General), Social Sciences, Sociology, Theology
ISBN Prefix(es): 973-28
Associate Companies: Societatea Comerciala Librariile Humanitas
Subsidiaries: Societatea Comerciala Librariile Humanitas; Societate franco romana de difuzare a cartii SA
Bookshop(s): Libraria Humanitas, Pasajul Kretzulescu CI Victoriei nr 45; Libraria din fundul curtii, Cl Victoriei nr 120, Bucharest

Iasi, imprint of The Center for Romanian Studies

Editura Institutul European+
17, Cronicar Mustea St, 6600 Iasi
Tel: (032) 230197; (032) 233731; (032) 233800 *Fax:* (032) 230-197
E-mail: rtvnova@mail.cccis.ro; euroedit@mail.dntis.ro
Key Personnel
President: Anca Untu-Dumitrescu
Editor-in-Chief: Sorin Parvu
Public Relations: Liliana Buruiana-Popovici
Founded: 1991
Membership(s): The Association of Romaniau Editors.
Subjects: Education, English as a Second Language, Government, Political Science, History, Literature, Literary Criticism, Essays, Medicine, Nursing, Dentistry, Philosophy, Religion - Other, Theology
ISBN Prefix(es): 973-9148; 973-95528; 973-586; 973-95671; 973-611; 973-95870
Distributed by Humanitas
Distributor for Ceu Press (Budapest)

Editura Junimea+
Bd Carol 1 nr 3-5, 6600 Isai
Tel: (032) 117290
Key Personnel
Dir: Nicolae Cretu
Administrative Dir: Constantin Ursache
Foreign Rights: Christian Tamas
Founded: 1969
Subjects: Literature, Literary Criticism, Essays, Technology
ISBN Prefix(es): 973-37

Editura Kriterion SA+
Str Justitiei 41-43, Ap 4, Sector 4, 70529 Bucharest
Tel: (01) 3366509 *Fax:* (01) 313 11 07
E-mail: krit@dnt.ro; kriterion@mail.dnt.cj.ro
Key Personnel
Manager & Dir: H Szabo Gyula *Tel:* (095) 1634377 *E-mail:* szabogyula@yahoo.com
Founded: 1969
Subjects: Art, Ethnicity, Fiction, History, Literature, Literary Criticism, Essays, Poetry
ISBN Prefix(es): 973-26
Number of titles published annually: 40 Print
Total Titles: 200 Print
Branch Office(s)
Kriterion Cluj, Str S Mict, MNr 12A Cluj
Tel: (064) 197450 *Fax:* (064) 197450
E-mail: kriterion@mail.dntej.ro

Lider Verlag+
Bd Libertati No 4, bl 117, et 111, ap7, sector 4, Bucharest 761061
Tel: (01) 337-33-067; (01) 3374881 *Fax:* (01) 337-48-22
Key Personnel
President & International Rights: Casandra Enescu
Founded: 1994
Subjects: Art, History, Language Arts, Linguistics, Literature, Literary Criticism, Essays, Medicine, Nursing, Dentistry, Philosophy, Romance
ISBN Prefix(es): 973-8117; 973-97836

Litera Publishing House
Piata Presei Libere nr 1, Bucharest
Tel: (01) 2331349; (01) 2332749 *Fax:* (01) 2231873
E-mail: info@litera.ro
Web Site: www.litera-publishing.com
Key Personnel
Manager: Gheorghe Buzatu
Subjects: Literature, Literary Criticism, Essays
ISBN Prefix(es): 973-43

MAST Verlag+
Str Craesti 2, bl A47, ap 10, Bucharest 77418
Tel: (01) 7786950 *Fax:* (01) 4104588
Key Personnel
Contact: Florin Mateescu
Founded: 1994
Subjects: Agriculture, Animals, Pets, Antiques, Astrology, Occult, Gardening, Plants, Medicine, Nursing, Dentistry, Veterinary Science
ISBN Prefix(es): 973-97297; 973-97867; 973-97868; 973-8011

Editura Medicala (Medical Publishing House)+
Bulevardul Pache Protopopescu, nr 131, sectoe 2, 131 Bucharest
Tel: (01) 25 25 186 *Fax:* (01) 25 25 189
E-mail: edmedicala@fx.ro
Web Site: www.ed-medicala.ro
Key Personnel
Man Dir: Alexandru Oproiu *E-mail:* oproiu@fx.ro
Founded: 1954
Medical Publishing House.
Subjects: Medicine, Nursing, Dentistry
ISBN Prefix(es): 973-39
Number of titles published annually: 30 Print

Mentor Kiado+
Member of Hungarian Book Guild From Romania
Str Paltinis nr 4, cod 4300, Targu-Mure, Mure
Tel: (0265) 256975 *Fax:* (0265) 256975
Key Personnel
Ed-in-Chief: Istvan Kiraly
Editor: Gyorgy Galfvi *Tel:* (065) 167091 *Fax:* (065) 167087; Andras Ferenc Kovacs *Tel:* (065) 167091 *Fax:* (065) 167087; Zsolt Lang *Tel:* (065) 167091 *Fax:* (065) 167087
Founded: 1993
Main mission is the publication of works of living Hungarian literature, particularly those of Transylvanian (province of Romania) writers. Special focus is the patronage of new writers & the Minomtates Mundi series, which presents the literary traditions of minority peoples.
Subjects: Art, Drama, Theater, Ethnicity, History, Literature, Literary Criticism, Essays, Philosophy, Poetry, Romance, Social Sciences, Sociology
ISBN Prefix(es): 973-95943; 973-96650; 973-97072; 973-9263
Total Titles: 5 Print

Editura Meridiane+
P-ta Presei Libere 1, 71341 Bucharest
Mailing Address: PO Box 33-47, 79729 Bucharest
Tel: (01) 222-33-93 *Fax:* (01) 222-30-37
Key Personnel
Dir: Elena Victoria Jiquidi
Senior Editor, Acquisitions & Foreign Rights: Livia Szasz Campeanu; Andrei Niculescu
Founded: 1952
Subjects: Anthropology, Archaeology, Architecture & Interior Design, Art, Biography, Drama,

Theater, Fashion, Film, Video, History, Language Arts, Linguistics, Literature, Literary Criticism, Essays, Medicine, Nursing, Dentistry, Music, Dance, Nonfiction (General), Religion - Other, Social Sciences, Sociology, Travel, Art History, Design, Cultural studies, Media
ISBN Prefix(es): 973-33
Number of titles published annually: 25 Print
Total Titles: 65 Print

Editura Militara+
Str Gen, Cristescu nr 5, 79735 Bucharest
Tel: (01) 3112191; (01) 6133601 *Fax:* (01) 3237822
Key Personnel
Dir: Cornel Barbulescu
Founded: 1950
Subjects: Education, Electronics, Electrical Engineering, Engineering (General), History, Military Science, Mysteries, Social Sciences, Sociology
ISBN Prefix(es): 973-32
Bookshop(s): Libraria Militara (Military Bookshop), Piate Natiunilor Unite nr 3, Bucharest

Editura Minerva+
Bdul Metalurgiei nr 32-34, sector 4, Bucharest
Tel: (01) 3308808; (01) 3308840 *Fax:* (01) 3308808; (01) 3308840
E-mail: desfacere@edituraaramis.ro
Founded: 1969
Subjects: Astrology, Occult, Biography, Computer Science, Education, Film, Video, Finance, Library & Information Sciences
ISBN Prefix(es): 973-21
Parent Company: Editura Minerva
Subsidiaries: Series Biblioteca Pentru Toti

Monitorul Oficial, Editura+
Palace of Parliament, 2-4 Izvor St, Sector 5 Bucharest
Tel: (01) 402-2173; (01) 402-2176; (01) 411-5833 *Fax:* (01) 312-0901; (01) 312-4703; (01) 410-7736
E-mail: ramomrk@bx.logicnet.ro
Key Personnel
Manager: Eugenia Clubancan
Founded: 1832
Subjects: Law
ISBN Prefix(es): 973-567
Distributed by Kubon & Sagner (Germany)
Bookshop(s): Str Blanduziei nr 1, sector 1, Bucharest

Editura Muzicala
Str Calea Victoriei nr 141, 79733 Bucharest
Tel: (01) 3129867 *Fax:* (01) 3129867
E-mail: editura_muzicala@hotmail.com
Key Personnel
Man Dir: Vlad Ulpiu; Marius Vasileanu
Founded: 1958
Books, musical scores, compact discs & CD-ROM's.
Subjects: Biography, Music, Dance
ISBN Prefix(es): 973-42
Orders to: Bucharest

Nemira Verlag+
Bdul Ion Mihalache nr 125, sector 1, Casa Presei Libere, corp D, etj 3, sector 1, Bucharest
Tel: (01) 2242156 *Fax:* (01) 2241600
E-mail: editura@nemira.ro
Key Personnel
Editorial Dir: Vlad T Popescu
International Rights: Iulia Stoica
Founded: 1991
Subjects: Accounting, Advertising, Economics, Education, Government, Political Science, Literature, Literary Criticism, Essays, Marketing, Science Fiction, Fantasy

ISBN Prefix(es): 973-569; 973-9301; 973-9144; 973-99576; 973-95169; 973-9177; 973-96255
Associate Companies: Nemira & Co; Nemira Multimedia
Bookshop(s): Edutura Nemira, PO Box 33-22, 71341 Bucharest
Book Club(s): Clubul cartii
Shipping Address: Edutura Nemira, PO Box 33-22, 71341 Bucharest
Warehouse: Edutura Nemira, PO Box 33-22, 71341 Bucharest
Orders to: Edutura Nemira, PO Box 33-22, 71341 Bucharest

Editura Niculescu+
Str Octav Cocarascu 79, Sector 1, 781821 Bucharest
Tel: (01) 2242898; (01) 2220372 *Fax:* (01) 2242898; (01) 2220372
E-mail: edit@niculescu.ro
Web Site: www.niculescu.ro
Key Personnel
President: Dr Christian Niculescu *Tel:* (09) 2342900
Marketing & Distribution: Lavona George
Founded: 1993
Subjects: Accounting, Biography, Biological Sciences, Business, Career Development, Child Care & Development, Cookery, Economics, Education, Engineering (General), English as a Second Language, Fiction, Film, Video, Gardening, Plants, Geography, Geology, Government, Political Science, Health, Nutrition, History, House & Home, Humor, Language Arts, Linguistics, Law, Management, Marketing, Mathematics, Mysteries, Natural History, Nonfiction (General), Outdoor Recreation, Philosophy, Physics, Science (General), Self-Help, Social Sciences, Sociology, Wine & Spirits, Reference Work
ISBN Prefix(es): 973-568
Number of titles published annually: 180 Print; 18 CD-ROM
Total Titles: 70 Print; 12 CD-ROM
Associate Companies: Clubul de Carte Niculescu, Str Octav Cocarascu 79, 78182 Bucharest *Tel:* (01) 224-24-80

Editura Orion+
Str Ion Brezoianu 51B, 70711 Bucharest
Tel: (01) 3125250 *Fax:* (01) 2104636
Key Personnel
President: Cristian Corneliu Bigica
Editor: Florin Lupescu
ISBN Prefix(es): 973-95052; 973-95532; 973-97273; 973-98353; 973-8020
Parent Company: Orion Enterprises Ltd

Oxford, *imprint of* The Center for Romanian Studies

Editura Paideia+
Str Tudor Arghezi nr 15, sector 2, Bucharest
Tel: (01) 2115804; (01) 2120347 *Fax:* (01) 2120348
E-mail: paideia@fx.ro
Key Personnel
President: Ion Bansoiu *Tel:* (01) 2529850
Founded: 1990
Non-profit organization.
Subjects: Literature, Literary Criticism, Essays, Philosophy, Religion - Other, Social Sciences, Sociology
ISBN Prefix(es): 973-9131; 973-95306; 973-9368; 973-9393; 973-8064; 973-596
Number of titles published annually: 60 Print; 10 CD-ROM
Total Titles: 30 Print; 6 CD-ROM; 4 Audio
Foreign Rep(s): Anca Chelaru (USA)
Foreign Rights: Radu Lungu (France)

Pallas-Akademia Editura
Str Petofi nr4, CP140 Miercurea-Ciuc
Tel: (066) 171036 *Fax:* (066) 171036
E-mail: pallas@nextra.ro
Key Personnel
Man Dir: Josef Gyula Tozser
Chief Editor: Maria Kozma
Copyright/Foreign Rights: Eva Herta
Founded: 1993
Subjects: Biography, Computer Science, Engineering (General), Ethnicity, Fiction, Journalism, Literature, Literary Criticism, Essays, Regional Interests, Religion - Catholic, Science (General), Social Sciences, Sociology, Technology, Art History
ISBN Prefix(es): 973-96702
Number of titles published annually: 30 Print
Distributed by Aligator kft Koenyvkereskedes (Cluj-Napoca, Romania); Babits Kiado (Szekszard, Hungary); Carthographia Kiado (Budapest, Hungary); Casa de Presa (Bucarest, Romania); Custos Koenyvkereskedes (Bucarest, Romania); Editura Humanitas (Bucarest, Romania); Editura Lyra (Targu-Mures, Romania); Sc Bon Ami (Stantu-Gheorghe, Romania); Sc Cartimpex Koenyvkeseskedes (Cluj-Napoca, Romania); Sc Libris srl (Satu-Mare, Romania); Sc Samlibris (Satu-Mare, Romania); Sc Zalanta Prest (Salonta, Romania)
Distributor for Akademiai Kiado (Budapest, Hungary); Babits Kiado (Szekszard, Hungary); Bagolyvar Kiado (Budapest, Hungary); Carthogrphia Kiado (Budapest, Hungary); Editura Dacia (Cluj-Napoca, Romania); Editura Humanita (Bucarest, Romania); Editura Ion Creanga (Bucharest, Romania); Editura Komp-Press (Cluj-Napoca, Romania); Editura Rao (Bucarest, Romania); Euro pa Kiado (Budapest, Hungary); Kossuth Kiado (Budapest, Hungary); Magveto Kiado (Budapest, Hungary); Magyar Koenyvklubb (Budapest, Hungary); Mentor Kiado (Targu-Mures, Romania); Mora Ferenc Kiado (Budapest, Hungary); Osiris Kiado (Budapest, Hungary); Park Kiado (Budapest, Hungary); Polis Kiado (Cluj-Napoca, Romania); Sprinter Koenyvkereskedes (Budapest, Hungary); Szent Istvan Tarsulat (Budapest, Hungary); Szukits Kiado (Szeged, Hungary)
Bookshop(s): str Petofi nr 4, Miercurea Ciuc 4100; P-ta Libertatii 5/A, Gheorgheni 4200; P-ta Marton Aron nr 2, Odorheiu-Secuiesc 4150; Str Koroesi Csoma Sandor nr 2, SPantu Gheorghe 4000; P-ta Trandafirilor nr 57, Targu-Mures 4300; Str M Sadoveanu nr 3, Brasov 2200; Str Universitatii nr 1, Cluj-Napoca 3400; Str Horea nr 6, Satu-Mare; Sindicatelor nr 7, Salonta 3650; Libraria Eminescu, Bul Elisabeta nr 5, Sector 5, Bucharest

Pandora Publishing House+
B-dulLacul Tei nr 123, bloc 4, Bucharest 723241
Tel: (021) 688 6739 *Fax:* (021) 243 3739
Key Personnel
Dir: Ion Monafu *E-mail:* editurapandora@hotmail.com
Associate Dir: Valer Monafu
E-mail: valmonafu@msn.com
Founded: 1991
Specialize in fiction, nonfiction, translation from contemporary foreign authors, science & children's books.
Subjects: Biography, Fiction, Humor, Literature, Literary Criticism, Essays, Nonfiction (General), Poetry, Science (General), Science Fiction, Fantasy
ISBN Prefix(es): 973-96336; 973-96932; 973-95148; 973-8147
Number of titles published annually: 15 Print
Total Titles: 120 Print
Associate Companies: Prolectura Foundation
Foreign Rep(s): Dan Monafu (Canada); Valer Monafu (USA)

ROMANIA

Petrion Verlag+
Calea Plevnei 124, sector 6, Bucharest 70700
Tel: (01) 3103407; (01) 3152641 *Fax:* (01) 3124525; (01) 3152641
E-mail: petrion@stranets.ro
Founded: 1990
Subjects: Education, Mathematics, Microcomputers, Physics
ISBN Prefix(es): 973-9116

Polirom Verlag+
4, Copou Blvd, PO Box 266, 6600 Iasi
Tel: (032) 214-100; (032) 214-111; (032) 217-440 *Fax:* (032) 214-100; (032) 214-111; (032) 217-440
E-mail: office@polirom.ro
Web Site: www.polirom.ro
Key Personnel
Manager: Silviu Lupescu
Founded: 1995
Subjects: Anthropology, Communications, History, Journalism, Literature, Literary Criticism, Essays, Management, Marketing, Medicine, Nursing, Dentistry, Philosophy, Psychology, Psychiatry, Social Sciences, Sociology
ISBN Prefix(es): 973-9248; 973-97108; 973-97410; 973-97522; 973-683

Portland, *imprint of* The Center for Romanian Studies

Editura RAO Bucuresti, *imprint of* Grupul Editorial RAO

Grupul Editorial RAO (RAO Publishing Group)+
Str Turda, Nr 117-119, Bl 6, parter, 78219 Bucharest
Tel: (01) 224-12-31; (01) 224-14-72; (01) 224-18-47; (01) 224-21-36 *Fax:* (01) 224-12-31; (01) 224-14-72; (01) 224-18-47; (01) 224-21-36
E-mail: office@raobooks.com; club@raobooks.com
Web Site: www.raobooks.com
Key Personnel
President: Anca Enculescu
Editorial Dir: Ondine Dascalita
Contact: Ovidiu Enculescu
Founded: 1993
Membership(s): AER & IBBY.
Subjects: Biography, Education, Fiction, History, Nonfiction (General), Science Fiction, Fantasy, Self-Help, Classic & Contemporary Fiction, Textbooks
ISBN Prefix(es): 973-576; 973-9460; 973-98762; 973-98626
Total Titles: 280 Print
Imprints: Editura Enciclopedia RAO; Editura Fahrenheit; Editura RAO Bucuresti; RAO International Publishing Co
Warehouse: Str Tiate Mics 4, Sibiu *Fax:* (069) 215605 *E-mail:* rao.sb@bx.logicnet.ro
Orders to: RAO International Publishing Co, PO Box 2-124, Bucharest, Contact: Catalina Manolache

RAO International Publishing Co, *imprint of* Grupul Editorial RAO

RAO International Publishing Co+
Imprint of Grupul Editorial RAO
125 Ion Mihalache Blvd, Bl 7, sc A, sector 1, Bucharest
Tel: (01) 224-1002; (01) 224-1704 *Fax:* (01) 222-8059
E-mail: rao.b@bx.logicnet.ro
Key Personnel
Dir: Ondine Dascalita
Subjects: Biography, Fiction, Literature, Literary Criticism, Essays, Mysteries, Nonfiction (General), Religion - Other, Romance, Science Fiction, Fantasy
ISBN Prefix(es): 973-576; 973-9164; 973-96203; 973-96204
Subsidiaries: Rao Educational
Book Club(s): Rao Buchklub

Realitatea Casa de Edituri Productie Audio-Video Film+
B-dul Dacia nr 126, 70267 Bucharest
Tel: (01) 6117105; (01) 6517105; (01) 6332468; (01) 6143793 *Fax:* (01) 2105411
E-mail: leu@dnt.ro
Key Personnel
President: Corneliu Leu
Editor: George Atanasiu; Leu Vlad
Founded: 1990
Specialize in film production & video cassettes.
Membership(s): Romanian Copyright Society.
Subjects: Education, Government, Political Science, Literature, Literary Criticism, Essays, Nonfiction (General), Philosophy, Romance
ISBN Prefix(es): 973-9025
Parent Company: Realitatea-Publishers & Producers Ltd
Branch Office(s)
Monolith Corporation, 37 4181 St, Suite A2, Jackson Heights, NY 11372, United States *Tel:* 718-507-2870
Bookshop(s): Bucharest, Timisoara, Iassi, Busteni (Romania)

Rentrop & Straton Verlagsgruppe und Wirtschaftsconsulting+
4, Natiunile Unite Blvd, Bloc 107A, sector 5, Bucharest 050122
Tel: (021) 337.4146 *Fax:* (021) 337.2211
E-mail: rs@rs.ro; office@rs.ro
Web Site: www.rs.ro
Key Personnel
General Editor: George Straton
International Rights: Violeta Carutasu
Founded: 1995
Subjects: Accounting, Advertising, Business, Career Development, Child Care & Development, Communications, Computer Science, Economics, Finance, How-to, Law, Management, Marketing, Nonfiction (General), Self-Help, Travel
ISBN Prefix(es): 973-97748; 973-98033; 973-8154
Associate Companies: VNR Verlag fur die Deutsche Wirtschaft AG, Bonn, Germany
Bookshop(s): Libraria Rentrop & Straton, 22-24, Cantemir Blvd, Bucharest, sector 4; Libraria Rentrop & Straton, ROMEXPO, pavilion35, 53-57, Marasti Blvd, Bucharest, sector 1

Saeculum IO+
Teodosie Rudeanu, 29, 011257 Bucharest
Tel: (021) 2228597 *Fax:* (021) 3452827; (021) 2228597
E-mail: saeculum@tcnet.ro
Web Site: www.saeculum.ro
Key Personnel
Proprietor: Prof Ionel Oprisan, PhD
Founded: 1994
Membership(s): SER (Publishers' Society of Romania).
Subjects: Anthropology, Art, Biography, Fiction, History, Literature, Literary Criticism, Essays, Mysteries, Parapsychology, Philosophy, Poetry, Romance, Theology
ISBN Prefix(es): 973-9211; 973-9399; 973-642
Parent Company: Saeculum IO
Associate Companies: Saeculum Vizual; Vestala; Ciucea, 5, bloc L19, Ap 216, 032522 Bucharest

Editura 'Scrisul Romanesc'
Str Mihai Viteazul 4, 1100 Craiova
Tel: (051) 419506
Key Personnel
Dir: Ilarie Hinoveanu
Founded: 1972
'Romanian Writing' Publishing House.
Subjects: Government, Political Science, Literature, Literary Criticism, Essays, Social Sciences, Sociology
ISBN Prefix(es): 973-38

Editura Signata+
Str Chiriac nr 26, 1900 Timisoara
Tel: (056) 153081
Key Personnel
Dir: Ioan Iancu
Founded: 1990
Membership(s): Romanian Writers' Association.
Subjects: Technology
ISBN Prefix(es): 973-551

Editura Stiintifica SA (Scientific Publishing House)+
Piata Presei Libere nr 1, 79737 Bucharest
Tel: (01) 3351654; (01) 3367442 *Fax:* (01) 3356499
Key Personnel
Man Dir: Dinu Grama
Founded: 1990
Subjects: Biological Sciences, Geography, Geology, History, Mathematics, Nonfiction (General), Philosophy, Psychology, Psychiatry, Science (General)
ISBN Prefix(es): 973-44

Editura Stiintifica si Enciclopedica (Scientific & Encyclopedia Publishing House)
Piata Presei Libere nr 1, 78737 Bucharest
Tel: (01) 175168
Key Personnel
Manager: Dinu Grama
Production Manager, Sales Dir: Alexandru Banciu
Founded: 1975 (by amalgamation of Romanian Encyclopaedic Publishing House & Scientific Publishing House)
The Foreign Encyclopedias Office supplies any encyclopedic materials, information, data, statistics, maps & illustrations concerning Romania required by foreign publishing houses.
Subjects: Language Arts, Linguistics, Literature, Literary Criticism, Essays, Science (General), Social Sciences, Sociology
ISBN Prefix(es): 973-29

Est-Samuel Tastet Verlag+
Bdul Uverturii nr 57-69, Bl 10, sc C, et 1, ap 87, sector 6, Bucharest
Mailing Address: ap 24, sector 1, Bucharest
Tel: (01) 6386250 *Fax:* (01) 3122012
Key Personnel
Contact: Samuel Tastet
Founded: 1995
Subjects: Art, Biography, Drama, Theater, Fiction, Literature, Literary Criticism, Essays, Poetry
ISBN Prefix(es): 973-96902; 973-98094

Editura Tehnica
Piata presei libere 1, 79738 Bucharest
Tel: (01) 222-33-21 *Fax:* (01) 222-37-76
Founded: 1950
Also book packager.
Subjects: Engineering (General), Science (General), Technology
ISBN Prefix(es): 973-31

Editura Teora+
Calea Mosilor 211, sector 2, Bucharest 70325
Tel: (021) 2106204 *Fax:* (021) 2103828
E-mail: mesaj@teora.ro
Web Site: www.teora.ro
Key Personnel
Dir: Teodor Raducanu
Founded: 1990

Subjects: Computer Science, Economics, Electronics, Electrical Engineering, Law, Medicine, Nursing, Dentistry, Philosophy, Psychology, Psychiatry, Science Fiction, Fantasy, Sports, Athletics, Technology
ISBN Prefix(es): 973-601

Editura Top Suspans
Aleea Terasei, Nr 6, Bl R2, Ap 5, Sect 4, Bucharest 75582
Tel: (01) 6830924; (01) 6103359
Key Personnel
Dir: Nicolae Carp
ISBN Prefix(es): 973-9060

Editura Univers SA+
Str Ionel Perlea nr 9, et 2, ap 4, int 24C, 79739 Bucharest
Tel: (01) 2244640; (01) 3104510 *Fax:* (01) 3104510
E-mail: univers@rnc.ro *Cable:* 1 PIATA PRESEI LIBERE, 79739 BUCHAREST
Key Personnel
General Dir: Prof Martin Mircea
Editor: Denisa Comanescu
Foreign Rights Editor: Adrian Mihaltianu
Founded: 1961
Subjects: Biography, Education, Fiction, Literature, Literary Criticism, Essays, Philosophy, Poetry, Romance, Science Fiction, Fantasy
ISBN Prefix(es): 973-34
Subsidiaries: Univers Informatic

Universal Dalsi+
Piata Presei Libere, corp b1, et 4, cam 379-380, sector 1, Bucharest
Tel: (01) 3355354; (01) 3371682 *Fax:* (01) 3373566; (01) 3129709
E-mail: marian@kappa.ro
Key Personnel
Dir: Maria Marian *Tel:* (01) 650 6091 *Fax:* (01) 312 9709
Founded: 1992
Private publishing house specialized in belles lettres in Romanian & other languages.
Subjects: Education, Fiction, Literature, Literary Criticism, Essays, Philosophy, Poetry, Science (General), Social Sciences, Sociology, Theology
ISBN Prefix(es): 973-9166; 973-8157; 973-95690; 973-96039; 973-9409
Total Titles: 10 Print
Distributor for Letos Mimai, Balasion

Editura Valahia SRL
Str Trivale, bloc 61, sc B, ap 9, Pitesti, Jud Arges
Tel: (097) 680948
Key Personnel
Dir: George Nitu
Founded: 1990
ISBN Prefix(es): 973-95049

Editura de Vest+
Piata Sf Gheorghe nr 3, 1900 Timisoara
Tel: (056) 191959 *Fax:* (056) 14212
Key Personnel
Dir: Vasile Popovici
Founded: 1972
Subjects: Art, Fiction, Science (General), Technology
ISBN Prefix(es): 973-36

Vestala Verlag+
Str Resita 2, bl P4, ap 20, sector 4, 74696 Bucharest
Tel: (01) 222-8597; (01) 345-2827 *Fax:* (01) 222-8597; (01) 345-2827
Key Personnel
Contact: Dr Ionel Oprisan
Founded: 1993
Membership(s): Publishers' Association of Romania (Asociatia Editorilor din Romania).
Subjects: Art, Biography, History, Literature, Literary Criticism, Essays, Mysteries, Parapsychology, Philosophy
ISBN Prefix(es): 973-9200; 973-96063; 973-96421; 973-96817; 973-9418
Number of titles published annually: 30 Print
Total Titles: 120 Print
Parent Company: Saeculum Verlag, 74696 Bucharest
Associate Companies: Saeculum i o Verlag
Distribution Center: Str Teodosie Rudeanu 29, Sect I, Bucharest

Vox Editura+
Str Petru Maior nr 32, sec 1, Bucharest 781232
Tel: (01) 2220213; (01) 2220214 *Fax:* (01) 2220213
E-mail: edituravox@hotmail.com
Key Personnel
General Manager: Lucia Ovezea
Founded: 1994
Subjects: Gardening, Plants
ISBN Prefix(es): 973-96922; 973-97848; 973-98159; 973-9381

Vremea Publishers Ltd+
Str Constantin Daniel 14, sect 1, 71121 Bucharest
Tel: (01) 3358131 *Fax:* (01) 3110219
E-mail: vremea@fx.ro
Key Personnel
President: Nicolae Henegariu
Vice President: Cristina Cantacuzino
Man Dir & Chief Editor: Silvia Colfescu
  Tel: (092) 226088
Copyright/Foreign Rights: Maria Giugariu
Founded: 1990
Membership(s): AER Romanian Publishers Association.
Subjects: Art, Astrology, Occult, Biography, Child Care & Development, Education, Fiction, Health, Nutrition, History, Literature, Literary Criticism, Essays, Medicine, Nursing, Dentistry, Parapsychology, Philosophy, Poetry, Religion - Other, Science Fiction, Fantasy, Social Sciences, Sociology
ISBN Prefix(es): 973-9162; 973-95063; 973-95581
Number of titles published annually: 45 Print
Total Titles: 250 Print

Russian Federation

General Information

Capital: Moscow
Language: Russian
Religion: Predominantly Christian (mostly Russian Orthodox), also Islam and Buddhist
Population: 149.5 million
Bank Hours: Generally open for short hours between 0930-1230 Monday-Friday
Shop Hours: Generally 0900-1800 Monday-Friday; often open weekends
Currency: 100 kopeks = 1 rubl
Export/Import Information: According to Ukrainian quotas and customs duties, companies engaged in trade should register with the Ukraine Ministry of Foreign Economic Relations. Licenses for export and import are also required for trade with Russia.
Copyright: UCC, Berne, Florence (see Copyright Conventions, pg xi)

Agni Publishing House
23 Michurin St, 443110 Samara
Tel: (08462) 70-32-87; (08462) 70-23-87 (ext 445 - Orders) *Fax:* (08462) 70-23-85
E-mail: cdk@transit.samara.ru; support@agniart.ru (distribution & ordering)
Web Site: www.agni.samara.ru
Key Personnel
Manager: Sergey Tyoply
Also producers of fine art reproductions of paintings by Russian artists, photo-landscapes, framing & art albums.
Subjects: History, Philosophy

Airis Press+
106 Prospekt Mira, Office 555, 129626 Moscow
Tel: (095) 9561684; (095) 7852925 *Fax:* (095) 9561684; (095) 7852925
E-mail: rolf@airis.ru
Web Site: www.airis.ru
Key Personnel
Marketing Dir: Igor Chesnokov *E-mail:* iches@airis.ru
Founded: 1993
Specialize in educational literature, books helping school-leavers & students to prepare for the exams, handbooks & textbooks in foreign languages, popular educational books, reference books.
Subjects: Business, Career Development, Child Care & Development, Cookery, Crafts, Games, Hobbies, Education, English as a Second Language, Gardening, Plants, Health, Nutrition, How-to, Language Arts, Linguistics, Medicine, Nursing, Dentistry
ISBN Prefix(es): 5-7836; 5-8112
Number of titles published annually: 70 Print; 3 Audio
Total Titles: 180 Print; 3 Audio
Distributor for Foulsham; New Market Press; Parenting Press

ARGO-RISK Publisher
ul Staryj Gaj 6-1-419, 111402 Moscow
Tel: (095) 4768538 *Fax:* (095) 2926511
E-mail: zayats@glas.apc.org
Key Personnel
Dir: Vladislav Artsatbanov
Editor-in-Chief: Dmitri Kuz'min
Founded: 1993
Subjects: Gay & Lesbian, Literature, Literary Criticism, Essays, Poetry
ISBN Prefix(es): 5-900506

Armada Publishing House+
Kronshtadtskii Blvd, 37b, 125499 Moscow
Tel: (095) 4544301; (095) 45431526 *Fax:* (095) 4542481
E-mail: riv@armada.msk.ru
Key Personnel
President: Dmitri Adamov
Editor: Anton Rybin
Foreign Rights: Olga Zasetskaya
Founded: 1992
Subjects: Animals, Pets, Fiction, Mysteries, Romance, Science Fiction, Fantasy
ISBN Prefix(es): 5-7632

Aspect Press Ltd+
ul Plehanova 23, corpus 3, Moscow 111398
Tel: (095) 3094062 *Fax:* (095) 3091166
E-mail: info@aspectpress.ru
Web Site: www.aspectpress.ru
Key Personnel
Dir & Owner: Leonid Shipov *E-mail:* shipov@aspectpress.ru
Founded: 1992
Specialize in university textbooks in humanities; Russian biographical dictionary in 33 vols.
Subjects: Economics, Government, Political Science, History, Philosophy, Social Sciences, Sociology
ISBN Prefix(es): 5-7567
Number of titles published annually: 50 Print

RUSSIAN FEDERATION

Total Titles: 110 Print
Distributed by Nauka Ltd (Japan)

Aurora Art Publishers+
7/9 Nevsky Prospect, 191065 St Petersburg
Tel: (0812) 312-3753 *Fax:* (0812) 312-5460
Telex: 121562 *Cable:* FOREIGN TRADE FIRM AURORA LENINGRAD
Key Personnel
President, Rights & Permissions: Boris Pidemsky
Commercial Dir: Zenobius Spetchinsky
Production: Faina Timofeeva
Founded: 1969
Publishes in foreign languages (English, French & German).
Subjects: Art
ISBN Prefix(es): 5-7300
Associate Companies: Aurora Design

N E Bauman Moscow State Technical University Publishers+
5, 2nd Baumanskaya, 107005 Moscow
Tel: (095) 263-67-98; (095) 263-60-45; (095) 265-37-97 *Fax:* (095) 265-42-98
E-mail: press@bmstu.ru
Web Site: www.bmstu.ru
Key Personnel
Dir: Tatyana I Popenchenko
Founded: 1989
Subjects: Biblical Studies, Business, Communications, Computer Science, Earth Sciences, Economics, Education, Electronics, Electrical Engineering, Energy, Engineering (General), Law, Management, Mathematics, Mechanical Engineering, Microcomputers, Physical Sciences, Science (General), Technology
ISBN Prefix(es): 5-7038
Parent Company: Moscow State Technical University

Beta-Service ZAO, see Mir Knigi Ltd

BLIC, russko-Baltijskij informaciionnyj centr, AO+
ul krasnogo flota 4, 190000 St Petersburg
Tel: (0812) 3112252 *Fax:* (0812) 3112252; (0812) 1135896
E-mail: blitz@blitz.spb.ru
Key Personnel
Press-Attache: Natalya Mikhailova *Tel:* (0812) 3121440
Founded: 1992
Specializes in various archival references, catalogs, historical books & monographies.
Subjects: Biography, Drama, Theater, Fiction, History, Maritime, Nonfiction (General), Poetry, Religion - Other, Romance, Science (General), Science Fiction, Fantasy, Sports, Athletics
ISBN Prefix(es): 5-86789
Total Titles: 70 Print
Branch Office(s)
Blumenstrape 126, 47798 Krefeld, Germany, Contact: Marina Potapova *Tel:* (0215) 1608453 *Fax:* (0215) 1608453
U.S. Office(s): 307 Mission Ave, San Rafael, CA 34901, United States, Contact: W Edward Nute *Tel:* 415-453-3579 *Fax:* 415-453-0343
E-mail: enute@igc.apc.org

Izdatelstvo Bolshaya Rossiyskaya Entsiklopedia
Pokrovskij bul'var' 8, 109817 Moscow
Tel: (095) 9177582; (095) 9179009 *Fax:* (095) 9177139
Key Personnel
Dir: Dr A Gorkin
Founded: 1925
The Great Encyclopedia of Russia Publishing House.
ISBN Prefix(es): 5-85270

CentrePolygraph Traders & Publishers Co+
18 Oktyabrskaya St, RU-127018 Moscow
Tel: (095) 2817411 *Fax:* (095) 2844074
Key Personnel
Editorial Dir: Igor Lazarev
Founded: 1991
Subjects: Astrology, Occult, Fiction, Mysteries, Science Fiction, Fantasy, Western Fiction
ISBN Prefix(es): 5-7001
Showroom(s): 20/1 Decabristov ul, Moscow
Bookshop(s): ul 32 Raspletina, Moscow
Warehouse: 70/1 Nizhegordoskaya ul, Moscow

Izdatel'stovo Dal'nevostonogo Gosudarstvennogo Universite (Far-East State University Press)+
Oktjabrskaja ul 27, 690600 Vladivostok
Tel: 57779 (Director) *Fax:* 257200
Telex: 213218 FESU SU
Key Personnel
Dir: Tatyana V Prudkoglyad
Founded: 1982
Subjects: Human Relations, Mathematics
ISBN Prefix(es): 5-7444
Bookshop(s): Fesupress Bookshop, Oktjabrskaja ul 27, 690600 Vladivostok

Izdatelstvo Detskaya Literatura+
Malyi Cherkasskij pereulok 1, 103720 Moscow
Tel: (095) 9280803 *Fax:* (095) 9213007
Key Personnel
Dir: Tamara M Shatunova
Foreign Rights, Sales: Tatyana P Vladimirskaya *Tel:* (095) 9213007
Founded: 1933
Children's Literature Publishing.
Subjects: Art, Fiction, History, Literature, Literary Criticism, Essays, Poetry
ISBN Prefix(es): 5-08
Subsidiaries: Detskaya Literatura Publishers
Branch Office(s)
Dom Detskoy Knigi, I Tverskaya-Yamskaya 13, Moscow

Dom, Izdatel'stvo sovetskogo deskkogo fonda im & I Lenina+
Armjanskij per, 11/2a, 101963 Moscow
Tel: (095) 9236661 *Fax:* (095) 9285322
Key Personnel
Editor-in-Chief: A Likhanov
Founded: 1989
Subjects: Child Care & Development, Cookery, Crafts, Games, Hobbies, Education, Fiction, House & Home, How-to, Women's Studies
ISBN Prefix(es): 5-85201

Druzhba Narodov+
ul Petrovka 26, 101409 Moscow
Tel: (095) 9258671
Key Personnel
Dir: Gennady S Gots
Editor-in-Chief: Leonid A Teracopyan
Commercial Manager: Mikhail A Malygin
Founded: 1990
Membership(s): the Association of Soviet Publishers.
Subjects: Crafts, Games, Hobbies, Theology
ISBN Prefix(es): 5-285
Parent Company: Ministry of Printing of Russian Federation
Associate Companies: Publishing houses of Russian Federation & other Soviet Republic All-Union Society "Book"; All-Union Culture Fund; Pushkin Fund

Izdatelstvo Ekologija
ul Kirova 40, 101000 Moscow
Tel: (095) 9287860
Key Personnel
Dir: L P Tizensgauzen
Editor-in-Chief: G P Dolgovykh

Founded: 1963
Forest Industry Publishing House.
Subjects: Environmental Studies
ISBN Prefix(es): 5-7120

Izdatelstvo 'Ekonomika'
Berezhkovskaia naberezhnaya 6, 123995 Moscow
Tel: (095) 240-4877; (095) 240-4848 *Fax:* (095) 240-4817
E-mail: info@economizdat.ru
Web Site: www.economizdat.ru
Key Personnel
Dir: E V Polievktova
Founded: 2000
Economics publishing house.
Subjects: Accounting, Agriculture, Business, Cookery, Economics, Education, Finance, Law, Literature, Literary Criticism, Essays, Management, Natural History, Science (General)
ISBN Prefix(es): 5-282

Nalchik Book Publishing House Elbrus, *imprint of* Kabardino-Balkarskoye knizhnoye izdatelstvo

Energoatomizdat
ul Rozdestvenka 5/7, 103031 Moscow
Tel: (095) 9259993 *Fax:* (095) 2356585
Key Personnel
Dir: A P Aleshkin
Editor-in-Chief: G G Malkin
Founded: 1963
Publishing House for Atomic Literature.
Subjects: Computer Science, Electronics, Electrical Engineering, Environmental Studies, Literature, Literary Criticism, Essays, Physics, Science (General), Technology
ISBN Prefix(es): 5-283

FGUP Izdatelstvo Mashinostroenie (Mashinostroenie Publishers)+
Stromynskij pereulok 4, 107076 Moscow
Tel: (095) 2683858 *Fax:* (095) 2694897
E-mail: mashpubl@mashin.ru
Web Site: www.mashin.ru
Key Personnel
Dir: Olga N Rumyantseva
Deputy Dir: Liubov I Kouzovkina *Tel:* (095) 268-4968 *E-mail:* kouzovkina@umail.ru
Founded: 1931
Publishing House for Mechanical Engineering.
Subjects: Aeronautics, Aviation, Automotive, Biography, Computer Science, Economics, Engineering (General), Environmental Studies, Mathematics, Mechanical Engineering, Technology
ISBN Prefix(es): 5-217
Associate Companies: Aspect

Finansy i Statistika Publishing House+
Cernyevskogo 7, 101000 Moscow
Tel: (095) 925-47-08 *Fax:* (095) 925-09-57
E-mail: mail@finstat.ru
Web Site: www.finstat.ru
Key Personnel
Man Dir & Editor-in-Chief: Alevtina N Zvonova
Translator: Margarita Ter-Oganian *Tel:* (095) 923 0483
Founded: 1924
Finance & Statistics Publishing House.
Membership(s): Russian Association of Book Publishers; Russian Association of Book Sellers; Guild of Russian Financiers.
Subjects: Accounting, Business, Career Development, Computer Science, Economics, Environmental Studies, Finance, Human Relations, Law, Library & Information Sciences, Management, Marketing, Mathematics, Microcomputers, Public Administration, Real Estate, Securities, Self-Help
ISBN Prefix(es): 5-279

Total Titles: 25 Print
Distributed by KnoRus
Distributor for KnoRus

Izdatelstvo Fizkultura i Sport+
ul Kaljaevskajastr 27, 101421 Moscow
Tel: (095) 2582690 *Fax:* (095) 2001217
Key Personnel
Dir: Valery L Shteinbakh
Editor-in-Chief: V I Vinokurov
Founded: 1923
Subjects: Outdoor Recreation, Sports, Athletics
ISBN Prefix(es): 5-278

Fizmatlit Publishing Co+
ul Profsojuznaja 90, 117997 Moscow
Tel: (095) 3347151 *Fax:* (095) 3360666
Key Personnel
Dir: L I Gladneva
Deputy Dir: A N Zotov
Founded: 1931
Subjects: Astronomy, Communications, Computer Science, Mathematics, Mechanical Engineering, Microcomputers, Physical Sciences, Physics
ISBN Prefix(es): 5-02
Parent Company: Nauka Publishers

Izdatelstvo Galart
ul Cernjahovskogo 4a, Moscow 125319
Tel: (095) 1512502; (095) 1514513 *Fax:* (095) 1513761
Key Personnel
Dir: V V Goryainov
Chief Editor: B Z Yashchina
Founded: 1969
Subjects: Art
ISBN Prefix(es): 5-269

Gidrometeoizdat+
ul Beringa 38, 199226 St Petersburg
Tel: (0812) 3520815 *Fax:* (0812) 3522688 *Cable:* LENINGRAD B-115 GIMIZ
Key Personnel
Dir: A I Ugriumov
Editor-in-Chief: Antonina S Andreeva
Publicity, Promotion: Sergey A Smoliakov
Founded: 1934
Subjects: Agriculture, Animals, Pets, Earth Sciences, Environmental Studies, Geography, Geology, Science (General)
ISBN Prefix(es): 5-286

Glas New Russian Writing+
PO Box 47, 119517 Moscow
Tel: (095) 441 9157 *Fax:* (095) 441 9157
Web Site: www.bham.ac.uk/glas; www.glas.msk.su
Key Personnel
Publisher & Editor: Natasha Perova
E-mail: perova@glas.msk.su
Founded: 1992
Specialize in contemporary Russian literature in English translation, bringing publishers & interested readers up to date on the latest hits in Russian literary fiction. Features various literary trends with a view to show the entire literary map of Russia today. More than 100 authors in 23 issues have come out to date.
Subjects: Fiction, Literature, Literary Criticism, Essays
ISBN Prefix(es): 1-56663; 5-7172
Number of titles published annually: 4 Print
Total Titles: 28 Print
Branch Office(s)
University of Birmingham, Russian Dept, Birmigham B15 TT, United Kingdom, Contact: Dr Arch Tait *Tel:* (0121) 414 6047 *Fax:* (0121) 414 6047 *E-mail:* a.l.tait@bham.ac.uk *Web Site:* www.bham.ac.uk/glas
U.S. Office(s): 1332 N Halsted St, Chicago, IL 60622-2694, United States, Contact: Ivan Dee *Tel:* (312) 787-6262 *Fax:* (312) 787-6269 *E-mail:* elephant@ivanrdee.com
Foreign Rep(s): Arch Tait (Worldwide); Ivan R Dee (USA) (Worldwide)
Shipping Address: National Book Network, 4720 Boston Way, Lanham, MD, United States *Tel:* (301) 459-3366 *Fax:* (301) 459-1705 *E-mail:* rfreese@nbnbooks.com
Warehouse: 15200 NBN Way, Blue Ridge Summit, PA 17214, United States
Distribution Center: Ivan R Dee, 1332 N Halsted St, Chicago, IL 60622-2694, United States, Contact: Alexander Dee *Tel:* (312) 787-6262 *Fax:* (312) 787-6269 *E-mail:* elephant@ivanrdee.com
Orders to: Central Books Ltd, 99 Wallis Rd, London E9 5LN, United Kingdom, Contact: Bill Norris *Tel:* (020) 8986 4854 *Fax:* (020) 8533 5821 *E-mail:* orders@centralbooks.com (only UK & Europe)
Northwestern University Press, Chicago Distribution Center, 11030 South Langley Ave, Chicago, IL 60628, United States *Tel:* (773) 568-1550 *Fax:* (773) 660-2235 (USA & Canada)

INFRA-M Izdatel'skij dom+
107 Dmitrovskoye Shosse, 127214 Moscow
Tel: (095) 4857077; (095) 4855918 *Fax:* (095) 4855918
E-mail: books@infra-m.ru
Web Site: www.infra-m.ru
Key Personnel
Dir General: Helen Valentinovn's Mel'chuk *Tel:* (095) 485-7077 *E-mail:* offiche@infra-m.ru
Editor-in-Chief: Prudnikov Vladmiir Mikhaylovich *Tel:* (095) 485-5779 *E-mail:* prudnik@orch.ru
Sales Manager: Ilyukhin Vyacheslav Yevgen'evich *Tel:* (095) 485-7400
Head of Sales: Anna Mikhaylonv's Tokmadzhyan *Tel:* (095) 485-7177
Foreign Rights Manager: Regina Bouglo *Tel:* (095) 4855918 *E-mail:* regina@orc.ru
Founded: 1992
Publisher of business books in accounting, management, law, public sector & produces audio & video courses of foreign languages.
Subjects: Accounting, Business, Computer Science, Economics, Education, Film, Video, Finance, Government, Political Science, Language Arts, Linguistics, Law, Management, Marketing, Technology
ISBN Prefix(es): 5-86225; 5-16
Distributed by Infra M Kniga

Interbook-Business AO
Spiridonevsky per 12/9, App 11, 103104 Moscow
Tel: (095) 2006462; (095) 956-37-52 *Fax:* (095) 956-37-52
E-mail: interbook@msk.tsi.ru
Key Personnel
Dir: Gennadi Popov
Founded: 1992
Subjects: Art, Cookery, Crafts, Games, Hobbies, Gardening, Plants, Health, Nutrition, History, Regional Interests, Sports, Athletics
ISBN Prefix(es): 5-89164

Izdatelstvo Iskusstvo+
Sobinovskij per 3, 103009 Moscow
Tel: (095) 2035872 *Fax:* (095) 2918882
Key Personnel
Dir: O A Makarov
Deputy Dir: Bodnarouk Tatyana; Yamshchikov Anatoly
Founded: 1938 (as Izogiz & Iskusstvo)
Publishing house for art literature.
Specialize in Art.
Subjects: Architecture & Interior Design, Art, Drama, Theater, Film, Video, History, Philosophy
ISBN Prefix(es): 5-210
Distributed by Calmann & King (UK)
Distributor for Booth-Clibborn Editions; Giunti (Italy); Jaca Book (Italy)

Izvestia Sovetov Narodnyh Deputatov Russian Federation (RF)
Pukinskaja pl 5, 103798 Moscow
Tel: (095) 2093738 *Fax:* (095) 2095394
Telex: 411121 Vesti SU
Key Personnel
Dir: Y F Yefremov
Subjects: Agriculture, Business, Economics, Government, Political Science, Law, Public Administration, Social Sciences, Sociology, Sports, Athletics
ISBN Prefix(es): 5-206

Kabardino-Balkarskoye knizhnoye izdatelstvo+
ul Malo-Kabardinskaja 1, 360000 Nalchik Kabardino Balkarskoye respublika
Tel: 54184
Key Personnel
Dir: Ibragim Matgerievich Gadiev
Chief Editor: Anatoly Muratovich Bitsuev
Founded: 1928
Subjects: Ethnicity
ISBN Prefix(es): 5-86778
Parent Company: Ministry of Press & Mass Informatio
Imprints: Nalchik Book Publishing House Elbrus

Kavkazskaya Biblioteka Publishing House+
prosp Karl Marksa 78, 355045 Stavropol'
Tel: (8652) 32314
Key Personnel
Dir: Eugen Panasko
Founded: 1990
Subjects: Fiction, Human Relations, Literature, Literary Criticism, Essays, Poetry, Science Fiction, Fantasy
ISBN Prefix(es): 5-8436
Distributor for Samarskiy Dom Pechaty & Sovremennic

Izdatelstvo Kazanskago Universiteta+
ul Lenina 18, 420008 Kazan Respublika Tatarstan
Tel: 325363
E-mail: kacimov@niimm.kazan.su
Key Personnel
Dir: Andrei Vatrushkin
Founded: 1957
Subjects: Chemistry, Chemical Engineering, Criminology, Economics, Environmental Studies, Mathematics
ISBN Prefix(es): 5-7464

Izdatelstvo Khudozhestvennaya Literatura+
Nov Basmannaya ul 19, 107882 Moscow
Tel: (095) 261-85-41 *Fax:* (095) 261-83-00
Key Personnel
Editor-in-Chief: V S Modestov *Tel:* (095) 261-38-64
Dir: A N Petzov *Tel:* (095) 261-88-65
Founded: 1930 (as The State Publishers of Fiction)
Publishing house for fiction, poetry & literary biography.
Subjects: Biography, Fiction, Literature, Literary Criticism, Essays, Music, Dance, Poetry
ISBN Prefix(es): 5-280

Izdatelstvo Kniga+
ul Tverskaja 50, 125047 Moscow
Tel: (095) 2516003 *Fax:* (095) 2500489
Telex: 411871
Key Personnel
Vice President: Vladimar Y Shvedov
Chairman of the Board, Dir: Viktor N Adamov
Editor-in-Chief: Ivan A Prokhorov
Founded: 1964

Subjects: Library & Information Sciences, Publishing & Book Trade Reference
ISBN Prefix(es): 5-212
Subsidiaries: Kniga Printshop (owned jointly-Kniga Publishers, Russia & Fargo Group, Toronto, Ontario, Canada); The Culture Center at Bol shaya Polianka (owned jointly-USSR & USA); Business Week- Russian Language Edition (jointly by McGraw-Hill Corp, USA Publishers & Kniga Publishers, Russia)

Izdatelstvo Knizhnaya Palata
ul. Oktjabr'skaja 4, Moscow 103009
Tel: (095) 2889247 *Fax:* (095) 1635827
Key Personnel
Dir: Alexey F Kurilko
Editor-in-Chief: V T Kabanov
Founded: 1987
Publishing House "Book Chamber".
Subjects: Fiction, Publishing & Book Trade Reference
ISBN Prefix(es): 5-7000

Izdatelskii Dom Kompozitor (Kompozitor Publishing House)
ul Sadovaja-Triumfalnaja, 12/14, 127006 Moscow
Tel: (095) 2092380; (095) 2094105 *Fax:* (095) 2095498
E-mail: music@sumail.ru
Key Personnel
Dir: G Voronov
Founded: 1957
Subjects: Biography, Education, Music, Dance
ISBN Prefix(es): 5-85285

KUbK Publishing House+
ul Gurjanova 5-134, 109548 Moscow
Tel: (095) 1640910; (095) 3679473 *Fax:* (095) 1528689
Key Personnel
President: Viktor Oubeiko
International Rights: Natalia Oubeiko
Founded: 1992
Subjects: Animals, Pets, Computer Science, Cookery, Romance
ISBN Prefix(es): 5-85554

Kul'tura redakcionno-izdatel skij kompleks
ul 35 Arbat, 121835 Moscow
Tel: (095) 2481151 *Fax:* (095) 2302180
ISBN Prefix(es): 5-8334
Branch Office(s)
Nevsky Pz, 15, St Petersburg

Ladomir Publishing House+
K-617, Korp 1435, Moscow 103617
Tel: (095) 530-9833; (095) 530-8477 *Fax:* (095) 537-4742-7870
Key Personnel
Editor-in-Chief: Yu Mirhailov
Founded: 1990
Subjects: Antiques, Asian Studies, Fiction, Government, Political Science, History, Philosophy, Religion - Buddhist, Religion - Hindu, Religion - Islamic, Science Fiction, Fantasy, Sports, Athletics
ISBN Prefix(es): 5-86218

Legprombytizdat
1-J Kadashevskii pereulok 12, 113035 Moscow
Tel: (095) 2330947
Key Personnel
Dir: T G Gromova
Editor-in-Chief: T P Drozdova
Founded: 1932
Light Industry & the Services Publishing House.
Subjects: Business, Labor, Industrial Relations, Social Sciences, Sociology
ISBN Prefix(es): 5-7088

Izdatelstvo Lenizdat+
ul Fontanka 59, 191023 St Petersburg
Tel: (0812) 3111451 *Fax:* (0812) 3151295
Telex: I22-693 IZDAT
Key Personnel
Gen Dir: V N Nabirukhin
Editor-in-Chief: V N Bunin
Founded: 1917
St Petersburg Publishing House.
Membership(s): the Association of Bookpublishers of Russia. Founder of Russian International Book Exchange.
Subjects: Agriculture, Art, Fiction, Government, Political Science, Science (General), Science Fiction, Fantasy, Technology
ISBN Prefix(es): 5-289
Parent Company: Ministry of the Press & Mass Media of the Russian Federation

Publishing House Limbus Press+
Izmailovsky pr , 14, 198005 St Petersburg
Tel: (0812) 1126547 *Fax:* (0812) 1126706
E-mail: limbuspr@rol.ru; limbus@limbuspress.ru
Web Site: www.limbuspress.ru
Key Personnel
Publisher: Konstantin Tublin
Editor-in-Chief: Victor Toporov
Foreign Rights: Julia Goumen
Subjects: Biography, Fiction, Nonfiction (General)
Number of titles published annually: 60 Print
Branch Office(s)
Moscow
Foreign Rep(s): Anna Benn (England); Catherine Fzagou (Greece); Anastasia Lester (France); Christian Marti-Menzel (Spain)

Izdatelstvo Malysh
ul Davydkovskaja 5, 121352 Moscow
Tel: (095) 4430654 *Fax:* (095) 4430655
Key Personnel
Dir: V M Maiiboroda
Editor-in-Chief: V A Rybin
Founded: 1957
Children's World Publishing House.
ISBN Prefix(es): 5-213

Izdatelstvo Medicina+
Petroverigskij pereulok 6/8, 103000 Moscow
Tel: (095) 9248785 *Fax:* (095) 9286003
Telex: 412282 MEDIZ SU
Key Personnel
Dir: A M Stochik *Tel:* (095) 9288648
Editor-in-Chief: N R Paleev *Tel:* (095) 9248785
Foreign Rights Manager: O H Sheshukova *Tel:* (095) 9239368
Founded: 1918
Publishing house for medicine.
Subjects: Health, Nutrition, Medicine, Nursing, Dentistry, Psychology, Psychiatry, Science (General)
ISBN Prefix(es): 5-225
Associate Companies: Association for Medical Literature
Bookshop(s): Komsomolski pr 25, Moscow; Begovaya, 11, Moscow

Izdatelstvo Metallurgiya+
2j Obydenskij pereulok 14, 119857 Moscow
Tel: (095) 2025532 *Fax:* (095) 2025752
Key Personnel
Dir: A G Belikov
Editor-in-Chief: N N Marchenko
Founded: 1939
Publishing house for metallurgy.
Subjects: Earth Sciences, Engineering (General), Technology
ISBN Prefix(es): 5-229

Izdatelstvo Mezdunarodnye Otnoshenia+
ul Sadovaja-Spasskaja 20, 107078 Moscow
Tel: (095) 2076793 *Fax:* (095) 2002204

Key Personnel
Chief Executive: B P Likhachev
Production: M Rodin
Founded: 1957
International relations publishing house.
Subjects: Biography, Government, Political Science
ISBN Prefix(es): 5-7133
Parent Company: Goscomizdat, Strastnoi bul 5, Moscow 101409

Middle Urals Publishing House, see Sredne-Uralskoye knizhnoye izatelstve (Middle Urals Publishing House)

Ministerstvo Kul 'tury RF+
Kitaijskij pr d 7, 103693 Moscow
Tel: 220 4560
E-mail: rnb@q1as.apc.org
Membership(s): IFLA.
Subjects: Genealogy, History, Library & Information Sciences, Social Sciences, Sociology
ISBN Prefix(es): 5-7196
Distributed by Kubon & Sagner

Izdatelstvo Mir (Mir Publishers)+
1-j Rizskij per 2, 129820 Moscow
Tel: (095) 286-17-83 *Fax:* (095) 288-95-22
Web Site: www.mir-pubs.dol.ru
Key Personnel
Dir: Dr Kh P Abdullaev *E-mail:* khpa@mir.msk.ru
Editor-in-Chief: Dr V I Propoi *Tel:* (095) 286 43 00 *E-mail:* vivp@mir.msk.ru
International Relations Supervisor: V V Gerasimovsky *Tel:* (095) 286 17 00 *E-mail:* vvg@mir.msk.ru
Founded: 1946 (under name Mir since 1964)
Translation & publication of scientific & technical books.
Membership(s): ASKI (Book Publishers Association of Russia), Association "Task Force Against Piracy".
Subjects: Aeronautics, Aviation, Animals, Pets, Astronomy, Biological Sciences, Chemistry, Chemical Engineering, Communications, Computer Science, Earth Sciences, Electronics, Electrical Engineering, Engineering (General), Environmental Studies, Fiction, Geography, Geology, Health, Nutrition, Mathematics, Mechanical Engineering, Microcomputers, Physical Sciences, Physics, Psychology, Psychiatry, Science (General), Science Fiction, Fantasy, Self-Help, Technology
ISBN Prefix(es): 5-03
Number of titles published annually: 50 Print
Total Titles: 170 Print

Mir Knigi Ltd+
ul Sadovaja-Spasskaja 6, 107045 Moscow
Tel: (095) 2083879 *Fax:* (095) 7428579
Key Personnel
Media Project Dir: Slovovieva Rimma *E-mail:* rimma@beta.ru
Founded: 1999
Publisher of *Mir Knigi* magazine.
Subjects: Fiction, Nonfiction (General)
ISBN Prefix(es): 5-7043
Owned by: Beta-Service

Izdatelstvo Molodaya Gvardia
ul Suscevskaja 21, 103030 Moscow
Tel: (095) 9722288 *Fax:* (095) 9720582
Key Personnel
General Dir: Valentin Yurkin
Founded: 1922
Young Guard Publishing House of the Young Communist League Central Committee.
Subjects: Art, Biography, Government, Political Science, History, Literature, Literary Criticism, Essays, Poetry, Social Sciences, Sociology, Sports, Athletics
ISBN Prefix(es): 5-235

Izdatelstvo Mordovskogo gosudar stvennogo
Sovetskaja 24, Saransk, Mordovskaja resp 430000
Tel: 74771 *Fax:* 74771
Telex: teletype srn87aelita
Key Personnel
Dir: Aleksander N Zernov
Founded: 1990
Specialize in scientific & educational publications for high school.
Subjects: Agriculture, Civil Engineering, Economics, Education, Engineering (General), Geography, Geology, History, Language Arts, Linguistics, Literature, Literary Criticism, Essays, Mathematics, Medicine, Nursing, Dentistry, Philosophy, Social Sciences, Sociology
ISBN Prefix(es): 5-7103
Total Titles: 1,098 Print
Parent Company: Mordovian State University
Bookshop(s): ul Bolshevitskya 68, 430000 Saransk

Moscow University Press+
B Nikitskaya St 5/7, 103009 Moscow
Tel: (095) 2295091; (095) 2297541 *Fax:* (095) 2036671; (095) 2297541
E-mail: kd_mgu@df.ru
Telex: 411483 MGUSU
Key Personnel
Dir: N S Timofeyev
Founded: 1756
Membership(s): University Press Council.
Subjects: Education, Mathematics, Medicine, Nursing, Dentistry, Science (General), Sports, Athletics
ISBN Prefix(es): 5-211
Branch Office(s)
Rights & Permissions: VAAP, Bolshaya Bronnaya 6a, Moscow 103670

Izdatelstvo Moskovskii Rabochii+
Cistoprudnyj bul'var' 8, 101854 Moscow
Tel: (095) 2210735 *Fax:* (095) 9254274
Key Personnel
President, All Moscow, Dir, Moskovskii Rabochiy: Dmitri V Evdokimov
General Dir, All Moscow: Ferdinand V Kaploun
Vice President: Oleg P Benukh; Alexei Vengerov
Editor-in-Chief: G I Broido
Founded: 1922
Moscow Worker Publishing House.
Subjects: Fiction, Nonfiction (General)
ISBN Prefix(es): 5-239; 5-7110
Branch Office(s)
Konstatin Evdokimov Bosmsco, 131 Beverly St, Boston, MA 02114, United States *Tel:* (617) 248-3988 *Fax:* (617) 248-3885

Izdatelstvo Muzyka+
14 Neglinnaya St, 103031 Moscow
Tel: (095) 921-51-70 *Fax:* (095) 928-33-04
E-mail: muzyka@insar.ru
Web Site: www.muzykaizd.ru
Key Personnel
Dir: I Savintsen
Chief Distributor: Aleksey Grebennikov
Founded: 1861
State Music Publishing House.
Subjects: Education, Music, Dance
ISBN Prefix(es): 5-7140
Number of titles published annually: 150 Print
Subsidiaries:
Distributor for Schott
Showroom(s): ul Petrovka 26, 103031 Moscow
Bookshop(s): Music World, ul B.Nikitskaja, 13, 103871 Moscow
Warehouse: Ul Petrovka 26, 103031 Moscow
Orders to: ul Petrovka 26, 103031 Moscow

Izdatelstvo Mysl+
Leninskj Prospect 15, II907I Moscow
Tel: (095) 2324248; (095) 952-5065; (095) 955-0458
Key Personnel
Dir: Timofeyev Yevgeny Alexeyevich
Founded: 1963
Subjects: Economics, Geography, Geology, History, Philosophy, Science (General)
ISBN Prefix(es): 5-244

Nauka Publishers+
ul Profsoyuznaya 90, 117997 Moscow
Tel: (095) 3347151 *Fax:* (095) 4202220
E-mail: nauka@naukaran.ru
Web Site: www.maik.rssi.ru
Telex: 411612 IZAN *Cable:* Moscow-485
Key Personnel
Dir: V Vasiliev
Editor-in-Chief: T Filippova *Tel:* (095) 336 1022
Head of International Department: Vitali Anishchenko *Tel:* (095) 336 0266
Sales: V Bogomolov *Tel:* (095) 334 7479 *Fax:* (095) 334 7479
Founded: 1727
Scientific books & journals in all fields of knowledge, university textbooks, popular science, academic monographs.
There are six self-supporting branches of Nauka in Moscow, two divisions in Novosibirsk & St Petersburg, Akademkniga Book selling firm & four printshops. The firm's other business activities include direct mail & advertising.
Subjects: Aeronautics, Aviation, Archaeology, Art, Asian Studies, Astronomy, Biological Sciences, Chemistry, Chemical Engineering, Communications, Computer Science, Earth Sciences, Economics, Education, Electronics, Electrical Engineering, Energy, Engineering (General), Environmental Studies, Geography, Geology, Government, Political Science, Health, Nutrition, History, Language Arts, Linguistics, Law, Library & Information Sciences, Literature, Literary Criticism, Essays, Management, Marketing, Mathematics, Mechanical Engineering, Medicine, Nursing, Dentistry, Microcomputers, Natural History, Physics, Psychology, Psychiatry, Radio, TV, Science (General), Social Sciences, Sociology, Technology
ISBN Prefix(es): 5-02
Number of titles published annually: 1,000 Print
Total Titles: 80 Print
Subsidiaries: Akademkniga Booktrading Co; Oriental Literature Publishing Co Nauka; Physical & Mathematical Literature Publishing Co Nauka
Divisions: Printshops Nauka
Branch Office(s)
Siberian Publishing Co Nauka, Sovetskaya Ul 18, Novosibirsk 63009, Dir: Ye A Lazarchuk *Tel:* (03832) 225 181 *Fax:* (03832) 233 502
St Petersburg Publishing Co Nauka, Mendeleevskaya Liniya 1, St Petersburg 199034, Dir: S V Valchuk *Tel:* (0812) 328 3912 *Fax:* (0812) 328 0051
Ural Publishing Co Nauka, Ul Amundsena 100, Yekaterinburg 620016, Dir: Yu Ye Kezhun *Tel:* (03432) 288 149 *Fax:* (03432) 678 872
Bookshop(s): Shubinsky Per 6, Moscow, GSP 121009 *Tel:* (095) 241 0309 *Fax:* (095) 241 0277 *E-mail:* akademkniga@g23.relcom.ru *Web Site:* www.ak-book.naukaran.ru
Shipping Address: Nauka-Export Booktrading Co, Profsoyuznaya Ul 90, Moscow 117997, Dir: V V Bogomolov *Tel:* (095) 334 7479; (095) 334 7140 *Fax:* (095) 334 7479; (095) 334 7140 *E-mail:* nauka@naukae.msk.ru

Izdatelstvo Nedra+
Tverskaja Zastava 3, 125047 Moscow
Tel: (095) 2505255 *Fax:* (095) 2502772
Key Personnel
Dir: V D Menshicov
Founded: 1963
Natural Resources Publishing House.
Subjects: Earth Sciences, Energy, Geography, Geology
ISBN Prefix(es): 5-247

Izdatel'stvo Nizhegorodskogo Gosudarstvennogo Univ
prosp Gagarina 23, kpmn 230, 603600 Nizhniy Novgorod
Tel: (08312) 657825 *Fax:* (08312) 658592
E-mail: rector@nnucnit.unn.ac.ru
Web Site: www.unn.ac.ru
Founded: 1990
Subjects: Archaeology, Biological Sciences, Chemistry, Chemical Engineering, Computer Science, Economics, Education, Electronics, Electrical Engineering, Engineering (General), English as a Second Language, Environmental Studies, Government, Political Science, History, Law, Marketing, Mathematics, Mechanical Engineering, Microcomputers, Philosophy, Physical Sciences, Physics, Psychology, Psychiatry, Social Sciences, Sociology
ISBN Prefix(es): 5-680; 5-85746

Novosti Izdatelstvo+
7 Bolsyuaya Of pochyutovaya st, 107082 Moscow
Tel: (095) 265-5008 *Fax:* (095) 975-2065; (095) 230-2119; (095) 230-2667
E-mail: novosty@df.ru
Web Site: www.novosty.ru
Telex: 7581; 7582
Key Personnel
Dir: Alexander Eidinov *Tel:* (095) 265-6335
Man Dir: Alexander Proskurin
Rights Dept: Alexei Triumfov *Tel:* (095) 265-5135
Founded: 1963
Subjects: Art, Economics, Fiction, Government, Political Science, History, Nonfiction (General), Philosophy, Social Sciences, Sociology
ISBN Prefix(es): 5-7020

Obdeestro Znanie+
Lubjanskij poezed 4, 101835 Moscow
Tel: (095) 9281531
Key Personnel
Dir & Editor-in-Chief: V C Beliakov
Founded: 1951
The Knowledge.
Subjects: Business, Child Care & Development, Fiction, Science (General), Science Fiction, Fantasy, Self-Help
ISBN Prefix(es): 5-07

Okoshko Ltd Publishers (Izdatelstvo)+
Zubovskij Blvd 17, 119859 Moskva
Tel: (095) 2450998 *Fax:* (095) 2053424
Key Personnel
Dir: Ivan A Logashin
Founded: 1993
Russian - Belgian Joint Publishing Venture
Also acts as an exclusive Zuidnederlandse Uitgeverij's representative in CIS & Baltic countries.
Subjects: Education, English as a Second Language, Language Arts, Linguistics
ISBN Prefix(es): 5-7400
Total Titles: 23 Print
Parent Company: Zuidnederlandse Uitgeverij NV, Belgium

Panorama Publishing House+
Bol Tishinskoj per 38, 123557 Moscow
Tel: (095) 2053707 *Fax:* (095) 2053708
Key Personnel
Dir: Valery S Buyanov
Founded: 1974
Subjects: Art, Child Care & Development, Fiction, Health, Nutrition, History, House & Home
ISBN Prefix(es): 5-85220

RUSSIAN FEDERATION

Izdatel'stvo Patriot
Olimpijskij prospekt 22, 129110 Moscow
Tel: (095) 2844904
Founded: 1951
Voluntary Society for the Promotion of the Army, Air Force & Navy.
Subjects: Military Science
ISBN Prefix(es): 5-7030

Pedagogika Press
Smolenskij Bulvar 4, 119034 Moscow
Tel: (095) 2465969 *Fax:* (095) 2465969
Key Personnel
Dir: V S Khelemendik
Founded: 1969
Subjects: Education, Science (General)
ISBN Prefix(es): 5-7155

Permskaja Kniga
ul K Marksa 30, 614000 Perm
Tel: (03422) 324245
Key Personnel
Editor-in-Chief: Almira G Zebzeeva
Subjects: Cookery, Crafts, Games, Hobbies, Fiction, Gardening, Plants, House & Home, Poetry, Romance
ISBN Prefix(es): 5-7625

Planeta Publishers+
ul Petrovka 8/11, Moscow 103031
Tel: (095) 9230470 *Fax:* (095) 2005246
Telex: 411733 *Cable:* PETROVKA 8/11 MOSCOW
Key Personnel
Dir: Vladimir Seredin
Editor-in-Chief: Gennadiy Alifanov
Founded: 1969
Subjects: Architecture & Interior Design
ISBN Prefix(es): 5-85250
Associate Companies: Interprint
Subsidiaries: Jupiter

Pressa Publishing House
ul Pravdy 24, 125867 Moscow
Tel: (095) 2573482 *Fax:* (095) 2505205
Key Personnel
Dir: VP Leontiev
Subjects: Earth Sciences, Fiction, Literature, Literary Criticism, Essays
ISBN Prefix(es): 5-253

Profizdat+
ul Kirova 13, 101000 Moscow
Tel: (095) 924-5740; (095) 924-8225 (books); (095) 924-4637 (periodicals) *Fax:* (095) 975-2329
E-mail: profizdat@profizdat.ru
Web Site: www.profizdat.ru
Key Personnel
Dir: Vladimir N Soloviev
Founded: 1930
Information & publishing house.
Subjects: Art, Cookery, Fiction, Gardening, Plants, Labor, Industrial Relations, Nonfiction (General), Poetry, Sports, Athletics
ISBN Prefix(es): 5-255

Progress Publishers
17 Zubovskij Blvd, 119847 Moscow
Tel: (095) 2469032 *Fax:* (095) 2302403
Telex: 411800 Kegl
Key Personnel
Dir: A K Avelitchev
Editor-in-Chief: V N Loskutov; B V Oreshkin
Production: Mikhail Pavlovich Kryakovkin
Founded: 1931
Subjects: Biography, Economics, Fiction, Government, Political Science, History, Language Arts, Linguistics, Law, Literature, Literary Criticism, Essays, Philosophy, Social Sciences, Sociology
ISBN Prefix(es): 5-01

Prometej Izdatelstvo
ul Usacheva 64, 119048 Moscow
Tel: (095) 2454495
Key Personnel
Dir: V N Bukreev
Founded: 1987
ISBN Prefix(es): 5-7042; 5-8300

Izdatelstvo Prosveshchenie (Prosveshcheniye Publishers)+
3-j proezd Marinoi Roshchi 41, 129846 Moscow 127521
Tel: (095) 789-30-29; (095) 789-30-40 *Fax:* (095) 200-42-66; (095) 289-33-98
E-mail: msamodwrova@prosv.ru
Web Site: www.prosv.ru
Telex: 111999 Park
Key Personnel
Dir General: Mr Alexander M Kondakov
Commercial Dir: Mr Mikhail Yu Kozhevnikov
Founded: 1930
Educational books & products.
Membership(s): EEPG.
Subjects: Astronomy, Biological Sciences, Chemistry, Chemical Engineering, Computer Science, Cookery, Crafts, Games, Hobbies, Earth Sciences, Education, Geography, Geology, History, Literature, Literary Criticism, Essays, Mathematics, Music, Dance, Physical Sciences, Physics, Poetry
ISBN Prefix(es): 5-09
Number of titles published annually: 700 Print; 10 CD-ROM; 20 Audio
Total Titles: 80,000 Print; 15 CD-ROM; 60 Audio
Associate Companies: Prosveshchenie Media

Izdatelstvo Radio i Svyaz+
Poctant, a/ja 693, 101000 Moscow
Mailing Address: ul Myasnizkaya 40, 101000 Moscow
Tel: (095) 2585351
Key Personnel
Dir: E N Salnikov
Founded: 1981
Communications Publishing House.
Subjects: Communications, Computer Science, Electronics, Electrical Engineering, Radio, TV
ISBN Prefix(es): 5-256

Raduga Publishers+
43 Sivtsev Vrazhek Lane, 121839 Moscow
Tel: (095) 2416815 *Fax:* (095) 2416353
E-mail: raduga@pol.ru
Web Site: www.raduga.express.ru *Cable:* MOSCOW TITUL
Key Personnel
Dir: Nina S Litvinets
Marketing Dir: Nikolai P Iamskoi
Founded: 1982
Subjects: Art, Biography, Cookery, Education, Fiction, History, Literature, Literary Criticism, Essays, Philosophy, Poetry, Romance, Science Fiction, Fantasy
ISBN Prefix(es): 5-05

Respublika
Politizdat lzd, Miusskaja pl 7, Moscow 125811
Tel: (095) 251-7956
Key Personnel
Dir: A P Poliakov
Editor-in-Chief: E P Loshkariev
Founded: 1918
Publishers of Political Literature.
Subjects: Government, Political Science, History
ISBN Prefix(es): 5-250

Russkaya Kniga Izdatelstvo (Publishers)+
Bolshoy Tishinsky pereulok, h 38, 123557 Moscow
Tel: (095) 2053377 *Fax:* (095) 2053424
Key Personnel
Dir: M F Nenashev
Founded: 1957
Russian Book State Publishing House.
Subjects: Art, Cookery, Fiction, Government, Political Science, Health, Nutrition, History
ISBN Prefix(es): 5-268

Russkij Jazyk+
Staropanskij pereulok 1/5, 103012 Moscow
Tel: (095) 9239705 *Fax:* (095) 9288906
Web Site: www.russyaz.ru
Key Personnel
Dir: V I Nazarov
Chief Editor: A A Alexeeva
Founded: 1974
Russian Language Publishers.
Subjects: English as a Second Language
ISBN Prefix(es): 5-200

St Andrew's Biblical Theological College+
Jerusalem St 3, Moscow 109316
Tel: (095) 2702200 *Fax:* (095) 2707644
E-mail: standrews@standrews.ru
Web Site: www.standrews.ru
Key Personnel
Contact: Dr Alexei Bodrov *E-mail:* abodrov@standrews.ru
Sales & Marketing Manager: German Utenov
Founded: 1990
Independent theological college publishing house. Textbooks on Biblical studies & themes & two journals. High quality religious & theological literature.
Subjects: Archaeology, Art, Biblical Studies, Child Care & Development, Education, History, Philosophy, Publishing & Book Trade Reference, Religion - Other, Theology
ISBN Prefix(es): 5-89647
Number of titles published annually: 25 Print
Total Titles: 100 Print

Scorpion Publishers+
Mozajskoe 9-41, 121471 Moscow
Tel: (095) 4436991
Key Personnel
President: Tatjana Piljajena
Founded: 1990
Membership(s): the Association of Pubishers; specialize in publishing & trade; also acts as agent of buying or selling international rights & editions.
Subjects: Animals, Pets, Crafts, Games, Hobbies, Health, Nutrition, Philosophy, Theology, Veterinary Science
ISBN Prefix(es): 5-86408
Distributed by Solutions Ltd (West Europe)

Izdatelstvo Sovetskii Pisatel
ul Sadoway Triumfalnaya 14-12, 103006 Moscow
Tel: (095) 209 2384; (095) 209 4105; (095) 209 1942 *Fax:* (095) 2023200
Key Personnel
Director: A N Zhukov
Chief Editor: V I Mussalitin
Founded: 1935
USSR Writer's Union Publishing House
Publishes monthly magazine *Soviet Motherland* in Yiddish.
Subjects: Art, Literature, Literary Criticism, Essays, Poetry
ISBN Prefix(es): 5-265

Sovremennik Publishers Too
Horosevskoe sosse 62, 123007 Moscow
Tel: (095) 9412992 *Fax:* (095) 9413544

Key Personnel
Dir: L A Frolov
Chief Editor: A P Karelin
Founded: 1970
Subjects: Drama, Theater, Fiction, Literature, Literary Criticism, Essays
ISBN Prefix(es): 5-270

SP Interbuk, Russian-Slovenien jv
ul Petrovka 26, 101409 Moscow
Tel: (095) 9245081 *Fax:* (095) 2002281; (095) 2302403
Key Personnel
Dir General: Alexander M Pershin
Editor-in-Chief: Sergei V Goncharenko
Commercial Dir: Mr Juri G Ivanov
15 in various cities of the former USSR.
Membership(s): the Board of All-Russian Publishers' Association, All-Russian Books Distributors Association, All-Russia Publishers Club, Board of Izdatbank, All-Russia Union of Independent Publishers, Advisory Board of the Ministry of Information.
ISBN Prefix(es): 5-7664
Subsidiaries: Alma-Ata; Donetsk; Drozdy; Ekaterinograd; Forest; Kiev; Logos; Sibir; Slavia; Slavutich; St Petersburg; Tjumen
Divisions: Commercial Centre; Interbook Business; Printing Centre; Advertising Centre
Showroom(s): Starosadsky per 7/10, str 5, 101000 Moscow
Shipping Address: Interbuk Transport & Depots, Russian-Slovenien jv ul Petrovka 26, 101409 Moscow *Tel:* (095) 9245081 *Fax:* (095) 2002281

Sredne-Uralskoye knizhnoye izatelstve (Middle Urals Publishing House)+
Malysheva 24, GSP-351, 620219 Sverdlovsk
Tel: (03432) 514162 *Fax:* (03432) 512859
Key Personnel
Dir: Victor J Selivanov
Founded: 1920
Subjects: Fiction, Literature, Literary Criticism, Essays
ISBN Prefix(es): 5-7529
Subsidiaries:
Warehouse: Artinskaya St 23B, 620046 Ekaterinburg

Izdatelstvo Standartov+
Novo presnenskij per 3, 123557 Moscow
Tel: (095) 252 0348 *Fax:* (095) 268-4724
E-mail: standard@online.ru
Key Personnel
Dir: N V Zen'kovich
Editor-in-Chief: V P Videneyev
Founded: 1926
Official publications of the state service on standard data.
Subjects: Advertising, Law
ISBN Prefix(es): 5-7050

Stroyizdat Publishing House
Dolgorukovskaya u 23 a, 101442 Moscow
Tel: (095) 2516967
Key Personnel
Dir: Vladimir A Kasatkin
Chief Editor: G A Zhigatcheva
Founded: 1932
Subjects: Architecture & Interior Design, Geography, Geology, Mechanical Engineering, Social Sciences, Sociology
ISBN Prefix(es): 5-274

Izdatelstvo Sudostroenie+
ul Gogolja 8, St Petersburg 191065
Tel: (0812) 3124479 *Fax:* (0812) 3120821
Key Personnel
Man Dir & Editor-in-Chief: Anatoly A Andreev
Founded: 1940
Publishing House for Shipbuilding.
Subjects: Advertising, Education, Engineering (General), History, Maritime, Mechanical Engineering, Military Science, Science (General), Technology, Transportation
ISBN Prefix(es): 5-7355
Bookshop(s): Varag, Malaja Morskaja 8, St Petersburg 191186

Teorija Verojatnostej i ee Primenenija+
ul Vavilova, 42, 117966 Moscow
Tel: (095) 1352380; (095) 3324410 *Fax:* (095) 1135125
E-mail: tvp@caravan.ru
Key Personnel
Dir & Partner: V I Khokhlov
Editor-in-Chief: Yu V Prokhorov
Founded: 1990
Worldwide except the territory of the former USSR
Specialize in Mathematical Applied Sciences; also acts as Research Laboratories & as a Distribution Center for Western Scientific & Professional Editions & Software.
Subjects: Communications, Economics, Mathematics, Military Science, Physics, Securities
ISBN Prefix(es): 5-85484
Subsidiaries: TEV PLC; TBIMC; TVP-Interkniga
Distributed by SIAM USA; VSP (Netherlands)
Distributor for Academic Press; Blackwell; Cambridge University Press; Chapman & Hall; Harcourt Brace; O'Reilly; Pitman; Prentice Hall; John Wiley & Sons (all Russia)
Showroom(s): TVP, 1921 Nakhimovskii prosp 47, 117418 Moscow
Orders to: TVP, 1921, Nakhimovskii props 47, 117418 Moscow

Text Publishers Ltd Too+
7 Cosmonavta Volkova St, 125299 Moscow
Tel: (095) 156-4202 *Fax:* (095) 150-0472
E-mail: textpub@windoms.sitek.net
Key Personnel
Editor-in-Chief: Mikhail Chernenko
President: Vitaly Babenko
Dir: Olgert Libkin
Commercial Dir: Valery Genkin
Art Dir: Vladimir Lubarov
Founded: 1988
Membership(s): Association of Russian Publishers.
ISBN Prefix(es): 5-7516
Shipping Address: 56 Proezd Cherepanovykh, 125183 Moscow
Warehouse: 56 Proezd Cherepanovykh, 125183 Moscow
Orders to: 56 Proezd Cherepanovykh, 125183 Moscow

Top Secret Collection Publishers
ul B Nikitzkaya 22 of 12, 103009 Moscow
Tel: (095) 2022011; (095) 2024531 *Fax:* (095) 2913885
E-mail: topsec@glasnet.ru
Key Personnel
Rts Mgr: Elena Pavlova
Founded: 1993
Subjects: Biography, Fiction, Nonfiction (General), Travel
ISBN Prefix(es): 5-85275

Izdatelstvo Transport
Basmannyj Tupik 6a, 103064 Moscow
Tel: (095) 2625964 *Fax:* (095) 2611322
Key Personnel
Dir: V G Peshkov
Founded: 1923
Subjects: Aeronautics, Aviation, Automotive, Maritime, Transportation
ISBN Prefix(es): 5-277

Izdatelstvo Ural' skogo+
Prosp Lenina 135, 620219 Ekaterinburg
Tel: (03432) 515448 *Fax:* (03432) 51-54-48
E-mail: info@idc.e-burg-ru
Key Personnel
Dir: Victor Kochkin
Chief Editor: Fiodor Eremeyev
Founded: 1986
Specialize in monographs & handbooks.
Subjects: Literature, Literary Criticism, Essays, Mathematics, Philosophy
ISBN Prefix(es): 5-7525

Voronezh State University Publishers
ul Engelsa SA8, Voronez 394000
Tel: (0732) 560481
Key Personnel
Dir: Olga D Tekutyeva
Founded: 1958
Subjects: Biological Sciences, Chemistry, Chemical Engineering, Economics, Geography, Geology, Language Arts, Linguistics, Literature, Literary Criticism, Essays, Mathematics, Social Sciences, Sociology
ISBN Prefix(es): 5-7455

Voyenizdat+
ul Zorge 1, 103160 Moscow
Tel: (095) 1950154 *Fax:* (095) 1952454
Key Personnel
Dir: U J Stadnyuk
Chief Editor: S P Kulichkin; N P Sinitzin
Founded: 1919
Publishing House, Ministry of Defence
ASCI publishing.
Subjects: Biography, Fiction, Government, Political Science, History, Military Science
ISBN Prefix(es): 5-203

Vsesoyuznii Molodejnii Knizhnii Centre
Petrovka 26, 101409 Moscow
Tel: (095) 924 7879
Key Personnel
Gen Dir: A D Tchavchanidze
Founded: 1989
All-Union Youth Book Centre.
Subjects: Fiction, Literature, Literary Criticism, Essays, Science (General)
ISBN Prefix(es): 5-7012

Vsesoyuznoe Obyedineniye Vneshtorgizdat
ul Fadeeva 1, 125047 Moscow
Tel: (095) 2505162 *Fax:* (095) 2539794
Telex: 411238 *Cable:* VNESHTORGIZDAT MOSCOW
Key Personnel
Dir-General: Vladimir I Prokopov
Chief Editor: Nickolai I Romanenko
Sales: Valentin A Sirotkin
Production: Vladimir A Melnichenko
Founded: 1925
Foreign Trade Publishing House
Publish Catalogs, Prospectuses & Advertising Material in Russian & Foreign Languages on Soviet exports. Execute foreign firms' orders for printing services, translation & publishing in Russian of maintenance & other documents.
Subjects: Business
ISBN Prefix(es): 5-85025

Izdatelstvo Vysshaya Shkola+
ul Neglinnaja 29/14, 101439 Moscow
Tel: (095) 2000456 *Fax:* (095) 2090350
Cable: 101430 GSP-4
Key Personnel
Dir: M I Kiselev
Chief Editor: A M Trubitsin
Founded: 1939
Higher School Publishing House.
Membership(s): Publishers' Association of Russian Federation.
Subjects: Biological Sciences, Chemistry, Chemical Engineering, Economics, History, Language

Arts, Linguistics, Literature, Literary Criticism, Essays, Philosophy, Physics, Technology
ISBN Prefix(es): 5-06

Rwanda

General Information

Capital: Kigali
Language: Kinyarwanda (a Bantu tongue) and French (both official) and Kiswahili
Religion: Traditional beliefs (about 50%), most of rest Roman Catholic
Bank Hours: 0800-1800 Monday-Friday; 0800-1300 Saturday
Shop Hours: 0800-1900 Monday-Saturday
Currency: 100 centimes = 1 Rwanda franc
Export/Import Information: No tariff on books and advertising, but Statistical tax. Import license, for statistical purposes, and Foreign Exchange License required. Application to National Bank, through authorized bank.
Copyright: UCC, Berne (see Copyright Conventions, pg xi)

Diocese de Kabjayi, see Imprimerie de Kabgayi

Government Printer (Imprimerie National du Rwanda)
BP 351, Kigali
Tel: 75350 *Fax:* 75820

Imprimerie de Kabgayi+
BP 66, Gitarama
Tel: 62252; 62877 *Fax:* 62345
Key Personnel
Man Dir: Thomas Habimana
Founded: 1932
Associate Companies: Diocese de Kabgayi ASBL, BP 66, Gitarama; Editions Bibliques et Liturgiques, BP 66, Gitarama

INADES (Institut Africain pour le Developpment Economique et Social)
15, rue Jean-Mermoz, Cocody, Abidjam 08
Mailing Address: BP 2088, Abidjan 08
Tel: (0225) 22404720; (0225) 2244 20 59 *Fax:* (0225) 44 84 38
E-mail: inades@africaonline.co.ci; inades@ci.refer.org
Web Site: www.inades.ci.refer.org
Key Personnel
Sales: Michel Guery
Founded: 1975
Subjects: Literature, Literary Criticism, Essays, Regional Interests, Religion - Other, Social Sciences, Sociology

Samoa

General Information

Capital: Apia
Language: Samoan, English
Religion: Predominantly Christian (Congregational, Roman Catholic & Methodist)
Population: 165,000
Bank Hours: 0930-1500 Monday-Friday
Shop Hours: 0800-1200, 1330-1630 Monday-Friday; 0800-1230 Saturday
Currency: 100 sene = 1 tala (western Samoan dollar)
Export/Import Information: No tariff on most books, printed advertising generally free but some subject to duty. No import license or exchange controls.

Institute for Research Extension and Training in Agriculture (IRETA)
The University of the South Pacific, Alafua Campus, PMB, Apia
Tel: (0685) 22372; (0685) 21882; (0685) 21671 *Fax:* (0685) 22347; (0685) 22933
E-mail: uspireta@samoa.usp.ac.fj
Telex: 251 USP SX
Key Personnel
Dir: Mohammed Umar *E-mail:* umar_m@samoa.usp.ac.fj
Parent Company: The University of the South Pacific

IRETA, see Institute for Research Extension and Training in Agriculture (IRETA)

Saudi Arabia

General Information

Capital: Riyadh
Language: Arabic (English widely understood)
Religion: Islamic (officially) with about 85% of the Sunni sect
Population: 16.9 million
Bank Hours: 0830-1200, 1700-1900 Saturday-Wednesday; 0830-1130 Thursday. During Ramadan: 1000-1330 Saturday-Thursday
Shop Hours: 0900-1200, 1600-2100 Saturday-Thursday. During Ramadan closed until sunset, then open until 0200
Currency: 100 halalahs = 20 qurush = 1 Saudi riyal
Export/Import Information: No tariffs on books; advertising matter subject to ad valorem duty but if total duty on one consignment is less than 50 riyals, matter can enter free. Catalogues distributed gratis, usually admitted free. All printed matter except textbooks subject to censorship. No import licenses required.
Copyright: UCC (see Copyright Conventions, pg xi)

Asam Establishment for Publishing & Distribution
PO Box 87782, Riyadh 11652
Tel: (01) 4453732 *Fax:* (01) 4412583
Key Personnel
General Manager, Owner: Fahed M Abo Rdoun
Subjects: Religion - Islamic
ISBN Prefix(es): 9960-714

Dar Al-Mirrikh (Mars Publishing House)
PO Box 10720, Riyadh 11443
Tel: (01) 464 7531; (01) 465 7939; (01) 4658523 *Fax:* (01) 465 7939
Telex: 403129
Key Personnel
President: Abdullah Majid
Vice President: Shams Zakaria
Contact: Mr Abdul Hameed Noor Mohd
ISBN Prefix(es): 9960-24

Dar Al-Rayah for Publishing & Distribution
PO Box 40124, Riyadh 11499
Tel: (01) 4931869 *Fax:* (01) 4911985
ISBN Prefix(es): 9960-661

Dar Al-Shareff for Publishing & Distribution+
PO Box 2479, Riyadh 11563
Tel: (01) 4779491

Key Personnel
President: Ibrahim Al-Hazemi
Founded: 1992
Subjects: Animals, Pets, Astronomy, Behavioral Sciences, Biography, Drama, Theater, History, Humor, Literature, Literary Criticism, Essays, Medicine, Nursing, Dentistry, Nonfiction (General), Philosophy, Religion - Islamic, Romance, Sports, Athletics, Veterinary Science, Women's Studies
ISBN Prefix(es): 9960-640; 9960-741

International Publications Agency (IPA)
PO Box 70, Dhahran Airport
Tel: (03) 8954925
Telex: 871229
Key Personnel
Manager: Said Salah
Subjects: Regional Interests

Al Jazirah Organization for Press, Printing, Publishing
Al-Nassiriah St, Riyadh 11411
Mailing Address: PO Box 354, Riyadh
Tel: (01) 4419999 *Fax:* (01) 4412536
Key Personnel
Dir General: Saleh Al-Ajroush
Editor-in-Chief: Khalid el Malek
Founded: 1964
Subjects: Government, Political Science, Law
ISBN Prefix(es): 9960-9190

King Saud University+
PO Box 2254, Riyadh 11451
Tel: (01) 4672832 *Fax:* (01) 4672894
Web Site: www.ksu.edu.sa
Telex: 461019 KSU SJ
Key Personnel
President: Prof Abdullah Al-Faisal
Vice President: Prof Ibrahim Al-Mish'Al
Vice President, Research & Higher Studies: Prof Khalid Al Hamoudi
Dir, Translation Center: Prof Ahmed A Almohandis
Dean, University Libraries: Dr Sulaiman S Al Ugla
Founded: 1957
Subjects: Agriculture, Behavioral Sciences, Biological Sciences, Chemistry, Chemical Engineering, Geography, Geology, Language Arts, Linguistics, Mathematics, Medicine, Nursing, Dentistry, Technology
ISBN Prefix(es): 9960-05

Saudi Publishing & Distributing House+
3rd Floor, Al-Jawhara Bldg No 1, Medina Rd, Baghdadiah, Jeddah 21451
Mailing Address: PO Box 899, Dammam
Tel: (03) 8334158 *Fax:* (03) 8335520
E-mail: info@spdh-sa.com
Web Site: www.spdh-sa.com *Cable:* NASHRADAR
Key Personnel
Chairman & Man Dir: Mohammed Salahuddin
Founded: 1966
Also act as importers & distributors of English & Arabic books (academic, reference & general).
Subjects: Literature, Literary Criticism, Essays, Religion - Other, Science (General)
ISBN Prefix(es): 9960-26
Branch Office(s)
PO Box 899, Riyadh *Tel:* (01) 464 7894
Bookshop(s): Hyat Plaza Complex, King Saud St, Dammam Dhahran St Near Governorate, Dannan *Tel:* (03) 8323515; Zouman Shopping Centre, opposite S Fakhee Hospital, Jeddah *Tel:* (02) 6608964

Senegal

General Information

Capital: Dakar
Language: French
Religion: About 90% Islamic, 5% Christian (mostly Roman Catholic), the rest follow traditional beliefs
Population: 8.2 million
Bank Hours: Generally 0800-1115, 1430-1630 Monday-Friday
Shop Hours: Vary, and some open Sunday morning, some close Monday morning. Generally are 0800-1200, 1430-1800 Monday-Saturday
Currency: 100 centimes = 1 CFA franc
Export/Import Information: Member of West African Economic Community. No tariff on books except atlases. Added taxes apply to atlases. Advertising matter (more than one copy) subject to fiscal and customs duty plus added taxes. Import licenses and exchange controls apply for imports from outside EEC, Franc Zone, USA and Canada.
Copyright: Berne, UCC (see Copyright Conventions, pg xi)

Nouvelles Editions Africaines du Senegal (NEAS)+
10, Rue El Hadj Amadou Assane-Ndoye, Dakar
Mailing Address: BP 260, Dakar
Tel: 8211381; 8221580 *Fax:* 8223604
Key Personnel
President: Souleymane Bachir Diagne
Dir General: Mr Doudou Ndiaye
Founded: 1989
Subjects: Literature, Literary Criticism, Essays, Social Sciences, Sociology
ISBN Prefix(es): 2-7236
Distributed by African Imprint Library Services

Agence de Distribution de Presse
BP 374, Dakar
Tel: (08) 320278 *Fax:* (08) 324915
E-mail: adpresse@telecomplus.sn
Key Personnel
Man Dir: Philipe Schorp
Founded: 1943
Affiliated to NMPP, Paris.
Parent Company: NMPP (Paris, France)

CAEC, see Centre Africain d'Animation et d'Echanges Culturels Editions Khoudia (CAEC)

Centre Africain d'Animation et d'Echanges Culturels Editions Khoudia (CAEC)+
HLM Fass-Paillote, Immeuble 7, Dakar
Tel: 211023 *Fax:* 215109
Key Personnel
Production Dir: Ms Aissatou Dia
Founded: 1989
Subjects: Anthropology, Drama, Theater, Education, Ethnicity, Fiction, Literature, Literary Criticism, Essays, Poetry
ISBN Prefix(es): 2-87895
Distributed by Edilis (Ivory Coast); Presence Africaine (France)
Distributor for Edilis (Ivory Coast); Haho (Togo)

Centre de Linguistique Appliquee
Universite de Dakar, Faculte des Lettres et Sciences Humaines, Fann Parc, Dakar
Tel: 230126
Subjects: Language Arts, Linguistics, Literature, Literary Criticism, Essays

CODESRIA (Council for the Development of Social Science Research in Africa)+
PO Box 3304, Dakar, Avenue Cheikh Anta Diop X Canal IV, Dakar
Tel: 8259814; 8259822 *Fax:* 8241289; 8640143
E-mail: codesria@sonatel.senet.net
Web Site: www.cordesria.org
Telex: 61339 Codes SG
Key Personnel
Head of Publications & Communications: Felicia Oyekanmi *E-mail:* felicia.oyekanmi@codesria.sn
Founded: 1973
Publish in four languages: English, French, Portuguese & Arab. Specialize in social sciences. Also acts as a coordinator of social science research in Africa.
Membership(s): International Research Councils.
Subjects: Behavioral Sciences, Developing Countries, Economics, Education, Environmental Studies, Ethnicity, Government, Political Science, History, Labor, Industrial Relations, Social Sciences, Sociology, Women's Studies
ISBN Prefix(es): 1-870784; 2-86978
Number of titles published annually: 10 Print
Total Titles: 186 Print
Warehouse: African Books Collective Ltd, The Jam Factory, 27 Park End St, Oxford OX1 1KU, United Kingdom *E-mail:* abc@africanbookscollective.com
Karthala, Edition Diffusion, 22-24 Blvd Arago, 75013 Paris, France

Council for the Development of Social Science Research in Africa, see CODESRIA (Council for the Development of Social Science Research in Africa)

Enda Tiers Monde
4 & 5 rue Kleber, Dakar
Mailing Address: BP 3370, Dakar
Tel: (0221) 821-60-27; (0221) 822-42-29 *Fax:* (0221) 822-26-95
E-mail: enda@enda.sn
Web Site: www.enda.sn
Telex: 51456SG
Key Personnel
President: Cheikh Hamidou Kane
Founded: 1972

Environment & Development Action in the Third World, see Enda Tiers Monde

Institut Fondamental d'Afrique Noire, Cheikh Anta Diop (Fundamental Institute of Black Africa, Sheik Anta Diop)
Campus universitaire, Dakar
Mailing Address: BP 206, Dakar
Tel: 825 00 90; 825 98 90; 825 71 24 *Fax:* 24 49 18
E-mail: bifan@telecomplus.sn
Web Site: www.refer.sn/ifan
Key Personnel
Dir: Prof Samb Djibril
Founded: 1936
Branch Office(s)
Musee de la Mer, Campus universitaire, BP 206 Dakar-Fann
Musee historique, Campus universitaire, BP 206 Dakar-Fann
Musees d'Art africain, Campus universitaire, BP 206 Dakar-Fann

IFAN, see Institut Fondamental d'Afrique Noire, Cheikh Anta Diop

NEAS, see Nouvelles Editions Africaines du Senegal (NEAS)

Les Nouvelles Editions Africaines du Senegal NEAS+
BP 260, 10 rue El Hadj Amadou Assane, Ndoye, Dakar
Tel: (08) 211381; (08) 221580 *Fax:* (08) 223604
E-mail: neas@sentoo.sn
Key Personnel
Dir General: Francois Boirot
Commercial Dir: Mamadou Kasse
Founded: 1972
Subjects: Biography, Education, Ethnicity, Fiction, History, Nonfiction (General), Philosophy, Poetry, Psychology, Psychiatry, Religion - Other, Science (General), Social Sciences, Sociology
ISBN Prefix(es): 2-7236
Number of titles published annually: 15 Print
Total Titles: 800 Print
Distributed by CEDA; Editions Donniya; Editions Jamana; Ganndal; NEI
Distributor for CEDA; Editions Donniya; Editions Jamana; Ganndal; NEI

Edition Sahel+
9 rue Thiong, BP 3683, Dakar
Tel: 212164
Telex: 469 teranga sg
Key Personnel
Contact: Niane Idrissa
Founded: 1982
ISBN Prefix(es): 2-906993

Societe Africaine d'Edition
14 Rue Jules Ferry, BP 1877, Dakar
Tel: 217977; 220284
Key Personnel
Man Dir: Pierre Biarnes
Founded: 1961
Subjects: Economics, Foreign Countries, Government, Political Science
Branch Office(s)
32 rue de l'Echiquier, 75010 Paris, France
Tel: 5230233

Societe d'Edition d'Afrique Nouvelle
10 rue El Hadj Amadou Assane Ndoye, BP 260, Dakar
Tel: (08) 211381; (08) 221580 *Fax:* (08) 223604
Telex: 21 450 NEA SG
Key Personnel
Man Dir: Athanase Ndong
Senior Editor, Rights & Permissions: Rene Odou
Subjects: Foreign Countries, Religion - Other
ISBN Prefix(es): 2-7236

Serbia and Montenegro

General Information

Capital: Belgrade
Language: Serbian, Albanian, Croation and Bosnian
Religion: Predominately Eastern Orthodox (65%), also Islamic, Roman Catholic and Protestant
Population: 10.8 million
Bank Hours: 0800-1500 Monday-Friday
Shop Hours: 0800-2000 Monday-Friday; 0800-1500 Saturday. Some open weekdays continuously and early Sunday morning
Currency: 100 paras = 1 Yugoslav New Dinar
Export/Import Information: No tariffs on books except on publications by publishers from Serbia and Montenegro printed abroad. Advertising catalogs for such books dutied, otherwise free; non-Serbian language advertising materials dutied. Special equalization tax, customs clearance charge and import surcharge when

SERBIA AND MONTENEGRO

goods are subject to duty. No import licenses required. Exchange controls. The basic commercial unit is known as an enterprise but there are no state monopolies.
Copyright: UCC, Berne (see Copyright Conventions, pg xi)

AGAPE+
Cara Dusana 4, 21000 Novi Sad
Tel: (021) 469-474 *Fax:* (021) 469-382
E-mail: agape@eunet.yu
Web Site: www.agape.yu
Key Personnel
President & International Rights: Karoly Harmath
E-mail: harmath@eunet.yu
Founded: 1977
Membership(s): ELCE; Association of Hungarian Catholic Publishers; International Association of Franciscan Publishers, UCIP.
Subjects: Religion - Catholic, Theology
ISBN Prefix(es): 86-463
Number of titles published annually: 50 Print
Parent Company: AGAPE Kft, Hu-Szeged, Matyas ter 26, 6725 Szeged, Hungary, Eva Balogh

Alfa-Narodna Knjiga
Safarikova 11, PO Box 247, 11000 Belgrade
Tel: (011) 3221-484; (011) 3227-426; (011) 3223-910 *Fax:* (011) 3227-946
E-mail: alfankkl@eunet.yu
Web Site: www.narodnaknjiga.co.yu
Key Personnel
Editor-in-Chief: Milicko Mijovic
Foreign Rights Mgr: Tea Jovanovic *Tel:* (011) 3227-426 *Fax:* (011) 3227-946 *E-mail:* tea@eunet.yu
Subjects: Art, Astrology, Occult, Child Care & Development, Cookery, Criminology, Fiction, Government, Political Science, Health, Nutrition, History, How-to, Journalism, Language Arts, Linguistics, Literature, Literary Criticism, Essays, Medicine, Nursing, Dentistry, Mysteries, Nonfiction (General), Philosophy, Poetry, Psychology, Psychiatry, Religion - Other, Science (General), Self-Help
ISBN Prefix(es): 86-331
Number of titles published annually: 300 Print
Total Titles: 1,000 Print
Foreign Rep(s): Tea Jovanovic (Worldwide)
Foreign Rights: Tea Jovanovic (World)

Association of Yugoslav Publishers & Booksellers
Kneza Milosa 25, 11000 Belgrade
Mailing Address: POB 570, 11000 Belgrade
Tel: (011) 642-533; (011) 642 248 *Fax:* (011) 646-339
E-mail: ognjenl@eunet.yu
Web Site: www.beobookfair.co.yu
Key Personnel
General Dir: Mr Ognjen Lakicevic
E-mail: ognjenl@eunet.yu
Publisher: Mrs Mirjana Popovic
Founded: 1954
Organizer of the International Book Fair in Belgrade.
Membership(s): IPA, Geneve.
ISBN Prefix(es): 86-7115

Beogradski Izdavacko-Graficki Zavod
Bulevar Vojvode Misica 17/VI, 11000 Belgrade
Tel: (011) 650-235; (011) 651-666 *Fax:* (011) 651-841
Web Site: www.suc.org/biz/BIGZ/
Telex: 11855 Yu Bigz *Cable:* BEOGRAF
Key Personnel
Man Dir: Gojko Zecar
Editorial Dir, Permissions: Vidosav Stevanovic
Founded: 1831
Subjects: Philosophy, Poetry, Social Sciences, Sociology

ISBN Prefix(es): 86-13
Imprints: BIGZ
Book Club(s): Book Lovers' Club

BIGZ, *imprint of* Beogradski Izdavacko-Graficki Zavod

Borba
Trg Marksa I Engelsa 7, Belgrade 11000
Tel: (011) 3243-437 *Fax:* (011) 3244-913
Web Site: www.borba.co.yu
Key Personnel
Dir: Novica Dukic
Founded: 1922
ISBN Prefix(es): 86-80105

Decje Novine, see Niro Decje Novine

Forum
Vojvode Misica 1, 22100 Novi Sad
Tel: (021) 57 286 *Fax:* (021) 57 691
Telex: yu-14199
Key Personnel
Dir: Kalman Petkovics
Subjects: Fiction, Government, Political Science
ISBN Prefix(es): 86-323

Gradevinska Knjiga
Trg Nikole Pasica 8/11, 11000 Belgrade
Tel: (011) 323 35 65; (011) 324 76 62 *Fax:* (011) 323 32 34
Key Personnel
Man Dir: Milan Visnic
Editor & Chief: Milica Dodic
Commercial Manager: Jovo Karadzic
Founded: 1948
Subjects: Architecture & Interior Design, Engineering (General)
ISBN Prefix(es): 86-395
Bookshop(s): Narodnog fronta 14, Belgrade; Student, 27 marta 78, Belgrade

Izdavacka preduzece Gradina+
Pobede 38, 18000 Nis
Tel: (018) 25 864; (018) 25 456 *Fax:* (018) 25 456
E-mail: gradinar@bankerinter.net
Key Personnel
Dir: Gordana Jovanovic
Subjects: Art, Science (General)
ISBN Prefix(es): 86-7129
Bookshop(s): ul pobede 113Y, Nis; Veljka Vlahovica 2, Nis; Dimitrija Tucovica bb, Nis

Jugoslavijapublik+
Knez Mihailova 10, 11000 Belgrade
Tel: (011) 633 266 *Fax:* (011) 622 858
Telex: 11125
Key Personnel
General Manager: Slobodan Zaric
Founded: 1962
Subjects: History, Philosophy, Religion - Other
ISBN Prefix(es): 86-7121

Jugoslovenska Revija
Karatordeva 41, 11000 Belgrade
Tel: (011) 625-829
Telex: 12954 Yurew
Key Personnel
Dir: Rajko Bobot
Permissions: Milovan Ignjatovic
Subjects: Art, Travel
ISBN Prefix(es): 86-7413

Tehnicka Knjiga (Technical Book)+
Vojvode Stepe 89, 11000 Belgrade
Tel: (011) 468 596 *Fax:* (011) 473 442
E-mail: tknjiga@eunet.yu
Web Site: www.tehknjiga.co.yu

Key Personnel
Editor-in-Chief: Mrdjenovic Dragi
Man Dir: Grbovic Radivoje
Sales Manager: Cosovic Llida
Subjects: Computer Science, Electronics, Electrical Engineering, Engineering (General), How-to, Science (General)
ISBN Prefix(es): 86-325

Kultura
XIV VUSB 4-6, 21470 Backi Petrovac
Tel: (021) 780-144 *Fax:* (021) 780-291 *Cable:* Obzor Novi Sad
Key Personnel
Dir: Anna Makanova
ISBN Prefix(es): 86-7103
Bookshop(s): Backi Petrovac Bodvis Jan

Libertatea
Zarka Zrenjanina 7, 26000 Pancevo
Tel: (013) 33-51; 13 346 447 *Fax:* (013) 46-447
Cable: Libertatea Pancevo
Key Personnel
Dir: Todor Gilezan
ISBN Prefix(es): 86-7001

Minerva
Trg 29 novembra 3, 24000 Subotica
Tel: (024) 28834; (024) 25712 *Fax:* (024) 23-208
Cable: Minerva Subotica
Key Personnel
Dir: Josip Prcic
Subjects: Science (General)
ISBN Prefix(es): 86-7099
Bookshop(s): ul oktobra 4, 24000 Subotica; Maksima Gorkog 20, 24000 Subotica; Put M Pijade 25, 24000 Subotica

MiS Sport IGP
Formerly Sportska Knjiga
Radnicka 24, 11030 Belgrade
Tel: (011) 3220226; (011) 3225361 *Cable:* Sportska Knjiga
Key Personnel
Dir: Dragoslav Bajic
Editor: Sava Bjelajac
Founded: 1949
Subjects: Sports, Athletics
ISBN Prefix(es): 86-7107

Narodna Biblioteka Srbije (National Library of Serbia)
ul Skerliceva 1, 11000 Belgrade
Tel: (011) 451 2429 *Fax:* (011) 451 289
E-mail: kovacevic@nbsbg.nbs.bg.ac.yu
Web Site: www.nbs.bg.ac.yu
Telex: NBS 12208
Key Personnel
Dir: Svetislav Duric
Founded: 1832
Subjects: History
ISBN Prefix(es): 86-7035

Naucna Knjiga+
Uzun Mirkova 5/1, 11000 Belgrade
Tel: (011) 635 819; (011) 637 868; (011) 637 230 *Fax:* (011) 638 070 *Cable:* NAUCNA KNJIGA
Key Personnel
Man Dir: Dr Blazo Perovic
Founded: 1947
Subjects: Education, Engineering (General), Medicine, Nursing, Dentistry, Science (General)
ISBN Prefix(es): 86-23; 86-321
Bookshop(s): Znanje, Gracanicka br 16, Belgrade; Naucna Knjiga, Knez Mihailova gr 19 & 40, Belgrade; Naucna knjiga, Jug Bogdanova 68, Prokuplje

Nio Pobjeda - Oour Izdavacko-Publicisticka Djelatnost
Bulevar revolucije 11, 81000 Podgorica

PUBLISHERS — SERBIA AND MONTENEGRO

Tel: (081) 45955; (081) 44433; (081) 44474
Fax: (081) 52803
Telex: 61243 YU pob
Key Personnel
Dir: Ljubo Buric
Publishing Dir: Mileta Radovanovic
Editor: Branko Banjevic; Djerdj Djokaj; Ratko Vujosevic; Vojislav Minic
Sales, Trade Dir: Miodrag Raonic
Founded: 1962
Subjects: Science (General)
ISBN Prefix(es): 86-309
Branch Office(s)
Safarikova 15, 21000 Novi Sad *Tel:* (021) 51086
Miladin Popovica bb, 38000 Pristina *Tel:* (038) 24062
Karadordev trg 7, 11080 Zemun *Tel:* (011) 600652

Niro Decje Novine
pf 24, Tihomira Matijevica 4, 32300 Gornji Milanovac
Tel: (032) 712246; (032) 712247; (032) 714970; (032) 711256; (032) 711248; (011) 3221476; (011) 342010 *Fax:* (032) 711248
Telex: 13731 GM, 12206 BGB
Subjects: Education
ISBN Prefix(es): 86-367

Nolit Publishing House+
Terazije 27/II, 11000 Belgrade
Tel: (011) 345 017; (011) 355 510 *Fax:* (011) 627 285 *Cable:* NOLIT BGD
Key Personnel
Man Dir: Radivoje Nesie
Editorial: Radivoje Mikic
Dir: Branko Nikezic
Founded: 1928
Subjects: Agriculture, Art, Fiction, History, Philosophy, Psychology, Psychiatry, Social Sciences, Sociology
ISBN Prefix(es): 86-19

Obod
Njegoseva 3, 81250 Cetinje
Tel: (086) 233-331 *Fax:* (086) 233-951
E-mail: ipobod@cg.ju *Cable:* OBOD CETINJE
Key Personnel
Dir: Vasko Jankovic
Founded: 1946
Membership(s): Association of Yugoslav Publishers & Booksellers.
Subjects: Education, Fiction, Language Arts, Linguistics, Nonfiction (General), Poetry, Science (General)
ISBN Prefix(es): 86-305
Number of titles published annually: 30 Print
Branch Office(s)
Dobracina 32, 11000 Belgrade *Tel:* (011) 626-553
Bookshop(s): Njegoseva 11, 11000 Belgrade

Izdavacka Organizacija Rad
Mose Pijade 12, 11000 Belgrade
Tel: (011) 3239-758; (011) 3239-998 *Fax:* (011) 3230-923
Key Personnel
Man Dir: Bravislav Milosevic
Sales Dir: Milovan Vlahovic
21 bookshops throughout Serbia and Montenegro.
Subjects: Biography, Economics, Engineering (General), Government, Political Science, Philosophy, Poetry, Social Sciences, Sociology
ISBN Prefix(es): 86-09
Bookshop(s): Papirus, Terazije 26, Belgrade; Frankopanska 5, Zagreb

Panorama NIJP/ID Grigorije Bozovic
Dom Stampe BB, 38000 Pristina
Tel: (038) 29 090; (038) 21 156; (038) 29 866
Fax: (038) 29 809 *Cable:* Jedinstvo Pristina
Key Personnel
Dir: Milan Seslija
Subjects: Government, Political Science, History, Medicine, Nursing, Dentistry, Philosophy, Social Sciences, Sociology
ISBN Prefix(es): 86-7019

Partenon MAM Sistem+
Simina 9a/1, 11000 Belgrade
Tel: (011) 632535; (011) 625942; (011) 633465 *Fax:* (011) 632535; (011) 2623980
E-mail: partenon@infosky.net
Key Personnel
Dir: Momcilo Mitrovic
Subjects: Agriculture, Fiction, Science (General), Linguistics
ISBN Prefix(es): 86-7157
Number of titles published annually: 30 Print

Izdavacko Preduzece Matice Srpske+
Ulica Matice srpske 1, 21000 Novi Sad
Tel: (021) 420 199; (021) 420 198 *Fax:* (021) 28 574; (021) 25 859
E-mail: bms@bms.ns.ac.yu
Web Site: www.bms.ns.ac.yu
Key Personnel
Dir: Milorad Grujic *E-mail:* m.grujic@sezampro.yu
Editor: Ivan Negrisorac; Milica Micic Dimovski; Dragan Mojovic
Founded: 1826
Subjects: History, Human Relations, Literature, Literary Criticism, Essays
ISBN Prefix(es): 86-363
Bookshop(s): Zmaj Jovina 4, Novi Sad, Milenko Ranin *Tel:* 29-436; Trg Toz Markovica 24, Novi Sad, Zdravko Gaseric *Tel:* 29-307

Privredni Pregled
Marsala Birjuzova 3, 11000 Belgrade
Tel: (011) 625522; (011) 628477 *Fax:* (011) 3281473; (011) 3281912
E-mail: novinska@hotmail.com; desk@grmec.co.yu
Web Site: www.grmec.co.yu
Telex: 11509 Yu Pp *Cable:* Privredni Pregled Bgd
Key Personnel
Dir: Toma Markovic
Contact: Dusan Jugovic; Stana Sehalic
Editor-in-Chief: Slobodan Kljajic
Subjects: Economics, Law, Management
ISBN Prefix(es): 86-315
Branch Office(s)
Orce Nikolova 79, Skopje
Mose Pijade, 21 Zagreb
Hala 'Tivoli', Ljubljana
Marsala Tita 86, Sarajevo

Prosveta
Cika Ljubina 1, 11000 Belgrade
Tel: (011) 629 843; (011) 631 566 *Fax:* (011) 182 581
Telex: 11609 Yu
Key Personnel
General Dir: Vidosav Stevanovic
Editor-in-Chief: Milisav Savic
Export Manager: Milutin Trifunovic
Rights & Permissions: Branka Simic
Founded: 1945
Subjects: Human Relations
ISBN Prefix(es): 86-07
Book Club(s): Prosveta

Radnicka Stampa
Trg Nikole Pasica 5/V, 11000 Belgrade
Mailing Address: Postanski fah 995, 11000 Belgrade
Tel: (011) 3230-927; (011) 3230-921; (011) 3236-259
E-mail: radstamp@sezampro.yu
Web Site: www.radnickastampa.co.yu/
Telex: RSNIRO YU 72638 *Cable:* Radnicka stampa Belgrade
Key Personnel
Dir: Radoslav Roso
Sales Manager: Cedo Males
Subjects: Economics, Government, Political Science, Social Sciences, Sociology
ISBN Prefix(es): 86-7073

Republicki Zavod za Unapredivanje Vaspitanja i Obrazovanja
Kneza Milosa 101, 11000 Belgrade
Tel: (011) 659322
Key Personnel
Chief Executive: Milivoje Brajove
Editor-in-Chief: Krsto Lekovie
Sales Manager: Radmila Miranovie
Founded: 1973
Republic Institution for the Improvement of Education.
Subjects: Education
ISBN Prefix(es): 86-80871
Bookshop(s): Knjizara Zavoda, Kneza Milosa 101, 11000 Belgrade

Savez Inzenjera i Tehnicara Jugoslavije (Union of Engineers & Technicians of Yugoslavia)+
Kneza Milosa 9, 11000 Belgrade
Tel: (011) 3243653; (011) 3243652 *Fax:* (011) 3243652
E-mail: internet@eunet.yu *Cable:* SITJ BEOGRAD
Key Personnel
President: Mihailo Milojevic, PhD
Vice President: Budimir Cetkovic; Radomir Simic, PhD
General Secretary: Milorad Terzic, PhD
Founded: 1919
Membership(s): World Federation of Engineering Organizations; World Federation of Scientific Workers; Regional Council of Coordination of Central & East-European Engineering Organizations.
Subjects: Civil Engineering, Communications, Economics, Electronics, Electrical Engineering, Engineering (General), Mechanical Engineering, Science (General), Technology
ISBN Prefix(es): 86-80067

Savremena Administracija
Crnotravska 7-9, 11000 Belgrade
Tel: (011) 668567; (011) 661913; (011) 667436 *Fax:* (011) 667436
Telex: 12233 Yu Sa
Key Personnel
Dir: Vojin Moraca
Contact: Miroslav Spasojevic
Founded: 1954
Subjects: Economics, Law
ISBN Prefix(es): 86-387

Sluzbeni List
Jovana Ristica 1, 11000 Belgrade
Tel: (011) 3060333; (011) 3060310 *Fax:* (011) 3060393
Telex: 11756 Yu Slist
Key Personnel
Dir: Dusan Masovic
Contact: Blagoje Nikolic
Subjects: Law
ISBN Prefix(es): 86-355
Bookshop(s): Prodavnica 1, Brankova 16, Belgrade, Croatia; Prodavnica 2, 9 Novembra 1a

Sportska Knjiga, see MiS Sport IGP

Srpska Knjizevna Zadruga (Serbian Literary Association)
Srpskih vladara 19/I, 11000 Belgrade
Tel: (011) 330 305 *Fax:* (011) 626-224
Founded: 1892

SERBIA AND MONTENEGRO

Subjects: History
ISBN Prefix(es): 86-379

Svetovi (The Worlds)+
Arse Teodorovica 11, 21000 Novi Sad
Tel: (021) 28032; (021) 28036 *Fax:* (021) 28036; (021) 28032
E-mail: aum.mar@eunet.yu
Key Personnel
Dir: Jovan Zivlak
Founded: 1951
Subjects: Anthropology, Art, Fiction, Philosophy, Poetry
ISBN Prefix(es): 86-7047
Number of titles published annually: 40 Print
Total Titles: 2,000 Print
Bookshop(s): Pasiceva 32, Novi Sad *Tel:* (021) 23-071

Tehnika, see Savez Inzenjera i Tehnicara Jugoslavije

Turisticka Stampa+
Dure Dakovica 100, 11000 Belgrade
Tel: (011) 750-740; (011) 759 076 *Fax:* (011) 762-236
Key Personnel
Man Dir & Editorial: Dragan Kankaras
Founded: 1953
Subjects: Art
ISBN Prefix(es): 86-7041

Vesti
Ljube Stojanovica 5, 31000 Uzice
Tel: (031) 513261; (031) 514263 *Fax:* (031) 511941
E-mail: redakcija@vesti.co.yu
Web Site: www.vesti.co.yu/onama.htm
Key Personnel
Dir: Zoran Lazic
ISBN Prefix(es): 86-7319

VINC, *imprint of* Vojnoizdavacki i novinski centar

Vojnoizdavacki i novinski centar+
Bircaninova 5, 11000 Belgrade
Tel: (011) 644 188; (011) 641 159 *Fax:* (011) 645 020
Key Personnel
President: Dr Nikola Popovic
Editor-in-Chief: Milisav Djordjevic
Editor, Foreign Writers' Edition: Novica Stevanovic
Founded: 1945
Subjects: Military Science
ISBN Prefix(es): 86-335; 86-80641
Imprints: VINC
Bookshop(s): Poslovni biro "Vojna Knjiga", Vase Carapica 22, 11000 Belgrade

Vuk Karadzic+
Bulevar Revolucije 77A, 11000 Belgrade
Tel: (011) 423-290; (011) 424-558; (011) 424-560 *Fax:* (011) 422-012 *Cable:* VUK KARADZIC BELGRADE
Key Personnel
Man Dir: Ancic Vojin
Founded: 1956
Subjects: Art, History, Philosophy, Psychology, Psychiatry, Science (General), Social Sciences, Sociology
ISBN Prefix(es): 86-307
Branch Office(s)
Dure Dakovica 5, Banja Luka *Tel:* (078) 60080
Bul 23, oktobra 35, Novi Sad *Tel:* (021) 611763
Francuska 10, Smederevska Palanka
Novosadska bb, Svetozarevo *Tel:* (035) 223313

Zavod za Izdavanje Udzbenika
Sremska 7, 21000 Novi Sad
Tel: (021) 22068 *Fax:* (021) 22069
Key Personnel
Man Dir: Vasilije Lalatovic
Contact: Slobodan Babic
Founded: 1965
Subjects: Education
ISBN Prefix(es): 86-413

Zavod za udzbenike i nastavna sredstva
(Publishing House for Textbooks & Teaching Aids)
Obilicev venac 5, 11000 Belgrade
Tel: (011) 635-142; (011) 3051-900 (sales) *Fax:* (011) 2390-072 (sales)
E-mail: prodaja@zavod.co.yu (sales)
Web Site: www.zavod.co.yu
Key Personnel
Manager: Dr Rados Ljusic *Tel:* (011) 638-463 *E-mail:* direktor@zavod.co.yu
Founded: 1957
Subjects: Education
ISBN Prefix(es): 86-17
Bookshop(s): Kosovska 45, 11000 Belgrade; Vukasoviceva 50, 11090 Belgrade

Sierra Leone

General Information

Capital: Freetown
Language: English
Religion: Predominantly traditional beliefs, also some Islamic and Christian
Population: 4.5 million
Bank Hours: 0800-1330 Monday-Thursday; 0800-1400 Friday
Shop Hours: 0800-1300, 1400-1830 Monday-Saturday
Currency: 100 cents = 1 leone
Export/Import Information: No tariff on books except children's picture books and advertising matter. Open general license. Exchange controls.

Macmillan Education
34-36 Rawdon St, Private Mail Bag 904, Freetown
Tel: (022) 225683 *Fax:* (022) 229186
E-mail: macmillan@sierratel.sl
Web Site: www.macmillan-africa.com
Key Personnel
General Manager: Kai Fomba
Parent Company: Macmillan Publishers Ltd, United Kingdom

Njala Educational Publishing Centre
Njala University PMB, Freetown

Sierra Leone University Press
Fourah Bay College, University of Sierra Leone, Mount Aureol, Freetown
Mailing Address: PO Box 87
Tel: (022) 27300; (022) 23494; (022) 27399; (022) 27323 *Cable:* Fourahbay
Key Personnel
Chairman & Honorary Editor: Prof Eldred Jones
Honorary Secretary, Rights & Permissions: Prof W S Marcus Jones
Founded: 1968
Subjects: Ethnicity, History, Nonfiction (General), Religion - Other, Social Sciences, Sociology

United Christian Council Literature Bureau
Bunumbu Press, Bo
Mailing Address: PO Box 28, Bo

Tel: 032462
Key Personnel
Man Dir: Joseph E Tucker

Singapore

General Information

Capital: Singapore
Language: Malay (national and official), also Chinese (Mandarin), Tamil and English (all official)
Religion: Daoism, Buddhist, Islamic, Christian, Hindu and Taoism
Population: 2.8 million
Bank Hours: 1000-1500 Monday-Friday; 930-1130 Saturday
Shop Hours: 0900-1800 Monday-Saturday
Currency: 100 cents = 1 Singapore dollar
Export/Import Information: No tariffs on books and advertising. Import licenses; no seditious publications permitted. Normal exchange control.
Copyright: Florence (see Copyright Conventions, pg xi)

K C Ang Publishing Pte Ltd+
Imprint of Bunny Books
93 Hitam Manis, Chip Bee Garden, Singapore 278503
Tel: 4741680 *Fax:* 2542002
Key Personnel
Man Dir: K C Ang
Founded: 1985
Specialize in children's books.
ISBN Prefix(es): 9971-974

APA Production Pte Ltd+
38 Joo Koon Rd, Singapore 628990
Tel: 8651600; 8651601 *Fax:* 8616438
E-mail: apasin@singnet.com.sg
Telex: RS 36201APASIN
Key Personnel
Man Dir: Hans Hoefer; Yinglock Chan
Founded: 1971
Subjects: Travel
ISBN Prefix(es): 9971-925; 9971-982; 981-234
Parent Company: Langenscheidt KG
Associate Companies: APA Publications (HK), Hong Kong
Imprints: Insight Guides; Insight Pocket Guides; Insight Topics
U.S. Office(s): Langenscheidt Publishers, Inc, 46-35 54 Rd, Maspeth, NY 11378, United States
Distributor for Langenscheidt (Asia)

APAC Publishers Services Pte Ltd+
05-03 Hiap Huat House, 70 Bedemeer Rd, Singapore 339940
Tel: 6844 7333 *Fax:* 6747 8916
E-mail: service@apacmedia.com.sg
Key Personnel
Man Dir: Steven Goh *E-mail:* sgohapac@singnet.com.sg
Founded: 1990
Subjects: Architecture & Interior Design, Business, Chemistry, Chemical Engineering, Civil Engineering, Computer Science, Economics, Engineering (General), Environmental Studies, Management, Medicine, Nursing, Dentistry, Science (General), Social Sciences, Sociology, Technology
ISBN Prefix(es): 981-3045
Total Titles: 6 Print
Distributor for American Medical Assn; American Society of Microbiology; Berg Publishers; Berghahn Publishers; Blackwell Publishing; CAB International; Columbia University Press;

Haworth Press; Health Press; Hong Kong University Press; Humana Press; Industrial Press; Institute of Chemical Engineers; John Hopkins University Press; S Karger; Lippincott Williams & Wilkins; Marcel Decker; New York University Press; W W Norton; Quality Medical Publishing; Lynne Rienner Publishers; Royal Society of Chemistry; Schattauer; M E Sharpe; Springer Publishing; Teachers College Press; Thomas Telford; UNSW Press; Woodhead Publishing

Aquanut Agencies Pte Ltd
305 Clementi Avenue 4, No 08-427, Singapore S 120305
Tel: 7753614 *Fax:* 7753614
E-mail: aquanut@singnet.com.sg
Web Site: www.aquanut.com.sg
Key Personnel
Dir: Mr Leslie Lung
Founded: 1998
To carry on the business of publisher, book & print sellers. Also consultant for print, publishing & publicity.
Subjects: Asian Studies, Behavioral Sciences, How-to, Human Relations, Humor, Nonfiction (General), Self-Help, Social Sciences, Sociology
Number of titles published annually: 12 Print
Total Titles: 3 Print
Distributed by Horizon Books Pte Ltd

Archipelago Press+
26 Bukit Pasoh Rd, Singapore 089840
Tel: 2248044 *Fax:* 2247400
E-mail: edm@pacific.net.sg
Key Personnel
Chairman: Didier Millet
Man Dir: Charles Orwin
Editorial Dir: Timothy Auger
Founded: 1989
Subjects: Architecture & Interior Design, Art, Asian Studies, Cookery, Crafts, Games, Hobbies, History, Natural History, Photography, Travel
ISBN Prefix(es): 981-3018
Imprints: Archipelago Press, Les Editions du Pacifique

Archipelago Press, Les Editions du Pacifique, *imprint of* Archipelago Press

Asiapac Books Pte Ltd+
996 Bendemeer Rd, No 06-08, Singapore 339944
Tel: 63928455 *Fax:* 63926455
E-mail: asiapacbooks@pacific.net.sg
Web Site: www.asiapacbooks.com
Key Personnel
President: Chong Shin-Kian
Publisher: Lim Li-Kok
Publishing Dir: Lydia Lum
Founded: 1982
Membership(s): Singapore Book Publishers Association; specialize in publishing & distribution.
Subjects: Asian Studies, History, Humor, Philosophy
ISBN Prefix(es): 9971-985; 981-3029; 981-3068; 981-229
Number of titles published annually: 50 Print
Total Titles: 400 Print; 4 Audio
Distributed by Asia Books Co Ltd (Thailand); Caves Books Ltd (Taiwan); China Book Import Centre (China); China Books (Australia); China Books & Periodicals Inc (US); China National Publications (China); Eastwind Books & Arts Inc (US); Eastwind Books of Berkeley (US); Eslite Bookstore (Taiwan); Eslite Corporation (Taiwan); Goodwill Trading Co Inc (Philippines); Kinokuniya Bookstores of Taiwan Co Ltd (Taiwan); Kyobo Book Centre Co Ltd (Korea); Marketing Services for Publishers (Philippines); National Bookstore Inc (Philippines); Peace Books Company Ltd (Hong Kong); P T Gramedia Asri Media (Indonesia)
Distributor for China Books & Periodicals Inc (US); Chinese Literature Press (SE Asia); CNPIEC (China); Foreign Languages Press (China); Millbank Books Ltd (UK); National Textbook Co (USA); Oriental Publications (Australia); Penton Overseas, Inc (USA); Sterling Publishing Co, Inc (USA)

Cannon International+
Legal Deposit Section, Singapore Resource Library, National Library Board, Stamford Rd, Singapore 178896
Tel: 6546 7271 *Fax:* 6546 7262
E-mail: legaldep@nlb.gov.sq
Web Site: www.nlb.gov.sg
Key Personnel
Chief Executive, Rights & Permissions: Wu Cheng Tan
Sales: Amirudin Bin Marzuki
Publicity: Pearlyn Peh
Founded: 1975
Subjects: Education, Language Arts, Linguistics, Literature, Literary Criticism, Essays
ISBN Prefix(es): 9971-84; 9971-83; 981-00; 9971-941; 9971-943
Imprints: Kingsway Publishers
Subsidiaries: Kingsway Publisher
Distributor for Robert Gibson (Singapore)

Marshall Cavendish Books, *imprint of* Times Media Pte Ltd

Marshall Cavendish Books
One New Industrial Rd, Singapore 536196
Tel: (065) 2848844 *Fax:* (065) 2854871
E-mail: te@corp.tpl.com.sg
Web Site: www.timesone.com.sg/te
Parent Company: Times Publishing Ltd

Marshall Cavendish Continuity Sets, *imprint of* Times Media Pte Ltd

Celebrity Educational Publishers
Block 474 Tampines St 43, No 01-108, Singapore 520474
Tel: (06) 7857274 *Fax:* (06) 7489108
Key Personnel
Man Dir, Editorial: Christopher S C Tan
Sales: Henry K H Ng
Production, Publicity: Lily Tay
Founded: 1983
Subjects: Language Arts, Linguistics, Science (General)
ISBN Prefix(es): 981-201
Subsidiaries: Willet Children's Books Australia

China Knowledge Press+
2 Tan Quee Lan St, 05 01 Primero Place, Singapore 188091
Tel: (065) 6310 8737 *Fax:* (065) 6310 8738
E-mail: info@chinaknowledge-press.com
Web Site: www.chinaknowledge-press.com
Key Personnel
Contact: Sharon Tang *E-mail:* sharon@chinaknowledge-press.com
Founded: 2000
Provides independent insight, analysis & information to foreign investors to help them explore opportunities & determine values in the China market.
Specializes in translation projects, investment & consultancy services for the China market.
Subjects: Business
ISBN Prefix(es): 981-04
Number of titles published annually: 6 Print
Total Titles: 3 Print; 2 Online
Branch Office(s)
20 Millstream Close, Hitchin, Herts SG4 0D4, United Kingdom, Contact: Ms Weai-Hunt Yap *Tel:* (0146) 442230 *E-mail:* ywhunt@chinaknowledge.com

Chopsons Pte Ltd+
Siglap PO Box 264, Singapore 914503
Tel: 64483634 *Fax:* 64481071
E-mail: chopsons@singnet.com.sg
Key Personnel
Man Dir: Mr N T S Chopra
Founded: 1969
Supplies publications from Southeast Asia to the libraries all over the world - monographs & journals/serials
Also acts as Literary Agent.
Subjects: Asian Studies, Education, Fiction, Government, Political Science, Poetry, Religion - Other, Science (General), Social Sciences, Sociology
ISBN Prefix(es): 9971-68
Distributor for Centre for Advanced Studies; Institute of Southeast Asian Studies; Singapore University Press; Sociology Department, National University of Singapore; World Scientific Publishing

Daiichi Media Pte Ltd
21 Kim Keat Rd, No 04-01, Singapore 328805
Tel: 6849 8666 *Fax:* 6256 5922
E-mail: info@daiichimedia.com.sg; sales@daiichimedia.com.sg
Web Site: www.daiichimedia.com
Key Personnel
Business Development Manager: Edward Poon *E-mail:* edward@daiichimedia.com
Founded: 1993
Subjects: Art, Geography, Geology, Health, Nutrition, History, Mathematics, Science (General)
Total Titles: 15 CD-ROM

Earlybird Books, *imprint of* Federal Publications (S) Pte Ltd

les editions du Pacifique, *imprint of* Times Media Pte Ltd

EPB, *imprint of* SNP Panpac Pacific Publishing Pte Ltd

EPB Publishers Pte Ltd+
Block 162, Bukit Merah Central, 04-3545, Singapore 150162
Tel: 278 0881 *Fax:* 278 2456
E-mail: epb@sbg.com.sg
Telex: EPB RS 56289 *Cable:* EDUPUBS
Key Personnel
General Manager: Au Pui Chuan
Marketing: Kenny Koh
Production: Steven Tan
Founded: 1967
Membership(s): Singapore Book Publishers' Association.
Subjects: Education
ISBN Prefix(es): 9971-0
Parent Company: Singapore National Printers Ltd, 303 Upper Serangoon Rd, Singapore 1334
Bookshop(s): EPB Bedok, North Street 1, 01-423 1646 *Tel:* 4437980; EPB Bukit Batok, 376 Bukit Batok St 31, 01-110 650376 *Tel:* 5624023; EPB Bukit Merah, 161 Bukit Merah Central, 01-3719 150161 *Tel:* 2730092; EPB Clementi Ave 3, 01-297 0512 *Tel:* 7770052; EPB Clementi West, 725 Clementi West St 2, 01-206 0521 *Tel:* 7788923; EPB Jurong West St 51, 01-213 2264 *Tel:* 5624106; 20 Outram Park, 02-187/213 0316 *Tel:* 2202377; EPB Tampine, 138 Tampines St 11, 01-132 1852 *Tel:* 7831939
Warehouse: PSA Multi Storey Complex, Blk 22 Pasir Pahjang Rd, No 06-29 Singapore

SINGAPORE

Europhone Language Institute (Pte) Ltd+
3 Coleman St No 04-33, Singapore 179803
Tel: 3373617; 3363992 *Fax:* 3374506 *Cable:* LANGUAGE SINGAPORE
Key Personnel
Chief Executive: K P Sivam
Founded: 1970
ISBN Prefix(es): 981-3019; 9971-9910; 9971-9912
Branch Office(s)
122 Campbell Complex, Kuala Lumpur, Malaysia

Federal Publications (S) Pte Ltd+
Times Centre, One New Industrial Rd, Singapore 536196
Tel: 62139288 *Fax:* 62844733
E-mail: tpl@tpl.com.sg
Web Site: www.tpl.com.sg
Telex: 35846 *Cable:* FEDPUBS, SINGAPORE
Key Personnel
General Manager: June Oei *E-mail:* juneoei@tpl.com.sg
Publisher & Editorial Manager: Joy Tan
Sales Manager: Marina Ooi
Founded: 1957
Subjects: Education
ISBN Prefix(es): 981-01; 9971-4
Parent Company: Times Publishing Ltd, Times Centre, One New Industrial Rd 536196
Associate Companies: Federal Publications (HK) Ltd, Hong Kong; Federal Publications Sdn Bhd, Malaysia
Imprints: Earlybird Books; Times Academic Press
Distributor for Chambers Harrap Publishers Ltd

FEP International Private Ltd
108 Pasir Panjand Rd, No 05-01A, Singapore 118535
Tel: 4743135 *Fax:* 4752389
Telex: Fep rs 25601 *Cable:* Bookmark
Key Personnel
Publishing Manager, Rights & Permissions: Wong Sek Ohn
Publishing, Science & Math: Dr S Ramalingam
Publishing, Language & Arts: Ms Goh Bee Choo
Founded: 1960
Firm is also a large offset printer specializing in color work.
ISBN Prefix(es): 9971-1
Branch Office(s)
Australia
Egypt (Arab Republic of Egypt)
Ghana
Hong Kong
India
Jamaica
Kenya
Lesotho
Malaysia
Nigeria
Pakistan
Philippines
Swaziland
Trinidad & Tobago
United Kingdom
Zimbabwe

Global Educational Services Pte Ltd+
4 Jalan Mata Ayer, Irving Industrial Bldg, Singapore 759147
Mailing Address: Blk 844 Sims Ave, No 01-706, Singapore 400844
Tel: 7585086 *Fax:* 7586172
E-mail: global@signet.com.sg
Key Personnel
Man Dir: Yoke Yin Ong
Founded: 1986
Joint projects with education institutions in design & publishing of educational materials; exclusive distributor for National University of Singapore on a series of operations research/management software for universities & management programs.
Specialize in Pre-school books design, Education Software, OEM Publishing projects, Operations Research Software.
Subjects: Language Arts, Linguistics, Mathematics, Science (General)
ISBN Prefix(es): 981-3006; 981-3032; 981-3059; 981-3098; 981-4106
Associate Companies: Global Educational Services Sdn Bhd, Malaysia
Subsidiaries: Global Educational Services Inc
Orders to: 222 Fourteenth St, Unit 5, Charlottesville, VA 22903, United States *Fax:* 434-979-0823

Gordon & Breach, *imprint of* International Publishers Distributor (S) Pte Ltd

Graham Brash Pte Ltd
Block 1, Level 2, 45 Kian Teck Dr, Singapore 628859
Mailing Address: Jurong Point Post Office, PO Box 884, Singapore 916430
Tel: 6262 4843 *Fax:* 6262 1519
E-mail: graham_brash@giro.com.sg
Web Site: www.grahambrash.com.sg
Telex: rs 23718 Feenix GB
Key Personnel
Chief Executive Officer: Chuan Campbell
Dir: Helene Campbell
General Manager: Evelyn Lee
Founded: 1926
Subjects: Business, Education, Ethnicity, Government, Political Science, Religion - Other, Self-Help
ISBN Prefix(es): 9971-947; 981-218; 9971-9901; 981-4115
Distributed by Asia Books Co Ltd (Taiwan); Bookazine (Thailand); Booker International (Brunei); Bookmark Inc (Philippines); Caves Books Ltd (Taiwan); China Books (Australia); The Commercial Press (HK) Ltd (Hong Kong); Dymocks Franchise Systems (Singapore); Far East Media (HK) Ltd (Singapore); Gazelle Book Services Ltd (UK); Goodwill Trading Co Inc (Philippines); Heian International Inc (US); Hong Kong Book Centre (Singapore); Hushion House (Canada); Java Books (Indonesia); Kelly & Walsh Ltd (Singapore); National Book Store Inc (Philippines); PageOne The Bookshop (Hong Kong & Philippines); Pansing Distribution Sdn Bhd (Singapore); Peace Book Co Ltd (Singapore); Editions le Printemps Ltd (Mauritius); SAP Group (Indonesia); W H Smith (Singapore); Swindon Book Co (Hong Kong); Times/Federal Publication (Singapore)

Harwood Academic Publishers, *imprint of* International Publishers Distributor (S) Pte Ltd

Hillview Publications Pte Ltd+
Blk 231 Bain St No 04-59, Bras Basah Complex, Singapore 3348996
Tel: 334 8996 *Fax:* 334 8997
Key Personnel
Man Dir: L M Ng
Contact: Ms Ng Lai Mien
Founded: 1984
Membership(s): Spore Book Publishers Association.
Subjects: Accounting, Economics, Education, English as a Second Language, Geography, Geology, Mathematics, Physics, Social Sciences, Sociology
ISBN Prefix(es): 981-202; 981-3052; 981-4013; 981-4041; 981-4073; 981-4099

Insight Guides, *imprint of* APA Production Pte Ltd

Insight Pocket Guides, *imprint of* APA Production Pte Ltd

Insight Topics, *imprint of* APA Production Pte Ltd

Institute of Southeast Asian Studies+
30 Heng Mui Keng Terrace, Pasir Panjang, Singapore 119614
Tel: (65) 6778 0955 *Fax:* (65) 6775 6259
E-mail: pubsunit@iseas.edu.sg
Web Site: bookshop.iseas.edu.sg
Key Personnel
Dir: K Kesavapany *Tel:* 6870 2405
Man Editor: Triena Ong *Tel:* 6870 2448
  E-mail: triena@iseas.edu.sg
Book Promotions & Secretary: Celina Kiong
  E-mail: celina@iseas.edu.sg
Founded: 1968
Scholarly publishers
Conduct post-doctoral research on politics, economics & social issues pertaining to the Asia-Pacific.
Subjects: Asian Studies, Economics, Energy, Environmental Studies, Finance, Foreign Countries, Government, Political Science, Social Sciences, Sociology
ISBN Prefix(es): 9971-902; 981-3035; 981-230
Number of titles published annually: 40 Print; 40 Online; 40 E-Book
Total Titles: 1,000 Print; 1 CD-ROM; 27 Online; 890 E-Book
Imprints: ISEAS
Distributed by Asia Books; James Bennett Library Services; Eurospan; Taylor & Francis Asia Pacific; United Publishers Services Ltd

Intellectual Publishing Co
113 Eunos Ave 3 04-08, Gordon Industrial Bldg, Singapore 409838
Tel: 7466025 *Fax:* 7489108
Telex: RS 55708 Ipccp *Cable:* IPC INTELLE
Key Personnel
Manager: B C Poh
Editorial, Rights & Permissions: B L Poh
Sales, Publicity: B S Poh
Founded: 1971
Subjects: Language Arts, Linguistics
ISBN Prefix(es): 9971-907; 9971-960; 981-200
Associate Companies: Intellectual Publishing Sdn Bhd, 29A 1st floor, Jalan Selimang, Taman Tenaga, Cheras 3 1/2 ms, Kuala Lumpur, Malaysia
Subsidiaries: Intellectual Publishing Co Ltd

International Publishers Distributor (S) Pte Ltd+
Kent Ridge, Singapore 911106
Mailing Address: PO Box 1180, 911106 Singapore
Tel: 741 6933 *Fax:* 741 6922
E-mail: ipdmktg@sg.gbhap.com
Key Personnel
Man Dir: K C Ang *E-mail:* kcang@singnet.com
Founded: 1989
Subjects: Art, STM
Total Titles: 3,000 Print
Parent Company: Gordon & Breach Publishing Group
Imprints: Gordon & Breach; Harwood Academic Publishers
U.S. Office(s): PO Box 20029, River Front Plaza Station, Newark, NJ 07102-0301, United States

IPD, see International Publishers Distributor (S) Pte Ltd

ISEAS, *imprint of* Institute of Southeast Asian Studies

Kingsway Publishers, *imprint of* Cannon International

PUBLISHERS — SINGAPORE

LexisNexis
3 Killiney Rd, No 08-08 Winsland House one, Singapore 239519
Tel: 6733 1380 *Fax:* 6773 1719
Web Site: www.lexisnexis.com.sg
Key Personnel
Man Dir: Michael Evans *Tel:* 6434 3800 *Fax:* 6339 0163
Regional Publishing Dir: Conita Leung *Tel:* 6434 3830
Publishing Manager: Balasakher Shunmugam *Tel:* 6434 3838
Man Editor: Zabrina Hamid *Tel:* 6434 3841; Andrew Yeoh *Tel:* 6434 3842
Senior Editor: Sharon Kaur *Tel:* 6434 3847; Yee See Mun *Tel:* 6434 3809
Regional Sales Dir: Bryan Barrington *Tel:* 6434 3850
Founded: 1982
Subjects: Law
Parent Company: Reed Elsevier
Associate Companies: LexisNexis, 12/F, Hennessy Centre, 500 Hennessy Rd, Causeway Bay, Hong Kong, Business Development Manager: Anisha Sakhrani *Tel:* 2965 1400 *Fax:* 2976 0840 *Web Site:* www.lexisnexis.com.hk; LexisNexis, Vijaya Bldg, 14th Floor, 17, Barakhamba Rd, New Delhi 110001, India, Publishing Manager: Ambika Nair *Tel:* (011) 373 9614 *Fax:* (011) 332 6456 *Web Site:* www.lexisnexis.co.in; Malayan Law Journal Sdn Bhd, Wisma HB, Unit A-5-1, 5th Floor, Megan Phileo Ave, 12 Jalan Yap Kwan Seng, 50450 Kuala Lumpur, Malaysia, Managing Editor, New Business Development: Julie Anne Thomas *Tel:* (03) 2162 2833 *Fax:* (03) 2162 3811 *Web Site:* www.mjl.com.my

Maruzen Asia (Pte) Ltd
391A Orchard Rd No 04-08, Singapore 238872
Tel: 7751577 *Fax:* 7351678
Telex: Mapore rs 26521 *Cable:* Maruzen Singapore
Key Personnel
Dir: Tadao Nireki
Man Dir, Editorial: Yuki Hatori
Marketing: David Tan
Founded: 1689
Subjects: Asian Studies, Medicine, Nursing, Dentistry, Social Sciences, Sociology, Technology
ISBN Prefix(es): 9971-954
Parent Company: Maruzen Co Ltd, Japan
Associate Companies: Maruzen International Co Ltd, NY, United States

Masagung Books Pte Ltd
41 Sixth Ave, Off Bukit Timah Rd, Singapore 276483
Tel: 4683276 *Fax:* 345000
Telex: rs 34500 A; B Gasing *Cable:* Gasing Singapore
Key Personnel
Chairman: Haji Masagung
Manager: Tan Tho Quek
Founded: 1980
Subjects: Foreign Countries
ISBN Prefix(es): 9971-927
Parent Company: CV Haji Masagung, Indonesia

McGallen & Bolden Associates+
Subsidiary of McGallen & Bolden PR Corporation
Maxwell House, Suite F, 20 Maxwell Rd, No 04-01F, Singapore 069113
Tel: 63246588 *Fax:* 63246966
E-mail: sales@mcgallen.com
Web Site: mcgallen.net
Founded: 1991
Subjects: Advertising, Art, Biography, Biological Sciences, Business, Chemistry, Chemical Engineering, Child Care & Development, Communications, Computer Science, Economics, Education, Fiction, Geography, Geology, History, Language Arts, Linguistics, Medicine, Nursing, Dentistry, Philosophy, Psychology, Psychiatry, Religion - Other, Social Sciences, Sociology
Number of titles published annually: 2 Print; 2 CD-ROM; 10 Online; 2 Audio
Total Titles: 10 Print; 6 CD-ROM; 13 Online; 5 Audio
U.S. Office(s): 1455 Tallevast Rd, Suite L1029, Sarasota, FL 34243, United States, Contact: Dr Seamus Phan *E-mail:* sales@mcgallen.com

McGraw-Hill Asia/India Group
Division of The McGraw-Hill Companies
60 Tuas Basin Link, Jurong 638775
Tel: 6863-1580 *Fax:* 6861-9296
Web Site: www.asia-mcgraw-hill.com.sg
Key Personnel
Group VP: Gunawan Hadi
Regional offices in Singapore, Hong Kong, Taiwan, Korea, Malaysia, Thailand, India, Philippines, Japan, China.

Newscom Pte Ltd+
Blk 105, Boon Keng Rd, No 04-17, Singapore 339776
Tel: 6291 9861 *Fax:* 6293 1445
E-mail: circulation@newscom-mail.com
Web Site: www.newscomonline.com
Key Personnel
Chairman: Austin Morais
Circulation Manager: Dinesh Charles *E-mail:* dineshcharles@newscom-mail.com
Founded: 1987
Acts as media representative.
Membership(s): the BPA & ABC (UK).
Subjects: Publishing & Book Trade Reference, Technology
Parent Company: NewSources Investments Ltd, Unit B, 19th floor, 133 Wanchai Rd, Wanchai, Hong Kong
Associate Companies: Newsteam SDN BHD, 87-89 Jalan Ipoh, 3rd floor, 51200 Kuala Lumpur, Malaysia *Tel:* (03) 4044-8599 *Fax:* (03) 4044-9599

Pan Pacific Publications (S) Pte Ltd+
16 Fan Yoong Rd, Singapore 629793
Tel: 2616288 *Fax:* 2616088
E-mail: ppps@pacific.net.sg
Telex: 36496
Key Personnel
Chairman: Steve Seow Kui Lim
General Manager: Catherine Ngien
Man Editor: Margaret Tan
Operations Manager: Brenda Goh
Founded: 1971
Membership(s): Publishers' Association (Singapore).
Subjects: Education
ISBN Prefix(es): 981-208; 9971-63
Parent Company: Pan Pacific Public Co Ltd
Associate Companies: Eastview Publications Sdn Bhd, Malaysia
Subsidiaries: Manhattan Press (S) Pte Ltd; Manhattan Press (HK) Ltd

Panpac, *imprint of* SNP Panpac Pacific Publishing Pte Ltd

Pearson Education Asia Pte Ltd
23/25 First Lok Yang Rd, Jurong 629734
Tel: 3199388 *Fax:* 3199175
E-mail: asia@pearsoned.com.sg
Web Site: www.pearsoned-asia.com
Key Personnel
Publishing Manager, Higher Education: Yew Kee Chiang
Dir, Singapore Education: Andrew Yeo
Founded: 1998
Subjects: Education
ISBN Prefix(es): 981-247; 981-4063; 981-4069; 981-4075; 981-4079; 981-4080; 981-4083; 981-4085; 981-4087; 981-4088; 981-4093; 981-4096; 981-4098; 981-4105; 981-4110; 981-4114; 981-4119
Parent Company: Pearson Education, One Lake St, Upper Saddle River, NJ 07458, United States

PG Medical Books+
6A Napier Rd, Gleneagles Annexe, Block No 02-38 Gleneagles Hospital, Singapore 258500
Tel: 4726339 *Fax:* 4728219
Telex: rs 39967 *Cable:* PG PUB
Key Personnel
Chief Executive, Rights & Permissions: Ms Chiam Soo Lee
Editorial & Production: Mrs Sook-Cheng Lim
International Marketing: Lew Kok Liat
Production: Mary Cho
Founded: 1982
Subjects: Medicine, Nursing, Dentistry
ISBN Prefix(es): 9971-909; 9971-973; 981-3096; 981-206
Bookshop(s): PG Lucky Plaza Medical Books

Printworld Services Pte Ltd
80 Genting Lane Na 09-07, Genting Blk Ruby Industrial Complex, Singapore 349565
Tel: 7442166 *Fax:* 7460845
E-mail: printw@mbox2.singnet.com.sg
Telex: 28990 (print)
Key Personnel
Man Dir: N T Nair
ISBN Prefix(es): 981-3093

Pustaka Nasional Pte Ltd
Joo Chiat Complex, Blk 2 Joo Chiat Rd No 05-1125, Singapore 420002
Tel: 7454321; 7454649 *Fax:* 7452417
E-mail: sales@pustaka.com.sg; mohamed@pustaka.com.sg
Web Site: www.pustaka.com.sg
Telex: rs 26746 Smcc Pn *Cable:* HUDAYA
Key Personnel
Manager: Mr Syed Ali Bin Syed Zain
Founded: 1965
Subjects: Foreign Countries, Religion - Islamic
ISBN Prefix(es): 9971-77
Associate Companies: Pustaka Islamiyah SDN BHD
Distributor for Dewan Bahasa Dan Pustaka (Malaysia)
Showroom(s): Blk 1, Jalan Pasar Baru, No 01-41, Singapore 402001

Reed Elsevier, South East Asia+
51 Changi Business Park, Central 2, No 07-01, The Signature, Singapore 486066
Tel: 6789 9900 *Fax:* 6789 9966
Web Site: www.reed-elsevier.com
Key Personnel
Executive Dir: Paul Beh
Founded: 1986
Membership(s): Singapore Book Publishers Association & Afro Asian Book Council.
Subjects: Biological Sciences, Chemistry, Chemical Engineering, Electronics, Electrical Engineering, Law, Physical Sciences, Physics, Science (General), Social Sciences, Sociology, Technology, Travel
ISBN Prefix(es): 9971-64
Parent Company: Reed Elsevier plc, 25 Victoria St, London SW1H 0EX, United Kingdom

Ridge Books, *imprint of* Singapore University Press Pte Ltd

Select Publishing Pte Ltd+
19 Tanglin Rd No 03-15, Tanglin Shopping Centre, Singapore 247909

SINGAPORE

Tel: 6732 1515 *Fax:* 6736 0855
E-mail: info@selectbooks.com.sg
Web Site: www.selectbooks.com.sg
Key Personnel
Man Dir: Lena U Wen Lim
Founded: 2000
Specialize in books on Southeast Asia.
Membership(s): Publishers Association (Singapore).
Subjects: Alternative, Architecture & Interior Design, Art, Asian Studies, Developing Countries, Drama, Theater, Fiction
ISBN Prefix(es): 981-4022
Total Titles: 30 Print
Distributed by Asia Books (Thailand)

The Shanghai Book Co (Pte) Ltd
Blk 231 Bain St, No 02-73, Bras Basah Complex, Singapore 180231
Tel: 336 0144 *Fax:* 336 0490
E-mail: shanghaibooks@sbg.com.sg
Key Personnel
Man Dir: Mong Hock Chen
  E-mail: chenmonghock@pacific.net.sg
Founded: 1925
ISBN Prefix(es): 9971-906
Associate Companies: Shanghai Book Co (KL) SDN BHD, No 63C Jalan Sultan, 50000 Kuala Lumpur, Malaysia *Tel:* (03) 2384642 *Fax:* (03) 2320700

Shing Lee Group Publishers+
120 Hillview Ave 05-06/07, Kewalran Hillview, Singapore 669594
Tel: 67601388 *Fax:* 67651506
E-mail: kongjing@shinglee.com.sg
Telex: rs 39255 Bai *Cable:* SHINGBOOK
Key Personnel
Marketing Dir: Mr Peh Chin Thye
Executive Dir: Soh-Ngoh Peh
Founded: 1985
Subjects: Cookery
ISBN Prefix(es): 9971-61
Subsidiaries: Booktree; Concorde Publishers Pte Ltd; Dragon Investment PL; Dragon Link Granite PL; First Dragon Development PL; Second Dragon Development PL; Shing Lee Bookstore Pte Ltd; Shing Lee Investment Pte Ltd; Shing Lee Publishers Pte Ltd; Shing Lee Realty Pte Ltd; Super Food Investment International PL; Tech Media; Third Dragon Development PL; Third Dragon Holdings PL; Qingdao Huashan International Country Club

Singapore University Press, *imprint of* Singapore University Press Pte Ltd

Singapore University Press Pte Ltd+
Yusof Ishak House, NUS, 31, Lower Kent Ridge Rd, Singapore 119260
Tel: 67761148; 68742382; 68742472; 68748186
  Fax: 67740652
E-mail: nusbooks@nus.edu.sg
Web Site: www.nus.edu.sg/npu
Telex: rs 51112 NUSBUR *Cable:* SINGPRESS
Key Personnel
Chairman: Prof Lim Seh Chun
Man Dir: Peter Schoppert
  E-mail: peter_schoppert@nus.edu.sg
Founded: 1971
Publishing House of the National University of Singapore.
Specialize in Southeast Asian & Asia-Pacific titles (scholarly & academic).
Membership(s): IASP; SBPA.
Subjects: Asian Studies, Economics, Environmental Studies, Finance, Government, Political Science, History, Language Arts, Linguistics, Law, Literature, Literary Criticism, Essays, Management, Maritime, Psychology, Psychiatry, Science (General), Social Sciences, Sociology, Medicine & Architecture

ISBN Prefix(es): 9971-69
Number of titles published annually: 30 Print
Total Titles: 1 CD-ROM; 1 Online; 100 E-Book
Ultimate Parent Company: National University of Singapore
Imprints: Ridge Books; Singapore University Press
Distributed by APD Singapore Pte Ltd (Southeast Asia only); World Scientific Publishing Co (for co-published titles only)
Foreign Rep(s): Europsan Ltd (Africa, Europe, Middle East); UNIREPS (Australia, New Zealand); United Publishers Services (Japan); University of Hawaii Press (Latin America, North America, South America)

SNP Panpac Pacific Publishing Pte Ltd+
Jurong Bldg, No 04-00 CPF, 21 Jurong East St, 13, Singapore 609646
Tel: 6261 6288 *Fax:* 6261 6088
Web Site: www.snp.com/sg
Key Personnel
General Manager: Rick Ang *E-mail:* rickang@snp.com.sg
Publisher & Sales: Lim Geok Leng
Sales & Marketing Manager: Kelvyn Chong
Customer Service Manager: Agnes Sim Hwee Bin
Man Editor: Zuraidah Jaffar
Subjects: Education
ISBN Prefix(es): 981-3001; 981-208
Associate Companies: SNP Eastview Publications Sdn Bhd, Lot 3, Jalan Saham, 23/3, Kawasan MIEL, Phase 8, 40675 Shah Alam, Selangor Darul Ehsan, Malaysia *Tel:* 5548 1088 *Fax:* 5548 1080 *E-mail:* yhchia@snpo.com.my; SNP Manhattan Press (Hong Kong) Ltd, Eastern Sea Industrial Bldg, 48-56 Tai Lin Pai Rd, Kwai Chung, Hong Kong *Tel:* 2481 1930 *Fax:* 2481 3379 *E-mail:* shumjeff@manhattanpress.com.hk
Imprints: EPB; Panpac
Bookshop(s): SNP Bookstores Pte Limited, Suntec City Mall, 3 Temasek Blvd, B1-025, Singapore 038983 *Tel:* 6 333 5976 *Fax:* 6 333 9236 *E-mail:* ashleyb@snp.com.sg

Stamford College Publishers/Authors-Publishers+
Legal Deposit Section, Singapore Resource LIbrary, National Library Board, Stamford Rd, Singapore 178896
Tel: 3323639 *Fax:* 3323273
E-mail: legaldep@nlb.gov.sq.hdtsdnl@technet.sq
Key Personnel
Man Dir, Publicity: L P Nicol
Editorial: L Thomas
Sales: J Dennis
Production: Mr Arangasamy
Founded: 1970
Subjects: Education
ISBN Prefix(es): 9971-83
Branch Office(s)
Stamford Executive Bookshop, Petaling Jaya, Malaysia

Success Publications Pte Ltd+
Blk 3013 Bedok Industrial Park E, No 04-2102, Bedok North Av 4, Singapore 489979
Tel: 4432003; 4430512 *Fax:* 4453156
E-mail: succpub@singnet.com.sg
Distributing, importing, exporting & publishing of educational books & materials; reading program; assessment books; Chinese.
Subjects: Education, English as a Second Language, Mathematics, Science (General)
ISBN Prefix(es): 981-216
Subsidiaries: Steven Tuition Centre
Orders to: Rest of the World, Bowker-Saur Ltd, Windsor Court, E Grinstead House, E Grinstead, West Sussex RH19 1XA, United Kingdom *Tel:* (01342) 326972 *Fax:* (01342) 336198

BOOK

Taylor & Francis Asia Pacific+
Member of Taylor & Francis Group
240 Macpherson Rd, No 08-01 Pines Industrial Bldg, Singapore 348574
Tel: 67415166 *Fax:* 67429356
E-mail: info@tandf.com.sg
Web Site: www.tandf.co.uk
Key Personnel
Man Dir: Barry D Clarke *E-mail:* barry.clarke@tandf.com.sg
Founded: 1998
Subjects: Architecture & Interior Design, Art, Asian Studies, Biological Sciences, Business, Child Care & Development, Criminology, Economics, Education, Engineering (General), Environmental Studies, Ethnicity, Government, Political Science, History, Library & Information Sciences, Management, Medicine, Nursing, Dentistry, Philosophy, Physical Sciences, Psychology, Psychiatry, Religion - Other, Science (General), Social Sciences, Sociology, Specialize in book distribution, publisher services, confrences & author support
Distributor for American Psychological Association (USA); Aslib (UK); Brookings Institution (USA); Earthscan (UK); Edinburgh University Press (UK); Edward Elgar (UK); Lawrence Erlbaum & Associates (USA); Free Press (USA); David Fulton (UK); Guilford Press (USA); Idea Group (UK); Information Age (USA); Institute International Economics (USA); Library Association (UK); Pluto Press (UK); Transaction Publishers (USA); Westview Press (USA); World Bank (USA)

Tech Publications Pte Ltd+
No B1-39 Sim Lim Tower, 10 Jalan Besar, Singapore 0820
Tel: 2763611 *Fax:* 2763622
E-mail: techpub@pacific.net.sg
Telex: 7449835
Key Personnel
President: Gyan Jain
Vice President & Marketing Manager: Rajiv Jain
Founded: 1984
Subjects: Computer Science, Electronics, Electrical Engineering
ISBN Prefix(es): 981-214; 981-3005; 981-3091
Associate Companies: Micro Tech Publications, Dubai, United Arab Emirates
Bookshop(s): 04-35 Funan Centre 179097
Warehouse: 211 Henderson Rd, Henderson Bldg No 02-11 159552

Tecman, *imprint of* Tecman Bible House

Tecman Bible House+
No 04-47 Bras Basah Complex, 231 Bain St, Singapore 180231
Tel: 6338-6764 *Fax:* 6338-8236
E-mail: tecman@tecman.com.sg
Web Site: www.tecman.com.sg
Key Personnel
President: Jane Tan
Founded: 1971
Import, export, retail & wholesale of Christian publications & products.
Subjects: Biblical Studies, Religion - Protestant, Theology
Imprints: Tecman

Times Academic Press, *imprint of* Federal Publications (S) Pte Ltd

Times Books International, *imprint of* Times Media Pte Ltd

Times Editions, *imprint of* Times Media Pte Ltd

Times Media Pte Ltd+
Times Centre, One New Industrial Rd, Singapore 536196
Tel: 62848844 *Fax:* 62771186
E-mail: te@corp.tpl.com.sg
Web Site: www.timesone.com.sg/te
Telex: RS25713 *Cable:* TIMES
Key Personnel
Deputy Publisher: David Yip *E-mail:* davidyip@tpl.com.sg
International Sales & Rights: Angeline Lim *Tel:* 62139404 *E-mail:* angelinelim@tpl.com.sg
Founded: 1979
Subjects: Art, Cookery, Gardening, Plants, Government, Political Science, Health, Nutrition, Literature, Literary Criticism, Essays, Travel, Culture, Heritage, International Interests, Parenting
ISBN Prefix(es): 981-204; 2-85700; 981-232
Parent Company: Times Publishing Group, One New Industrial Rd 536196
Associate Companies: Marshall Cavendish Books Ltd
Imprints: Marshall Cavendish Books; Marshall Cavendish Continuity Sets; les editions du Pacifique; Times Books International; Times Editions
Branch Office(s)
Bangunan Times Publishing, Lot 46, Subang Industrial Park, Bahu riga, 60000 Shah Alam, Malaysia, Contact: Christine Chong *Fax:* (03) 7354620
Times Books International, Malaysia

John Wiley & Sons (Asia) Pte Ltd+
2 Clementi Loop, No 02-01, Singapore 129809
Tel: 64632400 *Fax:* 64634605; 64634604
E-mail: enquiry@wiley.com.sg
Web Site: www.wiley.co.uk
Key Personnel
Vice President, Asia: Steven Miron
Publisher: Nick Wallwork
Foreign Rights Executive: Ira Tan
Number of titles published annually: 20 Print
Parent Company: John Wiley & Sons Inc, 111 River St, Hoboken, NJ 07030, United States
Associate Companies: John Wiley & Sons, Ltd, United Kingdom; Jacaranda Wiley, Ltd, Australia

World Scientific Publishing Co Pte Ltd+
5 Toh Tuck Link, Singapore 596224
Tel: 6467-5775 *Fax:* 6467-7667
E-mail: wspc@wspc.com.sg
Web Site: www.worldscientific.com
Key Personnel
Man Dir: Doreen Liu
Dir & Publisher: Mrs Sook Cheng Lim
Assistant Dir: Miss G K Tan
Manager, Sales: Ms Siew Lan Tan
Founded: 1980
Membership(s): STM; Pub Assoc (Spore).
Subjects: Asian Studies, Biological Sciences, Chemistry, Chemical Engineering, Civil Engineering, Computer Science, Economics, Electronics, Electrical Engineering, Engineering (General), Environmental Studies, Finance, Management, Mathematics, Mechanical Engineering, Medicine, Nursing, Dentistry, Physics, Technology
ISBN Prefix(es): 1-86094; 981-02; 9971-950; 9971-966; 9971-978; 981-238; 981-256
Number of titles published annually: 400 Print
Total Titles: 6,000 Print
Subsidiaries: Imperial College Press
Branch Office(s)
World Scientific Publishing (HK) Co Ltd, PO Box 72482, Kowloon Central Post Office, Kowloon, Hong Kong *Tel:* 2771-8791 *Fax:* 2771-8155 *E-mail:* wsped@pacific.net.hk
No 16 SW Boag Rd, T Nagar, Chennai 600 017, India *Tel:* (044) 520 71164 *E-mail:* sales-ind@wspc.com
5F-6, No 88, Sec 3, Hsin-Sheng S Rd, Taipei, Taiwan, Province of China *Tel:* (02) 2369-1366 *Fax:* (02) 2369-0460 *E-mail:* wsptw@ms13.hinet.net
World Scientific Publishing Co Ltd, 57 Shelton St, London WC2H 9HE, United Kingdom *Tel:* (020) 7836-0888 *Fax:* (020) 7836-2020 *E-mail:* sales@wspc.co.uk
U.S. Office(s): World Scientific Publishing Co Inc, 1060 Main St, Suite 202, River Edge, NJ 07661, United States *Tel:* 201-487-9655 *Fax:* 201-487-9656 *E-mail:* wspc@wspc.com
Web Site: www.worldscientific.com
Distributor for Imperial College Press (UK); The National Academy Press, USA (Asia-Pacific except Japan, Australia, New Zealand)

Slovakia

General Information

Capital: Bratislava
Language: Slovak
Religion: Predominantly Roman Catholic, some Lutheran
Population: 5.3 million
Currency: 100 Halerue = 1 koruna
Export/Import Information: There are plans to exabilish custom-free zones to stimulate foreign investment. 6% VAT on books.
Copyright: UCC, Berne (see Copyright Conventions, pg xi)

ARCHA sro Vydavatel'stro+
Staromestska 6, 813 36 Bratislava
Tel: (07) 5315586; (07) 54415609 *Fax:* (07) 5441586
E-mail: archa@internet.sk
Key Personnel
Editor-in-Chief: Marian Sapak
International Rights: Petra Bombikova
Subjects: Government, Political Science, History, Law, Philosophy, Science (General), Social Sciences, Sociology
ISBN Prefix(es): 80-7115

AV Studio Reklamno-vydavatel'ska agentura
Lykovcova 7, 841 04 Bratislava
Tel: (07) 726297 *Fax:* (07) 726297
Founded: 1993
Subjects: Health, Nutrition, Religion - Other
ISBN Prefix(es): 80-88779

Danubiaprint
Fucikova 22, 81580 Bratislava
Tel: (07) 309167 *Fax:* (07) 362613
Key Personnel
Dir: Viliam Kacer
Firm is the publishing house of the Central Committee of the Communist Party of Slovakia.
Subjects: Biography, Economics, Fiction, Government, Political Science, History, Law, Philosophy, Social Sciences, Sociology
ISBN Prefix(es): 80-218
Book Club(s): CKP (Clenska kniznica Pravdy)

Dom Techniky Zvazu Slovenskych Vedeckotechnickych Spolocnosti Ltd
Skultetyho 1, 83227 Bratislava
Tel: (02) 5022 4421 *Fax:* (02) 5542 4983
E-mail: zsvts@rainside.sk
Key Personnel
Dir: Dipl Ing Lubomir Mravec
Manager: Dipl Ing Anna Kamasova
Founded: 1974
Subjects: Business, Finance, Management, Marketing, Mechanical Engineering
ISBN Prefix(es): 80-230

Egmont Neografia spol sro+
Nevadzova 8, 827 99 Bratislava 27
Tel: (07) 02 4333 8064; (07) 02 4333 3933; (07) 295966 *Fax:* (07) 238755
E-mail: egmont@netlab.sk
Key Personnel
Man Dir: Stanislar Valko
Founded: 1990
Subjects: Humor
ISBN Prefix(es): 80-7134
Parent Company: Egmont Holding International, Denmark

Vydavatelstvo Junior sro Slovart Print+
Pekna cesta c 6, 83403 Bratislava
Tel: (02) 44872378; (02) 44872379 *Fax:* (02) 44872133
E-mail: obchod@junior.sk
Web Site: www.junior.sk
Key Personnel
Commercial Dir: Marta Horakova
Contact: Jaroslav Pijak *E-mail:* pijak@junior.sk
Founded: 1994
ISBN Prefix(es): 80-7146
Associate Companies: Nakladatelstvi Junior, Prague, Czech Republic
Distributor for Slowakei

Kalligram spol sro (Kalligram Ltd)+
Staromestska 6/d, 811 03 Bratislava
Tel: (02) 54415028 *Fax:* (02) 54410809
Web Site: www.kalligram.sk
Key Personnel
Dir: Laszlo Szigeti *E-mail:* szig@kalligram.sk
Contact: Attila Agoston *E-mail:* kiado@kalligram.sk
Founded: 1991
Subjects: Art, Fiction, Philosophy, Social Sciences, Sociology, Politics
ISBN Prefix(es): 80-7149
Number of titles published annually: 70 Print
Total Titles: 600 Print
Branch Office(s)
Pesti Kalligram Kft, Tuzolto utca 8, fe 2, 1094 Budapest, Hungary *Tel:* (01) 2157954 *Fax:* (01) 2166875 *E-mail:* kalligram@interware.hu
Orders to: Kalligram Publishers

Luc vydavatelske druzstvo+
Kozicova 2, 841 10 Bratislava
Mailing Address: PO Box 224, 811 06 Bratislava
Tel: (07) 65730331 *Fax:* (07) 65730331
Key Personnel
International Rights: Anna Kolkova
Founded: 1989
Membership(s): Association of Slovak Catholic Publishers, Publishers of Catholic Libraries of Europe.
Subjects: Biography, Education, History, Philosophy, Poetry, Religion - Catholic, Theology
ISBN Prefix(es): 80-7114

Mlade leta Spd sro
Sasinkova 5, 815 19 Bratislava 1
Tel: (07) 55 56 45 12; (07) 55 56 62 82 *Fax:* (07) 21 57 14
Web Site: www.mlade-leta.sk
Telex: 093421
Key Personnel
Man Dir: Oldrich Polak
Editorial: Magda Baloghova
Sales Dir: Jana Misikova
Production: Jozef Sipos
Publicity: Eva Hornisova
Founded: 1950
Young Miss: Slovak Publishing House of Children's Literature.
ISBN Prefix(es): 80-06
Distributed by Distribucna agentura Valko (Bratislava & Western Slovakia); Knizna distribucia Pezolt (Eastern Slovakia); Knizne Cen-

trum spol sro (Central Slovakia); Marcan spol sro (Bratislava & Western Slovakia); Modul spol sro (Bratislava & Western Slovakia); Sabol Marek - Marsab (Eastern Slovakia); Slovart - Store spol sro (Bratislava & Western Slovakia)
Bookshop(s): Detska Kniha, Hurbanovo nam 7, Bratislava (The Child's Book); Klincova 35, Bratislava, Slovenia *Tel:* (07) 55 56 65 08
Book Club(s): Club of Young Readers

Vydavatelstvo Obzor+
Spitalska 35, 81585 Bratislava
Tel: (07) 368395; (07) 55695; (07) 57015 *Fax:* (07) 368395 *Cable:* VYDAVATELSTVO OBZOR BRATISLAVA
Key Personnel
Acting Dir: Ing Richard Dame
Founded: 1953
Horizon: Slovak Book & Periodical Publishing House for People's Education.
Subjects: Archaeology, Art, Law, Literature, Literary Criticism, Essays, Mysteries, Parapsychology
ISBN Prefix(es): 80-215

Opus Records & Publishing House+
Mlynske Nivy 73, 827 99 Bratislava
Tel: (02) 58247560 *Fax:* (02) 53412447
E-mail: opus@ba.profinet.sk
Key Personnel
Man Dir: Prof Milos Jurkovic
Commercial Dir: Emilia Suta
Editorial: Slavka Dzadikova
Publicity: Dr Alena Jarosova
Founded: 1971
Membership(s): IFPI & Sound Carriers.
Subjects: Music, Dance
ISBN Prefix(es): 80-7093
Parent Company: Bonton Slovagcia
Associate Companies: Music-Video-Express

Vydavatel'stvo Osveta (Verlag Osveta)+
Osloboditelov 21, 036 01 Martin
Tel: (043) 4134 121 *Fax:* (0842) 35036
Key Personnel
Proprietor: Martin Farkas
Founded: 1953
Subjects: Education, Fiction, Medicine, Nursing, Dentistry, Nonfiction (General), Science (General), Travel
ISBN Prefix(es): 80-217; 80-88824; 80-967377
Bookshop(s): Spitalska 18, 811 08 Bratislava; Knihkupcetvi Klaty Klas, Osveta Exact Service, Lannova 6, 370 01 Ceske Budejovice, Czech Republic; M R Stefanika, 075 01 Trebisov
Warehouse: Expedicny Sklad Vydavatelstva Osveta, 038 41 Kost'any nad Turcom

Vydavatel'stvo SFVU Pallas
Trnavska 112, 82633 Bratislava
Mailing Address: PO Box 224, 82633 Bratislava
Tel: (07) 296627 *Fax:* (07) 294229; (07) 292820
Publishing House of the Slovak Fund of Fine Arts.
Subjects: Art, Biography, Literature, Literary Criticism, Essays
ISBN Prefix(es): 80-7095

Polygraf Print sro
Capajevova 44, 08001 Presov
Tel: (051) 44 13 280 *Fax:* (051) 77 13 241; (051) 77 13 270
E-mail: polygrafprint@polygrafprint.sk

Vydavatepstvo Praca spol sro+
Stefanikova 19, 812 71 Bratislava 1
Tel: (02) 5249 2890 *Fax:* (07) 392840; (07) 392853
Key Personnel
Dir: Miroslav Bernath
Founded: 1946
Praca Publishing House.
Subjects: Cookery, Crafts, Games, Hobbies, Finance, Law, Outdoor Recreation, Romance
ISBN Prefix(es): 80-7094
Divisions: Nakladatelstvo
Bookshop(s): Knizna predajna Praca, 81271 Bratislava, nam SNP 20

Priroda Publishing+
Kocelova 17, 82108 Bratislava
Tel: (02) 5556 4672 *Fax:* (02) 5556 4669
E-mail: priroda@priroda.sk
Web Site: www.priroda.sk
Key Personnel
Dir: Emilia Jankovitsova
Editorial: Jela Fellegiova
Founded: 1949
Publishing House.
Subjects: Business, Gardening, Plants, House & Home, How-to, Management, Outdoor Recreation, Self-Help, Travel, Veterinary Science, Nature
ISBN Prefix(es): 80-07
Number of titles published annually: 100 Print
Total Titles: 8,000 Print
Distributed by Aktis (Czech Republic); EUROMEDIA; Bertlesmann Group in Czech Republic
Warehouse: Plynarenska 6, 82109 Bratislava

Serafin+
Frantiskanska 2, 811 01 Bratislava
Tel: (02) 54434359 *Fax:* (02) 54434342
E-mail: vydserafin@gmx.net
Web Site: www.serafin.sk
Key Personnel
Contact: Adriana Alexyova; P Stefan Bankovic
Founded: 1990
Membership(s): Zdruzenie katolickych vydavatelstiev Slovenska.
Subjects: Foreign Countries, Poetry, Religion - Catholic, Medicine
ISBN Prefix(es): 80-88944
Number of titles published annually: 15 Print
Total Titles: 125 Print
Parent Company: Zdruzenie katolickych vydavatelstiev Slovenska
Bookshop(s): Frantisek

Slo Viet
Palarikova 21, 811 04 Bratislava
Tel: (07) 52494886
Founded: 1990
Membership(s): SSPOL & SSPUL.
Subjects: Asian Studies, Ethnicity, History, Language Arts, Linguistics, Poetry
ISBN Prefix(es): 80-900500
Number of titles published annually: 3 Print

Slovansky Tatran, Vydavatel'stro spoi sro
Michalska 9, 81582 Bratislava
Tel: (02) 54435849 *Fax:* (02) 54435777
Key Personnel
Man Dir: Eva Mladekova
Founded: 1947
Slovak Publishing House of Belles Lettres
Rights & Permissions, LITA, Slovak Literary Agency, Partizanska 21, 811 03 Bratislava.
Subjects: Art, Drama, Theater, Literature, Literary Criticism, Essays, Nonfiction (General), Poetry, Regional Interests
ISBN Prefix(es): 80-222

Slovenska Narodna Kniznica, Martin (Slovak National Library, Martin)+
Mudronova 26, 03652 Martin
Tel: (0842) 31861 *Fax:* (0842) 32993
E-mail: vms@esix.matica.sk
Key Personnel
Publicity Manager: Tomas Winkler
Founded: 1863
Subjects: Biography, Ethnicity
ISBN Prefix(es): 80-7090

Slovenske pedagogicke nakladateistvo (Slovak Pedagogical Publishing House)+
Sasinkova 5, 81560 Bratislava
Tel: (07) 55423892 *Fax:* (07) 55571894
E-mail: spn@spn.sk *Cable:* SPN BRATISLAVA
Key Personnel
General Dir: Maria Sedlakova
Sales Manager: Eva Sarandiova *Tel:* (07) 55563229
Founded: 1920
Slovak Publishing House for Educational Literature.
Subjects: Education, English as a Second Language, Ethnicity, History, Language Arts, Linguistics, Literature, Literary Criticism, Essays, Mathematics, Music, Dance, Physics, Psychology, Psychiatry, Social Sciences, Sociology, Sports, Athletics, Travel, Specializes in languages
ISBN Prefix(es): 80-08
Number of titles published annually: 160 Print; 1 CD-ROM
Total Titles: 1 CD-ROM
Parent Company: Media Trade sro, Krizna 28, Bratislava 1 81107
Bookshop(s): Krizna 47, Wagnerova, Contact: Andrej Martinka *Tel:* (02) 55425504
Orders to: Media Trade sro - SPN, Sasinkova 5, Bratislava *Tel:* (02) 55563229 *E-mail:* spn@spn.sk

Vydavatel'stvo Slovenskej akademie vied, see VEDA (Vydavatel'stvo Slovenskej akademie vied)

Slovensky Spisovatel Ltd as+
Andreja Plavku 12, 813 67 Bratislava
Tel: (02) 5249 9734 *Fax:* (02) 5249 9736
Key Personnel
Dir: Martin Chovanec *E-mail:* martin.ch@slovspis.sk
Editor-in-Chief: Stefan Strazay
Founded: 1951
Subjects: Fiction, Literature, Literary Criticism, Essays, Poetry
ISBN Prefix(es): 80-220
Bookshop(s): Laurinska 2, 81367 Bratislava
Book Club(s): KMP (Kruh milovnikov poezie); SPKK (Spolocnost' priatel'ov krasnych knih)
Warehouse: Vajnorska 128, 83292 Bratislava

Smena Publishing House
Prazska 11, 81284 Bratislava
Tel: (07) 491455; (07) 497171
Telex: 09341 *Cable:* BRATISLAVA SMENA
Key Personnel
Dir: Jaroslav Sisolak
Editor-in-Chief: Marie Caganova
Founded: 1949
Publishing House of Slovak.
Subjects: Biography, Crafts, Games, Hobbies, Fiction, History, Philosophy, Poetry, Psychology, Psychiatry, Social Sciences, Sociology
ISBN Prefix(es): 80-85686
Book Club(s): Maj

Sofa+
Vazskall, 82107 Bratislava 211
Tel: (02) 55422508 *Fax:* (02) 55422508
E-mail: sofa@ba.sknet.sk
Founded: 1992
Subjects: Child Care & Development, Economics, Health, Nutrition, Human Relations, Library & Information Sciences, Philosophy, Physics, Psychology, Psychiatry, Publishing & Book Trade Reference, Social Sciences, Sociology
ISBN Prefix(es): 80-85752

Sport Publishing House Ltd+
Vajnorska ulica 100/A, 83258 Bratislava
Tel: (07) 49249618 *Fax:* (07) 49249586
Key Personnel
Man Dir: Ludovit Svenk
Founded: 1957
Founded as publishing house of Slovak Central Committee of Czechoslovak Physical Culture Organization, 1992 transformed to Sport Publishing House Ltd.
Specializes in sports, travel & Western fiction.
Subjects: Fiction, Science Fiction, Fantasy, Sports, Athletics, Travel, Western Fiction
ISBN Prefix(es): 80-7096
Number of titles published annually: 6 Print
Total Titles: 2 Print

Technicka Univerzita
T G Masaryka 2117/24, 960 53 Zvolen
Tel: (045) 5206111 *Fax:* (0855) 20027
Telex: 72267 VSLDC
Founded: 1997
Subjects: Agriculture, Animals, Pets, Architecture & Interior Design, Economics, Education, Environmental Studies, Science (General), Technology
ISBN Prefix(es): 80-228

Ustav informacii a prognoz skolstva mladeze a telovychovy+
Stare Grunty 52, 842 44 Bratislava
Tel: (02) 6542 6521 *Fax:* (02) 6542 6521
E-mail: hrab@uip.sanet.sk
Founded: 1975
Subjects: Career Development, Computer Science, Education, Labor, Industrial Relations, Library & Information Sciences, Management, Microcomputers, Outdoor Recreation, Psychology, Psychiatry, Social Sciences, Sociology
ISBN Prefix(es): 80-7098
Associate Companies: Slovenska pedagogicka kniznica

VEDA (Vydavatel'stvo Slovenskej akademie vied)
Bradacova 7, 852 86 Bratislava
Tel: (02) 63831172 *Fax:* (02) 63835391; (02) 63832254
Web Site: www.veda-sav.sk
Telex: 93464 UKSAV *Cable:* VEDA BRATISLAVA
Key Personnel
Dir: Dr Milan Brnak
Editor-in-Chief: Emil Borcin
Sales & Marketing Manager: Anna Markova
  E-mail: markova@centrum.sk
Founded: 1953
Publishing House of the Slovak Academy of Sciences.
Subjects: Archaeology, Earth Sciences, History, Language Arts, Linguistics, Literature, Literary Criticism, Essays, Nonfiction (General), Philosophy, Psychology, Psychiatry, Regional Interests, Social Sciences, Sociology, Technology
ISBN Prefix(es): 80-224
Bookshop(s): Knihkupectvo VEDY, Stefanikova 3, 81106 Bratislava *Tel:* (02) 5249 8095

Vysoka Vojenska Skola Letecka
Rampova 7, 041 21 Kosice
Mailing Address: PO Box 26, 041 21 Kosice
Tel: (095) 6512183; (095) 6333851 *Fax:* (095) 333851
Key Personnel
Contact: Frantisek Olejnik
ISBN Prefix(es): 80-7166

Vydavatelstvo Wist sro+
Kozmonautov 35, 03601 Martin
Tel: (0842) 4289652 *Fax:* (0842) 4289652
E-mail: wist@enelux.sk
Key Personnel
President: Robert Schwandner
Editor-in-Chief: Tomasz Trancygier
  E-mail: ttran@enelux.sk
International Rights: Prava I Prevodi
Founded: 1993
Subjects: Fiction, Romance
ISBN Prefix(es): 80-8049
Number of titles published annually: 50 Print

Zilinska Univerzita
Moyzesova 20, 010 26 Zilina
Tel: (089) 625919; (089) 621247 *Fax:* (089) 620023
Web Site: www.utc.sk
Key Personnel
Manager: Miroslav Kopecky
Dir: Milan Dado; Pavol Kostial; Frantisek Schlosser
Founded: 1953
ISBN Prefix(es): 80-7100

ZSVTS, see Dom Techniky Zvazu Slovenskych Vedeckotechnickych Spolocnosti Ltd

Slovenia

General Information

Capital: Ljubljana
Language: Slovenian and Serbo-Croat
Religion: Predominantly Roman Catholic
Population: 2 million
Bank Hours: 0730-1800 Monday-Friday and 0730-1200 Saturday
Shop Hours: 0800-1900 Monday-Friday; 0800-1300 Saturday, some open Saturday afternoon
Currency: Tolar
Export/Import Information: 3% VAT on books.
Copyright: UCC, Berne (see Copyright Conventions, pg xi)

Cankarjeva Zalozba+
Kopitarjeva ul 2, 1512 Ljubljana
Tel: (01) 4323 144 *Fax:* (01) 2318 782
E-mail: knjigarna.oxford@cankarjeva-z.si
Web Site: www.cankarjeva-z.si
Telex: 31821 Yu Cankar
Key Personnel
Man Dir: Dr Martin Znidersic
Editor: Janez Stanic
Rights & Permissions: Dagmar Dolinar
Subjects: Biography, Cookery, Education, Fiction, History, How-to, Law, Philosophy, Poetry, Psychology, Psychiatry, Social Sciences, Sociology
ISBN Prefix(es): 86-361

Casopisni zavod Uradni list Republike Slovenije
Slovenska cesta 9, 1000 Ljubljana
Tel: (01) 1250 294 *Fax:* (01) 1251 418
E-mail: info@uradni-list.si
Web Site: www.uradni-list.si
Key Personnel
Chief Executive: Polutnik Marko
Editorial: Leskovic Alenka; Kurt Marija
Founded: 1946
Subjects: Law, Legislation
ISBN Prefix(es): 86-7085; 961-204

East West Operation (EWO) Ltd+
Cankarjeva 1, 1000 Ljubljana
Tel: (01) 4256 272 *Fax:* (01) 2517 348
E-mail: ewo-arkadna@siol.net
Key Personnel
General Manager: Slavko Pregl
Foreign Rights: Irene Motaln-Sezun
Founded: 1991
Subjects: Art, Economics, Gardening, Plants, Health, Nutrition, History, Wine & Spirits
ISBN Prefix(es): 961-207
Subsidiaries: EWO Buechhandel GmbH

Franc-Franc podjetje za promocijo kulture Murska Sobota d o o+
Stefana Kovaca 30, 9000 Murska Sobota
Mailing Address: PP 27, 9000 Murska Sobota
Tel: (06) 922501 *Fax:* (06) 922501
E-mail: franc.franc@siol.net
Key Personnel
Owner, Dir & International Rights: Franci Just
Owner: Feri Lainscek
Founded: 1992
Membership(s): Verbandes der Veleger und Buchhaendler Sloweniens. Specialize in Literature.
Subjects: Fiction, Journalism, Language Arts, Linguistics, Literature, Literary Criticism, Essays, Poetry, Regional Interests
ISBN Prefix(es): 961-219

Mladinska Knjiga International+
Slovenska cesta 29, 1000 Ljubljana
Tel: (01) 2413 284; (01) 2413 288 *Fax:* (01) 4252 294
E-mail: intsales@mkz-lj.si
Web Site: www.emka.si
Key Personnel
Man Dir: Majda Sikosek
Editor: Vasja Krasevec
Subjects: Art, Astrology, Occult, Biblical Studies, Biography, Biological Sciences, Chemistry, Chemical Engineering, Child Care & Development, Cookery, Crafts, Games, Hobbies, Drama, Theater, Education, Fiction, Gardening, Plants, Health, Nutrition, History, House & Home, How-to, Language Arts, Linguistics, Literature, Literary Criticism, Essays, Mathematics, Military Science, Mysteries, Nonfiction (General), Physics, Poetry, Psychology, Psychiatry, Regional Interests, Romance, Science (General), Science Fiction, Fantasy, Self-Help, Travel, Women's Studies
ISBN Prefix(es): 86-11

Moderna galerija Ljubljana/Museum of Modern Art+
Tomsiceva 14, 1000 Ljubljana
Tel: (01) 2416 800 *Fax:* (01) 2514 120
E-mail: info@mg-li.si
Web Site: www.mg-lj.si
Key Personnel
Dir: Ms Zdenka Badovinac
Founded: 1948
Subjects: Art
Total Titles: 5 Print

Pomurska zalozba
Lendavska 1, 9000 Murska Sobota
Tel: (069) 32-420 *Fax:* (069) 31-086
Telex: 35-229 Yu Zgpmsb
Key Personnel
Dir: Ludvik Socic
Editor-in-Chief: Joze Hradil
Subjects: Fiction, Literature, Literary Criticism, Essays, Poetry
ISBN Prefix(es): 86-7195; 86-80755
Bookshop(s): Dobra knjiga, Titova c, 69000 Murska Sobota; Knjigarna Gornja Radgona 69250, Serbia and Montenegro; Knjigarna Lendava 69220, Serbia and Montenegro; Knjigarna Ljutomer 69240, Serbia and Montenegro

Slovenska matica
Kongresni trg 8, 1001 Ljubljana
Tel: (01) 2514 200; (01) 2514 227; (01) 4263 190 *Fax:* (01) 2514 200
Key Personnel
President: Dr Joza Mahnic
Vice President: Peter Vodopivec
Publisher: Drago Jancar

Founded: 1864
Subjects: Literature, Literary Criticism, Essays, Philosophy
ISBN Prefix(es): 86-80933; 961-213

Univerza v Ljubljani Ekonomska Fakulteta+
Kardeljeva pl 17, 1000 Ljubljana
Tel: (061) 5892-400 *Fax:* (061) 5892-698
E-mail: joze.cibej@uni-lj.si
Web Site: www.ef.uni-lj.si
Key Personnel
International Rights: Dr Lea Bregar
Founded: 1946
Subjects: Accounting, Advertising, Business, Economics, Finance, Government, Political Science, Language Arts, Linguistics, Law, Management, Marketing, Mathematics, Securities
ISBN Prefix(es): 86-398; 961-6081; 961-6273

Zalozba Mihelac d o o+
Kersnikova 4, 1000 Ljubljana
Tel: (01) 4344 431 *Fax:* (01) 4344 431
Key Personnel
Contact: Mihelac Spela
Founded: 1990
Subjects: Art, Astrology, Occult, Astronomy, Biblical Studies, Child Care & Development, Communications, Drama, Theater, English as a Second Language, Fiction, Foreign Countries, Government, Political Science, History, Journalism, Language Arts, Linguistics, Literature, Literary Criticism, Essays, Medicine, Nursing, Dentistry, Parapsychology, Philosophy, Photography, Psychology, Psychiatry, Regional Interests, Religion - Buddhist, Religion - Catholic, Self-Help, Social Sciences, Sociology, Theology, Travel
ISBN Prefix(es): 961-6271
Showroom(s): Dunajska 23, 1000 Ljubljana
Bookshop(s): Dunajska 23, 1000 Ljubljana
Book Club(s): MOLJ
Orders to: Dunajska 23, 1000 Ljubljana

Zalozba Obzorja d d Maribor+
Partizanska 3-5, 2000 Maribor
Tel: (02) 2283116 *Fax:* (02) 2523213
E-mail: pivec@zalozba-obzorja.si
Web Site: www.zalozba-obzorja.si
Key Personnel
Chief Executive: Pavla Pece
Editor: Bojan Osterc
Founded: 1950
Subjects: Animals, Pets, Anthropology, Biography, Biological Sciences, Business, Chemistry, Chemical Engineering, Child Care & Development, Cookery, Crafts, Games, Hobbies, Criminology, Drama, Theater, Earth Sciences, Economics, Education, English as a Second Language, Environmental Studies, Fiction, Gardening, Plants, Gay & Lesbian, Health, Nutrition, History, Journalism, Language Arts, Law, Literature, Literary Criticism, Essays, Management, Marketing, Mathematics, Medicine, Nursing, Dentistry, Music, Dance, Nonfiction (General), Philosophy, Photography, Physics, Poetry, Psychology, Psychiatry, Regional Interests, Religion - Other, Science (General), Self-Help, Social Sciences, Sociology, Travel
ISBN Prefix(es): 86-377; 961-230
Divisions: Zalozba Obzorja p.o. Maribor
Bookshop(s): Zalozba Obzorja-Knjigarna, Gosposka 24 SLO, 2000 Maribor
Warehouse: Turnerjeva 17, SLO, 2000 Maribor

South Africa

General Information
Capital: Pretoria
Language: Afrikaans and English (both official) 11 other official languages exist
Religion: Predominatly Christian. Politically most important is the Dutch Reformed Church (about 30% of the white population). Also many Methodist, Anglican and African Independent Churches among African Christians
Population: 41.25 million
Bank Hours: 0900-1530 Monday-Friday
Shop Hours: Vary province to province. Often 0900-1700 Monday-Friday
Currency: 1 rand = 4.32 USDL (June 1996)
Export/Import Information: Printed books, brochures, leaflets and similar matter (tariff heading 49.01) are free of duty and surcharge with the exception of directories, guide books, year books, Christmas annuals and hand-books relating to South Africa which attract duty at a rate of 20% or 11c/Kg. No objectionable or undesirable literature permitted. No import permit required. Trade advertising matter, commercial catalogues and the like (tariff heading 4911.10.10 to 4911.10.30) are free of duty (otherwise 25% and 20% duty respectively). 5% surcharge is payable in all instances. 14% VAT on books. No import permit is required.

AA The Motorist Publications, *imprint of* Reader's Digest Southern Africa

Acacia Books, *imprint of* Nasou Via Afrika

Acorn Books+
PO Box 4845, Randburg 2125
Tel: (011) 8805768 *Fax:* (011) 8805768
E-mail: acorbook@iafrica.com
Key Personnel
Publisher: Eleanor-Mary Cadell
Founded: 1985
Specialize in natural history & African wildlife.
Subjects: Natural History, Travel, African Wildlife
ISBN Prefix(es): 1-874802
Total Titles: 6 Print

Addison Wesley, *imprint of* Maskew Miller Longman

Addison Wesley Longman, *imprint of* Pearson Education (Prentice Hall)

Africasouth Paperbacks, *imprint of* New Africa Books (Pty) Ltd

Afritech, *imprint of* Nasou Via Afrika

Afro, *imprint of* Nasou Via Afrika

Allyn & Bacon, *imprint of* Maskew Miller Longman

Anansi Uitgewers+
Forestweg 10, Oranjezicht, Capetown 8001
Tel: (021) 968411 *Fax:* (021) 969698
Key Personnel
Man Dir, Editorial: Dr Lydia Snyman
Man Dir, Financial: Andre Conradie
Founded: 1989
ISBN Prefix(es): 1-86843; 0-947454; 1-874885
Warehouse: c/o Newman and Swart Street, Durbanvile
Orders to: PO Box 559, Durbanville 7550
Tel: (021) 968411 *Fax:* (021) 969698

Appleton Lange, *imprint of* Pearson Education (Prentice Hall)

Ashanti Publishing+
PO Box 5091, Rivonia 2128
Tel: (011) 8032506 *Fax:* (011) 8035094
Key Personnel
Man Dir: Nicholas Combrinck
Founded: 1987
Subjects: Environmental Studies, Foreign Countries, Government, Political Science, Military Science, Sports, Athletics
ISBN Prefix(es): 1-874800; 1-919686
Parent Company: Ashanti International Films Ltd, Gibraltar
Subsidiaries: Gibraltar
Branch Office(s)
Daring Publishing Group, 913 Tuscarawas St W, Canton, OH 44702, United States

Atlas, *imprint of* Nasou Via Afrika

Jonathan Ball Publishers
Design Centre, 179 Loop St, Central, Capetown 8001
Mailing Address: PO Box 6836, Roggebaai, Cape Town 8012
Tel: (011) 622-2900 *Fax:* (011) 622-7610
Key Personnel
Publishing & Rights: Francine Blum
Marketing: Eugene Ashton
Sales: Alastair Steyn
Founded: 1977
Subjects: Biography, Government, Political Science, History, Literature, Literary Criticism, Essays, Sports, Athletics
ISBN Prefix(es): 1-86842
Parent Company: Nasionale Boekhandel
Ultimate Parent Company: Nasionale Pers
Imprints: Delta Books; Ad Donker Publications

Jossey Bass, *imprint of* Pearson Education (Prentice Hall)

Bateleur, *imprint of* Nasou Via Afrika

Benjamin Cummings, *imprint of* Maskew Miller Longman

Bible Society of South Africa
15 Anton Anreith Arcade, Cape Town 8001
Mailing Address: PO Box 6215, Roggebay, Cape Town 8012
Tel: (021) 421-2040 *Fax:* (021) 419-4846
E-mail: biblia@biblesociety.co.za
Web Site: www.biblesociety.co.za
Telex: 527964 *Cable:* Testaments Cape Town
Key Personnel
General Secretary: Rev Gerrit Kritzinger
Chief Executive, General Secretary, Rights & Permissions: Dr D Tolmie
Sales, Production: Rev A C Human
Publicity: N Turley
Founded: 1820 (as auxiliary of British & Foreign Bible Society, 1965 as autonomous body)
Subjects: Biblical Studies, Religion - Other
ISBN Prefix(es): 0-7982
Imprints: Bybelgenootskap
Branch Office(s)
220 Kimberley Rd, Bloemfontein 9301, PO Box 12149, Brandhof 9324, Regional Secretary: Rev Jan de Wet *Tel:* (051) 448-9451 *Fax:* (051) 448-9455 *E-mail:* bibbfn@biblesociety.co.za
J1776 Zinhlamvu St, PO Box 160, Esikhawini 3887, Regional Secretary: Dr Josiah Mazibuko *Tel:* (035) 796-1181 *Fax:* (035) 796-2028 *E-mail:* bibkwaz@biblesociety.co.za
Stand 5080 Zone 5, Pimbille, Private Bag X05, Kliptown 1812, Regional Secretary: Rev Sello Maboea *Tel:* (011) 938-1453 *Fax:* (011) 938-1561 *E-mail:* bibsow@biblesociety.co.za

PUBLISHERS

SOUTH AFRICA

18 Central Ave, PO Box 2002, Kempton Park 1620, Regional Secretary: Rev Kobie Krige *Tel:* (011) 970-4010 *Fax:* (011) 970-2506 *E-mail:* bibjhg@biblesociety.co.za
70-76 Ramsay Ave, PO Box 30801, Mayville 4058, Regional Secretary: Dr Andries Boshoff *Tel:* (031) 207-4933 *Fax:* (031) 207-1058 *E-mail:* bibdbn@biblesociety.co.za
31 Cotswold Ave, Cotswold, PO Box 7579, Newton Park 6055, Regional Secretary: Rev Ben Fourie *Tel:* (041) 364-1138 *Fax:* (041) 365-2634 *E-mail:* bibpe@biblesociety.co.za
15 Anton Anreith Arcade, Cape Town 8001, PO Box 6446, Roggebaai 8012, Regional Secretary: Rev Eugene Louw *Tel:* (021) 421-2040 *Fax:* (021) 419-4846 *E-mail:* bibcpt@biblesociety.co.za

Brabys Brochures
Formerly Caversham Brochures
Publishing House, 34 Kings Rd, Pinetown 3610
Mailing Address: PO Box 1426, Pinetown 3600
Tel: (031) 717 4000 *Fax:* (031) 717 4001
E-mail: brabys@brabys.com
Web Site: www.brabys.com
Key Personnel
Product Manager: P M Dahn *E-mail:* pam@brabys.co.za
Founded: 1904
Business directory publisher, maps, brochures, media sales & online advertising.
Subjects: Business
ISBN Prefix(es): 0-620; 1-86833; 1-874834
Parent Company: Brabys AC (Pty) Ltd, 12 Caversham Rd, Pinetown, 3600 KwaZulu-Natal

The Brenthurst Press (Pty) Ltd
PO Box 87184, Houghton, Johannesburg 2041
Tel: (011) 6466024 *Fax:* (011) 4861651
E-mail: orders@brenthurst.co.az
Web Site: www.brenthurst.org.za
Key Personnel
Sales Manager: Sally MacRoberts *E-mail:* sallymac@brenthurst.co.za
Founded: 1974
Subjects: History, Natural History, Regional Interests
ISBN Prefix(es): 0-909079

Bybelgenootskap, *imprint of* Bible Society of South Africa

Killie Campbell Africana Library, *imprint of* University of KwaZulu-Natal Press

Cape Provincial Library Service
PO Box 659, Cape Town 8000
Tel: (021) 5910095 *Fax:* (021) 4102261
Key Personnel
Contact: Mrs Liesel de Villiers *E-mail:* lieseldu@cpls.wcapc.gov.za
Founded: 1950
Subjects: Library & Information Sciences
ISBN Prefix(es): 0-7984

Caversham Brochures, see Brabys Brochures

Centaur, *imprint of* Heinemann Educational Publishers Southern Africa

Centre for Conflict Resolution
University of Cape Town, Private Bag, Rondebosch 7701
Tel: (021) 6502503; (021) 6502750 *Fax:* (021) 6852142; (021) 6504053
E-mail: ccr@uctvax.uct.ac.za
Web Site: www.uct.ac.za
Telex: 5-21439
Key Personnel
Executive Dir: Mr Laurie Nathan *Tel:* (021) 4222512 *Fax:* (021) 4222622 *E-mail:* lnathan@ccr.uct.ac.za
Founded: 1968
Specialize in conflict management.
Subjects: Human Relations, Social Sciences, Sociology
ISBN Prefix(es): 0-7992
Number of titles published annually: 10 Print
Total Titles: 24 Print

Charles Merrill, *imprint of* Maskew Miller Longman

Clever Books+
999 Arcadia St, Arcadia, Pretoria 0028
Mailing Address: PO Box 13816, Alkantrant, Hatfield 0005
Tel: (012) 3424715 *Fax:* (012) 432376
Key Personnel
Owner: J Steenhuisen
Founded: 1981
Specialize in educational books & worksheets.
Membership(s): S A Publishers Association & S A Book Dealers Association; also specialize in Study Guides.
Subjects: Biological Sciences, Education, English as a Second Language, Language Arts, Linguistics, Mathematics, Physical Sciences, Science (General)
ISBN Prefix(es): 0-947056; 0-77004
Total Titles: 1,200 Print; 12 CD-ROM
Book Club(s): Clever Book Club

CMP Reprints, *imprint of* Sasavona Publishers & Booksellers

Conflict Management; Africa; Peacemaking; Peacebuilding, see Centre for Conflict Resolution

CUM Books (Pty) Ltd, see Digma Publications

Benjamin Cummings, *imprint of* Pearson Education (Prentice Hall)

Daan Retief, *imprint of* HAUM - Daan Retief Publishers (Pty) Ltd

Daan Retief, *imprint of* Jacklin Enterprises (Pty) Ltd

De Jager Haum, *imprint of* Maskew Miller Longman

De Jager Publishers, see HAUM - De Jager Publishers

Delta Books, *imprint of* Jonathan Ball Publishers

Digma Publications
Division of Butterworth Publishers
PO Box 65042, Benmore 2010
Tel: (011) 8834854 *Fax:* (011) 8836540
Telex: 425847 *Cable:* Chrispub
Key Personnel
Chairman: J J M Jacobs
Publisher: Freddie Crous; Koos van Niekerk
Founded: 1939
Subjects: Law, Religion - Other
ISBN Prefix(es): 0-86984; 1-86829

Ad Donker (Pty) Ltd+
Imprint of Jonathan Ball Publishers (Pty) Ltd
PO Box 33977, Jeppestown 2043
Tel: (011) 622-2900 *Fax:* (011) 622-7610
Key Personnel
Publishing & Permissions: Francine Blum *E-mail:* fplum@jonathanball.co.za
Marketing: Eugene Ashton
Sales: Alastair Steyn
Founded: 1973
Subjects: Nonfiction (General), General South African
ISBN Prefix(es): 0-86852
Parent Company: Nasionale Boekhandel
Ultimate Parent Company: Nasionale Pers
Associate Companies: Delta Books (Pty) Ltd
Warehouse: Jonathan Ball Publishers (Pty) Ltd, 10-14 Watkins St, Denver Ext 4, Johannesburg 2094

Ad Donker Publications, *imprint of* Jonathan Ball Publishers

Educum, *imprint of* Maskew Miller Longman

Educum Publishers Ltd
PO Box 3068, Halfway House 1685
Tel: (011) 3153647 *Fax:* (011) 3152757
Key Personnel
Group Man Dir: P Greyling
Senior General Manager: W Struik
General Manager: W C De Wet
Sales: C Mahlaba
Founded: 1947
Subjects: Accounting, Agriculture, Art, Biblical Studies, Biological Sciences, Business, Chemistry, Chemical Engineering, Computer Science, Cookery, Economics, Education, Engineering (General), Geography, Geology, Government, Political Science, History, Literature, Literary Criticism, Essays, Mathematics, Music, Dance, Natural History, Physical Sciences, Physics, Poetry, Religion - Protestant, Science (General), Social Sciences, Sociology, Technology
ISBN Prefix(es): 0-7980
Parent Company: Perskor Books (Pty) Ltd
Associate Companies: Varia Publishers, PO Box 3068, Halfway House, 1685; Lex Patria Publishers, PO Box 845, Johannesburg 2000

Cassell Elt, *imprint of* Pearson Education (Prentice Hall)

Woodhead Faulkner, *imprint of* Pearson Education (Prentice Hall)

Fernwood Press (Pty) Ltd+
PO Box 15344, Vlaeberg, Capetown 8018
Tel: (021) 7948686 *Fax:* (021) 7948339
E-mail: ferpress@iafrica.com
Web Site: www.fernwoodpress.co.za
Key Personnel
Man Dir & International Rights: Pieter Struik
Founded: 1991
Subjects: Art, History, Natural History, Nonfiction (General), Regional Interests, Travel, Wine & Spirits
ISBN Prefix(es): 1-874950; 0-9583154
Number of titles published annually: 5 Print
Distributed by Central Books Ltd/Global Book Marketing

Financial Times, *imprint of* Maskew Miller Longman

Financial Times-Pitman, *imprint of* Pearson Education (Prentice Hall)

Flesch Financial Publications (Pty) Ltd+
4 Gordon St, Gardens, Cape Town 8001
Tel: (021) 4617472 *Fax:* (021) 4613758
E-mail: sflesch@aztec.co.za
Key Personnel
Man Dir: S Flesch *E-mail:* sflesch@iafrica.com
Editorial: M G K Maher
Sales Manager: Peter Duncan
Founded: 1966

Membership(s): Publishers Association of South Africa.
Subjects: Aeronautics, Aviation, Animals, Pets, Business, Maritime
ISBN Prefix(es): 0-949989
Total Titles: 3 Print; 1 CD-ROM
Associate Companies: W J Flesch & Partners (Pty) Ltd
Branch Office(s)
104 Greenway, Greenside 2193

Folio, *imprint of* Juventus/Femina Publishers

Russel Friedman Books
PO Box 73, Halfway House 1685
Tel: (011) 702-2300 *Fax:* (011) 702-1403
E-mail: rfbooks@iafrica.com
Web Site: www.rfbooks.co.za
Key Personnel
Contact: Russel Friedman
Founded: 1982
Subjects: Natural History
ISBN Prefix(es): 0-9583223; 1-875091
U.S. Office(s): 4651 Glenshire Pl, Atlanta, GA 30338, United States

Galago, *imprint of* Galago Publishing Pty Ltd

Galago Publishing Pty Ltd+
8 First Ave, Alberton North
Mailing Address: PO Box 1645, 1450 Alberton
Tel: (011) 9072029 *Fax:* (011) 8690890
E-mail: lemur@mweb.co.za
Web Site: www.galago.co.za
Key Personnel
Man Dir: Francis Stiff
Founded: 1982
Specialize in general nonfiction, military, hunting & Africa.
Membership(s): Publishers' Association South Africa.
Subjects: Aeronautics, Aviation, African American Studies, Biography, Foreign Countries, History, Military Science, Nonfiction (General), Hunting & Africa
Number of titles published annually: 6 Print
Total Titles: 20 Print
Parent Company: Lemur Books Pty Ltd
Imprints: Galago

Gecko Poetry, *imprint of* University of KwaZulu-Natal Press

Ginn, *imprint of* Heinemann Educational Publishers Southern Africa

GK Hall, *imprint of* Maskew Miller Longman

Government Printer
PO Box 571, Capetown 8000
Mailing Address: Private Bag X85, Pretoria 0001
Tel: (012) 323-9731; (012) 457-531; (021) 457-531 *Fax:* (012) 461-4404 *Cable:* QUAD
Subjects: Education, Geography, Geology
ISBN Prefix(es): 0-621
Branch Office(s)
Cape Town *Tel:* (021) 465-7531

Hadeda Books, *imprint of* University of KwaZulu-Natal Press

G K Hall, *imprint of* Pearson Education (Prentice Hall)

Harvester Wheatsheaf, *imprint of* Maskew Miller Longman

Harvester Wheatsheaf, *imprint of* Pearson Education (Prentice Hall)

HAUM - Daan Retief Publishers (Pty) Ltd+
PO Box 629, Pretoria 0001
Tel: (012) 3228474 *Fax:* (012) 3222424
Key Personnel
Man Dir, Production: M A C Jacklin
Editorial, Sales, Publicity, Rights & Permissions: Dr H J M Retief
Founded: 1973
Subjects: Education, Regional Interests
Parent Company: HAUM (Hollandsch Afrikaansche Uitgevers MaatschappIij)
Associate Companies: HAUM-De Jager Publishers
Imprints: Daan Retief
Book Club(s): Kinderklub; Young People's Book Club

De Jager Haum, *imprint of* Pearson Education (Prentice Hall)

HAUM - De Jager Publishers
PO Box 629, Pretoria 0001
Tel: (012) 3284620 *Fax:* (012) 3284706; (012) 3283809
Key Personnel
Man Dir: Chris Richter
General Manager, Publishing: Lena Kohler
General Manager, Marketing: Johann Verreynne
Founded: 1894 (as HAUM)
Subjects: Literature, Literary Criticism, Essays, Religion - Other
ISBN Prefix(es): 0-7986
Parent Company: HAUM (Hollandsch Afrikaansche Uitgevers Maatschappij)
Associate Companies: HAUM-Daan Retief Publishers (Pty) Ltd
Branch Office(s)
Blomfontein
Cape Town
Durban
King William's Town
Pietersburg
Pretoria
Vereeniging
Witwatersrand
Orders to: PO Box 12635, Clubview 0014

HAUM (Hollandsch Afrikaansche Uitgevers Maatschappij)+
PO Box 629, Pretoria 0001
Tel: (012) 32284620 *Fax:* (012) 3284706; (012) 3283809
Key Personnel
Manager, Publisher: Chris Richter
Subjects: Biography, Education, Ethnicity, Fiction, History, Nonfiction (General), Poetry
ISBN Prefix(es): 0-7986
Subsidiaries: HAUM-Daan Retief Publishers (Pty) Ltd; HAUM-De Jager Publishers; HAUM Educational Publishers; IKUT; Juventus/Femina Publishers; Rostrum
Bookshop(s): HAUM Academic Bookshop; HAUM Booksellers

Heinemann-Centaur, *imprint of* Heinemann Educational Publishers Southern Africa

Heinemann Educational Publishers Southern Africa+
66 Park Lane, Sandton, Gauteng, 2196 Johannesburg
Mailing Address: PO Box 781940, Sandton, Gauteng, 2146 Johannesburg
Tel: (011) 322 8600 *Fax:* (011) 322 8716
E-mail: customerliaison@heinemann.co.za
Web Site: www.heinemann.co.za
Key Personnel
Publishing Dir: Saul Molobi

Founded: 1986
Membership(s): South African Publishers Association.
Subjects: Economics, Education, English as a Second Language, Mathematics, Mechanical Engineering
ISBN Prefix(es): 0-435; 0-620
Parent Company: Reed Educational & Professional Publishing
Ultimate Parent Company: Reed Elsevier plc
Imprints: Ginn; Centaur; Heinemann-Centaur; Lexicon; Isando Books
Subsidiaries: Heinemann Higher and Further Education (Pty) Ltd

Heinemann Publishers (Pty) Ltd+
PO Box 781940, Sandton 2146
Tel: (011) 784 8619 *Fax:* (011) 784 8360
E-mail: bevw@heinemann.co.za
Key Personnel
Man Dir, Rights & Permissions: Kevin Kroeger
Publishing: Robert Sulley
Production: Angela Tuck
Publicity: Andrew Meyer
Founded: 1966
Subjects: Computer Science, Medicine, Nursing, Dentistry, Nonfiction (General), Science (General), Technology
ISBN Prefix(es): 1-86813; 0-908379; 0-947034; 0-947472; 1-86834; 1-86853; 1-874820; 1-874914

The Hippogriff Press CC+
PO Box 191, Parklands, Johannesburg 2121
Tel: (011) 6464229 *Fax:* (011) 6464229
Key Personnel
Contact: E M MacPhail
Founded: 1989
Membership(s): IPASA (Independent Publishers Association of South Africa).
Subjects: Fiction, Poetry
ISBN Prefix(es): 0-9583122

Homeros, *imprint of* Tafelberg Publishers Ltd

Ellis Horwood, *imprint of* Pearson Education (Prentice Hall)

Human & Rousseau (Pty) Ltd+
Waalburg Bldg, 1st Floor, 28 Wale St, Cape Town 8001
Mailing Address: PO Box 5050, Cape Town 8000
Tel: (021) 424 1320; (021) 424 1323 *Fax:* (021) 424 2510; (021) 426 5744
E-mail: rhauman@nbh.naspers.co.za
Web Site: www.humanrousseau.com
Key Personnel
General Manager: Kerneels Breytenbach
Operations Manager: Riel Hauman
Marketing Manager: Elsa Wolfaard
Founded: 1959
Subjects: Anthropology, Architecture & Interior Design, Art, Biography, Business, Child Care & Development, Communications, Cookery, Crafts, Games, Hobbies, Drama, Theater, Economics, Fiction, Gardening, Plants, History, House & Home, How-to, Language Arts, Linguistics, Literature, Literary Criticism, Essays, Management, Marketing, Music, Dance, Natural History, Nonfiction (General), Philosophy, Poetry, Religion - Protestant, Romance, Self-Help, Sports, Athletics
ISBN Prefix(es): 0-7981
Parent Company: Nasionale Boekhandel Ltd
Branch Office(s)
Johannesburg
Pretoria
Orders to: Nasionale Boekhandel, PO Box 487, Bellville 7535 *Tel:* (021) 918 8500 *Fax:* (021) 951 4903

PUBLISHERS — SOUTH AFRICA

Human Sciences Research Council+
134 Pretouris St, Pretoria 0002
Mailing Address: Private Bag X41, Pretoria 0001
Tel: (012) 302 2999 *Fax:* (012) 326 5362
Web Site: www.hsrc.ac.za
Key Personnel
Publisher: Mrs R Keet *E-mail:* rkeet@beauty.hsrc.ac.za
Founded: 1965
Research Institution, Human Sciences only. Publish own research, selected external authors & co-publish with one UK publisher.
Subjects: Behavioral Sciences, Career Development, Criminology, Education, Government, Political Science, Human Relations, Philosophy, Psychology, Psychiatry, Regional Interests, Social Sciences, Sociology, Women's Studies
ISBN Prefix(es): 0-7969; 0-86965
Total Titles: 274 Print
Branch Office(s)
CSIR Bldg, 359 King George V Ave, 4th Floor, Private Bag X07, Durban 4014 *Tel:* (031) 273 1400 *Fax:* (031) 273 1403
Plein Park Bldg, 69-83 Plein St, 14th Floor, Private Bag X9182, Cape Town 8000 *Tel:* (021) 467 4420 *Fax:* (021) 467 4424
Distributor for Zed Books (London)
Bookshop(s): HSRC Publishers, PO Box 5556, Petoria 0001, Contact: J Moagi *Tel:* (012) 3022004 *Fax:* (012) 3022933 *E-mail:* jels@beauty.hsrc.ac.za
Orders to: PO Box 5556, Pretoria 0001, Contact: J Moagi *Tel:* (012) 3022330 *Fax:* (012) 2022442 *E-mail:* jels@beauty.hsrc.ac.za

Institute for Reformational Studies CHE+
c/o Potchefstroom University for Christian Higher Education, Private Bag X6001, Potchefstroom 2520
Tel: (018) 299-1623 *Fax:* (018) 299-2799
E-mail: irsajvdw@puknet.puk.ac.za
Web Site: www.puk.ac.za
Telex: 346019 *Cable:* PUK
Key Personnel
Dir: Prof B J van der Walt
Editiorial: Rita Swanepoel
Administration: Dr A J van der Walt
Founded: 1962
Subjects: Anthropology, Art, Biblical Studies, Developing Countries, Education, Government, Political Science, Religion - Protestant, Theology, Women's Studies
ISBN Prefix(es): 0-86990; 1-86822
Parent Company: Potchefstroom University for Christian Higher Education

Isando Books, *imprint of* Heinemann Educational Publishers Southern Africa

Ithemba! Publishing+
PO Box 1048, Auckland Park 2006
Tel: (011) 726 6529 *Fax:* (011) 726 6529
E-mail: firechildren@icon.co.za
Web Site: www.icon.co.za/~firechildren/ithemba/ithemba.htm
Key Personnel
Man Dir: Bronwen Jones
Founded: 1994
Membership(s): Publishers Association of South Africa & Children's Book Forum. Publisher of South African produced books only.
Subjects: Biography, Fiction, Regional Interests
U.S. Office(s): Lucretia Humphrey, 3026 Fifth Ave N, Great Falls, MT 59401, United States
Distributed by Africa Book Centre; Lucretia Humphrey (USA); National Book Trust of India (Asia)

Ivy Publications+
PO Box 397, Pretoria 0001
Tel: (012) 218931 *Fax:* (012) 3255984
E-mail: therese@statelib-pww.gov.za

Key Personnel
Contact: Ian Bruton-Simmonds
Founded: 1989
Subjects: Education, English as a Second Language, Journalism, Language Arts, Linguistics, Literature, Literary Criticism, Essays, Management, Nonfiction (General), Romance
ISBN Prefix(es): 0-620

Jacana Education+
5 Saint Peter Rd, Bellevue, Gauteng 2198
Mailing Address: PO Box 2004, Houghton, Gauteng 2041
Tel: (011) 648 1157 *Fax:* (011) 648 5516
E-mail: marketing@jacana.co.za; production@jacana.co.za
Web Site: www.jacana.co.za
Founded: 1991
Subjects: Child Care & Development, Education, English as a Second Language, Environmental Studies, Gardening, Plants, Health, Nutrition, Medicine, Nursing, Dentistry, Travel
ISBN Prefix(es): 1-874955

Mike Jacklin, *imprint of* Jacklin Enterprises (Pty) Ltd

Jacklin Enterprises (Pty) Ltd+
PO Box 521, Parklands 2121
Tel: (011) 265 4200 *Fax:* (011) 314 2984
E-mail: mjacklin@jacklin.co.za
Web Site: www.jacklin.co.za
Key Personnel
Man Dir: Mike Jacklin *Tel:* (011) 6521802
Editorial, Rights & Permissions: Daleen Zaaiman
Sales: Marie Erasmus
Production: Bashir Ismail
Founded: 1992
Specialize in children's book clubs (5); mail order fulfillment for books, magazines & partworks.
Subjects: Fiction, Romance, Technology, Transportation
ISBN Prefix(es): 1-86839; 1-874927
Total Titles: 2,000 Print; 2 Audio
Imprints: Mike Jacklin; Kennis Onbeperk; Daan Retief
Divisions: Disney Book Club; Daan Retief Book Clubs; Read & Learn Programme; Partworks Subscriptions
Distributor for BBC; Eaglemoss; Fabbri; Marshall Cavendish; Orbis (all South Africa only)

Janssen Publishers CC
PO Box 404, Simon's Town 7995
Tel: (021) 7861548 *Fax:* (021) 7862468
E-mail: janssenp@iafrica.com
Web Site: www.janssenbooks.co.za
Founded: 1981
Specialize in photo & art books of the male nude.
Subjects: Art, Erotica, Gay & Lesbian, Photography
ISBN Prefix(es): 1-919901
Number of titles published annually: 10 Print
Total Titles: 120 Print
Distribution Center: SOVA-Sozialistische Verlagsauslieferung GmbH, Friesstr 20-24, 60388 Frankfurt, Germany *Tel:* (069) 410 211 *Fax:* (069) 410 280 *E-mail:* sovaffm@t-online.de
Weatherhill, Inc, 41 Monroe Turnpike, Trumbull, CT 06611, United States *Tel:* 203-459-5090 *Fax:* 203-459-5095

Jasmyn, *imprint of* Tafelberg Publishers Ltd

Johannesburg Art Gallery
PO Box 23561, Joubert Park, Johannesburg 2044
Tel: (011) 7253130; (011) 7253180 *Fax:* (011) 7206000
Web Site: www.saevents.co.za/gallery.htm

Key Personnel
Dir: Rochelle Keene
Curator of Publications: Sandy Shoolman
Founded: 1910
Membership(s): AAM, SAMA & ICOM.
Subjects: Art, Education, Photography
ISBN Prefix(es): 1-874836
Total Titles: 20 Print

Juta & Co+
Mercury Crescent, Hillstar Industria, Wetton, Cape Town 7779
Mailing Address: PO Box 14373, Lansdown 7779
Fax: (021) 797 5569 (orders only)
E-mail: books@juta.co.za
Web Site: www.juta.co.za *Cable:* JUTA
Key Personnel
Chief Executive Officer: Rory Wilson
 Tel: (021) 797 5101 *Fax:* (021) 797 0121
 E-mail: rwilson@juta.co.za
Corporate Marketing Manager: Navine Christian
 E-mail: nchristian@juta.co.za
Founded: 1853
Overseas Agents: Blackstone Press Ltd, 1st Floor, 104 Ebley St, Bondi Junction, Sydney, NSW 2022, Australia; BRAD, 244A London Rd, Hadleigh, Essex SS7 2DE, UK. Tel: (0702) 552912 Fax: (0702) 556095 (academic, medical & technical titles); Hammick's Law Bookshop, 191-192 Fleet St, London EC4A 2AH, UK (law titles).
Membership(s): ABSA & SAPA.
Subjects: Accounting, Business, Education, Law, Medicine, Nursing, Dentistry
ISBN Prefix(es): 0-7021
Number of titles published annually: 500 Print; 10 CD-ROM
Total Titles: 44 CD-ROM
Parent Company: Juta Holdings (Pty) Ltd
Associate Companies: Juta (UK) Ltd, The Kidlington Centre, Suite E, Oxford 0X52DL, United Kingdom; Jutastat (Pty) Ltd
Branch Office(s)
Mercury Crescent Kenwyn, Cape Town 7790
 Tel: (021) 7975101 *Fax:* (021) 7627424
PO Box 1010, Johannesburg 2000
Showroom(s): Madeira St, Umtata, Transkei
 Tel: (0471) 23634
Shipping Address: Hillstar Industrial Township, Wetton Cape, Jenny Newby *E-mail:* jnewby@juja.co.za
Warehouse: Hillstar Industrial Township, Wetton Cape, Winston Bell *Fax:* (021) 7616267 *E-mail:* wbell@juta.co.za

Juventus/Femina Publishers+
PO Box 629, Pretoria 0001
Tel: (012) 3284620 *Fax:* (012) 3283809
Telex: 30435
Key Personnel
Man Dir: Piet Scholtz
Manager, Editorial: Lena Kohler
Chief Publisher: Kobie Gouws
Sales: Robbie Goossen
Production: Manus Oberholzer
Publicity: Sas Klopper
Rights & Permissions: Hettie Scholtz
Founded: 1980
Subjects: Fiction, Nonfiction (General), Social Sciences, Sociology, Women's Studies
ISBN Prefix(es): 0-86816; 0-907996
Parent Company: HAUM (Hollandsch Afrikaansche Uitgevers Maatschappij)
Imprints: Folio

Kagiso, *imprint of* Maskew Miller Longman

Kagiso, *imprint of* Pearson Education (Prentice Hall)

Kennis Onbeperk, *imprint of* Jacklin Enterprises (Pty) Ltd

SOUTH AFRICA

Kima Global Publishers+
Kima Global House, 11 Columbine Rd, Rondebosch, Cape Town 7700
Mailing Address: PO Box 374, Rondebosch 7701
Tel: (021) 686-7154 *Fax:* (021) 686-9066
E-mail: info@kimaglobal.co.za
Web Site: www.kimaglobal.co.za
Key Personnel
Founder, Publisher & Man Dir: Mr Robin Beck
  E-mail: robin@kimaglobal.co.za
Founded: 1993
Independent company specializing in personal growth books.
Membership(s): PMA.
Subjects: Alternative, Astrology, Occult, Behavioral Sciences, How-to, Human Relations, Psychology, Psychiatry, Religion - Other, Self-Help
ISBN Prefix(es): 0-9584065; 0-9584261; 0-9584359; 0-958693
Number of titles published annually: 10 Print
Total Titles: 30 Print; 27 Online
U.S. Office(s): c/o Holistic Marketing Cooperative, 705-B SE Melody Lane, Suite 329, Lee's Summit, MO 64063, United States, Contact: Diana Trott *Tel:* 816-525-1802 *Fax:* 816-471-7091
Distributed by Banyan Tree Books (Australia); Deep Books Ltd (UK)
Distributor for Summit University Press
Foreign Rights: Katia Schumer (Spain & Portugal)
Warehouse: Packaging Dynamics, 8800 NE Undergroud Dr, Kansas City, MO 64108, United States
Orders to: Holistic Marketing Cooperative, 705B SE Melody Lane, Suite 329, Lee's Summit, MO 64063, United States, Contact: Diana Trott *Tel:* 816-525-1802 *E-mail:* diana@holisticmarketing.com

KZN Books, *imprint of* Nasou Via Afrika

Ladybird Books, *imprint of* Maskew Miller Longman

LAPA Publishers (Pty) Ltd+
380 Bosman St, Pretoria 0002
Mailing Address: PO Box 123, Pretoria 0001
Tel: (012) 401 0700 *Fax:* (012) 3255498
E-mail: lapa@atkv.org.za
Key Personnel
Publication & Administrative Officer: Esme Smith
  E-mail: esmes@atkv.org.za
Founded: 1943
Publisher & Bookseller.
Subjects: Fiction, Law, Nonfiction (General), Philosophy, Religion - Other
ISBN Prefix(es): 0-7993
Number of titles published annually: 140 Print
Ultimate Parent Company: ATKV, Dover St, Randburg 2194
Imprints: Symbol Books
Book Club(s): Eike-Boekklub; Keurbiblioteek; President Boekklub; Romankeur; Symbol; Treffer-Boekklub

Lexicon, *imprint of* Heinemann Educational Publishers Southern Africa

LexisNexis Butterworths South Africa
215 North Ridge Rd, Morningside, 4001 Durban
Mailing Address: PO Box 792, 4000 Durban
Tel: (031) 268 3111; (031) 268 3007 (customer service) *Fax:* (031) 268 3108; (021) 268 3109
Toll Free *Fax:* (031) 268 3102 (Marketing)
Web Site: www.lexisnexis.co.za
Key Personnel
Chief Executive Officer: Billy Last *Tel:* (031) 268 3253 *Fax:* (031) 29 8686
Sales & Marketing Dir: James Martens *Tel:* (031) 268 3246 *Fax:* (031) 268 3114
Electronic Publishing Dir: Chris Uniacke
  Tel: (031) 268 3256 *Fax:* (031) 268 3114
Publishing Dir: Theuns Viljoen *Tel:* (031) 268 3247 *Fax:* (031) 268 3114
National Sales Executive: Wendy de Sornay
  Tel: (031) 268 3261 *Fax:* (031) 268 3271
Marketing Manager: Shannon MacLennan
  Tel: (031) 268 3251
Marketing Coordinator: Tracy Naicker *Tel:* (031) 268 3243
Subjects: Economics, Education, Law
ISBN Prefix(es): 0-409
Parent Company: LexisNexis Butterworth & Co (Publishers) Ltd, United States
Ultimate Parent Company: Reed Elsevier plc, 25 Victoria St, London SW1H 0EX, United Kingdom
Branch Office(s)
F10 Centurion Business, Bosmansdam Rd, Milnerton, 7441 Capetown *Tel:* (021) 551 8900 *Fax:* (021) 551 5121
Grayston 66, 2 Norwich Close, Sandton, 2196 Johannesburg *Tel:* (011) 784 8009 *Fax:* (011) 883 6540
Distributor for Butterworth-Heinemann

Longman, *imprint of* Maskew Miller Longman

Longman, *imprint of* Pearson Education (Prentice Hall)

Maskew Miller Longman, *imprint of* Pearson Education (Prentice Hall)

Lux Verbi (Pty) Ltd+
33 Waterkant St, Cape Town 8000
Mailing Address: PO Box 5, Wellington 7654
Tel: (021) 8733851 *Fax:* (021) 8730069
E-mail: luxverbi.publ@kinglsey.co.za
Telex: 526922
Key Personnel
Executive Chairman: Willem J van Zijl
Publishing: Hester Venter
Marketing: Maryna Volschenk
Founded: 1956
Subjects: Religion - Other, Theology
ISBN Prefix(es): 0-86997; 0-7963
Subsidiaries: Waterkant-Uitgewers (Edms) Bpk
Bookshop(s): OK Centre Shop, 404 Murchison St, Ladysmith; Central Square 37, Union St, London; The Mall, c/o Malanand Sauer St, Vanderbijlpark
Book Club(s): New Day Readers Circle

MacMillan, *imprint of* Maskew Miller Longman

MacMillan Books, *imprint of* Maskew Miller Longman

MacMillan College, *imprint of* Maskew Miller Longman

MacMillan ELT, *imprint of* Maskew Miller Longman

MacMillan Reference, *imprint of* Maskew Miller Longman

Maskew Miller Longman+
Howard Drive, Pinelands, Cape Town 7405
Mailing Address: PO Box 396, Cape Town 8000
Tel: (021) 531 7750 *Fax:* (021) 531 4877
E-mail: firstname@mml.co.za
Web Site: www.mml.com
Telex: 526053 SA
Key Personnel
Chief Executive: Fathima Dada *E-mail:* fathima@mml.co.za
Publishing Dir: Japie Pienaar *E-mail:* japie@mmi.co.za
Dir, Trade & Adult: Orenna Krut
  E-mail: orenna@mml.co.za
Dir MML International: Graham van der Vyver
  E-mail: graham@mmo.co.za
Financial Dir: Ms Cornelius Vamvadelis
Dir, Publishing Services, Editorial & Production: Jeremy Boraine
Founded: 1893
Subjects: Education, Language Arts, Linguistics, Literature, Literary Criticism, Essays
ISBN Prefix(es): 0-623; 0-636
Parent Company: Pearson Education
Ultimate Parent Company: Pearson Plc
Imprints: Unibook; De Jager Haum; Educum; Kagiso; Longman; Pearson Education South Africa; Perskor; Phumelela; Sached; Vlaeberg; Addison Wesley; Allyn & Bacon; Benjamin Cummings; Charles Merrill; Financial Times; GK Hall; Harvester Wheatsheaf; Ladybird Books; MacMillan; MacMillan Books; MacMillan College; MacMillan ELT; MacMillan Reference; Prentice Hall; Prentice Hall Australia; Prentice Hall Europe; Prentice Hall South Africa; QUE College; Regents Prentice Hall; Scribner; Woodhead Faulkner
Branch Office(s)
Private Bag X08, Amethyst St, Bertsham, 2013 Johannesburg *Tel:* (011) 4961730 *Fax:* (011) 4961117

Mayibuye Books+
Private Bag X 17, Belville, 7535 Cape Town
Tel: (021) 9592529 *Fax:* (021) 9593411
E-mail: mayibuye@mweb.co.za
Key Personnel
Head, Marketing/Distribution: Lavona George
  E-mail: lavona@intekom.co.za
Dir: B Feinberg *E-mail:* bfeinberg@uwc.ac.za
Founded: 1992
A pioneering project helping to recover areas of South African history that have been neglected.
Subjects: Biography, History, Literature, Literary Criticism, Essays
ISBN Prefix(es): 1-86808
Total Titles: 94 Print; 1 CD-ROM

Media House Publications+
PO Box 782395, Sandton 2146
Tel: (011) 8826237 *Fax:* (011) 8829652
Key Personnel
Contact: K Everingham
Founded: 1983
Subjects: Humor, Nonfiction (General)

Charles Merrill, *imprint of* Pearson Education (Prentice Hall)

The Methodist Publishing House
Unit of The Methodist Church of Southern Africa
PO Box 708, Capetown 8000
Tel: (021) 4483640 *Fax:* (021) 4483716
Key Personnel
General Manager: D R Leverton *E-mail:* dave@methbooks.co.za
Founded: 1894
Christian Booktrade.
Subjects: Religion - Protestant
ISBN Prefix(es): 0-949942; 0-947450; 1-919883
Total Titles: 10 Print
Distributor for Abingdon (South Africa); Eagle (South Africa); Highland (South Africa); Upper Room Books (South Africa); WCC (South Africa); Westminster/John Knox (South Africa)
Bookshop(s): PO Box 1452, Benoni 1500 *E-mail:* benoni@methbooks.co.za; PO Box 130430, Bryanston 2074 *E-mail:* vicky@methbooks.co.za; PO Box 708, Cape Town 8000 *E-mail:* arnette@methbooks.co.za; PO Box 108, Durban 4000 *E-mail:* jackie@methbooks.co.za; PO Box 8508, Johannesburg 2000 *E-mail:* jhb@methbooks.co.za; PO

Box 1042, Kimberley 8300 *E-mail:* leahanne@methbooks.co.za; 164 Chapel St, Pietermaritzburg 3200 *E-mail:* roland@methbooks.co.za

Nasionale Boekhandel Ltd
386 Voortrekker Rd, Parow 7500
Mailing Address: PO Box 150, 7500 Parow
Tel: (021) 5911131
Telex: 526951 SA *Cable:* Nasboek
Key Personnel
Group Man Dir: P J Botha
Founded: 1950
Subjects: Education, Medicine, Nursing, Dentistry
Subsidiaries: Cape Booksellers Ltd; Human & Rousseau (Pty) Ltd; Nasboek (Natal) Ltd; Nasionale Boekwinkels Bpk; Nasou Ltd; Nasou Oudiovista; Natal Booksellers Ltd; J L van Schaik (Pty) Ltd; Van Schaik's Bookstore (Pty) Ltd; Tafelberg Publishers Ltd; Via Afrika Ltd; Via Afrika (Bophuthatswana) Ltd; Via Afrika (Ciskei) Ltd; Via Afrika (OFS) Ltd; Via Afrika (Transkei) Ltd, Umtata; Via Afrika (Lebowa) Ltd; Rygill's Educational Suppliers; Heer Printers (Pty) Ltd, Pretoria (all in Republic of South Africa); Nasionale Boekhandel (SWA) (Pty) Ltd
Book Club(s): Leserskring (Leisure Books)

Nasou Via Afrika+
40 Heerengracht, Cape Town 8001
Mailing Address: PO Box 5197, Cape Town 8000
Tel: (021) 406-3314; (021) 406-3005 (customer service) *Fax:* (021) 406-2922; (021) 406-3086
E-mail: mdewitt@nasou.com (customer service)
Web Site: www.nasou-viaafrika.com *Cable:* Via Afrika
Key Personnel
General Manager: D H Schroeder
  E-mail: dschroed@nasou.com
Senior Manager, Publishing: G Niebuhr
  E-mail: gniebuhr@nasou.com
Marketing Manager: T Priem *E-mail:* tpriem@nasou.com
Founded: 1970
Subjects: Fiction, Poetry, Science (General), Social Sciences, Sociology, Technology
ISBN Prefix(es): 0-77004; 0-625; 0-7994
Total Titles: 1,500 Print
Parent Company: Via Afrika
Ultimate Parent Company: NASPERS
Imprints: Acacia Books; Afritech; Afro; Atlas; Bateleur; KZN Books
Bookshop(s): PO Box 1058, Bloemfontein 9300 *Tel:* (051) 448-2345 *Fax:* (051) 448-4544 *E-mail:* bfn@afribooks.com; 15 Kraal St, East End, PO Box 1097, Bloemfontein 9300 *Tel:* (051) 447-5295 *Fax:* (051) 447-1754; PO Box 5485, Cape Town 8000 *Tel:* (021) 406-3880; (021) 406-3992 *Fax:* (021) 406-3371 *E-mail:* bvl@afribooks.com; 40 Heerengracht, PO Box 2834, Cape Town 8000 *Tel:* (021) 406-3313 *Fax:* (021) 406-2932; Loxford House, Hill St, 3rd floor, PO Box 1163, East London 5200 *Tel:* (043) 722-2464; (043) 742-0722 *Fax:* (043) 743-9914; PO Box 279, East London 5200 *Tel:* (043) 735-3888 *Fax:* (043) 735-4200 *E-mail:* el@afribooks.com; PO Box 82, George 6530 *Tel:* (044) 873-2812 *Fax:* (044) 873-2811 *E-mail:* grg@afribooks.com; Investec House, Hatfield Sq, 1st/2nd floor, 1115 Burnette St, PO Box 11943, Hatfield 0028 *Tel:* (012) 362-1141 *Fax:* (012) 362-4658 (Publishing); (012) 362-8671 (Marketing); Private Bag X5022, Kimberley 8300 *Fax:* (053) 832-9475; Tarentaal Trading Ctre, Cor Kaapsehoop Rd & N4, PO Box 2400, Nelspruit 1200 *Tel:* (013) 741-1936 *Fax:* (013) 741-3086; PO Box 556, Pinetown 3600 *Tel:* (031) 705-2417 *Fax:* (031) 701-8300 *E-mail:* ptn@afribooks.com; Ground floor, Charter House, Crompton St, PO Box 2505, Pinetown 3600 *Tel:* (031) 702-6184 *Fax:* (031) 702-6189; Nedbank Bldg, 10th floor, Office No 1001, 59-60 Landros Mare St, Polokwane 0699 *Tel:* (015) 291-4978; (015) 291-5328 *Fax:* (015) 291-5250; PO Box 95, Port Elizabeth 6000 *Tel:* (041) 363-1163 *Fax:* (041) 363-1183 *E-mail:* pe@afribooks.com; PO Box 3626, Randburg 2125 *Tel:* (011) 792-2213 *Fax:* (011) 792-2239 *E-mail:* rbg@afribooks.com; 49 Steen St, Room No 10, PO Box 9749, Rustenburg 0300 *Tel:* (014) 594-0514 *Fax:* (014) 594-0337

National Botanical Institute
Private Bag X7, Claremont 7735
Tel: (021) 799 8800 *Fax:* (021) 761 4687
E-mail: rpub@nbipre.nbi.ac.za
Web Site: www.nbi.ac.za
Key Personnel
Head Research, Support Services & Publications: M Joubert *E-mail:* mf@nbipre.nbi.ac.za
Directed toward research & conservation in the botanical field.
Subjects: Biological Sciences, Environmental Studies, Gardening, Plants, Natural History, Science (General)
ISBN Prefix(es): 0-9583205; 1-874907; 1-919684
Total Titles: 100 Print
Distributor for Briza Publications (South Africa)

New Africa Books (Pty) Ltd+
99 Garfield Rd, Claremont, Cape Town 7700
Mailing Address: PO Box 23317, Claremont, Cape Town 7735
Tel: (021) 67441387 *Fax:* (021) 6742920
E-mail: newafrica@nacp.co.za; orders@dpp.co.za (ordering)
Web Site: www.nacp.co.za
Key Personnel
Man Dir: Brian Wafawarowa
Marketing Manager: Dave Chislett
  E-mail: dave@dpp.co.za
Marketing Administrator: Erica Wicomb
  E-mail: erica@naep.co.za
Founded: 1971
Membership(s): PASA.
Subjects: Agriculture, Anthropology, Archaeology, Architecture & Interior Design, Biography, Child Care & Development, Cookery, Developing Countries, Drama, Theater, Economics, Education, English as a Second Language, Environmental Studies, Fiction, Government, Political Science, History, Humor, Literature, Literary Criticism, Essays, Natural History, Nonfiction (General), Photography, Poetry, Publishing & Book Trade Reference, Regional Interests, Women's Studies
ISBN Prefix(es): 1-919876; 0-86486
Ultimate Parent Company: New Africa Investments Ltd
Imprints: Africasouth Paperbacks; David Philip; New Africa Education; Spearhead
Branch Office(s)
PO Box 32328, Braamfontein 2017 *Tel:* (011) 727 7062 *Fax:* (011) 727 7063
526 16 Rd, Constantia Sq, Halfway House, Midrand, Johannesburg, Contact: Gillian Temple *Tel:* (011) 805-6096 *Fax:* (011) 805-1622 *E-mail:* patience.tsotetsi@jhb.dpp.co.za
Distributed by Africa Book Centre
Distributor for James Currey (Johannesburg); Christopher Hurst; Oneworld Publications; Zed Books

New Africa Education, *imprint of* New Africa Books (Pty) Ltd

Oceanographic Research Institute
PO Box 10712, Marine Parade, Durban 4056
Tel: (031) 3288222; (031) 3288238 *Fax:* (031) 3288188
E-mail: library@iru.org.za
Web Site: www.ori.org.za
Key Personnel
Dir: Prof R P van der Elst
Deputy Dir: Prof M H Schleyer
Librarian: Mrs A B Kleu
Founded: 1958
Library services, exchange of scientific publications.
Subjects: Biological Sciences, Environmental Studies, Natural History, Science (General), Marine Biology, Conservation, Fisheries, Coastal Management, Pollution Studies
ISBN Prefix(es): 0-86989
Total Titles: 1 Print
Parent Company: South African Association of Marine Biological Research
Associate Companies: Sea World, Durban *Tel:* (031) 3288222 *Fax:* (031) 3288188
Distributed by Oceanographic Research Institute

Peachpit Press, *imprint of* Pearson Education (Prentice Hall)

Pearson Education (Prentice Hall)
Mill St, 8010 Cape Town
Mailing Address: PO Box 12122, Cape Town 7700
Tel: (021) 686 6356 *Fax:* (021) 686 4590
E-mail: firstname@mml.co.za
Web Site: www.pearsoned.com
Key Personnel
Man Dir: Marian DeWet
Publisher, Higher Education: Hanli Venter
Founded: 1994
Distributes Prentice Hall titles in South Africa. Publish & distribute our subsidiaries. Specialize in higher education.
Subjects: Education
Parent Company: Pearson Plc
Associate Companies: Maskew Miller Longman (Pty) Ltd, Howard Dr, PO Box 96, Cape Town 8000, Man Dir: Fathima Dada *Tel:* (021) 5137750 *Fax:* (021) 5314049
Imprints: Addison Wesley Longman; Appleton Lange; Benjamin Cummings; Casselt Elt; Charles Merrill; De Jager Haum; Ellis Horwood; G K Hall; Harvester Wheatsheaf; Jossey Bass; Kagiso; Longman; Maskew Miller Longman; Peachpit Press; PH Macmillan ELT; PH Macmillan College; PH Macmillan Reference; Prentice Hall; Prentice Hall (Australia); Prentice Hall (Canada); Prentice Hall (Europe); Prentice Hall International; Prentice Hall (South Africa); Que College; Regents Prentice Hall; Schirmer; Scribner Reference; Woodhead Faulkner; Financial Times-Pitman
Showroom(s): Maskew Miller Longman (Midrand)

Pearson Education South Africa, *imprint of* Maskew Miller Longman

Perskor, *imprint of* Maskew Miller Longman

Perskor Books (Pty) Ltd
Postbus 3068, Halfway House 1685
Tel: (011) 315-3647 *Fax:* (011) 315-2757
E-mail: vlaeberg@icon.co.za
Telex: 83561; 87483 *Cable:* Vaderland
Key Personnel
Man Dir: F Wessels
Editorial, Rights & Permissions: P V Heerden
Sales: S J Fourie
Production: A Bothma
Publicity: S Kloppers
Founded: 1940
Subjects: Education, Law
ISBN Prefix(es): 0-628
Subsidiaries: Educum Publishers Ltd; Perskor Publishers
Bookshop(s): Johannesburgse Boekwinkel; Perskor Bookshop

SOUTH AFRICA

Book Club(s): Klub-Dagbreek; Klub 707; Klub Saffier
Orders to: Perskor-Boekwinkel, 4 Banfield Rd, Industrial North, Maraisburg 1700

PH Macmillan College, *imprint of* Pearson Education (Prentice Hall)

PH Macmillan ELT, *imprint of* Pearson Education (Prentice Hall)

PH Macmillan Reference, *imprint of* Pearson Education (Prentice Hall)

David Philip, *imprint of* New Africa Books (Pty) Ltd

Phumelela, *imprint of* Maskew Miller Longman

Prentice Hall, *imprint of* Maskew Miller Longman

Prentice Hall, *imprint of* Pearson Education (Prentice Hall)

Prentice Hall (Australia), *imprint of* Pearson Education (Prentice Hall)

Prentice Hall Australia, *imprint of* Maskew Miller Longman

Prentice Hall (Canada), *imprint of* Pearson Education (Prentice Hall)

Prentice Hall (Europe), *imprint of* Pearson Education (Prentice Hall)

Prentice Hall Europe, *imprint of* Maskew Miller Longman

Prentice Hall International, *imprint of* Pearson Education (Prentice Hall)

Prentice Hall (South Africa), *imprint of* Pearson Education (Prentice Hall)

Prentice Hall South Africa, *imprint of* Maskew Miller Longman

Publitoria Publishers+
PO Box 23334, Innesdale, Pretoria 0031
Tel: (012) 3290313 *Fax:* (012) 3290306
Key Personnel
Man Dir: L S van der Walt
Founded: 1982
Subjects: Education, Poetry
ISBN Prefix(es): 0-86880; 1-874991

QUE College, *imprint of* Maskew Miller Longman

Que College, *imprint of* Pearson Education (Prentice Hall)

Queillerie Publishers+
PO Box 879, Cape Town 8000
Tel: (021) 406 3326 *Fax:* (021) 406 3111
E-mail: queiller@nbh.naspers.co.za
Key Personnel
Manager: Frederik de Jager
Founded: 1992
Membership(s): Publishers Association of South Africa (PASA).

Subjects: Biography, Business, Cookery, Fiction, Gay & Lesbian, Human Relations, Labor, Industrial Relations, Nonfiction (General)
ISBN Prefix(es): 0-7958; 1-919710
Parent Company: Nasionale Boekhandel
Associate Companies: Jonathan Ball Publishers; Human & Rousseau Publishers; Kwela Books; Leisure Hour; Leo Books; Nasou Via Afrika; Tafelberg Publishers; Van Schaik Bookstore; J L Van Schaik
Shipping Address: Nasionale Boekhandel, PO Box 487, Bellville 7535
Warehouse: Nasionale Boekhandel, PO Box 487, Bellville 7535
Orders to: Nasionale Boekhandel, PO Box 487, Bellville 7535 *Tel:* (021) 918-8607 *Fax:* (021) 951-4903 *E-mail:* rdoman@naspers.com

Ravan Press (Pty) Ltd+
PO Box 32484, Braamfontein, Johannesburg 2017
Tel: (011) 4840916 *Fax:* (011) 48442631
Key Personnel
General Manager: Monica Seeber
Sales, Publicity & Rights: Ipuseng Kotsokoane
Book Design, Production: Matthew Seal
Founded: 1972
Membership(s): the Publishers Association of South Africa.
Subjects: Anthropology, Biography, Business, Economics, Education, Environmental Studies, Ethnicity, Fiction, Government, Political Science, History, Labor, Industrial Relations, Management, Music, Dance, Nonfiction (General), Social Sciences, Sociology, Women's Studies
ISBN Prefix(es): 0-86975; 1-86917
Parent Company: Hodder & Stoughton Educational Southern Africa
Distributed by Hodder & Stoughton Educationa (Europe & UK); Ohio University Press (USA)
Warehouse: PSD, PO Box 15016, Hurlyvale 1611

Reader's Digest Southern Africa+
21 Dreyer St, 1st fl, Sanclare Bldg, Claremont, 8000 Cape Town
Mailing Address: Private Bag 15, 8003 Capemail
Tel: (021) 670 6100 *Fax:* (021) 670 6200
E-mail: customer.sa@readersdigest.com
Web Site: www.readersdigest.co.za
Key Personnel
Man Dir: Barry Lloyd *Fax:* (021) 6706204 *E-mail:* barry@heritage.co.za
Editorial, Books & Rights & Permissions: D O Oakes *Tel:* (021) 6706252 *Fax:* (021) 6706203 *E-mail:* dongie.oakes@readersdigest.com
Editorial, Magazines: A Spencer-Smith *Tel:* (021) 6706182 *E-mail:* tony.spencer-smith@readersdigest.com
Financial Dir: Jeff Mann *Tel:* (021) 6702789 *Fax:* (021) 6706209 *E-mail:* jeff.mann@readersdigest.com
Marketing, Publicity, Dir: Philip Bateman *Tel:* (021) 6702690 *Fax:* (021) 618763 *E-mail:* philip@heritage.co.za
Sr Project Editor: Sandy Shepherd *Tel:* (021) 6706255 *E-mail:* sandy.shepherd@readersdigest.com
Direct mail books & catalogs.
Subjects: Computer Science, Cookery, Gardening, Plants, Health, Nutrition, Medicine, Nursing, Dentistry, Nonfiction (General), Travel
ISBN Prefix(es): 1-874912; 1-919750
Number of titles published annually: 5 Print
Total Titles: 53 Print
Parent Company: Reader's Digest Association, PO Box 235, Pleasantville, NY 10570, United States
Ultimate Parent Company: Heritage Collection Holdings Ltd
Imprints: AA The Motorist Publications
Branch Office(s)
Johannesburg Advertising Office, John Annandale *Tel:* (011) 799 2907 *Fax:* (011) 799 2999
Distributed by R D Vainons

Foreign Rights: Leigh Rautenbach (Southern Africa)
Warehouse: 8 Moorsom Ave, Epping 2 7475, Contact: Omar Kahaar *Fax:* (021) 548446 *E-mail:* omar-wdmkahaar@heritage.co.za

Regents Prentice Hall, *imprint of* Maskew Miller Longman

Regents Prentice Hall, *imprint of* Pearson Education (Prentice Hall)

Renaissance, *imprint of* Tafelberg Publishers Ltd

Rostrum, see HAUM (Hollandsch Afrikaansche Uitgevers Maatschappij)

Sable Media, see Struik Publishers (Pty) Ltd

Sached, *imprint of* Maskew Miller Longman

Sasavona Publishers & Booksellers
Private Bag X8, Braamfontein, Johannesburg 2017
Tel: (011) 4032502 *Fax:* (011) 3397274
Key Personnel
Manager: A E Kalteurider
Founded: 1974 (1875 as Swiss Mission Publishing)
Subjects: Education, Literature, Literary Criticism, Essays, Religion - Other
ISBN Prefix(es): 0-907985; 0-949985
Parent Company: Evangelical Presbyterian Church - Swiss Mission in SA, Private Bag X8, Braamfontein, Johannesburg 2017
Imprints: CMP Reprints; Sasavona Books; Swiss Mission Publications

Sasavona Books, *imprint of* Sasavona Publishers & Booksellers

Schirmer, *imprint of* Pearson Education (Prentice Hall)

Scribner, *imprint of* Maskew Miller Longman

Scribner Reference, *imprint of* Pearson Education (Prentice Hall)

Shuter & Shooter (Pty) Ltd
PO Box 109, Pietermaritzburg 3200
Tel: (033) 394 8881 *Fax:* (033) 342 7419 *Cable:* SHUSHOO
Key Personnel
Man Dir: Dave Ryder *E-mail:* dryder@shuter.co.za
Editorial, Rights & Permissions: J Inglis
Publicity: T Hepworth
Production: J Sharpe
Founded: 1925
Also Major Book Dealer.
Subjects: Biography, Ethnicity, History, Nonfiction (General), Science (General), Social Sciences, Sociology, Technology
ISBN Prefix(es): 0-947476; 0-7960; 0-86985
Parent Company: The Natal Witness (Pty) Ltd
Associate Companies: Ikhwezi Publishers, PO Box 648, Umtata 5100 *Tel:* (0471) 23988 *Fax:* (0471) 22786; Reach Out Publishers (at above address)
Subsidiaries: Shuter & Shooter (Gazankulu) (Pty) Ltd; Shuter & Shooter (Transkei) (Pty) Ltd
Branch Office(s)
219 Werdmuller Centre, Main Rd, Claremont, Cape Town 7700
Pharmacy House, 2nd floor, 26 Juta St, Braamfontein 2017
O & S Building, Shop 18E, 18 Witklip St, Ladanna 0704
19 Fifth Avenue, Walmer 6070

South African Institute of International Affairs+
University of the Witwatersrand, Jan Smuts House, East Campus, 2017 Johannesburg
Mailing Address: PO Box 31596, Braamfontein, Johannesburg 2017
Tel: (011) 339 2021 *Fax:* (011) 339 2154
E-mail: saiiagen@global.co.za
Web Site: www.wits.ac.za/saiia
Key Personnel
National Dir: Dr Greg Mills
Founded: 1934
Subjects: Economics, Foreign Countries, Government, Political Science, Military Science
ISBN Prefix(es): 1-874890
Branch Office(s)
Cape Town, Contact: Alan Harvey *Tel:* (021) 788-9295 *Fax:* (021) 788-9261
Durban, Contact: John Dickson *Tel:* (031) 201-4877 *Fax:* (031) 201-4914
Grahamstown
Pietermaritzburg
Port Elizabeth, Contact: Mr Peter Warmington *Tel:* (0331) 940381 *Fax:* (0331) 942332
Pretoria, Contact: Roland Henwood *Tel:* (012) 420-2687 *Fax:* (012) 420-3886
Witwatersrand, Contact: Philip Clayton *Tel:* (011) 636-2904 *Fax:* (011) 636-0512

South African Institute of Race Relations
PO Box 31044, Braamfontein, Johannesburg 2017
Tel: (011) 403-3600 *Fax:* (011) 403-3671; (011) 339-2061
E-mail: sairr@sairr.org.za
Web Site: www.sairr.org.za
Key Personnel
Dir: J S Kane-Berman
Marketing Manager: Joe Mpye
Founded: 1929
Specialize in human rights.
Subjects: Agriculture, Business, Ethnicity, Government, Political Science, Human Relations, Law, Public Administration, Social Sciences, Sociology, Human Rights
ISBN Prefix(es): 0-86982

Southern Book Publishers (Pty) Ltd+
PO Box 5563, Johannesburg 2128
Tel: (011) 3153633 *Fax:* (011) 3153810
E-mail: Southern@struik.co.za
Key Personnel
Man Dir: C F B Van Rooyen
Editorial, Rights & Permissions: Louise Grantham
Local Sales, Publicity: Jane Winters
Production: Renee Ferreira
Office Manager: Bernice Janse Van Rensburg *E-mail:* bernicejvr@struik.co.za
Founded: 1987
Subjects: Animals, Pets, Gardening, Plants, Health, Nutrition, How-to, Natural History, Nonfiction (General), Travel
ISBN Prefix(es): 1-86812
Distributed by New Holland Publishers
Warehouse: SDC, PO Box 193, Maitland
Orders to: SDC, PO Box 193, Maitland

Spearhead, *imprint of* New Africa Books (Pty) Ltd

Struik Publishers (Pty) Ltd+
Cornelis Struik House, 80 McKenzie St, Cape Town 8001
Tel: (021) 4624360 *Fax:* (021) 462-4379; (021) 461-9378
E-mail: admin@struik.co.za
Web Site: www.struik.co.za *Cable:* DEKENA CAPETOWN
Key Personnel
Man Dir: Steve Connolly
Sales Dir: Deone Maasch
Founded: 1962
Subjects: Business, Child Care & Development, Cookery, Environmental Studies, Fiction, Gardening, Plants, Humor, Natural History, Nonfiction (General), Travel, African Countries/Interests, Lifestyle, Women's Interest
ISBN Prefix(es): 0-86977; 0-947458
Parent Company: New Holland Publishing (South Africa) (Pty) Ltd, PO Box 1144, Cape Town 8000
Ultimate Parent Company: Johnnie Communications
Associate Companies: Struik Christian Books, PO Box 1144, Cape Town 8000
Imprints: Timmins Publishers (Pty) Ltd
Subsidiaries: Timmins; Struik-Winchester
Distributed by National Book Distributors; New Holland Publishers
Warehouse: Booksite Afrika, Graph Ave, Montague Gardens 7441 *Tel:* (021) 5295900 *Fax:* (021) 5511124 *Web Site:* www.booksite.co.za

Struik-Winchester, see Struik Publishers (Pty) Ltd

Swiss Mission Publications, *imprint of* Sasavona Publishers & Booksellers

Symbol Books, *imprint of* LAPA Publishers (Pty) Ltd

Tafelberg Publishers Ltd+
PO Box 879, Cape Town 8000
Tel: (021) 406 3033 *Fax:* (021) 4242510
E-mail: tafelbrg@tafelberg.com
Web Site: www.nb.co.za/tafelberg *Cable:* BOEKNUUS CAPE TOWN
Key Personnel
General Manager: Harres Van Zyl
Founded: 1950
Publishes forms in African literature, author & political publications, books for young children & young readers in all the official languages & a wide variety of illustrated nonfiction.
Subjects: Cookery, Crafts, Games, Hobbies, Fiction, Gardening, Plants, Literature, Literary Criticism, Essays, Nonfiction (General), Romance
ISBN Prefix(es): 0-624
Number of titles published annually: 100 Print; 1 CD-ROM
Total Titles: 1,200 Print; 1 CD-ROM
Parent Company: Nasionale Boekhandel Ltd
Ultimate Parent Company: Nasionale Publisher
Imprints: Homeros; Jasmyn; Renaissance
Orders to: Nasionale Boekhandel, PO Box 487, Bellville 7535 *Tel:* (021) 918-8500 *Fax:* (021) 951-4903 *E-mail:* rdoman@naspers.com

Target Publishers (Edms) Bpk
PO Box 22688, Klerksdorp 2570
Tel: (018) 4627556 *Fax:* (018) 4627557
ISBN Prefix(es): 0-9583132

Taurus+
PO Box 39400, Bramley 2018
Tel: 7860018
Key Personnel
Chief Executive: Tienie du Plessis; Hans Pienaar; Gerrit Olivier; John Miles; Ampie Coetzee
Founded: 1975
ISBN Prefix(es): 0-947046
Parent Company: Licomil Co (Pty) Ltd

Thomson Publications
PO Box 56182, Pinegowrie 2123
Tel: (011) 7892144 *Fax:* (011) 7893196
ISBN Prefix(es): 0-9583086; 0-9583865
Parent Company: Times Media Ltd

Timmins Publishers (Pty) Ltd, *imprint of* Struik Publishers (Pty) Ltd

Unibook, *imprint of* Maskew Miller Longman

Unisa Press+
University of South Africa, PO Box 392, Pretoria 0003
Tel: (012) 4293549 *Fax:* (012) 4293221
E-mail: kempg@alpha.unisa.ac.za
Web Site: www.unisa.ac.za/dept/press/index.html *Cable:* UNISA
Key Personnel
Head, Unisa Press: Mrs P Van Der Walt *Tel:* (012) 429 3051 *E-mail:* vdwp@alpha.unisa.ac.za
Head, Publishing & Secretary, International Rights: Ms S J Moolman *Tel:* (012) 429 3023 *E-mail:* moolms@alpha.unisa.ac.za
Founded: 1957
Specialize in academic publications.
Subjects: Economics, Education, History, Language Arts, Linguistics, Law, Nonfiction (General), Psychology, Psychiatry, Theology
ISBN Prefix(es): 0-86981; 1-86888
Total Titles: 128 Print
Parent Company: University of South Africa Pretonia
Orders to: The Business Section, Unisa Press, PO Box 392, Pretoria 0002

United Protestant Publishers (Pty) Ltd, see Lux Verbi (Pty) Ltd

University of Durban-Westville Library
PB X54001, Durban 4000
Tel: (031) 204 4111; (031) 204 5058 *Fax:* (031) 204 4383; (031) 204 4474
E-mail: mmoodley@pixie.udw.ac.za
Telex: 623228
Key Personnel
Chief Librarian: Mr M M Moodley *E-mail:* mmoodley@pixie.udw.ac.za
Founded: 1961
Subjects: Drama, Theater, Music, Dance
ISBN Prefix(es): 0-949947; 0-947445

University of KwaZulu-Natal Press+
Gate M14, Ridge Rd, Scottsville, Pietermaritzburg, KwaZulu-Natal 3201
Mailing Address: Private Bag X01, Scottsville, KwaZulu-Natal 3209
Tel: (033) 260 5226; (033) 260 5225 *Fax:* (033) 260 5801
E-mail: books@ukzn.ac.za
Web Site: www.ukznpress.co.za
Key Personnel
Publisher: Glenn Cowley
Founded: 1947
Membership(s): PASA (Publishers Association of South Africa).
Subjects: Biography, Biological Sciences, Education, Genealogy, Government, Political Science, Health, Nutrition, History, Literature, Literary Criticism, Essays, Poetry, Psychology, Psychiatry, Regional Interests, Social Sciences, Sociology, Women's Studies, Natural Science
ISBN Prefix(es): 0-86980; 1-86914
Number of titles published annually: 20 Print
Imprints: Killie Campbell Africana Library; Gecko Poetry; Hadeda Books
Distributed by Africa Book Centre (London); International Specialist Book Services (USA)

Van Schaik Publishers+
1064 Arcadia St, 1st floor, Hatfield 0083
Mailing Address: PO Box 12681, Hatfield 0028
Tel: (012) 342-2765 *Fax:* (012) 430-3563
E-mail: vanschaik@vanschaiknet.com
Web Site: www.vanschaiknet.com

SOUTH AFRICA

Key Personnel
Chief Executive Officer: Leanne Martini
  E-mail: lmartini@vanschaiknet.com
Founded: 1914
Specialize in publishing high-quality academic texts at affordable prices. Aim to provide academic content in any form, combination or format.
Subjects: Business, Economics, Education, Government, Political Science, History, Labor, Industrial Relations, Language Arts, Linguistics, Management, Medicine, Nursing, Dentistry, Public Administration, Social Sciences, Sociology, Natural Sciences
ISBN Prefix(es): 0-627; 0-86874
Number of titles published annually: 20 Print; 3 CD-ROM; 1 Online
Total Titles: 800 Print; 3 CD-ROM; 1 Online; 6 Audio
Parent Company: Via Afrika
Ultimate Parent Company: NASPERS
Imprints: Van Schaik Publishers Academica
Distributor for Jacana
Warehouse: On the Dot Distribution, PO Box 487, Bellville, Contact: Marietha Van Wyk
  Tel: (021) 918 8500 *Fax:* (021) 951 4903
  E-mail: mjvanwy@naspers.com
Orders to: PO Box 487, Bellville 7535, Contact: Cathleen Cloete *Tel:* (021) 918 8584 *Fax:* (021) 951 4903 *E-mail:* ccloete@naspers.com

Van Schaik Publishers Academica, *imprint of* Van Schaik Publishers

Vivlia Publishers & Booksellers+
One Amanda Ave, Lea Glen, Florida 1716
Mailing Address: PO Box 1040, Florida Hills 1716
Tel: (011) 472-3912 *Fax:* (011) 472-4904
E-mail: vivlia@icon.co.ta
Key Personnel
Man Dir: Albert N Nemukula
National Sales & Mktg: S Mota
Editorial Service Mgr: G Nose
Founded: 1990 (To serve the disadvantaged group & publish mainly South African, 11 official languages)
Services schools & libraries.
Subjects: Education, Literature, Literary Criticism, Essays, Mathematics, Science (General)
ISBN Prefix(es): 0-9583125; 1-86867; 1-874868
Total Titles: 15 Print
Branch Office(s)
PO Box 4180, Randburg 1716
Distributor for Africa World Press Inc (US)
Showroom(s): Africa Book Centre, 38 King St, London, United Kingdom, Contact: A W Zurburg *Tel:* (020) 7497 0309

Vlaeberg, *imprint of* Maskew Miller Longman

Waterkant-Uitgewers (Edms) Bpk
33 Waterkant St, Posbus 4539, Cape Town 8000
Tel: (021) 215540 *Fax:* (021) 4191865
Key Personnel
Man Dir: W J van Zijl
Publicity: Mrs E M Volschenk
Founded: 1980
Subjects: Religion - Other
ISBN Prefix(es): 0-907992; 1-875081
Parent Company: Lux Verbi (Pty) Ltd
Associate Companies: Waterkant Publishers

Who's Who of Southern Africa
PO Box 411697, Craighall, Johannesburg 2024
Tel: (011) 8802406 *Fax:* (011) 8802366
Key Personnel
Editor: S V Hayes *E-mail:* shayes@jonathanball.co.za
Founded: 1907

Total Titles: 1 Print
Parent Company: Jonathan Ball Publishers SA

Witwatersrand University Press+
23 Junction Ave, Parktown, Johannesburg
Mailing Address: PO Wits, Johannesburg 2050
Tel: (011) 4845907 *Fax:* (011) 4845971
Web Site: www.wits.ac.za/wup.html
Key Personnel
Publisher: Veronica Klipp *Tel:* (011) 4845910
Commissioning Editor: Maggie Mostert
Founded: 1922
Scholarly publisher specializing in the Humanities.
Member of Publisher's Association of South Africa.
Subjects: Anthropology, Archaeology, Biography, Business, Crafts, Games, Hobbies, Drama, Theater, Economics, Education, Ethnicity, Finance, Government, Political Science, History, Language Arts, Linguistics, Law, Literature, Literary Criticism, Essays, Medicine, Nursing, Dentistry, Natural History, Religion - Jewish, Science (General)
ISBN Prefix(es): 1-86814
Number of titles published annually: 20 Print
Total Titles: 160 Print
Distributed by Africa Book Centre (UK & Europe); Transaction Publishers
Orders to: Book Promotions, PO Box 5, Plumstead 7800, Contact: Rose Meny-Gibert
  Tel: (021) 706 0949 *Fax:* (021) 706 0941
  E-mail: orders@bookpro.ca.za

Woodhead Faulkner, *imprint of* Maskew Miller Longman

Zebra Press, see Struik Publishers (Pty) Ltd

Spain

General Information

Capital: Madrid
Language: Castilian Spanish (official) is the most widely used. Also Basque in the north, Catalan in the northeast, Galician in the northwest
Religion: Roman Catholic
Population: 40 million
Bank Hours: 0900-1400 Monday-Friday; 0900-1300 Saturday
Shop Hours: 0900-1300, 1700-2000 Monday-Saturday
Currency: 100 Eurocents = 1 Euro; 166.386 Spanish pesetas = 1 Euro
Export/Import Information: Member of European Economic Community. Tariffs on books same as other EEC members. 4% VAT on books. Import license not required; foreign books subject to censorship. No exchange controls.
Copyright: UCC, Berne, Florence (see Copyright Conventions, pg xi)

Aache Ediciones
Avda Constitucion, 33 bajo B, 19003 Guadalajara
SAN: 000-006X
Tel: (0949) 220 438 *Fax:* (0949) 220 438
E-mail: ediciones@aache.com
Web Site: aache.iberlibro.net
Key Personnel
Dir: Antonio Herrera Casado
Founded: 1990
Specialize in Guadalajara (Spain) books.
ISBN Prefix(es): 84-87743; 84-95179

Publicacions de l'Abadia de Montserrat
Ausias March, 92-98, Interior C, 08013 Barcelona
SAN: 004-668X
Tel: (093) 2450303; (093) 2657923; (093) 2430302 *Fax:* (093) 2473594
E-mail: pamsa@pamsa.com
Web Site: www.pamsa.com
Key Personnel
Administrator: Jordi Ubeda i Baulo
Dir: Josep Massot i Muntaner
Founded: 1914
Subjects: Biography, Fiction, History, Language Arts, Linguistics, Literature, Literary Criticism, Essays, Music, Dance, Philosophy, Religion - Catholic, Theology
ISBN Prefix(es): 84-7202; 84-7826

Academia de la Llingua Asturiana
C/Marques de Santa Cruz 6-2, Apartau de Correos 574, 33080 Uvieu/Oviedo Asturias
SAN: 000-0205
Tel: (0985) 211837 *Fax:* (0985) 226816
E-mail: alla@asturnet.es
Web Site: www.asturnet.es/alla
Key Personnel
President: Ana Maria Cano Gonzalez
Founded: 1981
Subjects: Anthropology, Language Arts, Linguistics, Literature, Literary Criticism, Essays
ISBN Prefix(es): 84-8168; 84-9750; 84-86936
Orders to: Albora Llibros, Pz Romualdo Alvargonzalez 5, 33202 Xixon *Tel:* 85354213 *Fax:* 85354213

Acantilado, see Sirmio

Acantilado+
Subsidiary of Quaderns Crema
Muntaner, 462 3 1, 08006 Barcelona
Tel: (093) 4144906 *Fax:* (093) 4147107
E-mail: correo@elacantilado.com
Web Site: www.elacantilado.com
Key Personnel
Man Dir: Jaume Vallcorba
Founded: 1999
Subjects: History, Literature, Literary Criticism, Essays, Poetry, Narratives
ISBN Prefix(es): 84-95359; 84-930657
Number of titles published annually: 50 Print
Total Titles: 100 Print

Editorial Acanto SA
Bertran, 113, 08023 Barcelona
SAN: 022-2322
Tel: (093) 4189093 *Fax:* (093) 4189088
E-mail: acantocb@dtinf.net
Key Personnel
Editor: Silvia Blume
Founded: 1987
Subjects: Cookery, Crafts, Games, Hobbies, Gardening, Plants, Health, Nutrition, Sports, Athletics
ISBN Prefix(es): 84-86673; 84-95376

Acento Editorial+
Joaquin Turina 39, 28004 Madrid
SAN: 000-0361
Tel: (091) 5088996; (091) 5085145; (091) 4228976 *Fax:* (091) 5089927; (091) 5084974
E-mail: informa@acento-editorial.com
Key Personnel
Contact: MaPaz Serrano
Founded: 1993
Subjects: Fiction, How-to, Music, Dance, Nonfiction (General), Science (General), Self-Help, Travel
ISBN Prefix(es): 84-483

Editorial Acervo SL+
Ronda General Mitre 200, 08006 Barcelona
SAN: 022-2349

Tel: (093) 2122664 *Fax:* (093) 4174425
E-mail: acervo25@hotmail.com
Key Personnel
Man Dir: Ana Perales
Founded: 1954
Subjects: History, Law, Literature, Literary Criticism, Essays, Science Fiction, Fantasy
ISBN Prefix(es): 84-7002
Total Titles: 1 Print

Editorial Acribia SA+
Royo Urieta 23, 50006 Zaragoza
SAN: 022-2357
Mailing Address: PO Box 466, 50080 Zaragoza
Tel: (0976) 232089 *Fax:* (0976) 219212
E-mail: acribia@infornet.es
Web Site: www.editorialacribia.com
Key Personnel
Man Dir & other offices: Pascual Lopez Lorenzo
Founded: 1957
Subjects: Agriculture, Medicine, Nursing, Dentistry, Natural History, Science (General), Veterinary Science
ISBN Prefix(es): 84-200
Number of titles published annually: 30 Print
Total Titles: 980 Print

Centro de Estudios Adams-Ediciones Valbuena SA
Alcala, 135, 28009 Barcelona
SAN: 002-046X
Tel: (093) 4465000; (0902) 333 543 *Fax:* (093) 4465004
E-mail: info@adams.es
Web Site: www.adams.es
Key Personnel
Dir General: Felix Perez Ruiz de Valbuena
Founded: 1957
Subjects: Accounting, Career Development, Computer Science, Labor, Industrial Relations, Psychology, Psychiatry, Public Administration, Transportation
ISBN Prefix(es): 84-7357; 84-8303; 84-9731

Editorial AEDOS SA+
Consell de Cent, 391, 08009 Barcelona
SAN: 022-2373
Tel: (093) 488 34 92 *Fax:* (093) 487 76 59
Web Site: www.mundiprensa.es
Key Personnel
Manager: Cristina Concellon
Founded: 1939
Subjects: Agriculture, Animals, Pets, Biological Sciences, Developing Countries, Earth Sciences, Economics, Energy, Environmental Studies, Foreign Countries, Human Relations, Labor, Industrial Relations, Management, Veterinary Science
ISBN Prefix(es): 84-7003
Parent Company: Mundiprensa Libros

AENOR (Asociacion Espanola de Normalizacion y Certificacion)+
Genova, 6, 28004 Madrid
Tel: (091) 4 32 60 00; (0902) 102 201 *Fax:* (091) 913 10 36 95
E-mail: info@aenor.es
Web Site: www.aenor.es
Key Personnel
President: Manual Lopez Cachero
General Dir: Ramon Naz Pajares
Dir, Operations: Avelino Brito Marquinas
Fax: (01) 913 10 31 72
Head, Publishing Dept: Silvia Sevilla
E-mail: ssevilla@aenor.es
Founded: 1986
Membership(s): ISO, IEC, CEN, CENELEC, ETSI, COPANT, IQNET & GENE.
Subjects: Standardization & Certification
ISBN Prefix(es): 84-8143

Editorial Afers, SL+
La Llibertat, 12, Apartat de Correus 267, 46470 Catarroja, Valencia
Tel: (0961) 26 86 54 *Fax:* (0961) 27 25 82
E-mail: afers@provicom.com
Web Site: www.provicom.com/afers
Key Personnel
Dir: Rafael Aracil i Marti i Josep Termes i Ardevol
Editorial Dir: Vicent S Olmos i Tamarit
E-mail: vicent.olmos@provicom.com
Promotion & Rights: Tremedal Ortiz
Founded: 1985
Subjects: History, Regional Interests, Social Sciences, Sociology
ISBN Prefix(es): 84-86574
Foreign Rep(s): Agusti Colomines

Agata, *imprint of* Libsa Editorial SA

Agencia Espanola de Cooperacion
Ave de los Reyes Catolicos, 4, 28040 Madrid
SAN: 001-6446
Tel: (091) 5838100; (091) 5838254; (091) 5838101; (091) 5838102 *Fax:* (091) 5838310; (091) 5838311; (091) 5838313
Key Personnel
Publishing Dir: Antonio Papell Cervera
Subjects: Art, Biography, Drama, Theater, Economics, Education, History, Law, Literature, Literary Criticism, Essays, Poetry, Social Sciences, Sociology
ISBN Prefix(es): 84-7232

Agora Editorial+
Carreteria 92, 29008 Malaga
SAN: 003-9683
Tel: (095) 2228699; (095) 2221847 *Fax:* (095) 2226411
Key Personnel
Publicity Dir: Antonio Gonzalez Alcalde
Commercial Dir: Jose Conzado Mora
Founded: 1979
Subjects: Literature, Literary Criticism, Essays, Mathematics
ISBN Prefix(es): 84-85698; 84-8160

Ediciones Agrotecnicas, SL
Plaza de Espana 10 5º Izq, 28008 Madrid
Tel: (091) 5473515 *Fax:* (091) 5474506
E-mail: agrotecnicas@agrotecnica.com
Web Site: www.agrotecnica.com
Subjects: Agriculture, Civil Engineering
ISBN Prefix(es): 84-87480
Subsidiaries: ISLA Agricola, SA

Editorial Aguaclara+
C/Rosello, 55, 03010 Alacant
SAN: 002-242X
Tel: (096) 524 00 64 *Fax:* (096) 525 93 02
E-mail: edit.aguaclara@natural.es
Key Personnel
Dir: Luis T Bonmati Gutierrez
Founded: 1982
Subjects: Fiction, Literature, Literary Criticism, Essays, Poetry, Religion - Catholic
ISBN Prefix(es): 84-86234

Aguilar SA de Ediciones
Torrelaguna, 60, 28043 Madrid
SAN: 000-0779
Tel: (091) 7449060 *Fax:* (091) 7449093
E-mail: limarquezes@santillana.es
Web Site: www.gruposantillana.es
Telex: 47137 Agata *Cable:* GUILARDITOR
Key Personnel
President: Jesus de Polanco Gutierrez
Vice President: Francisco Perez Gonzalez
Dir General: Ambrosio Maria Ochoa Vazquez
Editorial Dir: Jaime Salinas Bonmati; Mauricio Santos Arrabal
Dir, Children's Books: Miguel Azaola
Sales Dir: Miguel Lendinez
Publisher of nonfiction books in Spanish.
Subjects: Art, Fiction, Geography, Geology, History, How-to, Humor, Journalism, Language Arts, Linguistics, Medicine, Nursing, Dentistry, Nonfiction (General), Philosophy, Religion - Other, Science (General), Self-Help, Travel
ISBN Prefix(es): 84-03
Branch Office(s)
Aguilar SA, Argentina
Isla Negra SA, Chile
Libreria Cientifica, Colombia
Edidac, Ecuador
Aguilar SA, Mexico
La Familia y Studium, Peru
Itaca SA
Editemas y Dilae SA, Venezuela

AITIM (Asociacion de Investigacion Tecnica de las industrias de la Madera y Corcho)+
Flora 3-2, 28013 Madrid
Tel: (091) 5425864 *Fax:* (091) 5590512
E-mail: informame@aitim.es
Web Site: www.aitim.es
Key Personnel
Dir: Fernando Peraza Sanchez; J Enrique Peraza Sanchez *E-mail:* e.peraza@aitim.es
Founded: 1964

Ediciones Akal SA+
Sector Foresta, 1, 28760 Tres Cantos, Madrid
SAN: 001-5326
Tel: (091) 8061996 *Fax:* (091) 6564911; (091) 8044028
E-mail: pedidos.akal@akal.com (orders); edicion@akal.com; universidad@akal.com; educacion@akal.com; prensa@akal.com
Web Site: www.akal.com
Key Personnel
Editor: Ramon Acal
International Rights: Juan Barja
Subjects: Anthropology, Archaeology, Architecture & Interior Design, Art, Asian Studies, Behavioral Sciences, Economics, Education, English as a Second Language, Film, Video, Law, Philosophy, Psychology, Psychiatry, Social Sciences, Sociology
ISBN Prefix(es): 84-460; 84-406; 84-7339; 84-7600
Associate Companies: Ediciones Istmo

Editorial 'Alas'+
C/Villarroel Nº 124, 08011 Barcelona
SAN: 002-2446
Mailing Address: Apdo 36.274, 08080 Barcelona
Tel: (093) 4537506; (093) 3233445 *Fax:* (093) 4537506
E-mail: sala@editorial-alas.com
Web Site: www.editorial-alas.com
Key Personnel
Contact: Jordi Sala
Founded: 1923
Specialize in sports subjects with emphasis on martial arts.
Subjects: Health, Nutrition, Parapsychology, Religion - Buddhist, Sports, Athletics, Martial arts
ISBN Prefix(es): 84-203

Alba, *imprint of* Libsa Editorial SA

Alberdania SL+
Istillaga Plaza, 2 Behea C, 20304 Irun, Gipuzkoa
SAN: 000-1201
Tel: (0943) 63 28 14 *Fax:* (0943) 63 80 55
E-mail: alberdania@ctv.es
Key Personnel
Contact: Jorge Gimenez Bech
Founded: 1993
Subjects: Anthropology, Art, Literature, Literary Criticism, Essays
ISBN Prefix(es): 84-88669; 84-95589

El Aleph Editores, *imprint of* Grup 62

El Aleph Editores
Imprint of Grup 62
Peu de la Creu, 4, 08001 Barcelona
Tel: (093) 443 71 00 *Fax:* (093) 443 71 30
E-mail: correu@grup62.com
Web Site: www.grup62.com
Key Personnel
Rights Manager: Laura Pujol
ISBN Prefix(es): 84-931977

Alfaguara Ediciones SA - Grupo Santillana+
Torrelaguna, 60, 28043 Madrid
SAN: 001-5431
Tel: (091) 744 90 60 *Fax:* (091) 744 92 24
E-mail: loboan@santillana.es
Web Site: www.santillana.es
Telex: 47137 Agata *Cable:* GUARA MADRID
Key Personnel
Man Dir: Guillermo Schavelzon
Editor: Amaya Elezcano
Editor Assistant: Asun Lasaosa
Rights & Permissions: Rosa Arrizabalaga
Founded: 1960
Subjects: Fiction, Literature, Literary Criticism, Essays, Travel
ISBN Prefix(es): 84-204
Subsidiaries: Alfaguara; Aguilar; Attea; El Pais-Aguilar; Taurus
U.S. Office(s): Santillana Publishing Co, 901 W Walnut St, Bldg A, Compton, CA 90220, United States

Ediciones Alfar SA
Centro Andaluz del Libro, Pol Ind La Chaparrilla, parcela 34-36, Carretera Sevilla-Malaga, KM 3, 41016 Sevilla
SAN: 001-544X
Tel: (095) 4406100; (095) 4406366; (095) 4406614 *Fax:* (05) 4402580
Key Personnel
President: Manuel Angel Vazquez Medel
Dir General: Manuel Diaz Vargas
Founded: 1982
Subjects: Anthropology, Archaeology, Behavioral Sciences, Fiction, History, Literature, Literary Criticism, Essays, Mathematics, Medicine, Nursing, Dentistry, Philosophy, Social Sciences, Sociology
ISBN Prefix(es): 84-7898; 84-8248; 84-86256

Edicions Alfons el Magnanim, Institucio Valenciana d'Estudis i Investigacio+
Quevedo 10, 46001 Valencia
SAN: 002-0923
Tel: (096) 3883756 *Fax:* (096) 3883751
Web Site: www.alfonselmagnanim.com
Key Personnel
President: Fernando Giner
Vice President: Enrique Crespo
Dir: Ricardo Belleveser *Tel:* (0963) 88 3760 *Fax:* (0963) 88 3751 *E-mail:* ricardo.bellveser@diputacion.m400.gva.es
Subjects: Ethnicity, Government, Political Science, History, Social Sciences, Sociology
ISBN Prefix(es): 84-7822; 84-500; 84-398; 84-505
Warehouse: Corona, 36, 46002 Valencia *Tel:* (06) 3912561; 3912562
Orders to: LLIG, Pl Manises, 3, 46003 Valencia *Tel:* (06) 3866170

Editorial Algazara+
Lisboa, 48, 29006 Malaga
SAN: 002-2519
Tel: (095) 2358284 *Fax:* (095) 2333175
Founded: 1991
Membership(s): Editors Association of Andalucia
Subjects: History, Literature, Literary Criticism, Essays
ISBN Prefix(es): 84-87999

Alianza Editorial SA+
Division of General Edition
Juan Ignacio Luca de Tena, 15, 28027 Madrid
SAN: 000-1570
Tel: (091) 3938888 *Fax:* (091) 3207480
E-mail: alianza@anaya.es; mmorales@anaya.es
Web Site: www.alianzaeditorial.es
Key Personnel
Man Dir: Luis Sunen Garcia
Marketing: Ruth Zauner
Rights & Permissions: Laura Malejakis
Founded: 1966
Specialize in books for adults.
Subjects: Art, Fiction, Government, Political Science, History, Mathematics, Music, Dance, Philosophy, Poetry, Science (General), Social Sciences, Sociology
ISBN Prefix(es): 84-206
Parent Company: Grupo Anaya
Associate Companies: Alianza Editorial Argentina, Av Belgrano 355-Piso 10, Buenos Aires 1092, Argentina, Jorge Lafforgue *Tel:* (01) 4342 4426; Alianza Editorial Mexicana, 180 Remacimiento, Col San Juan Tlihuaca, Azcapotzalco 02400 DF, Mexico, Juan Carlos Arguelles *Tel:* (05) 561 8333 *Fax:* (05) 561 5231

Alinco SA - Aura Comunicacio
Placa Lesseps, 33, 08023 Barcelona
SAN: 000-5339
Tel: (093) 2172054 *Fax:* (093) 2373469
ISBN Prefix(es): 84-87711

Alta Fulla Editorial
Passatge d'Alio, 10, 08037 Barcelona
SAN: 000-1694
Tel: (093) 4590708; (093) 4591363 *Fax:* (093) 2075203
E-mail: altafulla@altafulla.com
Web Site: www.altafulla.com
Key Personnel
Editor & Dir: Josep J Moli Cambray
Founded: 1977
Specialize in linguistics & paperback books.
Subjects: Anthropology, Architecture & Interior Design, Cookery, Crafts, Games, Hobbies, Economics, Mythology, Social Sciences, Sociology, Antropologia, Artes y Oficios, Cultura Popular, Etnografia, Facsimiles de Libros Antiguos, Folklore
ISBN Prefix(es): 84-85403; 84-86556; 84-7900

Altea, Taurus, Alfaguara SA
Torrelaguna, 60, 28043 Madrid
SAN: 005-0881
Tel: (091) 744 90 60 *Fax:* (091) 744 92 24
E-mail: clientes@santillana.es
Web Site: www.alfaguara.santillana.es
Key Personnel
Man Dir: Ambrosio Ochoa
Editorial: Jose Antonio Millan; Luis Sunen
Publicity & Promotion: Maria de Calonje
Rights & Permissions: Rosa Arrizabalaga
Founded: 1956
Subjects: Anthropology, Art, Biography, Education, Government, Political Science, History, Language Arts, Linguistics, Literature, Literary Criticism, Essays, Music, Dance, Philosophy
ISBN Prefix(es): 84-306; 84-372; 84-204

Ediciones Altera SL+
Comte d'Urgell, 64 1r 1a, 08011 Barcelona
SAN: 006-3428
Tel: (093) 4519537 *Fax:* (093) 4517441
E-mail: editorial@altera.net
Key Personnel
Commerical Manager: Mr Guillermo Losada
Founded: 1995
Subjects: Literature, Literary Criticism, Essays
ISBN Prefix(es): 84-920659; 84-89779
Number of titles published annually: 8 Print

Total Titles: 34 Print
Orders to: Prologo Distribuciones, Mascado 35, Bajas, 08032 Barcelona

Ambit Serveis Editorials, SA+
Consell de Cent, 282 baixos, 08007 Barcelona
SAN: 000-183X
Tel: (093) 4881342 *Fax:* (093) 4874772
Key Personnel
Dir: Josep M A Benach Olivella
Founded: 1981
Subjects: Art, Cookery, Geography, Geology, Photography, Craftsmanship, Fine Arts, Nature
ISBN Prefix(es): 84-89681; 84-87342; 84-86147

Amnistia Internacional Editorial SL
Palmera, 15, 28029 Madrid
SAN: 002-2608
Tel: (091) 315 2851 *Fax:* (091) 323 2158
E-mail: amnistia.internacional@a-i.es
Key Personnel
Dir: Cristina Martinez
Founded: 1987
Subjects: Developing Countries, Education, Foreign Countries, Government, Political Science, Law, Nonfiction (General), Regional Interests, Social Sciences, Sociology
ISBN Prefix(es): 84-86874
U.S. Office(s): AI-USA, 304 Pennsylvania Ave SE, Washington, DC, DC 20003, United States
Distributed by La Catarata; El Pais Aguilar

AMV Ediciones, see Ediciones A Madrid Vicente

AMV Ediciones+
Calle Almansa, 94, 28040 Madrid
Tel: (091) 5336926; (091) 5349368 *Fax:* (091) 5530286
Web Site: www.amvediciones.com
Key Personnel
Manager: Antonio Madrid Vicente
  E-mail: amadrid@acta.es
Founded: 1986
Specialize also in cooling, heating & construction.
Subjects: Agriculture, Electronics, Electrical Engineering, Engineering (General), Gardening, Plants, Health, Nutrition, Medicine, Nursing, Dentistry, Science (General), Technology, Wine & Spirits, Food Technology
ISBN Prefix(es): 84-89922
Number of titles published annually: 15 Print; 110 Online; 1 E-Book
Total Titles: 110 Print; 10 CD-ROM; 110 Online; 1 E-Book

Editorial Anagrama
Pedro de la Creu, 58, 08034 Barcelona
SAN: 022-2616
Tel: (093) 2037652 *Fax:* (093) 2037738
E-mail: anagrama@anagrama-ed.es
Web Site: www.anagrama-ed.es
Telex: 98753 Agram E
Key Personnel
Editor & Dir: Jorge Herralde
Founded: 1968
Subjects: Anthropology, Literature, Literary Criticism, Essays, Philosophy, Psychology, Psychiatry, Social Sciences, Sociology
ISBN Prefix(es): 84-339

Ediciones Anaya SA+
Juan Ignacio Luca de Tena, 15, 28027 Madrid
Tel: (091) 393 86 00 *Fax:* (091) 320 91 29; (091) 742 66 31
E-mail: cga@anaya.es
Web Site: www.anaya.es
Telex: 22039 Anaya E *Cable:* Edinaya
Key Personnel
Chairman: Maria Isabel Andres Bravo

PUBLISHERS

SPAIN

Vice President: Juan Jose Losada
Man Dir: Enrique Coque
Editorial, Rights & Permissions: Ramiro Sanchez
Sales: Antonio Gutierrez
Founded: 1959
Subjects: Education
ISBN Prefix(es): 84-207
Parent Company: Grupo Anaya, Juan Ignacio, Luca de Tena 15, 28027 Madrid
Associate Companies: Credsa, Calabria 108, 08015 Barcelona; Algaida Editores SA, Avda de San Francisco Javier s/n, Edificio Hermes, 41005 Seville, Juan Ignacio, Luca de Tena 15, 28027 Madrid; Ediciones Generales Anaya, Anaya Multimedia, Juan Ignacio, Luca de Tena 15, 28027 Madrid; Edicions Xerais de Galicia, Doctor Maranon 10, 36211 Vigo; Ediciones Catedra SA; Ediciones Piramide SA; Ediciones Versal SA; Editorial Barcanova SA; Editorial Biblograf SA; Editorial Tecnos SA

Anaya Educacion
Juan Ignacio Luca de Tena, 15, 28027 Madrid
Tel: (091) 393 86 00 *Fax:* (091) 320 91 29; (091) 742 66 31
E-mail: cga@anaya.es
Web Site: www.anaya.es
Key Personnel
Marketing Dir: Alejandro Sanchez
    E-mail: asanchez@anaya.es
ISBN Prefix(es): 84-207

Anaya-Touring Club+
Unit of Grufo Anaya SA
Juan Ignacio Luca de Tena, 15, 28027 Madrid
Tel: (091) 393 86 00 *Fax:* (091) 742 66 31; (091) 320 91 29
E-mail: cga@anaya.es
Web Site: www.anaya.es
Key Personnel
Publisher: Pedro Pardo *Tel:* (01) 3938935
    Fax: (01) 3207022 *E-mail:* ppardo@anaya.es
International Rights: Luis Bartolome
Founded: 1989
Specialize in travel books, guides, phrase books.
Subjects: Travel
ISBN Prefix(es): 84-8165
Number of titles published annually: 30 Print
Total Titles: 280 Print
Imprints: Guia Viva; Guiarama; Guiatotal

Anglo-Didactica, SL Editorial+
Santiago de Compostela, 16, BAJO-B, 28034 Madrid
SAN: 002-2667
Tel: (091) 3780188 *Fax:* (091) 3780188
E-mail: anglodidac@aregen.net
Key Personnel
Chief Executive Officer & Administration: Ana Merino Olmos *E-mail:* anamerino@worldonline.es
Founded: 1986
Specialize in bilingual books (Spanish-English) for learning or teaching both English & Spanish.
Subjects: Education, English as a Second Language, Language Arts, Linguistics
ISBN Prefix(es): 84-86623
Number of titles published annually: 4 Print
Total Titles: 60 Print
Distributed by Bilingual Publications Co

Editorial Anthropos del Hombre+
Poligono Industrial Can Roses, nave 22, 08191 Rubi Barcelona
SAN: 000-2313
Tel: (093) 6972296 *Fax:* (093) 6972296
Key Personnel
Editorial Dir: Esteban Mate
Founded: 1981

ISBN Prefix(es): 84-7658; 84-85887
Distribution Center: Literal Book Distributors, PO Box 713, Adelphi, MD 20783, United States (USA), Contact: Jose Valencia

Arambol, SL+
Garcia de Paredes, 86, 28010 Madrid
SAN: 002-2713
Tel: (091) 3194057 *Fax:* (091) 3194057
E-mail: arambolsl@hotmail.com
Key Personnel
Administrator: Monica Guijarro
Founded: 1988
Subjects: Music, Dance
ISBN Prefix(es): 84-88128
Distributed by Piles; Seemsa
Distributor for Schell Music

Editorial Aranzadi SA
Ctra de Aoiz, Km 3, 5, 31486 Elcano
SAN: 002-273X
Tel: (0902) 444 144 *Fax:* (0948) 297 200
E-mail: clientes@aranzadi.es
Web Site: www.aranzadi.es
Key Personnel
President: Mariae de Aranzadi
General Dir: Jose Ruiz Cerrillo; Fernando Lopez Lorente
Sales & Marketing Dir: Rafael Rodiguez Galobart
Information Dir: Luis De La Guardia
Personnel Dir: Herminio De Vicente Medina
Publications Dir: Alberto Larrondo Ilondain
Sales Administrative Dir: Edurne Goni
Finance Dir: Pello Irujo Amezaga
Founded: 1929
Loose leaf publications, books & online products.
Subjects: Finance, Law, Management
ISBN Prefix(es): 84-7016; 84-8193; 84-9767; 84-8410
Total Titles: 25 CD-ROM; 15 Online
Branch Office(s)
Elcano Navarra
Geova
Madrid
Editorial Aranzadi Madrid, C/Genova 25, Madrid, Contact: Inigo Mosloso *Tel:* (091) 3080835 *Fax:* (091) 3101071 *E-mail:* clientes@aranzadi.es

Editorial Franciscana Aranzazu
Santuario de Aranzazu, 20567 Onati
SAN: 000-2682
Tel: (043) 780797; (043) 780951 *Fax:* (043) 783370
Key Personnel
Dir: Juan Ignacio Larrea
ISBN Prefix(es): 84-7240; 84-404; 84-398

Arco Libros SL+
Juan Bautista de Toledo, 28, 28002 Madrid
Tel: (091) 4153687; (091) 4161371 *Fax:* (091) 4135907
E-mail: arcolibros@arcomuralla.com
Web Site: www.arcomuralla.com
Key Personnel
Man Dir: Lidio Nieto Jimenez *Tel:* (091) 4161371
Founded: 1985
Subjects: History, Language Arts, Linguistics, Library & Information Sciences, Literature, Literary Criticism, Essays, Philology
ISBN Prefix(es): 84-7635

Arguval Editorial SA+
Heroes de Sostoa, 122, 29002 Malaga
SAN: 002-2780
Tel: (095) 2318784; (095) 2360213 *Fax:* (095) 2323715
E-mail: editorial@arguval.com
Web Site: www.arguval.com
Key Personnel
Dir: Francisco Arguelles

Founded: 1983
ISBN Prefix(es): 84-86167; 84-89672

Editorial Ariel SA+
Member of Planeta Group
Diagonal 662-664, 7a planta B, 08008 Barcelona
Tel: (093) 496 70 30 *Fax:* (093) 496 70 32
E-mail: editorial@ariel.es
Web Site: www.ariel.es
Key Personnel
General Manager: Jose Luis Castillejo
    E-mail: castillejo@ariel.es
Publisher, Foreign Rights: Asuncion Hernandez
    E-mail: ahernandez@ariel.es
Founded: 1941
Subjects: Economics, Geography, Geology, History, Literature, Literary Criticism, Essays, Philosophy, Psychology, Psychiatry, Science (General), Social Sciences, Sociology
ISBN Prefix(es): 84-344
Number of titles published annually: 80 Print; 80 Online; 80 E-Book
Total Titles: 700 Online; 700 E-Book
Associate Companies: Editorial Seix Barral SA
U.S. Office(s): Planeta Publishing Corp, 939 Crandon Blvd, Unidades 18 & 19, Key Biscayne, FL 33149, United States, Contact: Eugeni Roca *Tel:* 305-361-0053 *Fax:* 305-361-0054 *E-mail:* eroca@netrox.net

Asociacion de Investigacion Tecnica de las industrias de la Madera y Corcho, see AITIM (Asociacion de Investigacion Tecnica de las industrias de la Madera y Corcho)

Asociacion para el Progreso de la Direccion (APD)
Jose Maria Olabarri, 2, 48001 Bilbao
SAN: 000-3662
Tel: (094) 423 22 50 *Fax:* (094) 423 62 49
E-mail: apd@bil.apd.es
Web Site: www.apd.es
Key Personnel
Dir, Publications: Vidal Perez Herrero
Subjects: Business
ISBN Prefix(es): 84-7019

Editorial Astri SA+
Riera Can Pahissa, 14-18 Nave 11, Poligono Industrial CL PLA, 08750 Molins de Rei Barcelona
SAN: 002-2829
Tel: (093) 6801207 *Fax:* (093) 6803194
E-mail: astri@astri.es
Web Site: www.astri.es *Cable:* ASTRI
Key Personnel
Manager: Joaquin Minano
Founded: 1983
Subjects: Art, Astrology, Occult, Cookery, Crafts, Games, Hobbies, Fashion, Film, Video, Gardening, Plants, Health, Nutrition, House & Home, How-to, Nonfiction (General), Science Fiction, Fantasy, Self-Help, Western Fiction
ISBN Prefix(es): 84-7590; 84-469
Number of titles published annually: 80 Print
Bookshop(s): Passatje del Libre, Torret del Olla, 166, 08023 Barcelona

Sociedad de Educacion Atenas SA+
Mayor 81, 28013 Madrid
SAN: 004-9646
Tel: (091) 5480127 *Fax:* (091) 5591771
Key Personnel
Man Dir, Editorial: Santiago L de Vega
Founded: 1935
Subjects: Biography, Education, Psychology, Psychiatry, Religion - Other
ISBN Prefix(es): 84-7020

SPAIN

Ediciones Atril+
Ctrade Fuenlabrada a Pinto, Km 21, 800, 28320 Pinto Madrid
SAN: 001-5741
Tel: (091) 6911000 *Fax:* (091) 6916380
Key Personnel
General Dir: Antonio Zorita Garcia
Founded: 1989
Specialize in publishing of color graphic impressions. Print color books for other publishers or publicity companies.
Subjects: Health, Nutrition, Medicine, Nursing, Dentistry
ISBN Prefix(es): 84-87589

Atrium Group+
Ganduxer, 112, 1st Floor, 08022 Barcelona
SAN: 000-2801
Tel: (093) 2540099 *Fax:* (093) 2118139
E-mail: atrium@atriumgroup.org
Web Site: www.atriumbooks.com
Founded: 1993
Subjects: Architecture & Interior Design
ISBN Prefix(es): 84-8185
Imprints:
Distributed by

Augustinus Editorial, see Avgvstinvs

Biblioteca de Autores Cristianos+
Don Ramon de la Cruz, 57, 1° A-B, 28001 Madrid
SAN: 003-9004
Tel: (091) 3090862; (091) 3090973 *Fax:* (091) 3091980
E-mail: bac@planalfa.es
Key Personnel
Dir: D Bernardo Herradez Rubio
Sales: Manuel Garcia Hernandez
Publicity: Bartolome Parera Galmes
Founded: 1945
Subjects: Astrology, Occult, History, Philosophy, Religion - Other, Theology
ISBN Prefix(es): 84-7914; 84-220
Warehouse: Aragoneses, No 8, Poligono Industrial, 28100 Alcobendas

Avgvstinvs
General Davila 5, bajo D, 28003 Madrid
SAN: 000-443X
Tel: (091) 5342070 *Fax:* (091) 5544801
E-mail: revista@avgvstinvs.org
Web Site: www.avgvstinvs.org
Key Personnel
Dir: John J Oldfield *E-mail:* oar.sezeq@terra.es
Subjects: Theology
ISBN Prefix(es): 84-85096; 84-604; 84-605; 84-400; 84-300

Ayalga Ediciones SA+
Alcalde Luis Treillard, 14-16, 33400 Salinas Asturias
SAN: 000-4472
Tel: (085) 5500599; (085) 501299 *Fax:* (085) 5500869 *Cable:* AYALGA
Key Personnel
President: Francisco Javier Sitges
Vice President: Agustin Santarua
Man Dir: Ramon Baragano
Sales: Francisco Alzueta
Founded: 1976
Subjects: Regional Interests
ISBN Prefix(es): 84-7411; 84-400
Divisions: Ayalga Ediciones SA
Orders to: Gran Via Escultor Salzillo, 19-11, 300004 Murcia

Editorial Ayuso
San Bernardo 48, 28015 Madrid
SAN: 000-5193
Tel: (091) 2228080
Subjects: Social Sciences, Sociology
ISBN Prefix(es): 84-336

Ediciones B, SA+
Bailen, 84, 08009 Barcelona
SAN: 001-5911
Tel: (093) 484 66 00 *Fax:* (093) 232 46 60
Web Site: www.edicionesb.es; www.edicionesb.com
Telex: 53183
Key Personnel
Man Dir: Blanca Rosa Roca
Assistant Dir: Carlos Ramos
Production Dir: Jordi Omella
Head of Production: Jordi Aspa
Public Relations: Silvia Fernandez
Rights: Alejandra Segrelles
Founded: 1986
Subjects: Biography, Fiction, Humor, Nonfiction (General)
ISBN Prefix(es): 84-406; 84-7735

BAC, see Biblioteca de Autores Cristianos

Baile del Sol, Colectivo Cultural+
Apdo de Correos 133, 38280 Tegueste, Santa Cruz de Tenerife
SAN: 001-0103
Tel: 676438253
E-mail: bailesol@yahoo.com
Key Personnel
General Coordinator: Tito Exposito
Founded: 1992
Subjects: Alternative, History, Poetry, Self-Help
ISBN Prefix(es): 84-88671; 84-95309

Editorial Barath SA+
Blasco de Garay 15, 28015 Madrid
SAN: 002-2977
Tel: (091) 4496049
Key Personnel
Man Dir: Victorino del Pozo
Sales: Cinta Barrobes
Production: Jorge Vines
Founded: 1980
Subjects: Astrology, Occult, Human Relations
ISBN Prefix(es): 84-85799
Associate Companies: Distribuciones Alfaomega SA, Calle Calvo Asensio 13, 28015 Madrid

Editorial Barcanova SA+
Placa Lesseps, 33 entl, 08023 Barcelona
SAN: 022-2985
Tel: (093) 2172054; (093) 2172550 *Fax:* (093) 2373469
E-mail: barcanova@barcanova.es
Web Site: www.barcanova.es
Key Personnel
Dir General: Ramon Besora Oliva
Editorial: Jordi Galofre
Production: Enric Canut
Founded: 1981
Subjects: Education
ISBN Prefix(es): 84-7533; 84-489; 84-85923
Parent Company: Grupo Anaya, Madrid
Associate Companies: Ediciones Anaya SA

Editorial Barcino SA+
Montseny, 9 baixos, 08012 Barcelona
SAN: 002-3000
Tel: (093) 2186888 *Fax:* (093) 2186888
E-mail: ebarcino@editorialbarcino.com
Web Site: www.editorialbarcino.com
Key Personnel
Literary Dir: Amadeu J Soberanas i Lleo
Founded: 1924
Subjects: Literature, Literary Criticism, Essays
ISBN Prefix(es): 84-7226

Beascoa SA Ediciones
Pujades, 81, 08005 Barcelona
SAN: 001-5997
Tel: (093) 3196517; (093) 3934380 *Fax:* (093) 3107694; (093) 3934389
E-mail: info@beascoa.com
Key Personnel
President: Francisco Beascoa-Anton
ISBN Prefix(es): 84-488; 84-7546
Associate Companies: Sol-Jouem, Lisbon, Portugal
Subsidiaries: Beascoa Internacional

Ediciones Bellaterra SA
Navas de Tolosa, 289b, 08027 Barcelona
SAN: 001-6004
Tel: (093) 3390511; (093) 3499786 *Fax:* (093) 3520851
E-mail: bellaterra@retermail.es
Key Personnel
Man Dir: Felio Riera Domenech
Editorial: Jeannine Rochefort
Sales: Angeles Galan Gallego
Founded: 1972
Subjects: Science (General), Social Sciences, Sociology, Technology
ISBN Prefix(es): 84-7290

Beta Editorial SA
Roux 67, 08017 Barcelona
SAN: 000-5746
Tel: (093) 2804640 *Fax:* (093) 2806320
Founded: 1943
ISBN Prefix(es): 84-7091

Biblioteca 'NT', *imprint of* EUNSA (Ediciones Universidad de Navarra SA)

Editorial Biblioteca Nueva SL
Almagro, 38, 28010 Madrid
SAN: 002-3086
Tel: (091) 3100436 *Fax:* (091) 3198235
E-mail: editorial@bibliotecanueva.com
Web Site: www.bibliotecanueva.es
Key Personnel
Man Dir: Antonio Roche
Sales Dir: Paz Casas Ruiz-Castillo
Founded: 1920
Subjects: Biography, Economics, History, Poetry, Psychology, Psychiatry
ISBN Prefix(es): 84-7030; 84-9742
Number of titles published annually: 140 Print
Total Titles: 3,895 Print

Biografia Joven, *imprint of* Editorial Casals SA

Boletin Oficial del Estado
Ave de Manoteras, 54, 28050 Madrid
SAN: 000-6254
Tel: (091) 902 365 303 *Fax:* (091) 5382349
E-mail: info@docu.boe.es
Web Site: www.boe.es
Key Personnel
Dir General: Beatriz Martin
Founded: 1661
Subjects: Law, Public Administration
ISBN Prefix(es): 84-340

Bookbank SL Agencia Literaria+
San Martin de Porres 14, 28035 Madrid
Tel: (091) 3733539 *Fax:* (091) 3165591
E-mail: bookbank@nexo.es
Key Personnel
Dir: Alicia Gonzalez Sterling
Founded: 1983
Specialize in representing foreign publishers & agents in Spain & Latin America & Spanish authors worldwide.

Antoni Bosch Editor SA+
Manuel Girona, 61, 08034 Barcelona
Tel: (093) 206 07 30 *Fax:* (093) 206 07 31
E-mail: info@antonibosch.com

Web Site: www.antonibosch.com
Key Personnel
President: Antoni Bosch-Domenech
Production, Rights & Permissions & Man Dir: Isabel Cruz Saez *E-mail:* icruz@antonibosch.com
Founded: 1978
Subjects: Economics, Music, Dance, Science (General)
ISBN Prefix(es): 84-85855; 84-95348
Associate Companies: Bon Ton
Distributor for Bon Ton

Bosch Casa Editorial SA+
Comte d'Urgell, 51 bis, 08011 Barcelona
SAN: 000-6297
Tel: (093) 4548437; (093) 4544629; (093) 4521050 *Fax:* (093) 3236736
E-mail: bosch@boschce.es
Web Site: www.boschce.es
Key Personnel
President: Agustin Bosch Domenech
Man Dir: J Manuel Ianez
Marketing Manager: Albert Ferre
Founded: 1934
Membership(s): Publishers Association of Catalonia, focused in law books & legal matters.
Subjects: Criminology, Journalism, Language Arts, Linguistics, Law, Literature, Literary Criticism, Essays, Public Administration, Radio, TV
ISBN Prefix(es): 84-7162; 84-7676

J M Bosch Editor+
Ronda Universidad, 11, 08029 Barcelona
Tel: (093) 3175308 *Fax:* (093) 4122764
E-mail: jmb@libreriabosch.es
Web Site: www.libreriabosch.es/jmb
Key Personnel
Dir: Javier Bosch *E-mail:* direccion@libreriabosch.es
Founded: 1889
Subjects: Law
ISBN Prefix(es): 84-7698
Number of titles published annually: 35 Print
Total Titles: 530 Print
Parent Company: Libreria Bosch

Editorial M J Bosch, SL
Villarroel, 39-3r.3a, 08011 Barcelona
SAN: 006-6435
Tel: (093) 4512335
E-mail: mjbosch@colon.net
Key Personnel
Dir: Maria Jesus Bosch
Subjects: Criminology, Law
ISBN Prefix(es): 84-89591

Edicions Bromera SL+
Poligon Industrial I, Ronda Tintorers 117, Apartat de correus 147, 46600 Alzira
SAN: 002-0974
Tel: (096) 2402254 *Fax:* (096) 2403191
E-mail: illa@bromera.com; bromera@bromera.com
Web Site: www.bromera.com
Founded: 1986
Membership(s): the Valencia Publisher's Association.
Subjects: Literature, Literary Criticism, Essays
ISBN Prefix(es): 84-7660

Editorial Bruno+
Maestro Alonso, 21, 28028 Madrid
SAN: 002-3175
Tel: (091) 724 48 00 *Fax:* (091) 361 31 33
E-mail: informacion@editorial-bruno.es
Web Site: www.editorial-bruno.es
Key Personnel
Man Dir: Francisco Fernandez Cilleruelo
Founded: 1897
Subjects: Communications, Education, Religion - Catholic
ISBN Prefix(es): 84-216
Warehouse: Av Castilla, 15-17, Pol Ind S Fernando 1, 28850 Torrejon de Ardoz (Madrid)

Cabildo Insular de Gran Canaria Departamento de Ediciones
Calle Bravo Murillo 21, 35002 Las Palmas de Gran Canaria
SAN: 000-6793
Tel: (0928) 219421 *Fax:* (0928) 381627
E-mail: webadmin@grancanaria.com
Web Site: www.grancanaria.com
Key Personnel
Dept Head: Jesus Bombin Quintana
President: Jose Manuel Soria Lopez
Subjects: Geography, Geology, History, Natural History, Regional Interests
ISBN Prefix(es): 84-8103; 84-86127; 84-500; 84-505; 84-600

Caja de Ahorros del Mediterraneo-Obras Sociales
San Fernando, 40, 03001 Alicante
SAN: 000-6290
Tel: (06) 5906363; (06) 5905785 *Fax:* (06) 5905828
E-mail: cam@cam.es
Web Site: www.cam.es
ISBN Prefix(es): 84-7599; 84-88440

Calambur Editorial, SL+
Maria Teresa, 17-1° C, 28028 Madrid
Tel: (091) 913553033 *Fax:* (091) 913553033
E-mail: calambur@calambureditorial.com
Web Site: www.calambureditorial.com
Key Personnel
Man Dir: Fernando Saenz *E-mail:* fsaenz@calambureditorial.com
Founded: 1998
Membership(s): Emilio Torne, JF Escudero, Fernando Saenz.
Subjects: Fiction, Humor, Poetry
ISBN Prefix(es): 84-88015
Number of titles published annually: 12 Print
Total Titles: 86 Print

Calamo Editorial
C/Pintor Aparicio, 13, 03003 Alicante
SAN: 002-3213
Tel: (096) 5130581 *Fax:* (096) 5115345
E-mail: calamo@lobocom.es
Web Site: www.lobocom.es/~calamo
Key Personnel
Dir: Ana Cristina Baidal Lopez *E-mail:* anacris@lobocom.es
Founded: 1990
Subjects: Fiction, Human Relations, Literature, Literary Criticism, Essays, Religion - Islamic, Travel, Arab & Mediterranean Culture
ISBN Prefix(es): 84-87839

Calesa SA Editorial La+
Camino Viejo de Zaratan, km 1,5, 47610 Zaratan (Valladolid)
SAN: 002-5119
Mailing Address: Parque Tecnologico de Boecillo, Parcela 134, 47151 Boecillo (Valladolid)
Tel: (0983) 548 102 *Fax:* (0983) 548 024
E-mail: editorial@la-calesa.com
Web Site: www.la-calesa.com
Key Personnel
Manager: Jacinto Altes-Bustelo
Founded: 1989
Subjects: Language Arts, Linguistics, Mathematics
ISBN Prefix(es): 84-8105; 84-87463
Subsidiaries: Boecillo Editora Multimedia, SA

Edicions Camacuc+
Arquebisbe Olaetxea, 18-baux esq, Apdo de Correos 11007, 46080 Valencia
SAN: 002-0990
Tel: (096) 357 28 56 *Fax:* (096) 357 28 56
Key Personnel
Pastor: Amparo Sospedra
Founded: 1987
Subjects: History, Literature, Literary Criticism, Essays, Science Fiction, Fantasy
ISBN Prefix(es): 84-86970; 84-89938

Editorial Cantabrica SA+
Nervion 3-6, 48001 Bilbao
SAN: 002-3280
Tel: (04) 4245307 *Fax:* (04) 4231984
Key Personnel
Man Dir: Begona Grijelmo Mattern
Founded: 1960
Subjects: Cookery, Humor, Language Arts, Linguistics, Sports, Athletics
ISBN Prefix(es): 84-221
Warehouse: Andres Isasi, 11-3, 48012 Bilbao Vizcaya

Carroggio SA de Ediciones+
C Pelai, 28-30, 08001 Barcelona
SAN: 000-7439
Tel: (093) 4949922 *Fax:* (093) 4949923
E-mail: carroggio@carroggio.com
Web Site: www.carroggio.es
Key Personnel
General Administrator: Santiago Carroggio
Founded: 1911
Specialize in art & educational books.
Subjects: Art, History, Literature, Literary Criticism, Essays, Natural History
ISBN Prefix(es): 84-7254
Branch Office(s)
San Ignacio de Loyola, 4, 46006 Valencia
Tel: (096) 3854377 *Fax:* (096) 3820159

Instituto Cartografico Latino, *imprint of* Editorial Vicens-Vives

Casa de Velazquez+
C/de Paul Guinard, Ciudad Universitaria, 28040 Madrid
SAN: 000-7471
Tel: (091) 5433605 *Fax:* (091) 5446870
E-mail: bcv@bibli.cvz.es
Key Personnel
Dir: Gerard Chastagnaret
Head of Publishing: Vincent Lautie
Founded: 1928
Subjects: Archaeology, Geography, Geology, History, Language Arts, Linguistics, Literature, Literary Criticism, Essays, Social Sciences, Sociology
ISBN Prefix(es): 84-86839; 84-9750; 84-404; 84-500; 84-398; 84-300; 2-87634; 84-95555

Editorial Casals SA+
Casp 79, 08013 Barcelona
Tel: (093) 2449550 *Fax:* (093) 2656895
E-mail: casals@editorialcasals.com
Web Site: www.editorialcasals.com
Key Personnel
Man Dir: Ramon Casals *E-mail:* export@editorialcasals.com
Rights & Permissions: Angelica Regidor
Founded: 1870
Subjects: Art, Education, Literature, Literary Criticism, Essays, Mathematics, Music, Dance, Philosophy, Religion - Catholic, Science (General), Social Sciences, Sociology
ISBN Prefix(es): 84-218; 84-7552
Number of titles published annually: 200 Print
Total Titles: 1,800 Print
Associate Companies: Combel Editorial, SA; Editorial Magisterio Espanol, SA

Imprints: Biografia Joven; Punto Juvenil; Novelas y Cuentos
Warehouse: Juli Galve i Brusons 72-74, 08912 Badalona

Editorial Casariego+
c/Cristobal Bordiu, 3, 28003 Madrid
SAN: 002-3329
Tel: (091) 4424339; (091) 4425178; (091) 4411330; (091) 4416829 *Fax:* (091) 4426224
E-mail: casariego@infonegocio.com
Web Site: www.casariego.com
Key Personnel
Man Dir, Production, Rights & Permissions: Carmen Diaz-Casariego
Editorial, Sales: Isabel Rodriguez
Founded: 1959
Subjects: Art
ISBN Prefix(es): 84-86760
Bookshop(s): Libreria Facsimilia y Arte, Calle Cristobal Bordiu 36, 28003 Madrid

Casset Ediciones SL+
Pez Austral, 9, 28007 Madrid
SAN: 001-6225
Tel: (091) 5043584 *Fax:* (091) 2508841
Key Personnel
Editorial Dir: Javier Parra Alvarez
Founded: 1990
Subjects: Humor, Parapsychology
ISBN Prefix(es): 84-87859

Editorial Castalia
Zurbano, 39, 28010 Madrid
SAN: 002-3345
Tel: (091) 3195857 *Fax:* (091) 3102442
E-mail: castalia@infornet.es
Web Site: www.castalia.es
Key Personnel
Man Dir: Amparo Soler
Sales Dir: Federico Ibanez
Founded: 1941
Specialize in editions of the classics.
Subjects: Education, Literature, Literary Criticism, Essays
ISBN Prefix(es): 84-7039; 84-9740

Edicios do Castro
O Castro de Samoedo, 15168 Sada (A Coruna)
SAN: 001-4605
Tel: (0981) 621494; (0981) 620937; (0981) 620200 *Fax:* (0981) 623804
E-mail: edicios.ocastro@sargadelos.com
Web Site: www.sargadelos.com
Key Personnel
Dir: Isaac Diaz Pardo
Founded: 1963
Subjects: Art, Drama, Theater, Economics, Geography, Geology, History, Literature, Literary Criticism, Essays, Poetry, Science (General), Social Sciences, Sociology
ISBN Prefix(es): 84-7492; 84-8485; 84-85134
Imprints: Graficas do Castro/Moret

Graficas do Castro/Moret, *imprint of* Edicios do Castro

Catalogo, *imprint of* Ediciones Maeva

Biblioteca de Catalunya
Carrer de l'Hospital, 56, 08001 Barcelona
Tel: (093) 270 23 00 *Fax:* (093) 270 23 04
E-mail: bustia@bnc.es
Web Site: www.gencat.es/bc
Key Personnel
Dir: Mrs Vinyet Panyella *E-mail:* vinyetp@bnc.es
Chief of Difussion Area: Montserrat Fonoll
 E-mail: mfonoll@bnc.es
Founded: 1914

Subjects: Art, History, Library & Information Sciences, Literature, Literary Criticism, Essays, Music, Dance
ISBN Prefix(es): 84-7845
Number of titles published annually: 6 Print
Parent Company: Department of Culture
Ultimate Parent Company: Generalitat De Catalunya
Distribution Center: Les Punxes Distribuidora S L, Sardenya 75 81, 08018 Barcelona *Tel:* (093) 485-63-10 *Fax:* (093) 300-90-91

Ediciones Catedra SA+
Juan Ignacio Luca de Tena, nº 15, 28027 Madrid
SAN: 001-6144
Tel: (091) 3200119; (091) 3938800; (091) 3938787 *Fax:* (091) 7426631; (091) 7412118
E-mail: catedra@catedra.com
Web Site: www.catedra.com
Telex: 41071 MAEG
Key Personnel
Man Dir: Gustavo Dominguez Leon
Rights & Permissions: Marisa Barreno; Josune Garcia
Founded: 1973
Subjects: Art, Film, Video, History, Human Relations, Language Arts, Linguistics, Literature, Literary Criticism, Essays, Music, Dance, Philosophy, Poetry, Women's Studies
ISBN Prefix(es): 84-376
Parent Company: Grupo Anaya, Juan Ignacio, Luca de Tena 15, 28027 Madrid
Associate Companies: Ediciones Anaya SA; Tecnos; Piramide; Algaida
Bookshop(s): Iriarte 4, 28028 Madrid
Warehouse: Avda Ferrocarril s/n, 28346 Madrid
Orders to: Comercial Grupo Anaya, SA Calle Iriaste, 4, 28028 Madrid *Tel:* (01) 3597600 *Fax:* (01) 3559403

CCG, see Consello da Cultura Galega - CCG

Editorial CCS, see Central Catequistica Salesiana (CCS)

CEAC, Grupo Editorial SA+
Peru, 164, 08020 Barcelona
SAN: 003-3634
Tel: (093) 3073004 *Fax:* (093) 2660067
E-mail: atencioncliente@ceacedit.com; info@ceacedit.com
Web Site: www.ceacedit.com; www.editorialceac.com
Key Personnel
Man Dir: Santiago Pintanel
International Rights & Permissions Dir: Julia Esteve
Technical, Literary Dir: Norma Fenoglio
Founded: 1957
Membership(s): Publishers Association of Spain.
Subjects: Architecture & Interior Design, Education, Electronics, Electrical Engineering, Engineering (General), Fiction, Health, Nutrition, Photography, Science Fiction, Fantasy
ISBN Prefix(es): 84-329
Parent Company: Grupo Editorial Ceac SA
Associate Companies: Grupo Ceac SA
Subsidiaries: Editorial Timun Mas SA; Ediciones Vidorama SA
Branch Office(s)
Aconcagua Ediciones y Publicaciones SA, Xochicalco, 352 Col Narvarte, 03020 Mexico, DF, Mexico
Warehouse: Poligono Can Magarola calle, 08100 Mollet del Valles

Cedel, Ediciones Jose O Avila Monteso ES+
Mallorca, 257, 08008 Barcelona
SAN: 001-625X
Tel: (093) 2156039 *Fax:* (093) 2156088
E-mail: cedel@wbsite.es

Key Personnel
President: Sr Oriol Avila i Monteso, Sr
Man Dir, Rights & Permissions: Jose Avila
Founded: 1956
Subjects: Agriculture, Biological Sciences, Environmental Studies, Health, Nutrition
ISBN Prefix(es): 84-352

CEIC Alfons El Vell
Pza Rei en Jaume, 10, 46700 Gandia, Valencia
Tel: (06) 2876551 *Fax:* (06) 2875286
Key Personnel
Dir: Gabriel Garcia Frasquet

Celeste Ediciones+
Fernando VI, 8-1, 28004 Madrid
SAN: 000-7722
Tel: (091) 3100599; (002) 118298 *Fax:* (091) 3100459
E-mail: info@celesteediciones.com
Key Personnel
Manager: Miguel Angel San Jose
Dir of Export: Jesus Miranda
Rights: Cristina Fernandez Calderon
Founded: 1980
Subjects: Advertising, Architecture & Interior Design, Art, Economics, History, Mathematics, Music, Dance, Photography, Science (General), Travel
ISBN Prefix(es): 84-87553; 84-8211

Central Catequistica Salesiana (CCS)
Alcala, 166, 28028 Madrid
SAN: 002-3701
Tel: (091) 7252000 *Fax:* (091) 7262570
E-mail: apedidos@editorialccs.com; sei@editorialccs.com
Web Site: www.editorialccs.com
Founded: 1944
Subjects: Biblical Studies, Biography, Crafts, Games, Hobbies, Drama, Theater, Education, Religion - Catholic
ISBN Prefix(es): 84-7043; 84-8316

Centro de Cultura Tradicional
Plaza de Colon, 4, 37001 Salamanca
SAN: 000-7951
Tel: (0923) 293255 *Fax:* (0923) 293256
E-mail: cct@dipsanet.es
Web Site: www.dipsanet.es/cultura/culturatradicional/inicio.htm
Key Personnel
Dir: Angel Carril Ramos *Tel:* (0923) 293255
 E-mail: acarril@dipsanet.es
ISBN Prefix(es): 84-87339

Centro de Estudios Avanzados en Ciencias Sociales (CEACS) del Instituto Juan March de Estudios e Investigaciones
Castello, 77, 28006 Madrid
Tel: (091) 4354240 *Fax:* (091) 5763420
E-mail: webmast@mail.march.es
Web Site: www.march.es
Key Personnel
President: Juan March
Vice-President: Carlos March
Man Dir: Jose Luis Yuste Grijalba
Dir: Jose Maria Maravall

Centro de Estudios Politicos Y Constitucionales+
Plaza de la Marina Espanola, 9, 28071 Madrid
SAN: 000-8109
Tel: (091) 5401950 *Fax:* (091) 5419574
E-mail: cepc@cepc.es
Web Site: www.cepc.es
Key Personnel
Dir: Carmen Iglesias Cano
Assistant Dir: Feliciano Barrios Pintado
Founded: 1939

PUBLISHERS SPAIN

Subjects: Government, Political Science, History, Law, Philosophy, Social Sciences, Sociology
ISBN Prefix(es): 84-259

Centro UNESCO de San Sebastian
Urbieta, 11-1°, 20006 San Sebastian
Tel: (0943) 427003 *Fax:* (0943) 427003
E-mail: unescoeskola@retemail.es
Web Site: www.servicom.es/unesco
Key Personnel
Executive Dir: Juan Ignacio Martinez de Morentin de Goni
Founded: 1992
Specialize in Unesco training courses, manuals & student books.
Subjects: Education
Total Titles: 107 Print; 7 Online; 5 E-Book; 310 Audio
Parent Company: Unesco

Circe Ediciones, SA+
Milanesat, 25-27, 08017 Barcelona
SAN: 000-9865
Tel: (093) 2040990; (093) 2040659 *Fax:* (093) 2041183
E-mail: circe@oceano.com
Telex: 51735 Exit-E
Key Personnel
Editor: Silvia Lluis
Founded: 1986
Subjects: Biography, Fiction, Literature, Literary Criticism, Essays, Nonfiction (General)
ISBN Prefix(es): 84-7765

Cisneros
Joaquin Costa, 36, 28002 Madrid
SAN: 003-9799
Tel: (091) 5619900 *Fax:* (091) 5613990
Key Personnel
Contact: A Enrique Chacon
Founded: 1914
ISBN Prefix(es): 84-7047

Editorial Ciudad Nueva
Jose Picon 28, 28028 Madrid
Tel: (091) 725 95 30; (091) 356 96 12 *Fax:* (091) 713 04 52
E-mail: editorial@ciudadnueva.com
Web Site: www.ciudadnueva.com
Key Personnel
Editorial Dir: Jose Luis Romero
Founded: 1964
Membership(s): Espana.
Subjects: Religion - Other
ISBN Prefix(es): 84-86987; 84-85159; 84-89651; 84-9715
Parent Company: Citta Nuova Editrice, Italy
Subsidiaries: Ciutat Nova (Publicaciones en lengua Catalana)
U.S. Office(s): Living City Office, 99-28 64 Rd, Rego Park, NY 10465, United States

Civitas SA Editorial
Barbara de Braganza, 10, 28004 Madrid
SAN: 002-3205
Tel: (091) 902 011 787 *Fax:* (091) 725 26 73
E-mail: clientes@civitas.es
Web Site: www.civitas.es
Key Personnel
President & Counselor: Eduardo Garcia de Enterria
Founded: 1970
Subjects: Economics, Law, Public Administration
ISBN Prefix(es): 84-470; 84-7398
Bookshop(s): General Pardinas, 24, 28001 Madrid

Editorial Claret SA+
Roger de Lluria, 5, 08010 Barcelona
Tel: (093) 3010887 *Fax:* (093) 3174830
E-mail: editorial@claret.es; admin@claret.es
Web Site: www.claret.es

Key Personnel
Man Dir & Production: Pere Codina Mas
Editorial Manager: Marcel-Li Lopez Rodriguez
Sales: Carlos Delgado Martinez
Publicity: Luis Vinoles del val
Founded: 1926
Subjects: Religion - Other
ISBN Prefix(es): 84-7263

Editorial Clie+
Editorial Clie Galvani 113, 08224 Terrassa, Barcelona
SAN: 004-0010
Tel: (093) 7884262; (093) 7885722 *Fax:* (093) 7800514
E-mail: libros@clie.es
Web Site: www.clie.es
Key Personnel
Sales Manager: Deborah Vila
Founded: 1924
Subjects: Religion - Protestant
ISBN Prefix(es): 84-7645; 84-7228; 84-8267; 84-300
Book Club(s): Club de Lectores Clie

Climent, Eliseau Editor+
Perez Bayer 11, 46002 Valencia
SAN: 002-7936
Tel: (06) 3516492 *Fax:* (06) 3529872
E-mail: 3i4@arrakis.es
Key Personnel
Editor: Elisen Climent Corbera
Founded: 1968
ISBN Prefix(es): 84-85211; 84-7502

Cofas SA, *imprint of* Vinaches Lopez, Luisa

Ediciones Colegio De Espana (ECE)+
Compania, 65, 37008 Salamanca
Tel: (023) 21 47 88 *Fax:* (023) 21 87 91
E-mail: info@colesp.eurart.es
Web Site: www.eurart.es/emp/colesp
Key Personnel
Executive: Jose Luis de Celis
Founded: 1987
Subjects: Art, Language Arts, Linguistics, Literature, Literary Criticism, Essays
ISBN Prefix(es): 84-86408; 84-9750; 84-404; 84-604; 84-300
Number of titles published annually: 20 Print
Total Titles: 50 Print

COLEX, see Editorial Constitucion y Leyes SA - COLEX

Columna Edicions, Libres i Comunicacio, SA+
Viladomat 0135, 08015 Barcelona
SAN: 001-0391
Tel: (093) 4238761 *Fax:* (093) 4238761
Founded: 1985
Subjects: Fiction, Poetry
ISBN Prefix(es): 84-7809; 84-8300; 84-86433
Subsidiaries: Aea

Combel, *imprint of* Editorial Esin, SA

Combel Editorial SA+
Affiliate of Editorial Casals SA
c/Casp 79, 08013 Barcelona
Tel: (093) 2449550 *Fax:* (093) 2656895
E-mail: casals@editorialcasals.com
Key Personnel
Man Dir: Ramon Casals
Rights: Angelica Regidar
Founded: 1989
ISBN Prefix(es): 84-7864
Number of titles published annually: 50 Print
Total Titles: 500 Print
Foreign Rep(s): Independent Publishers Group-Chicago (USA)

Editora Comercial de Publicaciones+
Almirante Cadarso 11, 46005 Valencia
SAN: 001-0480
Tel: (096) 3952045; (096) 3957293 *Fax:* (096) 3952297
E-mail: edicep@nexo.net
Key Personnel
Man Dir: Mora Pilar Taroncher
Founded: 1979
Subjects: Biblical Studies, History, Law, Philosophy, Religion - Catholic
ISBN Prefix(es): 84-7050

Los Libros del Comienzo+
Arriaza, 14, 28008 Madrid
SAN: 004-0487
Tel: (091) 5481079 *Fax:* (091) 5400378
E-mail: buzon@libroscomienzo.com
Web Site: www.libroscomienzo.com
Key Personnel
Publisher: Eduardo Rosello
Founded: 1990
Subjects: Self-Help
ISBN Prefix(es): 84-87598

Compania Literaria+
Padilla, 56, 28006 Madrid
SAN: 001-0693
Tel: (091) 4015312 *Fax:* (091) 4015312
Key Personnel
Dir: Juan Bercelo
Founded: 1994
Subjects: Anthropology, Biography, History, Journalism, Literature, Literary Criticism, Essays, Nonfiction (General), Social Sciences, Sociology, Travel
ISBN Prefix(es): 84-8213

Ediciones de la Universidad Complutense de Madrid+
Donoso Cortes, 63-3 planta, 28015 Madrid
Tel: (091) 394 64 60; (091) 394 64 61 *Fax:* (091) 394 64 58
E-mail: ecsa@rect.ucm.es
Web Site: www.ucm.es/info/ecsa
Key Personnel
Dir General: D Juan Diego Perez Gonzalez
Founded: 1986
Subjects: Anthropology, Biological Sciences, Economics, History, Psychology, Psychiatry, Social Sciences, Sociology
ISBN Prefix(es): 84-7754
Parent Company: Grupo Anaya
Orders to: Grupo Distribuidor ED, Ferrer del Rio 35, 28028 Madrid

Complutense, SA Editorial+
Donoso Cortes, 63-3 planta, 28015 Madrid
Tel: (091) 3946460; (091) 3946461 *Fax:* (091) 3946458
E-mail: ecsa@eucmos.sim.ucm.es
Web Site: www.ucm.es/info/ecsa
Key Personnel
Council Delegate: Antonio de Juan Abad
Dir General: Miguel Saugar
Dir Editorial: Isabel Merino Pella
 E-mail: imerino@eucmos.sim.ucm.cs
Founded: 1995
Specialize in Biographics, Dictionaries, Medicine, Nursing.
Subjects: Anthropology, Art, Biography, History, Philosophy, Science (General), Social Sciences, Sociology, Women's Studies
ISBN Prefix(es): 84-89784; 84-89365; 84-7491; 84-600
Number of titles published annually: 50 Print
Bookshop(s): Libreria Complutense, c/Donoso Lortes 65, 28015 Madrid *Tel:* (091) 5437558 *Fax:* (091) 5437476 *E-mail:* ecsa3@interbook.net

Comunica Press SA+
c/Real 33, portal 15, 1º A, 28250 Madrid
SAN: 001-074X
Tel: (091) 8591604 *Fax:* (091) 8595269
E-mail: info@comunica.es
Web Site: www.comunica.es
Key Personnel
Dir General: Tito Drago
Founded: 1989
ISBN Prefix(es): 84-88817
Associate Companies: Inter Press Service
Subsidiaries: Comunica Press

Comunidad Autonoma de Madrid, Servicio de Documentacion y Publicaciones
Fortuny, 51, 28010 Madrid
SAN: 001-0820
Tel: (091) 702 76 21 *Fax:* (091) 319 85 68
Key Personnel
Contact: Gomez Garcia
Founded: 1983
Subjects: Agriculture, Animals, Pets, Archaeology, Architecture & Interior Design, Art, Biological Sciences, Business, Communications, Cookery, Crafts, Games, Hobbies, Economics, Education, Film, Video, Gardening, Plants, History, Law, Management, Medicine, Nursing, Dentistry, Music, Dance, Natural History, Poetry, Science (General), Sports, Athletics, Transportation, Travel, Wine & Spirits
ISBN Prefix(es): 84-451; 84-500; 84-505; 84-606

Consejo Superior de Investigaciones Cientificas+
Vitruvio, 8, 28006 Madrid
SAN: 001-1347
Tel: (091) 561-2833; (091) 5629633 *Fax:* (091) 5629634
E-mail: publ@orgc.csic.es
Web Site: www.csic.es/publica
Key Personnel
Contact: Teodoro Sacristan *E-mail:* t.sacristan@orgc.csic.es
Founded: 1911
D Teodoro Sacristan Santos, Servicio de Publicaciones CSIC, Vitruvio 8, 28006 Madrid.
Subjects: Science (General)
ISBN Prefix(es): 84-00

Consello da Cultura Galega - CCG
Pazo de Raxoi 2º Andar, 15705 Santiago de Compostela
SAN: 001-141X
Tel: (0981) 957202 *Fax:* (0981) 957205
E-mail: consello.cultura.galega@xunta.es
Web Site: www.consellodacultura.org
Key Personnel
President: Carlos Otero Diaz
Subjects: Anthropology, Architecture & Interior Design, Art, Biological Sciences, Journalism, Law, Photography
ISBN Prefix(es): 84-87172; 84-505

Editorial Constitucion y Leyes SA - COLEX
Sor Angela de la Cruz, nº 6-7a Pl, 28020 Madrid
Tel: (091) 5813485 *Fax:* (091) 5813490
E-mail: colexeditor@interbook.net
Web Site: www.colex.es
Key Personnel
Dir: Rosario Fonseca-Herrero Raimundo
Founded: 1981
Subjects: Economics, Government, Political Science, Law, Management
ISBN Prefix(es): 84-7879; 84-86123

Costaisa SA+
Pau Alcover, 33, 08017 Barcelona
Tel: (093) 536 100 *Fax:* (093) 057 917
E-mail: costaisa@costaisa.com
Web Site: www.costaisa.com

Key Personnel
Computer Science: Jordi Bisbe
Founded: 1968
Specialize in Multimedia, CD-ROM & the Internet.

Creaciones Monar Editorial
Escorial 26-28, 08024 Barcelona
SAN: 001-1894
Tel: (093) 2133928 *Fax:* (093) 2198460
Web Site: www.monar.com
Key Personnel
Contact: Vicente Monar Puerto
Founded: 1956
Subjects: Biblical Studies
ISBN Prefix(es): 84-85131; 84-89068

Ediciones Cristiandad+
Serrano 51-1 Izquierda, 28006 Madrid
Tel: (091) 781 99 70 *Fax:* (091) 781 99 77
E-mail: info@kgm.es
Web Site: www.edicionescristiandad.com
Subjects: Biblical Studies, History, Philosophy, Religion - Catholic, Social Sciences, Sociology
ISBN Prefix(es): 84-7057

Ediciones Cruilla SA+
Subsidiary of Ediciones SM
Balmes 245-4, 08006 Barcelona
Tel: (093) 2376344; (093) 2922172 *Fax:* (093) 2380116
Web Site: www.cruilla.com
Key Personnel
Man Dir: Josep Herrero Casanovas
Founded: 1984
Publishes only in the Catalan language.
ISBN Prefix(es): 84-7629; 84-8286
Total Titles: 1,152 Print

CSIC, see Consejo Superior de Investigaciones Cientificas

CTE-Centro de Tecnologia Educativa SA+
Via Augusta, 4 6a Planta, 08006 Barcelona
SAN: 000-9040
Tel: (093) 217 75 01 *Fax:* (093) 217 62 53
E-mail: cte@mx2.redestb.es.com
Web Site: www.centrocte.com
Key Personnel
Manager: Diego De Herrera Gimenez; Jose Luis Baron Sese
Founded: 1983
Specialize in technical books.
Membership(s): ANCED.
Subjects: Business, Education
ISBN Prefix(es): 84-7608
Warehouse: Puig-gari, 21, 08014 Barcelona

Ediciones la Cupula SL+
Plaza de las Beates, 3, 08003 Barcelona
SAN: 001-8066
Tel: (093) 268 28 05 *Fax:* (093) 268 07 65
E-mail: lacupula@eix.intercom.es
Web Site: www.lacupula.com
Key Personnel
Manager: Jose M Berenguer Sanchez
Subjects: Humor, Young & Adult Comics (Humor & Sex)

Curial Edicions Catalanes SA
Bruc 144, 08037 Barcelona
SAN: 001-2181
Tel: (093) 4588101 *Fax:* (093) 2077427
E-mail: curial@lix.intercom.es
Key Personnel
Administrator: Carmina Garcia I Roca
Subjects: Art, Ethnicity, Geography, Geology, History, Literature, Literary Criticism, Essays
ISBN Prefix(es): 84-7256

Rafael Dalmau, Editor
Carrer del Pi, 13-1-1, 08002 Barcelona
SAN: 004-7295
Tel: (093) 3173338 *Fax:* (093) 3173338
Founded: 1959
Subjects: Anthropology, Biography, Ethnicity, Geography, Geology, History
ISBN Prefix(es): 84-232
Distributor for Garsineu

Ediciones Daly S L (Daly Technical Books Publishers)+
Cordoba 11 - 2 F, 29640 Fuengirola, Malaga
SAN: 001-6527
Tel: (095) 2582569 *Fax:* (095) 2583619
E-mail: daly@edicionesdaly.com
Web Site: edicionesdaly.com
Key Personnel
Dir: David Fernandez Garcia
Manager: Hugo Armando Quiroga Capovilla
Founded: 1986
Membership(s): Association of Andalusia Publishers.
Subjects: Architecture & Interior Design, Art, Cookery, Crafts, Games, Hobbies, Education, Engineering (General), Gardening, Plants, Technology, Carpentry, Wrought iron
ISBN Prefix(es): 84-86584
Total Titles: 200 Print
Showroom(s): ABA, EEUU; Salones Internacionales del Libro; Bogota, Colombia; Frankfort, Germany; Guadalajara, Mexico; Liber; London, United Kingdom; Tokyo, Japan
Bookshop(s): Buenos Aires, Argentina
Warehouse: Poligono Industrial La Vega, Mijas, Malaga

Editorial Deimos, SL
Glorieta del Puente de Segovia, 3, 28011 Madrid
Tel: (091) 479-23-42 *Fax:* (091) 5438214
E-mail: editorial@deimos-es.com
Web Site: www.deimos-es.com
Key Personnel
Administrator: Paulina Pardo Castaneda
Subjects: History, Mathematics, Religion - Catholic
ISBN Prefix(es): 84-86379
Number of titles published annually: 6 Print
Total Titles: 46 Print

Editorial Revista de Derecho Privado Editorial de Derecho Financiero, *imprint of* EDERSA (Editoriales de Derecho Reunidas SA)

Espanola Desclee De Brouwer SA+
Henao, 6-3º Dcha, Apartado de Correos, 277, 48009 Bilbao
SAN: 002-4090
Tel: (094) 4233045; (094) 4246843 *Fax:* (094) 4237594
E-mail: info@desclee.com
Web Site: www.desclee.com
Key Personnel
Manager: Javier Gogeascoechea Arrien
Founded: 1958
Subjects: Biblical Studies, Management, Psychology, Psychiatry, Religion - Other
ISBN Prefix(es): 84-330

Ediciones Desnivel, SL
Calle San Victorino, 8, 28025 Madrid
SAN: 001-2858
Tel: (091) 3602242 *Fax:* (091) 3602264
E-mail: edicionesdesnivel@desnivel.com
Web Site: www.desnivel.com
Key Personnel
Coordinator: Ana Fernandez Soto
Editorial Dir: Dario Rodriguez
Editor: Hector del Campo; Jordi Pastor
Dir, Publicity: Ana Vinuesa
ISBN Prefix(es): 84-87746; 84-89969; 84-95760
Bookshop(s): Librerio Desnivel, c/Dmore de Dios, 11, 28011 Madrid

Ediciones Destino SA+
Provenza nº 260, 5a Planta, 08008 Barcelona
SAN: 001-6586
Tel: (093) 496 70 01 *Fax:* (093) 496 70 02
E-mail: edicionesdestino@stl.logiccontrol.es
Web Site: www.edestino.es
Key Personnel
President: Joaquin Palau Fau
Founded: 1942
Subjects: Architecture & Interior Design, Art, Fiction, History, Literature, Literary Criticism, Essays, Nonfiction (General)
ISBN Prefix(es): 84-233

Editorial Diagonal del grup 62+
Peu de la Creu 4, 08001 Barcelona
Tel: (093) 4437100 *Fax:* (093) 4437129
Key Personnel
President: Josep Maria Fortia Vinolas
General Dir: Jaime Igea Noguera
Founded: 1962
Specialize in literary work consultations.
Subjects: Geography, Geology, History
ISBN Prefix(es): 84-87254; 84-95808; 84-9762
Divisions: Catalana d'Ediciones SA
Warehouse: Joan d'Austria 57-59, 08005 Barcelona

Editorial Diagonal, *imprint of* Grup 62

Ediciones Diaz de Santos SA+
Dona Juana I de Castilla 22, Urb Quinta de los Molinos, 28027 Madrid
SAN: 001-6519
Tel: (091) 7434890 *Fax:* (091) 7434023
E-mail: librerias@diazdesantos.es
Web Site: www.diazdesantos.es
Telex: 45141 Dsan E ref Ediciones
Key Personnel
Man Dir: Joaquin Vioque Lozano
Sales: Antonio Vila Fernandez
Founded: 1983
Subjects: Business, Computer Science, Economics, Management, Medicine, Nursing, Dentistry, Science (General)
ISBN Prefix(es): 84-87189; 84-86251; 84-7978
Distributed by Grupo Editorial Iberoamerica (Mexico)
Bookshop(s): Diaz de Santos SA - Libreria Cientifico-Tecnica, Lagasca, 95, 28006 Madrid

Didaco Comunicacion y Didactica, SA+
Regas, 3 bajos, 08006 Barcelona
Tel: (093) 237 64 00 *Fax:* (093) 218 92 77
E-mail: didaco@cambrabcn.es
Web Site: www.didaco.es
Key Personnel
Manager: Lin Balague *E-mail:* lin@didaco.es
Administrator: Manuel Pastor *E-mail:* pastor@didaco.es
Publicity: Charo Latorre *E-mail:* charolatorre@didaco.es
International Sales: Victor Mesalles
  E-mail: vmesalles@didaco.es
National Sales: Alfonso R Salmeron
  E-mail: mail@didaco.es
Founded: 1986
Producers of multimedia English courses.
Subjects: Biological Sciences, English as a Second Language, Health, Nutrition, Language Arts, Linguistics, Nonfiction (General)
ISBN Prefix(es): 84-86983
Total Titles: 9 CD-ROM
Showroom(s): Bologna Children's Book Fair, Frankfurt Buchmesse, Liber, Barcelona

Dilagro SA
Comerc 48, 25007 Lleida
Tel: (0973) 24 51 00; (0973) 23 34 80
  Fax: (0973) 23 64 13
Web Site: www.dilagro.com
Key Personnel
Man Dir: Jorge Marimon
Subjects: Agriculture, Ethnicity, History, Regional Interests
ISBN Prefix(es): 84-7234
Bookshop(s): Libreria Tenica, Comercio 48, 25007 leida

Dinsic Publicacions Musicals
Santa Anna 10, E 3a, 08002 Barcelona
Tel: (093) 318 06 05 *Fax:* (093) 412 05 01
E-mail: dinsic@dinsic.com
Web Site: www.dinsic.com/
Key Personnel
International Rights: Francesca Galofre Mora
Founded: 1988
Subjects: Music, Dance
ISBN Prefix(es): 84-86949

Ediciones Diputacion de Salamanca
Division of Diputacion de Salamanca
Felipe Espino 1, 37002 Salamanca
SAN: 001-348X
Tel: (0923) 29 31 00 *Fax:* (0923) 29 31 29
E-mail: informacion@dipsanet.es
Web Site: www.dipsanet.es
Key Personnel
Dir: Jesus Garcia Cesteros
Founded: 1982
Subjects: Geography, Geology, History, Regional Interests
ISBN Prefix(es): 84-7797; 84-500; 84-505
Distributed by Distribuciones Breogan

Diputacion Provincial de Cordoba
Avda del Mediterraneo, s/n, 14011 Cordoba
SAN: 001-3307
Tel: (0957) 211392; (0957) 211323 *Fax:* (0957) 211387
Key Personnel
Administration: Delores Martinez Coca
ISBN Prefix(es): 84-8154; 84-87034; 84-500; 84-505

Diputacion Provincial de Malaga
Unit of Provincial Government
Av de los Guindos, 48, 29004 Malaga
Tel: (0952) 069 207 *Fax:* (0952) 069 215
E-mail: cedma@cedma.com
Web Site: cedma.com
Key Personnel
Publication Dir: Victoria Rosado
  E-mail: vrosado@cedma.com
Founded: 1973
Subjects: Anthropology, Archaeology, Art, Drama, Theater, Geography, Geology, History, Literature, Literary Criticism, Essays, Poetry
ISBN Prefix(es): 84-7785; 84-505
Number of titles published annually: 1 CD-ROM; 1 Online
Total Titles: 50 Print; 2 CD-ROM; 1 Online
Distributed by Atenea; Bitacora; Breogan
Warehouse: Avda-Guindos, 48, 29004 Malaga

Diputacion Provincial de Sevilla, Servicio de Publicaciones
Av Menendez y Pelayo, 32, 41004 Sevilla
SAN: 001-3501
Tel: (095) 4550029 *Fax:* (095) 4550050
E-mail: caba174@dipusevilla.es
Web Site: www.dipusevilla.es
Key Personnel
Dir: Carmen Barriga Guillen
Founded: 1967
Subjects: History, Literature, Literary Criticism, Essays, Social Sciences, Sociology
ISBN Prefix(es): 84-7798; 84-500; 84-505

Diseno Editorial SA
Estudiantes, 5, 28040 El Escorial, Madrid
Tel: (091) 5533168
Key Personnel
Dir: Ramon Nieto Alvarez-Uria
Founded: 1985
Books in Castellano & Catalan.
Subjects: Education, Literature, Literary Criticism, Essays
ISBN Prefix(es): 84-87666
Number of titles published annually: 4 Print
Total Titles: 2 Print
Warehouse: Colonia Guell, 08690 Sta Coloma De Cervello, Barcelona
Orders to: Exclusivas Escolares, Carretera Nacional II, km 593-4, 08740 Sant Andreu de la Barca, Barcelona *Tel:* (093) 635 1300

DOC 6, SA
Mallorca. 272, Planta 3a, 08037 Barcelona
Tel: (093) 215 43 13 *Fax:* (093) 488 36 21
E-mail: mail@doc6.es
Web Site: www.doc6.es

Ediciones Doce Calles SL
Apdo Correos 270, 28300 Aranjuez (Madrid)
SAN: 001-6659
Tel: (091) 902 197 501 *Fax:* (091) 925 137 060
E-mail: docecalles@infonegocio.com
Web Site: www.infonegocio.com/docecalles
Key Personnel
Dir General: Pedro Miguel Sanchez Moreno
Dir, Marketing: Isabel Santos Esteras
  E-mail: isantos@infonegocio.com
Founded: 1987
Subjects: Aeronautics, Aviation, African American Studies, Anthropology, Architecture & Interior Design, Civil Engineering, Health, Nutrition, History, Medicine, Nursing, Dentistry, Natural History
ISBN Prefix(es): 84-87111; 84-89796
Number of titles published annually: 6 Print
Total Titles: 105 Print
Foreign Rep(s): Puvill Libros SA

Editorial Don Quijote+
Compas del Porvenir, 6, 41013 Sevilla
SAN: 002-3817
Tel: (05) 4235080
Key Personnel
Man Dir: Manuel Barrera Blasco
Founded: 1981
Subjects: Drama, Theater, Fiction, History, Literature, Literary Criticism, Essays, Poetry
ISBN Prefix(es): 84-85933; 84-88767

Editorial Donostiarra SA+
Pokopandegi, 4, Pabellon Igaralde Barrio de Igara, Apdo 671, 20018 San Sebastian Guipuzcoa
SAN: 002-3825
Tel: (0943) 215 737; (0943) 213 011 *Fax:* (0943) 219 521
E-mail: info@donostiarra.com
Web Site: www.donostiarra.com
Key Personnel
President: Francisco Javier Rodriguez de Abajo
Marketing Dir: Jacobo Vidal Luzuriaga
Founded: 1965
Subjects: Accounting, Engineering (General), Film, Video, Finance, Health, Nutrition, Technology
ISBN Prefix(es): 84-7063
Distributor for EGA-Donostiarra-Profesores-Editores, SA; Larrauri Editorial SA
Book Club(s): Anele

Dorleta SA+
Nicolas Alcorta, 2, 48003 Bilbao
SAN: 001-4133
Tel: (094) 4218710 *Fax:* (094) 4322232
E-mail: dorletoi@sarenet.es
Key Personnel
Editor: Angel Tona
Dir: Jose Gondra
Dir, Commercial: Yolanda Domingo

Founded: 1985
Subjects: Sports, Athletics
ISBN Prefix(es): 84-87812; 84-404

Editorial Dossat SA
Plaza de Santa Ana 9, 28012 Madrid
SAN: 002-3833
Tel: (091) 3694011 *Fax:* (091) 3691398
Key Personnel
Man Dir: Barrera San Martin Eugeniano
Subjects: Architecture & Interior Design, Automotive, Civil Engineering, Disability, Special Needs, Electronics, Electrical Engineering, Engineering (General), Journalism, Medicine, Nursing, Dentistry, Science (General)
ISBN Prefix(es): 84-237

Ediciones Doyma SA+
Travesera de Gracia, 17-21, 08021 Barcelona
SAN: 001-6675
Tel: (093) 2000 711 *Fax:* (093) 2091 136
Web Site: www.doyma.es
Telex: 51964 Ink E
Key Personnel
Man Dir: Jose A Dotu
Journal Division Manager: Edgar Dotu
Book Division Manager: German Covas
Editorial Manager: Dr Oscar Vilarroya
Foreign Rights: Pilar Aparicio
Manager: Lorenzo Matas; Jose Latorre
Founded: 1971
Subjects: Medicine, Nursing, Dentistry
ISBN Prefix(es): 84-85285; 84-7592
Subsidiaries: AP (Americana de Publicaciones); Doyma Argentina SA; Doyma Andina SA; Doyma Mexicana SA CV; Ediciones Doyma de Venezuela CA

Durvan SA de Ediciones+
Subsidiary of Club Internacional Del Libro
Colon de Larreategui 13-3 izda, 48001 Bilbao, Vizcaya
SAN: 001-4214
Tel: (094) 4230777 *Fax:* (094) 4243832
E-mail: editorial@durvan.com
Web Site: www.durvan.com
Key Personnel
Man Dir: Lorenzo Portillo Sisniega *Tel:* (090) 2104020
Founded: 1960
ISBN Prefix(es): 84-85001; 84-7677
Number of titles published annually: 2 Print; 1 CD-ROM; 1 Online
Total Titles: 42 Print; 3 CD-ROM; 1 Online
Associate Companies: Durclub, SA de Ediciones
Distributor for Carroggio, SA de Ediciones; Club Internacional del Libro; Ediciones Rueda JM, SA; Urmo, SA
Warehouse: C/Nervion, 3-3, 48001 Bilbao

Dykinson SL+
Melendez Valdes 61, 28015 Madrid
Tel: (091) 544 28 46; (091) 544 28 69 *Fax:* (091) 544 60 40
E-mail: info@dykinson.com
Web Site: www.dykinson.es; www.dykinson.com
Key Personnel
Contact: Rafael Tigeras Sanchez
Founded: 1973
Subjects: Economics, Education, Law, Psychology, Psychiatry
ISBN Prefix(es): 84-88030; 84-8155; 84-86133; 84-88038; 84-9772
Total Titles: 850 Print

Ediciones Ebenezer+
Camelies 19, 08024 Barcelona
SAN: 001-6713
Tel: (093) 2133515 *Fax:* (093) 2131684
E-mail: 101745.1635@compuserve.com
Key Personnel
Manager: Carlos A Piedad
Libreria & Distribution.
Subjects: Film, Video, Music, Dance
ISBN Prefix(es): 84-87498
Associate Companies: Libreria Biblica ALFA & OMEGA, Apdo 20159, 08080 Barcelona
Distributor for Broadman & Holman; Clie; Ed Carribe; Spanish House

ECE, see Ediciones Colegio De Espana (ECE)

Editorial EDAF SA+
Jorge Juan 30, 28001 Madrid
SAN: 002-3884
Tel: (091) 435 82 60 *Fax:* (091) 431 52 81
E-mail: edaf@edaf.net
Web Site: www.edaf.es
Key Personnel
President: Luciano Fossati
Dir: Jose Antonio Fossati
Publicity: Gerardo Fossati
Founded: 1959
Subjects: Astrology, Occult, Health, Nutrition, History, Literature, Literary Criticism, Essays, Self-Help
ISBN Prefix(es): 84-414; 84-7166; 84-7640
Total Titles: 1,000 Print
Branch Office(s)
Edaf del Plata, Lavalle, 1646-piso 7°, oficina, 21, 1048 Buenos Aires, Argentina, Contact: Alfonso Barredo *Tel:* (011) 11 43 75 55 00 *Fax:* (011) 11 43 75 55 00 *E-mail:* edafall@interar.com.ar
Edaf Y Morales, SA, Oriente 180 n 279, Col Moctezuma 2a Sec, Delg Venustiano Carranza 15530, Mexico, Contact: Gildardo Morales *Tel:* (05) 55 785 19 51 *Fax:* (05) 55 785 27 51 *E-mail:* edaf@edaf-y-morales.com.mx
Warehouse: Poligno Azque, Ctra de Daganzo KM, 3400 Naves 2Y3-Alcala de Henares, Madrid, Contact: Horacio Mallo *Tel:* (091) 8809514 *Fax:* (091) 8893851

Edebe
Passeig Sant Joan Bosco 62, 08017 Barcelona
SAN: 001-4435
Tel: (093) 2037408 *Fax:* (093) 2054670
E-mail: editorial@edebe.com
Web Site: www.edebe.com
Key Personnel
Dir: Antonio Garrido Gonzalez
Publication Dir: Jose Luis Gomez Cutillas
Specialize in education & literature.
Subjects: Education, Fiction, Literature, Literary Criticism, Essays, Technology
ISBN Prefix(es): 84-236
Associate Companies: Editorial Don Bosco SA, Mexico; Editorial Edebe, Argentina

EDERSA (Editoriales de Derecho Reunidas SA)
Leganitos, 15 5°-1, 28013 Madrid
SAN: 001-4451
Tel: (091) 5477961 *Fax:* (091) 5478001
E-mail: dijusa@dijusa.es *Cable:* REVIPRIV
Key Personnel
Man Dir: Narciso Amoros Dorda
Marketing Dir: Narciso Amoros Koehler
Founded: 1913
Subjects: Biography, History, Law, Philosophy, Social Sciences, Sociology
ISBN Prefix(es): 84-7130; 84-400; 84-8494
Imprints: Ediciones Pegaso; Editorial Revista de Derecho Privado Editorial de Derecho Financiero

Edex, Centro de Recursos Comunitarios+
Indautxu n° 9, 48011 Bilboa, Vizcaya
Tel: (094) 442 57 84 *Fax:* (094) 441-7512
E-mail: edex@edex.es
Web Site: www.edex.es
Key Personnel
Editor: Claudia Alcepay
Subjects: Child Care & Development, Education

EDHASA (Editora y Distribuidora Hispano-Americana SA)+
Av Diagonal, 519-521, 2° piso, 08029 Barcelona
Tel: (093) 4949720 *Fax:* (093) 4194584
E-mail: info@edhasa.es
Web Site: www.edhasa.es
Key Personnel
Editorial Dir: Daniel Fernandez *E-mail:* d.fdez@edhasa.es
General Manager: Anna Ardid *E-mail:* a.ardid@edhasa.es
Rights Department: Esther Lopez *E-mail:* e.lopez@edhasa.es
Publisher's Assistant: Cecilia Asker *E-mail:* c.asker@edhasa.es
Founded: 1946
Subjects: Fiction, History, Literature, Literary Criticism, Essays
ISBN Prefix(es): 84-350
Number of titles published annually: 60 Print
Total Titles: 600 Print

Edi-Liber Irlan SA+
Corsega 314, 08037 Barcelona
SAN: 001-4516
Tel: (093) 4160641 *Fax:* (093) 4160774
E-mail: ediliber@mx3.redestb.es
Key Personnel
Editor & International Rights: Monica Bertran
Founded: 1983
Membership(s): Associacio D'Escriptors en Llengua Catalana.
Subjects: Cookery, Drama, Theater, Fiction, Literature, Literary Criticism, Essays, Poetry
ISBN Prefix(es): 84-7589
Distributor for L'arc de Bera'
Book Club(s): Club De Lectors Dels Paisos Catalans-Cercle De Lectors

Ediciones Ceac, *imprint of* Grupo Editorial CEAC SA

Ediciones Deusto SA
Alameda de Recalde, 27-7°, 48009 Bilbao Vizcaya
SAN: 001-6594
Tel: (094) 4356177 *Fax:* (094) 4356173
E-mail: edicio01@sarenet.es
Web Site: www.ediciones-deusto.es
Key Personnel
General Dir: Xavier Arrufat
Founded: 1960
Subjects: Accounting, Finance, Management
ISBN Prefix(es): 84-234

Ediciones El Almendro de Cordoba+
El Almendro 10, Castana 11, 28500 Arganda-Madrid
SAN: 001-6810
Tel: (0957) 082 789; (0957) 274 692 *Fax:* (0957) 274 692
E-mail: ediciones@elalmendro.com
Web Site: www.elalmendro.com
Key Personnel
Man Dir, Editorial: Jesus Pelaez del Rosal
Founded: 1982
Also book packager.
Subjects: Biblical Studies, Religion - Catholic, Religion - Jewish, Religion & Judaism
ISBN Prefix(es): 84-8005; 84-86077
Subsidiaries: PI El Guijar

Ediciones l'Isard, S L+
Affiliate of Gremi D'Editors de Catalunya
Corsega, 663-665, entl A, 08026 Barcelona
Tel: (093) 436 81 18 *Fax:* (093) 436 03 41

PUBLISHERS — SPAIN

E-mail: isard@isard.net
Web Site: www.isard.net
Key Personnel
Dir: Jordi Marti i Canellas
Founded: 1995
Subjects: Architecture & Interior Design, Art, Cookery, Health, Nutrition, Wine & Spirits
ISBN Prefix(es): 84-921314; 84-89931
Number of titles published annually: 4 Print
Total Titles: 20 Print

Ediciones y Distribuciones Universitarias SA, see Tres Torres Ediciones SA

Institut d'Edicions de la Diputacio de Barcelona
Londres, 55, 1r bis, 08036 Barcelona
SAN: 001-3188
Tel: (093) 4022 116 *Fax:* (093) 4022 290
E-mail: godovx@diba.es
Web Site: www.diba.es
Key Personnel
Dir: Josep Montanyes
Founded: 1991
ISBN Prefix(es): 84-7794

Edicola-62, *imprint of* Grup 62

Edicomunicacion SA+
Las Torres, 75-77, 08042 Barcelona
SAN: 002-1350
Tel: (093) 3590866 *Fax:* (093) 3590004
Key Personnel
Dir: Jose Luis Salgado
Subjects: Astrology, Occult, Humor, Nonfiction (General), Parapsychology, Poetry
ISBN Prefix(es): 84-7672

Edigol Ediciones SA+
Sant Gabriel, 50, 08950 Esplugues de Llobregat, Barcelona
SAN: 002-144X
Tel: (093) 372 63 04 *Fax:* (093) 371 76 32
E-mail: info@edigol.com
Web Site: www.edigol.com
Telex: Cllc E
Key Personnel
Man Dir: Jorge Onrubia
Sales: Joana Rius; Carmentxu Aparicio
Founded: 1976 (as Edigol Ediciones Cartograficas)
General service on Educational Cartography. Wall charts on drugs, anatomy, children's letters & numbers charts.
Subjects: Education, Geography, Geology, Educational Cartography, School Maps
ISBN Prefix(es): 84-85406
Parent Company: Industria Grafica Offset Lito SA, Sant Gabriel, 50, Esplugues de Llobregat, 08950 Barcelona

Edika-Med, SA+
Josep Tarradellas, 52, 08029 Barcelona
SAN: 002-1490
Tel: (093) 454 96 00 *Fax:* (093) 323 48 03
E-mail: info@edikamed.com
Web Site: www.edikamed.com
Key Personnel
Manager: Dolores Gandia
Founded: 1988
Membership(s): Grenio Publications; Specialize in Medical Literature.
Subjects: Medicine, Nursing, Dentistry, Psychology, Psychiatry
ISBN Prefix(es): 84-7877

Edilesa-Ediciones Leonesas SA+
Camino Cuesta Luzar, S/N, 24010 Trobajo del Camino, Leon
SAN: 001-8198
Tel: (0987) 80 11 16 *Fax:* (0987) 84 00 28
E-mail: edilesa@edilesa.es
Web Site: www.edilesa.es
Key Personnel
Dir: Jesus Vincente Pastor Benavides
Founded: 1981
Subjects: Architecture & Interior Design, Art, Cookery, Literature, Literary Criticism, Essays, Photography, Travel
ISBN Prefix(es): 84-8012; 84-86013
Distributor for Hullera Vasco-Leonesa y Fundacion Hullera Vasco-Leonesa
Book Club(s): Club Bibliofilo Leones

Edilux+
c/Juncos n° 7-bajo, 18006 Granada
SAN: 003-8245
Tel: (0958) 08 20 00; (0958) 184056 *Fax:* (0958) 184056; (0958) 082472
E-mail: ediluxsl@supercable.es
Founded: 1984
Subjects: Art, Photography, Travel
ISBN Prefix(es): 84-87282; 84-95856

EDIMSA - Editores Medicos SA+
Gabriela Mistral, 2, 28035 Madrid
SAN: 002-1601
Tel: (091) 376 81 40 *Fax:* (091) 373 99 07
E-mail: edimsa@edimsa.es
Web Site: www.edimsa.es
Key Personnel
General Dir: Carlos Gimenez Antolin
ISBN Prefix(es): 84-87054; 84-95076; 84-7714

Ediciones Edinford SA+
Marmolistas, 3 y 5, 29013 Malaga
SAN: 001-6748
Fax: (095) 254689
Key Personnel
Contact: Jose Luis Gonzalez Sodis
Founded: 1989
Subjects: College & Local Textbooks
ISBN Prefix(es): 84-87555; 84-404

Editorial Ediseis SA
Pza Ciudad de Salta 3, 28043 Madrid
SAN: 001-4443
Tel: (091) 4165511; (091) 4165218 *Fax:* (091) 4165411
Telex: 47088 Edse E
Key Personnel
Man Dir: Luis Maria Saiz Martinez
Founded: 1981
Subjects: Language Arts, Linguistics
ISBN Prefix(es): 84-85786; 84-7711; 84-389
Branch Office(s)
Ediseis M, Rosellon 55, 08029 Barcelona
Bookshop(s): The English Bookshop, Calaf 52, 08021 Barcelona

Editorial Editex SA+
Complejo Empresarial Atica 7 Edificio 3, Planta 3a, Oficina B via dos Castillas 33 Pozuelo de Alarcon, 28224 Madrid
SAN: 002-3914
Tel: (091) 7992040 *Fax:* (091) 7150444
E-mail: correo@editex.es
Web Site: www.editex.es
Key Personnel
Dir General: Severino Basarrate Elorrieta
Founded: 1946
Subjects: Child Care & Development, Health, Nutrition, Management
ISBN Prefix(es): 84-7131

Editora y Distribuidora Hispano Americana SA (EDHASA), see EDHASA (Editora y Distribuidora Hispano-Americana SA)

Editorial Everest SA+
Ctra Leon-La Coruna, Km 5, Apdo 339, 24080 Leon
Tel: (0987) 844200 *Fax:* (0987) 844202
E-mail: publicaciones@everest.es
Web Site: www.everest.es
Telex: 89916 *Cable:* EVEREST LEON
Key Personnel
Man Dir: Jose Antonio Lopez Martinez
Publication Dir: Raquel Lopez Varela
Export Dir: Severino Fernandez
Marketing Manager: Fernando Rodriguez Pereyra
Founded: 1958
Subjects: Animals, Pets, Astrology, Occult, Cookery, Crafts, Games, Hobbies, Gardening, Plants, History, Physics, Religion - Catholic
ISBN Prefix(es): 84-241
Associate Companies: Lectorum Publications Inc, 137 W 14th St, New York, NY 10011, United States (US Distributor)
Subsidiaries: Ediciones Gaviota SL
Orders to: Everest de Ediciones & Distribucion SL, Carretera Leon-Coruna, Km 5, Apdo 339, 24080 Leon, Manager: Javier Atienza

EDUNSA, see Tres Torres Ediciones SA

Ediciones Ega+
Juan de Garay, 15, 48003 Bilbao
SAN: 001-7124
Tel: (04) 4216787 *Fax:* (04) 4213010
Key Personnel
Dir & Editor: Jose Maria Gogeascoechea Arrien
Founded: 1988
Subjects: Religion - Other
ISBN Prefix(es): 84-7726

Egales (Editorial Gai y Lesbiana)+
Cervantes, 2, 08002 Barcelona
Tel: (093) 4127283 *Fax:* (093) 4127283
E-mail: egales@auna.com
Web Site: www.editorialegales.com
Key Personnel
Dir: Helle Bruun
International Rights: Connie Dagas
Founded: 1995
Subjects: Gay & Lesbian
ISBN Prefix(es): 84-95346
Total Titles: 84 Print
Distributed by Alamo Square Distributors (Only USA)

Publicaciones de El Ciervo, S.A., see EL Ciervo 96

EL Ciervo 96
Calvet 56, 08021 Barcelona
SAN: 004-6345
Tel: (093) 200 51 45; (093) 201 00 96 *Fax:* (093) 201 10 15
E-mail: redaccion@elciervo.es
Web Site: www.elciervo.es
Key Personnel
Dir: Lorenzo Gomis
ISBN Prefix(es): 84-87178

El Hogar y la Moda SA
Muntaner, 40-42, 08011 Barcelona
SAN: 002-7715
Tel: (093) 508 70 00 *Fax:* (093) 454 87 72
E-mail: hymsa@hymsa.com
Web Site: www.hymsa.com
Telex: 50482
Key Personnel
Man Dir: Xavier Elies
Editorial: Josep Sarret
Sales, Rights & Permissions: Carlos Elies
Production: Jordi Balmana
Founded: 1909
Subjects: Women's Studies
ISBN Prefix(es): 84-7183
Parent Company: Editorial Everest, SA, Muntaner, 40-42, 08011 Barcelona

Associate Companies: Sociedad General de Publicaciones, Carretera Montcada s/n, Poligono Industrial, Barcelona; ASMI SA, Calle Aribau 20 pral, Barcelona
Subsidiaries: Servicios Editoriales SA; Publiventa SA
Bookshop(s): Libreria Hogar y Moda, Muntaner, 40-42, 08011 Barcelona

El Viso, SA Ediciones
Lopez de Hoyos, 350, 28043 Madrid
SAN: 001-690X
Tel: (091) 5196576; (091) 5196583 *Fax:* (091) 5196583
E-mail: lvisoh@anexo.es
Key Personnel
Contact: Custodia Caballero
Founded: 1981
Subjects: Art, Photography
ISBN Prefix(es): 84-86022; 84-95241
Distributed by Les Punxes, SL; Visor Distibuciones, SL

Ediciones Elfos SL (Publishing Company ELFS)+
Alberes, 34, 08017 Barcelona
Tel: (093) 4069479 *Fax:* (093) 4069006
E-mail: eltos-ed@teleline.es
Web Site: www.edicioneselfos.com
Key Personnel
Man Dir: Rita Schnitzer
Founded: 1980
Subjects: Cookery, Health, Nutrition, Humor, Decorative Art
ISBN Prefix(es): 84-85791; 84-87251; 84-88990; 84-8423
Number of titles published annually: 18 Print
Orders to: Naturart, SA, Avda Mare de Deu de Lorda, 20, 08034 Barcelona *Tel:* (093) 2054000 *Fax:* (093) 2051441

Elkar, Euskal Liburu eta Kantuen Argitaldaria, SL+
Igara Bidea, 88 bis, 20003 San Sebastian
Tel: (943) 310327 *Fax:* (943) 310345
Key Personnel
Administrator: Jose Maria Sors
Founded: 1972
Specialize in student languages.
Subjects: Education
ISBN Prefix(es): 84-7529; 89-7917; 84-85485
Warehouse: Zabaltzen, Igarabidea, 88 bis, Donostia *Tel:* (043) 2122144/212033 *Fax:* (043) 212192

Emece Editores, see Publicaciones y Ediciones Salamandra SA

EmpresaActiva, *imprint of* Ediciones Urano, SA

Editorial Empuries, *imprint of* Grup 62

Editorial Empuries
Imprint of Grup 62
Provenca 278, 08008 Barcelona
Tel: (093) 4870062 *Fax:* (093) 4874147
Key Personnel
Rights Manager: Laura Pujol
Founded: 1983
ISBN Prefix(es): 84-7596

Enciclopedia Catalana, SA+
Diputacio, 250, 08007 Barcelona
Tel: (093) 412 0030 *Fax:* (093) 301 4863
Web Site: www.enciclopedia-catalana.com
Key Personnel
Foreign Rights Manager: Iolanda Bethencourt
  E-mail: ibethencourt@grec.com
Founded: 1965

Subjects: Art, Cookery, Education, Fiction, Geography, Geology, Health, Nutrition, History, Literature, Literary Criticism, Essays, Poetry, Publishing & Book Trade Reference, Religion - Catholic, Romance, Travel
ISBN Prefix(es): 84-412

Ediciones Encuentro SA+
Cedaceros, 3, 2°, 28014 Madrid
Tel: (091) 532 26 07 *Fax:* (091) 532 23 46
E-mail: encuentro@ediciones-encuentro.es
Web Site: www.ediciones-encuentro.es
Key Personnel
President: Jose Miguel Oriol
Man Dir: Carmina Salgado
Sales: Joan R De la Serna
Production: Norberto Moreno
Editorial, Rights & Permissions: Gabriel Lanzas
Founded: 1978
Subjects: Anthropology, Art, Economics, History, Literature, Literary Criticism, Essays, Philosophy, Social Sciences, Sociology, Theology
ISBN Prefix(es): 84-7490
Number of titles published annually: 50 Print
Total Titles: 700 Print
Foreign Rep(s): Bookstore Banquet Jose Cubas (Argentina); Bookstore Juan Pablo II (Dominican Republic); Bookstore Miraflores Time Shred of Union (Peru); Bookstore Prow Mac Iver (Chile); Bookstore Stadium (Ecuador); Bookstore the Apdo Internationa (Costa Rica); Byblos Editorial Eduardo (Uruguay); Catholic Bookstore (Panama); Catholic University of Puerto Rico Bookstore (Puerto Rico); Cost Hispamer This of the UCA (South America); Disliber-Spec-Mexico SA of CU (Mexico); Distributing Paulinas (USA); Distritexto Ltda (Colombia); El Libro (Ecuador); Interservice Distribution SA of CU Col Copilco University (Mexico); Paulinas Jr (Peru); Warp Editions (Venezuela); World Book Centre (Chile)

Ediciones Endymion
Marques deSanta Ana, 4, 28004 Madrid
SAN: 001-6977
Tel: (01) 5223668; (01) 5222210
Key Personnel
President: Jesus Moya Andrinal
Founded: 1986
Subjects: Poetry
ISBN Prefix(es): 84-7731

EOS Gabinete de Orientacion Psicologica
Avda Reina Victoria, 8, 2a Planta, 28003 Madrid
Tel: (091) 554 12 04 *Fax:* (091) 554 12 03
E-mail: eos@eos.es
Web Site: www.eos.es
Founded: 1971
Subjects: Psychology, Psychiatry
ISBN Prefix(es): 84-85851; 84-9727; 84-89967

Erein+
Tolosa Etorbidea 107, 20018 Donostia
SAN: 002-8436
Tel: (0943) 218300; (0943) 218211 *Fax:* (0943) 218311
E-mail: erein@erein.com
Web Site: www.erein.com
Key Personnel
Man Dir, Production, Rights & Permissions: Aramaio Julen Lizundia
Editorial: Beitia Inaki Aldecoa
Sales, Publicity: Arzamendi Pello Elzaburu
Founded: 1976
Subjects: Education, Literature, Literary Criticism, Essays, Poetry
ISBN Prefix(es): 84-7568; 84-85324; 84-400; 84-9746

Ediciones Eseuve SA
Batalla del Salado, 34, 28045 Madrid

SAN: 001-7027
Tel: (091) 539-01-03 *Fax:* (091) 528-87-59
Key Personnel
Contact: Angel Sabat Gomez
Founded: 1987
ISBN Prefix(es): 84-87301; 84-404
Parent Company: Ediciones Rialp SA
Subsidiaries: Esmon Publicidad SA

Esic Editorial
Avda de Valdenigrales, s/n, 28223 Pozuelo de Alarcon, Madrid
Tel: (091) 4524100 *Fax:* (091) 3528534
E-mail: info.madrid@esic.es
Web Site: www.esic.es
Key Personnel
Contact: Maria Jesus Merino Sanz
  E-mail: mariajesusmerino@esic.es
Founded: 1970
Specializes in economy, marketing & enterprise.
Subjects: Accounting, Economics
ISBN Prefix(es): 84-7356

ESIN, *imprint of* Editorial Esin, SA

Editorial Esin, SA+
Casp, 79, 08013 Barcelona
Tel: (093) 244 95 50 *Fax:* (093) 265 68 95
E-mail: combel@editorialcasals.com
Web Site: www.editorialcasals.com
Key Personnel
Man Dir: Casals Ramon
Founded: 1987
Subjects: Education, Fiction, Religion - Catholic
ISBN Prefix(es): 84-7864
Number of titles published annually: 50 Print
Total Titles: 400 Print
Associate Companies: Editorial Casals, SA
Imprints: Combel; ESIN
Warehouse: Juli Galve i Brussons, 72, 08912 Badalona

Editorial Espasa-Calpe SA+
Carreterade Irun, Km 12, 200, Apdo de correos, 547, 28049 Madrid
Tel: (091) 3589689 *Fax:* (091) 3589364; (091) 3589505
E-mail: sagerencias@espasa.es
Web Site: www.espasa.com
Telex: 48850 Espac E *Cable:* ESPACALPE
Key Personnel
General Manager: Jorge Hernandez
Editorial Dir: Rafael Gonzalez Cortes
Rights & Permissions: Carlos Ezponda Ibanez
Founded: 1925
Membership(s): Planeta Group (Spain).
Subjects: Art, Biography, Child Care & Development, Cookery, English as a Second Language, Fiction, History, Literature, Literary Criticism, Essays, Nonfiction (General), Science Fiction, Fantasy, Self-Help, Social Sciences, Sociology
ISBN Prefix(es): 84-339; 84-239; 84-670; 84-8326
Branch Office(s)
Roger de Lluria 33, 08009 Barcelona
Balbino Marron s/n, Edf Viapol portal A 5a, 41008 Sevilla
Simon Bolivar, 27 - dpto 34-35, 48013 Bilbao
Hebreista Perez Bayer, 9-10A, 46002 Valencia
Distributed by Planeta International S A (Restrictions Latin America)
Bookshop(s): Libreria Austral, Roger de Lluria 33, 08009 Barcelona; Casa del Libro Espasa-Calpe SA, Gran Via 29, 28013 Madrid; Casa del Libro, Maestro Victoria 3, 28013 Madrid; Casa del Libro, Colon de Larreategui 41, 48009 Bilbao; Casa del Libro, Paseo de Gracia 62, 08007 Barcelona

Editorial Espaxs SA
Rossello, 132, 08036 Barcelona

Tel: (093) 454 06 52 *Fax:* (093) 4510149
Telex: 50679 Espx E
Subjects: Medicine, Nursing, Dentistry
ISBN Prefix(es): 84-7179
Bookshop(s): Libreria Espaxs, Rosellon 132, 08036 Barcelona; Facultad de Medicina, 28804 Alcala de Henares, Madrid; Calle Zaragoza 5, 11003 Cadiz; Cami de Riudoms 6, local 2, 43201 Reus (Tarragona); Calle Fernando el Catolico 57, 50006 Zaragoza

Espiritualidad
Triana, 9, 28016 Madrid
Tel: (091) 350-49-22 *Fax:* (091) 350-49-22
E-mail: ede@edespiritualidad.org
Web Site: www.edespiritualidad.org
Founded: 1948
ISBN Prefix(es): 84-7068

Estudio de Bioinformacion, S L+
Embajador Vich, 22-4°-8a, 46002 Valencia
Tel: (096) 351 46 27 *Fax:* (096) 394 37 27
E-mail: bioinformacion@bioinformacion.com
Web Site: www.bioinformacion.com
Key Personnel
Dir: Ernesto Hanquet
Subjects: Psychology, Psychiatry
ISBN Prefix(es): 84-86772; 84-921862

Instituto de Estudios Fiscales+
Alcala 9, 1a planta, 28014 Madrid
Tel: (091) 5063740 (ext 51307) *Fax:* (091) 5273951
E-mail: ventas.campillo@sgt.meh.es
Web Site: www.minhac.es/ief
Key Personnel
Coordinator, Editorial Production: Alberto Romero Martin
Subjects: Accounting, Economics, Law, Public Administration
ISBN Prefix(es): 84-476
Parent Company: Ministerio de Economia y Hacienda
Warehouse: Centro de Publicaciones del Ministerio de Economia y Hacienda, Pza Campillo del Mundo Nuevo, 3-28005 Madrid
Orders to: Centro de Publicaciones del Ministerio de Economia y Hacienda Pza, Campillo del Mundo Nuevo, 3-28005 Madrid

Instituto de Estudios Riojanos
Muro de la Mata, 8 Principal, 26071 Logrono La Rioja
Tel: (0941) 262064; (0941) 262065 *Fax:* (0941) 246667
Key Personnel
Dir: Jose Miguel Delgado Idarreta
Founded: 1946
Membership(s): CECEL (Confederacioon Espanola de Centros de Estudios Locales).
Subjects: Archaeology, Art, Biological Sciences, Chemistry, Chemical Engineering, Earth Sciences, Geography, Geology, History, Language Arts, Linguistics, Literature, Literary Criticism, Essays, Mathematics, Physical Sciences, Regional Interests, Social Sciences, Sociology
ISBN Prefix(es): 84-87252; 84-89362; 84-89747

Institut d'Estudis Metropolitans de Barcelona
Bellaterra, 08193 Barcelona
Tel: (093) 691 83 61; (093) 691 97 97; (093) 691 91 82 *Fax:* (093) 580 65 72
E-mail: iermb@uab.es
Web Site: www.uab.es/iemb/
Key Personnel
Dir: Oriol Nel lo i Colom

Publicaciones Etea (ETEA Publishing)
Escritor Castilla Aguayo, 4, 14004 Cordoba
SAN: 002-8724
Tel: (0957) 222100 *Fax:* (0957) 222182
E-mail: comunica@etea.com
Web Site: www.etea.com
Key Personnel
Dir: Jesus N Ramirez Sobrino *E-mail:* jramirez@etea.com
Founded: 1963
University education.
Subjects: Business, Economics, Labor, Industrial Relations
ISBN Prefix(es): 84-86785; 84-9750
Number of titles published annually: 20 Print
Parent Company: ETEA - Institucion Universitaria de la Compenia de Jesus
Distributed by Desclee de Brouwer
Foreign Rights: Desclee de Brouwer (Spain)

Etu Ediciones SL+
Grau de Sant Andreu 415, 08030 Barcelona
Tel: (093) 2741671 *Fax:* (093) 2741671
E-mail: etu@arrakis.es
Key Personnel
Dir General: Tristan Llop
Founded: 1996 (Founded by Kabaleb's son)
Courses of occult sciences.
Subjects: Astrology, Occult, Religion - Other, Angels
Total Titles: 7 Print
Distributed by Indigo (Spain & South America)
Distributor for Alfaomega S L (Spain)

Eumo Editorial+
P de Miquel de Clariana, 3, 08500 Vic, Barcelona
SAN: 002-9351
Tel: (093) 889 28 18; (093) 889 29 61 *Fax:* (093) 889 35 41
E-mail: eumoeditorial@eumoeditorial.com
Web Site: www.eumoeditorial.com
Key Personnel
Dir General: Montse Ayats
Founded: 1979
Subjects: Archaeology, Education, Health, Nutrition, History, Library & Information Sciences, Literature, Literary Criticism, Essays, Nonfiction (General), Poetry, Women's Studies
ISBN Prefix(es): 84-7602; 84-9750; 84-300; 84-9766
Number of titles published annually: 25 Print
Total Titles: 1,100 Print
Distribution Center: Arc De Bera, C de Belgica 47-49, Poligon Montigala, 08911 Badalona, Contact: Pep Vila *Tel:* (093) 465 30 08 *Fax:* (093) 465 87 90

Ediciones Eunate+
Pintor Crispin, 12-7° G, 31008 Pamplona, Navarra
Tel: (0948) 272352 *Fax:* (0948) 172636
E-mail: eunate@cin.es
Web Site: www.cin.es
Key Personnel
Dir General: Pedro Llorente Apat
Founded: 1987
ISBN Prefix(es): 84-7768

EUNSA (Ediciones Universidad de Navarra SA)+
Plaza de los Sauces, 1-2, 31010 Baranain Navarra
Tel: (0948) 256850 *Fax:* (0948) 256854
E-mail: eunsa@cin.es
Web Site: www.eunsa.es
Key Personnel
Editorial Dir: Jose Martinez Echalar
Production: Abel del Rio
Chairman: Damaso Rico
Founded: 1967
Subjects: Architecture & Interior Design, Biological Sciences, Business, Economics, Education, Engineering (General), History, Journalism, Language Arts, Linguistics, Law, Library & Information Sciences, Literature, Literary Criticism, Essays, Medicine, Nursing, Dentistry, Philosophy, Religion - Other, Theology
ISBN Prefix(es): 84-313
Imprints: Biblioteca 'NT' (number of paperback series covering the arts & sciences, current affairs, religion & philosophy, etc)

Fondo de Cultura Economica de Espana, SL+
Via de los Poblados, s/n, Edif Indubuilding-Goico, 4-15, 28033 Madrid
SAN: 003-0562
Tel: (091) 7632800; (091) 7632766 *Fax:* (091) 7635133
E-mail: fcevent@interbook.es
Key Personnel
Man Dir: Arturo Azuela
Founded: 1934
Subjects: Anthropology, Economics, Government, Political Science, History, Language Arts, Linguistics, Law, Literature, Literary Criticism, Essays, Philosophy, Psychology, Psychiatry, Science (General), Social Sciences, Sociology, Technology
ISBN Prefix(es): 84-375
Parent Company: Fondo de Cultura Economica, Mexico
U.S. Office(s): Fondo de Cultura Economica, 2293 Verus St, San Diego, CA 92154, United States
Bookshop(s): Libreria Mexico, c/Fernando el Catolico, 86, 28015 Madrid

Miguel Font Editor
Pedro Ripoll Palov, 20, Apdo 128, E-07008 Palma de Mallorca, Baleares
SAN: 004-2196
Tel: (071) 477300 *Fax:* (071) 476805
E-mail: miquel@globalnet.es
Key Personnel
Manager: Miguel Font i Cirer
Founded: 1984
ISBN Prefix(es): 84-86366; 84-7967

Forum Artis, SA+
Serrano, 7-1 izda, 28001 Madrid
SAN: 003-0805
Tel: (091) 4353180; (091) 4350548 *Fax:* (091) 4355124
E-mail: forum@adenet.es
Key Personnel
Dir: Mario Antolin Paz
Founded: 1991
Subjects: Art
ISBN Prefix(es): 84-88836

Naipes Heraclio Fournier SA
Poligono Industrial de Gojain, Avda San Blas 19, 01171 Legutiano
SAN: 004-3400
Mailing Address: PO Box 94, 01006 Vitoria
Tel: (0945) 465525 *Fax:* (0945) 465543
E-mail: fournier@nhfournier.es
Web Site: www.nhfournier.es
Telex: 35510 *Cable:* FOURNIER
ISBN Prefix(es): 84-85074; 84-88928

Fragua Editorial
Andres Mellado, 64, 28015 Madrid
Tel: (091) 544 22 97; (091) 549 18 06 *Fax:* (091) 549 18 06
E-mail: fragua@fragua.com
Web Site: www.fragua.com
Key Personnel
Man Dir: Mariano Munoz Alonso
Founded: 1972
Subjects: Advertising, Communications, Journalism, Language Arts, Linguistics, Library & Information Sciences, Philosophy, Photography, Radio, TV, Technology
ISBN Prefix(es): 84-7074; 84-7974

Fundacio La Caixa
Avda Diagonal, 621-629 Torre II, pl 12, 08028 Barcelona
SAN: 003-1240
Tel: (093) 404 6079 *Fax:* (093) 3395703
E-mail: info@lacaixa.es
Web Site: portal1.lacaixa.es
Key Personnel
Vice President: Alejandro Plasencia
ISBN Prefix(es): 84-7664

Fundacion Biblioteca Alemana Gorres
Subsidiary of Fundacion Deutsche Stiftung
San Buenaventura, 9, 28005 Madrid
Tel: (091) 3668508; (091)3668509
Key Personnel
Dir: Hans Juretschke
Librarian: Jutta Ploss
Founded: 1955

Fundacion Coleccion Thyssen-Bornemisza
Paseo del Prado, 8, 28014 Madrid
Tel: (091) 420 39 44 *Fax:* (091) 4202780
E-mail: umseo.thyssen-bornemisza@offcampus.es
Key Personnel
Contact: Laura Estevez Couras *E-mail:* lestevez@umseothyssen.org
Subjects: Art
ISBN Prefix(es): 84-88474
Distributed by Lunwerg SA

Fundacion de Estudios Libertarios Anselmo Lorenzo
Paseo de Alberto Palacios, 2, 28021 Madrid
Tel: (091) 7970424 *Fax:* (091) 5052183
E-mail: fal@cnt.es
Web Site: www.cnt.es/fal
Key Personnel
President: Ignacio Soriano
Librarian: Manuel Carlos Garcia
Founded: 1986
Subjects: Biography, Economics, History, Labor, Industrial Relations, Literature, Literary Criticism, Essays, Social Sciences, Sociology, Anarchism, Trade Unionism
ISBN Prefix(es): 84-86864
Number of titles published annually: 4 Print
Distributed by Taluzma (Barcelona)
Distributor for Lucina; Nossa y Jara Editores

Fundacion de los Ferrocarriles Espanoles
Santa Isabel, 44, 28012 Madrid
Tel: (091) 1511 071 *Fax:* (091) 5284822; (091) 5391415
E-mail: fuccu20@ffe.es
Web Site: www.ffe.es
Key Personnel
Dir: Carlos Zapatero
Specialize in Railways.
ISBN Prefix(es): 84-404; 84-604; 84-398; 84-88675; 84-505

Fundacion Gratis Date
Apdo 2154, 31080 Pamplona
Tel: (0948) 123612 *Fax:* (0948) 123612
E-mail: fundacion@gratisdate.org
Web Site: www.gratisdate.org
Key Personnel
Dir: Jose Maria Iraburu
ISBN Prefix(es): 84-87903; 84-404

Fundacion Juan March
Castello, 77, 28006 Madrid
Tel: (091) 435 42 40 *Fax:* (091) 576 34 20
E-mail: webmast@mail.march.es
Web Site: www.march.es
Key Personnel
Dir General: Jose Luis Yuste
ISBN Prefix(es): 84-7075; 84-500; 84-400

Fundacion Marcelino Botin
Pedrueca, 1, 39003 Santander, Cantabria
Tel: (0942) 226072 *Fax:* (0942) 226045
E-mail: fmabotin@fundacionmbotin.org
Web Site: www.fundacionmbotin.org
Key Personnel
Dir: Rafael Benjumea Cabeza De Saca
Contact: Isabel Cubria *E-mail:* prensa@fundacionmbotin.org
Founded: 1990
Subjects: Archaeology, Art, Environmental Studies, History, Human Relations, Science (General)
ISBN Prefix(es): 84-87678; 84-95516; 84-404; 84-500; 84-398
Number of titles published annually: 12 Print
Distributed by Emiliano Garcia de la Torre (Spain)

Fundacion Rosacruz+
Apdo de Correos, 1219, 50080 Zaragoza
Tel: (076) 589100 *Fax:* (076) 589161
E-mail: correo@fundacionrosacruz.org
Web Site: www.fundacionrosacruz.org
Founded: 1993
Subjects: Literature, Literary Criticism, Essays, Mysteries, Philosophy, Religion - Other
ISBN Prefix(es): 84-87055
Parent Company: Stichting Rozkruis Pers, Netherlands
Associate Companies: Rozekruis Pers, France
Distributed by Totem (Balears Islands); Unicornio (Canary Islands)
Showroom(s): 49 bajos, Alicante *Tel:* (01) 5144805; del Oro, 23, Barcelona *Tel:* (093) 2184368; Porvenir, 12, entlo, Gerona; Tabares, 10 transversal izda. no2, La Cuesta (Tenerife); Santa Ana, 69, Leon *Tel:* (087) 213767; Francisco de Ricci, 7, Madrid *Tel:* (091) 5595992; Ladron de Guevara, 12, Malaga *Tel:* (05) 2253949; Goethe, 15 A, Palma De Mallorca *Tel:* (071) 285629; Po de la Pechina, 6 bajo, Valencia *Tel:* (06) 3910267; Santa Cruz, 8, Zaragoza *Tel:* (076) 574268

Editorial Fundamentos+
Caracas, 15-3 ctro dcha, 28010 Madrid
Tel: (091) 319 96 19 *Fax:* (091) 319 55 84
E-mail: fundamentos@editorialfundamentos.es
Web Site: www.editorialfundamentos.es
Key Personnel
Man Dir: Juan Serraller Ibanez
Editorial: Cristina Vizcaino
Founded: 1970
Subjects: Alternative, Crafts, Games, Hobbies, Drama, Theater, Fiction, Film, Video, Government, Political Science, Literature, Literary Criticism, Essays, Music, Dance, Philosophy, Psychology, Psychiatry, Social Sciences, Sociology
ISBN Prefix(es): 84-245

Galaxia SA Editorial+
Reconquista, 1, 36201 Vigo Pontevedra
Tel: (0986) 432100 *Fax:* (0986) 223205
E-mail: galaxia@editorialgalaxia.es
Web Site: www.editorialgalaxia.es
Key Personnel
Dir General: Carlos Casares
Founded: 1950
Subjects: Art, History, Literature, Literary Criticism, Essays, Philosophy, Poetry, Social Sciences, Sociology, Travel
ISBN Prefix(es): 84-7154; 84-8288
Warehouse: Trav Vigo, 71 (Sotano), 36206 Vigo Pontevedra

La Galera, SA Editorial+
Diputacio, 250, 08007 Barcelona
Tel: (093) 4120030 *Fax:* (093) 3173277; (093) 3014863
E-mail: lagalera@grec.com
Web Site: www.enciclopedia-catalana.com
Key Personnel
Man Dir: Roma Doria Forcada
Founded: 1963
Subjects: Education
ISBN Prefix(es): 84-246

Vicent Garcia Editores, SA
Guardia Civil, 22 Torre 3a, piso 1°, 3a, 46020 Valencia
SAN: 005-318X
Tel: (096) 361 9559; (096) 3691589; (096) 369 3246 *Fax:* (096) 393 00 57
E-mail: vgesa@combios.es
Web Site: www.vgesa.com
Key Personnel
Dir General: Ricardo J Vicent
Founded: 1974
Specialize in facsimiles of manuscripts, incunabula & ancient books.
Subjects: Antiques, Art, Gardening, Plants, History, Language Arts, Linguistics, Law, Religion - Catholic, Travel
ISBN Prefix(es): 84-85094; 84-87988; 84-400
Book Club(s): Club Konrad Haebler

Ediciones Gaviota SA+
Subsidiary of Editorial Everest SA
Manuel Tovar, 8, 28034 Madrid
Tel: (091) 358 01 08 *Fax:* (091) 729 38 58
E-mail: publicaciones@ediciones-gaviota.es
Web Site: www.everest.es
Key Personnel
Man Dir: Jose Antonio Lopez Martinez
Publication Dir: Matthew Todd Borgens
Export Dir: Severino Fernandez
Founded: 1980
Specialize in Children's & Juvenile Books.
ISBN Prefix(es): 84-392
Associate Companies: Lectorum Publications Inc, 137 West 14 St, New York, NY 10011, United States (US Distributor)
Subsidiaries: Everset de Ediciones y Distribucion
Orders to: Everset de Ediciones y Distribucion

Editorial Gedisa SA+
Bonanova Stroll, 9 1° 1a, 08022 Barcelona
Tel: (093) 253 09 04 *Fax:* (093) 253 09 05
E-mail: gedisa@gedisa.com
Web Site: www.gedisa.com
Key Personnel
Publisher: Victor Landman
Founded: 1977
Subjects: Biography, Education, Human Relations, Nonfiction (General), Philosophy, Psychology, Psychiatry, Social Sciences, Sociology, Sports, Athletics
ISBN Prefix(es): 84-7432
Subsidiaries: Editorial Celtia SA; Editorial Gedisa Mexicana SA

Generalitat de Catalunya Diari Oficial de la Generalitat vern
Carrer Rocafort, 120, 08015 Barcelona
Tel: (093) 302 64 62 *Fax:* (093) 318 62 21
E-mail: llibrbcn@gencat.net
Web Site: www.gencat.net/diari
Key Personnel
General Dir: Ricard Lobo
Founded: 1977
Subjects: Art, Education, Health, Nutrition, History, Law, Public Administration, Regional Interests
ISBN Prefix(es): 84-393
Bookshop(s): Llibreria de la Generalitat de Catalunya, Rambla dels Estudis 118, 08002 Barcelona *E-mail:* llibrgi@gencat.net; Llibreria de la Generalitat de Catalunya, Gran Via de Jaume 1, 38, 17001 Girona *Tel:* (0972) 22 72 67 *E-mail:* llibrgi@gencat.net; Llibreria de la Generalitat de Catalunya, Rambla

d'Arago, 43, 25003 Lleida *Tel:* (0973) 28 19 30 *E-mail:* llibrlle@gencat.net
Orders to: Llibreria de la Generalitat de Catalunya, Rambla dels Estudis 118, 08002 Barcelona *E-mail:* llibrcn@gencat.net

Ediciones Gestio 2000 SA+
Comte Borrell, 241, 08029 Barcelona
Tel: (093) 4106767 *Fax:* (093) 4109645
E-mail: info@gestion2000.com
Web Site: www.gestion2000.com
Key Personnel
Dir: Alexandre Amat *E-mail:* aamat@gestion2000.com
Founded: 1986
Specialize in Business Management.
Subjects: Accounting, Advertising, Career Development, Computer Science, Economics, Finance, Human Relations, Management, Marketing, Technology
ISBN Prefix(es): 84-86703; 84-8088; 84-86582
Total Titles: 400 Print; 10 CD-ROM
Bookshop(s): Libreria de la Empresa c/Muntaner, 90 08011 Barcelona *E-mail:* libreria.empresa@gestion2000.com

Instituto de Cultura Juan Gil-Albert+
Avda Estacion, 6, 03005 Alicante
Tel: (096) 5121 216; (096) 5121 300 *Fax:* (096) 5121 216
E-mail: galbert@dip-alicante.es
Web Site: www.dip-alicante.es/galbert/
Key Personnel
President: Antonio Mira Perceval
Dir: Emilio La Parra Lopez
Founded: 1983
Also acts as Council for scientific research.
Subjects: Art, Poetry, Social Sciences, Sociology
ISBN Prefix(es): 84-7784

Editorial Gustavo Gili SA+
Rossello, 87-89, 08029 Barcelona
Tel: (093) 3228161 *Fax:* (093) 3229205
E-mail: info@ggili.com
Web Site: www.ggili.com
Key Personnel
President: Gustavo Gili
Editor-in-Chief & Man Dir: Monica Gili
Man Dir & Sales General Manager: Gabriel Gili
Sales Export: Saskia Adriaensen; Pepita Sanchez
Production: Andreas Schweiger
Foreign Rights: Elena Llobera
Founded: 1902
Publisher specializing in architectural books & magazines
Also subscription & periodical publications.
Subjects: Architecture & Interior Design, Art, Communications, Photography, Technology, Travel
ISBN Prefix(es): 84-252
Number of titles published annually: 50 Print
Total Titles: 1,200 Print
Associate Companies: Ediciones G Gili, SA de CV, Avda Valle de Bravo, 21-53050, Mexico (ISBN: 968-887)
Distributor for Colegio De Arquitectos de Almeria; Collegi D'Arquitectes de Catalunya
Distribution Center: Trucatriche, 3800 Main St, Suite 8, Chula Vista, CA 91911, United States, Pedro Alonzo *Tel:* 619-426-2690 *Fax:* 619-426-2695 *E-mail:* info@trucatriche.com (International Orders - Attention: Gustavo Gili)

Gran Enciclopedia-Asturiana Silverio Canada
Menendez Valdes, 33-1, 33201 Gijon, Asturias
SAN: 004-9476
Tel: (0985) 170921; (0985) 349684 *Fax:* (0985) 349542
E-mail: gea.edi@teleline.es; gea_edi@yahoo.es
Web Site: www.enciclopediaasturiana.com
Telex: 89736 Edju E
Key Personnel
Man Dir, Editorial: Silverio Canada
Sales: Fernando Alvarez Conde
Production: Manuel Cardenas
Founded: 1970
Subjects: Regional Interests
ISBN Prefix(es): 84-7286
Orders to: Alto Atocha 7, Gijon

Grao Editorial+
Francesc Tarrega, 32-34, 08027 Barcelona
Tel: (093) 4080464; (093) 4050455 *Fax:* (093) 3524337
E-mail: grao@grao.com; editorial@grao.com
Web Site: www.grao.com
Key Personnel
Manager: Joaquim Mart
Editorial Dir: Cinta Vidal
Founded: 1977
Subjects: Education
ISBN Prefix(es): 84-7827
Number of titles published annually: 25 Print
Total Titles: 250 Print
Parent Company: Institut de Recursos I Investigacio per a la Foirmacio, SK (IRIF)

Grao Editorial+
Formerly Institut de Recursos I investigacio per a la Formacio SL (IRIF)
Francesc Tarrega, 32-34, 08027 Barcelona
Tel: (093) 4080464; (093) 4050455 *Fax:* (093) 3524337
E-mail: grao@grao.com
Web Site: www.grao.com
Key Personnel
Delegated Counselor: Antoni Zabala i Vidiella
Founded: 1977
Subjects: Education
ISBN Prefix(es): 84-7827
Number of titles published annually: 50 Print
Total Titles: 300 Print
Divisions: Grao Editorial; Interactiva

Editorial Gredos SA+
Sanchez Pacheco, 85, Apdo 2076, 28002 Madrid
Tel: (091) 7444920 *Fax:* (091) 5192033
E-mail: comercial@editorialgredos.com
Web Site: www.editorialgredos.com
Founded: 1944
Subjects: Economics, Education, History, Literature, Literary Criticism, Essays, Philosophy, Psychology, Psychiatry
ISBN Prefix(es): 84-249

Grijalbo Mondadon SA Junior+
Formerly Ediciones Junior SA
Arago 385, 08013 Barcelona
Tel: (093) 4767100 *Fax:* (093) 4767121
Key Personnel
President: Juan Grijalbo
Council Delegate: Jose Maria Vives
Assistant Council Delegate: Gonzalo Ponton
Manager: Josep Maria Pujol
Founded: 1974
Membership(s): Grupo & Grijalbo-Mondadori Publications in Barcelona.
Subjects: Humor
ISBN Prefix(es): 84-7419
Warehouse: Grijalbo Comercial, SA, Progreso, 274, Badelona (Barcelona)

Grijalbo Mondadori SA+
Arago 385, 08013 Barcelona
Tel: (093) 4767100 *Fax:* (093) 4767121
E-mail: marketing@grijalbo.com
Web Site: www.grijalbo.com
Key Personnel
General Manager: Riccardo Cavallero *Tel:* (093) 476 71 23 *Fax:* (093) 476 71 21 *E-mail:* ricky@grijalbo.com
General Editor: Claudio Lopez de Lamadrid *Tel:* (093) 476 71 03 *E-mail:* claudio@grijalbo.com
Editor: Cristina Arminana *Tel:* (093) 476 71 00 *E-mail:* cristina@grijalbo.com; Silvia Querini *Tel:* (093) 476 71 05 *E-mail:* silviaq@grijalbo.com
Rights: Isabelle Bordallo *Tel:* (093) 476 71 03 *E-mail:* bordallo@grijalbo.com; Dora Hernando *E-mail:* dora@grijalbo.com
Contact: Carmen Garrido Montero *E-mail:* carmen@grijalbo.com
Founded: 1962
Subjects: Architecture & Interior Design, Fiction, Gardening, Plants, Human Relations, Humor, Literature, Literary Criticism, Essays, Nonfiction (General), Poetry
ISBN Prefix(es): 84-253; 84-397; 84-7515; 84-8441
Number of titles published annually: 400 Print
Branch Office(s)
Grijalbo SA, Av Belgrano, 1256/64, 1093 Buenos Aires, Argentina *Tel:* (0383) 74 03, 49 40 *Fax:* (0381) 27 26 *E-mail:* info@grijalbo.com.ar
Distribuidora Exclusiva Grijalbo SA, Centro Industiral Eldorado, Calle 64, 88 A-06, interior 1-2, Bogota D E, Colombia *Tel:* (0224) 74 28; (0252) 26 75 *Fax:* (0252) 95 97 *E-mail:* grijalbo@cdl.telecom.com.co
Editorial Grijalbo SA, Almirante Barroso, 27, Santiago De Chile, Chile *Tel:* (0672) 30 27 *Fax:* (0672) 18 50 *E-mail:* mondador@entelchile.net
Editorial Grijalbo SA DE C V, Av Homero, No 544, Col Chapultepec-Morales, 11570 Mexico D F, Mexico *Tel:* (05) 2030660; (05) 2030955 *Fax:* (05) 2547683
Ap Correos, 106-62260 Chacao, Av Principal Diego Cisnero, Edificio colegial Bolivariana, piso 2, local 2-2 Los Ruices, Caracas, Venezuela *Tel:* (0238) 13 22 *Fax:* (0239) 03 08 *E-mail:* griven@etheron.net
Distributor for Dedicersa De Cervantes Ediciones SA; Editorial Amazonas SA; Electa Espana SA; Forza Editores Inc
Foreign Rights: Ros Ramsay (UK); Mary Anne Thompson

Editorial Grupo Cero
Duque de Osuna Nº 4 Locales, 28015 Madrid
Tel: (091) 758 19 40; (091) 5423349 *Fax:* (091) 758 19 41
E-mail: pedidos@editorialgrupocero.com
Web Site: www.editorialgrupocero.com
Key Personnel
Dir: Miguel Oscar Menassa
Founded: 1976
Subjects: Literature, Literary Criticism, Essays, Medicine, Nursing, Dentistry, Poetry, Psychology, Psychiatry, Social Sciences, Sociology
ISBN Prefix(es): 84-85498

Grupo Comunicar
Apdo Correos 527, 21080 Huelva
Tel: (0959) 248380 *Fax:* (0959) 248380
E-mail: info@grupocomunicar.com
Web Site: www.grupo-comunicar.com
Key Personnel
President: Jose Ignacio Aguaded Gomez
Vice President: Enrique Martinez-Salanova Sanchez
Founded: 1989
Subjects: Communications, Education
Number of titles published annually: 4 Print; 3 CD-ROM; 4 Online; 2 E-Book
Total Titles: 40 Print; 5 CD-ROM; 4 Online; 5 E-Book
Distributor for Abis & Books; Amares; A-Z Dislibros; Carrer de Llibres; Centro Andaluz del Libro; Andres Garcia; Grial; Ikuska; Lemus

Grupo Editorial, see Ediciones SM

Grupo Editorial CEAC SA+
Paseig Manel Girona, 71 Baixos, 08034 Barcelona
SAN: 003-357X
Tel: (093) 2472424 *Fax:* (093) 2315115
E-mail: atencioncliente@ceacedit.com
Web Site: www.ceacedit.com; www.editorialceac.com
Key Personnel
President: Guillermo Menal, Sr
Executive Manager: Jaume Pintanel
Dir, International: Esteve Julia
Editorial Dir: Isabel Marti *E-mail:* imarti@ceacedit.com; Jose Lopez Jara *Tel:* (093) 307 52 59 *E-mail:* jljara@caecedit.com
Subjects: Education, Science Fiction, Fantasy, Technology
Imprints: Ediciones Ceac; Timun Mas; Libros Cupula

Grupo Santillana de Ediciones SA+
Torrelaguna, 60, 28043 Madrid
Tel: (091) 7449060 *Fax:* (091) 3224475
E-mail: grupo@santillana.es
Web Site: www.gruposantillana.com
Key Personnel
President: Emiliano Martinez
Vice President: Francisco Perez Gonzalez; Ricardo Diez Hochleitner
Man Dir: Isabel de Polanco Moreno
Founded: 1960
Subjects: Education
ISBN Prefix(es): 84-294; 84-668
Associate Companies: Editorial Santillana, Argentina; Editorial Santillana, Bolivia; Editorial Santillana, Colombia; Editorial Santillana, Costa Rica; Editorial Santillana, Chile; Editorial Santillana, Ecuador; Editorial Santillana, El Salvador; Editorial Santillana, Guatemala; Editorial Santillana, Mexico; Editorial Santillana, Paraguay; Editorial Santillana, Peru; Editorial Santillana, Puerto Rico; Editorial Santillana, Dominican Republic; Editorial Santillana, Uruguay; Editorial Santillana, Venezuela
Divisions: Aguilar; Alfaguara; Altea; Taurus; Richmond
U.S. Office(s): Santillana Publishing Co, 2105 NW 86 Ave, Miami, FL 33112, United States

Guadalquivir SL Ediciones
Asuncion, 61, 41011 Sevilla
SAN: 003-3863
Tel: (095) 422 19 76; (095) 422 19 17 *Fax:* (095) 421 33 20
E-mail: guadalquivir.ed@svq.servicom.es
Founded: 1979
Subjects: Art, History, Literature, Literary Criticism, Essays
ISBN Prefix(es): 84-8093; 84-86080
Subsidiaries: Varflora
Orders to: Varflora, 17 Bajo, 41001 Seville

Guia Viva, *imprint of* Anaya-Touring Club

Guiarama, *imprint of* Anaya-Touring Club

Guiatotal, *imprint of* Anaya-Touring Club

Editorial Gulaab
Alquima, 6 (P 1 Los Rosales), 28933 Mostoles
Tel: (091) 6170867 *Fax:* (071) 61 86 55
E-mail: alfaomega@sew.es
Key Personnel
Editor: J M Beltran Alorda
Subjects: Human Relations, Philosophy, Religion - Buddhist, Religion - Hindu, Religion - Other, Women's Studies
ISBN Prefix(es): 84-86797

Distributed by Alfa Omego (Spain); Ed Cerro Manupuehue (Chile); Ed luz de Luna (Argentina); Ed Moderna (Colombia); Unicornio (Spain)

Harlequin Iberica SA
Hermosilla, 21, 28001 Madrid
SAN: 003-407X
Tel: (091) 4358623 *Fax:* (091) 4310484
E-mail: atencionalcliente@harlequiniberica.com
Web Site: www.harlequiniberica.com
Key Personnel
General Dir: Maria Teresa Villar
Founded: 1982
Subjects: Romance
ISBN Prefix(es): 84-396
Parent Company: Harlequin Enterprises Ltd, Toronto, ON, Canada

Heinemann Iberia SA, see Macmillan Heinemann ELT

Hercules de Ediciones, SA
Comandonte fontenes 6-1 AB, 15003 A Coruna La Coruna
Tel: (0981) 220585; (0981) 226443 *Fax:* (0981) 220717
E-mail: empg05052@empresas-galicia.com
Key Personnel
President: Francisco Rodriguez Iglesias
Manager: Nicolas Salvador Egido
Subjects: Anthropology, Child Care & Development, Education
ISBN Prefix(es): 84-87244; 84-89468
Branch Office(s)
Hercules Astur
Warehouse: Rua Chinto Crespo, 2, A Gandara, San Pedro, L A Coruna

Editorial Herder SA+
Provenca, 388, 08025 Barcelona
Tel: (093) 476 26 26 *Fax:* (093) 207 34 48
E-mail: editorialherder@herder-sa.com
Web Site: www.herder-sa.com
Telex: 54120 Hegr E *Cable:* HERDER
Key Personnel
Man Dir: Friedl Antonio Valtl
Publicity: Carlos Rey
Founded: 1943
Subjects: Economics, Education, Language Arts, Linguistics, Medicine, Nursing, Dentistry, Philosophy, Psychology, Psychiatry, Religion - Other, Social Sciences, Sociology, Theology
ISBN Prefix(es): 84-254
Associate Companies: Verlag Herder & Co, Austria; Verlag Herder GmbH & Co KG, Germany; Herder und Herder GmbH, Germany; Herder Editrice e Libreria, Italy; Herder AG, Switzerland
Branch Office(s)
Herder Editorial y Livreria, Calle 12, No 6/89, Apdo Aereo, 6855 Bogota, Colombia (Delegacione de Venta)
Hesperia SA Editorial y Libreria, Ave Callao 565, Buenos Aires, Argentina (Delegacione de Venta)
Bookshop(s): Libreria Herder

Ediciones Hiperion SL+
Salustiano Olozaga, 14, 28001 Madrid
Tel: (091) 577 60 15; (091) 577 60 16 *Fax:* (091) 435 86 90
E-mail: info@hiperion.com
Web Site: www.hiperion.com
Key Personnel
Man Dir, Editorial: Jesus Munarriz
Sales: Maite Merodio
Founded: 1976
Subjects: Language Arts, Linguistics, Literature, Literary Criticism, Essays, Poetry, Religion - Islamic, Religion - Jewish

ISBN Prefix(es): 84-7517; 84-85272
Number of titles published annually: 30 Print
Total Titles: 600 Print
Bookshop(s): Libreria Hiperion, Calle Salustiano Olozaga 14, 28001 Madrid *Tel:* (091) 577 60 15

Editorial Hispano Europea SA+
Bori i Fontesta, 6-8, 08021 Barcelona
Tel: (093) 2013709; (093) 2018500 *Fax:* (093) 4142635
E-mail: hispaneuropea@mx3.redestb.es
Telex: 98772 cllcE
Key Personnel
Man Dir, Editorial & Publicity: Jorge J Prat
Sales: Xavier Campillo
Production: Jose Madueno
Founded: 1956
Subjects: Animals, Pets, Business, Gardening, Plants, Health, Nutrition, Sports, Athletics
ISBN Prefix(es): 84-255
Number of titles published annually: 50 Print
Total Titles: 536 Print

Editorial Horsori SL
Rambla de Fabra i Puig 10-12 1 1a, 08030 Barcelona
Tel: (093) 3461997 *Fax:* (093) 3118498
E-mail: horsori@retemail.net
Web Site: www.horsori.es
Key Personnel
Contact: Francisco Segu
Subjects: Education, Philosophy
ISBN Prefix(es): 84-85840
Warehouse: MADE Av Catalonya sln Pol Ind Can Coll, 08185, Lliga de Vall Barcelona

Ibaizabal Edelvives SA
Barrio San Miguel, s/n, 48340 Amorebieta-Etxano, Vizcaya
Tel: (094) 6308036 *Fax:* (094) 6308028
E-mail: ibaizabal@ibaizabal.biz
Key Personnel
Dir: Jose Iraolagoitia Mendibe
Contact: Itziar Osa
Founded: 1990
Materials for school teaching literary editions.
Subjects: Education, Literature, Literary Criticism, Essays, Religion - Catholic
ISBN Prefix(es): 84-8325; 84-7992
Number of titles published annually: 123 Print
Total Titles: 1,436 Print
Warehouse: Edelvives, Barrio San Miguel S/A, 48340 Amorebieta-Etxano, Vizcaya *Tel:* (04) 4532009; (04) 4532174 *Fax:* (04) 4532091
Orders to: Edelvives, Barrio San Miguel S/A, 48340 Amorebieta-Etxano, Vizcaya *Tel:* (04) 4532009; (04) 4532174 *Fax:* (04) 4532091

Editorial Iberia, SA+
Plato, 26, 08006 Barcelona
Tel: (093) 2010599; (093) 2013807 *Fax:* (093) 2097362
E-mail: omega@ediciones-omega.es
Web Site: www.ediciones-omega.es
Telex: 98095
Key Personnel
Administrator: Antonio Paricio Larrea
Founded: 1945
Subjects: Art, Biography, Education, Fiction, Health, Nutrition, Literature, Literary Criticism, Essays, Physics, Psychology, Psychiatry, Science (General), Self-Help, Travel
ISBN Prefix(es): 84-7082
Parent Company: Ediciones Omega, SA
Associate Companies: Ediciones Medici, SL

Iberico Europea de Ediciones SA
Serrano, 44, 28001 Madrid
SAN: 003-4762
Tel: (091) 4357243

Founded: 1966
Subjects: Art, Biography, Business, How-to, Music, Dance, Social Sciences, Sociology
ISBN Prefix(es): 84-256

Icaria Editorial SA+
Ausias Marc, 16, 3r, 2a, 08010 Barcelona
Tel: (093) 3011723 *Fax:* (093) 3178242
Web Site: www.icariaeditorial.com
Key Personnel
Man Dir, Editorial, Rights & Permissions: Anna Monjo Omedes
Founded: 1977
Subjects: Anthropology, Cookery, Developing Countries, Economics, Energy, Environmental Studies, Literature, Literary Criticism, Essays, Poetry, Social Sciences, Sociology, Women's Studies, Analysis of International Politics, Critical Economy, Ecology, Relations of the North-South, Social Sciences, Voices & Proposals
ISBN Prefix(es): 84-7426
Warehouse: Lepanto, 135-7, 08013 Barcelona

Publicaciones ICCE (Calasanz Institute for Educational Sciences)+
Eraso 3, Madrid 28028
SAN: 003-6277
Tel: (091) 725 72 00 *Fax:* (091) 361 10 52
E-mail: info@ciberaula.net
Web Site: www.ciberaula.net
Key Personnel
Dir: Juan Yzuel *E-mail:* direccion@ciberaula.net
Publishing Dept Dir: Luis M Bandres
 E-mail: editorial@ciberaula.net
Founded: 1967
Subjects: Education, History, Psychology, Psychiatry, Religion - Other, Social Sciences, Sociology
ISBN Prefix(es): 84-7278
Number of titles published annually: 10 Print
Total Titles: 85 Print
Parent Company: Calasanzian Fathers

Icono Perpetuo Socorro, *imprint of* Editorial El Perpetuo Socorro

Idea Books, SA+
c/ Huelva 10, 08940 Cornella de Llobregat, Barcelona
Tel: (093) 4533002 *Fax:* (093) 4541895
E-mail: ideabooks@ideabooks.es
Web Site: www.ideabooks.es
Key Personnel
Co-owner & International Rights & Permissions: Jorge Fernandez
Founded: 1990
Publisher of nonfiction books for professionals, students & children. Specialize in woodworking, furniture, iron & construction.
Membership(s): Society of Editors.
Subjects: Agriculture, Biological Sciences, Child Care & Development, Crafts, Games, Hobbies, Earth Sciences, Education, Geography, Geology, Human Relations, Music, Dance, Philosophy, Physics, Religion - Other, Science (General)
ISBN Prefix(es): 84-8236; 84-87624
Number of titles published annually: 35 Print; 2 Audio
Imprints: Idea Musica; Idea Universitaria

Idea Musica, *imprint of* Idea Books, SA

Idea Universitaria, *imprint of* Idea Books, SA

Editorial Pablo Iglesias
Monte Esquinza, 30-3-D, 28010 Madrid
Tel: (091) 104 313 *Fax:* (091) 194 585
E-mail: administracion@fpi.es
Web Site: www.fpabloiglesias.es

Key Personnel
Dir: Manuel Ortuno Armas
ISBN Prefix(es): 84-85691

Imagen y Deporte, SL+
Marte, 1 bajo, 50012 Zaragoza
Tel: (0976) 75 40 00 *Fax:* (0976) 75 40 00
Web Site: www.imagenydeporte.com
Key Personnel
Man Dir: Carlos Torres *E-mail:* produccion@imagenydeporte.com
International Manager: Elena Rodrigo
 E-mail: internacional@imagenydeporte.com
National Sales: Elisa de Pedro *E-mail:* editorial@imagenydeporte.com
Production Manager: Jose Torres
 E-mail: imagenydeporte@imagenydeporte.com
Founded: 1988
Production & distribution company of educational products, domentines & books.
Subjects: Education, Sports, Athletics
ISBN Prefix(es): 84-89117

Impredisur, SL+
Cuesta Molinos, 7 bajo, 18008 Granada
Tel: (0958) 202955; (0958) 290577
Key Personnel
President: Ignacio Llamas Labella
Founded: 1990
Subjects: Law, Regional Interests
ISBN Prefix(es): 84-7933
Bookshop(s): Libros Adaiz, Colegios 3, 18001 Granada
Orders to: Apdo de Correos 878, 18080 Granada

Incafo Archivo Fotografico Editorial, SL
Castello, 59, 28001 Madrid
SAN: 002-4864
Tel: (091) 4313460; (091) 5780961 *Fax:* (091) 4313589
Telex: 42459 Icf E
Key Personnel
Man Dir, Editorial: Luis Blas Aritio
Production: Javier Echevarri
Rights & Permissions: Margarita Mendez de Vigo
Founded: 1973
Subjects: Art, Environmental Studies, Natural History
ISBN Prefix(es): 84-85389; 84-8089
Book Club(s): Club del Libro de la Naturaleza

INEF Madrid, see Instituto Nacional del Educacion Fisica Madrid (INEF-Madrid)

Institucion Fernando el Catolico de la Excma Diputacion de Zaragoza
Plaza de Espana, 2, 50071 Zaragoza
Tel: (0976) 28 88 78; (0976) 28 88 79
 Fax: (0976) 28 88 69
E-mail: info@ifc.dpz.es
Web Site: www.dpz.es
Key Personnel
President: D Javier Lamban
Dir: Dr Gonzalo Borras
Secretary: D Jose Barranco
Founded: 1943
Subjects: Agriculture, Archaeology, Art, Geography, Geology, History, Law, Literature, Literary Criticism, Essays, Music, Dance
ISBN Prefix(es): 84-7820
Branch Office(s)
Centro de Estudios Borjanos, Casa de Aguilar, Borja
Centro de Estudios Bibilitanos, Puerta de Terrer, Calatayud
Grupo Cultural Caspolino, Palacio Barberan, 50700 Caspe
Centro de Estudios Darocenses, Puerta Baja, 50360 Daroca

Centro de Estudios Cinco Villas, Ramon y Caja, 17, 50600 Ejea Caballeros
Centro de Estudios Turiasonenses, Apdo 39, 50500 Tarazona

Institut de Recursos I investigacio per a la Formacio SL (IRIF), see Grao Editorial

Instituto de Estudios Economicos (Institute for Economic Studies)
Castello, 128, 6a planta, 28006 Madrid
Tel: (091) 782 05 80 *Fax:* (091) 562 36 13
E-mail: iee@ieemadrid.com
Web Site: www.ieemadrid.com
Key Personnel
Administrator: D Jose Maria Goizueta Besga
Founded: 1979
Subjects: Economics, Social Sciences, Sociology
ISBN Prefix(es): 84-85719

Instituto Nacional de Administracion Publica
Calla Atocha, 106, 28012 Madrid
Tel: (091) 3493115; (091) 3493241 *Fax:* (091) 3493287
E-mail: cati.fuente@inap.map.es
Web Site: www.inap.map.es
ISBN Prefix(es): 84-7088; 84-500; 84-505
Branch Office(s)
Plaza de San Diego s/n, 28801 Alcala de Henares (Madrid) *Tel:* (091) 888 22 00 *Fax:* (091) 880 28 61
Calle de Jose Maranon, 12, 28010 Madrid
 Tel: (091) 594 97 00 *Fax:* (091) 445 08 39
Avenida del Doctor Marcelino Roca s/n, Peniscola (Casellon de la Plana) *Tel:* (0964) 48 08 25 *Fax:* (0964) 48 06 49

Instituto Nacional del Educacion Fisica Madrid (INEF-Madrid)
Martin Fierro, s/n, 28040 Madrid
Tel: (091) 336 4000 *Fax:* (091) 336 4032
E-mail: webmaster@inef.upm.es
Web Site: www.inef.com
Key Personnel
Subdirector INEF: Teresa Gonzales Aja
Founded: 1961

Instituto Nacional de Estadistica
Paseo de la Castellana, 183, 28071 Madrid
Tel: (091) 583 91 00 *Fax:* (091) 583 91 58
E-mail: info@ine.es
Web Site: www.ine.es
Key Personnel
President: Jose Ouevedo
Subjects: Mathematics
ISBN Prefix(es): 84-260
Distributed by Libreria Lines-Chiel; Mundi-Prensa Libros, SA

Instituto Nacional de la Salud
P° del Prado 18-20 (planta baja), 28014 Madrid
Tel: (0901) 400-100 *Fax:* (091) 5964480
E-mail: oiac@msc.es
Web Site: www.msc.es
Key Personnel
Dir General: Josep Bonet Bertomeu
Head of Documentation & Publications: Carmen Limon Mendizabal
Subjects: Health, Nutrition
ISBN Prefix(es): 84-351; 84-500; 84-505

Instituto Vasco de Criminologia
Villa Soroa Ategorrieta, 22, 20013 Donostia-San Sebastian
Tel: (0943) 321411; (0943) 321412 *Fax:* (0943) 321272
Web Site: www.sc.ehu.es
Key Personnel
Dir: Antonio Beristain
Founded: 1976
Subjects: Criminology, Human Rights
ISBN Prefix(es): 84-920328

Ediciones Internacionales Universitarias SA+
Pantoja 14, 28002 Madrid
Tel: (091) 5193907 *Fax:* (091) 4136808
E-mail: eiunsa@ibernet.com
Web Site: www.eunsa.es
Key Personnel
Contact: Damaso Rico
Founded: 1967
Subjects: Biography, Economics, Journalism, Nonfiction (General), Philosophy, Theology
ISBN Prefix(es): 84-87155; 84-8469; 84-89893
Holding Company: Plaza de los Sauces, 1-2, 31010 Baranain (Navarra) *Tel:* (0948) 256850 *Fax:* (0948) 256854 *E-mail:* eunsa@cin.es
Branch Office(s)
Pantoja 14, 28002 Madrid *Tel:* (091) 5193907 *Fax:* (091) 4136808 *E-mail:* eiunsa@inbernet.com

Intress, see Institut de Treball Social - Serveis Socials

IR Indo Edicions
Av Florida 30, 36210 Vigo, Galicia
Tel: (0986) 21 48 34 *Fax:* (0986) 21 11 33
E-mail: correo@irindo.com
Web Site: www.irindo.com; irindo.net
Key Personnel
Contact: Bieito Ledo
Founded: 1985
ISBN Prefix(es): 84-7680

Iralka Editorial SL+
Ametzagana, 21-Local 10, 20012 San Sebastian
Tel: (0943) 32 30 14 *Fax:* (0943) 32 30 22
E-mail: iralka@euskalnet.net
Web Site: www.euskalnet.net/iralka
Key Personnel
Editor: Manuel Muner Sorazu
Founded: 1993
Subjects: Anthropology, Literature, Literary Criticism, Essays, Philosophy, Poetry, Social Sciences, Sociology
ISBN Prefix(es): 84-89806; 84-605; 84-920202; 84-920963
Number of titles published annually: 5 Print
Total Titles: 40 Print
Distributed by Andalucia Rodriguez Santos; Bibliotecas y Exportacion Purvill Libros, S A; Catalunya Virus Editorial; Delegacion Granada; Euskal Herria Bitarte

IRIF, see Grao Editorial

Ediciones Irusa+
Roger de Flor, 91, 08013 Barcelona
Tel: (093) 2318032 *Fax:* (093) 2653670
Key Personnel
Contact: Xabier Etxarri
Founded: 1982
Subjects: Cookery, Humor
ISBN Prefix(es): 84-8065; 84-86819

Editorial Isidoriana, Libreria
Plaza de San Isidoro, 4, 24003 Leon
Mailing Address: Apdo 126, 24080 Leon
Tel: (0987) 876161 *Fax:* (0987) 876162
E-mail: sanisidoro@infonegocio.com
Key Personnel
Dir: Antonio Vinayo Gonzalez *Tel:* (0987) 876070 *Fax:* (0987) 876061

Ediciones Istmo SA+
Sector Foresta, 1, 28760 Tres Contos
SAN: 001-7817
Tel: (091) 8061996 *Fax:* (091) 8044028
Key Personnel
Man Dir: Eduardo Casado Martindela Camara
Founded: 1969
Subjects: Anthropology, Art, History, Language Arts, Linguistics, Literature, Literary Criticism, Essays, Philosophy, Social Sciences, Sociology
ISBN Prefix(es): 84-7090

Ediciones JJB
Perez Galdos 12, 4, Apdo 1084, 26002 Logrono, La Rioja
Tel: (041) 236928 *Fax:* (041) 226127
Key Personnel
Dir: Julian de Juan Berzosa
Founded: 1977
ISBN Prefix(es): 84-85305

Ediciones JLA+
PO Box 54122, 2080 Madrid
SAN: 001-8007
Tel: (091) 3158577 *Fax:* (091) 7336239
Key Personnel
Dir: Jose Luis Alvarez *Tel:* (091) 3864292 *Fax:* (091) 3161882 *E-mail:* vinilos@vinilos.com
Founded: 1975
Subjects: Radio, TV
ISBN Prefix(es): 84-7872; 84-86570
Warehouse: c/o Valdesahgil, 26-Local, 28039 Madrid

Joyas Bibliograficas SA
Fomento, 5, 28013 Madrid
SAN: 003-8210
Tel: (091) 5470220
Key Personnel
Administrator: Carlos Romero de Lecea
Subjects: History, Literature, Literary Criticism, Essays, Poetry
ISBN Prefix(es): 84-7094

Ediciones Jucar+
Menendez Valdes, 33-1, 33201 Gijon Asturias
Tel: (098) 5170921; (098) 5349684; (098) 5349684 *Fax:* (098) 55349545
Telex: 89736 Edju E
Key Personnel
Man Dir: Silverio Canada Acebal
Editorial: Maria de Calonje
Production: Manuel Cardenas
Founded: 1974
Subjects: Fiction, Government, Political Science, Literature, Literary Criticism, Essays, Music, Dance, Poetry
ISBN Prefix(es): 84-334
Orders to: Honesto Batalon 7, Gijon *Tel:* (985) 355790

Ediciones Junior SA, see Grijalbo Mondadon SA Junior

Junta de Castilla y Leon Consejeria de Educacion y Cultura
Avda de Soria, 15, 47071 La Disterniga (Valladolid)
Tel: (0983) 411587 *Fax:* (0983) 411527
E-mail: publicaciones.cec@pop-in.jcyl.es
Web Site: www.jcyl.es
Key Personnel
Dir: Agustin Garcia Simon *E-mail:* agustin.garcia@cec.jcyl.es
Founded: 1984
Subjects: Archaeology, Art, Biography, History, Literature, Literary Criticism, Essays, Poetry, Regional Interests, Science (General), Travel
ISBN Prefix(es): 84-7846; 84-9718; 84-500; 84-505
Distributor for Lidiza; Siglo

Editorial Juventud SA+
Provenza, 101, 08029 Barcelona
Tel: (093) 444 18 00 *Fax:* (093) 444 18 02
E-mail: juventud@bcn.servicom.es
Web Site: www.editorialjuventud.es *Cable:* JUVENTUD
Key Personnel
Dir General: Luis Zendrera Duniau
Founded: 1923
Subjects: Accounting, Aeronautics, Aviation, Animals, Pets, Architecture & Interior Design, Art, Biography, Fiction, History, Language Arts, Linguistics, Sports, Athletics, Travel
ISBN Prefix(es): 84-261
Associate Companies: Editorial Juventud SA, Mexico
Subsidiaries: Editorial Juventud de Espana Ltd
Distributed by Editorial Corimbo; Editorial Parsifal

Editorial Kairos SA+
Numancia, 117-121, Edificio Centro Planta 2a, puerta 3a, 08029 Barcelona
Tel: (093) 430-3746 *Fax:* (093) 410-5166
E-mail: kairos@sendanet.es *Cable:* KAIROS
Key Personnel
Man Dir: Salvador Paniker
Editorial, Rights & Permissions, Sales: Agustin Paniker
Production, Publicity: Pilar Tomas
Founded: 1966
Publishes a growing range of new consciousness titles.
Subjects: Philosophy, Psychology, Psychiatry, Religion - Other, Social Sciences, Sociology
ISBN Prefix(es): 84-7245

Laertes SA de Ediciones+
Virtud, 8, 08012 Barcelona
Tel: (093) 2187020; (093) 2185558 *Fax:* (093) 2174751
E-mail: laertes@jet.es
Key Personnel
Man Dir & Editorial: Eduardo Suarez Alonso
Sales, Publicity: Carmen Miret
Founded: 1975
Subjects: Anthropology, Archaeology, Biography, Education, Fiction, Film, Video, Gay & Lesbian, Literature, Literary Criticism, Essays, Philosophy, Travel, Medicine & Nursing
ISBN Prefix(es): 84-85346; 84-7584; 84-400
Total Titles: 525 Print
Foreign Rep(s): Ediciones Del Aguazul (Argentina); Ediciones Del Aguazul (Mexico)

Editorin Laiovento SL+
Rua do Horreo, 60, Apdo 1 072, 15072 Santiago de Compostela Galiza
Tel: (0981) 887570 *Fax:* (0981) 572239
E-mail: laiovento@laiovento.com
Web Site: www.laiovento.com
Key Personnel
President: Afonso Ribas Fraga
Founded: 1989
Subjects: Economics, Education, History, Literature, Literary Criticism, Essays, Poetry, Science (General), Science Fiction, Fantasy, Social Sciences, Sociology, Technology, Humanities & Social Sciences
ISBN Prefix(es): 84-87847; 84-89896
Imprints: Lengua Gallega Y Portuguesa
Distributor for Ninguna

Leandro Lara Editor+
Ave Antonio Gaudi, 76-126 NAVE 1 bis Pol Ind Rubi Sud, 08191 Rubi
Tel: (093) 6970036; (093) 6970364
E-mail: leandro@covnet.com
Key Personnel
Contact: Leandro Lara Merino
ISBN Prefix(es): 84-7699

Larousse Editorial SA+
Avda Diagonal 407 bis 10, 08008 Barcelona

Tel: (093) 2922666 *Fax:* (093) 2922162; (093) 2922163
E-mail: larousse@larousse.es
Key Personnel
Contact: Yolanda Portillo Jimenez
Founded: 1991
ISBN Prefix(es): 84-8016
Subsidiaries: Grandes De La Cite International

Las Ediciones de Arte (LEDA), see LEDA (Las Ediciones de Arte)

LEDA (Las Ediciones de Arte)+
Riera Sant Miguel 37 entl, 08006 Barcelona
Tel: (093) 2379389; (093) 2155273
Key Personnel
Man Dir: Daniel Basilio Bonet
Founded: 1942
Subjects: Advertising, Architecture & Interior Design, Art, Child Care & Development, Crafts, Games, Hobbies
ISBN Prefix(es): 84-7095

Edicions de l'Eixample, SA+
Mallorca 297, pral, 08037 Barcelona
Tel: (093) 4584600 *Fax:* (093) 2076248
Key Personnel
Council Delegates: Salvador Saura; Ramon Torrente
Dir: Isabel Segura
Founded: 1983
Subjects: Fiction
ISBN Prefix(es): 84-86279

Lengua Gallega Y Portuguesa, *imprint of* Editorin Laiovento SL

Liber Ediciones, SA
Travesia Bayona, 1, 31011 Pamplona
Tel: (0948) 177 488; (0902) 300 307 *Fax:* (0948) 176 667
E-mail: info@arsliber.com
Web Site: www.arsliber.com
Key Personnel
Contact: Juan Jose Izquierdo Broncano
Founded: 1989
Subjects: Art
ISBN Prefix(es): 84-89339

Ediciones Libertarias/Prodhufi SA+
C Bravo Murillo, 37-1 Dcha, 28015 Madrid
Tel: (091) 593 33 93 *Fax:* (091) 594 16 96
E-mail: libertarias@libertarias.com
Web Site: www.libertarias.com
Key Personnel
Publisher: Carmelo Martinez Garcia
Communication Dir: Annamaria Duran
Founded: 1979
Subjects: Cookery, Government, Political Science, Health, Nutrition, History, Literature, Literary Criticism, Essays, Poetry, Psychology, Psychiatry, Science Fiction, Fantasy, Social Sciences, Sociology
ISBN Prefix(es): 84-7954; 84-87095; 84-85641; 84-7683; 84-86943
Distributed by Conty SA de CV (Central America); Libertarias Prodhufi, SA

Libros Cupula, *imprint of* Grupo Editorial CEAC SA

Libsa, *imprint of* Libsa Editorial SA

Libsa Editorial SA+
San Rafael, 4, 28108 Alcobendas Madrid
Tel: (091) 657 25 80 *Fax:* (091) 657 25 83
E-mail: libsa@libsa.es
Web Site: www.libsa.es
Key Personnel
President: Amado Sanchez *E-mail:* rocio@libsa.redestb.es
Foreign Rights: Alberto Boix
Foreign Rights Manager: Francisco Saavedra
Founded: 1980
Subjects: Art, Cookery, Crafts, Games, Hobbies, Gardening, Plants, Health, Nutrition, House & Home, Language Arts, Linguistics, Literature, Literary Criticism, Essays, Nonfiction (General), Self-Help, Children/Adult lists, Leisure & Practical Guides
ISBN Prefix(es): 84-7630
Imprints: Agata; Alba; Libsa

LID Editorial Empresarial, SL (LID Business Publisher)+
Sopelana, 22, 28023 Madrid
SAN: 004-010X
Tel: (091) 372 90 03 *Fax:* (091) 372 85 14
E-mail: info@lideditorial.com
Web Site: www.lideditorial.com
Key Personnel
President: Marcelino Elosua
Editor: Isabel Saavedra; Mercedes Vidaurrazaga
Founded: 1993
Membership(s): Gremio de Editores de Madrid.
Subjects: Biography, Business, Career Development, Economics, Finance, Language Arts, Linguistics, Marketing, Self-Help, Economics & Business, Spanish Business History, Specialized Business Dictionaries
ISBN Prefix(es): 84-88717
Number of titles published annually: 12 Print; 1 CD-ROM
Total Titles: 50 Print; 2 CD-ROM
Distribution Center: LOGISTA (Spain)

Llibres del Segle+
La Rectoria, 17466 Gaueses Girona
Tel: (093) 795079; (093) 794023 *Fax:* (093) 210354
E-mail: costapau@releline.es
Key Personnel
Production: Rosa M Tries
Subjects: Art, Education, History, Literature, Literary Criticism, Essays, Nonfiction (General), Poetry, Social Sciences, Sociology
ISBN Prefix(es): 84-89885; 84-920952; 84-8128
Total Titles: 12 Print
Distributor for L'Arc de Bera

Loguez Ediciones+
Carretera de Madrid 90, Apdo 1, 37900 Santa Marta de Tormes (Salamanca)
SAN: 003-8849
Tel: (0923) 138541 *Fax:* (0923) 138586
E-mail: loguezediciones@eresmas.com
Key Personnel
Man Dir, Sales: L Rodriguez Lopez
Editorial, Publicity: Maribel G Martinez
Founded: 1978
Specialize in children's literature & musical books.
Subjects: Art, Earth Sciences, Education, Fiction, Gay & Lesbian, Literature, Literary Criticism, Essays, Music, Dance, Religion - Catholic, Religion - Other, Self-Help, Theology
ISBN Prefix(es): 84-85334; 84-89804
Number of titles published annually: 12 Print; 3 CD-ROM

Ediciones Luciernaga, *imprint of* Grup 62

Ediciones Luciernaga
Peu de la Creu 4, 08001 Barcelona
Tel: (093) 443 71 00 *Fax:* (093) 443 71 30
E-mail: correu@grup62.com
Web Site: www.grup62.com
Key Personnel
Rights Manager: Laura Pujol

Founded: 1963
ISBN Prefix(es): 84-87232; 84-89957

Editorial Luis Vives (Edelvives)+
63a Feria del Libro, 28034 Madrid
Tel: (091) 334 48 83 *Fax:* (091) 334 48 93
E-mail: jmarketing@edelvives.es
Web Site: www.grupoeditorialluisvives.com
    Cable: EDELVIVES
Key Personnel
Man Dir: Antonio Gimenez de Baguees
Editorial Dir: Jose Manuel Gomez Luque
Production Dir: Jesus Agudo
Commercial Dir: Jose Luis Illana
Founded: 1890
Subjects: Education
ISBN Prefix(es): 84-263
Number of titles published annually: 200 Print
Total Titles: 35,000 Print; 6 CD-ROM; 3 Audio
Associate Companies: Editorial Ibaizabal, Barrio de San Miguel s/n Euba-Amorebieta, 48290 Vizcaya *Tel:* (046) 308036 *Fax:* (046) 308028 *E-mail:* ibaizabal@euskalnet.net
Subsidiaries: Edicions Baula
Branch Office(s)
Poligono de Cranda s/n, 33199 Asturias
    Tel: (098) 579 46 16 *E-mail:* asturias@edelvives.es
Passeo Valldaura, 184, 08042 Barcelona
    Tel: (093) 354 03 99 *E-mail:* barcelona@endelvives.es
Ayagaures 8 Nave D, Urb Ind Lomo Blanco-Las Torres, 35010 Las Palmas de Gran Canaria 9 *Tel:* (0928) 48 12 47 *E-mail:* canarias@edelvives.es
Manuel Tovar, esq. Estrada, 28034 Madrid
    Tel: (091) 344 48 84 *E-mail:* madrid@edelvives.es
Veracruz, 32 (Pol. San Luis), 29006 Malaga
    Tel: (095) 236 3409 *E-mail:* malaga@edelvives.es
Via Apia, 32, (Pol. Ind. Fuentequintillo), 41089 Montequintille (Sevilla) *Tel:* (095) 4 129 180 *E-mail:* sevilla@edelvives.es
Avda Txori-Erri, 46 No, Modulo 4, Letra E, 48150 Sondika (Vizcaya) *Tel:* (094) 453 20 09 *E-mail:* bilbao@edelvives.es
Poligono 1-2 (Pol.Faea) Parcela 28, 45600 Talavera de la Reina (Toledo) *Tel:* (0925) 81 74 34 *E-mail:* toledo@edelvives.es
Avda Ausias March 222, Pista de Silla, 46026 Valencia *Tel:* (096) 375 98 11 *E-mail:* valencia@edelvives.es
Acero 4, (Pol San Cristobal), 47012 Valladolid *Tel:* (0983) 21 30 38 *E-mail:* valladolid@edelvives.es
Severino Cobas 142 (Lavadores), 36214 Vigo
    Tel: (0986) 27 20 13 *E-mail:* vigo@edelvives.es
Ctra de Madrid, km 315 700, 50012 Zaragoza
    Tel: (0976) 30 40 30 *E-mail:* zaragoza@edelvives.es
Distribution Center: Editorial Luis vives, Ctra de Madrid km 315 700, 50012 Zaragoza, Francisco Calleja *Tel:* (0976) 304030 *Fax:* (0976) 340630 *E-mail:* zaragoza@edelvives.es

Editorial Lumen SA+
Travessera de Gracia 47-5°-pl, 08021 Barcelona
Tel: (093) 3660300 *Fax:* (093) 3660013
E-mail: lumen@editoriallumen.com
Key Personnel
Man Dir: Esther Tusquets
Founded: 1939
Subjects: Art, Fiction, Humor, Literature, Literary Criticism, Essays, Poetry, Social Sciences, Sociology
ISBN Prefix(es): 84-264

Lunwerg Editores, SA+
Beethoven, 12, 08021 Barcelona
SAN: 004-072X

Tel: (093) 2015933 *Fax:* (093) 2011587
E-mail: lunwerg.mad@retemail.es
Key Personnel
Man Dir: Juan Carlos Luna
Rights & Permissions: Carmen Garcia
Founded: 1980
Subjects: Archaeology, Architecture & Interior Design, Art, Cookery, Drama, Theater, History, Maritime, Photography, Transportation, Travel, Wine & Spirits
ISBN Prefix(es): 84-7782; 84-85983; 84-9785
Number of titles published annually: 60 Print

Lynx Edicions
Montseny, 8, E-08193 Bellaterra, Barcelona
Tel: (093) 594 77 10 *Fax:* (093) 592 09 69
E-mail: pruizolalla@hbw.com
Web Site: www.hbw.com
Key Personnel
Contact: Pilar Ruiz-Olalla
Founded: 1989
Subjects: Animals, Pets, Natural History
ISBN Prefix(es): 84-87334
U.S. Office(s): Lynx Edicions, c/o Mail Management Group Inc, 81 N Forest Ave, Rockville Centre, NY 11570, United States

Antonio Machado, SA
Tomas Breton, 55, 28045 Madrid
Tel: (091) 4681398 *Fax:* (091) 4681098
E-mail: editorial@visordis.es
Key Personnel
Dir: Jose Miguel Garcia Sanchez
Books, Magazines, Journals, Newspapers.
Subjects: Architecture & Interior Design, Art, Drama, Theater, Education, Government, Political Science, History, Language Arts, Linguistics, Literature, Literary Criticism, Essays, Music, Dance, Philosophy, Psychology, Psychiatry, Publishing & Book Trade Reference, Regional Interests, Self-Help, Social Sciences, Sociology, Cultural History, Performing Arts
ISBN Prefix(es): 84-7644

Macmillan Heinemann ELT
Martin de Vargas 5, Esc C 1, 28005 Madrid
Tel: (091) 517 85 40 *Fax:* (091) 517 85 54
E-mail: madrid@mad.heinemann.es
Web Site: www.heinemann.es
Parent Company: Macmillan Publishers Ltd
Distributor for Language Teaching Publications (LTP); Max Hueber Verlag/Verlag Fuer Deutsch

Mad SL Editorial+
Polig Merka C/B, naves 1-3, 41500 Alcala de Guadaira Sevilla
Tel: (095) 5630820 *Fax:* (095) 5630713
E-mail: info@mad.es
Web Site: www.mad.es
Key Personnel
Administrator: Dolores Lopez-Jurado
Dir: Luis Abril Mula *E-mail:* luis@mad.es
Gen Dir: Narciso Sanchez-Valdenaura *E-mail:* nsv@mad.es
Founded: 1983
Subjects: Law
ISBN Prefix(es): 84-86526

Ediciones Maeva+
Benito de Castro 6, 28028 Madrid
Tel: (091) 355 95 69 *Fax:* (091) 355 19 47
E-mail: maeva@infornet.es
Web Site: www.maeva.es
Key Personnel
Contact: Cuadros Lopez Maite
Founded: 1985
Subjects: Anthropology, Biography, Foreign Countries, History, Literature, Literary Criticism, Essays, Nonfiction (General), Regional Interests, Travel

ISBN Prefix(es): 84-86478; 84-95354
Imprints: Catalogo
Subsidiaries: Editoriales Exclusivas
Orders to: SGEL, c/o Avda Valdelaparda, 29, Poligono Industrial, 28108 Alcobendas-Madrid
Tel: (091) 6576955 *Fax:* (091) 6576958

Editorial Magisterio Espanol SA+
Casp 79, 08013 Barcelona
Tel: (093) 902107007 *Fax:* (093) 6420086
Web Site: www.editorialcasals.com
Key Personnel
General Manager: Ramon Casals
Founded: 1866
Subjects: Education, Fiction, Literature, Literary Criticism, Essays, Philosophy, Religion - Catholic
ISBN Prefix(es): 84-265
Parent Company: Editorial Casals, SA

Magoria, *imprint of* Obelisco Ediciones S

Edicions de la Magrana SA+
Santa Perpetua, 10-12, 08012 Barcelona
Tel: (093) 2170088 *Fax:* (093) 2171174
E-mail: magrana@rba.es
Web Site: www.rbalibros.com
Key Personnel
Man Dir: Carles-Jordi Guardiola
Production: Lluis Baselga
Assistant Dir: Eva Eduardo
Founded: 1975
Subjects: Biography, Cookery, Fiction, Literature, Literary Criticism, Essays, Philosophy, Science (General), Social Sciences, Sociology
ISBN Prefix(es): 84-7410

Mandala Ediciones+
Escalinata, 9, 28013 Madrid
SAN: 004-1114
Tel: (091) 5840954 *Fax:* (091) 5480326
Key Personnel
Man Dir: Fernando Cabal *Tel:* (091) 5480954
Editorial: Gonzalo Rivero
Founded: 1980
Subjects: Architecture & Interior Design, Astrology, Occult, Behavioral Sciences, Cookery, Earth Sciences, Environmental Studies, Film, Video, Health, Nutrition, Medicine, Nursing, Dentistry, Music, Dance, Psychology, Psychiatry, Religion - Buddhist, Religion - Hindu, Religion - Islamic, Biological Agriculture, Biological Medicine, Chinese Medicine, Dietetic Natural, Ecological Architecture, Ecology, Fitoterapia, Homeopatia, Manual Medicine, Massage, Relaxation
ISBN Prefix(es): 84-86961; 84-88769; 84-95052
Total Titles: 210 Print

Editorial Mapfre SA
Paseo de Recoletos, 25, 28004 Madrid
Tel: (091) 581 53 60 *Fax:* (091) 581 18 83
E-mail: edimap@mapfre.com
Web Site: www2.mapfre.com
Key Personnel
Man Dir: Miguel Angel Gimeno
Subjects: Financial Security & Services, Insurances
ISBN Prefix(es): 84-7100

Marcial Pons Ediciones Juridicas SA
San Sotero, 6, 28037 Madrid
Tel: (091) 304 33 03 *Fax:* (091) 327 23 67; (091) 7541218
E-mail: librerias@marcialpons.es; ediciones@marcialpons.es
Web Site: www.marcialpons.es
Founded: 1990
Subjects: Economics, Law, Public Administration
ISBN Prefix(es): 84-7248; 84-9768

Number of titles published annually: 80 Print
Total Titles: 1,500 Print

Marcombo SA+
Gran Via, 594, 08007 Barcelona
Tel: (093) 3180079 *Fax:* (093) 3189339
E-mail: marcombo.boixareu@marcombo.es
Web Site: www.marcombo.es
Key Personnel
Man Dir: Josep M Boixareu Vilaplana
Marketing & Sales Manager: Jose Romero Gonzalez
Founded: 1945
Subjects: Anthropology, Automotive, Business, Civil Engineering, Communications, Computer Science, Economics, Electronics, Electrical Engineering, Energy, Finance, Management, Marketing, Mathematics, Microcomputers, Radio, TV
ISBN Prefix(es): 84-267
Branch Office(s)
Marcombo SA, Plaza de la Villa 1, 28005 Madrid
Distributed by Distribuciones Alba, S.A.; Alfaomego Grupo Editor (Colombia, Mexico, Guatemala, Costa Rica, Ecuador, Nicaragua, Honduras, El Salvador); Asturlibros, Poligono Silvota; Be Nvil, S.A. Llibres; Carrasco Libros, S.L.; Contemporanea de Ediciones (Venezuela); Distribuidora Cuspide, S.R.L. (Argentina); Galileo Libros, Ltd (Chile); Andres Libreros - Libro Tecnico; Lidiza, S.A.; Losa Libros Ltda (Uruguay); Marcombo, S.A.; Odon Molina, Distribuidor de Libros; Palma Distribucions, S.L.; Pato Libros; Distribuidora Del Sur; UNBE, S.A.; Unidisa, Demetrio Sillero; Viuber, S.L.Delegacion de Edit
Bookshop(s): Libreria Hispano Americana

Editorial Marfil SA+
Sant Eloi 17, 03804 Alcoi
Tel: (096) 5523311 *Fax:* (096) 5523496
E-mail: editorialmarfil@editorialmarfil.com
Web Site: www.editorialmarfil.com *Cable:* MARFIL
Key Personnel
Contact: Veronica Canto Domenych
Founded: 1947
Subjects: Education, Literature, Literary Criticism, Essays, Psychology, Psychiatry
ISBN Prefix(es): 84-268; 84-7816

Editorial Marin SA+
Avda San Julian, 234, Poligono Industrial El Congost, 08400 Granollers Barcelona
Tel: (093) 8468101 *Fax:* (093) 8468107
Cable: MARINEDI
Key Personnel
Administrator: Manuel Marin
Man Dir: Jorge Fernandez
Founded: 1900
Subjects: Art, Medicine, Nursing, Dentistry, Nonfiction (General)
ISBN Prefix(es): 84-7102
Branch Office(s)
Editorial Marin SA, Anaxagoras 1400, Colonia Santa Cruz Atoyac, 03310 Mexico, DF, Mexico
Warehouse: Calle Industria 5/n, Polzono Industrial, El Papiol

Ediciones Marova SL+
Cedaceros, 3, 28014 Madrid
SAN: 004-1610
Tel: (091) 5322606 *Fax:* (091) 5225123
E-mail: glanzas@infornet.es
Key Personnel
Man Dir: Jose Miguel Oriol
Founded: 1956
Subjects: Education, Psychology, Psychiatry, Religion - Other, Social Sciences, Sociology, Theology
ISBN Prefix(es): 84-269

PUBLISHERS   SPAIN

Ediciones Martinez-Roca SA+
Paseo de Recoletos, 4, 3a planta, 28001 Madrid
Tel: (091) 423 0314 *Fax:* (091) 423 0306
E-mail: info@ediciones-martinez-roca.es
Web Site: www.edicionesmartinezroca.com
Key Personnel
Man Dir: Fernando Calvo Aparicio
Founded: 1988
Subjects: Animals, Pets, Astrology, Occult, Biography, Crafts, Games, Hobbies, Fiction, Health, Nutrition, How-to, Literature, Literary Criticism, Essays, Nonfiction (General), Psychology, Psychiatry, Romance, Science Fiction, Fantasy, Self-Help, Sports, Athletics
ISBN Prefix(es): 84-270

La Mascara, SL Editorial+
Pza Juan Pablo II 5-B izda, 46015 Valencia
SAN: 002-5127
Tel: (096) 3486500 *Fax:* (096) 3487440
E-mail: lamascara@arrakis.es
Key Personnel
Commercial Dir: Celso Andres
Founded: 1991
Subjects: Biography, Music, Dance, Poetry
ISBN Prefix(es): 84-7974
Subsidiaries: La Mascara France, Sarl

McGraw-Hill/Interamericana de Espana SAU+
Basauri 17, Edificio Valrealty, Planta 1, 28023 Aravaca, Madrid
Tel: (091) 1803000
Web Site: www.mcgraw-hill.es
Telex: 43817 DIE
Key Personnel
Group Man Dir: Antonio Garcia-Maroto
  E-mail: agmaroto@attmail.com
Publisher, Business & Professional Division: Eduardo Susanna
Publisher, High School Vocational Technical Division: Wenceslao Ortega
Distributor & Book Store Sales Manager: Fernando Serrano
Controller & Business Manager: Jose Castellano
Production Manager: Jose Martinez Alaminos
EDP Manager: Miguel Angel de Dios
Founded: 1974
Iberian/Mercosur Peninsula Group. Markets served: Spain, Portugal, Argentina, Uruguay, Paraguay.
Subjects: Biological Sciences, Education, Health, Nutrition, Medicine, Nursing, Dentistry, Science (General), Technology
ISBN Prefix(es): 84-7615; 84-85240; 84-481; 84-486
Parent Company: The McGraw-Hill Companies, 1221 Avenue of the Americas, New York, NY 10020, United States
Branch Office(s)
Mercosur, Argentina, Suipacha 764, 1008 Buenos Aires, Argentina *Tel:* (011) 3228868 *Fax:* (011) 3223456 (Distribudora Cuspide)
Mercosur, Paraguay, Suipacha 764, 1008 Buenos Aires, Argentina *Tel:* (011) 3228868 *Fax:* (011) 3223456 (Distribudora Cuspide)
Mercosur, Uruguay, Suipacha 764, 1008 Buenos Aires, Argentina *Tel:* (011) 3228868 *Fax:* (011) 3223456 (Distribudora Cuspide)

ME Editores, SL+
Marcelina, 23, 28029 Madrid
SAN: 004-0908
Tel: (091) 3151008 *Fax:* (091) 3230844
Founded: 1992
ISBN Prefix(es): 84-495

Editorial Medica JIMS, SL
Balmes, 266, 08006 Barcelona
Tel: (093) 2188800 *Fax:* (093) 2188928
Cable: EDITOJIMS

Key Personnel
Man Dir, Editorial, Publicity: Antonio Jimenez Sanchez
Sales: Teresa Jimenez Sayo
Production: Luis Jimenez Sayo
Founded: 1956
Subjects: Medicine, Nursing, Dentistry
ISBN Prefix(es): 84-7092

Ediciones Medici SA+
Plato, 26, 08006 Barcelona
Tel: (093) 2 010 599; (093) 2 013 807; (093) 2 012 144 *Fax:* (093) 2 097 362
E-mail: omega@ediciones-omega.es
Web Site: www.ediciones-medici.es; www.ediciones-omega.es
Key Personnel
Man Dir: Ana Dexeus; Antonio Paricio; Gabriel Paricio
Founded: 1983
Subjects: Child Care & Development, Cookery, Education, Health, Nutrition, Human Relations, Medicine, Nursing, Dentistry, Nonfiction (General)
ISBN Prefix(es): 84-86193
Parent Company: Ediciones Omega SA
Orders to: Ediciones Omega/Medici, Plato, 26, 08006 Barcelona

Editorial Mediterrania SL+
Guillem Tell 15 - 17 entlo, 08006 Barcelona
Tel: (093) 218 34 58; (093) 237 86 65 *Fax:* (093) 237 22 10
E-mail: edit.med@retemail.es
Key Personnel
Man Dir & Sales: Eduard Fornes
Editorial, Rights & Permissions: Josep Abril
Production: Nuria Carpena
Publicity: Monica Estrich
Founded: 1980
Membership(s): Association of Editors in the Catalan Language & Editors Guild of Catalunya.
Subjects: Art, Health, Nutrition, History, Literature, Literary Criticism, Essays, Outdoor Recreation, Photography, Religion - Catholic, Sports, Athletics, Travel
ISBN Prefix(es): 84-8334

Ediciones Mensajero+
Sancho de Azpeitia, 2, Apdo 73, 48014 Bilbao
SAN: 001-852X
Tel: (094) 4 470 358 *Fax:* (094) 4 472 630
E-mail: mensajero@mensajero.com
Web Site: www.mensajero.com *Cable:* MENSAJERO
Key Personnel
Man Dir: Angel Antonio Perez
Editorial, Production: Josu Leguina
  E-mail: josuleguina@mensajero.com
Publicity & Sales: Jose Manuel Diaz
Founded: 1915
Subjects: Education, How-to, Philosophy, Psychology, Psychiatry, Religion - Other, Social Sciences, Sociology
ISBN Prefix(es): 84-271

Editorial Milenio Arts Grafiques Bobala, SL+
Sant Salvador 8, 25005 Lleida
Tel: (0973) 236 611 *Fax:* (0973) 240 795
E-mail: editorial.milenio@cambrescat.es
Web Site: www.edmilenio.com
Key Personnel
Dir: Lluis Pages i Marigot *Fax:* (0973) 740 795
Founded: 1996
Specialize in Spanish & Latin American books.
ISBN Prefix(es): 84-89790
Total Titles: 20 Print
Associate Companies: Pages Editors, SL
Distributed by Espana y America
Book Club(s): Eventualmente

Ministerio de Economia y Hacienda Secretario General Tecnica Centro de Publicaciones
Pza Campillo del Mundo Nuevo, 3, 28005 Madrid
SAN: 004-2315
Tel: (091) 5063740 (ext 51307) *Fax:* (091) 4682300
Key Personnel
Technical General Secretario: Rosa Rodriguez-Moreno
ISBN Prefix(es): 84-460; 84-476; 84-7196; 84-85482

Ministerio de Educacion y Culture Centro de Publicaciones
Ciudad Universitaria, 28071 Madrid
Tel: (091) 453 98 00 *Fax:* (091) 453 98 00
Web Site: www.mec.es/mec
Key Personnel
Editorial Control Head: Antonio Arenas Carrera
ISBN Prefix(es): 84-369

Ministerio de Justicia e Interior, Centro de Publicaciones
San Bernardo, 62 Planta baja, 28071 Madrid
Tel: (091) 390 44 29; (091) 390 20 83; (091) 390 20 97 *Fax:* (091) 390 20 92
Web Site: www.mju.es
Key Personnel
General Assistant Dir of Documentation & Publications: Gonzalo Puebla De Diego
Founded: 1947
Subjects: Law
ISBN Prefix(es): 84-7787; 84-500; 84-505
Distributed by BOE; DIJUSA; Diputacion de Barcelona; Edisofer, S.L.; Marcial Pons; Reydis Libros, Lazaro Pascual Yague S.L.; Tapia Libros, S.A.
Warehouse: C/Ocana, 151-28047 Madrid

Ministerio de Trabajo y Asuntos Sociales
Torrelaguna 73, 28027 Madrid
Tel: (091) 3634100 *Fax:* (091) 3634327
E-mail: sugerir@sta.mtas.es
Web Site: www.mtas.es/insht/index.htm
Key Personnel
Dir: Javier Gomez-Hortiguela Amillo
ISBN Prefix(es): 84-7425; 84-500; 84-400; 84-505

Ediciones Minotauro+
Adva Diagonal 662, 08034 Barcelona
Tel: (093) 492 8869 *Fax:* (093) 496 7041
E-mail: edicionesminotauro@arrakis.es
Web Site: www.edicionesminotauro.com
Key Personnel
Man Dir: Francisco Porrua
Founded: 1983
Subjects: Biography, Fiction, Literature, Literary Criticism, Essays, Science Fiction, Fantasy
ISBN Prefix(es): 84-450
Total Titles: 150 Print

Editores Mira, SA
Dalia 11, 50012 Zaragoza
Tel: (0976) 460505 *Fax:* (0976) 460446
E-mail: miraeditores@ctv.es
Web Site: www.miraeditores.com
ISBN Prefix(es): 84-86778; 84-88688; 84-89859

MK Ediciones y Publicaciones
Castello 30, 28001 Madrid
SAN: 004-3311
Tel: (091) 4316305 *Fax:* (091) 5754978
Key Personnel
Editorial Dir: Marta Ferre Pich
Founded: 1975
Specialize in Theater.
Subjects: Drama, Theater
ISBN Prefix(es): 84-7389

591

SPAIN

M Moleiro Editor, SA+
Travesera de Gracia, 17-21, 08021 Barcelona
Tel: (093) 414 20 10; (0902) 11 33 79 *Fax:* (093) 201 50 62
E-mail: mmoleiro@moleiro.com
Web Site: www.moleiro.com
Key Personnel
President: Manuel Moleiro
International Rights: Ms Monica Miro
Founded: 1992
Specialize in facsimile editions of medieval illuminated manuscripts, maps & atlases.
Subjects: Art, Biblical Studies, Medicine, Nursing, Dentistry
ISBN Prefix(es): 84-88526

Editorial Molino+
Calabria, 166, 08015 Barcelona
Tel: (093) 226 06 25 *Fax:* (093) 226 69 98
E-mail: molino@menta.net
Web Site: www.editorialmolino.es *Cable:* MOLINO BARCELONA
Key Personnel
Man Dir: Luis A del Molino
Founded: 1933
Subjects: Education, Fiction, Mysteries, Sports, Athletics
ISBN Prefix(es): 84-272
Number of titles published annually: 100 Print
Total Titles: 1,345 Print

Editorial Moll SL+
Can Valero, 25, Poligon Can Valero, 07011 Palma de Mallorca, Balearic Islands
Tel: (0971) 72 41 76 *Fax:* (0971) 72 62 52
E-mail: info@editorialmoll.es
Web Site: www.editorialmoll.es
Key Personnel
Man Dir: Francesc de B Moll
Founded: 1934
Also acts as book distributor to the Balearic Islands.
Subjects: Art, Biography, Fiction, History, Language Arts, Linguistics, Literature, Literary Criticism, Essays, Natural History, Poetry, Regional Interests, Social Sciences, Sociology, Travel
ISBN Prefix(es): 84-273
Number of titles published annually: 60 Print
Total Titles: 950 Print
Bookshop(s): Llibres Mallorca, Esglesia de Sta Eulalia, 11, 07001 Palma de Mallorca, Contact: Victor Moll *Tel:* (0971) 728453 *Fax:* (0971) 728453

Monograma Ediciones
Padre Bartolome Pou, 24, 07003 Palma de Mallorca, Baleares
SAN: 004-2617
Tel: (071) 754124; (071) 712593 *Fax:* (071) 712593
E-mail: totem@atlas-iap.es
Key Personnel
Dir General: Leonardo Sainz Fernandez
ISBN Prefix(es): 84-88777
Orders to: Palau Reial, No 3, 07001 Palma de Mallorca, Baleares

Editorial Monte Carmelo
Padre Silverio, 2, Apdo, 19, 09001 Burgos
Tel: (0947) 25 60 61 *Fax:* (0947) 25 60 62; (0947) 273265
E-mail: editorial@montecarmelo.com
Web Site: www.montecarmelo.com
Key Personnel
Dir: Alberto Pacho Polvorinos
Subjects: Religion - Catholic
ISBN Prefix(es): 84-7239

Ediciones Morata SL+
Mejia Lequerica, 12, 28004 Madrid
Tel: (091) 448 09 26 *Fax:* (091) 448 09 25
E-mail: morata@edmorata.es
Web Site: www.edmorata.es
Key Personnel
Man Dir: Florentina Gomez Morata
Founded: 1920
Subjects: Behavioral Sciences, Child Care & Development, Disability, Special Needs, Education, Human Relations, Philosophy, Psychology, Psychiatry, Self-Help, Social Sciences, Sociology, Women's Studies
ISBN Prefix(es): 84-7112
Total Titles: 300 Print
Distributed by Berriak - Comercial de Edit. S.L.; Cerezo Libros; Distriforma, S.A.; EA Libros; Andres Garcia Libros, S.L.; Gea Llibres, S.L.; Lemus, Distribuciones, CB; Modesto Alonso Estravis, Distribuciones; Nogara Libros, SA; Norte, Promociones y Distrib. S.L.; Les Punxes Distribuidora, S.L.; Serrano Libros; La Tierra Libros, SL

Anaya & Mario Muchnik+
Juan Ignacio Luca de Tena, 15, 28027 Madrid
Tel: (091) 393 86 00 *Fax:* (091) 320 91 29; (091) 742 66 31
E-mail: cga@anaya.es
Web Site: www.anaya.es
Key Personnel
General Dir: Victor Freixanes
Founded: 1990
Subjects: Literature, Literary Criticism, Essays
ISBN Prefix(es): 84-7979
Parent Company: Grupo Anaya SA
Distributor for America Latina

Instituto de la Mujer (Miniterio de Trabajo y Asuntos Sociales)
Condesa de Venadito, nº 34, 28027 Madrid
Tel: (091) 363 80 00
E-mail: inmujer@mtas.es
Web Site: www.mtas.es/mujer
Key Personnel
Dir General: Pilar Davila del Cerro
ISBN Prefix(es): 84-7799; 84-500; 84-505

Mundi-Prensa Libros SA+
Castello, 37, 28001 Madrid
Tel: (091) 4 36 37 00 *Fax:* (091) 5 75 39 98
E-mail: liberia@mundiprensa.es
Web Site: www.mundiprensa.es *Cable:* MUNDIPREN
Key Personnel
Man Dir: Jose Maria Hernandez
  E-mail: hernandez@mundiprensa.es
Manager: Ramon Reverte *E-mail:* resavbp@data.net.mx
Editorial & Publicity: Maria Isabel Hernandez
  E-mail: libreria@mundiprensa.es
Associate to Commercial Dir: Jose Chai
  E-mail: jchai@mundiprensa.es
International Agency of Subscriptions: Pilar Garcia Gil *E-mail:* pilargarcia@mundiprensa.es
Administration: Ana Lopez *E-mail:* lopez@mundiprensa.es
Sales Mgr: Mariano Estaban *E-mail:* barcelona@mundiprensa.es
Information: Joaquin Alcaniz
  E-mail: informatica@mundiprensa.es
Accounting: Agustin de las Heras
  E-mail: delasheras@mundiprensa.es
Founded: 1948
Subjects: Agriculture, Animals, Pets, Biological Sciences, Economics, Gardening, Plants, Mechanical Engineering, Technology, Veterinary Science
ISBN Prefix(es): 84-7114; 84-8476
Subsidiaries: Mundi-Prensa Mexico, SA de CV; Libreria Agricola; Editorial Aedos, SA
Divisions: Mundi-Prensa Barcelona
Bookshop(s): Libreria Mundi-Prensa; Libreria Agricola, Fernando VI 2, 28004 Madrid; Libreria Internacional, Aedos-Consejo de ciento 391, 08009 Barcelona

Mundo Negro Editorial+
Arturo Soria, 101, 28043 Madrid
SAN: 002-5690
Tel: (091) 4158115; (091) 4152412 *Fax:* (091) 5192550
E-mail: 100623.1651@compuserve.com
Key Personnel
Dir: Antonio Villarino
Founded: 1960
Subjects: Anthropology, Art, Biography, Developing Countries, Ethnicity, Foreign Countries, History, Religion - Catholic, Religion - Other, Theology
ISBN Prefix(es): 84-7295

Munoz Moya Editor+
28 de Febrero 8, 41310 Brenes
Tel: (05) 5653058
E-mail: editorial@mmoya.com; ediextre@mmoya.com
Web Site: www.mmoya.com
Key Personnel
Contact: Miguel Angel Munoz Moya
Founded: 1984
Specialize in Biblioteca Americana.
Subjects: Anthropology, Astrology, Occult, History, Literary Criticism, Essays, Mysteries, Poetry, Religion - Buddhist, Religion - Catholic, Religion - Jewish
ISBN Prefix(es): 84-8010; 84-86335; 84-931192
Number of titles published annually: 24 Online; 24 E-Book
Total Titles: 45 Online; 45 E-Book

Editorial la Muralla SA+
Constancia 33, 28002 Madrid
SAN: 002-5143
Tel: (091) 415 36 87; (091) 416 13 71 *Fax:* (091) 413 59 07
E-mail: arcolibros@arcomuralla.com
Web Site: www.arcomuralla.com
Key Personnel
Man Dir: Lidio Nieto
Publicity, Rights & Permissions: Nuria Nieto
Production: Julio Sanchez
Founded: 1968
Subjects: Art, Biological Sciences, Education, Geography, Geology, History, Language Arts, Linguistics, Literature, Literary Criticism, Essays, Mathematics, Music, Dance, Physical Sciences, Physics, Technology
ISBN Prefix(es): 84-7133; 84-404
Distributed by Distribudora Malaguena Atenea; Distribuciones Cimadevilla SA; Egatorre; Andres Garcia Libros; Grial; Carmen Fernandez Lappi; Libregus SL; LOGI; Lyra; Marcelino Perich Rasclosa; Odon Molina; Palma Distribucion SL; Pedidos; PROLOGO; La Tierra Libros; UNIDISA

Editorial Musica Moderna
Garcia Luna, 1 y 3, Apdo 2401, 28080 Madrid
SAN: 002-5356
Tel: (091) 416 91 81; (091) 415 37 78
Key Personnel
Editor, Dir: Francisco Carmona
Founded: 1935
Subjects: Music, Dance
ISBN Prefix(es): 84-86292

Naque Editora+
Pasaje Gutierrez Ortega, 1, 13001 Ciudad Real
Tel: (0926) 216714 *Fax:* (0926) 216714
E-mail: naque@naque.es
Web Site: www.naque.es

Key Personnel
Editor: Cristina Ruiz Perez
Founded: 1995
Specialize in bimonthly magazines & translations.
Subjects: Art, Drama, Theater, Education, Literature, Literary Criticism, Essays, Cultural Management, Pedagogy
ISBN Prefix(es): 84-89987
Number of titles published annually: 10 Print
Total Titles: 69 Print
Distributor for Arbole Marionetas; IGDEM

Narcea SA de Ediciones+
Av Dr Federico Rubio y Gali, 9, 28039 Madrid
Tel: (091) 554 64 84; (091) 554 61 02 *Fax:* (091) 554 64 87
E-mail: narcea@narceaediciones.es
Web Site: www.narceaediciones.es
Key Personnel
Editorial Dir: A de Miguel
Sales: N Nacher
Production: P Pazos
Rights & Permissions: C Vegas
Founded: 1968
Subjects: Education, Psychology, Psychiatry, Religion - Other, Social Sciences, Sociology
ISBN Prefix(es): 84-277

Ediciones Nauta Credito SA+
Loreto, 16, 08029 Barcelona
Tel: (093) 4392204 *Fax:* (093) 4107314
Telex: 54495 sele e *Cable:* EDINAUTA
Key Personnel
President: Jose Luis Ruiz de Villa Macho
Founded: 1962
Also book packager.
Subjects: Art, Nonfiction (General)
ISBN Prefix(es): 84-278
Warehouse: N Sra Montserrat 84-86, 08020 Barcelona

Navarra, Comunidad Autonoma, Servicio de Prensa, Publica Pamplona
Calle de las Navas de Tolosa, 21, 31002 Pamplona, Navarra
Tel: (0948) 427121 *Fax:* (0948) 427123
E-mail: fpubli01@cfnavarra.es
Web Site: www.cfnavarra.es/publicaciones
Key Personnel
Press Dir: Felix Carmona Salinas
ISBN Prefix(es): 84-235
Orders to: Fondo de Publicaciones Gobierno de Navarra

NER, *imprint of* Editorial El Perpetuo Socorro

Editorial Nerea SA+
San Bartolome, 2-5º dcha, 20007 San Sebastian (Guipuzcoa)
Tel: (0943) 432227 *Fax:* (0943) 433379
E-mail: nerea@nerea.net
Key Personnel
Editor: Nerea Atxega
Contact: Marta Casares
Founded: 1987
Subjects: Architecture & Interior Design, Art, History, Women's Studies, Art History
ISBN Prefix(es): 84-86763; 84-89569

Noguer y Caralt Editores SA+
Santa Amelia, 22 bajos, 08034 Barcelona
SAN: 004-0568
Tel: (093) 280 13 99 *Fax:* (093) 280 19 93
E-mail: noguer-caralt@mx2.redestb.es
Key Personnel
President: Emilio Ardevol
Founded: 1942
Subjects: Art, Astrology, Occult, Biography, Cookery, Fiction, Geography, Geology, History, Literature, Literary Criticism, Essays, Nonfiction (General), Outdoor Recreation
ISBN Prefix(es): 84-279; 84-217
Associate Companies: Editorial Noguer SA

Editorial Noray+
Cardenal Vives i Tuto, 59, bajos, 08034 Barcelona
Tel: (093) 280 59 66 *Fax:* (093) 280 61 90
E-mail: info@noray.es
Web Site: www.noray.es
Key Personnel
Man Dir: Pablo Zendrera Zariquiey
Editorial: Panxo Pi-Suner Canellas
Founded: 1978
Subjects: Crafts, Games, Hobbies, Fiction, Maritime, Sports, Athletics
ISBN Prefix(es): 84-7486
Number of titles published annually: 20 Print
Bookshop(s): Libreria Maritima Noray

Ediciones Norma SA+
Parque Europolis, C/V, nave 16B, Apto Postal 116, 28230 Las Rozas de Madrid
Tel: (091) 6370760; (091) 6377414 *Fax:* (091) 5470133; (091) 6370760
E-mail: norma-capitel@normacapitel.com
Web Site: www.norma-capitel.com
Key Personnel
Man Dir, Editorial, Rights & Permissions: Alonso Rafael Perez *E-mail:* rpa@norma-capitel.com
Founded: 1978
Subjects: Alternative, Career Development, Child Care & Development, Cookery, How-to, Medicine, Nursing, Dentistry, Self-Help
ISBN Prefix(es): 84-7487
Associate Companies: Ediciones Eilea SA
Subsidiaries: Eilea SA; Libros Gamma
Showroom(s): Ronda de la Plazuela 8, 28230 Las Rozas, Madrid
Bookshop(s): Ronda de la Plazuela 8, 28230 Las Rozas, Madrid
Shipping Address: Ronda de la Plazuela 8, 28230 Las Rozas, Madrid
Warehouse: Ronda de la Plazuela 8, 28230 Las Rozas, Madrid
Orders to: Ronda de la Plazuela 8, 28230 Las Rozas, Madrid

Novelas y Cuentos, *imprint of* Editorial Casals SA

Nuer Ediciones
Plaza Conde de Miranda 4 1º 4a, 28005 Madrid
Tel: (091) 674 92 21; (091) 902 118 298 *Fax:* (091) 655 71 01
E-mail: nuer@pasadizo.com; correo@pasadizo.com
Web Site: www.pasadizo.com
Key Personnel
Dir: Carlos Diaz Maroto *E-mail:* cdmaroto@pasadizo.com; Miguel San Jose Romano *E-mail:* miguel@pasadizo.com
ISBN Prefix(es): 84-8068

Nueva Acropolis+
Pizarro 19, Bajo dcha, 28004 Madrid
Tel: (091) 5228730 *Fax:* (091) 5312952
E-mail: oinaes@jet.es
Web Site: www.acropolis.org
Founded: 1957
Membership(s): the School of Philosophy.
Subjects: Anthropology, Archaeology, Astrology, Occult, Astronomy, History, Parapsychology, Philosophy, Religion - Other
ISBN Prefix(es): 84-85982; 84-400; 84-300

OASIS, Producciones Generales de Comunicacion+
Perez Galdos, 36, Barcelona 08012
Tel: (093) 2372020 *Fax:* (093) 2177378
Key Personnel
Contact: Tomas Mata; Ua Matthiasdottir
Founded: 1978
Subjects: Alternative, Cookery, Earth Sciences, Environmental Studies, Ethnicity, Health, Nutrition, Outdoor Recreation, Psychology, Psychiatry, Self-Help, Sports, Athletics
ISBN Prefix(es): 84-7901

Obelisco Ediciones S (Obelisco Publishing)+
Pedro IV, 78, 3º, 5, 08005 Barcelona
Tel: (093) 3098525 *Fax:* (093) 3098523
E-mail: comercial@edicionesobelisco.com; obelisco@edicionesobelisco.com
Web Site: www.edicionesobelisco.com
Key Personnel
Manager: Julio Peradejordi Salazar
Founded: 1981
Subjects: Alternative, Astrology, Occult, Biblical Studies, Crafts, Games, Hobbies, Health, Nutrition, How-to, Human Relations, Medicine, Nursing, Dentistry, Nonfiction (General), Parapsychology, Psychology, Psychiatry, Religion - Buddhist, Religion - Catholic, Religion - Hindu, Religion - Islamic, Religion - Jewish, Religion - Protestant, Religion - Other, Self-Help, Astrology, New Age, Occult, Spiritualism, Alternative psychology, Judaica
ISBN Prefix(es): 84-7720; 84-86000
Number of titles published annually: 60 Print
Total Titles: 900 Print
Imprints: Magoria
U.S. Office(s): Obelisco Publishing, 8871 SW 129th Terrace, Miami, FL 33176, United States *Tel:* 305-233-3365 *E-mail:* miami@edicionesurano.com
Distributed by Libreria Artemis Edinter SA (Guatemala); Ediciones Cruz Del Sur (Panama); Dellare (Guatemala); Distribuciones del Futuro (Argentina); Forsa Editions Inc (Puerto Rico); Endiciones Gaviota (Colombia); Gussi Libros (Uruguay); Lectorum Sa De CV (US); Los Andes (Costa Rica); Mr Books (Ecuador); Pomaire (Venezuela); Ediciones Urano (Chile); Corporacion Yupanqui SA (Peru)

Ediciones Oceano Grupo SA+
Milanesado, 21-23, 08017 Barcelona
Tel: (093) 280 20 20 *Fax:* (093) 203 17 91
E-mail: info@oceano.com
Telex: 51735 Exit E
Key Personnel
Man Dir: Jose Lluis Monreal
Editorial: Carlos Gispert
Sales: Roberto Niubo
Production: Jose Gay
Rights & Permissions: Marta Bueno
Founded: 1950
Subjects: Art, Education, Fiction, Geography, Geology, History, Literature, Literary Criticism, Essays, Management, Science (General)
ISBN Prefix(es): 84-7069
Associate Companies: Ediciones Centrum Tecnicas y Cientificas SA, Milanesat, 21-23, 08017 Barcelona; Circe Ediciones SA, Milanesat, 21-23, 08017 Barcelona; Ediciones Manfer SA, Milanesat, 21-23, 08017 Barcelona
Subsidiaries: Instituto Gallach de Libreria y Ediciones SL
Orders to: Ediciones Oceano, SA, Paseo de Gracia, 26, 08007 Barcelona

Ediciones Offo, SA
Los Mesejo 23, 28007 Madrid
SAN: 001-8929
Tel: (091) 5514214 *Fax:* (091) 5010699
Key Personnel
Council Delegate: Joaquin Zuazo Martinez
Founded: 1957
ISBN Prefix(es): 84-7117

Oikos-Tau SA Ediciones+
Montserrat 12-14, 08340 Vilassar de Mar, Barcelona

Tel: (093) 7590791 *Fax:* (093) 7506825
Key Personnel
Man Dir, Editorial: Jordi Garcia-Bosch
Sales: Climent Garcia-Bosch
Founded: 1963
Membership(s): Editors Guild of Cataluna & Federation of Editors of Spain.
Subjects: Agriculture, Anthropology, Architecture & Interior Design, Behavioral Sciences, Biography, Biological Sciences, Earth Sciences, Economics, Education, Geography, Geology, History, Language Arts, Linguistics, Literature, Literary Criticism, Essays, Marketing, Medicine, Nursing, Dentistry, Poetry, Psychology, Psychiatry, Social Sciences, Sociology
ISBN Prefix(es): 84-281

Ediciones Ojeda
c/Seneca, 12 bajos izquierda, 08006 Barcelona
Mailing Address: PO Box 34055, E-08080 Barcelona
Tel: (093) 2370009 *Fax:* (093) 4159845
E-mail: lib.europa@mx3.redestb.es
Key Personnel
International Rights: Angel Garcia Fuente de la Oyeda
ISBN Prefix(es): 84-920591; 84-931390

Ediciones Olimpic, SL+
Placa de Lesseps, 33, 08023 Barcelona
Tel: (093) 2382864
E-mail: edolimpic@worldonline.es
Key Personnel
Administrator: Rafael Barberan
Contact: Angels Gimeno *E-mail:* angelsgimeno@hotmail.com
Founded: 1987
Specialize in legal books for universities.
Subjects: Fiction, Science Fiction, Fantasy, Social Sciences, Sociology, Western Fiction
ISBN Prefix(es): 84-7750

Ediciones Omega SA+
Plato 26, 08006 Barcelona
Tel: (093) 2010599; (093) 2013807; (093) 2012144 *Fax:* (093) 2097362
E-mail: omega@ediciones-omega.es
Web Site: www.ediciones-omega.es
Key Personnel
Man Dir: Gabriel Paricio; Antonio Paricio
Founded: 1948
Also specialize in field guides.
Subjects: Agriculture, Biological Sciences, Chemistry, Chemical Engineering, Film, Video, Geography, Geology, Natural History, Photography, Science (General), Technology
ISBN Prefix(es): 84-282

Omnicon, SA+
Mendez Alvaro, 66-A - 5º C, 28045 Madrid
Tel: (091) 527 82 49 *Fax:* (091) 528 13 48
E-mail: omnicon@skios.es
Web Site: www.omnicon.es
Key Personnel
Dir & International Rights: Juan M Varela
Founded: 1988
Subjects: Photography, Photography & Imaging Technical Books
ISBN Prefix(es): 84-88914; 84-404; 84-604

Opera Tres Ediciones Musicales+
Cuesta de Santo Domingo, 11, 28013 Madrid
SAN: 004-4210
Tel: (091) 542 4320 *Fax:* (091) 541 0580; (091) 680 76 26
Key Personnel
Contact: Blanca R Garcia
Subjects: Music, Dance
ISBN Prefix(es): 84-7893

Ediciones Orbis SA
Av Diagonal, 652 Edif A, 6, 08034 Barcelona
Tel: (093) 2800512 *Fax:* (093) 2801472
E-mail: orbis@edorbis.es
Key Personnel
Dir: Monica Casetti
ISBN Prefix(es): 84-402; 84-7530; 84-7634

Ediciones del Oriente y del Mediterraneo
Prado Luis, 11, 28440 Guadarrama (Madrid)
Tel: (091) 854 34 28 *Fax:* (091) 854 83 52
E-mail: sicamor@teleline.es
Web Site: www.webdoce.com/orienteymediterraneo
Key Personnel
Dir: Fernando Garcia Burillo
Subjects: Asian Studies, Biography, Developing Countries, Education, Ethnicity, Fiction, Foreign Countries, History, Literature, Literary Criticism, Essays, Nonfiction (General), Philosophy, Poetry, Religion - Islamic, Social Sciences, Sociology, Women's Studies
ISBN Prefix(es): 84-87198
Number of titles published annually: 12 Print
Total Titles: 74 Print
Distributed by Distribuciones Gracia Alvarez, SL; Arcadia Libros, SL; Distribuciones Cimadevilla, SL; Comercial Kalandraka, SL; Gaia Libros, SL; Gea Llibres, SL; Icaro Distribuidora, SL; Ikuska Libros, SL; Antonio Machado Libros, SA; Marketing i Distribucio Editorial, SL; Nadales Libros, SL; Odon Molina Distribuidor de Libros, SL; Palma Distribucions, SL; Puvill Libros, SA
Distribution Center: L' Alebrije, c/Gosol, 39, 08017 Barcelona

Editorial Alfredo Ortells SL
Sagunto, nº 5, 46009 Valencia
SAN: 002-2500
Tel: (096) 347 10 00 *Fax:* (096) 347 39 10
E-mail: editorial@ortells.com
Web Site: www.ortells.com
Key Personnel
Man Dir: Alfredo Ortells
Founded: 1952
ISBN Prefix(es): 84-7189; 84-9748

Oxford University Press Espana SA+
c/o Parque Empresarial San Fernando, Edificio Atenas 1, 28831 San Fernando de Henares, Madrid
Tel: (091) 6602600 *Fax:* (091) 6602626; (091) 6602629
Key Personnel
Man Dir: Jesus Lezcano
Founded: 1991
Subjects: Education, Language Arts, Linguistics
ISBN Prefix(es): 84-8104
Total Titles: 93 Print
Parent Company: Oxford University Press, United Kingdom
Subsidiaries: Parque Empresarial San Fernando; Girona; Mayor; Plaza de los Alfeceres; Pintor Rodriguez Acosta; Linares Rivas; Don Cristian; Uria; Doctor Manuel Candela; Paseo de Zorrilla; Reina Fabiola; Marques De Nervion

Pages Editors, SL+
Sant Salvador, 8, 25005 Lleida
Tel: (0973) 23 66 11 *Fax:* (0973) 24 07 95
E-mail: ed.pages.editors@cambrescat.es; editorial.milenio@cambrescat.es
Key Personnel
Dir: Lluis Pages i Marigot
Editor: Ramon Badia
Founded: 1991
Specialize in Catalan & Spanish books.
Subjects: Agriculture, Anthropology, Drama, Theater, Ethnicity, Fiction, History, Nonfiction (General), Philosophy, Psychology, Psychiatry, Religion - Catholic, Social Sciences, Sociology

ISBN Prefix(es): 84-7935
Associate Companies: Editorial Milenio Arts Grafiques Bobala, SL *E-mail:* editorial.milenio@cambrescat.es

Ediciones Paidos Iberica SA+
Mariano Cubi, 92, 08021 Barcelona
Tel: (093) 241 92 50 *Fax:* (093) 202 29 54
E-mail: paidos@paidos.com
Web Site: www.paidos.com
Key Personnel
Man Dir: Javier Colomo
Production: Rosa Hurtado
Founded: 1945
Specialize in Social Sciences.
Subjects: Communications, Psychology, Psychiatry, Self-Help, Social Sciences, Sociology
ISBN Prefix(es): 84-7509
Parent Company: Editorial Paidos, Argentina
Associate Companies: Editorial Paidos Mexicana SA, Ruben Dario 118, Colonia Moderna, 03510 Mexico DF, Mexico

Editorial Paidotribo SL+
Consejo de Ciento, 245 bis 1º 1a, 08011 Barcelona
Tel: (093) 3233311 *Fax:* (093) 4535033
E-mail: paidotribo@paidotribo.com
Web Site: www.paidotribo.com
Key Personnel
Editor: Emilio Ortega Gomez
Founded: 1985
Subjects: Education, Health, Nutrition, Sports, Athletics, Anatomy
ISBN Prefix(es): 84-8019; 84-86475

Ediciones El Pais SA
Gran via 32-6 planta, 28013 Madrid
SAN: 001-6888
Tel: (091) 3301015 *Fax:* (091) 7449093
E-mail: elpaisaguilar@santillana.es
Key Personnel
Dir: Guillermo Schauelzon
Founded: 1976
Subjects: How-to, Journalism, Language Arts, Linguistics, Nonfiction (General), Self-Help, Travel, travel
ISBN Prefix(es): 84-86459; 84-95595

Pais Vasco Servicio Central de Publicaciones
Division of Gobierno VASCO
Libreria Donostia 1, 01010 Vitoria-Gazteiz
SAN: 003-2964
Tel: (0945) 01 68 66 *Fax:* (0945) 01 87 09
E-mail: hac-sabd@ej-gv.es
Web Site: www.ej-gv.net/publicaciones/cpa0/SCP.htm
Key Personnel
Contact: Pedro Castro Uribarren
Founded: 1980
Subjects: Agriculture, Art, Business, Education, Health, Nutrition, History, Law, Public Administration, Social Sciences, Sociology
ISBN Prefix(es): 84-457; 84-500; 84-7542
Number of titles published annually: 200 Print; 10 CD-ROM
Total Titles: 3,450 Print; 30 CD-ROM
Distributed by Bidea 2000 SL
Bookshop(s): Gobierno Vasco Dto de Hacienda y Administracion Publica Libreria, Duque de Wellington 2, Vitoria 01010 *Tel:* (0945) 018557 *Fax:* (0945) 078709 *E-mail:* hac-sabd@ej-gv.es
Orders to: Bidea 2000 SL, N Salcedo, 9, 48012 Bilbao *Tel:* (094) 4278177 *Fax:* (094) 4273745
Egartorre, Mirlo, 23, Madrid *Tel:* (01) 7116008 *Fax:* (01) 7116763
Zabaltzen, Portuetxe Kalea 88, 20009 San Sebastian *Tel:* (0943) 310301 *Fax:* (0943) 310452

El Paisaje Editorial+
Arrangoiti 8, Aranguren 48850
Tel: (04) 6390774

PUBLISHERS   SPAIN

Key Personnel
Dir General: Agustin Garcia Alonso
Founded: 1981
Subjects: Biography, Drama, Theater, Fiction, Literature, Literary Criticism, Essays, Music, Dance, Poetry
ISBN Prefix(es): 84-7697; 84-7541; 84-85956
Parent Company: El Paisaje, Urazurrutia, 37 Bajo 1: Centro, 48003 Bilbao
Branch Office(s)
Apdo 88, Cordoba
Bookshop(s): Centro Comercial del Libro, SA, Urbanizduion Torres de San Lamberto 3, 50011 Zaragoza

Ediciones Palabra SA+
Paseo de la Castellana, 210-2, 28046 Madrid
Tel: (091) 350 1179; (091) 350 7720 *Fax:* (091) 359 02 30
E-mail: ayuda@edicionespalabra.es
Web Site: www.edicionespalabra.es
Key Personnel
Chief Executive Officer: Belen Martin
    E-mail: belenmartin@edicionespalabra.es
Manager: Ricardo Regidor
    E-mail: ricardoregidor@edicionespalabra.es
Founded: 1963
Subjects: Biography, Education, History, Religion - Other, family & leisure time
ISBN Prefix(es): 84-7118; 84-8239
Number of titles published annually: 80 Print; 1 CD-ROM
Total Titles: 500 Print; 1 CD-ROM

Ediciones Paraiso, SL+
Munoz Degrain, 15, 33007 Oviedo
Tel: (0985) 203 789
E-mail: paraiso@seteas.com
Key Personnel
Owner, Dir: Maria Emilia Fernandez Garcia
ISBN Prefix(es): 84-88472; 84-604

Editorial Paraninfo SA+
Magallanes, 25, Madrid
Tel: (091) 4463350 *Fax:* (091) 4456218; (091) 14478892
E-mail: info@paraninfo.es
Web Site: www.paraninfo.es
Key Personnel
Man Dir: Alfonso Mangada Sanz
Sales Dir: Miguel Mangada Ferber; Manuel Montalban Velasco
Founded: 1948
Subjects: Biological Sciences, Business, Computer Science, How-to, Management, Physical Sciences, Science (General), Technology
ISBN Prefix(es): 84-283
Bookshop(s): Libreria Paraninfo, Magallanes 25, 28015 Madrid; Melendez Valdes 65, Madrid 28015

Parlamento Vasco
Becerro de Bengoa, s/n, 01005 Vitoria-Gasteiz, Alava
Tel: (0945) 004 000 *Fax:* (0945) 146 016
E-mail: protocol@parlam.euskadi.net
Web Site: parlamento.euskadi.net
Key Personnel
Dir: Juan Carols da Silva Ochoa
Subjects: History, Law, Social Sciences, Sociology
ISBN Prefix(es): 84-87122

Parramon Ediciones SA+
Ronda de Sant Pere, 5 4th Fl, 08010 Barcelona
Tel: (093) 289 27 20 *Fax:* (093) 426 37 30
E-mail: sales@parramon.es
Web Site: www.parramon.com
Key Personnel
Man Dir: Fernando Penuela
Foreign Rights Dir: Remei Piqueras
    E-mail: remei@parramon.es
Foreign Rights: Gemma Isus; Esther Serra
    E-mail: eserra@parramon.es
International Relations: Montse Soriano
Founded: 1958
Subjects: Art, Crafts, Games, Hobbies, Education, Health, Nutrition, How-to, Practical Art, Fiction & Non-Fiction Children & Juvenile Illustrated Books, Human Body, Parenting & Reference Books
ISBN Prefix(es): 84-342
Parent Company: Carvajal, SA
Warehouse: Parramon Ediciones, Pedrosa B, 29-31, Poligono Pedrosa, 08908 L'Hospitalet del LLobregat, Barcelona

Ediciones Partenon+
Paseo de la Habana 56, 28036 Madrid
SAN: 004-4903
Tel: (091) 5634450 *Fax:* (091) 5628405
Key Personnel
Man Dir: Rafael Torres Gorriz
Founded: 1969
Subjects: Language Arts, Linguistics, Literature, Literary Criticism, Essays, Social Sciences, Sociology
ISBN Prefix(es): 84-7119
U.S. Office(s): Ave Domenech 284, 00918 San Juan, Puerto Rico *Tel:* 787-753-8879 *Fax:* 787-754-8265 *E-mail:* proex@icepr.com

Editorial Parthenon Communication, SL+
Cami Del Pla de Can Sans No 24, Sant Andreu de Llavaneres, 08392 Barcelona
Tel: (093) 7952008 *Fax:* (093) 7952008
Founded: 1991
Specialize in graphics design.
Subjects: Architecture & Interior Design, Biography, Environmental Studies
ISBN Prefix(es): 84-88251

Centre de Pastoral Liturgica+
Rivadeneyra 6, 7, 08002 Barcelona
Tel: (093) 3022235 *Fax:* (093) 3184218
E-mail: cpl@tsai.es
Web Site: www.cpl.es/
Key Personnel
President: Josep Urdeix
Founded: 1966
Subjects: Literature, Literary Criticism, Essays, Religion - Other, Theology
ISBN Prefix(es): 84-7467
Warehouse: Pujudes, 77-79, Barcelona

Pearson Educacion S A+
Nunez de Balboa, 120, 28006 Madrid
SAN: 002-2527
Tel: (091) 5903432 *Fax:* (091) 5903448
E-mail: firstname.lastname@pearsoned-ema.com
Telex: 47688 Wxyz E *Cable:* EDIMBRASA
Key Personnel
President: Bill Anderson
Man Dir, Higher Education Division: Luis Collado
Man Dir, School Division & VP: Luisa Crespo
Editorial Dir, School Division: Concho Ordonez
Man Dir, Professional & Trade Division: Ricardo Mendiola
VP, Finance/Operations: Robert Meek
Founded: 1942
Subjects: Art, Education, History, Language Arts, Linguistics, Medicine, Nursing, Dentistry, Philosophy, Psychology, Psychiatry, Science (General)
ISBN Prefix(es): 84-205
Parent Company: Pearson Plc
Branch Office(s)
Enrique Granados 46, 08008 Barcelona
Iruna 12, 48014 Bilbao
Saturnino Calleja 1, 28002 Madrid
Calle Amores 2027 Editorial Alhambra Mexicana SA de CV, Colonia del Valle, 03100 Mexico, DF, Mexico
Plaza de las Descalzas 2, 18009 Granada
Pasadizo de Pernas 13, 15005 La Coruna
Tomas Morales 48, 35003 Las Palmas
General Porlier 14, 38004 Santa Cruz de Tenerife
Reina Mercedes 35, 41012 Seville
Cabillers 5, 46003 Valencia
Julio Ruiz de Alda 12, 47013 Valladolid
Concepcion Arenal 25, 50005 Zaragoza
Bookshop(s): Nunez de Balboa, 120, 28006 Madrid SAN: 002-2527

Ediciones Pegaso, *imprint of* EDERSA (Editoriales de Derecho Reunidas SA)

Ediciones Peninsula, *imprint of* Grup 62

Ediciones Peninsula
Imprint of Grup 62
Peu de la Creu, 4, 08001 Barcelona
Tel: (093) 443 71 00 *Fax:* (093) 443 71 30
E-mail: correu@grup62.com
Web Site: www.grup62.com
Key Personnel
Rights Manager: Laura Pujol
Founded: 1963

Pentalfa Ediciones+
Division of Grupo Helicon SA
Apdo de Correos 360, 33080 Oviedo
Tel: (0985) 985 386 *Fax:* (0985) 985 512
E-mail: pentalfa@helicon.es
Web Site: www.helicon.es/pentalfa.htm
Key Personnel
Dir: Gustavo Bueno Sanchez *Tel:* (0985) 245857 *Fax:* (0985) 245649 *E-mail:* gbs@fgbueno.es
Founded: 1974
Subjects: Anthropology, Philosophy
ISBN Prefix(es): 84-85422; 84-7848
Total Titles: 3 Print; 2 CD-ROM

Perea Ediciones+
Velazquez, 31, 13620 Pedro Munoz, Ciudad Real
Tel: (026) 568261 *Fax:* (026) 586386
Key Personnel
Manager: Jose Perea Ramirez
Founded: 1987
Subjects: Astrology, Occult, Literature, Literary Criticism, Essays
ISBN Prefix(es): 84-7729

Editorial Peregrino SL (Pilgrim Publications)+
Ctra CM-412, km 65, Apdo 19, 13350 Moral de Calatrava, Ciudad Real
Tel: (0926) 338 245 *Fax:* (0926) 338 042
E-mail: editorialperegrino@mac.com
Web Site: www.editorialperegrino.net
Key Personnel
Manager: Demetrio Canovas
Founded: 1979
Editing & distributing religious literature.
Subjects: Biblical Studies, Biography, Religion - Protestant
ISBN Prefix(es): 84-86589
Number of titles published annually: 10 Print
Total Titles: 60 Print
Parent Company: Evangelical Press
Distributed by Cristianismo Historico (USA); Distribuidora Bereana (USA)
Distributor for El Estandarte de la Verdad (Spain)
Book Club(s): Club Peregrino, Apdo 19, 13350 Moral de Calatrava, Ciudad Real

Editorial Perfils
Del Bages, 7, 25006 Lleida
Mailing Address: PO Box 794, 25080 Lleida
Tel: (0973) 242160 *Fax:* (0973) 221670
E-mail: perfils@arrakis.es

Key Personnel
Dir: Mario Arque Domingo *Tel:* (973) 234453
ISBN Prefix(es): 84-87695

Permanyer Publications+
Mallorca 310, 08037 Barcelona
Tel: (093) 207 59 20 *Fax:* (093) 457 66 42
E-mail: permanyer@permanyer.com
Web Site: www.dolor.es; www.aidsreviews.com
Key Personnel
Dir General & Editor: Ricard Permanyer
Founded: 1973
Journals & Books.
Subjects: Medicine, Nursing, Dentistry, Veterinary Science
Associate Companies: Permanyer Portugal, Av Duque d'Avila 92, Lisbon, Portugal

Editorial Perpetuo Socorro+
C/ Covarrubias, 19, 28010 Madrid
Tel: (091) 445 51 26 *Fax:* (091) 445 51 27
E-mail: perso@pseditorial.com
Web Site: www.pseditorial.com
Key Personnel
Dir: Antonio Manual C Baptista
Founded: 1946
Subjects: Education, Religion - Other, Theology
ISBN Prefix(es): 972-563

Editorial El Perpetuo Socorro
Covarrubias 19, 28010 Madrid
SAN: 002-399X
Tel: (091) 445 51 26 *Fax:* (091) 445 51 27
E-mail: ed-ps@planalfa.es
Key Personnel
Dir: Vidal Ayala Sacristan
Founded: 1943
Membership(s): AECE (Catholic Association of Publishers of Spain), Coedit Lit (Liturgical Coeditors of Spanish Episcopal Conference).
Subjects: Behavioral Sciences, Biblical Studies, Biography, Music, Dance, Religion - Catholic, Theology
ISBN Prefix(es): 84-284
Imprints: Icono Perpetuo Socorro; NER
Distributed by PPC
Distributor for Perpetuo Socorro (Mexico)

Ediciones Piramide SA+
Juan Ignacio Luca de Tena 15, 28007 Madrid
Tel: (091) 393 89 89 *Fax:* (091) 742 36 61
E-mail: piramide@anaya.es
Web Site: www.edicionespiramide.es
Telex: 41071 Maeg E
Key Personnel
Chairman: Maria Isabel Andres Bravo
Dir: Guillermo de Toca
Rights & Permissions: Paloma Rivero; Guillermo de Toca
Founded: 1973
Subjects: Business, Economics, Law, Psychology, Psychiatry, Science (General), Technology
ISBN Prefix(es): 84-368; 84-369
Parent Company: Grupo Anaya, Juan Ignacio, Luca de Tena 15, 28027 Madrid
Associate Companies: Ediciones Anaya

Pirene Editorial, sal+
Ausias March, 16, 3r. la., 08010 Barcelona
Tel: (093) 3178682 *Fax:* (093) 3178242
Key Personnel
Literary Dir: Francesc Boada
Founded: 1987
Editions in Spanish & Catalan
Specialize in Infant & Children's Books.
Subjects: Biography, Education, Fiction, Humor
ISBN Prefix(es): 84-7766

Editorial Planeta SA+
Edifici Planeta Diagonal 662-664, 08034 Barcelona
Tel: (093) 2285800 *Fax:* (093) 2177140; (093) 2177748
E-mail: marketing@planeta.es
Web Site: www.editorial.planeta.es
Telex: 93458 Edtp *Cable:* EDIPLAN
Key Personnel
Chairman: Jose Manuel Lara Hernandez
General Manager: Jose Manuel Lara Bosch
Publishing General Manager: Ymelda Navajo
Founded: 1952
Members of the Planate Group: Editorial Ariel SA; Credito Internacional del Libro SA (CILSA), Balmes 155, 08008 Barcelona; Editorial Seix Barral SA; Editorial Planeta Argentina SAIC, Viamonte 1451, Buenos Aires, Argentina; Editorial Planeta Chilena SA, Olivares 1229 - 4, Santiago, Chile; Planeta Colombiana Editorial SA, Calle 22, 6-27 3 piso Edificio Distral, Bogota DE, Colombia; Editorial Planeta del Ecuador, Ave Francisco de Orellana, 1811 y 10 de Agosto, Edificio El Cid Planta baja, Quito, Ecuador; Difusion Editorial SA, Clavijero, 70 Col Transito, 06820 Mexico DF, Mexico; Ediciones Andinas SA, Camino Real, 159 Oficina 600, San Isidro-Lima, Peru; Editorial Planeta Venezolana SA Calle Madrid-Quinta Toscanella entre New York y Trinidad, Las Mercedes, Caracas 1050, Venezuela.
Subjects: Fiction, Nonfiction (General)
ISBN Prefix(es): 84-320; 84-395; 84-08
Associate Companies: Planeta/Agostini (Forum y Fasciculos Planeta), Aribau 185, 08021 Barcelona; Sudamericana/Planeta SA (Editores), Argentina; Lord Cochrane SA, Ave Providencia 727, Santiago, Chile; Editorial Artemisa SA, Ave Cuauhtemoc 1236 - 4, Colonia Vertiz Narvarte, Delegacion Benito Juarez, 03600 Mexico, DF, Mexico; Editorial Joaquin Mortiz SA, Mexico

Plawerg Editores SA
Beethoven, 10, 1º, 2a, 08021 Barcelona
Tel: (093) 414 72 26 *Fax:* (093) 209 50 01
E-mail: info@plawerg.es
Web Site: www.plawerg.com
Key Personnel
Man Dir: Juan Carlos Brinardeli
Founded: 1994
Specialize in Multimedia Editions.
ISBN Prefix(es): 84-89351

Editorial Playor SA+
Alberto Boch, 10-2 dcha, 28014 Madrid
SAN: 002-6239
Tel: (091) 3690652 *Fax:* (091) 3694441
E-mail: playor@attglobal.net
Key Personnel
Man Dir: Carlos A Montaner
Manager: Linda Periut
Founded: 1971
Subjects: Education, History, Language Arts, Linguistics, Literature, Literary Criticism, Essays, Mathematics, Science (General)
ISBN Prefix(es): 84-359

Plaza y Janes Editores SA+
Travessera de Gracia 47-49, 08021 Barcelona
Tel: (093) 3660340 *Fax:* (093) 3660105
Web Site: www.plaza.es
Key Personnel
Man Dir: Manfred Grebe
Dir Sales Division: Juan Pascual
Editorial Dir: Nuria Tey
Founded: 1959
Subjects: Biography, Fiction, History, Nonfiction (General)
ISBN Prefix(es): 84-01
Number of titles published annually: 100 Print
Total Titles: 500 Print
Parent Company: Verlagsgruppe Bertelsmann International GmbH, Munich, Germany

Pleniluni Edicions+
Roger de Lluria, 5, 08010 Barcelona
Tel: (093) 301 08 87 *Fax:* (093) 3174830
Founded: 1979
Membership(s): Association of Editors in Llengua, Catalana & Gremi.
Subjects: Crafts, Games, Hobbies, Science Fiction, Fantasy, Sports, Athletics
ISBN Prefix(es): 84-85752

Editorial Pliegos+
Gobernador 29 4A, 28014 Madrid
SAN: 002-6247
Tel: (091) 4291545 *Fax:* (091) 4291545
Key Personnel
Dir: Cesar E Leante
Founded: 1983
Subjects: Drama, Theater, Fiction, Journalism, Literature, Literary Criticism, Essays, Poetry
ISBN Prefix(es): 84-88435; 84-86214; 84-96045

Polifemo, Ediciones
Avda de Bruselas, 44, 28028 Madrid
Tel: (091) 7257101 *Fax:* (091) 3556811
E-mail: libros@polifemo.com
Web Site: www.polifemo.com
Founded: 1985
Subjects: Anthropology, Archaeology, Asian Studies, History, Travel
ISBN Prefix(es): 84-86547
Total Titles: 45 Print

Editorial Popular SA+
Dr Esquerdo, 173 6 Izda, 28007 Madrid
SAN: 002-6263
Tel: (091) 409 35 73 *Fax:* (091) 573 41 73
E-mail: epopular@infornet.es
Web Site: www.editorialpopular.com
Key Personnel
Man Dir: Ricardo Herrero-Velarde
Dir: Mercedes Calero
Founded: 1972
Subjects: Education, Government, Political Science, Literature, Literary Criticism, Essays, Social Sciences, Sociology
ISBN Prefix(es): 84-85016; 84-86524; 84-7884

Editorial Portic SA+
Imprint of Enciclopedia Catalana, SA
Diputacio, 250, 08007 Barcelona
Tel: (093) 412 00 30 *Fax:* (093) 301 48 63
E-mail: hiperenciclopedia@grec.com
Web Site: www.enciclopedia-catalana.com
Key Personnel
Rights Department: Monica Rocamora
Founded: 1963
Subjects: Biography, Journalism, Literature, Literary Criticism, Essays
ISBN Prefix(es): 84-7306

PPC Editorial y Distribuidora, SA+
Impresores, 15, Urbanizacion Prado del Espino, 28660 Boadilla del Monte (Madrid)
Tel: (091) 4228800 *Fax:* (091) 4226117
E-mail: buzonppc@ppc-editorial.com
Web Site: www.ppc-editorial.com *Cable:* PEPECE
Key Personnel
President: Antonio Montero
Man Dir: Angel Alos
Sales Dir: Ignacio Martin
Rights & Permissions: Javier Cortes
Publicity: Monica Hernandez
Founded: 1955
Subjects: Education, Philosophy, Religion - Other
ISBN Prefix(es): 84-288; 84-400
Bookshop(s): Librerias PPC

Pre-Textos+
Luis Santangel, 10, 46005 Valencia
SAN: 001-4354
Tel: (096) 333 32 26 *Fax:* (096) 395 54 77
E-mail: info@pre-textos.com

Web Site: www.pre-textos.com
Key Personnel
Man Dir: D Manuel Borras Arana
Production Manager: Manuel Ramirez
Founded: 1976
Subjects: Biography, Fiction, Language Arts, Linguistics, Literature, Literary Criticism, Essays, Music, Dance, Nonfiction (General), Philosophy, Poetry
ISBN Prefix(es): 84-85081; 84-87101; 84-8191
Number of titles published annually: 50 Print
Total Titles: 600 Print
Warehouse: CELESA, Moratines 22, 28005 Madrid

Editorial Prensa Espanola
Padilla 6, 28006 Madrid
SAN: 002-6328
Tel: (091) 4462616
Key Personnel
Dir: Rogelio Gonzalez-Ubeda
Founded: 1905
Subjects: Fiction, Nonfiction (General)
ISBN Prefix(es): 84-287; 84-487

Prensas Universitarias de Zaragoza+
Edificio de Ciencias Geologicas Pedro Cerbuna, 12, 50009 Zaragoza
Tel: (0976) 761330 *Fax:* (0976) 761063
E-mail: spublica@posta.unizar.es
Web Site: wzar.unizar.es/spub/
Key Personnel
Editorial Dir: D Guillermo Perez Sarrion
  E-mail: gperez@posta.unizar.es
Founded: 1542
Subjects: History, Literature, Literary Criticism, Essays, Science (General), Social Sciences, Sociology, Academic
ISBN Prefix(es): 84-7733
Distributed by Bitacora

Editorial Presencia Gitana
Valderrodrigo 76 y 78, bajos A, 28039 Madrid
Tel: (091) 373 62 07 *Fax:* (091) 373 44 62
E-mail: anpregit@teleline.es
Key Personnel
Responsable Legal: Manuel Martin Ramirez
Founded: 1987
Membership(s): the European's Net Interface; specialize in gypsies.
Subjects: Anthropology, Biography, Education, Ethnicity, History, Humor, Social Sciences, Sociology, Antiracism, Gipsies (culture, language, story)
ISBN Prefix(es): 84-87347

Edicions Proa, SA+
Diputacio 250, 08007 Barcelona
Tel: (093) 4120030 *Fax:* (093) 3014863
E-mail: enciclo.catalan@bcn.servicom.es
Key Personnel
Literary Dir: Oriol Izquierdo Llopis
Founded: 1928
Subjects: Fiction, Literature, Literary Criticism, Essays, Poetry, Social Sciences, Sociology
ISBN Prefix(es): 84-8256
Parent Company: Enciclopedia Catalana, SA
Bookshop(s): Proa Espais, Diputacio 250, 08007 Barcelona

Progensa+
Parque Industrial PISA, c/Comercio 12, 41927 Mairena del Aljarafe, Sevilla
Tel: (0954) 186 200 *Fax:* (0954) 186 111
E-mail: progensa@progensa.com
Web Site: www.progensa.es
Key Personnel
Manager: Francisco Chica Gonzalez
Founded: 1980
Publishers of technical books.

Subjects: Electronics, Electrical Engineering, Energy, How-to, Technology
ISBN Prefix(es): 84-86505
Total Titles: 2 Print; 1 CD-ROM

Promocion Popular Cristiana, see PPC Editorial y Distribuidora, SA

Pronaos, SA Ediciones+
Mayor, 58-6, 28013 Madrid
SAN: 001-9364
Tel: (091) 5418199; (091) 5412766 *Fax:* (091) 4203429; (091) 5412766
E-mail: pronaos@teleline.es; jaire@teleline.es
Key Personnel
International Rights: Rosario Alberdi
Subjects: Architecture & Interior Design, Art, Gardening, Plants
ISBN Prefix(es): 84-85941
Total Titles: 2 CD-ROM
Bookshop(s): Naos-Libros, Quintana-12, 28013 Madrid *Tel:* (091) 5473916

Instituto Provincial de Investigaciones y Estudios Toledanos (IPIET)+
Pza de la Merced, 4, 45002 Toledo
SAN: 003-536X
Tel: (0925) 259367 *Fax:* (0925) 259348
E-mail: diputolepu@diputoledo.es
Key Personnel
President: Miguel A Ruiz Ayucar Alonso
Dir: Julio Porres de Mateo
Founded: 1963
Subjects: Archaeology, Art, Biological Sciences, Cookery, Drama, Theater, Ethnicity, Geography, Geology, History, Poetry, Social Sciences, Sociology
ISBN Prefix(es): 84-87103; 84-9750; 84-500; 84-505
Distributed by Pedro Alcantarilla (Spain)

Publicaciones de la Universidad de Alicante
Apdo de correos 99, 03080 Alicante
Tel: (0965) 909 576 *Fax:* (0965) 909 445
E-mail: publicaciones.ventas@ua.es
Web Site: publicaciones.ua.es
Key Personnel
Publication Dir: Jose Ramon Giner Mallol
  Tel: (0965) 90 34 80 *Fax:* (0965) 90 94 45
  E-mail: JRamon.Giner@ua.es
Subjects: Agriculture, Chemistry, Chemical Engineering, Economics, Literature, Literary Criticism, Essays, Medicine, Nursing, Dentistry, Regional Interests, Science (General), Social Sciences, Sociology
ISBN Prefix(es): 84-7908
Distributed by Distribuciones de Enlace SA; Resto del mundo; Servei del Llibre l'Estaquirot; Sudamerica
Orders to: L'Estaquirot, Mare de Deu del Coll, 53, 08023 Barcelona

Publicaciones de la Universidad Pontificia Comillas-Madrid
Universidad Pontificia Comillas de Madrid, Alberto Aguilera 23, 28015 Madrid
Tel: (091) 542 28 00 *Fax:* (091) 734 45 70
E-mail: edit@pub.upco.es
Web Site: www.upco.es
Key Personnel
Dir: Eusebio Gil Coria
Founded: 1975
Subjects: Economics, History, Law, Medicine, Nursing, Dentistry, Philosophy, Social Sciences, Sociology, Theology, Women's Studies
ISBN Prefix(es): 84-87840; 84-89708; 84-600; 84-8468
Distributed by Edisofer; Ikuska Libros; Melisa; Odon Molina; Sal Terrae; Sendra Marco

Publicaciones y Ediciones Salamandra SA+
Formerly Emece Editores
Mallorca, 237-Entlo, 1, 08008 Barcelona
Tel: (093) 2151199 *Fax:* (093) 2154636
E-mail: emece@ran.es
Key Personnel
Contact: Sigrid Kraus de Carril
Founded: 1989
Subjects: Child Care & Development, Fiction, History, Romance
ISBN Prefix(es): 84-7888
Parent Company: Emece Editores, Argentina
Distributed by Emece Editores Argentina SA; Emece Editores Mexico SA

Pulso Ediciones, SL+
Rambla del Celler, 117-119, 08190 Sant Cugat del Valles, Barcelona
Tel: (0935) 896 264 *Fax:* (0935) 895 077
E-mail: pulso@pulso.com
Web Site: www.pulso.com
Key Personnel
Manager: Gloria Pasias Lomelino
Founded: 1978
Subjects: Animals, Pets, Architecture & Interior Design, Behavioral Sciences, Computer Science, Health, Nutrition, Medicine, Nursing, Dentistry, Psychology, Psychiatry, Science (General), Veterinary Science
ISBN Prefix(es): 84-86671

Punto Juvenil, *imprint of* Editorial Casals SA

Quaderns Crema SA+
Muntaner, 462 3º 1a, 08006 Barcelona
Tel: (093) 4144906 *Fax:* (093) 4147107
E-mail: correo@acantilado.es
Web Site: www.quadernscrema.com
Key Personnel
Man Dir: Jaume Vallcorba
Founded: 1979
Subjects: History, Literature, Literary Criticism, Essays, Poetry, Narratives
ISBN Prefix(es): 84-85704; 84-7727
Number of titles published annually: 32 Print
Total Titles: 325 Print
Subsidiaries: Acantilado

RA-MA, Libreria y Editorial Microinformatica+
Jarama 3A, Poligno Industrial lgarsa, 28860 Paracuellos de Jarama, Madrid
Tel: (091) 658 42 80 *Fax:* (091) 662 81 39
E-mail: info@ra-ma.com
Web Site: www.ra-ma.com
Key Personnel
Contact: Jose L Ramirez *E-mail:* joselrc@ra-ma.com
Founded: 1984
Subjects: Computer Science, Microcomputers
ISBN Prefix(es): 84-86381; 84-7897

RACC-62, *imprint of* Grup 62

RACC-62
Imprint of Grup 62
Peu de la Creu, 4, 08001 Barcelona
Tel: (093) 443 71 00 *Fax:* (093) 443 71 30
E-mail: correu@grup62.com
Web Site: www.grup62.com
Key Personnel
Rights Manager: Laura Pujol

Editora Regional de Murcia - ERM
Isaac Albeniz, 4, 30009 Murcia
Tel: (068) 280246 *Fax:* (068) 298293
E-mail: editora.regional@carm.es
Web Site: www.carm.es
Founded: 1980
Subjects: Anthropology, Archaeology, Architecture & Interior Design, Art, Cookery, Crafts,

Games, Hobbies, Economics, Education, Environmental Studies, Gardening, Plants, Geography, Geology, History, Literature, Literary Criticism, Essays, Music, Dance, Outdoor Recreation, Philosophy, Poetry, Regional Interests, Religion - Islamic
ISBN Prefix(es): 84-7564
Distributed by Distribuidora M Atenea, SL; Carisma Libros; Distribuciones Cimadevilla; M Alonso Estravis Distribuidora; Herro Ediciones; Icaro Distribuidora, SL; Lidiza; Servei del Llibre; Distribuciones Lyra; Distribuidora Literaria de Editorial Siglo XXI; Miguel Sanchez Libros; La Tierra Libros; Troquel; Viuber
Orders to: Siglo XXI, c/Plaza 5, 28043 Madrid *Tel:* (091) 7591809

Editorial Reus SA
Calle Preciados, 23-2, 28013 Madrid
Tel: (091) 2213619; (091) 2223054 *Fax:* (091) 5312408
E-mail: reus@editorialreus.es
Web Site: www.editorialreus.es
Key Personnel
President: Jose Luis Allende y Garcia-Baxter
Founded: 1852
Subjects: Law
ISBN Prefix(es): 84-290
Distributed by Edisofer
Warehouse: Avda Democracia, Nave 305, 7- 28031 Madrid

Ediciones Luis Revenga
Travesia de Andres Mellado, 9, 28015 Madrid
SAN: 001-8317
Tel: (091) 5434646 *Fax:* (091) 5434706
E-mail: cuadcerv@elr.es
Key Personnel
Dir: Oscar Berdugo
ISBN Prefix(es): 84-87607; 84-398

Editorial Reverte SA+
Loreto 13-15 Local B, 08029 Barcelona
Mailing Address: Apdo de Correos 1237, 08029 Barcelona
Tel: (093) 419 33 36; (093) 419 32 76 *Fax:* (093) 419 51 89
E-mail: istz0125@tsai.es; prom.reverte@teleline.es
Web Site: www.ludosoft.net/reverte/present.htm
Cable: EDIREVER
Key Personnel
Dir: Felipe Reverte
Editorial: Amado J Sala
Sales: Pablo Reverte
Rights & Permissions: Marta Sala
Founded: 1947
Subjects: Engineering (General), Science (General)
ISBN Prefix(es): 84-291
Associate Companies: Marsala, SA, Ave Angel Gallardo 613, 1405 Buenos Aires, Argentina; Salvatore Conforti, SL, Calle 37, No 22-72, (Barrio La Soledad), Bogota DE, Colombia; REPLA SA, de CV, Rio Panuco, 141-A, 06500 Mexico DF, Mexico; Editorial Miro CA, Venezuela

Editorial Revista Agustiniana
Ramonet 3, 28033 Madrid
Tel: (091) 550-5000 *Fax:* (091) 550-5225
E-mail: revista@agustiniana.com
Web Site: www.agustiniana.com
Key Personnel
Dir: Rafael Lazcano
Founded: 1960
Subjects: Biblical Studies, Philosophy, Religion - Catholic
ISBN Prefix(es): 84-86898; 84-95745
Distributed by Ediciones Y Distribuciones Isla

Ediciones Rialp SA+
Alcala 290, 28027 Madrid
Tel: (091) 3260504 *Fax:* (091) 3261321
E-mail: ediciones@rialp.com
Web Site: www.rialp.com/
Telex: 43229 Coim E (abonado 701) *Cable:* RIALPSA
Key Personnel
President: Jaime Vicens
Vice President: Jesus Domingo Garcia
Editorial: Miguel Arango
Children's Editorial: Carmen Gomez de Aguero
Public Relations: Teresa Arregui; Alfonso Rascon
Rights & Permissions: Eva Rubira
Membership(s): Editors Association of Spain & Commerce Association of Spain.
Subjects: Cookery, Economics, Education, Gardening, Plants, Health, Nutrition, History, Literature, Literary Criticism, Essays, Military Science, Music, Dance, Philosophy, Poetry, Religion - Other, Science (General)
ISBN Prefix(es): 84-321
Branch Office(s)
Via Augusta, No 6, pral a 08006 Barcelona
Warehouse: Logistica de Ediciones, SA, Bembibre, 28-30, Polg Cobo Calleja, (28940 Fuenlabrada, Madrid *Tel:* (091) 6420086 *Fax:* (091) 6421696
Orders to: Cauce, Distribuidora de Ediciones SA, Sebastian Elcano, 30, 28012 Madrid *Tel:* (091) 4672666 *Fax:* (091) 5302537

Riquelme y Vargas Ediciones SL+
Avda de Andalucia 29, 23006 Jaen
Tel: (053) 270066 *Fax:* (053) 270066
Key Personnel
Contact: Elias Riquelme Ibanez
Founded: 1982
Subjects: Agriculture, Art, History, Law, Literature, Literary Criticism, Essays
ISBN Prefix(es): 84-86216; 84-300

Editorial Roasa SL
Carretera de Huetor Vega, Edif Roma, 5-1A, 18008 Granada
Tel: (058) 0227846 *Fax:* (058) 132530 *Cable:* APDO 2069
Key Personnel
Man Dir, Sales: Felix J Rodriguez
Editorial: Jorge Alonso
Production: Manuel Alonso
Founded: 1982
Membership(s): Association of Editions of Andalucia (AEA).
Subjects: Art, History
ISBN Prefix(es): 84-86043; 84-8042; 84-300

Ediciones Joaquin Rodrigo
General Yague 11, 28020 Madrid
Tel: (091) 555 2728 *Fax:* (091) 556 4334
E-mail: ediciones@joaquin-rodrigo.com
Web Site: www.joaquin-rodrigo.com
Key Personnel
General Manager: Cecilia Rodrigo
Specialize in Classical Music.
ISBN Prefix(es): 84-88558; 84-604

Ediciones ROL SA+
San Elias, 29 bajos, 08006 Barcelona
Tel: (093) 200 80 33 *Fax:* (093) 200 27 62
E-mail: rol@e-rol.es
Web Site: www.e-rol.es
Key Personnel
Man Dir: Julia Martinez Saavedra
Founded: 1977
Membership(s): The Spanish Association of Technical Press.
Subjects: Health, Nutrition, Human Relations, Medicine, Nursing, Dentistry, Psychology, Psychiatry, Science (General), Social Sciences, Sociology
ISBN Prefix(es): 84-85535

Josep Ruaix Editor
Av de la Vila 18, 08180 Moia, Barcelona
Tel: (093) 820 81 36; (093) 830 02 33
Web Site: www.ruaix.com/
Key Personnel
Contact: J Ruaix
Founded: 1976
Subjects: Language Arts, Linguistics
ISBN Prefix(es): 84-920619; 84-404; 84-604; 84-398; 84-400; 84-300; 84-89812
Number of titles published annually: 3 Print
Total Titles: 62 Print
Distributed by Gran Via Llibres; L'Arc de Bera, SA

Rueda, SL Editorial+
Fisicas 5, Pol Urtinsa II, 28923 Alcorcon, Madrid
Tel: (091) 619 27 79; (091) 619 25 64 *Fax:* (091) 610 28 55
E-mail: ed_rueda@infornet.es
Web Site: www.editorialrueda.es
Key Personnel
International Rights: Sanchez Rafael Rueda
Founded: 1970
Subjects: Agriculture, Architecture & Interior Design, Biological Sciences, Civil Engineering, Earth Sciences, Environmental Studies, Gardening, Plants, Geography, Geology
ISBN Prefix(es): 84-7207

Salvat Editores SA+
45, Calle Mallorca, 08029 Barcelona
Tel: (090) 2117547 *Fax:* (093) 4955710
E-mail: infosalvat@salvat.com
Web Site: www.salvat.es
Key Personnel
Financial Dir: Jean Paul Dupoizat
ISBN Prefix(es): 84-345
Parent Company: Hachette Livre SA, Paris, France
Divisions: Venta Directa; Fasciculos; Literatura

Editorial Miguel A Salvatella SA
Sant Domenec, 5, 08012 Barcelona
Tel: (093) 2189026 *Fax:* (093) 2177437
E-mail: editorial@salvatella.com
Web Site: www.salvatella.com
Founded: 1922
Subjects: Education, Origami
ISBN Prefix(es): 84-7210; 84-8412

Editorial San Martin+
Arenal 23, 28013 Madrid
SAN: 002-6654
Tel: (091) 8599964 *Fax:* (091) 8599964
Key Personnel
Man Dir: Jorge Tarazona
Founded: 1854
Subjects: Aeronautics, Aviation, History, Military Science
ISBN Prefix(es): 84-7140
Bookshop(s): Libreria San Martin, Puerta del Sol 6, 28013 Madrid
Warehouse: Libreria San Martin, Puerta del Sol, 6 28013 Madrid

San Pablo Ediciones+
Protasio Gomez 15, 28027 Madrid
SAN: 001-9739
Tel: (091) 7425113 *Fax:* (091) 7425723
E-mail: dir.editorial@sanpablo-ssp.es
Web Site: www.sanpablo-ssp.es
Key Personnel
President: Antonio Marono Pena *Fax:* (091) 305 2050 *E-mail:* ventao@sanpablo-ssp.es
Publication Dir: Ezequiel Varona
Administration: Antonio Diaz Martinez
Sales: Cecilio Ortiz
Production: Jose Maria Fernandez
Founded: 1936
Editorial.

Subjects: Biography, Education, Religion - Other, Theology
ISBN Prefix(es): 84-285
Number of titles published annually: 100 Print
Total Titles: 1,500 Print
Parent Company: Sociedad de San Pablo
Bookshop(s): Eight in Spain
Warehouse: Resina 1, 28021 Madrid
Orders to: Resina 1, 28021 Madrid

Ediciones San Pio X+
M de Mondejar, 32, 28028 Madrid
SAN: 001-9720
Tel: (091) 726.28.17; (091) 355 2727 *Fax:* (091) 726.28.17
E-mail: espx@planalfa.es
Key Personnel
Dir: Cesar Pallares Munoz
Founded: 1967
Subjects: Biblical Studies, Education, Philosophy, Religion - Catholic, Social Sciences, Sociology, Theology
ISBN Prefix(es): 84-7221
Number of titles published annually: 25 Print
Total Titles: 315 Print
Associate Companies: Bruno, Maestro Alonso, 21, 28028 Madrid *Tel:* (091) 3610448 *Fax:* (091) 3613133 *E-mail:* info@editorial.bruno.es
U.S. Office(s): 170-23 83 Ave, Jamaica, NY 11432, United States *Tel:* 212-291 9891 *Fax:* 212-291 9830

Universidad de Santiago de Compostela+
Campus Universitario Sur, 15782 Santiago de Compostela
SAN: 005-2728
Tel: (0981) 593 500 *Fax:* (0981) 593 963
E-mail: spublic@usc.es
Key Personnel
Technical Dir: Marisa Melon-Rodriguez
Technical Coordinator: Juan L Blanco Valdes
Founded: 1945
Membership(s): Association of Spanish Editorial University.
Subjects: Art, Education, Electronics, Electrical Engineering, Geography, Geology, History, Language Arts, Linguistics, Law, Philosophy, Physics, Science (General), Social Sciences, Sociology
ISBN Prefix(es): 84-7191; 84-8121; 84-9750
Number of titles published annually: 50 Print; 3 CD-ROM
Total Titles: 1,500 Print; 7 CD-ROM
Distributed by Klaus Dieter Vervuert (Europe)
Distributor for Breogan Distribuciones (Spain, Center); Editorial Galaxia (Galicia); L'Alebrije (South America); Libraria Couceiro (Portugal); Puvill Libros (Europe & America); Bitacora (Catalonia)

SARPE, see Axel Springer Publicaciones

Ediciones Scriba SA+
Affiliate of Libreria Martinez Perez
Valencia, 246, 08007 Barcelona
Tel: (093) 215 19 33 *Fax:* (093) 487 37 66
Telex: 98772 Cllc E (Scriba)
Key Personnel
Man Dir: Manuel Martinez Bravo *Tel:* (093) 2152089 *E-mail:* mmb@scriba.jazztel.es
Founded: 1890
Subjects: Art, Medicine, Nursing, Dentistry, Science (General)
ISBN Prefix(es): 84-85835
Bookshop(s): Libreria Martinez Perez, Valencia, 246, 08007 Barcelona *E-mail:* lmp@scriba.jazztel.es

Secretariado Trinitario+
Av Filiberto Villalobos 80, 37007 Salamanca
Tel: (0923) 23 56 02 *Fax:* (0923) 23 56 02
E-mail: secretrinitario@planalfa.es
Web Site: www.aecae.es/secretrinitario
Key Personnel
Man Dir: Nereo Silanes
Rights & Permissions: Laurentino Silanes
Founded: 1967
Subjects: Religion - Catholic, Religion - Other, Theology
ISBN Prefix(es): 84-88643; 84-85376; 84-500; 84-400
Parent Company: Orden de la Santisima Trinidad

Editorial Seix Barral SA+
Member of Planeta Group
Avda Diagonal 662-664 7a, 08034 Barcelona
Tel: (093) 496 7003 *Fax:* (093) 496 7004
E-mail: editorial@seix-barral.es
Web Site: www.seix-barral.es
Telex: 98255 Sxbl E
Key Personnel
Editorial Dir: Adolfo Garcia Ortega
  E-mail: agarcia@seix-barral.es
Editorial: Pere Gimferrer
General Manager: Julian Leon *E-mail:* jleon@planeta.es
Founded: 1911
Specialize in foreign language, drama, essay.
Membership(s): the Planeta Group (see Editorial Planeta SA).
Subjects: Fiction, Poetry
ISBN Prefix(es): 84-322
Number of titles published annually: 60 Print
Orders to: Editorial Planeta SA, Corcega 273, 08008 Barcelona

Selecta-Catalonia Ed
Ronda de Sant Pere, 3 pral, 08010 Barcelona
Tel: (093) 3172331; (093) 3185183 *Fax:* (093) 3024793
Key Personnel
Delegate, Advisor: Sebastia Borras i Tey
Founded: 1943
Publications in Catalonian language.
Subjects: Ethnicity, Literature, Literary Criticism, Essays, Regional Interests
ISBN Prefix(es): 84-7667
Bookshop(s): Libreria Catalonia SA, Ronda de Sant Pere, 3 pral, 08010 Barcelona

Ediciones del Serbal SA+
Francese Tarrega, 32, 08027 Barcelona
Mailing Address: Apartado de Correos 1386, 08080 Barcelona
Tel: (093) 408 08 34 *Fax:* (093) 408 07 92
E-mail: serbal@ed-serbal.es
Web Site: www.ed-serbal.es
Key Personnel
Man Dir, Editorial, Production: Jose Maria Riano de Castro
Publicity: Noelia Riano
Sales: Rafael Alvarez Luque
Founded: 1980
ISBN Prefix(es): 84-85800; 84-7628

Servicio de Publicaciones Universidad de Cadiz+
Dr Maranon, 3, 11002 Cadiz
Mailing Address: Apdo de Correos 439, 11080 Cadiz
Tel: (0956) 015268 *Fax:* (0056) 015634
E-mail: publicaciones@uca.es
Web Site: www.uca.es/serv/publicaciones
Key Personnel
Dir: Antonio Serrano Cueto *Tel:* (0956) 015 267
  E-mail: antonio.serrano@uca.es
Founded: 1980
Subjects: Chemistry, Chemical Engineering, Engineering (General), History, Law, Literature, Literary Criticism, Essays, Medicine, Nursing, Dentistry, Science (General)
ISBN Prefix(es): 84-7786; 84-398; 84-505; 84-300; 84-600
Distributed by Libreria Telmatica Espanola
Distributor for L'Alebrije (For America)
Distribution Center: Breogan Distribuciones, c/Lanuza, 11 Local Derecha, 28028 Madrid, Contact: Jose Miguel Ramos *Tel:* (01) 7130631 *Fax:* (01) 7130631

Servicio de Publicaciones Universidad de Cordoba+
Avda Menendez Pidal s/n, 14071 Cordoba
Tel: (0957) 21 81 25 *Fax:* (0957) 21 81 96; (057) 218666 (Director)
E-mail: publicaciones@uco.es; pal1gocag@lucano.uco.es (Director)
Web Site: www.uco.es/organiza/servicios/publica/presenta.htm
Key Personnel
Dir: Gustavo Gomez Castro
Founded: 1976
Subjects: Agriculture, Archaeology, Biological Sciences, Computer Science, Economics, Geography, Geology, Law, Veterinary Science
ISBN Prefix(es): 84-7801
Distributed by DOR SA; Francisco Baena SL

Servicio de Publicaciones y Produccion Documental de la Universidad de Las Palmas de Gran Canaria
Juan de Quesada, nº 30, 35001 Las Palmas de Gran Canaria
Tel: (0928) 451000; (0928) 451023 *Fax:* (0928) 451022
E-mail: universidad@ulpgc.es
Web Site: www.ulpgc.es
Key Personnel
Coordinator: German Santana Henriquez
ISBN Prefix(es): 84-89728; 84-88412; 84-606; 84-600; 84-95792; 84-95286

Ediciones Seyer+
Canizares 23, 29002 Malaga
SAN: 001-9798
Tel: (095) 2320887 *Fax:* (095) 2325511
Key Personnel
Dir: Antonio Abad
Founded: 1979
Subjects: Art, Literature, Literary Criticism, Essays, Maritime, Music, Dance, Poetry, Science Fiction, Fantasy, Sports, Athletics
ISBN Prefix(es): 84-86975
Warehouse: San Millan, 15 29013 Malaga

SGEL, see Sociedad General Espanola de Libreria SA - SGEL

Siglo XXI de Espana Editores SA+
Principe de Vergara 78, 28006 Madrid
Tel: (091) 562 37 23; (091) 561 77 48 *Fax:* (091) 561 58 19
E-mail: sigloxxi@sigloxxieditores.com
Web Site: www.sigloxxieditores.com *Cable:* SIGLOEDIT
Key Personnel
Man Dir, Production: Joaquin Garcia Ballestero
Sales: Eduardo Rivas
Man Dir: Javier Abasolo Fernandez
Founded: 1967
Subjects: Anthropology, Government, Political Science, History, Literature, Literary Criticism, Essays, Philosophy, Psychology, Psychiatry, Social Sciences, Sociology
ISBN Prefix(es): 84-323
Subsidiaries: Siglo XXI Editores SA de CV
Distributed by Distribuidora Literaria De Editorial Siglo XXI, SA

Signament I Comunicacio, SL Signament Edicions+
Enric Granados 11 entresol 1a, 08007 Barcelona
Tel: (093) 4516888 *Fax:* (093) 3234417

Key Personnel
Editor & Author: Xavier Escura-Dalmau
Founded: 1993
Subjects: History, Medicine, Nursing, Dentistry
ISBN Prefix(es): 84-921381

Ediciones Sigueme SA+
C/Garcia Tejado 23-27, Salamanca 37007
Tel: (0923) 21 82 03 *Fax:* (0923) 27 05 63
E-mail: sigueme@ctv.es *Cable:* SIGUEME SALAMANCA
Key Personnel
Man Dir, Editorial: Santiago L de Vega
Sales: Jose Maria Hernandez
Production: Jesus Pulido
Publicity: Jorge Sans Vila
Founded: 1958
Subjects: Biblical Studies, Biography, History, Philosophy, Religion - Catholic, Religion - Protestant, Theology
ISBN Prefix(es): 84-301
Bookshop(s): Libreria Sigueme, Francisco Garcia Tejado 23-27, 37007 Salamanca

Silex Ediciones+
Alcala 202, 28028 Madrid
Tel: (091) 356.69.09 *Fax:* (091) 361.00.75
E-mail: pedidosweb@silexediciones.com
Web Site: www.silexediciones.com
Key Personnel
President: D Eleonor Dominguez Ramirez
Founded: 1972
Subjects: Aeronautics, Aviation, Archaeology, Art, Biography, History, Maritime, Photography, Travel
ISBN Prefix(es): 84-85041; 84-7737

Editorial Sintes SA
Ronda Universitat 4, 08007 Barcelona
Tel: (093) 3182838
Key Personnel
Man Dir, Editorial: Luis Sintes Pros; Jorge Sintes Pros
Founded: 1968
Subjects: Health, Nutrition, Sports, Athletics
ISBN Prefix(es): 84-302
Bookshop(s): Libreria Sintes, Ronda Universitat 4, 08007 Barcelona

Editorial Sintesis, SA+
Vallehermoso, 34, 28015 Madrid
Tel: (091) 593 20 98 *Fax:* (091) 445 86 96
E-mail: sintesis@sintesis.com
Web Site: www.sintesis.com
Key Personnel
President: Felisa Cedenilla Lorente
Contact: Francisco Belloso Cruzado
Founded: 1986 (Editorial Sintesis was founded in 1986 to provide high quality scientific & academic texts for University students in all areas of study)
Subjects: Biography, Biological Sciences, Chemistry, Chemical Engineering, Communications, Computer Science, Earth Sciences, Economics, Education, Engineering (General), Geography, Geology, History, Journalism, Language Arts, Linguistics, Library & Information Sciences, Literature, Literary Criticism, Essays, Management, Mathematics, Mechanical Engineering, Nonfiction (General), Philosophy, Physical Sciences, Psychology, Psychiatry, Science (General), Social Sciences, Sociology, Travel
ISBN Prefix(es): 84-7738; 84-9756
Number of titles published annually: 100 Print
Foreign Rep(s): Colofon (Mexico); Proeme (Latin America, USA)

Equipo Sirius SA+
Avda Rafael Finat, 34, 28044 Madrid
Tel: (091) 710 73 49 *Fax:* (091) 705 43 04
E-mail: sirius@equiposirius.com
Web Site: www.equiposirius.com
Key Personnel
Contact: Carmen de Pablo Urcelay
Founded: 1985
Subjects: Archaeology, Astronomy, Crafts, Games, Hobbies, Education, Photography, Physical Sciences, Science (General)
ISBN Prefix(es): 84-86639; 84-95495
Distributed by Editorial Hispano Andina Ltda (Colombia); Cuspide Libros SA (Argentina); Libreria Escolar Editora (Portugal); Reverte Ediciones SA de CV; Sousa, Sobrinho y Freixo (Portugal)

Sirmio+
Formerly Acantilado
Ferrar Valls i Taberner 8, 08006 Barcelona
Tel: (093) 2123808 *Fax:* (093) 4182317
E-mail: qcrema@mito.ibernet.com
Key Personnel
Man Dir: Jaume Vallcorba
Founded: 1989
Subjects: Art, Fiction, History, Literature, Literary Criticism, Essays, Philosophy, Poetry
ISBN Prefix(es): 84-7769
Parent Company: Quaderns Crema

Ediciones Siruela SA+
Plaza de Manuel Becerra 15, 28028 Madrid
Tel: (091) 3555720; (091) 3554605; (091) 3552202 *Fax:* (091) 3552201
E-mail: siruela@siruela.com
Web Site: www.siruela.com
Key Personnel
Dir: Jacobo F J Stuart
Founded: 1982
Subjects: Animals, Pets, Art, Biography, Fiction, Humor, Literature, Literary Criticism, Essays, Mysteries, Nonfiction (General), Philosophy, Poetry, Religion - Buddhist, Religion - Catholic, Religion - Hindu, Religion - Islamic, Religion - Jewish, Religion - Other, Social Sciences, Sociology, Theology
ISBN Prefix(es): 84-7844; 84-85876

Edicions 62, *imprint of* Grup 62

Edicions 62+
Imprint of Grup 62
Peu de la Creu, 4, 08001 Barcelona
Tel: (093) 4437100 *Fax:* (093) 4437130
E-mail: correu@grup62.com
Web Site: www.grup62.com
Key Personnel
Man Dir: Juan Capdevila
Editorial Dir: Oriol Castanys
Sales & Publicity: Joaquim Sabria
Rights Manager: Laura Pujol
General Secretary: Josefina Revilla
Founded: 1962
Subjects: Art, Biography, Drama, Theater, Fiction, History, Literature, Literary Criticism, Essays, Music, Dance, Nonfiction (General), Philosophy, Poetry, Social Sciences, Sociology, Travel
ISBN Prefix(es): 84-297

Grup 62+
Peu de la Creu, 4, 08001 Barcelona
Tel: (093) 443 71 00 *Fax:* (093) 443 71 30
E-mail: correu@grup62.com
Web Site: www.grup62.com
Key Personnel
Man Dir: Pere Sureda Vinolas
Editorial Dir: Martina Ros
Literary Dir: Xavier Folch
Sales & Publicity: Sergi Martinez
Rights Manager: Laura Pujol
Subjects: Biography, Drama, Theater, Fiction, History, Language Arts, Linguistics, Literature, Literary Criticism, Essays, Nonfiction (General), Parapsychology, Philosophy, Poetry, Psychology, Psychiatry, Science (General), Travel
ISBN Prefix(es): 84-297 (Peninsula Edicions); 84-89999 (Difusio Editorial S L)
Imprints: El Aleph Editores; Editorial Diagonal; Edicola-62; Editorial Empuries; Ediciones Luciernaga; Ediciones Peninsula; RACC-62; Edicions 62
Foreign Rep(s): Grupo Editorial Norma (South America, USA)

Ediciones SM+
Joaquin Turina 39, 28044 Madrid
Tel: (091) 4228800 *Fax:* (091) 5089927
E-mail: jcabrerap@ediciones-sm.com
Telex: 44710 Edsm E
Key Personnel
Dir General: Jorge Delkader Teig
Production Dir: Ignacio Fernandez
Publication Dir, Scholarly: Fernando Lopez-Aranguren
Publication Dir, General: Jose A Camacho
Rights: NcPaz Serrano
Communications & Public Relations: Juan A Cabrera
Founded: 1950
Specialize in publication of children's, juveniles, young adults & textbooks.
Subjects: Biography, Education, Humor, Literature, Literary Criticism, Essays, Philosophy, Religion - Other, Social Sciences, Sociology, Theology
ISBN Prefix(es): 84-348
Parent Company: Editions SM
Associate Companies: Cruilla, Calle Balmes 245 - 4, pta 3, 08006 Barcelona
Subsidiaries: Acento Editorial; Cesma; Ediciones SM; Editorial Crvilla; PPC
Orders to: CESMA SA, Aguacate 25, 28044 Madrid

Sociedad General Espanola de Libreria SA - SGEL
Avda Valdelaparra 29, 28108 Alcobendas, Madrid
Tel: (091) 657 69 00; (091) 657 69 12 *Fax:* (091) 657 69 28; (091) 657 69 19
Web Site: www.sgel.es
Key Personnel
Dir General: Enrique Valles
Founded: 1914
Subjects: English as a Second Language
ISBN Prefix(es): 84-7143
Parent Company: HDS

Anna Soler-Pont Literary Agecy
Travessera de Gracia 22, 08021 Barcelona
Tel: (093) 201 90 90 *Fax:* (093) 201 90 90
E-mail: pontas@intercom.es
Founded: 1992
Subjects: Fiction, History, Literature, Literary Criticism, Essays, Women's Studies

Ramon Sopena SA+
Corcega, 60 bajos, 08029 Barcelona
Tel: (093) 3223703 *Fax:* (093) 3223703
Key Personnel
Man Dir, Rights & Permissions: Ramon Sopena Rimblas
Production: Ramon Sopena, Jr
Founded: 1894
Subjects: Art, History, Language Arts, Linguistics, Science (General)
ISBN Prefix(es): 84-303
Total Titles: 200 Print

SPES Editorial SL+
C/Aribau 197-199, 3a, 08021 Barcelona
SAN: 000-5975
Tel: (093) 2413505 *Fax:* (093) 2413511
E-mail: vox@vox.es
Web Site: www.vox.es

PUBLISHERS — SPAIN

Telex: 54155 Cvox E *Cable:* Biblograf
Key Personnel
Man Dir: Alberto Cliarlau
Founded: 1952
Subjects: Language Arts, Linguistics
ISBN Prefix(es): 84-7153; 84-8332
Parent Company: Grupo Anaya, Juan Ignacio Luca de Terra 15, 28027 Madrid
Associate Companies: Ediciones Anaya SA

Axel Springer Publicaciones+
Pedro Teixeira 8, 8 planta, 28020 Madrid
SAN: 000-4448
Tel: (091) 5140600 *Fax:* (091) 5140624
Telex: 46148 Srpe
Key Personnel
Man Dir: Alfredo Marron Gomez
Editorial: Marisa Perez Bodegas
Sales: Jose Aguilera Morena
Production: Andres Salcedo Pena
Publicity: Javier Jaen
Founded: 1952
Subjects: Art, Cookery, Crafts, Games, Hobbies, Gardening, Plants, History, Language Arts, Linguistics, Medicine, Nursing, Dentistry, Military Science, Music, Dance, Science (General), Sports, Athletics, Transportation
ISBN Prefix(es): 84-7291; 84-7700

Springer-Verlag Iberica, SA
Provenca, 388, 1 planta, 08025 Barcelona
Tel: (093) 4570227; (093) 4570759 *Fax:* (093) 4571502
E-mail: springer.bcn@springer.es
Key Personnel
Man Dir: Stephanie Van Duin
Founded: 1990
ISBN Prefix(es): 84-07
Parent Company: Springer-Verlag GmbH & Co KG, Heidelberger Platz 3, 14197 Berlin, Germany

Stanley Editorial+
Mendelu 15, 28280 Hondarribia
Tel: (0943) 64 04 12 *Fax:* (0943) 64 38 63
Web Site: www.libross.com
Key Personnel
Manager: Edward R Rosset *E-mail:* erossetc.stanley@nexo.es
Contact: Richard S Rosset *E-mail:* rrossety.stanley@nexo.es
Founded: 1998
Specialize in Languages.
Subjects: History, Language Arts, Linguistics
ISBN Prefix(es): 84-7873; 84-86859
Total Titles: 100 Print
Subsidiaries: Cosmos (Mexico)
Distributor for ELI; Express Publishing
Warehouse: Popigono Olivares, c/o Sierra de Albarracin 3, Arganda del Rey, Madrid 28500
Tel: (091) 195928 *Fax:* (091) 195551

Editorial Rudolf Steiner+
Guipuzcoa 11-1 izda, 28020 Madrid
SAN: 002-6603
Tel: (091) 5 531 481 *Fax:* (091) 5 531 481
E-mail: rudolfsteiner@teleline.es
Key Personnel
President: Isabel Novillo Gavin
Founded: 1977
Subjects: Agriculture, Education, Philosophy, Psychology, Psychiatry, Religion - Other
ISBN Prefix(es): 84-89197; 84-85370
Number of titles published annually: 12 Print

Suaver, Javier Presa Suarez
Gran Via, 8, 36203 Vigo, Pontevedra
SAN: 005-0288
Mailing Address: Apdo Postal n 427, 36280 Vigo
Tel: (086) 439507

Key Personnel
Dir: Javier Presa Suarez
Founded: 1990
Subjects: Poetry
ISBN Prefix(es): 84-88446; 84-604
Distributed by Puvill Libros SA

Ediciones Susaeta SA
Campezo 13, 28022 Madrid
SAN: 005-0431
Tel: (091) 3009100 *Fax:* (091) 3009110
E-mail: ediciones.susaeta@nexo.es
Telex: 22148 Ssta e
Key Personnel
Sales Dir: Jose Ignacio Susaeta Erburu
Subjects: Biblical Studies, Cookery, Crafts, Games, Hobbies, Fiction, Gardening, Plants, Travel
ISBN Prefix(es): 84-305

Ediciones Tabapress, SA+
Barquillo, 7, 28004 Madrid
SAN: 005-0644
Tel: (01) 5320876 *Fax:* (01) 5325890
E-mail: ediciones.tabapress@tsai.es
Key Personnel
Dir: Jesus Campos
Founded: 1988
Subjects: Art, History
ISBN Prefix(es): 84-7952; 84-86938; 84-500; 84-398

Ediciones Tarraco
San Francisco, 10, 43003 Tarragona
SAN: 002-0001
Tel: (077) 233813 *Fax:* (077) 233851
Key Personnel
Man Dir: Javier Elias
Founded: 1976
Subjects: Art, Education
ISBN Prefix(es): 84-7320
Parent Company: F Sugranes Editors SA, San Francisco, 10, 43003 Tarragona

TEA Ediciones SA+
Calle Fray Bernardino de Sahagun 24, 28036 Madrid
Tel: (091) 2 705 000 *Fax:* (091) 3 458 608
E-mail: madrid@teaediciones.com
Web Site: www.teaediciones.com
Telex: 22135 *Cable:* TEACEGOS
Key Personnel
Man Dir: Jaime Perena Brand
Sales: Milagros Anton
Production: Carlos Segura
Founded: 1957
Subjects: Psychology, Psychiatry
ISBN Prefix(es): 84-7174
Number of titles published annually: 15 Print
Total Titles: 300 Print
Parent Company: TEA-Cegos SA, Calle Fray Bernardino de Sahagun 24, 28036 Madrid
Branch Office(s)
Calle Paris, 211, 08008 Barcelona
Avda S Francisco Savier 21, 41005 Sevilla
Bidebarrieta 12, 48008 Bilbao
Bookshop(s): Paris 211, 08008 Barcelona

Ediciones Tecnicas Rede, SA
Ecuador, 91, 08029 Barcelona
Tel: (093) 4103097 *Fax:* (093) 4392813
Key Personnel
Founding Editor: Pascual Gomez Aparicio
Subjects: Electronics, Electrical Engineering
ISBN Prefix(es): 84-247

Editores Tecnicos Asociados SA
Loreto, 13-15, Local B, 08029 Barcelona
Tel: (093) 4193336
Key Personnel
Man Dir: Carlos Palomar

Founded: 1963
Subjects: Architecture & Interior Design, Computer Science, Engineering (General), How-to
ISBN Prefix(es): 84-7146

Instituto Tecnologico de Galicia, ITG
Pocomaco, Sector 1, Portal 5, 15190 A Coruna
Tel: (0981) 17 32 06 *Fax:* (0981) 17 32 23
E-mail: itg1@itg.es
Web Site: www.itg.es
Key Personnel
Manager: Carlos Bald Orosa
Founded: 1991
ISBN Prefix(es): 84-89473

Editorial Tecnos SA+
Juan Ignacio Luca de Tena 15, 28027 Madrid
Tel: (091) 3938800; (091) 393 86 86 *Fax:* (091) 7426631
Web Site: www.tecnos.es
Telex: Maeg 41071
Key Personnel
Man Dir, Editorial: Alejandro Sierra Benayas
Production: Mariano Moreno
Publicity, Rights & Permissions: Pilar Lagarma
Founded: 1947
Subjects: Art, Business, Economics, Education, History, Law, Literature, Literary Criticism, Essays, Philosophy, Psychology, Psychiatry, Science (General), Social Sciences, Sociology, Technology
ISBN Prefix(es): 84-309
Parent Company: Grupo Anaya, Ferrer del Rio 35, 28028 Madrid
Associate Companies: Ediciones Anaya SA
Sales Office(s): Grupo Distribuidor Editorial SA, D Ramon de la Cruz 67, 28001 Madrid

Editorial Teide SA
Viladomat 291, 08029 Barcelona
Tel: (093) 4398009 *Fax:* (093) 3224192
E-mail: info@editorialteide.es
Web Site: www.editorialteide.es
Key Personnel
Man Dir, Publicity, Rights & Permissions, Editorial, Sales: Federico Rahola
Founded: 1942
Subjects: Education
ISBN Prefix(es): 84-307
Branch Office(s)
Calle Hierbabuena 50, 28039 Madrid *Tel:* (091) 5707920
Warehouse: Tambor del Bruch 8, 08970 San Juan Despi

Editorial Augusto E Pila Telena SL+
Pozo Nuevo 12 bajos, 28430 Alpedrete, Madrid
Tel: (091) 857 28 88; (607) 25 20 82 *Fax:* (091) 857 28 80
E-mail: pilatena@arrakis.es
Web Site: www.arrakis.es/~pilatena
Key Personnel
Man Dir: Augusto E Pila Telena
Editorial: Augusto Pila
Sales: Raquel Laviste
Founded: 1972
Specialize in Physical Education.
Subjects: Sports, Athletics
ISBN Prefix(es): 84-85514; 84-400; 84-922803; 84-922838; 84-923778; 84-95353

Ediciones Temas de Hoy, SA+
Paseo de Recoletos, 4 planta, 28001 Madrid
Tel: (091) 4230318 *Fax:* (091) 4230309; (091) 5970654
E-mail: bnogueras@temasdehoy.es; info@temasdehoy.es
Web Site: www.temasdehoy.es
Key Personnel
Council Delegate: Ymelda Navajo Lazaro
Founded: 1987

Subjects: Biography, History, How-to, Humor, Literature, Literary Criticism, Essays, Self-Help
ISBN Prefix(es): 84-7880; 84-86675; 84-8460

Editorial Sal Terrae+
Poligolo de Raos, Parcela 14-1, 39600 Maliano (Cantabria)
Mailing Address: Section 77, 39080 Santander (Cantabria)
Tel: (0942) 369 198 *Fax:* (0942) 369 201
E-mail: salterrae@salterrae.es
Web Site: www.salterrae.es
Key Personnel
Man Dir: Jesus Garcia-Abril
Founded: 1919
Subjects: Anthropology, Biography, History, Literature, Literary Criticism, Essays, Philosophy, Psychology, Psychiatry, Religion - Other, Theology, Autobiography, memoirs, letters, bible, family & relationships, nursing, love & sexuality
ISBN Prefix(es): 84-293

Tesitex, SL
Melchor Cano 15, 37007 Salamanca
Tel: (0923) 255115 *Fax:* (0923) 258703
E-mail: tesitex@tesitex.es
Web Site: www.tesitex.es
Key Personnel
Dir General: Jose Antonio Romero
Founded: 1988
Specialize in Electronic Book & Congress.
Subjects: Nonfiction (General), Publishing & Book Trade Reference
ISBN Prefix(es): 84-89609; 84-920313

Tf Editores+
Aragoneses 2, Acceso 11, Poligono Industrial de Alcobendas, 28108 Alcobendas, Madrid
Tel: (091) 484 1870; (091) 484 1878 *Fax:* (091) 661 3594
E-mail: editorial@tfeditores.com
Web Site: www.tfeditores.com
Key Personnel
Contact: Titto Ferreira; Chusa Hernandez
Founded: 1994
Publication Company, Edition, Printers.
Subjects: Architecture & Interior Design, Art, Literature, Literary Criticism, Essays, Photography
ISBN Prefix(es): 84-95183
Number of titles published annually: 40 Print
Total Titles: 215 Print
Parent Company: Tf Artes Graficas

Thales Sociedad Andaluza de Educacion Matematica
Facultad de Matematicas, Apdo 1160, 41080 Sevilla
Tel: (095) 4623658 *Fax:* (095) 4236378
E-mail: thales@cica.es
Web Site: thales.cica.es
Key Personnel
President: Rescuing Guerrero Hidalgo
Vice President: Mountain Vicenta Gil
Founded: 1981
Subjects: Education, Mathematics
ISBN Prefix(es): 84-920056

Editorial Thassalia, SA
muntaner, 48-50-3, 08011 Barcelona
Tel: (093) 4511298 *Fax:* (093) 4511283
Key Personnel
Dir General: Joan Agut
Founded: 1994
Subjects: Fiction, History, Nonfiction (General), Religion - Buddhist, Religion - Hindu, Religion - Islamic, Spirituality
ISBN Prefix(es): 84-8237
Orders to: Distribuciones Prologo, Mascaro 35, 08032 Barcelona *Tel:* (093) 347 25 11 *Fax:* (093) 459 95 06

Timun Mas, *imprint of* Grupo Editorial CEAC SA

Tirant lo Blanch SL Libreriaa+
Artes Graficas 14, Bajo dcha, 46010 Valencia
SAN: 002-6964
Tel: (096) 3610048 *Fax:* (096) 3694151
E-mail: tlb@tirant.es
Web Site: www.tirant.es
Key Personnel
Manager: Candelaria Lopez-Quiles
Founded: 1976
Subjects: Criminology, Education, Labor, Industrial Relations, Law, Management, Social Sciences, Sociology
ISBN Prefix(es): 84-8002; 84-86558; 84-8442
Branch Office(s)
Campus Universitario Borrio, 12071 Castellon
Gravador Esteve, 5, 46021 Valencia *Tel:* (0034) 963749840 *Fax:* (0034) 963341835
Warehouse: Calle Mendez Nunez, 34, 46024 Valencia

Titania, *imprint of* Ediciones Urano, SA

Gregorio del Toro Editor
Hortaleza 81, 28004 Madrid
SAN: 003-3413
Tel: (091) 3080077; (091) 3190139 *Fax:* (091) 3080187
Subjects: Fiction, Nonfiction (General)
ISBN Prefix(es): 84-312

Ediciones de la Torre+
Espronceda 20, 28003 Madrid
Tel: (091) 692 20 34 *Fax:* (091) 692 20 34
E-mail: info@edicionesdelatorre.com
Web Site: www.edicionesdelatorre.com
Key Personnel
Manager: Jose Maria Gutierrez
Editorial: Rosa Perez
Founded: 1976
Subjects: Advertising, Child Care & Development, Communications, Drama, Theater, Education, Geography, Geology, History, Human Relations, Journalism, Literature, Literary Criticism, Essays, Nonfiction (General), Philosophy, Physics, Poetry, Radio, TV, Science (General), Social Sciences, Sociology
ISBN Prefix(es): 84-7960; 84-85866; 84-85277; 84-86587
Warehouse: C/Sorgo, 45, 28029 Madrid
Orders to: C/Sorgo, 454, 28029 Madrid

Torremozas SL Ediciones
Apdo de Correos 19032, 28080 Madrid
Tel: (091) 350 50 27; (091) 359 03 15 *Fax:* (091) 345 85 32
E-mail: ediciones@torremozas.com
Web Site: www.torremozas.com
Founded: 1982
Specialize in Poetry.
Subjects: Literature, Literary Criticism, Essays, Poetry, Women's Studies
ISBN Prefix(es): 84-7839; 84-86072
Distributed by Maidhisa SL

Trea Ediciones, SL+
Maria Gonzalez La Pondala, 98, Nave D Polig Indl de Somonte, 33393 Gijon, Asturias
Tel: (098) 5303801 *Fax:* (098) 5303717; (098) 5303712
E-mail: trea@trea.es
Key Personnel
Manager: Miguel A Blanco Vazquez
Editor: Alvaro Diaz Huici
International Rights: Ferwanda Poblet
Founded: 1990
Subjects: Art, Biological Sciences, Cookery, Education, Fiction, Geography, Geology, History, Library & Information Sciences, Literature, Literary Criticism, Essays, Nonfiction (General), Photography, Poetry, Public Administration, Travel
ISBN Prefix(es): 84-87733; 84-89427; 84-9704; 84-95178

Institut de Treball Social - Serveis Socials
Avda Diagonal, 482, 20, tercera, 08006 Barcelona
Tel: (093) 217 26 64 *Fax:* (093) 237 36 34
E-mail: intressbar@intress.org
Web Site: www.intress.org
Key Personnel
President: Rosa Domenech Ferrer
Founded: 1984
ISBN Prefix(es): 84-87400

Tres Torres Ediciones SA+
Formerly Ediciones y Distribuciones Universitarias SA
Viladomat, 247-249, 08029 Barcelona
SAN: 001-5091
Tel: (093) 3637450 *Fax:* (093) 3637452
Telex: 98772 CLLCE
Key Personnel
Administration Manager: Rufino Torres Castineira
Editorial Dir: Albert Ferre Cardona
Founded: 1985
Subjects: Art, Chemistry, Chemical Engineering, Language Arts, Linguistics, Marketing, Mathematics
ISBN Prefix(es): 84-7747; 84-85257

Trito Edicions, SL
Av de la Catedral 3, 08002 Barcelona
Mailing Address: Apartat de Correus, 2254, 08080 Barcelona
Tel: (093) 342 61 75 *Fax:* (093) 302 26 70
E-mail: info@trito.es
Web Site: www.trito.es
Founded: 1993
Subjects: Music, Dance
ISBN Prefix(es): 84-88955

Editorial Trivium, SA+
Molina, 20, 28029 Madrid
SAN: 002-7006
Tel: (091) 3147495 *Fax:* (091) 3153236
Key Personnel
President: Carlos Tapia Navarro
Founded: 1982
Subjects: Economics, Law
ISBN Prefix(es): 84-7855; 84-86440
Bookshop(s): Libreria Trivium, SA
Warehouse: Pintores, 30 (Polig Urtinsa II), 28925 Alcorcon Madrid

Trotta SA Editorial+
Ferraz, 55, 28008 Madrid
Tel: (091) 5430361 *Fax:* (091) 5431488
E-mail: editorial@trotta.es
Web Site: www.trotta.es
Key Personnel
President: Alejandro Sierra Benayas
General Secretary: Christiane Schwamborn
Founded: 1990
Hardcover & Paperback.
Subjects: History, Law, Literature, Literary Criticism, Essays, Philosophy, Psychology, Psychiatry, Religion - Catholic, Religion - Islamic, Religion - Jewish, Religion - Other, Social Sciences, Sociology, Theology
ISBN Prefix(es): 84-87699; 81-8164
Number of titles published annually: 60 Print
Total Titles: 700 Print

Ediciones Turner, see Turner Publicaciones

Turner Publicaciones+
Rafael Calvo 42-2 esc izda, 28010 Madrid
SAN: 002-029X
Tel: (091) 308 33 36 *Fax:* (091) 319 39 30

E-mail: turner@turnerlibros.com
Web Site: www.turnerlibros.com
Key Personnel
President: Andrea Nasi
Publisher: Manuel Arroyo
Chief Executive Officer: Santiago F de Cayela
  E-mail: sfcayela@turnerlibros.com
Editorial Dir: Juan G de Oteyza
  E-mail: jgoteyza@turnerlibros.com
Founded: 1973
Specialize in production of catalogues & illustrated books; publishes general nonfiction.
Subjects: Architecture & Interior Design, Art, History, Literature, Literary Criticism, Essays, Nonfiction (General), Philosophy, Photography, Poetry, Regional Interests, Museum Catalogues
ISBN Prefix(es): 84-7506; 84-85137
Number of titles published annually: 120 Print
Total Titles: 400 Print; 5 Audio
Subsidiaries: Editorial Turner de Mexico SA

Tursen, SA
Mazarredo, 4-5 B, 28005 Madrid
Tel: (091) 3667148 *Fax:* (091) 3653148
Key Personnel
Contact: Alicia Parrilla
Founded: 1990
Membership(s): la Camara, federacion y gremio de Editores; also acts as book illustrator.
Subjects: Advertising, Architecture & Interior Design, Art, Child Care & Development, Cookery, Crafts, Games, Hobbies, Disability, Special Needs, Environmental Studies, Gardening, Plants, Outdoor Recreation, Photography, Self-Help, Sports, Athletics, Travel
ISBN Prefix(es): 84-87756
Book Club(s): Circulo des Lectores
Warehouse: Poligono Industrial Las Monjas C/Invierno S/N Naves 14-15, Torrejon, Madrid

Tusquets Editores+
Cesare Cantu 8, 08017 Barcelona
Tel: (093) 2530400 *Fax:* (093) 4176703; (093) 4188698 (Rights & Editing)
E-mail: general@tusquets-editores.es
Web Site: www.tusquets-editores.com
Key Personnel
Man Dir: Beatriz de Moura; Antonio Lopez Lamadrid
Sales: Rosa Maria Segala
Publicity: Natalia Gil
Production: Orencio Sales
Foreign Rights & Permissions: Patricia Sanchez
  E-mail: rightspat@tusquets-editores.es
Foreign Rights Acquisitions: Carmen Corral
Founded: 1969
Subjects: Biography, Fiction, History, Literature, Literary Criticism, Essays, Science (General)
ISBN Prefix(es): 84-7223
Branch Office(s)
Tusquets Editores SA, Venezuela 1664, 1096 Buenos Aires, Argentina *Tel:* (011) 43814520 *Fax:* (011) 43811760 *E-mail:* tusquets@interar.com.ar
Tusquets Editores Mexico, SA de CV, Edgar Allan Poe 91, Col Polanco 11560, Mexico *Tel:* (055) 281 50 40; (055) 281 53 44 *Fax:* (055) 281 55 92 *E-mail:* tusquets@mail.nextgeninter.net.mx
Warehouse: Carretera del Prat 39, Poligono Industrial Almeda nave n 5, 08940 Cornella, Barcelona

Ediciones Tutor SA+
Marques de Urquijo, 34-2 izq, 28008 Madrid
SAN: 002-0303
Tel: (091) 5599832 *Fax:* (091) 5410235
E-mail: tutor@autovia.com
Key Personnel
President: Jesus Domingo Garcia
Editorial Dir & Rights & Permissions: David Domingo Yanes
Marketing, Public Relations: Vivas Francisco Rubira
Founded: 1989
Subjects: Animals, Pets, Career Development, Cookery, Crafts, Games, Hobbies, Gardening, Plants, Health, Nutrition, Humor, Outdoor Recreation, Sports, Athletics
ISBN Prefix(es): 84-7902
Associate Companies: Editorial El Drac SL
Warehouse: ADT, c/o Pelaya ue4, Poligono Industrial Rio de Janeiro, 28110 algete, Madrid *Tel:* (091) 6280606
Orders to: I Taca SA Distribuciones Editoriales, Lopez de Hoyos, 141, 28002 Madrid *Tel:* (091) 3224400 *Fax:* (091) 3224370

Ediciones 29 - Libros Rio Nuevo+
Francesc Vila, Nave 14, Poligono Industrial Can Magi, 08190 Sant Cugat del Valles, Barcelona
Tel: (093) 675 41 35 *Fax:* (093) 590 04 40
E-mail: ediciones29@comunired.com
Web Site: www.ediciones29.com
Key Personnel
Man Dir: Alfredo Llorente Diez
Founded: 1968
Subjects: Astrology, Occult, Cookery, Erotica, Literature, Literary Criticism, Essays, Poetry, Religion - Catholic, Self-Help
ISBN Prefix(es): 84-7175
Total Titles: 200 Print

Editorial Txertoa+
Plz de Olaeta (Ferrerias) s/n-bajo, 20011 San Sebastian
SAN: 002-7022
Tel: (0943) 45 97 57 *Fax:* (0943) 46 09 41
E-mail: txertoa@nexo.es
Key Personnel
Man Dir: Luis Aberasturi
Founded: 1968
Subjects: Anthropology, Art, Biography, Ethnicity, Geography, Geology, Language Arts, Linguistics, Literature, Literary Criticism, Essays, Regional Interests, Religion - Other, Science (General), Social Sciences, Sociology
ISBN Prefix(es): 84-7148
Number of titles published annually: 12 Print
Total Titles: 250 Print

Ultramar Editores SA
San Andres, 505, 08030 Barcelona
Tel: (093) 3460602 *Fax:* (093) 8412334
E-mail: ultramar@javajan.com
Telex: 53132 Saedi E
Key Personnel
Man Dir: Emilio Teixidor
Founded: 1973
Subjects: Biography, Fiction, Film, Video, Literature, Literary Criticism, Essays, Science Fiction, Fantasy
ISBN Prefix(es): 84-7386

Umbriel, *imprint of* Ediciones Urano, SA

Universidad de Granada
Antiguo Colegio Maximo, Campus Universitario de Cartuja, Universidad de Granada, 18015 Granada
Tel: (0958) 243025 *Fax:* (0958) 243066
Web Site: www.ugr.es
Key Personnel
Dir: Rafael G Peinado Santaella
Deputy Dir: Antonio Martin
Subjects: Anthropology, Archaeology, Art, Biological Sciences, Education, Geography, Geology, History, Law, Literature, Literary Criticism, Essays, Medicine, Nursing, Dentistry, Music, Dance, Philosophy, Science (General), Social Sciences, Sociology
ISBN Prefix(es): 84-338; 84-600

Universidad de Las Palmas de Gran Canaria, Escuela Universitaria de Informatica (ULPGC)
Campus Universitario de Tafira, 35017 Las Palmas de Gran Canaria
Tel: (0928) 45-87-81; (0928) 45-87-00 *Fax:* (0928) 45-87-11
E-mail: organizacion@sinf.ulpgc.es
Key Personnel
Dir: Eugenia Rua-Figueroa
ISBN Prefix(es): 84-8098

Universidad de Malaga+
Campus de Teatinos, Blvd Louis Pasteur 30, 29071 Malaga
SAN: 005-2310
Tel: (095) 213 29 17 *Fax:* (095) 213 29 18
E-mail: buzon@uma.es
Web Site: www.uma.es
Key Personnel
Dir: Juan Antonio Lacomba Avellan
Founded: 1978
Subjects: Agriculture, Art, Earth Sciences, Economics, Education, History, Law, Medicine, Nursing, Dentistry, Philosophy, Social Sciences, Sociology
ISBN Prefix(es): 84-7496; 84-9750
Distributed by Distribuciones de Enlace SA

Ediciones Universidad de Navarra SA, *see* EUNSA (Ediciones Universidad de Navarra SA)

Universidad de Navarra, Ediciones SA+
Plaza de los Sauces 1-2, 31010 Barainain, Navarra
Tel: (0948) 256850 *Fax:* (0948) 256854
E-mail: eunsa@cin.es
Web Site: www.eunsa.es
Key Personnel
President: Manuel de Muga
Sales: Juan de Muga
Founded: 1967
Subjects: Art
ISBN Prefix(es): 84-313

Universidad de Oviedo Servicio de Publicaciones
Arguelles 19, 33003 Oviedo
Tel: (0985) 210160; (0985) 222428 *Fax:* (0985) 218352
Web Site: www.uniovi.es
Key Personnel
Dir: Ubaldo Gomez
Subjects: Behavioral Sciences, Language Arts, Linguistics, Physical Sciences, Science (General), Social Sciences, Sociology
ISBN Prefix(es): 84-7468; 84-9750; 84-8317

Ediciones Universidad de Salamanca+
Plaza de San Benito, 23, Salamanca 37008
Tel: (0923) 294598 *Fax:* (0923) 262579
E-mail: eus@usal.es
Web Site: www3.usal.es
Key Personnel
Man Dir: Jose Manuel Bustos Gisbert
  E-mail: jbustos@gugu.usal.es
Founded: 1486
Subjects: Education, History, Literature, Literary Criticism, Essays, Philosophy, Science (General)
ISBN Prefix(es): 84-7481
Number of titles published annually: 100 Print
Bookshop(s): Salamanca

Universidad de Sevilla Secretariado de Publicaciones
Porvenir 27, 41013 Sevilla
Tel: (095) 487444; (095) 487442 *Fax:* (095) 487 7443
Web Site: publius.cica.es
Key Personnel
Dir: Enrique Valdivieso Gonzalez

ISBN Prefix(es): 84-472; 84-7405
Distributed by Distribuciones de Enlace SA; L'Alebrije; L'Estaquirot

Universidad de Valladolid Secretariado de Publicaciones e Intercambio Editorial+
c/Juan Mambrilla, 14, 47003 Valladolid
Tel: (0983) 187810 *Fax:* (0983) 187812
E-mail: spic@uva.es
Web Site: www.uva.es
Key Personnel
Dir: Palacio Zuniga
Founded: 1949
Subjects: Accounting, Archaeology, Architecture & Interior Design, Art, Business, Chemistry, Chemical Engineering, Computer Science, Economics, Education, Electronics, Electrical Engineering, Engineering (General), Geography, Geology, Government, Political Science, History, Law, Literature, Literary Criticism, Essays, Medicine, Nursing, Dentistry, Philosophy, Physics, Psychology, Psychiatry, Science (General), Social Sciences, Sociology
ISBN Prefix(es): 84-7762; 84-8448

Publicacions de la Universitat de Barcelona+
Gran Via de les Corts Catalanes 585, 08007 Barcelona
Tel: (093) 402 11 00 *Fax:* (093) 403 54 46
E-mail: srodon@pu.ges.ub.es
Web Site: www.ub.es
Key Personnel
Dir: Joan Duran i Fontanals
Editorial: Carmen Garcia Gonzalez
Founded: 1935
Membership(s): de Gremi d'Editors de Catalunya & de Asociacion Editoriales Universitarias Espanoles.
Subjects: Art, Economics, Education, History, Law, Mathematics, Science (General), Social Sciences, Sociology
ISBN Prefix(es): 84-475
Bookshop(s): Balmes-21, 08071 Barcelona
Warehouse: Baldiri I Reixac, s/n 08028 Barcelona

Universitat de Valencia Servei de Publicacions
Artes Graficas 13, 46010 Valencia
Tel: (096) 3864115 *Fax:* (096) 3864067
E-mail: publicacions@uv.es
Web Site: www.uv.es
Key Personnel
Editor: Maite Simon Mendez
Technical Editorial: Immaculada Mesa Ballester
Subjects: Biological Sciences, Economics, Education, History, Literature, Literary Criticism, Essays, Medicine, Nursing, Dentistry, Philosophy
ISBN Prefix(es): 84-370

Edicions de la Universitat Politecnica de Catalunya SL
Jordi Girona, 31, 08034 Barcelona
Tel: (093) 4016 883 *Fax:* (093) 4015 885
E-mail: edicions-upc@upc.es
Web Site: www.edicionsupc.es
Key Personnel
Publisher: Josep Maria Serra-Munoz
 E-mail: josep.maria.serra@upc.es
Founded: 1994
Subjects: Architecture & Interior Design, Chemistry, Chemical Engineering, Civil Engineering, Computer Science, Electronics, Electrical Engineering, Engineering (General), Science (General)
ISBN Prefix(es): 84-7653

Urano, *imprint of* Ediciones Urano, SA

Ediciones Urano, SA+
Aribau 142, pral, 08036 Barcelona
Tel: (093) 2375 564 *Fax:* (093) 4153 796
E-mail: atencion@edicionesurano.com
Web Site: www.edicionesurano.com
Key Personnel
Manager: Joaquin Sabate
Literary Dir & International Rights: Gregorio Vlastelica *E-mail:* edit@edicionesurano.com
Fiction Editor: Aranzazu Sumalla
Founded: 1984
Subjects: Alternative, Astrology, Occult, Business, Fiction, Health, Nutrition, How-to, Management, Mysteries, Psychology, Psychiatry, Romance, Self-Help
ISBN Prefix(es): 84-7953; 84-86344; 84-95618; 84-95752
Number of titles published annually: 74 Print
Total Titles: 561 Print
Imprints: EmpresaActiva; Titania; Umbriel; Urano
Branch Office(s)
Castillo 540, 1414 Buenos Aires, Argentina
 Tel: (011) 477 143 82 *Fax:* (011) 477 143 82
 E-mail: argentina@edicionesurano.com
Av Francisco Bilbao, 2809 Providencia, Santiago, Chile *Tel:* (02) 341 67 31 *Fax:* (02) 225 38 96
 E-mail: chile@edicionesurano.com
Transversal 43, No 97-75, Santafe de Bogota DC, Colombia *Tel:* (01) 253 24 88 *Fax:* (01) 226 24 73 *E-mail:* colombia@edicionesurano.com
Vito Alessio Robles, No 140, Col Florida, 01030 Alvaro Obregon, Mexico *Tel:* (05) 661 0774 *Fax:* (05) 661 7590 *E-mail:* mexico@edicionesurano.com
Avda Luis Roche-Edif Santa Clara, PB Altamira Sur, 1062 Caracas, Venezuela *Tel:* (02) 264 03 73 *Fax:* (02) 261 69 62 *E-mail:* venezuela@edicionesurano.com

Urmo SA de Ediciones+
Nervion 3-6, 48001 Bilbao
Tel: (094) 424 53 07 *Fax:* (094) 423 19 84
E-mail: urmo@infonegocio.com
Web Site: www.urmo.com
Key Personnel
Chairman: Federico Guillermo Grijelmo Ribechnnin
Contact: Begona Grijelmo Mattern
Founded: 1963
Subjects: Engineering (General), Microcomputers, Science (General)
ISBN Prefix(es): 84-314
Total Titles: 210 Print

Editorial De Vecchi SA
Balmes, 114, 1°, 08008 Barcelona
Tel: (093) 272 46 70 *Fax:* (093) 487 74 94
Founded: 1967
Subjects: Agriculture, Animals, Pets, Cookery, Crafts, Games, Hobbies, Sports, Athletics
ISBN Prefix(es): 84-315

Editorial Verbo Divino+
Ave de Pamplona 41, 31200 Estella Navarra
Tel: (0948) 55 65 05; (0948) 55 65 11
 Fax: (0948) 55 45 06
E-mail: ventas@verbodivino.es; evd@verbodivino.es
Web Site: www.verbodivino.es *Cable:* VERBODIVINO
Key Personnel
Man Dir: Father Tomas Langarica
Sales Dir: Martin Esparza
Advertising, Rights & Permissions: Maria Puy Larramendi
Founded: 1957
Subjects: Biblical Studies, Religion - Catholic, Social Sciences, Sociology, Theology
ISBN Prefix(es): 84-7151; 84-8169
Distributed by Alpa Libros (Spain); Bidea 2000 (Spain); Centro Biblico Verbo Divino (Ecuador); Centro Paulino (Venezuela); Claret Libreria (Spain); Comercial Gravi - Libros (Spain); Departamento Pastoral Biblica (Mexico); Distribucion Buho Azul (Spain); Distribucion Icaro (Spain); Distribucion Vilas Duran (Spain); Distribuciones Edit Lyra (Spain); Distriforma SA (Spain); Editorial Guadalupe (Argentina); Editorial Verbo Divino (Bolivia); Emaus Libros SL (Spain); Empresa Periodistica Mundo (Chile); Fundacion Editores Verbo Divino (Colombia); Libreria Catolica Gethesemani (United States); Libreria Centro Biblico Verbo Divino (Paraguay); Libreria Hispamer SA (Nicaragua); Libreria San Pablo (Venezuela); Libreria Verbum (Mexico); Libros D&D Unidisa (Spain); Manantial Cultura - Lib Loyola (Guatemala); Paulinas Distribuidora (United States); PPC Edit y Distribuidora SA (Spain); PPC Editorial y Distribuidora (Spain); Spanish Speaking Bookstore Distrib (United States)

Editorial Verbum SL+
Equilaz 6, 2° Derecha, 28010 Madrid
Tel: (091) 446 88 41 *Fax:* (091) 594 45 59
E-mail: verbum@globalnet.es
Key Personnel
Dir: Pio E Serrano
Administrator: Aurora Calvino
Founded: 1991
Specialize in Spanish for foreigners.
Subjects: Drama, Theater, Fiction, Language Arts, Linguistics, Literature, Literary Criticism, Essays, Music, Dance, Philosophy, Poetry
ISBN Prefix(es): 84-7962; 84-7926
Total Titles: 136 Print; 1 Audio
Foreign Rep(s): Sara Grecco Editoriales (Puerto Rico); Interlogos (Italy)
Warehouse: Calle del Pez 21, 28004 Madrid

Javier Vergara Editor SA
Fernando III 1-1E, 28670 Villaviciosa de Odon
SAN: 003-7613
Tel: 6163600 *Fax:* 6163708
Key Personnel
General Manager: Rodolfo Blanco
Publicity Manager: Maria Eugenia Delso
Founded: 1987
Subjects: Biography, Business, Fiction, History, Music, Dance, Nonfiction (General), Psychology, Psychiatry, Self-Help
ISBN Prefix(es): 84-7417
Parent Company: Javier Vergara Editor Argentina

Veron Editor+
Calle de la Torre, 17 local 1, 08006 Barcelona
Tel: (093) 4161643 *Fax:* (093) 4161433
E-mail: veron@veroneditor.com
Key Personnel
Man Dir, Sales, Rights & Permissions: Lluis Veron Jane
Founded: 1965
Subjects: Literature, Literary Criticism, Essays, Nonfiction (General)
ISBN Prefix(es): 84-7255

Ediciones Versal SA
Rosello, 41-45, 08029 Barcelona
Tel: (093) 494 85 90 *Fax:* (093) 419 02 97
E-mail: cga.barcelona@cga.es
Web Site: www.anaya.es
Telex: 54155 CVOX E
Key Personnel
Dir General & Editorial: Antoni Munne
Production: Blanca Marques
Founded: 1984
Subjects: Biography, Literature, Literary Criticism, Essays, Nonfiction (General)
ISBN Prefix(es): 84-86311; 84-86717; 84-7876
Parent Company: Grupo Anaya, Juan Ignacio Luca de Tena, 15, 28027 Madrid
Associate Companies: Ediciones Anaya SA
Orders to: Grupo Distribuidor Editorial SA, Ferrer del Rio, 35, 28028 Madrid

Gobierno de Canarias - Viceconsejeria de Cultura y Deportes
Comodoro Rolin, 1 casa de cultura, planta 5, 38007 Santa Cruz de Tenerife
SAN: 005-3171
Tel: (0922) 202202 *Fax:* (092) 2474165
Key Personnel
Director General: Horacio Umpierrez Sanchez
ISBN Prefix(es): 84-7947; 84-87137; 84-505; 84-87317
Distributed by Bitacora Servicios Editoriales (Spain); Dist Edit Breogan SL (Spain); Distribuciones Lemus (Spain); Rafael Roca Suarez E Hijos (Spain); Servei Del Llibre (Spain)

Vicens Basica, *imprint of* Editorial Vicens-Vives

Vicens Universidad, *imprint of* Editorial Vicens-Vives

Editorial Vicens-Vives+
Av de Sarria 130-132, 08017 Barcelona
Tel: (093) 2523700; (093) 2523703 *Fax:* (093) 2523710
E-mail: e@vicensvives.es
Web Site: www.vicensvives.es
Telex: 51425 Live E
Key Personnel
President: Roser Rahola; Pere Vicens
Dir: Albert Vicens; Anna Vicens
Founded: 1942
Subjects: Education, Ethnicity, Fiction, History, Mathematics, Science (General)
ISBN Prefix(es): 84-316
Imprints: Instituto Cartografico Latino; Vicens Basica; Vicens Universidad

Ediciones A Madrid Vicente+
Almansa, 94, 28040 Madrid
SAN: 000-2437
Tel: (091) 5336926 *Fax:* (091) 5330286
E-mail: amadrid@acta.es
Web Site: www.amvediciones.com
Key Personnel
Dir: Antonio Madrid Vicente
Founded: 1986
Subjects: Agriculture, Electronics, Electrical Engineering, Technology, Specialize in books about food technology, refrigeration, air conditioning, electricity, construction, coatings & pharmacy
ISBN Prefix(es): 84-89922; 84-87440; 84-398
Total Titles: 100 Print
Foreign Rep(s): Mundi Prensa Calle Castello 37 (Latin America, Portugal, Spain, USA)

Vinaches Lopez, Luisa+
Cervantes 34, 03570 Villajoyasa
Tel: (01) 3694488 *Fax:* (01) 3694488
Key Personnel
Dir: Lidia Falcon
International Rights: Elvira Siurana
Founded: 1976 (Vindicacion, 1997 Kira Edit)
Membership(s): Spanish Feminist party.
Subjects: Anthropology, Biography, Drama, Theater, Fiction, Literature, Literary Criticism, Essays, Nonfiction (General), Poetry, Women's Studies, Feminism
ISBN Prefix(es): 84-922067; 84-404; 84-604; 84-605
Parent Company: Vindicacion Feminista Publicaciones
Imprints: Cofas SA
Divisions: Aconcagua Publishing
Distributed by Aconcagia Publishing; Editorial Hacer; Kira Edit

Visor Distribuciones, SA+
Tomas Breton, 55, 28045 Madrid
Tel: (091) 4681248; (091) 4681011; (091) 4681102 *Fax:* (091) 4681098
E-mail: editorial@visordis.es
Web Site: www.visordis.es
Key Personnel
Dir: Jose Miguel Garcia Sanchez
Founded: 1987
Subjects: Art, Education, Literature, Literary Criticism, Essays, Philosophy, Psychology, Psychiatry
ISBN Prefix(es): 84-7774

Visor Libros+
Isacc Peral, 18, 28015 Madrid
Tel: (091) 5492655 *Fax:* (091) 544 86 95
E-mail: visor-libros@visor-libros.com
Web Site: www.visor-libros.com
Key Personnel
Contact: Jesus Garcia Sanchez
Founded: 1970
Subjects: Language Arts, Linguistics, Literature, Literary Criticism, Essays, Poetry
ISBN Prefix(es): 84-7522

VOSA, SL Ediciones
Hermosilla, 132-bajo, 28028 Madrid
Tel: (091) 7259430 *Fax:* (091) 7259430
E-mail: mauosa@terra.es
Founded: 1983
Subjects: Government, Political Science, History
ISBN Prefix(es): 84-8218; 84-86293
Number of titles published annually: 6 Print
Total Titles: 150 Print

Ediciones Vulcano+
Matilde Hernandez, 71, 28025 Madrid
SAN: 003-3812
Tel: (091) 500 16 49; (091) 461 44 58 *Fax:* (091) 461 44 58
E-mail: vulcano@vulcanoediciones.com
Web Site: www.vulcanoediciones.com
Key Personnel
Editor: Isidoro Correa
Founded: 1980
Subjects: Literature, Literary Criticism, Essays, Poetry, Technology, Travel
ISBN Prefix(es): 84-7828

Wolters Kluwer Espana SA
Collado Mediano 9, 28230 Lass Rozas Madrid
Tel: (091) 6020023 *Fax:* (091) 6020021
E-mail: pilarg@wke.es
Telex: 99020 EPWS
Key Personnel
Resident Dir: P C Minderhout
ISBN Prefix(es): 84-87670
Parent Company: Wolters Kluwer NV, Netherlands

Ediciones Xandro+
Apdo 40 020, Avda del Mediterraneo, 18, 28007 Madrid
SAN: 002-0591
Tel: (091) 5520261 *Fax:* (091) 5014145
Key Personnel
Contact: Belda German
Founded: 1987
Subjects: Psychology, Psychiatry
ISBN Prefix(es): 84-88665; 84-404; 84-604; 84-398; 84-400; 84-300

Xarait Libros SA
Paseo de San Francisco de Sales 32, 28003 Madrid
SAN: 005-3538
Tel: (091) 534 15 67 *Fax:* (091) 535 08 31
Key Personnel
Man Dir: Miguel Ortiz Martinez
Founded: 1973
Subjects: Architecture & Interior Design, Art
ISBN Prefix(es): 84-85434

Edicions Xerais de Galicia
Doctor Maranon, 12, 36211 Vigo
SAN: 001-4591
Tel: (0986) 214888 *Fax:* (0986) 201366
E-mail: xerais@xerais.es
Web Site: www.xerais.es
Key Personnel
Contact: Manuel Bragado Rodriguez
Founded: 1976
Subjects: Education, Fiction, History, Language Arts, Linguistics, Poetry, Social Sciences, Sociology
ISBN Prefix(es): 84-7507; 84-8302

Xunta de Galicia
Conselleria de Cultura Comunicacion Social e Turismo, San Caetano s-n, 15771 Santiago de Compostela
Tel: (081) 544816 *Fax:* (081) 544887
Key Personnel
Subdirector Xeral of Culture: Xabier Senin Fernandez
Conselleria de Cultura e Xuventude, Ed San Caetano, s/n.
Subjects: Agriculture, Animals, Pets, Art, Biological Sciences, Business, Economics, Education, Fiction, Finance, Geography, Geology, Health, Nutrition, History, Law, Literature, Literary Criticism, Essays, Management, Maritime, Marketing, Military Science, Public Administration, Science (General), Sports, Athletics, Design, graphic arts
ISBN Prefix(es): 84-453

Editorial Zendrera Zariquiey, SA+
Cardenal Vivesi Tuto 59 bajos, 08034 Barcelona
Tel: (093) 280 12 34 *Fax:* (093) 280 61 90
E-mail: info@editorialzendrera.com
Web Site: www.editorialzendrera.com
Key Personnel
Man Dir: Zendrera Zariquiey
International Rights: Ms Fabregat
Founded: 1997
Subjects: Computer Science, Cookery, Travel
ISBN Prefix(es): 84-8418; 84-89675
Total Titles: 120 Print
Associate Companies: Editorial Sirpus, SL

Sri Lanka

General Information

Capital: Colombo
Language: Sinhala & Tamila (official & national) & English (national)
Religion: Predominantly Buddhism
Population: 17.6 million
Bank Hours: 0900-1300 Monday-Friday
Shop Hours: 0800-1730 Monday-Friday
Currency: 100 cents = 1 Sri Lanka rupee
Export/Import Information: No tariff on books or advertising. Import license required for most book importation. Exchange controls.
Copyright: UCC, Berne, Florence (see Copyright Conventions, pg xi)

Buddhist Publication Society Inc
54 Sangharaja Mawatha, Kandy
Mailing Address: PO Box 61, Kandy
Tel: (08) 223679; (08) 237283 *Fax:* (08) 223679
E-mail: bps@ids.lk; bps@metta.lk
Web Site: www.metta.lk
Key Personnel
President, Editor: Bhikkhu Bodhi
 E-mail: venbodhi@metta.lk
Administrative Secretary: L B W Seneviratne
Founded: 1958
Subjects: Religion - Buddhist
ISBN Prefix(es): 955-24

SRI LANKA

Foreign Rep(s): Vipassana Research Publications of America (USA)
Foreign Rights: Dhamma Books (India); Wisdom Books (UK)

Business Directory of Lanka Ltd+
Ward Place, No 49, Colombo 07
Tel: (01) 2695095; (074) 721560; (074) 721561
Fax: (074) 721560
E-mail: info@lanka.com
Web Site: www.lanka.com
Key Personnel
Man Dir: Mangala Wickramarachchi
E-mail: kompass@itmin.com
Founded: 1994
Membership(s): Ceylon Chamber of Commerce.
ISBN Prefix(es): 955-9405
Subsidiaries: Kompass Lanka (Pvt) Ltd; Raffles Lanka (Pvt) Ltd

Calvary Press+
123 Highlevel Rd, Kirillapone, Colombo 6
Tel: (01) 553110
Subjects: Religion - Protestant
ISBN Prefix(es): 955-587

Department of Census & Statistics
PO Box 563, Colombo 7
Tel: (01) 675297 *Fax:* (01) 697594
E-mail: dcensus@lanka.ccom.lk
Web Site: www.statistics.gov.lk
Key Personnel
Dir General: Mr A G W Nanayakkara
ISBN Prefix(es): 955-577

The Ceylon Chamber of Commerce
50 Navam Mawatha, Colombo 02
Tel: (01) 2452183; (01) 2421745; (01) 2329143
Fax: (01) 2437477; (01) 2449352
E-mail: info@chamber.lk
Web Site: www.chamber.lk
Key Personnel
Chairman: Mr A C Gunasinghe
Vice Chairman: Mr P D Rodrigo
Deputy Chairman: Mr Tilak De Zoysa
Secretary General: Mr C G Jayasuriya
Founded: 1839
ISBN Prefix(es): 955-604

Colombo Book Association+
POB 1946, Colombo
Tel: (01) 686878; (01) 072270652 *Fax:* (01) 696578
Key Personnel
President: Dhammadesha Ambalampitiya
Founded: 1983
Successful UNESCO project devoted to develop the literacy.
Subjects: Education, English as a Second Language
ISBN Prefix(es): 955-588
Imprints: Denuma

Danuma, *imprint of* Danuma Prakashakayo

Danuma Prakashakayo+
84 Serpentine Rd, Borella, Colombo 8
Tel: (01) 686878 *Fax:* (01) 696578
Founded: 1983
Subjects: Literature, Literary Criticism, Essays, Poetry, Science Fiction, Fantasy
ISBN Prefix(es): 955-556
Imprints: Danuma
Subsidiaries: Colombo Children's Book Society
Orders to: 84 Leslie, Ranagala Mawatha, Colombo 8

Denuma, *imprint of* Colombo Book Association

Edirisooriya & Company
68, Elie House Rd, Colombo 15
Tel: (01) 522555; (01) 523216 *Fax:* (01) 446380; (01) 074618905
Telex: 21701 GLOBAL CE *Cable:* UNIMER
Key Personnel
Printing Manager: Lindwal Peiris *Tel:* (01) 074618905
Founded: 1985
Printing & binding of local circulation school books, web offset machines, etc.
Subjects: *Specialize in stickers, labels, diaries & calendars*
ISBN Prefix(es): 955-9228
Parent Company: S P Samy & Co (Pvt) Ltd
Subsidiaries: United Merchants Ltd
Branch Office(s)
Edirisooriya & Co, 30 Prince St, Colombo 11, Contact: Mr Ganesh *Tel:* (01) 441560; (01) 446380 *Fax:* (01) 446380

Gihan Book Shop
144C Hill St, Dehiwala
Key Personnel
Author: W O T Fernando
Founded: 1980
Subjects: Mathematics
ISBN Prefix(es): 955-593
Imprints: Sanjana Offset

M D Gunasena & Co Ltd
217 Olcott Mawatha, Colombo 11
Mailing Address: PO Box 246, Colombo 11
Tel: (01) 323981; (01) 323982; (01) 323983; (01) 323984 *Fax:* (01) 323336
E-mail: mdgunasena@mail.ewisl.net
Web Site: mdgunasena.com
Founded: 1913
Associated imprints include Ananda Books Ltd, Sirisara Vidyalaya.
ISBN Prefix(es): 955-21

Inter-Cultural Book Promoters+
21 G4 Peramuna Mawatha, Eldeniya, Kadawatha
Tel: 525359 *Fax:* 525359
E-mail: inculture@eureka.lk
Founded: 1985
Subjects: Language Arts, Linguistics, Philosophy, Religion - Buddhist, Religion - Catholic, Religion - Hindu, Religion - Islamic, Religion - Jewish, Religion - Protestant, Religion - Other
ISBN Prefix(es): 955-9036
Parent Company: Inter-cultural Research Center

International Centre for Ethnic Studies+
554/1 Peradeniya Rd, Kandy
Tel: (08) 234892 *Fax:* (08) 234892
E-mail: ices@slt.lk
Web Site: www.icescolombo.org
Key Personnel
Executive Dir: Dr Radhika Coomaraswamy
Librarian: Mr Ponudurai Thambirajah
Founded: 1982
A social science & policy research institute.
Subjects: Ethnicity, Women's Studies
ISBN Prefix(es): 955-580
Total Titles: 20 Print
Branch Office(s)
Kynsey Terrace, Colombo 8
Distributed by St Martin's Press
Distributor for Frances Pinter (UK)

J K Publications
J K 50, Katuwawala, Borelasgamuwa
Tel: (01) 518954
Key Personnel
Author: Jayasena Kottegoda
Subjects: Music, Dance
ISBN Prefix(es): 955-9438
Total Titles: 7 Print
Distributed by Godage; Gunasena; Lake House

Dayawansa Jayakody & Co+
101 Ven S Mahinda, Thero Mawatha, Colombo 10
Tel: (011) 2695773 *Fax:* (011) 2696653
E-mail: dayawansa@slt.lk
Key Personnel
Chairman: Dayawansa Jayakody
Man Dir: Veronica Damayanthi Jayakody
Founded: 1960
Membership(s): IPA; APPA; Sri Lanka Association of Publishers.
Subjects: Drama, Theater, Fiction, Literature, Literary Criticism, Essays, Poetry
ISBN Prefix(es): 955-551
Number of titles published annually: 84 Print
Total Titles: 4,200 Print
Associate Companies: Helabima Publishers
U.S. Office(s): Dayawansa Jayakody & Company (USA), 131 Banwell Lane, Mount Laurel, NJ 08054, United States *Tel:* 856-234-8001; 502-212-9154 *Fax:* 856-234-8001; 502-212-9154
E-mail: dayawanska@eureka.lk (US Sales)
Distributor for Helabima Publishers
Foreign Rep(s): Uditha Daminda Jayakody (USA)
Warehouse: 163/4, Siri Dhamma Mawatha, Colombo 10

Karunaratne & Sons Ltd+
647, Kuluratne Mawatha, Colombo 10
Tel: 692295 *Fax:* 229 9860
E-mail: info@calcey.com
Web Site: www.calcey.com
Key Personnel
Chief Executive Officer: Mangala Karunaratne
Founded: 1971
Membership(s): Sri Lanka Association of Publishers.
Subjects: Archaeology, Economics, Education, Ethnicity, History, Philosophy, Religion - Buddhist, Social Sciences, Sociology, Women's Studies
ISBN Prefix(es): 955-9098

KVG de Silva & Sons+
415 Galle Rd, Colombo 4
Tel: (01) 84146 *Fax:* (01) 586598
Key Personnel
Managing Partner: Mrs Devini Dias; K V N Silva; Mrs Veena Silva
Founded: 1898
Subjects: History, Regional Interests, Religion - Other
ISBN Prefix(es): 955-9112
Bookshop(s): Fort, Colombo & YMBA Shopping Complex, 44/9 YMBA Bldg, Borella, Colombo

Lake House Investments Ltd+
41 W A D Ramanayake Mawatha, Colombo 2
Tel: (01) 35175; (01) 33271 *Fax:* (01) 44 7848; (01) 44 9504
E-mail: lhl@srilanka.net
Telex: 21266 Lakexpo CE *Cable:* COLOMBO 2 SRI LANKA
Key Personnel
Chairman: R S Wijewardene
Manager: S M Aziz
Founded: 1965
Specialize in Text Books on Science & Law both in Sinhala & English.
Membership(s): The Book Publisher's Association of Sri Lanka.
Subjects: Education, Fiction, History, Law, Medicine, Nursing, Dentistry, Music, Dance, Science (General), Sports, Athletics
ISBN Prefix(es): 955-552
Associate Companies: Lake House Printers & Publishers Ltd
Divisions: Chitrafoto; Lake House Bookshop; Lakexpo
Bookshop(s): Columbo University Bookshop, Columbo University, Cumarathuga Munidasa

Mawatha, Columbo; Lake House Bookshop, 100 Chittampalam Gardinar Mawatha, Colombo 2

Law Publishers Association+
21 Sownders Court, Colombo 2
Tel: (01) 330363 *Fax:* (01) 436629
Founded: 1990
Subjects: Biography, Law
ISBN Prefix(es): 955-9210
Divisions: FAMYS
Orders to: FAMYS, 21 Sownders Court, Colombo 2

Ministry of Cultural Affairs
8th floor Sethsiripaya, Battaramulla
Tel: (01) 437328
E-mail: mcasec@sltnet.lk
Web Site: www.mca.gov.lk *Cable:* Sunlay
Key Personnel
Dir, Publications: R L Wimaladharma
Deputy Dir, Publications: K G Amaradasa
Editorial: Prof J D Dheerasekera; Prof D E Hettiaratchi; D P Ponnamperuma
Founded: 1971
Subjects: Art, Ethnicity, Literature, Literary Criticism, Essays, Religion - Other
ISBN Prefix(es): 955-9117
Bookshop(s): Jayanti Bookshop, 135 Dharmapala Mawatha, Colombo 7
Book Club(s): Book Club of the Ministry of Cultural Affairs of Sri Lanka

Ministry of Education+
Isurupaya, Sri Jayawardenapura Kotte, Battaramulla
Tel: 565141-5150
Key Personnel
Contact: Richard Pathirana
Subjects: Accounting, Agriculture, Chemistry, Chemical Engineering, Computer Science, Geography, Geology, Mathematics, Physics, Science (General)
ISBN Prefix(es): 955-28
Subsidiaries: Educational Publications Dept

National Children's Educational Foundation+
International Headquarters, Mulleriyawa New Town
Tel: 578090 *Fax:* 578090
ISBN Prefix(es): 955-9104

National Library & Documentation Centre
No 14, Independence Ave, Colombo 07
Mailing Address: PO Box 1764, Colombo 07
Tel: (01) 685198; (01) 685199; (01) 698847; (01) 685197 *Fax:* (01) 685201
E-mail: natlib@sltnet.lk
Web Site: www.natlib.lk
Key Personnel
Chairman: Ms Tissa Kariyawasam
Dir General: Mr M S U Amarasiri *Tel:* (01) 687581 *E-mail:* dg@mail.natlib.lk
Deputy Dir: M A Nalani
Founded: 1970
Membership(s): IFLA; COMLA; CDNLAO; ACCU; AMIC.
Subjects: Communications, Computer Science, Ethnicity, Human Relations, Library & Information Sciences, Literature, Literary Criticism, Essays, Regional Interests, Social Sciences, Sociology
ISBN Prefix(es): 955-9011
Total Titles: 2 CD-ROM

Department of National Museums
PO Box 854, Colombo 7
Tel: (01) 595366 *Fax:* (01) 595366
Key Personnel
Contact: W T T P Gunawardane
Subjects: Anthropology, Antiques, Natural History

ISBN Prefix(es): 955-578
Subsidiaries: National Museum (Galle); National Museum (Kandy); National Museum (Ratnapura); Folk Museum; Dutch Period Museum; National Museum of Natural History; School Science Museum; School Science Museum; School Science Museum; School Science Museum; Puppetry & Children's Museum; National Maritime Museum

Pradeepa Publishers+
34/34 Lawyers Off Complex, St Sebastian Hill, Colombo 12
Tel: (094) 435074; (094) 863261; (071) 735532 *Fax:* (094) 863261
Key Personnel
Author & Editor: K Jayatilake *E-mail:* kjayatie@hotmail.com
Founded: 1968
Membership(s): the Writers Association, Sri Lanka Book Publishers Association.
Subjects: Fiction, Literature, Literary Criticism, Essays, Religion - Buddhist
ISBN Prefix(es): 955-554

Saara Buddhi Publication
19/1, Haltotawatta Lane, Avissawella 10700
ISBN Prefix(es): 955-9415

Saman Saha Madara Publishers
194 Sri Jayawardenapura Mawatha, Welikada, Rajagiriya
Tel: (01) 2862055 *Fax:* (01) 2868071
E-mail: prince@eureka.lk
Key Personnel
President: Mahinda Ralapanawe
E-mail: ralapanawe@sltnet.lk
Founded: 1970
Subjects: Fiction, Literature, Literary Criticism, Essays
ISBN Prefix(es): 955-563
Total Titles: 2 Print

Samayawardena Printers Publishers & Booksellers+
53 Maligakanda Rd, Maradana, Colombo 10
Tel: (01) 694682 *Fax:* (01) 698977; (01) 683525
E-mail: samaya@applestr.lk
Founded: 1960
Membership(s): Sri Lanka Book Publishers Association & Asia Pacific Book Publishers Association.
Subjects: Education, English as a Second Language, Nonfiction (General), Philosophy, Religion - Buddhist
ISBN Prefix(es): 955-570
Bookshop(s): Samayawardhana Book Shop, 61 Maligakanda Rd, Colombo 10 *Tel:* (01) 677539 *Fax:* (01) 683986

Sanjana Offset, *imprint of* Gihan Book Shop

Somawathi Hewavitharana Fund
Mahabodhi Mandiraya, 130 Maligakanda Rd, Colombo 10
Mailing Address: 36/6 Rosmead Pl, Colombo 7
Tel: (01) 698079
Key Personnel
Trustee: Noel Wijenaike; Nanda Amerasinghe *Tel:* (01) 694026; Parinda Ranasinghe Tripitaka Publications.
Subjects: Religion - Buddhist
ISBN Prefix(es): 955-616
Number of titles published annually: 6 Print
Total Titles: 80 Print

Sri Lanka Jama'ath-e-Islami
77, Dematagoda Rd, Colombo 9
Tel: (01) 687091 *Fax:* (01) 686030

ISBN Prefix(es): 955-608
Bookshop(s): Sri Lanka Jama'ath-e-Islami Book Stall, 77, Dematagoda Rd, Colombo 9

State Printing Corp+
95 Sir Chittampalam Gardiner Mawatha, Colombo 2
Tel: (01) 503694 *Fax:* (01) 503694
Key Personnel
Marketing Manager: Jagath Gamanayake
ISBN Prefix(es): 955-610

Sunera Publishers+
64, Devala Rd, Nugegoda
Tel: 511527
Founded: 1989
Subjects: Career Development, Economics, Law, Management
ISBN Prefix(es): 955-9128

Swarna Hansa Foundation+
9 Windsor Ave, Dehiwala
Mailing Address: PO Box 16, Dehiwala
Tel: (01) 712566 *Fax:* (01) 733649
Key Personnel
Program Executive: Gallege Punyawardana
Founded: 1978
Branch Offices: Hasalaka; Hiniduma; Kalawana; Nikaweratiya; Regional Centres at Kandy.
Subjects: Agriculture, Education, Environmental Studies, Health, Nutrition, History, Journalism, Literature, Literary Criticism, Essays, Poetry, Religion - Buddhist, Social Sciences, Sociology, Women's Studies
ISBN Prefix(es): 955-560
Branch Office(s)
Hiniduma

Trumpet Publishers (Pvt) Ltd+
A-4, Perahera Mawatha, Colombo 3
Tel: (01) 447622
Web Site: www.lankawebdirectory.com
Specialize in printing.
ISBN Prefix(es): 955-565
Parent Company: T F & I Printers
Associate Companies: Tanatha Finance & Investment Co Ltd

Unigraphics (Pte) Ltd
732, Maradana Rd, Colombo 10
Tel: (01) 694538 *Fax:* (01) 693731
E-mail: uni.graphics@lanka.ccom.lk
ISBN Prefix(es): 955-619

Vidura Science Publishers
55/A First Lane, Medawelikada Rd, Rajagiriya
Tel: (091) 564713
Subjects: Science (General)
ISBN Prefix(es): 955-567
Subsidiaries: Anura C Printers

Warna Publishers+
Aluth Rd, Wennappuwa
Subjects: Chemistry, Chemical Engineering, Government, Political Science, Mathematics, Science (General), Science Fiction, Fantasy
ISBN Prefix(es): 955-9375
Branch Office(s)
New Rd, Wennappuwa
Distributed by Godage Bookshop; Gunasena Book Shop; Lake House Book Shop

Waruni Publishers+
72/15 A Second Lane, Pushpanada Mawatha, Kandy
Tel: (08) 24370 *Fax:* (08) 32343
Telex: 22787 Matsui CE
Key Personnel
Man Dir: K P Vimala Jharma
Subjects: Agriculture, Biography, Genealogy
ISBN Prefix(es): 955-566

Sudan

General Information

Capital: Khartoum
Language: Arabic (official), English also used
Religion: Muslims (north), Animists or Christians (south)
Population: 28.3 million
Bank Hours: 0830-1200 Sunday-Thursday
Shop Hours: 0800-1300, 1700-2000 Saturday-Thursday
Currency: 1,000 milliemes = 100 piastres = 1 Sudanese pound
Export/Import Information: No tariff on books; some advertising matter may be dutied. Import licenses required. Exchange controls; annual foreign exchange budget.

ACADI, see Arab Organization for Agricultural Development

AOAD, see Arab Organization for Agricultural Development

Arab Center for Agricultural Documentation, see Arab Organization for Agricultural Development

Arab Organization for Agricultural Development
St No 7 Amarat, Khartoum 11111
Mailing Address: PO Box 474, Khartoum
Tel: (011) 78760; (011) 78761; (011) 78762; (011) 78763 *Fax:* (011) 471402
E-mail: inquiry@aoad.org; info@aoad.org
Web Site: www.aoad.org
Telex: 22554SD *Cable:* AOAD
Founded: 1970
Parent Company: Arab League

Al-Ayam Press Co Ltd
Aboul Ela Bldgs, United Nations Sq, Khartoum
Mailing Address: PO Box 363, Khartoum
Web Site: www.alayam.com
Key Personnel
Man Dir: Beshir Muhammad Said
Founded: 1953
Subjects: Fiction, Nonfiction (General), Poetry

Khartoum University Press
Elbarlaman St, Khartoum
Mailing Address: PO Box 321, Khartoum
Tel: (011) 80558; (011) 81806 *Fax:* (011) 870558
Web Site: www.khartoumuniversity.edu
Key Personnel
Man Dir, General Editor: Ali El-Mak
Sales Manager: Abdel Raham Ibrahim
Editorial, Rights & Permissions: Jamal Abdel Malik; Judy El-Nagar
Founded: 1968
Subjects: Biography, Ethnicity, Fiction, History, Nonfiction (General), Philosophy, Poetry, Religion - Other, Science (General), Social Sciences, Sociology, Technology
Bookshop(s): University of Khartoum Bookshop

Suriname

General Information

Capital: Paramaribo
Language: Dutch. Hindustani and Javanese also spoken
Religion: Christian, Hindu & Islamic
Population: 410,000
Bank Hours: 0730-1400 Monday-Friday
Shop Hours: 0730-1630 Monday-Friday; 0730-1300 Saturday
Currency: 100 cents = 1 Suriname gulden or florin
Export/Import Information: No tariff on books except children's picture books; none on small quantities of advertising matter. Added taxes charged. Import licenses liberally granted. Exchange controls.
Copyright: Berne (see Copyright Conventions, pg xi)

Apollo's Reklame en Uitgeversburo
Toreniastraat 3, Paramaribo
Mailing Address: PO Box 574, Paramaribo
ISBN Prefix(es): 99914-908

NV Drukkerij Eldorado
Eldoradolaan 1, Paramaribo
Tel: (0597) 472362
ISBN Prefix(es): 99914-51

Groto Publikasi
Moengostr 75, Paramaribo
Tel: (0597) 493569
Specialize in Dutch & Suriname language publications.
ISBN Prefix(es): 99914-914

R Ishaak
Oranje Nassaustr 72, Nieuw Nickerie
Tel: 031917 *Fax:* 0231917
ISBN Prefix(es): 99914-924

C Kersten & Co
Steenbakkerijstraat 27, Paramaribo
Tel: 471150 *Fax:* 472320
E-mail: kersten@sr.net
Web Site: www.kersten.sr
Telex: 142
ISBN Prefix(es): 99914-52

Lutchman, Drs LFS+
Elizelaan 10, Paramaribo
Tel: 465558; 44/453419
Key Personnel
Editor & Author: Sylvia Singh
Specialize in Poetry.
Subjects: Fiction, Poetry
ISBN Prefix(es): 99914-918
Associate Companies: Buitenweg; Handelsdrukkery; dr S Redmondstr 70
Bookshop(s): Vaco NV, Domineestr 26-32, Paramaribo; C Kersten & Co, NV-Steenbakkerij str 27

Mavis A Noordwijk
Regentessestr 3, Paramaribo
Mailing Address: PO Box 2653, Paramaribo
Tel: (0597) 479402
ISBN Prefix(es): 99914-907

Dr C D Ooft
Dr H D Benjaminstr 28, Paramaribo
Tel: (0597) 499139
ISBN Prefix(es): 99914-910

Orchid Press
PO Box 28, Paramaribo
ISBN Prefix(es): 99914-904

Pro Media Productions
Domineestr 12 boven, Paramaribo
Tel: 479355
ISBN Prefix(es): 99914-912

Publishing Services Suriname (Gowtu Stari Publishing)+
Van Idsingastraat 133, Paramaribo
Tel: (0598) 472746; (0598) 455792 *Fax:* (0598) 410366
E-mail: pssmoniz@sr.net
Web Site: www.parbo.com
Key Personnel
Author, Publisher: I Krishnadath
Illustration, Publisher: A Slyngard
Founded: 1992
Specialize in Children's Books, Educational Matters, Surinamese literature.
ISBN Prefix(es): 99914-915; 99914-920; 99914-928
Total Titles: 20 Print
Associate Companies: Uitgeverij Lees Mee

Educatieve Uitgeverij Sorava
Latourweg 10, Paramaribo
Tel: 483879
Web Site: www.icpcredit.com
ISBN Prefix(es): 99914-906; 99914-57

Stichting Kinderkrant Suriname
PO Box 3013, Paramaribo
ISBN Prefix(es): 99914-53

Stichting Volksboekwinkel
Keizerstr 197, Paramaribo
Mailing Address: PO Box 3040, Paramaribo
Tel: 472469
ISBN Prefix(es): 99914-901; 99914-4

Stichting Wetenschappelijke Informatie+
Prins Hendrikstr 38, Paramaribo
Tel: 475232 *Fax:* 422195
E-mail: swin@sr.net
Key Personnel
Man Dir, Editorial, Production, Publicity: J K Menke
Sales: W Boedhoe
Founded: 1977
Subjects: Anthropology, Developing Countries, Ethnicity, Government, Political Science, History, Labor, Industrial Relations, Literature, Literary Criticism, Essays, Science (General), Social Sciences, Sociology, Women's Studies
ISBN Prefix(es): 99914-900
Distributor for Local Surinamese Publications

Vaco, *imprint of* Vaco NV Uitgeversmij

Vaco NV Uitgeversmij+
Domineestr 32 Boven, Paramaribo
Mailing Address: PO Box 1841, Paramaribo
Tel: (0597) 472545 *Fax:* (0597) 10563
E-mail: interf@sr.net
Telex: 123 INCO SN
Key Personnel
Man Dir: E Hogenboom
Publisher: J Trotman
Founded: 1952
Subjects: History, Regional Interests
ISBN Prefix(es): 99914-0
Parent Company: Interfund NV
Imprints: Vaco

Drs F H R Oedayrajsingh Varma+
PO Box 9192, Paramaribo
Key Personnel
Dir: Dr Ferdinand H Varma
Subjects: Regional Interests
ISBN Prefix(es): 99914-903
Branch Office(s)
Postbus 70225, 1007 KE Amsterdam, Netherlands
Tel: (020) 628163

M Waagmeester-Verkuyl
Naarstr 4, Paramaribo

Mailing Address: PO Box 9166, Paramaribo
Tel: (0597) 498356
ISBN Prefix(es): 99914-905; 99914-88

Swaziland

General Information

Capital: Mbabane
Language: Siswati, English used in business
Religion: Christian (about 60%), most others follow traditional beliefs
Population: 913,000
Bank Hours: Until 1100 Saturday
Shop Hours: 0700-1800
Currency: 100 cents = 1 lilangeni = 1 South African rand
Export/Import Information: Same as South Africa.

Boleswa, *imprint of* Macmillan Boleswa Publishers (Pty) Ltd

Macmillan Boleswa Publishers (Pty) Ltd
Plot 230/231, First Ave, Matsapa Industrial Estate, Manzini
Mailing Address: PO Box 1235, Manzini
Tel: 84533 *Fax:* 85247
E-mail: macmillan@iafrica.sz
Web Site: www.macmillansa.co.za; www.macmillan-africa.com
Telex: 2221 MACSW WD
Key Personnel
Man Dir: Elias Nwandwe
Founded: 1978
Subjects: Education
ISBN Prefix(es): 0-333; 0-7978
Parent Company: Macmillan Publishers Ltd, United Kingdom
Imprints: Boleswa
Subsidiaries: Macmillan Swaziland National Publishing Co; Macmillan Botswana Publishing Co
Branch Office(s)
Matsapa

Sweden

General Information

Capital: Stockholm
Language: Swedish. Some Finnish and Lapp also spoken
Religion: Evangelical Lutheran Church of Sweden
Population: 8.8 million
Bank Hours: 0930-1500 Monday-Friday
Shop Hours: 0900-1800 Monday-Friday (later Friday); 0900-1400 or 1600 Saturday
Currency: 100 oere = 1 Swedish korona
Export/Import Information: Member of the European Free Trade Association. No tariff on books. Advertising tax. 25% VAT on books. No import licenses. No exchange controls.
Copyright: UCC, Berne, Florence (see Copyright Conventions, pg xi)

Bokforlaget Atlantis AB+
Sturegatan 24, 11436 Stockholm
Tel: (08) 7830440 *Fax:* (08) 6617285
E-mail: mail@atlantis-publishers.se *Cable:* ATLANTISBOOKS
Key Personnel
Man Dir: Kjell Peterson
Production: Lennart Rolf
Marketing Dir & Rights & Permissions: Hans Bjornell
Founded: 1977
Subjects: Art, Cookery, Fiction, Health, Nutrition, History, Nonfiction (General)
ISBN Prefix(es): 91-7486
Associate Companies: Clio History Book Club
Book Club(s): Clio History Book Club

Acta Universitatis Gothoburgensis
Renstroemsgatan 4, 405 30 Gothenburg
Mailing Address: Box 222, Gothenburg 405 30
Tel: (031) 7731000 *Fax:* (031) 163797
E-mail: library@ub.gu.se
Web Site: www.ub.gu.se
Key Personnel
Man Dir: Jon Erik Norstrand
Publishes only works produced at or connected with Goteborg University.
Subjects: Art, Education, Language Arts, Linguistics, Literature, Literary Criticism, Essays, Social Sciences, Sociology, Women's Studies
ISBN Prefix(es): 91-7346
Parent Company: Goeteborgs Universitetsbibliotek

Akademiforlaget Corona AB
Box 5, 201 20 Malmo
Tel: (040) 286161 *Fax:* (040) 286162
E-mail: kundservice@cor.se
Web Site: www.cor.se
Key Personnel
Man Dir: Lars Welinder *E-mail:* lars.welinder@cor.se
Founded: 1961
Subjects: Education, Fiction, Nonfiction (General)
ISBN Prefix(es): 91-564; 91-7034

Akademiforlaget Goteborgslitteratur+
Esselte Studium, 402 23 Gothenburg
Mailing Address: Box 5103, 402 23 Gothenburg
Tel: (031) 81 34 10 *Fax:* (031) 81 14 92
E-mail: sales@akg.se
Key Personnel
Dir: Sven Holmberg
Founded: 1990
Subjects: Behavioral Sciences, Cookery, Education, English as a Second Language, Human Relations, Language Arts, Linguistics, Mathematics, Medicine, Nursing, Dentistry, Music, Dance, Philosophy, Technology
ISBN Prefix(es): 91-24

Albert Bonniers Forlag+
Division of The Bonnier Group
Box 3159, 103 63 Stockholm
Tel: (08) 696 86 20 *Fax:* (08) 696 8369; (08) 696 8347
E-mail: info@abforlag.bonnier.se
Web Site: www.albertbonniersforlag.com
Key Personnel
Publisher: Eva Bonnier
Man Dir: Kerstin Angelin
Rights & Permissions: Teresa Carlstrom
Founded: 1837
Publishing House.
Subjects: Fiction, Nonfiction (General)
ISBN Prefix(es): 91-7458; 91-0; 91-34; 91-85015
Parent Company: Bonnierforlagen AB

Alfabeta Bokforlag AB+
Svartensgatan 6, Stockholm
Mailing Address: PO Box 4284, 102 66 Stockholm
Tel: (08) 714 36 30 *Fax:* (08) 643 24 31
E-mail: info@alfamedia.se
Web Site: www.alfamedia.se *Cable:* ALFABETA STOCKHOLM
Key Personnel
Man Dir, Rights & Permissions: Dag Hernried
Sales & Production: Lena Spaulding
E-mail: lena@alfamedia.se
Founded: 1976
Subjects: Art, Ethnicity, Fiction, Film, Video, Music, Dance, Nonfiction (General), Psychology, Psychiatry, Travel
ISBN Prefix(es): 91-7712; 91-85328
Subsidiaries: Gammafon AB (audio cassettes)

Allt om Hobby AB+
Box 90133, 120 21 Stockholm
Tel: (08) 99 93 33 *Fax:* (08) 99 88 66
E-mail: order@hobby.se
Web Site: www.hobby.se
Key Personnel
Publisher: Freddy Stenbom *E-mail:* freddy.stenbom@hobby.se
Founded: 1966
Subjects: Aeronautics, Aviation, Communications, Crafts, Games, Hobbies, Electronics, Electrical Engineering, History, Maritime, Military Science, Photography, Transportation
ISBN Prefix(es): 91-85496; 91-7243
Book Club(s): Allt om Hobbys Bokklubb; Flygboklubben

Almquist & Wiksell, *imprint of* Liber AB

Almqvist och Wiksell International
PO Box 7634, 10394 Stockholm
Tel: (08) 613 61 00 *Fax:* (08) 24 25 43
E-mail: scand.mongr@awi.se
Web Site: www.akademibokhandeln.se
Key Personnel
Dir: Mats Thomasson
Sales Manager: Hans Linder
Affiliated to the Akademibokhandeln Group & publishers to the universities of Stockholm, Uppsala & Lund.
Subjects: Science (General)
ISBN Prefix(es): 91-22

Apotekarsocietetens Forlag
PO Box 1136, 111 81 Stockholm
Tel: (08) 7235000 *Fax:* (08) 205511
Key Personnel
Man Dir: Yvonne Andersson *E-mail:* andersson.y@swepharm.se

AB Arcanum+
Tollestorpsvagen 2H, S-443 03 Stenkullen
Tel: (0302) 242 70 *Fax:* (0302) 242 73
E-mail: info@arcanum-utbildning.se
Web Site: www.arcanum-utbildning.se
Key Personnel
Man Dir: Bo Ramme
Founded: 1970
Subjects: Medicine, Nursing, Dentistry
ISBN Prefix(es): 91-85690

Arkitektur Forlag AB
Fishargatan 8, 10266 Stockholm
Mailing Address: PO Box 4296, 10266 Stockholm
Tel: (08) 7027850 *Fax:* (08) 6115270
E-mail: redaktionen@arkitektur.se
Web Site: www.arkitektur.se
Key Personnel
Contact: Marianne Lundqvist *E-mail:* marianne.lundqvist@arkitektur.se
Founded: 1901
Subjects: Architecture & Interior Design
ISBN Prefix(es): 91-86050
Number of titles published annually: 4 Print

Bokforlaget Axplock+
Eskilsgatan 12B, 645 30 Strangnas
Mailing Address: Box 100, 645 22 Strangnas
Tel: (0152) 150 60 *Fax:* (0152) 151 40
E-mail: post@axplock.se
Web Site: www.axplock.se

Key Personnel
Publisher: Hans Richter
Founded: 1985
Subjects: Drama, Theater, Fiction, Gardening, Plants, History, How-to, Humor, Language Arts, Linguistics, Music, Dance, Mysteries, Nonfiction (General), Poetry, Self-Help
ISBN Prefix(es): 91-86436
Number of titles published annually: 10 Print
Total Titles: 90 Print

BBB Bokklubben Bra Bocker, *imprint of* Bokforlaget Bra Bocker AB

Berghs
PO Box 45084, 104 30 Stockholm
Tel: (08) 31 65 59 *Fax:* (08) 32 77 45
E-mail: info@berghsforlag.se
Web Site: www.berghsforlag.se
Key Personnel
Chairman: Anders Oehman
Man Dir: Carl Hafstroem
Editorial Dir: Eva Vider
Founded: 1954
Subjects: Crafts, Games, Hobbies, Nonfiction (General)
ISBN Prefix(es): 91-502
Orders to: Foerlagssystem, PO Box 30195, 10425 Stockholm *Tel:* (08) 6574510

BBT Bhaktivedanta Book Trust
c/o ISKCON, Korsnas gard, 147 92 Grodinge
Tel: (08) 530 257 72
E-mail: p.huy@t-online.de
Subjects: Cookery, Music, Dance, Philosophy, Religion - Hindu, Religion - Other
ISBN Prefix(es): 91-7149; 91-85580
U.S. Office(s): BBT, 3764 Watseka Ave, Los Angeles, CA 90034, United States *Tel:* 310-836-2676

Bibliotekstjaenst AB
Traktorvaegen 11, 221 82 Lund
Mailing Address: PO Box 200, 221 82 Lund
Tel: (046) 18 00 00 *Fax:* (046) 18 01 25
E-mail: btj@btj.se
Web Site: www.btj.se
Telex: 32200 btjlund s
Founded: 1951
Subjects: Library & Information Sciences
ISBN Prefix(es): 91-7018
Associate Companies: BTJ Europe, Belgium; BTJ Inc, United States; BTJ Norge, Norway
Subsidiaries: BTJ Tryck AB
Divisions: BTJ Database; BTJ Media

Bonnier Audio+
Box 3159, 103 63 Stockholm
Tel: (08) 6968700 *Fax:* (08) 6968757
E-mail: info@bonnieraudio.se
Web Site: www.bonnieraudio.se
Key Personnel
President & Publisher: Christina Andersson
    E-mail: christina.andersson@bonnieraudio.se
Founded: 1986
Specialize in audio books.
Subjects: Fiction
ISBN Prefix(es): 91-7950
Number of titles published annually: 35 Print
Total Titles: 350 Print
Parent Company: Bonnierfoerlagen

Bonnier Carlsen Bokforlag AB
Drottninggatan 82, 11183 Stockholm
Tel: (08) 59895500 *Fax:* (08) 59895545
Key Personnel
Man Dir: Pentti Molander
Sales: Johnny Gustafsson
Founded: 1968
Subjects: Animals, Pets, Erotica, Fiction, History, Mysteries, Romance, Science Fiction, Fantasy, Social Sciences, Sociology, Sports, Athletics, Cartoons, Child care, Comics, Fantasy, Fairy tales, Adventure, Classics, Health, Holidays, Horror & Ghost, Love & Sexuality, Social Situations
ISBN Prefix(es): 91-510; 91-48; 91-638
Parent Company: Bonnierforlagen AB

Bonnier Utbildning AB
Sveavagen 56, 103 63 Stockholm
Mailing Address: PO Box 3159, 103 63 Stockholm
Tel: (08) 696 85 90 *Fax:* (08) 696 86 55
E-mail: info@bonnierutbildning.se
Web Site: www.bonnierutbildning.se
Key Personnel
Publisher: Lars Malmius
Founded: 1987
Specialize in schoolbooks.
ISBN Prefix(es): 91-622
Parent Company: Bonnierforlagen AB

Albert Bonniers Forlag AB
PO Box 3159, 103 63 Stockholm
Tel: (08) 696 86 20 *Fax:* (08) 696 83 61
E-mail: info@abforlag.bonnier.se
Web Site: www.albertbonniersforlag.se *Cable:* BONNIERS
Key Personnel
Man Dir: Kerstin Angelin
Publishing Dir: Eva Bonnier
Publisher: Karl Otto Bonnier
Rights & Permissions & Production: Arne Bjoerkman
Rights & Permissions: Teresa Carlstroem
Production: Robert Hedberg
Publicity: Ingela Palmquist; Carina Soederman
Subjects: Art, Cookery, Fiction, Nonfiction (General)
ISBN Prefix(es): 91-0
Parent Company: Bonnierfoerlagen AB
Warehouse: Samdistribution, PO Box 449, S-19104 Sollentuna

BOOX+
Kammakargatan 35, 111 60 Stockholm
Tel: (08) 411 37 00 *Fax:* (08) 411 53 30
E-mail: transbok@algonet.se
Key Personnel
Editor & Man Dir: Monica Norberg
Photographer & Picture Editor: Michel Hjorth
Designer: Bo Ljungstrom
Founded: 1998
Packagers of ideas for the international publishing world.
Subjects: Art, Cookery, Crafts, Games, Hobbies, Gardening, Plants, Nonfiction (General), Photography, Wine & Spirits
ISBN Prefix(es): 91-973496
Total Titles: 1 Print

Bokforlaget Bra Bocker AB
Box 890, 201 80 Malmo
Tel: (040) 665 46 00 *Fax:* (040) 665 46 22
E-mail: kundservice@bbb.se
Web Site: www.bbb.se
Key Personnel
President & Marketing: Rolf Nilstam
Vice President, Production: Janson Anders
Editorial, Encyclopedia: Christer Engstoem
Editorial, Nonfiction: Lillemor Eagle
Editorial, Fiction: Goeran Green Claes
Founded: 1965
Subjects: Fiction, Geography, Geology, History
ISBN Prefix(es): 91-7024; 91-7119; 91-7133
Parent Company: International Masters Publishers AB, PO Box 814, 201 80 Malmoe
Imprints: BBB Bokklubben Bra Bocker

Brombergs Bokforlag AB+
Hantverkargatan 26, 112 98 Stockholm
Mailing Address: Box 12 886, 112 98 Stockholm
Tel: (08) 562 62 080 *Fax:* (08) 562 62 085
E-mail: info@brombergs.se
Web Site: www.brombergs.se
Telex: 12442 Fotex Bropublish S
Key Personnel
Man Dir, Publicity: Dorotea Bromberg
Production, Rights & Permissions: Ylva Aaberg
    E-mail: ylva.aberg@brombergs.se
Founded: 1973
Subjects: Fiction, Nonfiction (General)
ISBN Prefix(es): 91-7608
Number of titles published annually: 25 Print

Forlaget By och Bygd
PO Box 22087, 104 22 Stockholm
Tel: (08) 652 09 55
Key Personnel
Man Dir: Asa-Britt Karlsson
Subjects: Government, Political Science, Social Sciences, Sociology
ISBN Prefix(es): 91-85354

Byggforlaget+
Narvavaegen 19, 114 81 Stockholm
Mailing Address: PO Box 5456, 114 81 Stockholm
Tel: (08) 665 36 50 *Fax:* (08) 667 39 49
Web Site: www.byggforlaget.se
Key Personnel
Man Dir: Claes Dymling *Tel:* (08) 6653670
    E-mail: claes@byggforlaget.se
Founded: 1948
Subjects: Architecture & Interior Design
ISBN Prefix(es): 91-85194; 91-7988

Calago Foerlag, *imprint of* Ordfront Foerlag AB

Carlsson Bokfoerlag AB+
Stora Nygatan 31, 111 27 Stockholm
Tel: (08) 411 23 49 *Fax:* (08) 796 84 57
Key Personnel
Man Dir: Trygve Carlsson
Founded: 1983
Subjects: Anthropology, Art, Government, Political Science, History, Journalism, Literature, Literary Criticism, Essays, Travel, Women's Studies, Ethnology
ISBN Prefix(es): 91-7798; 91-7203
Warehouse: Foerlagssystem, Loevasvagen 26, 791 45 Falun

Citadell, *imprint of* Raben och Sjoegren Bokforlag

Rene Coeckelberghs Bokfoerlag AB
PO Box 45059, 104 30 Stockholm
Tel: (08) 7230880 *Fax:* (08) 7230311
Telex: 14277 reco S
Key Personnel
Man Dir: Rene Coeckelberghs
Subjects: Fiction, Nonfiction (General), Poetry
ISBN Prefix(es): 91-7250; 91-7103; 91-7212; 91-7640

Combi International AB, see Forlagshuset Norden AB

Bokforlaget Cordia AB+
Box 1723, 701 17 Orebro
Tel: (019) 333850 *Fax:* (019) 333859
E-mail: forlaget@cordia.se
Web Site: www.cordia.se
Key Personnel
President: Lars-G Stahl
Publisher: Goran Rask *E-mail:* g.rask@verbum.se
Founded: 1995
Subjects: History, Human Relations, Nonfiction (General), Spirituality
ISBN Prefix(es): 91-7085; 91-86082; 91-7080

PUBLISHERS

SWEDEN

Parent Company: Verbum AB
Associate Companies: Foerlagshuset Gothia; Gleerups Foerlag; Verbum Foerlag

Dahlia Books, International Publishers & Booksellers
Box 1025, 751 40 Uppsala
Tel: (018) 101098 *Fax:* (018) 100525
E-mail: dahlia@telia.com
Founded: 1973
Major function of this company is bookselling (antiquarian & new).
ISBN Prefix(es): 91-974094

Delta Forlags AB
Box 15123, 161 15 Bromma
Tel: (08) 25 47 81
Founded: 1973
Subjects: Fiction, Nonfiction (General), Science (General)
ISBN Prefix(es): 91-7228
Book Club(s): Delta Science Fiction Bok Klubb

Egmont Serieforlaget
Oestra Foerstadsgatan 34, 20508 Malmo
Tel: (040) 6939400 *Fax:* (040) 6939498
E-mail: egmont@egmont.com
Web Site: www.egmont.com
Telex: 32449 Hemmet S
Founded: 1920
Subjects: Fiction, Human Relations, Cartoons, Comics
ISBN Prefix(es): 91-7300; 91-7674; 91-7912
Parent Company: Gutenberghus Group, Denmark
Associate Companies: Ehapa-Verlag GmbH, Germany; Gutenberghus Publishing Service A/S, Denmark; NW Damm og Son A/S, Norway
Book Club(s): Part-owner of Kalle Ankas Pocket

Ekelunds Forlag AB+
Rasundav 160, 169 02 Solna
Mailing Address: PO Box 2050, 169 02 Solna
Tel: (08) 821320 *Fax:* (08) 832956
E-mail: education@ekelunds.se
Key Personnel
Contact: Marit Ekelund
Founded: 1981
Subjects: Education, English as a Second Language
ISBN Prefix(es): 91-7724; 91-646

Liber Ekonomi, *imprint of* Liber AB

Ekonomibok Forlag AB
Groentevaegen 5, 254 84 Helsingborg
Tel: (042) 929 50 *Fax:* (042) 929 50
Key Personnel
Man Dir: Maj-Britt Hallgren *E-mail:* hallgren@ekonomibok.se
Founded: 1973
Subjects: Business, Fiction, Finance
ISBN Prefix(es): 91-86406

Ellerstroms+
Fredsgatan 6, 222 20 Lund
Tel: (046) 323295 *Fax:* (046) 323295
E-mail: info@ellerstroms.se
Web Site: www.ellerstroms.se
Key Personnel
Editor: Erik Magnotorn *E-mail:* erik@ellerstroms.se
Founded: 1983
Publisher of fiction, prose & poetry. Swedish & translations.
Subjects: Fiction, Literature, Literary Criticism, Essays, Poetry
Number of titles published annually: 20 Print
Total Titles: 220 Print
Distribution Center: Postservice *Tel:* (411) 45400 *Fax:* (411) 45401

Energica Foerlags AB/Halsabocker+
PO Box 8, 794 93 Orsa
Tel: (0250) 55 20 00 *Fax:* (0250) 43191
Web Site: www.energica.com
Key Personnel
Man Dir: Monica Katarina Frisk
    E-mail: monica@energica.se
Founded: 1985
Subjects: Health, Nutrition, Psychology, Psychiatry
ISBN Prefix(es): 91-87056
Total Titles: 50 Print
Parent Company: Energica Foerlags AB

Eriksson & Lindgren Bokforlag+
St Eriksgatan 14, 102 23 Stockholm
Mailing Address: PO Box 12085, 102 23 Stockholm
Tel: (08) 6523226; (08) 6523227 *Fax:* (08) 6523223
E-mail: info@eriksson-lindgren.se
Key Personnel
Publisher & Man Dir: Claes Eriksson
Publisher: Marianne Eriksson
Founded: 1989
Subjects: Child Care & Development
ISBN Prefix(es): 91-87804; 91-87805; 91-87803; 91-85199
Number of titles published annually: 30 Print

Bokforlaget Fingraf AB+
PO Box 4084, 151 04 Soedertaelje
Tel: (08) 550 300 23 *Fax:* (08) 550 695 70
Key Personnel
Man Dir: Ossi Nikula
Editorial: Eivor Nikula
Founded: 1979
Subjects: Fiction, Humor, Medicine, Nursing, Dentistry
ISBN Prefix(es): 91-85964; 91-88556
Associate Companies: Fingraf Bookprinters AB, Forradsvagen 8, Box 4084, S-151 04 Soedertalje

Fischer & Co+
Norrlandsgatan 15, 111 43 Stockholm
Tel: (08) 242160 *Fax:* (08) 247825
E-mail: bokforlaget@fischer-co.se
Web Site: www.fischer-co.se
Key Personnel
Man Dir: Sara Nillson *E-mail:* sara@fischer-co.se
Founded: 1969
Subjects: Biography, Fiction, History, Nonfiction (General)
ISBN Prefix(es): 91-7054
Total Titles: 1 Audio
Book Club(s): Bockernas Klubb

Forlagshuset Norden AB+
PO Box 305, 201 23 Malmoe
Tel: (040) 93 42 50 *Fax:* (040) 93 01 56
Founded: 1931
ISBN Prefix(es): 91-86442
Subsidiaries: Combi International AB

Folkuniversitetets foerlag+
Magle Lilla Kyrkogata 4, 223 51 Lund
Tel: (046) 148720 *Fax:* (046) 132904
E-mail: info@folkuniversitetetsforlag.se
Web Site: www.folkuniversitetetsforlag.se
Key Personnel
Man Dir: Goran Fasth
Editorial, Production, Rights & Permissions: Kristin Nilsson
Sales, Publicity, Editor: Annalisa Mikaelsson
Founded: 1971
Subjects: Education, Language Arts, Linguistics
ISBN Prefix(es): 91-7434
Number of titles published annually: 10 Print
Total Titles: 140 Print

Foreningen Svenska Laromedelsproducenter (The Swedish Association of Educational Publishers)
Drottninggatan 97, 2tr, 113 60 Stockholm
Tel: (08) 736 19 40 *Fax:* (08) 736 19 44
E-mail: fsl@fsl.se
Web Site: www.fsl.se
Key Personnel
Man Dir: Lena Westerberg *Tel:* (08) 7361943
    E-mail: lena.westerberg@forlagskansli.se
Founded: 1974
ISBN Prefix(es): 91-85386

Bengt Forsbergs Foerlag AB+
Soedra Tullgatan 4, 211 40 Malmoe
Tel: (040) 763 20 *Fax:* (040) 303939
E-mail: info@forsbergsforlag.se
Web Site: www.forsbergsforlag.se *Cable:* GODBOK
Key Personnel
Man Dir: Joergen Forsberg
Rights: Claes Forsberg
Sales Dir: Matts Forsberg
Founded: 1944
Specialize in telephone sales.
Subjects: Animals, Pets, Art, History, Medicine, Nursing, Dentistry, Photography
ISBN Prefix(es): 91-7046
Subsidiaries: Editions Corniche

Bokforlaget Forum AB+
Gamla Brogatan 26, 107 23 Stockholm
Mailing Address: PO Box 70321, 107 23 Stockholm
Tel: (08) 696 84 40; (08) 6968410 (Orders)
    Fax: (08) 696 83 67
Key Personnel
Publisher, Man Dir: Karin Leijon
Publisher, Editorial: Viveca Peterson
Information: Anneli Eldh
Marketing: Irene Westin Ahlgren
Rights & Permissions: Birgitta Lindgren
Production: Bengt Permatz
Sr Editor: Kerstin Bergfors; Karin Linge Nordh
Founded: 1944
Subjects: Fiction, Nonfiction (General)
ISBN Prefix(es): 91-37
Parent Company: Bonnierforlagen

C E Fritzes AB
10647 Stockholm
Tel: (08) 6909190 *Fax:* (08) 6909191
E-mail: order.fritzes@liber.se
Web Site: www.fritzes.se
Key Personnel
Man Dir: Christer Bunge-Meyer *E-mail:* christer.bunge-meyer@liber.se
Founded: 1837
Official publications from Swedish government & authorities.
ISBN Prefix(es): 91-38
Parent Company: Wolters Kluwer Scandinavia
Orders to: Kundtjaenst, S-10647 Stockholm

Gedins Forlag+
Tysta Gatan 10, 115 20 Stockholm
Tel: (08) 662 15 51 *Fax:* (08) 6637073
E-mail: gedins@perigab.se
Key Personnel
Publisher: Per I Gedin
Founded: 1987
Subjects: Fiction, Nonfiction (General)
ISBN Prefix(es): 91-7964
Book Club(s): Part-owner of Manadens Bok
Orders to: Sam Distribution, PO Box 449, 19124 Sollentuna *Tel:* (08) 6968400 *Fax:* (08) 6968358

SK-Gehrmans Musikforlag AB+
Haelsingegatan 1, 102 31 Stockholm
Mailing Address: Box 6005, 102 31 Stockholm
Tel: (08) 6100600 *Fax:* (08) 6100628

E-mail: order@sk-gehrmans.se
Web Site: www.sk-gehrmans.se
Key Personnel
Man Dir: Kettil Skarby *E-mail:* kettil.skarby@sk-gehrmans.se
Secretary: Cecilia Strom *E-mail:* cecilia.strom@sk-gehrmans.se
Founded: 1999
Music publisher
Orchestral parts rental.
Subjects: Music, Dance, Folk music & ballads, music with Christian lyrics accordion music, orchestral music for brass & woodwinds, contemporary music, classical music, music for choirs, educational publications, sheet music publications & compilations, sheet whole sale distributions & printing plant
ISBN Prefix(es): 91-7748

Gidlunds Bokforlag
PO Box 123, 776 23 Hedemora
Tel: (0225) 77 11 55 *Fax:* (0255) 77 11 65
E-mail: utgivning@gidlunds.se
Web Site: www.gidlunds.se
Key Personnel
Man Dir: Krister Gidlund
Founded: 1984
Subjects: Art, Biography, History, Philosophy, Social Sciences, Sociology
ISBN Prefix(es): 91-7844

Foerlagshuset Gothia (Gothia Publishing House)+
Box 15169, 104 65 Stockholm
Tel: (08) 4622660 *Fax:* (08) 4620322
E-mail: info.gothia@verbum.se
Web Site: www.gothia.nu
Key Personnel
President, Publisher & Man Dir: Olle Sundling *E-mail:* olle.sundling@verbum.se
Rights & Permissions: Agneta Lundin
Founded: 1985
Subjects: Child Care & Development, Education, Health, Nutrition, Medicine, Nursing, Dentistry, Regional Interests, Social Care
ISBN Prefix(es): 91-526; 91-7205; 91-85174; 91-86028; 91-7728; 91-85232; 91-85660

Gothia Publishing House, see Foerlagshuset Gothia

Hagaberg AB+
PO Box 6471, 113 82 Stockholm
Tel: (08) 690 90 00 *Fax:* (08) 7021940
Key Personnel
Man Dir: Ingrid Olausson
Editorial: Rune Olausson
Founded: 1983
Subjects: Gardening, Plants, Philosophy, Psychology, Psychiatry, Theology
ISBN Prefix(es): 91-86584

Hallgren och Fallgren Studieforlag AB
Skolgatan 3, 753 12 Uppsala
Tel: (018) 50 71 00 *Fax:* (018) 12 72 70
E-mail: info@hallgren-fallgren.se
Web Site: www.hallgren-fallgren.se
Key Personnel
Man Dir, Editorial, Rights & Permissions: Daniel Aberg; Karin Hallgren
Founded: 1973
Subjects: Education, Science (General)
ISBN Prefix(es): 91-7382

Hanseproduktion AB (Hanse Production AB)
Tranhusgatan 29, 621 55 Visby
Tel: (0498) 24 93 18 *Fax:* (0498) 24 93 18
Key Personnel
Chief Executive: Thorbjoern Oedin
Founded: 1978

Subjects: Art, Regional Interests
ISBN Prefix(es): 91-85716

Bokforlaget Hegas AB
Box 201, 263 21 Hoeganaes
Tel: (042) 330 340 *Fax:* (042) 330 141
E-mail: kom.litt@helsingborg.se
Key Personnel
Contact: Lena Hultberg
ISBN Prefix(es): 91-86650; 91-86651; 91-973287; 91-973620; 91-973621

Liber Hermods, *imprint of* Liber AB

Hillelforlaget (Hillel Publishing House)+
Wahreudorfksgutau 3B, 11147 Stockholm
Mailing Address: Box 7427, 10391 Stockholm
Tel: (08) 587 858 04 *Fax:* (08) 587 858 58
Key Personnel
Man Dir: Marina Burstein *E-mail:* marina.burstein@hillel.nu
Founded: 1969
Subjects: Regional Interests, Religion - Jewish
ISBN Prefix(es): 91-85164
Number of titles published annually: 3 Print
Total Titles: 20 Print

Lars Hoekerbergs Bokfoerlag
Fleminggatan 21, S-11226 Stockholm
Tel: (08) 244360 *Fax:* (08) 6503984
E-mail: hokerbook@ebox.tninet.se
Key Personnel
Man Dir: Jan Hoekerberg
Founded: 1882
Subjects: Fiction, Nonfiction (General)
ISBN Prefix(es): 91-7084; 91-7157
Number of titles published annually: 1 Print
Total Titles: 3 Print

Hundskolan i Solleftea AB
Overgard Pl 7015, SE-881 93 Solleftea
Tel: (0620) 832 00 *Fax:* (0620) 832 29
E-mail: gundvald@hundskolan.se
Web Site: www.humanitydog.se
Key Personnel
Contact: Gunvald Andersen
ISBN Prefix(es): 91-971825

ICA bokforlag+
Stora gatan 41, 721 85 Vasteras
Tel: (021) 194278 *Fax:* (021) 194283
E-mail: bok@forlaget.ica.se
Web Site: www.forlaget.ica.se/bok
Telex: 40486 ica s *Cable:* ICAFOeRLAGET
Key Personnel
Publisher: Goran Sunehag *Tel:* (021) 192470 *E-mail:* goran.sunehag@forlaget.ica.se
Rights Manager: Ulla Joneby *E-mail:* ulla.joneby@forlaget.ica.se
Founded: 1945
Subjects: Animals, Pets, Cookery, Crafts, Games, Hobbies, Gardening, Plants, Health, Nutrition, House & Home, How-to, Self-Help
ISBN Prefix(es): 91-534
Number of titles published annually: 70 Print
Total Titles: 450 Print

Idrottsantikvariatet, *imprint of* Stroemberg B&T Forlag AB

Industrilitteratur Vindex, Forlags AB
Industrihuset, Storgatan 19, S-114 85 Stockholm
Mailing Address: Box 5527, 114 85 Stockholm
Tel: (08) 783 81 00 *Fax:* (08) 660 59 11
E-mail: aestan.orstadius@industrilitteratur.se
Founded: 1887
Publications section of the Swedish Trade Council.
Subjects: Ethnicity, Marketing, Public Administration

ISBN Prefix(es): 91-7548
Parent Company: Swedish Trade Council; Federation of Swedish Industry

Informationsfoerlaget AB
Sveavaegen 61, S-113 86 Stockholm
Mailing Address: Box 6884, 113 86 Stockholm
Tel: (08) 34 09 15 *Fax:* (08) 31 39 03
E-mail: red@informationsforlaget.se
Key Personnel
Man Dir: Ulf Heimdahl
Senior Editor: Ylva Aberg
Founded: 1979
Specialize in sponsored books in cooperation with Swedish industry and authorities.
Subjects: Cookery, How-to, Wine & Spirits
ISBN Prefix(es): 91-7736

Ingenjoersforlaget AB+
106 12 Stockholm
Tel: (08) 796 66 90 *Fax:* (08) 22 77 44
E-mail: redaktionen@miljorapporten.se
Telex: 17191 Tecnews S *Cable:* Ingforlag
Key Personnel
Man Dir: Hakan Ryden
Founded: 1970
Subjects: Science (General)
ISBN Prefix(es): 91-7284; 91-85804; 91-973810

Interculture+
Box 4160, 102 62 Stockholm
Tel: (08) 642 78 04 *Fax:* (08) 642 35 91
Telex: 909 Teleopr S attn Intconswed *Cable:* INTCONSWED
Key Personnel
Man Dir: Jan Valdelin
Founded: 1983
Subjects: Fiction, Film, Video
ISBN Prefix(es): 91-86608
Parent Company: ICS Interconsult Sweden A

International Bible Society
Box 205, 524 23 Herrljunga
Tel: (0513) 219 30 *Fax:* (0513) 215 01
Key Personnel
Executive Dir: Hans-Lennart Raask
ISBN Prefix(es): 91-7165; 91-87412
Parent Company: Colorado Springs, CO, United States
Subsidiaries: IBS

Internationella bibelsaellskapet, see International Bible Society

Interskol Forlag AB
Schaktugnsgatan 2, 216 16 Malmoe
Tel: (040) 51 01 95 *Fax:* (040) 15 06 25
E-mail: info@interskol.se
Web Site: www.interskol.se
Key Personnel
Dir: Kenneth Arvidsson
Founded: 1975
Specialize in school books.
ISBN Prefix(es): 91-7306

Invandrarfoerlaget+
Katrinedalsgatan 43, 504 51 Boras
Tel: (033) 13 60 70 *Fax:* (033) 13 60 75
E-mail: migrant@immi.se
Web Site: www.immi.se
Key Personnel
Editor: Miguel Benito
Founded: 1973
Subjects: Education, Ethnicity
ISBN Prefix(es): 91-85242; 91-7906
Number of titles published annually: 4 Print
Total Titles: 140 Print
Parent Company: Immigrant-institute, Katrinedalsgatan 43, 50451 Boras

ITK Laromedel AB+
Box 8071, 104 20 Stockholm

PUBLISHERS
SWEDEN

Tel: (08) 24 43 60 *Fax:* (08) 650 39 84
Key Personnel
Man Dir: Jan Hoekerberg
Contact: Annika Thiam
Founded: 1923
Subjects: Science (General), Technology
ISBN Prefix(es): 91-7084; 91-7157
Associate Companies: Lars Hoekerbergs Bokfoerlag

Iustus Forlag AB
Ostra Agatan 9, 753 22 Uppsala
Tel: (018) 693091 *Fax:* (018) 693099
E-mail: iustus@iustus.se
Web Site: www.iustus.se
Key Personnel
Man Dir: Eva Thorell *Tel:* (018) 693068
  E-mail: eva.thorell@iustus.se
Marketing: Ewa Waites *Tel:* (018) 693063
  E-mail: ewaw@iustus.se
Founded: 1973
Specialize in law books, aimed at both university level & practicing lawyers, judges, civil servants.
Subjects: Business, Economics, Finance, Government, Political Science, Law, Management, Public Administration
ISBN Prefix(es): 91-7678
Number of titles published annually: 40 Print
Total Titles: 200 Print

IVA, see Kungl Ingenjoersvetenskapsakademien (IVA)

Jannersten Forlag AB+
774 27 Avesta
Tel: (0226) 619 00 *Fax:* (0226) 10927
E-mail: bridge@jannersten.se
Web Site: www.jannersten.com
Key Personnel
Dir: Per Jannersten
Founded: 1939
Subjects: Crafts, Games, Hobbies
ISBN Prefix(es): 91-85024

Johnston & Streiffert Editions+
Soedermalmsgatan 35, 431 69 Moelndal
Tel: (031) 826160 *Fax:* (031) 825150
Key Personnel
President: Turlough Johnston *E-mail:* turlough.johnston@swipnet.se
Contact: Eleonore Wagner
Founded: 1985
Also acts as Print Broker & Agent.
Subjects: Animals, Pets, Automotive, Crafts, Games, Hobbies, How-to, Maritime, Sports, Athletics
ISBN Prefix(es): 91-87036
Number of titles published annually: 3 Print
Total Titles: 10 Print
Associate Companies: Streiffert Foerlag, Stockholm
Subsidiaries: Johnston Print Consultants

Liber Kartor, *imprint of* Liber AB

Klassikerforlaget
PO Box 45022, 104 30 Stockholm
Tel: (08) 457 03 00 *Fax:* (08) 457 03 34
E-mail: klassikerforlaget@raben.se
Key Personnel
Editor: Anders Stroem
Founded: 1953
Subjects: Literature, Literary Criticism, Essays
ISBN Prefix(es): 91-7102; 91-88680
Parent Company: P A Norstrdt & Soner AB

Konsultforlaget AB
PO Box 2070, 750 02 Uppsala
Tel: (018) 55 50 80 *Fax:* (018) 55 50 81
E-mail: info@uppsala-publishing.se
Web Site: www.uppsala-publishing.se
Key Personnel
Man Dir: Mats Josephson
ISBN Prefix(es): 91-7005

Kungl Ingenjoersvetenskapsakademien (IVA)
(Royal Swedish Academy of Engineering Sciences)
Grev Turegatan 14, 102 42 Stockholm SE
Mailing Address: PO Box 5073, 102 42 Stockholm
Tel: (08) 7912900 *Fax:* (08) 6115623
E-mail: info@iva.se
Web Site: www.iva.se *Cable:* Ivacademi
Key Personnel
President: Lena Torell
Editorial: Cissi Billgren Askwall
Editor: Eva Reinholdren *E-mail:* er@iva.se
Founded: 1919
Royal Swedish Academy of Engineering Sciences.
Subjects: Management, Science (General), Technology
ISBN Prefix(es): 91-7082

Hans Richter Laromedel+
Box 100, 645 22 Straengnaes
SAN: 105-0893
Tel: (0152) 150 60; (0200) 11 55 30 (orders)
  Fax: (0152) 151 40; (0200) 11 55 31 (orders)
E-mail: info@richter.d.se
Web Site: www.richter.d.se
Key Personnel
Dir: Hans Richter *E-mail:* post@richter.d.se
Founded: 1982
Also acts as Agent; Mail Order Distribution & Direct Marketing to Businesses & Schools.
Membership(s): Swedish Publishers Association; FSL.
Subjects: Education, English as a Second Language, Language Arts, Linguistics, Music, Dance
ISBN Prefix(es): 91-7884
Imprints: Nyforlaget
Subsidiaries: Bokforlaget Axplock
Distributor for Bokforlaget Axplock; Nyforlaget

Bokforlaget Robert Larson AB+
Box 6074, 121 06 Johanneshov
Tel: (08) 732 84 60 *Fax:* (08) 732 71 76
E-mail: info@larsonforlag.se
Web Site: www.larsonforlag.se *Cable:* LARSONBOOKS
Key Personnel
Dir: Birgitta Larson; Joakim Larson; Robert Larson
Founded: 1971
Subjects: Nonfiction (General)
ISBN Prefix(es): 91-514

Legenda, *imprint of* Bokfoerlaget Natur och Kultur

Liber AB+
Rasundavagen 18i Solna, 11398 Stockholm
Tel: (08) 6909200 *Fax:* (08) 6909458
E-mail: export@liber.se; infomaster@liber.se
Web Site: www.liber.se
Key Personnel
President: Jan Thurfell *E-mail:* hedwig.hermanson@liber.se
Subjects: Business, English as a Second Language, Geography, Geology, Health, Nutrition, History, Language Arts, Linguistics, Mathematics, Medicine, Nursing, Dentistry, Science (General), Social Sciences, Sociology, Technology
ISBN Prefix(es): 91-21; 91-40
Parent Company: Wolters Kluwer Scandinavia

Imprints: Almquist & Wiksell; Liber Ekonomi; Liber Hermods; Liber Kartor
Subsidiaries: Liber Distribution; Norstedts Tuvidik

Liber Hermods AB+
Besoksadress Norra Vallgatan 100, 205 10 Malmo
Tel: (040) 258600 *Fax:* (040) 304600
Web Site: www.liberhermods.se
Key Personnel
President: Per Bergknut
Founded: 1898
Specialize in educational & business publishing & distance education.
Membership(s): Euro Business Publishing Network.
ISBN Prefix(es): 91-23

Libris Bokforlaget+
PO Box 1213, 701 12 Oerebro
Tel: (019) 208400 *Fax:* (019) 208430
E-mail: info@libris.se
Web Site: www.libris.se
Key Personnel
Man Dir: Soren Liljedahl *E-mail:* soren.liljedahl@libris.se
Publicity Dir: Anna Stenlund
Rights & Permissions: Inger Lundin
Founded: 1916
Subjects: Fiction, Theology
ISBN Prefix(es): 91-7194
Parent Company: Libris Media AB
Book Club(s): Libris Bok & Musikklubb

Lidman Production AB+
Vaertavaegen 8, 115 24 Stockholm
Tel: (08) 6633615 *Fax:* (08) 6633590
E-mail: lidman@canit.se
Key Personnel
Publisher: Sven Lidman
Founded: 1973
Subjects: Education

Metodistkyrkans Foerlag, see Forlaget Sanctus (Metodistkyrkans Forlag)

Mezopotamya Publishing & Distribution+
Box 4036, 141 04 Huddinge
Tel: (08) 774 73 54 *Fax:* (08) 7110836
Key Personnel
Editor: Nedim Dagdeviren
Specialize in publishing & distribution of Kurdish books, children's books & musical productions.
Subjects: Asian Studies, Ethnicity, History, Language Arts, Linguistics
ISBN Prefix(es): 91-971307

Bokfoerlaget Natur och Kultur+
Karlavaegen 31, 102 54 Stockholm
Mailing Address: PO Box 27323, 102 54 Stockholm
Tel: (08) 4538600 *Fax:* (08) 4538790
E-mail: info@nok.se
Web Site: www.nok.se
Key Personnel
Man Dir & Chief Executive Officer: Lars Grahn
Editorial Dir, Academic Books, Fiction & Nonfiction: Christian Reimers
Editorial Dir, Textbooks: Lars Kaellquist
Rights & Permissions, Children's Books: Johanna Ringertz *E-mail:* johanna.ringertz@nok.se
Rights & Permissions, General Nonfiction & Fiction: Katarina Grip *E-mail:* katarina.grip@nok.se
IT & New Media: Christina Forsberg
Founded: 1922
Subjects: Biography, Fiction, History, Nonfiction (General), Psychology, Psychiatry, Science (General), Social Sciences, Sociology
ISBN Prefix(es): 91-27; 91-582
Number of titles published annually: 350 Print

Total Titles: 5,000 Print; 12 CD-ROM; 60 Audio
Imprints: Legenda (commercial fiction & suspense novels)
Subsidiaries: Natur och Kultur/Fakta etc
Book Club(s): Boeckernas Klubb, Box 3317, 103 66 Stockholm; Natur och Kultur Direkt
Warehouse: Foerlagsdistribution, Skarpraettarvaegen 1, PO Box 706, Jaerfaella 176 27

Natur och Kultur Fakta etc+
Ostermalmsgatan 45, 11426 Stockholm
Mailing Address: Box 27323, 10254 Stockholm
Tel: (08) 4538725 Fax: (08) 4538798
E-mail: info@nok.se
Web Site: www.nok.se
Key Personnel
Man Dir: Rolf Ellnebrand Tel: (08) 4538729 E-mail: rolf.ellnebrand@nok.se
Production Manager: Torbjorn Tesch Tel: (08) 4538728 E-mail: torbjorn.tesch@nok.se
Permissions: Viveka Pettersson Tel: (08) 4538733 E-mail: viveka.pettersson@nok.se
Founded: 1935
Subjects: Agriculture, Animals, Pets, Cookery, Crafts, Games, Hobbies, Gardening, Plants, Health, Nutrition, House & Home, Photography, Science (General)
ISBN Prefix(es): 91-27
Number of titles published annually: 30 Print
Total Titles: 300 Print; 300 Online
Parent Company: Bokfoerlaget Natur och Kultur

Nautiska Foerlaget AB+
Box 15410, 104 65 Stockholm
Tel: (08) 677 00 00 Fax: (08) 677 00 10
E-mail: nautiska.ab@nautiskamf.se Cable: Namco
Key Personnel
Manager: H Hultkrantz
The Nautical Publishing Co Ltd.
Subjects: Maritime
ISBN Prefix(es): 91-970094; 91-89564; 91-973537

Nordiska Bokhandelns
Broetvaegen 32, 161 39 Bromma
Tel: (08) 26 98 09 Fax: (08) 25 42 46 Cable: NORDBOK
Key Personnel
Man Dir: Hans Molander
Founded: 1851
ISBN Prefix(es): 91-516
Bookshop(s): AB Nordiska Bokhandeln

P A Norstedt & Soener AB
PO Box 2052, 10312 Stockholm
Tel: (08) 7893000 Fax: (08) 214006
Key Personnel
Chief Executive: Kjell Bohlund
Contact: Lise-Lott Olofsson Tel: (08) 7698711 E-mail: lise-lott.olofsson@norstedts.se
Founded: 1823
Subsidiaries: Norstedts Forlag; Norstedts Ordbok; Bokforlaget Prisma; Raben & Sjoegren; Tiden
Foreign Rights: Pan Agency
Book Club(s): Barnens Bokklubb (Partially owned); Boeckernas Klubb (Partially owned); Clio (Partially owned); Hem & Tradgard; Manadens Bok (Partially owned); Matt & Njutning

Norstedts Forlag+
Subsidiary of P A Norstedt & Soener AB
PO Box 2052, 103 12 Stockholm
Tel: (08) 769 88 50 Fax: (08) 769 88 64
E-mail: info.norstedts@liber.se
Web Site: www.norstedts.se
Key Personnel
Man Dir: Svante Weyler E-mail: svante.weyler@norstedts.se
Rights & Permissions: Agneta Markas E-mail: agneta.markas@norstedts.se
Secretary: Gerd Ronnberg E-mail: gerd.ronnberg@norstedts.se
Founded: 1823
Subjects: Fiction, Nonfiction (General)
ISBN Prefix(es): 91-1
Number of titles published annually: 100 Print

Norstedts Juridik
Haelsingeg 49, 113 82 Stockholm
Mailing Address: PO Box 6472, 113 82 Stockholm
Tel: (08) 690 91 00 Fax: (08) 6909070
Web Site: www.njab.se
Subjects: Law
ISBN Prefix(es): 91-7598

Norstedts Ordbok
Subsidiary of P A Norstedt & Soener AB
PO Box 45022, 10430 Stockholm
Tel: (08) 7698950
E-mail: info.orabok@norstedtordbok.se
Web Site: www.norstedtsordbok.se
Ultimate Parent Company: KF Media

Bokforlaget Nya Doxa AB+
Kungsgatan 5, 713 23 Nora
Mailing Address: Box 113, 713 23 Nora
Tel: (0587) 104 16 Fax: (0587) 142 57
E-mail: info@nya-doxa.se
Web Site: www.nya-doxa.se
Key Personnel
Publisher: Dr David Stansvik E-mail: david.stansvik@nya-doxa.se
International Rights: Karina Klok Madsen
Founded: 1991 (1974 as Bokfoerlaget Doxa AB)
Also distribution & sales for Bokfoerlaget Thales, Sweden.
Subjects: Art, Biblical Studies, Communications, Ethnicity, History, Literature, Literary Criticism, Essays, Nonfiction (General), Philosophy, Science (General), Social Sciences, Sociology, Theology, Women's Studies
ISBN Prefix(es): 91-88248; 91-578
Number of titles published annually: 30 Print
Total Titles: 200 Print

Nyforlaget, imprint of Hans Richter Laromedel

Bokforlaget Opal AB
Tegelbergsvaegen 31, 161 02 Bromma
Mailing Address: PO Box 20 113, 161 02 Bromma
Tel: (08) 6571990 Fax: (08) 6183470
E-mail: opal@opal.se
Web Site: www.opal.se
Key Personnel
Man Dir: Bengt Christell
Joint Publisher: Valborg Segerhjelm
Founded: 1973
Subjects: Animals, Pets, Fiction, Humor, Literature, Literary Criticism, Essays, Social Sciences, Sociology, Sports, Athletics, Adventure, Classics, Horror & Ghost, Nature
ISBN Prefix(es): 91-7270
Book Club(s): Barnens Bokklub (jointly owned)

Ordfront Foerlag AB (Ordfront Publishing House)+
PO Box 17506, 118 91 Stockholm
Tel: (08) 462 44 00 Fax: (08) 4624490
E-mail: forlaget@ordfront.se; info@ordfront.se
Web Site: www.ordfront.se Cable: ORDFRONT STOCKHOLM
Key Personnel
Man Dir: Leif Ericsson
Editorial, Rights & Permissions: Eva Stenberg E-mail: eva@ordfront.se
Vice President & Publishing Dir: Jan-Erik Pettersson
Founded: 1969
Membership(s): Swedish Publishers Association; Specialize in history, politics, journalism & fiction.
Subjects: Fiction, History, Journalism, Publishing & Book Trade Reference, Social Sciences, Sociology
ISBN Prefix(es): 91-7324
Total Titles: 50 Print
Imprints: Calago Foerlag
Book Club(s): Ordfront Bookclub
Distribution Center: Foerlagssystem AB, PO Box 30195, S-10425 Stockholm

Pagina Forlags AB+
PO Box 2103, 174 02 Sundbyberg
Tel: (08) 564 218 00 Fax: (08) 564 218 19
E-mail: info@pagina.se
Web Site: www.pagina.se
Key Personnel
President: Lauri Pappinen
Founded: 1979
Subjects: Computer Science
ISBN Prefix(es): 91-86200; 91-86201; 91-636
Parent Company: Pagina AB
Subsidiaries: Pagina Oy
Orders to: FoerlagsSystem AB, Box 13195, 104 25 Stockholm Tel: (08) 657 19 90 Fax: (08) 657 19 95 E-mail: order@fsys.se

Pandang, imprint of Raben och Sjoegren Bokforlag

Bokforlaget Plus AB
Sankt Eriksgatan 48, 112 34 Stockholm
Tel: (08) 654 74 08
Key Personnel
Man Dir: Bengt Svensson
Founded: 1976
Subjects: Fiction, Nonfiction (General)
ISBN Prefix(es): 91-7406

Bokforlaget Prisma+
Subsidiary of P A Norstedt & Soener AB
Tryckerigatan 4, SE-103 12 Stockholm
Mailing Address: PO Box 2052, S-103 12 Stockholm
Tel: (08) 7698900 Fax: (08) 241276
E-mail: prisma@prismabok.se
Web Site: www.prismabok.se
Key Personnel
Man Dir: Viveca Ekelund E-mail: viveca.ekelund@prismabok.se
Secretary: Gunnel Nordsater E-mail: gunnel.nordsater@prismabok.se
Founded: 1963
International Rights Contact: Pan Agency, PO Box 2052, SE-10312, Stockholm, Tel: (08) 769 8700, Fax: (08) 769 8804.
Subjects: Cookery, Fiction, Gardening, Plants, Health, Nutrition, History, House & Home
ISBN Prefix(es): 91-518
Foreign Rights: Pan Agency

Psykologifoerlaget AB+
Box 47054, 100 74 Stockholm
Tel: (08) 775 09 00; (08) 775 09 10 (orders) Fax: (08) 775 09 20
E-mail: info@psykologiforlaget.se
Web Site: www.psykologiforlaget.se
Key Personnel
Man Dir: Catharina Mabon
Founded: 1957
Subjects: Education, Psychology, Psychiatry
ISBN Prefix(es): 91-7418

R & S Books, imprint of Raben och Sjoegren Bokforlag

Raben och Sjoegren Bokforlag+
Subsidiary of P A Norstedt & Soener AB
Tryckerigatan 4, 103 12 Stockholm

PUBLISHERS

SWEDEN

Mailing Address: PO Box 2052, 103 12 Stockholm
Tel: (08) 7698800 *Fax:* (08) 7698813
E-mail: raben-sjogren@raben.se
Web Site: www.raben.se
Key Personnel
Publishing Dir: Suzanne Ohman-Sunden
  E-mail: suzanne.ohman-sunden@raben.se
Publisher: Birgitta Westin *E-mail:* birgitta.westin@raben.se
Secretary: Alva Settepassi *E-mail:* alva.settepassi@raben.se
Founded: 1942
Subjects: Nonfiction (General)
ISBN Prefix(es): 91-29
Imprints: Citadell; Pandang; R & S Books; Tiden
Book Club(s): Barnens Bokklubb (jointly owned)

Bokforlaget Rediviva, Facsimileforlaget
PO Box 15148, 161 15 Bromma
Tel: (08) 25 70 07
Key Personnel
Man Dir: Karin Skrutkowska
Founded: 1968
Subjects: Geography, Geology
ISBN Prefix(es): 91-7120

Richters Egmont
Sallerupsvaegen 9, 205 75 Malmoe
Tel: (040) 38 06 00 *Fax:* (040) 933708
E-mail: egmont@egmont.com
Web Site: www.egmont.com
Telex: 33180 richt S
Key Personnel
Man Dir, Rights & Permissions: Lars G Gustafsson
Editorial: Ia Atterholm; Annika Bladh
Sales: Lena Oeman; Ulf Ottosson
Production: Anders Enquist
Founded: 1942
Subjects: Fiction, Nonfiction (General), Comics/Cartoons
ISBN Prefix(es): 91-7705; 91-7706
Parent Company: Gutenberghus Group, Copenhagen, Denmark
Book Club(s): Kalle Ankas Bokklubb; Kokboksklubben God Mat; Laeslandet; Richters Bokklubb; Richters Ungdomsbokklub; Skoenhet och Haelsa; Spaenningsbokklubben

Samsprak Forlags AB
PO Box 247, 701 44 Oerebro
Tel: (019) 13 24 45 *Fax:* (019) 18 72 55
E-mail: info@samsprak.se
Web Site: www.samsprak.se
Key Personnel
Contact: Sven Olov Stalfelt
Founded: 1980
Subjects: Communications, Education
ISBN Prefix(es): 91-86020
Total Titles: 10 Print; 1 CD-ROM; 14 Audio

Forlaget Sanctus (Metodistkyrkans Forlag)
PO Box 45130, 104 30 Stockholm
Tel: (08) 31 55 70 *Fax:* (08) 31 55 79
Telex: 909 Teleopr S
Founded: 1873
The Publishing House of the United Methodist Church in Sweden.
Subjects: Religion - Protestant, Theology
ISBN Prefix(es): 91-7214

Schultz Forlag AB
Asogatan 164, 116 32 Stockholm
Fax: (08) 641 35 36
Key Personnel
Dir: Barbro Schultz-Lundestam *Tel:* (01) 43298392 *E-mail:* Lundest@attglobal.net
Founded: 1982
Specializes in film/video production & novels, artbooks & poetry.

Subjects: Art, Film, Video, Literature, Literary Criticism, Essays, Photography, Poetry
ISBN Prefix(es): 91-87370
Number of titles published annually: 4 Print
Total Titles: 30 Print
Associate Companies: Schultz Forlag SARL
Distributed by Printed Matter (New York)
Distribution Center: Amigo Musik AB, Fredrik Boquist *Tel:* (08) 5566970 *Fax:* (08) 55696979
Web Site: www.amigo.se

Bokforlaget Semic AB
Landsvaegen 57, 172 25 Sundbyberg
Mailing Address: Box 1243, 172 25 Sundbyberg
Tel: (08) 799 30 50 *Fax:* (08) 799 30 64
E-mail: bokforlaget@semic.se
Web Site: www.semic.se
Key Personnel
Publisher: Mans Gahrton *E-mail:* mans.gahrton@semic.se
Founded: 1945
Subjects: Animals, Pets, Architecture & Interior Design, Cookery, Crafts, Games, Hobbies, Gardening, Plants, House & Home, Sports, Athletics
ISBN Prefix(es): 91-552
Parent Company: Semic International AB

Semic Bokforlaget International AB+
Landsvaegen 57, 172 25 Sundbyberg
Mailing Address: Box 1243, 172 25 Sundbyberg
Tel: (08) 779 30 50 *Fax:* (08) 799 30 64
E-mail: bokforlaget@semic.se
Web Site: www.semic.se *Cable:* SEMICPRESS S
Key Personnel
Man Dir: Richard Ekstroem
Founded: 1950
Subjects: Cookery, Crafts, Games, Hobbies, Humor, Sports, Athletics
ISBN Prefix(es): 91-552
Parent Company: Bonnierforetagen, Torsgatan 21, 113 90 Stockholm
Subsidiaries: Bokfoerlaget Semic AB; Jultidningsfoerlaget AB; Kustannus Oy Semic; Semic Press AB

Bokforlaget Settern AB+
Florshult, 286 92 Oerkelljunga
Tel: (0435) 80470 *Fax:* (0435) 80400
E-mail: info@settern.se
Web Site: www.settern.se
Key Personnel
Man Dir: Magdalena Roenneholm
  E-mail: magdalena@settern.se
Sales, Publicity, Advertising Dir: Joergen Wahlen; Tomas Wahlen
Founded: 1974
Specialize in hunting & fishing books.
Membership(s): Svenska Forlaggare foreningen, NOFF.
Subjects: Nonfiction (General), Hunting & Fishing
ISBN Prefix(es): 91-7586
Number of titles published annually: 15 Print
Total Titles: 600 Print
Distribution Center: BTj Seelig & direct Bokforlaget Settern

Sjoestrands Foerlag
Box 1305, 172 26 Sundbyberg
Tel: (08) 29 99 32 *Fax:* (08) 98 46 45
Key Personnel
Man Dir: Ulla-Britt Sjoestrand
Editor: Mr Stellan Forsman
Founded: 1978
Subjects: Astrology, Occult, Fiction, Nonfiction (General), Science Fiction, Fantasy
ISBN Prefix(es): 91-7574

SNS Foerlag+
Skoeldungagatan 1-2, 114 27 Stockholm

Mailing Address: Box 5629, 114 86 Stockholm
Tel: (08) 507 025 00 *Fax:* (08) 507 025 15
E-mail: info@sns.se
Web Site: www.sns.se
Key Personnel
Man Dir: Torgny Wadensjoe
Founded: 1948
Subjects: Economics, Social Sciences, Sociology
ISBN Prefix(es): 91-7150

Sober Foerlags AB
10536 Stockholm
Tel: (08) 672 6000 *Fax:* (08) 672 6001
Key Personnel
Man Dir: Kjell E Johanson
Editorial: Ann-Marie Tjaernkvist
Founded: 1972
Subjects: Health, Nutrition, Social Sciences, Sociology
ISBN Prefix(es): 91-7296
Orders to: Sober Forlags AB, Metallvagen 4, 435 83 Molnlycke

Bokforlaget Spektra AB+
PO Box 7024, 300 07 Halmstad
Tel: (035) 360 30 *Fax:* (035) 361 77
Key Personnel
Man Dir: Ake Hallberg; Solveig Hallberg
Founded: 1965
Subjects: Computer Science, Crafts, Games, Hobbies, Fiction, How-to, Publishing & Book Trade Reference, Science (General)
ISBN Prefix(es): 91-7136
Associate Companies: Grafisk Kompetens, Spektra Studio AB, Box 7039, 300 07 Halmstad

Stenstroems Bokfoerlag AB+
Linnegatan 98, 115 23 Stockholm
Mailing Address: PO Box 24086, 104 50 Stockholm
Tel: (08) 6637601; (08) 662078028 *Fax:* (08) 6632201
Key Personnel
Publisher: Bengt Stenstroem
Founded: 1976
Specialize in reference books.
ISBN Prefix(es): 91-86448; 91-86600; 91-88970; 91-970221; 91-970393
Associate Companies: Interpublishing AB Stenstroem

Frank Stenvalls Forlag+
Foereningsgatan 67, 211 52 Malmoe
Mailing Address: Box 17111, 200 10 Malmoe
Tel: (040) 127703 *Fax:* (040) 127700
E-mail: fstenval@algonet.se
Key Personnel
Man Dir: Frank Stenvall
Founded: 1966
Subjects: Aeronautics, Aviation, Maritime, Transportation
ISBN Prefix(es): 91-7266
Number of titles published annually: 5 Print
Total Titles: 60 Print
Bookshop(s): Stenvalls
Book Club(s): Swedish Military Bookclub

Stiftelsen Kursverksamhetens Foerlag, see Folkuniversitetets foerlag

Streiffert Forlag AB
Karlavaegen 71, 102 47 Stockholm
Mailing Address: PO Box 5334, 102 47 Stockholm
Tel: (08) 661 58 80 *Fax:* (08) 783 04 33
E-mail: info@streiffert.se
Web Site: www.streiffert.se
Key Personnel
Man Dir: Bo Streiffert *E-mail:* bo@streiffert.se
Founded: 1985
Subjects: Travel
ISBN Prefix(es): 91-7886

Number of titles published annually: 8 Print
Total Titles: 41 Print

Stroemberg B&T Forlag AB+
Grimstagatan 170, 162 11 Vallingby
Tel: (08) 6201900 *Fax:* (08) 7399836
E-mail: bokforlaget@stromberg.se
Web Site: www.stromberg.se
Key Personnel
Publisher: Hanserik Tonnheim
Founded: 1990
Subjects: Art, History, Religion - Other, Sports, Athletics
ISBN Prefix(es): 91-7151; 91-7148; 91-7198; 91-85110; 91-86184
Imprints: Idrottsantikvariatet; Stroembergs Bokforlag
Warehouse: Johnson & Johnsonhuset, Staffausvag 2, 19184 Sollentuna

Stroembergs Bokforlag, *imprint of* Stroemberg B&T Forlag AB

Stromberg+
Grimstagatan 170, 162 11 Vaellingby
Tel: (08) 6201900 *Fax:* (08) 7399836
E-mail: bokforlaget@stromberg.se
Web Site: www.stromberg.se
Key Personnel
Publisher: Hanserik Tonnheim
Man Dir: Thomas Bjorklund
Founded: 1991
Subjects: Cookery, Economics, Education, Law, Nonfiction (General), Regional Interests
ISBN Prefix(es): 91-7151; 91-7148
Warehouse: Seelig & Co, Box 1308, Solna
Orders to: Seelig & Co, Box 1308, Solna

Studentlitteratur AB+
Akergraenden 1, 221 00 Lund
Mailing Address: PO Box 141, 221 00 Lund
Tel: (046) 312000 *Fax:* (046) 305338
E-mail: info@studentlitteratur.se
Web Site: www.studentlitteratur.se
Key Personnel
President: Stefan Persson
Publishing Dir: Robert Kipowski; Sven-Ake Lennung
Rights Manager: Kristina Karlssol
  E-mail: kristina.karlssol@studentlitteratur.se;
  Susanne Worning *E-mail:* susanne.worning@studentlitteratur.se
Production: Thomas Lundgren
Founded: 1963
Subjects: Accounting, Behavioral Sciences, Biological Sciences, Business, Chemistry, Chemical Engineering, Computer Science, Education, Engineering (General), Language Arts, Linguistics, Law, Management, Mathematics, Medicine, Nursing, Dentistry, Philosophy, Physical Sciences, Psychology, Psychiatry, Social Sciences, Sociology, Technology
ISBN Prefix(es): 91-44
Number of titles published annually: 200 Print
Total Titles: 2,500 Print
Parent Company: Bratt International A/B, Lund

Studieforlaget i Goteborg Stiftelsen Kursverksamhetens Forlag
Box 2542, 403 17 Gothenburg
Tel: (031) 106580 *Fax:* (031) 135359
E-mail: kursbokhandeln@folkuniversitetet.se
Key Personnel
Contact: Bo Nordell
ISBN Prefix(es): 91-7602

Svenska alliansmissionens (SAM) foerlage
Box 11054, 551 11 Joenkoeping
Tel: (036) 71 98 70 *Fax:* (036) 71 98 20
E-mail: info@sam.f.se
Web Site: www.sam.f.se *Cable:* SAM
Key Personnel
Man Dir: Torbjoern Wetteroe
Subjects: Religion - Other
ISBN Prefix(es): 91-7484

Svenska Arbetsgivareforeningens forlag
114 82 Stockholm
Tel: (08) 553 430 00 *Fax:* (08) 553 430 99
Cable: EMPLOYERS
Key Personnel
Manager: Kjell Frykhammar
ISBN Prefix(es): 91-7152

Svenska Foerlaget liv & ledarskap ab+
Box 3313, 103 66 Stockholm
Tel: (08) 412 27 00 *Fax:* (08) 411 41 30
E-mail: kundservice@svenskaforlaget.com
Web Site: www.svenskaforlaget.com
Key Personnel
President: Lena Kjellgren
Publisher: Peter Stenson
Founded: 1982
Subjects: Animals, Pets, Biography, Business, Career Development, History, Human Relations, Management, Nonfiction (General), Philosophy, Psychology, Psychiatry, Self-Help
ISBN Prefix(es): 91-7738
Parent Company: Schibsted ASA
Book Club(s): Bokklubben Liv & Ledarskap

Svenska Institutet+
Skeppsbron 2, Box 7434, 103 91 Stockholm
Tel: (08) 453 78 00 *Fax:* (08) 20 72 48
E-mail: si@si.se
Web Site: www.si.se
Founded: 1945
Specialize in information about Sweden-culture & society in many languages.
ISBN Prefix(es): 91-520

The Swedish Association of Educational Publishers (Foreningen Svenska Laromedelsproducenter), see Foreningen Svenska Laromedelsproducenter (The Swedish Association of Educational Publishers)

Teknografiska Institutet AB
PO Box 1243, 171 24 Solna
Tel: (08) 83 42 85 *Fax:* (08) 73 04 13
Key Personnel
Production: Ingrid Karpebaeck
Founded: 1946
ISBN Prefix(es): 91-7172

Tiden, *imprint of* Raben och Sjoegren Bokforlag

Timbro+
Grev Turegatan 19, 102 45 Stockholm
Mailing Address: PO Box 5234, 102 45 Stockholm
Tel: (08) 587 898 00 *Fax:* (08) 587 898 55
E-mail: info@timbro.se
Web Site: www.timbro.se
Key Personnel
President: Mattias Bengtsson
Production: Barbro Bengtson
Permissions & International Rights: Kristina von Unge *Tel:* (08) 587 898 34 *E-mail:* kristinau@timbro.se
Founded: 1978
Publishes a periodical for culture, politics & economics (Smedjan-www.smedjan.com).
Subjects: Economics, Government, Political Science, Nonfiction (General), Social Sciences, Sociology, Free Enterprise
ISBN Prefix(es): 91-7566
Parent Company: Stiftelsen Fritt Naringsliv

Tryckeriforlaget AB+
PO Box 7093, 183 07 Taby
Tel: (08) 756 74 45 *Fax:* (08) 756 03 95
E-mail: tidkort@tidkort.se
Key Personnel
Dir: Leif Lindberg
Subjects: Antiques, Business, Wine & Spirits
ISBN Prefix(es): 91-970081; 91-971201; 91-972765

Var Skola Foerlag AB+
Riddargatan 17, 114 57 Stockholm
Tel: (08) 662 33 51 *Fax:* (08) 6621843
E-mail: var.skola@pi.se
Key Personnel
Man Dir: Gunnel Radahl; Stig Radahl
Subjects: Nonfiction (General)
ISBN Prefix(es): 91-7396

Verbum Foerlag AB+
Goetgatan 22 A, Stockholm
Mailing Address: Box 15169, 104 65 Stockholm
Tel: (08) 743 65 00 *Fax:* (08) 641 45 85
E-mail: info.forlag@verbum.se
Web Site: www.verbum.se
Key Personnel
Man Dir: Johan F Dalman
Founded: 1911
Membership(s): FSL, SBF, IPA & Worlddidac.
Subjects: Music, Dance, Religion - Other, Theology
ISBN Prefix(es): 91-526
Parent Company: Verbum AB
Associate Companies: Gleerups Foerlag; Foerlagshuset Gothia
Subsidiaries: Libraria Konsthantverk AB
Divisions: Publishing, Stationery
Bookshop(s): V Hamngatan 21, Gothenburg

AB Wahlstroem & Widstrand+
Sturegatan 32, 114 85 Stockholm
Mailing Address: Box 5587, 114 85 Stockholm
Tel: (08) 696 84 80 *Fax:* (08) 696 83 80
E-mail: info@wwd.se
Web Site: www.wwd.se *Cable:* WAHLWID S
Key Personnel
Publisher & Man Dir: Unn Palm
Sales Dir: Bengt Hennings
Rights & Permissions: Marina Kosjanov
  E-mail: marina.kosjanov@wwd.se
Founded: 1884
Specialize in novels, poetry, illustrated nature books, travel guides, health, psychology.
Subjects: Fiction, Health, Nutrition, Nonfiction (General), Poetry, Psychology, Psychiatry
ISBN Prefix(es): 91-46
Parent Company: Bonnierforlagen AB

Wahlstrom & Widstrand
Sturegatan 32, 114 85 Stockholm
Mailing Address: PO Box 5587, 114 85 Stockholm
Tel: (08) 696 84 80 *Fax:* (08) 696 83 80
E-mail: info@wwd.se
Web Site: www.wwd.se *Cable:* Bebolag
Key Personnel
Man Dir: Unn Palm *Tel:* (08) 696 84 81
  E-mail: unn.palm@wwd.se
Subjects: Art, Biography, Cookery, Fiction, History, Nonfiction (General)
ISBN Prefix(es): 91-46; 91-500; 91-614

B Wahlstroms
Warfvinges vaeg 30, 104 25 Stockholm
Mailing Address: PO Box 30022, 104 25 Stockholm
Tel: (08) 619 86 00 *Fax:* (08) 618 97 61
E-mail: info@wahlstroms.se
Web Site: www.wahlstroms.se
Key Personnel
Chairman & Man Dir: Bertil Wahlstroem
Editor-in-Chief & Permissions: Brit-Marie Johansson
Founded: 1911
Subjects: Fiction, Nonfiction (General)

ISBN Prefix(es): 91-32
Parent Company: J A Lindblads Bokfoerlag AB
Bookshop(s): Kungsholmens Bokhandel AB, PO Box 49014, 100 28 Stockholm
Warehouse: Loevasvaegen 26, 791 29 Falun

Zindermans AB
1a Langgatan 6, 413 03 Gothenburg
Mailing Address: Box 31029, 400 32 Gothenburg
Tel: (031) 775 04 00 *Fax:* (031) 12 06 60 *Cable:* ZINDERMANS
Key Personnel
Man Dir: Leif Stigsjoeoe
Founded: 1960
Subjects: Biography, Fiction, Government, Political Science, History, How-to, Nonfiction (General), Psychology, Psychiatry, Social Sciences, Sociology
ISBN Prefix(es): 91-528

Switzerland

General Information

Capital: Berne
Language: 3 official: German, French and Italian
Religion: Protestant and Roman Catholic
Population: 6.8 million
Bank Hours: 0800 or 0830-1200 or 1230, 1300 or 1330-1630 Monday-Friday
Shop Hours: 0800-1200, 1330-1830 Monday-Friday; in most cities, closed Monday morning; 0800-1200, 1330-1600 or 1700 Saturday
Currency: 100 rappen (centimes) = 1 Swiss franc
Export/Import Information: Member of the European Free Trade Association. No tariff on books. Most books exempt from Turnover Tax. Advertising matter usually dutiable, some exempt from Turnover Tax. 2% VAT on books. No import licenses required. No exchange controls.
Copyright: UCC, Berne, Florence (see Copyright Conventions, pg xi)

Aare-Verlag+
Laurenzenvorstadt 89, 5001 Aarau
Tel: (062) 836 86 50 *Fax:* (062) 836 86 56
E-mail: bildung@sauerlaender.ch
Web Site: www.sauerlaender.ch
Key Personnel
Publishing Manager: Hans Christof Saueriaender
Editor: Barbara Kueper
International Rights: Claudia Kukla
Founded: 1953
Subjects: Education
ISBN Prefix(es): 3-7260
Subsidiaries: Verlag Sauerlaende
Orders to: Koch, Neff & Oetringer, Schockenriedstr 39, 70565 Stuttgart, Germany

AD, *imprint of* Editions Andre Delcourt & Cie

Editions Ad Solem
2, rue des Voisins, 1211 Geneva 12
Mailing Address: Postfach 479, 1211 Geneva 12
Tel: (022) 321 19 30 *Fax:* (022) 321 19 31
E-mail: office@adsolem.ch
Web Site: www.ad-solem.com
Subjects: Christian literature

ADIRA+
29, rue du Rhone, Geneve 1204
Tel: (022) 312 25 43 *Fax:* (022) 312 26 13
E-mail: adira@adira.net
Web Site: www.adira.net
Key Personnel
President: Dominique Mottas
Author: Michel Potay
Founded: 1974
Also acts as distributor.
Subjects: Philosophy, Religion - Other, Spirituality
ISBN Prefix(es): 2-901821
Number of titles published annually: 2 Print
Total Titles: 12 Print
Parent Company: Editions Michel Potay
Ultimate Parent Company: Maison de la Revelation
U.S. Office(s): ADIRA New York, 590 Madison Ave, 21st Floor, New York, NY 10022, United States
Distributed by Hervey's; Pathways

Adonia-Verlag+
Postfach 3060, 8800 Thalwil
Tel: (01) 7207712 *Fax:* (01) 9800622
Web Site: www.libroplus.ch
Founded: 1986
Membership(s): SBVV, SSV, Pen.
Subjects: Poetry, Women's Studies
ISBN Prefix(es): 3-905009

Editions L'Age d'Homme - La Cite
Rue de Geneve 10, 1000 Lausanne 9
Tel: (021) 312 00 95 *Fax:* (021) 320 84 40
E-mail: agedhomme@iprolink.ch
Key Personnel
Man Dir: Vladimir Dimitrijevic
Founded: 1966
Subjects: Art, Biography, Drama, Theater, Fiction, Film, Video, Literature, Literary Criticism, Essays, Music, Dance, Philosophy, Poetry, Psychology, Psychiatry, Regional Interests, Religion - Other, Science Fiction, Fantasy, Social Sciences, Sociology
ISBN Prefix(es): 2-8251
Branch Office(s)
5 rue Ferou, 75006 Paris, France *Tel:* (01) 46 34 18 51 *Fax:* (01) 40 51 71 02
Bookshop(s): Librairie la Proue, Escaliers du Marche 17, 1000 Lausanne; Librairie Le Rameau d'Or, 19 blvd Georges Favon, 1200 Geneva

J H Goehre Albanus Verlag
Hulfteggstr 10, 8401 Winterthur 1
Tel: (052) 293503
Key Personnel
Contact: J H Goehre
Founded: 1946
Membership(s): SBVV/VVDS.
ISBN Prefix(es): 3-85510

Amboss-Verlag E Widmer+
Postfach 404, 9434 Au SG
Tel: (071) 711236; (071) 714590 *Fax:* (071) 714590
Key Personnel
Contact: Charlotte Knoepfli-Widmer
Founded: 1968
ISBN Prefix(es): 3-85517

Ammann Verlag & Co+
Neptunstr 20, 8032 Zurich
Tel: (01) 268 10 40 *Fax:* (01) 268 10 50
E-mail: info@ammann.ch
Web Site: www.ammann.ch
Key Personnel
Publisher: Egon Ammann; Marie-Luise Flammersfeld
Sales, Marketing & Press: Patrik Zeller
Production: Beate Becker
Editor: Stephanie von Harrach
Editor, Rights & Permissions: Laurenz Bolliger
Founded: 1981
Subjects: Art, Biography, Fiction, History, Literature, Literary Criticism, Essays, Nonfiction (General), Poetry, Religion - Islamic, Science (General), Travel
ISBN Prefix(es): 3-250
Number of titles published annually: 20 Print
Orders to: Ammann Verlag, Buchzentrum AG, B2, 4601 Olten

Antonius-Verlag
Gaertnerstr 7, 4500 Solothurn
Tel: (065) 223912
Key Personnel
Contact: Maria Gasser
Subjects: Education, Medicine, Nursing, Dentistry, Psychology, Psychiatry
ISBN Prefix(es): 3-85520
Branch Office(s)
Testzentrale der Deutschen Psychologen, Robert-Bosch-Breite 25, 37079 Gottingen, Germany
Testzentrale der Schweizer Psychologen, Laenggassstr 76, Bern 9, Germany
Universitaetsverlag, Perolles 42, 1700 Fribourg

Arche Verlag AG, Raabe und Vitali+
Niederdorfstr 90, 8001 Zurich
Tel: (01) 252 24 10 *Fax:* (01) 261 11 15
E-mail: info@arche-verlag.com
Web Site: www.arche-verlag.com
Telex: 815239
Key Personnel
Owner: Elisabeth Raabe; Regina Vitali
Founded: 1944
Subjects: Biography, Fiction, Literature, Literary Criticism, Essays, Music, Dance, Poetry, Travel
ISBN Prefix(es): 3-7160
Divisions: Arche Verlag GmbH

Archivio Storico Ticinese
Via del Bramantino 3, 6500 Bellinzona
Tel: (091) 820 0101 *Fax:* (091) 825 1874
E-mail: casagrande@casagrande-online.ch
Web Site: www.casagrande-online.ch
Telex: 846266
Key Personnel
Man Dir: Virgilio Gilardoni
Sales, Production: Libero Casagrande
Founded: 1960
Subjects: Art, Economics, History, Literature, Literary Criticism, Essays
ISBN Prefix(es): 88-7714
Parent Company: Edizioni Casagrande SA

Ariston Editions+
Villa Bellevue, Hauptstr 14, Kreuzlingen 8280
Mailing Address: Postfach 6030, 1211 Geneve 6
Tel: (071) 6727218 *Fax:* (071) 6727219
E-mail: 106420.3235@compuserve.com
Telex: 413428 arve ch *Cable:* ARISTON
Key Personnel
Man Dir, Editorial & Sales: Dr Monika Roell
Founded: 1964
Subjects: How-to, Medicine, Nursing, Dentistry, Nonfiction (General), Parapsychology, Psychology, Psychiatry, Self-Help
ISBN Prefix(es): 3-7205
Branch Office(s)
Ariston Verlag GmbH und Co Verlagsservice, Boschetsriederstr 12, 81379 Munich, Germany *Tel:* (089) 7241034 *Fax:* (089) 7241718
Ariston-P R Presse, Hauptrasse 14, 8280 Kreuzlingen

Collection Artou, *imprint of* Editions Olizane

Ascona Presse
Passaggio San Pietro 7, 6612 Ascona
Tel: (091) 791 13 34 *Fax:* (091) 791 13 34
E-mail: info@rmeuter.ch
Web Site: www.rmeuter.ch
Founded: 1986
Subjects: Art

ASELF, see Association Suisse des Editeurs de Langue Francaise

SWITZERLAND

Association pour la Diffusion Internationale de la Revelation d'Ares, see ADIRA

Association Suisse des Editeurs de Langue Francaise (Swiss Publishers' Association (French Language))
2, Av Agassit, 1001 Lausanne
Tel: (021) 3197111 *Fax:* (021) 7963311
E-mail: pschibli@centrepatronal.ch
Key Personnel
President: Francine Bouchet
Subjects: Architecture & Interior Design, Business, Earth Sciences, Economics, Environmental Studies, Fiction, History, How-to, Law, Medicine, Nursing, Dentistry, Physics, Science (General), Self-Help, Coffee Table Books, Ecology, Environmental Science, Picture Books
ISBN Prefix(es): 2-88303

Astrodata AG+
Albisriederstr 232, 8047 Zurich
Tel: (043) 343 33 33 *Fax:* (043) 343 33 43
E-mail: info@astrodata.ch
Web Site: www.astrodata.ch
Key Personnel
President: Claude Weiss
Founded: 1978
Subjects: Astrology, Occult, Psychology, Psychiatry
ISBN Prefix(es): 3-907029
Distributor for Edition Astroterra

AT Verlag+
Division of AZ Fachverlage AG
Bahnhofstr 39-43, 5001 Aarau
Tel: (062) 836 6666 *Fax:* (062) 836 6667
E-mail: info.buchverlag@azag.ch
Web Site: www.at-verlag.ch
Key Personnel
Editorial Dir: Urs Hunziker *E-mail:* urs.hunziker@azag.ch
Editorial: Monika Schmidhofer *E-mail:* monika.schmidhofer@azag.ch
Production: Edith Guenter *E-mail:* edith.guenter@azag.ch; Adrian Pabst *E-mail:* adrian.pabst@azag.ch
Sales: Karin Asti *E-mail:* karin.asti@azag.ch; Christine Gutknecht *E-mail:* christine.gutknecht@azag.ch
Marketing: Eugen Jung *E-mail:* eugen.jung@azag.ch
Foreign Rights: Danielle Schwab *E-mail:* danielle.schwab@azag.ch
Founded: 1967
This is the book publishing section of the Aargauer Zeitung AG.
Subjects: Cookery, Health, Nutrition, How-to, Mysteries, Regional Interests
ISBN Prefix(es): 3-905214; 3-85502
Warehouse: Grafische Betriebe Aargauer Zeitung AG, Neumattstr 1/Betrieb Telli, 5004 Aarau

Athenaeum Verlag AG
Via Miravalle 23, 6900 Lugano-Massagno
Tel: (091) 571536 *Cable:* athenag
Key Personnel
Man Dir: J-E Nussbaumer
Administration: J Wuest-Wolfensberger
Editorial: J Steiner
Founded: 1972
Subjects: Art, Biography, Government, Political Science, History, Literature, Literary Criticism, Essays, Nonfiction (General), Science (General)
ISBN Prefix(es): 3-85532
Branch Office(s)
Buchauslieferung, Schweizer Buchzentrum, Olten

Atlantis Musikbuch+
Imprint of Schott Musik International
Tramstr 71, 8050 Zurich
Founded: 1976
Subjects: Music, Dance
ISBN Prefix(es): 3-254

Atlantis-Verlag AG
Kreuzstr 39, 8008 Zurich
Tel: (01) 2622717 *Fax:* (01) 2512615
Telex: 815987
Founded: 1930
Subjects: Art, Geography, Geology
ISBN Prefix(es): 3-7611
Branch Office(s)
Atlantis-Verlag GmbH & Co KG, Germany

Atrium Verlag AG+
Ruetistr 4, 8030 Zurich
Mailing Address: Post Box 262, 8030 Zurich
Tel: (01) 473035
Key Personnel
Contact: Uwe Weitendorf
Founded: 1936
Subjects: Fiction, Literature, Literary Criticism, Essays
ISBN Prefix(es): 3-85535

Augustin-Verlag
Bahnhofstr 20, 8240 Thayngen
Tel: (052) 6492340 *Fax:* (052) 649 31 94
E-mail: augustin@augustin.ch
Key Personnel
President & Publisher: Karl Augustin
Founded: 1911
Publish journals (weekly newspapers for village people named Heimatblatt).
Subjects: Geography, Geology, History, Regional Interests
ISBN Prefix(es): 3-85540; 3-905116; 3-9521861

Editions de la Baconniere SA+
Division of Medecine et Hygiene
46, chemin de la Mousse, 1225 Chene-Bourg
Tel: (022) 8690029 *Fax:* (022) 8690015
E-mail: DEB@medecinehygiene.ch
Key Personnel
Contact: Denis Bertholet
Founded: 1927
Subjects: Art, Biography, History, Music, Dance, Philosophy, Poetry, Social Sciences, Sociology
ISBN Prefix(es): 2-8252

U Baer Verlag+
Mainaustr 35, 8008 Zurich
Tel: (01) 3835500 *Fax:* (01) 3836883
Key Personnel
Man Dir: Dr Ulrich Baer
Editorial, Production: Marianne Widmer
Founded: 1971
Subjects: Art, Photography
ISBN Prefix(es): 3-905137

Barenreiter Verlag Basel AG+
Neuweilerstr 15, 4015 Basel
Tel: (061) 395898; (061) 395899 *Fax:* (061) 3079660
E-mail: info@baerenreiter.com
Web Site: www.baerenreiter.com
Key Personnel
President: Leonard Scheuch
Member Board: Peter G Isler
Founded: 1944
Membership(s): Swiss Society of Music Publishers.
Subjects: Music, Dance
ISBN Prefix(es): 3-7618
Parent Company: Baerenreiter Praha
Associate Companies: Baerenreiter Verlag GmbH & KO KG, Heinrich-Schutz-Allee 35, 34131 Kassel-Wilhelmshohe, Germany, Barbara Scheuch *Tel:* (0561) 3105-0 *Fax:* (0561) 3105-240 *E-mail:* info@baerenreiter.com

Buchhandlung Baeschlin+
Hauptstr 32, 8750 Glarus
Tel: (055) 6401125 *Fax:* (055) 6406594
Web Site: www.baeschlin.ch
Founded: 1853
ISBN Prefix(es): 3-85546

H R Balmer AG Verlag
Neugasse 12, 6301 Zug
Tel: (041) 726 9797 *Fax:* (041) 726 9798
E-mail: info@buecher-balmer.ch
Web Site: www.buecher-balmer.ch
Telex: 868812 buch ch
Key Personnel
Man Dir: Christoph Balmer
Founded: 1974
Subjects: History, Literature, Literary Criticism, Essays, Psychology, Psychiatry
ISBN Prefix(es): 3-85548
Warehouse: Boesch 41, 6331 Huenenberg

Bargezzi-Verlag AG+
Wasserwerksgasse 19, 3011 Bern
Mailing Address: Postfach 28, 3000 Berne 13
Tel: (031) 221380; (031) 211434 *Cable:* Bargezzi Berne
Key Personnel
Man Dir, Editorial, Sales, Publicity, Rights & Permissions: Josef Gruebel
Production: Werner F Waegli
Founded: 1948
Subjects: Literature, Literary Criticism, Essays, Religion - Other
ISBN Prefix(es): 3-85550

Bartschi Publishing
Sternenstr 20b, 8903 Birmensdorf
Tel: (01) 7373528
Key Personnel
Dir: Helen Bartschi
Founded: 1989
Subjects: Literature, Literary Criticism, Essays, Poetry, Psychology, Psychiatry
ISBN Prefix(es): 3-9520020

Basileia Verlag und Basler Missionsbuchhandlung
Missionsstr 21, 4003 Basel
Tel: (061) 251766 *Fax:* (061) 2688321; (061) 232523
Key Personnel
Man Dir: Rudolf Kellenberger
Subjects: Religion - Other, Social Sciences, Sociology
ISBN Prefix(es): 3-85555

Basilius Presse AG+
Gueterstr 86, 4002 Basel
Tel: (061) 228004; (061) 228005 *Fax:* (061) 232523 *Cable:* BASILIUS VERLAG
Key Personnel
Man Dir: P Weibel
Founded: 1957
Subjects: Art, Nonfiction (General), Science (General)
ISBN Prefix(es): 3-85560

Baumgartner Blicher, *imprint of* Terra Grischuna Verlag Buch-und Zeitschriftenverlag

Editions Belle Riviere
La Fontanelle, 1882 Gruyon
Tel: (024) 498 40 49 *Fax:* (024) 498 40 46
Key Personnel
Man Dir: Eugene Chave
Founded: 1974
ISBN Prefix(es): 2-88121

Benteli Verlag+
Seftigenstr, 310, 3084 Wabern-Bern
Tel: (031) 9608484 *Fax:* (031) 9617414
E-mail: info@benteliverlag.ch

Web Site: www.benteliverlag.ch
Key Personnel
Man Dir: Till Schapp
Founded: 1899
High quality books.
Subjects: Art, Photography
ISBN Prefix(es): 3-7165
Number of titles published annually: 35 Print
Total Titles: 350 Print

Benziger Verlag AG+
Bellerivstr 3, 8008 Zurich
Tel: (01) 2527050 *Fax:* (01) 2624792
Key Personnel
Contact: Christian Machalet
Founded: 1792
Subjects: Art, Music, Dance, Religion - Catholic, Religion - Protestant, Theology
ISBN Prefix(es): 3-545
Parent Company: Patmos Verlag

Beobachter Buchverlag
Foerrlibuckstr 10, Postfach, 8021 Zurich
Tel: (01) 8296111 *Fax:* (01) 8103791
Web Site: www.beobachter.ch
Key Personnel
Contact: H Hausherr *Tel:* (01) 4488984
  E-mail: hhausherr@beobachter.ch
ISBN Prefix(es): 3-85569
Total Titles: 60 Print
Branch Office(s)
Industriestr 54, Postfach 8152, Glattbrugg-Zurich

Berchtold Haller Verlag+
Nageligasse 9, 3000 Bern 7
Mailing Address: Postfach 15, 3000 Bern 7
Tel: (031) 334 03 03 *Fax:* (031) 334 03 06
Web Site: www.egw.ch
Key Personnel
Contact: Peter Schranz *E-mail:* schranz@theol-buch.ch
Founded: 1848
Subjects: Religion - Protestant, Romance
ISBN Prefix(es): 3-85570
Number of titles published annually: 3 Print
Total Titles: 40 Print; 13 Audio
Parent Company: Evangelisches Geweinschafhwerth EGW

Bergli Books AG+
Ruemelinplatz 19, 4001 Basel
Tel: (061) 373 27 77 *Fax:* (061) 373 27 78
E-mail: info@bergli.ch
Web Site: www.bergli.ch
Key Personnel
Man Dir: Dianne Dicks
Founded: 1990
Specialize in intercultural books on crossing cultures, emigration, intercultural marriages, bilingualism, short story anthologies.
Subjects: Behavioral Sciences, Ethnicity, Foreign Countries, Human Relations, Literature, Literary Criticism, Essays, Nonfiction (General), Travel, Women's Studies
ISBN Prefix(es): 3-9520002; 3-905252
Distributor for Survival Books; Travelers' Tales

Berichthaus Verlag, Dr Conrad Ulrich
Voltastr 43, 8044 Zurich
Tel: (01) 2526349 *Fax:* (01) 2526426
Subjects: History, History of Zurich & Switzerland
ISBN Prefix(es): 3-85572
Orders to: Schweiz Buchzentrum, 4601 Olten

Beroa-Verlag
Zellerstr 61, 8038 Zurich
Tel: (01) 4801313 *Fax:* (01) 4801312
Founded: 1957
Subjects: Biblical Studies
ISBN Prefix(es): 3-905335; 3-905336; 3-909337

Bettex, Editions Medicales Roland
2, rue de l Etrat, 1211 Geneva 4
Mailing Address: CP 456, 1211 Geneva 4
Tel: (022) 7029311 *Fax:* (022) 7029355
ISBN Prefix(es): 2-88113
Branch Office(s)
3, rue des Fontenalilles CP 193, 1000 Lausanne 13
Street 8, rue Copernic, 75116 Paris, France
  Tel: (0147) 271559

Editions Beyeler
Baeumleingasse 9, 4001 Basel
Tel: (061) 235412 *Fax:* (061) 229691
Key Personnel
Owner: Ernst Beyeler
Founded: 1967
Subjects: Art
ISBN Prefix(es): 3-85575; 3-9520156

Bibellesbund Verlag+
Flugplatzstr 5, Postfach, 8404 Winterthur
Tel: (052) 245 14 45 *Fax:* (052) 245 14 46
E-mail: info@bibellesebund.ch
Web Site: www.bibellesebund.ch
Key Personnel
Secretary-General, Switzerland: Andreas Zimmermann
Secretary-General, Germany: Reinhold Frey
Man Dir, Sales, Production, Publicity, Switzerland: Martin Wassmer
Man Dir, Sales, Production, Publicity, Germany: Karl-Martin Gunther
Founded: 1930
Scripture Union of Switzerland & Germany.
Subjects: Religion - Protestant
ISBN Prefix(es): 3-87982
Associate Companies: Bibellesebund eV Industriestr 2, Postfach, 51703 Marienheide-Roth, Germany *Tel:* (02264) 7045 *Fax:* (02264) 7155
  E-mail: info@bibellesebund.de
Distributed by Haenssler Verlag; Brunnen Verlag

Bibliographisches Institut & F A Brockhaus AG
Gubelstr 11, 6301 Zug
Mailing Address: Postfach 4531, 6304 Zug
Tel: (041) 7108375 *Fax:* (041) 7108325
Web Site: www.bifab.de
Key Personnel
Man Dir: Dr Ernst Grab
Founded: 1967
Subjects: Biological Sciences, Business, Chemistry, Chemical Engineering, Computer Science, Earth Sciences, Economics, Education, Environmental Studies, Geography, Geology, Health, Nutrition, History, Language Arts, Linguistics, Mathematics, Music, Dance, Nonfiction (General), Philosophy, Physics, Religion - Other, Science (General)
ISBN Prefix(es): 3-411; 3-7653
Parent Company: Bibliographisches Institut und F A Brockhaus AG, Germany

Verlag Bibliophile Drucke von Josef Stocker AG
Hasenbergstr 7, 8953 Dietikon
Mailing Address: PO Box 66, 8953 Dietikon
Tel: (01) 7404444
Key Personnel
Man Dir: Mr Stocker
Subjects: Poetry
ISBN Prefix(es): 3-85577; 3-7276
Parent Company: Verlag Stocker-Schmid AG
Bookshop(s): Buchhandlung Stocker-Schmid, Hasenbergstr 7, PO Box 66, 8953 Dietikon

La Bibliotheque des Arts+
55, Ave de Rumine, 1005 Lausanne
Tel: (021) 3123667 *Fax:* (021) 3123615
Web Site: www.archinform.net

Key Personnel
Dir: Mr Francois Daulte
Founded: 1952
Subjects: Art
ISBN Prefix(es): 2-85047; 2-88453
Subsidiaries: La Bibliotheque des Arts
Branch Office(s)
Archer Fields Inc, 636 Broadway, New York, NY 10012, United States

Birkhauser Verlag AG+
Viaduktstr 42, 4051 Basel
Mailing Address: PO Box 133, 4010 Basel
Tel: (061) 2050707 *Fax:* (061) 2050799
E-mail: info@birkhauser.ch; sales@birkhauser.ch
Web Site: www.birkhauser.ch *Cable:* EDITA
Key Personnel
General & Editorial Manager: Edward Mazenauer
Marketing Manager: Sven Steiner; Patrick Schneebeli
Rights & Licences: Liv Etienne *Tel:* (061) 2050707 *E-mail:* etienne@birkhauser.ch
Founded: 1879
Subjects: Architecture & Interior Design, Biological Sciences, Engineering (General), Environmental Studies, Mathematics, Physics
ISBN Prefix(es): 3-7643
Total Titles: 200 Print
Parent Company: Springer Science+Business Media, Tiergartenstrasse A7, Heidelberg 69121, Germany
Imprints: Birkhauser Verlag fuer Architektur
Subsidiaries: Birkhauser Boston Inc
U.S. Office(s): Birkhauser Boston Inc, c/o Springer-Verlag New York Inc, 175 Fifth Ave, New York, NY 10010, United States *Web Site:* www.birkhauser.com
Distributor for Princeton Architectural Press (USA, UK)
Warehouse: Springer Auslieferungs Gesellschaft, Haberstrasse 7, Heidelberg 69121, Germany
  Tel: (049) 6221345-0

Birkhauser Verlag fuer Architektur, *imprint of* Birkhauser Verlag AG

Blaukreuz-Verlag Bern+
Lindenrain 5a, 3001 Bern
Mailing Address: Postfach 5524, 3001 Bern
Tel: (031) 300 58 66 *Fax:* (031) 300 58 69
E-mail: verlag@blaueskreuz.ch
Web Site: www.blaueskreuz.ch *Cable:* BLAUKREUZVERLAG
Key Personnel
Man Dir: Ernst Zuercher
Founded: 1884
Publishes for the Blue Cross health & religious movement.
Subjects: Biography, Health, Nutrition, Religion - Protestant, Religion - Other
ISBN Prefix(es): 3-85580
Parent Company: Blaues Kreuz der deutschen Schweiz

Les Editions de la Fondation Martin Bodmer
Postfach, 1223 Cologny
Mailing Address: PO Box 7, 1223 Cologny-Geneva
Tel: (022) 7362370 *Fax:* (022) 7001540
Key Personnel
Contact: Dr Martin Bircher
Founded: 1971
Subjects: Language Arts, Linguistics
ISBN Prefix(es): 3-85682

Bohem Press Kinderbuchverlag+
Hardturmstr 122, 8005 Zurich
Tel: (01) 440 7000 *Fax:* (01) 440 7001
E-mail: art@bohem.ch
Web Site: www.bohem.ch

Key Personnel
Dir: O Bozejovsky v Rawennoff *Tel:* (01) 4407004
Publisher: Susanne Zeller
Founded: 1973
Subjects: Animals, Pets, Child Care & Development, Fiction
ISBN Prefix(es): 3-85581

Brunnen-Verlag Basel+
Wallstr 6, 4002 Basel
Tel: (061) 234406 *Fax:* (061) 2956069
E-mail: brunnen-verlag@bluewin.ch
Key Personnel
Man Dir: Hans-Peter Zueblin
Founded: 1921
Subjects: Biography, Child Care & Development, Fiction, How-to, Religion - Other, Self-Help
ISBN Prefix(es): 3-7655
Bookshop(s): Buchhandlung Pilgermission, Spalenberg 20, 4002 Basel; Brunnen-Buchhandlung, Marktgasse 31, 8180 Buelach; Brunnen-Buchhandlung, St Gallerstr 6, 8500 Frauenfeld; Libreria La Fonte, Viale Stazione 1, 6512 Giubiasco; Buechegge AG, Loewengasse 37, 8810 Horgen; Christlicher Buecherladen zur Arche, Amtshausgasse 10, 4410 Liestal; Evangelische Buchhandlung, Haupstr 25, 5734 Reinach AG; Christliche Buchhandlung, Ave Mercier de Molin 1, 3960 Sierre; Christliche Buchhandlung, Bahnhofstr 42, 6210 Sursee; Christliche Buchhandlung, Susann-Muellerstr 14, 9630 Wattwil; Christliche Buchhandlung "Brunne-Stube", Schmidstr 3, 8570 Weinfelden; Brunnen-Buchhandlung, untere Bahnofstr 20, 9500 Wil; Christliche Buchhandlung, HERTI-Zentrum, 6300 Zug; Sunnaewirbel, Buecher & Geschenke, Olympstr 4, 6440 Brunnen; Senfkorn-Laden, Hauptstr 33, 5262 Frick

Verlag Bucheli+
Baarerstr 43, 6304 Zug
Mailing Address: Postfach 4161, 6304 Zug
Tel: (041) 741 77 55 *Fax:* (041) 741 71 15
E-mail: info@bucheli-verlag.ch
Web Site: www.mueller-rueschlikon.ch/bucheli.htm
Key Personnel
Contact: Hans-Joerg Degen
Subjects: Automotive
ISBN Prefix(es): 3-7168

Buchhaus AG, see Office du Livre SA (Buchhaus AG)

Buchverlag Basler Zeitung
Hochbergerstr 15, 4002 Basel
Tel: (061) 6391315 *Fax:* (061) 6391343
E-mail: order@baz.ch
Web Site: www.baz.ch
Key Personnel
Marketing: Jasmine Gasser
ISBN Prefix(es): 3-85815
Book Club(s): SBVV

Bugra Suisse Burchler Grafino AG+
Seftigenstr 310, 3084 Wabern
Tel: (031) 548111 *Fax:* (031) 544562
Telex: 911934
Key Personnel
Man Dir, Rights & Permissions: Dr Rudolf Gysi
Marketing: Erich Hirschi
Editorial: Peter Wyss
Founded: 1886
Subjects: Art, Education, Regional Interests
ISBN Prefix(es): 3-7170

Cahiers de la Renaissance Vaudoise
One Place Grand-Saint-Jean, 1002 Lausanne
Mailing Address: Postfach 3414, 1002 Lausanne
Tel: (021) 3121914 *Fax:* (021) 3126714
E-mail: courrier@ligue-vaudoise.ch
Web Site: www.ligue-vaudoise.ch
Key Personnel
President: Olivier Delacretaz
Subjects: Government, Political Science, History
ISBN Prefix(es): 2-88017

Les Editions Camphill
Fondation Perceval, 1211 Saint-Prex
Tel: (021) 8062269 *Fax:* (021) 8061897
Key Personnel
Contact: John Byrde
Founded: 1979
Subjects: Anthropology, Education, Social Sciences, Sociology
ISBN Prefix(es): 2-8299

Carre d'Art Edition Archigraphie+
c/o NLDA, One Pl de l'le, 1204 Geneva
Tel: (022) 311 57 50 *Fax:* (022) 312 21 21
Founded: 1989
Subjects: Architecture & Interior Design
ISBN Prefix(es): 2-88287
Branch Office(s)
3 ruede Fribourg, 1201 Geneva

Edizioni Casagrande SA+
Via del Bramantino, 3, 6500 Bellinzona
Tel: (091) 820 0101 *Fax:* (091) 825 1874
E-mail: casagrande@casagrande-online.ch
Web Site: www.casagrande-online.ch
Telex: 846266
Key Personnel
Man Dir, Editorial: Libero Casagrande
Founded: 1972
Subjects: Art, History, Literature, Literary Criticism, Essays
ISBN Prefix(es): 88-7713
Subsidiaries: Archivio Storico Ticinese; Istituto Editoriale Ticinese (IET) SA; Istituto Grafico Casagrande SA
Bookshop(s): Libreria Casagrande, Viale Stazione, 6500 Bellinzona

Castle Publications SA
22, rue Centrale, 1248 Hermance
Tel: (022) 511036 *Fax:* (022) 7511111; (022) 7884240
Key Personnel
Man Dir: Nicolas Ferguson
Founded: 1972
Subjects: Communications, Language Arts, Linguistics
ISBN Prefix(es): 2-88344
Associate Companies: CEEL (Centre Experimental pour l'Enseignement des Langues)
Imprints: SAPL
Subsidiaries: Castle Mexico; Didasko (Castle Japan) 6-7-31-611 Itashibori; SAOL Publications, Canada; Castle France

Causa Verlag GmbH, see Tobler Verlag

Caux Books
Rue du Panorama, 1824 Caux
Tel: (021) 9629469 *Fax:* (021) 9629465
E-mail: info@caux.ch
Web Site: www.caux.ch
Subjects: Biography, Religion - Other, Social Sciences, Sociology
ISBN Prefix(es): 3-85601
Subsidiaries: Caux Edition SA

Caux Edition SA
Rue de Panorama, 1824 Caux
Tel: (021) 963 94 69 *Fax:* (021) 962 94 65
E-mail: info@caux.ch
Web Site: www.caux.ch
Key Personnel
Man Dir, Editorial: Chas Piguet
Founded: 1965
Subjects: Biography, Drama, Theater, Religion - Other, Social Sciences, Sociology
ISBN Prefix(es): 2-88037
Parent Company: Caux Verlag AG
Branch Office(s)
22, av Roche-Schuman, 92100 Boulogne-Billancourt, France *Tel:* (01) 41104050 *Fax:* (01) 41108067
Bookshop(s): Librairie de Caux, Rue de Panorama, 1824 Caux

Verlag Bo Cavefors
c/o Mardatropa AG, 8001 Zurich
Mailing Address: Postfach 5837, 8001 Zurich
Tel: (01) 2017200
Key Personnel
Man Dir: Bo Cavefors
Subjects: Fiction, Poetry, Religion - Catholic
ISBN Prefix(es): 3-85593

CEC-Cosmic Energy Connections+
Belsitostr 12, 8044 Zurich
Tel: (0761) 7059 632 *Fax:* (0761) 7059 633
Founded: 1985
Subjects: Education, Human Relations, Philosophy, Psychology, Psychiatry, Self-Help, Sports, Athletics
ISBN Prefix(es): 3-905276
Warehouse: Bailey Distribution Ltd, Lea Royd Rd, Mountfield Industrial Estate, New Romney, Kent TN28 8XU, United Kingdom *Tel:* (0679) 66905 *Fax:* (0679) 66638
Orders to: Bailey Distribution Ltd, Lea Royd Rd, Mountfield Industrial Estate, New Romney, Kent TN28 8XU, United Kingdom *Tel:* (0679) 66905 *Fax:* (0679) 66638

Cedilivre SA, see Editions Foma SA

Centre Experimental pour l'Enseignement des Langues, see Castle Publications SA

Chamaeleon Verlag AG
Weinbergstr 11, 8001 Zurich
Tel: (01) 2525497 *Fax:* (01) 2725282
Key Personnel
Manager: Mrs Andree Mathis
Founded: 1985
ISBN Prefix(es): 3-905274

Christiana-Verlag+
Postfach 95, 8260 Stein am Rhein
Tel: (052) 741 41 31 *Fax:* (052) 741 20 92
E-mail: info@christiana.ch
Web Site: www.christiana.ch
Key Personnel
Man Dir & International Rights: Arnold Guillet *Tel:* (052) 7414131
Founded: 1948
Subjects: Biological Sciences, Education, Philosophy, Religion - Catholic, Demonology, Angeology, Hagiographic
ISBN Prefix(es): 3-7171
Number of titles published annually: 12 Print
Branch Office(s)
Postfach 110, 78201 Singen, Germany *Tel:* (052) 741 41 31 *Fax:* (052) 741 20 92
Postfach 174, 8260 Stein am Rhein, Austria *Tel:* (052) 741 41 31 *Fax:* (052) 741 20 92
Distribution Center: Ennstaler GesmbH & Co KG, Stadtplatz 26, 4402 Steyr, Austria *Tel:* (07252) 5205320 *Fax:* (07252) 5205322
Marianne Pattloch, Lindenhof 3, Postfach 1254, 63825 Westerngrund, Germany *Tel:* (06024) 24 75 *Fax:* (06024) 26 07 (Germany)
Orders to: Postfach 110, 78201 Singen, Germany

Christoph Merian Verlag+
St Alban-Vorstadt 5, 4002 Basel
Tel: (061) 226 33 25 *Fax:* (061) 226 33 45

PUBLISHERS — SWITZERLAND

E-mail: verlag@merianstiftung.ch
Web Site: www.christoph-merian-verlag.ch
Key Personnel
Chief Executive, Editorial: Dr Beat von Wartburg
Chief Executive: Claus Donau
Marketing: Franzijka Nyffenegger
   E-mail: fnyffenegger@cmsbas.ch
Founded: 1976
Subjects: Art, History, Literature, Literary Criticism, Essays, Photography, Regional Interests
ISBN Prefix(es): 3-85616
Total Titles: 80 Print
Shipping Address: Schweizer Bridezentrum SBZ, Postbach, 4601 Olten, Contact: Yvonne Sardoz
Tel: (062) 209 2704 *Fax:* (062) 209 2788

Chronos Verlag+
Eisengasse 9, 8008 Zurich
Tel: (01) 265 4343 *Fax:* (01) 265 4344
E-mail: info@chronos-verlag.ch
Web Site: www.chronos-verlag.ch
Founded: 1985
Specialize in Gender studies, media & theatre studies.
Subjects: Fiction, Film, Video, History, Nonfiction (General), Social Sciences, Sociology
ISBN Prefix(es): 3-905312; 3-905314; 3-905315; 3-905313; 3-905311; 3-905310; 3-905278
Number of titles published annually: 50 Print
Total Titles: 350 Print
Orders to: AVA, Centralweg 16, Postfach 27, 8910 *Tel:* (01) 762 4260 *Fax:* (01) 762 4210 (Switzerland/Liechtenstein)
GVA, Postfach 2021, Goettingen, Germany *Tel:* (0551) 48 71 77 *Fax:* (0551) 4 13 92 (Germany/European Union)

Clairefontaine, Editions
Av Eglantine 3, 1006 Lausanne
Tel: (021) 323 08 79
Key Personnel
Contact: Albert Mermoud

Werner Classen Verlag
Spluegenstr 10, 8027 Zurich
Tel: (01) 2015606 *Cable:* CLASSENVERLAG ZURICH
Key Personnel
Dir: Werner Classen
Founded: 1945
Subjects: Humor, Music, Dance, Poetry, Psychology, Psychiatry
ISBN Prefix(es): 3-7172

De Clivo Press
Usterstr 126, 8600 Duebendorf
Tel: (01) 8201124
Telex: CH 55256 Serco *Cable:* Declivopress Duebendorf
Key Personnel
Proprietor: Dr Walter Amstutz
ISBN Prefix(es): 3-85634

Cockatoo Press (Schweiz), Thailand-Publikationen (Thailand Publications (Switzerland))+
Im Leeacher 30, 8132 Zurich
Tel: (01) 9841725 *Fax:* (01) 9843420
E-mail: cockatoo@thailine.com
Web Site: www.thailine.com
Founded: 1991
Specialize in publishing & promotion, information service.
Subjects: Antiques, Archaeology, Asian Studies, Business, Cookery, Foreign Countries, Language Arts, Linguistics, Mysteries, Religion - Buddhist, Social Sciences, Sociology, Travel
ISBN Prefix(es): 3-905302
Parent Company: Thailine 2000, Im Leeacher 30, Hinteregg ZH, 8132 Zurich, Mrs Ratanaporn Muller-Kaewdam
Associate Companies: Chiang Saen Internet Ltd Part
Subsidiaries: Thailand Publications Switzerland
Distributor for Editions Duang Kamol; Pilot Publishing; Suriwong Books; White Lotus Press

Rene Coeckelberghs Editions
Museggstr 7, 6004 Lucerne
Tel: (041) 515060 *Fax:* (041) 516645
Packagers.
Subjects: Nonfiction (General)
ISBN Prefix(es): 2-8310; 3-905285

Conseil oecumenique de Eglises, see World Council of Churches (WCC Publications)

Consejo Mundial de Iglesias, see World Council of Churches (WCC Publications)

Cosa-Verlag, Giusep Condrau SA+
Casa Desertina, 7180 Disentis
Mailing Address: Postfach 10, 7180 Disentis
Tel: (081) 947 64 64; (081) 947 63 52 *Fax:* (081) 947 63 52
E-mail: condrau@cosa.ch
Web Site: www.cosa.ch *Cable:* DESERTINA DISENTIS
Key Personnel
Man Dir, Rights & Editorial: Pius Condrau
Founded: 1953
Subjects: Art
ISBN Prefix(es): 3-9521636
Bookshop(s): Condrau, Disentis

Cosmic Energy Connections-CEC, see CEC-Cosmic Energy Connections

Cosmos-Verlag AG
Krayigenweg 2, CP 425, 3074 Muri BE
Mailing Address: PO Box 5776, 3001 Bern
Tel: (31) 9506464 *Fax:* (31) 9506460
E-mail: info@cosmosverlag.ch
Key Personnel
Contact: Regina Haener *E-mail:* haener@cosmosverlag.ch
Founded: 1923
Subjects: Accounting, Business, Fiction, Finance, Management, Regional Interests
ISBN Prefix(es): 3-85621; 2-8296; 3-305
Number of titles published annually: 12 Print

Comite international de la Croix-Rouge
19 Ave de la Paix, 1202 Geneva
Tel: (022) 734 60 01 *Fax:* (022) 733 20 57; (022) 730 27 68
Web Site: www.icrc.org
Telex: CICR 414226
Key Personnel
Head of Publishing Unit: Charles Pierrat
   Fax: (022) 73 8768
Founded: 1863
Subjects: Law
ISBN Prefix(es): 2-88145
Total Titles: 4 Print; 2,000 Online
U.S. Office(s): International Committee of the Red Cross, 780 Third Ave, 28th Floor, New York, NY 10017, United States

Cultur Prospectiv, Edition
Muehlebachstr 35, 8008 Zurich
Tel: (01) 260 69 01 *Fax:* (01) 260 69 29
E-mail: cedition@culturprospectiv.ch
Web Site: www.culturprospectiv.ch
Key Personnel
Contact: Dr Hans-Peter Meier
Founded: 1990
Subjects: Social Sciences, Sociology
ISBN Prefix(es): 3-905345

Edizioni Armando Dado, Tipografia Stazione
Via Orelli 29, 6600 Locarno
Tel: (091) 751 48 02 *Fax:* (091) 752 10 26
Key Personnel
Man Dir: Armando Dado
Subjects: Art, History, Literature, Literary Criticism, Essays, Photography
ISBN Prefix(es): 88-85115; 88-86315; 88-8281

Daimon Verlag AG+
Hauptstr 85, 8840 Einsiedeln
Tel: (055) 412 2266 *Fax:* (055) 412 2231
E-mail: daimon@compuserve.com
Web Site: www.daimon.ch
Key Personnel
Publisher: Dr Robert Hinshaw *E-mail:* r@daimon.ch
Founded: 1979
Specialize in Dream Interpretation.
Membership(s): SBVV.
Subjects: Environmental Studies, History, Poetry, Psychology, Psychiatry
ISBN Prefix(es): 3-85630
Distributor for Chiron; Eranos; Parabola; Sounds True Rec; Spring Publication & Spring Audio/Journal
Orders to: Bookworld Companies, 1941 Whitfield Park Loop, Sarasota, FL 34243, United States

Daphnis-Verlag
Kappelistr 15, 8002 Zurich
Tel: (01) 202 52 71 *Fax:* (01) 201 42 31
Key Personnel
Man Dir: J Fischlin
Founded: 1959
Subjects: Poetry
ISBN Prefix(es): 3-85631

De Vier Winstreken, *imprint of* Nord-Sued Verlag

Marcel Dekker AG+
Hutgasse 4, 4001 Basel
Mailing Address: Postfach 812, 4001 Basel
Tel: (061) 260 63 00 *Fax:* (061) 260 63 33
E-mail: intlcustserv@dekker.com
Web Site: www.dekker.com
Key Personnel
President: Bruno Baumgartner
Founded: 1975
Subjects: Business, Chemistry, Chemical Engineering, Civil Engineering, Earth Sciences, Electronics, Electrical Engineering, Mathematics, Medicine, Nursing, Dentistry
ISBN Prefix(es): 0-8247
Parent Company: Marcel Dekker Inc, 270 Madison Ave, New York, NY 10016, United States

Editions Delachaux et Niestle SA+
2, rue de l Etrat, 1027 Lonay 21
Mailing Address: Case Postale 44, 1000 Lausanne 21
Tel: (021) 8110711 *Fax:* (021) 8110712
E-mail: contact@delachaux-niestle.com
Key Personnel
Man Dir: David Perret
Sales, Permissions: Yvette Perret
Founded: 1861
Subjects: Earth Sciences, Education, Medicine, Nursing, Dentistry, Psychology, Psychiatry, Science (General), Social Sciences, Sociology
ISBN Prefix(es): 2-603; 2-8255
Subsidiaries: Delachaux Niestle, France SA
Branch Office(s)
4 rue Laferriere, 75009 Paris, France
82 rue de Courcelles, 75008 Paris, France
   Tel: (01) 48881239 *Fax:* (01) 48881277

Editions Andre Delcourt & Cie+
27, rue de la Borde, 1018 Lausanne
Mailing Address: CP 113, 1018 Lausanne
Tel: (021) 6479772 *Fax:* (021) 6478831

SWITZERLAND

Key Personnel
Publisher: Andre Delcourt
Founded: 1986
Subjects: Architecture & Interior Design, Art, Literature, Literary Criticism, Essays, Medicine, Nursing, Dentistry, Photography
ISBN Prefix(es): 2-88161
Imprints: AD; Delta; Delta et Spes; Spes

Delta, *imprint of* Editions Andre Delcourt & Cie

Delta et Spes, *imprint of* Editions Andre Delcourt & Cie

Verlag Harri Deutsch+
Riedstr 2, 3600 Thun
Tel: (033) 2223975 *Fax:* (033) 2223950
E-mail: verlag@harri-deutsch.de
Web Site: www.harri-deutsch.de
Key Personnel
Man Dir: Harri Deutsch
Editor: Bernd Mueller
Founded: 1971
Subjects: Astronomy, Biological Sciences, Chemistry, Chemical Engineering, Computer Science, Economics, Electronics, Electrical Engineering, Mathematics, Physics, Science (General), Sports, Athletics, Technology
ISBN Prefix(es): 3-87144; 3-8171
Total Titles: 900 Print; 7 CD-ROM; 5 Online; 5 E-Book
Parent Company: Verlag Harri Deutsch, Germany
Bookshop(s): Naturwiss Fachbuchhandlung an der Universitaet, Graefstr 47, 60486 Frankfurt, Germany *Tel:* (069) 775021 *Fax:* (069) 7073739
Web Site: www.harri-deutsch.de
Orders to: Brockhaus Commission, Postfach 1220, 70806 Kornwestheim, Germany *Tel:* (07) 154-132720 *Fax:* (07) 154-132710

Didax, *imprint of* Editions Foma SA

Diogenes Verlag AG+
Sprecherstr 8, CH 8032 Zurich
Tel: (01) 2548511 *Fax:* (01) 2528407
E-mail: info@diogenes.ch
Web Site: www.diogenes.ch *Cable:* DIOGENESVERLAG ZURICH
Key Personnel
Man Dir & Owner, Publisher: Daniel Keel
Man Dir & Owner, Administration & Finance: Rudolf C Bettschart
Man Dir, Organization & Marketing: Stefan Fritsch
Editorial Dir: Winfried Stephan
Publicity & Promotion: Ruth Geiger
Sales & Marketing: Ulrich Richter
Production: Res Schenk
Foreign Rights & Permissions: Susanne Bauknecht
Corporate Finance: Martha Pfyl
Founded: 1952
Subjects: Art, Drama, Theater, Fiction, Literature, Literary Criticism, Essays, Mysteries, Philosophy, Children's Books
ISBN Prefix(es): 3-257

Drei-D-World und Foto-World Verlag und Vertrieb+
Wartenbergstr 39, 4020 Basel
Tel: (061) 424917
Key Personnel
International Rights: David Haisch
Founded: 1982
Subjects: Art, Business, Communications, Ethnicity, Foreign Countries, How-to, Marketing, Photography, Real Estate, Travel
ISBN Prefix(es): 3-905450
Associate Companies: Pamelart
Subsidiaries: Icebear Group Branch

Branch Office(s)
Icebear Group, 103-2 Lewis Pl, CL-11500 Negoubo, Sri Lanka *Fax:* (031) 33862
Distributor for Pamelart

Librairie Droz SA+
11 rue Massot, 1211 Geneva 12
Mailing Address: PO Box 389, 1211 Geneva 12
Tel: (022) 3466666 *Fax:* (022) 3472391
E-mail: droz@droz.org
Web Site: www.droz.org
Key Personnel
Man Dir, Rights & Permissions: Max Engammare
Sales Dir: Mrs Burquier
Founded: 1924
Subjects: Antiques, History, Literature, Literary Criticism, Essays, Social Sciences, Sociology
ISBN Prefix(es): 2-600
Number of titles published annually: 80 Print; 2 CD-ROM; 2 E-Book
Total Titles: 80 Print; 4 CD-ROM; 2 E-Book

Duboux Editions SA+
Frutigenstr 6, 3600 Thun
Tel: (033) 2256060 *Fax:* (033) 2256066
E-mail: duboux-editions@duboux.ch
Web Site: www.duboux.ch
Key Personnel
President & Publisher: Jean-Pierre Duboux
Founded: 1988
Subjects: Cookery, Travel
ISBN Prefix(es): 3-907950
Distributed by Verlag Handwerk & Technik

Gottlieb Duttweiler Institute for Trends & Futures
Langhaldenstr 21, 8803 Rueschlikon, Zurich
Mailing Address: Postfach 531, 8803 Rueschlikon, Zurich
Tel: (01) 7246111 *Fax:* (01) 7246262
E-mail: biblio@gdi.ch
Web Site: www.gdi.ch *Cable:* GREEN MEADOW
Key Personnel
Chief Executive Officer: David Bosshart
Marketing: Karin Hartmann
Founded: 1963
Subjects: Economics, Management, Marketing, Social Sciences, Sociology
ISBN Prefix(es): 3-7184
Parent Company: Migros-Genossenschafts-Bund, Zurich
Imprints: GDI

Editions l'Eau Vive
13 rue de Monthoux, 1201 Geneva
Tel: (022) 7329847 *Fax:* (022) 7410482
Key Personnel
Man Dir: Rolande Gloor
Founded: 1960
Subjects: Biography, Religion - Other
ISBN Prefix(es): 2-88035

Eboris-Coda-Bompiani+
11 rue Maunoir, 167 Geneva
Tel: (022) 7188820 *Fax:* (022) 7079199
Key Personnel
President: Isabella Coda-Bompiani
Founded: 1994
Subjects: History, Literature, Literary Criticism, Essays, Photography
ISBN Prefix(es): 2-940121
Number of titles published annually: 30 Print; 35 E-Book
Total Titles: 130 Print; 140 E-Book

Editions Eboris SA, see Eboris-Coda-Bompiani

Eco Verlags AG+
Langstr 187, 8005 Zurich
Tel: (01) 440400

Key Personnel
Man Dir: Verena Stettler
Founded: 1976
Subjects: Literature, Literary Criticism, Essays, Nonfiction (General)
ISBN Prefix(es): 3-85647
Imprints: Literatheke; Neue Szene

Verlag ED Emmentaler Druck AG
Dorfstr, 3550 Langnau im Emmental
Tel: (035) 21911 *Fax:* (035) 0524642
Key Personnel
Man Dir, Sales: Paul Hartmann
Editorial & Publicity: Markus F Rubli
Founded: 1845
Subjects: Fiction, Photography, Regional Interests
ISBN Prefix(es): 3-85654

Editions Edita+
Route de Geneve, CP 85, 1000 Lausanne 9
Tel: (021) 6251392 *Fax:* (021) 6254291
Telex: 450296
Key Personnel
Contact: Michel Ferloni; Francois Mukundi
Founded: 1953
Subjects: Art, History
ISBN Prefix(es): 2-88001
Subsidiaries: Editions Office du Livre
Orders to: Office du Livre Distribution, 101 Route de Villars, 1701 Fribourg

Edition Epoca+
Werdstr 128, 8003 Zurich
Tel: (01) 4511717 *Fax:* (01) 4511717
E-mail: info@epoca.ch
Web Site: www.epoca.ch
Key Personnel
Contact: Urs Kummer; Adrian Stokar
Founded: 1995
Subjects: Fiction, Literature, Literary Criticism, Essays, Philosophy, Social Sciences, Sociology
ISBN Prefix(es): 3-905513
Number of titles published annually: 7 Print

eFeF-Verlag/Edition Ebersbach+
Klosterparkgaessli 8, 5430 Wettingen
Tel: (056) 4260618 *Fax:* (056) 4270461
E-mail: info@efefverlag.ch
Web Site: www.efefverlag.ch
Founded: 1984
Subjects: Biography, Fiction, Women's Studies
ISBN Prefix(es): 3-9521022
Orders to: Buch 2000, Obfeldstr 35, 8910 Affoltern

Drei Eidgenossen Verlag
Huegelweg 15, 4102 Binningen
Tel: (061) 475166 *Fax:* (061) 475166
Key Personnel
Man Dir: Mr Hosch
Founded: 1936
ISBN Prefix(es): 3-85643

Editions Eisele SA
Av de la Confrerie 42, 1008 Prilly/Lausanne
Tel: (021) 6256324 *Fax:* (021) 6236359
Web Site: www.eisele.ch
Key Personnel
International Rights: Jean-Luc Eisele
Subjects: Education, History, Science (General)
ISBN Prefix(es): 2-88002

ELCE Editeurs et Libraires Catholiques d'Europe
Hans-Walter Luthi, Wattstr 6, 9012 Saint Gallen
Tel: (071) 279580 *Fax:* (071) 279580
E-mail: hawas@mhs.ch
Key Personnel
Contact: Hans-Walter Luthi

Elektrowirtschaft Verlag
Militaerstr 36, 8021 Zurich
Mailing Address: Postfach 3080, 8021 Zurich
Tel: (01) 2994141 *Fax:* (01) 2994140
E-mail: redaktion@infel.ch
Web Site: www.infel.ch
Subjects: Electronics, Electrical Engineering
ISBN Prefix(es): 3-85651

Elvetica Edizioni SA+
CP 134, 6834 Morbio Inferiore
Tel: (091) 6835056 *Fax:* (091) 6837605
E-mail: info@swissfinance.com
Web Site: www.tinet.ch/swissfinance
Key Personnel
General Manageaer: Dr M G Grosso
Founded: 1967
Membership(s): Societa Editori Svizzera Italiana; Association Europeenne des Editeurs d'Annuaires; Schweizer Adressbuch Verleger Verband.
Subjects: Economics, Novels, Essays & Literature
ISBN Prefix(es): 88-86639
Total Titles: 1 CD-ROM; 1 E-Book

Erker-Verlag
Division of Erker-Galerie AG
Bahnhofstr 8, 9000 St Gallen
Tel: (071) 227979 *Fax:* (071) 227919
Key Personnel
Contact: Franze Larese; Juerg Janett
Founded: 1946
Subjects: Art, Literature, Literary Criticism, Essays, Philosophy, Poetry
ISBN Prefix(es): 3-905542; 3-905543; 3-905544; 3-905545; 3-905546
Distribution Center: Balmer Ag, Bucherlager, Bosch 41, Hunenberg (Switzerland)
Stuttgarter Verlagskontor SVK GmbH, Rotebuhlstr 77, D-70178 Stuttgart, Germany (Rest of the world)

Edition Hans Erpf Edition+
Postfach 6018, 3001 Bern
Tel: (037) 711385 *Fax:* (037) 711968 *Cable:* BUCHERPF
Key Personnel
Man Dir: Hans Erpf
Founded: 1966
Subjects: Humor, Literature, Literary Criticism, Essays
ISBN Prefix(es): 3-905517; 3-905520
Number of titles published annually: 20 Print

Espaces Photographiques, *imprint of* Editions Olizane

Editions Esprit Ouvert+
3 Chemin de Mornex, 1003 Lausanne
Tel: (021) 3208844 *Fax:* (021) 3235403
Founded: 1988
Subjects: Film, Video, Literature, Literary Criticism, Essays
ISBN Prefix(es): 2-88329

Eular Verlag (Eular Publishers)
Subsidiary of Friedrich Reinhardt AG
Missionsstr 36, 4012 Basel
Tel: (061) 251317 *Fax:* (061) 251286
E-mail: eular@reinhardt.ch
Key Personnel
Publisher & International Rights: Ruedi Reinhardt
Founded: 1977
Official publishers of The European League Against Rheumatism (EULAR).
Subjects: Health, Nutrition, Medicine, Nursing, Dentistry
ISBN Prefix(es): 3-7177
Orders to: Reinhardt Media-Service

Europa Verlag AG
Raemistr 5, 8024 Zurich
Tel: (01) 471629
Telex: 816534 fere ch *Cable:* Europaverlag Zurich
Key Personnel
Man Dir: Emmie Oprecht
Founded: 1933
Distributor for UNESCO, Paris.
Subjects: Art, Government, Political Science, History, Philosophy
ISBN Prefix(es): 3-85665
Associate Companies: Verlag Oprecht, Zurich (Theatrical)

Edition Exodus
Imprint of Societe Cooperative Edition Exodus
Bederstr 76, 8027 Zurich
Mailing Address: Postfach 8027, 8027 Zurich 5
Tel: (01) 2041774 *Fax:* (01) 2024933
E-mail: editionexodus@compuserve.com
Web Site: www.kath.ch/exodus
Key Personnel
Publisher: Markus Koferli
Founded: 1982
Subjects: History, Philosophy, Religion - Catholic, Religion - Protestant, Social Sciences, Sociology, Theology
ISBN Prefix(es): 3-905575

AZ Fachverlage AG, see AT Verlag

Faksimile Verlag AG
Maihofstr 25, 6000 Lucerne 9
Mailing Address: Postfach 177, 6000 Lucerne 9
Tel: (041) 4290820 *Fax:* (041) 4290840
E-mail: faksimile@faksimile.ch
Web Site: www.faksimile.ch
Subjects: Antiques, Art, History
ISBN Prefix(es): 3-85672

FEDA SA+
Via Frasca 8, 6900 Lugano
Tel: (091) 9235677 *Fax:* (091) 9220171
Founded: 1990
Subjects: Archaeology, Architecture & Interior Design, Art, Photography
ISBN Prefix(es): 88-7269
Associate Companies: Edizioni Gottardo SA, Lugano, Italy; Giampiero Casagrande Editore, Lugano, Italy
Imprints: FIDIA

Editions Francois Feij
Pl de l'Eglise, 1166 Perroy
Tel: (021) 8254675
Subjects: Law
ISBN Prefix(es): 2-88030

FIDIA, *imprint of* FEDA SA

Fidia Edizioni d'Arte, see FEDA SA

Fischer Media AG fur Verlag und Publishing
Bahnhofplatz 1, 3110 Muensingen
Tel: (031) 7205111 *Fax:* (031) 7205112
E-mail: info@fischerprint.ch
Web Site: www.fischergroup.ch
Key Personnel
Manager: Heinrich Gasser
ISBN Prefix(es): 3-85681
Parent Company: Fischer Druck AG

Maurice et Pierre Foetisch SA
6, rue de Bourg, 1002 Lausanne
Tel: (021) 3239444; (021) 3239445 *Fax:* (021) 3115011
Telex: 524227
Key Personnel
Man Dir & other offices: Jean-Claude Foetisch
Founded: 1947
Subjects: Education, Music, Dance, Radio, TV
Associate Companies: Disco SA

Editions Foma SA
5, Av Longemalle, 1020 Renens-Lausanne
Tel: (021) 6351361 *Fax:* (021) 6351704
Telex: CH-Cedil 25416
Key Personnel
Man Dir, Editorial: J-L Peverelli
Sales: M Sculati
Publicity: Ann-Mari Mingard
Rights & Permissions: F Buhler
Founded: 1948
Subjects: Film, Video, Literature, Literary Criticism, Essays, Photography, Psychology, Psychiatry, Sports, Athletics
ISBN Prefix(es): 2-88003
Imprints: Didax
Subsidiaries: 5 Continents, Cedilivre SA
Bookshop(s): Didax

Fondation de l'Encyclopedie de Geneve
Case Postale 3640, 1211 Geneva 3
Fax: (022) 3273391; (022) 3273365
Key Personnel
President: Catherine Santschi
Founded: 1979
Description of Geneva's past & present.
Subjects: History
ISBN Prefix(es): 2-940069
Total Titles: 11 Print

Fortuna Finanz-Verlag AG+
Bergholzweg 30, 8123 Ebmatingen
Tel: (01) 9103102 *Fax:* (01) 9103353
E-mail: info@goldseiten.de
Web Site: www.goldseiten.de
Key Personnel
Man Dir: Ueli Vonau
Founded: 1953
Subjects: Finance
ISBN Prefix(es): 3-85684

Fotorotar AG/EGG ZH, *imprint of* Schweizerisches Jugendschriftenwerk, SJW

Frobenius AG
Spalenring 31, 4012 Basel
Tel: (061) 7715677 *Fax:* (061) 7116218
Key Personnel
Publicity: Otto Rymann
Subjects: History, Law, Literature, Literary Criticism, Essays, Regional Interests
ISBN Prefix(es): 3-85695

G+B Arts International+
Postfach 91, 4004 Basel
Tel: (061) 2610138 *Fax:* (061) 2610173
Key Personnel
Contact: Linda Lowery-Stuart
Subjects: Architecture & Interior Design, Art, Drama, Theater, History, Photography
Associate Companies: Craftsman House; Fine Arts Press; Harwood Academic; Verlag der Kunst; Harvey Miller Publishers; neue bildende Kunst
Orders to: Marston Book Services Ltd, PO Box 269, Abingdon, Oxon 0X14 4YN, United Kingdom *Tel:* (01) 2354 65500 *Fax:* (01) 2354 65555

Verlag Gachnang & Springer, Bern-Berlin
Muristr 16, 3006 Bern
Tel: (031) 3518383 *Fax:* (031) 3518385
E-mail: verlag@gachnang-springer.com
Web Site: www.gachnang-springer.com
Key Personnel
President: Johannes Gachnang
Editor: Constance Lotz; Christine Meyer-Thoss
Founded: 1983
Subjects: Art, Philosophy
ISBN Prefix(es): 3-906127

Distributed by buch 2000 (Switzerland); DAP Distributed Art Publishers (USA, Canada); Buchhandlung Walther Koenig (Europe, excluding Switzerland)

Garuda-Verlag+
Sonneggstr 10, 8953 Dietikon
Tel: (01) 7411287 *Fax:* (056) 6401012
E-mail: garuda@bluewin.ch
Key Personnel
Dir: P Eisenegger; K Eisenegger
Founded: 1985
Also acts as book distributor & agent.
Subjects: Religion - Buddhist
ISBN Prefix(es): 3-906139
Distributor for Diamant Verlag; Fabri-Verlag; GARUDA-VERLAG

GC, *imprint of* Giampiero Casagrande Editore

GDI, *imprint of* Gottlieb Duttweiler Institute for Trends & Futures

Georg et Cie SA, see Georg Editeur SA

Georg Editeur SA+
chemin de la Mousse 46, 1225 Chene-Bourg
Tel: (022) 8690029 *Fax:* (022) 8690015
E-mail: livres@medecinehygiene.ch
Web Site: www.medecinehygiene.ch
Key Personnel
Man Dir: Henri Weissenbach *E-mail:* henri.weissenbach@medecinehygiene.ch; Jean-Francois Balavoine
Founded: 1857
Subjects: Economics, Environmental Studies, Ethnicity, Government, Political Science, History, Language Arts, Linguistics, Law, Music, Dance, Philosophy, Psychology, Psychiatry, Religion - Other, Science (General), Social Sciences, Sociology
ISBN Prefix(es): 2-8257
Number of titles published annually: 35 Print
Total Titles: 450 Print; 1 CD-ROM
Parent Company: Medecine & Hygiene
Associate Companies: Editions Eshel, Paris, France
Imprints: Editions Medecine et Hygiene
Distribution Center: Vilo Distribution, 25 rue Ginoux, 75015 Paris, France *Tel:* (01) 45770805 *Fax:* (01) 45757553

Giampiero Casagrande Editore+
Via Frasca 8, 6900 Lugano
Tel: (091) 9235677 *Fax:* (091) 9220171
Telex: 030
Founded: 1982
Subjects: Architecture & Interior Design, Art, History, Photography
ISBN Prefix(es): 88-7795
Imprints: GC
Subsidiaries: Fidia Edizioni d'Arte (FEDA SA)

Verlag Gleitschirm
Postfach 68, 7007 Chur
Tel: (081) 235241 *Fax:* (081) 221452
ISBN Prefix(es): 3-906334
Divisions: Gleitschirm-Reisen

Globi Verlag AG
Binzstr 15, 8045 Zurich
Tel: (01) 4552130 *Fax:* (01) 4552188
E-mail: info@globi.ch
Web Site: www.globi.ch
Telex: 813282 *Cable:* GLOBIVERLAG ZURICH
Key Personnel
Man Dir: Emil Herzog
Founded: 1944
Subjects: Humor

ISBN Prefix(es): 3-85703
Warehouse: B D Buecherdienst Einsiedeln, 8840 Einsiedeln

Goethe-Verlag, Godhard von Heydebrand
Worbstr 20, Postfach 38, 3067 Boll
Tel: (031) 833248
Key Personnel
Manager: Godhard von Heydebrand
Founded: 1955
ISBN Prefix(es): 3-85730

Victor Goldschmidt Verlagsbuchhandlung
Mostackerstr 17, 4003 Basel
Tel: (061) 236565 *Fax:* (061) 2616123
Key Personnel
Contact: Salomon Goldschmidt
Founded: 1902
Membership(s): Swiss Booksellers & Publishers Association.
Subjects: Religion - Jewish, "Judaica" & "Hebraica", Hebrew, German, English, French & Yiddish
ISBN Prefix(es): 3-85705

Pierre Gonin Editions d'Art
Ch Du Grand-Praz 1, 1012 Lausanne-Chailly
Tel: (021) 7285948 *Fax:* (021) 7285948
Web Site: www.lemeilleur.ch/editionsgonin
Key Personnel
Contact: Francoise Gonin
Founded: 1990
ISBN Prefix(es): 2-88016

Gotthelf-Verlag
Badenerstr 69, 8026 Zurich
Tel: (01) 2428155 *Fax:* (01) 2646486
E-mail: rms@reinhardt.ch
Key Personnel
Man Dir: Alfred Ruedisuehli
Founded: 1928
Subjects: Religion - Other
ISBN Prefix(es): 3-85706
Associate Companies: CVB Buch und Druck, Missionsstr 36, 4012 Basel

Govinda-Verlag (Govinda Press)+
Postfach 257, 8212 Neuhausen 2
Tel: (052) 6726677 *Fax:* (052) 6726678
E-mail: info@govinda.ch
Web Site: www.govinda.ch
Key Personnel
Manager: Ronald Zuerrer *E-mail:* rz@govinda.ch
Founded: 1989
Subjects: Astrology, Occult, Mysteries, Parapsychology, Philosophy, Poetry, Religion - Hindu, Religion - Other
ISBN Prefix(es): 3-906347
Number of titles published annually: 5 Print
Total Titles: 50 Print

Graduate Institute of International Studies+
132 rue de Lausanne, 1211 Geneva 21
Tel: (022) 9085700 *Fax:* (022) 9085710
E-mail: info@hei.unige.ch
Web Site: www.hei.unige.ch
Key Personnel
Dir, Publications Department: Vera Gowlland
Founded: 1927
Publishes only works originating from the Institute.
Subjects: Economics, History, Law
ISBN Prefix(es): 3-8288
U.S. Office(s): Columbia University Press, New York, NY, United States
Distributed by Kegan Paul International (UK); Kluwer (The Hague); Presses Universitaires de France (PUF) (France)

Editions du Grand-Pont
2 Place Bel Air, 1003 Lausanne

Tel: (021) 3123222 *Fax:* (021) 3113222
Founded: 1971
ISBN Prefix(es): 2-88148

Editions du Griffon (Neuchatel)
Faubourg du Lac 536, 2001 Neuchatel
Tel: (032) 7252204
Founded: 1944
Subjects: Art
ISBN Prefix(es): 2-88006

Editions Francois Grounauer
One rue du Belvedere, 1203 Geneva
Tel: (022) 447948
Founded: 1972
Subjects: Government, Political Science, History, Social Sciences, Sociology
ISBN Prefix(es): 2-88076

GSMBA, Edition Bruno Gasser
Kasernenstr 23, 4058 Basel
Tel: (061) 6811103 *Fax:* (061) 6811103
E-mail: gasser@dial-switch.ck
ISBN Prefix(es): 3-905504

Guides-Olizane, *imprint of* Editions Olizane

Th Gut Verlag
Seestr 86, 8712 Staefa
Tel: (01) 9285211 *Fax:* (01) 9285200
Web Site: www.gutverlag.ch/
Telex: 875668
Key Personnel
Contact, All offices: Ulrich Gut
Founded: 1943
Subjects: Ethnicity, Government, Political Science, Regional Interests
ISBN Prefix(es): 3-85717

GVA Publishers Ltd+
PO Box 135, Champel, 1211 Geneva 12
Tel: (022) 3112424 *Fax:* (022) 3112556
Key Personnel
Executive Vice President: Alain Nicollier
Founded: 1979
Membership(s): American Booksellers Association.
Subjects: Art, Travel
ISBN Prefix(es): 2-88115

Haffmans Verlag AG+
Seefeldstr 301, 8034 Zurich
Tel: (01) 386 4000 *Fax:* (01) 386 4001
E-mail: verlag@haffmans.ch *Cable:* HAFFMANS VERLAG
Key Personnel
Man Dir, Publisher: Gerd Haffmans
Man Dir, Finance Production: Urs Jakob
Editor: Heiko Arntz
Editor & International Rights: Sophie von Heppe
Sales: Constantin Ragusa
Founded: 1982
Subjects: Art, Fiction, Humor, Literature, Literary Criticism, Essays, Mysteries, Philosophy, Poetry, Science Fiction, Fantasy
ISBN Prefix(es): 3-251
Number of titles published annually: 60 Print; 10 Audio
Total Titles: 350 Print; 17 Audio

Hagenbach & Bender GMBH
Gutenbergstr 20, 3011 Bern
Tel: (31) 3816666 *Fax:* (31) 3816677
E-mail: rights@hagenbach-bender.com
Web Site: www.hagenbach-bender.com
Key Personnel
Contact: Dieter A Hagenbach *E-mail:* dieter@hagenbach-bender.com
Founded: 2001
Literary & media agency.

PUBLISHERS

SWITZERLAND

Hallwag Kuemmerly & Frey AG+
Nordring 4, 3000 Bern
Tel: (031) 423131 *Fax:* (031) 414133
Telex: 912661 Hawa CH *Cable:* HALLWAG BERNE
Key Personnel
President: Dr Juergen Schad
Editorial, Permissions: Beat Koelliker
Sales: Juerg Burri
Founded: 1912
Subjects: Animals, Pets, Art, Cookery, History, How-to, Nonfiction (General), Science (General), Travel
ISBN Prefix(es): 3-444
Branch Office(s)
Hallwag Verlagsgesellschaft mbH, Germany

Paul Haupt Bern+
Falkenplatz 14, 3001 Bern
Tel: (031) 3012425 *Fax:* (031) 3014669
E-mail: info@haupt.ch
Web Site: www.haupt.ch *Cable:* HAUPTBERN
Key Personnel
Man Dir, Permissions: Men Haupt
Production: Erich Hauri
Sales, Publicity: Cordula Frevel
Editor, Rights: Regina Balmer
Contact: Matthias Haupt
Founded: 1906
Subjects: Art, Crafts, Games, Hobbies, Economics, Education, How-to, Science (General), Social Sciences, Sociology
ISBN Prefix(es): 3-258
Total Titles: 2,500 Print; 5 CD-ROM
Foreign Rights: Gudruu Hebel (Scandinavia)
Bookshop(s): Hoeheweg 11, Interlaken 3800

Institut fuer Heilpaedagogik
Moosmattstr 12, 6005 Lucerne
Tel: (041) 3170033 *Fax:* (041) 3170034
E-mail: info@ihpl.ch
Web Site: www.ihpl.ch
Key Personnel
President: Anton Huber
ISBN Prefix(es): 3-85745

Max Heindel Verlag Rosenkreuzer Philosophie
(Max Heindel Publishing House Rosicrucian Philosophy)
La Motta Fex, 7514 Sils Maria/Fex
Tel: (081) 834 20 03 *Fax:* (081) 834 20 04
E-mail: max_heindel_verlag@bluewin.ch
Web Site: www.heindel-verlag.ch
Key Personnel
Contact: Annemarie Giovanoli-Troost *Tel:* (081) 834 2122 *Fax:* (081) 834 2124

Heinrich Hugendubel AG
Villa Bellevue, Hauptstr 14, 8280 Kreuzlingen
Tel: (071) 67711-90 *Fax:* (071) 67711-91

Helbing und Lichtenhahn Verlag AG+
Elisabethenstr 8, 4051 Basel
Tel: (061) 2289070 *Fax:* (061) 2289071
E-mail: info@helbing.ch
Web Site: www.helbing.ch
Key Personnel
Dir: Men Haupt
Founded: 1822
Subjects: Anthropology, Economics, Environmental Studies, Government, Political Science, History, Language Arts, Linguistics, Law, Management
ISBN Prefix(es): 3-7190
Associate Companies: Sauerlaender AG

Verlag Helvetica Chimica Acta
Hofwiesenstr 26, 8042 Zurich
Tel: (01) 3602434 *Fax:* (01) 3602435
E-mail: info@wiley-vch.ch
Web Site: www.wiley-vch.de

Key Personnel
Man Dir: Dr M V Kisakuerek
Subjects: Chemistry, Chemical Engineering
ISBN Prefix(es): 3-85727; 3-906390

Herder AG Basel
Muttenzerstr 109, 4133 Pratteln 1
Tel: (061) 8210900 *Fax:* (061) 8279067
E-mail: verkauf@herder.ch
Telex: 64358
Subjects: Philosophy, Religion - Other, Theology
ISBN Prefix(es): 3-906371; 3-906372
Associate Companies: Verlag Herder GmbH & Co KG, Germany; Verlag A G Ploetz GmbH & Co KG, Germany; Herder und Herder GmbH, Germany; Verlag Herder & Co, Austria; Herder Editrice e Libreria, Italy; Editorial Herder SA, Spain

Verlag Huber & Co AG+
Division of Huber & Co AG
Promenadenstr 16, Postfach 382, 8500 Frauenfeld
Tel: (052) 723 5617 *Fax:* (052) 723 5619
E-mail: buchverlag@huber.ch
Web Site: www.huber.ch
Key Personnel
Man Dir & Publisher: Hansrudolf Frey *Tel:* (052) 723 5618
Production: Arthur Miserez *Tel:* (052) 723 5656 *Fax:* (052) 721 4977
Marketing: Charlotte Krahenbuehl
Founded: 1809
Subjects: Agriculture, Art, Environmental Studies, Ethnicity, Government, Political Science, History, Language Arts, Linguistics, Regional Interests
ISBN Prefix(es): 3-7193; 3-274
Total Titles: 200 Print
Bookshop(s): Buchhandlung Huber & Co AG, Freiestr 8, 8501 Frauenfeld *Tel:* (052) 7235858 *E-mail:* info@huberbooks.ch *Web Site:* www.huberbooks.ch

Hug & Co+
Grossmuensterrplatz 7, 8001 Zurich
Mailing Address: Limmatquai 28-30, Postfach, 8022 Zurich
Tel: (01) 269 41 41 *Fax:* (01) 269 41 06
E-mail: info@hug-musikverlage.ch
Web Site: www.hug-musikverlage.ch
Telex: 829311 muvich
Key Personnel
Dir: Erika Hug
Founded: 1807
Subjects: Music, Dance
ISBN Prefix(es): 3-906415
Associate Companies: Edition Foetisch-Foetisch Freres, Case postale, 1002 Lausanne
Warehouse: Musica Vivam Flughofstr 61, 8152 Glattbrugg, Zurich
Orders to: Musica Vivam Flughofstr 61, 8152 Glattbrugg, Zurich

Editions Charles Huguenin Pro Arte
rue du Sapin 2a, 2114 Fleurier
Tel: (038) 61 27 27 *Fax:* (038) 61 37 19
Key Personnel
Man Dir: Jean-Charles Frochaux
Parent Company: Schola Cantorum-Triton
Associate Companies: Cantate Domino

Idegraf SA, Editions
route de Chancy, 28, 1213 Petit-Lancy
Tel: (022) 792 03 96 *Fax:* (022) 793 63 30
E-mail: 101512.3363@compuserve.com

Editions Ides et Calendes SA+
Evole 19, 2000 Neuchatel
Tel: (032) 725 38 61 *Fax:* (032) 725 58 80
E-mail: info@idesetcalendes.com; artides@artides.com; ides@livre.net

Web Site: www.artides.com; www.livre.net/ides
Key Personnel
Chief Executive: Alain Bouret
Founded: 1941
Subjects: Art, Law, Lives d'art & peiuture; photoarchive, photogalerie
ISBN Prefix(es): 2-8258

Verlag Industrielle Organisation+
Dietzingerstr 3, 8036 Zurich
Tel: (01) 4667711 *Fax:* (01) 4667412
E-mail: info@ofv.ch
Web Site: www.ofv.ch
Key Personnel
Contact: Gerhard Labitzke *Tel:* (01) 466 74 76 *E-mail:* glabitzke@ofv.ch
Founded: 1931
Subjects: Electronics, Electrical Engineering, Human Relations, Management, Marketing
ISBN Prefix(es): 3-85743
Parent Company: Orell Fussli Verlag

Interfrom AG Editions+
Scheideggstr 78, 8022 Zurich
Mailing Address: Postfach 5005, 8022 Zurich
Tel: (01) 2020900
Key Personnel
Publisher: Leo V Fromm
Executive Vice President & Editorial: A Harms-Hunold
Sales Manager: Annegret Busch
Public Relations: Ursula Malzahn
Founded: 1974
Popular Science by German-speaking Experts.
Subjects: Economics, Education, Environmental Studies, Ethnicity, Government, Political Science, History, Science (General), Social Sciences, Sociology
ISBN Prefix(es): 3-7201
Imprints: Zuerich
Branch Office(s)
Verlag A Fromm, Breiter Gang 10-16, 49076 Osnabrueck, Germany
U.S. Office(s): Fromm International Publ Corp, 560 Lexington Ave, New York, NY 10022, United States
Warehouse: Schweizer Buchzentrum, 4601 Olten
Orders to: Schweizer Buchzentrum, 4601 Olten

Iris Verlag AG
c/o Poly Laupen AG, Bahnweg 2, 3177 Laupen
Tel: (031) 7473300 *Fax:* (031) 7473301
E-mail: polyinfo@rentsch.ch
Web Site: www.poly-laupen.ch
Key Personnel
Man Dir: Horst Hochrein
Deputy Man Dir: Peter Konrad
ISBN Prefix(es): 3-85751

ISIOM Verlag fur Tondokumente, Weinreb Tonarchiv+
CP 362, 6600 Locarno
Tel: (091) 7513524 *Fax:* (091) 7516154
E-mail: isiom@bluewin.ch
Key Personnel
President: Hans Haessig-Tellenbach
Author: Friedrich Weinreb; Graf Duerckneim
Founded: 1974
Specialize in audio books.
Subjects: Ethnicity, Philosophy, Religion - Jewish, Theology
ISBN Prefix(es): 88-85151

Jordanverlag AG+
Steffenstr 1, 8052 Zurich
Tel: (01) 3023676
Key Personnel
Contact: Peter Buff
Founded: 1984
Subjects: Biblical Studies, Religion - Catholic, Religion - Protestant
ISBN Prefix(es): 3-906561

SWITZERLAND

Editions Jouvence+
CP 184, 1233 Bernex, Geneva
Tel: (022) 794 66 22 *Fax:* (022) 794 67 86
E-mail: info@editions-jouvence.com
Web Site: www.editions-jouvence.com
Key Personnel
Dir: Jacques Maire
Editorial Dir: Olivier Clerc *Tel:* (0450) 432862
 E-mail: olivier.clerc@usa.net
Founded: 1989
Subjects: Child Care & Development, Environmental Studies, Health, Nutrition, Psychology, Psychiatry, Self-Help, Social Sciences, Sociology
ISBN Prefix(es): 2-88353
Associate Companies: BP 7, 74161 St Julien-en-Genevois, France *Tel:* (0450) 43 28 60 *Fax:* (0450) 43 29 24

JPM Publications SA+
12 av William Fraisse, 1006 Lausanne
Tel: (021) 6177561 *Fax:* (021) 6161257
E-mail: information@jpmguides.com
Web Site: www.jpmguides.com
Key Personnel
Man Dir: Mr Jean-Paul Minder *Tel:* (021) 617 75 66 *E-mail:* jeanpaul.minder@jpmguides.com
Founded: 1992
Subjects: Travel
ISBN Prefix(es): 2-88452
U.S. Office(s): 245 E 19 St, 3D, New York, NY 10003, United States, Contact: Dorsey Smith
Distributed by Hunter Publishing

Jugend mit einer Mission Verlag+
Poststr 14, Postfach 144, 2500 Biel 8
Tel: (032) 418988 *Fax:* (032) 418920
Key Personnel
Publisher: Eva Stopper
Founded: 1991
Subjects: Biblical Studies, Education, Religion - Protestant, Theology
ISBN Prefix(es): 3-906568

Junod Nicolas
12 rue Robert-de-Traz, 1206 Geneva
Tel: (022) 347 02 42 *Fax:* (022) 347 02 42
Telex: 23381 trib ch
Key Personnel
Man Dir, Rights & Permissions: Henri Heizmann
Founded: 1977
Subjects: Art, Cookery, Government, Political Science, Health, Nutrition, History, Humor, Radio, TV
ISBN Prefix(es): 2-8297
Parent Company: SA de la Tribune de Geneve

Juris Druck & Verlag AG
Basteiplatz 5, 8953 Dietikon
Tel: (01) 2117727; (01) 2117747 *Fax:* (01) 7409019
E-mail: juris@swissonline.ch
Key Personnel
Man Dir: Markus Christen
Founded: 1945
Membership(s): SBVV.
Subjects: History, Law
ISBN Prefix(es): 3-260

Kalos-Verlag
Fritz Aerni-Schaffhauserstr 446, 8052 Zurich
Tel: (01) 3022751 *Fax:* (01) 3022751
ISBN Prefix(es): 3-906598

Kanisius Verlag+
ave de Beauregard 3, 1701 Fribourg
Mailing Address: Postfach 1052, 1701 Fribourg, Germany
Tel: (026) 425 87 40 *Fax:* (026) 425 87 38
Web Site: www.canisius.ch *Cable:* KANISIUSWERK FRIBOURG

Key Personnel
Man Dir, Publicity: Dr Barbara Evers-Greder
Production Manager: Peter Ledergerber
Founded: 1898
Subjects: Biblical Studies, Biography, Cookery, Religion - Catholic, Self-Help, Theology
ISBN Prefix(es): 3-85764
Bookshop(s): Kanisiusbuchhandlung,, Bahnhofplatz 6, 1701 Fribourg *Tel:* (037) 221345; Kanisiusbuchhandlung, Haengebrueckstr 16, 1702 Fribourg *Tel:* (037) 222954; Kanisiuswerk, Blarerstr 18, 78462 Konstanz, Germany

S Karger AG, Medical & Scientific Publishers+
Allschwilerstr 10, 4009 Basel
Tel: (061) 3061111 *Fax:* (061) 3061234
E-mail: karger@karger.ch
Web Site: www.karger.com
Key Personnel
President: Dr Thomas Karger
Man Dir: Steven Karger
Dir, Sales & Marketing: Mr Moritz Thommen
Rights & Permissions: Mrs Carmen Scaglia
Founded: 1890
Anatomy Atlas.
Subjects: Biological Sciences, Medicine, Nursing, Dentistry, Psychology, Psychiatry, Veterinary Science
ISBN Prefix(es): 3-8055
Associate Companies: Karger Japan, Inc, Yushima S Bldg 3F, 4-2-3, Yushima, Bunkyo-ku, Tokyo 113-0034, Japan *Tel:* (03) 3815-1800 *Fax:* (03) 3815-1802 *E-mail:* publisher@karger.jp; S Karger AG, 4 Rickett St, London SW6 1RU, United Kingdom *Tel:* (020) 7610 3331 *Fax:* (020) 7610 3337 *E-mail:* uk@karger.ch; S Karger Publishers Inc, 26 W Avon Rd, PO Box 529, Farmington, CT 06085, United States *Tel:* 860-675-7834 *Fax:* 860-675-7302 *E-mail:* karger@snet.net; Panther Publishers Private Ltd, 33 First Main, Koramangala First Block, Bangalore 560 034, India *Tel:* (080) 5505 836, 5505 837 *Fax:* (080) 5505 981 *E-mail:* panther_publishers@vsnl.com
Branch Office(s)
DA Information Services, 648 Whitehorse Rd, PO Box 163, Mitcham, Victoria 3132, Australia *Tel:* (03) 92107777 *Fax:* (03) 92107788 *E-mail:* service@dadirect.com.au *Web Site:* www.dadirect.com.au
Librairie Luginbuehl, 36 bd de Latour-Maubourg, 75007 Paris, France *Tel:* (01) 45514258 *Fax:* (01) 45560780 *E-mail:* liblug@club-internet.fr
APAC Publishers Service Pte Ltd, 70, Bendemeer Rd, 05-03 Hiap Huat House, 339940 Singapore, Singapore *Tel:* 6844 7333 *Fax:* 6747 8916 *E-mail:* service@apacmedia.com.sg
Bookshop(s): Karger Libri AG, Petersgraben 31, 4009 Basel *Tel:* (061) 306 1111 *Fax:* (061) 306 1516 *E-mail:* books@libri.karger.ch *Web Site:* www.libri.ch

KBV, see Kinderbuchverlag Luzern

Verlag Walter Keller, Dornach
Lehmenweg 5, 4143 Dornach 2
Tel: (061) 7015713 *Fax:* (061) 7015716
E-mail: info@verlag-walterkeller.ch
Web Site: www.verlag-walterkeller.ch
Key Personnel
Contact: Ingrid Bergmann *E-mail:* i-bergmann@verlag-walterkeller.ch
Founded: 1969
Specialize in Eurythmic.
Subjects: Art
ISBN Prefix(es): 3-906633
Distributed by Anthroposophic Press Inc

Editions Ketty & Alexandre+
1063 Chapelle-sur-Moudon

Tel: (021) 9051111 *Fax:* (021) 9056050
Key Personnel
Contact: Alexandre Gisiger
Founded: 1975
Subjects: History
ISBN Prefix(es): 2-88114

Kinderbuchfonds Baobab
Laufenstr 16, 4053 Basel
Tel: (061) 3332727 *Fax:* (061) 3332726
E-mail: baobab@access.ch
Web Site: www.baobabbooks.ch
Founded: 1983
Editor of children's books from Africa, Asia & Latin America.
Total Titles: 3 Print

Kinderbuchverlag Luzern+
Laurenzenvorstadt 89, 5001 Aarau
Tel: (062) 836 86 50 *Fax:* (062) 836 86 56
E-mail: sauerlaender@sauerlaender.de
Web Site: www.sauerlaender.ch
Key Personnel
Publisher: Hans Uristof
Editorial & Foreign Rights Dir: Jasua Zagovc
Founded: 1979
Subjects: Animals, Pets, Art, Natural History, Nonfiction (General)
ISBN Prefix(es): 3-276

Kindler Verlag AG
Nelkenstr 20, 8006 Zurich
Tel: (01) 3633007
Telex: 045 57608 *Cable:* Kindlerverlag Zurich
Key Personnel
Publisher: Helmut Kindler; Nina Kindler
Subjects: Anthropology, Psychology, Psychiatry
ISBN Prefix(es): 3-463

Klett und Balmer & Co Verlag
Baarerstr 95, 6302 Zug
Mailing Address: Postfach 2357, 6302 Zug
Tel: (041) 726 28 00 *Fax:* (041) 726 28 01
E-mail: info@klett.ch
Web Site: www.klett.ch
Key Personnel
Man Dir: Christoph Balmer; Michael Klett; Roland Klett; Dr Thomas Klett
Manager: Hans Egli
Founded: 1967
Subjects: Education, Government, Political Science, Philosophy, Science (General)
ISBN Prefix(es): 3-264
Parent Company: Ernst Klett KG, Stuttgart, Germany

Kober Verlag Bern AG
Hildegardstr 6, 3097 Liebefeld
Tel: (031) 9714687
E-mail: koberpress@mindspring.com
Web Site: www.kober.com/kvb.htm
Key Personnel
President: Harald Blum
Man Dir, Sales: Emil Zillig
Founded: 1816
Subjects: Philosophy, Religion - Other, Theology
ISBN Prefix(es): 3-85767
Associate Companies: The Kober Press, PO Box 2194, San Francisco, CA 94126, United States

Kolumbus-Verlag+
Muehlebuehlstr 10, 5737 Menziken
Tel: (064) 7711370 *Cable:* VDB MENZIKEN
Key Personnel
Man Dir: Dr G van den Bergh
Founded: 1945
Subjects: Language Arts, Linguistics, Philosophy
ISBN Prefix(es): 3-85769

Kommissionsverlag Leobuchhandling
Gallusstr 20, 9001 St Gallen

Tel: (071) 222917 *Fax:* (071) 220587
Key Personnel
Man Dir: Eugen Hettinger
Founded: 1918
ISBN Prefix(es): 3-85788; 3-9520218

Galerie Kornfeld & Co
Laupenstr 41, 3001 Bern
Tel: (031) 381 46 73 *Fax:* (031) 382 18 91
E-mail: galerie@kornfeld.ch
Web Site: www.kornfeld.ch
Key Personnel
Proprietor: Eberhard W Kornfeld
Founded: 1864
Subjects: Art
ISBN Prefix(es): 3-85773

Kossodo Verlag AG
av Lignon 27-28, 1219 Le Lignon
Tel: (022) 962230
Key Personnel
Dir: Martha Duessel
Founded: 1956
Subjects: Art
ISBN Prefix(es): 3-7208

Verlag Karl Kraemer & Co+
Postfach 1209, 8034 Zurich
Tel: (01) 2528454 *Fax:* (0711) 784960 (Germany)
E-mail: info@kraemerverlag.com
Web Site: www.kraemerverlag.com
Key Personnel
Publisher, President & Man Dir: Karl H Kraemer
 E-mail: karl.kraemer@kraemerverlag.com
International Rights: Mrs Gudrun Kraemer
Founded: 1962
Specialize in publishing books & magazines on architecture, town planning & building construction.
Subjects: Architecture & Interior Design
ISBN Prefix(es): 3-85774
Associate Companies: Kark Kraemer Verlag GmbH und Co, Schulze-Delitzsch-Str 15, 70565 Stuttgart, Germany *Tel:* (0711) 78 49 60 *Fax:* (0711) 78 49 620
Bookshop(s): Karl Kraemer Fachbuchhandlung, Rotebuehlstr 42, 70178 Stuttgart, Germany *Tel:* (0711) 66993-0 *Fax:* (0711) 628955

Verlag Rene Kramer AG+
33, via del Tiglio, 6906 Lugano-Cassarate
Tel: (091) 518941 *Cable:* Edikramer Lugan 06
Key Personnel
Man Dir, Publicity: Rene Kramer
Founded: 1962
Subjects: Cookery
ISBN Prefix(es): 2-88290

Kranich-Verlag, Dres AG & H R Bosch-Gwalter+
Dufourstr 30, 8702 Zollikon
Tel: (01) 3918484 *Fax:* (01) 3920884
E-mail: boschag@zik.ch
Founded: 1951
Specialize in Special Editions.
Subjects: Architecture & Interior Design, Art, Biblical Studies, Biography, Business, Economics, History, Language Arts, Linguistics, Law, Literature, Literary Criticism, Essays, Philosophy, Poetry, Psychology, Psychiatry, Religion - Catholic, Religion - Protestant, Theology, Travel
ISBN Prefix(es): 3-906640; 3-909194
Number of titles published annually: 5 Print
Total Titles: 115 Print; 2 CD-ROM

Kuemmerly & Frey (Geographischer Verlag)
Alpenstr 58, 3052 Zollikofen/Bern
Tel: (031) 9152211 *Fax:* (031) 9152210
E-mail: info@swissmaps.ch
Web Site: www.swissmaps.ch
Telex: 912765 *Cable:* KUMMERLYFREY
Key Personnel
Man Dir: Walter Frey
Founded: 1852
Subjects: Geography, Geology, Travel
ISBN Prefix(es): 3-259
Associate Companies: Kuemmerly & Frey Verlags-GmbH, Austria; BLay-Foldex, France; Kuemmerly & Frey Verlags-GmbH, Germany

Imprimerie A Kuendig
49 Chemin de l'Etang, CP 26, 1219 Chatelaine/Geneva
Tel: (022) 966013
Key Personnel
Manager: Georges Naef
Founded: 1923
ISBN Prefix(es): 2-88018

Edition Kunzelmann GmbH
Gruetstr 28, 8134 Adliswil
Tel: (01) 7103681 *Fax:* (01) 7103817
Web Site: www.kunzelmann.ch
Founded: 1945
Subjects: Music, Dance
ISBN Prefix(es): 3-85662; 3-9521049

Labor et Fides SA+
One rue Beauregard, 1204 Geneva
Tel: (022) 311 32 69 *Fax:* (022) 781 30 51
E-mail: contact@laboretfides.com
Web Site: www.laboretfides.com
Key Personnel
Chairman: Gabriel de Montmollin
Founded: 1924
Subjects: Religion - Other, Social Sciences, Sociology, Theology
ISBN Prefix(es): 2-8309

Herbert Lang & Cie AG, Buchhandlung, Antiquariat
Muenzgraben 2, Ecke Amthausgasse, 3000 Bern 9
Tel: (031) 3108484 *Fax:* (031) 3108494
Telex: 912867 lang ch *Cable:* Librilang
Key Personnel
President: Christoph H Lang
Founded: 1813 (re-formed 1921)
Agents for libraries throughout the world.
Subjects: Science (General)
ISBN Prefix(es): 3-261

Peter Lang AG+
Hochfeldstr 32, 3000 Bern 9
Mailing Address: PO Box 746, 3000 Bern 9
Tel: (031) 306 17 17 *Fax:* (031) 306 17 27
E-mail: info@peterlang.com
Web Site: www.peterlang.com
Key Personnel
Editorial: Tony Albala de Rivas
Founded: 1977
Specialize in academic publications.
Subjects: Art, History, Language Arts, Linguistics, Law, Literature, Literary Criticism, Essays, Philosophy, Social Sciences, Sociology, Theology
ISBN Prefix(es): 0-8204; 3-631; 3-906750; 3-906751; 3-906752; 3-906753; 3-906754; 3-906755; 3-906757; 3-906758; 3-906759; 3-906756; 3-906760; 3-906761; 3-906762; 3-906763; 3-906764; 3-906765; 3-906766; 3-906767; 3-906768; 3-906769
Subsidiaries: Peter Lang GmbH; Peter Lang Publishing, Inc; PIE-Peter Lang SA
Orders to: Moosstr 1, PO Box 350, 2542 Pieterlen *Tel:* (032) 376 17 17 *Fax:* (032) 376 17 27

Langenscheidt AG Zuerich-Zug
Gratis-Anrufumleitung n Zur, 8001 Zurich
Mailing Address: Postfach 326, 8021 Zurich
Tel: (01) 2115000 *Fax:* (01) 2122149
Key Personnel
Administration: Doctor Ernst Grub
Membership(s): the Langenscheidt Group, Germany.
Subjects: Language Arts, Linguistics
ISBN Prefix(es): 3-269; 3-906725
Parent Company: Langenscheidt KG, Germany

Franz Larese und Juerg Janett, see Erker-Verlag

Larousse (Suisse) SA
c/o Acces-Direct, 3 Route du Grand-Mont, 1052 Le Mont-sur-Lausanne
Tel: (021) 335336
Key Personnel
Man Dir: Jean-Claude Viatte
ISBN Prefix(es): 2-8276
Parent Company: Librairie Larousse, France

Lehrmittelverlag des Kantons Zurich+
Unit of State of Kanton Zurich
Raeffelstr 32, 8045 Zurich
Tel: (01) 465 85 85 *Fax:* (01) 465 85 86
E-mail: lehrmittelverlag@lmv.zh.ch
Web Site: www.access.ch/lmvzh
Key Personnel
Assistant Dir: Robert Fuchs *Tel:* (01) 4658507
Sales Manager: Engemann Beat *Tel:* (01) 4658540 *E-mail:* beat.engemann@lmv.ch
Founded: 1851
Subjects: Film, Video, Radio, TV

Lenos Verlag+
Spalentorweg 12, 4051 Basel
Tel: (061) 261 34 14 *Fax:* (061) 261 35 18
E-mail: lenos@lenos.ch
Web Site: www.lenos.ch
Key Personnel
Program Dir, Publicity: Heidi Sommerer
Sales: Tom Forrer
Founded: 1970
Subjects: Government, Political Science, Journalism, Nonfiction (General)
ISBN Prefix(es): 3-85787

Leonis Verlag+
Kirchenweg, 8034 Zurich
Tel: (01) 475565 *Fax:* (01) 262 48 81 *Cable:* LEONISVERLAG ZURICH
Key Personnel
Proprietor, Man Dir: Dr Wolfgang M Metz
Founded: 1976
Subjects: How-to, Religion - Other, Self-Help
ISBN Prefix(es): 3-7210; 3-85627
Associate Companies: Doulos Verlag

Bernard Letu Editeur+
2 rue Calvin, 1204 Geneva
Tel: (022) 204757 *Fax:* (022) 208492
Founded: 1973
Subjects: Art, Photography
ISBN Prefix(es): 2-88051

Lia rumantscha
Obere Plessurstr 47, 7001 Chur
Tel: (081) 258 3222 *Fax:* (081) 258 3223
E-mail: liarumantscha@rumantsch.ch
Web Site: www.liarumantscha.ch
Key Personnel
Dir: Gion A Derungs
Founded: 1919
Company also gives financial support to other publications in Romansh in the Romansh-speaking area.
Subjects: History, Language Arts, Linguistics, Literature, Literary Criticism, Essays, Music, Dance, Poetry, Regional Interests, Religion - Other
ISBN Prefix(es): 3-906680

SWITZERLAND

Die Libelle Verlag Ag Libellen Haus
Sternengarten 6, 8574 Lengwil
Tel: (071) 688 35 55 *Fax:* (071) 688 35 65
E-mail: info@libelle.ch
Web Site: www.libelle.ch
ISBN Prefix(es): 3-909081

Limmat Verlag+
Quellenstr 25, 8031 Zurich
Tel: (01) 445 80 80 *Fax:* (01) 445 80 88
E-mail: mail@limmatverlag.ch
Web Site: www.limmatverlag.ch
Key Personnel
Sales: Jurg Zimmerli *Tel:* (01) 445 80 81
    E-mail: zimmerli@limmatverlag.ch
Founded: 1975
Subjects: Art, Biography, Fiction, Government, Political Science, Literature, Literary Criticism, Essays, Social Sciences, Sociology, Women's Studies
ISBN Prefix(es): 3-85791
Total Titles: 400 Print

Literatheke, *imprint of* Eco Verlags AG

E Lopfe-Benz AG Rorschach, Graphische Anstalt und Verlag
Pestalozzistr 5, 9401 Rorschach
Tel: (071) 8440444 *Fax:* (071) 8440445
Key Personnel
Dir: Emil Enderle; Dieter Mildenberger
Editorial: Werner Meier
Sales: Peter Kruijsen
Advertising: Hans Schoebi; Peter Bick; Daniel Anderegg
Founded: 1875
Graphical Institute & Publisher.
Subjects: History, Humor, Poetry
ISBN Prefix(es): 3-85819; 3-906785; 3-9521222
Subsidiaries: Nebelspalter Verlag

Maihof Verlag
Sihlbruggstr 105A, 6341 Baar
Tel: (041) 767 76 80 *Fax:* (041) 767 76 77
E-mail: maihofdruck@logon.ch
Web Site: www.maihofdruck.ch
Key Personnel
Publisher: Margrit Boschung
Founded: 1959
Subjects: Biography, History, Maritime
ISBN Prefix(es): 3-9520027; 3-9520756

La Maison de la Bible+
Chemin de Praz-Roussy 4bis, 1032 Romanel-sur-Lausanne
Tel: (021) 867 10 10 *Fax:* (021) 867 10 15
E-mail: info@bible.ch
Web Site: www.bible.ch
Key Personnel
Chief Executive Dir & International Rights: Paul-Andre Eicher *Tel:* (021) 811 40 50
    E-mail: pae@bible.ch
Contact: Vivian Andre; Olivia Festal; Stefan Waldmann
Founded: 1917
Specialize in publishing & translating bibles, books, audio & CD-ROM.
Membership(s): CBA & ECPA.
Subjects: Biblical Studies, Biography, Human Relations, Religion - Protestant, Theology, Family
ISBN Prefix(es): 2-8260; 2-608
Number of titles published annually: 25 Print
Total Titles: 340 Print; 4 CD-ROM; 47 Audio
Parent Company: Geneva Bible Society
Imprints: Editions OURANIA
Divisions:
Distributed by Haenssler/Bolanz/C L Verlag (Germany); Service d'Orientation Biblique (Canada); Servidis (Switzerland)
Distributor for Crossway; Focus on the Family; Harvest House; Lion, OM; Moody (US); STL; Thomas Nelson (US); Zondervan (US)

Foreign Rep(s): Stephan Waldmann (Worldwide)
Foreign Rights: Olivia Festal (Worldwide)

Manesse Verlag GmbH
Badergasse 9, 8001 Zurich
Tel: (01) 2525551 *Fax:* (01) 2625347
E-mail: buch@dva.de
Web Site: www.manesse.ch
Key Personnel
Man Dir: Anne Marie Wells
International Rights: Angelika Rachor
Founded: 1944
Subjects: Fiction, History, Literature, Literary Criticism, Essays, Philosophy, Poetry
ISBN Prefix(es): 3-7175
Total Titles: 350 Print
Parent Company: Deutsche Verlags-Anstalt GmbH (DVA), Germany

Manus Verlag
Bergstr 90, 8708 Maennedorf
Tel: (01) 920 27 27 *Fax:* (01) 920 27 40
E-mail: manart@bluewin.ch
Web Site: www.manus.ch
Key Personnel
Manager: Kurt Borer
Founded: 1970
ISBN Prefix(es): 3-907003; 3-906982

Librairie-Editions J Marguerat+
2 pl St Francois, 1002 Lausanne
Tel: (021) 3237717 *Fax:* (021) 3126732
Key Personnel
Dir: Jean Bakker
Founded: 1940
Subjects: Ethnicity, Geography, Geology, History, Music, Dance, Travel
ISBN Prefix(es): 2-88008

MARKT & TECHNIK AG, see Pearson Education

MARP, see Muslim Architecture Research Program (MARP)

Viktoria-Verlag Peter Marti, see Viktoria-Verlag Peter Marti

Les Editions la Matze
One rue du Mont, 1951 Sion
Tel: (027) 3231652 *Fax:* (027) 3231652
Key Personnel
Man Dir, Sales: Guy Gessler
Founded: 1975
Subjects: Archaeology, Art, Fiction, History, Military Science
ISBN Prefix(es): 2-88025

Meandre
14 Stalden, 1700 Fribourg
Tel: (026) 322174 *Fax:* (026) 323287
Key Personnel
Contact: Gerard Bourgarel
ISBN Prefix(es): 2-88359

Medecine et Hygiene
78 ave de la Roseraie, 1211 Geneva 4
Tel: (022) 702 93 11 *Fax:* (022) 702 93 55
E-mail: direction@medecinehygiene.dr
Web Site: www.medhyg.ch
Key Personnel
Man Dir, Sales: P Y Balavoine
Publicity & Advertising Dir: G Antonietti
Editor-in-Chief: Dr B Kiefer
Founded: 1943
Subjects: Medicine, Nursing, Dentistry, Psychology, Psychiatry, Science (General)
ISBN Prefix(es): 3-88049

BOOK

Editions Medecine et Hygiene, *imprint of* Georg Editeur SA

Peter Meili & Co, Buchhandlung
Fronwagplatz 13, 8200 Schaffhausen
Tel: (053) 254144 *Fax:* (053) 254746
Telex: 76777 meibuch
Founded: 1838
Subjects: Government, Political Science, History, Language Arts, Linguistics, Regional Interests
ISBN Prefix(es): 3-85805
Bookshop(s): Buchhandlung Meili & Co

Memory/Cage Editions
Edenstr 12, 8045 Zurich
Tel: (01) 281 35 65 *Fax:* (01) 281 35 66
E-mail: mail@memorycage.com
Web Site: www.memorycage.com
Key Personnel
Publisher: Daniel Kurjakovic
    E-mail: kurjakovic@memorycage.com
Founded: 1994
Subjects: Art, Literature, Literary Criticism, Essays, Photography
ISBN Prefix(es): 3-907053
Orders to: DAP, 155 Sixth Ave, New York, NY 10013, United States, Contact: Amy Lozada *Tel:* 212-627-1999 *Fax:* 212-627-9484

Editions H Messeiller SA
11 St Nicolas, 2006 Neuchatel
Tel: (032) 7251296 *Fax:* (032) 7241937
Key Personnel
Dir: Cl-H Messeiller
Founded: 1887
Subjects: Art, Education, Law, Psychology, Psychiatry, Public Administration, Religion - Other
ISBN Prefix(es): 2-8261

Minervaverlag Bern+
Seftigenstr 25, 3001 Bern
Mailing Address: PO Box 6849, 3001 Bern
Tel: (031) 3726223 *Fax:* (031) 3726223
Key Personnel
Contact: Louis R Jenzer
Founded: 1991
Membership(s): Swiss Bookseller & Editera Association.
ISBN Prefix(es): 3-9520216
Total Titles: 2 Print; 8 Audio
Distributor for Prodest SA Lugano; WerdtVerlag Zuerich

Editions Minkoff
8 rue Eynard, 1211 Geneva 12
Mailing Address: CP 377, 1211 Geneva 12
Tel: (022) 310 46 60 *Fax:* (022) 310 28 57
E-mail: minkoff@minkoff-editions.com
Web Site: www.minkoff-editions.com
Key Personnel
Dir: Sylvie Minkoff *E-mail:* minkoff@ipzolink.ch
Founded: 1970 (in France, 1989)
Specialize in fac-similes
Also acts as agents for: Editions des Abbesses; Centre de Music Baroque de Versailles; Patrimoine Musical Regional francais; Editions Universite-Conservatrioe de Musique de Geneve; Editions EBL-La Borie en Limousin; New Grove Dictionary of Music & Musicians, London; Editions de l'Oiseau-Lyre, Monaco; Bibliotheque Nationale music publications, Claude Debussy Documentation Centre, CNRS music publications & the French Musicological Society, Paris.
Subjects: Art, Drama, Theater, History, Music, Dance
ISBN Prefix(es): 2-8266
Number of titles published annually: 50 Print
Total Titles: 1,200 Print
Parent Company: Minkoff France Editeur

Bookshop(s): A La Regle d'Or, Librairie Musicale, Minkoff France Editeur, 23 rue de Fleurus, 75006 Paris, France *Tel:* (01) 45449433 *Fax:* (01) 45449430

Mondo SA (Editions-Verlag-Edizioni)
St Antoine 7, 1800 Vevey
Tel: (021) 924 12 40 *Fax:* (021) 924 46 62
E-mail: info@mondo.ch
Web Site: www.mondo.ch
Telex: 452100 Spn Ch
Key Personnel
Dir: Arslan Alamir
ISBN Prefix(es): 2-88168

Motovun Book GmbH+
Grendelstr 15, 6004 Lucerne
Tel: (041) 4109515 *Fax:* (041) 4109516
E-mail: motovun@bluewin.ch
Web Site: www.motovun-group-association.org
Key Personnel
Man Dir & Publisher: Juergen Braunschweiger
Rights & Permissions: Brigitte Abeida
Founded: 1999
Also acts as publisher & packager.
Membership(s): Motovun Group Association; Swiss Publishers Association.
Subjects: Archaeology, Art, Crafts, Games, Hobbies, Geography, Geology, History, Religion - Other, Travel
Subsidiaries: Motovun Productions & Trade

Verlag Rudolf Muehlemann
Haus zu Lagerstr 6, 8570 Weinfelden
Tel: (071) 622 53 53 *Fax:* (071) 622 30 04
Founded: 1949
ISBN Prefix(es): 3-85809

Lars Mueller Publishers+
Klosterstr 42, 5430 Wettingen
Mailing Address: PO Box 912, 5401 Baden
Tel: (056) 4301740 *Fax:* (056) 4301741
E-mail: info@lars-mueller-publishers.com
Web Site: www.lars-mueller-publishers.com
Key Personnel
Manager: Lars Mueller
Founded: 1983
Subjects: Architecture & Interior Design, Art, Photography, Graphic design & typography
ISBN Prefix(es): 3-906700; 3-907044; 3-907078; 3-03778
Number of titles published annually: 20 Print
U.S. Office(s): Distributed Art Publishers Inc, 155 Sixth Ave, 2nd floor, New York, NY 10013-1507, United States, Contact: Donna Wingate *Tel:* 212-627-1999 *E-mail:* dwingate@dapinc.com

Mueller Rueschlikon Verlags AG+
Gewerbestr 10, 6330 Cham
Mailing Address: Postfach 4561, 6304 Zug
Tel: (041) 443040-42 *Fax:* (041) 417115
Key Personnel
Rights & Licenses: Monika Hess
Publicity: Roland Dietschi
Founded: 1938
Subjects: Animals, Pets, Cookery, Crafts, Games, Hobbies, Fiction, How-to, Outdoor Recreation, Wine & Spirits
ISBN Prefix(es): 3-275

Editions Musicales De La Schola Cantorum
Case postale 112, 1890 St-Maurice
Tel: (024) 485 24 80 *Fax:* (024) 485 34 60
E-mail: frochaux-schola@bluewin.ch; labatiaz@bluewin.ch
Key Personnel
Contact: Roulin Blaise
Founded: 1896
Specializes in choral music, organ & choral methods.

Membership(s): ASMEM.
Subjects: Music, Dance
Parent Company: Labatiaz
Associate Companies: Cantate Domino
Distributor for Gesseney; Labatiaz; Tales; Chorus (Pierre Kaelin); Musique Abbe Bovet; Henn

Muslim Architecture Research Program (MARP)+
Postfach 207, 8061 Zurich 4
Tel: (02) 4711228 *Fax:* (02) 4711228
Key Personnel
Contact: Alena Norod
Founded: 1973
Publisher of the first encyclopedia of architecture
Also acts as Archaeological Institute & Architectural Office.
Subjects: Archaeology, Architecture & Interior Design, Art
ISBN Prefix(es): 3-906995
Warehouse: Muenchenbuchsea
Ostrov, Czech Republic

Edito Georges Naef SA+
33 quai Wilson, 1211 Geneva 21
Mailing Address: Case Postale 256, 1211 Geneva 21
Tel: (022) 7380502 *Fax:* (022) 7384224
E-mail: naef@kister.ch
Web Site: www.kister.ch
Key Personnel
Contact: Georges Naef
Founded: 1986
Specialize in internet development.
ISBN Prefix(es): 2-8313
Total Titles: 24 CD-ROM
Parent Company: Kister SA
Subsidiaries: Naef Diffusion

Les Editions Nagel SA (Paris)
6 rue du Port, 1211 Geneva 7
Tel: (022) 734 17 30 *Fax:* (022) 7337424
E-mail: info@nagel.ch
Web Site: www.nagel.ch
Key Personnel
Man Dir: Guillaume Briquet
Founded: 1928
Subjects: Archaeology, Art, Government, Political Science, Philosophy, Travel
ISBN Prefix(es): 2-8263

Verlag Nagel & Kimche AG, Zurich+
Imprint of Sanssouci
Nordstr 9, Postfach, 8035 Zurich
Tel: (01) 366 66 80 *Fax:* (01) 366 66 88
E-mail: info@nagel-kimche.ch
Web Site: www.nagel-kimche.ch
Telex: 897522 naki
Key Personnel
International Rights: Monika Kemptner
Contact: Dr Dirk Vaihinger *E-mail:* vaihinger@nagel-kimche.ch
Founded: 1983
Subjects: Fiction
ISBN Prefix(es): 3-312
Ultimate Parent Company: Carl Hanser Verlag, Munich, Germany
Associate Companies: Zsolnay Verlag

Natura-Verlag Arlesheim
Pfeffingerweg 1, 4144 Arlesheim
Tel: (061) 717111 *Fax:* (061) 7064201
Subjects: Astrology, Occult, Education, Philosophy
ISBN Prefix(es): 3-85817

Nebelspalter-Verlag
Pestalozzistr 5, 9401 Rorschach
Tel: (071) 8440444 *Fax:* (071) 8440445
Key Personnel
Dir: E Enderle; D Mildenberger

Founded: 1875
Subjects: Humor
ISBN Prefix(es): 3-85819; 3-906785; 3-9521222
Parent Company: E Loepfe-Benz AG

Neptun-Verlag
Morellstr 6, 8280 Kreuzlingen
Mailing Address: Postfach 307, 8280 Kreuzlingen
Tel: (072) 727262
E-mail: neptun@bluewin.ch
Web Site: www.neptunart.ch
Telex: 882221 nept ch
Key Personnel
Manager: Herbert Berchtold
Founded: 1946
Subjects: History, Travel
ISBN Prefix(es): 3-85820

Neue Szene, *imprint of* Eco Verlags AG

Neue Zuercher Zeitung AG Buchverlag+
Zuercherstr 39, 8952 Schlieren
Tel: (01) 2581505 *Fax:* (01) 2581399
E-mail: buch.bestellung@nzz.ch
Web Site: www.nzz-buchverlag.ch
Key Personnel
Publicity Manager: Walter Koepfli *E-mail:* buch.verlag@nzz.ch
Book publishing division of Zurich daily newspaper.
ISBN Prefix(es): 3-85823; 3-03823
Total Titles: 200 Print; 10 CD-ROM

Verlag Arthur Niggli AG
Steinackerstr 8, 8583 Sulgen
Tel: (071) 6449111 *Fax:* (071) 6449190
E-mail: info@niggli.ch
Web Site: www.niggli.ch
Key Personnel
Man Dir: Bruno Waldburger
Founded: 1950
Subjects: Architecture & Interior Design, Art, Typography
ISBN Prefix(es): 3-7212

Les Editions Noir sur Blanc+
Le Motta, 1147 Montricher
Tel: (021) 8645931 *Fax:* (021) 8644026
E-mail: noirsurblanc@bluewin.ch *Cable:* EDINOBL
Key Personnel
Contact: Vera Michalski-Hoffmann
Founded: 1986
Subjects: Biography, Cookery, Drama, Theater, Fiction, History, Humor, Literature, Literary Criticism, Essays
ISBN Prefix(es): 2-88250
Branch Office(s)
123 blvd Saint Germain, 75006 Paris, France
Tel: (01) 43269846 *Fax:* (01) 40518792
ul Frascati 18, 00483 Warsaw, Poland

Editions Nord-Sud, *imprint of* Nord-Sued Verlag

Nord-Sud Edizioni, *imprint of* Nord-Sued Verlag

Nord-Sued Verlag
Industriestr 8, 8625 Gossau, Zurich
Tel: (01) 9366868 *Fax:* (01) 9366800 *Cable:* NORDSUED
Key Personnel
Dir: Davy Sidjanski
Editorial: Brigitte Hanhart Sidjanski; Jurgen Lassig
Public Relations: Sabine Reiner
Production: Ulrich Gaebler
Rights & Permissions: Monika Giuliani
Founded: 1961
ISBN Prefix(es): 3-85825; 3-314

Imprints: De Vier Winstreken; Editions Nord-Sud; North-South Books; Nord-Sud Edizioni
Divisions: Michael Neugebauer Verlag

North-South Books, imprint of Nord-Sued Verlag

Novalis Media AG
PO Box 1021, 8201 Schaffhausen
Tel: (052) 6201490 *Fax:* (052) 6201491
E-mail: info@novalis.ch
Web Site: www.novalis.ch *Cable:* Novalis Schaffhausen
Key Personnel
Contact: Eva Frensch *Tel:* (052) 932780 *Fax:* (052) 932784; Mr M Frensch *Tel:* 052 6201490
Founded: 1946
Subjects: Anthropology, Art, Education, History, Language Arts, Linguistics, Philosophy, Psychology, Psychiatry, Religion - Other, Social Sciences, Sociology, Theology
Number of titles published annually: 6 Print
Total Titles: 44 Print
Online services available through Novalis.
Branch Office(s)
PO Box 600, 78266 Buesingen, Contact: Mr Bracker *Tel:* (07734) 932780 *Fax:* (07734) 932781

NZN Buchverlag AG+
Hirschengraben 66, 8001 Zurich
Tel: (01) 266 12 92 *Fax:* (01) 266 12 93
E-mail: nzn@nzn.ch
Web Site: www.nzn.ch
Key Personnel
Editor-in-Chief: Magdalena Seibl
Founded: 1946
Subjects: Religion - Catholic
ISBN Prefix(es): 3-85827
Number of titles published annually: 4 Print

Objectif Terre, imprint of Editions Olizane

Octopus Verlag
Vazerolgasse 1, 7000 Chur
Tel: (081) 252 10 29 *Fax:* (081) 252 94 66
ISBN Prefix(es): 3-279

Oekumenischer Rat der Kirchen, see World Council of Churches (WCC Publications)

Oesch Verlag AG+
Jungholzstr 28, 8050 Zurich
Tel: (01) 305 70 60 *Fax:* (01) 305 70 66
E-mail: info@oeschverlag.ch
Web Site: www.oeschverlag.ch *Cable:* OESCH
Key Personnel
Dir: Martin Brugger
Editorial: Natasha Fischer *E-mail:* lektorat@oeschverlag.ch
Rights & Permissions: Anne Brugger
Founded: 1935
Subjects: Career Development, Fiction, Health, Nutrition, Management, Marketing, Nonfiction (General), Self-Help
ISBN Prefix(es): 3-85833; 3-0350
Number of titles published annually: 40 Print
Total Titles: 2 Audio
Associate Companies: Conzett Verlag *E-mail:* info@finanzbuch.ch *Web Site:* www.finanzbuch.ch; Jopp Verlag *E-mail:* info@oeschverlag.ch *Web Site:* www.joppverlag.ch

Office du Livre SA (Buchhaus AG)
ZI3, Corminboeuf, CP 1061, 1701 Fribourg
Mailing Address: PO Box 1152, 1701 Fribourg
Tel: (026) 4675111 *Fax:* (026) 4675455
E-mail: information@olf.ch
Web Site: www.olf.ch
Telex: 942291 Olf CH *Cable:* Livreoffice

Key Personnel
Dir: Jean-Marc Rod
Founded: 1947
Subjects: Antiques, Architecture & Interior Design, Art, Asian Studies, Crafts, Games, Hobbies, Sports, Athletics
ISBN Prefix(es): 3-7215; 2-8264

Editions Olizane+
11 rue des Vieux-Grenadiers, 1205 Geneva
Tel: (022) 328 52 52 *Fax:* (022) 328 57 96
E-mail: guides@olizane.ch
Web Site: www.olizane.ch
Key Personnel
Man Dir: Matthias Huber
Founded: 1981
Subjects: Ethnicity, Photography, Travel
ISBN Prefix(es): 2-88086
Imprints: Objectif Terre; Collection Artou; Espaces Photographiques; Guides-Olizane; Etudes Orientales
Foreign Rights: Gaia Media Basel (Germany)

Edition Olms AG+
Breitlenstr 11, 8634 Hombrechtikon/Zurich
Tel: (01) 2445030 *Fax:* (01) 2445031
E-mail: info@edition-olms.com
Web Site: www.edition-olms.com
Key Personnel
Man Dir & other offices: Manfred Olms
Founded: 1977
Subjects: Art, Film, Video, Humor, Music, Dance, Photography
ISBN Prefix(es): 3-283
Warehouse: VVA/Bertelsmann, DFA/B, attn: Mrs Pia Brenne, PO Box 7600, 33310 Guetersloh, Germany

Orell Fuessli Buchhandlungs AG+
Dietzingerstr 3, 8036 Zurich
Tel: (01) 466 77 11 *Fax:* (01) 466 74 12
E-mail: info@ofv.ch
Web Site: www.ofv.ch
Telex: 813021 orla ch *Cable:* ORELLVERLAG ZURICH
Key Personnel
Man Dir & Sales, Marketing: Dr Manfred Hiefner
Rights & Permissions: Pia Hiefner-Hug
Founded: 1519
Subjects: Accounting, Art, Biography, Business, Economics, Education, Geography, Geology, History, How-to, Law
ISBN Prefix(es): 3-280; 3-7249
Parent Company: Orell Fuessli Graphische Betriebe AG
Imprints: Eugen Rentsch Verlag AG
Bookshop(s): Orell Fuessli Buchhandlung, Pelikanstr 10, 8022 Zurich

Verlag Organisator AG
Loewenstr 16, Postfach, 8021 Zurich
Tel: (01) 2118155 *Fax:* (01) 4010815; (01) 4928758
Telex: 813834 *Cable:* orga/ch
Key Personnel
Man Dir, Editorial: F Borner
Sales, Publicity, Production: Bruno Waldburger
Founded: 1919
Subjects: Accounting, Government, Political Science, Labor, Industrial Relations
ISBN Prefix(es): 3-7220
Parent Company: Rudolf Haufe Verlag GmbH & Co KG, Germany
Bookshop(s): Basel; Lucerne; St Gallen; Schaffhausen; Winterthur; Zurich; others throughout Switzerland

Etudes Orientales, imprint of Editions Olizane

Origo Verlag+
Rathausgasse 30, 3011 Bern

Tel: (031) 3114480 *Fax:* (031) 3114470
Key Personnel
Proprietor & Man Dir: Alexander Wild
Founded: 1947
Subjects: Mysteries, Parapsychology, Philosophy, Psychology, Psychiatry, Religion - Buddhist, Religion - Jewish, Religion - Other, Theology
ISBN Prefix(es): 3-282; 3-85835
Associate Companies: Verlag Alexander Wild

Orte-Verlag
Centralweg 16, 8910 Affoltern aA
Tel: (01) 888 1556
E-mail: info@orteverlag.ch
Web Site: www.orteverlag.ch
Key Personnel
Man Dir: Werner Bucher
Publicity: Ruth Good-Ramp
Subjects: Poetry
ISBN Prefix(es): 3-85830

Ostschweiz Druck und Verlag
Hofstetstr 14, 9303 Wittenbach
Tel: (071) 2922929 *Fax:* (071) 2922938
Telex: 77393
Key Personnel
Man Dir, Sales: Dr Emil Daehler
Founded: 1892
Subjects: Art, History, Music, Dance, Poetry, Social Sciences, Sociology
ISBN Prefix(es): 3-85837; 3-9521313

Ott Verlag Thun (Ott Publishers, Inc)+
Laenggasse 57, 3607 Thun 7
Mailing Address: Postfach 802, 3607 Thun 7
Tel: (033) 225 39 39 *Fax:* (033) 225 39 33
E-mail: info@ott-verlag.ch
Web Site: www.ott-verlag.ch *Cable:* OTTPUBL THUN
Key Personnel
Man Dir: Hans M Ott
Founded: 1923
Specialize in printers & editors.
Subjects: Business, Earth Sciences, Economics, Gardening, Plants, Geography, Geology, Management, Military Science, Nonfiction (General), Sports, Athletics
ISBN Prefix(es): 3-7225
Associate Companies: Translegal Ltd (publishers of dictionaries)

Editions OURANIA, imprint of La Maison de la Bible

Editions du Panorama
CP 3511, 2500 Bielefeld 3
Tel: (032) 3581665 *Fax:* (032) 3581665
Key Personnel
Man Dir: Paul Thierrin
Founded: 1951
Subjects: Business, Fiction
ISBN Prefix(es): 2-88019

Panorama Verlag, see Tobler Verlag

Parkett Publishers Inc+
Quellenstr 27, 8031 Zurich
Tel: (01) 2718140 *Fax:* (01) 2724301
E-mail: info@parkettart.com
Web Site: www.parkettart.com
Key Personnel
Man Dir: Dieter von Graffenried; Bice Curiger
Founded: 1984
Subjects: Art
ISBN Prefix(es): 3-907509
U.S. Office(s): Parkett Publishers, 155 Avenue of the Americas, Spring St, New York, NY 10013, United States *Tel:* 212-673-2660 *Fax:* 212-271-0704 *E-mail:* info@parkettart.com

PUBLISHERS

SWITZERLAND

Editions Parole et Silence+
Le Muveran, 1888 Les Plans
Tel: (024) 6982301 *Fax:* (024) 6982311
Key Personnel
Contact: Sabine Larive
ISBN Prefix(es): 2-84573

Editions du Parvis
1648 Hauteville
Tel: (026) 915 93 93 *Fax:* (026) 915 93 99
E-mail: book@parvis.ch
Web Site: www.parvis.ch
Key Personnel
Executive: Jean-Marie Castella
Founded: 1970
Subjects: Health, Nutrition, Religion - Catholic
ISBN Prefix(es): 2-88022; 3-907523; 3-907525
Number of titles published annually: 20 Print
Distributed by Gallus (Austria)
Distributor for Centro Editoriale Valtortiano (Europe)

Foundation Simon I Patino, see Editions Patino

Editions Patino+
8, rue Giovanni Gambini, 1211 Geneva 25
Mailing Address: CP 182, 1211 Geneva 25
Tel: (022) 3470211 *Fax:* (022) 7891829
Key Personnel
Contact: John Dubouchet; Roger Guggisberg
Founded: 1986
Subjects: Fiction, Philosophy
ISBN Prefix(es): 2-88213
Orders to: Vilo L'Amateur, 25 rue Ginoux, 75015 Paris, France *Fax:* (1) 45757553

Paulus Verlag, see Editions Saint-Paul

Editions Payot Lausanne+
18 ave de la Gare, 1001 Lausanne
Mailing Address: CP 529, 1001 Lausanne
Tel: (021) 3290264 *Fax:* (021) 3290266
E-mail: ed.payot.nadir@bluewin.ch
Key Personnel
Publisher: Jacques Scherrer
Founded: 1875
Membership(s): ASELF.
Subjects: Anthropology, Archaeology, Architecture & Interior Design, History, Law, Literature, Literary Criticism, Essays, Medicine, Nursing, Dentistry, Music, Dance, Nonfiction (General), Philosophy, Regional Interests, Science (General), Social Sciences, Sociology
ISBN Prefix(es): 2-601
Total Titles: 490 Print
Parent Company: Nadir SA/Jacques Scherrer Editeur, Lausanne
Distributed by Doin Editeurs, Paris (for medical books in France, Belgium & Canada)
Distributor for Olympic Museum Publications (France & Belgium)
Orders to: Olf, ZI-3 Corminboeuf, 1701 Fribourg

Pearson Education+
Chollerstr 37, 6300 Zug
Tel: 747 4747 *Fax:* 747 4777
E-mail: firstname.lastname@pearson.ch; mailbox@pearson.ch
Web Site: www.pearson.ch
Key Personnel
Business Manager: Tobias Eberhart
Chairman: Gunther Frank *Tel:* (089) 46003 121 *Fax:* (089) 46003 120
Vice Chairman: Josef Grand
Member of the Board: Martin Frey *Tel:* (01) 384 1414 *Fax:* (01) 384 1284
Founded: 1983
Other Business Activities: Distribution of M&T Books & Software; Sub-distribution of Microsoft, Lotus, Novell & Others.
Subjects: Computer Science
Parent Company: Pearson Plc
Distributor for Adobe Press; BradyGAMES; Hayden Books; New Riders; Que; Sams; Sams.net; Waite Group Press; Ziff-Davis Press
Distribution Center: Pearson Education Schweiz AG, Chollerstrasse 37, CH-6301 Zug

Pedrazzini Tipografia
Via Varenna, 7, 6600 Locarno
Tel: (091) 751 7734 *Fax:* (091) 751 5118
E-mail: tipedra@webshuttle.ch
Key Personnel
Man Dir & other offices: Benedetto Pedrazzini
Founded: 1880
Subjects: Education, History, Literature, Literary Criticism, Essays, Publishing & Book Trade Reference, Religion - Other
ISBN Prefix(es): 88-7408

Pendo Verlag GmbH+
Forchstr 40, 8032 Zurich
Mailing Address: Postfach, 8032 Zurich
Tel: (01) 3897030 *Fax:* (01) 3897035
E-mail: info@pendo.ch
Web Site: www.pendo.ch
Key Personnel
Publisher: Ernst Piper *Tel:* (089) 13999252 *Fax:* (089) 13999170 *E-mail:* ernst.piper@t-online.de
Editor: Katrin Eckert *Tel:* (01) 3897032 *Fax:* (01) 3897035
Founded: 1971
Specialize in Literature, Contemporary History, Essays.
Subjects: Government, Political Science, History, Poetry, Religion - Other
ISBN Prefix(es): 3-85842
Number of titles published annually: 35 Print
Total Titles: 200 Print
Imprints: Politics
Branch Office(s)
Volkarstr 13, 80634 Munich, Germany *Tel:* (089) 13999252 *Fax:* (089) 13999170 *E-mail:* ernst.piper@online.de *Web Site:* www.ernst-piper.de

Perret Edition
Blutzwis 14, 8604 Volketswil
Tel: (01) 9972717 *Fax:* (01) 9972718
Founded: 1995
Subjects: Art, Photography
ISBN Prefix(es): 3-9520910

Verlag Die Pforte im Rudolf Steiner Verlag
Huegelweg 34, 4143 Dornach
Mailing Address: Postfach 135, 4143 Dornach
Tel: (061) 706 91 30 *Fax:* (061) 706 91 39
E-mail: verlag@rudolf-steiner.com
Web Site: www.rudolf-steiner.com
Key Personnel
International Rights: Benedikt Marzahn
Founded: 1960
Subjects: Anthropology, Philosophy
ISBN Prefix(es): 3-85636
Total Titles: 70 Print

Pharos-Verlag, Hansrudolf Schwabe AG
Therwilestr 5, 4011 Basel
Mailing Address: Postfach 68, 4011 Basel
Tel: (061) 541021 *Fax:* (061) 2797972
Key Personnel
Man Dir: Alexander Schwabe
Advertising Dir: Myrte Schwabe
Founded: 1958
Subjects: Transportation, Wine & Spirits
ISBN Prefix(es): 3-7230

Philosophisch-Anthroposophischer Verlag am Goetheanum+
Oberer Zielweg 60, 4143 Dornach 1
Tel: (061) 706 84 40 *Fax:* (061) 706 84 41
E-mail: anthrosuisse@bluewin.ch
Web Site: www.goetheanum.ch
Key Personnel
General Secretary: Otfried Doerfler
Founded: 1908
Subjects: Art, Education, Literature, Literary Criticism, Essays, Mathematics, Medicine, Nursing, Dentistry, Philosophy, Religion - Other, Science (General), Theology
ISBN Prefix(es): 3-7235
Subsidiaries: Rudolf Geering Verlag

Politics, imprint of Pendo Verlag GmbH

Editions Pourquoi Pas+
CP 60, 1247 Anieres, Geneve
Tel: (022) 7511031
Key Personnel
Contact: Astrid Mirabaud
Founded: 1981
Subjects: Literature, Literary Criticism, Essays
ISBN Prefix(es): 2-88173

Presses Polytechniques et Universitaires Romandes, PPUR+
EPFL-Ecublens, Centre Midi, 1015 Lausanne
Tel: (021) 693 41 31 *Fax:* (021) 693 40 27
E-mail: ppur@epfl.ch
Web Site: www.ppur.org
Telex: 450 456 attn. PPUR
Key Personnel
President: Pierre-Francois Pittet
Man Dir, Editorial: Olivier Babel
Production: Christophe Borlat
Promotion: Sylvain Collette
International Rights: Yasmine Babel-Sraih *Tel:* (021) 693 60 44 *E-mail:* yasmine.babel@epfl.ch
Founded: 1980
Also acts as book packager.
Subjects: Architecture & Interior Design, Biological Sciences, Chemistry, Chemical Engineering, Civil Engineering, Computer Science, Earth Sciences, Electronics, Electrical Engineering, Engineering (General), Management, Mathematics, Mechanical Engineering, Physics, Science (General), Technology
ISBN Prefix(es): 2-88074
Number of titles published annually: 30 Print
Distributed by Eyrolles-Geodif (France & Maroc); Patrimoine for Belgium (Benelux); PIP (Canada & USA)

Pro Juventute Verlag+
Seehofstr 15, 8032 Zurich
Tel: (01) 2567777 *Fax:* (01) 2567778
E-mail: info@projuventute.ch
Web Site: www.projuventute.ch
ISBN Prefix(es): 3-7152

Editions Pro Schola
3 Place Chauderon, 1003 Lausanne
Tel: (021) 323 66 55 *Fax:* (021) 323 67 77
E-mail: benedict@benedict-schools.com
Web Site: www.benedict-international.com
Key Personnel
Man Dir: Dr Jean J Benedict
Founded: 1928
Official distributor of the Benedict Method.
Membership(s): ASDEL.
Subjects: Education, English as a Second Language, Language Arts, Linguistics
ISBN Prefix(es): 2-88009
Total Titles: 85 Print
Distributed by Buchimport Peter Reimer
Warehouse: 24 Rue de Geneve, 1003 Lausanne

Promoedition SA+
35, rue des Bains, 1211 Geneva
Mailing Address: CP 5615, 1211 Geneva
Tel: (022) 8099460 *Fax:* (022) 7811414
Key Personnel
International Rights Contact: Thierry B Opplkofer

SWITZERLAND

Founded: 1972
Subjects: Business, Communications, Film, Video, Finance
ISBN Prefix(es): 2-88129

Psychosophische Gesellschaft
Schedlern, 9063 Stein
Tel: (071) 59 13 01
Subjects: Astrology, Occult, Education, Philosophy, Psychology, Psychiatry, Theology
ISBN Prefix(es): 3-85846

Punktum AG, Buchredaktion und Bildarchiv+
Klusstr 50, 8032 Zurich
Tel: (01) 422 45 40 *Fax:* (01) 422 48 13
Key Personnel
Contact: Dr Niklaus Flueeler; Marianne Flueeler-Grauwiter
Specialize in Swiss Topics.
Subjects: Art, Ethnicity, History, Travel
ISBN Prefix(es): 3-907577
Divisions: Punktum Buchredoktion (Packaging), Punktum Bildarchiv (Picture Library)

Rabe Verlag AG Zuerich
Frankengasse 6, 8001 Zurich
Tel: (01) 261 85 40 *Fax:* (01) 261 85 41 *Cable:* RABEVERLAG ZURICH
Key Personnel
Man Dir, Sales: Dr J Kanitz
Editorial, Rights & Permissions: Dr Elsa Kanitz
Production: Dr P Portmann
Founded: 1962
Subjects: Art
ISBN Prefix(es): 3-85852
U.S. Office(s): PAPYRUS Franchise Corp, 954 16 St, Oakland, CA 94608, United States
Warehouse: CH-8608 Bubikon Zurich/Dorfstr. 15-15a *Tel:* (055) 243 23 83

Robert Raeber, Buchhandlung am Schweizerhof
Schweizerhofquai 2, 6002 Lucerne
Mailing Address: Postfach 4170, 6002 Lucerne
Tel: (041) 512371
Key Personnel
Man Dir: Robert Raeber-Huber
Founded: 1973
Subjects: Fiction, Travel
ISBN Prefix(es): 3-7239
Bookshop(s): Raeber Buchhandlung, Schweizerhofquai 2, 6002 Lucerne

Raphael, Editions+
CP 1, 1801 Le Mont-Pelerin
Tel: (021) 9215230 *Fax:* (021) 9215237
Key Personnel
Dir: Mr Denis Ducatel *E-mail:* denis.ducatel@dplanet.ch
Founded: 1990
Subjects: Literature, Literary Criticism, Essays, Psychology, Psychiatry, Religion - Protestant
ISBN Prefix(es): 2-88417
Total Titles: 24 Print
Distributed by Editions Empreinte; Interlivres (Canada); Jeunesse en Mission Belgique (Belgium); Olbis

Rauhreif Verlag
Titlisstr 3, 4313 Moehlin
Tel: (061) 851 53 63
Subjects: Literature, Literary Criticism, Essays
ISBN Prefix(es): 3-907764

Verlag fuer Recht und Gesellschaft AG
Ringstr 75, 4106 Therwil
Tel: (061) 726 26 26 *Fax:* (061) 726 26 27
E-mail: info@vrg-verlag.ch
Web Site: www.vrg-verlag.ch *Cable:* REGES VERLAG
Key Personnel
Man Dir: Dr Peter J Amuer
Founded: 1933
Subjects: Accounting, Law
ISBN Prefix(es): 3-7242
Associate Companies: Sciamed Verlag AG, Ringstr 75, Postfach, 4106 Therwil

Recom, *imprint of* RECOM Verlag

RECOM Verlag
Missionsstr 36, 4012 Basel
Tel: (061) 2646480 *Fax:* (061) 2616213
Web Site: www.recom-pcc.de
Telex: 63755 rein ch
Key Personnel
Man Dir, Sales, Production, Publicity: Alfred Ruedisuehli
Founded: 1971 (1985)
Subjects: Medicine, Nursing, Dentistry
ISBN Prefix(es): 3-7245; 3-497
Parent Company: Friedrich Reinhardt AG
Imprints: Recom

Regenbogen Verlag+
Postfach 472, 8027 Zurich
Tel: (01) 454 3033 *Fax:* (01) 454 3035
E-mail: info@regenbogen-verlag.ch
Web Site: www.regenbogen-verlag.ch
Key Personnel
General Manager: Theo Ruff
Subjects: Art, Travel
ISBN Prefix(es): 3-85862
Orders to: Prolit Buchvertrieb GmbH, Siemensstr 18a, 35394 Giessen, Germany *Tel:* (0641) 77053

Reich Verlag AG+
Museggstr 12, 6004 Lucerne
Tel: (041) 4103721 *Fax:* (041) 4103227
Web Site: www.terramagica.de
Key Personnel
Man Dir: Alfons Wueest
Founded: 1974
Specialize in books of plates.
Subjects: Photography
ISBN Prefix(es): 3-7243
Number of titles published annually: 8 Print
Total Titles: 60 Print
Imprints: Terra Magica

Verlag Friedrich Reinhardt AG
Missionsstr 36, 4012 Basel
Tel: (061) 264 64 64 *Fax:* (061) 264 64 65
Web Site: www.reinhardt.ch *Cable:* Freinhardt Basle
Key Personnel
Man Dir, Rights & Permissions: Dr Ernst Reinhardt
Founded: 1900
Subjects: Art, Biography, Environmental Studies, Fiction, History, How-to, Religion - Other, Theology
ISBN Prefix(es): 3-7245; 3-497
Subsidiaries: Eular Verlag; Reinhardt Communications

Eugen Rentsch Verlag AG, *imprint of* Orell Fuessli Buchhandlungs AG

Rex Verlag
St Karliquai 12, 6000 Lucerne 5
Tel: (041) 4194700 *Fax:* (041) 4194711
E-mail: info@rex-freizyt.ch
Web Site: www.rex-freizyt.ch
Key Personnel
Man Dir: Markus Kappeler
Founded: 1931
Subjects: Education, Fiction, Religion - Catholic
ISBN Prefix(es): 3-7252
Bookshop(s): Rex Buchladen, St Karliquair 12, Postfach 5266, 6000 Lucerne

Rhein-Trio, Edition/Editions du Fou+
Drahtzugstr 10, 4057 Basel
Tel: (061) 6831635 *Fax:* (061) 6831635
E-mail: rhein-trio@usa.net
Founded: 1993
Specialize in comics.
Subjects: Art, Astrology, Occult, Humor, Mysteries, Poetry
ISBN Prefix(es): 3-9520470
Distributed by Comics Virt (Austria)
Distributor for Comicwelt

Editiones Roche
c/o F Hoffmann-La Roche Ltd, Grenzacherstr 124, 4070 Basel
Tel: (061) 688 3611 *Fax:* (061) 688 2775
Web Site: www.roche.com
Key Personnel
Publications Manager: Edith E Troxler
E-mail: basel.editiones_roche@roche.com
Founded: 1971
Subjects: Art, Health, Nutrition, Natural History, Science (General)
ISBN Prefix(es): 3-907046; 3-907770

Rodana Verlag AG, see Schweizer Spiegel Verlag Mit

Rodera-Verlag der Cardun AG+
Postfach 8411, Winterthur
Tel: (052) 292442 *Fax:* (052) 292592
Key Personnel
Contact: Franz H Duebi
Founded: 1991
Subjects: Biography, History, Literature, Literary Criticism, Essays, Theology
ISBN Prefix(es): 3-907803

Hans Rohr Verlag
Moehrlistr 130, 8006 Zurich 1
Tel: (01) 3614846 *Fax:* (01) 3639513
E-mail: buchhandlung.hans.rohr@dm.krinfo.ch
Key Personnel
Man Dir: Hans R Rohr
Founded: 1921
Subjects: Antiques, Film, Video, Language Arts, Linguistics, Regional Interests, Travel
ISBN Prefix(es): 3-85865

Rondo Verlag
Hittenbergstr 1, 8636 Wald
Tel: (055) 246 39 37 *Fax:* (055) 246 42 93
Web Site: www.rondo-verlag.ch
Key Personnel
Contact: Elisabeth Wild
ISBN Prefix(es): 3-907935

Roth et Sauter SA
La Pale, 1026 Denges-Lausanne
Tel: (021) 801 75 61 *Fax:* (021) 802 32 79
Telex: 458179 rsd ch
Key Personnel
Man Dir: Michel Logoz; Pierre Sauter
Founded: 1890
Subjects: Art
ISBN Prefix(es): 2-88075
Imprints: Editions du Verseau

Rotpunktverlag+
Freyastr 20, 8004 Zurich
Mailing Address: Postfach 2134, 8026 Zurich
Tel: (01) 2418434 *Fax:* (01) 2418474
E-mail: info@rotpunktverlag.ch
Web Site: www.rotpunktverlag.ch
Key Personnel
International Rights: Thomas Heilmann
Founded: 1977
Membership(s): SBVV.

Subjects: Alternative, Developing Countries, Fiction, Government, Political Science, History, Nonfiction (General), Outdoor Recreation, Travel
ISBN Prefix(es): 3-85869
Orders to: AS Verlagsservice Holler, Schaldorferstr 16, 8641 St Marien im Murzrtal, Austria *Tel:* (03864) 67 77 *Fax:* (03864) 38 88
Buch 2000/AVA, Postfach 27, 8910 Affoltern *Tel:* (01) 762 42 60 *Fax:* (01) 762 60 65
Prolit Verlagsauslieferung, Postfach 9, 35461 Fernwald, Germany *Tel:* (0641) 9439325 *Fax:* (0641) 9439329

Rotten-Verlags AG
Terbinerstr 2, 3930 Visp
Tel: (027) 948 30 32 *Fax:* (027) 948 30 33
E-mail: rottenverlag@mengis.ch
ISBN Prefix(es): 3-907816; 3-907624

Ruegger Verlag+
Division of Sudostschweiz Presse AG
Albisriederstr 80A, 8040 Zurich
Mailing Address: Postfach 1470, 8040 Zurich
Tel: (01) 4912130 *Fax:* (01) 4931176
E-mail: info@rueggerverlag.ch
Web Site: www.rueggerverlag.ch
Key Personnel
Secretary: Marianne Pearson *E-mail:* mpearson@rueggerverlag.ch
Publisher: Myriam Engler
Subjects: Business, Criminology, Economics, Education, Environmental Studies, Government, Political Science, Management, Psychology, Psychiatry, Social Sciences, Sociology, Women's Studies, Specialize in economics, politics, sociology, ecology & educational research
ISBN Prefix(es): 3-7253
Number of titles published annually: 30 Print
Distribution Center: Buendner Buchvertrieb, Postfach, Rossbodenstr 33, 7004 Chur

SAB Schweiz Arbeitsgemeinschaft fuer die Berggebiete+
Laurstr 10, 5200 Brugg
Mailing Address: Postfach 174, 5200 Brugg
Tel: (056) 411079 *Fax:* (056) 413642
Subjects: Agriculture, Architecture & Interior Design, Economics, Energy, Environmental Studies, Labor, Industrial Relations, Regional Interests, Social Sciences, Sociology
ISBN Prefix(es): 3-85873

Sabe AG Verlagsinstitut+
Gotthardstr 52, 8002 Zurich
Tel: (01) 2024477 *Fax:* (01) 2021932
E-mail: sabeverlag@access.ch
Key Personnel
Dir: Heinrich M Zweifel
Founded: 1969
Membership(s): Worlddidac & Swissdidac; Specialize in educational material of all kinds including software.
Subjects: Biological Sciences, Education, Geography, Geology, History, Language Arts, Linguistics, Mathematics, Natural History
ISBN Prefix(es): 3-252
Distributed by Heinevetter Verlag
Distributor for Verlag fuer Paedagogische Medien; Verlag an der Ruhr; Veritas Verlag

Editions Saint-Augustin+
4, rue Simplon, 1890 St-Maurice
Tel: (024) 486 05 04 *Fax:* (024) 486 05 23
E-mail: editions@staugustin.ch
Key Personnel
General Dir: Marc Larive
Founded: 1934
Subjects: Religion - Catholic, Theology
ISBN Prefix(es): 2-88011
Bookshop(s): Librairie La Procure-Le Passage, Rue de Carouge 53, 1205 Geneve; Librairie Saint-Augustin, 88 rue de Lausanne, 1700 Fribourg; Librairie Saint-Augustin, ave du Simplon 4, 1890 St-Maurice

Editions Saint-Paul
Perolles 42, 1705 Fribourg
Tel: (026) 4264111 *Fax:* (026) 4264531
E-mail: druckerei@st-paul.ch
Web Site: www.st-paul.ch
Key Personnel
Marketing Dir: Anton Scherer
Founded: 1873
Subjects: Education, Philosophy, Psychology, Psychiatry
ISBN Prefix(es): 3-7228; 2-88355
Parent Company: Imprimerie et Librairies Saint-Paul SA, 42, blvd Perolles, Case Postale 150, 1705 Fribourg
Associate Companies: Editions de la Sarine, 42, blvd Perolles, Case Postale 150, 1705 Fribourg; Editions Universitaires SA
Bookshop(s): Librairie Saint-Paul, Perolles 38, 1700 Fribourg; Librairie du Vieux Comte, rue de Vevey, 1630 Bulle

Salvioni arti grafiche SA
Via Ghiringhelli 9, 6500 Bellinzona
Tel: (091) 8211111 *Fax:* (091) 8211112
ISBN Prefix(es): 88-7967

SAPL, *imprint of* Castle Publications SA

Satyr-Verlag Dr Humbel+
Gotthardstr 25, 8002 Zurich
Tel: (01) 2810845 *Fax:* (01) 2810846
Key Personnel
Manager: Dr Humbel
Founded: 1985
Subjects: Humor, Literature, Literary Criticism, Essays
ISBN Prefix(es): 3-906420
Parent Company: Satyr-Verlag Dr Humbel, 12 rue du Chateu, F-90200 Grosmagny, France
Orders to: Satyr-Verlag, Postfach 6411, 8023 Zurich

Sauerlaender AG+
Laurenzenvorstadt 89 Postfach, 5001 Aarau
Tel: (062) 836 86 26 *Fax:* (062) 836 86 20
E-mail: sauerlaender@sauerlaender.ch
Web Site: www.sauerlaender.ch
Telex: 981195 SAG CH
Key Personnel
Publisher & Man Dir: Hans Christof Sauerlaender
Editorial: Hansten Doornkaat; Peter Egger; Paula Peretti
Man Dir, Sales & Marketing: Klaus Wilberg
Sales: Monika Roesler
Advertising Manager: Heike Ossenkop
Rights & Permissions: Kerstin Michaelis
Founded: 1807
Subjects: Education, Nonfiction (General)
ISBN Prefix(es): 3-7941
Total Titles: 600 Print; 6 CD-ROM
Associate Companies: SABE Verlag AG, Todistrasse 23, 8002 Zurich *Tel:* (01) 202-1932 *E-mail:* verlag@sabe.ch
Subsidiaries: Verlag Sauerlaender GmbH

Scherz Verlag AG+
Member of Verlagsgruppe Droemer Weltbild
Marktgasse 25, 3000 Bern 7
Mailing Address: Postfach 66, 3000 Bern 7
Tel: (031) 227337 *Fax:* (031) 3277171 *Cable:* SCHERZEDIT
Key Personnel
Editoral Dir: Peter Lohmann
Man Dir: Fuerg Zurlinden
Editorial Dept: Dorthe Binkert; Rachel Gratzfeld
Rights & Permissions: Barbara Frankhauser
Marketing Dir: Thomas Reisch
Contact: Isabella Milan *E-mail:* i.milan@scherzverlag.ch
Founded: 1938
Specialize in Hardcover fiction & nonfiction.
Subjects: Biography, History, Parapsychology, Philosophy, Psychology, Psychiatry
ISBN Prefix(es): 3-502
Total Titles: 1,200 Print
Subsidiaries: Otto Wilhelm Barth-Verlag KG

Schlaepfer & Co AG
Kasernenstr 64, 9100 Herisau
Tel: (071) 354 64 64 *Fax:* (071) 525126
Key Personnel
Man Dir: P Schlaepfer
Founded: 1974
ISBN Prefix(es): 3-85882
Orders to: Schlapfer & Co AG Buchverlag, CH-9100 Herisau

Schnellmann-Verlag+
Rotackerstr 49, 8645 Jona-Kempraten
Tel: (055) 2111472 *Fax:* (055) 2111477
Web Site: www.dictionaries.ch
Key Personnel
Dir: Hans Schnellmann
Founded: 1973
ISBN Prefix(es): 3-85542

Verlag fuer Schoene Wissenschaften
Unterer Zielweg 36, Postfach, 4143 Dornach 2
Tel: (061) 7013911 *Fax:* (061) 7011417
E-mail: schoene_wissenschaften@bluewin.ch
Key Personnel
Chief Executive: Dr Heinz Matile
Founded: 1928
Belles Lettres Publishing Co - Albert Steffen Foundation.
Subjects: Art, Fiction, Literature, Literary Criticism, Essays, Poetry
ISBN Prefix(es): 3-85889

A Schudel & Co AG, Verlag
Schopfgaesschen 8, 4125 Riehen 1
Mailing Address: Postfach 198, 4125 Riehen 1
Tel: (061) 671011 *Fax:* (061) 671363
E-mail: a.schudel@bluewin.ch
Key Personnel
Manager: Ch Schudel
ISBN Prefix(es): 3-85895

Schulthess Polygraphischer Verlag AG
Zwingliplatz 2, 8022 Zurich
Tel: (01) 251 93 36 *Fax:* (01) 261 63 94
Web Site: www.schulthess.com *Cable:* 2
Key Personnel
Dir, Advertising, Permissions: Werner Stocker
Founded: 1791
Firm has incorporated the former Leemann AG Druckerei/Verlag since 1978.
Subjects: Business, Law, Social Sciences, Sociology
ISBN Prefix(es): 3-7255

Schwabe & Co AG
Steinentorstr 13, 4010 Basel
Tel: (061) 278 95 65 *Fax:* (061) 272 95 66
E-mail: verlag@schwabe.ch
Web Site: www.schwabe.ch *Cable:* SCHWABECO BASEL
Key Personnel
Man Dir: Hans-Rudolf Bienz; Dr Urs Breitenstein
Founded: 1488
Subjects: Archaeology, Art, History, Literature, Literary Criticism, Essays, Medicine, Nursing, Dentistry, Philosophy, Photography, Psychology, Psychiatry, Theology
ISBN Prefix(es): 3-7965
Orders to: Verlag, 4132 Muttenz

Hansrudolf Schwabe AG, see Pharos-Verlag, Hansrudolf Schwabe AG

Verkehrshaus der Schweiz, see Verkehrshaus der Schweiz

Schweizer Spiegel Verlag Mit+
Raemistr 18, 8024 Zurich
Tel: (01) 472195 *Fax:* (01) 7502943
Key Personnel
Contact: Allan Guggenbuhl
Subjects: Education, Psychology, Psychiatry
ISBN Prefix(es): 3-7270; 3-85863

Schweizerische Stiftung fuer Alpine Forschungen
Binzstr 23, 8045 Zurich
Tel: (01) 461 01 47 *Fax:* (01) 461 07 11
E-mail: mail@alpinfo.ch
Web Site: www.alpineresearch.ch; www.alpinfo.ch
Key Personnel
President: Dr Juerg Marmet
Editorial: Dr Fritz Schwarzenbach
Founded: 1939
Swiss Foundation for Alpine Research.
Subjects: Earth Sciences, Geography, Geology
ISBN Prefix(es): 3-85515

Schweizerischen Gesellschaft fuer Volkskunde (Swiss Folklore Society), *imprint of* Verlagsbuchhandlung AG

Schweizerischer Verein fuer Schweisstechnik
St Alban-Vorstadt 95, 4006 Basel
Tel: (061) 233973 *Fax:* (061) 3178480
ISBN Prefix(es): 3-85896

Schweizerisches Jugendschriftenwerk, SJW+
Uetlibergstr 20, 8045 Zurich
Tel: (01) 462 49 40 *Fax:* (01) 462 69 13
E-mail: office@sjw.ch
Web Site: www.sjw.ch
Key Personnel
Dir: Tsultrin Shabga *E-mail:* t.shabga@sjw.ch
Art Dir: Hanna Burkard
Sales: Emilienne Eberia
Founded: 1956
ISBN Prefix(es): 3-7269
Number of titles published annually: 30 Print
Total Titles: 300 Print
Parent Company: Edition Fondation
Imprints: Fotorotar AG/EGG ZH
Orders to: BD Bucherdienst/Einsiel

Verlag Schweizerisches Katholisches Bibelwerk
Rue de l'hopital, 1700 Fribourg
Key Personnel
Dir: Othmar Keel
Membership(s): AMB.
Subjects: Religion - Catholic
ISBN Prefix(es): 3-7203

Schweizerisches Ost-Institut, see Verlag SOI (Schweizerisches Ost-Institut)

Sciamed Verlag AG
Wallstr 14, 4010 Basel
Mailing Address: Postfach 646, 4010 Basel
Tel: (061) 231775; (061) 235366 *Fax:* (061) 2722775 *Cable:* SCIAMED
Founded: 1983
Subjects: Medicine, Nursing, Dentistry
ISBN Prefix(es): 3-7242
Parent Company: Verlag fuer Recht und Gesellschaft AG

Editions Scriptar SA+
Creux de Corsy, 25, 1093 La Conversion-Lausanne
Tel: (021) 7911065 *Fax:* (021) 7914084
E-mail: info@jsh.ch
Web Site: www.jsh.ch
Key Personnel
Publicity Manager: F Mugnier *Tel:* (021) 7960097
Founded: 1946
Publisher of Swiss Watch & Jewelry Journal International Edition.
Subjects: Specializes in Watches & Jewelry
ISBN Prefix(es): 2-88012

Editions Du Signal Rene Gaillard
2-4, rue de Geneve, 1003 Lausanne
Tel: (021) 3290194 *Fax:* (021) 3290194
Key Personnel
Proprietor: Rene Gaillard
Founded: 1972
Subjects: Human Relations
ISBN Prefix(es): 2-88023

Sinwel-Buchhandlung Verlag
Lorrainestr 10, 3000 Bern 11
Tel: (031) 425205 *Fax:* (031) 3331376
Telex: 911469
Founded: 1978
Subjects: Crafts, Games, Hobbies, Outdoor Recreation
ISBN Prefix(es): 3-85911

SJW, see Schweizerisches Jugendschriftenwerk, SJW

SKAT (Swiss Centre for Development Cooperation in Technology & Management)
Vadianstr 42, 9000 St Gallen
Tel: (071) 2285454 *Fax:* (071) 2285455
E-mail: info@skat.ch
Web Site: www.skat.ch
Key Personnel
Head Information: Silvia Ndiaye *E-mail:* silvia.ndiaye@skat.ch
Founded: 1978
Consulting, documentation, & project implementation of water supply, sanitation & urban development.
Subjects: Manuals & reports
ISBN Prefix(es): 3-908001
Number of titles published annually: 10 Print
Total Titles: 66 Print
Distributed by IT Publications Ltd

Editions D'Art Albert Skira SA
Rue Quai des Bergues, 29, 1201 Geneva
Tel: (022) 906 80 00 *Fax:* (022) 3495535 *Cable:* Edart Geneva
Key Personnel
Man Dir, Editorial: Mrs R Skira
Sales, Production & Publicity: Jean-Michel Skira
Founded: 1928
Subjects: Art, Education
ISBN Prefix(es): 2-605

Slatkine Reprints
5, rue des Chaudronniers, 1211 Geneva 3
Tel: (022) 3100476 *Fax:* (022) 3107101
E-mail: librarie@slatkine.ch
Web Site: www.slatkine.ch
Key Personnel
Man Dir: Michel E Slatkine
Founded: 1918
ISBN Prefix(es): 2-05

Verlag SOI (Schweizerisches Ost-Institut)
Jubilaeumsstr 41, Postfach, 3000 Bern
Tel: (031) 431212 *Fax:* (031) 3513801
Telex: 32728 *Cable:* Schweizost
Key Personnel
Man Dir: Peter Sager
Sales Manager: Peter Burgunder
Production Manager: Peter Dolder
Founded: 1958
Subjects: Government, Political Science, History, Social Sciences, Sociology
ISBN Prefix(es): 3-85913
Bookshop(s): Buchhandlung SOI, Jubilaeumsstr 41, 3000 Berne

Speer -Verlag
Limmattalstr 130, 8049 Zurich
Tel: (01) 341 42 56; (01) 262 33 91 *Fax:* (01) 342 45 31 *Cable:* SPERVERLAG
Key Personnel
Man Dir: R Roemer
Founded: 1944
Subjects: Fiction, Mysteries, Philosophy, Poetry
ISBN Prefix(es): 3-85916

Spes, *imprint of* Editions Andre Delcourt & Cie

Sphinx Verlag AG
Andreaspl 12, 4051 Basel
Tel: (061) 2619292 *Fax:* (061) 2629221
Key Personnel
Dir: H C Sauerlaender
Founded: 1975
Subjects: Astrology, Occult, Fiction, Health, Nutrition, Philosophy, Psychology, Psychiatry, Science (General)
ISBN Prefix(es): 3-85914
Associate Companies: Sauerlaender AG

Staatskunde Verlag E Krattiger AG, see Tobler Verlag

Staempfli Verlag AG+
Hallerstr 7, 3001 Bern
Mailing Address: PO Box 8326, 3001 Bern
Tel: (031) 3006666 *Fax:* (031) 3006688
E-mail: verlag@staempfli.com
Web Site: www.staempfli.com
Key Personnel
President, Editor, Rights & Permissions: Dr Rudolf Staempfli
Editor, Sales & Advertising Dir: Ursula Merz
Editor: Stephan Grieb
Marketing: Susanne Farner
Founded: 1799
Membership(s): Law Books in Europe.
Subjects: Government, Political Science, Law
ISBN Prefix(es): 3-7272
Parent Company: Staempfli Holding AG
Bookshop(s): Buchstaempfli, Versandbuchhandlung, PO Box 560, 3000 Bern 9
Tel: (031) 3006677 *Fax:* (031) 3006688
E-mail: buchstaempfli@staempfli.com

Stahlbau Zentrum Schweiz (Swiss Institute of Steel Construction)
Seefeldstr 25, 8034 Zurich
Tel: (01) 261 89 80 *Fax:* (01) 262 09 62
E-mail: info@szs.ch
Web Site: www.szs.ch
Key Personnel
Man Dir: Urs Wyss
Swiss Institute of Steel Construction.
ISBN Prefix(es): 3-85920

Rudolf Steiner Verlag, see Verlag Die Pforte im Rudolf Steiner Verlag

Rudolf Steiner Verlag
Hugelweg 34, 4143 Dornach 1
Mailing Address: Postfach 135, 4143 Dornach 1
Tel: (061) 706 91 30 *Fax:* (061) 706 91 39
E-mail: verlag@rudolf-steiner.com
Web Site: www.rudolf-steiner.com
Key Personnel
Man Dir, Editorial: Benedikt Marzahn
Publicity, Sales: Winfried Altmann
Production: Carlo Frigeri; B Marzahn
Contact: Sabine Scherrer *Tel:* (061) 7069137
Founded: 1949

PUBLISHERS — SWITZERLAND

Administrators of the Rudolf Steiner Literary Estate.
Subjects: Philosophy
ISBN Prefix(es): 3-7274
Total Titles: 700 Print
Subsidiaries: Editrice Antroposofica SRL
Bookshop(s): Buchhandlung Duldeck, Haus Duldeck, Postfach 135, 4143 Dornach 1

Edition Stemmle AG+
Im Fischer, Seestr 16, 8800 Zurich
Mailing Address: Postfach 365, 8201 Schaffhausen
Tel: (01) 7235050 *Fax:* (01) 7235059
E-mail: info@editionstemmle.ch
Web Site: www.editionstemmle.com
Key Personnel
Publisher & President: Dr Thomas N Stemmle
Vice President & General Manager: Robert Zueblin
Vice President & Editorial Dir: Mirjam Ghisleni-Stemmle
Founded: 1993
Subjects: Architecture & Interior Design, Art, Photography
ISBN Prefix(es): 3-905514

Verlag Stocker-Schmid AG
Hasenbergstr 7, 8953 Dietikon
Mailing Address: Postfach 66, 8953 Dietikon
Tel: (01) 7404444
Subjects: Library & Information Sciences, Military Science, Regional Interests
ISBN Prefix(es): 3-85577; 3-7276
Subsidiaries: Verlag Bibliophile Drucke von Josef Stocker AG
Bookshop(s): Buchhandlung Stocker-Schmid

Strom-Verlag Luzern+
Staffelhof 21, 8055 Zurich 15
Tel: (041) 4408845 *Fax:* (041) 4408844
E-mail: pegasus.ebikon@edi.begasoft.ch
Key Personnel
Man Dir: Roland Grueter
Founded: 1956
Subjects: Ethnicity, Fiction, Natural History, Photography, Science (General), Travel
ISBN Prefix(es): 3-85921

Swedenborg - Verlag+
Apollostr 2, 8032 Zurich
Tel: (01) 2515945
Key Personnel
President: Helen Guedemann
Editor: Dr Friedemann Horn
Manager: Heinz Grob
Founded: 1952
Subjects: Theology
ISBN Prefix(es): 3-85927
Orders to: Schweizer Buchzentrum, Olten

Swiss Centre for Development Cooperation in Technology & Management, see SKAT (Swiss Centre for Development Cooperation in Technology & Management)

Tages-Anzeiger
Werdstr 21, Postfach, 8004 Zurich
Tel: (01) 248 44 11 *Fax:* (01) 248 44 71
E-mail: tamedia@tamedia.ch
Web Site: www.tages-anzeiger.ch
ISBN Prefix(es): 3-85932

Terra Grischuna Verlag Buch-und Zeitschriftenverlag+
Felsenaustr 5, 7004 Chur
Tel: (081) 2867050 *Fax:* (081) 2867057
E-mail: info@terra-grischuna.ch
Web Site: www.terra-grischuna.ch
Key Personnel
Owner: Reto Fetz
Founded: 1942
Subjects: Geography, Geology, Natural History, Regional Interests, Romance, Travel
ISBN Prefix(es): 3-7298
Imprints: Baumgartner Blicher
Distributed by Herold Verlags ausli efering

Terra Magica, *imprint of* Reich Verlag AG

Thailand Press, see Cockatoo Press (Schweiz), Thailand-Publikationen

Theologischer Verlag und Buchhandlungen AG+
Badenerstr 69, Postfach, 8026 Zurich
Tel: (01) 299 33 55 *Fax:* (01) 299 33 58
E-mail: tvz@ref.ch
Web Site: www.tvz.ref.ch
Key Personnel
Dir, Editorial: Werner Blum
Rights & Permissions: Mrs E Frick
Publicity: Reinhold Jost
Founded: 1934
Subjects: Biblical Studies, History, Religion - Other, Theology
ISBN Prefix(es): 3-290
Bookshop(s): Theologische Buchhandlung, Raeffelstr 20, 8045 Zurich (antiquarian bookshop)

Theseus - Verlag AG+
Im Eigeli 6A, 8700 Kystnacht
Tel: (01) 9109294 *Fax:* (01) 9108019
Founded: 1973
Subjects: Art, Fiction, Philosophy, Religion - Buddhist
ISBN Prefix(es): 3-85936
Subsidiaries: Theseus Verlag GmbH

3-D-World, see 3 Dimension World (3-D-World)

3 Dimension World (3-D-World)+
Wartenbergstr 39, 4020 Basel
Tel: (061) 424917
Key Personnel
Publishing Dir: Gerd A Haisch
Founded: 1982
Membership(s): SBVV/SGS.
Subjects: Art, Biography, Film, Video, Geography, Geology, Marketing, Travel
ISBN Prefix(es): 3-905450
Parent Company: Pamelart/Icebear-Group Inc

Istituto Editoriale Ticinese (IET) SA
Via del Bramantino, 3, 6500 Bellinzona
Tel: (091) 8200101 *Fax:* (091) 8251874
Telex: 846266
Key Personnel
Man Dir: Libero Casagrande
Founded: 1900
Subjects: Fiction, Literature, Literary Criticism, Essays, Poetry
ISBN Prefix(es): 88-7713
Parent Company: Edizioni Casagrande SA

Tipografia Stazione, see Edizioni Armando Dado, Tipografia Stazione

Tobler Verlag+
Trogenerstr 80, 9450 Altstaetten
Tel: (071) 755 6060 *Fax:* (071) 755 1254
E-mail: books@tobler-verlag.ch
Web Site: www.tobler-verlag.ch
Key Personnel
Publication Manager: Hans Joerg Tobler
Tobler Verlag has merged with Causa Verlag, Helion Verlag, Panorama Verlag & Staatskunde-Verlag E Krattiger AG.
Subjects: Health, Nutrition, Law, Management, Marketing, Nonfiction (General), Parapsychology, Philosophy, Photography, Psychology, Psychiatry
ISBN Prefix(es): 3-907506; 3-85612

Trachsel - Verlag AG+
Alpenblickweg 7, 3714 Frutigen
Mailing Address: Postfach 60, 3714 Frutigen
Tel: (33) 6711407 *Fax:* (33) 6712449
Key Personnel
Man Dir: Ernst Trachsel-Neukom
Founded: 1946
Subjects: Religion - Other
ISBN Prefix(es): 3-7271
Imprints: TVF

Trans Tech Publications SA
Brandrain 6, 8707 Zurich-uetikon
Tel: (01) 9221022 *Fax:* (01) 9221033
E-mail: ttp@ttp.net
Web Site: www.ttp.net
Key Personnel
Dir: T Wohlbier *E-mail:* t.wohlbier@ttp.net
Founded: 1967
Subjects: Chemistry, Chemical Engineering, Mechanical Engineering, Physics
ISBN Prefix(es): 0-87849; 3-908158
Number of titles published annually: 30 Print
Total Titles: 412 Print
Branch Office(s)
c/o Enfield P & D Co, Inc, PO Box 699, Enfield
Tel: 603-632-7377 *Fax:* 603-632-5611

Translegal AG
Laenggasse 57, 3600 Thun
Tel: (033) 221622 *Fax:* (033) 2253933
Key Personnel
Contact: Hans Ott
ISBN Prefix(es): 3-85942
Subsidiaries: Ott Verlag & Druck AG

Editions du Tricorne+
14, rue Lissignol, 1201 Geneva
Tel: (022) 7388366 *Fax:* (022) 7319749
E-mail: tricorne@freesurf.ch
Web Site: www.tricorne.org
Key Personnel
Man Dir: Serge Kaplun
Founded: 1976
Essays.
Subjects: Art, Crafts, Games, Hobbies, Economics, Management, Mathematics, Philosophy, Poetry, Psychology, Psychiatry, Regional Interests, Religion - Other, Social Sciences, Sociology
ISBN Prefix(es): 2-8293
Number of titles published annually: 12 Print
Total Titles: 234 Print
Parent Company: ASK
Distributed by Presses Universitaires de France (PUF)

Editions des Trois Collines Francois Lachenal
Sezegnin, 1285 Geneva
Tel: (022) 7561309 *Fax:* (022) 7561302
Key Personnel
Dir: Francois Lachenal
Founded: 1935
Subjects: Art, Government, Political Science, Philosophy, Psychology, Psychiatry
ISBN Prefix(es): 3-88013

TVF, *imprint of* Trachsel - Verlag AG

Editions 24 Heures
33, ave de la Gare, 1001 Lausanne
Tel: (021) 3494500 *Fax:* (021) 3494224
Telex: 455745 Vgh Ch
Key Personnel
Man Dir: P Lamuniere
Founded: 1969

SWITZERLAND

Subjects: Aeronautics, Aviation, Animals, Pets, Art, Automotive, Education, History, Military Science, Music, Dance, Transportation
ISBN Prefix(es): 2-8265; 2-88260

Werner Ulmer & Co
Mittlere Haltenstr 1, 3625 Heiligenschwendi
Tel: (033) 432220 *Fax:* (033) 434848
Key Personnel
Contact: Werner Ulmer
ISBN Prefix(es): 3-7222

Der Universitatsverlag Freiburg (University Editions of Freiburg)+
Perolles 42, 1705 Freiburg
Tel: (026) 426 43 11 *Fax:* (026) 426 43 00
E-mail: eduni@st-paul.ch
Web Site: www.st-paul.ch/uni-press-FR
Key Personnel
Dir: Anton Scherer
Production Manager: Adolf Muller
Promotion Manager: Maurice Greder
Sales Manager & Subscriptions: Bernadette Meister
Founded: 1953
Subjects: Art, Economics, Ethnicity, Government, Political Science, History, Law, Literature, Literary Criticism, Essays, Medicine, Nursing, Dentistry, Music, Dance, Philosophy, Psychology, Psychiatry, Religion - Other, Theology
ISBN Prefix(es): 3-7278; 2-8271
Parent Company: Imprimerie et Libraries Saint-Paul SA, 42, blvd de Perolles, 1705 Fribourg
Associate Companies: Editions Saint-Paul; Editions de la Sarine, 42, blvd de Perolles, 1705 Fribourg
Bookshop(s): Librairie et Edition de la Suisse Romande

Uranium Verlag Zug
Postfach 42, 6317 Oberwil b Zug
Tel: (042) 217744
Telex: Topaz 58280
Key Personnel
Man Dir, Sales: L Young
Editorial: Mrs Young
Founded: 1976
Subjects: Nonfiction (General)
ISBN Prefix(es): 3-294
Branch Office(s)
Atzelbergstr 22, 60389 Frankfurt am Main, Germany

VCH Verlags-AG
Hofwiesenstr 36, 8042 Zurich
Mailing Address: Postfach 465, 8042 Zurich
Tel: (01) 3602438 *Fax:* (01) 3602439
E-mail: info@wiley-vch.de
Web Site: www.wiley-vch.de
Telex: 911527 DMS CH
ISBN Prefix(es): 3-527
Parent Company: Wiley-VCH Verlag GmbH, Pappelallee 3, 69469 Weinheim, Germany

Vdf Hochschulverlag AG an der ETH Zurich
Voltastr 24, 8044 Zurich
Mailing Address: ETH Zentrum, 8092 Zurich
Tel: (01) 632 42 42 *Fax:* (01) 632 12 32
E-mail: verlag@vdf.ethz.ch
Web Site: www.vdf.ethz.ch
Key Personnel
Marketing: Claudia Signer *Tel:* (01) 632 77 72 *E-mail:* signer@vdf.ethz.ch
International Rights: Ernst Schaerer
Founded: 1992
Subjects: Agriculture, Architecture & Interior Design, Civil Engineering, Computer Science, Economics, Engineering (General), Environmental Studies, Management, Mathematics, Physics, Science (General)
ISBN Prefix(es): 3-7281

Number of titles published annually: 70 Print; 3 CD-ROM
Total Titles: 11 CD-ROM
Orders to: Brockhaus Kommissionsgeschaeft, Postfach 1220, 70806 Kornwestheim, Germany

Verbandsdruckerei AG
Laupenstr 7a, 3000 Bern
Tel: (031) 252911
Telex: 32255
Key Personnel
Man Dir: Markus Rubli
Founded: 1919
Book publishing branch of Grafino Grafische Betriebe AG (Grafino Printing House).
Subjects: Agriculture, Nonfiction (General), Regional Interests
ISBN Prefix(es): 3-7280

Verkehrshaus der Schweiz
Lidostr 5, 6006 Lucerne
Tel: (041) 370444 *Fax:* (041) 3706168
E-mail: mail@verkehrshaus.org
Web Site: www.verkehrshaus.ch
Key Personnel
Dir: Fredy Rey
Subjects: Communications, Transportation
ISBN Prefix(es): 3-85954
Branch Office(s)
Museum of Transportation & Communication

Verlagsbuchhandling AG
St Alban-Vorstadt 56, 4006 Basel
Tel: (061) 239723
Key Personnel
Dir: Franz Kaeser; Willy Kohler
Manager: Andre Horisberger
Founded: 1897
Subjects: Crafts, Games, Hobbies, Ethnicity, Music, Dance, Regional Interests
ISBN Prefix(es): 3-85775
Imprints: Schweizerischen Gesellschaft fuer Volkskunde (Swiss Folklore Society)
Orders to: Gesellschaft fuer Volkskunde, St Alban-Vorstadt 56, 4006 Basel

Editions Eliane Vernay+
79, rue des Eaux-Vives, 1207 Geneva
Tel: (022) 7350460 *Fax:* (022) 7350460
Key Personnel
Man Dir: Eliane Vernay
Founded: 1977
Subjects: Poetry
ISBN Prefix(es): 2-88291

Editions du Verseau, *imprint of* Roth et Sauter SA

Versus Verlag AG+
Merkurstr 45, 8032 Zurich
Tel: (044) 2510892 *Fax:* (044) 2626738
E-mail: info@versus.ch
Web Site: www.versus.ch
Key Personnel
Contact: Anne Buechi
Founded: 1993
Subjects: Accounting, Art, Business, Economics, Finance, Human Relations, Labor, Industrial Relations, Law, Management, Marketing, Public Administration
ISBN Prefix(es): 3-908143; 3-909066; 3-03909
Distribution Center: AVA Buch 2000 Affoltern

Verlag Alfred Vetter
Gartenstr 15, 8002 Zurich
Tel: (01) 2011184
ISBN Prefix(es): 3-85956

Vexer Verlag+
Bleichestr 3, 9000 Saint Gallen

BOOK

Tel: (071) 220986
E-mail: vexer@freesurf.ch
Key Personnel
Contact: Josef Felix Mueller
Founded: 1985
Subjects: Art, Film, Video, Literature, Literary Criticism, Essays
ISBN Prefix(es): 3-909090
Total Titles: 80 Print
Distributed by Buchhandlung Walther Konig

Viktoria-Verlag Peter Marti
Burgdorfstr 10, 3510 Konolfingen BE
Tel: (031) 7911932 *Fax:* (031) 7912564
Subjects: Humor, Regional Interests
ISBN Prefix(es): 3-85958

Editions Vivez Soleil SA+
15 rue Francois-Jacquier, Case Postale 313, 1225 Chene-Bourg, Geneva
Mailing Address: BP 18, 74103 Annemasse Cedex, France
Tel: (04) 50 87 27 09 *Fax:* (04) 50 87 27 13
Key Personnel
President: Dr Christian Tal Schaller
Dir: Mr Marcel-Diedier, VRAC
Founded: 1987
Subjects: Health, Nutrition, Human Relations, Parapsychology, Psychology, Psychiatry
ISBN Prefix(es): 2-88058
Orders to: 21, rue des Tournelles, 74100 Ville-La-Grand

Verlag A Vogel
Postfach 63, Haetschen, 9053 Teufen
Tel: (071) 335 66 66 *Fax:* (071) 334684
E-mail: vavch@access.ch
Web Site: www.verlag-avogel.ch
Key Personnel
Contact: Silvia Loher *Tel:* (071) 335 66 70
ISBN Prefix(es): 3-906404
Number of titles published annually: 1 Print

Vogt-Schild Ag, Druck und Verlag+
Zuchwilerstr 21, 45010 Solothurn 50
Tel: (032) 6247111 *Fax:* (032) 6247444
Telex: 934646 *Cable:* PRINTERS SOLEURE
Key Personnel
Dir: Dr Markus H Haefely
Public Relations: Hans A Roelli
Founded: 1906
Specialize in periodicals.
Subjects: Architecture & Interior Design, Chemistry, Chemical Engineering, Electronics, Electrical Engineering, Technology, Transportation
ISBN Prefix(es): 3-85962
Subsidiaries: Jeger Moll Druck und Verlag AG
Orders to: Vogt-Schild Ag

Verlag Die Waage+
Dorfstr 90, 8802 Kilchberg
Tel: (01) 7155569; (01) 7241969 *Fax:* (01) 7153380
Key Personnel
Publisher & International Rights: Felix M Wiesner
Founded: 1951
Subjects: Erotica, Fiction, History, Literature, Literary Criticism, Essays, Mysteries, Philosophy, Poetry, Religion - Jewish, Religion - Other, Romance, Social Sciences, Sociology, Theology, Women's Studies
ISBN Prefix(es): 3-85966

Verlag im Waldgut AG+
Eisenwerk Industriestr 21, 8500 Frauenfeld
Tel: (054) 222344 *Fax:* (054) 7288927
Key Personnel
President & Chief Editor: Beat Brechbuehl
Founded: 1980
Founded by Beat Brechbuehl, writer & publisher, in Wald near Zurich. In 1987 the publishing

house moved to Frauenfeld & expanded its program.
Subjects: Developing Countries, Education, Ethnicity, Foreign Countries, Poetry
ISBN Prefix(es): 3-7294

Walter Verlag AG+
Dorfstr 81, 8706 Meilen
Mailing Address: PO Box 121, 8706 Meilen
Tel: (062) 341188 *Fax:* (062) 321184
E-mail: info@walter-verlag.ch
Web Site: www.walter-verlag.ch
Key Personnel
Dir: Machalet Chnshan
Publicity: Charlotte Kraehenbuehl
Rights & Permissions: Erika Straumann
Founded: 1924
Subjects: Psychology, Psychiatry, Regional Interests, Religion - Other
ISBN Prefix(es): 3-530

WCC Publications, see World Council of Churches (WCC Publications)

Weber SA d'Editions
CP 109, 1224 Chene-Dorugeries
Tel: (07) 93104541
Key Personnel
Man Dir: Marcel Weber
Founded: 1951
Subjects: Architecture & Interior Design, Art, Health, Nutrition, Library & Information Sciences, Photography
ISBN Prefix(es): 2-7190; 2-88301; 3-295

Weka Informations Schriften Verlag AG+
Hermetschloostr 77, 8010 Zurich
Tel: (01) 4328432 *Fax:* (01) 4328201
Key Personnel
Man Dir: Robert Boss
Founded: 1978
Specialize in Loose-Leaf Publication.
Subjects: Computer Science, Law, Management
ISBN Prefix(es): 3-297
Parent Company: WEKA Firmengruppe GmbH, Roemerstr 4, 86438 Kissing, Germany

Weltrundschau Verlag AG+
Obermeuhofstr 1, 6341 Baar
Tel: (041) 761 54 31 *Fax:* (041) 761 44 04
E-mail: wrs@bluewin.ch
Web Site: www.wrs.ch *Cable:* WORLDREVIEW
Key Personnel
Man Dir: Franz Truniger
Editorial: E Gysling
Founded: 1959
Subjects: Government, Political Science, Sports, Athletics
ISBN Prefix(es): 3-7283
Associate Companies: Jeunesse Verlagsanstalt, Kirchstr 1, Vaduz, Liechtenstein (Rights & Permissions)

Weltwoche ABC-Verlag+
Edenstr 20, Postfach, 8021 Zurich
Tel: (01) 2078643; (01) 2078650; (01) 2078756 *Fax:* (01) 2078680
E-mail: order@baz.ch
Key Personnel
President: Rudolf Baechtold
Man Dir: Peter Zwicky
Founded: 1937
Subjects: Art, Nonfiction (General)
ISBN Prefix(es): 3-85504; 3-85975; 3-9520932
Book Club(s): SBVV

Wepf & Co AG
Eisengasse 5, 4001 Basel
Mailing Address: Postfach 2064, 4001 Basel
Tel: (061) 256377 *Fax:* (061) 253597
E-mail: wepf@dial.eunet.ch *Cable:* WEPFCO BASEL
Key Personnel
Dir: H Herrmann; M Weber
Manager: Hans Jo Pfeiffer
Founded: 1902
Subjects: Architecture & Interior Design, Earth Sciences, Ethnicity, Geography, Geology
ISBN Prefix(es): 3-85977
Number of titles published annually: 5 Print

Werner Druck AG
Kanonengasse 32, 4051 Basel
Tel: (061) 2710690 *Fax:* (061) 2710601
Web Site: www.wernerdruck.ch
Key Personnel
President & Co-Dir: Dr H G Hinderling
Co-Dir: N Werner
Founded: 1862
Subjects: Art
ISBN Prefix(es): 3-85979

Buchverlag der Druckerei Wetzikon AG
Rapperswilerstr 1, Postf, 8620 Wetzikon 1
Tel: (01) 9333111 *Fax:* (01) 9323232
Telex: 875547
Subjects: Environmental Studies
ISBN Prefix(es): 3-85981

Wiese Verlag AG+
Hochbergerstr 15, 4002 Basel
Tel: (061) 6391315 *Fax:* (061) 6391343
E-mail: order@baz.ch
Web Site: www.baz.ch
Key Personnel
Publisher: Peter Zwicky
Founded: 1988
Subjects: Architecture & Interior Design, Art, Crafts, Games, Hobbies
ISBN Prefix(es): 3-909158; 3-909164
Parent Company: Basler Zeitung
Book Club(s): SBVV

Verlag Alexander Wild+
Rathausgasse 30, 3011 Bern
Tel: (031) 3114480 *Fax:* (031) 3114470
Key Personnel
Man Dir, Owner: Alexander Wild
Founded: 1977
Subjects: Literature, Literary Criticism, Essays
ISBN Prefix(es): 3-7284; 3-85982
Associate Companies: Origo-Verlag
Distributor for Origo-Verlag

WMO, see World Meteorological Organization

J E Wolfensberger AG
Bederstr 109, 8027 Zurich
Tel: (01) 2857878 *Fax:* (01) 2857879
E-mail: prepress@wolfensberger-ag.ch
Web Site: www.wolfensberger-ag.ch
Key Personnel
Dir: Ulla Wolfensberger
Founded: 1905
Subjects: Art, Lithographs, Limited editions, signed & numbered
ISBN Prefix(es): 3-85987

World Council of Churches (WCC Publications)+
150 Route de Ferney, 1211 Geneva 2
Mailing Address: PO Box 2100, 1211 Geneva 2
Tel: (022) 7916379 *Fax:* (022) 7981346
E-mail: hs@wcc-coe.org
Web Site: www.wcc-coe.org
Telex: 415730 OIK CH *Cable:* OIKOUMENE, GENEVA
Key Personnel
General Secretary: Konrad Raiser
Dir & Publisher: Jan H Kok
International Rights: Heather Stunt *Tel:* (022) 7916379 *E-mail:* hs@wcc-coe.org
Founded: 1948
Subjects: Religion - Other, Theology
ISBN Prefix(es): 2-8254
Total Titles: 15 Print
U.S. Office(s): World Council of Churches, Room 915, 475 Riverside Dr, New York, NY 10015-0050, United States
Distributed by Asian Trading Co (India); Christian Literature Society of Korea; Conference of Churches in Aotearoa-New Zealand; Ecumenical Council of Denmark; Intercultural Publications (India); ISPCK (India); Korea Christian Book Service; Methodist Publishing House (South Africa); National Council of Churches in Australia; United Church Distribution Center (Canada)
Bookshop(s): Examiner Bookshop, Mumbai, India; Epworth Bookshop, Wellington, New Zealand
Shipping Address: Distribution Center, PO Box 348, Route 222 & Sharadin Rd, Kutztown, PA 19530-0348, United States *Fax:* (610) 683-5616

World Meteorological Organization
7 bis Ave de la Paix, CP 2300, 1211 Geneva 2
Mailing Address: CP 2300, 1211 Geneva 2
Tel: (022) 730 8111 *Fax:* (022) 730 8181
E-mail: pubsales@gateway.wmo.ch; ipa@www.wmo.ch
Web Site: www.wmo.ch
Telex: 414199 OMM CH; 23260 *Cable:* METEOMOND GENEVE
Subjects: Science (General), Technology
ISBN Prefix(es): 92-63

World Wild Life Films (Pty) Ltd
Eduard Zingg, Postfach 6586, 8023 Zurich
Tel: (01) 4331444 *Fax:* (01) 4331460
Web Site: www.kftu.com
Key Personnel
Man Dir: Eduard Zingg
ISBN Prefix(es): 3-85986

WOZ Die Wochenzeitung (WOZ The Weekly Paper)
Hardturmstr 66, 8031 Zurich
Tel: (01) 448 14 14 *Fax:* (01) 448 14 15
E-mail: woz@woz.ch
Web Site: www.woz.ch

Wyss Verlag AG Bern
Effingerstr 17, 3008 Bern
Tel: (031) 253715; (031) 254425 *Fax:* (031) 3814821; (031) 254821
Key Personnel
Dir: Christoph Wyss
Founded: 1849
Subjects: Art, History, Law
ISBN Prefix(es): 3-7285

Zbinden Druck und Verlag AG
St Alban-Vostadt 16, Postfach, 4006 Basel
Tel: (061) 2722105 *Fax:* (061) 2726722
Key Personnel
Man Dir: Kurt Krause
Subjects: Anthropology, Biography, Education, Poetry
ISBN Prefix(es): 3-85989

Ziegler Druck- und Verlags-AG, Gemsberg-Verlag, Foto & Schmalfilm-Verlag
Postfach 778, Garnmarkt 10, 8401 Winterthur
Tel: (052) 266 99 00 *Fax:* (052) 266 99 10
Web Site: www.zieglerdruck.ch
Key Personnel
Manager: Alfons Rueede
ISBN Prefix(es): 3-85701

Editions Zoe
11, rue des Moraines, 1227 Carouge, Geneva
Tel: (022) 309 36 06 *Fax:* (022) 309 36 03
E-mail: edzoe@iprolink.ch
Web Site: www.editionszoe.ch
Key Personnel
Man Dir: Marlyse Pietri-Bachmann
Founded: 1975
Subjects: History, Literature, Literary Criticism, Essays, Social Sciences, Sociology
ISBN Prefix(es): 2-88182

Zuerich, *imprint of* Interfrom AG Editions

Zumstein & Cie
Zeughausgasse 24, 3000 Bern 7
Tel: (031) 312 00 55 *Fax:* (031) 312 23 26
E-mail: post_zumstein@briefmarken.ch
Web Site: www.zumstein-cie.ch
Founded: 1905
Subjects: Crafts, Games, Hobbies
ISBN Prefix(es): 3-909278; 3-85994

Syrian Arab Republic

General Information

Capital: Damascus
Language: Arabic and some Kurdish.
Religion: Islamic (mostly of the Sunni sect) and Christian
Population: 13.7 million
Bank Hours: 0800-1400 Saturday-Thursday
Shop Hours: 1000-1900. Closed Friday. Generally long closing at lunchtime
Currency: 100 piastres = 1 Syrian pound
Export/Import Information: No tariffs on books except children's picture books, with additional taxes; most advertising matter is dutied. State organization for control and execution of publicity and advertising within Syria is Arab Advertising Organization, Damascus. The General Advertising Institute, 2842, must get samples of commercial advertising and promotional materials before distribution permitted. Import license must be submitted to Commercial Bank of Syria in order to obtain exchange license.
Copyright: No copyright conventions signed

Damascus University Press
Damascus University Library, Damascus, Baramkah
Tel: (011) 2215104; (011) 2215101 *Fax:* (011) 2236010
E-mail: info@damascus-online.com
Web Site: www.damascus-online/university.htm
Telex: 411971
Key Personnel
Dir: Dr Hussain Omran
Subjects: Accounting, Agriculture, Anthropology, Archaeology, Architecture & Interior Design, Art, Behavioral Sciences, Business, Chemistry, Chemical Engineering, Civil Engineering, Communications, Computer Science, Earth Sciences, Economics, Education, Electronics, Electrical Engineering, Engineering (General), English as a Second Language, Environmental Studies, Finance, Geography, Geology, Government, Political Science, Health, Nutrition, History, Journalism, Language Arts, Linguistics, Law, Library & Information Sciences, Marketing, Mathematics, Mechanical Engineering, Medicine, Nursing, Dentistry, Natural History, Philosophy, Physics, Poetry, Psychology, Psychiatry, Public Administration, Religion - Islamic, Science (General), Social Sciences, Sociology, Transportation
Publication(s): *Arab Journal for Pharmaceutics*; *Arab Universities Journal for Medical Research and Studies*; *Damascas University Journal for Engineering Sciences*; *Damascus University Journal*; *Damascus University Journal for Agricultural Sciences*; *Damascus University Journal for Arts and Human and Educational Sciences*; *Damascus University Journal for Medical Sciences*; *Damascus University Journal for the Basic Sciences*; *Damascus University Journal for the Economic Sciences*; *Damascus University Journal for the New in the Medical Sciences*

Dar Al Maarifah (House of Knowledge)
29 Ayar St, Damascus
Mailing Address: PO Box 30268, Damascus
Tel: (011) 44670278 *Fax:* (011) 2241615
E-mail: info@easyquran.com
Web Site: www.dar-al-maarifah.com; www.easyquran.com
Founded: 1986
Also printer & distributor.
Membership(s): Arab Publishers Association.
Number of titles published annually: 1 CD-ROM
Total Titles: 240 Print; 5 CD-ROM

Institut Francais d'Etudes Arabes de Damas
BP 344, Damascus
Tel: (011) 3330214; (011) 3331962 *Fax:* (011) 3327887
E-mail: ifead@net.sy
Web Site: www.lb.refer.org/ifead
Telex: 412.272 IFEAD SY
Key Personnel
Dir: Dominique Mallet
Founded: 1922
Specialize in academic publications.
Subjects: Anthropology, Archaeology, Geography, Geology, History, Language Arts, Linguistics, Literature, Literary Criticism, Essays, Philosophy, Religion - Islamic, Social Sciences, Sociology
ISBN Prefix(es): 2-901315; 2-84128
Number of titles published annually: 8 Print
Total Titles: 4 Print
Parent Company: Direction Generale des Relations Culturelles Scientifiques et Techniques, Ministere des affaires Etrangeres, Paris, France
Distributed by Al-Jaffan et al Jabi (Middle East)
Distribution Center: Leila Books, 39 Kasr El-Nil St, 2nd floor, Daher 11271 Cairo, Egypt (Arab Republic of Egypt) *E-mail:* leilabks@intouch.com
Librairie-Boutique de l'ima, One rue des Fosses, Saint-Bernard 75236 Cedex 05, Paris, France
E-mail: bookshop@imarabe.org
Orders to: Librairie d'Amerique et d'Orient (Adrien Maisonneuve), 11, rue St-Sulpice, F-75006 Paris, France *Tel:* (01) 43268635 *Fax:* (01) 43545954

Taiwan, Province of China

General Information

Capital: Taipei
Language: Northern Chinese (Mandarin)
Religion: Predominantly Buddhist, also Muslim, Daoist, & Christian
Population: 20.9 million
Bank Hours: 0900-1530 Monday-Friday; 0900-1200 Saturday
Shop Hours: 1000-2130 Monday-Saturday
Currency: 100 cents = 1 new Taiwan dollar
Export/Import Information: No tariffs on books and advertising. Import licenses required; exchange available when license is presented at authorized bank. Publications approved for import will not violate the Republic of China's basic national policy, undermine public morality or contravene special regulations.
Copyright: No copyright conventions signed. Copyright is protected by the Copyright Law. Companies and individuals, including foreigners, can register their works with the Ministry of the Interior for portection. An amendment broading the scope of the Republic of China's Copyright Law was passed 28 June 1985 by the Legislative Yuan and put into effect on 12 July 1985. The amendment, aimed at curbing pirating activities, sharply increases the maximum sentence for violating copyrights from three to five years and the maximum fine from US $75 to US $11,250, and brings computer software and video tapes under the scope of the law. Publications printed in Taiwan must acquire approval from the copyright holder before export.

Ai Chih Book Co Ltd
235 Chienfu St, Kaohsiung 806
Tel: (07) 8121571 *Fax:* (07) 8121534
Key Personnel
Contact: Yang Baong Min
Subjects: Child Care & Development, Literature, Literary Criticism, Essays
ISBN Prefix(es): 957-608

Arsorigo Co Ltd+
5D-24, No 5, Sec 5, Hsing Yi Rd, Taipei
Tel: (02) 2735-1274 *Fax:* (02) 2725-2387
Key Personnel
Chief Executive: Yuan ChiiShen

Art Book Co Ltd+
4F, 18, Lane 283, Roosevelt Rd, Section 3, Taipei
Tel: (02) 23620578 *Fax:* (02) 23623594
E-mail: artbook@ms43.hinet.net
Key Personnel
Publisher: Kung-shang Ho
Founded: 1972
Specialize in Fine Arts.
Subjects: Antiques, Art, History, How-to
ISBN Prefix(es): 957-672; 957-9045

The Artist Publishing Co
6F, 147, Chungching S Rd, Sec 1, 100 Taipei
Tel: (02) 23932780 *Fax:* (02) 23932012
E-mail: artvenue@tpts6.seed.net.tw
Key Personnel
Chief Executive: Ho Cheng-Kuang
Founded: 1975
Subjects: Art
ISBN Prefix(es): 957-9500; 957-8273; 957-9530

Asian Culture Co Ltd+
6F, No 21, Nanking E Rd, Sec 3, Taipei
Tel: (02) 2507-2606 *Fax:* (02) 2507-4260
E-mail: asian@asianculture.com.tw
Web Site: www.asianculture.com.tw
Key Personnel
President: Eric Tong-sheng Wu
International Rights: Mr Yuan-chun Ting
Designer: Cheng Fong-Pin
Founded: 1982
Subjects: Archaeology, Art, Asian Studies, Biography, Business, Fiction, Health, Nutrition, History, Law, Literature, Literary Criticism, Essays, Military Science, Philosophy, Photography, Romance, Self-Help, Women's Studies, Dance, Autobiography
ISBN Prefix(es): 957-8983; 957-9027; 957-9449

PUBLISHERS

Bookman Books Ltd+
2nd Fl-5, 88 Hsinsheng S Rd, Sec 3, Taipei
Tel: (02) 2368-7226; (02) 2365-8617 *Fax:* (02) 2363-6630; (02) 2365-3548
Web Site: www.bookman.com.tw
Key Personnel
Man Dir: Jerome (Cheng-lung) Su
Founded: 1977
Also acts as exclusive agents in Taiwan for W W Norton, USA, & Faber & Faber, UK.
Subjects: Literature, Literary Criticism, Essays, Social Sciences, Sociology
ISBN Prefix(es): 957-586

Campus Evangelical Fellowship, Literature Department+
22, Sec 4, Roosevelt Rd, Taipei 100
Tel: (02) 2368-2361 *Fax:* (02) 2367-2139
E-mail: info@cef.org.tw
Web Site: www.cef.org.tw
Key Personnel
Dir: Hui-Ping Peng
Vice Dir: Ruth Cha
Editor: Stephen Wu
Founded: 1965
Subjects: Biblical Studies, Biography, Child Care & Development, Human Relations, Religion - Protestant
ISBN Prefix(es): 957-587
U.S. Office(s): Overseas Campus Magazine, PO Box 638, Lomita, CA 90717-0638, United States

Cheng Chung Book Co, Ltd
20 Hengyang Rd, Taipei
Tel: (02) 2382-2815 *Fax:* (02) 2389-3571
Web Site: www.ccbc.com.tw
Subjects: Education
ISBN Prefix(es): 957-09

Cheng Wen Publishing Company
3F, No 227, Sec 3, Roosevelt Rd, Taipei 106
Tel: (02) 2362-8032 *Fax:* (02) 2366-0806
E-mail: ccicncwp@ms17.hinet.net
Key Personnel
Chief Executive & Publisher: Larry C Huang
Founded: 1964
Subjects: History, Literature, Literary Criticism, Essays, Philosophy
ISBN Prefix(es): 957-07

Cheng Yun Publishing Company Ltd+
Rm 612F, No 601, Chung Cheng Rd, Shihlin, Taipei 111
Tel: (02) 28117798 *Fax:* (02) 28123041
E-mail: toybook@ms34.hinet.net
Web Site: www.toybook.com.tw
Key Personnel
Chief Executive: Lai Yen-Ping
Founded: 1991
ISBN Prefix(es): 957-9241
Associate Companies: Seven Brocades Products Inc

Chien Chen Bookstore Publishing Company Ltd+
80, Liming Rd, Kaohsiung
Tel: (07) 3820363 *Fax:* (07) 3892816
Key Personnel
Chief Exec: Mu-Shiung Chang
Founded: 1977
Subjects: Accounting, Agriculture, Animals, Pets, Behavioral Sciences, Biological Sciences, Business, Career Development
ISBN Prefix(es): 957-9574; 957-704

Chin Chin Publications Ltd
4F, 125, Suhg Chinng Rd, Taipei 104
Tel: (02) 25084331 *Fax:* (02) 25074902
E-mail: we122179@ms13.hinet.net

Web Site: www.weichuan.org.tw
ISBN Prefix(es): 957-9427

China Law Magazine Ltd
130 Ch'ungch'ing S Rd Sec 1, Province of Taiwan, Taipei
Tel: (02) 23814211 *Fax:* (02) 23814211
E-mail: chinals@hk.china.com
ISBN Prefix(es): 957-99166
Parent Company: China Legal Service (UK) Ltd, United Kingdom

China Times Publishing Co+
5F, 240, Hoping West Rd Sec 3, Taipei
Tel: (02) 2304-7103 *Fax:* (02) 23027844
Web Site: www.chinatimes.com.tw
Founded: 1975
ISBN Prefix(es): 957-13

Chinese Christian Literature Council Taiwan Ltd
2F, 277, Hoping E Rd, Sec 2, Taipei
Tel: (02) 7080230 *Fax:* (02) 7551895
Key Personnel
Chief Executive: Lien-Hwa Chow
ISBN Prefix(es): 957-9186

Chu Liu Book Company+
Rm 312, No 25, Po-Ai Rd, Taipei 10035
Tel: (02) 2371 1031 *Fax:* (02) 3815823
E-mail: chuliu@ms13.hinet.net
Key Personnel
Off Manager: Paul Hsiung
Founded: 1973
Subjects: Art, Child Care & Development, Education, History, Human Relations, Literature, Literary Criticism, Essays, Philosophy, Psychology, Psychiatry, Social Sciences, Sociology
ISBN Prefix(es): 957-732; 957-9464

Chung Hwa Book Co Ltd+
5F, 8, Lane 181, Chiutsung Rd, Sec 2, Taipei 114
Tel: (02) 8797 8669 *Fax:* (02) 8797 8909 *Cable:* 2821 TAIPEI
Key Personnel
Man Dir: James C Hsiung
Vice President: Erica Hsiung
Founded: 1912
Subjects: Art, Biography, Education, Engineering (General), Fiction, History, Literature, Literary Criticism, Essays, Medicine, Nursing, Dentistry, Music, Dance, Philosophy, Poetry, Psychology, Psychiatry, Religion - Other, Science (General), Social Sciences, Sociology
ISBN Prefix(es): 957-43

Commonwealth Publishing Company Ltd+
2F, 1, Lane 93, Sung Chiang Rd, Taipei 104
Tel: (02) 2517-3688 *Fax:* (02) 2517-3686
Web Site: www.bookzone.com.tw
Key Personnel
President: Charles Kao
Publisher: Cora Wang
Founded: 1982
General trade & translated titles.
Subjects: Biography, Business, Child Care & Development, Economics, Fiction, Health, Nutrition, Management, Nonfiction (General), Science (General), Self-Help
ISBN Prefix(es): 957-621
Number of titles published annually: 150 Print
Associate Companies: CommonWealth Magazine, 4F, No 87, Sung Chiang Rd, Taipei 104 *Tel:* (02) 2507 8627; Global Views Monthly Magazine

Cynosure Publishing Inc+
4F, No 26, Alley 91, Sec 1, Nei Fo Rd, Taipei
Tel: 8862 2657 3275 *Fax:* (02) 2657 5300
E-mail: cynobook@tpts4.seed.net.tw

Key Personnel
Exec Dir: Jimmy C C Chen *Tel:* (02) 2657 3275 *Fax:* (02) 2657 5300
Founded: 1989
Also acts as Packager.
ISBN Prefix(es): 957-9158; 957-9430
Parent Company: Long Ken Corp Ltd
Book Club(s): Hello! Book Club Inc, 5F, No 203, Chung Hsiao E Rd, Sec 3, Taipei, ROC *Tel:* (02) 27401281 *Fax:* (02) 27401545 *E-mail:* heloclub@ms22.hinet.net *Web Site:* www.hellobookclub.com

Dayi Information Co
1F, 8-1, Jeikuang Rd, Taipei 114
Tel: (02) 5796800 *Fax:* (02) 5796805
Key Personnel
Contact: Jeff Wang
Founded: 1992
Subjects: Business
ISBN Prefix(es): 957-99775

Designer Publisher Inc
7F, 159-2, Shih-Ta Rd, Taipei
Tel: (02) 365 6268 *Fax:* (02) 365 6521
Key Personnel
Chief Executive: Wang Su-Chao
Founded: 1992
Subjects: Advertising, Communications, Graphics, Typography
ISBN Prefix(es): 957-9570
Imprints: Wang Su-Chao
Subsidiaries: Graphic Communications Monthly

Echo Publishing Company Ltd+
5-2 Pa Teh Rd, Sec 4, Ln 72, Alley 16, Taipei
Tel: (02) 763-1452 *Fax:* (02) 27568712
Key Personnel
Chief Executive: Ms Linda Wu
Founded: 1970
Subjects: Anthropology, Antiques, Archaeology, Architecture & Interior Design, Art, Asian Studies, Child Care & Development, Crafts, Games, Hobbies
ISBN Prefix(es): 957-588
Associate Companies: Echo Communications Co Ltd
Distributed by Charles E Tuttle Co (USA & UK)

Far East Book Co Ltd
66, Chungking S Rd, Sec 1, Taipei
Tel: (02) 2311 8740 *Fax:* (02) 2311 4184
E-mail: service@mail.fareast.com.tw
Web Site: www.fareast.com.tw *Cable:* 1418 TAIPEI
Key Personnel
Manager: Jonathan Riverbank
Founded: 1950
Subjects: Art, Education, History, Literature, Literary Criticism, Essays, Physics, Poetry
ISBN Prefix(es): 957-9666; 957-612
Distributed by U.S. International Inc.

Farseeing Publishing Company Ltd+
4F, 50-1, Hsinsheng S Rd, Section 1, Taipei
Tel: (02) 23921167 *Fax:* (02) 3225455
E-mail: fars@msb.ninet.net
Web Site: www.farseeing.com.tw
Key Personnel
Chief Executive: Hsiao Feng-Fu
Founded: 1983
Subjects: English as a Second Language, Health, Nutrition, Medicine, Nursing, Dentistry
ISBN Prefix(es): 957-640; 957-9506; 957-99215; 957-99266
Associate Companies: Weyfar Books Co Ltd
Subsidiaries: Farseeing Nursing Press
Divisions: Fayfar Publishing Co Ltd

Fuh-Wen Book Co+
63, Linsen Rd, Sec 2, Tainan

TAIWAN, PROVINCE OF CHINA

Tel: (06) 2744219; (06) 2351830 *Fax:* (06) 2347222
Key Personnel
President: Mr Chu Ho Wu
Vice President: James Chin
Editor: Shih Shu-Yen
Subjects: Accounting, Agriculture, Automotive, Chemistry, Chemical Engineering, Civil Engineering, Computer Science, Economics, Electronics, Electrical Engineering, Engineering (General), Environmental Studies, Finance, Marketing, Mathematics, Mechanical Engineering, Physical Sciences, Physics, Science (General)
ISBN Prefix(es): 957-536
Subsidiaries: Taiwan Fuh-Wen Sin-Yah Co Ltd
Branch Office(s)
985 Papen Rd, Bridgewater, NJ 08807, United States
Book Club(s): ABA
Shipping Address: The Kaohsiung Port
Warehouse: No 18 Alley 88 Lane 71, Fuh-Sin Rd, Yung-Kang Village, Tainan County

Grand East Enterprise, *imprint of* San Min Book Co Ltd

Great China Book Company
4F-2, 150, Chion First Rd, Chungho 235 Taipei
Tel: (02) 82263099 *Fax:* (02) 82265906
ISBN Prefix(es): 957-521

Grimm Press Ltd+
6F, No 20, Sec 2, Hsin-Sheng S Rd, Taipei 106
Tel: (02) 23517251 *Fax:* (02) 23517244
E-mail: ishbel@cite.com.tw
Key Personnel
Publisher: K T Hao
Editor: Joy Chao
Marketing Dir: Annie Lin
Rights Manager: Bruce Ishbel
International Rights: Catherine Van Hale
Publishes classic stories & modern tales from East & West.
Subjects: Animals, Pets, Biography, Fiction, History, Humor, Science (General), Technology
ISBN Prefix(es): 957-745

Chu Hai Publishing (Taiwan) Co Ltd
2F-1, 151, Anho Rd, Sec 2, Taipei 106
Tel: (02) 7080290 *Fax:* (02) 7084804
Key Personnel
International Rights: Gee H Luk
Subjects: Agriculture, Architecture & Interior Design, Art, Business, Civil Engineering, Computer Science, Engineering (General), Environmental Studies, Gardening, Plants, Health, Nutrition, Medicine, Nursing, Dentistry, Social Sciences, Sociology, Travel
ISBN Prefix(es): 957-657

Heavenly Lotus Publishing Co, Ltd
2F, 168, Chungch'eng Rd, Sec 2, Shih Lin, Taipei
Tel: (02) 2873-6629 *Fax:* (02) 8736709
Key Personnel
President: Yun-Pen Lee
Founded: 1975
Subjects: Religion - Buddhist
ISBN Prefix(es): 957-665; 957-9397

Hilit Publishing Co Ltd+
11F, No 28, Roosevelt Rd, Sec 3, Taipei 100
Tel: (02) 2362-6602 *Fax:* (02) 2365-2552
E-mail: hilit.publish@msa.hinet.net
Web Site: www.hilit.com.tw
Key Personnel
Chairman: Dixson Sung
Dir: Bob Wang
Representative: Joyce Wang
Founded: 1980

Subjects: Agriculture, Antiques, Art, Asian Studies, Cookery, Crafts, Games, Hobbies, Fiction, Gardening, Plants, How-to, Photography, Travel, diet
ISBN Prefix(es): 957-629
Associate Companies: Highlight International Co Ltd
Warehouse: 35, Lanc 142, Kun Yang St, Taipei

Ho-Chi Book Publishing Co+
No 322-2 An Kun Rd, Nei-Hu Area, Taipei 114
Tel: (02) 2974-0168 *Fax:* (02) 2792-4702
E-mail: hochi@ms12.hinet.net; hochi@email.gcn.net.tw
Key Personnel
Contact: Wu Kuei-tsung
Founded: 1956
Subjects: Behavioral Sciences, Biological Sciences, Child Care & Development, Health, Nutrition, Medicine, Nursing, Dentistry, Psychology, Psychiatry, Technology, Veterinary Science, Life Science
ISBN Prefix(es): 957-666; 957-9097
Distributor for Churchill Livingstone; Lippincott-Raven; McGraw-Hill; W B Saunders; Williams & Wilkins
Bookshop(s): Ho-Chi Book Store (Bei-yi Branch), Suite 249, Wu-Hsing St., Taipei 110 *Tel:* (02) 2723-9404 *Fax:* (02) 2723-0997; Tai-da Branch, Suite 7, Lane 12, Roosevelt Rd., Sec 4, Taipei 100 *Tel:* (02) 2365-1544 *Fax:* (02) 2367-1266; Rong-Zong Branch, Suite 120, Shih-Pai Rd, Sec 2, Taipei 112 *Tel:* (02) 2826-5375 *Fax:* (02) 2823-9604; Taichung Branch, Suite 24, Yu-Der Rd, Taichung *Tel:* (04) 203-0795 *Fax:* (04) 202-5093; Kaohsiung Branch, Suite 1, Pei-Peng 1st St, Kaohsiung 800 *Tel:* (07) 322-6177 *Fax:* (07) 323-5118

Hsiao Yuan Publication Co, Ltd+
20, Lane 333, Riisevekt Rd, Sec 3, Taipei 106
Tel: (02) 23676789 *Fax:* (02) 23628424
E-mail: vfafol30@ms5.hinet.net
Key Personnel
Vice President: Feng Chu Huang-Yu
Subjects: Business, Chemistry, Chemical Engineering, Computer Science, Electronics, Electrical Engineering, English as a Second Language, Literature, Literary Criticism, Essays, Mathematics, Physical Sciences, Technology
ISBN Prefix(es): 957-12
Bookshop(s): No 96-3, Sec 3, Hsin Sheng S Rd, Taipei

Hsin Yi Publications+
75, Chung-Chung S Rd, Sec 2, Taipei
Tel: (02) 23965303 *Fax:* (02) 23910799
Web Site: www.hsin-yi.org.tw
Key Personnel
Publisher: Show Chung Ho
Chief Editor: Sin-Ju Ho
Director: Jung-Chen Cheng *E-mail:* jung@hsin-yi.org.tw
Founded: 1978
Distributed by Shen's Books & Supplies, 8625 Hubbard Rd, Auburn, CA 95602.
ISBN Prefix(es): 957-642; 957-9526
Total Titles: 1,000 Print
Parent Company: Hsin Yi Foundation
Associate Companies: Hsinex International Corporation, 75 Sec 2, Chung-Chung S Rd, Taipei, Contact: Santee Wen *Tel:* (02) 23913384 *Fax:* (02) 23913384 *E-mail:* santee@hsin-hi.org.tw

Hu Yu She Culture Co Ltd, see HYS Culture Co Ltd

HYS Culture Co Ltd+
2, Alley 3, Lane 130, Paoan Rd, Yungan, Kaohsiung

Tel: (07) 6914310 *Fax:* (02) 6914311
E-mail: hysccl@msl.hinet.net
Web Site: www.hysbook.com.tw
Key Personnel
General Manager: Mr G L Hsu
Subjects: Animals, Pets
ISBN Prefix(es): 957-9561

Jillion Publishing Co+
2F, No 9, Lane 2, Nanking W Rd, Taipei 104
Tel: (02) 2571-0558 *Fax:* (02) 5231891
E-mail: lanbri@tpts.5.seed.net.tw
Key Personnel
Chief Exec: Ai Tien-Shi
Founded: 1985
Subjects: Career Development, English as a Second Language, How-to, Language Arts, Linguistics
ISBN Prefix(es): 957-9415; 957-786

Kuang Fu Book Co Ltd+
6F, No 38, Fushing N Rd, Taipei
Tel: (02) 2771-6622 *Fax:* (02) 7315982
E-mail: lolatiao@kfgroup.com.tw
Web Site: www.kfgroup.com.tw
Key Personnel
President: Mr C H Lin
Foreign Affairs Executive: Mr Hong-Long Lin
Foreign Rights & Manager: Ming-Yen Tiao *Tel:* (02) 2741-0415
Founded: 1962
Also specializing in distance learning.
Subjects: Art, Education, Fiction, Health, Nutrition, History, Literature, Literary Criticism, Essays, Medicine, Nursing, Dentistry, Science (General)
ISBN Prefix(es): 957-42
Total Titles: 2,000 Print; 80 CD-ROM
Imprints: Kwang Fu Book Enterprises Co, Ltd
Subsidiaries: Kwang Toong Book Department Store Co Ltd
U.S. Office(s): Tron Link Enterprises Co, Ltd, 9401 De Vry Dr, Irvine, CA, United States, Contact: Mr Hong-tien Lin *Tel:* 949-856-9769; 949-854-1569 *Fax:* 949-856-9769 *E-mail:* hongtien@aol.com
Book Club(s): New Reader's Book Club, Contact: Lola Tiao *Tel:* (02) 2771-6622 *E-mail:* bookclub@kfgroup.com.tw

Kuei Kuan Book Co Ltd, see Laureate Book Co Ltd

Kwang Fu Book Enterprises Co, Ltd, *imprint of* Kuang Fu Book Co Ltd

Laureate Book Co Ltd+
2F, No 542-3, Chung-Chun Rd, Hsien tien, Taipei 105
Tel: 8862 2219 3338 *Fax:* (02) 2218-2859
E-mail: laureate@ms10.hinet.net
Key Personnel
Manager: A-Shen Lai
Founded: 1975
Subjects: Anthropology, Behavioral Sciences, Business, Child Care & Development, Education, Government, Political Science, History, Literature, Literary Criticism, Essays, Management, Philosophy, Psychology, Psychiatry, Social Sciences, Sociology, Women's Studies
ISBN Prefix(es): 957-551

Lead Wave Publishing Company Ltd+
3F, No 2 Roosevelt Rd, Sec 4, Taipei
Tel: (02) 23650177 *Fax:* (02) 23656407
E-mail: customer@liwil.com.tw
Web Site: www.liwil.com.tw
Subjects: Computer Science, Microcomputers
ISBN Prefix(es): 957-9252
Parent Company: Liwei Publishing Co Ltd

Lee & Lee Communications+
16F-6, No 268, Liancheng Rd, Junghe City, Taipei County, 235 Taipei
Tel: (02) 8228-0518 *Fax:* (02) 8228-0618
E-mail: service@leelee.com; culture@leelee.com
Web Site: www.leelee.com
Key Personnel
Distribution Manager: Shumin Huang
Founded: 1988
Membership(s): Association of Multimedia, International.
Subjects: Antiques, Art
ISBN Prefix(es): 957-99049

Lien Ho Wen Hsueh Press Co Ltd, see UNITAS Publishing Co Ltd

Liming Cultural Enterprise Co Ltd
3F 49, Chungching S Rd Sec 1, Taipei
Tel: (02) 23821152 *Fax:* (02) 23821244
ISBN Prefix(es): 957-16
Subsidiaries: Tai-Chung Kaohsiung/Two Cities
Bookshop(s): 49 Chung-King S Rd, Section 1, Taipei 100
Warehouse: 19 Lane 482 Chung-Shan Rd, Section 2, Chung-Ho, Hsieh

Lin Pai Press Company Ltd+
1F, 15, Lane 71, Lungchiang Rd, Taipei
Tel: (02) 7765889 *Fax:* (02) 7712568
Membership(s): Republic of China Publisher's Association.
Subjects: Fiction, Journalism, Literature, Literary Criticism, Essays, Mysteries, Romance
ISBN Prefix(es): 957-593; 957-812
Parent Company: Lin Pai Publishing Co Ltd
Shipping Address: 271 Chungyang Rd, Nan Gang, Taipei
Warehouse: 6F3 Lane 327, Sec 2, Jongshan Rd, Jongher, Taipei Shiang

Linking Publishing Company Ltd+
555 Chunghsiao East Rd, Sec 4, Taipei 110
Tel: (02) 27634300 (ext 5040) *Fax:* (02) 27634590
E-mail: linkingp@udngroup.com.tw
Web Site: www.udngroup.com.tw/linkingp
Key Personnel
Editorial Dir: Linden T C Lin *E-mail:* linden@udngroup.com.tw
Founded: 1974
Subjects: Art, Asian Studies, Biography, Business, Career Development, Child Care & Development, Cookery, Economics, English as a Second Language, Fiction, Health, Nutrition, History, Human Relations, Literature, Literary Criticism, Essays, Management, Nonfiction (General), Self-Help, Travel, Wine & Spirits, Women's Studies
ISBN Prefix(es): 957-08

Liwil Publishing Co Ltd, see Lead Wave Publishing Company Ltd

Morning Star Publisher Inc+
No 1, 30 Road Industry Zone, Taichung 407
Tel: (04) 23595820 *Fax:* (04) 23597123
E-mail: morning@tcts.seed.net.tw
Web Site: www.morning-star.com.tw
Key Personnel
President: Ming-Min Chen
Founded: 1980
Subjects: Environmental Studies, Fiction, Health, Nutrition, How-to, Human Relations, Management, Regional Interests, Romance, Self-Help
ISBN Prefix(es): 957-583
U.S. Office(s): 21311 Espada Place, Diamond Bar City, CA 91765, United States *Tel:* 909-396-7811 *Fax:* 909-396-9511
Book Club(s): A B A

National Museum of History
49 Nanhai Rd, Taipei 10728
Tel: (02) 3610270-514 *Fax:* (02) 3610171
Subjects: Antiques, Art, Asian Studies, History

National Palace Museum
Publications Division, 221, Chihshan Rd, Sec 2, Taipei
Tel: (02) 8821230 *Fax:* (02) 8821440
E-mail: service@npm.gov.tw
Web Site: www.npm.gov.tw
Key Personnel
Director: Mr Cheng-shang Tu
Head of Publications Division: Ms Sai-lan Hu
Founded: 1983
Subjects: Antiques, Archaeology, Art, History
ISBN Prefix(es): 957-562
Bookshop(s): World Journal Book Store, 379 Broadway, New York, NY 10013, United States; Paragon Books, 1507 S Michigan Ave, Chicago, IL 60605, United States

Newton Publishing Company Ltd+
No 9, Alley 44, Shu Wei Rd, Taipei 106
Tel: (02) 2706-0336 *Fax:* (02) 2707 3759
E-mail: newton00@mslf.hinet.net
Key Personnel
Chairman: Kao Yuan Chin
President: Chun-Tus Liu
Dir, International Rights Dept: Kao Yung Hsin
Subjects: Biography, Management, Marketing, Mathematics, Medicine, Nursing, Dentistry, Nonfiction (General), Physical Sciences, Science (General), Social Sciences, Sociology
ISBN Prefix(es): 957-627
Subsidiaries: Little Newton Co; Newton Culture Viedeo Co
Distributed by Leader Books Co (Hong Kong); Transforma (Malaysia)

Pearson Education
5F, No 147, Chung-Ching S Rd, Sec 1, Taipei 100
Tel: (02) 2370 8168 *Fax:* (02) 2370 8169
E-mail: firstname@pearsoned.com.tw
Web Site: www.pearsoned.com.tw
Key Personnel
General Manager: Angela Yang
Sales Manager/HED: Anderson Ho
Finance/Administration Manager: Chris Chen
Sales Manager/ELT: Jeff Huang
Publishing Manager/TRSL: Stella Chou
Parent Company: Pearson Plc
Branch Office(s)
7F, No 245, Roosevelt Rd, Sec 3, Taipei
Tel: 2368 3904 *Fax:* 2367 3994

Petroleum Information Publishing Co
4F-16 12 Lane 609, Chunghsin Rd Sec 5, Sanchung 241
Tel: (02) 29996909 *Fax:* (02) 29996746
E-mail: pip@tptsl.seed.net.tw
Web Site: www.oil.net.tw
Key Personnel
Chief Executive: Hong Tse-Wen
Subjects: Chemistry, Chemical Engineering, Environmental Studies, Science (General), Technology
ISBN Prefix(es): 957-9694
Subsidiaries: Petroleum Information Magazine

San Min Book Co Ltd+
386 Fushing N Rd, Taipei 104
Tel: (02) 25006600 *Fax:* (02) 25064000
E-mail: editor@sanmin.com.tw
Web Site: www.sanmin.com.tw
Key Personnel
Publicity Manager: Chen-Chiang Liu
International Rights: Wang Yun-Fen
Editor: Allie Hwang
Founded: 1953
Also acts as Bookseller.
Subjects: Accounting, Advertising, Agriculture, Anthropology, Art, Computer Science, Economics, Education, Government, Political Science, Law, Literature, Literary Criticism, Essays, Mathematics, Music, Dance, Philosophy, Religion - Buddhist, Religion - Other, Science (General), Technology
ISBN Prefix(es): 957-14; 957-19
Number of titles published annually: 300 Print
Total Titles: 5,000 Print
Imprints: Grand East Enterprise
Branch Office(s)
No 61, Section 1, Chungking S Rd, Taipei 100

Senate Books Co Ltd+
6F-2, No 98, Jen Ai Rd, Sec 2, Taipei 100
Tel: (02) 23213054 *Fax:* (02) 23214041
E-mail: senatebooks@usa.net
Key Personnel
General Manager: Tiffany Lo *E-mail:* senate@ficnet.net
International Rights: James Peiscy
Founded: 1985
Subjects: Law
ISBN Prefix(es): 957-789
Distributor for Matthew Bender

Shuttle Multimedia Inc
1F, 8-1 Jei Kuang Rd, Taipei 114
Tel: (02) 87924088 *Fax:* (02) 87924089
Web Site: www.eduplus.com
Key Personnel
Contact: Jeff Wang
Founded: 1993
Develop & sell software, CD-title mainly.
Subjects: Education, English as a Second Language
ISBN Prefix(es): 957-99430

Shy Mau & Shy Chaur Publishing Co Ltd+
5F1, No 19, Ming-Sheng Rd, Shin-Diann City, Taipei Hsien
Tel: (02) 2218-3277 *Fax:* (02) 2218-3239
E-mail: carrol@coolbooks.com.tw
Web Site: www.coolbooks.com.tw
Key Personnel
President: Chien Tai-Hsiung
Assistant Dir: Chien Yu Shan
International Rights: Lin Cheng-Tsung
Founded: 1982
Subjects: Biological Sciences, Business, Child Care & Development, Computer Science, Gardening, Plants, Health, Nutrition, History, How-to, Journalism, Law, Management, Psychology, Psychiatry, Real Estate, Science (General), Self-Help, Social Sciences, Sociology, Travel, zoology, entertainment
ISBN Prefix(es): 957-776; 957-529

Sinorama Magazine Co+
5F, No 54, Chunghsiao, East Rd Sec 1, Taipei 100
Tel: (02) 2392-2256 *Fax:* (02) 2397-0655
E-mail: service@mail.sinorama.com.tw
Web Site: www.sinorama.com.tw
Key Personnel
Publisher: Jason Hu
Editor-in-Chief: Wang Jia-fong
Deputy Editor-in-Chief: Anna Y Wang
Founded: 1976
Subjects: English as a Second Language, Environmental Studies, History, Medicine, Nursing, Dentistry, cultural studies
ISBN Prefix(es): 957-9188
U.S. Office(s): Kwan Hwa Publishing (USA), Inc, 300 Wilshire Blvd, Suite 1510 A, Los Angeles, CA 90048, United States *Tel:* 213-782-8770 *Fax:* 213-782-8761

TAIWAN, PROVINCE OF CHINA

SMC Publishing Inc+
No 14, Alley 14, Lane 283, Roosevelt Rd, Sec 3, Taipei
Tel: (02) 2362-0190 *Fax:* (02) 3623834
Web Site: www.smcbook.com.tw
Key Personnel
Manager: Wei Te-wen
Founded: 1976
Publish in English & Chinese.
Subjects: Anthropology, Art, Asian Studies, Biological Sciences, History, Medicine, Nursing, Dentistry, Religion - Buddhist
ISBN Prefix(es): 957-638; 957-9482

The Third Wave Enterprise Co Ltd
Bl 18, Hsinyi Rd, Sec 5, Hsichih, Taipei 110
Tel: (02) 87803636 *Fax:* (02) 87805656
E-mail: AIWebmaster@acer.com.tw
Web Site: www.acertwp.com.tw
Key Personnel
International Information Dept Manager: David Tsai
Founded: 1981
ISBN Prefix(es): 957-23
Parent Company: Acer Inc
Associate Companies: Acer Advanced Inc; Acer Peripheral; Sertek
Distributor for Data Communication; LAN Times

Torch of Wisdom+
10, Lane 270, Chienkuo S Rd, Sec 1, 106 Taipei
Tel: (02) 7075802 *Fax:* (02) 7085054
E-mail: tow@ms2.hinet.net
Key Personnel
Contact: Pro Cheng Chen-Huang
Founded: 1951
Subjects: Asian Studies, Health, Nutrition, Religion - Buddhist
ISBN Prefix(es): 957-518

UNITAS Publishing Co Ltd+
10F 180 Chilung Rd Section 1, Taipei 100
Tel: (02) 27634300 *Fax:* (02) 27491208
E-mail: unitas@udngroup.com.tw
Web Site: www.udngroup.com.tw
Key Personnel
Chief Editor: Mr Ann-Ming Tsu
International Rights: Paula C Wang
Founded: 1984
Subjects: Fiction, Journalism, Literature, Literary Criticism, Essays, Nonfiction (General), Poetry, Romance, Women's Studies
ISBN Prefix(es): 957-522

Wang Su-Chao, *imprint of* Designer Publisher Inc

Wei-Chuan Publishing Company Ltd+
2F, 28 Jenai Rd, Sec 4, 106 Taipei
Tel: (02) 27021148 *Fax:* (02) 27042729
Key Personnel
Chief Executive: Huang Su-Huei
Founded: 1971
Subjects: Child Care & Development, Cookery, Crafts, Games, Hobbies, How-to
ISBN Prefix(es): 957-9285
Subsidiaries: Wei-Chuan's Publishing

World Book Co Ltd+
99 Chung Ching S Rd, Sec 1, Taipei
Tel: (02) 2311-0183 *Fax:* (02) 2331-7963
Key Personnel
President: Angela Chu Yen
Founded: 1921
Subjects: Art, Drama, Theater, History, Language Arts, Linguistics, Literature, Literary Criticism, Essays, Medicine, Nursing, Dentistry, Philosophy, Poetry, Social Sciences, Sociology, Chinese Classics
ISBN Prefix(es): 957-06

Wu Nan Book Co Ltd+
4F, No 339, Sec 2, Ho-Ping E Rd, 106 Taipei
Tel: (02) 2705-5066 *Fax:* (02) 2706-6100
E-mail: wunan@wunan.com.tw
Web Site: www.wunan.com.tw
Key Personnel
Manager of Planning Dept: Thomas Chen
Subjects: Anthropology, Biography, Biological Sciences, Business, Computer Science, Crafts, Games, Hobbies, Engineering (General), Environmental Studies, Finance, History, Language Arts, Linguistics, Law, Literature, Literary Criticism, Essays, Military Science, Religion - Other, Science (General), Technology, Geology, Games, Esoteric, Entertainment, Dance, Administration
ISBN Prefix(es): 957-11

Yee Wen Publishing Co Ltd+
4F-3, No 253, Sec 3, Roosevelt Rd, Taipei
Tel: (02) 2362-6012 *Fax:* (02) 2366-0977
E-mail: yeewen_us@yahoo.com
Key Personnel
Chief Executive: Feng-Chiao Yen
Sales Manager: Ming-Fang Tsai
Editorial Manager: Jammy Yen *Tel:* 650-367-5020 *Fax:* 650-364-0960
Founded: 1953
Subjects: Archaeology, Art, Asian Studies, Ethnicity, Geography, Geology, History, Literature, Literary Criticism, Essays, Philosophy, Regional Interests, Religion - Other, Science (General)
ISBN Prefix(es): 0-88691; 957-520
Number of titles published annually: 12 Print
Total Titles: 3,000 Print
U.S. Office(s): 518 Oak Park Way, Redwood City, CA 94062-4038, United States, Contact: Jammy Yen *Tel:* 650-367-5020 *Fax:* 650-364-0960 *E-mail:* yeewen_us@yahoo.com

Yi Hsien Publishing Co Ltd+
5F, No 1, Lane 7, Baugau Rd, Hsintien, Taipei
Tel: (02) 2918-2288 *Fax:* (02) 2917-2266
E-mail: yihsient@ms17.hinet.net
Web Site: www.yihsient.com.tw
Key Personnel
President & International Rights: Ed Tung
Founded: 1975
Subjects: Agriculture, Animals, Pets, Biological Sciences, Chemistry, Chemical Engineering, Earth Sciences, Health, Nutrition, Medicine, Nursing, Dentistry, Psychology, Psychiatry, Publishing & Book Trade Reference, Science (General), Veterinary Science
ISBN Prefix(es): 957-616
Bookshop(s): No 3, Lane 316, Roosevelt Rd, Sec 3, Taipei; No 178, Wu-ch'ang St, Taichung

Youth Cultural Publishing Co+
3F, 66-1 Chungking S Rd, Sec 1, Taipei
Tel: (02) 2311-2832 *Fax:* (02) 2311-3309
E-mail: youth@ms2.hinet.net
Web Site: www.youth.com.tw
Key Personnel
Chief Executive: Tchong-Koei Li
Contact: Ho Wei
Founded: 1958
Subjects: Cookery, Crafts, Games, Hobbies, Education, Fashion, Language Arts, Linguistics, Literature, Literary Criticism, Essays, Psychology, Psychiatry, Science (General), Travel, Entertainment, Food/Drink
ISBN Prefix(es): 957-530; 957-574
Parent Company: China Youth Corps
Showroom(s): No 219, Sung Chiang Rd, Taipei
Bookshop(s): No 6, Heng Yang Rd, Taipei; No 2-1, Feng Chia Rd, Taichung; No 157, Fu Hsing 2 Rd, Kaohsiung
Warehouse: No 21, Lane 111, Chung Ying St, Su Lin Town, Taipei

Yuan Liou Publishing Co, Ltd+
7F-5, No 184, Tingchow Rd, Sec 3, Taipei 100
Tel: (02) 2365-1212 *Fax:* (02) 2365 8989
E-mail: ylib@yuanliou.ylib.com.tw
Web Site: www.ylib.com.tw
Key Personnel
Publisher: Wang Jung-Wen
Founded: 1975
Subjects: Art, Business, Fiction, Health, Nutrition, History, How-to, Psychology, Psychiatry, Self-Help
ISBN Prefix(es): 957-32
Associate Companies: Meta Media International Co

Zen Now Press
3F, 6-2, Huaite St, Taipei 112
Tel: (02) 7182727 *Fax:* (02) 7174146
Key Personnel
President: Mr Su Chun-Jung
Subjects: Religion - Buddhist
ISBN Prefix(es): 957-9622
Distributed by Hsu Sheng Book Ltd

Tajikistan

General Information

Capital: Dushanbe
Language: Tajik
Population: 5.7 million
Bank Hours: Generally open for short hours between 0930-1230 Monday-Friday
Shop Hours: Generally 0900-1800 Monday-Friday; often open weekends
Currency: 100 kopeks = 1 rubl
Export/Import Information: According to Ukrainian quotas and customs duties, companies engaged in trade should register with the Ukraine Ministry of Foreign Economic Relations. Licenses for export and import are also required for trade with Russia.
Copyright: UCC (see Copyright Conventions, pg xi)

Irfon (Knowledge)
ul N Karabayeva 17, Dushanbe 734018
Tel: (03772) 33-39-06; (03772) 33-62-54
Key Personnel
Dir: J Sharifov
Editor-in-Chief: A Olimov
Founded: 1925
Subjects: Agriculture, Economics, Fiction, Government, Political Science, Medicine, Nursing, Dentistry, Philosophy, Social Sciences, Sociology, Technology
ISBN Prefix(es): 5-667

United Republic of Tanzania

General Information

Capital: Dar es Salem
Language: Swahili and English are both official languages
Religion: Islamic, Christian (mostly Roman Catholic), Hindu, the rest follow traditional beliefs
Population: 27.8 million

PUBLISHERS

Bank Hours: Mainland Tanzania: 0900-1200 Monday-Friday; 0900-1100 Saturday. Zanzibar: 0830-1130 Monday-Friday; 0830-1000 Saturday

Shop Hours: 0800-1200, 1400-1715 or 1800 Monday-Saturday

Currency: 100 cents = 1 Tanzanian shilling

Export/Import Information: No tariff on books or advertising matter. Import license and exchange controls.

Copyright: Berne, Florence (see Copyright Conventions, pg xi)

Africa Inland Church Literature Department, see Inland Publishers

Akajase Enterprises+
PO Box 7187, Dar Es Salaam
Tel: (051) 26121
Key Personnel
Dir: R A Akwilombe
Founded: 1988
Also bookseller.
Subjects: Fiction
ISBN Prefix(es): 9987-551

Ben and Company Ltd+
Samora Machel Ave, PO Box 3164, Plot 3, Dar Es Salaam
Tel: (812) 781421 *Fax:* (511) 12440
E-mail: siggers@pearsoned.ema.com
Telex: 41816
Key Personnel
Man Dir & Publicity: Ian Ben Moshi
Man Editor: James Odongo Ocholla
Senior Editor: Salim Kigenda
Sales & Marketing: Sadallah Sungura Alli
Founded: 1981
Specialize in Kiswahili, arts & crafts (life skills).
Membership(s): Publishers Association of Tanzania (PATA).
Subjects: English as a Second Language, Mathematics, Science (General)
ISBN Prefix(es): 9976-920
Total Titles: 72 Print

Benedictine Publications Ndanda, *imprint of* Ndanda Mission Press

Bilal Muslim Mission of Tanzania+
PO Box 20033, Dar Es Salaam
Tel: 21201111; 2112419; 2112420 *Fax:* 2116550
E-mail: bilal@raha.com
Telex: 41518 Geomic *Cable:* TABLIGH
Key Personnel
Chairman: Pyarali M Shivji *Tel:* (051) 114113
Editor: F H Abdullah
Chief Missionary: Sayid Saeed Akhtar Rizvi
 Tel: (051) 130345
Founded: 1968
An autonomous subsidiary of Shia Ithnaashery Supreme Council of Africa.
Subjects: Literature, Literary Criticism, Essays
ISBN Prefix(es): 9976-956

Bureau of Statistics+
PO Box 796, Dar Es Salaam
Tel: (051) 111634; (051) 111635 *Fax:* (051) 112352
E-mail: kento@raha.com
Telex: 41576 TASTAT TZ *Cable:* STATISTICS
Key Personnel
Publishing Officer: Eliab J C Chiduo
Founded: 1961
Subjects: Agriculture, Economics, Education

Central Tanganyika Press+
PO Box 15, Dodoma
Tel: (061) 22140 *Fax:* (061) 324565
Telex: 53328 TZ

Key Personnel
General Manager: James Lifa Chipaka
Marketing Sales Manager: David Tuppa
Founded: 1954
Subjects: Biblical Studies, Biography, Child Care & Development, Religion - Protestant
ISBN Prefix(es): 9976-66

DUP (1996) Ltd+
PO Box 35182, Dar Es Salaam
Tel: (051) 410300 *Fax:* (051) 410137
E-mail: director@dup.udsm.ac.tz
Telex: 41327 Uniscie *Cable:* UNIVERSITY DAR ES SALAAM
Key Personnel
Dir: N G Mwitta
Marketing Manager: L D T Minzi
Founded: 1979
Membership(s): Tanzania Publishers Association; also book packager.
Subjects: Accounting, Biological Sciences, Chemistry, Chemical Engineering, Civil Engineering, Developing Countries, Drama, Theater, Electronics, Electrical Engineering, History, Language Arts, Linguistics, Mathematics, Mechanical Engineering, Medicine, Nursing, Dentistry, Physical Sciences, Physics, Women's Studies
ISBN Prefix(es): 9976-60

East African Publishing House
PO Box 3209, Dar Es Salaam
Tel: (02) 557417; (02) 557788 *Cable:* Afrobooks Nairobi
Key Personnel
Man Dir: E N Wainaina
Chief Editor, Rights & Permissions: Gacheche Waruingi
Marketing, Publicity, Sales, Distribution: James K Muraya
Production: John Mwazo
Founded: 1965
Subjects: Biography, Education, Fiction, How-to, Nonfiction (General), Poetry, Regional Interests, Religion - Other, Science (General), Social Sciences, Sociology
ISBN Prefix(es): 9976-5
Parent Company: E A Cultural Trust
Associate Companies: Afropress Ltd, PO Box 30502, Nairobi

Eastern Africa Publications Ltd
PO Box 1002, Arusha
Tel: (057) 3176; (057) 26708
Telex: 42121 Concentre *Cable:* EAPL ARUSHA
Key Personnel
General Manager: Abdullah Saiwaad
Sales, Marketing: J J Kimpinga
Production: S M S Payowela
Founded: 1979
Subjects: Biography, Geography, Geology, Government, Political Science, History, Nonfiction (General), Poetry, Science (General)
ISBN Prefix(es): 9976-2
Parent Company: Tanzania Karatasi Associated Industries, PO Box 2418, Dar es Salaam
Branch Office(s)
PO Box 1408, Dar Es Salaam

Emmaus Bible School
PO Box 9322, Dodoma
Tel: (061) 354500 *Fax:* (061) 350911
E-mail: CMML-Dodoma@maf.org
Key Personnel
Dir: Hansjoerg Schaerer
Contact: Anna Guttke
Membership(s): TELM; Specialize in Correspondence Courses.
Subjects: Biblical Studies
ISBN Prefix(es): 9976-80
Associate Companies: Kanisa la Biblia (KLB) Publishers
Imprints: Emmaus Shule ya Biblia

UNITED REPUBLIC OF TANZANIA

Branch Office(s)
Emmaus Bible School, PO Box 9322, Dar es salaam *Tel:* (022) 2115920 *Fax:* (022) 2128767
Distributor for Everyday Publications Inc (Canada)

Emmaus Shule ya Biblia, *imprint of* Emmaus Bible School

General Publications Ltd+
PO Box 6804, Dar Es Salaam
Tel: (0741) 6195 85; (0741) 6231 82
Key Personnel
Man Dir: A A Macha
Founded: 1985
Specialize in primary level educational books for Tanzania schools & stationery sales.
Subjects: Education
ISBN Prefix(es): 9976-925
Number of titles published annually: 1 Print
Total Titles: 20 Print

Government Printer
PO Box 9124, Dar Es Salaam

Inland Publishers
PO Box 125, Mwanza
Tel: (068) 40064
Key Personnel
Dir: Rev S M Magesa
A publishing division of Africa Inland Church Literature Department.
Subjects: Nonfiction (General), Religion - Other
ISBN Prefix(es): 9976-906; 9976-70

Institute of Kiswahili Research
PO Box 35075, Dar Es Salaam
Tel: (051) 410376
E-mail: IKR@udsm.ac.tz
Web Site: www.uib.no/udsm/ucb/instiofkiswahili.html
Key Personnel
Dir: Prof David P B Massamba
Founded: 1930
Subjects: Language Arts, Linguistics, Literature, Literary Criticism, Essays
ISBN Prefix(es): 9976-911

Kajura Publications
PO Box 8692, Dar Es Salaam
Tel: (051) 866181
Subjects: Astrology, Occult, Government, Political Science, Science Fiction, Fantasy
ISBN Prefix(es): 9987-8855

Kanisa la Biblia Publishers (KLB)
One Pagala, Dodoma
Mailing Address: PO Box 1424, Dodoma
Tel: (026) 2354500 *Fax:* (026) 2350911
Key Personnel
Editor: Helmut Graef
Manager: Miss Inge Danzeisen
 E-mail: inge_danzeisen@yahoo.com
Founded: 1979
Specialize in Bible teaching books for lay people in Swahili.
Membership(s): TELM (Tanzania Evangelical Literature Ministry) & BSAT (Booksellers Association of Tanzania).
Subjects: Biblical Studies, Religion - Protestant, Theology
ISBN Prefix(es): 9976-74
Number of titles published annually: 2 Print
Total Titles: 33 Print; 2 Audio
Associate Companies: Emmaus Bible School, Box 1424, Dodoma
Distributor for Emmaus Bible School

Kisambo Publishers Ltd
PO Box 6542, Dar Es Salaam
Tel: (051) 114876; (051) 131382 *Fax:* (051) 112351

UNITED REPUBLIC OF TANZANIA

Founded: 1985
Subjects: Social Sciences, Sociology, Theology
ISBN Prefix(es): 9976-978
Imprints: Kiwavi; Tuitional Structures
Distributed by Diamond Publishers (Tepusa)
Distributor for Ben Co; CBP; Readit Books

Kiswahili, *imprint of* Press & Publicity Centre Ltd

Kiwavi, *imprint of* Kisambo Publishers Ltd

Ndanda Mission Press
PO Box 1004, Ndana, Mtwara
Fax: (682) 623 730; (059) 510 410
Key Personnel
Manager: Fr S Hoibeck
Founded: 1934
Subjects: Fiction, History, Medicine, Nursing, Dentistry, Religion - Catholic, Religion - Other, Social Sciences, Sociology, Theology
ISBN Prefix(es): 9976-63
Imprints: Benedictine Publications Ndanda; Peramiho, Tanzania
Distributed by Peramiko Publications; Tabora Mission Press

Northwestern Publishers+
PO Box 277, Bukoba
Founded: 1990
Subjects: Language Arts, Linguistics, Religion - Protestant, Theology
ISBN Prefix(es): 9987-569
Parent Company: Evangelical Lutheran Church in Tanzania, Northwestern Diocese
Distributor for Ben & Co (Oxford); Central Tanganyika Press; Dar University; Tanzania Publishing House
Bookshop(s): ELCT Church Bookshop

Nyota Publishers Ltd+
PO Box 3574, Dar Es Salaam
Tel: (051) 25547; (051) 25549
Key Personnel
Dir & Author: P A Mcharo
Dir: E B Wilson; J E Kishada; Mrs P E McHaro
Subjects: Accounting, Business, Education, English as a Second Language, Fiction, Medicine, Nursing, Dentistry
ISBN Prefix(es): 9987-556
Associate Companies: Nyota Consultancy Co Ltd

Oxford University Press
PO Box 5299, Dar Es Salaam
Tel: (051) 222 116389; (051) 222 113704
Fax: (051) 222 116614
E-mail: oxford@raha.com
Web Site: www.oup.com
Key Personnel
Manager: Salim Shaaban Salim
Founded: 1969
Subjects: Literature, Literary Criticism, Essays, Poetry
ISBN Prefix(es): 9976-4
Parent Company: Oxford University Press, United Kingdom

Peramiho Publications
PO Box 41, Peramiho
Tel: (054) 2730 *Fax:* (054) 2917
Key Personnel
Chief Executive: Fr Gerold Rupper
Contact: Bro Dominicus Weis; Bro Polycarr Stich
Founded: 1937
Local topics, printed mostly in Swahili.
Subjects: Agriculture, Religion - Other
ISBN Prefix(es): 9976-67
Associate Companies: Peramiho Printing Press
Subsidiaries: Benedictine Publication Ndanda/Peramiho
Divisions: Ndanda Mission Press

U.S. Office(s): Benedictine Priory, PO Box 528, Schuyler, NE 68661, United States *Tel:* 402-352-2127
Distributed by Ndanda Mission Press; TMP Tabora
Bookshop(s): Ndanda and Peramiho

Peramiho, Tanzania, *imprint of* Ndanda Mission Press

Press & Publicity Centre Ltd+
PO Box 20910, Dar Es Salaam
Tel: (051) 127765; (051) 122881; (051) 131078
Fax: (051) 113619; (051) 116749
Key Personnel
International Rights: Akberali Manji
Founded: 1981
Membership(s): Publishers Association of Tanzania (PATA).
Subjects: Agriculture, Astrology, Occult, Computer Science, Education, Environmental Studies, Fiction, Geography, Geology, Health, Nutrition, Language Arts, Linguistics, Literature, Literary Criticism, Essays, Science (General)
ISBN Prefix(es): 9976-916
Total Titles: 30 Print
Imprints: Kiswahili
Distributed by Tepusa
Distributor for Africa Book Collective Ltd (UK)
Bookshop(s): Aggrey Street Shop, Nkrumah St, Dar Es Salaam

Readit Books+
PO Box 21100, Dar es Salaam
Tel: (022) 2184077 *Fax:* (022) 2181077
E-mail: readit@raha.com
Key Personnel
Man Dir: Abdullah Saiwaad
Marketing Dir: Khalfan Abdallah
Founded: 1993
Subjects: Astronomy, Economics, Fiction, Science (General)
ISBN Prefix(es): 9987-21

South African Extension Unit
PO Box 70074, Dar Es Salaam
Tel: (051) 150314; (051) 150346 *Fax:* (051) 150346
E-mail: saeu@intafrica.com
Web Site: www.saide.org.za/worldbank/courtries/tanzania/saeu.htm
Key Personnel
Dir: Elizabeth Ligate
Founded: 1984
ISBN Prefix(es): 9976-73
Subsidiaries: South African Extension Uni

Tanzania Library Services Board
Unit of Ministry of Education & Culture
PO Box 9283, Dar es Salaam
Tel: (022) 215 09 23; (022) 215 00 48
E-mail: tlsb@africaonline.co.tz *Cable:* TANLIS
Key Personnel
Dir General: E A Mwinyimvua
Founded: 1963
Subjects: Library & Information Sciences
ISBN Prefix(es): 9976-65
Branch Office(s)
PO Box 1273, Arusha, Contact: Sophia M Labokhe *Tel:* (057) 502642
PO Box 321, Bukuoba, Contact: Mr Vedastus Muijage *Tel:* (066) 20460
PO Box 1900, Do Doma, Contact: John Mwelemi *Tel:* (061) 22063
PO Box 172, Iringa, Contact: Mr Metola Msusa Kanduru *Tel:* (061) 702421
PO Box 933, Kigoma, Contact: Rhoda Z Zamuye *Tel:* (0695) 3168
PO Box 443, Lindi, Contact: Geofrey Mushi *Tel:* (0525) 2156

PO Box 872, Mara/Musoma, Contact: Mr Hippolite Amin Latonge *Tel:* (068) 622183
PO Box 842, Mbeya, Contact: Emmanuel Luvands *Tel:* (065) 502589
PO Box 858, Mo Rogord, Contact: Leonard Ngowo *Tel:* (056) 602160
PO Box 863, Moshi, Contact: Mr Mariam Mundeme *Tel:* (055) 52432
PO Box 37, Mtwara, Contact: Emmanuel Herbert *Tel:* (059) 333352
PO Box 1363, Mwanza, Contact: Charles Katale *Tel:* (068) 41895
PO Box 804, Shinyanga, Contact: William Melale *Tel:* (08) 762151
PO Box 179, Songea, Contact: Mr Hezekia Chawe *Tel:* (065) 602041
PO Box 332, Sumbawanga, Contact: Peter Nkaki *Tel:* (065) 802259
PO Box 432, Tabora, Contact: Mr Carmilius C Nyigu *Tel:* (062) 3099
PO Box 5000, Tanga, Contact: Joseph Maginge *Tel:* (053) 43127

Tanzania Publishing House+
47 Samora Machel Ave, Dar Es Salaam
Mailing Address: PO Box 2138, Dar Es Salaam
Tel: (051) 32164 *Cable:* PUBLISH DAR ES SALAAM
Key Personnel
General Manager & International Rights: Primus Isidor Karugendo
Founded: 1966
Membership(s): Publishers Association of Tanzania-African Books Collective.
Subjects: Accounting, Agriculture, Animals, Pets, Art, Child Care & Development, Drama, Theater, English as a Second Language, Fiction, Gardening, Plants, Geography, Geology, Government, Political Science, Health, Nutrition, History, Journalism, Labor, Industrial Relations, Language Arts, Linguistics, Law, Management, Mathematics, Nonfiction (General), Photography, Physics, Poetry, Public Administration, Science (General), Sports, Athletics
ISBN Prefix(es): 9976-1
Parent Company: Tanzania Karatasi Associated Industries, Box 2418 DSM

Tema Publishers Ltd+
PO Box 63115, Dar es Salaam
Tel: (051) 113608 *Fax:* (051) 75422
Key Personnel
Chief Executive: T Maliyamkono
Founded: 1994
Membership(s): Publishers' Association of Tanzania (PATA).
Subjects: Education, Environmental Studies, Fiction, Nonfiction (General), Women's Studies
ISBN Prefix(es): 9987-25
Distributed by Tanzania Publishing House

Tuitional Structures, *imprint of* Kisambo Publishers Ltd

Thailand

General Information

Capital: Bangkok
Language: Thai is official language. English is widely used in government and commercial circles
Religion: Predominantly Buddhist of the Hinaya form
Population: 57.6 million
Bank Hours: 0830-1500 Monday-Friday
Shop Hours: Vary. Those catering to tourists generally open 0830-1800 or later
Currency: 100 satangs = 1 baht

PUBLISHERS

THAILAND

Export/Import Information: No tariff on books but Standard Profit Tax and Business Tax apply (also a Municipal Tax of percentage of Business Tax). Advertising subject to same taxes and ad valorem percentage of import duty. No import licenses for books, but special permit required by importer for orders over a certain sum. Certificate of payment (from Exchange Control Authority) required.
Copyright: Berne, Florence (see Copyright Conventions, pg xi)

Akson Charerntat (S/B Akson)
142 Phraeng Sapphasat Tanao Rd, Bangkok 10200
Tel: (02) 2214587 *Fax:* (02) 2255356
Key Personnel
Executive Dir: Surapon Dheva-Aksorn
ISBN Prefix(es): 974-405; 974-406

Bandansan
136-138 Nakhon Sawan Rd, Bangkok 10100
Tel: (02) 825511
ISBN Prefix(es): 974-225

Bannakhan
236 Woeng Nakhon Khasem, Bangkok 10100
Tel: (02) 227796
ISBN Prefix(es): 974-350

Bannakit Trading
34-42 Thanon Nakhonsawan Rd, Bangkok 10100
Tel: (02) 2825520; (02) 2827537; (02) 2814213
Fax: (02) 2820076
Subjects: Agriculture, Biography, Fiction
ISBN Prefix(es): 974-220

Chiang Mai University Library
239 Huay Kaew Rd, Muang District, Chiang Mai 50200
Tel: (053) 944501 *Fax:* (053) 222766
E-mail: prasit@lib.cmunet.edu
Web Site: www.lib.cmu.ac.th
Key Personnel
Dir: Mr Prasit Malumpong
ISBN Prefix(es): 974-565; 974-656; 974-657; 974-658

Chokechai Theues Shop+
Formerly Chokechai Thewet Co Ltd
59 Teethong Wang, Phra Nakhon, Bangkok 10200
Tel: (02) 2225-7877
Key Personnel
Man Dir: Wichai Rojjanaprapayon
Marketing Executive: Dr Wiwat Rojjanaprapayon
Founded: 1963
Subjects: Fiction, Romance, Science Fiction, Fantasy
ISBN Prefix(es): 974-420

Chokechai Thewet Co Ltd, see Chokechai Theues Shop

Office of Christian Education and Literature, *imprint of* Suriyaban Publishers

DK Book House Co Ltd
904 Gp 6 Srinakarin Nong Bon Prawet, Bangkok 10260
Tel: (02) 721-9190 *Fax:* (02) 247-1033
Telex: 81198 Frtmast Th
ISBN Prefix(es): 974-210
Parent Company: Duang Kamon Co, Ltd
Associate Companies: D K Today Co, Ltd
Subsidiaries: D K Mah Boon Krong Co Ltd
Divisions: Technical Books
Bookshop(s): Mah Boon Krong Centre, 3rd floor, Prathumwan, Bangkok

Duang Kamon Co Ltd
Khlong Toei Khlong, Toei, Bangkok 10110
Tel: (02) 252-6261; (02) 253-1766
ISBN Prefix(es): 974-210

Graphic Art (28) Co Ltd
105/19-21 Nares Si Phaya Bang Rak, Bangkok 10500
Tel: (02) 2330302
Telex: 20657 Graphic Th
Key Personnel
Chief Executive: Mrs Angkana Sajjaraktrakul
Export Manager: H J Weber
Founded: 1972
Subjects: Biological Sciences, Chemistry, Chemical Engineering, Electronics, Electrical Engineering, Language Arts, Linguistics, Philosophy, Photography, Physics, Regional Interests, Science Fiction, Fantasy
ISBN Prefix(es): 974-295
Subsidiaries: Pandora Publishing
Book Club(s): Science Fiction Magazine Club

Klang Withaya Publisher
724-6 Mahachai Rd, Bangkok 10200
Tel: (02) 2224546; (02) 2219331
Key Personnel
Manager: Prachark Chaovanabutvilai
ISBN Prefix(es): 974-205

New Generation Publishing Co Ltd+
486/70-73 Phetkasem 14 Thanon Petchburi Ratcha, Thewi Bangkok 10400
Tel: (02) 216 7393 5; (02) 2150677 *Fax:* (02) 611 0400
Key Personnel
Chief Executive: Kiatchai Prasertsrisak
Founded: 1990
Subjects: Animals, Pets, Art, English as a Second Language, Fiction, History, Natural History, Science (General)
ISBN Prefix(es): 974-7642
Parent Company: The Manager Media Group Public Co Ltd

Niyom Vidhya, see Niyom Witthaya

Niyom Witthaya
Formerly Niyom Vidhya
192 Thanon Bamrungmuang Rd, Bangkok 10200
Tel: (02) 217661
ISBN Prefix(es): 974-7278

Non
901 Soi Songpinong, Samrong Nua, Samutprakarn, Bangkok
Tel: (02) 90130
ISBN Prefix(es): 974-395

Odeon Store LP
860-2 Wangburapa, Phra Nakhon, Bangkok 10200
Tel: (02) 2210742 *Fax:* (02) 2253300 *Cable:* Odeonstore
Key Personnel
Man Dir: Vichai Praepanich
Founded: 1947
Subjects: Nonfiction (General)
ISBN Prefix(es): 974-275
Branch Office(s)
218/10-2 Siam Sq, Soi 1 Pathum Wan, Bangkok 10330 *Tel:* (02) 2514476

Pearson Education Indochina, Ltd
Rama 9, Suanluang, Bangkok 10250
Tel: (02) 731-7156-57; (02) 731-7150-51 (Hotline) *Fax:* (02) 731-7158
E-mail: cserv@pearson-indochina.com
Web Site: www.pearson-indochina.com
Key Personnel
President: Wong Wee Woon
Regional Manager: Narerat Ancharepirat *Tel:* (02) 722 7996
ELT Manager: Thansinee Thammapojsathid
ELT Marketing Executive: Udom Sathawara; Wanida Yingsiri
Publishing Manager: Sopis Rungruangvoratus
Founded: 1998
Formed through the merger of Simon & Schuster & Addison Wesley Longman.
Parent Company: Pearson Plc

Pikkhanet Kanphim
97-9 Soi Phrangsapasat, Tanao Rd, Bangkok 10200
Tel: (02) 222850
ISBN Prefix(es): 974-476

Pracha Chang & Co Ltd
87 Phaholyothin Rd, Bangkok 10100
Subjects: Education
ISBN Prefix(es): 974-7655

Prasan Mit
3382 New Phet Buri Rd, Bangkok 10310
Tel: (02) 3915287; (02) 3925230
ISBN Prefix(es): 974-467

Ruamsarn (1977) Co Ltd+
864 Burabha Palace, Mahachai Rd, Bangkok 10200
Tel: (02) 221-6483 *Fax:* (02) 222-2038
Key Personnel
Manager: Piya Taweevatanasarn
Founded: 1951
Subjects: Fiction, History
ISBN Prefix(es): 974-245

Sangdad Publishing Company Ltd+
320 Srivara Rd, Wangthonglang, Bangkok 10310
Tel: (02) 5385553; (02) 5387576 *Fax:* (02) 559-2643; (02) 5381499
E-mail: sangdad@asianet.co.th
Key Personnel
Chief Executive: Nidda Hongwiwat *Tel:* (02) 538 5553
President: Mr Thavitong Hongvivatana
Founded: 1984
Largest cookery book publisher in Thailand.
Subjects: Art, Child Care & Development, Cookery, History, Travel
Total Titles: 250 Print

Silkworm Books+
104/105 Chiang Mai, M 7, T Suthep, Muang, Chiang Mai 50100
Mailing Address: POB 217, Ratchadammoen Rd, Bangkok 10200
Tel: (053) 4765326 *Fax:* (053) 4765326
E-mail: silkedit@loxinfo.co.th
Web Site: www.silkwormbooks.com
Key Personnel
Publisher & Dir: Trasvin Jittidecharaks
Founded: 1991
Registered as Trasvin Publications Ltd, 54/1-5 Sridonchai Rd, Chiang Mai, Thailand.
Subjects: Asian Studies
ISBN Prefix(es): 974-7047
Distributed by University of Washington Press (North America)

Soemwit Barwakhan
222 Woeng Nakhonkasemm, Bangkok 10100
Tel: (02) 214541
ISBN Prefix(es): 974-270

Suksapan Panit (Business Organization of Teachers Council of Thailand)
Mansion 9, Rajdamnern Ave, Bangkok
Tel: (02) 811845
Web Site: www.suksapan.or.th
Telex: 72031 Suksapa Th

THAILAND

Key Personnel
Dir: Kamthon Sathirakul
Founded: 1950
ISBN Prefix(es): 974-8101

Suksit Siam Co Ltd
113, 115 Fung Nakorn Rd, Opp, Wat Rajbopith, Bangkok 10200
Tel: (02) 225-9531-2 *Fax:* (02) 222-5188
E-mail: sop@ffc.inet.co.th
Key Personnel
Manager, Publicity: Mrs Nilchawee Sivaraksa
Subjects: Government, Political Science, Social Sciences, Sociology
ISBN Prefix(es): 974-260

Suriyaban Publishers
14 Pramuan Rd, Bangkok 10500
Tel: (02) 2347991; (02) 2347992 *Cable:* CCT Office
Key Personnel
Man Dir: Pisnu Arkkapin
Founded: 1953
Subjects: Ethnicity, Literature, Literary Criticism, Essays, Religion - Other
ISBN Prefix(es): 974-500
Parent Company: Department of Christian Education and Literature, Church of Christ in Thailand
Imprints: Office of Christian Education and Literature
Bookshop(s): The Christian Bookstore

Sut Phaisan
683/8 Phra Chao Taksin Rd, Samre, Bangkok 10600
Tel: (02) 4682066; (02) 4675066
Subjects: Law
ISBN Prefix(es): 974-503

Thai Watana Panich Co, Ltd+
891 Rama One Prathymwan Pathum Wan, Bangkok 10330
Tel: (02) 215-0060-3 *Fax:* (02) 215-1360
E-mail: twpp@loxinfo.co.th
Web Site: www.twppress.com
Key Personnel
Man Dir: Thira T Suwan
Founded: 1935
Also acts as Distributor.
Subjects: Agriculture, Art, Biography, Education, Government, Political Science, Health, Nutrition, History, Language Arts, Linguistics, Management, Marketing, Mathematics, Music, Dance, Philosophy, Psychology, Psychiatry, Religion - Buddhist, Science (General), Social Sciences, Sociology
ISBN Prefix(es): 974-07
Distributor for Falcon; Kernerman; McGraw-Hills; Oxford; Pearson Education; Wendy Pye; Thomson Learning

Unesco Regional Office, Asia & the Pacific
PO Box 967, Prakhanong Post Office, Bangkok 10110
Tel: (02) 3910577 *Fax:* (02) 3910866
E-mail: bangkok@unesco.org
Web Site: www.unescobkk.org
Telex: 20591 *Cable:* UNESCO BANGKOK
Founded: 1961
Subjects: Communications, Education, Human Relations, Social Sciences, Sociology
ISBN Prefix(es): 974-680

Viratham
141 St Louis South Sathon Rd, Bangkok 10120
Tel: (02) 866848
ISBN Prefix(es): 974-380

Watthana Phanit
216-220 Bamrung Muang, Bangkok 10200
Tel: (02) 2217225
ISBN Prefix(es): 974-250; 974-02

White Lotus Co Ltd+
GPO Box 1141, Bangkok 10501
Tel: (02) 332-4915; (02) 741-6288; (02) 741-6289
Fax: (02) 311-4575; (02) 741-6287; (02) 741-6607
Web Site: thailine.com/lotus
Key Personnel
Chief Executive: D Ande *E-mail:* ande@loxinfo.ch.th
Founded: 1972
Out-of-print, new.
Specialize in books on Asia (Southeast).
Subjects: Art, Ethnicity, Natural History, Philosophy, Regional Interests, Religion - Other, Ceramics, ecology, flora & fauna, linguistics, performing arts, textiles
ISBN Prefix(es): 974-8495; 974-8496; 974-4800; 974-8434; 974-7534
Number of titles published annually: 30 Print

Togo

General Information

Capital: Lome
Language: French, Kabiye and Ewe are official languages
Religion: About half follow traditional beliefs, Christian (about 35%) and Muslim (about 15%).
Population: 4 million
Bank Hours: 0730-1130, 1430-1600 Monday-Friday
Shop Hours: 0800-1200, 1430 or 1500-1730 or 1800 Monday-Friday; 0730-1230 Saturday
Currency: 100 centimes = 1 CFA franc
Export/Import Information: No tariff on books; advertising catalogs dutied. Additional taxes: Tax Forfaitaire, Statistical Tax, and Customs Stamp Tax of percentage of duties and added taxes; Small Wharfage Tax. Import license required for goods from non-franc zones above a certain value; from franc zone, need authorization of Togolese Government Office. Exchange controls on non-franc zone.
Copyright: Berne (see Copyright Conventions, pg xi)

Editions Akpagnon+
BP 3531, Lome
Tel: 220244 *Fax:* 220244
Key Personnel
Man Dir: Yves-Emmanuel Dogbe
E-mail: yedogbe@yahoo.fr
Founded: 1979
Subjects: Biography, Developing Countries, Education, Literature, Literary Criticism, Essays, Parapsychology, Philosophy, Poetry, Self-Help, Social Sciences, Sociology
ISBN Prefix(es): 2-86427
Number of titles published annually: 10 Print
Total Titles: 5 Print
Orders to: CMD Claude M Diffusion Ltee, 1544 rue Villeray, Montreal, PQ H2E 1H1, Canada
L'Harmattan, 7 rue de l'Ecole Polytechnique, 75005 Paris, France
Nord-Sud Diffusion, 150 rue Berthelot, 1190 Brussels, Belgium
Presence Africaine, 25 bis, rue des Ecoles, 75005 Paris, France

Editogo
BP 891, Lome
Tel: (08) 21-37-18 *Fax:* (08) 21-14-89

Key Personnel
Man Dir: Kokou Amedegnato
Founded: 1962
Subjects: Education

Editions Haho, *imprint of* Maison d'Edition de la Librairie-Imprimerie Evangelique du Togo

Maison d'Edition de la Librairie-Imprimerie Evangelique du Togo
One rue du Commerce, BP 378, Lome
Tel: (08) 214582 *Fax:* (08) 216967
E-mail: ctce@cafe.tg
Key Personnel
Dir General: F K Agbobli
Editorial: W Y Aladji; J C van de Werk
ISBN Prefix(es): 2-906718
Imprints: Editions Haho
Bookshop(s): Librairie Evangelique, One Rue du Commerce, Lome *Tel:* (08) 212967

Les Nouvelles Editions Africaines du TOGO (NEA-TOGO)+
239 Bd du 13 Janvier, Lome
Mailing Address: BP 4862, Lome
Tel: (228) 21 67 61 *Fax:* (228) 22 10 03
E-mail: ctce@cafe.tg
Telex: 5393 NEAOM
Key Personnel
Dir: Yawo Agbeko Tsolenyanou; Mdme Christiane Tchotcho Ekue
Founded: 1990
Subjects: Fiction, Poetry
ISBN Prefix(es): 2-7236; 2-7412
Parent Company: Les Nouvelles Editions Africaines, Senegal
Associate Companies: Les Nouvelles Editions Africaines, Ivory Coast

Presses de l'Universite du Benin
BP 1515, Lome
Tel: (228) 21 30 27 *Fax:* (228) 21 85 95
E-mail: cafmicro@ub.tg
Web Site: www.ub.tg
Subjects: Medicine, Nursing, Dentistry, Science (General)
ISBN Prefix(es): 2-909886

Trinidad & Tobago

General Information

Capital: Port-of-Spain
Language: English (officially). French, Spanish, Hindi and Chinese also spoken
Religion: Roman Catholic and Anglican, also Hindu and Muslim
Population: 1.3 million
Bank Hours: 0800-1400 Monday-Thursday; 0800-1200, 1500-1700 Friday
Shop Hours: 0800-1630 Monday-Friday; 0800-1200 Saturday
Currency: 100 cents = 1 Trinidad and Tobago dollar
Export/Import Information: No tariff on books; duty and postal fee on advertising matter. No import license required for books; no obscene literature permitted. Exchange controls.
Copyright: UCC, Berne (see Copyright Conventions, pg xi)

Aquarela Galleries, see MacLean Art

Joan Bacchus-Xavier+
37 Tragarete Rd, Port-of-Spain
Tel: 6225588 *Fax:* 6251330

Founded: 1988
Subjects: Anthropology, History, Outdoor Recreation, Travel
ISBN Prefix(es): 976-8074

Caribbean Epidemiology Centre
16-18 Jamaica Blvd, Federation Park, Port-of-Spain
Mailing Address: PO Box 164, Port-of-Spain
Tel: (868) 622-4261; (868) 622-4262 *Fax:* (868) 622-2792
E-mail: postmaster@carec.paho.org
Web Site: www.carec.org
Telex: 22308
ISBN Prefix(es): 976-8114

Caribbean Telecommunications Union
Victoria Park Suites, 3rd floor, 14-17 Victoria Sq, Port-of-Spain
Tel: (868) 627-0281; (868) 627-0347 *Fax:* (868) 623-1523
E-mail: ctunion@c-t-u.org; secgen@c-t-u.org
Web Site: www.c-t-u.org
Founded: 1989
Governmental Agency responsible for telecommunications policy formulation for the Caribbean.
Subjects: Electronics, Electrical Engineering, Public Administration, Technology
ISBN Prefix(es): 976-8121

Charran's Educational Publishers+
58 Western Main Rd, St James
Mailing Address: PO Box 126, Port of Spain
Tel: (868) 622-3832 *Fax:* (868) 623-5829
Telex: 3000 Postlx Wg
Key Personnel
President: Mr Reginald Charran
Dir: Reginald Charran; Betty Charran
Sales: Terry R Ram
Founded: 1986
ISBN Prefix(es): 976-613
Bookshop(s): Muir Marshall Ltd, 64a Independence Sq, Port-of-Spain; Charran's Bookshop, 76 Henry St, Port-of-Spain; Charran's Bookshop (1978) Ltd, 58 Western Main Rd, St James; Charran's Wholesale Center, 58 Western Main Rd, St James; Charran's Arcade Book Shop, 12 Main Rd, Chaguanas *Tel:* (868) 671-1244; Charran's Book Stores, 53 Eastern Main Rd, Tunapuna *Tel:* (868) 663-1884

Economic & Business Research
10 Flament St, Port-of-Spain
Mailing Address: PO Box 708, Port-of-Spain
Tel: (868) 624-5064 *Fax:* (868) 623-4137
E-mail: maxifill@opus.co.tt
Web Site: www.opus.co.tt./maxifill
ISBN Prefix(es): 976-8008

Inprint Caribbean Ltd
35-37 Independence Sq, Port-of-Spain
Tel: 6271569; 6231711 *Fax:* 6271451
Telex: 22661 *Cable:* EXPRESS
Key Personnel
Manager: Kim Morton
Founded: 1975
Subjects: Economics, Education, Government, Political Science, History, Social Sciences, Sociology
ISBN Prefix(es): 976-608
Parent Company: Caribbean Communications Network (CCN)
Associate Companies: Prime Radio 106.1 FM; CCN TV6
Subsidiaries: Trinidad Express Newspapers Ltd

Jett Samm Publishing Ltd+
37 Newbury Hill, Glencoe
Tel: 637-9548
Web Site: jetsamm.com

Key Personnel
Editor-in-Chief: Nigel A Campbell
Founded: 1991
Subjects: Music, Dance, Travel
ISBN Prefix(es): 976-8106
Parent Company: Jett Samm Communications

MacLean Art+
Formerly Aquarela Galleries
No 3 Breezy Hill Ave, Cascade, Port of Spain
Tel: 622 8679 *Fax:* 622 7583
E-mail: gml@wow.net
Key Personnel
Manager: Geoffrey MacLean
Founded: 1984
Also acts as Dealers in Fine Art.
ISBN Prefix(es): 976-8066
Parent Company: Geoffrey MacLean Ltd
Associate Companies: MacLean Publishing Ltd

Moksha Institute of Caribbean Arts & Letters
One Sapphire Dr, Diego Martin
Mailing Address: PO Box 3254, Diego Martin
Tel: 6374516
Key Personnel
Editor & President: Anson Gonzalez
Founded: 1991
ISBN Prefix(es): 976-609
Imprints: New Voices

Multi-Media Ltd
4 Christina Court, Diego Martin
Mailing Address: PO Box 3290, Diego Martin
Tel: 6288637; 6226774 *Fax:* 6281903
ISBN Prefix(es): 976-8098

New Voices, *imprint of* Moksha Institute of Caribbean Arts & Letters

Systematics Studies Ltd
St Augustine Shopping Centre, Eastern Main Rd, St Augustine
Tel: (868) 645-8466 *Fax:* (868) 645-8467
E-mail: tobe@trinidad.net
Key Personnel
Manager: Shirley Dookeran
ISBN Prefix(es): 976-8034
Distributor for The Brookings Institution; Inter-American Development Bank; International Center for Economic Growth/Institute for Contemporary Studies; International Monetary Fund; Organization for Economic Co-operation & Development; United Nations; The World Bank; World Trade Organization

University of the West Indies (Trinidad & Tobago)
St Augustine
Tel: (868) 662 2002; (868) 662 3232 (ext 2132) *Fax:* 6639684
E-mail: infocentre@library.uwi.tt
Web Site: www.uwi.tt
Telex: (24520) (UWI-Wg) *Cable:* STOMATA
ISBN Prefix(es): 976-620

Tunisia

General Information

Capital: Tunis
Language: Arabic. French widely used
Religion: Islam
Population: 8.4 million
Bank Hours: 0800-1200/1400-1800 Monday-Friday
Shop Hours: 0800-1300/1500-1900 Monday-Saturday

Currency: 1,000 millimes = 1 Tunisian dinar
Export/Import Information: Tunisia had preferred tariffs and EEC agreement but most books are dutied. Advertising matter free. Custom formalities tax per 1,000 kg or less gross weight, with minimum rate. Consumption tax on and duty tax paid of percentage of duty and tax paid. Imports liberalized but in practice licenses granted dependent on foreign exchange position.
Copyright: UCC, Berne (see Copyright Conventions, pg xi)

Ben Abdallah Editions
Rue 8601 ZI Charguia, 2035 Tunis
Tel: (01) 237 011 *Fax:* (01) 786 290
Telex: 18 074 *Cable:* KARIM TN
Key Personnel
General Dir: M Mohamed Sellami
ISBN Prefix(es): 9973-707

Academie Tunisienne des Sciences, des Lettres et des Arts Beit El Hekma (Tunisian Academy of Sciences, Letters & Arts)+
25, Av de la Republique Carthage, Hanibal 2016
Tel: (71) 277 275; (71) 731 696; (71) 731 824 *Fax:* (71) 731 204
Key Personnel
President: Abdelwaheb Bouhdiba
Founded: 1983
Subjects: Art, Biography, Drama, Theater, Geography, Geology, History, Journalism, Language Arts, Linguistics, Law, Literature, Literary Criticism, Essays, Mathematics, Medicine, Nursing, Dentistry, Music, Dance, Philosophy, Physics, Poetry, Religion - Islamic, Social Sciences, Sociology, Veterinary Science
ISBN Prefix(es): 9973-929; 9973-911
Distributed by Afrique Culture; Dar Souhnoun; Demeter

Alyssa Editions
Rue Habib Thameur, 2026 Sidi Bou Saiid
Tel: 740989 *Fax:* 733659
Key Personnel
Dir Marketing: Sabria Beu Youssef
Founded: 1993
Subjects: Archaeology, Fiction, History, Mysteries, Regional Interests
ISBN Prefix(es): 9973-758

Les Editions de l'Arbre
17 rue Mohamed Karkoub (ex 7112), El Manar 2, 2092 Tunis Tunis
Tel: (01) 753 209 *Fax:* (01) 887 927
Key Personnel
Contact: A Beji
Founded: 1993
Subjects: Animals, Pets, Archaeology, Gardening, Plants, History, House & Home, Humor, Language Arts, Linguistics, Literature, Literary Criticism, Essays, Natural History, Outdoor Recreation, Poetry, Publishing & Book Trade Reference, Self-Help
ISBN Prefix(es): 9973-772

Arcs Editions+
32 Rue Charles de Gaulle, 1000 RP Tunis
Tel: (01) 351617
Key Personnel
Dir: Sihem Bensedrine
Assistant Dir: Afaf Bensedrine
Founded: 1988
Subjects: History
ISBN Prefix(es): 9973-740

Editions Bouslama+
15 Av de France, 1000 Tunis
Tel: (01) 245612 *Fax:* (01) 381100
Telex: 14230 *Cable:* Editions Bouslama

TUNISIA

Key Personnel
Man Dir, Rights & Permissions: Ali Bouslama
Sales: Hichem Bouslama
Production: Riadh Bouslama
Publicity: Hatem Bouslama
Founded: 1960
Subjects: History
ISBN Prefix(es): 9973-714
Branch Office(s)
15 bis rue Lamine el Abassi, Tunis

CAEU, *imprint of* Maison d'Edition Mohamed Ali Hammi

Dar Arabia Lil Kitab
Maison Arabe du Livre, Rue 7101, El-Manar 2 El-Menzah, 1004 Tunis
Tel: (01) 888255
Telex: 14966 Kitab
Key Personnel
Man Dir: Mahdi Ben Youssef
Founded: 1975
Subjects: Biography, Economics, Education, History, Language Arts, Linguistics, Literature, Literary Criticism, Essays, Religion - Other
ISBN Prefix(es): 9973-10
Parent Company: Dar Arabia Lil Kitab, ave Ghouma Mahmoud, BP 3185, Tripoli, Libyan Arab Jamahiriya

Dar El Afaq+
4, rue Ahmed Bayram, 1006 Tunis
Tel: (01) 265904 *Fax:* (01) 569035
Key Personnel
President: Nabil Rebai
Founded: 1989
Subjects: Government, Political Science, Literature, Literary Criticism, Essays, Religion - Islamic
ISBN Prefix(es): 9973-743
Showroom(s): 8, Rue Francoi, Boucher, 1006 Tunis
Bookshop(s): 8, Rue Francoi, Boucher 1006
Shipping Address: 8, Rue Francoi, Boucher, 1006 Tunis
Warehouse: 8, Rue Francoi, Boucher, 1006 Tunis

Demeter
36 av F Bourguiba, 2036 Soukra, Ariana
Tel: 71 94 52 42; 71 94 52 46 *Fax:* 71 94 51 99
ISBN Prefix(es): 9973-706

Faculte des Sciences Humaines et Sociales de Tunis
1029 Bab Saadoun, 1007 Tunis
Tel: (01) 560 950; 71 56 08 58 *Fax:* 71 56 75 51
Key Personnel
Dir: Mr Habib Dlala
Founded: 1956
Arabic & Latin languages.
Subjects: Archaeology, Ethnicity, Geography, Geology, History, Language Arts, Linguistics, Literature, Literary Criticism, Essays, Philosophy, Psychology, Psychiatry, Social Sciences, Sociology
ISBN Prefix(es): 9973-922

FTERSI, *see* Publications de la Fondation Temimi pour la Recherche Scientifique et L'Information

Government Printer (Imprimerie Officielle de la Republique Tunisienne - IORT)
Route de Rades, KM 2 Ave Farhat Hached, 2040 Rades
Tel: (01) 299914
Telex: 14939 TN
ISBN Prefix(es): 9973-906; 9973-946

Maison d'Edition Mohamed Ali Hammi+
3 Rue Dragut, 3001 Sfax El Jadida
Tel: 04224534 *Fax:* 74407441
E-mail: caeu@gnet.tn
Key Personnel
President: Abid Nouri
Founded: 1983
Subjects: History, Language Arts, Linguistics, Literature, Literary Criticism, Essays, Mathematics, Philosophy
ISBN Prefix(es): 9973-727
Imprints: CAEU
Distributor for Centre Culturel Arabic (Liban); El Farabi (Liban)

IORT (Imprimerie Officielle de la Republique Tunisienne), *see* Government Printer (Imprimerie Officielle de la Republique Tunisienne - IORT)

El-M'aaref Editions
7 rue de France, 4000 Sousse
Mailing Address: PO Box 215, Sousse 4000
Tel: (03) 256235 *Fax:* (03) 256530
ISBN Prefix(es): 9973-16; 9973-712
Parent Company: Dar El Maaref

Maison Tunisienne de l'Edition+
36, rue Babel Khadra, Bab Souika, 1006 Tunis
Tel: (01) 345333 *Fax:* (01) 353992
Telex: Mac 12032
Key Personnel
Man Dir: Larbi Azouz
Founded: 1966
Subjects: Agriculture, Anthropology, Archaeology, Biography, Drama, Theater, Education, History, Literature, Literary Criticism, Essays, Philosophy, Poetry, Public Administration, Religion - Islamic
ISBN Prefix(es): 9973-12

Publications de la Fondation Temimi pour la Recherche Scientifique et L'Information
BP 50, 1118 Zaghouan
Tel: (072) 676 446; (072) 680 110 *Fax:* (072) 676 710
E-mail: temimi.fond.@gnet.tn
Web Site: temimi.org (in Arabic); refer.org/6 (in French)
Key Personnel
Pres: Prof Abdeljelil Temimi
Founded: 1989
Subjects: Archaeology, History, Library & Information Sciences, Social Sciences, Sociology
ISBN Prefix(es): 9973-719
Number of titles published annually: 15 Print
Distributed by Geulhner & Rorin

Scientifique et l'Information-TRSI, *see* Publications de la Fondation Temimi pour la Recherche Scientifique et L'Information

Sud Editions
lter, rc Bernard, Tunis 1002
Tel: 71 79 80 64 *Fax:* 71 79 52 60
Telex: 12363 TN
Key Personnel
Man Dir: M Masmoudi
Editorial Dir: Nabil Asswad
Founded: 1976
Subjects: Art, Literature, Literary Criticism, Essays
ISBN Prefix(es): 9973-703
Warehouse: La Soukra, Km 15, 2036 Tunis

Editions Techniques Specialisees
2 bis, Rue du Reservoir, 1008 Tunis
Tel: (01) 71 74 61 61; (01) 71 74 70 04 *Fax:* (01) 71 74 61 60
E-mail: info@pagesjaunes.com.tn

Key Personnel
International Rights: Hajer Djilani
Founded: 1978
ISBN Prefix(es): 9973-711
Subsidiaries: Redaction

Societe Tunisienne de Diffusion
5, av de Carthage, 1000 RP Tunis
Tel: (01) 255000; (01) 261799 *Cable:* Studiffusion
ISBN Prefix(es): 9973-11

Turkey

General Information

Capital: Ankara
Language: Turkish
Religion: Predominantly Sunni Moslem
Population: 63.9 million
Bank Hours: 0900-1730 Monday-Friday
Shop Hours: 0800-1900 Monday-Saturday
Currency: Turkish lira
Export/Import Information: Books, magazines and similar publications are freely imported. International copyright laws enforced. 1% VAT on books.
Copyright: Berne, Florence (see Copyright Conventions, pg xi)

ABC Kitabevi AS
Tunel Meydani 1, Beyoglu, 80030 Istanbul
Tel: (0212) 27 62 404
Telex: 24094 Abck Tr
Key Personnel
Man Dir: Artun Altiparmak
Editorial: Oender Renkliyildirim
Sales: K Karakush
Production: Hasan Guenaydin
Publicity: Ferit Guersu
Rights & Permissions: Necip Inselel
Founded: 1976
Subjects: Education
ISBN Prefix(es): 975-09

Ada Press Publishers+
Istiklal Cd, 475/479 Beyoglu, Istanbul
Tel: (0212) 249 35 45
Key Personnel
Editor: Mr Ferit Edgue
Founded: 1976
Also acts as an art gallery.
ISBN Prefix(es): 975-438

Afa Yayincilik Sanayi Tic AS+
Istiklal Cad. Bekar Sk No 17, Taksim, Istanbul
Tel: (0212) 276 27 67 *Fax:* (0212) 2444362
Key Personnel
President: Atil Ant
International Rights: Dilek Basak
Founded: 1985
Subjects: Biography, Child Care & Development, Drama, Theater, Film, Video, Government, Political Science, Nonfiction (General)
ISBN Prefix(es): 975-414
Distributed by DaDa Ltd
Bookshop(s): AFA Kitabevi, Istiklal Cad, Bekar Sok No 17, Beyoglu/Istanbul

Akdeniz Yayincilik+
100 y1 Mah Matbaacilar Ve Ambarcilar Sitesi, No 83 Bagcilar, Istanbul
Tel: (0212) 629-0026 *Fax:* (0212) 629-0027
Key Personnel
President: H Mursit Ul
Editor: Filiztekin Ferhan
Founded: 1995

Specialize in geographical atlases, school books & dictionaries.
ISBN Prefix(es): 975-469
Parent Company: Altin Kitaplar Yayinevi Ve Ticaret As

Alkim Kitapcilik-Yayimcilik+
Za Zafer Carsisi 14, Kizilay/Ankara
Membership(s): Basar Arslan.
Subjects: Astrology, Occult, Business, Child Care & Development, Computer Science, Cookery, Crafts, Games, Hobbies, Drama, Theater, Economics, Finance, How-to, Law, Management, Marketing, Microcomputers, Nonfiction (General), Psychology, Psychiatry, Sports, Athletics
ISBN Prefix(es): 975-337

Altin Kitaplar Yayinevi
Celal Ferdi G Sk Nebioglu Han No 7/1, Cagaloglu, Istanbul 34440
Tel: (0212) 5206246; (0212) 5201588; (0212) 5268010 *Fax:* (0212) 5120266
E-mail: info@altinkitaplar.com.tr
Web Site: www.altinkitaplar.com.tr
Key Personnel
Vice President: Mursit Ul
Publisher: Batu Bozkurt
Production: Erden Heper
Editorial: Alpar Oya
Founded: 1959
Subjects: Criminology, Economics, Fiction, History, Nonfiction (General), Philosophy, Psychology, Psychiatry, Regional Interests, Science Fiction, Fantasy
ISBN Prefix(es): 975-7620
Showroom(s): Celal ferdi Goekcay SK, Nebio Is Hani, Istanbul

Arkadas Ltd+
Mithatpasa Cad No 28, Yenisehir, Ankara
Tel: (0312) 434 46 24 *Fax:* (0312) 435 60 57
Key Personnel
Chairman & Owner: Cumhur Ozdemir
 E-mail: cumhuro@arkadas.com.tr
Editor: Meltem Ozdemir *E-mail:* meltemo@arkadas.com.tr
Founded: 1979
Specialize in computer books, textbooks; also acts as Book Distributors, Bookshop. Authorized software replicator of Microsoft Co In MENA (Middle East & North Africa).
Subjects: Animals, Pets, Computer Science, Cookery, English as a Second Language, Environmental Studies, Mathematics, Music, Dance, Physics
ISBN Prefix(es): 975-509
Number of titles published annually: 100 Print
Total Titles: 300 Print
Distributor for Microsoft Press
Foreign Rep(s): Microsoft Press (Turkey)
Bookshop(s): ODTUU Alisveris Merkezi, Ankara

Arkeoloji Ve Sanat Yayinlari (Archaeology & Art Publications)+
Hayriye Cad, Corlu Apt 3/4, 80060 Galatasaray Istanbul
Tel: (212) 293 0378 *Fax:* (212) 245 6877
E-mail: info@arkeolojisanat.com
Web Site: www.arkeolojisanat.com
Key Personnel
Publisher: Nezih Basgelen
 E-mail: nezihbasgelen@superonline.com
Senior Editor: Brian Johnson
 E-mail: brianjohnson@superonline.com
Founded: 1978
Since 1978 Arkeoloji ve Sanat Yayinlari (Archaeology & Art Publications) has been publishing books on archaeology, history, & art history of Turkey. With titles in Turkish, English, German & French, the company's list includes publications ranging from specialized scholarly monographs to popular guides to Turkey's famed tourist sites. Besides books, the press publishes a bimonthly journal, Arkeoloji ve Sanat, presenting the academic contributions of the world's leading scholars of Anatolian archaeology & art.
Subjects: Anthropology, Antiques, Archaeology, Architecture & Interior Design, Art, History, Photography, Travel
ISBN Prefix(es): 975-7538
Number of titles published annually: 20 Print
Total Titles: 100 Print

Arkin Kitabevi
Ankara Cad No 60, 34410 Sirkeci, Istanbul
Tel: (0212) 522 92 24 *Fax:* (0212) 512 19 01
Telex: 28362 Rga Tr *Cable:* BIRARKINLAR ISTANBUL
Key Personnel
Owner: Ramazan Goikalp Arkin; Mefra Arkin
Dir: Tarik Kinali
Founded: 1942
Subjects: Education, Science (General)
ISBN Prefix(es): 975-402

Ataturk Kultur, Dil ve Tarih, Yusek Kurumu Baskanligi
Ataturk Bulvan No 217, Kavaklidere, Ankara
Tel: (0312) 428 61 00 *Fax:* (0312) 428 52 88
E-mail: bim@tdk.gov.tr
Web Site: www.tdk.gov.tr
Key Personnel
President: Prof Utkan Kocatuerk, PhD
Subjects: Archaeology, Ethnicity, History, Language Arts, Linguistics
ISBN Prefix(es): 975-16
Branch Office(s)
Atatuerk Research Ce
Turkish Culture Center
Turkish Historical Society
Turkish Language Society

Ataturk Universitesi+
25240 Erzurum
Tel: (0442) 231 11 11 *Fax:* (0442) 236 10 14
E-mail: webadmin@atauni.edu.tr
Web Site: www.atauni.edu.tr/
Key Personnel
Foreign Relations Coordinator: Dr Erol Cakmak
Founded: 1957
ISBN Prefix(es): 975-442

Aydin Yayincilik+
Nasuhi Akar Mahallesi, 1 Cad 25 SK No 12 A, Balgat/Ankara
Tel: (0312) 2873402; (0312) 2873403 *Fax:* (0312) 2873402
Subjects: Mathematics, Science (General)
ISBN Prefix(es): 975-7948
Subsidiaries: Aydin Web Tesisleri (printing)
Book Club(s): Yayincilar Birligi
Warehouse: 100 yil Bolvari, Gl sok, No 29, Ostim

Bilden Bilgisayar (Bilden Computer, Programming, Digital Publishing Ltd)
Ziverbey Kasap Ismail Sok, Sadikoglu Ys Merkezi No 13 Buro No 41, 81040 Kadikoy/Istanbul
Tel: (0216) 449 52 50 *Fax:* (0216) 449 52 51
E-mail: bilden@bilden.com.tr
Web Site: www.bilden.com.tr
Key Personnel
General Manager: Sukru Korman
Specializes in the development of educational software on CD-ROM for ages 3-18.
Subjects: Education, Language Arts, Linguistics, Mathematics, Science (General), Social Sciences, Sociology
Distributor for Encyclopedia Britannica Co; LangMaster

Birsen Yayinevi+
Cagaloglu Yokusu Evren Carsisi No 29/13, Cagaloglu, Istanbul 34440
Tel: (0212) 5278578; (0212) 5278522 *Fax:* (0212) 5270895
Web Site: www.geocities.com/birsen2us
Key Personnel
President: Mr Cengiz Algin
Vice President: Mr Bahadir Algin
Founded: 1973
ISBN Prefix(es): 975-511

Caglayan Kitabevi+
Galatasaray, Istiklal Cad 166, Tokatlyyan Yp hany Kat 1 No 7-8-9-21 Beyoglu, Istanbul
Tel: (0212) 2454433 *Fax:* (0212) 1491794
E-mail: info@caglayan.com
Key Personnel
President: Tuncay Caglayan
Founded: 1962 (Publishing since 1952)
Subjects: Chemistry, Chemical Engineering, Civil Engineering, Electronics, Electrical Engineering, Engineering (General), Management, Mathematics, Mechanical Engineering, Physics, Technology, Technical Books
ISBN Prefix(es): 975-436
Associate Companies: Caglayan Basimevi, Catalcesme Sokak 26, Cagaloglu, Istanbul; Caglayan Yayinev, PK 517, Beyoglu, Istanbul

CEP Kitaplari AS, *imprint of* Varlik Yayinlari AS

Cep Kitaplari AS+
Imprint of Varlik Yayinlari AS
Piyerloti Cad Ayberk Ap 7-9, Cemberlitas, 34400 Istanbul
Tel: (0212) 516 20 04 *Fax:* (0212) 516 20 05
Web Site: www.varlik.com.tr
Key Personnel
Editor-in-Chief: Osman Cetin Deniztekin
 Tel: (0212) 5162004 (ext 13) *E-mail:* varlik@isbank.net.tr
Founded: 1982
Membership(s): Turkish Publishers Association.
Subjects: Fiction, Nonfiction (General), Religion - Islamic, Science (General), Science Fiction, Fantasy, Women's Studies
ISBN Prefix(es): 975-434
Number of titles published annually: 5 Print
Total Titles: 60 Print
Distributed by Varlik Yayinlari AS

Dergah Yayinlari AS, see Ezel Erverdi (Dergah Yayinlari AS) Muessese Muduru

Dokuz Eylul Universitesi
Dokuzcesmeler Buca, Izmir
Tel: (0232) 420 41 80 *Fax:* (0232) 420 18 27
E-mail: hukuk@deu.edu.tr
Web Site: www.deu.edu.tr
Founded: 1982
ISBN Prefix(es): 975-441

Dost Kitabevi Yayinlari+
Karanfil Sokak 11/A, 06650 Kizilay Ankara
Tel: (0312) 4172901 *Fax:* (0312) 4199397
Key Personnel
Chief Executive Officer: Erdal Akalin *Tel:* (0312) 4252464 *Fax:* (0312) 4180355
Gen Mgr: Gunay Okumus *Tel:* (0312) 4188327 *Fax:* (0312) 4180355
Dir: Raul Mansur *Tel:* (0312) 4188772
 Fax: (0312) 4199397 *E-mail:* raulman@domi.net.tr
Editor-in-Chief: Levent Yilmaz *Tel:* (0312) 4188772 *Fax:* (0312) 4199397 *E-mail:* levent@easynet.fr
Founded: 1979
Chain of bookshops. Started publishing books in 1997. Co-editions with Dorling Kindersley, Franco Maria Ricci.

TURKEY

Membership(s): Turkish Publishers Association.
Subjects: History, Social Sciences, Sociology, Travel, Translated fiction
ISBN Prefix(es): 975-7501
Number of titles published annually: 60 Print
Total Titles: 80 Print
Branch Office(s)
105 Rue de l'Ouest, Paris, France, Mr Levent Yilmaz *Tel:* (01) 45410907 *E-mail:* levent@easynet.fr
Orders to: Dost Dagitim, Bayindir sokak 40/B, Kizilay Ankara 06650, Murat Duman *Tel:* (0312) 4324868 *Fax:* (0312) 4357596

Dost Yayinlari
Formerly Dost Yayinlari San Ve Tie Ltd
Tunel Gecidi Ishanib Blok 9/210, Beyoglu, Istanbul 80050
Tel: (0212) 245 31 41 *Fax:* (0212) 243 02 78
Key Personnel
Dir: Salim Sengil
Marketing Manager: Asli Sengil Cansever
Founded: 1947
Subjects: Art, Humor, Literature, Literary Criticism, Essays
ISBN Prefix(es): 975-95481; 975-7499

Dost Yayinlari San Ve Tie Ltd, see Dost Yayinlari

Eren Yayincilik ve Kitapcilik Ltd Sti+
Tunel, Istiklal Cad, Sofyali Sok No 34, 80050 Beyoglu-Istanbul
Tel: (0212) 251-2858
E-mail: eren@turk.net
Founded: 1983
Subjects: Engineering (General)
ISBN Prefix(es): 975-7622
Associate Companies: Ottomania
Branch Office(s)
Istanbul

Ezel Erverdi (Dergah Yayinlari AS) Muessese Muduru
Gedikpasa Cami Sk 57/1, 34490 Cemberlitas-Istanbul
Tel: (0212) 516 12 62; (0212) 516 00 47 *Fax:* (0212) 519 04 21
Web Site: www.dergahyayinlari.com
Key Personnel
Man Dir: Ezel Erverdi
Editorial: Mustafa Kutlu
Sales: Fatih Gokdag
Production: Kara Ismail
Publicity: Ashihan Erverdi
Founded: 1977
Subjects: Education, Ethnicity, Government, Political Science, History, Literature, Literary Criticism, Essays, Philosophy
ISBN Prefix(es): 975-7462; 975-7032
Subsidiaries: Ulke Yayin Haber Tic Ltd Sti; Emek matbaacilik ve ilancilik Ltd Sti
Bookshop(s): Ulke Yayin Haber Tic Ltd Sti, Ankara cad No 41/A Uygurhan Sirheci list

Iki Nokta Arastirma Basin Yayin Sanayi ve Ticaret Ltd Sti, *imprint of* IKI Nokta Research Press & Publications Industry & Trade Ltd

IKI Nokta Research Press & Publications Industry & Trade Ltd+
Moda Cad Usakligil Apt No 180/10, 81300 Kadikoy, Istanbul
Tel: (0216) 349 01 41 *Fax:* (0216) 337 67 56
E-mail: ikinokta@superonline.com; ikinokta@turkinfo.com; ikinokta@gisoturkey.com; ikinokta@turkgis.com; ikinokta@infoturk.com
Web Site: www.ikinokta.com
Key Personnel
President: Yuecel Yaman
International Rights: Kerem Ahmet

Founded: 1986
Specialize in database updating.
Subjects: Archaeology, Communications, Geography, Geology, History
ISBN Prefix(es): 975-340
Number of titles published annually: 130 Print; 5 CD-ROM; 1 Online; 1 E-Book
Imprints: Iki Nokta Arastirma Basin Yayin Sanayi ve Ticaret Ltd Sti

Iletisim Yayinlari+
Klodfarer Cad Iletisim Han 7/2, Cagaloglu, 34400 Istanbul
Tel: (0212) 516 22 60 *Fax:* (0212) 516 12 58
E-mail: iletisim@iletisim.com.tr
Web Site: www.iletisim.com.tr
Key Personnel
Contact: Nihat Tuna; Osman Yener
Founded: 1984
Subjects: Ethnicity, Fiction, Government, Political Science, History, Literature, Literary Criticism, Essays, Nonfiction (General), Philosophy, Science Fiction, Fantasy, Social Sciences, Sociology
ISBN Prefix(es): 975-470
Associate Companies: Birikim Yayinlari
Branch Office(s)
Selanik Cad 64/11 Yenisehir, 06640 Ankara
Bodrum
Ismir

Imge Kitabevi
Konur Sokak No: 17/12, 06650 Kizilay, Ankara
Tel: (0312) 419 46 10; (0312) 419 46 11 *Fax:* (0312) 425 29 87
E-mail: imge@www.imge.com.tr
Web Site: www.imgekitabevi.com
Key Personnel
Contact: Refik Tabakci
ISBN Prefix(es): 975-533
Parent Company: IImge Kitabevi Ltd
Divisions: IImge Kitabevi Yayinlari

Inkilap Publishers Ltd+
Ankara Cad No 99 Kat 1, 34410 Cataloglu, Istanbul
Tel: (0212) 5140611; (0212) 5140610 *Fax:* (0212) 5140612
Web Site: www.inkilap.com
Key Personnel
Man Dir: Nazar Fikri; Julia Fikri; Errol Fikri
Foreign Rights: Sema Diker *E-mail:* sdiker@inkilap.com
Founded: 1935
Subjects: Animals, Pets, Archaeology, Art, Business, Child Care & Development, Cookery, Drama, Theater, Economics, Electronics, Electrical Engineering, Fiction, Gardening, Plants, Humor, Management, Mathematics, Music, Dance, Philosophy, Photography, Physics, Poetry, Psychology, Psychiatry, Religion - Islamic
ISBN Prefix(es): 975-10
Parent Company: Anka Offset AS, Teknografik Matbaacilik AS, Ankara Cad 95, Sirkeci, Istanbul
Associate Companies: Inkas, Ingilizce Nesriyat Kitapcilik AS, Ankara Cad 95, Sirkeci, Istanbul
Branch Office(s)
Yeni Zaman Kitabevi, Ankara Cad 155, Sirkeci, Istanbul (correspondence to Inkilap)
Bookshop(s): Koerfez Mah Carrefour Ticaret Merkezi B-36, Ismit *Tel:* (0262) 335 31 91 *Fax:* (0262) 335 40 25; Yeni Havaalani Cad No 40 Kipa Alisveris Merkezi Cigli, Izmir *Tel:* (0232) 386 50 70 *Fax:* (0232) 386 50 70; Inkilap Mah B061 Carrefour Ticaret merkezi Uemraniye, Istanbul *Tel:* (0216) 525 12 95 *Fax:* (0216) 525 12 97; 100 Yil Mah 100 Evler Mevkii Carrefour Ticaret Merkezi B-51, Adana *Tel:* (0322) 256 54 65 *Fax:* (0322) 256 53 82

Isis Yayin Tic ve San Ltd+
Semsibey Sok 10, Beylerbeyi, 81210 Beylerbeyi/Istanbul
Tel: (0216) 3213851; (0216) 3213847; (0216) 3213847 *Fax:* (0216) 3218666
E-mail: isis@turk.net
Key Personnel
Dir: Sinan Kuneralp
Publishing: S Helvacioglu
Founded: 1983
Subjects: History, Social Sciences, Sociology
ISBN Prefix(es): 975-428

Kiyi Yayinlari+
Koca Aga Sokak No 6/1, T-80060 Beyoglu, Istanbul
Tel: (0212) 245 58 45 *Fax:* (0212) 245 40 09
E-mail: sbeygu@ibm.net
Web Site: www.kiyi.net
Key Personnel
Editor & Founder: Sahin Beygu *E-mail:* sbeygu@ibm.net
Founded: 1989
Membership(s): T Yay-Bir (Turkish Publishers Association).
Subjects: Fiction, Literature, Literary Criticism, Essays, Nonfiction (General), Poetry
ISBN Prefix(es): 975-444

Kok Yayincilik+
Incesu Cad, No 10, 06670 Kolej/Ankara
Tel: (0312) 4302622 *Fax:* (0312) 4350497
E-mail: kokbilgi@kokyayincilik.com.tr
Web Site: www.kokyayincilik.com.tr
Key Personnel
International Rights: Celal Musaoglu
Founded: 1987
Subjects: Animals, Pets, Child Care & Development, Education, Health, Nutrition, House & Home, Human Relations, Mathematics, Music, Dance
ISBN Prefix(es): 975-499
Imprints: Offset

Kubbealti Akademisi Kultur ve Sasat Vakfi+
Peykhane Sk No 3, 34400 Cemberlitas, Istanbul
Tel: (0212) 516 23 56 *Fax:* (0212) 517 14 60
Key Personnel
International Rights: Mrs Semahat Yuksel
Founded: 1978
Subjects: Architecture & Interior Design, Art, Biography, Environmental Studies, History, Literature, Literary Criticism, Essays, Music, Dance, Religion - Islamic, Culture
ISBN Prefix(es): 975-7663
Distributor for Istanbul Fetih Cemiyeti's Editions
Bookshop(s): Yeniceriler Cad No 43, 34490 Carsikapi, Istanbul

Metis Yayinlari (Metis Publishers)+
Ipek Sk No 9, Beyoglu, Istanbul
Tel: (0212) 245 45 19; (0212) 2454696 *Fax:* (0212) 2454519
E-mail: metis@turk.net
Web Site: www.metisbooks.com
Key Personnel
International, Foreign Rights: Ms Muege Guersoy Soekmen
Founded: 1982
Membership(s): Turkish Publishers' Association. Publisher of Psychiatry, Literature, Politics & Philosophy. Also acts as Verso agent in Turkey.
Subjects: Literature, Literary Criticism, Essays, Nonfiction (General), Philosophy, Poetry, Psychology, Psychiatry, Science Fiction, Fantasy, Social Sciences, Sociology, Western Fiction, Women's Studies, Political Studies
ISBN Prefix(es): 975-342; 975-7650
Number of titles published annually: 40 Print
Total Titles: 540 Print

PUBLISHERS

Nurdan YayinlariSanayi ve Ticaret Ltd Sti+
Prof Kazim Ysmail Guerkan Cad No 13 Kat 1, Cagaloglu-Istanbul
Tel: (0212) 522 55 04; (0212) 513 86 53
 Fax: (0212) 512 51 86
E-mail: info@nurdan.com.tr
Web Site: www.nurdan.com.tr
Key Personnel
Owner: Cetin Tuezuener
Dir: Nurdan Tuezuener
Editor: Faruk Cil
Founded: 1980
Membership(s): Turkish Publishers' Association.
Subjects: Regional Interests
ISBN Prefix(es): 975-527
Subsidiaries: Meydan Larousse Co; Nu-Do Publishing Distribution Co

Offset, *imprint of* Kok Yayincilik

Oguz Yayinlari
Babiali Cad 30/7, 34410 Cagaloglu, Istanbul
Tel: (0212) 5264745; (0212) 5113418 *Fax:* (0212) 5114695
Key Personnel
Editor: Sevgili Turan
Subjects: Religion - Islamic, Theology
ISBN Prefix(es): 975-538

Pan Yayincilik+
Barbaros Bulvari, 74/4, Besiktas, 80700 Istanbul
Tel: (0212) 2618072; (0212) 2275675 *Fax:* (0212) 2275674
E-mail: pan@pankitap.com
Web Site: www.pankitap.com
Key Personnel
Contact: Ferruh Gencer
Founded: 1986
Subjects: Fiction, Music, Dance, Science (General)
ISBN Prefix(es): 975-7652

Parantez Yayinlari Ltd+
Istiklal Cad 212, Alt Kat no 8, Beyoglu-Istanbul
Tel: (0212) 252 85 67 *Fax:* (0212) 252 85 67
E-mail: parantez@yahoo.com
Web Site: www.geocities.com/parantez
Key Personnel
International Rights: Metin Zeynioglu
Founded: 1991
Membership(s): Turkish Publishers Association & Turkish Pen Club.
Subjects: Biography, Fiction, Film, Video, Gay & Lesbian, Humor
ISBN Prefix(es): 975-7939

Payel Yayinevi+
Cagaloglu Yokusu Evren Han Kat 4 No 63, Cagaloglu, Istanbul
Tel: (0212) 511 82 83 *Fax:* (0212) 512 43 53
E-mail: shemsa@ttnet.net.tr *Cable:* PAYEL YAYINEVI-CAGALOGLU-ISTANBUL
Key Personnel
Editor & Owner: Ahmet Ozturk
Founded: 1966
Membership(s): Publishers Association of Turkey & Cumhuriyet Book Club.
Subjects: Archaeology, Film, Video, History, Literature, Literary Criticism, Essays, Psychology, Psychiatry, Science (General), Social Sciences, Sociology, Women's Studies
ISBN Prefix(es): 975-388
Book Club(s): Cumhuriyet Book Club

Pearson Education Turkey+
Koza Is Merkezi, "B" Blok Kat 4, Murbasan Sok Balmumcu, Istanbul
Tel: (0212) 288 6941 *Fax:* (0212) 267 1851
E-mail: firstname.lastname@pearsoned-ema.com
Web Site: www.pearsoneduc.com

Key Personnel
Regional Dir, East Med/Arab World: Christine Ozden
Sales Dir, East Med/Arab World: Necip Inselel
Founded: 1995
Branch offices in Adana, Ankara, Antalya, Bursa, & Izmir.
Subjects: English as a Second Language
ISBN Prefix(es): 975-7015
Parent Company: Pearson Education
Ultimate Parent Company: Pearson Plc
Branch Office(s)
Ankara
Adana
Antalya
Bursa
Izmir
Distributor for Langenscheidt

Redhouse Press+
SEV Matbaacilik ve Yayincilik AS, Rizapasa Yokusu No 50 Mercan, 34450 Istanbul
Tel: (0212) 520 7778; (0212) 520 2960; (0212) 520 0090 *Fax:* (0212) 522 1909
E-mail: info@redhouse.com.tr; sales@redhouse.com.tr
Web Site: www.redhouse.com.tr
Telex: 23554 Peettr
Key Personnel
Co-Dir: Cerina Logico Blakney; Richard Blakney
Editor: Charles Brown; Serap Bezmez
Sales: Sait Sermet
Founded: 1822
Subjects: Education
ISBN Prefix(es): 975-413
Bookshop(s): Redhouse Boolesbave

Remzi Kitabevi+
Selvili Mescit Sok No 3, 34440 Cagaloglu, Istanbul
Tel: (0212) 513 94 24; (0212) 513 94 25; (0212) 513 94 74; (0212) 513 94 75 *Fax:* (0212) 522 90 55
E-mail: post@remzi.com.tr
Web Site: www.remzi.com.tr *Cable:* REMZI KITABEVI ISTANBUL
Key Personnel
Man Dir: Erol Erduran
Dir: Ahmet Erduran
Production Manager: Oemer Erduran
Founded: 1927
Subjects: Art, Biography, Education, Fiction, History, Nonfiction (General), Philosophy, Psychology, Psychiatry, Science (General), Social Sciences, Sociology
ISBN Prefix(es): 975-14
Subsidiaries: Evrim Matbaacilik Ltd
Bookshop(s): Etiler Istanbul *Tel:* (0212) 282 2575 76 *Fax:* (0212) 282 2577; 44 Rumeli Caddesi, Nisantasi, Istanbul *Tel:* (0212) 234 5475-76 *Fax:* (0212) 232 5934; Erenkoy, Istanbul *Tel:* (0212) 448 0373-74 *Fax:* (0212) 448 0375; Akatlar, Istanbul *Tel:* (0212) 352 3355 *Fax:* (0212) 352 3356; Mecidiyekoy, Istanbul *Tel:* (0212) 217 1225 *Fax:* (0212) 216 8288; 452 Bagdat Cad, Suadiye, Istanbul *Tel:* (0212) 368 1491-92 *Fax:* (0212) 368 1467

Ruh ve Madde Yayinlari ve Saglik Hizmetleri AS (Spirit & Matter Publications)+
4/8 80060, Hasnun Galip Sok Pembe Cikmazi, Beyoglu, Istanbul
Tel: (0212) 2431814 *Fax:* (0212) 2520718
E-mail: bilyay@bilyay.org.tr
Web Site: www.ruhvemadde.com
Key Personnel
Foreign Rights: Yasemin Tokatli
Founded: 1994
Subjects: Alternative, Astrology, Occult, Earth Sciences, Nonfiction (General), Parapsychology, Philosophy, Religion - Islamic, Religion - Other, Self-Help

ISBN Prefix(es): 975-8007
Number of titles published annually: 25 Print
Total Titles: 300 Print
Parent Company: Foundation for Spreading the Knowledge to Unify Humanity
Associate Companies: Society for Research on the Nature of the Human Individual
Distributed by EGE META
Distributor for EGE META, META

Sabah Kitaplari+
Istiklal Cad No 192, Beyoglu/Istanbul
Tel: (0212) 5028410; (0212) 5028319
Key Personnel
Contact: Serpil Demirtas *E-mail:* sdemirtas@sabah.com.tr
Founded: 1974
Subjects: Biography, Business, Criminology, History, Management, Nonfiction (General)
ISBN Prefix(es): 975-579
Associate Companies: Suereli Yayinlar AS, Bueyuekdere Cad, Levent, Istanbul *Tel:* (01) 692420 (Periodical Press Inc)

Saray Medikal Yayin Tic Ltd Sti+
168 Sok No 5-7, Bornova/Izmir
Tel: (0232) 3394969 *Fax:* (0232) 3733700
E-mail: eozkarahan@novell.cs.eng.dev.edu.tr
Key Personnel
Contact: Cetin Gultekin
Founded: 1993
Membership(s): Turkish Publishers Association.
Subjects: Behavioral Sciences, Child Care & Development, Computer Science, Engineering (General), Medicine, Nursing, Dentistry, Philosophy, Self-Help, Social Sciences, Sociology
ISBN Prefix(es): 975-7816; 975-7074
Parent Company: Saray Medikal Yayin Sar ve Tic Ltd Sti
Subsidiaries: Bassaray Printing

Seckin Yayinevi+
Saglik Sok 19-B, 06410 Sihhiye, Ankara
Tel: (0312) 4353030 *Fax:* (0312) 4352472
E-mail: seckin@seckin.com.tr
Web Site: www.seckin.com.tr
Key Personnel
International Rights: Koray Seckin
Founded: 1959
Membership(s): Turkish Publishers Association.
Subjects: Accounting, Computer Science, Economics, Law
ISBN Prefix(es): 975-347
Number of titles published annually: 70 Print
Total Titles: 233 Print

Soez Yayin/Oyunajans+
4 Gazeteciler Sitesi, C-2 D 9 Levent, 80630 Istanbul
Mailing Address: P K 7 Levent, 80622 Istanbul
Tel: (0212) 2806701 *Fax:* (0212) 2806803
Web Site: www.oyunajans.com
Key Personnel
Contact: Mr Hueseyin Nevzat Erkmen
 E-mail: nerkmen@turk.net; Mr Ali Erkmen
 E-mail: aerkmen.@turk.net
Founded: 1983
Specialize in translations of Turkish literature into English.
Subjects: Advertising, Alternative, Art, Business, Career Development, Crafts, Games, Hobbies, Fiction, Film, Video, Finance, Health, Nutrition, How-to, Management, Psychology, Psychiatry, Self-Help
ISBN Prefix(es): 975-7190; 975-95491
Total Titles: 50 Print

Toker Yayinlari+
Ankara cad 46/14, Sirkeci, Istanbul 34420
Tel: (0212) 5223309

Key Personnel
President: Mr Yalcin Toker
Founded: 1962
Membership(s): Turkish Publishers Association.
Subjects: Ethnicity, History, Literature, Literary Criticism, Essays
ISBN Prefix(es): 975-445
U.S. Office(s): C E M Toker, PO Box 39652, Phoenix, AZ 85069, United States

Toros Yayinlari Ltd Co
Yenicarsi Cad Luks Apt 33/1, 80050 Galatasaray, Istanbul
Tel: (0212) 2444155 *Fax:* (0212) 2452858; (0212) 2444155
Key Personnel
Author: Ali Neyzi
Editor: Rasit Goekceli *E-mail:* rgokceli@escortnet.com; Sahin Beygu
Founded: 1981
Subjects: Literature, Literary Criticism, Essays
ISBN Prefix(es): 975-433

Turkish Republic - Ministry of Culture+
Ataturk Bulvari No 29, 06050 Opera Ankara-Turkiye
Tel: (0312) 309 08 50 *Fax:* (0312) 312-4359
E-mail: yayimlar@kutuphanelergm.gov.tr
Web Site: www.kultur.gov.tr
Key Personnel
Dir, Publications Dept: Ali Osman Guzel
Founded: 1973
Subjects: Archaeology, Art, Drama, Theater, History, Literature, Literary Criticism, Essays
ISBN Prefix(es): 975-17
Distributed by Dosimm

Varlik Yayinlari AS+
Cagaloglu, Yokusu 40/2, Istanbul
Tel: (0212) 5226924 *Fax:* (0212) 5162005
E-mail: varlik@varlik.com.tr; varlik@isbank.net.tr
Web Site: www.varlik.com.tr
Key Personnel
Publisher: Osman Deniztekin *Tel:* (0212) 5162004 ext 13 *E-mail:* osmand@netscape.net
Founded: 1946
Membership(s): Turkish Publishers Association.
Subjects: Fiction, Nonfiction (General), Poetry, Science (General), Self-Help, Social Sciences, Sociology, Women's Studies
ISBN Prefix(es): 975-434
Number of titles published annually: 20 Print
Total Titles: 200 Print
Imprints: CEP Kitaplari AS
Distributor for CEP Kitaplari AS

Yapi-Endustri Merkezi Yayinlari-Yem Yayin+
Cumhuriyet Cad 329, 80230 Harbiye/Istanbul
Tel: (0212) 2193939 *Fax:* (0212) 2256623
E-mail: yem-od@yunus.mam.tubitak.gov.tr; kitap@yem.net
Web Site: www.yem.net
Key Personnel
President: Dogan Hasol
Deputy General Manager: Bulent Kumral *E-mail:* bulent_kumral@yem.net
Founded: 1968
Membership(s): UICB. Also acts as bookshop & book importer.
Subjects: Architecture & Interior Design, Art, Civil Engineering
ISBN Prefix(es): 975-7438
Distributor for Melissa (Greece)

Kabalci Yayinevi
Prof Kazym Ysmail Gurkan Cad, Ortaklar Han No 12/3, Istanbul
Tel: (0212) 512 5602 *Fax:* (0212) 511 7794
E-mail: info@turkyaybir.com.tr
Web Site: www.turkyaybir.org.tr/kabalci.html

Key Personnel
Owner: Sabri Kabalci
Dir: Mustafa Kuepuesodlu
Founded: 1984
Subjects: Anthropology, Archaeology, Art, Drama, Theater, Fiction, History, Literature, Literary Criticism, Essays, Nonfiction (General), Philosophy, Poetry, Science (General), Social Sciences, Sociology, ABC series; contemporary French thought
ISBN Prefix(es): 975-7942
Bookshop(s): Ortabahce Cad 22/4, Besiktas-Istanbul

Alev Yayinlari+
Yenicarsi Cad 26/5, Galatasaray, Istanbul
Tel: (0212) 2921016 *Fax:* (0212) 2921017
Key Personnel
Contact: Alev Yayinlari
Founded: 1989
Specialize in Alevite-Islamic Culture & Philosophy.
Subjects: Ethnicity, Government, Political Science, Literature, Literary Criticism, Essays
ISBN Prefix(es): 975-335
Parent Company: Genel Ajans Ltd
Distributed by Baris; Papiruea; Say; Yoen
Distributor for CAN; Pencere
Book Club(s): Cumhuriyet Book Club

Yetkin Printing & Publishing Co Inc+
Strazburg Cad No 31/A, Sihhiye/Ankara
Tel: (0312) 4181273; (0312) 2314234
 Fax on Demand: (0312) 4174388
Key Personnel
President, Editor: Y Ziya Gwlkok
Founded: 1984
Subjects: Accounting, Computer Science, Law, Management
ISBN Prefix(es): 975-464
Divisions: Kazimkarahekir Cd (Printing)
Bookshop(s): Gulkok Bookstore, Kocabeyoglu Pst 74, Kizilay, Ankara

Yuce Reklam Yay Dagt AS+
PK 76, 34492 Beyazit, Istanbul
Tel: (01) 5227506 *Fax:* (01) 5163959
Telex: 22418 NEKTR
Key Personnel
Dir: Fahri Savasci; Ali Seven; Munip Oniz
Founded: 1982
Subjects: Computer Science, Electronics, Electrical Engineering, Medicine, Nursing, Dentistry
ISBN Prefix(es): 975-411
Subsidiaries: A F M Yayincilik-Tanitim
Warehouse: Dizdariye Cesme Sok 6 Emre Han, Kat: 1, Sultanahmet, 34400 Istanbul
Orders to: Yuce Yayin AS, PK 40 Beyazit, 34492 Istanbul

Turkmenistan

General Information

Capital: Ashkhabad
Language: Turkmen
Religion: Predominantly Sunni Muslim
Population: 3.8 million
Bank Hours: Generally open for short hours between 0930-1230 Monday-Friday
Shop Hours: Generally 0900-1800 Monday-Friday; often open weekends
Currency: 23 marats = 1 US dollar
Export/Import Information: Companies engaged in trade should register with the Turkmenistan Ministry of Foreign Affairs.

Izdatelstvo Turkmenistan
ul Atabaeva 20, 744000 Aschabad
Tel: (03632) 294275
Key Personnel
Dir: A M Dzhanmuradov
Chief Editor: A Allanazarov
Founded: 1965
Turkmenistan Publishing House.
Subjects: Agriculture, Fiction, Government, Political Science, Science (General), Social Sciences, Sociology
ISBN Prefix(es): 5-87228

Uganda

General Information

Capital: Kampala
Language: English is official language
Religion: Predominantly Christian (about 60%) and some Muslim
Population: 19.4 million
Bank Hours: 0830-1400 Monday-Friday
Shop Hours: 0830-1230, 1400-1630 or longer; 0800-1230 Saturday
Currency: 100 cents = 1 new Uganda shilling
Export/Import Information: No tariff on books or advertising matter but subject to sales tax. Import license and exchange controls (granted automatically with import licenses).

Centenary Publishing House Ltd+
PO Box 6246, Kampala
Tel: (041) 241599 *Fax:* (041) 250427
Key Personnel
Man Dir, Editorial, Production, Rights & Permissions: Rev Sam Kakiza
Sales, Publicity: V Kagga-Senyonga
Founded: 1977
Subjects: Education, Religion - Other
ISBN Prefix(es): 9970-9004
Parent Company: Church of Uganda, PO Box 14123, Kampala

Centre for Basic Research
Affiliate of Network of Ugandan Researchers & Research Users (NURRU)
15 Baskerville Ave, Kololo
Mailing Address: PO Box 9863, Kampala
Tel: (041) 231228; (041) 235533; (041) 342987 *Fax:* (041) 235413
E-mail: cbr@cbr-ug.org
Web Site: www.cbr-ug.org
Key Personnel
Executive Dir: Dr Bazaara Nyangabyaki
Senior Assistant Librarian: Judith Akello
Founded: 1988
New publications covering topics on Civil Society, Human Rights, Foreign Investment, Taxation Federalism in Uganda, Trade Unions & Gender. Formed a partnership with Action-Aid to undertake critical case studies on the Relevance, Access, Quality & Equity Dimensions of Universal Primary Education (UPE) in Uganda.
Membership(s): CODESRIA.
Subjects: Agriculture, Environmental Studies, Ethnicity, Geography, Geology, Government, Political Science, History, Labor, Industrial Relations, Law, Social Sciences, Sociology, Women's Studies, Social Sciences, Humanities
Total Titles: 121 Print

Fountain, *imprint of* Fountain Publishers Ltd

Fountain Publishers Ltd+
Fountain House, 55 Nkrumah Rd, Kampala

Mailing Address: PO Box 488, Kampala
Tel: (041) 259163; (041) 251112; (031) 263041; (031) 263042 *Fax:* (041) 251160
E-mail: fountain@starcom.co.ug
Web Site: www.fountainpublishers.co.ug
Key Personnel
Board Chairman & Man Dir: James Tumusiime
Business Manager: Moses Mugasa
Publishing Editor: Alex Bangirana
Marketing Manager: Paul Waddimba
Founded: 1988
Membership(s): Uganda Publishers & Booksellers Association (UPABA); African Publishers Network (APNET).
Subjects: Agriculture, Anthropology, Biography, Career Development, Cookery, Economics, Education, Fiction, Government, Political Science, Health, Nutrition, History, Humor, Language Arts, Linguistics, Mathematics, Nonfiction (General), Physical Sciences, Poetry, Psychology, Psychiatry, Science (General), Social Sciences, Sociology, Travel, Women's Studies
ISBN Prefix(es): 9970-02
Number of titles published annually: 30 Print
Total Titles: 400 Print
Imprints: Fountain
Distributed by African Books Collective (ABC) (Australia, Europe, UK & USA); James Currey Ltd (UK)
Distributor for James Currey Ltd (UK); Food Agricultural Organization (FAO) (Italy); Christopher Hurst (UK); Lion Publishers Plc (UK); Oxfam GB (UK); Princeton University Press; Scholastic Inc (USA); Zed Books Ltd (UK)
Foreign Rep(s): The African Books Collective (ABC) (Australia, Commonwealth, Europe, North America)
Foreign Rights: The African Books Collective (ABC) (Australia, Commonwealth, Europe, North America)
Bookshop(s): Bookpoint Ltd, PO Box 488, Kampala, Contact: Sara Namirembe *Tel:* (041) 346742 *Fax:* (041) 251160 *E-mail:* fountain@starcom.co.ut; University Bookshop Makerere, Contact: Catherine Tugaineyo *Tel:* (041) 543442

Roce (Consultants) Ltd
PO Box 1481, Kampala
Tel: (041) 106010 *Fax:* (041) 321062
Web Site: www.rutaagi.com
Key Personnel
Man Dir: Mr Robert K Rutaagi
Operations Dir: Celia K Rutaagi
Consulting Dir: Prof Ben Kiregyera
Founded: 1984
General Business, consultancy & publishing.
Membership(s): Uganda Publishers Booksellers Association Specialize in Poetry & Swahili.
Subjects: Management, Marketing, Poetry, Epigrams, Sayings, Swahili
ISBN Prefix(es): 9970-402
Number of titles published annually: 1 Print
Total Titles: 6 Print
Associate Companies: Roce Textiles & General Merchandise, Luwum St, Entebbe Airport, Kampala
Bookshop(s): Uganda Bookshop; Mukono Bookshop

T & E Publishers+
PO Box 5784, Kampala
Tel: (041) 542207 *Fax:* (041) 542207
Key Personnel
Chief Executive: Tobias Karindiriza
Subjects: Natural History
ISBN Prefix(es): 9970-9001

Ukraine

General Information
Capital: Kiev
Language: Ukrainian
Religion: Predominantly Christian (mostly Ukrainian Orthodox)
Population: 52 million
Bank Hours: Generally open for short hours between 0930-1230 Monday-Friday
Shop Hours: Generally 0900-1800 Monday-Friday; often open weekends
Currency: 100 kopeks = 1 rubl
Export/Import Information: According to Ukrainian quotas and customs duties, companies engaged in trade should register with the Ukraine Ministry of Foreign Economic Relations. 28% VAT on books. Licenses for export and import are also required for trade with Russia.
Copyright: UCC (see Copyright Conventions, pg xi)

ASK Ltd+
3 Nesterova St, 03057 Kyiv
Mailing Address: 2b Shamrylo-Str, PO Box 62, 04112 Kyiv
Tel: (044) 241-94-96; (044) 456-72-51 *Fax:* (044) 455-58-89
E-mail: ask.sale@i.com.ua
Key Personnel
Executive Dir: Lebedyev Oleg *E-mail:* ask.main@i.com.ua
Founded: 1991 (Founded by Lebedyev Oleg, Motzny Oleg, Sologub Igor, Sythevsky Oleg & Zyporucha Anatoliy)
Subjects: Accounting, Astrology, Occult, Biblical Studies, Business, Career Development, Child Care & Development, Computer Science, Cookery, Economics, English as a Second Language, Fiction, Gardening, Plants, Law, Marketing, Microcomputers, Nonfiction (General), Parapsychology, Science Fiction, Fantasy, Social Sciences, Sociology, Western Fiction
ISBN Prefix(es): 966-539
Number of titles published annually: 230 Print
Total Titles: 750 Print
Bookshop(s): 2 Sheljabov Str, 03057 Kyiv

Derzhavne Naukovo-Vyrobnyche Pidpryemstro Kartografia (State Scientific & Production Enterprise Kartographia)+
54 Popudrenka Str, Kyiv 02094
Tel: (044) 5524033 *Fax:* (044) 2388314
E-mail: admin@ukrmap.com.ua
Web Site: www.ukrmap.com.ua
Key Personnel
Dir: Rostyslav Sossa
Editor-in-Chief: Iryna Rudenko
Commercial Manager: Olexander Zacheshygryva
Founded: 1944
Development, production & realization of cartographic production.
Subjects: Geography, Geology
Parent Company: State Service of Geodesy, Cartography & Cadastre of Ukraine
Ultimate Parent Company: Ministry of Environment & Natural Resources of Ukraine
Distributed by Cartotravel (Germany); Kiwi Book Shop (Czech Republic); Omni Resources (US); Sklep Podroznika, InterMap (Poland)
Distributor for Freytag (Austria); GiziMap (Hungary); Hallwag (Switzerland); Ravenstein (Germany)

Dnipro
42 Volodymyrska St, 01034 Kyiv
Tel: (044) 224-31-82 *Fax:* (044) 224 41 57
Key Personnel
Dir: Mr Taras I Serhiychuk
Editor-in-Chief: S K Zholob
Founded: 1919
Subjects: Fiction, Literature, Literary Criticism, Essays, Folk-lore, modern Ukranian & foreign authors, world classics
ISBN Prefix(es): 5-308; 966-578

Kamenyar
3 Pidvalna St, 290000 Lviv
Tel: (0322) 72-19-49 *Fax:* (0322) 72-79-22
Key Personnel
Dir: Mr Dmytro I Sapiha
Brochures, "Dzvin" magazine, wholesale of printed materials.
ISBN Prefix(es): 5-7745; 966-7255

Lybid (University of Kyyiv Press)+
10 Khreshchatyk St, 252001 Kyiv
Tel: (044) 228-11-12; (044) 228-11-81 *Fax:* (044) 229-11-71
Telex: 131498 PTB SU
Key Personnel
Dir: Ms Olena O Boyko
Heritage of Ukranian people, national-cultural rebirth of independent Ukraine. Famous series: "Monuments of Historical Thought of Ukraine", "Literary Monuments of Ukraine".
Subjects: Education, Literature, Literary Criticism, Essays, Science (General)
ISBN Prefix(es): 5-325

Mystetstvo Publishers+
11 Zolotovoritska St, 252034 Kyiv
Tel: (044) 225-53-92; (044) 224-91-01 *Fax:* (044) 229-05-64
Key Personnel
Dir: Mrs Nina D Prybyeha
Founded: 1932
Subjects: Art, Drama, Theater, Ethnicity, Film, Video, History, Literature, Literary Criticism, Essays, Travel
ISBN Prefix(es): 5-7715; 966-577

Naukova Dumka Publishers
Division of National Acedemy of Sciences of Ukraine
Ul Tereshchenkivska 3, 01601 Kiev
Tel: (044) 2244068; (044) 2251042; (044) 2254170 *Fax:* (044) 2247060
E-mail: ndumka@ukrpost.net
Key Personnel
Dir & Editor-in-Chief: Alexeenko Igor
Founded: 1922
Subjects: Agriculture, Biological Sciences, Chemistry, Chemical Engineering, Computer Science, Earth Sciences, Economics, Environmental Studies, Geography, Geology, Health, Nutrition, History, Language Arts, Linguistics, Law, Literature, Literary Criticism, Essays, Mathematics, Mechanical Engineering, Medicine, Nursing, Dentistry, Natural History, Philosophy, Photography, Physical Sciences, Psychology, Psychiatry
ISBN Prefix(es): 966-00
Number of titles published annually: 60 Print
Total Titles: 12 Print
Distributed by ASK; Oberegi Publishers; Osnova

Osnova, Kharkov State University Press+
Ul Universitetskaya 16, 310003 Harkiv
Tel: (057) 224647
Key Personnel
Man Dir: Nikolay N Sorokun *Tel:* (057) 219268
Dir: Valery K Gorbat'ko
Founded: 1949
Subjects: Aeronautics, Aviation, Agriculture, Archaeology, Architecture & Interior Design, Biological Sciences, Business, Chemistry, Chemical Engineering
ISBN Prefix(es): 5-7768

UKRAINE

Osnovy Publishers+
5/18 Lykhachov Blv, 252133 Kyiv
Tel: (044) 295 25 82; (044) 295 86 36 *Fax:* (044) 295 25 82
Key Personnel
Dir: Ms Valentyna Kyrylova
Rights Contact: Victor Ruzhitsky
Founded: 1993
Subjects: Business, Economics, Finance, Government, Political Science, History, Law, Management, Philosophy, Poetry, Public Administration, Social Sciences, Sociology, Women's Studies
ISBN Prefix(es): 966-500
Total Titles: 150 Print

Osvita (Education)
Prosp Chornovola 4, 1st floor, 79019 Lviv
Mailing Address: PO Box 1596, Lviv 79019
Tel: (032) 297 1206 *Fax:* (032) 297 1794
E-mail: info@osvita.org
Web Site: www.osvita.org
Key Personnel
Center Dir: Andriy Hatalyak
Center Advisor: Angelina Belyakova
Founded: 1993
Membership(s): Pan Educational Publishers Club (PEP-Club).
Subjects: Biological Sciences, Chemistry, Chemical Engineering, Child Care & Development, Education, English as a Second Language, History, Literature, Literary Criticism, Essays, Mathematics, Music, Dance, Physical Sciences, Physics, German, French
ISBN Prefix(es): 966-04
Number of titles published annually: 108 Print
Total Titles: 500,000 Print

Urozaj
vul Uryc Kogo 45, 03035 Kiev 35
Tel: (044) 2440517
Key Personnel
Dir: Vasily G Prikhodko
Subjects: Agriculture, Environmental Studies, Gardening, Plants, House & Home, Technology, Veterinary Science
ISBN Prefix(es): 5-337

Veselka Publishers+
63 Melnykova St, 04655 Kyiv 55
Tel: (044) 213-95-01 *Fax:* (044) 213-33-59
E-mail: veskiev@iptelecom.net.ua
Key Personnel
Dir: Mr Yarema P Hoyan
Founded: 1934
Subjects: Fiction, Literature, Literary Criticism, Essays
ISBN Prefix(es): 5-301
Bookshop(s): Munich; Frankfurt am Main; Toronto; Prague; Chicago

United Arab Emirates

General Information

Capital: Abu Dhabi
Language: Arabic and English
Religion: Islamic
Population: 2.23 million
Bank Hours: 0800-1200 Saturday-Thursday (1100 Thursday in Abu Dhabi)
Shop Hours: Abu Dhabi: Summer: 0800-1300, 1600-dusk Saturday-Thursday; Winter: 0800-1300, 1530-1900 Saturday-Thursday. Northern Emirates: Summer: 0900-1300, 1630-2000 or 2100 Saturday-Thursday: Winter: 0900-1300, 1600-2000 or 2100 Saturday-Thursday
Currency: 100 fils = 1 UAE dirham
Export/Import Information: No tariff on books or advertising matter, except duty on imports in Dubai and ad valorem rates in Ras al Khaimah anf Sharjah. No import licenses requires except for obscene publications in Dubai.

Arabian Heritage Books, *imprint of* Motivate Publishing

Department of Culture & Information Government of Sharjah
Cultural Book Round About, Air Port Rd, Sharjah
Mailing Address: PO Box 5119, Sharjah
Tel: (06) 5671116; (06) 5673139 *Fax:* (06) 5662126; (06) 5660535
E-mail: shjbookfair@hotmail.com; cultural@emirates.net.ae
Web Site: shjbookfair.gov.ae
Telex: 68508 TOURSH *Cable:* THAQAFA
Key Personnel
Head: Mr Issam Bin Saqr Al Qassimi
Founded: 1982
Subjects: Poetry, Regional Interests

Gulf Business Books, *imprint of* Motivate Publishing

Motivate Publishing+
PO Box 2331, Dubai
Tel: (04) 282 4060 *Fax:* (04) 282 4436
E-mail: motivate@emirates.net.ae
Web Site: www.booksarabia.com
Key Personnel
Man Partner: Ian Fairservice
Founded: 1981
Subjects: Biography, Business, Cookery, Foreign Countries, History, Natural History, Travel
ISBN Prefix(es): 1-873544; 1-86063
Imprints: Arabian Heritage Books; Gulf Business Books
Subsidiaries: Stewart's Court
Orders to: Book Representation & Distribution Ltd, 244A London Rd, Hadleigh, Essex S57 2DE, United Kingdom *Tel:* (020) 7552912 *Fax:* (020) 7556095

United Kingdom

General Information

Capital: London
Language: English; Welsh in most of Wales (where it is used alongside English for official purposes). About 80,000 speak Scots Gaelic (in Highlands and Islands of Scotland). Irish is used in parts of Northern Ireland
Religion: Protestant (The Church of England) officially, Roman Catholic, Methodist, United Reformed and Baptist have significant numbers of adherents
Population: 57.8 million
Bank Hours: 0900-1730 Monday-Friday
Shop Hours: 0900-1730 Monday-Saturday
Currency: 100 pence = 1 pound sterling
Export/Import Information: Member of the European Union. No tariffs on books; advertising matter dutiable over a certain weight. No import licenses required; nominal exchange controls. Advertising in the UK is regulated by statutes and voluntary codes; for information contact The Advertising Standards Authority Ltd, Torrington Place, London, WC1E 7HW.
Copyright: UCC, Berne, Florence (see Copyright Conventions, pg xi)

A A Publishing+
Fanum House, 4th floor, Basingstoke, Hants RG21 2EA
Tel: (01256) 491522 *Fax:* (01256) 322575
E-mail: aapublish@theaa.com
Web Site: www.theaa.com; www.aanewsroom.com
Telex: 858538 AA BASG
Key Personnel
Editorial Dir: Michael Buttler *Tel:* (01250) 491573 *E-mail:* michael.buttler@theaa.com
Man Dir: John Howard
Sales & Marketing Manager: Graham Sowerby
Founded: 1908
Subjects: Travel
ISBN Prefix(es): 0-86145; 0-7495; 0-901088
Total Titles: 530 Print
Parent Company: AA
Warehouse: T B S Ltd, Brantham, Near Manningtree, Essex CO11 1NW, Mr Colchester *Tel:* (01206) 255804 *Fax:* (01206) 255848

A & C, *imprint of* Helm Information Ltd

A-Mail Academic
City Bridge House, 57 Southwark St, London SE1 1RU
Tel: (020) 7871 9139 *Fax:* (020) 7871 9140
E-mail: a-mail@djlb.co.uk
Web Site: www.a-mail.co.uk
Key Personnel
Division Manager: Duncan Copplestone *E-mail:* dcopplestone@djlb.co.uk
Business Development Executive: Vivienne Medway *E-mail:* vmedway@djlb.co.uk
Sales Account Executive: Ian Wordsworth *E-mail:* iwordsworth@djlb.co.uk
Sales Administrator: James Murtagh *E-mail:* jmurtagh@djlb.co.uk
Supplier of targeted worldwide academic & library mailing lists & data.
Parent Company: Dudley Jenkins Group plc ("Your partners in academic marketing")

Abacus, *imprint of* Time Warner Book Group UK

Abbotsford Publishing+
2A Brownsfield Rd, Lichfield WS13 6BT
Tel: (01543) 255749; (01543) 258903
Web Site: www.abbotsfordpublishing.com
Key Personnel
Partner: Kathy Simmons *E-mail:* ka.simmons@btopenworld.com; Howard Clayton
Founded: 1992
Membership(s): Independent Publishers Guild.
Subjects: History, Maritime, Natural History, Poetry, Regional Interests, Travel, Local History, Mind/Body/Spirit
ISBN Prefix(es): 1-899596; 0-9503563
Number of titles published annually: 3 Print; 3 Online
Total Titles: 12 Print; 12 Online

ABC-CLIO+
35A Great Clarendon St, Oxford OX2 6AT
Tel: (01865) 311350 *Fax:* (01865) 311358
E-mail: oxford@abc-clio.ltd.uk
Web Site: www.abc-clio.com
Key Personnel
Editorial: Simon Mason; Robert G Neville *E-mail:* bneville@abc-clio.ltd.uk
Marketing Manager: Suzanne Wheatley *E-mail:* swheatley@abc-clio.ltd.uk
Sales: Deborah Porter *E-mail:* dporter@abc-clio.ltd.uk
Founded: 1971

Specialize in abstracting services & bibliographies in print & electronic formats.
Subjects: Anthropology, Foreign Countries, History, Literature, Literary Criticism, Essays, Sports, Athletics
ISBN Prefix(es): 0-87436; 1-57607; 0-903450; 1-85109
Number of titles published annually: 18 Print; 10 CD-ROM; 1 E-Book
Total Titles: 350 Print; 30 CD-ROM; 3 E-Book
Parent Company: ABC-CLIO, 130 Cremona Dr, PO Box 1911, Santa Barbara, CA 93117, United States
Foreign Rep(s): DA Information Services Pty Ltd (India, South Africa); Disvan Enterprises (India); Andrew Durnell (Austria, Belgium, Croatia, Cyprus, Czech Republic, Denmark, Netherlands, Estonia, Finland, France, Germany, Greece, Hungary, Iceland, Italy, Latvia, Lithuania, Luxembourg, Malta, Monaco, Norway, Poland, Russia, Serbia and Montenegro, Slovak Republic, Slovenia, Sweden, Switzerland, Bosnia and Herzegovina); Iberian Book Services (Gibraltar, Portugal, Spain); Phambili Agencies CC (South Africa); Publishers Marketing Services Ltd (Brunei, Malaysia, Singapore); Publishers International Marketing (Asia, Middle East); I J Sagun Enterprises, Inc (Guam, Micronesia, Philippines); United Publishers Services Ltd (Japan)
Warehouse: Plymbridge Distributors Ltd, Estover Rd, Plymouth PL6 7PZ
Orders to: Plymbridge Distributors Ltd, Estover Rd, Plymouth PL6 7PZ *Tel:* (01752) 202301 *Fax:* (01752) 202333 *E-mail:* orders@plymbridge.com

ABG Professional Information
ABG Publications, c/o Croner CCH Group Ltd, 145 London Rd, Kingston upon Thames KT2 6SU
Tel: 08707 772906 *Fax:* 08702 404388
E-mail: info@abgpublications.co.uk
Web Site: www.abgpublications.co.uk
Key Personnel
Publications Dir: Sally Johnson
Subjects: Accounting, Business, Finance, Management
ISBN Prefix(es): 1-85355; 0-85291
Parent Company: Institute of Chartered Accountants (England & Wales)/Accountancy Business Group
Bookshop(s): Blackwells' as the Institute, Moorgate Place, Copthall Ave, London EC2R 7DJ
Warehouse: 21 Erica Rd, Stacey Bushes, Milton Keynes
Orders to: Accountancy Books of ICAEW, PO Box 620, Central Milton Keynes MK9 2JX

Abington Publishing, *imprint of* Woodhead Publishing Ltd

Absolute Press+
Scarborough House, 29 James St W, Bath BA1 2BT
Tel: (01225) 316 013 *Fax:* (01225) 445 836
E-mail: info@absolutepress.co.uk
Web Site: www.absolutepress.co.uk
Key Personnel
Man Dir, Publisher & International Rights: Jon Croft
Publicity: B Douglas
Founded: 1979
Also acts as agent in UK & Europe for Smith and Kraus & Streetwise Maps.
Subjects: Biography, Cookery, Gay & Lesbian, Travel, Wine & Spirits
ISBN Prefix(es): 0-948230; 0-9506785; 1-899791
Foreign Rep(s): Troika (UK)
Distribution Center: BHB International Inc, 302 West North Second St, Seneca, SC 29678, United States *Tel:* (864) 885-9444 *Fax:* (864) 885-1090 *E-mail:* bhbrackett@bellsouth.net
Web Site: www.bhbinternational.com (USA)
Central Books, 99 Wallis Rd, London E9 5LN *Tel:* (020) 8986 4854 *Fax:* (020) 8533 5821
E-mail: info@centralbooks.com
Peribo Pty Ltd, 58 Beaumont Rd, Mt Kuring-Gai, NSW 2080, Australia *Tel:* (02) 9457 0011 *Fax:* (02) 9457 0022 *E-mail:* peribomec@bigpond.com (Australia & New Zealand)

Academic Press, *imprint of* Elsevier Ltd

Acair Ltd+
7 James St, Stornoway, Isle of Lewis HS1 2QN
Tel: (01851) 703 020 *Fax:* (07880) 725 320
E-mail: enquiries@acairbooks.com
Web Site: www.acairbooks.com
Key Personnel
Chairman: Angus MacDonald
Founded: 1978
Publish a wide range of Gaelic, English & Bilingual books.
Subjects: Biography, Environmental Studies, Fiction, History, Poetry
ISBN Prefix(es): 0-86152

Access Press, *imprint of* HarperCollins UK

Ace Books, see Age Concern Books

Acorn Editions, *imprint of* James Clarke & Co Ltd

Acorn Editions, *imprint of* The Lutterworth Press

Act 3 Publishing+
67 Upper Berkeley St, London W1H 7QX
Tel: (020) 7402 5321
Key Personnel
Contact: R Keith Brian
Founded: 1985
Membership(s): Independent Publishers Guild.
Subjects: Alternative, Child Care & Development, Fiction, Film, Video, Human Relations, Humor, Nonfiction (General), Poetry, Psychology, Psychiatry, Self-Help
ISBN Prefix(es): 0-948068
Number of titles published annually: 1 Print
Total Titles: 1 Print

Actinic Press, *imprint of* Cressrelles Publishing Company Ltd

Actinic Press Ltd+
Imprint of Cressrelles Publishing Company Ltd
10 Station Rd, Industrial Estate, Colwall, Malvern WR13 6RN
Tel: (01684) 540154 *Fax:* (01684) 540154
Key Personnel
Man Dir: Leslie Smith
Founded: 1926
Specialize in Chiropody.
ISBN Prefix(es): 0-900024
Total Titles: 1 Print
Parent Company: Cressrelles Publishing Co Ltd

ACU, see Association of Commonwealth Universities (ACU)

Acumen Publishing Ltd+
15A Lewins Yard, East St, Chesham, Bucks HP5 1HQ
Tel: (01494) 794398 *Fax:* (01494) 784850
Web Site: www.acumenpublishing.co.uk
Key Personnel
Publisher: Steven Gerrard *E-mail:* steven.gerrard@acumenpublishing.co.uk
Founded: 1998
Independent publisher of academic books in philosophy, history & politics for students, lecturers & researchers in institutions of higher education worldwide.
Subjects: History, Philosophy
ISBN Prefix(es): 1-902683; 1-84465
Number of titles published annually: 15 Print
Total Titles: 60 Print
Shipping Address: Marston Book Services, 160 Milton Park, Abingdon, Oxon OX14 4YN
Warehouse: Marston Book Services, 160 Milton Park, Abingdon, Oxon OX14 4YN
Distribution Center: Marston Book Services, 160 Milton Park, Abingdon, Oxon OX14 4YN
Orders to: Marston Book Services, 160 Milton Park, Abingdon, Oxon OX14 4YN
Returns: Marston Book Services, 160 Milton Park, Abingdon, Oxon OX14 4YN

Adamantine Press Ltd+
Richmond Bridge House, 417-421 Richmond Rd, Twickenham TW1 2EX
Key Personnel
Dir: Jeremy Geelan
Founded: 1976
Subjects: Business, Communications
ISBN Prefix(es): 0-7449
Warehouse: Central Books Ltd, 99 Wallis Rd, London E9 5LN
Orders to: Central Books Ltd, 99 Wallis Rd, London E9 5LN

Addison-Wesley, *imprint of* Pearson Education Europe, Mideast & Africa

Adelphi Papers, *imprint of* International Institute for Strategic Studies

Adlard Coles Nautical+
Imprint of A & C Black Publishers Ltd
37 Soho Sq, London W1D 3QZ
Tel: (020) 7758 0200 *Fax:* (020) 7758 0222
E-mail: acn@acblack.com
Web Site: www.adlardcoles.com
Key Personnel
Dir: Janet Murphy
Rights Dir: Paul Langridge
Founded: 1947
Specialize in nautical books for the leisure market.
Subjects: Outdoor Recreation, Sports, Athletics
ISBN Prefix(es): 0-7136
Number of titles published annually: 40 Print
Total Titles: 320 Print; 1 CD-ROM
Associate Companies: Thomas Reed Publications
Distributor for Sheridan House
Warehouse: Macmillan Distribution Ltd, Howard Rd, Eaton Socon, Huntingdon, Cambs PE19 8EZ *Tel:* (01480) 223131

Adlib, *imprint of* Scholastic Ltd

Adobe Press, *imprint of* Pearson Education Europe, Mideast & Africa

Advisory Unit: Computers in Education+
126 Great North Rd, Hatfield, Herts AL9 5JZ
Tel: (01707) 266714 *Fax:* (01707) 273684
E-mail: sales@advisory-unit.org.uk
Web Site: www.advisory-unit.org.uk
Key Personnel
Export Sales Dir: M Aston *E-mail:* mike@kcited.demon.co.uk
Founded: 1991
Specialize in Educational Software.
Membership(s): ESPA, BESA & NAACE.
Subjects: Computer Science, Disability, Special Needs, Economics, Geography, Geology, Mathematics, Microcomputers, Technology
ISBN Prefix(es): 1-874164
Number of titles published annually: 4 Print
Total Titles: 20 Print; 8 CD-ROM; 1 E-Book

Distributed by Orfeus (Denmark & Scandinavia)
Distributor for Harvard Associates (North America)

A4 Publications Ltd
Hagley Chambers, Thornleigh, 35 Hagley Rd, Stourbridge DY8 1QR
Tel: (01384) 440591 *Fax:* (01384) 440582
Key Personnel
Publisher & Dir: Francesca Ash
  Tel: (01892) 783535 *Fax:* (01892) 783848
  E-mail: francesca.ash@a4publications.com
Advertising Sales: Julie Cruikshanks
  E-mail: nought2twelve@a4publications.com;
  Jerry Wooldridge *E-mail:* jerrywooldridge@a4publications.com
Founded: 1981
Membership(s): LIMA.
ISBN Prefix(es): 0-510; 0-946197; 0-9502363

Age Concern Books+
Astral House, 1268 London Rd, London SW16 4ER
Tel: (020) 8765 7200 *Fax:* (020) 8765 7211
E-mail: infodep@ace.org.uk
Web Site: www.ageconcern.org.uk
Key Personnel
Marketing Manager: Michael Addison
Publisher: Richard Holloway
Founded: 1971
Specialize in practical handbooks for older people & their careers & professionals working with older people; training packs for professional careers.
Subjects: Finance, Health, Nutrition
ISBN Prefix(es): 0-86242
Total Titles: 70 Print
Parent Company: Age Concern England
Orders to: Biblios Publishers Distribution Service Ltd, Star Rd, Partridge Green, West Sussex RH13 8LD

Ai Interactive Ltd
Larkhill House, Cemetery Rd, Abingdon, Oxon OX14 1AS
Tel: (01235) 529595 *Fax:* (01235) 520205
E-mail: medical@andromeda-interactive.co.uk
Web Site: www.andromeda-interactive.co.uk
Key Personnel
Editorial, Marketing: John Bradley *E-mail:* john@andromeda-interactive.co.uk
Rights, Finance: Mark Ritchie *E-mail:* mark@andromeda-interactive.co.uk
Sales: Clive Helmington *E-mail:* clive@andromeda-interactive.co.uk
Subjects: Medicine, Nursing, Dentistry, Graphic design
ISBN Prefix(es): 1-898137
Distribution Center: JA Majors, Texas

Airlife Publishing Ltd+
101 Longden Rd, Shrewsbury, Salop SY3 9EB
Tel: (01743) 235651 *Fax:* (01743) 232944
E-mail: info@airlifebooks.com
Web Site: www.airlifebooks.com
Key Personnel
Rights & Permissions: Anne Walker
  E-mail: anne@airlifebooks.com
Founded: 1976
Subjects: Aeronautics, Aviation, Military Science, Transportation
ISBN Prefix(es): 0-9504543; 0-906393; 1-85310; 1-84037
Number of titles published annually: 100 Print
Total Titles: 600 Print

AJ Press, *imprint of* Books International

AK Press & Distribution+
PO Box 12766, Edinburgh EH8 9YE
Tel: (0131) 5555165 *Fax:* (0131) 5555215
E-mail: help@akuk.com
Web Site: www.akuk.com
Founded: 1991
Mail order catalog available.
Subjects: Fiction, Philosophy, Poetry, Social Sciences, Sociology
ISBN Prefix(es): 1-873176; 1-902593
U.S. Office(s): 674-A 23rd St, Oakland, CA 94612, United States *Tel:* 510-208-1700 *Fax:* 510-208-1701
Distributed by Bookspeed (UK); Counter Productions (UK); Turnaround (UK)

Al-Shirkatul Islamiyyah, *imprint of* Islam International Publications Ltd

Aladdin Books Ltd+
28 Percy St, London W1P 0LD
Tel: (020) 7323 3319 *Fax:* (020) 7323 4829
E-mail: kerry.mciver@aladdinbooks.co.uk
Web Site: www.aladdinbooks.co.uk
Key Personnel
Dir: C V Nicholas; E P Whittaker
Founded: 1980
Subjects: Nonfiction (General)

Albyn Press
2 Caversham St, Chelsea, London SW3 4AH
Tel: (020) 7351 4995 *Fax:* (020) 7351 4995

Aldwych Press Ltd+
3 Henrietta St, Covent Garden, London WC2E 8LU
Tel: (020) 7240 0856 *Fax:* (020) 7379 0609
E-mail: info@eurospan.co.uk
Web Site: www.eurospan.co.uk
Key Personnel
Man Dir: Michael Geelan
Dir: Danny Maher
Marketing: Imogen Adams
Founded: 1979
Subjects: Economics, Government, Political Science, Law, Library & Information Sciences, Military Science, Philosophy, Social Sciences, Sociology
ISBN Prefix(es): 0-86172

Ian Allan Publishing Ltd+
Riverdene Business Park, Molesey Rd, Hersham, Surrey KT12 4RG
Tel: (01932) 266600 *Fax:* (01932) 266601
E-mail: info@ianallanpub.co.uk
Web Site: www.ianallan.com
Key Personnel
Chairman: David Allan
Man Dir: Tony Saunders
Dir Publishing: Bill Lucas
Production Director: Nicholas Lerwill
Retail Sales Manager: Wendy Myers
Publishing Manager: Peter Waller
Sales & Marketing Manager: Nigel Passmore
Founded: 1945
Subjects: Aeronautics, Aviation, Architecture & Interior Design, Automotive, Cookery, Gardening, Plants, Maritime, Photography, Transportation
ISBN Prefix(es): 0-7110
Parent Company: Ian Allan Group
Associate Companies: Ian Allan Motors; Ian Allan Travel; Chase Organics
Imprints: Dial House
Distributor for Mill Stream; Runpast; World of Transport; Yore Publications
Foreign Rep(s): Bill Bailey Publishers' Representatives (Austria, Belgium, Bulgaria, Croatia, Cyprus, Czech Republic, Netherlands, Estonia, France, Germany, Gibraltar, Greece, Hungary, Italy, Latvia, Liechtenstein, Lithuania, Luxembourg, Malta, Monaco, Poland, Portugal, Romania, Slovenia, Spain, Serbia and Montenegro); D Richard Bowen (Scandinavia); Combined Books (USA); DLS Australia Pty Ltd (Australia & New Zealand, Papua New Guinea); Electra Media Group Pty Ltd (Brunei, China, Hong Kong, Japan, Korea, Malaysia, Philippines, Singapore, Taiwan, Thailand, Eastern Asia); PIM (India, Middle East, Pakistan); Vanwell Publishing Ltd (Canada)
Bookshop(s): 47 Stephenson St, Birmingham *Tel:* (0121) 643 2496 *Fax:* (0121) 643 6855; Main Terminal Bldg, 3rd Floor, Birmingham International Airport, Birmingham B26 3QJ *Tel:* (0121) 781 0921 *Fax:* (0121) 781 0928; 45-46 Lower Marsh, London SE1 7SG *Tel:* (0207) 401 2100 *Fax:* (0207) 401 2887; Unit 5, Piccadilly Station Approach, Manchester M1 2GH *Tel:* (0161) 237 9840 *Fax:* (0161) 237 9921
Warehouse: Littlehampton Book Services Ltd, Faraday Close, Durrington, Worthing, West Sussex BN13 3RB *Tel:* (01903) 828800 *Fax:* (01903) 721596

Umberto Allemandi & Co Publishing+
70 S Lambeth Rd, London SW8 1RL
Tel: (020) 7735 3331 *Fax:* (020) 7735 3332
E-mail: contact@theartnewspaper.com
Web Site: www.theartnewspaper.com
Key Personnel
Editor-in-Chief: Cristina Ruiz *E-mail:* c.ruiz@theartnewspaper.com
Founded: 1982
Books on general culture; three newspapers.
Subjects: Architecture & Interior Design, Art, Gardening, Plants
ISBN Prefix(es): 88-422
Total Titles: 150 Print
Branch Office(s)
Via Mancini 8, Torino 10131, Italy, Contact: Nicole Kerr-Munslow *Tel:* (011) 8199111 *Fax:* (011) 8193090 *E-mail:* nicole.kerr.munslow@allemandi.com
Distributed by Antique Collectors Club (UK, USA & Australia only)

J A Allen, *imprint of* Robert Hale Ltd

Allen Lane, *imprint of* The Penguin Group UK

Allen Lane, *imprint of* Viking

Allied Mouse Ltd+
Mayfield, High St, Dingwall, Ross-shire IV15 9SS
Tel: (01349) 865400 *Fax:* (01349) 866066
E-mail: info@heartstone.co.uk
Web Site: www.heartstone.co.uk
Key Personnel
Dir: Sita Sidle; Nick Sidle
Founded: 1988
Subjects: Fiction
ISBN Prefix(es): 0-9513492
Membership(s): Publishers' Association

Allison & Busby+
Subsidiary of Editorial Prensa Iberica
Suite 111, Bon Marche Centre, 241-251 Ferndale Rd, London SW9 8BJ
Tel: (020) 7738 7888 *Fax:* (020) 7733 4244
E-mail: all@allisonbusby.co.uk
Web Site: www.allisonandbusby.com
Key Personnel
Publishing Dir: David Shelley *E-mail:* davids@allisonbusby.co.uk
Marketing: Fiona Hague
Editor: Debbie Hatfield
Founded: 1966
Subjects: Biography, Contemporary & Literary Fiction, Crime Fiction, Writers' Guides
ISBN Prefix(es): 0-7490 (Allison & Busby)
Number of titles published annually: 40 Print
Total Titles: 240 Print

PUBLISHERS — UNITED KINGDOM

Shipping Address: Turnaround Publisher Services, Olympia Trading Estate, Unit 3, Coburg Rd, London N22 6T2, Contact: Bill Godber *Tel:* (020) 8829 3000 *Fax:* (020) 8881 5088 *E-mail:* orders@turnaround-uk.com

Allyn & Bacon, *imprint of* Pearson Education Europe, Mideast & Africa

Almond Press, *imprint of* Sheffield Academic Press Ltd

Altamira Press, *imprint of* SAGE Publications Ltd

Alun Books
Imprint of Goldleaf Publishing
3 Crown St, Port Talbot, W Glam, Wales SA13 1BG
Tel: (01639) 886186
E-mail: enquiries@alunbooks.co.uk
Web Site: www.alunbooks.co.uk
Key Personnel
Editor: Sally Jones
Founded: 1977
Publish books about Wales &/or by Welsh authors.
Subjects: Biography, Fiction, History, Poetry, Travel
ISBN Prefix(es): 0-907117; 0-9505643
Total Titles: 56 Print
Imprints: Barn Owl Press (Children's Books); Goldleaf Publishing (Local History)
Distributor for Port Talbot Historical Society

Amadeus Press, *imprint of* Timber Press Inc

Amber Books Ltd+
Bradley's Close, 74-77 White Lion St, London N1 9PF
Tel: (020) 7520 7600 *Fax:* (020) 7520 7606; (020) 7520 7607
E-mail: enquiries@amberbooks.co.uk
Web Site: www.amberbooks.co.uk
Key Personnel
Rights & Operations Dir: Sara Ballard
Man Dir: Stasz Gynch
Founded: 1989
Subjects: Aeronautics, Aviation, Automotive, Crafts, Games, Hobbies, Criminology, How-to, Maritime, Military Science, Nonfiction (General), Parapsychology, Sports, Athletics, Transportation
ISBN Prefix(es): 1-897884
Total Titles: 120 Print
Parent Company: Brown Packaging Books Ltd

Amber Lane Press Ltd+
Cheorl House, Church St, Charlbury OX7 3PR
Tel: (01608) 810024 *Fax:* (01608) 810024
E-mail: info@amberlanepress.co.uk
Web Site: www.amberlanepress.co.uk
Key Personnel
Man Dir: Judith Scott
Founded: 1978
Subjects: Biography, Drama, Theater, Music, Dance
ISBN Prefix(es): 0-906399; 1-872868
Number of titles published annually: 3 Print
Total Titles: 100 Print

Amber Waves, *imprint of* Heartland Publishing Ltd

Amberwood Publishing Ltd+
Unit 4, Alpha House, Laser Quay, Culpeper Close, Medway City Estate, Rochester, Kent ME2 4HH
Tel: (01634) 290115 *Fax:* (01634) 290761
E-mail: books@amberwoodpublishing.com
Web Site: www.amberwoodpublishing.com
Key Personnel
Chairman: Henry Crisp *Fax:* (01483) 457101
Chief Executive: Victor Perfitt
Man Dir: June Crisp *Tel:* (01634) 290115 *Fax:* (01634) 290761
Sales: Bob Couchman *Tel:* (01634) 290115
Founded: 1991
Specialize in Natural/Health Publications, herbs, vitamins & minerals & self medication.
Subjects: Health, Nutrition, Aromatherapy, Herbal Medicine
ISBN Prefix(es): 1-899308; 0-9517723
Number of titles published annually: 3 Print
Total Titles: 32 Print

American Technical Publishers
27/29 Knowl Piece, Wilbury Way, Hitchin, Herts SG4 0SX
Tel: (01462) 437933 *Fax:* (01462) 433678
E-mail: atp@ameritech.co.uk
Web Site: www.ameritech.co.uk
Distributor for American Ceramic Society; American Concrete Institute; American Society for Civil Engineers; American Society for Mechanical Engineers; American Society for Testing & Materials; American Water Works Association; William Andrew; Asian Productivity Organisation; ASM International; Casti Publishing Inc; ICBO; Instrument Society of America; National Association of Corrosion Engineers; Noble Publishing Corporation; Pegasus Communications; Productivity Press; Quality Resources; Research Signpost/Transworld Research; Research Studies Press; Society for Mining, Metallurgy & Exploration; Society of Automotive Engineers; Society of Manufacturing Engineers; Synapse Information Resources Inc; Technical Association of the Pulp & Paper Industry; Water Environment Federation

Amistad, *imprint of* HarperCollins UK

Amnesty International Publications
99-119 Rosebery Ave, London EC1R 4RE
Tel: (020) 7814 6200 *Fax:* (020) 7833 1510
E-mail: information@amnesty.org.uk
Web Site: www.amnesty.org.uk *Cable:* AMNESTY LONDON WC1
Key Personnel
Marketing: Guy Montgomery
Founded: 1961
Subjects: Human Rights
ISBN Prefix(es): 0-86210; 0-900058
Branch Office(s)
80A Stranmillis Rd, Belfast BT9 5AD
Tel: (02890) 666 216/666 001 *Fax:* (02890) 666 164 *E-mail:* enquiriesni@amnesty.org.uk
6 Castle St, Edinburgh EH2 3AT *Tel:* (0131) 466 6200 *Fax:* (0131) 466 6201 *E-mail:* rburnett@edinburgh.amnesty.org.uk
Orders to: PO Box 4, Rugby, Warwickshire CV21 1RU *Tel:* (01788) 545553 *Fax:* (01788) 579244

Amsco Publications, *imprint of* Omnibus Press

Anchor, *imprint of* Transworld Publishers Ltd

Andersen Artists Greeting Cards, *imprint of* Andersen Press Ltd

Andersen Giants, *imprint of* Andersen Press Ltd

Andersen Paperback Picture Books, *imprint of* Andersen Press Ltd

Andersen Press Ltd+
Affiliate of Random House
20 Vauxhall Bridge Rd, London SW1V 2SA
Tel: (020) 7840 8701 *Fax:* (020) 7233 6263
E-mail: andersenpress@randomhouse.co.uk
Web Site: www.andersenpress.co.uk
Key Personnel
Publisher & Man Dir: Klaus Flugge *Tel:* (020) 7840 8702 *E-mail:* kflugge@randomhouse.co.uk
International Rights: Sarah Pakenham *Tel:* (020) 7840 8704 *E-mail:* spakenham@randomhouse.co.uk
Publicity Manager: Rebecca Garrill *Tel:* (020) 7840 8704 *E-mail:* rgarrill@randomhouse.co.uk
Founded: 1976
Subjects: Fiction
ISBN Prefix(es): 0-86264; 0-905478
Total Titles: 396 Print
Associate Companies: Random House
Imprints: Andersen Artists Greeting Cards; Andersen Giants; Andersen Young Readers Library; Tigers; Andersen Paperback Picture Books; Andersen Press Board Books
Distributed by General Publishing (Canada); Random House (Australia); Random House (South Africa); Random House (New Zealand)
Foreign Rep(s): General Publishing (Canada); Akiko Iwamoto (Japan); Random House (Guam, Indonesia, Malaysia, Philippines, Singapore, Thailand); Random House Australia Pty Ltd (Australia); Random House (NZ) Ltd (New Zealand); Random House of Canada Ltd (Hong Kong, South Korea, Taiwan); Random House of South Africa Pty Ltd (South Africa); Wei Zhao (China)
Warehouse: The Book Service Ltd, Colchester Rd, Frating Green, Colchester, Essex CO7 7DW *Tel:* (01206) 255678 *Fax:* (01206) 255930
Orders to: The Book Service Ltd, Colchester Rd, Frating Green, Colchester, Essex CO7 7DW *Tel:* (01206) 255678 *Fax:* (01206) 255930

Andersen Press Board Books, *imprint of* Andersen Press Ltd

Andersen Young Readers Library, *imprint of* Andersen Press Ltd

Anderson Rand Ltd
The Scotts Bindery, Russell Court, Cambridge CB2 1HL
Tel: (01223) 566640 *Fax:* (01223) 316144; (01223) 566643
E-mail: info@andrand.com
Web Site: www.andrand.com
Key Personnel
Man Dir: Dr R O Anderson *E-mail:* anderson.rand@usa.net
Founded: 1989
Comprehensive data on European book related organizations, mainly publishers, libraries & book sellers.
Subjects: Library & Information Sciences, Publishing & Book Trade Reference
ISBN Prefix(es): 1-873539
Total Titles: 4 Print; 4 CD-ROM

Andre Deutsch, *imprint of* Carlton Publishing Group

Chris Andrews Publications
15 Curtis Yard, North Hinksey Lane, Oxford OX2 0LX
Tel: (01865) 723404 *Fax:* (01865) 725294
E-mail: enquiries@cap-ox.com
Web Site: www.cap-ox.com
Key Personnel
Contact: C M Andrews
Founded: 1982
Membership(s): BAPLA & IPG.
Subjects: Travel, Oxford, Cotswolds, Thames & Chilterns
ISBN Prefix(es): 0-9509643

UNITED KINGDOM

Andromeda, *imprint of* Andromeda Oxford Ltd

Andromeda Oxford Ltd+
Kimber House, One Kimber Rd, Abingdon, Oxon OX14 1BZ
Tel: (01235) 550 296 *Fax:* (01235) 550 330
E-mail: mail@andromeda.co.uk
Web Site: www.andromeda.co.uk
Key Personnel
Man Dir: David Holyoak *E-mail:* david.holyoak@andromeda.co.uk
Publishing Dir: Graham Bateman *E-mail:* graham.bateman@andromeda.co.uk
Production Dir: Clive Sparling *E-mail:* clive.sparling@andromeda.co.uk
Sales & Marketing Dir (US, Canada, Germany & Australia): Christopher Collier *E-mail:* chris.collier@andromeda.co.uk
Sales Manager (UK, Europe & the Far East): Anne-Marie Hansen *E-mail:* anne-marie.hansen@andromeda.co.uk
Sales Executive: Hannah Longden *E-mail:* hannah.longden@andromeda.co.uk
Founded: 1986
Produce color illustrated, multi-volume reference works.
Subjects: Animals, Pets, Archaeology, Art, Behavioral Sciences, Earth Sciences, Gardening, Plants, Geography, Geology, History, Human Relations, Natural History, Religion - Islamic, Religion - Jewish, Science (General)
Total Titles: 500 Print
Parent Company: Mediainvest PLC
Imprints: Andromeda
Foreign Rights: D S Druck (Eastern Europe); Jacky Spigel (France & Germany)

Angels' Share, *imprint of* Neil Wilson Publishing Ltd

Anglo-German Foundation for the Study of Industrial Society (Deutsch Britische Stiftung)
34 Belgrave Sq, London SW1X 8DZ
Tel: (020) 7823 1123 *Fax:* (020) 7823 2324
E-mail: info@agf.org.uk
Web Site: www.agf.org.uk
Key Personnel
Dir: Keith Dobson *E-mail:* kd@agf.org.uk
Press & Publications Officer: Annette Birkholz *E-mail:* ab@agf.org.uk
Projects Manager: Ann Pfeiffer *E-mail:* ap@agf.org.uk
Founded: 1973
Subjects: Economics, Environmental Studies, Government, Political Science, Health, Nutrition, Labor, Industrial Relations, Management, Public Administration, Social Sciences, Sociology
ISBN Prefix(es): 0-905492; 1-900834
Number of titles published annually: 8 Print; 2 E-Book
Total Titles: 73 Print
Branch Office(s)
Humboldt Universitat Berlin/GBZ, Jagerstr 10/11, 10117 Berlin, Germany
Distributed by Palgrave (UK)
Orders to: YPS (York Publishing Services), 64 Hallfield Rd, Layerthorpe, York YO31 72Q *Tel:* (01904) 431213 *Fax:* (01904) 430868

Anthem Press, *imprint of* Wimbledon Publishing Company Ltd

Antique Collectors' Club Ltd+
Sandy Lane, Old Martlesham, Woodbridge, Suffolk IP12 4SD
Tel: (01394) 389950 *Fax:* (01394) 389999
E-mail: peter.hawk@antique-acc.com; sales@antique-acc.com
Web Site: www.antique-acc.com
Key Personnel
Man Dir: Diana Steel
Dir: Brian Cotton
Sales Dir: Mark Eastnent
Founded: 1966 (privately owned)
Subjects: Antiques, Architecture & Interior Design, Art, Gardening, Plants
ISBN Prefix(es): 1-85149; 0-907462; 0-902028
Number of titles published annually: 30 Print
Total Titles: 200 Print
Imprints: Garden Art Press Ltd
U.S. Office(s): Antique Collectors' Club, Market Street Industrial Park, Wappingers Falls, NY 12590, United States, Contact: Dan Farrell *Tel:* 914-297-0003 *Fax:* 914-297-0068 *E-mail:* sales@antique-cc.com

Antiques & Collectors Guides Ltd+
Righolm, 40 High Barholm, Kilbarchan, Strathclyde PA10 2EQ
Tel: (0141) 8480880 *Fax:* (0141) 8892063
Key Personnel
Editor & Author: Mr Loudon Temple
Founded: 1990
Subjects: Antiques
ISBN Prefix(es): 0-9514842

Anvil Books Ltd+
Unit 3, Olympia Trading Estate, Coburg Rd, London N22 6TZ
Tel: (020) 8829-3000 *Fax:* (020) 8881-5088
Cable: ANVIL
Key Personnel
Man Dir, Sales, Production, Publicity, Rights & Permissions: Rena Dardis
Editorial: Margaret Dardis
Founded: 1964
Subjects: Biography, History
ISBN Prefix(es): 0-900068; 0-947962; 1-901737
Associate Companies: The Children's Press, Ireland

Anvil Press Poetry Ltd
Neptune House, 70 Royal Hill, London SE10 8RF
Tel: (020) 8469 3033 *Fax:* (020) 8469 3363
E-mail: info@anvilpresspoetry.com
Web Site: www.anvilpresspoetry.com
Key Personnel
Founder & Editorial Dir: Peter Jay
Sales, Marketing & Promotion: Hamish Ironside
Administration & Rights: Kit Yee Wong
Founded: 1968
Subjects: Poetry
ISBN Prefix(es): 0-85646; 0-900977
Imprints: Poetica
Distributed by Littlehampton Book Services Ltd; Midpoint Trade Books
Warehouse: Littlehampton Book Services, Columbia Bldg, Faraday Close, Durrington, Worthing BN13 3HP
Distribution Center: Consortium (US Office)
Orders to: Littlehampton Book Services, Columbia Bldg, Faraday Close, Durrington, Worthing BN13 3HP

AP Information Services Ltd+
Marlborough House, 1st floor, 298 Regents Park Rd, London N3 2UU
Tel: (020) 8349 9988 *Fax:* (020) 8349 9797
E-mail: info@apinfo.co.uk
Web Site: www.apinfo.co.uk
Key Personnel
Man Dir: Alan Philipp *E-mail:* alan@apinfo.co.uk
Dir Finance & Personnel: Gail Philipp *E-mail:* gail@apinfo.co.uk
Editorial Manager, Business Publications: Helen Helmer *E-mail:* helen@apinfo.co.uk
Editorial Manager, Finance Directories: Debbie Robel *E-mail:* debbie@apinfo.co.uk
Head Sales & Marketing: Jacinta Tobin *E-mail:* jacinta@apinfo.co.uk
Marketing Manager: Philip Lowther *E-mail:* philip@apinfo.co.uk
Administrative Manager: Sally Rodohan *E-mail:* sally@apinfo.co.uk
Head of IT & Production: Kumar Divakaran *E-mail:* kumar@apinfo.co.uk
Founded: 1969
Membership(s): Directory Publishers Association.
Subjects: Business, Education, Finance
ISBN Prefix(es): 0-906247; 1-902202
Distributed by Money Market Directories (USA)

Apex Publishing Ltd
PO Box 7445, Colchester, Essex CO4 9UA
Tel: (0870) 242 0938 *Fax:* (0870) 046 6536
E-mail: enquiry@apexpublishing.co.uk
Web Site: www.apexpublishing.co.uk
Key Personnel
Man Dir: Susan Kidby
Founded: 2002
Subsidy publishing for unknown & unpublished authors.
Subjects: Education, Fiction, Health, Nutrition, Nonfiction (General), Philosophy, Poetry, Religion - Other, Science Fiction, Fantasy, Self-Help
ISBN Prefix(es): 1-904444

Apollos, *imprint of* Inter-Varsity Press

Apple Press+
Sheridan House, 112-116A Western Rd, Hove, East Sussex BN3 1DD
Tel: (01273) 727268 *Fax:* (01273) 727269
E-mail: information@quarto.com
Web Site: www.quarto.com
Key Personnel
UK Sales Manager: Marian Silvester
Key Accounts Manager: Stuart Henderson
Editorial Office Manager: Gail Norman *E-mail:* gailn@rotovision.com
Founded: 1984
Specialize in publishing illustrated nonfiction.
Subjects: Antiques, Art, Cookery, Crafts, Games, Hobbies, Fashion, Health, Nutrition, House & Home, Nonfiction (General), Photography, Transportation, Art Instruction, Beauty, Body/Mind/Spirit, Design, Diet, Fitness, Food & Drink, Lifestyle, Pets
ISBN Prefix(es): 1-85076; 1-84092
Number of titles published annually: 25 Print
Total Titles: 500 Print
Parent Company: Quarto Publishing PLC
Distributor for Walter Foster Publishing (UK & Europe only)
Orders to: Grantham Book Services, Isaac Newton Way, Alma Park Industrial Estate, Grantham, Lincs NG31 9SD *Tel:* (020) 754 1080 *Fax:* (020) 754 1061 *E-mail:* orders@gbs.tbs-ltd.co.uk

Appletree Press Ltd+
The Old Potato Station, 14 Howard St S, Belfast BT7 1AP
Tel: (028) 9024 3074 *Fax:* (028) 9024 6756
E-mail: reception@appletree.ie
Web Site: www.appletree.ie
Key Personnel
Man Dir, Rights & Permissions: John D Murphy
Editorial: J Brown
Sales & Marketing: M Elliott
Founded: 1974
Publishers of gift & guidebooks in eight languages, including French, Russian, Japanese, Greek & Spanish
Also acts as Book Packager.
Subjects: Art, Cookery, Crafts, Games, Hobbies, History, Literature, Literary Criticism, Essays, Music, Dance, Photography, Regional Interests, Social Sciences, Sociology
ISBN Prefix(es): 0-904651; 0-86281
Total Titles: 300 Print

PUBLISHERS

UNITED KINGDOM

Arcadia Books Ltd+
15-16 Nassau St, London W1W 7AB
Tel: (0207) 436 9898
E-mail: info@arcadiabooks.co.uk
Web Site: www.arcadiabooks.co.uk
Key Personnel
Publisher: Gary Pulsifer
Publishing Dir: Daniela de Groote
Founded: 1996
Subjects: Biography, Fiction, Gay & Lesbian, Travel, Autobiography, Crime, Gender Studies, Translated Fiction
ISBN Prefix(es): 1-900850
Number of titles published annually: 20 Print
Total Titles: 100 Print
Distribution Center: Independent Publishers Group, Chicago, IL, United States

Architectural Association Publications+
36 Bedford Sq, London WC1B 3ES
Tel: (020) 7887 4021; (020) 7887 4000
Fax: (020) 7414 0783
E-mail: publications@aaschool.ac.uk
Web Site: www.aaschool.ac.uk/publications
Key Personnel
Chairman: Mohsen Mostafavi
Publications Coordinator: Marilyn Sparrow
Founded: 1847
Also acts as a School of Architecture.
Subjects: Architecture & Interior Design
ISBN Prefix(es): 1-870890; 0-904503; 1-902902

Architectural Press, *imprint of* Elsevier Ltd

Arcturus Publishing Ltd+
26/27 Bickels Yard, 151-153 Bermondsey St, London SE1 3HA
Tel: (020) 7407 9400 *Fax:* (020) 7407 9444
E-mail: info@arcturuspublishing.com
Web Site: www.arcturuspublishing.com
Key Personnel
Man Dir: Ian McLellan
Founded: 1994
ISBN Prefix(es): 1-84193
Number of titles published annually: 70 Print
Total Titles: 300 Print; 2 Audio

Argentum, *imprint of* Aurum Press Ltd

Argo Spoken Word+
One Sussex Pl, London W6 9XS
Mailing Address: PO Box 1420, W6 9XS London
Tel: (020) 8910 5000 *Fax:* (020) 8910 3130
Key Personnel
Product Manager: Alex Mitchison
E-mail: alexandra.mitchison@umusic.com
Founded: 1950
Subjects: Nonfiction (General), Poetry
ISBN Prefix(es): 1-85849
Parent Company: Decca Music Group
Warehouse: EMI Music Services, Hermes Close, Tatchbrook Park, Leamington Spa CU34 6RP

Argyll Publishing
Glendaruel, Argyll PA22 3AE
Tel: (01369) 820229 *Fax:* (01369) 820372
E-mail: argyll.publishing@virgin.net
Web Site: www.skoobe.biz
Key Personnel
Publisher: Derek Rodger
Founded: 1992
Subjects: Biography, History, Poetry, Literature, Scottish Interest
ISBN Prefix(es): 1-874640; 1-902831
Distribution Center: Central Books, 99 Wallis Rd, London E9 5LN *Tel:* (020) 8986 4854 (England & Wales)
PD Meany, Box 118, Streetsville, ON L5M 2B7, Canada (North America)

Scottish Book Source, 137 Dundee St, Edinburgh EH11 1BG *Tel:* (0131) 229 6800 *E-mail:* enquiries@scottishbooks.org *Web Site:* www.scottishbooks.org (Scotland)

Arkana, *imprint of* Penguin Books Ltd

Arms and Armour Press, *imprint of* Cassell & Co

Arms & Armour Press+
Wellington House, 125 Strand, London WC2R 0BB
Tel: (020) 7420 5555 *Fax:* (020) 7420 7261
Telex: 9413701
Key Personnel
Chairman & Chief Executive: Philip Sturrock
Editorial Dir & Rights: Alison Goff
Sales Dir: Michelle Gustave
Founded: 1966
Subjects: Aeronautics, Aviation, Crafts, Games, Hobbies, Government, Political Science, History, Maritime, Military Science, Transportation, Naval Warfare
ISBN Prefix(es): 0-85368; 1-85409
Parent Company: Continuum International Publishing Group Ltd

Arnefold, *imprint of* George Mann Publications

Arnold+
338 Euston Rd, London NW1 3BH
Tel: (020) 7873 6000 *Fax:* (020) 7873 6325
E-mail: feedback.arnold@hodder.co.uk
Web Site: www.arnoldpublishers.com
Key Personnel
Chairman: Tim Hely-Hutchinson
Man Dir: Richard Stileman
Head of Marketing: Elizabeth Munn
STM Dir: Nick Dunton
Production Dir: Iain McWilliams
Foreign Rights & Permissions: Rebecca Duprey
Sales Dir: Andy White
Medical: Georgia Bentliff
Humanities: Christopher Wheeler
Marketing Assistant: Rachel Monk *Tel:* (020) 7873 6026 *E-mail:* rachel.monk@hodder.co.uk
Founded: 1890
Arnold is the academic, professional & medical division of Hodder Headline Plc.
Subjects: Environmental Studies, Geography, Geology, History, Human Relations, Language Arts, Linguistics, Literature, Literary Criticism, Essays, Medicine, Nursing, Dentistry, Psychology, Psychiatry, Social Sciences, Sociology, Cultural & Media Studies, Statistics
ISBN Prefix(es): 0-340; 0-7131; 0-85324
Parent Company: Hodder Headline Plc
Ultimate Parent Company: W H Smith
Branch Office(s)
Hodder & Stroughton (Australia) Pty Ltd, 12 Strathalbyn St, Kew East, Victoria 3102, Australia
Hodder Moa Becket, New Zealand
Hodder & Stoughton Educational, South Africa
Distributed by Bookpoint

Arrow, *imprint of* Random House UK Ltd

Art Books International Ltd+
Unit 14 Groves Business Centre Shipton Rd, Milton-under-Wychwood, Chipping Norton, Oxon OX7 6JP
Tel: (020) 7720 1503; (020) 7578 1222
Fax: (020) 7720 3158
E-mail: sales@art-bks.com
Web Site: www.artbooksinternational.co.uk
Key Personnel
Man Dir: Stanley Kekwick *E-mail:* stanley@art-bks.com
Founded: 1991

Specialize in distribution of art books.
Subjects: Antiques, Architecture & Interior Design, Art, Crafts, Games, Hobbies, Drama, Theater, Fashion, Music, Dance, Photography
ISBN Prefix(es): 1-874044
Total Titles: 12 Print
U.S. Office(s): Strauss Consultants, 45 Main St, Suite 611, Brooklyn, NY 11201-1021, United States, Contact: Karen Strauss *Tel:* 718-625-9382 *Fax:* 718-625-9386 *E-mail:* strausscon@aol.com
Distributor for Apex Publishing; Art Books International; BE-MA Editrice; Beaux Arts; Biblioteque del l'Image; Black Dog Publishing; Zelda Cheatle Press; Bernard Jacobson Gallery; Cygnet Press; Design Line; Edwards; Form; Hand Held; Kala Press; Editions Menges; Khosla; Magnus Edizioni; Manchester City Art Galleries; McCabe; Memory Cage; Momentum; Museum of London; National Gallery of Ireland; Pallas Athene Arts; Raab Gallery; Royal Academy; Salts Mill Estates; SPES; Station Press; UIAH; Ziggurat

The Art Newspaper, *see* Umberto Allemandi & Co Publishing

Art Sales Index Ltd+
194 Thorpe Lea Rd, Egham, Surrey TW20 8HA
Tel: (01784) 451145 *Fax:* (01784) 451144
E-mail: sales@art-sales-index.com
Web Site: www.art-sales-index.com
Key Personnel
Chairman: Richard Hislop *E-mail:* asi@art-sales-index.com
Man Editor & Technical Dir: Duncan Hislop
Founded: 1968
Also acts as International On-Line Service-Accessible World-Wide, 24 hours a day, 7 days a week.
Subjects: Art
ISBN Prefix(es): 0-903872

The Art Trade Press Ltd
9 Brockhampton Rd, Havant, Hants PO9 1NU
Tel: (023) 9248 4943
Key Personnel
Editorial, Sales: Mrs J M Curley
Founded: 1907
Subjects: Art
ISBN Prefix(es): 0-900083

Artech House+
46 Gillingham St, London SW1V 1AH
Tel: (020) 7596 8750 *Fax:* (020) 7630 0166
E-mail: artech-uk@artechhouse.com
Web Site: www.artechhouse.com
Key Personnel
Chief Executive: William M Bazzy
Dir, Sales & Marketing: Sharon J Horn
Senior Commissioning Editor: Dr Julie A Lancashire
Founded: 1969
Publisher of professional books for engineers & managers.
Subjects: Communications, Computer Science, Electronics, Electrical Engineering, Engineering (General), Management, Radio, TV, Science (General), Technology, Transportation
ISBN Prefix(es): 0-89006; 1-58053
Number of titles published annually: 70 Print; 5 CD-ROM
Parent Company: Artech House Inc, 685 Canton St, Norwood, MA 02062, United States
Associate Companies: Horizon House Publications, 46 Gillingham St, London SW1V 1HH
Warehouse: Mercury International, Yeomans Dr, Brickhill St, Blakelands TN9 1TD *Tel:* (01908) 218844

UNITED KINGDOM   BOOK

Artetech Publishing Co
54 Frome Rd, Bradford-on-Avon, Wilts BA15 1LD
Tel: (01225) 862482 *Fax:* (01225) 865601
Key Personnel
President: Dr G Terence Meaden *E-mail:* terence.meaden@torro.org.uk
Founded: 1975
Also publishes the monthly international Journal of Meteorology.
Subjects: Archaeology, Earth Sciences, Environmental Studies
ISBN Prefix(es): 0-9510590
Total Titles: 3 Print
Associate Companies: Tornado & Storm Research Organization
Imprints: Meteorology

Arthur James Ltd+
Imprint of John Hunt Publishing Ltd
46a West St, New Alresford, Hants SO24 9AU
Tel: (01962) 736880 *Fax:* (01962) 736881
E-mail: office@johnhunt-publishing.com
Web Site: www.johnhunt-publishing.com
Key Personnel
Contact: J Hunt *E-mail:* johnhuntpublishing@compuserve.com
Founded: 1935
Membership(s): Independent Publishers Guild.
Subjects: Philosophy, Psychology, Psychiatry, Religion - Buddhist, Religion - Catholic, Religion - Hindu, Religion - Jewish, Religion - Protestant, Social Sciences, Sociology, Theology, Meditation
ISBN Prefix(es): 0-85305
Total Titles: 300 Print
Associate Companies: Cairns Publications
Shipping Address: Unit 9 Amor Way, Durhams Lane, Letchworth, Herts SG6 1VA
Warehouse: Unit 9 Amor Way, Dunhams Lane, Letchworth, Herts SG6 1VA

Arts Council of England
14 Great Peter St, London SW1P 3NQ
Tel: (020) 7333 0100 *Fax:* (020) 7973 6590
E-mail: enquiries@artscouncil.org.uk
Web Site: www.artscouncil.org.uk
Key Personnel
Chairman: Gerry Robinson
Chief Executive: Peter Hewitt
Executive Dir, Communications: Wendy Andrews
Dir, Information: Michael Clark
Assistant Officer, Infomation: J Lomas *Tel:* 9736517 *E-mail:* jackie.lomas@artscouncil.org.uk
Founded: 1946
Specialize in arts policy, arts management & research.
Subjects: Art, Photography, Dance, Drama, Visual Arts
ISBN Prefix(es): 0-7287
Distributed by Marston Book Services Ltd

AS Publishing+
73 Montpelier Rise, London NW11 9DU
Tel: (020) 8458 3552 *Fax:* (020) 8458 0618
E-mail: asp@dircon.co.uk
Key Personnel
Editor: Angela Sheehan
Packager of children's information books.
Imprints: Cherrytree Books

Ashgate Publishing Ltd+
Gower House, Croft Rd, Aldershot, Hants GU11 3HR
Tel: (01252) 331551 *Fax:* (01252) 344405
E-mail: info@ashgatepub.co.uk
Web Site: www.ashgate.com
Key Personnel
Senior Administrator, Editorial & Production: Jacque Cox *E-mail:* jcox@ashgatepub.co.uk
Senior Editor, Academic Business & Economics: Brendan George *E-mail:* bgeorge@ashgatepub.co.uk
Senior Editor, International Relations & Politics: Kirstin Howgate *E-mail:* khowgate@ashgatepub.co.uk
Senior Editor, Sociology, Ethnic & Gender Studies, Social Policy & Social Work: Caroline Wintersgill *E-mail:* cwintersgill@ashgatepub.co.uk
Editor, Art & Architectural History: Pamela Edwardes
Editor, History: Thomas Gray *E-mail:* tgray@ashgatepub.co.uk
Editor, Human Geography, Environmental Studies, Planning & Transport: Valerie Rose *E-mail:* vrose@ashgatepub.co.uk
Editor, Librarianship & Information Management: Suzie Duke *E-mail:* dukesuz@aol.com; Alison Kirk *E-mail:* akirk@ashgatepub.co.uk
Editor, Music: Heidi May *E-mail:* hmay@ashgatepub.co.uk
Publishing Dir, Art Books: Lucy Myers *Tel:* (020) 7841 9800 *Fax:* (020) 7837 6322 *E-mail:* lmyers@ashgatepub.co.uk
Publishing Dir, Business & Management: Josephine Burges
Publisher, History & Variorum: John Smedley *E-mail:* jsmedley@ashgatepub.co.uk
Publisher, Music: Rachel Lynch
Publisher, Theology & Religious Studies: Sarah Lloyd *E-mail:* slloyd@ashgatepub.co.uk
Publisher, Training & Professional: Jonathan Norman
Consultant Publisher, Aviation: John Hindley *Tel:* (01483) 860336 *Fax:* (01483) 860336 *E-mail:* jhindley@ashgatepub.co.uk
Consultant Publisher, Law & Legal Studies: John Irwin *E-mail:* jirwin@ashgatepub.co.uk
Manager, International Sales Department: Richard Dowling *E-mail:* rdowling@ashgatepub.co.uk
Founded: 1967
Subjects: Architecture & Interior Design, Art, Business, Criminology, Economics, Environmental Studies, Government, Political Science, History, Law, Library & Information Sciences, Literature, Literary Criticism, Essays, Management, Marketing, Music, Dance, Philosophy, Public Administration, Social Sciences, Sociology, Theology, Transportation
ISBN Prefix(es): 0-566; 1-85742; 1-85628; 0-86078; 0-85972; 0-291; 0-7546; 1-85521
Number of titles published annually: 750 Print
Associate Companies: Dartmouth Publishing Co Ltd; Gower Publishing Co Ltd
Imprints: Dartmouth (Law & Legal Studies); Gower Publishing Ltd (Business books & training resources); Lund Humphries (Art, architecture & design); Variorum (Collected studies in history)
U.S. Office(s): Ashgate Publishing Co, 101 Cherry St, Suite 420, Burlington, VT 05401-4405, United States *Tel:* 802-865-7641 *Fax:* 802-865-7847 *E-mail:* info@ashgate.com
Foreign Rep(s): Ashgate-Gower Asia Pacific (Australia & New Zealand, China, Malaysia & Singapore); Ashgate Publishing Co (North America, South America); Book Bird (Pakistan); ICK (Information & Culture Korea) (Korea); IMA (Africa exc North & South Africa); IPL Technologies (S) Pte Ltd (Indonesia, Philippines); Maya Publishers PVT Ltd (India); Publishers International Marketing (Middle East); United Publishers Services Ltd (Japan)
Orders to: Bookpoint Limited, Ashgate Gower Customer Service, 39 Milton Park, Abingdon, Oxon OX14 4TD *Tel:* (01235) 827730 *Fax:* (01235) 400454 *E-mail:* orders@bookpoint.co.uk *Web Site:* pubeasy.books.bookpoint.co.uk
2252 Ridge Rd, Brookfield, VT 05036-9704, United States *Tel:* 802-276-3162 *Fax:* 802-276-3837 *E-mail:* orders@ashgate.com (North America)

Ashgrove Publishing+
27 John St, London WC1N 2BX
Tel: (020) 7831 5013 *Fax:* (020) 7831 5011
Web Site: www.ashgrovepublishing.com
Key Personnel
Owner: Brad Thompson
Founded: 1970
Subjects: Cookery, Health, Nutrition, Mysteries, Religion - Other, Self-Help
ISBN Prefix(es): 0-906798; 1-85398
Number of titles published annually: 6 Print
Total Titles: 30 Print
Parent Company: Hollydata Publishers Ltd
Distribution Center: Bookworld Companies, 1941 Whitfield Park Loop, Sarasota, FL 34243, United States (USA)

Ashmolean Museum Publications+
Beaumont St, Oxford OX1 2PH
Tel: (01865) 278010 *Fax:* (01865) 278018
E-mail: publications@ashmus.ox.ac.uk
Web Site: www.ashmol.ox.ac.uk/ash/publications
Key Personnel
Sales & Marketing Officer: Declan McCarthy
Founded: 1683
Publishing & Retailing.
Subjects: Archaeology, Art, Asian Studies, Crafts, Games, Hobbies, History, Regional Interests, Travel
ISBN Prefix(es): 0-907849; 1-85444; 0-900090
Number of titles published annually: 15 Print
Parent Company: University of Oxford
Imprints: Griffith Institute
Branch Office(s)
Scholarly Book Services Inc, Canadian Distribution, 77 Mowat Ave, Suite 403, Toronto, ON M6K 3E3, Canada
U.S. Office(s): Arthur Schwarz & Co Inc, US Distribution, 15 Meades Mountain Rd, Woodstock, NY 12498, United States
Warehouse: Gazelle, Unit 2-3, Hightown, LEL Industrial Estate, Whitecross Mills, Lancaster
Orders to: Gazelle Book Services Ltd, Falcon House, Queen St, Lancaster LA1 1RN *Tel:* (01524) 68765 *Fax:* (01524) 63232
Woodstocker Books, Arthur Schwartz & Co Inc, 15 Meads Mountain Rd, Woodstock, NY 12498, United States *Tel:* 845-679-4024 *Fax:* 845-679-4093 *E-mail:* aschwartz@aschwartzbooks.com *Web Site:* www.aschwartzbooks.com (US)

Ashton & Denton Publishing Co (CI) Ltd
3 Burlington House, Saint Savior's Rd, Saint Helier, Jersey JE2 4LA
Tel: (01534) 735461; (01534) 727976 *Fax:* (01534) 875805
Key Personnel
Man Dir & Sales: A D W Mackenzie
Editorial & Publicity: Mrs Y E Ashden *E-mail:* ashden@supanet.com
Production: M Mackenzie
Founded: 1948
Specialize in Channel Islands publications.
Subjects: Business, Finance, Regional Interests
ISBN Prefix(es): 0-85053
Number of titles published annually: 6 Print
Total Titles: 8 Print
U.S. Office(s): Ashton & Denton Publishing Co, PO Box 3, Cornish, UT, United States

Aslib, The Association for Information Management+
Temple Chambers, 3-7 Temple Ave, London EC4Y 0HP
Tel: (020) 7583 8900 *Fax:* (020) 7583 8401
E-mail: aslib@aslib.com; pubs@aslib.com

Web Site: www.aslib.co.uk
Key Personnel
Managing Editor: Diane Heath
Head of Publications: Sarah Blair
Marketing Manager: Chris Grandy
Founded: 1924
Membership(s): FID, ECIA, ALPSP, ICSTI.
Subjects: Business, Law, Library & Information Sciences, Management, Technology
ISBN Prefix(es): 0-85142
Distributed by DA Books & Journals Pty (Australia); Kinokuniyiya (Japan); Portland Press LD (Rest of World); Allied Publishers Pvt Ltd
Orders to: Portland Press Ltd, Commerce Way, Whitehall Industrial Estate, Colchester CO2 8HP

Aspect, *imprint of* Salamander Books Ltd

Aspect Guides, *imprint of* Peter Collin Publishing Ltd

Associated University Presses, *imprint of* Golden Cockerel Press Ltd

The Association for Information Management, see Aslib, The Association for Information Management

Association for Scottish Literary Studies+
c/o Dept of Scottish History, University of Glasgow, 9 University Gardens, Glasgow G12 8QH
Tel: (0141) 330 5309 *Fax:* (0141) 330 5309
Web Site: www.asls.org.uk
Key Personnel
President: Alan MacGillivray
Treasurer: Tom Ralph
Secretary: Lorna Smith
General Editorial: Dr Liam McIlvanney
General Manager: Duncan Jones *E-mail:* d.jones@scothist.arts.gla.ac.uk
Founded: 1970
ASLS is an educational charity supporting the study, teaching & writing of Scottish literature & language.
Subjects: Literature, Literary Criticism, Essays, Scottish Literature & Linguistics
ISBN Prefix(es): 0-948877; 0-9502629
Number of titles published annually: 6 Print
Orders to: Book Source, Cowlairs Estate, 32 Finlas St, Glasgow G22 5DU *Tel:* (0141) 557 0189 *E-mail:* orders@booksource.net

Association of Commonwealth Universities (ACU)
John Foster House, 36 Gordon Sq, London WC1H 0PF
Tel: (020) 7380 6700 *Fax:* (020) 7387 2655
E-mail: info@acu.ac.uk
Web Site: www.acu.ac.uk *Cable:* ACUMEN LONDON WC1
Key Personnel
Secretary General: Dr John Rowett
Head, Product Development: Sue Kirkland *Tel:* (020) 7380 6710 *E-mail:* s.kirkland@acu.ac.uk
Man Editor: Paul Turner
Founded: 1913
Specialize in promoting, in various practical ways, contact & cooperation between its member institutions.
Membership(s): 500 universities in 35 countries/regions in the Commonwealth; Directory & Database Publishers Association.
Subjects: Developing Countries, Education, Higher Education
ISBN Prefix(es): 0-85143
Number of titles published annually: 4 Print; 1 Online
Total Titles: 8 Print; 1 Online
Distributed by Palgrave Macmillan

Association for Science Education+
College Lane, Hatfield, Herts AL10 9AA
Tel: (01707) 283000 *Fax:* (01707) 266532
E-mail: info@ase.org.uk
Web Site: www.ase.org.uk
Key Personnel
Chief Executive: Dr Derek Bell
Deputy Chief Executive: John Lawrence
Publications Dir: Jane R Hanrott
Booksales Manager: Rob Oxley
Founded: 1901
Subjects: Biological Sciences, Chemistry, Chemical Engineering, Computer Science, Disability, Special Needs, Education, Energy, Physics, Science (General)
ISBN Prefix(es): 0-86357
Number of titles published annually: 12 Print; 1 CD-ROM
Total Titles: 25 Print; 1 CD-ROM

Astic, *imprint of* Gwasg Gwenffrwd

ATAPepperpot Gift, *imprint of* Colour Library Direct

Atelier Books
6 Dundas St, Edinburgh EH3 6HZ
Tel: (0131) 5574050 *Fax:* (0131) 5578382
E-mail: mail@bournefineart.co.uk
Web Site: www.bournefineart.co.uk/books.html
Key Personnel
Man Dir: Patrick Bourne *E-mail:* bournefineart@enterprise.net
ISBN Prefix(es): 1-873830
Orders to: Scottish Book Source, 137 Dundee St, Edinburgh EH11 1BG *Tel:* (0131) 229 6800 *Fax:* (0131) 229 9070 *Web Site:* www.scottishbooks.org

The Athlone Press Ltd+
The Continuum International Publishing Group Ltd, The Tower Bldg, 11 York Rd, London SE1 7NX
Tel: (020) 7922 0888 *Fax:* (020) 7922 0881
E-mail: athlonepress@btinternet.com
Web Site: www.transcomm.ox.ac.uk/wwwroot/athlone_press.htm
Key Personnel
Chairman: Brian Southam
Man Dir: Doris Southam
Editorial Dir: Tristan Palmer *E-mail:* tpalmer.athlonepress@btinternet.com
Production Manager: P J Albutt
Founded: 1949
Subjects: Anthropology, Archaeology, Art, Asian Studies, Economics, Film, Video, History, Law, Philosophy, Science (General), Social Sciences, Sociology, Academic
U.S. Office(s): The Athlone Press, 390 Campus Dr, Somerset, NJ 08873, United States *Tel:* 732-445-1245 *Fax:* 732-748-9801
Warehouse: Hoddle Doyle Meadows Ltd, Station Rd, Linton, Cambs CB1 69W
Orders to: c/o Book Systems Plus, BSP House, Station Rd, Linton, Cambs CB1 6NW *Tel:* (01223) 894870 *Fax:* (01223) 894871

Atlantic Transport Publishers
Trevithick House, West End, Penryn TR10 8HE
Tel: (01326) 373656 *Fax:* (01326) 378309; (01326) 373656
Key Personnel
Contact: David Joy *E-mail:* davjoy@aol.com
Founded: 1979
Subjects: History, Mechanical Engineering, Transportation
ISBN Prefix(es): 0-906899; 1-902827
Orders to: Atlantic Publishers, Trevithick House, West End, Penryn, Cornwall TR10 8HE

Atlas Press+
BCM Atlas Press, 27 Old Gloucester St, London WC1N 3XX
Tel: (020) 7490 8742 *Fax:* (021) 7490 8742
E-mail: enquiries@atlaspress.co.uk
Web Site: www.atlaspress.co.uk
Key Personnel
Partner: Alastair Brotchie; Malcolm Green
Partner & Rights Contact: Antony Melville
Copy Editor & Proofreader: Chris Allen
Founded: 1983
Accessible translations of key works of the European avant-garde of the last 100 years. Mostly previously untranslated & often unobtainable in their original languages; where possible, editing done in collaboration with living authors/groups/artists; concise introductions & annotation as necessary.
Subjects: Alternative, Art, Biography, Drama, Theater, Erotica, Fiction, European Avant-Garde Literature & Art, Art History, Limited Editions
ISBN Prefix(es): 0-947757; 1-900565
Number of titles published annually: 8 Print
Total Titles: 75 Print
Imprints: The Printed Head
Distributed by Exact Change (trade titles only); Marginal Distribution (Canada); Peribo Pty Ltd (Australia)
Distributor for Cymbalum Pataphysicum
Foreign Rep(s): Exact Exchange (USA)
Orders to: Consortium Inc, 1045 Westgate Dr, St Paul, MN 51140-0165, United States *Tel:* 612-221-9035 *Fax:* 612-221-0124
Turnaround Publisher Services, Olympia Trading Estate, Unit 3, Coburg Rd, London N22 6TZ, Contact: Bill Godber *Tel:* (020) 8829 3000 *Fax:* (020) 8881 5088

Atom, *imprint of* Time Warner Book Group UK

Attack!, *imprint of* Creation Books

Audio-Forum - The Language Source
POB 35488, St Johns Wood, London NW8 6WD
Tel: (020) 586 4499 *Fax:* (020) 722 1068
E-mail: microworld@ndirect.co.uk
Web Site: www.microworld.ndirect.co.uk
Subjects: Language Arts, Linguistics
Total Titles: 250 Print

Audiobooks, *imprint of* Random House UK Ltd

Augener, *imprint of* Stainer & Bell Ltd

Aulis Publishers
Imprint of David Percy Associates
25 Belsize Park, London NW3 4DU
Tel: (01672) 539 041 *Fax:* (01373) 452 888
E-mail: info@aulis.com
Web Site: www.aulis.com
Key Personnel
Director: David Percy
Founded: 1992
Specialize in videotapes on space.
Subjects: History, Physical Sciences
ISBN Prefix(es): 1-898541
Total Titles: 3 Print

Aurora Northern Classics, *imprint of* The Orkney Press Ltd

Aurum Press Ltd+
25 Bedford Ave, London WC1B 3AT
Tel: (020) 7637 3225 *Fax:* (020) 7580 2469
Web Site: www.aurumpress.co.uk
Key Personnel
Man Dir: Bill McCreadie *E-mail:* bill.mccreadie@aurumpress.co.uk
Editorial Dir: Piers Burnett *E-mail:* piers.burnett@aurumpress.co.uk

UNITED KINGDOM

Sr Editor: Graham Coster
Sales Dir: Graham Eanes
Founded: 1976
Subjects: Art, Biography, Film, Video, Military Science, Nonfiction (General), Photography, Sports, Athletics, Travel, General adult nonfiction
ISBN Prefix(es): 1-85410; 1-903221 (Jacqui Small); 1-902538 (Argentum); 1-84513
Number of titles published annually: 70 Print
Total Titles: 250 Print
Imprints: Argentum (Specialist photography); Jacqui Small (Books on interiors, lifestyle, gardens)
Warehouse: Littlehampton Book Services, Faraday Close, Durrington Worthing BN13 3HD
Tel: (01903) 828500 *Fax:* (01903) 828625

Authentic Lifestyle, *imprint of* Paternoster Publishing

Autumn Publishing Ltd
North Barn, Appledram Barns, Birdham Rd, Appledram, Chichester PO20 7EQ
Tel: (01243) 531660 *Fax:* (01243) 774433
E-mail: autumn@autumnpublishing.co.uk
Web Site: www.autumnpublishing.co.uk
Key Personnel
Man Dir: Campbell Goldsmid *E-mail:* campbell@autumnpublishing.co.uk
Founded: 1976
ISBN Prefix(es): 0-946593; 1-85997
Imprints: Byeway Books

Avero Publications Ltd+
20 Great North Rd, Newcastle-upon-Tyne NE2 4PS
Tel: (0191) 2615790 *Fax:* (0191) 2611209
E-mail: nstc@newcastle.ac.uk
Key Personnel
Man Dir: F J G Robinson
Dir: Gwen Averley
Founded: 1981
Specialize in CD-ROM.
Subjects: Biography, History
ISBN Prefix(es): 0-907977
Subsidiaries: Romulus Press Ltd

Avon, *imprint of* HarperCollins UK

Award Publications Ltd+
27 Longford St, 1st floor, London NW1 3DZ
Tel: (020) 7388 7800 *Fax:* (020) 7388 7887
E-mail: info@award.abel.co.uk
Key Personnel
Man Dir: R Wilkinson
Production Manager: Deborah Wadsworth
Contact: Anna Wilkinson
Founded: 1955
ISBN Prefix(es): 0-86163; 1-84135
Imprints: Horus Editions
Warehouse: Award Publications Ltd, The Old Riding School, Welbeck Estate, NR Workshop, Notts S80 3LS *Tel:* (01909) 478 170 *Fax:* (01909) 484 632
Orders to: Award Publications Ltd, The Old Riding School, Welbeck Estate, NR Workshop, Notts S80 3LS *Tel:* (01909) 478 170 *Fax:* (01909) 484 632

Azure, *imprint of* The Society for Promoting Christian Knowledge (SPCK)

b small publishing+
Pinewood, 3A Coombe Ridings, Kingston-Upon-Thames KT2 7JT
Tel: (020) 8974 6851 *Fax:* (020) 8974 6845
E-mail: info@bsmall.co.uk
Web Site: homepage.ntlworld.com/codework/welcome.htm

Key Personnel
Partner/Publisher: Catherine Bruzzone *E-mail:* cath@bsmall.co.uk
Founded: 1990
Specialize in general children's activity books & foreign language learning.
ISBN Prefix(es): 1-874735; 1-902915
Distributed by MacMillan Distribution Ltd (UK trade)

BAAF Adoption & Fostering+
Skyline House, 200 Union St, London SE1 0LX
Tel: (020) 7593 2000 *Fax:* (020) 7593 2001
E-mail: mail@baaf.org.uk
Web Site: www.baaf.org.uk
Key Personnel
Chief Executive: Felicity Collier
Dir, Publications: Shaila Shah
Commissioning Editor of Adoption & Fostering (Journal): Roger Bullock
Publications Promotions Officer: Marianne Harper *Tel:* (020) 7593 2037 *E-mail:* marianne.harper@baaf.org.uk
Founded: 1980
Registered charity promoting best practice in both adoption & fostering services. Umbrella body for member agencies & all those working with children in the UK care system.
Subjects: Child Care & Development, Psychology, Psychiatry, Social Sciences, Sociology, Adoption, Childcare, Fostering
ISBN Prefix(es): 0-903534; 1-873868; 0-9506807; 1-903699
Number of titles published annually: 15 Print
Total Titles: 120 Print

Bernard Babani (Publishing) Ltd+
The Grampians, Shepherds Bush Rd, London W6 7NF
Tel: (020) 7603 2581; (020) 7603 7296 *Fax:* (020) 7603 8203
E-mail: enquiries@babanibooks.com
Web Site: www.babanibooks.com *Cable:* RADIOBOOKS LONDON W6
Key Personnel
Man Dir, Edit: M H Babani
Sales, Rights & Permissions: S Babani
Production, Publicity: P Pragnell
Founded: 1977 (Babani Press 1971, Bernards Publishers 1942)
Subjects: Computer Science, Electronics, Electrical Engineering, Radio, TV
ISBN Prefix(es): 0-85934; 0-900162
Associate Companies: Babani Press

Babel Guides, *imprint of* Boulevard Books UK/The Babel Guides

Baha'i Publishing Trust+
4 Station Approach, Oakham, Rutland LE15 6QW
Tel: (01572) 722780 *Fax:* (01572) 724280
E-mail: sales@bahaibooks.co.uk
Web Site: www.bahai-publishing-trust.co.uk
Key Personnel
General Manager: Gordon James Kerr
Editorial Dir: George Ballentyne
Founded: 1937
Membership(s): International Association of Baha'i Publishers.
Subjects: Government, Political Science, Human Relations, Philosophy, Religion - Other, Social Sciences, Sociology
ISBN Prefix(es): 0-900125; 1-870987
Parent Company: NSA Baha'is of UK
Imprints: Nightingale Books
Shipping Address: The Maltings, Station Rd, Ketton, Near Stamford, Kent, Lincs PE9 3RQ
Warehouse: The Maltings, Station Rd, Ketton, Near Stamford, Lincs PE9 3RQ

Bill Bailey Publishers' Representatives
16 Devon Sq, Newton Abbot, Devon TQ12 2HR
Tel: (01626) 331079 *Fax:* (01626) 331080
E-mail: billbailey.pubrep@eclipse.co.uk
Key Personnel
Partner: W G Bailey; N Hammond; B J McGee; M J Parsons
Founded: 1981
Sales Representation in Europe
A partnership with all types of books.
Distributed by International Publishers Representatives Ltd (Eastern Mediterranean & Middle East); JAMCO Distribution Inc (US); Maclennan & Petty Pty Ltd (Australia); The South African Medical Association (South Africa)

Bailey Brothers & Swinfen Ltd
Units 1A/1B Learoyd Rd, Mountfield Industrial Estate, New Romney TN28 8XU
Tel: (01797) 366905 *Fax:* (01797) 366638
Key Personnel
Dir: R P Mortimore; H J Mortimore
Founded: 1937
ISBN Prefix(es): 0-561
Parent Company: Bailey & Swinfen Holdings Ltd
Subsidiaries: Bailey Distribution Ltd

Bailliere Tindall Ltd, *imprint of* Elsevier Ltd

The Banner of Truth Trust+
The Grey House, 3 Murrayfield Rd, Edinburgh EH12 6EL
Tel: (0131) 337 7310 *Fax:* (0131) 346 7484
E-mail: info@banneroftruth.co.uk
Web Site: www.banneroftruth.co.uk
Key Personnel
General Manager: John Rawlinson
Editorial Dir: Hywel Jones
Production Manager: Murdo MacLeod
Founded: 1957
Historic Christianity through literature.
Subjects: Religion - Protestant
ISBN Prefix(es): 0-85151
U.S. Office(s): PO Box 621, Carlisle, PA 17013, United States *Tel:* 717-249-5747 *Fax:* 717-249-0604 *E-mail:* info@banneroftruth.org
Warehouse: 17 Bankhead Dr, Sighthill Industrial Estate, Edinburgh EH11 4DW

Banson
Unit L, Gunnels Wood Park, Gunnels Wood Park Rd, Stevenage SG1 2BH
Tel: (020) 7729 7315; (020) 7613 1388 *Fax:* (020) 7729 7870
E-mail: banson@ourplanet.com
Key Personnel
Man Dir: Mr B Ullstein
Founded: 1987
Specialize in packaging for International Organizations.
Subjects: Environmental Studies

Bantam Paperbacks, *imprint of* Transworld Publishers Ltd

Bantam Press, *imprint of* Transworld Publishers Ltd

The Banton Press
Dippin Cottage, Kildonan, Isle of Arran KA27 8SB
Tel: (01770) 820231 *Fax:* (01770) 820231
E-mail: bantonpress@btinternet.com
Web Site: www.bantonpress.co.uk
Key Personnel
Contact: Mark E G Brown
Founded: 1988
Subjects: Astrology, Occult, History, Mysteries, Religion - Other
ISBN Prefix(es): 1-85652
Number of titles published annually: 4 Print
Total Titles: 176 Print

PUBLISHERS — UNITED KINGDOM

McCall Barbour+
28 George IV Bridge, Edinburgh EH1 1ES
Tel: (0131) 225-4816 *Fax:* (0131) 225-4816
E-mail: ashbethany43@hotmail.com
Key Personnel
Man Dir: Dr T C Danson-Smith
Founded: 1900
Christian Publishers.
Subjects: Religion - Protestant
ISBN Prefix(es): 0-7132
Total Titles: 2 Print

Barefoot Books
124 Walcot St, Bath BA1 5BG
Tel: (01225) 322400 *Fax:* (01225) 322499
E-mail: info@barefootbooks.co.uk
Web Site: www.barefootbooks.com
Founded: 1993
Branch Office(s)
2067 Massachusetts Ave, Cambridge, MA 02140, United States

Barmarick Publications
Enholmes Hall, Patrington, Hull, East Yorks HU12 0PR
Tel: (01964) 630033 *Fax:* (01964) 631716
Web Site: www.barmarick.co.uk
Key Personnel
Partner: Dr R Dobbins; A M Lunn; Dr B O Pettman *E-mail:* barrie.o.pettman@barmarick.co.uk
Founded: 1982
Subjects: Labor, Industrial Relations, Management, Social Sciences, Sociology
ISBN Prefix(es): 1-85385
Total Titles: 292 Print

Barn Dance Publications Ltd+
62 Beechwood Rd, Croydon CR2 0AA
Tel: (020) 8657 2813 *Fax:* (020) 8651 6080
E-mail: barndance@pubs.co.uk
Web Site: www.barndancepublications.co.uk
Key Personnel
Dir: Derek L Jones
Founded: 1984
Membership(s): Book Data.
Subjects: Music, Dance, Fold Dance
ISBN Prefix(es): 0-9514275; 1-874565
Total Titles: 18 Print; 13 Audio

Barn Owl Press (Children's Books), *imprint of* Alun Books

Barnabas, *imprint of* Bible Reading Fellowship

Bartsky Legal Texts Ltd, *imprint of* CyberClub

Basil Blackwell Ltd, see Blackwell Publishing Ltd

Batsford Ltd+
Division of Chrysalis Group
The Chrysalis Bldg, Bramley Rd, London W10 6SP
Tel: (020) 7221 2213; (020) 7314 1469 (sales) *Fax:* (020) 7221 6455; (020) 7314 1594 (sales)
E-mail: enquiries@chrysalis.com
Web Site: www.chrysalisbooks.co.uk/books/publisher/batsford
Key Personnel
Group Sales & Marketing Dir: Richard Samson *Tel:* (020) 7314 1459 *Fax:* (020) 7314 1549 *E-mail:* rsamson@chrysalisbooks.co.uk
Dir of Marketing: Kate Wood *Tel:* (020) 7314 1496 *E-mail:* kwood@chrysalisbooks.co.uk
Marketing & Publicity Manager: Rachel Armstrong *Tel:* (020) 7314 1605 *Fax:* (020) 7314 1549 *E-mail:* rarmstrong@chrysalisbooks.co.uk
Foreign Rights Manager: Emma O'Grady *Tel:* (020) 7314 1447 *E-mail:* eogrady@chrysalisbooks.co.uk
Permissions: Terry Forshaw *Tel:* (020) 7314 1607 *E-mail:* tforshaw@chrysalisbooks.co.uk
Founded: 1843
Subjects: Agriculture, Archaeology, Architecture & Interior Design, Art, Crafts, Games, Hobbies, Fashion, Film, Video, Gardening, Plants, History, House & Home, Nonfiction (General), Outdoor Recreation, Photography, Social Sciences, Sociology
ISBN Prefix(es): 0-7134
U.S. Office(s): 9 East 40 St, 10th floor, New York, NY, United States
Distributor for Chilton Book Co; Lennard/Queen Anne Press; Meredith Books (Europe); Taunton Press; Storey Books
Foreign Rights: Emma O'Grady (Eastern Europe, Italy, Latin America, Portugal, Russia, Spain)
Orders to: HarperCollins Distribution, Campsie View, Westerhill Rd, Bishopbriggs, Glasgow G64 2QT *Fax:* (087) 0787 1995 (Trade only)

Colin Baxter, *imprint of* Colin Baxter Photography Ltd

Colin Baxter Photography Ltd+
The Old Dairy, Woodlands Industrial Estate, Grantown-on-Spey, Morayshire PH26 3NA
Tel: (01479) 873999 *Fax:* (01479) 873888
E-mail: sales@colinbaxter.co.uk
Web Site: www.colinbaxter.co.uk; www.worldlifelibrary.co.uk
Key Personnel
Man Dir: Colin Baxter
Marketing Dir & Rights: Colin Kirkwood *E-mail:* colin.kirkwood@colinbaxter.co.uk
Editorial & Production Dir: Mike Rensner
Founded: 1984
Independent Private Company.
Subjects: Natural History, Photography, Travel
ISBN Prefix(es): 0-948661; 1-900455; 1-84107
Number of titles published annually: 20 Print
Total Titles: 80 Print
Imprints: Colin Baxter; Worldlife Library
Distributed by Voyageur Press (US)
Foreign Rep(s): Ted Dougherty (Austria, Belgium, Netherlands, France, Germany, Greece, Italy, Luxembourg, Switzerland); Theo Philips (Branei, Hong Kong, Malaysia, Philippines, Singapore, Thailand); Peter Prout (Spain); Voyageur Press Inc (USA)
Orders to: Freepost, PO Box 1, Grantown-on-Spey, Moray PH26 3YA

Bay View Books Ltd+
The Red House, 25-26 Bridgeland St, Bideford EX39 2PZ
Tel: (01237) 479225; (01237) 421285 *Fax:* (01237) 421286
Key Personnel
International Rights: Charles Herridge
Founded: 1986
Subjects: Automotive
ISBN Prefix(es): 1-870979; 1-901432
Warehouse: Bailey Distribution Ltd, Units 1A/B Learoyd Rd, Mountfield Industrial Estate, New Romney, Kent TN28 8XU
Orders to: Chris Lloyd Sales & Marketing, 463 Ashley Rd, Parkstone, Poole, Dorset BH14 0AX

BBC Audiobooks+
Windsor Bridge Rd, Bath BA2 3AX
Tel: (01672) 562255 *Fax:* (01672) 564634
E-mail: bbc@covertocover.co.uk
Web Site: bbcaudiobooks.com
Key Personnel
Man Dir: Paul Dempsey
Publishing Dir: Jan Paterson
Production & Publicity Manager: Lesley Barnes
Sales Manager: Mary Finch *E-mail:* mary@chivers.co.uk
Marketing Manager: Christine Graham *E-mail:* christine@chivers.co.uk
Founded: 1979
Specialize in Large Print Books, Audio Books (complete & unabridged) & Facsimile Reprints.
Subjects: Biography, Fiction, Mysteries, Nonfiction (General), Romance, Western Fiction
ISBN Prefix(es): 0-563; 0-7451; 0-85995; 0-85997; 0-86220; 0-85119; 1-85549
Number of titles published annually: 1,215 Print; 216 Audio
Total Titles: 4,300 Print; 2,500 Audio
Parent Company: BBC Worldwide, 80 Wood Lane, London W12 0TT
Imprints: Black Dagger; Cavalcade Story Cassettes; Camden Large Print; Chivers Children's Audio Books; Chivers Large Print; Galaxy Large Print; Gunsmoke Western; Paragon; Read-Along; Sterling Audio Books; Windsor Large Print Bestsellers; Word for Word Audio Books
U.S. Office(s): Chivers North America, One Lafayette Rd, Box 1450, Hampton, NH 03842-0015, United States, Contact: Jim Brannigan *Tel:* 603-926-8744 *Fax:* 603-929-3890
Foreign Rep(s): Booktalk Pty Ltd (audio books) (Southern Africa); Chivers North America (USA); Hargraves Library Service (Southern Africa); The Library Supply Co Ltd (New Zealand); Michael O'Brien (Ireland); Hargraves Library Service (large print) (Australia); Vanwell Publishing Ltd (Canada)

BBC Books, *imprint of* BBC Worldwide Publishers

BBC English+
Woodlands, 80 Wood Lane, London W12 0TT
Tel: (020) 8576 2221 *Fax:* (020) 8576 3040
Web Site: www.bbcenglish.com
Key Personnel
Dir: Charles Hyde
Dir, International Publishing: Be Lenthall
Founded: 1943
Subjects: English as a Second Language
ISBN Prefix(es): 1-85497; 0-946675
Parent Company: BBC Worldwide Ltd

BBC Worldwide Publishers+
Woodlands, 80 Wood Lane, London W12 0TT
Tel: (020) 8433 2000 *Fax:* (020) 8749 0538
E-mail: bbcsales@bbc.co.uk
Web Site: www.bbcworldwide.com
Telex: 934678 BBCENTG *Cable:* BROADCASTS LONDON
Key Personnel
Head of Book Publishing: Chris Weller
Head of Sales & Marketing: Stuart Biles
Production Manager: Brian Dickson
Sales & Marketing Dir: Kevin Harrington
International Sales & Marketing Dir: Charles Hyde
International Rights & Export Manager: Richard Gay
Founded: 1925
Subjects: Cookery, Gardening, Plants, History, Language Arts, Linguistics, Natural History
ISBN Prefix(es): 0-563
Parent Company: BBC Worldwide
Imprints: Network Books; BBC Books
Bookshop(s): 4-5 Langham Pl, Upper Regent St, London
Orders to: Exel-logistics Media Services, Invicta House, St Thomas Longley Rd, Medway City Industrial Estate, Rochester, Kent ME2 4DU *Tel:* (0634) 297123 *Fax:* (0634) 298000

BCA - Book Club Associates+
Greater London House, Hampstead Rd, Camden, London NW1 7TZ

Tel: (020) 7760 6500 *Fax:* (020) 7760 6501
Web Site: www.bca.co.uk
Key Personnel
Chief Executive: Alan Roe
Editorial Dir: Chris Holifield
Founded: 1966
Subjects: Aeronautics, Aviation, Animals, Pets, Antiques, Archaeology, Architecture & Interior Design, Art, Astrology, Occult, Automotive, Cookery, Crafts, Games, Hobbies, Fiction, Film, Video, Gardening, Plants, Geography, Geology, History, How-to, Humor, Literature, Literary Criticism, Essays, Microcomputers, Military Science, Music, Dance, Mysteries, Natural History, Nonfiction (General), Outdoor Recreation, Photography, Poetry, Romance, Science (General), Science Fiction, Fantasy, Self-Help, Sports, Athletics, Travel, Wine & Spirits
Ultimate Parent Company: Bertelsmann AG, Germany
Branch Office(s)
Guild House, Farnsby St, Swindon, Wilts SN1 5DD *Tel:* (01793) 512100 *Fax:* (01793) 567711
Book Club(s): Ancient & Medieval History; Arts Guild; bol.com; Book Club of Ireland; Books Direct; Books for Children; English Book Club; Escape Fiction; Fantasy & Science Fiction; History Guild; Home Softwave World; Just Good Books; Mango; Military & Aviation; Mind, Body & Spirit; Mystery & Thriller Guild; Quality Paperbacks Direct; Railway Book Club; Taste; TSP; World Books

BCP, *imprint of* Gerald Duckworth & Co Ltd

Beaconsfield, *imprint of* Beaconsfield Publishers Ltd

Beaconsfield Publishers Ltd+
20 Chiltern Hills Rd, Beaconsfield, Bucks HP9 1PL
Tel: (01494) 672118 *Fax:* (01494) 672118
E-mail: books@beaconsfield-publishers.co.uk
Web Site: www.beaconsfield-publishers.co.uk
Key Personnel
President, Editor & Man Dir: John Churchill
Founded: 1979
Carefully developed titles in medicine, nursing, patient care & homeopathy.
Subjects: Alternative, Health, Nutrition, Medicine, Nursing, Dentistry
ISBN Prefix(es): 0-906584
Number of titles published annually: 2 Print
Total Titles: 34 Print
Imprints: Beaconsfield
Foreign Rep(s): Astam Books (Australia); Viking Seven Seas (New Zealand)
Orders to: Jackson Distribution, 3 Gibsons Rd, Heaton Moor, Stockport SK4 4JX, Contact: Brian Jackson *Tel:* (0161) 947-9669 *Fax:* (0161) 947-9669 *E-mail:* jacksonpub@aol.com
Returns: Jackson Distribution, 3 Gibsons Rd, Heaton Moor, Stockport SK4 4JX, Contact: Brian Jackson *Tel:* (0161) 947-9669 *Fax:* (0161) 947-9669 *E-mail:* jacksonpub@aol.com
Membership(s): IPG

Ruth Bean Publishers+
Victoria Farmhouse, Carlton, Bedford MK43 7LP
Tel: (01234) 720356 *Fax:* (01234) 720590
E-mail: ruthbean@onetel.net.uk
Key Personnel
Dir: Nigel Bean; Ruth Bean
Founded: 1972
Specialize in needlecrafts & costume.
Membership(s): IPG.
Subjects: Anthropology, Crafts, Games, Hobbies, Drama, Theater, Fashion
ISBN Prefix(es): 0-903585

Beano Books, *imprint of* Geddes & Grosset

Mitchell Beazley+
2-4 Heron Quays, London E14 4JP
Tel: (020) 7531 8400; (020) 7531 8480 (UK sales); (020) 7531 8481 (special sales); (020) 7531 8479 (marketing); (020) 7531 8488 (publicity); (020) 7531 8482 (export sales); (020) 7531 8484 (foreign rights); (020) 7531 8476 (US sales) *Fax:* (020) 7531 8650
E-mail: enquiries@mitchell-beazley.co.uk
Web Site: www.mitchell-beazley.com
Key Personnel
Publisher & Man Dir: Jane Aspden
UK Sales & Marketing Dir: Mark Scott
International Sales & Marketing Dir: Kate Newton
Editorial Dir: Louise Dixon
Art Dir: Vivien Brar
Production Dir: Julie Young
Financial Controller: Paula Warrender
UK Sales Manager: Helen Twewus
Publicity Manager: Fiona Smith
Marketing Manager: Nicola Wright
Special Sales Executive: Clare Webb
Founded: 1969
High quality book publishers.
Subjects: Antiques, Cookery, Gardening, Plants, House & Home, Wine & Spirits
ISBN Prefix(es): 0-85533; 1-85732; 1-84000; 0-86134
Parent Company: Octopus Publishing Group
Orders to: Littlehampton Book Services Ltd, Faraday Close, Durrington, Worthing, West Sussex BN13 3RB *Tel:* (01933) 828800 *Fax:* (0193) 828802

BECTA, *imprint of* British Educational Communication & Technology Agency (BECTA)

BECTA, see British Educational Communication & Technology Agency (BECTA)

Belitha Press Ltd+
Division of Chrysalis Group
The Chrysalis Bldg, Bramley Rd, London W10 6SP
Tel: (020) 7221 2213; (020) 7314 1469 (sales) *Fax:* (020) 7221 6455; (020) 7314 1594 (sales)
E-mail: enquiries@chrysalis.com
Web Site: www.chrysalis.co.uk/childrens/publisher/belitha
Telex: 8950511 ONEONE
Key Personnel
Dir, Children's Sales & Marketing: Dennis McGuirk *Tel:* (020) 7314 1623 *E-mail:* dmcguirk@chrysalisbooks.co.uk
Marketing & Publicity Manager: Ben Cameron *Tel:* (020) 7314 1625 *E-mail:* bcameron@chrysalisbooks.co.uk
Publicity Officer: Tessa Arditti *Tel:* (020) 7314 1627 *E-mail:* tarditti@chrysalisbooks.co.uk
Foreign Rights Executive: Elisabeth Carlsson *Tel:* (020) 7314 1602 *E-mail:* ecarlsson@chrysalisbooks.co.uk
Founded: 1980
Publishers of high-quality illustrated children's books for the international market.
Subjects: Art, Biography, Crafts, Games, Hobbies, Environmental Studies, Foreign Countries, Geography, Geology, Mathematics, Music, Dance, Natural History, Nonfiction (General)
ISBN Prefix(es): 1-85561; 1-84138; 0-947553
Orders to: Littlehampton Book Services, Faraday Close, Off Columbia Dr, Durrington, West Sussex BN13 3HD *Tel:* (01903) 828800 *Fax:* (01903) 828802 *E-mail:* orders@lbsltd.co.uk (Trade only)

Belknap, *imprint of* Harvard University Press

Bellew Publishing Co Ltd+
Nightingale Centre, 8 Balham Hill, London SW12 9EA
Tel: (020) 8673 5611 *Fax:* (020) 8675 2142
E-mail: bellewsubs@hotmail.com
Key Personnel
Chief Executive & Man Dir: I B Bellew
Chairman: Ian Mcquordale
Founded: 1983
Also book packager.
Subjects: Architecture & Interior Design, Art, Crafts, Games, Hobbies, Environmental Studies, Fiction, History, Travel
ISBN Prefix(es): 0-947792; 1-85725
Imprints: Deirdre McDonald Ltd
Orders to: Plymbridge Distributors Ltd, Estover Rd, Plymouth PL6 7PZ

Belton Books, *imprint of* Stainer & Bell Ltd

BEN Gunn, *imprint of* SB Publications

David Bennett Books+
Division of Chrysalis Group
The Chrysalis Bldg, Bramley Rd, London W10 6SP
Tel: (020) 7221 2213; (020) 7314 1469 (sales) *Fax:* (020) 7221 6455; (020) 7314 1594 (sales)
E-mail: enquiries@chrysalis.com
Web Site: www.chrysalisbooks.co.uk/childrens/publisher/davidbennett
Key Personnel
Dir, Children's Sales & Marketing: Dennis McGuirk *Tel:* (020) 7314 1623 *E-mail:* dmcguirk@chrysalisbooks.co.uk
Marketing & Publicity Manager: Ben Cameron *Tel:* (020) 7314 1625 *E-mail:* bcameron@chrysalisbooks.co.uk
Publicity Officer: Tessa Arditti *Tel:* (020) 7314 1627 *E-mail:* tarditti@chrysalisbooks.co.uk
Foreign Rights Executive: Elisabeth Carlsson *Tel:* (020) 7314 1602 *E-mail:* ecarlsson@chrysalisbooks.co.uk
Founded: 1989
Specializes in picture books & novelties ages 0-7.
Orders to: Littlehampton Book Services, Faraday Close, Off Columbia Dr, Durrington, West Sussex BN13 3HD *Tel:* (01903) 828800 *Fax:* (01903) 828802 *E-mail:* orders@lbsltd.co.uk (Trade only)

Berg Publishers+
Imprint of Oxford International Publishers Ltd
Angel Court, 81 St Clements St, 1st floor, Oxford OX4 1AW
Tel: (01865) 245104 *Fax:* (01865) 791165
E-mail: enquiry@bergpublishers.com
Web Site: www.bergpublishers.com
Key Personnel
Man Dir: Kathryn Earle *E-mail:* kearle@bergpublishers.com
Production Manager: Ken Bruce *E-mail:* kbruce@bergpublishers.com
Founded: 1981
Academic publisher.
Subjects: Anthropology, Ethnicity, Fashion, Film, Video, Government, Political Science, History, Social Sciences, Sociology, Women's Studies
ISBN Prefix(es): 0-85496; 1-85973; 1-84520
Number of titles published annually: 60 Print; 3 Online; 30 E-Book
Total Titles: 800 Print; 3 Online; 75 E-Book
Imprints: Oswald Wolff Books
Distributed by Palgrave Macmillan (USA & Canada)
Foreign Rep(s): APAC Publishers Services PTE Ltd (Brunei, Burma, Cambodia, China, Hong Kong, Indonesia, Malaysia, Philippines, Singapore, Thailand, Vietnam); Andrew Durnell (Europe); Footprint Books Pty Ltd (Australia,

PUBLISHERS UNITED KINGDOM

Fiji, New Zealand, New Guinea); ICK (Information & Culture Korea) (Korea); IPS Middle East (Africa, Middle East); Maya Publishers (India); Troika (UK); Unifacmanu Trading Co Ltd (Taiwan); United Publishers Services Ltd (Japan)
Shipping Address: PSL Freight Ltd, Bathe Wharf, Station Rd, Maldon, Essex CM9 4GQ *Tel:* (01621) 854451 *Fax:* (01621) 840771
Warehouse: Orca Book Services, Stanley House, 3 Fleet Lane, BH15 3AJ Poole RH13 8LD *Tel:* (01202) 665432 *Fax:* (01202) 666219 *E-mail:* orders@orcabookservices.co.uk
Distribution Center: VHPS Fulfillment, 16365 James Madison Hwy, Gordonsville, VA 22942, United States
Orders to: VHPS Fulfillment, 16365 James Madison Hwy, Gordonsville, VA 22942, United States
Returns: VHPS Fulfillment, 16365 James Madison Hwy, Gordonsville, VA 22942, United States

Berghahn Books Ltd+
3 Newtec Pl, Magdalen Rd, Oxford OX4 1RE
Tel: (01865) 250011 *Fax:* (01865) 250056
E-mail: info@berghahnbooks.com
Web Site: www.berghahnbooks.com
Key Personnel
Publisher: Dr Marion Berghahn
Editorial: Mark Stanton
Marketing Manager: Chris McVeigh
Founded: 1994
Subjects: Anthropology, Economics, Government, Political Science, History, Literature, Literary Criticism, Essays, Military Science, Religion - Jewish, Social Sciences, Sociology, Women's Studies, Gender, Humanities, Migration
ISBN Prefix(es): 1-57181
Number of titles published annually: 100 Print; 15 Online
Total Titles: 600 Print; 1 CD-ROM; 15 Online
U.S. Office(s): Berghahn Books Inc, 604 W 115 St, New York, NY 10025, United States, Publisher: Dr Marion Berghahn *Tel:* 212-222-6502 *Fax:* 212-222-5209
Orders to: Berghahn Books Inc, PO Box 605, Herndon, VA 20172, United States *Tel:* 703-661-1500 *Fax:* 703-661-1501 *E-mail:* tod@booksintl.com
Marston Book Services, PO Box 269, Abingdon OX14 4YN, Contact: Patrick Wehmeier *Tel:* (01235) 465500 *Fax:* (01235) 465555 *E-mail:* direct.order@marston.co.uk

Berlitz (UK) Ltd+
Lincoln House, 296-302 High Holborn, London WC1 7JH
Tel: (020) 7611 9640 *Fax:* (020) 7611 9656
E-mail: publishing@berlitz.co.uk
Web Site: www.berlitz.co.uk; languagecenter.berlitz.com/holborn
Key Personnel
Man Dir: Roger Kirkpatrick *Tel:* (020) 7518 8304 *E-mail:* roger.kirkpatrick@berlitz.ie
Operations Dir: Anthony Finn *Tel:* (020) 7518 8306 *E-mail:* anthony.finn@berlitz.ie
Founded: 1970
Specialize in phrase books, dictionaries, audio, video & childrens language products, travel guides & language reference.
ISBN Prefix(es): 1-58592
Total Titles: 375 Print
Parent Company: Berlitz Publishing Company Ltd
Ultimate Parent Company: Berlitz International Inc
Distributed by Virgin Publishing Ltd (United Kingdom)

Bernards (Publishers) Ltd, see Bernard Babani (Publishing) Ltd

Betterway, *imprint of* David & Charles Ltd

BFBS, *imprint of* Bible Society

BFI Publishing+
21 Stephen St, London W1T 1LN
Tel: (020) 7957 4789 *Fax:* (020) 74367950; (020) 76362516
E-mail: publishing@bfi.org.uk
Web Site: www.bfi.org.uk
Key Personnel
Head of Publishing: Andrew Lockett
Marketing & Sales: Rebecca Watts *Tel:* (20) 79574817 *E-mail:* rebecca.watts@bfi.org.uk
Production, Rights & Permissions: Tom Cabot
Marketing & Promotions: Sarah Prosser
Founded: 1980
Subjects: Film, Video, Radio, TV, Social Sciences, Sociology, Women's Studies
ISBN Prefix(es): 0-85170
Number of titles published annually: 30 Print
Total Titles: 280 Print
Distributed by Indiana University Press (North America)
Warehouse: Plymbridge Distributors Ltd, Estover Rd, Plymouth PL6 7PZ *Tel:* (01752) 202301
Orders to: Plymbridge Distributors Ltd, Estover Rd, Plymouth PL6 7PZ *Tel:* (01752) 202301

Bible Distributors, *imprint of* Chapter Two

Bible Reading Fellowship+
Elsfield Hall, 1st floor, 15-17 Elsfield Way, Oxford OX2 8FG
Tel: (01865) 319700 *Fax:* (01865) 319701
E-mail: enquiries@brf.org.uk
Web Site: www.brf.org.uk
Key Personnel
Chief Executive Officer: Richard Fisher *E-mail:* richardfisher@brf.org.uk
Commissioning Editor: Sue Doggett *E-mail:* suedoggett@brf.org.uk; Naomi Starkey *E-mail:* naomi.starkey@brf.org.uk
Marketing & Operations Manager: Karen Laister *E-mail:* karen.laister@brf.org.uk
Founded: 1922
Subjects: Biblical Studies, Education, Religion - Protestant, Theology
ISBN Prefix(es): 0-7459; 1-84101
Total Titles: 200 Print; 1 E-Book
Imprints: Barnabas
Orders to: Marston Book Services, PO Box 269, Oxford OX14 4YN *Tel:* (01235) 46550 *Fax:* (01235) 465555 *Web Site:* www.marston.co.uk

Bible Society+
Stonehill Green, Westlea, Swindon SN5 7DG
Tel: (01793) 418100 *Fax:* (01793) 418118
E-mail: info@bfbs.org.uk
Web Site: www.biblesociety.org.uk
Telex: 44283
Key Personnel
Chief Executive: N Crosbie
Commercial Dir: Ashley Scott
Export: Janet Edwards
Production: D Hill
Rights & Permissions: Miss K Luckett
Founded: 1804
Subjects: Biblical Studies
ISBN Prefix(es): 0-564
Imprints: BFBS

Joseph Biddulph Publisher+
32 Stryd Ebeneser, Pontypridd CF37 5PB
Tel: (01443) 662559
Key Personnel
Sole Proprietor: Joseph Biddulph
Founded: 1991
Subjects: Architecture & Interior Design, Language Arts, Linguistics, Literature, Literary Criticism, Essays, Heraldry
ISBN Prefix(es): 1-89799; 0-948565
Number of titles published annually: 4 Print
Total Titles: 54 Print
Imprints: Languages Information Centre

Big Time, *imprint of* Peter Haddock Ltd

BILD Publications
Campion House, Green St, Kidderminster, Worcs DY10 1JL
Tel: (01562) 723010 *Fax:* (01562) 723029
E-mail: enquiries@bild.org.uk
Web Site: www.bild.org.uk
Key Personnel
Chief Executive: John Harris *E-mail:* g.pardoe@bild.org.uk
Founded: 1972
Subjects: Behavioral Sciences, Child Care & Development, Disability, Special Needs, Health, Nutrition
ISBN Prefix(es): 1-873791; 0-906054; 1-902519; 1-904082
Orders to: Book Source, 32 Finlas St, Cowlains Estate, Glasgow G22 5DU *Tel:* (0141) 558 1366 *Fax:* (0141) 557 0189

Binky (Childrens), *imprint of* Grange Books PLC

Bio Scientifica, *imprint of* Society for Endocrinology

Biocommerce Data Ltd
Subsidiary of PJB Publications
Suffield House, 9 Paradise Rd, Richmond, Surrey TW9 1SJ
Tel: (020) 8332 4660 *Fax:* (020) 8332 4666
E-mail: biocom@pjbpubs.com; custserv@biocom.com (orders)
Web Site: www.pjbpubs.com/bcd
Key Personnel
Publisher: Sarah Walkley *E-mail:* sarah.walkley@informa.com
Database Manager: Ruth Williams *E-mail:* ruth.williams@pjbpubs.com
Founded: 1990
Publish directories of companies involved in biotechnology.
Subjects: Agriculture, Biological Sciences, Medicine, Nursing, Dentistry
ISBN Prefix(es): 1-871393
Total Titles: 2 Print; 2 CD-ROM; 1 Online
Ultimate Parent Company: T&F Informa

BIOS Scientific Publishers Ltd+
Member of Taylor & Francis Group PLC
4 Park Sq, Milton Park, Abingdon, Oxfordshire OX14 4RN
Tel: (01235) 828600 *Fax:* (01235) 829011
E-mail: sales@bios.co.uk
Web Site: www.bios.co.uk
Key Personnel
Chairman: Derek Phillips
Man Dir & International Rights: Dr Jonathan Ray
Sales: Simon Watkins *E-mail:* simon.watkins@bios.co.uk
Founded: 1989
Publishers of Instant Notes, The Basics, Clinic Handbooks, Advanced Texts, Advanced Methods, Key Topics series, Genomes 2, Human Molecular Genetics 2, Clinic Intensive Care, Medical Mycology, Biotechnic & Histochemistry.
Membership(s): International Group of STM Publishers.
Subjects: Agriculture, Biological Sciences, Medicine, Nursing, Dentistry
ISBN Prefix(es): 1-872748; 1-85996

Distributed by Springer Verlag New York Inc (North America); University of New South Wales (Australia & New Zealand); Viva Books (India)
Distributor for Horizon Scientific Press; Experiemental Biology Reviews; Royal Microscopical Society (microscopy handbooks); Society of Experimental Biology
Foreign Rep(s): Academic Marketing Services (South Africa, Zimbabwe); APAC Publishers (SE Asia, Singapore); Durnell Marketing Ltd (Ireland, Europe, Northern Ireland); IPS (Middle East) Ltd (Middle East, North Africa); UNIREPS (Australia, New Zealand)
Orders to: Plymbridge Distributors Ltd, Estover Rd, Plymouth, Devon Tel: (01752) 202301 Fax: (01753) 202333 E-mail: orders@plymbridge.com
Springer-Verlag, PO Box 2485, Secaucus, NJ 07096-2485, United States Fax: 212-533-5587 E-mail: order@springer-ny.com

Birlinn Ltd+
West Newington House, 10 Newington Rd, Edinburgh EH9 1QS
Tel: (0131) 668 4371 Fax: (0131) 668 4466
E-mail: info@birlinn.co.uk
Web Site: www.birlinn.co.uk
Key Personnel
Man Dir & International Rights: Hugh Andrew
Office Manager: Sarah Tranter
Founded: 1992
Membership(s): Scottish Publishers Association.
Subjects: Fiction, History, Regional Interests
ISBN Prefix(es): 1-874744
Number of titles published annually: 80 Print
Associate Companies: Maclean Press
Imprints: Canongate Books "A" Ltd; John Donald Publishers Ltd; Polygon
Distributor for Maclean Press
Foreign Rep(s): Dufour Editions Distribution (North America)
Warehouse: Scottish Book Source, 32 Finlas St, Glasgow G22 5DU
Orders to: 137 Dundee St, Edinburgh, Scotland, Fiona Maxwell-Hoy Tel: (0131) 229 6800 Fax: (0131) 229 9070

Birmingham Books
Central Library, Chamberlain Sq, Birmingham B3 3HQ
Tel: (0121) 235 2868; (0121) 235 4511
Fax: (0121) 233 9702; (0121) 233 4458
ISBN Prefix(es): 0-7093

Birmingham Library Information Services
Main Library, Information Services, Edgbaston, Birmingham B15 2TT
Tel: (0121) 303 4511; (0121) 233 9702; (0121) 235 2868 Fax: (0121) 233 4458
E-mail: central.library@birmingham.gov.uk
Web Site: www.birmingham.gov.uk; www.is.bham.ac.uk
ISBN Prefix(es): 0-7093; 0-901011

Bishopsgate Press Ltd+
Bartholomew House, 15 Tonbridge Rd, Hiddenborough, Tonbridge, Kent TN11 9BH
Tel: (01732) 833778 Fax: (01732) 833090
Key Personnel
Chief Executive: Ian Straker
Publishing Manager: Bob Wilson
Founded: 1800
Subjects: Biography, Crafts, Games, Hobbies, Film, Video, Finance, Religion - Other
ISBN Prefix(es): 0-900873; 1-85219
Parent Company: Whitstable Litho Ltd, Milstrood Rd, Whitstable, Kent CT5 3PP

BLA Publishing Ltd+
BIC Ling Kee House, One Christopher Rd, East Grinstead, West Sussex RH19 3BT
Tel: (01342) 318980 Fax: (01342) 410980
Key Personnel
Chairman: Bak Ling Au
Contact: Penny Kitchenham
Founded: 1981
Specialist packagers (Illustrated Trade & Children's).
Subjects: Aeronautics, Aviation, Antiques, Biological Sciences, Crafts, Games, Hobbies, Maritime, Religion - Other
ISBN Prefix(es): 0-907733
Parent Company: Ling Kee (UK) Ltd
Associate Companies: Ward Lock Educational Co Ltd

A & C Black Publishers Ltd+
Subsidiary of Bloomsbury Publishing PLC
37 Soho Sq, London W1D 3QZ
Tel: (020) 7758 0200 Fax: (020) 7758 0222
E-mail: enquiries@acblack.co.uk
Web Site: www.acblack.co.uk
Key Personnel
Chairman: Nigel Newton
Dir: Charles Black
Man Dir: Jill Coleman
Production: Oscar Heini
Rights Dir: Paul Langridge
Distribution Dir: Terry Rouelett
Publicity: Rosanna Bortoli
Founded: 1807
Subjects: Art, Crafts, Games, Hobbies, Drama, Theater, Education, Maritime, Music, Dance, Natural History, Nonfiction (General), Sports, Athletics, Ornithology, Reference
ISBN Prefix(es): 0-7136; 0-212
Total Titles: 1,300 Print
Imprints: Andrew Brodie; Adlard Coles Nautical; Christopher Helm (Publishers) Ltd; Herbert Press Ltd; Pica Press; T & AD Poyser Ltd; Thomas Reed
Distributed by Midpoint Trade Books
Distributor for Magi Children's Books; Sheridan House; Sunflower Books; V&A Publications
Warehouse: Macmillan Distribution Ltd, Houndsmills, Basingstoke, Hants RG21 6XS Fax: (01256) 327 961 Web Site: www.macmillandistribution.co.uk
Orders to: Macmillan Distribution Ltd, Houndsmills, Basingstoke, Hants RG21 6XS Fax: (01256) 327 961 Web Site: www.macmillandistribution.co.uk

Black Ace Books+
PO Box 6557, Forfar DD8 2YS
Tel: (01307) 465096 Fax: (01307) 465494
Web Site: www.blackacebooks.com
Key Personnel
Dir: Hunter Steele; Boo Wood
Founded: 1991
Specialize in high quality fiction.
Subjects: Fiction, History, Philosophy
ISBN Prefix(es): 1-872988
Number of titles published annually: 5 Print
Total Titles: 30 Print
Parent Company: Black Ace Enterprises
Associate Companies: Maran Steele Music

Black Dagger, imprint of BBC Audiobooks

Black Lace, imprint of Virgin Publishing Ltd

Black Spring Press Ltd+
126 Cornwall Rd, 2nd floor, London SE1 8TQ
Tel: (020) 7401 2044 Fax: (020) 7401 2055
E-mail: bsp@blackspring.demon.co.uk
Key Personnel
Dir: M Prausnitz E-mail: maja@blackspring.demon.co.uk; S R J Pettifar E-mail: bsp@blackspring.demon.co.uk
Founded: 1984
Subjects: Fiction, Music, Dance
ISBN Prefix(es): 0-948238; 0-931181
Orders to: Airlift Book Co, 8 The Arena, Mollison Ave, Enfield EN3 7NJ Tel: (020) 8804 0400 Fax: (020) 8804 0044

Black Swan, imprint of Transworld Publishers Ltd

Blackbirch Press, imprint of Thomson Gale

Blackie Children's Books+
80 Strand, London WC2R 0RL
Tel: (020) 7010 3000 Fax: (020) 7010 6060
Telex: 917181
ISBN Prefix(es): 0-216
Parent Company: The Penguin Group
Shipping Address: Penguin Books, Bath Rd, Harmondsworth, Middx UB7 0DA
Warehouse: Penguin Books, Bath Rd, Harmondsworth, Middx UB7 0DA
Orders to: Penguin Books, Bath Rd, Harmondsworth, Middx UB7 0DA

Blackstaff Press+
Member of W & G Baird Group
Blackstaff House, Wildflower Way, Apollo Rd, Belfast BT12 6TA
Tel: (028) 9066 8074 Fax: (028) 9066 8207
E-mail: info@blackstaffpress.com
Web Site: www.blackstaffpress.com
Key Personnel
Chairman: Roy Bailie
Man Dir: Anne Tannahill
Marketing & Publicity Manager: Bairbre Ryan E-mail: marketing@blackstaffpress.com
Managing Editor: Patricia Horton
Production: Elizabeth McBlain
Rights: Susan Dalzell
Publicity: Sarah Harding E-mail: marketing@blackstaffpress.com
Founded: 1971
Subjects: Art, Biography, Cookery, Drama, Theater, Fiction, History, Humor, Literature, Literary Criticism, Essays, Music, Dance, Natural History, Nonfiction (General), Photography, Poetry, Regional Interests, Religion - Buddhist, Religion - Catholic, Religion - Hindu, Religion - Islamic, Religion - Jewish, Religion - Protestant, Religion - Other, Travel
ISBN Prefix(es): 0-85640
Orders to: Dufour Editions Inc, Byers Rd, PO Box 7, Chester Springs, PA 19425-0007, United States Tel: 610-458-5005 Fax: 610-458-7103 E-mail: info@dufoureditions.com
Gill & Macmillan Distribution, 10 Hume Ave, Park West, Dublin 12, Ireland Tel: (3531) 500 9500 Fax: (3531) 500 9599 E-mail: sales@gillmacmillan.ie Web Site: www.gillmacmillan.ie
Peter Hyde Associates (PTY) Ltd, PO Box 2856, Cape Town 8000, South Africa Tel: (021) 423 6692 Fax: (021) 422 0375 E-mail: peterhyde@intekom.co.za

Blackwell Business, imprint of Blackwell Publishing Ltd

Blackwell Finance, imprint of Blackwell Publishing Ltd

Blackwell Publishing Ltd+
Member of The Blackwell Group
108 Cowley Rd, Oxford OX4 1JF
Tel: (01865) 791100 Fax: (01865) 791347
Web Site: www.blackwellpublishers.co.uk
Telex: 837022 Cable: BOOKS OXFORD
Key Personnel
Publisher, Aquaculture & Fisheries, Food Science, Agriculture: Nigel Balmforth E-mail: nigel.balmforth@oxon.blackwellpublishing.com

Deputy Divisional Dir Engineering & Construction: Julia Burden E-mail: julia.burden@oxon.blackwellpublishing.com
Commissioning Editor, Philosophy: Nick Bellorini E-mail: nick.bellorini@oxon.blackwellpublishing.com
Commissioning Editor, Literature: Emma Bennett E-mail: emma.bennett@oxon.blackwellpublishing.com
Senior Commissioning Editor, Literature & Classical Studies: Al Bertrand E-mail: alfred.bertrand@oxon.blackwellpublishing.com
Commissioning Editor, Psychology & Education: Sarah Bird E-mail: sarah.bird@oxon.blackwellpublishing.com
Publisher, Nursing & Health Sciences: Griselda Campbell E-mail: griselda.campbell@oxon.blackwellpublishing.com
Academic & Science Books Director: Philip Carpenter E-mail: philip.carpenter@oxon.blackwellpublishing.com
Commissioning Editor, Dentistry & Health Sciences: Caroline Connelly E-mail: caroline.connelly@oxon.blackwellpublishing.com
Senior Commissioning Editor, Earth Sciences: Ian Francis E-mail: ian.francis@oxon.blackwellpublishing.com
Senior Commissioning Editor, Theology & Religious Studies: Rebecca Harkin E-mail: rebecca.harkin@oxon.blackwellpublishing.com
Associate Editorial Dir, History: Tessa Harvey E-mail: tessa.harvey@oxon.blackwellpublishing.com
Commissioning Editor, Nursing: Beth Knight E-mail: beth.knight@oxon.blackwellpublishing.com
Commissioning Editor: Elizabeth Marchant E-mail: elizabeth.marchant@oxon.blackwellpublishing.com
Senior Commissioning Editor, Engineering & Construction: Madeleine Metcalfe E-mail: madeleine.metcalfe@oxon.blackwellpublishing.com
Senior Commissioning Editor, Business & Management: Rosemary Nixon E-mail: rosemary.nixon@oxon.blackwellpublishing.com
Dir of Medical Publishing: Andrew Robinson E-mail: andrew.robinson@oxon.blackwellpublishing.com
Senior Commissioning Editor, Chemistry: Paul Sayer E-mail: paul.sayer@oxon.blackwellpublishing.com
Associate Publishing Dir, Veterinary Medicine: Antonia Seymour E-mail: antonia.seymour@oxon.blackwellpublishing.com
Commissioning Editor, Ecology & Evolution: Sarah Shannon E-mail: sarah.shannon@oxon.blackwellpublishing.com
Publisher, Human Geography, Sociology & Politics: Justin Vaughan E-mail: justin.vaughan@oxon.blackwellpublishing.com
Publisher, Modern History: Christopher Wheeler E-mail: christopher.wheeler@oxon.blackwellpublishing.com
Marketing & Sales Dir: Tom Gold-Blyth E-mail: tom.gold-blyth@oxon.blackwellpublishing.com
Marketing Manager, History, Classics, Anthropology, Archaeology, Sociology: Jennifer Howell E-mail: jennifer.howell@oxon.blackwellpublishing.com
Senior Marketing Controller, Business & Management, Economics & Finance, Psychology & Education: Eloise Keating E-mail: eloise.keating@oxon.blackwellpublishing.com
Nursing & Health Sciences: Sharon Kershaw E-mail: sharon.kershaw@oxon.blackwellpublishing.com
Senior Marketing Manager: Paul Millicheap E-mail: paul.millich@oxon.blackwellpublishing.com
Chemistry, Food, Aquaculture & Fisheries: Katie Moll E-mail: katie.moll@oxon.blackwellpublishing.com
Associate Divisional Marketing Manager, Literature & Philosophy: Laura Montgomery E-mail: laura.montgomery@oxon.blackwellpublishing.com
Veterinary Medicine & Agriculture: Sarah-Kate Powell E-mail: sarah-kate.powell@oxon.blackwellpublishing.com
Dir-Medical Marketing: Philip Saugman E-mail: philip.saugman@oxon.blackwellpublishing.com
Dentistry: Jennifer Stewart E-mail: jennifer.stewart@oxon.blackwellpublishing.com
Medical Sales Manager: Darren Webster E-mail: darren.webster@oxon.blackwellpublishing.com
Marketing Manager - Science, Geography, Politics & Social Policy: Katherine Wheatley E-mail: katherine.wheatley@lackwellpublishing.com
Field Sales Manager - Asia, India, Middle East & Africa: Alberto Barraclough E-mail: alberto.barraclough@oxon.blackwellpublishing.com
Account Manager: Stephen Barrett E-mail: stephen.barrett@oxon.blackwellpublishing.com
Trade Marketing Controller: Neil Burling E-mail: neil.burling@oxon.blackwellpublishing.com
Sales Dir: Edward Crutchley E-mail: edward.crutchley@oxon.blackwellpublishing.com
Regional Sales Manager - UK & Europe: Gavin Lythe E-mail: gavin.lythe@oxon.blackwellpublishing.com
Account Manager: Simon Mawdsley E-mail: simon.mawdsley@oxon.blackwellpublishing.com; Alan Sedgman E-mail: alan.sedgman@oxon.blackwellpublishing.com
Sales Assistant: Elly Thomson E-mail: helena.thomson@oxon.blackwellpublishing.com
Senior Sales Administrator: Pam Todd E-mail: pam.todd@oxon.blackwellpublishing.com
Account Manager: Ben Townsend E-mail: ben.townsend@oxon.blackwellpublishing.com
Sales Assistant: Rachel Wilkinson E-mail: rachel.wilkinson@oxon.blackwellpublishing.com
Founded: 1922
Allied Companies: Blackwell Scientific Publications Ltd; Polity Press; NCC Blackwell.
Subjects: Business, Computer Science, Economics, Finance, Geography, Geology, Government, Political Science, History, Labor, Industrial Relations, Language Arts, Linguistics, Law, Literature, Literary Criticism, Essays, Philosophy, Psychology, Psychiatry, Religion - Other, Social Sciences, Sociology, Women's Studies
ISBN Prefix(es): 0-631; 0-85520; 0-86216; 0-943205
Imprints: Blackwell Finance; Blackwell Reference; Blackwell Business
U.S. Office(s): Blackwell Publishers Inc, 238 Main Street, Cambridge, MA 02142, United States Tel: 617-547-7110 Fax: 617-547-0789
Warehouse: Marston Book Services Ltd, Osney Mead, Oxford OX2 0DT Tel: (01865) 791155 Fax: (01865) 791927

Blackwell Reference, imprint of Blackwell Publishing Ltd

Blackwell Science Ltd+
Osney Mead, Oxford OX2 0EL
Tel: (01865) 206206 Fax: (01865) 721205
E-mail: shona.macdonald@blacksci.co.uk
Telex: 83355 MEDBOK G
Key Personnel
Chairman: Nigel Blackwell
Man Dir: Robert Campbell
Finance Dir: Martin Wilkinson
Editorial Dir: Peter Saugman
Production Dir: John Strange
Sales Dir: Edward Crutchley
Founded: 1939
Subjects: Architecture & Interior Design, Behavioral Sciences, Chemistry, Chemical Engineering, Child Care & Development, Earth Sciences, Fashion, Geography, Geology, Health, Nutrition, Law, Medicine, Nursing, Dentistry, Psychology, Psychiatry, Science (General), Sports, Athletics, Veterinary Science
ISBN Prefix(es): 0-86542; 0-632
Subsidiaries: Blackwell MZV; Blackwell Science (Australia) Pty Ltd; Munksgaard, International Booksellers & Publishers Ltd; Arnette Blackwell; Blackwell Science (Japan); Blackwell Science Ltd; Blackwell Wissenschafts-Verlag GmbH; Blackwell Science Inc
Bookshop(s): Art & Poster Shop, Broad St, Oxford; MOMA, Pembroke St, Oxford
Shipping Address: Marston Book Services Ltd, Osney Mead, Oxford 0X2 0DT
Orders to: Marston Book Services Ltd, Osney Mead, Oxford 0X2 0DT

John Blake Publishing Ltd+
3 Bramber Court, 2 Bramber Rd, London W14 9PB
Tel: (020) 7381 0666 Fax: (020) 7381 6868
E-mail: words@blake.co.uk
Web Site: www.blake.co.uk
Key Personnel
Man Dir: John Blake E-mail: john@blake.co.uk
Deputy Man Dir: Rosie Ries E-mail: rosie@blake.co.uk
Executive Editor: Adam Parfitt E-mail: adam@blake.co.uk
Production Editor: Michelle Signore
Founded: 1991
Subjects: Biography, Criminology, Fiction, Nonfiction (General), Radio, TV
ISBN Prefix(es): 1-85782
Number of titles published annually: 60 Print
Imprints: Blake Publishing; Metro Publishing
Sales Office(s): Derek Searle Associates Ltd, The Coach House, Cippenham Lodge, Cippenham Lane, Slough, Berks SL1 5AN
Tel: (01753) 539 295 Fax: (01753) 551 863
E-mail: dsapublish@aol.com (UK & Europe)
U.S. Office(s): 82 Wall St, Suite 1105, New York, NY 10005, United States Fax: 212-968-7962
Distributed by Bookwise International (Australia); Hushion House Publishing Ltd (Canada); Forrester Books NZ Ltd (New Zealand); Peter Hyde Associates (South Africa); Seven Hills Book Distribtors (US)
Orders to: Little Hamptons, Faraday Close Durrington Worthing, West Sussex BN13 3RB
Tel: (01903) 828 500 Fax: (01903) 828 635
E-mail: lml@lbsltd.co.uk

Blake Publishing, imprint of John Blake Publishing Ltd

Blaketon Hall Ltd
Unit 1, 26 Marsh Green Rd, Marsh Barton, Exeter, Devon EX2 8PN
Tel: (01392) 210 602 Fax: (01392) 421 165
E-mail: sales@blaketonhall.co.uk
Web Site: www.blaketonhall.co.uk
Key Personnel
Man Dir: John Shillingford E-mail: martin@blaketonhall.co.uk
Dir: Pat Shillingford
Founded: 1976
Also acts as remainder dealer.
Subjects: Animals, Pets, Crafts, Games, Hobbies, How-to, Nonfiction (General)
ISBN Prefix(es): 0-907854

Blandford, imprint of Cassell & Co

UNITED KINGDOM

Blandford Publishing Ltd+
Stanley House, 3 Fleets Lane, Poole, Dorset BH15 3A1
Tel: (01202) 665432 *Fax:* (01202) 666219
Telex: 9413701
Key Personnel
Chairman & Chief Executive: Philip Sturrock
Editorial Dir, Rights & Special Sales: Alison Goff
Sales Dir: Finbarr McCabe
Founded: 1919
Subjects: Animals, Pets, Astrology, Occult, Crafts, Games, Hobbies, Criminology, History, Music, Dance, Natural History, Outdoor Recreation, Sports, Athletics
ISBN Prefix(es): 0-7137
Parent Company: Continuum International Publishing Group Ltd

Bloodaxe Books Ltd+
Highgreen, Tarset, Northumberland NE48 1RP
Tel: (01434) 240 500 *Fax:* (01434) 240 505
E-mail: editor@bloodaxebooks.demon.co.uk
Web Site: www.bloodaxebooks.com
Key Personnel
Chairman: Simon Thirsk
Editor: Neil Astley
Rights & Permissions Manager: Peg Osterman
Publicity: Christine MacGregor
Founded: 1978
Subjects: Poetry
ISBN Prefix(es): 0-906427; 1-85224
Number of titles published annually: 40 Print
U.S. Office(s): DuFour Editions Inc, PO Box 7, Chester Springs, PA 19425-0007, United States *Tel:* 610-458-5005 *Fax:* 610-458-7103 *E-mail:* dufour8023@aol.com
Orders to: Littlehampton Book Services, Centre Warehouse, Columbia Bldg, Faraday Durington Close, Worthing, West Sussex BN13 3RB *Tel:* (01903) 828 800 *Fax:* (01903) 828 801 *E-mail:* orders@lbsltd.co.uk

Bloomsbury Publishing PLC+
38 Soho Sq, London W1D 3HB
Tel: (020) 7494 2111 *Fax:* (020) 7434 0151
E-mail: csm@bloomsbury.com
Web Site: www.bloomsburymagazine.com
Key Personnel
Chairman & Man Dir: Nigel Newton
Publishing Dir, Fiction: Liz Calder
Publishing Dir, Reference: Kathy Rooney
Production Dir: Penny Edwards
Publicity Dir: Katie Bond
Editor-in-Chief: Alexandra Pringle
International Rights: Ruth Logan
Sales, UK: David Ward
Marketing: Minna Fry
Founded: 1987
Subjects: Biography, Career Development, Child Care & Development, Communications, Cookery, Crafts, Games, Hobbies, Drama, Theater, Economics, Fiction, Finance, History, How-to, Humor, Literature, Literary Criticism, Essays, Management, Marketing, Medicine, Nursing, Dentistry, Nonfiction (General), Self-Help
ISBN Prefix(es): 0-7475
Number of titles published annually: 1,000 Print
Subsidiaries: A & C Black Publishing Ltd
Orders to: Macmillan Distribution Ltd, Houndsmill, Basingstoke, Hants RG21 6XS

Blorenge Books+
Blorenge Cottage, Church Lane, Llan-ffwyst, Y Fenni NP7 9NG
Tel: (01873) 856114
Key Personnel
Proprietor: Chris Barber
Founded: 1985
Subjects: Fiction, History, Mysteries, Outdoor Recreation, Travel
Number of titles published annually: 3 Print
Total Titles: 12 Print

Blueprint, *imprint of* Routledge

Blueprint+
Leatherhead, Randalls Rd, Surrey KT22 7RU
Tel: (01372) 802080 *Fax:* (01372) 802079
E-mail: publications@pira.co.uk
Key Personnel
Publisher: Annabel Taylor
Subjects: Photography, Publishing & Book Trade Reference
Parent Company: Pira International

BMJ Publishing Group+
BMA House, Tavistock Sq, London WC1H 9JR
Tel: (020) 7387 4499; (020) 7383 6245
Fax: (020) 7383 6661; (020) 7383 6662
E-mail: customerservices@bmjbooks.com
Web Site: www.bmjpg.com
Key Personnel
Chief Executive & Editor: Dr Richard Smith
Business Development Dir: Maurice Long
Publisher: John Hudson *E-mail:* jhudson@bmjbooks.com
Publishing Dir, Specialist Journals: Alexandra Williamson
Production Executive: Nathan Harris *E-mail:* nharris@bmjbooks.com
Sales & Marketing Executive: Clair Grant-Salmon *E-mail:* cgrantsalmon@bmjbooks.com
Sales & Marketing Manager: Helen Robertson *E-mail:* hrobertson@bmjbooks.com
Rights Executive: Kate Webster *E-mail:* rights@bmjbooks.com
Books Division Manager, Rights & Permisssions: John Hudson
Commissioning Editor: Mary Banks *E-mail:* mbanks@bmjbooks.com
Development Editor: Christina Karaviotis *E-mail:* ckaraviotis@bmjbooks.com
Founded: 1857
Subjects: Medicine, Nursing, Dentistry
ISBN Prefix(es): 0-7279; 0-900221
Parent Company: British Medical Association
Imprints: PSP
Subsidiaries: Professional & Scientific Publications
Distributed by AMA Services (WA) Pty Ltd (Australia); American College of Physicians (USA, Mexico); Apac Publishers Services (Far East, excluding Japan & Taiwan); BMJ Books (USA); Canadian Medical Association (Canada); HWA Eng Trading Co (Taiwan); Jaypee Brothers (India); Medical Association of South Africa (South Africa); Nankodo Co Ltd (Japan); Phi Shoten (Japan); F K Schattauer (Germany)
Distributor for American Academy of Ophthalmology; American Academy of Physicians; British Dental Journal; Schattauer
Foreign Rep(s): Anthony Rudkin Associates (Cyprus, Greece, Middle East, North Africa, Turkey, Iran); Associated Marketing Services (France & Spain, Italy & Portugal); Brookside Publishing Services (Ireland); David Towle International (Baltic States, Scandinavia); John Wilde Partnership (Austria, Germany & Switzerland); Kelvin Van Hasselt (Africa, Caribbean)
Bookshop(s): Burton St, London WC1 *Tel:* (020) 7383 6244 *Fax:* (020) 7383 6455 *E-mail:* orders@bmjbookshop.com *Web Site:* www.bmjbookshop.com
Shipping Address: Unit 11c, North Orbital Trading Estate, Napsbury Lane, St Albans, Herts AL1 1XB
Warehouse: Unit 11c, North Orbital Trading Estate, Napsbury Lane, St Albans, Herts AL1 1XB

Boatswain Press, *imprint of* Kenneth Mason Publications Ltd

Bobcat Books, *imprint of* Omnibus Press

Bodley Head CHildrens, *imprint of* Random House UK Ltd

Book Club Associates, see BCA - Book Club Associates

The Book Guild Ltd+
Temple House, 25 High St, Lewes, East Sussex BN1 2LU
Tel: (01273) 472534 *Fax:* (01273) 476472
E-mail: info@bookguild.co.uk
Web Site: www.bookguild.co.uk
Key Personnel
Chairman: G M Nissen, CBE
Editorial Dir: Carol Biss
Founded: 1982
Subjects: Art, Biography, Fiction, History, Literature, Literary Criticism, Essays, Military Science, Travel
ISBN Prefix(es): 1-85776; 0-86332
Number of titles published annually: 100 Print
Orders to: Vine House Distribution, Waldenbury, North Common, Chailey, East Sussex BN8 4DR *Tel:* (01825) 723398 *Fax:* (01825) 724188 *E-mail:* sales@vinehouseuk.co.uk *Web Site:* www.vinehouseuk.co.uk
Returns: Vine House Distribution, Waldenbury, North Common, Chailey, East Sussex BN8 4DR
Membership(s): IPG; Publishers' Association

Book House, *imprint of* The Salariya Book Co Ltd

Book Marketing Ltd
7 John St, London WC1N 2ES
Tel: (020) 7440 8931 *Fax:* (020) 7242 7485
E-mail: bml@bookmarketing.co.uk
Web Site: www.bookmarketing.co.uk
Key Personnel
Man Dir: Jo Henry
Founded: 1990
Market research company.
Subjects: Publishing & Book Trade Reference
ISBN Prefix(es): 1-873517
Total Titles: 15 Print

Book Packaging & Marketing+
One Church St, Blakesley NN12 8RA
Tel: (01327) 861300 *Fax:* (01327) 861300
Key Personnel
Proprietor: Martin F Marix Evans *E-mail:* martin@marixevans.freeserve.co.uk
Founded: 1989
Book creator, authorship, photography, picture research, delivered as ready-for-press or film or printed books or as tiles for incorporation into website.
Specialize in Illustrated trade & reference books, editorial & authorship, picture research & production services.
Subjects: History, Military Science, Photography, Travel
Number of titles published annually: 4 Print; 1 Online
Total Titles: 50 Print; 3 Online

Bookmarks Publications+
One Bloomsbury St, London WC1B 3QE
Tel: (020) 7637 1848 *Fax:* (020) 7637 3416
E-mail: mailorder@bookmarks.uk.com
Web Site: www.bookmarks.uk.com
Key Personnel
Editorial: Emma Bircham *E-mail:* publications@bookmarks.uk.com
Founded: 1979
Publisher for the Socialist Workers' Party (GB).

PUBLISHERS UNITED KINGDOM

Subjects: Economics, Government, Political Science, History, Labor, Industrial Relations
ISBN Prefix(es): 0-906224; 1-898876
Branch Office(s)
GPO Box 1473N, Melbourne 3001, Australia

Books for Europe Ltd+
3 Sutton Court, Grange Rd, London W5 3PG
Tel: (020) 8840 6672 *Fax:* (020) 8840 6672
Key Personnel
Man Dir: Juliusz Komarnicki *Fax:* (020) 8966 7865 *E-mail:* juliusz.komarnicki@freesurf.ch
Founded: 1984
Also acts as sales agent in UK, European Community & Middle East for publishers.
Subjects: Accounting, Advertising, Aeronautics, Aviation, Antiques, Archaeology, Architecture & Interior Design, Art, Asian Studies
Associate Companies: Book Representation & Distribution Ltd
Branch Office(s)
CP 196, 6908 Massagno, Switzerland *Tel:* (091) 9671539 *Fax:* (091) 9667865

Books International+
101 Lynchford Rd, Farnborough, Hants GU14 6ET
Tel: (01252) 376564 *Fax:* (01252) 370181
E-mail: booksinter@aol.com
Web Site: www.books-international.co.uk/
Key Personnel
President: Mr Kris Machala
Founded: 1989
Subjects: Aeronautics, Aviation, Automotive, Crafts, Games, Hobbies, History, Maritime, Military Science, Publishing & Book Trade Reference, Transportation
ISBN Prefix(es): 0-9528867
Parent Company: Books International, Poland
Imprints: AJ Press
Branch Office(s)
Books International, ul Lubelska 30-32, 03-308 Warsaw, Poland
Distributor for AJ Press
Bookshop(s): 101 Lynchford Rd, Farnborough, Hants GU14 6ET

Books of Zimbabwe Publishing Co (Pvt) Ltd
130A South Rd, Haywards Heath, West Sussex RH16 4LP
Tel: (01444) 455549
E-mail: info@booksofzimbabwe.com
Web Site: www.booksofzimbabwe.com
Key Personnel
Rights & Permissions: Joan Hopcraft
Founded: 1968
Subjects: Biography, Education, Fiction, Foreign Countries, History, Nonfiction (General)
ISBN Prefix(es): 0-86920
Total Titles: 140 Print
Subsidiaries: Africana Book Society (Pty) Ltd

Books on Screen, *imprint of* Butterworths Tolley

Boosey & Hawkes Music Publishers Ltd+
295 Regent St, London W1B 2JH
Tel: (020) 7580 2060 *Fax:* (020) 7291 7109
E-mail: information@boosey.com
Web Site: www.boosey.com/publishing
Key Personnel
Chief Executive: Richard Holland
Sales & Marketing Dir: S A Richards
Founded: 1890
Also acts as a distributor for other music companies & book publishers of musical background books.
Subjects: Music, Dance
ISBN Prefix(es): 0-85162
Parent Company: Boosey & Hawkes PLC
Divisions: B & H Inc, Printed Music Division

U.S. Office(s): B & H Inc, 24 E 21 St, 2nd floor, New York, NY, United States *Tel:* 212-358-5302 *E-mail:* trade.uk@boosey.com
Orders to: The Hyde, Edgware Rd, London NW9 6JN *Tel:* (020) 8205 3861 *Fax:* (020) 8200 3737

Borland Press, *imprint of* Pearson Education Europe, Mideast & Africa

Borthwick Institute Publications
University of York, Heslington, York YO10 5DD
Tel: (01904) 321160
Web Site: www.york.ac.uk/borthwick
Founded: 1950
Subjects: Archaeology, Genealogy, History
Number of titles published annually: 10 Print
Total Titles: 100 Print

Boulevard Books UK, *imprint of* Boulevard Books UK/The Babel Guides

Boulevard Books UK/The Babel Guides+
71 Lytton Rd, Oxford OX4 3NY
Tel: (01865) 712931 *Fax:* (01865) 712931
E-mail: raybabel@dircon.co.uk
Web Site: www.babelguides.com
Key Personnel
Dir, Boulevard Books UK: Ray Keenoy
Rights & Marketing Mgr, Babel Guides to Fiction in English Translation: Clara Corona
Founded: 1989
Publish contemporary world fiction in English translation, popular guides to fiction in translation.
Subjects: Fiction, Literature, Literary Criticism, Essays
ISBN Prefix(es): 1-899460
Number of titles published annually: 4 Print
Total Titles: 30 Print
Imprints: Babel Guides; Boulevard Books UK
Distributed by Gazelle Book Services; ISBS (USA & Canada)

Bounty Books, *imprint of* Octopus Publishing Group

Bounty Books+
Division of The Octopus Group Ltd
2-4 Heron Quays, London E14 4JP
Tel: (020) 7531 8600 *Fax:* (020) 7531 8607
Web Site: www.bounty-publishing.co.uk
Key Personnel
Man Dir: Alison Golt
Publishing & International Sales Dir: Polly Manguel
UK National Accounts Manager: Tony Cartlidge
Export Sales Executive: Emma Harrison
Publisher of promotional titles.
Subjects: Animals, Pets, Antiques, Cookery, Crafts, Games, Hobbies, Fiction, Gardening, Plants, History, Natural History, Religion - Other, Sports, Athletics, Transportation
Distribution Center: Little Hampton Book Services *Tel:* (01903) 828800

Bowerdean Publishing Co Ltd
8 Abbotstone Rd, Putney, London SW15 1QR
Tel: (020) 8788 0938 *Fax:* (020) 8788 0938
Web Site: www.bowerdean.co.uk/
Key Personnel
Contact: Robert Dudley *E-mail:* rdudley@btinternet.com
Founded: 1993
Subjects: Management, Social Sciences, Sociology
ISBN Prefix(es): 0-906097
U.S. Office(s): c/o Kaimleen Hughes, IPM 22893 Quicksilver Dr, Dulles, VA 20166, United States *Tel:* 703-661-1500 *Fax:* 703-661-1501

Distributed by Central Books (UK); DA Information Services (Australia); International Publishers Marketing (USA & Canada); Phambili Agencies (South Africa)
Warehouse: Central Books, 99 Wallis Rd, London E95LN, Bill Wallis *Tel:* (020) 8986 4854 *Fax:* (020) 8533 5821

Bowker, see CSA (Cambridge Scientific Abstracts)

Boxtree, *imprint of* Pan Macmillan

Boxtree Ltd+
20 New Wharf Rd, London N1 9RR
Tel: (020) 7014 6000 *Fax:* (020) 7014 6001
Web Site: www.panmacmillan.com/imprints/boxtree.html
Founded: 1986
Subjects: Film, Video, Humor, Radio, TV, Science Fiction, Fantasy
ISBN Prefix(es): 1-85283; 0-7522
Parent Company: Pan Macmillan
Ultimate Parent Company: Macmillan Group
Distributor for Museum Quilts (UK); Piccadilly (UK); Rosendale (UK); Smith Gryphon (UK)
Warehouse: Little Hampton Book Services

Marion Boyars Publishers Ltd+
24 Lacy Rd, London SW15 1NL
Tel: (020) 8788 9522 *Fax:* (020) 8789 8122
Web Site: www.marionboyars.co.uk
Key Personnel
Man Dir, Rights & Permissions, Publicity, Production: Catheryn Kilgarriff *E-mail:* catheryn@marionboyars.com
Editorial Dir: Arthur Boyars
Editorial: Ken Hollings
Founded: 1975
Independent literary trade publisher
Please include return postage for unsolicited submissions.
Subjects: Drama, Theater, Fiction, Film, Video, Literature, Literary Criticism, Essays, Music, Dance, Philosophy
ISBN Prefix(es): 0-7145
Number of titles published annually: 20 Print
Total Titles: 527 Print
U.S. Office(s): Marion Boyars Publishers Inc, 237 E 39 St, New York, NY 10016, United States, Dir, Publicity & Subsidiary Rights: Franklin Dennis *Tel:* 212-697-9676 *Fax:* 212-808-0664 *E-mail:* fdennis@gc.cuny.edu
Distributor for Peribo Pty Ltd (Australia & New Zealand); Quartet Sales & Marketing (South Africa)
Foreign Rep(s): Peribo Pty (Australia)
Distribution Center: Consortium Book Sales Distribution Inc, 1045 Westgate Dr, Saint Paul, MN 55114-1065, United States *Fax:* 651-917-6406 (US)
Orders to: Central Books, 99 Wallis Rd, London E9 5LN *Tel:* (020) 8986 4854 *Fax:* (020) 8533 5821 *E-mail:* orders@centralbooks.com

Boydell & Brewer Ltd+
PO Box 9, Woodbridge IP12 3DF
Tel: (01394) 610 600 *Fax:* (01394) 610 316
E-mail: boydell@boydell.co.uk
Web Site: www.boydell.co.uk
Key Personnel
Man Dir: Dr R W Barber
Head of Sales & Marketing: Michael Richards
Founded: 1969
Publish & distribute academic & trade history & literature studies. Also publish Hispanic & German studies, plus music, philosophy, film & African studies.
Subjects: African American Studies, Film, Video, History, Literature, Literary Criticism, Essays, Music, Dance, Philosophy, Travel

669

UNITED KINGDOM

ISBN Prefix(es): 0-85115; 0-85993
Number of titles published annually: 200 Print; 5 CD-ROM
U.S. Office(s): Boydell & Brewer Inc, 668 Mount Hope Ave, Rochester, NY 14620-2731, United States *Tel:* 585-275-0419 *Fax:* 585-271-8778
Distributor for Almanach de Gotha; Burke's; Early English Text Society; Victoria County History
Foreign Rep(s): Nancy Bye (USA); Duke Hill/Marsha Martin (USA); Colin Flint (Baltic States, Denmark, Finland, Iceland, Norway, Sweden); Ben Greig (Baltic States, Scandinavia); Hushion House Publishing Inc (Canada); Iberian Book Services (Spain & Portugal); Inter Media Americana (Mexico, South Africa); Pat Malango (USA); Flavio Marcello (France, Italy); Publishers International Marketing; Publishers International Marketing (Korea, Middle East, North Africa, Philippines, Southeast Asia); Remley & Associates (USA); Roger Sauls (USA); Ben Schrager (USA); SHS (Austria, Germany & Switzerland); Siobhan Mullet (Ireland); TML (Pakistan)

BPP Publishing Ltd
Aldine Pl, London W12 8AA
Tel: (020) 8740 2222 *Fax:* (020) 8740 1111
E-mail: info@bpp.com
Web Site: www.bpp.com
Founded: 1976
Subjects: Accounting, Business, Economics, Marketing
ISBN Prefix(es): 0-7517; 0-86277; 1-871824

BPS Books (British Psychological Society)+
Division of British Psychological Society
St Andrews House, 48 Princess Rd E, Leicester LE1 7DR
Tel: (0116) 254 9568 *Fax:* (0116) 247 0787
E-mail: enquiry@bps.org.uk
Web Site: www.bps.org.uk
Key Personnel
Publisher: Joyce Collins
Senior Editor: Jon Reed
Founded: 1981
Membership(s): IPG (Independent Publishers Guild).
Subjects: Behavioral Sciences, Education, Management
ISBN Prefix(es): 0-901715; 1-85433
Total Titles: 100 Print
Imprints: BPS Multimedia
U.S. Office(s): Stylus Publishing Inc, 22883 Quicksilver Dr, Dulles, VA 20166, United States
Distributed by Paul H Brookes (USA)
Warehouse: Plymbridge Distributors Ltd, Estover, Plymouth PL6 7PZ

BPS Multimedia, *imprint of* BPS Books (British Psychological Society)

Dr Barry Bracewell-Milnes
26 Lancaster Court, Banstead, Surrey SM7 1RR
Tel: (01737) 350736 *Fax:* (01737) 371415
Key Personnel
Dir: J B Bracewell-Milnes *E-mail:* jim_1001@hotmail.com
Subjects: Economics, Finance, Taxation

Bradford Books, *imprint of* MIT Press Ltd

Bradt Travel Guides Ltd+
19 High St, Chalfont St Peter, Gerrards Cross SL9 9QE
Tel: (01753) 893444 *Fax:* (01753) 892333
E-mail: enquiries@bradt-travelguides.com
Web Site: www.bradtguides.com
Key Personnel
President: Hilary Bradt
Editor: Patricia Hayne
Office Manager: Debbie Hunter
Sales & Marketing Manager: Peter Webb
Founded: 1972
Subjects: Outdoor Recreation, Travel
ISBN Prefix(es): 0-946983; 1-898323; 1-84162
Total Titles: 59 Print
Associate Companies: The Globe Pequot Press, PO Box 480, 246 Goose Lane, Guilford, CT 06437-0480, United States *Tel:* 203-458-4500 *Fax:* 203-458-4601 *E-mail:* info@globe-pequot.com
Distributed by Altair (Spain); Camerapix Publishers International (East Africa); Cartotheque E G G (France); Craenen, bvba Mechelsesteenweg (Belgium); Eco Trip 2001 (Israel); Globe Pequot Press (North America); Greene Phoenix Marketing (New Zealand); InterMediaAmericana Ltd (Baltic States, West & Southern Africa, Indian Ocean, Middle East (Except Israel), South & Central America, Caribbean); Inter Orbis (Italy); Dennis Jones & Associates Pty Ltd (Australia); Nilsson & Lamm bv (Netherlands); OLF SA (Switzerland); Platypus (Sweden, Norway); Scanvik Books aps Esplanaden (Denmark, Norway); TransQuest Asia Publishers Pte Ltd (Spain); Wild Dog Press (South Africa)
Foreign Rep(s): Altair (Spain); Camerapix Publishers International (East Africa); Cartotheque E G G (France); Craenen, bvba Mechelsesteenweg (Belgium); Eco Trip 2001 (Israel); The Globe Pequot Press (Canada, USA); Greene Phoenix Marketing (New Zealand); Inter Orbis (Italy); InterMediaAmericana Ltd (Baltic States, Caribbean, Central/South America, Middle East exc Israel, South Africa); Dennis Jones & Associates Pty Ltd (Australia); Nilsson & Lamm bv (Netherlands); OLF SA (Switzerland); Platypus (Norway, Sweden); Scanvik Books aps Esplanaden (Denmark, Norway); TransQuest Asia Publishers Pte Ltd (Spain); Wild Dog Press (South Africa)
Orders to: Portfolio, Unit 5, Perivale Industrial Park, Horsenden Lane S, Greenford UB6 7RL
Tel: (020) 8997 9000 *Fax:* (020) 8997 9097
E-mail: sales@portfoliobooks.com

BradyGames, *imprint of* Pearson Education Europe, Mideast & Africa

Brassey's UK Ltd+
Division of Chrysalis Group
The Chrysalis Bldg, Bramley Rd, London W10 6SP
Tel: (020) 7221 2213; (020) 7314 1469 (sales) *Fax:* (020) 7221 6455; (020) 7314 1594 (sales)
E-mail: enquiries@chrysalis.com
Web Site: www.chrysalis.co.uk/books/publisher/brasseys
Key Personnel
Group Sales & Marketing Dir: Richard Samson *Tel:* (020) 7314 1459 *Fax:* (020) 7314 1549 *E-mail:* rsamson@chrysalisbooks.co.uk
Dir of Marketing: Kate Wood *Tel:* (020) 7314 1496 *E-mail:* kwood@chrysalisbooks.co.uk
Marketing & Publicity Manager: Rachel Armstrong *Tel:* (020) 7314 1605 *Fax:* (020) 7314 1549 *E-mail:* rarmstrong@chrysalisbooks.co.uk
Rights: Candida Buckley *Tel:* (01622) 863117 *Fax:* (01622) 863227 *E-mail:* candidabuckley@aol.com
Permissions: Terry Forshaw *Tel:* (020) 7314 1607 *E-mail:* tforshaw@chrysalisbooks.co.uk
Founded: 1886
Subjects: Aeronautics, Aviation, History, Maritime, Military Science
ISBN Prefix(es): 1-57488; 1-85753; 0-904609
Subsidiaries: Brassey's Inc
Divisions: Conway Maritime Press; Putnam Aeronautical
U.S. Office(s): Brassey's Inc, Suite 100, 22883 Quicksilver Dr, Dulles, VA 20166, United States
Orders to: HarperCollins Distribution, Campsie View, Westerhill Rd, Bishopbriggs, Glasgow G64 2QT *Fax:* (087) 0787 1995 (Trade only)

Nicholas Brealey Publishing+
3-5 Spafield St, Clerkenwell, London EC1R 4QB
Tel: (020) 7239 0360 *Fax:* (020) 7239 0370
E-mail: sales@nbrealey-books.com
Web Site: www.nbrealey-books.com
Key Personnel
Man Dir: Nicholas Brealey
Marketing & Publicity Dir: Angie Tainsh *E-mail:* angiet@nbrealey-books.com
International Rights: Sue Coll *E-mail:* rights@nbrealey-books.com
Founded: 1992
Subjects: Business, Career Development, Economics, Finance, Foreign Countries, Management, Self-Help, Foreign Countries
ISBN Prefix(es): 1-85788
Total Titles: 100 Print
U.S. Office(s): Intercultural Press Inc, 374 US Route One, PO Box 700, Yarmouth, ME 04096, United States, Publicity & Marketing: Terri Welch *Tel:* 207-846-5168 *Fax:* 207-846-5181 *E-mail:* books@interculturalpress.com (non-trade sales)
Distributor for Intercultural Press Inc (outside USA)
Warehouse: The Book Service, Colchester Rd, Frating, Frating Green, Essex C07 7DW
Tel: (01206) 256 000
Orders to: The Book Service, Colchester Rd, Frating, Frating Green, Essex C07 7DW
Tel: (01206) 256 000
Nicholas Brealey Publishing, c/o National Book Network, 15200 NBN Way, Blue Ridge Summit, PA 17214, United States
Membership(s): IPG

Breedon Books Publishing Company Ltd+
Division of Breedon Publishing Group
Breedon House, 3 The Parker Centre, Mansfield Rd, Derby DE21 4SZ
Tel: (01332) 384235 *Fax:* (01332) 292755
E-mail: sales@breedonpublishing.co.uk
Web Site: www.breedonbooks.co.uk
Key Personnel
Chairman: Caron Steve *E-mail:* steve.caron@breedonpublishing.co.uk
Customer Services Manager: Beverley Rushworth *E-mail:* beverley.rushworth@breedonpublishing.co.uk
Publicity Manager: Tom Cairns *E-mail:* tom.cairns@breedonpublishing.co.uk
Founded: 1980
Subjects: Biography, Criminology, Genealogy, History, Sports, Athletics
ISBN Prefix(es): 0-907969; 1-873626; 1-85983
Number of titles published annually: 40 Print
Total Titles: 500 Print
Associate Companies: Soccer Publishing Inc, PO Box 1417, Princeton, NJ 08540, United States
Imprints: Breedon Sport; Breedon Heritage
Sales Office(s): Derek Searle Associates Ltd, Unit 13, Progress Business Centre, Whittle Parkway, Burnham, Berks SL1 6DQ *Tel:* (01628) 559500 *Fax:* (01628) 663876 *E-mail:* dsapublish@aol.com

Breedon Heritage, *imprint of* Breedon Books Publishing Company Ltd

Breedon Sport, *imprint of* Breedon Books Publishing Company Ltd

Breese Books Ltd+
164 Kensington Park Rd, London W11 2ER

Tel: (020) 7727 9426 *Fax:* (020) 7229 3395
E-mail: mbreese999@aol.com
Web Site: www.sherlockholmes.co.uk
Key Personnel
Man Dir: Martin Breese
Founded: 1985
Subjects: Fiction
ISBN Prefix(es): 0-947533
Number of titles published annually: 20 Print
Total Titles: 300 Print
Imprints: The Dreamer's Guides
Foreign Rights: Cathy Miller, Foreign Rights Agency (World)
Orders to: Clipper Distribution Services Ltd, Windmill Grove, Portchester, Hants PO16 9HT *Tel:* (01705) 200080 *Fax:* (01705) 200090
Midpoint Trade Books, NY, 27 W 20 St, Suite 1102, New York, NY 10011, United States *Tel:* 212-727-0190 *Fax:* 212-727-0195

Breslich & Foss Ltd+
2a Union Court, 20-22 Union Rd, London SW4 6JP
Tel: (020) 7819 3990 *Fax:* (020) 7819 3998
E-mail: sales@breslichfoss.com
Key Personnel
Man Dir: Paula G Breslich
Foreign Sales: Janet Ravenscroft
Founded: 1978
Also acts as packager.
Subjects: Architecture & Interior Design, Art, Cookery, Crafts, Games, Hobbies, Gardening, Plants, Health, Nutrition, Wine & Spirits
ISBN Prefix(es): 1-85004

Brewin Books, *imprint of* Brewin Books Ltd

Brewin Books Ltd+
Doric House, 56 Alcester Rd, Studley, Warwicks B80 7LG
Tel: (01527) 854228 *Fax:* (01527) 852746
E-mail: enquiries@brewinbooks.com
Web Site: www.brewinbooks.com
Key Personnel
Dir: Alan Brewin
Founded: 1973
Subjects: Biography, Education, Fiction, Genealogy, Health, Nutrition, History, Military Science, Nonfiction (General), Regional Interests, Transportation, Travel, Publish a range of Midland Regional non-fiction titles on the regions history including hospital, health, housing, police, education, transport, local history, biographies, contemporary fiction & some military history. Distribute for several local authorities for walking guides & local history books
ISBN Prefix(es): 0-9505570; 0-947731; 1-85858
Number of titles published annually: 25 Print
Total Titles: 210 Print
Associate Companies: Supaprint (Redditch) Ltd, Enfield Estate, Unit 19, Redditch Worcs B97 6BZ, Manager: Mike Abbott *Tel:* (01527) 8562212 *Fax:* (01527) 8560451 *E-mail:* mike@supaprint.com
Imprints: Brewin Books; Alton Douglas Books; History-into-Print
Distributor for City of Birmingham Libraries & Leisure; Hereford City Council; Rosmini House (Philosophy)
Warehouse: Supaprint (Redditch) Ltd, Enfield Estate, Unit 19, Redditch Worcs B97 6BZ, Manager: Mike Abbott *Tel:* (01527) 8562212 *Fax:* (01527) 8560451 *E-mail:* mike@supaprint.com

Bridge Books+
61 Park Ave, Wrexham LL12 7AW
Tel: (01978) 358661 *Fax:* (01978) 262377
Key Personnel
Official Delegate, Partner: W A Williams
E-mail: waw@bridgebooks.co.uk
Founded: 1983
Subjects: Aeronautics, Aviation, Ethnicity, Genealogy, History, Military Science, Regional Interests
ISBN Prefix(es): 1-872424; 0-9508285
Number of titles published annually: 12 Print
Associate Companies: Maelor Interactive Publishing Ltd, Wrexham
Subsidiaries: Maelor Interactive Publishing Ltd

Brilliant Publications+
One Church View, Sparrow Hall Farm, Edlesborough, Dunstable LU6 2ES
Tel: (01525) 229720 *Fax:* (01525) 229725
E-mail: sales@brilliantpublications.co.uk
Web Site: www.brilliantpublications.co.uk
Key Personnel
Publisher: Priscilla Hannaford *E-mail:* priscilla@brilliantpublications.co.uk
Founded: 1993
Specialize in educational books for 3-13 year olds.
Subjects: Education
ISBN Prefix(es): 1-897675; 1-903893
Number of titles published annually: 20 Print
Total Titles: 100 Print
Membership(s): IPG; Publishers' Association

Brimax, *imprint of* Brimax Books

Brimax Books+
Division of The Octopus Publishing Group
Appledram Barns, Birdham Rd, Chichester PO20 7EQ
Tel: (01243) 792 489 *Fax:* (020) 7531 8607
Pre-school publisher.
Subjects: Fiction, Nonfiction (General), Traditional board books, innovative interactive, classic stories & fairy tales, early learning, reference, new fiction
ISBN Prefix(es): 1-85854; 0-86112; 0-900195; 0-904494
Imprints: Brimax
Orders to: Littlehampton Book Services Ltd, Faraday Close, Durington, Worthing, West Sussex NN10 6RZ *Tel:* (01933) 828801

Britannia Press, *imprint of* East-West Publications (UK) Ltd

British Academic Press, *imprint of* I B Tauris & Co Ltd

The British Academy+
10 Carlton House Terrace, London SW1Y 5AH
Tel: (020) 7969 5200 *Fax:* (020) 7969 5300
E-mail: secretary@britac.ac.uk
Web Site: www.britac.ac.uk
Telex: 263194
Key Personnel
Publications Officer: James Rivington
Rights & Permissions: Janet English
Founded: 1902
The British Academy is a Registered Charity, No 233176.
Subjects: Archaeology, Art, History, Literature, Literary Criticism, Essays, Philosophy, Social Sciences, Sociology
ISBN Prefix(es): 0-85672; 0-902732
Orders to: OUP Distribution Services, Saxon Way West, Corby, Northamptonshire NN18 9ES
Oxbow Books, Park End Place, Oxford OX1 1HN

The British & Foreign Bible Society, see Bible Society

British Association for Adoption & Fostering, see BAAF Adoption & Fostering

British Cement Association, see Concrete Information Ltd

The British Council, Design, Publishing & Print Department
10 Spring Gardens, London SW1A 2BN
Tel: (020) 7930 8466 *Fax:* (020) 7389 6347
E-mail: general.enquiries@britcoun.org
Web Site: www.britishcouncil.org
Telex: 8952201BRICONG
Key Personnel
Head of Dept: Christine Borell
Head of Editorial: Nichola Liu
Founded: 1934
Promotion abroad of a wider knowledge of Britain & the English language, development of closer cultural relations with other countries
Among book & journal titles published or co-published are *British Book News, Media in Education Development, English Language Teaching Journal, ELT Documents, Language Teaching, British Writers, How to Live in Britain, The British Council Collection 1938-84, TV English, Video English*.
Subjects: English as a Second Language, Human Relations, Regional Interests
ISBN Prefix(es): 0-86355; 0-900229; 0-901618
U.S. Office(s): The British Council, The Cultural Attache, British Embassy, 3100 Massachusetts Ave, Washington, DC 20008, United States

British Educational Communication & Technology Agency (BECTA)
Millburn Hill Rd, Science Park, Coventry CV4 7JJ
Tel: (024) 7641 6994 *Fax:* (024) 7641 1418
E-mail: becta@becta.org.uk
Web Site: www.becta.org.uk
Key Personnel
Chief Executive: Owen Lynch
Board Chair: Prof David Hargreaves
Press & Public Relations Officer: Nicola Newman
Founded: 1973
Subjects: Education, Government, Political Science, Technology
ISBN Prefix(es): 0-86184; 0-902204
Imprints: BECTA

British Film Institute, see BFI Publishing

British Horse Society
Stoneleigh Deer Park, Kenilworth, Warwicks CV8 2XZ
Tel: (08701) 202 244 *Fax:* (01926) 707 800
E-mail: enquiry@bhs.org.uk
Web Site: www.bhs.org.uk
Key Personnel
Chief Executive: Hywel Davies
ISBN Prefix(es): 0-900226
Subsidiaries: The British Horse Society Trading Company Ltd

The British Library
St Pancras, 96 Euston Rd, London NW1 2DB
Tel: (01937) 546585 *Fax:* (01937) 546586
E-mail: nbs-info@bl.uk
Web Site: www.bl.uk
Key Personnel
Dir: Robert Smith
Founded: 1973
ISBN Prefix(es): 0-7123
Parent Company: The British Library
Orders to: Turpin Distribution Services Ltd, Blackhorse Rd, Letchworth, Herts SG6 1HN *Tel:* (01462) 672555 *Fax:* (01462) 480947

British Library Document Supply Centre
Document Supply Centre, Boston Spa, Wetherby, West Yorks LS23 7BQ
Tel: (01937) 546060 *Fax:* (01937) 546333
E-mail: dsc-customer-services@bl.uk
Web Site: www.bl.uk

Key Personnel
Publications Officer: Dorothy Drydale
 E-mail: garth.frankland@bl.uk
Founded: 1962
ISBN Prefix(es): 0-7123; 0-9532; 0-904654; 0-900220
Parent Company: British Library, 96 Euston Rd, London NW1 2DB
Orders to: Turpin Distribution Services Ltd, Blackhorse Rd, Letchworth, Herts SG6 1HN *Tel:* (0146) 672555 *Fax:* (0146) 480947

British Library Publications+
96 Euston Rd, London NW1 2DB
Tel: (020) 7412 7000 *Fax:* (020) 7412 7768
E-mail: enquiries@bl.uk
Web Site: www.bl.uk
Key Personnel
Publishing Manager: David Way *Tel:* (020) 7412 7532 *E-mail:* david.way@bl.uk
Founded: 1979
Publishing & book trade reference.
Subjects: Art, History
ISBN Prefix(es): 0-7123
Number of titles published annually: 50 Print; 3 CD-ROM
Total Titles: 600 Print; 10 CD-ROM
Parent Company: The British Library
Distributed by University of Toronto Press (Canada & USA)
Orders to: Extenza-Turpin Distribution Ltd, Stratton Business Park, Pegasus Drive, Biggleswade, Beds SG18 8QB

British Museum Press+
46 Bloomsbury St, London WC1B 3QQ
Tel: (020) 7637 1292 *Fax:* (020) 7436 7315
E-mail: customerservices@bmcompany.co.uk; information@thebritishmuseum.ac.uk
Web Site: www.britishmuseum.co.uk
Telex: 28592 BMPUBS G
Key Personnel
Man Dir: Andrew Thatcher
Production: Susan Walby
Head of Sales, Marketing & Rights: Alasdair MacLeod *E-mail:* a.macleod@bmcompany.co.uk
Publicity: Penelope Vogler
Managing Editor: Teresa Francis
Founded: 1973
Subjects: Archaeology, Art, Asian Studies, Crafts, Games, Hobbies, Ethnicity
ISBN Prefix(es): 0-7141
Parent Company: The British Museum Co Ltd
Bookshop(s): British Museum Shop, Great Russell St, London WC1
Orders to: Thames & Hudson Ltd, 44 Clockhouse Rd, Farnborough, Hants

British Psychological Society, see BPS Books (British Psychological Society)

British Tourist Authority
Thames Tower, Black's Rd, London W6 9EL
Tel: (020) 8846 9000 *Fax:* (020) 8846 0302
Web Site: www.visitbritain.com
Key Personnel
Chief Executive: David Quarmby
Founded: 1969
Subjects: Travel
ISBN Prefix(es): 0-7095; 0-85630
Branch Office(s)
Buenos Aires, Argentina
Sydney, Australia
Brussels, Belgium
Ontario, Canada
Copenhagen, Denmark
Paris, France
Frankfurt, Germany
Hong Kong, Hong Kong
Dublin, Ireland
Milano, Italy
Rome, Italy
Osaka, Japan
Tokyo, Japan
Amsterdam, Netherlands
Auckland, New Zealand
Oslo, Norway
Lisbon, Portugal
Seoul, Republic of Korea
Singapore, Singapore
Craighall, South Africa
Madrid, Spain
Stockholm, Sweden
Zurich, Switzerland
Taipei, Taiwan, Province of China
U.S. Office(s): Chicago, IL, United States
New York, NY, United States

Andrew Brodie, *imprint of* A & C Black Publishers Ltd

Bronant Books, *imprint of* Gwasg Gwenffrwd

Brooklands Books Ltd
PO Box 146, Cobham, Surrey KT11 1LG
Tel: (01932) 865051 *Fax:* (01932) 868803
E-mail: info@brooklands-books.com
Web Site: www.brooklands-books.com
Key Personnel
Man Dir: Ian Dowdeswell
Marketing Dir: Barbara Cleveland
Membership(s): British Motor Heritage.
Subjects: Automotive, Motorcycles, Military, Racing
Number of titles published annually: 50 Print
Total Titles: 800 Print
Branch Office(s)
CarTech, 11605 Kost Dam Rd, North Branch, MN 55056, United States *Tel:* 651-583-3471 *Fax:* 651-583-2023
Distributor for Robert Bentley Inc

The Brown Reference Group PLC+
8 Chapel Pl, Rivington St, London EC2A 3DQ
Tel: (020) 7920 7500 *Fax:* (020) 7920 7501
E-mail: info@brownreference.com
Web Site: www.brownreference.com
Key Personnel
Chairman: Ashley Brown
Man Dir: Sharon Hutton *Tel:* (020) 7920 7508 *E-mail:* shutton@brownpartworks.co.uk
Founded: 1995
Packager of books, partworks & continuity series.
Subjects: Cookery, Crafts, Games, Hobbies, History, Music, Dance, Natural History, Science (General), Social Sciences, Sociology, Military History, Popular Culture
ISBN Prefix(es): 1-84044

Brown, Son & Ferguson, Ltd
4/10 Darnley St, Glasgow G41 2SD
Tel: (0141) 4291234 *Fax:* (0141) 4201694
E-mail: enquiry@skipper.co.uk
Web Site: www.skipper.co.uk *Cable:* SKIPPER GLASGOW
Key Personnel
Chief Executive, Editorial, Production: T Nigel Brown
Sales & Publicity: David H Provan
Rights & Permissions: L Ingram-Brown
Founded: 1832
Subjects: Drama, Theater, Maritime, Scottish Plays, Nautical Publications
ISBN Prefix(es): 0-85174
Number of titles published annually: 10 Print; 1 CD-ROM
Total Titles: 1 CD-ROM
Subsidiaries: James Munro & Co

Brown Wells & Jacobs Ltd
Foresters Hall, 25-27 Westow St, London SE19 3RY
Tel: (020) 8771 5115 *Fax:* (020) 8771 9994
E-mail: postmaster@popking.demon.co.uk
Web Site: www.bwj.org
Key Personnel
Man Dir: Graham Brown *Fax:* (020) 8771 9994
Founded: 1978
Subjects: Nonfiction (General)
Number of titles published annually: 15 Print
Total Titles: 35 Print
Associate Companies: Book Street Ltd

Brunner-Routledge, *imprint of* Taylor & Francis

Bryntirion Press+
Bryntirion, Bridgend CF31 4DX
Tel: (01656) 655886 *Fax:* (01656) 665919
E-mail: office@emw.org.uk
Web Site: www.evangelicalmvt-wales.org/books/bryntirionpress/default.htm
Key Personnel
Press Manager: Huw Kinsey
Founded: 1955
Publish books in Welsh & English
Also distribute for other publishers.
Subjects: Biblical Studies, Biography, History, Religion - Protestant, Theology
ISBN Prefix(es): 0-900898; 0-9502680; 1-85049
Total Titles: 80 Print
Parent Company: Evangelical Movement of Wales
Imprints: Evangelical Library of Wales
Distributed by Evangelical Press (English language titles)

Buildings of England, *imprint of* Penguin Books Ltd

Buildings of England, *imprint of* The Penguin Group UK

Burall Floraprint Ltd
Oldfield Lane, PO Box 29, Wisbech, Cambs PE13 2TH
Tel: (0870) 728 72 22 *Fax:* (0870) 728 72 77
E-mail: floraprint@burall.com
Web Site: www.bflora.com
Key Personnel
Man Dir: Brian Pinker
Founded: 1986
Promotional print for horticulture.
Subjects: Gardening, Plants
ISBN Prefix(es): 0-903001
Total Titles: 8 Print
Parent Company: Burall Ltd
Ultimate Parent Company: The Burall Group Ltd
Foreign Rep(s): John Markham Associates (Canada, USA)
Orders to: John Markham Associates, 11210 Elderberry Way, Rural Route 3, Sidney, BC V8L 5JD, Canada *Tel:* 604-655-1823 *Fax:* 604-655-1826 (Canada & USA)

Business Books, *imprint of* Random House UK Ltd

Business Monitor International+
Mermaid House, 2 Puddle Dock, Blackfriars, London EC4V 3DS
Tel: (020) 7248 0468 *Fax:* (020) 7248 0467
E-mail: subs@businessmonitor.com
Web Site: www.businessmonitor.com
Key Personnel
Agencies & Business Development Manager: Anne Wittman *Tel:* (020) 7557 7110 *E-mail:* awittman@businessmonitor.com
Publisher: Jonathan Feroze *Tel:* (020) 7557 7111 *E-mail:* jferoze@businessmonitor.com; Richard Londesborough *Tel:* (020) 7557 7105 *E-mail:* rlondesborough@businessmonitor.com

PUBLISHERS — UNITED KINGDOM

Head of Marketing, Books: Sarah Bennett *Tel:* (020) 7557 7106 *E-mail:* sbennett@businessmonitor.com
Market Analysis: Terry Alexander *E-mail:* talexander@businessmonitor.com
Syndication & Licensing: Andrew Leighton *E-mail:* aleighton@businessmonitor.com
Subscriptions: Joanna Miller *E-mail:* jmiller@businessmonitor.com
Consultant: Rob Anderson *E-mail:* randerson@businessmonitor.com
Technical Support: David Mulvaney *E-mail:* dmulvaney@businessmonitor.com
Macroeconomic Analysis: Matt Brooks *E-mail:* mbrooks@businessmonitor.com
Commercial Intelligence Service: Nick Jotischky *E-mail:* njotischky@businessmonitor.com
Founded: 1984
Specialize in essential news, data, analysis & forecasts on economic, business & political developments in global emerging markets countries.
Subjects: Business, Chemistry, Chemical Engineering, Developing Countries, Economics, Energy, Engineering (General), Finance, Foreign Countries, Government, Political Science, Journalism, Securities, Social Sciences, Sociology
Number of titles published annually: 80 Print; 28 CD-ROM; 68 Online
Total Titles: 80 Print; 28 CD-ROM; 68 Online
Associate Companies: Commercial Intelligence Service

Buster Books, *imprint of* Michael O'Mara Books Ltd

Butterworth Heinemann, *imprint of* Reed Educational & Professional Publishing

Butterworth Heinemann Ltd, *imprint of* Elsevier Ltd

Butterworths Direct, *imprint of* Butterworths Tolley

Butterworths Tolley+
2 Addiscombe Rd, Croydon CR9 5AF
Tel: (020) 8686 9141; (020) 8662 2000 (customer service) *Fax:* (020) 8686 3155; (020) 8662 2012 (customer service)
E-mail: customer-services@butterworths.com
Key Personnel
Man Dir: Paul Virik
Founded: 1818
Subjects: Accounting, Finance, Law
ISBN Prefix(es): 0-510; 0-406; 0-85459; 0-7545; 1-86012
Number of titles published annually: 120 Print; 10 CD-ROM
Total Titles: 1,000 Print; 50 CD-ROM; 25 E-Book
Parent Company: Reed Elsevier plc, 25 Victoria St, London SW1H 0EX
Associate Companies: Butterworths-Australia, Reed Elsevier Bldg, Tower 2, 475-495 Victoria Ave, Chatswood NSW 2067, Australia *Tel:* (02) 9422-2222 *Fax:* (02) 9422-2444; Butterworths-Canada, 75 Clegg Rd, Markham, ON L6G 1A1, Canada *Tel:* 905-479-2665 *Fax:* 905-479-2826; Butterworths-New Zealand, 205-207 Victoria St, Wellington, New Zealand *Tel:* (04) 385 1479 *Fax:* (04) 385 1598; Butterworths-Asia, N01 Temasek Ave, 17-01 Millenia Tower 039192, Singapore *Tel:* 336 9661 *Fax:* 336 9662; Butterworths-South Africa, 8 Walter Place, Mayville 4091 Natal, South Africa *Tel:* (031) 2683111 *Fax:* (031) 2683108
Imprints: Books on Screen; Butterworths Direct; Eclipse; Tolley
Branch Office(s)
Butterworths, 26 Upper Ormond Quay, Dublin 7, Ireland *Tel:* (03531) 873 1268 (editorial enquiries)
2, Addiscombe Rd, Croyden, Surrey CR9 5AF *Tel:* (020) 8686 9141 *Fax:* (020) 8686 3155
Butterworths LEXIS Direct, Globe House, Victoria Way, Woking, Surrey GU21 1DD *Tel:* (01483) 257725 (online publishing division)
Butterworths, 4 Hill St, Edinburgh EH2 3JZ, Dir: Philip Woods *Tel:* (0131) 225 7828 *Fax:* (0131) 220 1833 *E-mail:* sales.service@butterworths.co.uk
U.S. Office(s): Reed Elsevier Inc, 2 Park Ave, 2nd floor, New York, NY 10016, United States *Tel:* 212-448-2300 *Fax:* 212-448-2196
Bookshop(s): Butterworths Bookshop, 35 Chancery Lane, London WC2A 1EL *Tel:* (020) 7400 2868 *Fax:* (020) 7400 2870
Warehouse: Butterworths Warehouse, Unit 3, 2 Shipton Way, Express Park, Rusden, Northants NN10 6GL *Tel:* (01933) 411682 *Fax:* (01933) 411857
Orders to: Butterworths Warehouse, Unit 3, 2 Shipton Way, Express Park, Rusden, Northants NN10 6GL *Tel:* (01933) 411682 *Fax:* (01933) 411857

Bwrdd Croeso Cymru (Wales Tourist Board)
Brunel House, 2, Fitzalan Rd, Cardiff CF24 0UY
Tel: (029) 2047 5214 *Fax:* (029) 2048 5031
E-mail: info@visitwales.com
Web Site: www.visitwales.com
Key Personnel
Chief Executive: Jonathan Jones
Head of Production Services & Sales: Rhys Jones
Founded: 1969
Subjects: Travel
ISBN Prefix(es): 1-85013; 0-900784
Orders to: Jarrold Publishing, Whitefriars, Norwich NR3 1TR

Byeway Books, *imprint of* Autumn Publishing Ltd

Bygone Kent, *imprint of* Meresborough Books Ltd

CABI Publishing
Division of CAB International
Wallingford, Oxon OX10 8DE
Tel: (01491) 832111 *Fax:* (01491) 833508
E-mail: publishing@cabi.org
Web Site: www.cabi-publishing.org
Key Personnel
Publishing Dir: David Nicholson *E-mail:* d.nicholson@cabi.org
Book Publisher: Tim Hardwick *E-mail:* t.hardwick@cabi.org
Man Dir: Tony Llewellyn *E-mail:* t.llewellyn@cabi.org
Sales & Marketing Dir: Caroline McNamara *E-mail:* c.mcnamara@cabi.org
Commercial Dir: Mr Kelvin Tunley *E-mail:* k.tunley@cabi.org
Promotion Services Manager: Sarah Harris *E-mail:* s.harris@cabi.org
Founded: 1928
A nonprofit international organization dedicated to improving human welfare worldwide through the dissemination, application & generation of scientific knowledge in support of sustainable development.
Subjects: Agricultural Economics, Engineering & Entomology, Animal Breeding, Genetics, Nutrition & Production, Biodiversity, Biological Control, Crop Production & Protection, Dairy Science, Ecology & Environment, Entomology, Forestry, Horticulture, Human Nutrition, Leisure/Tourism, Medicinal Plants, Nematology, Parasitology & Infectious Diseases, Plant Biotechnology, Breeding, Genetic & Pathology, Postharvest, Rural Development, Sugar Industry, Veterinary Medicine, Weed Science
ISBN Prefix(es): 0-85198; 0-85199
Total Titles: 300 Print; 20 CD-ROM; 1 Online; 6 E-Book
U.S. Office(s): 875 Massachusetts Ave, 7th floor, Cambridge, MA 02139, United States *Tel:* (617) 395-4056 *Fax:* (617) 354-6875 *E-mail:* cabi-nao@cabi.org

Cadogan Guides+
Network House, One Ariel Way, London W12 7SL
Tel: (020) 8600 3550 *Fax:* (020) 8600 3599
E-mail: info@cadoganguides.com; editorial@cadoganguides.com; advertising@cadoganguides.com; publicity@cadoganguides.com; marketing@cadoganguides.com
Web Site: www.cadoganguides.com
Key Personnel
Editorial Dir: Vicki Ingle
Founded: 1985
Specialize in Travel Guides.
Subjects: Travel
ISBN Prefix(es): 0-947754; 0-946313; 1-86011
Parent Company: Morris Publications Ltd
U.S. Office(s): The Globe Pequot Press, 6 Business Park Rd, PO Box 833, Old Saybrook, CT 06475-0833, United States
Foreign Rep(s): Books for Europe (Austria, Czech Republic, France, Hungary, Poland, Switzerland); Capricorn Link (Aust) Pty Ltd (Australia); The Globe Pequot Press (Canada, USA); Peter Hyde & Associates (Pty) Ltd (South Africa); Inter Media Americans (IMA) (Caribbean, South America); Nicky La Touche (Italy); Pernille Larsen (Scandinavia); Nilsson & Lamm (Holland); Sandro Salucci (Croatia, Greece, Portugal, Slovenia, Spain)
Orders to: Grantham Book Services, Isaac Newton Way, Alma Park Industrial Estate, Grantham, Lincs NG31 9SD

Calder Publications Ltd+
51 The Cut, London SE1 8LF
Tel: (020) 7633 0599
E-mail: info@calderpublications.com
Web Site: www.calderpublications.com
Key Personnel
Manager, Publishing Dir: John Calder *Tel:* (020) 76333
Production, Editorial, Design, Sales, Rights & Permissions: Toby Fenton
Founded: 1949
Publishers of international literature & books on cultural subjects
No unsol mss considered.
Subjects: Art, Biography, Drama, Theater, Fiction, Literature, Literary Criticism, Essays, Music, Dance, Nonfiction (General), Philosophy, Poetry
ISBN Prefix(es): 0-7145
Number of titles published annually: 30 Print
Total Titles: 400 Print; 200 Online; 200 E-Book
Parent Company: The Calder Educational Trust, 51 The Cut, London SE1 8LF, Contact: John Calder
Associate Companies: Riverrun Press, 1200 County Road 523, Flemington, NJ 08822, United States
Imprints: Riverrun Press
Distributed by Whitehurst & Clark
Foreign Rep(s): Whitehurst & Clarke, Raritan Industrial (Canada, USA)
Warehouse: Combined Book Services, Units I-K Paddock, Wood Distribution Centre, Paddock Wood, Tonbridge, Kent TN12 6UU *Tel:* (01892) 837171 *Fax:* (01892) 837272 *E-mail:* orders@combook.co.uk

Cambridge Scientific Abstracts, see CSA (Cambridge Scientific Abstracts)

UNITED KINGDOM   BOOK

Cambridge University Press+
The Edinburgh Bldg, Shaftesbury Rd, Cambridge CB2 2RU
Tel: (01223) 312393 *Fax:* (01223) 315052
E-mail: information@cup.cam.ac.uk; uksales@cambridge.org (sales); editorial@cambridge.org (editorial enquiries); rights@cambridge.org (rights & permission); www@cambridge.org (web services)
Web Site: www.cambridge.org
Key Personnel
Chief Executive: S Bourne
Editorial Dir: R Barling; A M C Brown; A Gilfillan; M Y Holdsworth
International Dir: P Langworth
Production Dir: C Murray
Rights Sales Manager: Christina Roberts
Permissions: Linda Nicol
Founded: 1534
Subjects: Agriculture, Anthropology, Archaeology, Architecture & Interior Design, Art, Biblical Studies, Biography, Biological Sciences, Chemistry, Chemical Engineering, Computer Science, Drama, Theater, Earth Sciences, Economics, Education, Engineering (General), English as a Second Language, Environmental Studies, Geography, Geology, Government, Political Science, History, Language Arts, Linguistics, Law, Literature, Literary Criticism, Essays, Mathematics, Medicine, Nursing, Dentistry, Music, Dance, Philosophy, Physical Sciences, Psychology, Psychiatry, Social Sciences, Sociology, Theology
Number of titles published annually: 1,600 Print; 10 CD-ROM; 50 Audio
Imprints: Canto
Branch Office(s)
Cambridge University Press, 10 Stamford Rd, Oakleigh, Victoria 3166, Australia *Tel:* (03) 9568 0322 *Fax:* (03) 9563 1517 *E-mail:* info@cambridge.edu.au *Web Site:* www.cambridge.edu.au
Cambridge University Press, Ruiz De Alarcon 13, 28014 Madrid, Spain
Cambridge University Press, 40 W 20 St, New York, NY 10011-4211, United States (US Branches)
Cambridge University Press, 1 The Moorings, Portswood Ridge, Victoria & Alfred Waterfront, Capetown 8001, South Africa
Distributor for The Asser Press (Worldwide)
Foreign Rights: Bardon-Chinese Media Agency (Hong Kong & Macao, Taiwan); Bestun Korea Agency (Korea)
Showroom(s): One & 2 Trinity St, Cambridge CB2 1SU

Camden Large Print, *imprint of* BBC Audiobooks

Camden Press Ltd+
46 Colebrooke Row, London N1 8AF
Tel: (020) 7226 2061 *Fax:* (020) 7226 2418
Key Personnel
Chairman: Robert Borzello
Founded: 1985
Subjects: Art, Biography, Health, Nutrition, Social Sciences, Sociology, Women's Studies
ISBN Prefix(es): 0-948491

Camerapix Publishers International Ltd+
6 Alston Rd, Barnet, Herts EN5 4ET
Tel: (020) 8449 5503 *Fax:* (020) 8449 8120
E-mail: camerapixuk@btinternet.com
Web Site: www.camerapix.com
Key Personnel
Man Dir: Mrs Rukhsana Haq
Dir: Salim Amin
Publisher of travel guides & photographic travel books.
Subjects: Travel
ISBN Prefix(es): 1-874041
Number of titles published annually: 3 Print
Total Titles: 65 Print

Cameron & Hollis+
Imprint of Cameron Books
PO Box 1, Moffat, Dumfries DG10 9SU
Tel: (01683) 220808 *Fax:* (01683) 220012
E-mail: editorial@cameronbooks.co.uk; sales@cameronbooks.co.uk (orders)
Web Site: www.cameronbooks.co.uk
Key Personnel
Dir: Ian Cameron; Jill Hollis
Founded: 1976
Primarily packagers.
Subjects: Architecture & Interior Design, Art, Environmental Studies, Film, Video, Natural History
ISBN Prefix(es): 0-906506
Associate Companies: Movie
Subsidiaries: Edition, Cameron & Hollis

Campbell Books, *imprint of* Macmillan Children's Books

Campbell Books, *imprint of* Pan Macmillan

Candle Books, *imprint of* Angus Hudson Ltd

Candle Books, *imprint of* Lion Hudson PLC

Canongate Academic, *imprint of* Tuckwell Press Ltd

Canongate Books "A" Ltd, *imprint of* Birlinn Ltd

Canongate Books Ltd+
14 High St, Edinburgh EH1 1TE
Tel: (0131) 557 5111 *Fax:* (0131) 557 5211
E-mail: info@canongate.co.uk; customerservices@canongate.co.uk
Web Site: www.canongate.net
Key Personnel
Publisher: Jamie Byng
Production Dir: Caroline Gorham
Rights Manager: Polly Hutchison
Sales Manager: David Graham
Founded: 1973
Subjects: Biography, Fiction, History, Literature, Literary Criticism, Essays, Music, Dance, Non-fiction (General), Poetry, Regional Interests, Travel
ISBN Prefix(es): 0-86241; 1-84195
Number of titles published annually: 65 Print
Total Titles: 350 Print
Imprints: Canongate Classics
Distributed by Grove Atlantic (USA)
Orders to: Publishers Group West, 1700 Fourth St, Berkeley, CA 96710, United States *Tel:* 510-528-1444

Canongate Classics, *imprint of* Canongate Books Ltd

Canterbury Press, *imprint of* SCM-Canterbury Press Ltd

Canterbury Press Norwich, *imprint of* Hymns Ancient & Modern Ltd

Canto, *imprint of* Cambridge University Press

Capall Bann Publishing+
Auton Farm, Milverton Somerset TA4 1NE
Tel: (01823) 401528 *Fax:* (01823) 401529
E-mail: enquiries@capallbann.co.uk
Web Site: www.capallbann.co.uk
Key Personnel
Publisher: Jon Day; Julia Day
Founded: 1993
Family owned & run company.
Subjects: Alternative, Animals, Pets, Archaeology, Astrology, Occult, Education, Environmental Studies, Gardening, Plants, Maritime, Music, Dance, Mysteries, Parapsychology, Philosophy, Psychology, Psychiatry, Religion - Other, Self-Help, Women's Studies, Alternative Healing, Mind, Body & Spirit
ISBN Prefix(es): 1-898307; 1-86163
Number of titles published annually: 40 Print
Total Titles: 250 Print

Jonathan Cape, *imprint of* Random House UK Ltd

Jonathan Cape Childrens, *imprint of* Random House UK Ltd

Capstone Publishing Ltd+
Oxford Centre for Innovation, Mill St, Oxford OX2 0JX
Tel: (01865) 798623 *Fax:* (01865) 240941
E-mail: capstone_publishing@msn.com
Web Site: www.capstone.co.uk
Key Personnel
Dir: Mark Allin; Richard Burton
Sales & Marketing Dir: Simon Benham
 Tel: (0171) 6223082 *Fax:* (0171) 6223082
 E-mail: simonbenham@capstoneuk.fireserve.co.uk
Publishing Manager: Catherine Meyrick
Founded: 1996
Membership(s): IPG.
Subjects: Business, Economics, Management
ISBN Prefix(es): 1-900961; 1-84112
Number of titles published annually: 20 Print
Total Titles: 90 Print
Distributor for Bard Press
Foreign Rights: Susie Adams (UK exclusive)
Warehouse: Marston Book Services, PO Box 269, Abingdon, Oxon OX14 4YN *Tel:* (01235) 465600 *Fax:* (01235) 465655
LPG Group, 40 Commerce Park, Milford, CT 06460, United States *Tel:* 203-878-6417 *Fax:* 203-874-2308
Orders to: Marston Book Services, PO Box 269, Abingdon, Oxon OX14 4YN *Tel:* (01235) 465600 *Fax:* (01235) 465655

Carcanet Press Ltd+
Alliance House, 4th floor, Cross St, Manchester M2 7AP
Tel: (0161) 834 8730 *Fax:* (0161) 832 0084
E-mail: info@carcanet.u-net.com
Web Site: www.carcanet.co.uk
Key Personnel
Editorial & Man Dir: Michael Schmidt
Sales: Pamela Heaton *E-mail:* pam@carcanet.co.uk
Marketing & Publicity Manager: Angharad Jackson *E-mail:* angharad@carcanet.co.uk
Editorial & Production Manager: Judith Wilson *E-mail:* judith@carcanet.co.uk
Financial Director: Julie Munro *E-mail:* julie@carcanet.co.uk
Founded: 1969
Independent Poetry & fiction translation publisher.
Subjects: Fiction, Literature, Literary Criticism, Essays, Poetry
ISBN Prefix(es): 0-85635; 0-902145; 1-85754; 1-903039
Number of titles published annually: 45 Print
Total Titles: 700 Print
Parent Company: Folio Holdings
Associate Companies: Folio Society
Imprints: From The Portuguese; Fyfield Books; Oxford Poets

Distributed by Littlehampton Book Services
Orders to: Paul & Co, PO Box 442, Concord, MA 01742, United States *Tel:* 508-369-3049 *Fax:* 508-369-2385

Cardiff Academic Press+
St Fagans Rd, Fairwater, Cardiff CF5 3AE
Tel: (029) 2056 03 *Fax:* (029) 2055 4909
E-mail: drakegroup@btinternet.com
Key Personnel
Man Dir: Mr R G Drake
Founded: 1979
Subjects: Biography, Education, Literature, Literary Criticism, Essays, Regional Interests, Religion - Other, Social Sciences, Sociology, Women's Studies, Welsh Studies
ISBN Prefix(es): 1-899025; 1-870495
Parent Company: Drake Group
Imprints: Plantin Publishers
Distributor for ECW Press (Canada); ILSI Press (USA); Plantin Publishers (UK); TUNS Press (Canada)

Careers Research & Advisory Centre Ltd, see Hobsons

Careers & Occupational Information Centre (COIC)
Room W46, Moorfoot, Sheffield S1 4PQ
Tel: (0114) 259 4564 *Fax:* (0114) 259 3439
Key Personnel
Production Manager: David Baker
Founded: 1974
Subjects: Career Development
ISBN Prefix(es): 0-86110
Parent Company: Dept of Educational & Employment

Carfax Publishing, *imprint of* Taylor & Francis

Carfax Publishing
Member of Taylor & Francis Group
11 New Fetter Lane, London EC4P 4EE
Tel: (020) 7583 9855 *Fax:* (020) 7842 2298
E-mail: sales@carfax.co.uk
Web Site: www.carfax.co.uk
Key Personnel
Man Editor: Ian White
Contact: Stephen Entwistle
Founded: 1972
Branch Office(s)
ITPS, Cheriton House, Northway, Andover SP10 5BE *Tel:* (01264) 342 926 *Fax:* (01264) 343 005 *E-mail:* book.orders@tandf.co.uk (European customer service operation for books)
U.S. Office(s): 325 Chestnut St, Suite 800, Philadelphia, PA 19106, United States *Fax:* 215-625-8914

Carlton Books, *imprint of* Carlton Publishing Group

Carlton Publishing Group+
20 Mortimer St, London W1T 3JW
Tel: (020) 7612 0400 *Fax:* (020) 7612 0401
E-mail: enquires@carltonbooks.co.uk; sales@carltonbooks.co.uk; editorial@carltonbooks.co.uk
Web Site: www.carltonint.co.uk
Key Personnel
Man Dir: Jonathan Goodman
Editorial Dir: Piers Murray Hill
International Sales Dir: Fiona Langdon
Founded: 1992
Publisher of illustrated books.
Subjects: Antiques, Architecture & Interior Design, Art, Biography, Criminology, Erotica, Fashion, Film, Video, Health, Nutrition, History, Humor, Music, Dance, Natural History, Radio, TV, Sports, Athletics, Wine & Spirits
ISBN Prefix(es): 0-233; 1-85868; 1-85375; 1-84222
Number of titles published annually: 100 Print
Total Titles: 700 Print
Parent Company: Carlton Communications PLC
Associate Companies: Carlton TV; Carlton International
Imprints: Andre Deutsch; Carlton Books; Granada Media; Manchester United Books; Prion

Jon Carpenter, *imprint of* Jon Carpenter Publishing

Jon Carpenter Publishing+
Alder House, Market St, Charlbury OX7 3PH
Tel: (01608) 811969 *Fax:* (01608) 811969
Key Personnel
Publisher: Jon Carpenter *E-mail:* jon@joncarpenter.co.uk
Founded: 1992
Specialize in distribution & representation of overseas publishers.
Subjects: Animals, Pets, Cookery, Developing Countries, Economics, Environmental Studies, Government, Political Science, Health, Nutrition, History, Social Sciences, Sociology
ISBN Prefix(es): 1-897766; 1-902279
Number of titles published annually: 10 Print
Total Titles: 120 Print
Imprints: Jon Carpenter; Wychwood Press
Distributed by Envirobook (Australia); I P G; New Horizons (South Africa)
Distributor for Apex Press (USA); Bootstrap Press (USA); Envirobook (Australia); International Books (Netherlands)
Shipping Address: Central Books, 99 Wallis Rd, London E9 5LN
Warehouse: Central Books, 99 Wallis Rd, London E9 5LN
Orders to: Central Books, 99 Wallis Rd, London E9 5LN

Carrick Media
1/4 Galt House, 31 Bank St, Irvine KA12 0LL
Tel: (01294) 311322 *Fax:* (01294) 311322
E-mail: enquiries@carrickmedia.demon.co.uk
Key Personnel
Proprietor: Kenneth Roy
Production Editor: Fiona McDonald *E-mail:* fm@carrickmedia.demon.co.uk
Founded: 1983
Specialize in Scotland & British media.
ISBN Prefix(es): 0-946724

Carroll & Brown Ltd+
20 Lonsdale Rd, Queen's Park, London NW6 6RD
Tel: (020) 7372 0900 *Fax:* (020) 7372 0460
E-mail: mail@carrollandbrown.co.uk
Web Site: www.carrollandbrown.co.uk
Key Personnel
Man Dir: Amy Carroll
Publisher: Denise Brown
Art Dir: Chrissie Lloyd
Senior Sales Dir: Simonne Waud
International Sales: Kate Hill; Lucy Paine; Cathy Slater
Founded: 1989
Publisher & packager of illustrated reference books for the coedition market. Provides a bespoke packaging service for other publishers.
Subjects: Alternative, Child Care & Development, Cookery, Crafts, Games, Hobbies, Gardening, Plants, Health, Nutrition, How-to, Nonfiction (General), Religion - Other
ISBN Prefix(es): 1-903258
Number of titles published annually: 20 Print
Distributed by Grantham Book Services

The Cartoon Cave+
One Willoughby Drive, Empingham, Oakham, Leics LE15 8PY
Tel: (01780) 460689; (01780) 460757
Fax: (01780) 460689
Web Site: www.cartooncave.co.uk
Key Personnel
Contact: Larry Harris *E-mail:* larryh@cartooncave.co.uk
Founded: 1980 (*Larry Harris Productions Ltd*)
Publishes fiction for children between the ages of seven & fifteen.
ISBN Prefix(es): 0-9526834
Total Titles: 4 Print
Distributed by Gardners Books

Frank Cass Publishers+
Crown House, 47 Chase Side, London N14 5BP
Tel: (020) 8920 2100 *Fax:* (020) 8447 8548
E-mail: info@frankcass.com
Web Site: www.frankcass.com
Key Personnel
Man Dir: Frank Cass
Editorial: Andrew Humphreys
Production: Mike Moran
Publicity Books: Eliza Dunlop
Publicity, Journals: Anne Kidson
Trade Manager: Joanna Legg
Rights & Permissions: Amna Whiston
Founded: 1957
Publisher of social science & humanities journals, monographs & edited collections.
Subjects: Developing Countries, Economics, History, Law, Literature, Literary Criticism, Essays, Military Science, British & International History, International Relations, Military Science & Development Studies, Politics, Sports Studies
ISBN Prefix(es): 0-7146
Associate Companies: Irish Academic Press
Subsidiaries: Vallentine, Mitchell & Co Ltd; The Littman Library of Jewish Civilization
U.S. Office(s): ISBS, 5824 NE Hassalo St, Portland, OR 97213-3644, United States *Fax:* 503-280-8832 *E-mail:* cass@isbs.com (North America)
Warehouse: Biblios Distribution, Star Rd, Partridge Green, West Sussex RH13 8LD *Tel:* (0403) 710971 *Fax:* (0403) 711143
Orders to: Plymbridge Distributors Ltd, Estover Rd, Plymouth PL6 7PY *Tel:* (01752) 202301 *Fax:* (01752) 202331 *E-mail:* orders@plymbridge.com
ISBS, 5824 NE Hassalo St, Portland, OR 97213-3644, United States *Fax:* 503-280-8832 *E-mail:* orders@isbs.com (North America)

Cassell & Co+
Wellington House, 125 Strand, London WC2R 0BB
Tel: (020) 7420 5555 *Fax:* (020) 7240 7261; (020) 7240 8531
Telex: 9413701
Key Personnel
Chairman & Chief Executive: Philip Sturrock
Imprint Dir, Arms & Armour Press, Blandford, Ward Lock & Cassell: Alison Goff
Imprint Dir, Cassell Academic & Contemporary Studies: Janet Joyce
Imprint Dir, Victor Gollancz: Jane Blackstock
Imprint Dir, Religious & Professional: Ruth McCurry
UK Trade Sales, Cassell: Finbarr McCabe
UK Trade Sales, Gollancz: Adrienne Maguire
UK Trade Sales, Academic: Georgian Brindley
Sales & Marketing Dir, Academic Division: Anne Godfrey
International Sales, General: Michael Goff
International Sales, Academic: Becca Seymour
Rights & Permissions, Gollancz: Jane Blackstock
Founded: 1848
Overseas Representation: Australia: New Holland Publishers Pty Ltd, NSW Australia; Canada: Books Inc, North Vancouver, Canada; Caribbean: HRA, London, UK; Central Europe: European Marketing Services, London,

UK; Southern Europe: Penny Padovani, London, UK; Hong Kong, China, Korea, Taiwan: APS Ltd, Hong Kong; Hungary, Czech Republic, Slovakia, Croatia: CLB Marketing Services, Kecskemet, Hungary; India: Maya Publishers PVT Ltd, New Delhi, India; Japan: Ashton International Marketing Services, UK; Malaysia: APD Kuala Lumpur, Selangor Darul Ehsan, Malaysia; Middle East: Aston International Marketing Services, UK; Netherlands: Nilsson & Lamm, Netherlands; New Zealand: David Bateman, Auckland, New Zealand; Pakistan: Mackwin & Co, Karachi, Pakistan; Poland, Russia, Romania, Baltic States, Former USSR, Bulgaria: Bianca Katris, IMA, Greece; Singapore, Indonesia, Thailand: APD Singapore Ltd, Singapore; Scandinavia: PKB, Glostrup, Denmark; South America: HRA, London, UK; South Africa: Struik Book Distributors, Cape Town, South Africa; USA: Sterling Publishing Co Inc, New York, USA.

Subjects: Accounting, Advertising, Architecture & Interior Design, Art, Biblical Studies, Biography, Business, Career Development, Cookery, Crafts, Games, Hobbies, Developing Countries, Education, Environmental Studies, Fiction, Film, Video, Gardening, Plants, Gay & Lesbian, Geography, Geology, History, House & Home, How-to, Humor, Labor, Industrial Relations, Library & Information Sciences, Management, Marketing, Military Science, Music, Dance, Natural History, Nonfiction (General), Outdoor Recreation, Photography, Poetry, Publishing & Book Trade Reference, Religion - Catholic, Religion - Protestant, Science (General), Science Fiction, Fantasy, Social Sciences, Sociology, Sports, Athletics, Theology

ISBN Prefix(es): 0-304; 0-7137; 0-7063; 0-289; 1-85409; 1-85079; 0-575; 0-85493; 0-86187; 1-84188

Parent Company: Hachette Livre

Associate Companies: Sterling Publishing, 387 Park Ave S, New York, NY 10016-8810, United States *Tel:* 212-532-7160 *Fax:* 212-213-2495

Imprints: Arms and Armour Press; Blandford; Geoffrey Chapman; Leicester University Press; Mansell; Mowbray; New Orchard Editions; Pinter, Studio Vista; Tycooly; Victor Gollancz; Ward Lock; Wisley Handbooks; Witherby

Subsidiaries: Arms & Armour Press; Blandford Press; Geoffrey Chapman; Ward Lock Ltd; Mowbray; New Orchard Editions; Studio Vista; Victor Gollancz; Mansell; Pinter; Leicester University Press

Distributed by Sterling Publishing (USA & Canada only)

Orders to: Cassell, Stanley House, 3 Fleets Lane, Poole, Dorset BH15 3AJ *Tel:* (0202) 670581 *Fax:* (0202) 666219

Sterling Publishing, 387 Park Ave S, New York, NY 10016-8810, United States *Tel:* 212-532-7160 *Fax:* 212-213-2495

Cassell Illustrated, *imprint of* Octopus Publishing Group

Castle House Publications Ltd
Quint House, Nevill Ridge, Nevill Park, Tunbridge Wells, Kent TN4 8NN
Tel: (01892) 539606 *Fax:* (01892) 517773; (01892) 517005
E-mail: enquiries@castlehouse.co.uk
Web Site: www.castlehouse.co.uk
Key Personnel
Man Dir: Donald Reinders
Production Editor: Jo Lethaby
Founded: 1973
Specializes In: Medicine
Also run medical conferences.
Divisions: Castle House Medical Conferences

Castlemead Publications+
Raynham House, Broadmeads, Ware, Herts SG12 9HY
Tel: (01920) 465525 *Fax:* (01920) 465545
E-mail: sales@castlemeadpublications.fsnet.co.uk
Key Personnel
Proprietor: Susan D M Lee
Founded: 1982
Publisher of pediatric growth charts.
Membership(s): Publishers Association.
Subjects: Aeronautics, Aviation, Child Care & Development, Medicine, Nursing, Dentistry, Natural History, Regional Interests, Transportation
ISBN Prefix(es): 0-948555

Kyle Cathie Ltd+
122 Arlington Rd, London NW1 7HP
Tel: (020) 7692 7215 *Fax:* (020) 7692 7260
E-mail: general.enquiries@kyle-cathie.com
Web Site: www.kylecathie.co.uk
Key Personnel
Man Dir: Kyle Cathie *E-mail:* kcathie@aol.com
Editor: Caroline Taggart
Sales & Marketing Dir: Julia Barder *Tel:* (020) 7692 7233 *E-mail:* julia.barder@kyle-cathie.com
Rights Dir: Melanie Gray *Tel:* (020) 7692 7256 *E-mail:* melanie.gray@kyle-cathie.com
Founded: 1990
Subjects: Biography, Cookery, Gardening, Plants, Health, Nutrition, History, Natural History, Philosophy, Lifestyle, Health & Beauty, Mind, Body & Spirit
ISBN Prefix(es): 1-85626
Total Titles: 25 Print
Distributed by Simon & Schuster Pty Ltd (Australia); Whitecap (Canada); Reed Publishing NZ Ltd (New Zealand); Wild Dog (South America)
Foreign Rep(s): Frances Bucquet (Austria, Benelux, Eastern Europe, France, Germany, Italy, Switzerland); John Edgeler (Caribbean, Central & South America, Middle East, Southern Europe, Scandinavia); Gunnar Lie (Africa, Asia); Benji OCampo (Korea, Philippines); Pansing Distribution (Brunei, Malaysia & Singapore); Reed Publishing NZ Ltd (New Zealand); Simon & Schuster (Australia) Pty Ltd (Australia); Trafalgar Square (USA); Whitecap (Canada)
Orders to: Littlehampton Book Services Ltd, Faraday Close, Durrington, West Sussex BN13 3RB *Tel:* (01903) 828800 *Fax:* (01903) 828801 *E-mail:* orders@lbsltd.co.uk

Catholic Institute for International Relations+
Canonbury Yard, Unit 3, 190a New North Rd, London N1 7BJ
Tel: (020) 7354 0883 *Fax:* (020) 7359 0017
E-mail: ciir@ciir.org
Web Site: www.ciir.org
Key Personnel
Executive Dir: Christine Allen *E-mail:* christine@ciir.org
Production Editor: Adam Bradbury *E-mail:* adam@ciir.org
Press & Information Coordinator: Fiona Sinclair *E-mail:* fiona@ciir.org
Founded: 1940
Also acts as development agency.
Subjects: Developing Countries, Economics, Government, Political Science, Theology
ISBN Prefix(es): 0-904393; 0-946848; 1-85287
Orders to: Central Books, 99 Wallis Rd, London E9 5LN

The Catholic Truth Society+
40-46 Harleyford Rd, London SE11 5AY
Tel: (020) 7640 0042 *Fax:* (020) 7640 0046
E-mail: info@cts-online.org.uk
Web Site: www.cts-online.org.uk *Cable:* APOSTOLIC LONDON
Key Personnel
General Secretary: Fergal Martin
Founded: 1884
Subjects: Education, Religion - Catholic
ISBN Prefix(es): 0-85183; 1-86082
Imprints: CTS Publications
Distributor for Liberia Editrice Vaticana; L'Osservatore Romano Newspaper
Bookshop(s): 25 Ashley Pl, London SW1P 1LT
Book Club(s): CTS Readers Club

Caucasus World, *imprint of* RoutledgeCurzon

Causeway Press Ltd+
129 New Court Way, Ormskirk, Lancs L39 5HP
Mailing Address: PO Box 13, Ormskirk, Lancs L39 5HP
Tel: (01695) 576048; (01695) 577360 *Fax:* (01695) 570714
E-mail: davidalcorn.causewaypress@btinternet.com
Key Personnel
Editorial, Publicity, Rights & Permissions, Sales & Production: Michael Haralambos
Company Secretary: David Gray
Founded: 1982
Subjects: Business, Economics, Geography, Geology, Government, Political Science, Health, Nutrition, History, Mathematics, Psychology, Psychiatry, Social Sciences, Sociology, Technology
ISBN Prefix(es): 0-946183; 1-873929; 1-902796
Warehouse: The Trade Counter, Mendlesham, Suffolk IP14 5NA

Cavalcade Story Cassettes, *imprint of* BBC Audiobooks

Paul Cave Publications Ltd
74 Bedford Pl, Southampton SO15 2DF
Tel: (01703) 223591; (01703) 333457 *Fax:* (01703) 227190
E-mail: lanksmag@zone.co.uk
Key Personnel
Chairman & Editor: Paul Cave
Dir: Joan Cave
Founded: 1960
Membership(s): Periodical Publishers Association.
Subjects: Regional Interests
ISBN Prefix(es): 0-86146; 0-9501735

Marshall Cavendish Partworks Ltd
Member of Times Publishing Group
119 Wardour St, London W1F 0UW
Tel: (020) 7565 6000 *Fax:* (020) 7734 6221
E-mail: info@marshallcavendish.co.uk
Web Site: www.marshallcavendish.co.uk
Telex: 23880 *Cable:* MARCAV LONDON W1
Key Personnel
Acting Chief Executive: John Armour
Circulation Manager: Christopher Jenner
Subjects: Antiques, Art, Astrology, Occult, Cookery, Crafts, Games, Hobbies, Gardening, Plants, Health, Nutrition
ISBN Prefix(es): 0-7485
Associate Companies: ALP SNC, France; Marshall Cavendish Corporation, United States
Orders to: Circulation Department, 119 Wardour St, London W1V 3TD

Cavendish Publishing Ltd+
The Glass House, Wharton St, London WC1X 9PX
Tel: (020) 7278 8000 *Fax:* (020) 7278 8080
E-mail: info@cavendishpublishing.com
Web Site: www.cavendishpublishing.com
Key Personnel
Man Dir: Jeremy Stein *E-mail:* jeremystein@cavendishpublishing.com

Man Editor: Ms Cara Annett *E-mail:* caraannett@cavendishpublishing.com
Editor: Jon Lloyd *E-mail:* jonlloyd@cavendishpublishing.com; Ruth Massey *E-mail:* ruthmassey@cavendishpublishing.com
Commissioning Editor: Beverley Brown *E-mail:* beverleybrown@cavendishpublishing.com
Brand & Product Manager: Cathy Thornhill *E-mail:* cathythornhill@cavendishpublishing.com
Founded: 1990
Membership(s): Publishers Association of Great Britain.
Subjects: Criminology, Law, Medicine, Nursing, Dentistry, Securities, Social Sciences, Sociology
ISBN Prefix(es): 1-874241; 1-85941; 1-876213
Number of titles published annually: 100 Print
Total Titles: 500 Print
Subsidiaries: Cavendish Publishing (Australia) Pty Limited

Caxton Publishing Group Ltd, *imprint of* Verulam Publishing Ltd

CBD Research Ltd+
Chancery House, 15 Wickham Rd, Beckenham, Kent BR3 5JS
Tel: (020) 8650 7745 *Fax:* (020) 8650 0768
E-mail: cbd@cbdresearch.com
Web Site: www.cbdresearch.com
Key Personnel
Dir: Mrs S P Henderson; A J Henderson
Founded: 1961
Specialize in directory listings of associations, directories & official United Nations organizations.
Membership(s): Directory Publishers Association; Independent Publishers Guild.
ISBN Prefix(es): 0-900246
Total Titles: 16 Print; 2 CD-ROM; 1 E-Book
Subsidiaries: Chancery House Press
Membership(s): IPG

CCH Editions Ltd+
145 London Rd, Kingston Upon Thames, Surrey KT2 6SR
Tel: (020) 8547 3333 *Fax:* (020) 8547 1124
E-mail: customer.services@cch.co.uk
Web Site: www.cch.co.uk
Key Personnel
Man Dir: Hans Staal
Founded: 1982
Subjects: Business, Law
ISBN Prefix(es): 0-86325
Parent Company: Commerce Clearing House Inc, PO Box 5490, Chicago, IL 60680-5490, United States

Centaur Books, *imprint of* Old Vicarage Publications

Centaur Press (1954)
51 Achilles Rd, London NW6 1DZ
Tel: (020) 7431 4391 *Fax:* (020) 7431 5129
E-mail: books@opengatepress.co.uk
Web Site: www.opengatepress.co.uk
Key Personnel
Man Dir: T J L Wynne-Tyson
Founded: 1954
Linden Press at the above address has no connection with the Simon & Schuster imprint of the same name.
Subjects: Education, Environmental Studies
ISBN Prefix(es): 0-900000; 0-900001
Parent Company: Open Gate Press
Subsidiaries: The Linden Press
Bookshop(s): Keele's, Fontwell, Arundel, West Sussex BN18 0TA

Center for Advanced Welsh & Celtic Studies
National Library of Wales, Aberystwyth, Ceredigion SY23 3HH
Tel: (01970) 626717 *Fax:* (01970) 627066
E-mail: cawcs@wales.ac.uk
Web Site: www.aber.ac.uk/~awcwww/s/cyflwyniad.html
Key Personnel
Dir: Geraint H Jenkins *E-mail:* gcj@aber.ac.uk
Editorial Officer: Glenys Howells *E-mail:* glh@aber.ac.uk
Founded: 1985
Specialize in academic & celtic.
Parent Company: University of Wales

Centre for Alternative Technology+
Machynlleth, Powys SY20 9AZ
Tel: (01654) 705980; (01654) 705959 (mail order); (01654) 705993 (CAT shop) *Fax:* (01654) 702782; (01654) 705999 (mail order); (01654) 703605 (education & courses)
E-mail: pubs@cat.org.uk
Web Site: www.cat.org.uk
Key Personnel
Publisher: Caroline Oakley
Marketing Manager: Allan Shepherd
Production Manager: Graham Preston
Founded: 1974
Publisher of DIY Titles for environmentalists
Registered charity.
Subjects: Energy, Gardening, Plants, Nonfiction (General), Technology, Sustainable Lifestyles
Number of titles published annually: 4 Print
Distributed by New Society Publishers (USA & Canada)
Foreign Rep(s): New Society Publishers (Canada, USA)
Shipping Address: CAT Mail Order *Tel:* (01654) 705959 *Fax:* (01654) 705999 *E-mail:* mail.order@cat.org.uk (24-hour mail order)

Centre for Information on Language Teaching & Research (CILT)+
20 Bedfordbury, London WC2N 4LB
Tel: (020) 7379 5101; (020) 7379 5110 (resources library & information services) *Fax:* (020) 7379 5082
E-mail: publications@cilt.org.uk; library@cilt.org.uk (library information)
Web Site: www.cilt.org.uk
Key Personnel
Dir: Dr Lid King *E-mail:* lid.king@cilt.org.uk
Head of Publishing: Emma Rees *E-mail:* emma.rees@cilt.org.uk
Founded: 1966
Membership(s): Publishers Association.
Subjects: Education, Language Arts, Linguistics
ISBN Prefix(es): 0-948003; 0-903466; 1-874016; 0-9500528; 1-902031
Number of titles published annually: 25 Print; 4 Audio
Total Titles: 100 Print; 8 Audio
Orders to: Central Books Ltd, 99 Wallis Rd, London E9 5LN *Tel:* (020) 8458 9910 *Fax:* (020) 8533 5821 *E-mail:* mo@centralbooks.com

Century, *imprint of* Random House UK Ltd

Chadwyck-Healey Ltd+
The Quorum, Barnwell Rd, Cambridge CB5 8SW
Tel: (01223) 215512 *Fax:* (01223) 215514
E-mail: andrew.hall@proquest.co.uk
Web Site: www.proquest.co.uk
Key Personnel
Vice President of Publishing: Julie Carroll-Davis *E-mail:* julie.carroll-davis@proquest.co.uk
Rights & Contracts Manager: Caroline Gomm *E-mail:* caroline.gomm@proquest.co.uk
Founded: 1973
Specialize in electronic publishing.
Subjects: Art, Drama, Theater, Economics, Film, Video, History, Literature, Literary Criticism, Essays, Music, Dance, Radio, TV, Science (General), Social Sciences, Sociology, Humanities
ISBN Prefix(es): 0-85964
Parent Company: Proquest Information & Learning

Chambers Harrap Publishers Ltd+
Division of Lagardere
7 Hopetoun Crescent, Edinburgh EH7 4AY
Tel: (0131) 5565929 *Fax:* (0131) 5565313
E-mail: admin@chambers.co.uk; webmanager@chambers.co.uk
Web Site: www.chambersharrap.co.uk
Telex: 727967 Words G
Key Personnel
Man Dir: Maurice Shepherd
Publishing Manager: Patrick White *E-mail:* pwhite@chambersharrap.co.uk
Sales & Marketing Manager: Jane Camillin
Sales & Rights Manager: Stephanie Divens
Reference publisher.
ISBN Prefix(es): 0-550; 0-245
Number of titles published annually: 20 Print
Distributed by Allied Publishers Ltd (India); David Bateman Ltd (New Zealand); Andrew Betsis ELT (Greece); Bohemian Ventures (Czech Republic); Gemcraft Books (Australia); Houghton Mifflin (USA & English-speaking Canada); Inter Logos srl. (Italy); Larousse-Bordas (France & French-speaking countries); Ediciones Larousse SA (Mexico & Latin America); Livraria Martins (Brazil); The Macmillan Press (UK); Paramount Books (Pvt) Ltd (Pakistan); Quartet Sales & Marketing (South Africa); Readwide Bookshop Ltd (Ghana); Slovak Ventures (Slovakia); Spes SA (Spain); Times Media Private (Brunai, Malaysia, Singapore & Thailand)
Orders to: The Macmillan Press, Brunel Rd, Houndmills, Basingstoke, Hants RG21 6XS *Tel:* (01256) 406817 *Fax:* (01256) 812521

Chancellor Publications
32 Hatton Garden, 1st Floor, London EC1N 8DL
Tel: (020) 7269 9150 *Fax:* (020) 7269 9151
E-mail: mail@chancellorpublication.com
Web Site: www.chancellorpublication.com
Key Personnel
Man Dir: Jonathan Bloch *E-mail:* jbloch@globalnet.co.uk
Founded: 1994
Supplier of legal & financial texts for practitioners & laymen.
Subjects: Law
ISBN Prefix(es): 1-899217
Total Titles: 5 Print
U.S. Office(s): ISBS Inc, 920 NE 58th Ave, Suite 300, Portland, OR 97213-3644, United States *Fax:* 503-280-8832 *E-mail:* rod@isbs.com *Web Site:* www.isbs.com
Membership(s): IPG

Channel 4 Books, *imprint of* Pan Macmillan

Channel View Publications, *imprint of* Multilingual Matters Ltd

Chapman
4 Broughton Pl, Edinburgh EH1 3RX
Tel: (0131) 5572207 *Fax:* (0131) 5569565
E-mail: admin@chapman-pub.co.uk
Web Site: www.chapman-pub.co.uk
Key Personnel
Editor: Joy Hendry *E-mail:* editor@chapman.co.uk
Founded: 1970
Specialize in Scottish culture generally. Publish & develop Scottish literature in particular, also international writing. Quarterly magazine devoted to Scottish literature & arts. Features mainly poetry & plays.

Subjects: Drama, Theater, Literature, Literary Criticism, Essays, Poetry, Women's Studies
ISBN Prefix(es): 0-906772
Number of titles published annually: 4 Print
Total Titles: 60 Print; 1 Online; 1 E-Book

Geoffrey Chapman, *imprint of* Cassell & Co

Geoffrey Chapman, *imprint of* The Continuum International Publishing Group Ltd

Paul Chapman Publishing, *imprint of* SAGE Publications Ltd

Chapter Two
Fountain House, Conduit Mews, London SE18 7AP
Tel: (020) 8316 5389 *Fax:* (020) 8854 5963
E-mail: chapter2UK@aol.com
Web Site: www.chaptertwo.org.uk
Key Personnel
Dir: Edwin N Cross
Founded: 1976
Publisher & bookseller
Specialize in Plymouth Brethren Literature & their history.
Subjects: Language Arts, Linguistics, Religion - Protestant, Theology
ISBN Prefix(es): 1-85307; 0-947588
Number of titles published annually: 20 Print
Total Titles: 190 Print
Imprints: Bible Distributors
Distributed by Beroea Verlag (Switzerland)
Distribution Center: Believers Bookshelf, 5205 Regional Rd 81, Unit 3, Beamsville, ON L0R 1B3, Canada
Believers Bookshelf Inc, Box 261, Sunbury, PA 17801, United States
Bible & Book Depot, Box 25119, Christchurch 5, New Zealand
Bible, Book & Tract Depot, 23 Santa Rosa Ave, Ryde, NSW 2112, Australia
Bible House, Gateway Mall, 35 Tudor St, Bridgetown, Barbados
Bibles & Publications Chretiennes, 30 rue Chateauvert, 26000 Valence, France
Bible Treasury Bookstore, 46 Queen St, Dartmouth, NS B2Y 1G1, Canada
The Bookshelf, 263 St Heliers Bay Rd, Auckland 5, New Zealand
Chapter Two Bookshop, 199 Plumstead Common Rd, London SE18 2UJ
Christian Truth Bookroom, Paddisonpet, Tenali, 522 201 Andhra, Pradesh, India
CSV, An der Schlossfabrik 30, 42499 Hueckeswagen, Germany
Depot de Bibles et Traites Chretiens, 4 rue du Nord, 1800 Vevey, Switzerland
Echoes of Truth, No 11 Post Office Rd, PO Box 2637, Mushin, Lagos, Nigeria
El Ekhwa Library, 3 Anga Hanem St, Shoubra, Cairo, Egypt (Arab Republic of Egypt)
Grace & Truth Bookroom, 87 Chausee Rd, Castries, St Lucia, West Indies, Jamaica
HoldFast Bible & Tract Depot, 100 Camden Rd, Tunbridge Wells, Kent TN1 2QP
Kristen Litteratur, Tjosvoll ost, 4270 Akrehamn, Norway
Uit het Woord der Waarheid, Postbus 260, 7120 AG Aalten, Netherlands
Words of Life Trust, 3 Chuim, Khar Village, Mumbai 400052, India
Words of Truth, PO Box 147, Belfast BT8 4TT

Deborah Charles Publications+
173 Mather Ave, Liverpool L18 6JZ
Tel: (0151) 724 2500 *Fax:* (0151) 729 0371
E-mail: dcp@legaltheory.demon.co.uk
Web Site: www.legaltheory.demon.co.uk
Key Personnel
Prof: B S Jackson

Founded: 1988
Subjects: Law, Philosophy, Social Sciences, Sociology, Legal Theory
ISBN Prefix(es): 0-9513793; 0-9528938

Charnwood Library Series, see Ulverscroft Large Print Books Ltd

Chartered Institute of Bankers (CIB) Publications, *imprint of* Institute of Financial Services

The Chartered Institute of Building
Englemere, Kings Ride, Ascot, Berks SL5 7TB
Tel: (01344) 630700 *Fax:* (01344) 630777
E-mail: reception@ciob.org.uk
Web Site: www.ciob.org.uk
Key Personnel
Chief Executive: Keith Banbury
Editorial, Production, Rights & Permissions: David Petori
Bookshop: Sally Marsh *E-mail:* smarsh@englemer.co.uk
Librarian: Katherine Bowyer
Subjects: Architecture & Interior Design, Environmental Studies, Law, Management, Regional Interests
ISBN Prefix(es): 0-906600; 1-85380; 0-901822
Associate Companies: American Institute of Constructors

Chartered Institute of Library & Information Professionals in Scotland
Scottish Centre for Information & Library Services, Brandon Gate, Bldg C, 1st floor, Leechlee Rd, Hamilton ML3 6AU
Tel: (01698) 458888 *Fax:* (01698) 458899
E-mail: slic@slainte.org.uk
Web Site: www.slainte.org.uk
Key Personnel
Publications Officer: Alan Reid *Tel:* (0131) 271 3970 *Fax:* (0131) 440 4635 *E-mail:* alan.reid@midlothian.gov.uk
Founded: 1908
Membership(s): Scottish Publishers Association.
Subjects: History, Library & Information Sciences, Regional Interests
ISBN Prefix(es): 0-900649
Number of titles published annually: 3 Print
Total Titles: 12 Print
Orders to: Scottish Book Source, The Scottish Book Centre, 137 Dundee St, Edinburgh EH11 1BG *Tel:* (0131) 2296800 *Fax:* (0131) 2299070 *E-mail:* info@booksource.net *Web Site:* www.booksource.net

Chartered Institute of Personnel & Development+
CIPD House, Camp Rd Wimbledon, London SW19 4UX
Tel: (020) 8971 9000 *Fax:* (020) 8263 3333
E-mail: publish@cipd.co.uk
Web Site: www.cipd.co.uk
Key Personnel
Head of Publishing: Sarah Brown
Sales & Marketing Manager: Jim Ellis
Founded: 1913
Specialize in books & reports covering the whole range of training, personnel & development issues, from practical guides & texts for students to books on best practice & strategic issues.
Subjects: Business, Human Relations, Management
ISBN Prefix(es): 0-85292
Number of titles published annually: 35 Print
Warehouse: CIPD Distribution, c/o Plymbridge Distributors Ltd, Estover, Plymouth PL6 7PZ
Orders to: CIPD Distribution, c/o Plymbridge Distributors Ltd, Estover, Plymouth PL6 7PZ

The Chartered Institute of Public Finance & Accountancy
3 Robert St, London WC2N 6BH
Tel: (020) 7543 5600 *Fax:* (020) 7543 5607
E-mail: publications@cipfa.org
Web Site: www.cipfa.org.uk/shop
Key Personnel
Publications Manager: Sara Hackwood
Subjects: Accounting, Finance

Chatham House, see Royal Institute of International Affairs

Chatham House Papers, *imprint of* Royal Institute of International Affairs

Chatham Publishing+
Park House, 1 Russell Gardens, London NW11 9NN
Tel: (020) 8458 6314 *Fax:* (020) 8905 5245
E-mail: info@chathampublishing.com
Web Site: www.chathampublishing.com
Key Personnel
Editorial Dir: Julian Mannering *E-mail:* julian@chathampublishing.co.uk
Publisher: Robert Gardiner *E-mail:* robert@chathampublishing.co.uk
Founded: 1996
Small publishing house concerned principally with maritime history & narrative history.
Subjects: Maritime, Nonfiction (General), Nautical Archaeology, Naval or Mercantile History & Biography, Ship Modelling
ISBN Prefix(es): 1-86176
Number of titles published annually: 30 Print
Total Titles: 150 Print
Parent Company: Trident Publishing Ltd
Distributed by Grantham Book Services
Distribution Center: Peribo Pty Limited, 58 Beaumont Rd, Mount Kuring-Gai NSW 2080, Australia *Fax:* (02) 457 0022 *E-mail:* peribomec@bigpond.com
Publishers Marketing Services Pte Ltd, 10c Jalan Ampas, No 07-01, Warehouse, Ho Seng Lee Flatted 1232, Singapore *Tel:* 253 0008 *E-mail:* raymondlim@pms.com.sg
Vanwell Publishing Ltd, PO Box 2131, 1 Northrup Crescent, St Catharines L2R 7S2, ON, Canada *Tel:* (905) 937 3100 *Fax:* (905) 937 1760 *E-mail:* sales@vanwell.com
Titles SA, PO Box 411196, Craiighall 2024, South Africa *Fax:* (01) 1497 5377 *E-mail:* prenew@iafrica.com
Publishers Marketing Services Pte Ltd, 28a Jalan SS21/58, Damansara Utama, Petaling Jaya 47400, Malaysia *Fax:* (03) 718 7997
Stackpole Books, 5067 Ritter Rd, Mechanicsburg, PA 17055, United States *Tel:* (717) 796 0411 *Fax:* (717) 796 0412 *E-mail:* sales@stackpolebooks.com *Web Site:* www.stackpolebooks.com
South Pacific Books, PO Box 68097, Newton, Auckland 2, New Zealand *Fax:* (09) 376 2141 *E-mail:* sales@soupacbooks.co.nz

Chatto & Windus, *imprint of* Random House UK Ltd

The Chemical Society, see The Royal Society of Chemistry

Cherrytree, *imprint of* Evans Brothers Ltd

Cherrytree Books, *imprint of* AS Publishing

Cherrytree Books+
Imprint of Evans Brothers Ltd
2A Portman Mansions, Chiltern St, London W1U 6NR
Tel: (020) 7487 0920 *Fax:* (020) 7487 0921
E-mail: sales@evansbrothers.co.uk
Web Site: www.evansbooks.co.uk

Key Personnel
Man Dir: Julian Batson
Rights Manager: Britta Martins
Publisher: Angela Sheehan
Production Dir: Lesley Barnes
Founded: 1988
Publish illustrated information books for children ages 5-15 years, mainly for the school library.
ISBN Prefix(es): 0-7451; 0-7540
Associate Companies: Chivers Press Ltd; Evans Brothers Ltd; Zero to Ten Ltd
U.S. Office(s): Chivers North America Inc, One Lafayette Rd, Hampton, NH 03842, United States

Child's Play (International) Ltd+
Ashworth Rd, Bridgemead, Swindon, Wilts SN5 7YD
Tel: (01793) 616286 *Fax:* (01793) 512795
E-mail: allday@childs-play.com
Web Site: www.childs-play.com
Key Personnel
Chairman: Michael Twinn
UK Sales: Paul Gerrish
Publicity: Libby New
Editor: Sue Baker *Tel:* (01793) 616286
    E-mail: sue@childs-play.com
Education Officer: Imogen Cooper
Chief Executive Officer (Sales & Marketing): Richard Searle-Barnes *Tel:* (01793) 616286
    E-mail: richard@childs-play.com
Founded: 1972
Specialize in Early Years Education.
Membership(s): BTHMA & IPG.
ISBN Prefix(es): 0-85953; 1-904550
Total Titles: 400 Print; 7 Audio
Subsidiaries: Childs Play Australia
U.S. Office(s): Childs Play USA, 67 Minot Ave, Auburn, ME 04210, United States, Contact: Laurie Reynolds *Tel:* 207-784-7252 *Fax:* 207-784-7358 *E-mail:* cmpmaine@aol.com

Child's World Education Ltd
PO Box 1881, Gerrards Cross, Bucks SL9 9AN
Tel: (01753) 647060 *Fax:* (01753) 645522
Key Personnel
Contact: Susan Daughtrey
Subjects: Education
ISBN Prefix(es): 1-898696

Chivers Children's Audio Books, *imprint of* BBC Audiobooks

Chivers Large Print, *imprint of* BBC Audiobooks

Chorion IP+
Vernon House, 40 Shaftesbury Ave, London W1D 7ER
Tel: (020) 7434 1880 *Fax:* (020) 7434 1882
E-mail: info@enidblyton.co.uk
Web Site: www.chorion.co.uk
Founded: 1998
Crime novels.
Subjects: Fiction, Film, Video, Finance
Ultimate Parent Company: Chorion PLC, Aldwych House, 71-91 Aldwych, London WC2B 4HN

Chough Series (Educational Packs), *imprint of* Lodenek Press

Christian Education+
1020 Bristol Rd, Selly Oak, Birmingham B29 6LB
Tel: (0121) 472 4242 *Fax:* (0121) 472 7575
E-mail: enquiries@christianeducation.org.uk
Web Site: www.christianeducation.org.uk/cep/cep_about.htm

Key Personnel
Dir: Peter Fishpool *E-mail:* director@christianeducation.org.uk
Senior Editor: Elizabeth Bruce-Whitehorn
    E-mail: editorial@christianeducation.org.uk
Marketing: Lynette Adjei *E-mail:* marketing@christianeducation.org.uk
Sales: Jeanne Hayling *E-mail:* sales@christianeducation.org.uk
Consultant Editor: Colin Johnson *E-mail:* colin@cem.org.uk
Design & Production Editor: Liam Purcell
    E-mail: production@christianeducation.org.uk
Founded: 1809
Subjects: Biblical Studies, Crafts, Games, Hobbies, Drama, Theater, Education, Religion - Protestant
ISBN Prefix(es): 0-7197; 0-85213
Imprints: Hillside
Subsidiaries: International Bible Reading Association (IBRA)
Bookshop(s): NCEL Bookroom

Christian Education Movement, see Christian Education

Christian Focus, *imprint of* Christian Focus Publications Ltd

Christian Focus Publications Ltd+
Geanies House, Fearn, Tain, Ross-shire IV20 1TW
Tel: (01862) 871 011 *Fax:* (01862) 871 699
E-mail: info@christianfocus.com
Web Site: www.christianfocus.com
Key Personnel
Man Dir: William Mackenzie
    E-mail: whmmackenzie@christianfocus.com
General Manager: Ian Thompson *Tel:* (01862) 871 022 *E-mail:* ian.thompson@christianfocus.com
Production Manager: Jonathan Dunbar
    E-mail: jdunbar@christianfocus.com
Editorial Manager: Willie Mackenzie
    E-mail: Willie.Mackenzie@christianfocus.com
Children's Editor: Catherine Mackenzie
    E-mail: cmackenzie@christianfocus.com
Founded: 1979
Evangelical publisher.
Membership(s): Christian Booksellers Association & Evangelical Christian Publishing Association.
Subjects: Fiction, Religion - Protestant, Theology
ISBN Prefix(es): 0-906731; 1-871676; 1-85792
Number of titles published annually: 90 Print
Total Titles: 800 Print; 1 CD-ROM; 1 Audio
Parent Company: Balintore Holdings PLC
Imprints: Mentor; Christian Focus; Christian Heritage
U.S. Office(s): Riverside, 636 South Oak, Iowa Falls, IA 50126, United States *Fax:* 515-648-5106 *E-mail:* maureenr@riversidedistributors.com
Foreign Rep(s): Cook Communications Ministries (Canada); Family Reading (Australia); Publishers International Marketing (Asia); Struik Christian Books (Southern Africa); SU (New Zealand)

Christian Heritage, *imprint of* Christian Focus Publications Ltd

Christian Research Association
Vision Bldg, 4 Footscray Rd, Eltham, London SE9 2TZ
Tel: (020) 8294 1989 *Fax:* (020) 8294 0014
E-mail: admin@christian-research.org.uk
Web Site: www.christian-research.org.uk
Key Personnel
Executive Dir: Dr Peter Brierley
Founded: 1993

Provide resources & undertaking research for Christian leaders.
Subjects: Management, Religion - Catholic, Religion - Protestant
ISBN Prefix(es): 1-85321
Number of titles published annually: 5 Print; 1 Online
Total Titles: 19 Print; 1 Online

The Chrysalis Press+
7 Lower Ladyes Hills, Kenilworth, Warwicks CV8 2GN
Tel: (01926) 855223
E-mail: chrysalis@margaretbuckley.com
Key Personnel
Man Dir: Brian Boyd
Founded: 1992
Subjects: Biography, Fiction, Literature, Literary Criticism, Essays
ISBN Prefix(es): 1-897765
Number of titles published annually: 2 Print; 2 Online; 2 E-Book
Total Titles: 10 Print; 10 Online; 10 E-Book

Church House Publishing+
31 Great Smith St, London SW1P 3BN
Tel: (020) 7898 1300 *Fax:* (020) 7898 1305
E-mail: sales@c-of-e.org.uk
Web Site: www.chpublishing.co.uk
Key Personnel
Publishing Manager: Alan Mitchell *Tel:* (020) 7898 1450 *E-mail:* alan.mitchell@c-of-e.org.uk
Production Manager: Katharine Allenby
    Tel: (020) 7898 1452 *E-mail:* katharine.allenby@c-of-e.org.uk
Sales & Marketing Manager: Matthew Tickle
    Tel: (020) 7898 1454 *E-mail:* matthew.tickle@c-of-e.org.uk
Editorial & Copyright Manager: Sarah Roberts
    Tel: (020) 7898 1578 *E-mail:* sarah.roberts@c-of-e.org.uk
National Society Publications Off: Hamish Bruce
    Tel: (020) 7898 1453 *E-mail:* hamish.bruce@c-of-e.org.uk
Contact: Aderyn Watson *E-mail:* aderyn.watson@c-of-e.org.uk
Subjects: Religion - Other
ISBN Prefix(es): 0-7151; 0-901819
Number of titles published annually: 40 Print; 1 CD-ROM
Total Titles: 300 Print; 1 CD-ROM; 1 Audio
Parent Company: The Archbishops Council of the Church of England
Imprints: The National Society
Distributed by Novalis (Canada); Charles Paine Pty Ltd (Australia)
Distribution Center: Marston Book Services, PO Box 269, Abingdon, Oxon OX14 4YN
Tel: (01235) 465500 *Fax:* (01235) 465518
Orders to: The Canterbury Press, St Mary's Works, St Mary's Plain, Norwich NR3 3BH, Contact: Melanie Cole *Tel:* (01603) 612914 *Fax:* (01603) 624483

Church Literature Association, *imprint of* Church Union

Church Society
Dean Wace House, 16 Rosslyn Rd, Watford, Herts WD18 0NY
Tel: (01923) 235111 *Fax:* (01923) 800362
E-mail: enquiries@churchsociety.org
Web Site: www.churchsociety.org
Key Personnel
Publishing Secretary: David Phillips
Founded: 1835 (Present company started in 1950 as an amalgamation of two other similar organizations)
Specialize in books & booklets. Publishers 'Churchmen' quarterly since 1879. A society founded to keep the Church of England faithful to its formularies.

UNITED KINGDOM

Subjects: Religion - Protestant, Theology
ISBN Prefix(es): 0-85190
Total Titles: 4 Print

Church Times, *imprint of* Hymns Ancient & Modern Ltd

Church Union
Faith House, 7 Tufton St, London SW1P 3QN
Tel: (020) 7222 6952 *Fax:* (020) 7976 7180
E-mail: churchunion@care4free.net
Web Site: www.churchunion.care4free.net
Key Personnel
Contact: Julien Chilcott-Monk
Founded: 1859
Membership(s): Bookseller Association; specialize in religious books; also acts as Bookseller.
Subjects: Religion - Catholic, Religion - Protestant, Religion - Other
ISBN Prefix(es): 0-85191
Imprints: Church Literature Association; Tufton Books
Distributed by SCM - Canterbury Press
Bookshop(s): Faith House Bookshop, 7 Tufton St, London SW1P 3QN

Churchill Livingstone, *imprint of* Elsevier Ltd

Cicerone Press
2 Police Sq, Milnthorpe, Cumbria LA7 7PY
Tel: (01539) 562 069 *Fax:* (01539) 563 417
E-mail: info@cicerone.co.uk
Web Site: www.cicerone.co.uk
Key Personnel
Dir, Sales & Marketing: Mrs Lesley Williams *E-mail:* lesley@cicerone.demon.co.uk
Dir, Editorial, Production & Finance: Jonathan E Williams *E-mail:* jonathan@cicerone.demon.co.uk
Founded: 1969
Publish specialized guides to walking, trekking, climbing, mountaineering & biking in the UK, Europe & other world regions.
Subjects: Outdoor Recreation, Travel
ISBN Prefix(es): 0-902363; 1-85284
Number of titles published annually: 20 Print
Total Titles: 280 Print
Distributed by Alpenbooks (USA); Midpoint Trade Books (USA)
Warehouse: 2B Summerlands Industrial Estate, North Kendal, Cumbria

CILIPS, *see* Chartered Institute of Library & Information Professionals in Scotland

CILT, *see* Centre for Information on Language Teaching & Research (CILT)

Cinderella, *imprint of* Novello & Co Ltd

CIRIA
Classic House, 174-180 Old St, London EC1V 9BP
Tel: (020) 7549 3300 *Fax:* (020) 7253 0523
E-mail: enquiries@ciria.org.uk
Web Site: www.ciria.org.uk

CIWEM, *imprint of* Terence Dalton Ltd

Clarendon Press, *imprint of* Oxford University Press

Clarion, *imprint of* Elliot Right Way Books

James Clarke & Co Ltd+
PO Box 60, Cambridge CB1 2NT
Tel: (01223) 350865 *Fax:* (01223) 366951
E-mail: publishing@jamesclarke.co.uk
Web Site: www.jamesclarke.co.uk
Key Personnel
Man Dir: Adrian C Brink
Founded: 1859
Membership(s): IPG, Publishers' Association.
Subjects: Biblical Studies, Biography, History, Library & Information Sciences, Literature, Literary Criticism, Essays, Nonfiction (General), Philosophy, Publishing & Book Trade Reference, Religion - Catholic, Religion - Protestant, Theology
ISBN Prefix(es): 0-227
Number of titles published annually: 4 Print
Total Titles: 300 Print
Imprints: Acorn Editions; Patrick Hardy Books; Lutterworth Press
Distributed by Parkwest Publications Inc
Foreign Rep(s): Keith Ainsworth (Pty) Ltd (Australia); Applied Media (India, Sri Lanka); Catholic Supplies (NK) (New Zealand); CKK (Hong Kong, Indonesia, Malaysia, Philippines, Singapore, Thailand); Iberian Book Services (Portugal & Spain); Parkwest Publications Inc (USA); Kelvin van Hasselt Publishing Services (Africa, Caribbean)
Membership(s): IPG; Publishers' Association

Class Publishing+
Barb House, Barb Mews, London W6 7PA
Tel: (020) 7371 2119 *Fax:* (020) 7371 2878
E-mail: post@class.co.uk
Web Site: www.class.co.uk
Key Personnel
Manager: Richard Warner
Founded: 1989
Subjects: Health, Nutrition, Law, Medicine, Nursing, Dentistry
ISBN Prefix(es): 1-872362; 1-859590
Book Club(s): BCA
Warehouse: Plymbridge Distributors Ltd, Plymbridge House, Estover Rd, Plymouth, Devon PL6 7PY *Tel:* (01752) 202300 *Fax:* (01752) 202330 *E-mail:* enquiries@plymbridge.com
Web Site: www.plymbridge.com
Membership(s): IPG

Classey Books, *imprint of* E W Classey Ltd

E W Classey Ltd+
Oxford House, Marlborough St, Faringdon, Oxon SN7 7JP
Mailing Address: PO Box 93, Faringdon, Oxon SN7 7DR
Tel: (01367) 244700 *Fax:* (01367) 244800
E-mail: info@classeybooks.com
Web Site: www.abebooks.com/home/bugbooks; www.classeybooks.com
Key Personnel
Publisher: E W Classey
Contact: Mr P Classey
Founded: 1949
Subjects: Biological Sciences, Earth Sciences, Environmental Studies, Natural History, Science (General), Arachnology, Botany, Entomology, Geology, Natural History, Ornithology, Zoology
ISBN Prefix(es): 0-900848; 0-86096
Imprints: Classey Books; Ferendune; Hedera Press
Orders to: Bookmart-Classeybooks, PO Box 93, Faringdon, Oxon SN7 7DR *Tel:* (01367) 244800 *Fax:* (01367) 244700

Classics, *imprint of* The Penguin Group UK

CLB Books, *imprint of* Colour Library Direct

CLB Publishing, *imprint of* Colour Library Direct

Clever Clogs, *imprint of* Funfax Ltd

Cloverleaf, *imprint of* Evans Brothers Ltd

CMP Information Ltd
Riverbank House, Angel Lane, Tonbridge, Kent TN9 1SE
Tel: (01732) 377591 *Fax:* (01732) 377440
Web Site: www.cmpdata.co.uk
Subjects: Advertising, Architecture & Interior Design, Business, Energy, Film, Video, Health, Nutrition, Publishing & Book Trade Reference
ISBN Prefix(es): 0-86382
Number of titles published annually: 12 Print; 2 CD-ROM; 5 Online
Total Titles: 12 Print; 2 CD-ROM; 5 Online
Parent Company: United Business Media

Coachwise Ltd
Chelsea Close, Off Amberley Rd, Armley, Leeds LS12 4HP
Tel: (0113) 2311310 *Fax:* (0113) 2319606
E-mail: enquiries@coachwise.ltd.uk
Web Site: www.coachwise.ltd.uk
Key Personnel
Man Dir: Dr Tony Byrne
General Manager: Kath Leonard
Marketing Executive & International Rights Contact: Melanie Drake *E-mail:* mdrake@coachwise.ltd.uk
Founded: 1989
Specialize in leisure management & coaching targeting sports professionals.
Membership(s): Direct Marketing Association (UK) Ltd.
Subjects: Health, Nutrition, Music, Dance, Outdoor Recreation, Sports, Athletics
Total Titles: 40 Print; 1 CD-ROM; 1 Audio
Parent Company: National Coaching Foundation

Cockbird Press+
PO Box 356, Heathfield TN21 9QF
Tel: (01435) 830430 *Fax:* (01435) 830027
Key Personnel
Man Dir: Lucy Faridany
General Editor: Diane White
Founded: 1990
Publish prints through catalogues by mail order.
Subjects: Biography, History, Travel
ISBN Prefix(es): 1-873054
Distributed by Seven Hills Book Distributors (US distributor)

COIC, *see* Careers & Occupational Information Centre (COIC)

Adlard Coles Nautical, *imprint of* A & C Black Publishers Ltd

Rosica Colin Ltd+
One Clareville Grove Mews, London SW7 5AH
Tel: (020) 7370 1080 *Fax:* (020) 7244 6441
Key Personnel
Dir: Joanna Marston
Founded: 1949
Literary agents.

Peter Collin Publishing Ltd+
38 Soho Sq, London W1D 3HB
Tel: (020) 7494 2111 *Fax:* (020) 7434 0151
E-mail: order@petercollin.com
Web Site: www.petercollin.com
Key Personnel
Dir: S M H Collin; Peter Collin
Founded: 1985
Specialize in English & bilingual dictionaries.
ISBN Prefix(es): 0-948549; 1-901659
Imprints: Aspect Guides
U.S. Office(s): IPG, 814 N Franklin St, Chicago, IL 60610, United States *Tel:* 312-337-0747 *Fax:* 312-337-5985 *E-mail:* order@petercollin.com
Distributed by Foucher, Klett

Shipping Address: PO Box 1321, Oak Park, IL 60304, United States *Tel:* 708-366-9553 *Fax:* 708-366-9554 (USA)
Orders to: Marston Book Services, PO Box 269, Abingdon, Oxon OX14 4YN *Tel:* (01235) 465600 *Fax:* (01235) 465655 *E-mail:* sales@marston.co.uk

Colonsay Books, *imprint of* House of Lochar

ColorCards, *imprint of* Speechmark Publishing Ltd

Colour Library Direct+
Godalming Business Center, Catteshall Lane, Woolsack Way, Godalming GU7 1XW
Tel: (01483) 426777 *Fax:* (01483) 426947
E-mail: prod@quad-pub.co.uk
Key Personnel
Man Dir: Brian Phipps
Publishing Dir: Will Steeds
Sales, Rights, Promotions: Des Higgins
Production: Grame Proctor
Production Manager: Karen Staff
Founded: 1959
Subjects: Animals, Pets, Art, Cookery, Environmental Studies, Photography, Travel
ISBN Prefix(es): 0-906558; 0-86283; 0-904681; 1-84100; 1-85833
Parent Company: Quadrillion
Imprints: ATAPepperpot Gift; CLB Books; CLB Publishing; QPI Books
Divisions: Bramley Books; CLB Editions; CLB Publishing; CLD Direct Marketing; IMC Video; Pepperpot Gift & Stationary; QPI Publishing; Quadrillion Multimedia Ltd

Colourpoint Books+
Colourpoint House, Jubilee Business Park, 21 Jubilee Rd, Newtownards BT23 4YH
Tel: (028) 9182 0505 *Fax:* (028) 9182 1900
E-mail: info@colourpoint.co.uk; sales@colourpoint.co.uk
Web Site: www.colourpoint.co.uk
Key Personnel
Partner: Malcolm Johnston *E-mail:* malcolm@colourpoint.co.uk; Sheila M Johnston *E-mail:* sheila@colourpoint.co.uk; Wesley Johnston
Partner & International Rights: Norman Johnston *E-mail:* norman@colourpoint.co.uk
Administrator: Michelle Chambers
Sales Manager: Lawrence Greer
Founded: 1993
Specializes in educational textbooks/resources, transport titles, books of Irish interest.
Membership(s): Publishers Association & Irish Educational Publishers' Association.
Subjects: Biography, Disability, Special Needs, Education, Government, Political Science, History, Maritime, Religion - Other, Transportation
ISBN Prefix(es): 1-898392; 1-904242
Number of titles published annually: 30 Print
Total Titles: 120 Print
Distributed by Ian Allan Publishing (England, Scotland & Wales)
Distributor for Business Enthusiast Publishing; Nostalgia Road; Arthur Southern; Trans-Pennine Publishing

Combined Academic Publishers
15A Lewin's Yard, East St, Chesham, Bucks HP5 1HQ
Tel: (01494) 581601 *Fax:* (01494) 581602
Web Site: www.combinedacademic.co.uk
Key Personnel
Dir: Nicholas Esson *E-mail:* nickesson@combinedacademic.demon.co.uk
Marketing Manager: Julia Monk
Founded: 1997

Full service sales, marketing & distribution agency which serves the needs of university & academic presses seeking promotion/marketing, field sales representation & distribution in the UK & Europe.
Imprints: Duke University Press (UK & Europe); Indiana University Press (UK & Europe); McGill-Queens University Press (UK & Europe); University of Illinois Press (UK & Europe); University of Nebraska Press (UK & Europe); University of Texas Press (UK & Europe); University of Washington Press (UK & Europe)
Shipping Address: Marston Book Services Ltd, 160 Milton Park, PO Box 269, Abingdon, Oxon OX14 4YN *Tel:* (01235) 465500 *Fax:* (01235) 465555 *E-mail:* trade.orders@marston.co.uk

Comedia, *imprint of* Routledge

Commission for Racial Equality+
St Dunstan's House, 201-211 Borough High St, London SE1 1GZ
Tel: (020) 7939 0000 *Fax:* (020) 7939 0001
E-mail: info@cre.gov.uk
Web Site: www.cre.gov.uk
Key Personnel
Chairman: Trevor Phillips
Marketing, Production, Rights & Permissions: Desrie Thomson
Founded: 1976
Subjects: Human Relations
ISBN Prefix(es): 0-907920; 1-85442; 0-902355
Imprints: CRE
Branch Office(s)
Lancaster House, 3rd floor, 67 Newhall St, Birmingham B3 1NA *Tel:* (0121) 710 3000 *Fax:* (0121) 710 3001
Capital Tower, 3rd floor, Greyfriars Rd, Cardiff CF10 3AG *Tel:* (02920) 729 200 *Fax:* (02920) 729 220
The Tun, 12 Jackson's Entry off Holyrood Rd, Edinburgh EH8 8PJ *Tel:* (0131) 524 2000 *Fax:* (0131) 524 2001 *E-mail:* scotland@cre.gov.uk
Yorkshire Bank Chambers, 1st floor, Infirmary St, Leeds LS1 2JP *Tel:* (0113) 389 3600 *Fax:* (0113) 389 3601
Maybrook House, 5th floor, 40 Blackfiars St, M3 2EG Manchester *Tel:* (0161) 835 5500 *Fax:* (0161) 835 5501
Orders to: CRE Customer Services, PO Box 29, Norwich NR3 1GN *Tel:* (0870) 240 3697 *Fax:* (0870) 240 3698 *E-mail:* CRE@tso.co.uk

Commonwealth Secretariat+
Marlborough House, Pall Mall, London SW1Y 5HX
Tel: (020) 7747 6500 *Fax:* (020) 7930 0827
E-mail: info@commonwealth.int
Web Site: www.thecommonwealth.org
Key Personnel
Head of Publications: Mr R Jones-Parry *E-mail:* r.jones-parry@commonwealth.int
Founded: 1948
Intergovernmental organization with responsibility for the work & all activities of the Commonwealth.
Subjects: Agriculture, Developing Countries, Earth Sciences, Economics, Education, Energy, Environmental Studies, Finance, Government, Political Science, Law, Management, Public Administration, Social Sciences, Sociology, Technology, Women's Studies
ISBN Prefix(es): 0-85092
Number of titles published annually: 40 Print; 2 CD-ROM
Total Titles: 150 Print; 4 CD-ROM; 2 Audio
Foreign Rep(s): Addenda Ltd (New Zealand); Book Bird (Pakistan); Booker International (Brunei); Bookwell (India); Buma Kor & Co Ltd (Cameroon); DCS-Athens (Greece); E & D Limited (Tanzania); Globe Enterprises (Malaysia); Grassroots Bookshop (Zimbabwe); Hargraves Library Services (South Africa); Iberian Book Services (Spain); Karim International (Bangladesh); Barbie Keene (Zimbabwe); Prestige Books (Zimbabwe); Publishers Scandinavian Consultancy (Scandinavia); Reimmer Book Services (Ghana); Renouf Publishing Company Ltd (Canada); SARDC (Mozambique); Select Books Pte Ltd (Singapore); Stylus Inc USA (USA); Tausco Book Distributors (India); Transglobal Publishers Service Ltd (Hong Kong); TRIOPS (Germany)
Warehouse: York Publishing Services, 64 Hallfield Rd, Layerthorpe, York YO31 72Q, Contact: Duncan Beal *Tel:* (01904) 431 213 *Fax:* (01904) 430 868 *Web Site:* www.yps-publishing.co.uk
Orders to: York Publishing Services, 64 Hallfield Rd, Layerthorpe, York YO31 7ZQ *Tel:* (01904) 431 213 *Fax:* (01904) 430 868 *E-mail:* dbeal@yps-publishing.co.uk
Membership(s): Publishers' Association

Compass Equestrian Ltd+
Cadborough Farm, Oldberrow, Henley-in-Arden, Warwicks B95 5NX
Tel: (0156) 479 5136 *Fax:* (0156) 479 5136
E-mail: compbook@globalnet.co.uk
Web Site: www.users.globalnet.co.uk/~compbook
Key Personnel
Dir: Valerie Wofford Watson
Contact: Clare Harris
Founded: 1996
Specializes in books on Equestrian topics.
Subjects: Nonfiction (General)
ISBN Prefix(es): 1-900667
Total Titles: 13 Print
Distributed by Trafalgar Square Publishing

Compass Maps Ltd
The Coach House, Beech Court, Winford BS40 8DW
Tel: (01275) 474737 *Fax:* (01275) 474787
E-mail: info@papoutmaps.com
Web Site: www.mapgroup.net

Compendium Publishing+
43 Frith St, 1st Floor, London WIV 5TE
Tel: (020) 72874570 *Fax:* (020) 74940583
E-mail: compendium@compuserve.com
Key Personnel
Man Dir: Alan Greene
Editorial: Simon Forty
Founded: 1998
Subjects: Aeronautics, Aviation, African American Studies, Anthropology, Antiques, Architecture & Interior Design, Art, Asian Studies, Automotive, Cookery, Crafts, Games, Hobbies, Erotica, History, How-to, Maritime, Military Science, Nonfiction (General), Sports, Athletics, Transportation, Travel
ISBN Prefix(es): 1-902579
Imprints: Wag Books; Windrow & Greene
Divisions: Compendium Publishing Ltd

Computer Science Press, *imprint of* W H Freeman & Co Ltd

Computer Step+
Southfield Rd, Southam, Warwicks CV47 0FB
Tel: (01926) 817999 *Fax:* (01926) 817005
E-mail: publisher@ineasysteps.com
Web Site: www.ineasysteps.com
Key Personnel
Publisher: Harshad Kotecha
Partner & International Rights: Mrs Sevanti Kotecha *E-mail:* sevanti@computerstep.com
Founded: 1991

Subjects: Business, How-to, Technology, Computers, Educational Software
ISBN Prefix(es): 1-874029; 1-84078
Total Titles: 60 Print; 10 E-Book
Distributed by Computer Bookshops (UK non-booktrade); Federal Publications (Malaysia); IDG Books India (India, Pakistan, Bangladesh); Penguin Books (Australia, New Zealand, South Africa)

Concrete Information Ltd
Formerly British Cement Association
Riverside House, 4 Meadows Business Park, Station Approach, Blackwater, Camberley, Surrey GU17 9AB
Tel: (01276) 608770 *Fax:* (01276) 37369
E-mail: enquiries@concreteinfo.org
Web Site: www.concreteinfo.org
Key Personnel
Head of Information Service: Edwin Trout
 E-mail: etrout@concreteinfo.org
Founded: 1935
Subjects: Civil Engineering, Engineering (General), Cement, Concrete
ISBN Prefix(es): 0-7210

Condor Books, *imprint of* Souvenir Press Ltd

Connections, *imprint of* Eddison Sadd Editions Ltd

Conran Octopus, *imprint of* Octopus Publishing Group

Conran Octopus+
Imprint of Octopus Publishing Group
2-4 Heron Quays, London E14 4JP
Tel: (020) 7531 8400 *Fax:* (020) 7531 8627
E-mail: info@conran-octopus.co.uk
Web Site: www.conran-octopus.co.uk
Telex: 296249
Key Personnel
Sales & Marketing Dir: Catharine Snow
 E-mail: catharine.snow@conran-octopus.co.uk
Publishing Dir: Lorraine Dickey *E-mail:* lorraine.dickey@conran-octopus.co.uk
Creative Dir: Leslie Harrington *E-mail:* leslie.harrington@conran-octopus.co.uk
Publicity & Marketing Assistant: Virginia McIntosh *E-mail:* virginia.mcintosh@conran-octopus.co.uk
UK Sales & Marketing Dir: Martin Hunka
 Tel: (020) 7531 8625 *E-mail:* martin.hunka@conran-octopus.co.uk
Founded: 1984
Subjects: Architecture & Interior Design, Crafts, Games, Hobbies, Gardening, Plants
ISBN Prefix(es): 1-85029; 1-84091
Distribution Center: APD Singapore Ptd Limited, 52 Genting Lane #06-05, Hiangkie Complex 1, Singapore 349560, Singapore, Contact: Ian Pringle *Tel:* 749 3551 *Fax:* 749 3552 *E-mail:* apd@pacific.net.sg (Singapore, Malaysia, Indonesia, Vietnam, Burma, Laos & Thailand)
Asia Publishers Services Ltd, 16F Wing Fat Commercial Bldg, 218 Aberdeen Main Rd, Aberdeen, Hong Kong, Contact: Ed Summerson *Tel:* (02553) 2553 9289/9280 *Fax:* (02553) 2554 2912 *E-mail:* apshk@netvigator.com (Hong Kong, China & Taiwan)
Books for Europe, Vosberger Weg 22, 8181 JH, Heerde, Netherlands, Contact: Mr Robert Pleysier *Tel:* (0578) 696 596 *Fax:* (0578) 696 798 *E-mail:* r.j.pleysier.bfe@wxs.nl (Netherlands)
Books for Europe, Via Del Casagrande 22, 6930 Bregonzona, Canton Ticino, Switzerland, Contact: Juliusz Komarnicki *Tel:* (091) 967 1539 *Fax:* (091) 966 7865 *E-mail:* juliusz.komarnicki@freesurf.ch (France & Benelux)
CLB Marketing Services, Ktona Jozef utca 41 1/4, Budapest H-1137, Hungary, Contact: Csaba Lengyel de Bagota *Tel:* (01) 3405213 *Fax:* (01) 3405213 (Hungary, Czech Republic, Slovakia, Slovenia, Croatia & Poland)
HardieGrant Books, 12 Claremont St, 3141 South Yarra, Victoria, Australia *Tel:* (03) 9827 8377 *Fax:* (03) 9827 8766 *E-mail:* jodiemartin@hardiegarnt.com.au (Australia)
Gill Hess Ltd, 15 Church St, Skerries, Co Dublin, Ireland *Tel:* (01) 849 1801 *Fax:* (01) 849 2384 (Ireland)
HRA - Humphrys Roberts Associates, 24 High St, Wanstead, London EII 2AQ, Publishers' Consultant & Representative: Mr Chris Humphrys *Tel:* (020) 8530 5028 *Fax:* (020) 8530 7870 *E-mail:* humph4hra@aol.com (Central America)
HRA - Humphrys Roberts Associates, Caixa Postal 801, AG Jardim da Gloria, 06700/970 Cotia SP, Brazil, Publishers' Consultant & Representative: Mr Terry Roberts *Tel:* (011) 492 4496 *Fax:* (011) 492 6896 *E-mail:* hrabrasil@intercall.com.br (South America)
IKC Korea, 473 19 Deokyo-dong, Mapo-Ku, Seoul 121-210, Republic of Korea *Tel:* (02) 3141 4791 *Fax:* (02) 3141 7733 *E-mail:* ickseoul2@netsgo.com (Korea)
Inter Media Americana, 17 Jeffrey's Place, London NWI 9PP, Contact: Tony Moggach *Tel:* (020) 7267 8054 *Fax:* (020) 7485 8462 *E-mail:* ima@moggach.demon.co.uk (North Africa)
Inter Media Americana, 14 York Rise, London NW5 1ST, Contact: Tony Moggach *Tel:* (020) 7267 8054 *Fax:* (020) 7485 8462 *E-mail:* ima@moggach.demon.co.uk
Victoria Kalish, 1080 Shoreway St, Foster City, CA 94404, United States, Director of Special Markets: Victoria Kalish *Tel:* (650) 573-5732 *Fax:* (650) 618-1535 *E-mail:* VKalishOPG@aol.com (USA)
Marketing Services for Publishers, 57 Sta Teresita, Kapitolyo, Pasig City 1603, Philippines, Contact: Benjie Ocampo *Tel:* (02) 635 3592; 635 3593 *Fax:* (02) 631 4470 *E-mail:* benjie@compass.com.ph (Philippines)
Nilsson & Lamm: Stockholding, Pampuslaan 212, 1382 JS Weesp, Netherlands *Tel:* (0294) 464 949 *Fax:* (0294) 494 455 *E-mail:* nilam@euronet.nl (Netherlands)
Octopus India, PO Box 7208, First Floor, Arun House, 2/25 Ansari Rd, New Delhi 110 002, India, Contact: Ajay Parmer *Tel:* (011) 328 4894 *Fax:* (011) 328 1819 *E-mail:* aparmar@vsnl.com (India & Sri Lanka)
Octopus Publishing Group, 7/30 Hooper St, Randwick, 2031 NSW, Australia, Contact: Tina Gitsas *Tel:* (02) 9298 8624 *Fax:* (02) 9298 8624 *E-mail:* tinaoctopus.@bigpond.com (Australia - special sales)
Octopus Publishing Group, 4-7-16-106Kamiuma, Setagaya-ku, Tokyo 150-0011, Japan, Contact: Ms Noriko Skai *Tel:* (0813) 5433 7638 *Fax:* (0813) 5433 7639 *E-mail:* noriko@cool.email.ne.jp (Japan)
Publisher's Agent, 56 Rosebank, Holyport Rd, Fulham, London SW6 6LH, Contact: Penny Padovani *Tel:* (020) 381 3936 *E-mail:* padovanibooks@compuseve.com (Italy, Spain, Portugal & Gibraltar)
Publisher's Services, Ziegenhainer Strasse 169, 60433 Frankfurt, Germany, Contact: Gabrielle Kern *Tel:* (069) 510 694 *Fax:* (069) 510 695 *E-mail:* Gabriele.Kern@publishersservices.de (Germany, Austria & Switzerland)
Quartet Sales & Marketing, Struik House, 7 Wessel Rd, 12 Carmel Avenue, NorthCliff, Gaiteng, Johannesburg, South Africa *Tel:* (011) 782 2034 *Fax:* (011) 782 2053 *E-mail:* shirley.c@mweb.co.za (South Africa)
Reed Publishing (NZ) Ltd, 39 Rawene Rd, Private Bag, Auckland 10, New Zealand *Tel:* (09) 480 4950 *Fax:* (09) 419 1212 *E-mail:* JBrockie@reed.co.nz
Derek Searle Associates Ltd, Progress Business Centre, Unit 13, Whittel Parkway, Burnham, Bucks SL1 6DQ *Tel:* (08) 559 500 *Fax:* (08) 663 876 *E-mail:* Dsapublish@aol.com
Vollmer Communications: Stockholding, Bunsen Strage No 5, 82152, Martinsried Munich, Germany *Tel:* (089) 857 3862 *Fax:* (089) 857 5592 *E-mail:* wv@vollmer-communications.com (Germany)
Peter Ward Book Exports, 4-5 Academy Buildings, Fanshaw Road, London NI 6LQ *Tel:* (020) 7613 5533 *Fax:* (020) 7613 4433 *E-mail:* pwbookex@dircon.co.uk (Middle East, Greece, Israel, Cyprus & Malta)
Orders to: Littlehampton Bopok Services Ltd, Faraday Close, Durrington, Worthing, West Sussex BN13 3RB *Tel:* (01933) 828503

Conservative Policy Forum
32 Smith Sq Westminster, London SW1P 3HH
Tel: (020) 7222 9000
E-mail: cpf@conservatives.com
Web Site: www.conservatives.com
Key Personnel
Dir: Greg Clark
Assistant Dir: Tracy-Jane Malthouse
 E-mail: tmalthouse@conservatives.com
Founded: 1945 (as Conservative Political Forum)
Subjects: Economics, Government, Political Science
ISBN Prefix(es): 0-85070

Constable, *imprint of* Constable & Robinson Ltd

Constable & Robinson Ltd+
3 The Lanchester, 162 Fulham Palace Rd, London W6 9ER
Tel: (020) 8741 3663 *Fax:* (020) 8748 7562
E-mail: enquiries@constablerobinson.com
Web Site: www.constablerobinson.com
Telex: 27950 ref 830
Key Personnel
Man Dir: Nick Robinson
Editorial: Carol O'Brien *E-mail:* carol@constablerobinson.com
Sales Dir: Andrew Hayward *E-mail:* andrew@constablerobinson.com
Sales Manager: Andrew Sauerwine
 E-mail: andrews@constablerobinson.com
Rights Manager: Eryl Humphrey Jones
 E-mail: eryl@constablerobinson.com
Founded: 1896
Subjects: Archaeology, Art, Astrology, Occult, Behavioral Sciences, Criminology, Erotica, Gay & Lesbian, Health, Nutrition, History, Humor, Literature, Literary Criticism, Essays, Military Science, Nonfiction (General), Photography, Psychology, Psychiatry, Science Fiction, Fantasy, Travel, Current Affairs
ISBN Prefix(es): 1-85487; 0-09; 1-84119; 1-84529
Number of titles published annually: 130 Print
Imprints: Constable; Robinson; Robinson's Children
Distribution Center: TBS Direct, Colchester Rd, Frating Green, Colchester, Essex CO7 7DW *Tel:* (01206) 255 678 *Fax:* (01206) 255 930
Orders to: TBS Direct, Colchester Rd, Frating Green, Colchester, Essex CO7 7DW *Tel:* (01206) 255 777 *Fax:* (01206) 255 914

Consultants Bureau, *imprint of* Kluwer Academic/Plenum Publishers

The Continuum International Publishing Group Ltd
The Tower Bldg, 11 York Rd, London SE1 7NX
Tel: (0207) 922 0880 *Fax:* (0207) 922 0881
E-mail: info@continuum-books.com
Web Site: www.continuumbooks.com

PUBLISHERS — UNITED KINGDOM

Key Personnel
President (New York Office): Philip Sturrock
  E-mail: psturrock@continuumbooks.com
Executive Vice President & General Manager (New York): Ulla Schnell *E-mail:* ulla@continuum-books.com
Executive Vice President & Publishing Dir (New York): Nicholas Weir Williams
Vice President & Senior Editor: Frank Oveis
  E-mail: frank@continuumbooks.com
Publisher-at-Large at New York Operation: Werner Mark Linz
Finance Dir: Frank Roney *E-mail:* froney@continuumbooks.com
Editorial Dir: Janet Joyce
Sale & Marketing Dir: John Parsons
Production Manager: Ian Sherratt
Subjects: Business, Drama, Theater, Education, Government, Political Science, History, Literature, Literary Criticism, Essays, Nonfiction (General), Psychology, Psychiatry, Women's Studies
ISBN Prefix(es): 0-304; 0-7201; 0-8264; 0-7136; 0-225; 0-264; 0-7185; 1-85567; 0-567; 0-485; 1-84127; 1-85805 ('); 0-8044; 0-86175
Number of titles published annually: 300 Print
Imprints: Geoffrey Chapman; Leicester University Press; Mansell; Mowbray; Pinter; Tycooly
U.S. Office(s): The Continuum International Publishing Group Inc, 370 Lexington Ave, New York, NY 10017, United States *Tel:* 212-953-5858 *Fax:* 212-953-5944
Orders to: Orca Book Services, Stanley House, 3 Fleets Lane, Poole, Dorset BH15 3AJ *Tel:* (01202) 665432 *Fax:* (01202) 666219

Conway Maritime Press+
Division of Chrysalis Group
The Chrysalis Bldg, Bramley Rd, London W10 6SP
Tel: (020) 7221 2213; (020) 7314 1469 (sales)
Fax: (020) 7221 6455; (020) 7314 1594 (sales)
E-mail: enquiries@chrysalis.com
Web Site: www.chrysalisbooks.co.uk/books/publisher/conway
Key Personnel
Group Sales & Marketing Dir: Richard Samson
  Tel: (020) 7314 1459 *Fax:* (020) 7314 1549
  E-mail: rsamson@chrysalisbooks.co.uk
Dir of Marketing: Kate Wood *Tel:* (020) 7314 1496 *E-mail:* kwood@chrysalisbooks.co.uk
Marketing & Publicity Manager: Rachel Armstrong *Tel:* (020) 7314 1605 *Fax:* (020) 7314 1549 *E-mail:* rarmstrong@chrysalisbooks.co.uk
Rights: Candida Buckley *Tel:* (01622) 863117 *Fax:* (01622) 863227 *E-mail:* candidabuckley@aol.com
Permissions: Terry Forshaw *Tel:* (020) 7314 1607 *E-mail:* tforshaw@chrysalisbooks.co.uk
Founded: 1968
Subjects: Maritime
ISBN Prefix(es): 0-85177
Associate Companies: Putnam Aeronautical Books

Leo Cooper, *imprint of* Pen & Sword Books Ltd

Leo Cooper+
Imprint of Pen & Sword Books Ltd
47 Church St, Barnsley, South Yorks S70 2AS
Tel: (01226) 734555 *Fax:* (01226) 734438
E-mail: enquiries@pen-sword.demon.co.uk
Web Site: www.pen-and-sword.co.uk
Key Personnel
Man Dir: Charles Hewitt *E-mail:* charles@pen-and-sword.co.uk
Publishing Manager: Henry Wilson
  E-mail: henry@pen-and-sword.co.uk
Book Production Manager: Barbara Bramall
  E-mail: production@pen-and-sword.co.uk
Sales Manager: Paula Brennan *E-mail:* sales@pen-and-sword.co.uk
Marketing & Publicity: Jonathan Wright
  E-mail: marketing@pen-and-sword.co.uk
Founded: 1990
Subjects: Biography, History, Maritime, Military Science, Nonfiction (General), Travel
ISBN Prefix(es): 0-85052
Number of titles published annually: 100 Print
Total Titles: 350 Print
Associate Companies: Wharncliffe Publishing
Distributed by Combined Books (USA); Vanwell Publishing Ltd (Canada)

Co-operative Union, *imprint of* Holyoake Books

Copper Beech Publishing Ltd+
PO Box 159, East Grinstead, Sussex RH19 4HF
Tel: (01342) 314734 *Fax:* (01342) 314794
E-mail: sales@copperbeechpublishing.co.uk
Web Site: www.btinternet.com/~copperbeechpublishing
Key Personnel
Contact: Jan Barnes
Membership(s): IPG.
Subjects: Etiquette, Food & Drink, Victoriana
ISBN Prefix(es): 0-9516295; 1-898617

Cordee Ltd+
3a De Montfort St, Leicester LE1 7HD
Tel: (0116) 2543579 *Fax:* (0116) 2471176
E-mail: info@cordee.co.uk
Web Site: www.cordee.co.uk
Key Personnel
Contact: Ken Vickers *E-mail:* kenvickers@cordee.co.uk
Founded: 1973
Specialist publisher, distributor & wholesaler (worldwide).
Subjects: Outdoor Recreation, Travel
ISBN Prefix(es): 1-871890; 0-904405

Corgi, *imprint of* Transworld Publishers Ltd

Cornwall Books, *imprint of* Golden Cockerel Press Ltd

Corwin Press, *imprint of* SAGE Publications Ltd

Joanna Cotler Books, *imprint of* HarperCollins UK

Cottage Publications
Laurel Cottage, 15 Ballyhay Rd, Donaghadee, Co Down BT21 0NG
Tel: (01247) 888033; (0410) 057990 (mobile)
  Fax: (01247) 888063
E-mail: info@cottage-publications.com
Web Site: www.cottage-publications.com
Key Personnel
Contact: Timothy Johnston *E-mail:* tim@cottage-publications.com
Founded: 1990
Specialize in illustrated books on Ireland.
Subjects: Art, History, Regional Interests
ISBN Prefix(es): 0-9516402; 1-900935
Total Titles: 20 Print

Council for British Archaeology
Bowes Morrell House, 111 Walmgate, York YO1 9WA
Tel: (01904) 671417 *Fax:* (01904) 671384
E-mail: archaeology@compuserve.com; cbabooks@dial.pipex.com
Web Site: www.britarch.ac.uk
Key Personnel
Dir: George Lambrick *E-mail:* georgelambrick@britarch.ac.uk
Publications Officer: Kate Sleight
Founded: 1944
Subjects: Archaeology, Education
ISBN Prefix(es): 0-900312; 0-906780; 1-872414

Number of titles published annually: 12 Print
Total Titles: 65 Print

Countryside Books
2 Highfield Ave, Newbury, Berks RG14 5DS
Tel: (01635) 43816 *Fax:* (01635) 551004
E-mail: info@countrysidebooks.co.uk
Web Site: www.countrysidebooks.co.uk
Key Personnel
Man Dir, Editorial, Sales & Production: Nicholas Battle
Publicity, Rights & Permissions: Suzanne Battle
Founded: 1976
Publisher of regional interest books within UK
Specialize in walking guides.
Subjects: Genealogy, History, Regional Interests
ISBN Prefix(es): 0-905392; 0-86368; 1-85306
Number of titles published annually: 50 Print
Total Titles: 400 Print
Subsidiaries: Local Heritage Books

Countyvise Ltd+
14 Appin Rd, Birkenhead, Merseyside CH41 9HH
Tel: (0151) 6473333 *Fax:* (0151) 6478286
E-mail: info@countyvise.co.uk
Web Site: www.countyvise.co.uk
Key Personnel
Man Dir: John Emmerson *E-mail:* je@birkenheadpress.co.uk
Founded: 1981
Subjects: Biography, History, Maritime, Regional Interests, Sports, Athletics, Transportation
ISBN Prefix(es): 0-907768; 1-871201; 0-9516129; 1-873245; 1-901231
Number of titles published annually: 7 Print
Total Titles: 121 Print
Imprints: Liver Press; Merseyside Port Folios; Picton Press (Liverpool)

Covenant Publishing Co Ltd
8 Blades Court, Deodar Rd, London SW15 2NU
Tel: (020) 8877 9010 *Fax:* (020) 8871 4770
E-mail: admin@britishisrael.co.uk
Web Site: www.britishisrael.co.uk
Key Personnel
Chairman: M A Clark
Administrator: J B Dowse
Founded: 1922
Subjects: Religion - Other
ISBN Prefix(es): 0-85205

Richard & Erika Coward Writing & Publishing Partnership+
16 Sturgess Ave, London NW4 3TS
Tel: (0208) 202 9592
E-mail: info@writers.net
Key Personnel
Author: Richard Coward *E-mail:* richardcoward@onetel.net.uk
Business Manager: Erika Coward
ISBN Prefix(es): 0-9515019

CRAC, *imprint of* Hobsons

CRE, *imprint of* Commission for Racial Equality

Creation Books+
72/80 Leather Lane, 4th floor, London EC1N 7TR
Tel: (020) 7430 9878 *Fax:* (020) 7242 5527
E-mail: info@creationbooks.com
Web Site: www.creationbooks.com
Key Personnel
President: James Williamson *E-mail:* james@creationbooks.com
Dir: Laurence Raine *E-mail:* laurence@creationbooks.com
Publishing Executive & Rights: Miranda Filbee
  E-mail: miranda@creationbooks.com
Founded: 1989

UNITED KINGDOM

Subjects: Biography, Erotica, Fiction, Film, Video, Nonfiction (General), Photography
ISBN Prefix(es): 1-871592; 1-84068; 1-902588
Total Titles: 100 Print
Associate Companies: Glitter Books, 85 Clerkenwell Rd, Suite 403, London EC1R 5AR, Contact: James Williamson *Tel:* (020) 7430 9878 *Fax:* (020) 7242 5527 *E-mail:* glitter@creationbooks.com
Imprints: Attack!; Velvet
U.S. Office(s): PO Box 1137, New York, NY 10156, United States
c/o Subterranean Co, Box 160, Monroe, OR 97456, United States
Foreign Rep(s): Julian Ashton (Far East, Middle East); Creation Books Tokyo (Japan); Tower Books (Australia & New Zealand)
Distribution Center: Consortium Book Sales & Distribution, 1045 Westgate Dr, Saint Paul, MN 55114, United States *Tel:* 651-221-9035 *Fax:* 651-917-6406 *Web Site:* www.cbsd.com
Last Gasp, 777 Florida St, San Francisco, CA 94110, United States *Tel:* 415-824-6636 *Fax:* 415-824-1836 *Web Site:* www.lastgasp.com
Marginal Distribution, 277 George St, Unit 102, North Peterborough, ON K9J 3G9, Canada *Tel:* 705-745-2326 *Fax:* 705-745-2122 *Web Site:* www.marginalbook.com
Orders to: Book Clearing House, 45 Purdy St, Harrison, NY 10528, United States *Fax:* 914-835-0398 *E-mail:* bookch@aol.com *Web Site:* www.book-clearing-house.com (US & Canada mail order)
Turnaround, Olympia Trading Estate, Unit 3, Coburg Rd, Wood Green, London N22 6TZ *Tel:* (020) 8829 3000 *Fax:* (020) 8881 5088

Creative Monochrome, *imprint of* Creative Monochrome Ltd

Creative Monochrome Ltd
20 St Peter's Rd, Croydon CR0 1HD
Tel: (020) 8686 3282 *Fax:* (020) 8681 0662
E-mail: sales@cremono.com; roger@cremono.demon.co.uk
Key Personnel
Man Dir: Roger Maile *E-mail:* roger@cremono.com
Founded: 1992
Membership(s): IPG.
Subjects: Photography
ISBN Prefix(es): 1-873319
Total Titles: 24 Print
Imprints: Creative Monochrome; Digital Photoart; Photo Art International
Distribution Center: Ingrams & Small Changes Inc (USA & Canada)

Cressrelles Publishing Company Ltd+
Industrial Estate, 10 Station Rd, Colwall, Malvern, Herefordshire WR13 6RN
Tel: (01684) 540154 *Fax:* (01684) 540154
Key Personnel
Man Dir: Leslie Smith
Business Manager: Simon Smith
  E-mail: simonsmith@cressrelles4drama.fsbusiness.co.uk
Founded: 1973
Subjects: Drama, Theater
ISBN Prefix(es): 0-85956
Number of titles published annually: 3 Print
Total Titles: 48 Print
Imprints: Actinic Press (chiropody); Kenyon-Deane (plays); J Garnet Miller Ltd (plays); New Playwrights Network (plays)
Distributed by Empire Publishing Services
Distributor for Anchorage Press Inc; I E Clark Inc

Critical Studies in Latin American Culture, *imprint of* Verso

Paul H Crompton Ltd+
102 Felsham Rd, London SW15 1DQ
Tel: (020) 8780 1063 *Fax:* (020) 8780 1063
E-mail: cromptonph@aol.com
Key Personnel
Publicity & Rights: Paul Crompton
International Rights: Rose Brookhouse
Founded: 1968
Also produce martial arts videos.
Subjects: Cookery, Crafts, Games, Hobbies, Health, Nutrition
ISBN Prefix(es): 0-901764; 1-874250
Distributed by Talman Company (North America)
Orders to: c/o Airlift Book Co, 8 The Arena, Mollison Ave, Enfield, Middlesex EN3 7NJ *Tel:* (081) 8040400 *Fax:* (081) 8040044

Croner CCH Group Ltd
145 London Rd, Kingston-upon-Thames, Surrey KT2 6SR
Tel: (020) 85473333 *Fax:* (020) 85472637
E-mail: info@croner.co.uk
Web Site: www.croner.co.uk
Telex: 267778
Key Personnel
Man Dir: H F Staal
Production: George Rankin
Finance Dir: Peter Diggles
Founded: 1941
Subjects: Business, Finance, Health, Nutrition, Labor, Industrial Relations, Law, Transportation
ISBN Prefix(es): 0-900319; 1-85524
Parent Company: Wolters Kluwer (UK) PLC
Ultimate Parent Company: Wolters Kluwer NV, Netherlands
Subsidiaries: CCH Editions (Bicester)

Crossbridge Books+
345 Old Birmingham Rd, Bromsgrove B60 1NX
Tel: (0121) 447 7897 *Fax:* (0121) 445 1063
E-mail: crossbridgebooks@btinternet.com
Web Site: www.crossbridgebooks.com
Key Personnel
Publisher & International Rights Contact: Eileen Mohr
Founded: 1995
Publish Christian books.
Membership(s): Christian Booksellers Association; Independent Publishers Guild.
Subjects: Biography, Religion - Protestant, Self-Help
ISBN Prefix(es): 0-9524604
Number of titles published annually: 3 Print
Total Titles: 15 Print
Imprints: Mohr Books

Crossway, *imprint of* Inter-Varsity Press

Crown House Publishing Ltd+
Crown Buildings, Bancyfelin, Carmarthen SA33 5ND
Tel: (01267) 211345 *Fax:* (01267) 211882
E-mail: books@crownhouse.co.uk
Web Site: www.crownhouse.co.uk
Key Personnel
Dir: David Bowman
Marketing Dir: Caroline Lenton
Founded: 1998
Subjects: Business, Education, Psychology, Psychiatry
ISBN Prefix(es): 1-899836; 1-904424
Number of titles published annually: 20 Print
Total Titles: 110 Print
U.S. Office(s): 4 Berkeley St, 1st floor, Norwalk, CT 06850, United States
Foreign Rep(s): Everybody's Books (South Africa); Footprint Books (Australia); Mark Tracten (Canada, USA)
Orders to: PO Box 2223, Williston, VT 05495, United States *Tel:* 877-925-1213 *Fax:* 802-864-7626

The Crowood Press Ltd+
The Stable Block, Crowood Lane, Ramsbury, Marlborough, Wilts SN8 2HR
Tel: (01672) 520320 *Fax:* (01672) 520280
E-mail: enquiries@crowood.com
Web Site: www.crowood.com
Key Personnel
Publisher, Chief Executive: John F Dennis
Man Dir: Ken Hathaway
Sales Office Manager: Julie Sankey
  E-mail: admin@crowood.com
Rights Manager: Madeleine Hacking
Founded: 1982
Subjects: Aeronautics, Aviation, Animals, Pets, Automotive, Crafts, Games, Hobbies, Gardening, Plants, Maritime, Natural History, Outdoor Recreation, Sports, Athletics
ISBN Prefix(es): 0-946284; 1-85223; 1-86126
Imprints: Helmsman Guides
Distributed by Grantham Book Services (United Kingdom); Peter Hyde Associates (South Africa); Motorbooks International (US transport & military titles); Nilsson & Lamm (Netherlands); Peribo Pty Ltd (Australia & New Zealand); Publishers Marketing Services (Singapore); Publishers Marketing Services Pte Ltd (Malaysia); Trafalgar Square Publishing (USA); Vanwell Publishing Ltd (Canada)
Foreign Rep(s): Bookport Associates (Southern Europe); D Richard Bowen (Scandinavia); European Marketing Services (Austria, Belgium, France, Germany, Luxembourg, Switzerland)
Warehouse: Bookpoint Ltd, 39 Milton Park, Abingdon Oxon

G L Crowther
224 S Meadow Lane, Preston PR1 8JP
Tel: (01772) 257126
Key Personnel
Contact: G L Crowther
Founded: 1984
Specialize in maps showing all navigations, tramways & railways known to have existed in the UK.
Subjects: Geography, Geology, Transportation
ISBN Prefix(es): 1-85615
Number of titles published annually: 20 Print
Total Titles: 125 Print

Crucible Publishers
3 Town Barton, Norton St Philip, Bath BA2 7LN
Tel: (01373) 834900 *Fax:* (01373) 834900
E-mail: sales@cruciblepublishers.com
Web Site: www.cruciblepublishers.com
Key Personnel
Man Dir: Mr Robin Campbell
Founded: 2002
Also publish Crucible Classics.
Subjects: Ecology, Mind, Body & Spirit

Crux Press, *imprint of* Impart Books

CSA (Cambridge Scientific Abstracts)+
4640 Kingsgate, Cascade Way, Oxford Business Park South, Oxford OX4 2ST
Tel: (0441) 865 336250 *Fax:* (0441) 865 336258
E-mail: service@csa.com; tjones@csa.com (sales); marketing@bowker.uk.co
Web Site: www.csa.com
Key Personnel
Man Dir: Jacki Heppard *Tel:* (01342) 336043
  E-mail: jacki.heppard@bowker.com
Marketing Manager: Jo Grange *Tel:* (01342) 336143 *E-mail:* jo.grange@bowker.com
Sales Dir: Doug Macmillan *Tel:* (01342) 336157
  E-mail: doug.macmillan@bowker.co.uk
Founded: 1988
Publisher of reference tools & professional development texts for the library & information world & publishing industry.

Subjects: Library & Information Sciences, Publishing & Book Trade Reference
ISBN Prefix(es): 1-85739; 0-8352; 0-85935; 1-88387
Total Titles: 150 Print; 8 CD-ROM; 4 Online; 5 E-Book
Online services available through Dialog.
Parent Company: Cambridge Information Group
Distributed by D W Thorpe (Australia)
Distributor for R R Bowker LLC (UK, Europe, Middle East, Africa, Southeast Asia)

CTBI Publications
Inter-Church House, 35-41 Lower Marsh, London SE1 7SA
Tel: (020) 7523 2121 *Fax:* (020) 7928 0010
E-mail: info@ctbi.org.uk
Web Site: www.ctbi.org.uk
Key Personnel
International Rights: Rev D J Rudiger *Tel:* (020) 7523 2041
Publications Secretary: Rev Collin Davey, PhD *Tel:* (020) 7523 2154
Founded: 1940 (as BCC Publications)
Subjects: Biblical Studies, Biography, Education, Environmental Studies, History, Microcomputers, Religion - Catholic, Religion - Protestant, Religion - Other, Theology, Women's Studies
ISBN Prefix(es): 0-85169
Parent Company: Churches Together In Britain & Ireland
Distributor for World Council of Churches (UK & Ireland)
Bookshop(s): Church House Bookshop, 31 Great Smith St, London SW1P 3BN *Tel:* (020) 7898 1306 *Fax:* (020) 7898 1305 *E-mail:* bookshop@c-of-e.org.uk

CTS Publications, *imprint of* The Catholic Truth Society

Curiad
The Old Library, County Rd, Pen-y-Groes, Caernarfon, Gwynedd LL54 6EY
Tel: (01286) 882166 *Fax:* (01286) 882692
E-mail: curiad@curiad.co.uk
Web Site: www.curiad.co.uk
Key Personnel
Contact: Dyfed Wyn Edwards
Founded: 1992
Subjects: Music, Dance
ISBN Prefix(es): 1-897664

Current Science Group+
Middlesex House, 34-42 Cleveland St, London W1T 4LB
Tel: (020) 7323 0323 *Fax:* (020) 7580 1938
E-mail: info@current-science.com
Web Site: www.current-science-group.com
Key Personnel
Chairman: Vitek Tracz *E-mail:* vitek@sciencenow.com
Man Dir: Anne Greenwood *E-mail:* anne@sciencenow.com
Operations Dir: Mike Lennie
Marketing Dir: Daryl Rainer
Finance Dir: Brett Hassell *E-mail:* brett@sciencenow.com
Human Resources Manager: Cheryl Gambrill *E-mail:* cheryl@sciencenow.com
Subjects: Biological Sciences, Medicine, Nursing, Dentistry, Science (General)
ISBN Prefix(es): 1-870485; 1-85927
Subsidiaries: Current Drugs Ltd; Science Press
U.S. Office(s): 20 N Third St, Philadelphia, PA 19106-2113, United States *Tel:* 215-574-2266 *Fax:* 215-574-2270

James Currey Ltd+
73 Boxley Rd, Oxford OX2 0BS
Tel: (01865) 244 111 *Fax:* (01865) 246 454
E-mail: editorial@jamescurrey.co.uk
Web Site: www.jamescurrey.co.uk
Key Personnel
Chairman: James M Currey
Man & Editorial Dir: Dr Douglas H Johnson *E-mail:* douglas.johnson@jamescurrey.co.uk
Editorial Manager: Lynn Taylor *E-mail:* lynn.taylor@jamescurrey.co.uk
Founded: 1985
Subjects: Agriculture, Anthropology, Archaeology, Biography, Developing Countries, Drama, Theater, Economics, Education, Environmental Studies, Ethnicity, Foreign Countries, Government, Political Science, History, Law, Philosophy, Social Sciences, Sociology, Africa, Caribbean, Gender Studies, Literary Criticism, Theatre & Film, Third World Bibliographies
ISBN Prefix(es): 0-85255
Number of titles published annually: 50 Print
Total Titles: 360 Print
Imprints: Hans Zell Bibliographies
Foreign Rep(s): IMA (Africa); Intermedia Americana Ltd (Africa & Mideast exc South Africa & Israel, Africa exc South Africa); David Philip Publishers (Africa)
Orders to: Plymbridge Distributors Ltd, Estover, Plymouth PL6 7PZ *Tel:* (01752) 202301 *Fax:* (01752) 202333 *E-mail:* orders@plymbridge.com

CyberClub+
16 St John St, London EC1M 4AY
Tel: (020) 8731 6161 *Fax:* (020) 8905 5050
Web Site: www.astorlaw.com
Key Personnel
Contact: Richard Astor
Membership(s): Publishers Association (UK).
Subjects: Law
ISBN Prefix(es): 1-873994
Imprints: Bartsky Legal Texts Ltd

Cyfres y Gair, *imprint of* Cyhoeddiadau'r Gair

Cygnus Arts, *imprint of* Golden Cockerel Press Ltd

Cyhoeddiadau Barddas
Pen-Rhiw, 71 Ffordd Pentrepoeth, Treforys, Abertawe SA6 6AE
Tel: (01792) 792 829
Key Personnel
Contact: Alan Llwyd
Founded: 1976
Specializes in Welsh language & literature.
Subjects: Literature, Literary Criticism, Essays, Poetry
ISBN Prefix(es): 1-900437

Cyhoeddiadau FBA, *imprint of* Francis Balsom Associates

Cyhoeddiadau'r Gair (Work Publications)+
Cyngor Ysgolion Sul, Ysgol Addsg, Prifysgol Cymru Bangor, Safle'r Normal, Bangor, Gwynedd LL57 2PX
Tel: (01248) 382947 *Fax:* (01248) 383954
E-mail: eds00e@bangor.ac.uk
Web Site: www.ysgolsul.com
Key Personnel
Contact: Aled Davies *E-mail:* aled.davies@bangor.ac.uk
Founded: 1992
Specialize in Welsh language Christian books, cards & systems.
Subjects: Biblical Studies, Religion - Protestant
ISBN Prefix(es): 1-85994
Total Titles: 300 Print; 2 CD-ROM
Parent Company: Cyngor Ysgolion Sul
Imprints: Cyfres y Gair
Subsidiaries: Cardiau'r Gair gifts
Distributed by Welsh Books Council
Distributor for Curaid; Gwasg Efeng yl Aidd Cymru
Bookshop(s): Canolfan Addysg Grefyddol, Bangor
Warehouse: Libanus, Bontnewydd

Cymdeithas Lyfrau Ceredigion+
Ystafell B5, Y Coleg Diwinyddol, Stryd y Brenin, Aberystwyth, Ceredigion SY23 2LT
Tel: (01970) 617776 *Fax:* (01970) 624049; (01970) 625844
E-mail: clc.gyf@talk21.com
Key Personnel
Contact: Dylan Williams
Founded: 1954
Subjects: Ceredigion Interest
ISBN Prefix(es): 0-901410; 0-948930; 1-902416
Orders to: The Distribution Centre, Unit 16, Glan-yr-afon Industrial Estate, Hanbadarn Fawr, Aberystwyth, Ceredigion SY23 3AQ

Cynulliad Cenedlaethol Cymru, *imprint of* National Assembly for Wales

D&B Ltd
Holmers Farm Way, High Wycombe, Bucks HP12 4UL
Tel: (01494) 422000 *Fax:* (01494) 422260
E-mail: custserv@dnb.com
Web Site: www.dnb.com
Key Personnel
Man Dir: Claes Henckel
Sales: Nigel Dickinson
Publicity & Marketing: Barbara James
Founded: 1841
Membership(s): Directory Publishers Association, European Association of Directory Publishers, Booksellers Association & Business Information Network.
ISBN Prefix(es): 0-901491; 0-900714; 1-86071
Parent Company: D&B Corporation, 103 JFK Parkway, Short Hills, NJ 07078, United States
Branch Office(s)
Bangor
Birmingham
Glasgow
London
Manchester
Newport
Nottingham
Southampton

D C Thomson & Co Ltd
80 Kingsway East, Dundee DD4 8SL
Tel: (01382) 223131 *Fax:* (01382) 462097
E-mail: shout@dcthomson.co.uk
Web Site: www.dcthomson.co.uk
Key Personnel
Chairman: Brian H Thompson
Founded: 1905
Branch Office(s)
Courier Buildings, 2 Albert Sq, Dundee DD1 9QJ *Tel:* (01382) 223131 *Fax:* (01382) 322214
144 Port Dundas Rd, Glasgow G4 OHZ *Tel:* (0141) 332 9933 *Fax:* (0141) 331 1595
185 Fleet St, London EC4A 2HS *Tel:* (020) 7400 1030 *Fax:* (020) 7831 9440
137 Chapel St, Manchester M3 6AA *Tel:* (0161) 834 2831 *Fax:* (0161) 833 2884

Daily Telegraph (map service), *imprint of* Roger Lascelles

Dales Large Print Series, *imprint of* Magna Large Print Books

Terence Dalton Ltd+
Water St, Lavenham, Suffolk CO10 9RN
Tel: (01787) 249290 *Fax:* (01787) 248267
E-mail: tdl@lavenhamgroup.cp.uk
Web Site: www.terencedalton.co.uk

Key Personnel
Man Dir: Terence Dalton *E-mail:* terence@lavenhamgroup.co.uk
Dir: Mrs Lis Whitehair *E-mail:* lis@lavenhamgroup.co.uk
Marketing Manager: Erica Hammond *E-mail:* erica@lavenhamgroup.co.uk
Business Development Officer: Barney Goodrich *E-mail:* barney@lavenhamgroup.co.uk
Conference & Book Sales: Claire Smith *E-mail:* claire@lavenhamgroup.co.uk
Book Sales: Gail Moss *E-mail:* gail@lavenhamgroup.co.uk
Webmaster: Steve Lodge *E-mail:* steve@lavenhamgroup.co.uk
Founded: 1967
Contract publishers for CIWEM (Chartered Institution of Water & Environmental Management). Some East Anglian, maritime & aviation titles still available.
Subjects: Aeronautics, Aviation, Environmental Studies, Maritime, Regional Interests, Magazines
ISBN Prefix(es): 0-900963; 0-86138; 0-903214; 0-904623
Parent Company: The Lavenham Group PLC
Associate Companies: The Lavenham Press Ltd, Water St, Lavenham, C010 9RN Sudbury, Suffolk, Contact: Terence Dalton *Tel:* (01787) 247436 *Fax:* (01787) 248267 *E-mail:* postmaster@lavenhamgroup.co.uk
Imprints: CIWEM; Eastland Press; Mallard Reprints
Distributor for CIWEM

Dance Books Ltd+
The Old Bakery, 4 Lenten St, Alton, Hants GU34 1HG
Tel: (01420) 86138 *Fax:* (01420) 86142
E-mail: dl@dancebooks.co.uk
Web Site: www.dancebooks.co.uk
Key Personnel
Man Dir, Production, Rights & Permissions: David Leonard
Sales Dir: Richard Holland
Founded: 1960
Publishers & bookkeepers.
Subjects: Music, Dance
ISBN Prefix(es): 0-903102; 1-85273
Number of titles published annually: 10 Print
Total Titles: 130 Print
Distributed by Princeton Book Co; Astam Books
Distributor for Princeton Book Co

The C W Daniel Co Ltd+
One Church Path, Saffron Walden, Essex CB10 1JP
Tel: (01799) 521909; (01799) 526216 *Fax:* (01799) 513462
E-mail: cwdaniel@dial.pipex.com
Web Site: www.cwdaniel.com
Key Personnel
Man Dir: Ian Miller
Editorial, Rights & Permissions: Jane Miller
Accounts: Jane Goodacre
Marketing, Publicity: Genevieve Miller *Tel:* (01799) 521909
Founded: 1903
Publisher of Mind, Body & Spirit Paperbacks.
Subjects: Animals, Pets, Astrology, Occult, Health, Nutrition, Self-Help
ISBN Prefix(es): 0-85207; 0-85032; 0-85435; 0-85978; 0-85243
Number of titles published annually: 10 Print
Total Titles: 200 Print
Imprints: L N Fowler & Co Ltd; Health Science Press; Neville Spearman Publishers
Distributed by Alternative Books (UK); APA Publications (Singapore); Beekman Publishers Inc (USA); Gemcraft Books (UK); Homeopathic Educational Services; National Book Network (USA); The New Leaf Distributing Co (USA); The Nutri Book Corp (USA); Peaceful Living Publications (UK)
Distributor for Brotherhood of Life, NM; Haug Verlag, Germany
Foreign Rep(s): Angell Eurosales (Northern Europe, Scandinavia); Bookport Associates (Greece & Cyprus, Spain, Italy & Portugal); Kerim Colakoglu (Turkey); Donald MacDonald (Scotland); Tony Moggach (Africa, Eastern Europe, Middle East); National Book Network (Canada, USA); Theo Phillips (Hong Kong, Malaysia & Singapore, Philippines, Thailand); David Williams (South America)
Foreign Rights: Angell Euorsales (Northern Europe, Scandinavia); Angell Eurosales (Northern Europe, Scandinavia); Bookport Associates (Greece, Greece & Cyprus, Spain, Italy & Portugal); Kerim Colakoglu (Turkey); Donald MacDonald (Scotland); Genny Kelliher (Northern Ireland); Joe Portelli (Greece, Italy, Portugal, Spain); Tom Moggach (Africa); Tony Moggach (Eastern Europe, Middle East); National Book Network (Canada, USA); Theo Philips (Hong Kong, Malaysia & Singapore, Philippines, Thailand); The Segrue Partnership (London); David Williams (South America)
Warehouse: Unit 7, Saffron Business Centre, Elizabeth Close, off Elizabeth Way, Saffron Walden, Essex CB10 2BL

Darf Publishers Ltd
277 West End Lane, London NW6 1QS
Tel: (020) 7431 7009 *Fax:* (020) 7431 7655
E-mail: darf@freeuk.com
Web Site: home.freeuk.net/darf
Key Personnel
Chief Executive: M B Fergiani
Editorial: Usama Al Fergiani
Sales, Publicity: Ghassan Fergiani
Production: A Bentaleb
Manager & Rights & Permissions: John Cowen
Founded: 1983
Specialize in reprints of out-of-print & rare books written in the 18th & 19th centuries.
Subjects: Archaeology, History, Religion - Islamic, Travel
ISBN Prefix(es): 1-85077
Number of titles published annually: 10 Print
Total Titles: 200 Print
Parent Company: Dar Al Fergian, PO Box 132, Tripoli, Libyan Arab Jamahiriya
Subsidiaries: Dar Al Fergiani

Dartmouth, *imprint of* Ashgate Publishing Ltd

Darton, Longman & Todd Ltd+
One Spencer Court, 140-142 Wandsworth High St, London SW18 4JJ
Tel: (020) 8875 0155 *Fax:* (020) 8875 0133
E-mail: tradesales@darton-longman-todd.co.uk
Web Site: www.darton-longman-todd.co.uk
Key Personnel
Production: Leslie Kay
Sales & Marketing Dir: Alan Mordue
Editorial Dir: Brendan Walsh
Man Editor: Helen Porter
Rights & Permissions: Rachel Davis
Founded: 1959
Subjects: Biblical Studies, Religion - Catholic, Religion - Protestant, Religion - Other, Theology
ISBN Prefix(es): 0-232
Warehouse: 9 Amor Way, Dunhams Lane, Letchworth, Herts S96 1U9

Datapack Books, *imprint of* E J Morten (Publishers)

David & Charles Ltd+
Brunel House, Forde Close, Newton Abbot, Devon TQ12 4PU
Tel: (01626) 323200 *Fax:* (01626) 323319
E-mail: postermaster@davidandcharles.co.uk
Web Site: www.davidandcharles.co.uk
Telex: 42904 BOOKS G
Key Personnel
Sales & Marketing Dir: Susie Hallam
Non-Executive Dir: Neil McRae
Rights & Book Club Manager: Sue Narramore
Publishing Dir: Piers Spence
Operation Dir & Production Manager: Amanda Newton
Press & Promotions Officer: Susan Hallam
Founded: 1960
Subjects: Animals, Pets, Art, Cookery, Crafts, Games, Hobbies, Gardening, Plants, Health, Nutrition, How-to, Maritime, Outdoor Recreation, Photography, Transportation, Travel
ISBN Prefix(es): 0-7153; 0-907115; 1-85724; 0-276; 0-86438
Associate Companies: Levinson
Imprints: Betterway; How Design; North Light; Popular Woodworking; Writer's Digest
Divisions: The Readers' Union
Distributed by David Batemen Ltd (New Zealand); F & W Publications, Inc (USA & Canada); Kirby Book Distribution (Australia); Trinity Books (South Africa)
Foreign Rep(s): Angell Eurosales (Belgium, Denmark, Netherlands, Finland, France, Iceland, Norway, Sweden); Pat Bence (Botswana, Caribbean, Kenya, Mauritius, The Gambia); Candida Buckley (Denmark, Netherlands, Finland, Norway, Switzerland); Michelle Morrow Curreri (Asia, Latin America, Middle East); Lora Fountain (France); Gabriele Kern (Austria, Germany, Switzerland); Surit Mitra (Bangladesh, Indonesia, Nepal, Sri Lanka); Penny Padovani (France, Gibraltar, Greece, Italy, Spain); Marta Schooler (Asia, Latin America, Middle East)
Book Club(s): Readers Union Ltd
Orders to: Exel Logistics, DMS 3, Sheldon Way, Larkfield, Aylesford, Kent ME20 65E

Christopher Davies Publishers Ltd+
PO Box 403, Swansea SA1 4YF
Tel: (01792) 648825 *Fax:* (01792) 648825
E-mail: sales@cdaviesbookswales.com
Web Site: www.cdaviesbookswales.com
Key Personnel
Man Dir: Christopher Talfan Davies *E-mail:* chris@cdaviesbookswales.com
Founded: 1949
Subjects: Cookery, Health, Nutrition, History, Natural History
ISBN Prefix(es): 0-7154; 0-85339

Dawson Books+
Subsidiary of Dawson Holdings PLC
Foxhills House, Rushden, Northants NN10 6DB
Tel: (01933) 417500 *Fax:* (01933) 417501
E-mail: contactus@dawson.co.uk; bksales@dawsonbooks.co.uk
Web Site: www.dawson.co.uk
Key Personnel
Man Dir: Diane Kerr
Sales Manager: George Hammond
Customer Service Manager: Tina Atterbury
Senior Team Leader, Customer Service: Sally Barber
Team Leader, Customer Service: Jason Sinclair; Linda Finch
Distribution Manager: Margaret Beresford
Manager Standing Orders: Chris Wilson
IT Manager: Alan Benton
Content Manager: Mark Howard
Marketing Manager: Steven Welch
Founded: 1809
Specialize in international library & information (subscriptions, book, library software); news distribution.
ISBN Prefix(es): 0-946291; 0-9506540

PUBLISHERS UNITED KINGDOM

Associate Companies: Dawson Books España, Pasaje 26 y 28-Nave 4, 28230 Las Rozas (Madrid), Spain *Tel:* (091) 710-42-80 *Fax:* (091) 710-43-57 *E-mail:* libros@dawson.lci.es; Dawson France, 3, rue Galvani, 91745 Massy Cedex, France *Tel:* (01) 69 19 21 50 *Fax:* (01) 69 19 21 66 *E-mail:* librarie@dawson.fr; Quality Books Inc, 1003 W Pines Rd, Oregon, IL 61061-9680, United States *Fax:* 815-732-4499

Debrett's Ltd+
Brunel House, 55-57 N Wharf Rd, London W2 1LA
Tel: (020) 7915 9633 *Fax:* (020) 7753 4212
E-mail: people@debretts.co.uk
Web Site: www.debretts.co.uk
Key Personnel
Editorial, Peerage & Baronetage: Charles Kidd
Editorial: David Williamson
Operations Manager: Andrew Moulder
Business Development: Sharon Tidball
Founded: 1769
Subjects: Biography, Genealogy
ISBN Prefix(es): 1-870520; 0-905649
Orders to: Vinehouse Distribution Ltd, Waldenbury, North Common, Chailey, East Sussex BN27 3RP *Tel:* (01825) 723 398 *Fax:* (01825) 724 188

Decadence from Dedalus, *imprint of* Dedalus Ltd

Dedalus European Classics, *imprint of* Dedalus Ltd

Dedalus Ltd+
Langford Lodge, St Judith's Lane, Sawtry, Cambs PE28 5XE
Tel: (01487) 832382 *Fax:* (01487) 832382
E-mail: info@dedalusbooks.com
Web Site: www.dedalusbooks.com
Key Personnel
Chief Executive: Eric Lane
Chairman: Juri Gabriel
Editorial Dir: Robert Irwin
Founded: 1983
Subjects: Fiction, Literature, Literary Criticism, Essays
ISBN Prefix(es): 0-946626; 1-873982; 1-903517
Imprints: Dedalus European Classics; Decadence from Dedalus; Dedalus Nobel Prize Winner; Europe 1992-98; Empire of the Senses; Original English Language Fiction
U.S. Office(s): Subterranean Co, 265 S Fifth St, Monroe, OR 97651, United States
Distributed by Central Books
Foreign Rep(s): Richard D. Bowen (Scandinavia); Michael Geoghegan (Austria, Belgium, France, Germany, Switzerland, Holland); Marginal Distribution (Canada); Penny Padovani (Greece, Italy, Portugal, Spain); Peribo Pty Ltd (Australia, New Zealand); SCB Disributors (USA)

Dedalus Nobel Prize Winner, *imprint of* Dedalus Ltd

Defiant Publications
190 Yoxall Rd, Shirley, Solihull, West Midlands B90 3RN
Tel: (0121) 745 8421
E-mail: info@defiantpublications.co.uk
Key Personnel
Proprietor: Peter B Hands
Founded: 1980
Subjects: Humor, Transportation
ISBN Prefix(es): 0-946857

Delancey Press Ltd+
4 Delancey Passage, London NW1 7NN
Tel: (020) 7387 3544 *Fax:* (020) 8383 5314
E-mail: delanceypress@aol.com
Web Site: www.delanceypress.com
Key Personnel
Man Dir: Tatiana Wilson
Subjects: Fiction, Humor
ISBN Prefix(es): 0-9539119
Number of titles published annually: 2 Print
Total Titles: 4 Print
Distributed by The Book Guild Ltd
Orders to: Vine House Distribution

Delectation, *imprint of* Delectus Books

Delectus Books+
27 Old Gloucester St, London WC1N 3XX
Tel: (020) 8963 0979 *Fax:* (020) 8963 0502
Web Site: abebooks.com/home/delectus; www.delectusbooks.co.uk
Key Personnel
Publisher: Michael R Goss *E-mail:* mgdelectus@aol.com
Founded: 1988
Subjects: Anthropology, Criminology, Erotica, Gay & Lesbian, Psychology, Psychiatry, Dada, Decadence, Drugs & Alcohol, Ethnology, Fantasy, Folklore, Gothic & Horror, Occult & Witchcraft, Psychoanalysis, Scotland & Ireland, Sexology, Surrealism, Symbolists & the 1890's, True Crime, Vampires & Werewolves
ISBN Prefix(es): 1-897767
Number of titles published annually: 3 Print
Total Titles: 15 Print
Imprints: Delectation
Distributed by Marginal (Canada); Peribo (Australia & New Zealand); Turnaround (UK & Europe)
Orders to: Last Gasp of San Francisco, 777 Florida St, San Francisco, CA 94100, United States, Contact: Erick Gilbert *Tel:* 415-824-6636 *E-mail:* gasp@lastgasp.com

Delta Books (Pty) Ltd+
Imprint of Jonathan Ball Publishers (Pty) Ltd
Clarendon House, 52 Cornmarket St, Oxford OX1 3HJ
Mailing Address: PO Box 33977, Jeppestown 2043, South Africa
Tel: (01865) 304059 *Fax:* (01865) 304035
E-mail: mail@premierbookmarketing.com
Key Personnel
Publishing & Permissions: Francine Blum *E-mail:* fplum@jonathanball.co.za
Marketing: Eugene Ashton
Sales: Alastair Steyn
Founded: 1980
Subjects: Nonfiction (General), General South African
ISBN Prefix(es): 0-908387
Parent Company: Nasionale Boekhandel
Ultimate Parent Company: Nasionale Pers
Associate Companies: Ad Donker (Pty) Ltd
Warehouse: Jonathan Ball Publishers, 10-14 Watkins St, Denver Ext 4, Johannesburg 2094, South Africa

Denor Press+
PO Box 12913, London N12 ONP
Tel: (020) 8343 7368 *Fax:* (020) 8446 4504
E-mail: denor@dial.pipex.com
Web Site: www.xhf37.dial.pipex.com
Key Personnel
Rights Dir: Brendan Beder
Promotion & Marketing Executive: Elizabeth Plumstead
Founded: 1997
Membership(s): Publishers' Association.
Subjects: Fiction, Health, Nutrition, Medicine, Nursing, Dentistry, Music, Dance, Nonfiction (General), Promotion & marketing services
ISBN Prefix(es): 0-9526056
Total Titles: 4 Print; 4 Online; 4 E-Book
Ultimate Parent Company: Denor Press

Andre Deutsch Children's Books, *imprint of* Scholastic Ltd

Andre Deutsch Ltd+
20 Mortimer St, London W1N 7RD
Tel: (020) 7612 0400 *Fax:* (020) 7612 0401
Web Site: www.carlton.com
Founded: 1951
Subjects: Art, Biography, Government, Political Science, History, Humor, Music, Dance, Photography, Sports, Athletics, Travel
ISBN Prefix(es): 0-233; 1-85375 (Prion)
Parent Company: Carlton Books Ltd
Imprints: Prion
Warehouse: HarperCollins Publishers, PO Box, Glasgow G4 0NB *Tel:* (0141) 306 3100 *Fax:* (0141) 306 3767

Diagram Visual Information Ltd+
195 Kentish Town Rd, London NW5 2JU
Tel: (020) 7482 3633 *Fax:* (020) 7482 4932
E-mail: diagramvis@aol.com
Key Personnel
Dir & International Rights: Bruce Robertson
Founded: 1967
Book designer & creator.
Subjects: Art, Crafts, Games, Hobbies
ISBN Prefix(es): 1-900121
Number of titles published annually: 10 Print
Total Titles: 400 Print

Dial House, *imprint of* Ian Allan Publishing Ltd

Dickson Price Publishers Ltd
Unit 9 The Shipyard, Upper Brents, Faversham ME13 7DZ
Tel: (01795) 597800 *Fax:* (01795) 597800
Key Personnel
Man Dir, Editorial, Rights & Permissions: Mr K E Dickson
Production: D S Wanstall
Founded: 1980
Subjects: Computer Science, Electronics, Electrical Engineering
ISBN Prefix(es): 0-85380

Digital Photoart, *imprint of* Creative Monochrome Ltd

Digital Press, *imprint of* Elsevier Ltd

DIME, *imprint of* Tarquin Publications

Dinas, *imprint of* Y Lolfa Cyf

Discovers, *imprint of* Moonlight Publishing Ltd

Discovery Walking Guides Ltd+
10 Tennyson Close, Dallington, Northampton NN5 7HJ
Tel: (01604) 244869 *Fax:* (01604) 752576
Web Site: www.walking.demon.co.uk
Key Personnel
Company Secretary: David Brawn
Contact: Ros Brawn
Founded: 1993
Specialize in walking guides, botanical guides, tour & trail maps.
Subjects: Gardening, Plants, Travel
ISBN Prefix(es): 1-899554
Number of titles published annually: 8 Print
Total Titles: 45 Print
Imprints: Tour & Trail Maps; Warm Island Walking Guides
Distribution Center: Gardners Books, One Whittle Drive, Eastbourne BN23 6QH *Tel:* (01323) 521555 *Fax:* (01323) 525509
Membership(s): IPG

UNITED KINGDOM

Disney, *imprint of* Ladybird Books Ltd

DIY Publishing
PO Box 35488, St Johns Wood, London NW8 6WD
Tel: (020) 7586 4499 *Fax:* (020) 7722 1068
E-mail: info@diypublishing.com
Web Site: www.diypublishing.com
Service for authors to publish & sell their publications online.
Associate Companies: World Microfilms Publications Ltd

DMG Business Media Ltd
Queensway House, 2 Queensway, Redhill, Surrey RH1 1QS
Tel: (01737) 768611 *Fax:* (01737) 855477
Web Site: www.dmg.co.uk
Key Personnel
Managing Dir: Paul Camp
Subscriptions Mgr: Ben Martin *E-mail:* bmartin@dmg.co.uk
Subjects: Chemistry, Chemical Engineering, Civil Engineering, Communications, Engineering (General), Maritime, Publishing & Book Trade Reference, Radio, TV, Securities, Transportation
Parent Company: DMG World Media
Associate Companies: DMG Exhibition Group

Dobro Publishing
52 Howcroft Crescent, Finchley, London N3 1PB
Tel: (020) 8346 4010
E-mail: dobropublishing@aol.com
Web Site: www.drsandradelroy.com
Key Personnel
Contact: Dr Sandra Delroy
 E-mail: psychologist@drsandradelroy.com
Subjects: Health, Nutrition, Medicine, Nursing, Dentistry, Psychology, Psychiatry
ISBN Prefix(es): 0-9527520

The Dolmen Press Ltd, see Colin Smythe Ltd

Dolphin Paperbacks, *imprint of* Orion Children's Books

John Donald Publishers Ltd, *imprint of* Birlinn Ltd

John Donald Publishers Ltd+
Imprint of Birlinn Ltd
West Newington House, 10 Newington Rd, Edinburgh EH9 1QS
Tel: (0131) 668 4371 *Fax:* (0131) 668 4466
E-mail: info@birlinn.co.uk
Web Site: www.birlinn.co.uk
Key Personnel
Man Dir: Hugh Andrew
Founded: 1973
Subjects: History, Regional Interests, Sports, Athletics, Travel
ISBN Prefix(es): 0-85976
Number of titles published annually: 40 Print
Total Titles: 170 Print
Warehouse: Book Source, 32 Finlas St, Cowlairs Estate, Glasgow 922 SDU *Tel:* (0870) 240 2182 *Fax:* (0141) 557 0189
Orders to: Book Source, 32 Finlas St, Cowlairs Estate, Glasgow 922 SDU, Contact: Gerry McLean *Tel:* (0870) 240 2182 *Fax:* (0141) 557 0189 *E-mail:* orders@booksource.net

Donhead Publishing Ltd
Lower Coombe, Donhead St Mary, Shaftesbury, Dorset SP7 9LY
Tel: (01747) 828422 *Fax:* (01747) 828522
E-mail: sales@donhead.com
Web Site: www.donhead.com

Key Personnel
Dir: Jill Pearce
Founded: 1992
Subjects: Architecture & Interior Design, Architectural & Building Conservation, Heritage & Landscapes
ISBN Prefix(es): 1-873394
Number of titles published annually: 7 Print
Total Titles: 50 Print
Branch Office(s)
PRG Inc, PO Box 1768, Rockville, MD 20849, United States (North America only)
Membership(s): IPG

Dorling Kindersley Ltd+
80 Strand, London WC2R OLR
Tel: (020) 7010 3000 *Fax:* (020) 7010 6060
E-mail: customer.service@dk.com
Web Site: www.dk.com
Key Personnel
Chairman: Peter Kindersley
Deputy Chairman: Christopher Davis
International Sales Dir: Ruth Sandys
Group Sales & Marketing Dir: David Holmes
Man Dir, Multi-Media: Alan Buckingham
Production Dir: Martyn Longly
International Sales (Adults): Michael Devenish
Chief Exec: James Middlehurst
Founded: 1974
Subjects: Art, Child Care & Development, Cookery, Crafts, Games, Hobbies, Gardening, Plants, Health, Nutrition, History, House & Home, Music, Dance, Nonfiction (General), Photography, Self-Help, Sports, Athletics, Wine & Spirits
ISBN Prefix(es): 0-7894; 0-86318; 0-7513; 0-7547; 1-4053
Associate Companies: DK Inc (USA), United States
Subsidiaries: DKP Inc; DK Family Library
Branch Office(s)
DK Australia & New Zealand
DK Canada
DK France
DK Germany
DK Russia
DK South Africa
U.S. Office(s): DK Family Library Inc, 7566 Southland Executive Park, Orlando, FL 32809, United States
Dorling Kindersley Inc, 375 Hudson St, New York, NY 10014, United States *Tel:* 212-213-4800 *Fax:* 212-213-5240
Distributed by Penguin Books
Bookshop(s): 10-13 Knox St WC2E 8HN
Warehouse: International Book Distributors Ltd, Magna Park, Coventry Rd, Butterworth, Leics LE17 4XH

Doubleday, *imprint of* Transworld Publishers Ltd

Alton Douglas Books, *imprint of* Brewin Books Ltd

Drake Educational Associates Ltd+
Saint Fagans Road, Fairwater, Cardiff CF5 3AE
Tel: (029) 2056 0333 *Fax:* (029) 2055 4909
E-mail: info@drakeav.com
Web Site: www.drakegroup.co.uk
Key Personnel
Man Dir: Mr R G Drake
Founded: 1970
Specialize in literacy & languages.
Subjects: Disability, Special Needs, Education
ISBN Prefix(es): 0-86174
Parent Company: Drake Group
Distributor for Highsmith Press (USA); Pembroke Publishers (Canada)

Dramatic Lines Publishers+
PO Box 201, Twickenham, Middlesex TW2 5RQ

Tel: (020) 8296 9502 *Fax:* (020) 8296 9503
E-mail: mail@dramaticlines.co.uk
Web Site: www.dramaticlines.co.uk
Key Personnel
Managing Editor: John Nicholas
Founded: 1994
Drama publisher.
Membership(s): Publishers' Association.
Subjects: Drama, Theater, Education
ISBN Prefix(es): 0-9522224; 0-9537770; 1-9045571
Number of titles published annually: 6 Print

The Dreamer's Guides, *imprint of* Breese Books Ltd

Dref Wen, *imprint of* Gwasg y Dref Wen

Duck Editions, *imprint of* Gerald Duckworth & Co Ltd

Gerald Duckworth & Co Ltd+
90-93 Cowcross St, London EC1M 6BF
Tel: (020) 7490 7300 *Fax:* (020) 7490 0080
E-mail: info@duckworth-publishers.co.uk
Web Site: www.ducknet.co.uk
Key Personnel
Man Dir: Peter Mayer
Founded: 1898
Specialize in Greek & Latin classics.
Subjects: Fiction, Language Arts, Linguistics, Literature, Literary Criticism, Essays, Maritime, Nonfiction (General), Philosophy, Psychology, Psychiatry, Religion - Other, Science (General), Classics, Linguistics
ISBN Prefix(es): 0-7156; 1-85399; 0-8629
Number of titles published annually: 300 Print
Total Titles: 1,500 Print
Imprints: BCP; Duck Editions
Subsidiaries: Bristol Classical Press
Warehouse: Book Sellers International, PO Box 605, Herndon, VA 20172, United States *Tel:* 703-434-7064

Duke University Press, *imprint of* Combined Academic Publishers

Dun & Bradstreet Ltd, see D&B Ltd

Dunedin Academic Press+
Hudson House, 8 Albany St, Edinburgh EH1 3QB
Tel: (0131) 473 2397 *Fax:* (01250) 870920
E-mail: mail@dunedinacademicpress.co.uk
Web Site: www.dunedinacademicpress.co.uk
Key Personnel
Dir: Anthony Kinahan *E-mail:* anthony@dunedinacademicpress.co.uk
Founded: 2000
Membership(s): Scottish Publishers Association.
Subjects: Biography, Earth Sciences, Economics, Education, Geography, Geology, History, Law, Literature, Literary Criticism, Essays, Philosophy, Social Sciences, Sociology, Theology
ISBN Prefix(es): 1-903765
Number of titles published annually: 12 Print
Total Titles: 30 Print
Foreign Rep(s): International Specialized Book Services (Canada, USA)

Gwasg Dwyfor
Uned 8, Stad Ddlwydiannol, Penygroes, Caernarfon, Gwynedd LL55 6DB
Tel: (01286) 881911 *Fax:* (01286) 880120
E-mail: argraff@gwasgdwyfor.demon.co.uk
Key Personnel
Partner: J A Ellis; Dafydd Owen; M P Roberts
Founded: 1981
Subjects: Nonfiction (General)
ISBN Prefix(es): 1-870394

PUBLISHERS — UNITED KINGDOM

Eagle/Inter Publishing Service (IPS) Ltd+
6-7 Leapale Rd, Guildford, Surrey GU1 4JX
Tel: (01483) 306309 *Fax:* (01483) 579196
E-mail: eagle_indeprint@compuserve.com
Key Personnel
Man Dir: David Wavre
Editorial Manager: Lynne Barratt
Production Dir: James Ralton
Founded: 1990
Subjects: Religion - Catholic, Religion - Protestant, Religion - Other
ISBN Prefix(es): 0-86347
Orders to: STL, Kingstown Broadway, PO Box 300, Carlisle CA3 0QS

Eaglemoss Publications Ltd+
5 Cromwell Rd, London SW7 2HR
Tel: (020) 7590 8300 *Fax:* (020) 7590 8301
E-mail: enquiries@woodgt.co.uk
Web Site: www.eaglemoss.co.uk
Key Personnel
Chief Executive: Mark Stanley
Dir: E B Hilton
Commercial Dir: J D Sibley
Financial Dir: S P Rose
Editorial Dir: Maggie Calmels
Marketing Dir: Suzie Deeming
Trade Enquiries: Gary Neale *E-mail:* garyneale@eaglemoss.co.uk
Founded: 1979
Specialize in publication of Partworks.
Subjects: Art, Computer Science, Cookery, Crafts, Games, Hobbies, Criminology, Outdoor Recreation, Photography, Sports, Athletics, Transportation
Branch Office(s)
Australia
Malaysia
New Zealand
Singapore
South Africa

EAL, *imprint of* Training Publications Ltd

Earthlink, *imprint of* Simon & Schuster Ltd

Earthscan Publications Ltd+
120 Pentonville Rd, London N1 9JN
Tel: (020) 7278 0433 *Fax:* (020) 7278 1142
E-mail: earthinfo@earthscan.co.uk
Web Site: www.earthscan.co.uk
Key Personnel
Chief Executive: Jonathan Sinclair-Wilson
Sales Dir for Kogan Page: Julie McNair
Editorial: Frances McDermott
Production: Peter Chadwick
Publicity: Jeannette Hurdle
Marketing Issues/Bulk Orders: Helen Rose *E-mail:* hrose@earthscan.co.uk
Press/PR Enquiries: Martha Fumagalli *E-mail:* mfumagalli@kogan-page.co.uk
Press Review Copies: Helen Engstrand *E-mail:* engstrand@kogan-page.co.uk
Academic Inspection Copy Inquiries: Anna Murphy *E-mail:* amurphy@kogan-copy.co.uk
Founded: 1988
Subjects: Developing Countries, Environmental Studies
ISBN Prefix(es): 1-85383
Parent Company: Kogan Page Ltd, London
U.S. Office(s): Kogan Page, 163 Central Ave, Suite 2, Hopkins Professional Bldg, Dover, NH 03820, United States
Distributed by Island Press (USA)
Distributor for Island Press (outside North America)

East-West Publications (UK) Ltd+
2 Regent's Court King's Rd, Burnham-on-Crouch CM0 8PP
Tel: (01621) 782466 *Fax:* (01621) 782466
Key Personnel
Chairman: L W Carp
Founded: 1976
Subjects: Music, Dance, Religion - Other
ISBN Prefix(es): 0-85692; 1-872571
Associate Companies: Cromwell Book Services Ltd
Imprints: Britannia Press; Gallery Children's Books
Warehouse: East-West & Britannia, TBS, Frating Distribution Centre, Frating Green, Colchester CO7 7DW
Gallery: The Trade Counter, The Airfield, Norwich Rd, Mendlesham IP14 5NA

Eastland Press, *imprint of* Terence Dalton Ltd

Ebury, *imprint of* Random House UK Ltd

Ecco, *imprint of* HarperCollins UK

Eclipse, *imprint of* Butterworths Tolley

The Economist Books
58A Hatton Garden, London EC1N 8LX
Tel: (020) 7404 3001 *Fax:* (020) 7404 3003
E-mail: info@profilebooks.co.uk

The Economist Intelligence Unit+
15 Regent St, London SW1Y 4LR
Tel: (020) 7830 1007 *Fax:* (020) 7830 1023
E-mail: london@eiu.com
Web Site: www.eiu.com
Telex: 266353 *Cable:* EIUG
Key Personnel
Man Dir: Nigel Ludlow
Editorial Dir: Daniel Franklin
Founded: 1954
Subjects: Automotive, Business, Developing Countries, Economics, Finance, Management, Travel
ISBN Prefix(es): 0-85058; 0-86218; 0-900351
Parent Company: The Economist Group
Branch Office(s)
60/F Central Plaza, 18 Harbour Rd, Wanchai, Hong Kong *Tel:* 2802 7288; 2585 3888 *Fax:* 2802 7638; 2802 7720 *E-mail:* hongkong@eiu.com
Postbus 1254, 1300 BG Almere, Netherlands *Tel:* (036) 530 0749 *Fax:* (036) 530 1227 *E-mail:* cmf@eiu.com
No 23-01 PWC Bldg, No 8 Cross St 048424, Singapore *Tel:* 534 5177 *Fax:* 534 5077 *E-mail:* soniayao@eiu.com
U.S. Office(s): The Economist Bldg, 111 W 57th St, New York, NY 10019, United States *Tel:* 212-698-9745 *Fax:* 212-586-1181; 212-586-1182 *E-mail:* newyork@eiu.com
Foreign Rep(s): Agencia Estado Ltda (Brazil); Albertina icome Praha (Czech Republic & Slovakia); Alex Centre for Multimedia & Libraries (ACML) (Egypt); Bharat Book Bureau (India); Business Italy srl (Italy); e-Tech Solutions de Colombia Ltda (Colombia); e-Tech Solutions de Ecuador SA (Ecuador); Edutech Middle East (Gulf States, United Arab Emirates); Viktor Herman (Bulgaria, Croatia, Macedonia, Romania, Slovenia, Serbia and Montenegro, Bosnia and Herzegovina); IMA (India Pvt) Ltd (India); INFOESTRATEGICA (Mexico); InterOPTICS AEE (Greece & Cyprus); Dariusz Kuzminski (Poland, Ukraine); Latin Knowledge Consulting (Venezuela); Wanju Lee (South Korea); Quantec Research (Pty) Ltd (South Africa); Rayden Research Ltd (Japan); Rose Systems (CIS, Jordan, Iran, Syria); Sita International Information Services (India); Taiwan Asia Strategy Consulting (Taiwan); THAI-DTR Co Ltd (Thailand)

Bookshop(s): The Economist Bookshop, 25 St James St, London SW1A 1HG
Warehouse: PO Box 200, Harold Hill, Romford RM3 8UX

Eddison Sadd Editions Ltd+
St Chads House, 148 King's Cross Rd, London WC1X 9DH
Tel: (020) 7837 1968 *Fax:* (020) 7837 6844
E-mail: langel@eddisonsadd.co.uk
Key Personnel
Man Dir: Nick Eddison
Editorial Dir: Ian Jackson
Founded: 1982
Packagers of international co-editions.
Subjects: Nonfiction (General), Illustrated Books, Kits
Associate Companies: Connections Book Publishing
Imprints: Connections

Edinburgh City Libraries
Central Library, George IV Bridge, Edinburgh EH1 1EG
Tel: (0131) 242 8000
E-mail: eclis@edinburgh.gov.uk
Web Site: www.edinburgh.gov.uk/libraries

Edinburgh Project on Extensive Reading, see EPER

Edinburgh University Press Ltd+
22 George Sq, Edinburgh EH8 9LF
Tel: (0131) 650 4223
E-mail: marketing@eup.ed.ac.uk; journals@eup.ed.ac.uk (Orders)
Web Site: www.eup.ed.ac.uk
Key Personnel
Non-Executive Chair: Tim Rix *E-mail:* tim.rix@eup.ed.ac.uk
Man Dir, Sales & Marketing Dir: Timothy Wright *E-mail:* timothy.wright@eup.ed.ac.uk
Deputy Man Dir & Editorial Dir: Jackie Jones *Tel:* (0131) 6504217 *E-mail:* jackie.jones@eup.ed.ac.uk
Rights Manager: Alison Bowden *E-mail:* alison.bowden@eup.ed.ac.uk
Production Manager: Ian Davidson *E-mail:* ian.davidson@eup.ed.ac.uk
Finance Manager: Jan Thomson *E-mail:* jan.thomson@eup.ed.ac.uk
Senior Commissioning Editor: Nicola Carr *E-mail:* nicola.carr@eup.ed.ac.uk
Commissioning Editor: Sarah Edwards *E-mail:* sarah.edwards@eup.ed.ac.uk
Consultant Editor: John Davey *E-mail:* jcadavey@btinternet.com
Associate Editor: Roda Morrison *E-mail:* roda.morrison@eup.ed.ac.uk
Managing Desk Editor: Eddie Clark *E-mail:* edward.clark@eup.ed.ac.uk; James Dale *E-mail:* james.dale@eup.ed.ac.uk
Marketing Manager: Charlotte Maxwell *E-mail:* charlotte.maxwell@eup.ed.ac.uk; Douglas McNaughton *E-mail:* douglas.mcnaughton@eup.ed.ac.uk
Sales Administrator: Anna Skinner *E-mail:* anna.skinner@eup.ed.ac.uk
Founded: 1948
Subjects: Anthropology, Archaeology, Architecture & Interior Design, Art, Computer Science, Economics, Education, Environmental Studies, Film, Video, Government, Political Science, History, Literature, Literary Criticism, Essays, Music, Dance, Natural History, Philosophy, Public Administration, Religion - Islamic, Science (General), Social Sciences, Sociology, Theology, Women's Studies
ISBN Prefix(es): 0-85224; 0-7486
Parent Company: The University of Edinburgh
Distributed by Columbia University Press (USA & Canada)

Warehouse: Marston Book Services, PO Box 269, Abingdon, Oxon OX14 4YN *Tel:* (01235) 465500

Orders to: Marston Book Services, PO Box 269, Abingdon, Oxon OX14 4YN *Tel:* (01235) 465500 *Fax:* (01235) 465556

Edition XII
23 Arundel Gardens, London W11 2LW
Mailing Address: 10 Regents Wharf, 4th floor, All Saints St, London N1 9RL
Tel: (020) 7229 6471; (020) 7833 0120 *Fax:* (020) 7229 5239; (020) 7923 5500; (020) 7923 5505
E-mail: info@editionxii.co.uk
Web Site: www.editionxii.co.uk
Key Personnel
Man Dir: Edward More O'Ferrall
Marketing Manager: Simon Klemba
Specialize in academic publications.
Subjects: Business, Computer Science, Economics, Education, Engineering (General), Law, Social Sciences, Sociology
ISBN Prefix(es): 1-86149; 0-9520105; 1-899522
Parent Company: Lime House Media Group Ltd, The Lime House, Unit 2, Chase Side Works, Chelmsford Rd, Southgate, London N16 4JN
Orders to: Mike Sirott, 3691 S 3200 W, West Valley, UT 84119, United States
Baker & Taylor Books, 44 Kirby Ave, Somerville, NJ 08876, United States

Educational Explorers (Publishers) Ltd
11 Crown St, Reading, Berks RG1 2TQ
Mailing Address: PO Box 3391, Winnersh, Wokingham RG41 5ZD
Tel: (0118) 987 3101 *Fax:* (0118) 987 3103
E-mail: explorers@cuisenaire.co.uk
Web Site: www.cuisenaire.co.uk
Key Personnel
Chairman: D M Gattegno
Man Dir: M J Hollyfield *E-mail:* hollyfield@cuisenaire.co.uk
Founded: 1960
Subjects: Language Arts, Linguistics, Mathematics, Psychology, Psychiatry
ISBN Prefix(es): 0-85225
Parent Company: Educational Solutions (UK) Ltd of Reading
Associate Companies: Cuisenaire Co, 11 Crown St, Reading, Berks RG1 2TQ; Educational Explorers Film Co, 11 Crown St, Reading, Berks RG1 2TQ; Educational Solutions Inc, 99 University Pl, New York, NY 10003-4555, United States

EITB, *imprint of* Training Publications Ltd

Eland Publishing Ltd
61 Exmouth Market, 3rd floor, London EC1R 4QL
Tel: (020) 7833 0762 *Fax:* (020) 7833 4434
E-mail: info@travelbooks.co.uk
Web Site: www.travelbooks.co.uk
Key Personnel
Dir: Rose Baring
Subjects: Biography, Fiction, Travel
ISBN Prefix(es): 0-907871
Imprints: Sickle Moon Books
Warehouse: Grantham Book Services, Isaac Newton Way, Alma Park Industrial Estate, Grantham, Lincs NG31 9SD
Orders to: Grantham Book Services, Isaac Newton Way, Alma Park Industrial Estate, Grantham, Lincs NG31 9SD

ELC International
5 Five Mile Drive, Oxford OX2 8HT
Tel: (01865) 513186; (01865) 26520284 *Fax:* (01865) 513186; (01865) 26530180
E-mail: snyderpub@aol.com

Electronic Publishing Services Ltd (EPS)
26 Rosebery Ave, London EC1R 4SX
Tel: (020) 7837 3345 *Fax:* (020) 7837 8901
E-mail: eps@epsltd.com
Web Site: www.epsltd.com
Key Personnel
Chairman: David R Worlock
Dir: David J Powell
Founded: 1985
Research & consultancy company which specializes in electronic publishing strategy development & high-level market research.
Membership(s): The UK Publishers Association.
Subjects: Library & Information Sciences, Publishing & Book Trade Reference
ISBN Prefix(es): 0-9517344
Total Titles: 10 Print

Element Books Ltd+
Old School House, The Courtyard, Bell St, Shaftesbury, Dorset SP7 8BP
Tel: (01747) 851448 *Fax:* (01747) 855721
Key Personnel
Chairman: Michael Mann
Chief Executive: David Alexander
Man Dir: Julia McCutchen
Sales: Penny Stopa
Publicity: Jenny Carradice
Production Dir: Roger Lane *E-mail:* roger_lane@iconex.mactel.org
Founded: 1978
Subjects: Art, Astrology, Occult, Biography, Environmental Studies, Health, Nutrition, Literature, Literary Criticism, Essays, Management, Music, Dance, Philosophy, Psychology, Psychiatry, Religion - Other, Science (General), Self-Help, Travel, Women's Studies, Feminist Studies, Zen
ISBN Prefix(es): 1-85230; 1-86204; 0-906540
U.S. Office(s): Element Books Inc, 21 Broadway, Rockport, MA 01966, United States *Tel:* 508-546-1040
Distributed by India Book Distributors (Bombay) Ltd; India Book House Pvt Ltd; TBI Publishers' Distributors
Orders to: Penguin Books Ltd, Bath Rd, Harmondsworth, West Drayton, Middlesex UB7 0DA *Tel:* (0181) 8994000 *Fax:* (0181) 8994099

11:9, *imprint of* Neil Wilson Publishing Ltd

Elfande Ltd+
Surrey House, 31 Church St, Leatherhead, Surrey KT22 7HX
Tel: (01372) 220330 *Fax:* (01372) 220340
E-mail: sales@contact-uk.com
Web Site: www.contact-uk.com
Key Personnel
Man Dir: Nick Gould
Administration: Sarah Williams
Founded: 1985
Publish annual image source books in Europe.
Subjects: Architecture & Interior Design, Art, Photography
ISBN Prefix(es): 1-870458
Number of titles published annually: 6 Print; 3 CD-ROM
Total Titles: 6 Print; 3 CD-ROM; 3 E-Book
U.S. Office(s): Tonal Values, 133 N Montclair Ave, Dallas, TX, United States, Contact: Jill Peterson *Tel:* 214-943-2569 *Fax:* 214-942-6771 *E-mail:* info@tonalvalues.com

Edward Elgar Publishing Ltd
Glensanda House, Montpellier Parade, Cheltenham, Glos GL50 1UA
Tel: (01242) 226934 *Fax:* (01242) 262111
E-mail: info@e-elgar.co.uk
Web Site: www.e-elgar.co.uk
Key Personnel
Man Dir: Edward Elgar *E-mail:* edward@e-elgar.co.uk
Sales & Marketing Manager: Hilary Quinn
Contact: Sandy Elgar *E-mail:* sandy@e-elgar.co.uk
Founded: 1986
A privately owned scholarly publisher with a focus on economics.
Subjects: Business, Developing Countries, Economics, Environmental Studies, Finance, Government, Political Science, Labor, Industrial Relations
ISBN Prefix(es): 1-85898; 1-85278; 1-84064
Number of titles published annually: 250 Print
Total Titles: 1,360 Print
U.S. Office(s): Edward Elgar Publishing Inc, 136 West St, Suite 202, Northhampton, MA 01060, United States, Contact: Rick Henning *Tel:* 413-584-5551 *Fax:* 413-584-9933 *E-mail:* rhenning@e-elgar.com
Orders to: DA Book Information Services, 648 Whitehorse Rd, Mitcham, Victoria 3132, Australia *Tel:* (03) 9210 7777 *Fax:* (03) 9210 7788 *E-mail:* Service@dadirect.com.au
Edward Elgar Publishing Inc, 2 Winter Sport Lane, PO Box 574, Williston, VT 05495-0575, United States *Fax:* 802-864-7626 *E-mail:* rhenning@e-elgar.com
Marston Book Services, PO Box 269, Abingdon, Oxon OX14 4YN *Tel:* (01235) 465500 *Fax:* (01235) 465555 *E-mail:* trade@marston.co.uk
Taylor & Francis Asia Pacific, Pines Industrial Bldg, 240 Macpherson Rd 348574, Singapore, Man Dir: Barry Clarke *Tel:* 741 5166 *Fax:* 742 9356 *E-mail:* info@tandf.com.sg
United Publishers Services Limited, Kenkyu-Sha Bldg, 9 Kanda Surugadai 2-Chome, Chiyoda-Ku, Tokyo, Japan *Tel:* (03) 3291 4541 *Fax:* (03) 3292 8610

Elkin, *imprint of* Novello & Co Ltd

Elliot Right Way Books+
Kingswood Bldgs, Brighton Rd, Lower Kingswood, Tadworth, Surrey KT20 6TD
Tel: (01737) 832202 *Fax:* (01737) 830311
E-mail: info@right-way.co.uk
Web Site: www.right-way.co.uk
Key Personnel
Dir: A Clive Elliot; Malcolm G Elliot
Editor: Judith Mitchell
Founded: 1945 (by Andrew George Elliot, father of the present owners)
Independent Book Publisher.
Subjects: Animals, Pets, Business, Career Development, Cookery, Crafts, Games, Hobbies, Finance, Genealogy, Health, Nutrition, House & Home, How-to, Humor, Self-Help, Sports, Athletics, Transportation, Drawing, Driving, Family Reference, Fishing, Hobbies, Horses, Pets, Public & Social Speaking, Quizzes
ISBN Prefix(es): 0-7160; 1-899606
Number of titles published annually: 20 Print
Total Titles: 120 Print
Ultimate Parent Company: Andrew Elliot & Sons Ltd
Imprints: Clarion (Bargain Books); Right Way Books
Foreign Rep(s): Hushion House Publishing Ltd (Canada); Peribo (Australia); Theo Phillips (CKK Ltd) (Asia); Kelvin Van Hasselt (Africa, Caribbean); Peter Ward (Middle East)

Aidan Ellis Publishing+
Whinfield, Herbert Rd, Salcombe, South Devon TQ8 8HN
Tel: (01548) 842755
E-mail: mail@aidanellispublishing.co.uk
Web Site: www.demon.co.uk/aepub
Key Personnel
Partner: Aidan Ellis; Lucinda Ellis
Founded: 1971

Subjects: Art, Biography, Gardening, Plants, Literature, Literary Criticism, Essays, Maritime, Natural History, Nonfiction (General)
ISBN Prefix(es): 0-85628
Total Titles: 50 Print
Foreign Rep(s): Keith Ainsworth Pty Ltd (Australia & New Zealand)
Orders to: Orca Book Services, 3 Fleets Lane, Poole, Dorset BH15 3AJ Tel: (01202) 665 432 Fax: (01202) 666 219 E-mail: orders@orcabookservices.co.uk

Elm Publications+
Seaton House, Kings Ripton, Huntingdon, Cambs PE28 2NJ
Tel: (01487) 773254; (01487) 773238
E-mail: elm@elm-training.co.uk
Web Site: www.elm-training.co.uk
Key Personnel
Man Dir & Rights & Permissions: Sheila Ritchie E-mail: sritchie@elm-training.co.uk
Production: Lesley Taylor
Founded: 1977
Subjects: Business, History, Law, Library & Information Sciences, Management, Travel, Tourism
ISBN Prefix(es): 0-946139; 1-85450; 0-9505828
Number of titles published annually: 20 Print; 10 Online
Total Titles: 100 Print; 20 Online; 4 E-Book
Parent Company: Elm Consulting Ltd
Associate Companies: Elm Training

Elm Tree Books Ltd, see Hamish Hamilton Ltd

Elsevier, imprint of Elsevier Ltd

Elsevier Advanced Technology, imprint of Elsevier Ltd

Elsevier Advanced Technology+
The Boulevard, Langford Lane, Kidlington, Oxford OX5 1GB
Mailing Address: PO Box 150, Kidlington, Oxford OX5 1AS
Tel: (01865) 843848 Fax: (01865) 843010
E-mail: eatsales@elsevier.co.uk (sales)
Web Site: www.nepcon.co.uk/ex0210g.htm
Key Personnel
International Sales: Sophie Hayward
Contact: Philippa Sumner Tel: (01865) 843828 Fax: (01865) 843971 E-mail: p.sumner@elsevier.co.uk
Subjects: Business
Parent Company: Elsevier Science Ltd
Ultimate Parent Company: Reed Elsevier plc
Imprints: Trade and Technical Press
U.S. Office(s): Elsevier Science Inc, 655 Avenue of the Americas, New York, NY 10010-5107, United States Tel: 212-989-5800 Fax: 212-633-3990

Elsevier/Geo Abstracts, imprint of Elsevier Ltd

Elsevier Ltd+
Formerly Elsevier Science Ltd
The Boulevard, Langford Lane, Kidlington, Oxford OX5 1GB
Tel: (01865) 843000 Fax: (01865) 843010
E-mail: initial.surname@elsevier.com
Web Site: www.elsevier.com
Key Personnel
Chief Operating Officer: Gavin Howe
Publishing Support & Properties Dir: Anna Moon
CEO, Science & Technology (Books & Journals): Arie Jongejan
Man Dir: Philip Shaw
CEO Health Sciences (Books & Journals): Brian Nairn
Man Dir (Health Sciences UK/Netherlands): Dominic Vaughan
Founded: 1971
Subjects: Agriculture, Architecture & Interior Design, Behavioral Sciences, Biological Sciences, Business, Chemistry, Chemical Engineering, Communications, Computer Science, Earth Sciences, Economics, Education, Electronics, Electrical Engineering, Energy, Environmental Studies, Health, Nutrition, Library & Information Sciences, Mechanical Engineering, Medicine, Nursing, Dentistry, Technology
ISBN Prefix(es): 0-08; 0-7216; 0-7020; 0-85334; 1-85166; 0-7234; 0-4430; 0-323
Parent Company: Reed Elsevier, Netherlands
Imprints: Academic Press; Architectural Press; Bailliere Tindall Ltd; Butterworth Heinemann Ltd; Churchill Livingstone; Digital Press; Elsevier; Elsevier Advanced Technology; Focal Press; Elsevier/Geo Abstracts; Gulf Professional Press; Harcourt Publishers Ltd; JAI; Made Simple Books; Morgan Kauffman; Mosby; Newnes; North Holland; T & AD Poyser Ltd; Saunders
Branch Office(s)
Elsevier Ltd (Health Sciences), 32 Jamestown Rd, 111 Queen's Rd, London NW1 7BY
Elsevier Ltd (Health Sciences), Robert Stevenson House, 1-3 Baxters Place, Keith Walk, Edinburgh EH1 3AF
Elsevier Ltd (Science & Technology), 84 Theobald's Road, London WC1X 8RR
Elsevier Ltd (Science & Technology), Linacre House, Jordan Hill, Oxford OX2 8DP
Elsevier/Geo Abstracts, The Old Bakery, 111 Queen's Rd, Norwich NR1 3PL

Elsevier Science Ltd, see Elsevier Ltd

Emerald
60/62 Toller Lane, Bradford, West Yorks BD8 9BY
Tel: (01274) 777700 Fax: (01274) 785201
E-mail: info@emeraldinsight.com; information@emeraldinsight.com (academic sales); editorial@emeraldinsight.com (editorial)
Web Site: www.emeraldinsight.com
Key Personnel
Chairman: Dr Barrie Pettman
Man Dir: Dr Keith Howard
Head of Corporate Communications: Gillian Crawford E-mail: gcrawford@emeraldinsight.com
Productions, Rights & Permissions: Tracy Cogan
Publicity: Michelle Kelly
Customer Operations Manager: Suzanne Halliday E-mail: shalliday@emeraldinsight.com
Founded: 1969
Subjects: Business, Human Relations, Library & Information Sciences, Management, Marketing
ISBN Prefix(es): 0-86176; 0-905440; 0-903763

Empire of the Senses, imprint of Dedalus Ltd

Empiricus Books, imprint of Janus Publishing Co Ltd

Encyclopaedia Britannica (UK) International Ltd
Unity Wharf, 2nd floor, London SE1 2BH
Tel: (020) 7500 7800; (0845) 075 700 (orders CD or DVD inside UK); (0177) 901 3948 (orders CD or DVD outside UK); (0845) 075 8000 (order books inside UK); (0845) 901 3948 (order books outside UK) Fax: (020) 7500 7878
E-mail: enquiries@britannica.co.uk
Web Site: www.britannica.co.uk
Telex: 422084
Key Personnel
Man Dir: James Strachan
Marketing Manager: Marcus Missen
ISBN Prefix(es): 0-85229
Parent Company: Encyclopaedia Britannica Inc, Britannica Centre, 310 S Michigan Ave, Chicago, IL 60604, United States
Associate Companies: Encyclopaedia Britannica (Australia) Inc, Level 1, 90 Mount St, North Sydney NSW 2060, Australia Tel: (02) 9923 5600 Fax: (02) 9929 3758 E-mail: feedbackaccount@brittanica.com.au; Encyclopaedia Britannica (France) Ltd; Encyclopaedia Britannica (India) Pvt. Ltd., Britannica Centre, 55-56 Ydyog Vihar Phase 4, Gurgaon 122016, India Tel: (0124) 639 9933 Fax: (0124) 639 9942 E-mail: corporate@brittanicain.com Web Site: www.brittanicaindia.com; Encyclopaedia Britannica (Italy) Ltd; Encyclopaedia Britannica (Japan) Inc; Korea Britannica Corp; Encyclopaedia Britannica (Philippines) Inc; Encyclopaedia Britannica SA; Encyclopaedia Britannica de Espana, SA

The Energy Information Centre+
Rosemary House, Lanwades Business Park, Newmarket CB8 7PW
Tel: (01638) 751 400 Fax: (01638) 751 801
E-mail: info@eic.co.uk
Web Site: www.eic.co.uk
Key Personnel
Editorial Dir: Robert Buckley
Commercial Dir: Michael Southin
Founded: 1975
Subjects: Energy
ISBN Prefix(es): 0-905332
Parent Company: Cambridge Information & Research Services

English Teaching Professional
32-34 Great Peter St, London SW1P 2DB
Tel: (020) 7222 1155 Fax: (020) 7222 1551
E-mail: info@etprofessional.com
Web Site: www.etprofessional.com
Key Personnel
Editorial Dir: Peter Collin E-mail: peter@etprofessional.com
Editor: Helena Gomm E-mail: helenagomm@etprofessional.com
Subjects: English as a Second Language
Parent Company: First Person Publishing Limited
Distribution Center: Marston Lindsay Ross Distribution, Omega Centre Collett Didcot, Oxon OX11 7AW Tel: (01235) 515700 Fax: (01235) 515777

Enigma Books, imprint of Severn House Publishers Inc

Entra, imprint of Training Publications Ltd

Eos, imprint of HarperCollins UK

EPER
21 Hill Pl, Edinburgh EH8 9DP
Tel: (0131) 650 6200 Fax: (0131) 667 5927
E-mail: ials.enquiries@ed.ac.uk
Web Site: www.ials.ed.ac.uk
Key Personnel
Project Dir: David R Hill
Founded: 1984
Subjects: English as a Second Language, Language Arts, Linguistics
ISBN Prefix(es): 1-871914; 1-871019; 1-871035; 1-871027

Epworth Press+
Division of Methodist Publishing House
Methodist Publishing House, 4 John Wesley Rd, Werrington, Peterborough PE4 6ZP
Tel: (01733) 325002 Fax: (01733) 384180
E-mail: comm.editor@mph.org.uk
Web Site: www.mph.org.uk
Key Personnel
Chair of MPH Board: Dudley Coates

UNITED KINGDOM

Chief Executive: Martin Stowe
Commissioning Editor: Dr Natalie Watson
Founded: 1750
Subjects: Biblical Studies, Religion - Protestant, Religion - Other, Theology, Worship
ISBN Prefix(es): 0-7162
Number of titles published annually: 12 Print
Total Titles: 200 Print
Associate Companies: SCM-Canterbury Press
Sales Office(s): SCM Press Ltd
Distributed by SCM-Canterbury Press
Foreign Rights: SCM Press
Bookshop(s): Methodist Bookshop, 25 Marylebone Rd, London
Distribution Center: Hymns Ancient & Modern, Norwich
Methodist Publishing House, Peterborough

ERA Technology Ltd+
Cleeve Rd, Leatherhead, Surrey KT22 7SA
Tel: (01372) 367000 Fax: (01372) 367099
E-mail: info@era.co.uk
Web Site: www.era.co.uk
Key Personnel
Divisional Manager: R W H Stafford
Founded: 1920
Specialize in Contract R & D.
Subjects: Aeronautics, Aviation, Automotive, Communications, Computer Science, Electronics, Electrical Engineering, Environmental Studies, Technology, Air Pollution Control, Energy Efficiency, Power Generation
ISBN Prefix(es): 0-7008
Subsidiaries: ERA Technology (Asia) Pte Ltd; ERA Technology Inc

Ernest Press
17 Carleton Drive, Glasgow G46 6AQ
Tel: (0141) 637 5492 Fax: (0141) 637 5492
E-mail: sales@ernest-press.co.uk
Web Site: www.ernest-press.co.uk
Key Personnel
Proprietor: Peter Hodghiss
Subjects: Mountaineering, Mounting Biking Guides
ISBN Prefix(es): 0-948153
Warehouse: Cordee, 3A De Montfort St, Leicester LE1 7HD

Ernst & Young+
Becket House, One Lambeth Palace Rd, London SE1 7EU
Tel: (020) 7951 2000 Fax: (020) 7951 1345
Web Site: www.ey.com
Also chartered accountants & business advisers.
Subjects: Accounting, Foreign Countries, Management
ISBN Prefix(es): 0-9505745; 1-873278

The Erskine Press+
The Old Bakery, Banham, Norwich, Norfolk NR16 2HW
Tel: (01953) 88 72 77 Fax: (01953) 88 83 61
E-mail: erskpres@aol.com
Web Site: www.erskine-press.com
Key Personnel
Man Dir: Crispin de Boos
Consultant: Stephen Easton
Founded: 1986
Specialize in literature on Antarctic Exploration.
Membership(s): Independent Publishers Guild.
Subjects: Architecture & Interior Design, Art, Astronomy, Cookery, History, Travel
ISBN Prefix(es): 1-85297; 0-948285
Total Titles: 58 Print
Parent Company: Archival Facsimiles Ltd

estamp+
204 St Albans Ave, London W4 5JU
Tel: (020) 8994 2379 Fax: (020) 8994 2379
E-mail: st@estamp.demon.co.uk

Key Personnel
Director: Sylvie Turner
Founded: 1990
Specialize in art publishing, mail order, contemporary print making & paper.
ISBN Prefix(es): 1-871831
Total Titles: 17 Print
Shipping Address: Central Book, 199 Wallis Rd, London E9 SLN, Contact: Kirsty Tel: (020) 8986 7859 Fax: (020) 8533 5821
Membership(s): IPG

Estates Gazette
147-151 Wardour St, London W1V 4BN
Tel: (020) 8652 3500; (020) 7411 2540 (edit); (020) 7411 2626 (advertising); (01444) 445335 (subscriptions) Fax: (020) 7437 2432; (020) 7437 0294 (edit); (020) 7437 2432 (advertising); (01444) 445567 (subscriptions)
Key Personnel
Publisher & Man Dir: James Blazeby
Editorial Dir: Peter Bill E-mail: peter.bill@rbi.co.uk
Commissioning Editor: Alison Richards
Founded: 1858
Leading providers of property information.
ISBN Prefix(es): 0-7282; 0-900361
Parent Company: Reed Business Information Ltd
Orders to: Oakfield House, Perrymount Rd, Haywards Heath, West Sussex RH16 3DM

Ethics International Press Ltd+
St Andrews Castle, St Andrews St S, Bury St Edmunds, Suffolk IP33 3PH
Tel: (01223) 357458 Fax: (01223) 303598
E-mail: info@ethicspress.com
Web Site: www.ethicspress.com
Founded: 1993
Academic, business & government.
Subjects: Business, Environmental Studies, Film, Video, Government, Political Science, Law, Management, Philosophy, Public Administration, Social Sciences, Sociology
ISBN Prefix(es): 1-871891
Number of titles published annually: 3 Print; 6 CD-ROM; 6 E-Book
Total Titles: 10 Print; 6 CD-ROM; 6 E-Book

Eurobook Ltd+
PO Box 52, Wallingford, Oxon OX10 0XU
Tel: (01865) 858333 Fax: (01865) 858263; (01865) 340087
E-mail: eurobook@compuserve.com
Key Personnel
Man Dir, Rights & Permissions: Peter S Lowe
Editor: Ruth Spriggs
Sales, Publicity & Advertising: R McFarlane
International Rights: P S Lowe
Founded: 1968
Subjects: Animals, Pets, Gardening, Plants, Natural History, Nonfiction (General), Science (General)
ISBN Prefix(es): 0-85654
Imprints: Peter Lowe

Euromonitor PLC+
60-61 Britton St, London EC1M 5UX
Tel: (020) 7251 8024 Fax: (020) 7608 3149
E-mail: info@euromonitor.com
Web Site: www.euromonitor.com
Telex: 262433 Monref G
Key Personnel
Man Dir: Trevor Fenwick
Marketing Dir: David Gudgin
Chairman: Robert Senior
Founded: 1972
Membership(s): UK & European Directory Publishers Associations.
Subjects: Business, Economics, Marketing, Publishing & Book Trade Reference, Demographics, Macro-Economic Data, Market Research Reports

BOOK

ISBN Prefix(es): 0-903706; 0-86338; 1-84264
Number of titles published annually: 25 Print; 6 CD-ROM
Total Titles: 6 CD-ROM
Branch Office(s)
Euromonitor International (Asia) Pte Ltd, Singapore Technologies Bldg, 3 Lim Teck Kim Rd, No 08-02, Singapore 088934, Singapore Tel: 6429 0590 Fax: 6324 1855 E-mail: info@euromonitor.com.sg
Euromonitor International Brazil, Brazil Tel: (011) 3771 3490 Fax: (011) 5081 5290 E-mail: robert.listik@euromonitorintl.com Web Site: www.euromonitor.com
U.S. Office(s): Euromonitor International Inc, 122 S Michigan Ave, Suite 810, Chicago, IL 60603, United States Tel: 312-922-1115 Fax: 312-922-1157 E-mail: insight@euromonitorintl.com Web Site: www.euromonitor.com
Distributed by Gale Research

Europa, imprint of Taylor & Francis

Europa Publications
Member of Taylor & Francis Group
11 New Fetter Lane, London EC4P 4EE
Tel: (020) 7842 2110; (020) 7842 2133 (marketing & sales) Fax: (020) 7842 2249 (marketing & sales)
E-mail: info.europa@tandf.co.uk
Web Site: www.europapublications.com
Key Personnel
Editorial Dir: Paul Kelly Fax: (020) 7842 2391 E-mail: edit.europa@tandf.co.uk
Marketing Manager: Mary Sweny
Accounts Manager: Frances Bunting
Founded: 1926
Membership(s): Directory Publishers Association.
Subjects: Developing Countries, Economics, Education, Foreign Countries, Government, Political Science, Publishing & Book Trade Reference, International affairs
ISBN Prefix(es): 0-946653; 1-85743; 0-900362; 0-905118
Number of titles published annually: 30 Print

Europe 1992-98, imprint of Dedalus Ltd

European Schoolbooks Ltd
The Runnings, Cheltenham GL51 9PQ
Tel: (01242) 245252 Fax: (01242) 224137
E-mail: direct@esb.co.uk
Web Site: www.eurobooks.co.uk
Key Personnel
Man Dir: Frank A Preiss E-mail: fap@esb.co.uk
Founded: 1964
Also act as distributor for European publishers.
Subjects: Economics, Environmental Studies, Foreign Countries, Geography, Geology, Language Arts, Linguistics, Social Sciences, Sociology
ISBN Prefix(es): 0-85048
Subsidiaries: European Schoolbooks Publishing
Bookshop(s): The European Bookshop, 5 Warwick St, London W1R 5RA Tel: (020) 7734 5259 Fax: (020) 7287 1720; The Italian Bookshop, 7 Cecil Court, London WC2N 4EZ Tel: (020) 7240 1634 Fax: (020) 7240 1635 E-mail: italbookshop@freenet.co.uk

The Eurospan Group
3 Henrietta St, Covent Garden, London WC2E 8LU
Tel: (020) 7240 0856 Fax: (020) 7379 0609
E-mail: info@eurospan.co.uk
Web Site: www.eurospan.co.uk
Key Personnel
Group Man Dir: Michael Geelan
Chairman: Danny Maher
Operations Manager: Kate Symonds
Business Manager: Patrick Tay
Marketing: Imogen Adams; Sally Greene; Tina Moran; Clare Sutton
Founded: 1963

PUBLISHERS   UNITED KINGDOM

Subjects: Agriculture, Anthropology, Archaeology, Art, Asian Studies, Behavioral Sciences, Biblical Studies, Biography, Biological Sciences, Business, Chemistry, Chemical Engineering, Child Care & Development, Communications, Computer Science, Developing Countries, Disability, Special Needs, Drama, Theater, Earth Sciences, Economics, Education, Energy, Engineering (General), Environmental Studies, Ethnicity, Film, Video, Finance, Foreign Countries, Gay & Lesbian, Genealogy, Geography, Geology, Government, Political Science, Health, Nutrition, History, Human Relations, Journalism, Labor, Industrial Relations, Language Arts, Linguistics, Law, Library & Information Sciences, Literature, Literary Criticism, Essays, Management, Maritime, Marketing, Mathematics, Medicine, Nursing, Dentistry, Microcomputers, Military Science, Music, Dance, Natural History, Nonfiction (General), Philosophy, Physics, Poetry, Psychology, Psychiatry, Public Administration, Radio, TV, Regional Interests, Religion - Buddhist, Religion - Catholic, Religion - Hindu, Religion - Islamic, Religion - Jewish, Religion - Protestant, Religion - Other, Science (General), Science Fiction, Fantasy, Social Sciences, Sociology, Technology, Theology, Veterinary Science, Women's Studies

Distributor for AMS Press; Aldwych Press; American Academy of Orthopaedic Surgeons; American Enterprise Institute; American Institute for Aeronautics & Astronautics; American Library Association; American Psychiatric Press; American Psychological Association; Amsterdam University Press (The Netherlands); Auburn House; Austin & Winfield; Bergin & Garvey; Boyton/Cook; CSIRO Publishing (Australia); Catholic University of America Press; Da Capo Press; Lawrence Erlbaum Associates Inc; Fordham University Press; Greenwood Press; Hampton Press; Heinemann USA; Human Sciences Press; Idea Group Publishing; International Scholars Publications; Iowa State University Press; Jason Aronson Publishers; Kent State University Press; Krieger Publishing Co; Libraries Unlimited; Louisiana State University Press; Lynne Rienner Publishers; ME Sharpe Publishing; Narosa Publishing House (India); Neal-Schuman Publishers; Rutgers University Press; The New York Academy of Sciences; The University of North Carolina Press; Ohio State University Press; Open Court Publishing Co; PMA Publishing; Penn State Press; Popular Culture Ink; Praeger Publishers; Quorum Books; Scholarly Resources; The Oryx Press; SIR Publishing (New Zealand); Slack Inc; Southern Illinois University Press; Syracuse University Press; Teacher Ideas Press; Teachers College Press; Temple University Press; Thomas International Publishing Co; University of Alabama Press; University of Georgia Press; University of Massachusetts Press; University of Missouri Press; University of Nevada Press; University of Notre Dame Press; University of Pittsburgh Press; University Press of Florida; University Press of Kansas; University Press of Virginia; University of South Carolina Press; University of Wisconsin Press; Wayne State University Press; Who's Who in Italy (Italy); Facts on File (UK, Ireland & Europe)

Orders to: EDS, 3 Henrietta St, London WC2E 8LU

Evangelical Library of Wales, imprint of Bryntirion Press

Evangelical Press & Services Ltd+
Grange Close, Faverdale North, Darlington DL3 0PH
Tel: (01325) 380232 Fax: (01325) 466153
E-mail: sales@evangelicalpress.org
Web Site: www.evangelicalpress.org
Key Personnel
General Manager & International Rights: Anthony L Gosling E-mail: anthony.gosling@evangelicalpress.org
Founded: 1967
International publisher of christian, evangelical & reformed literature.
Subjects: Biblical Studies, Religion - Protestant, Theology
ISBN Prefix(es): 0-85234; 0-946462; 0-85479
Number of titles published annually: 25 Print
Total Titles: 300 Print
Subsidiaries: Europresse SARL (French Publisher)
U.S. Office(s): PO Box 825, Webster, NY 14580, United States E-mail: usa.sales@evangelicalpress.org
Distributor for Bryntirion Press; Carey Publications; Grace Publications Trust

Evans Brothers Ltd+
2A Portman Mansions, Chiltern St, London W1U 6NR
Tel: (020) 7487 0920 Fax: (020) 7487 0921
E-mail: sales@evansbrothers.co.uk
Web Site: www.evansbooks.co.uk
Telex: 8811713 Evbook G
Key Personnel
Dir: B D Jones; A Ojora
Man Dir: Stephen T Pawley E-mail: stephenp@evansbrothers.co.uk
Rights Manager: Britta Martins
Production Manager: Jenny Mulvanny
UK Publisher: Su Swallow
Founded: 1908
Subjects: Art, English as a Second Language, Geography, Geology, History, Library & Information Sciences, Mathematics, Music, Dance, Religion - Other, Science (General), Citizenship, Design & Technical, ICT, PSHE, R/E Multifaith, Social Issues
ISBN Prefix(es): 0-237; 1-84089; 1-84234
Number of titles published annually: 120 Print
Total Titles: 730 Print
Ultimate Parent Company: Imperial Securities
Associate Companies: Evans Brothers (Nigeria Publishers) Ltd, Nigeria
Imprints: Cherrytree; Cloverleaf
Subsidiaries: Evans Brothers (Kenya) Ltd; Zero to Ten Limited
Foreign Rep(s): The British Bookshop (Austria); The Educational Book Service (Botswana, Zambia); Evans Brothers Ltd (Brazil); Pansing Distribution Sdn Bhd (Brunei, Indonesia, Malaysia & Singapore); Reed Educational & Professional Publishing (Australia); Saunders Books Company (Canada); South Pacific Books (Imports) Ltd (New Zealand); TPL Corporation (HK) Ltd (Hong Kong); Trafalgar Square Publishing (USA)
Orders to: Thomson Publishing Services, Cheriton House, North Way, Andover, Hants SP10 5BE Tel: (01264) 343072 Fax: (01264) 342788 E-mail: carol.appleton@thomsonpublishingservices.co.uk Web Site: www.thomsonpublishingservices.co.uk

Ex Libris, imprint of Ex Libris Press

Ex Libris Press+
One The Shambles, Bradford on Avon, Wilts BA15 1JS
Tel: (01225) 863595 Fax: (01225) 863595
E-mail: roger.jonesW@ex-librisbooks.co.uk (orders)
Web Site: www.ex-librisbooks.co.uk
Key Personnel
Proprietor: Roger Jones E-mail: rogjones@hotmail.com
Founded: 1981
Local & regional press covering west country & Channel Islands, also list of book on country life & lore.
Subjects: Biography, Geography, Geology, History, Literature, Literary Criticism, Essays, Walking guides & countryside paperback & occasional hardback
ISBN Prefix(es): 0-9506563; 0-948578; 1-903341
Number of titles published annually: 8 Print
Total Titles: 70 Print
Imprints: Ex Libris; Seaflower Books
Distributed by Halsgrove (UK)
Membership(s): IPG

Helen Exley Giftbooks+
16 Chalk Hill, Watford, Herts WD19 4BG
Tel: (01923) 250505 Fax: (01923) 818733
Toll Free Fax: 800-440
E-mail: enquiry@exleypublications.co.uk
Key Personnel
Chairman: Richard Exley
Man Dir & Editorial Dir: Helen Exley
Rights Dir: Sonya Dougan Furnell E-mail: sonya@exleypublications.co.uk
Export Sales Manager: Michael Illingworth
Contact: Alyse Bunker E-mail: alyse.bunker@exleypublications.co.uk
Founded: 1976
Specializes in giftbooks, family & relationships, inspirational & biographies.
Subjects: Biography, Human Relations, Humor, Nonfiction (General)
ISBN Prefix(es): 1-85015; 1-86187; 0-905521
Total Titles: 400 Print
Associate Companies: Exley Handels GmbH, Schloss Merode, D52379 Langerwehe, Merode, Germany; Exley SA, 13 rue de Genval, B-1301 Bierges, Belgium
Subsidiaries: Exley Giftbooks
Distributed by Exley Handel GmbH (Germany); Exley SA (Belgium)

Exley Publications Ltd, see Helen Exley Giftbooks

Expert Books, imprint of Transworld Publishers Ltd

Express Newspapers+
Ludgate House, 245 Blackfriars Rd, London SE1 9UX
Tel: (020) 7928 8000 Fax: (020) 7922 7966
Key Personnel
Licensing Manager: Sue McGeever Tel: (020) 7922 7887 E-mail: sue.mcgeever@express.co.uk
Subjects: Business, Cookery, Humor, Management, Sports, Athletics
ISBN Prefix(es): 0-85079
Parent Company: Northern & Shell, Ludgate House, 245 Blackfriars Rd, London SE1 9UX

Eye Books
51 Boscombe Rd, London W12 9HT
Tel: (020) 8743 3276 Fax: (020) 8743 3276
E-mail: info@eye-books.com
Web Site: www.eye-books.com
Membership(s): IPG
Distributed by Bookwise (Australia & New Zealand); Grantham Book Services (UK)
Foreign Rep(s): Bookwise (Australia)

Fabbri (GE) Ltd+
Elme House, 133 Long Acre, London WC2E 9AW
Tel: (020) 7836 0519; (020) 7468 5600
Fax: (020) 7836 0280
E-mail: mailbox@gefabbri.co.uk
Web Site: www.gefabbri.co.uk
Key Personnel
Man Dir: Peter Edwards

693

Dir: Liz Glaze
International Dir: Philip Costick
Editorial Dir: Hilary Newstead
Editor-in-Chief: Katie Preston
Marketing Dir: Huw Thomas
Chief Accountant: Duncan Lewis
Founded: 1987
Imprints: GE Fabbri; GE Magazines
Subsidiaries: GE Fabbri; GE Magazines

Faber & Faber Ltd+
3 Queen Sq, London WC1N 3AU
Tel: (020) 7465 0045 *Fax:* (020) 7465 0034
Web Site: www.faber.co.uk *Cable:* FABBAF LONDON WC1
Key Personnel
Man Dir: Toby Faber
Publishing Dir: Joanna Mackle
Contract Manager: Alan Winwright
Publisher: Walter Donohue
Head of Sales: Chris McLaren
Founded: 1929
Also Distributor.
Subjects: Art, Biography, Drama, Theater, Fiction, Film, Video, History, How-to, Literature, Literary Criticism, Essays, Music, Dance, Philosophy, Poetry, Psychology, Psychiatry, Radio, TV, Religion - Other, Social Sciences, Sociology, Wine & Spirits
ISBN Prefix(es): 0-571
Parent Company: Geoffrey Faber Holdings
Subsidiaries: Faber Inc USA
U.S. Office(s): Faber & Faber Inc, 50 Cross St, Winchester, MA 01890, United States
Orders to: Macmillan Distribution Ltd, Brinel Rd Houndmills Ind Est, Baringstone Harts RG21 6XS *Tel:* (01256) 302692

Fabian Society
11 Dartmouth St, London SW1H 9BN
Tel: (020) 7227 4900 *Fax:* (020) 7976 7153
E-mail: info@fabian-society.org.uk
Web Site: www.fabian-society.org.uk
Key Personnel
Deputy General Secretary: Adrian Harvey *Tel:* (020) 7227 4908
Finance Officer: Margaret McGillen *Tel:* (020) 7227 4903
General Secretary: Sunder Katwala *Tel:* (020) 7227 4905
Administrator: Claire Willgress
Editorial Manager: Ellie Levenson
Local Societies Officer: Deborah Stoate
Membership Officer: Giles Wright
Events Manager: Emma Burnell
Founded: 1884
Subjects: Economics, Government, Political Science
ISBN Prefix(es): 0-7163
Subsidiaries: NCLC Publishing Society Ltd

Facet Publishing+
Imprint of Chartered Institute of Library & Information Professionals (CILIP)
7 Ridgmount St, London WC1E 7AE
Tel: (020) 7255 0590 *Fax:* (020) 7255 0591
E-mail: info@facetpublishing.co.uk
Web Site: www.facetpublishing.co.uk; www.cilip.org.uk
Key Personnel
Man Dir & International Rights: Janet Liebster
Publishing Dir: Helen Carley *Tel:* (020) 7255 0592 *E-mail:* helen.carley@facetpublishing.co.uk
Commissioning Editor: Rebecca Casey
Production Manager: Kathryn Beecroft
Sales Manager: Rohini Ramachandran
Founded: 1980
Specialize in library & information science.
Subjects: Computer Science, Library & Information Sciences, Management, Technology
ISBN Prefix(es): 0-85365; 0-85157; 1-85604

Warehouse: Bookpoint Ltd, 130 Milton Park, Abingdon OX14 4SB
Neal-Schuman, 100 William St, Suite 2003, New York, NY 10038-4512, United States (North American orders)
Orders to: Bookpoint Ltd, 130 Milton Park, Abingdon, Oxon OX14 4SB
Neal-Schuman Publishers Inc, 100 William St, Suite 2003, New York, NY 10038-4512, United States

The Factory Shop Guide
34 Park Hill, London SW4 9PB
Tel: (020) 7622 3722 *Fax:* (020) 7720 3536
E-mail: factshop@macline.co.uk
Key Personnel
Partners: Gillian Cutress; Rolf Stricker
Founded: 1985
Subjects: Gardening, Plants, Travel
ISBN Prefix(es): 0-948965

Fairacres Publication, *imprint of* SLG Press

Fairfield, *imprint of* Novello & Co Ltd

Falco, *imprint of* Hawk Books

Famedram Publishers Ltd+
PO Box 3, Ellon, Aberdeenshire AB41 9EA
Tel: (01651) 842429 *Fax:* (01651) 842180
E-mail: famedram@artwork.co.uk
Key Personnel
Man Dir: Bill Williams
Production: Eleanor Stewart
Editor (Artwork): Richard Carr
Advertising Sales: Sandra Moore *Tel:* (01436) 675743 *Fax:* (01436) 673327
Founded: 1971
Publisher of Artwork - bimonthly arts newspaper for Scotland & Northern England.
Subjects: Poetry, Travel, Wine & Spirits
ISBN Prefix(es): 0-905489; 0-9501944
Total Titles: 40 Print
Imprints: Northern Books

Family Law, *imprint of* Jordan Publishing Ltd

Family Walks, *imprint of* Scarthin Books

Fanny, *imprint of* Knockabout Comics

Farsight Press+
5 Lynette Ave, London SW4 9HE
Tel: (020) 8675 1693
Key Personnel
Dir & Sole Proprietor: Mr F Knox
Founded: 1996
Research & publication on criminology.
Subjects: Criminology
ISBN Prefix(es): 0-948669
Number of titles published annually: 4 Print
Total Titles: 4 Print

FBA Publications, *imprint of* Francis Balsom Associates

Feather Books
PO Box 438, Shrewsbury SY3 0WN
Tel: (01743) 872177 *Fax:* (01743) 872177
E-mail: john@waddysweb.freeuk.com
Web Site: www.waddysweb.com
Founded: 1984
Christian publisher.
Membership(s): Independent Publishers Guild.
Subjects: Drama, Theater, Fiction, Music, Dance, Poetry, Science Fiction, Fantasy, Hymns
ISBN Prefix(es): 0-947718; 1-84175
Number of titles published annually: 60 Print

Total Titles: 250 Print
Book Club(s): The Quill Hedgehog Club

Ferendune, *imprint of* E W Classey Ltd

Fernhurst Books+
Duke's Path, High St, Arundel, West Sussex BN18 9AJ
Tel: (01903) 882277 *Fax:* (01903) 882715
E-mail: sales@fernhurstbooks.co.uk
Web Site: www.fernhurstbooks.co.uk
Key Personnel
Man Dir: Tim Davison
Founded: 1979
Paperbacks on all aspects of water sports.
Subjects: Maritime
ISBN Prefix(es): 0-906754; 1-898660
Number of titles published annually: 14 Print
Total Titles: 106 Print; 1 CD-ROM
U.S. Office(s): Robert Hale, 1803 132 Ave NE, Suite 4, Bellevue, WA 98005, United States *Tel:* 425-881-5212 *Fax:* 425-881-0731
Warehouse: Clipper Distribution, Windmill Grove, Porchester, Hants P016 9HT *Tel:* (02392) 200080 *Fax:* (02392) 200090

FHG Publications Ltd
Abbey Mill Business Centre, Seedhill, Paisley PA1 1TJ
Tel: (0141) 8870428 *Fax:* (0141) 8897204
E-mail: fhg@ipcmedia.com
Web Site: www.holidayguides.com
Key Personnel
General Manager: George Pratt
Founded: 1947
Subjects: Travel
ISBN Prefix(es): 1-85055; 0-900365
Parent Company: IPC Media Ltd, King's Reach Tower, Stampford St, London SE19LS
U.S. Office(s): Hunter Publishing, 239 S Beach Rd, Hobe Sound, FL, United States

Sadie Fields Productions Ltd+
4C/D West Point, 36/37 Warple Way, London W3 0RQ
Tel: (020) 89969970 *Fax:* (020) 89969977
E-mail: edith@tangobooks.co.uk
Key Personnel
Dir: David Fielder; Sheri Safran
Founded: 1981
Also book packager, childrens novelty (popups, holograms, touch & feel etc).
Associate Companies: Sadie Fields Management Inc
Divisions: Tango Books

Financial Times Prentice Hall, *imprint of* Pearson Education Europe, Mideast & Africa

Financial Training Co
New London House, 6 London St, London EC3R 7LQ
Tel: (020) 7481 6050 *Fax:* (020) 7265 0337
Web Site: www.financial-training.com
Key Personnel
Man Dir: William Macpherson
Founded: 1978
Subjects: Accounting
ISBN Prefix(es): 1-85179
Branch Office(s)
Swift House, Market Place, Berkshire RG40 1AP *Tel:* (0118) 977 4922 *Fax:* (0118) 989 4029
7 Hill St, Centre City Tower, Birmingham B5 4UA *Tel:* (0121) 644 4700 *Fax:* (0121) 644 4701
Saint David's House, Wood St, Suite 5, Cardiff *Tel:* (029) 2038 8067 *Fax:* (029) 2023 7408
91 Mitchell St, Glasgow G1 3LN *Tel:* (0141) 248 8080 *Fax:* (0141) 298 8040
32a Castle Way, Southampton, Hampshire SO14 2AW *Tel:* (023) 8022 0852 *Fax:* (023) 8063 4379

The Sherethorn Centre, Prospect St, Hull HU2 8PX
49 Saint Pauls St, Leeds LS1 2TE *Tel:* (0113) 388 9310 *Fax:* (0113) 242 8889
66 London Rd, 3rd floor, Beckville House, Leicester LE2 0QD
Coopers Bldg, Church St, 3rd floor, Liverpool L1 3AA *Tel:* (0151) 708 8839 *Fax:* (0151) 709 4264
18-20 Crucifix Lane, London SE1 3JW *Tel:* (020) 7407 5000 *Fax:* (020) 7407 0101
7-13 Mellor St, London SE1 eQP *Tel:* (020) 7407 5000 *Fax:* (020) 7407 0101
One Angel Square, Torrens St, London EC1 V1 NY *Tel:* (0207) 520 1146
10-14 White Lion St, London N1 9PD *Tel:* (020) 7520 1125 *Fax:* (020) 7520 1120
Saint James Bldg, Oxford St, 6th floor, Manchester M1 6FQ, United Republic of Tanzania *Tel:* (0161) 237 3366 *Fax:* (0161) 236 9047
Provincial House, Northumberland St, Newcastle Upon Tyne NE1 7DQ *Tel:* (0191) 232 9365 *Fax:* (0191) 232 2115
5 Clumber St, Alan House, 3rd floor, Nottingham NG1 3ED *Tel:* (0115) 941 0723 *Fax:* (0115) 941 5779
463a Glossop Rd, Pegasus House, Sheffield S10 2QD *Tel:* (0114) 266 9265 *Fax:* (0114) 268 4084

Financial World Publishing, see Institute of Financial Services

Findhorn Press Inc+
305a The Park, Findhorn, Forres IV36 3TE
Tel: (01309) 690582 *Fax:* (01309) 690036
E-mail: info@findhornpress.com
Web Site: www.findhornpress.com
Key Personnel
Publisher: Thierry Bogliolo *Tel:* (0467) 283488 (France) *Fax:* (0467) 490419 (France) *E-mail:* thierry@findhornpress.com
Founded: 1971
Publishes books that bring hope, healing & inspiration to the world.
Subjects: Self-Help, Alternative Health, Spirituality
ISBN Prefix(es): 0-905242; 1-899171; 1-84409
Number of titles published annually: 20 Print
Total Titles: 90 Print; 2 Audio
Distributed by Anthroposophic Press (North America); Brumby Books (Australia); Deep Books (UK & Europe); New Horizons (South Africa); Peaceful Living Publications (New Zealand)
Foreign Rep(s): Findhorn Publishing Services (Worldwide)

Firebird Books Ltd+
PO Box 327, Poole, Dorset BH15 2RG
Tel: (01202) 715349 (sales); (01258) 454675 (editorial) *Fax:* (01202) 736191
E-mail: skboorh@bournemouth-net.co.uk
Key Personnel
Publisher: Stuart Booth
Production Dir: Kathryn Booth
Sales Dir: Chris Lloyd *E-mail:* chrlloyd@globalnet.co.uk
Founded: 1987
Subjects: History, Military Science
ISBN Prefix(es): 1-85314
Associate Companies: Wise Owl Quiz Promotions
Sales Office(s): Chris Lloyd Sales & Marketing, Poole *Tel:* (01202) 715349

First & Best in Education Ltd+
Earlstrees Court, Earlstrees Rd, Corby, Northants NN17 4HH
Tel: (01536) 399004 (editorial); (01536) 399005 (accounts) *Fax:* (01536) 399012
E-mail: anne@firstandbest.co.uk
Web Site: www.firstandbest.co.uk

Key Personnel
Man Dir & Marketing: Tony Attwood *Tel:* (01536) 399013 *E-mail:* tonyattwood@hamilton-house.com
Editor: Anne Cockburn
Founded: 1979
Specialize in publishing books on marketing & direct mail & copiable books for schools & software for schools.
Subjects: Business, Education
ISBN Prefix(es): 0-906888; 1-898091; 1-86083
Number of titles published annually: 30 Print; 25 CD-ROM
Total Titles: 600 Print; 200 CD-ROM
Ultimate Parent Company: Hamilton House Mailings plc
Imprints: School Improvement Reports

First Discovery, *imprint of* Moonlight Publishing Ltd

First Discovery-Art, *imprint of* Moonlight Publishing Ltd

Fishing News Books Ltd+
Osney Mead, Oxford OX2 0EL
Tel: (01865) 206206 *Fax:* (01865) 721205
E-mail: fishing.newsbooks@oxon.blackwellpublishing.com
Web Site: www.fishknowledge.com
Telex: 83355 MEDBOK G
Key Personnel
Publisher: Nigel Balmforth *E-mail:* nigel.balmforth@oxon.blackwellpublishing.com
Marketing: Katie Moll *E-mail:* katie.moll@oxon.blackwellpublishing.com
Founded: 1953
Subjects: Maritime
ISBN Prefix(es): 0-85238
Parent Company: Blackwell Scientific Publishing Ltd, Osney Mead, Oxford OX2 0EL
Bookshop(s): Blackwell Book Shops
Orders to: Blackwell Publishing Direct Orders, PO Box 269, Abingdon, Oxfordshire OX14 4YN *Tel:* (01235) 465500 *Fax:* (01235) 455556

The Fitzjames Press, *imprint of* Motor Racing Publications Ltd

Five Star, *imprint of* Thomson Gale

Flambard Press+
Stable Cottage, East Fourstones, Hexham, Northumberland NE47 5DX
Tel: (01434) 674360 *Fax:* (01434) 674178
Web Site: www.flambardpress.co.uk
Key Personnel
Managing Editor: Peter Lewis
Founded: 1990
Non-commercial publisher mainly for writers north of England.
Subjects: Fiction, Poetry
ISBN Prefix(es): 1-873226
Number of titles published annually: 7 Print
Total Titles: 68 Print
Warehouse: Central Books, London
Distribution Center: Central Books, London
Orders to: Central Books, London
Returns: Central Books, London

Flame Tree Publishing+
Crabtree Hall, Crabtree Lane, Fulham, London SW6 6TY
Tel: (020) 7386 4700 *Fax:* (020) 7386 4700
E-mail: info@flametreepublishing.com
Web Site: www.flametreepublishing.com
Key Personnel
Publisher: Nick Wells
Man Dir: Frances Bodiam
Sales Operations Manager: Helen Wall
Founded: 1992

Publishers of books & stationery.
Membership(s): Independent Publishers Guild.
Subjects: Art, Education, History, Music, Dance, Religion - Other
ISBN Prefix(es): 1-90404; 1-84451; 1-90381
Number of titles published annually: 25 Print
Total Titles: 200 Print
Parent Company: The Foundry Creative Media Co Ltd
Distribution Center: Marston Book Services

Flicks Books+
29 Bradford St, Trowbridge, Wilts BA14 9AN
Tel: (01225) 767 728 *Fax:* (01225) 760 418
E-mail: flicks.books@pipex.com
Key Personnel
Publisher: Matthew Stevens
Founded: 1986
Subjects: Film, Video, Cinema, TV
ISBN Prefix(es): 0-948911; 1-86236
Total Titles: 70 Print

Floris Books+
15 Harrison Gardens, Edinburgh EH11 1SH
Tel: (0131) 337 2372 *Fax:* (0131) 347 9919
E-mail: floris@floris.books.co.uk
Web Site: www.florisbooks.co.uk
Key Personnel
Editorial: Christopher Moore
Production, Rights & Permissions: Christian Maclean
Schools/Libraries: Angelique Fowlie
Contact: Joanne Moore
Founded: 1976
Membership(s): Scottish Publishers Association.
Subjects: Crafts, Games, Hobbies, Religion - Other, Science (General)
ISBN Prefix(es): 0-903540; 0-86315
Warehouse: Scottish Book Source, 32 Finlas St, Glasgow G22 5DU *Tel:* (0870) 240 2182 *E-mail:* orders@booksource.net

Focal Press, *imprint of* Elsevier Ltd

Fodors, *imprint of* Random House UK Ltd

Folens Ltd+
Boscombe Rd, Dunstable, Beds LU5 4RL
Tel: (0870) 609 1237 *Fax:* (0870) 609 1236
E-mail: folens@folens.com
Web Site: www.folens.com
Key Personnel
Man Dir: Malcolm Watson
Dir, Sales & Marketing: Adrian Cockell
Founded: 1986
Publishers of educational books for both teachers & children up to the age of 18 years.
Subjects: Education
ISBN Prefix(es): 1-85276; 1-84163; 1-84303; 0-94788; 1-84191; 1-86202
Number of titles published annually: 150 Print; 20 CD-ROM
Total Titles: 1,500 Print; 120 CD-ROM
Associate Companies: Educational Publishers
Distributed by Agius + Agius Limited (Malta); Al Kashkool Bookshop (Jordan); All Prints Distributors & Publishers (United Arab Emirates); Al Manahil Educational Consultancy (Oman); Bacon & Hughes Limited (Canada); Educational Supplies Pty Ltd (Australia); Incentive Publications Inc (USA); International Language Bookshop (Egypt); LKD Educational Resources (Jordan); Mars Publishing House (Saudi Arabia); Modern Teaching Aids (Australia); Proof Line (M) Sdn Bhd (Malaysia); Saeed & Samir Bookstore Co Ltd (Kuwait); September 21 Enterprise Pte Ltd (Singapore); Social Studies School Service (USA); South Pacific Books (Imports) Ltd (New Zealand); Southern Cross (Australia); Stanford House (ELT Resource Centre) (Hong Kong); TEK Books (Bookworld

UNITED KINGDOM

Espana) (Spain); University Book Store (M) Sdn Bhd (Malaysia)
Foreign Rep(s): IPR Beirut (Lebanon); IPR Cyprus (Cyprus)
Distribution Center: CES Holdings
E-mail: info@cesholdings.co.uk
Garnders Books *Tel:* (01323) 521 777 *Fax:* (01323) 521 666 *E-mail:* export@gardners.com

Food Trade Press, *imprint of* Food Trade Press Ltd

Food Trade Press Ltd+
Station House, Hortons Way, Westerham, Kent TN16 1BZ
Tel: (01959) 563944 *Fax:* (01959) 561285
E-mail: ftpbooks@aol.com
Web Site: foodtradepress.net
Key Personnel
Dir: Adrian M Binsted
Founded: 1944
Publisher, distributor & bookseller for the food trade.
Specialize in food production & technology.
ISBN Prefix(es): 0-900379; 0-903962
Number of titles published annually: 12 Print; 1 CD-ROM
Total Titles: 52 Print; 3 CD-ROM
Associate Companies: Attwood & Binsted Ltd
Imprints: Food Trade Press; Food Trade Review
Distributor for Campden & Chorleywood Food RA (UK); Chemical Publishing (USA); Chiriotti Editori (Italy); CTI Publications (USA); Food & Nutrition Press (USA); Leatherhead Food RA (UK)

Food Trade Review, *imprint of* Food Trade Press Ltd

Forbes Publications Ltd+
Abbott House, 1-2 Hanover Sq, London W1S 1YZ
Tel: (020) 7495 7945 *Fax:* (020) 7495 7916
E-mail: editorial@rapportgroup.com
Key Personnel
Dir: Judith Bloor; Mary Anne FitzGerald
Founded: 1947
Subjects: Business, Economics, Education, Health, Nutrition, Human Relations, Science (General), Technology
ISBN Prefix(es): 0-901762; 1-899527
Parent Company: The Rapport Group Ltd
Orders to: Plymbridge Distributors, Estover Rd, Plymouth, Devon PL6 7PZ *Tel:* (01752) 202300 *Fax:* (01752) 202330

Forensic Science Society
Clarke House, 18A Mount Parade, Harrogate HG1 1BX
Tel: (01423) 506068 *Fax:* (01423) 566391
E-mail: tracey@forensic-science-society.org.uk
Web Site: www.forensic-science-society.org.uk
Founded: 1959
Subjects: Forensic science

Forth Naturalist & Historian
University of Stirling, Biological Sciences, Stirling FK9 4LA
Mailing Address: 30 Dunmar Drive, Alloa, Clackmannan, Scotland FK10 2EH
Tel: (01786) 467755 *Fax:* (01786) 464994
Web Site: www.stir.ac.uk/departments/naturalsciences/forth_naturalist
Telex: 777557 Stuniv G
Key Personnel
Honorary Editor & Secretary: Lindsay Corbett *Tel:* (01259) 215091 *E-mail:* lindsay.corbett@stir.ac.uk
Chairman: Prof John Proctor
Founded: 1975
An informal charitable body of the University of Stirling to promote the environment, heritage & wildlife of Central Scotland. Specialize in maps & journals.
Membership(s): Scottish Publishers Association.
Subjects: Environmental Studies, History, Natural History
ISBN Prefix(es): 0-9506962; 0-9514147; 1-898008; 0-903650
Number of titles published annually: 1 Print
Total Titles: 30 Print
Ultimate Parent Company: University of Stirling
Distributed by Scottish Book Source; Scottish Publishers Association
Distributor for Clarkmannanshire Libraries; CFSS (Clarkmannanshire Field Studies Society); Creag Darach; Falkirk Local History Society; RIAS/Rutland Press; Stirling District Libraries

G T Foulis & Co, *imprint of* Haynes Publishing

Foulsham Publishers+
Brunel Rd, Houndmills, Basingstoke RG21 6XS
Tel: (01256) 329242 *Fax:* (01256) 812558; (01256) 812521
E-mail: mdl@macmillan.co.uk
Telex: 41671 TCS G
Key Personnel
Man Dir & Commissioning Editor: B A R Belasco *E-mail:* belasco@foulsham.com
Dir, Finance & Export Sales: Graham M Kitchen *E-mail:* kitchen@foulsham.com
Production Dir: Roy Mantel *E-mail:* mantel@foulsham.com
International Rights & Foreign Rights Manager (London): Cathy Miller
Editorial Dir: W Hobson *E-mail:* hobson@foulsham.com
Founded: 1819
Subjects: Alternative, Antiques, Astrology, Occult, Cookery, Crafts, Games, Hobbies, Education, Film, Video, Finance, Gardening, Plants, Health, Nutrition, House & Home, How-to, Humor, Self-Help, Technology, Travel, Wine & Spirits, Family Reference, Know How, Mind, Body, Spirit, Self Improvement
ISBN Prefix(es): 0-572
Number of titles published annually: 100 Print; 2 E-Book
Total Titles: 300 Print
Imprints: Quantum
Orders to: Associated Publishers Group, 1501 County Hospital Rd, Nashville, TN 37218, United States *Tel:* 615-254-2420 *Fax:* 615-254-2405

The Foundational Book Company for the John W Doorly Trust
The John Doorly Trust, PO Box 659, London SW3 6SJ
Tel: (020) 7584 1053
Founded: 1946
Subjects: Biblical Studies, Religion - Other
ISBN Prefix(es): 0-85241
Total Titles: 40 Print
Distribution Center: Rare Book Company, PO Box 6957, Freehold, NJ 07728, United States, Ann Beals *Tel:* 732-364-8043 *Fax:* 732-364-8043 *E-mail:* rarebooks@aol.com
The Bookmark, PO Box 801143, Santa Clarita, CA 91380-1143, United States *Tel:* 805-298 7767 *Fax:* 805-250 9227 *E-mail:* order@thebookmark.com

Foundery Press & Chester House Publications, *imprint of* Methodist Publishing House

Fountain Press, *imprint of* Newpro UK Ltd

Four Seasons Publishing Ltd+
16 Orchard Rise, Kingston on Thames, Surrey KT2 7EY
Tel: (020) 8942 4445 *Fax:* (020) 8942 4446
E-mail: info@fourseasons.net
Key Personnel
Man Dir: Christopher Shepheard-Walwyn *E-mail:* csw@fourseasons.net
Founded: 1988
Expanding range of nonfiction gift books & social stationery for the international co-edition market.
ISBN Prefix(es): 1-85645

Fourth Estate+
Division of HarperCollins UK
77-85 Fulham Palace Rd, London W6 8JB
Tel: (020) 8741 4414 *Fax:* (020) 8307 4466
E-mail: general@4thestate.co.uk
Web Site: www.4thestate.co.uk
Key Personnel
Chief Executive Officer & Publisher: Victoria Barnsley
Publishing Dir: Christopher Potter
Dep Man Dir: Stephen Page
Rights Dir: Susie Dunlop
Production: Graham Cook
Publicity Dir: Nicky Eaton
Founded: 1984
Subjects: Architecture & Interior Design, Biography, Cookery, Fiction, Gay & Lesbian, History, Humor, Literature, Literary Criticism, Essays, Radio, TV
ISBN Prefix(es): 0-947795; 1-872180; 1-84115; 1-85702
Imprints: Guardian Books
Distributor for John Brown Publishing; Duncan Baird Publisher (UK); Harvill Press (UK); Profile Books (UK)
Orders to: TBS, Frating Green, Colchester C07 7DW

L N Fowler & Co Ltd, *imprint of* The C W Daniel Co Ltd

W & G Foyle Ltd
113-119 Charing Cross Rd, London WC2H 0EB
Tel: (020) 7437 5660 *Fax:* (020) 7434 1574
E-mail: administration@foyles.co.uk
Web Site: www.foyles.co.uk *Cable:* FOYLIBRA LONDON WC2
Key Personnel
Chairman & Man Dir: WR Christopher Foyle
Marketing Dir: Bill Foyle Samuel *Tel:* (020) 7440 3226 *E-mail:* bill@foyles.co.uk
General Manager: Sharon Murray
Founded: 1903
General book store.
Divisions: Archaeology; Art; Astronomy; Autobiographies & Biographies; Children's Books - Fiction & Non-Fiction; Cinema; Computing; Cookery; Drama; Education; Engineering; English Language, EFL, Dictionaries & Reference; English Literature; Fiction - Hardback & Paperback; Foreign Languages; History; Humour; Maths & Physics; Medical, Nursing & Veterinary; Music; Natural History & Biology; Photography; Rare Books; Sociology; Sport; Technical; Theology; Transport; Travel

Francis Balsom Associates+
Unit 4, The Science Park, Aberystwyth SY23 3AH
Tel: (01970) 636400 *Fax:* (01970) 636414
E-mail: info@fbagroup.co.uk
Web Site: www.fbagroup.co.uk
Key Personnel
Man Dir: Sue Balsom
Chairman & Company Secretary: Denis Balsom
Business Manager: Priscilla Gibby
Founded: 1989

Subjects: Art, Government, Political Science, Health, Nutrition, Sports, Athletics
ISBN Prefix(es): 1-901862
Imprints: Cyhoeddiadau FBA; FBA Publications

The Fraser Press
182 Bath St, Glasgow G2 4HG
Tel: (0141) 3331992 *Fax:* (0141) 3331992
Key Personnel
Proprietor: M Hay
Founded: 1991
Subjects: Architecture & Interior Design, Art
ISBN Prefix(es): 1-873805

Free Association Books Ltd+
57 Warren St, London W1T 5NZ
Tel: (020) 7388 3182 *Fax:* (020) 7388 3187
E-mail: info@fabooks.com
Web Site: www.fabooks.com
Key Personnel
Chief Executive, Editorial & Man Dir: Tower Brown
Publisher: Trevor E Brown
Rights & Permissions: Cathy Miller
Sales & Marketing Manager: Elisabetta Minervini
Founded: 1983
Subjects: Behavioral Sciences, Child Care & Development, Ethnicity, Human Relations, Philosophy, Psychology, Psychiatry, Social Sciences, Sociology
ISBN Prefix(es): 0-946960; 1-85343
U.S. Office(s): NYUP, Elmer Holmes Bobst Library, 70 Washington Sq S, New York, NY 10012-1091, United States
Foreign Rep(s): Astam Books Pty ltd (Australia, New Zealand, Papua New Guinea); Bookworm (Israel); Richard Bowen (Scandinavia); Roy de Boo (Germany); ISBS (North America); Jordan Book Centre (Middle East); Kay Kato (Japan); Dineke Kemper (Benelux, France, Switzerland, Holland); Flavio Marcello (Italy, Portugal, Spain); STM Publishers Services Pte (Far East); Viva Books (India)
Foreign Rights: Cathy Miller Agency
Warehouse: The Trade Counter, Unit D, Trading Estate Rd, London NW10 7LU
Distribution Center: Astam Books Pty Ltd, 57-61 John St, Leichhardt NSW 2040, Australia, Contact: Chris Player *Tel:* (02) 9566 4400 *Fax:* (02) 9566 4411 *E-mail:* astam@interconnect.com.au
Roy de Boo, Diederik van Altenstraat 12, 5095 AP Hooge Mierde, Netherlands *Tel:* (13) 5096033 *Fax:* (13) 5096034 *E-mail:* roy.de.boo@inter.nl.net (Germany)
Bookworm, 30 Basel St, Tel Aviv 62744, Israel *Tel:* (972) 3546 2714 *Fax:* (972) 3546 2714 *E-mail:* bookworm@classnet.co.il
Richard Bowen, Post Box 30037, S 200 61 Malmo 30, Sweden (Scandinavia)
BR&D, Hadleigh Hall, London Rd, Hadleigh SS7 2DE *Tel:* (01702) 552912 *Fax:* (01702) 556095
Eleanor Cripps, 4 Lytes Cary Rd, Keynsham, Bristol BS18 1XD *Tel:* (0117) 983 7326 (Midlands, Southeast England, Mid & South Wales)
Peter Hampson, 19 Guest Rd, Prestwich, Manchester M25 3DG *Tel:* (0161) 773 9753 (North Wales, North England, Scotland)
ISBS, 5804 NE Hassalo St, Portland, OR 97213-3644, United States *Fax:* 503-280-8832 *E-mail:* fab@isbs.com (North America)
Jordan Book Centre, PO Box 301, Al-Jubeiha, Amman 11941, Jordan *Tel:* (6) 5151882 *Fax:* (6) 5152016 *E-mail:* jbc@go.com.jo
Kay Kato, 5-14 Gokurakuji, 1-Chome, Kamakura Kanagawa 248, Japan
Dineke Kemper, Kemper Couseil, Dr Beguinlaan 72, NL 2272 AL Voorburg, Netherlands *Tel:* (70) 3868031 *Fax:* (70) 3861498 *E-mail:* kemper_conseil@dataweb.nl (France, Holland, Switzerland, Benelux)
Flavio Marcello, Via Vicenza 36, 35138 Padova, Italy (Italy, Spain & Portugal)
Gareth Pottle, 27 Highbury Pl, London N5 1QP *Tel:* (0171) 359 0679 (South London, Home Counties (South, East Anglia, Northern Ireland, Eire))
STM Publishers Services Pte Ltd, 352 Lorong Chuan, #01-05 Laurel Park 556783, Singapore, Contact: Tony Poh Leong Wah *E-mail:* tonypoh@pacific.net.sg
Celia Stocks, 63 Bride St, London N7 8RN *Tel:* (0171) 607 4519 (North London, Home Counties (North))
Viva Books, 4325/3 Ansari Rd, Darya Ganj, New Delhi 110002, India, Contact: Vinod Vashishtha
Orders to: ISBS, 5804 NE Hassalo St, Portland, OR 97213-3644, United States *Fax:* 503-280-8832 *E-mail:* fab@isbs.com
Plymbridge Distributors Ltd, Estover, Plymouth PL6 7PZ *Tel:* (01752) 202301 *Fax:* (01752) 202333 *E-mail:* cservs@plymbridge.com (UK & Europe)

Free Press, *imprint of* Simon & Schuster Ltd

Freedom Ministries, *imprint of* Moorley's Print & Publishing Ltd

Freedom Press
Angel Alley, 84b Whitechapel High St, London E1 7QX
Tel: (020) 7247 9249 *Fax:* (020) 7377 9526
Key Personnel
Manager: Charles Crute; Vernon Richards
Founded: 1886 (Independent non-profit making publisher)
Subjects: Economics, Government, Political Science, History, Philosophy, Social Sciences, Sociology
ISBN Prefix(es): 0-900384
Number of titles published annually: 7 Print
Total Titles: 80 Print
Distributed by Active Distribution; AK Distribution; Left Bank Distribution
Distributor for AK Press; Calabria Press; Michael E Coughlin; Five Leaves Publications; Left Bank Distribution; Libertarian Education; Phoenix Press; Red Lion Press; See Sharp Press

W H Freeman, *imprint of* Palgrave Publishers Ltd

W H Freeman & Co Ltd
Brunel Rd, Houndmills, Basingstoke, Hants RG21 6XS
Tel: (01256) 329242 *Fax:* (01256) 330688
Web Site: www.whfreeman.co.uk
Key Personnel
Man Dir: Dominic Knight *Tel:* (01256) 302750
Founded: 1959
Subjects: Behavioral Sciences, Biological Sciences, Chemistry, Chemical Engineering, Child Care & Development, Computer Science, Earth Sciences, Economics, Electronics, Electrical Engineering, Environmental Studies, Geography, Geology, Mathematics, Medicine, Nursing, Dentistry, Physical Sciences, Psychology, Psychiatry, Science (General)
ISBN Prefix(es): 0-7167; 0-87893; 0-935702; 1-57259; 0-87901; 0-89454
Parent Company: W H Freeman & Co, 41 Madison Ave, 37th floor, New York, NY 10010, United States
Ultimate Parent Company: Verlagsgruppe Georg von Holtzbrinck GmbH, Germany
Holding Company: Scientific American, 41 Madison Ave, New York, NY 10014, United States
Imprints: Scientific American; Computer Science Press
Distributed by Palgrave (UK, Europe, Africa, Middle East, India & Pakistan)
Distributor for Sirauer Associates; Spectrum; University Science Books; Worth
Orders to: Marston Book Services, PO Box 87, Oxford OX4 1LB
W H Freeman & Co, 41 Madison Ave, New York, NY 10010, United States *Tel:* 212-576-9400 *Fax:* 212-481-1891 *Web Site:* www.whfreeman.com (North America & Far East)
Macmillan Education Publishers Australia Pty Ltd, Levels 4 & 5, 627 Chapel St, South Yarra, Victoria 3141, Australia *Tel:* (03) 9825 1025 *Fax:* (03) 9825 1010 *E-mail:* mea@macmillan.com.au *Web Site:* www.macmillan.com.au (Australia)

Samuel French Ltd
52 Fitzroy St, London W1T 5JR
Tel: (020) 7387 9373 *Fax:* (020) 7387 2161
E-mail: theatre@samuelfrench-london.co.uk
Web Site: www.samuelfrench-london.co.uk
Key Personnel
Chairman: Charles Van Nostrand
Man Dir: J W Bedding
Dir: Amanda Smith; Paul Taylor
Secretary to Man Dir: Vivien Goodwin
Founded: 1830
Subjects: Drama, Theater
ISBN Prefix(es): 0-573
Associate Companies: Samuel French (Canada) Ltd, 100 Lombard St, Lower Level, Toronto, ON, Canada; Samuel French Inc, 45 W 25 St, New York, NY 10010, United States; 7623 Sunset Blvd, Hollywood, CA 90046, United States
Bookshop(s): French's Theatre Bookshop, 52 Fitzroy St, London W1P 6JR

Sigmund Freud Copyrights
10 Brook St, Wivenhoe, Colchester CO7 9DS
Tel: (01206) 825433 *Fax:* (01206) 822990
E-mail: info@markpaterson.co.uk
Web Site: www.markpaterson.co.uk/sigmund.htm
Key Personnel
Dir: Mark Paterson *E-mail:* mark@markpaterson.co.uk
Archivist: Tom Roberts *E-mail:* tom@markpaterson.co.uk
Administrator: S Pearce
Associate Companies: Mark Paterson & Associates; Quentin Books Ltd

The Friendly Press
Member of Quakers Uniting in Publications Worldwide (QUIP)
26 Cleeve Hill, Bristol BS16 6UL
Tel: (0117) 908-2281 *Fax:* (0117) 908-2282
E-mail: phgassoc@aol.com
Key Personnel
Dir: Anne Hodkinson
Contact: E Anne Lang
Subjects: ELT Books & Materials, Religious Quaker
ISBN Prefix(es): 0-948728
Parent Company: PH Group

From The Portuguese, *imprint of* Carcanet Press Ltd

Frontier Publishing Ltd+
Windetts, Seething Rd, Kirkstead, Norwich NR15 1EG
Tel: (01508) 558174
E-mail: frontier.pub@macunlimited.net
Web Site: www.frontierpublishing.co.uk
Key Personnel
Principal: Mr R Barnes
Founded: 1986
Subjects: Art, History, Nonfiction (General), Photography, Poetry, Travel
ISBN Prefix(es): 0-85036; 1-872914; 0-9508701
Total Titles: 20 Print
Imprints: Frontier 2000 Series
Membership(s): IPG

UNITED KINGDOM

Frontier 2000 Series, *imprint of* Frontier Publishing Ltd

The FruitMarket Gallery
45 Market St, Edinburgh EH1 1DF
Tel: (0131) 225 2383 *Fax:* (0131) 220 3130
E-mail: fruitmarket@fruitmarket.co.uk
Web Site: www.fruitmarket.co.uk
Key Personnel
Dir: Dr Fiona Bradley
Design & Publishing Manager: Elizabeth McLean
Development Manager: Armida Taylor
Education Manager: Tracy Morgan
Finance Manager: Graham Mannerings
Media & Marketing Manager: Annie Woodman
Founded: 1984
Mission: to bring the work of leading artists worldwide to Scotland & to exhibit the work of Scottish artists in an international context, engaging with contemporary issues.
Subjects: Art
ISBN Prefix(es): 0-947912

David Fulton Publishers Ltd+
The Chiswick Centre, 414 Chiswick High Rd, London W4 5TF
Tel: (020) 8996 3610 *Fax:* (020) 8996 3622
E-mail: mail@fultonpublishers.co.uk
Web Site: www.fultonpublishers.co.uk
Key Personnel
Chairman: David Fulton *E-mail:* david.fulton@fultonpublishers.co.uk
Man Dir: David Hill *E-mail:* david.hill@fultonpublishers.co.uk
Marketing Dir: Rachael Robertson *E-mail:* rachael.robertson@fultonpublishers.co.uk
Publisher: Helen Fairlie *E-mail:* helen.fairlie@fultonpublishers.co.uk
Senior Commissioning Editor: Nina Stibbe *E-mail:* nina.stibbe@fultonpublishers.co.uk
Commissioning Editor (Special Education Needs): Jude Bowen *E-mail:* jude.bowen@fultonpublishers.co.uk
Commissioning Editor: Margaret Haigh *E-mail:* margaret.haigh@fultonpublishers.co.uk
Marketing Executive: Fred O'Connor *E-mail:* fred.oconnor@fultonpublishers.co.uk; Georgina Allan *E-mail:* georgina.allan@fultonpublishers.co.uk
Production Manager: Alan Worth *E-mail:* alan.worth@fultonpublishers.co.uk
Founded: 1987
Specialize in SEN books for teachers.
Subjects: Disability, Special Needs, Education
ISBN Prefix(es): 1-85346
U.S. Office(s): Taylor & Francis Inc, 1900 Frost Rd, Suite 101, Bristol, PA 19007-1598, United States *Tel:* 215-785-5800 *Fax:* 215-785-5515
Foreign Rep(s): Andrew Durnell (Ireland, Europe, Scandinavia); Karim International (Bangladesh); Viva Group (India); Yale Representation Ltd (England)
Foreign Rights: Book Promotions (Pty) Ltd (South Africa); Hemisphere Publication Services (Asia & the Pacific); Macmillan Academic & Reference (Australia); Macmillan Publishers New Zealand Ltd (New Zealand); Taylor & Francis Inc (North America)
Warehouse: Marston Book Services Ltd, PO Box 269, Abingdon, Oxon OX14 4YN
Orders to: Marston Book Services Ltd, PO Box 269, Abington, Oxon OX14 4YN

Fun Files, *imprint of* Funfax Ltd

Funfax Ltd+
9 Henrietta St, London WC2E 8PS
Tel: (020) 7836 5411 *Fax:* (020) 7836 7570
E-mail: clairrey@dk-uk.com
Key Personnel
Man Dir & Foreign Rights: Roger Priddy
Commercial Dir: Jonathan Mitchell
Sales Dir: Steve Evans
Chief Editor: Lisa Telford
Production Manager: Mike Kudar
Art Dir: Roger Tainsh
Founded: 1990
ISBN Prefix(es): 1-85597; 0-7547; 1-86208
Parent Company: Dorling Kindersley Ltd, 80 Strand, London WC2R ORL
Imprints: Clever Clogs; Fun Files; FX Pax; Junior Funfax; Know Alls; Lettermen; Mad Jack; Magic Joneuery; Microfax
U.S. Office(s): Dorling Kindersley Inc, 95 Madison Ave, New York, NY 10016, United States
Web Site: www.dk.com
Warehouse: International Book Distributors, Magna Park, Coventry Rd, Lutterworth, Lincs LE17

Furco Ltd
10 Jewry St, Winchester, Hants SO23 8RZ
Mailing Address: PO Box 6109, Harare, Zimbabwe
Tel: (04) 726795 *Fax:* (04) 726796
E-mail: info@africafilmtv.com
Web Site: www.africafilmtv.com
Key Personnel
Publisher & Editor: Russell Honeyman *E-mail:* russell@africafilmtv.com
Sales Dir: Newton Musara *E-mail:* newton@africafilmtv.com
Administration Manager: Martha Musekiwa *E-mail:* martha@africafilmtv.com
Founded: 1986
Publisher of *Africa Film & TV*, quarterly magazine & annual directory.
Subjects: Film, Video, Radio, TV

FX Pax, *imprint of* Funfax Ltd

Fyfield Books, *imprint of* Carcanet Press Ltd

Gaia Books, *imprint of* Octopus Publishing Group

Gaia Books Ltd+
66 Charlotte St, London W1T 4QE
Tel: (020) 7323 4010 *Fax:* (020) 7323 0435
E-mail: info@gaiabooks.com
Web Site: www.gaiabooks.co.uk
Key Personnel
Man Dir: Joss Pearson *E-mail:* jpearson@gaiabooks.com
Rights Dir: Rebecca Thurgur
UK Publisher: Cathy Grieve
Founded: 1982
Specialize in books that celebrate the vision of Gaia, the self-sustaining living Earth & seek to help their readers live in greater personal & planetary harmony; mainly four-color illustrated titles.
Subjects: Architecture & Interior Design, Environmental Studies, Gardening, Plants, Health, Nutrition, Mind, Body & Spirit, Natural Health & Living
ISBN Prefix(es): 1-85675
Number of titles published annually: 12 Print
Total Titles: 110 Print; 5 Audio
Branch Office(s)
20 High St, Stroud, Glos GL5 1AZ, UK Publisher: Lyn Hemming *Tel:* (01453) 752985 *Fax:* (01453) 752987 *E-mail:* addressee@gaiabooks.co.uk
Distributed by Simon & Schuster (USA, Canada, open market excluding Britain & Commonwealth)
Orders to: Grantham Book Services, Alma Park Industrial Estate, Isaac Newton Way, Lincolnshire NG31 9SD, Contact: Marilyn Baines *Tel:* (01476) 541080 *Fax:* (01476) 541061

Gairm Publications
29 Waterloo St, Glasgow G2 6BZ
Tel: (0141) 221 1971 *Fax:* (0141) 221 1971
Key Personnel
Editor: Derick S Thomson
Founded: 1952
Specialize in Scottish Gaelic publications.
Subjects: Biography, Fiction, Music, Dance, Poetry, Regional Interests
ISBN Prefix(es): 1-871901; 0-901771
Total Titles: 120 Print

Galaxy Large Print, *imprint of* BBC Audiobooks

Gale, *imprint of* Thomson Gale

Gale Research, see Thomson Gale

Gallery Children's Books, *imprint of* East-West Publications (UK) Ltd

Galliard, *imprint of* Stainer & Bell Ltd

Garden Art Press Ltd, *imprint of* Antique Collectors' Club Ltd

Garden Art Press Ltd+
Imprint of Antique Collectors' Club Ltd
5A Church St, Woodbridge IP12 1DS
Tel: (01394) 385501 *Fax:* (01394) 384434
Key Personnel
Man Dir: Diana Steel
Subjects: Gardening, Plants
ISBN Prefix(es): 1-870673

Walter H Gardner & Co
16 Chalton Dr, London N2 0QW
Tel: (20) 8458 3202 *Fax:* (20) 8458 8499
E-mail: walterhgardnerco@aol.com
Key Personnel
Man Partner: Walter H Gardner
Sales & Marketing: Mrs D Gardner
Founded: 2001
Also acts as remainder & periodical back issue dealer.

Garland Science, *imprint of* Taylor & Francis

Garnet Publishing Ltd+
8 Southern Court, South St, Reading, Berks RG1 4QS
Tel: (0118) 959 7847 *Fax:* (0118) 959 7356
E-mail: enquiries@garnet-ithaca.demon.co.uk (general enquiries); orders@garnet-ithaca.demon.co.uk (ordering)
Web Site: www.garnet-ithaca.co.uk
Key Personnel
Editorial Manager: Emma Hawker *E-mail:* emmahawker@garnet-ithaca.demon.co.uk
Editor: Anna Hines *E-mail:* annahines@garnet-ithaca.demon.co.uk
Founded: 1991
Subjects: Anthropology, Archaeology, Architecture & Interior Design, Art, Biography, Cookery, English as a Second Language, Foreign Countries, History, Literature, Literary Criticism, Essays, Photography, Religion - Islamic, Travel
ISBN Prefix(es): 1-85964; 1-873938
Total Titles: 300 Print
Imprints: Ithaca Press; South Street Press
Distributed by ISBS (US & Canada)

Gateway Books+
Imprint of Gill & Macmillan
The Hollies, Wellow, Bath BA2 8QJ
Tel: (01225) 835 127 *Fax:* (01225) 840 012
E-mail: sales@gatewaybooks.com

Founded: 1982
Subjects: Anthropology, Earth Sciences, Environmental Studies, Health, Nutrition, Mysteries, Philosophy, Psychology, Psychiatry, Religion - Other, Self-Help
ISBN Prefix(es): 0-946551; 1-85860
U.S. Office(s): Gateway Books at WPR, 2819 Tenth St, Berkeley, CA 94710, United States Tel: 510-841-9347
Distributor for Amethyst Books (Banbury, UK)
Orders to: Airlift Book Co, 8 The Arena, Mollison Ave, Enfield, Middlesex EN3 7NJ Tel: (0181) 8040 400 Fax: (0181) 8040 044

The Gay Men's Press, imprint of GMP Publishers Ltd

Gazelle Books, imprint of Angus Hudson Ltd

GE Fabbri, imprint of Fabbri (GE) Ltd

GE Magazines, imprint of Fabbri (GE) Ltd

Geddes & Grosset+
Subsidiary of D C Thomson & Co Ltd
David Dale House, Rosedale St, New Lanark, Lanark ML11 9DJ
Tel: (01555) 665000 Fax: (01555) 665694
E-mail: info@gandg.sol.co.uk
Key Personnel
Publisher: Ron B Grosset E-mail: ron@gandg.sol.co.uk; Mike Miller E-mail: mike@gandg.sol.co.uk
Founded: 1987
Specializes in popular reference & children's books for the mass market.
Membership(s): Scottish Publishers Association.
ISBN Prefix(es): 1-85534
Number of titles published annually: 80 Print
Imprints: Beano Books; Tarantula Books; Waverley Books
Distributed by Book Source; Peter Haddock Ltd

Geiser Productions+
7 The Corner, Grange Rd, London W5 3PQ
Tel: (020) 8579 4653 Fax: (020) 8567 6593
E-mail: geiser@gxn.co.uk
Web Site: www.geiserproductions.com; www.sidsjournal.com
Key Personnel
Dir & International Rights: N H Geiser
Dir: Sidney DuBroff
Founded: 1967
In-house producers of sponsored & commissioned works, who accept assignments in all areas - whether large or small. Areas of endeavour include serious fiction, politics & country sports.
Membership(s): IPG.
Subjects: Fiction, Government, Political Science, Journalism, Outdoor Recreation, Sports, Athletics
ISBN Prefix(es): 0-9503262

Gembooks
16 Green Park, 91 Manor Rd, East Cliff, Bournemouth BH1 3HR
Tel: (01202) 399729 Fax: (01202) 399729
E-mail: readbooks@onmail.co.uk
Key Personnel
Editor & Author: Peter G Read
Founded: 1995
Specialize in diamond fiction.
Subjects: Criminology, Fiction, Mysteries, Diamond Industry
ISBN Prefix(es): 0-9525315
Total Titles: 3 Print

Genesis Publications Ltd+
2 Jenner Rd, Guildford, Surrey GU1 3PL
Tel: (01483) 540970 Fax: (01483) 304709
E-mail: info@genesis-publications.com
Web Site: www.genesis-publications.com
Key Personnel
Publisher: Brian Roylance
Founded: 1972
Subjects: Art, History, Literature, Literary Criticism, Essays, Natural History, Poetry, Science (General)
ISBN Prefix(es): 0-904351

Geographers' A-Z Map Company Ltd
Fairfield Rd, Borough Green, Sevenoaks, Kent TN15 8PP
Tel: (01732) 781000 Fax: (01732) 780677
E-mail: tradesales@a-zmaps.co.uk
Web Site: www.azmaps.co.uk
Key Personnel
Man Dir: D W Churchill; K Palmer
Founded: 1936
ISBN Prefix(es): 0-85039
Showroom(s): 44 Gray's Inn Rd, London WC1X 8HX Tel: (020) 7440 9500 Fax: (020) 7440 9501 E-mail: shop@a-zmaps.co.uk

The Geographical Association+
160 Solly St, Sheffield S1 4BF
Tel: (0114) 296 0088 Fax: (0114) 296 7176
E-mail: ga@geography.org.uk
Web Site: www.geography.org.uk
Key Personnel
Marketing Manager: Richard Jones
Senior Administrator: Frances Soar
Founded: 1893
National association for geography teachers with a membership of over 10,000.
Also book packager.
Subjects: Geography, Geology
ISBN Prefix(es): 0-900395; 0-948512; 1-899085; 1-905448
Number of titles published annually: 25 Print
Total Titles: 120 Print
Branch Office(s)
Bedfordshire Branch, Contact: Mr David Cooper Tel: (01536) 710226
Berkhamstead Branch
Birmingham Branch, Contact: Julia Legg Tel: (0114) 2960088
Blackpool & District Branch, Blackpool Sixth Form College, Blackpool Old Road, Highfurlong, Blackpool, Contact: Joan M Clarke Tel: (01253) 761330
Bradford Branch, Contact: Mr D E Cotton
Brighton & District Branch, Contact: Julia Legg Tel: (0114) 2960088
Cambridge & District Branch, Contact: Richard Dilley Tel: (01480) 461857
Cardiff Branch, Contact: Julia Legg Tel: (0114) 2960088
Chester, Halton & Warrington Branch, Contact: Elaine Jackson Tel: (01928) 425489
Durham Branch, Contact: Adam Nichols Tel: (0191) 374 7821
Geographical Association Branch Network, President: Alison Bailey Web Site: www.digitalbristol.org/members/ga/
Guildford Branch, Contact: Mr R E J Seymour
Hampshire Branch, Contact: Kim Adams Tel: (01962) 852764 Web Site: www.mcnaughtweb.freeserve.co.uk/hantsga/index.htm
Hereford Branch, Contact: Julia Legg Tel: (0114) 2960088 E-mail: jlegg@geography.org.uk
Hertfordshire GTA Branch
High Weald Branch, Chairman: Peter Goddard Tel: (01580) 764917 Fax: (01580) 764917 E-mail: c.g.@tobermory.demon.co.uk
Huddersfield & Halifax Branch, Contact: Janet Clarkson Tel: (01484) 608599
Hull & District Branch, Contact: Richard Hurrell Tel: (01482) 711688 Fax: (01482) 798991
Isle of Thanet Branch, Chairman: Jan Ingram Tel: (01843) 862845
Kingston-upon-Thames Branch, Contact: Dr Annie Hughes
Leicester Branch, Contact: Malcolm Pollard
Lincoln Branch E-mail: steephill@btinternet.com
Liverpool & District Branch, Contact: David Chambers Tel: (0151) 420 4941 Fax: (0151) 330 3366
Manchester Branch, Contact: Mrs M Blackburn
Norfolk Branch, Contact: Kirsten Remer Web Site: www.norfolkga.org.uk/
North Staffordshire Branch, Alleyne, Stone, Staffordshire ST15 8DT, Honorary Secretary: Robert G Jones Tel: (01785) 354200 Fax: (01785) 354222 E-mail: robertgjones@yahoo.com
Oxford Branch, St Edwards School, Woodstock Road, Oxford OX2 7NN, Contact: Dr G Nagle Tel: (01865) 319231
Plymouth & District Branch, Contact: Miss N S M Paterson Tel: (01752) 668482
Ribblesdale Branch, Contact: Mike Pearson
Tyneside Branch, Inspection & Advisory Service, Education Department, County Hall, Durham DH1 5UJ, Contact: Trevor Hemsley Tel: (0191) 383 4558
Worcester Branch, Contact: Richard Yarwood Web Site: www.worc.ac.uk/departs/envman/worcGA/
York & District Branch, 14 St James' Mount, York YO23 1EL, Secretary: Hilary Arnold Tel: (01904) 655114
Foreign Rep(s): Drake International (Europe, USA)

Geological Society Publishing House
Unit 7, Brassmill Enterprise Centre, Brassmill Lane, Bath BA1 3JN
Tel: (01225) 445046 Fax: (01225) 442836
E-mail: rebecca.toop@geolsoc.org.uk
Web Site: www.geolsoc.org.uk
Key Personnel
Dir, Publishing: Neal Marriott E-mail: neal.marriott@geolsoc.org
Editor: Angharad Hills E-mail: angharad.hills@geolsoc.org.uk
Sales: Dawn Angel E-mail: dawn.angel@geolsoc.org.uk
Founded: 1807
Membership(s): European Federation of Geologists & Association of European Geological Societies.
Subjects: Civil Engineering, Earth Sciences, Geography, Geology, Science (General)
ISBN Prefix(es): 0-903317; 1-897799; 1-86239
Number of titles published annually: 30 Print
Total Titles: 250 Print; 2 CD-ROM
Parent Company: The Geological Society, Burlington House, Piccadilly, London W1J 0BG
Distributed by AAPG (North America)
Distributor for American Association of Petroleum Geologists (European distributor); Geological Society of America (European distributor); Society for Sedimentary Geology (European distributor)
Orders to: AAPG Bookstore, PO Box 979, Tulsa, OK 74101-0979, United States
Affiliated East-West Press PVT Ltd, G-1/16 Ansari Rd, New Delhi 110 002, India, Contact: Sunny Malik Tel: (011) 3279113 Fax: (011) 3260538
Kanda Book Trading Co, Cityhouse Tama 204, Tsurumaki 1-3-10, Tama-Shi, Tokyo 206-0034, Japan Tel: (04) 23577650 Fax: (04) 23577651

George Mann Publications+
8 Birnam Sq, Maidstone ME16 8UN
Tel: (01622) 759591 Fax: (01622) 209193
Web Site: www.gmp.co.uk
Key Personnel
Chairman: George Mann
Man Dir: John Arne
Founded: 1972

Subjects: Astrology, Occult, Biography, Fiction, Human Relations, Nonfiction (General), Philosophy
ISBN Prefix(es): 0-7041
Parent Company: Arnefold Editions
Imprints: Arnefold; George Mann; Recollections

Laura Geringer Books, *imprint of* HarperCollins UK

E J W Gibb Memorial Trust
2 Penarth Pl, Cambridge CB3 9LU
Tel: (01985) 213409 *Fax:* (01985) 212910
Web Site: www.arisandphillips.com
Key Personnel
Secretary to the Trustees: Robin Bligh
Founded: 1902
A charity which supports & publishes books on the literature, religions, philosophy & history of the Persian, Turks & Arab peoples.
Subjects: History, Literature, Literary Criticism, Essays, Philosophy, Religion - Other
ISBN Prefix(es): 0-906094
Orders to: c/o Oxbow Books, Park End Place, Oxford OX1 1HN

Stanley Gibbons Publications
5 Parkside, Christchurch Rd, Ringwood, Hants BH24 3SH
Tel: (01425) 472363 *Fax:* (01425) 470247
E-mail: sales@stangib.demon.co.uk
Web Site: www.stanleygibbons.com
Key Personnel
Dir: Richard Purkis *E-mail:* rpurkis@stanleygibbons.co.uk
Editor: Hugh Jeffries *E-mail:* hjeffries@stanleygibbons.co.uk
General Sales Manager: Brian Case
 E-mail: bcase@stanleygibbons.co.uk
Founded: 1856
Subjects: Crafts, Games, Hobbies, Philately
ISBN Prefix(es): 0-85259
Parent Company: Stanley Gibbons International Ltd, 399 Strand, London WC2R 0LX

Ginn & Company, *imprint of* Reed Educational & Professional Publishing

Ginn & Co Ltd+
PO Box 1127, Freepost (SCE 7554), Oxford OX2 8YY
Tel: (01865) 888000 *Fax:* (01865) 314222
E-mail: enquiries@ginn.co.uk
Web Site: www.ginn.co.uk
Key Personnel
Publishing Dir: Kath Donovan; Rod Theodorou; Stephen Fahey
Man Dir: Paul Shuter *Tel:* (01865) 311366
 E-mail: pshuter@ginn.co.uk
UK Sales Manager: Rachel Colyer *Tel:* (01865) 314096
Founded: 1862 (USA), 1920 (London)
Representation Outside the UK: Argentina: Kel Ediciones SA; Australia: Rigby Heinemann; Botswana, Lesotho & Swaziland: Heinemann Educational Botswana. Botswana; Brazil: Carlos Barbison; Canada: Irwin Publishing; Egypt: Cairo Trade Cuvae; India: Oxford University Press India; Jamaica: Schools Promotion Services; Kenya: Benjamin Kithyaka; New Zealand Reed Publishing (NZ) Ltd; Pakistan: Oxford University Press; Singapore & South East Asia: Susan Chua; South Africa: Heinemann Publishers Ltd; Uganda: Rotash Enterprises; Uruguay: Bookshop SA; Zimbabwe: Textbook Sales (PVT) Ltd; Reed Publishing Group (NZ) Ltd; Transglobal Publishers Service Ltd.
Subjects: Education
ISBN Prefix(es): 0-602

Parent Company: Reed Educational & Professional Publishing
Ultimate Parent Company: Reed Elsevier plc, 25 Victoria St, London SW1H 0EX
Foreign Rep(s): Agius & Agius Ltd (Europe); Basil Bonaparte (Grenada); Book Link Co Ltd (Thailand); Books & Bits (Chile); Brown Onduso (Kenya); Bushbooks (Australia); Cairo Trade Center - Alexandria (Egypt); Cairo Trade Center - Cairo (Egypt); Chris Chirwa (Southern Africa); Susan Chua (Brunei, Singapore, Sri Lanka); Crownbooks (Africa); George Davis (Jamaica); Drum Publishers (Tanzania); Editions de L' Ocean Indien Ltd (Africa); English Book Center (Colombia); Carole Ford (Europe, United Arab Emirates); R Yvonne Gaynes (Caribbean, Grenadines); Harcourt Canada (Canada); Heinemann Inc (USA); Heinemann Botswana (Southern Africa); Carroll Heinemann (Ireland); Heinemann Ed Books (Nigeria) Ltd (Nigeria); Heinemann Lesotho (Southern Africa); Heinemann South Africa (South Africa); Heinemann Southern Africa (Southern Africa); Heinemann Swaziland (Southern Africa); Heinneman UK (UK); Irwin Publishing (Canada); Louise Jacobs (Africa, Far East, Middle East); Jango Heinemann (Southern Africa); Ishmael M Khan & Sons Ltd (Trinadad & Tobago); Rufus Khodra (Caribbean); Mark Kuo (Cambodia, Indonesia, Korea, Latin America, Malaysia, Myanmar, Vietnam); Gerry McCullough (Southern Africa); Nzomo Educational Supplies Ltd (Kenya); Onganda Y' Omambo Bookshop (Southern Africa); Oxford University Press (Pakistan); Publishers Marketing Associates (Pakistan); Adam Quilter (Caribbean, Central & South America, World); R E D I (Africa); Rearden Book Suppliers (Lebanon); Reed Publishing Group (NZ) Ltd (New Zealand); F Reimmer Book Services (Ghana); Rigby Heinemann (Australia); Rorash Educational Publishers (Uganda); S Seshadra (India); Clare Symonette (Caribbean); Transglobal Publishers Service Ltd (Hong Kong); Julie White (Barbados)
Warehouse: Unit 1, Block H, Industrial Estate, Long Eaton, Nottingham NG10 1GG

IL Giornale dell'Arte, see Umberto Allemandi & Co Publishing

Glasgow City Libraries Publications+
The Mitchell Library, North St, Glasgow G3 7DN
Tel: (0141) 287 2846 *Fax:* (0141) 287 2815
Web Site: www.glasgowlibraries.org
Key Personnel
Commercial Manager: Verina Litster
 E-mail: verina.litster@cls.glasgow.gov.uk
Founded: 1980
Specialize in local history fact books.
Membership(s): Scottish Publishers' Association.
Subjects: History, Regional Interests
ISBN Prefix(es): 0-906169
Distribution Center: The Mitchell Library

Mary Glasgow Publications, *imprint of* Nelson Thornes Ltd

Global Oriental Ltd+
PO Box 219, Folkestone, Kent CT18 2WP
Tel: (01303) 226799 *Fax:* (01303) 243087
E-mail: info@globaloriental.co.uk
Web Site: www.globaloriental.co.uk
Key Personnel
Publisher & Man Dir: Paul Norbury
Sales Manager, International Sales-Marketing: Iris Warr
Founded: 1994
Subjects: Art, Biography, Education, Geography, Geology, Health, Nutrition, History, Language Arts, Linguistics, Literature, Literary Criticism, Essays, Religion - Other, Transportation, Travel, Comparative & Cultural Studies, Media & Cultural Studies, Korea-General Reference, Lafcadio Hearn Studies, Martial Arts, Memoirs
ISBN Prefix(es): 1-86034; 1-901903; 1-898823
Number of titles published annually: 12 Print
Total Titles: 52 Print
Imprints: Renaissance Books
Distributed by University of Hawaii Press (USA & Canada)
Foreign Rep(s): APD Singapore (Southeast Asia); Unifacmanu Trading Co (Taiwan); United Publishers Services Ltd (Japan)
Distribution Center: Orca Book Services, Stanley House, 3 Fleets Lane, Poole, Dorset BH15 3AJ *Tel:* (01202) 665432 *Fax:* (01202) 666219
 E-mail: orders@orcabookservices.co.uk
Orders to: Midpoint Trade Books, 1263 Southwest Blvd, Kansas City, KS 66103, United States *Tel:* 913-831-2233 *Fax:* 913-362-7401

Glowworm Books Ltd+
Unit 7, Greendykes Industrial Estate, Broxburn EH52 6PG
Tel: (01506) 857570 *Fax:* (01506) 858100
E-mail: admin@GlowwormBooks.co.uk; sales@amaising.co.uk (packaging); sales@glowwormbooks.co.uk (publishing & schools division)
Web Site: www.GlowwormBooks.co.uk
Key Personnel
Man Dir: Mrs K Allan
Operations Dir: Mr G Allan
Sales Manager: Mrs Marion Farish
Buyer: Annie Crighton
Founded: 1984
Specialize in publishing children's picture books, also a school supplier for text books & libraries (in Scotland only).
Membership(s): Booksellers Association & Scottish Publishers Association.
ISBN Prefix(es): 1-871512
Number of titles published annually: 3 Print
Total Titles: 43 Print

GMC Publications Ltd+
166 High St, Lewes, East Sussex BN7 1XU
Tel: (01273) 477374; (01273) 488005
 Fax: (01273) 478606
E-mail: pubs@thegmcgroup.com; theguild@thegmcgroup.com
Web Site: www.thegmcgroup.com/pubsweb/
Key Personnel
Senior Man Editor, Books: April McCroskie
 Fax: (01273) 487692 *E-mail:* aprilm@thegmcgroup.com
Publish magazines books & videos for general trade.
Subjects: Crafts, Games, Hobbies, Gardening, Plants, How-to, Photography
ISBN Prefix(es): 1-86108
Total Titles: 120 Print
Imprints: Guild of Master Publications Inc
Distributor for Sterling Publishing Co Inc; Taunton Press Publishers
Warehouse: Mail International Ltd, Braybon Business Park, Consort Way, Burgess Hill W Sussex

GMP Publishers Ltd+
99a Wallis Rd, London E9 5LN
Tel: (020) 8986 4854 *Fax:* (020) 8533 5821
E-mail: davidoraubrey@gmpub.demon.co.uk
Web Site: www.gmppubs.co.uk
Key Personnel
Dir, Editorial, Art & Photography: Aubrey Walter
Dir, Editorial, Fiction: David Fernbach
Founded: 1979
gay fiction & nonfiction.
Subjects: Art, Fiction, Gay & Lesbian, History, Nonfiction (General)
ISBN Prefix(es): 0-85449; 0-907040; 0-946097
Associate Companies: Heretic Books Ltd

Imprints: The Gay Men's Press; Editions Aubrey Walter
Distributed by LPC/Inbook (North America)
Orders to: Central Books Ltd, 99 Wallis Rd, London E9 5LN *Tel:* (020) 8986 4854 *Fax:* (020) 8533 5821

Godsfield Press, *imprint of* Octopus Publishing Group

Godsfield Press Ltd+
Division of David & Charles Ltd
Laurel House, Station Approach, Alresford SO24 9JH
Tel: (01962) 735633; (01626) 323200 (general enquiries) *Fax:* (01962) 735320; (01626) 323319 (general enquiries)
E-mail: mail@davidandcharles.co.uk
Web Site: www.davidandcharles.co.uk
Key Personnel
Proprietor: Debbie Thorpe *E-mail:* debbie@godsfield.com
Founded: 1995
Subjects: Health, Nutrition, Esoterics/New Age, Divination, Personal Growth, Sacred Living, Spiritual Wisdom
ISBN Prefix(es): 1-899434; 1-84181
Distributed by David & Charles (United Kingdom & Eire)
Orders to: HarperCollins Distribution Service, Glasgow GA ONB

Golden Cockerel Press Ltd+
16 Barter St, London WC1A 2AH
Tel: (020) 7405 7979 *Fax:* (020) 7404 3598
Telex: 23565
Key Personnel
Man Dir, UK: Andrew Lindesay; Tamar Lindesay *E-mail:* lindesay@btinternet.com
Founded: 1979
Subjects: Architecture & Interior Design, Art, Drama, Theater, Film, Video, Government, Political Science, History, Literature, Literary Criticism, Essays, Music, Dance, Philosophy, Social Sciences, Sociology, Theology
ISBN Prefix(es): 0-8453; 0-8387; 0-8386; 0-934223; 0-941664; 0-87413; 1-900541; 0-918016; 0-498
Associate Companies: Associated University Presses Inc, 440 Forsgate Dr, Cranbury, NJ 08512, United States
Imprints: Associated University Presses (UK, Europe, India, Australia & New Zealand); Cornwall Books; Cygnus Arts
Distributor for Associated University Presses (UK, Europe, India, Australia & New Zealand)
Orders to: Gazelle Book Services, Falcon House, Queen Square, Lancaster LA1 1RN *Tel:* (01524) 68765 *Fax:* (01524) 63232 *E-mail:* gazelle4go@aol.com

Golden Dawn, *imprint of* Mandrake of Oxford

Golden Handshake, *imprint of* Jay Landesman

Goldleaf Publishing (Local History), *imprint of* Alun Books

Victor Gollancz, *imprint of* Cassell & Co

Victor Gollancz Ltd, see Gollancz/Witherby

Gollancz/Witherby+
Orion House, 5 Upper St Martin's Lane, London WC2H 9EA
Tel: (020) 7240 3444 *Fax:* (020) 7240 4822
E-mail: info@orionbooks.co.uk
Web Site: www.orionbooks.co.uk
Telex: 9413701 CASPUB
Key Personnel
Sales Dir: Andrew Macmillan
Rights & Permissions: Jane Blackstock
Publisher: Liz Knights
Production: Elizabeth Dobson
Science Fiction: Richard Evans
Children's: Chris Kloet
Subjects: Architecture & Interior Design, Biography, Fiction, History, Music, Dance, Mysteries, Natural History, Nonfiction (General), Outdoor Recreation, Science (General), Science Fiction, Fantasy, Sports, Athletics, Travel
ISBN Prefix(es): 0-575; 0-85493
Parent Company: Orion Publishing Group

Gomer Press (J D Lewis & Sons Ltd)+
Gwasg Gomer, Llandysul, Ceredigion SA44 4JL
Tel: (01559) 362371 *Fax:* (01559) 363758
E-mail: gwasg@gomer.co.uk
Web Site: www.gomer.co.uk *Cable:* GOMER LLANDYSUL
Key Personnel
Man Dir & Rights & Permissions: Jonathan Lewis
Editorial: Mairwen Prys Jones
Sales & Publicity: Meinir Garnon James
Founded: 1892
Specialize in books from Wales, about Wales, in Welsh & in English.
Subjects: Education, Fiction, Language Arts, Linguistics, Nonfiction (General), Poetry, Regional Interests
ISBN Prefix(es): 0-86383; 0-85088; 1-85902; 1-84323
Number of titles published annually: 100 Print
Total Titles: 700 Print
Parent Company: J D Lewis & Sons Ltd
Imprints: Pont Books
Bookshop(s): Gomerian Press, Llandysul, Dyfed

Goodnight Sleeptight, *imprint of* Grandreams Ltd

A H Gordon
Priory Cottage, Chetwade, Buckingham MK18 4LB
Tel: (01280) 848 650
Key Personnel
President: Adam Gordon *E-mail:* adam@adamgordon.freeewire.co.uk
Founded: 1990
Specialize in Tramways, trolley buses & railways. Publisher of new books & dealer in second hand books & ephemera.
Subjects: Transportation, Buses, Railways, Christian
ISBN Prefix(es): 1-874422
Number of titles published annually: 6 Print
Total Titles: 41 Print

The Robert Gordon University
Garthdee, Aberdeen AB10 7QE
Tel: (01224) 262000 *Fax:* (01224) 263553
E-mail: sim@rgu.ac.uk
Web Site: www.rgu.ac.uk
Key Personnel
Assistant Dean, Aberdeen Business School: Ian M Johnson
Course Leader (Electronic Publishing): Sarah Pedersen
Course Leader (Publishing Studies): Josephine M Royle
Founded: 1967
Subjects: Publishing & Book Trade Education & Training

Gower Publishing Ltd, *imprint of* Ashgate Publishing Ltd

Gower Publishing Ltd+
Imprint of Ashgate Publishing Ltd
Gower House, Croft Rd, Aldershot, Hants GU11 3HR
Tel: (01252) 331551 *Fax:* (01252) 344405
E-mail: info@gowerpub.com
Web Site: www.gowerpub.com
Key Personnel
Man Dir: Christopher Simpson
Sales & Marketing Dir: Rachel Maund
Founded: 1967
Subjects: Business, Management
ISBN Prefix(es): 0-566
Associate Companies: Dartmouth Publishing Ltd
Orders to: Ashgate-Gower Asia Pacific, 3/303 Barrenjoey Rd, Newport, NSW 2107, Australia *Tel:* (02) 9999 2777 *Fax:* (02) 9999 3688 *E-mail:* info@ashgate.com.au (Australia, SE & NE Asia)
Ashgate Publishing Ltd, 2252 Ridge Rd, Brookfield, VT 05036-9704, United States *Tel:* 802-276-3162 *Fax:* 802-276-3837 *E-mail:* info@ashgate.com (North America & South America)
Bookpoint Ltd, Gower Publishing Customer Service, 130 Milton Park, Abingdon, Oxon OX14 4SB *Tel:* (01235) 827730 *Fax:* (01235) 400454 *E-mail:* orders@bookpoint.co.uk/enquiries@bookpoint.co.uk *Web Site:* pubeasy.books.bookpoint.co.uk (UK & Europe)

Gracewing Publishing
2 Southern Ave, Leominster HR6 0QF
Tel: (01568) 616835 *Fax on Demand:* (01568) 613289
E-mail: gracewingx@aol.com
Web Site: www.gracewing.co.uk
Subjects: Religion - Other, Theology, Church Biography, Ecclesiastical History
Distributed by Morehouse (US)
Distributor for Mercer University Press (in UK); Our Sunday Visitor; Smyth & Helwys; Source; Templegate

Graham & Whiteside, *imprint of* Thomson Gale

Graham-Cameron Publishing & Illustration+
The Studio, 23 Holt Rd, Sheringham, Norfolk NR26 8NB
Tel: (01263) 821 333 *Fax:* (01263) 821 334
E-mail: enquiry@graham-cameron-illustration.com
Web Site: www.graham-cameron-illustration.com
Key Personnel
Partner: Helen Graham-Cameron; Mike Graham-Cameron
Marketing Manager: Duncan Graham-Cameron
Founded: 1985 (Founded as a book publisher, became a packager & illustration agency)
Editorial & production assistance. Approximately 37 freelance professional illustrators under contract.
Membership(s): Independent Publishers Guild (IPG), Cambridge Book Association (CBA) & Publishers in Cambridge Association (PICA).
Subjects: Education, English as a Second Language, Language Arts, Linguistics
ISBN Prefix(es): 0-947672

W F Graham (Northampton) Ltd
2 Pondwood Close, Moulton Park Industrial Estate, Northampton, Northamptonshire NN3 6RT
Tel: (01604) 645537 *Fax:* (01604) 648414
Key Personnel
Man Dir: R F Graham
Sales Dir: T A Graham
Founded: 1952
ISBN Prefix(es): 1-85128

Gramophone, *imprint of* Wilmington Business Information Ltd

Granada Media, *imprint of* Carlton Publishing Group

UNITED KINGDOM   BOOK

Grandreams Ltd+
6 Old King St, Bath, Avon BA1 2JW
Tel: (01225) 429383 *Fax:* (01225) 428161
E-mail: wrrake@robert-frederick.co.uk
Key Personnel
Rights Manager: Catherine Lyn-Jones
Production Manager: Josie Strong
Founded: 1977
Specialize in international coeditions & mass market children's books; dictionaries, reference books, foreign language books, novelty books, pop-ups, board books, storybooks, sticker books, coloring books.
Subjects: Fiction, Nonfiction (General)
ISBN Prefix(es): 0-86227
Parent Company: Grandreams Ltd, 435-437 Edgware Rd, Little Venice, London W2 1TN
Imprints: Grandreams USA; Goodnight Sleeptight
Branch Office(s)
435-437 Edgware Rd, London W2 1TH
U.S. Office(s): 8 Arbour Dr, Wayne, NJ, United States

Grandreams USA, *imprint of* Grandreams Ltd

Grange Books PLC+
The Grange, Units 1-6, Kingsnorth Industrial Estate, Hoo, Nr Rochester, Kent ME3 9ND
Tel: (01634) 256 000 *Fax:* (01634) 255 500
E-mail: grangebooks@aol.com
Web Site: www.grangebooks.co.uk
Key Personnel
Marketing Manager: Bob Siwecki
General Sales Support & Coordination: Deborah Duthie *E-mail:* deborah.duthie@grangebooks.co.uk
Sales (North America): Stephen Ash
 E-mail: stephen.ash@grangebooks.co.uk
Sales (UK - Southwest & Ireland): Geoff Bailey
Sales (Australia, New Zealand, Far East, India & South Africa): John Norman *E-mail:* john.norman@grangebooks.co.uk
Sales (UK - Southeast, East Anglia & London): Don Peachey
Sales (Middle East, Central & Eastern Europe, Norway & Baltic States, Spain, Portugal, Central & South America): Bob Siwecki *E-mail:* bob.siwecki@grangebooks.co.uk
Sales (UK - Northern England, Scotland, Sweden, Finland, Denmark, Iceland, Holland & Belgium): Glenn Trueman
Founded: 1972
Discount & promotional book publisher & distributor.
Subjects: Aeronautics, Aviation, Animals, Pets, Architecture & Interior Design, Art, Astronomy, Automotive, Cookery, Crafts, Games, Hobbies, Gardening, Plants, Natural History, Nonfiction (General), Transportation, Travel, Wine & Spirits
ISBN Prefix(es): 1-85627
Imprints: Binky (Childrens); Park Lane (Art)
U.S. Office(s): Book Club of America, 230 Fifth Ave, Suite 1405, New York, NY, United States
Showroom(s): Bermondsey, Nr London Bridge Station *Tel:* (01634) 256 000

Grant & Cutler Ltd
55-57 Great Marlborough St, London W1F 7AY
Tel: (020) 7734 2012 *Fax:* (020) 7734 9272
E-mail: contactus@grantandcutler.com
Web Site: www.grantandcutler.com
Key Personnel
Dir: R C O Howard *Tel:* (020) 7494 3130
Founded: 1935
Specialize in bookselling & library supplies in Western European languages. Also specialize in Critical Guides to French, German, Tamesis texts, research bibliographies & checklists.
Membership(s): Booksellers Association.
Subjects: Foreign Countries, Literature, Literary Criticism, Essays

ISBN Prefix(es): 0-7293; 0-900411
Number of titles published annually: 10 Print
Total Titles: 270 Print

Granta Books+
2/3 Hanover Yard, Noel Rd, London N1 8BE
Tel: (020) 7704 9776 *Fax:* (020) 7704 0474
E-mail: info@granta.com
Web Site: www.granta.com
Key Personnel
Editor: Ian Jack *E-mail:* ijack@granta.com
Deputy Editor: Shophie Harrison
 E-mail: sharrison@granta.com
Associate Editor: Liz Jobey *E-mail:* ljobey@granta.com
Managing Editor: Fatema Ahmed
 E-mail: fahmed@granta.com
Sales Dir: Frances Hollingdale
 E-mail: fhollingdale@granta.com
Publicity: Louise Campbell *E-mail:* lcampbell@granta.com
Subjects: Biography, Fiction, History, Literature, Literary Criticism, Essays, Nonfiction (General), Travel
ISBN Prefix(es): 1-86207
Parent Company: Granta Publications
Imprints: Granta Magazine
U.S. Office(s): Granta US, 1755 Broadway, 5th floor, New York, NY 10019, United States
Distributed by Allen & Unwin (Australia & New Zealand); Penguin Books (India); Raincoast (Canada)
Foreign Rep(s): Allen & Unwin Pty Ltd (Australia); Jonathan Ball/Harper Collins (South Africa); Michael Geoghegan (Austria, Belgium, France, Germany, Switzerland); I M A (Africa, Caribbean, Central & South America, Cyprus, Eastern Europe, Middle East, Turkey); Adam Murray (England, Scotland); Nilsson & Lamm (Netherlands); Penny Padovani (Gibraltar, Greece, Italy, Portugal, Slovenia, Spain); Penguin Books India (Bangladesh, India, Nepal, Pakistan, Sri Lanka); Raincoast Books (Canada); Repforce Ireland (Ireland); Hanne Rotovnik (Scandinavia); Roger Ward (Far East)
Warehouse: Macmillan Distribution Ltd, Houndmills Basingstroke, Hants RG21 6XS
Distribution Center: Macmillan Distribution Ltd, Houndmills Basingstroke, Hants RG21 6XS
Tel: (01256) 302692 *Fax:* (01256) 812521
E-mail: mdl@macmillan.co.uk

Granta Magazine, *imprint of* Granta Books

The Greek Bookshop+
57a Nether St, North Finchley, London N12 7NP
Mailing Address: PO Box 29283, London NI3 5BJ
Tel: (020) 8446 1986 *Fax:* (020) 8446 1985
E-mail: info@thegreekbookshop.com
Web Site: www.thegreekbookshop.com
Key Personnel
Partner: Loui D Loizou
 E-mail: zenobooksellers@aol.com; Maria Loizou
Founded: 1944
Publish books in Greek & English about Greece & Cyprus. Specialize in books about Byzantium, Modern History of Greece & Cyprus.
Subjects: Archaeology, Art, Cookery, History, Literature, Literary Criticism, Essays, Philosophy, Poetry, Romance, Travel
ISBN Prefix(es): 0-900834; 0-7228; 0-9521246
Total Titles: 25 Print
Subsidiaries: Loizou Publications

Green Books Ltd+
Foxhole, Dartington, Totnes, Devon TQ9 6EB
Tel: (01803) 863260 *Fax:* (01803) 863843
E-mail: greenbooks@gn.apc.org
Web Site: www.greenbooks.co.uk

Key Personnel
Chairman: Satish Kumar
Publisher (Editorial, Production, Rights): John Elford
Sales & Marketing Manager: Paul Rossiter
Founded: 1987
Subjects: Agriculture, Economics, Environmental Studies, How-to, Philosophy, Self-Help, Ecological, Spiritual & Cultural Issues
ISBN Prefix(es): 1-870098; 1-900322; 0-9527302; 1-903998
Associate Companies: Resurgence Magazine
Imprints: Green Earth Books; Resurgence Books; Themis Books
Distributed by Banyan Tree Book Distributors (Australia); Ceres Books
Distributor for Chelsea Green Publishing Co (UK)
Distribution Center: Alton Logistics Ltd, Unit 4, Battle Rd, Heathfield, Newton Abbot, Devon TQ12 6RY *Tel:* (01626) 832225 *Fax:* (01626) 832398 (UK & Ireland)
Chelsea Green Publishing, Main St, White River Junction, VT 05001, United States *Tel:* 802-295-6300 *Fax:* 802-295-6444 (USA)

Green Earth Books, *imprint of* Green Books Ltd

Green Print, *imprint of* The Merlin Press Ltd

W Green, *imprint of* Sweet & Maxwell Ltd

W Green The Scottish Law Publisher+
21 Alva St, Edinburgh EH2 4PS
Tel: (0131) 225 4879 (orders); (0131) 225 4879 (marketing); (0207) 449 1104 (trade customers); (264) 342 828 (international book orders & information); (264) 342 766 (international subscription orders & information) *Fax:* (0131) 225 2104 (orders); (0131) 225 2104 (marketing); (0207) 449 1144 (trade customers); (264) 342 761 (international book orders & information); (264) 342 761 (international subscription orders & information)
E-mail: enquiries@thomson.com; trade.sales@sweetandmaxwell.co.uk (trade customers)
Web Site: www.wgreen.co.uk
Key Personnel
Marketing Manager: Mdme Jane Scott
Publisher: Miss Jill Barrington
Dir: Gilly Michie
Man Editor: Stephen Chubb
Marketing Executive: Lyn Minay *E-mail:* lyn.minay@wgreen.co.uk
Subjects: Law
ISBN Prefix(es): 0-414
Total Titles: 140 Print; 1 CD-ROM
Ultimate Parent Company: The Thomson Corporation, Suite 2706, Toronto Dominion Bank Tower, PO Box 24, Toronto Dominion Centre, Toronto, ON M5K 1A1, Canada
Sales Office(s): Contact: Vicki McGee
 Tel: (01578) 730780 *Fax:* (01578) 730780
 E-mail: vicki.mcgee@sweetandmaxwell.co.uk (customers in the Lothian, Tayside, Borders, Grampian & Fife areas; that is, postcoded areas: AB/DD/EH/KY/TD)
Contact: Stephen Wilson *Tel:* (01698) 320286 *Fax:* (01698) 320286 *E-mail:* stephen.wilson@sweetandmaxwell.co.uk (customers in the Central, Strathclyde, Dumfries & Galloway, Northern & Western Isles & Highlands & Islands areas; that is, postcoded areas: DG/G/HS/IV/KW/FK/KA/ML/PA/PH/ZE)
Foreign Rep(s): Barbara Gerken (Scotland)
Warehouse: W. Green - ITPS, Cheriton House, North Way, Andover Hants SP10 5BE
Orders to: W Green, 100 Ave Rd, Swiss Cottage, London NW3 3PF *Tel:* (020) 7449 1111 *Fax:* (020) 7449 1155 (customer service)

Greenhaven Press, *imprint of* Thomson Gale

PUBLISHERS UNITED KINGDOM

Greenhill Books/Lionel Leventhal Ltd+
Park House, One Russell Gardens, London NW11 9NN
Tel: (020) 8458 6314 *Fax:* (020) 8905 5245
E-mail: info@greenhillbooks.com; sales@greenhillbooks.com
Web Site: www.greenhillbooks.com
Key Personnel
Chief Executive, Man Dir: Lionel Leventhal
Sales Dir: Mark Wray *E-mail:* mark.wray@greenhillbooks.com
Founded: 1984
Also acts as international distribution agent for Presidio Press, Novato, CA; Stackpole Books, Mechanicsburg, PA; Proctor Jones Publishing, San Francisco, CA; Emperor's Press, Chicago, IL; Concord, Hong Kong; Casemate Publishing, Havertown, PA; RZM Imports, Southbury, CT; Medals of America, Fountain Inn, SC; Countrysport Press, Camden, ME.
Subjects: Aeronautics, Aviation, Automotive, History, Maritime, Military Science, Transportation, Military history
ISBN Prefix(es): 0-947898; 1-85367
Number of titles published annually: 30 Print
Total Titles: 200 Print
Parent Company: Lionel Leventhal Ltd
Distributed by Peribo Pty Ltd (Australia); Publishers Marketing Services Pte Ltd (Malaysia & Singapore); South Pacific Books (New Zealand); Stackpole Books (US); Vanwell Publishing Ltd (Canada)

Greenwich Editions, *imprint of* Ramboro Books Plc

Greenwillow Books, *imprint of* HarperCollins UK

Greenwood Heinemann, *imprint of* Reed Educational & Professional Publishing

Gregg International, *imprint of* Gregg Publishing Co

Gregg Revivals, *imprint of* Gregg Publishing Co

Gregg Publishing Co
The Old Hospital Ardingly Rd, Chapelfields, Cuckfield, Haywards Heath RH17 5JR
Tel: (01444) 445070 *Fax:* (01444) 445050
E-mail: Rdowling@gowerpub.com
Key Personnel
Contact: Tracy Daborn
Founded: 1960
Subjects: Social Sciences, Sociology
ISBN Prefix(es): 0-576; 0-86127
Associate Companies: Ashgate Publishing Group
Imprints: Gregg International; Gregg Revivals
Orders to: Ashgate Distribution Services, Unit 3, Lower Farnham Rd, Aldershot, Hants GU12 4DL

Gresham Books, *imprint of* Woodhead Publishing Ltd

Gresham Books Ltd+
46 Victoria Rd, Summertown, Oxford OX2 7QD
Tel: (01865) 513582 *Fax:* (01865) 512718
E-mail: info@gresham-books.co.uk
Web Site: www.gresham-books.co.uk
Key Personnel
Dir: M L Lewis; P A Lewis
Founded: 1979
Specialize in hymnals, prayer books & school histories.
Subjects: History, Music, Dance, Religion - Catholic, Religion - Protestant, Local History
ISBN Prefix(es): 0-905418; 0-946095; 0-9502121
Number of titles published annually: 30 Print
Total Titles: 260 Print

Griffith Institute, *imprint of* Ashmolean Museum Publications

Grub Street+
The Basement, 10 Chivalry Rd, London SW11 1HT
Tel: (020) 7924 3966; (020) 7738 1008
Fax: (020) 7738 1009
E-mail: post@grubstreet.co.uk
Web Site: www.grubstreet.co.uk
Key Personnel
Chief Executive & Rights & Permissions: John Davies *E-mail:* john@grubstreet.com.uk
Chief Executive: Anne Dolamore
Founded: 1986
Subjects: Cookery, Health, Nutrition, Nonfiction (General), Wine & Spirits, Military History/Aviation
ISBN Prefix(es): 0-948817; 1-898697; 1-902304
Number of titles published annually: 30 Print
Total Titles: 140 Print
Foreign Rep(s): Capricorn Link Pty Ltd (Australia); Forrester Books (New Zealand); Peter Hyde Associates (South Africa); Seven Hills Book Distributors (USA); Vanwell Publishing (Canada)
Warehouse: Littlehampton Book Service (LBS), Faraday Close, Durrington, Worlting, West Sussex BN13 3RB

Guardian Books, *imprint of* Fourth Estate

Guild of Master Publications Inc, *imprint of* GMC Publications Ltd

Guinness World Records Ltd
Division of Guinness Media Inc
338 Euston Rd, London NW1 3BD
Tel: (020) 7891 4567 *Fax:* (020) 7891 4501
Cable: MOSTEST ENFIELD
Key Personnel
Man Dir: Christopher Irwin
Sales Dir: Fred Buxton
Sales & Marketing Dir: Malcolm Roughead
National Sales Manager: Shaun Elder
Founded: 1954
Subjects: Military Science, Music, Dance, Sports, Athletics
ISBN Prefix(es): 0-900424; 0-85112; 1-892051
Parent Company: Diageo plc, 8 Henrietta Pl, London W1G 0NB
Warehouse: Macmillan Distribution, Unit 8, Lye Industrial Estate, Pontardulais, Swansea SA4 1QD

Gulf Professional Press, *imprint of* Elsevier Ltd

Gunsmoke Western, *imprint of* BBC Audiobooks

Gwasg Carreg Gwalch+
12 Iard Yr Orsaf, Llanrwst, Conwy LL26 0EH
Tel: (01492) 642 031 *Fax:* (01492) 641 502
E-mail: llyfrau@carreg-gwalch.co.uk
Web Site: www.carreg-gwalch.co.uk
Key Personnel
Dir: Myrddin ap Dafydd *E-mail:* myrddin@carreg-gwalch.co.uk
Founded: 1980
Privately owned publisher & printing company.
Subjects: Welsh & Celtic Interest, Welsh Language
ISBN Prefix(es): 0-86381
Number of titles published annually: 70 Print
Total Titles: 1,000 Print
Branch Office(s)
Ysgubor Plas, Llwyndyrys, Pwllheli, Gwynedd LL53 6NG *Tel:* (01758) 750440

Gwasg Gwenffrwd+
Hendre Bach, Cerrigydrudion, Corwen, Clwyd LL21 9TB
Tel: (01490) 420 560; (0845) 330 6754
Key Personnel
Man Dir: Dr Goronwy Alun Hughes
Founded: 1947
Specialize in Pacific Islands, Oceanic Languages & Wales.
Membership(s): BLDSC (ASTIC Research Associates).
Subjects: Anthropology, Biography, Foreign Countries, Genealogy, History, Language Arts, Linguistics, Poetry, Regional Interests, Oceanic Languages, Pacific Islands, Wales
ISBN Prefix(es): 0-9501861; 1-85651
Number of titles published annually: 6 Print
Total Titles: 50 Print
Imprints: Astic; Bronant Books; A & Z Hughes; Translations Wales

Gwasg y Dref Wen+
28 Church Rd, Yr Eglwys Newydd, Cardiff CF4 2EA
Tel: (01222) 617860 *Fax:* (01222) 610507
E-mail: gwil-drefwen@btinternet.com
Key Personnel
Man Dir, Editorial: Roger Boore
Publicity, Sales: Gwilym Boore
Founded: 1970
Welsh-language publishers.
Membership(s): Union of Welsh Publishers & Booksellers.
ISBN Prefix(es): 0-946962; 0-904910; 1-85596
Number of titles published annually: 50 Print; 4 Audio
Total Titles: 450 Print; 15 Audio
Imprints: Dref Wen

Peter Haddock Ltd+
Industrial Estate, Pinfold Lane, Bridlington, East Yorks YO16 6BT
Tel: (01262) 678121 *Fax:* (01262) 400043
E-mail: enquiries@peterhaddock.com
Web Site: www.phpublishing.co.uk
Key Personnel
Man Dir: Peter Haddock
Sales Manager: David Haddock
Founded: 1952
ISBN Prefix(es): 0-7105
Imprints: Big Time

Hakluyt Society
c/o Map Library, British Library, 96 Euston Rd, London NW1 2DB
Tel: (01428) 641850 *Fax:* (01428) 641933
E-mail: office@hakluyt.com
Web Site: www.hakluyt.com
Key Personnel
Administrator: Richard Bateman
Founded: 1846
A registered charity inspired by & named after Richard Hakluyt (1552-1616), the famous collector & editor of narratives of voyages & travels & other documents relating to English interests overseas.
Subjects: Geography, Geology, History, Travel
ISBN Prefix(es): 0-904180
Number of titles published annually: 2 Print
Total Titles: 55 Print
Distributed by Ashgate Publishing Direct Sales

Peter Halban Publishers Ltd+
22 Golden Sq, London W1F 9JW
Tel: (020) 7437 9300 *Fax:* (020) 7431 9512
E-mail: books@halbanpublishers.com
Web Site: www.halbanpublishers.com
Key Personnel
Man Dir: Martine Halban; Peter Halban
Founded: 1986
Membership(s): Independent Publishers Guild.
Subjects: Biography, Fiction, History, Philosophy, Religion - Other

703

UNITED KINGDOM

ISBN Prefix(es): 1-870015
Number of titles published annually: 10 Print
Total Titles: 60 Print
Foreign Rep(s): Orion (Export Sales Dept)
Shipping Address: Littlehampton Book Services, Faraday Close, Durrington, Worthing, West Sussex BN13 3RB, Contact: Tim Kinghorn *Tel:* (01903) 828800 *Fax:* (01903) 828801 *E-mail:* info@lbsltd.co.uk *Web Site:* www.lbsltd.co.uk
Warehouse: Littlehampton Book Services, Faraday Close, Durrington, Worthing, West Sussex BN13 3RB, Contact: Tim Kinghorn *Tel:* (01903) 828800 *Fax:* (01903) 828801 *E-mail:* info@lbsltd.co.uk *Web Site:* www.lbsltd.co.uk
Distribution Center: Littlehampton Book Services
Orders to: Littlehampton Book Services, Faraday Close, Durrington, Worthing, West Sussex BN13 3RB, Contact: Rose Mellish *Tel:* (01903) 828800 *Fax:* (01903) 828801 *E-mail:* info@lbsltd.co.uk *Web Site:* www.lbsltd.co.uk

Haldane Mason Ltd+
59 Chepstow Rd, London W2 5BP
Tel: (020) 8459 2131 *Fax:* (020) 8728 1216
E-mail: haldane.mason@dial.pipex.com
Subjects: Cookery, Health, Nutrition, Sports, Athletics, Lifestyle, New Age

Robert Hale Ltd+
Clerkenwell House, 45-47 Clerkenwell Green, London EC1R 0HT
Tel: (020) 7251 2661 *Fax:* (020) 7490 4958
E-mail: enquire@halebooks.com
Web Site: www.halebooks.com
Key Personnel
Man Dir & Senior Editor: John Hale
Marketing Dir: Martin Kendall
Rights & Permissions Manager: Florence Pinard
Production Dir: Robert Hale
Founded: 1936
Subjects: Art, Biography, Cookery, Fiction, Geography, Geology, History, How-to, Music, Dance, Philosophy, Poetry, Sports, Athletics, Women's Studies
ISBN Prefix(es): 0-85131; 0-7198; 0-7090; 0-7091
Imprints: J A Allen; Horse Books; NAG Press
Distributor for Aperture; International Jewelry; Phoenix
Warehouse: Combined Book Services, Units 1/K, Paddock Wood Distribution Centre, Paddock Wood, Tonbridge, Kent TN12 6UU

GK Hall & Co, *imprint of* Thomson Gale

Halldale Publishing & Media Ltd
84 Alexandra Rd, Farnborough, Hants GU14 6DD
Tel: (01252) 532000 *Fax:* (01252) 512714
Web Site: www.halldale.com
Key Personnel
Publisher: Andrew Smith *E-mail:* andy@halldale.com
General Manager: Janet Llewellyn
Business Manager: Stephen Marston *E-mail:* steve@halldale.com
Founded: 1993
Subjects: Aeronautics, Aviation, Maritime
U.S. Office(s): 301 E Pine St, Suite 150, Orlando, FL 32801, United States *Tel:* 407-835-3628

Halsted Press, *imprint of* Wiley Europe Ltd

Hambledon & London Ltd+
102 Gloucester Ave, London NW1 8HX
Tel: (020) 7586 0817 *Fax:* (020) 7586 9970
E-mail: office@hambledon.co.uk
Web Site: www.hambledon.co.uk
Key Personnel
Man Dir: Martin Sheppard *E-mail:* ms@hambledon.co.uk
Commissioning Editor: Tony Morris *Tel:* (020) 7482 2333 *E-mail:* ajm@hambledon.co.uk
Founded: 1981
Subjects: History
ISBN Prefix(es): 0-907628; 1-85285; 0-9506882
Number of titles published annually: 24 Print
Total Titles: 200 Print
Sales Office(s): Yale University Press, 23 Pond St, London NW3 2PN *Tel:* (020) 7431 4422 *Fax:* (020) 7431 3755 (UK)
Foreign Rep(s): Michael Geoghegay (Austria, Netherlands, Germany, Switzerland); Andrew Russell (Ireland)
Distribution Center: Hoddle, Doyle & Meadows, Station Rd, Linton, Cambs CB1 6UX *Tel:* (1223) 893855 *Fax:* (1223) 893852
Palgrave Macmillan, 175 Fifth Ave, New York, NY 10010, United States *Web Site:* www.palgrave-usa.com

Hamish Hamilton, *imprint of* Penguin Books Ltd

Hamish Hamilton, *imprint of* The Penguin Group UK

Hamish Hamilton Ltd+
80 Strand, London WCR 0RL
Tel: (020) 7010 3000 *Fax:* (020) 7010 6060
E-mail: customer.service@penguin.co.uk
Web Site: www.penguin.co.uk
Telex: 917181; 2
Key Personnel
Publisher: Simon Prosser
Export Sales: Max Adam *E-mail:* max.adam@penguin.co.uk
Founded: 1931
Subjects: Art, Biography, Fiction, History, Music, Dance
ISBN Prefix(es): 0-14
Parent Company: Penguin Books Ltd
Subsidiaries: Elm Tree Books Ltd; Hamish Hamilton Children's Books Ltd
Shipping Address: Bath Road, Harmondsworth, West Dayton, Middlesex UB7 0DA
Warehouse: Bath Road, Harmondsworth, West Dayton, Middlesex UB7 0DA

Hamlyn, *imprint of* Octopus Publishing Group

Hamlyn+
Imprint of Octopus Publishing Group
2-4 Heron Quays, London E14 4JP
Tel: (020) 7531 8400 *Fax:* (020) 7531 8650
Web Site: www.hamlyn.co.uk
Key Personnel
Publisher & Man Dir: Alison Goff *Tel:* (020) 7531 8410 *Fax:* (020) 7531 8562 *E-mail:* alison.goff@hamlyn.co.uk
Sales & Marketing Dir: David Inman *Tel:* (020) 7531 8573 *Fax:* (020) 7537 0514 *E-mail:* david.inman@hamlyn.co.uk
Publicity & Marketing Manager: Sue Bobbermein *Tel:* (020) 7531 8584 *Fax:* (020) 7537 0514 *E-mail:* sue.bobbermein@hamlyn.co.uk
Export Sales Manager: Caroline Babler *Tel:* (020) 7531 8574 *Fax:* (020) 7537 0514 *E-mail:* caroline.babler@hamlyn.co.uk
Foreign Rights Manager - France, Spain, Portugal & Italy: John Saunders-Griffiths *Tel:* (020) 7531 8586 *E-mail:* john.saunders-griffiths@hamlyn.co.uk
Area Rights Manager - Scandinavia: Sarah French *Tel:* (020) 7531 8587 *E-mail:* sarah.french@hamlyn.co.uk
Area Rights Manager - Germany, Holland, Greece, South Africa: Roly Allen *Tel:* (020) 7531 8576 *E-mail:* roly.allen@hamlyn.co.uk
Foreign Rights Executive - Central & Eastern Europe & Finland: Daniel Bouquet *Tel:* (020) 7531 8575 *E-mail:* daniel.bouquet@hamlyn.co.uk
North American Rights Manager: Nicole Stephens *Tel:* (020) 7531 8577 *Fax:* (020) 7537 0514 *E-mail:* nicole.stephens@hamlyn.co.uk
UK Sales Dir: Kevin Hawkins *Tel:* (020) 7531 8582; (0780) 129 2031 *Fax:* (020) 7537 0514 *E-mail:* kevin.hawkins@hamlyn.co.uk
Special Sales Manager: Rebecca Collold *Tel:* (020) 7531 8585 *E-mail:* rebecca.collold@hamlyn.co.uk
Premium Sales Executive: Stuart Airley *Tel:* (020) 7531 8580 *E-mail:* stuart.airley@hamlyn.co.uk
Founded: 1947
International publisher of high quality illustrated, nonfiction for the general market.
Subjects: Architecture & Interior Design, Cookery, Crafts, Games, Hobbies, Fashion, Film, Video, Gardening, Plants, Health, Nutrition, History, Music, Dance, Natural History, Nonfiction (General), Sports, Athletics
ISBN Prefix(es): 0-600; 0-601
Distribution Center: Little Hampton Book Services Ltd, Faraday Close, Durrington, Worthin, West Sussex BN13 3RB *Tel:* (01903) 825 500 *Fax:* (01903) 828 625

Handbag Books, *imprint of* Kenneth Mason Publications Ltd

The Handsel Press+
62 Toll Rd, Kincardine, by Alloa FK10 4QZ
Tel: (01202) 665432 *Fax:* (01202) 666219
E-mail: handsel@dial.pipex.com
Web Site: www.handselpress.co.uk
Key Personnel
Chairman: David F Wright
Editor: Rev Jock Stein *Tel:* (01236) 723204
Founded: 1976
Subjects: Theology
ISBN Prefix(es): 0-905312; 1-871828
Distributed by Orca Book Services
Orders to: Scottish Book Source, 137 Dundee St, Edinburgh EH11 2QU *Tel:* (0131) 229 6800 *Fax:* (0131) 229 9070

Hans Zell Bibliographies, *imprint of* James Currey Ltd

Happy Cat Books Ltd+
Fieldfares Mill Lane, Bradfield, Manningtree CO11 2UT
Tel: (01255) 870902 *Fax:* (01255) 870902
E-mail: mcwest@happycat.co.uk
Key Personnel
Man Dir: Martin C West *E-mail:* mcwest@happycat.co.uk
Founded: 1994
Publishing of board & picture books for ages under 6, fiction for 7-9 years.
ISBN Prefix(es): 1-899248; 1-903285
Number of titles published annually: 16 Print
Total Titles: 55 Print
Distributed by Star Bright Books (Distribution in USA only)
Orders to: Macmillan Distribution Ltd, Houndmills, Basingstoke, Hampshire RG21 6X6 *Tel:* (01256) 302692 *Fax:* (01256) 812558

Harcourt Publishers Ltd, *imprint of* Elsevier Ltd

Harden's Ltd
14 Buckingham St, London WC2N 6DF
Tel: (020) 7839 4763 *Fax:* (020) 7839 7561
E-mail: mail@hardens.com
Web Site: www.hardens.com
Key Personnel
Dir: Peter Harden; Richard Harden
Founded: 1991

PUBLISHERS UNITED KINGDOM

Publish consumer guides, restaurant guides in particular. Specialize in corporate gift editions.
Subjects: Foreign Countries, Travel
ISBN Prefix(es): 1-873721
Number of titles published annually: 5 Print; 2 E-Book
Total Titles: 10 Print; 2 E-Book
Membership(s): IPG

Patrick Hardy Books, *imprint of* James Clarke & Co Ltd

Patrick Hardy Books, *imprint of* The Lutterworth Press

Patrick Hardy Books+
Imprint of James Clarke & Co Ltd
PO Box 60, Cambridge CB1 2NT
Tel: (01223) 350865 *Fax:* (01223) 366951
E-mail: sales@lutterworth.com; publishing@lutterworth.com
Web Site: www.lutterworth.com
Key Personnel
Man Dir: Adrian Brink
Subjects: Fiction, Nonfiction (General), Religion - Other
ISBN Prefix(es): 0-7444
Distributed by Parkwest Publications Inc

Harley Books+
Martins, Great Horkesley, Colchester, Essex C06 4AH
Tel: (01206) 271216 *Fax:* (01206) 271182
E-mail: harley@keme.co.uk
Web Site: www.harleybooks.com
Key Personnel
Dir: Annette Harley
Founded: 1983
Specialize in natural history, especially entomology & botany.
Subjects: Biological Sciences, Environmental Studies, Natural History
ISBN Prefix(es): 0-946589
Number of titles published annually: 3 Print
Total Titles: 7 Print
Parent Company: BH & A Harley Ltd
Membership(s): IPG

HarperAudio, *imprint of* HarperCollins UK

HarperBusiness, *imprint of* HarperCollins UK

HarperCollins, *imprint of* HarperCollins UK

HarperCollins Children's Books, *imprint of* HarperCollins UK

HarperCollins UK+
Subsidiary of News Corporation
77-85 Fulham Palace Rd, Hammersmith, London W6 8JB
Tel: (020) 8741 7070 *Toll Free Tel:* (0870) 900 2050 (customer service) *Fax:* (020) 8307 4813 *Toll Free Fax:* (0141) 306 3767 (customer service)
E-mail: contact@harpercollins.co.uk
Web Site: www.harpercollins.co.uk
Key Personnel
Chief Executive Officer & Publisher: Victoria Barnsley
Chief Operating Officer: John Baillie
Man Dir, General Books: Amanda Ridout
Man Dir, Collins: Thomas Webster
Founded: 1819
Membership(s): Publishers Association.
Subjects: Animals, Pets, Anthropology, Art, Astrology, Occult, Behavioral Sciences, Biblical Studies, Biography, Business, Child Care & Development, Cookery, Crafts, Games, Hobbies, English as a Second Language, Fiction, Film, Video, Finance, Foreign Countries, Gardening, Plants, Gay & Lesbian, Government, Political Science, Health, Nutrition, History, House & Home, How-to, Human Relations, Literature, Literary Criticism, Essays, Management, Mysteries, Natural History, Nonfiction (General), Outdoor Recreation, Philosophy, Psychology, Psychiatry, Romance, Science Fiction, Fantasy, Self-Help, Sports, Athletics, Theology, Travel, Wine & Spirits, Women's Studies
ISBN Prefix(es): 0-00; 0-01; 0-246; 0-261; 0-586
Parent Company: HarperCollins
Imprints: Access Press; Amistad; Avon; Joanna Cotler Books; Ecco; Eos; Laura Geringer Books; Greenwillow Books; HarperAudio; HarperBusiness; HarperCollins; HarperCollins Children's Books; HarperEntertainment; HarperFestival; HarperLargePrint; HarperResource; HarperSanFrancisco; HarperTorch; HarperTrophy; William Morrow; Perennial; PerfectBound; Quill; Rayo; ReganBooks; Tempest
U.S. Office(s): 10 East 53 St, New York, NY 10022, United States *Tel:* (212) 207-7000
Warehouse: Westerhill Rd, Bishopbriggs, Glasgow G64 2QT *Tel:* (041) 7723200
Orders to: PO Box, Glasgow G4 0NB *Tel:* (0141) 7723200

HarperEntertainment, *imprint of* HarperCollins UK

HarperFestival, *imprint of* HarperCollins UK

HarperLargePrint, *imprint of* HarperCollins UK

HarperResource, *imprint of* HarperCollins UK

HarperSanFrancisco, *imprint of* HarperCollins UK

HarperTorch, *imprint of* HarperCollins UK

HarperTrophy, *imprint of* HarperCollins UK

Hart Advertising Charity Agency, *imprint of* Hymns Ancient & Modern Ltd

Hart Publishing
Salter's Boatyard, Folly Bridge, Abingdon Rd, Oxford OX1 4LB
Tel: (01865) 245533 *Fax:* (01865) 794882
E-mail: mail@hartpub.co.uk
Web Site: www.hartpub.co.uk; www.hartpublishingusa.com
Key Personnel
Man Dir: Richard Hart *E-mail:* richard@hartpub.co.uk
Sales & Marketing Dir: Jane Parker *E-mail:* jane@hartpub.co.uk
Customer Services Manager: Joanne Ledger *E-mail:* jo@hartpub.co.uk
Editorial & Production Manager: April Boffin *E-mail:* april@hartpub.co.uk
Finance Manager: Liam Barrett *E-mail:* liam@hartpub.co.uk
Journals Manager: Barbara Darling *E-mail:* barbara@hartpub.co.uk
Founded: 1996
Subjects: Law
Number of titles published annually: 60 Print
Distributed by Academic Marketing Services (Pty) Ltd (South Africa); Aditya Books Private Ltd (India); Roger Bayliss (Trade Representation (UK) - London, South East, South West, Scotland); Codasat Canada - University of Toronto Press Distribution (Canada); Charles Gibbes (Italy & France); International Specialized Book Services (North America); Intersentia Uitgevers NV (Benelux); IP Communications Pty Ltd (Australia & New Zealand); J & L Watt Publishing Consultants (Arab Middle East, Eastern Mediterranean & North Africa); Kay (Kaoru) Kato (Japan); STM Publisher Services Pte Ltd (China, Hong Kong, Korea, Philippines, Singapore, Taiwan, Thailand, Vietnam); UBS Books (New Zealand)
Foreign Rep(s): Colin Flint (Scandinavia); Iberian Book Services (Spain & Portugal)

Harvard University Press+
Fitzroy House, 11 Chenies St, London WC1E 7EY
Tel: (020) 7306 0603 *Fax:* (020) 7306 0604
E-mail: info@hup-mitpress.co.uk
Web Site: www.hup.harvard.edu
Key Personnel
General Manager: Ann Sexsmith
Publicity Manager: Lisa Jolliffe
Founded: 1913
Subjects: Anthropology, Asian Studies, Behavioral Sciences, Biological Sciences, Business, Earth Sciences, Economics, Education, Film, Video, Government, Political Science, History, Law, Literature, Literary Criticism, Essays, Medicine, Nursing, Dentistry, Natural History, Nonfiction (General), Philosophy, Psychology, Psychiatry, Religion - Jewish, Science (General), Social Sciences, Sociology, Women's Studies
ISBN Prefix(es): 0-674
Imprints: Belknap
Subsidiaries: The Loeb Classical Library
U.S. Office(s): 79 Garden St, Cambridge, MA 02138, United States *Tel:* 617-495-2480 *E-mail:* contact_hup@harvard.edu
Orders to: John Wiley & Sons Ltd, Southern Cross Trading Estate, 1 Oldlands Way, Bognor Regis, West Sussex PO22 9SA *Tel:* (01243) 779777 *Fax:* (01243) 820250

Harvey Map Services Ltd+
12-22 Main St, Doune, Perthshire FK16 6BJ
Tel: (01786) 841202 *Fax:* (01786) 841098
E-mail: winni@harveymaps.co.uk
Web Site: www.harveymaps.co.uk
Key Personnel
Sales Dir: Susan Harvey
Marketing: Catherine Nelson
Founded: 1977
Also acts as mapmakers.
Subjects: Education, Sports, Athletics
ISBN Prefix(es): 1-85137

Harvill, *imprint of* Random House UK Ltd

The Harvill Press+
Imprint of Random House UK Ltd
Random House, 20 Vauxhall Bridge Rd, London SW1V 2SA
Tel: (020) 7840 8893 *Fax:* (020) 7840 6117
E-mail: enquiries@randomhouse.co.uk
Web Site: www.randomhouse.co.uk/harvill/; www.harvill.com
Key Personnel
Publisher: Christopher MacLehose
Sales Dir: Katharina Bielenberg *E-mail:* k.bielenberg@harvill-press.com
Editorial Dir: Margaret Stead; Guido Waldman
Marketing Dir: Paul Baggaley
Founded: 1946
Subjects: Anthropology, Biography, Fiction, Gardening, Plants, History, Literature, Literary Criticism, Essays, Mathematics, Mythology, Natural History, Nonfiction (General), Philosophy, Photography, Poetry, Self-Help, Travel, African Studies, Anthology, Art History, Crime Fiction, Current Affairs, Letters, Memoirs, Politics, Russian Studies
ISBN Prefix(es): 1-86046
Total Titles: 800 Print

UNITED KINGDOM

Hassle Free Press, *imprint of* Knockabout Comics

Hawk Books+
Kernick House, Kernick Rd, Penryn, Cornwall TR10 9DT
Mailing Address: PO Box 30, Penryn TR10 9YP
Tel: (01326) 376633 *Fax:* (01326) 376669
Key Personnel
Dir: P Hawkey
Founded: 1987
Specialize in character merchandise.
Subjects: Art, Humor
ISBN Prefix(es): 0-948248; 1-899441
Imprints: Falco; Sparrowhawk
Orders to: Bookpoint Ltd, 39 Milton Park, Abingdon, Oxon OX14 4TD

Hawker Publications Ltd+
Culvert House, Culvert Rd, Battersea SW11 5DH
Tel: (020) 7720 2108 *Fax:* (020) 7498 3023
E-mail: hawker@hawkerpubs.demon.co.uk
Web Site: www.careinfo.org
Key Personnel
Editor-in-Chief: Dr Richard Hawkins
 E-mail: richard@hawkerpubs.demon.co.uk
Founded: 1985
Specialize in providing a wide range of information to professionals working with elderly people & in the children's nursery sector.
Subjects: Child Care & Development, Medicine, Nursing, Dentistry
ISBN Prefix(es): 1-874790
Number of titles published annually: 12 Print
Total Titles: 18 Print
Warehouse: Plymbridge, Estover Rd, Plymouth PL6 7P2 *Fax:* (01752) 202330

Hawthorn Press+
Hawthorn House, One Lansdown Lane, Stroud, Glos GL5 1BJ
Tel: (01453) 757040 *Fax:* (01453) 751138
E-mail: info@hawthornpress.com
Web Site: www.hawthornpress.com
Key Personnel
Dir: Judith Large; Martin Large
Sales & Accounts: Alan Lord
Project Management & Sales: Rachel Jenkins
Editor: Matthew Barton
Administration & Sales: Lynda McGill
Founded: 1980
Membership(s): Independent Publishers Guild.
Subjects: Behavioral Sciences, Child Care & Development, Crafts, Games, Hobbies, Education, Psychology, Psychiatry, Self-Help, Women's Studies
ISBN Prefix(es): 1-869890; 1-903458; 0-9507062; 1-902069
Number of titles published annually: 12 Print
Total Titles: 100 Print
Distributed by Anthroposophic Press (USA & North America); Astam Books Pty Ltd (Australia); Ceres Books (New Zealand); De Nieuwe Boekerij Import (Holland); Peter Hyde Associates (South Africa); New Leaf Distributing Co (USA & North America); Rudolf Steiner Publications (South Africa); Tri-fold Books (Canada)
Orders to: BookSource, 32 Finlas St, Glasgow G22 5DU *Tel:* (0141) 558 1366 *Fax:* (0141) 557 0189 *E-mail:* info@booksource.net

Hayden Books, *imprint of* Pearson Education Europe, Mideast & Africa

Haymarket, *imprint of* Verso

Haynes, *imprint of* Haynes Publishing

Haynes Publishing+
Sparkford, Yeovil, Somerset BA22 7JJ
Tel: (01963) 442030; (01963) 442080 (trade)
 Fax: (01963) 440001 (trade)
E-mail: sales@haynes.co.uk
Web Site: www.haynes.co.uk
Key Personnel
Chairman: John H Haynes
Group Chief Executive: Eric Oakley
Editorial Dir: Mark Hughes
Sales Dir, UK: Jeremy Yates-Round
Overseas Sales & Rights Dir: Graham Cook
Marketing Dir (Motortrade): David Hermelin
Production: Nigel Clements
Operations Dir: Jon Allen
Finance Dir: James Bunkum
Book Trade Sales Manager: Tony Kemp
Head, UK Sales: Mike Webb
Customer Marketing Mgr: Rebecca Nicholls
Founded: 1960
Subjects: Aeronautics, Aviation, Automotive, Computer Science, History, House & Home, How-to, Maritime, Outdoor Recreation, Technology, Transportation, Motoring, Motorsports, Car & Motorcycle Service & Repair, Restoration
ISBN Prefix(es): 1-85010; 0-85696; 1-56392
Number of titles published annually: 100 Print
Total Titles: 2,280 Print
Parent Company: Haynes Publishing Group PLC
Imprints: G T Foulis & Co; Haynes; Patrick Stephens Ltd
Subsidiaries: Editions Haynes SARL; Haynes Manuals Inc; Haynes Publishing Nordiska AB; Sutton Publishing Ltd
Distributor for David Bull Publishing; Duke 'Powersport' Videos; Hazleton Publishing; The Stationery Office
Foreign Rep(s): Graham Cook (world exc USA & Canada)

Hayward Gallery Publishing
Royal Festival Hall, Belvedere Rd, London SE1 8XX
Tel: (020) 7921 0826 *Fax:* (020) 7401 2664
E-mail: dpower@hayward.org.uk
Web Site: www.hayward.org.uk
Subjects: Architecture & Interior Design, Photography, Visual Arts
ISBN Prefix(es): 1-85332
Number of titles published annually: 8 Print
Distribution Center: Cornerhouse Publications, 70 Oxford St, Manchester M1 5NH

Hazleton Publishing Ltd+
Mermaid House, 5th floor, London EC4V 3DS
Tel: (020) 7332 2000 *Fax:* (020) 7332 2003
E-mail: info@hazletonpublishing.com
Web Site: www.hazletonpublishing.com
Key Personnel
Chairman: Richard Poulter
Dir: Steven Palmer
Publisher: Nick Poulter
Managing Editor: Robert Yarham
Founded: 1975
Specialize in Year Books & Calendars.
Subjects: Motor Sports, Tennis & Golf
ISBN Prefix(es): 0-905138; 1-874557; 1-903135
Total Titles: 10 Print
Parent Company: Profile Media Group PLC

HB Publications
PO Box 21660, London SW16 1WJ
Tel: (020) 8769 1585 *Fax:* (020) 8769 2320
E-mail: sales@hbpublications.com
Web Site: www.hbpublications.com
Key Personnel
Contact: Lascelles Hussey
Specializes in the production of books for public sector managers.
Subjects: Accounting, Business, Finance, Management, Marketing
ISBN Prefix(es): 1-899448
Parent Company: HB Consulting

Headline, *imprint of* Headline Book Publishing Ltd

Headline Book Publishing Ltd+
338 Euston Rd, London NW1 3BH
Tel: (020) 7873 6000 *Fax:* (020) 7873 6124
E-mail: headline.books@headline.co.uk
Web Site: www.madaboutbooks.com
Key Personnel
Chief Executive: Tim Hely Hutchinson
Man Dir: Martin Neild
Deputy Man Dir: Kerr Macrae
Dir, Non-fiction Publishing: Val Hudson
Dir, Production: Bryone Picton
Sales Dir: James Horobin
Dir, Marketing: Julie Manton
Dir, Publicity: Georgina Moore
Dir, Fiction Publishing: Jane Morpeth
Dir, Rights: Sarah Thomson
Dir, Export Sales: Peter Newson
Founded: 1986
Subjects: Biography, Cookery, Fiction, Gardening, Plants, History, Nonfiction (General), Sports, Athletics, Wine & Spirits
ISBN Prefix(es): 0-7472; 0-7553
Number of titles published annually: 410 Print
Parent Company: Hodder Headline Ltd
Ultimate Parent Company: WH Smith PLC, Greenbridge Rd, Swindon SN3 3LD
Imprints: Headline; Review
Orders to: Bookpoint Ltd, 130 Milton Trading Estate, Abingdon, Oxon OX14 4SB
 Tel: (01235) 400400 *Fax:* (01235) 400500

Headline Specials, *imprint of* Moorley's Print & Publishing Ltd

Headlions, *imprint of* Packard Publishing Ltd

Health Development Agency+
Holborn Gate, 330 High Holborn, London WC1V 7BA
Tel: (020) 7430 0850 *Fax:* (020) 7061 3390
E-mail: communications@hda-online.org.uk
Web Site: www.hda-online.org.uk
Key Personnel
General Manager & Publisher: Boyd Simon
 Tel: (020) 7413 1846 *Fax:* (020) 7413 2028 *E-mail:* simon.boyd@hea.org.uk
Publishing Manager: Chris Owen *Tel:* (020) 7413 1909 *Fax:* (020) 7413 2028 *E-mail:* chris.owen@hea.org.uk
Man Editor: Delphine Verroest *Tel:* (020) 7413 2613 *Fax:* (020) 7413 2028 *E-mail:* delphine.verroest@hea.org
Sales & Customer Care Manager: Dolores Ashton *Tel:* (020) 7413 1986 *Fax:* (020) 7413 2028 *E-mail:* dolores.ashton@hea.org.uk
Distribution Manager: John Billingham *Tel:* (020) 7413 1892 *Fax:* (020) 7413 2028 *E-mail:* john.billingham@hea.org.uk
New Media Editor & International Rights Contact: Andrea Horth *Tel:* (020) 7413 8986 *Fax:* (020) 7413 2028 *E-mail:* andrea.horth@hea.org.uk
Founded: 1987
Membership(s): Publisher's Association & Educational Publisher's Council.
Subjects: Child Care & Development, Health, Nutrition, Medicine, Nursing, Dentistry, Sports, Athletics, Women's Studies
ISBN Prefix(es): 0-7521; 0-903652; 1-85448
Total Titles: 500 Print
Warehouse: Marston Book Services, PO Box 269, Abingdon, Oxon OX14 4YN

Health Science Press, *imprint of* The C W Daniel Co Ltd

Heartland Publishing, *imprint of* Heartland Publishing Ltd

PUBLISHERS — UNITED KINGDOM

Heartland Publishing Ltd
PO Box 902, Sutton Valence, Kent ME17 3HY
Tel: (01622) 843040 *Fax:* (01622) 843040
E-mail: publish@heartland.co.uk
Web Site: www.heartland.co.uk
Key Personnel
Dir: Jeff Horne; Nick Evans
Founded: 1995
A small independent book publisher & visual media consultancy.
Membership(s): Independent Publishers Guild (IPG).
Subjects: Music, Dance, Poetry, Travel
ISBN Prefix(es): 0-9525187
Imprints: Amber Waves; Heartland Publishing

Hedera Press, *imprint of* E W Classey Ltd

Heinemann Educational Publishing+
Halley Court, Jordan Hill, Oxford OX2 8EJ
Tel: (01865) 888130 (General Inquiries)
Fax: (01865) 314290 (General inquiries)
E-mail: orders@heinemann.co.uk
Web Site: www.heinemann.co.uk
Key Personnel
Regional Manager: Dawn Davidson *Tel:* (01865) 3144295 *E-mail:* dawn.davidson@repp.co.uk; Julian Ross *Tel:* (01865) 3144214 *E-mail:* julian.ross@repp.co.uk; Deborah Steele *Tel:* (01865) 3144509 *E-mail:* deborah.steele@repp.co.uk
Executive Administrator: Christine Fisher *Tel:* (01865) 314592 *E-mail:* christine.fisher@repp.co.uk
Man Dir: Bob Osborne *Tel:* (01865) 314120 *Fax:* (01865) 314078 *E-mail:* bob.osborne@repp.co.uk
Editorial Manager, International Division: Ruth Hamilton-Jones *Tel:* (01865) 314159 *Fax:* (01865) 314169 *E-mail:* ruth.hamilton-jones@repp.uk.co
Marketing Dir: Sally Green *Tel:* (01865) 314667 *Fax:* (01865) 314169 *E-mail:* sally.green@repp.co.uk
International Marketing Manager: Charlotte Svensson *Tel:* (01865) 3144153 *E-mail:* charlotte.svensson@repp.co.uk; Ejemhen O'Connell *Tel:* (01865) 314618 *Fax:* (01865) 314169 *E-mail:* ejemhen.o'connell@repp.co.uk
International Marketing Coordinator: Hayley Scott *Tel:* (01865) 314074 *Fax:* (01865) 314169 *E-mail:* hayley.scott@repp.co.uk
Business Development Dir: David Johns *Tel:* (01865) 3144588 *E-mail:* david.johns@repp.co.uk
Sales Dir: Neil Morley *E-mail:* neil.morley@repp.co.uk
Founded: 1961
Subjects: Education, Fiction, Nonfiction (General)
ISBN Prefix(es): 0-435; 0-431
Parent Company: Reed Educational & Professional Publishing
Ultimate Parent Company: Reed Elsevier plc, 25 Victoria Rd, London SW1H 0EX
Imprints: Heinemann Library
Sales Office(s): 5 March Rd, Edinburgh EH4 7TD *Tel:* (0131) 332 5098 *Fax:* (0131) 315 2618 (Scotland)
Distributed by Bushbooks; Golf View; Heinemann Educational Botswana; Crown Books; Irwin Publishing; Cairo Trade Centre; F Reimmer Book Services; Transglobal; Reed Edcational & Professional; The Book Merchant; Jacaranda Designs; Jhango Heinemann; Mark Kuo Arenabuki Sdn Bhd; Editions de l'Ocean Indien Ltd; New Namibia Books (Pty) Ltd; Reed Publishing Group (NZ) Ltd; Heinemann Educational Books (Nigeria) Plc; Redi Ltd; Susan Chua; Heinemann South Africa; Ishmael M Khan & Sons Ltd; Rorash Educational Publishers; Heinemann; Insaka Press; Eunice Pfende
Orders to: Heinemann Publishers, Halley Court, Jordan Hill, Oxford OX2 8EJ (UK orders, enquiries & manuscript submissions)
School Orders Dept, Freepost, PO Box 969, Oxford *Tel:* (01865) 888020 *Fax:* (01865) 314091 *E-mail:* he.service@heinemann.co.uk

Heinemann Educational, *imprint of* Reed Educational & Professional Publishing

Heinemann/Ginn, *imprint of* Reed Educational & Professional Publishing

Heinemann Library, *imprint of* Heinemann Educational Publishing

Heinemann Library, *imprint of* Reed Educational & Professional Publishing

William Heinemann, *imprint of* Random House UK Ltd

William Heinemann Ltd+
Imprint of Random House UK Ltd
Random House, 20 Vauxhall Bridge Rd, London SW1V 2SA
Tel: (020) 7840 8548 *Fax:* (020) 7828 6127
Founded: 1890
Subjects: Biography, Fiction, Government, Political Science, History, Nonfiction (General), Travel
ISBN Prefix(es): 0-434; 0-437

Helicon Publishing Ltd+
Division of RM plc
RM plc, 183 Milton Park, Abingdon, Oxon OX14 4SE
Tel: (08709) 200200 *Fax:* (01235) 826999
E-mail: helicon@rm.com
Web Site: www.helicon.co.uk
Key Personnel
Man Dir: David Attwooll
Rights Dir: Clare Painter
Sales & Marketing Dir: Sheila Lambie *E-mail:* sheila@helicon.co.uk
Sales Administration Manager: Hilary Isaac
Founded: 1992
Publishers of general & subject encyclopedias & dictionaries in book, CD-ROM & online form. Text & illustrations on the database are continuously updated offering flexible licensing, coedition & packaging opportunities.
Subjects: Art, Biography, Computer Science, Government, Political Science, History, Language Arts, Linguistics, Music, Dance, Science (General)
ISBN Prefix(es): 0-09; 1-85986
Total Titles: 70 Print; 5 CD-ROM
Imprints: Hutchinson Reference
Distributed by Penguin
Warehouse: Bookpoint, 130 Milton Park, Abingdon, Oxon OX14 4SB
Orders to: Bookpoint, 130 Milton Park, Abingdon, Oxon OX14 4SB

Helion & Co
26 Willow Rd, Solihull, West Midlands B91 1UE
Tel: (0121) 705 3393 *Fax:* (0121) 711 4075
E-mail: info@helion.co.uk
Web Site: www.helion.co.uk
Key Personnel
Owner & Rts Contact: Duncan Rogers *E-mail:* duncan@helion.co.uk
Sales: Wilf Rogers *E-mail:* wilfrid@helion.co.uk
Founded: 1992
Specialize in military history; emphasis on German & Austrian history 1675-1945.
Subjects: Biography, History, Nonfiction (General)
ISBN Prefix(es): 1-874622
Total Titles: 15 Print

Christopher Helm (Publishers) Ltd, *imprint of* A & C Black Publishers Ltd

Christopher Helm (Publishers) Ltd+
Imprint of A & C Black Publishers Ltd
37 Soho Sq, London W1D 3QZ
Tel: (020) 7758 0200 *Fax:* (020) 7758 0222
E-mail: customerservice@acblack.com; ornithology@acblack.com
Key Personnel
Chairman: Nigel Newton
Man Dir: Jill Coleman
Commissioning Editor: Nigel Redman *E-mail:* nredman@acblack.com
Rights & Permissions: Paul Langridge
Sales: David Wightman
Production Dir: Oscar Heini
Founded: 1986
Subjects: Natural History, Birds
ISBN Prefix(es): 0-7136; 0-7470; 1-873403; 1-903206
Number of titles published annually: 20 Print
Total Titles: 200 Print
Ultimate Parent Company: Bloomsbury Publishing PLC
Imprints: Pica Press; T & AD Poyser Ltd
Shipping Address: Brunel Rd, Houndmills, Basingstoke, Hants RG21 6XS *Tel:* (01256) 302692 *E-mail:* mdl@macmillan.co.uk
Warehouse: Macmillan Distribution Ltd, Howard Rd, Eaton Socon, Huntingdon, Cambs PE19 3EZ
Distribution Center: Macmillan Distribution Ltd
Orders to: Brunel Rd, Houndmills, Basingstoke, Hants RG21 6XS *Tel:* (01256) 302692 *E-mail:* mdl@macmillan.co.uk

Helm Information Ltd+
The Banks, Mountfield, Nr Robertsbridge, East Sussex TN32 5JY
Tel: (01580) 880 561 *Fax:* (01580) 880 541
Web Site: www.helm-information.co.uk
Key Personnel
Dir: Amanda Helm *E-mail:* amandahelm@helm-information.co.uk; Christopher Helm *E-mail:* christopher.helm@helm-information.co.uk
Editorial, Ornithology: Roger Riddington
Permissions & Promotions Assistant: Elizabeth Imlay *E-mail:* permissions@helm-information.co.uk
Founded: 1990
Membership(s): IPG (Independent Publisher's Guild).
Subjects: History, Literature, Literary Criticism, Essays, Natural History
ISBN Prefix(es): 1-873403; 1-903206
Total Titles: 20 Print
Associate Companies: Helm Wood Publishers Pty Ltd, PO Box 666, Wembley WA 601A, Australia
Imprints: A & C

Helmsman Guides, *imprint of* The Crowood Press Ltd

Help Yourself Books, *imprint of* Hodder & Stoughton Religious

Hemming Information Services
32 Vauxhall Bridge Rd, London SW1V 2SS
Tel: (020) 7973 6694 *Fax:* (020) 7233 5052
E-mail: customer@hqluk.com
Web Site: www.h-info.co.uk
Key Personnel
Publishing Dir: Graham Bond
Publisher: Yvonne Phillips *E-mail:* y.phillips@hemmings-group.co.uk

Head of Marketing: Susan Kirby *E-mail:* s.kirby@hemmings-group.co.uk
Man Editor: Dean Wanless *E-mail:* d.wanless@hemmings-group.co.uk
Marketing: Phaedra Rees *E-mail:* p.rees@hemmings-group.co.uk
Advertising: David Morris *E-mail:* d.morris@hemmings-group.co.uk
Data Sales: Alethea Wiles *Tel:* (020) 7973 6624 *E-mail:* contacts@hemmings-group.co.uk
Founded: 1939
Membership(s): DMA, DPA & EADP.
Subjects: Cookery, Government, Political Science, Marketing
ISBN Prefix(es): 0-7079
Parent Company: Hemming Group Ltd

Hendon Publishing Co Ltd
Hendon Mill, Hallam Rd, Nelson, Lancs BB9 8AD
Tel: (01282) 613129; (01282) 697725 *Fax:* (01282) 870215
Key Personnel
Chief Executive, Sales: Henry Nelson
Editorial: Dorothy Nelson
Production: Jean Marsden
Publicity, Rights & Permissions: James Nelson
Founded: 1971
Subjects: Cookery, History
ISBN Prefix(es): 0-86067; 0-902907
Parent Company: Hendon Mill Co Ltd
Showroom(s): Bookmarket, 24 Parker Lane, Burnley, Lancs
Bookshop(s): Colne Book Shop, One Newtown St, Colne, Lancs; Bookmarket, 4-6 Market St, Colne, Lancs

Ian Henry Publications Ltd+
20 Park Dr, Romford, Essex RM1 4LH
Tel: (01708) 736213 *Fax:* (01621) 850862
Key Personnel
Man Dir: Ian Wilkes *E-mail:* iwilkes@ianhenry.fsnet.co.uk
Founded: 1975
Subjects: Drama, Theater, Fiction, Genealogy, History, Regional Interests
ISBN Prefix(es): 0-86025
Number of titles published annually: 10 Print
Total Titles: 120 Print
Branch Office(s)
PO Box 1132, Studio City 91614-10132, United States
Distributed by Players' Press (USA)
Distributor for Players' Press

Heraldry Today+
Parliament Piece, Ramsbury, Wilts SN8 2QH
Tel: (01672) 520617 *Fax:* (01672) 520183
E-mail: heraldry@heraldrytoday.co.uk
Web Site: www.heraldrytoday.co.uk
Key Personnel
Head of Firm: Rosemary Pinches
Founded: 1954
Membership(s): Antiquarian Booksellers' Association.
Subjects: Art, Genealogy, History, Armour, Armed Forces, Heraldry, Orders of Knighthood, Peerages, Royalties
ISBN Prefix(es): 0-900455
Distributor for Society of Antiquaries

Herbert Press Ltd, *imprint of* A & C Black Publishers Ltd

Herbert Press Ltd+
Imprint of A & C Black Publishers Ltd
37 Soho Sq, London W1D 3QZ
Tel: (020) 7758 0200 *Fax:* (020) 7758 0222
E-mail: customerservices@acblack.com
Web Site: www.acblack.com

Key Personnel
Publisher: Linda Lambert *Tel:* (020) 7758 0320 *E-mail:* llambert@acblack.com
Founded: 1975
Specialize in Crafts.
Subjects: Archaeology, Architecture & Interior Design, Art
ISBN Prefix(es): 0-7136; 0-906969; 1-871569
Number of titles published annually: 3 Print
Total Titles: 100 Print
Ultimate Parent Company: Bloomsbury Publishing PLC
Distributed by Allen & Unwin (Australia); Penguin (Europe & Far East)
Orders to: MDL (Macmillan Distribution), Houndmills, Basingstoke, Hants RG21 6XS *Tel:* (01256) 302 692

Heritage, *imprint of* Osborne Books Ltd

Heritage House Group Ltd
Heritage House, Lodge Lane, Derby DE1 3HE
Tel: (01332) 347087 *Fax:* (01332) 290688
E-mail: sales@hhgroup.co.uk
Web Site: www.hhgroup.co.uk
Key Personnel
Man Dir: B C Wood
Publications Manager: Nick McCann
Founded: 1950
Specialize in guidebooks to Stately Homes, Castles, Museums, Cathedrals etc, aimed at the tourist industry.
ISBN Prefix(es): 0-85101
Number of titles published annually: 6 Print
Total Titles: 88 Print

Heritage Press
4 Buckingham St, Brighton, Sussex BN1 3LT
Tel: (01273) 731296 *Fax:* (01273) 731296
Key Personnel
International Rights: Ann Dean
Founded: 1991
Heritage Art Guides; specialize in books & postcard books on Burne-Jones, William Morris Pre-Raphaelites Aubrey Beardsley listed on Book Data.
Subjects: Architecture & Interior Design, Art, Nonfiction (General), Art Travel, Art History, Decorative Arts, Stained Glass, especially William Morris & Burne-Jones
ISBN Prefix(es): 1-873089
Total Titles: 5 Print
Distributed by Strauss Consultants (Canada & USA)
Foreign Rep(s): Roger Ward; David Williams (Austria, Netherlands, Ireland, Far East, France, Germany, Italy, London, Northern Ireland, Southern Europe, Scandinavia, Spain); Bookport Associates; Books for Europe; Continent Books; Julian Cooper; Emma Ferguson; Hanne Rotovnik; IMA; Alan Levelle; Anthony Mcggach (Austria, UK, China, Far East, France, Germany, Greece, Italy, London, Northern Europe, Northern Ireland, Southern Europe, Scandinavia, Spain, Switzerland, Turkey, USA); Tom Moggagh; Hibernian Book Services; MTM; Terry Rule; Strauss Consultants (Canada, USA)
Orders to: Art Books International Ltd, One Stewart's Court, 220 Stewart's Rd, London SW8 4UD *Tel:* (020) 7720 1503 *Fax:* (020) 7720 3158 *E-mail:* artbooks@a-b-i.demon.co.uk *Web Site:* www.artbooksinternational.co.uk (all countries except USA & Canada)

Nick Hern Books Ltd+
The Glasshouse, 49a Goldhawk Rd, London W12 8QP
Tel: (020) 8749 4953 *Fax:* (020) 8735 0250
E-mail: info@nickhernbooks.demon.co.uk
Web Site: www.nickhernbooks.co.uk

Key Personnel
Publisher: Nick Hern *E-mail:* nick@nickhernbooks.demon.co.uk
Founded: 1988
Specialist performing arts publisher.
Subjects: Drama, Theater
ISBN Prefix(es): 1-85459
Number of titles published annually: 40 Print
Total Titles: 300 Print
Distributed by Currency Press (Australia); Playwrights Canada Press (Canada); Theatre Communications Group (USA)
Distributor for Drama Book Publishers (USA, Canada & Australia)
Shipping Address: Grantham Book Services, Isaac Newton Way, Alma Park Industria, Grantham Lincs NG31 9SD *Tel:* (01476) 54100 *Fax:* (01476) 541060
Warehouse: Grantham Book Services, Isaac Newton Way, Alma Park Industria, Grantham Lincs NG31 9SD *Tel:* (01476) 54100 *Fax:* (01476) 541060
Orders to: Grantham Book Services, Isaac Newton Way, Alma Park Industria, Grantham Lincs NG31 9SD *Tel:* (01476) 54100 *Fax:* (01476) 541060

Hertfordshire Publications, *imprint of* University of Hertfordshire Press

High Risk, *imprint of* Serpent's Tail Ltd

Highland Books Ltd+
2 High Pines Knoll Rd, Godalming GU7 2EP
Tel: (01483) 424560 *Fax:* (01483) 424388
E-mail: info@highlandbks.com
Web Site: www.highlandbks.com
Key Personnel
Dir: Philip Ralli
Founded: 1983
Publish books for Christian market, including "pick-me-ups" (books that encourage & restore).
Subjects: Biography, Religion - Protestant, Self-Help
ISBN Prefix(es): 0-946616; 1-897913
Number of titles published annually: 8 Print
Total Titles: 60 Print
Foreign Rep(s): Methodist Wholesale (South Africa); Scripture Union (New Zealand)
Shipping Address: STL Ltd, PO Box 300, Kingstown Broadway Carlisle *Tel:* (01228) 574949
Warehouse: STL Ltd, PO Box 300, Kingstown Broadway Carlisle *Tel:* (01228) 574949
Orders to: STL Ltd, PO Box 300, Kingstown Broadway Carlisle *Tel:* (01228) 574949

Hillside, *imprint of* Christian Education

Hilmarton Manor Press+
Calne, Wilts SN11 8SB
Tel: (01249) 760208 *Fax:* (01249) 760379
E-mail: mailorder@hilmartonpress.co.uk
Web Site: www.hilmartonpress.co.uk
Key Personnel
Man Dir: C Baile de Laperriere
Founded: 1969
Subjects: Antiques, Architecture & Interior Design, Art, Photography, Wine & Spirits
ISBN Prefix(es): 0-904722
Distributor for ADEC (France); Arte & Antiques Editions (Germany); Bibliotheque Des Arts (France & Switzerland); Edition Grund (France); Edition Mayer (France); Guide Emer (France); Servedit-Acatos (France); Tardy (France)

Hippo, *imprint of* Scholastic Ltd

PUBLISHERS

Hippopotamus Press+
22 Whitewell Rd, Frome, Somerset BA11 4EL
Tel: (01373) 466653 *Fax:* (01373) 466653
Key Personnel
Editor: R John *E-mail:* rjhippopress@aol.com; M Pargitter
Foreign Editor: A Martin
Founded: 1974
Subjects: Literature, Literary Criticism, Essays, Poetry
ISBN Prefix(es): 0-904179
Number of titles published annually: 6 Print
Total Titles: 105 Print

History-into-Print, *imprint of* Brewin Books Ltd

HLT Publications
Woolwich Rd, Charlton, London SE7 8LN
Tel: (020) 8317 6161 *Fax:* (020) 8317 6001
E-mail: obp@hltpublications.com
Web Site: www.holborncollege.ac.uk/OldbaileyPress.cfm
Key Personnel
Chairman: John Grenier
Chief Executive: Prof Cedric Bell
Founded: 1971
Membership(s): Publishers Association of Great Britain.
Subjects: Business, Law
ISBN Prefix(es): 1-85352; 0-7510; 1-85248
Parent Company: HLT Group Ltd
Imprints: Old Bailey Press; Wise Owl Books
Subsidiaries: Old Bailey Press Ltd
Sales Office(s): Amalgamated Book Services Ltd, Royal Star Arcade, Suite 1, High Street, Maidstone, Kent ME14 1JL *Tel:* (01622) 764 555 *Fax:* (01622) 763 197
Warehouse: Antony Rowe Ltd, Vincent Rd, Unit 6, Bumpers Farm Industrial Estate, Chippenham, Wilts SN14 6QA *Tel:* (0118) 950 3911 *Fax:* (0118) 950 5776

Hobsons+
159 173 Saint John St, London EC1V 4DR
Tel: (020) 7336 6633 *Fax:* (020) 7608 1034
E-mail: enquiries@hobsons.co.uk
Web Site: www.hobsons.com
Key Personnel
Chairman: Martin Morgan
Man Dir: Chris Letcher
Founded: 1974
Publishers under license for the Careers Research & Advisory Centre Ltd.
Subjects: Business, Career Development, Education, Science (General), Technology
ISBN Prefix(es): 1-86017; 0-86021; 1-85324; 0-903161
Parent Company: Daily Mail Trust
Imprints: CRAC
Warehouse: Biblios 2, Old London Rd, Washington NR Horsham, West Sussex RH20 3EN
Orders to: Biblios Publishers' Distribution Service Ltd, Star Rd, Partridge Green, West Sussex RH13 8LD

Hodder & Stoughton, *imprint of* Hodder & Stoughton Religious

Hodder & Stoughton General
338 Euston Rd, London NW1 3BH
Tel: (020) 7873 6000 *Fax:* (020) 7873 6024
Key Personnel
Man Dir: Jamie Hodder-Williams *Tel:* (020) 7873 6125 *Fax:* (020) 7873 6198
Dir, Sales: Lucy Hale *Tel:* (020) 7873 6159 *Fax:* (020) 7873 6194
Dir, Publicity: Karen Geary *Tel:* (020) 7873 6141 *Fax:* (020) 7873 6195
Publisher, Audio: Rupert Lancaster *Tel:* (020) 7873 6029
Publishing Dir: Nick Sayeo *Tel:* (020) 7873 6081 *Fax:* (020) 7873 6198; Carolyn Mays *Tel:* (020) 7873 6132 *Fax:* (020) 7873 6198
Publisher, Sceptre: Carole Welch *Tel:* (020) 7873 6129 *Fax:* (020) 7873 6196
Head of Rights: Briar Silich
Founded: 1868
Subjects: Biography, Child Care & Development, Cookery, Fiction, History, Humor, Military Science, Mysteries, Self-Help, Sports, Athletics, Travel
ISBN Prefix(es): 0-340; 0-450
Total Titles: 5,000 Print; 300 Audio
Parent Company: Hodder Headline LTD
Ultimate Parent Company: W H Smith PLC
Imprints: Sceptre; Mobius
Orders to: Bookpoint Ltd, 130 Milton Park, Abingdon, Oxon OX14 4SB

Hodder & Stoughton Religious+
338 Euston Rd, London NW1 3BH
Tel: (020) 7873 6000 *Fax:* (020) 7873 6059
E-mail: firstname.surname@hodder.co.uk
Web Site: www.headline.co.uk
Key Personnel
Man Dir: Charles Nettleton
Publishing Dir: Judith Longman
Manager, Publicity: Sarah Dennis
Founded: 1868
Subjects: Biography, Child Care & Development, Human Relations, Humor, Religion - Catholic, Religion - Protestant, Religion - Other, Self-Help, Theology
ISBN Prefix(es): 0-340
Parent Company: Hodder Headline Ltd
Ultimate Parent Company: WH Smith PLC
Imprints: Help Yourself Books; Hodder Christian Books; Hodder & Stoughton; NIV Bibles
Distribution Center: Bookpoint Ltd, 39 Milton Park, Abingdon, Oxon OX14 4BR *Tel:* (01235) 400 400 *Fax:* (01235) 400 500
Orders to: Bookpoint Ltd, 39 Milton Park, Abingdon, Oxon OX14 4BR *Tel:* (01235) 400 400 *Fax:* (01235) 400 500 *E-mail:* orders@bookpoint.co.uk

Hodder Children's Books+
338 Euston Rd, London NW1 3BH
Tel: (020) 7873 6000 *Fax:* (020) 7873 6225
Web Site: www.hodderheadline.co.uk
Key Personnel
Man Dir: Charles Nettleton
Dir, Publishing: Margaret Conroy
Dir, Marketing: Elisa Offord
Dir, Rights: Andrew Sharp
Dir Sales: Les Phipps
Dir, Fiction, Picture & Gift Publishing: Anne McNeil
Dir, Hodder Wayland: Anne Clarke
Founded: 1868
Subjects: Fiction, Nonfiction (General), Science Fiction, Fantasy
ISBN Prefix(es): 0-340
Parent Company: RM plc, Abingdon, Oxon
Imprints: Hodder Wayland
Orders to: Bookpoint Ltd, 39 Milton Park, Abingdon, Oxon OX14 4TD

Hodder Christian Books, *imprint of* Hodder & Stoughton Religious

Hodder Education
338 Euston Rd, London NW1 3BH
Tel: (020) 7873 6272 *Fax:* (020) 7873 6299
E-mail: joanne.craik@hodder.co.uk
Web Site: www.hodderheadline.co.uk
Key Personnel
Man Dir: Philip Walters
Dir, Consumer Education: Katie Roden
Dir, Schools Publishing: Lis Tribe
Production & Design Dir: Alyssum Ross
Sales & Marketing Dir: Catherine Newman
Dir, FE/HE, Journals & Reference Books, Health Sciences: Mary Attree
Founded: 1868
Subjects: Biblical Studies, Biological Sciences, Business, Career Development, Chemistry, Chemical Engineering, Computer Science, Crafts, Games, Hobbies, Engineering (General), Geography, Geology, Language Arts, Linguistics, Literature, Literary Criticism, Essays, Mathematics, Natural History, Photography, Physics, Science (General), Sports, Athletics, Theology
ISBN Prefix(es): 0-340; 0-7131; 0-450; 0-7122
Parent Company: Hodder Headline PLC
Imprints: Teach Yourself
Orders to: Bookpoint Ltd, 130 Milton Park, Abingdon, Oxon OX14 4TD

Hodder Headline Ltd
338 Euston Rd, London NW1 3BH
Tel: (020) 7873 6000 *Fax:* (020) 7873 6024
Web Site: www.hodderheadline.co.uk
Key Personnel
Group Chief Executive: Tim Hely Hutchinson
Man Dir, Headline Book Publishing: Martin Neild
Man Dir, Hodder & Stoughton General: Jamie Hodder-Williams
Man Dir, Hodder Children's Books: Mary Tapissier
Man Dir, Hodder & Stoughton Religious: Charles Nettleton
Man Dir, Bookpoint Ltd: Tony Bryars
Man Dir: Hodder Arnold; Philip Walters
Acting Man Dir, John Murray: Martin Neild
Group Financial Dir: Colin Fairbairn
Founded: 1986
ISBN Prefix(es): 0-340; 0-7131; 0-450; 0-7122
Associate Companies: Hodder Dargaud Ltd
Subsidiaries: Hodder Headline Australia Pty Ltd; Hodder Moa Becket Publishers Limited; Edward Arnold (Publishers) Limited; Bookpoint Limited; Headline Book Publishing Limited; Hodder & Stoughton Limited
Divisions: Arnold; Headline Book Publishing; Hodder Children's Books; Hodder & Stoughton Educational; Hodder & Stoughton General; Hodder & Stoughton Religious Books; Hodder Headline Audio
Orders to: Bookpoint Ltd, 130 Milton Park, Abingdon, Oxon OX14 4TD *Tel:* (01235) 835001 *Fax:* (01235) 832068

Hodder Wayland, *imprint of* Hodder Children's Books

Holland Enterprises Ltd
18 Bourne Court, Southend Rd, Woodford Green, Essex IG8 8HD
Tel: (020) 8551 7711 *Fax:* (020) 8551 1266
E-mail: sales@holland-enterprises.co.uk
Web Site: www.holland-enterprises.co.uk
Key Personnel
Chairman: William C Holland
Man Dir: Jonathan Holland
ISBN Prefix(es): 1-85038

Hollis Publishing Ltd
Harlequin House, 7 High St, Teddington, Middlesex TW11 8EL
Tel: (020) 8977 7711 *Fax:* (020) 8977 1133
E-mail: hollis@hollis-pr.co.uk; orders@hollis-pr.co.uk
Web Site: www.hollis-pr.co.uk
Key Personnel
Man Dir: Gary Zabel
Publishing Dir: Rosie Sarginson
Sales Dir: Jane Ireland
Membership(s): Directory Publishers Association.
Subjects: Advertising, Marketing, Publishing & Book Trade Reference

UNITED KINGDOM

Holyoake Books
Stanford Hall, Loughborough LE12 5QR
Tel: (01509) 852333 *Fax:* (01509) 856500
E-mail: info@co-opu.demon.co.uk
Key Personnel
Publisher & Chief Information Officer: I V Williamson
Founded: 1869 (co-operative union)
Subjects: Human Relations, Social Sciences, Sociology
ISBN Prefix(es): 0-85195
Parent Company: Co-operative Union Ltd
Imprints: Co-operative Union

Home Health Education Service
Alma Park, Grantham, Lincs NG31 9SL
Tel: (01476) 591700; (01476) 539900 (orders) *Fax:* (01476) 577144
E-mail: stanborg@aol.com
Key Personnel
Secretary: Paul Hammond
Founded: 1892
Subjects: Religion - Other
ISBN Prefix(es): 0-904748; 0-900703; 1-899505
Parent Company: Stanborough Press
U.S. Office(s): Review & Herald Publishing Association, Hagerstown, MD 21740, United States

Honeyglen Publishing Ltd+
56 Durrels House, Warwick Gardens, London W14 8QB
Tel: (020) 7602 2876 *Fax:* (020) 7602 2876
Key Personnel
Publisher: Nadja Poderegin
Founded: 1982
Subjects: Biography, Fiction, History, Philosophy of History
ISBN Prefix(es): 0-907855
Total Titles: 13 Print
Orders to: Vine House Distribution Ltd, Waldenbury, North Common, Chailey, East Sussex BN8 4DR, Contact: Richard Squibb *Tel:* (01825) 723398 *Fax:* (01825) 724188 *E-mail:* sales@vinehouseuk.co.uk
Membership(s): IPG

Honno Welsh Women's Press+
c/o Canolfan Merched y Wawr, Stryd yr Efail, Aberystwyth SY23 2JH
Tel: (01970) 623 150 *Fax:* (01970) 623 150
E-mail: post@honno.co.uk
Web Site: www.honno.co.uk
Key Personnel
Editor: Janet Thomas
Information Officer: Alyson Tyler
Editor: Gwenlian Dafydd
Marketing Officer: Heidi Kivekas
Founded: 1986
Specialize in writings by women living in Wales or having a Welsh connection.
Subjects: Biography, Fiction, Nonfiction (General), Poetry
ISBN Prefix(es): 1-870206
Number of titles published annually: 6 Print
Total Titles: 50 Print
Orders to: Turnaround Distribution, Unit 3, Olympia Trading Estate, Coburg Rd, London N22 6TZ *Tel:* (020) 8829 3000 *Fax:* (020) 8881 5088 *E-mail:* claire@turnaround-uk.com (England, Scotland, Ireland & overseas)
Welsh Books Council Distribution Centre, Glanyrafon Industrial Estate, Aberystwyth, Ceredigion SSY23 3AQ *Tel:* (01970) 624 455 *Fax:* (01970) 625 506 *E-mail:* canolfan.ddosbarthu@2cllc.org.uk (Wales)

Hoover's Business Press
5 Five Mile Dr, Oxford OX2 8HT
Tel: (01865) 513186 *Fax:* (01865) 513186
Web Site: www.hoovers-europe.com

Key Personnel
Man Dir: William Snyder *E-mail:* snyderpub@aol.com
ISBN Prefix(es): 1-57311

Horizon Scientific Press+
Rowan House, 28 Queens Rd, Hethersett, Norwich NR9 3DB
Mailing Address: PO Box 1, Wymondham, Norfolk NR18 0EH
Tel: (01953) 601106 *Fax:* (01953) 603068
E-mail: mail@horizonpress.com
Web Site: www.horizonpress.com
Key Personnel
Contact: Hugh Griffin
Founded: 1993
Specialize in academic journals & books.
Subjects: Biological Sciences, Medicine, Nursing, Dentistry, Science (General)
ISBN Prefix(es): 1-898486
Number of titles published annually: 8 Print
Total Titles: 30 Print; 2 Online

Horse Books, *imprint of* Robert Hale Ltd

Horus Editions, *imprint of* Award Publications Ltd

Hospitality Training Foundation+
International House, High St, 3rd floor, Ealing, London W5 5DB
Tel: (020) 8579 2400 *Fax:* (020) 8840 6217
E-mail: info@htf.org.uk
Web Site: www.htf.org.uk
Key Personnel
Marketing Dir: Paul Hickey
Subjects: Career Development, Hotel & Catering
ISBN Prefix(es): 0-7033
Branch Office(s)
PO Box 67, Carmarthern SA31 1YU
 E-mail: htfwales@htf.org.uk
28 Castle St, Edinburgh EH2 2HT
 E-mail: htfscotland@htf.org.uk

House of Lochar
Isle of Colonsay, Argyll PA61 7YR
Tel: (01951) 200232 *Fax:* (01951) 200232
E-mail: lochar@colonsay.org.uk
Web Site: www.houseoflochar.com
Key Personnel
Partner: Christa Byrne; Kevin Byrne
 E-mail: byrne@colonsay.org.uk; Sophie Byrne
ISBN Prefix(es): 1-899863
Imprints: Colonsay Books; West Highland Series
Distributed by Natural Heritage (Canada); Scottish Book Source

Hove Foto Books, *imprint of* Newpro UK Ltd

How Design, *imprint of* David & Charles Ltd

How To Books Ltd+
3 Newtec Pl, Magdalen Rd, Oxford OX4 1RE
Tel: (01865) 793806 *Fax:* (01865) 248780
E-mail: info@howtobooks.co.uk
Web Site: www.howtobooks.co.uk
Key Personnel
Man Dir: Giles Lewis
International Rights: Ros Loten
Founded: 1991
Reference publisher.
Subjects: Business, Career Development, How-to, Management, Self-Help, Living & Working Abroad, Small Business, Successful Writing
ISBN Prefix(es): 1-85703; 1-85876; 1-84528
Number of titles published annually: 50 Print
Total Titles: 300 Print
Parent Company: How To Ltd
Shipping Address: Grantham Book Distributors

Warehouse: Grantham Book Services
Orders to: Grantham Book Services, Grantham NG31 9SD

Angus Hudson Ltd+
Concorde House, Grenville Place, Mill Hill, London NW7 3SA
Tel: (020) 8959 3668 *Fax:* (020) 8959 3678
E-mail: sales@angushudson.com
Web Site: www.angushudson.com
Key Personnel
Production Dir: Stephen Price
Man Dir: Nicholas Jones *E-mail:* nickj@angushudson.com
Controller: Christopher Atkinson
Founded: 1976
Subjects: Cookery, Religion - Protestant, Theology, Travel
Imprints: Candle Books; Gazelle Books
Subsidiaries: Monarch Books
Orders to: S T L Wholesale, Kingstown Industrial Estate, Kingstown Broadway, Carlisle

A & Z Hughes, *imprint of* Gwasg Gwenffrwd

Hugo's Language Books Ltd+
80 Strand, London WC2R 0RL
Tel: (020) 7010 3000 *Fax:* (020) 7010 6060
E-mail: customerservice@dk.com
Web Site: uk.dk.com
Key Personnel
Dir Sales: Peter G Lock
Founded: 1875
Subjects: English as a Second Language, How-to, Language Arts, Linguistics
ISBN Prefix(es): 0-85285
Parent Company: Dorling Kindersley plc
Ultimate Parent Company: Penguin Group UK
Orders to: Penguin Direct, Pearson Customer Operations, Edinburgh Gate, Harlow, Essex CM20 2JE *Fax:* (020) 8757 4030 *Web Site:* pubeasy.books.penguin.co.uk
Returns: Penguin Books Ltd, Online Returns Department, Pearson Customer Operations, Edinburgh Gate, Harlow, Essex CM20 2JE

"Huh!" 1991, *imprint of* Pentathol Publishing

Human Horizons Series, *imprint of* Souvenir Press Ltd

Hunt and Thorpe, *imprint of* John Hunt Publishing Ltd

John Hunt Publishing Ltd+
46a West St, New Alresford, Hants SO24 9AU
Tel: (01962) 736880; (01962) 736888 (orders) *Fax:* (01962) 736881
E-mail: office@johnhunt-publishing.com
Web Site: www.johnhunt-publishing.com
Key Personnel
Publisher: John Hunt *Tel:* (01962) 736885
 E-mail: john@johnhuntpub.demon.co.uk
Sales Manager: Colin Nutt
Financial Controller: Sandra Geary
Edit Manager: Anne O'Rorke
Marketing Administrator: Maria Watson
Founded: 1989
Membership(s): Independent Publishers Guild.
Subjects: Religion - Other, Inspirational, Educational, Children's Books including Novelty & Pop ups
ISBN Prefix(es): 0-85305; 1-85608; 1-903019
Number of titles published annually: 50 Print
Total Titles: 400 Print
Imprints: Hunt and Thorpe; Arthur James Ltd; "O" Books
Orders to: STL, Customer Service, PO Box 300, Carlisle, Cumbria CA3 0QS *Tel:* (0800) 282728 *Fax:* (0800) 282530 (UK) *E-mail:* salesline@stl.org

PUBLISHERS — UNITED KINGDOM

C Hurst & Co (Publishers) Ltd+
Covent Garden, 38 King St, London WC2E 8JZ
Tel: (020) 7240 2666 *Fax:* (020) 7240 2667
E-mail: hurst@atlas.co.uk
Web Site: www.hurstpub.co.uk
Key Personnel
Man Dir: Christopher Hurst
Sales & Rights: Michael Dwyer
Founded: 1968
Subjects: Economics, Government, Political Science, History, Regional Interests, Religion - Other
ISBN Prefix(es): 0-905838; 0-903983; 0-900966; 1-85065
Distributed by Alkem Co (S) Pte Ltd (Southeast Asia); Phambili Agencies (South Africa); Unifacmanu Trading Co Ltd (Taiwan); United Publishers Services Ltd (Japan); University & Reference Publishers' Services (UNIREPS) (Australia & New Zealand); Vanguard Books Pvt (Pakistan)
Foreign Rep(s): Peter & Bella Dietschi (Greece); Colin Flint (Denmark, Finland, Iceland, Norway & Sweden); Charles Gibbes (Portugal, Southern France); Cristina de Lara Ruiz (Spain); Ewa Ledochowicz (Central & Eastern Europe); Missing Link (Germany); David Pickering (Italy); James Tovey (Paris, Northern France); Alma van Zaane (Netherlands)
Shipping Address: Marston Book Services, PO Box 269, Abingdon, Oxon OX14 4YN
Tel: (01235) 465500 *Fax:* (01235) 465555
E-mail: trade.order@marston.co.uk *Web Site:* www.marston.co.uk

Hutchinson, *imprint of* Random House UK Ltd

Hutchinson Reference, *imprint of* Helicon Publishing Ltd

Hutchinson Childrens, *imprint of* Random House UK Ltd

Alan Hutchison Ltd
9 Pembridge Studios, 27A Pembridge Villas, London W11 3EP
Tel: (020) 7221 0129
Telex: 9419283AHPLTD
Key Personnel
Man Dir: Jemima Haddock
Founded: 1979
Subjects: Art
ISBN Prefix(es): 0-905885; 1-85272
Parent Company: Crown Products Group PLC
U.S. Office(s): Putnam Pub, 200 Madison Ave, New York, NY, United States

Hutton Press Ltd
130 Canada Dr, Cherry Burton, Beverly, East Yorks HU17 7SB
Tel: (01964) 550573 *Fax:* (01964) 550573
Key Personnel
Man Dir: Charles F Brook
Founded: 1979
Subjects: History, Maritime, Regional Interests
ISBN Prefix(es): 0-907033; 1-872167; 1-902709

Hyden House Ltd+
The Sustainability Centre, East Meon, Hants GU32 1HR
Tel: (01730) 823311 *Fax:* (01730) 823322
E-mail: info@permaculture.co.uk
Web Site: www.permaculture.co.uk
Key Personnel
Man Dir: Madeleine Harland
Creative Dir: Tim Harland
Founded: 1990
Specialize in permaculture & sustainable agriculture.
Subjects: Agriculture, Earth Sciences, Environmental Studies, Gardening, Plants, Permaculture
ISBN Prefix(es): 1-85623
Number of titles published annually: 7 Print
Total Titles: 27 Print
Imprints: Permanent Publications
Distributed by Chelsea Green
Distributor for Candlelight Trust (Australia); Solar Survival Press (USA); Tagari Publications (Australia)

Hymns Ancient & Modern Ltd+
St Mary's Works, St Mary's Plain, Norwich NR3 3BH
Tel: (01603) 612914 *Fax:* (01603) 624483
E-mail: admin@scm-canterburypress.co.uk
Web Site: www.scm-canterburypress.co.uk
Key Personnel
Chief Executive Officer: Gordon Knights
  E-mail: gordon@scm-canterburypress.co.uk
Founded: 1861 (Public company 1975)
Subjects: Religion - Other
ISBN Prefix(es): 0-907547; 1-85311
Imprints: Canterbury Press Norwich; Church Times; Hart Advertising Charity Agency; Religious & Moral Education Press; SCM Press
Subsidiaries: G J Palmer & Sons Ltd; SCM-Canterbury Press Ltd
Distributed by Morehouse Publishing (US)
Foreign Rep(s): Churches Stores (New Zealand); Hugh Dunphy (Jamaica, West Indies); International Publishers Marketing (USA); Morehouse Publishing (USA); Novalis (Canada); Openbook Publishers (Australia); Charles Paine Pty Ltd (Australia); Publishers International Marketing (London)
Membership(s): IPG

Iaith Cyf
Parc Busnes Aberarad, Uned 3, Castell Newydd Emlyn, Carmarthenshire SA38 9DB
Tel: (01239) 711668 *Fax:* (01239) 711698
E-mail: ymhol@cwmni-iaith.com
Web Site: www.cwmni-iaith.com
Key Personnel
Executive Dir: Gareth Ioan
Founded: 1993
Subjects: Education, Welsh Language
ISBN Prefix(es): 0-9522905; 1-900563

IC Publications Ltd, see International Communications

ICC United Kingdom
12 Grosvenor Pl, London SW1X 7HH
Tel: (020) 7823 2811 *Fax:* (020) 7235 5447
E-mail: katharinehedger@iccorg.co.uk
Web Site: www.iccwbo.org; www.iccuk.net
Key Personnel
Chair: Phil Watts
Dir: Richard C I Bate
Policy Executive: Tania Baumann
Founded: 1919
Subjects: Advertising, Business, Communications, Economics, Environmental Studies, Finance, Government, Political Science, Law, Marketing
U.S. Office(s): US Council of the ICC, 1212 Avenue of the Americas, New York, NY 10036, United States

Icon Press+
One Huggetts Lane, Lower Willingdon, Eastbourne, East Sussex BN22 OLZ
Tel: (01323) 507270 *Fax:* (01323) 507270
E-mail: iconpress@philipbrown.screaming.net
Web Site: www.iconpress.co.uk
Key Personnel
Dir: Philip Brown
Founded: 1986
Publishers of art manuals, local history & poetry books.
Subjects: Art, Foreign Countries, History, Humor, Poetry, Regional Interests, Travel
ISBN Prefix(es): 1-873812
Number of titles published annually: 2 Print
Total Titles: 20 Print

ICP, *imprint of* Wilmington Business Information Ltd

ICSA Publishing Ltd
16 Park Crescent, London W1B 1AH
Tel: (020) 7612 7020 *Fax:* (020) 7323 1132
E-mail: icsa.pub@icsa.co.uk
Web Site: www.icsapublishing.co.uk
Founded: 1981
Subjects: Business, Law, Management, Public Administration
ISBN Prefix(es): 1-86072
Number of titles published annually: 20 Print
Total Titles: 70 Print
Shipping Address: Extenza-Turpin, Stratton Business Park, Pegasus Drive, Biggleswade, Beds SG18 8QB *Tel:* (01767) 604596
Warehouse: Extenza-Turpin, Stratton Business Park, Pegasus Drive, Biggleswade, Beds SG18 8QB *Tel:* (01767) 604596
Distribution Center: Extenza-Turpin, Stratton Business Park, Pegasus Drive, Biggleswade, Beds SG18 8QB *Tel:* (01767) 604596
Orders to: Extenza-Turpin, Stratton Business Park, Pegasus Drive, Biggleswade, Beds SG18 8QB *Tel:* (01767) 604596
Returns: Extenza-Turpin, Stratton Business Park, Pegasus Drive, Biggleswade, Beds SG18 8QB *Tel:* (01767) 604596

Idol, *imprint of* Virgin Publishing Ltd

IEE, *imprint of* Institution of Electrical Engineers

Illustrated History Paperbacks, *imprint of* Sutton Publishing Ltd

Imago Publishing Ltd
Member of Imago Group
Albury Court, Albury, Thame, Oxon OX9 2LP
Tel: (01844) 337000 *Fax:* (01844) 339935
E-mail: sales@imago.co.uk
Web Site: www.imago.co.uk
Key Personnel
Dir: Richard Hayes *E-mail:* richardh@imago.co.uk
Founded: 1980
Specialize in providing production services to publishers on a world-wide basis.
Parent Company: Imago Holdings Ltd
Ultimate Parent Company: Imago Investments Ltd
Branch Office(s)
Imago Australia, 14 Brown St, Suite 241, Chatswood, Sydney 2067, Australia, Contact: Emma Bell *Tel:* (02) 9415 2713 *Fax:* (02) 9415 2714 *E-mail:* ebell@imagoaus.com
Imago France, 6eme etage, 42 rue le Peletier, 75009 Paris, France, Contact: Matt Critchlow *Tel:* (01) 42 81 41 24 *Fax:* (01) 42 81 41 24 *E-mail:* mcritchlow@imagogroup.com
Imago Services (HK) Ltd, Tung Chung Factory Bldg, 6th floor, Flat B, 653-659 King's Rd, North Point, Hong Kong, China, Contact: Kendrick Cheung *Tel:* 2811 3316 *Fax:* 2597 5256 *E-mail:* kcheung@imago.com.hk
Imago Productions (FE) Pte Ltd, 5 Lorong Bakar Batu, No 05-01, Macpherson Industrial Complex, 348742 Singapore, Singapore, Contact: KC Ng *Tel:* 748 4433 *Fax:* 748 6082 *E-mail:* kng@imago.com.sg
U.S. Office(s): Imago Sales (USA) Inc, 1431 Broadway-Penthouse, New York, NY 10018, United States, Contact: Howard Musk *Tel:* 212-

921-4411 *Fax:* 212-921-8226 *E-mail:* hmusk@imagousa.com

Imago Sales (USA Mid West) Inc, 17 N Loomis St, No 4A, Chicago, IL 60607, United States, Contact: Joseph Braff *Tel:* 847-705-3821 *Fax:* 847-963-2341 *E-mail:* jbraff@imagousa.com

Imago Sales (USA West Coast) Inc, 31952 Camino Capistrano, Suite C22, San Juan Capistrano, CA 92675, United States, Contact: Greg Lee *Tel:* 949-661-5998 *Fax:* 949-661-8013 *E-mail:* glee@imagousa.com

Immediate Publishing
27 Church Rd, Hove BN3 2FA
Tel: (01273) 207259; (01273) 207411 *Fax:* (01273) 205612
Key Personnel
Contact: Luci Allmark *E-mail:* luci@erlbaum.co.uk
Founded: 1993
Subjects: Computer Science
ISBN Prefix(es): 1-898931
Warehouse: Taylor & Francis, Rankin Rd, Basingstoke, Hamps RG24 8PR
Orders to: Direct Distribution, 27 Palmeira Mansions, Church Rd, Hove, East Sussex

Impart Books+
Gwelfryn, Llanidloes Rd, Newtown, Powys SY16 4HX
Tel: (01686) 623484
E-mail: impart@books.mid-wales.net
Web Site: www.books.mid-wales.net
Key Personnel
Proprietor: Alick Hartley
Founded: 1988
Subjects: Accounting, English as a Second Language, Mathematics
ISBN Prefix(es): 1-874155
Number of titles published annually: 3 Print
Total Titles: 50 Print
Imprints: Crux Press

Imperial College Press+
57 Shelton St, London WC2H 9HE
Tel: (020) 7836 3954 *Fax:* (020) 7836 2002
E-mail: edit@icpress.co.uk
Web Site: www.icpress.co.uk
Key Personnel
Contact: Dr John Navas *E-mail:* john@icpress.demon.co.uk
Founded: 1995
STM Publisher of Books & Journals. Specialize in medicine.
Subjects: Biological Sciences, Chemistry, Chemical Engineering, Electronics, Electrical Engineering, Engineering (General), Mathematics, Medicine, Nursing, Dentistry, Physical Sciences, Science (General)
ISBN Prefix(es): 1-86094
Number of titles published annually: 85 Print; 2 CD-ROM
Total Titles: 175 Print; 2 CD-ROM
Distributed by World Scientific Publishing (Territory: United Kingdom); World Scientific Publishing Co Inc (Territory: United States); World Scientific Publishing Co Pte Ltd (Territories: India, Singapore, Taiwan); World Scientific Publishing (HK) Co Ltd (Territory: Hong Kong)
Orders to: World Scientific Publishing, 57 Shelton St, Covent Garden, London WC2H 9HE

In Old Photographs, *imprint of* Sutton Publishing Ltd

The In Pinn, *imprint of* Neil Wilson Publishing Ltd

Incorporated Catholic Truth Society, see The Catholic Truth Society

Independence Educational Publishers Ltd
PO Box 295, Cambridge CB1 3XP
Tel: (01223) 566 130 *Fax:* (01223) 566 131
E-mail: issues@independence.co.uk
Web Site: www.independence.co.uk
Key Personnel
Publisher: Craig Donnellan
Founded: 1989
Subjects: Social Issues
ISBN Prefix(es): 1-86168; 1-872995

Independent Voices, *imprint of* Souvenir Press Ltd

Independent Writers Publications Ltd+
97 Geary Rd, Dollis Hill, London NW10 1HS
Tel: (020) 8438 0179 *Fax:* (020) 8438 0179
Key Personnel
Contact: Alfred Shmueli
Founded: 1993
Subjects: Fiction
ISBN Prefix(es): 1-897894

Indiana University Press, *imprint of* Combined Academic Publishers

Informa Publishing Group Ltd
Mortimer House, 37-41 Mortimer St, London W1T 3JH
Tel: (020) 7453 1000
E-mail: publishing.customers@informa.com
Web Site: www.informa.com
Key Personnel
Executive Chairman: Peter Rigby
Chief Executive: David Gilbertson
Corporate Development Director: Peter Miller

INSPEC, *imprint of* Institution of Electrical Engineers

Institute for Fiscal Studies
7 Ridgmount St, 3rd floor, London WC1E 7AE
Tel: (020) 7291 4800 *Fax:* (020) 7323 4780
E-mail: mailbox@ifs.org.uk
Web Site: www.ifs.org.uk
Key Personnel
Dir: Robert Chote
Deputy Dir: Ian Crawford; Rachel Griffith
Research Dir: Richard Blundell
Deputy Research Dir: James Banks
External Relations Manager: Emma Hyman *Tel:* (020) 7291 4850 *E-mail:* emma_h@ifs.org.uk
Executive Administrator: Robert Markless
Founded: 1969
Independent research institute
Publish research findings on all aspects of taxation & economic public policy.
Subjects: Economics, Finance, Public Administration, Working Papers (online only)
ISBN Prefix(es): 1-873357
Number of titles published annually: 15 Print; 10 Online
Total Titles: 200 Print; 100 Online

Institute of Development Studies
University of Sussex, Falmer, Brighton, Sussex BN1 9RE
Tel: (01273) 606261 *Fax:* (01273) 621202; (01273) 691647
E-mail: ids@ids.ac.uk
Web Site: www.ids.ac.uk
Key Personnel
Head of Information Resource Unit: Geoffrey Barnard *E-mail:* g.barnard@ids.ac.uk
Communications Manager: Rosalind Goodrich

Rights & Permissions: Gary Edwards *Tel:* (01273) 678269 *Fax:* (01273) 621202 *E-mail:* g.edwards@ids.ac.uk
Founded: 1966
Subjects: Agriculture, Developing Countries, Economics, Education, Environmental Studies, Government, Political Science, Public Administration, Women's Studies
ISBN Prefix(es): 0-903354; 0-903715; 1-85864
Number of titles published annually: 50 Print
Total Titles: 500 Print

Institute of Economic Affairs+
2 Lord North St, London SW1P 3LB
Tel: (020) 7799 8900 *Fax:* (020) 7799 2137
E-mail: enquiries@iea.org.uk; iea@iea.org.uk
Web Site: www.iea.org.uk
Key Personnel
Dir General: John Blundell *Tel:* (020) 7799 8911 *E-mail:* jblundell@iea.org.uk
Editorial Dir: Prof Philip Booth *Tel:* (020) 7799 8912 *E-mail:* pbooth@iea.org.uk
Development Dir: Jacqueline Baer O'Mahony *Tel:* (020) 7799 8904 *E-mail:* jbaer@iea.org.uk
Dir, Marketing & Subscriptions: Adam Myers *Tel:* (020) 7799 8920 *E-mail:* amyers@iea.org.uk
Sales Manager: Bob Layson *Tel:* (020) 7799 8909 *E-mail:* books@iea.org.uk
Founded: 1955
Subjects: Economics, Education
ISBN Prefix(es): 0-255

Institute of Education, University of London+
20 Bedford Way, London WC1H 0AL
Tel: (020) 7612 6260 *Fax:* (020) 7612 6560
E-mail: info@ioe.ac.uk
Web Site: www.ioe.ac.uk/publications
Key Personnel
Dir: Prof Geoff Whitty
Publications Officer: Deborah Spring *E-mail:* d.spring@ioe.ac.uk
Founded: 1902
Subjects: Education
ISBN Prefix(es): 0-85473
Number of titles published annually: 15 Print
Total Titles: 80 Print
Orders to: Central Books, 99 Wallis Rd, London E9 5LN *Tel:* (020) 8986 4854 *Fax:* (020) 8533 5821

Institute of Employment Rights
177 Abbeville Rd, London SW4 9RL
Tel: (020) 7498 6919 *Fax:* (020) 7498 9080
E-mail: office@ier.org.uk
Web Site: www.ier.org.uk
Key Personnel
Dir: Carolyn Jones
Founded: 1989
Subjects: Disability, Special Needs, Economics, Ethnicity, Government, Political Science, Law, Women's Studies
ISBN Prefix(es): 0-9543781
Number of titles published annually: 8 Print

Institute of Financial Services+
Formerly Financial World Publishing
IFS House, 4-9 Burgate Lane, Canterbury, Kent CT1 2XJ
Tel: (01227) 818 687 *Fax:* (01227) 763 788
E-mail: institute@ifslearning.com
Web Site: www.ifslearning.com
Key Personnel
Publishing Manager: Philip Blake *E-mail:* pblake@ifslearning.co.uk
Mail Order Manager: Morton Griffiths *E-mail:* mgriffiths@ifslearning.co.uk
Founded: 1987 (as Bankers Books Ltd)
Publisher of student & practitioner audiences across the financial services.
Subjects: Business, Finance, Law, Management
ISBN Prefix(es): 0-85297

Number of titles published annually: 90 Print
Total Titles: 190 Print
Parent Company: Chartered Institute of Bankers
Imprints: Chartered Institute of Bankers (CIB) Publications
Bookshop(s): 90 Bishopsgate, London EC2N 4DQ
Orders to: IFS Mail Order, c/o The Chartered Institute of Bankers, Emmanual House, Burgate Lane, Canterbury, Kent CT1 2XJ

Institute of Food Science & Technology
5 Cambridge Court, 210 Shepherds Bush Rd, London W6 7NJ
Tel: (020) 7603 6316 *Fax:* (020) 7602 9936
E-mail: info@ifst.org
Web Site: www.ifst.org
Founded: 1964
Professional qualifying body & educational charity.
Subjects: Science (General), Technology
ISBN Prefix(es): 0-905367
Number of titles published annually: 2 Print; 1 Online
Total Titles: 10 Print; 1 Online

Institute of Governance
Chisholm House, High School Yards, Edinburgh EH1 1LZ
Tel: (0131) 650 2456 *Fax:* (0131) 650 6345
Web Site: www.institute-of-governance.org
Key Personnel
Business Manager: Lindsay Adams *E-mail:* ladams@ed.ac.uk
Founded: 1976
Subjects: Government, Political Science
ISBN Prefix(es): 0-9518053; 0-9509626

Institute of Irish Studies, The Queens University of Belfast+
8 Fitzwilliam St, Belfast BT9 6AW
Tel: (028) 9027 3386 *Fax:* (028) 9043 9238
E-mail: iispubs@qub.ac.uk
Web Site: www.qub.ac.uk/iis
Key Personnel
Editor: Margaret McNulty *E-mail:* m.mcnulty@qub.ac.uk
Founded: 1987
A small press & publishing company which publishes academic & semi-academic books relative to all aspects of Irish studies.
Subjects: Anthropology, Archaeology, Art, Biography, Ethnicity, Film, Video, Geography, Geology, Government, Political Science, History, Language Arts, Linguistics, Regional Interests, Religion - Catholic, Religion - Protestant
ISBN Prefix(es): 0-85389
Number of titles published annually: 10 Print
Total Titles: 150 Print
Distributed by Dufour Editions (USA); P D Meaney (1 title only)
Distributor for Van Gorcum (North Ireland & Irish Republic for 1 book only)
Foreign Rep(s): Robert Towers (Ireland); Russell Book Representation (UK)
Distribution Center: Central Books Ltd, 99 Wallis Rd, London E9 5LN *Tel:* (020) 8986 4854 *Fax:* (020) 8533 5821 *E-mail:* orders@centralbooks.com (Great Britain & Europe)
Irish Books & Media, Inc, 1433 Franklin Ave E, Minneapolis, MN 55404-2135, United States *Tel:* 612-871-3505 *Fax:* 612-871-3358 *E-mail:* irishbooks@aol.com

Institute of Physics Publishing+
Dirac House, Temple Back, Bristol BS1 6BE
Tel: (0117) 929 7481 *Fax:* (0117) 929 4318
E-mail: custserv@iop.org
Web Site: www.iop.org; www.iop.org/IOPP/ioppabout.html

Key Personnel
Man Dir: Jerry Cowhig *E-mail:* jerry.cowhig@iop.org
Business Dir: Ken Lillywhite *E-mail:* ken.lillywhite@iop.org
Operations Dir: Dr Kurt Paulus *Tel:* (117) 930 1057 *E-mail:* kurt.paulus@iop.org
Finance Dir: Michael Bray *E-mail:* mike.bray@iop.org
Publishing Dir: Richard Roe *E-mail:* richard.roe@iop.org
Head of Book Publishing: Nicki Dennis *E-mail:* nicki.dennis@iop.org
Rights: Brenda Trigg *E-mail:* brenda.trigg@iop.org
Sales: Nicola Newey *E-mail:* nicola.newey@iop.org
Founded: 1874
Membership(s): ALPSP, PA & STM.
Subjects: Astronomy, Biography, Computer Science, Electronics, Electrical Engineering, Mathematics, Physical Sciences, Physics, Science (General), Technology
ISBN Prefix(es): 0-85274; 0-85498
Number of titles published annually: 45 Print
Total Titles: 700 Print
Parent Company: Institute of Physics
Imprints: Research Studies Press Ltd (RSP)
Subsidiaries: IOP Publishing Inc
U.S. Office(s): Institute of Physics Publishing, Inc, Public Ledger Bldg, Suite 1035, 150 S Independence Mall W, Philadelphia, PA 19106, United States *Tel:* 215-627-0880 *Fax:* 215-627-0879 *E-mail:* info@ioppubusa.com
Warehouse: Marston Book Services Ltd, PO Box 269, Abingdon OX14 4YN *Tel:* (01235) 465 500 *Fax:* (01235) 465 555
Orders to: c/o AIDC, 2 Winter Sport Lane, PO Box 20, Williston, VT 05495-0020, United States

Institution of Chemical Engineers
Davis Bldg, 165-189 Railway Terrace, Rugby CV21 3HQ
Tel: (01788) 578214 *Fax:* (01788) 560833
E-mail: jcressey@icheme.org.uk
Web Site: www.icheme.org
Telex: 311780
Key Personnel
Chief Executive & Secretary: Dr T J Evans
Senior Marketing Officer: Jacqueline Cressey
Founded: 1922
Subjects: Chemistry, Chemical Engineering
ISBN Prefix(es): 0-8169; 0-85295
U.S. Office(s): American Institute of Chemical Engineers, 345 E 47 St, New York, NY, United States
Distributed by American Institute of Chemical Engineers (Canada & USA only)

Institution of Electrical Engineers+
Publishing Dept, Michael Faraday House, Six Hills Way, Stevenage, Herts SG1 2AY
Tel: (01438) 313311 *Fax:* (01438) 742792
E-mail: postmaster@iee.org.uk
Web Site: www.iee.org.uk/publish
Key Personnel
Man Dir: Steven Mair
Publishing Dir: Robin Mellors-Bourne
Marketing Enquiries: Janet Porter
Commissioning Editor: Roland Harwood
President: David Brown
Founded: 1871
Subjects: Aeronautics, Aviation, Business, Communications, Computer Science, Electronics, Electrical Engineering, Energy, History, Management, Physical Sciences, Technology
ISBN Prefix(es): 0-85296; 0-906048; 0-86341
Number of titles published annually: 30 Print
Total Titles: 240 Print
Parent Company: Savoy Pl, London WC2R 0BL
Imprints: IEE; INSPEC; Peter Peregrinus Ltd
Bookshop(s): IEE, Savoy Pl, London WC2R 0BL

Warehouse: Unit 7, Fulton Close, Argyle Way, Stevenage SG1 2AF *Tel:* (01438) 355029 *Fax:* (01438) 355034
Orders to: PO Box 96, Stevenage, Herts SG1 2SD *Tel:* (01438) 767328 *Fax:* (01438) 742792 *E-mail:* sales@ieee.org *Web Site:* www.iee.org/shop/ (Publications Sales Dept)

Institution of Mechanical Engineers, see Professional Engineering Publishing Ltd

The Intef Institute, *imprint of* Karnak House

Intellect Ltd+
PO Box 862, Bristol BS99 1DE
Tel: (0117) 9589910 *Fax:* (0117) 9589911
E-mail: mail@intellectbooks.com
Web Site: www.intellectbooks.com
Key Personnel
Chairman: Masoud Yazdani
Dir Journal Publishing: Robin Beecroft
Founded: 1984
A multidisciplinary publisher for individual & institutional readers.
Subjects: Computer Science, Drama, Theater, Film, Video, Language Arts, Linguistics, Regional Interests, Women's Studies
ISBN Prefix(es): 1-871516; 1-84150
Number of titles published annually: 25 Print; 25 E-Book
Total Titles: 450 Print; 100 E-Book
Online services available through ebrary, netLibrary.
Branch Office(s)
Bristol, The Mill, Parnall Rd, Fishponds, Bristol BS16 3JG, Contact: Robin Beecroft *Tel:* (0117) 9589910 *Fax:* (0117) 9589911 *E-mail:* robin@intellectbooks.com *Web Site:* www.intellectbooks.com
Distributed by Astam Books (Australasia); Gardners Books (UK); International Specialised Book Services, Inc (North America)
Foreign Rep(s): Astam Books (Australia); ISBS (USA); Kemper Conseil (Netherlands)
Membership(s): IPG

Inter-Varsity Press+
Norton St, Nottingham NG7 3HR
Tel: (0115) 978 1054 *Fax:* (0115) 942 2694
E-mail: sales@ivpbooks.com
Web Site: www.ivpbooks.com
Key Personnel
Chief Executive: B Wilson
Editorial: S Carter
Production: J Mansfield *Tel:* (0115) 978 1054 *Fax:* (0115) 942 2694 *E-mail:* jam@ivpbooks.com
Sales: T Banting *Tel:* (0115) 978 1054 *Fax:* (0115) 942 2694 *E-mail:* trb@ivpbooks.com
Personal Assistant to Chief Executive: Christine Ward *E-mail:* cw@uccf.org.uk
Marketing: V Smith-Dziuba *Tel:* (0115) 978 1054 *Fax:* (0115) 942 2694
Founded: 1928
Publisher of evangelical Christian books.
Subjects: Education, Religion - Other
ISBN Prefix(es): 0-85110; 0-85111
Number of titles published annually: 50 Print
Total Titles: 650 Print
Parent Company: UCCF
Imprints: Apollos (Academic books); Crossway (Popular books); IVP (General books)
Distributor for I V Press; DK Religious; Piquant; Third Way
Distribution Center: IVP Book Centre, Norton St, Nottingham NG7 3HR *Tel:* (0115) 9781054 *Fax:* (0115) 9422694 *Web Site:* www.ivpbooks.com
Orders to: IVP Book Centre, Norton St, Nottingham NG7 3HR *Tel:* (0115) 9781054 *Fax:* (0115) 9422694 *Web Site:* www.ivpbooks.com

UNITED KINGDOM

Intercept Ltd
PO Box 716, Andover, Hants SP10 1YG
Tel: (01264) 334748 *Fax:* (01264) 334058
E-mail: intercept@andover.co.uk
Web Site: www.intercept.co.uk
Key Personnel
Manager: Andrew Cook
Founded: 1983
Subjects: Agriculture, Biological Sciences, Environmental Studies, Gardening, Plants, Geography, Geology, Medicine, Nursing, Dentistry, Natural History, Science (General), Technology
ISBN Prefix(es): 0-946707; 1-898298
Parent Company: Lavoisier, 14 rue de Provigny, 94236 Cachan, France
Distributor for Exegetics; Natural History Museum (London); Erich Nelson Foundation; NRC Research Press; Polytechnic International Press; Ray Society
Warehouse: Unit 2B, Duke Close, West Way, Walworth Industrial Estate, Andover, Hants SP10 5AR

Interfisc Publishing
14 Coopers Row, London EC3N 2BH
Tel: (020) 7702 9799 *Fax:* (020) 7702 3583
E-mail: editor@interfisc.com
Web Site: www.interfisc.com
Key Personnel
Contact: Adrian Ogley *E-mail:* aogley@interfisc.com
Founded: 1993
Professional & academic books on international tax.
Membership(s): Association of Learned & Professional Society of Publishers.
Subjects: Business
ISBN Prefix(es): 0-9520442
Total Titles: 2 Print
Parent Company: Interfisc, 27 Old Gloucester St, London WC1N 3XX
Foreign Rep(s): American Distributor (Canada, USA)
Orders to: International Information Services Inc, PO Box 3490, Silver Spring, MD 20918, United States *Tel:* (301) 565-2975 *Fax:* (301) 565-2973 *E-mail:* orders@interfisc.com (USA & Canada)

Intermediate Technology Publications Ltd, see ITDG Publishing

International Affairs, *imprint of* Royal Institute of International Affairs

International Bee Research Association
18 North Rd, Cardiff CF10 3DT
Tel: (02920) 372409 *Fax:* (02920) 665522
E-mail: mail@cardiff.ac.uk
Web Site: www.cf.ac.uk/ibra
Key Personnel
Dir: Richard Jones
Deputy Dir & Editor: Pamela A Munn, PhD
Founded: 1949
World information specialists on bees.
Membership(s): IUBS.
Subjects: Agriculture, Biological Sciences, Education, Natural History, Bees, Bee Science, Pollination, Conservation
ISBN Prefix(es): 0-86098; 0-900149

International Biographical Centre, *imprint of* Melrose Press Ltd

International Communications
7 Coldbath Sq, London EC1R 4LQ
Tel: (020) 7713 7711 *Fax:* (020) 7713 7898; (020) 7713 7970
E-mail: icpubs@africasia.com
Web Site: www.africasia.com

Key Personnel
Dir: Emena Ben Yedder
Group Publisher: Ahmed Afif Ben Yedder
Sales: Shaunagh Cowell
Founded: 1974
Subjects: Art, Business, Sports, Athletics, Specializes in Current Affairs, Middle East & Africa
ISBN Prefix(es): 0-905268
Number of titles published annually: 4 Print
Subsidiaries: IC Publications

International Institute for Strategic Studies+
Arundel House, 13-15 Arundel St, Temple Pl, London WC2R 3DX
Tel: (020) 7379 7676 *Fax:* (020) 7836 3108
E-mail: iiss@iiss.org
Web Site: www.iiss.org
Telex: 94081492 G *Cable:* MLINK
Key Personnel
Dir: Dr John Chipman *E-mail:* chipman@iiss.org
Assistant Dir: Steven Simon *E-mail:* simon@iiss.org; Terence Taylor *E-mail:* taylor@iiss.org
Manager, Editorial Service: James Green *Tel:* (020) 7379 7676 *E-mail:* green@iiss.org
Founded: 1958
Subjects: Government, Political Science, Military Science
ISBN Prefix(es): 0-86079; 0-900492
Number of titles published annually: 12 Print
Associate Companies: Oxford University Press, Great Clarendon St, Oxford OX2 6DP *Tel:* (01865) 267907 *Fax:* (01865) 267485
Imprints: The Military Balance; Strategic Survey; Survival; Adelphi Papers; Strategic Comments
Distributed by Oxford University Press
Orders to: Oxford University Press, Journals Marketing, 2001 Evans Rd, Cary, NC 27513, United States
Oxford University Press, Great Clarendon St, Oxford OX2 6DP *Tel:* (01865) 267907 *Fax:* (01865) 267485

International Labour Office
Millbank Tower, 21-24 Millbank, London SW1P 4QP
Tel: (020) 7828 6401 *Fax:* (020) 7233 5925
E-mail: ipu@ilo-london.org.uk; london@ilo-london.org.uk
Web Site: www.ilo.org/london
Key Personnel
Dir: Juan Somavia
Publications Manager: Nick Evans *E-mail:* evansn@ilo-london.org.uk
Information Officer: Carl David
Founded: 1919
ISBN Prefix(es): 92-2
Parent Company: International Labour Organization, 4 Route des Morillons, 1211 Geneva 22, Switzerland

International Map Trade Association
5 Spinacre, Becton Lane, Barton on Sea, Hants BH25 7DF
Tel: 01425) 620532 *Fax:* (01425) 620532
E-mail: imtaeurope@compuserve.com
Web Site: www.maptrade.org
Key Personnel
Executive Dir: Mike Cranidge *E-mail:* mike.cranidge@btinternet.com

International Water Association Publishing, see IWA Publishing

Interpet Publishing+
Vincent Lane, Dorking, Surrey RH4 3YX
Tel: (01306) 881033 *Fax:* (01306) 885009
E-mail: publishing@interpet.co.uk
Key Personnel
Publisher: Kevin Kingham

Subjects: Animals, Pets, Gardening, Plants, Veterinary Science
ISBN Prefix(es): 0-948955; 1-86054; 1-84286; 1-902389; 1-903098

Investment Intelligence, *imprint of* Wilmington Business Information Ltd

IOM Communications Ltd
Subsidiary of The Institute of Materials
One Carlton House Terrace, London SW1Y 5DB
Tel: (020) 7451 7300 *Fax:* (020) 7839 1702
E-mail: admin@materials.org.uk
Web Site: www.materials.org.uk *Cable:* 451-7300
Key Personnel
Head of Publishing: Bill Jackson *Tel:* (020) 7451 7305 *E-mail:* bill_jackson@materials.org.uk
Managing Editor: Peter Danckwerts *Tel:* (020) 7451 7310 *E-mail:* peter_danckwerts@materials.org.uk
Marketing Manager: Peter Richardson *Tel:* (020) 7451 7372 *E-mail:* peter_richardson@materials.org.uk
Subjects: Chemistry, Chemical Engineering, Engineering (General)
ISBN Prefix(es): 0-904357; 0-900497; 0-901462; 0-901716; 1-86125

Iona Community, see Wild Goose Publications

IPS, see Eagle/Inter Publishing Service (IPS) Ltd

IRL Press, *imprint of* Oxford University Press

Isis Publishing Ltd+
7 Centremead, Osney Mead, Oxford OX2 0ES
Tel: (01865) 250 333 *Fax:* (01865) 790 358
E-mail: sales@isis-publishing.co.uk
Web Site: www.isis-publishing.co.uk
Key Personnel
International Rights: Emma Cumberland *E-mail:* emma.cumberland@isis-publishing.co.uk
Subjects: Biography, Fiction, Health, Nutrition, Mysteries, Nonfiction (General), Self-Help, Western Fiction
ISBN Prefix(es): 1-85089; 1-85695; 0-7531
Number of titles published annually: 192 Print; 192 Audio
U.S. Office(s): Ulverscroft Large Print (USA) Inc, 1881 Ridge Rd, PO Box 1230, West Seneca, NY 14224-1230, United States *Tel:* 716-674-4270 *Fax:* 716-674-4195

Islam International Publications Ltd+
Islamabad, Sheephatch Lane, Tilford, Farnham GU10 2AQ
Tel: (01252) 783155; (01252) 783823 *Fax:* (01252) 783148
Web Site: www.alislam.org
Key Personnel
Dir: Mr N A Qamar
Founded: 1889
Specialize in books on Islam, various translations & exegesis of Holy Quran in different languages.
Subjects: Religion - Islamic, Theology
ISBN Prefix(es): 1-85372
Imprints: Al-Shirkatul Islamiyyah
Subsidiaries: London Mosque Publications
U.S. Office(s): The Ahmadiyya Movement in Islam Inc, Masjid Bait-Ur-Rehman, 15000 Good Hope Rd, Silver Spring, MD 20905, United States *Tel:* (301) 879-0110 *Fax:* (301) 879-0115

Islamic Foundation Publications
Markfield Conference Centre, Ratby Lane, Markfield, Leics LE67 9SY

Tel: (01530) 244 944; (01530) 249 230 *Fax:* (01530) 244 946; (01530) 249 656
E-mail: info@islamic-foundation.org.uk; publications@islamic-foundation.com
Web Site: www.islamic-foundation.com; www.islamic-foundation.org.uk *Cable:* ISLAMFOUND LEICESTER UK
Key Personnel
Dir General, Editorial: Dr M M Ahsan
Dir Publications: Farooq Murad
Contact: Chowdhury Mueen-Uddin *E-mail:* c.mueen@islamic-foundation.org.uk
Founded: 1973
Research, publication, post-graduation education, training.
Subjects: Economics, Education, Government, Political Science, History, Religion - Islamic
ISBN Prefix(es): 0-86037; 0-9503954
Number of titles published annually: 10 Print
Imprints: Revival Publications
Distributed by International Institute of Islamic Thought (USA); IPS (Pakistan); Islamic Circle of North America (USA); Islamic Society of North America (USA); Sound Vision (USA)
Orders to: The Islamic Foundation Publications Unit, Markfield Dawah Center, Ratby Lane, Markfield, Leics LE67 9SY

The Islamic Texts Society+
22A Brooklands Ave, Cambridge CB2 2DQ
Tel: (01223) 314387 *Fax:* (01223) 324342
E-mail: info@its.org.uk
Web Site: www.its.org.uk
Key Personnel
Man Dir: Fatima Azzam *E-mail:* fazzam@its.org.uk
Founded: 1981
Specialize in Islamic literature.
Membership(s): Publishers' Association.
Subjects: Art, Biography, History, Law, Natural History, Nonfiction (General), Philosophy, Poetry, Religion - Islamic
ISBN Prefix(es): 0-946621
Number of titles published annually: 6 Print
Total Titles: 40 Print
Foreign Rep(s): The American University in Cairo Press (Egypt); Eleanor Brasch Enterprises (Australia); Richard Carman (Sub-Saharan Africa); Iberian Book Services (Spain & Portugal); International Specialized Book Services (Canada, USA); Publishers International Marketing (Middle East, Southeast Asia); Quantum Publishing Solutions Ltd (UK); Andrew Russell (Ireland, Northern Ireland); Murray Sutton (Denmark, Iceland, Scandinavia); Viva Marketing (India)
Warehouse: Orca Book Services, Fleets Industrial Estate, One Willis Way, Poole, Dorset BH15 3SS *Tel:* (01202) 785729 *Fax:* (01202) 666219
Orders to: Orca Book Services Ltd, Stanley House, 3 Fleets Lane, Poole, Dorset BH15 3AJ *Tel:* (01202) 665432 *Fax:* (01202) 666219
E-mail: orders@orcabookservices.co.uk

IT Publications, *imprint of* ITDG Publishing

ITDG Publishing+
Formerly Intermediate Technology Publications Ltd
Bourton Hall, Bourton-on-Dunsmore, Rugby CV23 9QZ
Tel: (01926) 634501 *Fax:* (01926) 634502
E-mail: marketing@itpubs.org.uk; itpubs@itpubs.org.uk
Web Site: www.itdgpublishing.org.uk; www.developmentbookshop.com
Key Personnel
Editorial, Rights & Permissions: Helen Marsden
Sales & Publicity: Toby Harris *E-mail:* tobyh@itpubs.org.uk
Founded: 1973
Subjects: Agriculture, Business, Developing Countries, Finance, Social Sciences, Sociology, Technology
ISBN Prefix(es): 0-903031; 0-946688; 1-85339
Number of titles published annually: 25 Print
Total Titles: 400 Print
Parent Company: Intermediate Technology Development Group
Imprints: IT Publications
Distributed by Amin al-Abini (Middle East & North Africa); Astam Books Pty Ltd (Australia); Richard Bowen (Finland, Norway, Sweden, Iceland, Denmark); Grassroots Books Pvt Ltd (Zimbabwe); Horizon Books Ltd; InterMedia Americana (Central Africa); Lake House Bookshop (Sri Lanka); Maya Publishers Plc (India); Publishers Marketing Services Plc (Malaysia, Singapore, Indonesia. Thailand, Brunei); STM Publishers Services (Taiwan, Korea, Vietnam, Philippines, Hong Kong, Thailand, China); Stylus Publishing Inc (USA)
Distributor for IDRC (Canada); KIT Press (Amsterdam, The Netherlands); SKAT (Switzerland)
Foreign Rep(s): Stylus (USA)
Orders to: Plymbridge Distributors Ltd, Estover Rd, Plymouth PL6 7PY

Ithaca Press, *imprint of* Garnet Publishing Ltd

IUCN-The World Conservation Union
Publications Services Unit, 219c Huntingdon Rd, Cambridge CB3 0DL
Tel: (01223) 277894 *Fax:* (01223) 277175
E-mail: books@iucn.org
Web Site: www.iucn.org
Key Personnel
Publications Officer: Deborah Murith *Tel:* (022) 999 0119 *Fax:* (022) 999 0010 *E-mail:* dem@iucn.org
Founded: 1948
ISBN Prefix(es): 2-8317
Divisions:
Distributed by Island Press
Distributor for Cites; Ramsar; World Conservation Monitoring Centre

IVP, *imprint of* Inter-Varsity Press

IWA Publishing
Subsidiary of International Water Association
Alliance House, 12 Caxton St, London SW1H 0QS
Tel: (020) 7654 5500 *Fax:* (020) 7654 5555
E-mail: publications@iwap.co.uk
Web Site: www.iwapublishing.com
Subjects: Civil Engineering, Earth Sciences, Environmental Studies, Hydrology, Wastewater, Water
ISBN Prefix(es): 1-84339
Number of titles published annually: 50 Print; 1 CD-ROM
Total Titles: 250 Print; 5 CD-ROM
Distributed by Portland Press
Foreign Rights: Tony Poh (China, Korea, Malaysia, Philippines, Singapore, Thailand, Vietnam)
Distribution Center: Portland Customer Services, Commerce Way, Colchester CO2 8HP *Tel:* (01206) 796351 *E-mail:* sales@portland-services.com
Returns: Portland Customer Services, Commerce Way, Colchester CO2 8HP *Tel:* (01206) 796351

JAI, *imprint of* Elsevier Ltd

JAI Press Ltd+
38 Tavistock St, Covent Garden, London WC2E 7PB
Tel: (020) 7379 8834 *Fax:* (020) 7379 8835
Web Site: www.jaipress.com
Key Personnel
Marketing in Sales: Della Sar
Founded: 1985
Specialize in research-level serials, monograph series, treatises & journals.
Subjects: Accounting, Behavioral Sciences, Biological Sciences, Business, Chemistry, Chemical Engineering, Child Care & Development, Economics, Education, Government, Political Science, Library & Information Sciences, Management, Psychology, Psychiatry, Social Sciences, Sociology
ISBN Prefix(es): 0-89232; 1-55938; 0-7623
Parent Company: Elsevier Science
Warehouse: Marston Book Services Ltd, PO Box 269, Abingdon OX14 4YN

James & James (Publishers) Ltd+
Gordon House Business Centre, 6 Lissenden Gardens, London NW5 1LX
Tel: (020) 7482 8888 *Fax:* (020) 7482 8889
E-mail: jxj@jamesxjames.co.uk
Web Site: www.jamesxjames.co.uk
Key Personnel
Man Dir: Hamish MacGibbon
Project Editor: Susie May
Marketing Manager: Ruth Weinberg
Founded: 1985
Publishers of illustrated books on history & the environment, specifically illustrated histories of companies, schools & other institutions.
Subjects: Business, Environmental Studies, History
ISBN Prefix(es): 0-907383
Total Titles: 10 Print
Associate Companies: James & James Science Publishers Ltd, Contact: Edward Milford *Tel:* (0171) 387 8558
Membership(s): IPG

James & James (Science Publishers) Ltd+
8-12 Camden High St, London NW1 0JH
Tel: (020) 7387 8558 *Fax:* (020) 7387 8998
E-mail: jxj@jxj.com
Web Site: www.jxj.com
Key Personnel
Publisher: Edward Milford *E-mail:* em@jxj.com
Founded: 1990
Subjects: Architecture & Interior Design, Electronics, Electrical Engineering, Energy, Environmental Studies, Physics
ISBN Prefix(es): 0-907383; 1-873936; 1-902916
Total Titles: 70 Print
U.S. Office(s): Stylus Publishing LLC, 22883 Quicksilver Drive, Sterling, VA 20166, United States *Tel:* 703-661-1581 *Fax:* 703-661-1501 *E-mail:* styluspub@aol.com
Distributed by A & I Ltd

Arthur James Ltd, *imprint of* John Hunt Publishing Ltd

Jane's Information Group
Sentinel House, 163 Brighton Rd, Coulsdon, Surrey CR5 2YH
Tel: (020) 8700 3700 *Fax:* (020) 8763 1006
E-mail: info.uk@janes.com
Web Site: www.janes.com
Key Personnel
Man Dir: Alfred Rolington *Tel:* (020) 8700 3701 *Fax:* (020) 8700 3704 *E-mail:* alfred.rolington@janes.com
Publishing Dir, Reference: Ian Kay *Tel:* (020) 8700 3796 *Fax:* (020) 8700 3788 *E-mail:* ian.kay@janes.com
Group Communications Manager: Claire Brunavs *Tel:* (020) 8700 3703 *E-mail:* claire.brunavs@janes.com
Founded: 1897
Specialize in police, security, geopolitics, risk assessment, technical & infrastructure information. Full online subscription access & CD-ROMS.

UNITED KINGDOM

Subjects: Aeronautics, Aviation, Foreign Countries, Maritime, Military Science, Transportation
ISBN Prefix(es): 0-7106; 0-309; 0-532; 0-265
Total Titles: 200 Print; 12 CD-ROM; 200 Online; 9 E-Book
Parent Company: The Woodbridge Co Ltd
Branch Office(s)
78 Shenton Way, No 10-02, Singapore 079120, Singapore, Contact: David Fisher *Tel:* 6325 0866 *Fax:* 6226 1185 *E-mail:* asiapacific@janes.com
PO Box 3502, Rozelle NSW 2039, Australia, Contact: Pauline Roberts *Tel:* (02) 8587 7900 *Fax:* (02) 8587 7901 *E-mail:* oceania@janes.com
U.S. Office(s): Jane's Information Group (US), 110 N Royal St, Suite 200, Alexandria, VA 22314, United States, Contact: Rahul Belani *Tel:* 703-683-3700 *Fax:* 703-836-0029 *E-mail:* rahul.belani@janes.com

Janus Books, *imprint of* Janus Publishing Co Ltd

Janus Publishing Co Ltd+
105-107 Gloucester Pl, London W1U 6BY
Tel: (020) 7580 7664 *Fax:* (020) 7636 5756
E-mail: sales@januspublishing.co.uk
Web Site: www.januspublishing.co.uk
Key Personnel
Man Dir: Sandy Leung
Production: S Legg
Publicity: N Cording
Marketing: S Hughes
Founded: 1991 (For authors overlooked by big publishing houses)
Publisher of radical ideas
Janus-subsidized publishing; *Empiricus*-non-subsidized.
Subjects: Alternative, Astrology, Occult, Biography, Education, Fiction, Film, Video, Health, Nutrition, Nonfiction (General), Philosophy, Poetry, Religion - Buddhist, Religion - Jewish, Science Fiction, Fantasy, Theology, Social, Academic & Spiritual
ISBN Prefix(es): 1-85756
Ultimate Parent Company: Junction Books Ltd
Imprints: Janus Books; Empiricus Books
U.S. Office(s): IPG, 140 Union St, Marshfield, MA 02050-6273, United States, Contact: David Gebhart *Tel:* (781) 834-9830
Foreign Rep(s): Richard Bowden (Scandinavia, Sweden); IPG (USA)
Membership(s): IPG

Japan Library, *imprint of* RoutledgeCurzon

Jarrold Publishing+
Division of Jarrold & Sons Ltd
Whitefriars, Norwich NR3 1TR
Tel: (01603) 763300 *Fax:* (01603) 662748
E-mail: info@jarrold.com
Web Site: www.jarrold-publishing.co.uk
Key Personnel
Man Dir, Rights & Permissions: Caroline Jarrold
Founded: 1770
Specialize in the publishing of books, calendars & stationery.
Subjects: Biography, History, Regional Interests, Travel
ISBN Prefix(es): 0-85306; 0-7117
Number of titles published annually: 30 Print
Total Titles: 250 Print
Imprints: Pathfinder
Distributor for MacMillan Way Association; Northern Ireland Tourist Board; Wales Tourist Board
Bookshop(s): Jarrolds, 5 London St, Norwich, Norfolk NR2 1JF *Web Site:* www.britguides.co.uk

John Wiley & Sons, *imprint of* Wiley Europe Ltd

Johnson Publications Ltd+
21 Picadilly, London W1J 0DQ
Tel: (020) 7486 6757 *Fax:* (020) 7487 5436
Key Personnel
Dir: M A Murray-Pearce; Z M Pauncefort
Subjects: Advertising, Biography, Marketing
ISBN Prefix(es): 0-85307
Orders to: Spring Court, Abbots Rd, Abbots Langley, Herts WD5 0BJ

Jones & Bartlett International+
Barb House, Barb Mews, London W6 7PA
Tel: (01892) 539356 *Fax:* (01892) 614944
E-mail: j&b@class.co.uk
Web Site: www.jbpub.com
Key Personnel
International Rights: Richard Warner
Founded: 1983
Subjects: Biological Sciences, Computer Science, Earth Sciences, Geography, Geology, Health, Nutrition, Mathematics, Medicine, Nursing, Dentistry
ISBN Prefix(es): 0-86720
Parent Company: Jones & Bartlett Publishers, Inc, 40 Tall Pine Dr, Sudbury, MA 01776, United States
Foreign Rep(s): Academic Marketing Services Ltd (South Africa); Alfaomega Grupo Editor (Mexico); Alkem Company (S) Pte Ltd (Indonesia); Blackwell Publishing Asia (Australia & New Zealand); Cranbury International LLC (Caribbean including Puerto Rico, South America); Delaney Global Publishers Services, Inc (Guam, Philippines); Benjamin Ho (China & Hong Kong, Korea, Singapore, Taiwan, Thailand); Interknowledge Books Inc (Japan); International Publishers Representatives (IPR) (Middle East, Iran); Jones & Bartlett Publishers (UK, Canada, Continental Europe); LIDEL - Edicoes Tecnicas Lda (Portugal); Premium Educational Group (Puerto Rico); Publicaciones Educativas (Central America, Mexico); United Publishers Services Ltd (Japan); University Bookstore (Malaysia)
Orders to: Plymbridge Distributors, Plymbridge House, Estover Rd, Plymouth, Devon PL6 7PZ *Tel:* (0752) 695745 *Fax:* (0752) 695699

John Jones Publishing Ltd+
Unit 12, Clwydfro Business Centre, Ruthin LL15 1NJ
Tel: (01824) 707255 *Fax:* (01824) 705272
E-mail: johnjonespublishing.ltd@virgin.net
Web Site: www.johnjonespublishing.ltd.uk
Key Personnel
Man Dir: John Idris Jones
Founded: 1979
Specialize in paperbacks for the tourist market & books in English with a Welsh background.
Membership(s): IPG.
Subjects: Biography, History, Travel
ISBN Prefix(es): 1-871083
Total Titles: 49 Print
Distributed by John Reed (Australia)
Foreign Rep(s): John Reed Book Distribution

Jordan Publishing Ltd
21 St Thomas St, Bristol BS1 6JS
Tel: (0117) 923 0600 *Fax:* (0117) 925 0486
E-mail: customerservice@jordanpublishing.co.uk
Web Site: www.jordanpublishing.co.uk
Telex: 449119
Key Personnel
Man Dir: Richard Hudson
Publishing Dir: Martin West
Managing Editor: Mollie Dickenson
Marketing Manager: David Chaplin
   E-mail: dchaplin@jordanpublishing.co.uk
Founded: 1863

Subjects: Accounting, Business, Law
ISBN Prefix(es): 0-85308
Parent Company: Jordan & Sons Ltd, Bristol
Imprints: Jordans; Family Law
Branch Office(s)
20-22 Bedford Row, London WC1R 4JS
   Tel: (020) 7400 3333 *Fax:* (020) 7400 3366

Jordans, *imprint of* Jordan Publishing Ltd

Michael Joseph, *imprint of* Penguin Books Ltd

Michael Joseph Ltd+
80 Strand, London WC2 0RN
Tel: (020) 7416 3000 *Fax:* (020) 7416 3099
Telex: 917181
Key Personnel
Publishing Dir: Tom Weldon
Marketing Dir: John Bond
Export Sales Dir: Max Adam *E-mail:* max.adam@penguin.co.uk
Rights Dir: Sophie Brewer
Founded: 1936
Subjects: Biography, Fiction, History
ISBN Prefix(es): 0-7181
Parent Company: Penguin Books Ltd
Imprints: Mermaid
Warehouse: Penguin Group Distribution Ltd, 27 Wrights Lane, London W8 5TZ
Orders to: Penguin Group Distribution Ltd, Bath Rd, Harmondsworth, Middlesex UB7 0DA

Richard Joseph Publishers Ltd
PO Box 15, Torrington, Devon EX38 8ZJ
Tel: (01805) 625750 *Fax:* (01805) 625376
E-mail: sheppardsdir@aol.com
Web Site: www.sheppardsworld.com
Key Personnel
Man Dir: Richard Joseph *E-mail:* rjoe01@aol.com
Advertising: Claire Brumham
Founded: 1990
Reference books for the secondhand & antiquarian trades.
ISBN Prefix(es): 1-872699
Total Titles: 26 Print; 1 CD-ROM
Imprints: Sheppard
U.S. Office(s): Richard Joseph Publishers, PO Box 1350, State College, PA 16804-1350, United States
Membership(s): IPG

Jossey-Bass, *imprint of* Wiley Europe Ltd

Junior Funfax, *imprint of* Funfax Ltd

Kahn & Averill
9 Harrington Rd, London SW7 3ES
Tel: (020) 8743 3278 *Fax:* (020) 8743 3278
Key Personnel
Man Dir: M Kahn
Founded: 1947
Subjects: Music, Dance
ISBN Prefix(es): 0-900707; 1-871082
Shipping Address: Bailey Distribution Ltd, Mountfield Industrial Estate, New Romney, Kent TN28 8XU
Warehouse: Bailey Distribution Ltd, Mountfield Industrial Estate, New Rowney, Kent TN28 8XU
Orders to: Bailey Distribution Ltd, Mountfield Industrial Estate, New Romney, Kent TN28 8XU

Karnac Books Ltd+
118 Finchley Rd, London NW3 5HT
Tel: (020) 8969 4454 *Fax:* (020) 8969 5585
E-mail: books@karnac.demon.co.uk
Web Site: www.karnacbooks.com
Key Personnel
Man Dir: Cesare D S Sacerdoti
Founded: 1950

Subjects: Psychology, Psychiatry, Social Sciences, Sociology
ISBN Prefix(es): 0-946439; 1-85575; 0-9501647; 0-9507146
Imprints: Maresfield Lib
Distributed by Taylor & Francis (USA)
Distributor for Analytic Press; Clunie Press; Institute of Marital Studies
Bookshop(s): 118 Finchley Rd, London NW3 5HJ
Tel: (020) 8969 4454 *Fax:* (020) 8969 5585
E-mail: shop@karnacbooks.com

Karnak House+
300 Westbourne Park Rd, London W11 1EH
Tel: (020) 7243 3620 *Fax:* (020) 7243 3620
E-mail: connection@karnakhouse.co.uk
Web Site: www.karnakhouse.co.uk
Key Personnel
Dir: A S Saakana; Seheri Stroude
Founded: 1979
Specialize in African & Caribbean studies worldwide.
Subjects: Anthropology, Education, History, Language Arts, Linguistics, Nonfiction (General), Philosophy, Religion - Other, Science (General), Egyptology
ISBN Prefix(es): 0-907015; 1-872596
Number of titles published annually: 10 Print
Total Titles: 100 Print
Imprints: The Intef Institute
Distributed by Turnaround
Orders to: 631 E 75 St, Chicago, IL 60619, United States, Contact: Ras Seko Tafari
Tel: 773-651-9888 *Fax:* 773-651-9850

Kegan Paul International Ltd+
121 Bedford Court Mansions, Bedford Ave, London WC1B 3SW
Mailing Address: PO Box 256, London WC1B 3SW
Tel: (020) 7580 5511 *Fax:* (020) 7436 0899
E-mail: books@keganpaul.com
Web Site: www.keganpaul.com
Key Personnel
Chairman: Peter Hopkins
Editorial Dir: Kaori O'Connor
Founded: 1871
Subjects: Archaeology, Architecture & Interior Design, Art, Photography, Travel, Africa, Arabic Linguistics, Asian Studies, China, Egyptology, Environmental Studies & Natural Science, International Studies & Law, Islam, Japan, Korea, Literature & Poetry, Middle East, Oriental Philosophy & Religion, Pacific
ISBN Prefix(es): 0-7103
Number of titles published annually: 40 Print
Total Titles: 520 Print
U.S. Office(s): Columbia University Press, 562 W 113 St, New York, NY 10025, United States *Tel:* 212-666-1000 *Fax:* 212-316-3100
Distributed by Turpin Distribution
Shipping Address: John Wiley & Sons Ltd, Southern Cross Trading Estate, One Oldlands Way, Bognor Regis, West Sussex PO22 9SA, Contact: Diana Butterly *Tel:* (01243) 779777 *Fax:* (01243) 843303
Warehouse: John Wiley & Sons Ltd, Southern Cross Trading Estate, Oldlands Way Bagnor Regis, West Sussex PO22 9SA, Contact: Lori Powell *Tel:* (01243) 843223 *Fax:* (01243) 820250
Orders to: John Wiley & Sons Ltd, Southern Cross Trading Estate, One Oldlands Way, Bognor Regis, West Sussex PO22 9SA, Contact: Diane Butterly *Tel:* (01243) 843273 *Fax:* (01243) 843303
Columbia University Press, 61 W 62nd St, New York, NY 10023, United States *Tel:* 914-591-9111 *E-mail:* ms1004@columbia.edu *Web Site:* www.columbia.edu/cu/cup (North America)

Kelly's
Windsor Court, East Grinstead House, East Grinstead, West Sussex RH19 1XA
Tel: (01342) 335862 *Fax:* (01342) 335825
E-mail: kellys.mktg@reedinfo.co.uk
Web Site: www.kellysearch.com
Telex: 95127
Key Personnel
Publishing Dr: Brian Gallagher
Founded: 1799
Membership(s): Directory Publishers Association & European Directory Publishers Association.
Subjects: Business
ISBN Prefix(es): 0-610
Warehouse: Vale Packaging, 420 Vale Rd, Tonbridge, Kent TN9 1TO

Kemps Publishing Ltd+
11 The Swan Courtyard, Charles Edward Rd, Yardley, Birmingham B26 1BU
Tel: (0121) 765 4144 *Fax:* (0121) 706 1408
E-mail: info@kempsgold.co.uk
Web Site: www.kempsgold.co.uk
Key Personnel
Contact: Marisha Gorcewicz
Founded: 1912
ISBN Prefix(es): 0-86259; 0-900273; 0-901268; 0-905255

The Kenilworth Press Ltd+
Addington, Buckingham, Bucks MK18 2JR
Tel: (01296) 715101 *Fax:* (01296) 715148
E-mail: customer.services@kenilworthpress.co.uk
Web Site: www.kenilworthpress.co.uk
Key Personnel
Man Dir: David Blunt *E-mail:* david.blunt@kenilworthpress.co.uk
Dir: Deirdre Blunt
Founded: 1989
Publisher of instructional equestrian books
Also acts as official publisher to The British Horse Society.
Subjects: Animals, Pets, Natural History, Sports, Athletics, Veterinary Science
ISBN Prefix(es): 1-872082; 0-901366; 1-872119
Number of titles published annually: 10 Print
Total Titles: 100 Print
Imprints: Threshold
Divisions: Threshold Books
Distributed by Half Halt Press Inc (USA)
Distributor for Half Halt Press Inc
Warehouse: Hoddle Doyle Meadows, Station Rd, Linton, Cambs CB1 6UX

Kenyon-Deane, *imprint of* Cressrelles Publishing Company Ltd

Kenyon-Deane+
Imprint of Cressrelles Publishing Company Ltd
Industrial Estate, 10 Station Rd, Colwall, Nr Malvern, Herefordshire WR13 6RN
Tel: (01684) 540154 *Fax:* (01684) 540154
Key Personnel
Man Dir: Leslie Smith
Founded: 1930
Specialize in plays for women.
Subjects: Drama, Theater
ISBN Prefix(es): 0-7155
Number of titles published annually: 6 Print
Total Titles: 400 Print
Parent Company: Cressrelles Publishing Co Ltd
Distributor for Anchorage Press (Europe)

Kidhaven Press, *imprint of* Thomson Gale

Hilda King Educational+
Ashwells Manor Dr, Penn, Bucks HP10 8EU
Tel: (01494) 813947; (01494) 817947 *Fax:* (01494) 813947
E-mail: hildaking@clara.co.uk; orders@hilda-king.co.uk
Web Site: www.hildaking.clara.net
Key Personnel
Dir: Ron King *E-mail:* ron@hilda-king.co.uk
Contact: Hilda King *E-mail:* hilda@hilda-king.co.uk
Founded: 1990
Specializes in photocopiable educational resources.
Membership(s): Publishers Association.
Subjects: Geography, Geology, History, Mathematics, Audio Tapes (phonics); English & French Language; English & French, nursery
ISBN Prefix(es): 1-873533
Total Titles: 100 Print; 8 Audio

Laurence King Publishing Ltd+
71 Great Russell St, London WC1B 3BP
Tel: (020) 7430 8850 *Fax:* (020) 7430 8880
E-mail: info@laurenceking.co.uk
Web Site: www.laurenceking.co.uk
Key Personnel
Chairman: Robin Hyman
Man Dir: Laurence King
Editorial Dir, Professional Trade Division: Philip Cooper
Editorial Dir, College & Fine Art: Lee Ripley Greenfield
Rights Manager: Janet Pilch *E-mail:* janet@laurenceking.co.uk
Foreign Rights: Sarah Davis *E-mail:* sarah@laurenceking.co.uk
Founded: 1976
Also acts as designer & producer of high-quality illustrated books
Specialize in international co-editions.
Subjects: Architecture & Interior Design, Art, Fashion, Film, Video, House & Home, Religion - Other
ISBN Prefix(es): 1-85669
Total Titles: 200 Print
Warehouse: Thames & Hudson Ltd, 44 Clockhouse Rd, Farnborough, Hants GU14 7QZ

Kingfisher Publications Plc+
New Penderel House, 283-288 High Holborn, London WC1V 7HZ
Tel: (020) 7903 9999 *Fax:* (020) 7242 5009
E-mail: rights@kingfisherpub.com
Web Site: www.kingfisherpub.com
Key Personnel
Finance Dir: Geraud de Durand
Production Dir: John Richards
Export Sales Manager: Melissa Johnson
International Sales Dir: Hilary Downie *E-mail:* hdownie@kingfisherpub.co.uk
Key Accounts Manager: Sheila O'Sullivan *Tel:* (01926) 864 816 *Fax:* (01926) 864 816
UK Trade, Export and Marketing Sales Dir: Robert Pearce
UK Rights and special sales Dir: Catherine Potter
Export Sales Manager: Melissa Johnson
Sales Office Assistant: Pachi Lopez
Founded: 1974
Subjects: Regional Interests
ISBN Prefix(es): 0-7523; 0-86272; 1-85697; 1-85296
Number of titles published annually: 85 Print
Parent Company: Houghton Mifflin Co, 222 Berkeley St, Boston, MA 02116, United States
Sales Office(s): Chameleon Group, 5 Milnyard Sq, Orton Southgate, Peterborough PE2 6AX *Tel:* (01733) 370606 *Fax:* (01733) 370607
Distributed by I K International Pvt Ltd (India); Macmillan Distribution Ltd (England); Pansing Distribution SDN BHD (Brunei, Indonesia, Malaysia, Singapore); Paramount Books (PVT) Ltd (Pakistan); Publishers Associates Ltd (Hong Kong); Quartet Sales & Marketing (South Africa); Scholastic Australia Ltd (Australia); South Pacific Books (Imports) 2001 Ltd (New Zealand); Westland Books Pvt Ltd (India)

UNITED KINGDOM

Foreign Rep(s): Ashton International Marketing Services (China, Japan, Korea, Taiwan, Thailand); Humphrys Roberts Associates (Central America, South America, West Indies); Walton Marketing Services (Europe, Israel); Peter Ward Book Exports (Middle East)
Warehouse: Macmillan Distribution Ltd, Brunel Rd, Houndsmill, Basingstoke, Hants R921 2XS
Orders to: Macmillan Distribution Ltd, Brunel Rd, Houndsmill, Basingstoke, Hants R921 2XS

King's Fund Publishing+
11-13 Cavendish Sq, London W1G 0AN
Tel: (020) 7307 2400 *Fax:* (020) 7307 2801
E-mail: libweb@kingsfund.org.uk
Web Site: www.kingsfund.org.uk
Key Personnel
Head of Communications & Marketing: Stephen Lustig *Tel:* (020) 7307 2584 *E-mail:* slustig@kingsfund.org.uk
Founded: 1897
Health & social care titles mainly for professionals, managers, academics & libraries
Not for profit charitable foundation.
Subjects: Health, Nutrition, Social Sciences, Sociology
ISBN Prefix(es): 1-85551; 1-85717; 1-870551; 1-870607; 1-873883
Number of titles published annually: 30 Print
Total Titles: 200 Print
Parent Company: King's Fund
U.S. Office(s): Transaction Publishers, Contact: Mary Curtis *Tel:* 908-445-2280 *E-mail:* mcurtis@transactionpub.com

Jessica Kingsley Publishers+
116 Pentonville Rd, London N1 9JB
Tel: (020) 7833 2307 *Fax:* (020) 7837 2917
E-mail: post@jkp.com
Web Site: www.jkp.com
Key Personnel
Man Dir & International Rights: Jessica Kingsley *E-mail:* jessica@jkp.com
Sales & Marketing: Petra Green
Founded: 1987
Membership(s): Independent Publishers Guild, Publishers Association.
Subjects: Behavioral Sciences, Child Care & Development, Criminology, Disability, Special Needs, Education, Medicine, Nursing, Dentistry, Psychology, Psychiatry, Social Sciences, Sociology
ISBN Prefix(es): 1-85302
Total Titles: 650 Print; 3 CD-ROM; 3 Audio
Imprints: Pentn Press
Distributed by Astam Books Pty Ltd (Australia & New Zealand); Book Promotions (Pty) Ltd (South Africa); Irwin Publishing (Canada); Publishers Marketing Services (Singapore, Malaysia, Brunei & Indonesia); Taylor & Francis Inc (USA); United Publishers Services (Japan); Viva Marketing (India)
Distributor for Paul H Brooke & MacLennan & Petty (UK); Love Publishing (UK)
Foreign Rep(s): Asia Publishers Service Ltd (China, Hong Kong, Korea, Philippines, Taiwan); Bill Baird (Scotland); Book Bird (Pakistan); Book Representation & Distribution (England, Northern Ireland); Brookside Publishing Services (Ireland); Andrew Durnell (Europe); STM Pte Ltd (Thailand)

Kingsway Publications+
26-28 Lottbridge Drove, Eastbourne, East Sussex BN23 6NT
Tel: (01323) 437700 *Fax:* (01323) 411970
E-mail: books@kingsway.co.uk
Web Site: www.kingsway.co.uk
Key Personnel
Chief Executive Officer: John Paculabo
Publishing Dir: Richard Herkes
List Administrator: Cathy Williams

Foreign Rights: Chris Jackson
Founded: 1977
Publisher & supplier of Christian books, music, crafts & children's ministry resources.
Membership(s): Publishers' Association.
Subjects: Religion - Protestant, Religion - Other, Theology
ISBN Prefix(es): 0-86065; 0-85476
Parent Company: Kingsway Communications Ltd
Associate Companies: David C Cook
Distributor for Barbour (USA/Canada); Bethany House (USA/Canada); Chariot Victor (USA/Canada)
Orders to: STL Wholesale, PO Box 300, Kingstown Industrial Estates, Kingstown Broadway, Carlisle CA3 0JH *Fax:* (01228) 514949

Kinship Library, see Centaur Press (1954)

Kluwer Academic/Human Sciences Press, *imprint of* Kluwer Academic/Plenum Publishers

Kluwer Academic/Plenum Publishers+
Imprint of Kluwer Academic Publishers
100 Borough High St, London SE1 1LB
Tel: (020) 7863 3000 *Fax:* (020) 7863 3314
E-mail: mail@plenum.co.uk
Web Site: www.wkap.nl
Key Personnel
Man Dir: Dr Ken Derham *E-mail:* k.derham@plenum.co.uk
Editor: Joanna Lawrence
Founded: 1960
European Editorial office of Kluwer academic/Plenum Publishers of New Turk.
Membership(s): PA & STM.
Subjects: Biological Sciences, Chemistry, Chemical Engineering, Communications, Computer Science, Electronics, Electrical Engineering, Mathematics, Physical Sciences, Physics, Social Sciences, Sociology
ISBN Prefix(es): 0-306
Imprints: Consultants Bureau (journals); Kluwer Academic/Human Sciences Press (journals); Maik Nauka/Interperiodica (journals)
U.S. Office(s): 233 Spring St, 7th floor, New York, NY 10013-1522, United States *Tel:* (212) 620-8000
Orders to: Distribution Center, PO Box 322, 3300AH Dordrecht, Netherlands *Tel:* (078) 6392392 *Fax:* (078) 6546474 *E-mail:* orderdept@wkap.nl *Web Site:* www.wkap.nl (Except North, South & Central America)
Kluwer Academic Publishers, Assinippi Park, 101 Philip Dr, Norwell, MA 02061, United States *Tel:* 781-871-6600 *Fax:* 781-871-6528 *E-mail:* kluwer@wkap.com *Web Site:* www.wkap.nl (North, South & Central America)
Returns: Distribution Center, PO Box 322, 3300AH Dordrecht, Netherlands *Tel:* (078) 6392392 *Fax:* (078) 6546474 *E-mail:* orderdept@wkap.nl *Web Site:* www.wkap.nl (Except North, South & Central America); Kluwer Academic Publishers, Assinippi Park, 101 Philip Dr, Norwell, MA 02061, United States *Tel:* 781-871-6600 *Fax:* 781-871-6528 *E-mail:* kluwer@wkap.com *Web Site:* www.wkap.nl (North, South & Central America)

Knockabout Comics+
Unit 24, 10 Acklam Rd, London W10 5QZ
Tel: (020) 8969 2945 *Fax:* (020) 8968 7614
E-mail: knockcomic@aol.com
Web Site: www.knockabout.com
Key Personnel
Man Dir: Tony Bennett *E-mail:* tonyknock@aol.com
Distribution Manager: Joe Toussaint

BOOK

International Rights: Lora Fountain *Tel:* (014) 3562196 *Fax:* (014) 3482272
Founded: 1975
Subjects: Gardening, Plants, Health, Nutrition, Humor, Social Sciences, Sociology, Specialize in comic books, graphic novels & drug information
ISBN Prefix(es): 0-86166
Number of titles published annually: 6 Print
Total Titles: 110 Print
Parent Company: Toskanex Ltd
Imprints: Fanny; Hassle Free Press
Distributor for Last Gasp (North America); American Archives (North America); Quick Trading Co (North America); Rip Off Press (excludes USA & Canada)
Foreign Rights: Lora Fountain (France & Spain, Germany, Holland)

Know Alls, *imprint of* Funfax Ltd

Kogan Page Ltd+
120 Pentonville Rd, London N1 9JN
Tel: (020) 7278 0433 *Fax:* (020) 7837 6348
E-mail: kpinfo@kogan-page.co.uk; kpsales@kogan-page.co.uk; orders@kogan-page.co.uk
Web Site: www.kogan-page.co.uk
Key Personnel
Man Dir: Philip Kogan
Editorial Dir, Business, Trade, Professional & Academic: Pauline Goodwin
Editorial Dir, Reference & Directories: Linda Batham
Editorial Dir, Training & Careers: Philip Mudd
Editorial & Production Dir: Peter Chadwick
Sales & Marketing Dir: Julie McNair *E-mail:* jmcnair@kogan-page.co.uk
Finance Dir: Gordon Watts
Rights Manager: Ben Heywood *Tel:* (020) 7843 1965 *E-mail:* bheywood@kogan-page.co.uk
Export Sales Manager: Lynda Moynihan *E-mail:* lmoynihan@kogan-page.co.uk
Founded: 1967
Specialize in periodicals.
Subjects: Business, Career Development, Education, Finance, Management, Marketing, Self-Help, Transportation
ISBN Prefix(es): 0-85038; 1-85091; 0-7494
Subsidiaries: Earthscan Publications Ltd (environmental)
Branch Office(s)
Kogan Page India, c/o Viva Books, 432713 Ansari Rd, New Delhi 10002, India
U.S. Office(s): Kogan Page USA Office, 22 Broad St, Suite 34, Milford, CT 06460, United States
Web Site: www.earthscan.co.uk
Distributed by Stylus Publishing Inc (USA)
Distributor for American Bankers Association (excluding North & South America)
Warehouse: Littlehampton Book Services Ltd, Faraday Close, Durrington, Worthing, West Sussex BN13 3RB *Tel:* (01903) 828 800 *Fax:* (01903) 828 801 *E-mail:* orders@lbsltd.co.uk

Kuperard+
Imprint of Bravo Ltd
59 Hutton Grove, London N12 8DS
Tel: (020) 8446 2440 *Fax:* (020) 8446 2441
E-mail: kuperard@bravo.clara.net
Web Site: www.kuperard.co.uk
Key Personnel
Publishing: J Kuperard *E-mail:* kuperard@grove.clara.net
Sales & Marketing: Martin Kaye *E-mail:* martin@bravo.clara.net
Subjects: Education, Travel
ISBN Prefix(es): 1-85733; 1-870668
Number of titles published annually: 30 Print
Total Titles: 300 Print
Distribution Center: Orca Book Services *Tel:* (01202) 665432 *Fax:* (01202) 666219 *E-mail:* orders@orca-book-services.co.uk

Ladybird, *imprint of* Penguin Books Ltd

Ladybird Books Ltd+
80 Strand, London WC2R 0RL
Tel: (020) 7010 2900 *Fax:* (01509) 234672
Web Site: www.ladybird.co.uk
Telex: 341347
Key Personnel
Man Dir: Michael Herridge
Art Dir: Douglas Wilson
Sales Manager, Regional Export & Rights & Coeditions Manager: Yvonne Francis
Sales Manager, Regional Export: Nina Bueno del Carpio
Sales Manager: Ingrid Little
Marketing Dir: Diana Olivant
International Sales Dir: David King
UK Sales Dir: Deborah Wright
Product Manager: Michelle Thurston
Founded: (s)
Children's book publisher.
Subjects: Education, English as a Second Language, Fiction, History, Natural History, Nonfiction (General)
ISBN Prefix(es): 0-7214
Parent Company: Penguin Group
Imprints: Disney
Divisions: Ladybird Disney Books
Foreign Rep(s): Penguin Books Deutchland (Austria, Germany); Penguin Books Netherlands (Holland); Penguin Books S A (Spain & Portugal); Penguin France (France); Penguin Italia (Italy); Sezai Selek Sokak 10/2 (Bulgaria, Romania, Turkey)

Jay Landesman+
8 Duncan Terrace, London N1 8BZ
Tel: (020) 7837 7290 *Fax:* (020) 7833 1925
Key Personnel
Man Dir: Jay Landesman
Founded: 1977
Subjects: Biography, Humor, Poetry
ISBN Prefix(es): 0-905150
Total Titles: 160 Print
Associate Companies: Polytantric Press
Imprints: Golden Handshake; Polytantric Press

Landy Publishing
Acorns, 3 Staining Rise, Staining, Blackpool, Lancs FY3 0BU
Tel: (01253) 895678 *Fax:* (01253) 895678
E-mail: bobdobson@amserve.com
Key Personnel
Owner: Bob Dobson
Founded: 1981
Book publisher of regional titles.
Subjects: History, Regional Interests
ISBN Prefix(es): 1-872895
Number of titles published annually: 6 Print
Total Titles: 90 Print

Allen Lane, *imprint of* Penguin Books Ltd

Lang Syne Publishers Ltd+
120 Carstairs St, Dalmarnock, Glasgow G40 4JD
E-mail: enquiries@scottish-memories.co.uk
Web Site: www.scottish-memories.co.uk/langsyne/
Key Personnel
Dir: Kenneth W Laird
Founded: 1975
Subjects: Business, History, Humor, Music, Dance, Mysteries
ISBN Prefix(es): 0-946264; 1-85217
Branch Office(s)
Scott's Highland Enterprises, 1646 Beckworth Ave, London, ON N5V 2K7, Canada *Tel:* 519-453-0892 *Fax:* 519-453-6303
Scottish Flair, Quean Beyan, NSW *Tel:* (06) 2977-8780

Language Teaching Publications+
High Holborn House, 50/51 Bedford Row, London WC1R 4LR
Tel: (020) 7067 2500 *Fax:* (020) 7067 2600
E-mail: ltp@ltpwebsite.com
Web Site: www.ltpwebsite.com
Telex: 250 Elc
Key Personnel
Man Dir: Michael Lewis; Jimmie Hill
Founded: 1978
Alta Book Center, 14 Adrian Court, Burlingame, CA, United States 94010; Delta Systems Inc, 1400 Miller Parkway, McHenry, IL, United States 60050-7030.
Subjects: English as a Second Language, English as a foreign language
ISBN Prefix(es): 0-906717; 1-899396
Parent Company: Heinle Publishers, 25 Thomson Pl, Boston, MA 02210, United States
Imprints: LTP
U.S. Office(s): Alta Book Center, 14 Adrian Court, Burlingame, CA 94010, United States
Delta systems Inc, 1400 Miller Parkway, McHenry, IL 60050-7030, United States
Orders to: Thomson Learning, Nihonjisyo Brooks Bldg 3-F, 1-4-1, Kudankita, Chiyoda-ku, Tokyo 102-0073, Japan *Tel:* (03) 3511-4390 *Fax:* (03) 3511-4391 (Japan)
Thomson Learning, Seneca 53, Colonia Polanco, 11560 Mexico DF, Mexico *Tel:* (055) 5281-2906 *Fax:* (055) 5281-2656 (Latin America)
Thomson Learning, UIC Bldg, 5 Shenton Way No 01-01 068808, Singapore *Tel:* 6410-1200 *Fax:* 6410-1208 (Asia)
Thomson Learning, Distribution Center, 10650 Toebben Dr, Independence, KY 41051, United States (US)

Languages Information Centre, *imprint of* Joseph Biddulph Publisher

Roger Lascelles+
47 York Rd, Brentford, Middlesex TW8 0QP
Tel: (0181) 8470935 *Fax:* (0181) 5683886
Key Personnel
Publisher: Roger Lascelles
Founded: 1970
Membership(s): International Map Trade Association.
Subjects: Travel
ISBN Prefix(es): 0-903909; 1-872815; 1-85879
Imprints: Daily Telegraph (map service)
Distributor for LAC (Italy); Ravenstein (Germany)

The Latchmere Press
6 Dundalk Rd, London SE4 2JL
Tel: (020) 7639 7282
Key Personnel
Dir: Angela Cornforth
Founded: 1996
Subjects: Education
ISBN Prefix(es): 1-901090

Laurel, *imprint of* Novello & Co Ltd

Lawpack Publishing Ltd
76-89 Alscot Rd, London SE1 3AW
Tel: (020) 7394 4040 *Fax:* (020) 7394 4041
E-mail: enquiries@lawpack.co.uk
Web Site: www.lawpack.co.uk
Key Personnel
Man Dir: Thomas Coles *Tel:* (02) 7394 4050
Editor: Jamie Ross
Founded: 1993
Self-help legal publisher.
Subjects: Business, How-to, Law, Management, Self-Help, Taxes
ISBN Prefix(es): 1-898217; 1-902646

Lawrence & Wishart+
99a Wallis Rd, London E9 5LN
Tel: (020) 8533 2506 *Fax:* (020) 8533 7369
E-mail: info@lwbooks.co.uk
Web Site: www.l-w-bks.co.uk
Key Personnel
Man Editor: Sally J Davison *E-mail:* sally@lwbooks.co.uk
Sales & Publicity: Lindsay Thomas
Financial Dir: Avis Greenaway *E-mail:* avis@lwbooks.co.uk
Permissions: Vanna Derosas *E-mail:* vanna@lwbooks.co.uk
Founded: 1936
Subjects: Economics, Education, Environmental Studies, Ethnicity, Film, Video, Gay & Lesbian, Human Relations, Labor, Industrial Relations, Social Sciences, Sociology
ISBN Prefix(es): 0-85315
Distributed by New York University Press
Warehouse: Central Books Ltd *Tel:* (020) 8986 4854 *Fax:* (020) 8533 5821 *E-mail:* orders@centralbooks.com
Orders to: Troika Ltd, United House, North Rd, London N7 9DP *Tel:* (020) 7619 0800 *Fax:* (020) 7619 0810

LCCIEB, see London Chamber of Commerce & Industry Examinations Board (LCCIEB)

LDA-Living & Learning (Cambridge) Ltd+
Abbeygate House, East Rd, Cambridge, Cambs CB1 1DB
Tel: (01223) 357788 *Fax:* (01223) 460557
E-mail: internationalsales@mcgraw-hill.com
Key Personnel
Man Dir: Carole Mills
Marketing Manager: Jayne Harris *E-mail:* jayne_harris@mcgraw-hill.com
Founded: 1973
Publisher of educational books, resources & games.
Subjects: Child Care & Development, Education
ISBN Prefix(es): 1-85503; 0-905114
Number of titles published annually: 60 Print
Total Titles: 2,000 Print
Parent Company: McGraw-Hill Children's Publishing
Imprints: LDA Multimedia
Branch Office(s)
Living & Learning, 5-7 Pembroke Ave, Waterbeach, Cambs, Anita Low *Tel:* (01223) 864886

LDA Multimedia, *imprint of* LDA-Living & Learning (Cambridge) Ltd

Learning Development Aids+
Abbeygate House, East Rd, Cambridge, Cambs CB1 1DB
Tel: (01223) 365445 *Fax:* (01223) 460557
E-mail: ldaorders@compuserve.com
Key Personnel
Man Dir: Carol Mills
Marketing Dir: Ms Catherine Jeffrey
Founded: 1980
Publish learning materials for numeracy, language, literacy & motivation for primary school children & those with special needs.
Subjects: Health, Nutrition
ISBN Prefix(es): 1-85503
Parent Company: Living & Learning (Cambridge) Ltd
U.S. Office(s): 4383 Hecktown Rd, Unit GA1, Bethelem, PA 18017, United States
Bookshop(s): Chris Lloyd Sales & Marketing Services, 463 Ashley Rd, Poole, Dorset BH14 0AX
Shipping Address: Duke St, Wisbech, Cambs PE13 2AE
Warehouse: Duke St, Wisbech, Cambs PE13 2AE
Orders to: Duke St, Wisbech, Cambs PE13 2AE

Learning Matters, Crucial, *imprint of* Learning Matters Ltd

Learning Matters Ltd
33 Southernhay E, Exeter EX1 1NX
Tel: (01392) 215560 *Fax:* (01392) 215561
E-mail: info@learningmatters.co.uk
Web Site: www.learningmatters.co.uk
Key Personnel
Dir: Jonathan Harris *E-mail:* jonathan@learningmatters.co.uk
Founded: 1999
Publishers of training resources for teachers & course books for university students.
Subjects: Business, Computer Science, Education, Psychology, Psychiatry, Social Sciences, Sociology
ISBN Prefix(es): 1-903300; 1-903337; 1-84445
Number of titles published annually: 25 Print
Total Titles: 120 Print
Imprints: Learning Matters, Crucial
Distribution Center: BEBC, Albion Close, Parkstone, Poole BH12 3LL *Tel:* (0845) 230 9000 *Fax:* (01202) 715 556
Membership(s): IPG

Learning Together+
23 Carlston Ave, Cultra, Co Down BT18 0NF
Tel: (028) 90402086 *Fax:* (028) 90402086
E-mail: info@learningtogether.co.uk
Web Site: www.learningtogether.co.uk
Key Personnel
Contact: Janet McConkey
Founded: 1989
Specialize in verbal & nonverbal reasoning.
Subjects: Education, Mathematics, Science (General)
ISBN Prefix(es): 1-873385
Orders to: Mallard Marketing, Woodside Church Hill, West End Southampton 5030 3AU *Tel:* (02380) 482528 *Fax:* (02380) 361855 *Web Site:* www.learningtogther.co.uk

Legal Action Group+
242 Pentonville Rd, London N1 9UN
Tel: (020) 7833 2931 *Fax:* (020) 7837 6094
E-mail: lag@lag.org.uk
Web Site: www.lag.org.uk
Key Personnel
Chief Executive: Andrew Heywood
International Rights: Jonathan Pearce *E-mail:* jpearce@lag.org.uk
Founded: 1972
Membership(s): Independent Publishers' Guild.
Subjects: Law
ISBN Prefix(es): 0-905099
Total Titles: 30 Print

Leicester University Press, *imprint of* Cassell & Co

Leicester University Press, *imprint of* The Continuum International Publishing Group Ltd

Lemos & Crane+
20 Pond Sq, London N6 6BA
Tel: (020) 8348 8263 *Fax:* (020) 8347 5740
E-mail: admin@lemosandcrane.co.uk
Web Site: www.lemosandcrane.co.uk
Key Personnel
Partner: Paul Crane
Partner & Marketing Manager: Carwyn Gravell
Partner: Gerard Lemos
Founded: 1996
Subjects: Law, Management
ISBN Prefix(es): 1-898001
Orders to: Plymbridge Distributors Ltd, Estover Rd, Plymouth PL6 7PZ

Lennard Publishing, *imprint of* Queen Anne Press

Lennard Publishing
Windmill Cottage, Mackerye End, Harpenden, Herts AL5 5DR
Tel: (01582) 715866 *Fax:* (01582) 715121
E-mail: lennard@lenqap.demon.co.uk

Letterbox Library
71-73 Allen Rd, Stoke Newington, London N16 8RY
Tel: (020) 7503 4801 *Fax:* (020) 7503 4800
E-mail: info@letterboxlibrary.com
Web Site: www.letterboxlibrary.com
Key Personnel
Dir: Maikim Stern
Publicity & Marketing: Kerry Mason
Founded: 1983
Specialize in mulitcultural & non-sexist books.
Subjects: Art, Developing Countries, Disability, Special Needs, English as a Second Language, Environmental Studies, Ethnicity, Fiction, Foreign Countries, Gay & Lesbian, Geography, Geology, Health, Nutrition, History, Human Relations, Nonfiction (General), Religion - Hindu, Religion - Islamic, Religion - Jewish, Religion - Protestant, Religion - Other

Letterland International Ltd
33 New Rd, Barton, Cambs CB3 7AY
Tel: (01223) 262675 *Fax:* (01223) 264126
E-mail: info@letterland.com
Web Site: www.letterland.com
Key Personnel
Man Dir: Mark Wendon
Founded: 1985
Subjects: Education, Language Arts, Linguistics
ISBN Prefix(es): 0-907345; 1-86209
Distributed by Harper Collins Publishers (UK & Eire)

Lettermen, *imprint of* Funfax Ltd

Letts Educational
Member of Granada Learning Group
The Chiswick Centre, 414 Chiswick High Rd, London W4 5TF
Tel: (0845) 602 1937 *Fax:* (020) 8742 8390
E-mail: mail@lettsed.co.uk
Web Site: www.lettsed.co.uk
Key Personnel
Man Dir: Richard Carr
Production Dir: Julia Millette
Administrative Dir: Andrew Riddle
Founded: 1972
Subjects: Accounting, Computer Science, Economics, Finance, Labor, Industrial Relations, Law, Library & Information Sciences, Management, Marketing, Mathematics
ISBN Prefix(es): 1-85805; 1-85758; 1-84315
Parent Company: BPP Holdings PLC, Aldine House, Aldine Pl, London W12 8 AW
Subsidiaries: LETTS Educational; BPP Publishing; Blackstone Press
Warehouse: c/o The Trade Counter Ltd, The Airfield, Mendlesham 1P14 5NA

J D Lewis & Sons Ltd, see Gomer Press (J D Lewis & Sons Ltd)

John Libbey & Co Ltd+
PO Box 276, Eastleigh SO50 5YS
Tel: (023) 8065 0208 *Fax:* (023) 8065 0259
E-mail: johnlibbey@aol.com
Key Personnel
Man Dir & Publisher: John Libbey
Marketing Manager: Angie Needs
Founded: 1979
Subjects: Film, Video, Medicine, Nursing, Dentistry, Cinema/Animation, Epilepsy, Neurology, Nuclear Medicine
ISBN Prefix(es): 0-86196; 1-86462
Total Titles: 100 Print
Subsidiaries: John Libbey Eurotext Ltd
Branch Office(s)
John Libbey & Co PTY Ltd, Level 10, 15-17 Young St, Sydney, NSW 2000, Australia *Tel:* (02) 9251 4099 *Fax:* (02) 9251 4428 *E-mail:* jlsydney@mpx.com.au
U.S. Office(s): John Libbey at Demos Medical Publishing, 386 Park Ave S, Suite 201, New York, NY 10016, United States *Tel:* 212-683-0072 *Fax:* 212-683-0118
Distributed by Butterworth-Heinemann (Medical titles only); Indiana University Press (North America - film/cinema/animation titles only); Tower Books Wholesalers Pty Ltd (Asia & Southern Hemisphere)
Orders to: Plymbridge Distributors Ltd, Plymbridge House, Estover Rd, Plymouth PL6 7PY *Tel:* (01752) 202301 *Fax:* (01752) 202333 *E-mail:* orders@plymbridge.com (Europe)

Liberty+
21 Tabard St, London SE1 4LA
Tel: (020) 7403 3888 *Fax:* (020) 7407 5354
E-mail: info@liberty-human-rights.org.uk
Web Site: www.liberty-human-rights.org.uk
Key Personnel
Dir: John Wadham
Founded: 1934
Subjects: Law
ISBN Prefix(es): 0-901108; 0-946088
Associate Companies: Civil Liberties Trust

Library & Information Statistics Unit, see LISU

Libris Ltd+
26 Lady Margaret Rd, London NW5 2XL
Tel: (020) 7482 2390 *Fax:* (020) 7485 2730
E-mail: libris@onetel.net.uk
Web Site: www.librislondon.co.uk
Key Personnel
Dir: Nicholas Jacobs
Founded: 1986
Specialize in German-language literature in translation (pre-1945, from Goethe) & in German author studies (biography, criticism, literary history); German dictionaries.
Subjects: Biography, Fiction, History, Literature, Literary Criticism, Essays, Poetry
ISBN Prefix(es): 1-870352
Number of titles published annually: 3 Print
Total Titles: 42 Print
Distributed by Independent Publishers Group (IPA)
Shipping Address: Bookshippers Association Inc, 38 Wilks Ave, Unit 3b, Dartford Trade Park, Hawley Rd, Dartford, Kent DA1 1JS *Tel:* (01322) 274414 *Fax:* (01322) 274415
Orders to: Central Books Ltd, 99 Wallis Rd, London E9 5LN, Bill Norris *Tel:* (020) 8986 4854 *Fax:* (020) 8533 5821 *E-mail:* orders@centralbooks.com

Frances Lincoln Ltd+
4 Torriano Mews, Torriano Ave, London NW5 2RZ
Tel: (020) 7284 4009 *Fax:* (020) 7485 0490
E-mail: reception@frances-lincoln.com
Web Site: www.franceslincoln.com
Telex: 21376
Key Personnel
Man Dir: John Nicoll
Editorial Dir, Adult Nonfiction: Anne Fraser
Editorial Dir, Children's: Janetta Otter-Barry
Production: Siobhan Egan; Kim Oliver
Sales Dir: Martin Oestreicher
Rights (Europe): Janet Martin
Rights (USA): Andrew Dunn
Founded: 1977
Subjects: Architecture & Interior Design, Art, Child Care & Development, Crafts, Games,

Hobbies, Gardening, Plants, Health, Nutrition, House & Home, Photography
ISBN Prefix(es): 0-7112; 0-906459
Number of titles published annually: 70 Print
Total Titles: 400 Print
Distributed by ACC (USA); Bookwise (Australia); PGW (USA); Raincoast (Canada); Walker Books (Australia)
Distributor for Allen & Unwin; Barn Owl; Tamarind
Orders to: Bookpoint Ltd, 130 Milton Park, Abingdon, Oxon OX14 4SB *Tel:* (01235) 400 400

Linden Press, see Centaur Press (1954)

Linen Hall Library+
17 Donegall Sq N, Belfast BT1 5GB
Tel: (028) 9032 1707 *Fax:* (028) 9043 8586
E-mail: info@linenhall.com
Web Site: www.linenhall.com
Key Personnel
President: Steve Mungavin
Librarian: John Gray
Librarian, Northern Ireland Political Collection: Yvonne Murphy
Deputy Librarian: John Killen
Irish & Reference Librarian: Mr Gerry Healey
Systems Librarian: Monica McErlane
General Services Manager: Patricia Saunders
Finance Officer: Susan Finlay
Founded: 1788
Subjects: Biography, History, Library & Information Sciences, Literature, Literary Criticism, Essays
ISBN Prefix(es): 0-9508985; 1-900921
Number of titles published annually: 3 Print
Total Titles: 20 Print; 1 CD-ROM

Linford Mystery Library Series, see Ulverscroft Large Print Books Ltd

Linford Romance Library Series, see Ulverscroft Large Print Books Ltd

Linford Western Library Series, see Ulverscroft Large Print Books Ltd

Linguaphone Institute Ltd+
Liongate Enterprise Park, 80 Morden Rd, Mitcham CR4 4PH
Tel: (020) 8687 6010 *Fax:* (020) 8687 6310
E-mail: ads@linguaphone.co.uk (advertising); cst@linguaphone.co.uk (customer support)
Web Site: www.linguaphone.co.uk
Key Personnel
Chief Executive Officer: Clive Sawkins
Man Dir: Richard Avery *E-mail:* ra@linguaphone.co.uk
Founded: 1924
Supplier of self-study language courses, products & services.
Subjects: Language Arts, Linguistics
ISBN Prefix(es): 0-7473
Number of titles published annually: 5 Print; 5 CD-ROM; 1 Audio
Total Titles: 50 Print; 10 CD-ROM; 5 Audio
Imprints: Linguatape
Subsidiaries: Linguapac Distributors Plc; Linguapac Distributors Sdn Bhd; Linguaphone Institute Ltd
Showroom(s): Cortina, Inc, 7 Hollyhock Lane, Wilton, CT 06897, United States *Tel:* 203-762-2510 *E-mail:* info@cortina_languages.com
Shipping Address: Cortina, Inc, 7 Hollyhock Lane, Wilton, CT 06897, United States *Tel:* 203-762-2510 *E-mail:* info@cortina_languages.com
Warehouse: Cortina, Inc, 7 Hollyhock Lane, Wilton, CT 06897, United States *Tel:* 203-762-2510 *E-mail:* info@cortina_languages.com
Distribution Center: Cortina, Inc, 7 Hollyhock Lane, Wilton, CT 06897, United States *Tel:* 203-762-2510 *E-mail:* info@cortina_languages.com
Orders to: Cortina, Inc, 7 Hollyhock Lane, Wilton, CT 06897, United States *Tel:* 203-762-2510 *E-mail:* info@cortina_languages.com
Returns: Cortina, Inc, 7 Hollyhock Lane, Wilton, CT 06897, United States *Tel:* 203-762-2510 *E-mail:* info@cortina_languages.com

Linguatape, *imprint of* Linguaphone Institute Ltd

Lion Hudson PLC+
Mayfield House, 256 Banbury Rd, Oxford OX2 7DH
Tel: (01865) 302750 *Fax:* (01865) 302757
E-mail: international@lionhudson.com
Web Site: www.lionhudson.com
Key Personnel
Man Dir: Paul Clifford *E-mail:* paulc@lionhudson.com
Deputy Man Dir: Nick Jones *E-mail:* nickj@lionhudson.com
International Rights Dir: Tony Wales *E-mail:* tonyw@lionhudson.com
Sales Dir: John O'Nions *E-mail:* johno@lionhudson.com
Publishing Dir: Rod Shepherd *E-mail:* rods@lionhudson.com
Production Dir: Stephen Price *E-mail:* stephenp@lionhudson.com
Senior International Rights: Paul Whitton *E-mail:* paulw@lionhudson.com
International Rights: Robert Seath *E-mail:* roberts@lionhudson.com
Export Sales Manager: Anne Rogers *E-mail:* anner@lionhudson.com; Robert Wendover *E-mail:* robw@lionhudson.com
Founded: 1971
Specialize in Adult Religion & Spirituality, Illustrated Reference, Biography, Health, Gift Books, Children's Books - Bible Stories & Prayers, Information & Reference, Activity, Novelty & Picture Books.
Subjects: Biblical Studies, Nonfiction (General), Religion - Catholic, Religion - Protestant, Self-Help, Theology
ISBN Prefix(es): 0-7459; 0-85648; 1-85424; 1-85985; 0-948902
Number of titles published annually: 200 Print
Total Titles: 800 Print
Imprints: Candle Books; Monarch Books
Distributed by ASAF Import (Netherlands - Candle/Monarch imprints only); Bookwise (Australia - Lion Adult/Children imprints only); Campus Crusade Asia (Singapore - Candle/Monarch imprints only); Horizon Books (Singapore - Lion Adult/Children imprints only); Koorong Books (Australia - Candle/Monarch imprints only); Kregel Publications (USA - Candle/Monarch imprints only); New Holland (New Zealand - Lion Adult/Children imprints only); Novalis (Canada - selected Lion Adult/Children titles only); Omega Distributors Ltd (New Zealand - Candle/Monarch imprints only); OMF Literature (Philippines - All imprints); Pearson (South Africa - Candle imprint only); Scripture Union New Zealand (New Zealand - Lion Adult/Children imprints only); Struik Christian Books (South Africa - Lion Adult/Children & Monarch imprints only); Trafalgar Square Publishing (USA - selected Lion Adult/Children titles only)
Foreign Rights: Bridge Communications (Thailand); Richard Carman (Botswana, Middle East); Infozone Ina Shinwon (Indonesia); Japan Uni Agency (Japan); Korea Copyright Centre (Korea); Motovun (Japan); Andrew Nurnberg Associates (Mainland China); Eric Yang Agency (Korea)
Distribution Center: Marston Book Services, 160 Milton Park Estate, Abingdon, Oxon OX14 4YN *Tel:* (01235) 465511 *Fax:* (01235) 465518

Lippincott Williams & Wilkins
250 Waterloo Rd, London SE1 8RD
Tel: (020) 7981 0500 *Fax:* (020) 7981 0501
Web Site: www.lww.co.uk
Key Personnel
Dir, Journals Publishing: Caroline Black
Sales & Marketing Dir: Ian Banbery *E-mail:* ibanbery@lww.co.uk
Founded: 1893
Subjects: Medicine, Nursing, Dentistry, Veterinary Science
ISBN Prefix(es): 0-316; 1-901831
Parent Company: Wolters Kluwer
Branch Office(s)
Lippincott Williams & Wilkins Pty Ltd, Suite 4, Level 2, 22-36 Mountain St, Broadway, NSW 2007, Australia *Tel:* (02) 9212-5955 *Fax:* (02) 9212-6966
Lippincott Williams & Wilkins Asia Ltd, Suite 907-910, New T&T Centre, Harbour City, 7 Canton Rd, Tsimshatsui, Kowloon, Hong Kong *Tel:* 2610-2339 *Fax:* 2421-1123
U.S. Office(s): 351 W Camden St, Baltimore, MD 21201, United States *Tel:* (410) 528-4000
16522 Hunters Green Parkway, Hagerstown, MD 21740, United States *Tel:* (301) 223-2300 *Fax:* (301) 223-2398 *E-mail:* orders@LWW.com
345 Hudson St, 16th floor, New York, NY 10014, United States *Tel:* (212) 886-1200 (healthcare group also)
530 Walnut St, Philadelphia, PA 19106-3621, United States *Tel:* (215) 521-8300 *Fax:* (215) 521-8902 (head office)
Springhouse, 1111 Bethlehem Pike, PO Box 808, Springhouse, PA 19477, United States *Tel:* (215) 646-8700 *Fax:* (215) 654-1328

LISU
Formerly Library & Information Statistics Unit
Loughborough University, Loughborough, Leics LE11 3TU
Tel: (01509) 263171
E-mail: lisu@lboro.ac.uk
Web Site: www.lboro.ac.uk/departments/dis/lisu/lisuhp.html
Key Personnel
Dir: Dr J Eric Davies *E-mail:* j.e.davies@lboro.ac.uk
Deputy Dir & Senior Statistician: Claire Creaser
Research Associate & Copyright Adviser: Dr Sally Maynard
Founded: 1987
Subjects: Library & Information Sciences, Management, Public Administration
ISBN Prefix(es): 0-948848; 0-904924; 1-901786
Total Titles: 40 Print; 5 Online
Parent Company: Department of Information Science
Ultimate Parent Company: Loughborough University

Little Brown & Co (UK), see Virago Press

Little Tiger Press, *imprint of* Magi Publications

The Littman Library of Jewish Civilization+
PO Box 645, Oxford OX2 0UJ
Tel: (01865) 514688 *Fax:* (01865) 514688
E-mail: enquiries@littman.co.uk; editorial@littman.co.uk; marketing@littman.co.uk
Web Site: www.littman.co.uk
Key Personnel
Chief Executive Officer: Ludo Craddock

UNITED KINGDOM

Tel: (01865) 722964 *E-mail:* ludo.craddock@littman.co.uk
Dir: Colette Littman; Roby Littman
Editorial: Connie Webber
Subjects: Art, Biography, Drama, Theater, Ethnicity, History, Literature, Literary Criticism, Essays, Philosophy, Poetry, Religion - Jewish, Theology
ISBN Prefix(es): 1-874774; 1-904113
U.S. Office(s): ISBS, 920 NE 58th Ave, Suite 300, Portland, OR 97213-3786, United States
Distributed by ISBS (Exclusive distributor for the USA & Canada)
Warehouse: NBN Plymbridge, Estover Rd, Plymouth PL6 7PY *Tel:* (01752) 202000 *Fax:* (01752) 202333 *E-mail:* orders@nbnplymbridge.com *Web Site:* www.nbnplymbridge.com

Liver Press, *imprint of* Countyvise Ltd

Liverpool University Press+
4 Cambridge St, Liverpool L69 7ZU
Tel: (0151) 794 2233; (0151) 794 2237
  Fax: (0151) 794 2235
E-mail: j.m.smith@liv.ac.uk
Web Site: www.liverpool-unipress.co.uk
Key Personnel
Publisher: Robin J C Bloxsidge *Tel:* (0151) 794 2231 *E-mail:* r.j.c.bloxsidge@liv.ac.uk
Sales & Marketing: Simon Bell *Tel:* (0151) 794 2234 *E-mail:* sbell@liv.ac.uk
Production: Andrew Kirk *E-mail:* andrewk@liv.ac.uk
Founded: 1899
Subjects: Archaeology, Architecture & Interior Design, Art, Education, Environmental Studies, Geography, Geology, History, Literature, Literary Criticism, Essays, Medicine, Nursing, Dentistry, Regional Interests, Science (General), Science Fiction, Fantasy, Social Sciences, Sociology, Veterinary Science, Art history, cultural affairs, current events, population studies, urban & regional planning
ISBN Prefix(es): 0-85323
Number of titles published annually: 40 Print
Total Titles: 200 Print
Distributed by International Specialized Book Distributors; University of Pennsylvania Press (USA & Canada)
Distributor for Fremantle Arts Centre Press (Australia)
Orders to: Marston Book Services, PO Box 269, Abingdon, Oxon OX14 4YN

Livewire, *imprint of* The Women's Press Ltd

LLP Ltd
69-77 Paul St, London EC2A 4LQ
Tel: (020) 7553 1000 *Fax:* (020) 7553 1109
E-mail: info@lloydslist.com
Web Site: www.lloydslist.com *Cable:* LLOYDSLIST LONDON EC3
Key Personnel
Publishing Dir: Ray Girvan *Tel:* (020) 7553 1751
Chief Executive: David Gilbertson
Executive Editor: Christopher Mayer *Tel:* (020) 7553 1402
Editor: Julian Bray *Tel:* (020) 7553 1374
Production Editor: Linda Roulston *Tel:* (020) 7553 1480
Advertising Director: Paul Hubbard *Tel:* (020) 7553 1324
Founded: 1973
Business to business international publishers.
Subjects: Finance, Law, Maritime, Insurance
ISBN Prefix(es): 1-85044
Parent Company: LLP Ltd, Sheepen Pl, Colchester CO3 3LP

U.S. Office(s): LLP Limited, c/o Distributech Fulfillment Services, 41-21 28 St, Unit D, Long Island City, NY 11101, United States *Tel:* 718-786-0076 *Fax:* 718-786-4252

Local Heritage Books, see Countryside Books

Ward Lock, *imprint of* Cassell & Co

Locomotion Papers, *imprint of* Oakwood Press

Lodenek Press
Trevinette, Chapel Amble, Wadebridge, Cornwall PL27 6ES
Tel: (01208) 880850
Key Personnel
Man Dir, Sales, Production, Rights & Permissions: D R Rawe
Editorial: H J Ingrey
Founded: 1970
Subjects: Regional Interests
ISBN Prefix(es): 0-902899; 0-946143
Total Titles: 18 Print
Imprints: Chough Series (Educational Packs)
Distributed by Tabb House (in Cornwall only)
Distributor for Tabb House

Y Lolfa Cyf+
Talybont, Ceredigion SY24 5AP
Tel: (01970) 832 304 *Fax:* (01970) 832 782
E-mail: ylolfa@ylolfa.com
Web Site: www.ylolfa.com
Key Personnel
Man Dir, Production: Garmon Gruffudd
  E-mail: garmon@ylolfa.com
Editorial: Lefi Gruffudd
Administration, Rights & Permissions: Nia Williams
Marketing & Publicity: Dilwyn Phillips
Founded: 1965
Publishers of Welsh books & English books of Welsh & Celtic interest.
Subjects: Cookery, Crafts, Games, Hobbies, Fiction, Language Arts, Linguistics, Music, Dance, Poetry, Regional Interests, Science Fiction, Fantasy
ISBN Prefix(es): 0-86243; 0-904864; 0-9500178
Number of titles published annually: 50 Print
Total Titles: 500 Print; 4 Audio
Imprints: Dinas

London Chamber of Commerce & Industry Examinations Board (LCCIEB)
Athena House, 112 Station Rd, Sidcup, Kent DA15 7BJ
Tel: (020) 8309 3000 *Fax:* (020) 8302 4169
E-mail: custserv@lccieb.org.uk
Web Site: www.lccieb.com
Key Personnel
Publishing Manager: Christine Winters
  E-mail: christinew@lccieb.org.uk
Publishing arm of the LCCI Examinations Board, publish support materials for students, candidates of LCCI exams (& their teachers), student financial textbooks & teachers handbooks. Specialize in English language for business & secretarial.
Subjects: Business, Finance
Number of titles published annually: 10 Print
Total Titles: 60 Print

Stacey London, *imprint of* Stacey International

Lonely Planet, UK+
72-82 Rosebery Ave, Clerkenwell, London EC1R 4RW
Tel: (020) 7841 9000 *Fax:* (020) 7841 9001
E-mail: go@lonelyplanet.co.uk
Web Site: www.lonelyplanet.com

Key Personnel
Publisher: Tony Wheeler; Maureen Wheeler
Dir: Jim Hart
Manager, UK: Charlotte Hindle
Founded: 1991
Subjects: Travel
ISBN Prefix(es): 0-86442; 2-84070
Parent Company: Lonely Planet Publications Pty Ltd, Melbourne, Australia
Divisions: Lonely Planet (Australia); Lonely Planet (France); Lonely Planet (United States)
Warehouse: Grantham Book Services, Issac Newton Way, Alma Park Industrial Estate, Grantham NU31 9SD
Orders to: World Leisure Marketing, West Meadows Industrial Estate, Derby DE2 6HA

Longman, *imprint of* Pearson Education Europe, Mideast & Africa

Lorenz Books+
Hermes House, 88-89 Blackfriars Rd, London SE1 8HA
Tel: (020) 7401 2077 *Fax:* (020) 7633 9499
E-mail: bsp2b@aol.com
Key Personnel
Contact: Paul Anness
International Contact: Denise Lie
Subjects: Animals, Pets, Cookery, Crafts, Games, Hobbies, Gardening, Plants, Health, Nutrition, How-to, New Age
ISBN Prefix(es): 1-85967; 0-7548
Imprints: Ultimate
Subsidiaries: Anness Publications Pty; Anness Publications
U.S. Office(s): Anness Publishing, 27 W 20 St, Suite 504, New York, NY 10011, United States
Distributed by Bateman (New Zealand); Five Mile Press (Australia); Raincoast (Canada)
Orders to: Aurum Press, 25 Bedford Ave, London WC1B 3AT

Lorna, *imprint of* Novello & Co Ltd

Loughborough University
Dept of Information Science, Ashby Rd, Loughborough, Leics LE11 3TU
Tel: (01509) 263171; (01509) 223052
  Fax: (01509) 223053
E-mail: dis@lboro.ac.uk
Web Site: www.lboro.ac.uk
Telex: 34319
Key Personnel
Dept Head: Prof Ron Summers
Prof: Christine L Borgman *Tel:* (01509) 223050 *E-mail:* r.summers@lboro.ac.uk; John Feather *Tel:* (01509) 223058 *E-mail:* j.p.feather@lboro.ac.uk; Cliff McKnight *Tel:* (01509) 223061 *E-mail:* c.mcknight@lboro.ac.uk; Jack Meadows *Tel:* (01509) 223082 *E-mail:* a.j.meadows@lboro.ac.uk; Charles Oppenheim *Tel:* (01509) 223065 *E-mail:* c.oppenheim@lboro.ac.uk
ISBN Prefix(es): 0-902761

Peter Lowe, *imprint of* Eurobook Ltd

LTP, *imprint of* Language Teaching Publications

Luath Press Ltd+
543/2 Castlehill, The Royal Mile, Edinburgh EH1 2ND
Tel: (0131) 225 4326 *Fax:* (0131) 225 4324
E-mail: sales@luath.co.uk
Web Site: www.luath.co.uk
Key Personnel
Dir: Gavin MacDougall *E-mail:* gavin.macdougall@luath.co.uk
Founded: 1981
Publisher of *On the Trail of* series.
Membership(s): Scottish Publishers Association.

Subjects: Biography, Fiction, Genealogy, History, Literature, Literary Criticism, Essays, Natural History, Nonfiction (General), Outdoor Recreation, Poetry, Regional Interests, Science Fiction, Fantasy, Sports, Athletics, Travel, Wine & Spirits
ISBN Prefix(es): 0-946487; 1-84282
Number of titles published annually: 30 Print
Total Titles: 80 Print
Distributed by Addenda (New Zealand); Hushion House (Canada); Midpoint Trade Books (USA only); Peribo (Australia); Petersen (Germany, Austria, Switzerland)
Shipping Address: Scottish Book Source, 32 Finlas St, Glasgow G22 5DU
Warehouse: Scottish Book Source, 32 Finlas St, Glasgow G22 5DU
Orders to: Scottish Book Source, 32 Finlas St, Glasgow G22 5DU, Contact: Gerry McLean *Tel:* (0141) 558 1366 *Fax:* (0141) 557 0189 *E-mail:* info@booksource.net *Web Site:* www.booksource.net
Returns: Scottish Book Source, 32 Finlas St, Glasgow G22 5DU

Lucent Books, *imprint of* Thomson Gale

Lucis Press Ltd
3 Whitehall Court, Suite 54, London SW1A 2EF
Tel: (020) 7839 4512; (020) 7839 4513
Fax: (020) 7839 5575
E-mail: london@lucistrust.org
Web Site: www.lucistrust.org
Key Personnel
General Secretary: Chris Morgan
Dir: Helen Durant *E-mail:* lucispress@lucistrust.org
Founded: 1938
Publisher of 24 books of Esoteric Philosophy by Alice A Bailey.
Subjects: Astrology, Occult, Education, Philosophy, Religion - Other, Social Sciences, Sociology
ISBN Prefix(es): 0-85330
Total Titles: 38 Print; 1 CD-ROM
Parent Company: Lucis Publishing Co, 120 Wall St, 24th floor, New York, NY 10005, United States, Sarah McKechnie
Associate Companies: Lucis Trust, One rue de Varembe 3e, Case Postale 31, 1211 Geneva 20, Switzerland *Tel:* (022) 734-1252 *Fax:* (022) 740-0911 *E-mail:* geneva@lucistrust.org (for European translations)
Distributed by Lucis Press SA (South Africa); Sydney Goodwill Unit of Service (Australia); The Triangle Centre (New Zealand)
Distributor for Agni Yoga Society

Lucky Duck Publishing Ltd
Solar House, Station Rd, Kingswood, Bristol BS15 4PH
Tel: (0117) 947 5150 *Fax:* (0117) 947 5152
E-mail: publishing@luckyduck.co.uk
Web Site: www.luckyduck.co.uk
Founded: 1988
Educational publisher.
Subjects: Education
ISBN Prefix(es): 1-904315
Number of titles published annually: 20 Print
Total Titles: 100 Print

Lund Humphries, *imprint of* Ashgate Publishing Ltd

Lund Humphries+
Imprint of Ashgate Publishing Ltd
Gower House, Croft Rd, Aldershot, Hants GU11 3HR
Tel: (01252) 331551 *Fax:* (01252) 344405
E-mail: info@lundhumphries.com
Web Site: www.lundhumphries.com
Key Personnel
Man Dir: Lucy Myers *Tel:* (020) 7841 9800 *Fax:* (020) 7837 6322 *E-mail:* lmyers@lundhumphries.com
Founded: 1943
Subjects: Architecture & Interior Design, Art, Crafts, Games, Hobbies, Photography
ISBN Prefix(es): 0-85331
Number of titles published annually: 20 Print
Total Titles: 70 Print
U.S. Office(s): Ashgate Publishing, 101 Cherry St, Suite 420, Burlington, VT 05401-4405, United States *Tel:* 802-865-7641 *Fax:* 802-865-7847 *E-mail:* info@ashgate.com
Distributor for Hartley & Marks (Europe only); Powerhouse Publishing, Powerhouse Museum, Sydney (Outside Australia & New Zealand)
Warehouse: Bookpoint Ltd, 130 Milton Park, Abingdon, Oxon OX14 4SB

Lutterworth Press, *imprint of* James Clarke & Co Ltd

The Lutterworth Press+
PO Box 60, Cambridge CB1 2NT
Tel: (01223) 350865 *Fax:* (01223) 366951
E-mail: publishing@lutterworth.com
Web Site: www.lutterworth.com
Key Personnel
Man Dir, Rights: Adrian C Brink
Sales Manager: Colin Lester
Founded: 1799
Subjects: Archaeology, Art, Biblical Studies, Biography, Crafts, Games, Hobbies, Education, History, Natural History, Nonfiction (General), Religion - Protestant, Theology
ISBN Prefix(es): 0-7444; 0-7188
Number of titles published annually: 15 Print
Total Titles: 600 Print
Parent Company: James Clarke & Co Ltd
Imprints: Acorn Editions; Patrick Hardy Books
Distributed by Parkwest Publications Inc (USA exclusive; Canada non-exclusive)
Membership(s): IPG; Publishers' Association

Luxor Press L, see Charles Skilton Ltd

Lyle Publications Ltd
4 Shepherds Mill, Selkirk, Selkirkshire TD7 5EA
Tel: (01750) 23355 *Fax:* (01750) 23388
E-mail: lyle.publications@talk21.com
Key Personnel
Dir: Tony Curtis; Annette Curtis
Subjects: Antiques, Art
ISBN Prefix(es): 0-86248; 0-902921

Thomas Lyster Ltd
Units 3/4a, Old Boundary Way Industrial Park, Ormskirk, Lancs L39 2YW
Tel: (01695) 575112 *Fax:* (01695) 570120
E-mail: books@tlyster.co.uk
Web Site: www.tlyster.co.uk
Key Personnel
General Manager: Ian Lyster
Founded: 1988
Specialize in offering distribution services to other smaller publishers.
Membership(s): IPG
ISBN Prefix(es): 1-871482
Total Titles: 15 Print
Parent Company: Plymbridge Distributors Ltd, Estover Rd, Plymouth DL6 7DY
Distributor for Aquila Books; Broadview Publishing; Colour Affects Ltd; Cornish Books; Enanef Ltd; Fort Publishing Ltd; Lancashire Books; Landscape Press; Pigeon Publications; Royal & Ancient Golf Club; Sheldrake Press; South Bank University (Distance Learning Centre); Taghan Publishing

Macgregor Science, *imprint of* Thistle Press

Macmillan, *imprint of* Pan Macmillan

Macmillan Audio Books+
18-21 Cavaye Pl, London SW10 9PG
Tel: (020) 7373 6070 *Fax:* (020) 7244 6379
Subjects: Art, Biography, Cookery, Fiction, History, Military Science, Mysteries, Natural History, Poetry
ISBN Prefix(es): 0-333
Parent Company: Macmillan Publishers Ltd

Macmillan Children's Books, *imprint of* Pan Macmillan

Macmillan Children's Books+
Imprint of Pan Macmillan
20 New Wharf Rd, London N1 9RR
Tel: (020) 7014 6124 *Fax:* (020) 7014 6142
Web Site: www.panmacmillan.com
Key Personnel
Man Dir: Kate Wilson
Sales & Marketing Dir: Emma Hopkin
Associate Publisher: Marion Lloyd
Publishing Dir: Sarah Davies
Editorial Dir: Suzanne Carnell
Editorial Dir, Campbell Books: Camilla Reid
Subjects: Fiction, Nonfiction (General), Poetry
ISBN Prefix(es): 0-330; 0-333; 1-405
Number of titles published annually: 200 Print
Total Titles: 2,500 Print
Imprints: Campbell Books; Young Picador
Divisions: Black & White Colour

Macmillan Heinemann ELT
Macmillan Oxford, Between Towns Rd, Oxford OX4 3PP
Tel: (01865) 405700 *Fax:* (01865) 405701
E-mail: elt@mhelt.com
Web Site: www.mhelt.com
Key Personnel
Man Dir (Education): Chris Harrison
E-mail: chris.harrison@mhelt.com
Publishing Dir: Sue Bale *E-mail:* sue.bale@mhelt.com
Finance Dir: Paul Emmett *E-mail:* paul.emmett@mhelt.com
Publishing Dir Educational: Alison Hurbert
Specialize in the publication of core curriculum texts for primary, JSS, SSS.
ISBN Prefix(es): 0-435; 0-333
Parent Company: Macmillan Education Ltd

Macmillan Ltd
The Macmillan Bldg, 4 Crinan St, London N1 9XW
Tel: (020) 7833 4000 *Fax:* (020) 7843 4640
Web Site: www.macmillan.com
Key Personnel
Chief Executive Officer: Richard Charkin
Finance Dir: Geoff Todd
Executive Dir: Mike Barnard; Chris Paterson; Dominic Knight; David North; Annette Thomas
Founded: 1843
An international company focusing on high quality academic, scholarly, education & trade publishing as well as publishsip services for third parties.
Subjects: Fiction, Nonfiction (General)
ISBN Prefix(es): 0-312; 0-330; 0-333; 0-283; 0-7522; 1-4039; 1-4050
Number of titles published annually: 5,000 Print; 20 CD-ROM; 1,000 Online; 100 Audio
Parent Company: Verlagsgruppe Georg von Holtzbrinck
U.S. Office(s): Holtzbinck Publishers USA
Distribution Center: von Holtzbrinck Publishing Services
Macmillan Distribution Services Pty Ltd (Australia)
Macmillan Distribution Ltd
Peninsula Production & Distribution Ltd

Macmillan Press Ltd, see Palgrave Publishers Ltd

Macmillan Publishers (UK) Ltd+
Division of Grove
Brunel Rd, Houndsmills, Basingstoke, Hants RG21 6XS
Tel: (01256) 329242 *Fax:* (01256) 812558
E-mail: mdl@macmillan.com
Web Site: www.macmillan.com
Key Personnel
Chief Executive: R D P Charkin
Rights Dir, Trade: Chantal Noel *E-mail:* c.noel@macmillan.co.uk
Founded: 1843
ISBN Prefix(es): 0-333
Parent Company: Verlagsgruppe Georg van Holtzbrink
Associate Companies: Macmillan India Ltd, India; Gill & Macmillan Ltd, Ireland; Macmillan Publishers Nigeria Ltd, Nigeria; The Northern Nigerian Publishing Co Ltd, Nigeria; The College Press plc, Zimbabwe; Pan Macmillan Ltd
Subsidiaries: Grove's Dictionaries of Music Ltd; Macmillan Education Ltd; Macmillan Magazines Ltd; Macmillan Press Ltd; Macmillan Distribution Ltd; Macmillan General Books Ltd; Macmillan Children's Books Ltd; Stockton Press Ltd; Stockton Press Netherlands BV; Macmillan Publishers Australia Pty Ltd; Macmillan Publishers Hong Kong Ltd; Macmillan Publishers China Ltd; Peninsula Production & Distribution Ltd; Macmillan Language House Co Ltd; Macmillan Shuppan KK; Nature Japan KK; Macmillan Kenya Publishers Ltd; Editorial Macmillan de Mexico SA de CV; Macmillan Publishers New Zealand Ltd; Pansing Distribution Sdn Bhd; Macmillan Boleswa Publishers Pty Ltd; Macmillan Swaziland National Publishing Co Ltd; Nature America Inc; St Martin's Press Inc; College Press Pvt Ltd; Stockton Press Netherlands Holdings BV
Orders to: Macmillan Distribution Ltd, Brunel Rd, Houndmills, Basingstoke, Hants RG21 2XS *Tel:* (0125) 6329242

Macmillan Reference Ltd
Brunel Rd, Houndsmills, Basingstoke, Hants RG21 6XS
Tel: (01256) 329242 *Fax:* (01256) 812558
E-mail: mdl@macmillan.co.uk
Web Site: www.macmillan.co.uk
Key Personnel
Man Dir: Ian Jacobs *E-mail:* i.jacobs@macmillan.co.uk
Science Publisher: Gina Fullerlove *E-mail:* g.fullerlove@macmillan.co.uk
Art Publisher: Jane Turner *E-mail:* j.turner@macmillan.co.uk
Humanities & Social Sciences Publisher: Sara Lloyd *E-mail:* s.lloyd@macmillan.co.uk
Marketing: Alex Lankester *E-mail:* a.lankester@macmillan.co.uk
Production: Jeremy Macdonald *E-mail:* j.macdonald@macmillan.co.uk
Subjects: Art, Economics, Finance, Government, Political Science, History, Human Relations, Music, Dance, Science (General), Social Sciences, Sociology
ISBN Prefix(es): 0-333

Macmillan Reference USA, *imprint of* Thomson Gale

Macmillan Technical Publishing USA, *imprint of* Pearson Education Europe, Mideast & Africa

Julia Macrae, *imprint of* Random House UK Ltd

Mad Jack, *imprint of* Funfax Ltd

Made Simple Books, *imprint of* Elsevier Ltd

Magi Publications+
One The Coda Centre, 189 Munster Rd, London SW6 6AW
Tel: (020) 7385 6333 *Fax:* (020) 7385 7333
E-mail: info@littletiger.co.uk
Web Site: www.littletigerpress.com
Key Personnel
Rights Manager: M S Bhatia
Founded: 1987
Specialize in co-production of children's picture books.
Subjects: English as a Second Language, Fiction
ISBN Prefix(es): 1-870271; 1-85430; 1-952246
Imprints: Little Tiger Press
Orders to: A & C Black, Howard Rd, Eaton Socon, Huntingdon, Cambs PE19 3EZ

Magic Joneuery, *imprint of* Funfax Ltd

Magna Large Print Books+
Magna House, Long Preston, Skipton, North Yorks BD23 4ND
Tel: (01729) 840 225; (01729) 840 526; (01729) 840 251 *Fax:* (01729) 840 683
E-mail: enquiries@ulverscroft.co.uk
Web Site: www.ulverscroft.co.uk
Key Personnel
Man Dir: John Cressey
Rights: Diane Allen
Founded: 1973
ISBN Prefix(es): 0-86009; 1-85057; 1-85389; 0-7505; 1-84137
Number of titles published annually: 240 Print; 72 Audio
Total Titles: 1,000 Print
Parent Company: The Ulverscroft Group Ltd
Imprints: Dales Large Print Series; Story Sound Audio Tapes
Branch Office(s)
Ulverscroft (Large Print USA Inc), Seneca Pl, 1881 Ridge Rd, West Seneca, NY 14224, United States
Distributed by Ulverscroft (USA)
Showroom(s): Cawdor Books, 96 Dykehead St, Queenslie, Glasgow G33 4AQ *Tel:* (01729) 840225 *Fax:* (01729) 840683

Maik Nauka/Interperiodica, *imprint of* Kluwer Academic/Plenum Publishers

Mainstream Publishing Co (Edinburgh) Ltd+
7 Albany St, Edinburgh EH1 3UG
Tel: (0131) 557 2959 *Fax:* (0131) 556 8720
E-mail: enquiries@mainstreampublishing.com
Web Site: www.mainstreampublishing.com
Key Personnel
Dir: Bill Campbell; Irina MacKenzie; Peter MacKenzie
Sales Manager: Raymond Cowie
Sales Administration: Elaine Scott
Founded: 1978
Subjects: Art, Biography, Government, Political Science, History, Literature, Literary Criticism, Essays, Photography, Sports, Athletics, Travel
ISBN Prefix(es): 1-85158; 1-84018
Distributed by Bill Bailey Publishers' Representatives (Europe); Capricorn Link (Australia) Pty Ltd (Australia); CKK Ltd (Southeast Asia); Hushion House Ltd (Canada); Phambili (South Africa); Trafalgar Square (USA); Peter Ward Book Exports (Middle East)
Orders to: Tiptree, St Luke's Chase, Tiptree, Colchester, Essex C05 0SR

Making Sense of Science, *imprint of* Portland Press Ltd

Mallard Reprints, *imprint of* Terence Dalton Ltd

Management Books 2000 Ltd+
Forge House, Limes Rd, Kemble, Cirencester, Glos GL7 6AD
Tel: (01285) 771441 *Fax:* (01285) 771055
E-mail: mb.2000@virgin.net
Web Site: www.mb2000.com
Key Personnel
Publisher: James Alexander
Founded: 1986
Publisher & distributor of management guides, textbooks & references.
Subjects: Business, Career Development, Management, Marketing, Real Estate
ISBN Prefix(es): 1-85251; 1-85252
Number of titles published annually: 24 Print
Total Titles: 200 Print
Imprints: Mercury Books
Orders to: Combined Book Services, Paddock Wood Distribution Centre, Paddock Wood Kent TN12 6UU *Tel:* (01892) 837171

Management Pocketbooks Ltd+
Laurel House, Station Approach, Alresford, Hants SO24 9JH
Tel: (01962) 735 573 *Fax:* (01962) 733 637
E-mail: sales@pocketbook.co.uk
Web Site: www.pocketbook.co.uk
Key Personnel
International Rights: Rosalind Baynes *E-mail:* ros@pocketbook.co.uk
Founded: 1987
Small, highly accessible management guides written by trainers, full of graphics, mnemonics, bullet points for clarity & ease of recall.
Membership(s): IPG (Independent Publishers Guild).
Subjects: Business, Education, Management
ISBN Prefix(es): 1-870471; 1-903776
Number of titles published annually: 10 Print
Total Titles: 85 Print; 2 Audio
U.S. Office(s): Stylus Publishing, 22883 Quicksilver Dr, Sterling, VA 20166-2012, United States, Contact: John von Knorring *Tel:* 703-661-1504; 703-661-1515 (editorial); 703-661-1581 (orders) *Fax:* 703-661-1501 *E-mail:* styluspub@aol.com
Distribution Center: Trade Counter, Unit D, Trading Estate Rd, London NW10 7LU, Denise Johnson *Tel:* (20) 8963 0322
Membership(s): IPG

Manchester United Books, *imprint of* Carlton Publishing Group

Manchester University Press+
Oxford Rd, Manchester M13 9NR
Tel: (0161) 275 2310 *Fax:* (0161) 274 3346
E-mail: mup@man.ac.uk
Web Site: www.manchesteruniversitypress.co.uk
Key Personnel
Chief Executive & Production Director: David Rodgers *E-mail:* d.rodgers@man.ac.uk
Editorial Dir: Matthew Frost *E-mail:* m.frost@man.ac.uk
Editor: Tony Mason *E-mail:* t.mason@man.ac.uk; Alison Welsby *E-mail:* a.welsby@man.ac.uk
Sales & Marketing Dir: Clare Blick *E-mail:* c.blick@man.ac.uk
Rights & Publicity: Alison Sparkes *E-mail:* a.sparkes@man.ac.uk
Founded: 1903
Subjects: Art, Economics, Film, Video, Government, Political Science, History, Literature, Literary Criticism, Essays, Radio, TV, Social Sciences, Sociology, Academic publishers
ISBN Prefix(es): 0-7190
Associate Companies: Palgrave, 257 Park Ave S, New York, NY 10010, United States
Imprints: Mandolin
Distributed by University of British Columbia Press (Canada)

Mandolin, *imprint of* Manchester University Press

Mandrake of Oxford+
PO Box 250, Oxford OX1 1AP
Mailing Address: Po Box 1589, Blaine, WA 98231, United States
Tel: (01865) 243671 *Fax:* (01865) 432929
E-mail: mandrake@mandrake.uk.net
Web Site: www.mandrake.uk.net
Key Personnel
Contact: M Morgan
Founded: 1986
Also acts as Bookseller & Mail-Order Subscription Agent.
Subjects: Art, Astrology, Occult, Fiction, Health, Nutrition, Parapsychology, Religion - Hindu, Religion - Other, Science (General), Science Fiction, Fantasy
ISBN Prefix(es): 1-869928
Number of titles published annually: 10 Print
Imprints: Golden Dawn; Nuit-Isis
Orders to: Gazelle, White Crown Mills, Hightown, Lancaster LA1 4XS *Tel:* (01524) 68765 *Fax:* (01424) 63232 *E-mail:* Gazelle4go@AOL.com
New Leaf, 401 Thornton Rd, Lithia Springs, GA 30057-1557, United States *Tel:* 770-948-7845 *Fax:* 770-944-2313 (Trade only)

Maney, *imprint of* Maney Publishing

Maney Publishing+
Hudson Rd, Leeds LS9 7DL
Tel: (0113) 249 7481 *Fax:* (0113) 248 6983
E-mail: maney@maney.co.uk
Web Site: www.maney.co.uk
Key Personnel
Man Dir: Michael Gallico *E-mail:* m.gallico@maney.co.uk
Marketing Manager: Lynne Medhurst *E-mail:* l.medhurst@maney.co.uk
Founded: 1900
Academic book & journal publisher.
Subjects: Antiques, Archaeology, Architecture & Interior Design, Art, Drama, Theater, Engineering (General), History, Language Arts, Linguistics, Library & Information Sciences, Literature, Literary Criticism, Essays, Natural History
Number of titles published annually: 25 Print
Total Titles: 300 Print
Imprints: Maney; Northern Universities Press; Modern Humanities Research Association; Pasold Research Fund

Mango Publishing
49 Carnabys St, London W1F 9PY
Tel: (020) 7292 9000 *Fax:* (020) 7434 1077
E-mail: info@mangomedia.net
Web Site: www.mangopublishing.net
Key Personnel
Contact: Richard Coury *Tel:* (020) 7471 1744 *E-mail:* richard@mangopublishing.net
Subjects: Biography, Literature, Literary Criticism, Essays, Poetry, Poetry, literature & biography by Caribbean heritage writers especially women; literary criticism of Caribbean literature
ISBN Prefix(es): 1-902294
Total Titles: 10 Print

George Mann, *imprint of* George Mann Publications

Mansell, *imprint of* Cassell & Co

Mansell, *imprint of* The Continuum International Publishing Group Ltd

The Mansk Svenska Publishing Co Ltd+
17 North View, Peel, Isle of Man 1M5 1DQ
Tel: (0162) 4842855 *Fax:* (0162) 844241
E-mail: hanneke@advsys.co.uk
Key Personnel
Man Dir: G V C Young, OBE
Founded: 1980
Subjects: Biography, Fiction, History
ISBN Prefix(es): 0-907715
Branch Office(s)
Spellinge Gard, S-590 20 Mantord, Sweden
Bookshop(s): 50 Michael St, Peel 1M5 1HD

Manson Publishing Ltd+
73 Corringham Rd, London NW11 7DL
Tel: (020) 8905 5150 *Fax:* (020) 8201 9233
E-mail: manson@mansonpublishing.com
Web Site: www.mansonpublishing.com
Key Personnel
Man Dir: Michael Manson
Publishing Coordinator: Clair Chaventre
Founded: 1992
Membership(s): IPG; Publishers' Association.
Subjects: Agriculture, Biological Sciences, Chemistry, Chemical Engineering, Earth Sciences, Medicine, Nursing, Dentistry, Veterinary Science, Microbiology, Plant Science
ISBN Prefix(es): 1-874545; 1-84076
Total Titles: 100 Print; 1 CD-ROM
Subsidiaries: Veterinary Press Ltd
Distributed by Nankodo Co Ltd (Japan - medicine & veterinary medicine books); United Publishers Services Ltd (Japan - Science books only)
Distributor for Schluetersche Verlagsgesellschaft mbH & Co (English-language titles only)
Orders to: Marston Book Services Ltd, Unit 160, Milton Park Industrial Centre, Abingdon *Tel:* (01235) 465500 *Fax:* (01235) 465555

Peter Marcan Publications
PO Box 3158, London SE1 4RA
Tel: (020) 7357 0368
Key Personnel
Proprietor: Peter Marcan
Founded: 1978
Membership(s): Author-Publisher Enterprise (UK).
Subjects: Art, History, Music, Dance
ISBN Prefix(es): 0-9510289; 1-871811; 0-9504211

Marcham Manor Press+
Appleford, Abingdon, Oxon OX14 4PB
Tel: (01235) 848319
Key Personnel
Chief Executive, Editorial: G E Duffield
Sales, Publicity: G Elwes
Production: E Collie
Founded: 1963
Subjects: Asian Studies, Biblical Sciences, Biography, History, Music, Dance, Philosophy, Religion - Catholic, Religion - Protestant, Theology
ISBN Prefix(es): 0-900531
Parent Company: Appleford Publishing Group
Associate Companies: Appleford Printers, Courtenay Bookroom
Divisions: Sutton Courtenay Press

Maresfield Lib, *imprint of* Karnac Books Ltd

Maritime Books
Lodge Hill, Liskeard, Cornwell PL14 4EL
Tel: (01579) 343663 *Fax:* (01579) 346747
E-mail: editor@navybooks.com
Web Site: www.navybooks.com
Key Personnel
Chief Executive: M Critchley
Manager: P Garnett
Founded: 1980
Subjects: Maritime
ISBN Prefix(es): 0-907771
Total Titles: 26 Print
Subsidiaries: Warship World Magazine

Market House Books Ltd+
Market House, Market Sq, Aylesbury, Bucks HP20 1TN
Tel: (01296) 484911 *Fax:* (01296) 437073
E-mail: information@mhbref.com
Web Site: www.mhbref.com
Key Personnel
Dir: Dr Alan Isaacs *E-mail:* isaacs@mhbref.com; Peter Sapsed
Dir & Production: Dr John Daintith *E-mail:* daintith@mhbref.com
Founded: 1969
Book producer & Packager.

The Market Research Society
15 Northburgh St, London EC1V 0JR
Tel: (020) 7490 4911 *Fax:* (020) 7490 0608
E-mail: info@mrs.org.uk
Web Site: www.mrs.org.uk
Key Personnel
Dir General: David Barr
Organization for professional researchers & others engaged or interested in market, social & opinion research.

Mars Business Associates Ltd
62 Kingsmead, Lechlade, Glos GL7 3BW
Tel: (01367) 252 506 *Fax:* (01367) 252 506
E-mail: sales@marspub.co.uk
Web Site: www.marspub.co.uk
Key Personnel
Contact: Dr John Robertson *E-mail:* johnr@cccp.net
Founded: 1988
Subjects: Accounting, Finance

Marshall Editions Ltd+
The Old Brewery, 6 Blundell St, London N7 9BH
Tel: (020) 7700 6764 *Fax:* (020) 7700 4191
E-mail: info@marshalleditions.com
Web Site: www.quarto.com/group/companies/marshalleditions.htm
Key Personnel
Chairman: Richard Harman *E-mail:* rharman@smediakey.u-net.com
Publisher: Barbara Marshall
Chief Executive: Nick Croydon
Sales Dir: Belinda Rasmussen
Founded: 1977
Also acts as book packager.
Subjects: Business, Crafts, Games, Hobbies, Gardening, Plants, Geography, Geology, Health, Nutrition, History, Management, Military Science, Natural History, Religion - Other, Science (General), Travel, Wine & Spirits
ISBN Prefix(es): 0-9507901
Parent Company: Quarto

Marston House, *imprint of* Marston House

Marston House+
Marston Magna, Yeovil, Somerset BA22 8DH
Tel: (01935) 851331 *Fax:* (01935) 851372
Key Personnel
Man Dir, Production: A E Birks-Hay
Editorial Dir: M L Birks-Hay
Founded: 1991
Subjects: Architecture & Interior Design, Art, Gardening, Plants, Nonfiction (General), crafts
ISBN Prefix(es): 0-9517700; 1-899296
Number of titles published annually: 3 Print
Total Titles: 20 Print
Parent Company: Alphabet & Image Ltd
Imprints: Marston House
Foreign Rep(s): Helmut Ecker (Australia, Germany, Switzerland)
Orders to: Chris Lloyd Sales & Marketing Services, Stanley House, 1st floor, 3 Fleets

UNITED KINGDOM

Lane, Poole, Dorset BH15 3AJ, Chris Lloyd
Tel: (01202) 649930 *Fax:* (01202) 649950
E-mail: chrlloyd@globalnet.co.uk

Martin Books, *imprint of* Simon & Schuster Ltd

Martin Dunitz, *imprint of* Taylor & Francis

Martin Dunitz Ltd, see Taylor & Francis Medical Books

Kenneth Mason Publications Ltd+
Dudley House, 12 North St, Emsworth PO10 7DQ
Tel: (01243) 377977; (01243) 377978
Fax: (01243) 379136
E-mail: boatswain@dial.pipex.com
Key Personnel
Chairman: Kenneth Mason
Man Dir: Piers Mason
Founded: 1958
Subjects: Astrology, Occult, Child Care & Development, Cookery, Health, Nutrition, House & Home, Law, Maritime, Self-Help
ISBN Prefix(es): 0-85937; 1-873432; 0-900534
Imprints: Handbag Books; Boatswain Press
Warehouse: Book Barn

Adam Matthew Publications
Pelham House, London Rd, Marlborough, Wilts SN8 2AA
Tel: (01672) 511921 *Fax:* (01672) 511663
E-mail: info@ampltd.co.uk
Web Site: www.adam-matthew-publications.co.uk
Key Personnel
Director: William Pidduck
 E-mail: adam_matthew@msn.com; David Tyler
 E-mail: amp_david@msn.com
Founded: 1990
Original manuscript collections, rare printed books & other primary source material in microform & electronic format.
Subjects: African American Studies, Asian Studies, Economics, Ethnicity, History, Music, Dance, Religion - Other, Science (General), Social Sciences, Sociology, Technology, Women's Studies
ISBN Prefix(es): 1-85711
Number of titles published annually: 1 CD-ROM; 1 Online
Distributed by Maruzen Co Ltd (Japan only)
Foreign Rep(s): Maruzen Co Ltd (Japan); Transmission Books Co Ltd (Taiwan)

Mayhew-McCrimmon Ltd, see McCrimmon Publishing Co Ltd

MCB University Press Ltd, see Emerald

McCrimmon Publishing Co Ltd+
10-12 High St, Great Wakering, Southend-on-Sea (Essex) SS3 0EQ
Tel: (01702) 218956 *Fax:* (01702) 216082
E-mail: sales@mccrimmons.com (sales); orders@mccrimmons.com (orders); permissions@mccrimmons.com (permission-related inquiries); clipart@mccrimmons.com (clip art); accounts@mccrimmons.com-accounts
Web Site: www.mccrimmons.com
Key Personnel
Dir: Donald McCrimmon; Joan McCrimmon
 E-mail: mccrimmon@dial.pipex.com
Founded: 1968
Membership(s): PRS, MCPS.
Subjects: Biblical Studies, Education, Music, Dance, Religion - Catholic, Religion - Other, Textbooks-Liturgy
ISBN Prefix(es): 0-85597
Number of titles published annually: 20 Print
Total Titles: 100 Print

Distributed by Liturgical Press (USA)
Distributor for Harcourt Brace; LTP Chicago (USA); Printery House (USA); St Michael's Altar Breads
Bookshop(s): All Saints Pastoral Centre Bookshop, London Colney, Herts
Warehouse: 10 Terminal Close, Shoeburyness

Deirdre McDonald Ltd, *imprint of* Bellew Publishing Co Ltd

McGill-Queens University Press, *imprint of* Combined Academic Publishers

McGraw-Hill Education Europe, Middle East & Africa Group
Division of The McGraw-Hill Companies
Shoppenhangers Rd, Maidenhead, Berks SL6 2QL
Tel: (016) 2850 2500 *Fax:* (016) 2877 7342
Web Site: www.mcgraw-hill.co.uk
Key Personnel
Man Dir, Europe/MEA: Simon Allen
Man Dir, Italy: Italo Raimondi
Dir, Higher Educational Division: Murray St Leger
Dir, Schools Division: Joanne Johnston
Dir, Trade/Professional/Reference Division: Derek Stordahl
Regional offices in the UK (Headquarters), Italy, Greece & Dubai with representatives also in Denmark, Germany, Norway, Netherlands, Sweden, Ireland, Poland, Turkey, Egypt, Lebanon, the United Arab Emirates & Iran.
ISBN Prefix(es): 0-07; 0-335

McGraw-Hill Publishing Company+
McGraw Hill House, Shoppenhangers Rd, Maidenhead, Berks SL6 2QL
Tel: (01) 628 502500 *Fax:* (01) 628 635895
Web Site: www.mcgraw-hill.co.uk
Telex: 848484 *Cable:* McGrawHill
Key Personnel
Group VP, Northern Europe/MEA: I Raimondi
Publishing Dir: A Waller
Founded: 1899
Subjects: Career Development, Computer Science, Engineering (General), Management, Mathematics, Medicine, Nursing, Dentistry, Psychology, Psychiatry, Science (General), Social Sciences, Sociology
ISBN Prefix(es): 0-07
Parent Company: The McGraw-Hill Companies, 1221 Avenue of the Americas, New York, NY 10020, United States
Associate Companies: McGraw-Hill Book Co Australia Pty Ltd, Australia; McGraw-Hill Ryerson Ltd, Canada; Editorial McGraw-Hill Latinoamericana SA, Colombia; Tata McGraw-Hill Publishing Co Ltd, India; McGraw-Hill Book Co Japan Ltd, Japan; Libros McGraw-Hill de Mexico SA de CV, Mexico; McGraw-Hill Book Co, New Zealand Ltd, New Zealand; Editora McGraw-Hill de Portugal Lda, Portugal; Editorial McGraw-Hill Latinoamericana SA, Puerto Rico; McGraw-Hill Interamericana de Espana SA, Spain
Distributed by Amacom (UK, Europe); Berrett-Koehler (UK, Europe); Harvard Business School Press (UK, Europe)

Meadowfield Press, *imprint of* Merrow Publishing Co Ltd

Media Research Publishing Ltd+
Lister House, 117 Milton Rd, Weston Super Mare, North Somerset BS23 2UX
Tel: (01934) 644 309 *Fax:* (01934) 644 402
Key Personnel
Chairman: Cliff Dane *E-mail:* cliffd@globalnet.co.uk

Founded: 1993
Specialize in financial aspects of the music industry.
Subjects: Accounting, Business, Music, Dance
ISBN Prefix(es): 0-9521414; 0-9534171
Total Titles: 2 Print

The Medici Society Ltd
Grafton House, Hyde Estate Rd, London NW9 6JZ
Tel: (020) 8205 2500 *Fax:* (020) 8205 2552
E-mail: info@medici.co.uk
Web Site: www.medici.co.uk
Key Personnel
Chief Executive: Bryan Robertson
Contact: David Hardstaff
Founded: 1908
Subjects: Art, Poetry, Fine Art
ISBN Prefix(es): 0-85503
Bookshop(s): The Medici Galleries, 7 Grafton St, London W1X 3LA; 26 Thurloe St, London SW7 2LT

Willem A Meeuws Publisher
126-B Milton Park, Abingdon-upon-Thames OX14 4SA
Tel: (01235) 821994 *Fax:* (01235) 821994
E-mail: thorntons@booknews.demon.co.uk
Web Site: www.thorntonsbooks.co.uk
Key Personnel
Publisher: Willem A Meeuws
Founded: 1968
Subjects: History
ISBN Prefix(es): 0-902672
Total Titles: 70 Print
Subsidiaries: Thorntons of Oxford Ltd
Distributor for Folio Society; Slavica (USA)
Orders to: Thorntons of Oxford Ltd, Oxford

Melrose Press Ltd+
St Thomas Pl, Ely, Cambs CB7 4GG
Tel: (01353) 646600 *Fax:* (01353) 646601
E-mail: tradesales@melrosepress.co.uk; info@melrosepress.co.uk
Web Site: www.melrosepress.co.uk
Key Personnel
Chairman: Richard Kay
Man Dir: Nicholas Law
Chief Executive: Jean Pearson
Editorial & Head of Research: Jon Gifford
Founded: 1969
Subjects: Biography
ISBN Prefix(es): 0-948875; 1-903986
Imprints: International Biographical Centre
Shipping Address: Bath Road, Harmondsworth, West Drayton, Middlesex UB7 0DA

Mentor, *imprint of* Christian Focus Publications Ltd

MEP, *imprint of* Professional Engineering Publishing Ltd

Mercat Press+
10 Coates Crescent, Edinburgh EH3 7AL
Tel: (0131) 225 5324 *Fax:* (0131) 226 6632
E-mail: enquiries@mercatpress.com
Web Site: www.mercatpress.com
Key Personnel
Man Dir: Sean Costello; Tom Johnstone
Founded: 1970
Membership(s): Scottish Publishers' Association.
Subjects: Cookery, Gardening, Plants, Literature, Literary Criticism, Essays, Music, Dance, Natural History, Nonfiction (General), Outdoor Recreation, Regional Interests
ISBN Prefix(es): 0-901824; 0-906664; 1-873644; 0-902347; 1-85752
Number of titles published annually: 30 Print
Total Titles: 250 Print
Parent Company: Mercat Press Ltd

Merchiston Publishing
School of Communication Arts, Napier University, Craighouse Rd, Edinburgh EH10 5LG
Tel: (0131) 455 6150 *Fax:* (0131) 455 6193
Key Personnel
Contact: Mairi Sutherland *E-mail:* m.sutherland@napier.ac.uk
Founded: 1987
Membership(s): Scottish Publishers' Association.
Subjects: Publishing & Book Trade Reference, Regional Interests
ISBN Prefix(es): 0-9511266; 1-872800

Mercury Books, *imprint of* Management Books 2000 Ltd

Meresborough Books Ltd
17-25 Station Rd, Rainham, Kent ME8 7RS
Tel: (01634) 371591 *Fax:* (01634) 262114
E-mail: shop@rainhambookshop.co.uk
Web Site: www.rainhambookshop.co.uk
Key Personnel
Dir: Hamish Mackay-Miller; Barbara Mackay-Miller
Founded: 1977
Subjects: Regional Interests
ISBN Prefix(es): 0-905270; 0-948193
Associate Companies: Rainham Bookshop
Imprints: Bygone Kent

Meridian Books
Highfield House, 2 Highfield Ave, Newbury RG14 5DS
Tel: (016) 3554 3816 *Fax:* (016) 3555 1004
E-mail: jennie@countrysidebooks.co.uk
Key Personnel
Contact: Peter Groves
Founded: 1983
Subjects: Travel, Walking
ISBN Prefix(es): 1-869922
Distributed by Local Heritage Books

The Merlin Press Ltd+
PO Box 30705, London WC2E 8QD
Tel: (020) 7836 3020 *Fax:* (020) 7497 0309
E-mail: info@merlinpress.co.uk
Web Site: www.merlinpress.co.uk
Key Personnel
Dir & Rights: Anthony W Zurbrugg *E-mail:* tz@merlinpress.co.uk
Founded: 1956
Subjects: Economics, Government, Political Science, History, Labor, Industrial Relations, Philosophy, Social Sciences, Sociology, Labor Studies
ISBN Prefix(es): 0-85036; 1-85425
Number of titles published annually: 10 Print
Imprints: Green Print
Distributed by Central Books Ltd (United Kingdom); Independent Publishers Group (USA)

Mermaid, *imprint of* Michael Joseph Ltd

Merrell Publishers Ltd+
42 Southwark St, London SE1 1UN
Tel: (020) 7403 2047 *Fax:* (020) 7407 1333
E-mail: mail@merrellpublishers.com; sales@merrellpublishers.com
Web Site: www.merrellpublishers.com
Key Personnel
Publisher: Hugh Merrell *E-mail:* hm@merrellpublishers.com
Editorial Dir: Julian Honer *E-mail:* jh@merrellpublishers.com
Sales & Marketing Dir: Emilie Amos *E-mail:* ea@merrellpublishers.com
Design Manager: Nicola Bailey *E-mail:* nb@merrellpublishers.com
Production Manager: Michelle Draycott *E-mail:* md@merrellpublishers.com
Founded: 1993
Specialize in all aspects of the visual arts.
Also publishes several exhibition catalogues in association with galleries in Europe & North America.
Subjects: Architecture & Interior Design, Art, Crafts, Games, Hobbies, Photography, Design
ISBN Prefix(es): 1-85894
Number of titles published annually: 35 Print
Total Titles: 90 Print
U.S. Office(s): Merrell Publishers USA, 49 W 24 St, New York, NY 10010, United States, Contact: Joan Louise Brookbank *Tel:* 212-929-8344 *Fax:* 212-926-8346 *E-mail:* info@merrellpublishersusa.com
Foreign Rep(s): Ashton International Marketing Services (Japan); Asia Publishers Services Ltd (China, Hong Kong, Korea, Taiwan); Books for Europe (Baltic States, Scandinavia); Bookwise International (Australia, New Zealand); Client Distribution Services (USA); Critiques Livres Distribution (France); Humphrys Roberts Associates (Caribbean, Central America, South America); Gabriele Kern (Austria, Germany, Switzerland); Csaba & Jackie Lengyel de Bagota (Eastern Europe); Nilsson & Lamm (Belgium, Netherlands, Luxembourg); Penny Padovani (Greece, Italy, Portugal, Spain); Quartet Books (Southern Africa); Peter Ward Book Exports (Cyprus, Israel, Malta, Middle East, Turkey)
Foreign Rights: Maya Publishers (Bangladesh, India, Nepal, Sri Lanka, Bhutan)
Orders to: Marston Book Services, PO Box 269, Abingdon, Oxon OX14 4YN *Tel:* (01235) 465500 *Fax:* (01235) 465555 *E-mail:* trade.order@marston.co.uk; trade.enq@marston.co.uk
Client Distribution Services, 193 Edwards Drive, Jackson, TN 38301, United States (US & Canada)
Returns: Marston Book Services, PO Box 269, Abingdon, Oxon OX14 4YN *Tel:* (01235) 465500 *Fax:* (01235) 465555; Client Distribution Services, 193 Edwards Drive, Jackson, TN 38301, United States (US & Canada)

Merrion Press
100 Hackford Rd, London SW9 0QU
Tel: (020) 7735 7791 *Fax:* (020) 77357 059
Key Personnel
Dir: Susan Shaw
Subjects: Art, Literature, Literary Criticism, Essays
ISBN Prefix(es): 0-903560

Merrow Publishing Co Ltd
22 Abbey Rd, Darlington, Co Durham DL3 8LR
Tel: (01325) 351661 *Fax:* (01325) 351661
Key Personnel
Man Dir & Rights: J Gordon Cook
Founded: 1951
Subjects: Mechanical Engineering, Science (General), Technology
ISBN Prefix(es): 0-900541; 0-904095
Associate Companies: Meadowfield Press Ltd
Imprints: Meadowfield Press

Merseyside Port Folios, *imprint of* Countyvise Ltd

Meteorology, *imprint of* Artetech Publishing Co

Methodist Publishing House
4 John Wesley Rd, Werrington, Peterborough PE4 6ZP
Tel: (01733) 325002 *Fax:* (01733) 384180
E-mail: sales@mph.org.uk
Web Site: www.mph.org.uk
Key Personnel
Chief Executive & Rights: Brian Thornton *E-mail:* chief.exec@mph.org.uk
Founded: 1733
Subjects: Biblical Studies, Religion - Protestant, Theology
ISBN Prefix(es): 0-7162; 0-901027; 0-946550; 1-85852
Number of titles published annually: 40 Print; 1 CD-ROM; 2 Audio
Total Titles: 200 Print; 1 CD-ROM; 10 Audio
Parent Company: The Methodist Church of Great Britain
Imprints: Foundery Press & Chester House Publications
Distributor for Upper Room

Methuen, *imprint of* Random House UK Ltd

Methuen+
Formerly Methuen Publishing Ltd
215 Vauxhall Bridge Rd, London SW1V 1EJ
Tel: (020) 7798 1600 *Fax:* (020) 7828 2098; (020) 7233 9827
Web Site: www.methuen.co.uk
Key Personnel
Man Dir: Peter Tummons *E-mail:* ptummons@methuen.co.uk
Publishing Dir: Max Eilenberg *E-mail:* maxe@methuen.co.uk
Founded: 1889
Subjects: Archaeology, Biography, Drama, Theater, Fiction, History, Humor, Music, Dance, Travel, Discovery, autobiography
ISBN Prefix(es): 0-413; 0-417
Total Titles: 500 Print
Subsidiaries: Methuen Drama Ltd
Warehouse: TBS Distribution Centre, Colchester Rd, Frating Green, Colchester, Essex CO7 7DW *Tel:* (01206) 255678 *Fax:* (01206) 255930

Methuen Publishing Ltd, see Methuen

Metro Books+
3 Bramber Court, 2 Bramber Rd, London W14 9PB
Tel: (020) 7381 0666 *Fax:* (020) 7381 6868
E-mail: words@blake.co.uk
Web Site: www.blake.co.uk
Founded: 1995
Subjects: Biography, Child Care & Development, Cookery, Gardening, Plants, Health, Nutrition, Nonfiction (General), Psychology, Psychiatry, Travel
ISBN Prefix(es): 1-900512
Parent Company: John Blake Publishing Ltd

Metro Publishing, *imprint of* John Blake Publishing Ltd

MGM+
10 Cumberland Court, Great Cumberland Pl, London W1H 7DP
Tel: (020) 7262 8386
Key Personnel
Contact: Marcus Gregory
Founded: 1996
Subjects: Poetry, Psychology, Psychiatry
ISBN Prefix(es): 0-9528799
Imprints: Our Wonderful Psychoneural Systems
U.S. Office(s): 4500 Seminary Rd, Alexandria, VA 22304-1533, United States, M Y Yassa

Micelle, *imprint of* Micelle Press

Micelle Press+
10-12 Ullswater Crescent, Weymouth, Dorset DT3 5HE
Tel: (01305) 781574 *Fax:* (01305) 781574
E-mail: tony@wdi.co.uk
Web Site: www.wdi.co.uk/micelle
Key Personnel
Proprietor: Anthony L L Hunting *E-mail:* tony@wdi.co.uk
Founded: 1984

A specialist publisher & bookseller of books on cosmetics, toiletries, perfumes, surfactants & other specialty materials. In addition to our own books, we publish on behalf of the International Federation of Societies of Cosmetic Chemists (IFSCC), & represent the Cosmetic, Toiletry & Fragrance Association (CTFA) in the EC, Quensen & Ourdas for Haarmann & Reimer books in the UK, & some other publishers.
Membership(s): Independent Publishers Guild.
Subjects: Biological Sciences, Chemistry, Chemical Engineering, Health, Nutrition, Natural History, Physical Sciences, Science (General), Technology
ISBN Prefix(es): 1-870228; 0-9608752
Total Titles: 20 Print
Imprints: Micelle
Divisions: Janet Barber Translations
U.S. Office(s): PO Box 1519, Port Washington, NY 11050-0306, United States, Contact: Art Candido Tel: 516-767-7171 Fax: 516-944-9824 E-mail: info@scholium.com
Distributed by Scholium International Inc (US & Canada); Springflex Aromatherapy Pty Ltd (Australia); Talulah Books (South Africa); United Books & Periodicals (India)
Distributor for CTFA Inc (US, restriction UK only); Quensen & Ourdas (Germany, restriction UK only); H Ziolkowsy GmbH (Germany, restriction not Germany)

Michael Joseph, *imprint of* The Penguin Group UK

Michelin Tyre PLC, Tourism Dept, Maps & Guides Division
Edward Hyde Bldg, 38 Clarendon Rd, Watford, Herts WD1 1SX
Tel: (01923) 415000 Fax: (01923) 415250
Web Site: www.michelin.co.uk
Key Personnel
Head of Tourism & Sales Manager: John Lewis
Founded: 1910
Subjects: Travel
ISBN Prefix(es): 0-206
Parent Company: Michelin et Cie, France
U.S. Office(s): Michelin Travel Publications - Michelin Tire Corp, One Parkway South, Greenville, SC 29615, United States

Microfax, *imprint of* Funfax Ltd

Microform Academic Publishers
Division of Microform Imaging Ltd
Main St, East Ardsley, Wakefield, West Yorks WF3 2AT
Tel: (01924) 825700 Fax: (01924) 871005
E-mail: info@microform.co.uk
Web Site: www.microform.co.uk
Subjects: Americana, Regional, Government, Political Science, History, Literature, Literary Criticism, Essays, Social Sciences, Sociology
Number of titles published annually: 6 CD-ROM
Total Titles: 10 CD-ROM

Middleton Press
Easebourne Lane, Midhurst, West Sussex GU29 9AZ
Tel: (01730) 813169 Fax: (01730) 812601
Web Site: www.middletonpress.co.uk
Key Personnel
President & Editor: Vic Mitchell
Founded: 1981
Produce books for the railway & tramway enthusiast & modeller.
Subjects: Military Science, Regional Interests, Transportation, Railways, Tramways, Trolleybuses
ISBN Prefix(es): 0-906520; 1-873793; 1-901706; 1-904474

Midland Publishing+
Imprint of Ian Allan Publishing Ltd
4 Watling Dr, Hinckley LE10 3EY
Tel: (01455) 233747 Fax: (01455) 233737
E-mail: midlandbooks@compuserve.com
Web Site: www.ianallan.com/publishing
Key Personnel
Publisher: N P Lewis
Founded: 1992
Subjects: Aeronautics, Aviation, Military Science, Transportation
ISBN Prefix(es): 1-85780
Distribution Center: Midland Counties Publications, 4 Waitling Dr, Hinckley, Lincs LE10 3EY, Sales Manager: Nigel Passmore Tel: (01455) 233747 Fax: (01455) 233737
E-mail: midlandbooks@compuserve.com

Miles Kelly Publishing Ltd+
Bardfield Centre, Great Bardfield CM7 4SL
Tel: (01371) 811309 Fax: (01371) 811393
E-mail: info@mileskelly.net
Web Site: www.mileskelly.net

The Military Balance, *imprint of* International Institute for Strategic Studies

Harvey Miller Publishers+
Imprint of Brepols Publishers NV
Box 269, 2300 Abingdon OX14 4YN
Tel: (01235) 465500 Fax: (01235) 465555
E-mail: harvey.miller@brepols.net
Key Personnel
Dir: Harvey Miller
Editorial Dir: Elly Miller
Founded: 1969
Subjects: Art, History
ISBN Prefix(es): 0-905203; 1-872501; 0-85602
Associate Companies: G+B Arts International
Distributed by International Publishers Distributor
Distribution Center: David Brown Book Co, 28 Main St, PO Box 511, Oakville, CT 06779, United States Tel: 860-945-9329 Fax: 860-945-9468 E-mail: david.brown.bk.co@snet.net (US & Canada)
Marston Book Services, PO Box 269, Abingdon, Oxon OX14 4YN Tel: (01235) 465500 Fax: (01235) 465555 (UK)

J Garnet Miller+
Imprint of Cressrelles Publishing Company Ltd
Industrial Estate, 10 Station Rd, Colwall, Malvern, Herefordshire WR13 6RN
Tel: (01684) 540154 Fax: (01684) 540154
Key Personnel
Man Dir: Leslie Smith
Business Manager: Simon Smith
Founded: 1955
Subjects: Drama, Theater
ISBN Prefix(es): 0-85343
Number of titles published annually: 10 Print
Total Titles: 250 Print
Parent Company: Cressrelles Publishing Co Ltd
Distributed by Empire Publishing Services (Restrictions, Africa & Asia)
Distributor for I E Clark Inc (UK & Europe)
Foreign Rights: Bakers Plays (USA); DALRO (Southern Africa); Play Bureau (New Zealand); Warners Chappel (Australia)

J Garnet Miller Ltd, *imprint of* Cressrelles Publishing Company Ltd

Miller, *imprint of* Octopus Publishing Group

Miller's Publications
c/o Excel Logistics, Warehouse 1, Sanders Lodge Ind Estate, Wellingborough Rd, Rushdon NN10 6BQ
Tel: (01933) 273411 Fax: (01933) 229330
Key Personnel
General Manager: Valerie Lewis
Executive Editor: Alison Starling
Subjects: Antiques, Architecture & Interior Design
ISBN Prefix(es): 0-85533; 1-85732; 1-84000; 0-86134; 0-905879
Parent Company: Octopus Publishing Group
Distributed by Antique Collectors Club (USA)

MIND Publications+
15-19 Broadway, London E15 4BQ
Tel: (020) 8519 2122 Fax: (020) 8522 1725; (020) 8534 6399 (orders)
E-mail: contact@mind.org.uk; publications@mind.org.uk (mail order)
Web Site: www.mind.org.uk
Key Personnel
Chief Executive: Richard Brook
Information Dir: Anny Brackx Tel: (020) 8221 9660 Fax: (020) 7221 9681 E-mail: a.brackx@mind.org.uk
Founded: 1946
Specialize in mental health, psychiatry, psychology.
Subjects: Psychology, Psychiatry, Self-Help, Women's Studies
ISBN Prefix(es): 1-874690; 0-900557
Number of titles published annually: 15 Print
Total Titles: 200 Print; 200 Online; 200 E-Book

MIT Press Ltd
Fitzroy House, 11 Chenies St, London WC1E 7EY
Tel: (020) 7306 0603 Fax: (020) 7306 0604
E-mail: info@hup-mitpress.co.uk
Web Site: mitpress.mit.edu
Key Personnel
General Manager: Ann Sexsmith
  E-mail: asexsmith@hup-mitpress.co.uk
Publicity Manager: Ann Twiselton
  E-mail: atwiselton@hup-mitpress.co.uk
Exhibits & Text Manager: Judith Bullent
  E-mail: jbullent@hup-mitpress.co.uk
Founded: 1932
Subjects: Architecture & Interior Design, Art, Behavioral Sciences, Computer Science, Earth Sciences, Economics, Environmental Studies, Finance, Language Arts, Linguistics, Philosophy, Psychology, Psychiatry, Science (General), Social Sciences, Sociology, Technology
ISBN Prefix(es): 0-262
Number of titles published annually: 250 Print
Parent Company: MIT Press
Imprints: Bradford Books; Semiotext(e); Zone Books
Orders to: Astam Books, 57-61 John St, Leichhardt, NSW 2040, Australia Tel: (02) 9566 4400 Fax: (02) 9566 4411
John Wiley & Sons Ltd, Southern Cross Trading Estate, One Oldlands Way, Bognor Regis, West Sussex PO22 9SA Tel: (01243) 779 777 Fax: (01243) 820 250 E-mail: cs-books@wiley.co.uk
c/o Triliteral, 100 Maple Ridge Drive, Cumberland, RI 02864, United States Tel: 401-658-4226 Fax: 401-531-2801 E-mail: mitpress-orders@mit.edu
Returns: John Wiley & Sons Ltd, Southern Cross Trading Estate, One Oldlands Way, Bognor Regis, West Sussex PO22 9SA Tel: (01243) 779 777 Fax: (01243) 820 250 E-mail: cs-books@wiley.co.uk

Mitchell Beazley, *imprint of* Octopus Publishing Group

Mobius, *imprint of* Hodder & Stoughton General

Modern Humanities Research Association, *imprint of* Maney Publishing

PUBLISHERS UNITED KINGDOM

Mohr Books, *imprint of* Crossbridge Books

Monarch Books, *imprint of* Lion Hudson PLC

Monarch Books+
Imprint of Lion Hudson plc
Mayfield House, 256 Banbury Rd, Oxford, London OX2 7DH
Tel: (01865) 302750 *Fax:* (01865) 302757
E-mail: monarch@lionhudson.com
Key Personnel
Editorial Dir: Tony Collins *E-mail:* tonyc@lionhudson.com
Founded: 1988
Christian publisher producing up-market paperbacks for the international market.
Subjects: Biblical Studies, Biography, Education, Fiction, Gay & Lesbian, Humor, Psychology, Psychiatry, Religion - Protestant, Self-Help, Theology
ISBN Prefix(es): 0-8254; 1-85424
Number of titles published annually: 35 Print
Total Titles: 100 Print
Distributed by Kregel Publications
Warehouse: Kregel Publications, PO Box 2607, Grand Rapids, MI 49501, United States
Tel: 616-451-4775 *Fax:* 616-451-9330
Orders to: Kregel Publications, PO Box 2607, Grand Rapids, MI 49501, United States
Tel: 616-451-4775 *Fax:* 616-451-9330
Marston Book Services Ltd, PO Box 269, Abingdon, Oxon OX14 4YN *Tel:* (01235) 465606 *Fax:* (01235) 465509 *E-mail:* salesuk@lionhudson.com

Monument, *imprint of* Witherby & Co Ltd

Moonlight First Encyclopedia, *imprint of* Moonlight Publishing Ltd

Moonlight Publishing Ltd
36 Stratford Rd, London W8 6QA
Tel: (020) 7376 0299 *Fax:* (020) 7937 8921
Key Personnel
Dir: Christine Baker; P Stanley Baker; Robin Baker
Founded: 1980
Subjects: Nonfiction (General)
ISBN Prefix(es): 1-85103; 0-907144
Imprints: Discovers; First Discovery; First Discovery-Art; Moonlight First Encyclopedia; Pocket Bears; Pocket Worlds; Tales of Heaven & Earth
Orders to: Ragged Bears Ltd, Ragged Appleshaw, Andover, Hants SP11 3HX *Tel:* (01264) 772269

Moorley's Print & Publishing Ltd+
23 Park Rd, Ilkeston, Derbyshire DE7 5DA
Tel: (0115) 9320643 *Fax:* (0115) 9320643
E-mail: info@moorleys.co.uk
Web Site: www.moorleys.co.uk
Key Personnel
Chairman & Man Dir: John R Moorley
E-mail: john@moorleys.co.uk
Founded: 1966
Subjects: Biblical Studies, Drama, Theater, Music, Dance, Poetry, Religion - Protestant, Theology
ISBN Prefix(es): 0-901495; 0-86071
Number of titles published annually: 12 Print
Total Titles: 320 Print
Associate Companies: Truedata Computer Services
Imprints: Freedom Ministries; Headline Specials
Distributor for Cliff College Publishing; Nimbus Press; Pustaka Sufes Sdn Bhd; Social Workers Christian Fellowship; T Young

Morgan Kauffman, *imprint of* Elsevier Ltd

Morgan Publishing, *imprint of* Welsh Academic Press

William Morrow, *imprint of* HarperCollins UK

E J Morten (Publishers)+
6 Warburton St, Didsbury, Manchester M20 6WA
Tel: (0161) 445 7629 *Fax:* (0161) 445 7629
E-mail: timlovat@aol.com
Key Personnel
Man Dir, Rights & Permissions: John Anthony Morten
Founded: 1969
Facsimile reprints undertaken.
Subjects: History, Regional Interests
ISBN Prefix(es): 0-85972; 0-901598
Parent Company: E J Morten (Booksellers), Didsbury, Manchester
Imprints: Datapack Books; Pride Publications
Divisions: Morten Hire

Mosby, *imprint of* Elsevier Ltd

Motilal (UK) Books of India
PO Box 324, Borehamwood, Herts WD6 1NB
Tel: (020) 8905 1244 *Fax:* (020) 8905 1108
E-mail: info@mlbduk.com
Web Site: www.mlbduk.com
Key Personnel
Man Dir: Ray McLennan
Founded: 1980
Comprehensive coverage of Indology subjects. Imports from all Indian publishers against special orders. Also acts as UK agent for Motilal Banarsidass, Sundeep Prakashan, Concept Publications, Kant Publications & South Asia Books (India).
Subjects: Archaeology, Architecture & Interior Design, Art, Asian Studies, Education, History, Language Arts, Linguistics, Literature, Literary Criticism, Essays, Philosophy, Religion - Buddhist, Religion - Hindu, Religion - Islamic, Romance, Social Sciences, Sociology, Women's Studies, Specializes in Indology, Hinduism, Buddhism, Jainism, Translations of Sanskrit & Pali texts
ISBN Prefix(es): 81-208; 0-946482
Total Titles: 8,000 Print
Ultimate Parent Company: Money Savers (London) Ltd

Motor Racing Publications Ltd+
PO Box 1318, Croydon CR9 5YP
Tel: (020) 8654 2711 *Fax:* (020) 8407 0339
E-mail: mrp.books@virgin.net
Web Site: www.motorracingpublications.co.uk
Key Personnel
Man Dir, Publicity, Rights & Permissions: John Blunsden
Editorial & Customer Services: John Plummer
Sales, Production: Jim Starr
Founded: 1948
Specialize in sports.
Subjects: Automotive, Technology, Transportation
ISBN Prefix(es): 0-900549; 0-947981; 0-948358; 1-899870
Number of titles published annually: 11 Print
Total Titles: 80 Print
Imprints: The Fitzjames Press
Distributed by Motorbooks International USA (overseas distribution); Vine House Distribution Ltd
Foreign Rep(s): Bookport Associates (Gibraltar, Italy, Malta, Portugal & Spain); Bookworld Wholesale; D Richard Bowen (Scandinavia); Dennis Buckingham; Patrick Bygate (Croatia & Slovenia, Greece); Juliusz Komarnicki (Austria, Czech Republic, France, Hungary, Poland, Slovak Republic, Switzerland); Mike Lapworth; Clive Malins; Robert J Pleysier (Benelux, Germany); Mike Ryba

Mowbray, *imprint of* Cassell & Co

Mowbray, *imprint of* The Continuum International Publishing Group Ltd

MQ Publications Ltd
12 The Ivories, 6-8 Northampton St, London N1 2HY
Tel: (020) 7359 2244 *Fax:* (020) 7359 1616
E-mail: mail@mqpublications.com
Web Site: gustocreative.dsvr.co.uk/mqp-site/home.html
Key Personnel
Man Dir: Susan Jenkins; Gerson Kesner
Specialize in gift books.
Subjects: Cookery, Crafts, Games, Hobbies, Health, Nutrition, History, Cultural Reference, Mind, Body & Spirit, Sex
Warehouse: Biblios, Star Rd, Patridge Green, West Sussex

MRP, *see* Motor Racing Publications Ltd

Multilingual Matters Ltd+
Frankfurt Lodge, Clevedon Hall, Victoria Rd, Clevedon BS21 7HH
Tel: (01275) 876519 *Fax:* (01275) 871673
E-mail: info@multilingual-matters.com
Web Site: www.multilingual-matters.com
Key Personnel
Man Dir: Mike Grover *E-mail:* mike@multilingual-matters.com
Editorial Manager: Marjukka Grover
E-mail: marjukka@multilingual-matters.com
Production Manager: Ken Hall *E-mail:* ken@multilingual-matters.com
Marketing Manager: Kathryn King
E-mail: kathryn@multilingual-matters.com
Dir Sales & Distribution: Tommi Grover
E-mail: tommi@multilingual-matters.com
Founded: 1982
Specialize in bilingualism & bilingual education, second & foreign language learning & translation studies, also tourism research.
Subjects: Education, Environmental Studies, Geography, Geology, Language Arts, Linguistics, Social Sciences, Sociology, Travel, Tourism Research
ISBN Prefix(es): 0-905028; 1-85359; 1-873150; 1-84541
Number of titles published annually: 35 Print
Total Titles: 440 Print
Imprints: Channel View Publications
Branch Office(s)
Channel View Publications, 5201 Dufferin St, North York, ON M3H 5T8, Canada
Tel: 416-667-7791 *Fax:* 416-667-7832
E-mail: utpbooks@utpress.utoronto.ca (American Distributors)
UTP, 5201 Dufferin St, North York, ON M3H 5T8, Canada *Tel:* 416-667-7791 *Fax:* 416-667-7832 *E-mail:* utpbooks@utpress.utoronto.ca
Orders to: Marston Book Services, PO Box 269, Abingdon, Oxon OX14 4YN *Tel:* (01235) 465500 *Fax:* (01235) 465555 *E-mail:* direct.order@marston.co.uk
Membership(s): IPG

James Munro & Co
4-10 Darnley St, Glasgow G41 2SD
Tel: (0141) 429 1234 *Fax:* (0141) 420 1694
E-mail: enquiry@skipper.co.uk; sales@skipper.co.uk (orders)
Web Site: www.skipper.co.uk
Key Personnel
Sales Dir: L Ingram-Brown
Founded: 1832
Subjects: Maritime
ISBN Prefix(es): 0-85174
Parent Company: Brown, Son & Ferguson, Ltd

Murchison's Pantheon Ltd+
Murray House, 45 Beech St, London EC2Y 8AD
Tel: (020) 7374 2828 *Fax:* (020) 7628 6270
E-mail: 100450.1105@compuserve.com
Key Personnel
Contact: Charles Blount *E-mail:* charlesblount@compuserve.com
Specialize in audio travel guides.
Subjects: History, Travel
ISBN Prefix(es): 1-900652

Murdoch Books UK Ltd
Erico House, 93-99 Upper Richmond Rd, 6th floor, Putney, London SW15 2TG
Tel: (020) 8785 5995 *Fax:* (020) 8785 5985

John Murray (Publishers) Ltd+
338 Euston Rd, London NW1 3BH
Tel: (020) 7873 6000 *Fax:* (020) 7873 6446
E-mail: enquiries@johnmurrays.co.uk
Web Site: www.madaboutbooks.co.uk
Key Personnel
Man Dir: Roland Philipps
Head of Rights: Jane Blackstock
Publishing Dir: Gordon Wise
Publicity Dir: Sam Evans
Sales & Marketing: Matt Richell
Founded: 1768
Subjects: Fiction, Nonfiction (General)
ISBN Prefix(es): 0-7195
Parent Company: Hodder Headline Ltd
Ultimate Parent Company: WHSmith PLC
Orders to: Bookpoint Ltd, 130 Milton Park, Abingdon, Oxon OX14 4TD *Tel:* (01235) 835001 *Fax:* (01235) 832068

Music Sales Ltd, see Omnibus Press

Muslim Welfare House London Publishers, see MWH London Publishers

Muze UK Ltd+
10 Baker's Yard, Baker's Row, London EC1R 3DD
Tel: (0870) 7277 256 *Fax:* (0870) 7277 257
E-mail: colin@muze.co.uk
Web Site: www.muze.com
Key Personnel
President: Colin Larkin
Research Editor: Nic Oliver
Administration: Susan Pipe
Founded: 1990
Subjects: Biography, Music, Dance
ISBN Prefix(es): 1-872747
Parent Company: Muze Inc, 304 Hudson St, 8th floor, New York, NY 10013, United States

MWH London Publishers+
233 Seven Sisters Rd, London N4 2DA
Tel: (020) 7263 3071 *Fax:* (020) 7281 12687
E-mail: info@mwht.org.uk
Web Site: www.mwht.org.uk
Telex: 8812176
Key Personnel
Man Dir: Mohamed Tamin
Founded: 1970
Subjects: Regional Interests
ISBN Prefix(es): 0-906194
Associate Companies: Muslim Information Centre
Orders to: MIC, London

NAG Press, *imprint of* Robert Hale Ltd

NAG Press+
Imprint of Robert Hale Ltd
Clerkenwell House, 45-47 Clerkenwell Green, London EC1R 0HT
Tel: (020) 7251 2661 *Fax:* (020) 7490 4958
E-mail: enquire@halebooks.com
Web Site: www.halebooks.com/n_a_g_press_files.html
Key Personnel
Dir: Martin Kendall
Founded: 1937
Subjects: Horological & Gemmological
ISBN Prefix(es): 0-7198
Total Titles: 100 Print
Warehouse: CBS, Units 1/K, Paddockwood Distribution Centre, Paddock Wood, Kent TN12 6UU, Contact: Alan Smith *Tel:* (01892) 837171 *Fax:* (01892) 837212 *E-mail:* orders@combook.co.uk

NATE, see National Association for the Teaching of English (NATE)

National Archives of Scotland
H M General Register House, 2 Princes St, Edinburgh EH1 3YY
Tel: (0131) 535 1334 *Fax:* (0131) 535 1328
E-mail: publications@nas.gov.uk; enquiries@nas.gov.uk
Web Site: www.nas.gov.uk
Key Personnel
Head of Publications & Education Branch: Rosemary Gibson
Publications Officer: Alison Lindsay *Tel:* (0131) 535 1353
Founded: 1787
General historical & educational publications designed to make the holdings of the NAS more accessible.
Membership(s): Scottish Publishers Association.
Subjects: History
ISBN Prefix(es): 1-870874
Number of titles published annually: 3 Print
Total Titles: 42 Print
Branch Office(s)
West Search Room, West Register House, Charlotte Square, Edinburgh EH2 4DJ *Tel:* (0131) 535 1413 *Fax:* (0131) 535 1411 *E-mail:* wsr@nas.gov.uk

National Assembly for Wales, *imprint of* National Assembly for Wales

National Assembly for Wales
Cardiff Bay, Cardiff CF99 1NA
Tel: (029) 20 825111 *Fax:* (029) 20 825350
E-mail: stats.pubs@wales.gsi.gov.uk
Web Site: www.wales.gov.uk
Key Personnel
Man Dir & General Editor: E Swires-Hennessy *Tel:* (029) 2082 5087 *Fax:* (029) 2082 5087 *E-mail:* ed.swires-hennessy@wales.gsi.gov.uk
Founded: 1981
Specialize in statistics on Wales.
Subjects: Business, Economics, Education, Government, Political Science, Health, Nutrition, Public Administration, Social Sciences, Sociology
ISBN Prefix(es): 0-7504
Total Titles: 35 Print
Imprints: Cynulliad Cenedlaethol Cymru; National Assembly for Wales

National Association for Mental Health, see MIND Publications

National Association for the Teaching of English (NATE)+
Broadfield Business Centre, 50 Broadfield Rd, Sheffield S8 0XJ
Tel: (0114) 255 5419 *Fax:* (0114) 255 5296
E-mail: info@nate.org.uk
Web Site: www.nate.org.uk
Key Personnel
Development & Communications Dir: Trevor Millum
Founded: 1963
Specialize in English teaching.
Membership(s): Publishers' Association.
Subjects: Drama, Theater, Education, English as a Second Language, Film, Video, Literature, Literary Criticism, Essays, Poetry, Literacy, Information & communication technology
ISBN Prefix(es): 0-901291
Number of titles published annually: 10 Print
Total Titles: 50 Print
Distributed by Australian Reading Association
Distributor for BELTA; Paul Chapman Publishing; Devon County Council; Drake Publishing; English & Media Centre; Falmer Press; Framework Press/Fultons; David Fulton; Garth Publishing; Nelsons; Open University Press; PCET Wallcharts; Thimble Press; Ward Lock

National Centre for Language & Literacy+
University of Reading, Bulmershe Court, Reading RG6 1HY
Tel: (0118) 378 8820 *Fax:* (0118) 378 6801
E-mail: ncll@reading.ac.uk
Web Site: www.ncll.org.uk
Key Personnel
Dir: Prof Viv Edwards *E-mail:* v.k.edwards@reading.ac.uk
Centre Administrator: Pam Brown
Publications: Judy Tallet
Founded: 1969
Specialize in language & literacy learning.
Subjects: Education, English as a Second Language, Language Arts, Linguistics
ISBN Prefix(es): 0-7049

National Childbirth Trust Publishing
25-27 High St, Chesterton, Cambridge CB4 1ND
Tel: (01223) 352790 *Fax:* (01223) 460718
E-mail: bpc@bpccam.co.uk
Web Site: www.bpccam.co.uk

National Computing Centre, see Blackwell Publishing Ltd

National Council for Voluntary Organisations (NCVO)+
Regent's Wharf, 8 All Saints St, London N1 9RL
Tel: (020) 7713 6161 *Fax:* (020) 7713 6300
E-mail: ncvo@ncvo-vol.org.uk
Web Site: www.ncvo-vol.org.uk
Key Personnel
Chief Executive: Stuart Etherington
Head of Marketing & Publications: Jim Minton
Marketing Officer: Lou Large
Online Development Manager: Simon Cope *Tel:* (0207) 520 2544 *E-mail:* simon.cope@ncvo-vol.org.uk
Founded: 1919 (NCVO), 1969 (BSP), 1991 (NCVO Publications)
Also publish in association with other organizations.
Subjects: Disability, Special Needs, Finance, Management, Public Administration
ISBN Prefix(es): 0-7199
Orders to: Hamilton House Mailings, 17 Staveley Way, Northampton NN6 7TX
Membership(s): IPG; Publishers' Association

National Extension College+
Michael Young Centre, Purbeck Rd, Cambridge CB2 2HN
Tel: (01223) 400 200 *Fax:* (01223) 400 399
E-mail: info@nec.ac.uk
Web Site: www.nec.ac.uk
Key Personnel
Executive Dir: Ros Morpeth
Assistant Dir: Roger Merritt
Founded: 1963
Membership(s): ICDE, NIACE & BAOL.
Subjects: Accounting, Business, Career Development, Education, English as a Second Language, Environmental Studies, Self-Help
ISBN Prefix(es): 0-86082; 1-85356; 0-902404
Imprints: NEC

PUBLISHERS — UNITED KINGDOM

National Foster Care Association+
87 Blackfriars Rd, London SE1 8HA
Tel: (020) 7620 6400 *Fax:* (020) 7620 6401
E-mail: nfca@fostercare.org.uk
Key Personnel
Executive Dir: Gerri McAndrew
Communications Manager: Katrina Phillips
Founded: 1976
Subjects: Child Care & Development
ISBN Prefix(es): 1-897869; 0-946015

National Foundation for Educational Research
The Mere Upton Park, Slough SL1 2DQ
Tel: (01753) 574123 *Fax:* (01753) 691632
E-mail: enquiries@nfer.ac.uk
Web Site: www.nfer.ac.uk
Key Personnel
Head of Publication: Dr Enver Carim
Founded: 1946
Subjects: Education
ISBN Prefix(es): 0-7005; 0-7087; 0-85633; 0-901225
Branch Office(s)
Slough Rd, Datchet, Berks SL3 9AU *Tel:* (01753) 574123 *Fax:* (01753) 691632 (Please do not send post to this address)
Genesis 4, York Science Park, University Rd, Heslington, York YO10 5DG *Tel:* (01904) 433435 *Fax:* (01904) 433436 *E-mail:* j.harland@nfer.ac.uk
Chestnut House, Tawe Business Village, Phoenix Way, Enterprise Park, Swansea SA7 9LA *Tel:* (01792) 459800 *Fax:* (01792) 797815 *E-mail:* scya@nfer.ac.uk

National Galleries of Scotland+
Publications Dept, The Dean Gallery, 73 Belford Rd, Edinburgh EH4 3DS
Tel: (0131) 624 6257; (0131) 624 6261
Fax: (0131) 315 2963
E-mail: publications@nationalgalleries.org
Web Site: www.nationalgalleries.org
Key Personnel
Head of Publications & Picture Library: Janis Adams *E-mail:* jadams@nationalgalleries.org
Subjects: Art, Photography
ISBN Prefix(es): 0-903598; 1-903278
Total Titles: 90 Print; 1 CD-ROM

National Institute of Adult Continuing Education (NIACE)+
Renaissance House, 20 Princess Rd W, Leicester LE1 6TP
Tel: (0116) 204 4200; (0116) 204 4201
Fax: (0116) 285-4514
E-mail: enquiries@niace.org.uk; niace@niace.org.uk
Web Site: www.niace.org.uk
Key Personnel
Dir: Alan Tuckett *E-mail:* alan.tuckett@niace.org.uk
Dir, Research, Development & Information: Peter Lavender *E-mail:* peter.lavender@niace.org.uk
Dir, Programmes & Policy: Sue Cara
Dir, Finance: Margaret Conner *E-mail:* margaret.conner@niace.org.uk
Founded: 1921
NIACE, the national organization for adult learning, has a broad remit to promote life long learning opportunities for adults. NIACE works to develop increased participation in education & training. It aims to do this for more who do not have easy access due to class, gender, age, race, language & culture, learning difficulties, disabilities or insufficient financial resources.
Subjects: Education
ISBN Prefix(es): 1-872941; 1-86201; 0-900559
Number of titles published annually: 40 Print
Total Titles: 100 Print
Branch Office(s)
NIACE Dysgu Cymru, 35 Cathedral Rd, Ground Floor, Cardiff, Wales CF11 9HB *Tel:* (0292) 0370900 *Fax:* (0292) 0370909 *E-mail:* enquiries@niacecy.demon.co.uk *Web Site:* www.niacedc.org.uk

National Library of Scotland
George IV Bridge, Edinburgh EH1 1EW
Tel: (0131) 226 4531 *Fax:* (0131) 622 4803
E-mail: enquiries@nls.uk
Web Site: www.nls.uk
Key Personnel
Librarian: Martyn Wade
Dir, Public Services: Dr Alan Marchbank *E-mail:* a.marchbank@nls.uk
Head of Public Programs: Dr Kenneth Gibson *E-mail:* k.gibson@nls.uk
Subjects: History, Regional Interests

National Library of Wales
Aberystwyth, Ceredigion SY23 3BU
Tel: (01970) 632 800 *Fax:* (01970) 615 709
E-mail: holi@llgc.org.uk
Web Site: www.llgc.org.uk
Key Personnel
President: R Brinley Jones
Vice President: John Phillips
Treasurer: Conrad L Bryant
Editor: Gwyn Jenkins
Librarian: Andrew M W Green
Founded: 1907
Copyright/Legal Deposit Library.
Subjects: Art, Genealogy, Government, Political Science, Library & Information Sciences, Literature, Literary Criticism, Essays, Photography, Publishing & Book Trade Reference
ISBN Prefix(es): 0-907158

National Museum & Gallery
Cathays Park, Cardiff CF10 3NP
Tel: (029) 2039 7951 *Fax:* (029) 2037 3219
E-mail: post@nmgw.ac.uk
Web Site: www.nmgw.ac.uk
Key Personnel
Contact: John Williams-Davies

National Museums of Scotland Publishing, see NMS Enterprises Ltd - Publishing

National Portrait Gallery Publications+
St Martin's Pl, London WC2H 0HE
Tel: (020) 7306 0055 (ext 266); (020) 7312 2482
Fax: (020) 7306 0092
Web Site: www.npg.org.uk
Key Personnel
Head of Trading: Robert Carr-Archer *E-mail:* rcarrarcher@npg.org.uk
Publishing Manager: Celia Joicey
Production Manager: Ruth Muller-Wirth *E-mail:* rmullerwirth@npg.org.uk
Senior Editor: Anjali Bulley *E-mail:* abulley@npg.org.uk
Sales & Marketing Officer: Pallavi Vadhia *E-mail:* pvadhia@npg.org.uk
Founded: 1976 (book publishing division)
Also acts as Picture Library.
Subjects: Art, Biography, History, Photography
ISBN Prefix(es): 0-904017; 1-85514
Number of titles published annually: 14 Print
Total Titles: 45 Print
U.S. Office(s): Antique Collector's Club, Market St, Industrial Park, Wappingers Falls, New York, NY 12590, United States *Fax:* 845-297-0068
Warehouse: Grantham Book Services, Isaac Newton Way, Alva Park Industrial Estate, Grantham, Lincs N931 9SD *Tel:* (01476) 541 080 *Fax:* (01476) 541 061

The National Society, *imprint of* Church House Publishing

National Trust+
36 Queen Anne's Gate, London SW1H 9AS
Tel: (0870) 609 5380 *Fax:* (020) 7222 5097
Web Site: www.nationaltrust.org.uk
Key Personnel
Publisher: Margaret Willes
Founded: 1987
Subjects: Art, Cookery, Gardening, Plants, History, Photography, Social Sciences, Sociology, Travel
ISBN Prefix(es): 0-7078
Number of titles published annually: 12 Print
Total Titles: 75 Print
Parent Company: National Trust Enterprises, The Stable Block, Heywood House, Westbury, Wilts BA13 4NA
Branch Office(s)
Rowallane House, Saintfield, Ballynahinch, Co Down, Northern Ireland BT24 7LH *Tel:* (028) 9751 0721 *Fax:* (028) 9751 1242
Wemyss House, 28 Charlotte Sq, Edinburgh EH2 4ET *Tel:* (0131) 243 9300 *Web Site:* www.nts.org.uk/
Hughenden Manor, High Wycombe, Bucks HP14 4LA *Tel:* (01494) 528051 *Fax:* (01494) 463310 *Web Site:* www.nationaltrust.org.uk/regions/thameschilterns/ (regional office for Thames & Solent)
The Hollens, Grasmere, Ambleside, Cumbria LA22 9QZ *Tel:* (0870) 609 5391 *Fax:* (015394) 35353 (regional office for the North West)
Killerton House, Broadclyst, Exeter EX5 3LE *Tel:* (01392) 881691 *Fax:* (01392) 881954 (regional office for Devon & Cornwall)
Blickling, Norwich NR11 6NF *Tel:* (0870) 609 5388 *Fax:* (01263) 734924 *Web Site:* www.nationaltrust.org.uk/regions/eastanglia/ (regional office for East Anglia)
Clumber Park Stableyard, Worksop, Notts S80 3BE *Tel:* (01909) 486411 *Fax:* (01909) 486377 (regional office for the East Midlands)
Attingham Park, Shrewsbury, Salop SY4 4TP *Tel:* (01743) 708100 *Fax:* (01743) 708150 *E-mail:* sevinfo@stmp.ntrust.org.uk *Web Site:* www.nationaltrust.org.uk/regions/westmidlands/ (regional office for the West Midlands)
Polesden Lacey, Dorking, Surrey RH5 6BO *Tel:* (01372) 453401 *Fax:* (01372) 452023 (regional office for the South East)
Eastleigh Court, Bishopstrow, Warminster, Wilts BA12 9HW *Tel:* (01985) 843600 *Fax:* (01985) 843624 *Web Site:* www.nationaltrust.org.uk/regions/wessex/ (regional office for Wessex)
Goddards, 27 Tadcaster Rd, Dringhouses, York Y024 1GG *Tel:* (01904) 702021 *Fax:* (01904) 771970 (regional office for Yorkshire & North East)
Trinity Sq, Llandudno, Wales LL30 2DE *Tel:* (01492) 860123 *Fax:* (01492) 860233
U.S. Office(s): Trafalgar Square Publishing, Howe Hill Rd, North Pomfret, VT 05053, United States
Warehouse: MacMillian Distribution Ltd, Houndmills, Basingstoke R921 GXS, Mrs Beverly Morris *Tel:* (01256) 329242 *Fax:* (01256) 812558
Orders to: MacMillian Distribution Ltd, Houndmills, Basingstoke R921 GXS, Hazel Maynard

National Youth Agency
17-23 Albion St, Leicester LE1 6GD
Tel: (0116) 285 3700 *Fax:* (0116) 285 3777
E-mail: nya@nya.org.uk
Web Site: www.nya.co.uk
ISBN Prefix(es): 0-86155
Number of titles published annually: 12 Print
Total Titles: 75 Print

NCVO, see National Council for Voluntary Organisations (NCVO)

NEC, *imprint of* National Extension College

UNITED KINGDOM

Negotiate Ltd+
99 Caiyside, Edinburgh EH10 7HR
Tel: (0131) 445 7571; (0131) 477 7858
Fax: (0131) 445 7572
E-mail: florence@negweb.com
Web Site: www.negotiate.co.uk
Key Personnel
Man Dir: Gavin Kennedy *E-mail:* gavin@negweb.com
Founded: 1986
Subsidiaries: Negotiate P S C

Neil Wilson Publishing Ltd+
Pentagon Centre, Suite 303, 36 Washington St, Glasgow G3 8AZ
Tel: (0141) 221 1117 *Fax:* (0141) 221 5363
E-mail: info@nwp.co.uk
Web Site: www.nwp.co.uk
Key Personnel
Man Dir: Neil Wilson *E-mail:* neil@nwp.sol.co.uk
Production Editor: Sallie Moffat *E-mail:* sallie@nwp.co.uk
Founded: 1992
Membership(s): Scottish Publishers Association.
Subjects: Biography, Cookery, Fiction, History, Humor, Music, Dance, Outdoor Recreation, Regional Interests, Sports, Athletics, Wine & Spirits
ISBN Prefix(es): 1-897784; 1-903238
Number of titles published annually: 15 Print
Total Titles: 100 Print
Imprints: Angels' Share; 11:9; The In Pinn; The Vital Spark
Distributed by Interlink Books (USA)
Foreign Rep(s): Interlink Publishing (USA); Murray Sutton (Scandinavia)
Warehouse: Book Source, 32 Finlas St, Cowlairs Estate, Glasgow G22 5DU *Tel:* (0870) 240 2182 *Fax:* (0141) 557 0189 *E-mail:* orders@booksource.net *Web Site:* www.booksource.net
Orders to: Book Source, 32 Finlas St, Cowlairs Estate, Glasgow G22 5DU *Tel:* (0870) 240 2182 *Fax:* (0141) 557 0189 *E-mail:* orders@booksource.net *Web Site:* www.booksource.net

Nelson Thornes Ltd+
Delta Pl, 27 Bath Rd, Cheltenham GL53 7TH
Tel: (01242) 267100; (01242) 267311
Fax: (01242) 267311
E-mail: export@nelsonthornes.com
Web Site: www.nelsonthornes.com
Key Personnel
Man Dir General Management: Fred Grainger
Founded: 1972
Subjects: Business, Child Care & Development, Education, Environmental Studies, Geography, Geology, History, Language Arts, Linguistics, Mathematics, Medicine, Nursing, Dentistry, Music, Dance, Physics, Religion - Other, Science (General), Social Sciences, Sociology, Technology
ISBN Prefix(es): 0-7487; 0-85950; 1-871402
Parent Company: Wolters Kluwer PLC
Ultimate Parent Company: Wolters Kluwer NV, Netherlands
Associate Companies: Moorhouse Black; Croner; Maps
Imprints: Mary Glasgow Publications
Warehouse: Alexandra Industrial Estate, Alexandra Way, Ashchurch, Tewkesbury GL20 8PE

Net.Works, *imprint of* Take That Ltd

Network Books, *imprint of* BBC Worldwide Publishers

Neville Spearman Publishers, *imprint of* The C W Daniel Co Ltd

New Cavendish Books+
3 Denbigh Rd, London W11 2SJ
Tel: (020) 7229 6765 *Fax:* (020) 7792 0027
E-mail: sales@cavbooks.demon.co.uk
Web Site: www.newcavendishbooks.co.uk
Key Personnel
Dir: Narisa Chakra *E-mail:* narisa@new-cav.demon.co.uk
Founded: 1973
Subjects: Nonfiction (General), Technology, Toys, collecting & popular culture
ISBN Prefix(es): 0-904568; 1-872727
Number of titles published annually: 4 Print
Total Titles: 70 Print
Imprints: White Mouse Editions
Distributed by Antique Collectors Club (UK & Europe); Antique Collectors Club (USA) (USA); Critiques Livres (France); Peribo Pty Ltd (Australia)

New Era Publications UK Ltd+
Saint Hill Manor, East Grinstead, Sussex RH19 4JY
Tel: (01342) 314 846 *Fax:* (01342) 314 857
E-mail: books@newerapublications.com
Web Site: www.newerapublications.com
Key Personnel
Man Dir: Margaret Blunden
Dir, Public Affairs: Robert Springall
Sales Dir: Nic Webb *E-mail:* nic@nrgw.demon.co.uk
Marketing Director: Robert Black
Founded: 1985
Subjects: Business, Education, Fiction, Health, Nutrition, Management, Nonfiction (General), Philosophy, Religion - Other, Science Fiction, Fantasy, Self-Help, Western Fiction
ISBN Prefix(es): 1-870451; 1-900944
Total Titles: 90 Print; 1 CD-ROM; 18 Audio
Parent Company: New Era Publications International ApS, Denmark
Associate Companies: Author Services Inc, 7051 Hollywood Blvd, Suite 400, Los Angeles, CA 90028, United States *Tel:* 213-466-3310 *E-mail:* asi@earthlink.net
Branch Office(s)
Continental Publications Pty Ltd, Budget House, 6th floor, 130 Main St, Johannesburg 2001, South Africa *Tel:* (0113) 316 621 *Fax:* (0113) 316 621
Nueva Era Dinamica SA, C/montera 20, 1 Dcha, 28013 Madrid, Spain *Tel:* (07) 77 0941
New Era Central Europe, Leonardo Da Vinci u 8-12, 1084 Budapest, Hungary *Tel:* (01) 210-3446 *Fax:* (01) 210-3501
New Era Publications Australia Pty Ltd, Ballarat House, Level 3, 68-72 Wentworth Ave, Surry Hills, NSW 2010, Australia *Tel:* (02) 211 0692 *Fax:* (02) 211 0686
New Era Publications Deutschland GmbH, Hittfelder Kirchweg 5, 21220 Seevetal-Maschen, Germany *Tel:* (04105) 68330 *Fax:* (04105) 683322 *E-mail:* buch@newerapublications.de
New Era Publications France EURL, 14, Rue des Moulins, 75001 Paris, France *Tel:* (01) 42 974250 *Fax:* (01) 42 974260 *E-mail:* librairie@newerapublications.com
New Era Publications Group, Bldg 1, Str Kasatkina, 16, 129301 Moscow, Russian Federation *Tel:* (095) 286 88 31 *Fax:* (095) 286 88 31
New Era Publications Italia, Via Cadorna, 61, 20090 Vimodrone (MI), Italy *Tel:* (02) 274 09271 *Fax:* (02) 274 09198 *E-mail:* sales@newera.it
New Era Publications Japan Inc, 4-38-15-2F Higashi Ikebukuro, Toshima-Ku, Tokyo 108, Japan *Tel:* (03) 5960 5660 *Fax:* (03) 5960 5561 *E-mail:* nepjp@newerapublications.com
Source Publications Co, 2nd Floor 65, Section 4, Min-Shen East Rd, Taipei ROC, Taiwan, Province of China *Tel:* (02) 25465851

U.S. Office(s): Bridge Publications, A751 Fountain Ave, Los Angeles, CA, United States
Warehouse: Bailey Distribution, Learoyd Rd, New Romney, Kent TN28 8XU

New European Publications Ltd+
14-16 Carroun Rd, London SW8 1JT
Tel: (020) 7582 3996 *Fax:* (020) 7582 7021
Key Personnel
Dir: Richard Body; John Coleman
Founded: 1987
Specialize in European affairs & subjects with a special interest in 'communitarian' politics.
Subjects: Aeronautics, Aviation, Government, Political Science, Travel
ISBN Prefix(es): 1-872410
Number of titles published annually: 5 Print
Total Titles: 23 Print
Orders to: Central Books Ltd, 99 Wallis Rd, London E9 5LN

New Holland, *imprint of* New Holland Publishers (UK) Ltd

New Holland Publishers (UK) Ltd+
Garfield House, 86-88 Edgware Rd, London W2 2EA
Tel: (020) 7724 7773 *Fax:* (020) 7724 6184
E-mail: postmaster@nhpub.co.uk
Web Site: www.newhollandpublishers.com
Key Personnel
Man Dir: John Beaufoy *E-mail:* john@nhpub.co.uk
Editorial: Jo Jennings; Yvonne McFarlane; Rosemary Wilkinson
Sales & Marketing Dir: Terry Shaughnessy *E-mail:* terry@nhpub.co.uk
Sales Office Manager: Alex Lattes *E-mail:* alex@nhpub.co.uk
Publicity & Promotions Manager: Yvonne Thynne *E-mail:* yvonnet@nhpub.co.uk
Rights Executive: Anna Thomas *E-mail:* anna@nhpub.co.uk
Founded: 1956
Specialize in illustrated books.
Subjects: Cookery, Crafts, Games, Hobbies, House & Home, How-to, Natural History, Travel
ISBN Prefix(es): 1-85368; 1-85974
Parent Company: The New Holland Struik Publishing Group (Pty) Ltd, South Africa
Imprints: New Holland
Subsidiaries: New Holland Australia
Distributor for Complete Dive Guides; Juicy Books; La Belle Aurore; Pilot Books; SCP Publishing; Southern Book Publishers (Europe, UK, North America & Asia); Stonebridge Press (Europe, UK & South Africa); Struik Publishers (Europe, UK & North America); Turtle Press; Weatherhill (Europe, UK & South Africa)
Shipping Address: F J Tytherleigh & Co Ltd, Hubert Rd, Brentwood, Essex CM14 4RF
Orders to: Littlehampton Book Services Ltd, Faraday Close, Durrington, West Sussex BN13 3RB *Tel:* (01903) 828500 *Fax:* (01903) 828625 *E-mail:* orders@lbsltd.co.uk

New Orchard Editions, *imprint of* Cassell & Co

New Playwrights Network, *imprint of* Cressrelles Publishing Company Ltd

New Playwrights' Network+
Imprint of Cressrelles Publishing Company Ltd
10 Station Rd Industrial Estate, Colwall, Malvern, Herefordshire WR13 6RN
Tel: (01684) 540154 *Fax:* (01684) 540154
Key Personnel
Managing Proprietor: L G Smith
Founded: 1972

PUBLISHERS — UNITED KINGDOM

Subjects: Drama, Theater
ISBN Prefix(es): 0-86319; 0-903653; 0-906660
Number of titles published annually: 5 Print
Total Titles: 400 Print

New Roders, *imprint of* Pearson Education Europe, Mideast & Africa

Newnes, *imprint of* Elsevier Ltd

Newpro UK Ltd+
Old Sawmills Rd, Faringdon, Oxon SN7 7DS
Tel: (01367) 242411 *Fax:* (01367) 241124
E-mail: sales@newprouk.co.uk
Key Personnel
Man Dir: Chris Coleman *E-mail:* chriscoleman@newprouk.co.uk
Founded: 1984
Also distributes for other photography publishers.
Subjects: Crafts, Games, Hobbies, History, Natural History, Photography
ISBN Prefix(es): 0-86343; 0-85245
Imprints: Fountain Press; Hove Foto Books

Nexus, *imprint of* Virgin Publishing Ltd

Nexus Special Interests+
Nexus House, Azalea Drive, Swanley, Kent BR8 8HU
Tel: (01322) 660070 *Fax:* (01322) 667633
Key Personnel
Books Manager & International Rights Contact: Bill Burkinshaw *Fax:* (01296) 738704
Customer Services Manager: Jayne Hewish
Specialize in hobby & craft books, magazines, plans, exhibitions & awards evenings.
Subjects: Crafts, Games, Hobbies, Engineering (General), Gardening, Plants, Wine & Spirits
ISBN Prefix(es): 1-87403; 0-85344; 1-85486; 0-85076; 0-85242; 0-900841
Total Titles: 130 Print
Parent Company: Nexus Media Ltd
Distributed by Chris Lloyd
Foreign Rep(s): Chris Lloyd
Warehouse: Cassell Warehouse, Fleets Industrial Estate, One, Willis Way, Poole, Dorset BH15 3SS

The NFER-NELSON Publishing Co Ltd+
The Chiswick Centre, 414 Chiswick High Rd, London W4 5TF
Tel: (020) 8996 8444; (020) 8996 8445 (international enquiries) *Toll Free Tel:* (0845) 602 1937 (customer service) *Fax:* (020) 8996 3660 (international enquiries)
E-mail: information@nfer-nelson.co.uk; edu&hsc@nfer-Nelson.co.uk (customer service)
Web Site: www.nfer-nelson.co.uk
Telex: 937400 ONECOM G ref 24966001
Key Personnel
Man Dir: Michael Jackson
Commercial Dir: Penn Fiona
Business Development Dir: Ian Florance
Founded: 1981
A joint venture of the National Foundation for Educational Research in England & Wales & the Thomson Corporation.
Subjects: Business, Child Care & Development, Education, Health, Nutrition, Psychology, Psychiatry
ISBN Prefix(es): 0-7005; 0-7087; 0-85633; 0-901225
Parent Company: Thomson Corporation
Associate Companies: Thomas Nelson & Sons Ltd, Routledge
Divisions: ASE
Warehouse: Units 1 & 2, Wyndham Rd, Hawkswoan Estate, Swindon, Wiltshire SN2 1BR
Distribution Center: Dansk Psykologisk Forlag, Copenhagen, Denmark
ETCC, Dublin, Ireland
Editions du Centre de Psychologie Appliquee, Paris, France
Malta Union of Professional Psychologists, Valletta, Malta
Nelson Canada, Scarborough, ON, Canada
Nelson Publishers (SEA) plc, Singapore
Norsk Psykologforening, Oslo, Norway
NZCER, Wellington, New Zealand
Occupational & Medical Suppliers, Johannesburg, South Africa
Organizzazioni Speciali, Florence, Italy
Psico, Lisbon, Portugal
Psykologien Kustannus Oy, Helsinki, Finland
PsykologiForlaget AB, Stockholm, Sweden
Stoelting, Dale Wood, IL, United States
Swets Test Services, Lisse, Netherlands
Testzentrale, Gottingen, Germany
Transgobal Publishers Service Ltd, Hong Kong
Universitets Forlaget, Oslo, Norway
HAD Center Ltd, Nicosia, Cyprus
Western Psychological Services, Los Angeles, CA, United States
PJ Professional Resources Ltd, Victoria, Australia
Par Inc, Odessa, FL, United States
NTI, Oman
Manasavan, Delhi, India
Testzentrale, Bern, Switzerland
Verlag Hans Huber AG, Bern, Switzerland
Unifacmanu Trading Co Ltd, Taipai, Taiwan, Province of China

NIACE, see National Institute of Adult Continuing Education (NIACE)

Nico Editions, *imprint of* Thoemmes Press

Nielsen BookData
Editorial Dept, 89-95 Queensway, Stevenage SG1 EA
Tel: (01438) 744100; (01483) 712244 (customer service) *Toll Free Tel:* (0870) 7778711 (customer service) *Fax:* (01438) 745578
E-mail: customerservices@nielsenbooknet.co.uk; helpdesk@nielsenbooknet.co.uk
Web Site: www.whitaker.co.uk; www.nielsenbookdata.com *Cable:* WHITMANACK LONDON WC1
Key Personnel
Man Dir: Francis Bennett
Editorial Dir: Michael Healy *E-mail:* michael.healy@nielsenbookdata.co.uk
Head of Sales (UK): Simon Skinner
Head of Marketing: Mo Siewcharran
Founded: 1841
Subjects: Publishing & Book Trade Reference
ISBN Prefix(es): 0-85021
Parent Company: VNU Business Media Inc
Associate Companies: Bookseller Publications
Subsidiaries: The Standard Book Numbering Agency Ltd; Teleordering Ltd; BookTrack Ltd

Nightingale Books, *imprint of* Baha'i Publishing Trust

Nightingale Press, *imprint of* Wimbledon Publishing Company Ltd

Nile & Mackenzie Ltd+
13 John Prince's St, London W1G 0JR
Tel: (020) 7493 0351 *Fax:* (020) 7495 0128
Key Personnel
Man Dir: Daljit Sehbai
Rights & Permissions: Donna Stewart
Founded: 1974
Subjects: Education
ISBN Prefix(es): 0-86031

James Nisbet & Co Ltd+
78 Tilehouse St, Hitchin, Herts SG5 2DY
Tel: (01462) 438331 *Fax:* (01462) 431528
Key Personnel
Chairman: E M Mackenzie-Wood
Founded: 1810
Subjects: Education
ISBN Prefix(es): 0-7202

NIV Bibles, *imprint of* Hodder & Stoughton Religious

NMS Enterprises Ltd - Publishing+
National Museums of Scotland, Chambers St, Edinburgh EH1 1JF
Tel: (0131) 247 4026 *Fax:* (0131) 247 4012
E-mail: publishing@nms.ac.uk
Web Site: www.nms.ac.uk
Key Personnel
Publishing Dir: Lesley A Taylor *Tel:* (0131) 247 4186 *E-mail:* ltaylor@nms.ac.uk
Marketing: Kate Blackadder
Administrator: Elizabeth Dewar
Founded: 1985 (as National Museums of Scotland Publishing)
Subjects: Archaeology, Art, Biography, Cookery, Geography, Geology, History, Natural History, Nonfiction (General), Poetry, Science (General), Technology, Scottish history & culture, photographic archive
ISBN Prefix(es): 0-948636; 1-901663
Number of titles published annually: 15 Print
Total Titles: 110 Print; 1 CD-ROM; 1 Audio
Distributed by BookSource (Scotland); Codasat Canada Ltd (Canada); Gazelle Book Services (UK except Scotland) & Europe); Arthur Schwartz & Co Inc (US)

No Exit Press, *imprint of* Oldcastle Books Ltd

No Exit Press, see Oldcastle Books Ltd

North Holland, *imprint of* Elsevier Ltd

North Light, *imprint of* David & Charles Ltd

North York Moors National Park
The Old Vicarage, Bondgate, Helmsley, Yorks YO62 5BP
Tel: (01439) 770657 *Fax:* (01439) 770691
E-mail: j.renney@northyorkmoors-npa.gov.uk
Web Site: www.northyorkmoors-npa.gov.uk
Subjects: Archaeology, Geography, Geology, Natural History, Regional Interests
ISBN Prefix(es): 1-904622; 0-907480

Northcote House Publishers Ltd+
Horndon House, Horndon, Tavistock, Devon PL19 9NQ
Tel: (01822) 810066 *Fax:* (01822) 810034
E-mail: northcote.house@virgin.net
Web Site: www.northcotehouse.com
Key Personnel
Publisher: Brian Hulme
Founded: 1985
Membership(s): IPG.
Subjects: Drama, Theater, Education, Literature, Literary Criticism, Essays, Music, Dance
ISBN Prefix(es): 0-7463
Number of titles published annually: 20 Print
Total Titles: 150 Print
Imprints: Writers & Their Work
Distributed by University Press of Mississippi (USA)
Orders to: Combined Book Services, Unit 1/K, Paddock Wood Distribution Centre, Paddock Wood, Tonbridge, Kent PL19 9WQ
Tel: (01892) 837171 *Fax:* (01892) 837272

Northern Books, *imprint of* Famedram Publishers Ltd

UNITED KINGDOM

Northern Universities Press, *imprint of* Maney Publishing

Norton & Liveright, Countryman Press, *imprint of* W W Norton & Company Ltd

W W Norton & Company Ltd+
Castle House, 75/76 Wells St, London W1T 3QT
Tel: (020) 7323 1579 *Toll Free Tel:* 800-233-4830 (orders) *Fax:* (020) 7436 4553 *Toll Free Fax:* 800-458-6515 (orders)
E-mail: office@wwnorton.co.uk
Web Site: www.wwnorton.co.uk
Key Personnel
President: W Drake McFeely
Man Dir: R A Cameron
Sales Manager: Judith Pamplin
Publicity: Ariadne Van de Ven
Marketing Manager: Victoria Keown-Boyd
Founded: 1980
Subjects: Architecture & Interior Design, Art, Biography, Economics, Government, Political Science, History, Literature, Literary Criticism, Essays, Maritime, Music, Dance, Photography, Psychology, Psychiatry
ISBN Prefix(es): 0-393
Number of titles published annually: 120 Print; 20 CD-ROM
Total Titles: 4,000 Print
Parent Company: W W Norton & Company Inc, 500 Fifth Ave, New York, NY 10110, United States
Imprints: Norton & Liveright, Countryman Press
Distributor for New Directions
Foreign Rep(s): APAC Publishers Services Pte Ltd (Indonesia, Malaysia & Singapore, Thailand); B K Norton Ltd (Korea & Taiwan); Delaney Global Publishers Service (Guam, Philippines); M K International Ltd (Japan); Pearson Education New Zealand (New Zealand); Transglobal Publishers Service Ltd (Hong Kong); US PubRep Inc (Caribbean, Mexico, South & Central America); John Wiley & Sons Australia, Ltd (Australia)
Orders to: John Wiley & Sons Ltd, One Oldlands Way, Bognor Regis, West Sussex PO22 9SA

Norwood Publishers Ltd
3 Chapel St, Norwood Green, Halifax, West Yorks HX3 8QU
Tel: (01274) 602454
Key Personnel
Dir: Mr M H Wolfenden
Secretary: A M Wolfenden
Founded: 1991 (as Norwood Publishers, 2002 as Norwood Publishers Ltd)
Subjects: Education, Health, Nutrition, Social Sciences, Sociology
ISBN Prefix(es): 1-873784

Novello & Co Ltd+
8-9 Frith St, London W1D 3JB
Tel: (020) 7434 0066 *Fax:* (020) 7287-6329
E-mail: music@musicsales.co.uk; media@musicsales.co.uk
Web Site: www.musicsales.co.uk; www.chesternovello.com
Key Personnel
Executive Dir: James Rushton *E-mail:* james.rushton@musicsales.co.uk
Managing Editor: Howard Friend *E-mail:* howard.friend@musicsales.co.uk
Head of Promotion: Gill Graham *E-mail:* gill.graham@musicsales.co.uk
Founded: 1811
Subjects: Music, Dance
ISBN Prefix(es): 0-85360
Parent Company: Music Sales Ltd
Imprints: Cinderella; Elkin; Fairfield; Laurel; Lorna; Paxton

Branch Office(s)
c/o Shawnee Press Inc, 49 Waring Drive, Delaware Gap, PA 18327-1099, United States
Orders to: Music Sales Ltd, Newmarket Rd, Bury St-Edmunds, Suffolk IP33 3YB *Tel:* (01284) 702600 *Fax:* (01284) 768301

NTC Research+
Farm Rd, Henley-on-Thames, Oxon RG9 1EJ
Tel: (01491) 411000 *Fax:* (01491) 571188
E-mail: info@ntc.co.uk
Web Site: www.ntc-research.com
Key Personnel
Man Dir: David Roberts *E-mail:* david_roberts@ntc.co.uk
Production Dir: Andrew Denham
Librarian: Alison Haan *E-mail:* alison_haan@ntc.co.uk
Founded: 1984
Membership(s): Periodical Publishers Association (PPA).
Subjects: Advertising, Economics, Government, Political Science, Marketing, Radio, TV
ISBN Prefix(es): 1-870562
Parent Company: Information Sciences Ltd
Divisions: NTC Conferences Ltd; NTC Research Ltd
U.S. Office(s): 1615 "L" St NW, Suite 1220, Washington, DC 20036, United States *Tel:* 202-778-0680 *Fax:* 202-778-4546

Nuit-Isis, *imprint of* Mandrake of Oxford

"O" Books, *imprint of* John Hunt Publishing Ltd

Oakwood Library of Railway History, *imprint of* Oakwood Press

Oakwood Press
PO Box 13, Usk, Monmouthshire NP15 1YS
Tel: (01291) 650444 *Fax:* (01291) 650484
E-mail: oakwood-press@dial.pipex.com
Web Site: www.oakwood-press.dial.pipex.com
Key Personnel
Proprietor, Man Dir & Rights: Jane Kennedy
Founded: 1934
Specialist transport publisher.
Subjects: History, Transportation
ISBN Prefix(es): 0-85361
Number of titles published annually: 20 Print
Total Titles: 150 Print
Imprints: Locomotion Papers; Oakwood Library of Railway History
Divisions: Oakwood Video Library

Oceano Grupo Editorial, *imprint of* Thomson Gale

Octagon Press Ltd+
PO Box 227, London N6 4EW
Tel: (020) 8341 5971 *Fax:* (020) 8348 9392
E-mail: octagon@schredds.demon.co.uk
Web Site: www.octagonpress.com
Key Personnel
Man Dir: George Schrager
Publicity: Patti Schneider
Founded: 1972
Subjects: Anthropology, Asian Studies, Behavioral Sciences, Education, Philosophy, Poetry, Psychology, Psychiatry, Religion - Islamic, Religion - Other, Travel, Sufis
ISBN Prefix(es): 0-900860
Number of titles published annually: 2 Print
Total Titles: 150 Print
Distributed by ISHK Book Service (US, North America, South America)
Warehouse: Suffolk

Octopus Publishing Group+
2-4 Heron Quays, London E14 4JP
Tel: (020) 7531 8400 *Fax:* (020) 7531 8650
Web Site: www.octopus-publishing.co.uk
Subjects: Aeronautics, Aviation, Antiques, Architecture & Interior Design, Automotive, Cookery, Crafts, Games, Hobbies, Drama, Theater, Fiction, Film, Video, Gardening, Plants, Geography, Geology, Health, Nutrition, Literature, Literary Criticism, Essays, Music, Dance, Mysteries, Natural History, Nonfiction (General), Photography, Poetry, Science Fiction, Fantasy, Sports, Athletics, Travel, Wine & Spirits
Parent Company: Hachette Livre
Imprints: Bounty Books; Gaia Books; Cassell Illustrated; Conran Octopus; Hamlyn; Miller; Mitchell Beazley; Philip; Godsfield Press
Orders to: Littlehamptom Book Services Ltd, Durrington Worthing, West Sussex BN13 3RB *Tel:* (01903) 828800

Oilfield Publications Ltd
PO Box 11, Ledbury, Herts HR8 1BN
Tel: (01531) 634563 *Fax:* (01531) 634239; (01531) 633744
E-mail: opl@oilpubs.com
Web Site: www.oilpubs.com
Key Personnel
Man Dir: Julia Lourd
Publish book & vessel registers for the international offshore oil & gas industry.
Subjects: Energy, Maritime
ISBN Prefix(es): 1-870945
U.S. Office(s): Oilfield Publications Inc, 888 W Sam Houston Parkway S, Suite 280, Houston, TX 77042, United States *Tel:* 713-334-8970 *Fax:* 713-334-8968 *E-mail:* oplusa@oilpubs.com

Old Bailey Press, *imprint of* HLT Publications

Old Pond Publishing
Dencora Business Centre, 36 White House Rd, Ipswich, Suffolk IP1 5LT
Tel: (01473) 238200 *Fax:* (01473) 238201
E-mail: info@oldpond.com
Web Site: www.oldpond.com
Founded: 1998
Subjects: Agriculture, Transportation, Veterinary Science
ISBN Prefix(es): 1-903366
Number of titles published annually: 15 Print
Total Titles: 100 Print

Old Vicarage Publications
The Old Vicarage, Reades Lane, Dane in Shaw, Congleton, Cheshire CW12 3LL
Tel: (01260) 279276 *Fax:* (01260) 298913
Key Personnel
Proprietor: William Ball *E-mail:* william.ball@btinternet.com
Founded: 1983
Subjects: Ethnicity, Film, Video, Regional Interests, Travel
ISBN Prefix(es): 0-900269; 0-947818; 0-9508635
Imprints: Centaur Books
U.S. Office(s): State Book & Periodical Service, New York, NY, United States

Oldcastle Books Ltd+
18 Coleswood Rd, Harpenden, Herts AL5 1EQ
Tel: (01582) 761264 *Fax:* (01582) 712244
E-mail: info@noexit.co.uk
Web Site: www.noexit.co.uk
Key Personnel
Dir & Foreign Rights: Ion Mills
  E-mail: ionmills@noexit.co.uk
Founded: 1985
No unsolicited manuscripts.
Subjects: Crafts, Games, Hobbies, Fiction, Mysteries, Noir Fiction, Gambling, Crime Fiction
ISBN Prefix(es): 0-948353; 1-874061; 1-901982
Imprints: No Exit Press
Sales Office(s): 21 Great Ormond St, London WC1N 3JB *Tel:* (020) 7430 1021 *Fax:* (020)

PUBLISHERS UNITED KINGDOM

7430 0021 *Web Site:* www.thebigbookshop.co.uk
Foreign Rep(s): Capricorn Link (Australia); Codasat (Canada); Four Walls Eight Windows/No Exit Press (North America); Michael Geoghegan (Belgium, France); Gill & Macmillan (Ireland); Gabriele Kern (Austria, Germany & Switzerland); Pernille Larson (Scandinavia); PIMS (Far East, Middle East); Peter Prout (Gibraltar, Spain); PSD Promotions (Pty) Ltd (South Africa); Southern Publishers Group (New Zealand); Trafalgar Square Publishing (USA); Turnaround (UK)
Foreign Rights: Shirley Stewart
Distribution Center: Turnaround, 3 Olympia Trading Estate, Coburg Rd, London N22 6TZ *Tel:* (020) 8829 3000 *Fax:* (020) 8881 5088 *E-mail:* julie@turnaround-uk.com

The Oleander Press+
16 Orchard St, Cambridge CB1 1JT
Tel: (01223) 357768
E-mail: editor@oleanderpress.com
Web Site: oleanderpress.com
Key Personnel
Man Dir: Dr Jerry Toner
Founded: 1960
Specialize in travel.
Subjects: Biography, Drama, Theater, History, Language Arts, Linguistics, Literature, Literary Criticism, Essays, Poetry, Regional Interests, Travel, Arabian Peninsula, Games, Monographs
ISBN Prefix(es): 0-900891; 0-902675; 0-906672
Number of titles published annually: 6 Print
Total Titles: 120 Print

Michael O'Mara Books Ltd+
9 Lion Yard, Tremadoc Rd, London SW4 7NQ
Tel: (020) 7720 8643 *Fax:* (020) 7627 8953 (Editorial); (020) 7627 4900 (Foreign Sales)
E-mail: enquiries@michaelomarabooks.com
Web Site: www.michaelomarabooks.com
Key Personnel
Chairman: Michael O'Mara
Man Dir: Lesley O'Mara
Editorial Dir: Toby Buchan
Editorial Dir (Commissioning): Lindsay Davies
UK Sales Dir: David Crombie
UK Sales Manager: Alison Parker
Foreign Sales Manager: Philippa Slater
Childrens Managing Editor: Philippa Wingate
Production Consultant: David Bann
Founded: 1985
Subjects: Biography, History, Humor, Nonfiction (General), Juvenile
ISBN Prefix(es): 1-85479; 0-948397; 1-84317; 1-904613
Number of titles published annually: 80 Print
Imprints: Buster Books (juvenile list)
Distributed by Andrews McMeel (USA); Littlehampton Book Services
Orders to: Grantham Book Services, Isaac Newton Way, Alma Park Industrial Estate, Grantham, Lincs NG31 9SD *Tel:* (01476) 541080 *Fax:* (01476) 541061/63

Omnibus Press+
8-9 Frith St, London W1D 3JB
Tel: (020) 7434 0066 *Fax:* (020) 7287 6329
E-mail: music@musicsales.co.uk
Web Site: www.musicsales.com
Telex: 21892
Key Personnel
Chairman & Man Dir: Robert Wise
Chief Operating Officer: Chris Butler
Finance Director: Malcolm Grabham
European Sales Dir, Music Sales Ltd: Hilary Power
President, Music Sales Corporation: Barrie Edwards
VP, G Schirmer Inc, Associated Music Publishers: Susan Feder
man Dir, Edition Wilhelm Hansen: Tine Birger Christensen
General Manager, Union Musical Ediciones: German Bartolome
Man Dir, Premiere Music: Claude Duvivier
Man Dir, Bosworth Music GMBH: Michael Ohst
Man Dir, Chester Mucis Ltd, Novello & Co Ltd: James Rushton
Business Development Dir, Music Sales Ltd: Ian Morgan
Dir of Distribution and IT, Music Sales Ltd: David Vass
Vice President, Administration and Operations, Music Sales Corporation: Denise Maurin
Head of Copyright, Music Sales Limited: Alex Batterbee
Dir of Sales and Marketing, Music Sales Corporation: Steve Wilson
Man Dir, Music in Print: Iain Davidson
Founded: 1979
Subjects: Biography, Music, Dance
ISBN Prefix(es): 0-7119; 0-86001; 0-9657122
Parent Company: Music Sales Ltd, London
Imprints: Amsco Publications; Bobcat Books; Proteus; WISE Publications; Zomba Books
Subsidiaries: Music Sales Corp; Music Sales Pty
Branch Office(s)
Music Sales Pty Ltd, c/o Bookwise, 54 Coultenden Rd, Fundon, Austria
U.S. Office(s): Music Sales Corp, 257 Park Ave S, New York, NY 10010, United States *Tel:* 212-254-2100 *Fax:* 212-254-2013 *E-mail:* info@musicsales.com *Web Site:* www.musicsales.com
Distributor for BBC Music Guides; Firefly; Gramophone; OZONE; Parker Mead; RED Independent Music Press; Rogan House; Showcase Publications
Warehouse: Book Sales Ltd, Newmarket Rd, Bury St, Edmunds, Suffolk IP33 3YB
Distribution Center: Newmarket Rd, Bury St, Edmonds, Suffolk IP33 3YB *Tel:* (0284) 702600 *Fax:* (0284) 768301
445 Bellvale Rd, PO Box 572, Chester, NY 10918, United States *Tel:* 845-469-2271 *Fax:* 845-469-6952

Oneworld Publications
185 Banbury Rd, Oxford OX2 7AR
Tel: (01865) 310597 *Fax:* (01865) 310598
E-mail: info@oneworld-publications.com
Web Site: www.oneworld.publications.com
Key Personnel
Partner: Novin Doostdar *E-mail:* ndoostdar@oneworld-publications.com; Juliet Mabey *E-mail:* jmabey@oneworld-publications.com
Man Dir: Helen Coward *E-mail:* hcoward@oneworld-publications.com
Founded: 1986
Subjects: Anthropology, Education, History, Philosophy, Psychology, Psychiatry, Religion - Buddhist, Religion - Catholic, Religion - Hindu, Religion - Islamic, Religion - Jewish, Religion - Protestant, Religion - Other, Self-Help
ISBN Prefix(es): 1-85168
Number of titles published annually: 40 Print
Total Titles: 200 Print
U.S. Office(s): PO Box 2510, Novato, CA 94948, United States
Distribution Center: APD Kuala Lumpur, 18 Jalan SS3/41 47300, PJ Selangor, Darul, Ehsan, Malaysia *Tel:* (3) 7776063 *Fax:* (3) 7773414 *E-mail:* apdkl@tm.net.my (South-East Asia)
APD Singapore Pte Ltd, 52 Genting Lane #06-05, Hiang Kie Complex 1 349560, Singapore *Tel:* 7493551 *Fax:* 7493552 *E-mail:* apd@pacific.net.sg (South-East Asia)
Richard Carman, 16 Chapel Close, Comberbach, Northwich, Cheshire CW9 6BA *Tel:* (1606) 891107 *Fax:* (1606) 891107 (Africa)
Jim Chalmers, 2 Cheviot Rd, Paisley *Tel:* (0141) 884 5322 *Fax:* (0141) 884 5322 *E-mail:* jim@jchalmersassociates.freeserve.co.uk (Scotland, North East UK)
Andy Cocks, 13 King Cole Rd, Lexden, Colchester, Essex CO3 5AG *Tel:* (01206) 548515 *E-mail:* acocks@aspects.net (UK)
Lale Colakoglu, Sezai Selek Sok. 10/2, Nisantas, Istanbul 80200, Turkey *Tel:* (212) 247 85 51 *Fax:* (212) 247 89 83 *E-mail:* colakoglu@turk.net (Turkey)
Caroline Day, 21 Holtom St, Stratford-on-Avon, Warwicks CV37 6DQ *Tel:* (01789) 266903 (UK)
Durnell Marketing, 2 Linden Close, Tunbridge Wells, Kent TN4 8HH, Andrew B Durnell *Tel:* (01892) 544272 *Fax:* (01892) 511152 *E-mail:* mail@durnell.co.uk (Europe & Ireland)
InterMedia Americana Limited, PO Box 8734, London SE21 7ZF, David Williams *Tel:* (0208) 761 5140 *Fax:* (0208) 761 5139 (South America, the Caribbean)
ITPS, Cheriton House, North Way, Andover, Hants SP10 5BE *Tel:* (1264) 342832 *Fax:* (1264) 342788 *E-mail:* oneworld@itps.co.uk (outside US & Canada)
Anwer Iqbal, GPO Box 518, Main Chambers, 3 Temples Rd, Lahore, Pakistan *Tel:* (42) 636 7325 *Fax:* (42) 636 1370 *E-mail:* bookbird@lhr.comsats.net.pk (Pakistan)
Debbie Jones, The Firs, 6 Whitchurch Rd, Tavistock, Devon *Tel:* (01822) 617223 *Fax:* (01822) 610406 (UK)
Felicity Knight, 10 Buckingham Mews, Shoreham-by-Sea, Sussex BN43 6AJ *Tel:* (01273) 453270 (UK)
National Book Network, 15200 NBN Way, Blue Ridge Summit, PA 17214, United States *Tel:* 717-794-3800 *E-mail:* custserv@nbnbooks.com (US & Canada)
Publishers International Marketing, 7 Melton Close, Storrington, West Sussex RH20 4QA *Tel:* (01903) 741 935 *Fax:* (01903) 741 079 *E-mail:* ray@pim1-uk.freeserve.co.uk (Middle East, Japan, Hong Kong)
Research Press, PO 7208, 1st floor, Arun House, 2/25 Ansari, New Delhi 110002, India *Tel:* (011) 328 4894 *Fax:* (011) 328 1819 *E-mail:* aparmar@vsnl.com (India)
The Segrue Partnership, 67B Brent St, Hendon, London NW4 2EA *Tel:* (020) 8202 9452 *Fax:* (020) 8203 9180 (UK)
Mike Wilson, Plas Berw, Pentre Berw, Anglesey LL60 6LL *Tel:* (01248) 421580; (07775) 501986 (mobile) *Fax:* (01248) 421952 (UK)

Onlywomen Press Ltd+
40 St Lawrence Terrace, London W10 5ST
Tel: (020) 8354 0796 *Fax:* (020) 8960 2817
E-mail: onlywomenpress@aol.com
Web Site: www.onlywomenpress.com
Key Personnel
Man Dir: Lilian Mohin
Founded: 1974
Subjects: Fiction, Gay & Lesbian, History, Poetry, Women's Studies
ISBN Prefix(es): 0-906500
Number of titles published annually: 3 Print
Total Titles: 40 Print
Distributed by Airlift Book Company (UK & Europe); Alamo Square Press (North America); Bulldog Books Pty Ltd (Australia)

Open Books Publishing Ltd
Willow Cottage, Cudworth, Ilminster TA19 0PS
Tel: (01460) 52565 *Fax:* (01460) 52565
Key Personnel
Man Dir: Patrick Taylor *E-mail:* patrickta@aol.com
Founded: 1974
Subjects: Gardening, Plants, Nonfiction (General)
ISBN Prefix(es): 0-7291

Open Gate Press+
51 Achilles Rd, London NW6 1DZ

Tel: (020) 7431 4391 *Fax:* (020) 7431 5129
E-mail: books@opengatepress.co.uk
Web Site: www.opengatepress.co.uk
Key Personnel
Contact: Jeannie Cohen
Founded: 1988
Subjects: Anthropology, Archaeology, Economics, Government, Political Science, Philosophy, Psychology, Psychiatry, Social Sciences, Sociology
ISBN Prefix(es): 1-871871
U.S. Office(s): Paul & Company Publishers Consoritum Inc, PO Box 442, Concord, MA 10742, United States
Distributor for Cambridge International Publishers
Orders to: Book Representation & Distribution Ltd, 244-A London Rd, Hadleigh, Essex SS7 2DE

Open University Press+
McGraw-Hill House, Shoppenhangers Rd, Maidenhead, Berks SL6 2QL
Tel: (01628) 502500; (01628) 502720 (customer service) *Fax:* (01628) 635895 (customer service)
E-mail: enquiries@openup.co.uk (general enquries); emea_orders@mcgraw-hill.com (orders); emea_queries@mcgraw-hill.com (customer service)
Web Site: mcgraw-hill.co.uk/openup
Key Personnel
Man Dir & Publisher: Simon Allen
Financial Dir: Alan Martin
Publishing Dir: Shona Mullen
 E-mail: shona_mullen@mcgraw-hill.com
Marketing Manager: Susannah Bowen
 E-mail: susannah_bowen@mcgraw-hill.com
Senior Production Manager: Max Elvey
 E-mail: max_elvey@mcgraw-hill.com
Senior Production Editor: Eleanor Hayes
 E-mail: eleanor_hayes@mcgraw-hill.com
Rights & International Sales Executive: Amy Blower *E-mail:* amy_blower@mcgraw-hill.com
Founded: 1977
Subjects: Behavioral Sciences, Criminology, Developing Countries, Education, Government, Political Science, Health, Nutrition, Management, Psychology, Psychiatry, Public Administration, Social Sciences, Sociology, Women's Studies
ISBN Prefix(es): 0-335
Parent Company: McGraw-Hill Education

Open University Worldwide+
Walton Hall, Milton Keynes MK7 6AA
Tel: (01908) 858785 *Fax:* (01908) 858787
E-mail: ouwenq@open.ac.uk
Web Site: www.open.ac.uk
Key Personnel
Dir: Bob Masterton
Marketing Manager: Katherine Bull
Rights & Permissions, Print: Sue Hitchen
Rights & Permissions, Audio Visual: Diana Rualt
Founded: 1977
Subjects: Architecture & Interior Design, Astronomy, Biological Sciences, Chemistry, Chemical Engineering, Computer Science, Developing Countries, Disability, Special Needs, Earth Sciences, Economics, Education, Electronics, Electrical Engineering
ISBN Prefix(es): 0-7492
Parent Company: The Open University
Branch Office(s)
40 University Rd, Belfast BT7 1SU, Ireland
 Tel: (028) 9024 5025 *Fax:* (028) 9023 0565
 E-mail: ireland@open.ac.uk
66 High St Harborne, Birmingham *Tel:* (0121) 426 1661 *Fax:* (0121) 427 9484 *E-mail:* west-midlands@open.ac.uk
Cintra House, 12 Hills Rd, Cambridge CB2 1PF
 Tel: (01223) 364721 *Fax:* (01223) 355207
 E-mail: east-of-england@open.ac.uk

24 Cathedral Rd, Cardiff, Wales CF11 9SA
 Tel: (029) 2039 7911 *Fax:* (029) 2022 7930
 E-mail: wales@open.ac.uk
St James's House, 150 London Rd, East Grinstead RH19 1HG *Tel:* (01342) 327821
 Fax: (01342) 317411 *E-mail:* south-east@open.ac.uk
10 Drumsheugh Gardens, Edinburgh, Scotland
 Tel: (0131) 226 3851 *Fax:* (0131) 220 6730
 E-mail: scotland@open.ac.uk
2 Trevelyan Sq, Boar Lane, Leeds LS1 6ED
 Tel: (0113) 2444431 *Fax:* (0113) 2341862
 E-mail: yorkshire@open.ac.uk
1-11 Hawley Crescent, Camden Town, London NW1 8NP *Tel:* (020) 7485 6597 *Fax:* (020) 7556 6196 *E-mail:* london@open.ac.uk
Eldon House, Regent Centre, Gosforth, New Castle Upon Tyne NE3 3PW *Tel:* (0191) 284 1611 *Fax:* (0191) 284 6592 *E-mail:* north@open.ac.uk
Foxcombe Hall, Boars Hill, Oxford OX1 5HR
 Tel: (01865) 327000 *Fax:* (01865) 736288
 E-mail: south@open.ac.uk
351 Altrincham Rd, Sharston, Manchester M22 4UN *Tel:* (0161) 998 7272 *Fax:* (0161) 945 3356 *E-mail:* north-west@open.ac.uk
Clarendon Park, Clumber Ave, Sherwood Rise, Nottingham NG5 1AH *Tel:* (0115) 962 5451 *Fax:* (0115) 971 5575 *E-mail:* east-midlands@open.ac.uk
Distribution Center: Open University Technical & Distribution Services, Unit 16 Denington Industrial Estate, Wellingborough, Northants NN8 2RF *Tel:* (01933) 224911 *Fax:* (01933) 441780

Opus Book Publishing Ltd
20 The Strand, Steeple Ashton, Trowbridge, Wilts BA14 6EP
Tel: (01380) 871354 *Fax:* (01380) 871354
E-mail: opus@dmac.co.uk
Key Personnel
Contact: Diana van der Klugt
Subjects: Maritime
ISBN Prefix(es): 1-898574

Opus Publishing Ltd
36 Camden Sq, London NW1 9XA
Tel: (020) 7267 1034 *Fax:* (020) 7267 6026
E-mail: opuspub@btconnect.com
Key Personnel
President: Martin Heller

Orbit, *imprint of* Time Warner Book Group UK

Orchard Books, see The Watts Publishing Group Ltd

Ordnance Survey
Customer Contact Centre, Ordnance Survey, Romsey Rd, Southampton SO16 4GU
Tel: (08456) 05 05 05 (customer information); (023) 8079 2912 (outside Britain); (023) 8030 5030 (business enquiries) *Fax:* (023) 8079 2615 (trade customer information); (023) 8079 2615 (outside Britain)
E-mail: customerservices@ordnancesurvey.co.uk
Web Site: www.ordnancesurvey.co.uk
Key Personnel
Dir General: Vanessa Lawrence
Head of Marketing: Eric Bates
Head of Sales: Phil Watts
Press Officer: Philip Round
Sales Office Manager: Nicky Long *Tel:* (023) 8030 5278 *E-mail:* nlong@ordsvy.gov.uk
ISBN Prefix(es): 0-319

Original English Language Fiction, *imprint of* Dedalus Ltd

Orion, *imprint of* Orion Publishing Group Ltd

Orion Children's Books+
c/o The Orion Publishing Group, Orion House, 5 Upper St Martins Lane, London WC2H 9EA
Tel: (020) 7240 3444 *Fax:* (020) 7240 4822
E-mail: info@orionbooks.co.uk
Web Site: www.orionbooks.co.uk
Key Personnel
Publisher: Fiona Kennedy
Founded: 1993
ISBN Prefix(es): 1-85881
Number of titles published annually: 50 Print
Imprints: Dolphin Paperbacks

Orion Publishing Group Ltd+
Orion House, 5 Upper St Martins Lane, London WC2H 9EA
Tel: (020) 7240 3444 *Fax:* (020) 7240 4822
E-mail: info@orionbooks.co.uk
Web Site: orionbooks.co.uk
Key Personnel
Chairman: Arnaud Nourry
Chief Executive: Peter Roche
Group Finance Dir: Pierre de Cacqueray
Founded: 1991
Subjects: Archaeology, Art, Biography, Biological Sciences, Business, Crafts, Games, Hobbies, Fiction, Film, Video, History, Management, Mysteries, Nonfiction (General), Poetry, Religion - Other, Romance, Science (General), Science Fiction, Fantasy, Self-Help, Sports, Athletics, Western Fiction
ISBN Prefix(es): 0-7528
Parent Company: Hachette Livre
Associate Companies: Dent Children; Everyman; Millenium; Phoenix; Phoenix House
Imprints: Orion
Subsidiaries: JM Dent & Sons; Orion Books; Weidenfeld & Nicolson
Warehouse: Littlehampton Book Service, 14 Eldon Way, Lineside Estate, Littlehampton, West Sussex BN17 7HE
Orders to: Littlehampton Book Service, 14 Eldon Way, Lineside Estate, Littlehampton, West Sussex BN17 7HE

The Orkney Press Ltd+
12 Craigiefield Park, St Ola, Kirkwall, Orkney KW15 1TE
Tel: (01856) 874058
Key Personnel
Sales Dir: Mrs Sidsel Firth
Founded: 1981
Subjects: Anthropology, Archaeology, History, Maritime, Natural History, Philosophy, Science (General)
ISBN Prefix(es): 0-907618
Imprints: Scottish Falcon; Aurora Northern Classics

Orpheus Books Ltd+
2 Church Green, Witney, Oxon OX28 4AW
Tel: (01993) 774949 *Fax:* (01993) 700330
E-mail: info@orpheusbooks.com
Web Site: www.orpheusbooks.com
Key Personnel
Chairman: Nicholas Harris *E-mail:* nicholas@orpheusbooks.com
Founded: 1992
Principally book packagers.
Subjects: Animals, Pets, Astronomy, Earth Sciences, Geography, Geology, History, Natural History, Science (General), Transportation
ISBN Prefix(es): 1-901323
Number of titles published annually: 12 Print

Osborne Books Ltd
Unit 1B, Everoak Estate, Bromyard Rd, St Johns, Worcester, Worcs WR2 5HP
Tel: (01905) 748071 *Fax:* (0190) 748952
E-mail: books@osborne.u-net.com
Web Site: www.osbornebooks.co.uk
Key Personnel
Contact: Michael Fardon

Founded: 1987
Subjects: Accounting, Business, History, Literature, Literary Criticism, Essays, Photography
ISBN Prefix(es): 1-872962; 0-9510650
Imprints: Heritage

Osprey Publishing Ltd+
Elms Court, Chapel Way, Botley, Oxford OX2 9LP
Mailing Address: PO Box 1, Osceola, WI 54020-0001, United States
Tel: (01933) 443863 *Toll Free Tel:* 800-826-6600 *Fax:* (01865) 727017
E-mail: info@ospreydirect.co.uk; info@ospreydirectusa.com (USA & Canada)
Web Site: www.ospreypublishing.com
Key Personnel
Man Dir: William Shepherd
Financial Dir: Sarah Lough
Sales & Marketing Dir: Joanna Sharland
Illustrated military history from around the world with all-time greatest battles of land & air, from antiquity to the present day.
Subjects: Aeronautics, Aviation, Crafts, Games, Hobbies, History, Military Science
ISBN Prefix(es): 1-85532; 0-85045; 0-540; 1-84176
Total Titles: 600 Print
U.S. Office(s): Specialty Book Marketing, 443 Park Ave S, New York, NY 10016, United States, Contact: Bill Corsa *Tel:* 212-685-5560 *Fax:* 212-685-5836 *E-mail:* ospreyusa@aol.com
Distributor for Compendium Publishing
Orders to: Grantham Book Services, Isaac Newton Way, Alma Park Industrial Estate, Grantham, Lincs NG31 9SD *Tel:* (01476) 541 080 *Fax:* (01476) 541 061
Motorbooks International, 729 Prospect Ave, Osceola, WI 54020-0001, United States *Tel:* 715-294-3345 *Fax:* 715-294-4448

Our Wonderful Psychoneural Systems, *imprint of* MGM

Overstone Press, *imprint of* Thoemmes Press

Peter Owen Ltd+
73 Kenway Rd, London SW5 0RE
Tel: (020) 7373 5628; (020) 7370 6093 *Fax:* (020) 7373 6760
E-mail: admin@peterowen.com
Web Site: www.peterowen.com
Key Personnel
Sales & Publicity: Daniel McCabe
    E-mail: daniel@peterowen.com; Tom Perrin
    E-mail: tom@peterowen.com
Editorial: Antonia Owen *E-mail:* antonia@peterowen.com
Editorial & Rights: Simon Smith
    E-mail: ssmith@peterowen.com
Rights: Peter Owen
Design & Production: Francesca Bechara; Keith Savage
Founded: 1950
Subjects: Art, Biography, Drama, Theater, Fiction, Gay & Lesbian, Language Arts, Linguistics, Literature, Literary Criticism, Essays, Music, Dance, Publishing & Book Trade Reference, Social Sciences, Sociology, Women's Studies
ISBN Prefix(es): 0-7206
Number of titles published annually: 25 Print; 30 Audio
Distribution Center: Central Books, 99 Wallis Rd, London E9 5CN *Tel:* (020) 8986 4854 *Fax:* (20) 8533 5821 *E-mail:* orders@centralbooks.com (UK)
Dufour Editions Inc, PO Box 7, Chester Springs, PA 19425-0007, United States *Tel:* 610-458-5005 *Fax:* 610-458-7103 *E-mail:* info@dufoureditions.com *Web Site:* www.dufoureditions.com (USA)

Oxfam+
Member of Oxfam International
Oxfam Supporter Services Dept, Oxfam House, 274 Banbury Rd, Oxford OX2 7DZ
Tel: (01865) 313744 *Fax:* (01865) 313713
E-mail: oxfam@oxfam.org.uk; publish@oxfam.org.uk
Web Site: www.oxfam.org.uk
Telex: 83610 *Cable:* OXFAMG OXFORD
Key Personnel
Publishing Executive: Robert Cornford *E-mail:* r.cornford@oxfam.org.uk
Marketing: Deborah Logan
Contact: Caroline Knowles
Founded: 1942
Subjects: Developing Countries, Economics, Government, Political Science, Social Sciences, Sociology, Women's Studies
ISBN Prefix(es): 0-85598
Total Titles: 130 Print
Distributed by David Philip Publishers (Southern Africa); Stylus Publishing LLC (US & Canada)
Orders to: BEBC, PO Box 1496, Parkstone, Dorset BH12 3YD

Oxford International Centre for Publishing Studies
School of Art, Publishing & Music, Oxford Brookes University, The Richard Hamilton Bldg, Headington Hill Campus, Oxford OX3 0BP
Tel: (01865) 484951 *Fax:* (01865) 484952
E-mail: publishing@brookes.ac.uk
Web Site: www.brookes.ac.uk/schools/apm/publishing
Key Personnel
Dir: Prof Paul Richardson *E-mail:* ptrichardson@brookes.ac.uk
Founded: 1994
A centre for publishing education, training, consulting & research.

Oxford Poets, *imprint of* Carcanet Press Ltd

Oxford University Press+
Great Clarendon St, Oxford OX2 6DP
Tel: (01865) 556767 *Fax:* (01865) 556646
Web Site: www.oup.co.uk
Telex: 837330 Oxpres G
Key Personnel
Man Dir, ELT: Peter R Mothersole
Man Dir, UK Academic Division: Ivan S Asquith
Group Finance Dir: R C Boning
Group Personal Dir: M J Havelock
Public Affairs Manager: Caroline Scotter Mainprize
Chief Executive: Henry Reece
Man Dir, UK Educational Division: Fiona Clarke
Man Dir, International Division: Susan Froud
President, OUP USA: Edward Barry
Man Dir, OUP Spain: Jesus Lazcano
Founded: 1478
Subjects: Art, Biography, Economics, Education, Engineering (General), Government, Political Science, History, Language Arts, Linguistics, Law, Literature, Literary Criticism, Essays, Mathematics, Medicine, Nursing, Dentistry, Military Science, Music, Dance, Philosophy, Poetry, Psychology, Psychiatry, Publishing & Book Trade Reference, Religion - Other, Science (General), Social Sciences, Sociology
ISBN Prefix(es): 0-19
Associate Companies: Cornelsen und Oxford University Press GmbH, Germany
Imprints: Clarendon Press; IRL Press
Subsidiaries: Oxford University Press Inc
Branch Office(s)
70 Wynford Dr, Don Mills, ON M3C 1J9, Canada
Warwick House, 18th Floor, Taikoo Place, 979 King's Rd, Hong Kong, China
Oxford University Press Espana SA, Pargue Empresarial San Fernando de Henares: Edificio Atenas la Plantz, San Fernando de Henares, 28830 Madrid, Spain
PO Box 43, New Delhi 110001, India
Oxford University Press KK (Japan), 2-4-8 Kanamecho, Toshima-ku, Toyko 171, Japan
PO Box 72532, Nairobi, Kenya
Penerbit Fajar Bakti Sdn Bhd, Malaysia
PO Box 13033, Karachi 75350, Pakistan
37 Jal an Pemimpin, No 03-03 Union Industrial Bldg B Block A, Singapore 577177, Singapore
PO Box 5299, Dar es Salaam, Thailand
PO Box 1141, Cape Town 8000, South Africa
GPO Box 2784Y, Melbourne, Victoria (Australia & New Zealand)
Bookshop(s): 116-117 High St, Oxford OX1 4BZ *Tel:* (01865) 242913
Orders to: OUP Distribution Services, Saxon Way West, Corby, Northamptonshire NN18 9ES *Tel:* (01536) 741519 *Fax:* (01536) 746337

Oxford University Press Children's Books
Great Clarendon St, Oxford OX2 6DP
Tel: (01865) 556767 *Fax:* (01865) 267732
E-mail: enquiry@oup.com
Web Site: www.oup.co.uk

Oyster Books Ltd+
4 Kirlea Farm, Badgworth, Axbridge, Somerset BS26 2QH
Tel: (01934) 732251 *Fax:* (01934) 732123
E-mail: pearls@oysterbooks.co.uk
Key Personnel
Man Dir: Tim Wood
Production Dir: Ali Brooks
Sales Dir: Donna Webber
Sales & Marketing: Rachel Holmes
    E-mail: rachel@oysterbooks.co.uk
Founded: 1985
Also acts as book packagers.
Subjects: Fiction, Nonfiction (General)
ISBN Prefix(es): 0-948240

P N Review, see Carcanet Press Ltd

Packard Publishing Ltd+
Forum House, Stirling Rd, Chichester, West Sussex PO19 7DN
Tel: (01243) 537977 *Fax:* (01243) 537977
E-mail: info@packardpublishing.co.uk
Web Site: www.packardpublishing.com
Key Personnel
Man Dir: Michael Packard
Founded: 1977
Academic book publisher & distributor.
Subjects: Agriculture, Architecture & Interior Design, Biological Sciences, Environmental Studies, Gardening, Plants, Geography, Geology, Language Arts, Linguistics, Natural History, Elementary English & French, Landscape Architecture
ISBN Prefix(es): 0-906527; 0-948690; 1-85341
Number of titles published annually: 6 Print
Total Titles: 20 Print
Imprints: Headlions; PPL
Distributed by Stipes Publishing LLC (USA)
Distributor for Librairie DuLiban (UK); Oxygraphics Ltd (UK)

Palgrave Publishers Ltd+
Brunel Rd, Houndmills, Basingstoke, Hants RG21 6XS
Tel: (01256) 329242 *Fax:* (01256) 479476
E-mail: orders@palgrave.com (ordering online); catalogue@palgrave.com (catalogue requests); conferences@palgrave.com (conference & exhibition information); rights@palgrave.com (copyright & permissions); lectureservices@palgrave.com (inspection copy service); reviews@palgrave.com (review copy requests); booksellers@palgrave.com (bookseller queries)
Web Site: www.palgrave.com

UNITED KINGDOM

Key Personnel
Man Dir: Dominic Knight *E-mail:* d.knight@palgrave.com
Publishing Dir, College Publishing Division (Business, Computer Science & Engineering): Christopher Glennie *E-mail:* c.glennie@palgrave.com
Publishing Dir, College Publishing Division (Humanities & Social Science): Frances Arnold *E-mail:* f.arnold@palgrave.com
Publishing Dir, College Publishing Division (Professional & Business Management): Stephen Rutt *E-mail:* s.rutt@palgrave.com
Publishing Dir, Academic Division: Josie Dixon *E-mail:* j.dixon@palgrave.com
Sales & Marketing Dir: Margaret Hewinson *E-mail:* m.hewinson@palgrave.com
Marketing Dir: Carol Monoyios *E-mail:* c.monoyios@palgrave.com
International Sales Dir: Alastair Gordon *E-mail:* a.gordon@palgrave.com
UK Sales Dir: Sam Burridge *E-mail:* s.burridge@palgrave.com
Publishing Services Dir: Tim Fox *E-mail:* t.fox@palgrave.com
Subjects: Business, Computer Science, Economics, Engineering (General), History, Human Relations, Management, Science (General), Social Sciences, Sociology, Technology
ISBN Prefix(es): 0-312; 0-333; 1-4039
Parent Company: Macmillan Ltd
Imprints: W H Freeman
U.S. Office(s): 175 Fifth Ave, New York, NY, NY 10010, United States *Tel:* 212-982-3900 *Fax:* 212-777-6359

Pallas Athene+
42 Spencer Rise, London NW5 1AP
Tel: (020) 7229 2798 *Fax:* (020) 7792 1067
Key Personnel
President & Publisher: Alexander Fyjis-Walker
Founded: 1991
Subjects: Art, Travel
ISBN Prefix(es): 1-873429; 0-9529986
Total Titles: 20 Print
Imprints: Pallas Guides; WOL Books
Foreign Rights: Vincent Vichet-Vadakan Agency (Worldwide)
Orders to: Trafalgar Square Publishing, PO Box 257, Howe Hill Rd, North Pomfret, VT 05053, United States
Vine House Distribution Ltd, Waldenbury, North Common, Chailey, East Sussex BN8 4DR

Pallas Guides, *imprint of* Pallas Athene

Pan, *imprint of* Pan Macmillan

Pan Books Ltd, see Pan Macmillan

Pan Macmillan+
25 Eccleston Place, London SW1W 9NF
Tel: (020) 7881 8000 *Fax:* (020) 7881 8001
Web Site: www.panmacmillan.com
Key Personnel
Man Dir & Chief Executive: Adrian Soar *E-mail:* a.soar@macmillan.co.uk
Marketing: Iain Chapple *E-mail:* i.chapple@macmillan.co.uk
Production: Daria Neklesa *E-mail:* d.neklesa@macmillan.co.uk
Publicity: Kate Wright-Morris *E-mail:* k.wright-morris@macmillan.co.uk
International Sales and Marketing: Davina Kimber *Tel:* (01256) 302942
Marketing Requests: Kate Eshelby *Tel:* (020) 7014 6093
Rights Requests: Michelle Taylor *Tel:* (020) 7014 6155
Special Sales Requests: Katherine Brewster *Tel:* (020) 7014 6084 *E-mail:* kbrewster@macmillan.co.uk
Founded: 1947
No unsolicited manuscripts. Query first for appropriate contact details & submission process. New authors & agents for children's books should go through an agent.
Subjects: Education, Nonfiction (General), Romance, Self-Help
ISBN Prefix(es): 0-330
Parent Company: Macmillan Ltd
Holding Company: Macmillan Ltd
Associate Companies: Macmillan General Books Ltd
Imprints: Boxtree; Campbell Books; Channel 4 Books; Macmillan; Macmillan Children's Books; Pan; Papermac; Picador; Sidgwick & Jackson
Subsidiaries: Pan Macmillan (Australia) Pty Ltd; Pan Books New Zealand Ltd; Pan Books Pty Ltd
Warehouse: Houndmills, Basingstoke, Hants *Tel:* (01256) 464481 *Fax:* (01256) 460675
Orders to: Houndmills, Basingstoke, Hants *Tel:* (01256) 464481 *Fax:* (01256) 460675

Panaf Books
75 Weston St, London SE1 3RS
Tel: (0870) 333 1192
E-mail: zakakembo@yahoo.co.uk
Web Site: www.panafbooks.com
Founded: 1968
Academic & general publications.
ISBN Prefix(es): 0-901787
Ultimate Parent Company: Panaf Ltd

Pandora Press, *imprint of* Rivers Oram Press

Panos Institute
9 White Lion St, London N1 9PD
Tel: (020) 7278 1111 *Fax:* (020) 7278 0345
E-mail: info@panoslondon.org.uk
Web Site: www.panos.org.uk
Key Personnel
Head of Information: Heather Budge-Reid
Subjects: Developing Countries, Environmental Studies
ISBN Prefix(es): 1-870670
Distributed by Fernwood Books Ltd (Canada); Ideas Centre (Australia); Paula & Co (USA); Russel Friedman Boks (South Africa)

Papermac, *imprint of* Pan Macmillan

Paperstyle Gift Line, *imprint of* Ryland Peters & Small Ltd

Paragon, *imprint of* BBC Audiobooks

Parapress, *imprint of* Parapress Ltd

Parapress Ltd+
9 Frant Rd, Tunbridge Wells, Kent TN2 5SD
Tel: (01892) 512118 *Fax:* (01892) 512118
E-mail: office@parapress.eclipse.co.uk
Web Site: www.parapress.co.uk
Key Personnel
Man Dir: Elizabeth Imlay *E-mail:* e.imlay.parapress@virgin.net
General Assistant: James Ewing
Publicity Assistant: David Walsh
Founded: 1999
Specialize in animals, biography, history & militaria.
Membership(s): IPG.
Subjects: Animals, Pets, Biography, Crafts, Games, Hobbies, Education, Health, Nutrition, History, How-to, Humor, Literature, Literary Criticism, Essays, Maritime, Military Science, Music, Dance, Nonfiction (General), Outdoor Recreation, Self-Help, Sports, Athletics, Women's Studies
ISBN Prefix(es): 1-898594
Number of titles published annually: 4 Print
Total Titles: 20 Print
Imprints: Parapress

PARAS+
64 Sheperds Hill, Unit 3, London N6 5RN
Tel: (020) 8342 9600 *Fax:* (020) 8342 9600
E-mail: paraspublishing@telco4u.net
Key Personnel
Contact: Deborah O'Brien
Founded: 1990
Subjects: Poetry, Spirituality
ISBN Prefix(es): 1-874292
Total Titles: 4 Print

Park Lane (Art), *imprint of* Grange Books PLC

Parthenon Publishing, see Taylor & Francis Medical Books

Parthian Books+
53 Colum Rd, Cardiff CF10 3EF
Tel: (2920) 341314 *Fax:* (2920) 341314
E-mail: parthianbooks@yahoo.co.uk
Web Site: www.parthianbooks.co.uk
Key Personnel
Dir & International Rights: Richard Davies
Founded: 1993
Translations In: English from Welsh & Membership In: Literary Publishers-Wales.
Subjects: Drama, Theater, Fiction
ISBN Prefix(es): 0-9521558; 1-902638
Number of titles published annually: 6 Print
Total Titles: 26 Print
Owned by: St Clair Press, PO Box 287, Rozella, NSW 2039, Australia
Distributed by Dufour Editions (US)
Foreign Rep(s): Dufour Editions Inc (USA)
Orders to: Dufour Editions, St Clair Press, PO Box 287, Rozella NSW 2039, Australia

Partridge Press, *imprint of* Transworld Publishers Ltd

Pasold Research Fund, *imprint of* Maney Publishing

PasTest
Egerton Court, Parkgate Estate, Knutsford, Cheshire WA16 8DX
Tel: (01565) 752000 *Fax:* (01565) 650264
E-mail: enquiries@pastest.co.uk
Web Site: www.pastest.co.uk
Key Personnel
Dir, Rights: Freydis Campbell
Founded: 1972
Subjects: Business, Medicine, Nursing, Dentistry
ISBN Prefix(es): 0-906896; 1-901198

Paternoster Periodicals, *imprint of* Paternoster Publishing

Paternoster Press, *imprint of* Paternoster Publishing

Paternoster Publishing+
Subsidiary of Send the Light Ltd
PO Box 300, Carlisle, Cumbria CA3 OQS
Tel: (01228) 512512 *Fax:* (01228) 514949
E-mail: orderline@stl.org
Web Site: www.paternoster-publishing.com
Key Personnel
Publisher: Mark Finnie *Tel:* (01228) 512512 ext 2249 *E-mail:* mark.finnie@paternoster-markpublishing.com
General Manager: Rob Cook *Tel:* (01228) 512512 ext 2253 *E-mail:* rob.cook@paternoster-publishing.com

US Sales Manager: John Lewis *Tel:* 706-554-5827 *E-mail:* john@omlit.om.org
Founded: 1935
Specialize in religious (Christian) books & periodicals.
Subjects: History, Philosophy, Religion - Other
ISBN Prefix(es): 0-85364
Total Titles: 200 Print
Imprints: Authentic Lifestyle; Paternoster Periodicals; Paternoster Press; Regnum; Rutherford House

Pathfinder, *imprint of* Jarrold Publishing

Pathfinder London+
47 The Cut, London SE1 8LF
Tel: (020) 7261 1354 *Fax:* (020) 7261 1354
E-mail: pathfinderlondon@compuserve.com
Web Site: www.pathfinderpress.com
Key Personnel
Man Dir: T Hunt
Subjects: Developing Countries, Economics, Government, Political Science, History, Labor, Industrial Relations, Social Sciences, Sociology, Women's Studies
ISBN Prefix(es): 0-87348
Book Club(s): Pathfinder Readers Club
Warehouse: Plymbridge, Estover, Plymouth PL6 7PZ
Distribution Center: Australia Pathfinder, Level 1, 3/281-287 Beamish St, Campsie, NSW 2194, Australia *Tel:* (02) 9718 9698 *Fax:* (02) 9718 0197 *E-mail:* pathfinder_sydney@bigpond.com (Australia, New Zealand, the Pacific, Southeast Asia)
Iceland Pathfinder, Skolavordustig 6B, PO Box 233, Reykjavik IS 121, Iceland *Tel:* 552 5502 *E-mail:* pathfind@mmedia.is
New Zealand Pathfinder, 7 Mason Ave, PO Box 3025, Otahuhu, Auckland, Australia *Tel:* (09) 276 8885 *Fax:* (09) 276 9995 *E-mail:* pathfinder.auck@actrix.co.nz
Pathfinder Press, PO Box 162767, Atlanta, GA 30321-2767, United States *Tel:* 404-669-0600 *Fax:* 707-667-1141 *E-mail:* pathfinderpress@compuserve.com (USA, Caribbean, Latin America, East Asia)
Pathfinder Press Distribution, 2761 Dundas St W, Toronto, ON M6P 1Y4, Canada *Tel:* 416-531-9119 *Fax:* 416-531-9393 *E-mail:* pathdistribcan@bellnet.ca (Canada)
Sweden Pathfinder, Domardrand 16, S-129 04 Hagersten, Sweden *Tel:* (08) 31 69 33 *Fax:* (08) 31 69 33 *E-mail:* pathfbkh@algonet.se
Orders to: Pathfinder, c/o Baker & Taylor International, 102 Longueville Rd, Suite 143, Lane Cove, NSW 2066, Australia *Tel:* (02) 9924 0505 *Fax:* (02) 9924 0515 (Australia, New Zealand, the Pacific, Southeast Asia)
Plymbridge Distributors Ltd, Estover Rd, Plymouth PL6 7PZ *Tel:* (01752) 202301 *Fax:* (01752) 202331 *E-mail:* orders@plymbridge.com (Europe, the Middle East, Africa, South Asia)

Pavilion Books Ltd+
Division of Chrysalis Group
The Chrysalis Bldg, Bramley Rd, London W10 6SP
Tel: (020) 7221 2213; (020) 7314 1469 (sales) *Fax:* (020) 7221 6455; (020) 7314 1594 (sales)
E-mail: info@chrysalisbooks.co.uk; enquiries@chrysalis.com
Web Site: www.chrysalisbooks.co.uk/books/publisher/pavilion
Key Personnel
Group Sales & Marketing Dir: Richard Samson *Tel:* (020) 7314 1459 *Fax:* (020) 7314 1549 *E-mail:* rsamson@chrysalisbooks.co.uk
Dir of Marketing: Kate Wood *Tel:* (020) 7314 1496 *E-mail:* kwood@chrysalisbooks.co.uk
Permissions: Terry Forshaw *Tel:* (020) 7314 1607 *E-mail:* tforshaw@chrysalisbooks.co.uk
Foreign Rights Manager: Emma O'Grady *Tel:* (020) 7314 1447 *E-mail:* eogrady@chrysalisbooks.co.uk
Founded: 1981
Subjects: Art, Biography, Cookery, Film, Video, Gardening, Plants, House & Home, Photography, Travel
ISBN Prefix(es): 1-85145; 1-85793; 0-907516; 1-86205
Total Titles: 200 Print
Foreign Rights: Frank Chambers (Denmark, Far East, Finland, France, Norway, Sweden); John Saunders-Griffiths (Canada, USA); Nina de la Mer (Belgium, Germany, Holland); Emma O'Grady (Eastern Europe, Italy, Latin America, Portugal, Russia, Spain)
Orders to: Littlehampton Book Services, Faraday Close, Off Columbia Dr, Durrington, West Sussex BN13 3HD *Tel:* (01903) 828800 *Fax:* (01903) 828802 *E-mail:* orders@lbsltd.co.uk

Pavilion Publishing (Brighton) Ltd
The Ironworks, Cheapside, Brighton, East Sussex BN1 4GD
Tel: (01273) 623222 *Fax:* (01273) 625526
E-mail: info@pavpub.co.uk
Web Site: www.pavpub.com
Subjects: Social Sciences, Sociology, Disability, Health, Nursing, Special Needs
ISBN Prefix(es): 1-84196; 1-900600
Distributed by Gizmo
Distributor for Gizmo; NEC

Paxton, *imprint of* Novello & Co Ltd

PC Publishing+
Division of Music Technology Books Limited
Keepers House, Merton, Thetford, Norfolk IP25 6QH
Tel: (01953) 889900 *Fax:* (01953) 889901
E-mail: info@pc-publishing.com
Web Site: www.pc-publishing.co.uk
Key Personnel
Publisher: Philip Chapman
Founded: 1988
Subjects: Computer Science, Electronics, Electrical Engineering, Music, Dance
ISBN Prefix(es): 1-870775
Number of titles published annually: 10 Print
Total Titles: 40 Print
Distributed by Cimino Publishing Group (USA); Keyfax (US & Canada); Music Books Plus (US & Canada); Music Software (Australia & New Zealand)
Orders to: Littlehampton Book Services, Faraday Close, Durrington, Worthing, W Sussex BN13 3RB *Tel:* (01903) 828800 *Fax:* (01903) 828801 *E-mail:* enquiries@lbsltd.co.uk *Web Site:* www.lbsltd.co.uk (UK)

PCR, *imprint of* Wilmington Business Information Ltd

Pearson Education
128 Long Acre, London WC2 9AN
Tel: (020) 7447 2000 *Fax:* (020) 7240 5771
E-mail: firstname.lastname@pearsoned-ema.com
Telex: 81259
Key Personnel
President Professional Education: Peter Marshall
Administration Manager, Prod Ed: Juliane Heineke
Finance Dir, Higher/Prof Ed: John Knight
Vice President, UK Sales & Marketing: Adrian Meillor
Editor-in-Chief, Business & Ref: Richard Stagg
Editor-in-Chief, Computing: Steve Temblett
Founded: 1724
Subjects: Accounting, Aeronautics, Aviation, Agriculture, Anthropology, Art, Biological Sciences, Business, Career Development, Chemistry, Chemical Engineering, Computer Science, Criminology, Economics, Education, Engineering (General), Environmental Studies, Geography, Geology, Government, Political Science, Health, Nutrition, History, Language Arts, Linguistics, Law, Literature, Literary Criticism, Essays, Management, Mathematics, Music, Dance, Natural History, Philosophy, Physics, Poetry, Psychology, Psychiatry, Religion - Other, Science (General), Social Sciences, Sociology, Veterinary Science, Women's Studies
ISBN Prefix(es): 0-582; 0-05
Parent Company: Pearson Plc
Branch Office(s)
Fourth Ave, Pinnacles, Harlow, Essex CM19 5AA *Tel:* (01279) 623623 *Fax:* (01279) 431067
Showroom(s): 5 Bentinck St, London W1M 5RN *Tel:* (020) 7935 0121 *Fax:* (020) 7486 4204
Distribution Center: Magna Park, Coventry Rd, Lutterworth, Leics LE17 4XH *Tel:* (01442) 881900 *Fax:* (01442) 882177

Pearson Education Europe, Mideast & Africa+
Edinburgh Gate, Harlow, Essex CM20 2JE
Tel: (01279) 62 3623 *Fax:* (01279) 41 4130
E-mail: firstname.lastname@pearsoned-ema.com
Web Site: www.pearsoned.co.uk
Key Personnel
President & Chief Executive Officer, Group Executive: Nigel Portwood
Chief Operating Officer, Group Executive: Brian Landers
Vice President, Finance, Group Executive: Lianne Gammon
President, Pearson Education Ltd: Rod Bristow
Rights & Contracts Dir, Pearson Education Ltd: Lynette Owen
VP, Finance, Pearson Education Ltd: John Knight
Senior Vice President, People & Change: Graham Abbey
President, ELT & Schools: Dugie Cameron
Man Dir, ELT Publishing: Gill Negas
Marketing Dir, ELT Marketing: Martha Ware
Man Dir, UK Schools: Jeff Andrew
Dir, International: Kern Roberts
Publishing Dir, International: Jenny Pares
Publishing Dir, UK Schools: Lorna Cocking
President, Higher Education: Jim Green
Vice President, Production: Colin Lander
Head of Facilities Management, Operations: John Fessey
Divisional Coordinator, FM Operations: Miranda Fishburn
Dir, Customer Service, Corporate Services: Jennie Heals
President, Schools EMA: John Penrose
Man Dir, Direct English, Consumer Language Learning: Clive Sawkins
Founded: 1998 (result of merger of Addison Wesley Longman, Financial Times Management & Prentice Hall Europe)
Subjects: Art, Business, Communications, Drama, Theater, Economics, Education, Government, Political Science, History, Language Arts, Linguistics, Medicine, Nursing, Dentistry, Music, Dance, Philosophy, Psychology, Psychiatry, Religion - Other, Science (General), Social Sciences, Sociology, Technology
ISBN Prefix(es): 1-84479
Parent Company: Pearson Education
Ultimate Parent Company: Pearson PLC
Imprints: Allyn & Bacon; Prentice Hall; Prentice Hall Europe; Prentice Hall Regents; Longman; Addison-Wesley; Financial Times Prentice Hall; Scott Foresman; Que; Que Lycos Books; Ziff-Davis Press; New Roders; Macmillan Technical Publishing USA; Que Education & Training; BradyGames; Sams Publishing; Sams.net; Borland Press; Hayden Books; Adobe Press; Waite Group Press

UNITED KINGDOM

Branch Office(s)
Pearson Education Software Publishing Division, 124 Cambridge Science Park, Milton Rd, Cambridge CB4 4ZS *Tel:* (01223) 425558 *Fax:* (01223) 425349 *E-mail:* info@logo.com
128 Longacre, London WC2 9AN *Tel:* (020) 7477 2000 *Fax:* (020) 7240 5771
Campus 400, Maylands Ave, Hemel Hempstead, Herts HP2 7EZ *Tel:* (01442) 881900 *Fax:* (01442) 882099
U.S. Office(s): Pearson Education, One Lake St, Upper Saddle River, NJ 07458, United States

Peartree Publications
61 Peartree Lane, Bexhill, East Sussex TN39 4RQ
Tel: 01424 844274
Key Personnel
Partner: Roger Stepney
Founded: 1986
Subjects: Music, Dance
ISBN Prefix(es): 1-85254
Total Titles: 6 Print; 2 Audio

Peepal Tree Press Ltd+
17 Kings Ave, Leeds LS6 1QS
Tel: (0113) 245 1703 *Fax:* (0113) 246 8368
E-mail: contact@peepaltreepress.com
Web Site: www.peepaltreepress.com
Key Personnel
Man Editor: Jeremy Poynting *E-mail:* jeremy@peepal.demon.co.uk
Marketing Manager: Hannah Bannister *E-mail:* hannah@peepal.demon.co.uk
Founded: 1985
Specialize in Caribbean, African, South Asian & Black British fiction, poetry & criticism.
Subjects: Education, Fiction, History, Literature, Literary Criticism, Essays, Poetry, Social Sciences, Sociology
ISBN Prefix(es): 0-948833; 0-900715
Imprints: South Asians Overseas Series
Orders to: Central Books, 99 Wallis Rd, London E9 5LN
Paul & Co PCS Data Processing Inc, 360 W 31 St, New York, NY 10001, United States

Pelican History of Art, *imprint of* Yale University Press London

Pen & Sword Books Ltd+
47 Church St, Barnsley, South Yorks S70 2AS
Tel: (01226) 734555 *Fax:* (01226) 734438
E-mail: enquiries@pen-and-sword.co.uk
Web Site: www.pen-and-sword.co.uk
Key Personnel
Chairman: Nicholas Hewitt
Man Dir: Charles Hewitt *E-mail:* charles@pen-and-sword.co.uk
Publishing Manager: Henry Wilson *E-mail:* hw@henrywilson.lawlite.net
Production Manager: Barbara Bramall *E-mail:* production@pen-and-sword.co.uk
Sales Manager: Paula Brennan *E-mail:* sales@pen-and-sword.co.uk
Marketing & Publicity: Jonathan Wright *E-mail:* marketing@pen-and-sword.co.uk
Founded: 1990
Subjects: Aeronautics, Aviation, History, Maritime, Military Science, Local History, Military History
ISBN Prefix(es): 0-85052; 1-871647
Imprints: Leo Cooper; Pen & Sword Paperbacks; Wharncliffe Books

Pen & Sword Paperbacks, *imprint of* Pen & Sword Books Ltd

Pencil Press, *imprint of* Roundhouse Group

Penguin, *imprint of* Penguin Books Ltd

Penguin Books Ltd+
80 Strand, London WC2R 0RL
Tel: (020) 7416 3000 *Fax:* (020) 7416 3099; (020) 7416 3293
Web Site: www.penguin.com
Telex: 917181
Key Personnel
Chief Executive Officer: Anthony Forbes Watson
President: David Wan
Man Dir, Penguin General Division: Helen Fraser
Man Dir, Penguin Press: Andrew Rosenheim
Man Dir, Puffin: Philippa Milnes Smith
Man Dir, Frederick Warne: Sally Floyer
Rights Division (Warne): Susan Winton
Rights Dir (Adult): Sophie Brewer
Publicity Dir: Joanna Prior
Founded: 1935
General trade publisher; baby & toddler titles through to adult.
ISBN Prefix(es): 0-14; 0-7207; 0-14; 0-670; 0-7181
Parent Company: Penguin Publishing Co Ltd
Ultimate Parent Company: Pearson
Imprints: Viking; Puffin Books; Arkana; Ladybird; Hamish Hamilton; Michael Joseph; Allen Lane; Frederick Warne; Buildings of England; Penguin; Ventura
Divisions: Rough Guides Ltd
Branch Office(s)
Penguin USA, 375 Hudson St, New York, NY 10014, United States
Orders to: Penguin Group Distribution Ltd, Bath Rd, Harmondsworth, Middlesex UB7 0DA

The Penguin Group UK+
80 Strand, London WC2R 0RN
Tel: (020) 7010 3000
E-mail: editor@penguin.co.uk
Web Site: www.penguin.co.uk
Key Personnel
Chief Executive Officer, The Penguin Group: John Makinson
Chief Executive Officer, The Penguin Group (UK): Anthony Forbes Watson
Man Dir, Penguin: Helen Fraser
Man Dir, Ventura/Warne: Sally Floyer
Man Dir, Puffin: Francesca Dow
Group Sales & Operations: Peter Brown
Man Dir, Dorling Kindersley: Andrew Welhan
Founded: 1935
ISBN Prefix(es): 0-14; 0-670; 0-7181
Parent Company: Pearson PLC
Imprints: Michael Joseph; Hamish Hamilton; Viking; Allen Lane; Rough Guides; Buildings of England; Classics; Puffin
Subsidiaries: LadyBird Books Ltd
Divisions: Penguin General Books; Penguin Press; Frederick Warne; Dorling Kindersley; Puffin
U.S. Office(s): Penguin Group (USA) Inc, 375 Hudson St, New York, NY 10014, United States
Distributor for Rough Guides; Wisden
Warehouse: Penguin Books Ltd, Bath Rd, Harmondsworth MDDX UB7 (customer services)
Orders to: Penguin Books Ltd, Bath Rd, Harmondsworth, Middlesex UB7 0DA

The Penguin Press, *imprint of* Viking

The Pensions Management Institute
PMI House, 4/10 Artillery Lane, London E1 7LS
Tel: (020) 7247 1452 *Fax:* (020) 7375 0603
E-mail: enquiries@pensions-pmi.org.uk
Web Site: www.pensions-pmi.org.uk
Key Personnel
President: Roger Cobley
ISBN Prefix(es): 0-946242; 1-898785

Pentathol Publishing+
40 Gibson St, Wrexham, Wrexham County LL13 7NS

Mailing Address: PO Box 92, Wrexham, Wrexham County LL13 7NS
Key Personnel
Contact: A E Cowen
Founded: 1991
Membership(s): Publishers Association.
Subjects: Poetry
ISBN Prefix(es): 1-873021
Number of titles published annually: 1 Print
Total Titles: 1 Print
Imprints: "Huh!" 1991

Pentn Press, *imprint of* Jessica Kingsley Publishers

Perennial, *imprint of* HarperCollins UK

PerfectBound, *imprint of* HarperCollins UK

Pergamon Flexible Learning+
Imprint of Butterworth-Heinemann
Linacre House, Jordan Hill, Oxford OX2 8DP
Tel: (01865) 310366; (01865) 388190 *Fax:* (01865) 314290
E-mail: bhmarketing@repp.co.uk
Web Site: www.bh.com/pergamonfl
Key Personnel
Dir: Kathryn Grant *E-mail:* kathryn.grant@repp.co.uk
Marketing Manager: Duncan Enright *E-mail:* duncanenright@repp.co.uk
International Marketing Manager: Jacquie Shanahan *E-mail:* jacquie.shanahan@repp.co.uk
UK Sales Manager: Mark Hunt *E-mail:* m.hunt@elsevier.com
Key Accounts Manager, Wholesaler/Library Supplier/Online: Nigel Berkeley *E-mail:* n.berkeley@elsevier.com
Key Accounts Manager, Retail: Chris Hossack *E-mail:* c.hossack@elsevier.com
Field Academic Manager, Scotland & Ireland: Karen McWhirter *E-mail:* k.mcwhirter@elsevier.com
Trade & Academic Representative, Greater London & Home Counties: Tom Waggitt *E-mail:* t.waggitt@elsevier.com
Trade & Academic Representative, South & West: Nicola Haden *E-mail:* n.haden@elsevier.com
Trade & Academic Representative, Midlands & North: Lynne Saunderson *E-mail:* l.saunderson@elsevier.com
National Account Manager, Pergamon Flexible Learning: David Lockley *E-mail:* d.lockley@elsevier.com
European Sales Manager: Rosanna Ramacciotti *E-mail:* r.ramacciotti@elsevier.com
Regional Sales Manager, Germany, Austria & Switzerland: Catherine Anderson *E-mail:* c.anderson@elsevier.com
Sales Representative, Austria & Switzerland: Kai Wuerfl-Davidek *E-mail:* k.wuerfl@elsevier.com
Area Sales Manager, Southern Europe: Miguel Sanchez Gatell *E-mail:* m.sanchez@elsevier.com
Sales Representative, Italy, France & Greece: Nadia Balavoine *E-mail:* n.balavoine@elsevier.com
Product Manager: Steve Brewster *E-mail:* s.brewster@elsevier.com
Internet Marketing Manager: Maddie Davis *E-mail:* m.davis@elsevier.com
Area Sales Manager, Benelux & Scandinavia: Robert Fairbrother *E-mail:* r.fairbrother@elsevier.com
Sales Representative, Scandinavia: Krista Leppiko *E-mail:* k.leppiko@elsevier.com
Sales Representative, South Germany: Christiane Leipersberger *E-mail:* c.leipersberger@elsevier.com
Area Sales Manager, Eastern Europe: Radek Janousek *E-mail:* r.janousek@elsevier.com

International Sales Manager, Middle East & Africa: Klaus Beran *E-mail:* k.beran@elsevier.com
Sales Office Manager: Emma Wyatt *E-mail:* e.wyatt@elsevier.com
Sales Office Coordinator: Emily Mander *E-mail:* e.mander@elsevier.com
Foreign Rights Manager: Adele Parker *E-mail:* a.parker@elsevier.com
Foreign Rights Assistant: Annette Fuhrmeister *E-mail:* a.fuhrmeister@elsevier.com
Special Sales Manager: Judy Chappell *E-mail:* j.chappell@elsevier.com
Special Sales Executive, Technical Books: Rosie Moss *E-mail:* r.moss@elsevier.com
Internet Marketing Manager: Maddie Davis *E-mail:* m.davis@elsevier.com
Founded: 1987
Subjects: Business, Education, Management, Marketing, Customer Service, Sales, Health & Safety, Training & Development, Open Learning Materials
ISBN Prefix(es): 0-08; 0-7506
Parent Company: Butterworth-Heinemann, Linacre House, Jordan Hill, Oxford OX2 8DP
Ultimate Parent Company: Reed
Associate Companies: Butterworth-Heinemann Inc, 313 Washington St, Newton, MA 02158, United States *Tel:* 617-928-2500 *Fax:* 617-928-2620

Permanent Publications, *imprint of* Hyden House Ltd

Perpetuity Press+
50 Queens Rd, Leicester LE2 1TU
Tel: (0116) 221 7778 *Fax:* (0116) 221 7171
E-mail: orders@perpetuitypress.com
Web Site: www.perpetuitypress.com
Key Personnel
Publisher: K A Gill
Founded: 1994
Membership(s): IPG.
Subjects: Business, Criminology, Law, Management, Maritime, Security Management, Risk Management & Policing, crime prevention
ISBN Prefix(es): 1-899287
Membership(s): IPG

Peter Peregrinus Ltd, *imprint of* Institution of Electrical Engineers

Pevsner Architectural Guides, *imprint of* Yale University Press London

Phaidon Press Ltd+
Regent's Wharf, All Saints St, London N1 9PA
Tel: (020) 7843 1234 *Fax:* (020) 7843 1111
E-mail: esales@phaidon.com
Web Site: www.phaidon.com
Key Personnel
Man Dir: Andrew Price
Export Sales Dir: Sheila McKenna
Operations Dir: Fran Johnson
Publisher: Richard Schlagman
Vice President Sales & Marketing, Phaidon Press Inc: Mary Albi
Deputy Publisher: Amanda Renshaw
Marketing Manager: Truda Spruyt
UK Sales Manager: Simon Kingsley
Sales & Marketing Dir: John Roberts
International Editions Manager: Helen Garrett
Founded: 1923
Subjects: Architecture & Interior Design, Art, Biography, Drama, Theater, History, Photography
ISBN Prefix(es): 0-7148
Subsidiaries: Phaidon Press Inc
U.S. Office(s): 3 Center Plaza, Boston, MA 02108, United States, Contact: Jeremy Raymondjack *E-mail:* ussales@phaidon.com
Warehouse: Unit 4, Lodge Causeway Trading Estate Fishponds, Bristol, Avon BS16 3JB

Pharmaceutical Press+
Division of The Royal Pharmaceutical Society
One Lamberth High St, London SE1 7JN
Tel: (020) 7735 9141 *Fax:* (020) 7572 2509
E-mail: pharmpress@rpsgb.org
Web Site: www.pharmpress.com
Key Personnel
Dir, Publications: Charles Fry *E-mail:* charles.fry@rpsgb.org
Editorial Production Manager: John Wilson *E-mail:* john.wilson@rpsgb.org
Head of Sales & Marketing: Colin Fenton *E-mail:* colin.fenton@rpsgb.org
Sales Manager, Electronic Products: Peter Goacher *Tel:* (0171) 735 9141 *E-mail:* peter.goacher@rpsgb.org
Contracts & Licensing Manager: Jane Mulholland *E-mail:* jane.mulholland@rpsgb.org
Founded: 1841
Subjects: Chemistry, Chemical Engineering, Health, Nutrition, Law, Medicine, Nursing, Dentistry, Veterinary Science, Pharmaceutical
ISBN Prefix(es): 0-85369
Number of titles published annually: 30 Print; 5 CD-ROM
Total Titles: 60 Print; 7 CD-ROM; 1 Online
U.S. Office(s): 100 S Atkinson Rd, Suite 206, Grayslake, IL 60030-7820, United States
Warehouse: Customer Services Dept, PO Box 151, Wallingford OX10 8QU
Orders to: Customer Services Dept, PO Box 151, Wallingford OX10 8QU
Returns: Customer Services Dept, PO Box 151, Wallingford OX10 8QU

Philip & Tacey Ltd
North Way, Andover, Hants SP10 5BA
Tel: (01264) 332171 *Fax:* (01264) 384808
E-mail: sales@philipandtacey.co.uk
Web Site: www.philipandtacey.co.uk
Key Personnel
Man Dir: Gerry Vaughan
Founded: 1829
Membership(s): BESA.
Subjects: Education
ISBN Prefix(es): 0-902073
Associate Companies: Philograph Publications Ltd, Pottington Industrial Estate, Riverside Rd, Barnstable EX31 1LR
U.S. Office(s): Didax Inc, 395 Main St, Rowley, MA 01969, United States

George Philip Ltd, see Philip's

Philip, *imprint of* Octopus Publishing Group

Philip's+
Formerly George Philip Ltd
Division of Hachette Livre (France)
11 Salvsbury Rd, London NW6 6RG
Tel: (020) 7644 6900 *Fax:* (020) 7644 6987
E-mail: philips@philips-maps.co.uk
Web Site: www.philips-maps.co.uk
Key Personnel
Man Dir & Publisher: John Gaisford *Tel:* (020) 7644 6901 *E-mail:* john.gaisford@philips-maps.co.uk
Mapping Director: David Gaylard *Tel:* (020) 7644 6902 *E-mail:* david.gaylard@philips-maps.co.uk
Trade Sales Dir: Roger Fox *E-mail:* roger.fox@philips-maps.co.uk
Trade Sales Administrator: Wendy Graham *E-mail:* wendy.graham@philips-maps.co.uk; Dimity Castellano *E-mail:* dimity.castellano@philips-maps.co.uk
Rights, Foreign Rights, Premiums & Data Sales Dir: Victoria Dawbarn *E-mail:* victoria.dawbarn@philips-maps.co.uk
Digital Data Sales: James Mann *E-mail:* james.mann@philips-maps.co.uk
Founded: 1834

Specialize in world atlases, road & street atlases, astronomy, encyclopedias & illustrated reference.
Membership(s): Royal Geographical Society; International Map Traders Association.
Subjects: Astronomy, Geography, Geology
ISBN Prefix(es): 0-540
Total Titles: 300 Print
Parent Company: Octopus Publishing Group
Ultimate Parent Company: Lagardere Group
Orders to: Littlehampton Book Services, Durrington, Worthing, West Sussex BN13 3RB *Tel:* (01903) 828500 *Fax:* (01903) 828625 *E-mail:* orders@lbsltd.co.uk *Web Site:* www.lbsltd.co.uk

Phillimore & Co Ltd+
Shopwyke Manor Barn, Chichester, West Sussex PO20 2BG
Tel: (01243) 787636 *Fax:* (01243) 787639
E-mail: bookshop@phillimore.co.uk
Web Site: www.phillimore.co.uk
Key Personnel
Chairman: Philip Harris
Manager & Editorial: Noel H Osborne
Founded: 1897
Subjects: Archaeology, Architecture & Interior Design, History, Regional Interests
ISBN Prefix(es): 0-85033; 0-900592; 1-86077; 0-900809
Associate Companies: British Association for Local History; Historical Publications Ltd

Philograph Publications Ltd
Riverside Rd, Barnstaple EX31 1LR
Tel: (01271) 345061 *Fax:* (01271) 23076
Key Personnel
Man Dir: Chris Tacey
Founded: 1829
Specialize in teaching aids & resources for primary schools.
ISBN Prefix(es): 0-85370
Parent Company: Philip & Tacey Ltd, North Way, Andover, Hants
U.S. Office(s): Didax Inc, 395 Main St, Rowley, MA 01969, United States
Orders to: Philip & Tracey Ltd, Riverside Rd, Pottington Industrial Estate, Devon EX31 1LR

Photo Art International, *imprint of* Creative Monochrome Ltd

Phronesis, *imprint of* Verso

Piatkus Books+
5 Windmill St, London W1T 2JA
Tel: (020) 7631 0710 *Fax:* (020) 7436 7137
E-mail: info@piatkus.co.uk
Web Site: www.piatkus.co.uk
Key Personnel
Man Dir: Judy Piatkus
Editorial Dir: Gill Bailey
Sales Dir: Philip Cotterell
Publicity Manager: Jana Sommerlad
Production Manager: Simon Colverson
Rights Manager: Jon Mitchell
Founded: 1979
An independent publishing company. Specialize in general trade nonfiction & popular fiction including mass market.
Subjects: Astrology, Occult, Biography, Business, Career Development, Cookery, Criminology, Fashion, Fiction, Health, Nutrition, Humor, Management, Nonfiction (General), Psychology, Psychiatry, Self-Help
ISBN Prefix(es): 0-7499; 0-86188
Number of titles published annually: 175 Print
Total Titles: 3,000 Print
Parent Company: Judy Piatkus (Publishers) Ltd

UNITED KINGDOM

Distributed by Angell Eurosales (Austria, Benelux, France, Germany, Iceland, Scandinavia, Switzerland); Ashton International Marketing Services (Middle East); David Bateman Ltd (New Zealand); Bookport Associates (Gibraltar, Greece, Italy, Malta, Portugal, Spain); General Publishing (Canada); Kelvin van Hasselt (Mauritius, Seychelles & West Africa); Hodder Headline (Australia) Pty Ltd (Australia); India Book Distribution (Bombay) Ltd (India); MTM; Pansing Distribution Sdn Bhd (Malaysia & Singapore); Penguin South Africa (Pty) Ltd (South Africa & Zimbabwe); Ralph & Sheila Summers (Far East)
Shipping Address: Grantham Book Services Ltd, Isaac Newton Way, Alma Park Industrial Estate, Grantham, Lincs NG31 9SD *Tel:* (01476) 541000 *Fax:* (01476) 590223
Warehouse: Grantham Book Services Ltd, Isaac Newton Way, Alma Park Industrial Estate, Grantham, Lincs N931 9SD *Tel:* (1476) 541000 *Fax:* (1476) 590223
Orders to: Grantham Book Services Ltd, Isaac Newton Way, Alma Park Industrial Estate, Grantham, Lincs NG31 9SD *Tel:* (01476) 541000 *Fax:* (01476) 590223

Pica Press, *imprint of* A & C Black Publishers Ltd

Pica Press, *imprint of* Christopher Helm (Publishers) Ltd

Picador, *imprint of* Pan Macmillan

Piccadilly Press+
5 Castle Rd, London NW1 8PR
Tel: (020) 7267 4492 *Fax:* (020) 7267 4493
E-mail: books@piccadillypress.co.uk
Web Site: www.piccadillypress.co.uk
Key Personnel
Man Dir & Publisher: Brenda Gardner
Senior Editor: Yasemin Ucar
Production: Geoff Barlow
Rights: Margot Edwards
Book Clubs & Special Sales: Lea Garton
Founded: 1983
Independent children's publisher specializing in picture books, teenage fiction, nonfiction & parental books.
Subjects: Fiction, Humor, Nonfiction (General), Parenting
ISBN Prefix(es): 1-85340
Number of titles published annually: 30 Print
Total Titles: 250 Print
Foreign Rights: Akcali Copyright (Turkey); Luigi Bernabo Associates (Italy); The English Agency (Japan) Ltd (Japan); JLM Literary Agency (Greece); KCC (Korea); Jacqueline Miller Agency (France); Andrew Nurnberg Associates (Czech Republic, Hungary, Poland, Romania, Russia); I Pikarski (Israel)
Orders to: Ashton International Marketing Services, PO Box 298, Sevenoaks, Kent TN13 1WU *Tel:* (01732) 746 093 *Fax:* (01732) 746 096 (Cambodia, China, Indonesia, Japan, Korea, Laos & Myanmar)
Fields & Associates Ltd, 1/F Prosperous Commercial Bldg, 54 Jardine Bazaar, Causeway Bay, Hong Kong (Hong Kong), Pauline Lau
Forrester Books NZ Ltd, 10 Tarndale Grove, Albany, Private Bag 102907, North Shore Mail Center, Auckland, New Zealand *Tel:* (09) 415 2080 *Fax:* (09) 415 2083 *E-mail:* cath@forrester.co.nz (New Zealand)
Grantham Book Services, Isaac Newton Way, Alma Park Industrial Estate, Grantham NG31 9SD *Tel:* (01476) 541 080 *Fax:* (01476) 541 061 *E-mail:* orders@gbs.tbs-ltd.co.uk (UK)
The Old Whaling House, The Walls, Berwick-upon-Tweed TD15 1HP *Tel:* (01289) 332 934 *Fax:* (01289) 332 935 (France, Benelux, Scandinavia & Iceland)
Peribo, 58 Beaumont Rd, Mount Kuring-Gai, NSW 2080, Australia *Tel:* (02) 9457 0011 *Fax:* (02) 9457 0022 *E-mail:* peribo@bigpond.com (Australia)
Publishers Marketing Service, Unit 509, Block E, Philco Dmansara 1, Jalan 16/11, Off Jalan Damansara, 46350 Petaling Jaya, Selango Darul Ehsan, Malaysia *Tel:* (03) 755 3588 *Fax:* (03) 755 3017 *E-mail:* pmsmal@po.jaring.my (Malaysia)
Publishers Marketing Services, 10c Jalan Ampas 07-01, Ho Seng Lee Flatted Warehouse, Singapore 329513, Singapore *Tel:* 256 5166 *Fax:* 253 0008 *E-mail:* pmssin@mbox3.singnet.com.sg (Singapore)
Rep Force Ireland, 12 Longford Terrace, Monkstown, Co Dublin, Ireland *Tel:* (01) 280 1552 *Fax:* (01) 280 1054 (Ireland)
TBS Ltd, Frating Green, Colchester Rd, Colchester, Essex C07 7DW *Tel:* (01206) 256 000 *Fax:* (01206) 255 715
Trinity Books, PO Box 242, Randburg 2125, South Africa *Tel:* (011) 787 4010; (011) 787 4011 *Fax:* (011) 787 8920 *E-mail:* trinity@africa.com (South Africa)

Pickering & Chatto Publishers Ltd+
21 Bloomsbury Way, London WC1A 2TH
Tel: (020) 7405 1005 *Fax:* (020) 7405 6216
E-mail: info@pickeringchatto.co.uk
Web Site: www.pickeringchatto.com
Key Personnel
Chairman: Lord Rees-Mogg
Man Dir: James Powell *E-mail:* james@pickeringchatto.co.uk
Editorial Dir: Mark Pollard *E-mail:* mark@pickeringchatto.co.uk
Senior Editor: Michael Middeke *E-mail:* michael@pickeringchatto.co.uk
Marketing Manager: Paul Boland *E-mail:* paul@pickeringchatto.co.uk
Founded: 1985
Also specialize in rare books & journals in facsimile.
Subjects: Business, Economics, History, Literature, Literary Criticism, Essays, Philosophy, Women's Studies, History of Science, Politics
ISBN Prefix(es): 1-85196
Number of titles published annually: 20 Print; 5 Online
Total Titles: 25 Online
Imprints: William Pickering
Distributed by Ashgate Publishing Co (North & South America); DA Information Services (Australia & New Zealand); Publishers International Marketing (Singapore, Hong Kong, Indonesia, Philippines, Malaysia & Thailand); Turpin Distribution; Unifacmanu Trading Co Ltd (Taiwan)
Foreign Rep(s): Applied Media (India); Iberian Book Services (Spain & Portugal); Japan Book Associates Co (Japan); Publishers International Marketing (China, Middle East, South Korea)
Warehouse: Extenza-Turpin, Stratton Business Park, Pegasus Drive, Biggleswade, Beds SG18 8QG *Tel:* (01767) 604951 *Fax:* (01767) 601640 *E-mail:* books@extenza-turpin.com
Membership(s): IPG

William Pickering, *imprint of* Pickering & Chatto Publishers Ltd

Picton Press (Liverpool), *imprint of* Countyvise Ltd

Picture Corgi, *imprint of* Transworld Publishers Ltd

Pimlico, *imprint of* Random House UK Ltd

Pine Forge Press, *imprint of* SAGE Publications Ltd

Pinter, *imprint of* The Continuum International Publishing Group Ltd

Pinter, Studio Vista, *imprint of* Cassell & Co

Pinwheel Ltd+
Subsidiary of Andromeda Holdings Ltd
Station House, 8-13 Swiss Terrace, London NW6 4RR
Tel: (020) 7586 5100 *Fax:* (020) 7483 1999
E-mail: sales@pinwheel.co.uk
Web Site: www.pinwheel.co.uk
Key Personnel
Sales Manager: Kristina Dahlqvist *E-mail:* kristina.dahlqvist@pinwheel.co.uk; Giovanna Franchina *E-mail:* giovanna.franchina@pinwheel.co.uk
European Sales Manager: Rachel Pidcock *E-mail:* rachel.pidcock@pinwheel.co.uk
Sales Administrator: Rosie Guard *E-mail:* rosie.guard@pinwheel.co.uk
Commissioning Editor: Shaheen Bilgrami *E-mail:* shaheen.bilgrami@pinwheel.co.uk
Art Dir: Ali Scrivens *E-mail:* ali.scrivens@pinwheel.co.uk
Production Manager: Martin Croshow *E-mail:* martin.croshow@pinwheel.co.uk
Production Editor: Caterina Boselli *E-mail:* caterina.boselli@pinwheel.co.uk
Designer: Ella Butler *E-mail:* ella.butler@pinwheel.co.uk
Founded: 1995
Children's novelty books for preschool age.
Number of titles published annually: 15 Print
Total Titles: 60 Print

Pion Ltd+
207 Brondesbury Park, London NW2 5JN
Tel: (020) 8459 0066 *Fax:* (020) 8451 6454
E-mail: sales@pion.co.uk
Web Site: www.pion.co.uk
Key Personnel
Dir: Dr Jonathan Briggs
Man Dir: Adam Gelbtuch
Senior Editor: Dr Jan Schubert
Sales & Rights Manager: Diana Harrop *E-mail:* sales@pion.co.uk
Founded: 1960
Journal publisher.
Membership(s): ALPSP.
Subjects: Geography, Geology, Mathematics, Physical Sciences, Physics, Psychology, Psychiatry
ISBN Prefix(es): 0-85086
Total Titles: 15 Print
Associate Companies: Turpin Ltd (Joint venture with Institute of Physics Publishing)
Foreign Rights: Japan Uni Agency (Japan)
Warehouse: Extenza-Turpin Ltd, Stratton Business Park, Pegasus Dr, Biggleswade, Beds SG18 8QB *Tel:* (01767) 604951 *Fax:* (01767) 601640 *E-mail:* books@extenza-turpin.com (Book orders & Turpion journal orders; Pion Journal orders contact publisher)
Orders to: Extenza-Turpin Ltd, Stratton Business Park, Pegasus Dr, Biggleswade, Beds SG18 8QB *Tel:* (01767) 604951 *Fax:* (01767) 601640 *E-mail:* books@extenza-turpin.com (Book orders & Turpion journal orders; Pion Journal orders contact publisher)
Membership(s): IPG

PIRA Intl
Randalls Rd, Leatherhead, Surrey KT22 7RU
Tel: (01372) 802000 *Fax:* (01372) 802238
E-mail: publications@pira.co.uk
Web Site: www.piranet.com
Key Personnel
Contact: Philip Swinden

PUBLISHERS UNITED KINGDOM

A consultancy business with major publishing & conference activities, serving the printing, publishing, packaging & paper industries.
Subjects: Publishing & Book Trade Reference, Technology
ISBN Prefix(es): 1-85802; 0-902799
U.S. Office(s): Books International, PO Box 605, Herndon, VA 20172, United States *Tel:* 703-689-4204

Pitkin Unichrome Ltd+
Healey House, Dene Rd, Andover, Hants SP10 2AA
Tel: (01264) 409200 *Fax:* (01264) 334110
E-mail: enquiries@pitkin-unichrome.com
Web Site: www.britguides.com
Key Personnel
Dir: Heather Hook
Founded: 1947
Subjects: Biography, History, Travel
ISBN Prefix(es): 0-85372; 0-85373; 1-871004
Number of titles published annually: 10 Print; 1 CD-ROM
Total Titles: 280 Print; 1 CD-ROM; 270 Online; 1 E-Book
Parent Company: Jarrold Publishing
Ultimate Parent Company: Jarrold & Sons Ltd

PJB Reference Sevices
Division of PJB Publications Ltd
Suffield House, 9 Paradise Rd, Richmond, Surrey TW9 1SJ
Tel: (020) 8332 8970 *Fax:* (020) 8332 8937
E-mail: pjbreference@pjbpubs.com
Web Site: www.pjbreference.com
Supplier of contact names for the pharmaceutical, biotechnical, medical device, diagnostics & service industries. Details of pharma, biotech, MD & service company addresses worldwide with named senior personnel.
Ultimate Parent Company: Informa Group

Planet+
PO Box 44, Aberystwyth, Ceredigion SY23 3ZZ
Tel: (01970) 611255 *Fax:* (01970) 611197
E-mail: planet.enquiries@planetmagazine.org.uk
Web Site: www.planetmagazine.org.uk
Key Personnel
Chairman & Dir: John Barnie
Founded: 1985
Publishing House.
Subjects: Art, Literature, Literary Criticism, Essays, Poetry
ISBN Prefix(es): 0-9505188
Total Titles: 7 Print
Parent Company: Berw Cyf

Plantin Publishers, *imprint of* Cardiff Academic Press

Plantin Publishers+
St Fagans Rd, Fairwater, Cardiff CF5 3AE
Tel: (029) 2056 0333 *Fax:* (029) 2055 4909
E-mail: drakegroup@btinternet.com
Web Site: www.drakeed.com/cap
Key Personnel
Man Dir: R G Drake
Founded: 1987
Specialize in publishing re-prints of out-of-print titles, usually out-of-copyright.
Subjects: Biography, Literature, Literary Criticism, Essays
Parent Company: Cardiff Academic Press

Platform 5 Publishing Ltd
3 Wyvern House, Sark Rd, Sheffield S2 4HG
Tel: (0114) 255 8000 *Fax:* (0114) 255 2471
E-mail: platform5@platfive.freeserve.co.uk
Key Personnel
Publisher & Editor-in-Chief: Peter Fox
Editor: David Haydock
Founded: 1984
Subjects: Transportation
ISBN Prefix(es): 0-906579; 1-872524; 1-902336
Distributor for Quail Map Co (UK, except South of England); South Coast Transport Publishing

The Playwrights Publishing Co
70 Nottingham Rd, Burton Joyce, Notts NG14 5AL
Tel: (01159) 313356
E-mail: playwrightspublishingco@yahoo.com
Web Site: www.geocities.com/playwrightspublishingco
Key Personnel
Dir: Liz Breeze; Tony Breeze
Founded: 1990
Publisher of one-act & full length plays.
Subjects: Drama, Theater
ISBN Prefix(es): 1-873130
Number of titles published annually: 12 Print; 12 E-Book
Total Titles: 45 Print; 12 E-Book

Plexus Publishing Ltd+
55a Clapham Common Southside, London SW4 9BX
Tel: (020) 7622 2440 *Fax:* (020) 7622 2441
E-mail: info@plexusuk.demon.co.uk
Web Site: www.plexusbooks.com
Key Personnel
Sales, Production: Terence Porter
Editorial, Rights & Permissions: Sandra Wake
Coordinator Editor: Rebecca Martin
Founded: 1973
Publish illustrated nonfiction books specializing in international co-editions with an emphasis on biography, popular music, rock 'n' roll, popular culture, art, photography & cinema.
Subjects: Biography, Drama, Theater, Fashion, Film, Video, Music, Dance, Photography, Radio, TV
ISBN Prefix(es): 0-85965
Number of titles published annually: 15 Print
Total Titles: 100 Print
Distributed by Publishers Group West (USA & Canada)
Warehouse: Bookpoint Ltd, 39 Milton Park, Abingdon, Oxon OX14 4TD *Tel:* (01235) 400 400 *Fax:* (01235) 832 068
Orders to: Bookpoint Ltd, 39 Milton Park, Abingdon, Oxon OX14 4TD *Tel:* (01235) 400 400 *Fax:* (01235) 832 068
Publishers Group West, 1700 Fourth St, Berkeley, CA 94710, United States *Tel:* 510-528-1444 *Fax:* 510-528-3444

Plough Publishing House of Bruderhof Communities in the UK+
Darvell Bruderhof, Robertsbridge, East Sussex TN32 5DR
Tel: (01580) 883 344 *Fax:* (01580) 883 317
Toll Free Fax: 800-018-3347
E-mail: contact@bruderhof.com
Web Site: www.plough.com
Key Personnel
Man Dir, Rights & Permissions: Josef Ben Eliezer
Sales, Publicity & Advertising Dir: Stefan Tietze
Founded: 1937
Firm is the Publishing House of the Bruderhof Communities in the UK.
Subjects: Fiction, Poetry, Religion - Other, Self-Help, Theology

Pluto Books Ltd+
345 Archway Rd, London N6 5AA
Tel: (020) 8348 2724 *Fax:* (020) 8348 9133
E-mail: pluto@plutobks.demon.co.uk
Web Site: www.plutobooks.com
Key Personnel
President: Roger van Zwanenberg
E-mail: rogervz@plutobooks.com
Editorial Dir: Anne Beech *E-mail:* beech@plutobooks.com
Sales Dir: Simon Liebesny *E-mail:* simon@plutobooks.com
Founded: 1987
Subjects: African American Studies, Anthropology, Developing Countries, Economics, Government, Political Science, History, Social Sciences, Sociology
ISBN Prefix(es): 0-7452
Number of titles published annually: 80 Print; 80 Online; 80 E-Book
Total Titles: 450 Print; 250 Online; 250 E-Book
Imprints: Pluto Press
Distributed by University of Michigan Press
Distributor for Autonomedia; Ocean Press; Paradigm; South End Press
Shipping Address: Chicago Distribution Center, 11030 S Langley Ave, Chicago, IL 60628, United States
Warehouse: Chicago Distribution Center, 11030 S Langley Ave, Chicago, IL 60628, United States
Distribution Center: Chicago Distribution Center, 11030 S Langley Ave, Chicago, IL 60628, United States
Orders to: Chicago Distribution Center, 11030 S Langley Ave, Chicago, IL 60628, United States
Returns: Chicago Distribution Center, 11030 S Langley Ave, Chicago, IL 60628, United States

Pluto Press, *imprint of* Pluto Books Ltd

Pluto Press+
Imprint of Pluto Books Ltd
345 Archway Rd, London N6 5AA
Tel: (020) 8348 2724 *Fax:* (020) 8348 9133
E-mail: pluto@plutobooks.com
Web Site: www.plutobooks.com
Key Personnel
Man Dir: Roger van Zwanenberg
Editorial Dir: Anne Beech
Managing Editor: Robert Webb
Head, Sales & Marketing: Simon Liebesny
Tel: (020) 8374 2188 *E-mail:* simon@plutobooks.com
Founded: 1970
Independent progressive publishing.
Subjects: African American Studies, Anthropology, Biography, Criminology, Developing Countries, Economics, Environmental Studies, Ethnicity, Government, Political Science, History, Journalism, Labor, Industrial Relations, Law, Philosophy, Social Sciences, Sociology, Women's Studies
ISBN Prefix(es): 0-85305; 0-86104; 0-7453; 0-902818; 0-904383
Number of titles published annually: 80 Print
Total Titles: 500 Print
Associate Companies: Journeyman Press
Distributed by Book Promotions/Horizon Books (South Africa); Footprint Books (Australia); Taylor & Francis Asia Pacific (Far East (excluding Japan)); UBC Press, University of British Columbia (Canada); United Publishers Services Ltd (Japan); University of Michigan Press (USA)
Distributor for Autonomedia Publishers; Ocean Press; Paradigm Publishers; South End Press
Foreign Rep(s): Durnell Marketing (Europe); IPR Publishers Representatives (Middle East); Maya Publishers Pvt Ltd (India); Vera Medeiros Book Business International (Latin America)
Distribution Center: University of Michigan Press, c/o Chicago Distribution Center, 11030 S Langley Ave, Chicago, IL 60628, United States *E-mail:* custserv@press.uchicago.edu
Orders to: ITPS, Cheriton House, North Way, Andover, Hants SP10 5BE *Tel:* (01264) 342832 *Fax:* (01264) 342788 *E-mail:* pluto@thomsonpublishingservices.co.uk

Pocket Bears, *imprint of* Moonlight Publishing Ltd

Pocket Biographies, *imprint of* Sutton Publishing Ltd

Pocket Books, *imprint of* Simon & Schuster Ltd

Pocket Classics, *imprint of* Sutton Publishing Ltd

Pocket ColorCards, *imprint of* Speechmark Publishing Ltd

Pocket Histories, *imprint of* Sutton Publishing Ltd

Pocket Worlds, *imprint of* Moonlight Publishing Ltd

Poetica, *imprint of* Anvil Press Poetry Ltd

Point, *imprint of* Scholastic Ltd

Police Review Publishing Company Ltd
5th Foor, Celcon House, 289-293 High Holborn, London WC1V 7HZ
Tel: (020) 7440 4700 *Fax:* (020) 7405 7167; (020) 7405 7163
Key Personnel
Publisher: Fabiana Angelini *E-mail:* fabiana.angelini@policereview.co.uk
Man Dir: Alfred Rolington
Founded: 1893
Subjects: Criminology, Law
ISBN Prefix(es): 0-7106; 0-309; 0-85164
Parent Company: The Thomson Corporation
Associate Companies: Jane's Information Group, 1340 Braddock Pl, Suite 300, Alexandria, VA 22314-1651, United States *Tel:* 703-683-3700 *Fax:* 703-836-1593

The Policy Press+
University of Bristol, Beacon House, 4th floor, Queen's Rd, Bristol BS8 1QU
Tel: (0117) 331 4054 *Fax:* (0117) 331 4093
E-mail: tpp-info@bristol.ac.uk
Web Site: www.policypress.org.uk
Key Personnel
Publishing Dir: Alison Shaw *Tel:* (0117) 331 4085 *E-mail:* ali.shaw@bristol.ac.uk
Marketing & Sales Manager: Julia Mortimer *Tel:* (0117) 331 4098 *E-mail:* julia.mortimer@bristol.ac.uk
Editorial Manager: Dawn Louise Rushen *Tel:* (0117) 331 4094 *E-mail:* dawn.l.rushen@bristol.ac.uk
Founded: 1996
A specialist policy studies publisher, publishing books, journals, reports & guides from leading academics & researchers. Publications provide the latest research in accessible formats, reaching those who formulate or implement policy at executive & grass-roots levels, as well as academics & students.
Subjects: Civil Engineering, Disability, Special Needs, Economics, Education, Ethnicity, Geography, Geology, Government, Political Science, Health, Nutrition, Labor, Industrial Relations, Management, Public Administration, Social Sciences, Sociology, Women's Studies
ISBN Prefix(es): 0-86922; 1-86134; 1-873575
Associate Companies: The Joseph Rowntree Foundation
Orders to: DA Information Services, 648 Whitehorse Rd, Mitcham, Victoria 3132, Australia *Tel:* (03) 9210 7777 *Fax:* (03) 9210 7788 *E-mail:* service@dadirect.com.au (Australia, New Zealand & Papua New Guinea)
ISBS (International Specialised Book Services), 5824 NE Hassals St, Portland, OR 97213-3644, United States *Fax:* 503-280-8832 *E-mail:* orders@isbs.com *Web Site:* www.isbs.com

Marston Book Services, PO Box 269, Abingdon, Oxon OX14 4YN *Tel:* (01235) 465500 *Fax:* (01235) 465556 *E-mail:* direct.orders@marston.co.uk
Unifacmanu Trading Co Ltd, 4F, 91, Ho-Ping East Rd Section 1, Taipei, Taiwan, Province of China

Policy Studies Institute (PSI)
Subsidiary of University of Westminster
100 Park Village E, London NW1 3SR
Tel: (020) 7468 0468 *Fax:* (020) 7388 0914
E-mail: website@psi.org.uk
Web Site: www.psi.org.uk
Key Personnel
Dir: Prof Jim Skea *E-mail:* j.skea@psi.org.uk
Founded: 1978
Subjects: Art, Business, Economics, Education, Environmental Studies, Government, Political Science, Labor, Industrial Relations, Public Administration, Social Sciences, Sociology
ISBN Prefix(es): 0-85374; 0-9503317
Orders to: BEBC Ltd, PO Box 1496, Poole, Dorset BH12 3YD

Polity Press, see Blackwell Publishing Ltd

Polo Publishing+
30 Chichester Close, Hampton, Middlesex TW12 3QJ
Tel: (020) 8783 1903 *Fax:* (020) 8979 9425
Key Personnel
Contact: Alan Symons
Subjects: History, Religion - Jewish
ISBN Prefix(es): 0-9523751
Distributed by Seven Hills

Polybooks Ltd+
2 Caversham St, London SW3 4AH
Tel: (020) 7351 4995 *Fax:* (020) 7351 4995
Key Personnel
Managing Editor: James Hughes
Founded: 1964
Book publishers.
Subjects: Art, Biography, Communications, Erotica, Fiction, History, Literature, Literary Criticism, Essays, Nonfiction (General), Wine & Spirits
ISBN Prefix(es): 0-284
Total Titles: 20 Print
Parent Company: Charles Skilton Publishers
Associate Companies: Christchurch Publishers Ltd; Luxor Press

Polygon, *imprint of* Birlinn Ltd

Polygon+
Imprint of Birlinn Ltd
West Newington House, 10 Newington Rd, Edinburgh EH9 1QS
Tel: (0131) 668 4371 *Fax:* (0131) 668 4466
E-mail: info@birlinn.co.uk
Web Site: www.birlinn.co.uk
Key Personnel
Man Dir & International Rights: Hugh Andrew
Founded: 1969
Publisher.
Subjects: Drama, Theater, Fiction, Film, Video, History, Humor, Literature, Literary Criticism, Essays, Music, Dance, Nonfiction (General), Philosophy, Poetry, Women's Studies
ISBN Prefix(es): 0-7486
Total Titles: 100 Print
Warehouse: Scottish Book Source, 32 Finlas St, Glasgow G22 5DU
Orders to: 137 Dundee St, Edinburgh *Tel:* (0131) 229 6800 *Fax:* (0131) 229 9070

Polytantric Press, *imprint of* Jay Landesman

Pomegranate Europe Ltd
Unit 1 Heathcote Business Centre, Hurlbutt Rd, Warwick, Warwicks CV34 6TD
Tel: (01926) 430111 *Fax:* (01926) 430888
E-mail: sales@pomeurope.co.uk; isb@pomeurope.co.uk
Web Site: www.pomegranate.com
Key Personnel
Sales Dir: Ms Ley Bricknell
Founded: 1985
Also acts as distributor of books, calendars, cards, postcards, posters & social stationery throughout Europe.
Subjects: Architecture & Interior Design, Art, Astrology, Occult, Environmental Studies, Ethnicity, Photography, Women's Studies
ISBN Prefix(es): 1-56640; 1-85257

Pont Books, *imprint of* Gomer Press (J D Lewis & Sons Ltd)

Pookie Productions Ltd+
PO Box 27018, Edinburgh EH10 5YU
Tel: (0131) 221868 *Fax:* (0131) 221868
Key Personnel
Author & Dir: Ivy Wallace
Man Dir & International Rights: Heather Bonning; Cherry Hope
Founded: 1994
Licensing agent & copyright holders specializing in the work of Ivy Wallace, author & illustrator of the Pookie series & the Animal Shelf series.
Subjects: Fiction
ISBN Prefix(es): 1-872885
Distributed by Scholastic (Australia, New Zealand, Papua New Guinea); Verbatim Distributors (South Africa)
Orders to: Biblios Publishers Distribution Services, Star Rd, Partridge Green, West Sussex RH13 8LD

Popular Woodworking, *imprint of* David & Charles Ltd

David Porteous Editions+
PO Box 5, Chudleigh, Newton Abbot TQ13 0YZ
Tel: (01626) 853310 *Fax:* (01626) 853663
E-mail: sales@davidporteous.com
Web Site: www.davidporteous.com
Key Personnel
Publisher: David Porteous
Founded: 1992
Subjects: Art, Crafts, Games, Hobbies, How-to
ISBN Prefix(es): 1-870586
Total Titles: 18 Print
Distributed by Keith Ainsworth Pty Ltd (Australia); Everybody's Books CC (Republic of South Africa); Forrester Books NZ Ltd (New Zealand); Vanwell Publishing Ltd (Canada)
Warehouse: Parkwest Publications Inc, 451 Communipaw Ave, Jersey City, NJ 07304, United States *Tel:* 201-432-3257 *Fax:* 201-432-3708 *E-mail:* parkwest@parkwestpubs.com *Web Site:* www.parkwestpubs.com
Orders to: Parkwest Publications Inc, 451 Communipaw Ave, Jersey City, NJ 07304, United States *Tel:* 201-432-3257 *Fax:* 201-432-3708 *E-mail:* parkwest@parkwestpubs.com *Web Site:* www.parkwestpubs.com
Membership(s): IPG

Porthill Publishers
36 West Way, Edgware, Middlesex HA8 9LB
Mailing Address: PO Box 311, Edgware, Middlesex HA9 9EA
Tel: (020) 89586783 *Fax:* (020) 89054516
Key Personnel
Publisher: Mr Radomir Putnikovich
Membership(s): British Publishers Association.
Subjects: Art, History, The History of Serbian Culture

ISBN Prefix(es): 1-870732
Foreign Rep(s): Aleksandar Gacic (USA)

Portland Press Ltd+
59 Portland Pl, London W1B 1QW
Tel: (020) 7637 5873 *Fax:* (020) 7323 1136
E-mail: editorial@portlandpress.com
Web Site: www.portlandpress.com
Key Personnel
Man Dir: Rhonda Oliver
Dir, Marketing & Customer Service: Adam Marshall *E-mail:* adam.marshall@portlandpress.com
Founded: 1990
Membership(s): ALPSP & UKSG.
Subjects: Biological Sciences, Chemistry, Chemical Engineering, Health, Nutrition, Medicine, Nursing, Dentistry, Physical Sciences, Science (General), Biochemistry & Molecular Biology, school to research level
ISBN Prefix(es): 1-85578; 0-904498
Number of titles published annually: 5 Print
Total Titles: 112 Print; 3 Online; 3 Audio
Parent Company: The Biochemical Society
Imprints: Making Sense of Science
Branch Office(s)
Portland Customer Services, Commerce Way, Colchester CO2 8HP, Dir, Marketing & Customer Services: Adam Marshall *Tel:* (01206) 796351 *Fax:* (01206) 799331 *E-mail:* sales@portland-services.com *Web Site:* www.portland-services.com
Distributed by Affiliated East-West Press Pvt Ltd (India); DA Information Services (Australia, New Zealand & Papua New Guinea)
Distributor for Bioscientifica Ltd; Energy Institute; Information Today, Inc (Europe); International Water Association Publishing; Society for Endocrinology
Orders to: Portland Customer Services, Commerce Way, Colchester CO2 8HP *Tel:* 01206 796351 *Fax:* 01206 799331 *E-mail:* sales@portland-services.com *Web Site:* www.portland-services.com
Membership(s): IPG

T & AD Poyser Ltd, *imprint of* A & C Black Publishers Ltd

T & AD Poyser Ltd, *imprint of* Elsevier Ltd

PPL, *imprint of* Packard Publishing Ltd

PRC Publishing Ltd+
The Chrysalis Bldg, Bramley Rd, London W10 6SP
Tel: (020) 7700 7799 *Fax:* (020) 7700 0635
E-mail: info@chrysalisbooks.co.uk
Web Site: www.chrysalisbooks.co.uk/books/publisher/prc
Key Personnel
Man Dir: Joanne Messham *E-mail:* jmessham@chrysalisbooks.co.uk
Comissioning Editor: Martin Howard *E-mail:* mhoward@chrysalisbooks.co.uk
Group Sales & Marketing Dir: Richard Samson *Tel:* (020) 7314 1459 *Fax:* (020) 7314 1549 *E-mail:* rsamson@chrysalisbooks.co.uk
Dir of Marketing: Kate Wood *Tel:* (020) 7314 1496 *Fax:* (020) 7314 1594 *E-mail:* kwood@chrysalisbooks.co.uk
Permissions: Terry Forshaw *Tel:* (020) 7314 1607 *E-mail:* tforshaw@chrysalisbooks.co.uk
Founded: 1990
Subjects: Architecture & Interior Design, Art, Cookery, Crafts, Games, Hobbies, Gardening, Plants, How-to, Military Science, Music, Dance, Natural History, Nonfiction (General), Transportation, Wine & Spirits
ISBN Prefix(es): 1-85648
Parent Company: Chrysalis Books

Prentice Hall, *imprint of* Pearson Education Europe, Mideast & Africa

Prentice Hall Europe, *imprint of* Pearson Education Europe, Mideast & Africa

Prentice Hall Regents, *imprint of* Pearson Education Europe, Mideast & Africa

Mathew Price Ltd+
The Old Glove Factory, Bristol Rd, Sherborne, Dorset DT9 4HP
Tel: (01935) 816010 *Fax:* (01935) 816310
E-mail: mathewp@mathewprice.com
Web Site: www.mathewprice.com
Key Personnel
President: Mathew Price
Production Manager: Alis Pugh
Administration Manager: Sarah Newton
Founded: 1983
Subjects: Fiction, Nonfiction (General)
Number of titles published annually: 25 Print
Total Titles: 300 Print

Pride Publications, *imprint of* E J Morten (Publishers)

Prim-Ed Publishing UK Ltd
PO Box 2840, Coventry CV6 5ZY
Tel: (0870) 876 0151 *Fax:* (0870) 876 0152
E-mail: sales@prim-ed.com
Web Site: www.prim-ed.com
Key Personnel
Administration Manager: Joanne Turnbull
Contact: Seamus McGuinness
Subjects: Education, History, Language Arts, Linguistics, Mathematics, Religion - Other, Science (General), Specialize in Geography
Total Titles: 350 Print

Primary Source Microfilm, *imprint of* Thomson Gale

Primrose Hill Press Ltd+
Stratton Audley Park, Bicester OX27 9AB
Tel: (01869) 277 000 *Fax:* (01869) 277 820
Web Site: www.primrosehillpress.co.uk
Key Personnel
Dir: William Butler
Man Dir: Brian Hill *E-mail:* bhill@shpub.win-uk.net
Founded: 1997
Specialize in books dedicated to the art & artists of fine wood engraving.
Subjects: Animals, Pets, Art, Gardening, Plants, Poetry, Fine Wood Engraving
ISBN Prefix(es): 1-901648
Number of titles published annually: 10 Print
Total Titles: 28 Print

The Printed Head, *imprint of* Atlas Press

Prion, *imprint of* Andre Deutsch Ltd

Prion, *imprint of* Carlton Publishing Group

Prion, *imprint of* Prion Books Ltd

Prion Books Ltd+
Imperial Works, Perren St, London NW5 3ED
Tel: (020) 7482 4248 *Fax:* (020) 7482 4203
E-mail: books@prion.co.uk
Key Personnel
Man Dir: Barry Winkleman
Founded: 1980
Specialize in humor, food & drink, literary & historical reprints, cultural travel, health & nutrition.
ISBN Prefix(es): 1-85375
Number of titles published annually: 50 Print
Total Titles: 200 Print
Imprints: Prion
Distributed by Peter Hyde-Verbatim (South Africa); Peribo (Australia); South Pacific (New Zealand); Trafalgar Square (USA)
Shipping Address: Macmillan, Basingstoke, Hants RG21 6XS
Warehouse: Macmillan, Houndmills, Basingstoke, Hampshire RG21 6XS

Prion-Multimedia, see Prion Books Ltd

Prism Press Book Publishers Ltd+
Stanley House, 3 Fleets Lane, Poole BH15 3AJ
Tel: (01202) 665432 *Fax:* (01202) 666219
E-mail: orders@orcabookservices.co.uk
Key Personnel
Dir: Diana King; Julian King
Founded: 1974
Subjects: Astrology, Occult, Cookery, Environmental Studies, Government, Political Science, Philosophy, Self-Help, Technology, Wine & Spirits
ISBN Prefix(es): 0-904727; 0-907061; 1-85327
U.S. Office(s): Associated Publishers Group, 1501 County Hospital Rd, Nashville, TN 37218, United States
Orders to: Bailey Distribution Ltd, Units 1A/1B, Learoyd Rd, Mountfield Industrial Estate, New Romney, Kent TN28 8XU

Professional Book Supplies Ltd
8 Station Yard, Steventon, Abingdon, Oxford OX13 6RX
Tel: (01235) 861234 *Fax:* (01235) 861601
E-mail: probooks@aol.com
Key Personnel
Man Dir & Dir of Sales & Marketing: Christopher Smith
Production Dir: Lyn Simister
Founded: 1965
Also acts as Second Hand Law Dealers & Book Manufacturers.
Subjects: Accounting, Law
ISBN Prefix(es): 0-86205; 0-903486

Professional Engineering Publishing Ltd+
Northgate Ave, Bury St Edmunds, Suffolk IP32 6BW
Tel: (01284) 763277 *Fax:* (01284) 718692 (sales)
E-mail: orders@pepublishing.com
Web Site: www.pepublishing.com
Key Personnel
Publications Dir, Publishing & Information Systems: Allan Singleton
Books Publisher: Sheril Leich *E-mail:* sherill@pepublishing.com
Academic Dir: Peter Williams *E-mail:* peterw@pepublishing.com
Production: Mick Spencer *E-mail:* micks@pepublishing.com
Journals Publisher: Rosie Grimes
E-mail: rosieg@pepublishing.com
Founded: 1974
Book, journal & magazine publisher.
Membership(s): ALPSP; UKSG; NAG.
Subjects: Energy, Engineering (General), Management, Mechanical Engineering, Technology, Transportation
ISBN Prefix(es): 0-85298; 1-86058
Number of titles published annually: 60 Print; 2 CD-ROM; 14 Online
Total Titles: 300 Print; 2 CD-ROM; 14 Online
Parent Company: Institution of Mechanical Engineers
Imprints: MEP
U.S. Office(s): American Society of Mechanical Engineers, New York, NY, United States
Distributed by ASME (USA & Canada)
Distributor for ASME (Europe)

UNITED KINGDOM

Professional, Managerial & Healthcare Publications
PO Box 100, Chichester, West Sussex PO18 8HD
Tel: (01243) 576444 *Fax:* (01243) 576456
E-mail: admin@pmh.uk.com
Web Site: www.pmh.uk.com
Key Personnel
Editor & Publisher: Peter Harkness
Founded: 1994
Number of titles published annually: 4 Print
Total Titles: 2 CD-ROM

Profile Books Ltd+
58A Hatton Garden, London EC1N 8LX
Tel: (020) 7404 3001 *Fax:* (020) 7404 3003
E-mail: info@profilebooks.co.uk
Web Site: www.profilebooks.co.uk
Key Personnel
Publisher & Man Dir: Andrew Franklin *E-mail:* andrew.franklin@profilebooks.co.uk
Editorial Dir: Stephen Brough *E-mail:* stephen.brough@profilebooks.co.uk
Editorial & International Rights: Penny Daniel *E-mail:* penny.daniel@profilebooks.co.uk
Publicity & Marketing: Kate Griffin *E-mail:* kate.griffin@profilebooks.co.uk; Ruth Killick *E-mail:* ruth.killick@profilebooks.co.uk
Sales: Claire Beaumont *E-mail:* claire.beamont@profilebooks.co.uk
Direct Sales: Corinne Anyika
Founded: 1996
Subjects: Biography, Business, Criminology, Developing Countries, Economics, Environmental Studies, Ethnicity, Finance, History, Management, Marketing, Nonfiction (General), Psychology, Psychiatry, Social Sciences, Sociology, Travel, Current Affairs
ISBN Prefix(es): 1-86197
Divisions: The Economist Books
Distributor for The Economist Books
Foreign Rep(s): Allen & Unwin (Australia); APD Singapore Pte Ltd (Malaysia, Singapore, Thailand, Vietnam); Asia Publishers Services Ltd (China, Hong Kong, Korea, Philippines, Taiwan, Macao); Jonathan Bell Publishers Pty Ltd (South Africa); Andrew B Durnell (Europe); Faber & Faber (UK); PIM (Japan, Middle East); Renouf Publishing (Canada, USA); Repforce Ireland (Northern Ireland, Republic of Ireland); Viva Books Ltd (Bangladesh, India, Nepal, Pakistan, Sri Lanka)
Orders to: TBS Ltd, Frating Distribution Centre, Colchester Rd, Frating Green, Colchester CO7 7DW *Tel:* (01206) 256 000; (01206) 255 678 *Fax:* (01206) 255 930

ProQuest Information & Learning
Division of ProQuest Co
The Quorum, Barnwell Rd, Cambridge CB5 8SW
Tel: (01223) 215512 *Fax:* (01223) 215514
E-mail: marketing@proquest.co.uk
Web Site: www.proquest.co.uk
Key Personnel
Sales Dir: Sue Orchard
Man Dir: Tim Smartt
Subjects: Business, Economics, Electronics, Electrical Engineering, Management, Marketing, Music, Dance, Physics, Science (General), Social Sciences, Sociology
ISBN Prefix(es): 0-576

Proteus, *imprint of* Omnibus Press

PSI, see Policy Studies Institute (PSI)

PSP, *imprint of* BMJ Publishing Group

Psychological Corporation Ltd
32 Jamestown Rd, London NW1 7BY
Tel: (01) 865888188 *Fax:* (01) 865314348
E-mail: tpc@harcourt.com
Web Site: www.tpc-international.com
Key Personnel
Contact: Jessica Spencer
Founded: 1921
Subjects: Disability, Special Needs, Language Arts, Linguistics, Psychology, Psychiatry
ISBN Prefix(es): 0-7491
U.S. Office(s): 55 Academic Court, San Antonio, TX, United States
Orders to: Chinese Behavioural Science Corp, 9F-1, 206, Nan-Chuan Rd, Sec 2, Taipei 100 *Tel:* (08862) 2365 6349 *Fax:* (08862) 2365 0525 *E-mail:* cbsc@cm1.hinet.net
Dansk Psykologisk Forlag, Stockholmsgade 29, Copenhagen, Denmark *Tel:* 3538 1655 *Fax:* 3538 1665 *E-mail:* dk-psych@dpf.dk *Web Site:* www.dpf.dk

Psychology Press, *imprint of* Taylor & Francis

Publishing Training Centre at BookHouse+
45 E Hill, Wandsworth, London SW18 2QZ
Tel: (020) 8874 2718 *Fax:* (020) 8870 8985; (020) 7207 5915 (bookings)
E-mail: publishing.training@bookhouse.co.uk
Web Site: www.train4publishing.co.uk
Key Personnel
Chief Executive: Dag Smith; John Whitley
Courses Development Manager: Graham Smith
Founded: 1980
Act as co-publisher with UNESCO & is a member of ABPTOE.
Subjects: Career Development, Publishing & Book Trade Reference
ISBN Prefix(es): 0-907706

Puffin, *imprint of* The Penguin Group UK

Puffin Books, *imprint of* Penguin Books Ltd

QPI Books, *imprint of* Colour Library Direct

Quadrille Publishing Ltd+
Alhambra House, 27-31 Charing Cross Rd, 5th floor, London WC2H 0LS
Tel: (020) 7839 7117 *Fax:* (020) 7839 7118
Web Site: www.quadrille.co.uk
Key Personnel
Man Dir: Alison Cathie
International Sales Manager: Sabine Leon-Dufour
Founded: 1994
Subjects: Architecture & Interior Design, Astrology, Occult, Cookery, Crafts, Games, Hobbies, Gardening, Plants, Health, Nutrition, How-to, Wine & Spirits
Number of titles published annually: 35 Print
Total Titles: 150 Print

Quaker Books
Quaker Book Shop, Friends House, 173-177 Euston Rd, London NW1 2BJ
Tel: (020) 7663 1000 *Fax:* (020) 7663 1008; (020) 7663 1001 (orders)
E-mail: bookshop@quaker.org.uk
Web Site: www.quaker.org.uk
Key Personnel
Book Publishing: Peter Daniels *Tel:* (020) 7663 1099 *E-mail:* peterd@quaker.org.uk
Founded: 1882
Subjects: Religion - Other
ISBN Prefix(es): 0-85245
Parent Company: Religious Society of Friends

Qualum Publishing+
665 Finchley Rd, London NW2 2HN
Tel: (020) 7431 7171 *Fax:* (020) 7681 1316
E-mail: info@qualum.com
Web Site: www.qualum.com
Key Personnel
Contact: Jonathan Stoppi
Founded: 1993
Subjects: Education, Technology
ISBN Prefix(es): 1-899168
Number of titles published annually: 1 Print
Total Titles: 5 Print
Book Club(s): Independent Publishers Group

Quantum, *imprint of* Foulsham Publishers

Quartet Books Ltd+
Member of Namara Group
27 Goodge St, London W1T 2LD
Tel: (020) 7636 3992; (020) 7636 0968 *Fax:* (020) 7637 1866
E-mail: quartetbooks@easynet.co.uk
Key Personnel
Chairman: Naim Attallah
Man Dir: Jeremy Beale
Publishing Dir: Stella Kane
Editor: Zelfa Hourani; Chris Parker
Publicity: Arielle Gottlieb
Founded: 1972
Subjects: Biography, Fiction, History, Music, Dance, Philosophy
ISBN Prefix(es): 0-7043
Parent Company: Namara Ltd
Associate Companies: Robin Clark Ltd
Subsidiaries: Namara Publications
Distributed by Southern Publishers Group (New Zealand); Tower Books (Australia); Trinity Books (South Africa)
Warehouse: Plymbridge Distributors Ltd, Estover Rd, Plymouth, Devon PL6 7PZ *Tel:* (01752) 202300
Orders to: Plymbridge Distributors Ltd, Estover Rd, Plymouth, Devon PL6 7PZ *Tel:* (01752) 202300 *Fax:* (01752) 202333 *E-mail:* orders@plymbridge.com

Quarto Publishing plc+
The Old Brewery, 6 Blundell St, London N7 9BH
Tel: (020) 7700 6700 *Fax:* (020) 7700 4191
E-mail: quarto@quarto.com
Web Site: www.quarto.com
Key Personnel
Chairman & Chief Executive: Laurence F Orbach
Deputy Chief Executive: Robert J Morley
Publisher: Piers Spence *E-mail:* pierss@quarto.com
Founded: 1976
International co-editions publisher.
Subjects: Alternative, Animals, Pets, Antiques, Art, Astrology, Occult, Crafts, Games, Hobbies, Gardening, Plants, Health, Nutrition, House & Home, How-to, Natural History, Nonfiction (General), Outdoor Recreation, Self-Help, Gardening; Illustrated, How-To; Interior Design & Reference
Number of titles published annually: 50 Print
Total Titles: 5,000 Print
Parent Company: Quarto Group Inc, 276 Fifth Ave, Suite 206, New York, NY 10001, United States
Subsidiaries: Apple Press Ltd; The Artists & Illustrators Magazine Ltd; Quarto Children's Books; Quintet Publishing Ltd

Quartz Editions+
Premier House, 112 Station Rd, Edgware HA8 7BJ
Tel: (020) 8951 5656 *Fax:* (020) 8904 1200
E-mail: quartzeditions@btconnect.com
Key Personnel
Dir: Susan Pinkus
Founded: 1992
Packager & publisher of high-quality, illustrated titles for the international market.
Subjects: Education, Fiction, Nonfiction (General)
ISBN Prefix(es): 0-9534241

Que, *imprint of* Pearson Education Europe, Mideast & Africa

PUBLISHERS

UNITED KINGDOM

Que Education & Training, *imprint of* Pearson Education Europe, Mideast & Africa

Que Lycos Books, *imprint of* Pearson Education Europe, Mideast & Africa

Queen Anne Press+
Windmill Cottage, Mackerye End, Harpenden, Herts AL5 5DR
Tel: (01582) 715866 *Fax:* (01582) 715121
E-mail: queenanne@lenqap.demon.co.uk
Key Personnel
Chairman, Man Dir & Editorial Rights: Adrian Stephenson *E-mail:* stephenson@lennardqap.co.uk
Editor: Celia Kent
Founded: 1976
Specialize in sports.
Subjects: Sports, Athletics
ISBN Prefix(es): 1-85291
Total Titles: 40 Print
Parent Company: Lennard Associates
Imprints: Lennard Publishing
Divisions: Lennard Books
Warehouse: TBS Book Distribution, Colchester Rd, Frating Green, Colchester Essex CO7 7DW *Tel:* (01206) 255600 *Fax:* (01206) 255930
Orders to: Virgin Books, Thames Wharf Studios, Rainville Rd, London W6 9HT *Tel:* (020) 7386 3300 *Fax:* (020) 7386 3360

Quentin Books Ltd
10 Brook St, Wivenhoe, Colchester CO7 9DS
Tel: (01206) 825433; (01206) 825434
Fax: (01206) 822990
Key Personnel
Man Dir & International Rights: Mark Paterson *E-mail:* markpaterson@compuserve.com
Founded: 1978
Also acts as book packager.
Subjects: Geography, Geology, History, Regional Interests
ISBN Prefix(es): 0-947614
Associate Companies: Sigmund Freud Copyrights; Mark Paterson & Associates
Showroom(s): Alma St, Wivenhoe CO7 9BE
Bookshop(s): Alma St, Wivenhoe CO7 9BE

Quill, *imprint of* HarperCollins UK

Quiller Press, *imprint of* Quiller Publishing Ltd

Quiller Publishing Ltd+
Wykey House, Wykey, Shrewsbury SY4 1JA
Tel: (01939) 261616 *Fax:* (01939) 261606
E-mail: info@quillerbooks.com
Key Personnel
Man Dir, Editor & Rights & Permissions: Andrew Johnston
Founded: 2001
Specialize in sponsored books & adult nonfiction.
Subjects: Biography, Business, Cookery, History, House & Home, Humor, Nonfiction (General), Outdoor Recreation, Travel, Country Sports, Equestrian, Falconry, Fishing, Shooting
ISBN Prefix(es): 0-907621; 1-899163; 1-85310; 1-870948; 0-948253; 1-904057
Total Titles: 200 Print
Imprints: Quiller Press; Sportman's Press; Swan Hill Press
Distributed by Peribo Pty Ltd (Australia); Stackpole Books (USA)
Warehouse: Grantham Book Services, Isaac Newton Way, Alma Park Industrial Estate, Grantham, Lincs NG31 9SD *Tel:* (01476) 541080 *Fax:* (01476) 541061
Orders to: Grantham Book Services, Isaac Newton Way, Alma Park Industrial Estate, Grantham, Lincs NG31 9SD *Tel:* (01476) 541080 *Fax:* (01476) 541061

Quintessence Publishing Co Ltd+
Quintessence House, Grafton Rd, New Malden Surrey KT3 3AB
Tel: (020) 89496087 *Fax:* (020) 83361484
E-mail: info@quintpub.co.uk
Web Site: www.quintpub.co.uk
Key Personnel
Dir: Joyce Ronald
Managing Dir: Linda Johnson *E-mail:* ljohnson@quintpub.co.uk
Publishing Dir: Paul Smith *E-mail:* psmith@quintpub.co.uk
Customer Services: Andy Johnson *E-mail:* ajohnson@quintpub.co.uk; Christine McKittrick *E-mail:* cmckittrick@quintpub.co.uk
Marketing & Promotions: Susan Tralls *E-mail:* stralls@quintpub.co.uk
Founded: 1948
Subjects: Medicine, Nursing, Dentistry
ISBN Prefix(es): 0-86715; 1-85097; 4-87417
Parent Company: Quintessenz Verlag Berlin, Germany
Associate Companies: Quintessence Publishing Inc, IL, United States; Quintessence Publishing Co, Ltd, Tokyo, Japan

Quintet Publishing Ltd+
Division of Quarto Publishing PLC
The Fitzpatrick Bldg, 188-194 York Way, London N7 9QR
Tel: (020) 7700 2001 *Fax:* (020) 7700 5785
E-mail: quintet@quarto.com
Web Site: www.quarto.com
Key Personnel
Chairman & Chief Executive: Laurence F Orbach
Publishing Dir: Oliver Salzmann *E-mail:* olivers@quarto.com
Founded: 1984
Publishes co-edition books.
Subjects: Crafts, Games, Hobbies, Fashion, Gardening, Plants, Geography, Geology, Health, Nutrition, History, House & Home, How-to, Maritime, Military Science, Music, Dance, Mysteries, Natural History, Outdoor Recreation, Photography, Sports, Athletics, Technology, Transportation, Travel, Wine & Spirits
Number of titles published annually: 60 Print
Total Titles: 750 Print

RAC Publishing+
RAC House, Bartlett St, South Croydon, Surrey CR2 6XW
Mailing Address: PO Box 100, South Croydon, Surrey CR2 6XW
Tel: (020) 8686 0088 *Fax:* (020) 8688 2882
Key Personnel
Publisher: Lynne Elder *E-mail:* lynne@west-one.com
Founded: 1904
Publishers of guides, handbooks & maps for motorists & travelers.
Subjects: Automotive
ISBN Prefix(es): 0-86211; 0-902628
Parent Company: RAC Enterprises
Orders to: Bookpoint Ltd, 39 Milton Park, Abingdon, Oxon OX14 4TD

Radcliffe Medical Press Ltd+
18 Marcham Rd, Abingdon, Oxon OX14 1AA
Tel: (01235) 528820 *Fax:* (01235) 528830
E-mail: contact.us@radcliffemed.com
Web Site: www.radcliffe-oxford.com
Key Personnel
Man Dir: Andrew Bax
Editorial Dir: Gill Nineham
Financial Dir: Margaret McKeown
Editorial Manager: Jamie Etherington *E-mail:* jetherington@radcliffemed.com
Head of Marketing: Gregory Moxon
Founded: 1987
Subjects: Medicine, Nursing, Dentistry

ISBN Prefix(es): 1-870905; 1-85775
Total Titles: 300 Print; 2 CD-ROM

Ragged Bears Ltd+
Ragged Appleshaw, Andover, Hants SP11 9HX
Tel: (01264) 772269 *Fax:* (01264) 772391
E-mail: books@ragged-bears.co.uk
Web Site: www.ragged-bears.co.uk
Key Personnel
Man Dir: Pamela Shirley
Dir, Editorial & Rights: Henrietta Stickland
Founded: 1985
ISBN Prefix(es): 1-85714; 1-870817
Imprints: Spindlewood
Distributor for ACC - Children's Classics; Allen & Unwin Children's Books; b small Publishing; David Bennett Books; Children's Corner; Chronicle Books; Clunie Press; Era Publications; Gallery Children's Books; Key Porter Books; Lemniscaat; Lothian Books; Matthew Price Children's Books; Moonlight Publishing; North-South Books; Owl Man; R&S Books; Siphano Picture Books; Star Bright Books; Templar Publishing; Tundra Books; Upland Books; The Wordhouse
Warehouse: c/o The Trade Counter, The Airfield, Norwich Rd, Mendlesham, Suffolk IP14 5NA

Rainham Bookshop, see Meresborough Books Ltd

Ramakrishna Vedanta Centre
Blind Lane, Bourne End, Bucks SL8 5LG
Tel: (01628) 526464
E-mail: vedantauk@talk21.com
Web Site: www.ramakrishna.org; www.vedantauk.com
Key Personnel
Book Sales Manager: Tony Leong
Founded: 1948
Subjects: Philosophy, Religion - Hindu
ISBN Prefix(es): 0-902479; 0-7025

Ramboro Books Plc
10 Blenheim Court, Brewery Rd, London N7 9NT
Tel: (020) 7700 7444 *Fax:* (020) 7700 4552
E-mail: enquiries@ramboro.co.uk
Key Personnel
Chairman: John Needleman
International Sales Dir: Tim Finch *E-mail:* tfinch@chrysalisbooks.co.uk
US Sales Dir: Robin Cortie
Founded: 1964
Also remainder dealer, promotion publisher.
Subjects: Art, Cookery, History, Transportation
ISBN Prefix(es): 0-86288; 0-905694
Associate Companies: Greenwich Editions
Imprints: Greenwich Editions

Ramsay Head Press+
15 Gloucester Pl, Edinburgh EH3 6EE
Tel: (0131) 225 5646
E-mail: ramsayhead@btinternet.com
Key Personnel
Editorial Dir & International Rights: Conrad K Wilson
Contact: Christine Wilson
Founded: 1968
Membership(s): Scottish Publishers Association.
Subjects: Architecture & Interior Design, Art, Biography, Fiction, History, Literature, Literary Criticism, Essays, Poetry
ISBN Prefix(es): 0-902859; 1-873921
Total Titles: 24 Print

Random House UK Ltd+
Member of The Random House Group
Random House, 20 Vauxhall Bridge Rd, London SW1V 2SA
Tel: (020) 7840 8400 *Fax:* (020) 7233 8791

UNITED KINGDOM

E-mail: enquiries@randomhouse.co.uk
Web Site: www.randomhouse.co.uk
Key Personnel
Chief Executive: Gail Rebuck
Group Deputy Chairman, General Books Division: Simon Master
President, International Sales Division: Brian Davies
Man Dir, Ebury Special Books Division: Amelia Thorpe
Financial Dir: Anthony McConnell
Group Operations Dir: David Pemberton
Group Sales Dir: Mike Broderick
Man Dir, Century, Hutchinson & Arrow Books: Simon King
Group Marketing Dir: Caroline Michel
Group Production Dir: Stephen Esson
International Dir: Simon Littlewood
Founded: 1987
Subjects: Art, Astrology, Occult, Biography, Cookery, Fashion, Fiction, Government, Political Science, Health, Nutrition, Humor, Nonfiction (General), Philosophy, Poetry, Travel
ISBN Prefix(es): 1-85686; 0-7126
Imprints: Arrow; Audiobooks; Bodley Head CHildrens; Business Books; Jonathan Cape; Jonathan Cape Childrens; Century; Chatto & Windus; Ebury; Fodors; Harvill; William Heinemann; Hutchinson; Hutchinson Childrens; Julia Macrae; Methuen; Pimlico; Red Fox; Rider; Secker & Warburg; Vermilion; Vintage; Yellow Jersey Press
Orders to: The Book Service Ltd, TBS Distribution Centre, Colchester Rd, Frating Green, Colchester, Essex C07 7DW *Tel:* (01206) 255678

Ransom Publishing Ltd+
Rose Cottage, Howe Hill, Watlington, Oxon OX49 5HB
Tel: (01491) 613 711 *Fax:* (01491) 613 733
E-mail: ransom@ransom.co.uk
Web Site: www.ransom.co.uk
Key Personnel
Man Dir: Jenny Ertle *E-mail:* jenny@ransom.co.uk
Founded: 1995
Children's multimedia CD-ROM & book publisher.
Subjects: Geography, Geology, Language Arts, Linguistics, English Language
ISBN Prefix(es): 1-86398; 1-900127
Number of titles published annually: 20 Print; 8 CD-ROM
Total Titles: 70 Print; 40 CD-ROM

Rapra Technology Ltd+
Shawbury, Shrewsbury, Salop SY4 4NR
Tel: (01939) 250383 *Fax:* (01939) 251118
E-mail: publications@rapra.net
Web Site: www.rapra.net; www.polymer-books.com
Key Personnel
Chief Executive: Andrew Ward
Publications Sales & Marketing Business Manager: Dr Sarah Ward
Produces books, reports, databases relating to all aspects of rubber & plastics processes, products & properties.
Subjects: Automotive, Chemistry, Chemical Engineering, Science (General), Technology, Polymer Science & Technology
ISBN Prefix(es): 1-85957
Number of titles published annually: 25 Print; 10 Online
Total Titles: 300 Print

Rationalist Press Association
One Gower St, London WC1E 6HD
Tel: (020) 7436 1151 *Fax:* (020) 7079 3588
E-mail: info@rationalist.org.uk
Web Site: www.rationalist.org.uk

Key Personnel
Editor-in-Chief: Jim Herrick *E-mail:* jim.herrick@rationalist.org.uk
Editor: Frank Jordans
Business Manager: John Metcalf
Founded: 1899
Publisher of *New Humanist* bimonthly magazine.
Subjects: Literature, Literary Criticism, Essays, Philosophy, Psychology, Psychiatry, Religion - Other, Science (General), Social Sciences, Sociology, From a Humanist Perspective
ISBN Prefix(es): 0-301

Ravette Publishing Ltd+
Unit 3, Tristar Centre, Star Rd, Partridge Green, Horsham RH13 8RA
Tel: (01403) 711443 *Fax:* (01403) 711554
E-mail: ravettepub@aol.com
Key Personnel
Man Dir: Margaret Lamb
Founded: 1980
Subjects: Animals, Pets, Education, Environmental Studies, Fiction, Foreign Countries, Humor, Nonfiction (General), Self-Help
ISBN Prefix(es): 0-906710; 0-948456; 1-85304; 1-84161
Number of titles published annually: 40 Print
Total Titles: 167 Print
Distribution Center: Orca Book Services, Stanley House, 3 Fleets Lane, Poole, Dorset BH15 3AJ, Contact: Jill Caldicott *Tel:* (01202) 785738 *Fax:* (01202) 672076

Rayo, *imprint of* HarperCollins UK

RCGP, see Royal College of General Practitioners (RCGP)

Read-Along, *imprint of* BBC Audiobooks

The Reader's Digest Association Ltd
11 Westferry Circus, Canary Wharf, London E14 4HE
Tel: (020) 7715 8000 *Fax:* (020) 7715 8181
Web Site: www.readersdigest.co.uk
Telex: 264631
Key Personnel
Marketing Dir: Martin Pasteiner
General Books Editor: Noel Buchanan
Ad Editor: Cortina Butler
Subjects: Animals, Pets, Antiques, Archaeology, Architecture & Interior Design, Cookery, Crafts, Games, Hobbies, Earth Sciences, Fiction, Film, Video, Gardening, Plants, Health, Nutrition, House & Home, How-to, Mysteries, Nonfiction (General), Science (General), Travel
ISBN Prefix(es): 0-276
Parent Company: The Reader's Digest Association Inc, Pleasantville, NY 10570, United States

Reader's Digest Children's Books+
King's Court, Parsonage Lane, Bath BA1 1ER
Tel: (01225) 312200 *Fax:* (01225) 460942
Key Personnel
Contact: Jill Eade *E-mail:* eade@readersdigest.co.uk
Founded: 1981
Subjects: Education
ISBN Prefix(es): 1-85724; 1-84088; 0-907874
Parent Company: Readers Digest Inc
Imprints: Readers Digest Young Families
U.S. Office(s): Readers Digest Young Families, 355 Riverside Ave, Westport, CT 06880, United States
Shipping Address: Littlehampton Book Services, 10-14 Eldon Way, Lineside Estate, Littlehampton, West Sussex BN17 7HE

Readers Digest Young Families, *imprint of* Reader's Digest Children's Books

Reaktion Books Ltd+
79 Farringdon Rd, London EC1M 3JU
Tel: (020) 7404 9930 *Fax:* (020) 7404 9931
E-mail: info@reaktionbooks.co.uk
Web Site: www.reaktionbooks.co.uk
Key Personnel
Editorial Dir: Michael R Leaman
Publicity & Rights Dir: Maria Kilcoyne *E-mail:* maria@reaktionbooks.co.uk
Production Manager: Ken MacPherson
Sales Manager: David Hoek
Designer: Simon McFadden
Picture Researcher: Harry Gilonis
Founded: 1985
Specialize in nonfiction.
Subjects: Architecture & Interior Design, Art, Asian Studies, Film, Video, Geography, Geology, Government, Political Science, History, Language Arts, Linguistics, Literature, Literary Criticism, Essays, Nonfiction (General), Photography, Travel
ISBN Prefix(es): 0-948462; 1-86189
Number of titles published annually: 40 Print
Total Titles: 170 Print
U.S. Office(s): US Marketing Office, PO Box 976, North Kingstown, RI 02852, United States *Fax:* 401-885-7996
Foreign Rep(s): APD Singapore Pte Ltd (Brunei, Cambodia, Indonesia, Philippines, Singapore, Thailand, Vietnam); APD Singapore (Malaysia) Ltd (Malaysia); Applied Media (India); Richard Carman (Africa); Consortium Book Sales & Distribution Inc (Canada, USA); Consul Books (Netherlands); Michael Geoghegan (Belgium, France); Pernille Larson (Denmark, Finland, Iceland, Norway, Sweden); LCK Korea (Korea); Ewa Ledocowicz (Croatia, Czech Republic, Estonia, Hungary, Poland, Romania, Slovak Republic, Slovenia); Maruzen Company Ltd (Japan); Penny Padovani (Greece, Italy, Portugal, Spain); Stephan Phillip (Pty) Ltd (South Africa); PS Publishers' Services (Austria, Germany, Switzerland); Southern Publishers Group (New Zealand); Unifacmanu Trading Co (Taiwan); Unireps (Australia); United Publishers Services (Japan)
Warehouse: Grantham Book Services Ltd, Isaac Newton Way, Alma Park Industrial Estate, Grantham, Lincs NG31 9SD *Tel:* (01476) 541 080 *Fax:* (01476) 541 061 *E-mail:* orders@gbs.tbs-ltd.co.uk

Reardon Publishing+
56 Upper Norwood St, Leckhampton, Cheltenham, Glos GL53 0DU
Tel: (01242) 231800
E-mail: reardon@bigfoot.com
Web Site: www.reardon.co.uk; www.coltswoldbookshop.com (bookshop)
Founded: 1976
Subjects: Asian Studies, Foreign Countries, Chinese Culture in America, Cotswolds England, Cycling, Exploring Antarctica, Walking
ISBN Prefix(es): 0-950867; 1-873877
Number of titles published annually: 10 Print; 1 CD-ROM
Total Titles: 100 Print; 2 CD-ROM

Recollections, *imprint of* George Mann Publications

RED, *imprint of* Wilmington Business Information Ltd

Red Fox, *imprint of* Random House UK Ltd

RED Publishing, see Retail Entertainment Data Publishing Ltd

PUBLISHERS

Redcliffe Press Ltd+
81G Pembroke Road, Clifton, Bristol BS8 3EA
Tel: (0117) 9737207 *Fax:* (0117) 9238991
Key Personnel
Man Dir: John Sansom
Rights & Permissions & Sales: Angela Sansom
Editorial: Clara Sansom
Founded: 1976
Subjects: Art, Literature, Literary Criticism, Essays, Regional Interests
ISBN Prefix(es): 0-905459; 0-948265; 1-872971; 1-900178
Imprints: White Tree Books

Redstone Press+
7a St Lawrence Terrace, London W10 5SU
Tel: (020) 7352 1594 *Fax:* (020) 7352 8749
Web Site: www.redstonepress.co.uk
Key Personnel
Proprietor: Julian Rothenstein *E-mail:* jr@redstonepress.co.uk
Founded: 1987
Subjects: Art
ISBN Prefix(es): 1-870003
Associate Companies: Shambhala Publications (USA)
Subsidiaries: Shambhala Redstone Editions
Distributed by Central Books Ltd; Distribuciones Loring (Spain); Idea Books (Japan & Europe, excluding Spain); Bo Rudin (Scandinavia); Signature Books (UK)
Orders to: Central Books Ltd, 99 Wallis Rd, London E9 5LN *Tel:* (020) 8986 4854 *Fax:* (020) 8533 5821 *E-mail:* orders@centralbooks.com

Reed Business Information
Quadrant House, The Quadrant, Sutton, Surrey SM2 5AS
Tel: (020) 8652 3500 *Fax:* (01342) 335960
E-mail: webmaster@rbi.co.uk
Web Site: www.reedbusiness.com
Key Personnel
Chief Executive: Keith Jones
Chief Operating Officer: Mark Kelsey
Man Dir: James Blazeby; Neil Stiles; Sandy Whetton
Marketing Dir: Jane Burgess
Finance Dir: Carolyn Pickering
ISBN Prefix(es): 0-610; 0-611; 0-948056
Parent Company: Reed Elsevier plc, 25 Victoria St, London SW1H 0EX
Branch Office(s)
Quadrant House, The Quadrant, Sutton, Surrey SM2 5AS *Tel:* (020) 8652 3500 *Fax:* (020) 8652 8932
Statham House, Talbot Rd, Stretford, Manchester M32 OFP *Tel:* (0161) 877 6399 *Fax:* (0161) 877 6288
24, rue de Milan, Paris 75009, France *Tel:* (01) 55 95 95 13 *Fax:* (01) 55 95 95 15
U.S. Office(s): 3730 Kirby Drive, Suite 1030, Houston, TX 77098, United States *Tel:* 713-525-2600 *Fax:* 713-525-2659

Reed Educational & Professional Publishing+
Halley Court, Jordan Hill, Oxford OX2 8EJ
Tel: (01865) 311366 *Fax:* (01865) 314641
E-mail: reededucational@repp.co.uk
Web Site: www.repp.com
Key Personnel
Chief Executive: John Philbin
Finance Dir: Graham Shaw
Group Financial Controller: Michael Sheehy *Tel:* (01865) 314-230 *E-mail:* michael.sheehy@repp.co.uk
Subjects: Education, English as a Second Language
Parent Company: Reed Elsevier plc, 25 Victoria St, London SW1H 0EX
Associate Companies: Rigby Heinemann, Australia; Heinemann Educational, Botswana; Rigby Education, United States; Heinemann Publishers Ltd, South Africa; Greenwood Heinemann; Reed Publishing, New Zealand
Imprints: Butterworth Heinemann; Ginn & Company; Greenwood Heinemann; Heinemann Educational; Heinemann Library; Rigby; Rigby Heinemann; Heinemann/Ginn

Reed Elsevier Group plc
Affiliate of Reed Elsevier NV
25 Victoria St, London SW1H 0EX
Tel: (020) 7222 8420 *Fax:* (020) 7227 5799
Web Site: www.reed-elsevier.com
Key Personnel
Chief Executive Officer: Crispin Davis
Chief Financial Officer: Mark Armour
Corporate headquarters, jointly owned by Reed Elsevier plc, London, UK & Reed Elsevier NV, Amsterdam, Netherlands.

Thomas Reed, *imprint of* A & C Black Publishers Ltd

William Reed Directories+
Broadfield Park, Crawley, West Sussex RH11 9RT
Tel: (01293) 613 400 *Fax:* (01293) 610 322
E-mail: directories@william-reed.co.uk
Web Site: www.william-reed.co.uk
Key Personnel
Man Dir: Mark de Lange *E-mail:* mark.delange@william-reed.co.uk
Editorial Manager: Sulann Staniford *E-mail:* sulann.staniford@william-reed.co.uk
Group Sales Manager: Simon Hughes
Marketing Executive: Tracy Larner *E-mail:* tracy.larner@william-reed.co.uk
Founded: 1991
Membership(s): DPA.
Subjects: Business, Catering, Food & Drink
ISBN Prefix(es): 0-901595
Parent Company: William Reed Publishing Ltd
Associate Companies: Knowledge Store; William Reed International

ReganBooks, *imprint of* HarperCollins UK

Regency House Publishing Ltd+
Niall House, Rear of 24-26 Boulton Rd, Stevenage, Herts SG1 4QX
Tel: (014383) 14488 *Fax:* (014383) 11303
E-mail: regencyhouse@btclick.com
Key Personnel
Man Dir: Nicolette Trodd
Publisher: Brian Trodd
Founded: 1992
Publisher & packager of mass-market nonfiction.
Subjects: Animals, Pets, Architecture & Interior Design, Art, Automotive, Cookery, Crafts, Games, Hobbies, Nonfiction (General), Photography, Poetry, Regional Interests, Transportation
ISBN Prefix(es): 1-85361
Parent Company: Grange Books PLC

Regency Press CP Ltd
Gordon House, Lissenden Gardens, London NW5 1LX
Tel: (020) 7404 4882 *Fax:* (020) 7404 4885
E-mail: info@regency.org
Web Site: www.regency.org
Key Personnel
Contact: Cristina Paiva *Tel:* (020) 7468 0220 *E-mail:* cp@regency.org
Founded: 1990
Publications intended for developing controls & emerging markets. Specialize in human rights, world health, poverty reduction & racial equality; books for refugees & helping children.
Subjects: Environmental Studies
ISBN Prefix(es): 0-9532905

UNITED KINGDOM

Number of titles published annually: 10 Print; 1 CD-ROM; 5 Online; 5 E-Book; 1 Audio
Total Titles: 40 Print; 1 CD-ROM; 30 Online; 6 E-Book; 1 Audio
Subsidiaries: The Regency Corporation Ltd
Branch Office(s)
Rua Frei Caneca 91 cj 42, 01307-001 Sao Paulo-SP, Brazil *Tel:* (011) 3259 9233 *Fax:* (011) 3259 9233 *E-mail:* info@telecentros.org.br *Web Site:* www.telecentros.org.br

Regnum, *imprint of* Paternoster Publishing

RELATE
Herbert Gray College, Little Church St, Rugby, Warwicks CV21 3AP
Tel: (01788) 573241 *Fax:* (01788) 535007
E-mail: enquires@relate.org.uk
Web Site: www.relate.org.uk
Key Personnel
Chief Executive: Sarah Bowler
Head of Publications: Suzy Powling
Founded: 1938
Subjects: Human Relations, Psychology, Psychiatry, Social Sciences, Sociology
ISBN Prefix(es): 0-85351

Religious & Moral Education Press, *imprint of* Hymns Ancient & Modern Ltd

Religious & Moral Education Press (RMEP), *imprint of* SCM-Canterbury Press Ltd

Renaissance Books, *imprint of* Global Oriental Ltd

Research Studies Press Ltd (RSP)+
Imprint of Institute of Physics Publishing
16 Coach House Cloisters, 10 Hitchin St, Baldock, Herts SG7 6AE
Tel: (01462) 895060 *Fax:* (01462) 892546
E-mail: info@research-studies-press.co.uk
Web Site: www.research-studies-press.co.uk
Key Personnel
Publisher: William G Askew
Publishing Dir: Caroline Holmes
Man Dir: Stephen Holmes *E-mail:* stephen@rspltd.demon.co.uk
Founded: 1983
Subjects: Automotive, Biological Sciences, Chemistry, Chemical Engineering, Civil Engineering, Communications, Computer Science, Electronics, Electrical Engineering, Energy, Engineering (General), Mathematics, Mechanical Engineering, Microcomputers, Military Science, Technology, Transportation, Botany, Forestry
ISBN Prefix(es): 0-86380
Number of titles published annually: 15 Print; 15 CD-ROM; 50 Online; 50 E-Book
Total Titles: 100 Print; 50 CD-ROM
Foreign Rep(s): Amin Al-abini (Middle East); Book Marketing Services (India); DA Information Services (Australia, New Zealand, Papua New Guinea); Durnell Marketing (Austria, Belgium, Denmark, Netherlands, Ireland, Finland, France, Germany, Greece, Iceland, Italy, Norway & Sweden, Spain & Portugal, Switzerland, UK & Europe); Eastern Book Service Inc (Japan); Humphrys Roberts Associates (Mexico & South & Central America); Macmillan (China) Ltd (China); Pak Book Corporation (Pakistan); Princeton Selling Group (USA); TransQuest Asia Publishers (Hong Kong, Malaysia, Taiwan, Thailand); TransQuest Publishers Pte Ltd (Brunei, Cambodia, Indonesia, Laos, Myanmar, Philippines, Singapore, Vietnam)
Orders to: AIDC, 50 Winter Sport Lane, PO Box 20, Williston, VT 05495, United States *Tel:* 802-862-0095 *Fax:* 802-864-7626 *E-mail:* orders@aidcvt.com (North America)

Marston Book Services Ltd, PO Box 269, Abingdon, Oxon OX14 4YN *Tel:* (01235) 465 500 *Fax:* (01235) 465 555 *E-mail:* direct.order@marston.co.uk (Worldwide (excluding North America))
Membership(s): IPG

Research Studies Press Ltd (RSP), *imprint of* Institute of Physics Publishing

Resurgence Books, *imprint of* Green Books Ltd

Retail Entertainment Data Publishing Ltd
Subsidiary of Wilmington Business Information Ltd
Paulton House, 8 Shepherdess Walk, London N1 7LB
Tel: (020) 7566 8216 *Fax:* (020) 7566 8259 (Inquiry); (020) 7566 8316 (Editorial)
E-mail: info@redpublishing.co.uk
Web Site: www.redpublishing.co.uk
Key Personnel
Publisher & Dir: Rory A Cornwell
Publisher: Doug Marshall *Tel:* (020) 7566 8261
    E-mail: dmarshall@redpublishing.co.uk
Editor: Matthew Garbutt
Sales Manager: Becca Bailey
Founded: 1971
Subjects: Music, Dance
ISBN Prefix(es): 0-904520; 1-900105
Bookshop(s): Music Sales, Newmarket Rd, Bury St Edmunds, Suffolk IP33 3YB

Review, *imprint of* Headline Book Publishing Ltd

Revival Publications, *imprint of* Islamic Foundation Publications

RIBA Publications+
Construction House, 56-64 Leonard St, London EC2A 4LT
Tel: (020) 7251 0791 *Fax:* (020) 7608 2375
Web Site: www.ribabookshop.com; www.ribac.co.uk
Key Personnel
Man Dir: Geoffrey Denner
Production Dir: M Stribbling
Editor: Mark Lane
Marketing Executive: Diane Williams
    E-mail: diane@ribabooks.com
Founded: 1967
Subjects: Architecture & Interior Design
ISBN Prefix(es): 0-900630; 0-947877; 1-85946
Parent Company: RIBA Companies Ltd, 66 Portland Place, London W1N 4AD
Associate Companies: RIBA Information Services National Building Specification
Bookshop(s): RIBA Bookshop, 66 Portland Place, London W1N 4AD

The Richmond Publishing Co Ltd+
PO Box 963, Slough SL2 3RS
Tel: (01753) 643104 *Fax:* (01753) 646553
E-mail: rpc@richmond.co.uk
Key Personnel
Man Dir: Mrs S J Davie
Founded: 1970
Subjects: Environmental Studies, Natural History
ISBN Prefix(es): 0-85546
Total Titles: 100 Print

RICS Books+
Surveyor Court, Westwood Business Park, Coventry CV4 8JE
Tel: (020) 7222 7000 (ext 698) *Fax:* (020) 7334 3851
E-mail: weborders@rics.org.uk
Web Site: www.ricsbooks.com

Key Personnel
Man Dir: Angela Hartland *E-mail:* ahartland@rics.org.uk
Customer Service Manager: Rita Sparrow *Tel:* (020) 7334 3868 *E-mail:* rsparrow@rics.org.uk
Managing Editor: Toni Gill *Tel:* (020) 7222 7000 (ext 686) *Fax:* (020) 7334 3840 *E-mail:* tgill@rics.org
Founded: 1981
Specialize in surveying, property, construction & environment
The Royal Institution of Chartered Surveyors (RICS).
Subjects: Architecture & Interior Design, Civil Engineering, Earth Sciences, Environmental Studies, Real Estate
ISBN Prefix(es): 0-85406
Parent Company: RICS Business Services Ltd, 12 Great George St, Westminster, London SW1P 3AD
Bookshop(s): 12 Great George St, Parliament Sq, London SW1P 3AD *Tel:* (020) 7334 3776 *Fax:* (020) 7222 9430 *E-mail:* bookshop@rics.org.uk

Rider, *imprint of* Random House UK Ltd

Rigby, *imprint of* Reed Educational & Professional Publishing

Rigby Heinemann, *imprint of* Reed Educational & Professional Publishing

Right Way Books, *imprint of* Elliot Right Way Books

Riverrun Press, *imprint of* Calder Publications Ltd

Rivers Oram Press+
144 Hemingford Rd, London N1 1DE
Tel: (020) 7607 0823 *Fax:* (020) 7609 2776
E-mail: ro@riversoram.demon.co.uk
Key Personnel
Publisher: Elizabeth Fidlom
Editorial Manager: Helen Armitage
Editor: Nicola Chalton
Administration: Margaret Brittain
Founded: 1990
Subjects: Anthropology, Biography, Child Care & Development, Fashion, Gay & Lesbian, Government, Political Science, History, Nonfiction (General), Psychology, Psychiatry, Women's Studies
ISBN Prefix(es): 0-86359; 1-85489
Number of titles published annually: 15 Print
Total Titles: 250 Print
Imprints: Pandora Press
Foreign Rep(s): ADDENDA Ltd (New Zealand); IPG (Independent Publishers Group) (Africa, Canada, Japan, South America, USA); UNIREPS (University & Reference Publishers' Services) (Australia)
Foreign Rights: Silvia Brunelli (Italy, Spain); Monica Heyum (Scandinavia); Asako Kawachi (Japan, Korea); Literarische Agentur Silke Weniger (Germany)
Shipping Address: Clipper Distribution, Windmill Grove, Portchester, Hants PO16 9HT *Tel:* (02392) 200080 *Fax:* (02392) 200090 *E-mail:* office@clipperdistribution.co.uk
Warehouse: Clipper Distribution, Windmill Grove, Portchester, Hants PO16 9HT *Tel:* (02392) 200080 *Fax:* (02392) 200090 *E-mail:* office@clipperdistribution.co.uk
Distribution Center: Clipper Distribution, Windmill Grove, Portchester, Hants PO16 9HT *Tel:* (02392) 200080 *Fax:* (02392) 200090 *E-mail:* office@clipperdistribution.co.uk

Orders to: Clipper Distribution, Windmill Grove, Portchester, Hants PO16 9HT *Tel:* (02392) 200080 *Fax:* (02392) 200090 *E-mail:* office@clipperdistribution.co.uk
Returns: Clipper Distribution, Windmill Grove, Portchester, Hants PO16 9HT *Tel:* (02392) 200080 *Fax:* (02392) 200090 *E-mail:* office@clipperdistribution.co.uk

Roadmaster Publishing
PO Box 176, Chatham, Kent ME5 9AQ
Tel: (01634) 862843 *Fax:* (01634) 201555
E-mail: susanwright@blueyonder.co.uk
Key Personnel
Contact: Malcolm Wright
Subjects: Automotive, Environmental Studies, Geography, Geology, History, Natural History, Regional Interests, Transportation

Robinson, *imprint of* Constable & Robinson Ltd

Robinson's Children, *imprint of* Constable & Robinson Ltd

The Robinswood Press Ltd
30 South Ave, Stourbridge, West Midlands DY8 3XY
Tel: (01384) 397475 *Fax:* (01384) 440443
E-mail: info@robinswoodpress.com
Web Site: www.robinswoodpress.com
Key Personnel
Man Dir: Christopher John Marshall
Founded: 1985
Subjects: Disability, Special Needs, Education, English as a Second Language, Fiction, Nonfiction (General)
Number of titles published annually: 12 Print
Total Titles: 12 Print

Robson Books+
Division of Chrysalis Group
The Chrysalis Bldg, Bramley Rd, London W10 6SP
Tel: (020) 7221 2213; (020) 7314 1469 (sales) *Fax:* (020) 7221 6455; (020) 7314 1594 (sales)
E-mail: robson@chrysalisbooks.co.uk
Web Site: www.chrysalisbooks.co.uk/books/publisher/robson
Key Personnel
Group Sales & Marketing Dir: Richard Samson *Tel:* (020) 7314 1459 *Fax:* (020) 7314 1549
    E-mail: rsamson@chrysalisbooks.co.uk
Dir of Marketing: Kate Wood *Tel:* (020) 7314 1496 *E-mail:* kwood@chrysalisbooks.co.uk
Marketing & Publicity Manager: Sharon Benjamin *Tel:* (020) 7314 1496
    E-mail: sbenjamin@chrysalisbooks.co.uk
Permissions: Terry Forshaw *Tel:* (020) 7314 1607
    E-mail: tforshaw@chrysalisbooks.co.uk
Founded: 1973
Subjects: Biography, Cookery, Government, Political Science, Humor, Military Science, Sports, Athletics, Travel
ISBN Prefix(es): 0-903895; 0-86051
Number of titles published annually: 75 Print
Total Titles: 800 Print
Orders to: HarperCollins Distribution, Campsie View, Westerhill Rd, Bishopbriggs, Glasgow G64 2QT *Fax:* (087) 0787 1995

George Ronald Publisher Ltd+
24 Gardiner Close, Abington, Oxon OX14 3YA
Tel: (01235) 529137
E-mail: sales@grbooks.com
Web Site: www.grbooks.com
Key Personnel
General Manager: Erica Leith *E-mail:* erica@grooks.com
Founded: 1947
Subjects: Religion - Other

ISBN Prefix(es): 0-85398
Branch Office(s)
8325 17 St North, St Petersburg, FL 33702, United States

Rooster Books Ltd
The Old Police Station, Priory Lane, Royston, Herts SG8 9DU
Tel: (01763) 242939 *Fax:* (01763) 243332
E-mail: rooster@solutions-for-business.co.uk
Web Site: www.solutions-for-books.co.uk/rooster
Key Personnel
Dir: Guy Garfit
Founded: 1978
Subjects: Business, Computer Science, Economics, Travel
ISBN Prefix(es): 1-871510
Number of titles published annually: 12 Print
Subsidiaries: Digital Colour Press; Solutions for Business

Rosendale Press Ltd+
8 Ponsonby Place, London SW1P 4PT
Tel: (020) 7834 1123 *Fax:* (020) 7834 1240
E-mail: info@rosendale.demon.co.uk
Key Personnel
Chairman: Timothy Green
Editorial Dir: Maureen Green *E-mail:* maureen@rosendale.demon.co.uk
Founded: 1987
Specialize in International co-editions.
Subjects: Cookery, Health, Nutrition, Human Relations, Self-Help
ISBN Prefix(es): 0-9509182; 1-872803
Warehouse: Littlehampton Book Services Ltd, 10-14 Eldon Way, Lineside Estate, Littlehampton, West Sussex BN17 7HE
Membership(s): IPG

RotoVision SA
Sheridan House, 112-116A Western Rd, Hove, East Sussex BN3 1DD
Tel: (01273) 727 268 *Fax:* (01273) 727 269
E-mail: sales@rotovision.com
Web Site: www.rotovision.com
Key Personnel
Chief Executive: Ken Fund *E-mail:* kenf@rotovision.com
Publisher: Aidan Walker *E-mail:* aidanw@rotovision.com
Founded: 1974
Subjects: Advertising, Architecture & Interior Design, Photography
ISBN Prefix(es): 2-88046

Rough Guides, *imprint of* The Penguin Group UK

Rough Guides Ltd+
Division of Penguin Books Ltd
80 Strand, London WC2R 0RL
Tel: (020) 7010 3000 *Fax:* (020) 7010 6767
E-mail: mail@roughguides.com
Web Site: www.roughguides.com
Key Personnel
Publisher: Mark Ellingham
Editorial Dir: Martin Dunford
Rights Dir: Richard Trillo
Founded: 1982
Specialize in worldwide travel guides for independently minded travelers, music & cultural reference books & maps.
Subjects: Developing Countries, Foreign Countries, Geography, Geology, History, Music, Dance, Outdoor Recreation, Travel
ISBN Prefix(es): 1-85828; 1-84353
Parent Company: Penguin Books
Ultimate Parent Company: Pearson
Branch Office(s)
345 Hudson St, 4th floor, New York, NY 10014, United States

Distributed by Penguin Companies
Orders to: Penguin Books Australia Ltd, 487 Maroondah Hwy, Ringwood, Victoria 3134, Australia
Penguin Books Canada Ltd, 10 Alcorn Ave, Siuite 300, Toronto, ON M4V 3B2, Canada
Viking Penguin USA, 375 Hudson St, New York, NY 10014-3657, United States

Roundhall Sweet & Maxwell, *imprint of* Sweet & Maxwell Ltd

Roundhouse, *imprint of* Roundhouse Group

Roundhouse Group
Millstone, Limers Lane, Northam, North Devon EX39 2RG
Tel: (01237) 474 474 *Fax:* (01237) 474 774
E-mail: roundhouse.group@ukgateway.net
Web Site: www.roundhouse.net
Key Personnel
President & Chief Executive: Alan T Goodworth
Founded: 1991
Distributor of small & medium publisher lists from the USA, Canada & Australia.
Also acts as agent & representative for English-language publishers. Full service representation & warehousing for publishers to UK, Europe, Middle East & Africa.
Subjects: Art, Asian Studies, Biography, Business, Cookery, Criminology, Drama, Theater, Erotica, Film, Video, Health, Nutrition, History, Language Arts, Linguistics, Literature, Literary Criticism, Essays, Medicine, Nursing, Dentistry, Music, Dance, Natural History, Philosophy, Photography, Psychology, Psychiatry, Radio, TV, Religion - Other, Self-Help, Social Sciences, Sociology, Sports, Athletics, Travel
ISBN Prefix(es): 1-85710
Parent Company: Roundhouse Publishing Ltd
Imprints: Pencil Press; Roundhouse
Subsidiaries: Pencil Press; Roundhouse Reference Books
Distributor for Allen & Unwin (Australia) (UK & Europe); Applause Cinema & Theatre Books (UK & Europe); Archipelago Press (selected titles); Bayeux Arts (UK & Europe); Carnot USA Books (UK & Europe); Chelsea House (UK & Europe); Creative Homeowner (UK & Europe); CSA Word Audio Books (UK & Europe); Editions Didier Millet (selected titles); Fairview Press (UK & Europe); Free Spirit Publishing (UK & Europe); Gambit Chess Books (UK & Europe); Ginkgo Press (UK & Europe); Global Exchange (UK & Europe); Gryphon House (UK & Europe); Hale & Iremonger (UK & Europe); Harcourt (selected titles); Hardie Grant Books (UK & Europe); Haworth Press (Selected titles); Home Planners (UK & Europe); Interlink Publishing (UK & Europe); Key Porter Books (UK & Europe); Listen & Live Audio (UK & Europe); Little Hills Press (UK & Europe); Lothian Books (UK & Europe); Mosaic Press (UK & Europe); Newmarket Press (UK & Europe); Paragon House (UK & Europe); Quality Medical Publishing (UK & Europe); RDR Books (UK & Europe); Roxbury Publishing (UK & Europe); Sarasota Press (UK & Europe); Scala/Riverside (UK & Ireland); Self-Counsel Press (UK & Europe); Seven Locks Press (UK & Europe); Sinclair-Stevenson (UK & Europe); Sourcebooks (UK & Europe); SPI Books (selected titles); Ulysses Travel Guides (UK & Europe); University Press of Mississippi (UK & Europe); Visible Ink (UK & Europe); Warwick Publishing (UK & Europe)
Shipping Address: Orca Book Services, Stanley House, Fleets Lane, Poole Dorset BH15 3AJ
Warehouse: Orca Book Services, Stanley House, Fleets Lane, Poole Dorset BH15 3AJ

Routledge, *imprint of* Taylor & Francis

Routledge+
Member of Taylor & Francis Group
11 New Fetter Lane, London EC4P 4EE
Tel: (020) 7583 9855 *Fax:* (020) 7842 2298
E-mail: info@routledge.co.uk
Web Site: www.routledge.com
Key Personnel
Chief Executive: A Selby
Publishing Dir: S Neil
IT: Tony Short
Founded: 1988
Represents the publishing interests & activities previously undertaken under the names of Routledge & Kegan Paul Ltd, Methuen Academic, Tavistock Publications Ltd, Croom Helm Ltd & Unwin Hyman Academic.
Subjects: Archaeology, Biography, Business, Communications, Developing Countries, Economics, Education, Film, Video, Geography, Geology, Government, Political Science, History, Language Arts, Linguistics, Law, Literature, Literary Criticism, Essays, Philosophy, Psychology, Psychiatry, Religion - Other, Social Sciences, Sociology, Women's Studies
ISBN Prefix(es): 0-415; 0-7448; 0-7099; 0-85664; 0-416; 0-85362; 0-422
Number of titles published annually: 1,000 Print
Total Titles: 7,000 Print
Imprints: Blueprint; Comedia
U.S. Office(s): 29 W 35th St, New York, NY 10001, United States *Tel:* 212-216-7800 *Fax:* 212-564-7854 *E-mail:* info@routledge-ny.com *Web Site:* www.routledge-ny.com
Orders to: Copp Clark, 2775 Matheson Blvd East, Mississauga, ON L4W 4P7, Canada
Taylor & Francis, 7625 Empire Dr, Florence, KY, United States *Tel:* 800-634-7064 *Fax:* 800-248-4724 *E-mail:* cserve@routledge-ny.com (US)
Taylor & Francis Customer Services, ITPS, Cheriton House, North Way, Andover, Hants SP10 5BE *Tel:* (01264) 343071 *Fax:* (01264) 343005 *E-mail:* book.orders@tandf.co.uk (UK, Europe & Asia)

RoutledgeCurzon, *imprint of* Taylor & Francis

RoutledgeCurzon
Member of Taylor & Francis Group
11 New Fetter Lane, London EC4P 4EE
Tel: (020) 7583 9855 *Fax:* (020) 7842 2298
E-mail: info@routledge.co.uk
Web Site: www.routledge.com
Key Personnel
Chairman: Malcolm Campbell
Dir: Martina Campbell
Marketing Executive: Digby Halsby
  E-mail: digby.halsby@tandf.co.uk
Senior Editor: Craig Fowlie *E-mail:* craig.fowlie@tandf.co.uk
Founded: 1970
Specialize in Asian & Middle Eastern studies.
Subjects: Anthropology, Asian Studies, Business, Developing Countries, Economics, Ethnicity, Foreign Countries, History, Language Arts, Linguistics, Philosophy, Regional Interests, Religion - Buddhist, Religion - Hindu, Religion - Islamic, Religion - Jewish, Religion - Other, Social Sciences, Sociology, Travel, Women's Studies
ISBN Prefix(es): 0-7007; 1-415
Number of titles published annually: 200 Print
Total Titles: 800 Print
Imprints: Caucasus World; Japan Library
U.S. Office(s): 29 W 35 St, New York, NY 10001, United States *Tel:* 212-216-7800 *Fax:* 212-564-7854 *Web Site:* www.routledge-ny.com
Distributed by Paul & Co (Canada & USA, Middle East titles only); University of Hawaii Press (Canada & USA except for Middle East titles)

UNITED KINGDOM

Distributor for Nordic Institute of Asian Studies (NIAS); University of Hawaii Press (UK, Europe, Africa, Middle East, South Asia)
Orders to: ITPS - International Thompson Publishing Service, Cheriton House, North Way, Andover, Hampshire SP10 5BE
Tel: (01264) 342 991 *Fax:* (01264) 364 418
E-mail: curzon@itps.co.uk

RoutledgeFalmer, *imprint of* Taylor & Francis

Joseph Rowntree Foundation
The Homestead, 40 Water End, York, North Yorks YO30 6WP
Tel: (01904) 629241 *Fax:* (01904) 620072
E-mail: julia.lewis@jrf.org.uk
Web Site: www.jrf.org.uk

Royal College of General Practitioners (RCGP)+
14 Princes Gate, Hyde Park, London SW7 1PU
Tel: (020) 7581 3232 *Fax:* (020) 7225 3047; (020) 7584 6716 (editorial)
E-mail: info@rcgp.org.uk
Web Site: www.rcgp.org.uk
Key Personnel
Publications Manager: Helen Farrelly
 E-mail: hfarrelly@rcgp.org.uk
Founded: 1952
Subjects: Education, Health, Nutrition, Medicine, Nursing, Dentistry, Psychology, Psychiatry
ISBN Prefix(es): 0-85084
Distributed by San Medrea (Spain)

Royal Genealogies, *imprint of* Stacey International

Royal Institute of International Affairs+
Chatham House, 10 St James's Sq, London SW1Y 4LE
Tel: (020) 7957 5700 *Fax:* (020) 7957 5710
E-mail: contact@riia.org
Web Site: www.riia.org
Key Personnel
Head, Publications: Margaret May *Tel:* (020) 7957 5704 *E-mail:* mmay@riia.org
Media Enquiries: Keith Burnet *Tel:* (020) 7314 2798 *E-mail:* kburnet@riia.org
Founded: 1920
Subjects: Asian Studies, Business, Developing Countries, Economics, Energy, Environmental Studies, Foreign Countries, Government, Political Science
ISBN Prefix(es): 0-905031; 1-86203
Imprints: Chatham House Papers; International Affairs; The World Today
U.S. Office(s): Cassell, PO Box 605, Herndon, VA 20172, United States
Chatham House Foundation, 16 Sutton Place 9/A, New York, NY 10022, United States, Contact: Richard W Murphy
Brookings Institution Press, 1775 Massachusetts Ave, NW, Washington, DC 20036, United States
Distributed by Brookings; Cambridge University Press; Cassell Academic; Oxford University Press; Routledge
Warehouse: Plymbridge Distributors Ltd, Plymbridge House, Estover Rd, Plymouth, Devon PL6 7PZ *Fax:* (01752) 202 3333
Orders to: Plymbridge Distributors Ltd, Plymbridge House, Estover Rd, Plymouth, Devon PL6 7PZ *Fax:* (01752) 202 3333

Royal Institution of Chartered Surveyors, see RICS Books

The Royal Society
6-9 Carlton House Terrace, London SW1Y 5AG
Tel: (020) 7839 5561 *Fax:* (020) 7930 2170
E-mail: info@royalsoc.ac.uk
Web Site: www.royalsoc.ac.uk
Key Personnel
President: Robert May
Executive Secretary: Stephen Cox
 E-mail: stephen.cox@royalsoc.ac.uk
Dir of Communications: Dr David Stewart Boak
 E-mail: david.boak@royalsoc.ac.uk
Head of Publishing: John Taylor *E-mail:* john.taylor@royalsoc.ac.uk
Founded: 1660
Subjects: Education, Energy, Engineering (General), Geography, Geology, Mathematics, Mechanical Engineering, Physical Sciences, Physics, Psychology, Psychiatry, Science (General)
ISBN Prefix(es): 0-85403

The Royal Society of Chemistry+
Burlington House, Piccadilly, London W1J 0BA
Tel: (020) 7437 8656 *Fax:* (020) 7437 8883
E-mail: sales@rsc.org
Web Site: www.rsc.org
Key Personnel
Head of Information Services: Robert Welham
Editorial, Books: Dr Robert Andrews
Editorial, Journals: Robert Parker
Editorial, Secondary Services: Sharon Bellard
Sales & Promotion: Barry Anderson; Jenny McCluskey
Production: John Futter
Founded: 1841
Subjects: Chemistry, Chemical Engineering, Engineering (General), Health, Nutrition, Mechanical Engineering
ISBN Prefix(es): 0-85186; 0-85404; 0-85990
Branch Office(s)
Thomas Graham House, Science Park, Milton Rd, Cambridge CB4 0WF *Tel:* (01223) 420066 *Fax:* (01223) 423623
Distributed by Springer-Verlag New York Inc (North America)
Orders to: Turpin Distribution Services Ltd, Blackhorse Rd, Letchworth, Herts SG6 1HN *Tel:* (01462) 672555 *Fax:* (01462) 480947

Royal Society of Medicine Press Ltd+
One Wimpole St, London W1G 0AE
Tel: (020) 7290 2921 *Fax:* (020) 7290 2929
E-mail: publishing@rsm.ac.uk
Web Site: www.rsmpress.co.uk
Key Personnel
Man Dir: Peter Richardson
Subjects: Medicine, Nursing, Dentistry
ISBN Prefix(es): 1-85315
Number of titles published annually: 35 Print; 1 E-Book
Total Titles: 500 Print; 1 E-Book
Distributed by Elsevier Australia (Australia, New Zealand & South Pacific); Panther Publishers (India); World Scientific Publishing Co (Japan, Korea & China)
Foreign Rep(s): Bernd Feldmann (Austria, Germany, Switzerland); Frans Janssen (Belgium, Netherlands, Luxembourg); Zoe Kaviani (Africa, Gulf States, Middle East); Jan Norbye (Denmark, Finland, Iceland, Norway, Sweden); Jim Osgerby (Southeast England exc London, Southern England); Judith Rushby (Scotland, Midlands, Northern England)
Distribution Center: Jamco Distribution Inc, 1401 Lakeway Drive, Lewisville, TX 75057, United States
Marston Book Services, PO Box 269, Abington, Oxon OX14 4YN (Europe & Middle East)

RSP, see Research Studies Press Ltd (RSP)

The Rubicon Press+
57 Cornwall Gardens, London SW7 4BE
Mailing Address: PO Box 147, Lytham St Annes, Lancs FY8 3WZ
Tel: (020) 7937 6813

Key Personnel
Partner: Juanita Homan; Robin A Page
 E-mail: robin.page@whsmithnet.co.uk
Founded: 1985
Specializing in Egyptology & English history.
Subjects: Antiques, Archaeology, Biography, Fiction, History, Literature, Literary Criticism, Essays, Travel, Women's Studies
ISBN Prefix(es): 0-948695
Book Club(s): Ancient & Medieval History Book Cl; Book Club Associates, Greater London House, Hampstead Rd, London NW1 7TZ, Contact: Michael Greenwood *Tel:* (020) 7760 6500 *Fax:* (020) 7760 6777; The History Guild
Membership(s): IPG

Michael Russell Publishing Ltd+
Wilby Hall, Wilby, Norwich NR16 2JP
Tel: (01953) 887776 *Fax:* (01953) 887762
Key Personnel
Man Dir: Michael Russell
 E-mail: michaelrussell@waitrose.com
Founded: 1976
Subjects: Nonfiction (General)
ISBN Prefix(es): 0-85955
Number of titles published annually: 15 Print
Total Titles: 135 Print

Rutherford House, *imprint of* Paternoster Publishing

The Rutland Press+
15 Rutland Sq, Edinburgh EH1 2BE
Tel: (0131) 229 7545 *Fax:* (0131) 228 2188
Web Site: www.rias.org.uk
Key Personnel
Sales & Marketing Manager: Eilidh Donaldson
Publishing Manager: Helen Leng *E-mail:* hleng@rias.org.uk
Publishing Coordinator: Susan Skinner
Founded: 1982
Subjects: Architecture & Interior Design, Travel
ISBN Prefix(es): 1-873190
Parent Company: Royal Incorporation of Architects in Scotland

Ryland Peters & Small Ltd+
Kirkman House, 12-14 Whitfield St, London W1T 2RP
Tel: (020) 7436 9090 *Fax:* (020) 7436 9790
E-mail: info@rps.co.uk
Web Site: www.rylandpeters.com
Key Personnel
Man Dir: David Peters
Rights Dir: Joanna Everard *E-mail:* joanna.everard@rps.co.uk
Art Dir: Gabriella Le Grazie
Publishing Dir: Alison Starling
Sales Manager: Jacqueline MacEachern
Founded: 1995
Publish high quality illustrated books for the international market.
Subjects: Architecture & Interior Design, Cookery, Gardening, Plants, Health, Nutrition, House & Home, Self-Help, Wine & Spirits, Lifestyle
ISBN Prefix(es): 1-84172
Number of titles published annually: 100 Print
Total Titles: 250 Print
Imprints: Paperstyle Gift Line
U.S. Office(s): Ryland Peters & Small Inc, 519 Broadway, 5th floor, New York, NY 10012, United States *Tel:* 646-613-8682; 646-613-8684; 646-613-8685 *Fax:* 646-613-8683 *E-mail:* info@rylandpeters.com
Warehouse: Macmillan Distribution Ltd, Brunel Rd, Houndmills, Basingstoke, Hants RG21 6XS *Tel:* (01256) 329 242 *Fax:* (01256) 327 961 *E-mail:* mdl@macmillam.co.uk
Distribution Center: COSI Toll Free *Tel:* 877-342-1478 *Fax:* 201-840-7242 *E-mail:* bookorders@cosi-us.com (US)

Macmillan Distribution Ltd, Brunel Rd, Houndmills, Basingstoke, Hants RG21 6XS *Tel:* (01256) 329 242 *Fax:* (01256) 327 961 *E-mail:* mdl@macmillan.co.uk

SAGE Publications Ltd+
1 Oliver's Yard, 55 City Rd, London EC1Y 1SP
Tel: (020) 7374 8500; (020) 7374 0645 (customer service) *Fax:* (020) 7374 8600
E-mail: info@sagepub.co.uk
Web Site: www.sagepub.co.uk
Key Personnel
Man Dir: Stephen Barr
Non-Executive Dir: Paul Chapman
Production Dir: Richard Fidczuk
Finance Dir: Katharine Jackson
Editorial Dir: Ziyad Marar
Human Resources Dir: Jane Quick
Founded: 1971
Membership(s): IPG.
Subjects: Anthropology, Behavioral Sciences, Biological Sciences, Business, Communications, Computer Science, Criminology, Economics, Education, Engineering (General), Environmental Studies, Ethnicity, Finance, Government, Political Science, Health, Nutrition, History, Human Relations, Language Arts, Linguistics, Management, Marketing, Medicine, Nursing, Dentistry, Philosophy, Psychology, Psychiatry, Religion - Protestant, Social Sciences, Sociology, Women's Studies
ISBN Prefix(es): 0-7591; 0-7619
Imprints: Altamira Press; Paul Chapman Publishing; Corwin Press; Pine Forge Press; Sage Science Press
Divisions: Scolari
Branch Office(s)
SAGE Publications India Pvt Ltd, B-42 Panchsheel Enclave, New Delhi 100 017, India *Tel:* (011) 2649 1290 *Fax:* (011) 2649 2117 *E-mail:* sage@vsnl.com *Web Site:* www.indiasage.com
U.S. Office(s): SAGE Publications USA, 2455 Teller Rd, Thousand Oaks, CA 91320, United States *Tel:* (805) 499-0721; (805) 499-9774 *Fax:* (805) 499-0871 *E-mail:* info@sagepub.com *Web Site:* www.sagepub.com

Sage Science Press, *imprint of* SAGE Publications Ltd

Sainsbury Publishing Ltd+
Auldearn Main St, Bleasby, Nottingham NG14 7GH
Tel: (01636) 830499 *Fax:* (01636) 830175
Key Personnel
Dir: George Sainsbury *E-mail:* george@gsbooks.demon.co.uk
Founded: 1987
Subjects: Humor, Natural History
ISBN Prefix(es): 1-870655

Saint Andrew Press+
121 George St, Edinburgh EH2 4YN
Tel: (0131) 225 5722 *Fax:* (0131) 220 3113
E-mail: standrewpress@cofscotland.org.uk
Web Site: www.churchofscotland.org.uk
Key Personnel
Head of Publishing: Ann Crawford
Sales & Production Manager: Derek Auld
Distribution: Ian Dunnet
Marketing & Publicity Officer: Alison Fleming
Founded: 1954
Membership(s): Scottish Publishers Association.
Subjects: History, Regional Interests, Religion - Protestant, Religion - Other, Theology
ISBN Prefix(es): 0-7152; 0-86153
Number of titles published annually: 12 Print
Total Titles: 100 Print
Parent Company: The Board of Communication of the Church of Scotland
Ultimate Parent Company: The Church of Scotland
Distributor for Church of Scotland Stationery; Pathway Productions; Wild Goose Publications

St David's Press, *imprint of* Welsh Academic Press

St George's Press
17 Ingatestone Rd, Woodford, Green Essex IG8 9AN
Tel: (020) 8504 1199 *Fax:* (020) 8559 0989
E-mail: sgp17@aol.com
Web Site: www.eppingforest.co.uk/stgeorgespress
Founded: 1969
Specialize in the works of Julian Fane, novelist, short story writer, memorialist & literary figure of distinction.
Subjects: Fiction, Literature, Literary Criticism, Essays
ISBN Prefix(es): 0-14; 0-902619

St James Press, *imprint of* Thomson Gale

St Jerome Publishing
2 Maple Rd W, Brooklands, Manchester M23 9HH
Tel: (0161) 973 9856 *Fax:* (0161) 905 3498
E-mail: stjerome@compuserve.com
Web Site: www.stjerome.co.uk
Key Personnel
Man Dir & International Rights: Ken Baker
Founded: 1994
Specialize in books on interpreting & related fields; intercultural communication.
Subjects: Language Arts, Linguistics, Cultural Studies, Literary Studies
ISBN Prefix(es): 1-900650
Number of titles published annually: 15 Print
Total Titles: 52 Print
Distributed by Binghamton University Press; European Institute for the Media; Exeter University Press; Kent State University Press; Multilingual Matters; Northern Illinois University Press; Rodopi; Routledge; Rutgers University Press
Membership(s): IPG; Publishers' Association

St Paul's Bibliographies Ltd+
17 Greenbanks, Lyminge, Kent CT18 8HG
Tel: (0130) 386 2258 *Fax:* (0130) 386 2660
E-mail: stpauls@stpaulsbib.com
Web Site: www.oakknoll.com/spbib.html
Key Personnel
Dir: J von Hoelle; R Fleck; C Reynard
Founded: 1979
ISBN Prefix(es): 0-906795; 0-946053; 1-873040
Parent Company: Oak Knoll Press, 414 Delaware St, New Castle, DE 19720, United States
Distributed by Oak Knoll Press
Distributor for Oak Knoll Press (USA)
Orders to: Scott Brinded, 106 Dover Rd, Folkestone, Kent CT20 1NN *Tel:* (01303) 220567 *Fax:* (01303) 220600

St Pauls Publishing+
187 Battersea Bridge Rd, London SW11 3AS
Tel: (020) 7978 4300 *Fax:* (020) 7978 4370
E-mail: editions@stpauls.org.uk
Web Site: www.stpauls.ie
Key Personnel
Man Dir & Rights & Permissions: Fr Andrew Pudussery *Tel:* (020) 79784300 *Fax:* (020) 79784370 *E-mail:* vpudussery@tiscali.org.uk
Founded: 1967
Subjects: Human Relations, Humor, Philosophy, Religion - Catholic, Religion - Other, Social Sciences, Sociology, Theology
ISBN Prefix(es): 0-85439
Number of titles published annually: 35 Print
Total Titles: 265 Print
Parent Company: Society of St Paul, Via della Fanella 39, 00148 Rome, Italy
Bookshop(s): St Pauls, Morpeth Terrace, Victoria, London SW1P 1EP, Sebastian Karamvelil *Tel:* (020) 7828 5582 *Fax:* (020) 7828 3329 *E-mail:* bookshop@stpauls.org.uk
Distribution Center: Moyglare Rd, Maynooth, Co Kildare, Ireland, Contact: Sergs Magbanua *Tel:* (01) 6285933 *Fax:* (01) 6289330 *E-mail:* sales@stpauls.ie *Web Site:* www.stpauls.ie

Salamander Books Ltd+
Division of Chrysalis Books
The Chrysalis Bldg, Bramley Rd, London W10 6SP
Tel: (020) 7314 1469 *Fax:* (020) 7314 1594
Web Site: www.chrysalisbooks.co.uk/books/publisher/salamander
Key Personnel
Group Sales & Marketing Dir: Richard Samson *E-mail:* rsamson@chrysalisbooks.co.uk
Dir of Marketing: Kate Wood *E-mail:* kwood@chrysalisbooks.co.uk
Sales Manager: Sharon Pitcher *E-mail:* spitcher@chrysalisbooks.co.uk
Foreign Rights: Candida Buckley *E-mail:* candidabuckley@aol.com
Permissions: Terry Forshaw *E-mail:* tforshaw@chrysalisbooks.co.uk
Founded: 1974
Subjects: Aeronautics, Aviation, Animals, Pets, Architecture & Interior Design, Cookery, Crafts, Games, Hobbies, Gardening, Plants, Health, Nutrition, History, House & Home, Native American Studies, Natural History, Sports, Athletics, Transportation, American History, US Cars & Motorbikes
ISBN Prefix(es): 0-86101; 1-84065
Imprints: Aspect; Vega
Orders to: HarperCollins Distribution, Campsie View, Westerhill Rd, Bishopbriggs, Glasgow *Fax:* (087) 0787 1995 (Trade only)

The Salariya Book Co Ltd+
25 Marlborough Pl, Brighton, East Sussex BN1 1UB
Tel: (01273) 603 306 *Fax:* (01273) 693 857
E-mail: salariya@salariya.com
Web Site: www.salariya.com
Key Personnel
Dir: David Salariya *E-mail:* david.salariya@salariya.com
Editor: Karen Barker Smith *E-mail:* karen.barkersmith@salariya.com; Michael Ford *E-mail:* michael.ford@salariya.com
Finance, Production & Rights: Jo Furse *E-mail:* jo.furse@salariya.com
Founded: 1989
Illustrated children's books for international co-edition market.
Subjects: Architecture & Interior Design, Fiction, Foreign Countries, Geography, Geology, History, Natural History, Science (General), Technology
Total Titles: 150 Print
Imprints: Book House

The Saltire Society
9 Fountain Close, 22 High St, Edinburgh EH1 1TF
Tel: (0131) 556 1836 *Fax:* (0131) 557 1675
E-mail: saltire@saltiresociety.org.uk
Web Site: www.saltiresociety.org.uk
Key Personnel
Administrator: Kathleen Munro
Founded: 1936
Subjects: History, Literature, Literary Criticism, Essays
ISBN Prefix(es): 0-85411
Branch Office(s)
Blvd Brand Whitlock 152, BTE 3, 1200 Brussels, Belgium, Convener: Alasdair Geater *Tel:* (02)

735 82 72 *Web Site:* www.amg1.net/scotland. htm (Brussels)
´Eredene´, Huntly Rd, Aboyne, Convener: Ian Kinniburgh *Tel:* (0133) 988 6484 *E-mail:* iankinniburgh@beeb.net (Aberdeen)
Feddans, Cardross G82 5IG, Chair: Alison Cowey *Tel:* (01436) 841 440 (Helensburgh)
Magdalene House, Lochmaben, Dumfries DG11 1PD, Convener: Mdme May McKerrell of Hillhouse *Tel:* (01387) 810439 (Dumfries & Galloway)
1/35 Bothwell House, Edinburgh EH7 5YL, Chairman: Ian MacDonald *Tel:* (0131) 659 6058 (Edinburgh)
14 Cleveden Drive, Glasgow, Convener: Kenneth Thomson *Tel:* (0141) 334 7773
Birchdale, 69 Culduthel Rd, Inverness IV2 4HH, Chairman: Dr Alastair Scott-Brown *Tel:* (01463) 223 294 *E-mail:* ardynsb@onetel. net.uk (Highland)
Lea Cottage, 16 Whiteside, Kirriemuir DD8 4HZ, Chairman: Betty Allan *Tel:* (01575) 574 134 (Kirriemuir)
Solwayside, Harbour Rd, Wigtown, Convener: Mary Norris *Tel:* (01988) 402253 (Galloway)
Warehouse: Scottish Book Source, 32 Finlas St, Glasgow G22 5DU
Orders to: Scottish Book Source, 32 Finlas St, Glasgow G22 5DU *Tel:* (0131) 229 6800 *Fax:* (0131) 229 9070

Salvationist Publishing & Supplies Ltd
One Tiverton St, London SE1 6NT
Tel: (020) 7367 6570; (020) 7367 6580 (mail orders) *Fax:* (020) 7367 6589
E-mail: mail_order@sp-s.co.uk
Web Site: www.archive.salvationarmy.org.uk
Key Personnel
Man Dir: Lieutenant General Michael Williams
Company Secretary: Gordon Camsey
Subjects: Music, Dance, Religion - Other
ISBN Prefix(es): 0-85412
Subsidiaries: S P & S Mail Order (also ordering)

Sams Publishing, *imprint of* Pearson Education Europe, Mideast & Africa

Sams.net, *imprint of* Pearson Education Europe, Mideast & Africa

Sangam Books Ltd+
57 London Fruit Exchange Brushfield St, London E1 6EP
Tel: (020) 7377-6399 *Fax:* (020) 7375-1230
E-mail: goatony@aol.com
Key Personnel
Chief Executive, Sales, Publicity: A A de Souza
Founded: 1981
Membership(s): Publishers Association UK.
Subjects: Fiction, Medicine, Nursing, Dentistry, Nonfiction (General), Science (General), Social Sciences, Sociology, Technology
ISBN Prefix(es): 0-86131; 0-86311; 0-86125; 0-86132
Number of titles published annually: 30 Print
Parent Company: Orient Longman Pvt Ltd, India

Sapphire, *imprint of* Virgin Publishing Ltd

Saqi Books+
26 Westbourne Grove, London W2 5RH
Tel: (020) 7221 9347 *Fax:* (020) 7229 7492
E-mail: info@saqibooks.com
Web Site: www.saqibooks.com
Key Personnel
Publisher: Andre Gaspard
Managing Editor: Penny Warburton
Publicity: Rebecca O'Connor
Commissioning Editor: Mitchell Albert
Founded: 1984

Subjects: Art, Asian Studies, Biography, Cookery, Developing Countries, Ethnicity, Fiction, Foreign Countries, Government, Political Science, History, Humor, Language Arts, Linguistics, Literature, Literary Criticism, Essays, Music, Dance, Nonfiction (General), Photography, Social Sciences, Sociology, Travel, Wine & Spirits, Balkan Studies, Middle Eastern Studies
ISBN Prefix(es): 0-86356
Number of titles published annually: 30 Print
Total Titles: 200 Print
Foreign Rep(s): Durnell Marketing (Europe); Horizon Books (Singapore & Malaysia); Palgrave Macmillan (Australia, USA)
Foreign Rights: La Nouvelle Agence (France); Pontas Agency (Spain)

Saunders, *imprint of* Elsevier Ltd

KG Saur, *imprint of* Thomson Gale

Steve Savage Publishers Ltd+
Old Truman Brewery, 91 Brick Lane, London E1 6QL
Tel: (020) 7770 6083
E-mail: mail@savagepublishers.com
Web Site: www.savagepublishers.com
Founded: 2001
Subjects: Fiction, Humor, Literature, Literary Criticism, Essays, Nonfiction (General)
ISBN Prefix(es): 0-903065
Orders to: Book Source, 32 Finlas St, Glasgow G22 5DU *Tel:* (0141) 558 1366 *Fax:* (0141) 557 0189 *E-mail:* orders@booksource.net

Savannah Publications
90 Dartmouth Rd, Forest Hill, London SE23 3HZ
Tel: (020) 8244 4350 *Fax:* (020) 8244 2448
E-mail: savpub@dircon.co.uk
Web Site: www.savannah-publications.com
Subjects: Publishers of military works of reference & military genealogy
ISBN Prefix(es): 1-902366
Total Titles: 100 Print

Savitri Books Ltd+
115J Cleveland St, London W1T 6PU
Tel: (020) 7436 9932 *Fax:* (020) 7580 6330
Key Personnel
Man Dir: M S Srivastava
Founded: 1983
Also acts as packagers.
Subjects: Crafts, Games, Hobbies, How-to, Natural History
ISBN Prefix(es): 0-9534103

SAWD Publications+
Suite 1, 62 Bell Rd, Sittingbourne, Kent ME10 4HE
Tel: (01795) 472 262 *Fax:* (01795) 422 633
E-mail: wainman@sawd.demon.co.uk
Key Personnel
Partners: Allison Wainman; Susannah Wainman
Founded: 1989
Subjects: Cookery, Gardening, Plants, Humor, Nonfiction (General)
ISBN Prefix(es): 1-872489

SB Publications+
19 Grove Rd, Seaford, East Sussex BN25 1TP
Tel: (01323) 893498 *Fax:* (01323) 893860
E-mail: sales@sbpublications.swinternet.co.uk
Key Personnel
Owner: Lindsay Woods
Founded: 1987
Membership(s): IPG.
Subjects: History, Maritime, Regional Interests, Transportation, Travel, UK local history & guides
ISBN Prefix(es): 1-85770; 1-870708
Number of titles published annually: 25 Print

Total Titles: 140 Print
Imprints: BEN Gunn

Scarthin Books+
The Promenade Scarthin, Cromford, Derbyshire DE4 3QF
Tel: (01629) 823272 *Fax:* (01629) 825094
E-mail: clare@scarthinbooks.demon.co.uk
Web Site: www.scarthinbooks.com; www.books.co.uk
Key Personnel
Proprietor: D J Mitchell
Marketing: G N Cooper
Founded: 1981
Membership(s): Booksellers Association of Great Britain & Ireland (BAGBI).
Subjects: History, Outdoor Recreation
ISBN Prefix(es): 0-907758
Number of titles published annually: 5 Print
Total Titles: 110 Print
Imprints: Family Walks

Sceptre, *imprint of* Hodder & Stoughton General

Schirmer Reference, *imprint of* Thomson Gale

Schofield & Sims Ltd+
Dogley Mill, Fenay Bridge, Huddersfield HD8 0NQ
Tel: (01484) 607080 *Fax:* (01484) 606815
E-mail: post@schofieldandsims.co.uk
Web Site: www.schofieldandsims.co.uk
Key Personnel
Chairman: John S Nesbitt
Man Dir: J Stephen Platts
Sales Dir: Jack Brierley
Founded: 1901
ISBN Prefix(es): 0-7217
Membership(s): IPG

Scholastic Ltd+
Westfield Rd, Southam, Leamington Spa, Warwicks CV47 0RA
Tel: (01926) 887799; (01926) 813910 (warehouse) *Fax:* (01926) 883331
E-mail: scholastic@tens.co.uk
Web Site: www.scholastic.co.uk
Key Personnel
Man Dir: David Kewley
Educational Publishing Dir: Annie Peel
Sales & Marketing Dir: Gavin Lang
Buying Dir, Direct Marketing: Victoria Birkett
Editorial Dir, Children's Books: David Fickling
Senior Commissioning Editor, Educational Books: Gina Nuttall
Editor, Book Clubs: Helen Ward
Editor, Hippo Books: Anne Finnis
Production: Doug Brown
Advertising: Chris Pratt
Finance, IT: Ian Bloodworth
Senior Trade Vice President: Michael Jacobs
Marketing Vice President: Jennifer Pasanen
Founded: 1964
Subjects: Fiction, Nonfiction (General)
ISBN Prefix(es): 0-590
Parent Company: Scholastic Inc, 557 Broadway, New York, NY 10012-3999, United States
Imprints: Adlib; Andre Deutsch Children's Books; Hippo; Point
Branch Office(s)
Scholastic Childrens Books, Commonwealth House, 1-19 New Oxford St, London WC1A 1NU *Tel:* (020) 7421 9000 *Fax:* (020) 7421 9001

School Improvement Reports, *imprint of* First & Best in Education Ltd

School Improvement Reports, see First & Best in Education Ltd

School of Oriental & African Studies+
Thornhaugh St, Russell Sq, London WC1H 0XG
Tel: (020) 7637 2388 *Fax:* (020) 7436 3844
E-mail: md2@soas.ac.uk; aol@soas.ac.uk
Web Site: www.soas.ac.uk *Cable:* SOASUL LONDON WC1
Key Personnel
Publications Manager: M J Daly
Publications: Andrew Osmond
Founded: 1916
Subjects: Art, History, Language Arts, Linguistics, Literature, Literary Criticism, Essays, Religion - Other, Asia & Africa
ISBN Prefix(es): 0-901877; 0-7286

SchoolPlay Productions Ltd+
15 Inglis Rd, Colchester, Essex CO3 3HU
Tel: (01206) 540111 *Fax:* (01206) 766944
E-mail: schoolplay@inglis-house.demon.co.uk
Web Site: www.schoolplayproductions.co.uk
Key Personnel
Man Dir: Jeremy Lucas *E-mail:* jrl@inglis-house.demon.co.uk
Founded: 1989
Specialize in publishing plays & musicals for performance by youth groups & schools; play scripts & musical scores.
Subjects: Drama, Theater, Music, Dance
ISBN Prefix(es): 1-872475; 1-902472
Number of titles published annually: 12 Print
Total Titles: 140 Print

Science & Technology Letters, *imprint of* Science Reviews Ltd

Science Reviews, *imprint of* Science Reviews Ltd

Science Reviews Ltd
PO Box 314, St Albans, Herts AL1 4ZG
Tel: (01727) 847322 *Fax:* (01727) 847323
E-mail: scilet@scilet.com
Web Site: www.scilet.com
Key Personnel
Publisher: Dr Peter J Farago
Founded: 1978
Subjects: Chemistry, Chemical Engineering, Environmental Studies, Medicine, Nursing, Dentistry, Science (General)
Associate Companies: Science & Technology Letters; Science Reviews Inc, 1115 S Plymouth Court, Suite 412, Chicago, IL 60605, United States *Tel:* 312-913-1404 (also orders)
Imprints: Science Reviews; Science & Technology Letters; Symposium Press

Scientific American, *imprint of* W H Freeman & Co Ltd

SCM-Canterbury Press Ltd+
Subsidiary of Hymns Ancient & Modern Ltd
9-17 St Albans Pl, London N1 0NX
Tel: (020) 7359 8033 *Fax:* (020) 7359 0049
E-mail: admin@scm-canterburypress.co.uk
Web Site: www.scm-canterburypress.co.uk
Key Personnel
Group Chief Executive Officer: Gordon Knights *Tel:* (01603) 612914 ext 203 *E-mail:* gordon@scm-canterburypress.co.uk
Group Financial Controller: Brenda Medhurst *Tel:* (01603) 612914 ext 208 *E-mail:* brenda@scm-canterburypress.co.uk
Customer Services Manager: Louise Hopcroft *Tel:* (01603) 612914 ext 207
Publishing Dir: Christine Smith *Tel:* (020) 7359 8033 *E-mail:* christine@scm-canterburypress.co.uk
Senior Commissioning Editor: Barbara Laing *Tel:* (020) 7354 6217 *E-mail:* barbara@scm-canterburypress.co.uk
Senior Marketing Manager: Michael Addison *Tel:* (020) 7354 6214 *E-mail:* michael@scm-canterburypress.co.uk
Senior Marketing Controller: Anita Manbodh *Tel:* (020) 7354 6292 *E-mail:* anita@scm-canterburypress.co.uk
Key Accounts & UK Sales Manager: Kevin Allard *Tel:* (01603) 612914 *E-mail:* kevin@scm-canterburypress.co.uk
Rights & Permissions Manager: Jenny Willis *Tel:* (020) 7354 6211 *E-mail:* jenny@scm-canterburypress.co.uk
Production Manager: Stephen Rogers *Tel:* (020) 7354 6218 *E-mail:* stephen@scm-canterburypress.co.uk
Friends Administrator: Margaret Tosh *Tel:* (020) 7359 8034 *E-mail:* margaret@scm-canterburypress.co.uk
Founded: 1929 (as SCM Press Ltd)
Membership(s): Publishers Association
Subjects: Biblical Studies, Biography, Religion - Catholic, Religion - Jewish, Religion - Protestant, Religion - Other, Theology
ISBN Prefix(es): 0-334; 0-7162; 0-907547; 0-900274; 1-85175; 1-85311
Number of titles published annually: 100 Print; 6 CD-ROM; 6 Audio
Total Titles: 3,000 Print; 12 CD-ROM; 12 Audio
Imprints: Canterbury Press; Religious & Moral Education Press (RMEP); SCM Press
Distributor for Deo Publishing (UK); Epworth Press (UK); Tufton Books (UK)
Foreign Rep(s): Columba Books (Ireland); Hugh Dunphy (West Indies); Durnell Marketing (Europe); Novalis (Canada); Openbook (Australia & New Zealand); Westminster John Knox (USA)
Shipping Address: St Mary's Works, St Mary's Plain, Norwich, Norfolk NR3 3BH *Tel:* (01603) 612914 *Fax:* (01603) 624483
Warehouse: St Mary's Works, St Mary's Plain, Norwich, Norfolk NR3 3BH *Tel:* (01603) 612914 *Fax:* (01603) 624483
Orders to: St Mary's Works, St Mary's Plain, Norwich, Norfolk NR3 3BH *Tel:* (01603) 612914 *Fax:* (01603) 624483
Returns: St Mary's Works, St Mary's Plain, Norwich, Norfolk NR3 3BH *Tel:* (01603) 612914 *Fax:* (01603) 624483

SCM Press, *imprint of* Hymns Ancient & Modern Ltd

SCM Press, *imprint of* SCM-Canterbury Press Ltd

Scott Foresman, *imprint of* Pearson Education Europe, Mideast & Africa

Scottish Braille Press
Division of Royal Blind Asylum & School
Craigmillar Park, Edinburgh EH16 5NB
Tel: (0131) 662 4445 *Fax:* (0131) 662 1968
E-mail: enquiries@scottish-braille-press.org
Web Site: www.scottish-braille-press.org
Key Personnel
Manager: John Donaldson *E-mail:* john.donaldson@scottish-braille-press.org
Sales & Marketing Manager: Stewart Connell *E-mail:* stewart.connell@scottish-braille-press.org
Founded: 1891
Also acts as Printer.

Scottish Council for Research in Education
61 Dublin St, Edinburgh EH3 6NL
Tel: (0131) 557 2944 *Fax:* (0131) 556 9454
E-mail: scre.info@scre.ac.uk; scre@scre.ac.uk
Web Site: www.scre.ac.uk
Key Personnel
Dir: Valerie Wilson *Tel:* (0131) 623 2964 *E-mail:* valerie.wilson@scre.ac.uk
Administrative Services: Moira Simpson
Information Services: John Lewin
Founded: 1932
Research in the service of education, using research series, research reviews & research reports.
ISBN Prefix(es): 0-901116; 0-947833; 1-86003
Total Titles: 153 Print

Scottish Cultural Press+
Imprint of SCP Publishers Ltd
Unit 6, Newbattle Abbey Business Annexe, Newbattle Rd, Dalkeith EH22 3LJ
Tel: (0131) 660-6366 (editorial); (0131) 660-4757 (editorial); (0131) 660-4666 (orders)
E-mail: info@scottishbooks.com
Web Site: www.scottishbooks.com
Key Personnel
Dir: Avril Gray
Dir & Company Secretary: Brian Pugh
Founded: 1992
Publisher of Scottish nonfiction & fiction.
Subjects: Archaeology, Biography, Environmental Studies, Fiction, History, Literature, Literary Criticism, Essays, Nonfiction (General), Poetry, Regional Interests, Social Sciences, Sociology
ISBN Prefix(es): 80-7239; 1-840170; 1-898827
Total Titles: 100 Print
Associate Companies: Scottish Children, Unit 13d, New Battle Abbey Business Annexe, New Battle Rd, Dalkeith EH22 3LT *Tel:* (0131) 660-4757, 660-6414 (Editorial); (0131) 660-4666 (orders) *Fax:* (0131) 660-6414 (editorial); (0131) 660-4666 (orders) *E-mail:* info@scottishbooks.com *Web Site:* www.scottishbooks.com
U.S. Office(s): Wilson & Associates, PO Box 2569, Alvin, TX 77512, United States *Tel:* 281-388-0196 *Fax:* 413-683-8503 *E-mail:* info@thebookdistribution.com *Web Site:* www.thebookdistribution.com (Canada & US)
Distributor for Scottish Children's Press; Scottish Cultural Press

Scottish Executive Library & Information Services
Saughton House, Broomhouse Dr, Edinburgh EH11 3XD
Tel: (0131) 244 4552 *Fax:* (0131) 244 4545
Web Site: www.scotland.gov.uk
Key Personnel
Contact: Colin Jardine *E-mail:* colin.jardine@scotland.gov.uk
Founded: 1984
Subjects: Agriculture, Criminology, Disability, Special Needs, Economics, Education, Energy, Environmental Studies, Finance, Government, Political Science, Health, Nutrition, Social Sciences, Sociology, Transportation
Distributed by HMSO Books

Scottish Falcon, *imprint of* The Orkney Press Ltd

Scottish Text Society+
27 George Sq, Edinburgh EH8 9LD
Mailing Address: School of English Studies, University of Nottingham, Nottingham NG7 2RD *Tel:* (0115) 951 5922
Tel: (0115) 951 5922
E-mail: sts@arts.gla.ac.uk
Web Site: www.scottishtextsociety.org
Key Personnel
Editorial Secretary: Nicola Royan *E-mail:* nicola.royan@nottingham.ac.uk
Founded: 1882
Subjects: Genealogy, History, Literature, Literary Criticism, Essays, Poetry, Religion - Protestant, Theology, Medieval Literature
ISBN Prefix(es): 0-9500245; 1-897976
Total Titles: 23 Print

Scribner, *imprint of* Simon & Schuster Ltd

UNITED KINGDOM

Charles Scribner's Sons, *imprint of* Thomson Gale

Scripta Technica, *imprint of* Wiley Europe Ltd

Scripture Union+
207-209 Queensway, Bletchley, Milton Keynes, Bucks MK2 2EB
Tel: (01908) 856000 *Fax:* (01908) 856111
E-mail: info@scriptureunion.org.uk
Web Site: www.scriptureunion.org.uk
Key Personnel
Publishing Dir: Malcolm Hall
  E-mail: malcolmh@scriptureunion.org.uk
Copyright Permissions, Overseas Rights Administration: Rosemary North *E-mail:* rosemaryn@scriptureunion.org.uk
Founded: 1867
Specialize in holiday club resources.
Subjects: Biblical Studies, Education, Religion - Protestant, Theology
ISBN Prefix(es): 0-85421; 0-86201
Number of titles published annually: 100 Print
Total Titles: 450 Print; 450 Online
Branch Office(s)
157 Albertbridge Rd, Belfast BT5 4PS, Ireland *Tel:* (028) 9045 4806 *Fax:* (028) 9073 9758 *E-mail:* admin@suni.co.uk *Web Site:* www.suni.co.uk (Northern Ireland)
87 Lower George's St, Dun Laoghaire, Co Dublin, Ireland *Tel:* (01) 280 2300 *Fax:* (01) 280 2409 *E-mail:* suirl@aol.ie *Web Site:* www.scriptureunion.ie (Republic of Ireland)
9 Canal St, Glasgow, Scotland G4 0ABD *Tel:* (0141) 332 1162 *Fax:* (0141) 332 1162 *E-mail:* info@scriptureunionscotland.org.uk *Web Site:* www.scriptureunionscotland.org.uk (Scotland)
Orders to: Scripture Union Mail Order, PO Box 5148, Milton Keynes, MLO MK2 2YZ *Tel:* (01908) 856006 *Fax:* (01908) 856020 *E-mail:* mailorder@scriptureunion.org.uk (UK & Wales)
Send the Light (STL) Ltd, PO Box 300, Kingstown Broadway, Carlisle, Cumbria CA3 0GS *Tel:* (01228) 611758

Seaflower Books, *imprint of* Ex Libris Press

Search Press Ltd+
Wellwood, North Farm Rd, Tunbridge Wells, Kent TN2 3DR
Tel: (01892) 510850 *Fax:* (01892) 515903
E-mail: searchpress@searchpress.com
Web Site: www.searchpress.com
Key Personnel
Man Dir: Martin de la Bedoyere
  E-mail: martind@searchpress.com
Commissioning Editor: Rosalind Dace
Production: Inger Arthur
Founded: 1970
Subjects: Art, Crafts, Games, Hobbies, Gardening, Plants, How-to
ISBN Prefix(es): 0-85532

Secker & Warburg, *imprint of* Random House UK Ltd

Martin Secker & Warburg+
Imprint of Random House
20 Vauxhall Bridge Rd, London SW1V 2SA
Tel: (020) 7840 8570 *Fax:* (020) 7233 6117
E-mail: enquiries@randomhouse.co.uk
Web Site: www.randomhouse.co.uk
Key Personnel
Editorial Dir: Geoff Mulligan *Fax:* (020) 7233 6117
Editor: David Milner
Founded: 1910
Subjects: Fiction, Nonfiction (General)

ISBN Prefix(es): 0-436
Ultimate Parent Company: Bertelsmann

SEDA Publications
Selly Wick House, 59-61 Selly Wick Rd, Selly Park, Birmingham B29 7JE
Tel: (0121) 415 6801 *Fax:* (0121) 415 6802
E-mail: office@seda.ac.uk
Web Site: www.seda.ac.uk/publications.htm
Subjects: Education, Professional Development
Number of titles published annually: 8 Print
Total Titles: 38 Print

Semiotext(e), *imprint of* MIT Press Ltd

Senate, *imprint of* Tiger Books International PLC

Seren+
Imprint of Poetry Wales Press Ltd
38-40 Nolton St, 1st & 2nd floors, Bridgend CF31 3BN
Tel: (01656) 663018 *Fax:* (01656) 649226
E-mail: general@seren-books.com
Web Site: www.seren-books.com
Key Personnel
Chief Executive, Editorial: Cary Archard
Man Dir & International Rights: Mick Felton
  E-mail: mickfelton@seren.force9.co.uk
Editor: Robert Minhinnick
Fiction Editor: Will Atkins
Poetry Editor: Amy Wack
Publicity Officer: Simon Hicks
Founded: 1982
Subjects: Art, Biography, Drama, Theater, Fiction, Government, Political Science, History, Literature, Literary Criticism, Essays, Music, Dance, Photography, Poetry, Sports, Athletics, Women's Studies, Anthologies
ISBN Prefix(es): 0-907476; 1-85411
Number of titles published annually: 30 Print
Total Titles: 200 Print; 1 CD-ROM; 1 Audio
Distributed by Eleanor Brasch Associates (Australia); IPG
Distribution Center: Central Books, 99 Wallis Rd, London E9 5LN *Tel:* (0208) 986 4854 *Fax:* (0208) 533 5821 *E-mail:* orders@centbks.demon.co.uk (Trade)
Welsh Books Council, Uned 16 Stad Glanyrafon, Llanbadarn, Aberystwyth SY23 3AQ *Tel:* (01970) 624455 *Fax:* (01970) 625506 *Web Site:* www.gwales.com (Trade)

Serif+
47 Strahan Rd, London E3 5DA
Tel: (020) 8981 3990 *Fax:* (020) 8981 3990
Key Personnel
Publisher & International Rights: Stephen Hayward *E-mail:* stephen@serif.demon.co.uk
Founded: 1993
Subjects: Cookery, Developing Countries, Foreign Countries, Government, Political Science, History
ISBN Prefix(es): 1-897959
Orders to: Central Books, 99 Wallis Rd, London E9 5LN
Interlink Publishing Group, 46 Crosby St, Northampton, MA 01060-1804, United States *Tel:* 413-582-7054 *Fax:* 413-582-7057 *E-mail:* sales@interlinkbooks.com *Web Site:* www.interlinkbooks.com

Serpent's Tail Ltd+
4 Blackstock Mews, London N4 2BT
Tel: (020) 7354-1949 *Fax:* (020) 7704-6467
E-mail: info@serpentstail.com
Web Site: www.serpentstail.com
Key Personnel
Editorial Dir: Peter Ayrton *E-mail:* pete@serpentstail.com
Production: Ruth Petrie
Publicity: Anna Vallois

Sales & Marketing: Jenny Boyce
Founded: 1986
Subjects: African American Studies, Asian Studies, Biography, Criminology, Ethnicity, Fiction, Gay & Lesbian, Literature, Literary Criticism, Essays, Music, Dance, Mysteries, Nonfiction (General), Women's Studies, High Risk/Cult
ISBN Prefix(es): 1-85242
Number of titles published annually: 40 Print
Total Titles: 350 Print
Imprints: High Risk
U.S. Office(s): Lisa Garbutt Book Promotion, PO Box 976, North Kingstown, RI 02852, United States *Tel:* 401-885-3482 *Fax:* 401-885-7996
Distributed by Quartet Sales & Marketing (South Africa); Tower Books Pty Ltd (Australia)
Orders to: LBS, Faraday Close, Durrington, Worthing, West Sussex BN13 3RB *Tel:* (01903) 828800 *Fax:* (01903) 828801

Severn House Publishers Inc+
9-15 High St, Sutton, Surrey SM1 1DF
Tel: (0208) 7703930 *Fax:* (0208) 7703850
E-mail: sales@severnhouse.com
Web Site: www.severnhouse.com
Key Personnel
Chairman: Edwin Buckhalter *E-mail:* edwin@severnhouse.com
Publisher: Amanda Stewart
Acquisitions Editor: Hugo Cox
Rights Manager: Michelle Duff
Founded: 1974
Membership(s): RNA; CWA; RWA; ALA.
Subjects: Fiction, Mysteries, Romance, Science Fiction, Fantasy
ISBN Prefix(es): 0-7278
Number of titles published annually: 120 Print
Total Titles: 400 Print
Parent Company: Severn House Books (Holdings) Ltd
Imprints: Enigma Books
U.S. Office(s): Mercedes Distribution Center, Brooklyn Navy Yard, Bldg 3, Brooklyn, NY 11205, United States *Tel:* (718) 534-3000 *Fax:* (718) 935-9647 (Regular print, large print)
595 Madison Ave, 15th floor, New York, NY 10022, United States *Tel:* 212-888-4042 *Fax:* 212-759-5422 *E-mail:* sales@severnhouse.com *Web Site:* www.severnhouse.com (large print)
Warehouse: Grantham Book Services Ltd, Isaac Newton Way, Alma Park Industrial Estate, Grantham, Lincs NG31 9SD *Tel:* (01476) 541080 *Fax:* (01476) 541061
Orders to: Grantham Book Services Ltd, Isaac Newton Way, Alma Park Industrial Estate, Grantham, Lincs NG31 9SD *Tel:* (01476) 541080 *Fax:* (01476) 541061

Shakti Communications Ltd
28a Popin Business Centre, South Way, Wembley HA9 0HF
Tel: (020) 8903 5442 *Fax:* (020) 8903 4684
E-mail: info@shakticom.com
Web Site: www.shakticom.com
Key Personnel
Man Dir: Mr Ravi Jain *E-mail:* ravi@shakticom.com
ISBN Prefix(es): 0-7128; 0-906666; 0-9505709

Shaw & Sons Ltd
Shaway House, 21 Bourne Park, Bourne Rd, Crayford, Kent DA1 4BZ
Tel: (01322) 621100 *Fax:* (01322) 550553
E-mail: sales@shaws.co.uk
Web Site: www.shaws.co.uk
Key Personnel
Publishing Dir: D Hubber
Publications Dir: Crispin Williams
  E-mail: crispin@shaws.co.uk
Sales, Publicity: Barbara Ferguson
Founded: 1750

PUBLISHERS

Subjects: Government, Political Science, Law, Nonfiction (General)
ISBN Prefix(es): 0-7219
Number of titles published annually: 10 Print
Total Titles: 60 Print
Membership(s): Publishers' Association

Shearwater Press Ltd
45 SlieauDhoo, Tromode Park, Douglas, Isle of Man IM2 5LG
Tel: (01624) 627727 *Fax:* (01624) 663627
Telex: 629824 Bell
Key Personnel
Man Dir, Editorial: Peter Crellin
Founded: 1973
Subjects: Art, Fiction, Geography, Geology, History, Regional Interests
ISBN Prefix(es): 0-904980

Sheed & Ward UK+
The Tower Bldg, 11 York Rd, London SE1 7NX
Tel: (020) 7922 0880 *Fax:* (020) 7922 0881
E-mail: info@breathemail.net
Web Site: www.continuumbooks.com
Key Personnel
Dir, UK Publishing Services: Benn Linfield
 E-mail: blinfield@econtinuumbokos.com
Founded: 1926
Subjects: History, Philosophy, Religion - Other
ISBN Prefix(es): 0-7220
Parent Company: Continuum International Publishing Group

Sheffield Academic Press Ltd+
Stanley House, 3 Fleets Lane, Poole BH15 3AJ
Tel: (01202) 665 432 *Fax:* (01202) 666 219
E-mail: orders@orcabookservices.co.uk
Web Site: www.sheffieldacademicpress.com
Key Personnel
Man Dir: Jean Allen
Dir: David J A Clines; Dr Philip R Davies; Michael M Mallett
Marketing Manager: Maureen Allum
 E-mail: mallum@sheffac.demon.co.uk
Founded: 1976
Subjects: Archaeology, Biblical Studies, Biological Sciences, Chemistry, Chemical Engineering, Drama, Theater, Foreign Countries, Language Arts, Linguistics, Literature, Literary Criticism, Essays, Medicine, Nursing, Dentistry, Religion - Jewish, Science (General), Technology, Theology
ISBN Prefix(es): 0-905774; 1-85075; 1-84127
Number of titles published annually: 110 Print
Total Titles: 850 Print
Imprints: Almond Press
Distributor for Worldwide-Semitic Study Aids Series of University of Birmingham
Foreign Rep(s): Trevor Brown Associates (Europe); Erickson Marketing; Korean Christian Book Service (Korea); Justin Moulder (UK); Brian Pugh (Ireland, Northern Ireland, Scotland); Russell Book Representation (UK); Sheffield Academic Press (Australia, Canada, New Zealand); Derek Walker (Northeast England)
Distribution Center: Cornell University Press Services, 750 Cascadilla St, PO Box 6525, Ithaca, NY 14851, United States

Sheldon Press, *imprint of* The Society for Promoting Christian Knowledge (SPCK)

Sheldon Press+
Imprint of The Society for Promoting Christian Knowledge (SPCK)
Holy Trinity Church, Marylebone Rd, London NW1 4DU
Tel: (020) 7643 0382 *Fax:* (020) 7643 0391
E-mail: director@sheldonpress.co.uk
Web Site: www.sheldonpress.co.uk *Cable:* FUTURITY LONDON NW1
Key Personnel
Publisher: Joanna Moriarty *E-mail:* jmoriarty@spck.org.uk
Sales Manager: Susan Kodicek
 E-mail: skodicek@spck.org.uk
Founded: 1973
Subjects: Health, Nutrition, Psychology, Psychiatry, Self-Help
ISBN Prefix(es): 0-85969
Number of titles published annually: 15 Print
Total Titles: 200 Print
Warehouse: Marston Book Services Ltd
Orders to: 160 Milton Park Estate, Oxford OX14 4YN *Tel:* (01235) 465500 *Fax:* (01235) 465555

Sheldrake Press+
Imprint of Sheldrake Publications Ltd
188 Cavendish Rd, London SW12 0DA
Tel: (020) 8675 1767; (01752) 202301 (orders); (01752) 202300 (warehouse) *Fax:* (020) 8675 7736
E-mail: mail@sheldrakepress.demon.co.uk
Web Site: www.sheldrakepress.co.uk
Key Personnel
Contact: Mr J S Rigge
Founded: 1979
Subjects: Architecture & Interior Design, Cookery, History, House & Home, Music, Dance, Nonfiction (General), Outdoor Recreation, Transportation, Travel
ISBN Prefix(es): 1-873329
Number of titles published annually: 2 Print
Total Titles: 30 Print
Ultimate Parent Company: Sheldrake Holdings Ltd
Distributed by Interlink
Distributor for Inmerc bv
Foreign Rep(s): Bill Baily Publishers (Croatia, Cyprus, Czech Republic, Europe, Gibraltar, Iceland, Malta, Russia, Slovenia, Turkey)
Distribution Center: NBN Plymbridge

Shelfmark Books
90 Wallis Rd, London E9 5LN
Tel: (020) 8986 4854 *Fax:* (020) 8533 5821
E-mail: orders@centralbooks.com
Key Personnel
Contact: John Wardroper
Founded: 1994
Subjects: History, Literature, Literary Criticism, Essays
ISBN Prefix(es): 0-9526093

Shepheard-Walwyn (Publishers) Ltd+
The Chandlery, 50 Westminster Bridge Rd, Suite 604, London SEI 7QY
Tel: (020) 7721 7666 *Fax:* (020) 7721 7667
E-mail: books@shepheard-walwyn.co.uk
Web Site: www.shepheard-walwyn.co.uk
Key Personnel
Man Dir & International Rights: Anthony Werner
Founded: 1971
Nonfiction book publishers.
Subjects: Biography, Economics, Government, Political Science, History, Nonfiction (General), Philosophy, Religion - Other
ISBN Prefix(es): 0-85683
Number of titles published annually: 5 Print
Total Titles: 95 Print
Foreign Rep(s): Independent Publishers Group, Chicago (North America, South America); John Reed Book Distribution, Sydney (Australia & New Zealand)
Shipping Address: BR&D, Unit 1A/1B Learoyd Rd, Mountfield Road Industrial Estate, New Romney TN28 8XU *Tel:* (01702) 552912 *Fax:* (01702) 556095 *E-mail:* mail@bookreps.com
Distribution Center: Book Representation & Distribution, Hadleigh Hall, London Rd, Hadleigh

UNITED KINGDOM

SS7 2DE *Tel:* (01702) 552912 *Fax:* (01702) 556095 *E-mail:* mail@bookreps.com
Membership(s): IPG

Sheppard, *imprint of* Richard Joseph Publishers Ltd

Sherbourne Publications+
Sherbourne, Trefonen Rd, Morda, Oswestery, Salop SY10 9AG
Tel: (01691) 657 853 *Fax:* (01691) 657 853
Key Personnel
Contact: Dorothy McNeil
Founded: 1989
Membership(s): Society of Authors & ALCS Independent Publishers Guild.
Subjects: Animals, Pets, Poetry
ISBN Prefix(es): 1-872547
Distributor for B Small Publishing (UK); Tarquin Publications (UK)

Sheridan Book Company, *imprint of* Tiger Books International PLC

Sherwood Publishing+
Subsidiary of A D International
Sherwood House, 7 Oxhey Rd, Watford, Herts WD19 4QF
Tel: (01923) 224737 *Fax:* (01923) 210648
E-mail: sherwood@adinternational.com
Web Site: www.sherwoodpublishing.com
Key Personnel
Chief Executive: Julie Hay
Founded: 1993
Subjects: Behavioral Sciences, Career Development, Education, Human Relations, Management, Psychology, Psychiatry, Self-Help, Personal development for trainers
ISBN Prefix(es): 0-9521964
U.S. Office(s): Sherwood Publishing, 4036 Kerry Court, Minnetonka, MN 55343, United States

Shire Publications Ltd+
Cromwell House, Church St, Princes Risborough, Bucks HP27 9AA
Tel: (01844) 344301 *Fax:* (01844) 347080
E-mail: shire@shirebooks.co.uk
Web Site: www.shirebooks.com
Key Personnel
Publisher: John Rotheroe
Sales & General Manager: Sue Ross
Publicity Manager: Patience Dizon
Founded: 1962
Subjects: Antiques, Archaeology, Architecture & Interior Design, Biography, Crafts, Games, Hobbies, Electronics, Electrical Engineering, Ethnicity, Gardening, Plants, Genealogy, History, House & Home, Labor, Industrial Relations, Maritime, Military Science, Music, Dance, Natural History, Photography, Social Sciences, Sociology, Sports, Athletics, Transportation, Canals, Coins & Medals, Costume & Fashion Accessories, Egyptology, London, Scottish Heritage, Furniture & Furnishings, Glass, Ceramics, Guide & Walking, Motoring, Railway & Steam, Toys, Collectables, Textile History
ISBN Prefix(es): 0-85263; 0-7478
Number of titles published annually: 30 Print
Total Titles: 500 Print

Sickle Moon Books, *imprint of* Eland Publishing Ltd

Sidgwick & Jackson, *imprint of* Pan Macmillan

Sidgwick & Jackson Ltd+
Imprint of Pan Macmillan
25 Eccleston Place, London SW1W 9NF
Tel: (020) 7881 8000 *Fax:* (020) 7881 8001

UNITED KINGDOM

Key Personnel
Man Dir: William Armstrong
Publicity: Phillipa McEwan
Promotions Officer: James Strachan
Founded: 1908
Subjects: Archaeology, Biography, Cookery, Economics, Fiction, Government, Political Science, History, Military Science, Music, Dance, Sports, Athletics, Travel
ISBN Prefix(es): 0-283
Orders to: Macmillan Distribution Ltd, Brunel Rd, Houndmills, Basingstoke, Hants RG21 6XS

Sigma Leisure, *imprint of* Sigma Press

Sigma Press+
5 Alton Rd, Wilmslow, Cheshire SK9 5DY
Tel: (01625) 531035 *Fax:* (01625) 531035
E-mail: info@sigmapress.co.uk
Web Site: www.sigmapress.co.uk
Key Personnel
Man Dir, Production: Graham Beech
Editorial: Diana Beech
Founded: 1980
Specialize in books on all aspects of leisure activities, particulary of the outdoors.
Membership(s): IPG.
Subjects: Crafts, Games, Hobbies, Music, Dance, Outdoor Recreation, Regional Interests, Sports, Athletics, Transportation
ISBN Prefix(es): 1-85058; 0-905104
Total Titles: 250 Print
Imprints: Sigma Leisure
Warehouse: Thomas Lyster & Co, Unit 9, Ormskirk Industrial Estate, Old Boundary Way, Burscough Rd, Ormskirk L39 2TW *Tel:* (01695) 575112 *Fax:* (01695) 570120

Silver Link Publishing Ltd+
The Trundle, Ringstead Rd, Great Addington, Kettering, Northamptonshire NN14 4BW
Tel: (01536) 330588 *Fax:* (01536) 330469
E-mail: sales@nostalgiacollection.com
Web Site: www.nostalgiacollection.com
Key Personnel
Man Dir: Peter Townsend
Company Secretary: Frances Townsend
Production Manager: Mick Sanders
Founded: 1985
Also acts as book packager.
Subjects: Animals, Pets, Biography, Business, Crafts, Games, Hobbies, Health, Nutrition, History, Humor, Maritime, Nonfiction (General), Transportation, Towns/Cities in the UK & Farming
ISBN Prefix(es): 0-947971; 1-85895; 1-85794
Associate Companies: Past & Present Publishing Ltd

Simon & Schuster Audio, *imprint of* Simon & Schuster Ltd

Simon & Schuster Ltd+
Division of Simon & Schuster Inc
Africa House, 4th floor, 64-78 Kingsway, London WC2B 6AH
Tel: (020) 7316 1900 *Fax:* (020) 7316 0332
E-mail: firstname.surname@simonandschuster.co.uk
Web Site: www.simonsays.co.uk
Telex: 21702
Key Personnel
Man Dir & Chief Executive Officer: Ian Chapman *Fax:* (020) 7316 0291
Publishing Dir, Trade: Susanne Baboneau
Senior Editor, Scribner: Tim Binding
Publisher, Nonfiction: Helen Gummer
Publishing Dir, Children's Books: Ingrid Selberg
Editorial Dir, Martin Books: Janet Copleston
International Publisher: Jonathan Atkins
Sales & Marketing Dir: James Kellow
Rights: Diane Spivey
Production: Karen Ellison
Publicity: Rachael Healey
Dir, Finance: Bob Ness
Founded: 1987
Subjects: Biography, Business, Fiction, Nonfiction (General), Science (General)
ISBN Prefix(es): 0-671; 0-689; 0-684; 0-7434; 0-7432
Total Titles: 200 Audio
Parent Company: Simon & Schuster, 1230 Avenue of the Americas, New York, NY 10020, United States
Ultimate Parent Company: Viacom Inc, 1515 Broadway, New York, NY 10036, United States
Associate Companies: Simon & Schuster Australia, 20 Barcoo St, East Roseville NSW 2069, Australia
Imprints: Earthlink; Free Press; Martin Books; Pocket Books; Scribner; Simon & Schuster Audio; Simon & Schuster's Children's; Touchstone
Divisions: Martin Books
Distributed by S&S Australia; Distieau
Distributor for Pocket Books (US & Europe)
Shipping Address: HarperCollins Publishing Ltd, Westerhill Rd, Bishopbriggs, Glasgow G64 2QT
Warehouse: IBD Ltd, Magna Park, Coventry Rd, Lutterworth, Leics LE17 4XH *Tel:* (01442) 887900
Orders to: HarperCollins Publishing Ltd, Westerhill Rd, Bishopbriggs, Glasgow G64 2Q1
Returns: HarperCollins, Westerhill Rd, Bishopbriggs, Glasgow G64 2Q1

Simon & Schuster's Children's, *imprint of* Simon & Schuster Ltd

Charles Skilton Ltd+
2 Caversham St, London SW3 4AH
Tel: (020) 7351 4995 *Fax:* (020) 7351 4995
Key Personnel
Man Editor: James Hughes
Publicity Manager: Leonard Holdsworth
Founded: 1943
Subjects: Antiques, Art, Biography, Cookery, Erotica, History, Poetry
ISBN Prefix(es): 0-284
Total Titles: 40 Print
Subsidiaries: Albyn Press Ltd; Fortune Press; Luxor Press Ltd; Polybooks Ltd

Skoob Esoterica, *imprint of* Skoob Russell Square

Skoob Pacifica, *imprint of* Skoob Russell Square

Skoob Russell Square+
10 Brunswick Centre, off Bernard St, London WC1N 1AE
Tel: (020) 7278 8760
E-mail: books@skoob.com
Web Site: www.skoob.com
Key Personnel
President & Editorial Dir: I K Ong *E-mail:* ike@skoob.com
Artistic Manager: Mark Lovell *E-mail:* mark@skoob.com
Founded: 1987
Independent & multi-media.
Subjects: Anthropology, Antiques, Art, Asian Studies, Astrology, Occult, Computer Science, Economics, Fiction, Government, Political Science, History, Literature, Literary Criticism, Essays, Mathematics, Philosophy, Poetry, Publishing & Book Trade Reference, Science (General), Technology, Secondhand academic books
ISBN Prefix(es): 1-871438
Total Titles: 48 Print
Imprints: Skoob Esoterica; Skoob Seriph; Skoob Pacifica
Distributed by APG (USA); Gazelle Book Services Ltd (UK)

Skoob Seriph, *imprint of* Skoob Russell Square

SLG Press ((Community of) The Sisters of the Love of God)+
Convent of the Incarnation, Fairacres, Oxford OX4 1TB
Tel: (01865) 721301 *Fax:* (01865) 790860
E-mail: editor@slgpress.co.uk; orders@slgpress.co.uk
Web Site: www.slgpress.co.uk
Key Personnel
Editor: Sr Isabel Mary
Founded: 1967
Subjects: Religion - Other, Theology
ISBN Prefix(es): 0-7283
Number of titles published annually: 6 Print
Total Titles: 74 Print
Parent Company: SLG Charitable Trust Limited
Imprints: Fairacres Publication
Distributed by SCM-Canterbury Press (Australia, UK); Cistercian Publications (USA & Canada)

SLS Legal Publications (NI)
School of Law, The Queen's University Belfast, 28 University Sq, Belfast BT7 1NN
Tel: (028) 9027 3451 *Fax:* (028) 9027 3376; (028) 9033 5040
E-mail: law-enquiries@qub.ac.uk
Web Site: www.law.qub.ac.uk
Key Personnel
Program Dir: Miriam Dudley *E-mail:* m.dudley@qub.ac.uk
Publications Editor: Sara Gamble *E-mail:* s.gamble@qub.ac.uk
Legal Editor: Deborah McBride *E-mail:* d.mcbride@qub.ac.uk
Founded: 1980
Subjects: Law
ISBN Prefix(es): 0-85389

Jacqui Small, *imprint of* Aurum Press Ltd

Smith-Gordon & Co Ltd+
13 Shalcomb St, London SW10 0HZ
Tel: (020) 7351 7042 *Fax:* (020) 7351 1250
E-mail: publisher@smithgordon.com
Key Personnel
Dir & Publisher: Eldred Smith-Gordon
Founded: 1988
Subjects: Health, Nutrition, Medicine, Nursing, Dentistry, Science (General), Technology
ISBN Prefix(es): 1-85463
Total Titles: 80 Print
U.S. Office(s): Books International Inc, PO Box 605, Herndon, VA 22106, United States
Orders to: Smith-Gordon, 47 Worthing Rd, East Preston, Nr Worthing, West Sussex BN16 1DE, Rosemary Harris *Tel:* (01903) 856646 *Fax:* (01903) 856646

Smith Settle Ltd+
23 Sheep St, Burford OX18 4LS
Tel: (01756) 701381 *Fax:* (01524) 251708
E-mail: editorial@dalesman.co.uk
Key Personnel
Man Dir: Kenneth Smith
Editorial Dir: Mark Whitley
Founded: 1986
Membership(s): IPG.
Subjects: Art, Biography, History, Humor, Nonfiction (General), Regional Interests
ISBN Prefix(es): 1-870071; 1-85825
Number of titles published annually: 12 Print
Total Titles: 120 Print
Distributor for Spredden Press (UK); Woodstock Books (UK)

PUBLISHERS   UNITED KINGDOM

Colin Smythe Ltd+
38 Mill Lane, Gerrards Cross, Bucks SL9 8BA
Mailing Address: PO Box 6, Gerrards Cross, Bucks SL9 8XA
Tel: (01753) 886000 *Fax:* (01753) 886469
E-mail: sales@colinsmythe.co.uk
Web Site: www.colinsmythe.co.uk
Key Personnel
Man Dir & International Rights: Colin Smythe
   E-mail: cs@colinsmythe.co.uk
Production Dir: Leslie Hayward
Founded: 1966
Book publishers & author's agent.
Subjects: Biography, Drama, Theater, Literature, Literary Criticism, Essays, Religion - Catholic, Folklore & Mysticism
ISBN Prefix(es): 0-900675; 0-901072; 0-905715; 0-86114; 0-85105
Number of titles published annually: 12 Print
Total Titles: 480 Print
Distributed by Dufour Editions (USA & Canada); Oxford University Press (USA & Canada)
Distributor for ELT Press (Europe); Tir Eolas (Britain & Europe)
Warehouse: c/o Clipper Distribution Services Ltd, Windmill Grove, Portchester, Hants PO16 9HT *Tel:* (02392) 200080 *Fax:* (02392) 200090
Membership(s): IPG; Publishers' Association

Snowbooks Ltd
239 Old St, London EC1V 9EY
Tel: (020) 7553 4473 *Fax:* (020) 7251 3130
E-mail: info@snowbooks.com
Web Site: www.snowbooks.com
Key Personnel
Man Dir: Emma Cahill *Tel:* (079) 0406 2414
   E-mail: emma@snowbooks.com
Founded: 2003
Publishes intelligent yet readable, needful fiction & nonfiction. Nonfiction categories include popular science, business & society.
Subjects: Biography, Business, Earth Sciences, Fiction, Government, Political Science, Management, Nonfiction (General), Philosophy, Physics, Psychology, Psychiatry, Science (General), Science Fiction, Fantasy
Shipping Address: 11 Theresas Walk, Sanderstead Surrey CR2 0AU
Warehouse: 11 Theresas Walk, Sanderstead Surrey CR2 0AU
Distribution Center: 11 Theresas Walk, Sanderstead Surrey CR2 0AU, Contact: Emma Cahill *Tel:* (079) 0406 *Toll Free Tel:* 2414 *Toll Free Fax:* (20) 7251 3130 *E-mail:* emma@snobooks.com
Returns: 11 Theresas Walk, Sanderstead Surrey CR2 0AU
Membership(s): IPG

William Snyder Publishing Associates
5 Five Mile Drive, Oxford OX2 8HT
Tel: (01865) 513186 *Fax:* (01865) 513186
Key Personnel
Man Dir: William Snyder *E-mail:* snyderpub@aol.com
ISBN Prefix(es): 0-948058
Associate Companies: ELC International

Society for Endocrinology, *imprint of* Society for Endocrinology

Society for Endocrinology
22 Apex Court, Woodlands, Bradley Stoke, Bristol BS32 4JT
Tel: (01454) 642200 *Fax:* (01454) 642222
E-mail: info@endocrinology.org; sales@endocrinology.org
Web Site: www.endocrinology.org
Key Personnel
Executive Dir: Sue Thorn *E-mail:* sue.thorn@endocrinology.org
Publications Dir: Steve Byford *E-mail:* steve.byford@endocrinology.org
Sales & Marketing Officer: Lesley Drake
Founded: 1946
Established to promote the study of the endocrine system, publishes journals, books, conference proceedings & newsletters & offers a publication service to pharmaceutical companies
Learned society.
ISBN Prefix(es): 1-898099
Total Titles: 12 Print
Imprints: Bio Scientifica; Society for Endocrinology
Distributed by Portland Press Ltd

The Society for Promoting Christian Knowledge (SPCK)+
Holy Trinity Church, Marylebone Rd, London NW1 4DU
Tel: (020) 7643 0382 *Fax:* (020) 7643 0391
E-mail: spck@spck.org.uk
Web Site: www.spck.org.uk
Key Personnel
Publishing Dir: Simon Kingston
   E-mail: skingston@spck.org.uk
Sales Manager: Susan Kodicek
   E-mail: skodicek@spck.org.uk
Publicity: Corinne Munday *E-mail:* cmunday@spck.org.uk
Founded: 1698
Throughout the UK 28 Outlets.
Subjects: Biblical Studies, Biography, Religion - Catholic, Religion - Protestant, Self-Help, Theology
ISBN Prefix(es): 0-85969; 0-281; 1-902694
Number of titles published annually: 80 Print
Total Titles: 500 Print
Imprints: Azure; Sheldon Press
Distributed by The Pilgrim Press (US)
Warehouse: Marston Christian Warehouse
Orders to: Marston Book Services, PO Box 269, Abingdon, Oxford OX14 47N *Tel:* (01235) 465511 *Fax:* (01235) 465518

Society for Research into Higher Education, see SRHE

The Society of Metaphysicians Ltd+
Archers' Court, Stonestile Lane, The Ridge, Hastings, East Sussex TN35 4PG
Tel: (01424) 751577 *Fax:* (01424) 751577
E-mail: newmeta@btinternet.com; info@metaphysicians.org.uk
Web Site: www.newmeta.btinternet.co.uk; www.metaphysicians.org.uk; www.metaphysicalresearchgroup.org.uk
Key Personnel
President: J J Williamson
Dir, Research: I D Cumberland
General Secretary: Eleanor Swift
Correspondence Education: Terrance Kiernan
Business Secretary: Trevor Sully
Founded: 1944
Publisher of *Neometaphysical Digest* (quarterly).
Subjects: Astrology, Occult, Earth Sciences, Electronics, Electrical Engineering, Environmental Studies, Government, Political Science, Human Relations, Parapsychology, Philosophy, Physical Sciences, Physics, Psychology, Psychiatry, Science (General), Social Sciences, Sociology, Neometaphysics, Paraphysics
ISBN Prefix(es): 1-85228; 1-85810; 0-900684
Number of titles published annually: 150 Print
Total Titles: 2,330 Print
Associate Companies: Istituto Italiano di Ricerche Metafisiche, Triesto, Italy *Tel:* (040) 630315 *Fax:* (040) 630315 *E-mail:* metaresearch@tin.it; Society of Metaphysicians; Society of Metaphysicians (Nigeria) Ltd
Divisions: Metaphysical Research Group
Distributor for Health Research (USA); Sun Books (USA)

Sophia Books, *imprint of* Rudolf Steiner Press

South Asians Overseas Series, *imprint of* Peepal Tree Press Ltd

South Street Press, *imprint of* Garnet Publishing Ltd

Southgate Publishers+
The Square, Sandford, Crediton, Devon EX17 4LW
Tel: (01363) 776888 *Fax:* (01363) 776889
E-mail: info@southgatepublishers.co.uk
Web Site: www.southgatepublishers.co.uk
Key Personnel
Dir: Drummond Johnstone *E-mail:* dj@southgatepublishers.co.uk
Founded: 1991
Specialize in resources for teachers, home learning & life-long learning.
Subjects: Education, Environmental Studies, Mathematics, Music, Dance, Science (General)
ISBN Prefix(es): 1-85741
Total Titles: 120 Print
Subsidiaries: Mosaic Educational Publications
Distributed by Bacon & Hughes (Canada)

Souvenir Press Ltd+
130 Milton Park, Abingdon OX14 4SB
Tel: (01235) 400400 *Fax:* (01235) 400500
E-mail: orders@bookpoint.co.uk *Cable:* PUBLISHER LONDON WC1
Key Personnel
Man Dir, Rights & Permissions: Ernest Hecht
Production: Ken Ruskin
Publicity Executive: James Doyle
Founded: 1951
Subjects: Art, Biography, Fiction, History, How-to, Medicine, Nursing, Dentistry, Music, Dance, Philosophy, Poetry, Psychology, Psychiatry, Religion - Other, Social Sciences, Sociology, Sports, Athletics
ISBN Prefix(es): 0-285
Number of titles published annually: 55 Print
Total Titles: 700 Print
Imprints: Condor Books; Human Horizons Series; Independent Voices; The Story-Tellers
Subsidiaries: Condor Books; Euro-Features Ltd; Pictorial Presentations Ltd; Pop-Universal Ltd; Souvenir Press (Educational & Academic) Ltd; Souvenir Press (Films) Ltd
Orders to: BookPoint Ltd, 39 Milton Trading Estate, Abingdon, Oxon OX14 4TD
   E-mail: orders@bookpoint.co.uk
Membership(s): Publishers' Association

Sovereign International Books, *imprint of* Sovereign World Ltd

Sovereign World Ltd+
Unit 5, Goblands Farm, Cemetry Lane, Hadlow, Kent TN11 0DP
Mailing Address: PO Box 777, Tonbridge, Kent TN11 0ZS
Tel: (01732) 850598 *Fax:* (01732) 851077
E-mail: sovereignworldbooks@compuserve.com
Web Site: www.sovereign-world.org
Key Personnel
President: Chris Mungeam
Man Dir: Tim Pettingale *E-mail:* tim@sovereign-world.com
Founded: 1986
Subjects: Religion - Protestant
ISBN Prefix(es): 1-85240
Imprints: Sovereign International Books

SPA Books Ltd+
PO Box 728, Crawley RH10 7WD
Tel: (01293) 552727 *Fax:* (01438) 310104
E-mail: strongoakpress@hotmail.com

Key Personnel
Man Dir: Stephen Apps
Founded: 1980
Also distributor & retailer.
Subjects: Art, Biography, History, Military Science, Nonfiction (General), Regional Interests, Travel
ISBN Prefix(es): 0-907590
Associate Companies: The Strong Oak Press
Imprints: Strong Oak Press

Sparrowhawk, *imprint of* Hawk Books

SPCK, see The Society for Promoting Christian Knowledge (SPCK)

Speechmark Editions, *imprint of* Speechmark Publishing Ltd

Speechmark Publishing Ltd+
Telford Rd, Bicester, Oxon OX26 4LQ
Tel: (01869) 244644 *Fax:* (01869) 320040
E-mail: info@speechmark.net
Web Site: www.speechmark.net
Key Personnel
Publisher: Ian Franklin *E-mail:* ianf@speechmark.net
Sales Manager: Sally Dickinson *E-mail:* sallyd@speechmark.net
Marketing Manager: Su Underhill *E-mail:* suu@speechmark.net
Publishing Manager: Sarah Miles
  E-mail: sarahm@speechmark.net
Customer Services Manager: Jan Jervis
  E-mail: janj@speechmark.net
Founded: 1984
Practical handbooks for teachers, speech & language therapists, psychologists, occupational therapists & nursing staff.
Subjects: Behavioral Sciences, Child Care & Development, Disability, Special Needs, Education, Health, Nutrition, Language Arts, Linguistics, Medicine, Nursing, Dentistry, Psychology, Psychiatry, Social Sciences, Sociology, Autism, Early Development, Gerontology, Mental Health, Special Needs, Speech & Language
ISBN Prefix(es): 0-86388
Number of titles published annually: 35 Print
Total Titles: 200 Print; 1 CD-ROM; 1 Online; 1 E-Book; 5 Audio
Imprints: ColorCards; Pocket ColorCards; Speechmark Editions
Distributed by Speechbin
Membership(s): IPG

Spellmount Ltd Publishers+
Units 1/K, Paddock Wood Distribution Centre, Paddock Wood, Tonbridge TN12 6UU
Tel: (01892) 837171 *Fax:* (01892) 837272
E-mail: enquiries@spellmount.com
Key Personnel
Publisher: Jamie Wilson
Editorial Dir: Jag Wilson
Founded: 1983
Also acts as book packager.
Subjects: Biography, History, Military Science, Nonfiction (General)
ISBN Prefix(es): 0-946771; 1-873376; 1-86227
Associate Companies: Tom Donovan Publishing; Howell Press; National Army Museum PUBLICATIONS; Ken Trotman Ltd
Warehouse: CBS Ltd, 406 Vale Rd, Tonbridge, Kent TN9 1XR
Orders to: Amalgamated Book Services, Royal Star Arcade, High St, Suite 1, Maidstone, Kent ME14 1JL ME14 1JL, Sales Manager: Frank McNamara *Tel:* (01622) 764 555 *Fax:* (01622) 763 197 (North & East Midlands, Scotland, UK & Ireland)

Ashton International Marketing Services, PO Box 298, Sevenoaks, Kent TN13 1WV *Tel:* (01732) 746 093 *Fax:* (01732) 746 096 (Middle East & Far East)
Barry Brittlebank, 17 Whitehall Crescent, Bradford Rd, Wakefield, West Yorkshire WF1 2AF *Tel:* (01622) 764 555 *Fax:* (01622) 763 197 (Northern UK)
Jonathon Brooks, 57 Greenway, Berkhamsted, Herts (London)
D Richard Brown, Post Box 30037, 5-20061 Malmo 30, Sweden *Tel:* (040) 161 200 *Fax:* (040) 161 208 (Denmark, Finland, Iceland, Norway, Sweden)
European Marketing Services, 55 Overhill Rd, Dulwich, London SE22 0PQ *Tel:* (020) 8516-5433 *Fax:* (020) 8516-5434 (Austria, Belgium, France, Germany & Switzerland)
Owen Hazell, 180 Vale Rd, Tonbridge, Kent TN9 1SP (Southeast, East Anglia)
Robin House, 37 From Park, Bartestree, Hereford HR1 4BF (Southwest, Midland & South Wales)
Iberian Book Services, Sector Islas, Bloque 12, 1, B, 28760 Tres Cantos, Madrid, Spain *Tel:* (09) 1803 49 18 *Fax:* (09) 1803 59 36 (Spain & Portugal)
Carr O'Connell, 342 North Circular Rd, Philsboro, Dublin 7, Ireland (Northern Ireland & Ireland)
Penny Padovani, 56 Rosebank, Holyport Rd, Fulham, London SW6 6LH *Tel:* (020) 7381-3936 (Italy & Greece)
Peribo Pty Ltd, 58 Beaumont Rd, Mount Kuringgai, NSW 2080, Australia, Contact: Andrew Coffey *Tel:* (02) 9457 0011 *Fax:* (02) 9457 0022 (Australia & New Zealand)

Spindlewood, *imprint of* Ragged Bears Ltd

Spokesman+
Imprint of Bertrand Russell Peace Foundation Ltd
Russell House, Bulwell Lane, Nottingham NG6 0BT
Tel: (0115) 9708318; (0115) 9784504 *Fax:* (0115) 9420433
E-mail: elfeuro@compuserve.com
Web Site: www.spokesmanbooks.com; www.russfound.org
Key Personnel
Editorial: Ken Coates
Publications Manager, Rights & Permissions: Anthony Simpson
Production: Ken Fleet
Founded: 1970
Subjects: Business, Economics, Environmental Studies, Government, Political Science, Labor, Industrial Relations, Social Sciences, Sociology, Peace & Human Rights
ISBN Prefix(es): 0-85124
Associate Companies: Russell Press Ltd, Radford Mill, Norton St, Nottingham NG7 3HN

Spon Press, *imprint of* Taylor & Francis

Spon Press
Member of Taylor & Francis Group
11 New Fetter Lane, London EC4P 4EE
Tel: (020) 7583 9855 *Fax:* (020) 7842 2298
E-mail: info@routledge.co.uk
Web Site: www.sponpress.com
Key Personnel
Man Dir: Marianne Russell
Editorial Dir: Phillip Read
Marketing Dir: Robert Creffield
Production: Gavin Macdonald
Sales Manager: Chris Hall
Area Sales Export: Graham Boaler; Mima Birks
Rights & Permissions: Anna Bisztyga
Founded: 1834
Subjects: Architecture & Interior Design, Civil Engineering, Crafts, Games, Hobbies, Environmental Studies, Real Estate, Sports, Athletics, Transportation
ISBN Prefix(es): 0-413; 0-419

Sportman's Press, *imprint of* Quiller Publishing Ltd

Sports Turf Research Institute (STRI)
St Ives Estate, Bingley, West Yorks BD16 1AU
Tel: (01274) 565131 *Fax:* (01274) 561891
E-mail: info@stri.co.uk
Web Site: www.stri.co.uk
Key Personnel
Chief Executive: Dr Gordon McKillop
  E-mail: gordon.mckillop@stri.co.uk
Founded: 1929
Independent consultancy & research organization specializing in natural turf grass & sports surfaces.
Subjects: Turfgrass Science for Sports Surfaces
Number of titles published annually: 4 Print; 1 CD-ROM
Total Titles: 2 CD-ROM

The Sportsman's Press+
25 King Charles Walk, London SW19 6JA
Tel: (020) 8789 0229 *Fax:* (020) 8789 0229
Key Personnel
Publisher & Rights: Kenneth Kemp
Founded: 1984
Subjects: Humor, Sports, Athletics, Equestrian, Country Sports
ISBN Prefix(es): 0-948253
Orders to: Vine House, Waldenbury, North Common, Chailey, BN8 4DR East Sussex *Tel:* (01825) 723398 *Fax:* (01825) 724188

Springer-Verlag London Ltd+
Sweetapple House, Catteshall Rd, Goldaming, Surrey GU7 3DJ
Tel: (0483) 418800; (01483) 418822 (sales) *Fax:* (01483) 415151; (01483) 415144
E-mail: orders@springer.de
Key Personnel
Man Dir: John Watson
Founded: 1987
Subjects: Astronomy, Computer Science, Engineering (General), Mathematics, Medicine, Nursing, Dentistry
ISBN Prefix(es): 1-85233
Parent Company: Springer-Verlag GmbH & Co KG, Heidelberger Platz 3, 14197 Berlin, Germany

Square One Publications+
The Tudor House, 16 Church St, Upton Office Services, Upton-upon Severn, Worcester WR8 OH7
Tel: (01684) 593704 *Fax:* (01684) 594640
Key Personnel
Contact: Mary Wilkinson *E-mail:* marywilk@rinyonline.co.uk
Founded: 1988
Subjects: Militaria, autobiographies
ISBN Prefix(es): 1-899955
Warehouse: Upton Office Services, 18 Riverside Close Upton-On Severn, Worcester WR8 0JN, Contact: Deidre Thompson *Tel:* (01684) 592035 *E-mail:* deidre@uptonjazz.farmcom.net

SRHE
76 Portland Pl, London W1B 1NT
Tel: (020) 7637 2766 *Fax:* (020) 7637 2781
E-mail: srheoffice@srhe.ac.uk
Web Site: www.srhe.ac.uk
Key Personnel
Dir: Prof Heather Eggins *E-mail:* heathereggins@srhe.ac.uk
Founded: 1965

The Society is a registered charity & publishes mainly in cooperation with Open University Press.
Subjects: Education
ISBN Prefix(es): 0-9510798

Stacey International+
128 Kensington Church St, W8 4BH London
Tel: (020) 7221 7166 *Fax:* (020) 7792 9288
E-mail: stacey-inter@btconnect.com
Web Site: www.stacey-international.co.uk
Key Personnel
Chairman: Tom Stacey
Chief Executive: Max Scott
Marketing Manager: Kitty Carruthers
Customer Service: Meave Beckett
 E-mail: meave@stacey-international.co.uk
Founded: 1974
Subjects: Archaeology, Architecture & Interior Design, Art, Business, Cookery, Education, Foreign Countries, Gardening, Plants, Genealogy, Geography, Geology, History, Natural History, Religion - Islamic, Travel
ISBN Prefix(es): 0-905743; 0-9503304; 0-900988
Total Titles: 40 Print
Parent Company: Stacey Arts Ltd
Imprints: Royal Genealogies; Stacey London
Distribution Center: Central Books, 99 Wallis Rd, London E9 5LN, Contact: Katie Sneyd *Tel:* (0845) 458 9911 *Fax:* (0845) 458 9912
 E-mail: orders@centralbooks.com
Interlink Publishing Group, 46 Crosby St, Northampton, MA 01060-1804, United States *Tel:* 413-582-7054 *Fax:* 413-582-7057
 E-mail: info@interlinkbooks.com
Portfolio, Unit 5 Perivale Industrial Park, Horsenden Lane S, Greenford, Middlesex UB6 7RL *Tel:* (020) 8997 9000 *Fax:* (020) 8997 9097 *E-mail:* sales@portfoliobooks.co.uk (travel & children's titles)
Orders to: Portfolio, Unit 5 Perivale Industrial Park, Horsenden Lane S, Greenford, Middlesex UB6 7RL *Tel:* (020) 8997 9000 *Fax:* (020) 8997 9097 *E-mail:* sales@portfoliobooks.co.uk

Staff & Educational Development Association, see SEDA Publications

Stainer & Bell Ltd
Victoria House, 23 Gruneisen Rd, London N3 1DZ
Mailing Address: PO Box 110, London N3 1DZ
Tel: (020) 8343 3303 *Fax:* (020) 8343 3024
E-mail: post@stainer.co.uk
Web Site: www.stainer.co.uk
Key Personnel
Joint Man Dir, Production: Carol Wakefield
 E-mail: carol@stainer.co.uk
Joint Man Dir, Publicity, Rights & Permissions: Keith Wakefield *E-mail:* keith@stainer.co.uk
Publishing Dir: Nicholas Williams
 E-mail: nicholas@stainer.co.uk
Founded: 1907
Subjects: Education, Music, Dance, Religion - Other
ISBN Prefix(es): 0-85249
Imprints: Augener; Belton Books; Galliard; A Weekes; Joseph Williams

Harold Starke Publishers Ltd
203 Bunyan Court, Barbican, London EC2Y 8DH
Tel: (01379) 388334; (020) 7588 5195
 Fax: (01379) 388335
E-mail: red@eclat.force9.co.uk
Key Personnel
Editorial, Rights & Permissions: Miss N Galinski
Export Sales: Harold Starke
Founded: 1960
Membership(s): the British Publishers Association.
Subjects: Medicine, Nursing, Dentistry

ISBN Prefix(es): 0-287; 1-872457
Distribution Center: Pixey Green, Stradbroke, Eye, Suffolk IP21 5NG

The Stationery Office, see TSO (The Stationery Office)

Rudolf Steiner Press+
Imprint of Anthroposophic Press Inc
35 Park Rd, London NW1 6XT
Mailing Address: Hillside House, The Square, Forest Row, East Sussex RH18 5ES
Tel: (01342) 824433 *Fax:* (01342) 826437
E-mail: office@rudolfsteinerpress.com; editorial@rudolfsteinerpress.com
Web Site: www.rudolfsteinerpress.com
Key Personnel
Chief Editor: Sevak Gulbekian
Marketing Assistant/Administrator: K Bernard
Founded: 1920
Subjects: Agriculture, Art, Biography, Education, Health, Nutrition, Music, Dance, Philosophy, Self-Help
ISBN Prefix(es): 0-85440; 1-85584
Number of titles published annually: 15 Print
Total Titles: 400 Print
Imprints: Sophia Books
Distributor for BookSource (USA); Mercury Arts Publications (UK); New Knowledge Books (UK)
Distribution Center: Anthroposophic Press, PO Box 960, Herndon, VA 20172-0960, United States *E-mail:* service@anthropress.org (US)
Ceres Books, PO Box 11-336, Ellerslie, Auckland 5, New Zealand *Tel:* (09) 574 3356 *Fax:* (09) 527 4513 *E-mail:* info@ceres.co.nz (New Zealand)
Rudolf Steiner Book Centre, 307 Sussex St, Sydney, NSW 2000, Australia *Tel:* (02) 9264 5169 *Fax:* (02) 9267 1225 (Australia)
Rudolf Steiner Publications, PO Box 71925, 235 Bryanston Drive, Bryanston 2021 *Tel:* (011) 706 8544 *Fax:* (011) 706 4136 *E-mail:* steinerp@netactive.co.za (South Africa)
Tri-fold Books, Box 32, Stn Main, Guelph, ON N1H 6J6, Canada *Tel:* 519-821-9901 *Fax:* 519-821-5333 (Canada)
Orders to: BookSource, Cowlairs Industrial Estate, 32 Finlas St, Glasgow G22 5DU *Tel:* (0141) 558 1366 *Fax:* (0141) 557 0189 *E-mail:* orders@booksource.net
Returns: BookSource, Cowlairs Industrial Estate, 32 Finlas St, Glasgow G22 5DU

Stenlake Publishing Ltd+
54-58 Mill Sq, Catrine, Ayrshire KA5 6RD
Tel: (01290) 551122 *Fax:* (01290) 551122
E-mail: info@stenlake.co.uk
Web Site: www.stenlake.co.uk
Founded: 1984
Subjects: History, Maritime, Regional Interests
ISBN Prefix(es): 1-872074; 1-84033
Number of titles published annually: 50 Print
Total Titles: 350 Print

Patrick Stephens Ltd, *imprint of* Haynes Publishing

Sterling Audio Books, *imprint of* BBC Audiobooks

Stobart & Son Ltd, *imprint of* Stobart Davies Ltd

Stobart Davies Ltd+
Stobart House Pontyclerc, Penybanc Rd, Ammanford SA18 3HP
Tel: (01269) 593100 *Fax:* (01269) 596116
E-mail: sales@stobartdavies.com
Web Site: www.stobartdavies.com

Key Personnel
Publicity: Jane Evans *E-mail:* jane@stobartdavies.com
Rights & Permissions: Nigel Evans
Founded: 1989
Subjects: Crafts, Games, Hobbies, How-to, Natural History, Woodwork, Craft & Forestry
ISBN Prefix(es): 0-85442
Number of titles published annually: 5 Print
Total Titles: 65 Print
Imprints: Stobart & Son Ltd

Stokesby House Publications+
Stokesby, Norfolk NR29 3ET
Tel: (01493) 750645 *Fax:* (01493) 750146
E-mail: stokesbyhouse@btinternet.com
Web Site: www.stokesbyhouse.co.uk
Key Personnel
Contact: Pamela Minett
Subjects: Biological Sciences, Environmental Studies
ISBN Prefix(es): 0-9514490; 1-873600

Story Sound Audio Tapes, *imprint of* Magna Large Print Books

The Story-Tellers, *imprint of* Souvenir Press Ltd

Stott's Correspondence College
POB 35488, St Johns Wood, London NW8 6WD
Tel: (020) 586 4499 *Fax:* (020) 722 1068
E-mail: microworld@ndirect.co.uk
Web Site: www.microworld.ndirect.co.uk
Specialize in correspondence courses.
Subjects: Health, Nutrition, Calligraphy, Dressmaking, Fitness, Locksmithing

Strategic Comments, *imprint of* International Institute for Strategic Studies

Strategic Survey, *imprint of* International Institute for Strategic Studies

STRI, see Sports Turf Research Institute (STRI)

Strong Oak Press, *imprint of* SPA Books Ltd

Studio Editions Ltd+
Random House, 20 Vauxhall Bridge Rd, London SWIV 2SA
Tel: (020) 7973 9690 *Fax:* (020) 7233 6057
Telex: 261212
Key Personnel
Chairman: Sonia Land
Dir: J Roderick Webb
Rights Dir: K T Forster
Founded: 1982
Subjects: Antiques, Architecture & Interior Design, Art
ISBN Prefix(es): 0-946495; 1-85170; 1-85891
Subsidiaries: BPL Remainders; Studio Designs
Warehouse: Grantham Book Services Ltd, Isaac Newton Way, Alma Park Industrial East, Grantham Lincs NG31 9SD

Sunflower Books
12 Kendrick Mews, London SW7 3HG
Tel: (020) 7589 1862 *Fax:* (020) 7589 1862
E-mail: mail@sunflowerbooks.co.uk
Web Site: www.sunflowerbooks.co.uk
Key Personnel
Joint Man Dir: John Seccombe *Tel:* (01392) 274686; Patricia Underwood
Founded: 1982
Subjects: Travel, Landscapes; walking & touring guides to (mainly) European destinations
ISBN Prefix(es): 0-948513; 1-85691
Number of titles published annually: 6 Print
Total Titles: 48 Print
Parent Company: P A Underwood Ltd

Distributed by Hunter Publishing (USA)
Orders to: Macmillan Distribution Ltd, Brunel Rd, Houndmills, Basingstoke RG21 6XS
Tel: (01256) 302692 *Fax:* (01256) 812558

Supportive Learning Publications+
23 West View, Chirk, Wrexham LL14 5HL
Tel: (01691) 774778 *Fax:* (01691) 774849
E-mail: sales@slpuk.demon.co.uk
Web Site: www.slpuk.demon.co.uk
Key Personnel
Contact: Phil Roberts
Founded: 1988
Subjects: Disability, Special Needs, Drama, Theater, Education, English as a Second Language, Geography, Geology, History, Humor, Mathematics, Poetry, Science (General)
ISBN Prefix(es): 1-86109; 1-871585
Distributed by Galt Educational; Hope Education; The Yorklshire Purchasing Group

Survival, *imprint of* International Institute for Strategic Studies

Sussex Publications
POB 35488, St Johns Wood, London NW8 6WD
Tel: (020) 586 4499 *Fax:* (020) 722 1068
E-mail: microworld@ndirect.co.uk
Web Site: www.microworld.ndirect.co.uk
Subjects: History, Music, Dance, English
ISBN Prefix(es): 1-86013; 0-905272
Total Titles: 400 Print; 2 CD-ROM

Sutton Publishing Ltd+
Subsidiary of Haynes Publishing
Phoenix Mill, Thrupp, Stroud, Glos GL5 2BU
Tel: (01453) 731114 *Fax:* (01453) 731117
E-mail: sales@sutton-publishing.co.uk; editorial@sutton-publishing.co.uk; publishing@sutton-publishing.co.uk
Web Site: www.suttonpublishing.co.uk
Key Personnel
Man Dir: Keith Fullman
Publishing Dir, Permissions: Peter Clifford
Sales & Marketing Dir: Jeremy Yates-Round
Foreign Rights Manager: Viktoria Tischer
Contact: Rachel Graham *Tel:* (01453) 732409 *E-mail:* rachelgraham@sutton-publishing.co.uk
Founded: 1979
Subjects: Agriculture, Archaeology, Architecture & Interior Design, Art, Biography, Business, Engineering (General), Fiction, Genealogy, History, House & Home, Human Relations, Labor, Industrial Relations, Literature, Literary Criticism, Essays, Maritime, Military Science, Nonfiction (General), Photography, Regional Interests, Religion - Protestant, Social Sciences, Sociology, Sports, Athletics, Technology, Transportation, Travel
ISBN Prefix(es): 0-86299; 0-904387; 0-7509
Number of titles published annually: 200 Print
Total Titles: 800 Print
Imprints: Pocket Classics; In Old Photographs; Illustrated History Paperbacks; Pocket Biographies; Pocket Histories
Distributor for Army Records Society; History of Parliament Trust
Distribution Center: Haynes Publishing, Sparkford, Near Yeoril, Somerset BA22 7JJ

Swan Hill Press, *imprint of* Quiller Publishing Ltd

Sweet & Maxwell, *imprint of* Sweet & Maxwell Ltd

Sweet & Maxwell Ltd+
Cheriton House, North Way, Andover SP10 5BE
Tel: (020) 7393 7000; (020) 7449 1104
Fax: (020) 7449 1144
E-mail: info@routledge.co.uk
Founded: 1799
Subjects: Law
ISBN Prefix(es): 0-421; 0-420; 0-414
Parent Company: Thomson Corporation Publishing Ltd
Ultimate Parent Company: The Thomson Corporation, Toronto Dominion Bank Tower, Suite 2706, PO Box 24, Toronto Dominion Centre, Toronto, ON M5K 1A1, Canada
Imprints: Sweet & Maxwell; W Green; Roundhall Sweet & Maxwell
Subsidiaries: W Green; Roundhall Sweet & Maxwell
Distributor for Carswell (Europe); LBC (Europe); WGL (Europe)
Orders to: Cheriton House, North Way, Andover, Hants SP10 5BE

Sydney Jary Ltd+
9 Upper Belgrave Rd, Clifton, Bristol BS8 2XH
Tel: (0117) 974-1640 *Fax:* (0117) 973-7116
E-mail: admin@s-jary.co.uk
Key Personnel
Contact: Michael C Ross
Founded: 1960
Subjects: Biography, Business, History, Management, Military Science
Associate Companies: Avon World Limited

Symposium Press, *imprint of* Science Reviews Ltd

T & AD Poyser Ltd, *imprint of* Christopher Helm (Publishers) Ltd

Ta Ha Publishers Ltd
One Wynne Rd, London SW9 0BB
Tel: (020) 7737 7266 *Fax:* (020) 7737 7267
E-mail: sales@taha.co.uk
Web Site: www.taha.co.uk
Subjects: Religion - Islamic
ISBN Prefix(es): 0-907461; 1-897940; 1-842000
Number of titles published annually: 30 Print
Total Titles: 270 Print; 120 Online
Bookshop(s): Islamic Bookstore.com
Distribution Center: Islamic Bookstore.com
Orders to: 2040-F Lord Baltimore Drive, Baltimore, MD 21244, United States

Tabb House+
7 Church St, Padstow, Cornwall PL28 8BG
Tel: (01841) 532316 *Fax:* (01841) 532316
E-mail: tabbhouse@connexions.co.uk; books@tabb-house.fsnet.co.uk
Key Personnel
Chief Executive, Dir: Caroline White
Founded: 1980
Book Publisher.
Subjects: Biography, Fiction, Literature, Literary Criticism, Essays, Nonfiction (General), Poetry, Children's Fiction
ISBN Prefix(es): 0-907018; 1-873951; 0-9534079
Number of titles published annually: 4 Print
Total Titles: 103 Print
Distributed by Tor Mark Press
Orders to: Gardeners Books Ltd, One Whittle Dr, Willington Dr, Eastbourne, Sussex BN23 6QH *Tel:* (01323) 521 555 *Fax:* (01323) 521 666 *E-mail:* sales@gardners.com *Web Site:* gardners.com

The TAFT Group, *imprint of* Thomson Gale

Taigh Na Teud Music Publishers
13 Upper Breakish, Isle of Skye IV42 8PY
Tel: (01471) 822528 *Fax:* (01471) 822811
E-mail: sales@scotlandsmusic.com
Web Site: www.scotlandsmusic.com
Key Personnel
Sales Manager: Alasdair Martin
Founded: 1985
Subjects: Music, Dance
ISBN Prefix(es): 1-871931
Number of titles published annually: 6 Print; 2 CD-ROM
Total Titles: 60 Print; 12 CD-ROM

Take That Ltd, *imprint of* Verulam Publishing Ltd

Take That Ltd+
Imprint of Verulam Publishing Ltd
PO Box 200, Harrogate HG1 2YR
Tel: (01423) 507545 *Fax:* (01423) 526035
E-mail: sales@takethat.co.uk
Web Site: www.takethat.co.uk
Key Personnel
Man Dir: Chris Brown
Founded: 1987
Subjects: Business, Computer Science, Finance, Media/Sport, Gambling
ISBN Prefix(es): 1-873668; 0-9516461; 0-9519489; 1-903994
Number of titles published annually: 15 Print; 6 E-Book
Total Titles: 55 Print; 12 E-Book
Imprints: Net.Works
Distributed by Trafalgar Square
Distributor for Cardoza (Europe); Maximedia (UK)
Foreign Rep(s): Trafalgar Square Publishing (USA)
Orders to: Verulam, 152a Park Street Lane, Park St, St Albans, Herts AL2 2AU

Tales of Heaven & Earth, *imprint of* Moonlight Publishing Ltd

Tango Books+
Division of Sadie Fields Productions Ltd
4 C/D West Point, 36-37 Warple Way, London W3 ORG
Tel: (020) 8996 9970 *Fax:* (020) 8996 9977
E-mail: edith@tangobooks.co.uk
Key Personnel
Dir: David Fielder *Tel:* (020) 8735 4935 *E-mail:* david@tangobooks.co.uk; Sheri Safran *Tel:* (020) 8735 4931 *E-mail:* sheri@tangobooks.co.uk
Founded: 1991
ISBN Prefix(es): 1-85707
Imprints: Tango Cards
Distributor for Innovative Kids; Soundprints; Van der Meer
Warehouse: The Trade Center Ltd, Mendlesham Industrial Estate, Norwich Rd, Mendlesham, Suffolk IP14 5NA

Tango Cards, *imprint of* Tango Books

Taprobane Ltd
PO Box 717, London W5 3EY
Tel: (020) 8998 3024 *Fax:* (020) 8810 5415
ISBN Prefix(es): 1-873344

Tarantula Books, *imprint of* Geddes & Grosset

Tarquin, *imprint of* Tarquin Publications

Tarquin Publications+
Stradbroke, Diss, Norfolk IP21 5JP
Tel: (01379) 384 218 *Fax:* (01379) 384 289
E-mail: enquiries@tarquin-books.demon.co.uk
Web Site: www.tarquin-books.demon.co.uk
Key Personnel
Chief Executive, Editorial, Rights & Permissions: Gerald Jenkins *E-mail:* gerald@tarquin-books.demon.co.uk
Sales: Margaret Jenkins
Founded: 1970

PUBLISHERS

UNITED KINGDOM

Subjects: Education, Mathematics, Science (General)
ISBN Prefix(es): 0-906212; 1-899618
Number of titles published annually: 7 Print
Total Titles: 99 Print
Imprints: Tarquin; DIME
Membership(s): IPG

Taschen Evergreen, *imprint of* Taschen UK Ltd

Taschen UK Ltd+
Subsidiary of Taschen GmbH
13 Old Burlington St, London W1S 3AJ
Tel: (020) 7437 4350 *Fax:* (020) 7437 4360
E-mail: contact@taschen.com
Web Site: www.taschen.com
Key Personnel
Public Relations: Christa Urbain *E-mail:* c.urbain@taschen.com
Founded: 1994
Subjects: Art, Fashion, Photography, Architecture, Design
ISBN Prefix(es): 3-8228
Associate Companies: TASHEN Deutschland, Hohenzollernring 53, 50672 Cologne, Germany, Public Relations: Dr Christine Waiblinger *Tel:* (0221) 201 80 170 *Fax:* (0221) 201 80 42 *E-mail:* c.waiblinger@taschen-deutschland.com; TASCHEN Espana, c/ Victor Hugo, 1, 2° Dcha, Madrid, Spain, Customer Services: Mr Fernando Gonzalez *Tel:* (091) 360 50 63 *Fax:* (091) 360 50 64 *E-mail:* f.gonzalez@taschen-espana.com; TASCHEN France, 82, Rue Mazarine, 75006 Paris, France, Customer Services: Ms Regina Masanes *Tel:* (01) 40 51 70 93 *Fax:* (01) 43 26 73 80 *E-mail:* r.masanes@taschen-france.com; TASCHEN Japan, Atelier Ark Bldg, 5-11-23, Minami Aoyama Minato-Ku, Tokyo 107-0062, Japan, Public Relations: Ms Asuka Shibata *Tel:* (03) 57 78 30 00 *Fax:* (03) 57 78 30 30 *E-mail:* order@taschen-japan.com
Imprints: Taschen Evergreen
U.S. Office(s): Taschen USA, 230 Fifth Ave, Suite 1411, New York, NY 10001, United States, Contact: Paul Norton
Warehouse: Grantham Book Services, Isaac Newton Way, Alma Park Industrial Estate, Grantham, Lincs N931 9SD *Tel:* (01476) 541000 (UK only)
Distribution Center: Grantham Book Services, Isaac Newton Way, Alma Park Industrial Estate, Grantham, Lincs N931 9SD (UK only)

Tate Publishing Ltd+
Millbank, London SW1P 4RG
Tel: (020) 7887 8000; (020) 7887 8008
Fax: (020) 7887 8878
E-mail: tp.enquiries@tate.org.uk
Web Site: www.tate.org.uk *Cable:* TATEGAL LONDON
Key Personnel
Chief Executive: Celia Clear *E-mail:* celia.clear@tate.org.uk
Editor: Judith Severne *Tel:* (020) 7887 8868
E-mail: judith.severne@tate.org.uk
Picture Rights: Chris Webster *Tel:* (020) 7887 8867 *Fax:* (020) 7887 8900 *E-mail:* chris.webster@tate.org.uk
Sales & Rights Dir: James Attlee *E-mail:* james.attlee@tate.org.uk
Publishing Dir: Roger Thorp *Tel:* (020) 7887 8617 *E-mail:* roger.thorp@tate.org.uk
Founded: 1931
Publishers of art books, exhibition catalogues & gallery guides of modern art & British art since 1550.
Subjects: Architecture & Interior Design, Art, Education, Art History
ISBN Prefix(es): 1-85437
Number of titles published annually: 30 Print
Total Titles: 150 Print
Parent Company: Tate Enterprises
Ultimate Parent Company: Tate Gallery
Subsidiaries: Tate Gallery Liverpool; Tate Gallery Modern; Tate Gallery St Ives
Distributed by Thames & Hudson Pty Ltd (Australia); Harry N Abrams Inc (USA & Canada)

Tauris Academic Studies, *imprint of* I B Tauris & Co Ltd

I B Tauris & Co Ltd+
6 Salem Rd, London W2 4BU
Tel: (020) 7243 1225 *Fax:* (01727) 856398
E-mail: mail@ibtauris.com
Web Site: www.ibtauris.com
Key Personnel
Chairman & Publisher: Iradj Bagherzade
E-mail: ibagherzade@ibtauris.com
Man Dir: Jonathan McDonnell
E-mail: jmcdonnell@ibtauris.com
Financial Controller: Liz Stuckey
E-mail: lstuckey@ibtauris.com
Production: N Denny *E-mail:* ndenny@ibtauris.com
Marketing Manager: Paul Davighi
E-mail: pdavighi@ibtauris.com
Editor: H Birks; P Brewster; L Crook; D Stonestreet; A Wright
Rights Manager & US Publishing Manager: Isabella Steer *E-mail:* isteer@ibtauris.com
International Sales Manager: Martin Ashworth
E-mail: mashworth@ibtauris.com
Publicist: Ben Usher *E-mail:* busher@ibtauris.com
Founded: 1983
Independent publisher of both scholarly & general interest books
Specialize in Middle East studies, history, politics, international relations, film & visual culture.
Subjects: Architecture & Interior Design, Asian Studies, Developing Countries, Film, Video, Government, Political Science, History, Nonfiction (General), Religion - Islamic, Cultural Studies, Middle East Studies
ISBN Prefix(es): 1-85043; 1-86064
Number of titles published annually: 175 Print
Imprints: British Academic Press; Tauris Academic Studies; Tauris Parke; Tauris Parke Paperbacks
U.S. Office(s): I B Tauris & Co Ltd, St Martin's Press, 175 Fifth Ave, New York, NY 10010, United States *Tel:* 212-982-3900 *Fax:* 212-777-6359
Palgrave Macmillan, 175 Fifth Ave, New York, NY 10010, United States *Tel:* 212-982-3900 *Fax:* 212-982-5562
Distributor for The Khalili Collection (Worldwide); Saqi Books (USA only); Philip Wilson Publishers (Worldwide)
Orders to: Thomson Publishing Services, Cheriton House, North Way, Andover SP10 5BE

Tauris Parke, *imprint of* I B Tauris & Co Ltd

Tauris Parke Paperbacks, *imprint of* I B Tauris & Co Ltd

Taylor & Francis, *imprint of* Taylor & Francis

Taylor & Francis+
Member of Taylor & Francis Group
4 Park Sq, Milton Park, Abingdon, Oxon OX14 4RN
Tel: (01235) 828600 *Fax:* (01235) 828900
E-mail: info@tandf.co.uk
Web Site: www.tandf.co.uk
Key Personnel
Chief Executive: Peter Rigby
Man Dir Books & Journals: Roger Horton
Journal Marketing Dir: Bev Acreman
Books Sales Dir: C Chesher
Man Dir Psychology Press: Mike Forster
Journal Sales: K R Courtney
Founded: 1798
Subjects: Accounting, Art, Business, Computer Science, Economics, Education, Engineering (General), Finance, Government, Political Science, History, Human Relations, Language Arts, Linguistics, Management, Mathematics, Medicine, Nursing, Dentistry, Physics, Psychology, Psychiatry, Religion - Other, Social Sciences, Sociology, Transportation
ISBN Prefix(es): 0-85066; 1-85000; 0-7484
Number of titles published annually: 3,000 Print
Parent Company: Taylor & Francis Informa
Imprints: Brunner-Routledge; Carfax Publishing; Europa; Garland Science; Martin Dunitz; Psychology Press; Routledge; RoutledgeCurzon; RoutledgeFalmer; Spon Press; Taylor & Francis; Taylor & Francis Asia Pacific
Subsidiaries: Routledge Inc
Foreign Rep(s): Routledge Inc (North America); Routledge India Liaison (India); Taylor & Francis Group (East Asia, North America); United Publishers Services (Japan)
Foreign Rights: David Barrett-Jolley (Botswana); Marco Castellan (Central America, France, Italy, Portugal, South America, Spain); Christoph Chesher (UK); Sandra Collins (Austria, Germany & Switzerland); Graham Crossley (UK); Peter Havinga (Belgium, Netherlands, Greece, Luxembourg); Sophie Hopkin (Israel); M Anwer Iqbal (Pakistan); Se-Yung Jun (Korea); Barbie Keene (Zimbabwe); Lillian Koe (Malaysia); Jeffrey Lim (China, Taiwan); Roy Mansell (Lesotho, Namibia, South Africa); Vera Medeiros (Brazil); Michelle Swinge (Australia, Asia); Chinke Ojiji (Nigeria); Nick Pepper (Denmark, Finland, Iceland, Norway, Sweden); Ian Pringle (Brunei, Indonesia, Singapore, Thailand); Sophie Rogers (London); I J Sagun (Philippines); Hema Shah (Eastern Europe); Ed Summerson (Hong Kong); Takahiko Kaneko (Japan); Rachel Zillig (Caribbean, Middle East, North Africa, West Indies)
Orders to: ITPS, Cheriton House Northway, Andover SP10 5BE *Tel:* (01264) 342926

Taylor & Francis Asia Pacific, *imprint of* Taylor & Francis

Taylor & Francis Medical Books+
Formerly Martin Dunitz Ltd; Parthenon Publishing
Member of Taylor & Francis Group
11 New Fetter Lane, London EC4P 4EE
Tel: (020) 7842 2244 *Fax:* (020) 7842 2300
Key Personnel
Head of Medical Publishing: Nick Dunton
E-mail: nick.dunton@tandf.co.uk
Man Dir: Martin Dunitz *E-mail:* martin.dunitz@tandf.co.uk
Editor Commissioning: Robert Peden
E-mail: robert.peden@tandf.co.uk
Commissioning Editor: Alan Burgess
E-mail: alan.burgess@tandf.co.uk
Man Editor: Alison Campbell *E-mail:* alison.campbell@tandf.co.uk
Production: Rosemary Allen *E-mail:* rosemary.allen@tandf.co.uk
Marketing Manager: Daniel Tomkins
E-mail: daniel.tomkins@tandf.co.uk
Journal Sales & Advertising: Ian Mellor
E-mail: ian.mellor@tandf.co.uk
Rights Manager: Carla Oliveira *E-mail:* carla.oliveira@tandf.co.uk
Head of Special Sales: Beth Bacchus
E-mail: beth.bacchus@tandf.co.uk
Journal Editorial Enquiries: Maire Collins
E-mail: maire.collins@2tankd.co.uk
Customer Services: Teresa Davey *E-mail:* teresa.davey@tandf.co.uk

UNITED KINGDOM

General Enquiries: Heather Cameron
E-mail: heather.cameron@tandf.co.uk
Founded: 1978 (by Ruth & Martin Dunitz)
Medical publishers of postgraduate books & journals.
Recipient of 1991 Queen's Award for Export Achievement.
Subjects: Medicine, Nursing, Dentistry, Psychology, Psychiatry
ISBN Prefix(es): 0-906348; 0-948269; 1-85317; 1-84184; 1-901865
Number of titles published annually: 130 Print
Total Titles: 420 Print; 1 CD-ROM
Associate Companies: Isis Medical Media
Distributed by Taylor & Francis Group plc
Distributor for Remedica
Warehouse: ITPS, Cheriton House, North Way, Andover Hants SP10 5BE *Tel:* (01264) 342937 *Fax:* (01264) 343005
Orders to: ITPS, Cheriton House, North Way, Andover Hants SP10 5BE *Tel:* (01264) 342937 *Fax:* (01264) 343005

Taylor Graham Publishing
48 Regent St, Cambridge CB2 1FD
Web Site: www.taylorgraham.com
Key Personnel
Dir: Peter J Taylor
Founded: 1984
Subjects: Computer Science, Library & Information Sciences, Management, Technology
ISBN Prefix(es): 0-947568
U.S. Office(s): PMB 187, 12021 Wilshire Blvd, Los Angeles, CA 90025, United States

Teach Yourself, *imprint of* Hodder Education

Teeney Books Ltd+
Arlington House, 72 Fore St, Trowbridge BA14 8HD
Tel: (01225) 775657 *Fax:* (01225) 775676
E-mail: teeneybo@primex.co.uk
Key Personnel
Man Dir: Tiny de Vries
Production Dir: Martyn Lewis
Founded: 1990
ISBN Prefix(es): 1-873338; 1-85952

Telegraph Books+
One Canada Sq, Canary Wharf, London E14 5DT
Tel: (020) 7538 5000 *Fax:* (020) 7538 6064
Web Site: www.telegraph.co.uk
Telex: 22874 Telldn G
Key Personnel
Publisher: Morven Knowles
Product Manager: Clare Sims *E-mail:* clare.sims@telegraph.co.uk
Founded: 1930
Subjects: Cookery, Education, Gardening, Plants, Health, Nutrition, How-to, Humor, Journalism, Law, Military Science, Self-Help, Sports, Athletics
ISBN Prefix(es): 0-86367; 0-901684
Number of titles published annually: 50 Print
Parent Company: Telegraph Group Ltd
Ultimate Parent Company: Hollinger
Book Club(s): Telegraph Books Direct (United Kingdom)
Warehouse: Units 5 & 6 Industrial Estate, Brecon, Powys LD3 8LA
Orders to: Telegraph Books Direct

Tempest, *imprint of* HarperCollins UK

Temple Lodge Publishing Ltd
Hillside House, The Square, Forest Row, East Sussex RH18 5ES
Tel: (01342) 824000 *Fax:* (01342) 826437
E-mail: office@templelodge.com
Web Site: www.templelodge.com
ISBN Prefix(es): 0-904693; 1-902636

Distributed by Anthroposophic Press (USA); Steinerbooks (New Zealand); Rudolf Steiner Book Centre (Australia); Rudolf Steiner Publications (South Africa); Tri-fold Books (Canada)
Orders to: BookSource, 32 Finlas St, Glasgow G22 5DU *Tel:* (0141) 558 1366 *Fax:* (0141) 557 0189 *E-mail:* orders@booksource.net
Returns: Scottish BookSource Distribution, 32 Finlas St, Cowlairs Industrial Estate, Glasgow G22 5DU

Tern Press
St Mary's Cottage, Great Hales St, Market Drayton, Salop TF9 1JN
Tel: (01630) 652153
Key Personnel
Rights: Mary Parry; Nicholas Parry
Founded: 1972
Subjects: Biblical Studies, Literature, Literary Criticism, Essays, Natural History, Poetry
Total Titles: 90 Print
Branch Office(s)
Joshua Heller Rare Books Inc, PO Box 39114, Washington, DC 20016-9114, United States (US Affiliate)

Texere Publishing Ltd
71-77 Leadenhall St, London EC3A 3DE
Tel: (020) 7204 3644 *Fax:* (020) 7208 6701
Web Site: www.etexere.com
Key Personnel
Man Dir: Martin Liu
Dir, Production & Operations: Pom Somkabcharti
Executive Editor: David Wilson
Sales Manager & Administrative Coordinator: James Coulson
Founded: 2000
Total Titles: 80 Print
U.S. Office(s): Texere LLC, 55 E 52 St, New York, NY 10055, United States *Tel:* 212-317-5511 *Fax:* 212-317-5178
Distributed by W W Norton

Textile & Art Publications Ltd+
12 Queen St, Mayfair, London W1J 5PG
Tel: (020) 7499 7979 *Fax:* (020) 7409 2596
E-mail: post@textile-art.com
Web Site: www.textile-art.com
Key Personnel
Publisher: Michael Franses
Founded: 1993
Subjects: Art, Asian Studies, Religion - Buddhist, Textile art
ISBN Prefix(es): 1-898406
Number of titles published annually: 2 Print
Total Titles: 4 Print

TFPL
17-18 Britton St, London EC1M 5TL
Tel: (020) 7251 5522 *Fax:* (020) 7251 8318
E-mail: central@tfpl.com
Web Site: www.tfpl.com
Key Personnel
Founder & Chief Executive: Nigel Oxbrow
Dir & Senior Advisor: Angela Abell
Marketing Executive: Carmel Boland
E-mail: carmel.boland@tfpl.com
Marketing Manager: Bindy Pease *E-mail:* bindy.pease@tfpl.com
Founded: 1987
Specialist in recruitment, advisory, research & training services company focusing on knowledge, library, information, records, web & content management.
Membership(s): Directory Publishers Association.
Subjects: Communications, Computer Science, Human Relations, Library & Information Sciences
ISBN Prefix(es): 1-870889
Distributor for TFPL Inc

Thames & Hudson Ltd+
181A High Holborn, London WC1V 7QX
Tel: (020) 7845 5000 *Fax:* (020) 7845 5050
E-mail: sales@thameshudson.co.uk
Web Site: www.thamesandhudson.com
Key Personnel
Man Dir: Thomas Neurath
Editorial: Jamie Camplin
Sales Dir: Trevor Naylor
Production: Neil Palfreyman
Marketing: Anna Vinegrad
Rights: Christian Frederking *E-mail:* c.frederking@thameshudson.co.uk
Publicity: Kate Burvill
Permissions: Naomi Pritchard
Founded: 1949
Subjects: Archaeology, Architecture & Interior Design, Art, Crafts, Games, Hobbies, Ethnicity, Fashion, History, Music, Dance, Philosophy, Photography, Psychology, Psychiatry, Religion - Other, Science (General), Technology, Travel, Graphics, Popular Culture
ISBN Prefix(es): 0-500
Associate Companies: Editions Thames & Hudson, 12 Rue du Seine, Paris 75006, France
Subsidiaries: Thames & Hudson Ltd (Eastern Mediterranean, Middle East, Pakistan, Italy, Spain, Portugal, Mexico & Central America); Thames & Hudson (S) Private Ltd (Malaysia, Singapore & South-East Asia); Thames & Hudson (Australia) Pty Ltd (Australia); Thames & Hudson (China) Ltd (China & Hong Kong)
U.S. Office(s): Thames & Hudson Inc, 500 Fifth Ave, New York, NY 10110, United States
Distributor for Aperture; British Museum Press; Co & Bear; Flammarion; Laurence King; MOMA; National Gallery of Australia; Royal Academy of Arts; Royal Collection Enterprises; Scalo Publishing; Scriptum Editions; Skira Editore; Steidl Verlag; Violette Editions
Orders to: 44 Clockhouse Rd, Farnborough, Hants GU14 7QZ *Tel:* (01252) 541602 *Fax:* (01252) 377380

Tharpa Publications
Conishead Priory, Ulverston, Cumbria LA12 9QQ
Tel: (01229) 588599 *Fax:* (01229) 483919
E-mail: tharpa@tharpa.com
Web Site: www.tharpa.com
Key Personnel
Dir: Hugh Clift
Founded: 1984
Subjects: Religion - Buddhist
ISBN Prefix(es): 0-948006
Associate Companies: Editions Tharpa, BP 278, 75525 Paris Cedex 11, France *Tel:* (01) 43 67 87 87 *Fax:* (01) 43 67 87 87 *E-mail:* info@tharpa.org *Web Site:* www.tharpa.org; Editorial Tharpa Brasil, Rua Mourato Coelho 910, Cep 10.41 7.001, Sao Paulo, SP, Brazil *Tel:* (011) 814 6326 *Fax:* (011) 814 6326 *E-mail:* jangchub@iconet.com.br; Editorial Tharpa Espana, C/Empecinado n2, atico derecha, 41004 Sevilla, Spain *Tel:* (05) 421 1415 *Fax:* (05) 421 1415 *E-mail:* tharpa@teleline.es; Editorial Tharpa Mexico, Madero No 687 Colonia Centro, CP44100 Guadalajara, Jalisco, Mexico *Tel:* (03) 825 1301 *Fax:* (03) 827 1026 *E-mail:* tharpa@closeup.com.mx; Tharpa Canada Inc, 2255-B Queen St E, Suite 147, Toronto, ON, Canada *Tel:* (416) 504 0966 *Fax:* (416) 504 0966 *E-mail:* 76467.262@compuserve.com; Tharpa Verlag, Dennlerstr 38, 8047 Zurich, Switzerland *Tel:* (01) 401 0220 *Fax:* (01) 401 0220 *E-mail:* tharpa@tharpa.org *Web Site:* www.tharpa.org
U.S. Office(s): Tharpa Books, PO Box 430, 47 Sweeney Rd, Glen Spey, NY 12737, United States *Tel:* 845-856-5102 *Fax:* 845-856-2110 *E-mail:* tharpabooks@aol.com
Distribution Center: Banyan Tree, 13 College Rd, Kent Town 5067, Australia *Tel:* (08) 8363 4244 *Fax:* (08) 8363 4255 *E-mail:* banyan@dove.net.au

Buddhist Merit & Wisdom Service, Shop A, Ground Floor, Jenny's Court, 241-3 Sai Yee St, Mongkok, Kowloon, Hong Kong *Tel:* 2391 8143 *Fax:* 2391 1002

Gondwana Books, PO Box 11684, Vorna Valley, Midrand 1686, South Africa *Tel:* (011) 805 6019 *Fax:* (011) 805 3746 *E-mail:* gondwana@hixnet.co.za

Ingram Book Co, PO Box 3006, One Igngram Blvd, La Vergne, TN 37086-1986, United States

Midpoint Trade Books, 1263 Southwest Blvd, Kansas City, KS 66103, United States *Tel:* 913-362-7400 ext 109 *Fax:* 913-362-7401 *E-mail:* julie@midpt.com

Peaceful Living Publications, PO Box 300, Tauranga, New Zealand *Tel:* (07) 571 8105 *Fax:* (07) 571 8513

PM Associates Pte Ltd, 130 Killiney Rd 239561, Singapore *Tel:* 732 9522 *Fax:* 7323 6076

Tharpa Canada Inc, 2255-B Queen St E, Suite 147, Toronto, ON M4E 1G3, Canada *Tel:* (416) 504 0966 *Fax:* (416) 504 0966 *E-mail:* tsepp@sympatico.ca

The Tarragon Press+
Moss Park, Ravenstone, Whithorn DG8 8DR
Tel: (01988) 850368 *Fax:* (01988) 850304
Key Personnel
Dir & Editor: David Sumner *E-mail:* dsummer@gn.apc.org
Founded: 1987
Membership(s): Scottish Publishers Association.
Subjects: Biological Sciences, Environmental Studies, Health, Nutrition, Medicine, Nursing, Dentistry, Physical Sciences, Science (General)
ISBN Prefix(es): 1-870781
Orders to: Lavis Marketing, 73 Lime Walk, Headington, Oxford OX3 7AD

Themis Books, *imprint of* Green Books Ltd

Thistle Press+
4 Old Mill Cottages, Culsalmond, Insch, Aberdeenshire AB52 6TS
Tel: (01464) 821053 *Fax:* (01464) 821053
E-mail: info@oldmilldesign.co.uk
Key Personnel
Partner & International Rights Contact: Dr Keith Nicholson
Partner: Angela Nicholson
Founded: 1992
Membership(s): Scottish Publishers Association.
Subjects: Archaeology, Biography, Earth Sciences, Environmental Studies, History, Outdoor Recreation, Regional Interests, Travel, Scottish Travel Guides
Total Titles: 10 Print
Associate Companies: Scottish Travel Books, West Bank, Western Rd, Insch AB52 6JR
Imprints: Macgregor Science

Thoemmes Press+
11 Great George St, Bristol BS1 5RR
Tel: (0117) 929 1377 *Fax:* (0117) 922 1918
E-mail: info@thoemmes.com
Web Site: www.thoemmes.com
Key Personnel
Publisher: Rudi Thoemmes *E-mail:* rthoemmes@thoemmes.com
Production: Alan Rutherford
    E-mail: arutherford@thoemmes.com
Financial Dir: Linda Keeble
Marketing Manager: Alison Lewis
    E-mail: alisonlewis@thoemmes.com
Editorial: Philip de Bary *E-mail:* philip@thoemmes.com; Merilyn Holme
    E-mail: mholme@thoemmes.com; Kirsten Robertson *E-mail:* kroberton@thoemmes.com
Founded: 1989
Specialize in reprints.
Subjects: Business, Education, Geography, Geology, History, Language Arts, Linguistics, Management, Philosophy, Science (General), Social Sciences, Sociology, Theology
ISBN Prefix(es): 1-85506; 1-84371
Number of titles published annually: 60 Print
Total Titles: 1,000 Print
Parent Company: Thoemmes Ltd
Imprints: Nico Editions; Overstone Press
Orders to: Alton Logistics Ltd, Battle Rd, Unit 4, Heathfeld, Newton Abbot TQ12 6RY
The University of Chicago Press, 1427 60 St, Chicago, IL 60637-2954, United States

Thomson Gale
Formerly Gale Research
50 Milford Rd, Reading, Berks RG1 8LJ
Tel: (01264) 342962 *Fax:* (01264) 342763
Web Site: www.gale.com
Telex: 47214 ITPG
Key Personnel
Marketing Manager: Claire Gilman
Head of Sales: Lynne Guthrie
Customer Services Manager: Steven Kempson
    Tel: (0118) 957 7233 *Fax:* (0118) 959 1325
    E-mail: steven.kempson@gale.com
Founded: 1989
Subjects: Architecture & Interior Design, Art, Biography, Business, Child Care & Development, Drama, Theater, Fashion, Genealogy, History, Literature, Literary Criticism, Essays, Music, Dance, Women's Studies
ISBN Prefix(es): 1-873477
Parent Company: Gale Research
Imprints: Blackbirch Press; Five Star; Gale; Graham & Whiteside; Greenhaven Press; GK Hall & Co; Kidhaven Press; Lucent Books; Macmillan Reference USA; Oceano Grupo Editorial; Primary Source Microfilm; KG Saur; St James Press; Schirmer Reference; Charles Scribner's Sons; The TAFT Group; Thorndike Press; Twayne Publishers; UXL
Shipping Address: PO Box 699, Andover, Hants SP10 5YE
Warehouse: PO Box 699, Andover, Hants SP10 5YE
Orders to: PO Box 699, Andover, Hants SP10 5YE

Thorndike Press, *imprint of* Thomson Gale

Thoth Publications+
64 Leopold St, Loughborough, Leics LE11 5DN
Tel: (01509) 210626 *Fax:* (01509) 238034
E-mail: enquiries@thoth.co.uk
Web Site: www.thothpublications.com; www.thoth.co.uk
Subjects: New Age
Number of titles published annually: 9 Print
Total Titles: 60 Print

Thrass (UK) Ltd
Units 1-3 Tarvin Sands, Barrow Lane, Tarvin, Chester CH3 8JF
Tel: (01829) 741413 *Fax:* (01829) 741419
E-mail: enquiries@thrass.demon.co.uk
Web Site: www.thrass.co.uk
Publish educational books, charts & software, audio & video cassettes.
Subjects: Education
ISBN Prefix(es): 1-904912; 1-876424

Threshold, *imprint of* The Kenilworth Press Ltd

Tiger Books International PLC+
26A York St, Twickenham, Middlesex TW1 3LJ
Tel: (0181) 8925577 *Fax:* (0181) 8916550
E-mail: gp@dial.pipex.com
Key Personnel
Dir: Grahame Parish; Sue Parish
Founded: 1985
Specialize in remainders & promotional reprints.
Subjects: Fiction, Nonfiction (General)
ISBN Prefix(es): 1-85501; 1-870461; 1-84056
Associate Companies: Sheridan Book Company Ltd
Imprints: Sheridan Book Company; Senate
Warehouse: Bartholomews Storage & Distribution Ltd, Woodside Rd, Boyatt Wood Industrial Estate, Eastleigh, Hants SO5 5XZ

Tigers, *imprint of* Andersen Press Ltd

Timber Press Inc+
2 Station Rd, Swavesey, Cambridge CB4 5QJ
Tel: (01954) 232959 *Fax:* (01954) 206040
E-mail: timberpressuk@btinternet.com
Web Site: www.timberpress.com
Key Personnel
Marketing Manager (UK): Pam Segers
Owner & Chief Executive Officer: Bob Conklin
Publisher: Jane Connor
Founded: 1978
Subjects: Agriculture, Gardening, Plants, Music, Dance
ISBN Prefix(es): 0-917304; 0-88192; 0-931340; 0-931146; 1-57467
Imprints: Amadeus Press
U.S. Office(s): Timber Press, 133 SW Second Ave, Suite 450, Portland, OR 97204, United States *Tel:* 503-227-2878 *Fax:* 503-227-3070 *E-mail:* info@timberpress.com

Time-Life (UK)+
Brettenham House, Lancaster Pl, London WC2E 7EN
Tel: (020) 7911 8000 *Fax:* (020) 7911 8100
E-mail: email@timelife.demon.co.uk; email.uk@timewarnerbooks.co.uk
Web Site: www.twbookmark.com; www.timewarnerbooks.co.uk
Key Personnel
Man Dir: Joseph Peckl
Rights & Permissions: Curtis Kopf
Dir, Marketing: Alison Lindsay *Tel:* (020) 7911 8062 *E-mail:* alison.lindsay@timewarnerbooks.co.uk
European Head Off: Time-Life Books BV, Netherlands.
ISBN Prefix(es): 0-8094; 0-7835; 0-7054; 0-900658
Parent Company: Time Warner Inc, United States
Branch Office(s)
Time Life Books, 777 Duke St, Alexandria, VA 22314, United States
Time Life Building, Rockefeller Center, New York, NY 10020, United States
Orders to: Bookpoint Ltd, 39 Milton Park, Abingdon, Oxon OX14 4TD *Tel:* (0235) 835001 *Fax:* (0235) 832068
Returns: AOLTWBG Returns, 322 S Enterprise Blvd, Lebanon, IN 46052, United States (Whole copy returns); WPS/Warner Returns, 3000 University Center Dr, Tampa, FL 33612, United States (Stripped returns only)

Time Out Group Ltd+
Universal House, 251 Tottenham Court Rd, London W1T 7AB
Tel: (020) 7813 3000 *Fax:* (020) 7323 3438
E-mail: net@timeout.co.uk
Web Site: www.timeout.com
Key Personnel
Publisher: Tony Elliott
Man Dir: Mike Hardwick; David Pepper
    E-mail: davidpepper@timeout.com
Financial Dir: Richard Waterlow
Editorial Dir: Pete Fiennes *E-mail:* pete@timeout.com
Group Commercial Dir: Lesley Gill
Marketing Dir: Christine Cort
Production Dir: Steve Proctor

Group General Manager: Nichola
  Coulthard *Tel:* (020) 7813 6103
  E-mail: nicholacoulthard@timeout.com
Editor, Time Out Magazine London: Laura Lee
  Davies
Editor, Time Out New York: Cyndi Stivers
Founded: 1968
Specialize in magazines & guidebooks.
Subjects: Art, Drama, Theater, Fashion, Film,
  Video, Gay & Lesbian, Poetry, Radio, TV,
  Travel
Number of titles published annually: 10 Print
Total Titles: 40 Print
Divisions: Time Out Guides; Time Out Magazine
U.S. Office(s): Time Out New York, 627 Broadway, 7th floor, New York, NY 10012, United
  States

Time Warner Book Group UK+
Brettenham House, Lancaster Pl, London WC2E
  7EN
Tel: (020) 7911 8000 *Fax:* (020) 7911 8100
E-mail: email.uk@twbg.co.uk
Web Site: www.twbg.co.uk
Key Personnel
Chief Executive: David Young
Publisher: Ursula Mackenzie
Group Sales Dir: David Kent
Publishing Dir: Richard Beswick
Editorial Dir: Barbara Daniel *Tel:* (020) 7911
  8030 *E-mail:* barbara.daniel@twbg.co.uk; Hilary Hale; Tim Holman
Finance Dir: Nigel Batt
Export Sales Dir: Richard Kitson
Dir of Marketing: Roger Cazalet; Alison Lindsay
Group Marketing Dir: Terry Jackson
Rights Dir: Diane Spivey
Publicity Dir: Alison Menzies
Group Publicity Dir: Rosalie MacFarlane
Group Commercial Dir: Karen Blewett
Founded: 1988
Also acts as book distributor.
Subjects: Biography, Business, Fiction, Mysteries, Nonfiction (General), Romance, Science
  Fiction, Fantasy, Travel
ISBN Prefix(es): 0-8212; 0-316; 0-7515; 1-85723;
  1-86049
Number of titles published annually: 400 Print;
  36 E-Book; 12 Audio
Parent Company: Time Warner Inc
Associate Companies: Little Brown & Co,
  Boston, MA, United States
Imprints: Abacus; Atom; Orbit; Virago
U.S. Office(s): Time-Life Bldg, 1271 Avenue of
  the Americas, New York 10020, United States
Orders to: TBS Distribution Centre, Colchester
  Rd, Frating Green, Colchester, Essex C07 7LW

Titan Books Ltd+
Titan House, 144 Southwark St, London SE1
  0UP
Tel: (020) 7620 0200 *Fax:* (020) 7620 0032
E-mail: readerfeedback@titanemail.com
Web Site: www.titanbooks.com
Key Personnel
Publisher: Nick Landau
Editorial, Rights & Permissions: Katy Wild
Sales & Publicity: Linda Beavis
Production: Robert Kelly
Founded: 1981
Subjects: Art, Biography, Film, Video, Radio, TV,
  Science Fiction, Fantasy
ISBN Prefix(es): 1-85286; 0-907610; 1-84023
Number of titles published annually: 150 Print
Parent Company: Titan Entertainment Group,
  London
Divisions: Titan Magazines; Titan Merchandise;
  Titan Studio
Bookshop(s): Birmingham; Cambridge; Coventry; Croydon; Edinburgh; Glasgow; Liverpool;
  London; Newcastle; Southampton

Tobin Music
The Old Malthouse, Knight St, Sawbridgeworth,
  Herts CM21 9AX
Tel: (01279) 726625
E-mail: candida@tobinmusic.co.uk
Web Site: www.candidatobin.co.uk
Key Personnel
Man Dir, Editorial: Candida Tobin
  E-mail: candida@tobinmusic.co.uk
Sales, Production, Publicity, Rights & Permissions: Christopher Dell
Founded: 1973
Music education books covering all musical theory & simple composition for home & school
  use for all ages & abilities.
A unique system of teaching using patterns &
  colors, tutors on various instruments.
Subjects: Education, Music, Dance, Nonfiction
  (General), Tutors, workbooks & information
  books *Specializes In:*Classroom music teaching
  recorder, classical guitar & piano
ISBN Prefix(es): 0-905684
Total Titles: 31 Print; 1 CD-ROM
Imprints: Tobin Music Books

Tobin Music Books, *imprint of* Tobin Music

Tolley, *imprint of* Butterworths Tolley

Toucan Press
White Cottage, Rue de Carteret, Guernsey GY5
  7YG
Tel: (01481) 57017
Key Personnel
Man Dir: G Stevens Cox
Founded: 1850
Subjects: History, Literature, Literary Criticism,
  Essays
ISBN Prefix(es): 0-85694; 0-900749
Total Titles: 90 Print

Touchstone, *imprint of* Simon & Schuster Ltd

Tour & Trail Maps, *imprint of* Discovery
  Walking Guides Ltd

Towy Publishing
PO Box 24, Carmarthen SA31 1YS
Tel: (01267) 236569 *Fax:* (01267) 220444
E-mail: towyfairs@btopenworld.com
Subjects: Antiques
Total Titles: 3 Print

TPL, *imprint of* Training Publications Ltd

Trade and Technical Press, *imprint of* Elsevier
  Advanced Technology

Training Publications, *imprint of* Training
  Publications Ltd

Training Publications Ltd
3 Finway Court, Whippendell Rd, Watford; Herts
  WD18 7EN
Tel: (01923) 243730 *Fax:* (01923) 213 144
Key Personnel
General Manager: Mr B Peck
Editorial, Rights & Permissions: Mrs Lesley Page
  E-mail: lpage@emta.org.uk
Warehouse, Distribution: Mr J A Atkinson
Founded: 1965
Subjects: Engineering (General)
ISBN Prefix(es): 0-85083; 1-84019
Parent Company: Engineering & Marine Training
  Authority
Imprints: EAL; EITB; Entra; TPL; Training Publications

Warehouse: PO Box 75, Stockport, Chesire SK4
  1PH *Tel:* (0161) 480 5285 *Fax:* (0161) 474
  7502
Orders to: PO Box 75, Stockport, Chesire SK4
  1PH *Tel:* (0161) 480 5285 *Fax:* (0161) 474
  7502

Transedition, *imprint of* Transedition Ltd

Transedition Ltd+
43 Henley Ave, Oxford OX4 4DJ
Tel: (01865) 396700 *Fax:* (01865) 712500
E-mail: enquiries@transed.co.uk
Web Site: www.translateabook.com
Key Personnel
Sales & Acquisitions: Ed Glover *E-mail:* ed@
  transed.co.uk
Production: Richard Johnson *Tel:* (020) 8969
  4817 *Fax:* (020) 8969 0487 *E-mail:* graphics@
  dircon.co.uk
Translations: Kathy Pearmain *Tel:* (01865)
  396700 *E-mail:* kathy@translateabook.com
Accounts: Yasmin Qureski *E-mail:* yas@transed.
  co.uk
Founded: 1992
Packaged books & translations, illustrated books.
Membership(s): Motouun.
Subjects: Cookery, Gardening, Plants, History,
  Religion - Other, Theology
ISBN Prefix(es): 1-898250
Number of titles published annually: 6 Print
Total Titles: 100 Print
Imprints: Transedition
Divisions: Translate-A-Book
Foreign Rights: Illustrata (Portugal, Spain)

Translations Wales, *imprint of* Gwasg
  Gwenffrwd

Transport Bookman Publications Ltd+
8 South St, Isleworth, Middlesex TW7 7BG
Tel: (020) 8560 2666 *Fax:* (020) 8569 8273
Key Personnel
Man Dir: C F Stroud
Founded: 1971
Membership(s): Book Data & Booksellers Association.
Subjects: Transportation
ISBN Prefix(es): 0-85184
Parent Company: Chater & Scott Ltd

Transworld Publishers Ltd
Division of Random House Group Ltd
61-63 Uxbridge Rd, London W5 5SA
Tel: (020) 8579 2652 *Fax:* (020) 8579 5479
E-mail: info@transworld-publishers.co.uk
Web Site: www.booksattransworld.co.uk
Telex: 267974
Key Personnel
Deputy Man Dir, Publishing & Bantam Press
  Publisher: Mark Barty-King
Deputy Man Dir: Patrick Janson-Smith
Editorial Dir, Bantam Press: Ursula Mackenzie
Editorial Dir, Doubleday: Marianne Velmans
Juvenile Editorial Dir: Philippa Dickinson
UK Sales Dir: Garry Prior
Marketing Dir: Larry Finlay
International Sales Dir: John Blake
Publicity Dir: Judy Turner
Rights Dir: Rebecca Winfield
Art Dir: Liz Laczynska
Founded: 1950
Subjects: Biography, Computer Science, Criminology, Fiction, Film, Video, Government,
  Political Science, Health, Nutrition, Humor,
  Nonfiction (General), Science Fiction, Fantasy,
  Sports, Athletics
ISBN Prefix(es): 0-552
Ultimate Parent Company: Bertelsmann AG, Germany

PUBLISHERS — UNITED KINGDOM

Associate Companies: Transworld Publishers (Australia) Pty Ltd; Bantam Books (Canada) Inc/Doubleday Canada Ltd, Toronto, ON, Canada; Transworld Publishers (New Zealand) Pty
Imprints: Anchor; Bantam Paperbacks; Bantam Press; Black Swan; Corgi; Doubleday; Expert Books; Picture Corgi; Partridge Press; Young Corgi
Warehouse: PO Box 17, Wellingborough, Northants NN8 4BU

Treehouse Children's Books Ltd+
The Old Brewhouse, 2nd floor, Lower Charlton Trading Estate, Shepton Mallet, Somerset BA4 5QE
Tel: (01749) 330529 *Fax:* (01749) 330544
E-mail: ca.baker@virgin.net
Key Personnel
Dir: Andrew Bailey; David Bailey; Deborah Bailey; Dawn Powell; Richard Powell *E-mail:* richard.powell4@virgin.net
Founded: 1989
ISBN Prefix(es): 1-85576; 1-872300
Associate Companies: Emma Books Ltd
Warehouse: Macmillan Distribution Ltd, Brunel Rd, Houndmills, Basingstoke, Hants RG21 GX5

Trentham Books Ltd+
Westview House, 734 London Rd, Oakhill, Stoke-on-Trent, Staffs ST4 5NP
Tel: (01782) 745567; (01782) 844699 *Fax:* (01782) 745553
E-mail: tb@trentham-books.co.uk
Web Site: www.trentham-books.co.uk
Key Personnel
Editorial Dir: Dr Gillian Klein *E-mail:* gillian@trentham-books.co.uk
Dir & Sales Manager: Barbara Wiggins
Production Manager: John Stipling
Founded: 1981
Membership(s): Publishers Association of UK.
Subjects: Child Care & Development, Drama, Theater, Education, Ethnicity, Humor, Law, Psychology, Psychiatry, Social Sciences, Sociology, Technology, Women's Studies, Inclusive Education
ISBN Prefix(es): 0-948080; 1-85856; 0-7287; 0-9507735; 1-897898; 1-904133
Number of titles published annually: 35 Print
Total Titles: 300 Print
Subsidiaries: Trentham Print Design Ltd
Distributor for Arts Council of England

Trigon Press+
117 Kent House Rd, Beckenham, Kent BR3 1JJ
Tel: (0181) 7780534 *Fax:* (0181) 7767525
E-mail: trigon@easynet.co.uk
Key Personnel
Man Dir, Sales & Partner: Roger Sheppard
Editorial, Production: Judith Sheppard
Publicity: Angela Roberts
Rights & Permissions: Pat Palmer
Designer: Jacqui Burton
Founded: 1974
Membership(s): Independent Publishers Guild, Bibliographical Society; also acts as distributors for US museums & galleries.
Subjects: Art, Library & Information Sciences, Literature, Literary Criticism, Essays, Science Fiction, Fantasy
ISBN Prefix(es): 0-904929
Total Titles: 4 Print
Subsidiaries: The London Office
Distributed by Oak Knoll Books

Triumph House
Imprint of Forward Press
Remus House, Coltsfoot Dr, Woodston, Peterborough PE2 9JX
Tel: (01733) 898102 *Fax:* (01733) 313524
E-mail: triumphhouse@forwardpress.co.uk
Web Site: www.forwardpress.co.uk
Publisher of religious poetry.
Subjects: Poetry, Religion - Other, Christianity
Number of titles published annually: 15 Print
Ultimate Parent Company: Forward Press Ltd

Trotman Publishing+
2 The Green, Richmond, Surrey TW9 1PL
Tel: (0870) 900 2665 *Fax:* (020) 8486 1161
E-mail: sales@trotman.demon.co.uk
Web Site: www.careers-portal.co.uk/trotmanpublishing
Key Personnel
Chairman: Andrew Fiennes Trotman *Tel:* (020) 8486 1170
Dir: Tom Lee *Tel:* (020) 8486 1157
Editorial Dir: Amanda Williams *Tel:* (020) 8486 1168
Man Editor: Rachel Lockhart *Tel:* (020) 8486 1213
Advertising Manager: Alistair Rogers *Tel:* (020) 8486 1164
Marketing Manager: Deborah Jones *Tel:* (020) 8486 1158
Sales & Distribution Manager: Sean McKone *Tel:* (020) 8486 1166
Sales & Distribution Coordinator: Tracy Deadman *Tel:* (020) 8486 1160
Press Officer: Lorna Damiani *Tel:* (020) 8486 1165
Trade Sales Manager: Mike Baggallay *Tel:* (020) 8486 1165
Production Manager: Francisca Perez *Tel:* (020) 8486 1203
Man Dir: Toby Trotman *Tel:* (020) 8486 1171
New Media Manager: Alexis Castillo-Soto *E-mail:* alexis@trotman.co.uk
Founded: 1971
Subjects: Career Development, Education
ISBN Prefix(es): 0-85660
Parent Company: Trotman & Co Ltd
Associate Companies: Trotman (Australia) Ltd, Sydney, Australia
Subsidiaries: Careers Consultants Ltd; Syston Publishing Co Ltd

True Crime, *imprint of* Virgin Publishing Ltd

TSO (The Stationery Office)+
51 Nine Elms Lane, London SW8 5DR
Tel: (020) 7873 8787
E-mail: customer.services@tso.co.uk
Web Site: www.tso.co.uk
Key Personnel
Chief Executive Officer: Tim Hailstone
Dir, Business Development: Kevan Lawton
Man Dir: Keith Burbage
Editorial: Philip Brooks *Tel:* (01603) 605532 *E-mail:* phil.brooks@theso.co.uk
Chairman: Rupert Pennant-Rea
Chief Financial Officer: Richard Dell
Man Dir: Jeremy Hook; Dr Shane O'Neill
Human Resources Dir: David Orr
Founded: 1786
UK sales agent for most major international organizations.
Subjects: Agriculture, Archaeology, Architecture & Interior Design, Business, Computer Science, Earth Sciences, Economics, Education, Energy, Environmental Studies, Finance, Government, Political Science, Health, Nutrition, History, Law, Library & Information Sciences, Medicine, Nursing, Dentistry, Social Sciences, Sociology, Technology, Transportation
ISBN Prefix(es): 0-10; 0-11; 0-337
Associate Companies: The Parliamentary Press - London, Mandela Way, London SE1 5SS *Tel:* (020) 7394 4200; TSO Wales, G50, Phase Two, Government Bldgs, Ty-Glas, Llanishen, Cardiff CF14 5ST *Tel:* (02920) 765892; TSO Content Solutions, 84-90 East St, Epsom, Surrey KT17 1HF *Tel:* (01372) 845700; TSO Ireland, 16 Arthur St, Belfast BT1 4GD, Ireland *Tel:* (02890) 238451 *Fax:* (02890) 235401 *E-mail:* belfast.bookshop@tso.co.uk; TSO - Norwich, St Crispins, Duke St, Norwich NR3 1PD *Tel:* (01603) 622211; TSO Scotland, 71-73 Lothian Rd, Edinburgh EH3 9AZ *Tel:* (0870) 6065566 *Fax:* (0870) 606 5588 *E-mail:* edinburgh.bookshop@tso.co.uk
Bookshop(s): 68-69 Bull St, Birmingham B4 6AD, Manager: James Furnival *Tel:* (0121) 236 9696 *Fax:* (0121) 236 9699 *E-mail:* birmingham.bookshop@tso.co.uk; 18-19 High St, Cardiff CF10 1PT *Tel:* (02920) 39 5548 *Fax:* (02920) 38 4347 *E-mail:* cardiff.bookshop@tso.co.uk; 123 Kingsway, London WC2B 6PQ, Manager: Tiffany Holt *Tel:* (020) 7242 6393; (020) 7242 6410 *Fax:* (020) 7242 6394 *E-mail:* london.bookshop@tso.co.uk; 9-21 Princess St, Albert Sq, Manchester M60 8AS, Manager: Ian Penney *Tel:* (0161) 834 7201 *Fax:* (0161) 833 0634 *E-mail:* manchester.bookshop@tso.co.uk; TSO Scotland, 71-73 Lothian Rd, Edinburgh, Scotland EH3 9AZ *Tel:* (0870) 6065566 *Fax:* (0870) 606 5588 *E-mail:* edinburgh.bookshop@tso.co.uk

Tuba Press+
Tunley Cottage, Tunley, Cirencester, Glos GL7 6LW
Tel: (01285) 760424 *Fax:* (01285) 760766
Key Personnel
Partner, Books: Peter Ellson
Partner, Magazines: Charles Graham
Founded: 1976
Specialize in poetry, chiefly unpublished authors.
Membership(s): Association of Little Presses & Small Press Group of Britain.
Subjects: Fiction, Poetry
ISBN Prefix(es): 0-907155; 0-9505956
Total Titles: 33 Print

Tuckwell Press Ltd+
The Mill House, Phantassie, East Linton, East Lothian EH40 3DG
Tel: (01620) 860 164 *Fax:* (01620) 860 164
E-mail: customerservices@tuckwellpress.co.uk
Web Site: www.tuckwellpress.co.uk
Key Personnel
Publishing Dir: John Tuckwell
International Rights: Val Tuckwell
Founded: 1995
Specialize in Scottish history; mainly academic with emphasis on Scotland & the North of England.
Subjects: Archaeology, Architecture & Interior Design, Biography, Environmental Studies, History, Literature, Literary Criticism, Essays, Religion - Protestant
ISBN Prefix(es): 1-898410; 1-86232
Number of titles published annually: 40 Print
Total Titles: 150 Print
Imprints: Canongate Academic
Distributed by Footprint (Australia & New Zealand); Hushion House (USA & Canada)
Warehouse: Scottish BookSource, 32 Finlas St, Glasgow G22 5DU
Orders to: Scottish BookSource, 137 Dundee St, Edinburgh EH11 1BG

Tufton Books, *imprint of* Church Union

Twayne Publishers, *imprint of* Thomson Gale

Twelveheads Press
PO Box 59, Chacewater, Truro, Cornwall TR4 8ZJ
E-mail: sales@twelveheads.com
Web Site: www.twelveheads.com
Founded: 1978
Subjects: Archaeology, Genealogy, History, Maritime, Regional Interests, Transportation
ISBN Prefix(es): 0-906294

Number of titles published annually: 4 Print
Total Titles: 34 Print
Distribution Center: Tor Mark Press, United Downs Industrial Estate, St Day, Redruth TR16 5HY

Two-Can Publishing Ltd+
15 New Bridge St, London EC4V 6AU
Tel: (020) 7583 5839 *Fax:* (020) 7664-1652
E-mail: helpline@two-canpublishing.com; sales@creativepub.com
Web Site: www.two-canpublishing.com
Key Personnel
Chairman: Andrew Jarvis
Marketing Dir: Ian Grant
International Rights: Helen Cross
Founded: 1987
Specialize in children's magazines, books & multimedia.
Subjects: Animals, Pets, Geography, Geology, History, Natural History, Physics, Science (General), Technology
ISBN Prefix(es): 1-85434
Orders to: Title Book Services, Church Rd, Tiptree, Colchester, Essex C05 0SR

Tycooly, *imprint of* Cassell & Co

Tycooly, *imprint of* The Continuum International Publishing Group Ltd

UCL Press Ltd+
Imprint of Taylor & Francis Group Ltd
11 New Fetter Lane, London EC4P 4EE
Tel: (020) 7583 9855 *Fax:* (020) 7842 2298
E-mail: info@tandf.co.uk
Web Site: www.tandf.co.uk
Key Personnel
Publishing Dir: Stephen B Neal *E-mail:* stephen.neal@tandf.co.uk
Senior Editor, Social & Political Sciences: Mari Shullaw
Founded: 1991
Subjects: Archaeology, Art, Environmental Studies, Geography, Geology, Government, Political Science, History, Human Relations, Philosophy, Social Sciences, Sociology, Technology
ISBN Prefix(es): 1-85728; 1-84142
Orders to: Taylor & Francis Ltd, Rankine Rd, Basingstoke, Hants RG24 8PR *Tel:* (01256) 813000 *Fax:* (01256) 479438

UK Academy of Science, see The Royal Society

Ulster Historical Foundation+
12 College Sq E, Belfast BT1 6DD
Tel: (028) 90 332288 *Fax:* (028) 90 239885
E-mail: enquiry@uhf.org.uk
Web Site: www.ancestryireland.com
Key Personnel
Chairman: David Clement
Executive Dir: Fintan Mullan
Research Dir: Dr Brian Trainor
Project Manager: Andrew Vaughan
Founded: 1956
Subjects: Education, Genealogy, History, Regional Interests, Conferences, Genealogy, Historical Publishing
ISBN Prefix(es): 0-901905

Ultimate, *imprint of* Lorenz Books

Ulverscroft Large Print Books Ltd+
The Green Bradgate Rd, Anstey, Leicester LE7 7FU
Tel: (0116) 236 4325 *Fax:* (0116) 234 0205
E-mail: sales@ulverscroft.co.uk
Web Site: www.ulverscroft.co.uk
Key Personnel
Chairman: D F Thorpe
Man Dir: Patricia Henderson
Founded: 1964
Publishers of Ulverscroft Large Print Books, Charnwood Library Series, Linford Mystery Library Series, Linford Romance Library Series, Linford Western Library Series.
Subjects: Biography, Fiction, Literature, Literary Criticism, Essays, Mysteries, Nonfiction (General), Romance, Travel, Western Fiction
ISBN Prefix(es): 0-85456; 0-7089
U.S. Office(s): Ulverscroft Large Print (USA) Inc, 1881 Ridge Rd, PO Box 1230, West Seneca, NY 14224-1230, United States
Distributor for Magna Large Print (Australia, Canada, New Zealand, South Africa, USA)
Showroom(s): Cawdor Books, 96 Dykehead St, Queenslie, Glasgow G33 4QA *Tel:* (01729) 840225 *Fax:* (01729) 840683

Unicorn Books
56 Rowlands Ave, Hatch End, Pinner HA5 4BP
Tel: (020) 8420 1091 *Fax:* (020) 8428 0125
Web Site: www.unicornbooks.co.uk/
Key Personnel
Man Dir: Raymond Green
Founded: 1985
Membership(s): Antiquarian Bookseller's Association & Provincial Bookseller's Fairs Association.
Subjects: Military Science, Music, Dance, Transportation
ISBN Prefix(es): 1-85241
Parent Company: Factwell Ltd
Subsidiaries: MSR Books
Distributor for Archway Publishing; John Hallewell Publications

United Writers Publications Ltd+
Ailsa, Castle Gate, Penzance, Cornwall TR20 8BG
Tel: (01736) 365954 *Fax:* (01736) 365954
E-mail: info@unitedwriters.co.uk
Key Personnel
Man Dir, Editorial, Sales: Malcolm Sheppard *E-mail:* malcolm@unitedwriters.co.uk
Production: Tina Sully
Publicity: Peter Keane
Rights & Permissions: Julian Tremayne
Founded: 1962
Subjects: Biography, Fiction, Sports, Athletics, Travel
ISBN Prefix(es): 0-901976; 1-85200
Number of titles published annually: 6 Print
Total Titles: 150 Print

Universitas, *imprint of* Voltaire Foundation Ltd

The University of Birmingham
Information Services, Edgbaston, Birmingham B15 2TT
Tel: (0121) 414 3344 *Fax:* (0121) 414 3971
Web Site: www.general.bham.ac.uk
Key Personnel
Dir: Michele Shoebridge *E-mail:* m.i.shoebridge@bham.ac.uk
ISBN Prefix(es): 0-7044; 0-85057; 0-903054

University of Exeter Press+
Reed Hall, Streatham Dr, Exeter EX4 4QR
Tel: (01392) 263066 *Fax:* (01392) 263064
E-mail: uep@ex.ac.uk
Web Site: www.ex.ac.uk/uep
Key Personnel
Publisher: Simon C Baker *E-mail:* s.c.baker@ex.ae.uk
Marketing & Sales Manager: Genevieve Davey *Tel:* (01392) 264364 *E-mail:* uepsales@exeter.ac.uk
Founded: 1956
Subjects: Archaeology, Drama, Theater, Education, Film, Video, History, Language Arts, Linguistics, Literature, Literary Criticism, Essays, Maritime, Philosophy, Poetry, Regional Interests
ISBN Prefix(es): 0-85989; 0-900771
Total Titles: 250 Print
Distributed by David Brown Book Co (North America)
Foreign Rep(s): Warren Bertram (Benelux); D Richard Bowen (Scandinavia); Eleanor Brasch Enterprises (Australia & New Zealand); Bernd Feldmann (Austria, Germany, Switzerland); Peter Prout (Gibraltar, Spain & Portugal); Roger Ward (China & Hong Kong, Indonesia, Japan, Korea & Taiwan, Malaysia & Singapore, Philippines, Thailand)
Orders to: Plymbridge Distributors Ltd, Estover Rd, Plymouth PL6 7PY *Tel:* (01752) 202301 *Fax:* (01752) 202333 *E-mail:* orders@plymbridge.com

University of Hertfordshire Press
University of Hertfordshire, Learning & Information Services, College Lane, Hatfield AL10 9AD
Tel: (01707) 284682 *Fax:* (01707) 284666
E-mail: uhpress@herts.ac.uk
Web Site: www.herts.ac.uk/uhpress
Key Personnel
Publisher: Jane Housham
Founded: 1992
Subjects: Biography, Drama, Theater, Education, History, Literature, Literary Criticism, Essays, Mathematics, Medicine, Nursing, Dentistry, Parapsychology
ISBN Prefix(es): 1-902806
Number of titles published annually: 12 Print
Total Titles: 50 Print
Imprints: Hertfordshire Publications

University of Illinois Press, *imprint of* Combined Academic Publishers

University of London Careers Service
49-51 Gordon Sq, London WC1H 0PN
Tel: (020) 7554 4500 *Fax:* (020) 7383 5876
E-mail: careers@lon.ac.uk
Web Site: www.careers.lon.ac.uk
Key Personnel
Dir: Anne-Marie Martin *E-mail:* directors.office@careers.lon.ac.uk
Communications Services Manager: Ingrid Ross *Tel:* (020) 7554 4521 *E-mail:* i.ross@careers.lon.ac.uk
Head of Systems & Resources: Yanina Hinrichsen
Subjects: Career Development, How to Change Your Career, How to Analyse & Promote Your Skills for Work, How to Complete an Application Form, How to Write a Curriculum Vitae, How to Succeed at Interviews & Other Selection Methods
ISBN Prefix(es): 0-7187
Number of titles published annually: 1 Print
Total Titles: 5 Print

University of Nebraska Press, *imprint of* Combined Academic Publishers

University of Newcastle Upon Tyne
Registrar's Office, 6 Kensington Terrace, Newcastle Upon Tyne NE1 7RU
Tel: (0191) 222 6000 *Fax:* (0191) 222 6229
Web Site: www.ncl.ac.uk
Key Personnel
Publications Officer: Dinah A Michie *E-mail:* dinah.michie@ncl.ac.uk
Founded: 1963
ISBN Prefix(es): 0-7017; 0-900565

University of Texas Press, *imprint of* Combined Academic Publishers

University of Wales Press (Gwasg Prifysgol Cymru)+
Member of Literary Publishers (Wales) Ltd
10 Columbus Walk, Brigantine Pl, Cardiff CF10 4UP
Tel: (029) 2049-6899 *Fax:* (029) 2049-6108
E-mail: press@press.wales.ac.uk
Web Site: www.wales.ac.uk/press
Key Personnel
Dir: Ashley Drake *E-mail:* a.drake@press.wales.ac.uk
Deputy Dir: Richard Houdmont *E-mail:* r.houdmont@press.wales.ac.uk
Editorial Manager: Ceinwen Jones *E-mail:* c.jones@press.wales.ac.uk
Production/Design Manager: Nicola Roper *E-mail:* n.roper@press.wales.ac.uk
Commissioning Editor: Sarah Lewis *E-mail:* s.lewis@press.wales.ac.uk
Sales Support Executive: Bethan James *E-mail:* b.james@press.wales.ac.uk
Founded: 1922
Membership(s): Independent Publishers Guild.
Subjects: Archaeology, Architecture & Interior Design, Art, Economics, Education, Geography, Geology, History, Language Arts, Linguistics, Literature, Literary Criticism, Essays, Philosophy, Social Sciences, Sociology, Theology, Women's Studies
ISBN Prefix(es): 0-7083; 0-900768
Number of titles published annually: 60 Print; 1 CD-ROM; 20 E-Book
Total Titles: 500 Print; 6 CD-ROM; 200 E-Book
Online services available through Ingenta, netLibrary.
Distributed by Eleanor Brasch (Australia); Independent Publishers Group (IPG) (USA & Canada); United Publishers Services (UPS) (Japan)

University of Washington Press, *imprint of* Combined Academic Publishers

University Presses of California, Columbia & Princeton Ltd
c/o John Wiley & Sons Ltd, Distribution Centre, One Oldlands Way, Bognor Regis, West Sussex PO22 9SA
Tel: (01243) 843291 *Fax:* (01243) 820250
E-mail: lois@upccp.demon.co.uk
Web Site: www.ucpress.edu
Key Personnel
Office Manager: Lois Edwards *E-mail:* lois@upccp.demon.co.uk
Founded: 1976
Subjects: Social Sciences, Sociology
ISBN Prefix(es): 0-520
Parent Company: Columbia University Press, New York, NY, United States

Uplands Books+
One The Uplands, Maze Hill, Saint Leonards TN38 0HL
Tel: (01424) 422306 *Fax:* (01424) 719879
E-mail: sales@uplands-books.com
Key Personnel
International Rights: Christopher Maxwell-Stewart
Founded: 1990
Specialize in children's books.
Membership(s): IPG.
ISBN Prefix(es): 1-897951; 0-9512246
Warehouse: Trade Counters, Mendelsham Industrial Estate, Norwich Rd, Mendelsham Suffolk 1P14 5NA
Distribution Center: Ragged Bears Ltd, Ragged Appleshaw, Andover, Hants SP11 9HX
Orders to: Ragged Bears
Returns: Ragged Bears

Usborne Publishing Ltd+
Usborne House, 83-85 Saffron Hill, London EC1N 8RT
Tel: (020) 7430 2800 *Fax:* (020) 7430 1562; (020) 7242 0974
E-mail: mail@usborne.co.uk
Web Site: www.usborne.com
Key Personnel
Man Dir: Peter Usborne
General Manager: Robert Jones
Production Manager: Garry Lewis
Publishing Dir: Jenny Tyler
International Rights: Elizabeth Wright
Founded: 1973
ISBN Prefix(es): 0-7460; 0-86020

UXL, *imprint of* Thomson Gale

Vacation Work Publications+
9 Park End St, Oxford OX1 1HJ
Tel: (01865) 241978 *Fax:* (01865) 790885
E-mail: info@vacationwork.co.uk
Web Site: www.vacationwork.co.uk
Key Personnel
Dir & Rights: Charles James
Publicity Dir: David Woodworth
Contact: Andrew James *E-mail:* andrew@vacationwork.co.uk
Founded: 1967
Publisher of books for students abroad, the working traveler.
Subjects: Advertising, Career Development, Crafts, Games, Hobbies, Developing Countries, Foreign Countries, Outdoor Recreation, Travel
ISBN Prefix(es): 0-907638; 1-85458; 0-901205
Total Titles: 55 Print
Distributed by Globe Pequot (USA)

Vacher Dod Publishing Ltd
One Douglas St, London SW1P 4PA
Tel: (020) 7828 7256 *Fax:* (020) 7828 7269
E-mail: politics@vacherdod.co.uk
Web Site: www.vacherdod.co.uk
Key Personnel
Publisher: Andrew Cox *E-mail:* andrewcox@vacherdod.co.uk; Edward Peck
Founded: 1832
Publisher of UK Parliamentary Reference.
Subjects: Foreign Countries, Government, Political Science
ISBN Prefix(es): 0-905702

Vallentine, Mitchell & Co Ltd+
Subsidiary of Frank Cass Publishers
Suite 314, Premier House, 112-114 Station Rd, Edgware, Middx HA8 7AQ
Tel: (020) 8952 9526 *Fax:* (020) 8952 9242
E-mail: info@vmbooks.com
Web Site: www.vmbooks.com
Key Personnel
Man Dir: Frank Cass
Editorial: Hilary Hewitts
Trade: Joanna Legg
Production: Ray Green
Publicity: Hayley Osen
Founded: 1950
Subjects: Cookery, History, Literature, Literary Criticism, Essays, Religion - Jewish, Theology, Military History, Political Science
ISBN Prefix(es): 0-85303
Associate Companies: Irish Academic Press; The Woburn Press
Warehouse: Biblios Distribution, Partridge Green, West Sussex RH13 8LD *Tel:* (0403) 710971 *Fax:* (0403) 711143
Orders to: ISBS, 5824 NE Hassalo St, Portland, OR 97213-3644, United States *Tel:* 503-287-3093 *Fax:* 503-280-8832 *E-mail:* orders@isbs.com
Plymbridge Distributors Ltd, Estover Rd, Plymouth PL6 7PZ *Tel:* (07152) 202301 *Fax:* (07152) 202331 *E-mail:* orders@plymbridge.com

ValuSource, *imprint of* Wiley Europe Ltd

Van Duren Publishers Ltd, see Colin Smythe Ltd

Van Molle Publishing+
PO Box 29, Aberteifi, Cardigan, Ceredigion SA43 1YN
Tel: (01239) 851482 *Fax:* (01239) 851482
Key Personnel
Contact: Cheryl Foster
Founded: 1995
Subjects: Fiction, Children's Picture Books, Adult Fiction (General)
ISBN Prefix(es): 0-9526925
Total Titles: 4 Print

Variorum, *imprint of* Ashgate Publishing Ltd

Vega, *imprint of* Salamander Books Ltd

The Vegetarian Society
Parkdale, Dunham Rd, Altrincham, Cheshire WA14 4QG
Tel: (0161) 925 2000 *Fax:* (0161) 926 9182
E-mail: info@vegsoc.org
Web Site: www.vegsoc.org
Key Personnel
Chief Executive Officer: Tina Fox *Tel:* (016) 925 2002 *E-mail:* tina@vegsoc.org
Head Public Affairs: Samantha Calvert *E-mail:* sam@vegsoc.org
Editor: Dave Bowler *E-mail:* editor@vegsoc.org
Founded: 1847
Registered educational charity
Also publish in association with Harper Collins, Sigma Press & other publishers.
Subjects: Cookery, Education
ISBN Prefix(es): 0-900774

Veloce Publishing Ltd+
33 Trinity St, Dorchester, Dorset DT1 1TT
Tel: (01305) 260068 *Fax:* (01305) 268864
E-mail: info@veloce.co.uk
Web Site: www.veloce.co.uk; www.velocebooks.com
Key Personnel
Publisher: Rod Grainger
Dir: Judith Brooks
Founded: 1991
Also specialize in motorsports & workshop manuals.
Subjects: Automotive, Biography, Mechanical Engineering, Outdoor Recreation, Transportation
ISBN Prefix(es): 1-874105; 1-901295; 1-903706; 1-904788
Number of titles published annually: 25 Print
Total Titles: 200 Print
Distributed by Motorbooks International Inc (USA)
Distributor for Porter Publishing (UK)

Velvet, *imprint of* Creation Books

Ventura, *imprint of* Penguin Books Ltd

Venture Press Ltd
16 Kent St, Birmingham B5 6RD
Tel: (0121) 622 3911 *Fax:* (0121) 622 4860
E-mail: info@basw.co.uk
Key Personnel
Assistant Dir: Sally Arkley
ISBN Prefix(es): 0-900102; 0-9501603; 1-86178; 1-873878

Verbatim+
PO Box 156, Chearsley, Aylesbury, Bucks HP18 0DQ
Tel: (01844) 208474
Web Site: www.verbatimbooks.com

UNITED KINGDOM

Key Personnel
Man Dir, Editorial: Laurence Urdang
Sales, Rights & Permissions: Hazel Hall
Founded: 1974
Subjects: Language Arts, Linguistics
ISBN Prefix(es): 0-930454
Total Titles: 17 Print
Parent Company: Laurence Urdang Inc
U.S. Office(s): Verbatim Books, 4 Laurel Heights, Old Lyme, CT 06371-1462, United States, Contact: Laurence Urdang *Tel:* 860-434-2104 *E-mail:* luverbatim@aol.com

Veritas Foundation Publication Centre+
63 Jeddo Rd, London W12 9EE
Tel: (020) 8749 4957; (020) 8749 4965
Fax: (020) 8749 4965
E-mail: veritas@polish.co.uk
Key Personnel
Man Dir & Rights: Thomas Wachowiak
E-mail: thomas@veritas.knsc.co.uk
Sales: A Zabihe
Founded: 1947
Also publishes weekly newspaper.
Subjects: Education, Religion - Other
ISBN Prefix(es): 0-948202; 0-901215

Vermilion, *imprint of* Random House UK Ltd

Verso+
6 Meard St, London W1F 0EG
Tel: (020) 7437 3546; (020) 7434 1704; (020) 7439 8194 *Fax:* (020) 7734 0059
E-mail: enquiries@verso.co.uk
Web Site: www.versobooks.com
Key Personnel
Executive Chairman: George Galfavi
International Rights: Gil McNeil
Founded: 1971
Subjects: Economics, Ethnicity, Film, Video, Government, Political Science, History, Literature, Literary Criticism, Essays, Nonfiction (General), Philosophy, Psychology, Psychiatry, Social Sciences, Sociology, Women's Studies
ISBN Prefix(es): 0-86091; 0-85984; 0-902308
Number of titles published annually: 70 Print
Parent Company: New Left Review
Imprints: Critical Studies in Latin American Culture; Haymarket; Phronesis
U.S. Office(s): 180 Varick St, 10th floor, New York, NY 10014-4606, United States
Tel: 212-807-9680 *Fax:* 212-807-9152
E-mail: versoinc@aol.com
Distributed by Penguin Books (Canada); W W Norton/National Book Company (United States)
Foreign Rep(s): APD Singapore Ptd Ltd (Brunei, Malaysia, Singapore, Thailand); IMA (South America); Macmillan Publishers Australia (Australia & New Zealand); Maya Publishers Pvt Ltd (India); Missing Link (Germany); B K Norton Ltd (China & Taiwan, Hong Kong, Korea); Stephans Philip Publishers Ltd (South Africa, Zimbabwe); Publishers European Sales Agency (Europe); Segment Book Distributors (India); United Publishers Services (Japan); James & Lorin Watt (Cyprus, Malta, Middle East, Turkey); John Wilde Partnership (Austria, Germany & Switzerland)
Orders to: Marston Book Services, Unit 160 Milton Park, Abingdon, Oxford OX14 4SD *Tel:* 01235 465500

Verulam Publishing Ltd
152A Park Street Lane, Park St, Saint Albans, Herts AL2 2AU
Tel: (01727) 872770 *Fax:* (01727) 873866
E-mail: verulampub@yahoo.com; sales@verulampub.demon.co.uk
Key Personnel
Man Dir: David Collins *E-mail:* david.collins@verulampub.demon.co.uk
Dir: Penny Collins *E-mail:* penny.collins@verulampub.demon.co.uk
Founded: 1991
Subjects: Advertising, Animals, Pets, Business, Cookery, Humor, Marketing, Photography, Sports, Athletics
ISBN Prefix(es): 1-873668; 1-85882; 1-903994; 1-86019; 1-84067; 1-84186
Imprints: Caxton Publishing Group Ltd; Take That Ltd (US)
Distributor for Caxton Publishing Group World (US); Cumberland Houe Publishers Europe (US); Eric Dobby Publishing Ltd (USA); Rutledge Hill Press (Europe); Take That Ltd (US); Top Floor Publishing Europe (US)
Distribution Center: Gazelle Book Services Ltd, White Cross Mills, Hightown, South Rd, Lancaster LA1 4XS *Tel:* (01524) 68765 *Fax:* (01524) 63232 *E-mail:* sales@gazellebooks.co.uk

Vif, *imprint of* Voltaire Foundation Ltd

Viking, *imprint of* Penguin Books Ltd

Viking, *imprint of* The Penguin Group UK

Viking+
27 Wrights Lane, London W8 5TZ
Tel: (020) 7416 3000 *Fax:* (020) 7416 3274
Telex: 917181
Key Personnel
Chief Executive: Peter Mayer
Editorial Dir: Claire Alexander
Production: Joy Harrison
Marketing Dir: Clare Harrington
Rights & Permissions: Ruth Salazar
Founded: 1969
Formerly Allen Lane.
Subjects: Art, Biography, Cookery, Fiction, History, Nonfiction (General), Social Sciences, Sociology, Travel
ISBN Prefix(es): 0-670
Parent Company: Penguin Books Ltd
Imprints: Allen Lane; The Penguin Press
U.S. Office(s): 375 Hudson St, New York, NY 10014, United States *Tel:* 212-366-2000
Orders to: Penguin Books, Bath Rd, Harmondsworth, Middlesex UB7 0DA *Tel:* (01) 7591984

Viking Children's Books+
27 Wright's Lane, London W8 5TZ
Tel: (020) 7416 3000 *Fax:* (020) 7416 3086
Telex: 917181
Key Personnel
Chief Executive: Peter Mayer
Editorial Dir: Phillipa Milnes-Smith
Publishing Dir: Elizabeth Attenborough
Rights & Permissions: Nikki Griffiths
Founded: 1969
ISBN Prefix(es): 0-670
Parent Company: Penguin Books Ltd
U.S. Office(s): Viking Children's Books, 375 Hudson St, New York, NY 10014, United States *Tel:* 212-366-2000
Orders to: Penguin Books, Bath Rd, Harmondsworth, Middlesex UB7 0DA *Tel:* (01) 7591984

Vintage, *imprint of* Random House UK Ltd

Virago, *imprint of* Time Warner Book Group UK

Virago Press+
Brettenham House, Lancaster Pl, London WC2E 7EN
Tel: (020) 7911 8000 *Fax:* (020) 7911 8100
E-mail: virago.press@timewarnerbooks.co.uk
Web Site: www.virago.co.uk
Telex: 885233
Key Personnel
Publisher: Ms Lennie Goodings
Senior Editor: Jill Foulston
Founded: 1973
Subjects: Biography, Education, Fiction, Government, Political Science, Health, Nutrition, History, Philosophy, Public Administration, Social Sciences, Sociology, Travel, Women's Studies
ISBN Prefix(es): 0-86068; 1-86049; 1-85381
Parent Company: Little Brown & Co

Virgin Publishing Ltd+
Thames Wharf Studios, Rainville Rd, London W6 9HA
Tel: (020) 7386 3300 *Fax:* (020) 7386 3360
E-mail: info@virgin-books.co.uk; info@virgin-pub.co.uk
Web Site: www.virginbooks.com
Key Personnel
Chairman: Robert Devereux
Man Dir: Rob Shreeve
Publicity Manager: Susan Atkinson
Marketing Manager: Amy Nelson-Bennett
Sales Dir: Ray Mudie
Export Sales: Natalie Rogers
International Sales & Rights Dir: K T Forster
Editorial Dir: Humphrey Price
Publishing Dir, Travel: Louise Cavanagh
Rights Manager: Helen Monroe
E-mail: hmonroe@virgin-pub.co.uk
Founded: 1990
Specialize in music.
Subjects: Astrology, Occult, Biography, Child Care & Development, Criminology, Erotica, Film, Video, History, Humor, Music, Dance, Nonfiction (General), Radio, TV, Science Fiction, Fantasy, Sports, Athletics, Travel
ISBN Prefix(es): 0-352; 0-426; 1-85227; 0-7535; 0-85031; 0-86369
Parent Company: Virgin Media Group, 20 Soho Square, London W1A 1BS
Imprints: Black Lace; Idol; Nexus; Sapphire; True Crime
Distributor for Berlitz Publishing (UK & export)
Foreign Rep(s): Ashton International Marketing Services (Far East, India, Middle East); IMA (Africa, Eastern Europe); MRA (Brazil, Central & South America, West Indies); Onslow Books (Europe)
Foreign Rights: ACER (Spain); Agence Literaire Lora Fountain (France); Akcali Copyright (Turkey); Bengt Nordin Agency (Scandinavia); Big Apple Tuttle Mori Agency (China & Taiwan, Thailand); BPA of Israel (Israel); Dilia Literary Agency (Czech Republic); Helfa A W Literary Agency (Poland); Interrights Literary & Translation Bulgaria); KCC (Korea); Lex Copyright (Hungary); Lijnkamp Literary Agency (Netherlands); Living Agency (Italy); Motovun Co Ltd (Japan); Read 'n' Right Agency (Greece); Thomas Schluck GmbH (Germany); Synopsis Literary Agency (Russia); Eric Yang Agency (Korea)

The Vital Spark, *imprint of* Neil Wilson Publishing Ltd

VNU Business Publications
VNU House, 32-34 Broadwick St, London W1A 2HG
Tel: (020) 7316 9000 *Fax:* (020) 7316 9440
Web Site: www.vnu.co.uk
Key Personnel
Publishing Dir: Guy Phillips
Associate Publisher: Emma Devine
Man Dir: Brin Bucknor
Production Editor: Francis Abberley
Founded: 1980
Subjects: Accounting, Business, Communications, Computer Science, Economics, Finance, Management, Technology
ISBN Prefix(es): 0-86271

PUBLISHERS — UNITED KINGDOM

Parent Company: VNU Business Publications, Netherlands
Subsidiaries: Learned Information (Europe)
Orders to: Booksales Dept, VNU House, 32-34 Broadwick St, London W1A 2HG

Voltaire Foundation, *imprint of* Voltaire Foundation Ltd

Voltaire Foundation Ltd+
University of Oxford, 99 Banbury Rd, Oxford OX2 6JX
Tel: (01865) 284600 *Fax:* (01865) 284610
E-mail: email@voltaire.ox.ac.uk
Web Site: www.voltaire.ox.ac.uk
Key Personnel
Dir: Dr Nicholas Cronk *Tel:* (01865) 284602 *E-mail:* nicholas.cronk@voltaire.ox.ac.uk
Publisher: Clare Fletcher *Tel:* (01865) 284601 *E-mail:* clare.fletcher@voltaire.ox.ac.uk
Deputy Publisher: Janet Godden *Tel:* (01865) 284606 *E-mail:* janet.godden@voltaire-foundation.oxford.ac.uk
Electronic Publishing Manager: Dr Robert McNamee *Tel:* (01865) 284603 *E-mail:* robert.mcnamee@voltaire.ox.ac.uk
Founded: 1971
Publishing & seminars on the European Enlightenment. Specialize in works by & about Voltaire & other enlightenment writers.
Subjects: History, Language Arts, Linguistics, Literature, Literary Criticism, Essays, Philosophy
ISBN Prefix(es): 0-7294; 0-903588; 0-9502162
Number of titles published annually: 20 Print
Total Titles: 400 Print, 1 CD-ROM; 100 Online
Parent Company: University of Oxford
Imprints: Universitas; Vif; Voltaire Foundation
Foreign Rep(s): Aux Amateurs de Livres International (France)
Warehouse: Marston Book Services, 160 Milton Park, PO Box 269, Abingdon, Oxon OX14 4YN *Tel:* (01235) 465500 *Fax:* (01235) 465556 *E-mail:* direct.orders@marston.co.uk *Web Site:* www.marston.co.uk
Orders to: Marston Book Services, 160 Milton Park, PO Box 269, Abingdon, Oxon OX14 4YN *Tel:* (01235) 465500 *Fax:* (01235) 465556 *E-mail:* direct.orders@marston.co.uk
Returns: Marston Book Services, 160 Milton Park, PO Box 269, Abingdon, Oxon OX14 4YN

Wag Books, *imprint of* Compendium Publishing

Waite Group Press, *imprint of* Pearson Education Europe, Mideast & Africa

John Waite Ltd+
Tower House, Ivychurch, Romney Marsh TN29 0AX
Tel: (1797) 344 283 *Fax:* (01892) 784156
Key Personnel
Man Dir: John A Waite
Founded: 1983
Publisher of spoken work CDs & nonfiction.
Subjects: Nonfiction (General)
ISBN Prefix(es): 0-946714
Number of titles published annually: 2 Print

Walker Books Ltd+
Brunel Rd, Houndmills, Basingstoke RG21 6XS
Tel: (01256) 329242 *Fax:* (01256) 812558; (01256) 812521
E-mail: enquiry@walker.co.uk
Web Site: www.walkerbooks.co.uk
Key Personnel
Chairman & Editorial: David Lloyd
Man Dir: David Heatherwick
Merchandising: Judy Burdsall
Publicity Manager: Charlie Price
Foreign Rights: Caroline Muir
Art Dir: Amelia Edwards
Sales, UK: Ian Spanton
Sales & Marketing Dir: Henryk Wesolowski
Founded: 1978
Subjects: Fiction, Nonfiction (General)
ISBN Prefix(es): 1-56402; 0-7636; 0-7445
U.S. Office(s): Candlewick Press, 2067 Massachusetts Ave, Cambridge, MA 02140, United States *Tel:* 617- 661-3330 *Fax:* 617-661-0565 *E-mail:* licensing@candlewick.com *Web Site:* www.candlewick.com
Orders to: Faber Book Services, Burnt Mill, Elizabeth Way, Harlow, Essex CM20 2HX

Editions Aubrey Walter, *imprint of* GMP Publishers Ltd

The Warburg Institute+
University of London, Woburn Sq, London WC1H 0AB
Tel: (020) 7862 8949 *Fax:* (020) 7862 8955
E-mail: warburg@sas.ac.uk
Web Site: www.sas.ac.uk/warburg/
Key Personnel
Secretary: Anita Pollard
Founded: 1921
The Institute is a non-commercial organization.
Subjects: Art, History, Philosophy, Science (General)
ISBN Prefix(es): 0-85481
Number of titles published annually: 2 Print
Total Titles: 37 Print
Parent Company: University of London
Distributed by Nino Aragno Editore

Ward Lock Educational Co Ltd+
Bic Ling Kee House, One Christopher Rd, East Grinstead, West Sussex RH19 3BT
Tel: (01342) 318980 *Fax:* (01342) 410980
E-mail: wle@lingkee.com
Web Site: www.wardlockeducational.com
Key Personnel
Chairman: Bak Ling Au
General Manager: Penny Kitchenham *E-mail:* psk@lingkee.com
Founded: 1952
Subjects: Computer Science, Geography, Geology, History, Mathematics, Music, Dance, Poetry, Religion - Other, Science (General)
ISBN Prefix(es): 0-7062
Parent Company: Ling Kee Ltd
Associate Companies: B L A Publishing Ltd

Ward Lock Ltd+
Wellington House, 125 Strand, London WC2R OBB
Tel: (020) 7420 5555 *Fax:* (020) 7240 7261
Telex: 9413701
Key Personnel
Chairman & Chief Executive: Philip Sturrock
Publishing Dir: Alison Goff
Founded: 1854
Overseas Representation: Australia: New Holland Publishers Pty Ltd, NSW Australia 2086; Canada: Cavendish Books Inc, North Vancouver, Canada; Caribbean: HRA, London, UK; Central Europe: European Marketing Services, London, UK; Southern Europe: Penny Padovani, London, UK; Hong Kong, China, Korea, Taiwan: APS Ltd, Hong Kong; Hungary, Czech Republic, Slovakia, Croatia: CLB Marketing Services, Kecskemet, Hungary; India: Maya Publishers PVT Ltd, New Dehli, India; Japan: Ashton International Marketing Services, UK; Malaysia: APD Kuala Lumpur, Selangor Darul Ehsan, Malaysia; Middle East: Ashton International Marketing Services, UK; Netherlands: Netherlands: Nilsson & Lamm, Netherlands; New Zealand: David Bateman, Auckland, New Zealand; Pakistan: Mackwin & Co, Karachi, Pakistan; Poland, Russia, Romania, Baltic States, Former USSR, Bulgaria: Bianca Katris, IMA, Greece; Singapore, Indonesia, Thailand: APD Singapore Ltd, Singapore; Scandinavia: PKB, Glostrup, Denmark; South America: HRA, London, UK; South Africa: Struik Book Distributors, Cape Town, South Africa; USA: Sterling Publishing Co Inc, New York, USA.
Subjects: Cookery, Gardening, Plants, Health, Nutrition, House & Home, How-to, Nonfiction (General), Outdoor Recreation, Self-Help, Sports, Athletics
ISBN Prefix(es): 0-7063
Parent Company: Continuum International Publishing Group Ltd

Warm Island Walking Guides, *imprint of* Discovery Walking Guides Ltd

Frederick Warne, *imprint of* Penguin Books Ltd

Frederick Warne Publishers Ltd+
80 Strand, London WC2R 0RL
Tel: (020) 7010 3000 *Fax:* (020) 7010 6706
Key Personnel
Chief Executive: Anthony Forbes-Watson
Marketing: Gill Thomas
Production: Alan Lee
Man Dir: Sally Floyer
Founded: 1865
Specializes in classic characters & licensed merchandise programs.
ISBN Prefix(es): 0-7232
Parent Company: Penguin Books Ltd
U.S. Office(s): Penguin USA, 375 Hudson St, New York, NY 10014, United States *Tel:* 212-366-2000
Orders to: Penguin Books Ltd, Bath Rd, Harmondsworth, West Drayton, Middlesex UB7 0DA *Tel:* (02) 208 757 4000

Waterlow, *imprint of* Wilmington Business Information Ltd

A P Watt Ltd
20 John St, London WC1N 2DR
Tel: (020) 7405 6774 *Fax:* (020) 7831 2154
E-mail: apw@apwatt.co.uk
Web Site: www.apwatt.co.uk
Key Personnel
Man Dir: Derek Johns; Caradoc King
Dir: Sheila Crowley; Natasha Fairweather; Georgia Garrett
Foreign Rights Dir: Linda Shaughnessy
Media: Nick Harris
Founded: 1875

Franklin Watts, see The Watts Publishing Group Ltd

The Watts Publishing Group Ltd+
96 Leonard St, London EC2A 4XD
Tel: (020) 7739 2929 *Fax:* (020) 7739 2181
E-mail: gm@wattspub.co.uk
Web Site: www.wattspub.co.uk
Key Personnel
Group Man Dir: Marlene Johnson
Deputy Publishing Dir, Orchard Books: Rosemary Davies
Publishing Dir, Franklin Watts: Philippa Stewart
Publishing Dir, Orchard Books: Francesca Dow
Trade Sales Dir, Watts Publishing Group: George Spicer
Promotions & Marketing Associate Director: Linda Banner
Royalties & Contracts Manager: Marian Head
Rights Director: Claire Hurst
Founded: 1969
The Watts Group is comprised of Franklin Watts & Orchard Books.
Subjects: Fiction, Nonfiction (General)

ISBN Prefix(es): 0-7496; 1-85213; 1-86039; 0-85166; 1-84121; 0-86313
Parent Company: Hachette Livre
Subsidiaries: Grolier Australia Pty
U.S. Office(s): 387 Park Ave S, New York, NY 10016, United States
Orders to: Littlehampton Book Services, Worthing, West Sussex, Colchester, Essex C05 0SR

Waverley Books, *imprint of* Geddes & Grosset

Weatherbys Allen Ltd+
Sanders Rd, Wellingborough, Northamptonshire NN8 4BX
Tel: (01933) 440077 (ext 351) *Fax:* (01933) 270300
E-mail: turfnews@weatherbys-group.com
Web Site: www.weatherbys-allen.com
Key Personnel
Chief Executive: Caroline Burt
Founded: 1926
Subjects: Animals, Pets, Sports, Athletics
ISBN Prefix(es): 0-85131
Associate Companies: Mannin Industries Ltd, Isle of Man
Subsidiaries: The Caduceus Press
Distributor for The Pony Club (UK)
Bookshop(s): 4 Lower Grosvenor Place, London
Warehouse: The Trade Counter Ltd, 16 Airfield Norwich Rd, Mendlesham, Suffolk PI4 5NA

Webb & Bower (Publishers) Ltd+
9 Duke St, Dartmouth TQ6 9PY
Tel: (01803) 835525 *Fax:* (01803) 835552
Key Personnel
Man Dir: Richard Webb
Founded: 1975
Subjects: Nonfiction (General)
ISBN Prefix(es): 0-86350
Parent Company: R W Ltd
Associate Companies: Country Diary of an Edwardian Lady Ltd

Adrian Webster Ltd, see Websters International Publishers Ltd

Websters International Publishers Ltd+
Axe & Bottle Court, 70 Newcomen St, London SE1 1YT
Tel: (020) 7940 4700 *Fax:* (020) 7940 4701
E-mail: info@websters.co.uk
Web Site: www.websters.co.uk; www.ozclarke.com
Key Personnel
Chairman & Publisher: Adrian Webster
 E-mail: adrianqwe@msmail.websters.eurkom.ie
Man Dir: Jean-Luc Barbanneau
Financial Dir: Alan Fennell
Production Manager: Sara Granger
 E-mail: saragr@websters.co.uk
Editor-in-Chief: Susannah Webster
Founded: 1983
Specialize in wine information in all formats.
Subjects: Cookery, Health, Nutrition, Travel, Wine & Spirits
ISBN Prefix(es): 1-870604; 1-85320
Number of titles published annually: 6 Print; 1 CD-ROM
Total Titles: 20 Print
Associate Companies: Adrian Webster Ltd; Websters Multimedia Ltd
Distributed by Little Brown & Co (UK) Ltd
Foreign Rights: Elizabeth Brayne Foreign Rights Agency (all territories)

Websters Multimedia Ltd, see Websters International Publishers Ltd

A Weekes, *imprint of* Stainer & Bell Ltd

Welsh Academic Press+
PO Box 733, Cardiff CF14 2YX
Tel: (029) 2056 0343 *Fax:* (029) 2056 1631
E-mail: post@ashley.drake.com
Web Site: www.welsh-academic-press.co.uk
Key Personnel
Man Dir: Ashley Drake
Dir: Norman Drake; Siwan Drake
Founded: 1994
Specialize in the publishing of scholarly & academic books. that are also accessible to the general reader, "International in Outlook...Welsh in Identity".
Membership(s): Publishers' Association.
Subjects: Biography, Government, Political Science, History, Literature, Literary Criticism, Essays, Celtic Studies
ISBN Prefix(es): 1-86057
Number of titles published annually: 15 Print
Total Titles: 40 Print
Parent Company: Ashley Drake Publishing Ltd
Imprints: Morgan Publishing; St David's Press
Foreign Rep(s): Marika Janouskova (Eastern Europe); Cranbury International (Caribbean, South & Central America); Cristina de Lara Ruiz (Spain); Ted Dougherty (Austria, Benelux, Germany & Switzerland); Fathima News Enterprise (Singapore); Charles Gibbes (Greece); Globe Enterprises (Malaysia); Golden Book Services (Philippines); International Specialized Book Services (USA); Maya Publishers Pvt Ltd (India); Tony Moggach Associates (Sub-Saharan Africa); Mullet & Fitzpatrick (Ireland); Onslow Books (Scandinavia); Victor Osorio (Portugal); David Pickering (Italy); Anthony Rudkin Associates (Middle East); St. Clair Press (Australia); James Tovey (France); University of Toronto Press (Canada)
Warehouse: International Specialized Book Services, Hassalo St, Portland, OR, United States
Orders to: International Specialized Book Services, Hassalo St, Portland, OR, United States
Orca Book Services Ltd, 3 Fleets Lane, Poole, Dorset BH15 3AJ *Tel:* (01202) 665432 *Fax:* (01202) 666219 *E-mail:* orders@orcabookservices.co.uk (Order processing dept)

Welsh Womens Press, see Honno Welsh Women's Press

West Highland Series, *imprint of* House of Lochar

Westview Press
PO Box 317, Oxford OX2 9RU
Tel: (01865) 865466 *Fax:* (01865) 862763
E-mail: perseus@oppuk.co.uk
Web Site: www.westviewpress.com
Telex: 2 39479 WVP UR
Key Personnel
Vice President, Sales & Marketing - Perseus Books Group: Matthew Goldberg *Tel:* 212-207-7604 *E-mail:* matty.goldberg@perseusbooks.com
Manager: Gary Hall; Sue Miller
Founded: 1990
Subjects: Agriculture, Art, Economics, Environmental Studies, Government, Political Science, History, Social Sciences, Sociology
ISBN Prefix(es): 0-89158; 0-86531; 0-8133
Parent Company: Westview Press, 5500 Central Ave, Boulder, CO 80301, United States, Contact: Cathleen Tetro
Distributed by HarperCollins Publishers Order Department (New York)
Orders to: Perseus Books Group, PO Box 317, Oxford OX2 9RU *Tel:* (01865) 865466 *Fax:* (01865) 862763 *E-mail:* perseus@oppuk.co.uk
Perseus Books Group Customer Service, 5500 Central Ave, Boulder, CO 80301, United States *Fax:* 303-449-3356 *E-mail:* westview.orders@perseusbooks.com

Wharncliffe Books, *imprint of* Pen & Sword Books Ltd

Wharncliffe Publishing Ltd+
Imprint of Pen & Sword Books Ltd
47 Church St, Barnsley, South Yorks S70 2AS
Tel: (01226) 734222 *Fax:* (01226) 734438
E-mail: sales@pen-and-sword.co.uk
Key Personnel
Man Dir: Mr C Hewitt *Tel:* (01226) 734555
Founded: 1988
Subjects: History, Outdoor Recreation, Regional Interests, Local History, Countryside Books, Military History
Parent Company: Barnsley Chronicle Holdings Ltd
Distributed by Casemate
Distributor for National Archives (UK)
Membership(s): IPG

Which? Books, *imprint of* Which? Ltd

Which? Ltd+
2 Marylebone Rd, London NW1 4DF
Tel: (020) 7770 7000 *Fax:* (020) 7770 7485; (020) 7770 7600
E-mail: editor@which.net
Web Site: www.which.net
Telex: 918197
Key Personnel
Head of Publishing: Gill Rowley *Tel:* (020) 7830 7585 *E-mail:* rowleyg@which.co.uk
Founded: 1957
Subjects: Business, Computer Science, Finance, Gardening, Plants, Health, Nutrition, Law, Self-Help, Travel, Consumer Advice (Law, Finance, Practical), Accommodation & Restaurant Guides, Do-It-Yourself
ISBN Prefix(es): 0-85202
Total Titles: 80 Print
Parent Company: Consumers' Association
Imprints: Which? Books
Showroom(s): Castlemead, Gascoyne Way, Hertford SG14 1YB
Warehouse: Castlemead, Gascoyne Way, Hertford SG14 1YB *Fax:* (0171) 830 8585
Distribution Center: Penguin Books Ltd, 27 Wrights Lane, London W8 5TZ
Orders to: Castlemead, Gascoyne Way, Hertford SG14 1YB
Penguin Books Ltd, 27 Wrights Lane, London W8 5TZ
Membership(s): Publishers' Association

White Cockade Publishing+
71 Lonsdale Rd, Oxford OX2 7ES
Tel: (01865) 510411
E-mail: mail@whitecockade.co.uk
Web Site: www.whitecockade.co.uk
Key Personnel
Dir: Ms Perilla Kinchin
Founded: 1988
Membership(s): Independent Publishers Guild.
Subjects: Antiques, Architecture & Interior Design, Crafts, Games, Hobbies, History, Regional Interests, Social Sciences, Sociology, Women's Studies, Design History
ISBN Prefix(es): 0-9513124; 1-873487
Number of titles published annually: 1 Print
Total Titles: 12 Print

White Eagle Publishing Trust+
New Lands, Brewells Lane, Liss, Hants GU33 7HY
Tel: (01730) 893300 *Fax:* (01730) 892235
E-mail: enquiries@whiteagle.org
Web Site: www.whiteaglelodge.org
Key Personnel
Man Dir: Ylana Hayward

Foreign Rights: Geoffrey Dent *E-mail:* geoffrey@whiteagle.org
Founded: 1953
Subjects: Astrology, Occult, Religion - Other
ISBN Prefix(es): 0-85487
Total Titles: 46 Print; 10 Audio
Parent Company: White Eagle Lodge
Distributed by De Vorss & Co Inc (North America)

White Mouse Editions, *imprint of* New Cavendish Books

White Tree Books, *imprint of* Redcliffe Press Ltd

Whiting & Birch Ltd+
Forest Hill, 90 Dartmouth Rd, London SE23 3HZ
Tel: (020) 8244 2421 *Fax:* (020) 8244 2448
E-mail: savpub@dircon.co.uk
Web Site: www.whitingbirch.com
Key Personnel
Man Dir: David Whiting
Founded: 1987
Subjects: Child Care & Development, Criminology, Education, Ethnicity, Language Arts, Linguistics, Literature, Literary Criticism, Essays, Social Sciences, Sociology
ISBN Prefix(es): 1-871177; 1-86177
Number of titles published annually: 8 Print
Total Titles: 50 Print
Foreign Rep(s): Independent Publishers Group (IPG) (world exc Europe)
Foreign Rights: Independent Publishers Group (IPG) (world exc Europe)
Distribution Center: Independent Publishers Group (IPG), 814 N Franklin St, Chicago, IL 60610, United States *Tel:* 312-337-0747 *Fax:* 312-337-5785 *E-mail:* frontdesk@ipgbook.com *Web Site:* www.ipgbook.com (North America)

Whittet Books Ltd+
Hill Farm, Stonham Rd, Cotton, Stowmarket, Suffolk IP14 4RQ
Tel: (01449) 781877 *Fax:* (01449) 781898
Web Site: www.whittetbooks.com
Key Personnel
Chairman: A Whittet
Man Dir: Annabel Whittet *E-mail:* annabel@whittet.dircon.co.uk
Founded: 1976
Subjects: Animals, Pets, Natural History, Horses
ISBN Prefix(es): 0-905483; 1-873580
Parent Company: A Whittet & Co Ltd
Distributed by Diamond Farm Book Publishers (Canada & USA)
Warehouse: Biblios, Star Rd, Partridge Green, Horsham, Horsham, West Sussex RH13 8LD

Whittles Publishing+
Roseleigh House, Harbour Rd, Latheronwheel, Caithness KW5 6DW
Tel: (01593) 741240 *Fax:* (01593) 741360
E-mail: info@whittlespublishing.com
Web Site: www.whittlespublishing.com
Key Personnel
Publisher & Dir: Dr Keith Whittles
Promotions Coordinator: Sue Steven
Founded: 1986
Specialize in engineering, geomatics, surveying, applied science, nature writing & maritime. Also selected fiction noted in the land.
Membership(s): Scottish Publishers Association.
Subjects: Civil Engineering, Maritime, Natural History, Regional Interests, Geomatics
ISBN Prefix(es): 1-870325; 1-904445
Number of titles published annually: 20 Print
Total Titles: 60 Print
Foreign Rep(s): Academic Books (Austria, Germany & Switzerland); Avicenna Partnership (Greece, Middle East, Turkey, Iran); Roy de Boo (Belgium, Netherlands, Luxembourg); DA Information Services Pty Ltd (Australia & New Zealand, Papua New Guinea); Insat Books & Periodicals (India); Marcello sas (France & Spain, Italy & Portugal); STM Publishers Services Pte Ltd (Southeast Asia, Northeast Asia); David Towle International (Baltic States, Scandinavia); John W Wilson (North America)
Orders to: BookSource, 32 Finlas St, Cowlairs Industrial Estate, Glasgow G22 5DU
Tel: (0141) 558 1355 *Fax:* (0141) 557 0189
E-mail: customerservices@booksource.net

Whurr Publishers Ltd+
19B Compton Terrace, London N1 2UN
Tel: (020) 7359 5979 *Fax:* (020) 7226 5290
E-mail: info@whurr.co.uk
Web Site: www.whurr.co.uk
Key Personnel
Man Dir & Publisher: Colin Whurr
Company Secretary: Lynn Brett
Founded: 1987
Subjects: Business, Education, Medicine, Nursing, Dentistry, Psychology, Psychiatry
Total Titles: 400 Print
Subsidiaries: Cole & Whurr Ltd
Distributed by Elsevier Australia (Australia & New Zealand); Taylor & Francis (exclusive for North America)
Orders to: Extenza-Turpin Distribution Services Ltd, Stratton Business Park, Pegasus Drive, Biggleswade, Beds SG18 8QB *Tel:* (01767) 604965 *Fax:* (01767) 601640 *E-mail:* books@extenza-turpin.com *Web Site:* www.extenza-turpin.com

WI Enterprises Ltd
104 New Kings Rd, London SW6 4LY
Tel: (020) 7371 9300 *Fax:* (020) 7471 9300
E-mail: d.page@nfwi.org.uk
Web Site: www.womens-institute.co.uk/shop/policies/about.shtml
Key Personnel
Chairman: Barbara Gill
Group Manager: Mark Linacre
Sales & Marketing Manager: Dahla Page *E-mail:* d.page@nfwi.org.ok
Company Secretary: David Wood
Founded: 1977
Subjects: Cookery, Crafts, Games, Hobbies, Economics, Gardening, Plants, Women's Studies
ISBN Prefix(es): 0-947990; 0-900556
Parent Company: National Federation of Women's Institutes
Warehouse: WI Enterprises Ltd, Penzance TR93 0WW *Tel:* (01736) 333 333

Wild Goose Publications+
Savoy House, 4th floor, 140 Sauchiehall St, Glasgow G2 3DH
Tel: (0141) 332 6292 *Fax:* (0141) 332 1090
E-mail: admin@ionabooks.com
Web Site: www.ionabooks.com
Key Personnel
Publishing Manager: Sandra Kramer *E-mail:* sandra@ionabooks.com
Production Manager: Jane Riley *E-mail:* jane@ionabooks.com
Assistant Publishing Manager: Alex O'Neill *E-mail:* alex@ionabooks.com
Editorial Assistant: Neil Paynter
Administrator: Tri Boi Ta
Founded: 1985
Produces books on social justice, political & peace issues, holistic spirituality, healing & innovative approaches to worship. Part of the IONA community established in the Celtic Christian tradition of Saint Columba.
Membership(s): IPG.
Subjects: Biblical Studies, Government, Political Science, Music, Dance, Religion - Catholic, Religion - Protestant, Theology
ISBN Prefix(es): 0-947988; 1-901557
Number of titles published annually: 10 Print; 2 Audio
Total Titles: 125 Print; 25 Audio
Parent Company: The Iona Community
Distributed by GIA Publications (North America); Novalis Publishing (Canada); Pleroma Christian Supplies (New Zealand); Willow Connection Pty Ltd (Australia)
Orders to: Saint Andrew Press, 121 George St, Edinburgh EH2 4YN *Tel:* (0131) 225 5722 *Fax:* (0131) 220 3113

Wiley Europe Ltd+
The Atrium, Southern Gate, Chichester, West Sussex PO19 8SQ
Tel: (01243) 779777 *Fax:* (01243) 775878
E-mail: customer@wiley.co.uk
Web Site: www.wiley.co.uk
Key Personnel
Man Dir: Dr John Jarvis
Publishing Dir: Dr Steven Mair
STM Book Publishing Dir & Dir of Planning: Dr Ernest Kirkwood
Publisher, Technology: Dr Ann-Marie Halligan
Dir, New Media Development: Dr Rosemary Altoft
STM Journal Publishing Dir: Dr Michael Davis
Publisher, Medicine: Dr Deborah Reece
Publisher, College Division: Dr Simon Plumtree
Publisher, Chemistry: Dr Helen McPherson
Publisher, Medicine: Dr Richard Edelstein
Publisher, Life/Science: Dr Charlotte Brabants
Commercial Dir: Dr Sarah Stevens
Publisher, Psychology: Dr Michael Coombs
Dir Sales, Marketing & Publicity: Dr Robert Long
Publicity & Exhibition Man: Dr Julia Lampam
Production Dir: Helen Balley
Finance Dir: Jim Dicks
IT & Customer Service Dir: Peter Ferris
Marketing Development Dir: Paul Holmes
Sales Dir: Philip Kisray
Publishing Technologies Dir: Cliff Morgan
Human Resource Dir: Angela Poulter
Customer Service Dir: Margaret Radbourne
Distribution Dir: Mike Ridge
Publisher, Earth/Environmental Science: Sally Wilkinson
Senior Publishing Editor, Architecture: Maggie Toy
Founded: 1960
Other Main Office: WILEY-VCH, Pappelallee 3, 69469 Weinheim, Germany. Tel: (06201) 6060; Fax: (06201) 606328
2000 titles in print.
Subjects: Accounting, Architecture & Interior Design, Biological Sciences, Business, Chemistry, Chemical Engineering, Computer Science, Cookery, Earth Sciences, Economics, Finance, Management, Marketing, Mathematics, Mechanical Engineering, Medicine, Nursing, Dentistry, Physics, Psychology, Psychiatry, Religion - Other, Technology
Total Titles: 11,000 Print; 300 E-Book
Parent Company: John Wiley & Sons Inc, 111 River St, Hoboken, NJ 07030, United States
Associate Companies: John Wiley & Sons Australia Ltd, Australia *Tel:* (07) 3859 9755 *Fax:* (07) 3859 9715; John Wiley & Sons Canada Ltd, ON, Canada *Tel:* (416) 236-4433 *Fax:* (416) 236-4447; WILEY-VCH, Germany *Tel:* (06201) 606 0 *Fax:* (06201) 606 328 *E-mail:* info@wiley-vch.de; John Wiley & Sons (Asia) Pte Ltd, Singapore *Tel:* 463-2400 *Fax:* 463-4603; Tokyo Liaison Office, Kudonshita Tokyu Shin-Sakura, Bldg 6F, 1-3-3 Kudan-Kita, Chiyoda-ku Tokyo 102-0073, Japan *Tel:* (03) 3556 9762 *Fax:* (03) 3556 9763 *E-mail:* fwga5479@mb.infoweb.or.jp
Imprints: Wiley-Interscience; Wiley Liss; John Wiley & Sons; Halsted Press; Scripta Technica; Wiley-Heyden; ValuSource; Jossey-Bass

UNITED KINGDOM BOOK

Distributor for California, Columbia & Princeton University Press (Europe, Middle East, Africa); Indiana University Press (Continental Europe); Kegan Paul International Ltd (Europe); W W Norton & Co Ltd (Europe, Middle East, Africa, Asia, West Indies); O'Reilly UK Ltd (Europe, Middle East, Africa, Asia, West Indies); Research Studies Press Ltd (Europe, Middle East, Africa); Sybex International Corp (Continental Europe); The University of Chicago Press (Europe); Yale University Press (Europe, Middle East, Africa); Harvard University Press/MIT Press Ltd & LOEB Classical Library (Europe, Middle East, Africa)
Orders to: John Wiley & Sons Ltd Distribution Center, Southern Cross Trading Estate, One Oldlands Way, Bognor Regis, West Sussex PO22 9SA *Tel:* (01243) 779777 *Fax:* (01243) 820250

Wiley-Heyden, *imprint of* Wiley Europe Ltd

Wiley-Interscience, *imprint of* Wiley Europe Ltd

Wiley Liss, *imprint of* Wiley Europe Ltd

Joseph Williams, *imprint of* Stainer & Bell Ltd

Wilmington Business Information Ltd+
Paulton House, 8 Shepherdess Walk, London N1 7LB
Tel: (020) 7549 8704 *Fax:* (020) 7490 2979
Web Site: www.waterlow.com/signature/
Key Personnel
Dir: Rory A Conwell; Brian Gilbert; Michael Harrington; Paul Holden; Peter Lunn; Ahmed Zahedieh
Business Services Manager: E M Dutta *Tel:* (020) 7566 8277 *E-mail:* sdutta@waterlow.com
Founded: 1843
Membership(s): Directory & Database Publishers Association.
Subjects: Business, Disability, Special Needs, Drama, Theater, Fiction, Finance, Law, Music, Dance
Parent Company: Wilmington Group PLC
Associate Companies: Wilmington Publishing Ltd
Imprints: Gramophone; ICP; Investment Intelligence; PCR; RED; Waterlow
Subsidiaries: Retail Entertainment Data Publishing Ltd; Waterlow Specialist Information Publishing Ltd
Divisions: International Company Profile; Investment Intelligence; RED; Waterlow Co Services; Waterlow Professional Publishing; Waterlow Signature: Waterlow Direct Mail

Philip Wilson Publishers+
109 The Timber Yard, Drysdale St, London N1 6ND
Tel: (020) 7033 9900 *Fax:* (020) 7033 9922
E-mail: sales@philip-wilson.co.uk
Web Site: www.philip-wilson.co.uk
Key Personnel
Man Dir: Philip Wilson *E-mail:* pwilson@monoclick.co.uk
Sales & Publicity Manager: Juliana Powney *E-mail:* jpowney@monoclick.co.uk
Commissioning Editor: Anne Jackson *E-mail:* ajackson@monoclick.co.uk
Production Man: Norman Turpin *E-mail:* nturpin@monoclick.co.uk
Founded: 1975
Subjects: Antiques, Archaeology, Architecture & Interior Design, Art, Fashion
ISBN Prefix(es): 0-85667
Number of titles published annually: 16 Print
Total Titles: 150 Print
Distributed by Antique Collectors Club
Foreign Rep(s): APD Singapore Pte Ltd (Brunei, Indonesia, Malaysia, Singapore, Thailand); Asia Publishers Services Ltd (China & Hong Kong, Japan, Korea, Taiwan, Macao); Consul Books (Netherlands); Csaba Lengyel de bagota (Croatia, Czech Republic, Hungary, Romania, Slovak Republic, Slovenia, Serbia and Montenegro, Bosnia and Herzegovina); Exhibitions International (Belgium); Interart SRL (France); Livraria Gaudi Ltda (Brazil); Peter Hyde Associates (South Africa); Thames & Hudson (Australia); The Art Book Studio (India)
Foreign Rights: Michael Geoghegan (Austria, Germany, Switzerland); Michael Morris Associates (Middle East); Penny Padovani (Greece, Italy, Portugal, Spain); Hanne Rotovnik (Finland, Iceland, Scandinavia); David Wine (Israel)

Wimbledon Publishing Company Ltd+
75-76 Blackfriars Rd, London SE1 8HA
Tel: (020) 7401 4200 *Fax:* (020) 7928 4201
E-mail: enquiries@wpcpress.com
Web Site: www.wpcpress.com
Key Personnel
Man Dir: Mr K Sood
Sales & Marketing: Mr N McPherson
Editor, Nightingale Press: Mr L Chaput
Founded: 1993
Specialize in political science & humanities plus gift & humor books for the discerning wit.
Subjects: Biography, Biological Sciences, Business, Economics, Government, Political Science, Health, Nutrition, History, Humor, Language Arts, Linguistics, Literature, Literary Criticism, Essays, Self-Help, Women's Studies
ISBN Prefix(es): 1-898855; 1-903222
Number of titles published annually: 50 Print
Total Titles: 150 Print
Imprints: Anthem Press (Academic humanities); Nightingale Press (Gift books & humor); WPC Classics (School & college classics); WPC School Books (Secondary education textbooks)
U.S. Office(s): 4117 Hillsboro Pike, Suite 103-106, Nashville, TN 37215, United States *Tel:* 801-749-2983 *Fax:* 801-749-2983 *E-mail:* enquiries@wpcpress.com
Orders to: Pathway Book Service, 4 White Brook Lane, Gilsum, NH 03348, United States *Tel:* 603-357-0236 *Fax:* 603-357-2073 *E-mail:* pbs@pathwaybooks.com

Windhorse Publications+
11 Park Rd, Moseley, Birmingham B13 8AB
Tel: (0121) 449 9191 *Fax:* (0121) 449 9191
E-mail: info@windhorsepublications.com
Web Site: www.windhorsepublications.com
Key Personnel
Sales & Marketing Manager: Carol Bois
Founded: 1976
Subjects: Religion - Buddhist
ISBN Prefix(es): 0-904766; 1-899579
Number of titles published annually: 9 Print
Total Titles: 100 Print
Associate Companies: Windhorse Books, PO Box 574, Newtown, NSW 2042, Australia, Contact: Ratnajyoti *Tel:* (02) 9519 8826 *Fax:* (02) 9519 8826 *E-mail:* books@windhorse.com.au *Web Site:* www.windhorse.com.au (Australia)
Distributed by Booksource; Weatherhill Inc (North America)
Orders to: Weatherhill Inc, 41 Monroe Turnpike, Trumbull, CT 06611, United States *Tel:* 800-437-7840 *Fax:* 800-557-5601 *E-mail:* weatherhill@weatherhill.com *Web Site:* www.weatherhill.com (USA)

Windrow & Greene, *imprint of* Compendium Publishing

The Windrush Press Ltd+
Windrush House, 12 Main St, Adlestrop, Moreton-in-Marsh, Glos GL56 0LL
Tel: (01608) 658758 *Fax:* (01608) 659345
E-mail: info@windrushpublishingservices.com
Web Site: www.windrushpress.com
Key Personnel
Founding Dir: John Goulding
Man Dir: Geoffrey Smith
Publishing Dir: Victoria Huxley *E-mail:* victoriama.huxley@btinternet.com
Founded: 1987
Specialize in military history & ancient mysteries.
Subjects: Biography, History, Humor, Mysteries, Nonfiction (General), Travel
ISBN Prefix(es): 0-900075; 1-900624
Total Titles: 50 Print
Parent Company: Orion Group, 5 Upper St Martin's Lane, London WC2H 9EA
Distributor for Windrush Publishing Services
Orders to: Littlehampton Book Services, Faraday Close, Durrington, West Sussex BN13 3RB *Tel:* (01903) 828890 *Fax:* (01903) 828802

Windsor Books International
The Boundary, Wheatley Rd, Garsington, Oxford, Oxon OX44 9EJ
Tel: (01865) 361122 *Fax:* (01865) 361133
E-mail: sales@windsorbooks.co.uk
Web Site: www.windsorbooks.co.uk
Key Personnel
Man Dir: A Geoff Cowen *E-mail:* geoffcowen@windsorbooks.co.uk
Founded: 1991
Also acts as distributor in the UK & Europe for publishers in the US & other countries.
Subjects: Architecture & Interior Design, Art, Music, Dance, Radio, TV, Travel
ISBN Prefix(es): 1-874111
Subsidiaries: Springfield Books
Distributor for Allworth Press, New York (UK & Europe); Billboard Music Books, New York (UK & Europe); Creative Publishing International, Minnesota (UK & Europe); C & T Publishing, California (UK & Europe); Getty Publications, California (UK & Europe); The Globe Pequot Press, Connecticut (UK); Hudson Hills Press, New York (UK & Europe); Hunter Publishing, Florida (UK & Europe); The Lyons Press, Connecticut (UK); Meyer & Meyer, Aachen (UK); Sally Milner Publishing, Australia (UK & Europe); Open Road Publishing, New York (UK & Europe); Watson-Guptill Publications, New York (UK & Europe)

Windsor Large Print Bestsellers, *imprint of* BBC Audiobooks

Wise Owl Books, *imprint of* HLT Publications

WISE Publications, *imprint of* Omnibus Press

Wisley Handbooks, *imprint of* Cassell & Co

WIT Press+
Ashurst Lodge, Ashurst, Southampton SO40 7AA
Tel: (023) 8029 3223 *Fax:* (023) 8029 2853
E-mail: witpress@witpress.com
Web Site: www.witpress.com
Key Personnel
Chief Executive, Man Dir & Publicity: Prof C Brebbia
Marketing Manager: Helen Arnold *E-mail:* marketing@witpress.com
Sales Manager: Graham Presland *E-mail:* gpresland@witpress.com
Customer Services: Loraine Carter *E-mail:* lcarter@witpress.com
Founded: 1976
Publisher in advanced engineering subjects, including environmental engineering, engineering analysis & computational methods. Also publishes the proceedings of conferences organized by the Wessex Institute of Technology, edited/authored volumes & journals.

Subjects: Architecture & Interior Design, Automotive, Biological Sciences, Civil Engineering, Computer Science, Earth Sciences, Electronics, Electrical Engineering, Engineering (General), Environmental Studies, Maritime, Mathematics, Mechanical Engineering, Technology, Transportation, Acoustics, Biomedicine, Earthquake Engineering, Environmental & Ecological Engineering, Fluid Mechanics, Fracture Mechanics, Heat Transfer, Marine Engineering, Transport Engineering
ISBN Prefix(es): 0-931215; 0-945824; 1-56252; 1-85312; 0-905451
Number of titles published annually: 50 Print
Total Titles: 500 Print; 6 CD-ROM
Parent Company: Computational Mechanics International
U.S. Office(s): Computational Mechanics, 25 Bridge St, Billerica, MA 01821, United States *Tel:* 978-667-5841 *Fax:* 978-667-7582 *E-mail:* infousa@witpress.com

Witherby, *imprint of* Cassell & Co

Witherby & Co Ltd+
Book Dept, 2nd floor, 32-36 Aylesbury St, London EC1R 0ET
Tel: (020) 7251 5341 *Fax:* (020) 7251 1296
E-mail: books@witherbys.co.uk
Web Site: www.witherbys.com
Key Personnel
Man Dir: Alan Witherby
Founded: 1740
Membership(s): Bookseller Association; Institute of Experts.
Subjects: Business, Economics, Management, Maritime, Technology, Transportation
ISBN Prefix(es): 0-900886; 1-85609
Number of titles published annually: 20 Print; 2 Audio
Total Titles: 250 Print; 1 CD-ROM; 2 Audio
Imprints: Monument
Bookshop(s): 20 Aldermanbury, London EC2V 7HY, Contact: Christine Burge *Tel:* (020) 7417 4431 *Fax:* (020) 7417 4431 *E-mail:* books@witherbys.co.uk

H F & G Witherby Ltd, see Gollancz/Witherby

The Woburn Press+
Member of Taylor & Francis Group
Subsidiary of Frank Cass Publishers
Crown House, 47 Chase Side, London N14 5BP
Tel: (020) 8920 2100 *Fax:* (020) 8447 8548
E-mail: info@woburnpress.com
Web Site: www.frankcass.com/wp
Key Personnel
Man Dir: Stewart Cass
Editorial: Andrew Humphreys
Trade: Joanna Legg
Production: Daphna Weiss
Publicity: Hayley Osen
Founded: 1969
Subjects: Education
ISBN Prefix(es): 0-7130
Associate Companies: Vallentine, Mitchell & Co Ltd; Irish Academic Press
U.S. Office(s): 5824 NE Hassalo St, Portland, OR 97213-3644, United States *Tel:* 503-287-3093 *Fax:* 503-280-8832 *E-mail:* wp@isbs.com
Warehouse: Biblios Distributions, Star Rd, Partridge Green, West Sussex RH13 8LD *Tel:* (0403) 710971 *Fax:* (0403) 711143

WOL Books, *imprint of* Pallas Athene

Oswald Wolff Books, *imprint of* Berg Publishers

The Women's Press Ltd+
Member of Namara Group
27 Goodge St, London W1T 2LD
Tel: (020) 7636 3992 *Fax:* (020) 7637 1866
E-mail: sales@the-womens-press.com
Web Site: www.the-womens-press.com
Key Personnel
Man Dir: Emma Drew *E-mail:* emma@the-womens-press.com
Founded: 1977
Subjects: Alternative, Art, Biography, Disability, Special Needs, Environmental Studies, Ethnicity, Fiction, Gay & Lesbian, Government, Political Science, Health, Nutrition, Literature, Literary Criticism, Essays, Music, Dance, Nonfiction (General), Psychology, Psychiatry, Self-Help, Women's Studies
ISBN Prefix(es): 0-7043
Number of titles published annually: 36 Print
Imprints: Livewire (books for teenagers & young women)
Distributed by Codasat (Canada); Ted Dougherty (Europe-excluding Spain & Portugal); Iberian Book Services (Spain & Portugal); IMA (Africa, Eastern Europe, Caribbean & Latin America); Quartet (South Africa); Hanne Rotovnik (Scandinavia); Southern Publishers Group (New Zealand); Tower Books (Australia); Trafalgar Square (US)
Foreign Rights: Writer's House (USA)
Orders to: Plymbridge Distributors Ltd, Estover Rd, Estover, Plymouth PL6 7PZ *Tel:* (01752) 202301 *Fax:* (01752) 202331 *E-mail:* control@plymbridge.com

Woodhead Publishing Ltd+
Abington Hall, Abington, Cambs CB1 6AH
Tel: (01223) 891358 *Fax:* (01223) 893694
E-mail: wp@woodhead-publishing.com; info@woodhead-publishing.com
Web Site: www.woodhead-publishing.com
Key Personnel
Man Dir: Martin J Woodhead *Tel:* (01223) 891358 (ext 16) *E-mail:* martinw@woodhead-publishing.com
Editorial Dir: Francis Dodds *Tel:* (01223) 891358 (ext 15) *E-mail:* francisd@woodhead-publishing.com
Editorial & Production: Mary Campbell; Kristine Swift
Marketing Manager: Neil MacLeod *Tel:* (01223) 891358 (ext 33) *E-mail:* neilm@woodhead-publishing.com
Finance Dir: Rob Burleigh *Tel:* (01223) 891358 (ext 11) *E-mail:* robb@woodhead-publishing.com
Sales Administrator: Jenny Wheeler *Tel:* (01223) 891358 (ext 28)
Founded: 1989
Specialize in engineering materials, welding, food science, food technology, textiles, environment, finance & investment.
Subjects: Energy, Engineering (General), Finance, Health, Nutrition, Technology, Food Science
ISBN Prefix(es): 1-85573
Number of titles published annually: 45 Print; 2 CD-ROM; 30 Online; 30 E-Book
Total Titles: 400 Print; 4 CD-ROM; 100 Online; 100 E-Book
Imprints: Abington Publishing; Gresham Books
Distributed by CRC Press LLC
Distributor for American Welding Society
Warehouse: Combined Book Services Ltd, Units I/K, Paddock Wood Distribution Centre, Paddock Wood, Tonbridge TN12 6UU *Tel:* (01892) 837171 *Fax:* (01892) 837272
Membership(s): IPG

Word for Word Audio Books, *imprint of* BBC Audiobooks

Wordsworth Editions, *imprint of* Wordsworth Editions Ltd

Wordsworth Editions Ltd+
Cumberland House, Crib Street, Ware, Herts SG12 9ET
Tel: (01920) 465167 *Fax:* (01920) 462267
E-mail: enquiries@wordsworth-editions.com
Web Site: www.wordsworth-editions.co.uk/distributors.htm
Founded: 1987
Specialize in Wordsworth Editions & Classics with CD-ROM, folklore, myths & legends.
Subjects: History, Literature, Literary Criticism, Essays, Poetry
ISBN Prefix(es): 1-85326; 1-84022
Number of titles published annually: 50 Print; 20 CD-ROM
Total Titles: 700 Print; 10 CD-ROM
Imprints: Wordsworth Editions; Wordsworth Education
Distributed by Agius & Agius Ltd (Malta & Gozo); Allphy Book Distributors Ltd (New Zealand & Fiji); Bohemian Ventures sro (Czech Republic); Copernicus Diffusion (France); Inter Orbis Media Dist srl Ed (Italy); NTC/Contemporary (USA); OM Books International (India); Peribo Pty Ltd (Australia & Papua New Guinea); Readwide Bookshop Ltd (Ghana, The Gambia, Liberia, Cameroon & Sierra Leone); Ribera Libros SL (Spain); Slovak Ventures sro (Slovak Republic); Taschenbuch-Vertrieb Ingeborg Blank GmbH Lager und Buro (Germany & Austria)
Foreign Rep(s): Don O'Mahoney (Ireland); Advanced Global Distribution (USA); IMA (Caribbean, South America); Publishers International Marketing (Far East, Middle East)
Showroom(s): Cumberland House, Crib Street, Ware, Herts SG12 9ET
Warehouse: Wordsworth Editions, The Airfield, Mendlesham, Suffolk IP14 5NA

Wordsworth Education, *imprint of* Wordsworth Editions Ltd

Wordwright Books, *imprint of* Wordwright Publishing

Wordwright Publishing+
25 Oakford Rd, London NW5 1AJ
Tel: (020) 7284 0056 *Fax:* (020) 7284 0041
E-mail: wordwright@clara.co.uk
Key Personnel
Dir, International Rights: Charles Perkins *E-mail:* cfp@wordwright.clara.co.uk
Dir: Veronica Davis
Founded: 1987
Also book packager.
Membership(s): Book Packagers Association.
Subjects: Art, Cookery, Gardening, Plants, Geography, Geology, History, Humor, Natural History, Nonfiction (General), Social Sciences, Sociology, Sports, Athletics, Women's Studies
ISBN Prefix(es): 0-9527128
Total Titles: 40 Print
Imprints: Wordwright Books

World Microfilms Publications Ltd+
PO Box 35488, St Johns Wood, London NW8 6WD
Tel: (020) 7586 4499; (0845) 606 0612 *Fax:* (020) 7722 1068
E-mail: microworld@ndirect.co.uk
Web Site: www.microworld.ndirect.co.uk
Key Personnel
Man Dir: Stephen C Albert
Founded: 1969
Subjects: Architecture & Interior Design, Art, Drama, Theater, Economics, Film, Video, History, Music, Dance, Religion - Other, Science (General), Self-Help, Microfilm Collections
ISBN Prefix(es): 1-85035; 1-86013; 0-905272
Number of titles published annually: 10 Print
Total Titles: 700 Print; 3 CD-ROM; 400 Audio

UNITED KINGDOM

Associate Companies: Audio-Forum; Pidgeon Audio Visual; Sussex Tapes; Sussex Video; Stotts Correspondence College
Foreign Rep(s): Norman Ross Publishing Inc (Canada, USA)

World of Information+
2 Market St, Saffron Walden, Essex CB10 1HZ
Tel: (01799) 521150 *Fax:* (01799) 524805
E-mail: queries@worldinformation.com
Web Site: www.worldinformation.com
Key Personnel
Man Dir & Rights: Anthony Axon
Founded: 1972
Subjects: Business, Economics, Government, Political Science
ISBN Prefix(es): 1-86217
Number of titles published annually: 140 Print; 1 CD-ROM
Total Titles: 160 Print; 3 CD-ROM
Subsidiaries: Central European Business Ltd
Distribution Center: Storgatan 7 B, S-753 31, Uppsala, Sweden *Tel:* (0) 18 13 36 33 *Fax:* (0) 18 12 36 63

World of Islam Altajir Trust+
33 Thurloe Place, London SW7 2HQ
Tel: (020) 7581 3522 *Fax:* (020) 7584 1977
Key Personnel
Dir: Alistair Duncan
Founded: 1974
Subjects: Archaeology, Art, Religion - Islamic, Theology
ISBN Prefix(es): 0-905035; 1-901435
Orders to: Fox Communications & Publications, 39 Chelmsford Rd, London E18 2PW *Tel:* (020) 8498 9768 *Fax:* (020) 8504 2558

The World Today, *imprint of* Royal Institute of International Affairs

Worldlife Library, *imprint of* Colin Baxter Photography Ltd

WPC Classics, *imprint of* Wimbledon Publishing Company Ltd

WPC School Books, *imprint of* Wimbledon Publishing Company Ltd

Writers & Their Work, *imprint of* Northcote House Publishers Ltd

Writer's Digest, *imprint of* David & Charles Ltd

Wychwood Press, *imprint of* Jon Carpenter Publishing

Y Cyfarwyddwr Urdd Gobaith Cymru
Swyddfa'r Urdd, Ffordd Llanbadarn, Aberystwyth, Ceredigion SY23 1EN
Tel: (01970) 613100 *Fax:* (01970) 626120
E-mail: urdd@urdd.org
Web Site: www.urdd.org
Key Personnel
Chief Executive: Jim O'Rourke *E-mail:* jim@urdd.org
Founded: 1923

Yale English Monarchs, *imprint of* Yale University Press London

Yale University Press London+
47 Bedford Sq, London WC1B 3DP
Tel: (020) 7079 4900 *Fax:* (020) 7079 4901
E-mail: sales@yaleup.co.uk
Web Site: www.yalebooks.co.uk

Key Personnel
Man Dir: Robert Baldock *E-mail:* robert.baldock@yaleup.co.uk
Editorial Dir: Gillian Malpass *E-mail:* gillian.malpass@yaleup.co.uk
Sales & Marketing Dir: Kate Pocock *E-mail:* kate.pocock@yaleup.co.uk
Publicity: Hazel Hutchison
Sales: Andrew Jarmain
Rights: Anne Bihan
Editor: Sally Salvesen
Founded: 1961
Subjects: Anthropology, Architecture & Interior Design, Art, Asian Studies, Biography, Environmental Studies, Government, Political Science, History, Language Arts, Linguistics, Law, Literature, Literary Criticism, Essays, Music, Dance, Natural History, Nonfiction (General), Philosophy, Photography, Physical Sciences, Psychology, Psychiatry, Religion - Jewish, Social Sciences, Sociology, Theology, Women's Studies
ISBN Prefix(es): 0-300
Parent Company: Yale University Press, 302 Temple St, PO Box 209040, New Haven, CT 06520-9040, United States
Imprints: Pelican History of Art; Pevsner Architectural Guides; Yale English Monarchs
Subsidiaries: Yale Representation Ltd
Distributor for Metropolitan Museum of Art; National Gallery Publications
Orders to: John Wiley & Sons Ltd Distribution Centre, Southern Cross Trading Estate, Bognor Regis, West Sussex PO22 9SA

Yellow Jersey Press, *imprint of* Random House UK Ltd

Anglia Young Books+
Imprint of Motivation in Learning Ltd (Bangor)
Durham's Farmhouse, Ickleton, Saffron Walden, Essex CB10 1SR
Tel: (01799) 531192 *Fax:* (01799) 531192
Web Site: www.btinternet.com/~r.hayes
Key Personnel
Contact: Rosemary Hayes *E-mail:* r.hayes@btinternet.com
Founded: 1989
Subjects: Disability, Special Needs, Fiction, History, Religion - Other
ISBN Prefix(es): 1-871173
Distributor for Kallisto Ltd
Orders to: Broadgali House, 72 Church St, Deeping St James, Peterborough PE6 8HD

Young Corgi, *imprint of* Transworld Publishers Ltd

Young Picador, *imprint of* Macmillan Children's Books

Zed Books Ltd+
7 Cynthia St, London N1 9JF
Tel: (020) 7837 4014; (020) 7837 0384 *Fax:* (020) 7833 3960
E-mail: zedbooks@zedbooks.demon.co.uk
Web Site: zedweb.hypermart.net/zed/contact.htm
Key Personnel
Sales: Farouk Sohawon
Editor: Robert Molteno; Michael Pallis
Editor, Rights & Permissions: Mohammed Umar *E-mail:* mohammed@zedbooks.demon.co.uk
Marketing: Julian Hosie
Production: Anne Rodford
Founded: 1976
Subjects: Environmental Studies, Social Sciences, Sociology, Women's Studies, Development Studies
ISBN Prefix(es): 0-905762; 0-86232; 1-85649; 1-84277
Total Titles: 350 Print

Distributed by St Martin's Press/Palgrave (USA)
Shipping Address: Plymbridge, Estover, Plymouth PL6 7PZ
Warehouse: Plymbridge, Estover, Plymouth PL6 7PZ

Zeno Booksellers, see The Greek Bookshop

Ziff-Davis Press, *imprint of* Pearson Education Europe, Mideast & Africa

Zomba Books, *imprint of* Omnibus Press

Zone Books, *imprint of* MIT Press Ltd

Zwemmer Holdings Co Ltd
10 Stratton St, 6th floor, London W1J 8LG
Tel: (020) 7297 4555 *Fax:* (020) 7836 7049
E-mail: sales@zwemmer.com
Web Site: www.zwemmer.com
Key Personnel
Man Dir: Rupert Gather
Founded: 1921
Subjects: Architecture & Interior Design, Art, Film, Video, Photography, Performing Arts
ISBN Prefix(es): 0-302
Bookshop(s): OUP Bookshop, 72 Charing Cross Rd, London WC2H OBE; Whitechapel Art Gallery, Whitechapel High St, London E1 7QX; Zwemmers, 80 Charing Cross Rd, London WC2

Uruguay

General Information

Capital: Montevideo
Language: Spanish
Religion: Predominantly Roman Catholic
Population: 3.1 million
Bank Hours: 1300-1700 Monday-Friday
Shop Hours: 0900-1200, 1400-1900 Monday-Friday; 0900-1230 Saturday
Currency: 100 centesimos = 1 new Uruguayan peso
Export/Import Information: Member Southern Cone Common Market (MERCOSUR) No tariffs on books or single copies catalogues but surcharge on advertising matter. Additional surcharge on all imports, plus VAT Cif, plus Stamp Tax of percentage of total invoice value. No import licenses. No exchange controls.
Copyright: UCC, Berne, Buenos Aires (see Copyright Conventions, pg xi)

Albe Libros Technicos
Cerrito 564/566, Casilla Correos, 1601, Montevideo 11100
Tel: (02) 915 75 28; (02) 915 74 85 *Fax:* (02) 915 75 28
Web Site: www.bosch.es/puntos_internacional.asp
Key Personnel
Contact: Daniel Aljanati
Branch Office(s)
Albe Libros Technicos-Salto, Joaquin Suarez 28, Salto

Editorial Arca SRL+
Bartolome Mitre 1413, Montevideo 11100
Tel: (02) 9166966 int 110 *Fax:* (02) 901887; (02) 930188
E-mail: saroya@st.com.uy
Key Personnel
Man Dir: Claudio Rama
Founded: 1964
Subjects: Anthropology, Drama, Theater, Economics, Geography, Geology, Health, Nutrition,

History, Humor, Music, Dance, Poetry, Regional Interests, Religion - Other, Technology
ISBN Prefix(es): 9974-40

Arpoador+
Roque Graseras 693, Montevideo 11300
Tel: (02) 707826 *Fax:* (02) 717278
Key Personnel
Contact: Martha Paulick
Founded: 1995
Subjects: Economics, History, Literature, Literary Criticism, Essays
ISBN Prefix(es): 9974-7533

Barreiro y Ramos SA
Juan Carlos Gomez, PO Box 15, 11100 Montevideo
Tel: (02) 98 66 21 *Fax:* (02) 96 23 58 *Cable:* BAREIRAMOS
Key Personnel
Man Dir: Dr Gaston Barreiro Zorrilla
Sales Dir: Raul Catelli
Founded: 1871
Subjects: Literature, Literary Criticism, Essays, Religion - Other
ISBN Prefix(es): 84-8292; 9974-33

Cotidiano Mujer
San Jose 1436, 11200 Montevideo
Tel: (02) 9018782; (02) 9020393 *Fax:* (02) 4095651
E-mail: cotidian@chasque.apc.org.uy
Web Site: chasque.chasque.apc.org/cotidian/
Key Personnel
Contact: Elena Fonseca
Founded: 1985
Subjects also include ecology, feminism & human rights.
Subjects: Journalism, Women's Studies

Ediciones de Juan Darien+
Hocquart 1771, 11800 Montevideo
Tel: (02) 2090223
E-mail: dayraq@chasque.apc.org
Key Personnel
Contact: Dayman Cabrera
Founded: 1990
Subjects: Art, Cookery, Economics, Education, History, Literature, Literary Criticism, Essays, Nonfiction (General), Poetry, Social Sciences, Sociology
ISBN Prefix(es): 9974-580

Instituto del Tercer Mundo+
Juan D Jackson 1136, Montevideo 11200
Mailing Address: PO Box 1539, Montevideo 11000
Tel: (02) 419 6192 *Fax:* (02) 411 9222
E-mail: item@chasque.apc.org; item@item.org.uy
Web Site: www.chasque.apc.org/item/
Key Personnel
Dir: Roberto Bissio
Editor: Victor Bacchetta *E-mail:* victorb@chasque.apc.org
Founded: 1986
New Zealand/Aotearoa
Membership(s): Association for Progressive Communications (APC).
Subjects: Human Relations, Civil Society
ISBN Prefix(es): 9974-574
U.S. Office(s): Humanities Press International Inc, 165 First Ave, Atlantic Highlands, NJ 07716, United States *Tel:* 908-872-1441 *Fax:* 908-872-0717
DHL, 8424 NW 56 St, Suite MVD 023040, Miami, FL 33166, United States
Distributed by Andenbuch-Romanische Buchhandlung (Alemania); Arning Publications (Norway); CEDIB (Bolivia); Fondo de Cultura Economica (Peru); Hillco Media Group (Sweden); Humanities Press International Inc (US); Ibercultura GmbH (Switzerland); IEPALA (Spain); Instituto del Tercer Mundo (Uruguay); Lamuv Verlag (Germany); Leer Ltda (Colombia); Libreria De La Paz (Argentina); Libreria Lectura SA (Venezuela); Libreria Milnovecientos (Chile); Libri Mundi (Ecuador); MARCIAL PONS Libreros (Spain); Mellemfolkeligt Samvirke (Denmark); NCOS (Belgium); New Internationalist Aotearoa; New Internationalist (Australia); New Internationalist Canada (Canada); New Internationalist Publications (UK); Novib Publications (Netherlands); Oxfam Publications (UK); Sipro (Servicios Informativos Procesados AC) (Mexico); Tyron SA (Argentina)
Distributor for Revista delsur; Social Watch
Orders to: Hersilia Fonseca/Marketing

Departemento de Publicaciones de la Universidad de la Republica
Jose Enrique Rodo 1827, 11200 Montevideo
Tel: (02) 408 2906; (02) 408 5714 *Fax:* (02) 408 0303
E-mail: infoed@edic.edu.uy
Web Site: www.rau.edu.uy
Key Personnel
Dir: Daniel Cabalero
ISBN Prefix(es): 9974-0

Editorial Dismar+
18 de Julio 2172/308, 11200 Montevideo
Tel: (02) 407946
Key Personnel
Editor: Martha Campos
Founded: 1989
Membership(s): Camara Uruguaya del Libro.
Subjects: Journalism, Medicine, Nursing, Dentistry, Psychology, Psychiatry
ISBN Prefix(es): 9974-560

EQ Opciones en Educacion
Casilla del Correo 16035, 11600 Montevideo
Tel: (02) 4808720 *Fax:* (02) 4873965
E-mail: opciones@distrinet.com.uy
Key Personnel
Contact: Esperanza Querol
Founded: 1995
Membership(s): Camara Uruguaya del Libro; Specialize in educational material; Also acts as importer, seller & distributor.
Subjects: Astronomy, Education, Language teaching methods
Distributor for Editora Nova Fronteira; Editora Pedagogica Universitario; Hachette Livre
Distribution Center: CLE International, Paris, France

Editorial Libreria Amalio M Fernandez
25 de Mayo 589, 11000 Montevideo
Tel: (02) 9151782; (02) 295 26 84 *Fax:* (02) 295 17 82
Key Personnel
Man Dir & Editorial: Carlos W Deamestoy Perez
Sales: Jorge M Garcia
Founded: 1951
Subjects: Law, Social Sciences, Sociology
ISBN Prefix(es): 84-8293

La Flor del Itapebi+
Luis Piera 1917/401, 11300 Montevideo
Tel: (02) 710 92 67 *Fax:* (02) 710 92 67
E-mail: itapebi@itapebi.com
Web Site: www.itapebi.com
Key Personnel
Contact: Sra Isabel Grompone
Founded: 1992
Subjects: Computer Science, Fiction, Mathematics
ISBN Prefix(es): 9974-592
Parent Company: Olmer SA

Fundacion de Cultura Universitaria+
25 de Mayo 568, Casilla de Correo 1155, 11000 Montevideo
Tel: (02) 9152532; (02) 959038; (02) 9168360
Fax: (02) 9152549
E-mail: administrador@fcu.com.uy
Web Site: www.fcu.com.uy
Key Personnel
Man Dir: Carlos (Fallecido) Fuques
Administrator: Jorge Mahy
Founded: 1968
Subjects: Accounting, Criminology, Economics, Finance, Government, Political Science, History, Law, Regional Interests, Romance, Social Sciences, Sociology
Branch Office(s)
Artigas N 1251, regional Norte-Salto

Hemisferio Sur Edicion Agropecuaria
Buenos Aires 335, 11000 Montevideo
Tel: (02) 916 45 15; (02) 916 45 20 *Fax:* (02) 916 45 20
E-mail: librperi@adinet.com.uy
Key Personnel
Contact: Sra Margarita Peri
Subjects: Biological Sciences, Natural History
ISBN Prefix(es): 9974-556

Linardi y Risso Libreria
Juan Carlos Gomez 1435, Montevideo 11000
Tel: (02) 915 71 29; (02) 915 73 28 *Fax:* (02) 915 74 31
E-mail: lyrbooks@linardiyrisso.com
Web Site: www.linardiyrisso.com/
Founded: 1944
Specialize in Latin American books.
Subjects: Government, Political Science, History, Literature, Literary Criticism, Essays
ISBN Prefix(es): 9974-559
Orders to: Linardi Y Risso, 4405 NW 73 Ave, Suite 12-333 4567, Miami, FL 33166-6400, United States

A Monteverde y Cia SA+
Treinta y Tres 1475, 11000 Montevideo
Tel: (02) 915 2012; (02) 915 2939; (02) 915 8748
Fax: (02) 915 2012
E-mail: monteverde@monteverde.com.uy
Web Site: www.monteverde.com.uy/
Key Personnel
Man Dir: Daniel Mussini
Sales Dir: Liliana Mussini
Founded: 1879
Subjects: Astronomy, Biological Sciences, Chemistry, Chemical Engineering, Earth Sciences, Geography, Geology, History, Literature, Literary Criticism, Essays, Mathematics, Music, Dance, Natural History, Philosophy, Physical Sciences, Physics
ISBN Prefix(es): 9974-34
Subsidiaries: Cion; Encuaderna; Impresos; Talleres Graficos
Bookshop(s): Palacio del Libro
Orders to: Trienta y Tres 1475, 11000 Montevideo *Tel:* (02) 952939

Mosca Hermanos
18 de Julio 1578, Montevideo 11100
SAN: 004-2757
Tel: (02) 4093141; (02) 4011111 *Fax:* (02) 200 0588
E-mail: empresas@mosca.com.uy
Web Site: www.mosca.com.uy/ *Cable:* Moscaher
Key Personnel
Man Dir: Gustavo Mosca
Sales Dir: Gonzalo Mosca
Founded: 1888
Subjects: Literature, Literary Criticism, Essays, Religion - Other
ISBN Prefix(es): 9974-555; 84-89275

URUGUAY

Nordan-Comunidad+
Millan 4113, 12900 Montevideo
Tel: (02) 305 5609 *Fax:* (02) 308 1640
E-mail: nordan@nordan.com.uy; pedidos@nordan.com.uy; info@nordan.com.uy
Web Site: www.chasque.net/nordan/; www.nordan.com.uy
Key Personnel
Editor: Prieto Ruben
Coordinator: Zaya Arremyr *E-mail:* admin@nordan.com.uy
Subjects: Agriculture, Alternative, Anthropology, Architecture & Interior Design, Communications, Developing Countries, Economics, Education, Environmental Studies, Foreign Countries, Government, Political Science, Health, Nutrition, Language Arts, Linguistics, Literature, Literary Criticism, Essays, Philosophy, Poetry, Psychology, Psychiatry, Radio, TV, Social Sciences, Sociology, Women's Studies
ISBN Prefix(es): 9974-42

Prensa Medica Latinoamericana+
Guayabo 1790, apdo 504, 11200 Montevideo
Mailing Address: Casilla de Correo 6135, Montevideo
Tel: (02) 707 91 09 *Fax:* (02) 707 91 09
E-mail: prensmed@adinet.com.uy
Founded: 1988
Subjects: Child Care & Development, Health, Nutrition, Medicine, Nursing, Dentistry, Psychology, Psychiatry
ISBN Prefix(es): 9974-568

Punto de Encuentro Ediciones
Andresito Guacarary 1836, 11200 Montevideo
Tel: (02) 405167
Key Personnel
Editorial: Marylin Dias Capo
Founded: 1989
Subjects: Art, Literature, Literary Criticism, Essays
ISBN Prefix(es): 9974-603

Luis A Retta Libros
Paysandu 1827, 11200 Montevideo
Mailing Address: PO Box 591042, Miami, FL 33159-1042, United States
Tel: (02) 400-0766 *Fax:* (02) 409-0174
E-mail: rettalib@chasque.apc.org
Founded: 1975
Subjects: Anthropology, History, Literature, Literary Criticism, Essays, Poetry, Women's Studies
ISBN Prefix(es): 9974-557

Rosebud Ediciones+
Liber Arce 3089, 11300 Montevideo
Tel: (02) 771773 *Fax:* (02) 6287111
E-mail: zapican@adinet.com.uy
Key Personnel
Contact: Jacqueline Listur
Founded: 1993
Subjects: Biography, Ethnicity, Fiction, History, Humor, Nonfiction (General), Poetry, Self-Help
ISBN Prefix(es): 9974-638

Ediciones Sol del Sur+
Gral Prim 3145, 11600 Montevideo
Tel: (02) 621627
Key Personnel
Marketing Dir: Daniel Gonzalez Moras
Founded: 1968
Specializes in Poetry & Essay Writing.
Subjects: History, Literature, Literary Criticism, Essays, Regional Interests
Showroom(s): Barreiro y Ramos, SA, Juan Carlos Gomez, 1430 Montevideo
Bookshop(s): Linardi y Risso, Juan Carlos Gomez 1435
Orders to: Retta Libros, Paysandu 1827, Montevideo *Fax:* (02) 4090174

Ediciones Trilce+
Casilla de correos 12203, 11300 Montevideo
SAN: 002-0230
Mailing Address: Durazno 1888, 11200 Montevideo
Tel: (02) 412 77 22; (02) 412 76 62 *Fax:* (02) 412 76 62; (02) 412 77 22
E-mail: trilce@adinet.com.uy; infoventas@trilce.com.uy
Web Site: www.trilce.com.uy
Key Personnel
Dir: Pablo Harari
Founded: 1985
Subjects: Anthropology, Architecture & Interior Design, Biography, Communications, Developing Countries, Economics, Education, Fiction, Government, Political Science, History, Humor, Literature, Literary Criticism, Essays, Music, Dance, Poetry, Psychology, Psychiatry, Regional Interests, Religion - Other, Science (General), Social Sciences, Sociology, Technology, Women's Studies
ISBN Prefix(es): 9974-32; 84-89269

La Urpila Editores
Casilla 5088, Suc 1, Montevideo
Tel: (02) 9085347
Key Personnel
Dir: Prof Norma Suiffet
Founded: 1979
Subjects: Literature, Literary Criticism, Essays, Poetry
ISBN Prefix(es): 9974-566
Parent Company: Casa del Poeta Latinoamericano

Editia Uruguay+
Bartolome Mitre 1377, 11000 Montevideo
Tel: (02) 915-9633; (02) 915-9759 *Fax:* (02) 916-4419
E-mail: edita@adinet.com.uy
Web Site: www.editia.com
Key Personnel
Contact: Ernesto Sanjines
Founded: 1970
Specialize in computer science & technical books. Also a distributor & wholesaler.
Subjects: Computer Science
ISBN Prefix(es): 9974-621
Distributed by Diana (Mexico, USA, Central America & Colombia)
Distributor for Diana; Editores Mexicanos Unidos (Uruguay, Paraguay & Bolivia); GYR (Uruguay); Marcombo; Prentice Hall

Vinten Editor+
Hocquart 1771, 11800 Montevideo
Tel: (02) 2090223 *Fax:* (02) 290223
E-mail: dayraq@chasque.apc.org
Web Site: www.chasque.apc.org/dayraq/vinten
Key Personnel
Contact: Dayman Cabrera
Founded: 1976
Subjects: Art, Economics, Education, Literature, Literary Criticism, Essays, Nonfiction (General), Poetry, Social Sciences, Sociology
ISBN Prefix(es): 9974-570

Uzbekistan

General Information

Capital: Tashkent
Language: Uzbek
Religion: Predominantly Islamic (mostly Sunni Muslim)
Population: 21.6 million
Bank Hours: Generally open for short hours between 0930-1230 Monday-Friday
Shop Hours: Generally 0900-1800 Monday-Friday; often open weekends
Currency: 100 kopeks = 1 rubl

Izdatelstvo Literatury i isskustva
ul Navoi 30, 700129 Taskent
Tel: (0371) 445172
Key Personnel
Dir: Sh Z Usmanhodjayev
Editor-in-Chief: H T Turabekov
Founded: 1926
Subjects: Literature, Literary Criticism, Essays
ISBN Prefix(es): 5-638

Izdatelstvo Uzbekistan+
ul Navoi 30, 700129 Taskent
Tel: (0371) 443810
Key Personnel
Dir: Shomukhitdin Sh Mansurov
Chief Editor: Zufar A Juraev
Founded: 1924
Uzbek Publishing House.
Subjects: Art, Economics, Government, Political Science, History, Law
ISBN Prefix(es): 5-640
Associate Companies: Matbaa Uzbek-Turkey JV Rastr Uzbek-Britain JV

Venezuela

General Information

Capital: Caracas
Language: Spanish
Religion: Predominantly Roman Catholic
Population: 20.7 million
Bank Hours: 0830-1130, 1400-1630 Monday-Friday
Shop Hours: 0900-1300, 1500-1900 Monday-Saturday
Currency: 100 centimos = 1 bolivar
Export/Import Information: Member of the Latin American Free Trade Association.
Copyright: UCC, Berne (see Copyright Conventions, pg xi)

Academia Nacional de la Historia
Av Universidad, Bolsa a San Francisco, Palacio de las Academias, Caracas 1010-A
Tel: (02) 481-34-13; (02) 483-94-35; (02) 482-67-20; (02) 486720 *Fax:* (02) 481-75-47
E-mail: anhistoria@cantv.net
Telex: 27252
Key Personnel
Dir: Rafael Fernandez Heres
Founded: 1888
ISBN Prefix(es): 980-222

Alfadil Ediciones+
Calle Las Flores con calle Paraiso, Edificio Paraiso, PB, Sabana Grande, Caracas 1050
Mailing Address: Apdo 50304, Caracas 1050
Tel: (02) 762-3036; (02) 761-3576; (02) 763-5676 *Fax:* (02) 762-0210
E-mail: contacto@alfagrupo.com
Web Site: www.alfagrupo.com
Key Personnel
Executive President: Leonardo Milla Alcacer *E-mail:* leonardomilla@alfagrupo.com
General Administrative: Yolanda de Anuel *E-mail:* administracion@alfagrupo.com
Founded: 1978
Subjects: Astrology, Occult, Economics, Fiction, Geography, Geology, History, Journalism, Literature, Literary Criticism, Essays, Music, Dance, Nonfiction (General), Philosophy, Poetry, Self-Help, Social Sciences, Sociology
ISBN Prefix(es): 980-6005; 980-354
Parent Company: Alfa, Grupo Editorial

PUBLISHERS — VENEZUELA

Associate Companies: Distribuidora de Ediciones Noray, CA
Subsidiaries: Libreria Ludens
Bookshop(s): Ludens, SRL, Torre Polar, Local F, Plaza Venezuela, Caracas

Armitano Editores CA+
Cuarta Transversal de la Av principal de Boleita, paralela a la Av Romulo Gallegos, Edificio Centro Industrial Piso 1, Apdo 50853, Caracas 1070
Tel: (02) 2342565; (02) 2340870; (02) 2340865
Fax: (02) 2341647
E-mail: armiedit@telcel.net.ve
Web Site: www.armitano.com *Cable:* ARMITPRESS CARACAS VENEZUELA
Key Personnel
Man Dir: E Armitano
Sales Dir: P Salazar
Founded: 1957
Membership(s): Graphic Arts Association of Venezuela.
Subjects: Anthropology, Architecture & Interior Design, Art, Environmental Studies, History
ISBN Prefix(es): 980-216
Number of titles published annually: 12 Print
Total Titles: 350 Print

Editorial Ateneo de Caracas
Edificio Ateneo de Caracas, Piso 5, Caracas 1010-A
SAN: 000-4197
Mailing Address: Apdo 662, Caracas 101-A
Tel: (02) 5734622; (02) 5734400; (02) 5734600
Fax: (02) 5754475
E-mail: webmaster@ateneo.org.ve
Key Personnel
President: Maria Teresa Castillo
Editorial Dir, Sales, Production: Antonio Polo
Founded: 1978
Subjects: Art, Government, Political Science, History, Literature, Literary Criticism, Essays, Poetry, Psychology, Psychiatry, Science (General)
ISBN Prefix(es): 980-255; 84-8350
Bookshop(s): Libreria Ateneo de Caracas, Edificio Ateneo de Caracas 5 piso, Plaza Morelos Apdo 662, Caracas 1010

Monte Avila Editores Latinoamericana CA+
Av Eugenio Mendoza Con Lera Transversal, Qta Cristina, La Castellana, Caracas 1070
Mailing Address: Apdo 70712, Caracas 1070
Tel: (02) 265-6020; (02) 265-9871
E-mail: maelca@telcel.net.ve
Telex: 24220 Conac
Key Personnel
Man Dir & President: Alexis Marquez Rodriguez
Editorial, Rights & Permissions: Wilfredo Machado
Sales: Glenda Sanchez
Production: Mirna Ferrer
Founded: 1968
Tenemos Una Distribuidora En New York Lectorum Publications Inc, 111 Eighth Ave, Suite 804, New York, NY: Gerente Teresa Mlawer; Libros Sin Fronteras, PO Box 2085, Olympia, WA 98507-2085: Contact Michael Shapiro.
Subjects: Anthropology, Art, Economics, Education, Fiction, Geography, Geology, Government, Political Science, History, Literature, Literary Criticism, Essays, Music, Dance, Philosophy, Poetry, Psychology, Psychiatry, Regional Interests, Science (General), Social Sciences, Sociology
ISBN Prefix(es): 980-01
Distributed by Anahuac (Madrid)
Distributor for Editorial Anthropos Y Visor Libros De Espana; Editorial Montesinos; En Venezuela; Monte Avila Distribuye

Biblioteca Ayacucho
Av Urdaneta, Animas a PI Espana, Centro Financiero Latino Piso 12, Ofc 1, 2, 3, Caracas 1010-A
Mailing Address: Apdo 14413/2122, Caracas 1010-A
Tel: (02) 5644402; (02) 5643583 *Fax:* (02) 5634223
Telex: 26217 B1A4A *Cable:* BIAYACUCHO
Key Personnel
President of Editorial Commission, Editorial, Rights & Permissions: Dr Jose Ramon Medina
Editorial Dir: Oswaldo Teejo
Sales, Publicity: Miriam Valdez
Founded: 1975
Subjects: Anthropology, Architecture & Interior Design, Art, Developing Countries, Drama, Theater, Fiction, History, Literature, Literary Criticism, Essays, Philosophy, Photography, Poetry
ISBN Prefix(es): 980-276

Editorial Biosfera CA+
Ave Chama, Qta Coral, PB de Colinas de Bello Monte, Caracas 1050-A
Mailing Address: Apdo 50634, Caracas 1050-A
Tel: (02) 751 9119; (02) 753 8892 *Fax:* (02) 751 9320
Key Personnel
Man Dir, Editorial: Dr Serafin Mazparrote
Founded: 1979
Subjects: Art, Biological Sciences, Language Arts, Linguistics, Mathematics, Nonfiction (General), Science (General)
ISBN Prefix(es): 980-210
Subsidiaries: Litho-Mundo SA
Bookshop(s): Ediciones Amanecer (Libreria) Centro Polo, Av Principal, Colinas de Bello Monte

Sociedad Fondo Editorial Cenamec
Esquina de Salas-Edificio Sede del Ministerio de Educacion, Piso 5, Cultura y Deportes, Caracas 1080-A
Mailing Address: Apdo 75055, Caracas 1080-A
Tel: (02) 563-2591; (02) 563-3542; (02) 563-5597; (02) 563-8155; (02) 563-9997; (02) 563-8244
E-mail: cenamec@reacciun.ve
Web Site: www.cenamec.org.ve/
Key Personnel
President: Dr Enrique Planchart
Vice President: Prof Tania Calderin
Founded: 1974
Subjects: Biological Sciences, Chemistry, Chemical Engineering, Mathematics, Physics
ISBN Prefix(es): 980-218

Colegial Bolivariana CA
Av Diego Cisneros (Principal) Los Ruices, Edif CO-BO, Piso 1, Caracas 1071-A
Mailing Address: PO Box 70324, Caracas 1071-A
Tel: (02) 2391055; (02) 2391244; (02) 2391377; (02) 2391166; (02) 2391944; (02) 2391433; (02) 2391777; (02) 2391555 *Fax:* (02) 2396502; (02) 2379942
Web Site: co-bo.com *Cable:* COLEGIAL
Key Personnel
Man Dir: Hans L Schnell
Founded: 1961
ISBN Prefix(es): 980-262
Branch Office(s)
Puente Yanes A Tracabordo, Edificio BEL-VEL, Planta Baja, Caracas 1011
Ave Constitucion, Local No 28, Pto La Cruz 6023 Edo Anzoategui
Calle 97 (Bolivar) No 6-48, Apdo de Correos 834, Maracaibo 4001-A Edo Zulia

Ediciones Ekare+
Final Ave Luis Roche, Edif Banco del Libro, Altamira Sur 1062
SAN: 001-6780
Mailing Address: Apdo 68284, Caracas 1062
Tel: (02) 263 00 80; (02) 263 61 70 *Fax:* (02) 263 00 91 *Fax on Demand:* (02) 263 32 91
Key Personnel
President: Carmen Diana Dearden
Edit Dir & Foreign Rights: Maria Francisca Majobre
Marketing & Sales Manager: Maria Cristina Serrano
Founded: 1978
Specialize in children's picture books. Publish in Spanish only.
Subjects: Fiction
ISBN Prefix(es): 980-257; 84-8351
Subsidiaries: Ekare Sur; Ekare Espana

Fundacion Centro Gumilla
Edif Centro Valores PB Local 2, Esquina de La Luneta-Altagracia, Caracas 1010-A
Mailing Address: Apdo 4838, Caracas 1010-A
Tel: (02) 564 98 03; (02) 564 58 71; (02) 562 75 31 *Fax:* (02) 564 75 57
E-mail: comunicacion@gumilla.org.ve; centro@gumilla.org.ve
Web Site: www.gumilla.org.ve
Key Personnel
Contact: Klaus Vathroder SJ *E-mail:* vathroder@gumilla.org.ve
Subjects: Economics, Education, Government, Political Science, Labor, Industrial Relations, Religion - Catholic, Social Sciences, Sociology, Theology
ISBN Prefix(es): 980-250

Fundacion Servicio para el Agricultor
Av Francisco de Miranda, Edificio Cavendes, Piso 8 Ofc 806, Los Palos Grandes, Caracas 1062
Mailing Address: Apdo 2224, Caracas 1062
Tel: (02) 2843089; (02) 2841134; (02) 2852016 *Fax:* (02) 2853946
E-mail: izamora@etheron.net
Key Personnel
Contact: Dario Boscan; Jorge M Gonzalez
Founded: 1952
Subjects: Agriculture
ISBN Prefix(es): 980-260

Grijalbo SA
2 da Av de Campo Claro, Qta Harminia, Caracas
Mailing Address: Ap Correos, 106-62260, Chacao
Tel: (02) 238 15 42; (02) 238 17 32 *Fax:* (02) 239 03 08
E-mail: griven@etheron.net
Key Personnel
Man Dir: Manuel Morales
Founded: 1964
ISBN Prefix(es): 980-293
Parent Company: Ediciones Grijalbo SA, Spain

Editorial Kapelusz Venezolana SA
Ave Cajigal No 29, QTa K, San Bernadino, Apdo 14234, Caracas 1011-A
Tel: (02) 517601; (02) 526281
Telex: 24039 Ekave VC *Cable:* KAPELUSZ
Key Personnel
Man Dir: Horacio Perotti Beraldo
Founded: 1963
ISBN Prefix(es): 980-285
Parent Company: Editorial Kapelusz SA, Argentina

Editorial Labor de Venezuela SA
Ave Andres Bello, Edificio Garten, Caracas
Tel: (02) 7811398; (02) 7815819
Key Personnel
Man Dir: Jaime Salgado Palacio

VENEZUELA

McGraw-Hill de Venezuela
2 da Calle de Bello Monte, entre Av Casanova y Blvd de Sabana Grande, Local G-2, Caracas 1050
Mailing Address: Apdo 50785, Caracas 1050
Tel: (02) 238 3494; (02) 761 8181; (02) 761 6992 *Fax:* (02) 238 2374; (02) 761 6993
E-mail: dpmail@attmail.com
Telex: 29976
Key Personnel
Man Dir, Bogata: Carlos Marquez
General Manager: Mauricio Mikan
 E-mail: mikan@attmail.com
Controller-Business Manager: Rafael Ramos
College Division Manager: Javier Lindarte
Market Served: Venezuela.
ISBN Prefix(es): 980-6168
Parent Company: The McGraw-Hill Companies, 1221 Avenue of the Americas, New York, NY 10020, United States
Associate Companies: Libros McGraw-Hill de Mexico SA de CV, Bogota, Colombia

Ministerio de Educacion Biblioteca Central
Esq de Salas, Edif Ministerio, Torre de Servicio, Edif sede, Carmelitas, Caracas 1010
Tel: (02) 5628970 (ext 8149); (02) 5621767; (02) 5640025 *Fax:* (02) 5641224
Telex: 21943
Key Personnel
Dir: Lozada Bernarda
ISBN Prefix(es): 980-02

Editorial Nueva Sociedad+
Edificio IASA, piso 6 oficina 606, Plaza La Castellana, Caracas
Mailing Address: Apartado 61712, Caracas 1060-A
Tel: (02) 2659975; (02) 2650593 *Fax:* (02) 2673397
E-mail: nuso@nuevasoc.org.ve; nusoven@nuevasoc.org.ve
Web Site: www.nuevasoc.org.ve
Telex: 24163
Key Personnel
Dir: Dietmar Dirmoser *E-mail:* dirmoser@nuevasor.org.ve
Man Editor: Sergio Chejfec *E-mail:* chejfec@nuevasoc.org.ve
Books Coordinator: Helena Gonzalez
 E-mail: helena@nuevasoc.org.ve
Sales, Promotion: Ester de Rodriguez
 E-mail: ester@nuevasoc.org.ve
Founded: 1972
Subjects: Developing Countries, Economics, Environmental Studies, Ethnicity, Government, Political Science, Social Sciences, Sociology, Technology, Women's Studies
ISBN Prefix(es): 980-6110; 980-317

OCEI (Oficina Central de Estadistica e Informatica)
Edif Foundacion La Salle, PB, Av Boyaca, Mariperez, Caracas
Mailing Address: Apdo 4593, San Martin, Caracas 101
Tel: (02) 782 11 33; (02) 782 12 12; (02) 782 19 45; (02) 782 10 31; (02) 793 71 91; (02) 782 11 67 *Fax:* (02) 782 97 55
Telex: 21241
Key Personnel
Chief, Main Directory: Gustavo Jose Mendez Boiler *E-mail:* gmendez@platino.gov.ve
General Dir: Miguel Bolivar Chollett
Dir, Social Communication: Ana Maria Rodriguez
Founded: 1978
Specialize in the production of national statistics & policy information.
ISBN Prefix(es): 980-280
Warehouse: O C E I, Sotano 2

Oficina Central de Estadistics e Informatica, see OCEI (Oficina Central de Estadistica e Informatica)

Editorial Planeta Venezolana
Calle Madrid Entre New York Y Trinidad, Qta,Toscanella, Las Mercedes, 1050 Caracas
Mailing Address: Apdo 51285, Caracas 1050
Tel: (02) 913982; (02) 924872 *Fax:* (02) 913792
E-mail: planeta@viptel.com
Web Site: www.editorialplaneta.com.ve
Telex: 29944
ISBN Prefix(es): 980-271

Editorial Pomaire Venezuela SA
Ave Luis Roche, Edif Santa Clara, PB Altamira Sur, Apdo 51.960, Caracas 1062
Tel: (02) 2622122; (02) 2621253 *Fax:* (02) 2616962
Key Personnel
Man Dir: Jose Luis Garcia Froiz
ISBN Prefix(es): 980-290
Parent Company: Editorial Pomaire SA, Spain

Editorial Reverte Venezolana SA
Peligro a Pele el Ojo, Edificio Torre Carabobo, Local 2, La Candelaria, Caracas 1010
Mailing Address: Apdo 14520, Caracas 1010
Tel: (02) 572 44 68; (02) 572 66 70 *Fax:* (02) 572 25 98
ISBN Prefix(es): 980-294
Associate Companies: Editorial Reverte SA, Spain

Teduca, Tecnicas Educativas, CA
Av Romulo Gallegos, Edificio Zulia, Sector Montecristo, piso 1, Caracas 1062
Mailing Address: Apdo 1071, Caracas 1062
Tel: (02) 235 58 78; (02) 235 43 95; (02) 235 62 65 *Fax:* (02) 239 79 52
Telex: 27876 Cpbth Vc
Key Personnel
Chairman: Eduardo Robles Piquer
General Manager: Enrique de Polanco Soutullo
Founded: 1977
Subjects: Education
ISBN Prefix(es): 980-275
Associate Companies: Santillana SA de Ediciones, Spain
Orders to: Urbanizacion Industrial Cloris, Ave 2, Local 84-03 Ave Norte, Guarenas, Edo, Miranda

Ediciones Tripode
Calle Terepaima, Urb El Marques, Piso 3, Caracas 1070-A
Mailing Address: Apdo 75003, Caracas 1070-A
Tel: (02) 2378860; (02) 2378972 *Fax:* (02) 2377697
E-mail: tripode@comsis.com.ve
Web Site: www.comsis.com.ve/tripode/
Key Personnel
Dir: P Carlos Vitolo
Consultant: Padre Cesareo Gil
Manager: Coralia Salcedo R
Founded: 1972
Subjects: Religion - Catholic, Religion - Other
ISBN Prefix(es): 980-208

Universidad de los Andes, Consejo de Publicaciones
Edificio Administrativo, Piso 4, Merida
Tel: (074) 401111 ext 1998 *Fax:* (074) 274240 ext 1998
E-mail: dsia@ula.ve
Web Site: www.ula.ve
Key Personnel
Man Dir: Dr Eduardo Zuleto
Sales, Production: Macario Molina
Publicity: Ana Allegue de Pietri
Rights & Permissions: Asunta Briceno

Coordinator: Roberto Donoso Torres
Founded: 1977
Subjects: Medicine, Nursing, Dentistry, Regional Interests, Science (General), Social Sciences, Sociology, Technology
ISBN Prefix(es): 980-221

Vadell Hermanos Editores CA+
Esquina Peligro a Pele el Ojo, Edificio Golden, Sotano La Candelaria, Caracas
Tel: (02) 5723108; (02) 5778110 *Fax:* (02) 5725243
Web Site: www.vadellhermanos.com/
Key Personnel
General Manager: Dr Manuel M Vadell Graterol
Founded: 1973
Membership(s): Association Venezuelan Editors.
Subjects: Computer Science, Economics, Education, Geography, Geology, Psychology, Psychiatry, Science (General), Social Sciences, Sociology, Technology
ISBN Prefix(es): 980-212

Ediciones Vega SRL
Av Universitaria Edif Odeon, PB Los Chaguaramos, Apdo 51662, Caracas 1010-A
Tel: (02) 6622092; (02) 6621397 *Cable:* EDIVEGA
Key Personnel
Man Dir: Fernando Vega Alonso
Founded: 1965
ISBN Prefix(es): 980-6044
Bookshop(s): Libreria Tecnica Vega

Viet Nam

General Information

Capital: Hanoi
Language: Vietnamese
Religion: Predominantly Buddhist
Population: 69 million
Currency: 100 xu = 1 new dong
Export/Import Information: None available at present.
Copyright: Florence (see Copyright Conventions, pg xi)

Giao Duc Publishing House
81 Tran Huan Dao, Hanoi
Tel: (04) 268151 *Fax:* (04) 262010
Key Personnel
Dir: Nguyen Si Ty
Founded: 1957
Subjects: Education

Lao Dong (Labor) Publishing House
31, Hai Ba Trung St, Hanoi
Tel: (04) 253972

Pho Thong (Popularization) Publishing House
Hanoi

Popular Army Publishing House
Hanoi
Subjects: Military Science

Science & Technics Publishing House (Nha Xuat Ban Khoa Hoc Va Ky Thuat)+
70 Tran Hung Dao St, Hanoi 84-4
Tel: (04) 9 424 786; (04) 9 423 172; (04) 8220682; (04) 9423132; (04) 9423128; (04) 9423543; (04) 9423171 *Fax:* (04) 8 220 658
E-mail: nxbkhkt@hn.vnn.vn
Web Site: www.nxbkhkt.com.vn

Key Personnel
Dir: Prof To Dang Hai, PhD *E-mail:* todanghai@hn.vnn.vn
Founded: 1960
Membership(s): Vietnam Publishers Association.
Subjects: Accounting, Advertising, Aeronautics, Aviation, Agriculture, Animals, Pets, Archaeology, Architecture & Interior Design, Astronomy, Automotive, Behavioral Sciences, Biological Sciences, Business, Career Development, Chemistry, Chemical Engineering, Civil Engineering, Communications, Computer Science, Crafts, Games, Hobbies, Earth Sciences, Economics, Education, Electronics, Electrical Engineering, Energy, Engineering (General), English as a Second Language, Environmental Studies, Finance, Gardening, Plants, Geography, Geology, Health, Nutrition, How-to, Management, Maritime, Marketing, Mathematics, Mechanical Engineering, Medicine, Nursing, Dentistry, Microcomputers, Natural History, Physical Sciences, Physics, Radio, TV, Science (General), Securities, Technology, Transportation, Veterinary Science
Number of titles published annually: 280 Print
Total Titles: 10,000 Print
Branch Office(s)
28 Dong Khoi St, Q 1 Ho Chi Minh City 84-8 *Tel:* (08) 8 225 062; (08) 8 296 628 *E-mail:* chinhanhkhkt@hcm.fpt.vn
Bookshop(s): 31-33 Yen Bai St, Danang City *Tel:* (04) 8 220 686; 40 Ngo Quyen St, Hanoi *Tel:* (04) 9 349 147; 28 Dong Khoi St, Q1, Ho Chi Minh City *Tel:* (08) 8 225 062

Su Hoc (Historical) Publishing House
Hanoi
Subjects: Government, Political Science, Philosophy

Su That (Truth) Publishing House
24 Quang Trung St, Hanoi
Tel: (04) 252008
Founded: 1945
(Under the Central Committee of the Communist Party of Viet Nam).
Subjects: Government, Political Science, Philosophy, Social Sciences, Sociology

Trung-Tam San Xuat Hoc-Lieu
Tran-binh-Trong 240, Ho Chi Minh City 5

Y Hoc Publishing House
4 Le Thanh Ton, Hanoi
Tel: (04) 253274
Subjects: Medicine, Nursing, Dentistry

Zambia

General Information

Capital: Lusaka
Language: English is official language
Religion: Most follow traditional animist beliefs (70%), about 20% Christian (Protestant and Roman Catholic)
Population: 8.7 million
Bank Hours: 0815-1245 Monday, Tuesday, Wednesday, Friday; 0815-1200 Thursday; 0815-1100 Saturday
Shop Hours: Generally 0800-1700 Monday-Friday; 0800-1300 Saturday
Currency: 100 ngwee = 1 Zambian kwacha
Export/Import Information: No tariffs on books but all imports subject to sales tax. Single copies of advertising free. Import license required. Exchange controls.
Copyright: UCC, Berne (see Copyright Conventions, pg xi)

Aafzam Ltd+
PO Box 31012, Lusaka
Tel: (01) 223261
Key Personnel
Chairman: H Earl Johnson
Founded: 1971
Subjects: Biography, Business, Developing Countries, Government, Political Science, Music, Dance, Wine & Spirits
ISBN Prefix(es): 9982-9903
Associate Companies: A Afzamwines Ltd; Satis Suppliers Ltd

Apple Books+
PO Box 35687, Lusaka 10101
Tel: (01) 211216 *Fax:* (01) 224855
Key Personnel
Man Dir: G B Mwangilwa
General Manager: Rodrick Chris Chibesa
Founded: 1987
Membership(s): Booksellers & Publishers Association of Zambia; specialize in book exports; also acts as Literary Agent.
Subjects: Biography, Fiction, History, Humor
ISBN Prefix(es): 9982-06
Parent Company: Virgo Ltd

Bookworld Ltd+
Box 31838, Lusaka 10101
Tel: (01) 225 282 *Fax:* (01) 225 195
E-mail: bookwld@zamtel.zm
Founded: 1991
Membership(s): Booksellers & Publishers Association of Zambia.
Subjects: Education
ISBN Prefix(es): 9982-16

Wilfred Bwalya Chilangwa Publications+
Private Bag CH 50, Chelston, Lusaka
Tel: (01) 282998
E-mail: hope@samnet.zm
Key Personnel
Contact: Wilfred B Chilangwa
Founded: 1995
Subjects: Education, Human Relations
ISBN Prefix(es): 9982-827

Government Printer
PO Box 30136, 10100 Lusaka
Tel: (01) 215401; (01) 215805; (01) 215685; (01) 216972
ISBN Prefix(es): 9982-10

Historical Association of Zambia
PO Box 30680, Lusaka
Key Personnel
Chairman: Dr Y A Chondoka
Founded: 1969
Subjects: Agriculture, Anthropology, History
ISBN Prefix(es): 9982-802

Lundula Publishing House+
Mzenga Banda, Lusaka
Mailing Address: Private Bag E 708, Lusaka
Tel: (01) 96758496
E-mail: nlundula@yahoo.com
Key Personnel
Man Dir: Ngand 'Osamba Lundula
Founded: 1991
Not interested in buying international rights, sells only.
Membership(s): US & British Library & Zambian Book Sellers & Printers Association.
Subjects: Education, English as a Second Language, Language Arts, Linguistics, Social Sciences, Sociology
ISBN Prefix(es): 9982-9904
Number of titles published annually: 1 Print; 1 CD-ROM
Total Titles: 1 Print; 1 CD-ROM
Parent Company: Editions Passou, BP 236, Lubumbashi, The Democratic Republic of the Congo
Distributed by Zambia Educational Publishing House; Book World in Zambia; University of Zambia Bookshop
Distributor for Editions Passou (Democratic Republic of the Congo)
Book Club(s): US & British Libraries in Zambia; Writer's Association of Zambia

M & M Management & Labour Consultants Ltd+
PO Box 35128, Lusaka
Tel: (01) 217218 *Fax:* (01) 224495
Telex: ZA 40618
Key Personnel
Managing Consultant: Tresford K Mwaba
Founded: 1987
Also management consultants.
Subjects: Human Relations, Labor, Industrial Relations, Management
ISBN Prefix(es): 9982-805

Macmillan Publishers (Zambia) Ltd
Plot 8357, Sentor Investments Complex, Great North Rd, Luska
Mailing Address: PO Box 320199, Lusaka
Tel: (01) 223 669 *Fax:* (01) 223 657; (01) 641 018
E-mail: macpub@zamnet.zm
Web Site: www.macmillan-africa.com
Key Personnel
Man Dir: Miles Banda *E-mail:* mkbanda@zamnet.zm
Sales Manager: Elijah Chimbongwe
Educational publishers.
Parent Company: Macmillan Publishers Ltd, United Kingdom
Branch Office(s)
Plot No 22, Nawaitwika Rd, Northrise, Ndola

MFK Management Consultants Services+
Luangwa House, Cairo Rd, PO Box 31411, Lusaka
Tel: (01) 223530; (01) 252934
Key Personnel
Author: Frederick K Mwanza
Subjects: Business, Developing Countries, Economics, Finance, Government, Political Science, Management, Philosophy, Social Sciences, Sociology
ISBN Prefix(es): 9982-823

Movement for Multi-Party Democracy+
c/o Goodwin Bwalya Mwangilwa, MMD Secretariat, Private Bag E365, Lusaka
Tel: (01) 224850; (01) 224851; (01) 224852; (01) 224853 *Fax:* (01) 224855
Founded: 1991
Subjects: Government, Political Science, Public Administration
ISBN Prefix(es): 9982-17

Multimedia Zambia+
PO Box 320199, Lusaka
Tel: (01) 253666 *Fax:* (01) 363050
Telex: 40630 ZA
Key Personnel
Executive Dir: Mr Jumbe Ngoma
Founded: 1971
Subjects: Biography, Communications, Cookery, Fiction, Religion - Other, Social Sciences, Sociology
ISBN Prefix(es): 9982-30
Parent Company: Christian Council of Zambia/Zambia Episcopal Conference

Shipping Address: African Books Collective Ltd, The Jam Factory, 27 Park End St, Oxford OX1 1KU, United Kingdom
Warehouse: African Books Collective Ltd, The Jam Factory, 27 Park End St, Oxford OX1 1KU, United Kingdom
Orders to: African Books Collective Ltd, The Jam Factory, 27 Park End St, Oxford OX1 1KU, United Kingdom

Printpak (Z) Ltd
PO Box 70069, Ndola
Tel: (01) 611001; (01) 611002; (01) 600113; (01) 612027 *Fax:* (01) 617096
Telex: 41860
Key Personnel
Contact: J Muyuni
ISBN Prefix(es): 9982-13

University of Zambia Press (UNZA Press)
PO Box 32379, Lusaka 10101
Tel: (01) 213221; (01) 293058; (01) 292884; (01) 293580; (01) 219624; (01) 252514 *Fax:* (01) 253952
Telex: ZA 44370 *Cable:* UNZAS
Key Personnel
Publisher: Miss M A Sifuniso
Editorial: Christopher Bwalya; Samuel Kasankha
Production: John C Mukuka
Founded: 1938
Subjects: Education, Social Sciences, Sociology
ISBN Prefix(es): 9982-03
Parent Company: University of Zambia Company
Bookshop(s): University Bookshop

Yorvik Publishing Ltd+
Plot 531, David Kaunda Rd, Chingola
Mailing Address: PO Box 10583, Chingola
Tel: (02) 311628; (02) 312852; (02) 313707 *Fax:* (02) 311628
Key Personnel
Man Dir: A M Morton
Founded: 1993
Subjects: Special Education, Secondary School Sciences
ISBN Prefix(es): 9982-20
Associate Companies: Anthony Morton Ltd
Bookshop(s): AML Graphics, Armshal Rd, Noola

Zambia Association for Research & Development (ZARD)
Zard House Plot No 16, Manchinchi Rd, Northmead, Lusaka
Tel: (01) 224536; (01) 222883 *Fax:* (01) 222883
E-mail: zard@zamnet.zm; zard@zamtel.zm
Web Site: www.zard.org.zm
Key Personnel
Contact: Mercy Khozi
Founded: 1984
ZARD's aim is to promote & advance gender development & empowerment of women through research, training & advocacy.
Subjects: Government, Political Science, Health, Nutrition, Social Sciences, Sociology, Women's Studies
ISBN Prefix(es): 9982-818
Book Club(s): Booksellers & Publishers Association of Zambia

Zambia Educational Publishing House+
Chishango Rd, Lusaka 10101
Mailing Address: PO Box 32708, Lusaka 10101
Tel: (01) 229490; (01) 229211 *Fax:* (01) 225073
E-mail: zpa@zamnet.zm
Telex: ZA 40056 *Cable:* HOUSE LUSAKA
Key Personnel
Acting Man Dir: Beninco Mulota
Publishing Manager: R Munamwimbu
Marketing Manager: Alfred Sikabanga
Founded: 1967
Membership(s): Booksellers & Publishers Association of Zambia.
Subjects: Agriculture, Biography, Drama, Theater, Education, Ethnicity, Fiction, Government, Political Science, History, Language Arts, Linguistics, Literature, Literary Criticism, Essays, Poetry, Social Sciences, Sociology
ISBN Prefix(es): 9982-00; 9982-01
Distributed by Dzuka Publishing Co (Malawi); Gamsberg Publishers (Namibia)
Distributor for Longman Zambia; Macmillan Zambia; Multimedia Zambia; Printpak Ltd
Book Club(s): Read-a-Book Club

Zambia Printing Company Ltd (ZPC)+
Publicity House, Plot No 2349/50, Kabelenga Rd, Fairview, Lusaka
Mailing Address: PO Box 34798, Lusaka
Tel: (01) 227673; (01) 227674; (01) 227675 *Fax:* (01) 225026
Telex: ZA 40068
Key Personnel
Marketing Officer: Langson Siwale
Founded: 1988
Commercial Printing also.
Subjects: Agriculture, Child Care & Development, Drama, Theater, Education, Environmental Studies, Gardening, Plants, History, Women's Studies
ISBN Prefix(es): 9982-02
Parent Company: Zambia Printing Co Ltd

Zambian Ornithological Society (ZOS)
PO Box 33944, Lusaka 10101
E-mail: zos@zamnet.zm
Web Site: www.fisheagle.org
Subjects: Natural History
ISBN Prefix(es): 9982-811

ZARD, see Zambia Association for Research & Development (ZARD)

ZEPH, see Zambia Educational Publishing House

ZOS, see Zambian Ornithological Society (ZOS)

ZPC, see Zambia Printing Company Ltd (ZPC)

Zimbabwe

General Information
Capital: Harare
Language: English is the official language. Chishona and Sindebele are major African languages.
Religion: Majority (55%) Christian, most of the rest follow traditional beliefs
Population: 10 million
Bank Hours: 0830-1400 Monday, Tuesday, Thursday, Friday; 0830-1200 Wednesday; 0830-1100 Saturday
Shop Hours: 0800 or 0830-1700 Monday-Friday; 0800-1300 Saturday
Currency: 100 cents = 1 Zimbabwe dollar
Export/Import Information: Surcharge duty of 20% CIF to order, and 12 1/2% tax on retail sales on books. Advertising matter in bulk has duty and VAT charged. Import license is normally required for books and printed matter. Exchange controls.
Copyright: Berne (see Copyright Conventions, pg xi)

Academic Books (Pvt) Ltd+
28 South Ave, Harare
Mailing Address: PO Box 567, Harare
Tel: (04) 755034; (04) 754224 *Fax:* (04) 781913
Key Personnel
Editorial Dir: Irene Staunton
Membership(s): Zimbabwe Publisher's Association.
Subjects: Art, Education, Fiction, Geography, Geology, History, Literature, Literary Criticism, Essays, Nonfiction (General), Science (General)
ISBN Prefix(es): 0-949229; 0-908311
Parent Company: F E I C Ltd
Divisions: Baobab Books
Distributed by ABC (England); David Philip (South Africa)
Warehouse: 4 Conald Rd, Graniteside, Harare

Action Magazine+
PO Box Gt 1274, Graniteside, Harare
Tel: (04) 747217 *Fax:* (04) 747409
E-mail: action@action.co.zw
Web Site: www.action.co.zw
Key Personnel
Coordinator: Steve Murray
Founded: 1987
Developing & producing environment & health education materials, training in environmental education.
Subjects: Environmental Studies, Health, Nutrition
Parent Company: NGO, Zimbabwe Trust, 4 Lanark Rd, Harare

Books for Africa Publishing House+
21 Inez Terrace, Harare
Mailing Address: PO Box 3471, Harare
Tel: (04) 794329 *Fax:* (04) 61881
Telex: 22386
Key Personnel
Publishing Manager: Chris Nyabezi
Founded: 1979
Membership(s): the Book Publishers Association.
ISBN Prefix(es): 0-949933

Anvil Press+
78 Kaguvi St, Harare
Mailing Address: PO Box 4209, Harare
Tel: (04) 73-9681; (04) 78-1770; (04) 78-1771; (04) 792551 *Fax:* (04) 75-1202
Key Personnel
Man Dir: Paul Brickhill
Manager: Felix Nyabadza
Founded: 1987
Subjects: Drama, Theater, Environmental Studies, Literature, Literary Criticism, Essays, Social Sciences, Sociology
ISBN Prefix(es): 0-7974
Associate Companies: Grassroots Books
Bookshop(s): Grassroots Books, Africa House, 100 J Moyo Ave, Box A267, Avondale

Argosy Press
PO Box 2677, Harare 704715
Tel: (04) 704715; (04) 704766 *Fax:* (04) 752162
Telex: 26334
ISBN Prefix(es): 0-7974; 0-908309
Associate Companies: Modus Publications Pvt Ltd

Bold ADS
PO Box 1027, Harare
Tel: (04) 62-1321; (04) 62-1326 *Fax:* (04) 62-1328
E-mail: shunidzarira@boldads.co.zw
Telex: 26013
Key Personnel
General Manager: L M Manduku
Production Manager: N Magadzine
Sales & Marketing: L Ndlovu
Founded: 1950
Subjects: Foreign Countries
Parent Company: Zimbabwe Newspapers (Pvt) Ltd

Subsidiaries: B & T Directories (Pvt) Ltd; Publications (C A) (pvt) Ltd
Branch Office(s)
PO Box 1027, Bulawayo

Christian Audio-Visual Action (CAVA)
Box 649, Harare
Tel: (04) 752233 *Fax:* (04) 727030
E-mail: cava@mango.zw
Key Personnel
Contact: Rev H W Murray
Founded: 1977
Subjects: Biblical Studies, Theology

College Press Publishers (Pvt) Ltd+
Subsidiary of Macmillan Publishers Ltd
15 Douglas Rd, Workington, Harare
Mailing Address: PO Box 3041
Tel: (04) 754145; (04) 773231; (04) 773236; (04) 757153; (04) 754255 *Fax:* (04) 754256
E-mail: nellym@collegepress.co.zw
Telex: 22558 colprs zw *Cable:* LIBRIS
Key Personnel
Man Dir: Benias Benison Mugabe
Sales Dir: Cletus Jack Ngwaru
Publishing Manager: Cynthia Sithole *Tel:* (04) 754255 *Fax:* (04) 757150
Production Dir & International Division: Engelbert Lemon Luphahla
Financial Dir: Edwin Busangabanye
Founded: 1968
Primarily an educational publisher.
Membership(s): Zimbabwe Book Publishers Association & APNET
Subjects: Accounting, Agriculture, Biblical Studies, Biography, Biological Sciences, Business, Chemistry, Chemical Engineering, Child Care & Development, Cookery, Drama, Theater, Economics, English as a Second Language, Environmental Studies, Fiction, Geography, Geology, History, Mathematics, Physics, Poetry, Science (General), Teachers Education
ISBN Prefix(es): 0-86925; 1-77900
Number of titles published annually: 30 Print
Total Titles: 700 Print
Imprints: Scholastic Books; Ventures
Branch Office(s)
PO Box 298, Bulawayo, Contact: G Ndlovu
 Tel: (09) 74174
PO Box 1239, Gweru, Contact: G K Madzime
 Tel: (054) 23457
PO Box 355, Masvingo, Contact: G Muzenda
 Tel: (039) 62264
PO Box 963, Mutare, Contact: S J Chikuse
 Tel: (020) 64211
Distributed by Macmillan Publishers (Worldwide)
Distributor for Macmillan Publishers
Foreign Rep(s): Macmillan Publishers (Worldwide)
Orders to: College Press Publishers, Contact: Cletus Ngwaru

Dorothy Duncan Braille & Transcription Library
119 Fife Ave, Harare
Mailing Address: Box CY 1551 Causeway, Harare
Tel: (04) 251116; (04) 251117 *Fax:* (04) 251117
E-mail: chiedza@samara.co.zw
Key Personnel
Coordinator: Sister Catherine Jackson
Contact: Ster C Jackson
Founded: 1963
Parent Company: Dorothy Duncan Centre for the Blind & Physically Handicapped

Farm-level Applied Methods for East & Southern Africa (FARMESA)
Robinson House, 9th floor, Union Ave, Harare
Mailing Address: PO Box 3730, Harare
Tel: (04) 758051-4 *Fax:* (04) 758055
E-mail: fspzim@internet.co.zw; fspzim@harare.iafrica.com
Web Site: www.farmesa.co.zw
Key Personnel
Project Coordinator: Dr John Dixon *E-mail:* john.dixon@farmesa.co.zw
Information Officer: Margaret Zunguze
 E-mail: margaret.zunguze@farmesa.co.zw
Subjects: Agriculture

FARMESA, see Farm-level Applied Methods for East & Southern Africa (FARMESA)

Flame Lily, *imprint of* The Literature Bureau

Geological Survey Department
PO Box CY210, Causeway, Harare
Tel: (04) 790701; (04) 726342; (04) 726343; (04) 252016; (04) 252017 *Fax:* (04) 739601
E-mail: zimeosv@africaonline.co.zw; zgs@samara.co.zw
Web Site: www.geosurvey.co.zw
Telex: 22416 MINESZW *Cable:* MINES
Key Personnel
Dir: Dr J L Orpen
Founded: 1910
Subjects: Geography, Geology
Parent Company: Ministry of Mines, Zimbabwe, P Bag 7709, Causeway, Harrare

The Graham Publishing Company (Pvt) Ltd
PO Box 2931, Harare
Tel: (04) 706207 *Fax:* (04) 752439
Key Personnel
Man Dir: Gordon M Graham
Founded: 1968
Subjects: Fiction, History, Nonfiction (General), Travel
ISBN Prefix(es): 0-86921

HarperCollins Publishers Zimbabwe Pvt Ltd+
Union Ave, Harare
Mailing Address: PO Box UA 201, Union Ave, Harare
Tel: (04) 755408; (04) 710017; (04) 755409; (04) 710018 *Fax:* (04) 72-1413; (04) 710019
E-mail: harpcoll@icon.co.zw
Key Personnel
General Manager: Susan D McMillan
Founded: 1964 (formerly William Collins International)
Subjects: Accounting, Business, Education, English as a Second Language, Law
ISBN Prefix(es): 1-77902; 1-77904; 0-86923

Journal on Social Change
Mass Media House, 3rd floor, 19 Selous Ave, Harare
Mailing Address: PO Box 4405, Harare
Tel: (04) 72-0417; (04) 70-0047 *Fax:* (04) 73-0808
E-mail: schange@africaonline.co.zw
Key Personnel
Chairperson of Editorial Board: Joyce Kazembe
Coordinating Editor: John Vrekis
Founded: 1981 (Founded one year after independence to complement govt efforts to transform & reconstruct Zimbabwean society)
Non-profit, independent organization
Publishes quarterly journals.
Subjects: Art, Developing Countries, Economics, Government, Political Science, Labor, Industrial Relations, Social Sciences, Sociology, Analysis of National & Regional Current Affairs
Number of titles published annually: 4 Print

Legal Resources Foundation Publications Unit
Blue Bridge, 5th floor, Second St, Eastgate, Harare
Mailing Address: PO Box 918, Harare
Tel: (04) 251170; (04) 251174 *Fax:* (04) 728213
E-mail: lrfhre@mweb.co.zw
Web Site: site.mweb.co.zw/lrf
Key Personnel
National Dir: Eileen Sawyer
National Administrator: Deborah Barron
 E-mail: lrfbyo@mweb.co.zw
Founded: 1984
Subjects: Law
ISBN Prefix(es): 0-908312

The Literature Bureau
Ministry of Education, Sport & Culture, Causeway, Harare
Mailing Address: PO Box CY121, Causeway, Harare
Tel: (04) 726929; (04) 729120 *Cable:* LITBURO
Key Personnel
Chief Publications Officer: B C Chitsike
Principal Editorial Officers: E Tafa; E Bhala
Founded: 1954
Subjects: Animals, Pets, Drama, Theater, Literature, Literary Criticism, Essays, Poetry
ISBN Prefix(es): 0-86926
Imprints: Flame Lily
Branch Office(s)
PO Box 828, Bulawayo
Book Club(s): Shona Readers' Book Club

Longman Zimbabwe (Pvt) Ltd+
Tourle Rd, Southerton, Harare
Mailing Address: PO Box ST 125, Harare Southerton
Tel: (04) 621 661; (04) 621 667 *Fax:* (04) 621670
E-mail: customeralicek@longman.co.zw
Web Site: www.pearsoned.co.uk/contactus/worldwideoffices/africa
Telex: 225666 LONZIM *Cable:* Longman Harare Zimbabwe
Key Personnel
General Manager: Emily Chandauka
 E-mail: emilyc@longman.co.zw
Founded: 1964
Subjects: Accounting, Agriculture, Business, Cookery, Economics, Education, English as a Second Language, Environmental Studies, History, Mathematics, Natural History, Poetry, Religion - Other, Science (General)
ISBN Prefix(es): 0-582; 0-908308; 0-908310; 1-77903
Total Titles: 700 Print
Parent Company: Pearson Education, United Kingdom
Ultimate Parent Company: Pearson Plc

Mambo Press+
Senga Rd, Gweru
Mailing Address: PO Box 779, Gweru
Tel: (054) 24016; (054) 25807; (054) 24017; (054) 28351 *Fax:* (054) 21991
E-mail: mambo@icon.co.zw
Web Site: www.rutenga.com/mambo.htm
Key Personnel
General Manager: Fr R Gentile
Editor: Emmanuel Makadho
Marketing Manager: Charles Zhou
Founded: 1958
Subjects: Fiction, History, Natural History, Nonfiction (General), Poetry, Religion - Other
ISBN Prefix(es): 0-86922
Number of titles published annually: 12 Print
Total Titles: 320 Print
Foreign Rep(s): Africa B/Centre (UK); Botswana B/Cecntre (Botswana); Botswana B/Centre (USA); Pauline Multimedia (Zambia)
Bookshop(s): Mambo Bookshop, Speke Ave/First St, PO Box UA 320, Harare, Contact: Mrs R Mabuza *Tel:* (04) 705899; Mambo Bookshop, PO Box 1010, Masvingo, Contact: Mr H Muromo *Tel:* (039) 64566; Mambo Bookshop, Bulawayo, PO Box FM 87, Bulawayo, Contact: Mrs S Kamutingondo *Tel:* (09) 61162

ZIMBABWE

Manhattan Publications
30 Montgomery Rd, Highlands, Harare
Mailing Address: PO Box 5, Harare
Tel: (04) 442827; (04) 498206 *Fax:* (04) 496292
E-mail: nchudy@zol.co.zw
Key Personnel
Proprietor: Alexander Katz
Founded: 1983
Zimbabwe economics.
Subjects: Business, Economics
Number of titles published annually: 2 Print
Total Titles: 15 Print
Parent Company: Manhattan Realty (Pvt) Ltd

Mercury Press Pvt Ltd+
PO Box 2373, Harare
Tel: (04) 75-1515; (04) 75-1084 *Fax:* (04) 73-7670 *Cable:* TUTORIAL
Key Personnel
Man Dir & International Rights: D F Sutherland
Founded: 1972
Subjects: Education, English as a Second Language, Language Arts, Linguistics, Poetry
ISBN Prefix(es): 0-7974
Parent Company: Central African Correspondence College P/L, Gickon House 22, Kaguvi St, Harare
Associate Companies: Phoenix Printers P/L, Gickon House 22, Kaguvi St, Harare

National Archives of Zimbabwe+
Borrowdale Rd, Harare
Mailing Address: Private Bag 7729, Causeway, Harare
Tel: (04) 792 741 *Fax:* (04) 792 398
E-mail: nat.archives@gta.gov.zw
Web Site: www.gta.gov.zw
Founded: 1935
Subjects: Ethnicity, Genealogy, History, Nonfiction (General), Social Sciences, Sociology
ISBN Prefix(es): 0-908302

NAZ, see National Archives of Zimbabwe

Nehanda Publishers+
Union Ave, Harare
Mailing Address: PO Box UA517, Harare
Tel: (04) 734415; (04) 727077 *Fax:* (04) 734415
E-mail: lenneiye@mweb.co.zw
Key Personnel
President: Dr L M Lenneiye
Vice President: Dr Kimani Gecau
Founded: 1984
Subjects: Economics, Environmental Studies, Foreign Countries, Government, Political Science, Literature, Literary Criticism, Essays, Regional Interests
ISBN Prefix(es): 0-908305

Phantom Publishers+
PO Box BW59, Borrowdale, Harare
Tel: (04) 737241
Key Personnel
Author & Publisher: Jeremy Ford
Founded: 1988
Subjects: Poetry
ISBN Prefix(es): 0-7974
Orders to: Nationwide, PO Box 1819, Harare

Sapes Trust Ltd+
4 Deary Ave, Belgravia, Harare
Mailing Address: PO Box MP111, Mount Pleasant, Harare
Tel: (04) 252962; (04) 252963; (04) 252965 *Fax:* (04) 252963
E-mail: administrator@sapes.org.zw
Web Site: www.sapes.co.zw
Telex: 26464 AAPS 2W
Key Personnel
Chairperson: Dr Ibbo Mandaza
Head of Publications Division: Mrs J L Kazembe
Founded: 1989
Research, training & publications.
Subjects: Developing Countries, Economics, Environmental Studies, Government, Political Science, Public Administration, Social Sciences, Sociology
ISBN Prefix(es): 1-77905
Number of titles published annually: 5 Print; 1 CD-ROM
Subsidiaries: Southern Africa Publishing & Printing Houses (SAPPHO)
Distributed by African Books Collective
Distributor for CODESRIA

SAZ, see Standards Association of Zimbabwe (SAZ)

Scholastic Books, *imprint of* College Press Publishers (Pvt) Ltd

Social Change & Development, see Journal on Social Change

Standards Association of Zimbabwe (SAZ)
Northridge Park, Northend Close, Borrowdale, Harare
Mailing Address: PO Box 2259, Harare
Tel: (04) 885511; (04) 885512; (04) 882021; (04) 882022 *Fax:* (04) 882020
E-mail: sazlabs@mall.pcl.co.zw
Key Personnel
Dir General: M P Mutasa *Tel:* (04) 885517 *Fax:* (04) 882581 *E-mail:* standards@mail.pci.co.zw
Dir, Operations: Dr O Chinyanakobver *Tel:* (04) 753800; (04) 753802 *Fax:* (04) 749181 *E-mail:* sazlabs@mweb.co.zw
Founded: 1957
Subjects: Agriculture, Automotive, Chemistry, Chemical Engineering, Civil Engineering, Electronics, Electrical Engineering, Energy, Engineering (General), Mechanical Engineering
ISBN Prefix(es): 0-86928
Number of titles published annually: 96 Print
Total Titles: 1,173 Print
Branch Office(s)
PO Box 591, Mutare, Contact: Mr P Chiadzwa *Tel:* (020) 60516, (020) 656130 *Fax:* (020) 66252 *E-mail:* sazmutare@technopark.co.zw
PO Box RY 129, Raylton, Bulawayo, Contact: Mr A G Ncube *Tel:* (09) 70447, (09) 71876 *Fax:* (09) 70447 *E-mail:* sazbyo@acacia.mweb.co.zw

Thomson Publications Zimbabwe (Pvt) Ltd
130 Harare St, Harare 217373WE
Mailing Address: PO Box 1683, Harare
Tel: (04) 736835 *Fax:* (04) 749803
E-mail: tpubl@mweb.co.zw
Telex: 4705 ZW
Key Personnel
General Manager: Brian Gamble *Tel:* (04) 749741
Founded: 1954
Subjects: Accounting, Agriculture, Automotive, Business, Communications, Economics
ISBN Prefix(es): 0-7974
Total Titles: 7 Print
Subsidiaries: Amalgamated Publications

University of Zimbabwe Library
PO Box MP 45, Mount Pleasant, Harare
Tel: (04) 303211 *Fax:* (04) 335383
E-mail: mainlib@uzlib.uz.zw; infocentre@uzlib.uz.ac.zw
Web Site: www.uz.ac.zw/library
Key Personnel
Librarian: Dr B Mbambo
Founded: 1957
Number of titles published annually: 14,300 Print
Total Titles: 597,356 Print
Parent Company: National University of Science & Technology
Associate Companies: Africa University; Solusi University College
Divisions: National University of Science & Technology Library

University of Zimbabwe Publications+
Main Admin Bldg, 1st floor, West Wing, Mount Pleasant, Harare
Mailing Address: PO Box MP 167, Mount Pleasant, Harare
Tel: (04) 303211 (ext 1236 or 1662) *Fax:* (04) 333407
E-mail: uzpub@admin.uz.ac.zn
Web Site: www.uz.ac.zw/publications/
Telex: 26580 UNIVZ ZW *Cable:* UNIVERSITY
Key Personnel
Dir, Publications: M S Mtetwa
Founded: 1969
Subjects: History, Language Arts, Linguistics, Literature, Literary Criticism, Essays, Medicine, Nursing, Dentistry, Philosophy, Religion - Other, Science (General), Social Sciences, Sociology, Technology
ISBN Prefix(es): 0-908307; 1-77920; 0-86924
Distributed by African Books Collective (UK)

Ventures, *imprint of* College Press Publishers (Pvt) Ltd

Vision Publications+
753 Senga 2, Gweru
Founded: 1996
Subjects: Education, Fiction, Language Arts, Linguistics, Literature, Literary Criticism, Essays, Nonfiction (General), Poetry, Religion - Protestant, Theology
Parent Company: Vision Enterprises

ZEB, *imprint of* Zimbabwe Publishing House (Pvt) Ltd

Zimbabwe Foundation for Education with Production (ZIMFEP)+
Central Ave, Harare
Mailing Address: PO Box 54, Harare
Tel: (04) 755991; (04) 771833; (04) 771844; (04) 771834; (04) 771845; (04) 795679 *Fax:* (04) 749147
E-mail: zimfep@africaonline.co.zw
Key Personnel
Dir: Patrick Ndlovu
Founded: 1981
Membership(s): Zimbabwe Book Publishers Association.
Subjects: Drama, Theater, Education
ISBN Prefix(es): 0-908303

Zimbabwe International Book Fair+
Harare Gardens, J Nyerere Way, Harare
Mailing Address: PO Box CY 1179, Causeway, Harare
Tel: (04) 702104; (04) 702108 *Fax:* (04) 702129
E-mail: execdir@zibf.org.zw
Web Site: www.zibf.org.zw
Key Personnel
Executive Dir: Samuel Matsangaise *Tel:* (04) 704112
Subjects: Developing Countries
Foreign Rep(s): Becky Clarke (Caribbean, Europe, North America); Vikas Ghai (Asia); Marilyn Mevana (Lesotho, South Africa, Swaziland); Serah Mwanyiky (East Africa); Akoss Ofori-Mensah (West Africa)

Zimbabwe Publishing House (Pvt) Ltd+
183 Arcturus Rd, Kamfinsa Centre, Greendale
Mailing Address: PO Box GD 510, Harre
Tel: (04) 495335; (04) 497555 *Fax:* (04) 497554
E-mail: trade@zph.co.zw
Telex: 6035 Zph Zw

Key Personnel
Chairman: Mr D Martin
General Manager: Mwazvita Madondo
Editorial Manager & Rights & Permissions: Promise Mayo
Founded: 1981
Subjects: Cookery, Education, Geography, Geology, History, Literature, Literary Criticism, Essays, Mathematics, Natural History, Science (General)
ISBN Prefix(es): 0-949225; 0-949932; 0-908300; 1-77901
Total Titles: 187 Print
Associate Companies: African Publishing Group, PO Box 90150, Contact: Helena Perry *Tel:* (04) 497 55518 *Fax:* (04) 497 5554 *E-mail:* apg@ld.co.zw
Imprints: ZEB; ZPH
Subsidiaries: Zimbabwe Educational Books
Branch Office(s)
PO Box 1442, Bulawayo, Contact: Zwelithini Mpofu *Tel:* (04) 74666
PO Box 384, Masvingo, Contact: Stephan Rubaba *Tel:* (034) 68137
PO Box 1029, Mutare, Contact: Absalom Kunzwu *Tel:* (020) 08716
PO Box 1191, Gweru *Tel:* (054) 24978

Bookshop(s): Frontline Bookshop, PO Box 350, Harare
Warehouse: 97 Coventry Rd, Workington Harare *Tel:* (04) 667170

Zimbabwe Women Writers+
78 Kaguvi St, Harare
Mailing Address: PO Box 4209, Harare
Tel: (04) 774261 *Fax:* (04) 750282
E-mail: zww@telco.co.zw
Key Personnel
Contact: Keresia Chateuka
Founded: 1990
Subjects: Nonfiction (General), Poetry
Orders to: PO Box 4209, Harare

Zimbabwe Women's Bureau+
43 Hillside Rd, Cranborne, Harare
Mailing Address: PO Box CR 120, Cranborne, Harare
Tel: (04) 747905; (04) 747809; (04) 747433; (263) 720575 *Fax:* (04) 747905
E-mail: zwbtc@africaonline.co.zw
Key Personnel
Dir: Fiona Mwashita

Founded: 1978
Subjects: Agriculture, Education, Finance, Health, Nutrition, Human Relations

ZIMFEP, see Zimbabwe Foundation for Education with Production (ZIMFEP)

ZPH, *imprint of* Zimbabwe Publishing House (Pvt) Ltd

ZRD Trust+
107, Leopold Takawira St, Harare
Mailing Address: PO Box 2054, Harare
Tel: (04) 774775; (04) 744519 *Fax:* (04) 774764
Telex: 2033 ZW
Key Personnel
Editor & Publisher: R S Roberts *E-mail:* rsrob@mweb.co.zw
Founded: 1970
Specialize in reference works.
Membership(s): Central Africa Historical Association; Historical Association of Zimbabwe; Zimbabwe Independent Publishers.
Subjects: History, Zimbabwe
ISBN Prefix(es): 0-908306
Number of titles published annually: 2 Print
Total Titles: 15 Print

Type of Publication Index

ASSOCIATION PRESSES

Australia
Centenary of Technical Education in Bairnsdale Group, pg 17

Austria
Verband der Wissenschaftlichen Gesellschaften Oesterreichs (VWGOe), pg 59

Belgium
Documenta CV, pg 66

Chile
Alfabeta Impresores Ltda, pg 98

China
Sichuan Science & Technology Publishing House, pg 108

Czech Republic
Kalich SRO, pg 124

France
Groupement d'Information Promotion Presse Edition (GIPPE), pg 166
La Voix du Regard, pg 189

Germany
Blaukreuz-Verlag Wuppertal, pg 202
Chmielorz GmbH Verlag, pg 208
Verlag Deutsche Unitarier, pg 212
Deutscher Psychologen Verlag GmbH (DPV), pg 213
Dr Ernst Hauswedell & Co, pg 235
Lebenshilfe-Verlag Marburg, Verlag der Bundesvereinigung Lebenshilfe fuer Menschen mit geistiger Behinderung eV, pg 253
Neuland-Verlagsgesellschaft mbH, pg 264
Philipp Reclam Jun Verlag GmbH, pg 269
Premop Verlag GmbH, pg 271
Sax-Verlag Beucha, pg 278
Verlag Stahleisen GmbH, pg 286
Wiley-VCH Verlag GmbH, pg 300

Greece
Nomiki Bibliothiki, pg 310

Hong Kong
Ta Kung Pao (HK) Ltd, pg 319

India
Addison-Wesley Pte Ltd, pg 327

Italy
AIB Associazione Italiana Bibliotheche, pg 374
Belforte Editore Libraio srl, pg 377

Republic of Korea
Anam Publishing Co, pg 437
Korean Publishers Association, pg 440

The Former Yugoslav Republic of Macedonia
Mi-An Knigoizdatelstvo, pg 452

Morocco
Association de la Recherche Historique et Sociale, pg 474

Nigeria
Riverside Communications, pg 507

Russian Federation
N E Bauman Moscow State Technical University Publishers, pg 544
BLIC, russko-Baltijskij informaciionnyj centr, AO, pg 544

Spain
Aguilar SA de Ediciones, pg 571
Oikos-Tau SA Ediciones, pg 593

Turkey
Iletisim Yayinlari, pg 650

United Kingdom
Portland Press Ltd, pg 745

AUDIO BOOKS

Australia
Bible Society in Australia National Headquarters, pg 14
Boinkie Publishers, pg 15
Bolinda Publishing Pty Ltd, pg 15
Louis Braille Audio, pg 16
Greater Glider Productions Australia Pty Ltd, pg 24
F H Halpern, pg 24
Hodder Headline Australia, pg 26
Barry Long Books, pg 29
Narkaling Inc, pg 33
New Creation Publications Ministries & Resource Centre, pg 33
Tarka Publishing, pg 42

Austria
Edition S der OSD, pg 50
Niederosterreichisches Pressehaus Druck- und Verlagsgesellschaft mbH, pg 54
oebv & hpt Verlagsgesellschaft mbH & Co KG, pg 55

Barbados
Business Tutors, pg 62

Belgium
Editions De Boeck-Larcier SA, pg 66

Benin
Les Editions du Flamboyant, pg 75

Brazil
Editora Elevacao, pg 81
Editora Moderna Ltda, pg 86
Paulus Editora, pg 88

Chile
Instituto Geografico Militar, pg 99

China
Beijing Publishing House, pg 101
China Braille Publishing House, pg 102
Chinese Pedagogics Publishing House, pg 103
Fudan University Press, pg 104
Qingdao Publishing House, pg 107
Shanghai Educational Publishing House, pg 108
Tsinghua University Press, pg 109

Costa Rica
Ediciones Promesa, pg 116

Czech Republic
Karmelitanske Nakladatelstvi, pg 124
Karolinum, nakladatelstvi, pg 124
Knihovna A Tiskarna Pro Nevidome, pg 124

Denmark
Forlaget alokke AS, pg 129
Dansk Historisk Handbogsforlag ApS, pg 130
Kaleidoscope Publishers Ltd, pg 132
New Era Publications International ApS, pg 133

France
Editions Amrita SA, pg 146
Emgleo Breiz, pg 151
Brud Nevez, pg 151
Editions Des Femmes, pg 163

French Polynesia
Simone Sanchez, pg 190

Germany
Assimil GmbH, pg 195
Campus Verlag GmbH, pg 207
Deutsche Blinden-Bibliothek, pg 211
Verlagsgruppe Droemer Knaur GmbH & Co KG, pg 216
Egmont vgs verlagsgesellschaft mbH, pg 218
Eichborn AG, pg 219
Esogetics GmbH, pg 221
Guenther Butkus, pg 231
Heinz-Theo Gremme Verlag, pg 236
Verlag Herder GmbH & Co KG, pg 236
Klaus Isele, pg 242
KBV Verlags-und Medien - GmbH, pg 245
Kidemus Verlag GmbH, pg 245
Kleiner Bachmann Verlag fur Kinder und Umwelt, pg 246
Koptisch-Orthodoxes Zentrum, pg 249
Verlag Antje Kunstmann GmbH, pg 251
Lahn-Verlag GmbH, pg 251
Ingrid Langner, pg 252
Gustav Luebbe Verlag, pg 256
Verlagsgruppe Luebbe GmbH & Co KG, pg 256
Naumann & Goebel Verlagsgesellschaft mbH, pg 263
Verlag Friedrich Oetinger GmbH, pg 266
Osho Verlag GmbH, pg 267
Verlag Parzeller GmbH & Co KG, pg 268
Patmos Verlag GmbH & Co KG, pg 268
Pendragon Verlag, pg 269
Philipp Reclam Jun Verlag GmbH, pg 269
Reader's Digest Deutschland Verlag Das Beste GmbH, pg 274
Schirner Verlag, pg 280
TR - Verlagsunion GmbH, pg 291
Verlag und Studio fuer Hoerbuchproduktionen, pg 295
Vier Tuerme GmbH Verlag Klosterbetriebe, pg 295
Verlag Klaus Wagenbach, pg 297

Ghana
World Literature Project, pg 305

Greece
Hestia-I D Hestia-Kollaros & Co Corporation, pg 308
Pagoulatos Bros, pg 311
Pagoulatos G-G P Publications, pg 311
Patakis Publishers, pg 311
Scripta Theofilus Palevratzis-Ashover, pg 312
Toubis M, pg 312

Hong Kong
Benefit Publishing Co, pg 315
The Dharmasthiti Buddist Institute Ltd, pg 317
Joint Publishing (HK) Co Ltd, pg 317
Witman Publishing Co (HK) Ltd, pg 320

India
Addison-Wesley Pte Ltd, pg 327
Star Publications (P) Ltd, pg 350

Indonesia
PT Indira, pg 355

Ireland
Clo Iar-Chonnachta Teo, pg 358
Roberts Rinehart Publishers, pg 363

Israel
Breslov Research Institute, pg 365

Italy
Editrice Eraclea, pg 388
In Dialogo, pg 393
Editoriale Olimpia SpA, pg 401
RAI-ERI, pg 405

Rossato, pg 406
Ruggenti Editore, pg 406

Japan
Hyoronsha Publishing Co Ltd, pg 418
Seibido Shuppan Company Ltd, pg 426
Shincho-Sha Co Ltd, pg 427

Kenya
Jacaranda Designs Ltd, pg 434

Republic of Korea
Gim-Yeong Co, pg 438
Ke Mong Sa Publishing Co Ltd, pg 440
Koreaone Press Inc, pg 440
Moon Jin Media Co Ltd, pg 441
YBM/Si-sa, pg 443

The Former Yugoslav Republic of Macedonia
Medis, Skopje, pg 452

Martinique
George Lise-Huyghes des Etages, pg 460

Mexico
Libra Editorial SA de CV, pg 467
Ediciones Promesa, SA de CV, pg 470
Editorial Turner de Mexico, pg 472

Netherlands
Uitgeverij De Toorts, pg 490

New Zealand
Taylor Books, pg 501

Norway
Ariel Lydbokforlag, pg 508
Fono Forlag, pg 509

Peru
Instituto de Estudios Peruanos, pg 517

Philippines
Anvil Publishing Inc, pg 518

Poland
Wydawnictwo Podsiedlik-Raniowski i Spolka, pg 525
Wydawnictwo RTW, pg 526

Russian Federation
INFRA-M Izdatel'skij dom, pg 545

Singapore
Asiapac Books Pte Ltd, pg 555
Europhone Language Institute (Pte) Ltd, pg 556
McGallen & Bolden Associates, pg 557

Slovenia
Mladinska Knjiga International, pg 561
Zalozba Mihelac d o o, pg 562
Zalozba Obzorja d d Maribor, pg 562

Spain
Aguilar SA de Ediciones, pg 571
Consello da Cultura Galega - CCG, pg 578
Didaco Comunicacion y Didactica, SA, pg 579
Edilux, pg 581
Editorial la Muralla SA, pg 592
Editorial Verbum SL, pg 604

Switzerland
Bergli Books AG, pg 619
ISIOM Verlag fur Tondokumente, Weinreb Tonarchiv, pg 625
Theologischer Verlag und Buchhandlungen AG, pg 635

Taiwan, Province of China
Campus Evangelical Fellowship, Literature Department, pg 639
Echo Publishing Company Ltd, pg 639
Zen Now Press, pg 642

Turkey
IKI Nokta Research Press & Publications Industry & Trade Ltd, pg 650

United Kingdom
Barefoot Books, pg 663
Berlitz (UK) Ltd, pg 665
Bible Reading Fellowship, pg 665
Cherrytree Books, pg 678
Chorion IP, pg 679
George Mann Publications, pg 699
Grandreams Ltd, pg 702
Gwasg y Dref Wen, pg 703
HarperCollins UK, pg 705
Hawk Books, pg 706
Headline Book Publishing Ltd, pg 706
Hodder & Stoughton General, pg 709
Hodder Children's Books, pg 709
Hodder Headline Ltd, pg 709
Hugo's Language Books Ltd, pg 710
Isis Publishing Ltd, pg 714
Kuperard, pg 718
Ladybird Books Ltd, pg 719
Letterbox Library, pg 720
Macmillan Ltd, pg 723
Magna Large Print Books, pg 724
Murchison's Pantheon Ltd, pg 730
New Era Publications UK Ltd, pg 732
Orion Publishing Group Ltd, pg 736
Penguin Books Ltd, pg 740
The Penguin Group UK, pg 740
The Reader's Digest Association Ltd, pg 748
Roundhouse Group, pg 751
Telegraph Books, pg 764
World Microfilms Publications Ltd, pg 775

Zimbabwe
Christian Audio-Visual Action (CAVA), pg 783

AV MATERIALS

Australia
Art Gallery of South Australia Bookshop, pg 12
Artmoves Inc, pg 12
Board of Studies, pg 15
R J Cleary Publishing, pg 18

Encyclopaedia Britannica (Australia) Inc, pg 21
Greater Glider Productions Australia Pty Ltd, pg 24
Hampden Press, pg 24
Ready-Ed Publications, pg 39
RMIT Publishing, pg 39
Wizard Books Pty Ltd, pg 47

Austria
Oesterreichischer Bundesverlag Gmbh, pg 55

Belgium
Carto BVBA, pg 64

Brazil
A & A & A Edicoes e Promocoes Internacionais Ltda, pg 76
Empresa Brasileira de Pesquisa Agropecuaria, pg 81

Burundi
Editions Intore, pg 98

Chile
Instituto Geografico Militar, pg 99

China
China Machine Press (CMP), pg 102
People's Education Press, pg 106
Wuhan University Press, pg 109

Colombia
Consejo Episcopal Latinoamericano (CELAM), pg 110
Universidad Nacional Abierta y a Distancia, pg 113

Costa Rica
Centro Agronomico Tropical de Investigacion y Ensenanza (CATIE), pg 115

Denmark
Gyldendalske Boghandel - Nordisk Forlag A/S, pg 131
IBIS, pg 132
Kaleidoscope Publishers Ltd, pg 132
Square Dance Partners Forlag, pg 135
Systime, pg 135

Estonia
Eesti Rahvusraamatukogu, pg 139

Fiji
University of the South Pacific, pg 141

Finland
Otava Publishing Co Ltd, pg 143
Werner Soederstrom Osakeyhtio (WSOY), pg 145

France
Editions Belin, pg 149
Codes Rousseau, pg 155
Editions J Dupuis, pg 159
INRA Editions (Institut National de la Recherche Agronomique), pg 168
IRD Editions, pg 169
Editions MDI (La Maison des Instituteurs), pg 175

Germany
Belser Wissenschaftlicher Dienst, pg 199
Calwer Verlag GmbH, pg 207
Carl-Auer-Systeme Verlag, pg 207
Egmont vgs verlagsgesellschaft mbH, pg 218
Filmfaust Verlag - Internationale Filmzeitschrift, pg 224
Lehrmittelverlag Wilhelm Hagemann GmbH, pg 233
kopaed verlagsgmbh, pg 249
Kulturbuch-Verlag GmbH, pg 250
Lahn-Verlag GmbH, pg 251
Langenscheidt KG, pg 252
Ingrid Langner, pg 252
Libertas- Europaeisches Institut GmbH, pg 254
Medien-Verlag Bernhard Gregor GmbH, pg 258
Missio eV, pg 260
Nusser Verlag, pg 266
TR - Verlagsunion GmbH, pg 291
Ziethen-Panorama Verlag GmbH, pg 302

Greece
Ekdoseis Domi AE, pg 306

Hong Kong
The Chinese University Press, pg 316

Iceland
Namsgagnastofnun, pg 326

Israel
Rolnik Publishers, pg 371

Italy
IHT Gruppo Editoriale SRL, pg 393
Istituto della Enciclopedia Italiana, pg 393
Casa Editrice Maccari (CEM), pg 396
Scala Group spa, pg 407

Japan
AVACO - Christian Mass Communications Center, pg 415
International Society for Educational Information (ISEI), pg 419
Ongaku No Tomo Sha Corporation, pg 425
President Inc, pg 425
Seibido, pg 426
Seibundo Shinkosha Publishing Co Ltd, pg 426
Sekai Bunka-Sha, pg 427

Republic of Korea
Korea Britannica Corp, pg 440
Twenty-First Century Publishers, Inc, pg 443
YBM/Si-sa, pg 443

Malta
Media Centre, pg 460

Mexico
Ediciones Culturales Internacionales SA de CV Edicion Compra y Venta de Libros, Casetes, Videos, pg 463
Organizacion Cultural LP SA de CV, pg 469

PUBLISHERS

Netherlands
Ministerie van Verkeer en Waterstaat, pg 486

New Zealand
Learning Media Ltd, pg 498

Philippines
Our Lady of Manaoag Publisher, pg 520

Poland
PZWL Wydawnictwo Lekarskie Ltd, pg 526

Portugal
Paulinas, pg 534

Reunion
Association des Ecrivains Reunionnais (ADER), pg 537

Romania
Editura Cronos SRL, pg 539

Russian Federation
Airis Press, pg 543
BLIC, russko-Baltijskij informaciionnyj centr, AO, pg 544
Okoshko Ltd Publishers (Izdatelstvo), pg 547

Singapore
McGallen & Bolden Associates, pg 557

Slovenia
Franc-Franc podjetje za promocijo kulture Murska Sobota d o o, pg 561

Spain
Anaya Educacion, pg 573
Editorial Astri SA, pg 573
Central Catequistica Salesiana (CCS), pg 576
Editorial Claret SA, pg 577
Comunidad Autonoma de Madrid, Servicio de Documentacion y Publicaciones, pg 578
Didaco Comunicacion y Didactica, SA, pg 579
Edebe, pg 580
Erein, pg 582
Imagen y Deporte, SL, pg 587
Editorial la Muralla SA, pg 592
Pearson Educacion S A, pg 595
Editorial De Vecchi SA, pg 604

Sweden
Mezopotamya Publishing & Distribution, pg 613
Bokfoerlaget Natur och Kultur, pg 613
Verbum Foerlag AB, pg 616

Switzerland
Bibellesbund Verlag, pg 619

United Republic of Tanzania
Kanisa la Biblia Publishers (KLB), pg 643

United Kingdom
Barn Dance Publications Ltd, pg 663
BBC English, pg 663
Books of Zimbabwe Publishing Co (Pvt) Ltd, pg 669
Coachwise Ltd, pg 680
Drake Educational Associates Ltd, pg 688
Encyclopaedia Britannica (UK) International Ltd, pg 691
Hodder Education, pg 709
Islamic Foundation Publications, pg 714
Moorley's Print & Publishing Ltd, pg 729
Pavilion Publishing (Brighton) Ltd, pg 739
Pergamon Flexible Learning, pg 740
Ramakrishna Vedanta Centre, pg 747
World Microfilms Publications Ltd, pg 775

Viet Nam
Trung-Tam San Xuat Hoc-Lieu, pg 781

Zimbabwe
Christian Audio-Visual Action (CAVA), pg 783
National Archives of Zimbabwe, pg 784

BELLES LETTRES

Albania
Botimpex Publications Import-Export Agency, pg 1

Algeria
Enterprise Nationale du Livre (ENAL), pg 2

Argentina
Editorial Acme SA, pg 3
Ada Korn Editora SA, pg 3
Editorial Atlantida SA, pg 3
Ediciones Corregidor SAICI y E, pg 4
Ediciones de la Flor SRL, pg 6
Ediciones de Arte Gaglianone, pg 6
Editorial Losada SA, pg 7
Marymar Ediciones SA, pg 7
Editorial Sopena Argentina SACI e I, pg 9

Australia
Access Press, pg 10
AHB Publications, pg 11
Dragon Press, pg 20
Hat Box Press, pg 25
New Endeavour Press, pg 33
Spinifex Press, pg 42

Austria
Aarachne Verlag, pg 48
Aeneas Verlagsgesellschaft GmbH, pg 48
Amalthea-Verlag, pg 48
Astor-Verlag, Willibald Schlager, pg 48
DachsVerlag GmbH, pg 49
Denkmayr GmbH Druck & Verlag, pg 50
Doecker Verlag GmbH & Co KG, pg 50
Literature Verlag Droschl, pg 50
Edition S der OSD, pg 50

TYPE OF PUBLICATION INDEX

Ennsthaler GesmbH & Co KG, pg 50
Edition Ergo Sum, pg 50
Guthmann & Peterson Liber Libri, Edition, pg 51
Haymon-Verlag GesmbH, pg 51
Johannes Heyn GmbH & Co KG, pg 52
Leopold Stocker Verlag, pg 53
Literas-Verlag GmbH, pg 53
Merbod Verlag, pg 54
Thomas Mlakar Verlag, pg 54
Otto Mueller Verlag, pg 54
oebv & hpt Verlagsgesellschaft mbH & Co KG, pg 55
Richard Pils Publication PN°1, pg 56
Georg Prachner KG, pg 56
Residenz Verlag GmbH, pg 57
Ritter Druck und Verlags KEG, pg 57
Verlag Roeschnar, pg 57
Verlag Styria, pg 58
Verlag Anton Schroll & Co, pg 59
Wieser Verlag, pg 60
Paul Zsolnay Verlag GmbH, pg 60

Azerbaijan
Sada, Literaturno-Izdatel'skij Centr, pg 60

Belarus
Kavaler Publishers, pg 62

Belgium
Libraire Ancienne Noel Anselot, pg 63
Le Cri Editions, pg 66
Maison d'Editions Claude Dejaie, pg 66
Editions les Eperonniers, pg 67
Imprimerie Hayez SPRL, pg 68
Editions Labor, pg 69
Lansman Editeur, pg 69
La Longue Vue, pg 70
Paradox Pers vzw, pg 71
La Part de L'Oeil, pg 71
Imprimeur - Editeur Vaillant-Carmanne SA, pg 74
Vita, pg 74
Editions Luce Wilquin, pg 74

Bolivia
Gisbert y Cia SA, pg 75

Bosnia and Herzegovina
Svjetlost, pg 76

Brazil
Ars Poetica Editora Ltda, pg 78
Livraria Martins Fontes Editora Ltda, pg 81
Imago Editora Importacao e Exportacao Ltda, pg 84
Editora Nova Alexandria Ltda, pg 87
Editora Nova Fronteira SA, pg 87
Ediuoro Publicacoes, SA, pg 89
Editora Revan Ltda, pg 89
Livraria Sulina Editora, pg 91
34 Literatura S/C Ltda, pg 91
Editora da Universidade de Sao Paulo, pg 91
Vozes Editora Ltda, pg 92

Bulgaria
Andina Publishing House, pg 93
Bulgarski Pissatel, pg 93
EA EOOD, pg 94
Fama, pg 94

Interpres, pg 95
Pejo K Javorov Publishing House, pg 95
Kibea Publishing Co, pg 95
Kralica MAB, pg 95
Narodna Kultura, pg 96
Ivan Vazov Publishing House, pg 97

Burundi
Editions Intore, pg 98

Chile
Ediciones Bat, pg 99

China
China Theatre Publishing House, pg 103
Fudan University Press, pg 104
Jinan Publishing House, pg 105

Colombia
Instituto Caro y Cuervo, pg 111
Editorial Santillana SA, pg 112

The Democratic Republic of the Congo
Centre Protestant d'Editions et de Diffusion (CEDI), pg 114
Presses Universitaires du Zaiire (PUZ), pg 114

Costa Rica
Ediciones Promesa, pg 116
Editorial de la Universidad de Costa Rica, pg 116
Editorial Universitaria Centroamericana (EDUCA), pg 117

Croatia
AGM doo, pg 117
ALFA dd za izdavacke, graficke i trgovacke poslove, pg 117
ArTresor naklada, pg 117
Durieux d o o, pg 118
Faust Vrani, pg 118
Graficki zavod Hrvatske, pg 118
Knjizevni Krug Split, pg 118
Matica hrvatska, pg 118
Mladost d d Izdavacku graficku i informaticku djelatnost, pg 119
Skolska Knjiga, pg 119
Znanje d d, pg 119

Cuba
Holguin, Ediciones, pg 120
Editorial Oriente, pg 120
Union de Escritores y Artistas de Cuba, pg 121

Czech Republic
Atlantis sro, pg 122
Aurora, pg 122
Bakalar spol sro, pg 122
Columbus, pg 123
Euromedia Group-Odeon, pg 123
Horacek Ladislav-Paseka, pg 123
Josef Hribal, pg 124
Nakladatelstvi Jota spol sro, pg 124
Kalich SRO, pg 124
Karmelitanske Nakladatelstvi, pg 124
Konsultace spol sro, pg 125
Labyrint, pg 125
Lidove Noviny Publishing House, pg 125
Josef Lukasik A Spol sro, pg 125
Mariadan, pg 125
Melantrich, akc spol, pg 125

789

TYPE OF PUBLICATION INDEX — BOOK

Nase vojsko, nakladatelstvi a knizni obchod, pg 126
Prostor, nakladatelstvi sro, pg 127
NS Svoboda spol sro, pg 127
Svoboda Servis GmbH, pg 127
Vitalis sro, pg 128
Votobia sro, pg 128

Denmark

Grevas Forlag, pg 131
Gyldendalske Boghandel - Nordisk Forlag A/S, pg 131
Politisk Revy, pg 133
Det Schonbergske Forlag A/S, pg 134
Forlaget Vindrose A/S, pg 135
Wisby & Wilkens, pg 135

Egypt (Arab Republic of Egypt)

Al Arab Publishing House, pg 137
General Egyptian Book Organization, pg 138
Middle East Book Centre, pg 138
Senouhy Publishers, pg 138

Estonia

Ilmamaa, pg 139
Olion Publishers, pg 140
Oue Eesti Raamat, pg 140
Perioodika, pg 140
Tuum, pg 140

Finland

Fenix-Kustannus Oy, pg 142
Schildts Forlags AB, pg 144
Soderstroms Forlag, pg 144

France

Editions Al Liamm, pg 146
Alsatia SA, pg 146
L'Amitie par le Livre, pg 146
Editions Arcam, pg 147
Armenia Editions, pg 147
Editions Atlantica Seguier, pg 148
Editions Aubier-Montaigne SA, pg 148
Autrement Editions, pg 148
Berg International Editeur, pg 149
William Blake & Co, pg 150
De Boccard Edition-Diffusion, pg 150
Emgleo Breiz, pg 151
Editions du Cadratin, pg 151
Cicero Editeurs, pg 154
Editions de Compostelle, pg 155
Editions Jose Corti, pg 156
Nouvelles Editions Debresse, pg 157
La Delirante, pg 157
Les Editeurs Reunis, pg 160
Editions Pierre Fanlac, pg 162
Editions Fata Morgana, pg 162
FBT de R Editions, pg 163
Librairie Fischbacher, International Art Book Distribution (import-export), pg 163
Editions Galilee, pg 164
Editions Gallimard, pg 164
Librairie Guenegaud, pg 166
Editions Hatier SA, pg 167
Editions de l'Herne, pg 167
Pierre Horay Editeur, pg 168
Editions Infrarouge, pg 168
Les Editions Interferences, pg 169
Editions J'ai Lu, pg 169
Editions Klincksieck, pg 170
Langues & Mondes-L'Asiatheque, pg 171
Editions Fernand Lanore Sarl, pg 171
Lettres Vives Editions, pg 172

Editions des Limbes d'Or FBT de R Editions, pg 172
Mercure de France SA, pg 175
Librairie Minard, pg 176
Nil Editions, pg 177
Librairie A-G Nizet Sarl, pg 177
Noir Sur Blanc, pg 177
Nouvelles Editions Latines, pg 177
Editions Odile Jacob, pg 177
Editions de l'Orante, pg 178
Editions Paradigme, pg 178
Editions Jean Picollec, pg 179
Editions Christian Pirot, pg 180
Le Pre-aux-clercs, pg 180
Presence Africaine Editions, pg 180
Editions Sand et Tchou SA, pg 184
Editions Scala, pg 184
Editions Seghers, pg 184
Editions de Septembre, pg 184
Editions Le Serpent a Plumes, pg 184
Service Technique pour l'Education, pg 184
Editions Andre Silvaire Sarl, pg 185
Societe des Editions Grasset et Fasquelle, pg 185
Association d'Editions Sorg, pg 186
Editions Stock, pg 186
Les Editions de la Table Ronde, pg 186
Editions Tallandier, pg 187
Publications de l'Universite de Pau, pg 188
La Vague a l'ame, pg 188
Editions Verdier, pg 188

Germany

A Francke Verlag (Tubingen und Basel), pg 190
Verlag und Antiquariat Frank Albrecht, pg 192
Alpha Literatur Verlag/Alpha Presse, pg 192
Anabas-Verlag Guenter Kaempf GmbH & Co KG, pg 192
Verlag APHAIA Svea Haske, Sonja Schumann GbR, pg 193
arani-Verlag GmbH, pg 193
Ars Vivendi Verlag, pg 194
Asso Verlag, pg 195
Atelier Verlag Andernach (AVA), pg 195
Aufbau-Verlag GmbH, pg 195
J J Augustin Verlag GmbH, pg 195
Verlag der Autoren GmbH & Co KG, pg 196
AvivA Britta Jurgs GmbH, pg 196
Dr Bachmaier Verlag GmbH, pg 196
Dr Wolfgang Baur Verlag Kunst & Alltag, pg 198
be.bra verlag GmbH, pg 198
Bechtle Graphische Betriebe und Verlagsgesellschaft GmbH und Co KG, pg 198
Beck & Gluckler Verlag GmbH & Co KG, pg 198
Verlag C H Beck oHG, pg 198
Beerenverlag, pg 198
Belser Wissenschaftlicher Dienst, pg 199
Bergstadtverlag Wilhelm Gottlieb Korn GmbH Wuerzburg, pg 199
C Bertelsmann Verlag GmbH, pg 199
Edition Klaus Blahak Dr Fredric Kroll, pg 202
Blanvalet VerlagGmbH, pg 202
Bleicher Verlag GmbH, pg 202
Brandes & Apsel Verlag GmbH, pg 204
Brigg Verlag Franz-Joset Buchler KG, pg 204

Brunnen-Verlag GmbH, pg 205
Fachverlag Hans Carl GmbH, pg 207
Christusbruderschaft Selbitz ev, Abt Verlag, pg 209
Claassen Verlag GmbH, pg 209
ComMedia & Arte Verlag Bernd Mayer, pg 209
J G Cotta'sche Buchhandlung Nachfolger GmbH, pg 210
CTL-Presse Clemens-Tobias Lange, pg 210
Dagmar Dreves Verlag, pg 210
Dana Verlag, pg 210
Das Arsenal, Verlag fuer Kultur und Politik GmbH, pg 210
Deutsche Verlags-Anstalt GmbH (DVA), pg 212
Deutscher Literatur-Verlag, pg 213
Deutscher Taschenbuch Verlag GmbH & Co KG (dtv), pg 213
Edition Dia, pg 214
Dieterichsche Verlagsbuchhandlung Mainz, pg 214
Maximilian Dietrich Verlag, pg 214
Dolling und Galitz Verlag GmbH, pg 215
Droste Verlag GmbH, pg 216
Karl Elser Druck GmbH, pg 216
Echter Wurzburg Frankische Gesellschaftsdruckerei und Verlag GmbH, pg 217
Econ Taschenbuchverlag, pg 218
Econ Verlag GmbH, pg 218
Egmont vgs verlagsgesellschaft mbH, pg 218
Ehrenwirth Verlag GmbH, pg 218
Eichborn AG, pg 219
EinfallsReich Verlagsgesellschaft MbH, pg 219
Engelhorn Verlag GmbH, pg 220
Verlag Peter Engstler, pg 220
Eremiten-Presse und Verlag GmbH, pg 220
Europa Verlag GmbH, pg 222
Extent Verlag und Service Wolfgang M Flamm, pg 223
Fabel-Verlag Gudrun Liebchen, pg 223
Wolfgang Fietkau Verlag, pg 224
Karin Fischer Verlag GmbH, pg 225
Fleischhauer & Spohn GmbH & Co, pg 225
FVA-Frankfurter Verlagsanstalt GmbH, pg 226
Frieling & Partner GmbH, pg 227
GLB Parkland Verlags-und Vertriebs GmbH, pg 229
Cornelia Goethe Literaturverlag, pg 230
Wilhelm Goldmann Verlag GmbH, pg 230
Grabert-Verlag, pg 230
Haag und Herchen Verlag GmbH, pg 232
Hansa Verlag Ingwert Paulsen Jr, pg 234
Carl Hanser Verlag, pg 234
Siegfried Haring Literatten-Verlag Ulm, pg 234
Heinz-Theo Gremme Verlag, pg 236
Heliopolis-Verlag, pg 236
Hellerau-Verlag Dresden GmbH, pg 236
F A Herbig Verlagsbuchhandlung GmbH, pg 236
Hans-Alfred Herchen & Co Verlag KG, pg 236
Verlag Peter Hoell, pg 238
Hoffmann und Campe Verlag GmbH, pg 238
Horlemann Verlag, pg 239

Husum Druck- und Verlagsgesellschaft mbH Co KG, pg 240
Iudicium Verlag GmbH, pg 242
Jan Thorbecke Verlag GmbH & Co, pg 243
KBV Verlags-und Medien - GmbH, pg 245
Martin Kelter Verlag GmbH u Co, pg 245
Kidemus Verlag GmbH, pg 245
Verlag Kiepenheuer & Witsch, pg 245
Gustav Kiepenheuer Verlag GmbH, pg 245
Verlag Kleine Schritte Ursula Dahm & Co, pg 246
Klosterhaus-Verlagsbuchhandlung Dr Grimm KG, pg 247
Albrecht Knaus Verlag GmbH, pg 247
Kolibri-Verlag GmbH, pg 249
KONTEXTverlag, pg 249
Karin Kramer Verlag, pg 250
Krug & Schadenberg, pg 250
Verlag Antje Kunstmann GmbH, pg 251
Verlag Langewiesche-Brandt KG, pg 252
Ingrid Langner, pg 252
Leibniz-Buecherwarte, pg 253
Dr Gisela Lermann, pg 253
Libertas- Europaeisches Institut GmbH, pg 254
Linden-Verlag, pg 254
Logos-Verlag Literatur & Layout GmbH, pg 255
Luchterhand Literaturverlag GmbH/ Verlag Volk & Welt GmbH, pg 255
Lutherische Verlagsgesellschaft mbH, pg 256
Annemarie Maeger, pg 256
Mannerschwarm Skript Verlag GmbH, pg 257
Edition Maritim GmbH, pg 257
Matthes und Seitz Verlag GmbH, pg 258
Merlin Verlag Andreas Meyer Verlags GmbH und Co KG, pg 259
Merz & Solitude - Akademie Schloss Solitude, pg 259
Miranda-Verlag Stefan Ehlert, pg 260
Missio eV, pg 260
Mitteldeutscher Verlag GmbH, pg 261
Monia Verlag, pg 261
Nebel Verlag GmbH, pg 263
Neue Erde Verlags GmbH, pg 264
Verlag Neues Leben GmbH, pg 264
New Era Publications Deutschland GmbH, pg 265
Nie/Nie/Sagen-Verlag, pg 265
C W Niemeyer Buchverlage GmbH, pg 265
Rainar Nitzsche Verlag, pg 265
nymphenburger, pg 266
Orlanda Frauenverlag, pg 267
Osho Verlag GmbH, pg 267
Ostfalia-Verlag Jurgen Schierer, pg 267
Pandion-Verlag, Ulrike Schmoll, pg 268
Paranus Verlag - Bruecke Neumuenster GmbH, pg 268
Passavia Druckerei GmbH, Verlag, pg 268
Pfaffenweiler Presse, pg 269
Pfalzische Verlagsanstalt GmbH, pg 269

PUBLISHERS

Philipp Reclam Jun Verlag GmbH, pg 269
Pollner Verlag, pg 271
Projektion J Buch- und Musikverlag GmbH, pg 272
Propylaeen Verlag, Zweigniederlassung Berlin der Ullstein Buchverlage GmbH, pg 272
Quintessenz Verlags-GmbH, pg 273
Reclam Verlag Leipzig, pg 274
Rogner und Bernhard GmbH & Co Verlags KG, pg 276
Rowohlt Verlag GmbH, pg 277
Ruetten & Loening Berlin GmbH, pg 277
Eugen Salzer-Verlag GmbH & Co KG, pg 278
Richard Scherpe Verlag GmbH, pg 279
Schneekluth Verlag, pg 280
Schoeffling & Co, pg 281
Carl Ed Schuenemann KG, pg 281
Theodor Schuster, pg 282
Buchkonzept Simon KG, pg 283
Adolf Sponholtz Verlag, pg 284
Steidl Verlag, pg 287
Verlag Stendel, pg 287
Steyler Verlag, pg 288
Suedverlag GmbH, pg 288
Suedwest Verlag GmbH & Co KG, pg 289
Otto Teich, pg 289
Druck-und Verlagshans Thiele & Schwarz GmbH, pg 290
Thienemann Verlag GmbH, pg 291
Verlag Theodor Thoben, pg 291
Hans Thoma Verlag GmbH Kunst und Buchverlag, pg 291
Tomus Verlag GmbH, pg 291
Treves Editions Verein Zur Foerderung der Kuenstlerischen Taetigkeiten, pg 292
Ullstein Heyne List GmbH & Co KG, pg 293
Ulrike Helmer Verlag, pg 293
Unrast Verlag e V, pg 293
Verlag Volk & Welt GmbH, pg 296
W Ludwig Verlag GmbH, pg 297
Friedenauer Presse Katharina Wagenbach-Wolff, pg 297
Weidler Buchverlag Berlin, pg 298
Rosa Winkel Verlag GmbH, pg 300
Wolf's-Verlag Berlin, pg 301
Wolgang Fietkau, pg 301
The World of Books Literaturverlag, pg 301
Das Wunderhorn Verlag GmbH, pg 301
Wunderlich Verlag, pg 301
Zambon Verlag, pg 302
Zebulon Verlag GmbH & Co KG, pg 302

Ghana
Anowuo Educational Publications, pg 303
Ghana Publishing Corporation, pg 304
Moxon Paperbacks, pg 304
Waterville Publishing House, pg 305

Greece
Bergadis, pg 306
Boukoumanis' Editions, pg 306
Denise Harvey, pg 308
Hestia-I D Hestia-Kollaros & Co Corporation, pg 308
Minoas SA, pg 310
Sigma, pg 312
Stochastis, pg 312

Guadeloupe
JASOR, pg 313

Guatemala
Grupo Editorial RIN-78, pg 313

Haiti
Editions Caraibes SA, pg 314

Holy See (Vatican City State)
Biblioteca Apostolica Vaticana, pg 314

Hong Kong
Research Centre for Translation, pg 319

Hungary
Europa Konyvkiado, pg 321
Helikon Kiado, pg 321
Jelenkor Verlag, pg 322
Magveto Koenyvkiado, pg 322
Park Konyvkiado Kft (Park Publisher), pg 324
Szepirodalmi Koenyvkiado Kiado, pg 324

Iceland
Almenna Bokafelagid, pg 325
Forlagid, pg 325

India
Ananda Publishers Pvt Ltd, pg 328
Atma Ram & Sons, pg 329
Geeta Prakashan, pg 335
Arnold Heinman Publishers (India) Pvt Ltd, pg 335
Intertrade Publications Pvt Ltd, pg 338
Jaico Publishing House, pg 338
People's Publishing House (P) Ltd, pg 345

Indonesia
Pustaka Utama Grafiti, PT, pg 356

Israel
Am Oved Publishers Ltd, pg 365
The Bialik Institute, pg 365
Boostan Publishing House, pg 365
Classikaletet, pg 366
DAT Publications, pg 366
Gvanim Publishing House, pg 367
Hakibbutz Hameuchad Publishing House Ltd, pg 367
The Institute for the Translation of Hebrew Literature, pg 368
Karni Publishers Ltd, pg 369
Massada Press Ltd, pg 370
Schocken Publishing House Ltd, pg 371
Sifriat Poalim Ltd, pg 372
Y L Peretz Publishing Co, pg 373
Zmora-Bitan, Publishers Ltd, pg 374

Italy
Adelphi Edizioni SpA, pg 374
Bollati Boringhieri Editore, pg 378
Bonsignori Editore SRL, pg 378
Book Editore, pg 378
Campanotto, pg 379
Cappelli Editore, pg 380
M d'Auria Editore SAS, pg 384
Giulio Einaudi Editore SpA, pg 387
Giangiacomo Feltrinelli SpA, pg 389
Festina Lente Edizioni, pg 389
Arnaldo Forni Editore SRL, pg 389
Istituto Geografico de Agostini SpA, pg 390
Gius Laterza e Figli SpA, pg 391
Ugo Guanda Editore, pg 392
Edizioni Internazionali di Letteratura e Scienze, pg 393
Linea d'Ombra Libri, pg 395
Longanesi & C, pg 396
La Luna, pg 396
Tommaso Marotta Editore Srl, pg 397
Il Minotauro, pg 398
Arnoldo Mondadori Editore SpA, pg 398
Edumond Le Monnier, pg 399
Gruppo Ugo Mursia Editore SpA, pg 400
Newton & Compton Editori, pg 400
Nuova Coletti Editore Roma, pg 401
Leo S Olschki, pg 401
Paideia Editrice, pg 402
Palatina Editrice, pg 402
Neri Pozza Editore, pg 404
RAI-ERI, pg 405
Rara Istituto Editoriale di Bibliofilia e Reprints, pg 405
RCS Rizzoli Libri SpA, pg 405
Riccardo Ricciardi Editore SpA, pg 405
Salerno Editrice SRL, pg 406
Edizioni San Paolo SRL, pg 407
SEMAR Publishers SRL, pg 408
Studio Bibliografico Adelmo Polla, pg 409
Edizioni Studio Tesi SRL, pg 409
Sugarco Edizioni SRL, pg 409
UTET (Unione Tipografico-Editrice Torinese), pg 411
Viviani Editore srl, pg 412

Japan
Chuokoron-Shinsha Inc, pg 416
The Hokuseido Press, pg 418
Iwanami Shoten, Publishers, pg 419
Kodansha International Ltd, pg 421
Charles E Tuttle Publishing Co Inc, pg 430
Yushodo Shuppan, pg 431

Kenya
Foundation Books Ltd, pg 434
Transafrica Press, pg 436

Republic of Korea
Hollym Corporation; Publishers, pg 439
Hw Moon Publishing Co, pg 439
Iljisa Publishing House, pg 439
Jeong-eum Munhwasa, pg 439
Mirinae, pg 441
Sejong Daewang Kinyom Saophoe, pg 442

Latvia
Artava Ltd, pg 444
Nordik/Tapals Publishers Ltd, pg 445
Preses Nams, pg 445
Vaidelote, SIA, pg 445

Liechtenstein
Liechtenstein Verlag AG, pg 448

Lithuania
AS Narbuto Leidykla (AS Narbutas' Publishers), pg 448
Baltos Lankos, pg 449
Lietuvos Rasytoju Sajungos Leidykla, pg 449
Tyto Alba Publishers, pg 450
Vaga Ltd, pg 450

Luxembourg
Editions APESS ASBL, pg 450
Cahiers Luxembourgeois, pg 451
Eiffes Romain, pg 451
Op der Lay, pg 451
Editions Phi, pg 451

The Former Yugoslav Republic of Macedonia
Detska radost, pg 452
Makedonska kniga (Knigoizdatelstvo), pg 452
Mi-An Knigoizdatelstvo, pg 452
Strk Publishing House, pg 453
Zumpres Publishing Firm, pg 453

Malaysia
Holograms (M) Sdn Bhd, pg 456

Mali
EDIM SA, pg 460

Mexico
Ediciones Era SA de CV, pg 465
Fondo de Cultura Economica, pg 465
Editorial Hermes SA, pg 466
Phillip Richard Conover Lazo, pg 467
Ediciones Promesa, SA de CV, pg 470
Universidad Veracruzana Direccion General Editorial y de Publicaciones, pg 472
Universo Editorial SA de CV Edicion de Libros Revistas y Periodicos, pg 473

Monaco
Les Editions du Rocher, pg 474
Rondeau Giannipiero a Monaco, pg 474

Netherlands
Uitgeverij Arena BV, pg 478
De Bezige Bij B V Uitgeverij, pg 479
Callenbach BV, pg 480
Castrum Peregrini Presse, pg 480
Uitgeverij en boekhandel Van Gennep BV, pg 482
HES & De Graaf Publishers BV, pg 483
Historische Uitgeverij, pg 483
Uitgeverij Holland, pg 483
Uitgeverij J H Kok BV, pg 485
Nijgh & Van Ditmar Amsterdam, pg 487
Em Querido's Uitgeverij BV, pg 488
A J G Strengholt's Boeken, Anno 1928, BV, pg 489
Uitgeverij G A van Oorschot bv, pg 491
Wereldbibliotheek, pg 492

New Zealand
The Caxton Press, pg 495
Outrigger Publishers, pg 499

Nigeria
Aromolaran Publishing Co Ltd, pg 503
Black Academy Press, pg 503
Cross Continent Press Ltd, pg 504
Heritage Books, pg 505

791

TYPE OF PUBLICATION INDEX

BOOK

Longman Nigeria Plc, pg 505
New Horn Press Ltd, pg 506
Northern Nigerian Publishing Co Ltd, pg 506
Nwamife Publishers Ltd, pg 506
Onibon-Oje Publishers, pg 506
University Publishing Co, pg 507

Norway

Det Norske Samlaget, pg 508
Gyldendal Norsk Forlag A/S, pg 509

Philippines

Anvil Publishing Inc, pg 518
Cacho Publishing House, Inc, pg 518
Marren Publishing House, Inc, pg 519
Philippine Education Co Inc, pg 520
University of the Philippines Press, pg 521

Poland

Spoldzielnia Wydawnicza 'Czytelnik', pg 522
Wydawnictwo Dolnoslaskie, pg 522
Instytut Wydawniczy Pax, Inco-Veritas, pg 523
Iskry - Publishing House Ltd spotka zoo, pg 523
KAW Krajowa Agencja Wydawnicza, pg 523
'Ksiazka i Wiedza' Spotdzielnia Wydawniczo-Handlowa, pg 524
Wydawnictwo Literackie, pg 524
Wydawnictwo Lodzkie, pg 524
Wydawnictwo Lubelskie, pg 524
Muza SA, pg 524
Panstwowy Instytut Wydawniczy (PIW), pg 525
Wydawnictwo SIC, pg 526
'Slask' Ltd, pg 526
Spoleczny Instytut Wydawniczy Znak, pg 526
Spotdzielna Anagram, pg 526
Videograf II Sp z o o Zaklad Poracy Chronionej, pg 527
Wydawnictwo WAB, pg 527

Portugal

Bezerr-Editorae e Distribuidora de Abel Antonio Bezerra, pg 529
Brasilia Editora (J Carvalho Branco), pg 529
Editora Classica, pg 530
Edicoes Colibri, pg 530
DIFEL - Difusao Editorial SA, pg 530
Editorial Estampa, Lda, pg 531
Publicacoes Europa-America Lda, pg 531
Fenda Edicoes, pg 531
Chaves Ferreira Publicacoes SA, pg 531
Editorial Inquerito Lda, pg 532
Latina Livraria Editora, pg 532
Publicacoes Dom Quixote Lda, pg 535
Realizacoes Artis, pg 535
Sa da Costa Livraria, pg 535
Solivros, pg 536
Almerinda Teixeira, pg 536

Puerto Rico

University of Puerto Rico Press (EDUPR), pg 537

Romania

Ars Longa Publishing House, pg 538
Editura Clusium, pg 539
Editure Ion Creanga, pg 539
Editura Dacia, pg 539
Editura Excelsior Art, pg 539
Hasefer, pg 540
Editura Kriterion SA, pg 540
Mentor Kiado, pg 540
Editura Militara, pg 541
Editura Minerva, pg 541
Nemira Verlag, pg 541
Editura Niculescu, pg 541
Pallas-Akademia Editura, pg 541
Pandora Publishing House, pg 541
Polirom Verlag, pg 542
RAO International Publishing Co, pg 542
Saeculum IO, pg 542
Editura Signata, pg 542
Est-Samuel Tastet Verlag, pg 542
Editura Univers SA, pg 543

Russian Federation

ARGO-RISK Publisher, pg 543
Armada Publishing House, pg 543
BLIC, russko-Baltijskij informaciionnyj centr, AO, pg 544
Druzhba Narodov, pg 544
Kabardino-Balkarskoye knizhnoye izdatelstvo, pg 545
Kavkazskaya Biblioteka Publishing House, pg 545
KUbK Publishing House, pg 546
Ladomir Publishing House, pg 546
Publishing House Limbus Press, pg 546
Mir Knigi Ltd, pg 546
Panorama Publishing House, pg 547
Profizdat, pg 548
Raduga Publishers, pg 548
Russkaya Kniga Izdatelstvo (Publishers), pg 548
Izdatelstvo Sovetskii Pisatel, pg 548
Voyenizdat, pg 549

Senegal

Centre Africain d'Animation et d'Echanges Culturels Editions Khoudia (CAEC), pg 551
Les Nouvelles Editions Africaines du Senegal NEAS, pg 551

Serbia and Montenegro

Alfa-Narodna Knjiga, pg 552
Association of Yugoslav Publishers & Booksellers, pg 552
Beogradski Izdavacko-Graficki Zavod, pg 552
Izdavacka preduzece Gradina, pg 552
Jugoslavijapublik, pg 552
Nio Pobjeda - Oour Izdavacko-Publicisticka Djelatnost, pg 552
Obod, pg 553
Izdavacka Organizacija Rad, pg 553
Panorama NIJP/ID Grigorije Bozovic, pg 553
Partenon MAM Sistem, pg 553
Izdavacko Preduzece Matice Srpske, pg 553
Srpska Knjizevna Zadruga, pg 553
Svetovi, pg 554

Slovakia

Kalligram spol sro, pg 559
Luc vydavatelske druzstvo, pg 559
Vydavatelstvo Obzor, pg 560
Vydavatepstvo Praca spol sro, pg 560
Slovansky Tatran, Vydavatel 'stro spoi sro, pg 560
Slovensky Spisovatel Ltd as, pg 560
Smena Publishing House, pg 560

Slovenia

Cankarjeva Zalozba, pg 561
Franc-Franc podjetje za promocijo kulture Murska Sobota d o o, pg 561
Zalozba Mihelac d o o, pg 562
Zalozba Obzorja d d Maribor, pg 562

South Africa

HAUM (Hollandsch Afrikaansche Uitgevers Maatschappij), pg 564
Human & Rousseau (Pty) Ltd, pg 564
Nasou Via Afrika, pg 567
Queillerie Publishers, pg 568

Spain

Aguilar SA de Ediciones, pg 571
Ediciones Akal SA, pg 571
Ediciones Alfar SA, pg 572
Alianza Editorial SA, pg 572
Ambit Serveis Editorials, SA, pg 572
Editorial Biblioteca Nueva SL, pg 574
Calamo Editorial, pg 575
Editorial Castalia, pg 576
Complutense, SA Editorial, pg 577
Edilesa-Ediciones Leonesas SA, pg 581
Ediciones Encuentro SA, pg 582
Editorial Grupo Cero, pg 585
Ediciones Hiperion SL, pg 586
Institucion Fernando el Catolico de la Excma Diputacion de Zaragoza, pg 587
Editorial Lumen SA, pg 589
Editorial Milenio Arts Grafiques Bobala, SL, pg 591
Editorial Moll SL, pg 592
Editorial la Muralla SA, pg 592
Nueva Acropolis, pg 593
Editora Regional de Murcia - ERM, pg 597
Editorial Seix Barral SA, pg 599
Sirmio, pg 600
Torremozas SL Ediciones, pg 602
Trea Ediciones, SL, pg 602
Turner Publicaciones, pg 602
Tursen, SA, pg 603
Publicacions de la Universitat de Barcelona, pg 604
Editorial Verbum SL, pg 604
Visor Libros, pg 605

Sudan

Al-Ayam Press Co Ltd, pg 608
Khartoum University Press, pg 608

Sweden

Ellerstroms, pg 611
Samsprak Forlags AB, pg 615

Switzerland

Editions L'Age d'Homme - La Cite, pg 617
Ammann Verlag & Co, pg 617
Arche Verlag AG, Raabe und Vitali, pg 617
Atrium Verlag AG, pg 618
Editions de la Baconniere SA, pg 618
Verlag Bibliophile Drucke von Josef Stocker AG, pg 619
Blaukreuz-Verlag Bern, pg 619
Werner Classen Verlag, pg 621
Cosa-Verlag, Giusep Condrau SA, pg 621
Cosmos-Verlag AG, pg 621
Daphnis-Verlag, pg 621
eFeF-Verlag/Edition Ebersbach, pg 622
Erker-Verlag, pg 623
Edition Hans Erpf Edition, pg 623
Europa Verlag AG, pg 623
Giampiero Casagrande Editore, pg 624
Haffmans Verlag AG, pg 624
Editions Ides et Calendes SA, pg 625
Jordanverlag AG, pg 625
Kranich-Verlag, Dres AG & H R Bosch-Gwalter, pg 627
Lia rumantscha, pg 627
Limmat Verlag, pg 628
Manesse Verlag GmbH, pg 628
Librairie-Editions J Marguerat, pg 628
Editions H Messeiller SA, pg 628
Minervaverlag Bern, pg 628
Verlag Nagel & Kimche AG, Zurich, pg 629
Les Editions Noir sur Blanc, pg 629
Orte-Verlag, pg 630
Ostschweiz Druck und Verlag, pg 630
Editions du Panorama, pg 630
Verlag Friedrich Reinhardt AG, pg 632
Rex Verlag, pg 632
Roth et Sauter SA, pg 632
Rotpunktverlag, pg 632
Sinwel-Buchhandlung Verlag, pg 634
Speer-Verlag, pg 634
Strom-Verlag Luzern, pg 635
Editions des Trois Collines Francois Lachenal, pg 635
Editions 24 Heures, pg 635
Viktoria-Verlag Peter Marti, pg 636
Verlag Die Waage, pg 636
Verlag im Waldgut AG, pg 636
Buchverlag der Druckerei Wetzikon AG, pg 637
Zbinden Druck und Verlag AG, pg 637

Taiwan, Province of China

Chien Chen Bookstore Publishing Company Ltd, pg 639
Chung Hwa Book Co Ltd, pg 639

United Republic of Tanzania

East African Publishing House, pg 643

Togo

Editions Akpagnon, pg 646
Les Nouvelles Editions Africaines du TOGO (NEA-TOGO), pg 646

Tunisia

Academie Tunisienne des Sciences, des Lettres et des Arts Beit El Hekma, pg 647
Les Editions de l'Arbre, pg 647
Maison Tunisienne de l'Edition, pg 648
Editions Techniques Specialisees, pg 648

PUBLISHERS

Turkey
Altin Kitaplar Yayinevi, pg 649
Kabalci Yayinevi, pg 652

Ukraine
Osnova, Kharkov State University Press, pg 653
Osnovy Publishers, pg 654

United Kingdom
Books for Europe Ltd, pg 669
Canongate Books Ltd, pg 674
Carcanet Press Ltd, pg 674
The Chrysalis Press, pg 679
Andre Deutsch Ltd, pg 687
Aidan Ellis Publishing, pg 690
Faber & Faber Ltd, pg 694
GMP Publishers Ltd, pg 700
The Greek Bookshop, pg 702
Robert Hale Ltd, pg 704
The Harvill Press, pg 705
Northcote House Publishers Ltd, pg 733
Octopus Publishing Group, pg 734
Peter Owen Ltd, pg 737
Parapress Ltd, pg 738
Planet, pg 743
St George's Press, pg 753
Seren, pg 756
Souvenir Press Ltd, pg 759
Telegraph Books, pg 764
Tuba Press, pg 767
Frederick Warne Publishers Ltd, pg 771
The Windrush Press Ltd, pg 774

Uruguay
La Flor del Itapebi, pg 777
Ediciones Trilce, pg 778

Venezuela
Biblioteca Ayacucho, pg 779

Zimbabwe
Anvil Press, pg 782

BIBLES

Albania
NL SH, pg 1

Argentina
Argentine Bible Society, pg 3
Editorial Ruy Diaz SAEIC, pg 5
Editorial Guadalupe, pg 6
Ediciones Preescolar SA, pg 8
San Pablo, pg 9

Australia
Bible Society in Australia National Headquarters, pg 14
Hodder Headline Australia, pg 26
St Pauls Publications, pg 40

Austria
Oesterreichisches Katholisches Bibelwerk, pg 55

Belgium
NV Uitgeverij Altiora Averbode, pg 63

Brazil
Action Editora Ltda, pg 76
Associacao Arvore da Vida, pg 78
Edicoes Loyola SA, pg 85
Editora Mundo Cristao, pg 87

Paulinas Editorial, pg 88
Paulus Editora, pg 88
Ediouro Publicacoes, SA, pg 89
Editora Scipione Ltda, pg 90

Bulgaria
Sluntse Publishing House, pg 97

Colombia
Eurolibros Ltda, pg 111
Instituto Misionerao Hijas De San Pablo, pg 112
Editorial Panamericana, pg 112

Czech Republic
Ceska Biblicka Spolecnost, pg 123

Denmark
Det Danske Bibelselskab, pg 130
Scandinavia Publishing House, pg 134

Estonia
Eesti Piibliselts, pg 139

Finland
Forsamlingsforbundets Forlags AB, pg 142
Lasten Keskus Oy, pg 143

France
Editions Al Liamm, pg 146
Societe Biblique Francaise, pg 150
Editions du Cerf, pg 153
Editions Le Laurier, pg 171
Editions Mediaspaul, pg 175
Muller Edition, pg 176
Editions Le Sarment, pg 184

Germany
Agentur des Rauhen Hauses Hamburg GmbH, pg 191
Bertelsmann Lexikon Verlag GmbH, pg 200
R Brockhaus Verlag, pg 204
Deutsche Bibelgesellschaft, pg 211
Evangelische Haupt-Bibelgesellschaft und von Cansteinsche Bibelanstalt, pg 222
Grass-Verlag, pg 231
Verlag Katholisches Bibelwerk GmbH, pg 245
Verlag Parzeller GmbH & Co KG, pg 268
Pattloch Verlag GmbH & Co KG, pg 268
Silberburg-Verlag Titus Haeussermann GmbH, pg 283
Steyler Verlag, pg 288
Verein der Benediktiner zu Beuron-Beuroner Kunstverlag, pg 294

Ghana
Ghana Institute of Linguistics Literacy & Bible Translation (GILLBT), pg 304
World Literature Project, pg 305

Greece
Alamo Hellas, pg 305
Apostoliki Diakonia tis Ekklisias tis Hellados, pg 305
Chrysi Penna - Golden Pen Books, pg 306
Logos, pg 309

Hungary
Advent Kiado, pg 320
Agape Ferences Nyomda es Konyvkiado Kft, pg 320

India
Dolphin Publications, pg 333
Satprakashan Sanchar Kendra, pg 348

Indonesia
Nusa Indah, pg 356

Ireland
Dominican Publications, pg 359
Four Courts Press Ltd, pg 360

Israel
Carta, The Israel Map & Publishing Co Ltd, pg 365
Koren Publishers Jerusalem Ltd, pg 369
Rolnik Publishers, pg 371

Italy
Centro Biblico, pg 381
Citta Nuova Editrice, pg 382
Cittadella Editrice, pg 382
Elle Di Ci - Libreria Dottrina Cristiana, pg 387
Piero Gribaudi Editore, pg 391
In Dialogo, pg 393
Lubrina, pg 396
Giuseppe Maimone Editore, pg 397
Editrice Massimo SAS di Crespi Cesare e C, pg 397
Paideia Editrice, pg 402
Edizioni Piemme SpA, pg 403
Sardini Editrice, pg 407
Societa Editrice Internazionale - SEI, pg 408
Editrice Uomini Nuovi, pg 411

Japan
Japan Bible Society, pg 419
Myrtos Inc, pg 423

Kenya
Paulines Publications-Africa, pg 435

Republic of Korea
Kukmin Doseo Publishing Co Ltd, pg 440
St Pauls, pg 442
Word of Life Press, pg 443

Lebanon
Dar-El-Machreq Sarl, pg 446
Librairie Orientale sal, pg 446

Malta
Gozo Press, pg 460
Media Centre, pg 460

Mexico
Ediciones Dabar, SA de CV, pg 464
Fernandez Editores SA de CV, pg 465
Editorial Limusa SA de CV, pg 467
Naves Internacional de Ediciones SA, pg 469
Organizacion Cultural LP SA de CV, pg 469
Palabra Ediciones S A de C V, pg 469

TYPE OF PUBLICATION INDEX

Netherlands
Boekencentrum BV, pg 479
Katholieke Bijbelstichting, pg 484
Narratio Theologische Uitgeverij, pg 486
Telos Boeken, pg 490

Pakistan
Sheikh Muhammad Ashraf Publishers, pg 511

Philippines
Communication Foundation for Asia Media Group (CFAMG), pg 518
Logos (Divine Word) Publications Inc, pg 519
Our Lady of Manaoag Publisher, pg 520

Poland
Instytut Wydawniczy Pax, Inco-Veritas, pg 523
Vocatio Publishing House, pg 527

Serbia and Montenegro
AGAPE, pg 552

Singapore
Tecman Bible House, pg 558

South Africa
Institute for Reformational Studies CHE, pg 565

Spain
Publicacions de l'Abadia de Montserrat, pg 570
Editorial Claret SA, pg 577
Editora Comercial de Publicaciones, pg 577
Complutense, SA Editorial, pg 577
Ediciones Cristiandad, pg 578
Idea Books, SA, pg 587
Ediciones Mensajero, pg 591
San Pablo Ediciones, pg 598
Ediciones San Pio X, pg 599
Ediciones Sigueme SA, pg 600
Editorial Verbo Divino, pg 604

Sweden
International Bible Society, pg 612

Switzerland
Berchtold Haller Verlag, pg 619
Beroa-Verlag, pg 619
La Maison de la Bible, pg 628

Taiwan, Province of China
Campus Evangelical Fellowship, Literature Department, pg 639

United Republic of Tanzania
Northwestern Publishers, pg 644
Peramiho Publications, pg 644

United Kingdom
McCall Barbour, pg 663
Bible Society, pg 665
Cambridge University Press, pg 674
Chapter Two, pg 678
Christian Education, pg 679
Cyhoeddiadau'r Gair, pg 685
Darton, Longman & Todd Ltd, pg 686
HarperCollins UK, pg 705
Hodder & Stoughton Religious, pg 709

793

TYPE OF PUBLICATION INDEX   BOOK

Hodder Headline Ltd, pg 709
Angus Hudson Ltd, pg 710
The Islamic Texts Society, pg 715
Marcham Manor Press, pg 725
Oxford University Press, pg 737
St Pauls Publishing, pg 753
Tern Press, pg 764

Zimbabwe
Christian Audio-Visual Action (CAVA), pg 783

BIBLIOGRAPHIES

Albania
Botimpex Publications Import-Export Agency, pg 1
NL SH, pg 1

Argentina
Alfagrama SRL ediciones, pg 3
Ediciones Corregidor SAICI y E, pg 4
Instituto Nacional de Ciencia y Tecnica Hidrica (INCYTH), pg 7
Theoria SRL Distribuidora y Editora, pg 9

Australia
Australian Institute of Family Studies (AIFS), pg 13
Australian Scholarly Publishing, pg 13
Chingchic Publishers, pg 17
Magpie Books, pg 30
Mulini Press, pg 32
National Library of Australia, pg 33
Thorpe-Bowker, pg 43

Austria
Akademische Druck-u Verlagsanstalt Dr Paul Struzl GmbH, pg 48
Universitaetsverlag Wagner GmbH, pg 59
Zirkular - Verlag der Dokumentationsstelle fuer neuere oesterreichische Literatur, pg 60

Bangladesh
The University Press Ltd, pg 61

Belgium
Maison d'Editions Baha'ies ASBL, pg 63
Bourdeaux-Capelle SA, pg 64
Brepols Publishers NV, pg 64
La Charte Editions juridiques, pg 65
Maison d'Editions Claude Dejaie, pg 66
Dexia Bank, pg 66
Claude Lefrancq Editeur, pg 70
Zuid En Noord VZW, pg 75

Botswana
National Library Service, pg 76

Brazil
Edicon Editora e Consultorial Ltda, pg 81
Fundacao Joaquim Nabuco-Editora Massangana, pg 82
Edicoes Loyola SA, pg 85
Livraria Sulina Editora, pg 91

Bulgaria
Hristo G Danov State Publishing House, pg 93
Prohazka I Kacarmazov, pg 96

China
Qingdao Publishing House, pg 107
Shandong Friendship Publishing House, pg 107
Shanghai Far East Publishers, pg 108

Colombia
Editorial Santillana SA, pg 112

The Democratic Republic of the Congo
Facultes Catoliques de Kinshasa, pg 114

Costa Rica
Centro Agronomico Tropical de Investigacion y Ensenanza (CATIE), pg 115
Litografia Artex, SA, pg 115

Cote d'Ivoire
Les Nouvelles Editions Ivoiriennes, pg 117

Croatia
AGM doo, pg 117
Leksikografski Zavod Miroslav Krleza, pg 118
Matica hrvatska, pg 118

Cyprus
Chrysopolitissa Publishers, pg 121

Czech Republic
Divadelni Ustav, pg 123
Nakladatelstvi Jota spol sro, pg 124
Karmelitanske Nakladatelstvi, pg 124
Statni Vedecka Knihovna Usti Nad Labem, pg 127

Denmark
Borgens Forlag A/S, pg 129
Dansk Biblioteks Center, pg 130
Forlaget Forum, pg 131

Estonia
Academic Library of Tallinn Pedagogical University, pg 139
Eesti Entsuklopeediakirjastus, pg 139
Eesti Rahvusraamatukogu, pg 139
Estonian Academy Publishers, pg 139

Finland
Scriptum Forlags AB, pg 144
Suomalaisen Kirjallisuuden Seura, pg 144

France
Academie Nationale de Reims, pg 145
Actes-Graphiques, pg 145
ADPF Publications, pg 145
Agence Bibliographique de l'Enseignement Superieur, pg 146
Armenia Editions, pg 147
Editions Bertout, pg 149
Bibliotheque Nationale de France, pg 150
Editions Andre Bonne, pg 150
Editions du Cadratin, pg 151
Editions des Cahiers Bourbonnais, pg 151
CERDIC-Publications, pg 153

Chadwyck-Healey France (CHF), pg 153
CTNERHI - Centre Technique National d'Etudes et de Recherches sur les Handicaps et les Inadaptations, pg 156
Electre, pg 161
Institut d'Etudes Slaves IES, pg 162
Sarl Editions Jean Grassin, pg 166
Hachette Livre, pg 167
Institut International de la Marionnette, pg 169
Lettres Modernes Minard, pg 172
Maisonneuve et Larose, pg 174
Librairie Minard, pg 176
Librairie F de Nobele, pg 177
OGC Michele Broutta Editeur, pg 177
Editions A et J Picard SA, pg 179
Jean-Michel Place, pg 180
Le Pre-aux-clercs, pg 180
PRODIG, pg 182
References cf, pg 183
Service des Publications Scientifiques du Museum National d'Histoire Naturelle, pg 184
Universitas, pg 188

French Polynesia
Scoop/Au Vent des Iles, pg 189

Germany
Verlag und Antiquariat Frank Albrecht, pg 192
ARCult Media, pg 193
Barenreiter-Verlag Karl-Votterle GmbH & Co KG, pg 197
Bertelsmann Lexikon Verlag GmbH, pg 200
Biblio Verlag, pg 200
Edition Klaus Blahak Dr Fredric Kroll, pg 202
Buchverlage Langen-Mueller/Herbig, pg 205
Centaurus-Verlagsgesellschaft GmbH, pg 207
Cicero Presse Verlag & Antiquariat, pg 209
Copress Verlag, pg 209
Degener & Co, Manfred Dreiss Verlag, pg 211
Karl Elser Druck GmbH, pg 216
Dumjahn Verlag, pg 217
Duncker und Humblot GmbH, pg 217
Fraunhofer IRB Verlag Fraunhofer Informationszentrum Raum und Bau, pg 226
Friedrich Frommann Verlag, pg 227
Guetersloher Verlagshaus, pg 232
Harrassowitz Verlag, pg 234
Dr Ernst Hauswedell & Co, pg 235
Anton Hiersemann, Verlag, pg 237
Friedrich Hofmeister Musikverlag, pg 238
Edition ID-Archiv/ID-Verlag, pg 240
Iudicium Verlag GmbH, pg 242
JKL Publikationen GmbH, pg 243
Keip GmbH, pg 245
Vittorio Klostermann GmbH, pg 247
K F Koehler Verlag GmbH, pg 248
Verlag Valentin Koerner GmbH, pg 248
Koptisch-Orthodoxes Zentrum, pg 249
Institut fuer Landes- und Stadtentwicklungsforschung des Landes Nordrhein-Westfalen, pg 251

Dr Gisela Lermann, pg 253
Merlin Verlag Andreas Meyer Verlags GmbH und Co KG, pg 259
Musikantiquariat und Dr Hans Schneider Verlag GmbH, pg 262
MVB Marketing- und Verlagsservice des Buchhandels GmbH, pg 263
Verlag Neue Musik GmbH, pg 264
C W Niemeyer Buchverlage GmbH, pg 265
Max Niemeyer Verlag GmbH, pg 265
Georg Olms Verlag AG, pg 267
Pawel Panpresse, pg 268
Guido Pressler Verlag, pg 271
Rossipaul Kommunikation GmbH, pg 277
Eugen Salzer-Verlag GmbH & Co KG, pg 278
K G Saur Verlag GmbH, A Gale/Thomson Learning Company, pg 278
Sax-Verlag Beucha, pg 278
Schott Musik International GmbH & Co KG, pg 281
Stadt Duisburg - Amt Fuer Statistik, Stadtforschung und Europaangelegenheiten, pg 286
C A Starke Verlag, pg 287
Suedverlag GmbH, pg 288
Treves Editions Verein Zur Foerderung der Kuenstlerischen Taetigkeiten, pg 292
Trotzdem-Verlags Genossenschaft eG, pg 292
Ulrike Helmer Verlag, pg 293
Edition Curt Visel, pg 296
VWB-Verlag fur Wissenschaft & Bildung, Amand Aglaster, pg 297
Das Wunderhorn Verlag GmbH, pg 301

Ghana
Bureau of Ghana Languages, pg 303

Greece
Hestia-I D Hestia-Kollaros & Co Corporation, pg 308

Guatemala
Grupo Editorial RIN-78, pg 313

Haiti
Editions Caraibes SA, pg 314

Hong Kong
The Chinese University Press, pg 316
Sun Mui Press, pg 319

Hungary
Europa Konyvkiado, pg 321
Jelenkor Verlag, pg 322

India
Agricole Publishing Academy, pg 327
Disha Prakashan, pg 333
Gyan Publishing House, pg 335
Heritage Publishers, pg 335
Indian Documentation Service, pg 337
Natraj Prakashan, Publishers & Exporters, pg 343
Reliance Publishing House, pg 346
Vidya Puri, pg 352
Vidyarthi Mithram Press, pg 352

PUBLISHERS

Ireland
Sean Ros Press, pg 363

Israel
Ben-Zvi Institute, pg 365
The Institute for the Translation of Hebrew Literature, pg 368
The Magnes Press, pg 370
Misgav Yerushalayim, pg 370
Yad Izhak Ben-Zvi Press, pg 373
The Zalman Shazar Center, pg 374

Italy
AIB Associazione Italiana Bibliotheche, pg 374
Umberto Allemandi & C SRL, pg 375
Rosellina Archinto Editore, pg 376
Belforte Editore Libraio srl, pg 377
Editrice Bibliografica SpA, pg 378
Bonsignori Editore SRL, pg 378
Edizioni Bora SNC di E Brandani & C, pg 379
Casalini Libri, pg 380
Istituto Centrale per il Catalogo Unico delle Biblioteche Italiane e per le Informazioni Bibliografiche, pg 381
Colonnese Editore, pg 383
Arnaldo Forni Editore SRL, pg 389
Frati Editori di Quaracchi, pg 389
Lalli Editore SRL, pg 394
Angelo Longo Editore, pg 396
Lubrina, pg 396
OCTAVO Produzioni Editoriali Associate, pg 401
Leo S Olschki, pg 401
Maria Pacini Fazzi Editore, pg 402
Rubbettino Editore, pg 406
Salerno Editrice SRL, pg 406
Edizioni Rosminiane Sodalitas, pg 408
Editrice Uomini Nuovi, pg 411

Japan
Rinsen Book Co Ltd, pg 425
Toho Book Store, pg 429

Republic of Korea
Gim-Yeong Co, pg 438
Ke Mong Sa Publishing Co Ltd, pg 440
Korean Publishers Association, pg 440
Kukmin Doseo Publishing Co Ltd, pg 440

Latvia
Bibliography Institute of the National Library of Latvia, pg 444

Lebanon
Publitec Publications, pg 447

Liechtenstein
Topos Verlag AG, pg 448

Lithuania
Klaipedos Universiteto Leidykla, pg 449
Lithuanian National Museum Publishing House, pg 449
Martynas Mazvydas National Library of Lithuania, pg 449

Luxembourg
Service Central des Imprimes et des Fournitures de Bureau de l'Etat, pg 451

The Former Yugoslav Republic of Macedonia
St Clement of Ohrid National & University Library, pg 453

Malaysia
Geetha Publishers Sdn Bhd, pg 456

Malta
Fondazzjoni Patrimonju Malti, pg 460

Mexico
Centro de Estudios Mexicanos y Centroamericanos, pg 463
Instituto Nacional de Antropologia e Historia, pg 469

Morocco
Association de la Recherche Historique et Sociale, pg 474

Netherlands
APA (Academic Publishers Associated), pg 477
B M Israel BV, pg 478
De Graaf Publishers, pg 481
HES & De Graaf Publishers BV, pg 483
Philo Press (APA), pg 487

New Zealand
Cape Catley Ltd, pg 495

Nigeria
Evans Brothers (Nigeria Publishers) Ltd, pg 504

Pakistan
Academy of Education Planning & Management (AEPAM), pg 511
National Institute of Historical & Cultural Research, pg 514
Sang-e-Meel Publications, pg 514

Papua New Guinea
National Research Institute of Papua New Guinea, pg 515
Office of Libraries & Archives, Papua New Guinea, pg 516

Peru
Instituto de Estudios Peruanos, pg 517

Poland
Biblioteka Narodowa, pg 522
Wydawnictwo DiG, pg 522
Katolicki Uniwersytet Wydawniczo -Redakcja, pg 523
Ossolineum Zaklad Narodowy im Ossolinskich - Wydawnictwo, pg 525
Oficyna Wydawnicza Szkoly Glownej Handlowej w Warszawie Oficyna Wydawnicza SGH, pg 527
Towarzystwo Naukowe w Toruniu, pg 527
Wydawnictwa Uniwersytetu Warszawskiego, pg 527

Portugal
Biblioteca Geral da Universidade de Coimbra, pg 529
Edicoes Colibri, pg 530
Edicoes Cosmos, pg 530
Imprensa Nacional-Casa da Moeda, pg 532
Instituto de Investigacao Cientifica Tropical, pg 532
Edicoes Ora & Labora, pg 534
Paulinas, pg 534
Edicoes Talento, pg 536

Romania
Editura Academiei Romane, pg 538
Editura Excelsior Art, pg 539
Humanitas Publishing House, pg 540
Editura Niculescu, pg 541
Saeculum IO, pg 542
Vestala Verlag, pg 543

Russian Federation
BLIC, russko-Baltijskij informaciionnyj centr, AO, pg 544
Izdatelstvo Kniga, pg 545
Izdatelstvo Knizhnaya Palata, pg 546
Izdatelskii Dom Kompozitor, pg 546
Ministerstvo Kul'tury RF, pg 546
Izdatelstvo Mordovskogo gosudar stvennogo, pg 547
Izdatelstvo Ural' skogo, pg 549

Senegal
CODESRIA (Council for the Development of Social Science Research in Africa), pg 551

Serbia and Montenegro
Narodna Biblioteka Srbije, pg 552

Slovakia
Slovenska Narodna Kniznica, Martin, pg 560

South Africa
New Africa Books (Pty) Ltd, pg 567
South African Institute of International Affairs, pg 569

Spain
Arco Libros SL, pg 573
Editorial Casariego, pg 576
Biblioteca de Catalunya, pg 576
Editora Comercial de Publicaciones, pg 577
Instituto de Estudios Riojanos, pg 583
EUNSA (Ediciones Universidad de Navarra SA), pg 583
Joyas Bibliograficas SA, pg 588
Junta de Castilla y Leon Consejeria de Educacion y Cultura, pg 588
Editorial Monte Carmelo, pg 592
Mundo Negro Editorial, pg 592
Oikos-Tau SA Ediciones, pg 593
Pre-Textos, pg 596
Editorial Revista Agustiniana, pg 598
Trea Ediciones, SL, pg 602
Ediciones Xandro, pg 605

Sri Lanka
National Library & Documentation Centre, pg 607

Sweden
Dahlia Books, International Publishers & Booksellers, pg 611
Invandrarfoerlaget, pg 612
Mezopotamya Publishing & Distribution, pg 613
Bokforlaget Rediviva, Facsimileforlaget, pg 615

Switzerland
Librairie Droz SA, pg 622
Garuda-Verlag, pg 624
Presses Polytechniques et Universitaires Romandes, PPUR, pg 631

Taiwan, Province of China
Campus Evangelical Fellowship, Literature Department, pg 639

Tunisia
Academie Tunisienne des Sciences, des Lettres et des Arts Beit El Hekma, pg 647
Dar Arabia Lil Kitab, pg 648

Turkey
Ataturk Kultur, Dil ve Tarih, Yusek Kurumu Baskanligi, pg 649
IKI Nokta Research Press & Publications Industry & Trade Ltd, pg 650

United Kingdom
ABC-CLIO, pg 654
Arts Council of England, pg 660
Ashgate Publishing Ltd, pg 660
Aslib, The Association for Information Management, pg 660
Avero Publications Ltd, pg 662
The British Library, pg 671
British Library Document Supply Centre, pg 671
British Library Publications, pg 672
Cambridge University Press, pg 674
Chadwyck-Healey Ltd, pg 677
CTBI Publications, pg 685
Flicks Books, pg 695
The Geographical Association, pg 699
GMP Publishers Ltd, pg 700
Grant & Cutler Ltd, pg 702
Gwasg Gwenffrwd, pg 703
Hilmarton Manor Press, pg 708
Angus Hudson Ltd, pg 710
Institute of Development Studies, pg 712
International Bee Research Association, pg 714
Manchester University Press, pg 724
Peter Marcan Publications, pg 725
Melrose Press Ltd, pg 726
National Library of Scotland, pg 731
Pen & Sword Books Ltd, pg 740
Plough Publishing House of Bruderhof Communities in the UK, pg 743
The Reader's Digest Association Ltd, pg 748
St Paul's Bibliographies Ltd, pg 753
School of Oriental & African Studies, pg 755
Taylor & Francis, pg 763
Thistle Press, pg 765
Thomson Gale, pg 765
Transport Bookman Publications Ltd, pg 766
Trigon Press, pg 767
Philip Wilson Publishers, pg 774

TYPE OF PUBLICATION INDEX — BOOK

Venezuela
Biblioteca Ayacucho, pg 779

Zimbabwe
National Archives of Zimbabwe, pg 784

BRAILLE BOOKS

China
China Braille Publishing House, pg 102
Qingdao Publishing House, pg 107

Czech Republic
Knihovna A Tiskarna Pro Nevidome, pg 124

Germany
Deutsche Blinden-Bibliothek, pg 211
Verlag Esoterische Philosophie GmbH, pg 221
Sturtz Verlag GmbH, pg 288

India
Nem Chand & Brothers, pg 343

Lithuania
Svietimo ir mokslo ministerijos Leidybos centras, pg 449

United Kingdom
Scottish Braille Press, pg 755

Zimbabwe
Dorothy Duncan Braille & Transcription Library, pg 783

CD-ROM, ELECTRONIC BOOKS

Albania
State Textbook Publishing House, pg 1

Argentina
Abeledo-Perrot SAE e I, pg 2
Laffont Ediciones Electronicas SA, pg 7
San Pablo, pg 9

Australia
Artmoves Inc, pg 12
Australian Institute of Family Studies (AIFS), pg 13
Blackwell Publishing Asia, pg 15
Board of Studies, pg 15
Butterworths Australia Ltd, pg 16
China Books, pg 17
Chiron Media, pg 17
CSIRO Publishing (Commonwealth Scientific & Industrial Research Organisation), pg 19
D&B Marketing Pty Ltd, pg 19
Emerald City Books, pg 21
Encyclopaedia Britannica (Australia) Inc, pg 21
Era Publications, pg 21
Flora Publications International Pty Ltd, pg 22
Gangan Publishing, pg 23
Hampden Press, pg 24
Law Book Co Information Services, pg 28
New Creation Publications Ministries & Resource Centre, pg 33
Pascal Press, pg 36
Price Publishing, pg 37
Rankin Publishers, pg 39
Reed Educational Publishing Australia, pg 39
Regency Publishing, pg 39
Spinifex Press, pg 42
Standards Association of Australia, pg 42
State Library of NSW Press, pg 42
Thames & Hudson (Australia) Pty Ltd, pg 43
Thorpe-Bowker, pg 43

Austria
Abakus Verlag GmbH, pg 48
Braintrust Marketing Services Ges mbH Verlag, pg 49
Compass-Verlag GmbH, pg 49
Herold Business Data AG, pg 52
Linde Verlag Wien GmbH, pg 53
Verlag der Oesterreichischen Akademie der Wissenschaften (OEAW), pg 55
Verlag des Oesterreichischen Gewerkschaftsbundes GmbH, pg 55
Oesterreichischer Kunst und Kulturverlag, pg 55

Bangladesh
Gatidhara, pg 61

Belgium
Brepols Publishers NV, pg 64
Etablissements Emile Bruylant SA, pg 64
Campinia Media VZW, pg 64
Editions De Boeck-Larcier SA, pg 66
Easy Computing NV, pg 67
Koepel van de Vlaamse Noord - Zuidbeweging 11.11.11, pg 69
Uitgeverij Lannoo NV, pg 69
Larcier-Department of De Boeck & Larcier SA, pg 70
Wolters Kluwer Belgie NV, pg 74

Brazil
Comissao Nacional de Energia Nuclear (CNEN), pg 80
Editora Companhia das Letras/Editora Schwarcz Ltda, pg 80
Companhia Editora Forense, pg 81
Empresa Brasileira de Pesquisa Agropecuaria, pg 81
Hemus Editora Ltda, pg 83
Horus Editora Ltda, pg 83
Libreria Editora Ltda, pg 85
Editora Moderna Ltda, pg 86
Editora Nova Fronteira SA, pg 87
Saraiva SA, Livreiros Editores, pg 90

Bulgaria
Ciela Publishing House, pg 93
DATAMAP - Europe, pg 94
Interpres, pg 95

Chile
Norma de Chile, pg 99

China
Aviation Industry Press, pg 101
Beijing Publishing House, pg 101
Chemical Industry Press, pg 101
China Ocean Press, pg 102
Cultural Relics Publishing House, pg 103
Electronics Industry Publishing House, pg 104
Fudan University Press, pg 104
Higher Education Press, pg 105
Jilin Science & Technology Publishing House, pg 105
Patent Documentation Publishing House, pg 106
People's Education Press, pg 106
Qingdao Publishing House, pg 107
Shandong University Press, pg 108
Shanghai Foreign Language Education Press, pg 108
Tsinghua University Press, pg 109
Wuhan University Press, pg 109

Colombia
Centro Regional para el Fomento del Libro en America Latina y el Caribe, pg 110

Costa Rica
Centro Agronomico Tropical de Investigacion y Ensenanza (CATIE), pg 115
Union Mundial para la Naturaleza (UICN), Oficina Regional para Mesoamerica, pg 116

Croatia
Masmedia, pg 118

Cuba
Casa Editora Abril, pg 120
Instituto de Informacion Cientifica y Tecnologica (IDICT), pg 120

Czech Republic
Diderot sro, pg 123
Libri spol sro, pg 125
Narodni Knihovna CR, pg 126
Cesky normalizacni institut, pg 126

Denmark
Atuakkiorfik A/S Det Greenland Publishers, pg 129
Djof Publishing Jurist-og Okonomforbundets Forlag, pg 130
Christian Ejlers' Forlag aps, pg 131
Gads Forlag, pg 131
Kraks Forlag AS, pg 132
Scandinavia Publishing House, pg 134
Schultz Information, pg 134
A/S Skattekartoteket, pg 134
Systime, pg 135
Forlaget Thomson A/S, pg 135

Estonia
Academic Library of Tallinn Pedagogical University, pg 139
Eesti Piibliselts, pg 139
Eesti Rahvusraamatukogu, pg 139

Finland
Building Information Ltd, pg 141
Kirja-Leitzinger, pg 142
Otava Publishing Co Ltd, pg 143

France
ACR Edition, pg 145
Agence Bibliographique de l'Enseignement Superieur, pg 146
Editions de l'Atelier, pg 148
Atelier National de Reproduction des Theses, pg 148
Bibliotheque Nationale de France, pg 150
Cirad, pg 154
Codes Rousseau, pg 155
Editions Dalloz Sirey, pg 157
Editions La Decouverte, pg 157
Elsevier SAS (Editions Scientifiques et Medicales Elsevier), pg 161
Encyclopedia Universalis France SA, pg 161
Flammarion SA, pg 163
Association Frank, pg 164
Hachette Education, pg 166
Joly Editions, pg 169
Le Livre de Paris, pg 173
Editions de la Reunion des Musees Nationaux, pg 176
Association d'Editions Sorg, pg 186
Editions Springer France, pg 186
Sybex, pg 186

Germany
A Francke Verlag (Tubingen und Basel), pg 190
ABC der Deutschen Wirtschaft, Verlagsgesellschaft mbH, pg 190
ARCult Media, pg 193
Asgard-Verlag Dr Werner Hippe GmbH, pg 194
Bank-Verlag GmbH, pg 197
Verlag C H Beck oHG, pg 198
Verlag Beleke KG, pg 198
Belser Wissenschaftlicher Dienst, pg 199
Bergverlag Rother GmbH, pg 199
Bertelsmann Lexikon Verlag GmbH, pg 200
W Bertelsmann Verlag GmbH & Co KG, pg 200
Bibliographisches Institut & F A Brockhaus AG, pg 200
BW Bildung und Wissen Verlag und Software GmbH, pg 201
Blackwell Wissenschafts-Verlag GmbH, pg 201
Bock und Herchen Verlag, pg 202
Born-Verlag, pg 203
Oscar Brandstetter Verlag GmbH & Co KG, pg 204
R Brockhaus Verlag, pg 204
Bundesanzeiger Verlagsgesellschaft, pg 206
Chmielorz GmbH Verlag, pg 208
Compact Verlag GmbH, pg 209
Cornelsen Verlag GmbH & Co OHG, pg 210
Cornelsen Verlag Scriptor GmbH & Co KG, pg 210
Corona Verlag, pg 210
Data Becker GmbH & Co KG, pg 210
Datacom Buchverlag GmbH, pg 211
Degener & Co, Manfred Dreiss Verlag, pg 211
Verlag Horst Deike KG, pg 211
Verlag Harri Deutsch, pg 211
Deutsche Blinden-Bibliothek, pg 211
Deutscher Adressbuch-Verlag fuer Wirtschaft und Verkehr GmbH, pg 212
Deutscher Apotheker Verlag Dr Roland Schmiedel GmbH & Co, pg 212
Deutscher Instituts-Verlag GmbH, pg 213
Die Verlag H Schafer GmbH, pg 214
DSI Data Service & Information, pg 217
Ecomed Verlagsgesellschaft AG & Co KG, pg 218
Econ Taschenbuchverlag, pg 218

PUBLISHERS

Econ Verlag GmbH, pg 218
Egmont vgs verlagsgesellschaft mbH, pg 218
Elsevier GmbH/Urban & Fischer Verlag, pg 219
Europ Export Edition GmbH, pg 221
Extent Verlag und Service Wolfgang M Flamm, pg 223
Festo Didactic GmbH & Co KG, pg 224
Verkehrs-Verlag J Fischer GmbH & Co KG, pg 224
Verlag Franz Vahlen GmbH, pg 226
Fraunhofer IRB Verlag Fraunhofer Informationszentrum Raum und Bau, pg 226
Betriebswirtschaftlicher Verlag Dr Th Gabler, pg 228
Verlag Ernst und Werner Gieseking GmbH, pg 229
Govi-Verlag Pharmazeutischer Verlag, pg 230
Walter de Gruyter GmbH & Co KG, pg 231
Carl Hanser Verlag, pg 234
Rudolf Haufe Verlag GmbH & Co KG, pg 235
Dr Ernst Hauswedell & Co, pg 235
F A Herbig Verlagsbuchhandlung GmbH, pg 236
Hestra-Verlag Hernichel & Dr Strauss GmbH & Co KG, pg 237
Carl Heymanns Verlag KG, pg 237
S Hirzel Verlag GmbH und Co, pg 238
Hoppenstedt GmbH & Co KG, pg 239
Huss-Medien GmbH, pg 240
Huss-Verlag GmbH, pg 240
Huthig GmbH & Co KG, pg 240
Impuls-Theater-Verlag, pg 241
Industrieschau Verlagsgesellschaft mbH, pg 241
International Thomson Publishing (ITP), pg 242
Iudicium Verlag GmbH, pg 242
SachBuchVerlag Kellner, pg 245
Verlag im Kilian GmbH, pg 246
Klages-Verlag, pg 246
Vittorio Klostermann GmbH, pg 247
Knowledge Media International, pg 247
W Kohlhammer GmbH, pg 248
kopaed verlagsgmbh, pg 249
Lahn-Verlag GmbH, pg 251
Logophon Verlag und Bildungsreisen GmbH, pg 255
Hermann Luchterhand Verlag GmbH, pg 255
Matthias-Gruenewald-Verlag GmbH, pg 258
Medpharm Scientific Publishers, pg 258
C F Mueller Verlag, Huethig GmbH & Co, pg 262
Munzinger-Archiv GmbH Archiv fuer publizistische Arbeit, pg 262
MVB Marketing- und Verlagsservice des Buchhandels GmbH, pg 263
Verlag Stephanie Naglschmid, pg 263
Naumann & Goebel Verlagsgesellschaft mbH, pg 263
Nebel Verlag GmbH, pg 263
Net World Vision GmbH, pg 263
Verlag Neue Wirtschafts-Briefe GmbH & Co, pg 264
Verlag Friedrich Oetinger GmbH, pg 266
Georg Olms Verlag AG, pg 267
Patmos Verlag GmbH & Co KG, pg 268
Pearson Education Deutschland GmbH, pg 268
Philipp Reclam Jun Verlag GmbH, pg 269
Philippka-Sportverlag, pg 269
pmi Verlag, pg 270
Polygraph Verlag GmbH, pg 271
Reed Elsevier Deutschland GmbH, pg 274
Rossipaul Kommunikation GmbH, pg 277
Verlag Werner Sachon GmbH & Co, pg 277
K G Saur Verlag GmbH, A Gale/Thomson Learning Company, pg 278
Schaeffer-Poeschel Verlag fuer Wirtschaft Steuern Recht, pg 279
Verlag der Schillerbuchhandlung Hans Banger OHG, pg 279
Schirner Verlag, pg 280
Verlag Dr Otto Schmidt KG, pg 280
Erich Schmidt Verlag GmbH & Co, pg 280
Siegler & Co Verlag fuer Zeitarchive GmbH, pg 283
Johannes Sonntag Verlagsbuchhandlung GmbH, pg 284
Springer Science+Business Media GmbH & Co KG, pg 284
Springer Science+Business Media GmbH & Co KG, Berlin, pg 285
Staatliche Museen Kassel, pg 286
Straelener Manuskripte Verlag GmbH, pg 288
Sybex Verlag GmbH, pg 289
Konrad Theiss Verlag GmbH, pg 290
Georg Thieme Verlag KG, pg 291
TR - Verlagsunion GmbH, pg 291
Trotzdem-Verlags Genossenschaft eG, pg 292
UNO-Verlag GmbH, pg 293
Friedr Vieweg & Sohn Verlag, pg 296
Vista Point Verlag GmbH, pg 296
Vogel Medien GmbH & Co KG, pg 296
Voggenreiter-Verlag, pg 296
Walhalla Fachverlag GmbH & Co KG Praetoria, pg 297
Waxmann Verlag GmbH, pg 297
WEKA Firmengruppe GmbH & Co KG, pg 298
Wer liefert was? GmbH, pg 299
Wiley-VCH Verlag GmbH, pg 300

Greece

Apostoliki Diakonia tis Ekklisias tis Hellados, pg 305
Ekdotike Athenon SA, pg 307
Hestia-I D Hestia-Kollaros & Co Corporation, pg 308
Kalentis & Sia, pg 308
Kastaniotis Editions SA, pg 309
Editions Moressopoulos, pg 310
Nomiki Bibliothiki, pg 310
Pagoulatos Bros, pg 311
Patakis Publishers, pg 311
Sakkoulas Publications SA, pg 312
Toubis M, pg 312

Hong Kong

The Chinese University Press, pg 316
Chung Hwa Book Co (HK) Ltd, pg 316
Joint Publishing (HK) Co Ltd, pg 317
Research Centre for Translation, pg 319
Witman Publishing Co (HK) Ltd, pg 320

Hungary

Aranyhal Konyvkiado Goldfish Publishing, pg 320
Balassi Kiado Kft, pg 321
KJK-Kerszov, pg 322
Kossuth Kiado RT, pg 322
Nemzeti Tankoenyvkiado, pg 323
Novorg International Szervezo es Kiado kft, pg 323
Panem, pg 324
Polgar Kiado Kft, pg 324

Iceland

Mal og menning, pg 326
Namsgagnastofnun, pg 326

India

Affiliated East West Press Pvt Ltd, pg 327
Law Publishers, pg 340
Nem Chand & Brothers, pg 343
Research Signpost, pg 347
Sita Books & Periodicals Pvt Ltd, pg 349
Spectrum Publications, pg 350
Transworld Research Network, pg 351
Vidyarthi Mithram Press, pg 352
A H Wheeler & Co Ltd, pg 353

Indonesia

Gramedia, pg 355
PT Indira, pg 355
Lembaga Demografi Fakultas Ekonomi Universitas Indonesia, pg 355

Ireland

Cathedral Books Ltd, pg 358

Israel

Academy of the Hebrew Language, pg 364
Agudat Sabah, pg 364
Bitan Publishers Ltd, pg 365
Carta, The Israel Map & Publishing Co Ltd, pg 365
Doko Video Ltd, pg 366
Israel Music Institute (IMI), pg 368
K Dictionaries Ltd, pg 369
Kernerman Publishing Ltd, pg 369
Open University of Israel, pg 371
Rolnik Publishers, pg 371
R Sirkis Publishers Ltd, pg 372

Italy

Umberto Allemandi & C SRL, pg 375
Editore Armando Armando SRL, pg 376
Arsenale Editrice SRL, pg 376
Casa Editrice Bonechi, pg 378
Bonsignori Editore SRL, pg 378
Istituto Centrale per il Catalogo Unico delle Biblioteche Italiane e per le Informazioni Bibliografiche, pg 381
Centro Biblico, pg 381
Centro Scientifico Torinese, pg 381
CIC Edizioni Internazionali, pg 381
Il Cigno Galileo Galilei-Edizioni di Arte e Scienza, pg 382
D'Anna, pg 384
Edizioni Studio Domenicano (ESD), pg 387
Editoriale Fernando Folini, pg 389
Gangemi Editore spa, pg 390
Istituto Geografico de Agostini SpA, pg 390
Liguori Editore SRL, pg 395
Manifestolibri, pg 397
Editoriale Olimpia SpA, pg 401
RAI-ERI, pg 405
Rusconi Libri Srl, pg 406
Il Saggiatore, pg 406
Sardini Editrice, pg 407
Scala Group spa, pg 407
SEMAR Publishers SRL, pg 408
Edizioni Librarie Siciliane, pg 408
Vivere In SRL, pg 412
Zanichelli Editore SpA, pg 412

Japan

Dobunshoin Publishers Co, pg 416
Gakken Co Ltd, pg 417
Igaku-Shoin Ltd, pg 419
International Society for Educational Information (ISEI), pg 419
Iwanami Shoten, Publishers, pg 419
Kinokuniya Co Ltd (Publishing Department), pg 421
Nakayama Shoten Co Ltd, pg 423
Nosangyoson Bunka Kyokai, pg 424
Ongaku No Tomo Sha Corporation, pg 425
Sanshusha Publishing Co, Ltd, pg 426
Seibido Shuppan Company Ltd, pg 426
Shincho-Sha Co Ltd, pg 427
Shogakukan Inc, pg 427
Springer-Verlag Tokyo, pg 428
Toho Book Store, pg 429
Tokyo Shoseki Co Ltd, pg 430
Yakuji Nippo Ltd, pg 431
Zeimukeiri-Kyokai, pg 431

Republic of Korea

Cheong-mun-gag Publishing Co, pg 438
Chung Rim Publishing Co Ltd, pg 438
Gim-Yeong Co, pg 438
Korea Britannica Corp, pg 440
Maeil Gyeongje, pg 441
Moon Jin Media Co Ltd, pg 441
Woongjin.com Co Ltd, pg 443
YBM/Si-sa, pg 443

Liechtenstein

Rheintal Handelsgesellschaft Anstalt, pg 448

Lithuania

Lithuanian National Museum Publishing House, pg 449
TEV Leidykla, pg 450

Luxembourg

Edition Objectif Lune, pg 451
Editions Promoculture, pg 451

The Former Yugoslav Republic of Macedonia

Medis, Skopje, pg 452

Malaysia

Malayan Law Journal Sdn Bhd, pg 456
Pustaka Cipta Sdn Bhd, pg 458

Mexico

Ibcon SA, pg 466
Instituto Nacional de Antropologia e Historia, pg 469

TYPE OF PUBLICATION INDEX   BOOK

Instituto Nacional de Estadistica, Geographia e Informatica, pg 469
Organizacion Cultural LP SA de CV, pg 469
Pearson Educacion de Mexico, SA de CV, pg 470
SCRIPTA - Distribucion y Servicios Editoriales, SA de CV, pg 471

Netherlands

Brill Academic Publishers, pg 479
A W Bruna Uitgevers BV, pg 480
Elmar BV, pg 482
Uitgeverij Elzenga, pg 482
Hagen & Stam Uitgeverij Ten, pg 483
Katholieke Bijbelstichting, pg 484
Kluwer Academic Publishers, pg 484
Kluwer Law International, pg 485
Koninklijke Vermande bv, pg 485
Uitgeverij Lemma BV, pg 485
Uitgeverij Leopold BV, pg 485
Uitgeverij H Nelissen BV, pg 486
Tirion Uitgevers BV, pg 490
Van Dale Lexicografie BV, pg 491

New Zealand

Brookers Ltd, pg 494
CCH New Zealand Ltd, pg 495
Learning Media Ltd, pg 498
Nelson Price Milburn Ltd, pg 499

Norway

Elanders Publishing AS, pg 509
Fono Forlag, pg 509

Paraguay

Instituto de Ciencias de la Computacion (NCR), pg 516

Poland

Wydawnictwo DiG, pg 522
Polish Scientific Publishers PWN, pg 525
PZWL Wydawnictwo Lekarskie Ltd, pg 526
Wydawnictwa Szkolne i Pedagogiczne, pg 527

Portugal

Constancia Editores, SA, pg 530

Romania

Alcor-Edimpex (Verlag) Ltd, pg 538
The Center for Romanian Studies, pg 539
Editura Militara, pg 541
Editura Muzicala, pg 541
Rentrop & Straton Verlagsgruppe und Wirtschaftsconsulting, pg 542

Russian Federation

FGUP Izdatelstvo Mashinostroenie, pg 544
INFRA-M Izdatel'skij dom, pg 545
Izdatelstvo Prosveshchenie, pg 548

Serbia and Montenegro

Izdavacko Preduzece Matice Srpske, pg 553

Singapore

Archipelago Press, pg 555
Daiichi Media Pte Ltd, pg 555
LexisNexis, pg 557
McGallen & Bolden Associates, pg 557

Shing Lee Group Publishers, pg 558
Tecman Bible House, pg 558

Slovakia

Ustav informacii a prognoz skolstva mladeze a telovychovy, pg 561

Slovenia

Mladinska Knjiga International, pg 561

South Africa

Juta & Co, pg 565
South African Institute of International Affairs, pg 569
Van Schaik Publishers, pg 569

Spain

Editorial AEDOS SA, pg 571
Ediciones Agrotecnicas, SL, pg 571
Anaya Educacion, pg 573
Editorial Aranzadi SA, pg 573
Editorial Astri SA, pg 573
Bosch Casa Editorial SA, pg 575
Calesa SA Editorial La, pg 575
CEAC, Grupo Editorial SA, pg 576
Complutense, SA Editorial, pg 577
Didaco Comunicacion y Didactica, SA, pg 579
Durvan SA de Ediciones, pg 580
Esic Editorial, pg 582
Editorial Espasa-Calpe SA, pg 582
Fundacion Coleccion Thyssen-Bornemisza, pg 584
Ibaizabal Edelvives SA, pg 586
Idea Books, SA, pg 587
Larousse Editorial SA, pg 588
LID Editorial Empresarial, SL, pg 589
Editorial Luis Vives (Edelvives), pg 589
Marcombo SA, pg 590
Mundi-Prensa Libros SA, pg 592
Editorial Parthenon Communication, SL, pg 595
Pentalfa Ediciones, pg 595
Pronaos, SA Ediciones, pg 597
Pulso Ediciones, SL, pg 597
San Pablo Ediciones, pg 598
Servicio de Publicaciones Universidad de Cordoba, pg 599
Editorial Sal Terrae, pg 602
Tesitex, SL, pg 602

Sweden

Ekelunds Forlag AB, pg 611
Hallgren och Fallgren Studieforlag AB, pg 612
Hans Richter Laromedel, pg 613
Norstedts Juridik, pg 614
Norstedts Ordbok, pg 614
Studentlitteratur AB, pg 616

Switzerland

Bibellesbund Verlag, pg 619
Verlag Harri Deutsch, pg 622
Helbing und Lichtenhahn Verlag AG, pg 625
Verlag Industrielle Organisation, pg 625
La Maison de la Bible, pg 628
Presses Polytechniques et Universitaires Romandes, PPUR, pg 631
Verlag fuer Recht und Gesellschaft AG, pg 632
Schwabe & Co AG, pg 633
Schweizerisches Jugendschriftenwerk, SJW, pg 634

Theologischer Verlag und Buchhandlungen AG, pg 635
Vdf Hochschulverlag AG an der ETH Zurich, pg 636

Taiwan, Province of China

Kuang Fu Book Co Ltd, pg 640
Lead Wave Publishing Company Ltd, pg 640
Lee & Lee Communications, pg 641
Shuttle Multimedia Inc, pg 641
Sinorama Magazine Co, pg 641
The Third Wave Enterprise Co Ltd, pg 642
Wu Nan Book Co Ltd, pg 642

United Republic of Tanzania

Bureau of Statistics, pg 643

Thailand

Thai Watana Panich Co, Ltd, pg 646

Tunisia

Editions Techniques Specialisees, pg 648

Turkey

Alkim Kitapcilik-Yayimcilik, pg 649
Bilden Bilgisayar, pg 649
IKI Nokta Research Press & Publications Industry & Trade Ltd, pg 650
Soez Yayin/Oyunajans, pg 651

United Kingdom

ABC-CLIO, pg 654
Advisory Unit: Computers in Education, pg 655
Ai Interactive Ltd, pg 656
Umberto Allemandi & Co Publishing, pg 656
Anderson Rand Ltd, pg 657
Arnold, pg 659
Art Sales Index Ltd, pg 659
Aslib, The Association for Information Management, pg 660
Avero Publications Ltd, pg 662
BBC English, pg 663
Belitha Press Ltd, pg 664
Berlitz (UK) Ltd, pg 665
Blackwell Science Ltd, pg 667
Books for Europe Ltd, pg 669
Business Monitor International, pg 672
Chadwyck-Healey Ltd, pg 677
Chambers Harrap Publishers Ltd, pg 677
Chapter Two, pg 678
The Chartered Institute of Public Finance & Accountancy, pg 678
Child's World Education Ltd, pg 679
Chorion IP, pg 679
Coachwise Ltd, pg 680
Peter Collin Publishing Ltd, pg 680
Computer Step, pg 681
Croner CCH Group Ltd, pg 684
CSA (Cambridge Scientific Abstracts), pg 684
D&B Ltd, pg 685
The Economist Intelligence Unit, pg 689
Electronic Publishing Services Ltd (EPS), pg 690
Encyclopaedia Britannica (UK) International Ltd, pg 691
Estates Gazette, pg 692
Ethics International Press Ltd, pg 692

First & Best in Education Ltd, pg 695
Folens Ltd, pg 695
Geological Society Publishing House, pg 699
W Green The Scottish Law Publisher, pg 702
HarperCollins UK, pg 705
Helicon Publishing Ltd, pg 707
Hobsons, pg 709
Lawpack Publishing Ltd, pg 719
Letterbox Library, pg 720
Linguaphone Institute Ltd, pg 721
Macmillan Ltd, pg 723
Mandrake of Oxford, pg 725
McCrimmon Publishing Co Ltd, pg 726
Microform Academic Publishers, pg 728
National Council for Voluntary Organisations (NCVO), pg 730
NMS Enterprises Ltd - Publishing, pg 733
Oilfield Publications Ltd, pg 734
Orion Publishing Group Ltd, pg 736
Pavilion Publishing (Brighton) Ltd, pg 739
Pharmaceutical Press, pg 741
PJB Reference Sevices, pg 743
The Playwrights Publishing Co, pg 743
Plough Publishing House of Bruderhof Communities in the UK, pg 743
ProQuest Information & Learning, pg 746
Rapra Technology Ltd, pg 748
Retail Entertainment Data Publishing Ltd, pg 750
RICS Books, pg 750
Roundhouse Group, pg 751
The Rutland Press, pg 752
SAGE Publications Ltd, pg 753
Silver Link Publishing Ltd, pg 758
Sports Turf Research Institute (STRI), pg 760
Stainer & Bell Ltd, pg 761
Sweet & Maxwell Ltd, pg 762
Taylor & Francis, pg 763
Telegraph Books, pg 764
TFPL, pg 764
Thomson Gale, pg 765
Tobin Music, pg 766
TSO (The Stationery Office), pg 767
Two-Can Publishing Ltd, pg 768
University of Wales Press, pg 769
VNU Business Publications, pg 770
Websters International Publishers Ltd, pg 772
Wilmington Business Information Ltd, pg 774
World Microfilms Publications Ltd, pg 775
Yale University Press London, pg 776

Uruguay

EQ Opciones en Educacion, pg 777
La Flor del Itapebi, pg 777

Viet Nam

Science & Technics Publishing House, pg 780

CHILDREN'S BOOKS

Albania

Fan Noli Verlag Rexhep Hida, pg 1
NL SH, pg 1

PUBLISHERS

Algeria
Les Editions Algeriennes En-Nahdha, pg 2

Argentina
Editorial Abril SA, pg 2
Editorial Albatros SACI, pg 3
Argentine Bible Society, pg 3
Editorial Atlantida SA, pg 3
Beas Ediciones SRL, pg 4
Bonum Editorial SACI, pg 4
Editorial Caymi SACI, pg 4
Cesarini Hermanos, pg 4
Editorial Ciudad Nueva de la Sefoma, pg 4
Diana Argentina SA, Editorial, pg 5
Editorial Ruy Diaz SAEIC, pg 5
Ediciones Don Bosco Argentina, pg 5
Ediciones del Eclipse, pg 5
Emece Editores SA, pg 5
Errepar SA, pg 5
Angel Estrada y Cia SA, pg 5
Ediciones de la Flor SRL, pg 6
Editorial Guadalupe, pg 6
Libreria Huemul SA, pg 6
Librograf Editora, pg 7
Editorial Losada SA, pg 7
Ediciones LR SA, pg 7
Editorial Norte SA, pg 8
Editorial Plus Ultra SA, pg 8
Ediciones Preescolar SA, pg 8
San Pablo, pg 9
Editorial Sigmar SACI, pg 9
Editorial Sopena Argentina SACI e I, pg 9
Editorial Sudamericana SA, pg 9

Armenia
Arevik, pg 10

Australia
ABC Books (Australian Broadcasting Corporation), pg 10
Aboriginal Studies Press, pg 10
Access Press, pg 10
Allen & Unwin Pty Ltd, pg 11
Bandicoot Books, pg 14
Bible Society in Australia National Headquarters, pg 14
Boinkie Publishers, pg 15
Childerset Publishers, pg 17
China Books, pg 17
R J Cleary Publishing, pg 18
Coolabah Publishing, pg 18
Crawford House Publishing Pty Ltd, pg 18
Crossroad Distributors Pty Ltd, pg 18
D'Artagnan Publishing, pg 19
Dragon Press, pg 20
Edwina Publishing, pg 21
Egan Publishing Pty Ltd, pg 21
David Ell Press Pty Ltd, pg 21
Encyclopaedia Britannica (Australia) Inc, pg 21
Era Publications, pg 21
The Five Mile Press Pty Ltd, pg 22
Fremantle Arts Centre Press, pg 23
Great Western Press Pty Ltd, pg 24
Greater Glider Productions Australia Pty Ltd, pg 24
Geoffrey Hamlyn-Harris, pg 24
HarperCollinsReligious, pg 25
Hartys Creek Press, pg 25
Roland Harvey Studios, pg 25
Hodder Headline Australia, pg 26
Institute of Aboriginal Development (IAD Press), pg 27
Kangaroo Press, pg 28
Little Red Apple Publishing, pg 29
Thomas C Lothian Pty Ltd, pg 29
Macmillan Education Australia, pg 30
Magabala Books Aboriginal Corporation, pg 30
Margaret Hamilton Books Pty Ltd, pg 30
J M McGregor Pty Ltd, pg 31
Mimosa Publications Pty Ltd, pg 32
Mountain House Press, pg 32
New Era Publications Australia Pty Ltd, pg 33
Newman Centre Publications, pg 33
Off the Shelf Publishing, pg 34
Omnibus Books, pg 34
Pan Macmillan Australia Pty Ltd, pg 35
Papyrus Publishing, pg 35
Pearson Education Australia, pg 36
Penguin Group (Australia), pg 36
Plantagenet Press, pg 37
Rainforest Publishing, pg 38
Rams Skull Press, pg 38
Random House Australia, pg 38
Reed Educational Publishing Australia, pg 39
Reed for Kids, pg 39
St Joseph Publications, pg 40
St Pauls Publications, pg 40
Simon & Schuster (Australia) Pty Ltd, pg 41
Social Club Books, pg 41
Tarka Publishing, pg 42
Troll Books of Australia, pg 44
University of Queensland Press, pg 45
University of Western Australia Press, pg 45
The Useful Publishing Co, pg 45
Vista Publications, pg 45
Vital Publications, pg 45
Franklin Watts Australia, pg 46
Windhorse Books, pg 47
Wizard Books Pty Ltd, pg 47

Austria
Astor-Verlag, Willibald Schlager, pg 48
Annette Betz Verlag im Verlag Carl Ueberreuter, pg 48
DachsVerlag GmbH, pg 49
Denkmayr GmbH Druck & Verlag, pg 50
Development News Ltd, pg 50
Edition Ergo Sum, pg 50
Edition Graphischer Zirkel, pg 51
Verlag Jungbrunnen - Wiener Spielzeugschachtel GesellschaftmbH, pg 52
Verlag Kerle im Verlag Herder & Co, pg 53
Edition Koenigstein, pg 53
Mangold Kinderbucher, pg 53
Edition Neues Marchen, pg 54
Niederosterreichisches Pressehaus Druck- und Verlagsgesellschaft mbH, pg 54
Obelisk-Verlag, pg 55
oebv & hpt Verlagsgesellschaft mbH & Co KG, pg 55
Oesterreichischer Kunst und Kulturverlag, pg 55
Richard Pils Publication PN°1, pg 56
J Steinbrener OHG, pg 58
Edition Thurnhof KEG, pg 58
Verlag Carl Ueberreuter GmbH, pg 58

Azerbaijan
Sada, Literaturno-Izdatel'skij Centr, pg 60

Bangladesh
Ankur Prakashani, pg 61
Bangladesh Publishers, pg 61
Gatidhara, pg 61
Agamee Prakashani, pg 61
The University Press Ltd, pg 61

Belarus
Interdigest Publishing House, pg 62
Kavaler Publishers, pg 62
Narodnaya Asveta, pg 62

Belgium
Abimo, pg 62
Altina, pg 63
Maison d'Editions Baha'ies ASBL, pg 63
Bakermat NV, pg 63
Editions Gerard Blanchart & Cie SA, pg 63
Caramel, Uitgeverij, pg 64
Editions Casterman SA, pg 65
Editions Chantecler, pg 65
Uitgeverij Clavis, pg 65
Conservart SA, pg 65
Davidsfonds Uitgeverij NV, pg 66
Editions Delta SA, pg 66
Uitgeverij de Eenhoorn, pg 67
Facet NV, pg 67
Graton Editeur NV, pg 68
Editions Hemma, pg 68
IMPS SA, pg 68
Koepel van de Vlaamse Noord - Zuidbeweging 11.11.11, pg 69
Uitgeverij Lannoo NV, pg 69
Claude Lefrancq Editeur, pg 70
Parasol NV, pg 71
Rainbow Grafics Intl - Baronian Books SC, pg 72
Scaillet, SA, pg 73
Uitgeverij De Sikkel NV, pg 73
Standaard Uitgeverij, pg 73
Uitgeverij Averbode NV, pg 74
Zuid En Noord VZW, pg 75
Zuid-Nederlandse Uitgeverij NV/Central Uitgeverij, pg 75

Benin
Les Editions du Flamboyant, pg 75

Bermuda
The Bermudian Publishing Co, pg 75

Bosnia and Herzegovina
Bemust, pg 76

Brazil
A & A & A Edicoes e Promocoes Internacionais Ltda, pg 76
Agalma Psicanalise Editora Ltda, pg 77
AGIR S/A Editora, pg 77
Livraria Alema Ltda Brasileitura, pg 77
Editora Alfa Omega Ltda, pg 77
Editora Antroposofica Ltda, pg 77
Ao Livro Tecnico Industria e Comercio Ltda, pg 77
Associacao Arvore da Vida, pg 78
Editora Atica SA, pg 78
Editora Brasil-America (EBAL) SA, pg 79
Brinque Book Editora de Livros Ltda, pg 79
Callis Editora Ltda, pg 79
Centro de Estudos Juridicosdo Para (CEJUP), pg 79
Editora Companhia das Letras/Editora Schwarcz Ltda, pg 80
Concordia Editora Ltda, pg 80
Conquista, Empresa de Publicacoes Ltda, pg 80
Edicon Editora e Consultorial Ltda, pg 81
Editora Elevacao, pg 81
Livraria Martins Fontes Editora Ltda, pg 81
Formato Editorial ltda, pg 82
Global Editora e Distribuidora Ltda, pg 82
Editora Globo SA, pg 82
Editora e Grafica Carisio Ltda, Minas Editora, pg 83
Grafica Editora Primor Ltda, pg 83
Editora Harbra Ltda, pg 83
Imago Editora Importacao e Exportacao Ltda, pg 84
Editora Kuarup Ltda, pg 84
Editora Leitura Ltda, pg 84
Livraria Nobel S/A, pg 85
Edicoes Loyola SA, pg 85
Editora Manole Ltda, pg 86
Editora Meca Ltda, pg 86
Editora Melhoramentos Ltda, pg 86
Memorias Futuras Edicoes Ltda, pg 86
Editora Mercado Aberto Ltda, pg 86
Editora Moderna Ltda, pg 86
Editora Mundo Cristao, pg 87
Companhia Editora Nacional, pg 87
Editora Nova Fronteira SA, pg 87
Edit Palavra Magica, pg 88
Pallas Editora e Distribuidora Ltda, pg 88
Paulinas Editorial, pg 88
Paulus Editora, pg 88
Livraria Pioneira Editora/Enio Matheus Guazzelli e Cia Ltd, pg 88
Editora Primor Ltda, pg 89
Ediouro Publicacoes, SA, pg 89
Qualitymark Editora Ltda, pg 89
Editora Revan Ltda, pg 89
RHJ Livros Ltda, pg 89
Editora Rocco Ltda, pg 89
Salamandra Consultoria Editorial SA, pg 89
Editora Santuario, pg 90
Editora Scipione Ltda, pg 90
Editora Sinodal, pg 90
Sobrindes Linha Grafica E Editora Ltda, pg 90
Thex Editora e Distribuidora Ltda, pg 91
34 Literatura S/C Ltda, pg 91
Totalidade Editora Ltda, pg 91
Editora Vigilia Ltda, pg 92
Zip Editora Ltda, pg 92

Bulgaria
Abagar Pablioing, pg 92
Aleks Print Publishing House, pg 93
Antroposofsko Izdatelstvo Dimo R Daskalov OOD, pg 93
Bulgarski Houdozhnik Publishers, pg 93
Hristo G Danov State Publishing House, pg 93
Fama, pg 94
Fondacija Zlatno Kljuce, pg 94
Hermes Publishing House, pg 94
Heron Press Publishing House, pg 94
Izdatelstvo Lettera, pg 95
Pejo K Javorov Publishing House, pg 95
Kibea Publishing Co, pg 95
Kralica MAB, pg 95
MATEX, pg 95
Mladezh IK, pg 95
Musica Publishing House Ltd, pg 95

TYPE OF PUBLICATION INDEX   BOOK

Pet Plus, pg 96
Prosveta Publishers AS, pg 96
Prozoretz Ltd Publishing House, pg 96
Sanra Book Trust, pg 96
Seven Hills Publishers, pg 96
Slavena, pg 97
Sluntse Publishing House, pg 97
Svetra Publishing House, pg 97
TEMTO, pg 97
Trud - Izd kasta, pg 97
Ivan Vazov Publishing House, pg 97
Zunica, pg 97

Burundi
Editions Intore, pg 98

Cameroon
Editions Buma Kor & Co Ltd, pg 98

Chile
Arrayan Editores, pg 98
Norma de Chile, pg 99
Editorial Patris SA, pg 100
Pehuen Editores Ltda, pg 100
J.C. Saez Editor, pg 100
Ediciones Universitarias de Valparaiso, pg 100
Zig-Zag SA, pg 101

China
Anhui Children's Publishing House, pg 101
Beijing Juvenile & Children's Books Publishing House, pg 101
Beijing Publishing House, pg 101
China Film Press, pg 102
China Ocean Press, pg 102
Dolphin Books, pg 104
Education Science Publishing House, pg 104
Foreign Languages Press, pg 104
Fujian Children's Publishing House, pg 104
Guizhou Education Publishing House, pg 105
Heilongjiang Science & Technology Press, pg 105
Jilin Science & Technology Publishing House, pg 105
Jinan Publishing House, pg 105
Language Publishing House, pg 106
Morning Glory Press, pg 106
People's Education Press, pg 106
People's Fine Arts Publishing House, pg 106
Qingdao Publishing House, pg 107
Science Press, pg 107
Shandong Friendship Publishing House, pg 107
Shanghai Educational Publishing House, pg 108
Shanghai People's Fine Arts Publishing House, pg 108
Tomorrow Publishing House, pg 109
Writers' Publishing House, pg 109
Zhejiang Education Publishing House, pg 109

Colombia
Amazonas Editores Ltda, pg 110
Eurolibros Ltda, pg 111
Kapelusz Ltda Editorial, pg 111
Lito Technion Ltda, pg 112
Migema Ediciones Ltda, pg 112
Editorial Norma SA, pg 112
Editorial Oveja Negra Ltda, pg 112
Editorial Panamericana, pg 112

Editorial Santillana SA, pg 112
Carlos Valencia Editores, pg 113

The Democratic Republic of the Congo
Saint-Paul, pg 114

Costa Rica
Ediciones Promesa, pg 116
Editorial de la Universidad de Costa Rica, pg 116
Editorial Universitaria Centroamericana (EDUCA), pg 117

Cote d'Ivoire
Akohi Editions, pg 117
Centre de Publications Evangeliques, pg 117

Croatia
ALFA dd za izdavacke, graficke i trgovacke poslove, pg 117
Graficki zavod Hrvatske, pg 118
Matica hrvatska, pg 118
Nasa Djeca Publishing, pg 119
Znaci Vremena, Institut Za Istrazivanje Biblije, pg 119
Znanje d d, pg 119

Cuba
Casa Editora Abril, pg 120
Editorial Gente Nueva, pg 120
Editorial Oriente, pg 120

Czech Republic
Albatros AS, pg 122
Aurora, pg 122
Aventinum Nakladatelstvi spol sro, pg 122
Bakalar spol sro, pg 122
Ceska Biblicka Spolecnost, pg 123
Doplnek, pg 123
Erika spol sro, pg 123
Granit sro, pg 123
Iuventus, pg 124
Nakladatelstvi Jan Vasut, pg 124
Nakladatelstvi Jota spol sro, pg 124
Kalich SRO, pg 124
Karmelitanske Nakladatelstvi, pg 124
Konsultace spol sro, pg 125
Mariadan, pg 125
Mlada fronta, pg 125
Nava, pg 126
Pressfoto Vydavatelstvi Ceske Tiskove Kancelare, pg 127
NS Svoboda spol sro, pg 127
Touzimsky & Moravec, pg 127
Ladislav Vasicek, pg 128

Denmark
Agertofts Forlag A/S, pg 128
Alinea A/S, pg 128
Alma, pg 128
Forlaget alokke AS, pg 129
Forlaget Apostrof ApS, pg 129
Aschehoug Dansk Forlag A/S, pg 129
Atuakkiorfik A/S Det Greenland Publishers, pg 129
Bierman og Bierman I/S, pg 129
Bogfabrikken Fakta ApS, pg 129
Bonnier Publications A/S, pg 129
Borgens Forlag A/S, pg 129
Bornegudstjeneste-Forlaget, pg 129
Forlaget Carlsen A/S, pg 130
The Danish Literature Centre, pg 130
Egmont Serieforlaget A/S, pg 130

Forlaget Forum, pg 131
P Haase & Sons Forlag A/S, pg 131
Forlaget Hjulet, pg 132
Host & Son Publishers Ltd, pg 132
Forlaget Klematis A/S, pg 132
Lohse Forlag, pg 132
Mellemfolkeligt Samvirke, pg 133
Scandinavia Publishing House, pg 134
Sommer & Sorensen, pg 134
Unitas Forlag, pg 135
Wisby & Wilkens, pg 135

Egypt (Arab Republic of Egypt)
Al Arab Publishing House, pg 137
Dar Al-Kitab Al-Masri, pg 137
Dar Al-Matbo at Al-Gadidah, pg 138
Dar Al-Thakafia Publishing, pg 138
Dar El Shorouk, pg 138
The Egyptian Society for the Dissemination of Universal Culture and Knowledge (ESDUCK), pg 138
Elias Modern Publishing House, pg 138
Dar Al Maaref, pg 138

El Salvador
Clasicos Roxsil Editorial SA de CV, pg 138

Estonia
Eesti Entsuklopeediakirjastus, pg 139
Eesti Piibliselts, pg 139
Kirjastus Kunst, pg 139
Kupar Publishers, pg 139
Oue Eesti Raamat, pg 140
Sinisukk, pg 140
Tuum, pg 140
Valgus Publishers, pg 140

Finland
Forsamlingsforbundets Forlags AB, pg 142
Kustannus Oy Kolibri, pg 143
Kustannus Oy Semic, pg 143
Kustannus Oy Uusi Tie, pg 143
Kustannusosakeyhtio Tammi, pg 143
Lasten Keskus Oy, pg 143
Otava Publishing Co Ltd, pg 143
Schildts Forlags AB, pg 144
SV-Kauppiaskanava Oy, pg 144

France
Actes-Graphiques, pg 145
Editions d'Annabelle, pg 147
Armenia Editions, pg 147
Editions de l'Atelier, pg 148
Autrement Editions, pg 148
Editions A Barthelemy, pg 149
Societe Biblique Francaise, pg 150
Editions Andre Bonne, pg 150
Bookmaker, pg 150
Emgleo Breiz, pg 151
Editions BRGM, pg 151
Brud Nevez, pg 151
Editions Buchet-Chastel Pierre Zech Editeur, pg 151
Editions Casterman, pg 152
Editions du Cerf, pg 153
Dargaud, pg 157
Jean-P Delville Editions, pg 157
Dessain et Tolra SA, pg 158
Les Editions des Deux Coqs d'Or, pg 158
Les Devenirs Visuels, pg 158
Disney Hachette Edition, pg 158
Editions ELOR, pg 160

Editions Farel, pg 162
FBT de R Editions, pg 163
Librairie Fischbacher, International Art Book Distribution (import-export), pg 163
Flammarion SA, pg 163
Editions Fleurus, pg 163
Gammaprim, pg 165
Editions Jean Paul Gisserot, pg 165
Editions Grandir, pg 166
Hachette Jeunesse Image, pg 166
Hachette Jeunesse Roman, pg 166
L'Harmattan, pg 167
Editions Hatier SA, pg 167
Editions Kaleidoscope, pg 170
Editions Larousse, pg 171
Editions des Limbes d'Or FBT de R Editions, pg 172
Editions Lito, pg 172
Les Livres du Dragon d'Or, pg 173
LLB France (Ligue pour la Lecture de la Bible), pg 173
Editions Josette Lyon, pg 173
Editions Mango, pg 174
Editions Mediaspaul, pg 175
Editions Memo, pg 175
Editions Albin Michel, pg 175
Editions de la Reunion des Musees Nationaux, pg 176
Editions Nord-Sud, pg 177
Association Paris-Musees, pg 179
Editions du Centre Pompidou, pg 180
Les Presses d'Ile-de-France Sarl, pg 181
Editions du Rouergue, pg 183
Association d'Editions Sorg, pg 186
Ulisse Editions, pg 188
La Vague a l'ame, pg 188
Librairie Vuibert, pg 189

French Polynesia
Scoop/Au Vent des Iles, pg 189
Haere Po Editions, pg 189
Simone Sanchez, pg 190

Germany
Abakus Musik Barbara Fietz, pg 190
Agentur des Rauhen Hauses Hamburg GmbH, pg 191
Albarello Verlag GmbH, pg 191
Altberliner Verlag GmbH, pg 192
Anrich Verlag GmbH, pg 192
Antex Verlag-Hans Joachin Schuhmacher, pg 192
Antiquariats-Union Vertriebs GmbH & Co KG, pg 193
Arena Verlag GmbH, pg 193
Ars Edition GmbH, pg 194
Asso Verlag, pg 195
Auer Verlag GmbH, pg 195
Beerenverlag, pg 198
Berliner Handpresse Wolfgang Joerg und Erich Schonig, pg 199
Bertelsmann Lexikon Verlag GmbH, pg 200
Bibliographisches Institut & F A Brockhaus AG, pg 200
Bolanz Verlag fur Alle, pg 203
Born-Verlag, pg 203
Brigg Verlag Franz-Joset Buchler KG, pg 204
R Brockhaus Verlag, pg 204
Brunnen-Verlag GmbH, pg 205
Buchergilde Gutenberg Verlagsgesellschaft mbH, pg 205
Anita und Klaus Buscher B & B Verlag, pg 206
Butzon & Bercker GmbH, pg 206
Carlsen Verlag GmbH, pg 207

PUBLISHERS

Christophorus-Verlag GmbH, pg 208
CMA Edition, pg 209
Compact Verlag GmbH, pg 209
Coppenrath Verlag, pg 209
Corona Verlag, pg 210
Delphin Verlag GmbH, pg 211
Deutsche Bibelgesellschaft, pg 211
Deutscher Taschenbuch Verlag GmbH & Co KG (dtv), pg 213
Dipa-Verlag GmbH, pg 215
Domino Verlag, Guenther Brinek GmbH, pg 215
Echter Wurzburg Frankische Gesellschaftsdruckerei und Verlag GmbH, pg 217
Egmont EHAPA Verlag GmbH, pg 218
Egmont Franz Schneider Verlag GmbH, pg 218
Egmont Pestalozzi-Verlag, pg 218
Egmont vgs verlagsgesellschaft mbH, pg 218
Verlag Heinrich Ellermann GmbH & Co KG, pg 219
Engel & Bengel Verlag, pg 220
Ensslin und Laiblin Verlag GmbH & Co KG, pg 220
ERF-Verlag GmbH, pg 220
Espresso Verlag GmbH, pg 221
Esslinger Verlag J F Schreiber GmbH, pg 221
Christa Falk-Verlag, pg 223
Favorit-Verlag Huntemann und Markus & Co GmbH, pg 223
Finken Verlag GmbH, pg 224
Verlag der Francke Buchhandlung GmbH, pg 226
Franckh-Kosmos Verlags-GmbH & Co, pg 226
Verlag Freies Geistesleben, pg 227
Margarethe Freudenberger - selbstverlag fur jedermann, pg 227
Genius Verlag, pg 228
Gerstenberg Verlag, pg 228
Gerth Medien GmbH, pg 229
GLB Parkland Verlags-und Vertriebs GmbH, pg 229
Cornelia Goethe Literaturverlag, pg 230
Grass-Verlag, pg 231
Lehrmittelverlag Wilhelm Hagemann GmbH, pg 233
Carl Hanser Verlag, pg 234
F A Herbig Verlagsbuchhandlung GmbH, pg 236
Verlag Herder GmbH & Co KG, pg 236
Max Hieber KG, pg 237
Dieter Hoffmann Verlag, pg 238
Horlemann Verlag, pg 239
Johannis, pg 243
Jowi-Verlag, pg 243
Karl-May-Verlag Lothar Schmid GmbH, pg 244
Verlag Katholisches Bibelwerk GmbH, pg 245
Verlag Ernst Kaufmann GmbH, pg 245
Verlag Kerle im Verlag Herder, pg 245
Kidemus Verlag GmbH, pg 245
Kleiner Bachmann Verlag fur Kinder und Umwelt, pg 246
Knowledge Media International, pg 247
Koptisch-Orthodoxes Zentrum, pg 249
Roman Kovar Verlag, pg 249
Lahn-Verlag GmbH, pg 251
Lappan Verlag GmbH, pg 252
Leibniz-Buecherwarte, pg 253

Lentz Verlag, pg 253
Siegbert Linnemann Verlag, pg 254
Logos-Verlag Literatur & Layout GmbH, pg 255
Johannes Loriz Verlag der Kooperative Duernau, pg 255
Verlag Waldemar Lutz, pg 256
Menschenkinder Verlag und Vertrieb GmbH, pg 259
Karl-Heinz Metz, pg 259
Gertraud Middelhauve Verlag GmbH & Co KG, pg 260
Missio eV, pg 260
Moritz Verlag, pg 261
Verlag Karl Mueller GmbH, pg 262
Naumann & Goebel Verlagsgesellschaft mbH, pg 263
Nebel Verlag GmbH, pg 263
Verlag Neue Stadt GmbH, pg 264
Neuer Honos Verlag GmbH, pg 264
Verlag Neues Leben GmbH, pg 264
Oekotopia Verlag, Wolfgang Hoffman GmbH & Co KG, pg 266
Verlag Friedrich Oetinger GmbH, pg 266
Oncken Verlag KG, pg 267
Patmos Verlag GmbH & Co KG, pg 268
Pattloch Verlag GmbH & Co KG, pg 268
Pelikan Vertriebsgesellschaft mbH & Co KG, pg 269
Ravensburger Buchverlag Otto Maier GmbH, pg 274
Konrad Reich Verlag GmbH, pg 274
Verlag an der Ruhr GmbH, pg 277
Saatkorn-Verlag GmbH, pg 277
Verlag der Sankt-Johannis-Druckerei C Schweickhardt, pg 278
Scheffler-Verlag, pg 279
Agora Verlag Manfred Schlosser, pg 280
Siebert Verlag GmbH, pg 283
Tangens Systemverlag GmbH, pg 289
Thienemann Verlag GmbH, pg 291
Tipress Dienstleistungen fur das Verlagswesen GmbH, pg 291
Titania-Verlag Ferdinand Schroll, pg 291
Treves Editions Verein Zur Foerderung der Kuenstlerischen Taetigkeiten, pg 292
Verlag Beltz & Gelberg, pg 295
Voggenreiter-Verlag, pg 296
Ellen Vogt Garbe Verlag, pg 296
A Weichert Verlag GmbH & Co KG, pg 298
Friedrich Wittig Verlag GmbH, pg 301
Verlag DAS WORT GmbH, pg 301
Xenos Verlagsgesellschaft mbH, pg 301

Ghana

Adwinsa Publications (Ghana) Ltd, pg 303
Afram Publications (Ghana) Ltd, pg 303
Africa Christian Press, pg 303
Asempa Publishers, pg 303
Beginners Publishers, pg 303
Black Mask Ltd, pg 303
Educational Press & Manufacturers Ltd, pg 303
Ekab Business Ltd, pg 303
EPP Books Services, pg 304
Frank Publishing Ltd, pg 304
Goodbooks Publishing Co, pg 304
Kwamfori Publishing Enterprise, pg 304
Manhill Publication, pg 304

Quick Service Books Ltd, pg 304
Sam Woode Ltd, pg 304
Sedco Publishing Ltd, pg 305
Sub-Saharan Publishers, pg 305
Woeli Publishing Services, pg 305
World Literature Project, pg 305

Greece

AE Expaideftikon Vivlion Kai Diskon, pg 305
Akritas, pg 305
Anixis Publications, pg 305
Apostoliki Diakonia tis Ekklisias tis Hellados, pg 305
Athina, Mary Mavrogiannis, pg 306
Atlantis M Pechlivanides & Co SA, pg 306
Axiotelis G, pg 306
Boukoumanis' Editions, pg 306
Chrysi Penna - Golden Pen Books, pg 306
Chryssos Typos AE Ekodeis, pg 306
Dorikos Publishing House, pg 306
Elliniki Leschi Tou Vivliou, pg 307
Giovanis Publications, Pangosmios Ekdotikos Organismos, pg 307
Govostis Publishing SA, pg 307
Harmi-Press Publications, Haroula D Papadimitriou G P, pg 308
Hestia-I D Hestia-Kollaros & Co Corporation, pg 308
I Prooptiki, Ekdoseis, pg 308
Institute of Neohellenic Studies, Manolis Triantaphyllidis Foundation, pg 308
Kalentis & Sia, pg 308
Ilias Kambanas Publishing Organization, SA, pg 309
Kastaniotis Editions SA, pg 309
Kedros Publishers, pg 309
Logos, pg 309
Editions Moressopoulos, pg 310
Nakas Music House, pg 310
Odysseas Publications Ltd, pg 311
Orfanidis Publications, pg 311
Pagoulatos Bros, pg 311
Pagoulatos G-G P Publications, pg 311
Kyr I Papadopoulos E E, pg 311
Patakis Publishers, pg 311
M Psaropoulos & Co EE, pg 311
Psichogios Publications SA, pg 311
Rossi, E Kdoseis Eleni Rossi-Petsiou, pg 312
Sigma, pg 312
D & J Vardikos Vivliotechnica Hellas, pg 313
Vlassis, pg 313
S J Zacharopoulos SA Publishing Co, pg 313

Guyana

Roraima Publishers Ltd, pg 314

Haiti

Editions Caraibes SA, pg 314

Hong Kong

Benefit Publishing Co, pg 315
CFW Publications Ltd, pg 316
Chinese Christian Literature Council Ltd, pg 316
Christian Communications Ltd, pg 316
Island Press, pg 317
Joint Publishing (HK) Co Ltd, pg 317
Peace Book Co Ltd, pg 318
SCMP Book Publishing Ltd, pg 319
Sesame Publication Co, pg 319

Sun Ya Publications (HK) Ltd, pg 319
Times Publishing (Hong Kong) Ltd, pg 319

Hungary

Advent Kiado, pg 320
Aranyhal Konyvkiado Goldfish Publishing, pg 320
Idegenforgalmi Propaganda es Kiado Vallalat, pg 321
Ifjusagi Lap-eskonyvkiado Vallalat, pg 321
Lang Kiado, pg 322
Mora Ferenc Ifjusagi Koenyvkiado Rt, pg 323
Officina Nova Konyvek, pg 323
Park Konyvkiado Kft (Park Publisher), pg 324
Tevan Kiado Vallalat, pg 324

Iceland

AEskan, pg 325
Almenna Bokafelagid, pg 325
Fjolvi, pg 325
Forlagid, pg 325
Frjals fjolmiolun hf-Urvalsbaekur, pg 325
Idunn, pg 325
Mal og menning, pg 326
Setberg, pg 326
Skjaldborg Ltd, pg 326

India

Addison-Wesley Pte Ltd, pg 327
Advaita Ashrama, pg 327
Allied Publishers Pvt Ltd, pg 328
Ambar Prakashan, pg 328
Ananda Publishers Pvt Ltd, pg 328
Baha'i Publishing Trust of India, pg 329
Bani Mandir, Book-Sellers, Publishers & Educational Suppliers, pg 329
Bharat Publishing House, pg 330
Bhawan Book Service, Publishers & Distributors, pg 330
Children's Book Trust, pg 332
Dastane Ramchandra & Co, pg 333
DC Books, pg 333
Diamond Comics (P) Ltd, pg 333
Dolphin Publications, pg 333
Dreamland Publications, pg 333
Dutta Publishing Co Ltd, pg 333
Frank Brothers & Co Publishers Ltd, pg 334
HarperCollins Publishers India Pty Ltd, pg 335
Hindi Pracharak Sansthan, pg 336
Indian Book Depot, pg 336
Islamic Publishing House, pg 338
Lancer Publisher's & Distributors, pg 340
Laxmi Publications Pvt Ltd, pg 340
Learners Press Private Ltd, pg 340
Sri Ramakrishna Math, pg 341
A Mukherjee & Co Pvt Ltd, pg 342
M/S Gulshan Nanda Publications, pg 342
Naresh Publishers, pg 342
Nem Chand & Brothers, pg 343
Omsons Publications, pg 344
Paico Publishing House, pg 344
Paramount Sales (India) Pvt Ltd, pg 344
Parimal Prakashan, pg 345
Pitambar Publishing Co (P) Ltd, pg 345
Prabhat Prakashan, pg 345
Pratibha Pratishthan, pg 345
Rajpal & Sons, pg 346
M C Sarkar & Sons (P) Ltd, pg 348

TYPE OF PUBLICATION INDEX — BOOK

Sasta Sahitya Mandal, pg 348
Sat Sahitya Prakashan, pg 348
Satprakashan Sanchar Kendra, pg 348
Scientific Book Agency, pg 348
Shaibya Prakashan Bibhag, pg 349
Sharda Prakashan, pg 349
Shiksha Bharati, pg 349
Somaiya Publications Pvt Ltd, pg 349
Spectrum Publications, pg 350
Star Publications (P) Ltd, pg 350
Tara Publishing, pg 351
Vidya Puri, pg 352
Vidyarthi Mithram Press, pg 352
Vikas Publishing House Pvt Ltd, pg 352
Vivek Prakashan, pg 353

Indonesia
Mandira Jaya Abadi, pg 353
Angkasa CV, pg 353
PT Pustaka Antara Publishing & Printing, pg 353
Aurora, pg 353
Balai Pustaka, pg 353
Bina Rena Pariwara, pg 354
PT Dian Rakyat, pg 354
Dunia Pustaka Jaya PT, pg 354
Fortunajaya, pg 355
Gramedia, pg 355
PT Indira, pg 355
Karya Anda, CV, pg 355
Mizan, pg 355
Pustaka Utama Grafiti, PT, pg 356
Yayasan Obor Indonesia, pg 357

Ireland
An Gum, pg 358
Clo Iar-Chonnachta Teo, pg 358
Gill & Macmillan Ltd, pg 360
Kerryman Ltd, pg 361
Mercier Press Ltd, pg 362
The O'Brien Press Ltd, pg 362
Poolbeg Press Ltd, pg 363
Publishers Group South West (Ireland), pg 363
Roberts Rinehart Publishers, pg 363
Wolfhound Press Ltd, pg 364

Israel
Achiever, pg 364
Amichai Publishing House Ltd, pg 365
Bitan Publishers Ltd, pg 365
Breslov Research Institute, pg 365
Classikaletet, pg 366
Dekel Publishing House, pg 366
Dvir Publishing Ltd, pg 366
Feldheim Publishers Ltd, pg 367
Gefen Publishing House Ltd, pg 367
Hadar Publishing House Ltd, pg 367
Hakibbutz Hameuchad Publishing House Ltd, pg 367
Inbal Publishers, pg 368
The Institute for the Translation of Hebrew Literature, pg 368
Ma'ariv Book Guild (Sifriat Ma'ariv), pg 370
Modan Publishers Ltd, pg 370
Pitspopany Press, pg 371
Rolnik Publishers, pg 371
Saar Publishing House, pg 371
Schocken Publishing House Ltd, pg 371
R Sirkis Publishers Ltd, pg 372
Y Sreberk, pg 372
Steimatzky Group Ltd, pg 372
Urim Publications, pg 373
Yad Vashem - The Holocaust Martyrs' & Heroes' Remembrance Authority, pg 373
Yavneh Publishing House Ltd, pg 373
Yedioth Ahronoth Books, pg 373
Zakheim Publishing House, pg 373
Zmora-Bitan, Publishers Ltd, pg 374

Italy
Alba, pg 375
Rosellina Archinto Editore, pg 376
Edizioni Arka SRL, pg 376
Editore Armando Armando SRL, pg 376
Bovolenta, pg 379
Campanotto, pg 379
Edizioni Cartedit SRL, pg 380
Casa Musicale Edizioni Carrara SRL, pg 380
Casa Editrice Castalia, pg 380
Centro Biblico, pg 381
Edizioni Centro Studi Erickson, pg 381
Citta Nuova Editrice, pg 382
La Coccinella Editrice SRL, pg 383
Colonnese Editore, pg 383
Continental SRL Editrice, pg 383
Dami Editore SRL, pg 384
G De Bono Editore, pg 384
Edizioni E - Elle SRL, pg 385
Edizioni EBE, pg 385
Edizioni Il Punto d'Incontro SAS, pg 386
Editrice Eraclea, pg 388
Fatatrac, pg 388
Feguagiskia' Studios, pg 389
Istituto Geografico de Agostini SpA, pg 390
In Dialogo, pg 393
Edizioni Internazionali di Letteratura e Scienze, pg 393
Editoriale Jaca Book SpA, pg 394
Editrice Janus SpA, pg 394
Linea d'Ombra Libri, pg 395
Vincenzo Lo Faro Editore, pg 395
Macro Edizioni, pg 397
Giuseppe Maimone Editore, pg 397
Casa Editrice Menna di Sinisgalli Menna Giuseppina, pg 398
Messaggero di San Antonio, pg 398
Motta Junior Srl, pg 399
Edizioni Piemme SpA, pg 403
Edizioni Primavera SRL, pg 404
Il Punto D Incontro, pg 404
RAI-ERI, pg 405
Rara Istituto Editoriale di Bibliofilia e Reprints, pg 405
Editori Riuniti, pg 405
Rubbettino Editore, pg 406
Rugginenti Editore, pg 406
Adriano Salani Editore srl, pg 406
Lo Scarabeo Srl, pg 407
Editoriale Scienza, pg 407
Societa Editrice Internazionale - SEI, pg 408
Edizioni Sonda, pg 409
Editrice Uomini Nuovi, pg 411
Zanfi-Logos, pg 412

Jamaica
Carib Publishing Ltd, pg 413
Eureka Press Ltd, pg 413
Institute of Jamaica Publications, pg 413
LMH Publishing Ltd, pg 414
Twin Guinep Ltd, pg 414

Japan
Alice-Kan, pg 415
Child Honsha Co Ltd, pg 416
Dainippon Tosho Publishing Co, Ltd, pg 416
Dohosha Publishing Co Ltd, pg 417
Froebel - kan Co Ltd, pg 417
Fukuinkan Shoten Publishers Inc, pg 417
Fuzambo Publishing Co, pg 417
Gakken Co Ltd, pg 417
Hyoronsha Publishing Co Ltd, pg 418
International Society for Educational Information (ISEI), pg 419
Iwanami Shoten, Publishers, pg 419
Kaisei-Sha Publishing Co Ltd, pg 420
Kin-No-Hoshi Sha Co Ltd, pg 421
Kokudo-Sha Co Ltd, pg 421
Kosei Publishing Co Ltd, pg 421
Nagaoka Shoten Co Ltd, pg 423
Nishimura Co Ltd, pg 424
Obunsha Co Ltd, pg 424
Ongaku No Tomo Sha Corporation, pg 425
Poplar Publishing Co Ltd, pg 425
Saela Shobo (Librairie Ca et La), pg 425
Seibido Shuppan Company Ltd, pg 426
Shiko-Sha Co Ltd, pg 427
Shingakusha Co Ltd, pg 427
Akane Shobo Co Ltd, pg 427
Soryusha, pg 428
Tokyo Shoseki Co Ltd, pg 430
Yugaku-sha Ltd, pg 431
Zoshindo JukenKenkyusha, pg 431

Jordan
Al-Tanwir Al Ilmi (Scientific Enlightenment Publishing House), pg 432

Kenya
Africa Book Services (EA) Ltd, pg 433
Danmar Publishers, pg 433
Evangel Publishing House, pg 433
Focus Publications Ltd, pg 433
Heinemann Kenya Ltd (EAEP), pg 434
Jacaranda Designs Ltd, pg 434
Kenway Publications Ltd, pg 434
Kenya Literature Bureau, pg 434
Kenya Quality & Productivity Institute, pg 435
Lake Publishers & Enterprises Ltd, pg 435
Macmillan Kenya Publishers Ltd, pg 435
Paulines Publications-Africa, pg 435
Phoenix Publishers Ltd, pg 435
Sasa Sema Publications Ltd, pg 435
Space Sellers Ltd, pg 436
Sudan Literature Centre, pg 436
Uzima Press Ltd, pg 436

Democratic People's Republic of Korea
Grand People's Study House, pg 436

Republic of Korea
Ba-reunsa Publishing Co, pg 437
Biryongso Publishing Co, pg 437
Bo Ri Publishing Co Ltd, pg 437
Borim Publishing Co, pg 437
Dae Won Sa Co Ltd, pg 438
Dong-A Publishing & Printing Co Ltd, pg 438
Dong Hwa Publishing Co, pg 438
Haseo Publishing Co, pg 439
Hollym Corporation; Publishers, pg 439
Iljisa Publishing House, pg 439
Jigyungsa Ltd, pg 440
Jung-ang Munhwa Sa, pg 440
Ke Mong Sa Publishing Co Ltd, pg 440
Korea Britannica Corp, pg 440
Koreaone Press Inc, pg 440
Kukmin Doseo Publishing Co Ltd, pg 440
Kukminseokwan Publishing Co Ltd, pg 440
Kumsung Publishing Co Ltd, pg 440
Kyohaksa Publishing Co Ltd, pg 440
Literature Academy Publishing, pg 441
Minjisa Publishing Co, pg 441
Moon Jin Media Co Ltd, pg 441
Omun Gak, pg 441
St Pauls, pg 442
Samhwa Publishing Co Ltd, pg 442
Samseong Publishing Co Ltd, pg 442
Twenty-First Century Publishers, Inc, pg 443
Woongjin Media Corporation, pg 443
Woongjin.com Co Ltd, pg 443
Word of Life Press, pg 443
YBM/Si-sa, pg 443
Yearimdang Publishing Co, pg 443

Latvia
Alberts XII, pg 444
Artava Ltd, pg 444
Egmont Latvia SIA, pg 444
Hermess Ltd, pg 444
Madris, pg 445
Preses Nams, pg 445
Spriditis Publishers, pg 445
Vaidelote, SIA, pg 445
Zvaigzne ABC Publishers Ltd, pg 445

Lebanon
Arab Institute for Research & Publishing, pg 445
Dar Al-Kitab Al-Loubnani, pg 445
Dar El Ilm Lilmalayin, pg 446
Librairie du Liban Publishers (Sal), pg 446
Librairie Orientale sal, pg 446
Naufal Group Sarl, pg 447
World Book Publishing, pg 447

Liechtenstein
Frank P van Eck Publishers, pg 448

Lithuania
Alma Littera, pg 448
Dargenis Publishers, pg 449
Egmont Lietuva, pg 449
Lietus Ltd, pg 449
Lietuvos Rasytoju Sajungos Leidykla, pg 449
Margi Rastai Publishers, pg 449
Sviesa Publishers, pg 449
Vaga Ltd, pg 450
Victoria Publishers, pg 450
Vyturys Vyturio leidykla, UAB, pg 450

Luxembourg
Editions Emile Borschette, pg 450
Op der Lay, pg 451
Editions Saint-Paul, pg 451
Varkki Verghese, pg 452

PUBLISHERS

The Former Yugoslav Republic of Macedonia

Detska radost, pg 452
Nov svet (New World), pg 453
Prosvetno Delo Publishing House, pg 453

Madagascar

Maison d'Edition Protestante ANTSO, pg 453
Foibe Filan-Kevitry NY Mpampianatra (FOFIPA), pg 453
Librarie Mixte, pg 453

Malawi

Dzuka Publishing Co Ltd, pg 454
Popular Publications, pg 454

Malaysia

S Abdul Majeed & Co, pg 454
Amiza Associate Malaysia Sdn Bhd, pg 455
Associated Educational Distributors (M) Sdn Bhd, pg 455
Darulfikir, pg 455
Dewan Bahasa dan Pustaka, pg 455
Dewan Pustaka Islam, pg 455
Eastview Productions Sdn Bhd, pg 455
Federal Publications Sdn Bhd, pg 455
FEP International Sdn Bhd, pg 456
Forum Publications, pg 456
IBS Buku Sdn Bhd, pg 456
Mahir Publications Sdn Bhd, pg 456
Mecron Sdn Bhd, pg 457
Oscar Book International, pg 457
Pearson Education Malaysia Sdn Bhd, pg 457
Penerbit Jayatinta Sdn Bhd, pg 458
Penerbit Prisma Sdn Bhd, pg 458
Penerbitan Pelangi Sdn Bhd (Pelangi Publishing Pte Ltd), pg 458
Penerbitan Tinta, pg 458
Perfect Frontier Sdn Bhd, pg 458
Pustaka Cipta Sdn Bhd, pg 458
Pustaka Delta Pelajaran Sdn Bhd, pg 458
Pustaka Sistem Pelajaran Sdn Bhd, pg 458
Tempo Publishing (M) Sdn Bhd, pg 458
Tropical Press Sdn Bhd, pg 459
Utusan Publications & Distributors Sdn Bhd, pg 459
Vinpress Sdn Bhd, pg 459

Maldive Islands

Non-Formal Education Centre, pg 459

Malta

Merlin Library Ltd, pg 460
Publishers' Enterprises Group (PEG) Ltd, pg 460

Mauritius

Editions Capucines, pg 461
Golden Publications, pg 461
Editions de l'Ocean Indien Ltd, pg 461
Vizavi Editions, pg 461

Mexico

Adivinar y Multiplicar, SA de CV, pg 461
Editorial Avante SA de Cv, pg 462
Comision Nacional Forestal, pg 463
Ediciones Corunda SA de CV, pg 463
Ediciones Culturales Internacionales SA de CV Edicion Compra y Venta de Libros, Casetes, Videos, pg 463
Editorial Diana SA de CV, pg 464
Entretenlibro SA de CV, pg 465
Fernandez Editores SA de CV, pg 465
Fondo de Cultura Economica, pg 465
Editorial Hermes SA, pg 466
Editorial Iztaccihuatl SA, pg 467
Ediciones Larousse SA de CV, pg 467
Libros y Revistas SA de CV, pg 467
Editorial Limusa SA de CV, pg 467
Naves Internacional de Ediciones SA, pg 469
Organizacion Cultural LP SA de CV, pg 469
Panorama Editorial, SA, pg 470
Editorial Patria SA de CV, pg 470
Ediciones Cientificas La Prensa Medica Mexicana SA de CV, pg 470
Editorial Progreso SA de C V, pg 470
Ediciones Promesa, SA de CV, pg 470
Sayrols Editorial SA de CV, pg 471
Sistemas Tecnicos de Edicion SA de CV, pg 472
Ediciones Suromex SA, pg 472
Editorial Trillas SA de CV, pg 472

Republic of Moldova

Editura Hyperion, pg 473
Editura Lumina, pg 473

Morocco

Edition Diffusion de Livre au Maroc, pg 474
Editions Okad, pg 475

Nepal

International Standards Books & Periodicals (P) Ltd, pg 476

Netherlands

Ars Scribendi bv Uitgeverij, pg 478
Big Balloon BV, pg 479
Cadans, pg 480
Callenbach BV, pg 480
Uitgeverij Christofoor, pg 480
East-West Publications Fonds BV, pg 481
Educatieve Uitgeverij Edu'Actief BV, pg 481
Eekhoorn BV Uitgeverij, pg 482
Uitgeverij Elzenga, pg 482
Uitgeverij De Fontein BV, pg 482
Van Goor BV, pg 483
Gottmer Uitgevers Groep, pg 483
De Harmonie Uitgeverij, pg 483
Katholieke Bijbelstichting, pg 484
Kimio Uitgeverij bv, pg 484
LCG Malmberg BV, pg 485
Uitgeverij Leopold BV, pg 485
Meander Uitgeverij BV, pg 485
Mirran, pg 486
Narratio Theologische Uitgeverij, pg 486
Nederlands Literair Produktie-en Vertalingen Fonds (NLPVF), pg 486
Omega Boek BV, pg 487
Uitgeverij Ploegsma BV, pg 487
Prometheus, pg 488
Em Querido's Uitgeverij BV, pg 488
Rebo Productions BV, pg 488
Sjaloom Uitgeverijen, pg 489
Telos Boeken, pg 490
Uitgeverij De Toorts, pg 490
Uitgeverij Altamira-Becht BV, pg 490
Unieboek BV, pg 490
Van Buuren Uitgeverij BV, pg 491
Uitgeverij Vassallucci bv, pg 491
Uitgeverij De Vuurbaak BV, pg 492
Uitgeverij Westers, pg 492

New Zealand

Brick Row Publishing Co Ltd, pg 494
Bush Press Communications Ltd, pg 494
Cape Catley Ltd, pg 495
Craig Printing Co Ltd, pg 495
HarperCollins Publishers (New Zealand) Ltd, pg 497
Huia Publishers, pg 497
Learning Media Ltd, pg 498
Magari Publishing, pg 498
Mallinson Rendel Publishers Ltd, pg 498
Maori Publications Unit, pg 498
Nelson Price Milburn Ltd, pg 499
Reed Publishing (NZ) Ltd, pg 500
RSVP Publishing Co Ltd, pg 500
Shearwater Associates Ltd, pg 501
Shortland Publications Ltd, pg 501
Sunshine Books International Ltd, pg 501

Nigeria

ABIC Books & Equipment Ltd, pg 503
Adebara Publishers Ltd, pg 503
Evans Brothers (Nigeria Publishers) Ltd, pg 504
Fourth Dimension Publishing Co Ltd, pg 504
International Publishing & Research Company, pg 505
Literamed Publications Nigeria Ltd, pg 505
New Era Publishers, pg 506
Northern Nigerian Publishing Co Ltd, pg 506
Obobo Books, pg 506
Saros International Publishers, pg 507
Tabansi Press Ltd, pg 507
Tana Press Ltd & Flora Nwapa Books Ltd, pg 507
Joe-Tolalu & Associates, pg 507
Vantage Publishers International Ltd, pg 507
West African Book Publishers Ltd, pg 507

Norway

Ariel Lydbokforlag, pg 508
Atheneum Forlag A/S, pg 508
Det Norske Samlaget, pg 508
John Grieg Forlag AS, pg 509
Gyldendal Norsk Forlag A/S, pg 509
Lunde Forlag AS, pg 509
Luther Forlag A/S, pg 509
Sandviks Bokforlag, pg 510
Chr Schibsteds Forlag A/S, pg 510
Snofugl Forlag, pg 510
Solum Forlag A/S, pg 510
Stabenfeldt A/S, pg 510

Pakistan

Hamdard Foundation Pakistan, pg 512
Islamic Publications (Pvt) Ltd, pg 513
Malik Sirajuddin & Sons, pg 513
Maqbool Academy, pg 513
National Book Foundation, pg 513
Sang-e-Meel Publications, pg 514
Sh Ghulam Ali & Sons (Pvt) Ltd, pg 514

Papua New Guinea

Kristen Press, pg 515

Peru

Asociacion Editorial Bruno, pg 516
Carvajal SA, pg 516
Ediciones Peisa (Promocion Editorial Inca SA), pg 517
Tarea Asociacion de Publicaciones Educativas, pg 517

Philippines

Abiva Publishing House Inc, pg 518
Anvil Publishing Inc, pg 518
Bookman Printing & Publishing House Inc, pg 518
Bookmark Inc, pg 518
Cacho Publishing House, Inc, pg 518
Communication Foundation for Asia Media Group (CFAMG), pg 518
Marren Publishing House, Inc, pg 519
New Day Publishers, pg 520
Our Lady of Manaoag Publisher, pg 520
Philippine Baptist Mission SBC FMB Church Growth International, pg 520
Rex Bookstores & Publishers, pg 520

Poland

Wydawnictwo Dolnoslaskie, pg 522
Instytut Wydawniczy Pax, Inco-Veritas, pg 523
Iskry - Publishing House Ltd spotka zoo, pg 523
Ludowa Spoldzielnia Wydawnicza, pg 524
Muza SA, pg 524
Wydawnictwo Nasza Ksiegarnia Sp zoo, pg 524
Wydawnictwa Normalizacyjne Alfa-Wero, pg 525
Wydawnictwo Podsiedlik-Raniowski i Spolka, pg 525
Przedsiebiorstwo Wydawniczo-Handlowe Wydawnictwo Siedmiorog, pg 526
Res Polona, pg 526
Wydawnictwo RTW, pg 526
'Slask' Ltd, pg 526
Spotdzielna Anagram, pg 526
Vocatio Publishing House, pg 527
Wydawnictwo Wilga sp zoo, pg 527
Wydawn Na Sprawa' Wydawniczo-Oswiatowa Spotdzielnia Inwalidow, pg 528

Portugal

Edicoes Afrontamento, pg 528
Livraria Arnado Lda, pg 528
Contexto Editora, pg 530
Dinalivro, pg 530
Distri Cultural Lda, pg 530
Editorial Estampa, Lda, pg 531
Publicacoes Europa-America Lda, pg 531

TYPE OF PUBLICATION INDEX　　　　　　　　　　　　　　　　　　　　　　　BOOK

Europress Editores e Distribuidores de Publicacoes Lda, pg 531
Everest Editora, pg 531
Girassol Edicoes, LDA, pg 532
Gradiva-Publicacnoes Lda, pg 532
Livros Horizonte Lda, pg 533
Meriberica/Liber, pg 533
Editorial Noticias, pg 534
Editorial O Livro Lda, pg 534
Paulinas, pg 534
Perspectivas e Realidades, Artes Graficas, Lda, pg 534
Porto Editora Lda, pg 535
Portugalmundo, pg 535
Editorial Presenca, pg 535
Publicacoes Dom Quixote Lda, pg 535
Puma Editora Lda, pg 535
Editora Replicacao Lda, pg 535
Teorema, pg 536
Texto Editora, pg 536
Publicacoes Trevo Lda, pg 536
Vega-Publicacao e Distribuicao de Livros e Revistas, Lda, pg 536

Romania

Editura Aius, pg 538
Alcor-Edimpex (Verlag) Ltd, pg 538
Editora All, pg 538
Editura Clusium, pg 539
Coresi SRL, pg 539
Corint Publishing Group, pg 539
Editure Ion Creanga, pg 539
Editura Dacia, pg 539
Editura DOINA SRL, pg 539
Enzyklopadie Verlag, pg 539
Euro Print Verlag, pg 539
Editura Excelsior Art, pg 539
FF Press, pg 540
Editura Kriterion SA, pg 540
Lider Verlag, pg 540
MAST Verlag, pg 540
Mentor Kiado, pg 540
Editura Minerva, pg 541
Nemira Verlag, pg 541
Editura Niculescu, pg 541
Pandora Publishing House, pg 541
Grupul Editorial RAO, pg 542
RAO International Publishing Co, pg 542
Saeculum IO, pg 542
Vox Editura, pg 543

Russian Federation

Airis Press, pg 543
CentrePolygraph Traders & Publishers Co, pg 544
Dom, Izdatel'stvo sovetskogo deskkogo fonda im & I Lenina, pg 544
Druzhba Narodov, pg 544
Finansy i Statistika Publishing House, pg 544
Kabardino-Balkarskoye knizhnoye izdatelstvo, pg 545
Izdatelstvo Khudozhestvennaya Literatura, pg 545
KUbK Publishing House, pg 546
Ladomir Publishing House, pg 546
Publishing House Limbus Press, pg 546
Izdatelstvo Malysh, pg 546
Obdeestvo Znanie, pg 547
Okoshko Ltd Publishers (Izdatelstvo), pg 547
Panorama Publishing House, pg 547
Permskaja Kniga, pg 548
Izdatelstvo Prosveshchenie, pg 548
Raduga Publishers, pg 548
Russkaya Kniga Izdatelstvo (Publishers), pg 548
Scorpion Publishers, pg 548
Sredne-Uralskoye knizhnoye izdatelstve (Middle Urals Publishing House), pg 549
Izdatelstvo Sudostroenie, pg 549
Text Publishers Ltd Too, pg 549

Saudi Arabia

Dar Al-Shareeff for Publishing & Distribution, pg 550
Saudi Publishing & Distributing House, pg 550

Senegal

Centre Africain d'Animation et d'Echanges Culturels Editions Khoudia (CAEC), pg 551

Serbia and Montenegro

Alfa-Narodna Knjiga, pg 552
Minerva, pg 552
Obod, pg 553
Izdavacko Preduzece Matice Srpske, pg 553
Svetovi, pg 554
Vuk Karadzic, pg 554

Singapore

K C Ang Publishing Pte Ltd, pg 554
Asiapac Books Pte Ltd, pg 555
Cannon International, pg 555
Celebrity Educational Publishers, pg 555
Europhone Language Institute (Pte) Ltd, pg 556
Federal Publications (S) Pte Ltd, pg 556
FEP International Private Ltd, pg 556
Global Educational Services Pte Ltd, pg 556
Graham Brash Pte Ltd, pg 556
Pan Pacific Publications (S) Pte Ltd, pg 557
Pustaka Nasional Pte Ltd, pg 557
Shing Lee Group Publishers, pg 558
SNP Panpac Pacific Publishing Pte Ltd, pg 558
Success Publications Pte Ltd, pg 558
Tecman Bible House, pg 558

Slovakia

ARCHA sro Vydavatel'stro, pg 559
AV Studio Reklamno-vydavatel 'ska agentura, pg 559
Egmont Neografia spol sro, pg 559
Vydavatelstvo Junior sro Slovart Print, pg 559
Kalligram spol sro, pg 559
Luc vydavatelske druzstvo, pg 559
Mlade leta Spd sro, pg 559
Vydavatelstvo Obzor, pg 560
Vydavatel'stvo Osveta (Verlag Osveta), pg 560
Priroda Publishing, pg 560
Slo Viet, pg 560
Slovansky Tatran, Vydavatel 'stro spoi sro, pg 560
Sofa, pg 560

Slovenia

East West Operation (EWO) Ltd, pg 561
Franc-Franc podjetje za promocijo kulture Murska Sobota d o o, pg 561
Mladinska Knjiga International, pg 561
Zalozba Mihelac d o o, pg 562
Zalozba Obzorja d d Maribor, pg 562

South Africa

Anansi Uitgewers, pg 562
Educum Publishers Ltd, pg 563
HAUM - Daan Retief Publishers (Pty) Ltd, pg 564
HAUM - De Jager Publishers, pg 564
Human & Rousseau (Pty) Ltd, pg 564
Ithemba! Publishing, pg 565
Jacklin Enterprises (Pty) Ltd, pg 565
Maskew Miller Longman, pg 566
New Africa Books (Pty) Ltd, pg 567
Publitoria Publishers, pg 568
Ravan Press (Pty) Ltd, pg 568
Struik Publishers (Pty) Ltd, pg 569
Tafelberg Publishers Ltd, pg 569
Vivlia Publishers & Booksellers, pg 570

Spain

Publicacions de l'Abadia de Montserrat, pg 570
Editorial Acanto SA, pg 570
Editorial Aguaclara, pg 571
Aguilar SA de Ediciones, pg 571
Alberdania SL, pg 571
Alinco SA - Aura Comunicacio, pg 572
Anaya Educacion, pg 573
Editorial Astri SA, pg 573
Ediciones Atril, pg 574
Ediciones B, SA, pg 574
Editorial Barcanova SA, pg 574
Beascoa SA Ediciones, pg 574
Edicions Bromera SL, pg 575
Editorial Bruno, pg 575
Calamo Editorial, pg 575
Edicions Camacuc, pg 575
Editorial Casals SA, pg 575
CEAC, Grupo Editorial SA, pg 576
Editorial Claret SA, pg 577
Combel Editorial SA, pg 577
Compania Literaria, pg 577
Creaciones Monar Editorial, pg 578
Ediciones Cruilla SA, pg 578
Ediciones Daly S L, pg 578
Ediciones Destino SA, pg 579
Didaco Comunicacion y Didactica, SA, pg 579
Ediciones Ebenezer, pg 580
Editorial EDAF SA, pg 580
Edebe, pg 580
Editorial Everest SA, pg 581
El Hogar y la Moda SA, pg 581
Ediciones Elfos SL, pg 582
Elkar, Euskal Liburu eta Kantuen Argitaldaria, SL, pg 582
Enciclopedia Catalana, SA, pg 582
Erein, pg 582
Editorial Esin, SA, pg 582
Editorial Espasa-Calpe SA, pg 582
Fundacion Coleccion Thyssen-Bornemisza, pg 584
Fundacion Rosacruz, pg 584
Galaxia SA Editorial, pg 584
La Galera, SA Editorial, pg 584
Ediciones Gaviota SA, pg 584
Grijalbo Mondadori SA, pg 585
Grupo Editorial CEAC SA, pg 586
Grupo Santillana de Ediciones SA, pg 586
Editorial Gulaab, pg 586
Hercules de Ediciones, SA, pg 586
Ediciones Hiperion SL, pg 586
Ibaizabal Edelvives SA, pg 586
Idea Books, SA, pg 587
Ediciones JJB, pg 588
Ediciones JLA, pg 588
Editorial Juventud SA, pg 588
LEDA (Las Ediciones de Arte), pg 589
Libsa Editorial SA, pg 589
Llibres del Segle, pg 589
Loguez Ediciones, pg 589
Editorial Luis Vives (Edelvives), pg 589
Editorial Magisterio Espanol SA, pg 590
Edicions de la Magrana SA, pg 590
Editorial Marfil SA, pg 590
Editorial Marin SA, pg 590
Editorial Mediterrania SL, pg 591
Editorial Molino, pg 592
Editorial Moll SL, pg 592
Obelisco Ediciones S, pg 593
Editorial Alfredo Ortells SL, pg 594
Parramon Ediciones SA, pg 595
Pearson Educacion S A, pg 595
Editorial Peregrino SL, pg 595
Pirene Editorial, sal, pg 596
Editorial Playor SA, pg 596
Plaza y Janes Editores SA, pg 596
Ediciones Rialp SA, pg 598
Editorial Miguel A Salvatella SA, pg 598
San Pablo Ediciones, pg 598
Ediciones San Pio X, pg 599
Ediciones Seyer, pg 599
Silex Ediciones, pg 600
Equipo Sirius SA, pg 600
Ediciones Siruela SA, pg 600
Grup 62, pg 600
Ediciones SM, pg 600
Ramon Sopena SA, pg 600
Ediciones Susaeta SA, pg 601
Ediciones de la Torre, pg 602
Editorial Verbo Divino, pg 604
Veron Editor, pg 604
Edicions Xerais de Galicia, pg 605
Xunta de Galicia, pg 605
Editorial Zendrera Zariquiey, SA, pg 605

Sri Lanka

Colombo Book Association, pg 606
Danuma Prakashakayo, pg 606
Dayawansa Jayakody & Co, pg 606
Lake House Investments Ltd, pg 606
Pradeepa Publishers, pg 607
Saman Saha Madara Publishers, pg 607
Sunera Publishers, pg 607
Swarna Hansa Foundation, pg 607
Warna Publishers, pg 607

Sweden

Alfabeta Bokforlag AB, pg 609
Bokforlaget Axplock, pg 609
Bonnier Audio, pg 610
Bonnier Carlsen Bokforlag AB, pg 610
Egmont Serieforlaget, pg 611
Eriksson & Lindgren Bokforlag, pg 611
Hagaberg AB, pg 612
Hallgren och Fallgren Studieforlag AB, pg 612
Bokforlaget Hegas AB, pg 612
Mezopotamya Publishing & Distribution, pg 613
Bokfoerlaget Natur och Kultur, pg 613
Bokforlaget Opal AB, pg 614
Raben och Sjoegren Bokforlag, pg 614
Richters Egmont, pg 615
Bokforlaget Semic AB, pg 615

PUBLISHERS — TYPE OF PUBLICATION INDEX

Semic Bokforlaget International AB, pg 615
Sjoestrands Foerlag, pg 615

Switzerland
Association Suisse des Editeurs de Langue Francaise, pg 618
Bibellesbund Verlag, pg 619
Blaukreuz-Verlag Bern, pg 619
Bohem Press Kinderbuchverlag, pg 619
Caux Edition SA, pg 620
Christoph Merian Verlag, pg 620
Cosa-Verlag, Giusep Condrau SA, pg 621
Diogenes Verlag AG, pg 622
Editions Esprit Ouvert, pg 623
Jugend mit einer Mission Verlag, pg 626
Verlag Walter Keller, Dornach, pg 626
Kinderbuchverlag Luzern, pg 626
Lia rumantscha, pg 627
La Maison de la Bible, pg 628
Minervaverlag Bern, pg 628
Motovun Book GmbH, pg 629
Verlag Nagel & Kimche AG, Zurich, pg 629
Neptun-Verlag, pg 629
Nord-Sued Verlag, pg 629
Orell Fuessli Buchhandlungs AG, pg 630
Pro Juventute Verlag, pg 631
Rex Verlag, pg 632
Rodera-Verlag der Cardun AG, pg 632
Sauerlaender AG, pg 633
Schlaepfer & Co AG, pg 633
Strom-Verlag Luzern, pg 635
Uranium Verlag Zug, pg 636

Taiwan, Province of China
Ai Chih Book Co Ltd, pg 638
Campus Evangelical Fellowship, Literature Department, pg 639
Cheng Yun Publishing Company Ltd, pg 639
Chien Chen Bookstore Publishing Company Ltd, pg 639
Commonwealth Publishing Company Ltd, pg 639
Cynosure Publishing Inc, pg 639
Echo Publishing Company Ltd, pg 639
Grimm Press Ltd, pg 640
Hilit Publishing Co Ltd, pg 640
Hsin Yi Publications, pg 640
HYS Culture Co Ltd, pg 640
Kuang Fu Book Co Ltd, pg 640
Linking Publishing Company Ltd, pg 641
Newton Publishing Company Ltd, pg 641
Youth Cultural Publishing Co, pg 642
Yuan Liou Publishing Co, Ltd, pg 642

United Republic of Tanzania
Ben and Company Ltd, pg 643
Central Tanganyika Press, pg 643
DUP (1996) Ltd, pg 643
General Publications Ltd, pg 643
Kisambo Publishers Ltd, pg 643
Ndanda Mission Press, pg 644
Nyota Publishers Ltd, pg 644
Press & Publicity Centre Ltd, pg 644
Readit Books, pg 644
Tanzania Publishing House, pg 644
Tema Publishers Ltd, pg 644

Thailand
Bannakit Trading, pg 645
New Generation Publishing Co Ltd, pg 645
Suriyaban Publishers, pg 646
Thai Watana Panich Co, Ltd, pg 646

Togo
Editions Akpagnon, pg 646

Trinidad & Tobago
Charran's Educational Publishers, pg 647
Inprint Caribbean Ltd, pg 647

Tunisia
Les Editions de l'Arbre, pg 647
Arcs Editions, pg 647
Editions Bouslama, pg 647
Dar Arabia Lil Kitab, pg 648
Maison d'Edition Mohamed Ali Hammi, pg 648
Maison Tunisienne de l'Edition, pg 648

Turkey
Afa Yayincilik Sanayi Tic AS, pg 648
Altin Kitaplar Yayinevi, pg 649
Arkadas Ltd, pg 649
Arkin Kitabevi, pg 649
Aydin Yayincilik, pg 649
Ezel Erverdi (Dergah Yayinlari AS) Muessese Muduru, pg 650
Inkilap Publishers Ltd, pg 650
Kiyi Yayinlari, pg 650
Kok Yayincilik, pg 650
Nurdan YayinlariSanayi ve Ticaret Ltd Sti, pg 651
Pan Yayincilik, pg 651
Redhouse Press, pg 651
Remzi Kitabevi, pg 651
Sabah Kitaplari, pg 651
Saray Medikal Yayin Tic Ltd Sti, pg 651
Soez Yayin/Oyunajans, pg 651
Turkish Republic - Ministry of Culture, pg 652
Varlik Yayinlari AS, pg 652
Kabalci Yayinevi, pg 652

Uganda
Centenary Publishing House Ltd, pg 652
Fountain Publishers Ltd, pg 652

Ukraine
ASK Ltd, pg 653
Mystetstvo Publishers, pg 653
Veselka Publishers, pg 654

United Arab Emirates
Department of Culture & Information Government of Sharjah, pg 654
Motivate Publishing, pg 654

United Kingdom
Acair Ltd, pg 655
Act 3 Publishing, pg 655
Aladdin Books Ltd, pg 656
Allied Mouse Ltd, pg 656
Alun Books, pg 657
Andersen Press Ltd, pg 657
Andromeda Oxford Ltd, pg 658
Apple Press, pg 658
Arcturus Publishing Ltd, pg 659
Argo Spoken Word, pg 659
AS Publishing, pg 660
Autumn Publishing Ltd, pg 662
Award Publications Ltd, pg 662
b small publishing, pg 662
BAAF Adoption & Fostering, pg 662
Baha'i Publishing Trust, pg 662
Barefoot Books, pg 663
Barn Dance Publications Ltd, pg 663
BCA - Book Club Associates, pg 663
Belitha Press Ltd, pg 664
David Bennett Books, pg 664
Bible Reading Fellowship, pg 665
BLA Publishing Ltd, pg 666
A & C Black Publishers Ltd, pg 666
Blackie Children's Books, pg 666
Bloomsbury Publishing PLC, pg 668
Books for Europe Ltd, pg 669
Breslich & Foss Ltd, pg 671
Brimax Books, pg 671
British Museum Press, pg 672
Brown Wells & Jacobs Ltd, pg 672
Bryntirion Press, pg 672
Cassell & Co, pg 675
Cherrytree Books, pg 678
Child's Play (International) Ltd, pg 679
Chorion IP, pg 679
Christian Education, pg 679
Christian Focus Publications Ltd, pg 679
Church Union, pg 680
Colour Library Direct, pg 681
Constable & Robinson Ltd, pg 682
Crossbridge Books, pg 684
Cyhoeddiadau'r Gair, pg 685
Cymdeithas Lyfrau Ceredigion, pg 685
Delancey Press Ltd, pg 687
Dorling Kindersley Ltd, pg 688
Gwasg Dwyfor, pg 688
East-West Publications (UK) Ltd, pg 689
Encyclopaedia Britannica (UK) International Ltd, pg 691
Eurobook Ltd, pg 692
Evans Brothers Ltd, pg 693
Express Newspapers, pg 693
Faber & Faber Ltd, pg 694
Feather Books, pg 694
Sadie Fields Productions Ltd, pg 694
Floris Books, pg 695
W H Freeman & Co Ltd, pg 697
Funfax Ltd, pg 698
Gairm Publications, pg 698
Geddes & Grosset, pg 699
The Geographical Association, pg 699
Stanley Gibbons Publications, pg 700
Glowworm Books Ltd, pg 700
Gollancz/Witherby, pg 701
Gomer Press (J D Lewis & Sons Ltd), pg 701
Graham-Cameron Publishing & Illustration, pg 701
W F Graham (Northampton) Ltd, pg 701
Grandreams Ltd, pg 702
Grange Books PLC, pg 702
Gwasg y Dref Wen, pg 703
Peter Haddock Ltd, pg 703
Happy Cat Books Ltd, pg 704
Patrick Hardy Books, pg 705
HarperCollins UK, pg 705
Hawk Books, pg 706
Hodder Children's Books, pg 709
Hodder Headline Ltd, pg 709
Holland Enterprises Ltd, pg 709
Honno Welsh Women's Press, pg 710
Angus Hudson Ltd, pg 710
Islamic Foundation Publications, pg 714
The Kenilworth Press Ltd, pg 717
Kingfisher Publications Plc, pg 717
Kuperard, pg 718
Ladybird Books Ltd, pg 719
LDA-Living & Learning (Cambridge) Ltd, pg 719
Learning Together, pg 720
Letterbox Library, pg 720
Letterland International Ltd, pg 720
Frances Lincoln Ltd, pg 720
Lion Hudson PLC, pg 721
Y Lolfa Cyf, pg 722
Lorenz Books, pg 722
The Lutterworth Press, pg 723
Macmillan Children's Books, pg 723
Macmillan Heinemann ELT, pg 723
Macmillan Ltd, pg 723
Magi Publications, pg 724
The Mansk Svenska Publishing Co Ltd, pg 725
McCrimmon Publishing Co Ltd, pg 726
The Medici Society Ltd, pg 726
Methodist Publishing House, pg 727
National Foster Care Association, pg 731
New Era Publications UK Ltd, pg 732
NMS Enterprises Ltd - Publishing, pg 733
Octopus Publishing Group, pg 734
Michael O'Mara Books Ltd, pg 735
Opus Book Publishing Ltd, pg 736
Orion Children's Books, pg 736
Orion Publishing Group Ltd, pg 736
Orpheus Books Ltd, pg 736
Oyster Books Ltd, pg 737
Pan Macmillan, pg 738
Pavilion Books Ltd, pg 739
Penguin Books Ltd, pg 740
The Penguin Group UK, pg 740
Philip & Tacey Ltd, pg 741
Philograph Publications Ltd, pg 741
Piccadilly Press, pg 742
Pinwheel Ltd, pg 742
Pookie Productions Ltd, pg 744
Porthill Publishers, pg 744
Portland Press Ltd, pg 745
Mathew Price Ltd, pg 745
Quarto Publishing plc, pg 746
Quartz Editions, pg 746
Ramboro Books Plc, pg 747
Random House UK Ltd, pg 747
Ransom Publishing Ltd, pg 748
Ravette Publishing Ltd, pg 748
The Reader's Digest Association Ltd, pg 748
Reader's Digest Children's Books, pg 748
Regency House Publishing Ltd, pg 749
The Robinswood Press Ltd, pg 750
Saint Andrew Press, pg 753
St Pauls Publishing, pg 753
Salamander Books Ltd, pg 753
The Salariya Book Co Ltd, pg 753
Sangam Books Ltd, pg 754
Scholastic Ltd, pg 754
Scottish Cultural Press, pg 755
Scripture Union, pg 756
Seren, pg 756
Sherbourne Publications, pg 757
Speechmark Publishing Ltd, pg 760
Stacey International, pg 761
Studio Editions Ltd, pg 761
Supportive Learning Publications, pg 762

TYPE OF PUBLICATION INDEX BOOK

Tabb House, pg 762
Tango Books, pg 762
Tarquin Publications, pg 762
Teeney Books Ltd, pg 764
Tiger Books International PLC, pg 765
Transworld Publishers Ltd, pg 766
Treehouse Children's Books Ltd, pg 767
Two-Can Publishing Ltd, pg 768
Uplands Books, pg 769
Usborne Publishing Ltd, pg 769
Van Molle Publishing, pg 769
Viking Children's Books, pg 770
Walker Books Ltd, pg 771
Frederick Warne Publishers Ltd, pg 771
The Watts Publishing Group Ltd, pg 771
WI Enterprises Ltd, pg 773
Wordsworth Editions Ltd, pg 775
Y Cyfarwyddwr Urdd Gobaith Cymru, pg 776
Anglia Young Books, pg 776

Uruguay
A Monteverde y Cia SA, pg 777
Nordan-Comunidad, pg 778
Rosebud Ediciones, pg 778

Venezuela
Alfadil Ediciones, pg 778
Editorial Ateneo de Caracas, pg 779
Ediciones Ekare, pg 779

Viet Nam
Science & Technics Publishing House, pg 780

Zambia
Apple Books, pg 781
Yorvik Publishing Ltd, pg 782
Zambia Educational Publishing House, pg 782
Zambia Printing Company Ltd (ZPC), pg 782

Zimbabwe
Academic Books (Pvt) Ltd, pg 782
Anvil Press, pg 782
College Press Publishers (Pvt) Ltd, pg 783
The Literature Bureau, pg 783
Longman Zimbabwe (Pvt) Ltd, pg 783
Mambo Press, pg 783
Mercury Press Pvt Ltd, pg 784
Vision Publications, pg 784
Zimbabwe Publishing House (Pvt) Ltd, pg 784
ZRD Trust, pg 785

DATABASES

Argentina
Alfagrama SRL ediciones, pg 3
Instituto Nacional de Ciencia y Tecnica Hidrica (INCYTH), pg 7

Australia
Australasian Medical Publishing Company Ltd (AMPCO), pg 12
Curriculum Corporation, pg 19
Encyclopaedia Britannica (Australia) Inc, pg 21

Austria
Compass-Verlag GmbH, pg 49

Azerbaijan
Sada, Literaturno-Izdatel'skij Centr, pg 60

Belgium
Brepols Publishers NV, pg 64
Uitgeverij Lannoo NV, pg 69
Wolters Kluwer Belgie NV, pg 74

Brazil
Comissao Nacional de Energia Nuclear (CNEN), pg 80
Editora Nova Fronteira SA, pg 87

Bulgaria
DATAMAP - Europe, pg 94

China
Chemical Industry Press, pg 101
China Machine Press (CMP), pg 102
Electronics Industry Publishing House, pg 104
Fudan University Press, pg 104
Higher Education Press, pg 105
Patent Documentation Publishing House, pg 106

The Democratic Republic of the Congo
Facultes Catoliques de Kinshasa, pg 114

Costa Rica
Centro Agronomico Tropical de Investigacion y Ensenanza (CATIE), pg 115
Union Mundial para la Naturaleza (UICN), Oficina Regional para Mesoamerica, pg 116

Croatia
Masmedia, pg 118

Cuba
Instituto de Informacion Cientifica y Tecnologica (IDICT), pg 120

Czech Republic
Divadelni Ustav, pg 123
Libri spol sro, pg 125
Cesky normalizacni institut, pg 126

Denmark
Dansk Biblioteks Center, pg 130
Schultz Information, pg 134
Systime, pg 135

Estonia
Eesti Rahvusraamatukogu, pg 139
Ilmamaa, pg 139

France
Agence Bibliographique de l'Enseignement Superieur, pg 146
CERDIC-Publications, pg 153
Les Editions ESF, pg 160
Editions Legislatives, pg 171
Guide Rosenwald, pg 183
Editions Springer France, pg 186

Germany
AOL-Verlag Frohmut Menze, pg 193
ARCult Media, pg 193
AZ Bertelsmann Direct GmbH, pg 196

Verlag Beleke KG, pg 198
BW Bildung und Wissen Verlag und Software GmbH, pg 201
Fachverlag Hans Carl GmbH, pg 207
Carl Link Verlag-Gesellschaft mbH Fachverlag fur Verwaltungsrecht, pg 207
Chmielorz GmbH Verlag, pg 208
Deutscher Adressbuch-Verlag fuer Wirtschaft und Verkehr GmbH, pg 212
Deutscher Apotheker Verlag Dr Roland Schmiedel GmbH & Co, pg 212
Die Verlag H Schafer GmbH, pg 214
DSI Data Service & Information, pg 217
Ecomed Verlagsgesellschaft AG & Co KG, pg 218
Feltron-Elektronik Zeissler & Co GmbH, pg 223
Fraunhofer IRB Verlag Fraunhofer Informationszentrum Raum und Bau, pg 226
Gesundheits-Dialog Verlag GmbH, pg 229
Verlag Ernst und Werner Gieseking GmbH, pg 229
Gmelin Verlag GmbH, pg 230
Carl Hanser Verlag, pg 234
Hoppenstedt GmbH & Co KG, pg 239
Klages-Verlag, pg 246
K F Koehler Verlag GmbH, pg 248
Munzinger-Archiv GmbH Archiv fuer publizistische Arbeit, pg 262
pmi Verlag, pg 270
Reed Elsevier Deutschland GmbH, pg 274
Verlag Werner Sachon GmbH & Co, pg 277
K G Saur Verlag GmbH, A Gale/Thomson Learning Company, pg 278
Springer Science+Business Media GmbH & Co KG, pg 284
Springer Science+Business Media GmbH & Co KG, Berlin, pg 285
Georg Thieme Verlag KG, pg 291
UNO-Verlag GmbH, pg 293
Wer liefert was? GmbH, pg 299
Verlag fuer Wirtschaft & Verwaltung Hubert Wingen GmbH & Co KG, pg 300
Wison Verlag GmbH, pg 300

Greece
Hestia-I D Hestia-Kollaros & Co Corporation, pg 308

Hungary
Polgar Kiado Kft, pg 324
Typotex Kft Elektronikus Kiado, pg 324

India
Asia Pacific Business Press Inc, pg 328
National Institute of Industrial Research (NIIR), pg 343

Ireland
European Foundation for the Improvement of Living & Working Conditions, pg 360
Royal Irish Academy, pg 363

Israel
The Institute for the Translation of Hebrew Literature, pg 368
MAP-Mapping & Publishing Ltd, pg 370

Japan
Toyo Keizai Shinpo-Sha, pg 430

Kenya
Academy Science Publishers, pg 432
Kenya Meteorological Department, pg 435

Republic of Korea
Chung Rim Publishing Co Ltd, pg 438
Korea Britannica Corp, pg 440
Maeil Gyeongje, pg 441

Latvia
Bibliography Institute of the National Library of Latvia, pg 444
S/A Tiesiskas informacijas cerfus, pg 445

Lithuania
Centre of Legal Information, pg 449
Lithuanian National Museum Publishing House, pg 449

The Former Yugoslav Republic of Macedonia
Medis, Skopje, pg 452

Malaysia
Malayan Law Journal Sdn Bhd, pg 456

Mexico
Ibcon SA, pg 466
Mercametrica Ediciones SA Edicion de Libros, pg 468

Morocco
Access International Services, pg 474
Office Marocain D'Annonces-OMA, pg 475

Netherlands
A W Bruna Uitgevers BV, pg 480
IOS Press BV, pg 484

New Zealand
Universal Business Directories, Australia Pty Ltd, pg 502

Oman
Apex Press & Publishing, pg 511

Poland
Wydawnictwo DiG, pg 522
Instytut Meteorologii i Gospodarki Wodnej, pg 523

Romania
Editura Excelsior Art, pg 539

Russian Federation
BLIC, russko-Baltijskij informaciionnyj centr, AO, pg 544

PUBLISHERS

Senegal

CODESRIA (Council for the Development of Social Science Research in Africa), pg 551

Singapore

LexisNexis, pg 557
Tecman Bible House, pg 558

Slovakia

Ustav informacii a prognoz skolstva mladeze a telovychovy, pg 561

South Africa

Centre for Conflict Resolution, pg 563
Jacklin Enterprises (Pty) Ltd, pg 565

Spain

Editorial Aranzadi SA, pg 573

Sweden

Bibliotekstjaenst AB, pg 610

Switzerland

Cockatoo Press (Schweiz), Thailand-Publikationen, pg 621

Taiwan, Province of China

Chien Chen Bookstore Publishing Company Ltd, pg 639
Wu Nan Book Co Ltd, pg 642

United Republic of Tanzania

Bureau of Statistics, pg 643

Tunisia

Faculte des Sciences Humaines et Sociales de Tunis, pg 648

Turkey

IKI Nokta Research Press & Publications Industry & Trade Ltd, pg 650
Saray Medikal Yayin Tic Ltd Sti, pg 651

United Kingdom

ABC-CLIO, pg 654
Advisory Unit: Computers in Education, pg 655
Anderson Rand Ltd, pg 657
Art Sales Index Ltd, pg 659
Chadwyck-Healey Ltd, pg 677
Electronic Publishing Services Ltd (EPS), pg 690
Encyclopaedia Britannica (UK) International Ltd, pg 691
EPER, pg 691
Euromonitor PLC, pg 692
First & Best in Education Ltd, pg 695
Foulsham Publishers, pg 696
Hobsons, pg 709
Institute of Physics Publishing, pg 713
Institution of Electrical Engineers, pg 713
James & James (Science Publishers) Ltd, pg 715
Jane's Information Group, pg 715
Macmillan Ltd, pg 723
National Council for Voluntary Organisations (NCVO), pg 730
Nielsen BookData, pg 733
Oilfield Publications Ltd, pg 734

ProQuest Information & Learning, pg 746
William Reed Directories, pg 749
Thomson Gale, pg 765
Trigon Press, pg 767
VNU Business Publications, pg 770
Wilmington Business Information Ltd, pg 774

DICTIONARIES, ENCYCLOPEDIAS

Albania

Fan Noli Verlag Rexhep Hida, pg 1
NL SH, pg 1
State Textbook Publishing House, pg 1

Algeria

Enterprise Nationale du Livre (ENAL), pg 2

Argentina

Abeledo-Perrot SAE e I, pg 2
Editorial Caymi SACI, pg 4
Editorial Claridad SA, pg 4
Editorial Ruy Diaz SAEIC, pg 5
Angel Estrada y Cia SA, pg 5
Editorial Kier SACIFI, pg 7
Laffont Ediciones Electronicas SA, pg 7
Ediciones Larousse Argentina SA, pg 7
Librograf Editora, pg 7
Instituto Nacional de Ciencia y Tecnica Hidrica (INCYTH), pg 7
Ediciones Preescolar SA, pg 8
Editorial Sopena Argentina SACI e I, pg 9
Tipografica Editora Argentina, pg 9

Australia

Robert Berthold Photography, pg 14
Bridgeway Publications, pg 16
Butterworths Australia Ltd, pg 16
China Books, pg 17
Encyclopaedia Britannica (Australia) Inc, pg 21
Era Publications, pg 21
Flora Publications International Pty Ltd, pg 22
Great Western Press Pty Ltd, pg 24
Illert Publications, pg 26
Institute of Aboriginal Development (IAD Press), pg 27
Rams Skull Press, pg 38
Reed Educational Publishing Australia, pg 39
Wileman Publications, pg 46
John Wiley & Sons Australia, Ltd, pg 46

Austria

Akademische Druck-u Verlagsanstalt Dr Paul Struzl GmbH, pg 48
Fassbaender Verlag, pg 50
Edition Dr Heinrich Fuchs, pg 51
Oesterreichischer Bundesverlag Gmbh, pg 55

Belarus

Belaruskaya Encyklapedyya, pg 62
Interdigest Publishing House, pg 62
Kavaler Publishers, pg 62
Narodnaya Asveta, pg 62

TYPE OF PUBLICATION INDEX

Belgium

Brepols Publishers NV, pg 64
Editions De Boeck-Larcier SA, pg 66
Dexia Bank, pg 66
Intersentia Uitgevers NV, pg 68
Maklu, pg 70
La Renaissance du Livre, pg 72
Standaard Uitgeverij, pg 73
Vlaamse Esperantobond VZW, pg 74

Bosnia and Herzegovina

Bemust, pg 76
Svjetlost, pg 76

Brazil

Abril SA, pg 76
Agalma Psicanalise Editora Ltda, pg 77
Ao Livro Tecnico Industria e Comercio Ltda, pg 77
Editora Campus Ltda, pg 79
Edicon Editora e Consultorial Ltda, pg 81
EDUSC - Editora da Universidade do Sagrado Coracao, pg 81
Livraria Martins Fontes Editora Ltda, pg 81
Editora Globo SA, pg 82
Hemus Editora Ltda, pg 83
IBRASA (Instituicao Brasileira de Difusao Cultural Ltda), pg 83
Libreria Editora Ltda, pg 85
Edicoes Loyola SA, pg 85
Editora Meca Ltda, pg 86
Editora Melhoramentos Ltda, pg 86
Editora Moderna Ltda, pg 86
Editora Nova Fronteira SA, pg 87
Pallas Editora e Distribuidora Ltda, pg 88
Paulus Editora, pg 88
Ediouro Publicacoes, SA, pg 89
Saraiva SA, Livreiros Editores, pg 90
Editora Scipione Ltda, pg 90
Tempus Editores, pg 91
Thex Editora e Distribuidora Ltda, pg 91
Editora Vigilia Ltda, pg 92

Bulgaria

Abagar Pablioing, pg 92
Abagar, Veliko Tarnovo, pg 93
Dolphin Press Group Ltd, pg 94
EA EOOD, pg 94
Hermes Publishing House, pg 94
Izdatelstvo Lettera, pg 95
Kibea Publishing Co, pg 95
LIK Izdanija, pg 95
Litera Prima, pg 95
Naouka i Izkoustvo, Ltd, pg 95
Nov Covek Publishing House, pg 96
Pensoft Publishers, pg 96
Prozoretz Ltd Publishing House, pg 96
Reporter, pg 96
Seven Hills Publishers, pg 96
Sluntse Publishing House, pg 97
Technica, pg 97

Chile

Arrayan Editores, pg 98
Norma de Chile, pg 99
Publicaciones Lo Castillo SA, pg 100

China

Anhui People's Publishing House, pg 101
Beijing Education Publishing House, pg 101
Beijing Juvenile & Children's Books Publishing House, pg 101
Beijing Publishing House, pg 101
Beijing University Press, pg 101
Chemical Industry Press, pg 101
China Foreign Economic Relations & Trade Publishing House, pg 102
China Light Industry Press, pg 102
China Machine Press (CMP), pg 102
China Materials Management Publishing House, pg 102
China Ocean Press, pg 102
China Theatre Publishing House, pg 103
China Translation & Publishing Corp, pg 103
CITIC Publishing House, pg 103
Electronics Industry Publishing House, pg 104
Encyclopedia of China Publishing House, pg 104
Fudan University Press, pg 104
Guizhou Education Publishing House, pg 105
Heilongjiang Science & Technology Press, pg 105
Higher Education Press, pg 105
Inner Mongolia Science & Technology Publishing House, pg 105
Jilin Science & Technology Publishing House, pg 105
Jinan Publishing House, pg 105
Language Publishing House, pg 106
The People's Communications Publishing House, pg 106
Qingdao Publishing House, pg 107
Science Press, pg 107
Shandong Friendship Publishing House, pg 107
Shandong Literature & Art Publishing House, pg 107
Shanghai Far East Publishers, pg 108
Shanghai Foreign Language Education Press, pg 108
Sichuan University Press, pg 108
Tianjin Science & Technology Publishing House, pg 108
Wuhan University Press, pg 109
Zhejiang Education Publishing House, pg 109
Zhong Hua Book Co, pg 110

Colombia

Asociacion Instituto Linguistico de Verano, pg 110
Eurolibros Ltda, pg 111
Editorial Libros y Libres SA, pg 112
Ediciones Monserrate, pg 112
Editorial Panamericana, pg 112
Pearson Educacion de Colombia LTDA, pg 112
Editorial Santillana SA, pg 112

Croatia

Globus-Nakladni zavod, pg 118
Graficki zavod Hrvatske, pg 118
Informator dd, pg 118
Leksikografski Zavod Miroslav Krleza, pg 118
Masmedia, pg 118
Matica hrvatska, pg 118

TYPE OF PUBLICATION INDEX BOOK

Mladost d d Izdavacku graficku i informaticku djelatnost, pg 119
Vitagraf, pg 119

Cuba

Instituto de Informacion Cientifica y Tecnologica (IDICT), pg 120

Czech Republic

Academia, pg 122
Barrister & Principal, pg 122
Ceska Biblicka Spolecnost, pg 123
Columbus, pg 123
Diderot sro, pg 123
Divadelni Ustav, pg 123
Granit sro, pg 123
Horacek Ladislav-Paseka, pg 123
Nakladatelstvi Jan Vasut, pg 124
Karmelitanske Nakladatelstvi, pg 124
Karolinum, nakladatelstvi, pg 124
Libri spol sro, pg 125
Lidove Noviny Publishing House, pg 125
Maxdorf Ltd, pg 125
Nase vojsko, nakladatelstvi a knizni obchod, pg 126
Omnipress Praha, pg 126
Prostor, nakladatelstvi sro, pg 127
SystemConsult, pg 127
Votobia sro, pg 128

Denmark

Aschehoug Dansk Forlag A/S, pg 129
Gads Forlag, pg 131

Dominican Republic

Sociedad Editorial Americana, pg 136

Ecuador

Biblioteca Ecuatoriana Aurelio Espinosa Polit', pg 136
CIESPAL (Centro Internacional de Estudios Superiores de Comunicacion para America Latina), pg 136
Corporacion Editora Nacional, pg 136

Egypt (Arab Republic of Egypt)

Al Arab Publishing House, pg 137
Dar El Shorouk, pg 138
Elias Modern Publishing House, pg 138

Estonia

Eesti Entsuklopeediakirjastus, pg 139
Eesti Piibliselts, pg 139
Eesti Rahvusraamatukogu, pg 139
Ilmamaa, pg 139
Perioodika, pg 140
TEA Kirjastus, pg 140
Valgus Publishers, pg 140

Ethiopia

Addis Ababa University Press, pg 140

Finland

Otava Publishing Co Ltd, pg 143
Suomalaisen Kirjallisuuden Seura, pg 144
Tietoteos Publishing Co, pg 144
Werner Soederstrom Osakeyhtio (WSOY), pg 145
Yliopistopaino/Helsinki University Press, pg 145

France

Editions Al Liamm, pg 146
Armenia Editions, pg 147
Editions de l'Atelier, pg 148
Editions Belin, pg 149
Editions Bordas, pg 150
Emgleo Breiz, pg 151
Bureau des Longitudes, pg 151
Chasse Maree, pg 153
Counseil International de la Langue Francaise, pg 156
Editions Dalloz Sirey, pg 157
Editions du Dauphin, pg 157
Les Devenirs Visuels, pg 158
Les Dossiers d'Aquitaine, pg 159
Encyclopedia Universalis France SA, pg 161
L'Esprit Du Temps, pg 162
Institut d'Etudes Slaves IES, pg 162
Paul Geuthner Librairie Orientaliste, pg 165
Hachette Education, pg 166
Editions Hazan, pg 167
INRA Editions (Institut National de la Recherche Agronomique), pg 168
Joly Editions, pg 169
Karthala Editions-Diffusion, pg 170
Editions Lacour-Olle, pg 170
Langues & Mondes-L'Asiatheque, pg 171
Editions Larousse, pg 171
Editions Legislatives, pg 171
Letouzey et Ane Editeurs, pg 171
Le Livre de Paris, pg 173
LLB France (Ligue pour la Lecture de la Bible), pg 173
La Maison du Dictionnaire, pg 173
Editions Mango, pg 174
Masson-Williams et Wilkins, pg 174
Editions de la Reunion des Musees Nationaux, pg 176
Editions Fernand Nathan, pg 176
Editions du Centre Pompidou, pg 180
Presses Universitaires de France (PUF), pg 181
Le Robert, pg 183
Editions Technip SA, pg 187
Universitas, pg 188
Editions de Vegeures, pg 188
Editions Philateliques Yvert et Tellier, pg 189

Germany

AOL-Verlag Frohmut Menze, pg 193
J J Augustin Verlag GmbH, pg 195
Axel Juncker Verlag Jacobi KG, pg 196
Barenreiter-Verlag Karl-Votterle GmbH & Co KG, pg 197
Bauverlag GmbH, pg 198
Verlag C H Beck oHG, pg 198
Bertelsmann Lexikon Verlag GmbH, pg 200
Verlag Beruf und Schule Belz KG, pg 200
Bibliographisches Institut & F A Brockhaus AG, pg 200
Bibliographisches Institut GmbH, pg 201
Verlag Hermann Boehlaus Nachfolger Weimar GmbH & Co, pg 203
Oscar Brandstetter Verlag GmbH & Co KG, pg 204
F A Brockhaus GmbH, pg 204
Helmut Buske Verlag GmbH, pg 206
Calwer Verlag GmbH, pg 207
Marianne Cieslik, pg 209
Compact Verlag GmbH, pg 209
Verlag Darmstaedter Blaetter Schwarz und Co, pg 210
Deutscher Taschenbuch Verlag GmbH & Co KG (dtv), pg 213
Verlagsgruppe Droemer Knaur GmbH & Co KG, pg 216
Ecomed Verlagsgesellschaft AG & Co KG, pg 218
Elpis Verlag GmbH, pg 219
Encyclopedia Britannica, pg 219
Verlag Esoterische Philosophie GmbH, pg 221
Fachbuchverlag Pfanneberg & Co, pg 223
Festo Didactic GmbH & Co KG, pg 224
Harald Fischer Verlag GmbH, pg 224
Verlag Franz Vahlen GmbH, pg 226
Betriebswirtschaftlicher Verlag Dr Th Gabler, pg 228
Gebrueder Borntraeger Science Publishers, pg 228
Walter de Gruyter GmbH & Co KG, pg 231
Harenberg Kommunikation Verlags- und Medien-GmbH & Co KG, pg 234
Verlag Herder GmbH & Co KG, pg 236
Ernst Klett Verlag GmbH, pg 247
Verlag Fritz Knapp GmbH, pg 247
Knowledge Media International, pg 247
W Kohlhammer GmbH, pg 248
Laaber-Verlag, pg 251
Langenscheidt Fachverlag GmbH, pg 252
Langenscheidt KG, pg 252
Magnus Verlag, pg 256
Margraf Verlag, pg 257
Neuer Honos Verlag GmbH, pg 264
Max Niemeyer Verlag GmbH, pg 265
Georg Olms Verlag AG, pg 267
Polyglott-Verlag, pg 271
Polygraph Verlag GmbH, pg 271
Propylaeen Verlag, Zweigniederlassung Berlin der Ullstein Buchverlage GmbH, pg 272
Quintessenz Verlags-GmbH, pg 273
Dr Ludwig Reichert Verlag, pg 274
E Reinhold Verlag, pg 275
Reise Know-How Verlag Peter Rump GmbH, pg 275
Verlagsgruppe Reise Know-How, pg 275
Romiosini Verlag, pg 276
K G Saur Verlag GmbH, A Gale/Thomson Learning Company, pg 278
Schott Musik International GmbH & Co KG, pg 281
Theodor Schuster, pg 282
E Schweizerbart'sche Verlagsbuchhandlung (Naegele und Obermiller), pg 282
Silberburg-Verlag Titus Haeussermann GmbH, pg 283
Springer Science+Business Media GmbH & Co KG, pg 284
Verlag Stahleisen GmbH, pg 286
Straelener Manuskripte Verlag GmbH, pg 288
Wachholtz Verlag GmbH, pg 297
Wiley-VCH Verlag GmbH, pg 300
Xenos Verlagsgesellschaft mbH, pg 301

Ghana

Bureau of Ghana Languages, pg 303
EPP Books Services, pg 304

Greece

Alamo Hellas, pg 305
Athina, Mary Mavrogiannis, pg 306
Diavlos, pg 306
Dodoni Publications, pg 306
Ekdoseis Domi AE, pg 306
Ekdotike Athenon SA, pg 307
Eleftheroudakis, GCSA International Bookstore, pg 307
Hestia-I D Hestia-Kollaros & Co Corporation, pg 308
Hiotellis P, pg 308
I Prooptiki, Ekdoseis, pg 308
Institute of Neohellenic Studies, Manolis Triantaphyllidis Foundation, pg 308
Kalentis & Sia, pg 308
Ilias Kambanas Publishing Organization, SA, pg 309
Kastaniotis Editions SA, pg 309
Kyriakidis Vasileios, pg 309
Nakas Music House, pg 310
Pagoulatos Bros, pg 311
Pagoulatos G-G P Publications, pg 311
Patakis Publishers, pg 311
Rossi, E Kdoseis Eleni Rossi-Petsiou, pg 312
Sakkoulas Publications SA, pg 312
Michalis Sideris, pg 312
J Vassiliou Bibliopolein, pg 313
S J Zacharopoulos SA Publishing Co, pg 313

Haiti

Editions Caraibes SA, pg 314

Hong Kong

The Chinese University Press, pg 316
Chung Hwa Book Co (HK) Ltd, pg 316
Commercial Press (Hong Kong) Ltd, pg 316
Joint Publishing (HK) Co Ltd, pg 317
Peace Book Co Ltd, pg 318

Hungary

Akademiai Kiado, pg 320
Aranyhal Konyvkiado Goldfish Publishing, pg 320
Balassi Kiado Kft, pg 321
Greger-Delacroix, pg 321
Joszoveg Muhely Kiado, pg 322
Kossuth Kiado RT, pg 322
Novorg International Szervezo es Kiado kft, pg 323
Officina Nova Konyvek, pg 323
Panem, pg 324

Iceland

Bokautgafan Orn og Orlygur ehf, pg 325
Isafoldarprentsmidja hf, pg 326
Mal og menning, pg 326

India

Addison-Wesley Pte Ltd, pg 327
Agam Kala Prakashan, pg 327

PUBLISHERS

Agricole Publishing Academy, pg 327
Allied Publishers Pvt Ltd, pg 328
Ananda Publishers Pvt Ltd, pg 328
Anmol Publications Pvt Ltd, pg 328
Asian Educational Services, pg 329
Avinash Reference Publications, pg 329
Bani Mandir, Book-Sellers, Publishers & Educational Suppliers, pg 329
Bharat Publishing House, pg 330
Book Circle, pg 330
BR Publishing Corporation, pg 331
Cosmo Publications, pg 332
Diamond Comics (P) Ltd, pg 333
DK Printworld (P) Ltd, pg 333
Dutta Publishing Co Ltd, pg 333
General Book Depot, pg 335
Gyan Publishing House, pg 335
Heritage Publishers, pg 335
International Book Distributors, pg 338
Islamic Publishing House, pg 338
Law Publishers, pg 340
Munshiram Manoharlal Publishers Pvt Ltd, pg 342
National Book Organization, pg 342
Natraj Prakashan, Publishers & Exporters, pg 343
Omsons Publications, pg 344
Oxford University Press, pg 344
Parimal Prakashan, pg 345
Pitamber Publishing Co (P) Ltd, pg 345
Prabhat Prakashan, pg 345
Pratibha Pratishthan, pg 345
Publications & Information Directorate, CSIR, pg 345
Pustak Mahal, pg 345
Rahul Publishing House, pg 346
Rajendra Publishing House Pvt Ltd, pg 346
Rajpal & Sons, pg 346
Reliance Publishing House, pg 346
M C Sarkar & Sons (P) Ltd, pg 348
Sat Sahitya Prakashan, pg 348
Scientific Book Agency, pg 348
Shaibya Prakashan Bibhag, pg 349
Shiksha Bharati, pg 349
Sita Books & Periodicals Pvt Ltd, pg 349
Star Publications (P) Ltd, pg 350
Vidya Puri, pg 352
Vidyarthi Mithram Press, pg 352

Indonesia

PT Indira, pg 355
Karya Anda, CV, pg 355
Mizan, pg 355
Nusa Indah, pg 356

Ireland

An Gum, pg 358
Irish Texts Society (Cumann Na Scribeann nGaedhilge), pg 361
Topaz Publications, pg 364

Israel

Academy of the Hebrew Language, pg 364
Achiasaf Publishing House Ltd, pg 364
Achiever, pg 364
Amichai Publishing House Ltd, pg 365
The Bialik Institute, pg 365
Carta, The Israel Map & Publishing Co Ltd, pg 365
Classikaletet, pg 366
Dvir Publishing Ltd, pg 366
Gefen Publishing House Ltd, pg 367
Hakibbutz Hameuchad Publishing House Ltd, pg 367
Intermedia Audio, Video Book Publishing Ltd, pg 368
The Jerusalem Publishing House Ltd, pg 369
K Dictionaries Ltd, pg 369
Kernerman Publishing Ltd, pg 369
Keter Publishing House Ltd, pg 369
Kiryat Sefer, pg 369
Ma'ariv Book Guild (Sifriat Ma'ariv), pg 370
MAP-Mapping & Publishing Ltd, pg 370
Massada Press Ltd, pg 370
Misgav Yerushalayim, pg 370
M Mizrahi Publishers, pg 370
Prolog Publishing House, pg 371
Rolnik Publishers, pg 371
Rubin Mass Ltd, pg 371
Schlesinger Institute, pg 371
Schocken Publishing House Ltd, pg 371
Talmudic Encyclopedia Publications, pg 372
Yad Vashem - The Holocaust Martyrs' & Heroes' Remembrance Authority, pg 373
Yavneh Publishing House Ltd, pg 373
Zakheim Publishing House, pg 373

Italy

De Agostini Scolastica, pg 374
Alba, pg 375
Bompiani-RCS Libri, pg 378
Edizioni Bora SNC di E Brandani & C, pg 379
Casa Editrice Libraria Ulrico Hoepli SpA, pg 380
Citta Nuova Editrice, pg 382
Cittadella Editrice, pg 382
Editrice Eraclea, pg 388
Edi.Ermes srl, pg 388
Esselibri, pg 388
Federico Motta Editore SpA, pg 389
Festina Lente Edizioni, pg 389
Arnaldo Forni Editore SRL, pg 389
Garzanti Libri, pg 390
Istituto Geografico de Agostini SpA, pg 390
Edizioni del Girasole srl, pg 390
Giunti Gruppo Editoriale, pg 390
Ernesto Gremese Editore srl, pg 391
Istituto della Enciclopedia Italiana, pg 393
Editoriale Jaca Book SpA, pg 394
Casa Editrice Le Lettere SRL, pg 395
Librex, pg 395
Vincenzo Lo Faro Editore, pg 395
Loescher Editore SRL, pg 396
Angelo Longo Editore, pg 396
Macmillan Heinemann ELT, pg 396
Tommaso Marotta Editore Srl, pg 397
Edumond Le Monnier, pg 399
OCTAVO Produzioni Editoriali Associale, pg 401
Editoriale Olimpia SpA, pg 401
Leo S Olschki, pg 401
Paravia Bruno Mondadori Editori, pg 402
Edizioni Piemme SpA, pg 403
Amilcare Pizzi SpA, pg 403
RCS Libri SpA, pg 405
Editori Riuniti, pg 405
SAIE Editrice SRL, pg 406
Edizioni San Paolo SRL, pg 407
Sansoni-RCS Libri, pg 407
Edizioni Librarie Siciliane, pg 408
Societa Editrice Internazionale - SEI, pg 408
Nicola Teti e C Editore SRL, pg 410
Who's Who In Italy srl, pg 412
Zanichelli Editore SpA, pg 412

Japan

Bunkashobo-Hakubun-Sha, pg 415
Dogakusha Inc, pg 416
Dohosha Publishing Co Ltd, pg 417
Fumaido Publishing Company Ltd, pg 417
Fuzambo Publishing Co, pg 417
Gakken Co Ltd, pg 417
Hakusui-Sha Co Ltd, pg 417
Hakutei-Sha, pg 418
Hakuyu-Sha, pg 418
Heibonsha Ltd, Publishers, pg 418
Hirokawa Publishing Co, pg 418
Hokuryukan Co Ltd, pg 418
Ishihara Publishing Co Ltd, pg 419
Itaria Shobo Ltd, pg 419
Iwanami Shoten, Publishers, pg 419
Kadokawa Shoten Publishing Co Ltd, pg 420
Kaitakusha, pg 420
Maruzen Co Ltd, pg 422
Meiji Shoin Co Ltd, pg 422
Nagaoka Shoten Co Ltd, pg 423
Nakayama Shoten Co Ltd, pg 423
Nan'un-Do Co Ltd, pg 423
Nensho-Sha, pg 423
Nigensha Publishing Co Ltd, pg 423
Obunsha Co Ltd, pg 424
Ohmsha Ltd, pg 424
Ongaku No Tomo Sha Corporation, pg 425
Rinsen Book Co Ltd, pg 425
Sankyo Publishing Company Ltd, pg 426
Sanseido Co Ltd, pg 426
Sanshusha Publishing Co, Ltd, pg 426
Seishin Shobo, pg 427
Shimizu-Shoin, pg 427
Shincho-Sha Co Ltd, pg 427
Shokokusha Publishing Co Ltd, pg 428
Surugadai-Shuppan Sha, pg 429
Takahashi Shoten Co Ltd, pg 429
TBS-Britannica Co Ltd, pg 429
Toho Book Store, pg 429
Tokyo Shoseki Co Ltd, pg 430

Kenya

Heinemann Kenya Ltd (EAEP), pg 434
Kenway Publications Ltd, pg 434
Lake Publishers & Enterprises Ltd, pg 435
Macmillan Kenya Publishers Ltd, pg 435
Phoenix Publishers Ltd, pg 435
Sudan Literature Centre, pg 436

Democratic People's Republic of Korea

Grand People's Study House, pg 436
Korea Science and Encyclopedia Publishing House, pg 436

Republic of Korea

Chung Rim Publishing Co Ltd, pg 438
Dong-A Publishing & Printing Co Ltd, pg 438
Hollym Corporation; Publishers, pg 439
Ke Mong Sa Publishing Co Ltd, pg 440
Ki Moon Dang, pg 440
Korea Britannica Corp, pg 440
Kukmin Doseo Publishing Co Ltd, pg 440
Kukminseokwan Publishing Co Ltd, pg 440
Kyohaksa Publishing Co Ltd, pg 440
Min Jung Seo Rim Publishing Co, pg 441
Panmun Book Co Ltd, pg 442
Samseong Publishing Co Ltd, pg 442
YBM/Si-sa, pg 443
Yearimdang Publishing Co, pg 443

Latvia

Avots, pg 444
Nordik/Tapals Publishers Ltd, pg 445
Preses Nams, pg 445
Vaidelote, SIA, pg 445

Lebanon

Arab Institute for Research & Publishing, pg 445
Dar Al-Kitab Al-Loubnani, pg 445
Dar El Ilm Lilmalayin, pg 446
Dar-El-Machreq Sarl, pg 446
Librairie du Liban Publishers (Sal), pg 446
Librairie Orientale sal, pg 446
Naufal Group Sarl, pg 447

Lithuania

Alma Littera, pg 448
Eugrimas, pg 449
Lithuanian National Museum Publishing House, pg 449
Mokslo ir enciklopediju leidybos institutas, pg 449
Margi Rastai Publishers, pg 449
Sviesa Publishers, pg 449
TEV Leidykla, pg 450
Tyto Alba Publishers, pg 450
Vaga Ltd, pg 450
Victoria Publishers, pg 450

The Former Yugoslav Republic of Macedonia

Detska radost, pg 452
Murgorski Zoze, pg 453
Strk Publishing House, pg 453

Malaysia

S Abdul Majeed & Co, pg 454
Eastview Productions Sdn Bhd, pg 455
Federal Publications Sdn Bhd, pg 455
FEP International Sdn Bhd, pg 456
Mahir Publications Sdn Bhd, pg 456
MDC Publishers Printers Sdn Bhd, pg 457
Minerva Publications, pg 457
Pelanduk Publications (M) Sdn Bhd, pg 457
Penerbit Jayatinta Sdn Bhd, pg 458
Perfect Frontier Sdn Bhd, pg 458
Pustaka Delta Pelajaran Sdn Bhd, pg 458
Times Educational Co Sdn Bhd, pg 459
Utusan Publications & Distributors Sdn Bhd, pg 459

TYPE OF PUBLICATION INDEX — BOOK

Mexico
Editora Cientifica Medica Latinoamerican SA de CV, pg 463
Ediciones Culturales Internacionales SA de CV Edicion Compra y Venta de Libros, Casetes, Videos, pg 463
Maria Esther De Fleischmann, pg 464
Editorial Diana SA de CV, pg 464
Entretenlibro SA de CV, pg 465
Editorial Esfinge SA de CV, pg 465
Editorial Fata Morgana SA de CV, pg 465
Fernandez Editores SA de CV, pg 465
Fondo de Cultura Economica, pg 465
Grupo Editorial Iberoamerica, SA de CV, pg 466
Ediciones Larousse SA de CV, pg 467
Libros y Revistas SA de CV, pg 467
Editorial Limusa SA de CV, pg 467
Naves Internacional de Ediciones SA, pg 469
Nova Grupo Editorial SA de CV, pg 469
Organizacion Cultural LP SA de CV, pg 469
Pangea Editores, Sa de CV, pg 470
Panorama Editorial, SA, pg 470
Plaza y Valdes SA de CV, pg 470
Salvat Editores de Mexico, pg 471
SCRIPTA - Distribucion y Servicios Editoriales, SA de CV, pg 471
Sistemas Tecnicos de Edicion SA de CV, pg 472
Ediciones Suromex SA, pg 472

Republic of Moldova
Editura Cartea Moldovei, pg 473
Editura Lumina, pg 473

Morocco
Editions Okad, pg 475

Myanmar
Sarpay Beikman Public Library, pg 476

Netherlands
APA (Academic Publishers Associated), pg 477
BoekWerk, pg 479
Brill Academic Publishers, pg 479
Elmar BV, pg 482
Kluwer Technische Boeken BV, pg 485
The Pepin Press, pg 487
Reed Elsevier Nederland BV, pg 488
Uitgeverij Het Spectrum BV, pg 489
Van Dale Lexicografie BV, pg 491

New Zealand
Auckland University Press, pg 493
David Bateman Ltd, pg 494
HarperCollins Publishers (New Zealand) Ltd, pg 497

Nigeria
Evans Brothers (Nigeria Publishers) Ltd, pg 504
Nigerian Trade Review, pg 506
Riverside Communications, pg 507

Norway
J W Cappelens Forlag A/S, pg 508
N W Damm og Son A/S, pg 508
Det Norske Samlaget, pg 508
Elanders Publishing AS, pg 509
Gyldendal Norsk Forlag A/S, pg 509
Kunnskapsforlaget ANS, pg 509

Pakistan
The Book House, pg 512
Ferozsons (Pvt) Ltd, pg 512
Jang Publishers, pg 513
Maqbool Academy, pg 513
Nashiran-e-Quran Pvt Ltd, pg 513
Sang-e-Meel Publications, pg 514

Paraguay
Intercontinental Editora, pg 516

Peru
Ediciones Brown SA, pg 516

Philippines
Anvil Publishing Inc, pg 518
J C Palabay Enterprises, pg 519
Marren Publishing House, Inc, pg 519
Our Lady of Manaoag Publisher, pg 520
Rex Bookstores & Publishers, pg 520

Poland
Wydawnictwo DiG, pg 522
Energeia sp zoo Wydawnictwo, pg 523
Instytut Wydawniczy Pax, Inco-Veritas, pg 523
Iskry - Publishing House Ltd spotka zoo, pg 523
Ksiaznica Publishing Ltd, pg 524
Ludowa Spoldzielnia Wydawnicza, pg 524
Magnum Publishing House Ltd, pg 524
Muza SA, pg 524
Wydawnictwa Naukowo-Techniczne, pg 524
Ossolineum Zaklad Narodowy im Ossolinskich - Wydawnictwo, pg 525
Polish Scientific Publishers PWN, pg 525
Wydawnictwo Prawnicze Co, pg 526
PZWL Wydawnictwo Lekarskie Ltd, pg 526
Oficyna Wydawnicza Read Me, pg 526
Res Polona, pg 526
Wydawnictwo RTW, pg 526
'Slask' Ltd, pg 526
Videograf II Sp z o o Zaklad Poracy Chronionej, pg 527
'Wiedza Powszechna' Panstwowe Wydawnictwo, pg 527
Wydawnictwo Wilga sp zoo, pg 527

Portugal
Publicacoes Alfa SA, pg 528
Bertrand Editora Lda, pg 529
Editora Classica, pg 530
Editorial Confluencia Lda, pg 530
Constancia Editores, SA, pg 530
Edicoes Cosmos, pg 530
DIFEL - Difusao Editorial SA, pg 530
Dinalivro, pg 530
Europress Editores e Distribuidores de Publicacoes Lda, pg 531
Everest Editora, pg 531
Empresa Literaria Fluminense, Lda, pg 531
Latina Livraria Editora, pg 532
Livraria Apostolado da Imprensa, pg 533
Editora McGraw-Hill de Portugal Lda, pg 533
Melhoramentos de Portugal Editora, Lda, pg 533
Editorial Noticias, pg 534
Planeta Editora, LDA, pg 534
Porto Editora Lda, pg 535
Editorial Presenca, pg 535
Quimera Editores Lda, pg 535
Editora Replicacao Lda, pg 535
Edicioes Joao Sa da Costa Lda, pg 535
Edicoes 70 Lda, pg 535
Teorema, pg 536
Editorial Verbo SA, pg 536

Romania
Editura Academiei Romane, pg 538
Editura Aius, pg 538
Editora All, pg 538
Artemis Verlag, pg 538
The Center for Romanian Studies, pg 539
Editura Clusium, pg 539
Coresi SRL, pg 539
Corint Publishing Group, pg 539
Enzyklopadie Verlag, pg 539
Editura Excelsior Art, pg 539
FF Press, pg 540
Editura Gryphon, pg 540
Hasefer, pg 540
Humanitas Publishing House, pg 540
Editura Kriterion SA, pg 540
Lider Verlag, pg 540
Editura Meridiane, pg 540
Nemira Verlag, pg 541
Editura Niculescu, pg 541
Pallas-Akademia Editura, pg 541
Grupul Editorial RAO, pg 542
RAO International Publishing Co, pg 542
Rentrop & Straton Verlagsgruppe und Wirtschaftsconsulting, pg 542
Saeculum IO, pg 542
Editura Stiintifica SA, pg 542
Editura Stiintifica si Enciclopedica, pg 542
Est-Samuel Tastet Verlag, pg 542
Editura Tehnica, pg 542
Editura Teora, pg 542
Vestala Verlag, pg 543
Vox Editura, pg 543
Vremea Publishers Ltd, pg 543

Russian Federation
Airis Press, pg 543
Aspect Press Ltd, pg 543
Izdatelstvo Bolshaya Rossiyskaya Entsiklopedia, pg 544
FGUP Izdatelstvo Mashinostroenie, pg 544
Finansy i Statistika Publishing House, pg 544
Izdatelstvo Iskusstvo, pg 545
Izdatelskii Dom Kompozitor, pg 546
KUbK Publishing House, pg 546
Ladomir Publishing House, pg 546
Publishing House Limbus Press, pg 546
Izdatelstvo Mir, pg 546
Mir Knigi Ltd, pg 546
Izdatelstvo Muzyka, pg 547
Izdatelstvo Prosveshchenie, pg 548
Raduga Publishers, pg 548
Respublika, pg 548
Russkij Jazyk, pg 548
Izdatelstvo Sudostroenie, pg 549
Teorija Verojatnostej i ee Primenenija, pg 549
Text Publishers Ltd Too, pg 549
Izdatelstvo Ural' skogo, pg 549
Voronezh State University Publishers, pg 549

Saudi Arabia
King Saud University, pg 550

Senegal
Nouvelles Editions Africaines du Senegal (NEAS), pg 551
Les Nouvelles Editions Africaines du Senegal NEAS, pg 551

Serbia and Montenegro
Alfa-Narodna Knjiga, pg 552
Beogradski Izdavacko-Graficki Zavod, pg 552
Tehnicka Knjiga, pg 552
Minerva, pg 552
Obod, pg 553
Izdavacko Preduzece Matice Srpske, pg 553
Radnicka Stampa, pg 553
Vuk Karadzic, pg 554

Singapore
Archipelago Press, pg 555
Chopsons Pte Ltd, pg 555
Federal Publications (S) Pte Ltd, pg 556
FEP International Private Ltd, pg 556
Shing Lee Group Publishers, pg 558
Taylor & Francis Asia Pacific, pg 558

Slovakia
Priroda Publishing, pg 560
Slo Viet, pg 560
Slovenske pedagogicke nakladateistvo, pg 560
Ustav informacii a prognoz skolskej mladeze a telovychovy, pg 561
VEDA (Vydavatel'stvo Slovenskej akademie vied), pg 561

Slovenia
Cankarjeva Zalozba, pg 561
Mladinska Knjiga International, pg 561
Zalozba Mihelac d o o, pg 562
Zalozba Obzorja d d Maribor, pg 562

South Africa
Educum Publishers Ltd, pg 563
New Africa Books (Pty) Ltd, pg 567
Sasavona Publishers & Booksellers, pg 568
Tafelberg Publishers Ltd, pg 569
Witwatersrand University Press, pg 570

Spain
Ediciones Akal SA, pg 571
Anaya Educacion, pg 573
Anglo-Didactica, SL Editorial, pg 573
Arco Libros SL, pg 573
Calambur Editorial, SL, pg 575
Editorial Claret SA, pg 577

PUBLISHERS — TYPE OF PUBLICATION INDEX

Editora Comercial de Publicaciones, pg 577
Curial Edicions Catalanes SA, pg 578
Ediciones Daly S L, pg 578
Didaco Comunicacion y Didactica, SA, pg 579
Durvan SA de Ediciones, pg 580
Ediciones l'Isard, S L, pg 580
Edicomunicacion SA, pg 581
Editorial Everest SA, pg 581
El Hogar y la Moda SA, pg 581
Elkar, Euskal Liburu eta Kantuen Argitaldaria, SL, pg 582
Enciclopedia Catalana, SA, pg 582
Editorial Espasa-Calpe SA, pg 582
EUNSA (Ediciones Universidad de Navarra SA), pg 583
Forum Artis, SA, pg 583
Galaxia SA Editorial, pg 584
Gran Enciclopedia-Asturiana Silverio Canada, pg 585
Editorial Gredos SA, pg 585
Grijalbo Mondadori SA, pg 585
Hercules de Ediciones, SA, pg 586
Ediciones Istmo SA, pg 588
Editorial Juventud SA, pg 588
Larousse Editorial SA, pg 588
Libsa Editorial SA, pg 589
LID Editorial Empresarial, SL, pg 589
Lynx Edicions, pg 590
Editorial Marin SA, pg 590
Editorial Moll SL, pg 592
Anaya & Mario Muchnik, pg 592
Mundi-Prensa Libros SA, pg 592
Ediciones Norma SA, pg 593
Ediciones Oceano Grupo SA, pg 593
Oikos-Tau SA Ediciones, pg 593
Editorial Alfredo Ortells SL, pg 594
Editorial Paidotribo SL, pg 594
Editorial Paraninfo SA, pg 595
Parramon Ediciones SA, pg 595
Editorial Parthenon Communication, SL, pg 595
Ediciones Piramide SA, pg 596
Pulso Ediciones, SL, pg 597
Ediciones Rialp SA, pg 598
Josep Ruaix Editor, pg 598
San Pablo Ediciones, pg 598
Edicions 62, pg 600
Grup 62, pg 600
Ramon Sopena SA, pg 600
SPES Editorial SL, pg 600
Stanley Editorial, pg 601
Editorial De Vecchi SA, pg 604
Editorial Verbo Divino, pg 604
Editorial Verbum SL, pg 604
Veron Editor, pg 604

Sri Lanka

Lake House Investments Ltd, pg 606
Warna Publishers, pg 607

Sweden

Bokforlaget Bra Bocker AB, pg 610
Forlagshuset Norden AB, pg 611
Informationsfoerlaget AB, pg 612
Lidman Production AB, pg 613
Mezopotamya Publishing & Distribution, pg 613
Bokfoerlaget Natur och Kultur, pg 613
Norstedts Ordbok, pg 614
Psykologiforlaget AB, pg 614
Bokfoerlaget Rediviva, Facsimileforlaget, pg 615

Switzerland

Cockatoo Press (Schweiz), Thailand-Publikationen, pg 621
Comite international de la Croix-Rouge, pg 621
Marcel Dekker AG, pg 621
Verlag Harri Deutsch, pg 622
Duboux Editions SA, pg 622
Kinderbuchverlag Luzern, pg 626
Kindler Verlag AG, pg 626
Larousse (Suisse) SA, pg 627
Muslim Architecture Research Program (MARP), pg 629
Edition Olms AG, pg 630
Ott Verlag Thun, pg 630
Punktum AG, Buchredaktion und Bildarchiv, pg 632
Schnellmann-Verlag, pg 633
Schwabe & Co AG, pg 633
Weltrundschau Verlag AG, pg 637

Taiwan, Province of China

Chien Chen Bookstore Publishing Company Ltd, pg 639
Chung Hwa Book Co Ltd, pg 639
Far East Book Co Ltd, pg 639
Hsiao Yuan Publication Co, Ltd, pg 640
Kuang Fu Book Co Ltd, pg 640
Laureate Book Co Ltd, pg 640
Linking Publishing Company Ltd, pg 641
San Min Book Co Ltd, pg 641
World Book Co Ltd, pg 642
Wu Nan Book Co Ltd, pg 642

United Republic of Tanzania

Ben and Company Ltd, pg 643

Thailand

Suksapan Panit (Business Organization of Teachers Council of Thailand), pg 645
Thai Watana Panich Co, Ltd, pg 646

Tunisia

Academie Tunisienne des Sciences, des Lettres et des Arts Beit El Hekma, pg 647
Dar Arabia Lil Kitab, pg 648

Turkey

ABC Kitabevi AS, pg 648
Afa Yayincilik Sanayi Tic AS, pg 648
Altin Kitaplar Yayinevi, pg 649
Arkadas Ltd, pg 649
Arkin Kitabevi, pg 649
Ataturk Kultur, Dil ve Tarih, Yusek Kurumu Baskanligi, pg 649
Ezel Erverdi (Dergah Yayinlari AS) Muessese Muduru, pg 650
IKI Nokta Research Press & Publications Industry & Trade Ltd, pg 650
Iletisim Yayinlari, pg 650
Inkilap Publishers Ltd, pg 650
Kiyi Yayinlari, pg 650
Pearson Education Turkey, pg 651
Remzi Kitabevi, pg 651
Sabah Kitaplari, pg 651
Yapi-Endustri Merkezi Yayinlari-Yem Yayin, pg 652

Uganda

Fountain Publishers Ltd, pg 652

Ukraine

ASK Ltd, pg 653
Naukova Dumka Publishers, pg 653
Osvita, pg 654

United Kingdom

ABC-CLIO, pg 654
Andromeda Oxford Ltd, pg 658
Arms & Armour Press, pg 659
Art Sales Index Ltd, pg 659
AS Publishing, pg 660
Ashgate Publishing Ltd, pg 660
BCA - Book Club Associates, pg 663
Berlitz (UK) Ltd, pg 665
Blandford Publishing Ltd, pg 668
Bloomsbury Publishing PLC, pg 668
Blueprint, pg 668
Book Packaging & Marketing, pg 668
Books for Europe Ltd, pg 669
Butterworths Tolley, pg 673
Cambridge University Press, pg 674
Cassell & Co, pg 675
Chambers Harrap Publishers Ltd, pg 677
James Clarke & Co Ltd, pg 680
Peter Collin Publishing Ltd, pg 680
Constable & Robinson Ltd, pg 682
Leo Cooper, pg 683
CTBI Publications, pg 685
Christopher Davies Publishers Ltd, pg 686
Diagram Visual Information Ltd, pg 687
Encyclopaedia Britannica (UK) International Ltd, pg 691
Fishing News Books Ltd, pg 695
Flame Tree Publishing, pg 695
Flicks Books, pg 695
Gairm Publications, pg 698
Geddes & Grosset, pg 699
Graham-Cameron Publishing & Illustration, pg 701
W Green The Scottish Law Publisher, pg 702
Guinness World Records Ltd, pg 703
HarperCollins UK, pg 705
Helicon Publishing Ltd, pg 707
Hilmarton Manor Press, pg 708
Institute of Physics Publishing, pg 713
International Bee Research Association, pg 714
The Islamic Texts Society, pg 715
Kegan Paul International Ltd, pg 717
Kingfisher Publications Plc, pg 717
Letterbox Library, pg 720
The Lutterworth Press, pg 723
Macmillan Heinemann ELT, pg 723
Macmillan Ltd, pg 723
The Mansk Svenska Publishing Co Ltd, pg 725
Melrose Press Ltd, pg 726
Motilal (UK) Books of India, pg 729
Oneworld Publications, pg 735
Orpheus Books Ltd, pg 736
Packard Publishing Ltd, pg 737
Pearson Education, pg 739
Penguin Books Ltd, pg 740
Philip's, pg 741
Portland Press Ltd, pg 745
Quartz Editions, pg 746
The Reader's Digest Association Ltd, pg 748
Roundhouse Group, pg 751
Routledge, pg 751
RoutledgeCurzon, pg 751
St Pauls Publishing, pg 753
Salamander Books Ltd, pg 753
Stacey International, pg 761
Sweet & Maxwell Ltd, pg 762
I B Tauris & Co Ltd, pg 763
Taylor & Francis, pg 763
Thoemmes Press, pg 765
Thomson Gale, pg 765
University of Wales Press, pg 769
Verbatim, pg 769
Witherby & Co Ltd, pg 775
Wordsworth Editions Ltd, pg 775

Venezuela

Biblioteca Ayacucho, pg 779

Viet Nam

Science & Technics Publishing House, pg 780

Zimbabwe

The Literature Bureau, pg 783
Zimbabwe Publishing House (Pvt) Ltd, pg 784
ZRD Trust, pg 785

DIRECTORIES, REFERENCE BOOKS

Argentina

Alfagrama SRL ediciones, pg 3
Editorial Atlantida SA, pg 3
Oikos, pg 8

Armenia

Ajstan Publishers, pg 10

Australia

Australasian Medical Publishing Company Ltd (AMPCO), pg 12
Australian Marine Conservation Society Inc (AMCS), pg 13
Australian Scholarly Publishing, pg 13
Board of Studies, pg 15
Bridgeway Publications, pg 16
Cambridge University Press, pg 16
Casket Publications, pg 17
China Books, pg 17
CHOICE Magazine, pg 17
Church Archivists Press, pg 18
Currency Press Pty Ltd, pg 19
D&B Marketing Pty Ltd, pg 19
Encyclopaedia Britannica (Australia) Inc, pg 21
Flora Publications International Pty Ltd, pg 22
Ginninderra Press, pg 23
Hargreen Publishing Co, pg 24
HarperCollinsReligious, pg 25
Hodder Headline Australia, pg 26
The Images Publishing Group Pty Ltd, pg 26
Jesuit Publications, pg 27
Kingsclear Books, pg 28
Kookaburra Technical Publications Pty Ltd, pg 28
Library of Australian History, pg 29
Lowden Publishing Co, pg 30
Macmillan Publishers Australia Pty Ltd, pg 30
The Macquarie Library Pty Ltd, pg 30
Magpie Books, pg 30
Magpie Publications, pg 30
Melway Publishing Pty Ltd, pg 32
Moonlight Publishing, pg 32
Mulavon Press Pty Ltd, pg 32
National Library of Australia, pg 33
Navarine Publishing, pg 33

TYPE OF PUBLICATION INDEX — BOOK

Nimrod Publications, pg 33
Anne O'Donovan Pty Ltd, pg 34
Online Information Resources, pg 34
Pacific Publications (Australia) Pty Ltd, pg 35
Pandani Press, pg 35
Pearson Education Australia, pg 36
Priestley Consulting, pg 37
Queen Victoria Museum & Art Gallery Publications, pg 38
Queensland Art Gallery, pg 38
Rams Skull Press, pg 38
Rankin Publishers, pg 39
Reader's Digest (Australia) Pty Ltd, pg 39
Saltwater Publications, pg 40
Seanachas Press, pg 40
Skills Publishing, pg 41
Standards Association of Australia, pg 42
Thorpe-Bowker, pg 43
Three Sisters Publications Pty Ltd, pg 43
Tudor Australia Press, pg 44
Turton & Armstrong Pty Ltd Publishers, pg 44
Universal Press Pty Ltd, pg 44
University of Western Australia Press, pg 45
Villamonta Publishing Services Inc, pg 45
Wileman Publications, pg 46
Winetitles, pg 47
Zoe Publishing Pty Ltd, pg 47

Austria

Autorensolidaritat - Verlag der Interessengemeinschaft osterreichischer Autorinnen und Autoren, pg 48
Buchkultur Verlags GmbH Zeitschrift fuer Literatur & Kunst, pg 49
Compass-Verlag GmbH, pg 49
Cura Verlag GmbH, pg 49
Ferdinand Berger und Sohne, pg 50
Herold Business Data AG, pg 52
Johannes Heyn GmbH & Co KG, pg 52
Hollinek Bruder & Co mbH Gesellschaftsdruckerei & Verlagsbuchhandring, pg 52
Thomas Mlakar Verlag, pg 54
Pinguin-Verlag, Pawlowski GmbH, pg 56
Verlag Styria, pg 58
Zirkular - Verlag der Dokumentationsstelle fuer neuere oesterreichische Literatur, pg 60

Azerbaijan

Sada, Literaturno-Izdatel'skij Centr, pg 60

Bangladesh

The University Press Ltd, pg 61

Belarus

Belaruskaya Encyklapedyya, pg 62
Kavaler Publishers, pg 62
Publishing Center of Belarus State University, pg 62

Belgium

Editions Gerard Blanchart & Cie SA, pg 63
Editions du CEFAL, pg 65
Editions De Boeck-Larcier SA, pg 66
Editions Delta SA, pg 66

Documenta CV, pg 66
Ediblanchart sprl, pg 67
Girault Gilbert bvba, pg 67
Heideland-Orbis NV, pg 68
Editions Labor, pg 69
La Renaissance du Livre, pg 72
Paul Schiltz, pg 73
Scoop Infotex NV, pg 73
Snoeck-Ducaju en Zoon NV, pg 73

Bosnia and Herzegovina

Veselin Maslesa, pg 76
Svjetlost, pg 76

Brazil

Abril SA, pg 76
Editora do Brasil SA, pg 79
Editora Campus Ltda, pg 79
Centro de Estudos Juridicosdo Para (CEJUP), pg 79
Editora Expressao e Cultura-Exped Ltda, pg 81
Editora Globo SA, pg 82
Grafica Editora Primor Ltda, pg 83
Hemus Editora Ltda, pg 83
Livro Ibero-Americano Ltda, pg 83
LISA (Livros Irradiantes SA), pg 85
Livraria Kosmos Editora Ltda, pg 85
Edicoes Loyola SA, pg 85
Editora Melhoramentos Ltda, pg 86
Editora Nova Fronteira SA, pg 87
Paulus Editora, pg 88
Ediouro Publicacoes, SA, pg 89
Editora Rideel Ltda, pg 89
Editora Vecchi SA, pg 92
Editora Verbo Ltda, pg 92

Bulgaria

Abagar Pabloiing, pg 92
Gea-Libris Publishing House, pg 94
LIK Izdanija, pg 95
Prozoretz Ltd Publishing House, pg 96
Technica, pg 97

Chile

Publicaciones Lo Castillo SA, pg 100
Editorial Texido Ltda, pg 100

China

Anhui People's Publishing House, pg 101
Beijing Publishing House, pg 101
Chemical Industry Press, pg 101
China Foreign Economic Relations & Trade Publishing House, pg 102
China Machine Press (CMP), pg 102
China Materials Management Publishing House, pg 102
China Ocean Press, pg 102
China Social Sciences Publishing House, pg 103
China Theatre Publishing House, pg 103
China Translation & Publishing Corp, pg 103
Chinese Pedagogics Publishing House, pg 103
CITIC Publishing House, pg 103
Foreign Language Teaching & Research Press, pg 104
Guizhou Education Publishing House, pg 105
Higher Education Press, pg 105
Inner Mongolia Science & Technology Publishing House, pg 105

Jinan Publishing House, pg 105
Knowledge Press, pg 106
Lanzhou University Press, pg 106
Nanjing University Press, pg 106
National Defence Industry Press, pg 106
Patent Documentation Publishing House, pg 106
The People's Communications Publishing House, pg 106
Qingdao Publishing House, pg 107
Science Press, pg 107
Shandong Education Publishing House, pg 107
Shandong Friendship Publishing House, pg 107
Shanghai Calligraphy & Painting Publishing House, pg 108
Shanghai Educational Publishing House, pg 108
South China University of Science & Technology Press, pg 108
Tsinghua University Press, pg 109
World Affairs Press, pg 109
Xinhua Publishing House, pg 109
Zhong Hua Book Co, pg 110

Colombia

Centro Regional para el Fomento del Libro en America Latina y el Caribe, pg 110
Instituto Caro y Cuervo, pg 111
Editorial Santillana SA, pg 112

The Democratic Republic of the Congo

Presses Universitaires du Zaiire (PUZ), pg 114

Costa Rica

Editorial Nacional de Salud y Seguridad Social Ednass, pg 116

Cote d'Ivoire

Centre d'Edition et de Diffusion Africaines, pg 117
Heritage Publishing Co, pg 117

Croatia

AGM doo, pg 117
Graficki zavod Hrvatske, pg 118
Masmedia, pg 118
Mladost d d Izdavacku graficku i informaticku djelatnost, pg 119
Otokar Kersovani, pg 119
Skolska Knjiga, pg 119
Tehnicka Knjiga, pg 119

Cuba

Instituto de Informacion Cientifica y Tecnologica (IDICT), pg 120

Czech Republic

Barrister & Principal, pg 122
Divadelni Ustav, pg 123
Karolinum, nakladatelstvi, pg 124
Cesky normalizacni institut, pg 126
Omnipress Praha, pg 126
Statisticke a evidencni vydavatelstvi tiskopisu (SEVT), pg 127
SystemConsult, pg 127

Denmark

Ascheoug Dansk Forlag A/S, pg 129
Dansk Historisk Handbogsforlag ApS, pg 130
Gyldendalske Boghandel - Nordisk Forlag A/S, pg 131
Holkenfeldt 3, pg 132

Ingenioeren/Boger, pg 132
IT-og Telestyrelsen, pg 132
Kraks Forlag AS, pg 132
Mellemfolkeligt Samvirke, pg 133
Nyt Nordisk Forlag Arnold Busck A/S, pg 133
Joergen Paludan Forlag ApS, pg 133
Det Schonbergske Forlag A/S, pg 134
Systime, pg 135

Dominican Republic

Sociedad Editorial Americana, pg 136

Egypt (Arab Republic of Egypt)

American University in Cairo Press, pg 137
The Egyptian Society for the Dissemination of Universal Culture and Knowledge (ESDUCK), pg 138

Estonia

Eesti Entsuklopeediakirjastus, pg 139
Eesti Rahvusraamatukogu, pg 139
Olion Publishers, pg 140

Finland

Kirja-Leitzinger, pg 142
Schildts Forlags AB, pg 144
Soderstroms Forlag, pg 144
Weilin & Goos Oy, pg 144
Yritystieto Oy - Foretagsdata AB, pg 145

France

ADPF Publications, pg 145
Agence Bibliographique de l'Enseignement Superieur, pg 146
Editions Aubier-Montaigne SA, pg 148
Beauchesne Editeur, pg 149
Berg International Editeur, pg 149
La Bibliotheque des Arts, pg 150
Bibliotheque Nationale de France, pg 150
Editions Bordas, pg 150
Bureau des Longitudes, pg 151
Editions La Decouverte, pg 157
Editions Denoel, pg 157
Doin Editeurs, pg 159
Les Dossiers d'Aquitaine, pg 159
Editions Grund, pg 160
Elsevier SAS (Editions Scientifiques et Medicales Elsevier), pg 161
Editions Farel, pg 162
Librairie Artheme Fayard, pg 163
Editions Fivedit, pg 163
Folklore Comtois, pg 164
Association Frank, pg 164
Editions Jean Paul Gisserot, pg 165
Groupement d'Information Promotion Presse Edition (GIPPE), pg 166
Hachette Education, pg 166
Hachette Livre, pg 167
Hachette Pratiques, pg 167
Editions Hazan, pg 167
Hermann editeurs des Sciences et des Arts SA, pg 167
INRA Editions (Institut National de la Recherche Agronomique), pg 168
Institut International de la Marionnette, pg 169
Editions Klincksieck, pg 170
Editions Lacour-Olle, pg 170
Editions Larousse, pg 171

812

PUBLISHERS   TYPE OF PUBLICATION INDEX

Editions Lavoisier, pg 171
Librarie Maritime Outremer, pg 172
Le Livre de Paris, pg 173
Masson-Williams et Wilkins, pg 174
Editions Franck Mercier, pg 175
Editions Fernand Nathan, pg 176
Editions A et J Picard SA, pg 179
Editions Jean Picollec, pg 179
Jean-Michel Place, pg 180
Point Hors Ligne Editions, pg 180
Les Editions du Point Veterinaire, pg 180
Presence Africaine Editions, pg 180
Presses de la Sorbonne Nouvelle/PSN, pg 181
Presses Universitaires de France (PUF), pg 181
PRODIG, pg 182
References cf, pg 183
Guide Rosenwald, pg 183
Editions Sand et Tchou SA, pg 184
Selection du Reader's Digest SA, pg 184
Service Technique pour l'Education, pg 184
Sofiac (Societe Francaise des Imprimeries Administratives Centrales), pg 185
Editions Springer France, pg 186
Editions Tallandier, pg 187
Terre Vivante, pg 187
UNESCO Publishing, pg 188
Editions Vilo SA, pg 189
Librairie Philosophique J Vrin, pg 189

Germany

ABC der Deutschen Wirtschaft, Verlagsgesellschaft mbH, pg 190
Angelika und Lothar Binding, pg 192
AOL-Verlag Frohmut Menze, pg 193
ARCult Media, pg 193
Arnoldsche Verlagsanstalt GmbH, pg 194
Axel Juncker Verlag Jacobi KG, pg 196
Verlag C H Beck oHG, pg 198
Verlag Beleke KG, pg 198
Biblio Verlag, pg 200
Bibliographisches Institut & F A Brockhaus AG, pg 200
Bleicher Verlag GmbH, pg 202
Bouvier Verlag, pg 203
R Brockhaus Verlag, pg 204
F Bruckmann Munchen Verlag & Druck GmbH & Co Produkt KG, pg 204
Verlag C J Bucher GmbH, pg 205
Buchverlage Langen-Mueller/Herbig, pg 205
Bundesanzeiger Verlagsgesellschaft, pg 206
Calwer Verlag GmbH, pg 207
Compact Verlag GmbH, pg 209
Copress Verlag, pg 209
Verlag Darmstaedter Blaetter Schwarz und Co, pg 210
Verlag Werner Dausien, pg 211
Degener & Co, Manfred Dreiss Verlag, pg 211
Verlag Harri Deutsch, pg 211
Deutsche Blinden-Bibliothek, pg 211
Deutsche Landwirtschafts-Gesellschaft VerlagsgesGmbH, pg 212
Deutscher Adresbuch-Verlag fuer Wirtschaft und Verkehr GmbH, pg 212
Deutscher Taschenbuch Verlag GmbH & Co KG (dtv), pg 213

Verlagsgruppe Droemer Knaur GmbH & Co KG, pg 216
Dumjahn Verlag, pg 217
DuMont Reiseverlag GmbH & Co KG, pg 217
Dustri-Verlag Dr Karl Feistle, pg 217
Econ Verlag GmbH, pg 218
Eichborn AG, pg 219
Elsevier GmbH/Urban & Fischer Verlag, pg 219
Europ Export Edition GmbH, pg 221
Festland Verlag GmbH, pg 224
Verlagsgruppe J Fink GmbH & Co KG, pg 224
S Fischer Verlag GmbH, pg 225
Fischer Taschenbuch Verlag GmbH, pg 225
Focus-Verlag Gesellschaft mbH, pg 225
Franckh-Kosmos Verlags-GmbH & Co, pg 226
Verlag Franz Vahlen GmbH, pg 226
Fraunhofer IRB Verlag Fraunhofer Informationszentrum Raum und Bau, pg 226
GeoCenter Touristik Medienservice GmbH, pg 228
Gerth Medien GmbH, pg 229
Graefe und Unzer Verlag GmbH, pg 230
Gunter Olzog Verlag GmbH, pg 231
Walter Haedecke Verlag, pg 232
Rudolf Haufe Verlag GmbH & Co KG, pg 235
Dr Ernst Hauswedell & Co, pg 235
G Henle Verlag, pg 236
F A Herbig Verlagsbuchhandlung GmbH, pg 236
Anton Hiersemann, Verlag, pg 237
Hoppenstedt GmbH & Co KG, pg 239
Humboldt-Taschenbuch Verlag Jacobi KG, pg 240
Huss-Verlag GmbH, pg 240
Edition ID-Archiv/ID-Verlag, pg 240
Industrie- und Handelsverlag & Co KG, pg 241
Industrieschau Verlagsgesellschaft mbH, pg 241
Kastell Verlag GmbH, pg 244
Keip GmbH, pg 245
Verlag im Kilian GmbH, pg 246
Unterwegs Verlag, Manfred Klemann, pg 246
Vittorio Klostermann GmbH, pg 247
Verlag Fritz Knapp GmbH, pg 247
Knowledge Media International, pg 247
Roman Kovar Verlag, pg 249
Alfred Kroner Verlag, pg 250
Verlag Ernst Kuhn, pg 250
Ambro Lacus, Buch- und Bildverlag Walter A Kremnitz, pg 251
Leitfadenverlag Verlag Dieter Sudholt, pg 253
Dr Gisela Lermann, pg 253
Maeander Verlag GmbH, pg 256
Magnus Verlag, pg 256
Mairs Geographischer Verlag, pg 256
Matthiesen Verlag Ingwert Paulsen Jr, pg 258
Midena Verlag, pg 260
Mitteldeutscher Verlag GmbH, pg 261
Mosaik Verlag GmbH, pg 262
Motorbuch-Verlag, pg 262

MVB Marketing- und Verlagsservice des Buchhandels GmbH, pg 263
Neuer Honos Verlag GmbH, pg 264
R Oldenbourg Verlag GmbH, pg 267
Edition Parabolis, pg 268
Pendragon Verlag, pg 269
Jens Peters Publikationen, pg 269
Philipp Reclam Jun Verlag GmbH, pg 269
pmi Verlag, pg 270
Polygraph Verlag GmbH, pg 271
Presse Verlagsgesellschaft mbH, pg 271
Projektion J Buch- und Musikverlag GmbH, pg 272
Dr Josef Raabe-Verlags GmbH, pg 273
Dr Ludwig Reichert Verlag, pg 274
R V Reise- und Verkehrsverlag GmbH, pg 275
Rombach GmbH Druck und Verlagshaus & Co, pg 276
Verlag Werner Sachon GmbH & Co, pg 277
Eugen Salzer-Verlag GmbH & Co KG, pg 278
K G Saur Verlag GmbH, A Gale/Thomson Learning Company, pg 278
Sax-Verlag Beucha, pg 278
Verlag der Schillerbuchhandlung Hans Banger OHG, pg 279
Max Schmidt-Roemhild Verlag, pg 280
Verlag Schnell und Steiner GmbH, pg 281
Schwaneberger Verlag GmbH, pg 282
Springer Science+Business Media GmbH & Co KG, pg 284
Staatsbibliothek zu Berlin - Preussischer Kulturbesitz, pg 286
Stadler Verlagsgesellschaft mbH, pg 286
Verlag Stahleisen GmbH, pg 286
C A Starke Verlag, pg 287
Stattbuch Verlag GmbH, pg 287
Conrad Stein Verlag GmbH, pg 287
Stollfuss Verlag Bonn GmbH & Co KG, pg 288
Suedwest Verlag GmbH & Co KG, pg 289
Telex-Verlag Jaeger & Waldmann GmbH, pg 289
B G Teubner Verlag, pg 290
edition Text & Kritik im Richard Boorberg Verlag GmbH & Co, pg 290
Georg Thieme Verlag KG, pg 291
Tipress Dienstleistungen fur das Verlagswesen GmbH, pg 291
Tomus Verlag, pg 291
Transpress Verlagsgesellschaft mbH, pg 292
Trias Verlag in MVS Medizinverlage Stuttgart GmbH & Co KG, pg 292
Tuebinger Vereinigung fur Volkskunde eV (TVV), pg 292
Ullstein Heyne List GmbH & Co KG, pg 293
Verlag Eugen Ulmer GmbH & Co, pg 293
Dorothea van der Koelen, pg 294
Curt R Vincentz Verlag, pg 296
Voggenreiter-Verlag, pg 296
W Ludwig Verlag GmbH, pg 297
Weidler Buchverlag Berlin, pg 298
WEKA Firmengruppe GmbH & Co KG, pg 298

Werner Verlag GmbH & Co KG, pg 299
Wiley-VCH Verlag GmbH, pg 300
Verlagshaus Wohlfarth, pg 301
Xenos Verlagsgesellschaft mbH, pg 301

Ghana

Anowuo Educational Publications, pg 303
Ghana Publishing Corporation, pg 304
Moxon Paperbacks, pg 304
World Literature Project, pg 305

Greece

Alamo Hellas, pg 305
Beta Medical Publishers, pg 306
Chrysi Penna - Golden Pen Books, pg 306
Giovanis Publications, Pangosmios Ekdotikos Organismos, pg 307
Logos, pg 309
Minoas SA, pg 310
Nakas Music House, pg 310
Nomiki Bibliothiki, pg 310

Honduras

Editorial Guaymuras, pg 315

Hong Kong

Benefit Publishing Co, pg 315
Chung Hwa Book Co (HK) Ltd, pg 316
Joint Publishing (HK) Co Ltd, pg 317
Peace Book Co Ltd, pg 318
Ta Kung Pao (HK) Ltd, pg 319

Hungary

Akademiai Kiado, pg 320
Greger-Delacroix, pg 321
Kossuth Kiado RT, pg 322
Novorg International Szervezo es Kiado kft, pg 323
Pro Natura, pg 324

Iceland

Bokautgafan Orn og Orlygur ehf, pg 325
Idunn, pg 325
Setberg, pg 326

India

Academic Book Corporation, pg 327
Agam Kala Prakashan, pg 327
Amar Prakashan, pg 328
Asia Pacific Business Press Inc, pg 328
Asian Educational Services, pg 329
Associated Publishing House, pg 329
Atma Ram & Sons, pg 329
Bharat Law House Pvt Ltd, pg 330
BR Publishing Corporation, pg 331
Chowkhamba Sanskrit Series Office, pg 332
Cosmo Publications, pg 332
DC Books, pg 333
Disha Prakashan, pg 333
DK Printworld (P) Ltd, pg 333
Eastern Book Co, pg 333
Geeta Prakashan, pg 335
General Book Depot, pg 335
Gyan Publishing House, pg 335
Arnold Heinman Publishers (India) Pvt Ltd, pg 335
Heritage Publishers, pg 335

813

TYPE OF PUBLICATION INDEX BOOK

IBD Publisher & Distributors, pg 336
International Book Distributors, pg 338
Intertrade Publications Pvt Ltd, pg 338
Jaico Publishing House, pg 338
Kalyani Publishers, pg 339
Law Publishers, pg 340
Ministry of Information & Broadcasting, pg 341
National Institute of Industrial Research (NIIR), pg 343
Navajivan Trust, pg 343
Nem Chand & Brothers, pg 343
Newspread International, pg 343
Oxford University Press, pg 344
Oxonian Press (P) Ltd, pg 344
Panjab University Publication Bureau, pg 344
Parimal Prakashan, pg 345
Pitambar Publishing Co (P) Ltd, pg 345
Pointer Publishers, pg 345
Promilla & Publishers, pg 345
Rahul Publishing House, pg 346
Reliance Publishing House, pg 346
Scientific Book Agency, pg 348
Sita Books & Periodicals Pvt Ltd, pg 349
Small Industry Research Institute (SIRI), pg 349
Spectrum Publications, pg 350
Sri Satguru Publications, pg 350
Sterling Publishers Pvt Ltd, pg 350
Today & Tomorrow's Printers & Publishers, pg 351
Vidya Puri, pg 352
Vidyarthi Mithram Press, pg 352

Indonesia

Angkasa CV, pg 353
Lembaga Demografi Fakultas Ekonomi Universitas Indonesia, pg 355
Nusa Indah, pg 356
Pustaka Utama Grafiti, PT, pg 356
Tintamas Indonesia PT, pg 356

Ireland

An Gum, pg 358
Ballinakella Press, pg 358
Dee-Jay Publications, pg 359
Flyleaf Press, pg 360
Gill & Macmillan Ltd, pg 360
Institute of Public Administration, pg 361
Irish Management Institute, pg 361
On Stream Publications Ltd, pg 362
Royal Irish Academy, pg 363

Israel

Achiasaf Publishing House Ltd, pg 364
Am Oved Publishers Ltd, pg 365
Amichai Publishing House Ltd, pg 365
The Bialik Institute, pg 365
Carta, The Israel Map & Publishing Co Ltd, pg 365
Dekel Publishing House, pg 366
Edanim Publishers Ltd, pg 366
Encyclopedia Judaica, pg 366
Feldheim Publishers Ltd, pg 367
Intermedia Audio, Video Book Publishing Ltd, pg 368
Israel Exploration Society, pg 368
Israel Universities Press, pg 368
The Jerusalem Publishing House Ltd, pg 369
Karni Publishers Ltd, pg 369
Keter Publishing House Ltd, pg 369

Ma'ariv Book Guild (Sifriat Ma'ariv), pg 370
MAP-Mapping & Publishing Ltd, pg 370
Massada Press Ltd, pg 370
Massada Publishers Ltd, pg 370
Medcom Ltd, pg 370
Saar Publishing House, pg 371
Sadan Publishing Ltd, pg 371
Steimatzky Group Ltd, pg 372
Tcherikover Publishers Ltd, pg 372
Yad Vashem - The Holocaust Martyrs' & Heroes' Remembrance Authority, pg 373
Yedioth Ahronoth Books, pg 373

Italy

AIB Associazione Italiana Bibliotheche, pg 374
L'Airone Editrice, pg 375
Umberto Allemandi & C SRL, pg 375
Arcanta Aries Gruppo Editoriale, pg 375
Gruppo Editoriale Armenia SpA, pg 376
Editrice Bibliografica SpA, pg 378
Cappelli Editore, pg 380
Casa Editrice Libraria Ulrico Hoepli SpA, pg 380
Centro Di, pg 381
Citta Nuova Editrice, pg 382
Edizioni Cremonese SRL, pg 383
Direzione Generale Archivi, pg 385
Edagricole - Edizioni Agricole, pg 385
Editrice Eraclea, pg 388
Giangiacomo Feltrinelli SpA, pg 389
Garzanti Libri, pg 390
Istituto Geografico de Agostini SpA, pg 390
Giunti Gruppo Editoriale, pg 390
Gius Laterza e Figli SpA, pg 391
Ernesto Gremese Editore srl, pg 391
Gremese International srl, pg 391
Istituto della Enciclopedia Italiana, pg 393
Librex, pg 395
LIM Editrice SRL, pg 395
Arnoldo Mondadori Editore SpA, pg 398
Giorgio Mondadori & Associati, pg 399
Gruppo Ugo Mursia Editore SpA, pg 400
Newton & Compton Editori, pg 400
Nuova Alfa Editoriale, pg 401
La Nuova Italia Editrice SpA, pg 401
Leo S Olschki, pg 401
Paravia Bruno Mondadori Editori, pg 402
Pontifico Istituto Orientale, pg 404
RCS Libri SpA, pg 405
RCS Rizzoli Libri SpA, pg 405
Franco Maria Ricci Editore (FMR), pg 405
Il Saggiatore, pg 406
SAIE Editrice SRL, pg 406
Edizioni San Paolo SRL, pg 407
UTET (Unione Tipografico-Editrice Torinese), pg 411
Societa Editrice Vannini, pg 411
Zanichelli Editore SpA, pg 412

Jamaica

American Chamber of Commerce of Jamaica, pg 413

Japan

The American Chamber of Commerce in Japan, pg 415
Dogakusha Inc, pg 416
GakuseiSha Publishing Co Ltd, pg 417
Heibonsha Ltd, Publishers, pg 418
Hirokawa Publishing Co, pg 418
Hokuryukan Co Ltd, pg 418
Hyoronsha Publishing Co Ltd, pg 418
Iwanami Shoten, Publishers, pg 419
The Japan Times Ltd, pg 420
Kaitakusha, pg 420
Kenkyusha Ltd, pg 421
Kinokuniya Co Ltd (Publishing Department), pg 421
Kodansha International Ltd, pg 421
Kodansha Ltd, pg 421
Kodansha Scientific Ltd, pg 421
Nagaoka Shoten Co Ltd, pg 423
Nanzando Co Ltd, pg 423
Nigensha Publishing Co Ltd, pg 423
Nihon Bunka Kagakusha Co Ltd, pg 423
Nihon Tosho Center Co Ltd, pg 423
Obunsha Co Ltd, pg 424
Ohmsha Ltd, pg 424
Rinsen Book Co Ltd, pg 425
Sanseido Co Ltd, pg 426
Sanshusha Publishing Co, Ltd, pg 426
Seibido, pg 426
Seibido Shuppan Company Ltd, pg 426
Shimizu-Shoin, pg 427
Shogakukan Inc, pg 427
Shueisha Inc, pg 428
Tokyo Shoseki Co Ltd, pg 430
Toyo Keizai Shinpo-Sha, pg 430
Tsukiji Shokan Publishing Co, pg 430
University of Tokyo Press, pg 430
Zoshindo JukenKenkyusha, pg 431

Kenya

Africa Book Services (EA) Ltd, pg 433
Bookman Consultants Ltd, pg 433
Kenya Energy & Environment Organisation, Kengo, pg 434
Transafrica Press, pg 436

Republic of Korea

DanKook University Press, pg 438
Ke Mong Sa Publishing Co Ltd, pg 440
Korean Publishers Association, pg 440
Maeil Gyeongje, pg 441
Woongjin Media Corporation, pg 443
YBM/Si-sa, pg 443

Latvia

Avots, pg 444

Lebanon

Arab Institute for Research & Publishing, pg 445
Dar El Ilm Lilmalayin, pg 446
Librairie du Liban Publishers (Sal), pg 446
Librairie Orientale sal, pg 446
Publitec Publications, pg 447

Liechtenstein

Bonafides Verlags-Anstalt, pg 447

Lithuania

Eugrimas, pg 449
Lithuanian National Museum Publishing House, pg 449
TEV Leidykla, pg 450
Vaga Ltd, pg 450

Luxembourg

Service Central de la Statistique et des Etudes Economiques (STATEC), pg 451

The Former Yugoslav Republic of Macedonia

Prosvetno Delo Publishing House, pg 453
St Clement of Ohrid National & University Library, pg 453

Madagascar

Madagascar Print & Press Company, pg 453
Societe Malgache d'Edition, pg 454

Malaysia

Amiza Associate Malaysia Sdn Bhd, pg 455
Berita Publishing Sdn Bhd, pg 455
Dewan Bahasa dan Pustaka, pg 455
Federal Publications Sdn Bhd, pg 455
FEP International Sdn Bhd, pg 456
Geetha Publishers Sdn Bhd, pg 456
MDC Publishers Printers Sdn Bhd, pg 457
Oscar Book International, pg 457
Pearson Education Malaysia Sdn Bhd, pg 457
Penerbit Fajar Bakti Sdn Bhd, pg 457
Penerbitan Pelangi Sdn Bhd (Pelangi Publishing Pte Ltd), pg 458
Pustaka Cipta Sdn Bhd, pg 458
Trix Corporation Sdn Bhd, pg 459
Vinpress Sdn Bhd, pg 459

Maldive Islands

Novelty Printers & Publishers, pg 459

Mexico

Libreria y Ediciones Botas SA, pg 462
Editorial Edicol SA, pg 464
Ibcon SA, pg 466
Informatica Cosmos SA de CV, pg 466
Medios y Medios, Sa de CV, pg 468
Mercametrica Ediciones SA Edicion de Libros, pg 468
Nova Grupo Editorial SA de CV, pg 469
Ediciones Roca, SA, pg 471

Morocco

Access International Services, pg 474
Association de la Recherche Historique et Sociale, pg 474
Office Marocain D'Annonces-OMA, pg 475
Editions Services et Informations pour Etudiants, pg 475

PUBLISHERS

Netherlands
Uitgeversmaatschappij Agon B V, pg 477
APA (Academic Publishers Associated), pg 477
Ars Scribendi bv Uitgeverij, pg 478
B M Israel BV, pg 478
John Benjamins BV, pg 479
De Graaf Publishers, pg 481
BV Uitgeversbedryf Het Goede Boek, pg 482
HES & De Graaf Publishers BV, pg 483
Uitgeverij Holland, pg 483
Uitgeverij J H Kok BV, pg 485
Pearson Education Netherlands, pg 487
Reed Elsevier Nederland BV, pg 488
A J G Strengholt's Boeken, Anno 1928, BV, pg 489
Tirion Uitgevers BV, pg 490
Unieboek BV, pg 490

New Caledonia
Savannah Editions SARL, pg 493

New Zealand
David Bateman Ltd, pg 494
Brookers Ltd, pg 494
Current Pacific Ltd, pg 495
David's Marine Books, pg 495
Eton Press (Auckland) Ltd, pg 496
Evagean Publishing, pg 496
GCL Publishing (1997) Ltd, pg 496
HarperCollins Publishers (New Zealand) Ltd, pg 497
Landcare Research NZ, pg 497
Learning Guides (Writers & Publishers Ltd), pg 497
Legislation Direct, pg 498
New Zealand Council for Educational Research, pg 499
Oxford University Press, pg 499
Reed Publishing (NZ) Ltd, pg 500
Shoal Bay Press Ltd, pg 501
Statistics New Zealand, pg 501
Universal Business Directories, Australia Pty Ltd, pg 502

Nigeria
ABIC Books & Equipment Ltd, pg 503
Adebara Publishers Ltd, pg 503
Daily Times of Nigeria Ltd (Publication Division), pg 504
Ibadan University Press, pg 505
Longman Nigeria Plc, pg 505
Obafemi Awolowo University Press Ltd, pg 506
West African Book Publishers Ltd, pg 507
John West Publications Co Ltd, pg 507

Norway
Andresen & Butenschon AS, pg 508
H Ascheoug & Co (W Nygaard) A/S, pg 508
J W Cappelens Forlag A/S, pg 508
Gyldendal Norsk Forlag A/S, pg 509
Chr Schibsteds Forlag A/S, pg 510
Teknologisk Forlag, pg 510
Tiden Norsk Forlag, pg 511
Universitetsforlaget, pg 511

Oman
Apex Press & Publishing, pg 511

Pakistan
Jang Publishers, pg 513
Publishers United Pvt Ltd, pg 514
Sang-e-Meel Publications, pg 514
Shibil Publications (Pvt) Ltd, pg 514

Panama
Focus Publications International SA, pg 515

Papua New Guinea
IMPS Research Ltd, pg 515
National Research Institute of Papua New Guinea, pg 515

Peru
Editorial Desarrollo SA, pg 517

Philippines
Abiva Publishing House Inc, pg 518
Bright Concepts Printing House, pg 518
Communication Foundation for Asia Media Group (CFAMG), pg 518
J C Palabay Enterprises, pg 519
National Museum of the Philippines, pg 520
New Day Publishers, pg 520
Philippine Baptist Mission SBC FMB Church Growth International, pg 520
SIBS Publishing House Inc, pg 521
Solidaridad Publishing House, pg 521

Poland
Laumann-Polska, pg 524
Wydawnictwo Medyczne Urban & Partner, pg 524
Wydawnictwo Normalizacyjne Alfa-Wero, pg 525
Wydawnictwa Przemyslowe WEMA, pg 526
Oficyna Wydawnicza Read Me, pg 526
Wydawnictwo RTW, pg 526
'Slask' Ltd, pg 526
Spotdzielna Anagram, pg 526

Portugal
Publicacoes Alfa SA, pg 528
Difusao Cultural, pg 530
Publicacoes Europa-America Lda, pg 531
Gradiva-Publicacnoes Lda, pg 532
Instituto de Investigacao Cientifica Tropical, pg 532
Editora McGraw-Hill de Portugal Lda, pg 533
Editorial Presenca, pg 535
Publicacoes Dom Quixote Lda, pg 535
Edicoes 70 Lda, pg 535
Almerinda Teixeira, pg 536

Puerto Rico
University of Puerto Rico Press (EDUPR), pg 537

Romania
Editura Academiei Romane, pg 538
Alcor-Edimpex (Verlag) Ltd, pg 538
The Center for Romanian Studies, pg 539
Editura Cronos SRL, pg 539
Enzyklopadie Verlag, pg 539
Editura Excelsior Art, pg 539
Editura Gryphon, pg 540

Hasefer, pg 540
Editura Meridiane, pg 540
Pallas-Akademia Editura, pg 541
Polirom Verlag, pg 542
Editura Stiintifica si Enciclopedica, pg 542
Editura Tehnica, pg 542
Vestala Verlag, pg 543

Russian Federation
N E Bauman Moscow State Technical University Publishers, pg 544
BLIC, russko-Baltijskij informaciionnyj centr, AO, pg 544
Izdatelstvo Bolshaya Rossiyskaya Entsiklopedia, pg 544
FGUP Izdatelstvo Mashinostroenie, pg 544
Izdatelstvo Galart, pg 545
Izdatelskii Dom Kompozitor, pg 546
KUbK Publishing House, pg 546
Izdatelstvo Mezhdunarodnye Otnoshenia, pg 546
Ministerstvo Kul'tury RF, pg 546
Moscow University Press, pg 547
Izdatelstvo Muzyka, pg 547
Pedagogika Press, pg 548
Raduga Publishers, pg 548
Respublika, pg 548
Russkij Jazyk, pg 548
Izdatelstvo Standartov, pg 549
Izdatelstvo Ural' skogo, pg 549
Vsesoyuznii Molodejnii Knizhnii Centre, pg 549

Saudi Arabia
King Saud University, pg 550

Senegal
Agence de Distribution de Presse, pg 551

Serbia and Montenegro
Association of Yugoslav Publishers & Booksellers, pg 552
Narodna Biblioteka Srbije, pg 552
Naucna Knjiga, pg 552
Privredni Pregled, pg 553
Savremena Administracija, pg 553
Turisticka Stampa, pg 554
Vuk Karadzic, pg 554

Singapore
APA Production Pte Ltd, pg 554
China Knowledge Press, pg 555
Chopsons Pte Ltd, pg 555
Federal Publications (S) Pte Ltd, pg 556
FEP International Private Ltd, pg 556
LexisNexis, pg 557
Reed Elsevier, South East Asia, pg 557
SNP Panpac Pacific Publishing Pte Ltd, pg 558
Taylor & Francis Asia Pacific, pg 558

Slovenia
Cankarjeva Zalozba, pg 561
Zalozba Obzorja d d Maribor, pg 562

South Africa
Brabys Brochures, pg 563
Ad Donker (Pty) Ltd, pg 563
Flesch Financial Publications (Pty) Ltd, pg 563

TYPE OF PUBLICATION INDEX

Human & Rousseau (Pty) Ltd, pg 564
National Botanical Institute, pg 567
New Africa Books (Pty) Ltd, pg 567
Queillerie Publishers, pg 568
Reader's Digest Southern Africa, pg 568
Southern Book Publishers (Pty) Ltd, pg 569
Struik Publishers (Pty) Ltd, pg 569
Thomson Publications, pg 569
Unisa Press, pg 569
Van Schaik Publishers, pg 569
Who's Who of Southern Africa, pg 570

Spain
Ediciones Agrotecnicas, SL, pg 571
Aguilar SA de Ediciones, pg 571
Anaya Educacion, pg 573
Anglo-Didactica, SL Editorial, pg 573
Arco Libros SL, pg 573
Carroggio SA de Ediciones, pg 575
Comunidad Autonoma de Madrid, Servicio de Documentacion y Publicaciones, pg 578
Enciclopedia Catalana, SA, pg 582
Editorial Espasa-Calpe SA, pg 582
Fundacion Marcelino Botin, pg 584
Generalitat de Catalunya Diari Oficial de la Generalitat vern, pg 584
Grijalbo Mondadori SA, pg 585
Editorial Herder SA, pg 586
Idea Books, SA, pg 587
Ediciones Istmo SA, pg 588
Editorial Kairos SA, pg 588
Editorial Marin SA, pg 590
Ediciones Nauta Credito SA, pg 593
Editorial Noray, pg 593
Parramon Ediciones SA, pg 595
Pearson Educacion S A, pg 595
Plaza y Janes Editores SA, pg 596
Polifemo, Ediciones, pg 596
Ediciones Scriba SA, pg 599
Ramon Sopena SA, pg 600
Tesitex, SL, pg 602
Trea Ediciones, SL, pg 602
Veron Editor, pg 604
Vinaches Lopez, Luisa, pg 605
Xunta de Galicia, pg 605

Sri Lanka
Business Directory of Lanka Ltd, pg 606
National Library & Documentation Centre, pg 607
Waruni Publishers, pg 607

Sudan
Al-Ayam Press Co Ltd, pg 608
Khartoum University Press, pg 608

Sweden
Bibliotekstjaenst AB, pg 610
Forlagshuset Norden AB, pg 611
Informationsfoerlaget AB, pg 612
Klassikerforlaget, pg 613
Norstedts Ordbok, pg 614
Psykologifoerlaget AB, pg 614
Richters Egmont, pg 615
Bokforlaget Spektra AB, pg 615
Wahlstrom & Widstrand, pg 616

Switzerland
Aare-Verlag, pg 617
Editions de la Baconniere SA, pg 618
U Baer Verlag, pg 618

TYPE OF PUBLICATION INDEX BOOK

Bibliographisches Institut & F A Brockhaus AG, pg 619
Verlag Bibliophile Drucke von Josef Stocker AG, pg 619
Bugra Suisse Burchler Grafino AG, pg 620
Cockatoo Press (Schweiz), Thailand-Publikationen, pg 621
Cosa-Verlag, Giusep Condrau SA, pg 621
Editions Delachaux et Niestle SA, pg 621
Larousse (Suisse) SA, pg 627
Maihof Verlag, pg 628
Motovun Book GmbH, pg 629
Presses Polytechniques et Universitaires Romandes, PPUR, pg 631
Rex Verlag, pg 632
Der Universitatsverlag Freiburg, pg 636

Syrian Arab Republic

Damascus University Press, pg 638

Taiwan, Province of China

Chien Chen Bookstore Publishing Company Ltd, pg 639
Chung Hwa Book Co Ltd, pg 639
Designer Publisher Inc, pg 639
Kuang Fu Book Co Ltd, pg 640
Petroleum Information Publishing Co, pg 641
San Min Book Co Ltd, pg 641
Shy Mau & Shy Chaur Publishing Co Ltd, pg 641
Wu Nan Book Co Ltd, pg 642

United Republic of Tanzania

Ben and Company Ltd, pg 643
East African Publishing House, pg 643
Eastern Africa Publications Ltd, pg 643
Kanisa la Biblia Publishers (KLB), pg 643
Oxford University Press, pg 644

Thailand

Ruamsarn (1977) Co Ltd, pg 645
Thai Watana Panich Co, Ltd, pg 646

Trinidad & Tobago

Jett Samm Publishing Ltd, pg 647

Tunisia

Editions Techniques Specialisees, pg 648

Turkey

ABC Kitabevi AS, pg 648
Arkadas Ltd, pg 649
Arkin Kitabevi, pg 649
Remzi Kitabevi, pg 651
Sabah Kitaplari, pg 651
Yapi-Endustri Merkezi Yayinlari-Yem Yayin, pg 652
Yetkin Printing & Publishing Co Inc, pg 652

Uganda

Fountain Publishers Ltd, pg 652

Ukraine

Lybid (University of Kyyiv Press), pg 653
Naukova Dumka Publishers, pg 653

United Kingdom

A A Publishing, pg 654
ABC-CLIO, pg 654
Act 3 Publishing, pg 655
Adamantine Press Ltd, pg 655
A4 Publications Ltd, pg 656
Aldwych Press Ltd, pg 656
Umberto Allemandi & Co Publishing, pg 656
Anderson Rand Ltd, pg 657
Antique Collectors' Club Ltd, pg 658
Appletree Press Ltd, pg 658
Arms & Armour Press, pg 659
Art Sales Index Ltd, pg 659
The Art Trade Press Ltd, pg 659
Arts Council of England, pg 660
Ashgate Publishing Ltd, pg 660
Aslib, The Association for Information Management, pg 660
Association of Commonwealth Universities (ACU), pg 661
Association for Science Education, pg 661
Barn Dance Publications Ltd, pg 663
BBC Worldwide Publishers, pg 663
Mitchell Beazley, pg 664
Biocommerce Data Ltd, pg 665
BIOS Scientific Publishers Ltd, pg 665
BLA Publishing Ltd, pg 666
A & C Black Publishers Ltd, pg 666
Blackstaff Press, pg 666
Blackwell Publishing Ltd, pg 666
Blandford Publishing Ltd, pg 668
Bloomsbury Publishing PLC, pg 668
Blueprint, pg 668
Book Marketing Ltd, pg 668
Books for Europe Ltd, pg 669
Boulevard Books UK/The Babel Guides, pg 669
Bradt Travel Guides Ltd, pg 670
Brassey's UK Ltd, pg 670
Bridge Books, pg 671
British Library Publications, pg 672
British Museum Press, pg 672
Brooklands Books Ltd, pg 672
Business Monitor International, pg 672
Cambridge University Press, pg 674
Canongate Books Ltd, pg 674
Cassell & Co, pg 675
Castlemead Publications, pg 676
Kyle Cathie Ltd, pg 676
Paul Cave Publications Ltd, pg 676
CBD Research Ltd, pg 677
Chadwyck-Healey Ltd, pg 677
Chatham Publishing, pg 678
Christian Research Association, pg 679
Cicerone Press, pg 680
James Clarke & Co Ltd, pg 680
E W Classey Ltd, pg 680
CMP Information Ltd, pg 680
Compendium Publishing, pg 681
Computer Step, pg 681
Constable & Robinson Ltd, pg 682
The Continuum International Publishing Group Ltd, pg 682
Croner CCH Group Ltd, pg 684
CSA (Cambridge Scientific Abstracts), pg 684
CTBI Publications, pg 685
D&B Ltd, pg 685
The C W Daniel Co Ltd, pg 686
David & Charles Ltd, pg 686
Debrett's Ltd, pg 687
Andre Deutsch Ltd, pg 687
DMG Business Media Ltd, pg 688
Donhead Publishing Ltd, pg 688
East-West Publications (UK) Ltd, pg 689
Edition XII, pg 690
ELC International, pg 690
Edward Elgar Publishing Ltd, pg 690
Elsevier Ltd, pg 691
Encyclopaedia Britannica (UK) International Ltd, pg 691
estamp, pg 692
Estates Gazette, pg 692
Euromonitor PLC, pg 692
Europa Publications, pg 692
The Eurospan Group, pg 692
Faber & Faber Ltd, pg 694
Facet Publishing, pg 694
The Factory Shop Guide, pg 694
FHG Publications Ltd, pg 694
First & Best in Education Ltd, pg 695
Flicks Books, pg 695
Folens Ltd, pg 695
Forbes Publications Ltd, pg 696
Foulsham Publishers, pg 696
Fourth Estate, pg 696
Francis Balsom Associates, pg 696
Samuel French Ltd, pg 697
Geddes & Grosset, pg 699
Stanley Gibbons Publications, pg 700
Greenhill Books/Lionel Leventhal Ltd, pg 703
Guinness World Records Ltd, pg 703
Robert Hale Ltd, pg 704
Hamlyn, pg 704
Harden's Ltd, pg 704
Harley Books, pg 705
HarperCollins UK, pg 705
Harvard University Press, pg 705
Helicon Publishing Ltd, pg 707
Helm Information Ltd, pg 707
Hendon Publishing Co Ltd, pg 708
Heraldry Today, pg 708
Heritage Press, pg 708
Hilmarton Manor Press, pg 708
Hobsons, pg 709
Hodder Education, pg 709
Hodder Headline Ltd, pg 709
Hollis Publishing Ltd, pg 709
Hoover's Business Press, pg 710
How To Books Ltd, pg 710
Hugo's Language Books Ltd, pg 710
ICC United Kingdom, pg 711
Institute of Physics Publishing, pg 713
International Communications, pg 714
The Islamic Texts Society, pg 715
James & James (Science Publishers) Ltd, pg 715
Jane's Information Group, pg 715
Michael Joseph Ltd, pg 716
Richard Joseph Publishers Ltd, pg 716
Kegan Paul International Ltd, pg 717
Kelly's, pg 717
Kemps Publishing Ltd, pg 717
Kingfisher Publications Plc, pg 717
Kogan Page Ltd, pg 718
Ladybird Books Ltd, pg 719
Lawpack Publishing Ltd, pg 719
Lion Hudson PLC, pg 721
LISU, pg 721
LLP Ltd, pg 722
The Lutterworth Press, pg 723
Lyle Publications Ltd, pg 723
Macmillan Audio Books, pg 723
Macmillan Ltd, pg 723
Macmillan Reference Ltd, pg 724
Management Books 2000 Ltd, pg 724
Peter Marcan Publications, pg 725
Market House Books Ltd, pg 725
Kenneth Mason Publications Ltd, pg 726
Adam Matthew Publications, pg 726
McGraw-Hill Publishing Company, pg 726
Media Research Publishing Ltd, pg 726
Melrose Press Ltd, pg 726
Methodist Publishing House, pg 727
Muze UK Ltd, pg 730
NAG Press, pg 730
National Assembly for Wales, pg 730
National Council for Voluntary Organisations (NCVO), pg 730
National Foundation for Educational Research, pg 731
National Library of Scotland, pg 731
National Portrait Gallery Publications, pg 731
Nile & Mackenzie Ltd, pg 733
NTC Research, pg 734
Oilfield Publications Ltd, pg 734
The Oleander Press, pg 735
Open University Press, pg 736
Opus Book Publishing Ltd, pg 736
Oxfam, pg 737
Oxford University Press, pg 737
Palgrave Publishers Ltd, pg 737
Panos Institute, pg 738
Pen & Sword Books Ltd, pg 740
Penguin Books Ltd, pg 740
The Penguin Group UK, pg 740
Philip's, pg 741
PIRA Intl, pg 742
PJB Reference Sevices, pg 743
Professional Book Supplies Ltd, pg 745
Professional Engineering Publishing Ltd, pg 745
Quarto Publishing plc, pg 746
Queen Anne Press, pg 747
RAC Publishing, pg 747
Ramsay Head Press, pg 747
Rapra Technology Ltd, pg 748
The Reader's Digest Association Ltd, pg 748
William Reed Directories, pg 749
Retail Entertainment Data Publishing Ltd, pg 750
Rough Guides Ltd, pg 751
Routledge, pg 751
RoutledgeCurzon, pg 751
The Rutland Press, pg 752
SAGE Publications Ltd, pg 753
St Paul's Bibliographies Ltd, pg 753
Salamander Books Ltd, pg 753
Saqi Books, pg 754
Savannah Publications, pg 754
Shaw & Sons Ltd, pg 756
Sheed & Ward UK, pg 757
Silver Link Publishing Ltd, pg 758
Charles Skilton Ltd, pg 758
Colin Smythe Ltd, pg 759
Stacey International, pg 761
Harold Starke Publishers Ltd, pg 761
Sutton Publishing Ltd, pg 762
Sweet & Maxwell Ltd, pg 762
I B Tauris & Co Ltd, pg 763
Taylor & Francis, pg 763
Telegraph Books, pg 764
Thomson Gale, pg 765
Transport Bookman Publications Ltd, pg 766
Trigon Press, pg 767
TSO (The Stationery Office), pg 767

PUBLISHERS

Vacation Work Publications, pg 769
Vacher Dod Publishing Ltd, pg 769
Veloce Publishing Ltd, pg 769
Verbatim, pg 769
Verulam Publishing Ltd, pg 770
Virago Press, pg 770
VNU Business Publications, pg 770
The Watts Publishing Group Ltd, pg 771
Websters International Publishers Ltd, pg 772
Wilmington Business Information Ltd, pg 774
Philip Wilson Publishers, pg 774
Wordsworth Editions Ltd, pg 775

Uruguay

Instituto del Tercer Mundo, pg 777
Ediciones Trilce, pg 778

Viet Nam

Science & Technics Publishing House, pg 780

Zimbabwe

Bold ADS, pg 782
Mercury Press Pvt Ltd, pg 784
Thomson Publications Zimbabwe (Pvt) Ltd, pg 784
University of Zimbabwe Publications, pg 784
Vision Publications, pg 784
ZRD Trust, pg 785

FINE EDITIONS, ILLUSTRATED BOOKS

Albania

NL SH, pg 1

Argentina

Ediciones de Arte Gaglianone, pg 6
Editorial Quetzal-Domingo Cortizo, pg 8

Australia

Aeolian Press, pg 11
Art Gallery of South Australia Bookshop, pg 12
Artmoves Inc, pg 12
Cornford Press, pg 18
Crawford House Publishing Pty Ltd, pg 18
Dragon Press, pg 20
Gangan Publishing, pg 23
The Images Publishing Group Pty Ltd, pg 26
Incunabula Press, pg 26
Laurel Press, pg 28
Mountain House Press, pg 32
New Endeavour Press, pg 33
NMA Publications, pg 33
Pandani Press, pg 35
Plantagenet Press, pg 37
Raincloud Productions, pg 38
Rams Skull Press, pg 38
Random House Australia, pg 38
Rankin Publishers, pg 39
State Library of NSW Press, pg 42
State Publishing Unit of State Print SA, pg 42
Wellington Lane Press Pty Ltd, pg 46
Yanagang Publishing, pg 47

Austria

Annette Betz Verlag im Verlag Carl Ueberreuter, pg 48
Buchkultur Verlags GmbH Zeitschrift fuer Literatur & Kunst, pg 49
Carinthia Verlag, pg 49
Czernin Verlag Ltd, pg 49
Development News Ltd, pg 50
Diotima Presse, pg 50
Gangan Verlag, pg 51
Edition Graphischer Zirkel, pg 51
Haymon-Verlag GesmbH, pg 51
Karolinger Verlag GmbH & Co KG, pg 52
Edition Koenigstein, pg 53
Verlag Monte Verita, pg 54
Oesterreichischer Kunst und Kulturverlag, pg 55
E Perlinger Naturprodukte Handelsgesellschaft mbH, pg 56
Verlag Anton Pustet, pg 56
Thanhaeuser Edition, pg 58
Edition Thurnhof KEG, pg 58
Trauner Verlag, pg 58
Tyrolia Verlagsanstalt GmbH, pg 58
Universitaetsverlag Wagner GmbH, pg 59
Herbert Weishaupt Verlag, pg 59

Belarus

Belarus (The Belorussia), pg 62
Interdigest Publishing House, pg 62
Kavaler Publishers, pg 62

Belgium

Alamire vzw, Music Publishers, pg 63
Uitgeverij Clavis, pg 65
Editions De Boeck-Larcier SA, pg 66
Dexia Bank, pg 66
Glenat Benelux SA, pg 67
Groeninghe NV, pg 68
King Baudouin Foundation, pg 69
Uitgeverij Lannoo NV, pg 69
Claude Lefrancq Editeur, pg 70
Mercatorfonds NV, pg 71
La Renaissance du Livre, pg 72

Bermuda

The Bermudian Publishing Co, pg 75

Brazil

Abril SA, pg 76
Action Editora Ltda, pg 76
AGIR S/A Editora, pg 77
Conquista, Empresa de Publicacoes Ltda, pg 80
Editora Elevacao, pg 81
Empresa Brasileira de Pesquisa Agropecuaria, pg 81
Livraria Martins Fontes Editora Ltda, pg 81
Editora Globo SA, pg 82
Grafica Editora Primor Ltda, pg 83
LDA Editores Ltda, pg 84
Editora Manole Ltda, pg 86
Editora Marco Zero Ltda, pg 86
Companhia Editora Nacional, pg 87
Editora Nova Fronteira SA, pg 87
Editora Primor Ltda, pg 89
Rede Das Artes (Boccato Editores Collector's), pg 89
Editora Revan Ltda, pg 89
Spala Editora Ltda, pg 90
Talento Publicacoes Editora e Grafica Ltda, pg 91
Editora da Universidade de Sao Paulo, pg 91

Bulgaria

Abagar Pablioing, pg 92
Abagar, Veliko Tarnovo, pg 93
Bulgarski Houdozhnik Publishers, pg 93
Fondacija Zlatno Kljuce, pg 94
Hermes Publishing House, pg 94
Heron Press Publishing House, pg 94
Izdatelstvo Lettera, pg 95
Kibea Publishing Co, pg 95
Publishing House Narodno delo OOD, pg 96

Chile

Editorial Cuarto Propio, pg 99
Museo Chileno de Arte Precolombino, pg 99

China

Beijing Arts & Crafts Publishing House, pg 101
Beijing Juvenile & Children's Books Publishing House, pg 101
Beijing Publishing House, pg 101
China Film Press, pg 102
Cultural Relics Publishing House, pg 103
Dolphin Books, pg 104
Fudan University Press, pg 104
Fujian Science & Technology Publishing House, pg 104
Morning Glory Press, pg 106
People's Sports Publishing House, pg 107
Qingdao Publishing House, pg 107
Science Press, pg 107
Shandong Education Publishing House, pg 107
Shanghai Far East Publishers, pg 108
Yunnan University Press, pg 109

Colombia

Editorial Santillana SA, pg 112

The Democratic Republic of the Congo

Facultes Catoliques de Kinshasa, pg 114

Costa Rica

Litografia Artex, SA, pg 115
Ediciones Promesa, pg 116
Editorial de la Universidad de Costa Rica, pg 116

Croatia

ALFA dd za izdavacke, graficke i trgovacke poslove, pg 117
ArTresor naklada, pg 117
Matica hrvatska, pg 118

Cuba

Editorial Letras Cubanas, pg 120

Czech Republic

AULOS sro, pg 122
Chvojkova nakladatelstvi, pg 123
Lyra Pragensis Obecne Prospelna Spolecnost, pg 125

Denmark

Borgens Forlag A/S, pg 129
Carit Andersens Forlag A/S, pg 130
Christian Ejlers' Forlag aps, pg 131
Forlaget Hovedland, pg 132
Mallings ApS, pg 132

TYPE OF PUBLICATION INDEX

Egypt (Arab Republic of Egypt)

Dar El Shorouk, pg 138

Estonia

Eesti Rahvusraamatukogu, pg 139
Ilmamaa, pg 139
Kirjastus Kunst, pg 139
Kupar Publishers, pg 139

Finland

Kustannus Oy Kolibri, pg 143
Kustannusosakeyhtio Tammi, pg 143

France

ACR Edition, pg 145
Actes-Graphiques, pg 145
Adrian, pg 145
Adverbum SARL, pg 146
Editions Alternatives, pg 146
L'Amitie par le Livre, pg 146
Edition Anthese, pg 147
Armenia Editions, pg 147
Editions Art & Metiers Du Livre, pg 147
Editions Atlantica Seguier, pg 148
ATP - Packager, pg 148
Editions A Barthelemy, pg 149
Editions Bertout, pg 149
La Bibliotheque des Arts, pg 150
Bibliotheque Nationale de France, pg 150
Adam Biro Editions, pg 150
William Blake & Co, pg 150
Editions Andre Bonne, pg 150
Editions du Cadratin, pg 151
Editions Caracteres, pg 152
Editions Cenomane, pg 152
Chasse Maree, pg 153
Editions du Chene, pg 154
Le Cherche Midi Editeur, pg 154
Communication Par Livre (CPL), pg 155
Compagnie Francaise des Arts Graphiques SA, pg 155
La Delirante, pg 157
Editions Denoel, pg 157
Editions Dis Voir, pg 158
Du May, pg 159
Editions Edisud, pg 159
Editions ELOR, pg 160
Editions Grund, pg 160
Editions Terrail/Finest SA, pg 160
Editions Unes, pg 160
EPA (Editions Pratiques Automobiles), pg 161
Editions de l'Epargne, pg 161
Editions Errance, pg 162
Editions Pierre Fanlac, pg 162
Editions Fata Morgana, pg 162
FBT de R Editions, pg 163
Editions Filipacchi-Sonodip, pg 163
Editions Fleurus, pg 163
Folklore Comtois, pg 164
Editions du Garde-Temps, pg 165
Hachette Pratiques, pg 167
Editions Hazan, pg 167
Herscher, pg 168
Indigo & Cote-Femmes Editions, pg 168
Les Editions Interferences, pg 169
Editions du Jaguar, pg 169
Editions Klincksieck, pg 170
Editions des Limbes d'Or FBT de R Editions, pg 172
Editions Loubatieres, pg 173
Editions Lyonnaises d'Art et d'Histoire, pg 173
Editions Mango, pg 174
Editions Marie-Noelle, pg 174
Editions Marval, pg 174

817

TYPE OF PUBLICATION INDEX BOOK

Masson-Williams et Wilkins, pg 174
Editions Medianes, pg 175
Editions Memo, pg 175
Editions Memoire des Arts, pg 175
Editions Menges, pg 175
Nanga, pg 176
Editions Norma, pg 177
OGC Michele Broutta Editeur, pg 177
Editions J H Paillet et B Drouaud, pg 178
Editions Parentheses, pg 179
Editions Christian Pirot, pg 180
Editions Plume, pg 180
Editions du Centre Pompidou, pg 180
Presses de l'Ecole Nationale des Ponts et Chaussees, pg 181
Editions Ramsay, pg 182
Revue Noire, pg 183
Yves Riviere Editeur, pg 183
Editions Scala, pg 184
Editions du Seuil, pg 184
Societe Nouveaux Loisirs, pg 185
Somogy editions d'art, pg 185
Souffles, pg 186
Editions Stil, pg 186
Editions Thames & Hudson, pg 187
Alain Thomas Editeur, pg 187
Ulisse Editions, pg 188
Publications de l'Universite de Pau, pg 188
Editions Vague Verte, pg 188
Editions Van de Velde, pg 188
Galerie Lucie Weill-Seligmann, pg 189

Germany

Verlag und Antiquariat Frank Albrecht, pg 192
Arnoldsche Verlagsanstalt GmbH, pg 194
Ars Edition GmbH, pg 194
Babel Verlag Kevin Perryman, pg 196
Dr Bachmaier Verlag GmbH, pg 196
Edition Balance Marion Guenther Bonsack, pg 196
Bartkowiaks Forum Book Art, pg 197
Dr Wolfgang Baur Verlag Kunst & Alltag, pg 198
Verlag C H Beck oHG, pg 198
Edition Monika Beck, pg 198
Beerenverlag, pg 198
Berliner Handpresse Wolfgang Joerg und Erich Schonig, pg 199
Bibliographisches Institut & F A Brockhaus AG, pg 200
Brigg Verlag Franz-Josef Buchler KG, pg 204
F Bruckmann Munchen Verlag & Druck GmbH & Co Produkt KG, pg 204
Brunnen-Verlag GmbH, pg 205
Christian Verlag GmbH, pg 208
CTL-Presse Clemens-Tobias Lange, pg 210
Die Deutsche Bibliothek/Deutsche Buecherei Leipzig, pg 211
Dieterichsche Verlagsbuchhandlung Mainz, pg 214
Maximilian Dietrich Verlag, pg 214
Droste Verlag GmbH, pg 216
DuMont monte Verlag GmbH & Co KG, pg 217
DuMont Reiseverlag GmbH & Co KG, pg 217
Egmont vgs verlagsgesellschaft mbH, pg 218
Ellert & Richter Verlag GmbH, pg 219

Verlag Esoterische Philosophie GmbH, pg 221
Extent Verlag und Service Wolfgang M Flamm, pg 223
Fahrner & Fahrner, pg 223
Frederking & Thaler Verlag GmbH, pg 226
Verlag Freies Geistesleben, pg 227
Friedrich Frommann Verlag, pg 227
G Braun (vormals G Braun'sche Hofbuchdruckerei und Verlag) Gmbh, pg 227
Gerstenberg Verlag, pg 228
Gondrom Verlag GmbH & Co KG, pg 230
Graefe und Unzer Verlag GmbH, pg 230
Greven Verlag Koeln GmbH, pg 231
Walter Haedecke Verlag, pg 232
Harenberg Kommunikation Verlags- und Medien-GmbH & Co KG, pg 234
Hatje Cantz Verlag, pg 234
Dr Ernst Hauswedell & Co, pg 235
Heigl Verlag, Horst Edition, pg 235
G Henle Verlag, pg 236
Axel Hertenstein, Hertenstein-Presse, pg 237
Hestra-Verlag Hernichel & Dr Strauss GmbH & Co KG, pg 237
Wilhelm Heyne Verlag, pg 237
Anton Hiersemann, Verlag, pg 237
Hirmer Verlag GmbH, pg 238
Hoffmann und Campe Verlag GmbH, pg 238
Hyperion - Verlag, pg 240
Jan Thorbecke Verlag GmbH & Co, pg 243
Jovis Verlag GmbH, pg 243
Knesebeck Verlag, pg 247
Knowledge Media International, pg 247
W Kohlhammer GmbH, pg 248
KONTEXTverlag, pg 249
Koptisch-Orthodoxes Zentrum, pg 249
Ambro Lacus, Buch- und Bildverlag Walter A Kremnitz, pg 251
Karl Robert Langewiesche Nachfolger Hans Koester KG, pg 252
Verlag fuer Lehrmittel Poessneck GmbH, pg 253
Leipziger Universitaetsverlag GmbH, pg 253
Edition Libri Illustri GmbH, pg 254
Maro Verlag und Druck, Benno Kasmayr, pg 257
Mergus Verlag GmbH Hans A Baensch, pg 259
Merlin Verlag Andreas Meyer Verlags GmbH und Co KG, pg 259
Merz & Solitude - Akademie Schloss Solitude, pg 259
Moderne Buchkunst und Graphie Wolfgang Tiessen, pg 261
modo verlag GmbH, pg 261
Mueller & Schindler Verlag ek, pg 262
C W Niemeyer Buchverlage GmbH, pg 265
Nusser Verlag, pg 266
Edition Octopus & Okeanos Presse, pg 266
Verlag Friedrich Oetinger GmbH, pg 266
Pendragon Verlag, pg 269
Pfaffenweiler Presse, pg 269
Podzun-Pallas Verlag GmbH, pg 270
Prasenz Verlag der Jesus Bruderschaft eV, pg 271

Guido Pressler Verlag, pg 271
Verlag fur Regionalgeschichte, pg 274
Regura Verlag, pg 274
Dr Ludwig Reichert Verlag, pg 274
E Reinhold Verlag, pg 275
Rosenheimer Verlagshaus GmbH & Co KG, pg 276
Sax-Verlag Beucha, pg 278
Verlag Th Schaefer im Vicentz Verlag KG, pg 278
Richard Scherpe Verlag GmbH, pg 279
Rudolf Schneider Verlag, pg 280
Verlag Schnell und Steiner GmbH, pg 281
Theodor Schuster, pg 282
Dr Wolfgang Schwarze Verlag, pg 282
Sigloch Edition Helmut Sigloch GmbH & Co KG, pg 283
Silberburg-Verlag Titus Haeussermann GmbH, pg 283
L Staackmann Verlag KG, pg 286
Staatliche Museen Kassel, pg 286
Stapp Verlag Wolfgang Stapp, pg 286
Steiger Verlag, pg 287
Edition Gunter Stoberlein, pg 288
Straelener Manuskripte Verlag GmbH, pg 288
Svato Zapletal, pg 289
teNeues Verlag GmbH & Co KG, pg 290
Tipress Dienstleistungen fur das Verlagswesen GmbH, pg 291
Titania-Verlag Ferdinand Schroll, pg 291
Dorothea van der Koelen, pg 294
Verein der Benediktiner zu Beuron-Beuroner Kunstverlag, pg 294
Edition Curt Visel, pg 296
Verlag Klaus Wagenbach, pg 297
Uwe Warnke Verlag, pg 297
Wartburg Verlag GmbH, pg 297
Ziethen-Panorama Verlag GmbH, pg 302
Zweipunkt Verlag K Kaiser KG, pg 302

Ghana

World Literature Project, pg 305

Greece

Akritas, pg 305
Vefa Alexiadou Editions, pg 305
Apostoliki Diakonia tis Ekklisias tis Hellados, pg 305
Beta Medical Publishers, pg 306
Diachronikes Ekdoseis, pg 306
Ekdotike Athenon SA, pg 307
Evrodiastasi, pg 307
Govostis Publishing SA, pg 307
Hestia-I D Hestia-Kollaros & Co Corporation, pg 308
Kastaniotis Editions SA, pg 309
Melissa Publishing House, pg 310
Orfanidis Publications, pg 311
Patakis Publishers, pg 311
To Rodakio, pg 312

Hungary

Aranyhal Konyvkiado Goldfish Publishing, pg 320
Kiiarat Konyvdiado, pg 322
Officina Nova Konyvek, pg 323

Iceland

Forlagid, pg 325
Mal og menning, pg 326
Setberg, pg 326

India

Addison-Wesley Pte Ltd, pg 327
Brijbasi Printers Pvt Ltd, pg 331
India Book House Pvt Ltd, pg 336
Reliance Publishing House, pg 346
Roli Books Pvt Ltd, pg 347

Ireland

Tir Eolas, pg 363

Israel

Bitan Publishers Ltd, pg 365
DAT Publications, pg 366
Dvir Publishing Ltd, pg 366
Inbal Publishers, pg 368

Italy

A & A, pg 374
Adea Edizioni, pg 374
L'Airone Editrice, pg 375
Alberti Libraio Editore, pg 375
Umberto Allemandi & C SRL, pg 375
Gruppo Editoriale Armenia SpA, pg 376
Arsenale Editrice SRL, pg 376
Artema, pg 376
Artioli Editore, pg 377
Belforte Editore Libraio srl, pg 377
BeMa, pg 377
Biblos srl, pg 378
Giuseppe Bonanno Editore, pg 378
Casa Editrice Bonechi, pg 378
Bonechi-Edizioni Il Turismo Srl, pg 378
Edizioni Bora SNC di E Brandani & C, pg 379
Campanotto, pg 379
Canova SRL, pg 379
Edizioni del Capricorno, pg 380
Editrice Il Castoro, pg 380
Il Cigno Galileo Galilei-Edizioni di Arte e Scienza, pg 382
Citta Nuova Editrice, pg 382
Colonnese Editore, pg 383
Edizioni Della Torre di Salvatore Fozzi & C SAS, pg 385
Di Baio Editore SpA, pg 385
Direzione Generale Archivi, pg 385
EDIFIR SRL, pg 386
Edizioni d'Arte Antica e Moderna EDAM, pg 386
L'Erma di Bretschneider SRL, pg 388
Essegi, pg 388
ETR (Editrice Trasporti su Rotaie), pg 388
Federico Motta Editore SpA, pg 389
Fenice 2000, pg 389
Festina Lente Edizioni, pg 389
Edizioni Frassinelli SRL, pg 389
Edizioni Futuro SRL, pg 389
Grafica e Arte srl, pg 391
Ernesto Gremese Editore srl, pg 391
Gremese International srl, pg 391
Idea Books, pg 392
Editoriale Jaca Book SpA, pg 394
Jandi-Sapi Editori, pg 394
Kaos Edizioni SRL, pg 394
Laruffa Editore SRL, pg 394
Levante Editori, pg 395
Lindau, pg 395
Linea d'Ombra Libri, pg 395
Angelo Longo Editore, pg 396
Luni, pg 396
Magnus Edizioni SpA, pg 397
Edizioni Mediterranee SRL, pg 398
Giorgio Mondadori & Associati, pg 399
Moretti & Vitali Editori srl, pg 399
Giorgio Nada Editore SRL, pg 400
NodoLibri, pg 400

PUBLISHERS   TYPE OF PUBLICATION INDEX

OCTAVO Produzioni Editoriali Associale, pg 401
Leo S Olschki, pg 401
Maria Pacini Fazzi Editore, pg 402
Franco Cosimo Panini Editore SpA, pg 402
Amilcare Pizzi SpA, pg 403
Il Pomerio, pg 404
Priuli e Verlucca, Editori, pg 404
RAI-ERI, pg 405
RCS Rizzoli Libri SpA, pg 405
Reverdito Edizioni, pg 405
Rossato, pg 406
Rubbettino Editore, pg 406
Salerno Editrice SRL, pg 406
Sardini Editrice, pg 407
Scala Group spa, pg 407
SEMAR Publishers SRL, pg 408
Sicania, pg 408
Silvana Editoriale SpA, pg 408
Edizioni Rosminiane Sodalitas, pg 408
Tappeiner, pg 409
Turris, pg 410
Vaccari SRL, pg 411
Vinciana Editrice sas, pg 412
Vivere In SRL, pg 412
Viviani Editore srl, pg 412

Japan
Genko-Sha, pg 417
Hoikusha Publishing Co Ltd, pg 418
Hokuryukan Co Ltd, pg 418
Nigensha Publishing Co Ltd, pg 423
Seibido Shuppan Company Ltd, pg 426
Shincho-Sha Co Ltd, pg 427
Tankosha Publishing Co Ltd, pg 429

Kenya
Camerapix Publishers International Ltd, pg 433
Kenway Publications Ltd, pg 434

Democratic People's Republic of Korea
Korea Science and Encyclopedia Publishing House, pg 436

Republic of Korea
Omun Gak, pg 441
Youlhwadang Publisher, pg 444

Latvia
Madris, pg 445
Preses Nams, pg 445

Liechtenstein
Frank P van Eck Publishers, pg 448

Lithuania
AS Narbuto Leidykla (AS Narbutas' Publishers), pg 448
Lietus Ltd, pg 449
Lithuanian National Museum Publishing House, pg 449

Luxembourg
Editions Emile Borschette, pg 450
Edition Objectif Lune, pg 451
Editions Phi, pg 451

Macau
Livros Do Oriente, pg 452
Museu Maritimo, pg 452

The Former Yugoslav Republic of Macedonia
St Clement of Ohrid National & University Library, pg 453
Zumpres Publishing Firm, pg 453

Mauritius
Editions de l'Ocean Indien Ltd, pg 461
Vizavi Editions, pg 461

Mexico
Editorial AGATA SA de CV, pg 462
Artes de Mexico y del Mundo SA de CV, pg 462
Ediciones Culturales Internacionales SA de CV Edicion Compra y Venta de Libros, Casetes, Videos, pg 463
Editorial Diana SA de CV, pg 464
Edamex SA de CV, pg 464
Editorial Edicol SA, pg 464
Ediciones Era SA de CV, pg 465
Fondo Editorial de la Plastica Mexicana, pg 466
Editorial Jilguero, SA de CV, pg 467
Editorial Limusa SA de CV, pg 467
Instituto Nacional de Antropologia e Historia, pg 469
Naves Internacional de Ediciones SA, pg 469
Promociones de Mercados Turisticos SA de CV, pg 471
SCRIPTA - Distribucion y Servicios Editoriales, SA de CV, pg 471
Editorial Turner de Mexico, pg 472

Monaco
Editions EGC, pg 473

Morocco
Editions Le Fennec, pg 474
Editions Oum, pg 475

Netherlands
Gaberbocchus Press, pg 482
De Harmonie Uitgeverij, pg 483
HES & De Graaf Publishers BV, pg 483
Heuff Amsterdam Uitgever, pg 483
Hotei Publishing, pg 484
Miland Publishers, pg 486
Mondria Publishers, pg 486
Omega Boek BV, pg 487
The Pepin Press, pg 487
Koninklijke Smeets Offset, pg 489
Uitgeverij Het Spectrum BV, pg 489
Stedelijk Van Abbemuseum, pg 489
Steltman Editions, pg 489
Twente University Press, pg 490

New Zealand
The Caxton Press, pg 495
David Ling Publishing, pg 498

Norway
Andresen & Butenschon AS, pg 508

Oman
Apex Press & Publishing, pg 511

Pakistan
Sang-e-Meel Publications, pg 514

Peru
Ediciones Peisa (Promocion Editorial Inca SA), pg 517

Philippines
Cacho Publishing House, Inc, pg 518

Poland
Wydawnictwo Baturo, pg 522
Biblioteka Narodowa, pg 522
BOSZ scp, pg 522
Ludowa Spoldzielnia Wydawnicza, pg 524
Norbertinum, pg 524
Rosikon Press, pg 526
Videograf II Sp z o o Zaklad Poracy Chronionej, pg 527

Portugal
Arvore Coop de Actividades Artisticas, CRL, pg 528
Contexto Editora, pg 530
Difusao Cultural, pg 530
Dinalivro, pg 530
Distri Cultural Lda, pg 530
Edicoes ELO, pg 531
Editorial Estampa, Lda, pg 531
Gradiva-Publicacnoes Lda, pg 532
Imprensa Nacional-Casa da Moeda, pg 532
Latina Livraria Editora, pg 532
Editorial Presenca, pg 535
Quimera Editores Lda, pg 535
Edicioes Joao Sa da Costa Lda, pg 535
Solivros, pg 536
Teorema, pg 536

Romania
Alcor-Edimpex (Verlag) Ltd, pg 538
Enzyklopadie Verlag, pg 539
Humanitas Publishing House, pg 540
Mentor Kiado, pg 540
Editura Meridiane, pg 540
Editura Minerva, pg 541
Editura Paideia, pg 541
Saeculum IO, pg 542
Est-Samuel Tastet Verlag, pg 542
Vestala Verlag, pg 543

Russian Federation
Interbook-Business AO, pg 545
Izdatelstvo Iskusstvo, pg 545
Izvestia Sovetov Narodnyh Deputatov Russian Federation (RF), pg 545
Izdatelstvo Khudozhestvennaya Literatura, pg 545
Izdatelstvo Kniga, pg 545
Izdatelstvo Mir, pg 546
Obdeestro Znanie, pg 547
Panorama Publishing House, pg 547
Permskaja Kniga, pg 548
Planeta Publishers, pg 548
Profizdat, pg 548
Izdatelstvo Prosveshchenie, pg 548

Serbia and Montenegro
Alfa-Narodna Knjiga, pg 552

Singapore
Aquanut Agencies Pte Ltd, pg 555
Archipelago Press, pg 555
Marshall Cavendish Books, pg 555
McGallen & Bolden Associates, pg 557
Select Publishing Pte Ltd, pg 557

Slovenia
Mladinska Knjiga International, pg 561

South Africa
The Brenthurst Press (Pty) Ltd, pg 563
Fernwood Press (Pty) Ltd, pg 563
Human & Rousseau (Pty) Ltd, pg 564
Janssen Publishers CC, pg 565
Johannesburg Art Gallery, pg 565
New Africa Books (Pty) Ltd, pg 567
Reader's Digest Southern Africa, pg 568
Struik Publishers (Pty) Ltd, pg 569

Spain
Editorial Acanto SA, pg 570
Editorial Algazara, pg 572
Alinco SA - Aura Comunicacio, pg 572
Ambit Serveis Editorials, SA, pg 572
Calambur Editorial, SL, pg 575
Carroggio SA de Ediciones, pg 575
Editorial Casariego, pg 576
Celeste Ediciones, pg 576
Editora Comercial de Publicaciones, pg 577
Compania Literaria, pg 577
Consello da Cultura Galega - CCG, pg 578
Ediciones Daly S L, pg 578
Diputacion Provincial de Malaga, pg 579
Ediciones Doce Calles SL, pg 579
Ediciones l'Isard, S L, pg 580
Edilesa-Ediciones Leonesas SA, pg 581
El Viso, SA Ediciones, pg 582
Ediciones Elfos SL, pg 582
Ediciones Encuentro SA, pg 582
Naipes Heraclio Fournier SA, pg 583
Vicent Garcia Editores, SA, pg 584
Grijalbo Mondadori SA, pg 585
Hercules de Ediciones, SA, pg 586
Idea Books, SA, pg 587
Editorial Juventud SA, pg 588
Editorin Laiovento SL, pg 588
Liber Ediciones, SA, pg 589
Lunwerg Editores, SA, pg 589
Editorial Mediterrania SL, pg 591
M Moleiro Editor, SA, pg 592
Editorial Noray, pg 593
Ediciones del Oriente y del Mediterraneo, pg 594
Instituto Provincial de Investigaciones y Estudios Toledanos (IPIET), pg 597
Rueda, SL Editorial, pg 598
Universidad de Santiago de Compostela, pg 599
Silex Ediciones, pg 600
Equipo Sirius SA, pg 600
Ediciones Siruela SA, pg 600
Edicions 62, pg 600
Grup 62, pg 600
Tesitex, SL, pg 602
Tf Editores, pg 602
Trea Ediciones, SL, pg 602
Turner Publicaciones, pg 602
Publicacions de la Universitat de Barcelona, pg 604

Sweden
Bokforlaget Atlantis AB, pg 609
BOOX, pg 610
Bokforlaget Bra Bocker AB, pg 610

819

TYPE OF PUBLICATION INDEX — BOOK

Byggforlaget, pg 610
Bengt Forsbergs Foerlag AB, pg 611
Natur och Kultur Fakta etc, pg 614
Bokforlaget Settern AB, pg 615
Wahlstrom & Widstrand, pg 616

Switzerland

Ammann Verlag & Co, pg 617
AT Verlag, pg 618
U Baer Verlag, pg 618
Benteli Verlag, pg 618
Christoph Merian Verlag, pg 620
Diogenes Verlag AG, pg 622
Erker-Verlag, pg 623
FEDA SA, pg 623
Verlag Gachnang & Springer, Bern-Berlin, pg 623
Giampiero Casagrande Editore, pg 624
Pierre Gonin Editions d'Art, pg 624
Junod Nicolas, pg 626
Galerie Kornfeld & Co, pg 627
Kossodo Verlag AG, pg 627
Kranich-Verlag, Dres AG & H R Bosch-Gwalter, pg 627
Bernard Letu Editeur, pg 627
Lars Mueller Publishers, pg 629
Neue Zuercher Zeitung AG Buchverlag, pg 629
Orell Fuessli Buchhandlungs AG, pg 630
Parkett Publishers Inc, pg 630
Editiones Roche, pg 632
Editions Scriptar SA, pg 634
Edition Stemmle AG, pg 635
Versus Verlag AG, pg 636
Verlag im Waldgut AG, pg 636
Werner Druck AG, pg 637
J E Wolfensberger AG, pg 637

Taiwan, Province of China

Art Book Co Ltd, pg 638
Designer Publisher Inc, pg 639
Echo Publishing Company Ltd, pg 639
Hilit Publishing Co Ltd, pg 640
Kuang Fu Book Co Ltd, pg 640

United Republic of Tanzania

Central Tanganyika Press, pg 643

Thailand

Sangdad Publishing Company Ltd, pg 645

Tunisia

Maison Tunisienne de l'Edition, pg 648

Turkey

Arkeoloji Ve Sanat Yayinlari, pg 649
Dost Yayinlari, pg 650

Ukraine

Mystetstvo Publishers, pg 653

United Arab Emirates

Motivate Publishing, pg 654

United Kingdom

Abbotsford Publishing, pg 654
Umberto Allemandi & Co Publishing, pg 656
Architectural Association Publications, pg 659
Art Books International Ltd, pg 659
Ashgate Publishing Ltd, pg 660
Ashmolean Museum Publications, pg 660
Atlas Press, pg 661
Mitchell Beazley, pg 664
Blackstaff Press, pg 666
Blandford Publishing Ltd, pg 668
Book Packaging & Marketing, pg 668
Books for Europe Ltd, pg 669
Books of Zimbabwe Publishing Co (Pvt) Ltd, pg 669
Bridge Books, pg 671
British Library Publications, pg 672
Camerapix Publishers International Ltd, pg 674
Canongate Books Ltd, pg 674
Carlton Publishing Group, pg 675
Carroll & Brown Ltd, pg 675
Cockbird Press, pg 680
Conran Octopus, pg 682
Conway Maritime Press, pg 683
Leo Cooper, pg 683
Cottage Publications, pg 683
Defiant Publications, pg 687
Elfande Ltd, pg 690
The Erskine Press, pg 692
Faber & Faber Ltd, pg 694
Flame Tree Publishing, pg 695
The Fraser Press, pg 697
Garnet Publishing Ltd, pg 698
Genesis Publications Ltd, pg 699
Hamlyn, pg 704
The Harvill Press, pg 705
Hawk Books, pg 706
Alan Hutchison Ltd, pg 711
The Islamic Texts Society, pg 715
James & James (Publishers) Ltd, pg 715
Michael Joseph Ltd, pg 716
Kegan Paul International Ltd, pg 717
Mainstream Publishing Co (Edinburgh) Ltd, pg 724
Manchester University Press, pg 724
Marcham Manor Press, pg 725
Merrell Publishers Ltd, pg 727
National Portrait Gallery Publications, pg 731
New Cavendish Books, pg 732
Newpro UK Ltd, pg 733
Octopus Publishing Group, pg 734
Osprey Publishing Ltd, pg 737
Parapress Ltd, pg 738
Pavilion Books Ltd, pg 739
Phaidon Press Ltd, pg 741
Philip's, pg 741
Piatkus Books, pg 741
Pickering & Chatto Publishers Ltd, pg 742
Plexus Publishing Ltd, pg 743
Prion Books Ltd, pg 745
Quadrille Publishing Ltd, pg 746
Quentin Books Ltd, pg 747
Reaktion Books Ltd, pg 748
Reardon Publishing, pg 748
RotoVision SA, pg 751
Ryland Peters & Small Ltd, pg 752
Salamander Books Ltd, pg 753
Saqi Books, pg 754
Sheldrake Press, pg 757
Shepheard-Walwyn (Publishers) Ltd, pg 757
The Society for Promoting Christian Knowledge (SPCK), pg 759
Harold Starke Publishers Ltd, pg 761
Sutton Publishing Ltd, pg 762
Taschen UK Ltd, pg 763
I B Tauris & Co Ltd, pg 763
Tern Press, pg 764
Textile & Art Publications Ltd, pg 764
Transedition Ltd, pg 766
Trigon Press, pg 767
Veloce Publishing Ltd, pg 769
Webb & Bower (Publishers) Ltd, pg 772
Websters International Publishers Ltd, pg 772
Wordwright Publishing, pg 775

Uzbekistan

Izdatelstvo Literatury i isskustva, pg 778

FOREIGN LANGUAGE & BILINGUAL BOOKS

Afghanistan

Ministry of Education, Department of Educational Publications, pg 1
Pushtu Toulana, Afghan Academy, pg 1

Albania

State Textbook Publishing House, pg 1

Argentina

Editorial Idearium de la Universidad de Mendoza (EDIUM), pg 6
Ediciones Preescolar SA, pg 8

Armenia

Arevik, pg 10

Australia

Bayda Books, pg 14
Boinkie Publishers, pg 15
Boombana Publications, pg 16
China Books, pg 17
CIS Publishers, pg 18
Curriculum Corporation, pg 19
Flora Publications International Pty Ltd, pg 22
Gangan Publishing, pg 23
Illert Publications, pg 26
The Images Publishing Group Pty Ltd, pg 26
Institute of Aboriginal Development (IAD Press), pg 27
INT Press, pg 27
Little Red Apple Publishing, pg 29
Lonely Planet Publications Pty Ltd, pg 29
Magabala Books Aboriginal Corporation, pg 30
Mimosa Publications Pty Ltd, pg 32
Owl Publishing, pg 35
Pearson Education Australia, pg 36
State Library of NSW Press, pg 42
Tom Publications, pg 43

Austria

Gangan Verlag, pg 51
Langenscheidt-Verlag GmbH, pg 53
Merbod Verlag, pg 54
Thomas Mlakar Verlag, pg 54
oebv & hpt Verlagsgesellschaft mbH & Co KG, pg 55
Oesterreichischer Bundesverlag Gmbh, pg 55
Richard Pils Publication PN°1, pg 56
Roetzer Druck GmbH & Co KG, pg 57
Andreas Schnider Verlags-Atelier, pg 57
Edition Thurnhof KEG, pg 58
Verlag Mag Wanzenbock, pg 59
Wieser Verlag, pg 60

Azerbaijan

Sada, Literaturno-Izdatel'skij Centr, pg 60

Bangladesh

Ankur Prakashani, pg 61

Belarus

Kavaler Publishers, pg 62
Izdatelstvo Mastatskaya Litaratura, pg 62
Narodnaya Asveta, pg 62
Publishing Center of Belarus State University, pg 62

Belgium

Assimil NV, pg 63
Brepols Publishers NV, pg 64
Ediblanchart sprl, pg 67
Editions Hemma, pg 68
King Baudouin Foundation, pg 69
Marabout, pg 71
Uitgeverij Peeters Leuven (Belgie), pg 71
Stichting Ons Erfdeel VZW, pg 73
Uitgeverij De Garve, pg 74
Vander Editions, SA, pg 74
Vita, pg 74
Vlaamse Esperantobond VZW, pg 74
Zuid-Nederlandse Uitgeverij NV/Central Uitgeverij, pg 75

Brazil

Ao Livro Tecnico Industria e Comercio Ltda, pg 77
Ars Poetica Editora Ltda, pg 78
Callis Editora Ltda, pg 79
Editorial Dimensao Ltda, pg 80
E P U Editora Pedagogica e Universitaria Ltd, pg 81
Hemus Editora Ltda, pg 83
Editora Kuarup Ltda, pg 84
Waldir Lima Editora, pg 85
Editora Mundo Cristao, pg 87
Companhia Editora Nacional, pg 87
Editora Nova Alexandria Ltda, pg 87
Editora Revan Ltda, pg 89

Bulgaria

Abagar Pabloing, pg 92
Factor-Alias, pg 94
Hriker, pg 94
Interpres, pg 95
Kibea Publishing Co, pg 95
Naouka i Izkoustvo, Ltd, pg 95
Prohazka I Kacarmazov, pg 96
Prosveta Publishers AS, pg 96
Prozoretz Ltd Publishing House, pg 96
Seven Hills Publishers, pg 96
Svetra Publishing House, pg 97

Chile

Arrayan Editores, pg 98

China

Beijing Publishing House, pg 101
Beijing University Press, pg 101
Chemical Industry Press, pg 101
China Film Press, pg 102
China Ocean Press, pg 102
China Translation & Publishing Corp, pg 103
Chinese Pedagogics Publishing House, pg 103
CITIC Publishing House, pg 103
Education Science Publishing House, pg 104

PUBLISHERS

Foreign Language Teaching & Research Press, pg 104
Foreign Languages Press, pg 104
Fudan University Press, pg 104
Guizhou Education Publishing House, pg 105
Heilongjiang Science & Technology Press, pg 105
Higher Education Press, pg 105
Inner Mongolia Science & Technology Publishing House, pg 105
Jilin Science & Technology Publishing House, pg 105
Lanzhou University Press, pg 106
Liaoning People's Publishing House, pg 106
Morning Glory Press, pg 106
Nanjing University Press, pg 106
The Nationalities Publishing House, pg 106
New Times Press, pg 106
Qingdao Publishing House, pg 107
Science Press, pg 107
Shandong Friendship Publishing House, pg 107
Shandong University Press, pg 108
Shanghai Educational Publishing House, pg 108
Shanghai Foreign Language Education Press, pg 108
Tianjin Science & Technology Publishing House, pg 108
World Affairs Press, pg 109
Wuhan University Press, pg 109
Yunnan University Press, pg 109
Zhejiang Education Publishing House, pg 109
Zhejiang University Press, pg 109
Zhong Hua Book Co, pg 110

Colombia

Asociacion Instituto Linguistico de Verano, pg 110
Editorial Panamericana, pg 112
Pearson Educacion de Colombia LTDA, pg 112
Editorial Santillana SA, pg 112

The Democratic Republic of the Congo

Centre Protestant d'Editions et de Diffusion (CEDI), pg 114
Facultes Catoliques de Kinshasa, pg 114

Costa Rica

Centro Agronomico Tropical de Investigacion y Ensenanza (CATIE), pg 115
Ediciones Promesa, pg 116
Editorial Texto Ltda, pg 116
Union Mundial para la Naturaleza (UICN), Oficina Regional para Mesoamerica, pg 116

Croatia

ArTresor naklada, pg 117
Durieux d o o, pg 118
Faust Vrani, pg 118
Edit Niro (Novinska-izdavacka radna organizacija), pg 119
Sveucilisna tiskara doo, pg 119
Vitagraf, pg 119

Cuba

Editora Politica, pg 120

Czech Republic

Aventinum Nakladatelstvi spol sro, pg 122
Karmelitanske Nakladatelstvi, pg 124
Konias, pg 124
Lyra Pragensis Obecne Prospelna Spolecnost, pg 125
Votobia sro, pg 128

Denmark

Kaleidoscope Publishers Ltd, pg 132
Samfundslitteratur, pg 134
Systime, pg 135

Egypt (Arab Republic of Egypt)

Al Arab Publishing House, pg 137
Dar Al-Kitab Al-Masri, pg 137
Dar al-Nahda al Arabia, pg 138
Elias Modern Publishing House, pg 138
Dar Al Maaref, pg 138
Ummah Press, pg 138

Estonia

Eesti Entsuklopeediakirjastus, pg 139
Perioodika, pg 140

Finland

Kaantopiiri Oy, pg 142
Kirja-Leitzinger, pg 142
Yliopistopaino/Helsinki University Press, pg 145

France

Editions Al Liamm, pg 146
Armenia Editions, pg 147
Editions Assimil SA, pg 148
Aubanel Editions, pg 148
Editions Bertout, pg 149
William Blake & Co, pg 150
Emgleo Breiz, pg 151
Brud Nevez, pg 151
Editions Buchet-Chastel Pierre Zech Editeur, pg 151
Editions Caracteres, pg 152
Editions Jose Corti, pg 156
Counseil International de la Langue Francaise, pg 156
La Delirante, pg 157
Editions Dis Voir, pg 158
Les Editeurs Reunis, pg 160
Editions Terrail/Finest SA, pg 160
Institut d'Etudes Slaves IES, pg 162
Editions Farel, pg 162
Flammarion SA, pg 163
Association Frank, pg 164
Paul Geuthner Librairie Orientaliste, pg 165
Hachette Livre, pg 167
L'Harmattan, pg 167
Indigo & Cote-Femmes Editions, pg 168
Langues & Mondes-L'Asiatheque, pg 171
Editions Larousse, pg 171
Magnard, pg 173
Noir Sur Blanc, pg 177
Editions Norma, pg 177
Editions Ophrys, pg 177
Peeters-France, pg 179
Presses de la Sorbonne Nouvelle/ PSN, pg 181
Editions Prosveta, pg 182
Realisations pour l'Enseignement Multilingue International (REMI), pg 183
Service des Publications Scientifiques du Museum National d'Histoire Naturelle, pg 184
UNESCO Publishing, pg 188
YMCA-Press, pg 189

French Polynesia

Scoop/Au Vent des Iles, pg 189

Georgia

Merani Publishing House, pg 190

Germany

A Francke Verlag (Tubingen und Basel), pg 190
AOL-Verlag Frohmut Menze, pg 193
ARCult Media, pg 193
Arnoldsche Verlagsanstalt GmbH, pg 194
Ars Edition GmbH, pg 194
Aschendorffsche Verlagsbuchhandlung GmbH & Co KG, pg 194
Aulis Verlag Deubner & Co KG, pg 195
Babel Verlag Kevin Perryman, pg 196
Bauverlag GmbH, pg 198
C Bertelsmann Verlag GmbH, pg 199
Bertelsmann Lexikon Verlag GmbH, pg 200
Bibliographisches Institut & F A Brockhaus AG, pg 200
Helmut Buske Verlag GmbH, pg 206
Dr Cantz'sche Druckerei GmbH & Co, pg 207
Compact Verlag GmbH, pg 209
Copress Verlag, pg 209
Cornelsen Verlag GmbH & Co OHG, pg 210
CTL-Presse Clemens-Tobias Lange, pg 210
Deutscher Taschenbuch Verlag GmbH & Co KG (dtv), pg 213
Dieterichsche Verlagsbuchhandlung Mainz, pg 214
Domowina Verlag GmbH, pg 215
Verlag Duerr & Kessler GmbH, pg 217
N G Elwert Verlag, pg 219
Festo Didactic GmbH & Co KG, pg 224
Konkursbuch Verlag Claudia Gehrke, pg 228
Verlag der Stiftung Gralsbotschaft GmbH, pg 231
Walter de Gruyter GmbH & Co KG, pg 231
Siegfried Haring Literatten-Verlag Ulm, pg 234
Horlemann Verlag, pg 239
Max Hueber Verlag GmbH & Co KG, pg 239
Hyperion - Verlag, pg 240
IKO Verlag fur Interkulterelle Kommunikation, pg 241
Insel Verlag, pg 241
Klaus Isele, pg 242
Iudicium Verlag GmbH, pg 242
Jovis Verlag GmbH, pg 243
Ernst Klett Verlag GmbH, pg 247
Koptisch-Orthodoxes Zentrum, pg 249
Karin Kramer Verlag, pg 250
Kunstverlag Weingarten GmbH, pg 251
Laaber-Verlag, pg 251
Langenscheidt KG, pg 252
Libertas- Europaeisches Institut GmbH, pg 254
Hildegard Liebaug-Dartmann, pg 254
Logophon Verlag und Bildungsreisen GmbH, pg 255
Karin Mader, pg 256
Merz & Solitude - Akademie Schloss Solitude, pg 259
Monia Verlag, pg 261
Verlag Stephanie Naglschmid, pg 263
Neuthor - Verlag, pg 265
Verlag Friedrich Oetinger GmbH, pg 266
Osho Verlag GmbH, pg 267
Erich Roeth-Verlag, pg 276
Romiosini Verlag, pg 276
Ruhland Verlag Gimblt, pg 277
Verlag Otto Sagner, pg 278
Verlag Schnell und Steiner GmbH, pg 281
Stadler Verlagsgesellschaft mbH, pg 286
Verlag Stahleisen GmbH, pg 286
Stauffenburg Verlag Brigitte Narr GmbH, pg 287
Tipress Dienstleistungen fur das Verlagswesen GmbH, pg 291
Turkischer Schulbuchverlag Onel Cengiz, pg 293
Dorothea van der Koelen, pg 294
Vervuert Verlagsgesellschaft, pg 295
Vogel Medien GmbH & Co KG, pg 296
Zambon Verlag, pg 302
Ziethen-Panorama Verlag GmbH, pg 302

Ghana

Anowuo Educational Publications, pg 303
Bureau of Ghana Languages, pg 303
Ghana Institute of Linguistics Literacy & Bible Translation (GILLBT), pg 304
Ghana Publishing Corporation, pg 304
Sedco Publishing Ltd, pg 305

Greece

Akritas, pg 305
Athina, Mary Mavrogiannis, pg 306
Eleftheroudakis, GCSA International Bookstore, pg 307
Hestia-I D Hestia-Kollaros & Co Corporation, pg 308
Kalentis & Sia, pg 308
Nakas Music House, pg 310
Pagoulatos G-G P Publications, pg 311
Scripta Theofilus Palevratzis-Ashover, pg 312
Michalis Sideris, pg 312
Spyropoulos A, pg 312
S J Zacharopoulos SA Publishing Co, pg 313

Guadeloupe

JASOR, pg 313

Hong Kong

The Chinese University Press, pg 316
Chopsticks Publications Ltd, pg 316
Commercial Press (Hong Kong) Ltd, pg 316
The Dharmasthiti Buddist Institute Ltd, pg 317

TYPE OF PUBLICATION INDEX

BOOK

Hong Kong University Press, pg 317
Island Press, pg 317
Joint Publishing (HK) Co Ltd, pg 317
Ling Kee Publishing Group, pg 318
Research Centre for Translation, pg 319
Shanghai Book Co Ltd, pg 319

Hungary

Balassi Kiado Kft, pg 321
Corvina Books Ltd, pg 321
Joszoveg Muhely Kiado, pg 322
Nemzeti Tankoenyvkiado, pg 323

India

Asian Educational Services, pg 329
Bharat Publishing House, pg 330
Bharatiya Vidya Bhavan, pg 330
Bihar Hindi Granth Akademi, pg 330
Brijbasi Printers Pvt Ltd, pg 331
S Chand & Co Ltd, pg 331
Diamond Comics (P) Ltd, pg 333
General Book Depot, pg 335
Gyan Publishing House, pg 335
Kitab Ghar, pg 339
Sri Ramakrishna Math, pg 341
Motilal Banarsidass Publishers Pvt Ltd, pg 341
Neeta Prakashan, pg 343
Sri Satguru Publications, pg 348, 350
Star Publications (P) Ltd, pg 350
Suman Prakashan Pvt Ltd, pg 351
N M Tripathi Pvt Ltd Publishers & Booksellers, pg 351

Indonesia

Bina Aksara Parta, pg 354

Iraq

National House for Publishing, Distributing & Advertising, pg 357

Ireland

Ballinakella Press, pg 358
Clo Iar-Chonnachta Teo, pg 358
The Educational Company of Ireland, pg 359
On Stream Publications Ltd, pg 362

Israel

Achiasaf Publishing House Ltd, pg 364
Agudat Sabah, pg 364
Breslov Research Institute, pg 365
Carta, The Israel Map & Publishing Co Ltd, pg 365
Dekel Publishing House, pg 366
Eretz Hemdah Institute for Advanced Jewish Studies, pg 366
Gefen Publishing House Ltd, pg 367
(JDC) Brookdale Institute of Gerontology & Adult Human Development in Israel, pg 369
Prolog Publishing House, pg 371
Rubin Mass Ltd, pg 371
Schlesinger Institute, pg 371
Urim Publications, pg 373
Y L Peretz Publishing Co, pg 373

Italy

Umberto Allemandi & C SRL, pg 375
BeMa, pg 377
Bonacci editore, pg 378

Campanotto, pg 379
Cideb Editrice SRL, pg 382
Ciranna - Roma, pg 382
Cittadella Editrice, pg 382
CLUEB (Cooperativa Libraria Universitaria Editrice Bologna), pg 382
Costa e Nolan SpA, pg 383
M d'Auria Editore SAS, pg 384
Editrice Edisco, pg 386
Edistudio, pg 386
L'Erma di Bretschneider SRL, pg 388
Ernesto Gremese Editore srl, pg 391
Gruppo Editoriale Faenza Editrice SpA, pg 391
Guerra Edizioni GURU srl, pg 392
Kompass Fleischmann, pg 394
Levante Editori, pg 395
Lybra Immagine, pg 396
Macmillan Heinemann ELT, pg 396
Giorgio Nada Editore SRL, pg 400
Istituto Nazionale di Studi Romani, pg 400
OCTAVO Produzioni Editoriali Associale, pg 401
Pizzicato Edizioni Musicali, pg 403
Pontificio Istituto Orientale, pg 404
Priuli e Verlucca, Editori, pg 404
Psicologica Editrice, pg 404
Riccardo Ricciardi Editore SpA, pg 405
Rossato, pg 406
Editoriale San Giusto SRL Edizioni Parnaso, pg 406
SEMAR Publishers SRL, pg 408
Vaccari SRL, pg 411
Vianello Libri, pg 411

Japan

Baberu Inc, pg 415
Chuo-Tosho Co Ltd, pg 416
Contex Corporation, pg 416
Hakusui-Sha Co Ltd, pg 417
Hayakawa Publishing Inc, pg 418
Hoikusha Publishing Co Ltd, pg 418
The Hokuseido Press, pg 418
Hyoronsha Publishing Co Ltd, pg 418
Itaria Shobo Ltd, pg 419
Japan Broadcast Publishing Co Ltd, pg 419
The Japan Times Ltd, pg 420
Kaitakusha, pg 420
Myrtos Inc, pg 423
Nippon Hoso Shuppan Kyokai (NHK Publishing), pg 424
Nosangyoson Bunka Kyokai, pg 424
Obunsha Co Ltd, pg 424
Rinsen Book Co Ltd, pg 425
Sanshusha Publishing Co, Ltd, pg 426
Seibido, pg 426
Shufunotomo Co Ltd, pg 428
Surugadai-Shuppan Sha, pg 429
3A Corporation, pg 429
Toho Book Store, pg 429
Tsukiji Shokan Publishing Co, pg 430
Yakuji Nippo Ltd, pg 431
Yohan Shuppan, pg 431

Kazakstan

Kazakhstan, Izd-Vo, pg 432
Zazusy, Izd-Vo, pg 432

Kenya

Focus Publications Ltd, pg 433
Sasa Sema Publications Ltd, pg 435
Sudan Literature Centre, pg 436

Democratic People's Republic of Korea

The Foreign Language Press Group, pg 436
Foreign Languages Publishing House, pg 436

Republic of Korea

Gim-Yeong Co, pg 438
Hollym Corporation; Publishers, pg 439
Hongik Media Plus Ltd, pg 439
Koreaone Press Inc, pg 440
Kukmin Doseo Publishing Co Ltd, pg 440
Moon Jin Media Co Ltd, pg 441
Omun Gak, pg 441
Oriental Books, pg 441
Pyeong-hwa Chulpansa, pg 442
Twenty-First Century Publishers, Inc, pg 443
Word of Life Press, pg 443
YBM/Si-sa, pg 443

Latvia

Nordik/Tapals Publishers Ltd, pg 445

Lebanon

Arab Institute for Research & Publishing, pg 445
Dar Al-Kitab Al-Loubnani, pg 445
Dar Al-Maaref-Liban Sarl, pg 446
Librairie Orientale sal, pg 446
World Book Publishing, pg 447

Lesotho

Mazenod Book Centre, pg 447

Lithuania

AS Narbuto Leidykla (AS Narbutas' Publishers), pg 448
Dargenis Publishers, pg 449
Lietuvos Rasytoju Sajungos Leidykla, pg 449
Mokslo ir enciklopediju leidybos institutas, pg 449
Margi Rastai Publishers, pg 449
Sviesa Publishers, pg 449
Vaga Ltd, pg 450

Luxembourg

Cahiers Luxembourgeois, pg 451
Varkki Verghese, pg 452

Macau

Museu Maritimo, pg 452

The Former Yugoslav Republic of Macedonia

Detska radost, pg 452
Medis, Skopje, pg 452
Murgorski Zoze, pg 453
St Clement of Ohrid National & University Library, pg 453

Madagascar

Foibe Filan-Kevitry NY Mpampianatra (FOFIPA), pg 453
Librarie Mixte, pg 453
Imprimerie Takariva, pg 454

Malaysia

Penerbit Fajar Bakti Sdn Bhd, pg 457

Martinique

George Lise-Huyghes des Etages, pg 460

Mexico

Centro de Estudios Mexicanos y Centroamericanos, pg 463
Editorial Diana SA de CV, pg 464
Ediciones Euroamericanas, pg 465
Lasser Press Mexicana SA de CV, pg 467
Phillip Richard Conover Lazo, pg 467
Editorial Limusa SA de CV, pg 467
Ediciones Promesa, pg 470
Sistemas Tecnicos de Edicion SA de CV, pg 472

Republic of Moldova

Editura Lumina, pg 473

Monaco

Editions EGC, pg 473

Morocco

Editions La Porte, pg 475

Myanmar

Hanthawaddy Book House, pg 475

Namibia

Gamsberg Macmillan Publishers (Pty) Ltd, pg 476

Netherlands

Uitgeverij Jan van Arkel, pg 478
H W Blok Uitgeverij BV, pg 479
BoekWerk, pg 479
BZZTOH Publishers, pg 480
J M Meulenhoff bv, pg 486
Prometheus, pg 488
Servire BV Uitgevers, pg 489
Sociaal en Cultureel Planbureau, pg 489
Uitgeverij G A van Oorschot bv, pg 491

New Zealand

Maori Publications Unit, pg 498
Shearwater Associates Ltd, pg 501

Nigeria

Alliance West African Publishers & Co, pg 503
Hudanuda Publishing Co Ltd, pg 505
Longman Nigeria Plc, pg 505
Thomas Nelson (Nigeria) Ltd, pg 505
Northern Nigerian Publishing Co Ltd, pg 506
Nwamife Publishers Ltd, pg 506
Onibon-Oje Publishers, pg 506
Riverside Communications, pg 507
University Publishing Co, pg 507

Norway

NKI Forlaget, pg 510

Pakistan

HMR Publishing Co, pg 512

Panama

Focus Publications International SA, pg 515

PUBLISHERS

Peru
Ediciones Brown SA, pg 516
Ediciones Peisa (Promocion Editorial Inca SA), pg 517

Philippines
De La Salle University, pg 519
Sonny A Mendoza, pg 519

Poland
Energeia sp zoo Wydawnictwo, pg 523
Katolicki Uniwersytet Wydawniczo-Redakcja, pg 523
Wydawnictwo Literackie, pg 524
Wydawnictwo Lodzkie, pg 524
Oficyna Wydawnicza Politechniki Wroclawskiej, pg 525
Rosikon Press, pg 526
'Slask' Ltd, pg 526
Wydawnictwo TPPR Wspolpraca, pg 527
Wydawnictwa Uniwersytetu Warszawskiego, pg 527
Wydawn Na Sprawa' Wydawniczo-Oswiatowa Spotdzielnia Inwalidow, pg 528

Portugal
Atica, SA Editores e Livreiros, pg 529
Bertrand Editora Lda, pg 529
Brasilia Editora (J Carvalho Branco), pg 529
Edicoes Colibri, pg 530
Contexto Editora, pg 530
Didactica Editora, pg 530
DIFEL - Difusao Editorial SA, pg 530
Dinalivro, pg 530
Edicoes ELO, pg 531
Editora Replicacao Lda, pg 535
Solivros, pg 536

Puerto Rico
Editorial Cordillera Inc, pg 537
Ediciones Huracan Inc, pg 537
Piedras Press, Inc, pg 537
Publishing Resources Inc, pg 537
University of Puerto Rico Press (EDUPR), pg 537

Romania
Editura Academiei Romane, pg 538
Alcor-Edimpex (Verlag) Ltd, pg 538
Ars Longa Publishing House, pg 538
Editura Cronos SRL, pg 539
Editura Didactica si Pedagogica, pg 539
Editura Eminescu, pg 539
Enzyklopadie Verlag, pg 539
Editura Excelsior Art, pg 539
Humanitas Publishing House, pg 540
Editura Institutul European, pg 540
Editura Junimea, pg 540
Editura Kriterion SA, pg 540
MAST Verlag, pg 540
Editura Militara, pg 541
Monitorul Oficial, Editura, pg 541
Editura Niculescu, pg 541
Editura Paideia, pg 541
Pandora Publishing House, pg 541
Polirom Verlag, pg 542
Est-Samuel Tastet Verlag, pg 542
Editura Teora, pg 542

Russian Federation
Airis Press, pg 543
BLIC, russko-Baltijskij informaciionnyj centr, AO, pg 544
Finansy i Statistika Publishing House, pg 544
INFRA-M Izdatel 'skij dom, pg 545
Interbook-Business AO, pg 545
Izdatelstvo Iskusstvo, pg 545
Izdatelstvo Khudozhestvennaya Literatura, pg 545
Izdatelstvo Muzyka, pg 547
Okoshko Ltd Publishers (Izdatelstvo), pg 547
Progress Publishers, pg 548
Izdatelstvo Prosveshchenie, pg 548
Raduga Publishers, pg 548
Russkij Jazyk, pg 548
Izdatelstvo Vysshaya Shkola, pg 549

Saudi Arabia
King Saud University, pg 550
Saudi Publishing & Distributing House, pg 550

Senegal
Centre de Linguistique Appliquee, pg 551
CODESRIA (Council for the Development of Social Science Research in Africa), pg 551

Serbia and Montenegro
Forum, pg 552
Libertatea, pg 552
Obod, pg 553
Sluzbeni List, pg 553

Sierra Leone
United Christian Council Literature Bureau, pg 554

Singapore
Aquanut Agencies Pte Ltd, pg 555
Archipelago Press, pg 555
Chopsons Pte Ltd, pg 555
Europhone Language Institute (Pte) Ltd, pg 556
Graham Brash Pte Ltd, pg 556
McGallen & Bolden Associates, pg 557
Pustaka Nasional Pte Ltd, pg 557

Slovakia
Vydavatelstvo Obzor, pg 560
Priroda Publishing, pg 560
Slo Viet, pg 560
Slovenske pedagogicke nakladateistvo, pg 560
Sofa, pg 560

Slovenia
Franc-Franc podjetje za promocijo kulture Murska Sobota d o o, pg 561
Zalozba Mihelac d o o, pg 562

South Africa
HAUM - De Jager Publishers, pg 564
HAUM (Hollandsch Afrikaansche Uitgevers Maatschappij), pg 564
Ithemba! Publishing, pg 565
LAPA Publishers (Pty) Ltd, pg 566
Maskew Miller Longman, pg 566
The Methodist Publishing House, pg 566

TYPE OF PUBLICATION INDEX

Nasou Via Afrika, pg 567
Shuter & Shooter (Pty) Ltd, pg 568
Taurus, pg 569
Van Schaik Publishers, pg 569
Vivlia Publishers & Booksellers, pg 570

Spain
Editorial AEDOS SA, pg 571
Aguilar SA de Ediciones, pg 571
Anglo-Didactica, SL Editorial, pg 573
Editorial Ariel SA, pg 573
Editorial Barcanova SA, pg 574
Editorial Clie, pg 577
Ediciones Daly S L, pg 578
Didaco Comunicacion y Didactica, SA, pg 579
Ediciones Doce Calles SL, pg 579
Edilesa-Ediciones Leonesas SA, pg 581
Edilux, pg 581
Editorial Gulaab, pg 586
Ediciones Hiperion SL, pg 586
Icaria Editorial SA, pg 587
Idea Books, SA, pg 587
Incafo Archivo Fotografico Editorial, SL, pg 587
Larousse Editorial SA, pg 588
LID Editorial Empresarial, SL, pg 589
Lynx Edicions, pg 590
Antonio Machado, SA, pg 590
Macmillan Heinemann ELT, pg 590
Editorial Moll SL, pg 592
Ediciones del Oriente y del Mediterraneo, pg 594
Publicaciones y Ediciones Salamandra SA, pg 597
Silex Ediciones, pg 600
Sociedad General Espanola de Libreria SA - SGEL, pg 600
Stanley Editorial, pg 601
Ediciones 29 - Libros Rio Nuevo, pg 603
Universidad de Navarra, Ediciones SA, pg 603
Editorial Verbum SL, pg 604
Vinaches Lopez, Luisa, pg 605

Sri Lanka
Gihan Book Shop, pg 606
Inter-Cultural Book Promoters, pg 606
Lake House Investments Ltd, pg 606

Sudan
Al-Ayam Press Co Ltd, pg 608
Khartoum University Press, pg 608

Sweden
Ekelunds Forlag AB, pg 611
Folkuniversitetets foerlag, pg 611
Hallgren och Fallgren Studieforlag AB, pg 612
Invandrarfoerlaget, pg 612
Hans Richter Laromedel, pg 613
Bokforlaget Rediviva, Facsimileforlaget, pg 615
Frank Stenvalls Forlag, pg 615

Switzerland
Birkhauser Verlag AG, pg 619
Castle Publications SA, pg 620
Cockatoo Press (Schweiz), Thailand-Publikationen, pg 621
Edizioni Armando Dado, Tipografia Stazione, pg 621
Drei-D-World und Foto-World Verlag und Vertrieb, pg 622

Duboux Editions SA, pg 622
GVA Publishers Ltd, pg 624
Kolumbus-Verlag, pg 626
Lia rumantscha, pg 627
Lars Mueller Publishers, pg 629
Editions du Panorama, pg 630
Parkett Publishers Inc, pg 630
Editions Patino, pg 631
Editions Pro Schola, pg 631
Schweizerisches Jugendschriftenwerk, SJW, pg 634
Editions Scriptar SA, pg 634
Viktoria-Verlag Peter Marti, pg 636

Taiwan, Province of China
Hilit Publishing Co Ltd, pg 640
Hsiao Yuan Publication Co, Ltd, pg 640
Jillion Publishing Co, pg 640
Youth Cultural Publishing Co, pg 642

United Republic of Tanzania
East African Publishing House, pg 643
Eastern Africa Publications Ltd, pg 643
Inland Publishers, pg 643
Institute of Kiswahili Research, pg 643
Oxford University Press, pg 644

Thailand
Bandansan, pg 645
Bannakhan, pg 645
Duang Kamon Co Ltd, pg 645
Graphic Art (28) Co Ltd, pg 645
Klang Withaya Publisher, pg 645
Non, pg 645
Pikkhanet Kanphim, pg 645
Sangdad Publishing Company Ltd, pg 645
Soemwit Barwakhan, pg 645
Suksit Siam Co Ltd, pg 646
Sut Phaisan, pg 646
Thai Watana Panich Co, Ltd, pg 646
Viratham, pg 646

Tunisia
Academie Tunisienne des Sciences, des Lettres et des Arts Beit El Hekma, pg 647
Maison Tunisienne de l'Edition, pg 648

Turkey
ABC Kitabevi AS, pg 648
Inkilap Publishers Ltd, pg 650
Redhouse Press, pg 651
Saray Medikal Yayin Tic Ltd Sti, pg 651
Yapi-Endustri Merkezi Yayinlari-Yem Yayin, pg 652

Uganda
Roce (Consultants) Ltd, pg 653

Ukraine
ASK Ltd, pg 653
Dnipro, pg 653
Osvita, pg 654

United Arab Emirates
Motivate Publishing, pg 654

TYPE OF PUBLICATION INDEX — BOOK

United Kingdom
Acair Ltd, pg 655
Arnold, pg 659
Atlas Press, pg 661
BBC English, pg 663
Berlitz (UK) Ltd, pg 665
Bible Society, pg 665
Bloodaxe Books Ltd, pg 668
Books for Europe Ltd, pg 669
Books International, pg 669
Bridge Books, pg 671
Centre for Information on Language Teaching & Research (CILT), pg 677
Chambers Harrap Publishers Ltd, pg 677
Chapter Two, pg 678
Peter Collin Publishing Ltd, pg 680
Ethics International Press Ltd, pg 692
European Schoolbooks Ltd, pg 692
The Greek Bookshop, pg 702
Gwasg Gwenffrwd, pg 703
Gwasg y Dref Wen, pg 703
HarperCollins UK, pg 705
Haynes Publishing, pg 706
Hilmarton Manor Press, pg 708
Angus Hudson Ltd, pg 710
Hugo's Language Books Ltd, pg 710
ICC United Kingdom, pg 711
Impart Books, pg 712
International Bee Research Association, pg 714
Islam International Publications Ltd, pg 714
The Islamic Texts Society, pg 715
Kingfisher Publications Plc, pg 717
Letterbox Library, pg 720
Linguaphone Institute Ltd, pg 721
Y Lolfa Cyf, pg 722
Macmillan Heinemann ELT, pg 723
Magi Publications, pg 724
Willem A Meeuws Publisher, pg 726
Nelson Thornes Ltd, pg 732
Octopus Publishing Group, pg 734
Old Vicarage Publications, pg 734
Packard Publishing Ltd, pg 737
Pathfinder London, pg 739
Pearson Education Europe, Mideast & Africa, pg 739
St Pauls Publishing, pg 753
School of Oriental & African Studies, pg 755
Textile & Art Publications Ltd, pg 764
Verulam Publishing Ltd, pg 770
Voltaire Foundation Ltd, pg 771
World Microfilms Publications Ltd, pg 775

Uruguay
EQ Opciones en Educacion, pg 777
A Monteverde y Cia SA, pg 777

Uzbekistan
Izdatelstvo Literatury i isskustva, pg 778

Venezuela
Armitano Editores CA, pg 779

Viet Nam
Science & Technics Publishing House, pg 780

Zambia
Lundula Publishing House, pg 781

Zimbabwe
College Press Publishers (Pvt) Ltd, pg 783

GENERAL TRADE BOOKS - HARDCOVER

Argentina
Colmegna SA, pg 4
Ediciones Minotauro SA, pg 7

Australia
Aerospace Publications Pty Ltd, pg 11
Allen & Unwin Pty Ltd, pg 11
Australian Scholarly Publishing, pg 13
Barbara Beckett Publishing Pty Ltd, pg 14
Cookery Book, pg 18
Crawford House Publishing Pty Ltd, pg 18
Enterprise Publications, pg 21
Florilegium, pg 22
Hale & Iremonger Pty Ltd, pg 24
Histec Publications, pg 25
Hodder Headline Australia, pg 26
Hyland House Publishing Pty Ltd, pg 26
Institute of Aboriginal Development (IAD Press), pg 27
Joval Publications, pg 28
Gregory Kefalas Publishing, pg 28
Lansdowne Publishing Pty Ltd, pg 28
Life Planning Foundation of Australia, Inc, pg 29
Magabala Books Aboriginal Corporation, pg 30
Media East Press, pg 31
Melbourne University Press, pg 32
Mulini Press, pg 32
Navarine Publishing, pg 33
New Era Publications Australia Pty Ltd, pg 33
Anne O'Donovan Pty Ltd, pg 34
Off the Shelf Publishing, pg 34
Pascal Press, pg 36
Pearson Education Australia, pg 36
Penguin Group (Australia), pg 36
Queensland Art Gallery, pg 38
R & R Publications Pty Ltd, pg 38
Random House Australia, pg 38
Slouch Hat Publications, pg 41
Social Club Books, pg 41
State Library of NSW Press, pg 42
The Text Publishing Company Pty Ltd, pg 43
Thames & Hudson (Australia) Pty Ltd, pg 43
Caroline Thornton, pg 43
Turton & Armstrong Pty Ltd Publishers, pg 44
University of Western Australia Press, pg 45
Vital Publications, pg 45
Windhorse Books, pg 47

Austria
Christian Brandstaetter Verlagsgesellschaft mbH, pg 49
Buchkultur Verlags GmbH Zeitschrift fuer Literatur & Kunst, pg 49
Carinthia Verlag, pg 49
Czernin Verlag Ltd, pg 49
Verlag Harald Denzel, Auto- und Freizeitfuehrer, pg 50
Franz Deuticke Verlagsgesmbh, pg 50
Development News Ltd, pg 50
Edition S der OSD, pg 50
Edition Ergo Sum, pg 50
Verlag Lynkeus/H Hakel Gesellschaft, pg 51
Herold Business Data AG, pg 52
Kremayr & Scheriau Verlag, pg 53
Leopold Stocker Verlag, pg 53
Linde Verlag Wien GmbH, pg 53
Niederosterreichisches Pressehaus Druck- und Verlagsgesellschaft mbH, pg 54
Verlag Orac im Verlag Kremayr & Scheriau, pg 56
Verlag des Osterr Kneippbundes GmbH, pg 56
Promedia Verlagsges mbH, pg 56
Verlag Anton Pustet, pg 56
Studien Verlag Gmbh, pg 58

Belarus
Interdigest Publishing House, pg 62

Belgium
Altina, pg 63
Etablissements Emile Bruylant SA, pg 64
Claude Lefrancq Editeur, pg 70
Michelin Editions des Voyages, pg 71
Pelckmans NV, De Nederlandsche Boekhandel, pg 72
Prodim SPRL, pg 72

Benin
Les Editions du Flamboyant, pg 75

Brazil
Companhia Editora Forense, pg 81
Editora Forense Universitaria Ltda, pg 81
Ordem do Graal na Terra, pg 83
Editora Harbra Ltda, pg 83
LDA Editores Ltda, pg 84
Madras Editora, pg 86
Companhia Editora Nacional, pg 87
Editora Nova Fronteira SA, pg 87
Pallas Editora e Distribuidora Ltda, pg 88

Bulgaria
Abagar Pablioing, pg 92
Aratron, IK, pg 93
Dolphin Press Group Ltd, pg 94
Kibea Publishing Co, pg 95
Nov Covek Publishing House, pg 96
Reporter, pg 96

Burundi
Editions Intore, pg 98

Chile
Pontificia Universidad Catolica de Chile, pg 100

China
China Foreign Economic Relations & Trade Publishing House, pg 102
China Materials Management Publishing House, pg 102
Fudan University Press, pg 104
Kunlun Publishing House, pg 106
Qingdao Publishing House, pg 107
Shanghai Far East Publishers, pg 108

Colombia
Editorial Panamericana, pg 112

The Democratic Republic of the Congo
Centre de Vulgarisation Agricole, pg 114

Costa Rica
Academia de Centro America, pg 114
Litografia Artex, SA, pg 115
Editorial Texto Ltda, pg 116

Cote d'Ivoire
Universite d'Abidjan, pg 117

Croatia
Znaci Vremena, Institut Za Istrazivanje Biblije, pg 119

Czech Republic
Aventinum Nakladatelstvi spol sro, pg 122
Granit sro, pg 123
Horacek Ladislav-Paseka, pg 123
Nakladatelstvi Jota spol sro, pg 124
Mlada fronta, pg 125
Pavla Momcilova, pg 125
Prostor, nakladatelstvi sro, pg 127

Denmark
Atuakkiorfik A/S Det Greenland Publishers, pg 129
Borgens Forlag A/S, pg 129
Christian Ejlers' Forlag aps, pg 131
Gads Forlag, pg 131
P Haase & Sons Forlag A/S, pg 131
Forlaget Hjulet, pg 132
Holkenfeldt 3, pg 132
New Era Publications International ApS, pg 133
Politisk Revy, pg 133
Samlerens Forlag A/S, pg 134
Scandinavia Publishing House, pg 134
Det Schonbergske Forlag A/S, pg 134
Unitas Forlag, pg 135

Egypt (Arab Republic of Egypt)
The Egyptian Society for the Dissemination of Universal Culture and Knowledge (ESDUCK), pg 138

Estonia
Kirjastus Kunst, pg 139
Mats Publishers Ltd, pg 140

Finland
Herattaja-yhdistys Ry, pg 142
Karisto Oy, pg 142
Koala-Kustannus Oy, pg 143
Otava Publishing Co Ltd, pg 143
Recallmed Oy, pg 144

France
Actes-Graphiques, pg 145
Editions Alternatives, pg 146
L'Amitie par le Livre, pg 146
Editions Amrita SA, pg 146
Association pour la Recherche et l'Information demographiques (APRD), pg 147
ATP - Packager, pg 148
Editions de l'Aube, pg 148
Autrement Editions, pg 148
Editions A Barthelemy, pg 149
Editions Bertout, pg 149
Pierre Bordas & Fils, Editions, pg 150

PUBLISHERS

Editions Buchet-Chastel Pierre Zech Editeur, pg 151
Editions du Cadratin, pg 151
Editions des Cahiers Bourbonnais, pg 151
Editions Casterman, pg 152
Editions Cenomane, pg 152
Editions Jacqueline Chambon, pg 153
Editions Chiron, pg 154
Communication Par Livre (CPL), pg 155
De Vecchi Editions SA, pg 157
Editions Edisud, pg 159
Edition1, pg 160
Editions Terrail/Finest SA, pg 160
EPA (Editions Pratiques Automobiles), pg 161
Editions Pierre Fanlac, pg 162
Federation Francaise de la Randonnee Pedestre, pg 163
Editions Filipacchi-Sonodip, pg 163
Flammarion SA, pg 163
Les Editions Franciscaines SA, pg 164
Editions du Garde-Temps, pg 165
Editions Viviane Hamy, pg 167
L'Harmattan, pg 167
Editions Hazan, pg 167
Editions du Jaguar, pg 169
Editions Jean-Claude Lattes, pg 169
Editions Universitaires LCF, pg 171
Editions Loubatieres, pg 173
Editions Josette Lyon, pg 173
Editions Mango, pg 174
Editions Medianes, pg 175
Editions Mediaspaul, pg 175
Editions Franck Mercier, pg 175
Editions A M Metailie, pg 175
Editions Albin Michel, pg 175
Nil Editions, pg 177
Editions Norma, pg 177
Editions Odile Jacob, pg 177
Editions Christian Pirot, pg 180
Presses de la Cite, pg 180
Les Presses du Management, pg 181
Editions Saint-Michel SA, pg 183
Editions Le Serpent a Plumes, pg 184
Somogy editions d'art, pg 185
Editions Stock, pg 186
Alain Thomas Editeur, pg 187
Editions Tiresias Michel Reynaud, pg 187

French Polynesia

Scoop/Au Vent des Iles, pg 189

Germany

AOL-Verlag Frohmut Menze, pg 193
Arbeiterpresse Verlags- und Vertriebsgesellschaft mbH, pg 193
ARCult Media, pg 193
Ars Edition GmbH, pg 194
Augustus Verlag, pg 195
Autovision Verlag Guenther & Co, pg 196
Aviatic Verlag GmbH, pg 196
Dr Wolfgang Baur Verlag Kunst & Alltag, pg 198
Verlag Beleke KG, pg 198
Bergverlag Rother GmbH, pg 199
Bertelsmann Lexikon Verlag GmbH, pg 200
BLV Verlagsgesellschaft mbH, pg 202
Verlag Georg D W Callwey GmbH & Co, pg 207
Campus Verlag GmbH, pg 207
Dr Cantz'sche Druckerei GmbH & Co, pg 207
CartoTravel Verlag GmbH & Co KG, pg 207
Chmielorz GmbH Verlag, pg 208
Verlag Deutsche Unitarier, pg 212
Deutscher Apotheker Verlag Dr Roland Schmiedel GmbH & Co, pg 212
Dharma Edition, Tibetisches Zentrum, pg 214
Dietz Verlag Berlin GmbH, pg 215
Christoph Dohr, pg 215
Donat Verlag, pg 215
Drei Brunnen Verlag GmbH & Co, pg 216
Verlagsgruppe Droemer Knaur GmbH & Co KG, pg 216
DRW-Verlag Weinbrenner-GmbH & Co, pg 216
Ehrenwirth Verlag, pg 218
Elektor-Verlag GmbH, pg 219
Verlag am Eschbach GmbH, pg 221
Esogetics Verlag, pg 221
Eulenhof-Verlag Wolfgang Ehrhardt Heinold, pg 221
Fabel-Verlag Gudrun Liebchen, pg 223
Fachbuchverlag Pfanneberg & Co, pg 223
Franz Ferzak World & Space Publications, pg 224
Flechsig Buchvertrieb, pg 225
Franz-Sales-Verlag, pg 226
Frederking & Thaler Verlag GmbH, pg 226
Friedrich Kiehl Verlag GmbH, pg 227
Gatzanis Verlags GmbH, pg 228
Genius Verlag, pg 228
H Gietl Verlag & Publikationsservice GmbH, pg 229
GLB Parkland Verlags-und Vertriebs GmbH, pg 229
Cornelia Goethe Literaturverlag, pg 230
Graefe und Unzer Verlag GmbH, pg 230
Verlag der Stiftung Gralsbotschaft GmbH, pg 231
Gunter Olzog Verlag GmbH, pg 231
Walter Haedecke Verlag, pg 232
Heel Verlag GmbH, pg 235
Heigl Verlag, Horst Edition, pg 235
S Hirzel Verlag GmbH und Co, pg 238
Horlemann Verlag, pg 239
Jovis Verlag GmbH, pg 243
SachBuchVerlag Kellner, pg 245
Kleiner Bachmann Verlag fur Kinder und Umwelt, pg 246
Knesebeck Verlag, pg 247
Knowledge Media International, pg 247
Koehler & Amelang Verlagsgesellschaft, pg 248
Konradin-Verlagsgruppe, pg 249
Adam Kraft Verlag, pg 250
Kunstverlag Weingarten GmbH, pg 251
Karl Robert Langewiesche Nachfolger Hans Koester KG, pg 252
Libertas- Europaeisches Institut GmbH, pg 254
Gustav Luebbe Verlag, pg 256
Verlagsgruppe Luebbe GmbH & Co KG, pg 256
Lusatia Verlag-Dr Stuebner & Co KG, pg 256
Maro Verlag und Druck, Benno Kasmayr, pg 257
Matthias-Gruenewald-Verlag GmbH, pg 258
Medpharm Scientific Publishers, pg 258
Metropolis- Verlag fur Okonomie, Gesellschaft und Politik GmbH, pg 259
J B Metzlersche Verlagsbuchhandlung, pg 260
Meyer & Meyer Verlag, pg 260
Midena Verlag, pg 260
NaturaViva Verlags GmbH, pg 263
New Era Publications Deutschland GmbH, pg 265
Hans-Nietsch-Verlag, pg 265
Nusser Verlag, pg 266
Osho Verlag GmbH, pg 267
Ostfalia-Verlag Jurgen Schierer, pg 267
Palmyra Verlag, pg 268
Verlag Parzeller GmbH & Co KG, pg 268
Pfalzische Verlagsanstalt GmbH, pg 269
Polygraph Verlag GmbH, pg 271
Propylaeen Verlag, Zweigniederlassung Berlin der Ullstein Buchverlage GmbH, pg 272
Rake Verlag GmbH, pg 273
Reader's Digest Deutschland Verlag Das Beste GmbH, pg 274
Rowohlt Berlin Verlag GmbH, pg 277
J D Sauerlaender's Verlag, pg 278
Verlag der Schillerbuchhandlung Hans Banger OHG, pg 279
Schoeffling & Co, pg 281
Schwabenverlag Aktiengesellschaft, pg 282
Siedler Verlag, pg 283
Silberburg-Verlag Titus Haeussermann GmbH, pg 283
Springer Science+Business Media GmbH & Co KG, pg 284
Stadler Verlagsgesellschaft mbH, pg 286
C A Starke Verlag, pg 287
Steidl Verlag, pg 287
Steiger Verlag, pg 287
teNeues Verlag GmbH & Co KG, pg 290
Konrad Theiss Verlag GmbH, pg 290
Tipress Dienstleistungen fur das Verlagswesen GmbH, pg 291
Traditionell Bogenschiessen Verlag Angelika Hornig, pg 292
Verlag Moderne Industrie AG & Co KG, pg 295
Vier Tuerme GmbH Verlag Klosterbetriebe, pg 295
Verlag Klaus Wagenbach, pg 297
Weidlich Verlag, pg 298
Verlag Wissenschaft und Politik, pg 300
Verlagshaus Wohlfarth, pg 301
Verlag im Ziegelhaus Ulrich Gohl, pg 302

Ghana

Afram Publications (Ghana) Ltd, pg 303
Educational Press & Manufacturers Ltd, pg 303
World Literature Project, pg 305

Greece

Ekdotikos Oikos Adelfon Kyriakidi A E, pg 307
Kritiki Publishing, pg 309
Orfanidis Publications, pg 311
Patakis Publishers, pg 311
Proskinio Spyros Ch Marinis, pg 311
Toubis M, pg 312

Hong Kong

Book Marketing Ltd, pg 315
Commercial Press (Hong Kong) Ltd, pg 316
Joint Publishing (HK) Co Ltd, pg 317
Ling Kee Publishing Group, pg 318
Research Centre for Translation, pg 319
Ta Kung Pao (HK) Ltd, pg 319
Unicorn Books Ltd, pg 320
Vista Productions Ltd, pg 320

Hungary

Novorg International Szervezo es Kiado kft, pg 323
Officina Nova Konyvek, pg 323
Panem, pg 324

Iceland

Bokaforlag Birtingur, pg 325
Forlagid, pg 325
Skjaldborg Ltd, pg 326

India

Academic Book Corporation, pg 327
Addison-Wesley Pte Ltd, pg 327
Agam Kala Prakashan, pg 327
Allied Book Centre, pg 328
Bani Mandir, Book-Sellers, Publishers & Educational Suppliers, pg 329
Cosmo Publications, pg 332
Daya Publishing House, pg 333
Eastern Law House Pvt Ltd, pg 334
Frank Brothers & Co Publishers Ltd, pg 334
Gyan Publishing House, pg 335
Indus Publishing Co, pg 338
Kali For Women, pg 339
Konark Publishers Pvt Ltd, pg 339
Law Publishers, pg 340
Oxford University Press, pg 344
Rahul Publishing House, pg 346
Rajesh Publications, pg 346
Regency Publications, pg 346
Reliance Publishing House, pg 346
SABDA, pg 347
Scientific Book Agency, pg 348
Somaiya Publications Pvt Ltd, pg 349
Vidya Puri, pg 352
Vision Books Pvt Ltd, pg 352

Indonesia

Angkasa CV, pg 353
PT BPK Gunung Mulia, pg 355

Ireland

The Collins Press, pg 358
Dee-Jay Publications, pg 359
Gill & Macmillan Ltd, pg 360
The Hannon Press, pg 361
Mount Eagle Publications Ltd, pg 362
New Writers' Press, pg 362
The O'Brien Press Ltd, pg 362
Relay Books, pg 363
Roberts Rinehart Publishers, pg 363
Town House & Country House, pg 364
Wolfhound Press Ltd, pg 364

TYPE OF PUBLICATION INDEX

BOOK

Israel
Classikaletet, pg 366
DAT Publications, pg 366
L B Publishing Co, pg 369
Rubin Mass Ltd, pg 371
Schocken Publishing House Ltd, pg 371
R Sirkis Publishers Ltd, pg 372
Urim Publications, pg 373

Italy
Adea Edizioni, pg 374
L'Airone Editrice, pg 375
Artioli Editore, pg 377
Casa Editrice Astrolabio-Ubaldini Editore, pg 377
Belforte Editore Libraio srl, pg 377
Canova SRL, pg 379
La Cultura Sociologica, pg 384
Edizioni Dedalo SRL, pg 384
EDIFIR SRL, pg 386
Edizioni Studio Domenicano (ESD), pg 387
EDT Edizioni di Torino, pg 387
Ernesto Gremese Editore srl, pg 391
Gremese International srl, pg 391
Ibis, pg 392
Kaos Edizioni SRL, pg 394
Edizioni Lavoro SRL, pg 394
Edizioni Piemme SpA, pg 403
Edition Raetia Srl-GmbH, pg 405
Red/Studio Redazionale, pg 405
Rossato, pg 406
Il Saggiatore, pg 406
Samaya SRL, pg 406
Sperling e Kupfer Editori SpA, pg 409
Marco Tropea Editore, pg 410
Turris, pg 410

Jamaica
Carib Publishing Ltd, pg 413
Institute of Jamaica Publications, pg 413
LMH Publishing Ltd, pg 414

Japan
Bijutsu Shuppan-Sha, Ltd, pg 415
Chijin Shokan Co Ltd, pg 416
Chikuma Shobo Publishing Co Ltd, pg 416
Diamond Inc, pg 416
Dohosha Publishing Co Ltd, pg 417
Fuzambo Publishing Co, pg 417
Hakuyo-Sha, pg 418
Institute for Financial Affairs Inc-KINZAI, pg 419
Kinokuniya Co Ltd (Publishing Department), pg 421
KINZAI Corporation, pg 421
Kosei Publishing Co Ltd, pg 421
Kyodo-Isho Shuppan Co Ltd, pg 422
Mirai-Sha, pg 422
Nippon Hoso Shuppan Kyokai (NHK Publishing), pg 424
Nippon Jitsugyo Publishing Co Ltd, pg 424
Nosangyoson Bunka Kyokai, pg 424
Ongaku No Tomo Sha Corporation, pg 425
President Inc, pg 425
Reimei-Shobo Co Ltd, pg 425
Shincho-Sha Co Ltd, pg 427
Shufunotomo Co Ltd, pg 428
Soshisha Co Ltd, pg 428
Toho Shuppan, pg 429
Tokyo Shoseki Co Ltd, pg 430

Kenya
Heinemann Kenya Ltd (EAEP), pg 434
Kenway Publications Ltd, pg 434

Republic of Korea
Chung Rim Publishing Co Ltd, pg 438
Koreaone Press Inc, pg 440
Min-eumsa Publishing Co Ltd, pg 441
O Neul Publishing Co, pg 441
Woongjin.com Co Ltd, pg 443
Word of Life Press, pg 443

Latvia
Alberts XII, pg 444
Madris, pg 445

Lebanon
Librairie Orientale sal, pg 446
World Book Publishing, pg 447

Luxembourg
Editions Emile Borschette, pg 450
Editions Tousch, pg 452

Malawi
Central Africana Ltd, pg 454

Malaysia
Darulfikir, pg 455
Dewan Bahasa dan Pustaka, pg 455
Federal Publications Sdn Bhd, pg 455
MDC Publishers Printers Sdn Bhd, pg 457
Pearson Education Malaysia Sdn Bhd, pg 457
Penerbit Jayatinta Sdn Bhd, pg 458
Pustaka Cipta Sdn Bhd, pg 458
Pustaka Delta Pelajaran Sdn Bhd, pg 458
Tempo Publishing (M) Sdn Bhd, pg 458
Tropical Press Sdn Bhd, pg 459

Maldive Islands
Novelty Printers & Publishers, pg 459

Malta
Fondazzjoni Patrimonju Malti, pg 460

Martinique
Editions Gondwana, pg 460
George Lise-Huyghes des Etages, pg 460

Mauritius
Editions de l'Ocean Indien Ltd, pg 461

Mexico
Ediciones Eca SA de CV, pg 464
Edamex SA de CV, pg 464
Editorial Limusa SA de CV, pg 467
Pearson Educacion de Mexico, SA de CV, pg 470

Morocco
Dar Nachr Al Maarifa Pour L'Edition et La Distribution, pg 474

Netherlands
Uitgeverij Arena BV, pg 478
Uitgeverij Balans, pg 478
Business Contact BV, pg 480
BZZTOH Publishers, pg 480
Uitgeverij Cantecleer BV, pg 480
BV Uitgeversbedryf Het Goede Boek, pg 482
Mets & Schilt Uitgevers en Distributeurs, pg 486
Uitgeverij Mingus, pg 486
Prometheus, pg 488
Servire BV Uitgevers, pg 489
SWP, BV Uitgeverij, pg 490
Uitgeverij Terra bv, pg 490
Tirion Uitgevers BV, pg 490
Van Buuren Uitgeverij BV, pg 491

New Caledonia
Editions du Santal, pg 493

New Zealand
Auckland University Press, pg 493
David Bateman Ltd, pg 494
Bush Press Communications Ltd, pg 494
David's Marine Books, pg 495
Exisle Publishing Ltd, pg 496
Gnostic Press Ltd, pg 496
Godwit Publishing Ltd, pg 496
Halcyon Publishing Ltd, pg 496
HarperCollins Publishers (New Zealand), pg 497
Hazard Press Ltd, pg 497
Hodder Moa Beckett Publishers Ltd, pg 497
Huia Publishers, pg 497
Magari Publishing, pg 498
Nielsen BookData, pg 499
Otago Heritage Books, pg 499
R P L Books, pg 500
Resource Books Ltd, pg 500
Shoal Bay Press Ltd, pg 501
Southern Press Ltd, pg 501
Tandem Press, pg 501
Bridget Williams Books Ltd, pg 502

Nigeria
Riverside Communications, pg 507

Norway
Andresen & Butenschon AS, pg 508
Det Norske Samlaget, pg 508
Ex Libris Forlag A/S, pg 509
Pax Forlag A/S, pg 510

Pakistan
National Book Foundation, pg 513
Sang-e-Meel Publications, pg 514

Panama
Focus Publications International SA, pg 515

Peru
Ediciones Peisa (Promocion Editorial Inca SA), pg 517

Philippines
De La Salle University, pg 519
Rex Bookstores & Publishers, pg 520

Poland
Ksiaznica Publishing Ltd, pg 524
Magnum Publishing House Ltd, pg 524
Muza SA, pg 524

Portugal
Editorial Estampa, Lda, pg 531
Internationale Nouvelle Acropole, pg 534
Planeta Editora, LDA, pg 534

Puerto Rico
University of Puerto Rico Press (EDUPR), pg 537

Romania
The Center for Romanian Studies, pg 539
Editura Cronos SRL, pg 539
Humanitas Publishing House, pg 540
Editura Meridiane, pg 540
Monitorul Oficial, Editura, pg 541

Russian Federation
Armada Publishing House, pg 543
N E Bauman Moscow State Technical University Publishers, pg 544
Izdatelstvo Mir, pg 546
Izdatelstvo Muzyka, pg 547
Novosti Izdatelstvo, pg 547
Obdeestvo Znanie, pg 547
Permskaja Kniga, pg 548
Profizdat, pg 548
Russkaya Kniga Izdatelstvo (Publishers), pg 548
Text Publishers Ltd Too, pg 549
Top Secret Collection Publishers, pg 549

Serbia and Montenegro
Alfa-Narodna Knjiga, pg 552

Singapore
Aquanut Agencies Pte Ltd, pg 555
Archipelago Press, pg 555
Hillview Publications Pte Ltd, pg 556
McGallen & Bolden Associates, pg 557
Select Publishing Pte Ltd, pg 557

Slovakia
Vydavatepstvo Praca spol sro, pg 560
Serafin, pg 560
Sofa, pg 560

South Africa
Fernwood Press (Pty) Ltd, pg 563
Flesch Financial Publications (Pty) Ltd, pg 563
Galago Publishing Pty Ltd, pg 564
Human & Rousseau (Pty) Ltd, pg 564
New Africa Books (Pty) Ltd, pg 567
Southern Book Publishers (Pty) Ltd, pg 569

Spain
Alberdania SL, pg 571
CEAC, Grupo Editorial SA, pg 576
Comunidad Autonoma de Madrid, Servicio de Documentacion y Publicaciones, pg 578
Ediciones Daly S L, pg 578
EDHASA (Editora y Distribuidora Hispano-Americana SA), pg 580
Edilesa-Ediciones Leonesas SA, pg 581
Enciclopedia Catalana, SA, pg 582
Editorial Gustavo Gili SA, pg 585

PUBLISHERS

Grijalbo Mondadori SA, pg 585
Grupo Comunicar, pg 585
Idea Books, SA, pg 587
Ediciones Libertarias/Prodhufi SA, pg 589
Ediciones Maeva, pg 590
Ediciones Medici SA, pg 591
Obelisco Ediciones S, pg 593
Editorial El Perpetuo Socorro, pg 596
Editorial Presencia Gitana, pg 597
Instituto Provincial de Investigaciones y Estudios Toledanos (IPIET), pg 597
Grup 62, pg 600
Tursen, SA, pg 603
Tusquets Editores, pg 603
Ediciones Urano, SA, pg 604

Sri Lanka
Buddhist Publication Society Inc, pg 605

Sweden
Allt om Hobby AB, pg 609
Bokforlaget Axplock, pg 609
Fischer & Co, pg 611
ICA bokforlag, pg 612
Bokforlaget Nya Doxa AB, pg 614
Ordfront Foerlag AB, pg 614
Bokforlaget Settern AB, pg 615
Sjoestrands Foerlag, pg 615
Frank Stenvalls Forlag, pg 615
Tryckeriforlaget AB, pg 616

Switzerland
ADIRA, pg 617
Ammann Verlag & Co, pg 617
Benziger Verlag AG, pg 619
Bergli Books AG, pg 619
Christoph Merian Verlag, pg 620
Rene Coeckelberghs Editions, pg 621
Diogenes Verlag AG, pg 622
eFeF-Verlag/Edition Ebersbach, pg 622
Edition Exodus, pg 623
Haffmans Verlag AG, pg 624
Oesch Verlag AG, pg 630
Ott Verlag Thun, pg 630
Editions du Parvis, pg 631
Editions Payot Lausanne, pg 631
Perret Edition, pg 631
Verlag Die Pforte im Rudolf Steiner Verlag, pg 631
Rudolf Steiner Verlag, pg 634
Verlag im Waldgut AG, pg 636

Taiwan, Province of China
Asian Culture Co Ltd, pg 638
Echo Publishing Company Ltd, pg 639
Hilit Publishing Co Ltd, pg 640
Linking Publishing Company Ltd, pg 641

United Republic of Tanzania
Nyota Publishers Ltd, pg 644
Tanzania Publishing House, pg 644

Thailand
Chokechai Theues Shop, pg 645

Tunisia
Maison Tunisienne de l'Edition, pg 648

Turkey
Sabah Kitaplari, pg 651

United Arab Emirates
Motivate Publishing, pg 654

United Kingdom
Abbotsford Publishing, pg 654
Act 3 Publishing, pg 655
Adamantine Press Ltd, pg 655
Allison & Busby, pg 656
Amber Books Ltd, pg 657
Andromeda Oxford Ltd, pg 658
AP Information Services Ltd, pg 658
Apple Press, pg 658
Arcturus Publishing Ltd, pg 659
Arms & Armour Press, pg 659
Art Books International Ltd, pg 659
Arthur James Ltd, pg 660
Association for Scottish Literary Studies, pg 661
Atlantic Transport Publishers, pg 661
Aurum Press Ltd, pg 661
The Banner of Truth Trust, pg 662
Colin Baxter Photography Ltd, pg 663
Bay View Books Ltd, pg 663
Ruth Bean Publishers, pg 664
Black Ace Books, pg 666
Blackstaff Press, pg 666
John Blake Publishing Ltd, pg 667
Blandford Publishing Ltd, pg 668
Bloomsbury Publishing PLC, pg 668
Blueprint, pg 668
The Book Guild Ltd, pg 668
Book Packaging & Marketing, pg 668
Books for Europe Ltd, pg 669
Bounty Books, pg 669
Boxtree Ltd, pg 669
Boydell & Brewer Ltd, pg 669
Brassey's UK Ltd, pg 670
Nicholas Brealey Publishing, pg 670
Breedon Books Publishing Company Ltd, pg 670
Breslich & Foss Ltd, pg 671
Brewin Books Ltd, pg 671
Bryntirion Press, pg 672
Calder Publications Ltd, pg 673
Cameron & Hollis, pg 674
Canongate Books Ltd, pg 674
Capstone Publishing Ltd, pg 674
Carroll & Brown Ltd, pg 675
Cassell & Co, pg 675
Cockbird Press, pg 680
Colourpoint Books, pg 681
Compass Equestrian Ltd, pg 681
Compendium Publishing, pg 681
Conran Octopus, pg 682
Constable & Robinson Ltd, pg 682
Conway Maritime Press, pg 683
Leo Cooper, pg 683
Cressrelles Publishing Company Ltd, pg 684
Crossbridge Books, pg 684
Crown House Publishing Ltd, pg 684
The Crowood Press Ltd, pg 684
Dance Books Ltd, pg 686
Delectus Books, pg 687
Gerald Duckworth & Co Ltd, pg 688
Aidan Ellis Publishing, pg 690
Eurobook Ltd, pg 692
Helen Exley Giftbooks, pg 693
Faber & Faber Ltd, pg 694
Flame Tree Publishing, pg 695
Forbes Publications Ltd, pg 696
Four Seasons Publishing Ltd, pg 696
Fourth Estate, pg 696
Frontier Publishing Ltd, pg 697
Garden Art Press Ltd, pg 698
Garnet Publishing Ltd, pg 698
George Mann Publications, pg 699
GMC Publications Ltd, pg 700
Gollancz/Witherby, pg 701
Granta Books, pg 702
HarperCollins UK, pg 705
Harvard University Press, pg 705
The Harvill Press, pg 705
Headline Book Publishing Ltd, pg 706
Christopher Helm (Publishers) Ltd, pg 707
Helm Information Ltd, pg 707
Hippopotamus Press, pg 709
Hodder & Stoughton General, pg 709
Hodder & Stoughton Religious, pg 709
Hodder Headline Ltd, pg 709
ICC United Kingdom, pg 711
The Islamic Texts Society, pg 715
Janus Publishing Co Ltd, pg 716
The Kenilworth Press Ltd, pg 717
Lawpack Publishing Ltd, pg 719
Lion Hudson PLC, pg 721
The Littman Library of Jewish Civilization, pg 721
LLP Ltd, pg 722
Luath Press Ltd, pg 722
The Lutterworth Press, pg 723
Macmillan Ltd, pg 723
Management Books 2000 Ltd, pg 724
Marston House, pg 725
Mercat Press, pg 726
Metro Books, pg 727
Middleton Press, pg 728
Multilingual Matters Ltd, pg 729
John Murray (Publishers) Ltd, pg 730
National Portrait Gallery Publications, pg 731
Neil Wilson Publishing Ltd, pg 732
New Era Publications UK Ltd, pg 732
New European Publications Ltd, pg 732
NMS Enterprises Ltd - Publishing, pg 733
Octagon Press Ltd, pg 734
Octopus Publishing Group, pg 734
Old Pond Publishing, pg 734
Michael O'Mara Books Ltd, pg 735
Open Gate Press, pg 735
Orion Publishing Group Ltd, pg 736
The Orkney Press Ltd, pg 736
Peter Owen Ltd, pg 737
Parapress Ltd, pg 738
Pavilion Books Ltd, pg 739
Pen & Sword Books Ltd, pg 740
Penguin Books Ltd, pg 740
The Penguin Group UK, pg 740
Plough Publishing House of Bruderhof Communities in the UK, pg 743
Pluto Press, pg 743
Polybooks Ltd, pg 744
David Porteous Editions, pg 744
Profile Books Ltd, pg 746
Quadrille Publishing Ltd, pg 746
Quarto Publishing plc, pg 746
Queen Anne Press, pg 747
Quiller Publishing Ltd, pg 747
Quintet Publishing Ltd, pg 747
Reaktion Books Ltd, pg 748
Reardon Publishing, pg 748
Regency House Publishing Ltd, pg 749
Rivers Oram Press, pg 750
The Rubicon Press, pg 752
Ryland Peters & Small Ltd, pg 752
Sainsbury Publishing Ltd, pg 753

TYPE OF PUBLICATION INDEX

Saqi Books, pg 754
Steve Savage Publishers Ltd, pg 754
SCM-Canterbury Press Ltd, pg 755
Severn House Publishers Inc, pg 756
Shepheard-Walwyn (Publishers) Ltd, pg 757
Silver Link Publishing Ltd, pg 758
Skoob Russell Square, pg 758
Smith Settle Ltd, pg 758
Rudolf Steiner Press, pg 761
Stobart Davies Ltd, pg 761
Sutton Publishing Ltd, pg 762
Tabb House, pg 762
I B Tauris & Co Ltd, pg 763
Telegraph Books, pg 764
Thistle Press, pg 765
Time Warner Book Group UK, pg 766
Titan Books Ltd, pg 766
Transworld Publishers Ltd, pg 766
University of Hertfordshire Press, pg 768
Veloce Publishing Ltd, pg 769
Verso, pg 770
Virago Press, pg 770
Ward Lock Ltd, pg 771
White Cockade Publishing, pg 772
White Eagle Publishing Trust, pg 772
Whittet Books Ltd, pg 773
Wiley Europe Ltd, pg 773
Witherby & Co Ltd, pg 775
The Women's Press Ltd, pg 775
Wordwright Publishing, pg 775

Viet Nam
Science & Technics Publishing House, pg 780

Zimbabwe
Academic Books (Pvt) Ltd, pg 782
The Graham Publishing Company (Pvt) Ltd, pg 783
Zimbabwe Publishing House (Pvt) Ltd, pg 784
ZRD Trust, pg 785

JUVENILE & YOUNG ADULT BOOKS

Albania
NL SH, pg 1

Algeria
Enterprise Nationale du Livre (ENAL), pg 2

Argentina
Editorial Acme SA, pg 3
Aguilar Altea Taurus Alfaguara SA de Ediciones, pg 3
Editorial Atlantida SA, pg 3
Beas Ediciones SRL, pg 4
Bonum Editorial SACI, pg 4
Centro Editor de America Latina SA, pg 4
Editorial Ciudad Nueva de la Sefoma, pg 4
Ediciones Don Bosco Argentina, pg 5
Ediciones del Eclipse, pg 5
Errepar SA, pg 5
Editorial Guadalupe, pg 6
Kapelusz Editora SA, pg 7
Ediciones Minotauro SA, pg 7
Editorial Norte SA, pg 8
Editora Patria Grande, pg 8
Ediciones Preescolar SA, pg 8

TYPE OF PUBLICATION INDEX

BOOK

San Pablo, pg 9
Editorial Sigmar SACI, pg 9

Armenia
Arevik, pg 10

Australia
ABC Books (Australian Broadcasting Corporation), pg 10
Access Press, pg 10
Allen & Unwin Pty Ltd, pg 11
Beazer Publishing Company Pty Ltd, pg 14
Boinkie Publishers, pg 15
Louis Braille Audio, pg 16
Cole Publications, pg 18
Coolabah Publishing, pg 18
Crawford House Publishing Pty Ltd, pg 18
D'Artagnan Publishing, pg 19
Encyclopaedia Britannica (Australia) Inc, pg 21
Fremantle Arts Centre Press, pg 23
Greater Glider Productions Australia Pty Ltd, pg 24
Hodder Headline Australia, pg 26
Hunter Books, pg 26
Hyland House Publishing Pty Ltd, pg 26
Jarrah Publications, pg 27
Little Red Apple Publishing, pg 29
Magabala Books Aboriginal Corporation, pg 30
Pearson Education Australia, pg 36
Penguin Group (Australia), pg 36
Random House Australia, pg 38
Scholastic Australia Pty Ltd, pg 40
Tarka Publishing, pg 42
Transworld Publishers Pty Ltd, pg 44
University of Queensland Press, pg 45
Weather Press, pg 46
Wizard Books Pty Ltd, pg 47

Austria
BSE Verlag Dr Bernhard Schuttengruber, pg 49
DachsVerlag GmbH, pg 49
Danubia Werbung und Verlagsservice, pg 49
Denkmayr GmbH Druck & Verlag, pg 50
Development News Ltd, pg 50
Alois Goschl & Co, pg 51
Johannes Heyn GmbH & Co KG, pg 52
Verlag Jungbrunnen - Wiener Spielzeugschachtel GesellschaftmbH, pg 52
Verlag Kerle im Verlag Herder & Co, pg 53
Edition Neues Marchen, pg 54
Niederosterreichisches Pressehaus Druck- und Verlagsgesellschaft mbH, pg 54
oebv & hpt Verlagsgesellschaft mbH & Co KG, pg 55
Verlag Oesterreich GmbH, pg 55
Richard Pils Publication PN°1, pg 56
Pinguin-Verlag, Pawlowski GmbH, pg 56
Andreas Schnider Verlags-Atelier, pg 57
J Steinbrener OHG, pg 58
Tyrolia Verlagsanstalt GmbH, pg 58
Verlag Carl Ueberreuter GmbH, pg 58
Dr Otfried Weise Verlag Tabula Smaragdina, pg 59

Bangladesh
Gatidhara, pg 61

Belgium
NV Uitgeverij Altiora Averbode, pg 63
Maison d'Editions Baha'ies ASBL, pg 63
Editions Gerard Blanchart & Cie SA, pg 63
Uitgeverij Clavis, pg 65
Conservart SA, pg 65
Daphne Diffusion SA, pg 66
Editions Hemma, pg 68
Infoboek NV, pg 68
Infotex NV, pg 68
Uitgeverij J van In, pg 69
Uitgeverij Lannoo NV, pg 69
Lansman Editeur, pg 69
Claude Lefrancq Editeur, pg 70
Ligue pour la lecture de la Bible, pg 70
Editeurs de Litterature Biblique, pg 70
Les Editions du Lombard SA, pg 70
La Longue Vue, pg 70
Editions Memor, pg 71
Michelin Editions des Voyages, pg 71
Uitgeverij Pelckmans NV, pg 72
Henri Proost & Co, Pvba, pg 72
Standaard Uitgeverij, pg 73
Uitgeverij Averbode NV, pg 74
Les Editions Vie ouvriere ASBL, pg 74
C De Vries Brouwers BVBA, pg 74
Zuid-Nederlandse Uitgeverij NV/Central Uitgeverij, pg 75

Benin
Les Editions du Flamboyant, pg 75

Bosnia and Herzegovina
Veselin Maslesa, pg 76
Svjetlost, pg 76

Brazil
A & A & A Edicoes e Promocoes Internacionais Ltda, pg 76
AGIR S/A Editora, pg 77
Livraria Alema Ltda Brasileitura, pg 77
Editora Alfa Omega Ltda, pg 77
Editora Antroposofica Ltda, pg 77
Ao Livro Tecnico Industria e Comercio Ltda, pg 77
Associacao Arvore da Vida, pg 78
Editora Brasil-America (EBAL) SA, pg 79
Editora do Brasil SA, pg 79
Editora Brasiliense SA, pg 79
Centro de Estudos Juridicosdo Para (CEJUP), pg 79
Editora Companhia das Letras/Editora Schwarcz Ltda, pg 80
Concordia Editora Ltda, pg 80
Dumara Distribuidora de Publicacoes Ltda, pg 81
Edicon Editora e Consultorial Ltda, pg 81
Livraria Martins Fontes Editora Ltda, pg 81
Editora Forense Universitaria Ltda, pg 81
Formato Editorial ltda, pg 82
Editora Globo SA, pg 82
Editora e Grafica Carisio Ltda, Minas Editora, pg 83
Grafica Editora Primor Ltda, pg 83
Hemus Editora Ltda, pg 83
Editora Kuarup Ltda, pg 84
Editora Leitura Ltda, pg 84
Editora Mantiqueira de Ciencia e Arte, pg 86
Editora Marco Zero Ltda, pg 86
Editora Melhoramentos Ltda, pg 86
Memorias Futuras Edicoes Ltda, pg 86
Editora Mercuryo Ltda, pg 86
Editora Moderna Ltda, pg 86
Companhia Editora Nacional, pg 87
Editora Nova Alexandria Ltda, pg 87
Editora Nova Fronteira SA, pg 87
Olho D'Agua Comercio e Servicos Editoriais Ltda, pg 87
Edit Palavra Magica, pg 88
Paulinas Editorial, pg 88
Livraria Pioneira Editora/Enio Matheus Guazzelli e Cia Ltd, pg 88
Ediouro Publicacoes, SA, pg 89
Distribuidora Record de Servicos de Imprensa SA, pg 89
Editora Revan Ltda, pg 89
RHJ Livros Ltda, pg 89
Editora Rideel Ltda, pg 89
Editora Rocco Ltda, pg 89
Salamandra Consultoria Editorial SA, pg 89
Editora Santuario, pg 90
Saraiva SA, Livreiros Editores, pg 90
Editora Scipione Ltda, pg 90
Sobrindes Linha Grafica E Editora Ltda, pg 90
Livraria Sulina Editora, pg 91
Thex Editora e Distribuidora Ltda, pg 91
34 Literatura S/C Ltda, pg 91
Editora Vecchi SA, pg 92
Editora Verbo Ltda, pg 92
Editora Vida Crista Ltda, pg 92
Editora Vigilia Ltda, pg 92
Zip Editora Ltda, pg 92

Bulgaria
EA EOOD, pg 94
Fama, pg 94
Hermes Publishing House, pg 94
Kibea Publishing Co, pg 95
Mladezh IK, pg 95
Sluntse Publishing House, pg 97

Cameroon
Editions CLE, pg 98

Chile
Arrayan Editores, pg 98
Editorial Andres Bello/Editorial Juridica de Chile, pg 99
Norma de Chile, pg 99
Pehuen Editores Ltda, pg 100
J.C. Saez Editor, pg 100
Editorial Texido Ltda, pg 100
Zig-Zag SA, pg 101

China
Anhui People's Publishing House, pg 101
Beijing Juvenile & Children's Books Publishing House, pg 101
Beijing Publishing House, pg 101
China Film Press, pg 102
China Materials Management Publishing House, pg 102
Foreign Language Teaching & Research Press, pg 104
Fujian Science & Technology Publishing House, pg 104
Guizhou Education Publishing House, pg 105
Inner Mongolia Science & Technology Publishing House, pg 105
Jinan Publishing House, pg 105
Lanzhou University Press, pg 106
Morning Glory Press, pg 106
People's Literature Publishing House, pg 106
Shandong Education Publishing House, pg 107
Shandong Friendship Publishing House, pg 107
Shanghai Educational Publishing House, pg 108
Shanghai Far East Publishers, pg 108

Colombia
Bedout Editores SA, pg 110
Eurolibros Ltda, pg 111
Editorial Norma SA, pg 112
Editorial Oveja Negra Ltda, pg 112
Editorial Panamericana, pg 112
Editorial Santillana SA, pg 112

The Democratic Republic of the Congo
Centre Protestant d'Editions et de Diffusion (CEDI), pg 114
Saint-Paul, pg 114

Costa Rica
Editorial de la Universidad de Costa Rica, pg 116

Cote d'Ivoire
Centre d'Edition et de Diffusion Africaines, pg 117
Les Nouvelles Editions Ivoiriennes, pg 117

Croatia
ALFA dd za izdavacke, graficke i trgovacke poslove, pg 117
Mladost d d Izdavacku graficku i informaticku djelatnost, pg 119
Skolska Knjiga, pg 119
Znaci Vremena, Institut Za Istrazivanje Biblije, pg 119
Znanje d d, pg 119

Cuba
Casa Editora Abril, pg 120
Editorial Gente Nueva, pg 120
Editorial Oriente, pg 120
Editora Politica, pg 120

Czech Republic
Albatros AS, pg 122
Bakalar spol sro, pg 122
Erika spol sro, pg 123
Granit sro, pg 123
Kalich SRO, pg 124
Lyra Pragensis Obecne Prospelna Spolecnost, pg 125
Nase vojsko, nakladatelstvi a knizni obchod, pg 126
Nakladatelstvi Olympia AS, pg 126
Portal spol sro, pg 126
NS Svoboda spol sro, pg 127
Ladislav Vasicek, pg 128
Votobia sro, pg 128
Vysehrad spol sro, pg 128

Denmark
Alma, pg 128
Aschehoug Dansk Forlag A/S, pg 129
Atuakkiorfik A/S Det Greenland Publishers, pg 129

PUBLISHERS — TYPE OF PUBLICATION INDEX

Bogfabrikken Fakta ApS, pg 129
Borgens Forlag A/S, pg 129
Egmont Serieforlaget A/S, pg 130
Forlaget Forum, pg 131
Fremad A/S, pg 131
Grevas Forlag, pg 131
Gyldendalske Boghandel - Nordisk Forlag A/S, pg 131
P Haase & Sons Forlag A/S, pg 131
Hernovs Forlag, pg 132
Forlaget Hjulet, pg 132
Holkenfeldt 3, pg 132
Interpresse A/S, pg 132
Kaleidoscope Publishers Ltd, pg 132
Lohse Forlag, pg 132
Mallings ApS, pg 132
Scandinavia Publishing House, pg 134
Sommer & Sorensen, pg 134
Wisby & Wilkens, pg 135

Dominican Republic

Pontificia Universidad Catolica Madre y Maestra, pg 136

Egypt (Arab Republic of Egypt)

Elias Modern Publishing House, pg 138

Estonia

Eesti Entsuklopeediakirjastus, pg 139
Ilmamaa, pg 139
Kirjastus Kunst, pg 139
Kupar Publishers, pg 139
Tuum, pg 140
Valgus Publishers, pg 140

Finland

Karisto Oy, pg 142
Kustannus Oy Semic, pg 143
Kustannusosakeyhtio Tammi, pg 143
Lasten Keskus Oy, pg 143
Otava Publishing Co Ltd, pg 143
Schildts Forlags AB, pg 144
Scriptum Forlags AB, pg 144
Soderstroms Forlag, pg 144
SV-Kauppiaskanava Oy, pg 144
Werner Soederstrom Osakeyhtio (WSOY), pg 145

France

L'Amitie par le Livre, pg 146
Editions des Beatitudes, Pneumatheque, pg 149
Editions Belin, pg 149
Berger-Levrault Editions SAS, pg 149
Editions Andre Bonne, pg 150
Pierre Bordas & Fils, Editions, pg 150
Bragelonne, pg 151
Emgleo Breiz, pg 151
Editions BRGM, pg 151
Editions Casterman, pg 152
Editions Chardon Bleu, pg 153
Editions Circonflexe, pg 154
Codes Rousseau, pg 155
Dargaud, pg 157
Dessain et Tolra SA, pg 158
Les Editions des Deux Coqs d'Or, pg 158
Les Devenirs Visuels, pg 158
Editions J Dupuis, pg 159
Editions de l'Ecole, pg 159
Editions ELOR, pg 160
Editions Grund, pg 160
Editions Farel, pg 162
Editions Des Femmes, pg 163

France-Loisirs, pg 164
Editions Gallimard, pg 164
Editions Gamma, pg 165
Gammaprim, pg 165
Hachette Education, pg 166
Hachette Jeunesse Image, pg 166
Hachette Jeunesse Roman, pg 166
Hachette Livre, pg 167
Editions Hatier SA, pg 167
Pierre Horay Editeur, pg 168
Editions l'Instant Durable, pg 169
Editions Larousse, pg 171
Editions Le Laurier, pg 171
Editions Lito, pg 172
Le Livre de Paris, pg 173
Les Livres du Dragon d'Or, pg 173
LLB France (Ligue pour la Lecture de la Bible), pg 173
Editions Loubatieres, pg 173
Magnard, pg 173
Editions Mango, pg 174
Editions MDI (La Maison des Instituteurs), pg 175
Editions Albin Michel, pg 175
Editions Fernand Nathan, pg 176
Editions Ophrys, pg 177
Les Presses d'Ile-de-France Sarl, pg 181
Publi-Fusion, pg 182
Rageot Editeur, pg 182
Editions Le Sarment, pg 184
Editions Scala, pg 184
Selection du Reader's Digest SA, pg 184
Service Technique pour l'Education, pg 184
Editions du Seuil, pg 184
Societe des Editions Grasset et Fasquelle, pg 185
Association d'Editions Sorg, pg 186
Editions Tarmeye, pg 187
Librairie Pierre Tequi et Editions Tequi, pg 187
La Vague a l'ame, pg 188
Editions Vague Verte, pg 188
Les Editions Vaillant-Miroir-Sprint Publications, pg 188
Vents d'Ouest, pg 188

French Polynesia

Simone Sanchez, pg 190

Germany

Abakus Musik Barbara Fietz, pg 190
Agentur des Rauhen Hauses Hamburg GmbH, pg 191
Alibaba Verlag GmbH, pg 192
Anrich Verlag GmbH, pg 192
Arena Verlag GmbH, pg 193
Asso Verlag, pg 195
Aussaat Verlag, pg 195
Baken-Verlag Walter Schnoor, pg 196
Julius Beltz GmbH & Co KG, pg 199
C Bertelsmann Verlag GmbH, pg 199
Bertelsmann Lexikon Verlag GmbH, pg 200
Bibliographisches Institut & F A Brockhaus AG, pg 200
R Brockhaus Verlag, pg 204
Buchverlag Junge Welt GmbH, pg 205
Buchergilde Gutenberg Verlagsgesellschaft mbH, pg 205
Bund-Verlag GmbH, pg 206
Campus Verlag GmbH, pg 207
Carlsen Verlag GmbH, pg 207
Christliches Verlagshaus GmbH, pg 208

Cornelsen Verlag Scriptor GmbH & Co KG, pg 210
Verlag Werner Dausien, pg 211
Delphin Verlag GmbH, pg 211
Deutsche Bibelgesellschaft, pg 211
Deutscher Literatur-Verlag, pg 213
Deutscher Taschenbuch Verlag GmbH & Co KG (dtv), pg 213
Dreisam Ratgeber in der Rutsker Verlag GmbH, pg 216
Cecilie Dressler Verlag GmbH & Co KG, pg 216
Echter Wurzburg Frankische Gesellschaftsdruckerei und Verlag GmbH, pg 217
Egmont EHAPA Verlag GmbH, pg 218
Egmont Franz Schneider Verlag GmbH, pg 218
Egmont Pestalozzi-Verlag, pg 218
Egmont vgs verlagsgesellschaft mbH, pg 218
Verlag Heinrich Ellermann GmbH & Co KG, pg 219
Ensslin und Laiblin Verlag GmbH & Co KG, pg 220
Espresso Verlag GmbH, pg 221
Esslinger Verlag J F Schreiber GmbH, pg 221
Extent Verlag und Service Wolfgang M Flamm, pg 223
Fabel-Verlag Gudrun Liebchen, pg 223
FN-Verlag der Deutschen Reiterlichen Vereinigung GmbH, pg 225
Franckh-Kosmos Verlags-GmbH & Co, pg 226
Franz-Sales-Verlag, pg 226
Verlag Freies Geistesleben, pg 227
Margarethe Freudenberger - selbstverlag fur jedermann, pg 227
Gatzanis Verlags GmbH, pg 228
Verlag Junge Gemeinde E Schwinghammer GmbH & Co KG, pg 228
Gerstenberg Verlag, pg 228
Gerth Medien GmbH, pg 229
Gmelin Verlag GmbH, pg 230
Gondrom Verlag GmbH & Co KG, pg 230
Verlag der Stiftung Gralsbotschaft GmbH, pg 231
Grass-Verlag, pg 231
Guetersloher Verlagshaus, pg 232
Verlag des Gustav-Adolf-Werks, pg 232
Carl Hanser Verlag, pg 234
Heinz-Theo Gremme Verlag, pg 236
Edition Hentrich Druck & Verlag Gebr Hentrich und Tank GmbH & Co KG, pg 236
Herold Verlag Dr Wetzel, pg 236
Max Hieber KG, pg 237
Verlag Wolfgang Hoelker, pg 238
Horlemann Verlag, pg 239
J Ch Mellinger Verlag GmbH, pg 242
Julius Klinkhardt Verlagsbuchhandlung, pg 243
KBV Verlags-und Medien - GmbH, pg 245
Verlag Kerle im Verlag Herder, pg 245
Verlag im Kilian GmbH, pg 246
Kinderbuchverlag, pg 246
Kleiner Bachmann Verlag fur Kinder und Umwelt, pg 246
Klens Verlag GmbH, pg 246
Erika Klopp Verlag GmbH, pg 247
Knowledge Media International, pg 247

Verlag Knut Reim, Jugendpresseverlag, pg 247
Koptisch-Orthodoxes Zentrum, pg 249
Roman Kovar Verlag, pg 249
Verlag Antje Kunstmann GmbH, pg 251
Lahn-Verlag GmbH, pg 251
Lentz Verlag, pg 253
Loewe Verlag KG, pg 255
Logos-Verlag Literatur & Layout GmbH, pg 255
Karl-Heinz Metz, pg 259
Gertraud Middelhauve Verlag GmbH & Co KG, pg 260
Monia Verlag, pg 261
Naumann & Goebel Verlagsgesellschaft mbH, pg 263
Verlag Neue Stadt GmbH, pg 264
Neuer Honos Verlag GmbH, pg 264
Oekotopia Verlag, Wolfgang Hoffman GmbH & Co KG, pg 266
Verlag Friedrich Oetinger GmbH, pg 266
Oncken Verlag KG, pg 267
Pandion-Verlag, Ulrike Schmoll, pg 268
J Pfeiffer Verlag, pg 269
Projektion J Buch- und Musikverlag GmbH, pg 272
Ravensburger Buchverlag Otto Maier GmbH, pg 274
Konrad Reich Verlag GmbH, pg 274
Verlag an der Ruhr GmbH, pg 277
Saatkorn-Verlag, pg 277
Eugen Salzer-Verlag GmbH & Co KG, pg 278
Verlag der Sankt-Johannis-Druckerei C Schweickhardt, pg 278
Verlag Sauerlaender GmbH, pg 278
Scheffler-Verlag, pg 279
Richard Scherpe Verlag GmbH, pg 279
Agora Verlag Manfred Schlosser, pg 280
Verlag Karl Waldemar Schuetz, pg 281
Verlag Stendel, pg 287
Steyler Verlag, pg 288
Suedverlag, pg 288
Druck-und Verlagshans Thiele & Schwarz GmbH, pg 290
Thienemann Verlag GmbH, pg 291
Tipress Dienstleistungen fur das Verlagswesen GmbH, pg 291
Transpress Verlagsgesellschaft mbH, pg 292
Treves Editions Verein Zur Foerderung der Kuenstlerischen Taetigkeiten, pg 292
Turkischer Schulbuchverlag Onel Cengiz, pg 293
Unrast Verlag e V, pg 293
Verlag Beltz & Gelberg, pg 295
Voggenreiter-Verlag, pg 296
A Weichert Verlag GmbH & Co KG, pg 298
The World of Books Literaturverlag, pg 301
Xenos Verlagsgesellschaft mbH, pg 301

Ghana

Afram Publications (Ghana) Ltd, pg 303
Anowuo Educational Publications, pg 303
Beginners Publishers, pg 303
Ghana Publishing Corporation, pg 304
Moxon Paperbacks, pg 304

Waterville Publishing House, pg 305
World Literature Project, pg 305

Greece
Bergadis, pg 306
Chrysi Penna - Golden Pen Books, pg 306
Dodoni Publications, pg 306
Eleftheroudakis, GCSA International Bookstore, pg 307
Elliniki Leschi Tou Vivliou, pg 307
Ekdoseis Filon, pg 307
Hestia-I D Hestia-Kollaros & Co Corporation, pg 308
Kalentis & Sia, pg 308
Ilias Kambanas Publishing Organization, SA, pg 309
Kastaniotis Editions SA, pg 309
Katoptro Publications, pg 309
Kedros Publishers, pg 309
Mamuth Comix EPE, pg 310
Medusa/Selas Publishers, pg 310
Minoas SA, pg 310
Pagoulatos G-G P Publications, pg 311
Kyr I Papadopoulos E E, pg 311
Patakis Publishers, pg 311
Psichogios Publications SA, pg 311
Siamantas VA A Ouvas, pg 312
J Sideris OE Ekdoseis, pg 312
Sigma, pg 312
D & J Vardikos Vivliotechnika Hellas, pg 313

Haiti
Editions Caraibes SA, pg 314

Hong Kong
Breakthrough Ltd - Breakthrough Publishers, pg 315
Chung Hwa Book Co (HK) Ltd, pg 316
Joint Publishing (HK) Co Ltd, pg 317
SCMP Book Publishing Ltd, pg 319
Sun Ya Publications (HK) Ltd, pg 319
Witman Publishing Co (HK) Ltd, pg 320

Hungary
Advent Kiado, pg 320
Aranyhal Konyvkiado Goldfish Publishing, pg 320
Ifjusagi Lap-eskonyvkiado Vallalat, pg 321
Marton Aron Kiado Publishing House, pg 323
Mora Ferenc Ifjusagi Koenyvkiado Rt, pg 323
Park Konyvkiado Kft (Park Publisher), pg 324

Iceland
AEskan, pg 325
Almenna Bokafelagid, pg 325
Bokautgafan Orn og Orlygur ehf, pg 325
Frjals fjolmiolun hf-Urvalsbaekur, pg 325
Idunn, pg 325
Mal og menning, pg 326
Setberg, pg 326
Skjaldborg Ltd, pg 326

India
Ananda Publishers Pvt Ltd, pg 328
Atma Ram & Sons, pg 329
Bhawan Book Service, Publishers & Distributors, pg 330
Chowkhamba Sanskrit Series Office, pg 332
Dolphin Publications, pg 333
Frank Brothers & Co Publishers Ltd, pg 334
Ministry of Information & Broadcasting, pg 341
People's Publishing House (P) Ltd, pg 345
Pitambar Publishing Co (P) Ltd, pg 345
Rajkamal Prakashan Pvt Ltd, pg 346
Rajpal & Sons, pg 346
Regency Publications, pg 346
Shaibya Prakashan Bibhag, pg 349
Shiksha Bharati, pg 349
Tara Publishing, pg 351
Vidya Puri, pg 352
Vidyarthi Mithram Press, pg 352

Indonesia
Aurora, pg 353
Bina Rena Pariwara, pg 354
PT Bulan Bintang, pg 354
Djambatan PT, pg 354
Gaya Favorit Press, pg 355
Mizan, pg 355
Mutiara Sumber Widya PT, pg 356
Yayasan Obor Indonesia, pg 357

Ireland
An Gum, pg 358
Attic Press Ltd, pg 358
Ballinakella Press, pg 358
The Children's Press, pg 358
Clo Iar-Chonnachta Teo, pg 358
The O'Brien Press Ltd, pg 362
Roberts Rinehart Publishers, pg 363

Israel
Achiasaf Publishing House Ltd, pg 364
Am Oved Publishers Ltd, pg 365
Amichai Publishing House Ltd, pg 365
Boostan Publishing House, pg 365
Breslov Research Institute, pg 365
Dalia Peled Publishers, Division of Modan, pg 366
DAT Publications, pg 366
Dekel Publishing House, pg 366
Dvir Publishing Ltd, pg 366
Feldheim Publishers Ltd, pg 367
Gefen Publishing House Ltd, pg 367
Hakibbutz Hameuchad Publishing House Ltd, pg 367
The Institute for the Translation of Hebrew Literature, pg 368
Karni Publishers Ltd, pg 369
Keter Publishing House Ltd, pg 369
Kiryat Sefer, pg 369
Ma'ariv Book Guild (Sifriat Ma'ariv), pg 370
Machbarot Lesifrut, pg 370
Massada Press Ltd, pg 370
Massada Publishers Ltd, pg 370
M Mizrahi Publishers, pg 370
Pitspopany Press, pg 371
Rubin Mass Ltd, pg 371
Schocken Publishing House Ltd, pg 371
Sifriat Poalim Ltd, pg 372
Samuel Simson Ltd, pg 372
Y Sreberk, pg 372
Steimatzky Group Ltd, pg 372
Yad Vashem - The Holocaust Martyrs' & Heroes' Remembrance Authority, pg 373
Yavneh Publishing House Ltd, pg 373

Italy
Editrice Ancora, pg 375
Editore Armando Armando SRL, pg 376
Bompiani-RCS Libri, pg 378
Edizioni Borla SRL, pg 379
Cappelli Editore, pg 380
Edizioni Cartedit SRL, pg 380
Casa Editrice Libraria Ulrico Hoepli SpA, pg 380
Centro Biblico, pg 381
Citta Nuova Editrice, pg 382
Elle Di Ci - Libreria Dottrina Cristiana, pg 387
Feguagiskia' Studios, pg 389
Giangiacomo Feltrinelli SpA, pg 389
Garzanti Libri, pg 390
Istituto Geografico de Agostini SpA, pg 390
Giunti Gruppo Editoriale, pg 390
Piero Gribaudi Editore, pg 391
In Dialogo, pg 393
Edizioni Internazionali di Letteratura e Scienze, pg 393
Editoriale Jaca Book SpA, pg 394
Lalli Editore SRL, pg 394
Librex, pg 395
Lusva Editrice, pg 396
Editrice Massimo SAS di Crespi Cesare e C, pg 397
Milano Libri, pg 398
Minerva Italica SpA, pg 398
Arnoldo Mondadori Editore SpA, pg 398
Edumond Le Monnier, pg 399
Motta Junior Srl, pg 399
Gruppo Ugo Mursia Editore SpA, pg 400
Nardini Editore srl, pg 400
La Nuova Italia Editrice SpA, pg 401
Franco Cosimo Panini Editore, pg 402
Edizioni Piemme SpA, pg 403
Piero Manni srl, pg 403
RCS Libri SpA, pg 405
RCS Rizzoli Libri SpA, pg 405
SAIE Editrice SRL, pg 406
Edizioni San Paolo SRL, pg 407
Editrice la Scuola SpA, pg 407
Edizioni Sonda, pg 409
Nicola Teti e C Editore SRL, pg 410
Transeuropa, pg 410
Editrice Uomini Nuovi, pg 411
UTET (Unione Tipografico-Editrice Torinese), pg 411
Vallardi Industrie Grafiche, pg 411
Zanichelli Editore SpA, pg 412

Jamaica
Carib Publishing Ltd, pg 413

Japan
Akita Shoten Publishing Co Ltd, pg 415
Bunkasha Publishing Co Ltd, pg 415
Chikuma Shobo Publishing Co Ltd, pg 416
Child Honsha Co Ltd, pg 416
Dainippon Tosho Publishing Co, Ltd, pg 416
Froebel - kan Co Ltd, pg 417
Fukuinkan Shoten Publishers Inc, pg 417
Fuzambo Publishing Co, pg 417
Gakken Co Ltd, pg 417
GakuseiSha Publishing Co Ltd, pg 417
Hikarinokuni Ltd, pg 418
Hoikusha Publishing Co Ltd, pg 418
Hokuryukan Co Ltd, pg 418
Holp Book Co Ltd, pg 418
Hyoronsha Publishing Co Ltd, pg 418
Ie-No-Hikari Association, pg 419
Iwanami Shoten, Publishers, pg 419
Iwasaki Shoten Publishing Co Ltd, pg 419
Kodansha Ltd, pg 421
Komine Shoten Co Ltd, pg 421
Nosangyoson Bunka Kyokai, pg 424
Obunsha Co Ltd, pg 424
Saela Shobo (Librairie Ca et La), pg 425
The Sailor Publishing Co, Ltd, pg 426
Seibido Shuppan Company Ltd, pg 426
Seibundo Shinkosha Publishing Co Ltd, pg 426
Sekai Bunka-Sha, pg 427
Shingakusha Co Ltd, pg 427
Akane Shobo Co Ltd, pg 427
Shogakukan Inc, pg 427
Shueisha Inc, pg 428
Shufu-to-Seikatsu Sha Ltd, pg 428
Takahashi Shoten Co Ltd, pg 429
Tamagawa University Press, pg 429
Tokuma Shoten Publishing Co Ltd, pg 429
Tokyo Shoseki Co Ltd, pg 430
Charles E Tuttle Publishing Co Inc, pg 430
Yuki Shobo, pg 431
Zoshindo JukenKenkyusha, pg 431

Kenya
Focus Publications Ltd, pg 433
Foundation Books Ltd, pg 434
Heinemann Kenya Ltd (EAEP), pg 434
Kenway Publications Ltd, pg 434
Kenya Quality & Productivity Institute, pg 435
Phoenix Publishers Ltd, pg 435
Sasa Sema Publications Ltd, pg 435
Transafrica Press, pg 436

Democratic People's Republic of Korea
The Foreign Language Press Group, pg 436

Republic of Korea
Chung Rim Publishing Co Ltd, pg 438
Dai Hak Publishing Co, pg 438
Gim-Yeong Co, pg 438
Hanjin Publishing Co, pg 439
Hollym Corporation; Publishers, pg 439
Hw Moon Publishing Co, pg 439
Hyein Publishing House, pg 439
Ke Mong Sa Publishing Co Ltd, pg 440
Korea Britannica Corp, pg 440
Koreaone Press Inc, pg 440
Literature Academy Publishing, pg 441
Munye Publishing Co, pg 441
Seoul International Publishing House, pg 443
Sohaksa, pg 443
Woongjin Media Corporation, pg 443
Woongjin.com Co Ltd, pg 443
Yearimdang Publishing Co, pg 443

PUBLISHERS

Latvia
Alberts XII, pg 444
Artava Ltd, pg 444
Egmont Latvia SIA, pg 444
Nordik/Tapals Publishers Ltd, pg 445
Patmos, izdevnieciba, pg 445
Spriditis Publishers, pg 445
Zvaigzne ABC Publishers Ltd, pg 445

Lebanon
Dar El Ilm Lilmalayin, pg 446
Khayat Book and Publishing Co Sarl, pg 446
Librairie du Liban Publishers (Sal), pg 446
Librairie Orientale sal, pg 446

Liechtenstein
Frank P van Eck Publishers, pg 448

Lithuania
Egmont Lietuva, pg 449
Lietus Ltd, pg 449
Sviesa Publishers, pg 449
Tyto Alba Publishers, pg 450
Victoria Publishers, pg 450

The Former Yugoslav Republic of Macedonia
Detska radost, pg 452
Makedonska kniga (Knigoizdatelstvo), pg 452
Prosvetno Delo Publishing House, pg 453

Madagascar
Maison d'Edition Protestante ANTSO, pg 453

Malawi
Christian Literature Association in Malawi, pg 454

Malaysia
Berita Publishing Sdn Bhd, pg 455
Penerbit Jayatinta Sdn Bhd, pg 458
Penerbitan Tinta, pg 458
Pustaka Cipta Sdn Bhd, pg 458
Pustaka Delta Pelajaran Sdn Bhd, pg 458
Tempo Publishing (M) Sdn Bhd, pg 458
Uni-Text Book Co, pg 459

Maldive Islands
Non-Formal Education Centre, pg 459

Mauritius
Editions de l'Ocean Indien Ltd, pg 461
Vizavi Editions, pg 461

Mexico
Aconcagua Ediciones y Publicaciones SA, pg 461
Ediciones Alpe, pg 462
Ediciones Corunda SA de CV, pg 463
Ediciones Culturales Internacionales SA de CV Edicion Compra y Venta de Libros, Casetes, Videos, pg 463
Editorial Diana SA de CV, pg 464
Edamex SA de CV, pg 464
Entretenlibro SA de CV, pg 465
Editorial Esfinge SA de CV, pg 465
Fernandez Editores SA de CV, pg 465
Fondo de Cultura Economica, pg 465
Ediciones Larousse SA de CV, pg 467
Libra Editorial SA de CV, pg 467
Editorial Limusa SA de CV, pg 467
Nova Grupo Editorial SA de CV, pg 469
Organizacion Cultural LP SA de CV, pg 469
Pangea Editores, Sa de CV, pg 470
Panorama Editorial, SA, pg 470
Plaza y Valdes SA de CV, pg 470
Salvat Editores de Mexico, pg 471
Sistemas Tecnicos de Edicion SA de CV, pg 472
Ediciones Suromex SA, pg 472
Editorial Trillas SA de CV, pg 472

Morocco
Editions Al-Fourkane, pg 474
Editions Okad, pg 475
Editions Services et Informations pour Etudiants, pg 475

Myanmar
Kyi-Pwar-Ye Book House, pg 475
Smart & Mookerdum, pg 476

Netherlands
Ark Boeken, pg 478
Ars Scribendi bv Uitgeverij, pg 478
BV Uitgevery NZV (Nederlandse Zondagsschool Vereniging), pg 480
Cadans, pg 480
Callenbach BV, pg 480
Casterman NV, pg 480
Uitgeverij Christoffoor, pg 480
Uitgeverij Elzenga, pg 482
Frank Fehmers Productions, pg 482
Uitgeverij De Fontein BV, pg 482
Gottmer Uitgevers Groep, pg 483
De Harmonie Uitgeverij, pg 483
Hemma Holland BV, pg 483
Heuff Amsterdam Uitgever, pg 483
Uitgeverij Holland, pg 483
Uitgeverij Kluitman Alkmaar BV, pg 484
Uitgeverij J H Kok BV, pg 485
LCG Malmberg BV, pg 485
Lemniscaat, pg 485
Uitgeverij Leopold BV, pg 485
Meander Uitgeverij BV, pg 485
Mulder Holland BV, pg 486
Uitgeverij Ploegsma BV, pg 487
Em Querido's Uitgeverij BV, pg 488
Rebo Productions BV, pg 488
Sjaloom Uitgeverijen, pg 489
Uitgeverij Altamira-Becht BV, pg 490
Unieboek BV, pg 490
Uitgeverij De Vuurbaak BV, pg 492
Uitgeverij Zwijsen BV, pg 493

Netherlands Antilles
Bredero, pg 493

New Zealand
David Bateman Ltd, pg 494
Cape Catley Ltd, pg 495
Wendy Crane Books, pg 495
HarperCollins Publishers (New Zealand) Ltd, pg 497
Longacre Press, pg 498
Magari Publishing, pg 498
Nelson Price Milburn Ltd, pg 499
Shearwater Associates Ltd, pg 501

Nigeria
Aromolaran Publishing Co Ltd, pg 503
Cross Continent Press Ltd, pg 504
Ethiope Publishing Corporation, pg 504
Evans Brothers (Nigeria Publishers) Ltd, pg 504
Fourth Dimension Publishing Co Ltd, pg 504
Longman Nigeria Plc, pg 505
Nwamife Publishers Ltd, pg 506
Onibon-Oje Publishers, pg 506
Saros International Publishers, pg 507
University Publishing Co, pg 507
West African Book Publishers Ltd, pg 507

Norway
H Aschehoug & Co (W Nygaard) A/S, pg 508
Atheneum Forlag A/S, pg 508
J W Cappelens Forlag A/S, pg 508
N W Damm og Son A/S, pg 508
J W Eides Forlag A/S, pg 509
Fonna Forlag L/L, pg 509
Lunde Forlag AS, pg 509
Luther Forlag A/S, pg 509
Chr Schibsteds Forlag A/S, pg 510
Solum Forlag A/S, pg 510
Stabenfeldt A/S, pg 510

Pakistan
Sheikh Muhammad Ashraf Publishers, pg 511
Ferozsons (Pvt) Ltd, pg 512
Hamdard Foundation Pakistan, pg 512
Maqbool Academy, pg 513
National Book Foundation, pg 513

Papua New Guinea
Kristen Press, pg 515

Peru
Ediciones Brown SA, pg 516
Asociacion Editorial Bruno, pg 516
Carvajal SA, pg 516
Ediciones Peisa (Promocion Editorial Inca SA), pg 517
Tassorello, SA, pg 517

Philippines
Anvil Publishing Inc, pg 518
Bookman Printing & Publishing House Inc, pg 518
Sonny A Mendoza, pg 519
National Book Store Inc, pg 519
Our Lady of Manaoag Publisher, pg 520

Poland
Wydawnictwo Dolnoslaskie, pg 522
Instytut Wydawniczy Pax, Inco-Veritas, pg 523
Iskry - Publishing House Ltd spotka zoo, pg 523
KAW Krajowa Agencja Wydawnicza, pg 523
Wydawnictwo Lubelskie, pg 524
Wydawnictwo Nasza Ksiegarnia Sp zoo, pg 524
Ossolineum Zaklad Narodowy im Ossolinskich - Wydawnictwo, pg 525
'Slask' Ltd, pg 526
Spotdzielna Anagram, pg 526
Videograf II Sp z o o Zaklad Poracy Chronionej, pg 527
Wydawn Na Sprawa' Wydawniczo-Oswiatowa Spotdzielnia Inwalidow, pg 528

Portugal
Livraria Arnado Lda, pg 528
Bertrand Editora Lda, pg 529
Editorial Caminho SARL, pg 529
Livraria Civilizacao (Americo Fraga Lamares & Ca Lda), pg 529
Editora Classica, pg 530
DIFEL - Difusao Editorial SA, pg 530
Editorial Estampa, Lda, pg 531
Europress Editores e Distribuidores de Publicacoes Lda, pg 531
Everest Editora, pg 531
Editorial Franciscana, pg 531
Girassol Edicoes, LDA, pg 532
Gradiva-Publicacnoes Lda, pg 532
Editorial Inquerito Lda, pg 532
Edicoes ITAU (Instituto Tecnico de Alimentacao Humana) Lda, pg 532
Livros Horizonte Lda, pg 533
Livraria Tavares Martins, pg 533
Melhoramentos de Portugal Editora, Lda, pg 533
Nova Arrancada Sociedade Editora SA, pg 534
Paulinas, pg 534
Platano Editora SA, pg 534
Portugalmundo, pg 535
Editorial Presenca, pg 535
Puma Editora Lda, pg 535
Editora Replicacao Lda, pg 535
Edicoes Salesianas, pg 535
Almerinda Teixeira, pg 536
Vega-Publicacao e Distribuicao de Livros e Revistas, Lda, pg 536
Editorial Verbo SA, pg 536
Livraria Verdade e Vida Editora, pg 536

Romania
Editura Excelsior Art, pg 539
Nemira Verlag, pg 541
Editura Niculescu, pg 541
Pandora Publishing House, pg 541
RAO International Publishing Co, pg 542
Saeculum IO, pg 542
Vox Editura, pg 543

Russian Federation
Armada Publishing House, pg 543
Izdatelstvo Detskaya Literatura, pg 544
Druzhba Narodov, pg 544
Finansy i Statistika Publishing House, pg 544
Ladomir Publishing House, pg 546
Izdatelstvo Lenizdat, pg 546
Obdeestvo Znanie, pg 547
Raduga Publishers, pg 548
Russkaya Kniga Izdatelstvo (Publishers), pg 548

Saudi Arabia
Dar Al-Shareff for Publishing & Distribution, pg 550

Senegal
Centre Africain d'Animation et d'Echanges Culturels Editions Khoudia (CAEC), pg 551
Les Nouvelles Editions Africaines du Senegal NEAS, pg 551

TYPE OF PUBLICATION INDEX — BOOK

Serbia and Montenegro
Alfa-Narodna Knjiga, pg 552
Beogradski Izdavacko-Graficki Zavod, pg 552
Niro Decje Novine, pg 553
Nolit Publishing House, pg 553
Obod, pg 553
Partenon MAM Sistem, pg 553

Singapore
Asiapac Books Pte Ltd, pg 555
Hillview Publications Pte Ltd, pg 556
Pustaka Nasional Pte Ltd, pg 557

Slovakia
AV Studio Reklamno-vydavatel'ska agentura, pg 559
Egmont Neografia spol sro, pg 559
Mlade leta Spd sro, pg 559
Vydavatelstvo Obzor, pg 560
Smena Publishing House, pg 560

Slovenia
Mladinska Knjiga International, pg 561
Zalozba Mihelac d o o, pg 562
Zalozba Obzorja d d Maribor, pg 562

South Africa
HAUM (Hollandsch Afrikaansche Uitgevers Maatschappij), pg 564
Heinemann Educational Publishers Southern Africa, pg 564
Human & Rousseau (Pty) Ltd, pg 564
Johannesburg Art Gallery, pg 565
Juventus/Femina Publishers, pg 565
LAPA Publishers (Pty) Ltd, pg 566
New Africa Books (Pty) Ltd, pg 567
Queillerie Publishers, pg 568
Tafelberg Publishers Ltd, pg 569

Spain
Publicacions de l'Abadia de Montserrat, pg 570
Acento Editorial, pg 570
Alberdania SL, pg 571
Alinco SA - Aura Comunicacio, pg 572
Anaya Educacion, pg 573
Ediciones Atril, pg 574
Ediciones B, SA, pg 574
Beascoa SA Ediciones, pg 574
Edicions Bromera SL, pg 575
Edicions Camacuc, pg 575
Editorial Cantabrica SA, pg 575
Editorial Casals SA, pg 575
CEAC, Grupo Editorial SA, pg 576
Celeste Ediciones, pg 576
Central Catequistica Salesiana (CCS), pg 576
Editorial Claret SA, pg 577
Editora Comercial de Publicaciones, pg 577
Creaciones Monar Editorial, pg 578
Ediciones Daly S L, pg 578
Ediciones Destino SA, pg 579
Didaco Comunicacion y Didactica, SA, pg 579
Ediciones Diputacion de Salamanca, pg 579
Diseno Editorial SA, pg 579
Ediciones Ebenezer, pg 580
Edebe, pg 580
Edi-Liber Irlan SA, pg 580
Editorial Everest SA, pg 581
Elkar, Euskal Liburu eta Kantuen Argitaldaria, SL, pg 582
Enciclopedia Catalana, SA, pg 582
Erein, pg 582
Editorial Espasa-Calpe SA, pg 582
Eumo Editorial, pg 583
Galaxia SA Editorial, pg 584
Grijalbo Mondadori SA, pg 585
Grupo Editorial CEAC SA, pg 586
Harlequin Iberica SA, pg 586
Hercules de Ediciones, SA, pg 586
Ibaizabal Edelvives SA, pg 586
Ediciones Internacionales Universitarias SA, pg 588
Ediciones JLA, pg 588
Editorial Juventud SA, pg 588
Laertes SA de Ediciones, pg 588
LEDA (Las Ediciones de Arte), pg 589
Libsa Editorial SA, pg 589
Llibres del Segle, pg 589
Loguez Ediciones, pg 589
Editorial Luis Vives (Edelvives), pg 589
Editorial Lumen SA, pg 589
Edicions de la Magrana SA, pg 590
Editorial Marfil SA, pg 590
La Mascara, SL Editorial, pg 591
Editorial Mediterrania SL, pg 591
Ediciones Mensajero, pg 591
Editorial Molino, pg 592
Editorial Moll SL, pg 592
Mundo Negro Editorial, pg 592
Narcea SA de Ediciones, pg 593
Ediciones Olimpic, SL, pg 594
Editorial Alfredo Ortells SL, pg 594
Parramon Ediciones SA, pg 595
Editorial El Perpetuo Socorro, pg 596
Editorial Perpetuo Socorro, pg 596
Pirene Editorial, sal, pg 596
Editorial Playor SA, pg 596
Pre-Textos, pg 596
Edicions Proa, SA, pg 597
Publicaciones y Ediciones Salamandra SA, pg 597
San Pablo Ediciones, pg 598
Ediciones San Pio X, pg 599
Signament I Comunicacio, SL Signament Edicions, pg 599
Equipo Sirius SA, pg 600
Ediciones Siruela SA, pg 600
Grup 62, pg 600
Ediciones SM, pg 600
Ramon Sopena SA, pg 600
Ediciones Susaeta SA, pg 601
Editorial Sal Terrae, pg 602
Gregorio del Toro Editor, pg 602
Ediciones de la Torre, pg 602
Tursen, SA, pg 603
Ultramar Editores SA, pg 603
Xunta de Galicia, pg 605

Sri Lanka
Dayawansa Jayakody & Co, pg 606
Sunera Publishers, pg 607
Warna Publishers, pg 607

Sweden
Akademiforlaget Corona AB, pg 609
Allt om Hobby AB, pg 609
Berghs, pg 610
Bonnier Carlsen Bokforlag AB, pg 610
Egmont Serieforlaget, pg 611
Ekonomibok Forlag AB, pg 611
Gidlunds Bokforlag, pg 612
Foerlagshuset Gothia, pg 612
Bokforlaget Hegas AB, pg 612
Invandrarfoerlaget, pg 612
Libris Bokforlaget, pg 613
Bokfoerlaget Natur och Kultur, pg 613
Bokforlaget Opal AB, pg 614
Bokforlaget Plus AB, pg 614
Raben och Sjoegren Bokforlag, pg 614
Richters Egmont, pg 615
Sjoestrands Foerlag, pg 615
Var Skola Foerlag AB, pg 616
Verbum Foerlag AB, pg 616
B Wahlstroms, pg 616

Switzerland
Aare-Verlag, pg 617
Atrium Verlag AG, pg 618
Basilius Presse AG, pg 618
Bibellesbund Verlag, pg 619
Blaukreuz-Verlag Bern, pg 619
Werner Classen Verlag, pg 621
Editions Delachaux et Niestle SA, pg 621
Drei Eidgenossen Verlag, pg 622
Editions Eisele SA, pg 622
Globi Verlag AG, pg 624
Gotthelf-Verlag, pg 624
Junod Nicolas, pg 626
E Lopfe-Benz AG Rorschach, Graphische Anstalt und Verlag, pg 628
La Maison de la Bible, pg 628
Orell Fuessli Buchhandlungs AG, pg 630
Pharos-Verlag, Hansrudolf Schwabe AG, pg 631
Verlag Friedrich Reinhardt AG, pg 632
Rex Verlag, pg 632
Rodera-Verlag der Cardun AG, pg 632
Sauerlaender AG, pg 633
Schweizerisches Jugendschriftenwerk, SJW, pg 634
Speer-Verlag, pg 634
Editions 24 Heures, pg 635
J E Wolfensberger AG, pg 637

Taiwan, Province of China
Asian Culture Co Ltd, pg 638
Campus Evangelical Fellowship, Literature Department, pg 639
Chien Chen Bookstore Publishing Company Ltd, pg 639
Chung Hwa Book Co Ltd, pg 639
Echo Publishing Company Ltd, pg 639
Grimm Press Ltd, pg 640
Jillion Publishing Co, pg 640
Laureate Book Co Ltd, pg 640
Linking Publishing Company Ltd, pg 641
Morning Star Publisher Inc, pg 641
Youth Cultural Publishing Co, pg 642

United Republic of Tanzania
East African Publishing House, pg 643
Nyota Publishers Ltd, pg 644
Tanzania Publishing House, pg 644

Thailand
Suksapan Panit (Business Organization of Teachers Council of Thailand), pg 645

Togo
Editions Akpagnon, pg 646
Les Nouvelles Editions Africaines du TOGO (NEA-TOGO), pg 646

Tunisia
Les Editions de l'Arbre, pg 647
Maison Tunisienne de l'Edition, pg 648

Turkey
Altin Kitaplar Yayinevi, pg 649
Arkin Kitabevi, pg 649
Inkilap Publishers Ltd, pg 650
Soez Yayin/Oyunajans, pg 651
Kabalci Yayinevi, pg 652

Uganda
Fountain Publishers Ltd, pg 652

Ukraine
Veselka Publishers, pg 654

United Kingdom
Acair Ltd, pg 655
Act 3 Publishing, pg 655
Aladdin Books Ltd, pg 656
Andersen Press Ltd, pg 657
Andromeda Oxford Ltd, pg 658
Apex Publishing Ltd, pg 658
Appletree Press Ltd, pg 658
Arcturus Publishing Ltd, pg 659
AS Publishing, pg 660
Award Publications Ltd, pg 662
BBC Worldwide Publishers, pg 663
Belitha Press Ltd, pg 664
Blackie Children's Books, pg 666
Bloomsbury Publishing PLC, pg 668
The Book Guild Ltd, pg 668
Books for Europe Ltd, pg 669
Boxtree Ltd, pg 669
Cambridge University Press, pg 674
Canongate Books Ltd, pg 674
The Cartoon Cave, pg 675
Cassell & Co, pg 675
Christian Education, pg 679
Church Union, pg 680
Diagram Visual Information Ltd, pg 687
Dramatic Lines Publishers, pg 688
Encyclopaedia Britannica (UK) International Ltd, pg 691
Eurobook Ltd, pg 692
Helen Exley Giftbooks, pg 693
Feather Books, pg 694
W H Freeman & Co Ltd, pg 697
Gollancz/Witherby, pg 701
Gomer Press (J D Lewis & Sons Ltd), pg 701
Graham-Cameron Publishing & Illustration, pg 701
Grandreams Ltd, pg 702
Grange Books PLC, pg 702
Gwasg y Dref Wen, pg 703
Hamish Hamilton Ltd, pg 704
HarperCollins UK, pg 705
Hodder Children's Books, pg 709
Hodder Headline Ltd, pg 709
Angus Hudson Ltd, pg 710
Islamic Foundation Publications, pg 714
The Islamic Texts Society, pg 715
Janus Publishing Co Ltd, pg 716
Kingfisher Publications Plc, pg 717
Letterbox Library, pg 720
Lion Hudson PLC, pg 721
Y Lolfa Cyf, pg 722
The Lutterworth Press, pg 723
Macmillan Audio Books, pg 723
Macmillan Children's Books, pg 723
Macmillan Heinemann ELT, pg 723
Macmillan Ltd, pg 723
The Medici Society Ltd, pg 726

PUBLISHERS

New Era Publications UK Ltd, pg 732
Norwood Publishers Ltd, pg 734
Octopus Publishing Group, pg 734
Orion Publishing Group Ltd, pg 736
Orpheus Books Ltd, pg 736
Oxford University Press, pg 737
Parapress Ltd, pg 738
Penguin Books Ltd, pg 740
The Penguin Group UK, pg 740
Piccadilly Press, pg 742
Porthill Publishers, pg 744
Portland Press Ltd, pg 745
Quarto Publishing plc, pg 746
Quartz Editions, pg 746
Ragged Bears Ltd, pg 747
Ravette Publishing Ltd, pg 748
The Salariya Book Co Ltd, pg 753
Salvationist Publishing & Supplies Ltd, pg 754
Scholastic Ltd, pg 754
SchoolPlay Productions Ltd, pg 755
Scripture Union, pg 756
Sherbourne Publications, pg 757
Souvenir Press Ltd, pg 759
Supportive Learning Publications, pg 762
Tabb House, pg 762
Telegraph Books, pg 764
Transedition Ltd, pg 766
Two-Can Publishing Ltd, pg 768
Ward Lock Ltd, pg 771
The Women's Press Ltd, pg 775

Venezuela
Alfadil Ediciones, pg 778
Colegial Bolivariana CA, pg 779
Ediciones Ekare, pg 779
Universidad de los Andes, Consejo de Publicaciones, pg 780

Viet Nam
Science & Technics Publishing House, pg 780

Zambia
Zambia Printing Company Ltd (ZPC), pg 782

LARGE PRINT BOOKS

Australia
Bolinda Publishing Pty Ltd, pg 15
Pearson Education Australia, pg 36
Veritas Press, pg 45

Austria
Czernin Verlag Ltd, pg 49

Belarus
Interdigest Publishing House, pg 62

Belgium
Van Hemeldonck NV, pg 68

Bulgaria
Abagar Pablioing, pg 92
Abagar, Veliko Tarnovo, pg 93

China
China Light Industry Press, pg 102
Cultural Relics Publishing House, pg 103
Foreign Language Teaching & Research Press, pg 104

Czech Republic
Granit sro, pg 123

Dominican Republic
Editorama SA, pg 135

Ecuador
Corporacion de Estudios y Publicaciones, pg 136

Estonia
Estonian Academy Publishers, pg 139

France
Editions des Beatitudes, Pneumatheque, pg 149
Editions Chardon Bleu, pg 153
Jean-Michel Place, pg 180
Editions Saint-Michel SA, pg 183

Germany
Agentur des Rauhen Hauses Hamburg GmbH, pg 191
Butzon & Bercker GmbH, pg 206
Deutscher Taschenbuch Verlag GmbH & Co KG (dtv), pg 213
Karl Elser Druck GmbH, pg 216
Econ Verlag GmbH, pg 218
Fabel-Verlag Gudrun Liebchen, pg 223
Margarethe Freudenberger - selbstverlag fur jedermann, pg 227
Verlag der Stiftung Gralsbotschaft GmbH, pg 231
Koptisch-Orthodoxes Zentrum, pg 249
Lahn-Verlag GmbH, pg 251
Verlag der Sankt-Johannis-Druckerei C Schweickhardt, pg 278
K G Saur Verlag GmbH, A Gale/Thomson Learning Company, pg 278
Steyler Verlag, pg 288
Tipress Dienstleistungen fur das Verlagswesen GmbH, pg 291
Wichern Verlag GmbH, pg 299

Ghana
World Literature Project, pg 305

Greece
Akritas, pg 305
Evrodiastasi, pg 307
Zyrichidi Bros, pg 313

Hong Kong
Joint Publishing (HK) Co Ltd, pg 317
Peace Book Co Ltd, pg 318

India
B I Publications Pvt Ltd, pg 329
Reliance Publishing House, pg 346
Star Publications (P) Ltd, pg 350
Vidyarthi Mithram Press, pg 352

Italy
Centro Biblico, pg 381
Cittadella Editrice, pg 382
Edizioni Cultura della Pace, pg 383
Damanhur Edizioni, pg 384
Effata Editrice, pg 387
Museo storico in Trento, pg 400
Casa Editrice Roberto Napoleone, pg 400
Piero Manni srl, pg 403
Vianello Libri, pg 411
Vinciana Editrice sas, pg 412

Japan
Bunkasha Publishing Co Ltd, pg 415
Tankosha Publishing Co Ltd, pg 429

Republic of Korea
YBM/Si-sa, pg 443

Malaysia
Penerbitan Tinta, pg 458

New Zealand
Taylor Books, pg 501

Pakistan
Islamic Publications (Pvt) Ltd, pg 513
National Book Foundation, pg 513

Poland
'Slask' Ltd, pg 526

Portugal
Planeta Editora, LDA, pg 534
Editora Replicacao Lda, pg 535

Russian Federation
CentrePolygraph Traders & Publishers Co, pg 544

Saudi Arabia
Dar Al-Shareef for Publishing & Distribution, pg 550

South Africa
HAUM - Daan Retief Publishers (Pty) Ltd, pg 564
Jacklin Enterprises (Pty) Ltd, pg 565
Publitoria Publishers, pg 568

Spain
Ediciones Alfar SA, pg 572
Edicions Camacuc, pg 575
CEAC, Grupo Editorial SA, pg 576
Ediciones l'Isard, S L, pg 580
Edilesa-Ediciones Leonesas SA, pg 581
Fundacion Marcelino Botin, pg 584
Instituto Provincial de Investigaciones y Estudios Toledanos (IPIET), pg 597
Trea Ediciones, SL, pg 602

Switzerland
Comite international de la Croix-Rouge, pg 621

Taiwan, Province of China
National Museum of History, pg 641

United Kingdom
Bible Reading Fellowship, pg 665
Isis Publishing Ltd, pg 714
Magna Large Print Books, pg 724
Severn House Publishers Inc, pg 756
Ulverscroft Large Print Books Ltd, pg 768

Zimbabwe
Dorothy Duncan Braille & Transcription Library, pg 783

TYPE OF PUBLICATION INDEX

MAPS, ATLASES

Albania
NL SH, pg 1
State Textbook Publishing House, pg 1

Argentina
Aguilar Altea Taurus Alfaguara SA de Ediciones, pg 3
Editorial Ruy Diaz SAEIC, pg 5
Angel Estrada y Cia SA, pg 5
Instituto Nacional de Ciencia y Tecnica Hidrica (INCYTH), pg 7
Oikos, pg 8
Ediciones Preescolar SA, pg 8

Australia
Casket Publications, pg 17
China Books, pg 17
Crawford House Publishing Pty Ltd, pg 18
Encyclopaedia Britannica (Australia) Inc, pg 21
Hema Maps Pty Ltd, pg 25
INT Press, pg 27
Lonely Planet Publications Pty Ltd, pg 29
Melway Publishing Pty Ltd, pg 32
Outdoor Press Pty Ltd, pg 35
Reed Educational Publishing Australia, pg 39
See Australia Guides P/L, pg 40
Universal Press Pty Ltd, pg 44
John Wiley & Sons Australia, Ltd, pg 46

Austria
Freytag-Berndt und Artaria, Kartographische Anstalt, pg 51
Kuemmerly und Frey Verlags GmbH, pg 53
Oesterreichischer Kunst und Kulturverlag, pg 55
Universitaetsverlag Wagner GmbH, pg 59

Belgium
Abimo, pg 62
Carto BVBA, pg 64
Editions De Boeck-Larcier SA, pg 66
Geocart Uitg Cartogr AG Claus BVBA, pg 67
Girault Gilbert bvba, pg 67
Koepel van de Vlaamse Noord - Zuidbeweging 11.11.11, pg 69
Michelin Editions des Voyages, pg 71
Uitgeverij De Sikkel NV, pg 73
Standaard Uitgeverij, pg 73

Botswana
The Botswana Society, pg 76

Brazil
Fundacao Instituto Brasileiro de Geografia e Estatistica (IBGE - CDDI/DECOP), pg 82
Editora Harbra Ltda, pg 83
Libreria Editora Ltda, pg 85
Editora Scipione Ltda, pg 90
Editora Vigilia Ltda, pg 92

Bulgaria
Abagar Pablioing, pg 92
DATAMAP - Europe, pg 94
Prosveta Publishers AS, pg 96
Prozoretz Ltd Publishing House, pg 96

TYPE OF PUBLICATION INDEX

BOOK

Chile
Instituto Geografico Militar, pg 99
Zig-Zag SA, pg 101

China
Chengdu Maps Publishing House, pg 101
China Cartographic Publishing House, pg 102
China Ocean Press, pg 102
The People's Communications Publishing House, pg 106
Science Press, pg 107
Xi'an Cartography Publishing House, pg 109

Colombia
Eurolibros Ltda, pg 111
Migema Ediciones Ltda, pg 112
Editorial Santillana SA, pg 112

Costa Rica
Litografia Artex, SA, pg 115
Union Mundial para la Naturaleza (UICN), Oficina Regional para Mesoamerica, pg 116

Croatia
ALFA dd za izdavacke, graficke i trgovacke poslove, pg 117
Leksikografski Zavod Miroslav Krleza, pg 118
Masmedia, pg 118

Czech Republic
Karmelitanske Nakladatelstvi, pg 124
Kartografie Praha, pg 124

Denmark
Kraks Forlag AS, pg 132
Scan-Globe A/S, pg 134

Egypt (Arab Republic of Egypt)
Lehnert & Landrock Bookshop, pg 138

Estonia
Eesti Entsuklopeediakirjastus, pg 139
Eesti Piibliselts, pg 139
Sinisukk, pg 140

France
Autrement Editions, pg 148
Blay Foldex, pg 150
Blondel La Rougery SARL, pg 150
Editions BRGM, pg 151
Editions du Cadratin, pg 151
Cirad, pg 154
Les Devenirs Visuels, pg 158
Encyclopedia Universalis France SA, pg 161
Librairie Artheme Fayard, pg 163
Federation Francaise de la Randonnee Pedestre, pg 163
Editions Jean Paul Gisserot, pg 165
Groupe Hatier International, pg 166
Hachette Education, pg 166
INRA Editions (Institut National de la Recherche Agronomique), pg 168
Institut Geographique National IGN, pg 169
IRD Editions, pg 169
Editions Marcus, pg 174
Editions MDI (La Maison des Instituteurs), pg 175
Editions Memo, pg 175
Editions Franck Mercier, pg 175
Michelin Editions des Voyages, pg 175
Publications de l'Universite de Rouen, pg 182
Selection du Reader's Digest SA, pg 184
Societe Nouveaux Loisirs, pg 185
Taride Editions, pg 187
Editions Technip SA, pg 187
Editions Vilo SA, pg 189

Germany
Aufstieg-Verlag GmbH, pg 195
Bayerischer Schulbuch-Verlag GmbH, pg 198
Berndtson & Berndtson GmbH Verlag-Publishing, pg 199
Bertelsmann Lexikon Verlag GmbH, pg 200
Bibliographisches Institut & F A Brockhaus AG, pg 200
Bielefelder Verlagsanstalt GmbH & Co KG Richard Kaselowsky, pg 201
Bollmann-Bildkarten-Verlag GmbH & Co KG, pg 203
Kartographischer Verlag Busche GmbH, pg 206
CartoTravel Verlag GmbH & Co KG, pg 207
Columbus Verlag Paul Oestergaard GmbH, pg 209
Cornelsen Verlag GmbH & Co OHG, pg 210
Verlagsgruppe Droemer Knaur GmbH & Co KG, pg 216
Emil Fink Verlag, pg 224
Franckh-Kosmos Verlags-GmbH & Co, pg 226
Gebrueder Borntraeger Science Publishers, pg 228
GeoCenter Touristik Medienservice GmbH, pg 228
Gloatz, Hille GmbH & Co KG fur Mehrfarben und Zellglasdruck, pg 229
Axel Hertenstein, Hertenstein-Presse, pg 237
Karto + Grafik Verlagsgesellschaft (K & G Verlagsgesellschaft), pg 244
Kartographischer Verlag Reinhard Ryborsch, pg 244
Ernst Klett Verlag GmbH, pg 247
Knowledge Media International, pg 247
Karin Mader, pg 256
Mairs Geographischer Verlag, pg 256
Mairs Geographischer Verlag Kurt Mair GmbH & Co, pg 257
Naumann & Goebel Verlagsgesellschaft mbH, pg 263
Nelles Verlag GmbH, pg 263
Neuer Honos Verlag GmbH, pg 264
Justus Perthes Verlag Gotha GmbH, pg 269
Ravenstein Verlag GmbH, pg 274
Dr Ludwig Reichert Verlag, pg 274
E Reinhold Verlag, pg 275
Verlagsgruppe Reise Know-How, pg 275
R V Reise- und Verkehrsverlag GmbH, pg 275
E Schweizerbart'sche Verlagsbuchhandlung (Naegele und Obermiller), pg 282
Springer Science+Business Media GmbH & Co KG, pg 284
Staedte-Verlag, E v Wagner und J Mitterhuber GmbH, pg 286
Steiger Verlag, pg 287
Stiefel Eurocart GmbH, pg 288
Guenter Albert Ulmer Verlag, pg 293
Wachholtz Verlag GmbH, pg 297
Weidlich Verlag, pg 298
Westermann Schulbuchverlag GmbH, pg 299
Herbert Wichmann Verlag, pg 299

Ghana
Unimax Macmillan Ltd, pg 305

Greece
Anixis Publications, pg 305
Dodoni Publications, pg 306
Ekdoseis Domi AE, pg 306
Giovanis Publications, Pangosmios Ekdotikos Organismos, pg 307
Hestia-I D Hestia-Kollaros & Co Corporation, pg 308
Ianos, pg 308
Ilias Kambanas Publishing Organization, SA, pg 309
Patakis Publishers, pg 311
Toubis M, pg 312

Haiti
Editions Caraibes SA, pg 314

Hong Kong
Chung Hwa Book Co (HK) Ltd, pg 316
Geocarto International Centre, pg 317
Lands Department, Survey & Mapping Office, pg 318
Ling Kee Publishing Group, pg 318

Hungary
Cartographia Ltd, pg 321
Officina Nova Konyvek, pg 323
Szarvas Andras Cartographic Agency, pg 324

Iceland
Mal og menning, pg 326
Namsgagnastofnun, pg 326

India
Addison-Wesley Pte Ltd, pg 327
Indian Book Depot, pg 336
Kali For Women, pg 339
National Book Organization, pg 342
Rajendra Publishing House Pvt Ltd, pg 346
Scientific Book Agency, pg 348

Indonesia
Bina Aksara Parta, pg 354
Djambatan PT, pg 354
Mutiara Sumber Widya PT, pg 356
PATCO, pg 356

Ireland
An Gum, pg 358
Royal Irish Academy, pg 363
Tir Eolas, pg 363

Israel
Carta, The Israel Map & Publishing Co Ltd, pg 365
Kiryat Sefer, pg 369
MAP-Mapping & Publishing Ltd, pg 370
Steimatzky Group Ltd, pg 372
Steinhart-Katzir Publishers, pg 372
Terra Sancta Arts, pg 372
Yavneh Publishing House Ltd, pg 373

Italy
De Agostini Scolastica, pg 374
Gruppo Editoriale Armenia SpA, pg 376
Athesia Verlag Bozen, pg 377
Capone Editore SRL, pg 379
Edizioni Cartografiche Milanesi, pg 380
Centro Biblico, pg 381
Editrice Eraclea, pg 388
EuroGeoGrafiche Mencattini, pg 388
Istituto Geografico de Agostini SpA, pg 390
Bruno Ghigi Editore, pg 390
Editoriale Jaca Book SpA, pg 394
Kompass Fleischmann, pg 394
LAC - Litografia Artistica Cartografica Srl, pg 394
Leo S Olschki, pg 401
Red/Studio Redazionale, pg 405
Edizioni del Riccio SAS di G Bernardi, pg 405
Lo Scarabeo Srl, pg 407
Vallardi Industrie Grafiche, pg 411

Jamaica
American Chamber of Commerce of Jamaica, pg 413
Carib Publishing Ltd, pg 413

Japan
Japan Travel Bureau Inc, pg 420
Rinsen Book Co Ltd, pg 425
Shobunsha Publications Inc, pg 427
Teikoku-Shoin Co Ltd, pg 429
Tokyo Shoseki Co Ltd, pg 430

Kenya
Heinemann Kenya Ltd (EAEP), pg 434
Kenway Publications Ltd, pg 434
Macmillan Kenya Publishers Ltd, pg 435
Transafrica Press, pg 436

Democratic People's Republic of Korea
Academy of Sciences Publishing House, pg 436
Korea Science and Encyclopedia Publishing House, pg 436

Republic of Korea
Korea Britannica Corp, pg 440

Kuwait
Ministry of Information, pg 444

Latvia
Preses Nams, pg 445

Lebanon
GEOprojects Sarl, pg 446
Khayat Book and Publishing Co Sarl, pg 446

Luxembourg
Service Central de la Statistique et des Etudes Economiques (STATEC), pg 451

Malaysia
Panther Publishing, pg 457
Penerbit Fajar Bakti Sdn Bhd, pg 457

PUBLISHERS

Mexico
Editorial Avante SA de Cv, pg 462
Editorial Diana SA de CV, pg 464
Fernandez Editores SA de CV, pg 465
Fondo de Cultura Economica, pg 465
Organizacion Cultural LP SA de CV, pg 469
Instituto Panamericano de Geografia e Historia, pg 469
Ediciones Suromex SA, pg 472

Morocco
Dar Nachr Al Maarifa Pour L'Edition et La Distribution, pg 474

Namibia
Desert Research Foundation of Namibia (DRFN), pg 476

Netherlands
Buijten en Schipperheijn BV Drukkerij en Uitgeversmaatschappij, pg 480
Wegener Falkplan BV, pg 492

New Caledonia
Savannah Editions SARL, pg 493

New Zealand
Hodder Moa Beckett Publishers Ltd, pg 497
Southern Press Ltd, pg 501

Norway
J W Cappelens Forlag A/S, pg 508

Oman
Apex Press & Publishing, pg 511

Pakistan
Sang-e-Meel Publications, pg 514

Peru
Carvajal SA, pg 516
Editorial Lima 2000 SA, pg 517

Philippines
Bookman Printing & Publishing House Inc, pg 518

Poland
Biblioteka Narodowa, pg 522
Instytut Meteorologii i Gospodarki Wodnej, pg 523
Panstwowe Przedsiebiorstwo Wydawnictw Kartograficznych, pg 525
'Slask' Ltd, pg 526

Portugal
Constancia Editores, SA, pg 530
Distri Cultural Lda, pg 530
Everest Editora, pg 531
Imprensa Nacional-Casa da Moeda, pg 532
Instituto de Investigacao Cientifica Tropical, pg 532
Porto Editora Lda, pg 535
Ediciões Joao Sa da Costa Lda, pg 535
Turinta-Turismo Internacional, pg 536

Romania
Editura Academiei Romane, pg 538
Corint Publishing Group, pg 539
Editura Didactica si Pedagogica, pg 539
Editura Militara, pg 541
Vox Editura, pg 543

Russian Federation
Gidrometeoizdat, pg 545
Izdatelstvo Prosveshchenie, pg 548

Serbia and Montenegro
Naucna Knjiga, pg 552
Turisticka Stampa, pg 554

Slovenia
Mladinska Knjiga International, pg 561

South Africa
Brabys Brochures, pg 563
Jacana Education, pg 565
New Africa Books (Pty) Ltd, pg 567
Struik Publishers (Pty) Ltd, pg 569

Spain
Aguilar SA de Ediciones, pg 571
Ediciones Akal SA, pg 571
Anaya Educacion, pg 573
Anaya-Touring Club, pg 573
Arco Libros SL, pg 573
Editorial Bruno, pg 575
Comunidad Autonoma de Madrid, Servicio de Documentacion y Publicaciones, pg 578
Ediciones Diputacion de Salamanca, pg 579
Edebe, pg 580
Edigol Ediciones SA, pg 581
Edilesa-Ediciones Leonesas SA, pg 581
Editorial Everest SA, pg 581
Enciclopedia Catalana, SA, pg 582
Erein, pg 582
Editorial Espasa-Calpe SA, pg 582
Generalitat de Catalunya Diari Oficial de la Generalitat vern, pg 584
Editorial Herder SA, pg 586
Institucion Fernando el Catolico de la Excma Diputacion de Zaragoza, pg 587
Ediciones Istmo SA, pg 588
Larousse Editorial SA, pg 588
Editorial la Muralla SA, pg 592
Ediciones Nauta Credito SA, pg 593
Instituto Provincial de Investigaciones y Estudios Toledanos (IPIET), pg 597
Grup 62, pg 600
Ramon Sopena SA, pg 600
Tursen, SA, pg 603

Sri Lanka
Colombo Book Association, pg 606

Suriname
Vaco NV Uitgeversmij, pg 608

Switzerland
Ammann Verlag & Co, pg 617
Cockatoo Press (Schweiz), Thailand-Publikationen, pg 621
Hallwag Kuemmerly & Frey AG, pg 625
Kuemmerly & Frey (Geographischer Verlag), pg 627
Schweizerische Stiftung fuer Alpine Forschungen, pg 634
Verlag Stocker-Schmid AG, pg 635
World Meteorological Organization, pg 637

United Republic of Tanzania
Ben and Company Ltd, pg 643
Tanzania Publishing House, pg 644

Thailand
Thai Watana Panich Co, Ltd, pg 646
White Lotus Co Ltd, pg 646

Trinidad & Tobago
Joan Bacchus-Xavier, pg 646

Turkey
Altin Kitaplar Yayinevi, pg 649
Arkeoloji Ve Sanat Yayinlari, pg 649
Arkin Kitabevi, pg 649
Eren Yayincilik ve Kitapcilik Ltd Sti, pg 650
IKI Nokta Research Press & Publications Industry & Trade Ltd, pg 650
Iletisim Yayinlari, pg 650
Inkilap Publishers Ltd, pg 650
Remzi Kitabevi, pg 651
Saray Medikal Yayin Tic Ltd Sti, pg 651

Ukraine
Derzhavne Naukovo-Vyrobnyche Pidpryemstro Kartografia, pg 653

United Kingdom
A A Publishing, pg 654
Absolute Press, pg 655
Advisory Unit: Computers in Education, pg 655
Ian Allan Publishing Ltd, pg 656
Andromeda Oxford Ltd, pg 658
AS Publishing, pg 660
BCA - Book Club Associates, pg 663
Belitha Press Ltd, pg 664
Books for Europe Ltd, pg 669
Books of Zimbabwe Publishing Co (Pvt) Ltd, pg 669
Bwrdd Croeso Cymru, pg 673
Compass Maps Ltd, pg 681
Leo Cooper, pg 683
G L Crowther, pg 684
Discovery Walking Guides Ltd, pg 687
Dorling Kindersley Ltd, pg 688
Encyclopaedia Britannica (UK) International Ltd, pg 691
Express Newspapers, pg 693
The Factory Shop Guide, pg 694
Folens Ltd, pg 695
Forth Naturalist & Historian, pg 696
Garnet Publishing Ltd, pg 698
Geographers' A-Z Map Company Ltd, pg 699
Grange Books PLC, pg 702
The Greek Bookshop, pg 702
Greenhill Books/Lionel Leventhal Ltd, pg 703
HarperCollins UK, pg 705
Harvey Map Services Ltd, pg 705
Angus Hudson Ltd, pg 710
Islamic Foundation Publications, pg 714
Kuperard, pg 718
Roger Lascelles, pg 719
Lonely Planet, UK, pg 722

Macmillan Heinemann ELT, pg 723
Michelin Tyre PLC, Tourism Dept, Maps & Guides Division, pg 728
National Library of Wales, pg 731
New Holland Publishers (UK) Ltd, pg 732
Octopus Publishing Group, pg 734
Oilfield Publications Ltd, pg 734
Old Vicarage Publications, pg 734
Ordnance Survey, pg 736
Orpheus Books Ltd, pg 736
Oxford University Press, pg 737
Pearson Education, pg 739
Pen & Sword Books Ltd, pg 740
Philip's, pg 741
RAC Publishing, pg 747
The Reader's Digest Association Ltd, pg 748
Rough Guides Ltd, pg 751
Shire Publications Ltd, pg 757
Telegraph Books, pg 764

Uruguay
EQ Opciones en Educacion, pg 777
A Monteverde y Cia SA, pg 777

Venezuela
Armitano Editores CA, pg 779

Zimbabwe
National Archives of Zimbabwe, pg 784

MICROCOMPUTER SOFTWARE

Australia
Bible Society in Australia National Headquarters, pg 14
R J Cleary Publishing, pg 18

Austria
Oesterreichischer Bundesverlag Gmbh, pg 55

Belgium
Easy Computing NV, pg 67
Marabout, pg 71
Uitgeverij De Sikkel NV, pg 73
Wolters Kluwer Belgie NV, pg 74

Brazil
Livraria Alema Ltda Brasileitura, pg 77
Editora Campus Ltda, pg 79
Livraria Pioneira Editora/Enio Matheus Guazzelli e Cia Ltd, pg 88

Bulgaria
Aleks Soft, pg 93
Foi-Commerce, pg 94
Makros 2000 - Plovdiv, pg 95
Pensoft Publishers, pg 96

Chile
Edeval (Universidad de Valparaiso), pg 99

China
Aviation Industry Press, pg 101
Beijing University Press, pg 101
China Machine Press (CMP), pg 102
Electronics Industry Publishing House, pg 104
Fudan University Press, pg 104

TYPE OF PUBLICATION INDEX — BOOK

Guizhou Education Publishing House, pg 105
Jilin Science & Technology Publishing House, pg 105
Shandong University Press, pg 108
Shanghai Educational Publishing House, pg 108
Southwest China Jiaotong University Press, pg 108
Tianjin Science & Technology Publishing House, pg 108
Wuhan University Press, pg 109

Colombia
Pearson Educacion de Colombia LTDA, pg 112

Croatia
Skolska Knjiga, pg 119

Cuba
Apocalipis Digital, pg 120
Instituto de Informacion Cientifica y Tecnologica (IDICT), pg 120
Editora Politica, pg 120

Denmark
Schultz Information, pg 134
Systime, pg 135

Finland
Docendo Finland Oy, pg 141

France
Agence Bibliographique de l'Enseignement Superieur, pg 146
IRD Editions, pg 169
Sybex, pg 186

Germany
ARCult Media, pg 193
Data Becker GmbH & Co KG, pg 210
Deutscher Adressbuch-Verlag fuer Wirtschaft und Verkehr GmbH, pg 212
expert verlag GmbH, Fachverlag fuer Wirtschaft & Technik, pg 222
Feltron-Elektronik Zeissler & Co GmbH, pg 223
Ferd Dummler's Verlag, pg 223
Verlag Ernst und Werner Gieseking GmbH, pg 229
Hans Holzmann Verlag GmbH und Co KG, pg 239
Langenscheidt KG, pg 252
Verlag Neue Wirtschafts-Briefe GmbH & Co, pg 264
Sybex Verlag GmbH, pg 289
Wiley-VCH Verlag GmbH, pg 300

Greece
Hestia-I D Hestia-Kollaros & Co Corporation, pg 308
Kleidarithmos, Ekdoseis, pg 309
Scripta Theofilus Palevratzis-Ashover, pg 312

Iceland
Namsgagnastofnun, pg 326

India
Affiliated East West Press Pvt Ltd, pg 327
Nem Chand & Brothers, pg 343
Pitambar Publishing Co (P) Ltd, pg 345

Scientific Book Agency, pg 348
Vidyarthi Mithram Press, pg 352

Indonesia
Dinastindo, pg 354
Gramedia, pg 355
PT Indira, pg 355

Israel
Rolnik Publishers, pg 371

Italy
Sardini Editrice, pg 407
Societa Editrice Internazionale - SEI, pg 408
Societa Stampa Sportiva, pg 408

Japan
Gakken Co Ltd, pg 417
Hokuryukan Co Ltd, pg 418
Nippon Jitsuyo Publishing Co Ltd, pg 424
Shingakusha Co Ltd, pg 427

Republic of Korea
Ke Mong Sa Publishing Co Ltd, pg 440

The Former Yugoslav Republic of Macedonia
Medis, Skopje, pg 452

Mexico
Editora Cientifica Medica Latinoamerican SA de CV, pg 463
Ventura Ediciones, SA de CV, pg 473

Netherlands
Elmar BV, pg 482
Hagen & Stam Uitgeverij Ten, pg 483
LCG Malmberg BV, pg 485

Norway
Kunnskapsforlaget ANS, pg 509

Paraguay
Instituto de Ciencias de la Computacion (NCR), pg 516

Poland
Biblioteka Narodowa, pg 522
Oficyna Wydawnicza Read Me, pg 526

Portugal
FCA Editora de Informatica, pg 531
Lua Viajante-Edicao e Distribuicao de Livros e Material Audiovisual, Lda, pg 533

Romania
Editura Militara, pg 541
Editura Teora, pg 542

Russian Federation
N E Bauman Moscow State Technical University Publishers, pg 544
Izdatelstvo Mir, pg 546

Slovakia
Ustav informacii a prognoz skolstva mladeze a telovychovy, pg 561

Spain
Marcombo SA, pg 590
Pentalfa Ediciones, pg 595
Pulso Ediciones, SL, pg 597

Taiwan, Province of China
Dayi Information Co, pg 639
Lead Wave Publishing Company Ltd, pg 640
Shuttle Multimedia Inc, pg 641

Turkey
Alkim Kitapcilik-Yayimcilik, pg 649
Arkadas Ltd, pg 649
Kok Yayincilik, pg 650

Ukraine
ASK Ltd, pg 653

United Kingdom
Advisory Unit: Computers in Education, pg 655
British Educational Communication & Technology Agency (BECTA), pg 671
Castlemead Publications, pg 676
Computer Step, pg 681
Elm Publications, pg 691
First & Best in Education Ltd, pg 695
The NFER-NELSON Publishing Co Ltd, pg 733
Oxford University Press, pg 737
Telegraph Books, pg 764
Wiley Europe Ltd, pg 773

PAPERBACK BOOKS - MASS MARKET

Algeria
Enterprise Nationale du Livre (ENAL), pg 2

Argentina
Editorial Acme SA, pg 3
Ada Korn Editora SA, pg 3
Alianza Editorial de Argentina SA, pg 3
Argentine Bible Society, pg 3
Beas Ediciones SRL, pg 4
Emece Editores SA, pg 5
Ediciones de la Flor SRL, pg 6
Editorial Galerna SRL, pg 6
Editorial Kier SACIFI, pg 7
Editorial Sopena Argentina SACI e I, pg 9

Australia
Aletheia Publishing, pg 11
Allen & Unwin Pty Ltd, pg 11
Ashling Books, pg 12
Austed Publishing Co, pg 12
Candlelight Trust T/A Candlelight Farm, pg 17
R J Cleary Publishing, pg 18
Cornford Press, pg 18
Crossroad Distributors Pty Ltd, pg 18
David Ell Press Pty Ltd, pg 21
Extraordinary People Press, pg 22
Garr Publishing, pg 23
Garradunga Press, pg 23
Hale & Iremonger Pty Ltd, pg 24
HarperCollinsReligious, pg 25
Hartys Creek Press, pg 25
Hodder Headline Australia, pg 26
In-Tune Books, pg 26
Joval Publications, pg 28

Levanter Publishing & Associates, pg 29
Little Hills Press Pty Ltd, pg 29
Magabala Books Aboriginal Corporation, pg 30
Matthias Media, pg 31
Mayne Publishing, pg 31
Media East Press, pg 31
New Creation Publications Ministries & Resource Centre, pg 33
New Endeavour Press, pg 33
New Era Publications Australia Pty Ltd, pg 33
Nimrod Publications, pg 33
Parabel Place, pg 35
Pascoe Publishing Pty Ltd, pg 36
Penguin Group (Australia), pg 36
Pinevale Publications, pg 36
Plantagenet Press, pg 37
Playlab Press, pg 37
Pluto Press Australia Pty Ltd, pg 37
Raincloud Productions, pg 38
Random House Australia, pg 38
Rankin Publishers, pg 39
St Pauls Publications, pg 40
Scholastic Australia Pty Ltd, pg 40
Scroll Publishers, pg 40
Simon & Schuster (Australia) Pty Ltd, pg 41
Tarka Publishing, pg 42
Transworld Publishers Pty Ltd, pg 44
Tropicana Press, pg 44
University of Queensland Press, pg 45
The Useful Publishing Co, pg 45
Veritas Press, pg 45
Vista Publications, pg 45

Austria
DachsVerlag GmbH, pg 49
Johannes Heyn GmbH & Co KG, pg 52

Belarus
Interdigest Publishing House, pg 62

Belgium
EPO Publishers, Printers, Booksellers, pg 67
Editions Hemma, pg 68
Claude Lefrancq Editeur, pg 70
Marabout, pg 71
Roularta Books NV, pg 72
Scoop Infotex NV, pg 73
Sonneville Press (Uitgeverij) VTW, pg 73

Bermuda
The Bermudian Publishing Co, pg 75

Bolivia
Gisbert y Cia SA, pg 75

Brazil
Editora Agora Ltda, pg 77
Editora Aquariana Ltda, pg 77
Editora Campus Ltda, pg 79
Editora Forense Universitaria Ltda, pg 81
Editora Melhoramentos Ltda, pg 86
MG Editores Associados Ltda, pg 86
Ediouro Publicacoes, SA, pg 89
Summus Editorial Ltda, pg 91
Zip Editora Ltda, pg 92

PUBLISHERS

Bulgaria

Aratron, IK, pg 93
DA-Izdatelstvo Publishers, pg 93
EA EOOD, pg 94
Eurasia Academic Publishers, pg 94
Pejo K Javorov Publishing House, pg 95
Kibea Publishing Co, pg 95
Kralica MAB, pg 95
Litera Prima, pg 95
Naouka i Izkoustvo, Ltd, pg 95
Prozoretz Ltd Publishing House, pg 96
Sluntse Publishing House, pg 97
Svetra Publishing House, pg 97
TEMTO, pg 97
Trud - Izd kasta, pg 97
Ivan Vazov Publishing House, pg 97
Zunica, pg 97

Cameroon

Centre d'Edition et de Production pour l'Enseignement et la Recherche (CEPER), pg 98
Editions Semences Africaines, pg 98

Chile

Edeval (Universidad de Valparaiso), pg 99
Editorial Texido Ltda, pg 100
Zig-Zag SA, pg 101

China

Anhui People's Publishing House, pg 101
Beijing Publishing House, pg 101
China Materials Management Publishing House, pg 102
CITIC Publishing House, pg 103
Foreign Language Teaching & Research Press, pg 104
Guangdong Science & Technology Press, pg 105
Heilongjiang Science & Technology Press, pg 105
Inner Mongolia Science & Technology Publishing House, pg 105
Jilin Science & Technology Publishing House, pg 105
Language Publishing House, pg 106
Lanzhou University Press, pg 106
Science Press, pg 107
Shanghai Far East Publishers, pg 108
World Affairs Press, pg 109
Writers' Publishing House, pg 109

Colombia

Editorial Oveja Negra Ltda, pg 112
RAM Editores, pg 112

The Democratic Republic of the Congo

Centre Protestant d'Editions et de Diffusion (CEDI), pg 114
Presses Universitaires du Zaiire (PUZ), pg 114

Costa Rica

Editorial Universitaria Centroamericana (EDUCA), pg 117

Cote d'Ivoire

Akohi Editions, pg 117
Centre de Publications Evangeliques, pg 117
Centre d'Edition et de Diffusion Africaines, pg 117

Croatia

Skolska Knjiga, pg 119

Cuba

Editora Politica, pg 120

Czech Republic

Pavla Momcilova, pg 125
Svoboda Servis GmbH, pg 127

Denmark

Bogan's Forlag, pg 129
Bonnier Publications A/S, pg 129
Borgens Forlag A/S, pg 129
Forlaget Forum, pg 131
Gyldendalske Boghandel - Nordisk Forlag A/S, pg 131
Hekla Forlag, pg 131
Holkenfeldt 3, pg 132
Interpresse A/S, pg 132
Lindhardt og Ringhof Forlag A/S, pg 132
Nyt Nordisk Forlag Arnold Busck A/S, pg 133
Joergen Paludan Forlag ApS, pg 133
Rosenkilde & Bagger, pg 134
Scandinavia Publishing House, pg 134
Det Schonbergske Forlag A/S, pg 134
Forlaget Vindrose A/S, pg 135

Dominican Republic

Pontificia Universidad Catolica Madre y Maestra, pg 136

Egypt (Arab Republic of Egypt)

Middle East Book Centre, pg 138

Estonia

Kupar Publishers, pg 139
Olion Publishers, pg 140
Sinisukk, pg 140

Finland

Kirja-Leitzinger, pg 142

France

Alsatia SA, pg 146
Berger-Levrault Editions SAS, pg 149
Editions du Cerf, pg 153
Editeurs Crepin-Leblond, pg 156
Editions Des Femmes, pg 163
Editions First, pg 163
Editions Gerard de Villiers, pg 165
Editions Jean Paul Gisserot, pg 165
Hachette Livre, pg 167
Harlequin SA, pg 167
Editions Hazan, pg 167
Editions J'ai Lu, pg 169
Editions Larousse, pg 171
Editions Dominique Leroy, pg 171
Editions Lito, pg 172
Le Livre de Poche-L G F (Librairie Generale Francaise), pg 173
Presence Africaine Editions, pg 180
Presses Universitaires de France (PUF), pg 181
Editions Sand et Tchou SA, pg 184
Editions Seghers, pg 184
Editions Andre Silvaire Sarl, pg 185
Editions Tallandier, pg 187
10/18, pg 187

Germany

Anabas-Verlag Guenter Kaempf GmbH & Co KG, pg 192
Arena Verlag GmbH, pg 193
Argument-Verlag, pg 194
Aufbau Taschenbuch Verlag GmbH, pg 195
Aufbau-Verlag GmbH, pg 195
Aussaat Verlag, pg 195
J P Bachem Verlag GmbH, pg 196
Bastei Luebbe Taschenbuecher, pg 197
Bastei Verlag, pg 197
Beerenverlag, pg 198
Bertelsmann Lexikon Verlag GmbH, pg 200
Bock und Herchen Verlag, pg 202
Gustav Bosse GmbH & Co KG, pg 203
R Brockhaus Verlag, pg 204
Catia Monser Eggcup-Verlag, pg 207
Christliches Verlagshaus GmbH, pg 208
Verlag Harri Deutsch, pg 211
Deutscher Taschenbuch Verlag GmbH & Co KG (dtv), pg 213
Verlagsgruppe Droemer Knaur GmbH & Co KG, pg 216
DuMont Reiseverlag GmbH & Co KG, pg 217
Dustri-Verlag Dr Karl Feistle, pg 217
Econ Verlag GmbH, pg 218
Eremiten-Presse und Verlag GmbH, pg 220
Rita G Fischer Verlag, pg 225
S Fischer Verlag GmbH, pg 225
Verlag Freies Geistesleben, pg 227
Verlag A Fromm im Druck- u Verlagshaus Fromm GmbH & Co KG, pg 227
Grabert-Verlag, pg 230
Gunter Olzog Verlag GmbH, pg 231
Guetersloher Verlagshaus, pg 232
Haag und Herchen Verlag GmbH, pg 232
Hohenrain-Verlag GmbH, pg 239
Humboldt-Taschenbuch Verlag Jacobi KG, pg 240
KBV Verlags-und Medien - GmbH, pg 245
SachBuchVerlag Kellner, pg 245
Koptisch-Orthodoxes Zentrum, pg 249
Verlagsgruppe Luebbe GmbH & Co KG, pg 256
Philipp Reclam Jun Verlag GmbH, pg 269
Propylaeen Verlag, Zweigniederlassung Berlin der Ullstein Buchverlage GmbH, pg 272
Radius-Verlag GmbH, pg 273
Rake Verlag GmbH, pg 273
Ravensburger Buchverlag Otto Maier GmbH, pg 274
Rowohlt Verlag GmbH, pg 277
Verlag an der Ruhr GmbH, pg 277
Scheffler-Verlag, pg 279
Steiger Verlag, pg 287
J F Steinkopf Verlag GmbH, pg 287
Tetra Verlag Gmbh, pg 290
B G Teubner Verlag, pg 290
Tipress Dienstleistungen fur das Verlagswesen GmbH, pg 291
Trotzdem-Verlags Genossenschaft eG, pg 292

TYPE OF PUBLICATION INDEX

Tuebinger Vereinigung fur Volkskunde eV (TVV), pg 292
Verlag Eugen Ulmer GmbH & Co, pg 293
VDI Verlag GmbH, pg 294
Walhalla Fachverlag GmbH & Co KG Praetoria, pg 297
Georg Westermann Verlag GmbH, pg 299
Xenos Verlagsgesellschaft mbH, pg 301

Ghana

Africa Christian Press, pg 303
Anowuo Educational Publications, pg 303
Ghana Publishing Corporation, pg 304
Moxon Paperbacks, pg 304
Waterville Publishing House, pg 305

Greece

Chrysi Penna - Golden Pen Books, pg 306
Ekdotikos Oikos Adelfon Kyriakidi A E, pg 307
Harlenic Hellas Publishing SA, pg 308
Kalentis & Sia, pg 308
Kedros Publishers, pg 309
Logos, pg 309
Proskinio Spyros Ch Marinis, pg 311

Guadeloupe

JASOR, pg 313

Guatemala

Grupo Editorial RIN-78, pg 313

Hong Kong

Design Human Resources Training & Development, pg 317
Joint Publishing (HK) Co Ltd, pg 317
Ming Pao Publications Ltd, pg 318
Research Centre for Translation, pg 319
SCMP Book Publishing Ltd, pg 319

Hungary

Agape Ferences Nyomda es Konyvkiado Kft, pg 320
Magveto Koenyvkiado, pg 322
Szepirodalmi Koenyvkiado Kiado, pg 324
Tajak Korok Muzeumok Egyesuelet, pg 324

Iceland

Frjals fjolmiolun hf-Urvalsbaekur, pg 325

India

Addison-Wesley Pte Ltd, pg 327
Amar Prakashan, pg 328
Atma Ram & Sons, pg 329
Diamond Comics (P) Ltd, pg 333
Galgotia Publications Pvt Ltd, pg 334
Geeta Prakashan, pg 335
General Book Depot, pg 335
Arnold Heinman Publishers (India) Pvt Ltd, pg 335
Hindi Pracharak Sansthan, pg 336
Indian Book Depot, pg 336
Indian Council of Agricultural Research, pg 336
Kali For Women, pg 339

TYPE OF PUBLICATION INDEX BOOK

Lancer Publisher's & Distributors, pg 340
Mehta Publishers, pg 341
Natraj Prakashan, Publishers & Exporters, pg 343
Orient Paperbacks, pg 344
People's Publishing House (P) Ltd, pg 345
Popular Prakashan Pvt Ltd, pg 345
Rajkamal Prakashan Pvt Ltd, pg 346
Reliance Publishing House, pg 346
SABDA, pg 347
Sasta Sahitya Mandal, pg 348
Scientific Book Agency, pg 348
Star Publications (P) Ltd, pg 350
Sterling Information Technologies, pg 350
Sterling Publishers Pvt Ltd, pg 350
Tata McGraw-Hill Publishing Co Ltd, pg 351
Vision Books Pvt Ltd, pg 352

Indonesia
PT Indira, pg 355

Ireland
Ballinakella Press, pg 358
Brandon Book Publishers Ltd, pg 358
The Collins Press, pg 358
Emerald Publications, pg 359
The Hannon Press, pg 361
Mount Eagle Publications Ltd, pg 362
New Writers' Press, pg 362
The O'Brien Press Ltd, pg 362
On Stream Publications Ltd, pg 362

Israel
Am Oved Publishers Ltd, pg 365
Bitan Publishers Ltd, pg 365
Schocken Publishing House Ltd, pg 371
Sifriat Poalim Ltd, pg 372
Steimatzky Group Ltd, pg 372

Italy
Cappelli Editore, pg 380
Casa Editrice Libraria Ulrico Hoepli SpA, pg 380
Crisalide, pg 383
Edizioni Dedalo SRL, pg 384
Ediciclo Editore SRL, pg 386
Edizioni del Centro Camuno di Studi Preistorici, pg 386
EDT Edizioni di Torino, pg 387
Giulio Einaudi Editore SpA, pg 387
Giangiacomo Feltrinelli SpA, pg 389
Garzanti Libri, pg 390
Gius Laterza e Figli SpA, pg 391
Ernesto Gremese Editore srl, pg 391
Piero Gribaudi Editore, pg 391
Ugo Guanda Editore, pg 392
Longanesi & C, pg 396
La Luna, pg 396
Macro Edizioni, pg 397
Manifestolibri, pg 397
Editrice Massimo SAS di Crespi Cesare e C, pg 397
Arnoldo Mondadori Editore SpA, pg 398
Franco Muzzio Editore, pg 400
NodoLibri, pg 400
La Nuova Italia Editrice SpA, pg 401
Amilcare Pizzi SpA, pg 403
RCS Rizzoli Libri SpA, pg 405
Edizioni San Paolo SRL, pg 407
Edizioni Segno SRL, pg 407
Sperling e Kupfer Editori SpA, pg 409
Studio Bibliografico Adelmo Polla, pg 409
Marco Tropea Editore, pg 410
Edizioni Ubulibri SAS, pg 410
Edizioni La Vita Felice, pg 412
Zanichelli Editore SpA, pg 412

Jamaica
Institute of Jamaica Publications, pg 413

Japan
Chuokoron-Shinsha Inc, pg 416
Gakken Co Ltd, pg 417
Hayakawa Publishing Inc, pg 418
Iwanami Shoten, Publishers, pg 419
Japan Publications Inc, pg 419
Kosei Publishing Co Ltd, pg 421
Nanzando Co Ltd, pg 423
Nippon Hoso Shuppan Kyokai (NHK Publishing), pg 424
Nosangyoson Bunka Kyokai, pg 424
Reimei-Shobo Co Ltd, pg 425
Sanseido Co Ltd, pg 426
Seibido Shuppan Company Ltd, pg 426
Shincho-Sha Co Ltd, pg 427
Shufunotomo Co Ltd, pg 428
Sogensha Publishing Co Ltd, pg 428
Tsukiji Shokan Publishing Co, pg 430
Yohan Shuppan, pg 431

Kenya
Cosmopolitan Publishers Ltd, pg 433
Evangel Publishing House, pg 433
Foundation Books Ltd, pg 434
Heinemann Kenya Ltd (EAEP), pg 434
Kenway Publications Ltd, pg 434
Kenya Quality & Productivity Institute, pg 435
Life Challenge AFRICA, pg 435
Paulines Publications-Africa, pg 435

Democratic People's Republic of Korea
Grand People's Study House, pg 436

Republic of Korea
Bum-Woo Publishing Co, pg 437
Chung Rim Publishing Co Ltd, pg 438
Gim-Yeong Co, pg 438
Hakgojae Publishing Inc, pg 439
Hanul Publishing Co, pg 439
Korea Psychological Testing Institute, pg 440
Koreaone Press Inc, pg 440
Woongjin.com Co Ltd, pg 443
YBM/Si-sa, pg 443
Yeha Publishing Co, pg 443

Latvia
Artava Ltd, pg 444
Patmos, izdevnieciba, pg 445
Preses Nams, pg 445

Lithuania
Egmont Lietuva, pg 449
Mokslo ir enciklopediju leidybos institutas, pg 449

The Former Yugoslav Republic of Macedonia
Macedonia Prima Publishing House, pg 452

Madagascar
Imprimerie Takariva, pg 454
Trano Printy Fiangonana Loterana Malagasy (TPFLM)-(Imprimerie Lutherienne), pg 454

Malawi
Christian Literature Association in Malawi, pg 454

Malaysia
Darulfikir, pg 455
Mahir Publications Sdn Bhd, pg 456
Pustaka Cipta Sdn Bhd, pg 458

Mali
EDIM SA, pg 460

Mauritius
Editions de l'Ocean Indien Ltd, pg 461

Mexico
Aconcagua Ediciones y Publicaciones SA, pg 461
Editorial AGATA SA de CV, pg 462
Ediciones Alpe, pg 462
Colegio de Postgraduados en Ciencias Agricolas, pg 463
Centro de Estudios Monetarios Latinoamericanos (CEMLA), pg 465
Editorial Limusa SA de CV, pg 467
Naves Internacional de Ediciones SA, pg 469
Panorama Editorial, SA, pg 470
Selector SA de CV, pg 471
Sistemas Tecnicos de Edicion SA de CV, pg 472

Netherlands
BoekWerk, pg 479
A W Bruna Uitgevers BV, pg 480
BZZTOH Publishers, pg 480
Callenbach BV, pg 480
Uitgeversmaatschappij Ad Donker BV, pg 481
Uitgeverij Homeovisie BV, pg 483
Uitgeverij J H Kok BV, pg 485
Meander Uitgeverij BV, pg 485
Mets & Schilt Uitgevers en Distributeurs, pg 486
Uitgeverij Mingus, pg 486
Mirananda Publishers BV, pg 486
Uitgeverij Maarten Muntinga, pg 486
Narratio Theologische Uitgeverij, pg 486
Nijgh & Van Ditmar Amsterdam, pg 487
Prometheus, pg 488
Em Querido's Uitgeverij BV, pg 488

New Zealand
Cape Catley Ltd, pg 495
Church Mouse Press, pg 495
David's Marine Books, pg 495
Hazard Press Ltd, pg 497
Moss Associates Ltd, pg 498
Orca Publishing Services Ltd, pg 499
River Press, pg 500
RSVP Publishing Co Ltd, pg 500

Nigeria
Cross Continent Press Ltd, pg 504
Evans Brothers (Nigeria Publishers) Ltd, pg 504
Fourth Dimension Publishing Co Ltd, pg 504
Goldland Business Co Ltd, pg 505
Heritage Books, pg 505
JAD Publishers Ltd, pg 505
Longman Nigeria Plc, pg 505
New Horn Press Ltd, pg 506
Nwamife Publishers Ltd, pg 506
Onibon-Oje Publishers, pg 506
Saros International Publishers, pg 507
Joe-Tolalu & Associates, pg 507
West African Book Publishers Ltd, pg 507
John West Publications Co Ltd, pg 507

Norway
H Aschehoug & Co (W Nygaard) A/S, pg 508
Atheneum Forlag A/S, pg 508
Bladkompaniet A/S, pg 508
J W Cappelens Forlag A/S, pg 508
Det Norske Samlaget, pg 508
Gyldendal Norsk Forlag A/S, pg 509
Tiden Norsk Forlag, pg 511

Pakistan
Islamic Publications (Pvt) Ltd, pg 513
Sang-e-Meel Publications, pg 514

Peru
Ediciones Brown SA, pg 516

Philippines
Anvil Publishing Inc, pg 518
Books for Pleasure Inc, pg 518
Bright Concepts Printing House, pg 518
De La Salle University, pg 519
Estrella Publishing, pg 519
Marren Publishing House, Inc, pg 519
Sonny A Mendoza, pg 519
National Book Store Inc, pg 519
Our Lady of Manaoag Publisher, pg 520

Poland
Arlekin-Wydawnictwo Harlequin Enterprises sp zoo, pg 522
Spoldzielnia Wydawnicza 'Czytelnik', pg 522
Gdanskie Wydawnictwo Psychologiczne SC, pg 523
Ksiaznica Publishing Ltd, pg 524

Portugal
Comissao para a Igualdade e Direitos das Mulheres, pg 530
Difusao Cultural, pg 530
Dinalivro, pg 530
Publicacoes Europa-America Lda, pg 531
Gradiva-Publicacnoes Lda, pg 532
Planeta Editora, LDA, pg 534
Editorial Presenca, pg 535
Puma Editora Lda, pg 535
Editora Replicacao Lda, pg 535
Edicoes Salesianas, pg 535

PUBLISHERS

Edicoes 70 Lda, pg 535
Editora Ulisseia Lda, pg 536

Puerto Rico

University of Puerto Rico Press (EDUPR), pg 537

Romania

Artemis Verlag, pg 538
Editura Clusium, pg 539
Corint Publishing Group, pg 539
Editura Institutul European, pg 540
Nemira Verlag, pg 541
Editura Niculescu, pg 541
Grupul Editorial RAO, pg 542
RAO International Publishing Co, pg 542

Russian Federation

N E Bauman Moscow State Technical University Publishers, pg 544
Izdatelstvo Mir, pg 546
Izdatelstvo Mordovskogo gosudar stvennogo, pg 547
Izdatelstvo Muzyka, pg 547
Novosti Izdatelstvo, pg 547
Panorama Publishing House, pg 547
Profizdat, pg 548
Raduga Publishers, pg 548

Senegal

Centre Africain d'Animation et d'Echanges Culturels Editions Khoudia (CAEC), pg 551
Les Nouvelles Editions Africaines du Senegal NEAS, pg 551

Serbia and Montenegro

Alfa-Narodna Knjiga, pg 552
Izdavacka Organizacija Rad, pg 553

Singapore

McGallen & Bolden Associates, pg 557
Tecman Bible House, pg 558

Slovakia

Smena Publishing House, pg 560
Vydavatelstvo Wist sro, pg 561

South Africa

Educum Publishers Ltd, pg 563
Galago Publishing Pty Ltd, pg 564
The Hippogriff Press CC, pg 564
Institute for Reformational Studies CHE, pg 565
Kima Global Publishers, pg 566
LAPA Publishers (Pty) Ltd, pg 566
Maskew Miller Longman, pg 566
New Africa Books (Pty) Ltd, pg 567

Spain

Acento Editorial, pg 570
Editorial Aguaclara, pg 571
Alberdania SL, pg 571
Amnistia Internacional Editorial SL, pg 572
Anglo-Didactica, SL Editorial, pg 573
Editorial Aranzadi SA, pg 573
Editorial Astri SA, pg 573
Edicions Bromera SL, pg 575
Calambur Editorial, SL, pg 575
Biblioteca de Catalunya, pg 576
Ediciones Catedra SA, pg 576
Ediciones de la Universidad Complutense de Madrid, pg 577

Complutense, SA Editorial, pg 577
Comunidad Autonoma de Madrid, Servicio de Documentacion y Publicaciones, pg 578
Rafael Dalmau, Editor, pg 578
Ediciones Daly S L, pg 578
Didaco Comunicacion y Didactica, SA, pg 579
Ediciones Diputacion de Salamanca, pg 579
Edi-Liber Irlan SA, pg 580
Egales (Editorial Gai y Lesbiana), pg 581
Ediciones Encuentro SA, pg 582
Instituto de Estudios Fiscales, pg 583
Fundacion de Estudios Libertarios Anselmo Lorenzo, pg 584
Editorial Fundamentos, pg 584
Galaxia SA Editorial, pg 584
Editorial Gedisa SA, pg 584
Generalitat de Catalunya Diari Oficial de la Generalitat vern, pg 584
Grijalbo Mondadori SA, pg 585
Institucion Fernando el Catolico de la Excma Diputacion de Zaragoza, pg 587
Ediciones Internacionales Universitarias SA, pg 588
Junta de Castilla y Leon Consejeria de Educacion y Cultura, pg 588
Libsa Editorial SA, pg 589
Editorial Lumen SA, pg 589
Ediciones Maeva, pg 590
Ediciones Martinez-Roca SA, pg 591
La Mascara, SL Editorial, pg 591
Editorial Mediterrania SL, pg 591
Editorial Milenio Arts Grafiques Bobala, SL, pg 591
Editorial Molino, pg 592
Anaya & Mario Muchnik, pg 592
Munoz Moya Editor, pg 592
Noguer y Caralt Editores SA, pg 593
Editorial Noray, pg 593
OASIS, Producciones Generales de Comunicacion, pg 593
Editorial Paidotribo SL, pg 594
Pais Vasco Servicio Central de Publicaciones, pg 594
Editorial El Perpetuo Socorro, pg 596
Plaza y Janes Editores SA, pg 596
Edicions Proa, SA, pg 597
Publicaciones y Ediciones Salamandra SA, pg 597
Ediciones San Pio X, pg 599
Servicio de Publicaciones Universidad de Cadiz, pg 599
Ediciones Seyer, pg 599
Ediciones Siruela SA, pg 600
Edicions 62, pg 600
Grup 62, pg 600
Ramon Sopena SA, pg 600
Editorial Thassalia, SA, pg 602
Torremozas SL Ediciones, pg 602
Trotta SA Editorial, pg 602
Tursen, SA, pg 603
Ediciones 29 - Libros Rio Nuevo, pg 603
Ultramar Editores SA, pg 603
Editorial Verbum SL, pg 604

Sri Lanka

Samayawardena Printers Publishers & Booksellers, pg 607
Sunera Publishers, pg 607

Sudan

Al-Ayam Press Co Ltd, pg 608
Khartoum University Press, pg 608

Suriname

Vaco NV Uitgeversmij, pg 608

Sweden

Bokforlaget Nya Doxa AB, pg 614
Bokforlaget Settern AB, pg 615
B Wahlstroms, pg 616

Switzerland

CEC-Cosmic Energy Connections, pg 620
Werner Classen Verlag, pg 621
Scherz Verlag AG, pg 633
Editions D'Art Albert Skira SA, pg 634
Verlag Die Waage, pg 636

Taiwan, Province of China

Chung Hwa Book Co Ltd, pg 639
Morning Star Publisher Inc, pg 641
Shy Mau & Shy Chaur Publishing Co Ltd, pg 641
Zen Now Press, pg 642

United Republic of Tanzania

Central Tanganyika Press, pg 643
DUP (1996) Ltd, pg 643
East African Publishing House, pg 643
Inland Publishers, pg 643

Thailand

Bannakit Trading, pg 645
Chokechai Theues Shop, pg 645
Odeon Store LP, pg 645
Sangdad Publishing Company Ltd, pg 645

Tunisia

Faculte des Sciences Humaines et Sociales de Tunis, pg 648

Turkey

Ataturk Kultur, Dil ve Tarih, Yusek Kurumu Baskanligi, pg 649
Cep Kitaplari AS, pg 649
Iletisim Yayinlari, pg 650
Inkilap Publishers Ltd, pg 650
Pan Yayincilik, pg 651
Parantez Yayinlari Ltd, pg 651
Varlik Yayinlari AS, pg 652

Uganda

Fountain Publishers Ltd, pg 652

Ukraine

ASK Ltd, pg 653

United Kingdom

Act 3 Publishing, pg 655
Age Concern Books, pg 656
Allison & Busby, pg 656
Appletree Press Ltd, pg 658
Arcturus Publishing Ltd, pg 659
Arthur James Ltd, pg 660
Bernard Babani (Publishing) Ltd, pg 662
BBC Worldwide Publishers, pg 663
Berlitz (UK) Ltd, pg 665
Blackstaff Press, pg 666
Blackwell Publishing Ltd, pg 666
John Blake Publishing Ltd, pg 667
Bloomsbury Publishing PLC, pg 668
Books for Europe Ltd, pg 669
Bounty Books, pg 669
Boxtree Ltd, pg 669

Breedon Books Publishing Company Ltd, pg 670
Bryntirion Press, pg 672
Canongate Books Ltd, pg 674
Capall Bann Publishing, pg 674
Cassell & Co, pg 675
Compass Equestrian Ltd, pg 681
Computer Step, pg 681
Constable & Robinson Ltd, pg 682
Leo Cooper, pg 683
The C W Daniel Co Ltd, pg 686
Defiant Publications, pg 687
Discovery Walking Guides Ltd, pg 687
Eagle/Inter Publishing Service (IPS) Ltd, pg 689
Elliot Right Way Books, pg 690
Faber & Faber Ltd, pg 694
Famedram Publishers Ltd, pg 694
Forth Naturalist & Historian, pg 696
Fourth Estate, pg 696
Geddes & Grosset, pg 699
Gembooks, pg 699
Gollancz/Witherby, pg 701
W F Graham (Northampton) Ltd, pg 701
Robert Hale Ltd, pg 704
HarperCollins UK, pg 705
Hawthorn Press, pg 706
Headline Book Publishing Ltd, pg 706
Heartland Publishing Ltd, pg 707
Hobsons, pg 709
Hodder & Stoughton General, pg 709
Hodder Headline Ltd, pg 709
Hutton Press Ltd, pg 711
The Islamic Texts Society, pg 715
Lawpack Publishing Ltd, pg 719
Letterbox Library, pg 720
Lion Hudson PLC, pg 721
Y Lolfa Cyf, pg 722
Lonely Planet, UK, pg 722
Macmillan Children's Books, pg 723
Macmillan Ltd, pg 723
Marston House, pg 725
Kenneth Mason Publications Ltd, pg 726
Meridian Books, pg 727
Metro Books, pg 727
Monarch Books, pg 729
Moorley's Print & Publishing Ltd, pg 729
New Era Publications UK Ltd, pg 732
New Playwrights' Network, pg 732
Octopus Publishing Group, pg 734
Orion Publishing Group Ltd, pg 736
Oxford University Press, pg 737
Pan Macmillan, pg 738
Parapress Ltd, pg 738
Pathfinder London, pg 739
Pearson Education Europe, Mideast & Africa, pg 739
Penguin Books Ltd, pg 740
The Penguin Group UK, pg 740
Pentathol Publishing, pg 740
Polygon, pg 744
Ramakrishna Vedanta Centre, pg 747
Ravette Publishing Ltd, pg 748
Regency House Publishing Ltd, pg 749
Retail Entertainment Data Publishing Ltd, pg 750
The Robinswood Press Ltd, pg 750
George Ronald Publisher Ltd, pg 750
Scottish Executive Library & Information Services, pg 755
Sheldon Press, pg 757
Sherwood Publishing, pg 757
Shire Publications Ltd, pg 757

TYPE OF PUBLICATION INDEX — BOOK

Simon & Schuster Ltd, pg 758
SLG Press, pg 758
Rudolf Steiner Press, pg 761
Sunflower Books, pg 761
Time Warner Book Group UK, pg 766
Titan Books Ltd, pg 766
Transport Bookman Publications Ltd, pg 766
University Presses of California, Columbia & Princeton Ltd, pg 769
Van Molle Publishing, pg 769
Virago Press, pg 770
Ward Lock Ltd, pg 771
Wild Goose Publications, pg 773
Windhorse Publications, pg 774
Witherby & Co Ltd, pg 775
The Women's Press Ltd, pg 775
Wordsworth Editions Ltd, pg 775

Uruguay

Rosebud Ediciones, pg 778
Editia Uruguay, pg 778

Viet Nam

Science & Technics Publishing House, pg 780

Zimbabwe

Anvil Press, pg 782
The Graham Publishing Company (Pvt) Ltd, pg 783
Longman Zimbabwe (Pvt) Ltd, pg 783
Manhattan Publications, pg 784
Vision Publications, pg 784

PAPERBACK BOOKS - TRADE

Argentina

Colmegna SA, pg 4
Ediciones de la Flor SRL, pg 6

Australia

ABC Books (Australian Broadcasting Corporation), pg 10
Aerospace Publications Pty Ltd, pg 11
Allen & Unwin Pty Ltd, pg 11
Ashling Books, pg 12
Australian Broadcasting Authority, pg 13
Boombana Publications, pg 16
CHOICE Magazine, pg 17
R J Cleary Publishing, pg 18
Cookery Book, pg 18
Covenanter Press, pg 18
Crawford House Publishing Pty Ltd, pg 18
Crossroad Distributors Pty Ltd, pg 18
Currency Press Pty Ltd, pg 19
Dellasta Publishing, pg 19
Extraordinary People Press, pg 22
Fernfawn Publications, pg 22
Finch Publishing, pg 22
Fraser Publications, pg 22
Fremantle Arts Centre Press, pg 23
Ginninderra Press, pg 23
Hale & Iremonger Pty Ltd, pg 24
Geoffrey Hamlyn-Harris, pg 24
Hampden Press, pg 24
Histec Publications, pg 25
Hodder Headline Australia, pg 26
Hyland House Publishing Pty Ltd, pg 26
Indra Publishing, pg 27
Instauratio Press, pg 27
Institute of Aboriginal Development (IAD Press), pg 27
Jarrah Publications, pg 27
Gregory Kefalas Publishing, pg 28
Killara Press, pg 28
Kingsclear Books, pg 28
Barry Long Books, pg 29
Melbourne University Press, pg 32
K & Z Mostafanejad, pg 32
Mulini Press, pg 32
National Library of Australia, pg 33
New Endeavour Press, pg 33
New Era Publications Australia Pty Ltd, pg 33
Nimrod Publications, pg 33
NMA Publications, pg 33
Pearson Education Australia, pg 36
Penguin Group (Australia), pg 36
Playbox Theatre Co, pg 37
Pluto Press Australia Pty Ltd, pg 37
Pollitecon Publications, pg 37
Quakers Hill Press, pg 38
Random House Australia, pg 38
The Real Estate Institute of Australia, pg 39
Simon & Schuster (Australia) Pty Ltd, pg 41
South Head Press, pg 41
Spacevision Publishing, pg 41
Spectrum Publications, pg 41
Spinifex Press, pg 42
State Library of NSW Press, pg 42
Stirling Press, pg 42
Terania Rainforest Publishing, pg 43
The Text Publishing Company Pty Ltd, pg 43
Turton & Armstrong Pty Ltd Publishers, pg 44
Villamonta Publishing Services Inc, pg 45
Wakefield Press Pty Ltd, pg 46
John Wiley & Sons Australia, Ltd, pg 46
Windhorse Books, pg 47
Women's Health Advisory Service, pg 47
Worsley Press, pg 47
Wrightbooks Pty Ltd, pg 47

Austria

Verlag Harald Denzel, Auto- und Freizeitfuehrer, pg 50
Development News Ltd, pg 50
Ennsthaler GesmbH & Co KG, pg 50
Verlag Monte Verita, pg 54
Verlag Anton Pustet, pg 56
Verlag St Gabriel, pg 57
Studien Verlag Gmbh, pg 58

Belarus

Interdigest Publishing House, pg 62

Belgium

Etablissements Emile Bruylant SA, pg 64
Uitgeverij de Eenhoorn, pg 67
Georeto-Geogidsen, pg 67
Claude Lefrancq Editeur, pg 70
Scoop Infotex NV, pg 73

Brazil

Editora Agora Ltda, pg 77
Editora Aquariana Ltda, pg 77
Camara Dos Deputados Coordenacao De Publicacoes, pg 79
Editora Campus Ltda, pg 79
Companhia Editora Forense, pg 81
EDUSC - Editora da Universidade do Sagrado Coracao, pg 81
Editora Elevacao, pg 81
Editora Forense Universitaria Ltda, pg 81
Fundacao Cultural Avatar, pg 82
Ordem do Graal na Terra, pg 83
LDA Editores Ltda, pg 84
Madras Editora, pg 86
Editora Marco Zero Ltda, pg 86
Editora Melhoramentos Ltda, pg 86
Editora Mercado Aberto Ltda, pg 86
Editora Mercuryo Ltda, pg 86
Editora Mundo Cristao, pg 87
Editora Nova Fronteira SA, pg 87
Editora Objetiva Ltda, pg 87
Pearson Education Do Brasil, pg 88
Ediouro Publicacoes, SA, pg 89
Raboni Editora Ltda, pg 89
Summus Editorial Ltda, pg 91

Bulgaria

Antroposofsko Izdatelstvo Dimo R Daskalov OOD, pg 93
Aratron, IK, pg 93
EA EOOD, pg 94
Hermes Publishing House, pg 94
Kibea Publishing Co, pg 95
Kralica MAB, pg 95
MATEX, pg 95
Nov Covek Publishing House, pg 96
Reporter, pg 96
Ivan Vazov Publishing House, pg 97

Burundi

Editions Intore, pg 98

Chile

Red Internacional Del Libro, pg 100
Editorial Texido Ltda, pg 100

China

China Foreign Economic Relations & Trade Publishing House, pg 102
China Materials Management Publishing House, pg 102
Chinese Pedagogics Publishing House, pg 103
Foreign Language Teaching & Research Press, pg 104
Guangdong Science & Technology Press, pg 105
Heilongjiang Science & Technology Press, pg 105
Inner Mongolia Science & Technology Publishing House, pg 105
New Times Press, pg 106
Shanghai Calligraphy & Painting Publishing House, pg 108
Shanghai Far East Publishers, pg 108

Colombia

Fondo Educativo Interamericano SA, pg 111
RAM Editores, pg 112

Costa Rica

Editorial Texto Ltda, pg 116

Cote d'Ivoire

Centre de Publications Evangeliques, pg 117

Croatia

Durieux d o o, pg 118
Skolska Knjiga, pg 119
Znaci Vremena, Institut Za Istrazivanje Biblije, pg 119

Cuba

Editora Politica, pg 120

Czech Republic

Barrister & Principal, pg 122
Melantrich, akc spol, pg 125
Mlada fronta, pg 125
Cesky normalizacni institut, pg 126

Denmark

Akademisk Forlag A/S, pg 128
Borgens Forlag A/S, pg 129
Gyldendalske Boghandel - Nordisk Forlag A/S, pg 131
P Haase & Sons Forlag A/S, pg 131
Holkenfeldt 3, pg 132
Forlaget Hovedland, pg 132
Lindhardt og Ringhof Forlag A/S, pg 132
Politisk Revy, pg 133
Samfundslitteratur, pg 134
Samlerens Forlag A/S, pg 134
Scandinavia Publishing House, pg 134
Square Dance Partners Forlag, pg 135
Unitas Forlag, pg 135

Egypt (Arab Republic of Egypt)

Dar El Shorouk, pg 138
The Egyptian Society for the Dissemination of Universal Culture and Knowledge (ESDUCK), pg 138

Estonia

Estonian Academy Publishers, pg 139
Ilmamaa, pg 139
Mats Publishers Ltd, pg 140

Finland

Kaantopiiri Oy, pg 142
Karisto Oy, pg 142
Koala-Kustannus Oy, pg 143
Kustannusosakeyhtio Tammi, pg 143
Otava Publishing Co Ltd, pg 143

France

ADPF Publications, pg 145
Editions de l'Aube, pg 148
La Bibliotheque des Arts, pg 150
Bragelonne, pg 151
Editions La Decouverte, pg 157
Editions de l'Ecole, pg 159
Ecole Nationale Superieure des Beaux-Arts, pg 159
Editions Edisud, pg 159
Editions Farel, pg 162
Flammarion SA, pg 163
Editions Ganymede, pg 165
Editions Gerard de Villiers, pg 165
Hermann editeurs des Sciences et des Arts SA, pg 167
Pierre Horay Editeur, pg 168
Jouvence Editions, pg 170
Editions Mediaspaul, pg 175
Mille et Une Nuits, pg 175
Editions Odile Jacob, pg 177
Presses Universitaires de France (PUF), pg 181
Editions Prosveta, pg 182
Editions Le Sarment, pg 184
Editions Le Serpent a Plumes, pg 184
Editions Andre Silvaire Sarl, pg 185
Alain Thomas Editeur, pg 187

PUBLISHERS

TYPE OF PUBLICATION INDEX

French Polynesia
Scoop/Au Vent des Iles, pg 189
Haere Po Editions, pg 189

Germany
AOL-Verlag Frohmut Menze, pg 193
ARCult Media, pg 193
Aussaat Verlag, pg 195
Dr Bachmaier Verlag GmbH, pg 196
Bank-Verlag GmbH, pg 197
Bergverlag Rother GmbH, pg 199
Bertelsmann Lexikon Verlag GmbH, pg 200
Blaukreuz-Verlag Wuppertal, pg 202
BLV Verlagsgesellschaft mbH, pg 202
Carlsen Verlag GmbH, pg 207
Chmielorz GmbH Verlag, pg 208
Claudius Verlag, pg 209
Data Becker GmbH & Co KG, pg 210
Verlag Deutsche Unitarier, pg 212
Deutscher Apotheker Verlag Dr Roland Schmiedel GmbH & Co, pg 212
Deutscher Taschenbuch Verlag GmbH & Co KG (dtv), pg 213
Donat Verlag, pg 215
Verlagsgruppe Droemer Knaur GmbH & Co KG, pg 216
Emons Verlag, pg 219
Englisch Verlag GmbH, pg 220
Erlanger Verlag Fuer Mission und Okumene, pg 220
EVT Energy Video Training & Verlag GmbH, pg 222
Karin Fischer Verlag GmbH, pg 225
S Fischer Verlag GmbH, pg 225
Flensburger Hefte Verlag GmbH, pg 225
Focus-Verlag Gesellschaft mbH, pg 225
Franz-Sales-Verlag, pg 226
G Braun (vormals G Braun'sche Hofbuchdruckerei und Verlag) Gmbh, pg 227
Gatzanis Verlags GmbH, pg 228
Genius Verlag, pg 228
Gesellschaft fuer Organisationswissenschaft e V, pg 229
Gieck-Verlag GmbH, pg 229
Cornelia Goethe Literaturverlag, pg 230
Graefe und Unzer Verlag, pg 230
Grafit Verlag GmbH, pg 231
Verlag der Stiftung Gralsbotschaft GmbH, pg 231
Walter Haedecke Verlag, pg 232
Heel Verlag GmbH, pg 235
Heigl Verlag, Horst Edition, pg 235
Himmelsturmer Verlag, pg 237
S Hirzel Verlag GmbH und Co, pg 238
Junfermann-Verlag, pg 243
Verlag Kiepenheuer & Witsch, pg 245
Verlag im Kilian GmbH, pg 246
Verlag Kleine Schritte Ursula Dahm & Co, pg 246
Kolibri-Verlag GmbH, pg 249
Konradin-Verlagsgruppe, pg 249
Karin Kramer Verlag, pg 250
Institut fuer Landes- und Stadtentwicklungsforschung des Landes Nordrhein-Westfalen, pg 251

Karl Robert Langewiesche Nachfolger Hans Koester KG, pg 252
Dr Gisela Lermann, pg 253
LEU-VERLAG Wolfgang Leupelt, pg 254
Matthias-Gruenewald-Verlag GmbH, pg 258
Medpharm Scientific Publishers, pg 258
mentis Verlag GmbH, pg 259
Peter Meyer Verlag (pmv), pg 260
Midena Verlag, pg 260
MM-Verlagsgesellschaft mbH, pg 261
NaturaViva Verlags GmbH, pg 263
Neues Literaturkontor, pg 264
Hans-Nietsch-Verlag, pg 265
Oekobuch Verlag & Versand GmbH, pg 266
Verlag Parzeller GmbH & Co KG, pg 268
J Pfeiffer Verlag, pg 269
Piper Verlag GmbH, pg 270
Propylaeen Verlag, Zweigniederlassung Berlin der Ullstein Buchverlage GmbH, pg 272
Psychosozial-Verlag, pg 272
Werner Rau Verlag, pg 273
Reader's Digest Deutschland Verlag Das Beste GmbH, pg 274
Regura Verlag, pg 274
E Reinhold Verlag, pg 275
Reise Know-How Verlag Peter Rump GmbH, pg 275
Verlagsgruppe Reise Know-How, pg 275
Schott Musik International GmbH & Co KG, pg 281
Siegler & Co Verlag fuer Zeitarchive GmbH, pg 283
Silberburg-Verlag Titus Haeussermann GmbH, pg 283
teNeues Verlag GmbH & Co KG, pg 290
Tetra Verlag Gmbh, pg 290
Konrad Theiss Verlag GmbH, pg 290
Tipress Dienstleistungen fur das Verlagswesen GmbH, pg 291
Traditionell Bogenschiessen Verlag Angelika Hornig, pg 292
Treves Editions Verein Zur Foerderung der Kuenstlerischen Taetigkeiten, pg 292
Tuebinger Vereinigung fur Volkskunde eV (TVV), pg 292
UNO-Verlag GmbH, pg 293
Verlag Moderne Industrie AG & Co KG, pg 295
Vier Tuerme GmbH Verlag Klosterbetriebe, pg 295
Friedr Vieweg & Sohn Verlag, pg 296
VS Verlag fur Sozialwissenschaften, pg 297
Verlag Klaus Wagenbach, pg 297
Wartburg Verlag GmbH, pg 297
Wehr & Wissen Verlagsgesellschaft mbH, pg 298
Verlag Wissenschaft und Politik, pg 300

Ghana
Asempa Publishers, pg 303
Educational Press & Manufacturers Ltd, pg 303

Greece
Chrysi Penna - Golden Pen Books, pg 306
Ekdotike Athenon SA, pg 307

Harlenic Hellas Publishing SA, pg 308
Hestia-I D Hestia-Kollaros & Co Corporation, pg 308
Idmon Publications, pg 308
Kalentis & Sia, pg 308
Kritiki Publishing, pg 309
Medusa/Selas Publishers, pg 310
Minoas SA, pg 310
Ed Nea Acropolis, pg 310
Opera, pg 311
Patakis Publishers, pg 311
Sigma, pg 312

Hong Kong
Book Marketing Ltd, pg 315
Design Human Resources Training & Development, pg 317
Joint Publishing (HK) Co Ltd, pg 317
Lea Publications Ltd, pg 318
Sun Mui Press, pg 319

Hungary
Joszoveg Muhely Kiado, pg 322
Kiiarat Konyvdiado, pg 322
Magyar Kemikusok Egyesulete, pg 323
Szepirodalmi Koenyvkiado Kiado, pg 324
Typotex Kft Elektronikus Kiado, pg 324

Iceland
Bokaforlag Birtingur, pg 325
Mal og menning, pg 326

India
Addison-Wesley Pte Ltd, pg 327
Anmol Publications Pvt Ltd, pg 328
BR Publishing Corporation, pg 331
CICC Book House, Leading Publishers & Booksellers, pg 332
Eastern Law House Pvt Ltd, pg 334
Frank Brothers & Co Publishers Ltd, pg 334
Geeta Prakashan, pg 335
Gyan Publishing House, pg 335
India Book House Pvt Ltd, pg 336
Indus Publishing Co, pg 338
Konark Publishers Pvt Ltd, pg 339
Law Publishers, pg 340
Orient Paperbacks, pg 344
Oxford University Press, pg 344
People's Publishing House (P) Ltd, pg 345
Reliance Publishing House, pg 346
Sterling Publishers Pvt Ltd, pg 350
Stree, pg 350
Vidya Puri, pg 352
Vision Books Pvt Ltd, pg 352

Indonesia
Mizan, pg 355
Nusa Indah, pg 356
Tintamas Indonesia PT, pg 356

Ireland
A & A Farmar, pg 357
Brandon Book Publishers Ltd, pg 358
The Children's Press, pg 358
Clo Iar-Chonnachta Teo, pg 358
The Columba Book Service, pg 359
The Columba Press, pg 359
Dee-Jay Publications, pg 359
Estragon Press Ltd, pg 359
Gill & Macmillan Ltd, pg 360
Mercier Press Ltd, pg 362
Mount Eagle Publications Ltd, pg 362

Oak Tree Press, pg 362
The O'Brien Press Ltd, pg 362
On Stream Publications Ltd, pg 362
Roberts Rinehart Publishers, pg 363
Town House & Country House, pg 364
Veritas Co Ltd, pg 364
Wolfhound Press Ltd, pg 364

Israel
Bitan Publishers Ltd, pg 365
Boostan Publishing House, pg 365
Breslov Research Institute, pg 365
DAT Publications, pg 366
Dekel Publishing House, pg 366
Hakibbutz Hameuchad Publishing House Ltd, pg 367
The Institute for Israeli Arabs Studies, pg 368
L B Publishing Co, pg 369
Massada Press Ltd, pg 370
Mirkam Publishers, pg 370
Pitspopany Press, pg 371
R Sirkis Publishers Ltd, pg 372
Urim Publications, pg 373

Italy
Adelphi Edizioni SpA, pg 374
L'Airone Editrice, pg 375
Canova SRL, pg 379
Edizioni Carmelitane, pg 380
Il Castello srl, pg 380
Centro Biblico, pg 381
CIC Edizioni Internazionali, pg 381
Edizioni Dedalo SRL, pg 384
Edizioni Della Torre di Salvatore Fozzi & C SAS, pg 385
Ediciclo Editore SRL, pg 386
Edizioni del Centro Camuno di Studi Preistorici, pg 386
Edizioni Il Punto d'Incontro SAS, pg 386
Edizioni Qiqajon, pg 387
Giulio Einaudi Editore SpA, pg 387
l'Eta dell'Acquario, pg 388
Fanucci, pg 388
Garolla, pg 390
Garzanti Libri, pg 390
Piero Gribaudi Editore, pg 391
Gruppo Editoriale Faenza Editrice SpA, pg 391
IHT Gruppo Editoriale SRL, pg 393
Kaos Edizioni SRL, pg 394
Edizioni Lavoro SRL, pg 394
Lindau, pg 395
Lusva Editrice, pg 396
Edizioni Mediterranee SRL, pg 398
Arnoldo Mondadori Editore SpA, pg 398
NodoLibri, pg 400
La Nuova Italia Editrice SpA, pg 401
Il Saggiatore, pg 406
Editoriale San Giusto SRL Edizioni Parnaso, pg 406
Servitium, pg 408
Sorbona, pg 409
TEA Tascabili degli Editori Associati SpA, pg 409
Transeuropa, pg 410
Marco Tropea Editore, pg 410

Jamaica
Ian Randle Publishers Ltd, pg 414

Japan
AVACO - Christian Mass Communications Center, pg 415
Chikuma Shobo Publishing Co Ltd, pg 416
Dohosha Publishing Co Ltd, pg 417

841

TYPE OF PUBLICATION INDEX

BOOK

Hakuyo-Sha, pg 418
Hoikusha Publishing Co Ltd, pg 418
Hyoronsha Publishing Co Ltd, pg 418
International Society for Educational Information (ISEI), pg 419
Japan Publications Inc, pg 419
Kyodo-Isho Shuppan Co Ltd, pg 422
Nippon Hoso Shuppan Kyokai (NHK Publishing), pg 424
Shincho-Sha Co Ltd, pg 427
Shufunotomo Co Ltd, pg 428
Toho Shuppan, pg 429
Yohan Shuppan, pg 431

Kenya

Heinemann Kenya Ltd (EAEP), pg 434
Phoenix Publishers Ltd, pg 435
Sasa Sema Publications Ltd, pg 435

Republic of Korea

Gim-Yeong Co, pg 438
Hollym Corporation; Publishers, pg 439
Koreaone Press Inc, pg 440
Kukmin Doseo Publishing Co Ltd, pg 440
O Neul Publishing Co, pg 441
Prompter Publications, pg 442
Woongjin.com Co Ltd, pg 443
Word of Life Press, pg 443
Yeha Publishing Co, pg 443

Latvia

Alberts XII, pg 444
Artava Ltd, pg 444
Preses Nams, pg 445

Luxembourg

Essay und Zeitgeist Verlag, pg 451
Op der Lay, pg 451

Malaysia

S Abdul Majeed & Co, pg 454
Holograms (M) Sdn Bhd, pg 456
MDC Publishers Printers Sdn Bhd, pg 457
Pustaka Cipta Sdn Bhd, pg 458

Malta

Fondazzjoni Patrimonju Malti, pg 460

Mauritius

Hemco Publications, pg 461

Mexico

Colegio de Postgraduados en Ciencias Agricolas, pg 463
Del Verbo Emprender SA de CV, pg 464
Editorial Diana SA de CV, pg 464
Ediciones Eca SA de CV, pg 464
Edamex SA de CV, pg 464
Ediciones Era SA de CV, pg 465
Ediciones Euroamericanas, pg 465
Hoja Casa Editorial SA de CV, pg 466
Libra Editorial SA de CV, pg 467
Editorial Limusa SA de CV, pg 467
Editorial Minutiae Mexicana SA, pg 468
Naves Internacional de Ediciones SA, pg 469
Panorama Editorial, SA, pg 470

Monaco

Editions EGC, pg 473

Netherlands

Uitgeverij de Arbeiderspers, pg 477
Uitgeverij Arena BV, pg 478
Buijten en Schipperheijn BV Drukkerij en Uitgeversmaatschappij, pg 480
Business Contact BV, pg 480
BZZTOH Publishers, pg 480
Cadans, pg 480
Callenbach BV, pg 480
Uitgeverij De Fontein BV, pg 482
De Harmonie Uitgeverij, pg 483
Uitgeverij Holland, pg 483
Uitgeverij J H Kok BV, pg 485
Uitgeverij Leopold BV, pg 485
Uitgeverij Meinema, pg 485
Mets & Schilt Uitgevers en Distributeurs, pg 486
Uitgeverij Mingus, pg 486
Nijgh & Van Ditmar Amsterdam, pg 487
Servire BV Uitgevers, pg 489
A J G Strengholt's Boeken, Anno 1928, BV, pg 489
Telos Boeken, pg 490
Tirion Uitgevers BV, pg 490
Uitgeverij G A van Oorschot bv, pg 491

New Zealand

Aoraki Press Ltd, pg 493
Auckland University Press, pg 493
Brick Row Publishing Co Ltd, pg 494
Bush Press Communications Ltd, pg 494
Canterbury University Press, pg 494
Cape Catley Ltd, pg 495
Exisle Publishing Ltd, pg 496
Fraser Books, pg 496
Gondwanaland Press, pg 496
Graphic Educational Publications, pg 496
Halcyon Publishing Ltd, pg 496
HarperCollins Publishers (New Zealand) Ltd, pg 497
Hazard Press Ltd, pg 497
Heritage Press Ltd, pg 497
Hodder Moa Beckett Publishers Ltd, pg 497
Huia Publishers, pg 497
Lincoln University Press, pg 498
David Ling Publishing, pg 498
Longacre Press, pg 498
Magari Publishing, pg 498
Orca Publishing Services Ltd, pg 499
Otago Heritage Books, pg 499
R P L Books, pg 500
Resource Books Ltd, pg 500
Shoal Bay Press Ltd, pg 501
Southern Press Ltd, pg 501
Tandem Press, pg 501
Te Waihora Press, pg 501
University of Otago Press, pg 502
Bridget Williams Books Ltd, pg 502

Nigeria

Riverside Communications, pg 507
Joe-Tolalu & Associates, pg 507
University Publishing Co, pg 507
Vantage Publishers International Ltd, pg 507

Norway

J W Cappelens Forlag A/S, pg 508
Ex Libris Forlag A/S, pg 509
Pax Forlag A/S, pg 510

Peru

Ediciones Peisa (Promocion Editorial Inca SA), pg 517

Philippines

Anvil Publishing Inc, pg 518
Bookmark Inc, pg 518
Bright Concepts Printing House, pg 518
De La Salle University, pg 519
Marren Publishing House, Inc, pg 519
New Day Publishers, pg 520
Rex Bookstores & Publishers, pg 520

Poland

Arlekin-Wydawnictwo Harlequin Enterprises sp zoo, pg 522
Gdanskie Wydawnictwo Psychologiczne SC, pg 523
Ksiaznica Publishing Ltd, pg 524
Oficyna Wydawnicza Read Me, pg 526

Portugal

Editorial Estampa, Lda, pg 531
Publicacoes Europa-America Lda, pg 531
Gradiva-Publicacnoes Lda, pg 532
Planeta Editora, LDA, pg 534
Edicoes 70 Lda, pg 535

Puerto Rico

Modern Guides Company, pg 537

Romania

Editora All, pg 538
Editura Clusium, pg 539
Humanitas Publishing House, pg 540
Lider Verlag, pg 540
Editura Niculescu, pg 541
Polirom Verlag, pg 542

Russian Federation

N E Bauman Moscow State Technical University Publishers, pg 544
Glas New Russian Writing, pg 545
Publishing House Limbus Press, pg 546
Novosti Izdatelstvo, pg 547
Obdeestro Znanie, pg 547
Panorama Publishing House, pg 547
Text Publishers Ltd Too, pg 549
Izdatelstvo Ural' skogo, pg 549

Senegal

Centre Africain d'Animation et d'Echanges Culturels Editions Khoudia (CAEC), pg 551

Serbia and Montenegro

AGAPE, pg 552
Alfa-Narodna Knjiga, pg 552

Singapore

Aquanut Agencies Pte Ltd, pg 555
Chopsons Pte Ltd, pg 555
McGallen & Bolden Associates, pg 557
Select Publishing Pte Ltd, pg 557
Taylor & Francis Asia Pacific, pg 558
Tecman Bible House, pg 558

Slovakia

Priroda Publishing, pg 560
Serafin, pg 560
Smena Publishing House, pg 560

South Africa

Educum Publishers Ltd, pg 563
Fernwood Press (Pty) Ltd, pg 563
Galago Publishing Pty Ltd, pg 564
Heinemann Educational Publishers Southern Africa, pg 564
Johannesburg Art Gallery, pg 565
Kima Global Publishers, pg 566
Maskew Miller Longman, pg 566
New Africa Books (Pty) Ltd, pg 567
Queillerie Publishers, pg 568
Ravan Press (Pty) Ltd, pg 568
Southern Book Publishers (Pty) Ltd, pg 569

Spain

Alberdania SL, pg 571
Alianza Editorial SA, pg 572
CEAC, Grupo Editorial SA, pg 576
Complutense, SA Editorial, pg 577
Comunidad Autonoma de Madrid, Servicio de Documentacion y Publicaciones, pg 578
Rafael Dalmau, Editor, pg 578
Ediciones Destino SA, pg 579
Ediciones Diaz de Santos SA, pg 579
Didaco Comunicacion y Didactica, SA, pg 579
Diputacion Provincial de Malaga, pg 579
EDHASA (Editora y Distribuidora Hispano-Americana SA), pg 580
Edicomunicacion SA, pg 581
Edilesa-Ediciones Leonesas SA, pg 581
Elkar, Euskal Liburu eta Kantuen Argitaldaria, SL, pg 582
Enciclopedia Catalana, SA, pg 582
Fundacion Rosacruz, pg 584
Editorial Gustavo Gili SA, pg 585
Grijalbo Mondadori SA, pg 585
Impredisur, SL, pg 587
LEDA (Las Ediciones de Arte), pg 589
Ediciones Libertarias/Prodhufi SA, pg 589
Ediciones Maeva, pg 590
Ediciones Martinez-Roca SA, pg 591
Ediciones Medici SA, pg 591
Noguer y Caralt Editores SA, pg 593
Obelisco Ediciones S, pg 593
Omnicon, SA, pg 594
Editorial Peregrino SL, pg 595
Editorial El Perpetuo Socorro, pg 596
Polifemo, Ediciones, pg 596
Editorial Popular SA, pg 596
Equipo Sirius SA, pg 600
Grup 62, pg 600
Tirant lo Blanch SL Libreriaa, pg 602
Tursen, SA, pg 603
Tusquets Editores, pg 603
Ediciones 29 - Libros Rio Nuevo, pg 603
Ediciones Urano, SA, pg 604
Vinaches Lopez, Luisa, pg 605

Sri Lanka

Buddhist Publication Society Inc, pg 605
Inter-Cultural Book Promoters, pg 606

PUBLISHERS

Sweden
Allt om Hobby AB, pg 609
Delta Forlags AB, pg 611

Switzerland
ADIRA, pg 617
Ammann Verlag & Co, pg 617
Bergli Books AG, pg 619
Christoph Merian Verlag, pg 620
Cosmos-Verlag AG, pg 621
Cultur Prospectiv, Edition, pg 621
Diogenes Verlag AG, pg 622
Edition Exodus, pg 623
Peter Lang AG, pg 627
Oesch Verlag AG, pg 630
Editions Payot Lausanne, pg 631
Verlag Die Pforte im Rudolf Steiner Verlag, pg 631
Editions D'Art Albert Skira SA, pg 634
Rudolf Steiner Verlag, pg 634
Verlag im Waldgut AG, pg 636

Taiwan, Province of China
Chung Hwa Book Co Ltd, pg 639
Linking Publishing Company Ltd, pg 641
Petroleum Information Publishing Co, pg 641
Youth Cultural Publishing Co, pg 642
Yuan Liou Publishing Co, Ltd, pg 642

United Republic of Tanzania
Kanisa la Biblia Publishers (KLB), pg 643
Tanzania Publishing House, pg 644

Tunisia
Alyssa Editions, pg 647
Maison Tunisienne de l'Edition, pg 648

Turkey
Cep Kitaplari AS, pg 649
Inkilap Publishers Ltd, pg 650
Metis Yayinlari, pg 650
Pan Yayincilik, pg 651
Sabah Kitaplari, pg 651
Toros Yayinlari Ltd Co, pg 652
Varlik Yayinlari AS, pg 652

Ukraine
ASK Ltd, pg 653

United Arab Emirates
Motivate Publishing, pg 654

United Kingdom
Abbotsford Publishing, pg 654
Act 3 Publishing, pg 655
Adamantine Press Ltd, pg 655
Allison & Busby, pg 656
Andromeda Oxford Ltd, pg 658
Anvil Books Ltd, pg 658
Apex Publishing Ltd, pg 658
Arcturus Publishing Ltd, pg 659
Arms & Armour Press, pg 659
Art Books International Ltd, pg 659
Arthur James Ltd, pg 660
Ashgrove Publishing, pg 660
Aslib, The Association for Information Management, pg 660
Association for Scottish Literary Studies, pg 661
Association for Science Education, pg 661
Atlantic Transport Publishers, pg 661
Atlas Press, pg 661
Aulis Publishers, pg 661
The Banner of Truth Trust, pg 662
The Banton Press, pg 662
Colin Baxter Photography Ltd, pg 663
Bay View Books Ltd, pg 663
BBC Worldwide Publishers, pg 663
Ruth Bean Publishers, pg 664
BFI Publishing, pg 665
Bible Reading Fellowship, pg 665
Birlinn Ltd, pg 666
Black Ace Books, pg 666
Blackstaff Press, pg 666
John Blake Publishing Ltd, pg 667
Blandford Publishing Ltd, pg 668
Bloodaxe Books Ltd, pg 668
Bloomsbury Publishing PLC, pg 668
Blorenge Books, pg 668
Blueprint, pg 668
The Book Guild Ltd, pg 668
Book Packaging & Marketing, pg 668
Books for Europe Ltd, pg 669
Boulevard Books UK/The Babel Guides, pg 669
Bowerdean Publishing Co Ltd, pg 669
Boydell & Brewer Ltd, pg 669
Nicholas Brealey Publishing, pg 670
Breese Books Ltd, pg 670
Brewin Books Ltd, pg 671
Calder Publications Ltd, pg 673
Canongate Books Ltd, pg 674
Capstone Publishing Ltd, pg 674
Jon Carpenter Publishing, pg 675
Carroll & Brown Ltd, pg 675
Cassell & Co, pg 675
Centre for Alternative Technology, pg 677
Christian Education, pg 679
Cockbird Press, pg 680
Computer Step, pg 681
Concrete Information Ltd, pg 682
Constable & Robinson Ltd, pg 682
Leo Cooper, pg 683
Countyvise Ltd, pg 683
Creation Books, pg 683
Cressrelles Publishing Company Ltd, pg 684
Crossbridge Books, pg 684
Crown House Publishing Ltd, pg 684
The Crowood Press Ltd, pg 684
CTBI Publications, pg 685
Dance Books Ltd, pg 686
The C W Daniel Co Ltd, pg 686
Christopher Davies Publishers Ltd, pg 686
Dedalus Ltd, pg 687
Delectus Books, pg 687
DMG Business Media Ltd, pg 688
Eagle/Inter Publishing Service (IPS) Ltd, pg 689
Elliot Right Way Books, pg 690
Aidan Ellis Publishing, pg 690
Eurobook Ltd, pg 692
Express Newspapers, pg 693
Fabian Society, pg 694
Feather Books, pg 694
Findhorn Press Inc, pg 695
Flambard Press, pg 695
Fourth Estate, pg 696
George Mann Publications, pg 699
GMC Publications Ltd, pg 700
GMP Publishers Ltd, pg 700
Granta Books, pg 702
W Green The Scottish Law Publisher, pg 702
Harden's Ltd, pg 704
HarperCollins UK, pg 705
Harvard University Press, pg 705
The Harvill Press, pg 705
Haynes Publishing, pg 706
Headline Book Publishing Ltd, pg 706
Health Development Agency, pg 706
Heartland Publishing Ltd, pg 707
Christopher Helm (Publishers) Ltd, pg 707
Heritage Press, pg 708
Hodder & Stoughton General, pg 709
Hodder & Stoughton Religious, pg 709
Hodder Headline Ltd, pg 709
Honno Welsh Women's Press, pg 710
How To Books Ltd, pg 710
Institute of Food Science & Technology, pg 713
The Islamic Texts Society, pg 715
Janus Publishing Co Ltd, pg 716
Michael Joseph Ltd, pg 716
Lang Syne Publishers Ltd, pg 719
Lawrence & Wishart, pg 719
Lion Hudson PLC, pg 721
Luath Press Ltd, pg 722
The Lutterworth Press, pg 723
Macmillan Audio Books, pg 723
Macmillan, pg 723
Management Books 2000 Ltd, pg 724
Mandrake of Oxford, pg 725
Marston House, pg 725
Mercat Press, pg 726
The Merlin Press Ltd, pg 727
Metro Books, pg 727
J Garnet Miller, pg 728
Monarch Books, pg 729
Moorley's Print & Publishing Ltd, pg 729
Neil Wilson Publishing Ltd, pg 732
New Era Publications UK Ltd, pg 732
New European Publications Ltd, pg 732
NMS Enterprises Ltd - Publishing, pg 733
Octagon Press Ltd, pg 734
Octopus Publishing Group, pg 734
Old Pond Publishing, pg 734
The Oleander Press, pg 735
Michael O'Mara Books Ltd, pg 735
Onlywomen Press Ltd, pg 735
Open Gate Press, pg 735
Orion Publishing Group Ltd, pg 736
The Orkney Press Ltd, pg 736
Osprey Publishing Ltd, pg 737
Peter Owen Ltd, pg 737
Pan Macmillan, pg 738
Parthian Books, pg 738
PC Publishing, pg 739
Pearson Education Europe, Mideast & Africa, pg 739
Pen & Sword Books Ltd, pg 740
Penguin Books Ltd, pg 740
The Penguin Group UK, pg 740
Piatkus Books, pg 741
Plexus Publishing Ltd, pg 743
Police Review Publishing Company Ltd, pg 744
The Policy Press, pg 744
Polybooks Ltd, pg 744
Polygon, pg 744
David Porteous Editions, pg 744
Prion Books Ltd, pg 745
Profile Books Ltd, pg 746
Quadrille Publishing Ltd, pg 746
Quartet Books Ltd, pg 746
Quiller Publishing Ltd, pg 747
Quintet Publishing Ltd, pg 747
Rapra Technology Ltd, pg 748
Reaktion Books Ltd, pg 748
Reardon Publishing, pg 748
Retail Entertainment Data Publishing Ltd, pg 750
Rivers Oram Press, pg 750
Rooster Books Ltd, pg 751
Rough Guides Ltd, pg 751
Roundhouse Group, pg 751
The Rubicon Press, pg 752
Sainsbury Publishing Ltd, pg 753
Saint Andrew Press, pg 753
St Pauls Publishing, pg 753
Saqi Books, pg 754
Steve Savage Publishers Ltd, pg 754
SAWD Publications, pg 754
SCM-Canterbury Press Ltd, pg 755
Scottish Cultural Press, pg 755
Seren, pg 756
Serif, pg 756
Serpent's Tail Ltd, pg 756
Sheldon Press, pg 757
Shelfmark Books, pg 757
Sigma Press, pg 758
Silver Link Publishing Ltd, pg 758
Simon & Schuster Ltd, pg 758
Skoob Russell Square, pg 758
Colin Smythe Ltd, pg 759
Snowbooks Ltd, pg 759
The Society for Promoting Christian Knowledge (SPCK), pg 759
Spokesman, pg 760
Stenlake Publishing Ltd, pg 761
Stobart Davies Ltd, pg 761
Sutton Publishing Ltd, pg 762
Ta Ha Publishers Ltd, pg 762
Tabb House, pg 762
Take That Ltd, pg 762
I B Tauris & Co Ltd, pg 763
Telegraph Books, pg 764
The Tarragon Press, pg 765
Thistle Press, pg 765
Time Warner Book Group UK, pg 766
Titan Books Ltd, pg 766
Triumph House, pg 767
University of Hertfordshire Press, pg 768
University of London Careers Service, pg 768
Verso, pg 770
Ward Lock Ltd, pg 771
White Cockade Publishing, pg 772
White Eagle Publishing Trust, pg 772
The Windrush Press Ltd, pg 774

Uruguay
Nordan-Comunidad, pg 778
Editia Uruguay, pg 778

Viet Nam
Science & Technics Publishing House, pg 780

Zimbabwe
Sapes Trust Ltd, pg 784

PERIODICALS, JOURNALS

Afghanistan
Government Press, pg 1

Albania
NL SH, pg 1

TYPE OF PUBLICATION INDEX

BOOK

Argentina
Libreria Akadia Editorial, pg 3
Diario la Voz del Interior, pg 5
Editorial Idearium de la Universidad de Mendoza (EDIUM), pg 6
Editorial Polemos SA, pg 8
Editoria Universitaria de la Patagonia, pg 9

Australia
ACHPER Inc (Australian Council for Health, Physical Education & Recreation), pg 10
Aerospace Publications Pty Ltd, pg 11
Australasian Medical Publishing Company Ltd (AMPCO), pg 12
Australian Academic Press Pty Ltd, pg 13
Australian Institute of Family Studies (AIFS), pg 13
Bernal Publishing, pg 14
Blackwell Publishing Asia, pg 15
Book Collectors' Society of Australia, pg 15
David Boyce Publishing, pg 16
Bureau of Resource Sciences, pg 16
Butterworths Australia Ltd, pg 16
China Books, pg 17
Covenanter Press, pg 18
CSIRO Publishing (Commonwealth Scientific & Industrial Research Organisation), pg 19
Fernfawn Publications, pg 22
Gangan Publishing, pg 23
Illert Publications, pg 26
Instauratio Press, pg 27
James Nicholas Publishers Pty Ltd, pg 27
Jesuit Publications, pg 27
Law Book Co Information Services, pg 28
Magpies Magazine Pty Ltd, pg 30
Matthias Media, pg 31
Melbourne Institute of Applied Economic & Social Research, pg 31
Mulini Press, pg 32
National Gallery of Victoria, pg 33
NMA Publications, pg 33
Jill Oxton Publications Pty Ltd, pg 35
Papyrus Publishing, pg 35
Pearson Education Australia, pg 36
Priestley Consulting, pg 37
Queen Victoria Museum & Art Gallery Publications, pg 38
Royal Society of New South Wales, pg 40
Skills Publishing, pg 41
Somerset Publications, pg 41
Thorpe-Bowker, pg 43
University of Queensland Press, pg 45
Windhorse Books, pg 47
Winetitles, pg 47

Austria
Autorensolidaritat - Verlag der Interessengemeinschaft osterreichischer Autorinnen und Autoren, pg 48
Boehlau Verlag GmbH & Co KG, pg 48
Bohmann Druck und Verlag GmbH & Co KG, pg 49
Buchkultur Verlags GmbH Zeitschrift fuer Literatur & Kunst, pg 49
DachsVerlag GmbH, pg 49
Doecker Verlag GmbH & Co KG, pg 50
Edition Ergo Sum, pg 50
Ferdinand Berger und Sohne, pg 50
Globus Buchvertrieb, pg 51
Guthmann & Peterson Liber Libri, Edition, pg 51
Horst Knapp Finanznachrichten, pg 53
Linde Verlag Wien GmbH, pg 53
Medien & Recht, pg 54
Verlag der Oesterreichischen Akademie der Wissenschaften (OEAW), pg 55
Verlag des Oesterreichischen Gewerkschaftsbundes GmbH, pg 55
Oesterreichischer Agrarverlag, Druck- und Verlags- GmbH, pg 55
Oesterreichischer Bundesverlag Gmbh, pg 55
Oesterreichischer Kunst und Kulturverlag, pg 55
Resch Verlag, pg 56
Dr A Schendl GmbH und Co KG, pg 57
Andreas Schnider Verlags-Atelier, pg 57
Springer-Verlag Wien, pg 58
Studien Verlag Gmbh, pg 58
Edition Thurnhof KEG, pg 58
Universitaetsverlag Wagner GmbH, pg 59
WUV/Facultas Universitaetsverlag, pg 60
Zirkular - Verlag der Dokumentationsstelle fuer neuere oesterreichische Literatur, pg 60

Azerbaijan
Sada, Literaturno-Izdatel'skij Centr, pg 60

Bangladesh
Gono Prakashani, Gono Shasthya Kendra, pg 61
The University Press Ltd, pg 61

Belgium
Centre Aequatoria, pg 63
NV Uitgeverij Altiora Averbode, pg 63
Bourdeaux-Capelle SA, pg 64
Brepols Publishers NV, pg 64
Etablissements Emile Bruylant SA, pg 64
Cremers (Schoollandkaarten) PVBA, pg 66
Documenta CV, pg 66
Editions Dupuis SA, pg 66
Uitgeverij de Eenhoorn, pg 67
Espace de Libertes, pg 67
Huis Van Het Boek, pg 68
Institut Royal des Relations Internationales, pg 68
Intersentia Uitgevers NV, pg 68
IPIS vzw (International Peace Information Service), pg 69
Uitgeverij J van In, pg 69
Koepel de Vlaamse Noord - Zuidbeweging 11.11.11, pg 69
Koninklijke Vlaamse Academie van Belgie voor Wetenschappen en Kunsten, pg 69
Larcier-Department of De Boeck & Larcier SA, pg 70
Editeurs de Litterature Biblique, pg 70
Maklu, pg 70
La Part de L'Oeil, pg 71
Uitgeverij Peeters Leuven (Belgie), pg 71
Sonneville Press (Uitgeverij) VTW, pg 73
Stichting Ons Erfdeel VZW, pg 73
UGA Editions (Uitgeverij), pg 73
Wolters Kluwer Belgie NV, pg 74

Benin
Office National d'Edition de Presse et d'Imprimerie (ONEPI), pg 75

Bosnia and Herzegovina
Svjetlost, pg 76

Botswana
The Botswana Society, pg 76

Brazil
Action Editora Ltda, pg 76
Agalma Psicanalise Editora Ltda, pg 77
Editora Alfa Omega Ltda, pg 77
Antenna Edicoes Tecnicas Ltda, pg 77
Editora Brasil-America (EBAL) SA, pg 79
Concordia Editora Ltda, pg 80
Companhia Editora Forense, pg 81
EDUSC - Editora da Universidade do Sagrado Coracao, pg 81
Empresa Brasileira de Pesquisa Agropecuaria, pg 81
Fundacao Instituto Brasileiro de Geografia e Estatistica (IBGE - CDDI/DECOP), pg 82
Fundacao Sao Paulo, EDUC, pg 82
Editora Globo SA, pg 82
Editora Kuarup Ltda, pg 84
Edicoes Loyola SA, pg 85
Oliveira Rocha-Comercio e Servics Ltda, pg 87
Ediouro Publicacoes, SA, pg 89
Qualitymark Editora Ltda, pg 89
Rede Das Artes (Boccato Editores Collector's), pg 89
Selecoes Eletronicas Editora Ltda, pg 90
Editora Sinodal, pg 90
Spala Editora Ltda, pg 90
Editora UNESP, pg 91
Fundacao Getulio Vargas, pg 92
Editora Vecchi SA, pg 92
Editora Vida Crista Ltda, pg 92

Bulgaria
Agencija Za Ikomomicesko Programirane i Razvitie, pg 93
Foi-Commerce, pg 94
Gea-Libris Publishing House, pg 94
Hriker, pg 94
Interpres, pg 95
LIK Izdanija, pg 95
Litera Prima, pg 95
Makros 2000 - Plovdiv, pg 95
Publishing House Narodno delo OOD, pg 96
Pensoft Publishers, pg 96
Prohazka I Kacarmazov, pg 96
Sibi, pg 97
Sila & Zivot, pg 97

Burundi
Editions Intore, pg 98

Cameroon
Presses Universitaires d'Afrique, pg 98

Chile
Ediciones Bat, pg 99
Ediciones Universitarias de Valparaiso, pg 100

China
Beijing Publishing House, pg 101
Chemical Industry Press, pg 101
China Film Press, pg 102
China Foreign Economic Relations & Trade Publishing House, pg 102
China Machine Press (CMP), pg 102
China Ocean Press, pg 102
China Oil & Gas Periodical Office, pg 102
China Tibetology Publishing House, pg 103
China Translation & Publishing Corp, pg 103
China Youth Publishing House, pg 103
Foreign Language Teaching & Research Press, pg 104
Higher Education Press, pg 105
Inner Mongolia Science & Technology Publishing House, pg 105
Language Publishing House, pg 106
The People's Communications Publishing House, pg 106
Printing Industry Publishing House, pg 107
Science Press, pg 107
Shanghai Calligraphy & Painting Publishing House, pg 108
Shanghai Foreign Language Education Press, pg 108
Tianjin Science & Technology Publishing House, pg 108
World Affairs Press, pg 109

Colombia
Centro Regional para el Fomento del Libro en America Latina y el Caribe, pg 110
Consejo Episcopal Latinoamericano (CELAM), pg 110
Editorial Norma SA, pg 112
Editorial Santillana SA, pg 112
Universidad de los Andes Editorial, pg 113

The Democratic Republic of the Congo
Connaissance et Pratique du Droit Zairos (CDPZ), pg 114
Facultes Catoliques de Kinshasa, pg 114

Costa Rica
Centro Agronomico Tropical de Investigacion y Ensenanza (CATIE), pg 115
Litografia Artex, SA, pg 115

Cote d'Ivoire
Universite d'Abidjan, pg 117
Akohi Editions, pg 117

Croatia
Drzavna Uprava za Zastitu Prirode i Okolisa (State Directorate for the Protection of Nature & Environment), pg 118
Faust Vrani, pg 118
Filozofski Fakultet Sveucilista u Zagrebu, pg 118
Hrvatsko filozofsko drustvo, pg 118
Knjizevni Krug Split, pg 118

PUBLISHERS   TYPE OF PUBLICATION INDEX

Krscanska sadasnjost, pg 118
Matica hrvatska, pg 118
Nasa Djeca Publishing, pg 119
Tehnicka Knjiga, pg 119
Vitagraf, pg 119
Znaci Vremena, Institut Za Istrazivanje Biblije, pg 119

Cuba
Casa Editora Abril, pg 120
Pueblo y Educacion Editorial (PE), pg 121

Cyprus
Action Publications, pg 121
Omilos Pnevmatikis Ananeoseos, pg 121

Czech Republic
AMA nakladatelstvi, pg 122
Divadelni Ustav, pg 123
Nakladatelstvi Jota spol sro, pg 124
Karolinum, nakladatelstvi, pg 124
Labyrint, pg 125
Lidove Noviny Publishing House, pg 125
Narodni Knihovna CR, pg 126
Narodni Muzeum, pg 126
Cesky normalizacni institut, pg 126
Portal spol sro, pg 126

Denmark
Bonnier Publications A/S, pg 129
Borgens Forlag A/S, pg 129
The Danish Literature Centre, pg 130
Dansk Psykologisk Forlag, pg 130
Djof Publishing Jurist-og Okonomforbundets Forlag, pg 130
Egmont International Holding A/S, pg 130
FADL's Forlag A/S, pg 131
Fremad A/S, pg 131
Interpresse A/S, pg 132
Mellemfolkeligt Samvirke, pg 133
Museum Tusculanum Press, pg 133
A/S Skattekartoteket, pg 134
Syddansk Universitetsforlag, pg 135

Dominican Republic
Pontificia Universidad Catolica Madre y Maestra, pg 136
Editora Taller, pg 136

Ecuador
Centro de Planificacion y Estudios Sociales (CEPLAES), pg 136
CIESPAL (Centro Internacional de Estudios Superiores de Comunicacion para America Latina), pg 136
Corporacion Editora Nacional, pg 136

Egypt (Arab Republic of Egypt)
American University in Cairo Press, pg 137
Al Arab Publishing House, pg 137
Dar Al Hilal Publishing Institution, pg 138
Ummah Press, pg 138

El Salvador
Editorial Universitaria de la Universidad de El Salvador, pg 139

Estonia
Estonian Academy Publishers, pg 139
Kirjastus Kunst, pg 139
Tael Ltd, pg 140

Finland
Forsamlingsforbundets Forlags AB, pg 142
Kustannus Oy Uusi Tie, pg 143

France
Editions Al Liamm, pg 146
Editions Arcam, pg 147
Editions Art & Metiers Du Livre, pg 147
Editions de l'Atelier, pg 148
Autrement Editions, pg 148
Editions l'Avant-Scene de Prette Technique, pg 149
La Bartavelle, pg 149
Editions Belin, pg 149
Editions Bertout, pg 149
Emgleo Breiz, pg 151
Brud Nevez, pg 151
Editions des Cahiers Bourbonnais, pg 151
Editions Casterman, pg 152
CERDIC-Publications, pg 153
Editions Champ Vallon, pg 153
Cirad, pg 154
CTNERHI - Centre Technique National d'Etudes et de Recherches sur les Handicaps et les Inadaptations, pg 156
Editions Dalloz Sirey, pg 157
La Documentation Francaise, pg 158
Doin Editeurs, pg 159
Les Dossiers d'Aquitaine, pg 159
Dunod Editeur, pg 159
Editions de l'Ecole des Hautes Etudes en Sciences Sociales (EHESS), pg 159
Editions et Publications de l'Ecole Lacanienne (EPEL), pg 159
Editions Edisud, pg 159
Les Editeurs Reunis, pg 160
Les Editions ESF, pg 160
Editions rue d'Ulm, pg 160
EDP Sciences, pg 161
Elf Exploration Production, pg 161
Elsevier SAS (Editions Scientifiques et Medicales Elsevier), pg 161
Editions Entente, pg 161
L'Ere Nouvelle, pg 161
Editions Eres, pg 162
Editions Errance, pg 162
Editions Eska, pg 162
L'Esprit Du Temps, pg 162
Institut d'Etudes Augustiniennes, pg 162
Folklore Comtois, pg 164
Association Frank, pg 164
Futuribles SARL, pg 164
Editions Ganymede, pg 165
Paul Geuthner Librairie Orientaliste, pg 165
Hachette Livre International, pg 167
L'Harmattan, pg 167
Editions Hermes Science Publications, pg 167
Editions d'Histoire Sociale (EDHIS), pg 168
INRA Editions (Institut National de la Recherche Agronomique), pg 168
Institut International de la Marionnette, pg 169
IRD Editions, pg 169
Editions Klincksieck, pg 170
Editions Universitaires LCF, pg 171

Editions Legislatives, pg 171
LLB France (Ligue pour la Lecture de la Bible), pg 173
Editions de la Maison des Sciences de l'Homme, Paris, pg 173
Masson Editeur, pg 174
Editions Medianes, pg 175
Presses Universitaires du Mirail, pg 176
Editions Ophrys, pg 177
Opsys Operating System, pg 178
Ouest Editions, pg 178
Editions du Papyrus, pg 178
Editions Parentheses, pg 179
Editions Pedone, pg 179
Peeters-France, pg 179
Jean-Michel Place, pg 180
Les Editions du Point Veterinaire, pg 180
Editions du Centre Pompidou, pg 180
Presses Universitaires de Caen, pg 181
Presses Universitaires de France (PUF), pg 181
Presses Universitaires de Grenoble, pg 181
Presses Universitaires de Nancy, pg 181
PRODIG, pg 182
Editions Publications de l'Ecole Moderne Francaise sa (PEMF), pg 182
Publications de l'Universite de Rouen, pg 182
Editions Revue EPS, pg 183
Revue Espaces et Societes, pg 183
Revue Noire, pg 183
Sepia Editions, pg 184
Editions Le Serpent a Plumes, pg 184
Service des Publications Scientifiques du Museum National d'Histoire Naturelle, pg 184
Societe Mathematique de France - Institut Henri Poincare, pg 185
Editions Springer France, pg 186
SUD, pg 186
Editions Techniques et Scientifiques Francaises, pg 187
Terre Vivante, pg 187
Transeuropeennes/RCE, pg 188
Publications de l'Universite de Pau, pg 188
La Vague a l'ame, pg 188
Editions Vague Verte, pg 188
La Voix du Regard, pg 189

Germany
A Francke Verlag (Tubingen und Basel), pg 190
Accedo Verlagsgesellschaft mbH, pg 190
Akademie Verlag GmbH, pg 191
E Albrecht Verlags-KG, pg 192
ALS-Verlag GmbH, pg 192
Antiqua-Verlag GmbH, pg 193
AOL-Verlag Frohmut Menze, pg 193
Arbeiterpresse Verlags- und Vertriebsgesellschaft mbH, pg 193
ARCult Media, pg 193
Ardey-Verlag GmbH, pg 193
Aschendorffsche Verlagsbuchhandlung GmbH & Co KG, pg 194
Asgard-Verlag Dr Werner Hippe GmbH, pg 194
J J Augustin Verlag GmbH, pg 195
Aussaat Verlag, pg 195
Aviatic Verlag GmbH, pg 196

J P Bachem Verlag GmbH, pg 196
Bank-Verlag GmbH, pg 197
Barenreiter-Verlag Karl-Votterle GmbH & Co KG, pg 197
Verlag Dr Albert Bartens KG, pg 197
Bastei Verlag, pg 197
Baumann GmbH & Co KG, pg 197
Bauverlag GmbH, pg 198
Beacon Verlag Koerber OHG, pg 198
Ludwig Bechauf Verlag, pg 198
Verlag C H Beck oHG, pg 198
Verlag Beleke KG, pg 198
Berliner Debatte Wissenschafts Verlag, GSFP-Gesellschaft fur Sozialwissen-schaftliche Forschung und Publizistik mbH & Co KG, pg 199
Bertelsmann Lexikon Verlag GmbH, pg 200
W Bertelsmann Verlag GmbH & Co KG, pg 200
Bibliomed - Medizinische Verlagsgesellschaft mbH, pg 201
Blackwell Wissenschafts-Verlag GmbH, pg 201
Blaukreuz-Verlag Wuppertal, pg 202
BLV Verlagsgesellschaft mbH, pg 202
Verlag Erwin Bochinsky GmbH & Co KG, pg 202
Bock und Herchen Verlag, pg 202
Boehlau-Verlag GmbH & Cie, pg 202
Verlag Hermann Boehlaus Nachfolger Weimar GmbH & Co, pg 203
CB-Verlag Carl Boldt, pg 203
Born-Verlag, pg 203
Brandes & Apsel Verlag GmbH, pg 204
F Bruckmann Munchen Verlag & Druck GmbH & Co Produkt KG, pg 204
BuchMarkt Verlag K Werner GmbH, pg 205
Buchverlag Junge Welt GmbH, pg 205
Buechse der Pandora Verlags-GmbH, pg 205
Bund fuer deutsche Schrift und Sprache, pg 206
Bund-Verlag GmbH, pg 206
Bundesanzeiger Verlagsgesellschaft, pg 206
Aenne Burda Verlag, pg 206
Verlag Georg D W Callwey GmbH & Co, pg 207
Calwer Verlag GmbH, pg 207
Campusbooks Medien AG, pg 207
Fachverlag Hans Carl GmbH, pg 207
Carl Link Verlag-Gesellschaft mbH Fachverlag fur Verwaltungsrecht, pg 207
Centaurus-Verlagsgesellschaft GmbH, pg 207
Chmielorz GmbH Verlag, pg 208
Chr Belser AG fur Verlagsgeschaefte und Co KG, pg 208
Christliches Verlagshaus GmbH, pg 208
Marianne Cieslik, pg 209
Charles Coleman Verlag GmbH & Co KG, pg 209
Compact Verlag GmbH, pg 209
Connection Medien GmbH, pg 209
J G Cotta'sche Buchhandlung Nachfolger GmbH, pg 210
Data Becker GmbH & Co KG, pg 210

845

TYPE OF PUBLICATION INDEX — BOOK

Degener & Co, Manfred Dreiss Verlag, pg 211
Verlag Horst Deike KG, pg 211
Deutsche Landwirtschafts-Gesellschaft VerlagsgesGmbH, pg 212
Verlag Deutsche Unitarier, pg 212
Deutsche Verlags-Anstalt GmbH (DVA), pg 212
Deutscher Apotheker Verlag Dr Roland Schmiedel GmbH & Co, pg 212
Deutscher Drucker Verlagsgesellschaft mbH & Co KG, pg 212
Deutscher EC-Verband, pg 212
Deutscher Fachverlag GmbH, pg 212
Deutscher Gemeindeverlag GmbH, pg 212
Deutscher Instituts-Verlag GmbH, pg 213
Deutscher Kunstverlag GmbH, pg 213
Deutscher Psychologen Verlag GmbH (DPV), pg 213
Deutscher Verlag fur Kunstwissenschaft GmbH, pg 213
Deutscher Wirtschaftsdienst John von Freyend GmbH, pg 214
Diagonal-Verlag GbR Rink-Schweer, pg 214
Die Verlag H Schafer GmbH, pg 214
Dietrich zu Klampen Verlag, pg 214
Verlag J H W Dietz Nachf GmbH, pg 214
Dietz Verlag Berlin GmbH, pg 215
Edition Diskord, pg 215
DLV Deutscher Landwirtschaftsverlag GmbH, pg 215
Christoph Dohr, pg 215
Domino Verlag, Guenther Brinek GmbH, pg 215
Domowina Verlag GmbH, pg 215
Duncker und Humblot GmbH, pg 217
Dustri-Verlag Dr Karl Feistle, pg 217
Echter Wurzburg Frankische Gesellschaftsdruckerei und Verlag GmbH, pg 217
Ecomed Verlagsgesellschaft AG & Co KG, pg 218
Egmont EHAPA Verlag GmbH, pg 218
Elektor-Verlag GmbH, pg 219
Verlag Peter Engstler, pg 220
Eppinger-Verlag OHG, pg 220
Erasmus Grasser-Verlag GmbH, pg 220
Ergebnisse Verlag GmbH, pg 220
Ernst, Wilhelm & Sohn, Verlag Architektur und technische Wissenschaft GmbH & Co, pg 221
Verlag Esoterische Philosophie GmbH, pg 221
Eulenhof-Verlag Wolfgang Ehrhardt Heinold, pg 221
Europa Union Verlag GmbH, pg 222
Verlag Europaeische Wehrkunde, pg 222
Evangelische Verlagsanstalt GmbH, pg 222
Evangelischer Presseverband fuer Baden eV, pg 222
Evangelischer Presseverband fuer Bayern eV, pg 222
Fachverlag fur das graphische Gewerbe GmbH, pg 223

Fachverlag Schiele & Schoen GmbH, pg 223
Ferd Dummler's Verlag, pg 223
Ferdinand Enke Verlag, pg 224
Harald Fischer Verlag GmbH, pg 224
Franz-Sales-Verlag, pg 226
Verlag Franz Vahlen GmbH, pg 226
Fraunhofer IRB Verlag Fraunhofer Informationszentrum Raum und Bau, pg 226
Verlag A Fromm im Druck- u Verlagshaus Fromm GmbH & Co KG, pg 227
Friedrich Frommann Verlag, pg 227
G Braun (vormals G Braun'sche Hofbuchdruckerei und Verlag) Gmbh, pg 227
Verlagsbuchhandlung Megapress, Franz-J Gaber, pg 228
Betriebswirtschaftlicher Verlag Dr Th Gabler, pg 228
Gebrueder Borntraeger Science Publishers, pg 228
Konkursbuch Verlag Claudia Gehrke, pg 228
Verlag Junge Gemeinde E Schwinghammer GmbH & Co KG, pg 228
Alfons W Gentner Verlag GmbH & Co KG, pg 228
Germanisches Nationalmuseum, pg 228
Gesundheits-Dialog Verlag GmbH, pg 229
H Gietl Verlag & Publikationsservice GmbH, pg 229
Gildefachverlag GmbH & Co KG, pg 229
Gilles und Francke Verlag, pg 229
Govi-Verlag Pharmazeutischer Verlag GmbH, pg 230
Grass-Verlag, pg 231
Walter de Gruyter GmbH & Co KG, pg 231
Verlag des Gustav-Adolf-Werks, pg 232
Dr Curt Haefner-Verlag GmbH, pg 233
Carl Hanser Verlag, pg 234
Harenberg Kommunikation Verlags- und Medien-GmbH & Co KG, pg 234
Harrassowitz Verlag, pg 234
Haufe Mediengruppe, pg 235
Rudolf Haufe Verlag GmbH & Co KG, pg 235
Karl F Haug Verlag GmbH & Co, pg 235
Heel Verlag GmbH, pg 235
Verlag Herder GmbH & Co KG, pg 236
Hestra-Verlag Hernichel & Dr Strauss GmbH & Co KG, pg 237
Carl Heymanns Verlag KG, pg 237
F Hirthammer Verlag GmbH, pg 238
S Hirzel Verlag GmbH und Co, pg 238
Verlag Karl Hofmann GmbH & Co, pg 238
Hoppenstedt GmbH & Co KG, pg 239
Horlemann Verlag, pg 239
Edition Humanistische Psychologie (EHP), pg 240
Edition Hundertmark, pg 240
Huss-Medien GmbH, pg 240
Huss-Medien GmbH, pg 240
Huthig GmbH & Co KG, pg 240
IKO Verlag fur Interkulturelle Kommunikation, pg 241

Verlag fuer Internationale Politik GmbH, pg 242
Klaus Isele, pg 242
Iudicium Verlag GmbH, pg 242
Verlag J P Peter, Gebr Holstein GmbH & Co KG, pg 242
Jahreszeiten-Verlag GmbH, pg 242
Jan Thorbecke Verlag GmbH & Co, pg 243
Janus Verlagsgesellschaft, Dr Norbert Meder & Co, pg 243
Junfermann-Verlag, pg 243
Junius Verlag GmbH, pg 244
Jutta Pohl Verlag, pg 244
Juventa Verlag GmbH, pg 244
Kallmeyer'sche Verlagsbuchhandlung GmbH, pg 244
Katzmann Verlag KG, pg 245
Kirschbaum Verlag GmbH, pg 246
Vittorio Klostermann GmbH, pg 247
Verlagsgruppe Koehler/Mittler, pg 248
Koehlers Verlagsgesellschaft mbH, pg 248
Koesler Verlag GmbH, pg 248
W Kohlhammer GmbH, pg 248
Kolibri-Verlag GmbH, pg 249
Konradin-Verlagsgruppe, pg 249
kopaed verlagsgmbh, pg 249
Koptisch-Orthodoxes Zentrum, pg 249
Krafthand Verlag Walter Schultz GmbH, pg 250
Verlag Waldemar Kramer, pg 250
Laaber-Verlag, pg 251
Peter Lang GmbH Europaeischer Verlag der Wissenschaften, pg 252
Michael Lassleben Verlag und Druckerei, pg 252
J Latka Verlag GmbH, pg 253
Leipziger Universitaetsverlag GmbH, pg 253
Verlag Otto Lembeck, pg 253
Antiquariat Oskar Loewe, pg 255
Logos-Verlag Literatur & Layout GmbH, pg 255
Hermann Luchterhand Verlag GmbH, pg 255
Lucius & Lucius Verlagsgesellschaft mbH, pg 255
Verlagsgruppe Luebbe GmbH & Co KG, pg 256
Institut fuer Marxistische Studien und Forschungen eV (IMSF), pg 257
Mattes Verlag GmbH, pg 257
Matthias-Gruenewald-Verlag GmbH, pg 258
Medizinisch-Literarische Verlagsgesellschaft mbH, pg 258
Meisenbach Verlag GmbH, pg 258
Meyer & Meyer Verlag, pg 260
Missio eV, pg 260
E S Mittler und Sohn GmbH, pg 261
mode information Heinz Kramer GmbH, pg 261
Modellsport Verlag GmbH, pg 261
Mohr Siebeck, pg 261
C F Mueller Verlag, Huethig Gmb H & Co, pg 262
Verlag Norbert Mueller AG & Co KG, pg 262
Munzinger-Archiv GmbH Archiv fuer publizistische Arbeit, pg 262
MVB Marketing- und Verlagsservice des Buchhandels GmbH, pg 263

Verlag Natur & Wissenschaft Harro Hieronimus & Dr Jurgen Schmidt, pg 263
Verlag Neue Stadt GmbH, pg 264
Verlag Neue Wirtschafts-Briefe GmbH & Co, pg 264
Max Niemeyer Verlag GmbH, pg 265
Nomos Verlagsgesellschaft mbH und Co KG, pg 265
Oeko-Test Verlag GmbH & Co KG Betriebsgesellschaft, pg 266
Verlag Offene Worte, pg 266
R Oldenbourg Verlag GmbH, pg 267
Georg Olms Verlag AG, pg 267
Edition Parabolis, pg 268
Paranus Verlag - Bruecke Neumuenster GmbH, pg 268
Justus Perthes Verlag Gotha GmbH, pg 269
Verlag Dr Friedrich Pfeil, pg 269
Richard Pflaum Verlag GmbH & Co KG, pg 269
Physica-Verlag, pg 270
pmi Verlag, pg 270
Podzun-Pallas Verlag GmbH, pg 270
Polygraph Verlag GmbH, pg 271
Possev-Verlag GmbH, pg 271
Premop Verlag GmbH, pg 271
Presse Verlagsgesellschaft mbH, pg 271
Projektion J Buch- und Musikverlag GmbH, pg 272
Psychiatrie-Verlag GmbH, pg 272
Psychosozial-Verlag, pg 272
Verlag Friedrich Pustet GmbH & Co Kg, pg 272
Quintessenz Verlags-GmbH, pg 273
Dr Josef Raabe-Verlags GmbH, pg 273
Radius-Verlag GmbH, pg 273
Reader's Digest Deutschland Verlag Das Beste GmbH, pg 274
Verlag Recht und Wirtschaft GmbH, pg 274
Dr Ludwig Reichert Verlag, pg 274
Richardi Helmut Verlag GmbH, pg 276
Ritterbach Verlag GmbH, pg 276
Rossipaul Kommunikation GmbH, pg 277
Verlag Werner Sachon GmbH & Co, pg 277
J D Sauerlaender's Verlag, pg 278
K G Saur Verlag GmbH, A Gale/Thomson Learning Company, pg 278
M & H Schaper GmbH & Co KG, pg 279
Schiffahrts-Verlag, pg 279
Schild-Verlag GmbH, pg 279
Verlag Dr Otto Schmidt KG, pg 280
Verlag Schnell und Steiner GmbH, pg 281
Verlag Hans Schoener GmbH, pg 281
Schott Musik International GmbH & Co KG, pg 281
Schueren Verlag GmbH, pg 281
Schulz-Kirchner Verlag GmbH, pg 282
Verlag R S Schulz GmbH, pg 282
Otto Schwartz Fachbochhandlung GmbH, pg 282
E Schweizerbart'sche Verlagsbuchhandlung (Naegele und Obermiller), pg 282
Siegler & Co Verlag fuer Zeitarchive GmbH, pg 283

PUBLISHERS — TYPE OF PUBLICATION INDEX

Georg Siemens Verlagsbuchhandlung, pg 283
Silberburg-Verlag Titus Haeussermann GmbH, pg 283
Spektrum der Wissenschaft Verlagsgesellschaft mbH, pg 284
Spiegel-Verlag Rudolf Augstein GmbH & Co KG, pg 284
Springer Science+Business Media GmbH & Co KG, pg 284
Springer Science+Business Media GmbH & Co KG, Berlin, pg 285
Verlag Stahleisen GmbH, pg 286
C A Starke Verlag, pg 287
Stauffenburg Verlag Brigitte Narr GmbH, pg 287
Franz Steiner Verlag Wiesbaden GmbH, pg 287
Dr Dietrich Steinkopff Verlag GmbH & Co, pg 287
Terra-Verlag GmbH, pg 290
Tetra Verlag Gmbh, pg 290
Tetzlaff Verlag, pg 290
edition Text & Kritik im Richard Boorberg Verlag GmbH & Co, pg 290
Thalacker Medien GmbH Co KG, pg 290
Druck-und Verlagshans Thiele & Schwarz GmbH, pg 290
Georg Thieme Verlag KG, pg 291
TR - Verlagsunion GmbH, pg 291
Traditionell Bogenschiessen Verlag Angelika Hornig, pg 292
Trans Tech Publications, pg 292
Treves Editions Verein Zur Foerderung der Kuenstlerischen Taetigkeiten, pg 292
Trotzdem-Verlags Genossenschaft eG, pg 292
Verlag Eugen Ulmer GmbH & Co, pg 293
Ulrike Helmer Verlag, pg 293
UNO-Verlag GmbH, pg 293
Urban & Vogel Medien und Medizin Verlagsgesellschaft mbH & Co KG, pg 294
UVK Universitatsverlag Konstanz GmbH, pg 294
UVK Verlagsgesellschaft mbH, pg 294
Dorothea van der Koelen, pg 294
Vandenhoeck & Ruprecht, pg 294
VDI Verlag GmbH, pg 294
Verein der Benediktiner zu Beuron-Beuroner Kunstverlag, pg 294
Vereinigte Fachverlage GmbH, pg 295
Verlag fuer die Frau GmbH, pg 295
Verlag fur die Rechts- und Anwaltspraxis GmbH & Co, pg 295
Verlag fur Schweissen und Verwandte Verfahren, pg 295
Verlag und Druckkontor Kamp GmbH, pg 295
Vervuert Verlagsgesellschaft, pg 295
Friedr Vieweg & Sohn Verlag, pg 296
Curt R Vincentz Verlag, pg 296
Edition Curt Visel, pg 296
Vogel Medien GmbH & Co KG, pg 296
Dokument und Analyse Verlag Bogislaw von Randow, pg 296
VS Verlag fur Sozialwissenschaften, pg 297
VVF Verlag V Florentz GmbH, pg 297
VWB-Verlag fur Wissenschaft & Bildung, Amand Aglaster, pg 297
Wachholtz Verlag GmbH, pg 297

Walhalla Fachverlag GmbH & Co KG Praetoria, pg 297
Uwe Warnke Verlag, pg 297
Wartburg Verlag GmbH, pg 297
Waxmann Verlag GmbH, pg 297
WEKA Firmengruppe GmbH & Co KG, pg 298
Verlagsgruppe Weltbild GmbH, pg 298
Georg Westermann Verlag GmbH, pg 299
Westholsteinische Verlagsanstalt und Verlagsdruckerei Boyens & Co, pg 299
Wichern Verlag GmbH, pg 299
Herbert Wichmann Verlag, pg 299
Wiley-VCH Verlag GmbH, pg 300
Wissenschaftliche Verlagsgesellschaft mbH, pg 300
Verlag Konrad Wittwer GmbH, pg 301
Verlagshaus Wohlfarth, pg 301
WRS Verlag Wirtschaft, Recht und Steuern GmbH & Co KG, pg 301
Verlag Philipp von Zabern, pg 302
Verlag Zeitschrift fur Naturforschung, pg 302

Ghana

Black Mask Ltd, pg 303
Educational Press & Manufacturers Ltd, pg 303
World Literature Project, pg 305

Greece

Apostoliki Diakonia tis Ekklisias tis Hellados, pg 305
Beta Medical Publishers, pg 306
Ekdoseis Domi AE, pg 306
Exandas Publishers, pg 307
Govostis Publishing SA, pg 307
Harmi-Press Publications, Haroula D Papadimitriou G P, pg 308
Hestia-I D Hestia-Kollaros & Co Corporation, pg 308
Katoptro Publications, pg 309
Logos, pg 309
Editions Moressopoulos, pg 310
Ed Nea Acropolis, pg 310
Nomiki Bibliothiki, pg 310
M Psaropoulos & Co EE, pg 311
Sakkoulas Publications SA, pg 312
Society for Macedonian Studies, pg 312
Stochastis, pg 312
Technical Chamber of Greece, pg 312

Guatemala

Grupo Editorial RIN-78, pg 313

Guinea-Bissau

Instituto Nacional de Estudos e Pesquisa (INEP), pg 314

Guyana

The Hamburgh Register, pg 314

Hong Kong

Adsale Publishing Co Ltd, pg 315
Celeluck Co Ltd, pg 316
The Chinese University Press, pg 316
Electronic Technology Publishing Co Ltd, pg 317
Friends of the Earth (Charity) Ltd, pg 317
Geocarto International Centre, pg 317
Joint Publishing (HK) Co Ltd, pg 317

Modern Electronic & Computing Publishing Co Ltd, pg 318
Photoart Ltd, pg 318
Research Centre for Translation, pg 319
Technology Exchange Ltd, pg 319
Thomson Corporation, pg 319
Times Publishing (Hong Kong) Ltd, pg 319
Wellday Ltd, pg 320
Yazhou Zhoukan Ltd, pg 320

Hungary

Agape Ferences Nyomda es Konyvkiado Kft, pg 320
Foldmuvelesugyi Miniszterium Muszaki Intezet, pg 321
Ifjusagi Lap-eskonyvkiado Vallalat, pg 321
KJK-Kerszov, pg 322
Marton Aron Kiado Publishing House, pg 323
Mueszaki Koenyvkiado Ltd, pg 323
Mult es Jovo Kiado, pg 323
Nemzetkozi Szinhazi Intezet Magyar Kozpontja, pg 323
Officina Nova Konyvek, pg 323

Iceland

Haskolautgafan - University of Iceland Press, pg 325
Mal og menning, pg 326
Stofnun Arna Magnussonar a Islandi, pg 326

India

Advaita Ashrama, pg 327
Allied Book Centre, pg 328
Bani Mandir, Book-Sellers, Publishers & Educational Suppliers, pg 329
Bharatiya Vidya Bhavan, pg 330
Doaba Publications, pg 333
Eastern Book Co, pg 333
Hindi Pracharak Sansthan, pg 336
Indian Council of Agricultural Research, pg 336
Indian Council of Social Science Research (ICSSR), pg 336
Indian Museum, pg 337
B Jain Publishers (P) Ltd, pg 339
Law Publishers, pg 340
Sri Ramakrishna Math, pg 341
National Council of Applied Economic Research, Publications Division, pg 342
Publications & Information Directorate, CSIR, pg 345
Reliance Publishing House, pg 346
Research Signpost, pg 347
SAGE Publications India Pvt Ltd, pg 347
Satprakashan Sanchar Kendra, pg 348
Scientific Book Agency, pg 348
Shaibya Prakashan Bibhag, pg 349
Sita Books & Periodicals Pvt Ltd, pg 349
South Asian Publishers Pvt Ltd, pg 350
Spectrum Publications, pg 350
Theosophical Publishing House, pg 351
Transworld Research Network, pg 351
Vidya Puri, pg 352

Indonesia

PT Dian Rakyat, pg 354
Lembaga Demografi Fakultas Ekonomi Universitas Indonesia, pg 355

Ireland

Cathedral Books Ltd, pg 358
Cork University Press, pg 359
The Economic & Social Research Institute, pg 359
Gandon Editions, pg 360
Government Publications Ireland, pg 360
Institute of Public Administration, pg 361
Round Hall Sweet & Maxwell, pg 363
Royal Irish Academy, pg 363

Israel

Academy of the Hebrew Language, pg 364
Bar Ilan University Press, pg 365
Ben-Zvi Institute, pg 365
Bitan Publishers Ltd, pg 365
Freund Publishing House Ltd, pg 367
Gefen Publishing House Ltd, pg 367
Habermann Institute for Literary Research, pg 367
Haifa University Press, pg 367
Hanitzotz A-Sharara Publishing House, pg 367
The Institute for the Translation of Hebrew Literature, pg 368
Israel Antiquities Authority, pg 368
Israel Exploration Society, pg 368
Israel Music Institute (IMI), pg 368
Jerusalem Center for Public Affairs, pg 369
Maaliyot-Institute for Research Publications, pg 370
Rubin Mass Ltd, pg 371
Schlesinger Institute, pg 371
Tirosh Communication Ltd, pg 372
Yad Vashem - The Holocaust Martyrs' & Heroes' Remembrance Authority, pg 373
The Zalman Shazar Center, pg 374

Italy

AIB Associazione Italiana Bibliotheche, pg 374
Alba, pg 375
All'Insegna del Giglio, pg 375
Umberto Allemandi & C SRL, pg 375
Editore Armando Armando SRL, pg 376
Associazione Internazionale di Archeologia Classica, pg 377
Athesia Verlag Bozen, pg 377
Baha'i, pg 377
Belforte Editore Libraio srl, pg 377
Giuseppe Bonanno Editore, pg 378
Edizioni Bora SNC di E Brandani & C, pg 379
Edizioni Borla SRL, pg 379
Edizioni Bucalo SNC, pg 379
Campanotto, pg 379
Edizioni Cantagalli, pg 379
Edizioni Carmelitane, pg 380
Casa Musicale Edizioni Carrara SRL, pg 380
Editrice Il Castoro, pg 380
CEDAM (Casa Editrice Dr A Milani), pg 380
Istituto Centrale per il Catalogo Unico delle Biblioteche Italiane e per le Informazioni Bibliografiche, pg 381
Centro Scientifico Torinese, pg 381
Edizioni Centro Studi Erickson, pg 381
Centro Studi Terzo Mondo, pg 381
CIC Edizioni Internazionali, pg 381

TYPE OF PUBLICATION INDEX

BOOK

La Cultura Sociologica, pg 384
Edizioni Dedalo SRL, pg 384
Edizioni Dehoniane Bologna (EDB), pg 384
Direzione Generale Archivi, pg 385
Editoriale Domus SpA, pg 385
Edizioni d'Arte Antica e Moderna EDAM, pg 386
Edizioni del Centro Camuno di Studi Preistorici, pg 386
EDT Edizioni di Torino, pg 387
Elle Di Ci - Libreria Dottrina Cristiana, pg 387
ERGA SNC di Carla Ottino Merli & C (Edizioni Realizzazioni Grafiche - Artigiana), pg 388
L'Erma di Bretschneider SRL, pg 388
Edi.Ermes srl, pg 388
Etas Libri, pg 388
ETR (Editrice Trasporti su Rotaie), pg 388
EuroGeoGrafiche Mencattini, pg 388
Feguagiskia' Studios, pg 389
Arnaldo Forni Editore SRL, pg 389
Edizioni del Girasole srl, pg 390
Giunti Gruppo Editoriale, pg 390
Gruppo Editoriale Faenza Editrice SpA, pg 391
Herder Editrice e Libreria, pg 392
IHT Gruppo Editoriale SRL, pg 393
In Dialogo, pg 393
International University Press Srl, pg 393
Jandi-Sapi Editori, pg 394
Il Lavoro Editoriale, pg 395
LED - Edizioni Universitarie di Lettere Economia Diritto, pg 395
Casa Editrice Le Lettere SRL, pg 395
Liguori Editore SRL, pg 395
LIM Editrice SRL, pg 395
Lybra Immagine, pg 396
Macro Edizioni, pg 397
Giuseppe Maimone Editore, pg 397
Milella di Lecce Spazio Vivo srl, pg 398
Giorgio Mondadori & Associati, pg 399
Moretti & Vitali Editori srl, pg 399
Societa Editrice Il Mulino, pg 399
Museo storico in Trento, pg 400
Casa Editrice Roberto Napoleone, pg 400
New Magazine Edizioni, pg 400
Editoriale Olimpia SpA, pg 401
Leo S Olschki, pg 401
Palatina Editrice, pg 402
G B Palumbo & C Editore SpA, pg 402
Franco Cosimo Panini Editore SpA, pg 402
Piero Manni srl, pg 403
Pitagora Editrice SRL, pg 403
Pontificio Istituto Orientale, pg 404
Priuli e Verlucca, Editori, pg 404
RAI-ERI, pg 405
Franco Maria Ricci Editore (FMR), pg 405
Rirea Casa Editrice della Rivista Italiana di Ragioneria e di Economia Aziendale, pg 405
Rubbettino Editore, pg 406
Sardini Editrice, pg 407
Salvatore Sciascia Editore, pg 407
Edizioni Segno SRL, pg 407
Segretariato Nazionale Apostolato della Preghiera, pg 408
SEMAR Publishers SRL, pg 408
Servitium, pg 408
Sicania, pg 408
Edizioni Librarie Siciliane, pg 408

Societa Napoletana Storia Patria Napoli, pg 408
Societa Stampa Sportiva, pg 408
Edizioni Rosminiane Sodalitas, pg 408
Sorbona, pg 409
Edizioni del Teresianum, pg 410
Tilgher-Genova sas, pg 410
Vaccari SRL, pg 411
Vivalda Editori SRL, pg 412
Vivere In SRL, pg 412
Zanfi-Logos, pg 412

Jamaica

American Chamber of Commerce of Jamaica, pg 413
Institute of Jamaica Publications, pg 413
The Jamaica Bauxite Institute, pg 413
UWI Publishers' Association, pg 414

Japan

Akita Shoten Publishing Co Ltd, pg 415
The American Chamber of Commerce in Japan, pg 415
Bijutsu Shuppan-Sha, Ltd, pg 415
Daiichi Shuppan Co Ltd, pg 416
Dobunshoin Publishers Co, pg 416
Dohosha Publishing Co Ltd, pg 417
Genko-Sha, pg 417
Heibonsha Ltd, Publishers, pg 418
Hokuryukan Co Ltd, pg 418
Ie-No-Hikari Association, pg 419
Igaku-Shoin Ltd, pg 419
Iwanami Shoten, Publishers, pg 419
Kodansha Ltd, pg 421
Kosei Publishing Co Ltd, pg 421
Maruzen Co Ltd, pg 422
Mejikaru Furendo-sha, pg 422
Minerva Shobo Co Ltd, pg 422
Nigensha Publishing Co Ltd, pg 423
Nihon Rodo Kenkyu Kiko, pg 423
Nippon Jitsugyo Publishing Co Ltd, pg 424
Obunsha Co Ltd, pg 424
Ohmsha Ltd, pg 424
Ongaku No Tomo Sha Corporation, pg 425
Rinsen Book Co Ltd, pg 425
Shinkenchiku-Sha Co Ltd, pg 427
Shueisha Inc, pg 428
Springer-Verlag Tokyo, pg 428
Tankosha Publishing Co Ltd, pg 429
Toyo Keizai Shinpo-Sha, pg 430
Universal Academy Press, Inc, pg 430
Yohan Shuppan, pg 431
Yushodo Shuppan, pg 431
Zeimukeiri-Kyokai, pg 431

Jordan

Al-Tanwir Al Ilmi (Scientific Enlightenment Publishing House), pg 432

Kazakstan

Gylym, Izd-Vo, pg 432

Kenya

Africa Book Services (EA) Ltd, pg 433
British Institute in Eastern Africa, pg 433
Gaba Publications Amecea, Pastoral Institute, pg 434
International Centre for Research in Agroforestry (ICRAF), pg 434

Kenya Energy & Environment Organisation, Kengo, pg 434
Kenya Medical Research Institute (KEMRI), pg 435
Kenya Meteorological Department, pg 435
Shirikon Publishers, pg 436
Space Sellers Ltd, pg 436
Gideon S Were Press, pg 436

Democratic People's Republic of Korea

The Foreign Language Press Group, pg 436
Foreign Languages Publishing House, pg 436
Korea Science and Encyclopedia Publishing House, pg 436

Republic of Korea

Chung Rim Publishing Co Ltd, pg 438
Hak Won Publishing Co, pg 439
Ke Mong Sa Publishing Co Ltd, pg 440
Korean Publishers Association, pg 440
Literature Academy Publishing, pg 441
Nanam Publications Co, pg 441
Prompter Publications, pg 442
YBM/Si-sa, pg 443

Latvia

Artava Ltd, pg 444
Egmont Latvia SIA, pg 444
Preses Nams, pg 445

Lebanon

Dar-El-Machreq Sarl, pg 446
Institute for Palestine Studies, Publishing & Research Organization (IPS), pg 446

Liechtenstein

Botanisch-Zoologische Gesellschaft, pg 447
Topos Verlag AG, pg 448

Lithuania

Academia, pg 448
AS Narbuto Leidykla (AS Narbutas' Publishers), pg 448
Baltos Lankos, pg 449
Egmont Lietuva, pg 449
Martynas Mazvydas National Library of Lithuania, pg 449
TEV Leidykla, pg 450

Luxembourg

Editions APESS ASBL, pg 450
Cahiers Luxembourgeois, pg 451
Editions Saint-Paul, pg 451
Service Central de la Statistique et des Etudes Economiques (STATEC), pg 451

Macau

Livros Do Oriente, pg 452

The Former Yugoslav Republic of Macedonia

Detska radost, pg 452
Medis, Skopje, pg 452
Mi-An Knigoizdatelstvo, pg 452
St Clement of Ohrid National & University Library, pg 453

Madagascar

Maison d'Edition Protestante ANTSO, pg 453
Foibe Filan-Kevitry NY Mpampianatra (FOFIPA), pg 453
JEAG, pg 453
Madagascar Print & Press Company, pg 453
Societe Malgache d'Edition, pg 454

Malawi

Central Africana Ltd, pg 454

Malaysia

Berita Publishing Sdn Bhd, pg 455
Dewan Bahasa dan Pustaka, pg 455
Mahir Publications Sdn Bhd, pg 456
Malayan Law Journal Sdn Bhd, pg 456
The Malaysian Current Law Journal Sdn Bhd, pg 457
Pustaka Cipta Sdn Bhd, pg 458
Tropical Press Sdn Bhd, pg 459
University of Malaya, Department of Publications, pg 459

Maldive Islands

Non-Formal Education Centre, pg 459

Malta

Fondazzjoni Patrimonju Malti, pg 460

Mexico

Editorial AGATA SA de CV, pg 462
Grupo Editorial Armonia, pg 462
Centro de Estudios Mexicanos y Centroamericanos, pg 463
Colegio de Postgraduados en Ciencias Agricolas, pg 463
Editorial El Manual Moderno SA de CV, pg 464
Ediciones Era SA de CV, pg 465
Centro de Estudios Monetarios Latinoamericanos (CEMLA), pg 465
Fondo de Cultura Economica, pg 465
Instituto Indigenista Interamericano, pg 466
Janibi Editores SA de CV, pg 467
Editorial Jilguero, SA de CV, pg 467
Ediciones Libra, SA de CV, pg 467
Instituto Nacional de Antropologia e Historia, pg 469
Editorial Nova, SA de CV, pg 469
Instituto Panamericano de Geografia e Historia, pg 469
Plaza y Valdes SA de CV, pg 470
Universo Editorial SA de CV Edicion de Libros Revistas y Periodicos, pg 473

Morocco

Access International Services, pg 474
Editions Al-Fourkane, pg 474
Office Marocain D'Annonces-OMA, pg 475

Myanmar

Sarpay Beikman Public Library, pg 476

Namibia

Desert Research Foundation of Namibia (DRFN), pg 476

PUBLISHERS

Nepal
International Standards Books & Periodicals (P) Ltd, pg 476

Netherlands
John Benjamins BV, pg 479
Boom Uitgeverij, pg 479
Brill Academic Publishers, pg 479
BZZTOH Publishers, pg 480
Castrum Peregrini Presse, pg 480
Delft University Press, pg 481
Historische Uitgeverij, pg 483
IOS Press BV, pg 484
Kluwer Academic Publishers, pg 484
Kluwer Law International, pg 485
Uitgeverij J H Kok BV, pg 485
Uitgeverij Lemma BV, pg 485
Narratio Theologische Uitgeverij, pg 486
Nijgh & Van Ditmar Amsterdam, pg 487
Reed Elsevier Nederland BV, pg 488
Segment BV, pg 488
Semic Junior Press, pg 489
Uitgeverij SUN, pg 489
Swets & Zeitlinger Publishers, pg 489
SWP, BV Uitgeverij, pg 490
V S P International Science Publishers, pg 491
Uitgeverij G A van Oorschot bv, pg 491
Uitgeverij Verloren, pg 492

New Zealand
Brick Row Publishing Co Ltd, pg 494
Brookers Ltd, pg 494
Commonwealth Council for Educational Administration & Management, pg 495
New Zealand Council for Educational Research, pg 499
Outrigger Publishers, pg 499
Paerangi Books, pg 500
Publishing Solutions Ltd, pg 500
Resource Books Ltd, pg 500
SIR Publishing, pg 501
Southern Press Ltd, pg 501

Nigeria
Ahmadu Bello University Press Ltd, pg 503
Aromolaran Publishing Co Ltd, pg 503
Fourth Dimension Publishing Co Ltd, pg 504
Heritage Books, pg 505
JAD Publishers Ltd, pg 505
Nigerian Institute of International Affairs, pg 506
Riverside Communications, pg 507
University Publishing Co, pg 507
Vantage Publishers International Ltd, pg 507

Norway
Bladkompaniet A/S, pg 508
Gyldendal Norsk Forlag A/S, pg 509
Ernst G Mortensens Forlag A/S, pg 510
Novus Forlag, pg 510
Erik Sandberg, pg 510
Universitetsforlaget, pg 511

Pakistan
Centre for South Asian Studies, pg 512
Hamdard Foundation Pakistan, pg 512
HMR Publishing Co, pg 512
Islamic Research Institute, pg 513
Pakistan Institute of Development Economics (PIDE), pg 514
Sh Ghulam Ali & Sons (Pvt) Ltd, pg 514

Panama
Focus Publications International SA, pg 515

Papua New Guinea
Melanesian Institute, pg 515
National Research Institute of Papua New Guinea, pg 515

Peru
Carvajal SA, pg 516
Instituto Frances de Estudios Andinos, IFEA, pg 517
Sur Casa de Estudios del Socialismo, pg 517

Philippines
Bright Concepts Printing House, pg 518
De La Salle University, pg 519
Our Lady of Manaoag Publisher, pg 520
Philippine Baptist Mission SBC FMB Church Growth International, pg 520
San Carlos Publications, pg 521
SIBS Publishing House Inc, pg 521
Solidaridad Publishing House, pg 521
UST Publishing House, pg 521

Poland
Biblioteka Narodowa, pg 522
Wydawnictwo DiG, pg 522
Drukarnia I Ksiegarnia Swietego Wojciecha, Dziat Wydawniczy, pg 522
Instytut Historii Nauki PAN, pg 523
Instytut Meteorologii i Gospodarki Wodnej, pg 523
Wydawnictwo Medyczne Urban & Partner, pg 524
Wydawnictwa Normalizacyjne Alfa-Wero, pg 525
Ossolineum Zaklad Narodowy im Ossolinskich - Wydawnictwo, pg 525
Panstwowe Wydawnictwo Rolnicze i Lesne, pg 525
Polish Scientific Publishers PWN, pg 525
Oficyna Wydawnicza Politechniki Wroclawskiej, pg 525
Wydawnictwo Prawnicze Co, pg 526
Wydawnictwa Szkolne i Pedagogiczne, pg 527
Towarzystwo Naukowe w Toruniu, pg 527
Wydawnictwa Uniwersytetu Warszawskiego, pg 527
Wydawnictwo Uniwersytetu Wroclawskiego SP ZOO, pg 527

Portugal
Biblioteca Geral da Universidade de Coimbra, pg 529
Centro Estudos Geograficos, pg 529
Editora Classica, pg 530
Edicoes Colibri, pg 530
Comissao para a Igualdade e Direitos das Mulheres, pg 530
Edicoes Cosmos, pg 530
Difusao Cultural, pg 530
Impala, pg 532
Instituto de Investigacao Cientifica Tropical, pg 532
Latina Livraria Editora, pg 532
Meriberica/Liber, pg 533
Edicoes Ora & Labora, pg 534
Revista Penteado, pg 535
Edicoes Talento, pg 536

Romania
Editura Academiei Romane, pg 538
Editura Clusium, pg 539
Editura Excelsior Art, pg 539
Editura Gryphon, pg 540
Editura Medicala, pg 540
Rentrop & Straton Verlagsgruppe und Wirtschaftsconsulting, pg 542
Editura Univers SA, pg 543

Russian Federation
ARGO-RISK Publisher, pg 543
N E Bauman Moscow State Technical University Publishers, pg 544
BLIC, russko-Baltiskij informaciionnyj centr, AO, pg 544
Druzhba Narodov, pg 544
FGUP Izdatelstvo Mashinostroenie, pg 544
INFRA-M Izdatel'skij dom, pg 545
Izvestia Sovetov Narodnyh Deputatov Russian Federation (RF), pg 545
Izdatelskii Dom Kompozitor, pg 546
Moscow University Press, pg 547
Nauka Publishers, pg 547
Profizdat, pg 548
Russkaya Kniga Izdatelstvo (Publishers), pg 548
St Andrew's Biblical Theological College, pg 548
Izdatelstvo Standartov, pg 549
Izdatelstvo Sudostroenie, pg 549
Teorija Verojatnostej i ee Primenenija, pg 549

Senegal
Centre Africain d'Animation et d'Echanges Culturels Editions Khoudia (CAEC), pg 551
Centre de Linguistique Appliquee, pg 551
CODESRIA (Council for the Development of Social Science Research in Africa), pg 551
Societe d'Edition d'Afrique Nouvelle, pg 551

Serbia and Montenegro
AGAPE, pg 552
Beogradski Izdavacko-Graficki Zavod, pg 552
Forum, pg 552
Izdavacka preduzece Gradina, pg 552
Jugoslovenska Revija, pg 552
Libertatea, pg 552
Privredni Pregled, pg 553
Savez Inzenjera i Tehnicara Jugoslavije, pg 553
Sluzbeni List, pg 553
Turisticka Stampa, pg 554
Vuk Karadzic, pg 554

Singapore
Chopsons Pte Ltd, pg 555
LexisNexis, pg 557
Newscom Pte Ltd, pg 557
Reed Elsevier, South East Asia, pg 557
Singapore University Press Pte Ltd, pg 558
World Scientific Publishing Co Pte Ltd, pg 559

Slovakia
Egmont Neografia spol sro, pg 559
Vydavatelstvo Obzor, pg 560
Sofa, pg 560
Ustav informacii a prognoz skolstva mladeze a telovychovy, pg 561

Slovenia
Mladinska Knjiga International, pg 561
Zalozba Mihelac d o o, pg 562
Zalozba Obzorja d d Maribor, pg 562

South Africa
Cape Provincial Library Service, pg 563
Centre for Conflict Resolution, pg 563
Flesch Financial Publications (Pty) Ltd, pg 563
Institute for Reformational Studies CHE, pg 565
Jacklin Enterprises (Pty) Ltd, pg 565
National Botanical Institute, pg 567
Oceanographic Research Institute, pg 567
Thomson Publications, pg 569
Unisa Press, pg 569
University of Durban-Westville Library, pg 569

Spain
Publicacions de l'Abadia de Montserrat, pg 570
Editorial AEDOS SA, pg 571
Editorial Afers, SL, pg 571
Editorial 'Alas', pg 571
Ediciones Alfar SA, pg 572
Arco Libros SL, pg 573
Editorial Astri SA, pg 573
Edicions Camacuc, pg 575
Central Catequistica Salesiana (CCS), pg 576
Diputacion Provincial de Malaga, pg 579
Dorleta SA, pg 579
Ediciones Deusto SA, pg 580
Ediciones El Almendro de Cordoba, pg 580
Erein, pg 582
Instituto de Estudios Riojanos, pg 583
EUNSA (Ediciones Universidad de Navarra SA), pg 583
Fundacion de Estudios Libertarios Anselmo Lorenzo, pg 584
Galaxia SA Editorial, pg 584
Grao Editorial, pg 585
Harlequin Iberica SA, pg 586
Incafo Archivo Fotografico Editorial, SL, pg 587
Instituto Vasco de Criminologia, pg 587
Ediciones JLA, pg 588
Llibres del Segle, pg 589
Editorial Moll SL, pg 592
Editorial Noray, pg 593
Nueva Acropolis, pg 593

TYPE OF PUBLICATION INDEX — BOOK

OASIS, Producciones Generales de Comunicacion, pg 593
Omnicon, SA, pg 594
Editorial Peregrino SL, pg 595
Editorial El Perpetuo Socorro, pg 596
Instituto Provincial de Investigaciones y Estudios Toledanos (IPIET), pg 597
Pulso Ediciones, SL, pg 597
Editorial Revista Agustiniana, pg 598
Ediciones Rialp SA, pg 598
Ediciones ROL SA, pg 598
Universidad de Santiago de Compostela, pg 599
Secretariado Trinitario, pg 599
Servicio de Publicaciones Universidad de Cordoba, pg 599
Equipo Sirius SA, pg 600
Ediciones Siruela SA, pg 600
Ediciones Tecnicas Rede, SA, pg 601
Editorial Sal Terrae, pg 602
Tesitex, SL, pg 602
Vinaches Lopez, Luisa, pg 605

Sri Lanka
International Centre for Ethnic Studies, pg 606
Department of National Museums, pg 607
Swarna Hansa Foundation, pg 607

Sweden
Allt om Hobby AB, pg 609
Almqvist och Wiksell International, pg 609
Bibliotekstjaenst AB, pg 610
Iustus Forlag AB, pg 613
Mezopotamya Publishing & Distribution, pg 613
Semic Bokforlaget International AB, pg 615
Var Skola Foerlag AB, pg 616

Switzerland
Birkhauser Verlag AG, pg 619
Blaukreuz-Verlag Bern, pg 619
CEC-Cosmic Energy Connections, pg 620
Marcel Dekker AG, pg 621
Verlag ED Emmentaler Druck AG, pg 622
Editions Eisele SA, pg 622
Eular Verlag, pg 623
G+B Arts International, pg 623
Haffmans Verlag AG, pg 624
Helbing und Lichtenhahn Verlag AG, pg 625
S Karger AG, Medical & Scientific Publishers, pg 626
Peter Lang AG, pg 627
Lia rumantscha, pg 627
E Lopfe-Benz AG Rorschach, Graphische Anstalt und Verlag, pg 628
Maihof Verlag, pg 628
Medecine et Hygiene, pg 628
Nebelspalter-Verlag, pg 629
Verlag Arthur Niggli AG, pg 629
Verlag Organisator AG, pg 630
Parkett Publishers Inc, pg 630
Editions du Parvis, pg 631
Pedrazzini Tipografia, pg 631
Promoedition SA, pg 631
Verlag fuer Recht und Gesellschaft AG, pg 632
RECOM Verlag, pg 632
Sauerlaender AG, pg 633
Schulthess Polygraphischer Verlag AG, pg 633

Schwabe & Co AG, pg 633
Editions Scriptar SA, pg 634
Staempfli Verlag AG, pg 634
Terra Grischuna Verlag Buch-und Zeitschriftenverlag, pg 635
Trans Tech Publications SA, pg 635
Verlagsbuchhandlung AG, pg 636

Syrian Arab Republic
Damascus University Press, pg 638

Taiwan, Province of China
Designer Publisher Inc, pg 639
Echo Publishing Company Ltd, pg 639
Laureate Book Co Ltd, pg 640
Petroleum Information Publishing Co, pg 641
Sinorama Magazine Co, pg 641
Torch of Wisdom, pg 642
Yi Hsien Publishing Co Ltd, pg 642
Youth Cultural Publishing Co, pg 642
Zen Now Press, pg 642

Tunisia
Faculte des Sciences Humaines et Sociales de Tunis, pg 648

Turkey
Altin Kitaplar Yayinevi, pg 649
Arkeoloji Ve Sanat Yayinlari, pg 649
Ataturk Kultur, Dil ve Tarih, Yusek Kurumu Baskanligi, pg 649
Iletisim Yayinlari, pg 650
Kiyi Yayinlari, pg 650
Kok Yayincilik, pg 650
Metis Yayinlari, pg 650
Sabah Kitaplari, pg 651
Varlik Yayinlari AS, pg 652
Yapi-Endustri Merkezi Yayinlari-Yem Yayin, pg 652

Ukraine
Urozaj, pg 654

United Kingdom
A4 Publications Ltd, pg 656
Umberto Allemandi & Co Publishing, pg 656
Architectural Association Publications, pg 659
Arnold, pg 659
Artetech Publishing Co, pg 660
Arthur James Ltd, pg 660
Ashgate Publishing Ltd, pg 660
Aslib, The Association for Information Management, pg 660
Association for Scottish Literary Studies, pg 661
Association for Science Education, pg 661
BAAF Adoption & Fostering, pg 662
Berghahn Books Ltd, pg 665
BIOS Scientific Publishers Ltd, pg 665
Blackwell Publishing Ltd, pg 666
Borthwick Institute Publications, pg 669
Bryntirion Press, pg 672
Business Monitor International, pg 672
Butterworths Tolley, pg 673
Cambridge University Press, pg 674
Cavendish Publishing Ltd, pg 676
Chadwyck-Healey Ltd, pg 677
Chapman, pg 677
Chapter Two, pg 678

Church Society, pg 679
Church Union, pg 680
E W Classey Ltd, pg 680
Concrete Information Ltd, pg 682
Paul H Crompton Ltd, pg 684
CSA (Cambridge Scientific Abstracts), pg 684
CTBI Publications, pg 685
Terence Dalton Ltd, pg 685
Dawson Books, pg 686
Donhead Publishing Ltd, pg 688
Electronic Publishing Services Ltd (EPS), pg 690
Elsevier Ltd, pg 691
The Energy Information Centre, pg 691
English Teaching Professional, pg 691
Estates Gazette, pg 692
European Schoolbooks Ltd, pg 692
The Eurospan Group, pg 692
Fabian Society, pg 694
Famedram Publishers Ltd, pg 694
Feather Books, pg 694
Forensic Science Society, pg 696
Forth Naturalist & Historian, pg 696
Freedom Press, pg 697
Geological Society Publishing House, pg 699
W Green The Scottish Law Publisher, pg 702
Greenhill Books/Lionel Leventhal Ltd, pg 703
Gwasg Gwenffrwd, pg 703
Halldale Publishing & Media Ltd, pg 704
Hawker Publications Ltd, pg 706
Hobsons, pg 709
Hodder Headline Ltd, pg 709
Immediate Publishing, pg 712
Imperial College Press, pg 712
Institute for Fiscal Studies, pg 712
Institute of Development Studies, pg 712
Institute of Financial Services, pg 712
Institute of Food Science & Technology, pg 713
Institute of Governance, pg 713
Institute of Physics Publishing, pg 713
Institution of Electrical Engineers, pg 713
Intellect Ltd, pg 713
International Bee Research Association, pg 714
International Communications, pg 714
International Institute for Strategic Studies, pg 714
IOM Communications Ltd, pg 714
Islamic Foundation Publications, pg 714
ITDG Publishing, pg 715
IWA Publishing, pg 715
JAI Press Ltd, pg 715
James & James (Science Publishers) Ltd, pg 715
Jane's Information Group, pg 715
Kluwer Academic/Plenum Publishers, pg 718
Lang Syne Publishers Ltd, pg 719
Lawrence & Wishart, pg 719
Lippincott Williams & Wilkins, pg 721
Liverpool University Press, pg 722
LLP Ltd, pg 722
Macmillan Ltd, pg 723
Manchester University Press, pg 724
Maney Publishing, pg 725
Methodist Publishing House, pg 727
Multilingual Matters Ltd, pg 729

National Council for Voluntary Organisations (NCVO), pg 730
National Foster Care Association, pg 731
National Library of Wales, pg 731
New European Publications Ltd, pg 732
NTC Research, pg 734
Osprey Publishing Ltd, pg 737
Oxfam, pg 737
Oxford University Press, pg 737
Packard Publishing Ltd, pg 737
Paternoster Publishing, pg 738
Pathfinder London, pg 739
Perpetuity Press, pg 741
Pharmaceutical Press, pg 741
Pion Ltd, pg 742
PIRA Intl, pg 742
Planet, pg 743
Police Review Publishing Company Ltd, pg 744
The Policy Press, pg 744
Portland Press Ltd, pg 745
Professional Engineering Publishing Ltd, pg 745
Quintessence Publishing Co Ltd, pg 747
Radcliffe Medical Press Ltd, pg 747
Ramakrishna Vedanta Centre, pg 747
Random House UK Ltd, pg 747
Rapra Technology Ltd, pg 748
Rivers Oram Press, pg 750
Royal College of General Practitioners (RCGP), pg 752
Royal Institute of International Affairs, pg 752
The Royal Society, pg 752
Royal Society of Medicine Press Ltd, pg 752
SAGE Publications Ltd, pg 753
St Jerome Publishing, pg 753
Scottish Braille Press, pg 755
Scottish Executive Library & Information Services, pg 755
Scripture Union, pg 756
Sheffield Academic Press Ltd, pg 757
Sherwood Publishing, pg 757
SLS Legal Publications (NI), pg 758
Sports Turf Research Institute (STRI), pg 760
Take That Ltd, pg 762
Taylor & Francis, pg 763
Taylor & Francis Medical Books, pg 763
Taylor Graham Publishing, pg 764
Time Out Group Ltd, pg 765
Trentham Books Ltd, pg 767
TSO (The Stationery Office), pg 767
Two-Can Publishing Ltd, pg 768
University of Wales Press, pg 769
Voltaire Foundation Ltd, pg 771
Whiting & Birch Ltd, pg 773
Wiley Europe Ltd, pg 773
Wilmington Business Information Ltd, pg 774
Woodhead Publishing Ltd, pg 775
World Microfilms Publications Ltd, pg 775

Uruguay
Cotidiano Mujer, pg 777
Instituto del Tercer Mundo, pg 777
Nordan-Comunidad, pg 778
Prensa Medica Latinoamericana, pg 778
La Urpila Editores, pg 778

Venezuela
Fundacion Centro Gumilla, pg 779
Editorial Nueva Sociedad, pg 780

PUBLISHERS

Zambia

Historical Association of Zambia, pg 781

Zimbabwe

Journal on Social Change, pg 783
Sapes Trust Ltd, pg 784
Thomson Publications Zimbabwe (Pvt) Ltd, pg 784
University of Zimbabwe Publications, pg 784
Zimbabwe Foundation for Education with Production (ZIMFEP), pg 784
ZRD Trust, pg 785

PROFESSIONAL BOOKS

Albania

State Textbook Publishing House, pg 1

Argentina

Abeledo-Perrot SAE e I, pg 2
Editorial Acme SA, pg 3
Aguilar Altea Taurus Alfaguara SA de Ediciones, pg 3
Editorial Astrea de Alfredo y Ricardo Depalma SRL, pg 3
Editorial Claridad SA, pg 4
Cosmopolita SRL, pg 4
Editorial Ruy Diaz SAEIC, pg 5
Errepar SA, pg 5
EUDEBA (Editorial Universitaria de Buenos Aires), pg 5
Editorial Hemisferio Sur SA, pg 6
Editorial Idearium de la Universidad de Mendoza (EDIUM), pg 6
Juris Editorial, pg 6
Editorial Medica Panamericana SA, pg 7
Instituto Nacional de Ciencia y Tecnica Hidrica (INCYTH), pg 7
Instituto de Publicaciones Navales, pg 8
Editorial Paidos SAICF, pg 8
Tipografica Editora Argentina, pg 9
Editoria Universitaria de la Patagonia, pg 9
Victor P de Zavalia SA, pg 10
Editorial Zeus SRL, pg 10

Armenia

Arevik, pg 10

Australia

ACER Press, pg 10
ACHPER Inc (Australian Council for Health, Physical Education & Recreation), pg 10
Appropriate Technology Development Group (Inc) WA, pg 11
Art on the Move, pg 12
Ausmed Publications Pty Ltd, pg 12
Australian Academic Press Pty Ltd, pg 13
Australian Broadcasting Authority, pg 13
Australian Film Television & Radio School, pg 13
Australian Institute of Family Studies (AIFS), pg 13
Blackwell Publishing Asia, pg 15
Bureau of Resource Sciences, pg 16
Butterworths Australia Ltd, pg 16
Candlelight Trust T/A Candlelight Farm, pg 17
Chiron Media, pg 17
Cole Publications, pg 18

Cookery Book, pg 18
Crawford House Publishing Pty Ltd, pg 18
Crista International, pg 18
Deakin University Press, pg 19
Elsevier Australia, pg 21
Extraordinary People Press, pg 22
The Federation Press, pg 22
Fernfawn Publications, pg 22
Flora Publications International Pty Ltd, pg 22
Fraser Publications, pg 22
Ginninderra Press, pg 23
Gnostic Editions, pg 23
H&H Publishing, pg 24
Histec Publications, pg 25
The Images Publishing Group Pty Ltd, pg 26
Law Book Co Information Services, pg 28
MacLennan & Petty Pty Ltd, pg 30
Macmillan Education Australia, pg 30
McGraw-Hill Australia Pty Ltd, pg 31
National Gallery of Victoria, pg 33
OTEN (Open Training & Education Network), pg 34
Oxfam Community Aid Abroad, pg 35
Pacific Publications (Australia) Pty Ltd, pg 35
Pademelon Press, pg 35
Pearson Education Australia, pg 36
Pluto Press Australia Pty Ltd, pg 37
Press for Success, pg 37
Priestley Consulting, pg 37
RMIT Publishing, pg 39
St Clair Press, pg 40
Strucmech Publishing, pg 42
Tarka Publishing, pg 42
Tertiary Press, pg 43
Turton & Armstrong Pty Ltd Publishers, pg 44
Veritas Press, pg 45
Villamonta Publishing Services Inc, pg 45
Vista Publications, pg 45
Wildscape Australia, pg 46
Yanagang Publishing, pg 47

Austria

Autorensolidaritat - Verlag der Interessengemeinschaft osterreichischer Autorinnen und Autoren, pg 48
Braintrust Marketing Services Ges mbH Verlag, pg 49
Georg Fromme und Co, pg 51
Helbling Verlags-Gesellschaft mbH, pg 51
IAEA - International Atomic Energy Agency, pg 52
IG Autorinnen Autoren, pg 52
Verlag Lafite, pg 53
Leopold Stocker Verlag, pg 53
Linde Verlag Wien GmbH, pg 53
Verlag des Oesterreichischen Gewerkschaftsbundes GmbH, pg 55
Oesterreichischer Bundesverlag Gmbh, pg 55
Studien Verlag Gmbh, pg 58
Verlag Mag Wanzenbock, pg 59
Dr Otfried Weise Verlag Tabula Smaragdina, pg 59

Azerbaijan

Sada, Literaturno-Izdatel'skij Centr, pg 60

Bangladesh

Gatidhara, pg 61
The University Press Ltd, pg 61

Barbados

Business Tutors, pg 62

Belarus

Interdigest Publishing House, pg 62
Kavaler Publishers, pg 62

Belgium

Academia Press, pg 62
Vanden Broele NV, pg 64
Editions du CEFAL, pg 65
Conservart SA, pg 65
Editions De Boeck-Larcier SA, pg 66
Documenta CV, pg 66
Intersentia Uitgevers NV, pg 68
King Baudouin Foundation, pg 69
Koepel van de Vlaamse Noord - Zuidbeweging 11.11.11, pg 69
Uitgeverij Lannoo NV, pg 69
Larcier-Department of De Boeck & Larcier SA, pg 70
Maklu, pg 70
Toulon Uitgeverij, pg 73
UGA Editions (Uitgeverij), pg 73
Uitgeverij De Garve, pg 74
Imprimeur - Editeur Vaillant-Carmanne SA, pg 74
Wolters Kluwer Belgie NV, pg 74

Bolivia

Gisbert y Cia SA, pg 75

Brazil

A & A & A Edicoes e Promocoes Internacionais Ltda, pg 76
Editora Agora Ltda, pg 77
Aide Editora e Comercio de Livros Ltda, pg 77
Antenna Edicoes Tecnicas Ltda, pg 77
Editora Antroposofica Ltda, pg 77
ARTMED Editora, pg 78
Berkeley Brasil Editora Ltda, pg 78
Editora Edgard Blucher Ltda, pg 79
Editora Campus Ltda, pg 79
Alzira Chagas Carpigiani, pg 79
Centro de Estudos Juridicosdo Para (CEJUP), pg 79
Editora Contexto (Editora Pinsky Ltda), pg 80
Companhia Editora Forense, pg 81
Editora Elevacao, pg 81
Empresa Brasileira de Pesquisa Agropecuaria, pg 81
Editora FCO Ltda, pg 81
Editora Forense Universitaria Ltda, pg 81
Livraria Freitas Bastos Editora SA, pg 82
Fundacao Sao Paulo, EDUC, pg 82
Editora Guanabara Koogan SA, pg 83
Editora Harbra Ltda, pg 83
Hemus Editora Ltda, pg 83
Imago Editora Importacao e Exportacao Ltda, pg 84
Livraria Editora Infobook SA, pg 85
LTC-Livros Tecnicos e Cientificos Editora S/A, pg 85
Editora Lucre Comercio e Representacoes, pg 85
Madras Editora, pg 86
Editora Manole Ltda, pg 86
Editora Manuais Tecnicos de Seguros Ltda, pg 86

TYPE OF PUBLICATION INDEX

Medicina Panamericana Editora Do Brasil Ltda, pg 86
Medsi - Editora Medica e Cientifica Ltda, pg 86
Oliveira Rocha-Comercio e Servics Ltda, pg 87
Editora Ortiz SA, pg 88
Pearson Education Do Brasil, pg 88
Ediouro Publicacoes, SA, pg 89
Qualitymark Editora Ltda, pg 89
Editora Revan Ltda, pg 89
Livraria Editora Revinter Ltda, pg 89
Saraiva SA, Livreiros Editores, pg 90
Editora Scipione Ltda, pg 90
Selecoes Eletronicas Editora Ltda, pg 90
Livraria Sulina Editora, pg 91
Summus Editorial Ltda, pg 91
Talento Publicacoes Editora e Grafica Ltda, pg 91
Editora Universidade Federal do Rio de Janeiro, pg 92

Bulgaria

Ciela Publishing House, pg 93
DA-Izdatelstvo Publishers, pg 93
Dolphin Press Group Ltd, pg 94
EA EOOD, pg 94
Fondacija Zlatno Kljuce, pg 94
Makros 2000 - Plovdiv, pg 95
MATEX, pg 95
Musica Publishing House Ltd, pg 95
Pensoft Publishers, pg 96
Sibi, pg 97
Sila & Zivot, pg 97
Sita-MB, pg 97
TEMTO, pg 97
Todor Kableshkov University of Transport, pg 97

Cameroon

Presses Universitaires d'Afrique, pg 98

Chile

Edeval (Universidad de Valparaiso), pg 99
Norma de Chile, pg 99
Editorial Universitaria SA, pg 100
Ediciones Universitarias de Valparaiso, pg 100

China

Anhui People's Publishing House, pg 101
Chemical Industry Press, pg 101
China Agriculture Press, pg 102
China Film Press, pg 102
China Foreign Economic Relations & Trade Publishing House, pg 102
China Forestry Publishing House, pg 102
China Machine Press (CMP), pg 102
China Ocean Press, pg 102
China Theatre Publishing House, pg 103
China Tibetology Publishing House, pg 103
CITIC Publishing House, pg 103
Cultural Relics Publishing House, pg 103
Foreign Language Teaching & Research Press, pg 104
Fudan University Press, pg 104
Guangdong Science & Technology Press, pg 105

851

TYPE OF PUBLICATION INDEX — BOOK

Heilongjiang Science & Technology Press, pg 105
Henan Science & Technology Publishing House, pg 105
Higher Education Press, pg 105
Inner Mongolia Science & Technology Publishing House, pg 105
International Academic Publishers (IAP), pg 105
Language Publishing House, pg 106
Lanzhou University Press, pg 106
Nanjing University Press, pg 106
National Defence Industry Press, pg 106
New Times Press, pg 106
Patent Documentation Publishing House, pg 106
Printing Industry Publishing House, pg 107
Science Press, pg 107
Shandong University Press, pg 108
Shanghai Calligraphy & Painting Publishing House, pg 108
Shanghai College of Traditional Chinese Medicine Press, pg 108
Shanghai Far East Publishers, pg 108
Sichuan University Press, pg 108
South China University of Science & Technology Press, pg 108
Tianjin Science & Technology Publishing House, pg 108
Water Resources and Electric Power Press (CWPP), pg 109
Yunnan University Press, pg 109

Colombia
Centro Regional para el Fomento del Libro en America Latina y el Caribe, pg 110
Consejo Episcopal Latinoamericano (CELAM), pg 110
Fundacion Universidad de la Sabana Ediciones INSE, pg 111
Pearson Educacion de Colombia LTDA, pg 112
Tercer Mundo Editores SA, pg 113
Universidad Nacional Abierta y a Distancia, pg 113

Costa Rica
Academia de Centro America, pg 114
Centro Agronomico Tropical de Investigacion y Ensenanza (CATIE), pg 115
Editorial Nacional de Salud y Seguridad Social Ednass, pg 116
Editorial Tecnologica de Costa Rica, pg 116
Union Mundial para la Naturaleza (UICN), Oficina Regional para Mesoamerica, pg 116
Editorial de la Universidad de Costa Rica, pg 116

Cote d'Ivoire
Universite d'Abidjan, pg 117

Croatia
ALFA dd za izdavacke, graficke i trgovacke poslove, pg 117
Izdavacka Delatnost Hrvatske Akademije Znanosti I Umjetnosti, pg 118
Hrvatsko filozofsko drustvo, pg 118
Vitagraf, pg 119

Cuba
Editorial Oriente, pg 120
Editora Politica, pg 120
Pueblo y Educacion Editorial (PE), pg 121

Czech Republic
Grada Publishing, pg 123
Nakladatelstvi Jota spol sro, pg 124
Pavla Momcilova, pg 125
Narodni Knihovna CR, pg 126
Cesky normalizacni institut, pg 126
Psychoanalyticke Nakladatelstvi, pg 127
Votobia sro, pg 128

Denmark
Dansk Psykologisk Forlag, pg 130
Djof Publishing Jurist-og Okonomforbundets Forlag, pg 130
Christian Ejlers' Forlag aps, pg 131
FADL's Forlag A/S, pg 131
Gads Forlag, pg 131
Ingenioeren/Boger, pg 132
Mellemfolkeligt Samvirke, pg 133
Samfundslitteratur, pg 134
Schultz Information, pg 134
A/S Skattekarttoteket, pg 134
Systime, pg 135
Forlaget Thomson A/S, pg 135

Dominican Republic
Pontificia Universidad Catolica Madre y Maestra, pg 136

Ecuador
Centro de Planificacion y Estudios Sociales (CEPLAES), pg 136

Estonia
Academic Library of Tallinn Pedagogical University, pg 139
Eesti Rahvusraamatukogu, pg 139
Kirjastus Kunst, pg 140
Olion Publishers, pg 140
Valgus Publishers, pg 140

Finland
Building Information Ltd, pg 141
Kustannus Oy Duodecim, pg 141
Forsamlingsforbundets Forlags AB, pg 142
Kauppakaari Oyj, pg 142
Tietoteos Publishing Co, pg 144
Yliopistopaino/Helsinki University Press, pg 145

France
Adverbum SARL, pg 146
Arnette, pg 147
Editions BRGM, pg 151
Cepadues Editions SA, pg 153
Editions Chiron, pg 154
Chotard et Associes Editeurs, pg 154
Codes Rousseau, pg 155
CTIF (Center Technique Industriel de la Fonderie), pg 156
CTNERHI - Centre Technique National d'Etudes et de Recherches sur les Handicaps et les Inadaptations, pg 156
Editions Dalloz Sirey, pg 157
De Vecchi Editions SA, pg 157
Editions Delmas, pg 157
Institut pour le Developpement Forestier, pg 158
Doin Editeurs, pg 159
Dunod Editeur, pg 159
Editions d'Organisation, pg 160
EDP Sciences, pg 161
Elf Exploration Production, pg 161
Ellipses - Edition Marketing SA, pg 161
Editions de l'Epargne, pg 161
Editions Errance, pg 162
L'Esprit Du Temps, pg 162
Editions Fleurus, pg 163
Groupe de Recherche et d'Echanges Technologiques (GRET), pg 166
INRA Editions (Institut National de la Recherche Agronomique), pg 168
IRD Editions, pg 169
Joly Editions, pg 169
Editions Lavoisier, pg 171
Editions Legislatives, pg 171
LiTec (Librairies Techniques SA), pg 172
LT Editions-Jacques Lanore, pg 173
Masson Editeur, pg 174
Masson-Williams et Wilkins, pg 174
Maxima Laurent du Mesnil Editeur, pg 174
Editions du Papyrus, pg 178
Editions Parentheses, pg 179
Pearson Education France, pg 179
Editions Pedone, pg 179
Peeters-France, pg 179
Les Editions du Point Veterinaire, pg 180
Polytechnica SA, pg 180
Presses de l'Ecole Nationale des Ponts et Chaussees, pg 181
Les Presses du Management, pg 181
Editions Revue EPS, pg 183
Editions Saint-Michel SA, pg 183
Societe Mathematique de France - Institut Henri Poincare, pg 185
Sofiac (Societe Francaise des Imprimeries Administratives Centrales), pg 185
Editions Springer France, pg 186
Sybex, pg 186
Editions Technip SA, pg 187
Editions Techniques et Scientifiques Francaises, pg 187
TOP Editions, pg 188
Editions Village Mondial, pg 189

Germany
A Francke Verlag (Tubingen und Basel), pg 190
E Albrecht Verlags-KG, pg 192
AOL-Verlag Frohmut Menze, pg 193
Verlag APHAIA Svea Haske, Sonja Schumann GbR, pg 193
ARCult Media, pg 193
Asgard-Verlag Dr Werner Hippe GmbH, pg 194
Bank-Verlag GmbH, pg 197
Verlag Dr Albert Bartens KG, pg 197
Ludwig Bechauf Verlag, pg 198
Verlag C H Beck oHG, pg 198
Bertelsmann Lexikon Verlag GmbH, pg 200
Verlag Bertelsmann Stiftung, pg 200
W Bertelsmann Verlag GmbH & Co KG, pg 200
Verlag Beruf und Schule Belz KG, pg 200
BW Bildung und Wissen Verlag und Software GmbH, pg 201
BLV Verlagsgesellschaft mbH, pg 202
Verlag Erwin Bochinsky GmbH & Co KG, pg 202
Verlag Georg D W Callwey GmbH & Co, pg 207
Chmielorz GmbH Verlag, pg 208
Christusbruderschaft Selbitz ev, Abt Verlag, pg 209
Marianne Cieslik, pg 209
Charles Coleman Verlag GmbH & Co KG, pg 209
J G Cotta'sche Buchhandlung Nachfolger GmbH, pg 210
Deutsche Blinden-Bibliothek, pg 211
Deutsche Gesellschaft fuer Eisenbahngeschichte eV, pg 212
Deutsche Landwirtschafts-Gesellschaft VerlagsgesGmbH, pg 212
Deutscher Fachverlag GmbH, pg 212
Deutscher Instituts-Verlag GmbH, pg 213
Deutscher Psychologen Verlag GmbH (DPV), pg 213
Deutscher Verlag fur Grundstoffindustrie GmbH, pg 213
Christoph Dohr, pg 215
Donat Verlag, pg 215
DRW-Verlag Weinbrenner-GmbH & Co, pg 216
Ecomed Verlagsgesellschaft AG & Co KG, pg 218
Econ Verlag GmbH, pg 218
Elektor-Verlag GmbH, pg 219
Emons Verlag, pg 219
Verlag Esoterische Philosophie GmbH, pg 221
expert verlag GmbH, Fachverlag fuer Wirtschaft & Technik, pg 222
Extent Verlag und Service Wolfgang M Flamm, pg 223
Fachbuchverlag Pfanneberg & Co, pg 223
Fachverlag fur das graphische Gewerbe GmbH, pg 223
Festo Didactic GmbH & Co KG, pg 224
FN-Verlag der Deutschen Reiterlichen Vereinigung GmbH, pg 225
Verlag Franz Vahlen GmbH, pg 226
Fraunhofer IRB Verlag Fraunhofer Informationszentrum Raum und Bau, pg 226
Friedrich Kiehl Verlag GmbH, pg 227
Frieling & Partner GmbH, pg 227
Verlag A Fromm im Druck- u Verlagshaus Fromm GmbH & Co KG, pg 227
Betriebswirtschaftlicher Verlag Dr Th Gabler, pg 228
Gebrueder Borntraeger Science Publishers, pg 228
Alfons W Gentner Verlag GmbH & Co KG, pg 228
Gesundheits-Dialog Verlag GmbH, pg 229
Gildefachverlag GmbH & Co KG, pg 229
Gmelin Verlag GmbH, pg 230
Govi-Verlag Pharmazeutischer Verlag GmbH, pg 230
Wolfgang G Haas - Musikverlag Koeln ek, pg 232
Alfred Hammer, pg 233
Hardt und Worner Marketing fur das Buch, pg 234
Haschemi Edition Cologne Kunstverlag fuer Fotografie, pg 234
Hestra-Verlag Hernichel & Dr Strauss GmbH & Co KG, pg 237
Carl Heymanns Verlag KG, pg 237

PUBLISHERS

Hans Holzmann Verlag GmbH und Co KG, pg 239
Edition Humanistische Psychologie (EHP), pg 240
Huss-Medien GmbH, pg 240
Huss-Verlag GmbH, pg 240
Idea Verlag GmbH, pg 240
IKO Verlag fur Interkulturelle Kommunikation, pg 241
Informationsstelle Suedliches Afrika eV (ISSA), pg 241
International Thomson Publishing (ITP), pg 242
Iudicium Verlag GmbH, pg 242
Kallmeyer'sche Verlagsbuchhandlung GmbH, pg 244
Katzmann Verlag KG, pg 245
Verlag im Kilian GmbH, pg 246
Klages-Verlag, pg 246
Verlagsanstalt Alexander Koch GmbH, pg 247
R Koenig GmbH, pg 248
W Kohlhammer GmbH, pg 248
Kolibri-Verlag GmbH, pg 249
kopaed verlagsgmbh, pg 249
Krafthand Verlag Walter Schultz GmbH, pg 250
Laaber-Verlag, pg 251
Landbuch-Verlagsgesellschaft mbH, pg 251
Peter Lang GmbH Europaeischer Verlag der Wissenschaften, pg 252
LEU-VERLAG Wolfgang Leupelt, pg 254
Libertas- Europaeisches Institut GmbH, pg 254
Logos-Verlag Literatur & Layout GmbH, pg 255
Hermann Luchterhand Verlag GmbH, pg 255
Edition Maritim GmbH, pg 257
Max Schimmel Verlag, pg 258
Medien-Verlag Bernhard Gregor GmbH, pg 258
Medizinisch-Literarische Verlagsgesellschaft mbH, pg 258
mode information Heinz Kramer GmbH, pg 261
Verlag Norbert Mueller AG & Co KG, pg 262
Musikantiquariat und Dr Hans Schneider Verlag GmbH, pg 262
MVB Marketing- und Verlagsservice des Buchhandels GmbH, pg 263
Verlag Stephanie Naglschmid, pg 263
Verlag Natur & Wissenschaft Harro Hieronimus & Dr Jurgen Schmidt, pg 263
Neuland-Verlagsgesellschaft mbH, pg 264
Nusser Verlag, pg 266
Edition Parabolis, pg 268
Pearson Education Deutschland GmbH, pg 268
Richard Pflaum Verlag GmbH & Co KG, pg 269
Philippka-Sportverlag, pg 269
Physica-Verlag, pg 270
pmi Verlag, pg 270
Psychologie Verlags Union GmbH, pg 272
Psychosozial-Verlag, pg 272
Quintessenz Verlags-GmbH, pg 273
Verlag Recht und Wirtschaft GmbH, pg 274
Reed Elsevier Deutschland GmbH, pg 274
E Reinhold Verlag, pg 275
Ritterbach Verlag GmbH, pg 276

Ruhland Verlag Gimblt, pg 277
Ryvellus Medienagentur Dopfer, pg 277
I H Sauer Verlag GmbH, pg 278
K G Saur Verlag GmbH, A Gale/Thomson Learning Company, pg 278
Verlag Th Schaefer im Vicentz Verlag KG, pg 278
Schaeffer-Poeschel Verlag fuer Wirtschaft Steuern Recht, pg 279
Schapen Edition, H W Louis, pg 279
M & H Schaper GmbH & Co KG, pg 279
Schiffahrts-Verlag, pg 279
Verlag Dr Otto Schmidt KG, pg 280
E Schweizerbart'sche Verlagsbuchhandlung (Naegele und Obermiller), pg 282
Springer Science+Business Media GmbH & Co KG, pg 284
Springer Science+Business Media GmbH & Co KG, Berlin, pg 285
Franz Steiner Verlag Wiesbaden GmbH, pg 287
Dr Dietrich Steinkopff Verlag GmbH & Co, pg 287
Sternberg-Verlag bei Ernst Franz, pg 288
Suin Buch-Verlag, pg 289
Tetra Verlag Gmbh, pg 290
Thalacker Medien GmbH Co KG, pg 290
Georg Thieme Verlag KG, pg 291
Tipress Dienstleistungen fur das Verlagswesen GmbH, pg 291
Wirtschaftsverlag Carl Ueberreuter, pg 293
UNO-Verlag GmbH, pg 293
UVK Verlagsgesellschaft mbH, pg 294
Dorothea van der Koelen, pg 294
VAS-Verlag fuer Akademische Schriften, pg 294
Vereinigte Fachverlage GmbH, pg 295
Verlag fur Schweissen und Verwandte Verfahren, pg 295
Friedr Vieweg & Sohn Verlag, pg 296
Curt R Vincentz Verlag, pg 296
VS Verlag fur Sozialwissenschaften, pg 297
Werner Verlag GmbH & Co KG, pg 299
Dr Dieter Winkler, pg 300
Wison Verlag GmbH, pg 300
Xenos Verlagsgesellschaft mbH, pg 301

Ghana

Black Mask Ltd, pg 303
Building & Road Research Institute (BRRI), pg 303
World Literature Project, pg 305

Greece

Diavlos, pg 306
Govostis Publishing SA, pg 307
Hestia-I D Hestia-Kollaros & Co Corporation, pg 308
Kalentis & Sia, pg 308
Knossos Publications, pg 309
Nomiki Bibliothiki, pg 310
Alex Siokis & Co, pg 312

Haiti

Editions Caraibes SA, pg 314

Holy See (Vatican City State)

Pontificia Academia Scientiarum, pg 314

Hong Kong

Hong Kong University Press, pg 317
Joint Publishing (HK) Co Ltd, pg 317

Hungary

Kossuth Kiado RT, pg 322
Mezogazda Kiado, pg 323
Nemzetkozi Szinhazi Intezet Magyar Kozpontja, pg 323
Novorg International Szervezo es Kiado kft, pg 323
Panem, pg 324
Planetas Kiadoi es Kereskedelmi Kft, pg 324
Saldo Penzugyi Tanacsado es Informatikai Rt, pg 324
Szabvanykiado, pg 324

Iceland

Stofnun Arna Magnussonar a Islandi, pg 326

India

Academic Book Corporation, pg 327
Addison-Wesley Pte Ltd, pg 327
Agricole Publishing Academy, pg 327
B I Publications Pvt Ltd, pg 329
Book Circle, pg 330
BS Publications, pg 331
Daya Publishing House, pg 333
Eastern Book Co, pg 333
Eastern Law House Pvt Ltd, pg 334
Galgotia Publications Pvt Ltd, pg 334
International Book Distributors, pg 338
B Jain Publishers Overseas, pg 338
Law Publishers, pg 340
Laxmi Publications Pvt Ltd, pg 340
Multitech Publishing Co, pg 342
Munshiram Manoharlal Publishers Pvt Ltd, pg 342
National Council of Applied Economic Research, Publications Division, pg 342
Parimal Prakashan, pg 345
Reliance Publishing House, pg 346
Research Signpost, pg 347
SAGE Publications India Pvt Ltd, pg 347
Scientific Book Agency, pg 348
Sita Books & Periodicals Pvt Ltd, pg 349
Somaiya Publications Pvt Ltd, pg 349
South Asian Publishers Pvt Ltd, pg 350
Sterling Information Technologies, pg 350
Transworld Research Network, pg 351
Vastu Gyan Publication, pg 352
Vision Books Pvt Ltd, pg 352
Viva Books Pvt Ltd, pg 352
A H Wheeler & Co Ltd, pg 353

Indonesia

PT Bulan Bintang, pg 354
PT BPK Gunung Mulia, pg 355
CV Yasaguna, pg 357

Ireland

The Columba Book Service, pg 359
The Columba Press, pg 359
The Economic & Social Research Institute, pg 359
European Foundation for the Improvement of Living & Working Conditions, pg 360
Gandon Editions, pg 360
Gill & Macmillan Ltd, pg 360
Irish Management Institute, pg 361
Oak Tree Press, pg 362
On Stream Publications Ltd, pg 362
Relay Books, pg 363
Round Hall Sweet & Maxwell, pg 363

Israel

Ben-Zvi Institute, pg 365
The Bialik Institute, pg 365
Dekel Publishing House, pg 366
Freund Publishing House Ltd, pg 367
Gefen Publishing House Ltd, pg 367
Hakibbutz Hameuchad Publishing House Ltd, pg 367
Intermedia Audio, Video Book Publishing Ltd, pg 368
Israel Antiquities Authority, pg 368
Israel Exploration Society, pg 368
Israel Music Institute (IMI), pg 368

Italy

Adea Edizioni, pg 374
AIB Associazione Italiana Biblioteche, pg 374
Umberto Allemandi & C SRL, pg 375
Franco Angeli SRL, pg 375
Apimondia, pg 375
Editore Armando Armando SRL, pg 376
BeMa, pg 377
Editrice Bibliografica SpA, pg 378
Editore Giorgio Bretschneider, pg 379
Edizioni Bucalo SNC, pg 379
CEDAM (Casa Editrice Dr A Milani), pg 380
Istituto Centrale per il Catalogo Unico delle Biblioteche Italiane e per le Informazioni Bibliografiche, pg 381
Centro Biblico, pg 381
Centro Scientifico Torinese, pg 381
CG Ediz Medico-Scientifiche, pg 381
CIC Edizioni Internazionali, pg 381
Edizioni Dedalo SRL, pg 384
DEI Tipographia del Genio Civile, pg 384
Edizioni del Centro Camuno di Studi Preistorici, pg 386
Edi.Ermes srl, pg 388
Esselibri, pg 388
Etas Libri, pg 388
Gruppo Editoriale Faenza Editrice SpA, pg 391
Casa Editrice Libraria Idelson di G Gnocchi, pg 392
Idelson-Gnocchi Edizioni Scientifiche, pg 393
IHT Gruppo Editoriale SRL, pg 393
Edizioni Internazionali di Letteratura e Scienze, pg 393
Itaca, pg 393
Edizioni Lavoro SRL, pg 394
Linea d'Ombra Libri, pg 395
Lybra Immagine, pg 396
Milella di Lecce Spazio Vivo srl, pg 398

Mucchi Editore SRL, pg 399
New Magazine Edizioni, pg 400
Edizioni Olivares, pg 401
Franco Cosimo Panini Editore SpA, pg 402
Piccin Nuova Libraria SpA, pg 403
Pitagora Editrice SRL, pg 403
Pizzicato Edizioni Musicali, pg 403
Pontificio Istituto di Archeologia Cristiana, pg 404
Psicologica Editrice, pg 404
Rirea Casa Editrice della Rivista Italiana di Ragioneria e di Economia Aziendale, pg 405
Editrice San Marco SRL, pg 407
Societa Stampa Sportiva, pg 408
Sorbona, pg 409
Tomo Edizioni srl, pg 410
Transeuropa, pg 410
Vinciana Editrice sas, pg 412

Japan

The American Chamber of Commerce in Japan, pg 415
Bun-ichi Sogo Shuppan, pg 415
Daiichi Shuppan Co Ltd, pg 416
Dohosha Publishing Co Ltd, pg 417
Fumaido Publishing Company Ltd, pg 417
Hakutei-Sha, pg 418
Hokuryukan Co Ltd, pg 418
Igaku-Shoin Ltd, pg 419
Iwanami Shoten, Publishers, pg 419
Kaibundo Shuppan, pg 420
Kazamashobo Co Ltd, pg 420
Keigaku Publishing Co Ltd, pg 420
Kindai Kagaku Sha Co Ltd, pg 421
Maruzen Co Ltd, pg 422
Nakayama Shoten Co Ltd, pg 423
Nikkagiren Shuppan-Sha (JUSE Press Ltd), pg 424
Nippon Jitsugyo Publishing Co Ltd, pg 424
Nosangyoson Bunka Kyokai, pg 424
Ohmsha Ltd, pg 424
Sangyo-Tosho Publishing Co Ltd, pg 426
Seibido, pg 426
Shokokusha Publishing Co Ltd, pg 428
Shorin-Sha Co ltd, pg 428
Shufunotomo Co Ltd, pg 428
Sobun-Sha, pg 428
Toho Book Store, pg 429
Toho Shuppan, pg 429
Tokyo Kagaku Dojin Co Ltd, pg 429
Toppan Co Ltd, pg 430
Tsukiji Shokan Publishing Co, pg 430
Zeimukeiri-Kyokai, pg 431
Zenkoku Kyodo Shuppan, pg 431

Kenya

Action Publishers, pg 433
African Centre for Technology Studies (ACTS), pg 433
Focus Publications Ltd, pg 433
Heinemann Kenya Ltd (EAEP), pg 434
Kenway Publications Ltd, pg 434
Kenya Energy & Environment Organisation, Kengo, pg 434
Lake Publishers & Enterprises Ltd, pg 435
Midi Teki Publishers, pg 435
Shirikon Publishers, pg 436

Democratic People's Republic of Korea

Korea Science and Encyclopedia Publishing House, pg 436

Republic of Korea

Bal-eon, pg 437
Bi-bong Publishing Co, pg 437
Gim-Yeong Co, pg 438
Hakmunsa Publishing Co, pg 439
Korea Psychological Testing Institute, pg 440
Koreaone Press Inc, pg 440
Maeil Gyeongje, pg 441
Nanam Publications Co, pg 441
Prompter Publications, pg 442
Pyeong-hwa Chulpansa, pg 442
Samho Music Publishing Co Ltd, pg 442
Twenty-First Century Publishers, Inc, pg 443
Yeha Publishing Co, pg 443

Latvia

Nordik/Tapals Publishers Ltd, pg 445
Preses Nams, pg 445

Lebanon

Institute for Palestine Studies, Publishing & Research Organization (IPS), pg 446

Lithuania

AS Narbuto Leidykla (AS Narbutas' Publishers), pg 448
Centre of Legal Information, pg 449
Eugrimas, pg 449
Lietus Ltd, pg 449
Lithuanian National Museum Publishing House, pg 449
Martynas Mazvydas National Library of Lithuania, pg 449
Mokslo ir enciklopediju leidybos institutas, pg 449
Scena, pg 449
Svietimo ir mokslo ministerijos Leidybos centras, pg 449

Luxembourg

Editions Emile Borschette, pg 450
Editions Promoculture, pg 451
Varkki Verghese, pg 452

The Former Yugoslav Republic of Macedonia

Detska radost, pg 452
Macedonia Prima Publishing House, pg 452
Medis, Skopje, pg 452

Madagascar

Madagascar Print & Press Company, pg 453
Societe Malgache d'Edition, pg 454

Malaysia

IBS Buku Sdn Bhd, pg 456
Malayan Law Journal Sdn Bhd, pg 456
Minerva Publications, pg 457
Oscar Book International, pg 457

Malta

Publishers' Enterprises Group (PEG) Ltd, pg 460

Mauritius

Hemco Publications, pg 461

Mexico

Editorial AGATA SA de CV, pg 462
Alfaomega Grupo Editor SA de CV, pg 462
Editorial Azteca SA, pg 462
Colegio de Postgraduados en Ciencias Agricolas, pg 463
Ediciones Contables y Administrativas SA, pg 463
Publicaciones Cruz O SA, pg 463
Editorial Diana SA de CV, pg 464
El Colegio de Michoacan A C, pg 464
Editorial El Manual Moderno SA de CV, pg 464
Centro de Estudios Monetarios Latinoamericanos (CEMLA), pg 465
Editorial Fata Morgana SA de CV, pg 465
Editorial Herrero SA, pg 466
Editorial Limusa SA de CV, pg 467
Naves Internacional de Ediciones SA, pg 469
Organizacion Cultural LP SA de CV, pg 469
Panorama Editorial, SA, pg 470
Pearson Educacion de Mexico, SA de CV, pg 470
Editorial Trillas SA de CV, pg 472

Morocco

Dar Nachr Al Maarifa Pour L'Edition et La Distribution, pg 474

Myanmar

Shumawa Publishing House, pg 476

Namibia

Desert Research Foundation of Namibia (DRFN), pg 476

Netherlands

Backhuys Publishers BV, pg 478
Business Contact BV, pg 480
Uitgeverij Coutinho BV, pg 481
Educatieve Partners Nederland bv, pg 481
Hagen & Stam Uitgeverij Ten, pg 483
Uitgeverij Homeovisie BV, pg 483
IOS Press BV, pg 484
Katholieke Bijbelstichting, pg 484
Kluwer Law International, pg 485
Uitgeverij H Nelissen BV, pg 486
Samsom BedrijfsInformatie BV, pg 488
Scriptum, pg 488
SDU Juridische & Fiscale Uitgeverij, pg 488
Segment BV, pg 488
Sociaal en Cultureel Planbureau, pg 489
Swets & Zeitlinger Publishers, pg 489
Uitgeverij de Tijdstroom BV, pg 490

New Zealand

Brookers Ltd, pg 494
Butterworths New Zealand Ltd, pg 494
CCH New Zealand Ltd, pg 495
Fraser Books, pg 496
Learning Media Ltd, pg 498
Legislation Direct, pg 498
Reach Publications, pg 500

Southern Press Ltd, pg 501
Spinal Publications New Zealand Ltd, pg 501

Nigeria

Evans Brothers (Nigeria Publishers) Ltd, pg 504
Fourth Dimension Publishing Co Ltd, pg 504
Goldland Business Co Ltd, pg 505
New Africa Publishing Company Ltd, pg 505
Obafemi Awolowo University Press Ltd, pg 506
Riverside Communications, pg 507

Norway

Universitetsforlaget, pg 511
Vett & Viten AS, pg 511

Pakistan

Academy of Education Planning & Management (AEPAM), pg 511
The Book House, pg 512
HMR Publishing Co, pg 512
Sang-e-Meel Publications, pg 514
Vanguard Books Ltd, pg 515

Panama

Editorial Universitaria, pg 515

Paraguay

Intercontinental Editora, pg 516

Philippines

Ateneo de Manila University Press, pg 518
Our Lady of Manaoag Publisher, pg 520
Rex Bookstores & Publishers, pg 520
Salesiana Publishers Inc, pg 521
SIBS Publishing House Inc, pg 521
UST Publishing House, pg 521

Poland

Wydawnictwo DiG, pg 522
Polskie Wydawnictwo Ekonomiczne PWE SA, pg 522
Impuls, pg 523
Instytut Meteorologii i Gospodarki Wodnej, pg 523
Wydawnictwa Naukowo-Techniczne, pg 524
Ossolineum Zaklad Narodowy im Ossolinskich - Wydawnictwo, pg 525
Wydawnictwo Prawnicze Co, pg 526
Oficyna Wydawnicza Szkoly Glownej Handlowej w Warszawie Oficyna Wydawnicza SGH, pg 527
Instytut Techniki Budowlanej, Dzial Wydawniczo- Poligraficzny, pg 527
Wydawnictwa Uniwersytetu Warszawskiego, pg 527

Portugal

Edicoes Cetop, pg 529
Edicoes Colibri, pg 530
Difusao Cultural, pg 530
Dinalivro, pg 530
Instituto de Investigacao Cientifica Tropical, pg 532
Livraria Luzo-Espanhola Lda, pg 533

Editora McGraw-Hill de Portugal Lda, pg 533
Monitor-Projectos e Edicoes, LDA, pg 533
Petrony Livraria, pg 534
Quid Juris - Sociedade Editora, pg 535
Edicoes Salesianas, pg 535
Vega-Publicacao e Distribuicao de Livros e Revistas, Lda, pg 536

Puerto Rico

McGraw-Hill Intermericana del Caribe, Inc, pg 537

Romania

Editora All, pg 538
Editura Clusium, pg 539
FF Press, pg 540
Editura Gryphon, pg 540
Humanitas Publishing House, pg 540
Editura Meridiane, pg 540
Monitorul Oficial, Editura, pg 541
Editura Niculescu, pg 541
Polirom Verlag, pg 542
Rentrop & Straton Verlagsgruppe und Wirtschaftsconsulting, pg 542
Editura 'Scrisul Romanesc', pg 542

Russian Federation

FGUP Izdatelstvo Mashinostroenie, pg 544
Finansy i Statistika Publishing House, pg 544
Fizmatlit Publishing Co, pg 545
Gidrometeoizdat, pg 545
Izvestia Sovetov Narodnyh Deputatov Russian Federation (RF), pg 545
Izdatelstvo Kazanskago Universiteta, pg 545
Izdatelskii Dom Kompozitor, pg 546
Izdatelstvo Metallurgiya, pg 546
Izdatelstvo Mir, pg 546
Izdatelstvo Mordovskogo gosudar stvennogo, pg 547
Izdatelstvo Muzyka, pg 547
Nauka Publishers, pg 547
Profizdat, pg 548
Izdatelstvo Prosveshchenie, pg 548
Izdatelstvo Sudostroenie, pg 549
Voyenizdat, pg 549
Izdatelstvo Vysshaya Shkola, pg 549

Senegal

CODESRIA (Council for the Development of Social Science Research in Africa), pg 551

Serbia and Montenegro

Partenon MAM Sistem, pg 553
Privredni Pregled, pg 553
Savez Inzenjera i Tehnicara Jugoslavije, pg 553

Singapore

APAC Publishers Services Pte Ltd, pg 554
China Knowledge Press, pg 555
LexisNexis, pg 557
Maruzen Asia (Pte) Ltd, pg 557
McGallen & Bolden Associates, pg 557
Singapore University Press Pte Ltd, pg 558
World Scientific Publishing Co Pte Ltd, pg 559

Slovakia

Dom Techniky Zvazu Slovenskych Vedeckotechnickych Spolocnosti Ltd, pg 559
Priroda Publishing, pg 560
Slo Viet, pg 560
Sofa, pg 560

Slovenia

Zalozba Obzorja d d Maribor, pg 562

South Africa

Human Sciences Research Council, pg 565
Institute for Reformational Studies CHE, pg 565
Johannesburg Art Gallery, pg 565
Juta & Co, pg 565
LexisNexis Butterworths South Africa, pg 566
National Botanical Institute, pg 567
New Africa Books (Pty) Ltd, pg 567
Oceanographic Research Institute, pg 567
Van Schaik Publishers, pg 569

Spain

Centro de Estudios Adams-Ediciones Valbuena SA, pg 571
Editorial AEDOS SA, pg 571
AENOR (Asociacion Espanola de Normalizacion y Certificacion), pg 571
Ediciones Agrotecnicas, SL, pg 571
AMV Ediciones, pg 572
Arambol, SL, pg 573
Arco Libros SL, pg 573
Atrium Group, pg 574
Bosch Casa Editorial SA, pg 575
J M Bosch Editor, pg 575
CEAC, Grupo Editorial SA, pg 576
Cedel, Ediciones Jose O Avila Monteso ES, pg 576
Celeste Ediciones, pg 576
Civitas SA Editorial, pg 577
Editorial Constitucion y Leyes SA - COLEX, pg 578
Ediciones Daly S L, pg 578
Ediciones Diaz de Santos SA, pg 579
Ediciones Doce Calles SL, pg 579
Editorial Dossat SA, pg 580
Dykinson SL, pg 580
Edebe, pg 580
EDERSA (Editoriales de Derecho Reunidas SA), pg 580
Edex, Centro de Recursos Comunitarios, pg 580
Edika-Med, SA, pg 581
EOS Gabinete de Orientacion Psicologica, pg 582
Instituto de Estudios Fiscales, pg 583
Etu Ediciones SL, pg 583
Fundacion Marcelino Botin, pg 584
Generalitat de Catalunya Diari Oficial de la Generalitat vern, pg 584
Ediciones Gestio 2000 SA, pg 585
Editorial Gustavo Gili SA, pg 585
Grao Editorial, pg 585
Editorial Grupo Cero, pg 585
Grupo Comunicar, pg 585
Idea Books, SA, pg 587
Ediciones Internacionales Universitarias SA, pg 588
LEDA (Las Ediciones de Arte), pg 589

Ediciones Libertarias/Prodhufi SA, pg 589
LID Editorial Empresarial, SL, pg 589
Mad SL Editorial, pg 590
Marcial Pons Ediciones Juridicas SA, pg 590
Marcombo SA, pg 590
Ediciones Medici SA, pg 591
Ediciones Morata SL, pg 592
Mundi-Prensa Libros SA, pg 592
Editorial la Muralla SA, pg 592
Naque Editora, pg 592
Navarra, Comunidad Autonoma, Servicio de Prensa, Publica Pamplona, pg 593
Editorial Noray, pg 593
Ediciones Norma SA, pg 593
Ediciones Oceano Grupo SA, pg 593
Ediciones Olimpic, SL, pg 594
Omnicon, SA, pg 594
Editorial Paidotribo SL, pg 594
Pais Vasco Servicio Central de Publicaciones, pg 594
Progensa, pg 597
Pulso Ediciones, SL, pg 597
RA-MA, Libreria y Editorial Microinformatica, pg 597
Editorial Reus SA, pg 598
Ediciones ROL SA, pg 598
Rueda, SL Editorial, pg 598
Servicio de Publicaciones Universidad de Cordoba, pg 599
Signament I Comunicacio, SL Signament Edicions, pg 599
Editorial Sintes SA, pg 600
Editorial Sintesis, SA, pg 600
Ediciones Tecnicas Rede, SA, pg 601
Editores Tecnicos Asociados SA, pg 601
Tesitex, SL, pg 602
Tirant lo Blanch SL Libreriaa, pg 602
Ediciones de la Torre, pg 602
Trea Ediciones, SL, pg 602
Xunta de Galicia, pg 605

Sri Lanka

International Centre for Ethnic Studies, pg 606
National Library & Documentation Centre, pg 607
Sunera Publishers, pg 607

Sweden

Almqvist och Wiksell International, pg 609
Forlagshuset Norden AB, pg 611
Ingenjoersforlaget AB, pg 612
Iustus Forlag AB, pg 613
Norstedts Juridik, pg 614
Studentlitteratur AB, pg 616
Teknografiska Institutet AB, pg 616

Switzerland

Werner Classen Verlag, pg 621
Cockatoo Press (Schweiz), Thailand-Publikationen, pg 621
Marcel Dekker AG, pg 621
Drei-D-World und Foto-World Verlag und Vertrieb, pg 622
Eular Verlag, pg 623
Helbing und Lichtenhahn Verlag AG, pg 625
Verlag Industrielle Organisation, pg 625
JPM Publications SA, pg 626
S Karger AG, Medical & Scientific Publishers, pg 626
Editions Scriptar SA, pg 634

Sinwel-Buchhandlung Verlag, pg 634
3 Dimension World (3-D-World), pg 635
Vdf Hochschulverlag AG an der ETH Zurich, pg 636
Versus Verlag AG, pg 636
Vexer Verlag, pg 636

Taiwan, Province of China

Art Book Co Ltd, pg 638
Chien Chen Bookstore Publishing Company Ltd, pg 639
Farseeing Publishing Company Ltd, pg 639
Fuh-Wen Book Co, pg 639
Chu Hai Publishing (Taiwan) Co Ltd, pg 640
Ho-Chi Book Publishing Co, pg 640
Hsiao Yuan Publication Co, Ltd, pg 640
Laureate Book Co Ltd, pg 640
San Min Book Co Ltd, pg 641
Wei-Chuan Publishing Company Ltd, pg 642
Yi Hsien Publishing Co Ltd, pg 642

United Republic of Tanzania

Bureau of Statistics, pg 643
DUP (1996) Ltd, pg 643
Tanzania Publishing House, pg 644

Thailand

Bannakit Trading, pg 645
Niyom Witthaya, pg 645

Tunisia

Maison Tunisienne de l'Edition, pg 648

Turkey

Ataturk Kultur, Dil ve Tarih, Yusek Kurumu Baskanligi, pg 649
Birsen Yayinevi, pg 649
Inkilap Publishers Ltd, pg 650
Seckin Yayinevi, pg 651
Yapi-Endustri Merkezi Yayinlari-Yem Yayin, pg 652
Yetkin Printing & Publishing Co Inc, pg 652

Uganda

Centre for Basic Research, pg 652
Fountain Publishers Ltd, pg 652

Ukraine

ASK Ltd, pg 653
Naukova Dumka Publishers, pg 653
Osnova, Kharkov State University Press, pg 653
Osnovy Publishers, pg 654
Urozaj, pg 654

United Kingdom

ABG Professional Information, pg 655
Act 3 Publishing, pg 655
Actinic Press Ltd, pg 655
Adamantine Press Ltd, pg 655
Arnold, pg 659
Arts Council of England, pg 660
Ashgate Publishing Ltd, pg 660
Aslib, The Association for Information Management, pg 660
Association for Scottish Literary Studies, pg 661
Association for Science Education, pg 661

TYPE OF PUBLICATION INDEX — BOOK

BAAF Adoption & Fostering, pg 662
BILD Publications, pg 665
Blackwell Science Ltd, pg 667
Blueprint, pg 668
Books for Europe Ltd, pg 669
BPP Publishing Ltd, pg 670
BPS Books (British Psychological Society), pg 670
Brassey's UK Ltd, pg 670
Nicholas Brealey Publishing, pg 670
Brilliant Publications, pg 671
Business Monitor International, pg 672
Butterworths Tolley, pg 673
Capstone Publishing Ltd, pg 674
Cardiff Academic Press, pg 675
Jon Carpenter Publishing, pg 675
Cassell & Co, pg 675
Cavendish Publishing Ltd, pg 676
Centre for Information on Language Teaching & Research (CILT), pg 677
Chancellor Publications, pg 677
The Chartered Institute of Public Finance & Accountancy, pg 678
Christian Research Association, pg 679
Computer Step, pg 681
The Continuum International Publishing Group Ltd, pg 682
Crown House Publishing Ltd, pg 684
CSA (Cambridge Scientific Abstracts), pg 684
Donhead Publishing Ltd, pg 688
Edition XII, pg 690
Elsevier Advanced Technology, pg 691
Elsevier Ltd, pg 691
EPER, pg 691
Ernst & Young, pg 692
Estates Gazette, pg 692
Ethics International Press Ltd, pg 692
Euromonitor PLC, pg 692
The Eurospan Group, pg 692
Fishing News Books Ltd, pg 695
Flicks Books, pg 695
Free Association Books Ltd, pg 697
W H Freeman & Co Ltd, pg 697
David Fulton Publishers Ltd, pg 698
Garnet Publishing Ltd, pg 698
The Geographical Association, pg 699
Geological Society Publishing House, pg 699
Gomer Press (J D Lewis & Sons Ltd), pg 701
Gower Publishing Ltd, pg 701
W Green The Scottish Law Publisher, pg 702
Harley Books, pg 705
Harvard University Press, pg 705
Haynes Publishing, pg 706
Health Development Agency, pg 706
Hobsons, pg 709
Hodder Headline Ltd, pg 709
Horizon Scientific Press, pg 710
ICC United Kingdom, pg 711
ICSA Publishing Ltd, pg 711
Institute for Fiscal Studies, pg 712
Institute of Education, University of London, pg 712
Institute of Employment Rights, pg 712
Institute of Food Science & Technology, pg 713
Institution of Electrical Engineers, pg 713
Interfisc Publishing, pg 714
IOM Communications Ltd, pg 714
ITDG Publishing, pg 715
IWA Publishing, pg 715
JAI Press Ltd, pg 715
James & James (Science Publishers) Ltd, pg 715
Jane's Information Group, pg 715
Karnac Books Ltd, pg 716
Jessica Kingsley Publishers, pg 718
Kluwer Academic/Plenum Publishers, pg 718
Kogan Page Ltd, pg 718
The Latchmere Press, pg 719
Learning Matters Ltd, pg 720
Legal Action Group, pg 720
Lemos & Crane, pg 720
LISU, pg 721
LLP Ltd, pg 722
Lucky Duck Publishing Ltd, pg 723
Macmillan Ltd, pg 723
Management Books 2000 Ltd, pg 724
Management Pocketbooks Ltd, pg 724
Manchester University Press, pg 724
Manson Publishing Ltd, pg 725
Marcham Manor Press, pg 725
Media Research Publishing Ltd, pg 726
The Merlin Press Ltd, pg 727
Micelle Press, pg 727
Multilingual Matters Ltd, pg 729
National Association for the Teaching of English (NATE), pg 730
National Centre for Language & Literacy, pg 730
National Council for Voluntary Organisations (NCVO), pg 730
National Foster Care Association, pg 731
National Foundation for Educational Research, pg 731
National Institute of Adult Continuing Education (NIACE), pg 731
Nelson Thornes Ltd, pg 732
Old Pond Publishing, pg 734
Open University Press, pg 736
Oxfam, pg 737
Parapress Ltd, pg 738
Pavilion Publishing (Brighton) Ltd, pg 739
Pearson Education Europe, Mideast & Africa, pg 739
Pergamon Flexible Learning, pg 740
Perpetuity Press, pg 741
Phaidon Press Ltd, pg 741
Pharmaceutical Press, pg 741
PIRA Intl, pg 742
Police Review Publishing Company Ltd, pg 744
The Policy Press, pg 744
Portland Press Ltd, pg 745
Professional Engineering Publishing Ltd, pg 745
Publishing Training Centre at BookHouse, pg 746
Quiller Publishing Ltd, pg 747
Quintessence Publishing Co Ltd, pg 747
Radcliffe Medical Press Ltd, pg 747
Rapra Technology Ltd, pg 748
Reed Educational & Professional Publishing, pg 749
Research Studies Press Ltd (RSP), pg 749
RIBA Publications, pg 750
RICS Books, pg 750
The Robinswood Press Ltd, pg 750
Rooster Books Ltd, pg 751
Royal College of General Practitioners (RCGP), pg 752
Royal Institute of International Affairs, pg 752
Royal Society of Medicine Press Ltd, pg 752
SAGE Publications Ltd, pg 753
St Jerome Publishing, pg 753
Science Reviews Ltd, pg 755
Shaw & Sons Ltd, pg 756
Sheldon Press, pg 757
Sherwood Publishing, pg 757
SLS Legal Publications (NI), pg 758
Southgate Publishers, pg 759
Speechmark Publishing Ltd, pg 760
Spon Press, pg 760
Sports Turf Research Institute (STRI), pg 760
Stainer & Bell Ltd, pg 761
Rudolf Steiner Press, pg 761
Stobart Davies Ltd, pg 761
Take That Ltd, pg 762
I B Tauris & Co Ltd, pg 763
Taylor & Francis, pg 763
Taylor & Francis Medical Books, pg 763
TFPL, pg 764
Thistle Press, pg 765
Trentham Books Ltd, pg 767
TSO (The Stationery Office), pg 767
Whiting & Birch Ltd, pg 773
Whittles Publishing, pg 773
WIT Press, pg 774
Woodhead Publishing Ltd, pg 775

Uruguay
La Flor del Itapebi, pg 777
Editia Uruguay, pg 778

Venezuela
Ediciones Vega SRL, pg 780

Viet Nam
Science & Technics Publishing House, pg 780

Zimbabwe
Longman Zimbabwe (Pvt) Ltd, pg 783

REPRINTS

Argentina
Oikos, pg 8

Armenia
Arevik, pg 10

Australia
Boombana Publications, pg 16
Cookery Book, pg 18
Elsevier Australia, pg 21
Geoffrey Hamlyn-Harris, pg 24
Instauratio Press, pg 27
Little Red Apple Publishing, pg 29
Navarine Publishing, pg 33
Protestant Publications, pg 38
St Pauls Publications, pg 40
Veritas Press, pg 45
Windhorse Books, pg 47

Austria
Czernin Verlag Ltd, pg 49
DachsVerlag GmbH, pg 49
Development News Ltd, pg 50
Ennsthaler GesmbH & Co KG, pg 50
Oesterreichischer Kunst und Kulturverlag, pg 55

Azerbaijan
Sada, Literaturno-Izdatel'skij Centr, pg 60

Belarus
Belaruskaya Encyklapedyya, pg 62
Kavaler Publishers, pg 62

Belgium
Marabout, pg 71

Benin
Office National d'Edition de Presse et d'Imprimerie (ONEPI), pg 75

Brazil
Agalma Psicanalise Editora Ltda, pg 77
Centro de Estudos Juridicosdo Para (CEJUP), pg 79
Concordia Editora Ltda, pg 80
Edicon Editora e Consultorial Ltda, pg 81
Livraria Freitas Bastos Editora SA, pg 82
Fundacao Cultural Avatar, pg 82
Fundacao Sao Paulo, EDUC, pg 82
Editora Logosofica, pg 85
Pallas Editora e Distribuidora Ltda, pg 88
Qualitymark Editora Ltda, pg 89
Editora Revan Ltda, pg 89
Editora UNESP, pg 91

Bulgaria
Kralica MAB, pg 95
Seven Hills Publishers, pg 96
Svetra Publishing House, pg 97

China
Anhui People's Publishing House, pg 101
Chemical Industry Press, pg 101
China Film Press, pg 102
China Materials Management Publishing House, pg 102
Language Publishing House, pg 106
Lanzhou University Press, pg 106
The People's Communications Publishing House, pg 106
Shandong University Press, pg 108
South China University of Science & Technology Press, pg 108

Croatia
ArTresor naklada, pg 117
Matica hrvatska, pg 118
Znaci Vremena, Institut Za Istrazivanje Biblije, pg 119

Cuba
Editorial Letras Cubanas, pg 120
Editora Politica, pg 120
Pueblo y Educacion Editorial (PE), pg 121

Czech Republic
Euromedia Group-Odeon, pg 123
Cesky normalizacni institut, pg 126
Portal spol sro, pg 126

Denmark
Borgens Forlag A/S, pg 129
Dansk Historisk Handbogsforlag ApS, pg 130
Holkenfeldt 3, pg 132
Rosenkilde & Bagger, pg 134
Scandinavia Publishing House, pg 134

PUBLISHERS — TYPE OF PUBLICATION INDEX

Dominican Republic

Pontificia Universidad Catolica Madre y Maestra, pg 136

Ecuador

Corporacion Editora Nacional, pg 136

El Salvador

Editorial Universitaria de la Universidad de El Salvador, pg 139

Estonia

Estonian Academy Publishers, pg 139

Finland

Suomalaisen Kirjallisuuden Seura, pg 144

France

Editions Philippe Auzou, pg 148
Editions Bertout, pg 149
Bragelonne, pg 151
Editions des Cahiers Bourbonnais, pg 151
Chasse Maree, pg 153
Doin Editeurs, pg 159
Editions Jacques Gabay, pg 164
Jouvence Editions, pg 170
Editions Christian Pirot, pg 180
Jean-Michel Place, pg 180
Presses Universitaires de Caen, pg 181
Editions de Septembre, pg 184
Editions Springer France, pg 186

French Polynesia

Scoop/Au Vent des Iles, pg 189
Haere Po Editions, pg 189

Germany

Antiqua-Verlag GmbH, pg 193
AOL-Verlag Frohmut Menze, pg 193
Aufstieg-Verlag GmbH, pg 195
Belser Wissenschaftlicher Dienst, pg 199
Biblio Verlag, pg 200
Boehlau-Verlag GmbH & Cie, pg 202
BRUEN-Verlag, Gorenflo, pg 205
Degener & Co, Manfred Dreiss Verlag, pg 211
Engelhorn Verlag GmbH, pg 220
Verlag Esoterische Philosophie GmbH, pg 221
Esslinger Verlag J F Schreiber GmbH, pg 221
Harald Fischer Verlag GmbH, pg 224
Friedrich Frommann Verlag, pg 227
GLB Parkland Verlags-und Vertriebs GmbH, pg 229
Liselotte Hamecher, pg 233
Litteraturverlag Karlheinz Hartmann, pg 234
Edition Hentrich Druck & Verlag Gebr Hentrich und Tank GmbH & Co KG, pg 236
Keip GmbH, pg 245
Koptisch-Orthodoxes Zentrum, pg 249
Karin Kramer Verlag, pg 250
Laaber-Verlag, pg 251
Karl Robert Langewiesche Nachfolger Hans Koester KG, pg 252
Edition Libri Illustri GmbH, pg 254

Maro Verlag und Druck, Benno Kasmayr, pg 257
Mueller & Schindler Verlag ek, pg 262
Musikantiquariat und Dr Hans Schneider Verlag GmbH, pg 262
Neuthor - Verlag, pg 265
C W Niemeyer Buchverlage GmbH, pg 265
Georg Olms Verlag AG, pg 267
Orbis Verlag fur Publizistik GmbH, pg 267
Patio, Galerie und Druckwerkstatt, pg 268
Konrad Reich Verlag GmbH, pg 274
Roehrig Universitaets Verlag Gmbh, pg 276
Sachsenbuch Verlagsgesellschaft Mbh, pg 277
Verlag Th Schaefer im Vicentz Verlag KG, pg 278
Ulrich Schiefer bahn Verlag, pg 279
Schmidt Periodicals GmbH, pg 280
Verlag Schnell und Steiner GmbH, pg 281
Theodor Schuster, pg 282
Scientia Verlag und Antiquariat Schilling OHG, pg 282
Spieth-Verlag Verlag fuer Symbolforschung, pg 284
Stern-Verlag Janssen & Co, pg 288
Druck-und Verlagshans Thiele & Schwarz GmbH, pg 290
Transpress Verlagsgesellschaft mbH, pg 292
Trotzdem-Verlags Genossenschaft eG, pg 292
VWB-Verlag fur Wissenschaft & Bildung, Amand Aglaster, pg 297
Wachholtz Verlag GmbH, pg 297
Weidmannsche Verlagsbuchhandlung GmbH, pg 298

Ghana

Building & Road Research Institute (BRRI), pg 303
EPP Books Services, pg 304
World Literature Project, pg 305

Greece

Denise Harvey, pg 308
Ianos, pg 308
Dionysuis P Karavias Ekdoseis, pg 309
Panepistimio Ioanninon, pg 311

Hong Kong

Lea Publications Ltd, pg 318
Philopsychy Press, pg 318

Hungary

Aranyhal Konyvkiado Goldfish Publishing, pg 320
Kossuth Kiado RT, pg 322

India

Affiliated East West Press Pvt Ltd, pg 327
Agam Kala Prakashan, pg 327
Allied Publishers Pvt Ltd, pg 328
Associated Publishing House, pg 329
B I Publications Pvt Ltd, pg 329
Book Faith India, pg 330
BR Publishing Corporation, pg 331
Cosmo Publications, pg 332
Daya Publishing House, pg 333
Dutta Publishing Co Ltd, pg 333
Eastern Law House Pvt Ltd, pg 334

Eurasia Publishing House Private Ltd, pg 334
General Book Depot, pg 335
Gyan Publishing House, pg 335
International Book Distributors, pg 338
B Jain Publishers (P) Ltd, pg 339
Law Publishers, pg 340
Laxmi Publications Pvt Ltd, pg 340
Multitech Publishing Co, pg 342
Munshiram Manoharlal Publishers Pvt Ltd, pg 342
National Council of Applied Economic Research, Publications Division, pg 342
Navrang Booksellers & Publishers, pg 343
Omsons Publications, pg 344
Rahul Publishing House, pg 346
Reliance Publishing House, pg 346
Scientific Book Agency, pg 348
DB Taraporevala Sons & Co Pvt Ltd, pg 351
Theosophical Publishing House, pg 351

Ireland

Ballinakella Press, pg 358
Clo Iar-Chonnachta Teo, pg 358
The Collins Press, pg 358
Irish Times Ltd, pg 361
Mercier Press Ltd, pg 362
Mount Eagle Publications Ltd, pg 362
Ossian Publications, pg 363

Israel

Hakibbutz Hameuchad Publishing House Ltd, pg 367

Italy

Alberti Libraio Editore, pg 375
All'Insegna del Giglio, pg 375
Umberto Allemandi & C SRL, pg 375
Belforte Editore Libraio srl, pg 377
Giuseppe Bonanno Editore, pg 378
Bonsignori Editore SRL, pg 378
Edizioni Brenner, pg 379
Centro Scientifico Torinese, pg 381
CIC Edizioni Internazionali, pg 381
Cittadella Editrice, pg 382
Colonnese Editore, pg 383
Edizioni Cultura della Pace, pg 383
Edizioni del Centro Camuno di Studi Preistorici, pg 386
Festina Lente Edizioni, pg 389
Arnaldo Forni Editore SRL, pg 389
In Dialogo, pg 393
Casa Editrice Le Lettere SRL, pg 395
Maria Pacini Fazzi Editore, pg 402
Pheljna Edizioni d'Arte e Suggestione, pg 403
Priuli e Verlucca, Editori, pg 404
Rara Istituto Editoriale di Bibliofilia e Reprints, pg 405
Sardini Editrice, pg 407
Societa Napoletana Storia Patria Napoli, pg 408
Studio Bibliografico Adelmo Polla, pg 409
Nicola Teti e C Editore SRL, pg 410
Turris, pg 410
Vaccari SRL, pg 411

Jamaica

Eureka Press Ltd, pg 413

Japan

Hakutei-Sha, pg 418
Holp Book Co Ltd, pg 418
Rinsen Book Co Ltd, pg 425
Sobun-Sha, pg 428
Yohan Shuppan, pg 431

Kenya

Focus Publications Ltd, pg 433
Heinemann Kenya Ltd (EAEP), pg 434
Kenway Publications Ltd, pg 434
Life Challenge AFRICA, pg 435
Paulines Publications-Africa, pg 435
Phoenix Publishers Ltd, pg 435
Gideon S Were Press, pg 436

Latvia

Vaidelote, SIA, pg 445

Lebanon

The International Documentary Centre of Arab Manuscripts, pg 446

Liechtenstein

Topos Verlag AG, pg 448

Luxembourg

Editions Emile Borschette, pg 450
Varkki Verghese, pg 452

Madagascar

Maison d'Edition Protestante ANTSO, pg 453

Malaysia

S Abdul Majeed & Co, pg 454
MDC Publishers Printers Sdn Bhd, pg 457
Penerbit Jayatinta Sdn Bhd, pg 458
Pustaka Cipta Sdn Bhd, pg 458
Pustaka Delta Pelajaran Sdn Bhd, pg 458
Tempo Publishing (M) Sdn Bhd, pg 458

Mexico

Editorial AGATA SA de CV, pg 462
AGT Editor SA, pg 462
Centro de Estudios Mexicanos y Centroamericanos, pg 463
Editorial Diana SA de CV, pg 464
Fondo de Cultura Economica, pg 465

Netherlands

APA (Academic Publishers Associated), pg 477
John Benjamins BV, pg 479
Philo Press (APA), pg 487
Rebo Productions BV, pg 488
Tirion Uitgevers BV, pg 490

New Zealand

Brick Row Publishing Co Ltd, pg 494
CCH New Zealand Ltd, pg 495
Nagare Press, pg 499
River Press, pg 500
Shoal Bay Press Ltd, pg 501

Nigeria
Fourth Dimension Publishing Co Ltd, pg 504
Vantage Publishers International Ltd, pg 507
West African Book Publishers Ltd, pg 507

Pakistan
The Book House, pg 512
National Book Foundation, pg 513
National Institute of Historical & Cultural Research, pg 514
Royal Book Co, pg 514
Sang-e-Meel Publications, pg 514

Philippines
Ateneo de Manila University Press, pg 518
Bright Concepts Printing House, pg 518
De La Salle University, pg 519
J C Palabay Enterprises, pg 519
New Day Publishers, pg 520
UST Publishing House, pg 521

Poland
Wydawnictwa Artystyczne i Filmowe, pg 522
Biblioteka Narodowa, pg 522
Wydawnictwo Prawnicze Co, pg 526

Portugal
Livraria Apostolado da Imprensa, pg 533

Romania
Editura Institutul European, pg 540
Editura Militara, pg 541
Editura Paideia, pg 541
Saeculum IO, pg 542

Russian Federation
Aspect Press Ltd, pg 543
Izdatelstvo Khudozhestvennaya Literatura, pg 545
Ladomir Publishing House, pg 546
Ministerstvo Kul'tury RF, pg 546
Panorama Publishing House, pg 547
Planeta Publishers, pg 548

Senegal
CODESRIA (Council for the Development of Social Science Research in Africa), pg 551

Serbia and Montenegro
Alfa-Narodna Knjiga, pg 552
Libertatea, pg 552
Savez Inzenjera i Tehnicara Jugoslavije, pg 553

Singapore
Archipelago Press, pg 555
Cannon International, pg 555

Slovenia
East West Operation (EWO) Ltd, pg 561
Zalozba Mihelac d o o, pg 562

South Africa
Fernwood Press (Pty) Ltd, pg 563
Galago Publishing Pty Ltd, pg 564
Human Sciences Research Council, pg 565
Institute for Reformational Studies CHE, pg 565
Oceanographic Research Institute, pg 567
University of KwaZulu-Natal Press, pg 569

Spain
Editorial Afers, SL, pg 571
Editorial Algazara, pg 572
Ediciones Atril, pg 574
Ediciones Doce Calles SL, pg 579
Vicent Garcia Editores, SA, pg 584
Grijalbo Mondadori SA, pg 585
Institucion Fernando el Catolico de la Excma Diputacion de Zaragoza, pg 587
Ediciones JLA, pg 588
Ediciones Maeva, pg 590
Pentalfa Ediciones, pg 595
Editorial Peregrino SL, pg 595
Editorial El Perpetuo Socorro, pg 596
Instituto Provincial de Investigaciones y Estudios Toledanos (IPIET), pg 597
Publicaciones y Ediciones Salamandra SA, pg 597
Universidad de Santiago de Compostela, pg 599
Tursen, SA, pg 603
Editorial Txertoa, pg 603

Sri Lanka
Dayawansa Jayakody & Co, pg 606
Swarna Hansa Foundation, pg 607

Sweden
Bokforlaget Axplock, pg 609
Ordfront Foerlag AB, pg 614
Bokforlaget Rediviva, Facsimileforlaget, pg 615

Switzerland
Editions L'Age d'Homme - La Cite, pg 617
Cockatoo Press (Schweiz), Thailand-Publikationen, pg 621
Rene Coeckelberghs Editions, pg 621
Drei-D-World und Foto-World Verlag und Vertrieb, pg 622
Lars Mueller Publishers, pg 629
Edition Olms AG, pg 630
3 Dimension World (3-D-World), pg 635

Taiwan, Province of China
Cheng Wen Publishing Company, pg 639
Laureate Book Co Ltd, pg 640
Yi Hsien Publishing Co Ltd, pg 642

United Republic of Tanzania
Central Tanganyika Press, pg 643
General Publications Ltd, pg 643
Tanzania Publishing House, pg 644

Thailand
Sangdad Publishing Company Ltd, pg 645

Turkey
Arkeoloji Ve Sanat Yayinlari, pg 649
Ataturk Kultur, Dil ve Tarih, Yusek Kurumu Baskanligi, pg 649
Isis Yayin Tic ve San Ltd, pg 650
Varlik Yayinlari AS, pg 652

Uganda
Fountain Publishers Ltd, pg 652

United Kingdom
Arthur James Ltd, pg 660
Award Publications Ltd, pg 662
The Banton Press, pg 662
BCA - Book Club Associates, pg 663
Birlinn Ltd, pg 666
Books of Zimbabwe Publishing Co (Pvt) Ltd, pg 669
Breedon Books Publishing Company Ltd, pg 670
Bridge Books, pg 671
Canongate Books Ltd, pg 674
Chadwyck-Healey Ltd, pg 677
Chapter Two, pg 678
Christian Education, pg 679
Christian Focus Publications Ltd, pg 679
E W Classey Ltd, pg 680
Leo Cooper, pg 683
Crown House Publishing Ltd, pg 684
Darf Publishers Ltd, pg 686
John Donald Publishers Ltd, pg 688
Elliot Right Way Books, pg 690
The Erskine Press, pg 692
Flicks Books, pg 695
The Fraser Press, pg 697
Walter H Gardner & Co, pg 698
Garnet Publishing Ltd, pg 698
George Mann Publications, pg 699
GMP Publishers Ltd, pg 700
A H Gordon, pg 701
Grange Books PLC, pg 702
The Greek Bookshop, pg 702
W Green The Scottish Law Publisher, pg 702
Gregg Publishing Co, pg 703
Hilmarton Manor Press, pg 708
Hodder Headline Ltd, pg 709
Institute of Physics Publishing, pg 713
International Bee Research Association, pg 714
The Islamic Texts Society, pg 715
Janus Publishing Co Ltd, pg 716
Karnac Books Ltd, pg 716
Landy Publishing, pg 719
Lang Syne Publishers Ltd, pg 719
The Lutterworth Press, pg 723
Peter Marcan Publications, pg 725
Octopus Publishing Group, pg 734
Oneworld Publications, pg 735
Peter Owen Ltd, pg 737
Packard Publishing Ltd, pg 737
Plough Publishing House of Bruderhof Communities in the UK, pg 743
ProQuest Information & Learning, pg 746
Regency House Publishing Ltd, pg 749
Rivers Oram Press, pg 750
Royal College of General Practitioners (RCGP), pg 752
The Rubicon Press, pg 752
Skoob Russell Square, pg 758
Smith Settle Ltd, pg 758
The Society of Metaphysicians Ltd, pg 759
I B Tauris & Co Ltd, pg 763
Textile & Art Publications Ltd, pg 764
Thistle Press, pg 765
Thoemmes Press, pg 765
Tiger Books International PLC, pg 765
Transport Bookman Publications Ltd, pg 766
Veloce Publishing Ltd, pg 769
Verso, pg 770
VNU Business Publications, pg 770

Viet Nam
Science & Technics Publishing House, pg 780

Zambia
Apple Books, pg 781
Zambia Association for Research & Development (ZARD), pg 782

Zimbabwe
College Press Publishers (Pvt) Ltd, pg 783
The Literature Bureau, pg 783
Longman Zimbabwe (Pvt) Ltd, pg 783

SCHOLARLY BOOKS

Albania
NL SH, pg 1

Argentina
Alfagrama SRL ediciones, pg 3
Beatriz Viterbo Editora, pg 4
Editorial Claridad SA, pg 4
Editorial Hemisferio Sur SA, pg 6
Editorial Idearium de la Universidad de Mendoza (EDIUM), pg 6
Juris Editorial, pg 6
Oikos, pg 8
Editorial Paidos SAICF, pg 8
Ediciones Preescolar SA, pg 8
Editorial Troquel SA, pg 9
Victor P de Zavalia SA, pg 10

Armenia
Arevik, pg 10

Australia
AHB Publications, pg 11
Aletheia Publishing, pg 11
Art Gallery of Western Australia, pg 12
Artmoves Inc, pg 12
Athena Press, pg 12
Ausmed Publications Pty Ltd, pg 12
Australian Academy of Science, pg 13
Australian Film Television & Radio School, pg 13
Australian Institute of Family Studies (AIFS), pg 13
Australian Scholarly Publishing, pg 13
Bio Concepts Publishing, pg 14
Blackwell Publishing Asia, pg 15
Board of Studies, pg 15
Boombana Publications, pg 16
Crawford House Publishing Pty Ltd, pg 18
Crystal Publishing, pg 19
CSIRO Publishing (Commonwealth Scientific & Industrial Research Organisation), pg 19
Deakin University Press, pg 19
Dragon Press, pg 20
Dryden Press, pg 20
Freshet Press, pg 23
Gnostic Editions, pg 23
Hunter House Publications, pg 26
Illert Publications, pg 26
James Nicholas Publishers Pty Ltd, pg 27
Law Book Co Information Services, pg 28
Lucasville Press, pg 30

PUBLISHERS

Magpie Books, pg 30
Melbourne Institute of Applied Economic & Social Research, pg 31
Melbourne University Press, pg 32
K & Z Mostafanejad, pg 32
National Gallery of Victoria, pg 33
National Library of Australia, pg 33
Navarine Publishing, pg 33
Nimrod Publications, pg 33
OTEN (Open Training & Education Network), pg 34
Pearson Education Australia, pg 36
Pluto Press Australia Pty Ltd, pg 37
Pollitecon Publications, pg 37
Power Publications, pg 37
Quakers Hill Press, pg 38
Rams Skull Press, pg 38
Rumsby Scientific Publishing, pg 40
Ruskin Rowe Press, pg 40
St Joseph Publications, pg 40
Spaniel Books, pg 41
Spinifex Press, pg 42
State Library of NSW Press, pg 42
Tarka Publishing, pg 42
Threshold Publishing, pg 43
University of Queensland Press, pg 45
Veritas Press, pg 45
Wileman Publications, pg 46
Windhorse Books, pg 47

Austria

Boehlau Verlag GmbH & Co KG, pg 48
Carinthia Verlag, pg 49
Development News Ltd, pg 50
Doecker Verlag GmbH & Co KG, pg 50
Fassbaender Verlag, pg 50
Guthmann & Peterson Liber Libri, Edition, pg 51
Helbling Verlags-Gesellschaft mbH, pg 51
Verlag Hoelder-Pichler-Tempsky, pg 52
Ibera VerlagsgesmbH, pg 52
International Institute for Applied Systems Analysis (IIASA), pg 52
Verlag Monte Verita, pg 54
Mueller-Speiser Wissenschaftlicher Verlag, pg 54
Verlag der Oesterreichischen Akademie der Wissenschaften (OEAW), pg 55
Oesterreichischer Bundesverlag Gmbh, pg 55
Oesterreichischer Kunst und Kulturverlag, pg 55
Oesterreichisches Katholisches Bibelwerk, pg 55
Verlag des Osterr Kneippbundes GmbH, pg 56
Promedia Verlagsges mbH, pg 56
Resch Verlag, pg 56
Verlag der Salzburger Druckerei, pg 57
Andreas Schnider Verlags-Atelier, pg 57
Springer-Verlag Wien, pg 58
Verband der Wissenschaftlichen Gesellschaften Oesterreichs (VWGOe), pg 59
Verlag Veritas Mediengesellschaft mbH, pg 59
Universitaetsverlag Wagner GmbH, pg 59
WUV/Facultas Universitaetsverlag, pg 60
WUV/Service Fachverlag, pg 60
Zirkular - Verlag der Dokumentationsstelle fuer neuere oesterreichische Literatur, pg 60

Azerbaijan

Sada, Literaturno-Izdatel'skij Centr, pg 60

Bangladesh

Agamee Prakashani, pg 61
The University Press Ltd, pg 61

Belarus

Belaruskaya Encyklapedyya, pg 62
Narodnaya Asveta, pg 62

Belgium

Abimo, pg 62
Alamire vzw, Music Publishers, pg 63
De Boeck et Larcier SA, pg 64
Brepols Publishers NV, pg 64
Editions De Boeck-Larcier SA, pg 66
Dessain - Departement de De Boeck & Larcier SA, pg 66
Editions Hemma, pg 68
Koninklijke Vlaamse Academie van Belgie voor Wetenschappen en Kunsten, pg 69
Leuven University Press, pg 70
La Part de L'Oeil, pg 71
Pelckmans NV, De Nederlandsche Boekhandel, pg 72

Brazil

Agalma Psicanalise Editora Ltda, pg 77
Editora Alfa Omega Ltda, pg 77
Alzira Chagas Carpigiani, pg 79
Editora Companhia das Letras/ Editora Schwarcz Ltda, pg 80
Concordia Editora Ltda, pg 80
Companhia Editora Forense, pg 81
EDUSC - Editora da Universidade do Sagrado Coracao, pg 81
Empresa Brasileira de Pesquisa Agropecuaria, pg 81
Editora FCO Ltda, pg 81
Livraria Martins Fontes Editora Ltda, pg 81
Livraria Freitas Bastos Editora SA, pg 82
Fundacao Sao Paulo, EDUC, pg 82
Editora Harbra Ltda, pg 83
Editora Manole Ltda, pg 86
Editora Moderna Ltda, pg 86
Editora Nova Alexandria Ltda, pg 87
Editora Nova Fronteira SA, pg 87
Ediouro Publicacoes, SA, pg 89
Editora Revan Ltda, pg 89
Saraiva SA, Livreiros Editores, pg 90
34 Literatura S/C Ltda, pg 91
Editora UNESP, pg 91
Editora da Universidade de Sao Paulo, pg 91
Editora Universidade Federal do Rio de Janeiro, pg 92
Editora Vigilia Ltda, pg 92
Jorge Zahar Editor, pg 92

Bulgaria

Agencija Za Ikonomicesko Programirane i Razvitie, pg 93
Bulvest 2000 Ltd, pg 93
Ciela Publishing House, pg 93
Eurasia Academic Publishers, pg 94
Fondacija Zlatno Kljuce, pg 94
Izdatelstvo Lettera, pg 95
LIK Izdanija, pg 95
Makros 2000 - Plovdiv, pg 95
Musica Publishing House Ltd, pg 95
Naouka i Izkoustvo, Ltd, pg 95
Pensoft Publishers, pg 96
Regalia 6 Publishing House, pg 96
Todor Kableshkov University of Transport, pg 97
Zunica, pg 97

Chile

Ediciones Cieplan, pg 99
Editorial Cuarto Propio, pg 99
Edeval (Universidad de Valparaiso), pg 99
Publicaciones Lo Castillo SA, pg 100
Red Internacional Del Libro, pg 100
Ediciones Universitarias de Valparaiso, pg 100

China

Anhui People's Publishing House, pg 101
Chemical Industry Press, pg 101
China Film Press, pg 102
China Machine Press (CMP), pg 102
China Ocean Press, pg 102
China Theatre Publishing House, pg 103
China Tibetology Publishing House, pg 103
Dalian Maritime University Press, pg 104
Electronics Industry Publishing House, pg 104
Foreign Language Teaching & Research Press, pg 104
Fudan University Press, pg 104
Heilongjiang Science & Technology Press, pg 105
Henan Science & Technology Publishing House, pg 105
Higher Education Press, pg 105
Jinan Publishing House, pg 105
Language Publishing House, pg 106
Lanzhou University Press, pg 106
Nanjing University Press, pg 106
National Defence Industry Press, pg 106
Science Press, pg 107
Shandong Education Publishing House, pg 107
Shandong University Press, pg 108
Shanghai College of Traditional Chinese Medicine Press, pg 108
Shanghai Foreign Language Education Press, pg 108
Sichuan University Press, pg 108
South China University of Science & Technology Press, pg 108
Southwest China Jiaotong University Press, pg 108
Universidade de Macau, Centro de Publicacoes, pg 109
World Affairs Press, pg 109
Wuhan University Press, pg 109
Yunnan University Press, pg 109
Zhejiang Education Publishing House, pg 109
Zhong Hua Book Co, pg 110

Colombia

Asociacion Instituto Linguistico de Verano, pg 110
Consejo Episcopal Latinoamericano (CELAM), pg 110
Fondo Educativo Interamericano SA, pg 111
RAM Editores, pg 112
Editorial Santillana SA, pg 112
Tercer Mundo Editores SA, pg 113
Universidad de los Andes Editorial, pg 113
Universidad Nacional Abierta y a Distancia, pg 113

The Democratic Republic of the Congo

Facultes Catoliques de Kinshasa, pg 114

Costa Rica

Academia de Centro America, pg 114
Asamblea Legislativa, Biblioteca Monsenor Sanabria, pg 115
Centro Agronomico Tropical de Investigacion y Ensenanza (CATIE), pg 115
Litografia Artex, SA, pg 115
Editorial Porvenir, pg 116
Ediciones Promesa, pg 116
Editorial Tecnologica de Costa Rica, pg 116
Editorial de la Universidad de Costa Rica, pg 116

Cote d'Ivoire

Universite d'Abidjan, pg 117

Croatia

ALFA dd za izdavacke, graficke i trgovacke poslove, pg 117
ArTresor naklada, pg 117
Knjizevni Krug Split, pg 118

Cuba

Editora Politica, pg 120

Czech Republic

Barrister & Principal, pg 122
Kalich SRO, pg 124
SystemConsult, pg 127
Trizonia, pg 128
Vydavatelstvi Cesky Geologicky Ustav, pg 128

Denmark

Aarhus Universitetsforlag, pg 128
Dansk Psykologisk Forlag, pg 130
P Haase & Sons Forlag A/S, pg 131
Forlaget Hovedland, pg 132
Mellemfolkeligt Samvirke, pg 133
Museum Tusculanum Press, pg 133
Samfundslitteratur, pg 134
Scandinavia Publishing House, pg 134
Wisby & Wilkens, pg 135

Dominican Republic

Pontificia Universidad Catolica Madre y Maestra, pg 136

Ecuador

Centro de Planificacion y Estudios Sociales (CEPLAES), pg 136

Egypt (Arab Republic of Egypt)

Dar El Shorouk, pg 138
Sphinx Publishing Co, pg 138

El Salvador

UCA Editores, pg 138
Editorial Universitaria de la Universidad de El Salvador, pg 139

TYPE OF PUBLICATION INDEX — BOOK

Estonia
Estonian Academy Publishers, pg 139
Olion Publishers, pg 140
Tuum, pg 140
Valgus Publishers, pg 140

Ethiopia
Addis Ababa University Press, pg 140

Finland
Abo Akademis forlag - Abo Akademi University Press, pg 141
Suomalaisen Kirjallisuuden Seura, pg 144
Osuuskunta Vastapaino, pg 144
Yliopistopaino/Helsinki University Press, pg 145

France
Academie Nationale de Reims, pg 145
Adverbum SARL, pg 146
Armenia Editions, pg 147
Atelier National de Reproduction des Theses, pg 148
Editions Atlantica Seguier, pg 148
Berg International Editeur, pg 149
William Blake & Co, pg 150
Editions Buchet-Chastel Pierre Zech Editeur, pg 151
Editions des Cahiers Bourbonnais, pg 151
Editions Jacqueline Chambon, pg 153
Chasse Maree, pg 153
Cicero Editeurs, pg 154
Editions de Compostelle, pg 155
De Vecchi Editions SA, pg 157
Editions de l'Eclat, pg 159
Editions de l'Ecole des Hautes Etudes en Sciences Sociales (EHESS), pg 159
Editions Edisud, pg 159
Editions Recherche sur les Civilisations (ERC), pg 160
Editions Errance, pg 162
Editions Pierre Fanlac, pg 162
Editions Fata Morgana, pg 162
FBT de R Editions, pg 163
Federation d'Activities Culturelles, Fac Editions, pg 163
Editions Filipacchi-Sonodip, pg 163
Librairie Fischbacher, International Art Book Distribution (import-export), pg 163
Folklore Comtois, pg 164
Paul Geuthner Librairie Orientaliste, pg 165
Hachette Education, pg 166
L'Harmattan, pg 167
Editions Herault, pg 167
Kailash Editions, pg 170
Editions Klincksieck, pg 170
Langues & Mondes-L'Asiatheque, pg 171
P Lethielleux Editions, pg 171
Letouzey et Ane Editeurs, pg 171
Lettres Modernes Minard, pg 172
Editions des Limbes d'Or FBT de R Editions, pg 172
Macula, pg 174
Editions Marie-Noelle, pg 174
Editions Medianes, pg 175
Librairie Minard, pg 176
Presses Universitaires du Mirail, pg 176
Nil Editions, pg 177
Presses Universitaires de Strasbourg, pg 182

Publications de l'Universite de Rouen, pg 182
Publications Orientalistes de France (POF), pg 182
Somogy editions d'art, pg 185
Universitas, pg 188

French Polynesia
Scoop/Au Vent des Iles, pg 189
Haere Po Editions, pg 189

Germany
A Francke Verlag (Tubingen und Basel), pg 190
Accedo Verlagsgesellschaft mbH, pg 190
Akademie Verlag GmbH, pg 191
AOL-Verlag Frohmut Menze, pg 193
ARCult Media, pg 193
Argument-Verlag, pg 194
J J Augustin Verlag GmbH, pg 195
Augustinus-Verlag Wurzburg Inh Augustinerprovinz, pg 195
Bank-Verlag GmbH, pg 197
Barenreiter-Verlag Karl-Votterle GmbH & Co KG, pg 197
Bayerische Akademie der Wissenschaften, pg 198
Verlag Beleke KG, pg 198
Berliner Debatte Wissenschafts Verlag, GSFP-Gesellschaft fur Sozialwissen-schaftliche Forschung und Publizistik mbH & Co KG, pg 199
Berliner Wissenschafts-Verlag GmbH (BWV), pg 199
W Bertelsmann Verlag GmbH & Co KG, pg 200
Beuth Verlag GmbH, pg 200
Blackwell Wissenschafts-Verlag GmbH, pg 201
Edition Klaus Blahak Dr Fredric Kroll, pg 202
Verlag Die Blaue Eule, pg 202
Boehlau-Verlag GmbH & Cie, pg 202
Verlag Hermann Boehlaus Nachfolger Weimar GmbH & Co, pg 203
Klaus Boer Verlag, pg 203
Breitkopf & Hartel, pg 204
BRUEN-Verlag, Gorenflo, pg 205
Buechse der Pandora Verlags-GmbH, pg 205
Helmut Buske Verlag GmbH, pg 206
Catia Monser Eggcup-Verlag, pg 207
Centaurus-Verlagsgesellschaft GmbH, pg 207
Compact Verlag GmbH, pg 209
Das Arsenal, Verlag fuer Kultur und Politik GmbH, pg 210
Data Becker GmbH & Co KG, pg 210
Deutsche Bibelgesellschaft, pg 211
Deutscher Verlag fur Grundstoffindustrie GmbH, pg 213
Diagonal-Verlag GbR Rink-Schweer, pg 214
Verlag J H W Dietz Nachf GmbH, pg 214
Dietz Verlag Berlin GmbH, pg 215
Edition Diskord, pg 215
agenda Verlag Thomas Dominikowski, pg 215
Donat Verlag, pg 215
Duncker und Humblot GmbH, pg 217
Echo Verlag, pg 217

Elsevier GmbH/Urban & Fischer Verlag, pg 219
Erlanger Verlag Fuer Mission und Okumene, pg 220
Verlagsgesellschaft des Erziehungsvereins GmbH, pg 221
Europa Union Verlag GmbH, pg 222
Evangelische Verlagsanstalt GmbH, pg 222
Evangelischer Presseverband fuer Bayern eV, pg 222
Karin Fischer Verlag GmbH, pg 225
Flensburger Hefte Verlag GmbH, pg 225
FN-Verlag der Deutschen Reiterlichen Vereinigung GmbH, pg 225
Franz-Sales-Verlag, pg 226
Fraunhofer IRB Verlag Fraunhofer Informationszentrum Raum und Bau, pg 226
Friedrich Kiehl Verlag GmbH, pg 227
Friedrich Frommann Verlag, pg 227
Gebrueder Borntraeger Science Publishers, pg 228
Germanisches Nationalmuseum, pg 228
Verlag fuer Geschichte der Naturwissenschaften und der Technik, pg 229
Gesundheits-Dialog Verlag GmbH, pg 229
Goldschneck Verlag, pg 230
Govi-Verlag Pharmazeutischer Verlag GmbH, pg 230
Grote'sche Verlagsbuchhandlung GmbH & Co KG, pg 231
Walter de Gruyter GmbH & Co KG, pg 231
Gunter Olzog Verlag GmbH, pg 231
Guetersloher Verlagshaus, pg 232
Verlag des Gustav-Adolf-Werks, pg 232
Wolfgang G Haas - Musikverlag Koeln ek, pg 232
Liselotte Hamecher, pg 233
Carl Hanser Verlag, pg 234
Harrassowitz Verlag, pg 234
von Hase & Koehler Verlag KG, pg 234
Hellerau-Verlag Dresden GmbH, pg 236
G Henle Verlag, pg 236
Edition Hentrich Druck & Verlag Gebr Hentrich und Tank GmbH & Co KG, pg 236
Verlag Herder GmbH & Co KG, pg 236
Anton Hiersemann, Verlag, pg 237
F Hirthammer Verlag GmbH, pg 238
Verlag Peter Hoell, pg 238
Hofbauer, Christoph und Trojanow Ilia, Akademischer Verlag Muenchen, pg 238
Holos Verlag, pg 239
Horlemann Verlag, pg 239
Edition Humanistische Psychologie (EHP), pg 240
Huss-Medien GmbH, pg 240
Huss-Verlag GmbH, pg 240
Huthig GmbH & Co KG, pg 240
Edition ID-Archiv/ID-Verlag, pg 240
IKO Verlag fur Interkulturelle Kommunikation, pg 241
Klaus Isele, pg 242
Iudicium Verlag GmbH, pg 242
Janus Verlagsgesellschaft, Dr Norbert Meder & Co, pg 243
Juventa Verlag GmbH, pg 244

Keip GmbH, pg 245
Kirschbaum Verlag GmbH, pg 246
Vittorio Klostermann GmbH, pg 247
W Kohlhammer GmbH, pg 248
KONTEXTverlag, pg 249
kopaed verlagsgmbh, pg 249
Karin Kramer Verlag, pg 250
Alfred Kroner Verlag, pg 250
Verlag Ernst Kuhn, pg 250
Institut fuer Landes- und Stadtentwicklungsforschung des Landes Nordrhein-Westfalen, pg 251
Peter Lang GmbH Europaeischer Verlag der Wissenschaften, pg 252
Karl Robert Langewiesche Nachfolger Hans Koester KG, pg 252
Michael Lassleben Verlag und Druckerei, pg 252
Lebenshilfe-Verlag Marburg, Verlag der Bundesvereinigung Lebenshilfe fuer Menschen mit geistiger Behinderung eV, pg 253
Leipziger Universitaetsverlag GmbH, pg 253
Anton G Leitner Verlag (AGLV), pg 253
Verlag Otto Lembeck, pg 253
LEU-VERLAG Wolfgang Leupelt, pg 254
Libertas- Europaeisches Institut GmbH, pg 254
Hildegard Liebaug-Dartmann, pg 254
Robert Lienau GmbH & Co KG, pg 254
Luther-Verlag GmbH, pg 256
Verlag Waldemar Lutz, pg 256
Annemarie Maeger, pg 256
Mannerschwarm Skript Verlag GmbH, pg 257
Manutius Verlag, pg 257
Margraf Verlag, pg 257
Edition Marhold, pg 257
Mattes Verlag GmbH, pg 257
Medizinisch-Literarische Verlagsgesellschaft mbH, pg 258
Felix Meiner Verlag GmbH, pg 258
Merlin Verlag Andreas Meyer Verlags GmbH und Co KG, pg 259
Mohr Siebeck, pg 261
Verlag Stephanie Naglschmid, pg 263
Verlag Neue Wirtschafts-Briefe GmbH & Co, pg 264
Verlag Neuer Weg, pg 264
Neuland-Verlagsgesellschaft mbH, pg 264
Neuthor - Verlag, pg 265
Max Niemeyer Verlag GmbH, pg 265
Rainar Nitzsche Verlag, pg 265
Nusser Verlag, pg 266
Oekobuch Verlag & Versand GmbH, pg 266
R Oldenbourg Verlag GmbH, pg 267
Georg Olms Verlag AG, pg 267
Pahl-Rugenstein Verlag Nachfolger-GmbH, pg 267
Justus Perthes Verlag Gotha GmbH, pg 269
Philipps-Universitaet Marburg, pg 270
pmi Verlag, pg 270
Guido Pressler Verlag, pg 271
Psychologie Verlags Union GmbH, pg 272

PUBLISHERS — TYPE OF PUBLICATION INDEX

Verlag Friedrich Pustet GmbH & Co Kg, pg 272
Quintessenz Verlags-GmbH, pg 273
Verlag Recht und Wirtschaft GmbH, pg 274
REGENSBERG Druck & Verlag GmbH & Co, pg 274
Verlag fur Regionalgeschichte, pg 274
Dr Ludwig Reichert Verlag, pg 274
Roehrig Universitaets Verlag Gmbh, pg 276
Heidi Rogner, pg 276
Romiosini Verlag, pg 276
scaneg Verlag, pg 278
Schelzky & Jeep, Verlag fuer Reisen und Wissen, pg 279
Verlag Dr Otto Schmidt KG, pg 280
Verlag Schnell und Steiner GmbH, pg 281
Ferdinand Schoeningh Verlag GmbH, pg 281
Schott Musik International GmbH & Co KG, pg 281
Schueren Verlag GmbH, pg 281
Schulz-Kirchner Verlag GmbH, pg 282
E Schweizerbart'sche Verlagsbuchhandlung (Naegele und Obermiller), pg 282
Dr Arthur L Sellier & Co KG-Walter de Gruyter GmbH & Co KG OHG, pg 283
Edition Sigma e.Kfm, pg 283
Springer Science+Business Media GmbH & Co KG, pg 284
Verlag Stahleisen GmbH, pg 286
Stauffenburg Verlag Brigitte Narr GmbH, pg 287
Franz Steiner Verlag Wiesbaden GmbH, pg 287
Stern-Verlag Janssen & Co, pg 288
Steyler Verlag, pg 288
Edition Temmen, pg 290
edition Text & Kritik im Richard Boorberg Verlag GmbH & Co, pg 290
Tipress Dienstleistungen fur das Verlagswesen GmbH, pg 291
Trautvetter & Fischer Nachf, pg 292
Ulrike Helmer Verlag, pg 293
Universitaetsverlag Winter GmbH Heidelberg GmbH, pg 293
Unrast Verlag e V, pg 293
Urban & Vogel Medien und Medizin Verlagsgesellschaft mbH & Co KG, pg 294
UVK Universitatsverlag Konstanz GmbH, pg 294
UVK Verlagsgesellschaft mbH, pg 294
Dorothea van der Koelen, pg 294
Vandenhoeck & Ruprecht, pg 294
VAS-Verlag fuer Akademische Schriften, pg 294
Vereinte Evangelische Mission, Abt Verlag, pg 295
Verlag fur die Rechts- und Anwaltspraxis GmbH & Co, pg 295
Verlag fur Schweissen und Verwandte Verfahren, pg 295
Vervuert Verlagsgesellschaft, pg 295
Votum Verlag GmbH, pg 297
VWB-Verlag fur Wissenschaft & Bildung, Amand Aglaster, pg 297
Wachholtz Verlag GmbH, pg 297
Waxmann Verlag GmbH, pg 297
Weidler Buchverlag Berlin, pg 298
Weidmannsche Verlagsbuchhandlung GmbH, pg 298

Verlag Westfaelisches Dampfboot, pg 299
Westholsteinische Verlagsanstalt und Verlagsdruckerei Boyens & Co, pg 299
Herbert Wichmann Verlag, pg 299
Wiley-VCH Verlag GmbH, pg 300
Dr Dieter Winkler, pg 300
Wissenschaftliche Buchgesellschaft, pg 300
Verlag Konrad Wittwer GmbH, pg 301
Verlag Philipp von Zabern, pg 302

Ghana
Ghana Universities Press (GUP), pg 304
Sedco Publishing Ltd, pg 305
Woeli Publishing Services, pg 305
World Literature Project, pg 305

Greece
Anixis Publications, pg 305
Athina, Mary Mavrogiannis, pg 306
Editions Athina-Mavrogianni, pg 306
Ecole francaise d'Athenes, pg 307
Etaireia Spoudon Neoellinikou Politismou Kai Genikis Paideias, pg 307
Denise Harvey, pg 308
Hiotellis P, pg 308
Kardamitsa A, pg 309
Nea Thesis - Evrotas, pg 310
Pagoulatos Bros, pg 311
Panepistimio Ioanninon, pg 311
Michalis Sideris, pg 312

Guadeloupe
JASOR, pg 313

Guatemala
Grupo Editorial RIN-78, pg 313

Guyana
The Hamburgh Register, pg 314

Honduras
Editorial Guaymuras, pg 315

Hong Kong
The Chinese University Press, pg 316
Chung Hwa Book Co (HK) Ltd, pg 316
The Dharmasthiti Buddist Institute Ltd, pg 317
Hong Kong University Press, pg 317
Joint Publishing (HK) Co Ltd, pg 317
Philopsychy Press, pg 318
Research Centre for Translation, pg 319

Hungary
Aranyhal Konyvkiado Goldfish Publishing, pg 320
Atlantisz Kiado, pg 320
Balassi Kiado Kft, pg 321
Janus Pannonius Tudomanyegyetem, pg 322
Jelenkor Verlag, pg 322
Marton Aron Kiado Publishing House, pg 323
Mezogazda Kiado, pg 323
Nemzeti Tankoenyvkiado, pg 323
Planetas Kiadoi es Kereskedelmi Kft, pg 324

Iceland
Haskolautgafan - University of Iceland Press, pg 325

India
Advaita Ashrama, pg 327
Agam Kala Prakashan, pg 327
Agricole Publishing Academy, pg 327
Allied Publishers Pvt Ltd, pg 328
Amar Prakashan, pg 328
Ananda Publishers Pvt Ltd, pg 328
Anmol Publications Pvt Ltd, pg 328
Asian Educational Services, pg 329
Authorspress, pg 329
BR Publishing Corporation, pg 331
The Christian Literature Society, pg 332
Concept Publishing Co, pg 332
Cosmo Publications, pg 332
Daya Publishing House, pg 333
DK Printworld (P) Ltd, pg 333
Dutta Publishing Co Ltd, pg 333
Full Circle Publishing, pg 334
Gyan Publishing House, pg 335
Hindi Pracharak Sansthan, pg 336
Indian Institute of Advanced Study, pg 337
Indus Publishing Co, pg 338
Jaipur Publishing House, pg 339
Kerala University, Department of Publications, pg 339
Law Publishers, pg 340
Minerva Associates (Publications) Pvt Ltd, pg 341
Mudrak Publishers & Distributors, pg 342
Munshiram Manoharlal Publishers Pvt Ltd, pg 342
National Council of Applied Economic Research, Publications Division, pg 342
Oxford & IBH Publishing Co Pvt Ltd, pg 344
Oxford University Press, pg 344
Panchasheel Prakashan, pg 344
Panjab University Publication Bureau, pg 344
Pitambar Publishing Co (P) Ltd, pg 345
Rahul Publishing House, pg 346
Rastogi Publications, pg 346
Regency Publications, pg 346
Rekha Prakashan, pg 346
Reliance Publishing House, pg 346
SABDA, pg 347
SAGE Publications India Pvt Ltd, pg 347
Sasta Sahitya Mandal, pg 348
Scientific Book Agency, pg 348
Somaiya Publications Pvt Ltd, pg 349
South Asian Publishers Pvt Ltd, pg 350
Sterling Publishers Pvt Ltd, pg 350
Stree, pg 350

Indonesia
Angkasa CV, pg 353
Katalis PT Bina Mitra Plaosan, pg 355
Lembaga Demografi Fakultas Ekonomi Universitas Indonesia, pg 355
Mizan, pg 355
Nusa Indah, pg 356
PT Pustaka LP3ES Indonesia, pg 356

Ireland
The Columba Press, pg 359
Cork University Press, pg 359

Dee-Jay Publications, pg 359
Flyleaf Press, pg 360
Four Courts Press Ltd, pg 360
Gandon Editions, pg 360
The Goldsmith Press Ltd, pg 360
Herodotus Press, pg 361
Irish Academic Press, pg 361
Irish Management Institute, pg 361
The Lilliput Press Ltd, pg 361
On Stream Publications Ltd, pg 362
Relay Books, pg 363
Round Hall Sweet & Maxwell, pg 363
Tir Eolas, pg 363
Wolfhound Press Ltd, pg 364

Israel
Academon Publishing House, pg 364
Academy of the Hebrew Language, pg 364
Bar Ilan University Press, pg 365
Ben-Zvi Institute, pg 365
The Bialik Institute, pg 365
Breslov Research Institute, pg 365
Dekel Publishing House, pg 366
Dyonon/Papyrus Publishing House of the Tel-Aviv, pg 366
Gefen Publishing House Ltd, pg 367
Habermann Institute for Literary Research, pg 367
Haifa University Press, pg 367
Hakibbutz Hameuchad Publishing House Ltd, pg 367
The Institute for Israeli Arabs Studies, pg 368
The Israel Academy of Sciences & Humanities, pg 368
Israel Antiquities Authority, pg 368
Israel Exploration Society, pg 368
(JDC) Brookdale Institute of Gerontology & Adult Human Development in Israel, pg 369
K Dictionaries Ltd, pg 369
Kivunim-Arsan Publishing House, pg 369
Maaliyot-Institute for Research Publications, pg 370
MAP-Mapping & Publishing Ltd, pg 370
Misgav Yerushalayim, pg 370
The Moshe Dayan Center for Middle Eastern & African Studies, pg 371
Nehora Press, pg 371
Open University of Israel, pg 371
Schlesinger Institute, pg 371
University Publishing Projects Ltd, pg 373
Urim Publications, pg 373
Yad Izhak Ben-Zvi Press, pg 373
Yad Vashem - The Holocaust Martyrs' & Heroes' Remembrance Authority, pg 373
The Zalman Shazar Center, pg 374

Italy
Editore Armando Armando SRL, pg 376
Athesia Verlag Bozen, pg 377
Bastogi, pg 377
Bertello Edizioni, pg 377
BMG Ricordi SpA, pg 378
Bovolenta, pg 379
Edizioni Bucalo SNC, pg 379
Campanotto, pg 379
Edizioni Cantagalli, pg 379
Casa Editrice Lint Srl, pg 380
Casa Musicale Edizioni Carrara SRL, pg 380
CEDAM (Casa Editrice Dr A Milani), pg 380

Centro Programmazione Editoriale (CPE), pg 381
Edizioni Centro Studi Erickson, pg 381
Ciranna e Ferrara, pg 382
Direzione Generale Archivi, pg 385
Editrice Edisco, pg 386
Editori Laterza, pg 386
Edizioni del Centro Camuno di Studi Preistorici, pg 386
Edizioni di Storia e Letteratura, pg 386
Edizioni Qiqajon, pg 387
L'Erma di Bretschneider SRL, pg 388
Esselibri, pg 388
Arnaldo Forni Editore SRL, pg 389
Istituto Geografico de Agostini SpA, pg 390
Editrice Innocenti SNC, pg 393
Editoriale Jaca Book SpA, pg 394
Editrice Janus SpA, pg 394
Jouvence, pg 394
LED - Edizioni Universitarie di Lettere Economia Diritto, pg 395
LIM Editrice SRL, pg 395
Angelo Longo Editore, pg 396
Nicola Milano Editore, pg 398
Edumond Le Monnier, pg 399
New Magazine Edizioni, pg 400
Leo S Olschki, pg 401
G B Paravia & C SpA, pg 402
Pontificio Istituto Orientale, pg 404
Editoriale San Giusto SRL Edizioni Parnaso, pg 406
Editrice San Marco SRL, pg 407
Sansoni-RCS Libri, pg 407
Sardini Editrice, pg 407
Societa Stampa Sportiva, pg 408
Tappeiner, pg 409
Tilgher-Genova sas, pg 410
Casa Editrice Luigi Trevisini, pg 410

Jamaica
Institute of Jamaica Publications, pg 413
The Jamaica Bauxite Institute, pg 413
The Press, pg 414
Ian Randle Publishers Ltd, pg 414
University of the West Indies Press, pg 414

Japan
Business Center for Academic Societies Japan, pg 416
Chikuma Shobo Publishing Co Ltd, pg 416
Dobunshoin Publishers Co, pg 416
Eichosha Company Ltd, pg 417
Fumaido Publishing Company Ltd, pg 417
Kaitakusha, pg 420
Kazamashobo Co Ltd, pg 420
Keisuisha Publishing Company Ltd, pg 420
Kindai Kagaku Sha Co Ltd, pg 421
Koyo Shobo, pg 422
Myrtos Inc, pg 423
Nikkagiren Shuppan-Sha (JUSE Press Ltd), pg 424
Nippon Hoso Shuppan Kyokai (NHK Publishing), pg 424
Rinsen Book Co Ltd, pg 425
Seibido, pg 426
Seibundo Shuppan, pg 426
Sobun-Sha, pg 428
Taimeido Publishing Co Ltd, pg 429
Tamagawa University Press, pg 429
Thomson Learning Japan, pg 429
Toho Book Store, pg 429

Toyo Keizai Shinpo-Sha, pg 430
United Nations University Press, pg 430
Zoshindo JukenKenkyusha, pg 431

Kenya
Academy Science Publishers, pg 432
Action Publishers, pg 433
African Centre for Technology Studies (ACTS), pg 433
British Institute in Eastern Africa, pg 433
Evangel Publishing House, pg 433
Heinemann Kenya Ltd (EAEP), pg 434
Kenway Publications Ltd, pg 434
Lake Publishers & Enterprises Ltd, pg 435
Nairobi University Press, pg 435
Paulines Publications-Africa, pg 435
Phoenix Publishers Ltd, pg 435
Shirikon Publishers, pg 436
Gideon S Were Press, pg 436

Republic of Korea
Bi-bong Publishing Co, pg 437
Chung Rim Publishing Co Ltd, pg 438
Gim-Yeong Co, pg 438
Hakmunsa Publishing Co, pg 439
Hanul Publishing Co, pg 439
Iljo-gag Publishers, pg 439
Koreaone Press Inc, pg 440
Minjisa Publishing Co, pg 441
Munye Publishing Co, pg 441
Prompter Publications, pg 442
St Pauls, pg 442
Seogwangsa, pg 442
Sohaksa, pg 443
Yonsei University Press, pg 444

Latvia
Nordik/Tapals Publishers Ltd, pg 445

Lebanon
Dar-El-Machreq Sarl, pg 446
Librairie Orientale sal, pg 446

Libyan Arab Jamahiriya
Al-Fatah University, General Administration of Libraries, Printing & Publications, pg 447

Liechtenstein
Verlag der Liechtensteinischen Akademischen Gesellschaft, pg 448

Lithuania
Baltos Lankos, pg 449
Mokslo ir enciklopediju leidybos institutas, pg 449
Margi Rastai Publishers, pg 449

Luxembourg
Editions APESS ASBL, pg 450
Thesen Verlag Vowinckel, pg 452
Editions Tousch, pg 452
Varkki Verghese, pg 452

Macau
Instituto Portugues Oriente, pg 452

The Former Yugoslav Republic of Macedonia
St Clement of Ohrid National & University Library, pg 453

Madagascar
Editions Ambozontany, pg 453

Malaysia
Penerbit Universiti Sains Malaysia, pg 458
Pustaka Cipta Sdn Bhd, pg 458
Pustaka Sistem Pelajaran Sdn Bhd, pg 458
Penerbit Universiti Teknologi Malaysia, pg 459
University of Malaya, Department of Publications, pg 459

Mexico
Alfaomega Grupo Editor SA de CV, pg 462
Centro de Estudios Mexicanos y Centroamericanos, pg 463
Colegio de Postgraduados en Ciencias Agricolas, pg 463
Publicaciones Cruz O SA, pg 463
Ediciones Eca SA de CV, pg 464
Ediciones Era SA de CV, pg 465
Editorial Esfinge SA de CV, pg 465
Centro de Estudios Monetarios Latinoamericanos (CEMLA), pg 465
Ediciones Euroamericanas, pg 465
Fondo de Cultura Economica, pg 465
Editorial Limusa SA de CV, pg 467
Instituto Nacional de Antropologia e Historia, pg 469
Nova Grupo Editorial SA de CV, pg 469
Pangea Editores, Sa de CV, pg 470
Plaza y Valdes SA de CV, pg 470
Ediciones Promesa, SA de CV, pg 470
Sistemas Tecnicos de Edicion SA de CV, pg 472
Universidad Nacional Autonoma de Mexico (National University of Mexico), pg 472
Universidad Veracruzana Direccion General Editorial y de Publicaciones, pg 472

Republic of Moldova
Editura Lumina, pg 473

Monaco
Rondeau Giannipiero a Monaco, pg 474

Namibia
Multi-Disciplinary Research Centre Library, pg 476

Netherlands
APA (Academic Publishers Associated), pg 477
Backhuys Publishers BV, pg 478
A A Balkema Uitgevers BV, pg 478
Brill Academic Publishers, pg 479
Buijten en Schipperheijn BV Drukkerij en Uitgeversmaatschappij, pg 480
Delft University Press, pg 481
HES & De Graaf Publishers BV, pg 483
Historische Uitgeverij, pg 483
Holland University Press BV (APA), pg 483
Hotei Publishing, pg 484
IOS Press BV, pg 484
KIT - Royal Tropical Institute Publishers, pg 484

KITLV Press Royal Institute of Linguistics & Anthropology, pg 484
Koninklijke Vermande bv, pg 485
Uitgeverij Lemma BV, pg 485
The Pepin Press, pg 487
Philo Press (APA), pg 487
Swets & Zeitlinger Publishers, pg 489
Uitgeverij Verloren, pg 492
VU Boekhandel/Uitgeverij BV, pg 492

New Zealand
Aoraki Press Ltd, pg 493
Auckland University Press, pg 493
Canterbury University Press, pg 494
Clerestory Press, pg 495
Heritage Press Ltd, pg 497
Outrigger Publishers, pg 499
Paerangi Books, pg 500
Te Waihora Press, pg 501
University of Otago Press, pg 502
Bridget Williams Books Ltd, pg 502

Nigeria
Adebara Publishers Ltd, pg 503
Ahmadu Bello University Press Ltd, pg 503
Evans Brothers (Nigeria Publishers) Ltd, pg 504
Fourth Dimension Publishing Co Ltd, pg 504
Goldland Business Co Ltd, pg 505
Heritage Books, pg 505
Ibadan University Press, pg 505
International Publishing & Research Company, pg 505
JAD Publishers Ltd, pg 505
New Africa Publishing Company Ltd, pg 505
New Era Publishers, pg 506
Nigerian Institute of International Affairs, pg 506
Riverside Communications, pg 507
Vantage Publishers International Ltd, pg 507

Norway
Solum Forlag A/S, pg 510
Universitetsforlaget, pg 511

Pakistan
Academy of Education Planning & Management (AEPAM), pg 511
ASR Publications, pg 512
Centre for South Asian Studies, pg 512
Islamic Publications (Pvt) Ltd, pg 513
National Book Foundation, pg 513
Pakistan Institute of Development Economics (PIDE), pg 514
Sang-e-Meel Publications, pg 514
Vanguard Books Ltd, pg 515

Papua New Guinea
Kristen Press, pg 515
National Research Institute of Papua New Guinea, pg 515
Papua New Guinea Institute of Medical Research, pg 516

Paraguay
Instituto de Ciencias de la Computacion (NCR), pg 516

PUBLISHERS

Peru

Centro de la Mujer Peruana Flora Tristan, pg 516
Instituto de Estudios Peruanos, pg 517
Instituto Frances de Estudios Andinos, IFEA, pg 517
Sur Casa de Estudios del Socialismo, pg 517
Tarea Asociacion de Publicaciones Educativas, pg 517
Universidad de Lima-Fondo de Desarollo Editorial, pg 517

Philippines

Ateneo de Manila University Press, pg 518
De La Salle University, pg 519
Logos (Divine Word) Publications Inc, pg 519
New Day Publishers, pg 520
Our Lady of Manaoag Publisher, pg 520
San Carlos Publications, pg 521
UST Publishing House, pg 521

Poland

Wydawnictwo DiG, pg 522
Energeia sp zoo Wydawnictwo, pg 523
Wydawnictwa Geologiczne, pg 523
Instytut Historii Nauki PAN, pg 523
Impuls, pg 523
Iskry - Publishing House Ltd spotka zoo, pg 523
Katolicki Uniwersytet Wydawniczo-Redakcja, pg 523
Wydawnictwo Medyczne Urban & Partner, pg 524
Wydawnictwa Naukowo-Techniczne, pg 524
Ossolineum Zaklad Narodowy im Ossolinskich - Wydawnictwo, pg 525
Wydawnictwo Prawnicze Co, pg 526
Przedsiebiorstwo Wydawniczo-Handlowe Wydawnictwo Siedmiorog, pg 526
PZWL Wydawnictwo Lekarskie Ltd, pg 526
Oficyna Wydawnicza Read Me, pg 526
'Slask' Ltd, pg 526
Wydawnictwa Szkolne i Pedagogiczne, pg 527
Towarzystwo Naukowe w Toruniu, pg 527

Portugal

Livraria Arnado Lda, pg 528
Centro Estudos Geograficos, pg 529
Coimbra Editora Lda, pg 530
Edicoes Colibri, pg 530
Empresa Literaria Fluminense, Lda, pg 531
Gradiva-Publicacnoes Lda, pg 532
Imprensa Nacional-Casa da Moeda, pg 532
Instituto de Investigacao Cientifica Tropical, pg 532
Lua Viajante-Edicao e Distribuicao de Livros e Material Audiovisual, Lda, pg 533
Perspectivas e Realidades, Artes Graficas, Lda, pg 534
Editora Replicacao Lda, pg 535
Edicoes Silabo, pg 536
Vega-Publicacao e Distribuicao de Livros e Revistas, Lda, pg 536

Puerto Rico

Piedras Press, Inc, pg 537

Romania

Editura Academiei Romane, pg 538
Editura Aius, pg 538
The Center for Romanian Studies, pg 539
Editura Clusium, pg 539
Editura Dacia, pg 539
Humanitas Publishing House, pg 540
Editura Institutul European, pg 540
Editura Kriterion SA, pg 540
Mentor Kiado, pg 540
Editura Meridiane, pg 540
Editura Niculescu, pg 541
Petrion Verlag, pg 542
Saeculum IO, pg 542
Editura Stiintifica SA, pg 542
Editura Teora, pg 542

Russian Federation

Airis Press, pg 543
Aspect Press Ltd, pg 543
N E Bauman Moscow State Technical University Publishers, pg 544
BLIC, russko-Baltijskij informaciionnyj centr, AO, pg 544
FGUP Izdatelstvo Mashinostroenie, pg 544
Finansy i Statistika Publishing House, pg 544
Fizmatlit Publishing Co, pg 545
Izdatelstvo Iskusstvo, pg 545
Kabardino-Balkarskoye knizhnoye izdatelstvo, pg 545
Izdatelstvo Khudozhestvennaya Literatura, pg 545
Izdatelskii Dom Kompozitor, pg 546
Ministerstvo Kul 'tury RF, pg 546
Izdatelstvo Mir, pg 546
Moscow University Press, pg 547
Izdatelstvo Muzyka, pg 547
Nauka Publishers, pg 547
St Andrew's Biblical Theological College, pg 548
Izdatelstvo Ural' skogo, pg 549
Voronezh State University Publishers, pg 549
Izdatelstvo Vysshaya Shkola, pg 549

Saudi Arabia

King Saud University, pg 550

Serbia and Montenegro

Obod, pg 553

Singapore

APAC Publishers Services Pte Ltd, pg 554
Federal Publications (S) Pte Ltd, pg 556
Graham Brash Pte Ltd, pg 556
Institute of Southeast Asian Studies, pg 556
McGallen & Bolden Associates, pg 557
Select Publishing Pte Ltd, pg 557
Singapore University Press Pte Ltd, pg 558
Taylor & Francis Asia Pacific, pg 558
World Scientific Publishing Co Pte Ltd, pg 559

Slovakia

ARCHA sro Vydavatel'stro, pg 559
Dom Techniky Zvazu Slovenskych Vedeckotechnickych Spolocnosti Ltd, pg 559
Priroda Publishing, pg 560

Slovenia

Franc-Franc podjetje za promocijo kulture Murska Sobota d o o, pg 561
Zalozba Obzorja d d Maribor, pg 562

South Africa

The Brenthurst Press (Pty) Ltd, pg 563
Centre for Conflict Resolution, pg 563
Educum Publishers Ltd, pg 563
Human Sciences Research Council, pg 565
Institute for Reformational Studies CHE, pg 565
Ivy Publications, pg 565
Johannesburg Art Gallery, pg 565
Maskew Miller Longman, pg 566
Nasionale Boekhandel Ltd, pg 567
Oceanographic Research Institute, pg 567
Ravan Press (Pty) Ltd, pg 568
South African Institute of Race Relations, pg 569
University of KwaZulu-Natal Press, pg 569
Witwatersrand University Press, pg 570

Spain

Publicacions de l'Abadia de Montserrat, pg 570
Centro de Estudios Adams-Ediciones Valbuena SA, pg 571
Editorial Afers, SL, pg 571
Ediciones Akal SA, pg 571
Ediciones Alfar SA, pg 572
Arco Libros SL, pg 573
Editorial Bruno, pg 575
Biblioteca de Catalunya, pg 576
Ediciones Catedra SA, pg 576
Central Catequistica Salesiana (CCS), pg 576
Civitas SA Editorial, pg 577
Ediciones Colegio De Espana (ECE), pg 577
Compania Literaria, pg 577
Ediciones de la Universidad Complutense de Madrid, pg 577
Complutense, SA Editorial, pg 577
Dinsic Publicacions Musicals, pg 579
Ediciones El Almendro de Cordoba, pg 580
Enciclopedia Catalana, SA, pg 582
Ediciones Encuentro SA, pg 582
Esic Editorial, pg 582
Editorial Espasa-Calpe SA, pg 582
Instituto de Estudios Riojanos, pg 583
Grupo Comunicar, pg 585
Impredisur, SL, pg 587
Institucion Fernando el Catolico de la Excma Diputacion de Zaragoza, pg 587
Joyas Bibliograficas SA, pg 588
Editorial Juventud SA, pg 588
Editorial Moll SL, pg 592
Editorial la Muralla SA, pg 592
Naque Editora, pg 592
Oikos-Tau SA Ediciones, pg 593
Pages Editors, SL, pg 594
Polifemo, Ediciones, pg 596
Editorial Popular SA, pg 596
Publicaciones de la Universidad de Alicante, pg 597
Secretariado Trinitario, pg 599
Servicio de Publicaciones Universidad de Cadiz, pg 599
Ediciones Seyer, pg 599
Editorial Sintesis, SA, pg 600
Sirmio, pg 600
Ediciones SM, pg 600
Tirant lo Blanch SL Libreriaa, pg 602
Ediciones de la Torre, pg 602
Trotta SA Editorial, pg 602
Universidad de Malaga, pg 603
Ediciones Universidad de Salamanca, pg 603
Universidad de Valladolid Secretariado de Publicaciones e Intercambio Editorial, pg 604
Edicions de la Universitat Politecnica de Catalunya SL, pg 604
Editorial Verbum SL, pg 604

Sri Lanka

Inter-Cultural Book Promoters, pg 606
International Centre for Ethnic Studies, pg 606
Pradeepa Publishers, pg 607
Samayawardena Printers Publishers & Booksellers, pg 607
Somawathi Hewavitharana Fund, pg 607
Swarna Hansa Foundation, pg 607
Waruni Publishers, pg 607

Suriname

Stichting Wetenschappelijke Informatie, pg 608

Sweden

Carlsson Bokfoerlag AB, pg 610
Dahlia Books, International Publishers & Booksellers, pg 611
Hillelforlaget, pg 612
ITK Laromedel AB, pg 612
Bokforlaget Nya Doxa AB, pg 614
Studentlitteratur AB, pg 616

Switzerland

Augustin-Verlag, pg 618
Les Editions de la Fondation Martin Bodmer, pg 619
Edizioni Casagrande SA, pg 620
Marcel Dekker AG, pg 621
Librairie Droz SA, pg 622
eFeF-Verlag/Edition Ebersbach, pg 622
Garuda-Verlag, pg 624
Paul Haupt Bern, pg 625
Peter Lang AG, pg 627
Parkett Publishers Inc, pg 630
Editions Payot Lausanne, pg 631
Pedrazzini Tipografia, pg 631
Staempfli Verlag AG, pg 634
Vdf Hochschulverlag AG an der ETH Zurich, pg 636
Versus Verlag AG, pg 636

Syrian Arab Republic

Damascus University Press, pg 638

Taiwan, Province of China

Asian Culture Co Ltd, pg 638
Cheng Wen Publishing Company, pg 639

TYPE OF PUBLICATION INDEX — BOOK

Chien Chen Bookstore Publishing Company Ltd, pg 639
Chu Liu Book Company, pg 639
Chung Hwa Book Co Ltd, pg 639
Laureate Book Co Ltd, pg 640
Linking Publishing Company Ltd, pg 641
San Min Book Co Ltd, pg 641
SMC Publishing Inc, pg 642
Torch of Wisdom, pg 642
UNITAS Publishing Co Ltd, pg 642
World Book Co Ltd, pg 642
Yee Wen Publishing Co Ltd, pg 642
Yuan Liou Publishing Co, Ltd, pg 642

United Republic of Tanzania

DUP (1996) Ltd, pg 643
Press & Publicity Centre Ltd, pg 644
Tanzania Publishing House, pg 644
Tema Publishers Ltd, pg 644

Thailand

Pracha Chang & Co Ltd, pg 645
Sangdad Publishing Company Ltd, pg 645

Tunisia

Maison Tunisienne de l'Edition, pg 648

Turkey

Arkeoloji Ve Sanat Yayinlari, pg 649
Aydin Yayincilik, pg 649
Isis Yayin Tic ve San Ltd, pg 650
Kubbealti Akademisi Kultur ve Sasat Vakfi, pg 650

Uganda

Centre for Basic Research, pg 652
Fountain Publishers Ltd, pg 652
Roce (Consultants) Ltd, pg 653

Ukraine

ASK Ltd, pg 653
Naukova Dumka Publishers, pg 653
Osnovy Publishers, pg 654
Osvita, pg 654

United Kingdom

Act 3 Publishing, pg 655
Acumen Publishing Ltd, pg 655
Adamantine Press Ltd, pg 655
Umberto Allemandi & Co Publishing, pg 656
Anglo-German Foundation for the Study of Industrial Society, pg 658
Ashgate Publishing Ltd, pg 660
Ashmolean Museum Publications, pg 660
Atlantic Transport Publishers, pg 661
Atlas Press, pg 661
BAAF Adoption & Fostering, pg 662
Ruth Bean Publishers, pg 664
Berg Publishers, pg 664
Berghahn Books Ltd, pg 665
BFI Publishing, pg 665
Joseph Biddulph Publisher, pg 665
BIOS Scientific Publishers Ltd, pg 666
Birlinn Ltd, pg 666
Black Ace Books, pg 666
Books for Europe Ltd, pg 669
Borthwick Institute Publications, pg 669
Boydell & Brewer Ltd, pg 669
Bridge Books, pg 671
The British Academy, pg 671
Cameron & Hollis, pg 674
Cardiff Academic Press, pg 675
Cassell & Co, pg 675
Cavendish Publishing Ltd, pg 676
Church Union, pg 680
James Clarke & Co Ltd, pg 680
Commonwealth Secretariat, pg 681
The Continuum International Publishing Group Ltd, pg 682
James Currey Ltd, pg 685
John Donald Publishers Ltd, pg 688
Drake Educational Associates Ltd, pg 688
Gerald Duckworth & Co Ltd, pg 688
Dunedin Academic Press, pg 688
Educational Explorers (Publishers) Ltd, pg 690
Edward Elgar Publishing Ltd, pg 690
Elsevier Ltd, pg 691
The Erskine Press, pg 692
estamp, pg 692
Ethics International Press Ltd, pg 692
The Eurospan Group, pg 692
Facet Publishing, pg 694
Flicks Books, pg 695
Free Association Books Ltd, pg 697
Garden Art Press Ltd, pg 698
Garnet Publishing Ltd, pg 698
The Geographical Association, pg 699
Geological Society Publishing House, pg 699
GMP Publishers Ltd, pg 700
The Greek Bookshop, pg 702
Gregg Publishing Co, pg 703
Gwasg Gwenffrwd, pg 703
Hakluyt Society, pg 703
Harley Books, pg 705
Harvard University Press, pg 705
Christopher Helm (Publishers) Ltd, pg 707
Helm Information Ltd, pg 707
Heraldry Today, pg 708
Hodder Education, pg 709
Horizon Scientific Press, pg 710
Icon Press, pg 711
Immediate Publishing, pg 712
Imperial College Press, pg 712
Independent Writers Publications Ltd, pg 712
Institute of Education, University of London, pg 712
Institute of Irish Studies, The Queens University of Belfast, pg 713
Institute of Physics Publishing, pg 713
Institution of Electrical Engineers, pg 713
Intellect Ltd, pg 713
International Institute for Strategic Studies, pg 714
IOM Communications Ltd, pg 714
The Islamic Texts Society, pg 715
JAI Press Ltd, pg 715
James & James (Science Publishers) Ltd, pg 715
Kegan Paul International Ltd, pg 717
Hilda King Educational, pg 717
Jessica Kingsley Publishers, pg 718
Kluwer Academic/Plenum Publishers, pg 718
Kogan Page Ltd, pg 718
Landy Publishing, pg 719
Lawrence & Wishart, pg 719
The Littman Library of Jewish Civilization, pg 721
Liverpool University Press, pg 722
The Lutterworth Press, pg 723
Macmillan Ltd, pg 723
Macmillan Reference Ltd, pg 724
Manchester University Press, pg 724
Maney Publishing, pg 725
Manson Publishing Ltd, pg 725
Marcham Manor Press, pg 725
Merrow Publishing Co Ltd, pg 727
Micelle Press, pg 727
Motilal (UK) Books of India, pg 729
Multilingual Matters Ltd, pg 729
National Archives of Scotland, pg 730
National Library of Wales, pg 731
National Portrait Gallery Publications, pg 731
New European Publications Ltd, pg 732
NMS Enterprises Ltd - Publishing, pg 733
Northcote House Publishers Ltd, pg 733
Norwood Publishers Ltd, pg 734
Octagon Press Ltd, pg 734
Octopus Publishing Group, pg 734
The Oleander Press, pg 735
Oneworld Publications, pg 735
Open Gate Press, pg 735
Open University Press, pg 736
Oxfam, pg 737
Packard Publishing Ltd, pg 737
Parapress Ltd, pg 738
Peepal Tree Press Ltd, pg 740
Perpetuity Press, pg 741
Phaidon Press Ltd, pg 741
Pickering & Chatto Publishers Ltd, pg 742
Pion Ltd, pg 742
Pluto Press, pg 743
The Policy Press, pg 744
Portland Press Ltd, pg 745
Quintessence Publishing Co Ltd, pg 747
Reaktion Books Ltd, pg 748
Research Studies Press Ltd (RSP), pg 749
Rivers Oram Press, pg 750
Rooster Books Ltd, pg 751
Roundhouse Group, pg 751
RoutledgeCurzon, pg 751
Royal Institute of International Affairs, pg 752
SAGE Publications Ltd, pg 753
St Jerome Publishing, pg 753
SCM-Canterbury Press Ltd, pg 755
Scottish Cultural Press, pg 755
Scottish Text Society, pg 755
Sheffield Academic Press Ltd, pg 757
Shepheard-Walwyn (Publishers) Ltd, pg 757
Skoob Russell Square, pg 758
SLS Legal Publications (NI), pg 758
Colin Smythe Ltd, pg 759
Speechmark Publishing Ltd, pg 760
Stacey International, pg 761
Stainer & Bell Ltd, pg 761
Sutton Publishing Ltd, pg 762
Tate Publishing Ltd, pg 763
I B Tauris & Co Ltd, pg 763
Taylor & Francis, pg 763
Taylor Graham Publishing, pg 764
Textile & Art Publications Ltd, pg 764
Thistle Press, pg 765
Thoemmes Press, pg 765
Trentham Books Ltd, pg 767
TSO (The Stationery Office), pg 767
Tuckwell Press Ltd, pg 767
UCL Press Ltd, pg 768
University of Exeter Press, pg 768
University of Hertfordshire Press, pg 768
University Presses of California, Columbia & Princeton Ltd, pg 769
Verso, pg 770
Voltaire Foundation Ltd, pg 771
The Warburg Institute, pg 771
White Cockade Publishing, pg 772
Whiting & Birch Ltd, pg 773
Wimbledon Publishing Company Ltd, pg 774
Windhorse Publications, pg 774
WIT Press, pg 775
World of Islam Altajir Trust, pg 776
Yale University Press London, pg 776
Zed Books Ltd, pg 776

Uruguay

Fundacion de Cultura Universitaria, pg 777
Nordan-Comunidad, pg 778
Ediciones Trilce, pg 778

Venezuela

Biblioteca Ayacucho, pg 779
Editorial Nueva Sociedad, pg 780

Viet Nam

Science & Technics Publishing House, pg 780

Zambia

Historical Association of Zambia, pg 781
MFK Management Consultants Services, pg 781

Zimbabwe

Academic Books (Pvt) Ltd, pg 782
Anvil Press, pg 782
ZRD Trust, pg 785

SIDELINES

Argentina

Juegos & Co SRL, pg 6

Australia

Dynamo House P/L, pg 20

Brazil

Brinque Book Editora de Livros Ltda, pg 79
Ediouro Publicacoes, SA, pg 89
Rede Das Artes (Boccato Editores Collector's), pg 89

Colombia

Eurolibros Ltda, pg 111
RAM Editores, pg 112
Editorial Santillana SA, pg 112

Cuba

Casa Editora Abril, pg 120

Czech Republic

Cesky normalizacni institut, pg 126

Germany

Artcolor, pg 194
Coppenrath Verlag, pg 209
Esslinger Verlag J F Schreiber GmbH, pg 221

PUBLISHERS

Margarethe Freudenberger - selbstverlag fur jedermann, pg 227
Edition Hentrich Druck & Verlag Gebr Hentrich und Tank GmbH & Co KG, pg 236
Friedrich W Heye Verlag GmbH, pg 237
Lorber-Verlag & Turm-Verlag Otto Zluhan, pg 255
teNeues Verlag GmbH & Co KG, pg 290
Dorothea van der Koelen, pg 294

Greece
Toubis M, pg 312

Israel
Schocken Publishing House Ltd, pg 371

Mexico
Fernandez Editores SA de CV, pg 465
Ediciones Libra, SA de CV, pg 467
Sayrols Editorial SA de CV, pg 471
Ediciones Suromex SA, pg 472

Serbia and Montenegro
Izdavacka preduzece Gradina, pg 552

Singapore
Aquanut Agencies Pte Ltd, pg 555

Spain
Editorial 'Alas', pg 571
Editorial Astri SA, pg 573
Pirene Editorial, sal, pg 596
Editorial Miguel A Salvatella SA, pg 598
Equipo Sirius SA, pg 600
Stanley Editorial, pg 601

Ukraine
Mystetstvo Publishers, pg 653

United Kingdom
Four Seasons Publishing Ltd, pg 696

SUBSCRIPTION & MAIL ORDER BOOKS

Argentina
Beatriz Viterbo Editora, pg 4
Juris Editorial, pg 6
Instituto de Publicaciones Navales, pg 8

Australia
ACER Press, pg 10
Artmoves Inc, pg 12
Ashling Books, pg 12
Australian Broadcasting Authority, pg 13
Bernal Publishing, pg 14
Blackwell Publishing Asia, pg 15
Board of Studies, pg 15
Bridge To Peace Publications, pg 16
Butterworths Australia Ltd, pg 16
Covenanter Press, pg 18
Crista International, pg 18
Encyclopaedia Britannica (Australia) Inc, pg 21
Gould Genealogy, pg 23
Hartys Creek Press, pg 25
Instauratio Press, pg 27

Jarrah Publications, pg 27
Law Book Co Information Services, pg 28
Matthias Media, pg 31
Jill Oxton Publications Pty Ltd, pg 35
Papyrus Publishing, pg 35
Pascoe Publishing Pty Ltd, pg 36
Pollitecon Publications, pg 37
Priestley Consulting, pg 37
The Real Estate Institute of Australia, pg 39
Skills Publishing, pg 41
Slouch Hat Publications, pg 41
Threshold Publishing, pg 43
Veritas Press, pg 45
Vista Publications, pg 45

Austria
Andreas Schnider Verlags-Atelier, pg 57

Azerbaijan
Sada, Literaturno-Izdatel'skij Centr, pg 60

Belgium
Editions De Boeck-Larcier SA, pg 66
Koepel van de Vlaamse Noord - Zuidbeweging 11.11.11, pg 69
Wolters Kluwer Belgie NV, pg 74

Brazil
Abril SA, pg 76
Empresa Brasileira de Pesquisa Agropecuaria, pg 81
Fundacao Cultural Avatar, pg 82
Talento Publicacoes Editora e Grafica Ltda, pg 91

Bulgaria
Ciela Publishing House, pg 93
Hriker, pg 94
Publishing House Narodno delo OOD, pg 96

Chile
Arrayan Editores, pg 98

China
Foreign Language Teaching & Research Press, pg 104
Lanzhou University Press, pg 106
The People's Communications Publishing House, pg 106

Costa Rica
Editorial Texto Ltda, pg 116

Croatia
Vitagraf, pg 119

Cuba
Pueblo y Educacion Editorial (PE), pg 121

Czech Republic
Nakladatelstvi Jota spol sro, pg 124
Lyra Pragensis Obecne Prospelna Spolecnost, pg 125
Nase vojsko, nakladatelstvi a knizni obchod, pg 126

Denmark
Schultz Information, pg 134

TYPE OF PUBLICATION INDEX

Dominican Republic
Editora Taller, pg 136

Egypt (Arab Republic of Egypt)
Al Arab Publishing House, pg 137

France
L'Amitie par le Livre, pg 146
Editions Amrita SA, pg 146
Editions Canope, pg 152
Editeurs Crepin-Leblond, pg 156
Editions ELOR, pg 160
L'Harmattan, pg 167
Editions Le Laurier, pg 171
Muller Edition, pg 176
Jean-Michel Place, pg 180
Association d'Editions Sorg, pg 186

Germany
Chmielorz GmbH Verlag, pg 208
Data Becker GmbH & Co KG, pg 210
Dietrich zu Klampen Verlag, pg 214
H Gietl Verlag & Publikationsservice GmbH, pg 229
Heel Verlag GmbH, pg 235
Edition Hentrich Druck & Verlag Gebr Hentrich und Tank GmbH & Co KG, pg 236
Kerber Verlag, pg 245
Koptisch-Orthodoxes Zentrum, pg 249
Laaber-Verlag, pg 251
Edition Libri Illustri GmbH, pg 254
mode information Heinz Kramer GmbH, pg 261
Verlag Norbert Mueller AG & Co KG, pg 262
Edition Octopus & Okeanos Presse, pg 266
Springer Science+Business Media GmbH & Co KG, pg 284
C A Starke Verlag, pg 287
Tipress Dienstleistungen fur das Verlagswesen GmbH, pg 291
Trans Tech Publications, pg 292
Dorothea van der Koelen, pg 294

Ghana
World Literature Project, pg 305

Greece
Beta Medical Publishers, pg 306
Nomiki Bibliothiki, pg 310

Hong Kong
Breakthrough Ltd - Breakthrough Publishers, pg 315
Hong Kong China Tourism Press, pg 317
Press Mark Media Ltd, pg 318

Hungary
Novorg International Szervezo es Kiado kft, pg 323

India
International Book Distributors, pg 338
Law Publishers, pg 340
Sri Ramakrishna Math, pg 341
Reliance Publishing House, pg 346

Indonesia
PT Indira, pg 355

Ireland
Ballinakella Press, pg 358
Government Publications Ireland, pg 360
Oak Tree Press, pg 362

Israel
Hanitzotz A-Sharara Publishing House, pg 367

Italy
Apimondia, pg 375
BeMa, pg 377
Edizioni Carmelitane, pg 380
Electa, pg 387
Macro Edizioni, pg 397
Edizioni Piemme SpA, pg 403
Edizioni Segno SRL, pg 407
Sorbona, pg 409

Japan
Shufunotomo Co Ltd, pg 428

Kenya
Gideon S Were Press, pg 436

Republic of Korea
Korea Britannica Corp, pg 440
YBM/Si-sa, pg 443

Mexico
Artes de Mexico y del Mundo SA de CV, pg 462
Editora Cientifica Medica Latinoamerican SA de CV, pg 463
Colegio de Postgraduados en Ciencias Agricolas, pg 463
Instituto Nacional de Estadistica, Geographia e Informatica, pg 469

Netherlands
Hagen & Stam Uitgeverij Ten, pg 483

New Zealand
Aspect Press, pg 493
CCH New Zealand Ltd, pg 495
Southern Press Ltd, pg 501

Nigeria
Goldland Business Co Ltd, pg 505

Pakistan
The Book House, pg 512
International Educational Services, pg 512

Papua New Guinea
Melanesian Institute, pg 515

Paraguay
Intercontinental Editora, pg 516

Philippines
Our Lady of Manaoag Publisher, pg 520

Poland
Wydawnictwo Medyczne Urban & Partner, pg 524
Wydawnictwo Prawnicze Co, pg 526

TYPE OF PUBLICATION INDEX — BOOK

Portugal
Imprensa Nacional-Casa da Moeda, pg 532
Latina Livraria Editora, pg 532
Revista Penteado, pg 535
Solivros, pg 536

Romania
Humanitas Publishing House, pg 540
Editura Militara, pg 541
Editura Niculescu, pg 541
RAO International Publishing Co, pg 542

Russian Federation
N E Bauman Moscow State Technical University Publishers, pg 544
Finansy i Statistika Publishing House, pg 544
Mir Knigi Ltd, pg 546
Izdatelstvo Muzyka, pg 547
Profizdat, pg 548
St Andrew's Biblical Theological College, pg 548

Slovenia
Zalozba Mihelac d o o, pg 562

South Africa
Institute for Reformational Studies CHE, pg 565
Jacklin Enterprises (Pty) Ltd, pg 565
Juta & Co, pg 565
South African Institute of Race Relations, pg 569

Spain
Ediciones Agrotecnicas, SL, pg 571
Editorial Astri SA, pg 573
Ediciones l'Isard, S L, pg 580
Joyas Bibliograficas SA, pg 588
Lynx Edicions, pg 590
Edicions Proa, SA, pg 597
Instituto Provincial de Investigaciones y Estudios Toledanos (IPIET), pg 597
Secretariado Trinitario, pg 599
Vinaches Lopez, Luisa, pg 605

Sweden
Bokforlaget Axplock, pg 609
Hans Richter Laromedel, pg 613

Switzerland
Bergli Books AG, pg 619
Cosmos-Verlag AG, pg 621
Parkett Publishers Inc, pg 630
Weltrundschau Verlag AG, pg 637

Taiwan, Province of China
Senate Books Co Ltd, pg 641
Torch of Wisdom, pg 642
Yuan Liou Publishing Co, Ltd, pg 642

United Republic of Tanzania
Bureau of Statistics, pg 643
Emmaus Bible School, pg 643

Thailand
Sangdad Publishing Company Ltd, pg 645

Turkey
Iletisim Yayinlari, pg 650

Uganda
Centre for Basic Research, pg 652

United Kingdom
ABG Professional Information, pg 655
AK Press & Distribution, pg 656
Ian Allan Publishing Ltd, pg 656
Arts Council of England, pg 660
Association for Science Education, pg 661
Atlas Press, pg 661
BCA - Book Club Associates, pg 663
Bible Reading Fellowship, pg 665
Bridge Books, pg 671
Business Monitor International, pg 672
Chapman, pg 677
Christian Education, pg 679
E W Classey Ltd, pg 680
Leo Cooper, pg 683
Croner CCH Group Ltd, pg 684
The Energy Information Centre, pg 691
Epworth Press, pg 691
Free Association Books Ltd, pg 697
Freedom Press, pg 697
The Greek Bookshop, pg 702
Greenhill Books/Lionel Leventhal Ltd, pg 703
Hawk Books, pg 706
Hobsons, pg 709
Institute for Fiscal Studies, pg 712
ITDG Publishing, pg 715
Lang Syne Publishers Ltd, pg 719
Legal Action Group, pg 720
Letterbox Library, pg 720
Macmillan Ltd, pg 723
Kenneth Mason Publications Ltd, pg 726
Moorley's Print & Publishing Ltd, pg 729
National Association for the Teaching of English (NATE), pg 730
National Centre for Language & Literacy, pg 730
Oilfield Publications Ltd, pg 734
Osprey Publishing Ltd, pg 737
Parapress Ltd, pg 738
Perpetuity Press, pg 741
The Policy Press, pg 744
Ramakrishna Vedanta Centre, pg 747
The Reader's Digest Association Ltd, pg 748
Royal College of General Practitioners (RCGP), pg 752
The Royal Society, pg 752
SchoolPlay Productions Ltd, pg 755
Sheffield Academic Press Ltd, pg 757
Spokesman, pg 760
Stainer & Bell Ltd, pg 761
Take That Ltd, pg 762
Taylor & Francis, pg 763
TSO (The Stationery Office), pg 767
VNU Business Publications, pg 770
Wilmington Business Information Ltd, pg 774

Uruguay
Ediciones de Juan Darien, pg 777
Fundacion de Cultura Universitaria, pg 777
La Urpila Editores, pg 778
Vinten Editor, pg 778

Venezuela
Editorial Nueva Sociedad, pg 780

TEXTBOOKS - ELEMENTARY

Afghanistan
Ministry of Education, Department of Educational Publications, pg 1

Albania
NL SH, pg 1

Argentina
Editorial Acme SA, pg 3
AZ Editora SA, pg 3
Bonum Editorial SACI, pg 4
Cesarini Hermanos, pg 4
Ediciones Don Bosco Argentina, pg 5
Edicial SA, pg 5
Angel Estrada y Cia SA, pg 5
Gram Editora, pg 6
Libreria Huemul SA, pg 6
Kapelusz Editora SA, pg 7
Ediciones Preescolar SA, pg 8

Armenia
Arevik, pg 10

Australia
Board of Studies, pg 15
Boinkie Publishers, pg 15
Cambridge University Press, pg 16
China Books, pg 17
R J Cleary Publishing, pg 18
Coolabah Publishing, pg 18
Curriculum Corporation, pg 19
Dabill Publications, pg 19
Dellasta Publishing, pg 19
Educational Advantage, pg 20
Era Publications, pg 21
Hawker Brownlow, pg 25
Macmillan Education Australia, pg 30
Horwitz Martin Education, pg 31
McGraw-Hill Australia Pty Ltd, pg 31
Mimosa Publications Pty Ltd, pg 32
Pearson Education Australia, pg 36
Phoenix Education Pty Ltd, pg 36
Ready-Ed Publications, pg 39
Reed Educational Publishing Australia, pg 39
RIC Publications Pty Ltd, pg 39
Scholastic Australia Pty Ltd, pg 40
South Australian Government-Department of Education, Employment & Training, pg 41
University of Western Australia Press, pg 45
Windhorse Books, pg 47
Wizard Books Pty Ltd, pg 47

Austria
DachsVerlag GmbH, pg 49
Development News Ltd, pg 50
Herold Druck-und Verlagsgesellschaft mbH, pg 52
Johannes Heyn GmbH & Co KG, pg 52
Verlag Hoelder-Pichler-Tempsky, pg 52
Niederosterreichisches Pressehaus Druck- und Verlagsgesellschaft mbH, pg 54
Oesterreichischer Bundesverlag Gmbh, pg 55
Roetzer Druck GmbH & Co KG, pg 57

Bangladesh
Mullick Bros, pg 61
The University Press Ltd, pg 61

Belarus
Kavaler Publishers, pg 62
Narodnaya Asveta, pg 62

Belgium
Carto BVBA, pg 64
La Charte Editions juridiques, pg 65
Editions De Boeck-Larcier SA, pg 66
Uitgeverij J van In, pg 69
Editions Labor, pg 69
Editions Lumen Vitae ASBL, pg 70
Uitgeverij Pelckmans NV, pg 72
Uitgeverij De Sikkel NV, pg 73
Wolters Plantyn Educatieve Uitgevers, pg 74

Benin
Les Editions du Flamboyant, pg 75

Bolivia
Editorial Don Bosco, pg 75

Bosnia and Herzegovina
Bemust, pg 76

Botswana
Maskew Miller Longman, pg 76

Brazil
A & A & A Edicoes e Promocoes Internacionais Ltda, pg 76
Livraria Francisco Alves Editora SA, pg 77
Ao Livro Tecnico Industria e Comercio Ltda, pg 77
Editora Atica SA, pg 78
Editora Brasil-America (EBAL) SA, pg 79
Centro de Estudos Juridicosdo Para (CEJUP), pg 79
Conquista, Empresa de Publicacoes Ltda, pg 80
Editora Contexto (Editora Pinsky Ltda), pg 80
Editora Harbra Ltda, pg 83
Livro Ibero-Americano Ltda, pg 83
Waldir Lima Editora, pg 85
Edicoes Loyola SA, pg 85
Modulo Editora e Desenvolvimento Educacional Ltda, pg 87
Edit Palavra Magica, pg 88
Ediouro Publicacoes, SA, pg 89
Distribuidora Record de Servicos de Imprensa SA, pg 89
Saraiva SA, Livreiros Editores, pg 90
Editora Scipione Ltda, pg 90
Editora Vigilia Ltda, pg 92

Bulgaria
Bulvest 2000 Ltd, pg 93
Eurasia Academic Publishers, pg 94
Gea-Libris Publishing House, pg 94
Izdatelstvo Lettera, pg 95
Makros 2000 - Plovdiv, pg 95
Musica Publishing House Ltd, pg 95
Pensoft Publishers, pg 96

PUBLISHERS

Prohazka I Kacarmazov, pg 96
Prosveta Publishers AS, pg 96

Burundi
Editions Intore, pg 98

Cameroon
Editions CLE, pg 98
Editions Buma Kor & Co Ltd, pg 98
Editions Semences Africaines, pg 98

Chile
Instituto Geografico Militar, pg 99
J.C. Saez Editor, pg 100
Zig-Zag SA, pg 101

China
Beijing Education Publishing House, pg 101
Beijing Publishing House, pg 101
Chinese Pedagogics Publishing House, pg 103
Foreign Language Teaching & Research Press, pg 104
Language Publishing House, pg 106
People's Education Press, pg 106
People's Fine Arts Publishing House, pg 106
Shandong Education Publishing House, pg 107
Shanghai Calligraphy & Painting Publishing House, pg 108
Shanghai Educational Publishing House, pg 108
Shanghai Far East Publishers, pg 108
Shanghai Foreign Language Education Press, pg 108
Yunnan University Press, pg 109
Zhejiang Education Publishing House, pg 109
Zhejiang University Press, pg 109

Colombia
Ediciones Cultural Colombiana Ltda, pg 110
Eurolibros Ltda, pg 111
Kapelusz Ltda Editorial, pg 111
Editorial Libros y Libres SA, pg 112
Migema Ediciones Ltda, pg 112
Editorial Santillana SA, pg 112
Editorial Voluntad SA, pg 113

The Democratic Republic of the Congo
Centre de Recherche, et Pedagogie Appliquee, pg 114

Costa Rica
Litografia Artex, SA, pg 115
Editorial de la Universidad de Costa Rica, pg 116

Cote d'Ivoire
Centre d'Edition et de Diffusion Africaines, pg 117
Les Nouvelles Editions Ivoiriennes (NEI), pg 117

Croatia
ALFA dd za izdavacke, graficke i trgovacke poslove, pg 117
Skolska Knjiga, pg 119

Cuba
Pueblo y Educacion Editorial (PE), pg 121

Denmark
Alinea A/S, pg 128
Forlaget alokke AS, pg 129
Aschehoug Dansk Forlag A/S, pg 129
Dafolo Forlag, pg 130
Djof Publishing Jurist-og Okonomforbundets Forlag, pg 130
Gyldendalske Boghandel - Nordisk Forlag A/S, pg 131
P Haase & Sons Forlag A/S, pg 131
Holkenfeldt 3, pg 132
Forlaget Hovedland, pg 132
Kaleidoscope Publishers Ltd, pg 132
Forlaget Modtryk AMBA, pg 133
Nyt Nordisk Forlag Arnold Busck A/S, pg 133
Det Schonbergske Forlag A/S, pg 134
Wisby & Wilkens, pg 135

El Salvador
Clasicos Roxsil Editorial SA de CV, pg 138
Editorial Universitaria de la Universidad de El Salvador, pg 139

Estonia
Valgus Publishers, pg 140

Finland
Otava Publishing Co Ltd, pg 143
Soderstroms Forlag, pg 144

France
Alsatia SA, pg 146
Editions Belin, pg 149
Editions Buchet-Chastel Pierre Zech Editeur, pg 151
Cle International, pg 154
Armand Colin, Editeur, pg 155
Decanord, pg 157
Editions de l'Ecole, pg 159
Groupe Hatier International, pg 166
Hachette Education, pg 166
Hachette Livre International, pg 167
Editions Hatier SA, pg 167
Magnard, pg 173
Editions MDI (La Maison des Instituteurs), pg 175
Presence Africaine Editions, pg 180
Editions Spratbrow, pg 186

Germany
ALS-Verlag GmbH, pg 192
AOL-Verlag Frohmut Menze, pg 193
Auer Verlag GmbH, pg 195
C Bange GmbH & Co KG, pg 196
Bayerischer Schulbuch-Verlag GmbH, pg 198
Julius Beltz GmbH & Co KG, pg 199
Gustav Bosse GmbH & Co KG, pg 203
Christliche Verlagsgesellschaft mbH, pg 208
Cornelsen und Oxford University Press GmbH & Co, pg 210
Cornelsen Verlag GmbH & Co OHG, pg 210
Verlag Darmstaedter Blaetter Schwarz und Co, pg 210
Diesterweg, Moritz Verlag, pg 214
Verlag Duerr & Kessler GmbH, pg 217
Ferd Dummler's Verlag, pg 223
Finken Verlag GmbH, pg 224
Alfons W Gentner Verlag GmbH & Co KG, pg 228
Lehrmittelverlag Wilhelm Hagemann GmbH, pg 233
Verlag Otto Heinevetter Lehrmittel GmbH, pg 235
Horlemann Verlag, pg 239
Impuls-Theater-Verlag, pg 241
Kallmeyer'sche Verlagsbuchhandlung GmbH, pg 244
Ernst Klett Verlag GmbH, pg 247
Konkordia Verlag GmbH, pg 249
Lahn-Verlag GmbH, pg 251
Lucius & Lucius Verlagsgesellschaft mbH, pg 255
Manz G J Verlag und Druckerei, pg 257
Militzke Verlag, pg 260
Karl Heinrich Moeseler Verlag, pg 261
Oekotopia Verlag, Wolfgang Hoffman GmbH & Co KG, pg 266
Patmos Verlag GmbH & Co KG, pg 268
Verlag Sigrid Persen, pg 269
Philipp Reclam Jun Verlag GmbH, pg 269
Quelle und Meyer Verlag GmbH & Co, pg 273
Verlag an der Ruhr GmbH, pg 277
Schott Musik International GmbH & Co KG, pg 281
Tipress Dienstleistungen fur das Verlagswesen GmbH, pg 291
Turkischer Schulbuchverlag Onel Cengiz, pg 293
Verlag und Druckkontor Kamp GmbH, pg 295
Voggenreiter-Verlag, pg 296
Volk und Wissen Verlag GmbH & Co, pg 296
Westermann Schulbuchverlag GmbH, pg 299
Dr Dieter Winkler, pg 300

Ghana
Afram Publications (Ghana) Ltd, pg 303
Asempa Publishers, pg 303
Black Mask Ltd, pg 303
Educational Press & Manufacturers Ltd, pg 303
EPP Books Services, pg 304
Frank Publishing Ltd, pg 304
Ghana Publishing Corporation, pg 304
Sam Woode Ltd, pg 304
Sedco Publishing Ltd, pg 305
Sub-Saharan Publishers, pg 305
Unimax Macmillan Ltd, pg 305
Waterville Publishing House, pg 305

Greece
Athina, Mary Mavrogiannis, pg 306
Editions Athina-Mavrogianni, pg 306
Etaireia Spoudon Neoellinikou Politismou Kai Genikis Paideias, pg 307
I Prooptiki, Ekdoseis, pg 308
Ilias Kambanas Publishing Organization, SA, pg 309
Katoptro Publications, pg 309
Nakas Music House, pg 310
Patakis Publishers, pg 311
Rossi, E Kdoseis Eleni Rossi-Petsiou, pg 312

Guadeloupe
JASOR, pg 313

TYPE OF PUBLICATION INDEX

Guatemala
Fundacion para la Cultura y el Desarrollo, pg 313

Haiti
Editions Caraibes SA, pg 314

Hong Kong
Joint Publishing (HK) Co Ltd, pg 317
Ling Kee Publishing Group, pg 318
Times Publishing (Hong Kong) Ltd, pg 319
Witman Publishing Co (HK) Ltd, pg 320

Hungary
Corvina Books Ltd, pg 321
Mueszaki Koenyvkiado Ltd, pg 323
Nemzeti Tankoenyvkiado, pg 323

Iceland
Mal og menning, pg 326
Namsgagnastofnun, pg 326

India
Addison-Wesley Pte Ltd, pg 327
Ambar Prakashan, pg 328
B I Publications Pvt Ltd, pg 329
The Bangalore Printing & Publishing Co Ltd, pg 329
Bani Mandir, Book-Sellers, Publishers & Educational Suppliers, pg 329
Bharat Publishing House, pg 330
Bhawan Book Service, Publishers & Distributors, pg 330
Chowkhamba Sanskrit Series Office, pg 332
Frank Brothers & Co Publishers Ltd, pg 334
General Book Depot, pg 335
Arnold Heinman Publishers (India) Pvt Ltd, pg 335
Hindi Pracharak Sansthan, pg 336
Indian Book Depot, pg 336
Naresh Publishers, pg 342
National Council of Educational Research & Training, Publication Department, pg 343
Omsons Publications, pg 344
Oxford University Press, pg 344
Paico Publishing House, pg 344
Paramount Sales (India) Pvt Ltd, pg 344
Pitambar Publishing Co (P) Ltd, pg 345
Sasta Sahitya Mandal, pg 348
Scientific Book Agency, pg 348
Shaibya Prakashan Bibhag, pg 349
Shiksha Bharati, pg 349
Somaiya Publications Pvt Ltd, pg 349
Sree Rama Publishers, pg 350
Sterling Information Technologies, pg 350
Suman Prakashan Pvt Ltd, pg 351
A H Wheeler & Co Ltd, pg 353

Indonesia
Bina Rena Pariwara, pg 354
PT BPK Gunung Mulia, pg 355
PT Pradnya Paramita, pg 356

Ireland
An Gum, pg 358
C J Fallon, pg 360
Veritas Co Ltd, pg 364

TYPE OF PUBLICATION INDEX
BOOK

Israel
Am Oved Publishers Ltd, pg 365
The Bialik Institute, pg 365
Classikaletet, pg 366
Feldheim Publishers Ltd, pg 367
Karni Publishers Ltd, pg 369
Kiryat Sefer, pg 369
Ma'alot Publishing Company Ltd, pg 370
Modan Publishers Ltd, pg 370

Italy
De Agostini Scolastica, pg 374
Cappelli Editore, pg 380
Edizioni Centro Studi Erickson, pg 381
Edizioni Dehoniane Bologna (EDB), pg 384
Organizzazione Didattica Editoriale Ape, pg 385
Garzanti Libri, pg 390
Istituto Geografico de Agostini SpA, pg 390
Ghisetti e Corvi Editori, pg 390
Hora, pg 392
Nicola Milano Editore, pg 398
Minerva Italica SpA, pg 398
RCS Libri SpA, pg 405
Editrice la Scuola SpA, pg 407
Societa Editrice Internazionale - SEI, pg 408
Le Stelle Scuola, pg 409

Jamaica
Carib Publishing Ltd, pg 413
Carlong Publishers (Caribbean) Ltd, pg 413
Twin Guinep Ltd, pg 414

Japan
Dainippon Tosho Publishing Co, Ltd, pg 416
Dogakusha Inc, pg 416
Kaitakusha, pg 420
Nihon-Bunkyo Shuppan (Japan Educational Publishing Co Ltd), pg 423
Sanshusha Publishing Co, Ltd, pg 426
Shingakusha Co Ltd, pg 427
Thomson Learning Japan, pg 429
Tokyo Shoseki Co Ltd, pg 430
Zoshindo JukenKenkyusha, pg 431

Kenya
Africa Book Services (EA) Ltd, pg 433
Cosmopolitan Publishers Ltd, pg 433
Dhillon Publishers Ltd, pg 433
Focus Publications Ltd, pg 433
Foundation Books Ltd, pg 434
Heinemann Kenya Ltd (EAEP), pg 434
Kenya Literature Bureau, pg 434
The Jomo Kenyatta Foundation, pg 435
Macmillan Kenya Publishers Ltd, pg 435
Phoenix Publishers Ltd, pg 435
Shirikon Publishers, pg 436
Transafrica Press, pg 436
Gideon S Were Press, pg 436

Republic of Korea
Kyohaksa Publishing Co Ltd, pg 440
Moon Jin Media Co Ltd, pg 441
YBM/Si-sa, pg 443

Latvia
Lielvards Ltd, pg 445
Zvaigzne ABC Publishers Ltd, pg 445

Lebanon
Librairie Orientale sal, pg 446
World Book Publishing, pg 447

Lesotho
Mazenod Book Centre, pg 447
Saint Michael's Mission Social Centre, pg 447

Lithuania
Margi Rastai Publishers, pg 449
Sviesa Publishers, pg 449
Svietimo ir mokslo ministerijos Leidybos centras, pg 449
Tyto Alba Publishers, pg 450

Luxembourg
Editions Emile Borschette, pg 450
Service Central des Imprimes et des Fournitures de Bureau de l'Etat, pg 451

The Former Yugoslav Republic of Macedonia
St Clement of Ohrid National & University Library, pg 453

Madagascar
Centre National de Production de Materiel Didactique (CNAPMAD), pg 453
Foibe Filan-Kevitry NY Mpampianatra (FOFIPA), pg 453
Librarie Mixte, pg 453
Societe Malgache d'Edition, pg 454
Trano Printy Fiangonana Loterana Malagasy (TPFLM)-(Imprimerie Lutherienne), pg 454

Malawi
Dzuka Publishing Co Ltd, pg 454

Malaysia
Dewan Bahasa dan Pustaka, pg 455
Federal Publications Sdn Bhd, pg 455
FEP International Sdn Bhd, pg 456
Pearson Education Malaysia Sdn Bhd, pg 457
Penerbit Fajar Bakti Sdn Bhd, pg 457
Penerbitan Pelangi Sdn Bhd (Pelangi Publishing Pte Ltd), pg 458
Penerbitan Tinta, pg 458
Pustaka Cipta Sdn Bhd, pg 458
Utusan Publications & Distributors Sdn Bhd, pg 459

Maldive Islands
Non-Formal Education Centre, pg 459

Mali
EDIM SA, pg 460

Malta
Media Centre, pg 460

Mauritius
Golden Publications, pg 461
Editions de l'Ocean Indien Ltd, pg 461
EDITIONS Le Printemps, pg 461

Mexico
Adivinar y Multiplicar, SA de CV, pg 461
Editorial Avante SA de Cv, pg 462
Edamex SA de CV, pg 464
Editorial Esfinge SA de CV, pg 465
Fernandez Editores SA de CV, pg 465
Fondo de Cultura Economica, pg 465
Ediciones Larousse SA de CV, pg 467
Editorial Limusa SA de CV, pg 467
Nova Grupo Editorial SA de CV, pg 469
Palabra Ediciones S A de C V, pg 469
Editorial Patria SA de CV, pg 470
Pearson Educacion de Mexico, SA de CV, pg 470
Plaza y Valdes SA de CV, pg 470
Editorial Progreso SA de C V, pg 470
Publicaciones Cultural SA de CV, pg 471
Sistemas Tecnicos de Edicion SA de CV, pg 472
Ediciones Suromex SA, pg 472
Editorial Trillas SA de CV, pg 472

Republic of Moldova
Editura Lumina, pg 473

Morocco
Dar Nachr Al Maarifa Pour L'Edition et La Distribution, pg 474

Namibia
Desert Research Foundation of Namibia (DRFN), pg 476

Nepal
International Standards Books & Periodicals (P) Ltd, pg 476

Netherlands
Educatieve Partners Nederland bv, pg 481
Katholieke Bijbelstichting, pg 484
LCG Malmberg BV, pg 485
Pearson Education Netherlands, pg 487
Stenvert Systems & Service BV, pg 489
Wolters-Noordhoff B V, pg 492
Uitgeverij Zwijsen BV, pg 493

New Zealand
Wendy Crane Books, pg 495
ESA Publications (NZ) Ltd, pg 496
Eton Press (Auckland) Ltd, pg 496
Huia Publishers, pg 497
Legislation Direct, pg 498
Macmillan Publishers New Zealand Ltd, pg 498
Nelson Price Milburn Ltd, pg 499
Oxford University Press, pg 499
Pearson Education (PENZ) Ltd, pg 500
Reed Publishing (NZ) Ltd, pg 500
Sunshine Books International Ltd, pg 501

Nigeria
African Universities Press, pg 503
Africana-FEP Publishers Ltd, pg 503
Alliance West African Publishers & Co, pg 503
Aromolaran Publishing Co Ltd, pg 503
Cross Continent Press Ltd, pg 504
CSS Bookshops, pg 504
Educational Research & Study Group, pg 504
Evans Brothers (Nigeria Publishers) Ltd, pg 504
Fourth Dimension Publishing Co Ltd, pg 504
JAD Publishers Ltd, pg 505
Kola Sanya Publishing Enterprise, pg 505
Longman Nigeria Plc, pg 505
New Era Publishers, pg 506
Northern Nigerian Publishing Co Ltd, pg 506
Nwamife Publishers Ltd, pg 506
Onibon-Oje Publishers, pg 506
Riverside Communications, pg 507
Tabansi Press Ltd, pg 507
University Publishing Co, pg 507
Vantage Publishers International Ltd, pg 507
West African Book Publishers Ltd, pg 507

Norway
H Aschehoug & Co (W Nygaard) A/S, pg 508
J W Eides Forlag A/S, pg 509
Forlaget Fag og Kultur, pg 509
Gyldendal Norsk Forlag A/S, pg 509
Universitetsforlaget, pg 511

Pakistan
Sheikh Shaukat Ali & Sons, pg 511
The Book House, pg 512
Islamic Book Centre, pg 512
Islamic Publications (Pvt) Ltd, pg 513
Jang Publishers, pg 513
Maqbool Academy, pg 513

Papua New Guinea
Kristen Press, pg 515

Peru
Asociacion Editorial Bruno, pg 516
Tarea Asociacion de Publicaciones Educativas, pg 517
Tassorello, SA, pg 517

Philippines
Abiva Publishing House Inc, pg 518
Ateneo de Manila University Press, pg 518
Bookman Printing & Publishing House Inc, pg 518
Bookmark Inc, pg 518
J C Palabay Enterprises, pg 519
Marren Publishing House, Inc, pg 519
National Book Store Inc, pg 519
Our Lady of Manaoag Publisher, pg 520
Rex Bookstores & Publishers, pg 520
Saint Mary's Publishing Corp, pg 520
Salesiana Publishers Inc, pg 521
SIBS Publishing House Inc, pg 521
UST Publishing House, pg 521

PUBLISHERS

Poland
Impuls, pg 523
PZWL Wydawnictwo Lekarskie Ltd, pg 526
Res Polona, pg 526
Wydawnictwa Szkolne i Pedagogiczne, pg 527
Wydawn Na Sprawa' Wydawniczo-Oswiatowa Spotdzielnia Inwalidow, pg 528

Portugal
Livraria Arnado Lda, pg 528
Constancia Editores, SA, pg 530
Dinalivro, pg 530
Europress Editores e Distribuidores de Publicacoes Lda, pg 531
Lua Viajante-Edicao e Distribuicao de Livros e Material Audiovisual, Lda, pg 533
Editorial O Livro Lda, pg 534
Platano Editora SA, pg 534
Porto Editora Lda, pg 535
Editorial Presenca, pg 535
Almerinda Teixeira, pg 536
Texto Editora, pg 536

Puerto Rico
McGraw-Hill Intermericana del Caribe, Inc, pg 537

Romania
Editora All, pg 538
Editura Clusium, pg 539
Editura Didactica si Pedagogica, pg 539
Humanitas Publishing House, pg 540
Editura Niculescu, pg 541
Polirom Verlag, pg 542
RAO International Publishing Co, pg 542

Russian Federation
Airis Press, pg 543
INFRA-M Izdatel 'skij dom, pg 545
Izdatelstvo Mir, pg 546
Izdatelstvo Muzyka, pg 547
Okoshko Ltd Publishers (Izdatelstvo), pg 547
Izdatelstvo Prosveshchenie, pg 548

Senegal
Les Nouvelles Editions Africaines du Senegal NEAS, pg 551

Serbia and Montenegro
Republicki Zavod za Unapredivanje Vaspitanja i Obrazovanja, pg 553

Sierra Leone
Njala Educational Publishing Centre, pg 554

Singapore
Federal Publications (S) Pte Ltd, pg 556
Hillview Publications Pte Ltd, pg 556

Slovakia
Slo Viet, pg 560
Slovenske pedagogicke nakladateistvo, pg 560
Ustav informacii a prognoz skolstva mladeze a telovychovy, pg 561

Slovenia
Mladinska Knjiga International, pg 561
Zalozba Mihelac d o o, pg 562
Zalozba Obzorja d d Maribor, pg 562

South Africa
Educum Publishers Ltd, pg 563
Heinemann Educational Publishers Southern Africa, pg 564
Heinemann Publishers (Pty) Ltd, pg 564
Ivy Publications, pg 565
Maskew Miller Longman, pg 566
Nasou Via Afrika, pg 567
Publitoria Publishers, pg 568
Shuter & Shooter (Pty) Ltd, pg 568
Vivlia Publishers & Booksellers, pg 570

Spain
Publicacions de l'Abadia de Montserrat, pg 570
Ediciones Akal SA, pg 571
Ediciones Anaya SA, pg 572
Anaya Educacion, pg 573
Editorial Bruno, pg 575
Editorial Casals SA, pg 575
CEAC, Grupo Editorial SA, pg 576
Editorial Claret SA, pg 577
Edebe, pg 580
Editorial Everest SA, pg 581
Elkar, Euskal Liburu eta Kantuen Argitaldaria, SL, pg 582
Enciclopedia Catalana, SA, pg 582
Erein, pg 582
Eumo Editorial, pg 583
Grupo Comunicar, pg 585
Grupo Santillana de Ediciones SA, pg 586
Ibaizabal Edelvives SA, pg 586
Ediciones JJB, pg 588
Editorial Luis Vives (Edelvives), pg 589
Editorial Magisterio Espanol SA, pg 590
Editorial Marfil SA, pg 590
Editorial Moll SL, pg 592
Editorial la Muralla SA, pg 592
Oikos-Tau SA Ediciones, pg 593
Pearson Educacion S A, pg 595
Editorial Playor SA, pg 596
Editorial Miguel A Salvatella SA, pg 598
San Pablo Ediciones, pg 598
Ediciones Seyer, pg 599
Ediciones SM, pg 600
Editorial Teide SA, pg 601
Thales Sociedad Andaluza de Educacion Matematica, pg 602
Editorial Verbum SL, pg 604

Sri Lanka
M D Gunasena & Co Ltd, pg 606
Ministry of Education, pg 607

Suriname
Vaco NV Uitgeversmij, pg 608

Sweden
Ekelunds Forlag AB, pg 611
SK-Gehrmans Musikforlag AB, pg 611
Hillelforlaget, pg 612
Hans Richter Laromedel, pg 613
Liber AB, pg 613
Bokfoerlaget Natur och Kultur, pg 613

Switzerland
Aare-Verlag, pg 617
Editions Foma SA, pg 623
Sabe AG Verlagsinstitut, pg 633
Sauerlaender AG, pg 633
Tobler Verlag, pg 635
Verlag Alexander Wild, pg 637

Taiwan, Province of China
Chien Chen Bookstore Publishing Company Ltd, pg 639
Chung Hwa Book Co Ltd, pg 639
Newton Publishing Company Ltd, pg 641
San Min Book Co Ltd, pg 641
Wu Nan Book Co Ltd, pg 642

United Republic of Tanzania
Ben and Company Ltd, pg 643
DUP (1996) Ltd, pg 643
East African Publishing House, pg 643
Eastern Africa Publications Ltd, pg 643
General Publications Ltd, pg 643
Nyota Publishers Ltd, pg 644
Oxford University Press, pg 644
Press & Publicity Centre Ltd, pg 644
Readit Books, pg 644
Tanzania Publishing House, pg 644

Thailand
Thai Watana Panich Co, Ltd, pg 646

Togo
Editions Akpagnon, pg 646

Tunisia
Maison Tunisienne de l'Edition, pg 648

Turkey
Altin Kitaplar Yayinevi, pg 649
Arkadas Ltd, pg 649
Arkin Kitabevi, pg 649
Aydin Yayincilik, pg 649
Inkilap Publishers Ltd, pg 650
Pearson Education Turkey, pg 651

Ukraine
ASK Ltd, pg 653
Osvita, pg 654

United Kingdom
Arcturus Publishing Ltd, pg 659
Association for Science Education, pg 661
Blackwell Science Ltd, pg 667
Boosey & Hawkes Music Publishers Ltd, pg 669
Cambridge University Press, pg 674
Child's World Education Ltd, pg 679
Colourpoint Books, pg 681
Curiad, pg 685
Educational Explorers (Publishers) Ltd, pg 690
Evans Brothers Ltd, pg 693
First & Best in Education Ltd, pg 695
Folens Ltd, pg 695
Forbes Publications Ltd, pg 696
Francis Balsom Associates, pg 696
W H Freeman & Co Ltd, pg 697
The Geographical Association, pg 699
Ginn & Co Ltd, pg 700

TYPE OF PUBLICATION INDEX

Graham-Cameron Publishing & Illustration, pg 701
Gwasg y Dref Wen, pg 703
HarperCollins UK, pg 705
Heinemann Educational Publishing, pg 707
Hodder Education, pg 709
Hodder Headline Ltd, pg 709
Home Health Education Service, pg 710
Impart Books, pg 712
LDA-Living & Learning (Cambridge) Ltd, pg 719
Learning Development Aids, pg 719
Learning Together, pg 720
Letterland International Ltd, pg 720
Lion Hudson PLC, pg 721
Macmillan Heinemann ELT, pg 723
McCrimmon Publishing Co Ltd, pg 726
National Association for the Teaching of English (NATE), pg 730
Nelson Thornes Ltd, pg 732
James Nisbet & Co Ltd, pg 733
Oxford University Press, pg 737
Prim-Ed Publishing UK Ltd, pg 745
Quartz Editions, pg 746
Reed Educational & Professional Publishing, pg 749
SAGE Publications Ltd, pg 753
Schofield & Sims Ltd, pg 754
Scholastic Ltd, pg 754
Southgate Publishers, pg 759
Supportive Learning Publications, pg 762
Tobin Music, pg 766
Ward Lock Educational Co Ltd, pg 771
Wimbledon Publishing Company Ltd, pg 774

Uruguay
A Monteverde y Cia SA, pg 777

Uzbekistan
Izdatelstvo Uzbekistan, pg 778

Venezuela
Colegial Bolivariana CA, pg 779
Editorial Kapelusz Venezolana SA, pg 779

Zambia
Wilfred Bwalya Chilangwa Publications, pg 781
Multimedia Zambia, pg 781
Zambia Printing Company Ltd (ZPC), pg 782

Zimbabwe
College Press Publishers (Pvt) Ltd, pg 783
Longman Zimbabwe (Pvt) Ltd, pg 783
Zimbabwe Foundation for Education with Production (ZIMFEP), pg 784
Zimbabwe Publishing House (Pvt) Ltd, pg 784

TEXTBOOKS - SECONDARY

Afghanistan
Ministry of Education, Department of Educational Publications, pg 1

TYPE OF PUBLICATION INDEX

BOOK

Albania
NL SH, pg 1

Algeria
Enterprise Nationale du Livre (ENAL), pg 2

Argentina
Editorial Acme SA, pg 3
AZ Editora SA, pg 3
Cesarini Hermanos, pg 4
Ediciones Don Bosco Argentina, pg 5
Ediciones del Eclipse, pg 5
Edicial SA, pg 5
Angel Estrada y Cia SA, pg 5
Gram Editora, pg 6
Libreria Huemul SA, pg 6
Kapelusz Editora SA, pg 7
Editorial Losada SA, pg 7

Armenia
Arevik, pg 10

Australia
AHB Publications, pg 11
Edward Arnold (Australia) Pty Ltd, pg 12
Austed Publishing Co, pg 12
Beri Publishing, pg 14
Board of Studies, pg 15
Boinkie Publishers, pg 15
Cambridge University Press, pg 16
Candlelight Trust T/A Candlelight Farm, pg 17
Chalkface Press Pty Ltd, pg 17
China Books, pg 17
R J Cleary Publishing, pg 18
Cookery Book, pg 18
Curriculum Corporation, pg 19
Dabill Publications, pg 19
Dellasta Publishing, pg 19
Educational Advantage, pg 20
Emerald City Books, pg 21
Illert Publications, pg 26
Jarrah Publications, pg 27
Macmillan Education Australia, pg 30
Macmillan Publishers Australia Pty Ltd, pg 30
McGraw-Hill Australia Pty Ltd, pg 31
Pearson Education Australia, pg 36
Phoenix Education Pty Ltd, pg 36
Reed Educational Publishing Australia, pg 39
Scholastic Australia Pty Ltd, pg 40
Science Press, pg 40
South Australian Government-Department of Education, Employment & Training, pg 41
Tarka Publishing, pg 42
Thornbill Press, pg 43
University of Queensland Press, pg 45
Wileman Publications, pg 46
John Wiley & Sons Australia, Ltd, pg 46
Windhorse Books, pg 47
Wizard Books Pty Ltd, pg 47
Woodlands Publications, pg 47

Austria
DachsVerlag GmbH, pg 49
Development News Ltd, pg 50
Herold Druck-und Verlagsgesellschaft mbH, pg 52
Johannes Heyn GmbH & Co KG, pg 52
Verlag Hoelder-Pichler-Tempsky, pg 52
Niederosterreichisches Pressehaus Druck- und Verlagsgesellschaft mbH, pg 54
Oesterreichischer Bundesverlag Gmbh, pg 55
Oesterreichischer Gewerbeverlag GmbH, pg 55
Verlag Oldenbourg, pg 56
Roetzer Druck GmbH & Co KG, pg 57
Universitaetsverlag Wagner GmbH, pg 59
Verlag Mag Wanzenbock, pg 59

Bangladesh
Bangladesh Publishers, pg 61
Mullick Bros, pg 61
The University Press Ltd, pg 61

Belarus
Belaruskaya Encyklapedyya, pg 62
Kavaler Publishers, pg 62
Narodnaya Asveta, pg 62

Belgium
De Boeck et Larcier SA, pg 64
Carto BVBA, pg 64
La Charte Editions juridiques, pg 65
Editions De Boeck-Larcier SA, pg 66
Uitgeverij J van In, pg 69
Editions Labor, pg 69
Editions Lumen Vitae ASBL, pg 70
Uitgeverij Pelckmans NV, pg 72
Uitgeverij De Sikkel NV, pg 73
Les Editions Vie ouvriere ASBL, pg 74
Wolters Plantyn Educatieve Uitgevers, pg 74

Benin
Les Editions du Flamboyant, pg 75

Bolivia
Editorial Don Bosco, pg 75

Botswana
Maskew Miller Longman, pg 76

Brazil
Livraria Francisco Alves Editora SA, pg 77
Ao Livro Tecnico Industria e Comercio Ltda, pg 77
Editora Atica SA, pg 78
Centro de Estudos Juridicosdo Para (CEJUP), pg 79
Editora Harbra Ltda, pg 83
Livro Ibero-Americano Ltda, pg 83
Waldir Lima Editora, pg 85
Edicoes Loyola SA, pg 85
Editora Moderna Ltda, pg 86
Olho D'Agua Comercio e Servicos Editoriais Ltda, pg 87
Edit Palavra Magica, pg 88
Ediouro Publicacoes, SA, pg 89
Saraiva SA, Livreiros Editores, pg 90
Editora Scipione Ltda, pg 90
Editora Vigilia Ltda, pg 92

Bulgaria
Bulvest 2000 Ltd, pg 93
Eurasia Academic Publishers, pg 94
Gea-Libris Publishing House, pg 94
Izdatelstvo Lettera, pg 95
Makros 2000 - Plovdiv, pg 95
Musica Publishing House Ltd, pg 95
Pensoft Publishers, pg 96
Prosveta Publishers AS, pg 96

Burundi
Editions Intore, pg 98

Cameroon
Centre d'Edition et de Production pour l'Enseignement et la Recherche (CEPER), pg 98
Editions Buma Kor & Co Ltd, pg 98
Editions Semences Africaines, pg 98

Chile
Arrayan Editores, pg 98
Instituto Geografico Militar, pg 99

China
Anhui People's Publishing House, pg 101
Beijing Education Publishing House, pg 101
Beijing Publishing House, pg 101
Chemical Industry Press, pg 101
China Materials Management Publishing House, pg 102
Chinese Pedagogics Publishing House, pg 103
Electronics Industry Publishing House, pg 104
Foreign Language Teaching & Research Press, pg 104
Language Publishing House, pg 106
People's Education Press, pg 106
People's Fine Arts Publishing House, pg 106
Shandong Education Publishing House, pg 107
Shanghai Educational Publishing House, pg 108
Shanghai Far East Publishers, pg 108
Shanghai Foreign Language Education Press, pg 108
Yunnan University Press, pg 109
Zhejiang Education Publishing House, pg 109
Zhejiang University Press, pg 109

Colombia
Ediciones Cultural Colombiana Ltda, pg 110
Kapelusz Ltda Editorial, pg 111
Editorial Libros y Libres SA, pg 112
Migema Ediciones Ltda, pg 112
Pearson Educacion de Colombia LTDA, pg 112
Editorial Santillana SA, pg 112
Editorial Voluntad SA, pg 113

The Democratic Republic of the Congo
Centre de Recherche, et Pedagogie Appliquee, pg 114
Facultes Catoliques de Kinshasa, pg 114

Costa Rica
Jose Alfonso Sandoval Nunez, pg 115
Litografia Artex, SA, pg 115
Editorial de la Universidad de Costa Rica, pg 116
Editorial Universidad Nacional (EUNA), pg 116

Cote d'Ivoire
Akohi Editions, pg 117
Centre d'Edition et de Diffusion Africaines, pg 117
Les Nouvelles Editions Ivoiriennes (NEI), pg 117

Croatia
ALFA dd za izdavacke, graficke i trgovacke poslove, pg 117
Skolska Knjiga, pg 119

Cuba
Pueblo y Educacion Editorial (PE), pg 121

Czech Republic
Barrister & Principal, pg 122
NS Svoboda spol sro, pg 127
Svoboda Servis GmbH, pg 127
SystemConsult, pg 127

Denmark
Alinea A/S, pg 128
Forlaget alokke AS, pg 129
Dafolo Forlag, pg 130
Gyldendalske Boghandel - Nordisk Forlag A/S, pg 131
P Haase & Sons Forlag A/S, pg 131
Holkenfeldt 3, pg 132
Kaleidoscope Publishers Ltd, pg 132
Forlaget Modtryk AMBA, pg 133
Nyt Nordisk Forlag Arnold Busck A/S, pg 133
Det Schonbergske Forlag A/S, pg 134
Wisby & Wilkens, pg 135

Dominican Republic
Pontificia Universidad Catolica Madre y Maestra, pg 136

Ecuador
Corporacion Editora Nacional, pg 136

Egypt (Arab Republic of Egypt)
Middle East Book Centre, pg 138

El Salvador
Clasicos Roxsil Editorial SA de CV, pg 138
Editorial Universitaria de la Universidad de El Salvador, pg 139

Estonia
Valgus Publishers, pg 140

Finland
Otava Publishing Co Ltd, pg 143
Sairaanhoitajien Koulutussaatio, pg 144
Soderstroms Forlag, pg 144

France
Editions Al Liamm, pg 146
Aubanel Editions, pg 148
Editions Belin, pg 149
Emgleo Breiz, pg 151
Brud Nevez, pg 151
Cepadues Editions SA, pg 153
Cle International, pg 154
Armand Colin, Editeur, pg 155
Editions Dalloz Sirey, pg 157
Decanord, pg 157
Doin Editeurs, pg 159

PUBLISHERS

Editions de l'Ecole, pg 159
Gammaprim, pg 165
Groupe Hatier International, pg 166
Hachette Education, pg 166
Hachette Livre International, pg 167
Editions Hatier SA, pg 167
Editions Fernand Lanore Sarl, pg 171
Magnard, pg 173
Editions MDI (La Maison des Instituteurs), pg 175
Editions Ophrys, pg 177
Editions Roudil SA, pg 183
Editions Spratbrow, pg 186

Germany

ALS-Verlag GmbH, pg 192
AOL-Verlag Frohmut Menze, pg 193
Auer Verlag GmbH, pg 195
C Bange GmbH & Co KG, pg 196
Bayerischer Schulbuch-Verlag GmbH, pg 198
C C Buchners Verlag GmbH & Co KG, pg 205
Cornelsen und Oxford University Press GmbH & Co, pg 210
Cornelsen Verlag GmbH & Co OHG, pg 210
Verlag Darmstaedter Blaetter Schwarz und Co, pg 210
Diesterweg, Moritz Verlag, pg 214
Verlag Duerr & Kessler GmbH, pg 217
Ferd Dummler's Verlag, pg 223
Festo Didactic GmbH & Co KG, pg 224
Friedrich Kiehl Verlag GmbH, pg 227
Betriebswirtschaftlicher Verlag Dr Th Gabler, pg 228
Lehrmittelverlag Wilhelm Hagemann GmbH, pg 233
Verlag Handwerk und Technik GmbH, pg 233
Max Hieber KG, pg 237
Horlemann Verlag, pg 239
Impuls-Theater-Verlag, pg 241
Ernst Klett Verlag GmbH, pg 247
Konkordia Verlag GmbH, pg 249
Lahn-Verlag GmbH, pg 251
Hildegard Liebaug-Dartmann, pg 254
Robert Lienau GmbH & Co KG, pg 254
J Lindauer Verlag, pg 254
Lucius & Lucius Verlagsgesellschaft mbH, pg 255
Manz G J Verlag und Druckerei, pg 257
Militzke Verlag, pg 260
Karl Heinrich Moeseler Verlag, pg 261
Verlag Sigrid Persen, pg 269
Philipp Reclam Jun Verlag GmbH, pg 269
Quelle und Meyer Verlag GmbH & Co, pg 273
Verlag an der Ruhr GmbH, pg 277
Schott Musik International GmbH & Co KG, pg 281
B G Teubner Verlag, pg 290
Tipress Dienstleistungen fur das Verlagswesen GmbH, pg 291
Turkischer Schulbuchverlag Onel Cengiz, pg 293
Voggenreiter-Verlag, pg 296
Volk und Wissen Verlag GmbH & Co, pg 296
Westermann Schulbuchverlag GmbH, pg 299
Dr Dieter Winkler, pg 300

Ghana

Afram Publications (Ghana) Ltd, pg 303
Anowuo Educational Publications, pg 303
Asempa Publishers, pg 303
Black Mask Ltd, pg 303
Educational Press & Manufacturers Ltd, pg 303
EPP Books Services, pg 304
Frank Publishing Ltd, pg 304
Ghana Publishing Corporation, pg 304
Sam Woode Ltd, pg 304
Sedco Publishing Ltd, pg 305
Waterville Publishing House, pg 305
World Literature Project, pg 305

Greece

Athina, Mary Mavrogiannis, pg 306
Chrysi Penna - Golden Pen Books, pg 306
Ilias Kambanas Publishing Organization, SA, pg 309
Katoptro Publications, pg 309
Nakas Music House, pg 310
Patakis Publishers, pg 311
Rossi, E Kdoseis Eleni Rossi-Petsiou, pg 312

Guadeloupe

JASOR, pg 313

Guatemala

Fundacion para la Cultura y el Desarrollo, pg 313

Haiti

Editions Caraibes SA, pg 314

Hong Kong

Book Marketing Ltd, pg 315
Breakthrough Ltd - Breakthrough Publishers, pg 315
Joint Publishing (HK) Co Ltd, pg 317
Lea Publications Ltd, pg 318
Ling Kee Publishing Group, pg 318
Macmillan Publishers (China) Ltd, pg 318
Shanghai Book Co Ltd, pg 319
Times Publishing (Hong Kong) Ltd, pg 319
Vision Pub Co Ltd, pg 320
Witman Publishing Co (HK) Ltd, pg 320

Hungary

Corvina Books Ltd, pg 321
Mueszaki Koenyvkiado Ltd, pg 323
Nemzeti Tankoenyvkiado, pg 323
Novorg International Szervezo es Kiado kft, pg 323

Iceland

Almenna Bokafelagid, pg 325
Mal og menning, pg 326

India

Addison-Wesley Pte Ltd, pg 327
Ambar Prakashan, pg 328
B I Publications Pvt Ltd, pg 329
The Bangalore Printing & Publishing Co Ltd, pg 329
Bani Mandir, Book-Sellers, Publishers & Educational Suppliers, pg 329
Bhawan Book Service, Publishers & Distributors, pg 330
Chowkhamba Sanskrit Series Office, pg 332
Dastane Ramchandra & Co, pg 333
Frank Brothers & Co Publishers Ltd, pg 334
General Book Depot, pg 335
General Printers & Publishers, pg 335
Arnold Heinman Publishers (India) Pvt Ltd, pg 335
Hindi Pracharak Sansthan, pg 336
Laxmi Publications Pvt Ltd, pg 340
National Council of Educational Research & Training, Publication Department, pg 343
Oxford University Press, pg 344
Paico Publishing House, pg 344
Pitambar Publishing Co (P) Ltd, pg 345
Rajesh Publications, pg 346
Sasta Sahitya Mandal, pg 348
Scientific Book Agency, pg 348
Shiksha Bharati, pg 349
Somaiya Publications Pvt Ltd, pg 349
Sree Rama Publishers, pg 350
Sultan Chand & Sons Pvt Ltd, pg 350
DB Taraporevala Sons & Co Pvt Ltd, pg 351
A H Wheeler & Co Ltd, pg 353

Indonesia

PT Pustaka Antara Publishing & Printing, pg 353
Bina Rena Pariwara, pg 354
PT BPK Gunung Mulia, pg 355
PT Pradnya Paramita, pg 356

Ireland

An Gum, pg 358
C J Fallon, pg 360
Gill & Macmillan Ltd, pg 360
Veritas Co Ltd, pg 364

Israel

Am Oved Publishers Ltd, pg 365
The Bialik Institute, pg 365
Feldheim Publishers Ltd, pg 367
Karni Publishers Ltd, pg 369
Kernerman Publishing Ltd, pg 369
Kiryat Sefer, pg 369
Ma'alot Publishing Company Ltd, pg 370
MAP-Mapping & Publishing Ltd, pg 370
Modan Publishers Ltd, pg 370
Rubin Mass Ltd, pg 371
Yad Vashem - The Holocaust Martyrs' & Heroes' Remembrance Authority, pg 373

Italy

De Agostini Scolastica, pg 374
Archimede Edizioni, pg 376
Bianco, pg 377
Canova SRL, pg 379
Cappelli Editore, pg 380
Casa Editrice Giuseppe Principato Spa, pg 380
Casa Editrice Libraria Ulrico Hoepli SpA, pg 380
Cideb Editrice SRL, pg 382
Citta Nuova Editrice, pg 382
Edizioni Cremonese SRL, pg 383
D'Anna, pg 384
Edizioni Dehoniane Bologna (EDB), pg 384
Editrice Edisco, pg 386
Esselibri, pg 388
Garzanti Libri, pg 390
Istituto Geografico de Agostini SpA, pg 390
Ghisetti e Corvi Editori, pg 390
Gius Laterza e Figli SpA, pg 391
Loescher Editore SRL, pg 396
Editrice Massimo SAS di Crespi Cesare e C, pg 397
Minerva Italica SpA, pg 398
Arnoldo Mondadori Editore SpA, pg 398
La Nuova Italia Editrice SpA, pg 401
G B Palumbo & C Editore SpA, pg 402
Paravia Bruno Mondadori Editori, pg 402
Principato, pg 404
RCS Libri SpA, pg 405
Editrice San Marco SRL, pg 407
Editrice la Scuola SpA, pg 407
Societa Editrice Internazionale - SEI, pg 408
Le Stelle Scuola, pg 409
Societa Editrice Vannini, pg 411
Zanichelli Editore SpA, pg 412

Jamaica

Carib Publishing Ltd, pg 413
Carlong Publishers (Caribbean) Ltd, pg 413

Japan

Chikuma Shobo Publishing Co Ltd, pg 416
Chuo-Tosho Co Ltd, pg 416
Dainippon Tosho Publishing Co, Ltd, pg 416
Dogakusha Inc, pg 416
Eichosha Company Ltd, pg 417
Gakken Co Ltd, pg 417
Kaitakusha, pg 420
Nihon-Bunkyo Shuppan (Japan Educational Publishing Co Ltd), pg 423
Ongaku No Tomo Sha Corporation, pg 425
Sanshusha Publishing Co, Ltd, pg 426
Shimizu-Shoin, pg 427
Shingakusha Co Ltd, pg 427
Teikoku-Shoin Co Ltd, pg 429
Thomson Learning Japan, pg 429
Tokyo Shoseki Co Ltd, pg 430
Yamaguchi Shoten, pg 431
Zoshindo JukenKenkyusha, pg 431

Jordan

Jordan House for Publication, pg 432

Kenya

Africa Book Services (EA) Ltd, pg 433
Dhillon Publishers Ltd, pg 433
Focus Publications Ltd, pg 433
Foundation Books Ltd, pg 434
Heinemann Kenya Ltd (EAEP), pg 434
Kenya Literature Bureau, pg 434
The Jomo Kenyatta Foundation, pg 435
Macmillan Kenya Publishers Ltd, pg 435
Phoenix Publishers Ltd, pg 435
Shirikon Publishers, pg 436
Transafrica Press, pg 436
Gideon S Were Press, pg 436

TYPE OF PUBLICATION INDEX BOOK

Republic of Korea
Cheong-mun-gag Publishing Co, pg 438
Hakmunsa Publishing Co, pg 439
Koreaone Press Inc, pg 440
Kyohaksa Publishing Co Ltd, pg 440
Moon Jin Media Co Ltd, pg 441
Sohaksa, pg 443
YBM/Si-sa, pg 443

Latvia
Lielvards Ltd, pg 445
Zvaigzne ABC Publishers Ltd, pg 445

Lebanon
Librairie Orientale sal, pg 446

Lesotho
Mazenod Book Centre, pg 447
Saint Michael's Mission Social Centre, pg 447

Lithuania
Alma Littera, pg 448
Baltos Lankos, pg 449
Margi Rastai Publishers, pg 449
Sviesa Publishers, pg 449
Svietimo ir mokslo ministerijos Leidybos centras, pg 449
TEV Leidykla, pg 450
Tyto Alba Publishers, pg 450

Luxembourg
Editions APESS ASBL, pg 450
Editions Emile Borschette, pg 450
Editions Promoculture, pg 451
Service Central des Imprimes et des Fournitures de Bureau de l'Etat, pg 451

Macau
Instituto Portugues Oriente, pg 452

The Former Yugoslav Republic of Macedonia
St Clement of Ohrid National & University Library, pg 453

Madagascar
Centre National de Production de Materiel Didactique (CNAPMAD), pg 453
Foibe Filan-Kevitry NY Mpampianatra (FOFIPA), pg 453
Librarie Mixte, pg 453
Societe Malgache d'Edition, pg 454
Imprimerie Takariva, pg 454
Trano Printy Fiangonana Loterana Malagasy (TPFLM)-(Imprimerie Lutherienne), pg 454

Malawi
Dzuka Publishing Co Ltd, pg 454

Malaysia
Darulfikir, pg 455
Dewan Bahasa dan Pustaka, pg 455
Federal Publications Sdn Bhd, pg 455
FEP International Sdn Bhd, pg 456
Mahir Publications Sdn Bhd, pg 456
Pearson Education Malaysia Sdn Bhd, pg 457
Penerbit Fajar Bakti Sdn Bhd, pg 457
Penerbit Jayatinta Sdn Bhd, pg 458

Penerbitan Pelangi Sdn Bhd (Pelangi Publishing Pte Ltd), pg 458
Penerbitan Tinta, pg 458
Pustaka Cipta Sdn Bhd, pg 458
Pustaka Delta Pelajaran Sdn Bhd, pg 458
Times Educational Co Sdn Bhd, pg 459
Tropical Press Sdn Bhd, pg 459
Utusan Publications & Distributors Sdn Bhd, pg 459

Mali
EDIM SA, pg 460

Malta
Media Centre, pg 460

Mauritius
Editions Capucines, pg 461
Editions de l'Ocean Indien Ltd, pg 461
EDITIONS Le Printemps, pg 461

Mexico
Edamex SA de CV, pg 464
Editorial Esfinge SA de CV, pg 465
Fernandez Editores SA de CV, pg 465
Fondo de Cultura Economica, pg 465
Grupo Editorial Iberoamerica, SA de CV, pg 466
Editorial Jus SA de CV, pg 467
Ediciones Larousse SA de CV, pg 467
Editorial Limusa SA de CV, pg 467
Nova Grupo Editorial SA de CV, pg 469
Palabra Ediciones S A de C V, pg 469
Editorial Patria SA de CV, pg 470
Pearson Educacion de Mexico, SA de CV, pg 470
Editorial Progreso SA de C V, pg 470
Publicaciones Cultural SA de CV, pg 471
Sistemas Tecnicos de Edicion SA de CV, pg 472
Editorial Trillas SA de CV, pg 472

Republic of Moldova
Editura Lumina, pg 473

Morocco
Cabinet Conseil CCMLA, pg 474
Dar Nachr Al Maarifa Pour L'Edition et La Distribution, pg 474

Mozambique
Empresa Moderna Lda, pg 475
Editora Minerva Central, pg 475

Nepal
International Standards Books & Periodicals (P) Ltd, pg 476

Netherlands
Educatieve Partners Nederland bv, pg 481
Katholieke Bijbelstichting, pg 484
LCG Malmberg BV, pg 485
Uitgeverij Lemma BV, pg 485
Pearson Education Netherlands, pg 487

Twente University Press, pg 490
Wolters-Noordhoff B V, pg 492

New Zealand
ABA Books, pg 493
Aoraki Press Ltd, pg 493
The Caxton Press, pg 495
Wendy Crane Books, pg 495
Dunmore Press Ltd, pg 495
ESA Publications (NZ) Ltd, pg 496
Eton Press (Auckland) Ltd, pg 496
Huia Publishers, pg 497
Learning Guides (Writers & Publishers Ltd), pg 497
Macmillan Publishers New Zealand Ltd, pg 498
Nelson Price Milburn Ltd, pg 499
New House Publishers Ltd, pg 499
Oxford University Press, pg 499
Pearson Education (PENZ), pg 500
Reed Publishing (NZ) Ltd, pg 500
Resource Books Ltd, pg 500

Nigeria
African Universities Press, pg 503
Africana-FEP Publishers Ltd, pg 503
Alliance West African Publishers & Co, pg 503
Aromolaran Publishing Co Ltd, pg 503
Cross Continent Press Ltd, pg 504
CSS Bookshops, pg 504
Educational Research & Study Group, pg 504
Ethiope Publishing Corporation, pg 504
Evans Brothers (Nigeria Publishers) Ltd, pg 504
Fourth Dimension Publishing Co Ltd, pg 504
JAD Publishers Ltd, pg 505
Kola Sanya Publishing Enterprise, pg 505
Longman Nigeria Plc, pg 505
New Africa Publishing Company Ltd, pg 505
New Era Publishers, pg 506
Northern Nigerian Publishing Co Ltd, pg 506
Nwamife Publishers Ltd, pg 506
Onibon-Oje Publishers, pg 506
Riverside Communications, pg 507
Tabansi Press Ltd, pg 507
University Publishing Co, pg 507
Vantage Publishers International Ltd, pg 507
West African Book Publishers Ltd, pg 507

Norway
H Aschehoug & Co (W Nygaard) A/S, pg 508
J W Eides Forlag A/S, pg 509
Forlaget Fag og Kultur, pg 509
Gyldendal Norsk Forlag A/S, pg 509
NKI Forlaget, pg 510
Universitetsforlaget, pg 511
Vett & Viten AS, pg 511

Pakistan
Sheikh Shaukat Ali & Sons, pg 511
The Book House, pg 512
Islamic Book Centre, pg 512
Jang Publishers, pg 513
Maqbool Academy, pg 513

Peru
Ediciones Brown SA, pg 516
Asociacion Editorial Bruno, pg 516

Tarea Asociacion de Publicaciones Educativas, pg 517
Tassorello, SA, pg 517

Philippines
Abiva Publishing House Inc, pg 518
Ateneo de Manila University Press, pg 518
Bookman Printing & Publishing House Inc, pg 518
Bookmark Inc, pg 518
J C Palabay Enterprises, pg 519
Marren Publishing House, Inc, pg 519
National Book Store Inc, pg 519
Our Lady of Manaoag Publisher, pg 520
Rex Bookstores & Publishers, pg 520
Saint Mary's Publishing Corp, pg 520
Salesiana Publishers Inc, pg 521
SIBS Publishing House Inc, pg 521
UST Publishing House, pg 521

Poland
Impuls, pg 523
Instytut Meteorologii i Gospodarki Wodnej, pg 523
Wydawnictwa Naukowo-Techniczne, pg 524
Oficyna Wydawnicza Politechniki Wroclawskiej, pg 525
PZWL Wydawnictwo Lekarskie Ltd, pg 526
Res Polona, pg 526
Wydawnictwa Szkolne i Pedagogiczne, pg 527

Portugal
Livraria Arnado Lda, pg 528
Constancia Editores, SA, pg 530
Didactica Editora, pg 530
Dinalivro, pg 530
Europress Editores e Distribuidores de Publicacoes Lda, pg 531
Livraria Minerva, pg 533
Lua Viajante-Edicao e Distribuicao de Livros e Material Audiovisual, Lda, pg 533
Editora McGraw-Hill de Portugal Lda, pg 533
Editorial O Livro Lda, pg 534
Platano Editora SA, pg 534
Porto Editora Lda, pg 535
Editorial Presenca, pg 535
Editora Replicacao Lda, pg 535
Texto Editora, pg 536

Puerto Rico
Editorial Cultural Inc, pg 537
McGraw-Hill Intermericana del Caribe, Inc, pg 537

Romania
Editora All, pg 538
Editura Clusium, pg 539
Editura Didactica si Pedagogica, pg 539
Editura Militara, pg 541
Editura Niculescu, pg 541
Polirom Verlag, pg 542

Russian Federation
Airis Press, pg 543
Fizmatlit Publishing Co, pg 545
INFRA-M Izdatel 'skij dom, pg 545
Izdatelstvo Mir, pg 546
Izdatelstvo Mordovskogo gosudar stvennogo, pg 547
Izdatelstvo Muzyka, pg 547

PUBLISHERS

Okoshko Ltd Publishers (Izdatelstvo), pg 547
Izdatelstvo Prosveshchenie, pg 548

Senegal

Les Nouvelles Editions Africaines du Senegal NEAS, pg 551

Serbia and Montenegro

Republicki Zavod za Unapredivanje Vaspitanja i Obrazovanja, pg 553

Sierra Leone

Njala Educational Publishing Centre, pg 554

Singapore

Chopsons Pte Ltd, pg 555
Federal Publications (S) Pte Ltd, pg 556
Hillview Publications Pte Ltd, pg 556
Shing Lee Group Publishers, pg 558

Slovakia

Priroda Publishing, pg 560
Slovenske pedagogicke nakladateistvo, pg 560
Ustav informacii a prognoz skolstva mladeze a telovychovy, pg 561

Slovenia

Mladinska Knjiga International, pg 561
Zalozba Mihelac d o o, pg 562
Zalozba Obzorja d d Maribor, pg 562

South Africa

Educum Publishers Ltd, pg 563
Heinemann Educational Publishers Southern Africa, pg 564
Heinemann Publishers (Pty) Ltd, pg 564
Ivy Publications, pg 565
Maskew Miller Longman, pg 566
Nasou Via Afrika, pg 567
Publitoria Publishers, pg 568
Ravan Press (Pty) Ltd, pg 568
Shuter & Shooter (Pty) Ltd, pg 568
Vivlia Publishers & Booksellers, pg 570

Spain

Editorial Aguaclara, pg 571
Ediciones Akal SA, pg 571
Ediciones Alfar SA, pg 572
Ediciones Anaya SA, pg 572
Anaya Educacion, pg 573
Editorial Bruno, pg 575
Editorial Casals SA, pg 575
Editorial Claret SA, pg 577
Diseno Editorial SA, pg 579
Editorial Donostiarra SA, pg 579
Edebe, pg 580
Editorial Everest SA, pg 581
Elkar, Euskal Liburu eta Kantuen Argitaldaria, SL, pg 582
Enciclopedia Catalana, SA, pg 582
Erein, pg 582
Eumo Editorial, pg 583
Grupo Comunicar, pg 585
Grupo Santillana de Ediciones SA, pg 586
Hercules de Ediciones, SA, pg 586
Editorial Herder SA, pg 586
Ibaizabal Edelvives SA, pg 586
Ediciones Istmo SA, pg 588
Ediciones JJB, pg 588

Editorial Luis Vives (Edelvives), pg 589
Editorial Magisterio Espanol SA, pg 590
Editorial Marfil SA, pg 590
McGraw-Hill/Interamericana de Espana SAU, pg 591
Editorial Moll SL, pg 592
Editorial la Muralla SA, pg 592
Naque Editora, pg 592
Oikos-Tau SA Ediciones, pg 593
Editorial Paidotribo SL, pg 594
Editorial Paraninfo SA, pg 595
Pearson Educacion S A, pg 595
Editorial Playor SA, pg 596
Editorial Reverte SA, pg 598
San Pablo Ediciones, pg 598
Ediciones Seyer, pg 599
Ediciones SM, pg 600
Editorial Teide SA, pg 601
Editorial Augusto E Pila Telena SL, pg 601
Thales Sociedad Andaluza de Educacion Matematica, pg 602
Gregorio del Toro Editor, pg 602
Editorial Trivium, SA, pg 602
Editorial Verbum SL, pg 604

Sri Lanka

M D Gunasena & Co Ltd, pg 606
Ministry of Education, pg 607
Warna Publishers, pg 607

Sudan

Khartoum University Press, pg 608

Suriname

Vaco NV Uitgeversmij, pg 608

Sweden

Akademiforlaget Goteborgslitteratur, pg 609
Ekelunds Forlag AB, pg 611
Folkuniversitetets foerlag, pg 611
SK-Gehrmans Musikforlag AB, pg 611
Hans Richter Laromedel, pg 613
Liber AB, pg 613
Studentlitteratur AB, pg 616

Switzerland

Editions Foma SA, pg 623
Paul Haupt Bern, pg 625
Editions du Panorama, pg 630
Editions Payot Lausanne, pg 631
Editions Pro Schola, pg 631
Sabe AG Verlagsinstitut, pg 633
Sauerlaender AG, pg 633
Tobler Verlag, pg 635
Der Universitatsverlag Freiburg, pg 636
Verlag Alexander Wild, pg 637

Taiwan, Province of China

Chien Chen Bookstore Publishing Company Ltd, pg 639
Chung Hwa Book Co Ltd, pg 639
Farseeing Publishing Company Ltd, pg 639
Lead Wave Publishing Company Ltd, pg 640
Newton Publishing Company Ltd, pg 641
San Min Book Co Ltd, pg 641
World Book Co Ltd, pg 642
Wu Nan Book Co Ltd, pg 642
Youth Cultural Publishing Co, pg 642

United Republic of Tanzania

Ben and Company Ltd, pg 643
DUP (1996) Ltd, pg 643
East African Publishing House, pg 643
Eastern Africa Publications Ltd, pg 643
General Publications Ltd, pg 643
Ndanda Mission Press, pg 644
Nyota Publishers Ltd, pg 644
Oxford University Press, pg 644
Press & Publicity Centre Ltd, pg 644
Readit Books, pg 644
Tanzania Publishing House, pg 644

Thailand

Bannakit Trading, pg 645
Thai Watana Panich Co, Ltd, pg 646

Togo

Editions Akpagnon, pg 646
Les Nouvelles Editions Africaines du TOGO (NEA-TOGO), pg 646

Tunisia

Maison d'Edition Mohamed Ali Hammi, pg 648
Maison Tunisienne de l'Edition, pg 648

Turkey

Altin Kitaplar Yayinevi, pg 649
Arkadas Ltd, pg 649
Arkin Kitabevi, pg 649
Inkilap Publishers Ltd, pg 650
Pearson Education Turkey, pg 651

Uganda

Roce (Consultants) Ltd, pg 653

Ukraine

ASK Ltd, pg 653
Osvita, pg 654

United Kingdom

Association for Scottish Literary Studies, pg 661
Association for Science Education, pg 661
BBC Worldwide Publishers, pg 663
Blackwell Science Ltd, pg 667
Boosey & Hawkes Music Publishers Ltd, pg 669
BPS Books (British Psychological Society), pg 670
Cambridge University Press, pg 674
Cassell & Co, pg 675
Causeway Press Ltd, pg 676
Cavendish Publishing Ltd, pg 676
Child's World Education Ltd, pg 679
Colourpoint Books, pg 681
Computer Step, pg 681
CTBI Publications, pg 685
Curiad, pg 685
Educational Explorers (Publishers) Ltd, pg 690
European Schoolbooks Ltd, pg 692
Evans Brothers Ltd, pg 693
First & Best in Education Ltd, pg 695
Folens Ltd, pg 695
Forbes Publications Ltd, pg 696
W H Freeman & Co Ltd, pg 697
The Geographical Association, pg 699

TYPE OF PUBLICATION INDEX

Gomer Press (J D Lewis & Sons Ltd), pg 701
Graham-Cameron Publishing & Illustration, pg 701
HarperCollins UK, pg 705
Heinemann Educational Publishing, pg 707
Hobsons, pg 709
Hodder Education, pg 709
Hodder Headline Ltd, pg 709
Home Health Education Service, pg 710
Hugo's Language Books Ltd, pg 710
Impart Books, pg 712
Institute of Financial Services, pg 712
Institute of Physics Publishing, pg 713
LDA-Living & Learning (Cambridge) Ltd, pg 719
Learning Development Aids, pg 719
Macmillan Heinemann ELT, pg 723
McCrimmon Publishing Co Ltd, pg 726
McGraw-Hill Publishing Company, pg 726
John Murray (Publishers) Ltd, pg 730
National Association for the Teaching of English (NATE), pg 730
Nelson Thornes Ltd, pg 732
James Nisbet & Co Ltd, pg 733
Old Pond Publishing, pg 734
The Oleander Press, pg 735
Osborne Books Ltd, pg 736
Oxford University Press, pg 737
Packard Publishing Ltd, pg 737
PC Publishing, pg 739
Portland Press Ltd, pg 745
Reed Educational & Professional Publishing, pg 749
SAGE Publications Ltd, pg 753
Schofield & Sims Ltd, pg 754
Sigma Press, pg 758
Stokesby House Publications, pg 761
Tobin Music, pg 766
Verulam Publishing Ltd, pg 770
Ward Lock Educational Co Ltd, pg 771
Wimbledon Publishing Company Ltd, pg 774
Windhorse Publications, pg 774

Uruguay

Ediciones de Juan Darien, pg 777
EQ Opciones en Educacion, pg 777
La Flor del Itapebi, pg 777
A Monteverde y Cia SA, pg 777
Vinten Editor, pg 778

Uzbekistan

Izdatelstvo Uzbekistan, pg 778

Venezuela

Alfadil Ediciones, pg 778
Colegial Bolivariana CA, pg 779
Editorial Kapelusz Venezolana SA, pg 779

Zambia

Wilfred Bwalya Chilangwa Publications, pg 781
Lundula Publishing House, pg 781
Multimedia Zambia, pg 781
Zambia Printing Company Ltd (ZPC), pg 782

TYPE OF PUBLICATION INDEX — BOOK

Zimbabwe
Academic Books (Pvt) Ltd, pg 782
College Press Publishers (Pvt) Ltd, pg 783
Longman Zimbabwe (Pvt) Ltd, pg 783
Mercury Press Pvt Ltd, pg 784
Zimbabwe Foundation for Education with Production (ZIMFEP), pg 784
Zimbabwe Publishing House (Pvt) Ltd, pg 784

TEXTBOOKS - COLLEGE

Afghanistan
Government Press, pg 1

Albania
NL SH, pg 1

Algeria
Les Editions Algeriennes En-Nahdha, pg 2

Argentina
Abeledo-Perrot SAE e I, pg 2
Editorial Abril SA, pg 2
Editorial Acme SA, pg 3
Alianza Editorial de Argentina SA, pg 3
Editorial Astrea de Alfredo y Ricardo Depalma SRL, pg 3
Beatriz Viterbo Editora, pg 4
Editorial Cangallo SACI, pg 4
Cesarini Hermanos, pg 4
Editorial Claridad SA, pg 4
Club de Lectores, pg 4
Libreria del Colegio SA, pg 4
Depalma SRL, pg 5
Ediciones del Eclipse, pg 5
Edicial SA, pg 5
Editorial Hemisferio Sur SA, pg 6
Libreria Huemul SA, pg 6
Editorial Idearium de la Universidad de Mendoza (EDIUM), pg 6
Inter-Medica, pg 6
Juris Editorial, pg 6
Kapelusz Editora SA, pg 7
Editorial Medica Panamericana SA, pg 7
Editorial Paidos SAICF, pg 8
Editorial Plus Ultra SA, pg 8
Editorial Stella, pg 9
Tipografica Editora Argentina, pg 9
Editoria Universitaria de la Patagonia, pg 9
Victor P de Zavalia SA, pg 10
Editorial Zeus SRL, pg 10

Australia
AHB Publications, pg 11
Edward Arnold (Australia) Pty Ltd, pg 12
Ausmed Publications Pty Ltd, pg 12
Australasian Medical Publishing Company Ltd (AMPCO), pg 12
Australian Film Television & Radio School, pg 13
Australian Scholarly Publishing, pg 13
Beri Publishing, pg 14
Bio Concepts Publishing, pg 14
Blackwell Publishing Asia, pg 15
Boombana Publications, pg 16
Butterworths Australia Ltd, pg 16
Cambridge University Press, pg 16
China Books, pg 17
Cookery Book, pg 18
Crystal Publishing, pg 19
Dellasta Publishing, pg 19
Elsevier Australia, pg 21
The Federation Press, pg 22
Kerri Hamer, pg 24
H&H Publishing, pg 24
Hospitality Books, pg 26
Illert Publications, pg 26
Institute of Aboriginal Development (IAD Press), pg 27
James Nicholas Publishers Pty Ltd, pg 27
Jarrah Publications, pg 27
Landarc Publications, pg 28
Law Book Co Information Services, pg 28
MacLennan & Petty Pty Ltd, pg 30
Macmillan Education Australia, pg 30
Macmillan Publishers Australia Pty Ltd, pg 30
McGraw-Hill Australia Pty Ltd, pg 31
OTEN (Open Training & Education Network), pg 34
Pearson Education Australia, pg 36
Pluto Press Australia Pty Ltd, pg 37
Pollitecon Publications, pg 37
Press for Success, pg 37
Quakers Hill Press, pg 38
Regency Publishing, pg 39
RMIT Publishing, pg 39
Rumsby Scientific Publishing, pg 40
Spaniel Books, pg 41
Strucmech Publishing, pg 42
Tarka Publishing, pg 42
Tertiary Press, pg 43
University of Queensland Press, pg 45
University of Western Australia Press, pg 45
Vista Publications, pg 45
Wileman Publications, pg 46
John Wiley & Sons Australia, Ltd, pg 46
Windhorse Books, pg 47
Winetitles, pg 47
Woodlands Publications, pg 47

Austria
Boehlau Verlag GmbH & Co KG, pg 48
Development News Ltd, pg 50
Fassbaender Verlag, pg 50
Georg Fromme und Co, pg 51
Herold Druck-und Verlagsgesellschaft mbH, pg 52
Johannes Heyn GmbH & Co KG, pg 52
Verlag Hoelder-Pichler-Tempsky, pg 52
Ibera VerlagsgesmbH, pg 52
Innverlag + Gatt, pg 52
Leopold Stocker Verlag, pg 53
Leykam Buchverlagsges mbH, pg 53
MANZ'sche Verlags- und Universitaetsbuchhandlung GMBH, pg 54
Niederosterreichisches Pressehaus Druck- und Verlagsgesellschaft mbH, pg 54
Oesterreichischer Bundesverlag Gmbh, pg 55
Verlag Oldenbourg, pg 56
Paul Sappl, Schulbuch- und Lehrmittelverlag, pg 57
Springer-Verlag Wien, pg 58
Trauner Verlag, pg 58
Tyrolia Verlagsanstalt GmbH, pg 58
Universitaetsverlag Wagner GmbH, pg 59
WUV/Facultas Universitaetsverlag, pg 60
WUV/Service Fachverlag, pg 60

Bangladesh
Bangladesh Publishers, pg 61
The University Press Ltd, pg 61

Belarus
Belaruskaya Encyklapedyya, pg 62
Publishing Center of Belarus State University, pg 62

Belgium
Academia Press, pg 62
Aurelia Books PVBA, pg 63
De Boeck et Larcier SA, pg 64
Etablissements Emile Bruylant SA, pg 64
Campinia Media VZW, pg 64
La Charte Editions juridiques, pg 65
Uitgeverij Contact NV, pg 65
Cremers (Schoollandkaarten) PVBA, pg 66
Editions De Boeck-Larcier SA, pg 66
Diligentia-Uitgeverij, pg 66
Garant Publishers Ltd, pg 67
Infoboek NV, pg 68
Uitgeverij J van In, pg 69
Editions Labor, pg 69
Nauwelaerts Edition SA, pg 71
Uitgeverij Peeters Leuven (Belgie), pg 71
Uitgeverij Pelckmans NV, pg 72
Presses Universitaires de Bruxelles asbl, pg 72
Uitgeverij De Sikkel NV, pg 73
Uitgeverij De Garve, pg 74
Les Editions Vie ouvriere ASBL, pg 74
Wolters Plantyn Educatieve Uitgevers, pg 74

Bolivia
Gisbert y Cia SA, pg 75

Bosnia and Herzegovina
Svjetlost, pg 76

Brazil
Aide Editora e Comercio de Livros Ltda, pg 77
Editora Alfa Omega Ltda, pg 77
Livraria Francisco Alves Editora SA, pg 77
Ao Livro Tecnico Industria e Comercio Ltda, pg 77
Ars Poetica Editora Ltda, pg 78
ARTMED Editora, pg 78
Editora Atica SA, pg 78
Editora Atlas SA, pg 78
Bloch Editores SA, pg 79
Editora Edgard Blucher Ltda, pg 79
Editora Campus Ltda, pg 79
Alzira Chagas Carpigiani, pg 79
Centro de Estudos Juridicosdo Para (CEJUP), pg 79
CEPA - Centro Editor de Psicologia Aplicada Ltda, pg 80
Editora Companhia das Letras/Editora Schwarcz Ltda, pg 80
Conquista, Empresa de Publicacoes Ltda, pg 80
Editora Contexto (Editora Pinsky Ltda), pg 80
Livraria Duas Cidades Ltda, pg 80
Dumara Distribuidora de Publicacoes Ltda, pg 81
E P U Editora Pedagogica e Universitaria Ltd, pg 81
Edipro-Edicoes Profissionais Ltda, pg 81
Companhia Editora Forense, pg 81
Empresa Brasileira de Pesquisa Agropecuaria, pg 81
Editora FCO Ltda, pg 81
Livraria Martins Fontes Editora Ltda, pg 81
Livraria Freitas Bastos Editora SA, pg 82
Editora FTD SA, pg 82
Fundacao de Assistencia ao Estudante, pg 82
Fundacao Sao Paulo, EDUC, pg 82
Editora Guanabara Koogan SA, pg 83
Editora Harbra Ltda, pg 83
Hemus Editora Ltda, pg 83
Livro Ibero-Americano Ltda, pg 83
Imago Editora Importacao e Exportacao Ltda, pg 84
Waldir Lima Editora, pg 85
LISA (Livros Irradiantes SA), pg 85
Edicoes Loyola SA, pg 85
LTC-Livros Tecnicos e Cientificos Editora S/A, pg 85
Editora Lucre Comercio e Representacoes, pg 85
Madras Editora, pg 86
Makron Books do Brasil Editora Ltda, pg 86
Editora Manole Ltda, pg 86
Medicina Panamericana Editora Do Brasil Ltda, pg 86
Medsi - Editora Medica e Cientifica Ltda, pg 86
Editora Mercado Aberto Ltda, pg 86
Editora Moderna Ltda, pg 86
Cia Editora Nacional, pg 87
Olho D'Agua Comercio e Servicos Editoriais Ltda, pg 87
Editora Ortiz SA, pg 88
Pearson Education Do Brasil, pg 88
Livraria Pioneira Editora/Enio Matheus Guazzelli e Cia Ltd, pg 88
Ediouro Publicacoes, SA, pg 89
Qualitymark Editora Ltda, pg 89
Editora Revan Ltda, pg 89
Saraiva SA, Livreiros Editores, pg 90
Livraria Sulina Editora, pg 91
Edicoes Tabajara, pg 91
Tempus Editores, pg 91
34 Literatura S/C Ltda, pg 91
Editora da Universidade de Sao Paulo, pg 91
Editora Universidade Federal do Rio de Janeiro, pg 92
Fundacao Getulio Vargas, pg 92
Jorge Zahar Editor, pg 92

Bulgaria
Bulvest 2000 Ltd, pg 93
Darzhavno Izdatelstvo Zemizdat, pg 93
Dolphin Press Group Ltd, pg 94
Eurasia Academic Publishers, pg 94
Gea-Libris Publishing House, pg 94
Heron Press Publishing House, pg 94
Izdatelstvo Lettera, pg 95
Makros 2000 - Plovdiv, pg 95
MATEX, pg 95
Musica Publishing House Ltd, pg 95
Nov Covek Publishing House, pg 96
Pensoft Publishers, pg 96
Prosveta Publishers AS, pg 96
Slavena, pg 97

PUBLISHERS / TYPE OF PUBLICATION INDEX

Technica, pg 97
Todor Kableshkov University of Transport, pg 97

Cameroon

Centre d'Edition et de Production pour l'Enseignement et la Recherche (CEPER), pg 98

Chile

Arrayan Editores, pg 98
Editorial Andres Bello/Editorial Juridica de Chile, pg 99
Edeval (Universidad de Valparaiso), pg 99
Instituto Geografico Militar, pg 99
Pontificia Universidad Catolica de Chile, pg 100
J.C. Saez Editor, pg 100
Editorial Universitaria SA, pg 100
Ediciones Universitarias de Valparaiso, pg 100

China

Anhui People's Publishing House, pg 101
Aviation Industry Press, pg 101
Beijing University Press, pg 101
Chemical Industry Press, pg 101
China Film Press, pg 102
China Forestry Publishing House, pg 102
China Machine Press (CMP), pg 102
China Materials Management Publishing House, pg 102
Chinese Pedagogics Publishing House, pg 103
Cultural Relics Publishing House, pg 103
Foreign Language Teaching & Research Press, pg 104
Fudan University Press, pg 104
Higher Education Press, pg 105
Jilin Science & Technology Publishing House, pg 105
Language Publishing House, pg 106
Metallurgical Industry Press (MIP), pg 106
Nanjing University Press, pg 106
The People's Communications Publishing House, pg 106
People's Medical Publishing House (PMPH), pg 107
Printing Industry Publishing House, pg 107
Shandong University Press, pg 108
Shanghai College of Traditional Chinese Medicine Press, pg 108
Shanghai Far East Publishers, pg 108
Shanghai Foreign Language Education Press, pg 108
Sichuan University Press, pg 108
South China University of Science & Technology Press, pg 108
Wuhan University Press, pg 109
Yunnan University Press, pg 109
Zhejiang University Press, pg 109

Colombia

Bedout Editores SA, pg 110
Consejo Episcopal Latinoamericano (CELAM), pg 110
Universidad Externado de Colombia, pg 111
Fondo Educativo Interamericano SA, pg 111
Kapelusz Ltda Editorial, pg 111
McGraw-Hill Colombia, pg 112
Migema Ediciones Ltda, pg 112
Editorial Norma SA, pg 112
Pearson Educacion de Colombia LTDA, pg 112
Editorial Santillana SA, pg 112
Tercer Mundo Editores SA, pg 113
Universidad de los Andes Editorial, pg 113
Universidad Nacional Abierta y a Distancia, pg 113

The Democratic Republic of the Congo

Centre de Recherche, et Pedagogie Appliquee, pg 114
Facultes Catoliques de Kinshasa, pg 114
Presses Universitaires du Zaiire (PUZ), pg 114

Costa Rica

Garcia Hermanos Imprenta y Litografia, pg 115
Jose Alfonso Sandoval Nunez, pg 115
Editorial de la Universidad de Costa Rica, pg 116
Editorial Universidad Estatal a Distancia (EUNED), pg 116

Cote d'Ivoire

Universite d'Abidjan, pg 117
Akohi Editions, pg 117
Les Nouvelles Editions Ivoiriennes, pg 117

Croatia

Narodne Novine, pg 119
Skolska Knjiga, pg 119
Sveucilisna tiskara doo, pg 119

Cuba

ISCAH Fructuoso Rodriguez, pg 120
Pueblo y Educacion Editorial (PE), pg 121

Czech Republic

Academia, pg 122
Amosium Servis, pg 122
Barrister & Principal, pg 122
Horacek Ladislav-Paseka, pg 123
Karolinum, nakladatelstvi, pg 124
Melantrich, akc spol, pg 125
Mendelova zemedelska a lesnicka univerzita v Brne, pg 125
Portal spol sro, pg 126
Slon Sociologicke Nakladatelstvi, pg 127
NS Svoboda spol sro, pg 127
Votobia sro, pg 128

Denmark

Aarhus Universitetsforlag, pg 128
Akademisk Forlag A/S, pg 128
Borgens Forlag A/S, pg 129
Dansk Psykologisk Forlag, pg 130
FADL's Forlag A/S, pg 131
Fremad A/S, pg 131
Gads Forlag, pg 131
Forlaget GMT, pg 131
Gyldendalske Boghandel - Nordisk Forlag A/S, pg 131
Holkenfeldt 3, pg 132
Forlaget Hovedland, pg 132
Kaleidoscope Publishers Ltd, pg 132
Nyt Nordisk Forlag Arnold Busck A/S, pg 133
Polyteknisk Boghandel & Forlag, pg 133
C A Reitzel Boghandel & Forlag A/S, pg 134
Samfundslitteratur, pg 134

Dominican Republic

Pontificia Universidad Catolica Madre y Maestra, pg 136

Egypt (Arab Republic of Egypt)

Cairo University Press, pg 137
Dar Al-Kitab Al-Masri, pg 137
Dar Al-Matbo at Al-Gadidah, pg 138
The Egyptian Society for the Dissemination of Universal Culture and Knowledge (ESDUCK), pg 138
Dar Al Maaref, pg 138
Middle East Book Centre, pg 138

El Salvador

Clasicos Roxsil Editorial SA de CV, pg 138
UCA Editores, pg 138
Editorial Universitaria de la Universidad de El Salvador, pg 139

Estonia

Valgus Publishers, pg 140

Finland

Akateeminen Kustannusliike Oy, pg 141
Kirjayhtyma Oy, pg 142
Kustannuskiila Oy, pg 143
Otava Publishing Co Ltd, pg 143
Schildts Forlags AB, pg 144
Soderstroms Forlag, pg 144
Suomalaisen Kirjallisuuden Seura, pg 144
Osuuskunta Vastapaino, pg 144
Werner Soederstrom Osakeyhtio (WSOY), pg 145
Yliopistopaino/Helsinki University Press, pg 145

France

Adverbum SARL, pg 146
Association pour la Recherche et l'Information demographiques (APRD), pg 148
Atelier National de Reproduction des Theses, pg 148
Editions Aubier-Montaigne SA, pg 148
Editions Belin, pg 149
Societe d'Edition Les Belles Lettres, pg 149
Presses Universitaires de Bordeaux (PUB), pg 150
Editions Breal, pg 151
Editions BRGM, pg 151
Brud Nevez, pg 151
Cepadues Editions SA, pg 153
Editions Chiron, pg 154
Chotard et Associes Editeurs, pg 154
Cle International, pg 154
Armand Colin, Editeur, pg 155
Editions Cujas, pg 156
Editions Dalloz Sirey, pg 157
De Vecchi Editions SA, pg 157
Editions Desvigne, pg 158
Doin Editeurs, pg 159
Dunod Editeur, pg 159
Editions de l'Ecole, pg 159
Editions rue d'Ulm, pg 160
Elf Exploration Production, pg 161
Editions de l'Epargne, pg 161
Editions Errance, pg 162
Editions Galilee, pg 164
Paul Geuthner Librairie Orientaliste, pg 165
Groupe Hatier International, pg 166
Hachette Education, pg 166
Hachette Livre, pg 167
Hachette Livre International, pg 167
Editions Hatier SA, pg 167
Hermann editeurs des Sciences et des Arts SA, pg 167
Editions Hermes Science Publications, pg 167
INRA Editions (Institut National de la Recherche Agronomique), pg 168
Editions INSERM, pg 168
IRD Editions, pg 169
Editions Larousse, pg 171
Editions Universitaires LCF, pg 171
Les Editions LGDJ-Montchrestien, pg 172
Librairie Scientifique et Technique Albert Blanchard, pg 172
LiTec (Librairies Techniques SA), pg 172
Magnard, pg 173
Masson Editeur, pg 174
Masson-Williams et Wilkins, pg 174
Maxima Laurent du Mesnil Editeur, pg 174
Editions Modernes Media, pg 176
Editions de la Reunion des Musees Nationaux, pg 176
Editions Fernand Nathan, pg 176
Editions Ophrys, pg 177
Pearson Education France, pg 179
Editions Pedone, pg 179
Editions A et J Picard SA, pg 179
Polytechnica SA, pg 180
Presses de l'Ecole Nationale des Ponts et Chaussees, pg 181
Presses Universitaires de Caen, pg 181
Presses Universitaires de France (PUF), pg 181
Presses Universitaires de Grenoble, pg 181
Editions Roudil SA, pg 183
Editions du Seuil, pg 184
Editions Spratbrow, pg 186
Editions Tarmeye, pg 187
Librairie Philosophique J Vrin, pg 189
Librairie Vuibert, pg 189

Germany

A Francke Verlag (Tubingen und Basel), pg 190
AOL-Verlag Frohmut Menze, pg 193
Aschendorffsche Verlagsbuchhandlung GmbH & Co KG, pg 194
C Bange GmbH & Co KG, pg 196
Baumann GmbH & Co KG, pg 197
Bayerischer Schulbuch-Verlag GmbH, pg 198
Verlag C H Beck oHG, pg 198
Julius Beltz GmbH & Co KG, pg 199
Berliner Wissenschafts-Verlag GmbH (BWV), pg 199
Bernard und Graefe Verlag, pg 199
Biblio Verlag, pg 200
Blackwell Wissenschafts-Verlag GmbH, pg 201
Verlag Die Blaue Eule, pg 202
Boehlau-Verlag GmbH & Cie, pg 202
Buechse der Pandora Verlags-GmbH, pg 205
Burckhardthaus-Laetare Verlag GmbH, pg 206

TYPE OF PUBLICATION INDEX
BOOK

Fachverlag Hans Carl GmbH, pg 207
Centaurus-Verlagsgesellschaft GmbH, pg 207
Claudius Verlag, pg 209
Compact Verlag GmbH, pg 209
Cornelsen und Oxford University Press GmbH & Co, pg 210
Cornelsen Verlag GmbH & Co OHG, pg 210
Cornelsen Verlag Scriptor GmbH & Co KG, pg 210
Verlag Werner Dausien, pg 211
Verlag Harri Deutsch, pg 211
Deutscher Apotheker Verlag Dr Roland Schmiedel GmbH & Co, pg 212
Deutscher Verlag fur Grundstoffindustrie GmbH, pg 213
Dipa-Verlag GmbH, pg 215
Verlag Duerr & Kessler GmbH, pg 217
Duncker und Humblot GmbH, pg 217
Elsevier GmbH/Urban & Fischer Verlag, pg 219
Verlag Europa-Lehrmittel GmbH & Co KG, pg 221
Exil Verlag, pg 222
Fachbuchverlag Pfanneberg & Co, pg 223
Ferdinand Enke Verlag, pg 224
Festo Didactic GmbH & Co KG, pg 224
Verlag Reinhard Fischer, pg 225
Rita G Fischer Verlag, pg 225
Focus-Verlag Gesellschaft mbH, pg 225
Verlag Franz Vahlen GmbH, pg 226
Friedrich Kiehl Verlag GmbH, pg 227
Betriebswirtschaftlicher Verlag Dr Th Gabler, pg 228
Gebrueder Borntraeger Science Publishers, pg 228
Govi-Verlag Pharmazeutischer Verlag GmbH, pg 230
Walter de Gruyter GmbH & Co KG, pg 231
Gunter Olzog Verlag GmbH, pg 231
Guetersloher Verlagshaus, pg 232
Haag und Herchen Verlag GmbH, pg 232
Hamburger Lesehefte Verlag Iselt & Co Nfl mbH, pg 233
Carl Hanser Verlag, pg 234
Harrassowitz Verlag, pg 234
Rudolf Haufe Verlag GmbH & Co KG, pg 235
Verlag Herder GmbH & Co KG, pg 236
Hippokrates-Verlag GmbH, pg 238
S Hirzel Verlag GmbH und Co, pg 238
Hogrefe Verlag GmbH & Co Kg, pg 238
Huss-Medien GmbH, pg 240
Huss-Verlag GmbH, pg 240
Huthig GmbH & Co KG, pg 240
IKO Verlag fur Interkulturelle Kommunikation, pg 241
Impuls-Theater-Verlag, pg 241
ITpress Verlag, pg 242
Iudicium Verlag GmbH, pg 242
Ernst Klett Verlag GmbH, pg 247
W Kohlhammer GmbH, pg 248
kopaed verlagsgmbh, pg 249
Peter Lang GmbH Europaeischer Verlag der Wissenschaften, pg 252
Langenscheidt-Hachette, pg 252
Langenscheidt KG, pg 252

Verlag fuer Lehrmittel Poessneck GmbH, pg 253
Libertas- Europaeisches Institut GmbH, pg 254
Lucius & Lucius Verlagsgesellschaft mbH, pg 255
Manz G J Verlag und Druckerei, pg 257
Margraf Verlag, pg 257
Matthiesen Verlag Ingwert Paulsen Jr, pg 258
Meyer & Meyer Verlag, pg 260
Karl Heinrich Moeseler Verlag, pg 261
Mohr Siebeck, pg 261
Morsak Verlag, pg 261
Verlag Neue Wirtschafts-Briefe GmbH & Co, pg 264
Max Niemeyer Verlag GmbH, pg 265
Patmos Verlag GmbH & Co KG, pg 268
Philipp Reclam Jun Verlag GmbH, pg 269
Psychiatrie-Verlag GmbH, pg 272
Psychologie Verlags Union GmbH, pg 272
Quelle und Meyer Verlag GmbH & Co, pg 273
Quintessenz Verlags-GmbH, pg 273
Dr Ludwig Reichert Verlag, pg 274
Ritterbach Verlag GmbH, pg 276
Roehrig Universitaets Verlag Gmbh, pg 276
Rombach GmbH Druck und Verlagshaus & Co, pg 276
Romiosini Verlag, pg 276
Schaeffer-Poeschel Verlag fuer Wirtschaft Steuern Recht, pg 279
Verlag Dr Otto Schmidt KG, pg 280
Ferdinand Schoeningh Verlag GmbH, pg 281
Schott Musik International GmbH & Co KG, pg 281
Schulz-Kirchner Verlag GmbH, pg 282
Otto Schwartz Fachbochhandlung GmbH, pg 282
E Schweizerbart'sche Verlagsbuchhandlung (Naegele und Obermiller), pg 282
Springer Science+Business Media GmbH & Co KG, pg 284
Verlag H Stam GmbH, pg 286
Franz Steiner Verlag Wiesbaden GmbH, pg 287
B G Teubner Verlag, pg 290
Tipress Dienstleistungen fur das Verlagswesen GmbH, pg 291
Tuduv Verlagsgesellschaft mbH, pg 292
Tuebinger Vereinigung fur Volkskunde eV (TVV), pg 292
Wirtschaftsverlag Carl Ueberreuter, pg 293
Verlag Eugen Ulmer GmbH & Co, pg 293
UVK Universitatsverlag Konstanz GmbH, pg 294
UVK Verlagsgesellschaft mbH, pg 294
Vandenhoeck & Ruprecht, pg 294
Verlag fur Schweissen und Verwandte Verfahren, pg 295
Verlag Moderne Industrie AG & Co KG, pg 295
Verlag und Druckkontor Kamp GmbH, pg 295
Friedr Vieweg & Sohn Verlag, pg 296
VS Verlag fur Sozialwissenschaften, pg 297
Weidler Buchverlag Berlin, pg 298

Werner Verlag GmbH & Co KG, pg 299
Westermann Schulbuchverlag GmbH, pg 299
Herbert Wichmann Verlag, pg 299
Wiley-VCH Verlag GmbH, pg 300
Dr Dieter Winkler, pg 300
Winklers Verlag Gebrueder Grimm, pg 300
Verlag Konrad Wittwer GmbH, pg 301
Wochenschau Verlag, Dr Kurt Debus GmbH, pg 301

Ghana

Afram Publications (Ghana) Ltd, pg 303
Black Mask Ltd, pg 303
Bureau of Ghana Languages, pg 303
Educational Press & Manufacturers Ltd, pg 303
EPP Books Services, pg 304
Ghana Publishing Corporation, pg 304
Ghana Universities Press (GUP), pg 304
Sedco Publishing Ltd, pg 305
Unimax Macmillan Ltd, pg 305

Greece

Diavlos, pg 306
Ilias Kambanas Publishing Organization, SA, pg 309
Kleidarithmos, Ekdoseis, pg 309
Kritiki Publishing, pg 309
Nakas Music House, pg 310
Panepistimio Ioanninon, pg 311
Papazissis Publishers SA, pg 311
Patakis Publishers, pg 311

Guadeloupe

JASOR, pg 313

Guatemala

Grupo Editorial RIN-78, pg 313

Haiti

Editions Caraibes SA, pg 314

Hong Kong

Commercial Press (Hong Kong) Ltd, pg 316
Good Earth Publishing Co Ltd, pg 317
Hong Kong University Press, pg 317
Joint Publishing (HK) Co Ltd, pg 317
Philopsychy Press, pg 318
Times Publishing (Hong Kong) Ltd, pg 319
Union Press Ltd, pg 320
Witman Publishing Co (HK) Ltd, pg 320

Hungary

Akademiai Kiado, pg 320
Atlantisz Kiado, pg 320
Corvina Books Ltd, pg 321
Greger-Delacroix, pg 321
Janus Pannonius Tudomanyegyetem, pg 322
Joszoveg Muhely Kiado, pg 322
Mueszaki Koenyvkiado Ltd, pg 323
Nemzeti Tankoenyvkiado, pg 323
Panem, pg 324
Pro Natura, pg 324
Typotex Kft Elektronikus Kiado, pg 324

Iceland

Haskolautgafan - University of Iceland Press, pg 325
Namsgagnastofnun, pg 326

India

Academic Publishers, pg 327
Addison-Wesley Pte Ltd, pg 327
Affiliated East West Press Pvt Ltd, pg 327
Anmol Publications Pvt Ltd, pg 328
Arya Medi Publishing House, pg 328
Atma Ram & Sons, pg 329
B I Publications Pvt Ltd, pg 329
The Bangalore Printing & Publishing Co Ltd, pg 329
Bani Mandir, Book-Sellers, Publishers & Educational Suppliers, pg 329
Bhawan Book Service, Publishers & Distributors, pg 330
Book Circle, pg 330
BS Publications, pg 331
Charotar Publishing House, pg 332
Chowkhamba Sanskrit Series Office, pg 332
Concept Publishing Co, pg 332
Dastane Ramchandra & Co, pg 333
Dutta Publishing Co Ltd, pg 333
Eastern Law House Pvt Ltd, pg 334
Eurasia Publishing House Private Ltd, pg 334
Geeta Prakashan, pg 335
General Book Depot, pg 335
Goel Prakashen, pg 335
Arnold Heinman Publishers (India) Pvt Ltd, pg 335
Indian Council of Agricultural Research, pg 336
Intertrade Publications Pvt Ltd, pg 338
Khanna Publishers, pg 339
Konark Publishers Pvt Ltd, pg 339
Law Publishers, pg 340
Laxmi Publications Pvt Ltd, pg 340
Omsons Publications, pg 344
Oxford & IBH Publishing Co Pvt Ltd, pg 344
Oxford University Press, pg 344
Oxonian Press (P) Ltd, pg 344
Paico Publishing House, pg 344
Panjab University Publication Bureau, pg 344
People's Publishing House (P) Ltd, pg 345
Pitambar Publishing Co (P) Ltd, pg 345
Rajasthan Hindi Granth Academy, pg 346
Rajesh Publications, pg 346
Rajpal & Sons, pg 346
Rastogi Publications, pg 346
Regency Publications, pg 346
Reliance Publishing House, pg 346
Sasta Sahitya Mandal, pg 348
Scientific Book Agency, pg 348
Selina Publishers, pg 349
South Asian Publishers Pvt Ltd, pg 350
Sterling Information Technologies, pg 350
Sterling Publishers Pvt Ltd, pg 350
Sultan Chand & Sons Pvt Ltd, pg 350
DB Taraporevala Sons & Co Pvt Ltd, pg 351
Tata McGraw-Hill Publishing Co Ltd, pg 351
Today & Tomorrow's Printers & Publishers, pg 351
Vakils Feffer & Simons Ltd, pg 352

PUBLISHERS

S Viswanathan (Printers & Publishers) Pvt Ltd, pg 352
A H Wheeler & Co Ltd, pg 353

Indonesia

Andi Offset, pg 353
Angkasa CV, pg 353
Balai Pustaka, pg 353
PT Bulan Bintang, pg 354
Bumi Aksara PT, pg 354
Diponegoro CV, pg 354
Djambatan PT, pg 354
Institut Teknologi Bandung, pg 355
Nusa Indah, pg 356
PT Bhakti Baru, pg 356
PT Pradnya Paramita, pg 356

Islamic Republic of Iran

Amir Kabir Book Publishing & Distribution Co, pg 357
University of Tehran Publications & Printing Organization, pg 357

Ireland

An Gum, pg 358
The Economic & Social Research Institute, pg 359
Gill & Macmillan Ltd, pg 360
Herodotus Press, pg 361
Institute of Public Administration, pg 361
Irish Management Institute, pg 361
Oak Tree Press, pg 362
On Stream Publications Ltd, pg 362
Ossian Publications, pg 363
Round Hall Sweet & Maxwell, pg 363
Royal Irish Academy, pg 363
Veritas Co Ltd, pg 364

Israel

Achiasaf Publishing House Ltd, pg 364
Am Oved Publishers Ltd, pg 365
Amichai Publishing House Ltd, pg 365
The Bialik Institute, pg 365
Dvir Publishing Ltd, pg 366
Feldheim Publishers Ltd, pg 367
Otzar Hamore, pg 367
Israel Universities Press, pg 368
The Magnes Press, pg 370
Massada Publishers Ltd, pg 370
Open University of Israel, pg 371
Schocken Publishing House Ltd, pg 371
Y Sreberk, pg 372
Steimatzky Group Ltd, pg 372
Tcherikover Publishers Ltd, pg 372
Tel Aviv University, pg 372
Yad Eliahu Kitov, pg 373
Yavneh Publishing House Ltd, pg 373

Italy

De Agostini Scolastica, pg 374
Libreria Alfani Editrice SRL, pg 375
Archimede Edizioni, pg 376
Editore Armando Armando SRL, pg 376
Bianco, pg 377
Bollati Boringhieri Editore, pg 378
Bonacci editore, pg 378
Giuseppe Bonanno Editore, pg 378
Bulzoni Editore SRL (Le Edizioni Universitarie d'Italia), pg 379
Cappelli Editore, pg 380
Casa Editrice Giuseppe Principato Spa, pg 380
Celuc Libri, pg 381
CLEUP - Cooperative Libraria Editrice dell 'Universita di Padova, pg 382
Edizioni Cremonese SRL, pg 383
Edizioni Curci SRL, pg 384
G De Bono Editore, pg 384
DEI Tipographia del Genio Civile, pg 384
Casa Editrice Istituto della Santa, pg 385
ECIG, pg 385
EDIFIR SRL, pg 386
Editrice Edisco, pg 386
Editori Laterza, pg 386
Edizioni del Centro Camuno di Studi Preistorici, pg 386
Giulio Einaudi Editore SpA, pg 387
Edi.Ermes srl, pg 388
Esselibri, pg 388
Etas Libri, pg 388
Giangiacomo Feltrinelli SpA, pg 389
Editoriale Fernando Folini, pg 389
Fratelli Conte Editori SRL, pg 389
Istituto Geografico de Agostini SpA, pg 390
Gius Laterza e Figli SpA, pg 391
Herbita Editrice di Leonardo Palermo, pg 392
LED - Edizioni Universitarie di Lettere Economia Diritto, pg 395
Levante Editori, pg 395
Levrotto e Bella Libreria Editrice Universitaria SAS, pg 395
Liguori Editore SRL, pg 395
Loescher Editore SRL, pg 396
Loffredo Editore Napoli SpA®, pg 396
Masson SpA, pg 397
Minerva Italica SpA, pg 398
Mucchi Editore SRL, pg 399
Societa Editrice Il Mulino, pg 399
Gruppo Ugo Mursia Editore SpA, pg 400
Nagard, pg 400
La Nuova Italia Editrice SpA, pg 401
Paideia Editrice, pg 402
Paravia Bruno Mondadori Editori, pg 402
Piccin Nuova Libraria SpA, pg 403
Principato, pg 404
RCS Rizzoli Libri SpA, pg 405
Edizioni Universitarie Romane, pg 406
Casa Editrice Marietti Scuola SpA, pg 407
Edizioni Librarie Siciliane, pg 408
Societa Editrice Internazionale - SEI, pg 408
Societa Editrice la Goliardica Pavese SRL, pg 408
Edizioni Studium SRL, pg 409
Nicola Teti e C Editore SRL, pg 410
Edizioni Unicopli SpA, pg 411
Unipress, pg 411
UTET (Unione Tipografico-Editrice Torinese), pg 411
Valmartina Editore SRL, pg 411
Zanichelli Editore SpA, pg 412
Edizioni Zara, pg 412

Jamaica

CFM Publications, pg 413
The Press, pg 414

Japan

Bun-ichi Sogo Shuppan, pg 415
Dobunshoin Publishers Co, pg 416
Dogakusha Inc, pg 416
Eichosha Company Ltd, pg 417
The Eihosha Ltd, pg 417
Hakutei-Sha, pg 418
Hirokawa Publishing Co, pg 418
Hokuryukan Co Ltd, pg 418
Hyoronsha Publishing Co Ltd, pg 418
Igaku-Shoin Ltd, pg 419
Iwanami Shoten, Publishers, pg 419
The Japan Times Ltd, pg 420
Kaitakusha, pg 420
Kindai Kagaku Sha Co Ltd, pg 421
Kodansha Scientific Ltd, pg 421
Kyoritsu Shuppan Co Ltd, pg 422
Maruzen Co Ltd, pg 422
Mejikaru Furendo-sha, pg 422
Minerva Shobo Co Ltd, pg 422
Morikita Shuppan Co Ltd, pg 423
Nakayama Shoten Co Ltd, pg 423
Nanzando Co Ltd, pg 423
Nihon-Bunkyo Shuppan (Japan Educational Publishing Co Ltd), pg 423
Nikkagiren Shuppan-Sha (JUSE Press Ltd), pg 424
Nippon Hoso Shuppan Kyokai (NHK Publishing), pg 424
Obunsha Co Ltd, pg 424
Ohmsha Ltd, pg 424
Ongaku No Tomo Sha Corporation, pg 425
Reimei-Shobo Co Ltd, pg 425
Sagano Shoin, pg 426
Sanseido Co Ltd, pg 426
Sanshusha Publishing Co, Ltd, pg 426
Seibido, pg 426
Shokokusha Publishing Co Ltd, pg 428
Sobun-Sha, pg 428
Sogensha Publishing Co Ltd, pg 428
Tamagawa University Press, pg 429
Thomson Learning Japan, pg 429
Toho Book Store, pg 429
Tokyo Kagaku Dojin Co Ltd, pg 429
Tsukiji Shokan Publishing Co, pg 430
University of Tokyo Press, pg 430
Zeimukeiri-Kyokai, pg 431

Jordan

Jordan House for Publication, pg 432

Kenya

Action Publishers, pg 433
Africa Book Services (EA) Ltd, pg 433
African Centre for Technology Studies (ACTS), pg 433
Book Sales (K) Ltd, pg 433
Cosmopolitan Publishers Ltd, pg 433
Focus Publications Ltd, pg 433
Foundation Books Ltd, pg 434
Heinemann Kenya Ltd (EAEP), pg 434
Kenway Publications Ltd, pg 434
Kenya Literature Bureau, pg 434
Macmillan Kenya Publishers Ltd, pg 435
Midi Teki Publishers, pg 435
Nairobi University Press, pg 435
Shirikon Publishers, pg 436
Gideon S Were Press, pg 436

Democratic People's Republic of Korea

Educational Books Publishing House, pg 436

Republic of Korea

Bi-bong Publishing Co, pg 437
Bo Moon Dang, pg 437
Cheong-mun-gag Publishing Co, pg 438
Chung Rim Publishing Co Ltd, pg 438
Daeyoung Munhwasa, pg 438
Dong-A Publishing & Printing Co Ltd, pg 438
Hakmunsa Publishing Co, pg 439
Hanul Publishing Co, pg 439
Iljo-gag Publishers, pg 439
Jung-ang Munhwa Sa, pg 440
Koreaone Press Inc, pg 440
Kukminseokwan Publishing Co Ltd, pg 440
Kyohaksa Publishing Co Ltd, pg 440
Literature Academy Publishing, pg 441
Minjisa Publishing Co, pg 441
Moon Jin Media Co Ltd, pg 441
Nanam Publications Co, pg 441
Omun Gak, pg 441
Panmun Book Co Ltd, pg 442
Pearson Education Korea Ltd, pg 442
PoChinChai Printing Co Ltd, pg 442
Prompter Publications, pg 442
Sohaksa, pg 443
Yearimdang Publishing Co, pg 443
Yonsei University Press, pg 444

Kuwait

Ministry of Information, pg 444

Latvia

Lielvards Ltd, pg 445
Zvaigzne ABC Publishers Ltd, pg 445

Lebanon

Dar Al-Kitab Al-Loubnani, pg 445
Dar Al-Maaref-Liban Sarl, pg 446
Librairie du Liban Publishers (Sal), pg 446
Librairie Orientale sal, pg 446
World Book Publishing, pg 447

Lithuania

Eugrimas, pg 449
Klaipedos Universiteto Leidykla, pg 449
Mokslo ir enciklopediju leidybos institutas, pg 449
Margi Rastai Publishers, pg 449
Svietimo ir mokslo ministerijos Leidybos centras, pg 449
TEV Leidykla, pg 450

Luxembourg

Editions Promoculture, pg 451

Macau

Instituto Portugues Oriente, pg 452

The Former Yugoslav Republic of Macedonia

Detska radost, pg 452
Prosvetno Delo Publishing House, pg 453
St Clement of Ohrid National & University Library, pg 453

Madagascar

Foibe Filan-Kevitry NY Mpampianatra (FOFIPA), pg 453
Societe Malgache d'Edition, pg 454

TYPE OF PUBLICATION INDEX

BOOK

Malawi
Dzuka Publishing Co Ltd, pg 454

Malaysia
AMK Interaksi Sdn Bhd, pg 455
Berita Publishing Sdn Bhd, pg 455
Dewan Bahasa dan Pustaka, pg 455
Eastview Productions Sdn Bhd, pg 455
Federal Publications Sdn Bhd, pg 455
Geetha Publishers Sdn Bhd, pg 456
K Publishing & Distributors Sdn Bhd, pg 456
The Malaya Press Sdn Bhd, pg 456
Malayan Law Journal Sdn Bhd, pg 456
Panther Publishing, pg 457
Pearson Education Malaysia Sdn Bhd, pg 457
Penerbit Fajar Bakti Sdn Bhd, pg 457
Penerbit Universiti Sains Malaysia, pg 458
Preston Corporation Sdn Bhd, pg 458
Pustaka Cipta Sdn Bhd, pg 458
Text Books Malaysia Sdn Bhd, pg 459
Times Educational Co Sdn Bhd, pg 459
Utusan Publications & Distributors Sdn Bhd, pg 459

Mali
EDIM SA, pg 460

Martinique
Editions Gondwana, pg 460

Mauritania
Imprimerie Commerciale et Administrative de Mauritanie, pg 461

Mauritius
Editions Capucines, pg 461
EDITIONS Le Printemps, pg 461

Mexico
Aconcagua Ediciones y Publicaciones SA, pg 461
Alfaomega Grupo Editor SA de CV, pg 462
El Colegio de Mexico AC, pg 463
Colegio de Postgraduados en Ciencias Agricolas, pg 463
Compania Editorial Continental SA de CV, pg 463
Publicaciones Cruz O SA, pg 463
Editorial Diana SA de CV, pg 464
Editorial El Manual Moderno SA de CV, pg 464
Editorial Esfinge SA de CV, pg 465
Centro de Estudios Monetarios Latinoamericanos (CEMLA), pg 465
Fernandez Editores SA de CV, pg 465
Grupo Editorial Iberoamerica, SA de CV, pg 466
Editorial Herrero SA, pg 466
Editorial Jus SA de CV, pg 467
Phillip Richard Conover Lazo, pg 467
Editorial Limusa SA de CV, pg 467
Instituto Nacional de Antropologia e Historia, pg 469
Pearson Educacion de Mexico, SA de CV, pg 470

Plaza y Valdes SA de CV, pg 470
Publicaciones Cultural SA de CV, pg 471
Sistemas Tecnicos de Edicion SA de CV, pg 472
Sistemas Universales, SA, pg 472
Editorial Trillas SA de CV, pg 472
Universidad Nacional Autonoma de Mexico (National University of Mexico), pg 472
Universidad Veracruzana Direccion General Editorial y de Publicaciones, pg 472
Universo Editorial SA de CV Edicion de Libros Revistas y Periodicos, pg 473

Republic of Moldova
Editura Lumina, pg 473

Morocco
Cabinet Conseil CCMLA, pg 474
Dar Nachr Al Maarifa Pour L'Edition et La Distribution, pg 474

Mozambique
Empresa Moderna Lda, pg 475
Editora Minerva Central, pg 475

Myanmar
Hanthawaddy Book House, pg 475

Namibia
Desert Research Foundation of Namibia (DRFN), pg 476
Gamsberg Macmillan Publishers (Pty) Ltd, pg 476

Nepal
International Standards Books & Periodicals (P) Ltd, pg 476
Sajha Prakashan, Co-operative Publishing Organization, pg 477

Netherlands
Uitgeverij Jan van Arkel, pg 478
A A Balkema Uitgevers BV, pg 478
Uitgeverij Coutinho BV, pg 481
De Graaf Publishers, pg 481
Katholieke Bijbelstichting, pg 484
Uitgeverij J H Kok BV, pg 485
Uitgeverij Lemma BV, pg 485
Uitgeverij Meinema, pg 485
Uitgeverij H Nelissen BV, pg 486
Oriental Press BV (APA), pg 487
A J G Strengholt's Boeken, Anno 1928, BV, pg 489
ThiemeMeulenhoff, pg 490
Twente University Press, pg 490
Van Gorcum & Comp BV, pg 491
Wolters-Noordhoff B V, pg 492

New Zealand
Aoraki Press Ltd, pg 493
Brookers Ltd, pg 494
Butterworths New Zealand Ltd, pg 494
Dunmore Press Ltd, pg 495
ESA Publications (NZ) Ltd, pg 496
Learning Guides (Writers & Publishers Ltd), pg 497
Legislation Direct, pg 498
Macmillan Publishers New Zealand Ltd, pg 498
Moss Associates Ltd, pg 498
Oxford University Press, pg 499
Pearson Education (PENZ), pg 500
Reach Publications, pg 500

RSVP Publishing Co Ltd, pg 500
University of Otago Press, pg 502

Nigeria
ABIC Books & Equipment Ltd, pg 503
African Universities Press, pg 503
Africana-FEP Publishers Ltd, pg 503
Ahmadu Bello University Press Ltd, pg 503
Albah Publishers, pg 503
Aromolaran Publishing Co Ltd, pg 503
Cross Continent Press Ltd, pg 504
Ethiope Publishing Corporation, pg 504
Evans Brothers (Nigeria Publishers) Ltd, pg 504
Fourth Dimension Publishing Co Ltd, pg 504
Goldland Business Co Ltd, pg 505
Ibadan University Press, pg 505
Longman Nigeria Plc, pg 505
Thomas Nelson (Nigeria) Ltd, pg 505
New Africa Publishing Company Ltd, pg 505
New Horn Press Ltd, pg 506
Northern Nigerian Publishing Co Ltd, pg 506
Nwamife Publishers Ltd, pg 506
Obafemi Awolowo University Press Ltd, pg 506
Onibon-Oje Publishers, pg 506
Riverside Communications, pg 507
Tabansi Press Ltd, pg 507
University of Lagos Press, pg 507
Vantage Publishers International Ltd, pg 507
West African Book Publishers Ltd, pg 507

Norway
J W Cappelens Forlag A/S, pg 508
Det Norske Samlaget, pg 508
J W Eides Forlag A/S, pg 509
Gyldendal Norsk Forlag A/S, pg 509
NKI Forlaget, pg 510
Erik Sandberg, pg 510
Teknologisk Forlag, pg 510
Universitetsforlaget, pg 511
Vett & Viten AS, pg 511

Pakistan
The Book House, pg 512
HMR Publishing Co, pg 512
Islamic Book Centre, pg 512
Jang Publishers, pg 513
National Book Foundation, pg 513
West-Pakistan Publishing Co (Pvt) Ltd, pg 515

Papua New Guinea
Kristen Press, pg 515

Paraguay
Intercontinental Editora, pg 516

Peru
Ediciones Brown SA, pg 516
Asociacion Editorial Bruno, pg 516
Carvajal SA, pg 516
Instituto de Estudios Peruanos, pg 517
Libreria Studium SA, pg 517
Universidad de Lima-Fondo de Desarollo Editorial, pg 517

Universidad Nacional Mayor de San Marcos, pg 517
Editorial Universo SA, pg 517

Philippines
Ateneo de Manila University Press, pg 518
Bookman Printing & Publishing House Inc, pg 518
Bright Concepts Printing House, pg 518
Communication Foundation for Asia Media Group (CFAMG), pg 518
De La Salle University, pg 519
Garotech, pg 519
Marren Publishing House, Inc, pg 519
National Book Store Inc, pg 519
New Day Publishers, pg 520
Our Lady of Manaoag Publisher, pg 520
Philippine Education Co Inc, pg 520
Rex Bookstores & Publishers, pg 520
Salesiana Publishers Inc, pg 521
SIBS Publishing House Inc, pg 521
Sinag-Tala Publishers Inc, pg 521
UST Publishing House, pg 521

Poland
Wydawnictwo DiG, pg 522
Polskie Wydawnictwo Ekonomiczne PWE SA, pg 522
Gdanskie Wydawnictwo Psychologiczne SC, pg 523
Impuls, pg 523
Katolicki Uniwersytet Wydawniczo-Redakcja, pg 523
Wydawnictwo Medyczne Urban & Partner, pg 524
Wydawnictwa Naukowo-Techniczne, pg 524
Panstwowe Wydawnictwo Rolnicze i Lesne, pg 525
Polish Scientific Publishers PWN, pg 525
Oficyna Wydawnicza Politechniki Wroclawskiej, pg 525
PZWL Wydawnictwo Lekarskie Ltd, pg 526
Res Polona, pg 526
Wydawnictwa Szkolne i Pedagogiczne, pg 527
Wydawnictwa Uniwersytetu Warszawskiego, pg 527
Wydawnictwo Uniwersytetu Wroclawskiego SP ZOO, pg 527

Portugal
Livraria Almedina, pg 528
Livraria Arnado Lda, pg 528
Basica Editora, pg 529
Biblioteca Geral da Universidade de Coimbra, pg 529
Centro Estudos Geograficos, pg 529
Edicoes Colibri, pg 530
Edicoes Cosmos, pg 530
Dinalivro, pg 530
Publicacoes Europa-America Lda, pg 531
Europress Editores e Distribuidores de Publicacoes Lda, pg 531
Imprensa Nacional-Casa da Moeda, pg 532
Livraria Apostolado da Imprensa, pg 533
Livraria Luzo-Espanhola Lda, pg 533
Livraria Minerva, pg 533
Livros Horizonte Lda, pg 533

Lua Viajante-Edicao e Distribuicao de Livros e Material Audiovisual, Lda, pg 533
Editora McGraw-Hill de Portugal Lda, pg 533
Internationale Nouvelle Acropole, pg 534
Porto Editora Lda, pg 535
Editorial Presenca, pg 535
Quid Juris - Sociedade Editora, pg 535
Quimera Editores Lda, pg 535
Edicioes Joao Sa da Costa Lda, pg 535
Sa da Costa Livraria, pg 535
Edicoes 70 Lda, pg 535
Edicoes Silabo, pg 536
Almerinda Teixeira, pg 536
Vega-Publicacao e Distribuicao de Livros e Revistas, Lda, pg 536

Puerto Rico
Editorial Cultural Inc, pg 537
Libros-Ediciones Homines, pg 537
Ediciones Huracan Inc, pg 537
McGraw-Hill Intermericana del Caribe, Inc, pg 537
Piedras Press, Inc, pg 537
University of Puerto Rico Press (EDUPR), pg 537

Romania
Editura Academiei Romane, pg 538
Editora All, pg 538
The Center for Romanian Studies, pg 539
Editura Ceres, pg 539
Editura Clusium, pg 539
Editura Dacia, pg 539
Editura Didactica si Pedagogica, pg 539
Editura Medicala, pg 540
Editura Niculescu, pg 541
Editura Paideia, pg 541
Polirom Verlag, pg 542
Editura Stiintifica SA, pg 542

Russian Federation
Airis Press, pg 543
Aspect Press Ltd, pg 543
N E Bauman Moscow State Technical University Publishers, pg 544
Izdatelstvo 'Ekonomika', pg 544
FGUP Izdatelstvo Mashinostroenie, pg 544
Finansy i Statistika Publishing House, pg 544
Fizmatlit Publishing Co, pg 545
Gidrometeoizdat, pg 545
INFRA-M Izdatel 'skij dom, pg 545
Izdatelstvo Kazanskago Universiteta, pg 545
Izdatelstvo Medicina, pg 546
Izdatelstvo Metallurgiya, pg 546
Izdatelstvo Mir, pg 546
Izdatelstvo Muzyka, pg 547
Nauka Publishers, pg 547
Planeta Publishers, pg 548
Izdatelstvo Prosveshchenie, pg 548
Russkij Jazyk, pg 548
St Andrew's Biblical Theological College, pg 548
Izdatelstvo Standartov, pg 549
Voronezh State University Publishers, pg 549
Izdatelstvo Vysshaya Shkola, pg 549

Saudi Arabia
King Saud University, pg 550

Senegal
Les Nouvelles Editions Africaines du Senegal NEAS, pg 551

Serbia and Montenegro
Beogradski Izdavacko-Graficki Zavod, pg 552
Gradevinska Knjiga, pg 552
Libertatea, pg 552
Minerva, pg 552
Naucna Knjiga, pg 552
Obod, pg 553
Izdavacka Organizacija Rad, pg 553
Privredni Pregled, pg 553
Radnicka Stampa, pg 553
Sluzbeni List, pg 553
Zavod za Izdavanje Udzbenika, pg 554
Zavod za udzbenike i nastavna sredstva, pg 554

Sierra Leone
Njala Educational Publishing Centre, pg 554
Sierra Leone University Press, pg 554

Singapore
APAC Publishers Services Pte Ltd, pg 554
Cannon International, pg 555
Chopsons Pte Ltd, pg 555
FEP International Private Ltd, pg 556
Hillview Publications Pte Ltd, pg 556
Institute of Southeast Asian Studies, pg 556
LexisNexis, pg 557
Pan Pacific Publications (S) Pte Ltd, pg 557
SNP Panpac Pacific Publishing Pte Ltd, pg 558
Taylor & Francis Asia Pacific, pg 558
World Scientific Publishing Co Pte Ltd, pg 559

Slovakia
Vydavatel'stvo Osveta (Verlag Osveta), pg 560
Slo Viet, pg 560
Ustav informacii a prognoz skolstva mladeze a telovychovy, pg 561

Slovenia
Mladinska Knjiga International, pg 561
Zalozba Mihelac d o o, pg 562
Zalozba Obzorja d d Maribor, pg 562

South Africa
Educum Publishers Ltd, pg 563
HAUM - Daan Retief Publishers (Pty) Ltd, pg 564
HAUM - De Jager Publishers, pg 564
HAUM (Hollandsch Afrikaansche Uitgevers Maatschappij), pg 564
Heinemann Educational Publishers Southern Africa, pg 564
Heinemann Publishers (Pty) Ltd, pg 564
Ivy Publications, pg 565
LAPA Publishers (Pty) Ltd, pg 566
LexisNexis Butterworths South Africa, pg 566
Maskew Miller Longman, pg 566
Nasou Via Afrika, pg 567
New Africa Books (Pty) Ltd, pg 567
Ravan Press (Pty) Ltd, pg 568
Unisa Press, pg 569
Van Schaik Publishers, pg 569
Witwatersrand University Press, pg 570

Spain
Editorial Acribia SA, pg 571
Agora Editorial, pg 571
Editorial Aguaclara, pg 571
Ediciones Akal SA, pg 571
Ediciones Alfar SA, pg 572
AMV Ediciones, pg 572
Ediciones Anaya SA, pg 572
Arco Libros SL, pg 573
Editorial Ariel SA, pg 573
Editorial Barcanova SA, pg 574
Antoni Bosch Editor SA, pg 574
Editorial Casals SA, pg 575
Celeste Ediciones, pg 576
Central Catequistica Salesiana (CCS), pg 576
Civitas SA Editorial, pg 577
Editorial Claret SA, pg 577
Ediciones de la Universidad Complutense de Madrid, pg 577
Complutense, SA Editorial, pg 577
Editorial Constitucion y Leyes SA - COLEX, pg 578
Ediciones Daly S L, pg 578
Editorial Deimos, SL, pg 578
Ediciones Diaz de Santos SA, pg 579
Editorial Don Quijote, pg 579
Editorial Donostiarra SA, pg 579
Editorial Dossat SA, pg 580
Dykinson SL, pg 580
Edebe, pg 580
EDERSA (Editoriales de Derecho Reunidas SA), pg 580
Ediciones Edinford SA, pg 581
Enciclopedia Catalana, SA, pg 582
Publicaciones Etea, pg 583
Eumo Editorial, pg 583
Grupo Comunicar, pg 585
Grupo Santillana de Ediciones SA, pg 586
Editorial Herder SA, pg 586
Editorial Horsori SL, pg 586
Icaria Editorial SA, pg 587
Ediciones Istmo SA, pg 588
Laertes SA de Ediciones, pg 588
Ediciones Libertarias/Prodhufi SA, pg 589
Editorial Luis Vives (Edelvives), pg 589
Macmillan Heinemann ELT, pg 590
Marcial Pons Ediciones Juridicas SA, pg 590
McGraw-Hill/Interamericana de Espana SAU, pg 591
Mundi-Prensa Libros SA, pg 592
Editorial la Muralla SA, pg 592
Narcea SA de Ediciones, pg 593
Ediciones Norma SA, pg 593
Oikos-Tau SA Ediciones, pg 593
Ediciones Omega SA, pg 594
El Paisaje Editorial, pg 594
Editorial Paraninfo SA, pg 595
Ediciones Partenon, pg 595
Pearson Educacion S A, pg 595
Editorial Playor SA, pg 596
Editorial Pliegos, pg 596
PPC Editorial y Distribuidora, SA, pg 596
Progensa, pg 597
Publicaciones de la Universidad Pontificia Comillas-Madrid, pg 597
Editorial Reus SA, pg 598
Editorial Reverte SA, pg 598
Rueda, SL Editorial, pg 598
San Pablo Ediciones, pg 598
Universidad de Santiago de Compostela, pg 599
Ediciones Scriba SA, pg 599
Secretariado Trinitario, pg 599
Servicio de Publicaciones Universidad de Cadiz, pg 599
Servicio de Publicaciones Universidad de Cordoba, pg 599
Ediciones Seyer, pg 599
Silex Ediciones, pg 600
Editorial Sintesis, SA, pg 600
Editores Tecnicos Asociados SA, pg 601
Editorial Teide SA, pg 601
Editorial Augusto E Pila Telena SL, pg 601
Editorial Sal Terrae, pg 602
Tirant lo Blanch SL Libreriaa, pg 602
Editorial Trivium, SA, pg 602
Trotta SA Editorial, pg 602
Universidad de Malaga, pg 603
Universidad de Oviedo Servicio de Publicaciones, pg 603
Ediciones Universidad de Salamanca, pg 603
Universidad de Valladolid Secretariado de Publicaciones e Intercambio Editorial, pg 604
Publicacions de la Universitat de Barcelona, pg 604
Edicions de la Universitat Politecnica de Catalunya SL, pg 604
Urmo SA de Ediciones, pg 604
Editorial Verbo Divino, pg 604
Editorial Verbum SL, pg 604
Editorial Vicens-Vives, pg 605

Sri Lanka
M D Gunasena & Co Ltd, pg 606
Inter-Cultural Book Promoters, pg 606
Ministry of Education, pg 607
Samayawardena Printers Publishers & Booksellers, pg 607
Warna Publishers, pg 607

Sudan
Khartoum University Press, pg 608

Sweden
Akademiforlaget Corona AB, pg 609
Akademiforlaget Goteborgslitteratur, pg 609
Ekelunds Forlag AB, pg 611
Ekonomibok Forlag AB, pg 611
SK-Gehrmans Musikforlag AB, pg 611
Hans Richter Laromedel, pg 613
Liber AB, pg 613
Bokfoerlaget Natur och Kultur, pg 613
Norstedts Juridik, pg 614
Bokforlaget Nya Doxa AB, pg 614
Studentlitteratur AB, pg 616
Var Skola Foerlag AB, pg 616
Verbum Foerlag AB, pg 616

Switzerland
Augustin-Verlag, pg 618
Editions de la Baconniere SA, pg 618
Birkhauser Verlag AG, pg 619
Verlag Bo Cavefors, pg 620
Marcel Dekker AG, pg 621
Verlag Harri Deutsch, pg 622

TYPE OF PUBLICATION INDEX
BOOK

Maurice et Pierre Foetisch SA, pg 623
Paul Haupt Bern, pg 625
Helbing und Lichtenhahn Verlag AG, pg 625
Editions Ides et Calendes SA, pg 625
Klett und Balmer & Co Verlag, pg 626
Kolumbus-Verlag, pg 626
Peter Lang AG, pg 627
Larousse (Suisse) SA, pg 627
Lehrmittelverlag des Kantons Zurich, pg 627
Medecine et Hygiene, pg 628
Editions H Messeiller SA, pg 628
Neue Zuercher Zeitung AG Buchverlag, pg 629
Editions Payot Lausanne, pg 631
Presses Polytechniques et Universitaires Romandes, PPUR, pg 631
Editions Pro Schola, pg 631
RECOM Verlag, pg 632
Sauerlaender AG, pg 633
Schulthess Polygraphischer Verlag AG, pg 633
Staempfli Verlag AG, pg 634
Tobler Verlag, pg 635
Trans Tech Publications SA, pg 635
Der Universitatsverlag Freiburg, pg 636

Syrian Arab Republic
Damascus University Press, pg 638

Taiwan, Province of China
Bookman Books Ltd, pg 639
Chien Chen Bookstore Publishing Company Ltd, pg 639
Chu Liu Book Company, pg 639
Chung Hwa Book Co Ltd, pg 639
Far East Book Co Ltd, pg 639
Farseeing Publishing Company Ltd, pg 639
Fuh-Wen Book Co, pg 639
Great China Book Company, pg 640
Chu Hai Publishing (Taiwan) Co Ltd, pg 640
Hsiao Yuan Publication Co, Ltd, pg 640
Laureate Book Co Ltd, pg 640
Newton Publishing Company Ltd, pg 641
San Min Book Co Ltd, pg 641
Torch of Wisdom, pg 642
World Book Co Ltd, pg 642
Wu Nan Book Co Ltd, pg 642
Yee Wen Publishing Co Ltd, pg 642
Yi Hsien Publishing Co Ltd, pg 642
Youth Cultural Publishing Co, pg 642

United Republic of Tanzania
DUP (1996) Ltd, pg 643
East African Publishing House, pg 643
Emmaus Bible School, pg 643
Oxford University Press, pg 644
Press & Publicity Centre Ltd, pg 644
Readit Books, pg 644
Tanzania Publishing House, pg 644

Thailand
Akson Charerntat (S/B Akson), pg 645
Graphic Art (28) Co Ltd, pg 645
Odeon Store LP, pg 645
Prasan Mit, pg 645
Ruamsarn (1977) Co Ltd, pg 645
Suksapan Panit (Business Organization of Teachers Council of Thailand), pg 645
Thai Watana Panich Co, Ltd, pg 646
Watthana Phanit, pg 646

Togo
Editions Akpagnon, pg 646

Trinidad & Tobago
Charran's Educational Publishers, pg 647

Tunisia
Academie Tunisienne des Sciences, des Lettres et des Arts Beit El Hekma, pg 647
Maison Tunisienne de l'Edition, pg 648

Turkey
Alkim Kitapcilik-Yayimcilik, pg 649
Altin Kitaplar Yayinevi, pg 649
Arkadas Ltd, pg 649
Caglayan Kitabevi, pg 649
Inkilap Publishers Ltd, pg 650
Pearson Education Turkey, pg 651
Yetkin Printing & Publishing Co Inc, pg 652

Uganda
Fountain Publishers Ltd, pg 652
Roce (Consultants) Ltd, pg 653

Ukraine
ASK Ltd, pg 653
Osnova, Kharkov State University Press, pg 653
Osvita, pg 654

United Kingdom
Acumen Publishing Ltd, pg 655
Aslib, The Association for Information Management, pg 660
Association for Scottish Literary Studies, pg 661
BAAF Adoption & Fostering, pg 662
Berg Publishers, pg 664
BILD Publications, pg 665
BIOS Scientific Publishers Ltd, pg 665
Blackwell Science Ltd, pg 667
Blueprint, pg 668
Books for Europe Ltd, pg 669
BPS Books (British Psychological Society), pg 670
Butterworths Tolley, pg 673
Cambridge University Press, pg 674
Jon Carpenter Publishing, pg 675
Cassell & Co, pg 675
Causeway Press Ltd, pg 676
Cavendish Publishing Ltd, pg 676
Colourpoint Books, pg 681
Computer Step, pg 681
CTBI Publications, pg 685
Curiad, pg 685
Elm Publications, pg 691
Estates Gazette, pg 692
Ethics International Press Ltd, pg 692
European Schoolbooks Ltd, pg 692
The Eurospan Group, pg 692
Facet Publishing, pg 694
Financial Training Co, pg 694
Flicks Books, pg 695
Forbes Publications Ltd, pg 696
W H Freeman & Co Ltd, pg 697
David Fulton Publishers Ltd, pg 698
The Geographical Association, pg 699
W Green The Scottish Law Publisher, pg 702
HarperCollins UK, pg 705
Hodder Headline Ltd, pg 709
Horizon Scientific Press, pg 710
ICC United Kingdom, pg 711
ICSA Publishing Ltd, pg 711
Immediate Publishing, pg 712
Impart Books, pg 712
Imperial College Press, pg 712
Institute of Financial Services, pg 712
Institute of Physics Publishing, pg 713
IOM Communications Ltd, pg 714
ITDG Publishing, pg 715
Jones & Bartlett International, pg 716
Laurence King Publishing Ltd, pg 717
Kluwer Academic/Plenum Publishers, pg 718
Learning Matters Ltd, pg 720
Liverpool University Press, pg 722
Macmillan Heinemann ELT, pg 723
Macmillan, pg 723
Management Books 2000 Ltd, pg 724
Manchester University Press, pg 724
Marcham Manor Press, pg 725
Mars Business Associates Ltd, pg 725
McGraw-Hill Publishing Company, pg 726
The Merlin Press Ltd, pg 727
Micelle Press, pg 727
Motilal (UK) Books of India, pg 729
Multilingual Matters Ltd, pg 729
National Association for the Teaching of English (NATE), pg 730
Nelson Thornes Ltd, pg 732
Open University Press, pg 736
Osborne Books Ltd, pg 736
Oxford University Press, pg 737
Packard Publishing Ltd, pg 737
Palgrave Publishers Ltd, pg 737
PC Publishing, pg 739
Pearson Education Europe, Mideast & Africa, pg 739
Pergamon Flexible Learning, pg 740
Pharmaceutical Press, pg 741
Portland Press Ltd, pg 745
Professional Engineering Publishing Ltd, pg 745
Ramakrishna Vedanta Centre, pg 747
Reardon Publishing, pg 748
Reed Educational & Professional Publishing, pg 749
RoutledgeCurzon, pg 751
SCM-Canterbury Press Ltd, pg 755
Seren, pg 756
Colin Smythe Ltd, pg 759
The Society for Promoting Christian Knowledge (SPCK), pg 759
Spon Press, pg 760
Stokesby House Publications, pg 761
Sweet & Maxwell Ltd, pg 762
I B Tauris & Co Ltd, pg 763
Taylor & Francis, pg 763
Taylor & Francis Medical Books, pg 763
The Tarragon Press, pg 765
Trentham Books Ltd, pg 767
University of Wales Press, pg 769
Verulam Publishing Ltd, pg 770
Whittles Publishing, pg 773
Windhorse Publications, pg 774
WIT Press, pg 774

Uruguay
Barreiro y Ramos SA, pg 777
Ediciones de Juan Darien, pg 777
EQ Opciones en Educacion, pg 777
Fundacion de Cultura Universitaria, pg 777
Mosca Hermanos, pg 777
Prensa Medica Latinoamericana, pg 778
Vinten Editor, pg 778

Venezuela
Alfadil Ediciones, pg 778
Editorial Biosfera CA, pg 779
Ediciones Vega SRL, pg 780

Viet Nam
Science & Technics Publishing House, pg 780
Trung-Tam San Xuat Hoc-Lieu, pg 781

Zambia
Historical Association of Zambia, pg 781
Lundula Publishing House, pg 781
Zambia Printing Company Ltd (ZPC), pg 782

Zimbabwe
Academic Books (Pvt) Ltd, pg 782
College Press Publishers (Pvt) Ltd, pg 783
Mercury Press Pvt Ltd, pg 784
University of Zimbabwe Publications, pg 784
Zimbabwe Foundation for Education with Production (ZIMFEP), pg 784
Zimbabwe Publishing House (Pvt) Ltd, pg 784

TRANSLATIONS

Albania
Botimpex Publications Import-Export Agency, pg 1
NL SH, pg 1
State Textbook Publishing House, pg 1

Argentina
Ada Korn Editora SA, pg 3
Beatriz Viterbo Editora, pg 4
Ediciones Minotauro SA, pg 7
Instituto de Publicaciones Navales, pg 8
Oikos, pg 8

Armenia
Arevik, pg 10

Australia
Aeolian Press, pg 11
Bayda Books, pg 14
Boombana Publications, pg 16
Bridge To Peace Publications, pg 16
Gangan Publishing, pg 23
Gnostic Editions, pg 23
Illert Publications, pg 26
Owl Publishing, pg 35
Papyrus Publishing, pg 35
Pearson Education Australia, pg 36
Pollitecon Publications, pg 37
Regency Publishing, pg 39

PUBLISHERS — TYPE OF PUBLICATION INDEX

Austria
Annette Betz Verlag im Verlag Carl Ueberreuter, pg 48
Doecker Verlag GmbH & Co KG, pg 50
Literature Verlag Droschl, pg 50
Ennsthaler GesmbH & Co KG, pg 50
Gangan Verlag, pg 51
Haymon-Verlag GesmbH, pg 51
oebv & hpt Verlagsgesellschaft mbH & Co KG, pg 55
Springer-Verlag Wien, pg 58
Dr Otfried Weise Verlag Tabula Smaragdina, pg 59

Bangladesh
Gatidhara, pg 61
Gono Prakashani, Gono Shasthya Kendra, pg 61

Belarus
Interdigest Publishing House, pg 62

Belgium
EPO Publishers, Printers, Booksellers, pg 67
Koepel van de Vlaamse Noord - Zuidbeweging 11.11.11, pg 69
La Longue Vue, pg 70
Zuid-Nederlandse Uitgeverij NV/Central Uitgeverij, pg 75

Bosnia and Herzegovina
Bemust, pg 76

Brazil
Agalma Psicanalise Editora Ltda, pg 77
Editora Agora Ltda, pg 77
Editora Alfa Omega Ltda, pg 77
Editora Antroposofica Ltda, pg 77
Ao Livro Tecnico Industria e Comercio Ltda, pg 77
Editora Campus Ltda, pg 79
Centro de Estudos Juridicosdo Para (CEJUP), pg 79
Editora Companhia das Letras/ Editora Schwarcz Ltda, pg 80
Dumara Distribuidora de Publicacoes Ltda, pg 81
Companhia Editora Forense, pg 81
EDUSC - Editora da Universidade do Sagrado Coracao, pg 81
Fundacao Cultural Avatar, pg 82
Fundacao Sao Paulo, EDUC, pg 82
Editora Harbra Ltda, pg 83
Imago Editora Importacao e Exportacao Ltda, pg 84
LDA Editores Ltda, pg 84
Editora Logosofica, pg 85
Editora Marco Zero Ltda, pg 86
Medicina Panamericana Editora Do Brasil Ltda, pg 86
Editora Mercuryo Ltda, pg 86
Editora Mundo Cristao, pg 87
Editora Nova Alexandria Ltda, pg 87
Editora Nova Fronteira SA, pg 87
Paulinas Editorial, pg 88
Pearson Education Do Brasil, pg 88
Ediouro Publicacoes, SA, pg 89
Qualitymark Editora Ltda, pg 89
Editora Revan Ltda, pg 89
Livraria Editora Revinter Ltda, pg 89
Summus Editorial Ltda, pg 91
Tempus Editores, pg 91
34 Literatura S/C Ltda, pg 91
Triom Centro de Estudos Marina e Martin Hawey Editorial e Comercial Ltda, pg 91
Editora UNESP, pg 91
Editora Universidade Federal do Rio de Janeiro, pg 92
Jorge Zahar Editor, pg 92

Bulgaria
Abagar, Veliko Tarnovo, pg 93
Aratron, IK, pg 93
DA-Izdatelstvo Publishers, pg 93
Dolphin Press Group Ltd, pg 94
EA EOOD, pg 94
Eurasia Academic Publishers, pg 94
Fama, pg 94
Gea-Libris Publishing House, pg 94
Hermes Publishing House, pg 94
Heron Press Publishing House, pg 94
Hriker, pg 94
Pejo K Javorov Publishing House, pg 95
Kibea Publishing Co, pg 95
Kralica MAB, pg 95
LIK Izdanija, pg 95
MATEX, pg 95
Musica Publishing House Ltd, pg 95
Naouka i Izkoustvo, Ltd, pg 95
Narodna Kultura, pg 96
Nov Covek Publishing House, pg 96
Prosveta Publishers AS, pg 96
Prozoretz Ltd Publishing House, pg 96
Seven Hills Publishers, pg 96
Sila & Zivot, pg 97

Chile
Editorial Cuatro Vientos, pg 99

China
Beijing Publishing House, pg 101
Beijing University Press, pg 101
Chemical Industry Press, pg 101
China Film Press, pg 102
China Machine Press (CMP), pg 102
China Translation & Publishing Corp, pg 103
Chinese Pedagogics Publishing House, pg 103
Cultural Relics Publishing House, pg 103
Electronics Industry Publishing House, pg 104
Foreign Languages Press, pg 104
Fudan University Press, pg 104
Guizhou Education Publishing House, pg 105
Heilongjiang Science & Technology Press, pg 105
Higher Education Press, pg 105
Inner Mongolia Science & Technology Publishing House, pg 105
Kunlun Publishing House, pg 106
Lanzhou University Press, pg 106
Morning Glory Press, pg 106
Shandong Friendship Publishing House, pg 107
Shandong University Press, pg 108
Shanghai College of Traditional Chinese Medicine Press, pg 108
Shanghai Foreign Language Education Press, pg 108
South China University of Science & Technology Press, pg 108
Tianjin Science & Technology Publishing House, pg 108
World Affairs Press, pg 109
Writers' Publishing House, pg 109
Yunnan University Press, pg 109
Zhong Hua Book Co, pg 110

Colombia
Asociacion Instituto Linguistico de Verano, pg 110
Universidad Externado de Colombia, pg 111
Editorial Oveja Negra Ltda, pg 112
Editorial Panamericana, pg 112
Tercer Mundo Editores SA, pg 113

The Democratic Republic of the Congo
Saint-Paul, pg 114

Costa Rica
Editorial Texto Ltda, pg 116

Cote d'Ivoire
Heritage Publishing Co, pg 117

Croatia
ArTresor naklada, pg 117
Durieux d o o, pg 118
Faust Vrani, pg 118
Matica hrvatska, pg 118
Znaci Vremena, Institut Za Istrazivanje Biblije, pg 119

Czech Republic
Atlantis sro, pg 122
Aurora, pg 122
Barrister & Principal, pg 122
Chvojkova nakladatelstvi, pg 123
Columbus, pg 123
Horacek Ladislav-Paseka, pg 123
Nakladatelstvi Jota spol sro, pg 124
Kalich SRO, pg 124
Karmelitanske Nakladatelstvi, pg 124
Karolinum, nakladatelstvi, pg 124
Lidove Noviny Publishing House, pg 125
Lyra Pragensis Obecne Prospelna Spolecnost, pg 125
Mariadan, pg 125
Pavla Momcilova, pg 125
Cesky normalizacni institut, pg 126
Portal spol sro, pg 126
Prostor, nakladatelstvi sro, pg 127
Psychoanalyticke Nakladatelstvi, pg 127
Slon Sociologicke Nakladatelstvi, pg 127
Svoboda Servis GmbH, pg 127
Votobia sro, pg 128

Denmark
Forlaget alokke AS, pg 129
Dansk Psykologisk Forlag, pg 130
P Haase & Sons Forlag A/S, pg 131
Holkenfeldt 3, pg 132
Forlaget Hovedland, pg 132
New Era Publications International ApS, pg 133
Samfundslitteratur, pg 134
Samlerens Forlag A/S, pg 134
Wisby & Wilkens, pg 135

Egypt (Arab Republic of Egypt)
Dar El Shorouk, pg 138
Elias Modern Publishing House, pg 138

Estonia
Kirjastus Kunst, pg 139
Olion Publishers, pg 140
Perioodika, pg 140
Sinisukk, pg 140
Tuum, pg 140
Valgus Publishers, pg 140

Finland
Kaantopiiri Oy, pg 142
Koala-Kustannus Oy, pg 143
Lasten Keskus Oy, pg 143
Otava Publishing Co Ltd, pg 143
Yliopistopaino/Helsinki University Press, pg 145

France
ATP - Packager, pg 148
Editions de l'Aube, pg 148
Editions des Beatitudes, Pneumatheque, pg 149
Editions Andre Bonne, pg 150
Bragelonne, pg 151
Emgleo Breiz, pg 151
Alain Brethes Editions, pg 151
Brud Nevez, pg 151
Editions Buchet-Chastel Pierre Zech Editeur, pg 151
CERDIC-Publications, pg 153
Editions Jose Corti, pg 156
Editions La Decouverte, pg 157
Doin Editeurs, pg 159
Dunod Editeur, pg 159
Les Editeurs Reunis, pg 160
Association Frank, pg 164
Editions Infrarouge, pg 168
Les Editions Interferences, pg 169
Jouvence Editions, pg 170
Langues & Mondes-L'Asiatheque, pg 171
P Lethielleux Editions, pg 171
Macula, pg 173
Masson-Williams et Wilkins, pg 174
Editions A M Metailie, pg 175
Noir Sur Blanc, pg 177
Editions Odile Jacob, pg 177
Presses de la Sorbonne Nouvelle/ PSN, pg 181
Les Presses du Management, pg 181
Presses Universitaires de Caen, pg 181
Publications Orientalistes de France (POF), pg 182
Editions de Septembre, pg 184
Editions Stock, pg 186
Terre Vivante, pg 187
Editions Thames & Hudson, pg 187
TOP Editions, pg 188

French Polynesia
Haere Po Editions, pg 189

Germany
A Francke Verlag (Tubingen und Basel), pg 190
ARCult Media, pg 193
Ars Edition GmbH, pg 194
Babel Verlag Kevin Perryman, pg 196
Beck & Gluckler Verlag GmbH & Co KG, pg 198
Blaukreuz-Verlag Wuppertal, pg 202
BLV Verlagsgesellschaft mbH, pg 202
Claudius Verlag, pg 209
ComMedia & Arte Verlag Bernd Mayer, pg 209
J G Cotta'sche Buchhandlung Nachfolger GmbH, pg 210
Deutscher Taschenbuch Verlag GmbH & Co KG (dtv), pg 213
Donat Verlag, pg 215
Egmont vgs verlagsgesellschaft mbH, pg 218
Europa Verlag GmbH, pg 222

TYPE OF PUBLICATION INDEX

BOOK

Genius Verlag, pg 228
GLB Parkland Verlags-und Vertriebs GmbH, pg 229
Carl Hanser Verlag, pg 234
Heel Verlag GmbH, pg 235
Edition Hentrich Druck & Verlag Gebr Hentrich und Tank GmbH & Co KG, pg 236
Anton Hiersemann, Verlag, pg 237
Edition Humanistische Psychologie (EHP), pg 240
Huthig GmbH & Co KG, pg 240
Edition ID-Archiv/ID-Verlag, pg 240
Klaus Isele, pg 242
Iudicium Verlag GmbH, pg 242
Keip GmbH, pg 245
Kolibri-Verlag GmbH, pg 249
KONTEXTverlag, pg 249
Krug & Schadenberg, pg 250
Verlag Ernst Kuhn, pg 250
Matthias-Gruenewald-Verlag GmbH, pg 258
mentis Verlag GmbH, pg 259
Merlin Verlag Andreas Meyer Verlags GmbH und Co KG, pg 259
Midena Verlag, pg 260
Mohr Siebeck, pg 261
Neuthor - Verlag, pg 265
nymphenburger, pg 266
Palmyra Verlag, pg 268
Propylaeen Verlag, Zweigniederlassung Berlin der Ullstein Buchverlage GmbH, pg 272
Psychologie Verlags Union GmbH, pg 272
Quintessenz Verlags-GmbH, pg 273
Verlagsgruppe Reise Know-How, pg 275
Romiosini Verlag, pg 276
Ruetten & Loening Berlin GmbH, pg 277
Schoeffling & Co, pg 281
Springer Science+Business Media GmbH & Co KG, pg 284
Steiger Verlag, pg 287
Franz Steiner Verlag Wiesbaden GmbH, pg 287
Straelener Manuskripte Verlag GmbH, pg 288
Transpress Verlagsgesellschaft mbH, pg 292
Trotzdem-Verlags Genossenschaft eG, pg 292
Unrast Verlag e V, pg 293
Vervuert Verlagsgesellschaft, pg 295
Friedr Vieweg & Sohn Verlag, pg 296
Verlag Klaus Wagenbach, pg 297
Wiley-VCH Verlag GmbH, pg 300
Das Wunderhorn Verlag GmbH, pg 301

Ghana

Ghana Institute of Linguistics Literacy & Bible Translation (GILLBT), pg 304

Greece

Beta Medical Publishers, pg 306
Chrysi Penna - Golden Pen Books, pg 306
Diavlos, pg 306
Govostis Publishing SA, pg 307
Denise Harvey, pg 308
Hestia-I D Hestia-Kollaros & Co Corporation, pg 308
Hiotellis P, pg 308
Kalentis & Sia, pg 308
Kastaniotis Editions SA, pg 309

Kedros Publishers, pg 309
Kritiki Publishing, pg 309
Editions Moressopoulos, pg 310
Morfotiko Idryma Ethnikis Trapezas, pg 310
Nakas Music House, pg 310
Odysseas Publications Ltd, pg 311
Opera, pg 311
Patakis Publishers, pg 311
Psichogios Publications SA, pg 311

Hong Kong

The Chinese University Press, pg 316
Peace Book Co Ltd, pg 318
Philopsychy Press, pg 318
Research Centre for Translation, pg 319
Sun Mui Press, pg 319

Hungary

Advent Kiado, pg 320
Aranyhal Konyvkiado Goldfish Publishing, pg 320
Atlantisz Kiado, pg 320
Balassi Kiado Kft, pg 321
Jelenkor Verlag, pg 322
Joszoveg Muhely Kiado, pg 322
Mora Ferenc Ifjusagi Koenyvkiado Rt, pg 323
Panem, pg 324
Park Konyvkiado Kft (Park Publisher), pg 324
Polgar Kiado Kft, pg 324

Iceland

Frjals fjolmiolun hf-Urvalsbaekur, pg 325
Mal og menning, pg 326

India

Addison-Wesley Pte Ltd, pg 327
Agricole Publishing Academy, pg 327
Bani Mandir, Book-Sellers, Publishers & Educational Suppliers, pg 329
Dutta Publishing Co Ltd, pg 333
Islamic Publishing House, pg 338
Kali For Women, pg 339
Oxford University Press, pg 344
Parimal Prakashan, pg 345
Pitambar Publishing Co (P) Ltd, pg 345
Prabhat Prakashan, pg 345
Pratibha Pratishthan, pg 345
Sasta Sahitya Mandal, pg 348
Tara Publishing, pg 351

Indonesia

Andi Offset, pg 353
PT Indira, pg 355
Institut Teknologi Bandung, pg 355
Karya Anda, CV, pg 355
Mizan, pg 355
Nusa Indah, pg 356
Yayasan Obor Indonesia, pg 357

Ireland

Clo Iar-Chonnachta Teo, pg 358
The Goldsmith Press Ltd, pg 360

Israel

The Bialik Institute, pg 365
Bitan Publishers Ltd, pg 365
Breslov Research Institute, pg 365
DAT Publications, pg 366
Gefen Publishing House Ltd, pg 367

Hakibbutz Hameuchad Publishing House Ltd, pg 367
The Institute for Israeli Arabs Studies, pg 368
The Institute for the Translation of Hebrew Literature, pg 368
Israel Exploration Society, pg 368
Mirkam Publishers, pg 370
Nehora Press, pg 371
Schocken Publishing House Ltd, pg 371
Shalem Press, pg 372
Steinhart-Katzir Publishers, pg 372
Urim Publications, pg 373

Italy

Editore Armando Armando SRL, pg 376
BeMa, pg 377
Centro Biblico, pg 381
Edizioni Centro Studi Erickson, pg 381
CIC Edizioni Internazionali, pg 381
Cittadella Editrice, pg 382
Edizioni Dedalo SRL, pg 384
Edistudio, pg 386
Edizioni Qiqajon, pg 387
ERGA SNC di Carla Ottino Merli & C (Edizioni Realizzazioni Grafiche - Artigiana), pg 388
Jouvence, pg 394
Kaos Edizioni SRL, pg 394
Levante Editori, pg 395
La Luna, pg 396
Luni, pg 396
Pitagora Editrice SRL, pg 403
Rubbettino Editore, pg 406
Societa Stampa Sportiva, pg 408
Transeuropa, pg 410

Japan

Bunkasha Publishing Co Ltd, pg 415
Chikuma Shobo Publishing Co Ltd, pg 416
Contex Corporation, pg 416
The Hokuseido Press, pg 418
Iwanami Shoten, Publishers, pg 419
Japan Broadcast Publishing Co Ltd, pg 419
Kosei Publishing Co Ltd, pg 421
Myrtos Inc, pg 423
Nakayama Shoten Co Ltd, pg 423
Nigensha Publishing Co Ltd, pg 423
Nippon Hoso Shuppan Kyokai (NHK Publishing), pg 424
Ohmsha Ltd, pg 424
Pearson Education Japan, pg 425
President Inc, pg 425
Sanshusha Publishing Co, Ltd, pg 426
Shincho-Sha Co Ltd, pg 427
Shufunotomo Co Ltd, pg 428
Sobun-Sha, pg 428
Tamagawa University Press, pg 429
Toho Book Store, pg 429
Toppan Co Ltd, pg 430
Tsukiji Shokan Publishing Co, pg 430
Yohan Shuppan, pg 431

Jordan

Al-Tanwir Al Ilmi (Scientific Enlightenment Publishing House), pg 432

Kenya

Focus Publications Ltd, pg 433
Heinemann Kenya Ltd (EAEP), pg 434
Kenway Publications Ltd, pg 434

Life Challenge AFRICA, pg 435
Paulines Publications-Africa, pg 435

Democratic People's Republic of Korea

The Foreign Language Press Group, pg 436
Grand People's Study House, pg 436

Republic of Korea

B & B, pg 437
Cheong-mun-gag Publishing Co, pg 438
Chung Rim Publishing Co Ltd, pg 438
Gim-Yeong Co, pg 438
Iljo-gag Publishers, pg 439
Koreaone Press Inc, pg 440
Minjisa Publishing Co, pg 441
Nanam Publications Co, pg 441
Woongjin.com Co Ltd, pg 443
YBM/Si-sa, pg 443
Yeha Publishing Co, pg 443

Latvia

Alberts XII, pg 444
Artava Ltd, pg 444
Hermess Ltd, pg 444
Nordik/Tapals Publishers Ltd, pg 445
Patmos, izdevnieciba, pg 445
Preses Nams, pg 445
Vaidelote, SIA, pg 445
Vieda, SIA, pg 445

Lebanon

Dar El Ilm Lilmalayin, pg 446
Librairie Orientale sal, pg 446
World Book Publishing, pg 447

Liechtenstein

Frank P van Eck Publishers, pg 448

Lithuania

Andrena Publishers, pg 448
Dargenis Publishers, pg 449
Klaipedos Universiteto Leidykla, pg 449
Lietus Ltd, pg 449
Lietuvos Rasytoju Sajungos Leidykla, pg 449
Margi Rastai Publishers, pg 449
Scena, pg 449
Sviesa Publishers, pg 449
Svietimo ir mokslo ministerijos Leidybos centras, pg 449
TEV Leidykla, pg 450
Tyto Alba Publishers, pg 450

Luxembourg

Varkki Verghese, pg 452

The Former Yugoslav Republic of Macedonia

Detska radost, pg 452
Mi-An Knigoizdatelstvo, pg 452
Strk Publishing House, pg 453
Zumpres Publishing Firm, pg 453

Malaysia

Darulfikir, pg 455
Federal Publications Sdn Bhd, pg 455
MDC Publishers Printers Sdn Bhd, pg 457
Penerbit Jayatinta Sdn Bhd, pg 458
Penerbit Universiti Sains Malaysia, pg 458

PUBLISHERS

Penerbitan Tinta, pg 458
Pustaka Cipta Sdn Bhd, pg 458
Pustaka Delta Pelajaran Sdn Bhd, pg 458
Tempo Publishing (M) Sdn Bhd, pg 458
Tropical Press Sdn Bhd, pg 459

Maldive Islands
Non-Formal Education Centre, pg 459

Malta
Media Centre, pg 460

Mauritius
Editions de l'Ocean Indien Ltd, pg 461

Mexico
AGT Editor SA, pg 462
Centro de Estudios Mexicanos y Centroamericanos, pg 463
Editorial Diana SA de CV, pg 464
Edamex SA de CV, pg 464
Editorial El Manual Moderno SA de CV, pg 464
Ediciones Exclusivas SA, pg 465
Editorial Fata Morgana SA de CV, pg 465
Fondo de Cultura Economica, pg 465
Libra Editorial SA de CV, pg 467
Sistemas Tecnicos de Edicion SA de CV, pg 472
Editorial Trillas SA de CV, pg 472
Universidad Veracruzana Direccion General Editorial y de Publicaciones, pg 472

Morocco
Association de la Recherche Historique et Sociale, pg 474

Namibia
Desert Research Foundation of Namibia (DRFN), pg 476

Netherlands
Uitgeverij Arena BV, pg 478
Uitgeverij Jan van Arkel, pg 478
Erven J Bijleveld, pg 479
Business Contact BV, pg 480
BZZTOH Publishers, pg 480
Cadans, pg 480
De Harmonie Uitgeverij, pg 483
Historische Uitgeverij, pg 483
Katholieke Bijbelstichting, pg 484
J M Meulenhoff bv, pg 486
Nederlands Literair Produktie-en Vertalingen Fonds (NLPVF), pg 486
Podium Uitgeverij, pg 487
Prometheus, pg 488
Scriptum, pg 488
Swets & Zeitlinger Publishers, pg 489
Telos Boeken, pg 490
Tirion Uitgevers BV, pg 490
Uitgeverij G A van Oorschot bv, pg 491

New Zealand
Spinal Publications New Zealand Ltd, pg 501

Nigeria
Riverside Communications, pg 507

Norway
Pax Forlag A/S, pg 510
Solum Forlag A/S, pg 510

Pakistan
Islamic Publications (Pvt) Ltd, pg 513
Maqbool Academy, pg 513
Sang-e-Meel Publications, pg 514
Vanguard Books Ltd, pg 515

Peru
Instituto de Estudios Peruanos, pg 517

Philippines
Ateneo de Manila University Press, pg 518
De La Salle University, pg 519

Poland
Wydawnictwo Dolnoslaskie, pg 522
Gdanskie Wydawnictwo Psychologiczne SC, pg 523
Ksiaznica Publishing Ltd, pg 524
Wydawnictwo Literackie, pg 524
Magnum Publishing House Ltd, pg 524
Wydawnictwo Medyczne Urban & Partner, pg 524
Wydawnictwa Naukowo-Techniczne, pg 524
Ossolineum Zaklad Narodowy im Ossolinskich - Wydawnictwo, pg 525
Wydawnictwo Podsiedlik-Raniowski i Spolka, pg 525
Wydawnictwa Przemyslowe WEMA, pg 526
Oficyna Wydawnicza Read Me, pg 526
'Slask' Ltd, pg 526
Videograf II Sp z o o Zaklad Poracy Chronionej, pg 527
Wydawnictwo WAB, pg 527

Portugal
Edicoes Cetop, pg 529
Editora Classica, pg 530
Edicoes Colibri, pg 530
Dinalivro, pg 530
Editorial Estampa, Lda, pg 531
Europress Editores e Distribuidores de Publicacoes Lda, pg 531
Gradiva-Publicacnoes Lda, pg 532
Livraria Apostolado da Imprensa, pg 533
Livraria Minerva, pg 533
Quimera Editores Lda, pg 535
Editora Replicacao Lda, pg 535
Edicoes 70 Lda, pg 535
Edicoes Talento, pg 536

Romania
Editura Academiei Romane, pg 538
Editura Aius, pg 538
Ars Longa Publishing House, pg 538
Artemis Verlag, pg 538
Editura Clusium, pg 539
Editura Dacia, pg 539
Editura Didactica si Pedagogica, pg 539
Enzyklopadie Verlag, pg 539
Editura Excelsior Art, pg 539
FF Press, pg 540
Humanitas Publishing House, pg 540
Editura Institutul European, pg 540
Editura Kriterion SA, pg 540

Lider Verlag, pg 540
Mentor Kiado, pg 540
Editura Meridiane, pg 540
Editura Niculescu, pg 541
Polirom Verlag, pg 542
Grupul Editorial RAO, pg 542
RAO International Publishing Co, pg 542
Rentrop & Straton Verlagsgruppe und Wirtschaftsconsulting, pg 542
Saeculum IO, pg 542
Editura Stiintifica SA, pg 542
Editura Teora, pg 542
Editura Univers SA, pg 543

Russian Federation
Armada Publishing House, pg 543
Aspect Press Ltd, pg 543
BLIC, russko-Baltijskij informaciionnyj centr, AO, pg 544
CentrePolygraph Traders & Publishers Co, pg 544
Finansy i Statistika Publishing House, pg 544
Fizmatlit Publishing Co, pg 545
Glas New Russian Writing, pg 545
Interbook-Business AO, pg 545
Izdatelskii Dom Kompozitor, pg 546
Ladomir Publishing House, pg 546
Publishing House Limbus Press, pg 546
Izdatelstvo Medicina, pg 546
Izdatelstvo Mir, pg 546
Izdatelstvo Muzyka, pg 547
Nauka Publishers, pg 547
Panorama Publishing House, pg 547
Profizdat, pg 548
Raduga Publishers, pg 548
St Andrew's Biblical Theological College, pg 548
Teorija Verojatnostej i ee Primenenija, pg 549
Text Publishers Ltd Too, pg 549
Top Secret Collection Publishers, pg 549
Izdatelstvo Ural' skogo, pg 549

Saudi Arabia
King Saud University, pg 550

Serbia and Montenegro
Alfa-Narodna Knjiga, pg 552
Savez Inzenjera i Tehnicara Jugoslavije, pg 553

Slovakia
ARCHA sro Vydavatel'stro, pg 559
Kalligram spol sro, pg 559
Vydavatelstvo Obzor, pg 560
Vydavatel'stvo Osveta (Verlag Osveta), pg 560
Vydavatepstvo Praca spol sro, pg 560
Priroda Publishing, pg 560
Serafin, pg 560
Slo Viet, pg 560

Slovenia
Zalozba Mihelac d o o, pg 562
Zalozba Obzorja d d Maribor, pg 562

South Africa
Human & Rousseau (Pty) Ltd, pg 564
Institute for Reformational Studies CHE, pg 565

TYPE OF PUBLICATION INDEX

Spain
Editorial Acribia SA, pg 571
Ediciones Akal SA, pg 571
Anglo-Didactica, SL Editorial, pg 573
Ediciones Atril, pg 574
CEAC, Grupo Editorial SA, pg 576
Complutense, SA Editorial, pg 577
Diputacion Provincial de Malaga, pg 579
Edi-Liber Irlan SA, pg 580
Egales (Editorial Gai y Lesbiana), pg 581
Elkar, Euskal Liburu eta Kantuen Argitaldaria, SL, pg 582
Erein, pg 582
Fundacion de Estudios Libertarios Anselmo Lorenzo, pg 584
Fundacion Rosacruz, pg 584
Galaxia SA Editorial, pg 584
Editorial Gustavo Gili SA, pg 585
Editorial Gulaab, pg 586
Ediciones Hiperion SL, pg 586
Ibaizabal Edelvives SA, pg 586
Llibres del Segle, pg 589
Edicions de la Magrana SA, pg 590
Ediciones Minotauro, pg 591
Editorial Moll SL, pg 592
Anaya & Mario Muchnik, pg 592
Obelisco Ediciones S, pg 593
Ediciones del Oriente y del Mediterraneo, pg 594
Editorial Peregrino SL, pg 595
Pre-Textos, pg 596
Edicions Proa, SA, pg 597
Publicaciones y Ediciones Salamandra SA, pg 597
Universidad de Santiago de Compostela, pg 599
Editorial Thassalia, SA, pg 602
Ediciones de la Torre, pg 602
Trea Ediciones, SL, pg 602
Tursen, SA, pg 603
Publicacions de la Universitat de Barcelona, pg 604
Universitat de Valencia Servei de Publicacions, pg 604
Ediciones Urano, SA, pg 604
Editorial Verbum SL, pg 604
Vinaches Lopez, Luisa, pg 605

Sri Lanka
Dayawansa Jayakody & Co, pg 606
Pradeepa Publishers, pg 607
Swarna Hansa Foundation, pg 607

Sweden
Ellerstroms, pg 611
Hillelforlaget, pg 612
Bokforlaget Nya Doxa AB, pg 614

Switzerland
Ammann Verlag & Co, pg 617
CEC-Cosmic Energy Connections, pg 620
Cockatoo Press (Schweiz), Thailand-Publikationen, pg 621
Edition Epoca, pg 622
Haffmans Verlag AG, pg 624
Kanisius Verlag, pg 626
Verlag Nagel & Kimche AG, Zurich, pg 629
Editions Patino, pg 631
Rodera-Verlag der Cardun AG, pg 632
Rotpunktverlag, pg 632
Verlag im Waldgut AG, pg 636

Syrian Arab Republic
Damascus University Press, pg 638

883

TYPE OF PUBLICATION INDEX

BOOK

Taiwan, Province of China
Cheng Wen Publishing Company, pg 639
Chu Liu Book Company, pg 639
Fuh-Wen Book Co, pg 639
Hsiao Yuan Publication Co, Ltd, pg 640
Laureate Book Co Ltd, pg 640
Lead Wave Publishing Company Ltd, pg 640
Lin Pai Press Company Ltd, pg 641
Linking Publishing Company Ltd, pg 641
San Min Book Co Ltd, pg 641
Sinorama Magazine Co, pg 641
World Book Co Ltd, pg 642
Yee Wen Publishing Co Ltd, pg 642
Yi Hsien Publishing Co Ltd, pg 642
Youth Cultural Publishing Co, pg 642
Yuan Liou Publishing Co, Ltd, pg 642

United Republic of Tanzania
Northwestern Publishers, pg 644
Press & Publicity Centre Ltd, pg 644
Tanzania Publishing House, pg 644

Thailand
Bannakit Trading, pg 645
Sangdad Publishing Company Ltd, pg 645

Tunisia
Academie Tunisienne des Sciences, des Lettres et des Arts Beit El Hekma, pg 647
Maison Tunisienne de l'Edition, pg 648

Turkey
Alkim Kitapcilik-Yayimcilik, pg 649
Arkadas Ltd, pg 649
Arkeoloji Ve Sanat Yayinlari, pg 649
Iletisim Yayinlari, pg 650
Inkilap Publishers Ltd, pg 650
Kubbealti Akademisi Kultur ve Sasat Vakfi, pg 650
Metis Yayinlari, pg 650
Sabah Kitaplari, pg 651
Varlik Yayinlari AS, pg 652

Ukraine
ASK Ltd, pg 653
Osnova, Kharkov State University Press, pg 653
Osnovy Publishers, pg 654
Veselka Publishers, pg 654

United Kingdom
Umberto Allemandi & Co Publishing, pg 656
Atlas Press, pg 661
Boulevard Books UK/The Babel Guides, pg 669
Calder Publications Ltd, pg 673
Canongate Books Ltd, pg 674
Carcanet Press Ltd, pg 674
Dedalus Ltd, pg 687
Discovery Walking Guides Ltd, pg 687
Aidan Ellis Publishing, pg 690
Facet Publishing, pg 694
Garnet Publishing Ltd, pg 698
Gomer Press (J D Lewis & Sons Ltd), pg 701
Gwasg Gwenffrwd, pg 703
Gwasg y Dref Wen, pg 703

Peter Halban Publishers Ltd, pg 703
HarperCollins UK, pg 705
The Harvill Press, pg 705
Icon Press, pg 711
Institute of Physics Publishing, pg 713
International Bee Research Association, pg 714
Islam International Publications Ltd, pg 714
The Islamic Texts Society, pg 715
Kegan Paul International Ltd, pg 717
The Littman Library of Jewish Civilization, pg 721
Manchester University Press, pg 724
Motilal (UK) Books of India, pg 729
Octagon Press Ltd, pg 734
The Oleander Press, pg 735
Peter Owen Ltd, pg 737
Planet, pg 743
Profile Books Ltd, pg 746
Reaktion Books Ltd, pg 748
The Rubicon Press, pg 752
St Jerome Publishing, pg 753
Saqi Books, pg 754
SCM-Canterbury Press Ltd, pg 755
Seren, pg 756
Serpent's Tail Ltd, pg 756
Skoob Russell Square, pg 758
Veloce Publishing Ltd, pg 769
Verso, pg 770
The Women's Press Ltd, pg 775

Uruguay
Ediciones Trilce, pg 778

Viet Nam
Science & Technics Publishing House, pg 780

Zimbabwe
Christian Audio-Visual Action (CAVA), pg 783
The Literature Bureau, pg 783
Zimbabwe Publishing House (Pvt) Ltd, pg 784
Zimbabwe Women Writers, pg 785

UNIVERSITY PRESSES

Albania
NL SH, pg 1

Algeria
Enterprise Nationale du Livre (ENAL), pg 2

Argentina
EUDEBA (Editorial Universitaria de Buenos Aires), pg 5

Australia
AHB Publications, pg 11
Australian Scholarly Publishing, pg 13
Butterworths Australia Ltd, pg 16
Deakin University Press, pg 19
Hayes Publishing Co, pg 25
Macmillan Publishers Australia Pty Ltd, pg 30
Melbourne University Press, pg 32
University of New South Wales Press Ltd, pg 44

Austria
Abakus Verlag GmbH, pg 48
Linde Verlag Wien GmbH, pg 53

Oesterreichischer Kunst und Kulturverlag, pg 55
Andreas Schnider Verlags-Atelier, pg 57
Verband der Wissenschaftlichen Gesellschaften Oesterreichs (VWGOe), pg 59
WUV/Facultas Universitaetsverlag, pg 60
WUV/Service Fachverlag, pg 60

Bangladesh
Bangladesh Publishers, pg 61

Belgium
Academia-Bruylant, pg 62
Academia Press, pg 62
Artel, pg 63
Campinia Media VZW, pg 64
Editions De Boeck-Larcier SA, pg 66
King Baudouin Foundation, pg 69
Uitgeverij Lannoo NV, pg 69
Editions Lessius ASBL, pg 70
Leuven University Press, pg 70
La Part de L'Oeil, pg 71
Presses Universitaires de Namur ASBL, pg 72
Publications des Facultes Universitaires Saint Louis, pg 72
VUB Brussels University Press, pg 74

Bosnia and Herzegovina
Bemust, pg 76

Brazil
Alzira Chagas Carpigiani, pg 79
EDUSC - Editora da Universidade do Sagrado Coracao, pg 81
Thex Editora e Distribuidora Ltda, pg 91
Editora UNESP, pg 91
Editora da Universidade de Sao Paulo, pg 91
Editora Universidade Federal do Rio de Janeiro, pg 92

Bulgaria
Abagar, Veliko Tarnovo, pg 93
Ciela Publishing House, pg 93
Heron Press Publishing House, pg 94
Kralica MAB, pg 95
Sita-MB, pg 97
TEMTO, pg 97
Todor Kableshkov University of Transport, pg 97

Cameroon
Presses Universitaires d'Afrique, pg 98

Chile
Edeval (Universidad de Valparaiso), pg 99
Ediciones Universitarias de Valparaiso, pg 100

China
Beijing Medical University Press, pg 101
China Materials Management Publishing House, pg 102
Chongqing University Press, pg 103
East China University of Science & Technology Press, pg 104
Foreign Language Teaching & Research Press, pg 104

Nanjing University Press, pg 106
Shandong University Press, pg 108
Shanghai Foreign Language Education Press, pg 108
South China University of Science & Technology Press, pg 108
Southwest China Jiaotong University Press, pg 108
Universidade de Macau, Centro de Publicacoes, pg 109
Wuhan University Press, pg 109
Yunnan University Press, pg 109
Zhejiang University Press, pg 109

Colombia
Universidad Externado de Colombia, pg 111
Universidad de Antioquia, Division Publicaciones, pg 113

Costa Rica
Editorial Universidad Nacional (EUNA), pg 116
Editorial Universitaria Centroamericana (EDUCA), pg 117

Cote d'Ivoire
Universite d'Abidjan, pg 117

Croatia
Matica hrvatska, pg 118

Czech Republic
Doplnek, pg 123
Karolinum, nakladatelstvi, pg 124
Mendelova zemedelska a lesnicka univerzita v Brne, pg 125
Psychoanalyticke Nakladatelstvi, pg 127

Denmark
Aarhus Universitetsforlag, pg 128
Dansk Psykologisk Forlag, pg 130
FADL's Forlag A/S, pg 131
Museum Tusculanum Press, pg 133
Samfundslitteratur, pg 134

Dominican Republic
Pontificia Universidad Catolica Madre y Maestra, pg 136

Egypt (Arab Republic of Egypt)
Al Arab Publishing House, pg 137

Finland
Abo Akademis forlag - Abo Akademi University Press, pg 141
Osuuskunta Vastapaino, pg 144
Yliopistopaino/Helsinki University Press, pg 145

France
Association pour la Recherche et l'Information demographiques (APRD), pg 148
Autrement Editions, pg 148
Presses Universitaires de Bordeaux (PUB), pg 150
Comite National d'Evaluation (CNE), pg 155
Editions Dalloz Sirey, pg 157
Editions de l'Ecole des Hautes Etudes en Sciences Sociales (EHESS), pg 159
Editions rue d'Ulm, pg 160
ELLUG (Editions Litteraires et Linguistiques de l'Universite de Grenoble III), pg 161

PUBLISHERS

Institut d'Etudes Slaves IES, pg 162
Paul Geuthner Librairie Orientaliste, pg 165
Editions Jean Paul Gisserot, pg 165
Hachette Education, pg 166
L'Harmattan, pg 167
Editions de la Maison des Sciences de l'Homme, Paris, pg 173
Presses Universitaires du Mirail, pg 176
Editions Ophrys, pg 177
Editions Paradigme, pg 178
Presses de la Sorbonne Nouvelle/PSN, pg 181
Presses Universitaires de Caen, pg 181
Presses Universitaires du Septentrion, pg 182
Publications de l'Universite de Rouen, pg 182
Publications Orientalistes de France (POF), pg 182
Publications de la Sorbonne, pg 185
Universitas, pg 188
Publications de l'Universite de Pau, pg 188

French Polynesia
Scoop/Au Vent des Iles, pg 189

Germany
A Francke Verlag (Tubingen und Basel), pg 190
Campusbooks Medien AG, pg 207
Degener & Co, Manfred Dreiss Verlag, pg 211
Diesterweg, Moritz Verlag, pg 214
ITpress Verlag, pg 242
Iudicium Verlag GmbH, pg 242
Justus-Liebig-Universitat Giessen, pg 244
kopaed verlagsgmbh, pg 249
Michael Lassleben Verlag und Druckerei, pg 252
Leipziger Universitaetsverlag GmbH, pg 253
mentis Verlag GmbH, pg 259
Musikantiquariat und Dr Hans Schneider Verlag GmbH, pg 262
Nusser Verlag, pg 266
Edition Parabolis, pg 268
Philipps-Universitaet Marburg, pg 270
Roehrig Universitaets Verlag Gmbh, pg 276
Sax-Verlag Beucha, pg 278
Springer Science+Business Media GmbH & Co KG, Berlin, pg 285
Stauffenburg Verlag Brigitte Narr GmbH, pg 287
Trotzdem-Verlags Genossenschaft eG, pg 292
UVK Universitatsverlag Konstanz GmbH, pg 294
Waxmann Verlag GmbH, pg 297
Weidler Buchverlag Berlin, pg 298

Greece
Beta Medical Publishers, pg 306
Ekdotikos Oikos Adelfon Kyriakidi A E, pg 307
Hestia-I D Hestia-Kollaros & Co Corporation, pg 308
Kardamitsa A, pg 309
Panepistimio Ioanninon, pg 311
Sakkoulas Publications SA, pg 312

Hong Kong
The Chinese University Press, pg 316
Hong Kong University Press, pg 317

Hungary
Atlantisz Kiado, pg 320
Balassi Kiado Kft, pg 321
Kiiarat Konyvdiado, pg 322

Iceland
Haskolautgafan - University of Iceland Press, pg 325

India
Oxford University Press, pg 344
Reliance Publishing House, pg 346
Scientific Book Agency, pg 348

Indonesia
Institut Teknologi Bandung, pg 355
Karya Anda, CV, pg 355

Ireland
Cork University Press, pg 359
Gandon Editions, pg 360

Israel
Bar Ilan University Press, pg 365
Bezalel Academy of Arts & Design, pg 365
The Bialik Institute, pg 365
Dekel Publishing House, pg 366
Dyonon/Papyrus Publishing House of the Tel-Aviv, pg 366
Haifa University Press, pg 367
Hakibbutz Hameuchad Publishing House Ltd, pg 367
Open University of Israel, pg 371

Italy
All'Insegna del Giglio, pg 375
Franco Angeli SRL, pg 375
Arcipelago Edizioni di Chiani Marisa, pg 376
Editore Armando Armando SRL, pg 376
Associazione Internazionale di Archeologia Classica, pg 377
Belforte Editore Libraio srl, pg 377
BeMa, pg 377
Giuseppe Bonanno Editore, pg 378
Bonsignori Editore SRL, pg 378
Book Editore, pg 378
Editore Giorgio Bretschneider, pg 379
Campanotto, pg 379
Edizioni Cantagalli, pg 379
Casa Editrice Libraria Ulrico Hoepli SpA, pg 380
CEDAM (Casa Editrice Dr A Milani), pg 380
CELID, pg 381
Centro Italiano Studi Alto Medioevo, pg 381
Centro Studi Terzo Mondo, pg 381
Il Cigno Galileo Galilei-Edizioni di Arte e Scienza, pg 382
Cittadella Editrice, pg 382
CLUEB (Cooperativa Libraria Universitaria Editrice Bologna), pg 382
CLUT Editrice, pg 383
La Cultura Sociologica, pg 384
M d'Auria Editore SAS, pg 384
Ecole Francaise de Rome, pg 385
EDIFIR SRL, pg 386
Edizioni del Centro Camuno di Studi Preistorici, pg 386
EGEA (Edizioni Giuridiche Economiche Aziendali), pg 387
Edi.Ermes srl, pg 388
Esselibri, pg 388
Etas Libri, pg 388
Festina Lente Edizioni, pg 389
G Giappichelli Editore SRL, pg 390
Giuseppe Laterza Editore, pg 391
Instituti Editoriali E Poligrafici Internazionali SRL, pg 393
Ist Patristico Augustinianum, pg 393
Editoriale Jaca Book SpA, pg 394
Editrice LAS, pg 394
LED - Edizioni Universitarie di Lettere Economia Diritto, pg 395
Lindau, pg 395
Linea d'Ombra Libri, pg 395
Lubrina, pg 396
Milella di Lecce Spazio Vivo srl, pg 398
Monduzzi Editore SpA, pg 399
Moretti & Vitali Editori srl, pg 399
Nuova Coletti Editore Roma, pg 401
Maria Pacini Fazzi Editore, pg 402
Palatina Editrice, pg 402
G B Palumbo & C Editore SpA, pg 402
Paravia Bruno Mondadori Editori, pg 402
Pitagora Editrice SRL, pg 403
Rara Istituto Editoriale di Bibliofilia e Reprints, pg 405
Edizioni Universitarie Romane, pg 406
SEMAR Publishers SRL, pg 408
Sicania, pg 408
Edizioni Librarie Siciliane, pg 408
Sorbona, pg 409
Istituto Storico Italiano per l'Eta Moderna e Contemporanea, pg 409
Editrice Tirrenia Stampatori SAS, pg 410
Transeuropa, pg 410
Unipress, pg 411
Urbaniana University Press, pg 411
Vita e Pensiero, pg 412

Jamaica
The Press, pg 414

Japan
Hakutei-Sha, pg 418
Tamagawa University Press, pg 429
Waseda University Press, pg 431

Kazakhstan
Al-Farabi Kazakh National University, pg 432

Kenya
Nairobi University Press, pg 435

Democratic People's Republic of Korea
Grand People's Study House, pg 436

Republic of Korea
Suhagsa, pg 443
Yonsei University Press, pg 444

Lithuania
Klaipedos Universiteto Leidykla, pg 449
TEV Leidykla, pg 450

TYPE OF PUBLICATION INDEX

Malaysia
Penerbit Universiti Sains Malaysia, pg 458
University of Malaya, Department of Publications, pg 459

Mexico
Colegio de Postgraduados en Ciencias Agricolas, pg 463
Publicaciones Cruz O SA, pg 463
El Colegio de Michoacan A C, pg 464
Instituto Nacional de Antropologia e Historia, pg 469
Ediciones Promesa, SA de CV, pg 470

Republic of Moldova
Editura Lumina, pg 473

Morocco
Association de la Recherche Historique et Sociale, pg 474

Namibia
Multi-Disciplinary Research Centre Library, pg 476

Netherlands
Uitgeverij Jan van Arkel, pg 478
Backhuys Publishers BV, pg 478
Delft University Press, pg 481
KITLV Press Royal Institute of Linguistics & Anthropology, pg 484
Koninklijke Vermande bv, pg 485
Pearson Education Netherlands, pg 487
Tilburg University Press, pg 490
Twente University Press, pg 490

New Zealand
Auckland University Press, pg 493
Canterbury University Press, pg 494
Lincoln University Press, pg 498
University of Otago Press, pg 502

Norway
Glydendal Akademisk, pg 509

Peru
Instituto de Estudios Peruanos, pg 517
Universidad de Lima-Fondo de Desarollo Editorial, pg 517

Philippines
Ateneo de Manila University Press, pg 518
De La Salle University, pg 519
UST Publishing House, pg 521

Poland
Gdanskie Wydawnictwo Psychologiczne SC, pg 523
Impuls, pg 523
Katolicki Uniwersytet Wydawniczo-Redakcja, pg 523
'Slask' Ltd, pg 526
Oficyna Wydawnicza Szkoly Glownej Handlowej w Warszawie Oficyna Wydawnicza SGH, pg 527
Wydawnictwa Uniwersytetu Warszawskiego, pg 527

Portugal
Edicoes Colibri, pg 530
Dinalivro, pg 530
Editorial Estampa, Lda, pg 531
Imprensa Nacional-Casa da Moeda, pg 532
Planeta Editora, LDA, pg 534
Edicoes Silabo, pg 536
Usus Editora, pg 536

Puerto Rico
Libros-Ediciones Homines, pg 537

Romania
Editura Dacia, pg 539
Editura Excelsior Art, pg 539
Editura Minerva, pg 541
Editura Niculescu, pg 541
Polirom Verlag, pg 542

Russian Federation
N E Bauman Moscow State Technical University Publishers, pg 544
FGUP Izdatelstvo Mashinostroenie, pg 544
Finansy i Statistika Publishing House, pg 544
Izdatelstvo Kazanskago Universiteta, pg 545
Izdatelstvo Mordovskogo gosudar stvennogo, pg 547
Izdatel'stvo Nizhegorodskogo Gosudarstvennogo Univ, pg 547
St Andrew's Biblical Theological College, pg 548
Teorija Verojatnostej i ee Primenenija, pg 549
Izdatelstvo Ural' skogo, pg 549
Voronezh State University Publishers, pg 549

Singapore
Institute of Southeast Asian Studies, pg 556
Singapore University Press Pte Ltd, pg 558

Slovakia
Priroda Publishing, pg 560
Ustav informacii a prognoz skolstva mladeze a telovychovy, pg 561
Zilinska Univerzita, pg 561

South Africa
Human Sciences Research Council, pg 565
Institute for Reformational Studies CHE, pg 565
Unisa Press, pg 569
University of KwaZulu-Natal Press, pg 569
Witwatersrand University Press, pg 570

Spain
Ediciones Akal SA, pg 571
Editorial Deimos, SL, pg 578
Diputacion Provincial de Malaga, pg 579
Dykinson SL, pg 580
Publicaciones Etea, pg 583
Grupo Comunicar, pg 585
Editorial Horsori SL, pg 586
Idea Books, SA, pg 587
Ediciones Libertarias/Prodhufi SA, pg 589
Ediciones Morata SL, pg 592
Editorial Popular SA, pg 596

Prensas Universitarias de Zaragoza, pg 597
Servicio de Publicaciones Universidad de Cadiz, pg 599
Servicio de Publicaciones Universidad de Cordoba, pg 599
Tesitex, SL, pg 602
Trea Ediciones, SL, pg 602
Universidad de Malaga, pg 603
Universidad de Oviedo Servicio de Publicaciones, pg 603
Universidad de Valladolid Secretariado de Publicaciones e Intercambio Editorial, pg 604

Sweden
Acta Universitatis Gothoburgensis, pg 609

Switzerland
Birkhauser Verlag AG, pg 619
Helbing und Lichtenhahn Verlag AG, pg 625
Verlag Industrielle Organisation, pg 625
Editions Payot Lausanne, pg 631
Trans Tech Publications SA, pg 635
Vdf Hochschulverlag AG an der ETH Zurich, pg 636

Syrian Arab Republic
Institut Francais d'Etudes Arabes de Damas, pg 638

Taiwan, Province of China
World Book Co Ltd, pg 642

United Republic of Tanzania
DUP (1996) Ltd, pg 643

Tunisia
Faculte des Sciences Humaines et Sociales de Tunis, pg 648

Turkey
Alkim Kitapcilik-Yayimcilik, pg 649
Soez Yayin/Oyunajans, pg 651

Ukraine
Osnova, Kharkov State University Press, pg 653

United Kingdom
The Athlone Press Ltd, pg 661
Books for Europe Ltd, pg 669
Borthwick Institute Publications, pg 669
Boydell & Brewer Ltd, pg 669
Commonwealth Secretariat, pg 681
Ethics International Press Ltd, pg 692
Harvard University Press, pg 705
Imperial College Press, pg 712
Institute of Irish Studies, The Queens University of Belfast, pg 713
Liverpool University Press, pg 722
Manchester University Press, pg 724
Marcham Manor Press, pg 725
McGraw-Hill Publishing Company, pg 726
Motilal (UK) Books of India, pg 729
Open University Press, pg 736
Pearson Education Europe, Mideast & Africa, pg 739
Pluto Press, pg 743
The Policy Press, pg 744
Rivers Oram Press, pg 750

St Jerome Publishing, pg 753
University of Exeter Press, pg 768
University of Hertfordshire Press, pg 768
University of Wales Press, pg 769
Yale University Press London, pg 776

VIDEO CASSETTES

Argentina
San Pablo, pg 9

Australia
Bolinda Publishing Pty Ltd, pg 15
Bridge To Peace Publications, pg 16
Deakin University Press, pg 19
Encyclopaedia Britannica (Australia) Inc, pg 21
Fraser Publications, pg 22
Hampden Press, pg 24
Lonely Planet Publications Pty Ltd, pg 29
Barry Long Books, pg 29
New Creation Publications Ministries & Resource Centre, pg 33
OTEN (Open Training & Education Network), pg 34
Oxfam Community Aid Abroad, pg 35
Regency Publishing, pg 39
RMIT Publishing, pg 39
South Australian Government-Department of Education, Employment & Training, pg 41

Austria
Edition S der OSD, pg 50
Oesterreichischer Bundesverlag Gmbh, pg 55
Oesterreichischer Kunst und Kulturverlag, pg 55
Verlag des Osterr Kneippbundes GmbH, pg 56

Belgium
Uitgeverij De Sikkel NV, pg 73

Brazil
A & A & A Edicoes e Promocoes Internacionais Ltda, pg 76
Horus Editora Ltda, pg 83
Paulus Editora, pg 88

Bulgaria
Izdatelstvo Lettera, pg 95

China
Beijing Publishing House, pg 101
Beijing University Press, pg 101
China Film Press, pg 102
China Machine Press (CMP), pg 102
Foreign Language Teaching & Research Press, pg 104
Fudan University Press, pg 104
People's Education Press, pg 106
Shanghai Educational Publishing House, pg 108
Southwest China Jiaotong University Press, pg 108
Tsinghua University Press, pg 109

Colombia
Consejo Episcopal Latinoamericano (CELAM), pg 110

Costa Rica
Centro Agronomico Tropical de Investigacion y Ensenanza (CATIE), pg 115
Ediciones Promesa, pg 116

Cuba
Casa Editora Abril, pg 120

Czech Republic
Karmelitanske Nakladatelstvi, pg 124

Denmark
Forlaget alokke AS, pg 129
Kaleidoscope Publishers Ltd, pg 132
Kraks Forlag AS, pg 132
Mellemfolkeligt Samvirke, pg 133
Scandinavia Publishing House, pg 134
Systime, pg 135

Fiji
University of the South Pacific, pg 141

France
Editions Amrita SA, pg 146
Cirad, pg 154
Institut d'Etudes Augustiniennes, pg 162
Folklore Comtois, pg 164
INRA Editions (Institut National de la Recherche Agronomique), pg 168
Le Livre de Paris, pg 173
Editions Memoire des Arts, pg 175
Editions de la Reunion des Musees Nationaux, pg 176
Editions du Centre Pompidou, pg 180
Editions Prosveta, pg 182

Germany
Alouette Verlag, pg 192
AOL-Verlag Frohmut Menze, pg 193
Verlag Beleke KG, pg 198
Bibliographisches Institut & F A Brockhaus AG, pg 200
Buechse der Pandora Verlags-GmbH, pg 205
Carl-Auer-Systeme Verlag, pg 207
Cornelsen Verlag GmbH & Co OHG, pg 210
Datacom Buchverlag GmbH, pg 211
Deutscher Apotheker Verlag Dr Roland Schmiedel GmbH & Co, pg 212
Falken-Verlag GmbH, pg 223
FN-Verlag der Deutschen Reiterlichen Vereinigung GmbH, pg 225
Franckh-Kosmos Verlags-GmbH & Co, pg 226
Lehrmittelverlag Wilhelm Hagemann GmbH, pg 233
Happy Mental Buch- und Musik Verlag, pg 234
Hayit Reisefuhrer in der Rutsker Verlag GmbH, pg 235
Huss-Medien GmbH, pg 240
Knowledge Media International, pg 247
Verlagsgruppe Koehler/Mittler, pg 248
kopaed verlagsgmbh, pg 249
Koptisch-Orthodoxes Zentrum, pg 249
Lahn-Verlag GmbH, pg 251

PUBLISHERS

Medizinisch-Literarische Verlagsgesellschaft mbH, pg 258
Naumann & Goebel Verlagsgesellschaft mbH, pg 263
Nusser Verlag, pg 266
Georg Olms Verlag AG, pg 267
Osho Verlag GmbH, pg 267
Pollner Verlag, pg 271
Polyband Gesellschaft fur Bild Tontraeger mbH & Co Betriebs KG, pg 271
Quintessenz Verlags-GmbH, pg 273
Ulrich Schiefer bahn Verlag, pg 279
Schulz-Kirchner Verlag GmbH, pg 282
Silberburg-Verlag Titus Haeussermann GmbH, pg 283
Springer Science+Business Media GmbH & Co KG, pg 284
TR - Verlagsunion GmbH, pg 291
Turkischer Schulbuchverlag Onel Cengiz, pg 293
UNO-Verlag GmbH, pg 293
Verlag fur Schweissen und Verwandte Verfahren, pg 295
Curt R Vincentz Verlag, pg 296
Vista Point Verlag GmbH, pg 296
Voggenreiter-Verlag, pg 296
Verlagsgruppe Weltbild GmbH, pg 298

Greece
Apostoliki Diakonia tis Ekklisias tis Hellados, pg 305
Pagoulatos Bros, pg 311

Guyana
Guyana Community Based Rehabilitation Progeamme, pg 314

Hong Kong
Christian Communications Ltd, pg 316
Witman Publishing Co (HK) Ltd, pg 320

Hungary
Nemzeti Tankoenyvkiado, pg 323
Polgar Kiado Kft, pg 324

Iceland
Namsgagnastofnun, pg 326

India
Nem Chand & Brothers, pg 343
Spectrum Publications, pg 350
Theosophical Publishing House, pg 351

Ireland
Cathedral Books Ltd, pg 358
Ossian Publications, pg 363

Israel
Doko Video Ltd, pg 366
Hanitzotz A-Sharara Publishing House, pg 367
Prolog Publishing House, pg 371
R Sirkis Publishers Ltd, pg 372

Italy
Umberto Allemandi & C SRL, pg 375
Baha'i, pg 377
CIC Edizioni Internazionali, pg 381
Elle Di Ci - Libreria Dottrina Cristiana, pg 387
Edi.Ermes srl, pg 388
Istituto Geografico de Agostini SpA, pg 390
Ernesto Gremese Editore srl, pg 391
IHT Gruppo Editoriale SRL, pg 393
Museo storico in Trento, pg 400
G B Palumbo & C Editore SpA, pg 402
RAI-ERI, pg 405
Red/Studio Redazionale, pg 405
Societa Stampa Sportiva, pg 408
Editrice Uomini Nuovi, pg 411
Vivalda Editori SRL, pg 412

Jamaica
Association of Development Agencies, pg 413
Institute of Jamaica Publications, pg 413

Japan
AVACO - Christian Mass Communications Center, pg 415
Iwanami Shoten, Publishers, pg 419
Kosei Publishing Co Ltd, pg 421
Myrtos Inc, pg 423
Nigensha Publishing Co Ltd, pg 423
Nosangyoson Bunka Kyokai, pg 424
Ongaku No Tomo Sha Corporation, pg 425
Seibido, pg 426
Shogakukan Inc, pg 427
Tokyo Shoseki Co Ltd, pg 430
Yohan Shuppan, pg 431

Kenya
Jacaranda Designs Ltd, pg 434
Life Challenge AFRICA, pg 435

Republic of Korea
Korea Britannica Corp, pg 440
Moon Jin Media Co Ltd, pg 441
YBM/Si-sa, pg 443

Maldive Islands
Non-Formal Education Centre, pg 459

Mexico
Ediciones Culturales Internacionales SA de CV Edicion Compra y Venta de Libros, Casetes, Videos, pg 463
Editorial Jilguero, SA de CV, pg 467
Organizacion Cultural LP SA de CV, pg 469
Ediciones Promesa, SA de CV, pg 470
SCRIPTA - Distribucion y Servicios Editoriales, SA de CV, pg 471

Namibia
Desert Research Foundation of Namibia (DRFN), pg 476

Netherlands
Elmar BV, pg 482
Uitgeverij Lemma BV, pg 485

New Zealand
Learning Media Ltd, pg 498

Philippines
Communication Foundation for Asia Media Group (CFAMG), pg 518
Rex Bookstores & Publishers, pg 520

Poland
Polish Scientific Publishers PWN, pg 525

Romania
Editura Minerva, pg 541
Rentrop & Straton Verlagsgruppe und Wirtschaftsconsulting, pg 542

Russian Federation
INFRA-M Izdatel'skij dom, pg 545

Singapore
McGallen & Bolden Associates, pg 557

Slovenia
Mladinska Knjiga International, pg 561
Zalozba Obzorja d d Maribor, pg 562

South Africa
Reader's Digest Southern Africa, pg 568

Spain
Alinco SA - Aura Comunicacio, pg 572
Editorial Astri SA, pg 573
Editorial Casals SA, pg 575
Editorial Claret SA, pg 577
Didaco Comunicacion y Didactica, SA, pg 579
Edilux, pg 581
Fundacion de Estudios Libertarios Anselmo Lorenzo, pg 584
Ibaizabal Edelvives SA, pg 586
Editorial la Muralla SA, pg 592
Pulso Ediciones, SL, pg 597
San Pablo Ediciones, pg 598
Publicacions de la Universitat de Barcelona, pg 604

Sweden
Folkuniversitetets foerlag, pg 611
Hans Richter Laromedel, pg 613

Switzerland
CEC-Cosmic Energy Connections, pg 620
Vexer Verlag, pg 636
Editions Vivez Soleil SA, pg 636

Taiwan, Province of China
Echo Publishing Company Ltd, pg 639

Thailand
Thai Watana Panich Co, Ltd, pg 646

Turkey
Soez Yayin/Oyunajans, pg 651

United Kingdom
Abbotsford Publishing, pg 654
Ian Allan Publishing Ltd, pg 656
Umberto Allemandi & Co Publishing, pg 656
BBC English, pg 663
BCA - Book Club Associates, pg 663
Chorion IP, pg 679
E W Classey Ltd, pg 680
Coachwise Ltd, pg 680
Dorling Kindersley Ltd, pg 688
Encyclopaedia Britannica (UK) International Ltd, pg 691
Ethics International Press Ltd, pg 692
GMC Publications Ltd, pg 700
Imperial College Press, pg 712
New Era Publications UK Ltd, pg 732
Old Pond Publishing, pg 734
Pavilion Publishing (Brighton) Ltd, pg 739
Phaidon Press Ltd, pg 741
Plough Publishing House of Bruderhof Communities in the UK, pg 743
Portland Press Ltd, pg 745
The Reader's Digest Association Ltd, pg 748
SAGE Publications Ltd, pg 753
Sports Turf Research Institute (STRI), pg 760
Telegraph Books, pg 764
World Microfilms Publications Ltd, pg 775
World of Islam Altajir Trust, pg 776

Subject Index

ACCOUNTING

Albania
NL SH, pg 1
State Textbook Publishing House, pg 1

Argentina
Diana Argentina SA, Editorial, pg 5
Ediciones Don Bosco Argentina, pg 5
EUDEBA (Editorial Universitaria de Buenos Aires), pg 5

Australia
Edward Arnold (Australia) Pty Ltd, pg 12
Austed Publishing Co, pg 12
Butterworths Australia Ltd, pg 16
The Images Publishing Group Pty Ltd, pg 26
Law Book Co Information Services, pg 28
Macmillan Education Australia, pg 30
McGraw-Hill Australia Pty Ltd, pg 31
OTEN (Open Training & Education Network), pg 34
Pearson Education Australia, pg 36
Prospect Media Pty Ltd, pg 37
The Real Estate Institute of Australia, pg 39
RMIT Publishing, pg 39
Tertiary Press, pg 43
VCTA Publishing, pg 45

Austria
Linde Verlag Wien GmbH, pg 53
WUV/Service Fachverlag, pg 60

Azerbaijan
Sada, Literaturno-Izdatel'skij Centr, pg 60

Bangladesh
Bangladesh Publishers, pg 61

Belgium
Academia-Bruylant, pg 62
Editions de la Chambre de Commerce et d'Industrie SA (ECCI), pg 65
Editions De Boeck-Larcier SA, pg 66
Intersentia Uitgevers NV, pg 68
Wolters Kluwer Belgie NV, pg 74

Brazil
Editora Atlas SA, pg 78
Livraria Freitas Bastos Editora SA, pg 82
Editora Ortiz SA, pg 88
Pearson Education Do Brasil, pg 88
Livraria Pioneira Editora/Enio Matheus Guazzelli e Cia Ltd, pg 88
Saraiva SA, Livreiros Editores, pg 90
Fundacao Getulio Vargas, pg 92

Bulgaria
Ciela Publishing House, pg 93
Foi-Commerce, pg 94

Chile
Arrayan Editores, pg 98

China
Anhui People's Publishing House, pg 101
China Foreign Economic Relations & Trade Publishing House, pg 102
CITIC Publishing House, pg 103
Fudan University Press, pg 104
Jilin Science & Technology Publishing House, pg 105
Qingdao Publishing House, pg 107
Shandong University Press, pg 108
Shanghai Far East Publishers, pg 108
Sichuan University Press, pg 108
Zhejiang University Press, pg 109

Colombia
McGraw-Hill Colombia, pg 112
Universidad Nacional Abierta y a Distancia, pg 113

The Democratic Republic of the Congo
Centre de Recherche, et Pedagogie Appliquee, pg 114

Denmark
Samfundslitteratur, pg 134
Systime, pg 135
Forlaget Thomson A/S, pg 135

Dominican Republic
Pontificia Universidad Catolica Madre y Maestra, pg 136

France
Editions Bertrand-Lacoste, pg 149
Editions Breal, pg 151
Centre de Librairie et d'Editions Techniques (CLET), pg 152
Editions Delmas, pg 157
Editions Foucher, pg 164
LiTec (Librairies Techniques SA), pg 172
Ouest Editions, pg 178
Presses Universitaires de Caen, pg 181
Presses Universitaires de Grenoble, pg 181
Sofiac (Societe Francaise des Imprimeries Administratives Centrales), pg 185
TOP Editions, pg 188

Germany
Cornelsen Verlag GmbH & Co OHG, pg 210
Betriebswirtschaftlicher Verlag Dr Th Gabler, pg 228
Rudolf Haufe Verlag GmbH & Co KG, pg 235
IDW-Verlag GmbH, pg 241
Industria-Verlagsbuchhandlung GmbH, pg 241
Verlag Neue Wirtschafts-Briefe GmbH & Co, pg 264
Schaeffer-Poeschel Verlag fuer Wirtschaft Steuern Recht, pg 279
Erich Schmidt Verlag GmbH & Co, pg 280
Stollfuss Verlag Bonn GmbH & Co KG, pg 288
Wirtschaftsverlag Carl Ueberreuter, pg 293
WRS Verlag Wirtschaft, Recht und Steuern GmbH & Co KG, pg 301

Ghana
EPP Books Services, pg 304

Greece
Ekdotikos Oikos Adelfon Kyriakidi A E, pg 307

Hong Kong
SCMP Book Publishing Ltd, pg 319

Hungary
Saldo Penzugyi Tanacsado es Informatikai Rt, pg 324

India
Academic Publishers, pg 327
APH Publishing Corp, pg 328
Eastern Law House Pvt Ltd, pg 334
Frank Brothers & Co Publishers Ltd, pg 334
Pitambar Publishing Co (P) Ltd, pg 345
Pointer Publishers, pg 345
Reliance Publishing House, pg 346
Scientific Book Agency, pg 348
Sita Books & Periodicals Pvt Ltd, pg 349
Sultan Chand & Sons Pvt Ltd, pg 350
Vidya Puri, pg 352
A H Wheeler & Co Ltd, pg 353

Indonesia
Andi Offset, pg 353
Bumi Aksara PT, pg 354
Gramedia, pg 355

Ireland
Irish Management Institute, pg 361
Oak Tree Press, pg 362

Israel
Open University of Israel, pg 371

Italy
CLUEB (Cooperativa Libraria Universitaria Editrice Bologna), pg 382
Rirea Casa Editrice della Rivista Italiana di Ragioneria e di Economia Aziendale, pg 405

Jamaica
CFM Publications, pg 413

Japan
Institute for Financial Affairs Inc-KINZAI, pg 419
Nippon Jitsugyo Publishing Co Ltd, pg 424
Zeimukeiri-Kyokai, pg 431

Kenya
Africa Book Services (EA) Ltd, pg 433
Focus Publications Ltd, pg 433
Heinemann Kenya Ltd (EAEP), pg 434
Midi Teki Publishers, pg 435
Nairobi University Press, pg 435
Shirikon Publishers, pg 436

Republic of Korea
Chung Rim Publishing Co Ltd, pg 438

Lebanon
Librairie Orientale sal, pg 446

Liechtenstein
Bonafides Verlags-Anstalt, pg 447

Luxembourg
Editions Emile Borschette, pg 450
Editions Promoculture, pg 451

Madagascar
Foibe Filan-Kevitry NY Mpampianatra (FOFIPA), pg 453

Malaysia
SBT Professional Publications, pg 458

Mauritius
Editions de l'Ocean Indien Ltd, pg 461

Mexico
Ediciones Contables y Administrativas SA, pg 463
Ediciones Eca SA de CV, pg 464
Editorial Esfinge SA de CV, pg 465
Editorial Limusa SA de CV, pg 467
Organizacion Cultural LP SA de CV, pg 469
Sistemas Universales, SA, pg 472

Morocco
Cabinet Conseil CCMLA, pg 474

Netherlands
Business Contact BV, pg 480
Koninklijke Vermande bv, pg 485

New Zealand
Brookers Ltd, pg 494
CCH New Zealand Ltd, pg 495
Dunmore Press Ltd, pg 495
ESA Publications (NZ) Ltd, pg 496
Nelson Price Milburn Ltd, pg 499
New House Publishers Ltd, pg 499

Nigeria
Abisega Publishers (Nigeria) Ltd, pg 503
Evans Brothers (Nigeria Publishers) Ltd, pg 504

Norway
Glydendal Akademisk, pg 509

Pakistan
National Book Foundation, pg 513
Publishers United Pvt Ltd, pg 514

Peru
Editorial Desarrollo SA, pg 517
Tassorello, SA, pg 517

Philippines
Mutual Book Inc, pg 519
Rex Bookstores & Publishers, pg 520

Poland
Polskie Wydawnictwo Ekonomiczne PWE SA, pg 522

Portugal
Dinalivro, pg 530

Romania
Nemira Verlag, pg 541
Editura Niculescu, pg 541
Rentrop & Straton Verlagsgruppe und Wirtschaftsconsulting, pg 542

Russian Federation
Izdatelstvo 'Ekonomika', pg 544
Finansy i Statistika Publishing House, pg 544
INFRA-M Izdatel'skij dom, pg 545

Singapore
Hillview Publications Pte Ltd, pg 556

Slovenia
Univerza v Ljubljani Ekonomska Fakulteta, pg 562

South Africa
Educum Publishers Ltd, pg 563
Juta & Co, pg 565

Spain
Centro de Estudios Adams-Ediciones Valbuena SA, pg 571
Editorial Donostiarra SA, pg 579
Ediciones Deusto SA, pg 580
Esic Editorial, pg 582
Instituto de Estudios Fiscales, pg 583
Ediciones Gestio 2000 SA, pg 585
Editorial Juventud SA, pg 588
Universidad de Valladolid Secretariado de Publicaciones e Intercambio Editorial, pg 604

Sri Lanka
Ministry of Education, pg 607

Sweden
Studentlitteratur AB, pg 616

Switzerland
Cosmos-Verlag AG, pg 621
Orell Fuessli Buchhandlungs AG, pg 630
Verlag Organisator AG, pg 630
Verlag fuer Recht und Gesellschaft AG, pg 632
Versus Verlag AG, pg 636

Syrian Arab Republic
Damascus University Press, pg 638

Taiwan, Province of China
Chien Chen Bookstore Publishing Company Ltd, pg 639
Fuh-Wen Book Co, pg 639
San Min Book Co Ltd, pg 641

United Republic of Tanzania
DUP (1996) Ltd, pg 643
Nyota Publishers Ltd, pg 644
Tanzania Publishing House, pg 644

Turkey
Seckin Yayinevi, pg 651
Yetkin Printing & Publishing Co Inc, pg 652

Ukraine
ASK Ltd, pg 653

United Kingdom
ABG Professional Information, pg 655
Books for Europe Ltd, pg 669
BPP Publishing Ltd, pg 670
Butterworths Tolley, pg 673
Cassell & Co, pg 675
The Chartered Institute of Public Finance & Accountancy, pg 678
Ernst & Young, pg 692
Financial Training Co, pg 694
HB Publications, pg 706
Impart Books, pg 712
JAI Press Ltd, pg 715
Jordan Publishing Ltd, pg 716
Letts Educational, pg 720
Mars Business Associates Ltd, pg 725
Media Research Publishing Ltd, pg 726
National Extension College, pg 730
Osborne Books Ltd, pg 736
Pearson Education, pg 739
Professional Book Supplies Ltd, pg 745
Taylor & Francis, pg 763
VNU Business Publications, pg 770
Wiley Europe Ltd, pg 773

Uruguay
Fundacion de Cultura Universitaria, pg 777

Viet Nam
Science & Technics Publishing House, pg 780

Zimbabwe
College Press Publishers (Pvt) Ltd, pg 783
HarperCollins Publishers Zimbabwe Pvt Ltd, pg 783
Longman Zimbabwe (Pvt) Ltd, pg 783
Thomson Publications Zimbabwe (Pvt) Ltd, pg 784

ADVERTISING

Albania
NL SH, pg 1

Australia
The Images Publishing Group Pty Ltd, pg 26
McGraw-Hill Australia Pty Ltd, pg 31
Priestley Consulting, pg 37
The Real Estate Institute of Australia, pg 39

Belarus
Kavaler Publishers, pg 62

Brazil
Livraria Nobel S/A, pg 85
Livraria Pioneira Editora/Enio Matheus Guazzelli e Cia Ltd, pg 88
Summus Editorial Ltda, pg 91
Talento Publicacoes Editora e Grafica Ltda, pg 91

Bulgaria
Global Kontakts Balgarija, pg 94
Interpres, pg 95
Publishing House Narodno delo OOD, pg 96
Reporter, pg 96
Svetra Publishing House, pg 97
TEMTO, pg 97
Todor Kableshkov University of Transport, pg 97

China
Anhui People's Publishing House, pg 101
Chengdu Maps Publishing House, pg 101
China Film Press, pg 102
Fudan University Press, pg 104
Heilongjiang Science & Technology Press, pg 105
Jilin Science & Technology Publishing House, pg 105
Qingdao Publishing House, pg 107

Costa Rica
Litografia Artex, SA, pg 115

Cuba
Casa Editora Abril, pg 120

Czech Republic
PressArt Nakladatelstvi, pg 127

Denmark
Forlaget alokke AS, pg 129
Samfundslitteratur, pg 134

France
Blondel La Rougery SARL, pg 150
Editions Breal, pg 151
Communication Par Livre (CPL), pg 155
Editions Dalloz Sirey, pg 157
Institute Editeur, pg 160

Germany
AOL-Verlag Frohmut Menze, pg 193
Art Directors Club Verlag GmbH, pg 194
Cornelsen Verlag GmbH & Co OHG, pg 210
Deutscher Fachverlag GmbH, pg 212
Friedrich Kiehl Verlag GmbH, pg 227
Heinze GmbH, pg 236
Rossipaul Kommunikation GmbH, pg 277
Verlag Moderne Industrie AG & Co KG, pg 295
WRS Verlag Wirtschaft, Recht und Steuern GmbH & Co KG, pg 301

Ghana
World Literature Project, pg 305

Greece
Vivliothiki Eftychia Galeou, pg 313

Hong Kong
SCMP Book Publishing Ltd, pg 319
Wellday Ltd, pg 320

India
Reliance Publishing House, pg 346
Sita Books & Periodicals Pvt Ltd, pg 349
South Asia Publications, pg 349
A H Wheeler & Co Ltd, pg 353

Indonesia
Yayasan Obor Indonesia, pg 357

Italy
Arcipelago Edizioni di Chiani Marisa, pg 376
EGEA (Edizioni Giuridiche Economiche Aziendali), pg 387

Republic of Korea
Chung Rim Publishing Co Ltd, pg 438
Daehan Printing & Publishing Co Ltd, pg 438
Nanam Publications Co, pg 441

Latvia
Egmont Latvia SIA, pg 444

Lithuania
Algarve, pg 448

Mexico
Aguilar Altea Taurus Alfaguara SA de CV, pg 462
Editorial Diana SA de CV, pg 464
Fondo de Cultura Economica, pg 465
Editorial Limusa SA de CV, pg 467
Medios Publicitarios Mexicanos SA de CV Editora de Directorios de Medios, pg 468
Medios y Medios, Sa de CV, pg 468
Naves Internacional de Ediciones SA, pg 469
Editorial Nova, SA de CV, pg 469

Morocco
Access International Services, pg 474

Netherlands
Samsom BedrijfsInformatie BV, pg 488

Nigeria
West African Book Publishers Ltd, pg 507

PUBLISHERS   SUBJECT INDEX

Pakistan
International Educational Services, pg 512

Poland
Polskie Wydawnictwo Ekonomiczne PWE SA, pg 522
'Slask' Ltd, pg 526

Portugal
Edicoes Cetop, pg 529

Romania
Editura Cronos SRL, pg 539
Nemira Verlag, pg 541
Rentrop & Straton Verlagsgruppe und Wirtschaftsconsulting, pg 542

Russian Federation
Izdatelstvo Standartov, pg 549
Izdatelstvo Sudostroenie, pg 549

Singapore
McGallen & Bolden Associates, pg 557

Slovenia
Univerza v Ljubljani Ekonomska Fakulteta, pg 562

Spain
Celeste Ediciones, pg 576
Fragua Editorial, pg 583
Ediciones Gestio 2000 SA, pg 585
LEDA (Las Ediciones de Arte), pg 589
Ediciones de la Torre, pg 602
Tursen, SA, pg 603

Taiwan, Province of China
Designer Publisher Inc, pg 639
San Min Book Co Ltd, pg 641

Turkey
Soez Yayin/Oyunajans, pg 651

United Kingdom
Books for Europe Ltd, pg 669
Cassell & Co, pg 675
CMP Information Ltd, pg 680
Hollis Publishing Ltd, pg 709
ICC United Kingdom, pg 711
Johnson Publications Ltd, pg 716
NTC Research, pg 734
RotoVision SA, pg 751
Vacation Work Publications, pg 769
Verulam Publishing Ltd, pg 770

Viet Nam
Science & Technics Publishing House, pg 780

AERONAUTICS, AVIATION

Albania
NL SH, pg 1

Australia
Aerospace Publications Pty Ltd, pg 11
Chingchic Publishers, pg 17
Kookaburra Technical Publications Pty Ltd, pg 28
McGraw-Hill Australia Pty Ltd, pg 31

OTEN (Open Training & Education Network), pg 34
Turton & Armstrong Pty Ltd Publishers, pg 44

Austria
Herbert Weishaupt Verlag, pg 59

Brazil
Action Editora Ltda, pg 76

China
Aviation Industry Press, pg 101
National Defence Industry Press, pg 106
Qingdao Publishing House, pg 107

Czech Republic
Svet Kridel, pg 125

Finland
Koala-Kustannus Oy, pg 143

France
ATP - Packager, pg 148
Cepadues Editions SA, pg 153
Le Cherche Midi Editeur, pg 154
Editions Chiron, pg 154
Jean-P Delville Editions, pg 157
EPA (Editions Pratiques Automobiles), pg 161
Editions Eska, pg 162
Editions Jean Paul Gisserot, pg 165
Association d'Editions Sorg, pg 186

Germany
Air Gallery Edition, Helmut Kreuzer, pg 191
Aviatic Verlag GmbH, pg 196
Flugzeug Publikations GmbH, pg 225
Alfred Hammer, pg 233
Heel Verlag GmbH, pg 235
Kartographischer Verlag Reinhard Ryborsch, pg 244
Verlagsgruppe Koehler/Mittler, pg 248
Nara Verlag Josef Krauthaeuser, pg 250
E S Mittler und Sohn GmbH, pg 261
Motorbuch-Verlag, pg 262
Neckar Verlag GmbH, pg 263
Palazzi Verlag GmbH, pg 268
Paul Pietsch Verlage GmbH & Co, pg 270
UNO-Verlag GmbH, pg 293
Herbert Wichmann Verlag, pg 299

Greece
D & J Vardikos Vivliotechnica Hellas, pg 313

India
Affiliated East West Press Pvt Ltd, pg 327
Heritage Publishers, pg 335
Himalayan Books, pg 336
Sita Books & Periodicals Pvt Ltd, pg 349

Ireland
Avoca Publications, pg 358

Israel
Bitan Publishers Ltd, pg 365
Freund Publishing House Ltd, pg 367

Italy
Edizioni Cremonese SRL, pg 383
Editoriale Domus SpA, pg 385
Fenice 2000, pg 389
Editoriale Olimpia SpA, pg 401

Malaysia
Penerbit Universiti Teknologi Malaysia, pg 459

Mexico
Editorial Limusa SA de CV, pg 467

Netherlands
BV Uitgeversbedryf Het Goede Boek, pg 482

New Zealand
Craig Printing Co Ltd, pg 495
David Ling Publishing, pg 498
Southern Press Ltd, pg 501

Poland
Iskry - Publishing House Ltd spotka zoo, pg 523
Wydawnictwa Komunikacji i Lacznosci Co Ltd, pg 524

Portugal
Dinalivro, pg 530
Latina Livraria Editora, pg 532

Russian Federation
FGUP Izdatelstvo Mashinostroenie, pg 544
Izdatelstvo Mir, pg 546
Nauka Publishers, pg 547
Izdatelstvo Transport, pg 549

South Africa
Flesch Financial Publications (Pty) Ltd, pg 563
Galago Publishing Pty Ltd, pg 564

Spain
Ediciones Doce Calles SL, pg 579
Editorial Juventud SA, pg 588
Editorial San Martin, pg 598
Silex Ediciones, pg 600

Sweden
Allt om Hobby AB, pg 609
Frank Stenvalls Forlag, pg 615

Switzerland
Editions 24 Heures, pg 635

Ukraine
Osnova, Kharkov State University Press, pg 653

United Kingdom
Airlife Publishing Ltd, pg 656
Ian Allan Publishing Ltd, pg 656
Amber Books Ltd, pg 657
Arms & Armour Press, pg 659
BCA - Book Club Associates, pg 663
BLA Publishing Ltd, pg 666
Books for Europe Ltd, pg 669
Books International, pg 669
Brassey's UK Ltd, pg 670
Bridge Books, pg 671
Castlemead Publications, pg 676
Compendium Publishing, pg 681
The Crowood Press Ltd, pg 684
Terence Dalton Ltd, pg 685

ERA Technology Ltd, pg 692
Grange Books PLC, pg 702
Greenhill Books/Lionel Leventhal Ltd, pg 703
Halldale Publishing & Media Ltd, pg 704
Haynes Publishing, pg 706
Institution of Electrical Engineers, pg 713
Jane's Information Group, pg 715
Midland Publishing, pg 728
New European Publications Ltd, pg 732
Octopus Publishing Group, pg 734
Osprey Publishing Ltd, pg 737
Pearson Education, pg 739
Pen & Sword Books Ltd, pg 740
Salamander Books Ltd, pg 753

Viet Nam
Science & Technics Publishing House, pg 780

AFRICAN AMERICAN STUDIES

Brazil
Francisco J Laissue Livraria, pg 84
Pallas Editora e Distribuidora Ltda, pg 88

Cuba
Editorial Oriente, pg 120

France
Revue Noire, pg 183

Germany
Franz Steiner Verlag Wiesbaden GmbH, pg 287

Kenya
Nairobi University Press, pg 435
Sasa Sema Publications Ltd, pg 435

Poland
Wydawnictwa Uniwersytetu Warszawskiego, pg 527

South Africa
Galago Publishing Pty Ltd, pg 564

Spain
Ediciones Doce Calles SL, pg 579

United Kingdom
Boydell & Brewer Ltd, pg 669
Compendium Publishing, pg 681
Adam Matthew Publications, pg 726
Pluto Books Ltd, pg 743
Pluto Press, pg 743
Serpent's Tail Ltd, pg 756

AGRICULTURE

Albania
NL SH, pg 1

Argentina
Editorial Albatros SACI, pg 3
Cosmopolita SRL, pg 4
Editorial Hemisferio Sur SA, pg 6
Editoria Universitaria de la Patagonia, pg 9

SUBJECT INDEX BOOK

Armenia
Ajstan Publishers, pg 10

Australia
Bernal Publishing, pg 14
Bureau of Resource Sciences, pg 16
Candlelight Trust T/A Candlelight Farm, pg 17
Cornucopia Press, pg 18
CSIRO Publishing (Commonwealth Scientific & Industrial Research Organisation), pg 19
Department of Primary Industries, Queensland, pg 20
OTEN (Open Training & Education Network), pg 34
Pacific Publications (Australia) Pty Ltd, pg 35
Transpareon Press, pg 44
Winetitles, pg 47

Austria
CEEBA Publications Antenne d'Autriche, pg 49
Development News Ltd, pg 50
IAEA - International Atomic Energy Agency, pg 52
Leopold Stocker Verlag, pg 53
Oesterreichischer Agrarverlag, Druck- und Verlags- GmbH, pg 55
Georg Prachner KG, pg 56

Azerbaijan
Azernesr, pg 60

Bangladesh
The University Press Ltd, pg 61

Belarus
Belaruskaya Encyklapedyya, pg 62

Belgium
Campinia Media VZW, pg 64
King Baudouin Foundation, pg 69
Leuven University Press, pg 70
Presses agronomiques de Gembloux ASBL, pg 72

Brazil
Editora Antroposofica Ltda, pg 77
Instituto Campineiro de Ensino Agricola Ltda, pg 79
Empresa Brasileira de Pesquisa Agropecuaria, pg 81
Livro Ibero-Americano Ltda, pg 83
Icone Editora Ltda, pg 83
Livraria Nobel S/A, pg 85
Editora Ortiz SA, pg 88
Livraria Pioneira Editora/Enio Matheus Guazzelli e Cia Ltd, pg 88

Bulgaria
Darzhavno Izdatelstvo Zemizdat, pg 93
Pensoft Publishers, pg 96
TEMTO, pg 97

China
Beijing Publishing House, pg 101
Chemical Industry Press, pg 101
China Agriculture Press, pg 102
China Forestry Publishing House, pg 102
East China University of Science & Technology Press, pg 104
Fujian Science & Technology Publishing House, pg 104
Guangdong Science & Technology Press, pg 105
Heilongjiang Science & Technology Press, pg 105
Higher Education Press, pg 105
Inner Mongolia Science & Technology Publishing House, pg 105
International Academic Publishers (IAP), pg 105
Jilin Science & Technology Publishing House, pg 105
Jinan Publishing House, pg 105
Qingdao Publishing House, pg 107
Shandong Science & Technology Press, pg 107
Shanghai Scientific & Technical Publishers, pg 108
Shanghai Scientific & Technological Literature Press, pg 108
Sichuan Science & Technology Publishing House, pg 108
South China University of Science & Technology Press, pg 108
Tianjin Science & Technology Publishing House, pg 108
Zhejiang University Press, pg 109

Colombia
Universidad Nacional Abierta y a Distancia, pg 113

The Democratic Republic of the Congo
Centre de Vulgarisation Agricole, pg 114

Costa Rica
Academia de Centro America, pg 114
Centro Agronomico Tropical de Investigacion y Ensenanza (CATIE), pg 115
Instituto Interamericano de Cooperacion para la Agricultura (IICA), pg 115
Editorial de la Universidad de Costa Rica, pg 116
Editorial Universidad Estatal a Distancia (EUNED), pg 116

Croatia
Matica hrvatska, pg 118

Cuba
ISCAH Fructuoso Rodriguez, pg 120

Czech Republic
Mendelova zemedelska a lesnicka univerzita v Brne, pg 125

Dominican Republic
Pontificia Universidad Catolica Madre y Maestra, pg 136

Ecuador
Centro de Planificacion y Estudios Sociales (CEPLAES), pg 136
SECAP, pg 137

Egypt (Arab Republic of Egypt)
Dar Al-Matbo at Al-Gadidah, pg 138

Estonia
Eesti Entsuklopeediakirjastus, pg 139
Valgus Publishers, pg 140

France
Editions J B Bailliere, pg 149
Bottin SA, pg 151
Editions des Cahiers Bourbonnais, pg 151
Cemagref Editions, pg 152
Cirad, pg 154
Counseil International de la Langue Francaise, pg 156
Institut pour le Developpement Forestier, pg 158
Editions Edisud, pg 159
Folklore Comtois, pg 164
Groupe de Recherche et d'Echanges Technologiques (GRET), pg 166
INRA Editions (Institut National de la Recherche Agronomique), pg 168
Editions Lavoisier, pg 171
Editions Legislatives, pg 171
Editions John Libbey Eurotext, pg 172
Maisonneuve et Larose, pg 174
Editions Pedone, pg 179
Polytechnica SA, pg 180
Editions Sang de la Terre, pg 184
Terre Vivante, pg 187

Georgia
Sakartvelo Publishing House, pg 190

Germany
Badischer Landwirtschafts-Verlag GmbH, pg 196
Verlag Dr Albert Bartens KG, pg 197
Blackwell Wissenschafts-Verlag GmbH, pg 201
BLV Verlagsgesellschaft mbH, pg 202
Deutsche Landwirtschafts-Gesellschaft VerlagsgesGmbH, pg 212
Deutscher Fachverlag GmbH, pg 212
DLV Deutscher Landwirtschaftsverlag GmbH, pg 215
Hessisches Ministerium fuer Umwelt, Landwirtschaft und Forsten, pg 237
Justus-Liebig-Universitat Giessen, pg 244
Landbuch-Verlagsgesellschaft mbH, pg 251
Margraf Verlag, pg 257
Nusser Verlag, pg 266
J D Sauerlaender's Verlag, pg 278
Springer Science+Business Media GmbH & Co KG, pg 284
Thalacker Medien GmbH Co KG, pg 290
Verlag Eugen Ulmer GmbH & Co, pg 293
UNO-Verlag GmbH, pg 293
UTB fuer Wissenschaft Uni Taschenbuecher GmbH, pg 294

Ghana
Ghana Universities Press (GUP), pg 304
Sam Woode Ltd, pg 304
Sedco Publishing Ltd, pg 305
Unimax Macmillan Ltd, pg 305

Greece
Gartaganis D, pg 307

Guinea-Bissau
Instituto Nacional de Estudos e Pesquisa (INEP), pg 314

Haiti
Editions Caraibes SA, pg 314

Hong Kong
Friends of the Earth (Charity) Ltd, pg 317

Hungary
Foldmuvelesugyi Miniszterium Muszaki Intezet, pg 321
Mezogazda Kiado, pg 323
Pro Natura, pg 324

India
Affiliated East West Press Pvt Ltd, pg 327
Agricole Publishing Academy, pg 327
Allied Book Centre, pg 328
Allied Publishers Pvt Ltd, pg 328
APH Publishing Corp, pg 328
Avinash Reference Publications, pg 329
The Bangalore Printing & Publishing Co Ltd, pg 329
Bhawan Book Service, Publishers & Distributors, pg 330
Book Circle, pg 330
BR Publishing Corporation, pg 331
BSMPS - M/s Bishen Singh Mahendra Pal Singh, pg 331
Cosmo Publications, pg 332
Daya Publishing House, pg 333
Gyan Publishing House, pg 335
Heritage Publishers, pg 335
IBD Publisher & Distributors, pg 336
Indian Council of Agricultural Research, pg 336
Indus Publishing Co, pg 338
Inter-India Publications, pg 338
International Book Distributors, pg 338
Law Publishers, pg 340
Mehta Publishers, pg 341
Minerva Associates (Publications) Pvt Ltd, pg 341
National Book Organization, pg 342
National Council of Applied Economic Research, Publications Division, pg 342
Naya Prokash, pg 343
Nem Chand & Brothers, pg 343
Omsons Publications, pg 344
Oxford & IBH Publishing Co Pvt Ltd, pg 344
Pointer Publishers, pg 345
Rajasthan Hindi Granth Academy, pg 346
Rastogi Publications, pg 346
Regency Publications, pg 346
Reliance Publishing House, pg 346
Research Signpost, pg 347
Sasta Sahitya Mandal, pg 348
Scientific Book Agency, pg 348
Scientific Publishers India, pg 349
Sita Books & Periodicals Pvt Ltd, pg 349
Somaiya Publications Pvt Ltd, pg 349
South Asia Publications, pg 349
Sterling Publishers Pvt Ltd, pg 350
Today & Tomorrow's Printers & Publishers, pg 351
Transworld Research Network, pg 351

PUBLISHERS

Indonesia
Bhratara Karya Aksara, pg 354
Bumi Aksara PT, pg 354
Karya Anda, CV, pg 355
CV Yasaguna, pg 357

Iraq
National House for Publishing, Distributing & Advertising, pg 357

Ireland
On Stream Publications Ltd, pg 362

Israel
Hakibbutz Hameuchad Publishing House Ltd, pg 367

Italy
Apimondia, pg 375
CLUEB (Cooperativa Libraria Universitaria Editrice Bologna), pg 382
Giovanni De Vecchi Editore SpA, pg 384
Demetra SRL, pg 385
Edagricole - Edizioni Agricole, pg 385
Gangemi Editore spa, pg 390
Laruffa Editore SRL, pg 394
Patron Editore SrL, pg 402
Red/Studio Redazionale, pg 405
Editrice San Marco SRL, pg 407
Unipress, pg 411

Japan
Chikyu-sha Co Ltd, pg 416
Hakuyu-Sha, pg 418
Hokuryukan Co Ltd, pg 418
Ie-No-Hikari Association, pg 419
Japan Publications Inc, pg 419
Nosangyoson Bunka Kyokai, pg 424
Seibido Shuppan Company Ltd, pg 426
Taimeido Publishing Co Ltd, pg 429
Yokendo Ltd, pg 431
Zenkoku Kyodo Shuppan, pg 431

Kenya
African Centre for Technology Studies (ACTS), pg 433
Heinemann Kenya Ltd (EAEP), pg 434
International Centre for Research in Agroforestry (ICRAF), pg 434
Kenya Energy & Environment Organisation, Kengo, pg 434
Kenya Literature Bureau, pg 434

Democratic People's Republic of Korea
Korea Science and Encyclopedia Publishing House, pg 436

Republic of Korea
Daehan Printing & Publishing Co Ltd, pg 438
Hyangmunsa Publishing Co, pg 439
Korea University Press, pg 440

Latvia
Preses Nams, pg 445

Lithuania
Academia, pg 448
Klaipedos Universiteto Leidykla, pg 449
Mokslo ir enciklopediju leidybos institutas, pg 449
Margi Rastai Publishers, pg 449

Luxembourg
Service Central de la Statistique et des Etudes Economiques (STATEC), pg 451

Madagascar
Foibe Filan-Kevitry NY Mpampianatra (FOFIPA), pg 453

Malawi
Dzuka Publishing Co Ltd, pg 454

Maldive Islands
Non-Formal Education Centre, pg 459

Martinique
Editions Gondwana, pg 460

Mauritius
Editions de l'Ocean Indien Ltd, pg 461

Mexico
AGT Editor SA, pg 462
Colegio de Postgraduados en Ciencias Agricolas, pg 463
Fondo de Cultura Economica, pg 465
Grupo Editorial Iberoamerica, SA de CV, pg 466
Editorial Limusa SA de CV, pg 467
Plaza y Valdes SA de CV, pg 470

Republic of Moldova
Editura Cartea Moldovei, pg 473

Myanmar
Sarpay Beikman Public Library, pg 476

Namibia
Desert Research Foundation of Namibia (DRFN), pg 476
Multi-Disciplinary Research Centre Library, pg 476

Nepal
International Standards Books & Periodicals (P) Ltd, pg 476

Netherlands
KIT - Royal Tropical Institute Publishers, pg 484
Wageningen Academic Publishers, pg 492

New Zealand
Fraser Books, pg 496
Oxford University Press, pg 499
SIR Publishing, pg 501
Statistics New Zealand, pg 501

Nigeria
Evans Brothers (Nigeria Publishers) Ltd, pg 504
Ibadan University Press, pg 505
West African Book Publishers Ltd, pg 507

Pakistan
National Book Foundation, pg 513
Pakistan Institute of Development Economics (PIDE), pg 514
Publishers United Pvt Ltd, pg 514
Sang-e-Meel Publications, pg 514

Papua New Guinea
Kristen Press, pg 515

Peru
Instituto Frances de Estudios Andinos, IFEA, pg 517

Philippines
Communication Foundation for Asia Media Group (CFAMG), pg 518
International Rice Research Institute (IRRI), pg 519
Rex Bookstores & Publishers, pg 520

Poland
Ludowa Spoldzielnia Wydawnicza, pg 524
Panstwowe Wydawnictwo Rolnicze i Lesne, pg 525
Polish Scientific Publishers PWN, pg 525
Wydawnictwa Uniwersytetu Warszawskiego, pg 527

Portugal
Publicacoes Ciencia e Vida Lda, pg 529
Instituto de Investigacao Cientifica Tropical, pg 532
Editora McGraw-Hill de Portugal Lda, pg 533
Almerinda Teixeira, pg 536

Romania
Editura Ceres, pg 539
MAST Verlag, pg 540

Russian Federation
Izdatelstvo 'Ekonomika', pg 544
Gidrometeoizdat, pg 545
Izvestia Sovetov Narodnyh Deputatov Russian Federation (RF), pg 545
Izdatelstvo Lenizdat, pg 546
Izdatelstvo Mordovskogo gosudarstvennogo, pg 547

Saudi Arabia
King Saud University, pg 550

Serbia and Montenegro
Nolit Publishing House, pg 553
Partenon MAM Sistem, pg 553

Slovakia
Technicka Univerzita, pg 561

South Africa
Educum Publishers Ltd, pg 563
New Africa Books (Pty) Ltd, pg 567
South African Institute of Race Relations, pg 569

Spain
Editorial Acribia SA, pg 571
Editorial AEDOS SA, pg 571
Ediciones Agrotecnicas, SL, pg 571
AMV Ediciones, pg 572

SUBJECT INDEX

Cedel, Ediciones Jose O Avila Monteso ES, pg 576
Comunidad Autonoma de Madrid, Servicio de Documentacion y Publicaciones, pg 578
Dilagro SA, pg 579
Idea Books, SA, pg 587
Institucion Fernando el Catolico de la Excma Diputacion de Zaragoza, pg 587
Mundi-Prensa Libros SA, pg 592
Oikos-Tau SA Ediciones, pg 593
Ediciones Omega SA, pg 594
Pages Editors, SL, pg 594
Pais Vasco Servicio Central de Publicaciones, pg 594
Publicaciones de la Universidad de Alicante, pg 597
Riquelme y Vargas Ediciones SL, pg 598
Rueda, SL Editorial, pg 598
Servicio de Publicaciones Universidad de Cordoba, pg 599
Editorial Rudolf Steiner, pg 601
Universidad de Malaga, pg 603
Editorial De Vecchi SA, pg 604
Ediciones A Madrid Vicente, pg 605
Xunta de Galicia, pg 605

Sri Lanka
Ministry of Education, pg 607
Swarna Hansa Foundation, pg 607
Waruni Publishers, pg 607

Sweden
Natur och Kultur Fakta etc, pg 614

Switzerland
Verlag Huber & Co AG, pg 625
SAB Schweiz Arbeitsgemeinschaft fuer die Berggebiete, pg 633
Vdf Hochschulverlag AG an der ETH Zurich, pg 636
Verbandsdruckerei AG, pg 636

Syrian Arab Republic
Damascus University Press, pg 638

Taiwan, Province of China
Chien Chen Bookstore Publishing Company Ltd, pg 639
Fuh-Wen Book Co, pg 639
Chu Hai Publishing (Taiwan) Co Ltd, pg 640
Hilit Publishing Co Ltd, pg 640
San Min Book Co Ltd, pg 641
Yi Hsien Publishing Co Ltd, pg 642

Tajikistan
Irfon, pg 642

United Republic of Tanzania
Bureau of Statistics, pg 643
Peramiho Publications, pg 644
Press & Publicity Centre Ltd, pg 644
Tanzania Publishing House, pg 644

Thailand
Bannakit Trading, pg 645
Thai Watana Panich Co, Ltd, pg 646

Tunisia
Maison Tunisienne de l'Edition, pg 648

SUBJECT INDEX

Turkmenistan
Izdatelstvo Turkmenistan, pg 652

Uganda
Centre for Basic Research, pg 652
Fountain Publishers Ltd, pg 652

Ukraine
Naukova Dumka Publishers, pg 653
Osnova, Kharkov State University Press, pg 653
Urozaj, pg 654

United Kingdom
Batsford Ltd, pg 663
Biocommerce Data Ltd, pg 665
BIOS Scientific Publishers Ltd, pg 665
Cambridge University Press, pg 674
Commonwealth Secretariat, pg 681
James Currey Ltd, pg 685
Elsevier Ltd, pg 691
The Eurospan Group, pg 692
Green Books Ltd, pg 702
Hyden House Ltd, pg 711
Institute of Development Studies, pg 712
Intercept Ltd, pg 714
International Bee Research Association, pg 714
ITDG Publishing, pg 715
Manson Publishing Ltd, pg 725
Old Pond Publishing, pg 734
Packard Publishing Ltd, pg 737
Pearson Education, pg 739
Scottish Executive Library & Information Services, pg 755
Rudolf Steiner Press, pg 761
Sutton Publishing Ltd, pg 762
Timber Press Inc, pg 765
TSO (The Stationery Office), pg 767
Westview Press, pg 772

Uruguay
Nordan-Comunidad, pg 778

Venezuela
Fundacion Servicio para el Agricultor, pg 779

Viet Nam
Science & Technics Publishing House, pg 780

Zambia
Historical Association of Zambia, pg 781
Zambia Educational Publishing House, pg 782
Zambia Printing Company Ltd (ZPC), pg 782

Zimbabwe
College Press Publishers (Pvt) Ltd, pg 783
Farm-level Applied Methods for East & Southern Africa (FARMESA), pg 783
Longman Zimbabwe (Pvt) Ltd, pg 783
Standards Association of Zimbabwe (SAZ), pg 784
Thomson Publications Zimbabwe (Pvt) Ltd, pg 784
Zimbabwe Women's Bureau, pg 785

ALTERNATIVE

Australia
Allen & Unwin Pty Ltd, pg 11
Appropriate Technology Development Group (Inc) WA, pg 11
Bio Concepts Publishing, pg 14
Bridge To Peace Publications, pg 16
Gnostic Editions, pg 23
Hihorse Publishing Pty Ltd, pg 25
In-Tune Books, pg 26
Rams Skull Press, pg 38
Scroll Publishers, pg 40
Simon & Schuster (Australia) Pty Ltd, pg 41
Spinifex Press, pg 42
Tomorrow Publications, pg 44

Austria
Verlag des Osterr Kneippbundes GmbH, pg 56

Belgium
Altina, pg 63
Vita, pg 74

Brazil
Editora Aquariana Ltda, pg 77
Triom Centro de Estudos Marina e Martin Hawey Editorial e Comercial Ltda, pg 91

Bulgaria
Kibea Publishing Co, pg 95

China
Qingdao Publishing House, pg 107

Cuba
ISCAH Fructuoso Rodriguez, pg 120

Czech Republic
Chvojkova nakladatelstvi, pg 123
Nakladatelstvi Jota spol sro, pg 124
Votobia sro, pg 128

Denmark
Borgens Forlag A/S, pg 129
Politikens Forlag A/S, pg 133

France
Editions Alternatives, pg 146

Germany
EVT Energy Video Training & Verlag GmbH, pg 222
IKO Verlag fur Interkulturelle Kommunikation, pg 241
Karin Kramer Verlag, pg 250
Medizinisch-Literarische Verlagsgesellschaft mbH, pg 258
Die Silberschnur Verlag GmbH, pg 283
Suin Buch-Verlag, pg 289
Trotzdem-Verlags Genossenschaft eG, pg 292
Weber Zucht & Co, pg 298

India
Concept Publishing Co, pg 332
Firma KLM Privatee Ltd, Publishers & International Booksellers, pg 334
B Jain Publishers Overseas, pg 338

Italy
Edizioni GB, pg 390
Macro Edizioni, pg 397
Edizioni Mediterranee SRL, pg 398
Il Punto D Incontro, pg 404

Democratic People's Republic of Korea
Grand People's Study House, pg 436

Luxembourg
Varkki Verghese, pg 452

Netherlands
Servire BV Uitgevers, pg 489

New Zealand
RSVP Publishing Co Ltd, pg 500

Norway
Ex Libris Forlag A/S, pg 509
Hilt & Hansteen A/S, pg 509

Singapore
Select Publishing Pte Ltd, pg 557

South Africa
Kima Global Publishers, pg 566

Spain
Baile del Sol, Colectivo Cultural, pg 574
Editorial Fundamentos, pg 584
Ediciones Norma SA, pg 593
OASIS, Producciones Generales de Comunicacion, pg 593
Obelisco Ediciones S, pg 593
Ediciones Urano, SA, pg 604

Switzerland
Rotpunktverlag, pg 632

Turkey
Ruh ve Madde Yayinlari ve Saglik Hizmetleri AS, pg 651
Soez Yayin/Oyunajans, pg 651

United Kingdom
Act 3 Publishing, pg 655
Atlas Press, pg 661
Beaconsfield Publishers Ltd, pg 664
Capall Bann Publishing, pg 674
Carroll & Brown Ltd, pg 675
Foulsham Publishers, pg 696
Janus Publishing Co Ltd, pg 716
Quarto Publishing plc, pg 746
The Women's Press Ltd, pg 775

Uruguay
Nordan-Comunidad, pg 778

AMERICANA, REGIONAL

Albania
NL SH, pg 1

Mexico
El Colegio de Michoacan A C, pg 464
Instituto Nacional de Antropologia e Historia, pg 469

New Zealand
Barkfire Press, pg 494

Poland
Wydawnictwa Uniwersytetu Warszawskiego, pg 527

United Kingdom
Microform Academic Publishers, pg 728

ANIMALS, PETS

Albania
NL SH, pg 1
State Textbook Publishing House, pg 1

Argentina
Editorial Albatros SACI, pg 3
Editorial Caymi SACI, pg 4
Diana Argentina SA, Editorial, pg 5
Editorial Hemisferio Sur SA, pg 6
Ediciones Lidiun, pg 7

Australia
Austed Publishing Co, pg 12
Bandicoot Books, pg 14
Chiron Media, pg 17
D'Artagnan Publishing, pg 19
Department of Primary Industries, Queensland, pg 20
Egan Publishing Pty Ltd, pg 21
Hyland House Publishing Pty Ltd, pg 26
Lansdowne Publishing Pty Ltd, pg 28
Tom Roberts (Pat Roberts), pg 39
Simon & Schuster (Australia) Pty Ltd, pg 41
The Watermark Press, pg 46

Austria
Development News Ltd, pg 50
Verlag Carl Ueberreuter GmbH, pg 58

Belarus
Interdigest Publishing House, pg 62

Belgium
Editions Gerard Blanchart & Cie SA, pg 63
Ediblanchart sprl, pg 67
Marabout, pg 71
Zuid-Nederlandse Uitgeverij NV/Central Uitgeverij, pg 75

Brazil
Livraria Nobel S/A, pg 85
Editora Mantiqueira de Ciencia e Arte, pg 86
Ediouro Publicacoes, SA, pg 89

Bulgaria
Gea-Libris Publishing House, pg 94

China
China Agriculture Press, pg 102
China Braille Publishing House, pg 102
China Forestry Publishing House, pg 102
Jilin Science & Technology Publishing House, pg 105
Qingdao Publishing House, pg 107

PUBLISHERS SUBJECT INDEX

Science Press, pg 107
Shanghai Far East Publishers, pg 108

Colombia

Editorial Santillana SA, pg 112

Costa Rica

Editorial Texto Ltda, pg 116

Czech Republic

Aventinum Nakladatelstvi spol sro, pg 122
Granit sro, pg 123
Mendelova zemedelska a lesnicka univerzita v Brne, pg 125
Narodni Muzeum, pg 126

Denmark

Borgens Forlag A/S, pg 129

Egypt (Arab Republic of Egypt)

Dar Al-Matbo at Al-Gadidah, pg 138

Estonia

Sinisukk, pg 140
Valgus Publishers, pg 140

Finland

Weilin & Goos Oy, pg 144

France

Editions d'Annabelle, pg 147
ATP - Packager, pg 148
Editions Bornemann, pg 150
Le Cherche Midi Editeur, pg 154
Editeurs Crepin-Leblond, pg 156
De Vecchi Editions SA, pg 157
Les Editions des Deux Coqs d'Or, pg 158
Editions Grund, pg 160
Editions Jean Paul Gisserot, pg 165
Hachette Pratiques, pg 167
Le Jour, Editeur, pg 169
Editions Larousse, pg 171
Maisonneuve et Larose, pg 174
Les Editions du Point Veterinaire, pg 180
Editions Sang de la Terre, pg 184

Germany

Augustus Verlag, pg 195
Blackwell Wissenschafts-Verlag GmbH, pg 201
BLV Verlagsgesellschaft mbH, pg 202
DLV Deutscher Landwirtschaftsverlag GmbH, pg 215
Echo Verlag, pg 217
Egmont vgs verlagsgesellschaft mbH, pg 218
Engel & Bengel Verlag, pg 220
Franckh-Kosmos Verlags-GmbH & Co, pg 226
Graefe und Unzer Verlag GmbH, pg 230
F Hirthammer Verlag GmbH, pg 238
Knowledge Media International, pg 247
Kunstverlag Weingarten GmbH, pg 251
Kynos Verlag Dr Dieter Fleig GmbH, pg 251
Landbuch-Verlagsgesellschaft mbH, pg 251

Mergus Verlag GmbH Hans A Baensch, pg 259
Karl-Heinz Metz, pg 259
Mosaik Verlag GmbH, pg 262
Verlag Natur & Wissenschaft Harro Hieronimus & Dr Jurgen Schmidt, pg 263
Naumann & Goebel Verlagsgesellschaft mbH, pg 263
Neuer Honos Verlag GmbH, pg 264
Neumann Verlag, pg 264
Oertel & Sporer GmbH & Co, pg 266
Orbis Verlag fur Publizistik GmbH, pg 267
Heidi Rogner, pg 276
M & H Schaper GmbH & Co KG, pg 279
Adolf Sponholtz Verlag, pg 284
Tetra Verlag Gmbh, pg 290
Tomus Verlag GmbH, pg 291
Verlag Eugen Ulmer GmbH & Co, pg 293
Verlagsgruppe Weltbild GmbH, pg 298

Greece

Chrysi Penna - Golden Pen Books, pg 306
Hestia-I D Hestia-Kollaros & Co Corporation, pg 308
Editions Moressopoulos, pg 310
Kyr I Papadopoulos E E, pg 311

Hong Kong

SCMP Book Publishing Ltd, pg 319
Sesame Publication Co, pg 319

Hungary

Aranyhal Konyvkiado Goldfish Publishing, pg 320
Mezogazda Kiado, pg 323

Iceland

Skjaldborg Ltd, pg 326

India

Allied Book Centre, pg 328
Dolphin Publications, pg 333
Indian Council of Agricultural Research, pg 336
International Book Distributors, pg 338
Rastogi Publications, pg 346
Sasta Sahitya Mandal, pg 348
Vidya Puri, pg 352

Indonesia

Gramedia, pg 355

Italy

Edizioni Arka SRL, pg 376
Gruppo Editoriale Armenia SpA, pg 376
Dami Editore SRL, pg 384
Giovanni De Vecchi Editore SpA, pg 384
Edagricole - Edizioni Agricole, pg 385
Fatatrac, pg 388
Fenice 2000, pg 389
Kompass Fleischmann, pg 394
Editoriale Olimpia SpA, pg 401
Editoriale Scienza, pg 407

Japan

Froebel - kan Co Ltd, pg 417
Hakuyo-Sha, pg 418
Kaisei-Sha Publishing Co Ltd, pg 420

Nagaoka Shoten Co Ltd, pg 423
Seibido Shuppan Company Ltd, pg 426

Kenya

Kenway Publications Ltd, pg 434
Kenya Literature Bureau, pg 434

Democratic People's Republic of Korea

Korea Science and Encyclopedia Publishing House, pg 436

Republic of Korea

Borim Publishing Co, pg 437

Latvia

Nordik/Tapals Publishers Ltd, pg 445
Preses Nams, pg 445
Vaidelote, SIA, pg 445
Zvaigzne ABC Publishers Ltd, pg 445

Lebanon

Arab Institute for Research & Publishing, pg 445
Librairie du Liban Publishers (Sal), pg 446
Librairie Orientale sal, pg 446

Liechtenstein

Botanisch-Zoologische Gesellschaft, pg 447

Lithuania

Victoria Publishers, pg 450

Maldive Islands

Novelty Printers & Publishers, pg 459

Mexico

Editorial Diana SA de CV, pg 464
Fernandez Editores SA de CV, pg 465
Editorial Jilguero, SA de CV, pg 467
Sistemas Tecnicos de Edicion SA de CV, pg 472
Ediciones Suromex SA, pg 472

Netherlands

BZZTOH Publishers, pg 480
Callenbach BV, pg 480
Uitgeverij Christofoor, pg 480
Rebo Productions BV, pg 488
Tirion Uitgevers BV, pg 490
Unieboek BV, pg 490
Wageningen Academic Publishers, pg 492
Zuid Boekprodukties BV, pg 493

Poland

Wydawnictwo Baturo, pg 522
'Ksiazka i Wiedza' Spotdzielnia Wydawniczo-Handlowa, pg 524
Wydawnictwo RTW, pg 526

Portugal

Publicacoes Ciencia e Vida Lda, pg 529
Editorial Presenca, pg 535
Edicoes 70 Lda, pg 535

Romania

Editura Ceres, pg 539
MAST Verlag, pg 540

Russian Federation

Armada Publishing House, pg 543
Gidrometeoizdat, pg 545
KUbK Publishing House, pg 546
Izdatelstvo Mir, pg 546
Scorpion Publishers, pg 548

Saudi Arabia

Dar Al-Shareff for Publishing & Distribution, pg 550

Slovakia

Technicka Univerzita, pg 561

Slovenia

Zalozba Obzorja d d Maribor, pg 562

South Africa

Flesch Financial Publications (Pty) Ltd, pg 563
Southern Book Publishers (Pty) Ltd, pg 569

Spain

Editorial AEDOS SA, pg 571
Comunidad Autonoma de Madrid, Servicio de Documentacion y Publicaciones, pg 578
Editorial Everest SA, pg 581
Editorial Hispano Europea SA, pg 586
Editorial Juventud SA, pg 588
Lynx Edicions, pg 590
Ediciones Martinez-Roca SA, pg 591
Mundi-Prensa Libros SA, pg 592
Pulso Ediciones, SL, pg 597
Ediciones Siruela SA, pg 600
Ediciones Tutor SA, pg 603
Editorial De Vecchi SA, pg 604
Xunta de Galicia, pg 605

Sweden

Bonnier Carlsen Bokforlag AB, pg 610
Bengt Forsbergs Foerlag AB, pg 611
ICA bokforlag, pg 612
Johnston & Streiffert Editions, pg 613
Natur och Kultur Fakta etc, pg 614
Bokforlaget Opal AB, pg 614
Bokforlaget Semic AB, pg 615
Svenska Foerlaget liv & ledarskap ab, pg 616

Switzerland

Bohem Press Kinderbuchverlag, pg 619
Hallwag Kuemmerly & Frey AG, pg 625
Kinderbuchverlag Luzern, pg 626
Mueller Rueschlikon Verlags AG, pg 629
Editions 24 Heures, pg 635

Taiwan, Province of China

Chien Chen Bookstore Publishing Company Ltd, pg 639
Grimm Press Ltd, pg 640
HYS Culture Co Ltd, pg 640
Yi Hsien Publishing Co Ltd, pg 642

United Republic of Tanzania

Tanzania Publishing House, pg 644

895

SUBJECT INDEX

Thailand
New Generation Publishing Co Ltd, pg 645

Tunisia
Les Editions de l'Arbre, pg 647

Turkey
Arkadas Ltd, pg 649
Inkilap Publishers Ltd, pg 650
Kok Yayincilik, pg 650

United Kingdom
Andromeda Oxford Ltd, pg 658
BCA - Book Club Associates, pg 663
Blaketon Hall Ltd, pg 667
Blandford Publishing Ltd, pg 668
Bounty Books, pg 669
Capall Bann Publishing, pg 674
Jon Carpenter Publishing, pg 675
Colour Library Direct, pg 681
The Crowood Press Ltd, pg 684
The C W Daniel Co Ltd, pg 686
David & Charles Ltd, pg 686
Elliot Right Way Books, pg 690
Eurobook Ltd, pg 692
Grange Books PLC, pg 702
HarperCollins UK, pg 705
Interpet Publishing, pg 714
The Kenilworth Press Ltd, pg 717
Lorenz Books, pg 722
Orpheus Books Ltd, pg 736
Parapress Ltd, pg 738
Primrose Hill Press Ltd, pg 745
Quarto Publishing plc, pg 746
Ravette Publishing Ltd, pg 748
The Reader's Digest Association Ltd, pg 748
Regency House Publishing Ltd, pg 749
Salamander Books Ltd, pg 753
Sherbourne Publications, pg 757
Silver Link Publishing Ltd, pg 758
Two-Can Publishing Ltd, pg 768
Verulam Publishing Ltd, pg 770
Weatherbys Allen Ltd, pg 772
Whittet Books Ltd, pg 773

Viet Nam
Science & Technics Publishing House, pg 780

Zimbabwe
The Literature Bureau, pg 783

ANTHROPOLOGY

Albania
NL SH, pg 1

Argentina
Alianza Editorial de Argentina SA, pg 3
Amorrortu Editores SA, pg 3
Editorial Guadalupe, pg 6
Editorial Kier SACIFI, pg 7
Theoria SRL Distribuidora y Editora, pg 9
Tipografica Editora Argentina, pg 9

Australia
Aboriginal Studies Press, pg 10
Australian Rock Art Research Association, pg 13
Crawford House Publishing Pty Ltd, pg 18
Deakin University Press, pg 19
Emperor Publishing, pg 21
Gnostic Editions, pg 23
Illert Publications, pg 26
Institute of Aboriginal Development (IAD Press), pg 27
Magabala Books Aboriginal Corporation, pg 30
McGraw-Hill Australia Pty Ltd, pg 31
New Endeavour Press, pg 33
Pearson Education Australia, pg 36
Pollitecon Publications, pg 37
Queen Victoria Museum & Art Gallery Publications, pg 38
Simon & Schuster (Australia) Pty Ltd, pg 41
Summer Institute of Linguistics, Australian Aborigines Branch, pg 42
Transpareon Press, pg 44
Unity Press, pg 44
Veritas Press, pg 45

Austria
Akademische Druck-u Verlagsanstalt Dr Paul Struzl GmbH, pg 48
CEEBA Publications Antenne d'Autriche, pg 49
Development News Ltd, pg 50
Ferdinand Berger und Sohne, pg 50
Promedia Verlagsges mbH, pg 56
Springer-Verlag Wien, pg 58
Edition Va Bene, pg 59

Bangladesh
Ankur Prakashani, pg 61
The University Press Ltd, pg 61

Belgium
Academia-Bruylant, pg 62
Centre Aequatoria, pg 63
Editions De Boeck-Larcier SA, pg 66
EPO Publishers, Printers, Booksellers, pg 67
Koepel van de Vlaamse Noord - Zuidbeweging 11.11.11, pg 69
Claude Lefrancq Editeur, pg 70

Brazil
Agalma Psicanalise Editora Ltda, pg 77
Editora Alfa Omega Ltda, pg 77
Ars Poetica Editora Ltda, pg 78
Associacao Palas Athena do Brasil, pg 78
Editora Bertrand Brasil Ltda, pg 78
Editora Companhia das Letras/Editora Schwarcz Ltda, pg 80
Dumara Distribuidora de Publicacoes Ltda, pg 81
Fundacao Joaquim Nabuco-Editora Massangana, pg 82
Fundacao Sao Paulo, EDUC, pg 82
Global Editora e Distribuidora Ltda, pg 82
Francisco J Laissue Livraria, pg 84
Edicoes Loyola SA, pg 85
Editora Mercado Aberto Ltda, pg 86
Pallas Editora e Distribuidora Ltda, pg 88
Editora Revan Ltda, pg 89
Editora Rocco Ltda, pg 89
34 Literatura S/C Ltda, pg 91
Editora UNESP, pg 91
Editora da Universidade de Sao Paulo, pg 91
Editora Universidade Federal do Rio de Janeiro, pg 92
Jorge Zahar Editor, pg 92

Bulgaria
Kibea Publishing Co, pg 95
LIK Izdanija, pg 95
Litera Prima, pg 95

Chile
Arrayan Editores, pg 98
Ediciones Mil Hojas Ltda, pg 99

China
China Tibetology Publishing House, pg 103
Cultural Relics Publishing House, pg 103
Foreign Languages Press, pg 104
Jilin Science & Technology Publishing House, pg 105
Qingdao Publishing House, pg 107
Yunnan University Press, pg 109
Zhong Hua Book Co, pg 110

Colombia
Siglo XXI Editores de Colombia Ltda, pg 112
Tercer Mundo Editores SA, pg 113

The Democratic Republic of the Congo
Facultes Catoliques de Kinshasa, pg 114

Costa Rica
Ediciones Promesa, pg 116
Editorial de la Universidad de Costa Rica, pg 116

Czech Republic
Narodni Muzeum, pg 126
Slon Sociologicke Nakladatelstvi, pg 127

Denmark
Aarhus Universitetsforlag, pg 128
Museum Tusculanum Press, pg 133

Ecuador
Ediciones Abya-Yala, pg 136
Centro de Planificacion y Estudios Sociales (CEPLAES), pg 136
Pontificia Universidad Catolica del Ecuador, Centro de Publicaciones, pg 137

Egypt (Arab Republic of Egypt)
American University in Cairo Press, pg 137

Finland
Suomalaisen Kirjallisuuden Seura, pg 144

France
Adverbum SARL, pg 146
Anako Editions, pg 146
Editions Anthropos, pg 147
Autrement Editions, pg 148
Berg International Editeur, pg 149
Presses Universitaires de Bordeaux (PUB), pg 150
Editions de l'Ecole des Hautes Etudes en Sciences Sociales (EHESS), pg 159
Editions Edisud, pg 159
Editions Recherche sur les Civilisations (ERC), pg 160
Paul Geuthner Librairie Orientaliste, pg 165
Editions Jean Paul Gisserot, pg 165
Groupe de Recherche et d'Echanges Technologiques (GRET), pg 166
Editions Imago, pg 168
Indigo & Cote-Femmes Editions, pg 168
Kailash Editions, pg 170
Karthala Editions-Diffusion, pg 170
Editions de la Maison des Sciences de l'Homme, Paris, pg 173
Editions A M Metailie, pg 175
Editions Parentheses, pg 179
Payot & Rivages, pg 179
Peeters-France, pg 179
Jean-Michel Place, pg 180
Revue Espaces et Societes, pg 183

French Polynesia
Haere Po Editions, pg 189

Germany
Verlag C H Beck oHG, pg 198
Bertelsmann Lexikon Verlag GmbH, pg 200
Boehlau-Verlag GmbH & Cie, pg 202
Brandes & Apsel Verlag GmbH, pg 204
Dareschta Consulting und Handels GmbH, pg 210
Verlag Esoterische Philosophie GmbH, pg 221
Europaeische Verlagsanstalt GmbH & Rotbuch Verlag GmbH & Co KG, pg 222
Guetersloher Verlagshaus, pg 232
Verlag Peter Hoell, pg 238
Hofbauer, Christoph und Trojanow Ilia, Akademischer Verlag Muenchen, pg 238
Holos Verlag, pg 239
IKO Verlag fur Interkulturelle Kommunikation, pg 241
Iudicium Verlag GmbH, pg 242
Dr Anton Kovac Slavica Verlag, pg 249
Idime Verlag Inge Melzer, pg 259
Merlin Verlag Andreas Meyer Verlags GmbH und Co KG, pg 259
Preubmpassling Verlag Gisela Meussling, pg 260
Palmyra Verlag, pg 268
Edition Parabolis, pg 268
Philipps-Universitaet Marburg, pg 270
Dietrich Reimer Verlag GmbH, pg 274
Renate Schenk Verlag, pg 279
E Schweizerbart'sche Verlagsbuchhandlung (Naegele und Obermiller), pg 282
Spieth-Verlag Verlag fuer Symbolforschung, pg 284
Steyler Verlag, pg 288
Suin Buch-Verlag, pg 289
VWB-Verlag fur Wissenschaft & Bildung, Amand Aglaster, pg 297
Verlag Clemens Zerling, pg 302

Ghana
Ghana Institute of Linguistics Literacy & Bible Translation (GILLBT), pg 304

Greece
Hestia-I D Hestia-Kollaros & Co Corporation, pg 308
Kastaniotis Editions SA, pg 309
Kritiki Publishing, pg 309
Ed Nea Acropolis, pg 310
Panepistimio Ioanninon, pg 311

PUBLISHERS

Patakis Publishers, pg 311
Society for Macedonian Studies, pg 312

Guinea-Bissau

Instituto Nacional de Estudos e Pesquisa (INEP), pg 314

Guyana

The Hamburgh Register, pg 314

Honduras

Editorial Guaymuras, pg 315

Hong Kong

Hong Kong University Press, pg 317

Hungary

Osiris Kiado, pg 323

India

Affiliated East West Press Pvt Ltd, pg 327
Agam Kala Prakashan, pg 327
Ajanta Publications (India), pg 327
Ananda Publishers Pvt Ltd, pg 328
Asian Educational Services, pg 329
K P Bagchi & Co, pg 329
Bani Mandir, Book-Sellers, Publishers & Educational Suppliers, pg 329
Books & Books, pg 331
BR Publishing Corporation, pg 331
Chowkhamba Sanskrit Series Office, pg 332
Concept Publishing Co, pg 332
Cosmo Publications, pg 332
Gyan Publishing House, pg 335
Indian Council of Social Science Research (ICSSR), pg 336
Indian Museum, pg 337
Inter-India Publications, pg 338
Manohar Publishers & Distributors, pg 340
Minerva Associates (Publications) Pvt Ltd, pg 341
Munshiram Manoharlal Publishers Pvt Ltd, pg 342
National Book Organization, pg 342
Omsons Publications, pg 344
Popular Prakashan Pvt Ltd, pg 345
Rahul Publishing House, pg 346
Regency Publications, pg 346
Reliance Publishing House, pg 346
SAGE Publications India Pvt Ltd, pg 347
Scientific Book Agency, pg 348
Somaiya Publications Pvt Ltd, pg 349
South Asia Publications, pg 349
South Asian Publishers Pvt Ltd, pg 350
Spectrum Publications, pg 350
Vision Books Pvt Ltd, pg 352

Indonesia

Karya Anda, CV, pg 355
Pustaka Utama Grafiti, PT, pg 356

Ireland

Irish Texts Society (Cumann Na Scribeann nGaedhilge), pg 361
Roberts Rinehart Publishers, pg 363
Tir Eolas, pg 363

Israel

Agudat Sabah, pg 364
The Institute for Israeli Arabs Studies, pg 368
Schocken Publishing House Ltd, pg 371
Zmora-Bitan, Publishers Ltd, pg 374

Italy

Adelphi Edizioni SpA, pg 374
Franco Angeli SRL, pg 375
Editore Armando Armando SRL, pg 376
Edizioni Borla SRL, pg 379
Centro Studi Terzo Mondo, pg 381
il Cerchio Iniziative Editoriali, pg 381
Edizioni Cultura della Pace, pg 383
Edizioni Dedalo SRL, pg 384
Editori Laterza, pg 386
Edizioni del Centro Camuno di Studi Preistorici, pg 386
Essegi, pg 388
Gangemi Editore spa, pg 390
Edizioni GB, pg 390
Grafo, pg 391
Edizioni Guerini e Associati SpA, pg 392
Hermes Edizioni SRL, pg 392
Ibis, pg 392
Instituti Editoriali E Poligrafici Internazionali SRL, pg 393
Editoriale Jaca Book SpA, pg 394
Liguori Editore SRL, pg 395
La Luna, pg 396
Editrice Missionaria Italiana (EMI), pg 398
Newton & Compton Editori, pg 400
Leo S Olschki, pg 401
Priuli e Verlucca, Editori, pg 404
Rubbettino Editore, pg 406
Il Saggiatore, pg 406
Sellerio Editore, pg 408
SEMAR Publishers SRL, pg 408
Servitium, pg 408
Edizioni Librarie Siciliane, pg 408
Urbaniana University Press, pg 411
Zanichelli Editore SpA, pg 412

Jamaica

University of the West Indies Press, pg 414

Japan

Tosui Shobo Publishers, pg 430
Tsukiji Shokan Publishing Co, pg 430
Waseda University Press, pg 431

Kenya

Gaba Publications Amecea, Pastoral Institute, pg 434
Kenway Publications Ltd, pg 434
Shirikon Publishers, pg 436
Gideon S Were Press, pg 436

Republic of Korea

Iljo-gag Publishers, pg 439
Seogwangsa, pg 442
Sohaksa, pg 443

Lesotho

Saint Michael's Mission Social Centre, pg 447

Macau

Livros Do Oriente, pg 452

The Former Yugoslav Republic of Macedonia

Zumpres Publishing Firm, pg 453

Malaysia

Forum Publications, pg 456

Mexico

Centro de Estudios Mexicanos y Centroamericanos, pg 463
El Colegio de Mexico AC, pg 463
El Colegio de Michoacan A C, pg 464
Ediciones Euroamericanas, pg 465
Editorial Extemporaneos SA, pg 465
Fondo de Cultura Economica, pg 465
Instituto Indigenista Interamericano, pg 466
Editorial Jilguero, SA de CV, pg 467
Phillip Richard Conover Lazo, pg 467
Editorial Minutiae Mexicana SA, pg 468
Instituto Nacional de Antropologia e Historia, pg 469
Editorial Nueva Imagen SA, pg 469
Instituto Panamericano de Geografia e Historia, pg 469
Pangea Editores, Sa de CV, pg 470
Plaza y Valdes SA de CV, pg 470
Ediciones Promesa, SA de CV, pg 470
Siglo XXI Editores SA de CV, pg 472
Universidad Nacional Autonoma de Mexico (National University of Mexico), pg 472
Universidad Veracruzana Direccion General Editorial y de Publicaciones, pg 472

Morocco

Societe Ennewrasse Service Librairie et Imprimerie, pg 475

Nepal

International Standards Books & Periodicals (P) Ltd, pg 476

Netherlands

KIT - Royal Tropical Institute Publishers, pg 484
KITLV Press Royal Institute of Linguistics & Anthropology, pg 484
Podium Uitgeverij, pg 487
Uniepers BV, pg 491
Van Gorcum & Comp BV, pg 491

New Zealand

Outrigger Publishers, pg 499
University of Otago Press, pg 502
Victoria University Press, pg 502

Nigeria

Riverside Communications, pg 507

Pakistan

Pakistan Institute of Development Economics (PIDE), pg 514
Publishers United Pvt Ltd, pg 514
Sang-e-Meel Publications, pg 514

SUBJECT INDEX

Papua New Guinea

Melanesian Institute, pg 515
National Research Institute of Papua New Guinea, pg 515
Papua New Guinea Institute of Medical Research, pg 516
Summer Institute of Linguistics, pg 516

Peru

Instituto de Estudios Peruanos, pg 517
Fondo Editorial de la Pontificia Universidad Catolica del Peru, pg 517
Instituto Frances de Estudios Andinos, IFEA, pg 517
Editorial Horizonte, pg 517
Sur Casa de Estudios del Socialismo, pg 517

Philippines

Ateneo de Manila University Press, pg 518
Heritage Publishing House, pg 519
National Museum of the Philippines, pg 520
New Day Publishers, pg 520
Our Lady of Manaoag Publisher, pg 520
Rex Bookstores & Publishers, pg 520
San Carlos Publications, pg 521

Poland

Wydawnictwa Uniwersytetu Warszawskiego, pg 527

Portugal

Edicoes Cosmos, pg 530
Editorial Estampa, Lda, pg 531
Gradiva-Publicacnoes Lda, pg 532
Imprensa Nacional-Casa da Moeda, pg 532
Instituto de Investigacao Cientifica Tropical, pg 532
Internationale Nouvelle Acropole, pg 534
Edicoes Ora & Labora, pg 534
Edicoes 70 Lda, pg 535
Teorema, pg 536
Vega-Publicacao e Distribuicao de Livros e Revistas, Lda, pg 536

Puerto Rico

Instituto de Cultura Puertorriquena, pg 537

Romania

Editura Academiei Romane, pg 538
Aion Verlag, pg 538
Editura Excelsior Art, pg 539
Editura Meridiane, pg 540
Polirom Verlag, pg 542
Saeculum IO, pg 542

Senegal

Centre Africain d'Animation et d'Echanges Culturels Editions Khoudia (CAEC), pg 551

Serbia and Montenegro

Svetovi, pg 554

Slovenia

Zalozba Obzorja d d Maribor, pg 562

SUBJECT INDEX

BOOK

South Africa
Human & Rousseau (Pty) Ltd, pg 564
Institute for Reformational Studies CHE, pg 565
New Africa Books (Pty) Ltd, pg 567
Ravan Press (Pty) Ltd, pg 568
Witwatersrand University Press, pg 570

Spain
Academia de la Llingua Asturiana, pg 570
Ediciones Akal SA, pg 571
Alberdania SL, pg 571
Ediciones Alfar SA, pg 572
Alta Fulla Editorial, pg 572
Altea, Taurus, Alfaguara SA, pg 572
Editorial Anagrama, pg 572
Compania Literaria, pg 577
Ediciones de la Universidad Complutense de Madrid, pg 577
Complutense, SA Editorial, pg 577
Consello da Cultura Galega - CCG, pg 578
Rafael Dalmau, Editor, pg 578
Diputacion Provincial de Malaga, pg 579
Ediciones Doce Calles SL, pg 579
Ediciones Encuentro SA, pg 582
Fondo de Cultura Economica de Espana, SL, pg 583
Hercules de Ediciones, SA, pg 586
Icaria Editorial SA, pg 587
Iralka Editorial SL, pg 588
Ediciones Istmo SA, pg 588
Laertes SA de Ediciones, pg 588
Ediciones Maeva, pg 590
Marcombo SA, pg 590
Mundo Negro Editorial, pg 592
Munoz Moya Editor, pg 592
Nueva Acropolis, pg 593
Oikos-Tau SA Ediciones, pg 593
Pages Editors, SL, pg 594
Pentalfa Ediciones, pg 595
Polifemo, Ediciones, pg 596
Editorial Presencia Gitana, pg 597
Editora Regional de Murcia - ERM, pg 597
Siglo XXI de Espana Editores SA, pg 599
Editorial Sal Terrae, pg 602
Editorial Txertoa, pg 603
Universidad de Granada, pg 603
Vinaches Lopez, Luisa, pg 605

Sri Lanka
Department of National Museums, pg 607

Suriname
Stichting Wetenschappelijke Informatie, pg 608

Sweden
Carlsson Bokfoerlag AB, pg 610

Switzerland
Les Editions Camphill, pg 620
Helbing und Lichtenhahn Verlag AG, pg 625
Kindler Verlag AG, pg 626
Novalis Media AG, pg 630
Editions Payot Lausanne, pg 631
Verlag Die Pforte im Rudolf Steiner Verlag, pg 631
Zbinden Druck und Verlag AG, pg 637

Syrian Arab Republic
Damascus University Press, pg 638
Institut Francais d'Etudes Arabes de Damas, pg 638

Taiwan, Province of China
Echo Publishing Company Ltd, pg 639
Laureate Book Co Ltd, pg 640
San Min Book Co Ltd, pg 641
SMC Publishing Inc, pg 642
Wu Nan Book Co Ltd, pg 642

Trinidad & Tobago
Joan Bacchus-Xavier, pg 646

Tunisia
Maison Tunisienne de l'Edition, pg 648

Turkey
Arkeoloji Ve Sanat Yayinlari, pg 649
Kabalci Yayinevi, pg 652

Uganda
Fountain Publishers Ltd, pg 652

United Kingdom
ABC-CLIO, pg 654
The Athlone Press Ltd, pg 661
Ruth Bean Publishers, pg 664
Berg Publishers, pg 664
Berghahn Books Ltd, pg 665
Cambridge University Press, pg 674
Compendium Publishing, pg 681
James Currey Ltd, pg 685
Delectus Books, pg 687
Edinburgh University Press Ltd, pg 689
The Eurospan Group, pg 692
Garnet Publishing Ltd, pg 698
Gateway Books, pg 698
Gwasg Gwenffrwd, pg 703
HarperCollins UK, pg 705
Harvard University Press, pg 705
The Harvill Press, pg 705
Institute of Irish Studies, The Queens University of Belfast, pg 713
Karnak House, pg 717
Octagon Press Ltd, pg 734
Oneworld Publications, pg 735
Open Gate Press, pg 735
The Orkney Press Ltd, pg 736
Pearson Education, pg 739
Pluto Books Ltd, pg 743
Pluto Press, pg 743
Rivers Oram Press, pg 750
RoutledgeCurzon, pg 751
SAGE Publications Ltd, pg 753
Skoob Russell Square, pg 758
Yale University Press London, pg 776

Uruguay
Editorial Arca SRL, pg 776
Nordan-Comunidad, pg 778
Luis A Retta Libros, pg 778
Ediciones Trilce, pg 778

Venezuela
Armitano Editores CA, pg 779
Monte Avila Editores Latinoamericana CA, pg 779
Biblioteca Ayacucho, pg 779

Zambia
Historical Association of Zambia, pg 781

ANTIQUES

Albania
NL SH, pg 1

Australia
Carter's (Antiques & Collectibles) P/L, pg 17
Oriental Publications, pg 34

Austria
Oesterreichischer Kunst und Kulturverlag, pg 55

Belgium
Editions Chanlis, pg 65
Glenat Benelux SA, pg 67

Brazil
Edicon Editora e Consultorial Ltda, pg 81

China
Beijing Publishing House, pg 101
Cultural Relics Publishing House, pg 103
Qingdao Publishing House, pg 107
Shanghai Calligraphy & Painting Publishing House, pg 108
Sichuan University Press, pg 108

Colombia
Editorial Santillana SA, pg 112

Denmark
Museum Tusculanum Press, pg 133

France
Societe Nouvelle Rene Baudouin, pg 149
Adam Biro Editions, pg 150
Editions Casterman, pg 152
ELLUG (Editions Litteraires et Linguistiques de l'Universite de Grenoble III), pg 161
Institut d'Etudes Augustiniennes, pg 162
Paul Geuthner Librairie Orientaliste, pg 165
Macula, pg 173
Editions de la Reunion des Musees Nationaux, pg 176
Editions A et J Picard SA, pg 179
Presses Universitaires de Caen, pg 181
Editions Scala, pg 184
Somogy editions d'art, pg 185

Germany
Arnoldsche Verlagsanstalt GmbH, pg 194
GLB Parkland Verlags-und Vertriebs GmbH, pg 229
Dr Ernst Hauswedell & Co, pg 235
Kunstverlag Weingarten GmbH, pg 251
Karl Robert Langewiesche Nachfolger Hans Koester KG, pg 252
J B Metzlersche Verlagsbuchhandlung, pg 260
Mosaik Verlag GmbH, pg 262
Musikantiquariat und Dr Hans Schneider Verlag GmbH, pg 262
Georg Olms Verlag AG, pg 267
Patmos Verlag GmbH & Co KG, pg 268
Saarbrucker Druckerei und Verlag GmbH (SDV), pg 277
Schild-Verlag GmbH, pg 279
Dr Wolfgang Schwarze Verlag, pg 282
Staatliche Museen Kassel, pg 286
Weidmannsche Verlagsbuchhandlung GmbH, pg 298

Greece
D Papadimas, pg 311

Hong Kong
Chung Hwa Book Co (HK) Ltd, pg 316
Ling Kee Publishing Group, pg 318
SCMP Book Publishing Ltd, pg 319
Unicorn Books Ltd, pg 320

Hungary
Officina Nova Konyvek, pg 323

India
Agam Kala Prakashan, pg 327
Rahul Publishing House, pg 346

Indonesia
Gramedia, pg 355

Italy
Umberto Allemandi & C SRL, pg 375
Artioli Editore, pg 377
Bardi Editore srl, pg 377
Belforte Editore Libraio srl, pg 377
BeMa, pg 377
M d'Auria Editore SAS, pg 384
Giovanni De Vecchi Editore SpA, pg 384
Edipuglia, pg 386
Edizioni d'Arte Antica e Moderna EDAM, pg 386
Edizioni del Centro Camuno di Studi Preistorici, pg 386
Essegi, pg 388
Arnaldo Forni Editore SRL, pg 389
Ist Patristico Augustinianum, pg 393
Giorgio Mondadori & Associati, pg 399
OCTAVO Produzioni Editoriali Associale, pg 401
Pontifico Istituto Orientale, pg 404
Priuli e Verlucca, Editori, pg 404
Edizioni Librarie Siciliane, pg 408

Japan
Tankosha Publishing Co Ltd, pg 429

Republic of Korea
Dae Won Sa Co Ltd, pg 438
Daehan Printing & Publishing Co Ltd, pg 438
Youlhwadang Publisher, pg 444

Malta
Fondazzjoni Patrimonju Malti, pg 460

Mexico
Editorial Jilguero, SA de CV, pg 467
Instituto Nacional de Antropologia e Historia, pg 469

PUBLISHERS

Monaco
Les Editions du Rocher, pg 474

Morocco
Association de la Recherche Historique et Sociale, pg 474
Societe Ennewrasse Service Librairie et Imprimerie, pg 475

Netherlands
Castrum Peregrini Presse, pg 480
The Pepin Press, pg 487
Scriptum, pg 488
Uniepers BV, pg 491
Uitgeverij Waanders BV, pg 492

Norway
Andresen & Butenschon AS, pg 508
Aschehoug Forlag, pg 508
H Aschehoug & Co (W Nygaard) A/S, pg 508

Pakistan
The Book House, pg 512
Publishers United Pvt Ltd, pg 514

Poland
Wydawnictwo Arkady, pg 522
Wydawnictwo DiG, pg 522

Portugal
Camara Municipal de Castelo, pg 529
Editorial Estampa, Lda, pg 531

Romania
Enzyklopadie Verlag, pg 539
MAST Verlag, pg 540

Russian Federation
Ladomir Publishing House, pg 546

Spain
Vicent Garcia Editores, SA, pg 584

Sri Lanka
Department of National Museums, pg 607

Sweden
Tryckeriforlaget AB, pg 616

Switzerland
Cockatoo Press (Schweiz), Thailand-Publikationen, pg 621
Librairie Droz SA, pg 622
Faksimile Verlag AG, pg 623
Office du Livre SA (Buchhaus AG), pg 630
Hans Rohr Verlag, pg 632

Taiwan, Province of China
Art Book Co Ltd, pg 638
Echo Publishing Company Ltd, pg 639
Hilit Publishing Co Ltd, pg 640
Lee & Lee Communications, pg 641
National Museum of History, pg 641
National Palace Museum, pg 641

Turkey
Arkeoloji Ve Sanat Yayinlari, pg 649

United Kingdom
Antique Collectors' Club Ltd, pg 658
Antiques & Collectors Guides Ltd, pg 658
Apple Press, pg 658
Art Books International Ltd, pg 659
BCA - Book Club Associates, pg 663
Mitchell Beazley, pg 664
BLA Publishing Ltd, pg 666
Books for Europe Ltd, pg 669
Bounty Books, pg 669
Carlton Publishing Group, pg 675
Marshall Cavendish Partworks Ltd, pg 676
Compendium Publishing, pg 681
Foulsham Publishers, pg 696
Hilmarton Manor Press, pg 708
Lyle Publications Ltd, pg 723
Maney Publishing, pg 725
Miller's Publications, pg 728
Octopus Publishing Group, pg 734
Quarto Publishing plc, pg 746
The Reader's Digest Association Ltd, pg 748
The Rubicon Press, pg 752
Shire Publications Ltd, pg 757
Charles Skilton Ltd, pg 758
Skoob Russell Square, pg 758
Studio Editions Ltd, pg 761
Towy Publishing, pg 766
White Cockade Publishing, pg 772
Philip Wilson Publishers, pg 774

ARCHAEOLOGY

Albania
NL SH, pg 1

Argentina
EUDEBA (Editorial Universitaria de Buenos Aires), pg 5
Tipografica Editora Argentina, pg 9

Australia
Aboriginal Studies Press, pg 10
Australian Rock Art Research Association, pg 13
Gnostic Editions, pg 23
Queen Victoria Museum & Art Gallery Publications, pg 38
Thames & Hudson (Australia) Pty Ltd, pg 43
Three Sisters Publications Pty Ltd, pg 43
Veritas Press, pg 45

Austria
Akademische Druck-u Verlagsanstalt Dr Paul Struzl GmbH, pg 48
Carinthia Verlag, pg 49
Doecker Verlag GmbH & Co KG, pg 50
Ferdinand Berger und Sohne, pg 50
Verlag der Oesterreichischen Akademie der Wissenschaften (OEAW), pg 55
Andreas Schnider Verlags-Atelier, pg 57
Verband der Wissenschaftlichen Gesellschaften Oesterreichs (VWGOe), pg 59
Universitaetsverlag Wagner GmbH, pg 59

Bangladesh
The University Press Ltd, pg 61

SUBJECT INDEX

Belarus
Belaruskaya Encyklapedyya, pg 62

Belgium
Brepols Publishers NV, pg 64
Editions Chanlis, pg 65
Groeninghe NV, pg 68
Leuven University Press, pg 70
Uitgeverij Peeters Leuven (Belgie), pg 71

Botswana
The Botswana Society, pg 76

Brazil
Ars Poetica Editora Ltda, pg 78
Hemus Editora Ltda, pg 83
Francisco J Laissue Livraria, pg 84
Editora Melhoramentos Ltda, pg 86

Bulgaria
Litera Prima, pg 95
Pensoft Publishers, pg 96

Chile
Arrayan Editores, pg 98
Museo Chileno de Arte Precolombino, pg 99

China
China Tibetology Publishing House, pg 103
Cultural Relics Publishing House, pg 103
Foreign Languages Press, pg 104
Qingdao Publishing House, pg 107
Science Press, pg 107

Colombia
Amazonas Editores Ltda, pg 110

Costa Rica
Editorial de la Universidad de Costa Rica, pg 116

Croatia
Knjizevni Krug Split, pg 118
Matica hrvatska, pg 118
Znaci Vremena, Institut Za Istrazivanje Biblije, pg 119

Czech Republic
Academia, pg 122
Barrister & Principal, pg 122
Libri spol sro, pg 125
Lidove Noviny Publishing House, pg 125
Mariadan, pg 125
Narodni Muzeum, pg 126

Denmark
Aarhus Universitetsforlag, pg 128
Museum Tusculanum Press, pg 133
Syddansk Universitetsforlag, pg 135

Dominican Republic
Pontificia Universidad Catolica Madre y Maestra, pg 136

Ecuador
Corporacion Editora Nacional, pg 136
Pontificia Universidad Catolica del Ecuador, Centro de Publicaciones, pg 137

Egypt (Arab Republic of Egypt)
Lehnert & Landrock Bookshop, pg 138

Estonia
Tael Ltd, pg 140
Valgus Publishers, pg 140

Finland
Scriptum Forlags AB, pg 144

France
ATP - Packager, pg 148
De Boccard Edition-Diffusion, pg 150
Editions des Cahiers Bourbonnais, pg 151
Editions Casterman, pg 152
CNRS Editions, pg 155
Editions du Comite des Travaux Historiques et Scientifiques (CTHS), pg 155
Editions du Demi-Cercle, pg 157
Editions Edisud, pg 159
Editions Recherche sur les Civilisations (ERC), pg 160
Editions rue d'Ulm, pg 160
Editions Terrail/Finest SA, pg 160
Editions Errance, pg 161
Institut d'Ethnologie du Museum National d'Histoire Naturelle, pg 162
Institut d'Etudes Augustiniennes, pg 162
Editions Jean Paul Gisserot, pg 165
IRD Editions, pg 169
Kailash Editions, pg 170
Editions Klincksieck, pg 170
LLB France (Ligue pour la Lecture de la Bible), pg 173
Editions Lyonnaises d'Art et d'Histoire, pg 173
Editions de la Maison des Sciences de l'Homme, Paris, pg 173
Muller Edition, pg 176
Editions de la Reunion des Musees Nationaux, pg 176
Editions Pardes, pg 179
Peeters-France, pg 179
Editions A et J Picard SA, pg 179
Editions Pygmalion, pg 182
Sepia Editions, pg 184
Somogy editions d'art, pg 185
Publications de la Sorbonne, pg 185
Editions Thames & Hudson, pg 187

Germany
Verlag C H Beck oHG, pg 198
Biblio Verlag, pg 200
Boehlau-Verlag GmbH & Cie, pg 202
DuMont Reiseverlag GmbH & Co KG, pg 217
Wilhelm Fink GmbH & Co Verlags-KG, pg 224
Frederking & Thaler Verlag GmbH, pg 226
Germanisches Nationalmuseum, pg 228
Walter de Gruyter GmbH & Co KG, pg 231
Dr Rudolf Habelt GmbH, pg 232
Hirmer Verlag GmbH, pg 238
Holos Verlag, pg 239
Ikarus - Buchverlag, pg 241
Jan Thorbecke Verlag GmbH & Co, pg 243
Verlag Koenigshausen und Neumann GmbH, pg 248

SUBJECT INDEX

Karl Robert Langewiesche Nachfolger Hans Koester KG, pg 252
Michael Lassleben Verlag und Druckerei, pg 252
Gustav Luebbe Verlag, pg 256
Lukas Verlag fur Kunst- und Geistesgeschichte, pg 256
Maeander Verlag GmbH, pg 256
Gebr Mann Verlag GmbH & Co, pg 257
Orbis Verlag fur Publizistik GmbH, pg 267
Philipps-Universitaet Marburg, pg 270
Verlag Friedrich Pustet GmbH & Co Kg, pg 272
Dr Ludwig Reichert Verlag, pg 274
RVBG Rheinland-Verlag-und Betriebsgesellschaft des Landschaftsverbandes Rheinland mbH, pg 276
Saarbrucker Druckerei und Verlag GmbH (SDV), pg 277
Verlag Schnell und Steiner GmbH, pg 281
E Schweizerbart'sche Verlagsbuchhandlung (Naegele und Obermiller), pg 282
Scientia Verlag und Antiquariat Schilling OHG, pg 282
Franz Steiner Verlag Wiesbaden GmbH, pg 287
Konrad Theiss Verlag GmbH, pg 290
Traditionell Bogenschiessen Verlag Angelika Hornig, pg 292
UVK Universitatsverlag Konstanz GmbH, pg 294
Wachholtz Verlag GmbH, pg 297
Ernst Wasmuth Verlag GmbH & Co, pg 297
Wissenschaftliche Buchgesellschaft, pg 300
Verlag Philipp von Zabern, pg 302

Greece
Ecole francaise d'Athenes, pg 307
Ekdotike Athenon SA, pg 307
Evrodiastasi, pg 307
Hestia-I D Hestia-Kollaros & Co Corporation, pg 308
Kardamitsa A, pg 309
A G Leventis Foundation, pg 309
Morfotiko Idryma Ethnikis Trapezas, pg 310
Ed Nea Acropolis, pg 310
Nea Thesis - Evrotas, pg 310
Panepistimio Ioanninon, pg 311
D Papadimas, pg 311
Society for Macedonian Studies, pg 312

Guatemala
Grupo Editorial RIN-78, pg 313

Guyana
The Hamburgh Register, pg 314

Hungary
Akademiai Kiado, pg 320
Tajak Korok Muzeumok Egyesulet, pg 324

India
Abhinav Publications, pg 326
Agam Kala Prakashan, pg 327
Ajanta Publications (India), pg 327
APH Publishing Corp, pg 328
Asian Educational Services, pg 329
Books & Books, pg 331
BR Publishing Corporation, pg 331
Chowkhamba Sanskrit Series Office, pg 332
Cosmo Publications, pg 332
DK Printworld (P) Ltd, pg 333
Full Circle Publishing, pg 334
Gyan Publishing House, pg 335
Indian Museum, pg 337
Indus Publishing Co, pg 338
Intellectual Publishing House, pg 338
Inter-India Publications, pg 338
Mapin Publishing Pvt Ltd, pg 341
Munshiram Manoharlal Publishers Pvt Ltd, pg 342
National Book Organization, pg 342
Navrang Booksellers & Publishers, pg 343
Parimal Prakashan, pg 345
Rahul Publishing House, pg 346
Regency Publications, pg 346
Reliance Publishing House, pg 346
Scientific Book Agency, pg 348
Somaiya Publications Pvt Ltd, pg 349

Ireland
The Collins Press, pg 358
Cork University Press, pg 359
Gandon Editions, pg 360
Herodotus Press, pg 361
Morrigan Book Co, pg 362
Royal Irish Academy, pg 363
Tir Eolas, pg 363
Town House & Country House, pg 364

Israel
Bar Ilan University Press, pg 365
The Bialik Institute, pg 365
Carta, The Israel Map & Publishing Co Ltd, pg 365
Gefen Publishing House Ltd, pg 367
Haifa University Press, pg 367
Hakibbutz Hameuchad Publishing House Ltd, pg 367
Israel Antiquities Authority, pg 368
Israel Exploration Society, pg 368
The Jerusalem Publishing House Ltd, pg 369
The Magnes Press, pg 370
Sadan Publishing Ltd, pg 371
R Sirkis Publishers Ltd, pg 372

Italy
Mario Adda Editore SNC, pg 374
All'Insegna del Giglio, pg 375
Umberto Allemandi & C SRL, pg 375
Associazione Internazionale di Archeologia Classica, pg 377
Bardi Editore srl, pg 377
Bibliopolis - Edizioni di Filosofia e Scienze Srl, pg 378
Bonechi-Edizioni Il Turismo Srl, pg 378
Bonsignori Editore SRL, pg 378
Editore Giorgio Bretschneider, pg 379
Calosci, pg 379
Campanotto, pg 379
Colonnese Editore, pg 383
M d'Auria Editore SAS, pg 384
Edizioni Della Torre di Salvatore Fozzi & C SAS, pg 385
Ecole Francaise de Rome, pg 385
Edipuglia, pg 386
Editori Laterza, pg 386
Edizioni del Centro Camuno di Studi Preistorici, pg 386
L'Erma di Bretschneider SRL, pg 388
Essegi, pg 388
Flaccovio Editore, pg 389
Arnaldo Forni Editore SRL, pg 389
Adriano Gallina Editore sas, pg 389
Gangemi Editore spa, pg 390
Garolla, pg 390
Edizioni del Girasole srl, pg 390
Gius Laterza e Figli SpA, pg 391
Grafo, pg 391
Herbita Editrice di Leonardo Palermo, pg 392
Herder Editrice e Libreria, pg 392
Ila - Palma, Tea Nova, pg 393
Instituti Editoriali E Poligrafici Internazionali SRL, pg 393
ISAL (Istituto Storia dell'Arte Lombarda), pg 393
Editoriale Jaca Book SpA, pg 394
Jouvence, pg 394
Laruffa Editore SRL, pg 394
Angelo Longo Editore, pg 396
Edizioni de Luca SRL, pg 396
Macro Edizioni, pg 397
Edizioni Mediterranee SRL, pg 398
Accademia Naz dei Lincei, pg 400
Newton & Compton Editori, pg 400
OCTAVO Produzioni Editoriali Associate, pg 401
Leo S Olschki, pg 401
Osanna Venosa, pg 402
Franco Cosimo Panini Editore SpA, pg 402
Pontificio Istituto di Archeologia Cristiana, pg 404
Pontifico Istituto Orientale, pg 404
Edizioni Quasar di Severino Tognon SRL, pg 404
Edizioni Quattroventi SNC, pg 404
Scala Group spa, pg 407
Schena Editore, pg 407
Sellerio Editore, pg 408
SEMAR Publishers SRL, pg 408
Edizioni Librarie Siciliane, pg 408
Studio Bibliografico Adelmo Polla, pg 409
Tappeiner, pg 409

Japan
GakuseiSha Publishing Co Ltd, pg 417
Koyo Shobo, pg 422
Myrtos Inc, pg 423
Rinsen Book Co Ltd, pg 425
Toho Book Store, pg 429
Tosui Shobo Publishers, pg 430
Tsukiji Shokan Publishing Co, pg 430
Waseda University Press, pg 431

Kazakstan
Al-Farabi Kazakh National University, pg 432

Kenya
British Institute in Eastern Africa, pg 433

Democratic People's Republic of Korea
The Foreign Language Press Group, pg 436

Republic of Korea
Hakgojae Publishing Inc, pg 439
Iljisa Publishing House, pg 439
Sohaksa, pg 443

Lebanon
Librairie Orientale sal, pg 446

Liechtenstein
Historischer Verein fur das Furstentum Liechtenstein, pg 448

Lithuania
Klaipedos Universiteto Leidykla, pg 449
Lithuanian National Museum Publishing House, pg 449

Luxembourg
Service Central des Imprimes et des Fournitures de Bureau de l'Etat, pg 451

The Former Yugoslav Republic of Macedonia
Macedonia Prima Publishing House, pg 452
Zumpres Publishing Firm, pg 453

Malta
Fondazzjoni Patrimonju Malti, pg 460

Martinique
Editions Gondwana, pg 460

Mexico
Centro de Estudios Mexicanos y Centroamericanos, pg 463
Editorial Diana SA de CV, pg 464
El Colegio de Michoacan A C, pg 464
Ediciones Euroamericanas, pg 465
Fondo de Cultura Economica, pg 465
Editorial Jilguero, SA de CV, pg 467
Editorial Minutiae Mexicana SA, pg 468
Instituto Nacional de Antropologia e Historia, pg 469
Instituto Panamericano de Geografia e Historia, pg 469
Pangea Editores, Sa de CV, pg 470
Plaza y Valdes SA de CV, pg 470
Universidad Nacional Autonoma de Mexico (National University of Mexico), pg 472

Morocco
Association de la Recherche Historique et Sociale, pg 474
Edition Diffusion de Livre au Maroc, pg 474

Nepal
International Standards Books & Periodicals (P) Ltd, pg 476

Netherlands
A A Balkema Uitgevers BV, pg 478
Brill Academic Publishers, pg 479
The Pepin Press, pg 487
Tirion Uitgevers BV, pg 490
Uniepers BV, pg 491

New Zealand
Auckland University Press, pg 493
Bush Press Communications Ltd, pg 494
Clerestory Press, pg 495
Outrigger Publishers, pg 499
Southern Press Ltd, pg 501

PUBLISHERS

Pakistan
Publishers United Pvt Ltd, pg 514

Peru
Librerias ABC SA, pg 516
Instituto de Estudios Peruanos, pg 517
Fondo Editorial de la Pontificia Universidad Catolica del Peru, pg 517
Instituto Frances de Estudios Andinos, IFEA, pg 517

Philippines
National Museum of the Philippines, pg 520
Rex Bookstores & Publishers, pg 520
San Carlos Publications, pg 521

Poland
Wydawnictwo DiG, pg 522
Ossolineum Zaklad Narodowy im Ossolinskich - Wydawnictwo, pg 525
Towarzystwo Naukowe w Toruniu, pg 527
Wydawnictwa Uniwersytetu Warszawskiego, pg 527

Portugal
Camara Municipal de Castelo, pg 529
Edicoes Colibri, pg 530
Imprensa Nacional-Casa da Moeda, pg 532
Instituto de Investigacao Cientifica Tropical, pg 532
Internationale Nouvelle Acropole, pg 534

Romania
Editura Academiei Romane, pg 538
Enzyklopadie Verlag, pg 539
Editura Excelsior Art, pg 539
Editura Meridiane, pg 540

Russian Federation
Nauka Publishers, pg 547
Izdatel'stvo Nizhegorodskogo Gosudarstvennogo Univ, pg 547
St Andrew's Biblical Theological College, pg 548

Slovakia
Vydavatelstvo Obzor, pg 560
VEDA (Vydavatel'stvo Slovenskej akademie vied), pg 561

South Africa
New Africa Books (Pty) Ltd, pg 567
Witwatersrand University Press, pg 570

Spain
Ediciones Akal SA, pg 571
Ediciones Alfar SA, pg 572
Casa de Velazquez, pg 575
Comunidad Autonoma de Madrid, Servicio de Documentacion y Publicaciones, pg 578
Diputacion Provincial de Malaga, pg 579
Instituto de Estudios Riojanos, pg 583
Eumo Editorial, pg 583
Fundacion Marcelino Botin, pg 584

Institucion Fernando el Catolico de la Excma Diputacion de Zaragoza, pg 587
Junta de Castilla y Leon Consejeria de Educacion y Cultura, pg 588
Laertes SA de Ediciones, pg 588
Lunwerg Editores, SA, pg 589
Nueva Acropolis, pg 593
Polifemo, Ediciones, pg 596
Instituto Provincial de Investigaciones y Estudios Toledanos (IPIET), pg 597
Editora Regional de Murcia - ERM, pg 597
Servicio de Publicaciones Universidad de Cordoba, pg 599
Silex Ediciones, pg 600
Equipo Sirius SA, pg 600
Universidad de Granada, pg 603
Universidad de Valladolid Secretariado de Publicaciones e Intercambio Editorial, pg 604

Sri Lanka
Karunaratne & Sons Ltd, pg 606

Switzerland
Cockatoo Press (Schweiz), Thailand-Publikationen, pg 621
FEDA SA, pg 623
Les Editions la Matze, pg 628
Motovun Book GmbH, pg 629
Muslim Architecture Research Program (MARP), pg 629
Les Editions Nagel SA (Paris), pg 629
Editions Payot Lausanne, pg 631
Schwabe & Co AG, pg 633

Syrian Arab Republic
Damascus University Press, pg 638
Institut Francais d'Etudes Arabes de Damas, pg 638

Taiwan, Province of China
Asian Culture Co Ltd, pg 638
Echo Publishing Company Ltd, pg 639
National Palace Museum, pg 641
Yee Wen Publishing Co Ltd, pg 642

Tunisia
Alyssa Editions, pg 647
Les Editions de l'Arbre, pg 647
Faculte des Sciences Humaines et Sociales de Tunis, pg 648
Maison Tunisienne de l'Edition, pg 648
Publications de la Fondation Temimi pour la Recherche Scientifique et L'Information, pg 648

Turkey
Arkeoloji Ve Sanat Yayinlari, pg 649
Ataturk Kultur, Dil ve Tarih, Yusek Kurumu Baskanligi, pg 649
IKI Nokta Research Press & Publications Industry & Trade Ltd, pg 650
Inkilap Publishers Ltd, pg 650
Payel Yayinevi, pg 651
Turkish Republic - Ministry of Culture, pg 652
Kabalci Yayinevi, pg 652

Ukraine
Osnova, Kharkov State University Press, pg 653

United Kingdom
Andromeda Oxford Ltd, pg 658
Artetech Publishing Co, pg 660
Ashmolean Museum Publications, pg 660
The Athlone Press Ltd, pg 661
Batsford Ltd, pg 663
BCA - Book Club Associates, pg 663
Books for Europe Ltd, pg 669
Borthwick Institute Publications, pg 669
The British Academy, pg 671
British Museum Press, pg 672
Cambridge University Press, pg 674
Capall Bann Publishing, pg 674
Constable & Robinson Ltd, pg 682
Council for British Archaeology, pg 683
James Currey Ltd, pg 685
Darf Publishers Ltd, pg 686
Edinburgh University Press Ltd, pg 689
The Europspan Group, pg 692
Garnet Publishing Ltd, pg 698
The Greek Bookshop, pg 702
Herbert Press Ltd, pg 708
Institute of Irish Studies, The Queens University of Belfast, pg 713
Kegan Paul International Ltd, pg 717
Liverpool University Press, pg 722
The Lutterworth Press, pg 723
Maney Publishing, pg 725
Methuen, pg 727
Motilal (UK) Books of India, pg 729
NMS Enterprises Ltd - Publishing, pg 733
North York Moors National Park, pg 733
Open Gate Press, pg 735
Orion Publishing Group Ltd, pg 736
The Orkney Press Ltd, pg 736
Phillimore & Co Ltd, pg 741
The Reader's Digest Association Ltd, pg 748
Routledge, pg 751
The Rubicon Press, pg 752
Scottish Cultural Press, pg 755
Sheffield Academic Press Ltd, pg 757
Shire Publications Ltd, pg 757
Sidgwick & Jackson Ltd, pg 757
Stacey International, pg 761
Sutton Publishing Ltd, pg 762
Thames & Hudson Ltd, pg 764
Thistle Press, pg 765
TSO (The Stationery Office), pg 767
Tuckwell Press Ltd, pg 767
Twelveheads Press, pg 767
UCL Press Ltd, pg 768
University of Exeter Press, pg 768
University of Wales Press, pg 769
Philip Wilson Publishers, pg 774
World of Islam Altajir Trust, pg 776

Viet Nam
Science & Technics Publishing House, pg 780

ARCHITECTURE & INTERIOR DESIGN

Albania
NL SH, pg 1

SUBJECT INDEX

Argentina
EUDEBA (Editorial Universitaria de Buenos Aires), pg 5
Fundacion Editorial de Belgrano, pg 6
Editorial Idearium de la Universidad de Mendoza (EDIUM), pg 6
Marymar Ediciones SA, pg 7
Ediciones Nueva Vision SAIC, pg 8

Australia
Art on the Move, pg 12
CHOICE Magazine, pg 17
The Images Publishing Group Pty Ltd, pg 26
McGraw-Hill Australia Pty Ltd, pg 31
Press for Success, pg 37
Ruskin Rowe Press, pg 40
Thames & Hudson (Australia) Pty Ltd, pg 43
University of New South Wales Press Ltd, pg 44
The Watermark Press, pg 46

Austria
Christian Brandstaetter Verlagsgesellschaft mbH, pg 49
Haymon-Verlag GesmbH, pg 51
Loecker Verlag, pg 53
Modulverlag, pg 54
Oesterreichischer Kunst und Kulturverlag, pg 55
Passagen Verlag GmbH, pg 56
Promedia Verlagsges mbH, pg 56
Verlag Anton Pustet, pg 56
Ritter Druck und Verlags KEG, pg 57
Salzburger Nachrichten Verlagsgesellschaft mbH & Co KG, pg 57
Andreas Schnider Verlags-Atelier, pg 57
Springer-Verlag Wien, pg 58
Edition Tusch, pg 58

Bangladesh
The University Press Ltd, pg 61

Belarus
Belaruskaya Encyklapedyya, pg 62

Belgium
Brepols Publishers NV, pg 64
Conservart SA, pg 65
King Baudouin Foundation, pg 69
Uitgeverij Lannoo NV, pg 69
Mardaga, Pierre, Editeur, pg 71
Mercatorfonds NV, pg 71
Presses Universitaires de Bruxelles asbl, pg 72
Editions Racine, pg 72
Roularta Books NV, pg 72
Stichting Kunstboek bvba, pg 73

Brazil
AGIR S/A Editora, pg 77
ARTMED Editora, pg 78
Hemus Editora Ltda, pg 83
LDA Editores Ltda, pg 84
Livraria Nobel S/A, pg 85
Livraria Pioneira Editora/Enio Matheus Guazzelli e Cia Ltd, pg 88
Spala Editora Ltda, pg 90
Editora Universidade Federal do Rio de Janeiro, pg 92

Bulgaria
TEMTO, pg 97

901

SUBJECT INDEX

BOOK

China
Beijing Publishing House, pg 101
China Machine Press (CMP), pg 102
Guangdong Science & Technology Press, pg 105
Heilongjiang Science & Technology Press, pg 105
Henan Science & Technology Publishing House, pg 105
Higher Education Press, pg 105
Jilin Science & Technology Publishing House, pg 105
Qingdao Publishing House, pg 107
Shandong Science & Technology Press, pg 107
Shandong University Press, pg 108
Shanghai People's Fine Arts Publishing House, pg 108
Tianjin Science & Technology Publishing House, pg 108
Tsinghua University Press, pg 109

Colombia
Amazonas Editores Ltda, pg 110
Escala Ltda, pg 111
Siglo XXI Editores de Colombia Ltda, pg 112

Costa Rica
Editorial de la Universidad de Costa Rica, pg 116

Czech Republic
Karolinum, nakladatelstvi, pg 124
Libri spol sro, pg 125
Moravska Galerie v Brno, pg 126

Denmark
Arkitektens Forlag, pg 129
Christian Ejlers' Forlag aps, pg 131

Dominican Republic
Pontificia Universidad Catolica Madre y Maestra, pg 136

Egypt (Arab Republic of Egypt)
American University in Cairo Press, pg 137

Estonia
Kirjastus Kunst, pg 139
Valgus Publishers, pg 140

Finland
Building Information Ltd, pg 141
Rakentajain Kustannus Oy (Building Publications Ltd), pg 143
Otava Publishing Co Ltd, pg 143
Rakennustieto Oy, pg 144

France
Action Artistique de la Ville de Paris, pg 145
Editions Alternatives, pg 146
Edition Anthese, pg 147
Armenia Editions, pg 147
Berger-Levrault Editions SAS, pg 149
La Bibliotheque des Arts, pg 150
Adam Biro Editions, pg 150
William Blake & Co, pg 150
Editions Casterman, pg 152
CEP Editions, pg 153
Editions du Chene, pg 154
Editions Citadelles & Mazenod, pg 154
CLD, pg 154
Communication Par Livre (CPL), pg 155
Counseil International de la Langue Francaise, pg 156
Editions du Demi-Cercle, pg 157
Dessain et Tolra SA, pg 158
Editions Dis Voir, pg 158
Editions Edisud, pg 159
Institute Editeur, pg 160
Editions Terrail/Finest SA, pg 160
EPA (Editions Pratiques Automobiles), pg 161
Editions de l'Epargne, pg 161
Editions Eyrolles, pg 162
Flammarion SA, pg 163
Editions Fleurus, pg 163
Folklore Comtois, pg 164
Editions Jean Paul Gisserot, pg 165
Groupe Express-Expansion, pg 166
Hachette Livre, pg 167
Editions Hatier SA, pg 167
Editions Hazan, pg 167
Editions l'Instant Durable, pg 169
Librairie Leonce Laget, pg 171
LT Editions-Jacques Lanore, pg 173
Editions Charles Massin et Cie, pg 174
Editions du Moniteur, pg 176
Editions de la Reunion des Musees Nationaux, pg 176
Editions Norma, pg 177
Editions Parentheses, pg 179
Association Paris-Musees, pg 179
Editions A et J Picard SA, pg 179
Editions du Centre Pompidou, pg 180
Revue Noire, pg 183
Selection du Reader's Digest SA, pg 184
Societe Nouveaux Loisirs, pg 185
Somogy editions d'art, pg 185
Editions Thames & Hudson, pg 187
Ulisse Editions, pg 188
Editions Vilo SA, pg 189

Germany
Ardey-Verlag GmbH, pg 193
Aries-Verlag Paul Johannes Muller, pg 194
Arnoldsche Verlagsanstalt GmbH, pg 194
Augustus Verlag, pg 195
Bauverlag GmbH, pg 198
be.bra verlag GmbH, pg 198
Beuth Verlag GmbH, pg 200
Eberhard Blottner Verlag GmbH, pg 202
Verlag Hermann Boehlaus Nachfolger Weimar GmbH & Co, pg 203
Verlag Busse und Seewald GmbH, pg 206
Verlag Georg D W Callwey GmbH & Co, pg 207
Dr Cantz'sche Druckerei GmbH & Co, pg 207
Christian Verlag GmbH, pg 208
Hans Christians Druckerei und Verlag GmbH & Co KG, pg 208
Coppenrath Verlag, pg 209
Deutsche Verlags-Anstalt GmbH (DVA), pg 212
Dolling und Galitz Verlag GmbH, pg 215
DuMont monte Verlag GmbH & Co KG, pg 217
Ellert & Richter Verlag GmbH, pg 219
Ernst, Wilhelm & Sohn, Verlag Architektur und technische Wissenschaft GmbH & Co, pg 221
Europaeische Verlagsanstalt GmbH & Rotbuch Verlag GmbH & Co KG, pg 222
Forum Verlag GmbH & Co, pg 225
Fraunhofer IRB Verlag Fraunhofer Informationszentrum Raum und Bau, pg 226
Gerstenberg Verlag, pg 228
GLB Parkland Verlags-und Vertriebs GmbH, pg 229
Heinz-Jurgen Hausser, pg 233
Harenberg Kommunikation Verlags- und Medien-GmbH & Co KG, pg 234
Hatje Cantz Verlag, pg 234
Edition Hoffmann & Co, pg 238
Huthig GmbH & Co KG, pg 240
Jahreszeiten-Verlag GmbH, pg 242
Junius Verlag GmbH, pg 244
Kerber Verlag, pg 245
Knesebeck Verlag, pg 247
Knowledge Media International, pg 247
Verlagsanstalt Alexander Koch GmbH, pg 247
Koehler & Amelang Verlagsgesellschaft, pg 248
Koenemann Verlagesellschaft mbH, pg 248
W Kohlhammer GmbH, pg 248
Konradin-Verlagsgruppe, pg 249
Karl Kraemer Verlag GmbH und Co, pg 249
Verlag der Kunst/G+B Fine Arts Verlag GmbH, pg 251
Kunstverlag Weingarten GmbH, pg 251
Institut fuer Landes- und Stadtentwicklungsforschung des Landes Nordrhein-Westfalen, pg 251
Karl Robert Langewiesche Nachfolger Hans Koester KG, pg 252
Edition Lidiarte, pg 254
Gebr Mann Verlag GmbH & Co, pg 257
Edition Axel Menges, pg 259
Merz & Solitude - Akademie Schloss Solitude, pg 259
mode information Heinz Kramer GmbH, pg 261
modo verlag GmbH, pg 261
Mosaik Verlag GmbH, pg 262
C F Mueller Verlag, Huethig GmbH & Co, pg 262
Neuthor - Verlag, pg 265
Nicolaische Verlagsbuchhandlung Beuermann GmbH, pg 265
C W Niemeyer Buchverlage GmbH, pg 265
Oekobuch Verlag & Versand GmbH, pg 266
Oktagon Verlagsgesellschaft mbH, pg 267
Prestel Verlag, pg 271
Propylaeen Verlag, Zweigniederlassung Berlin der Ullstein Buchverlage GmbH, pg 272
Ritterbach Verlag GmbH, pg 276
Verlag Th Schaefer im Vicentz Verlag KG, pg 278
Schelzky & Jeep, Verlag fuer Reisen und Wissen, pg 279
Verlag R S Schulz GmbH, pg 282
Dr Wolfgang Schwarze Verlag, pg 282
Springer Science+Business Media GmbH & Co KG, pg 284
Springer Science+Business Media GmbH & Co KG, Berlin, pg 285
Staatliche Museen Kassel, pg 286
TASCHEN GmbH, pg 289
teNeues Verlag GmbH & Co KG, pg 290
TR - Verlagsunion GmbH, pg 291
Verlag Dr Alfons Uhl, pg 293
Vice Versa Verlag, pg 295
Ernst Wasmuth Verlag GmbH & Co, pg 297
WEKA Firmengruppe GmbH & Co KG, pg 298
Verlag fuer Wirtschaft & Verwaltung Hubert Wingen GmbH & Co KG, pg 300
Verlagshaus Wohlfarth, pg 301

Ghana
Building & Road Research Institute (BRRI), pg 303

Greece
Ecole francaise d'Athenes, pg 307
Forma Edkotiki E P E, pg 307
Giourdas Moschos, pg 307
Hestia-I D Hestia-Kollaros & Co Corporation, pg 308
Kastaniotis Editions SA, pg 309
Kleidarithmos, Ekdoseis, pg 309
Melissa Publishing House, pg 310

Hong Kong
Joint Publishing (HK) Co Ltd, pg 317
Press Mark Media Ltd, pg 318

Hungary
Kiiarat Konyvdiado, pg 322
Mueszaki Koenyvkiado Ltd, pg 323
Tajak Korok Muzeumok Egyesuelet, pg 324

India
Abhinav Publications, pg 326
APH Publishing Corp, pg 328
Book Circle, pg 330
Books & Books, pg 331
Chowkhamba Sanskrit Series Office, pg 332
Heritage Publishers, pg 335
Himalayan Books, pg 336
India Book House Pvt Ltd, pg 336
Manohar Publishers & Distributors, pg 340
Mapin Publishing Pvt Ltd, pg 341
Marg Publications, pg 341
Mudgala Trust, pg 342
Munshiram Manoharlal Publishers Pvt Ltd, pg 342
National Book Organization, pg 342
Nem Chand & Brothers, pg 343
Pustak Mahal, pg 345
Reliance Publishing House, pg 346
Scientific Book Agency, pg 348
Sita Books & Periodicals Pvt Ltd, pg 349
Vastu Gyan Publication, pg 352

Ireland
Ballinakella Press, pg 358
Gandon Editions, pg 360
The Lilliput Press Ltd, pg 361
The O'Brien Press Ltd, pg 362

Israel
Bezalel Academy of Arts & Design, pg 365

Italy
Mario Adda Editore SNC, pg 374
Alinea, pg 375

Umberto Allemandi & C SRL, pg 375
Arcadia Edizioni Srl, pg 375
L'Archivolto, pg 376
Edizioni ARES, pg 376
Arsenale Editrice SRL, pg 376
Artioli Editore, pg 377
Automobilia srl, pg 377
Bardi Editore srl, pg 377
Casa Editrice Luigi Battei, pg 377
BeMa, pg 377
Biblos srl, pg 378
Giuseppe Bonanno Editore, pg 378
Bonsignori Editore SRL, pg 378
Calosci, pg 379
CELID, pg 381
CLUEB (Cooperativa Libraria Universitaria Editrice Bologna), pg 382
Edizioni di Comunita SpA, pg 383
Edizioni Dedalo SRL, pg 384
DEI Tipographia del Genio Civile, pg 384
Di Baio Editore SpA, pg 385
Editoriale Domus SpA, pg 385
Ediart Editrice, pg 386
EDIFIR SRL, pg 386
Edizioni d'Arte Antica e Moderna EDAM, pg 386
Electa, pg 387
L'Erma di Bretschneider SRL, pg 388
Essegi, pg 388
Esselibri, pg 388
Federico Motta Editore SpA, pg 389
Festina Lente Edizioni, pg 389
Flaccovio Editore, pg 389
Arnaldo Forni Editore SRL, pg 389
Gangemi Editore spa, pg 390
Edizioni GB, pg 390
Gius Laterza e Figli SpA, pg 391
Gruppo Editoriale Faenza Editrice SpA, pg 391
Idea Books, pg 392
Editoriale Jaca Book SpA, pg 394
Laruffa Editore SRL, pg 394
Lybra Immagine, pg 396
Magnus Edizioni SpA, pg 397
Giuseppe Maimone Editore, pg 397
Edizioni Gabriele Mazzotta SRL, pg 397
Edizioni Medicea SRL, pg 398
Giorgio Mondadori & Associati, pg 399
Moretti & Vitali Editori srl, pg 399
Istituto Nazionale di Studi Romani, pg 400
OCTAVO Produzioni Editoriali Associate, pg 401
Officina Edizioni di Aldo Quinti, pg 401
Leo S Olschki, pg 401
Franco Cosimo Panini Editore SpA, pg 402
Il Pomerio, pg 404
Edizioni Riposte, pg 405
SAGEP Libri & Comunicazione Srl, pg 406
Sapere 2000 SRL, pg 407
Schena Editore, pg 407
Edizioni Scientifiche Italiane, pg 407
Edizioni Librarie Siciliane, pg 408
Silvana Editoriale SpA, pg 408
Il Sole 24 Ore Pirola, pg 409
Tappeiner, pg 409
Giovanni Tranchida Editore, pg 410
Transeuropa, pg 410
UTET (Unione Tipografico-Editrice Torinese), pg 411
Vianello Libri, pg 411
Zanichelli Editore SpA, pg 412

Japan
ADA Edita Tokyo Co Ltd, pg 415
Bijutsu Shuppan-Sha, Ltd, pg 415
Dohosha Publishing Co Ltd, pg 417
Kajima Institute Publishing Co Ltd, pg 420
Kogyo Chosakai Publishing Co Ltd, pg 421
Maruzen Co Ltd, pg 422
Shakai Shiso-Sha, pg 427
Shinkenchiku-Sha Co Ltd, pg 427
Mitsumura Suiko Shoin, pg 428
Shokokusha Publishing Co Ltd, pg 428
Shufunotomo Co Ltd, pg 428
Tankosha Publishing Co Ltd, pg 429

Democratic People's Republic of Korea
Korea Science and Encyclopedia Publishing House, pg 436

Republic of Korea
Bal-eon, pg 437
Bo Moon Dang, pg 437
Dae Won Sa Co Ltd, pg 438
Daehan Printing & Publishing Co Ltd, pg 438
Hakgojae Publishing Inc, pg 439
Youlhwadang Publisher, pg 444

Lebanon
Arab Institute for Research & Publishing, pg 445

The Former Yugoslav Republic of Macedonia
Zumpres Publishing Firm, pg 453

Mexico
Artes de Mexico y del Mundo SA de CV, pg 462
Edamex SA de CV, pg 464
Editorial Edicol SA, pg 464
Editorial Extemporaneos SA, pg 465
Fondo de Cultura Economica, pg 465
Editorial Jilguero, SA de CV, pg 467
Editorial Limusa SA de CV, pg 467
Naves Internacional de Ediciones SA, pg 469
Ediciones Promesa, SA de CV, pg 470
Servicios Especiales Maciel SA de CV, pg 472
Siglo XXI Editores SA de CV, pg 472
Editorial Trillas SA de CV, pg 472
Universidad Nacional Autonoma de Mexico (National University of Mexico), pg 472

Nepal
International Standards Books & Periodicals (P) Ltd, pg 476

Netherlands
Architectura & Natura, pg 478
BIS Publishers, pg 479
De Walburg Pers, pg 481
Delft University Press, pg 481
Hagen & Stam Uitgeverij Ten, pg 483
Nai Publishers, pg 486
The Pepin Press, pg 487
Uitgeverij SUN, pg 489
Uitgeverij Terra bv, pg 490

Thoth Publishers, pg 490
Unieboek BV, pg 490
Uniepers BV, pg 491
Uitgeverij 010, pg 493

New Zealand
Barkfire Press, pg 494
Craig Potton Publishing, pg 495
Hodder Moa Beckett Publishers Ltd, pg 497
Te Waihora Press, pg 501
Victoria University Press, pg 502

Norway
Andresen & Butenschon AS, pg 508
Aschehoug Forlag, pg 508
H Aschehoug & Co (W Nygaard) A/S, pg 508

Panama
Editorial Universitaria, pg 515

Philippines
Ateneo de Manila University Press, pg 518
UST Publishing House, pg 521

Poland
Aritbus et Historiae, Rivista Internationale di arti visive ecinema, Institut IRSA - Verlagsanstalt, pg 522
Wydawnictwo Arkady, pg 522
Wydawnictwo Baturo, pg 522
BOSZ scp, pg 522
Ossolineum Zaklad Narodowy im Ossolinskich - Wydawnictwo, pg 525
Oficyna Wydawnicza Politechniki Wroclawskiej, pg 525

Portugal
Armenio Amado Editora de Simoes, Beirao & Ca Lda, pg 528
Arvore Coop de Actividades Artisticas, CRL, pg 528
Camara Municipal de Castelo, pg 529
Dinalivro, pg 530
Distri Cultural Lda, pg 530
Editorial Estampa, Lda, pg 531
Latina Livraria Editora, pg 532
Editora McGraw-Hill de Portugal Lda, pg 533
Editorial Presenca, pg 535
Edicoes 70 Lda, pg 535
Vega-Publicacao e Distribuicao de Livros e Revistas, Lda, pg 536

Puerto Rico
McGraw-Hill Intermericana del Caribe, Inc, pg 537

Romania
Editura Meridiane, pg 540

Russian Federation
Izdatelstvo Iskusstvo, pg 545
Planeta Publishers, pg 548
Stroyizdat Publishing House, pg 549

Serbia and Montenegro
Gradevinska Knjiga, pg 552

Singapore
APAC Publishers Services Pte Ltd, pg 554
Archipelago Press, pg 555

Select Publishing Pte Ltd, pg 557
Taylor & Francis Asia Pacific, pg 558

Slovakia
Technicka Univerzita, pg 561

South Africa
Human & Rousseau (Pty) Ltd, pg 564
New Africa Books (Pty) Ltd, pg 567

Spain
Ediciones Akal SA, pg 571
Alta Fulla Editorial, pg 572
Atrium Group, pg 574
CEAC, Grupo Editorial SA, pg 576
Celeste Ediciones, pg 576
Comunidad Autonoma de Madrid, Servicio de Documentacion y Publicaciones, pg 578
Consello da Cultura Galega - CCG, pg 578
Ediciones Daly S L, pg 578
Ediciones Destino SA, pg 579
Ediciones Doce Calles SL, pg 579
Editorial Dossat SA, pg 580
Ediciones l'Isard, S L, pg 580
Edilesa-Ediciones Leonesas SA, pg 581
EUNSA (Ediciones Universidad de Navarra SA), pg 583
Editorial Gustavo Gili SA, pg 585
Grijalbo Mondadori SA, pg 585
Editorial Juventud, pg 588
LEDA (Las Ediciones de Arte), pg 589
Lunwerg Editores, SA, pg 589
Antonio Machado, SA, pg 590
Mandala Ediciones, pg 590
Editorial Nerea SA, pg 593
Oikos-Tau SA Ediciones, pg 593
Editorial Parthenon Communication, SL, pg 595
Pronaos, SA Ediciones, pg 597
Pulso Ediciones, SL, pg 597
Editora Regional de Murcia - ERM, pg 597
Rueda, SL Editorial, pg 598
Editores Tecnicos Asociados SA, pg 601
Tf Editores, pg 602
Turner Publicaciones, pg 602
Tursen, SA, pg 603
Universidad de Valladolid Secretariado de Publicaciones e Intercambio Editorial, pg 604
Edicions de la Universitat Politecnica de Catalunya SL, pg 604
Xarait Libros SA, pg 605

Sweden
Arkitektur Forlag AB, pg 609
Byggforlaget, pg 610
Bokforlaget Semic AB, pg 615

Switzerland
Association Suisse des Editeurs de Langue Francaise, pg 618
Birkhauser Verlag AG, pg 619
Carre d'Art Edition Archigraphie, pg 620
Editions Andre Delcourt & Cie, pg 621
FEDA SA, pg 623
G+B Arts International, pg 623
Giampiero Casagrande Editore, pg 624
Verlag Karl Kraemer & Co, pg 627

SUBJECT INDEX

Kranich-Verlag, Dres AG & H R Bosch-Gwalter, pg 627
Lars Mueller Publishers, pg 629
Muslim Architecture Research Program (MARP), pg 629
Verlag Arthur Niggli AG, pg 629
Office du Livre SA (Buchhaus AG), pg 630
Editions Payot Lausanne, pg 631
Presses Polytechniques et Universitaires Romandes, PPUR, pg 631
SAB Schweiz Arbeitsgemeinschaft fuer die Berggebiete, pg 633
Edition Stemmle AG, pg 635
Vdf Hochschulverlag AG an der ETH Zurich, pg 636
Vogt-Schild Ag, Druck und Verlag, pg 636
Weber SA d'Editions, pg 637
Wepf & Co AG, pg 637
Wiese Verlag AG, pg 637

Syrian Arab Republic

Damascus University Press, pg 638

Taiwan, Province of China

Echo Publishing Company Ltd, pg 639
Chu Hai Publishing (Taiwan) Co Ltd, pg 640

Turkey

Arkeoloji Ve Sanat Yayinlari, pg 649
Kubbealti Akademisi Kultur ve Sasat Vakfi, pg 650
Yapi-Endustri Merkezi Yayinlari-Yem Yayin, pg 652

Ukraine

Osnova, Kharkov State University Press, pg 653

United Kingdom

Ian Allan Publishing Ltd, pg 656
Umberto Allemandi & Co Publishing, pg 656
Antique Collectors' Club Ltd, pg 658
Architectural Association Publications, pg 659
Art Books International Ltd, pg 659
Ashgate Publishing Ltd, pg 660
Batsford Ltd, pg 663
BCA - Book Club Associates, pg 663
Bellew Publishing Co Ltd, pg 664
Joseph Biddulph Publisher, pg 665
Blackwell Science Ltd, pg 667
Books for Europe Ltd, pg 669
Breslich & Foss Ltd, pg 671
Cambridge University Press, pg 674
Cameron & Hollis, pg 674
Carlton Publishing Group, pg 675
Cassell & Co, pg 675
The Chartered Institute of Building, pg 678
CMP Information Ltd, pg 680
Compendium Publishing, pg 681
Conran Octopus, pg 682
Donhead Publishing Ltd, pg 688
Edinburgh University Press Ltd, pg 689
Elfande Ltd, pg 690
Elsevier Ltd, pg 691
The Erskine Press, pg 692
Fourth Estate, pg 696
The Fraser Press, pg 697
Gaia Books Ltd, pg 698
Garnet Publishing Ltd, pg 698

Golden Cockerel Press Ltd, pg 701
Gollancz/Witherby, pg 701
Grange Books PLC, pg 702
Hamlyn, pg 704
Hayward Gallery Publishing, pg 706
Herbert Press Ltd, pg 708
Heritage Press, pg 708
Hilmarton Manor Press, pg 708
James & James (Science Publishers) Ltd, pg 715
Kegan Paul International Ltd, pg 717
Laurence King Publishing Ltd, pg 717
Frances Lincoln Ltd, pg 720
Liverpool University Press, pg 722
Lund Humphries, pg 723
Maney Publishing, pg 725
Marston House, pg 725
Merrell Publishers Ltd, pg 727
Miller's Publications, pg 728
MIT Press Ltd, pg 728
Motilal (UK) Books of India, pg 729
W W Norton & Company Ltd, pg 734
Octopus Publishing Group, pg 734
Open University Worldwide, pg 736
Packard Publishing Ltd, pg 737
Phaidon Press Ltd, pg 741
Phillimore & Co Ltd, pg 741
Pomegranate Europe Ltd, pg 744
PRC Publishing Ltd, pg 745
Quadrille Publishing Ltd, pg 746
Ramsay Head Press, pg 747
The Reader's Digest Association Ltd, pg 748
Reaktion Books Ltd, pg 748
Regency House Publishing Ltd, pg 749
RIBA Publications, pg 750
RICS Books, pg 750
RotoVision SA, pg 751
The Rutland Press, pg 752
Ryland Peters & Small Ltd, pg 752
Salamander Books Ltd, pg 753
The Salariya Book Co Ltd, pg 753
Sheldrake Press, pg 757
Shire Publications Ltd, pg 757
Spon Press, pg 760
Stacey International, pg 761
Studio Editions Ltd, pg 761
Sutton Publishing Ltd, pg 762
Tate Publishing Ltd, pg 763
I B Tauris & Co Ltd, pg 763
Thames & Hudson Ltd, pg 764
Thomson Gale, pg 765
TSO (The Stationery Office), pg 767
Tuckwell Press Ltd, pg 767
University of Wales Press, pg 769
White Cockade Publishing, pg 772
Wiley Europe Ltd, pg 773
Philip Wilson Publishers, pg 774
Windsor Books International, pg 774
WIT Press, pg 774
World Microfilms Publications Ltd, pg 775
Yale University Press London, pg 776
Zwemmer Holdings Co Ltd, pg 776

Uruguay

Nordan-Comunidad, pg 778
Ediciones Trilce, pg 778

Venezuela

Armitano Editores CA, pg 779
Biblioteca Ayacucho, pg 779

Viet Nam

Science & Technics Publishing House, pg 780

ART

Albania

NL SH, pg 1
State Textbook Publishing House, pg 1

Argentina

Centro Editor de America Latina SA, pg 4
Diana Argentina SA, Editorial, pg 5
Emece Editores SA, pg 5
EUDEBA (Editorial Universitaria de Buenos Aires), pg 5
Laffont Ediciones Electronicas SA, pg 7
Ediciones Nueva Vision SAIC, pg 8
Editorial Quetzal-Domingo Cortizo, pg 8
Manrique Zago Ediciones SRL, pg 9

Australia

Aboriginal Studies Press, pg 10
Aeolian Press, pg 11
Allen & Unwin Pty Ltd, pg 11
Art Gallery of South Australia Bookshop, pg 12
Art Gallery of Western Australia, pg 12
Art on the Move, pg 12
Artmoves Inc, pg 12
Australian Rock Art Research Association, pg 13
Barbara Beckett Publishing Pty Ltd, pg 14
Boolarong Press, pg 15
Dangaroo Press, pg 19
D'Artagnan Publishing, pg 19
Edwina Publishing, pg 21
David Ell Press Pty Ltd, pg 21
Encyclopaedia Britannica (Australia) Inc, pg 21
Experimental Art Foundation, pg 22
Fine Art Publishing Pty Ltd, pg 22
Fremantle Arts Centre Press, pg 23
Granrott Press, pg 24
Hartys Creek Press, pg 25
The Images Publishing Group Pty Ltd, pg 26
In-Tune Press, pg 26
Incunabula Press, pg 26
Institute of Aboriginal Development (IAD Press), pg 27
Magabala Books Aboriginal Corporation, pg 30
McGraw-Hill Australia Pty Ltd, pg 31
Mountain House Press, pg 32
National Gallery of Australia, pg 33
National Gallery of Victoria, pg 33
New Endeavour Press, pg 33
Oriental Publications, pg 34
Pandani Press, pg 35
Power Publications, pg 37
Press for Success, pg 37
Queen Victoria Museum & Art Gallery Publications, pg 38
Queensland Art Gallery, pg 38
Reed Educational Publishing Australia, pg 39
Ruskin Rowe Press, pg 40
Spinifex Press, pg 42
State Library of NSW Press, pg 42
Thames & Hudson (Australia) Pty Ltd, pg 43
Unity Press, pg 44

Wakefield Press Pty Ltd, pg 46
Wellington Lane Press Pty Ltd, pg 46
Wileman Publications, pg 46
Yanagang Publishing, pg 47

Austria

Akademische Druck-u Verlagsanstalt Dr Paul Struzl GmbH, pg 48
Amalthea-Verlag, pg 48
Verlag Der Apfel, pg 48
Boehlau Verlag GmbH & Co KG, pg 48
Christian Brandstaetter Verlagsgesellschaft mbH, pg 49
Camera Austria, pg 49
Carinthia Verlag, pg 49
CEEBA Publications Antenne d'Autriche, pg 49
DachsVerlag GmbH, pg 49
Danubia Werbung und Verlagsservice, pg 49
Literature Verlag Droschl, pg 50
Ferdinand Berger und Sohne, pg 50
Edition Dr Heinrich Fuchs, pg 51
Edition Graphischer Zirkel, pg 51
Graz Stadtmuseum, pg 51
Haymon-Verlag GesmbH, pg 51
Herold Druck-und Verlagsgesellschaft mbH, pg 52
Johannes Heyn GmbH & Co KG, pg 52
Edition E Hilger, pg 52
Edition Koenigstein, pg 53
Kremayr & Scheriau Verlag, pg 53
Leykam Buchverlagsges mbH, pg 53
Loecker Verlag, pg 53
LOG-Internationale Zeitschrift fuer Literatur, pg 53
Modulverlag, pg 54
Paul Neff Verlag KG, pg 54
Passagen Verlag GmbH, pg 56
Verlag Sankt Peter, pg 56
Richard Pils Publication PN°1, pg 56
Pinguin-Verlag, Pawlowski GmbH, pg 56
Georg Prachner KG, pg 56
Verlag Anton Pustet, pg 56
Residenz Verlag GmbH, pg 57
Ritter Druck und Verlags KEG, pg 57
Verlag fuer Sammler, pg 57
Andreas Schnider Verlags-Atelier, pg 57
Springer-Verlag Wien, pg 58
Edition Thurnhof KEG, pg 58
Edition Tusch, pg 58
Verlag Carl Ueberreuter GmbH, pg 58
Verlag Anton Schroll & Co, pg 59
Weilburg Verlag, pg 59
Verlag Galerie Welz Salzburg, pg 59
Kunstverlag Wolfrum, pg 60
WUV/Facultas Universitaetsverlag, pg 60

Bangladesh

The University Press Ltd, pg 61

Belarus

Belarus (The Belorussia), pg 62
Belaruskaya Encyklapedyya, pg 62

Belgium

Libraire Ancienne Noel Anselot, pg 63
NV Artis-Historia, pg 63
Bartleby & Co, pg 63

Editions Gerard Blanchart & Cie SA, pg 63
Brepols Publishers NV, pg 64
Centre International de Recherches 'Primitifs Flamands' ASBL, pg 65
Editions Chanlis, pg 65
Conservart SA, pg 65
Uitgeverij Contact NV, pg 65
Le Daily-Bul, pg 66
Davidsfonds Uitgeverij NV, pg 66
Editions De Boeck-Larcier SA, pg 66
Maison d'Editions Claude Dejaie, pg 66
Editions Delta SA, pg 66
Dexia Bank, pg 66
Glenat Benelux SA, pg 67
Groeninghe NV, pg 68
Koninklijke Vlaamse Academie van Belgie voor Wetenschappen en Kunsten, pg 69
Uitgeverij Lannoo NV, pg 69
Lansman Editeur, pg 69
Editions Lessius ASBL, pg 70
Mercatorfonds NV, pg 71
Petraco-Pandora NV, pg 71
La Part de L'Oeil, pg 71
Uitgeverij Peeters Leuven (Belgie), pg 71
Editions Racine, pg 72
La Renaissance du Livre, pg 72
Roularta Books NV, pg 72
Sonneville Press (Uitgeverij) VTW, pg 73
Stichting Kunstboek bvba, pg 73
Stichting Ons Erfdeel VZW, pg 73
Marc Van de Wiele bvba, pg 74
Editions Luce Wilquin, pg 74

Botswana
The Botswana Society, pg 76

Brazil
AGIR S/A Editora, pg 77
Callis Editora Ltda, pg 79
Editora Campus Ltda, pg 79
Conquista, Empresa de Publicacoes Ltda, pg 80
Edicon Editora e Consultorial Ltda, pg 81
Livraria Martins Fontes Editora Ltda, pg 81
Grafica Editora Primor Ltda, pg 83
Livro Ibero-Americano Ltda, pg 83
Editora Index Ltda, pg 84
Edicoes Loyola SA, pg 85
Editora Mantiqueira de Ciencia e Arte, pg 86
Editora Melhoramentos Ltda, pg 86
Editora Mercuryo Ltda, pg 86
Editora Nova Fronteira SA, pg 87
Pallas Editora e Distribuidora Ltda, pg 88
Rede Das Artes (Boccato Editores Collector's), pg 89
Editora Revan Ltda, pg 89
Salamandra Consultoria Editorial SA, pg 89
Spala Editora Ltda, pg 90
Totalidade Editora Ltda, pg 91
Editora da Universidade de Sao Paulo, pg 91
Editora Universidade Federal do Rio de Janeiro, pg 92
Editora Verbo Ltda, pg 92
Jorge Zahar Editor, pg 92

Bulgaria
Abagar Pablioing, pg 92
Abagar, Veliko Tarnovo, pg 93
Fondacija Zlatno Kljuce, pg 94

Hriker, pg 94
Kibea Publishing Co, pg 95
Makros 2000 - Plovdiv, pg 95
Musica Publishing House Ltd, pg 95
Naouka i Izkoustvo, Ltd, pg 95
Seven Hills Publishers, pg 96
Slavena, pg 97
Svetra Publishing House, pg 97
Zunica, pg 97

Chile
Arrayan Editores, pg 98
Editorial Andres Bello/Editorial Juridica de Chile, pg 99
Ediciones Mil Hojas Ltda, pg 99
Museo Chileno de Arte Precolombino, pg 99
Norma de Chile, pg 99
Pontificia Universidad Catolica de Chile, pg 100
Ediciones Universitarias de Valparaiso, pg 100

China
Beijing Arts & Crafts Publishing House, pg 101
Beijing Publishing House, pg 101
China Braille Publishing House, pg 102
China Film Press, pg 102
China Light Industry Press, pg 102
Chinese Literature Press, pg 103
Cultural Relics Publishing House, pg 103
Encyclopedia of China Publishing House, pg 104
Foreign Languages Press, pg 104
Fudan University Press, pg 104
Fujian Children's Publishing House, pg 104
Guizhou Education Publishing House, pg 105
Morning Glory Press, pg 106
People's Fine Arts Publishing House, pg 106
Qingdao Publishing House, pg 107
Shanghai Calligraphy & Painting Publishing House, pg 108
Shanghai Far East Publishers, pg 108
Shanghai People's Fine Arts Publishing House, pg 108
Universidade de Macau, Centro de Publicacoes, pg 109
Yunnan University Press, pg 109
Zhejiang University Press, pg 109

Colombia
Amazonas Editores Ltda, pg 110
Dosmil Editora, pg 110
El Ancora Editores, pg 111
Escala Ltda, pg 111
Editorial Santillana SA, pg 112
Siglo XXI Editores de Colombia Ltda, pg 112
Universidad de Antioquia, Division Publicaciones, pg 113
Carlos Valencia Editores, pg 113
Villegas Editores Ltda, pg 113
Editorial Voluntad SA, pg 113

The Democratic Republic of the Congo
Facultes Catoliques de Kinshasa, pg 114

Costa Rica
Ediciones Promesa, pg 116
Editorial de la Universidad de Costa Rica, pg 116

Cote d'Ivoire
Les Nouvelles Editions Ivoiriennes, pg 117
Les Nouvelles Editions Ivoiriennes (NEI), pg 117

Croatia
AGM doo, pg 117
Globus-Nakladni zavod, pg 118
Graficki zavod Hrvatske, pg 118
Krscanska sadasnjost, pg 118
Matica hrvatska, pg 118
Mladost d d Izdavacku graficku i informaticku djelatnost, pg 119
Naklada Ljevak doo, pg 119
Skolska Knjiga, pg 119

Cuba
Casa de las Americas, pg 120
Holguin, Ediciones, pg 120
Editorial Letras Cubanas, pg 120
Union de Escritores y Artistas de Cuba, pg 121

Czech Republic
Aurora, pg 122
Aventinum Nakladatelstvi spol sro, pg 122
Brody, pg 122
Euromedia Group-Odeon, pg 123
Horacek Ladislav-Paseka, pg 123
Karolinum, nakladatelstvi, pg 124
Labyrint, pg 125
Lidove Noviny Publishing House, pg 125
Mariadan, pg 125
Maxdorf Ltd, pg 125
Mlada fronta, pg 125
Moravska Galerie v Brno, pg 126
Narodni Muzeum, pg 126
Prazske nakladatelstvi Pluto, pg 127
Votobia sro, pg 128

Denmark
Arnkrone Forlaget A/S, pg 129
Atuakkiorfik A/S Det Greenland Publishers, pg 129
Borgens Forlag A/S, pg 129
Christian Ejlers' Forlag aps, pg 131
Grevas Forlag, pg 131
Gyldendalske Boghandel - Nordisk Forlag A/S, pg 131
Edition Wilhelm Hansen AS, pg 131
Museum Tusculanum Press, pg 133
New Era Publications International ApS, pg 133
Nyt Nordisk Forlag Arnold Busck A/S, pg 133
Det Schonbergske Forlag A/S, pg 134

Ecuador
CIDAP, pg 136
Pontificia Universidad Catolica del Ecuador, Centro de Publicaciones, pg 137

Egypt (Arab Republic of Egypt)
American University in Cairo Press, pg 137

Estonia
Eesti Entsuklopeediakirjastus, pg 139
Eesti Rahvusraamatukogu, pg 139
Kirjastus Kunst, pg 139

Finland
Otava Publishing Co Ltd, pg 143
Schildts Forlags AB, pg 144
Soderstroms Forlag, pg 144
Weilin & Goos Oy, pg 144

France
ACR Edition, pg 145
Action Artistique de la Ville de Paris, pg 145
ADPF Publications, pg 145
Editions Alternatives, pg 146
Editions de l'Amateur, pg 146
Editions d'Amerique et d'Orient, Adrien Maisonneuve, pg 146
Editions Amez, pg 146
Editions Amrita SA, pg 146
Edition Anthese, pg 147
L'Arbalete, pg 147
Editions Arcam, pg 147
L'Arche Editeur, pg 147
Editions de l'Armancon, pg 147
Armenia Editions, pg 147
Editions Art & Metiers Du Livre, pg 147
Atelier National de Reproduction des Theses, pg 148
Editions Atlantica Seguier, pg 148
Editions Philippe Auzou, pg 148
Societe Nouvelle Rene Baudouin, pg 149
Bayard Presse, pg 149
Editions Belin, pg 149
Berger-Levrault Editions SAS, pg 149
La Bibliotheque des Arts, pg 150
Adam Biro Editions, pg 150
William Blake & Co, pg 150
De Boccard Edition-Diffusion, pg 150
Editions Andre Bonne, pg 150
Bookmaker, pg 150
Pierre Bordas & Fils, Editions, pg 150
Editions Bornemann, pg 150
Editions Buchet-Chastel Pierre Zech Editeur, pg 151
Editions du Buot, pg 151
Editions du Cadratin, pg 151
Editions des Cahiers Bourbonnais, pg 151
Editions Cahiers d'Art, pg 151
Editions Canope, pg 152
Editions Casteille, pg 152
Editions Casterman, pg 152
Editions Cenomane, pg 152
Editions Cercle d'Art SA, pg 153
Editions Jacqueline Chambon, pg 153
Chasse Maree, pg 153
Editions du Chene, pg 154
Cicero Editeurs, pg 154
Editions Circonflexe, pg 154
Editions Citadelles & Mazenod, pg 154
CNRS Editions, pg 155
Editions du Comite des Travaux Historiques et Scientifiques (CTHS), pg 155
Communication Par Livre (CPL), pg 155
Compagnie Francaise des Arts Graphiques SA, pg 155
Editions Denoel, pg 157
Dessain et Tolra SA, pg 158
Editions de la Difference, pg 158
Editions Dis Voir, pg 158
La Documentation Francaise, pg 158
Dreamland Editeur, pg 159
Ecole Nationale Superieure des Beaux-Arts, pg 159

Editions Edisud, pg 159
Editions Grund, pg 160
Editions Terrail/Finest SA, pg 160
Editions de l'Epargne, pg 161
Editions Pierre Fanlac, pg 162
Editions Fata Morgana, pg 162
FBT de R Editions, pg 163
Editions Des Femmes, pg 163
Librairie Fischbacher, International Art Book Distribution (import-export), pg 163
Flammarion SA, pg 163
Editions Fleurus, pg 163
Editions Fragments, pg 164
France-Loisirs, pg 164
Editions Galilee, pg 164
Editions Gallimard, pg 164
Imprimerie Librairie Gardet, pg 165
Paul Geuthner Librairie Orientaliste, pg 165
Editions Jean Paul Gisserot, pg 165
Editions Grandir, pg 166
Editions d'Art Albert Guillot, pg 166
Hachette Livre, pg 167
Pierre Hautot Editions, pg 167
Editions Hazan, pg 167
Hermann editeurs des Sciences et des Arts SA, pg 167
Editions de l'Herne, pg 167
Herscher, pg 168
Editions Hoebeke, pg 168
Pierre Horay Editeur, pg 168
Image/Magie, pg 168
Indigo & Cote-Femmes Editions, pg 168
Editions l'Instant Durable, pg 169
Institut International de la Marionnette, pg 169
Editions du Jaguar, pg 169
Editions Jannink, SARL, pg 169
Editions du Jeu de Paume, pg 169
Kailash Editions, pg 170
Editions Klincksieck, pg 170
Librairie Leonce Laget, pg 171
Editions du Laquet, pg 171
Editions Larousse, pg 171
Editions Dominique Leroy, pg 171
Liana Levi Editions, pg 172
Editions des Limbes d'Or FBT de R Editions, pg 172
Le Livre de Paris, pg 173
Editions Loubatieres, pg 173
Macula, pg 173
Editions Mango, pg 174
Editions Marval, pg 174
Editions Charles Massin et Cie, pg 174
Editions Medianes, pg 175
Editions Memo, pg 175
Editions Memoire des Arts, pg 175
Editions Albin Michel, pg 175
Gerard Monfort Editeur Sarl, pg 176
Editions de la Reunion des Musees Nationaux, pg 176
Nanga, pg 176
Librairie F de Nobele, pg 177
Editions Norma, pg 177
Nouvelles Editions Francaises, pg 177
OGC Michele Broutta Editeur, pg 177
Editions Parentheses, pg 179
Association Paris-Musees, pg 179
Editions Phebus, pg 179
Editions A et J Picard SA, pg 179
Jean-Michel Place, pg 180
Editions du Centre Pompidou, pg 180
Le Pre-aux-clercs, pg 180
Presses Universitaires de France (PUF), pg 181

Presses Universitaires de Strasbourg, pg 182
Propos de Campagne, pg 182
Editions Pygmalion, pg 182
References cf, pg 183
Revue Noire, pg 183
Yves Riviere Editeur, pg 183
Editions Scala, pg 184
Selection du Reader's Digest SA, pg 184
Editions Selection J Jacobs SA, pg 184
Sepia Editions, pg 184
Service Technique pour l'Education, pg 184
Editions du Seuil, pg 184
Societe Nouveaux Loisirs, pg 185
Somogy editions d'art, pg 185
Publications de la Sorbonne, pg 185
Editions Stil, pg 186
Editions Tallandier, pg 187
Editions Thames & Hudson, pg 187
Transedition ASBL, pg 188
Transeuropeennes/RCE, pg 188
Ulisse Editions, pg 188
UNESCO Publishing, pg 188
Publications de l'Universite de Pau, pg 188
Editions Vague Verte, pg 188
Editions de Vergeures, pg 188
Editions Vilo SA, pg 189
La Voix du Regard, pg 189

Germany

Accedo Verlagsgesellschaft mbH, pg 190
F A Ackermanns Kunstverlag GmbH, pg 190
AGIS Verlag GmbH, pg 191
Aisthesis Verlag, pg 191
akg-images gmbh, pg 191
Alibaba Verlag GmbH, pg 192
ALS-Verlag GmbH, pg 192
Anabas-Verlag Guenter Kaempf GmbH & Co KG, pg 192
AOL-Verlag Frohmut Menze, pg 193
Verlag APHAIA Svea Haske, Sonja Schumann GbR, pg 193
Aquamarin Verlag, pg 193
ARCult Media, pg 193
Ardey-Verlag GmbH, pg 193
Aries-Verlag Paul Johannes Muller, pg 194
Arkana Verlag Tete Boettger Rainer Wunderlich GmbH, pg 194
Arnoldsche Verlagsanstalt GmbH, pg 194
Ars Edition GmbH, pg 194
Artcolor, pg 194
Verlag Atelier im Bauernhaus Fischerhude Wolf-Dietmar Stock, pg 195
Atelier Verlag Andernach (AVA), pg 195
AvivA Britta Jurgs GmbH, pg 196
Edition Balance Marion Guenther Bonsack, pg 196
Bartkowiaks Forum Book Art, pg 197
Basilisken-Presse, pg 197
Dr Wolfgang Baur Verlag Kunst & Alltag, pg 198
Verlag C H Beck oHG, pg 198
Edition Monika Beck, pg 198
Bergstadtverlag Wilhelm Gottlieb Korn GmbH Wuerzburg, pg 199
Berliner Handpresse Wolfgang Joerg und Erich Schonig, pg 199
C Bertelsmann Verlag GmbH, pg 199
Bertelsmann Lexikon Verlag GmbH, pg 200

Betzel Verlag GmbH, pg 200
Biblio Verlag, pg 200
Verlag Die Blaue Eule, pg 202
Boehlau-Verlag GmbH & Cie, pg 202
Verlag Hermann Boehlaus Nachfolger Weimar GmbH & Co, pg 203
Klaus Boer Verlag, pg 203
Bonifatius GmbH Druck-Buch-Verlag, pg 203
Verlag Das Brennglas, pg 204
F Bruckmann Munchen Verlag & Druck GmbH & Co Produkt KG, pg 204
BRUEN-Verlag, Gorenflo, pg 205
Buch- und Kunstverlag Kleinheinrich, pg 205
Verlag C J Bucher GmbH, pg 205
Buchheim-Verlag, pg 205
Buchergilde Gutenberg Verlagsgesellschaft mbH, pg 205
Buechse der Pandora Verlags-GmbH, pg 205
Dr Cantz'sche Druckerei GmbH & Co, pg 207
Fachverlag Hans Carl GmbH, pg 207
Chorus-Verlag, pg 208
Chr Belser AG fur Verlagsgeschaefte und Co KG, pg 208
Hans Christians Druckerei und Verlag GmbH & Co KG, pg 208
Christusbruderschaft Selbitz ev, Abt Verlag, pg 209
Coppenrath Verlag, pg 209
CTL-Presse Clemens-Tobias Lange, pg 210
Daco Verlag Guenter Blase oHG, pg 210
Das Arsenal, Verlag fuer Kultur und Politik GmbH, pg 210
Verlag Werner Dausien, pg 211
Verlag Horst Deike KG, pg 211
Delp'sche Verlagsbuchhandlung, pg 211
Deutscher Kunstverlag GmbH, pg 213
Deutscher Taschenbuch Verlag GmbH & Co KG (dtv), pg 213
Deutscher Verlag fur Kunstwissenschaft GmbH, pg 213
Dieterichsche Verlagsbuchhandlung Mainz, pg 214
Dolling und Galitz Verlag GmbH, pg 215
Donat Verlag, pg 215
Droste Verlag GmbH, pg 216
DuMont monte Verlag GmbH & Co KG, pg 217
DuMont Reiseverlag GmbH & Co KG, pg 217
Echter Wurzburg Frankische Gesellschaftsdruckerei und Verlag GmbH, pg 217
Edition Aragon-Verlagsgesellschaft mbH, pg 218
Egmont vgs verlagsgesellschaft mbH, pg 218
EinfallsReich Verlagsgesellschaft MbH, pg 219
Ellert & Richter Verlag GmbH, pg 219
Englisch Verlag GmbH, pg 220
Verlag Peter Engstler, pg 220
EOS Verlag der Benediktiner der Erzabtei St. Ottilien, pg 220
Eremiten-Presse und Verlag GmbH, pg 220
Verlag am Eschbach GmbH, pg 221
Espresso Verlag GmbH, pg 221
Eulen Verlag, pg 221

Extent Verlag und Service Wolfgang M Flamm, pg 223
Fackeltrager-Verlag GmbH, pg 223
Fahrner & Fahrner, pg 223
Ferdinand Enke Verlag, pg 224
Emil Fink Verlag, pg 224
Wilhelm Fink GmbH & Co Verlags-KG, pg 224
Franz-Sales-Verlag, pg 226
Frederking & Thaler Verlag GmbH, pg 226
Verlag Freies Geistesleben, pg 227
Margarethe Freudenberger - selbstverlag fur jedermann, pg 227
Erhard Friedrich Verlag, pg 227
G Braun (vormals G Braun'sche Hofbuchdruckerei und Verlag) Gmbh, pg 227
Galerie Der Spiegel-Dr E Stunke Nachfolge GmbH, pg 228
Gatzanis Verlags GmbH, pg 228
Germanisches Nationalmuseum, pg 228
GLB Parkland Verlags-und Vertriebs GmbH, pg 229
Wilhelm Goldmann Verlag GmbH, pg 230
Gondrom Verlag GmbH & Co KG, pg 230
Grabert-Verlag, pg 230
Greven Verlag Koeln GmbH, pg 231
Guenther Butkus, pg 231
Verlag Klaus Guhl, pg 232
Verlag H M Hauschild GmbH, pg 232
Hachmeister Verlag, pg 232
Haenssler Verlag GmbH, pg 233
Heinz-Jurgen Hausser, pg 233
Harenberg Kommunikation Verlags- und Medien-GmbH & Co KG, pg 234
Hatje Cantz Verlag, pg 234
Dr Ernst Hauswedell & Co, pg 235
Heigl Verlag, Horst Edition, pg 235
Edition Hentrich Druck & Verlag Gebr Hentrich und Tank GmbH & Co KG, pg 236
F A Herbig Verlagsbuchhandlung GmbH, pg 236
Anton Hiersemann, Verlag, pg 237
Hirmer Verlag GmbH, pg 238
Edition Hoffmann & Co, pg 238
Hoffmann und Campe Verlag GmbH, pg 238
Hohenrain-Verlag GmbH, pg 239
Volker Huber Edition & Galerie, pg 239
Edition Hundertmark, pg 240
Insel Verlag, pg 241
Klaus Isele, pg 242
Iudicium Verlag GmbH, pg 242
Jan Thorbecke Verlag GmbH & Co, pg 243
Jonas Verlag fuer Kunst und Literatur GmbH, pg 243
Jovis Verlag GmbH, pg 243
Katzmann Verlag KG, pg 245
Kerber Verlag, pg 245
Albrecht Knaus Verlag GmbH, pg 247
Koehler & Amelang Verlagsgesellschaft, pg 248
Koenemann Verlagesellschaft mbH, pg 248
Verlag Valentin Koerner GmbH, pg 248
Anton H Konrad Verlag, pg 249
KONTEXTverlag, pg 249
Roman Kovar Verlag, pg 249
Karin Kramer Verlag, pg 250
Verlag Waldemar Kramer, pg 250

PUBLISHERS

Hubert Kretschmar Leipziger Verlagsgesellschaft, pg 250
Verlag Hubert Kretschmer, pg 250
Alfred Kroner Verlag, pg 250
Kulturstiftung der deutschen Vertriebenen, pg 250
Verlag der Kunst/G+B Fine Arts Verlag GmbH, pg 251
Kunstverlag Weingarten GmbH, pg 251
Kupfergraben Verlagsgesellschaft mbH, pg 251
Karl Robert Langewiesche Nachfolger Hans Koester KG, pg 252
LIT Verlag, pg 255
Lusatia Verlag-Dr Stuebner & Co KG, pg 256
Maeander Verlag GmbH, pg 256
Gebr Mann Verlag GmbH & Co, pg 257
Manutius Verlag, pg 257
Matthes und Seitz Verlag GmbH, pg 258
Matzker Verlag DiA, pg 258
Edition Axel Menges, pg 259
Merlin Verlag Andreas Meyer Verlags GmbH und Co KG, pg 259
Merz & Solitude - Akademie Schloss Solitude, pg 259
J B Metzlersche Verlagsbuchhandlung, pg 260
Mitteldeutscher Verlag GmbH, pg 261
modo verlag GmbH, pg 261
Mueller & Schindler Verlag ek, pg 262
Multi Media Kunst Verlag Dresden, pg 262
Munich, Edition, Verlag, Handels- und Dienstleistungskontar GmbH, pg 262
Naumann & Goebel Verlagsgesellschaft mbH, pg 263
Edition Nautilus Verlag, pg 263
Net World Vision GmbH, pg 263
Verlag Neue Kritik KG, pg 264
Verlag Neue Musikzeitung GmbH, pg 264
Nicolaische Verlagsbuchhandlung Beuermann GmbH, pg 265
C W Niemeyer Buchverlage GmbH, pg 265
Nieswand-Verlag GmbH, pg 265
Nusser Verlag, pg 266
nymphenburger, pg 266
Edition Octopus & Okeanos Presse, pg 266
Oekumenischer Verlag Dr R-F Edel, pg 266
Oktagon Verlagsgesellschaft mbH, pg 267
Pandion-Verlag, Ulrike Schmoll, pg 268
Paranus Verlag - Bruecke Neumuenster GmbH, pg 268
Patmos Verlag GmbH & Co KG, pg 268
Pawel Panpresse, pg 268
Pendragon Verlag, pg 269
Pfalzische Verlagsanstalt GmbH, pg 269
Philipp Reclam Jun Verlag GmbH, pg 269
Galerie Eva Poll, pg 271
Portikus, pg 271
Prasenz Verlag der Jesus Bruderschaft eV, pg 271
Guido Pressler Verlag, pg 271
Prestel Verlag, pg 271
Propylaeen Verlag, Zweigniederlassung Berlin der Ullstein Buchverlage GmbH, pg 272
Verlag Friedrich Pustet GmbH & Co Kg, pg 272
edition q Berlin Edition in der Quintessenz Verlags-GmbH, pg 272
Ravensburger Buchverlag Otto Maier GmbH, pg 274
Verlag fur Regionalgeschichte, pg 274
Regura Verlag, pg 274
Konrad Reich Verlag GmbH, pg 274
Dr Ludwig Reichert Verlag, pg 274
Dietrich Reimer Verlag GmbH, pg 274
Ritterbach Verlag GmbH, pg 276
Erich Roeth-Verlag, pg 276
Rogner und Bernhard GmbH & Co Verlags KG, pg 276
Rombach GmbH Druck und Verlagshaus & Co, pg 276
Verlag an der Ruhr GmbH, pg 277
Saarbrucker Druckerei und Verlag GmbH (SDV), pg 277
Sachsenbuch Verlagsgesellschaft Mbh, pg 277
Verlag der Sankt-Johannis-Druckerei C Schweickhardt, pg 278
K G Saur Verlag GmbH, A Gale/Thomson Learning Company, pg 278
scaneg Verlag, pg 278
Verlag Th Schaefer im Vicentz Verlag KG, pg 278
Schillinger Verlag GmbH, pg 279
Schirmer/Mosel Verlag, pg 279
Verlag Hermann Schmidt Universitatsdruckerei GmbH & Co, pg 280
Wilhelm Schmitz Verlag, pg 280
Verlag Schnell und Steiner GmbH, pg 281
Verlag Silke Schreiber, pg 281
Carl Ed Schuenemann KG, pg 281
H O Schulze KG, pg 282
Schwabenverlag Aktiengesellschaft, pg 282
Dr Wolfgang Schwarze Verlag, pg 282
Siebenberg-Verlag, pg 283
Rudolf G Smend, pg 283
Societaets-Verlag, pg 283
Spee Buchverlag GmbH, pg 284
Springer Science+Business Media GmbH & Co KG, pg 284
Staatliche Museen Kassel, pg 286
Stadler Verlagsgesellschaft mbH, pg 286
Steidl Verlag, pg 287
Franz Steiner Verlag Wiesbaden GmbH, pg 287
J F Steinkopf Verlag GmbH, pg 287
Steintor Verlag GmbH, pg 287
Steinweg-Verlag, Jurgen vomHoff, pg 287
Stiebner Verlag GmbH, pg 288
Edition Gunter Stoberlein, pg 288
Sueddeutsche Verlagsgesellschaft mbH, pg 288
Svato Zapletal, pg 289
TASCHEN GmbH, pg 289
teNeues Verlag GmbH & Co KG, pg 290
Konrad Theiss Verlag GmbH, pg 290
Hans Thoma Verlag GmbH Kunst und Buchverlag, pg 291
Treves Editions Verein Zur Foerderung der Kuenstlerischen Taetigkeiten, pg 292
Tuduv Verlagsgesellschaft mbH, pg 292
Verlag Dr Alfons Uhl, pg 293
Ullstein Heyne List GmbH & Co KG, pg 293
Dorothea van der Koelen, pg 294
Verein der Benediktiner zu Beuron-Beuroner Kunstverlag, pg 294
Vice Versa Verlag, pg 295
Edition Curt Visel, pg 296
VWB-Verlag fur Wissenschaft & Bildung, Amand Aglaster, pg 297
W Ludwig Verlag GmbH, pg 297
Wachholtz Verlag GmbH, pg 297
Verlag Klaus Wagenbach, pg 297
Uwe Warnke Verlag, pg 297
Wartburg Verlag GmbH, pg 297
Ernst Wasmuth Verlag GmbH & Co, pg 297
Verlagsgruppe Weltbild GmbH, pg 298
Weltkunst Verlag GmbH, pg 299
Wissenschaftliche Buchgesellschaft, pg 300
Verlag Claus Wittal, pg 301
Friedrich Wittig Verlag GmbH, pg 301
Das Wunderhorn Verlag GmbH, pg 301
Verlag Philipp von Zabern, pg 302
Zettner Verlag GmbH & Co KG, pg 302

Ghana

Ghana Academy of Arts & Sciences, pg 304

Greece

Akritas, pg 305
Atlantis M Pechlivanides & Co SA, pg 306
Chryssos Typos AE Ekodeis, pg 306
Ecole francaise d'Athenes, pg 307
Ekdotike Athenon SA, pg 307
Evrodiastasi, pg 307
Exandas Publishers, pg 307
Govostis Publishing SA, pg 307
Gutenberg Publications, pg 307
Hestia-I D Hestia-Kollaros & Co Corporation, pg 308
Idryma Meleton Chersonisou tou Aimou, pg 308
Kastaniotis Editions SA, pg 309
A G Leventis Foundation, pg 309
Medusa/Selas Publishers, pg 310
Melissa Publishing House, pg 310
Minoas SA, pg 310
Oceanida, pg 310
Patakis Publishers, pg 311
Sigma, pg 312
To Rodakio, pg 312

Holy See (Vatican City State)

Biblioteca Apostolica Vaticana, pg 314
Libreria Editrice Vaticana, pg 315

Hong Kong

Asia 2000 Ltd, pg 315
Benefit Publishing Co, pg 315
The Chinese University Press, pg 316
Chung Hwa Book Co (HK) Ltd, pg 316
Commercial Press (Hong Kong) Ltd, pg 316
FormAsia Books Ltd, pg 317
Hong Kong University Press, pg 317
Joint Publishing (HK) Co Ltd, pg 317
Steve Lu Publishing Ltd, pg 318
Press Mark Media Ltd, pg 318
Tai Yip Co, pg 319

Hungary

Akademiai Kiado, pg 320
Balassi Kiado Kft, pg 321
Corvina Books Ltd, pg 321
Helikon Kiado, pg 321
Jelenkor Verlag, pg 322
Vince Kiado Kft, pg 322
Magveto Koenyvkiado, pg 322
Officina Nova Konyvek, pg 323
Park Konyvkiado Kft (Park Publisher), pg 324
Planetas Kiadoi es Kereskedelmi Kft, pg 324
Tajak Korok Muzeumok Egyesuelet, pg 324

Iceland

Hid Islenzka Bokmenntafelag, pg 325
Iceland Review, pg 325

India

Abhinav Publications, pg 326
Advaita Ashrama, pg 327
Agam Kala Prakashan, pg 327
Ajanta Publications (India), pg 327
Ananda Publishers Pvt Ltd, pg 328
Associated Publishing House, pg 329
Atma Ram & Sons, pg 329
Bharatiya Vidya Bhavan, pg 330
Books & Books, pg 331
BR Publishing Corporation, pg 331
Brijbasi Printers Pvt Ltd, pg 331
S Chand & Co Ltd, pg 331
Chowkhamba Sanskrit Series Office, pg 332
Cosmo Publications, pg 332
DK Printworld (P) Ltd, pg 333
Dutta Publishing Co Ltd, pg 333
Frank Brothers & Co Publishers Ltd, pg 334
Goel Prakashen, pg 335
Gyan Publishing House, pg 335
Arnold Heinman Publishers (India) Pvt Ltd, pg 335
Heritage Publishers, pg 335
Himalaya Publishing House, pg 335
India Book House Pvt Ltd, pg 336
Indian Council for Cultural Relations, pg 336
Indian Museum, pg 337
Intellectual Publishing House, pg 338
Inter-India Publications, pg 338
Kali For Women, pg 339
Lalit Kala Akademi, pg 339
Manohar Publishers & Distributors, pg 340
Mapin Publishing Pvt Ltd, pg 341
Marg Publications, pg 341
Ministry of Information & Broadcasting, pg 341
Mudgala Trust, pg 342
Munshiram Manoharlal Publishers Pvt Ltd, pg 342
National Museum, pg 343
Navrang Booksellers & Publishers, pg 343
Paramount Sales (India) Pvt Ltd, pg 344
Prabhat Prakashan, pg 345
Pratibha Pratishthan, pg 345
Promilla & Publishers, pg 345

Rahul Publishing House, pg 346
Rajasthan Hindi Granth Academy, pg 346
Regency Publications, pg 346
Rekha Prakashan, pg 346
Reliance Publishing House, pg 346
Roli Books Pvt Ltd, pg 347
Rupa & Co, pg 347
Samkaleen Prakashan, pg 348
Sat Sahitya Prakashan, pg 348
Sri Satguru Publications, pg 348
South Asia Publications, pg 349
Sterling Publishers Pvt Ltd, pg 350
Suman Prakashan Pvt Ltd, pg 351
Tara Publishing, pg 351
DB Taraporevala Sons & Co Pvt Ltd, pg 351
Vakils Feffer & Simons Ltd, pg 352

Indonesia
PT Bulan Bintang, pg 354
Djambatan PT, pg 354
Dunia Pustaka Jaya PT, pg 354
Pustaka Utama Grafiti, PT, pg 356
Yayasan Lontar, pg 357

Ireland
An Gum, pg 358
The Columba Press, pg 359
Four Courts Press Ltd, pg 360
Gandon Editions, pg 360
The Goldsmith Press Ltd, pg 360
Irish Academic Press, pg 361
O'Brien Educational, pg 362
Roberts Rinehart Publishers, pg 363
Town House & Country House, pg 364

Israel
Bezalel Academy of Arts & Design, pg 365
The Bialik Institute, pg 365
Gefen Publishing House Ltd, pg 367
Hakibbutz Hameuchad Publishing House Ltd, pg 367
Keter Publishing House Ltd, pg 369
The Magnes Press, pg 370
Massada Press Ltd, pg 370
Massada Publishers Ltd, pg 370
Misgav Yerushalayim, pg 370
Rolnik Publishers, pg 371
Sifriat Poalim Ltd, pg 372
R Sirkis Publishers Ltd, pg 372
Steimatzky Group Ltd, pg 372
Tcherikover Publishers Ltd, pg 372
Y L Peretz Publishing Co, pg 373

Italy
Mario Adda Editore SNC, pg 374
Aesthetica, pg 374
Alba, pg 375
Alinari Fratelli SpA Istituto di Edizioni Artistiche, pg 375
Alinea, pg 375
Umberto Allemandi & C SRL, pg 375
Arcadia Edizioni Srl, pg 375
Archivio Guido Izzi Edizioni, pg 376
L'Archivolto, pg 376
Edizioni Arka SRL, pg 376
Arnaud Editore SRL, pg 376
Arsenale Editrice SRL, pg 376
Artema, pg 376
Edi.Artes srl, pg 376
Artioli Editore, pg 377
Associazione Internazionale di Archeologia Classica, pg 377
Athesia Verlag Bozen, pg 377
Automobilia srl, pg 377

Belforte Editore Libraio srl, pg 377
Bianco, pg 377
Biblos srl, pg 378
BMG Ricordi SpA, pg 378
Bompiani-RCS Libri, pg 378
Giuseppe Bonanno Editore, pg 378
Casa Editrice Bonechi, pg 378
Bonechi-Edizioni Il Turismo Srl, pg 378
Bonsignori Editore SRL, pg 378
Edizioni Bora SNC di E Brandani & C, pg 379
Bulzoni Editore SRL (Le Edizioni Universitarie d'Italia), pg 379
Edizioni Cadmo SRL, pg 379
Calosci, pg 379
Campanotto, pg 379
Canova SRL, pg 379
Capone Editore SRL, pg 379
Cappelli Editore, pg 380
Casa Editrice Libraria Ulrico Hoepli SpA, pg 380
Casa Editrice Lint Srl, pg 380
Il Castello srl, pg 380
Centro Di, pg 381
Centro Italiano Studi Alto Medioevo, pg 381
il Cerchio Iniziative Editoriali, pg 381
Il Cigno Galileo Galilei-Edizioni di Arte e Scienza, pg 382
Ciranna - Roma, pg 382
CLUEB (Cooperativa Libraria Universitaria Editrice Bologna), pg 382
Edizioni di Comunita SpA, pg 383
Costa e Nolan SpA, pg 383
D'Anna, pg 384
Edizioni Dedalo SRL, pg 384
Edizioni Della Torre di Salvatore Fozzi & C SAS, pg 385
Editoriale Domus SpA, pg 385
Ecole Francaise de Rome, pg 385
Ediart Editrice, pg 386
Editalia (Edizioni d'Italia), pg 386
Edizioni d'Arte Antica e Moderna EDAM, pg 386
Edizioni del Centro Camuno di Studi Preistorici, pg 386
Edizioni l'Arciere SRL, pg 387
Giulio Einaudi Editore SpA, pg 387
Electa, pg 387
Edizioni dell'Elefante, pg 387
ERGA SNC di Carla Ottino Merli & C (Edizioni Realizzazioni Grafiche - Artigiana), pg 388
L'Erma di Bretschneider SRL, pg 388
Edi.Ermes srl, pg 388
Essegi, pg 388
Edizioni Europa, pg 388
Fatatrac, pg 388
Federico Motta Editore SpA, pg 389
Giangiacomo Feltrinelli SpA, pg 389
Fenice 2000, pg 389
Festina Lente Edizioni, pg 389
Flaccovio Editore, pg 389
Arnaldo Forni Editore SRL, pg 389
Edizioni Frassinelli SRL, pg 389
Edizioni Futuro SRL, pg 389
Adriano Gallina Editore sas, pg 389
Gangemi Editore spa, pg 390
Garolla, pg 390
Garzanti Libri, pg 390
Istituto Geografico de Agostini SpA, pg 390
Giancarlo Politi Editore, pg 390
Edizioni del Girasole srl, pg 390
Giunti Gruppo Editoriale, pg 390
Gius Laterza e Figli SpA, pg 391
Grafica e Arte srl, pg 391
Grafo, pg 391

Ernesto Gremese Editore srl, pg 391
Gremese International srl, pg 391
Gruppo Editoriale Faenza Editrice SpA, pg 391
Ugo Guanda Editore, pg 392
Herbita Editrice di Leonardo Palermo, pg 392
Hopeful Monster Editore, pg 392
Idea Books, pg 392
IHT Gruppo Editoriale SRL, pg 393
Ila - Palma, Tea Nova, pg 393
ISAL (Istituto Storia dell'Arte Lombarda), pg 393
Istituto della Enciclopedia Italiana, pg 393
Editoriale Jaca Book SpA, pg 394
Jandi-Sapi Editori, pg 394
L Japadre Editore, pg 394
Lalli Editore SRL, pg 394
Il Lavoro Editoriale, pg 395
Editrice Liguria SNC di Norberto Sabatelli & C, pg 395
Linea d'Ombra Libri, pg 395
Vincenzo Lo Faro Editore, pg 395
Longanesi & C, pg 396
Angelo Longo Editore, pg 396
Edizioni de Luca SRL, pg 396
La Luna, pg 396
Magnus Edizioni SpA, pg 397
Giuseppe Maimone Editore, pg 397
Manfrini Editori, pg 397
Tommaso Marotta Editore Srl, pg 397
Marsilio Editori SpA, pg 397
Edizioni Gabriele Mazzotta SRL, pg 397
McRae Books, pg 398
Edizioni Mediterranee SRL, pg 398
Minerva Italica SpA, pg 398
Arnoldo Mondadori Editore SpA, pg 398
Giorgio Mondadori & Associati, pg 399
Mondolibro Editore SNC, pg 399
Moretti & Vitali Editori srl, pg 399
Gruppo Ugo Mursia Editore SpA, pg 400
Nardini Editore srl, pg 400
Accademia Naz dei Lincei, pg 400
Istituto Nazionale di Studi Romani, pg 400
NodoLibri, pg 400
Novecento Editrice Srl, pg 401
Nuova Alfa Editoriale, pg 401
La Nuova Italia Editrice SpA, pg 401
Nuovi Sentieri Editore, pg 401
OCTAVO Produzioni Editoriali Associale, pg 401
Officina Edizioni di Aldo Quinti, pg 401
Leo S Olschki, pg 401
Maria Pacini Fazzi Editore, pg 402
Paideia Editrice, pg 402
Palatina Editrice, pg 402
Fratelli Palombi SRL, pg 402
Franco Cosimo Panini Editore SpA, pg 402
Patron Editore SrL, pg 402
Pheljna Edizioni d'Arte e Suggestione, pg 403
Daniela Piazza Editore, pg 403
Amilcare Pizzi SpA, pg 403
Istituto Poligrafico e Zecca dello Stato, pg 403
Il Pomerio, pg 404
Neri Pozza Editore, pg 404
Priuli e Verlucca, Editori, pg 404
Psicologica Editrice, pg 404
Il Quadrante SRL, pg 404
Edizioni Quasar di Severino Tognon SRL, pg 404
Edizioni Quattroventi SNC, pg 404

Edition Raetia Srl-GmbH, pg 405
RAI-ERI, pg 405
RCS Libri SpA, pg 405
RCS Rizzoli Libri SpA, pg 405
Franco Maria Ricci Editore (FMR), pg 405
Edizioni Riposte, pg 405
Editori Riuniti, pg 405
Rubbettino Editore, pg 406
SAGEP Libri & Comunicazione Srl, pg 406
Il Saggiatore, pg 406
SAIE Editrice SRL, pg 406
Edizioni San Paolo SRL, pg 407
Sardini Editrice, pg 407
Scala Group spa, pg 407
Lo Scarabeo Srl, pg 407
Schena Editore, pg 407
Salvatore Sciascia Editore, pg 407
Edizioni Scientifiche Italiane, pg 407
Sellerio Editore, pg 408
SEMAR Publishers SRL, pg 408
Sicania, pg 408
Edizioni Librarie Siciliane, pg 408
Silvana Editoriale SpA, pg 408
Spirali Edizioni, pg 409
Stampa Alternativa - Nuovi Equilibri, pg 409
Studio Editoriale Programma, pg 409
Tappeiner, pg 409
Tassotti Editore, pg 409
TEA Tascabili degli Editori Associati, pg 409
Tema Celeste, pg 410
Tomo Edizioni srl, pg 410
Trainer International Editore-I Libri del Bargello, pg 410
Turris, pg 410
Editoriale Umbra SAS di Carnevali e, pg 411
UTET (Unione Tipografico-Editrice Torinese), pg 411
Vinciana Editrice sas, pg 412
Viviani Editore srl, pg 412

Jamaica
Ian Randle Publishers Ltd, pg 414

Japan
Bijutsu Shuppan-Sha, Ltd, pg 415
Chuokoron-Shinsha Inc, pg 416
Dohosha Publishing Co Ltd, pg 417
Fuzambo Publishing Co, pg 417
Gakken Co Ltd, pg 417
Genko-Sha, pg 417
Hakusui-Sha Co Ltd, pg 417
Hayakawa Publishing Inc, pg 418
Heibonsha Ltd, Publishers, pg 418
Hoikusha Publishing Co Ltd, pg 418
Holp Book Co Ltd, pg 418
International Society for Educational Information (ISEI), pg 419
Iwanami Shoten, Publishers, pg 419
Iwasaki Shoten Publishing Co Ltd, pg 419
Japan Broadcast Publishing Co Ltd, pg 419
Kadokawa Shoten Publishing Co Ltd, pg 420
Kaisei-Sha Publishing Co Ltd, pg 420
Kawade Shobo Shinsha Publishers, pg 420
Kinokuniya Co Ltd (Publishing Department), pg 421
Kodansha International Ltd, pg 421
Kodansha Ltd, pg 421
Kosei Publishing Co Ltd, pg 421
Koyo Shobo, pg 422

Mejikaru Furendo-sha, pg 422
Misuzu Shobo Ltd, pg 422
Nigensha Publishing Co Ltd, pg 423
Nihon-Bunkyo Shuppan (Japan Educational Publishing Co Ltd), pg 423
Nippon Hoso Shuppan Kyokai (NHK Publishing), pg 424
Nishimura Co Ltd, pg 424
Sekai Bunka-Sha, pg 427
Shakai Shiso-Sha, pg 427
Shibun-Do, pg 427
Shogakukan Inc, pg 427
Mitsumura Suiko Shoin, pg 428
Shokokusha Publishing Co Ltd, pg 428
Shueisha Inc, pg 428
Shufu-to-Seikatsu Sha Ltd, pg 428
Sogensha Publishing Co Ltd, pg 428
Tamagawa University Press, pg 429
Tankosha Publishing Co Ltd, pg 429
TBS-Britannica Co Ltd, pg 429
Toho Book Store, pg 429
Toho Shuppan, pg 429
Tokai University Press, pg 429
Tokuma Shoten Publishing Co Ltd, pg 429
Tokyo Shoseki Co Ltd, pg 430
Tokyo Sogensha Co Ltd, pg 430
Charles E Tuttle Publishing Co Inc, pg 430
Yohan Shuppan, pg 431

Kenya

Camerapix Publishers International Ltd, pg 433
Heinemann Kenya Ltd (EAEP), pg 434

Democratic People's Republic of Korea

The Foreign Language Press Group, pg 436
Korea Science and Encyclopedia Publishing House, pg 436
Literature and Art Publishing House, pg 436

Republic of Korea

Ahn Graphics, pg 437
Bal-eon, pg 437
Chung Rim Publishing Co Ltd, pg 438
Dae Won Sa Co Ltd, pg 438
Daehan Printing & Publishing Co Ltd, pg 438
Dong Hwa Publishing Co, pg 438
Ewha Womans University Press, pg 438
Hak Won Publishing Co, pg 439
Hakgojae Publishing Inc, pg 439
Hanjin Publishing Co, pg 439
Haseo Publishing Co, pg 439
Hollym Corporation; Publishers, pg 439
Ki Moon Dang, pg 440
Korea Textbook Co Ltd, pg 440
Kwangmyong Publishing Co, pg 440
Literature Academy Publishing, pg 441
Munhag-gwan, pg 441
Munye Publishing Co, pg 441
Nanam Publications Co, pg 441
PoChinChai Printing Co Ltd, pg 442
Samho Music Publishing Co Ltd, pg 442
Samhwa Publishing Co Ltd, pg 442
Samseong Publishing Co Ltd, pg 442
Seoul International Publishing House, pg 443
Seoul National University Press, pg 443
Yonsei University Press, pg 444
Youlhwadang Publisher, pg 444

Kuwait

Ministry of Information, pg 444

Laos People's Democratic Republic

Lao-phanit, pg 444

Latvia

Preses Nams, pg 445

Lebanon

Arab Institute for Research & Publishing, pg 445
Khayat Book and Publishing Co Sarl, pg 446

Liechtenstein

Verlag HP Gassner AG, pg 447
Kliemand Verlag, pg 448
Megatrade AG, pg 448
Saendig Reprint Verlag, Hans-Rainer Wohlwend, pg 448
Frank P van Eck Publishers, pg 448

Lithuania

Academia, pg 448
AS Narbuto Leidykla (AS Narbutas' Publishers), pg 448
Baltos Lankos, pg 449
Klaipedos Universiteto Leidykla, pg 449
Scena, pg 449
Tyto Alba Publishers, pg 450
Vaga Ltd, pg 450

Luxembourg

Editions APESS ASBL, pg 450
Galerie Editions Kutter, pg 451
Editions Phi, pg 451
Service Central des Imprimes et des Fournitures de Bureau de l'Etat, pg 451
Editions Tousch, pg 452

The Former Yugoslav Republic of Macedonia

Macedonia Prima Publishing House, pg 452
Makedonska kniga (Knigoizdatelstvo), pg 452
Nov svet (New World), pg 453
Zumpres Publishing Firm, pg 453

Malaysia

Penerbitan Pelangi Sdn Bhd (Pelangi Publishing Pte Ltd), pg 458
Pustaka Cipta Sdn Bhd, pg 458

Malta

Fondazzjoni Patrimonju Malti, pg 460

Mauritius

Editions de l'Ocean Indien Ltd, pg 461

Mexico

Artes de Mexico y del Mundo SA de CV, pg 462
Libreria y Ediciones Botas SA, pg 462
Cuernavaca Editorial S A, pg 463
Ediciones Culturales Internacionales SA de CV Edicion Compra y Venta de Libros, Casetes, Videos, pg 463
Edamex SA de CV, pg 464
Ediciones Era SA de CV, pg 465
Editorial Extemporaneos SA, pg 465
Fondo de Cultura Economica, pg 465
Fondo Editorial de la Plastica Mexicana, pg 466
Editorial Hermes SA, pg 466
Editorial Herrero SA, pg 466
Editorial Limusa SA de CV, pg 467
Galeria de Arte Misrachi SA, pg 469
Instituto Nacional de Antropologia e Historia, pg 469
Naves Internacional de Ediciones SA, pg 469
Editorial Nueva Imagen SA, pg 469
Pearson Educacion de Mexico, SA de CV, pg 470
SCRIPTA - Distribucion y Servicios Editoriales, SA de CV, pg 471
Servicios Especiales Maciel SA de CV, pg 472
Siglo XXI Editores SA de CV, pg 472
Ediciones Suromex SA, pg 472
Editorial Turner de Mexico, pg 472
Universidad Veracruzana Direccion General Editorial y de Publicaciones, pg 472

Republic of Moldova

Editura Hyperion, pg 473

Monaco

Rondeau Giannipiero a Monaco, pg 474
Editions Andre Sauret SA, pg 474

Morocco

Access International Services, pg 474
Association de la Recherche Historique et Sociale, pg 474
Edition Diffusion de Livre au Maroc, pg 474
Editions Oum, pg 475

Myanmar

Knowledge Press & Bookhouse, pg 475
Kyi-Pwar-Ye Book House, pg 475
Smart & Mookerdum, pg 476

Nepal

International Standards Books & Periodicals (P) Ltd, pg 476
Royal Nepal Academy, pg 477

Netherlands

APA (Academic Publishers Associated), pg 477
B M Israel BV, pg 478
John Benjamins BV, pg 479
BoekWerk, pg 479
Uitgeverij Cantecleer BV, pg 480
Davaco Publishers, pg 481
Uitgeverij Vrij Geestesleven, pg 482
Uitgeverij en boekhandel Van Gennep BV, pg 482
Heuff Amsterdam Uitgever, pg 483
Hotei Publishing, pg 484
KIT - Royal Tropical Institute Publishers, pg 484
Mets & Schilt Uitgevers en Distributeurs, pg 486
Mirananda Publishers BV, pg 486
Nai Publishers, pg 486
Omega Boek BV, pg 487
The Pepin Press, pg 487
Philo Press (APA), pg 487
Picaron Editions, pg 487
De Prom, pg 488
Em Querido's Uitgeverij BV, pg 488
Scriptum, pg 488
Koninklijke Smeets Offset, pg 489
Stedelijk Van Abbemuseum, pg 489
Steltman Editions, pg 489
Thoth Publishers, pg 490
Uniepers BV, pg 491
Uitgeverij Waanders BV, pg 492
Uitgeverij 010, pg 493

New Zealand

Auckland University Press, pg 493
Barkfire Press, pg 494
David Bateman Ltd, pg 494
Bush Press Communications Ltd, pg 494
Cicada Press, pg 495
Craig Potton Publishing, pg 495
Godwit Publishing Ltd, pg 496
HarperCollins Publishers (New Zealand) Ltd, pg 497
Hazard Press Ltd, pg 497
Huia Publishers, pg 497
David Ling Publishing, pg 498
Oxford University Press, pg 499
Resource Books Ltd, pg 500
Saint Publishing, pg 501
University of Otago Press, pg 502

Nigeria

Aromolaran Publishing Co Ltd, pg 503
New Africa Publishing Company Ltd, pg 505

Norway

Andresen & Butenschon AS, pg 508
Aschehoug Forlag, pg 508
H Aschehoug & Co (W Nygaard) A/S, pg 508
Atheneum Forlag A/S, pg 508
J W Eides Forlag A/S, pg 509
Gyldendal Norsk Forlag A/S, pg 509
Tell Forlag, pg 511

Oman

Apex Press & Publishing, pg 511

Pakistan

Classic, pg 512
Publishers United Pvt Ltd, pg 514
Sang-e-Meel Publications, pg 514

Panama

Editorial Universitaria, pg 515

Peru

Librerias ABC SA, pg 516
Editorial Horizonte, pg 517

Philippines

Heritage Publishing House, pg 519
National Book Store Inc, pg 519

SUBJECT INDEX

National Museum of the Philippines, pg 520
Our Lady of Manaoag Publisher, pg 520
Philippine Education Co Inc, pg 520
SIBS Publishing House Inc, pg 521
University of the Philippines Press, pg 521
Vera-Reyes Inc, pg 521

Poland

Aritbus et Historiae, Rivista Internationale di arti visive ecinema, Institut IRSA - Verlagsanstatt, pg 522
Wydawnictwo Arkady, pg 522
Wydawnictwa Artystyczne i Filmowe, pg 522
BOSZ scp, pg 522
Wydawnictwo DiG, pg 522
Wydawnictwo Dolnoslaskie, pg 522
Wydawnictwo Literackie, pg 524
Muza SA, pg 524
Ossolineum Zaklad Narodowy im Ossolinskich - Wydawnictwo, pg 525
Polish Scientific Publishers PWN, pg 525
Rosikon Press, pg 526
Towarzystwo Naukowe w Toruniu, pg 527

Portugal

Arvore Coop de Actividades Artisticas, CRL, pg 528
Assirio & Alvim, pg 528
Bertrand Editora Lda, pg 529
Camara Municipal de Castelo, pg 529
Livraria Civilizacao (Americo Fraga Lamares & Ca Lda), pg 529
Constancia Editores, SA, pg 530
Difusao Cultural, pg 530
Dinalivro, pg 530
Distri Cultural Lda, pg 530
Edicoes ELO, pg 531
Editorial Estampa, Lda, pg 531
Publicacoes Europa-America Lda, pg 531
Chaves Ferreira Publicacoes SA, pg 531
Editorial Franciscana, pg 531
Imprensa Nacional-Casa da Moeda, pg 532
Latina Livraria Editora, pg 532
Livros Horizonte Lda, pg 533
Livraria Tavares Martins, pg 533
Editora Pergaminho Lda, pg 534
Editorial Presenca, pg 535
Quatro Elementos Editores, pg 535
Quetzal Editores, pg 535
Quimera Editores Lda, pg 535
Realizacoes Artis, pg 535
Edicoes 70 Lda, pg 535
SocTip SA, pg 536
Solivros, pg 536
Vega-Publicacao e Distribuicao de Livros e Revistas, Lda, pg 536

Puerto Rico

University of Puerto Rico Press (EDUPR), pg 537

Romania

Editura Academiei Romane, pg 538
Alcor-Edimpex (Verlag) Ltd, pg 538
Artemis Verlag, pg 538
Casa Editoriala Independenta Europa, pg 538
Editura Clusium, pg 539
Editure Ion Creanga, pg 539
Editura Gryphon, pg 540

Editura Kriterion SA, pg 540
Lider Verlag, pg 540
Mentor Kiado, pg 540
Editura Meridiane, pg 540
Saeculum IO, pg 542
Est-Samuel Tastet Verlag, pg 542
Editura de Vest, pg 543
Vestala Verlag, pg 543
Vremea Publishers Ltd, pg 543

Russian Federation

Aurora Art Publishers, pg 544
Izdatelstvo Detskaya Literatura, pg 544
Izdatelstvo Galart, pg 545
Interbook-Business AO, pg 545
Izdatelstvo Iskusstvo, pg 545
Izdatelstvo Lenizdat, pg 546
Izdatelstvo Molodaya Gvardia, pg 546
Nauka Publishers, pg 547
Novosti Izdatelstvo, pg 547
Panorama Publishing House, pg 547
Profizdat, pg 548
Raduga Publishers, pg 548
Russkaya Kniga Izdatelstvo (Publishers), pg 548
St Andrew's Biblical Theological College, pg 548
Izdatelstvo Sovetskii Pisatel, pg 548

Serbia and Montenegro

Alfa-Narodna Knjiga, pg 552
Izdavacka preduzece Gradina, pg 552
Jugoslovenska Revija, pg 552
Nolit Publishing House, pg 553
Svetovi, pg 554
Turisticka Stampa, pg 554
Vuk Karadzic, pg 554

Singapore

Archipelago Press, pg 555
Daiichi Media Pte Ltd, pg 555
International Publishers Distributor (S) Pte Ltd, pg 556
McGallen & Bolden Associates, pg 557
Select Publishing Pte Ltd, pg 557
Taylor & Francis Asia Pacific, pg 558
Times Media Pte Ltd, pg 559

Slovakia

Kalligram spol sro, pg 559
Vydavatelstvo Obzor, pg 560
Vydavatel'stvo SFVU Pallas, pg 560
Slovansky Tatran, Vydavatel 'stro spoi sro, pg 560

Slovenia

East West Operation (EWO) Ltd, pg 561
Mladinska Knjiga International, pg 561
Moderna galerija Ljubljana/Museum of Modern Art, pg 561
Zalozba Mihelac d o o, pg 562

South Africa

Educum Publishers Ltd, pg 563
Fernwood Press (Pty) Ltd, pg 563
Human & Rousseau (Pty) Ltd, pg 564
Institute for Reformational Studies CHE, pg 565
Janssen Publishers CC, pg 565
Johannesburg Art Gallery, pg 565

Spain

Agencia Espanola de Cooperacion, pg 571
Aguilar SA de Ediciones, pg 571
Ediciones Akal SA, pg 571
Alberdania SL, pg 571
Alianza Editorial SA, pg 572
Altea, Taurus, Alfaguara SA, pg 572
Ambit Serveis Editorials, SA, pg 572
Editorial Astri SA, pg 573
Carroggio SA de Ediciones, pg 575
Editorial Casals SA, pg 575
Editorial Casariego, pg 576
Edicios do Castro, pg 576
Biblioteca de Catalunya, pg 576
Ediciones Catedra SA, pg 576
Celeste Ediciones, pg 576
Ediciones Colegio De Espana (ECE), pg 577
Complutense, SA Editorial, pg 577
Comunidad Autonoma de Madrid, Servicio de Documentacion y Publicaciones, pg 578
Consello da Cultura Galega - CCG, pg 578
Curial Edicions Catalanes SA, pg 578
Ediciones Daly S L, pg 578
Ediciones Destino SA, pg 579
Diputacion Provincial de Malaga, pg 579
Ediciones l'Isard, S L, pg 580
Edilesa-Ediciones Leonesas SA, pg 581
Edilux, pg 581
El Viso, SA Ediciones, pg 582
Enciclopedia Catalana, SA, pg 582
Ediciones Encuentro SA, pg 582
Editorial Espasa-Calpe SA, pg 582
Instituto de Estudios Riojanos, pg 583
Forum Artis, SA, pg 583
Fundacion Coleccion Thyssen-Bornemisza, pg 584
Fundacion Marcelino Botin, pg 584
Galaxia SA Editorial, pg 584
Vicent Garcia Editores, SA, pg 584
Generalitat de Catalunya Diari Oficial de la Generalitat vern, pg 584
Instituto de Cultura Juan Gil-Albert, pg 585
Editorial Gustavo Gili SA, pg 585
Guadalquivir SL Ediciones, pg 586
Editorial Iberia, SA, pg 586
Iberico Europea de Ediciones SA, pg 586
Incafo Archivo Fotografico Editorial, SL, pg 587
Institucion Fernando el Catolico de la Excma Diputacion de Zaragoza, pg 587
Ediciones Istmo SA, pg 588
Junta de Castilla y Leon Consejeria de Educacion y Cultura, pg 588
Editorial Juventud SA, pg 588
LEDA (Las Ediciones de Arte), pg 589
Liber Ediciones, SA, pg 589
Libsa Editorial SA, pg 589
Llibres del Segle, pg 589
Loguez Ediciones, pg 589
Editorial Lumen SA, pg 589
Lunwerg Editores, SA, pg 589
Antonio Machado, SA, pg 590
Editorial Marin SA, pg 590
Editorial Mediterrania SL, pg 591
M Moleiro Editor, SA, pg 592
Editorial Moll SL, pg 592
Mundo Negro Editorial, pg 592
Editorial la Muralla SA, pg 592
Naque Editora, pg 592

Ediciones Nauta Credito SA, pg 593
Editorial Nerea SA, pg 593
Noguer y Caralt Editores SA, pg 593
Ediciones Oceano Grupo SA, pg 593
Pais Vasco Servicio Central de Publicaciones, pg 594
Parramon Ediciones SA, pg 595
Pearson Educacion S A, pg 595
Pronaos, SA Ediciones, pg 597
Instituto Provincial de Investigaciones y Estudios Toledanos (IPIET), pg 597
Editora Regional de Murcia - ERM, pg 597
Riquelme y Vargas Ediciones SL, pg 598
Editorial Roasa SL, pg 598
Universidad de Santiago de Compostela, pg 599
Ediciones Scriba SA, pg 599
Ediciones Seyer, pg 599
Silex Ediciones, pg 600
Sirmio, pg 600
Ediciones Siruela SA, pg 600
Edicions 62, pg 600
Ramon Sopena SA, pg 600
Axel Springer Publicaciones, pg 601
Ediciones Tabapress, SA, pg 601
Ediciones Tarraco, pg 601
Editorial Tecnos SA, pg 601
Tf Editores, pg 602
Trea Ediciones, SL, pg 602
Tres Torres Ediciones SA, pg 602
Turner Publicaciones, pg 602
Tursen, SA, pg 603
Editorial Txertoa, pg 603
Universidad de Granada, pg 603
Universidad de Malaga, pg 603
Universidad de Navarra, Ediciones SA, pg 603
Universidad de Valladolid Secretariado de Publicaciones e Intercambio Editorial, pg 604
Publicacions de la Universitat de Barcelona, pg 604
Visor Distribuciones, SA, pg 605
Xarait Libros SA, pg 605
Xunta de Galicia, pg 605

Sri Lanka

Ministry of Cultural Affairs, pg 607

Sweden

Bokforlaget Atlantis AB, pg 609
Acta Universitatis Gothoburgensis, pg 609
Alfabeta Bokforlag AB, pg 609
Albert Bonniers Forlag AB, pg 610
BOOX, pg 610
Carlsson Bokfoerlag AB, pg 610
Bengt Forsbergs Foerlag AB, pg 611
Gidlunds Bokforlag, pg 612
Hanseproduktion AB, pg 612
Bokforlaget Nya Doxa AB, pg 614
Schultz Forlag AB, pg 615
Stroemberg B&T Forlag AB, pg 616
Wahlstrom & Widstrand, pg 616

Switzerland

Editions L'Age d'Homme - La Cite, pg 617
Ammann Verlag & Co, pg 617
Archivio Storico Ticinese, pg 617
Ascona Presse, pg 617
Athenaeum Verlag AG, pg 618
Atlantis-Verlag AG, pg 618
Editions de la Baconniere SA, pg 618

PUBLISHERS

U Baer Verlag, pg 618
Basilius Presse AG, pg 618
Benteli Verlag, pg 618
Benziger Verlag AG, pg 619
Editions Beyeler, pg 619
La Bibliotheque des Arts, pg 619
Bugra Suisse Burchler Grafino AG, pg 620
Edizioni Casagrande SA, pg 620
Christoph Merian Verlag, pg 620
Cosa-Verlag, Giusep Condrau SA, pg 621
Edizioni Armando Dado, Tipografia Stazione, pg 621
Editions Andre Delcourt & Cie, pg 621
Diogenes Verlag AG, pg 622
Drei-D-World und Foto-World Verlag und Vertrieb, pg 622
Editions Edita, pg 622
Erker-Verlag, pg 623
Europa Verlag AG, pg 623
Faksimile Verlag AG, pg 623
FEDA SA, pg 623
G+B Arts International, pg 623
Verlag Gachnang & Springer, Bern-Berlin, pg 623
Giampiero Casagrande Editore, pg 624
Editions du Griffon (Neuchatel), pg 624
GVA Publishers Ltd, pg 624
Haffmans Verlag AG, pg 624
Hallwag Kuemmerly & Frey AG, pg 625
Paul Haupt Bern, pg 625
Verlag Huber & Co AG, pg 625
Editions Ides et Calendes SA, pg 625
Junod Nicolas, pg 626
Verlag Walter Keller, Dornach, pg 626
Kinderbuchverlag Luzern, pg 626
Galerie Kornfeld & Co, pg 627
Kossodo Verlag AG, pg 627
Kranich-Verlag, Dres AG & H R Bosch-Gwalter, pg 627
Peter Lang AG, pg 627
Bernard Letu Editeur, pg 627
Limmat Verlag, pg 628
Les Editions la Matze, pg 628
Memory/Cage Editions, pg 628
Editions H Messeiller SA, pg 628
Editions Minkoff, pg 628
Motovun Book GmbH, pg 629
Lars Mueller Publishers, pg 629
Muslim Architecture Research Program (MARP), pg 629
Les Editions Nagel SA (Paris), pg 629
Verlag Arthur Niggli AG, pg 629
Novalis Media AG, pg 630
Office du Livre SA (Buchhaus AG), pg 630
Edition Olms AG, pg 630
Orell Fuessli Buchhandlungs AG, pg 630
Ostschweiz Druck und Verlag, pg 630
Parkett Publishers Inc, pg 630
Perret Edition, pg 631
Philosophisch-Anthroposophischer Verlag am Goetheanum, pg 631
Punktum AG, Buchredaktion und Bildarchiv, pg 632
Rabe Verlag AG Zuerich, pg 632
Regenbogen Verlag, pg 632
Verlag Friedrich Reinhardt AG, pg 632
Rhein-Trio, Edition/Editions du Fou, pg 632
Editiones Roche, pg 632
Roth et Sauter SA, pg 632
Verlag fuer Schoene Wissenschaften, pg 633
Schwabe & Co AG, pg 633
Editions D'Art Albert Skira SA, pg 634
Edition Stemmle AG, pg 635
Theseus - Verlag AG, pg 635
3 Dimension World (3-D-World), pg 635
Editions du Tricorne, pg 635
Editions des Trois Collines Francois Lachenal, pg 635
Editions 24 Heures, pg 635
Der Universitatsverlag Freiburg, pg 636
Versus Verlag AG, pg 636
Vexer Verlag, pg 636
Weber SA d'Editions, pg 637
Weltwoche ABC-Verlag, pg 637
Werner Druck AG, pg 637
Wiese Verlag AG, pg 637
J E Wolfensberger AG, pg 637
Wyss Verlag AG Bern, pg 637

Syrian Arab Republic

Damascus University Press, pg 638

Taiwan, Province of China

Art Book Co Ltd, pg 638
The Artist Publishing Co, pg 638
Asian Culture Co Ltd, pg 638
Chu Liu Book Company, pg 639
Chung Hwa Book Co Ltd, pg 639
Echo Publishing Company Ltd, pg 639
Far East Book Co Ltd, pg 639
Chu Hai Publishing (Taiwan) Co Ltd, pg 640
Hilit Publishing Co Ltd, pg 640
Kuang Fu Book Co Ltd, pg 640
Lee & Lee Communications, pg 641
Linking Publishing Company Ltd, pg 641
National Museum of History, pg 641
National Palace Museum, pg 641
San Min Book Co Ltd, pg 641
SMC Publishing Inc, pg 642
World Book Co Ltd, pg 642
Yee Wen Publishing Co Ltd, pg 642
Yuan Liou Publishing Co, Ltd, pg 642

United Republic of Tanzania

Tanzania Publishing House, pg 644

Thailand

New Generation Publishing Co Ltd, pg 645
Sangdad Publishing Company Ltd, pg 645
Thai Watana Panich Co, Ltd, pg 646
White Lotus Co Ltd, pg 646

Tunisia

Academie Tunisienne des Sciences, des Lettres et des Arts Beit El Hekma, pg 647
Sud Editions, pg 648

Turkey

Arkeoloji Ve Sanat Yayinlari, pg 649
Dost Yayinlari, pg 650
Inkilap Publishers Ltd, pg 650
Kubbealti Akademisi Kultur ve Sasat Vakfi, pg 650
Remzi Kitabevi, pg 651
Soez Yayin/Oyunajans, pg 651
Turkish Republic - Ministry of Culture, pg 652
Yapi-Endustri Merkezi Yayinlari-Yem Yayin, pg 652
Kabalci Yayinevi, pg 652

Ukraine

Mystetstvo Publishers, pg 653

United Kingdom

Umberto Allemandi & Co Publishing, pg 656
Andromeda Oxford Ltd, pg 658
Antique Collectors' Club Ltd, pg 658
Apple Press, pg 658
Appletree Press Ltd, pg 658
Art Books International Ltd, pg 659
Art Sales Index Ltd, pg 659
The Art Trade Press Ltd, pg 659
Arts Council of England, pg 660
Ashgate Publishing Ltd, pg 660
Ashmolean Museum Publications, pg 660
The Athlone Press Ltd, pg 661
Atlas Press, pg 661
Aurum Press Ltd, pg 661
Batsford Ltd, pg 663
BCA - Book Club Associates, pg 663
Belitha Press Ltd, pg 664
Bellew Publishing Co Ltd, pg 664
A & C Black Publishers Ltd, pg 666
Blackstaff Press, pg 666
The Book Guild Ltd, pg 668
Books for Europe Ltd, pg 669
Breslich & Foss Ltd, pg 671
The British Academy, pg 671
British Library Publications, pg 672
British Museum Press, pg 672
Calder Publications Ltd, pg 673
Cambridge University Press, pg 674
Camden Press Ltd, pg 674
Cameron & Hollis, pg 674
Carlton Publishing Group, pg 675
Cassell & Co, pg 675
Marshall Cavendish Partworks Ltd, pg 676
Chadwyck-Healey Ltd, pg 677
Colour Library Direct, pg 681
Compendium Publishing, pg 681
Constable & Robinson Ltd, pg 682
Cottage Publications, pg 683
David & Charles Ltd, pg 686
Andre Deutsch Ltd, pg 687
Diagram Visual Information Ltd, pg 687
Dorling Kindersley Ltd, pg 688
Eaglemoss Publications Ltd, pg 689
Edinburgh University Press Ltd, pg 689
Element Books Ltd, pg 690
Elfande Ltd, pg 690
Aidan Ellis Publishing, pg 690
The Erskine Press, pg 692
The Eurospan Group, pg 692
Evans Brothers Ltd, pg 693
Faber & Faber Ltd, pg 694
Flame Tree Publishing, pg 695
Francis Balsom Associates, pg 696
The Fraser Press, pg 697
Frontier Publishing Ltd, pg 697
The FruitMarket Gallery, pg 698
Garnet Publishing Ltd, pg 698
Genesis Publications Ltd, pg 699
Global Oriental Ltd, pg 700
GMP Publishers Ltd, pg 700
Golden Cockerel Press Ltd, pg 701
Grange Books PLC, pg 702
The Greek Bookshop, pg 702
Robert Hale Ltd, pg 704
Hamish Hamilton Ltd, pg 704
HarperCollins UK, pg 705
Hawk Books, pg 706
Helicon Publishing Ltd, pg 707
Heraldry Today, pg 708
Herbert Press Ltd, pg 708
Heritage Press, pg 708
Hilmarton Manor Press, pg 708
Alan Hutchison Ltd, pg 711
Icon Press, pg 711
Institute of Irish Studies, The Queens University of Belfast, pg 713
International Communications, pg 714
The Islamic Texts Society, pg 715
Kegan Paul International Ltd, pg 717
Laurence King Publishing Ltd, pg 717
Letterbox Library, pg 720
Frances Lincoln Ltd, pg 720
The Littman Library of Jewish Civilization, pg 721
Liverpool University Press, pg 722
Lund Humphries, pg 723
The Lutterworth Press, pg 723
Lyle Publications Ltd, pg 723
Macmillan Audio Books, pg 723
Macmillan Reference Ltd, pg 724
Mainstream Publishing Co (Edinburgh) Ltd, pg 724
Manchester University Press, pg 724
Mandrake of Oxford, pg 725
Maney Publishing, pg 725
Peter Marcan Publications, pg 725
Marston House, pg 725
The Medici Society Ltd, pg 726
Merrell Publishers Ltd, pg 727
Merrion Press, pg 727
Harvey Miller Publishers, pg 728
MIT Press Ltd, pg 728
Motilal (UK) Books of India, pg 729
National Galleries of Scotland, pg 731
National Library of Wales, pg 731
National Portrait Gallery Publications, pg 731
National Trust, pg 731
NMS Enterprises Ltd - Publishing, pg 733
W W Norton & Company Ltd, pg 734
Orion Publishing Group Ltd, pg 736
Peter Owen Ltd, pg 737
Oxford University Press, pg 737
Pallas Athene, pg 738
Pavilion Books Ltd, pg 739
Pearson Education, pg 739
Pearson Education Europe, Mideast & Africa, pg 739
Phaidon Press Ltd, pg 741
Planet, pg 743
Policy Studies Institute (PSI), pg 744
Polybooks Ltd, pg 744
Pomegranate Europe Ltd, pg 744
David Porteous Editions, pg 744
Porthill Publishers, pg 744
PRC Publishing Ltd, pg 745
Primrose Hill Press Ltd, pg 745
Quarto Publishing plc, pg 746
Ramboro Books Plc, pg 747
Ramsay Head Press, pg 747
Random House UK Ltd, pg 747
Reaktion Books Ltd, pg 748
Redcliffe Press Ltd, pg 749
Redstone Press, pg 749
Regency House Publishing Ltd, pg 749
Roundhouse Group, pg 751
Saqi Books, pg 754

School of Oriental & African Studies, pg 755
Search Press Ltd, pg 756
Seren, pg 756
Shearwater Press Ltd, pg 757
Charles Skilton Ltd, pg 758
Skoob Russell Square, pg 758
Smith Settle Ltd, pg 758
Souvenir Press Ltd, pg 759
SPA Books Ltd, pg 759
Stacey International, pg 761
Rudolf Steiner Press, pg 761
Studio Editions Ltd, pg 761
Sutton Publishing Ltd, pg 762
Taschen UK Ltd, pg 763
Tate Publishing Ltd, pg 763
Taylor & Francis, pg 763
Textile & Art Publications Ltd, pg 764
Thames & Hudson Ltd, pg 764
Thomson Gale, pg 765
Time Out Group Ltd, pg 765
Titan Books Ltd, pg 766
Trigon Press, pg 767
UCL Press Ltd, pg 768
University of Wales Press, pg 769
Viking, pg 770
The Warburg Institute, pg 771
Westview Press, pg 772
Philip Wilson Publishers, pg 774
Windsor Books International, pg 774
The Women's Press Ltd, pg 775
Wordwright Publishing, pg 775
World Microfilms Publications Ltd, pg 775
World of Islam Altajir Trust, pg 776
Yale University Press London, pg 776
Zwemmer Holdings Co Ltd, pg 776

Uruguay

Ediciones de Juan Darien, pg 777
Punto de Encuentro Ediciones, pg 778
Vinten Editor, pg 778

Uzbekistan

Izdatelstvo Uzbekistan, pg 778

Venezuela

Armitano Editores CA, pg 779
Editorial Ateneo de Caracas, pg 779
Monte Avila Editores Latinoamericana CA, pg 779
Biblioteca Ayacucho, pg 779
Editorial Biosfera CA, pg 779

Zimbabwe

Academic Books (Pvt) Ltd, pg 782
Journal on Social Change, pg 783

ASIAN STUDIES

Australia

Allen & Unwin Pty Ltd, pg 11
Edward Arnold (Australia) Pty Ltd, pg 12
China Books, pg 17
Crawford House Publishing Pty Ltd, pg 18
Hale & Iremonger Pty Ltd, pg 24
Hawker Brownlow, pg 25
Hyland House Publishing Pty Ltd, pg 26
Illert Publications, pg 26
Indra Publishing, pg 27
On The Stone, pg 34
Oriental Publications, pg 34
Queensland Art Gallery, pg 38
Spinifex Press, pg 42
Windhorse Books, pg 47

Austria

Verlag der Oesterreichischen Akademie der Wissenschaften (OEAW), pg 55
Edition Va Bene, pg 59

Azerbaijan

Sada, Literaturno-Izdatel'skij Centr, pg 60

Bangladesh

Ankur Prakashani, pg 61

Belgium

Brepols Publishers NV, pg 64
Uitgeverij Peeters Leuven (Belgie), pg 71

Brazil

Fundacao Cultural Avatar, pg 82
Editora Ground Ltda, pg 83
Francisco J Laissue Livraria, pg 84

Bulgaria

Eurasia Academic Publishers, pg 94

China

China Tibetology Publishing House, pg 103
Cultural Relics Publishing House, pg 103
Fudan University Press, pg 104
Qingdao Publishing House, pg 107
Shanghai College of Traditional Chinese Medicine Press, pg 108

Czech Republic

Narodni Muzeum, pg 126

Denmark

Aarhus Universitetsforlag, pg 128
Museum Tusculanum Press, pg 133

Finland

Kirja-Leitzinger, pg 142

France

De Boccard Edition-Diffusion, pg 150
Editions de l'Ecole des Hautes Etudes en Sciences Sociales (EHESS), pg 159
Editions Fata Morgana, pg 162
Kailash Editions, pg 170
Karthala Editions-Diffusion, pg 170
Langues & Mondes-L'Asiatheque, pg 171

Germany

J J Augustin Verlag GmbH, pg 195
Dieterichsche Verlagsbuchhandlung Mainz, pg 214
Duncker und Humblot GmbH, pg 217
Egmont vgs verlagsgesellschaft mbH, pg 218
Erlanger Verlag Fuer Mission und Okumene, pg 220
Harrassowitz Verlag, pg 234
Horlemann Verlag, pg 239
IKO Verlag fur Interkulturelle Kommunikation, pg 241
Iudicium Verlag GmbH, pg 242
Kolibri-Verlag GmbH, pg 249
LIT Verlag, pg 255
Nusser Verlag, pg 266
Dr Ludwig Reichert Verlag, pg 274
Schillinger Verlag GmbH, pg 279
Siebenberg-Verlag, pg 283
Buchkonzept Simon KG, pg 283
Rudolf G Smend, pg 283
Franz Steiner Verlag Wiesbaden GmbH, pg 287

Hong Kong

Asia 2000 Ltd, pg 315
Celeluck Co Ltd, pg 316
The Chinese University Press, pg 316
Chung Hwa Book Co (HK) Ltd, pg 316
Hong Kong Publishing Co Ltd, pg 317
Hong Kong University Press, pg 317
Joint Publishing (HK) Co Ltd, pg 317
Peace Book Co Ltd, pg 318
Research Centre for Translation, pg 319
South China Morning Post Ltd, pg 319
Yazhou Zhoukan Ltd, pg 320

India

Agam Kala Prakashan, pg 327
Asian Educational Services, pg 329
Authorspress, pg 329
Book Circle, pg 330
Book Faith India, pg 330
Chowkhamba Sanskrit Series Office, pg 332
The Christian Literature Society, pg 332
Concept Publishing Co, pg 332
Cosmo Publications, pg 332
DK Printworld (P) Ltd, pg 333
Full Circle Publishing, pg 334
Gyan Publishing House, pg 335
Inter-India Publications, pg 338
Lancer Publisher's & Distributors, pg 340
Mapin Publishing Pvt Ltd, pg 341
Mehta Publishers, pg 341
Minerva Associates (Publications) Pvt Ltd, pg 342
Munshiram Manoharlal Publishers Pvt Ltd, pg 342
Oxford & IBH Publishing Co Pvt Ltd, pg 344
Rahul Publishing House, pg 346
Reliance Publishing House, pg 346
SABDA, pg 347
SAGE Publications India Pvt Ltd, pg 347
Somaiya Publications Pvt Ltd, pg 349
South Asian Publishers Pvt Ltd, pg 350
Spectrum Publications, pg 350
Sri Satguru Publications, pg 350
Sterling Publishers Pvt Ltd, pg 350
Stree, pg 350
Tara Publishing, pg 351

Indonesia

Aurora, pg 353
Mizan, pg 355
Yayasan Obor Indonesia, pg 357

Italy

Editrice Atanor SRL, pg 377
Herder Editrice e Libreria, pg 392
Editoriale Jaca Book SpA, pg 394
Jouvence, pg 394
Paideia Editrice, pg 402
Pontificio Istituto Orientale, pg 404
Il Saggiatore, pg 406
SEMAR Publishers SRL, pg 408

Japan

Dohosha Publishing Co Ltd, pg 417
Japan Publications Inc, pg 419
The Japan Times Ltd, pg 420
Keisuisha Publishing Company Ltd, pg 420
Kokushokankokai Co Ltd, pg 421
Rinsen Book Co Ltd, pg 425
Shibun-Do, pg 427
Sobun-Sha, pg 428
Toho Book Store, pg 429
Toho Shuppan, pg 429
Charles E Tuttle Publishing Co Inc, pg 430
United Nations University Press, pg 430
Yohan Shuppan, pg 431
Yushodo Shuppan, pg 431

Kazakstan

Al-Farabi Kazakh National University, pg 432

Democratic People's Republic of Korea

Foreign Languages Publishing House, pg 436
Grand People's Study House, pg 436

Republic of Korea

Hakgojae Publishing Inc, pg 439
Hanul Publishing Co, pg 439
Oruem Publishing House, pg 442
Seogwangsa, pg 442

Luxembourg

Varkki Verghese, pg 452

Macau

Museu Maritimo, pg 452
Instituto Portugues Oriente, pg 452

Malaysia

S Abdul Majeed & Co, pg 454

Mauritius

Editions Capucines, pg 461

Mexico

El Colegio de Mexico AC, pg 463

Netherlands

APA (Academic Publishers Associated), pg 477
Brill Academic Publishers, pg 479
De Driehoek BV, Uitgeverij, pg 481
Hotei Publishing, pg 484
KITLV Press Royal Institute of Linguistics & Anthropology, pg 484
Oriental Press BV (APA), pg 487
The Pepin Press, pg 487
Philo Press (APA), pg 487

New Zealand

Barkfire Press, pg 494
Graphic Educational Publications, pg 496

Pakistan

Centre for South Asian Studies, pg 512
Maqbool Academy, pg 513

PUBLISHERS

Publishers United Pvt Ltd, pg 514
Sang-e-Meel Publications, pg 514
Vanguard Books Ltd, pg 515

Philippines

Ateneo de Manila University Press, pg 518
De La Salle University, pg 519
New Day Publishers, pg 520
Our Lady of Manaoag Publisher, pg 520
UST Publishing House, pg 521

Poland

Wydawnictwa Uniwersytetu Warszawskiego, pg 527

Portugal

Gradiva-Publicacnoes Lda, pg 532
Edicoes Manuel Lencastre, pg 532

Russian Federation

Ladomir Publishing House, pg 546
Nauka Publishers, pg 547

Singapore

Aquanut Agencies Pte Ltd, pg 555
Archipelago Press, pg 555
Asiapac Books Pte Ltd, pg 555
Chopsons Pte Ltd, pg 555
Institute of Southeast Asian Studies, pg 556
Maruzen Asia (Pte) Ltd, pg 557
Select Publishing Pte Ltd, pg 557
Singapore University Press Pte Ltd, pg 558
Taylor & Francis Asia Pacific, pg 558
World Scientific Publishing Co Pte Ltd, pg 559

Slovakia

Slo Viet, pg 560

Spain

Ediciones Akal SA, pg 571
Ediciones del Oriente y del Mediterraneo, pg 594
Polifemo, Ediciones, pg 596

Sweden

Mezopotamya Publishing & Distribution, pg 613

Switzerland

Cockatoo Press (Schweiz), Thailand-Publikationen, pg 621
Office du Livre SA (Buchhaus AG), pg 630

Taiwan, Province of China

Asian Culture Co Ltd, pg 638
Echo Publishing Company Ltd, pg 639
Hilit Publishing Co Ltd, pg 640
Linking Publishing Company Ltd, pg 641
National Museum of History, pg 641
SMC Publishing Inc, pg 642
Torch of Wisdom, pg 642
Yee Wen Publishing Co Ltd, pg 642

Thailand

Silkworm Books, pg 645

United Kingdom

Ashmolean Museum Publications, pg 660
The Athlone Press Ltd, pg 661
Books for Europe Ltd, pg 669
British Museum Press, pg 672
Compendium Publishing, pg 681
The Eurospan Group, pg 692
Harvard University Press, pg 705
Marcham Manor Press, pg 725
Adam Matthew Publications, pg 726
Motilal (UK) Books of India, pg 729
Octagon Press Ltd, pg 734
Reaktion Books Ltd, pg 748
Reardon Publishing, pg 748
Roundhouse Group, pg 751
RoutledgeCurzon, pg 751
Royal Institute of International Affairs, pg 752
Saqi Books, pg 754
Serpent's Tail Ltd, pg 756
Skoob Russell Square, pg 758
I B Tauris & Co Ltd, pg 763
Textile & Art Publications Ltd, pg 764
Yale University Press London, pg 776

ASTROLOGY, OCCULT

Argentina

Editorial Albatros SACI, pg 3
Editorial Caymi SACI, pg 4
Errepar SA, pg 5
EUDEBA (Editorial Universitaria de Buenos Aires), pg 5
Editorial Kier SACIFI, pg 7

Australia

Angel Publications, pg 11
Dynamo House P/L, pg 20
Gnostic Editions, pg 23
Hihorse Publishing Pty Ltd, pg 25
Social Club Books, pg 41
Spinifex Press, pg 42
Unity Press, pg 44
Veritas Press, pg 45

Austria

E Perlinger Naturprodukte Handelsgesellschaft mbH, pg 56
Pinguin-Verlag, Pawlowski GmbH, pg 56
Verlag Carl Ueberreuter GmbH, pg 58
Dr Otfried Weise Verlag Tabula Smaragdina, pg 59

Azerbaijan

Sada, Literaturno-Izdatel'skij Centr, pg 60

Barbados

Business Tutors, pg 62

Belgium

Altina, pg 63
Marabout, pg 71
Parsifal BVBA, pg 71

Brazil

Editora Agora Ltda, pg 77
Livraria Francisco Alves Editora SA, pg 77
Editora Bertrand Brasil Ltda, pg 78
Edicon Editora e Consultorial Ltda, pg 81
Fundacao Cultural Avatar, pg 82
Editora Ground Ltda, pg 83
Hemus Editora Ltda, pg 83
Horus Editora Ltda, pg 83
Icone Editora Ltda, pg 83
Editora Kuarup Ltda, pg 84
Francisco J Laissue Livraria, pg 84
Madras Editora, pg 86
Editora Nova Fronteira SA, pg 87
Livraria Pioneira Editora/Enio Matheus Guazzelli e Cia Ltd, pg 88
Totalidade Editora Ltda, pg 91
Triom Centro de Estudos Marina e Martin Hawey Editorial e Comercial Ltda, pg 91
Editora Vecchi SA, pg 92

Bulgaria

Antroposofsko Izdatelstvo Dimo R Daskalov OOD, pg 93
Aratron, IK, pg 93
Kibea Publishing Co, pg 95
Kralica MAB, pg 95
Sila & Zivot, pg 97
Sluntse Publishing House, pg 97

Chile

Ediciones Mil Hojas Ltda, pg 99

China

Qingdao Publishing House, pg 107

Colombia

RAM Editores, pg 112
Tercer Mundo Editores SA, pg 113

Czech Republic

Aventinum Nakladatelstvi spol sro, pg 122
Chvojkova nakladatelstvi, pg 123
Vodnar, pg 128
Votobia sro, pg 128

Denmark

Bogan's Forlag, pg 129
Borgens Forlag A/S, pg 129

Estonia

Perioodika, pg 140
Sinisukk, pg 140

France

Editions Amrita SA, pg 146
Alain Brethes Editions, pg 151
Editions du Chariot, pg 153
Le Cherche Midi Editeur, pg 154
CNRS Editions, pg 155
De Vecchi Editions SA, pg 157
Nouvelles Editions Debresse, pg 157
Editions Jacques Grancher, pg 165
Hachette Pratiques, pg 167
Harlequin SA, pg 167
Le Jour, Editeur, pg 169
Editions Lacour-Olle, pg 170
Maisonneuve et Larose, pg 174
Medius Editions, pg 175
Mercure de France SA, pg 175
Editions Pardes, pg 179
Editions Saint-Michel SA, pg 183
Editions Sand et Tchou SA, pg 184

Germany

Aquamarin Verlag, pg 193
Arun-Verlag, pg 194
Otto Wilhelm Barth-Verlag KG, pg 197
Verlag Hermann Bauer Gmbh & Co KG, pg 197
Chiron-Verlag Reinhardt Stiehle, pg 208
Verlag Esoterische Philosophie GmbH, pg 221
EVT Energy Video Training & Verlag GmbH, pg 222
Extent Verlag und Service Wolfgang M Flamm, pg 223
Wilhelm Goldmann Verlag GmbH, pg 230
Heigl Verlag, Horst Edition, pg 235
Wilhelm Heyne Verlag, pg 237
AIG I Hilbinger Verlag GmbH, pg 237
F Hirthammer Verlag GmbH, pg 238
Verlag Peter Hoell, pg 238
Heinrich Hugendubel Verlag GmbH, pg 240
Verlag Kleine Schritte Ursula Dahm & Co, pg 246
Koenigsfurt Verlag, Evelin Buerger et Johannes Fiebig, pg 248
Edition Octopus & Okeanos Presse, pg 266
Reichl Verlag Der Leuchter, pg 274
Dieter Ruggeberg Verlagsbuchhandlung, pg 277
Die Silberschnur Verlag GmbH, pg 283
Spieth-Verlag Verlag fuer Symbolforschung, pg 284
Thauros Verlag GmbH, pg 290
Verlag Clemens Zerling, pg 302

Greece

Chrysi Penna - Golden Pen Books, pg 306
Govostis Publishing SA, pg 307
Hestia-I D Hestia-Kollaros & Co Corporation, pg 308
Kastaniotis Editions SA, pg 309
Orfanidis Publications, pg 311

Hong Kong

SCMP Book Publishing Ltd, pg 319

Hungary

Advent Kiado, pg 320

Iceland

Bokaforlag Birtingur, pg 325
Skjaldborg Ltd, pg 326

India

Asian Educational Services, pg 329
Chowkhamba Sanskrit Series Office, pg 332
DK Printworld (P) Ltd, pg 333
Full Circle Publishing, pg 334
Gyan Publishing House, pg 335
Jaico Publishing House, pg 338
Munshiram Manoharlal Publishers Pvt Ltd, pg 342
Orient Paperbacks, pg 344
Parimal Prakashan, pg 345
Pustak Mahal, pg 345
Reliance Publishing House, pg 346
Somaiya Publications Pvt Ltd, pg 349
Sterling Publishers Pvt Ltd, pg 350

Israel

Astrolog Publishing House, pg 365

Italy

Adea Edizioni, pg 374
L'Airone Editrice, pg 375
Arcanta Aries Gruppo Editoriale, pg 375

Arktos, pg 376
Gruppo Editoriale Armenia SpA, pg 376
Editrice Atanor SRL, pg 377
Crisalide, pg 383
Damanhur Edizioni, pg 384
Giovanni De Vecchi Editore SpA, pg 384
Edizioni Il Punto d'Incontro SAS, pg 386
Arnaldo Forni Editore SRL, pg 389
Ernesto Gremese Editore srl, pg 391
Gremese International srl, pg 391
Edizioni Mediterranee SRL, pg 398
Mundici - Zanetti, pg 400
Il Punto D Incontro, pg 404

Japan
Gakken Co Ltd, pg 417
Koseisha-Koseikaku Co Ltd, pg 422
Seibido Shuppan Company Ltd, pg 426

Latvia
Alberts XII, pg 444
Nordik/Tapals Publishers Ltd, pg 445
Preses Nams, pg 445
Vieda, SIA, pg 445
Zvaigzne ABC Publishers Ltd, pg 445

Lithuania
AS Narbuto Leidykla (AS Narbutas' Publishers), pg 448

The Former Yugoslav Republic of Macedonia
Strk Publishing House, pg 453
Zumpres Publishing Firm, pg 453

Mexico
Centro Editorial Mexicano Osiris SA, pg 463
Ediciones CUPSA, Centro de Comunicacion Cultural CUPSA, AC, pg 463
Editorial Diana SA de CV, pg 464
Hoja Casa Editorial SA de CV, pg 466
Libra Editorial SA de CV, pg 467
Editorial Orion, pg 469
Pangea Editores, Sa de CV, pg 470
Sayrols Editorial SA de CV, pg 471
Ediciones Suromex SA, pg 472

Monaco
Les Editions du Rocher, pg 474

Netherlands
Ankh-Hermes BV, pg 477
BZZTOH Publishers, pg 480
Mirananda Publishers BV, pg 486
Semic Junior Press, pg 489
Servire BV Uitgevers, pg 489
Uitgeverij Het Spectrum BV, pg 489

New Zealand
Brookfield Press, pg 494
RSVP Publishing Co Ltd, pg 500

Portugal
Brasilia Editora (J Carvalho Branco), pg 529
Editorial Estampa, Lda, pg 531
Edicoes Manuel Lencastre, pg 532
Internationale Nouvelle Acropole, pg 534

Planeta Editora, LDA, pg 534
Editorial Presenca, pg 535
Editora Replicacao Lda, pg 535
Edicoes 70 Lda, pg 535
Vega-Publicacao e Distribuicao de Livros e Revistas, Lda, pg 536

Romania
Editura Dacia, pg 539
MAST Verlag, pg 540
Editura Minerva, pg 541
Vremea Publishers Ltd, pg 543

Russian Federation
CentrePolygraph Traders & Publishers Co, pg 544

Serbia and Montenegro
Alfa-Narodna Knjiga, pg 552

Slovenia
Mladinska Knjiga International, pg 561
Zalozba Mihelac d o o, pg 562

South Africa
Kima Global Publishers, pg 566

Spain
Editorial Astri SA, pg 573
Biblioteca de Autores Cristianos, pg 574
Editorial Barath SA, pg 574
Editorial EDAF SA, pg 580
Edicomunicacion SA, pg 581
Editorial Everest SA, pg 581
Etu Ediciones SL, pg 583
Mandala Ediciones, pg 590
Ediciones Martinez-Roca SA, pg 591
Munoz Moya Editor, pg 592
Noguer y Caralt Editores SA, pg 593
Nueva Acropolis, pg 593
Obelisco Ediciones S, pg 593
Perea Ediciones, pg 595
Ediciones 29 - Libros Rio Nuevo, pg 603
Ediciones Urano, SA, pg 604

Sweden
Sjoestrands Foerlag, pg 615

Switzerland
Astrodata AG, pg 618
Govinda-Verlag, pg 624
Natura-Verlag Arlesheim, pg 629
Psychosophische Gesellschaft, pg 632
Rhein-Trio, Edition/Editions du Fou, pg 632
Sphinx Verlag AG, pg 634

United Republic of Tanzania
Kajura Publications, pg 643
Press & Publicity Centre Ltd, pg 644

Turkey
Alkim Kitapcilik-Yayimcilik, pg 649
Ruh ve Madde Yayinlari ve Saglik Hizmetleri AS, pg 651

Ukraine
ASK Ltd, pg 653

United Kingdom
The Banton Press, pg 662
BCA - Book Club Associates, pg 663
Blandford Publishing Ltd, pg 668
Capall Bann Publishing, pg 674
Marshall Cavendish Partworks Ltd, pg 676
Constable & Robinson Ltd, pg 682
The C W Daniel Co Ltd, pg 686
Element Books Ltd, pg 690
Foulsham Publishers, pg 696
George Mann Publications, pg 699
HarperCollins UK, pg 705
Janus Publishing Co Ltd, pg 716
Lucis Press Ltd, pg 723
Mandrake of Oxford, pg 725
Kenneth Mason Publications Ltd, pg 726
Piatkus Books, pg 741
Pomegranate Europe Ltd, pg 744
Prism Press Book Publishers Ltd, pg 745
Quadrille Publishing Ltd, pg 746
Quarto Publishing plc, pg 746
Random House UK Ltd, pg 747
Skoob Russell Square, pg 758
The Society of Metaphysicians Ltd, pg 759
Virgin Publishing Ltd, pg 770
White Eagle Publishing Trust, pg 772

Venezuela
Alfadil Ediciones, pg 778

ASTRONOMY

Albania
NL SH, pg 1

Australia
Spinifex Press, pg 42

Brazil
Editora Nova Fronteira SA, pg 87
Editora Scipione Ltda, pg 90

Bulgaria
Litera Prima, pg 95
Makros 2000 - Plovdiv, pg 95

Chile
Arrayan Editores, pg 98

China
Inner Mongolia Science & Technology Publishing House, pg 105
Jilin Science & Technology Publishing House, pg 105
Qingdao Publishing House, pg 107

Czech Republic
Mariadan, pg 125
Mlada fronta, pg 125

Denmark
Fremad A/S, pg 131

Estonia
Eesti Entsuklopeediakirjastus, pg 139

France
Bookmaker, pg 150
EDP Sciences, pg 161
Editions Jacques Gabay, pg 164

Editions Jean Paul Gisserot, pg 165
Librairie Scientifique et Technique Albert Blanchard, pg 172
Editions Springer France, pg 186

Germany
BLV Verlagsgesellschaft mbH, pg 202
Columbus Verlag Paul Oestergaard GmbH, pg 209
Deutsche Verlags-Anstalt GmbH (DVA), pg 212
Deutscher Taschenbuch Verlag GmbH & Co KG (dtv), pg 213
Franz Ferzak World & Space Publications, pg 224
Franckh-Kosmos Verlags-GmbH & Co, pg 226
F A Herbig Verlagsbuchhandlung GmbH, pg 236
Anton Hiersemann, Verlag, pg 237
Springer Science+Business Media GmbH & Co KG, pg 284
Steiger Verlag, pg 287

Greece
Diavlos, pg 306

India
Chowkhamba Sanskrit Series Office, pg 332
Gyan Publishing House, pg 335
Heritage Publishers, pg 335
Rajendra Publishing House Pvt Ltd, pg 346
Reliance Publishing House, pg 346
Scientific Book Agency, pg 348

Italy
Il Castello srl, pg 380
Essegi, pg 388
Arnaldo Forni Editore SRL, pg 389
Editrice Massimo SAS di Crespi Cesare e C, pg 397
Leo S Olschki, pg 401
Editoriale Scienza, pg 407

Japan
Koseisha-Koseikaku Co Ltd, pg 422
Mita Press, Mita Industrial Co Ltd, pg 422
Nippon Hoso Shuppan Kyokai (NHK Publishing), pg 424

Lebanon
Librairie du Liban Publishers (Sal), pg 446

The Former Yugoslav Republic of Macedonia
Zumpres Publishing Firm, pg 453

Malaysia
Federal Publications Sdn Bhd, pg 455

Mexico
Editorial Limusa SA de CV, pg 467
Organizacion Cultural LP SA de CV, pg 469
Pangea Editores, Sa de CV, pg 470
Ediciones Suromex SA, pg 472

Netherlands
V S P International Science Publishers, pg 491

PUBLISHERS

Poland
Instytut Historii Nauki PAN, pg 523

Portugal
Constancia Editores, SA, pg 530
Dinalivro, pg 530
Gradiva-Publicacnoes Lda, pg 532
Impala, pg 532
Planeta Editora, LDA, pg 534

Romania
Editura Academiei Romane, pg 538

Russian Federation
Fizmatlit Publishing Co, pg 545
Izdatelstvo Mir, pg 546
Nauka Publishers, pg 547
Izdatelstvo Prosveshchenie, pg 548

Saudi Arabia
Dar Al-Shareff for Publishing & Distribution, pg 550

Slovenia
Zalozba Mihelac d o o, pg 562

Spain
Nueva Acropolis, pg 593
Equipo Sirius SA, pg 600

Switzerland
Verlag Harri Deutsch, pg 622

United Republic of Tanzania
Readit Books, pg 644

United Kingdom
The Erskine Press, pg 692
Grange Books PLC, pg 702
Institute of Physics Publishing, pg 713
Open University Worldwide, pg 736
Orpheus Books Ltd, pg 736
Philip's, pg 741
Springer-Verlag London Ltd, pg 760

Uruguay
EQ Opciones en Educacion, pg 777
A Monteverde y Cia SA, pg 777

Viet Nam
Science & Technics Publishing House, pg 780

AUTOMOTIVE

Argentina
Editorial Caymi SACI, pg 4

Australia
David Boyce Publishing, pg 16
CHOICE Magazine, pg 17
Graffiti Publications, pg 23
Gregory Kefalas Publishing, pg 28
McGraw-Hill Australia Pty Ltd, pg 31
OTEN (Open Training & Education Network), pg 34
Turton & Armstrong Pty Ltd Publishers, pg 44
Universal Press Pty Ltd, pg 44

Austria
Bohmann Druck und Verlag GmbH & Co KG, pg 49
Universitaetsverlag Wagner GmbH, pg 59

Belarus
Interdigest Publishing House, pg 62

Belgium
Uitgevery Gelbis NV, pg 67
Glenat Benelux SA, pg 67

China
China Machine Press (CMP), pg 102
China Materials Management Publishing House, pg 102
Jilin Science & Technology Publishing House, pg 105
National Defence Industry Press, pg 106
The People's Communications Publishing House, pg 106
Qingdao Publishing House, pg 107

Czech Republic
Cesky normalizacni institut, pg 126

Ecuador
SECAP, pg 137

Estonia
Mats Publishers Ltd, pg 140

France
ATP - Packager, pg 148
Editions Chiron, pg 154
Jean-P Delville Editions, pg 157
EPA (Editions Pratiques Automobiles), pg 161
Publi-Fusion, pg 182
Editions Soline, pg 185
Editions Technip SA, pg 187
Editions Vilo SA, pg 189

Germany
Autovision Verlag Guenther & Co, pg 196
CartoTravel Verlag GmbH & Co KG, pg 207
Delius, Klasing und Co, pg 211
Verlag Europa-Lehrmittel GmbH & Co KG, pg 221
Alfons W Gentner Verlag GmbH & Co KG, pg 228
Heel Verlag GmbH, pg 235
Huss-Verlag GmbH, pg 240
Jahreszeiten-Verlag GmbH, pg 242
Kirschbaum Verlag GmbH, pg 246
Moby Dick Verlag, pg 261
Motorbuch-Verlag, pg 262
Paul Pietsch Verlage GmbH & Co, pg 270
Verlag Walter Podszun Burobedarf-Bucher Abt, pg 270
Transpress Verlagsgesellschaft mbH, pg 292
Vogel Medien GmbH & Co KG, pg 296

Greece
Kleidarithmos, Ekdoseis, pg 309
Orfanidis Publications, pg 311

Hong Kong
Adsale Publishing Co Ltd, pg 315

India
Heritage Publishers, pg 335
Sita Books & Periodicals Pvt Ltd, pg 349

Indonesia
PT Indira, pg 355
Karya Anda, CV, pg 355

Italy
Automobilia srl, pg 377
Editoriale Domus SpA, pg 385
Giorgio Nada Editore SRL, pg 400

Japan
Gakken Co Ltd, pg 417
Nigensha Publishing Co Ltd, pg 423
Seibido Shuppan Company Ltd, pg 426

Kenya
Heinemann Kenya Ltd (EAEP), pg 434
Space Sellers Ltd, pg 436

Lebanon
Arab Scientific Publishers BP, pg 445

Mexico
Editorial Limusa SA de CV, pg 467
Sayrols Editorial SA de CV, pg 471
Sistemas Universales, SA, pg 472

New Zealand
GCL Publishing (1997) Ltd, pg 496

Russian Federation
FGUP Izdatelstvo Mashinostroenie, pg 544
Izdatelstvo Transport, pg 549

Spain
Editorial Dossat SA, pg 580
Marcombo SA, pg 590

Sweden
Johnston & Streiffert Editions, pg 613

Switzerland
Verlag Bucheli, pg 620
Editions 24 Heures, pg 635

Taiwan, Province of China
Fuh-Wen Book Co, pg 639

United Kingdom
Ian Allan Publishing Ltd, pg 656
Amber Books Ltd, pg 657
Bay View Books Ltd, pg 663
BCA - Book Club Associates, pg 663
Books International, pg 669
Brooklands Books Ltd, pg 672
Compendium Publishing, pg 681
The Crowood Press Ltd, pg 684
The Economist Intelligence Unit, pg 689
ERA Technology Ltd, pg 692
Grange Books PLC, pg 702
Greenhill Books/Lionel Leventhal Ltd, pg 703
Haynes Publishing, pg 706
Motor Racing Publications Ltd, pg 729
Octopus Publishing Group, pg 734

SUBJECT INDEX

RAC Publishing, pg 747
Rapra Technology Ltd, pg 748
Regency House Publishing Ltd, pg 749
Research Studies Press Ltd (RSP), pg 749
Roadmaster Publishing, pg 750
Veloce Publishing Ltd, pg 769
WIT Press, pg 774

Viet Nam
Science & Technics Publishing House, pg 780

Zimbabwe
Standards Association of Zimbabwe (SAZ), pg 784
Thomson Publications Zimbabwe (Pvt) Ltd, pg 784

BEHAVIORAL SCIENCES

Argentina
Editorial Polemos SA, pg 8

Australia
Allen & Unwin Pty Ltd, pg 11
Edward Arnold (Australia) Pty Ltd, pg 12
Ausmed Publications Pty Ltd, pg 12
Australian Academic Press Pty Ltd, pg 13
Australian Institute of Family Studies (AIFS), pg 13
Extraordinary People Press, pg 22
Kerri Hamer, pg 24
Macmillan Education Australia, pg 30
Mayne Publishing, pg 31
McGraw-Hill Australia Pty Ltd, pg 31
Mouse House Press, pg 32
Pearson Education Australia, pg 36
Jurriaan Plesman, pg 37
Wileman Publications, pg 46

Austria
WUV/Facultas Universitaetsverlag, pg 60

Bangladesh
Gatidhara, pg 61

Belgium
Campinia Media VZW, pg 64
Editions De Boeck-Larcier SA, pg 66
Marabout, pg 71

Brazil
Editora Alfa Omega Ltda, pg 77
ARTMED Editora, pg 78
Editora Bertrand Brasil Ltda, pg 78
Editora Harbra Ltda, pg 83
Editora Logosofica, pg 85
MG Editores Associados Ltda, pg 86
Editora Objetiva Ltda, pg 87
Olho D'Agua Comercio e Servicos Editoriais Ltda, pg 87
Edit Palavra Magica, pg 88
Pearson Education Do Brasil, pg 88
Livraria Pioneira Editora/Enio Matheus Guazzelli e Cia Ltd, pg 88
Editora Revan Ltda, pg 89
Summus Editorial Ltda, pg 91
Jorge Zahar Editor, pg 92

915

SUBJECT INDEX

Bulgaria
EA EOOD, pg 94
Todor Kableshkov University of Transport, pg 97

China
Anhui People's Publishing House, pg 101
Beijing Publishing House, pg 101
China Materials Management Publishing House, pg 102
Fudan University Press, pg 104
Lanzhou University Press, pg 106
Qingdao Publishing House, pg 107
Shandong University Press, pg 108
Shanghai College of Traditional Chinese Medicine Press, pg 108

Colombia
Editorial Libros y Libres SA, pg 112

Costa Rica
Editorial Nacional de Salud y Seguridad Social Ednass, pg 116
Ediciones Promesa, pg 116
Editorial de la Universidad de Costa Rica, pg 116

Denmark
Borgens Forlag A/S, pg 129

Egypt (Arab Republic of Egypt)
Dar El Shorouk, pg 138

Finland
Osuuskunta Vastapaino, pg 144
Yliopistopaino/Helsinki University Press, pg 145

France
Adverbum SARL, pg 146
Autrement Editions, pg 148
Editions Saint-Michel SA, pg 183

Germany
Deutscher Taschenbuch Verlag GmbH & Co KG (dtv), pg 213
Rainar Nitzsche Verlag, pg 265
Osho Verlag GmbH, pg 267
Psychologie Verlags Union GmbH, pg 272
Springer Science+Business Media GmbH & Co KG, pg 284
WEKA Firmengruppe GmbH & Co KG, pg 298

Greece
Hestia-I D Hestia-Kollaros & Co Corporation, pg 308

Hong Kong
Hong Kong University Press, pg 317

India
Agricole Publishing Academy, pg 327
Concept Publishing Co, pg 332
Jaico Publishing House, pg 338
National Book Organization, pg 342
Omsons Publications, pg 344
Reliance Publishing House, pg 346
SAGE Publications India Pvt Ltd, pg 347
Scientific Book Agency, pg 348
Somaiya Publications Pvt Ltd, pg 349
Sultan Chand & Sons Pvt Ltd, pg 350
A H Wheeler & Co Ltd, pg 353

Indonesia
Karya Anda, CV, pg 355

Ireland
On Stream Publications Ltd, pg 362

Israel
Ach Publishing House, pg 364
Bar Ilan University Press, pg 365
Dyonon/Papyrus Publishing House of the Tel-Aviv, pg 366
Freund Publishing House Ltd, pg 367
Schocken Publishing House Ltd, pg 371

Italy
Editore Armando Armando SRL, pg 376
Belforte Editore Libraio srl, pg 377
Giuseppe Bonanno Editore, pg 378
Edizioni Centro Studi Erickson, pg 381
Piero Gribaudi Editore, pg 391

Japan
Zeimukeiri-Kyokai, pg 431

Kenya
Nairobi University Press, pg 435

Republic of Korea
Chung Rim Publishing Co Ltd, pg 438

Latvia
Preses Nams, pg 445

The Former Yugoslav Republic of Macedonia
Strk Publishing House, pg 453
Zumpres Publishing Firm, pg 453

Malaysia
Penerbit Universiti Teknologi Malaysia, pg 459

Martinique
George Lise-Huyghes des Etages, pg 460

Mexico
El Colegio de Michoacan A C, pg 464
Fondo de Cultura Economica, pg 465
Editorial Limusa SA de CV, pg 467
Sistemas Tecnicos de Edicion SA de CV, pg 472

Namibia
Desert Research Foundation of Namibia (DRFN), pg 476

Netherlands
Boom Uitgeverij, pg 479
Brill Academic Publishers, pg 479
Kluwer Academic Publishers, pg 484
Tilburg University Press, pg 490
Uitgeverij De Toorts, pg 490

Nigeria
JAD Publishers Ltd, pg 505

Norway
Universitetsforlaget, pg 511

Pakistan
National Book Foundation, pg 513

Philippines
Ateneo de Manila University Press, pg 518
New Day Publishers, pg 520
Our Lady of Manaoag Publisher, pg 520
Rex Bookstores & Publishers, pg 520

Poland
Polish Scientific Publishers PWN, pg 525
Wydawnictwa Uniwersytetu Warszawskiego, pg 527

Portugal
Editora Classica, pg 530
Difusao Cultural, pg 530
Gradiva-Publicacnoes Lda, pg 532
Vega-Publicacao e Distribuicao de Livros e Revistas, Lda, pg 536

Puerto Rico
Libros-Ediciones Homines, pg 537

Saudi Arabia
Dar Al-Shareff for Publishing & Distribution, pg 550
King Saud University, pg 550

Senegal
CODESRIA (Council for the Development of Social Science Research in Africa), pg 551

Singapore
Aquanut Agencies Pte Ltd, pg 555

South Africa
Human Sciences Research Council, pg 565
Kima Global Publishers, pg 566

Spain
Ediciones Akal SA, pg 571
Ediciones Alfar SA, pg 572
Mandala Ediciones, pg 590
Ediciones Morata SL, pg 592
Oikos-Tau SA Ediciones, pg 593
Editorial El Perpetuo Socorro, pg 596
Pulso Ediciones, SL, pg 597
Universidad de Oviedo Servicio de Publicaciones, pg 603

Sweden
Akademiforlaget Goteborgslitteratur, pg 609
Studentlitteratur AB, pg 616

Switzerland
Bergli Books AG, pg 619

Syrian Arab Republic
Damascus University Press, pg 638

Taiwan, Province of China
Chien Chen Bookstore Publishing Company Ltd, pg 639
Ho-Chi Book Publishing Co, pg 640
Laureate Book Co Ltd, pg 640

Turkey
Saray Medikal Yayin Tic Ltd Sti, pg 651

United Kingdom
Andromeda Oxford Ltd, pg 658
BILD Publications, pg 665
Blackwell Science Ltd, pg 667
BPS Books (British Psychological Society), pg 670
Constable & Robinson Ltd, pg 682
Elsevier Ltd, pg 691
The Eurospan Group, pg 692
Free Association Books Ltd, pg 697
W H Freeman & Co Ltd, pg 697
HarperCollins UK, pg 705
Harvard University Press, pg 705
Hawthorn Press, pg 706
JAI Press Ltd, pg 715
Jessica Kingsley Publishers, pg 718
MIT Press Ltd, pg 728
Octagon Press Ltd, pg 734
Open University Press, pg 736
SAGE Publications Ltd, pg 753
Sherwood Publishing, pg 757
Speechmark Publishing Ltd, pg 760

Viet Nam
Science & Technics Publishing House, pg 780

BIBLICAL STUDIES

Albania
NL SH, pg 1

Argentina
Argentine Bible Society, pg 3
San Pablo, pg 9

Australia
Aletheia Publishing, pg 11
Aquila Press, pg 11
Bible Society in Australia National Headquarters, pg 14
Bridgeway Publications, pg 16
Catholic Institute of Sydney, pg 17
Crossroad Distributors Pty Ltd, pg 18
HarperCollinsReligious, pg 25
New Creation Publications Ministries & Resource Centre, pg 33
St Pauls Publications, pg 40
Vital Publications, pg 45

Belgium
Editions Gerard Blanchart & Cie SA, pg 63
Brepols Publishers NV, pg 64
Editions Lessius ASBL, pg 70
La Longue Vue, pg 70
Editions Lumen Vitae ASBL, pg 70
Uitgeverij Peeters Leuven (Belgie), pg 71

Brazil
Associacao Arvore da Vida, pg 78
Editora Cidade Nova, pg 80
Editora Companhia das Letras/Editora Schwarcz Ltda, pg 80
Editora Elevacao, pg 81

PUBLISHERS

Imago Editora Importacao e Exportacao Ltda, pg 84
Koinonia Comunidade Edicoes Ltda (Editora Koinonia Ltda), pg 84
Edicoes Loyola SA, pg 85
Editora Mercuryo Ltda, pg 86
Editora Mundo Cristao, pg 87
Paulinas Editorial, pg 88
Paulus Editora, pg 88

Bulgaria

Antroposofsko Izdatelstvo Dimo R Daskalov OOD, pg 93
Nov Covek Publishing House, pg 96
Sila & Zivot, pg 97
Svetra Publishing House, pg 97

China

Qingdao Publishing House, pg 107

Colombia

Consejo Episcopal Latinoamericano (CELAM), pg 110

The Democratic Republic of the Congo

Facultes Catoliques de Kinshasa, pg 114

Cote d'Ivoire

Centre de Publications Evangeliques, pg 117

Croatia

Krscanska sadasnjost, pg 118
Znaci Vremena, Institut Za Istrazivanje Biblije, pg 119

Czech Republic

Ceska Biblicka Spolecnost, pg 123
Karmelitanske Nakladatelstvi, pg 124

Denmark

Aarhus Universitetsforlag, pg 128
Lohse Forlag, pg 132
Scandinavia Publishing House, pg 134
Unitas Forlag, pg 135

Dominican Republic

Pontificia Universidad Catolica Madre y Maestra, pg 136

Estonia

Eesti Piibliselts, pg 139

Finland

Forsamlingsforbundets Forlags AB, pg 142
Herattaja-yhdistys Ry, pg 142
Lasten Keskus Oy, pg 143
Suomen Pipliaseura RY, pg 144

France

Adverbum SARL, pg 146
Editions de l'Atelier, pg 148
Editions Buchet-Chastel Pierre Zech Editeur, pg 151
Editions du Cerf, pg 153
Editions du Chalet, pg 153
Paul Geuthner Librairie Orientaliste, pg 165
P Lethielleux Editions, pg 171
Letouzey et Ane Editeurs, pg 171
Editions Mediaspaul, pg 175

Peeters-France, pg 179
Les Editions de la Source Sarl, pg 186

Germany

Aussaat Verlag, pg 195
Deutsche Bibelgesellschaft, pg 211
Echter Wurzburg Frankische Gesellschaftsdruckerei und Verlag GmbH, pg 217
Evangelische Verlagsanstalt GmbH, pg 222
Genius Verlag, pg 228
Guetersloher Verlagshaus, pg 232
Verlag Herder GmbH & Co KG, pg 236
Johannis, pg 243
Verlag Katholisches Bibelwerk GmbH, pg 245
Naumann & Goebel Verlagsgesellschaft mbH, pg 263
Verlag Neue Stadt GmbH, pg 264
Neuer Honos Verlag GmbH, pg 264
Oekumenischer Verlag Dr R-F Edel, pg 266
Verlag Schnell und Steiner GmbH, pg 281
J F Steinkopf Verlag GmbH, pg 287
Sternberg-Verlag bei Ernst Franz, pg 288
Thauros Verlag GmbH, pg 290
Verein der Benediktiner zu Beuron-Beuroner Kunstverlag, pg 294
Verlag und Studio fuer Hoerbuchproduktionen, pg 295
Friedrich Wittig Verlag GmbH, pg 301

Ghana

Asempa Publishers, pg 303
Ghana Institute of Linguistics Literacy & Bible Translation (GILLBT), pg 304
World Literature Project, pg 305

Greece

Alamo Hellas, pg 305
Apostoliki Diakonia tis Ekklisias tis Hellados, pg 305
Hestia-I D Hestia-Kollaros & Co Corporation, pg 308

Hong Kong

Christian Communications Ltd, pg 316
Philopsychy Press, pg 318
Times Publishing (Hong Kong) Ltd, pg 319

Hungary

Advent Kiado, pg 320

India

The Christian Literature Society, pg 332
Dolphin Publications, pg 333
Indian Society for Promoting Christian Knowledge (ISPCK), pg 337
Satprakashan Sanchar Kendra, pg 348

Indonesia

Aurora, pg 353
Nusa Indah, pg 356

Ireland

Cathedral Books Ltd, pg 358
Veritas Co Ltd, pg 364

Israel

Bar Ilan University Press, pg 365
The Bialik Institute, pg 365
Breslov Research Institute, pg 365
DAT Publications, pg 366
Gefen Publishing House Ltd, pg 367
Haifa University Press, pg 367
Hakibbutz Hameuchad Publishing House Ltd, pg 367
Israel Exploration Society, pg 368
Koren Publishers Jerusalem Ltd, pg 369
Open University of Israel, pg 371
Rolnik Publishers, pg 371
Rubin Mass Ltd, pg 371
Sadan Publishing Ltd, pg 371
Terra Sancta Arts, pg 372
Urim Publications, pg 373

Italy

Edizioni Cantagalli, pg 379
Edizioni Carmelitane, pg 380
Centro Biblico, pg 381
Citta Nuova Editrice, pg 382
Cittadella Editrice, pg 382
Claudiana Editrice, pg 382
Edizioni Dehoniane Bologna (EDB), pg 384
Edizioni del Centro Camuno di Studi Preistorici, pg 386
Elle Di Ci - Libreria Dottrina Cristiana, pg 387
Piero Gribaudi Editore, pg 391
In Dialogo, pg 393
Editrice LAS, pg 394
Lubrina, pg 396
Macro Edizioni, pg 397
Casa Editrice Marietti SpA, pg 397
Editrice Massimo SAS di Crespi Cesare e C, pg 397
Nuova Coletti Editore Roma, pg 401
Leo S Olschki, pg 401
Paideia Editrice, pg 402
Edizioni Piemme SpA, pg 403
Pontificio Istituto Orientale, pg 404
Editrice Queriniana, pg 404
Edizioni Segno SRL, pg 407
Edizioni del Teresianum, pg 410
Editrice Uomini Nuovi, pg 411
Urbaniana University Press, pg 411
Vivere In SRL, pg 412
Voce della Bibbia, pg 412

Japan

Sobun-Sha, pg 428

Kenya

Gaba Publications Amecea, Pastoral Institute, pg 434
Paulines Publications-Africa, pg 435
Shirikon Publishers, pg 436

Democratic People's Republic of Korea

Grand People's Study House, pg 436

Republic of Korea

St Pauls, pg 442

Latvia

Patmos, izdevnieciba, pg 445
Spriditis Publishers, pg 445

Lebanon

Dar-El-Machreq Sarl, pg 446

SUBJECT INDEX

The Former Yugoslav Republic of Macedonia

Zumpres Publishing Firm, pg 453

Madagascar

Maison d'Edition Protestante ANTSO, pg 453

Malawi

Popular Publications, pg 454

Malta

Media Centre, pg 460

Mexico

Ediciones CUPSA, Centro de Comunicacion Cultural CUPSA, AC, pg 463
Editorial Jus SA de CV, pg 467

Netherlands

APA (Academic Publishers Associated), pg 477
Buijten en Schipperheijn BV Drukkerij en Uitgeversmaatschappij, pg 480
Callenbach BV, pg 480
Uitgeverij Christvoor, pg 480
Uitgeverij Ten Have, pg 483
Katholieke Bijbelstichting, pg 484
Narratio Theologische Uitgeverij, pg 486
Philo Press (APA), pg 487
Tilburg University Press, pg 490

New Zealand

Church Mouse Press, pg 495
Outrigger Publishers, pg 499

Nigeria

Vantage Publishers International Ltd, pg 507

Papua New Guinea

Kristen Press, pg 515

Philippines

Claretian Communications Inc, pg 518
Communication Foundation for Asia Media Group (CFAMG), pg 518
New Day Publishers, pg 520
Our Lady of Manaoag Publisher, pg 520
Philippine Baptist Mission SBC FMB Church Growth International, pg 520
UST Publishing House, pg 521

Poland

Drukarnia I Ksiegarnia Swietego Wojciecha, Dziat Wydawniczy, pg 522
Instytut Wydawniczy Pax, Inco-Veritas, pg 523
Katolicki Uniwersytet Wydawniczo -Redakcja, pg 523
Pallottinum Wydawnictwo Stowarzyszenia Apostolstwa Katolickiego, pg 525
Vocatio Publishing House, pg 527

Portugal

Paulinas, pg 534
Planeta Editora, LDA, pg 534

SUBJECT INDEX

Puerto Rico
Publicaciones Voz de Gracia, pg 537

Romania
Editura Excelsior Art, pg 539
Hasefer, pg 540

Russian Federation
N E Bauman Moscow State Technical University Publishers, pg 544
St Andrew's Biblical Theological College, pg 548

Singapore
Tecman Bible House, pg 558

Slovenia
Mladinska Knjiga International, pg 561
Zalozba Mihelac d o o, pg 562

South Africa
Bible Society of South Africa, pg 562
Educum Publishers Ltd, pg 563
Institute for Reformational Studies CHE, pg 565

Spain
Central Catequistica Salesiana (CCS), pg 576
Editora Comercial de Publicaciones, pg 577
Creaciones Monar Editorial, pg 578
Ediciones Cristiandad, pg 578
Espanola Desclee De Brouwer SA, pg 578
Ediciones El Almendro de Cordoba, pg 580
M Moleiro Editor, SA, pg 592
Obelisco Ediciones S, pg 593
Editorial Peregrino SL, pg 595
Editorial El Perpetuo Socorro, pg 596
Editorial Revista Agustiniana, pg 598
Ediciones San Pio X, pg 599
Ediciones Sigueme SA, pg 600
Ediciones Susaeta SA, pg 601
Editorial Verbo Divino, pg 604

Sweden
Bokforlaget Nya Doxa AB, pg 614

Switzerland
Beroa-Verlag, pg 619
Jordanverlag AG, pg 625
Jugend mit einer Mission Verlag, pg 626
Kanisius Verlag, pg 626
Kranich-Verlag, Dres AG & H R Bosch-Gwalter, pg 627
La Maison de la Bible, pg 628
Theologischer Verlag und Buchhandlungen AG, pg 635

Taiwan, Province of China
Campus Evangelical Fellowship, Literature Department, pg 639

United Republic of Tanzania
Central Tanganyika Press, pg 643
Emmaus Bible School, pg 643
Kanisa la Biblia Publishers (KLB), pg 643

Ukraine
ASK Ltd, pg 653

United Kingdom
Bible Reading Fellowship, pg 665
Bible Society, pg 665
Bryntirion Press, pg 672
Cambridge University Press, pg 674
Cassell & Co, pg 675
Christian Education, pg 679
James Clarke & Co Ltd, pg 680
CTBI Publications, pg 685
Cyhoeddiadau'r Gair, pg 685
Darton, Longman & Todd Ltd, pg 686
Epworth Press, pg 691
The Eurospan Group, pg 692
Evangelical Press & Services Ltd, pg 693
The Foundational Book Company for the John W Doorly Trust, pg 696
HarperCollins UK, pg 705
Hodder Education, pg 709
Lion Hudson PLC, pg 721
The Lutterworth Press, pg 723
Marcham Manor Press, pg 725
McCrimmon Publishing Co Ltd, pg 726
Methodist Publishing House, pg 727
Monarch Books, pg 729
Moorley's Print & Publishing Ltd, pg 729
SCM-Canterbury Press Ltd, pg 755
Scripture Union, pg 756
Sheffield Academic Press Ltd, pg 757
The Society for Promoting Christian Knowledge (SPCK), pg 759
Tern Press, pg 764
Wild Goose Publications, pg 773

Zimbabwe
Christian Audio-Visual Action (CAVA), pg 783
College Press Publishers (Pvt) Ltd, pg 783

BIOGRAPHY

Albania
Botimpex Publications Import-Export Agency, pg 1
NL SH, pg 1

Algeria
Enterprise Nationale du Livre (ENAL), pg 2

Argentina
Editorial Acme SA, pg 3
Centro Editor de America Latina SA, pg 4
Editorial Ciudad Nueva de la Sefoma, pg 4
Editorial Claridad SA, pg 4
Diana Argentina SA, Editorial, pg 5
Emece Editores SA, pg 5
Ediciones de la Flor SRL, pg 6
Editorial Losada SA, pg 7
Instituto de Publicaciones Navales, pg 8
Editorial Planeta Argentina SAIC, pg 8
Editorial Quetzal-Domingo Cortizo, pg 8
Editorial Sudamericana SA, pg 9
Theoria SRL Distribuidora y Editora, pg 9
Javier Vergara Editor SA, pg 9

Australia
Aboriginal Studies Press, pg 10
Access Press, pg 10
Athena Press, pg 12
Bernal Publishing, pg 14
Boolarong Press, pg 15
Louis Braille Audio, pg 16
Casket Publications, pg 17
Church Archivists Press, pg 18
Cornford Press, pg 18
Crawford House Publishing Pty Ltd, pg 18
Emperor Publishing, pg 21
Fremantle Arts Centre Press, pg 23
Ginninderra Press, pg 23
Hale & Iremonger Pty Ltd, pg 24
Histec Publications, pg 25
The Images Publishing Group Pty Ltd, pg 26
Indra Publishing, pg 27
Institute of Aboriginal Development (IAD Press), pg 27
Kangaroo Press, pg 28
Little Red Apple Publishing, pg 29
Thomas C Lothian Pty Ltd, pg 29
Lowden Publishing Co, pg 30
Lucasville Press, pg 30
Magabala Books Aboriginal Corporation, pg 30
Melbourne University Press, pg 32
Mulini Press, pg 32
Ocean Press, pg 34
Ollif Publishing, pg 34
Outback Books - CQU Press, pg 34
Pan Macmillan Australia Pty Ltd, pg 35
Penguin Group (Australia), pg 36
Pinevale Publications, pg 36
The Polding Press, pg 37
Quakers Hill Press, pg 38
Ruskin Rowe Press, pg 40
St Pauls Publications, pg 40
Single X Publications, pg 41
Spectrum Publications, pg 41
State Library of NSW Press, pg 42
The Text Publishing Company Pty Ltd, pg 43
Transpareon Press, pg 44
Turton & Armstrong Pty Ltd Publishers, pg 44
University of New South Wales Press Ltd, pg 44
University of Queensland Press, pg 45
University of Western Australia Press, pg 45
Vista Publications, pg 45
Wakefield Press Pty Ltd, pg 46

Austria
Akademische Druck-u Verlagsanstalt Dr Paul Struzl GmbH, pg 48
Astor-Verlag, Willibald Schlager, pg 48
Christian Brandstaetter Verlagsgesellschaft mbH, pg 49
Doecker Verlag GmbH & Co KG, pg 50
Verlag Lynkeus/H Hakel Gesellschaft, pg 51
Haymon-Verlag GesmbH, pg 51
Johannes Heyn GmbH & Co KG, pg 52
Milena Verlag, pg 54
Paul Neff Verlag KG, pg 54
Verlag Neues Leben, pg 54
Niederosterreichisches Pressehaus Druck- und Verlagsgesellschaft mbH, pg 54
Verlag der Oesterreichischen Akademie der Wissenschaften (OEAW), pg 55
Promedia Verlagsges mbH, pg 56

Verlag Styria, pg 58
Edition Tau u Tau Type Druck Verlags-und Handels GmbH, pg 58
Verlag Carl Ueberreuter GmbH, pg 58
Wieser Verlag, pg 60
Zirkular - Verlag der Dokumentationsstelle fuer neuere oesterreichische Literatur, pg 60
Paul Zsolnay Verlag GmbH, pg 60

Bangladesh
The University Press Ltd, pg 61

Belarus
Belaruskaya Encyklapedyya, pg 62
Interdigest Publishing House, pg 62

Belgium
Centre Aequatoria, pg 63
Libraire Ancienne Noel Anselot, pg 63
Maison d'Editions Baha'ies ASBL, pg 63
Le Cri Editions, pg 66
Editions Delta SA, pg 66
EPO Publishers, Printers, Booksellers, pg 67
Espace de Libertes, pg 67
Editions Labor, pg 69
Uitgeverij Lannoo NV, pg 69
Claude Lefrancq Editeur, pg 70
Editions Lessius ASBL, pg 70
Scoop Infotex NV, pg 73
Standaard Uitgeverij, pg 73
Uitgeverij De Garve, pg 74
Zuid En Noord VZW, pg 75

Brazil
AGIR S/A Editora, pg 77
Editora Alfa Omega Ltda, pg 77
Ars Poetica Editora Ltda, pg 78
Artes e Oficios Editora Ltda, pg 78
Editora Bertrand Brasil Ltda, pg 78
Editora Companhia das Letras/ Editora Schwarcz Ltda, pg 80
Companhia Editora Forense, pg 81
Editora Elevacao, pg 81
Fundacao Cultural Avatar, pg 82
Global Editora e Distribuidora Ltda, pg 82
Editora Globo SA, pg 82
Editora Harbra Ltda, pg 83
Icone Editora Ltda, pg 83
Imago Editora Importacao e Exportacao Ltda, pg 84
LDA Editores Ltda, pg 84
Livraria Nobel S/A, pg 85
Editora Marco Zero Ltda, pg 86
Editora Mercuryo Ltda, pg 86
Editora Mundo Cristao, pg 87
Editora Nova Alexandria Ltda, pg 87
Editora Nova Fronteira SA, pg 87
Editora Objetiva Ltda, pg 87
Pallas Editora e Distribuidora Ltda, pg 88
Paulinas Editorial, pg 88
Ediouro Publicacoes, SA, pg 89
Distribuidora Record de Servicos de Imprensa SA, pg 89
Editora Revan Ltda, pg 89
Editora Rocco Ltda, pg 89
Spala Editora Ltda, pg 90
Editora Vecchi SA, pg 92
Jorge Zahar Editor, pg 92

Bulgaria

EA EOOD, pg 94
Publishing House Hristo Botev, pg 94
Kibea Publishing Co, pg 95
Makros 2000 - Plovdiv, pg 95
Musica Publishing House Ltd, pg 95
Pet Plus, pg 96
Reporter, pg 96
Sluntse Publishing House, pg 97
Trud - Izd kasta, pg 97
Ivan Vazov Publishing House, pg 97

Chile

Arrayan Editores, pg 98
Ediciones Bat, pg 99
Pehuen Editores Ltda, pg 100

China

Beijing Publishing House, pg 101
China Film Press, pg 102
China Ocean Press, pg 102
Foreign Languages Press, pg 104
Fudan University Press, pg 104
Jilin Science & Technology Publishing House, pg 105
Kunlun Publishing House, pg 106
Nanjing University Press, pg 106
People's Fine Arts Publishing House, pg 106
Qingdao Publishing House, pg 107
SDX (Shenghuo-Dushu-Xinzhi) Joint Publishing Co, pg 107
Shanghai Calligraphy & Painting Publishing House, pg 108
Shanghai Far East Publishers, pg 108
World Affairs Press, pg 109
Xinhua Publishing House, pg 109

Colombia

Editorial Oveja Negra Ltda, pg 112
Editorial Panamericana, pg 112

The Democratic Republic of the Congo

Centre Protestant d'Editions et de Diffusion (CEDI), pg 114
Presses Universitaires du Zaiire (PUZ), pg 114

Costa Rica

Ediciones Promesa, pg 116

Cote d'Ivoire

Universite d'Abidjan, pg 117
Centre d'Edition et de Diffusion Africaines, pg 117
Heritage Publishing Co, pg 117

Croatia

Graficki zavod Hrvatske, pg 118
Otokar Kersovani, pg 119
Skolska Knjiga, pg 119

Cuba

Holguin, Ediciones, pg 120
Editora Politica, pg 120

Cyprus

Andreou Chr Publishers, pg 121

Czech Republic

Atlantis sro, pg 122
Columbus, pg 123
Doplnek, pg 123
Euromedia Group-Odeon, pg 123
Horacek Ladislav-Paseka, pg 123
Nakladatelstvi Jota spol sro, pg 124
Jan Kanzelsberger Praha, pg 124
Karmelitanske Nakladatelstvi, pg 124
Knihovna A Tiskarna Pro Nevidome, pg 124
Lidove Noviny Publishing House, pg 125
Melantrich, akc spol, pg 125
Mlada fronta, pg 125
Prostor, nakladatelstvi sro, pg 127
Vitalis sro, pg 128
Votobia sro, pg 128

Denmark

Aschehoug Dansk Forlag A/S, pg 129
Dansk Historisk Handbogsforlag ApS, pg 130
Christian Ejlers' Forlag aps, pg 131
Grevas Forlag, pg 131
Gyldendalske Boghandel - Nordisk Forlag A/S, pg 131
Forlaget Hovedland, pg 132
Nyt Nordisk Forlag Arnold Busck A/S, pg 133
Scandinavia Publishing House, pg 134
Det Schonbergske Forlag A/S, pg 134
Unitas Forlag, pg 135

Dominican Republic

Pontificia Universidad Catolica Madre y Maestra, pg 136

Ecuador

CIESPAL (Centro Internacional de Estudios Superiores de Comunicacion para America Latina), pg 136
Corporacion Editora Nacional, pg 136

Egypt (Arab Republic of Egypt)

Dar El Shorouk, pg 138
Middle East Book Centre, pg 138

El Salvador

Clasicos Roxsil Editorial SA de CV, pg 138

Estonia

Eesti Entsuklopeediakirjastus, pg 139
Kirjastus Kunst, pg 139
Olion Publishers, pg 140
Oue Eesti Raamat, pg 140
Sinisukk, pg 140

Ethiopia

Addis Ababa University Press, pg 140

Finland

Recallmed Oy, pg 144
Schildts Forlags AB, pg 144
Soderstroms Forlag, pg 144

France

Academie Nationale de Reims, pg 145
Editions Actes Sud, pg 145
ADPF Publications, pg 145
Alsatia SA, pg 146
Editions ALTESS, pg 146
L'Amitie par le Livre, pg 146
Edition Anthese, pg 147
L'Arche Editeur, pg 147
Editions de l'Archipel, pg 147
Editions de l'Armancon, pg 147
Armenia Editions, pg 147
Editions de l'Atelier, pg 148
Editions Atlantica Seguier, pg 148
Editions Balland, pg 149
Beauchesne Editeur, pg 149
Editions Andre Bonne, pg 150
Editions Calmann-Levy SA, pg 152
Editions Canope, pg 152
Editions Champ Vallon, pg 153
Le Cherche Midi Editeur, pg 154
Corsaire Editions, pg 156
Editions Criterion, pg 156
Culture et Bibliotheque pour Tous, pg 156
Les Dossiers d'Aquitaine, pg 159
Edition1, pg 160
Librairie Artheme Fayard, pg 163
Editions Des Femmes, pg 163
Editions Gallimard, pg 164
Paul Geuthner Librairie Orientaliste, pg 165
Editions Jean Paul Gisserot, pg 165
Librairie Guenegaud, pg 166
Hachette Pratiques, pg 167
Editions Herault, pg 167
Pierre Horay Editeur, pg 168
Indigo & Cote-Femmes Editions, pg 168
Kailash Editions, pg 170
Michel Lafon Publishing, pg 171
Letouzey et Ane Editeurs, pg 171
Le Livre de Poche-L G F (Librairie Generale Francaise), pg 173
Editions Lyonnaises d'Art et d'Histoire, pg 173
Editions Medianes, pg 175
Mercure de France SA, pg 175
Editions Albin Michel, pg 175
Nil Editions, pg 177
Noir Sur Blanc, pg 177
Editions Odile Jacob, pg 177
Payot & Rivages, pg 179
Editions Jean Picollec, pg 179
Editions Christian Pirot, pg 180
Le Pre-aux-clercs, pg 180
Presses de la Cite, pg 180
Presses de la Renaissance, pg 181
Presses Universitaires de France (PUF), pg 181
Editions Pygmalion, pg 182
Editions Sand et Tchou SA, pg 184
Editions de Septembre, pg 184
Service Technique pour l'Education, pg 184
Editions du Seuil, pg 184
Somogy editions d'art, pg 185
Editions Stock, pg 186
Les Editions de la Table Ronde, pg 186
Editions Tiresias Michel Reynaud, pg 187
Editions Vague Verte, pg 188

French Polynesia

Scoop/Au Vent des Iles, pg 189

Germany

Asclepios Edition Lothar Baus, pg 194
Bechtle Graphische Betriebe und Verlagsgesellschaft GmbH und Co KG, pg 198
Verlag Beleke KG, pg 198
Bergstadtverlag Wilhelm Gottlieb Korn GmbH Wuerzburg, pg 199
C Bertelsmann Verlag GmbH, pg 199
Bertelsmann Lexikon Verlag GmbH, pg 200
Edition Klaus Blahak Dr Fredric Kroll, pg 202
Blanvalet VerlagGmbH, pg 202
Brandenburgisches Verlagshaus in der Dornier Medienholding GmbH, pg 204
R Brockhaus Verlag, pg 204
Hans Christians Druckerei und Verlag GmbH & Co KG, pg 208
Claassen Verlag GmbH, pg 209
CMA Edition, pg 209
Deutsche Verlags-Anstalt GmbH (DVA), pg 212
Deutscher Taschenbuch Verlag GmbH & Co KG (dtv), pg 213
Edition Dia, pg 214
Maximilian Dietrich Verlag, pg 214
Dietz Verlag Berlin GmbH, pg 215
Edition Diskord, pg 215
Drei Ulmen Verlag GmbH, pg 216
Verlagsgruppe Droemer Knaur GmbH & Co KG, pg 216
Karl Elser Druck GmbH, pg 216
Duncker und Humblot GmbH, pg 217
Egmont vgs verlagsgesellschaft mbH, pg 218
Ehrenwirth Verlag GmbH, pg 218
Engelhorn Verlag GmbH, pg 220
Ernst Kabel Verlag GmbH, pg 221
Europa Verlag GmbH, pg 222
Europaeische Verlagsanstalt GmbH & Rotbuch Verlag GmbH & Co KG, pg 222
Evangelische Verlagsanstalt GmbH, pg 222
Fischer Taschenbuch Verlag GmbH, pg 225
FVA-Frankfurter Verlagsanstalt GmbH, pg 226
Franz-Sales-Verlag, pg 226
Verlag Freies Geistesleben, pg 227
Gatzanis Verlags GmbH, pg 228
Genius Verlag, pg 228
Gerth Medien GmbH, pg 229
Wilhelm Goldmann Verlag GmbH, pg 230
Grabert-Verlag, pg 230
Guetersloher Verlagshaus, pg 232
von Hase & Koehler Verlag KG, pg 234
Edition Hentrich Druck & Verlag Gebr Hentrich und Tank GmbH & Co KG, pg 236
F A Herbig Verlagsbuchhandlung GmbH, pg 236
Wilhelm Heyne Verlag, pg 237
Anton Hiersemann, Verlag, pg 237
Hoffmann und Campe Verlag GmbH, pg 238
Hohenrain-Verlag GmbH, pg 239
Iudicium Verlag GmbH, pg 242
J Ch Mellinger Verlag GmbH, pg 242
JKL Publikationen GmbH, pg 243
Verlag Kiepenheuer & Witsch, pg 245
Gustav Kiepenheuer Verlag GmbH, pg 245
Verlag Kleine Schritte Ursula Dahm & Co, pg 246
Albrecht Knaus Verlag GmbH, pg 247
Knesebeck Verlag, pg 247
Koehler & Amelang Verlagsgesellschaft, pg 248
K F Koehler Verlag GmbH, pg 248
Anton H Konrad Verlag, pg 249
Karin Kramer Verlag, pg 250
Verlag Ernst Kuhn, pg 250
Dr Gisela Lermann, pg 253
Liebenzeller Mission, GmbH, Abt. Verlag, pg 254

Christoph Links Verlag - LinksDruck GmbH, pg 254
Gustav Luebbe Verlag, pg 256
Verlagsgruppe Luebbe GmbH & Co KG, pg 256
Matthias-Gruenewald-Verlag GmbH, pg 258
Medien-Verlag Bernhard Gregor GmbH, pg 258
Merlin Verlag Andreas Meyer Verlags GmbH und Co KG, pg 259
Militzke Verlag, pg 260
Miranda-Verlag Stefan Ehlert, pg 260
Monia Verlag, pg 261
Munzinger-Archiv GmbH Archiv fuer publizistische Arbeit, pg 262
Musikantiquariat und Dr Hans Schneider Verlag GmbH, pg 262
Muster-Schmidt Verlag, pg 263
Edition Nautilus Verlag, pg 263
Verlag Neue Stadt GmbH, pg 264
Verlag Neues Leben GmbH, pg 264
Neuthor - Verlag, pg 265
Nicolaische Verlagsbuchhandlung Beuermann GmbH, pg 265
nymphenburger, pg 266
Georg Olms Verlag AG, pg 267
Oreos Verlag GmbH, pg 267
Pahl-Rugenstein Verlag Nachfolger-GmbH, pg 267
Pal Verlagsgesellschaft mbH, pg 267
Pfalzische Verlagsanstalt GmbH, pg 269
Piper Verlag GmbH, pg 270
Propylaeen Verlag, Zweigniederlassung Berlin der Ullstein Buchverlage GmbH, pg 272
Verlag Friedrich Pustet GmbH & Co Kg, pg 272
Quell Verlag, pg 273
Quintessenz Verlags-GmbH, pg 273
Reclam Verlag Leipzig, pg 274
E Reinhold Verlag, pg 275
Eugen Salzer-Verlag GmbH & Co KG, pg 278
Verlag der Sankt-Johannis-Druckerei C Schweickhardt, pg 278
K G Saur Verlag GmbH, A Gale/Thomson Learning Company, pg 278
Sax-Verlag Beucha, pg 278
Verlag Schnell und Steiner GmbH, pg 281
Schoeffling & Co, pg 281
Ferdinand Schoeningh Verlag GmbH, pg 281
Schott Musik International GmbH & Co KG, pg 281
Schueren Verlag GmbH, pg 281
Siedler Verlag, pg 283
Sonnentanz-Verlag Roland Kron, pg 284
Springer Science+Business Media GmbH & Co KG, pg 284
Stapp Verlag Wolfgang Stapp, pg 286
C A Starke Verlag, pg 287
Steidl Verlag, pg 287
Stern-Verlag Janssen & Co, pg 288
Sternberg-Verlag bei Ernst Franz, pg 288
Steyler Verlag, pg 288
Suedverlag GmbH, pg 288
Suhrkamp Verlag, pg 289
Thauros Verlag GmbH, pg 290
Toleranz Verlag, Nielsen Frederic W, pg 291
Trotzdem-Verlags Genossenschaft eG, pg 292

Tuduv Verlagsgesellschaft mbH, pg 292
Ullstein Heyne List GmbH & Co KG, pg 293
Edition Curt Visel, pg 296
Weber Zucht & Co, pg 298
Wichern Verlag GmbH, pg 299
Das Wunderhorn Verlag GmbH, pg 301
Wunderlich Verlag, pg 301
Verlag Clemens Zerling, pg 302

Ghana

Africa Christian Press, pg 303
Asempa Publishers, pg 303
Bureau of Ghana Languages, pg 303
Ghana Publishing Corporation, pg 304
Waterville Publishing House, pg 305

Greece

D I Arsenidis Publications, pg 306
Dorikos Publishing House, pg 306
Govostis Publishing SA, pg 307
Denise Harvey, pg 308
Hestia-I D Hestia-Kollaros & Co Corporation, pg 308
Ianos, pg 308
Irini Publishing House - Vassilis G Katsikeas SA, pg 308
Kastaniotis Editions SA, pg 309
Kedros Publishers, pg 309
Knossos Publications, pg 309
Minoas SA, pg 310
Odysseas Publications Ltd, pg 311
Pagoulatos Bros, pg 311
Patakis Publishers, pg 311
Vlassis, pg 313

Hong Kong

Hong Kong University Press, pg 317
Ming Pao Publications Ltd, pg 318

Hungary

Europa Konyvkiado, pg 321
Zenemukiado Vallalat, pg 325

Iceland

Almenna Bokafelagid, pg 325
Bokautgafan Orn og Orlygur ehf, pg 325
Idunn, pg 325
Skjaldborg Ltd, pg 326

India

Ananda Publishers Pvt Ltd, pg 328
APH Publishing Corp, pg 328
Asian Educational Services, pg 329
The Bangalore Printing & Publishing Co Ltd, pg 329
Bharatiya Vidya Bhavan, pg 330
Chowkhamba Sanskrit Series Office, pg 332
The Christian Literature Society, pg 332
Disha Prakashan, pg 333
Enkay Publishers Pvt Ltd, pg 334
Geeta Prakashan, pg 335
Gyan Publishing House, pg 335
HarperCollins Publishers India Pty Ltd, pg 335
Heritage Publishers, pg 335
Hind Pocket Books Private Ltd, pg 336
Indian Society for Promoting Christian Knowledge (ISPCK), pg 337
Intertrade Publications Pvt Ltd, pg 338

Islamic Publishing House, pg 338
Jaico Publishing House, pg 338
Kairali Children's Book Trust, pg 339
Kairalee Mudralayam, pg 339
Kali For Women, pg 339
Kitab Ghar, pg 339
Sri Ramakrishna Math, pg 341
Ministry of Information & Broadcasting, pg 341
Natraj Prakashan, Publishers & Exporters, pg 343
Navajivan Trust, pg 343
Omsons Publications, pg 344
Oxford University Press, pg 344
Panjab University Publication Bureau, pg 344
People's Publishing House (P) Ltd, pg 345
Popular Prakashan Pvt Ltd, pg 345
Prabhat Prakashan, pg 345
Pratibha Pratishthan, pg 345
Promilla & Publishers, pg 345
Pustak Mahal, pg 345
Reliance Publishing House, pg 346
Sasta Sahitya Mandal, pg 348
Sat Sahitya Prakashan, pg 348
Shaibya Prakashan Bibhag, pg 349
Sharda Prakashan, pg 349
Sterling Publishers Pvt Ltd, pg 350
Theosophical Publishing House, pg 351
UBS Publishers Distributors Ltd, pg 351
Vidya Puri, pg 352
Vidyarthi Mithram Press, pg 352

Indonesia

Pustaka Utama Grafiti, PT, pg 356
Tintamas Indonesia PT, pg 356

Ireland

Attic Press Ltd, pg 358
Ballinakella Press, pg 358
Brandon Book Publishers Ltd, pg 358
Edmund Burke Publisher, pg 358
The Children's Press, pg 358
The Collins Press, pg 358
Dee-Jay Publications, pg 359
Dominican Publications, pg 359
Gill & Macmillan Ltd, pg 360
The Hannon Press, pg 361
The Lilliput Press Ltd, pg 361
Mercier Press Ltd, pg 362
Mount Eagle Publications Ltd, pg 362
The O'Brien Press Ltd, pg 362
On Stream Publications Ltd, pg 362
Roberts Rinehart Publishers, pg 363
Tir Eolas, pg 363
Town House & Country House, pg 364
Veritas Co Ltd, pg 364
Wolfhound Press Ltd, pg 364

Israel

Am Oved Publishers Ltd, pg 365
Bitan Publishers Ltd, pg 365
Boostan Publishing House, pg 365
Breslov Research Institute, pg 365
Edanim Publishers Ltd, pg 366
Feldheim Publishers Ltd, pg 367
Freund Publishing House Ltd, pg 367
Gefen Publishing House Ltd, pg 367
Hakibbutz Hameuchad Publishing House Ltd, pg 367
Karni Publishers Ltd, pg 369
Ma'ariv Book Guild (Sifriat Ma'ariv), pg 370

The Magnes Press, pg 370
Massada Press Ltd, pg 370
Rav Kook Institute, pg 371
Rubin Mass Ltd, pg 371
Steimatzky Group Ltd, pg 372
Urim Publications, pg 373
Yad Vashem - The Holocaust Martyrs' & Heroes' Remembrance Authority, pg 373
Zmora-Bitan, Publishers Ltd, pg 374

Italy

Adea Edizioni, pg 374
Adelphi Edizioni SpA, pg 374
Rosellina Archinto Editore, pg 376
Baha'i, pg 377
Belforte Editore Libraio srl, pg 377
Edizioni Bora SNC di E Brandani & C, pg 379
Cappelli Editore, pg 380
Editrice Il Castoro, pg 380
Cittadella Editrice, pg 382
Edizioni Cultura della Pace, pg 383
Edizioni la Scala, pg 387
Edizioni l'Arciere SRL, pg 387
Arnaldo Forni Editore SRL, pg 389
Edizioni Frassinelli SRL, pg 389
Edizioni Futuro SRL, pg 389
Galzerano Editore, pg 390
Garzanti Libri, pg 390
Gius Laterza e Figli SpA, pg 391
Piero Gribaudi Editore, pg 391
Kaos Edizioni SRL, pg 394
Lalli Editore SRL, pg 394
Longanesi & C, pg 396
Lubrina, pg 396
Giuseppe Maimone Editore, pg 397
Tommaso Marotta Editore Srl, pg 397
Editrice Massimo SAS di Crespi Cesare e C, pg 397
Edizioni Mediterranee SRL, pg 398
Messaggero di San Antonio, pg 398
Arnoldo Mondadori Editore SpA, pg 398
Edumond Le Monnier, pg 399
Moretti & Vitali Editori srl, pg 399
Gruppo Ugo Mursia Editore SpA, pg 400
Nardini Editore srl, pg 400
La Nuova Italia Editrice SpA, pg 401
Editrice Nuovi Autori, pg 401
Passigli Editori, pg 402
Daniela Piazza Editore, pg 403
Pizzicato Edizioni Musicali, pg 403
Il Quadrante SRL, pg 404
RCS Rizzoli Libri SpA, pg 405
Rusconi Libri Srl, pg 406
Salerno Editrice SRL, pg 406
Edizioni San Paolo SRL, pg 407
Sperling e Kupfer Editori SpA, pg 409
Sugarco Edizioni SRL, pg 409
Edizioni del Teresianum, pg 410
Editrice Uomini Nuovi, pg 411
Vivere In SRL, pg 412
Viviani Editore srl, pg 412
Who's Who In Italy srl, pg 412

Jamaica

Eureka Press Ltd, pg 413
Jamaica Publishing House Ltd, pg 414
Ian Randle Publishers Ltd, pg 414

Japan

Chikuma Shobo Publishing Co Ltd, pg 416
Hayakawa Publishing Inc, pg 418
Hoikusha Publishing Co Ltd, pg 418

PUBLISHERS

The Hokuseido Press, pg 418
Iwanami Shoten, Publishers, pg 419
Kaisei-Sha Publishing Co Ltd, pg 420
Kinokuniya Co Ltd (Publishing Department), pg 421
Kokudo-Sha Co Ltd, pg 421
Poplar Publishing Co Ltd, pg 425
Shimizu-Shoin, pg 427
Shincho-Sha Co Ltd, pg 427
Tokyo Tosho Co Ltd, pg 430

Kenya

Foundation Books Ltd, pg 434
Kenway Publications Ltd, pg 434
Paulines Publications-Africa, pg 435
Sasa Sema Publications Ltd, pg 435
Transafrica Press, pg 436

Democratic People's Republic of Korea

The Foreign Language Press Group, pg 436
Grand People's Study House, pg 436

Republic of Korea

Chung Rim Publishing Co Ltd, pg 438
Hongik Media Plus Ltd, pg 439
Hw Moon Publishing Co, pg 439
Ke Mong Sa Publishing Co Ltd, pg 440
Koreaone Press Inc, pg 440

Latvia

Artava Ltd, pg 444
Nordik/Tapals Publishers Ltd, pg 445
Preses Nams, pg 445

Lesotho

Saint Michael's Mission Social Centre, pg 447

Lithuania

Baltos Lankos, pg 449
Tyto Alba Publishers, pg 450
Vaga Ltd, pg 450

Luxembourg

Guy Binsfeld & Co Sarl, pg 450
Cahiers Luxembourgeois, pg 451

Macau

Livros Do Oriente, pg 452

The Former Yugoslav Republic of Macedonia

Strk Publishing House, pg 453
Zumpres Publishing Firm, pg 453

Malawi

Christian Literature Association in Malawi, pg 454
Dzuka Publishing Co Ltd, pg 454

Malaysia

Pelanduk Publications (M) Sdn Bhd, pg 457
Pustaka Cipta Sdn Bhd, pg 458
University of Malaya, Department of Publications, pg 459

Mali

EDIM SA, pg 460

Malta

Fondazzjoni Patrimonju Malti, pg 460

Mauritius

Editions de l'Ocean Indien Ltd, pg 461
EDITIONS Le Printemps, pg 461
Vizavi Editions, pg 461

Mexico

Aguilar Altea Taurus Alfaguara SA de CV, pg 462
Editorial Avante SA de Cv, pg 462
Publicaciones Cruz O SA, pg 463
Editorial Diana SA de CV, pg 464
Edamex SA de CV, pg 464
Lasser Press Mexicana SA de CV, pg 467
Pangea Editores, Sa de CV, pg 470
Editorial Patria SA de CV, pg 470
Ediciones Promesa, SA de CV, pg 470
Ediciones Suromex SA, pg 472
Javier Vergara Editor SA de CV, pg 473

Monaco

Les Editions du Rocher, pg 474

Morocco

Editions Al-Fourkane, pg 474
Association de la Recherche Historique et Sociale, pg 474

Myanmar

Sarpay Beikman Public Library, pg 476

Netherlands

Uitgeverij Ambo BV, pg 477
Uitgeverij Anthos, pg 477
Uitgeverij de Arbeiderspers, pg 477
Uitgeverij Arena BV, pg 478
Uitgeverij Balans, pg 478
De Boekerij BV, pg 479
Uitgeverij Bohn Stafleu Van Loghum BV, pg 479
BZZTOH Publishers, pg 480
Castrum Peregrini Presse, pg 480
Uitgeverij Christofoor, pg 480
Uitgeverij Conserve, pg 481
Uitgeversmaatschappij Ad Donker BV, pg 481
Elmar BV, pg 482
Uitgeverij Vrij Geesteslevan, pg 482
Mets & Schilt Uitgevers en Distributeurs, pg 486
J M Meulenhoff bv, pg 486
Uitgeverij Maarten Muntinga, pg 486
De Prom, pg 488
Em Querido's Uitgeverij BV, pg 488
A J G Strengholt's Boeken, Anno 1928, BV, pg 489
Tirion Uitgevers BV, pg 490
Uitgeverij Verloren, pg 492

New Zealand

Auckland University Press, pg 493
Brick Row Publishing Co Ltd, pg 494
Canterbury University Press, pg 494
Cape Catley Ltd, pg 495
The Caxton Press, pg 495
Clerestory Press, pg 495
Exisle Publishing Ltd, pg 496
Fraser Books, pg 496
Graphic Educational Publications, pg 496
HarperCollins Publishers (New Zealand) Ltd, pg 497
Hazard Press Ltd, pg 497
Heritage Press Ltd, pg 497
Hodder Moa Beckett Publishers Ltd, pg 497
Huia Publishers, pg 497
David Ling Publishing, pg 498
Longacre Press, pg 498
Nestegg Books, pg 499
Oxford University Press, pg 499
R P L Books, pg 500
Reed Publishing (NZ) Ltd, pg 500
University of Otago Press, pg 502
Bridget Williams Books Ltd, pg 502

Nigeria

Adebara Publishers Ltd, pg 503
Ahmadu Bello University Press Ltd, pg 503
Alliance West African Publishers & Co, pg 503
Aromolaran Publishing Co Ltd, pg 503
Black Academy Press, pg 503
Cross Continent Press Ltd, pg 504
CSS Bookshops, pg 504
Delta Publications (Nigeria) Ltd, pg 504
Educational Research & Study Group, pg 504
Fourth Dimension Publishing Co Ltd, pg 504
JAD Publishers Ltd, pg 505
Longman Nigeria Plc, pg 505
New Africa Publishing Company Ltd, pg 505
Nwamife Publishers Ltd, pg 506
Obafemi Awolowo University Press Ltd, pg 506
Obobo Books, pg 506
Onibon-Oje Publishers, pg 506
Joe-Tolalu & Associates, pg 507
University of Lagos Press, pg 507
University Publishing Co, pg 507
Vantage Publishers International Ltd, pg 507
John West Publications Co Ltd, pg 507

Norway

Andresen & Butenschon AS, pg 508
Atheneum Forlag A/S, pg 508
Det Norske Samlaget, pg 508
Fonna Forlag L/L, pg 509
Genesis Forlag, pg 509
Gyldendal Norsk Forlag A/S, pg 509
Lunde Forlag AS, pg 509
Luther Forlag A/S, pg 509
Chr Schibsteds Forlag A/S, pg 510
Snofugl Forlag, pg 510

Pakistan

Sheikh Muhammad Ashraf Publishers, pg 511
East & West Publishing Co, pg 512
Hamdard Foundation Pakistan, pg 512
Malik Sirajuddin & Sons, pg 513
National Institute of Historical & Cultural Research, pg 514
Publishers United Pvt Ltd, pg 514

Papua New Guinea

Kristen Press, pg 515

SUBJECT INDEX

Philippines

Communication Foundation for Asia Media Group (CFAMG), pg 518
Galleon Publications, pg 519
New Day Publishers, pg 520
Solidaridad Publishing House, pg 521

Poland

Spoldzielnia Wydawnicza 'Czytelnik', pg 522
Wydawnictwo DiG, pg 522
Instytut Historii Nauki PAN, pg 523
Iskry - Publishing House Ltd spotka zoo, pg 523
'Ksiazka i Wiedza' Spotdzielnia Wydawniczo-Handlowa, pg 524
Wydawnictwo Literackie, pg 524
Wydawnictwo Lodzkie, pg 524
Ludowa Spoldzielnia Wydawnicza, pg 524
Magnum Publishing House Ltd, pg 524
Norbertinum, pg 524
Ossolineum Zaklad Narodowy im Ossolinskich - Wydawnictwo, pg 525
Panstwowy Instytut Wydawniczy (PIW), pg 525
Wydawnictwa Uniwersytetu Warszawskiego, pg 527
Videograf II Sp z o o Zaklad Poracy Chronionej, pg 527

Portugal

Apostolado da Oracao Secretariado Nacional, pg 528
Brasilia Editora (J Carvalho Branco), pg 529
Publicacoes Europa-America Lda, pg 531
Editorial Franciscana, pg 531
Impala, pg 532
Imprensa Nacional-Casa da Moeda, pg 532
Livraria Apostolado da Imprensa, pg 533
Editora Livros do Brasil Sarl, pg 533
Livraria Tavares Martins, pg 533
Edicoes Ora & Labora, pg 534
Paulinas, pg 534
Editorial Presenca, pg 535
Quimera Editores Lda, pg 535
Realizacoes Artis, pg 535
Edicoes Salesianas, pg 535
Edicoes Talento, pg 536
Vega-Publicacao e Distribuicao de Livros e Revistas, Lda, pg 536
Livraria Verdade e Vida Editora, pg 536

Puerto Rico

Editorial Cultural Inc, pg 537

Romania

Artemis Verlag, pg 538
The Center for Romanian Studies, pg 539
Editura Clusium, pg 539
Editure Ion Creanga, pg 539
Editura DOINA SRL, pg 539
Enzyklopadie Verlag, pg 539
Editura Excelsior Art, pg 539
Humanitas Publishing House, pg 540
Editura Meridiane, pg 540
Editura Minerva, pg 541
Editura Muzicala, pg 541
Editura Niculescu, pg 541
Pallas-Akademia Editura, pg 541

SUBJECT INDEX — BOOK

Pandora Publishing House, pg 541
Grupul Editorial RAO, pg 542
RAO International Publishing Co, pg 542
Saeculum IO, pg 542
Est-Samuel Tastet Verlag, pg 542
Editura Univers SA, pg 543
Vestala Verlag, pg 543
Vremea Publishers Ltd, pg 543

Russian Federation

BLIC, russko-Baltijskij informaciionnyj centr, AO, pg 544
FGUP Izdatelstvo Mashinostroenie, pg 544
Izdatelstvo Khudozhestvennaya Literatura, pg 545
Izdatelskii Dom Kompozitor, pg 546
Publishing House Limbus Press, pg 546
Izdatelstvo Mezdunarodnye Otnoshenia, pg 546
Izdatelstvo Molodaya Gvardia, pg 546
Progress Publishers, pg 548
Raduga Publishers, pg 548
Top Secret Collection Publishers, pg 549
Voyenizdat, pg 549

Saudi Arabia

Dar Al-Shareff for Publishing & Distribution, pg 550

Senegal

Les Nouvelles Editions Africaines du Senegal NEAS, pg 551

Serbia and Montenegro

Izdavacka Organizacija Rad, pg 553

Singapore

McGallen & Bolden Associates, pg 557

Slovakia

Danubiaprint, pg 559
Luc vydavatelske druzstvo, pg 559
Vydavatel'stvo SFVU Pallas, pg 560
Slovenska Narodna Kniznica, Martin, pg 560
Smena Publishing House, pg 560

Slovenia

Cankarjeva Zalozba, pg 561
Mladinska Knjiga International, pg 561
Zalozba Obzorja d d Maribor, pg 562

South Africa

Jonathan Ball Publishers, pg 562
Galago Publishing Pty Ltd, pg 564
HAUM (Hollandsch Afrikaansche Uitgevers Maatschappij), pg 564
Human & Rousseau (Pty) Ltd, pg 564
Ithemba! Publishing, pg 565
Mayibuye Books, pg 566
New Africa Books (Pty) Ltd, pg 567
Queillerie Publishers, pg 568
Ravan Press (Pty) Ltd, pg 568
Shuter & Shooter (Pty) Ltd, pg 568
University of KwaZulu-Natal Press, pg 569
Witwatersrand University Press, pg 570

Spain

Publicacions de l'Abadia de Montserrat, pg 570
Agencia Espanola de Cooperacion, pg 571
Altea, Taurus, Alfaguara SA, pg 572
Sociedad de Educacion Atenas SA, pg 573
Ediciones B, SA, pg 574
Editorial Biblioteca Nueva SL, pg 574
Central Catequistica Salesiana (CCS), pg 576
Circe Ediciones, SA, pg 577
Compania Literaria, pg 577
Complutense, SA Editorial, pg 577
Rafael Dalmau, Editor, pg 578
EDERSA (Editoriales de Derecho Reunidas SA), pg 580
Editorial Espasa-Calpe SA, pg 582
Fundacion de Estudios Libertarios Anselmo Lorenzo, pg 584
Editorial Gedisa SA, pg 584
Editorial Iberia, SA, pg 586
Iberico Europea de Ediciones SA, pg 586
Ediciones Internacionales Universitarias SA, pg 588
Junta de Castilla y Leon Consejeria de Educacion y Cultura, pg 588
Editorial Juventud SA, pg 588
Laertes SA de Ediciones, pg 588
LID Editorial Empresarial, SL, pg 589
Ediciones Maeva, pg 590
Edicions de la Magrana SA, pg 590
Ediciones Martinez-Roca SA, pg 591
La Mascara, SL Editorial, pg 591
Ediciones Minotauro, pg 591
Editorial Moll SL, pg 592
Mundo Negro Editorial, pg 592
Noguer y Caralt Editores SA, pg 593
Oikos-Tau SA Ediciones, pg 593
Ediciones del Oriente y del Mediterraneo, pg 594
El Paisaje Editorial, pg 594
Ediciones Palabra SA, pg 595
Editorial Parthenon Communication, SL, pg 595
Editorial Peregrino SL, pg 595
Editorial El Perpetuo Socorro, pg 596
Pirene Editorial, sal, pg 596
Plaza y Janes Editores SA, pg 596
Editorial Portic SA, pg 596
Pre-Textos, pg 596
Editorial Presencia Gitana, pg 597
San Pablo Ediciones, pg 598
Ediciones Sigueme SA, pg 600
Silex Ediciones, pg 600
Editorial Sintesis, SA, pg 600
Ediciones Siruela SA, pg 600
Edicions 62, pg 600
Grup 62, pg 600
Ediciones SM, pg 600
Ediciones Temas de Hoy, SA, pg 601
Editorial Sal Terrae, pg 602
Tusquets Editores, pg 603
Editorial Txertoa, pg 603
Ultramar Editores SA, pg 603
Javier Vergara Editor SA, pg 604
Ediciones Versal SA, pg 604
Vinaches Lopez, Luisa, pg 605

Sri Lanka

Law Publishers Association, pg 607
Waruni Publishers, pg 607

Sudan

Khartoum University Press, pg 608

Sweden

Fischer & Co, pg 611
Gidlunds Bokforlag, pg 612
Bokfoerlaget Natur och Kultur, pg 613
Svenska Foerlaget liv & ledarskap ab, pg 616
Wahlstrom & Widstrand, pg 616
Zindermans AB, pg 617

Switzerland

Editions L'Age d'Homme - La Cite, pg 617
Ammann Verlag & Co, pg 617
Arche Verlag AG, Raabe und Vitali, pg 617
Athenaeum Verlag AG, pg 618
Editions de la Baconniere SA, pg 618
Blaukreuz-Verlag Bern, pg 619
Brunnen-Verlag Basel, pg 620
Caux Books, pg 620
Caux Edition SA, pg 620
Editions l'Eau Vive, pg 622
eFeF-Verlag/Edition Ebersbach, pg 622
Kanisius Verlag, pg 626
Kranich-Verlag, Dres AG & H R Bosch-Gwalter, pg 627
Limmat Verlag, pg 628
Maihof Verlag, pg 628
La Maison de la Bible, pg 628
Les Editions Noir sur Blanc, pg 629
Orell Fuessli Buchhandlungs AG, pg 630
Verlag Friedrich Reinhardt AG, pg 632
Rodera-Verlag der Cardun AG, pg 632
Scherz Verlag AG, pg 633
3 Dimension World (3-D-World), pg 635
Zbinden Druck und Verlag AG, pg 637

Taiwan, Province of China

Asian Culture Co Ltd, pg 638
Campus Evangelical Fellowship, Literature Department, pg 639
Chung Hwa Book Co Ltd, pg 639
Commonwealth Publishing Company Ltd, pg 639
Grimm Press Ltd, pg 640
Linking Publishing Company Ltd, pg 641
Newton Publishing Company Ltd, pg 641
Wu Nan Book Co Ltd, pg 642

United Republic of Tanzania

Central Tanganyika Press, pg 643
East African Publishing House, pg 643
Eastern Africa Publications Ltd, pg 643

Thailand

Bannakit Trading, pg 645
Thai Watana Panich Co, Ltd, pg 646

Togo

Editions Akpagnon, pg 646

Tunisia

Academie Tunisienne des Sciences, des Lettres et des Arts Beit El Hekma, pg 647
Dar Arabia Lil Kitab, pg 648
Maison Tunisienne de l'Edition, pg 648

Turkey

Afa Yayincilik Sanayi Tic AS, pg 648
Kubbealti Akademisi Kultur ve Sasat Vakfi, pg 650
Parantez Yayinlari Ltd, pg 651
Remzi Kitabevi, pg 651
Sabah Kitaplari, pg 651

Uganda

Fountain Publishers Ltd, pg 652

United Arab Emirates

Motivate Publishing, pg 654

United Kingdom

Absolute Press, pg 655
Acair Ltd, pg 655
Allison & Busby, pg 656
Alun Books, pg 657
Amber Lane Press Ltd, pg 657
Anvil Books Ltd, pg 658
Arcadia Books Ltd, pg 659
Argyll Publishing, pg 659
Atlas Press, pg 661
Aurum Press Ltd, pg 661
Avero Publications Ltd, pg 662
BBC Audiobooks, pg 663
Belitha Press Ltd, pg 664
Bishopsgate Press Ltd, pg 666
Blackstaff Press, pg 666
John Blake Publishing Ltd, pg 667
Bloomsbury Publishing PLC, pg 668
The Book Guild Ltd, pg 668
Books of Zimbabwe Publishing Co (Pvt) Ltd, pg 669
Breedon Books Publishing Company Ltd, pg 670
Brewin Books Ltd, pg 671
Bryntirion Press, pg 672
Calder Publications Ltd, pg 673
Cambridge University Press, pg 674
Camden Press Ltd, pg 674
Canongate Books Ltd, pg 674
Cardiff Academic Press, pg 675
Carlton Publishing Group, pg 675
Cassell & Co, pg 675
Kyle Cathie Ltd, pg 676
The Chrysalis Press, pg 679
James Clarke & Co Ltd, pg 680
Cockbird Press, pg 680
Colourpoint Books, pg 681
Leo Cooper, pg 683
Countyvise Ltd, pg 683
Creation Books, pg 683
Crossbridge Books, pg 684
CTBI Publications, pg 685
James Currey Ltd, pg 685
Debrett's Ltd, pg 687
Andre Deutsch Ltd, pg 687
Dunedin Academic Press, pg 688
Eland Publishing Ltd, pg 690
Element Books Ltd, pg 690
Aidan Ellis Publishing, pg 690
The Eurospan Group, pg 692
Ex Libris Press, pg 693
Helen Exley Giftbooks, pg 693
Faber & Faber Ltd, pg 694
Fourth Estate, pg 696
Gairm Publications, pg 698
Garnet Publishing Ltd, pg 698
George Mann Publications, pg 699

PUBLISHERS

Global Oriental Ltd, pg 700
Gollancz/Witherby, pg 701
Granta Books, pg 702
Gwasg Gwenffrwd, pg 703
Peter Halban Publishers Ltd, pg 703
Robert Hale Ltd, pg 704
Hamish Hamilton Ltd, pg 704
HarperCollins UK, pg 705
The Harvill Press, pg 705
Headline Book Publishing Ltd, pg 706
William Heinemann Ltd, pg 707
Helicon Publishing Ltd, pg 707
Helion & Co, pg 707
Highland Books Ltd, pg 708
Hodder & Stoughton General, pg 709
Hodder & Stoughton Religious, pg 709
Honeyglen Publishing Ltd, pg 710
Honno Welsh Women's Press, pg 710
Institute of Irish Studies, The Queens University of Belfast, pg 713
Institute of Physics Publishing, pg 713
Isis Publishing Ltd, pg 714
The Islamic Texts Society, pg 715
Janus Publishing Co Ltd, pg 716
Jarrold Publishing, pg 716
Johnson Publications Ltd, pg 716
John Jones Publishing Ltd, pg 716
Michael Joseph Ltd, pg 716
Jay Landesman Ltd, pg 719
Libris Ltd, pg 720
Linen Hall Library, pg 721
The Littman Library of Jewish Civilization, pg 721
Luath Press Ltd, pg 722
The Lutterworth Press, pg 723
Macmillan Audio Books, pg 723
Mainstream Publishing Co (Edinburgh) Ltd, pg 724
Mango Publishing, pg 725
The Mansk Svenska Publishing Co Ltd, pg 725
Marcham Manor Press, pg 725
Melrose Press Ltd, pg 726
Methuen, pg 727
Metro Books, pg 727
Monarch Books, pg 729
Muze UK Ltd, pg 730
National Portrait Gallery Publications, pg 731
Neil Wilson Publishing Ltd, pg 732
NMS Enterprises Ltd - Publishing, pg 733
W W Norton & Company Ltd, pg 734
The Oleander Press, pg 735
Michael O'Mara Books Ltd, pg 735
Omnibus Press, pg 735
Orion Publishing Group Ltd, pg 736
Peter Owen Ltd, pg 737
Oxford University Press, pg 737
Parapress Ltd, pg 738
Pavilion Books Ltd, pg 739
Phaidon Press Ltd, pg 741
Piatkus Books, pg 741
Pitkin Unichrome Ltd, pg 743
Plantin Publishers, pg 743
Plexus Publishing Ltd, pg 743
Pluto Press, pg 743
Polybooks Ltd, pg 744
Profile Books Ltd, pg 746
Quartet Books Ltd, pg 746
Quiller Publishing Ltd, pg 747
Ramsay Head Press, pg 747
Random House UK Ltd, pg 747
Rivers Oram Press, pg 750
Robson Books, pg 750
Roundhouse Group, pg 751

Routledge, pg 751
The Rubicon Press, pg 752
Saqi Books, pg 754
SCM-Canterbury Press Ltd, pg 755
Scottish Cultural Press, pg 755
Seren, pg 756
Serpent's Tail Ltd, pg 756
Shepheard-Walwyn (Publishers) Ltd, pg 757
Shire Publications Ltd, pg 757
Sidgwick & Jackson Ltd, pg 757
Silver Link Publishing Ltd, pg 758
Simon & Schuster Ltd, pg 758
Charles Skilton Ltd, pg 758
Smith Settle Ltd, pg 758
Colin Smythe Ltd, pg 759
Snowbooks Ltd, pg 759
The Society for Promoting Christian Knowledge (SPCK), pg 759
Souvenir Press Ltd, pg 759
SPA Books Ltd, pg 759
Spellmount Ltd Publishers, pg 760
Rudolf Steiner Press, pg 761
Sutton Publishing Ltd, pg 762
Sydney Jary Ltd, pg 762
Tabb House, pg 762
Thistle Press, pg 765
Thomson Gale, pg 765
Time Warner Book Group UK, pg 766
Titan Books Ltd, pg 766
Transworld Publishers Ltd, pg 766
Tuckwell Press Ltd, pg 767
Ulverscroft Large Print Books Ltd, pg 768
United Writers Publications Ltd, pg 768
University of Hertfordshire Press, pg 768
Veloce Publishing Ltd, pg 769
Viking, pg 770
Virago Press, pg 770
Virgin Publishing Ltd, pg 770
Welsh Academic Press, pg 772
Wimbledon Publishing Company Ltd, pg 774
The Windrush Press Ltd, pg 774
The Women's Press Ltd, pg 775
Yale University Press London, pg 776

Uruguay

Rosebud Ediciones, pg 778
Ediciones Trilce, pg 778

Zambia

Aafzam Ltd, pg 781
Apple Books, pg 781
Multimedia Zambia, pg 781
Zambia Educational Publishing House, pg 782

Zimbabwe

College Press Publishers (Pvt) Ltd, pg 783

BIOLOGICAL SCIENCES

Albania

NL SH, pg 1
State Textbook Publishing House, pg 1

Argentina

Editorial Hemisferio Sur SA, pg 6
Editorial Medica Panamericana SA, pg 7
Editoria Universitaria de la Patagonia, pg 9

SUBJECT INDEX

Australia

Aboriginal Studies Press, pg 10
Australian Academy of Science, pg 13
Australian Marine Conservation Society Inc (AMCS), pg 13
Robert Berthold Photography, pg 14
Bureau of Resource Sciences, pg 16
CSIRO Publishing (Commonwealth Scientific & Industrial Research Organisation), pg 19
Emerald City Books, pg 21
Encyclopaedia Britannica (Australia) Inc, pg 21
Illert Publications, pg 26
McGraw-Hill Australia Pty Ltd, pg 31
Pearson Education Australia, pg 36
Queen Victoria Museum & Art Gallery Publications, pg 38
Three Sisters Publications Pty Ltd, pg 43
University of New South Wales Press Ltd, pg 44

Austria

Bethania Verlag, pg 48
IAEA - International Atomic Energy Agency, pg 52
Verlag der Oesterreichischen Akademie der Wissenschaften (OEAW), pg 55
Oesterreichischer Bundesverlag Gmbh, pg 55
Springer-Verlag Wien, pg 58

Belarus

Belaruskaya Encyklapedyya, pg 62
Narodnaya Asveta, pg 62

Belgium

Artel, pg 63
Campinia Media VZW, pg 64
Editions De Boeck-Larcier SA, pg 66
Leuven University Press, pg 70
Presses agronomiques de Gembloux ASBL, pg 72

Brazil

ARTMED Editora, pg 78
Editora Edgard Blucher Ltda, pg 79
Centro de Estudos Juridicosdo Para (CEJUP), pg 79
EDUSC - Editora da Universidade do Sagrado Coracao, pg 81
Empresa Brasileira de Pesquisa Agropecuaria, pg 81
Fundacao Sao Paulo, EDUC, pg 82
Editora Guanabara Koogan SA, pg 83
Editora Harbra Ltda, pg 83
Interlivros Edicoes Ltda, pg 84
Editora Nova Fronteira SA, pg 87
Pearson Education Do Brasil, pg 88
Editora Scipione Ltda, pg 90

Bulgaria

Gea-Libris Publishing House, pg 94
Makros 2000 - Plovdiv, pg 95
Medicina i Fizkultura EOOD, pg 95
Pensoft Publishers, pg 96

Chile

Arrayan Editores, pg 98
Pontificia Universidad Catolica de Chile, pg 100

China

Beijing Medical University Press, pg 101
Beijing University Press, pg 101
Chemical Industry Press, pg 101
China Agriculture Press, pg 102
China Forestry Publishing House, pg 102
China Ocean Press, pg 102
Fudan University Press, pg 104
Henan Science & Technology Publishing House, pg 105
Higher Education Press, pg 105
International Academic Publishers (IAP), pg 105
Jilin Science & Technology Publishing House, pg 105
Nanjing University Press, pg 106
Qingdao Publishing House, pg 107
Science Press, pg 107
South China University of Science & Technology Press, pg 108
Tianjin Science & Technology Publishing House, pg 108
Wuhan University Press, pg 109
Zhejiang University Press, pg 109

Colombia

Fundacion Universidad de la Sabana Ediciones INSE, pg 111
Editorial Libros y Libres SA, pg 112
McGraw-Hill Colombia, pg 112
Universidad Nacional Abierta y a Distancia, pg 113

Costa Rica

Centro Agronomico Tropical de Investigacion y Ensenanza (CATIE), pg 115
Editorial Nacional de Salud y Seguridad Social Ednass, pg 116
Union Mundial para la Naturaleza (UICN), Oficina Regional para Mesoamerica, pg 116
Editorial de la Universidad de Costa Rica, pg 116

Czech Republic

Aventinum Nakladatelstvi spol sro, pg 122
Granit sro, pg 123
Mendelova zemedelska a lesnicka univerzita v Brne, pg 125
Narodni Muzeum, pg 126

Denmark

FADL's Forlag A/S, pg 131
Gads Forlag, pg 131

Dominican Republic

Pontificia Universidad Catolica Madre y Maestra, pg 136

Estonia

Academic Library of Tallinn Pedagogical University, pg 139
Eesti Entsuklopeediakirjastus, pg 139
Valgus Publishers, pg 140

Finland

Yliopistopaino/Helsinki University Press, pg 145

France

Editions Breal, pg 151
CNRS Editions, pg 155
Corsaire Editions, pg 156
Doin Editeurs, pg 159

923

Editions Espaces 34, pg 162
L'Expansion Scientifique Francaise, pg 162
Gammaprim, pg 165
Editions Hatier SA, pg 167
INRA Editions (Institut National de la Recherche Agronomique), pg 168
Editions INSERM, pg 168
InterEditions, pg 169
IRD Editions, pg 169
Editions Lavoisier, pg 171
Masson-Williams et Wilkins, pg 174
Ouest Editions, pg 178
Polytechnica SA, pg 180
Presses Universitaires de Caen, pg 181
Librairie Vuibert, pg 189

Germany

AOL-Verlag Frohmut Menze, pg 193
Aulis Verlag Deubner & Co KG, pg 195
Bayerischer Schulbuch-Verlag GmbH, pg 198
Blackwell Wissenschafts-Verlag GmbH, pg 201
Cornelsen Verlag GmbH & Co OHG, pg 210
Dareschta Consulting und Handels GmbH, pg 210
Verlag Harri Deutsch, pg 211
Dreisam Ratgeber in der Rutsker Verlag GmbH, pg 216
Ecomed Verlagsgesellschaft AG & Co KG, pg 218
Fachverlag Schiele & Schoen GmbH, pg 223
Franckh-Kosmos Verlags-GmbH & Co, pg 226
Gebrueder Borntraeger Science Publishers, pg 228
Walter de Gruyter GmbH & Co KG, pg 231
Lehrmittelverlag Wilhelm Hagemann GmbH, pg 233
Verlag Waldemar Kramer, pg 250
Logos-Verlag Literatur & Layout GmbH, pg 255
Margraf Verlag, pg 257
Verlag Stephanie Naglschmid, pg 263
Verlag Natur & Wissenschaft Harro Hieronimus & Dr Jurgen Schmidt, pg 263
Neumann Verlag, pg 264
Rainar Nitzsche Verlag, pg 265
Nusser Verlag, pg 266
Verlag Dr Friedrich Pfeil, pg 269
pmi Verlag, pg 270
Psychologie Verlags Union GmbH, pg 272
Quelle und Meyer Verlag GmbH & Co, pg 273
E Schweizerbart'sche Verlagsbuchhandlung (Naegele und Obermiller), pg 282
Springer Science+Business Media GmbH & Co KG, pg 284
Stiefel Eurocart GmbH, pg 288
Georg Thieme Verlag KG, pg 291
Urania Verlag mit Ravensburger Ratgebern, pg 294
UTB fuer Wissenschaft Uni Taschenbuecher GmbH, pg 294
Volk und Wissen Verlag GmbH & Co, pg 296
VWB-Verlag fur Wissenschaft & Bildung, Amand Aglaster, pg 297
Wiley-VCH Verlag GmbH, pg 300
Wissenschaftliche Verlagsgesellschaft mbH, pg 300
Verlag Zeitschrift fur Naturforschung, pg 302

Ghana

Ghana Universities Press (GUP), pg 304
Sedco Publishing Ltd, pg 305

Greece

Athina, Mary Mavrogiannis, pg 306
Kalentis & Sia, pg 308

Holy See (Vatican City State)

Pontificia Academia Scientiarum, pg 314

Hong Kong

Hong Kong University Press, pg 317
Times Publishing (Hong Kong) Ltd, pg 319

Hungary

Akademiai Kiado, pg 320
Nemzeti Tankoenyvkiado, pg 323

India

Addison-Wesley Pte Ltd, pg 327
Affiliated East West Press Pvt Ltd, pg 327
Agricole Publishing Academy, pg 327
Allied Book Centre, pg 328
Arihant Publishers, pg 328
B I Publications Pvt Ltd, pg 329
Bani Mandir, Book-Sellers, Publishers & Educational Suppliers, pg 329
BS Publications, pg 331
BSMPS - M/s Bishen Singh Mahendra Pal Singh, pg 331
Daya Publishing House, pg 333
Frank Brothers & Co Publishers Ltd, pg 334
IBD Publisher & Distributors, pg 336
International Book Distributors, pg 338
Narosa Publishing House, pg 342
Oxford & IBH Publishing Co Pvt Ltd, pg 344
Pointer Publishers, pg 345
Publications & Information Directorate, CSIR, pg 345
Rastogi Publications, pg 346
Regency Publications, pg 346
Reliance Publishing House, pg 346
Scientific Book Agency, pg 348
Scientific Publishers India, pg 349
Sita Books & Periodicals Pvt Ltd, pg 349
South Asian Publishers Pvt Ltd, pg 350
Sultan Chand & Sons Pvt Ltd, pg 350
Vidya Puri, pg 352
Vidyarthi Mithram Press, pg 352
S Viswanathan (Printers & Publishers) Pvt Ltd, pg 352

Ireland

Royal Dublin Society, pg 363
Royal Irish Academy, pg 363

Israel

Hakibbutz Hameuchad Publishing House Ltd, pg 367
The Israel Academy of Sciences & Humanities, pg 368
Open University of Israel, pg 371

Italy

Apimondia, pg 375
Archimede Edizioni, pg 376
Casa Editrice Giuseppe Principato Spa, pg 380
CEDAM (Casa Editrice Dr A Milani), pg 380
CG Ediz Medico-Scientifiche, pg 381
La Cultura Sociologica, pg 384
Demetra SRL, pg 385
Edagricole - Edizioni Agricole, pg 385
Edi.Ermes srl, pg 388
Editoriale Fernando Folini, pg 389
Edizioni GB, pg 390
Ibis, pg 392
Casa Editrice Libraria Idelson di G Gnocchi, pg 392
Casa Editrice Maccari (CEM), pg 396
Monduzzi Editore SpA, pg 399
Accademia Naz dei Lincei, pg 400
Editoriale Olimpia SpA, pg 401
Paravia Bruno Mondadori Editori, pg 402
Piccin Nuova Libraria SpA, pg 403
Edizioni Universitarie Romane, pg 406
Editrice San Marco SRL, pg 407
Editoriale Scienza, pg 407
Societa Editrice la Goliardica Pavese SRL, pg 408
Tilgher-Genova sas, pg 410
Transeuropa, pg 410
Unipress, pg 411
Zanichelli Editore SpA, pg 412

Japan

Baifukan Co Ltd, pg 415
Bun-ichi Sogo Shuppan, pg 415
CMC Publishing Co Ltd, pg 416
Hirokawa Publishing Co, pg 418
Hokuryukan Co Ltd, pg 418
Kyoritsu Shuppan Co Ltd, pg 422
Maruzen Co Ltd, pg 422
Mita Press, Mita Industrial Co Ltd, pg 422
Nakayama Shoten Co Ltd, pg 423
Nippon Hoso Shuppan Kyokai (NHK Publishing), pg 424
Sangyo-Tosho Publishing Co Ltd, pg 426
Tokai University Press, pg 429
Tokyo Kagaku Dojin Co Ltd, pg 429
Toppan Co Ltd, pg 430
Tsukiji Shokan Publishing Co, pg 430

Kazakstan

Gylym, Izd-Vo, pg 432
Al-Farabi Kazakh National University, pg 432

Kenya

African Centre for Technology Studies (ACTS), pg 433
Heinemann Kenya Ltd (EAEP), pg 434
Kenya Medical Research Institute (KEMRI), pg 435
Lake Publishers & Enterprises Ltd, pg 435

Democratic People's Republic of Korea

Academy of Sciences Publishing House, pg 436
Korea Science and Encyclopedia Publishing House, pg 436

Latvia

Lielvards Ltd, pg 445
Preses Nams, pg 445

Lebanon

Arab Scientific Publishers BP, pg 445

Lithuania

Academia, pg 448
Klaipedos Universiteto Leidykla, pg 449
Mokslo ir enciklopediju leidybos institutas, pg 449

The Former Yugoslav Republic of Macedonia

Medis, Skopje, pg 452

Malaysia

Penerbit Universiti Sains Malaysia, pg 458

Mexico

AGT Editor SA, pg 462
Centro de Estudios Mexicanos y Centroamericanos, pg 463
Colegio de Postgraduados en Ciencias Agricolas, pg 463
Editorial El Manual Moderno SA de CV, pg 464
Fondo de Cultura Economica, pg 465
Editorial Limusa SA de CV, pg 467
Editorial Minutiae Mexicana SA, pg 468
Organizacion Cultural LP SA de CV, pg 469
Pangea Editores, Sa de CV, pg 470
Pearson Educacion de Mexico, SA de CV, pg 470
Ediciones Cientificas La Prensa Medica Mexicana SA de CV, pg 470
Sistemas Tecnicos de Edicion SA de CV, pg 472
Universo Editorial SA de CV Edicion de Libros Revistas y Periodicos, pg 473

Republic of Moldova

Editura Lumina, pg 473

Namibia

Desert Research Foundation of Namibia (DRFN), pg 476

Netherlands

Backhuys Publishers BV, pg 478
A A Balkema Uitgevers BV, pg 478
Brill Academic Publishers, pg 479
Elsevier Science BV, pg 482
Hagen & Stam Uitgeverij Ten, pg 483
IOS Press BV, pg 484
LCG Malmberg BV, pg 485
V S P International Science Publishers, pg 491
VU Boekhandel/Uitgeverij BV, pg 492

PUBLISHERS

New Zealand
Canterbury University Press, pg 494
Craig Potton Publishing, pg 495
Wendy Crane Books, pg 495
ESA Publications (NZ) Ltd, pg 496
Landcare Research NZ, pg 497
Nelson Price Milburn Ltd, pg 499
SIR Publishing, pg 501

Nigeria
JAD Publishers Ltd, pg 505
Riverside Communications, pg 507
Vantage Publishers International Ltd, pg 507

Norway
Universitetsforlaget, pg 511

Pakistan
HMR Publishing Co, pg 512
National Book Foundation, pg 513
Publishers United Pvt Ltd, pg 514

Philippines
National Museum of the Philippines, pg 520
Rex Bookstores & Publishers, pg 520
San Carlos Publications, pg 521
SIBS Publishing House Inc, pg 521
UST Publishing House, pg 521

Poland
Instytut Historii Nauki PAN, pg 523
Ossolineum Zaklad Narodowy im Ossolinskich - Wydawnictwo, pg 525
Polish Scientific Publishers PWN, pg 525
PZWL Wydawnictwo Lekarskie Ltd, pg 526
Towarzystwo Naukowe w Toruniu, pg 527
Wydawnictwa Uniwersytetu Warszawskiego, pg 527

Portugal
Constancia Editores, SA, pg 530
Dinalivro, pg 530
Gradiva-Publicacnoes Lda, pg 532
Instituto de Investigacao Cientifica Tropical, pg 532
Editora McGraw-Hill de Portugal Lda, pg 533
Editora Replicacao Lda, pg 535

Romania
Editura Academiei Romane, pg 538
Editura Dacia, pg 539
Enzyklopadie Verlag, pg 539
Editura Niculescu, pg 541
Editura Stiintifica SA, pg 542

Russian Federation
Izdatelstvo Mir, pg 546
Nauka Publishers, pg 547
Izdatel'stvo Nizhegorodskogo Gosudarstvennogo Univ, pg 547
Izdatelstvo Prosveshchenie, pg 548
Voronezh State University Publishers, pg 549
Izdatelstvo Vysshaya Shkola, pg 549

Saudi Arabia
King Saud University, pg 550

Singapore
McGallen & Bolden Associates, pg 557
Reed Elsevier, South East Asia, pg 557
Taylor & Francis Asia Pacific, pg 558
World Scientific Publishing Co Pte Ltd, pg 559

Slovenia
Mladinska Knjiga International, pg 561
Zalozba Obzorja d d Maribor, pg 562

South Africa
Clever Books, pg 563
Educum Publishers Ltd, pg 563
National Botanical Institute, pg 567
Oceanographic Research Institute, pg 567
University of KwaZulu-Natal Press, pg 569

Spain
Editorial AEDOS SA, pg 571
Cedel, Ediciones Jose O Avila Monteso ES, pg 576
Ediciones de la Universidad Complutense de Madrid, pg 577
Comunidad Autonoma de Madrid, Servicio de Documentacion y Publicaciones, pg 578
Consello da Cultura Galega - CCG, pg 578
Didaco Comunicacion y Didactica, SA, pg 579
Instituto de Estudios Riojanos, pg 583
EUNSA (Ediciones Universidad de Navarra SA), pg 583
Idea Books, SA, pg 587
McGraw-Hill/Interamericana de Espana SAU, pg 591
Mundi-Prensa Libros SA, pg 592
Editorial la Muralla SA, pg 592
Oikos-Tau SA Ediciones, pg 593
Ediciones Omega SA, pg 594
Editorial Paraninfo SA, pg 595
Instituto Provincial de Investigaciones y Estudios Toledanos (IPIET), pg 597
Rueda, SL Editorial, pg 598
Servicio de Publicaciones Universidad de Cordoba, pg 599
Editorial Sintesis, SA, pg 600
Trea Ediciones, SL, pg 602
Universidad de Granada, pg 603
Universitat de Valencia Servei de Publicacions, pg 604
Xunta de Galicia, pg 605

Sweden
Studentlitteratur AB, pg 616

Switzerland
Bibliographisches Institut & F A Brockhaus AG, pg 619
Birkhauser Verlag AG, pg 619
Christiana-Verlag, pg 620
Verlag Harri Deutsch, pg 622
S Karger AG, Medical & Scientific Publishers, pg 626
Presses Polytechniques et Universitaires Romandes, PPUR, pg 631
Sabe AG Verlagsinstitut, pg 633

Taiwan, Province of China
Chien Chen Bookstore Publishing Company Ltd, pg 639
Ho-Chi Book Publishing Co, pg 640
Shy Mau & Shy Chaur Publishing Co Ltd, pg 641
SMC Publishing Inc, pg 642
Wu Nan Book Co Ltd, pg 642
Yi Hsien Publishing Co Ltd, pg 642

United Republic of Tanzania
DUP (1996) Ltd, pg 643

Thailand
Graphic Art (28) Co Ltd, pg 645

Ukraine
Naukova Dumka Publishers, pg 653
Osnova, Kharkov State University Press, pg 653
Osvita, pg 654

United Kingdom
Association for Science Education, pg 661
Biocommerce Data Ltd, pg 665
BIOS Scientific Publishers Ltd, pg 665
BLA Publishing Ltd, pg 666
Cambridge University Press, pg 674
E W Classey Ltd, pg 680
Current Science Group, pg 685
Elsevier Ltd, pg 691
The Eurospan Group, pg 692
W H Freeman & Co Ltd, pg 697
Harley Books, pg 705
Harvard University Press, pg 705
Hodder Education, pg 709
Horizon Scientific Press, pg 710
Imperial College Press, pg 712
Intercept Ltd, pg 714
International Bee Research Association, pg 714
JAI Press Ltd, pg 715
Jones & Bartlett International, pg 716
Kluwer Academic/Plenum Publishers, pg 718
Manson Publishing Ltd, pg 725
Micelle Press, pg 727
Open University Worldwide, pg 736
Orion Publishing Group Ltd, pg 736
Packard Publishing Ltd, pg 737
Pearson Education, pg 739
Portland Press Ltd, pg 745
Research Studies Press Ltd (RSP), pg 749
SAGE Publications Ltd, pg 753
Sheffield Academic Press Ltd, pg 757
Stokesby House Publications, pg 761
The Tarragon Press, pg 765
Wiley Europe Ltd, pg 773
Wimbledon Publishing Company Ltd, pg 774
WIT Press, pg 774

Uruguay
Hemisferio Sur Edicion Agropecuaria, pg 777
A Monteverde y Cia SA, pg 777

Venezuela
Editorial Biosfera CA, pg 779
Sociedad Fondo Editorial Cenamec, pg 779

Viet Nam
Science & Technics Publishing House, pg 780

Zimbabwe
College Press Publishers (Pvt) Ltd, pg 783

SUBJECT INDEX

BUSINESS

Albania
NL SH, pg 1
State Textbook Publishing House, pg 1

Argentina
Editorial Cangallo SACI, pg 4
Depalma SRL, pg 5
Diana Argentina SA, Editorial, pg 5
Javier Vergara Editor SA, pg 9

Australia
Allen & Unwin Pty Ltd, pg 11
Boolarong Press, pg 15
Butterworths Australia Ltd, pg 16
Crista International, pg 18
D&B Marketing Pty Ltd, pg 19
Deakin University Press, pg 19
Dryden Press, pg 20
Elsevier Australia, pg 21
Emerald City Books, pg 21
The Federation Press, pg 22
Hale & Iremonger Pty Ltd, pg 24
James Nicholas Publishers Pty Ltd, pg 27
Law Book Co Information Services, pg 28
Thomas C Lothian Pty Ltd, pg 29
Marketing Focus, pg 30
Nimaroo Publishers, pg 33
OTEN (Open Training & Education Network), pg 34
Pearson Education Australia, pg 36
Press for Success, pg 37
Prospect Media Pty Ltd, pg 37
The Real Estate Institute of Australia, pg 39
RMIT Publishing, pg 39
Stirling Press, pg 42
Tertiary Press, pg 43
Thorpe-Bowker, pg 43
VCTA Publishing, pg 45
Woodlands Publications, pg 47
Worsley Press, pg 47
Wrightbooks Pty Ltd, pg 47

Austria
Bohmann Druck und Verlag GmbH & Co KG, pg 49
Compass-Verlag GmbH, pg 49
Horst Knapp Finanznachrichten, pg 53
Linde Verlag Wien GmbH, pg 53
Springer-Verlag Wien, pg 58
Verband der Wissenschaftlichen Gesellschaften Oesterreichs (VWGOe), pg 59
WUV/Service Fachverlag, pg 60

Azerbaijan
Sada, Literaturno-Izdatel'skij Centr, pg 60

Barbados
Business Tutors, pg 62

Belarus
Kavaler Publishers, pg 62

SUBJECT INDEX

Belgium
Academia Press, pg 62
Editions de la Chambre de Commerce et d'Industrie SA (ECCI), pg 65
Creadif, pg 65
Editions De Boeck-Larcier SA, pg 66
Documenta CV, pg 66
Roularta Books NV, pg 72
Scoop Infotex NV, pg 73
Wolters Kluwer Belgie NV, pg 74

Bermuda
The Bermudian Publishing Co, pg 75

Bosnia and Herzegovina
Svjetlost, pg 76

Botswana
Morula Press, Business School of Botswana, pg 76

Brazil
Editora Atlas SA, pg 78
Berkeley Brasil Editora Ltda, pg 78
Editora Elevacao, pg 81
Editora Globo SA, pg 82
Livraria Nobel S/A, pg 85
Makron Books do Brasil Editora Ltda, pg 86
Cia Editora Nacional, pg 87
Editora Nova Fronteira SA, pg 87
Editora Ortiz SA, pg 88
Pearson Education Do Brasil, pg 88
Livraria Pioneira Editora/Enio Matheus Guazzelli e Cia Ltd, pg 88
Distribuidora Record de Servicos de Imprensa SA, pg 89
Saraiva SA, Livreiros Editores, pg 90
Summus Editorial Ltda, pg 91
Fundacao Getulio Vargas, pg 92

Bulgaria
Aratron, IK, pg 93
Ciela Publishing House, pg 93
Dolphin Press Group Ltd, pg 94
Foi-Commerce, pg 94
Interpres, pg 95
Makros 2000 - Plovdiv, pg 95
Naouka i Izkoustvo, Ltd, pg 95
Pensoft Publishers, pg 96
Seven Hills Publishers, pg 96
Todor Kableshkov University of Transport, pg 97

China
Beijing Publishing House, pg 101
China Foreign Economic Relations & Trade Publishing House, pg 102
China Labour Publishing House, pg 102
China Machine Press (CMP), pg 102
China Materials Management Publishing House, pg 102
China Textile Press, pg 103
CITIC Publishing House, pg 103
Fudan University Press, pg 104
Heilongjiang Science & Technology Press, pg 105
Jilin Science & Technology Publishing House, pg 105
Qingdao Publishing House, pg 107
Shandong Science & Technology Press, pg 107
Shandong University Press, pg 108
Shanghai Far East Publishers, pg 108
Shanghai Foreign Language Education Press, pg 108
Yunnan University Press, pg 109
Zhejiang University Press, pg 109

Colombia
McGraw-Hill Colombia, pg 112
Editorial Oveja Negra Ltda, pg 112
Editorial Panamericana, pg 112
Universidad Nacional Abierta y a Distancia, pg 113

Costa Rica
Academia de Centro America, pg 114

Croatia
Masmedia, pg 118
Prosvjeta, pg 119

Czech Republic
Karolinum, nakladatelstvi, pg 124
Pragma 4, pg 126
PressArt Nakladatelstvi, pg 127
Svoboda Servis GmbH, pg 127
SystemConsult, pg 127

Denmark
Fremad A/S, pg 131
Ingenioeren/Boger, pg 132
Samfundslitteratur, pg 134
Schultz Information, pg 134
Forlaget Thomson A/S, pg 135

Dominican Republic
Pontificia Universidad Catolica Madre y Maestra, pg 136

Egypt (Arab Republic of Egypt)
Dar El Shorouk, pg 138
Ummah Press, pg 138

Estonia
Olion Publishers, pg 140

Finland
Kauppakaari Oyj, pg 142
Yritystieto Oy - Foretagsdata AB, pg 145

France
Bottin SA, pg 151
Editions des Cahiers Bourbonnais, pg 151
De Vecchi Editions SA, pg 157
Editions d'Organisation, pg 160
Les Editions ESF, pg 160
InterEditions, pg 169
Editions Legislatives, pg 171
Maxima Laurent du Mesnil Editeur, pg 174
Pearson Education France, pg 179
Les Presses du Management, pg 181
Sofiac (Societe Francaise des Imprimeries Administratives Centrales), pg 185

Germany
AZ Bertelsmann Direct GmbH, pg 196
Bank-Verlag GmbH, pg 197
Bayerischer Schulbuch-Verlag GmbH, pg 198
Verlag Beleke KG, pg 198
Berliner Wissenschafts-Verlag GmbH (BWV), pg 199
Bertelsmann Lexikon Verlag GmbH, pg 200
Campus Verlag GmbH, pg 207
Chmielorz GmbH Verlag, pg 208
Compact Verlag GmbH, pg 209
Deutscher Adressbuch-Verlag fuer Wirtschaft und Verkehr GmbH, pg 212
Deutscher Betriebswirte-Verlag GmbH, pg 212
Deutscher Fachverlag GmbH, pg 212
Deutscher Wirtschaftsdienst John von Freyend GmbH, pg 214
Verlagsgruppe Droemer Knaur GmbH & Co KG, pg 216
Eppinger-Verlag OHG, pg 220
Fachbuchverlag Pfanneberg & Co, pg 223
Fachverlag fur das graphische Gewerbe GmbH, pg 223
Friedrich Kiehl Verlag GmbH, pg 227
Betriebswirtschaftlicher Verlag Dr Th Gabler, pg 228
Alfons W Gentner Verlag GmbH & Co KG, pg 228
Graefe und Unzer Verlag GmbH, pg 230
Dr Curt Haefner-Verlag GmbH, pg 233
Haufe Mediengruppe, pg 235
Rudolf Haufe Verlag GmbH & Co KG, pg 235
Hofbauer, Christoph und Trojanow Ilia, Akademischer Verlag Muenchen, pg 238
Hans Holzmann Verlag GmbH und Co KG, pg 239
Huss-Verlag GmbH, pg 240
Huthig GmbH & Co KG, pg 240
IDW Verlag GmbH, pg 241
IKO Verlag fur Interkulturelle Kommunikation, pg 241
Inno Vatio Verlags AG, pg 241
Koelner Universitaets-Verlag GmbH, pg 248
W Kohlhammer GmbH, pg 248
Leitfadenverlag Verlag Dieter Sudholt, pg 253
Libertas- Europaeisches Institut GmbH, pg 254
Logophon Verlag und Bildungsreisen GmbH, pg 255
Hermann Luchterhand Verlag GmbH, pg 255
Metropolis- Verlag fur Okonomie, Gesellschaft und Politik GmbH, pg 259
Verlag Neue Wirtschafts-Briefe GmbH & Co, pg 264
Nomos Verlagsgesellschaft mbH und Co KG, pg 265
Physica-Verlag, pg 270
Psychologie Verlags Union GmbH, pg 272
Rationalisierungs-Kuratorium der Deutschen Wirtschaft eV (RKW), pg 273
Verlag Norman Rentrop, pg 275
Ruhland Verlag Gimblt, pg 277
Schaeffer-Poeschel Verlag fuer Wirtschaft Steuern Recht, pg 279
Verlag Dr Otto Schmidt KG, pg 280
Erich Schmidt Verlag GmbH & Co, pg 280
Schulz-Kirchner Verlag GmbH, pg 282
Societaets-Verlag, pg 283
Springer Science+Business Media GmbH & Co KG, pg 284
Telex-Verlag Jaeger & Waldmann GmbH, pg 289
Wirtschaftsverlag Carl Ueberreuter, pg 293
UTB fuer Wissenschaft Uni Taschenbuecher GmbH, pg 294
Verlag Moderne Industrie AG & Co KG, pg 295
Verlagsgruppe Jehle-Rehm GmbH, pg 295
Walhalla Fachverlag GmbH & Co KG Praetoria, pg 297
WEKA Firmengruppe GmbH & Co KG, pg 298
Wer liefert was? GmbH, pg 299
WRS Verlag Wirtschaft, Recht und Steuern GmbH & Co KG, pg 301
Fachbuchverlag Armin W Wuth, pg 301

Greece
Hestia-I D Hestia-Kollaros & Co Corporation, pg 308
Kastaniotis Editions SA, pg 309
Kritiki Publishing, pg 309
Patakis Publishers, pg 311
Sakkoulas Publications SA, pg 312
Vivliothiki Eftychia Galeou, pg 313

Haiti
Editions Caraibes SA, pg 314

Hong Kong
The Chinese University Press, pg 316
Chung Hwa Book Co (HK) Ltd, pg 316
Joint Publishing (HK) Co Ltd, pg 317
Ming Pao Publications Ltd, pg 318
SCMP Book Publishing Ltd, pg 319
Wellday Ltd, pg 320
Yazhou Zhoukan Ltd, pg 320

Hungary
KJK-Kerszov, pg 322
Kossuth Kiado RT, pg 322
Lang Kiado, pg 322
Novorg International Szervezo es Kiado kft, pg 323

India
Academic Publishers, pg 327
Addison-Wesley Pte Ltd, pg 327
Asia Pacific Business Press Inc, pg 328
Associated Publishing House, pg 329
S Chand & Co Ltd, pg 331
Frank Brothers & Co Publishers Ltd, pg 334
General Book Depot, pg 335
Himalaya Publishing House, pg 335
Indian Council of Social Science Research (ICSSR), pg 336
Law Publishers, pg 340
National Council of Applied Economic Research, Publications Division, pg 342
National Institute of Industrial Research (NIIR), pg 343
Omsons Publications, pg 344
Orient Paperbacks, pg 344
Oxford University Press, pg 344
Reliance Publishing House, pg 346
Roli Books Pvt Ltd, pg 347
SAGE Publications India Pvt Ltd, pg 347
Scientific Book Agency, pg 348
Sita Books & Periodicals Pvt Ltd, pg 349

PUBLISHERS

Somaiya Publications Pvt Ltd, pg 349
South Asia Publications, pg 349
Sultan Chand & Sons Pvt Ltd, pg 350
Tata McGraw-Hill Publishing Co Ltd, pg 351
N M Tripathi Pvt Ltd Publishers & Booksellers, pg 351
Vidya Puri, pg 352
Viva Books Pvt Ltd, pg 352
A H Wheeler & Co Ltd, pg 353

Indonesia

PT Bulan Bintang, pg 354
Bumi Aksara PT, pg 354
Dinastindo, pg 354
PT Indira, pg 355
Pustaka Utama Grafiti, PT, pg 356
Yayasan Obor Indonesia, pg 357

Iraq

National House for Publishing, Distributing & Advertising, pg 357

Ireland

A & A Farmar, pg 357
The Educational Company of Ireland, pg 359
Gill & Macmillan Ltd, pg 360
The Hannon Press, pg 361
Irish Management Institute, pg 361
Oak Tree Press, pg 362
O'Brien Educational, pg 362
The O'Brien Press Ltd, pg 362

Israel

Dyonon/Papyrus Publishing House of the Tel-Aviv, pg 366
Intermedia Audio, Video Book Publishing Ltd, pg 368

Italy

Franco Angeli SRL, pg 375
Bancaria Editrice SpA, pg 377
Ciranna - Roma, pg 382
CLUEB (Cooperativa Libraria Universitaria Editrice Bologna), pg 382
Giovanni De Vecchi Editore SpA, pg 384
Casa Editrice Istituto della Santa, pg 385
Esselibri, pg 388
Etas Libri, pg 388
Isper SRL, pg 393
Itaca, pg 393
Edizioni Olivares, pg 401
RCS Libri SpA, pg 405
Edizioni Universitarie Romane, pg 406
Il Sole 24 Ore Pirola, pg 409
Tecniche Nuove SpA, pg 410
Who's Who In Italy srl, pg 412

Jamaica

Carlong Publishers (Caribbean) Ltd, pg 413

Japan

The American Chamber of Commerce in Japan, pg 415
CMC Publishing Co Ltd, pg 416
Diamond Inc, pg 416
Dobunshoin Publishers Co, pg 416
Gakken Co Ltd, pg 417
GakuseiSha Publishing Co Ltd, pg 417
Hayakawa Publishing Inc, pg 418
Kaibundo Shuppan, pg 420
Koyo Shobo, pg 422
Nihon Keizai Shimbun Inc Publications Bureau, pg 423
Nikkagiren Shuppan-Sha (JUSE Press Ltd), pg 424
The Nikkan Kogyo Shimbun Ltd, pg 424
Nippon Hoso Shuppan Kyokai (NHK Publishing), pg 424
Nippon Jitsugyo Publishing Co Ltd, pg 424
Pearson Education Japan, pg 425
PHP Institute Inc, pg 425
President Inc, pg 425
Sagano Shoin, pg 426
Seibido Shuppan Company Ltd, pg 426
Seibundo, pg 426
Seibundo Shinkosha Publishing Co Ltd, pg 426
Shincho-Sha Co Ltd, pg 427
The Simul Press Inc, pg 428
Sobun-Sha, pg 428
Toyo Keizai Shinpo-Sha, pg 430
Zeimukeiri-Kyokai, pg 431

Jordan

Jordan Book Centre Co Ltd, pg 432

Kazakhstan

Al-Farabi Kazakh National University, pg 432

Kenya

Focus Publications Ltd, pg 433
Heinemann Kenya Ltd (EAEP), pg 434
Midi Teki Publishers, pg 435
Shirikon Publishers, pg 436
Space Sellers Ltd, pg 436

Democratic People's Republic of Korea

Industrial Publishing House, pg 436

Republic of Korea

Bi-bong Publishing Co, pg 437
Chung Rim Publishing Co Ltd, pg 438
Gim-Yeong Co, pg 438
Hakmunsa Publishing Co, pg 439
Koreaone Press Inc, pg 440
Kyohaksa Publishing Co Ltd, pg 440
Maeil Gyeongje, pg 441
Oruem Publishing House, pg 442
Samseong Publishing Co Ltd, pg 442
Twenty-First Century Publishers, Inc, pg 443
Woongjin Media Corporation, pg 443
Woongjin.com Co Ltd, pg 443
Yeha Publishing Co, pg 443

Latvia

Preses Nams, pg 445

Lebanon

Arab Institute for Research & Publishing, pg 445
Dar El Ilm Lilmalayin, pg 446

Liechtenstein

Megatrade AG, pg 448

Lithuania

Tyto Alba Publishers, pg 450

Luxembourg

Service Central de la Statistique et des Etudes Economiques (STATEC), pg 451

Malawi

Dzuka Publishing Co Ltd, pg 454

Malaysia

Amiza Associate Malaysia Sdn Bhd, pg 455
Berita Publishing Sdn Bhd, pg 455
MDC Publishers Printers Sdn Bhd, pg 457
Minerva Publications, pg 457
Pelanduk Publications (M) Sdn Bhd, pg 457
Penerbitan Tinta, pg 458
Utusan Publications & Distributors Sdn Bhd, pg 459

Mauritius

Editions de l'Ocean Indien Ltd, pg 461

Mexico

Editorial Banca y Comercio SA de CV, pg 462
El Colegio de Mexico AC, pg 463
Ediciones Contables y Administrativas SA, pg 463
Ediciones Eca SA de CV, pg 464
Ibcon SA, pg 466
Editorial Limusa SA de CV, pg 467
McGraw-Hill Interamericana Editores, SA de CV, pg 468
Panorama Editorial, SA, pg 470
Editorial Pax Mexico, pg 470
Pearson Educacion de Mexico, SA de CV, pg 470
Sayrols Editorial SA de CV, pg 471
SCRIPTA - Distribucion y Servicios Editoriales, SA de CV, pg 471
Editorial Trillas SA de CV, pg 472
Editorial Turner de Mexico, pg 472
Javier Vergara Editor SA de CV, pg 473

Morocco

Access International Services, pg 474
Societe Ennewrasse Service Librairie et Imprimerie, pg 475

Nepal

International Standards Books & Periodicals (P) Ltd, pg 476

Netherlands

BoekWerk, pg 479
Business Contact BV, pg 480
Frank Fehmers Productions, pg 482
Kluwer Bedrijfswetenschappen, pg 485
Uitgeverij Lemma BV, pg 485
Mets & Schilt Uitgevers en Distributeurs, pg 486
Uitgeverij H Nelissen BV, pg 486
Pearson Education Netherlands, pg 487
Samsom BedrijfsInformatie BV, pg 488
Scriptum, pg 488
VNU Business Press Group BV, pg 492

New Zealand

David Bateman Ltd, pg 494
Brookers Ltd, pg 494

SUBJECT INDEX

Current Pacific Ltd, pg 495
Dunmore Press Ltd, pg 495
Exisle Publishing Ltd, pg 496
Hodder Moa Beckett Publishers Ltd, pg 497
Learning Guides (Writers & Publishers Ltd), pg 497
Moss Associates Ltd, pg 498
Nahanni Publishing Ltd, pg 499
Nelson Price Milburn Ltd, pg 499
Pursuit Publishing, pg 500
Shoal Bay Press Ltd, pg 501
Statistics New Zealand, pg 501
Tandem Press, pg 501
Universal Business Directories, Australia Pty Ltd, pg 502

Nigeria

Adebara Publishers Ltd, pg 503
Fourth Dimension Publishing Co Ltd, pg 504
Goldland Business Co Ltd, pg 505
New Africa Publishing Company Ltd, pg 505
Vantage Publishers International Ltd, pg 507

Norway

Ascheoug Forlag, pg 508
H Ascheoug & Co (W Nygaard) A/S, pg 508
Glydendal Akademisk, pg 509
Universitetsforlaget, pg 511

Oman

Apex Press & Publishing, pg 511

Pakistan

International Educational Services, pg 512
National Book Foundation, pg 513

Papua New Guinea

Kristen Press, pg 515

Peru

Editorial Desarrollo SA, pg 517

Philippines

Bright Concepts Printing House, pg 518
De La Salle University, pg 519
Garotech, pg 519
Logos (Divine Word) Publications Inc, pg 519
Mutual Book Inc, pg 519
New Day Publishers, pg 520
Our Lady of Manaoag Publisher, pg 520
Rex Bookstores & Publishers, pg 520
Sinag-Tala Publishers Inc, pg 521
University of the Philippines Press, pg 521
UST Publishing House, pg 521

Poland

Polskie Wydawnictwo Ekonomiczne PWE SA, pg 522
Polish Scientific Publishers PWN, pg 525

Portugal

Edicoes Cetop, pg 529
Editora Classica, pg 530
GECTI (Gabinete de Especializacao e Cooperacao Tecnica Internacional L), pg 531

SUBJECT INDEX BOOK

Editora McGraw-Hill de Portugal Lda, pg 533
Editorial Presenca, pg 535

Puerto Rico

McGraw-Hill Intermericana del Caribe, Inc, pg 537

Romania

Editura Cronos SRL, pg 539
Editura Excelsior Art, pg 539
Editura Niculescu, pg 541
Rentrop & Straton Verlagsgruppe und Wirtschaftsconsulting, pg 542

Russian Federation

Airis Press, pg 543
N E Bauman Moscow State Technical University Publishers, pg 544
Izdatelstvo 'Ekonomika', pg 544
Finansy i Statistika Publishing House, pg 544
INFRA-M Izdatel 'skij dom, pg 545
Izvestia Sovetov Narodnyh Deputatov Russian Federation (RF), pg 545
Legprombytizdat, pg 546
Obdeestro Znanie, pg 547
Vsesoyuznoe Obyedineniye Vneshtorgizdat, pg 549

Singapore

APAC Publishers Services Pte Ltd, pg 554
China Knowledge Press, pg 555
Graham Brash Pte Ltd, pg 556
McGallen & Bolden Associates, pg 557
Taylor & Francis Asia Pacific, pg 558

Slovakia

Dom Techniky Zvazu Slovenskych Vedeckotechnickych Spolocnosti Ltd, pg 559
Priroda Publishing, pg 560

Slovenia

Univerza v Ljubljani Ekonomska Fakulteta, pg 562
Zalozba Obzorja d d Maribor, pg 562

South Africa

Brabys Brochures, pg 563
Educum Publishers Ltd, pg 563
Flesch Financial Publications (Pty) Ltd, pg 563
Human & Rousseau (Pty) Ltd, pg 564
Juta & Co, pg 565
Queillerie Publishers, pg 568
Ravan Press (Pty) Ltd, pg 568
South African Institute of Race Relations, pg 569
Struik Publishers (Pty) Ltd, pg 569
Van Schaik Publishers, pg 569
Witwatersrand University Press, pg 570

Spain

Asociacion para el Progreso de la Direccion (APD), pg 573
Comunidad Autonoma de Madrid, Servicio de Documentacion y Publicaciones, pg 578
CTE-Centro de Tecnologia Educativa SA, pg 578

Ediciones Diaz de Santos SA, pg 579
Publicaciones Etea, pg 583
EUNSA (Ediciones Universidad de Navarra SA), pg 583
Editorial Hispano Europea SA, pg 586
Iberico Europea de Ediciones SA, pg 586
LID Editorial Empresarial, SL, pg 589
Marcombo SA, pg 590
Pais Vasco Servicio Central de Publicaciones, pg 594
Editorial Paraninfo SA, pg 595
Ediciones Piramide SA, pg 596
Editorial Tecnos SA, pg 601
Universidad de Valladolid Secretariado de Publicaciones e Intercambio Editorial, pg 604
Ediciones Urano, SA, pg 604
Javier Vergara Editor SA, pg 604
Xunta de Galicia, pg 605

Sweden

Ekonomibok Forlag AB, pg 611
Iustus Forlag AB, pg 613
Liber AB, pg 613
Studentlitteratur AB, pg 616
Svenska Foerlaget liv & ledarskap ab, pg 616
Tryckeriforlaget AB, pg 616

Switzerland

Association Suisse des Editeurs de Langue Francaise, pg 618
Bibliographisches Institut & F A Brockhaus AG, pg 619
Cockatoo Press (Schweiz), Thailand-Publikationen, pg 621
Cosmos-Verlag AG, pg 621
Marcel Dekker AG, pg 621
Drei-D-World und Foto-World Verlag und Vertrieb, pg 622
Kranich-Verlag, Dres AG & H R Bosch-Gwalter, pg 627
Orell Fuessli Buchhandlungs AG, pg 630
Ott Verlag Thun, pg 630
Editions du Panorama, pg 630
Promoedition SA, pg 631
Ruegger Verlag, pg 633
Schulthess Polygraphischer Verlag AG, pg 633
Versus Verlag AG, pg 636

Syrian Arab Republic

Damascus University Press, pg 638

Taiwan, Province of China

Asian Culture Co Ltd, pg 638
Chien Chen Bookstore Publishing Company Ltd, pg 639
Commonwealth Publishing Company Ltd, pg 639
Dayi Information Co, pg 639
Chu Hai Publishing (Taiwan) Co Ltd, pg 640
Hsiao Yuan Publication Co, Ltd, pg 640
Laureate Book Co Ltd, pg 640
Linking Publishing Company Ltd, pg 641
Shy Mau & Shy Chaur Publishing Co Ltd, pg 641
Wu Nan Book Co Ltd, pg 642
Yuan Liou Publishing Co, Ltd, pg 642

United Republic of Tanzania

Nyota Publishers Ltd, pg 644

Turkey

Alkim Kitapcilik-Yayimcilik, pg 649
Inkilap Publishers Ltd, pg 650
Sabah Kitaplari, pg 651
Soez Yayin/Oyunajans, pg 651

Ukraine

ASK Ltd, pg 653
Osnova, Kharkov State University Press, pg 653
Osnovy Publishers, pg 654

United Arab Emirates

Motivate Publishing, pg 654

United Kingdom

ABG Professional Information, pg 655
Adamantine Press Ltd, pg 655
AP Information Services Ltd, pg 658
Ashgate Publishing Ltd, pg 660
Ashton & Denton Publishing Co (CI) Ltd, pg 660
Aslib, The Association for Information Management, pg 660
Blackwell Publishing Ltd, pg 666
BPP Publishing Ltd, pg 670
Nicholas Brealey Publishing, pg 670
Business Monitor International, pg 672
Capstone Publishing Ltd, pg 674
Cassell & Co, pg 675
Causeway Press Ltd, pg 676
CCH Editions Ltd, pg 677
Chartered Institute of Personnel & Development, pg 678
CMP Information Ltd, pg 680
Computer Step, pg 681
The Continuum International Publishing Group Ltd, pg 682
Croner CCH Group Ltd, pg 684
Crown House Publishing Ltd, pg 684
The Economist Intelligence Unit, pg 689
Edition XII, pg 690
Edward Elgar Publishing Ltd, pg 690
Elliot Right Way Books, pg 690
Elm Publications, pg 691
Elsevier Advanced Technology, pg 691
Elsevier Ltd, pg 691
Emerald, pg 691
Ethics International Press Ltd, pg 692
Euromonitor PLC, pg 692
The Eurospan Group, pg 692
Express Newspapers, pg 693
First & Best in Education Ltd, pg 695
Forbes Publications Ltd, pg 696
Gower Publishing Ltd, pg 701
HarperCollins UK, pg 705
Harvard University Press, pg 705
HB Publications, pg 706
HLT Publications, pg 709
Hobsons, pg 709
Hodder Education, pg 709
How To Books Ltd, pg 710
ICC United Kingdom, pg 711
ICSA Publishing Ltd, pg 711
Institute of Financial Services, pg 712
Institution of Electrical Engineers, pg 713
Interfisc Publishing, pg 714
International Communications, pg 714
ITDG Publishing, pg 715

JAI Press Ltd, pg 715
James & James (Publishers) Ltd, pg 715
Jordan Publishing Ltd, pg 716
Kelly's, pg 717
Kogan Page Ltd, pg 718
Lang Syne Publishers Ltd, pg 719
Lawpack Publishing Ltd, pg 719
Learning Matters Ltd, pg 720
London Chamber of Commerce & Industry Examinations Board (LCCIEB), pg 722
Management Books 2000 Ltd, pg 724
Management Pocketbooks Ltd, pg 724
Marshall Editions Ltd, pg 725
Media Research Publishing Ltd, pg 726
National Assembly for Wales, pg 730
National Extension College, pg 730
Nelson Thornes Ltd, pg 732
New Era Publications UK Ltd, pg 732
The NFER-NELSON Publishing Co Ltd, pg 733
Orion Publishing Group Ltd, pg 736
Osborne Books Ltd, pg 736
Palgrave Publishers Ltd, pg 737
PasTest, pg 738
Pearson Education, pg 739
Pearson Education Europe, Mideast & Africa, pg 739
Pergamon Flexible Learning, pg 740
Perpetuity Press, pg 741
Piatkus Books, pg 741
Pickering & Chatto Publishers Ltd, pg 742
Policy Studies Institute (PSI), pg 744
Profile Books Ltd, pg 746
ProQuest Information & Learning, pg 746
Quiller Publishing Ltd, pg 747
William Reed Directories, pg 749
Rooster Books Ltd, pg 751
Roundhouse Group, pg 751
Routledge, pg 751
RoutledgeCurzon, pg 751
Royal Institute of International Affairs, pg 752
SAGE Publications Ltd, pg 753
Silver Link Publishing Ltd, pg 758
Simon & Schuster Ltd, pg 758
Snowbooks Ltd, pg 759
Spokesman, pg 760
Stacey International, pg 761
Sutton Publishing Ltd, pg 762
Sydney Jary Ltd, pg 762
Take That Ltd, pg 762
Taylor & Francis, pg 763
Thoemmes Press, pg 765
Thomson Gale, pg 765
Time Warner Book Group UK, pg 766
TSO (The Stationery Office), pg 767
Verulam Publishing Ltd, pg 770
VNU Business Publications, pg 770
Which? Ltd, pg 772
Whurr Publishers Ltd, pg 773
Wiley Europe Ltd, pg 773
Wilmington Business Information Ltd, pg 774
Wimbledon Publishing Company Ltd, pg 774
Witherby & Co Ltd, pg 775
World of Information, pg 776

Viet Nam

Science & Technics Publishing House, pg 780

PUBLISHERS

Zambia
Aafzam Ltd, pg 781
MFK Management Consultants Services, pg 781

Zimbabwe
College Press Publishers (Pvt) Ltd, pg 783
HarperCollins Publishers Zimbabwe Pvt Ltd, pg 783
Longman Zimbabwe (Pvt) Ltd, pg 783
Manhattan Publications, pg 784
Thomson Publications Zimbabwe (Pvt) Ltd, pg 784

CAREER DEVELOPMENT

Albania
NL SH, pg 1

Australia
Edward Arnold (Australia) Pty Ltd, pg 12
Hale & Iremonger Pty Ltd, pg 24
The Useful Publishing Co, pg 45
VCTA Publishing, pg 45
Woodlands Publications, pg 47
Wrightbooks Pty Ltd, pg 47

Austria
Braintrust Marketing Services Ges mbH Verlag, pg 49
Verlag des Oesterreichischen Gewerkschaftsbundes GmbH, pg 55
Oesterreichischer Bundesverlag Gmbh, pg 55
Oesterreichischer Gewerbeverlag GmbH, pg 55
WUV/Service Fachverlag, pg 60

Belarus
Interdigest Publishing House, pg 62

Belgium
Marabout, pg 71
Scoop Infotex NV, pg 73

Brazil
Hemus Editora Ltda, pg 83
Editora Lucre Comercio e Representacoes, pg 85
Qualitymark Editora Ltda, pg 89

Bulgaria
Dolphin Press Group Ltd, pg 94
Regalia 6 Publishing House, pg 96

China
China Film Press, pg 102
Jilin Science & Technology Publishing House, pg 105
Shanghai Far East Publishers, pg 108
Yunnan University Press, pg 109

Costa Rica
Editorial de la Universidad de Costa Rica, pg 116

Croatia
Narodne Novine, pg 119

Cuba
Instituto de Informacion Cientifica y Tecnologica (IDICT), pg 120

Denmark
Det Schonbergske Forlag A/S, pg 134

Dominican Republic
Pontificia Universidad Catolica Madre y Maestra, pg 136

France
Le Jour, Editeur, pg 169
Librairie Leonce Laget, pg 171
Editions Legislatives, pg 171
LT Editions-Jacques Lanore, pg 173
Maxima Laurent du Mesnil Editeur, pg 174
Les Presses du Management, pg 181
TOP Editions, pg 188

Germany
E Albrecht Verlags-KG, pg 192
AOL-Verlag Frohmut Menze, pg 193
Bertelsmann Lexikon Verlag GmbH, pg 200
W Bertelsmann Verlag GmbH & Co KG, pg 200
Verlag Beruf und Schule Belz KG, pg 200
BW Bildung und Wissen Verlag und Software GmbH, pg 201
Campus Verlag GmbH, pg 207
Charles Coleman Verlag GmbH & Co KG, pg 209
Cornelsen Verlag GmbH & Co OHG, pg 210
Deutscher Wirtschaftsdienst John von Freyend GmbH, pg 214
Dreisam Ratgeber in der Rutsker Verlag GmbH, pg 216
Econ Taschenbuchverlag, pg 218
Eppinger-Verlag OHG, pg 220
Fachbuchverlag Pfanneberg & Co, pg 223
Festo Didactic GmbH & Co KG, pg 224
Friedrich Kiehl Verlag GmbH, pg 227
Genius Verlag, pg 228
Alfons W Gentner Verlag GmbH & Co KG, pg 228
Verlag Gruppenpaedagogischer Literatur, pg 231
Verlag Handwerk und Technik GmbH, pg 233
Heckners Verlag, pg 235
HelfRecht Verlag und Druck, pg 236
Huss-Medien GmbH, pg 240
Kallmeyer'sche Verlagsbuchhandlung GmbH, pg 244
Mosaik Verlag GmbH, pg 262
Verlag Neue Wirtschafts-Briefe GmbH & Co, pg 264
Polygraph Verlag GmbH, pg 271
Quintessenz Verlags-GmbH, pg 273
Ritterbach Verlag GmbH, pg 276
Rossipaul Kommunikation GmbH, pg 277
I H Sauer Verlag GmbH, pg 278
Verlag Moderne Industrie AG & Co KG, pg 295
Verlag und Studio fuer Hoerbuchproduktionen, pg 295
Walhalla Fachverlag GmbH & Co KG Praetoria, pg 297
WEKA Firmengruppe GmbH & Co KG, pg 298
Winklers Verlag Gebrueder Grimm, pg 300

Ghana
Sam Woode Ltd, pg 304

Greece
Hestia-I D Hestia-Kollaros & Co Corporation, pg 308

Hong Kong
Chung Hwa Book Co (HK) Ltd, pg 316
SCMP Book Publishing Ltd, pg 319

Hungary
Mueszaki Koenyvkiado Ltd, pg 323

India
Dastane Ramchandra & Co, pg 333
General Book Depot, pg 335
Gyan Publishing House, pg 335
Nem Chand & Brothers, pg 343
Omsons Publications, pg 344
Orient Paperbacks, pg 344
Parimal Prakashan, pg 345
Reliance Publishing House, pg 346
Sultan Chand & Sons Pvt Ltd, pg 350
Viva Books Pvt Ltd, pg 352
A H Wheeler & Co Ltd, pg 353

Indonesia
Dinastindo, pg 354
PT Indira, pg 355
Katalis PT Bina Mitra Plaosan, pg 355

Ireland
Careers & Educational Publishers Ltd, pg 358
The Educational Company of Ireland, pg 359
Oak Tree Press, pg 362
O'Brien Educational, pg 362

Italy
Giovanni De Vecchi Editore SpA, pg 384
EGEA (Edizioni Giuridiche Economiche Aziendali), pg 387

Japan
Diamond Inc, pg 416
Seibido Shuppan Company Ltd, pg 426
Shufunotomo Co Ltd, pg 428

Kenya
Action Publishers, pg 433
Space Sellers Ltd, pg 436

Republic of Korea
Anam Publishing Co, pg 437
Ario Company Ltd, pg 437
Chung Rim Publishing Co Ltd, pg 438
Hongik Media Plus Ltd, pg 439
Koreaone Press Inc, pg 440

Liechtenstein
Rheintal Handelsgesellschaft Anstalt, pg 448

SUBJECT INDEX

Lithuania
Sviesa Publishers, pg 449

Luxembourg
Editions Emile Borschette, pg 450

Malaysia
Federal Publications Sdn Bhd, pg 455
IBS Buku Sdn Bhd, pg 456
Minerva Publications, pg 457
Trix Corporation Sdn Bhd, pg 459

Mauritius
Editions de l'Ocean Indien Ltd, pg 461

Mexico
Editorial Diana SA de CV, pg 464
Grupo Editorial Iberoamerica, SA de CV, pg 466
Editorial Limusa SA de CV, pg 467
Editorial Pax Mexico, pg 470

Morocco
Office Marocain D'Annonces-OMA, pg 475

Nepal
International Standards Books & Periodicals (P) Ltd, pg 476

Netherlands
Business Contact BV, pg 480
Twente University Press, pg 490
VNU Business Press Group BV, pg 492

New Zealand
Legislation Direct, pg 498
Moss Associates Ltd, pg 498

Pakistan
National Book Foundation, pg 513

Philippines
New Day Publishers, pg 520
Our Lady of Manaoag Publisher, pg 520

Portugal
Edicoes Cetop, pg 529
Impala, pg 532
Monitor-Projectos e Edicoes, LDA, pg 533

Romania
Coresi SRL, pg 539
Editura Niculescu, pg 541
Rentrop & Straton Verlagsgruppe und Wirtschaftsconsulting, pg 542

Russian Federation
Airis Press, pg 543
Finansy i Statistika Publishing House, pg 544

Slovakia
Ustav informacii a prognoz skolstva mladeze a telovychovy, pg 561

South Africa
Human Sciences Research Council, pg 565

SUBJECT INDEX

Spain
Centro de Estudios Adams-Ediciones Valbuena SA, pg 571
Ediciones Gestio 2000 SA, pg 585
LID Editorial Empresarial, SL, pg 589
Ediciones Norma SA, pg 593
Ediciones Tutor SA, pg 603

Sri Lanka
Sunera Publishers, pg 607

Sweden
Svenska Foerlaget liv & ledarskap ab, pg 616

Switzerland
Oesch Verlag AG, pg 630

Taiwan, Province of China
Chien Chen Bookstore Publishing Company Ltd, pg 639
Jillion Publishing Co, pg 640
Linking Publishing Company Ltd, pg 641

Turkey
Soez Yayin/Oyunajans, pg 651

Uganda
Fountain Publishers Ltd, pg 652

Ukraine
ASK Ltd, pg 653

United Kingdom
Bloomsbury Publishing PLC, pg 668
Nicholas Brealey Publishing, pg 670
Careers & Occupational Information Centre (COIC), pg 675
Cassell & Co, pg 675
Elliot Right Way Books, pg 690
Hobsons, pg 709
Hodder Education, pg 709
Hospitality Training Foundation, pg 710
How To Books Ltd, pg 710
Kogan Page Ltd, pg 718
Management Books 2000 Ltd, pg 724
McGraw-Hill Publishing Company, pg 726
National Extension College, pg 730
Pearson Education, pg 739
Piatkus Books, pg 741
Publishing Training Centre at BookHouse, pg 746
Sherwood Publishing, pg 757
Trotman Publishing, pg 767
University of London Careers Service, pg 768
Vacation Work Publications, pg 769

Viet Nam
Science & Technics Publishing House, pg 780

CHEMISTRY, CHEMICAL ENGINEERING

Albania
NL SH, pg 1

Argentina
EUDEBA (Editorial Universitaria de Buenos Aires), pg 5

Armenia
Arevik, pg 10

Australia
Australian Academy of Science, pg 13
CSIRO Publishing (Commonwealth Scientific & Industrial Research Organisation), pg 19
EA Books, pg 20
Emerald City Books, pg 21
McGraw-Hill Australia Pty Ltd, pg 31
Reed Educational Publishing Australia, pg 39
Royal Society of New South Wales, pg 40
Standards Association of Australia, pg 42

Austria
Bethania Verlag, pg 48
IAEA - International Atomic Energy Agency, pg 52
Oesterreichischer Bundesverlag Gmbh, pg 55
Springer-Verlag Wien, pg 58

Belgium
Conservart SA, pg 65
Editions De Boeck-Larcier SA, pg 66

Bolivia
Editorial Don Bosco, pg 75

Brazil
LTC-Livros Tecnicos e Cientificos Editora S/A, pg 85
Editora Scipione Ltda, pg 90

Bulgaria
Gea-Libris Publishing House, pg 94
Makros 2000 - Plovdiv, pg 95

Chile
Arrayan Editores, pg 98

China
Beijing University Press, pg 101
Chemical Industry Press, pg 101
China Forestry Publishing House, pg 102
China Ocean Press, pg 102
Fudan University Press, pg 104
Guizhou Education Publishing House, pg 105
Henan Science & Technology Publishing House, pg 105
International Academic Publishers (IAP), pg 105
Jiangsu Science & Technology Publishing House, pg 105
Jilin Science & Technology Publishing House, pg 105
Metallurgical Industry Press (MIP), pg 106
Nanjing University Press, pg 106
Printing Industry Publishing House, pg 107
Science Press, pg 107
Shandong University Press, pg 108
South China University of Science & Technology Press, pg 108
Tianjin Science & Technology Publishing House, pg 108
Tsinghua University Press, pg 109
Wuhan University Press, pg 109
Zhejiang University Press, pg 109

Colombia
McGraw-Hill Colombia, pg 112
Universidad Nacional Abierta y a Distancia, pg 113

Czech Republic
Academia, pg 122
Cesky normalizacni institut, pg 126
Vydavatelstvi Cesky Geologicky Ustav, pg 128

Denmark
Systime, pg 135

Dominican Republic
Pontificia Universidad Catolica Madre y Maestra, pg 136

Ethiopia
Addis Ababa University Press, pg 140

France
CNRS Editions, pg 155
Doin Editeurs, pg 159
Editions Jacques Gabay, pg 164
Gammaprim, pg 165
Hermann editeurs des Sciences et des Arts SA, pg 167
Editions Hermes Science Publications, pg 167
InterEditions, pg 169
Editions Lavoisier, pg 171
Librairie Scientifique et Technique Albert Blanchard, pg 172
Ouest Editions, pg 178
Polytechnica SA, pg 180
Presses Universitaires de Grenoble, pg 181
Editions Springer France, pg 186
Editions Technip SA, pg 187
Librairie Vuibert, pg 189

Germany
AOL-Verlag Frohmut Menze, pg 193
Aulis Verlag Deubner & Co KG, pg 195
Bayerischer Schulbuch-Verlag GmbH, pg 198
Verlag Beruf und Schule Belz KG, pg 200
Beuth Verlag GmbH, pg 200
Oscar Brandstetter Verlag GmbH & Co KG, pg 204
Fachverlag Hans Carl GmbH, pg 207
Cornelsen Verlag GmbH & Co OHG, pg 210
Verlag Harri Deutsch, pg 211
Deutscher Verlag fur Grundstoffindustrie GmbH, pg 213
Ecomed Verlagsgesellschaft AG & Co KG, pg 218
Ferd Dummler's Verlag, pg 223
Franckh-Kosmos Verlags-GmbH & Co, pg 226
S Hirzel Verlag GmbH und Co, pg 238
Huthig GmbH & Co KG, pg 240
Konradin-Verlagsgruppe, pg 249
Springer Science+Business Media GmbH & Co KG, pg 284
Verlag Stahleisen GmbH, pg 286
B G Teubner Verlag, pg 290
Georg Thieme Verlag KG, pg 291
Trans Tech Publications, pg 292
UTB fuer Wissenschaft Uni Taschenbuecher GmbH, pg 294
Curt R Vincentz Verlag, pg 296
Vogel Medien GmbH & Co KG, pg 296
Volk und Wissen Verlag GmbH & Co, pg 296
Vulkan-Verlag GmbH, pg 297
Wiley-VCH Verlag GmbH, pg 300
Verlag Zeitschrift fur Naturforschung, pg 302

Ghana
Sedco Publishing Ltd, pg 305

Greece
Ekdotikos Oikos Adelfon Kyriakidi A E, pg 307
Panepistimio Ioanninon, pg 311

Holy See (Vatican City State)
Pontificia Academia Scientiarum, pg 314

Hungary
Magyar Tudomanyos Akademia Koezponti Fizikai Kutato Intezet Koenyvtara, pg 322
Mueszaki Koenyvkiado Ltd, pg 323

India
Addison-Wesley Pte Ltd, pg 327
Affiliated East West Press Pvt Ltd, pg 327
APH Publishing Corp, pg 328
Asia Pacific Business Press Inc, pg 328
B I Publications Pvt Ltd, pg 329
Bani Mandir, Book-Sellers, Publishers & Educational Suppliers, pg 329
Bhawan Book Service, Publishers & Distributors, pg 330
BS Publications, pg 331
Goel Prakashen, pg 335
Heritage Publishers, pg 335
Multitech Publishing Co, pg 342
Narosa Publishing House, pg 342
National Institute of Industrial Research (NIIR), pg 343
Pitambar Publishing Co (P) Ltd, pg 345
Publications & Information Directorate, CSIR, pg 345
Rajasthan Hindi Granth Academy, pg 346
Scientific Book Agency, pg 348
Sita Books & Periodicals Pvt Ltd, pg 349
South Asian Publishers Pvt Ltd, pg 350
Sultan Chand & Sons Pvt Ltd, pg 350
Vidya Puri, pg 352
Vidyarthi Mithram Press, pg 352
Vikas Publishing House Pvt Ltd, pg 352
S Viswanathan (Printers & Publishers) Pvt Ltd, pg 352
Viva Books Pvt Ltd, pg 352

Indonesia
Andi Offset, pg 353
Institut Teknologi Bandung, pg 355

PUBLISHERS

Israel
Dyonon/Papyrus Publishing House of the Tel-Aviv, pg 366
Freund Publishing House Ltd, pg 367
Medcom Ltd, pg 370
Open University of Israel, pg 371

Italy
Casa Editrice Giuseppe Principato Spa, pg 380
D'Anna, pg 384
Editrice Edisco, pg 386
Giunti Gruppo Editoriale, pg 390
Loescher Editore SRL, pg 396
Masson SpA, pg 397
Monduzzi Editore SpA, pg 399
Nagard, pg 400
Principato, pg 404
Edizioni Universitarie Romane, pg 406
Societa Editrice la Goliardica Pavese SRL, pg 408
Sorbona, pg 409
Unipress, pg 411
Zanichelli Editore SpA, pg 412

Japan
Baifukan Co Ltd, pg 415
Dainippon Tosho Publishing Co, Ltd, pg 416
Hirokawa Publishing Co, pg 418
Kyoritsu Shuppan Co Ltd, pg 422
Maruzen Co Ltd, pg 422
Nippon Hoso Shuppan Kyokai (NHK Publishing), pg 424
Sangyo-Tosho Publishing Co Ltd, pg 426
Sankyo Publishing Company Ltd, pg 426
Sanyo Shuppan Boeki Co Inc, pg 426
Tokyo Kagaku Dojin Co Ltd, pg 429

Kazakstan
Gylym, Izd-Vo, pg 432
Al-Farabi Kazakh National University, pg 432

Democratic People's Republic of Korea
Academy of Sciences Publishing House, pg 436
Korea Science and Encyclopedia Publishing House, pg 436

Republic of Korea
Bo Moon Dang, pg 437
Prompter Publications, pg 442

Latvia
Lielvards Ltd, pg 445

Lithuania
Academia, pg 448
Klaipedos Universiteto Leidykla, pg 449

Malaysia
Penerbit Universiti Sains Malaysia, pg 458
Penerbit Universiti Teknologi Malaysia, pg 459

Mexico
Editorial Esfinge SA de CV, pg 465
Grupo Editorial Iberoamerica, SA de CV, pg 466
Editorial Limusa SA de CV, pg 467
Pearson Educacion de Mexico, SA de CV, pg 470
Universidad Nacional Autonoma de Mexico (National University of Mexico), pg 472

Republic of Moldova
Editura Lumina, pg 473

Nepal
International Standards Books & Periodicals (P) Ltd, pg 476

Netherlands
Delft University Press, pg 481
Elsevier Science BV, pg 482
Hagen & Stam Uitgeverij Ten, pg 483
IOS Press BV, pg 484
LCG Malmberg BV, pg 485
V S P International Science Publishers, pg 491

New Zealand
ABA Books, pg 493
ESA Publications (NZ) Ltd, pg 496
Nelson Price Milburn Ltd, pg 499
New House Publishers Ltd, pg 499

Nigeria
Riverside Communications, pg 507
West African Book Publishers Ltd, pg 507

Norway
Elanders Publishing AS, pg 509
NKI Forlaget, pg 510

Pakistan
National Book Foundation, pg 513
Publishers United Pvt Ltd, pg 514
Quaid-i-Azam University Department of Biological Sciences, pg 514

Philippines
UST Publishing House, pg 521

Poland
Instytut Historii Nauki PAN, pg 523
Wydawnictwa Naukowo-Techniczne, pg 524
Polish Scientific Publishers PWN, pg 525
PZWL Wydawnictwo Lekarskie Ltd, pg 526
Wydawnictwa Uniwersytetu Warszawskiego, pg 527

Portugal
Constancia Editores, SA, pg 530
Europress Editores e Distribuidores de Publicacoes Lda, pg 531
Editora McGraw-Hill de Portugal Lda, pg 533

Romania
Editura Academiei Romane, pg 538
Editura Dacia, pg 539

Russian Federation
Izdatelstvo Kazanskago Universiteta, pg 545
Izdatelstvo Mir, pg 546
Nauka Publishers, pg 547
Izdatel'stvo Nizhegorodskogo Gosudarstvennogo Univ, pg 547
Izdatelstvo Prosveshchenie, pg 548
Voronezh State University Publishers, pg 549
Izdatelstvo Vysshaya Shkola, pg 549

Saudi Arabia
King Saud University, pg 550

Singapore
APAC Publishers Services Pte Ltd, pg 554
McGallen & Bolden Associates, pg 557
Reed Elsevier, South East Asia, pg 557
World Scientific Publishing Co Pte Ltd, pg 559

Slovenia
Mladinska Knjiga International, pg 561
Zalozba Obzorja d d Maribor, pg 562

South Africa
Educum Publishers Ltd, pg 563

Spain
Instituto de Estudios Riojanos, pg 583
Ediciones Omega SA, pg 594
Publicaciones de la Universidad de Alicante, pg 597
Servicio de Publicaciones Universidad de Cadiz, pg 599
Editorial Sintesis, SA, pg 600
Tres Torres Ediciones SA, pg 602
Universidad de Valladolid Secretariado de Publicaciones e Intercambio Editorial, pg 604
Edicions de la Universitat Politecnica de Catalunya SL, pg 604

Sri Lanka
Ministry of Education, pg 607
Warna Publishers, pg 607

Sweden
Studentlitteratur AB, pg 616

Switzerland
Bibliographisches Institut & F A Brockhaus AG, pg 619
Marcel Dekker AG, pg 621
Verlag Harri Deutsch, pg 622
Verlag Helvetica Chimica Acta, pg 625
Presses Polytechniques et Universitaires Romandes, PPUR, pg 632
Trans Tech Publications SA, pg 635
Vogt-Schild Ag, Druck und Verlag, pg 636

Syrian Arab Republic
Damascus University Press, pg 638

Taiwan, Province of China
Fuh-Wen Book Co, pg 639
Hsiao Yuan Publication Co, Ltd, pg 640
Petroleum Information Publishing Co, pg 641
Yi Hsien Publishing Co Ltd, pg 642

United Republic of Tanzania
DUP (1996) Ltd, pg 643

Thailand
Graphic Art (28) Co Ltd, pg 645

Turkey
Caglayan Kitabevi, pg 649

Ukraine
Naukova Dumka Publishers, pg 653
Osnova, Kharkov State University Press, pg 653
Osvita, pg 654

United Kingdom
Association for Science Education, pg 661
Blackwell Science Ltd, pg 667
Business Monitor International, pg 672
Cambridge University Press, pg 674
DMG Business Media Ltd, pg 688
Elsevier Ltd, pg 691
The Eurospan Group, pg 692
W H Freeman & Co Ltd, pg 697
Hodder Education, pg 709
Imperial College Press, pg 712
Institution of Chemical Engineers, pg 713
IOM Communications Ltd, pg 714
JAI Press Ltd, pg 715
Kluwer Academic/Plenum Publishers, pg 718
Manson Publishing Ltd, pg 725
Micelle Press, pg 727
Open University Worldwide, pg 736
Pearson Education, pg 739
Pharmaceutical Press, pg 741
Portland Press Ltd, pg 745
Rapra Technology Ltd, pg 748
Research Studies Press Ltd (RSP), pg 749
The Royal Society of Chemistry, pg 752
Science Reviews Ltd, pg 755
Sheffield Academic Press Ltd, pg 757
Wiley Europe Ltd, pg 773

Uruguay
A Monteverde y Cia SA, pg 777

Venezuela
Sociedad Fondo Editorial Cenamec, pg 779

Viet Nam
Science & Technics Publishing House, pg 780

Zimbabwe
College Press Publishers (Pvt) Ltd, pg 783
Standards Association of Zimbabwe (SAZ), pg 784

CHILD CARE & DEVELOPMENT

Albania
NL SH, pg 1

Argentina
Editorial Paidos SAICF, pg 8

SUBJECT INDEX

Australia
Crossroad Distributors Pty Ltd, pg 18
Finch Publishing, pg 22
Hale & Iremonger Pty Ltd, pg 24
Hampden Press, pg 24
Little Red Apple Publishing, pg 29
McGraw-Hill Australia Pty Ltd, pg 31
OTEN (Open Training & Education Network), pg 34
Pademelon Press, pg 35
Pearson Education Australia, pg 36
Priestley Consulting, pg 37
RMIT Publishing, pg 39
Simon & Schuster (Australia) Pty Ltd, pg 41
Tertiary Press, pg 43
University of New South Wales Press Ltd, pg 44
Zoe Publishing Pty Ltd, pg 47

Austria
Development News Ltd, pg 50
Verlag des Osterr Kneippbundes GmbH, pg 56

Azerbaijan
Sada, Literaturno-Izdatel'skij Centr, pg 60

Bangladesh
Gatidhara, pg 61
Gono Prakashani, Gono Shasthya Kendra, pg 61

Belarus
Interdigest Publishing House, pg 62

Belgium
Koepel van de Vlaamse Noord - Zuidbeweging 11.11.11, pg 69
Marabout, pg 71
Zuid-Nederlandse Uitgeverij NV/Central Uitgeverij, pg 75

Brazil
A & A & A Edicoes e Promocoes Internacionais Ltda, pg 76
Agalma Psicanalise Editora Ltda, pg 77
Editora Antroposofica Ltda, pg 77
ARTMED Editora, pg 78
EDUSC - Editora da Universidade do Sagrado Coracao, pg 81
Editora Marco Zero Ltda, pg 86
Editora Mundo Cristao, pg 87
Paulinas Editorial, pg 88

Bulgaria
Fondacija Zlatno Kljuce, pg 94
Musica Publishing House Ltd, pg 95
Nov Covek Publishing House, pg 96
Reporter, pg 96
Sila & Zivot, pg 97
Sluntse Publishing House, pg 97

China
Anhui Children's Publishing House, pg 101
Beijing Juvenile & Children's Books Publishing House, pg 101
Beijing Publishing House, pg 101
China Braille Publishing House, pg 102
Guizhou Education Publishing House, pg 105
Jilin Science & Technology Publishing House, pg 105
Shandong Education Publishing House, pg 107
Shanghai Educational Publishing House, pg 108
Shanghai Far East Publishers, pg 108
Tianjin Science & Technology Publishing House, pg 108

Colombia
Consejo Episcopal Latinoamericano (CELAM), pg 110

Costa Rica
Ediciones Promesa, pg 116

Czech Republic
Pavla Momcilova, pg 125
Portal spol sro, pg 126

Denmark
Borgens Forlag A/S, pg 129
Fremad A/S, pg 131

Ecuador
Centro de Planificacion y Estudios Sociales (CEPLAES), pg 136

Egypt (Arab Republic of Egypt)
Dar Al-Thakafia Publishing, pg 138

Estonia
Sinisukk, pg 140
Valgus Publishers, pg 140

Finland
Lasten Keskus Oy, pg 143

France
Disney Hachette Edition, pg 158
Editions Larousse, pg 171
LT Editions-Jacques Lanore, pg 173
Editions Mango, pg 174
Editions Albin Michel, pg 175
Editions Stock, pg 186

Germany
AOL-Verlag Frohmut Menze, pg 193
Ars Edition GmbH, pg 194
Beust Verlag GmbH, pg 200
Carl-Auer-Systeme Verlag, pg 207
J G Cotta'sche Buchhandlung Nachfolger GmbH, pg 210
Deutscher Taschenbuch Verlag GmbH & Co KG (dtv), pg 213
Gatzanis Verlags GmbH, pg 228
Gesundheits-Dialog Verlag GmbH, pg 229
Verlag Gruppenpaedagogischer Literatur, pg 231
Dr Curt Haefner-Verlag GmbH, pg 233
Verlag im Kilian GmbH, pg 246
Knowledge Media International, pg 247
Midena Verlag, pg 260
Mosaik Verlag GmbH, pg 262
nymphenburger, pg 266
Psychologie Verlags Union GmbH, pg 272
Ernst Reinhardt Verlag GmbH & Co KG, pg 275
Springer Science+Business Media GmbH & Co KG, pg 284

Ghana
World Literature Project, pg 305

Greece
Akritas, pg 305
Anixis Publications, pg 305
Chrysi Penna - Golden Pen Books, pg 306
Govostis Publishing SA, pg 307
Hestia-I D Hestia-Kollaros & Co Corporation, pg 308
Kalentis & Sia, pg 308
Kastaniotis Editions SA, pg 309
Kedros Publishers, pg 309
Odysseas Publications Ltd, pg 311
Patakis Publishers, pg 311

Guyana
Guyana Community Based Rehabilitation Progeamme, pg 314

Hong Kong
The Chinese University Press, pg 316
Hong Kong University Press, pg 317
Ming Pao Publications Ltd, pg 318
SCMP Book Publishing Ltd, pg 319
Sesame Publication Co, pg 319
Unicorn Books Ltd, pg 320

Hungary
Aranyhal Konyvkiado Goldfish Publishing, pg 320
Kossuth Kiado RT, pg 322
Park Konyvkiado Kft (Park Publisher), pg 324

India
Full Circle Publishing, pg 334
Gyan Publishing House, pg 335
National Book Organization, pg 342
Pointer Publishers, pg 345
Reliance Publishing House, pg 346
Sita Books & Periodicals Pvt Ltd, pg 349
Vidyarthi Mithram Press, pg 352
Viva Books Pvt Ltd, pg 352

Indonesia
Advent Indonesia Publishing, pg 353
Gramedia, pg 355
Lembaga Demografi Fakultas Ekonomi Universitas Indonesia, pg 355
Yayasan Obor Indonesia, pg 357

Ireland
A & A Farmar, pg 357
Gill & Macmillan Ltd, pg 360
Irish YouthWork Press, pg 361
Tivenan Publications, pg 364
Veritas Co Ltd, pg 364

Israel
Bitan Publishers Ltd, pg 365
Classikaletet, pg 366
Dyonon/Papyrus Publishing House of the Tel-Aviv, pg 366
Schocken Publishing House Ltd, pg 371
R Sirkis Publishers Ltd, pg 372

Italy
Gruppo Abele, pg 374
Editore Armando Armando SRL, pg 376
Belforte Editore Libraio srl, pg 377
Edizioni Centro Studi Erickson, pg 381
Elle Di Ci - Libreria Dottrina Cristiana, pg 387
Fatatrac, pg 388
Feguagiskia' Studios, pg 389
In Dialogo, pg 393
Red/Studio Redazionale, pg 405
Samaya SRL, pg 406

Japan
Alice-Kan, pg 415
Gakken Co Ltd, pg 417
Japan Publications Inc, pg 419
Kokudo-Sha Co Ltd, pg 421
Kosei Publishing Co Ltd, pg 421
Minerva Shobo Co Ltd, pg 422
Reimei-Shobo Co Ltd, pg 425
Seibido Shuppan Company Ltd, pg 426
Shufunotomo Co Ltd, pg 428
Tsukiji Shokan Publishing Co, pg 430

Kenya
Paulines Publications-Africa, pg 435

Democratic People's Republic of Korea
The Foreign Language Press Group, pg 436
Grand People's Study House, pg 436

Republic of Korea
Bo Ri Publishing Co Ltd, pg 437
Chung Rim Publishing Co Ltd, pg 438
Hak Won Publishing Co, pg 439
Hakmunsa Publishing Co, pg 439
Minjisa Publishing Co, pg 441
O Neul Publishing Co, pg 441

Latvia
Preses Nams, pg 445
Zvaigzne ABC Publishers Ltd, pg 445

Lebanon
Librairie du Liban Publishers (Sal), pg 446
Librairie Orientale sal, pg 446

Lithuania
Dargenis Publishers, pg 449
Sviesa Publishers, pg 449
Victoria Publishers, pg 450

Malaysia
S Abdul Majeed & Co, pg 454
Federal Publications Sdn Bhd, pg 455
Tropical Press Sdn Bhd, pg 459

Maldive Islands
Non-Formal Education Centre, pg 459

Mexico
Ediciones Culturales Internacionales SA de CV Edicion Compra y Venta de Libros, Casetes, Videos, pg 463
Del Verbo Emprender SA de CV, pg 464
Editorial Diana SA de CV, pg 464
Fernandez Editores SA de CV, pg 465

Libra Editorial SA de CV, pg 467
Editorial Limusa SA de CV, pg 467
Organizacion Cultural LP SA de CV, pg 469
Ediciones Promesa, SA de CV, pg 470
Selector SA de CV, pg 471
Editorial Trillas SA de CV, pg 472

Republic of Moldova

Editura Lumina, pg 473

Netherlands

Erven J Bijleveld, pg 479
De Boekerij BV, pg 479
Boom Uitgeverij, pg 479
Uitgeverij Christofoor, pg 480
Uitgeverij Ploegsma BV, pg 487
Sociaal en Cultureel Planbureau, pg 489
SWP, BV Uitgeverij, pg 490
Tirion Uitgevers BV, pg 490
Uitgeverij De Toorts, pg 490
Unieboek BV, pg 490

New Zealand

Nagare Press, pg 499
Nelson Price Milburn Ltd, pg 499
Reach Publications, pg 500
Shoal Bay Press Ltd, pg 501
Words Work, pg 502

Nigeria

Evans Brothers (Nigeria Publishers) Ltd, pg 504
West African Book Publishers Ltd, pg 507

Norway

Aschehoug Forlag, pg 508
H Aschehoug & Co (W Nygaard) A/S, pg 508

Philippines

Bookmark Inc, pg 518
Our Lady of Manaoag Publisher, pg 520
Rex Bookstores & Publishers, pg 520

Poland

PZWL Wydawnictwo Lekarskie Ltd, pg 526

Portugal

Difusao Cultural, pg 530
Direccao Geral Familia, pg 530
Impala, pg 532
Editorial Presenca, pg 535
Vega-Publicacao e Distribuicao de Livros e Revistas, Lda, pg 536

Romania

Editura Niculescu, pg 541
Rentrop & Straton Verlagsgruppe und Wirtschaftsconsulting, pg 542
Vremea Publishers Ltd, pg 543

Russian Federation

Airis Press, pg 543
Dom, Izdatel'stvo sovetskogo deskkogo fonda im & I Lenina, pg 544
Obdeestro Znanie, pg 547
Panorama Publishing House, pg 547
St Andrew's Biblical Theological College, pg 548

Serbia and Montenegro

Alfa-Narodna Knjiga, pg 552

Singapore

McGallen & Bolden Associates, pg 557
Taylor & Francis Asia Pacific, pg 558

Slovakia

Sofa, pg 560

Slovenia

Mladinska Knjiga International, pg 561
Zalozba Mihelac d o o, pg 562
Zalozba Obzorja d d Maribor, pg 562

South Africa

Human & Rousseau (Pty) Ltd, pg 564
Jacana Education, pg 565
New Africa Books (Pty) Ltd, pg 567
Struik Publishers (Pty) Ltd, pg 569

Spain

Edex, Centro de Recursos Comunitarios, pg 580
Editorial Editex SA, pg 581
Editorial Espasa-Calpe SA, pg 582
Hercules de Ediciones, SA, pg 586
Idea Books, SA, pg 587
LEDA (Las Ediciones de Arte), pg 589
Ediciones Medici SA, pg 591
Ediciones Morata SL, pg 592
Ediciones Norma SA, pg 593
Publicaciones y Ediciones Salamandra SA, pg 597
Ediciones de la Torre, pg 602
Tursen, SA, pg 603

Sweden

Eriksson & Lindgren Bokforlag, pg 611
Foerlagshuset Gothia, pg 612

Switzerland

Bohem Press Kinderbuchverlag, pg 619
Brunnen-Verlag Basel, pg 620
Editions Jouvence, pg 626

Taiwan, Province of China

Ai Chih Book Co Ltd, pg 638
Campus Evangelical Fellowship, Literature Department, pg 639
Chu Liu Book Company, pg 639
Commonwealth Publishing Company Ltd, pg 639
Echo Publishing Company Ltd, pg 639
Ho-Chi Book Publishing Co, pg 640
Laureate Book Co Ltd, pg 640
Linking Publishing Company Ltd, pg 641
Shy Mau & Shy Chaur Publishing Co Ltd, pg 641
Wei-Chuan Publishing Company Ltd, pg 642

United Republic of Tanzania

Central Tanganyika Press, pg 643
Tanzania Publishing House, pg 644

Thailand

Sangdad Publishing Company Ltd, pg 645

Turkey

Afa Yayincilik Sanayi Tic AS, pg 648
Alkim Kitapcilik-Yayimcilik, pg 649
Inkilap Publishers Ltd, pg 650
Kok Yayincilik, pg 650
Saray Medikal Yayin Tic Ltd Sti, pg 651

Ukraine

ASK Ltd, pg 653
Osvita, pg 654

United Kingdom

Act 3 Publishing, pg 655
BAAF Adoption & Fostering, pg 662
BILD Publications, pg 665
Blackwell Science Ltd, pg 667
Bloomsbury Publishing PLC, pg 668
Carroll & Brown Ltd, pg 675
Castlemead Publications, pg 676
Dorling Kindersley Ltd, pg 688
The Eurospan Group, pg 692
Free Association Books Ltd, pg 697
W H Freeman & Co Ltd, pg 697
HarperCollins UK, pg 705
Hawker Publications Ltd, pg 706
Hawthorn Press, pg 706
Health Development Agency, pg 706
Hodder & Stoughton General, pg 709
Hodder & Stoughton Religious, pg 709
JAI Press Ltd, pg 715
Jessica Kingsley Publishers, pg 718
LDA-Living & Learning (Cambridge) Ltd, pg 719
Frances Lincoln Ltd, pg 720
Kenneth Mason Publications Ltd, pg 726
Metro Books, pg 727
National Foster Care Association, pg 731
Nelson Thornes Ltd, pg 732
The NFER-NELSON Publishing Co Ltd, pg 733
Rivers Oram Press, pg 750
Speechmark Publishing Ltd, pg 760
Thomson Gale, pg 765
Trentham Books Ltd, pg 767
Virgin Publishing Ltd, pg 770
Whiting & Birch Ltd, pg 773

Uruguay

Prensa Medica Latinoamericana, pg 778

Zambia

Zambia Printing Company Ltd (ZPC), pg 782

Zimbabwe

College Press Publishers (Pvt) Ltd, pg 783

CIVIL ENGINEERING

Australia

EA Books, pg 20
H&H Publishing, pg 24
The Images Publishing Group Pty Ltd, pg 26
OTEN (Open Training & Education Network), pg 34
Standards Association of Australia, pg 42
Strucmech Publishing, pg 42

Austria

Springer-Verlag Wien, pg 58

Brazil

ARTMED Editora, pg 78
Editora Campus Ltda, pg 79
Editora FCO Ltda, pg 81
Hemus Editora Ltda, pg 83

Bulgaria

Todor Kableshkov University of Transport, pg 97

China

Chemical Industry Press, pg 101
China Ocean Press, pg 102
Higher Education Press, pg 105
Jilin Science & Technology Publishing House, pg 105
Knowledge Press, pg 106
The People's Communications Publishing House, pg 106
South China University of Science & Technology Press, pg 108
Southwest China Jiaotong University Press, pg 108
Tsinghua University Press, pg 109
Water Resources and Electric Power Press (CWPP), pg 109
Zhejiang University Press, pg 109

Costa Rica

Editorial de la Universidad de Costa Rica, pg 116

Dominican Republic

Pontificia Universidad Catolica Madre y Maestra, pg 136

Finland

Docendo Finland Oy, pg 141

France

Editions Hermes Science Publications, pg 167
Ouest Editions, pg 178
Presses de l'Ecole Nationale des Ponts et Chaussees, pg 181
Editions Springer France, pg 186

Germany

Bauverlag GmbH, pg 198
Chmielorz GmbH Verlag, pg 208
Ernst, Wilhelm & Sohn, Verlag Architektur und technische Wissenschaft GmbH & Co, pg 221
Ferd Dummler's Verlag, pg 223
Fraunhofer IRB Verlag Fraunhofer Informationszentrum Raum und Bau, pg 226
Hestra-Verlag Hernichel & Dr Strauss GmbH & Co KG, pg 237
Huthig GmbH & Co KG, pg 240
Institut fuer Baustoffe, Massivbau und Brandschutz/Bibliothek, pg 241
Kirschbaum Verlag GmbH, pg 246
Krafthand Verlag Walter Schultz GmbH, pg 250
Oekobuch Verlag & Versand GmbH, pg 266

Springer Science+Business Media GmbH & Co KG, pg 284
Verlag Stahleisen GmbH, pg 286
Suin Buch-Verlag, pg 289
B G Teubner Verlag, pg 290
Trans Tech Publications, pg 292
Friedr Vieweg & Sohn Verlag, pg 296
Vogel Medien GmbH & Co KG, pg 296
WEKA Firmengruppe GmbH & Co KG, pg 298
Verlag fuer Wirtschaft & Verwaltung Hubert Wingen GmbH & Co KG, pg 300

Ghana
Building & Road Research Institute (BRRI), pg 303

Greece
Kleidarithmos, Ekdoseis, pg 309

India
Addison-Wesley Pte Ltd, pg 327
Affiliated East West Press Pvt Ltd, pg 327
Charotar Publishing House, pg 332
Heritage Publishers, pg 335
Khanna Publishers, pg 339
Laxmi Publications Pvt Ltd, pg 340
Oxford & IBH Publishing Co Pvt Ltd, pg 344
Scientific Book Agency, pg 348
Sita Books & Periodicals Pvt Ltd, pg 349
South Asian Publishers Pvt Ltd, pg 350
Viva Books Pvt Ltd, pg 352
A H Wheeler & Co Ltd, pg 353

Italy
Edizioni Cremonese SRL, pg 383
DEI Tipographia del Genio Civile, pg 384
New Magazine Edizioni, pg 400

Japan
Chikyu-sha Co Ltd, pg 416
Corona Publishing Co Ltd, pg 416
Kajima Institute Publishing Co Ltd, pg 420
Maruzen Co Ltd, pg 422

Democratic People's Republic of Korea
Korea Science and Encyclopedia Publishing House, pg 436

Republic of Korea
Bo Moon Dang, pg 437

Latvia
Preses Nams, pg 445

Malaysia
Penerbit Universiti Teknologi Malaysia, pg 459

Mexico
Editorial Limusa SA de CV, pg 467

Netherlands
A A Balkema Uitgevers BV, pg 478
Delft University Press, pg 481
Hagen & Stam Uitgeverij Ten, pg 483

New Zealand
Southern Press Ltd, pg 501

Nigeria
Evans Brothers (Nigeria Publishers) Ltd, pg 504

Pakistan
National Book Foundation, pg 513

Poland
Polish Scientific Publishers PWN, pg 525
Instytut Techniki Budowlanej, Dzial Wydawniczo- Poligraficzny, pg 527

Portugal
Editora McGraw-Hill de Portugal Lda, pg 533

Romania
Editura Gryphon, pg 540

Russian Federation
Izdatelstvo Mordovskogo gosudarstvennogo, pg 547

Serbia and Montenegro
Savez Inzenjera i Tehnicara Jugoslavije, pg 553

Singapore
APAC Publishers Services Pte Ltd, pg 554
World Scientific Publishing Co Pte Ltd, pg 559

Spain
Ediciones Agrotecnicas, SL, pg 571
Ediciones Doce Calles SL, pg 579
Editorial Dossat SA, pg 580
Marcombo SA, pg 590
Rueda, SL Editorial, pg 598
Edicions de la Universitat Politecnica de Catalunya SL, pg 604

Switzerland
Marcel Dekker AG, pg 621
Presses Polytechniques et Universitaires Romandes, PPUR, pg 631
Vdf Hochschulverlag AG an der ETH Zurich, pg 636

Syrian Arab Republic
Damascus University Press, pg 638

Taiwan, Province of China
Fuh-Wen Book Co, pg 639
Chu Hai Publishing (Taiwan) Co Ltd, pg 640

United Republic of Tanzania
DUP (1996) Ltd, pg 643

Turkey
Caglayan Kitabevi, pg 649
Yapi-Endustri Merkezi Yayinlari-Yem Yayin, pg 652

United Kingdom
Concrete Information Ltd, pg 682
DMG Business Media Ltd, pg 688
Geological Society Publishing House, pg 699
IWA Publishing, pg 715
The Policy Press, pg 744
Research Studies Press Ltd (RSP), pg 749
RICS Books, pg 750
Spon Press, pg 760
Whittles Publishing, pg 773
WIT Press, pg 774

Viet Nam
Science & Technics Publishing House, pg 780

Zimbabwe
Standards Association of Zimbabwe (SAZ), pg 784

COMMUNICATIONS

Albania
State Textbook Publishing House, pg 1

Argentina
Diana Argentina SA, Editorial, pg 5
Edicial SA, pg 5
Editorial Paidos SAICF, pg 8

Australia
Australian Broadcasting Authority, pg 13
Finch Publishing, pg 22
Kerri Hamer, pg 24
James Nicholas Publishers Pty Ltd, pg 27
Pearson Education Australia, pg 36
Standards Association of Australia, pg 42
VCTA Publishing, pg 45
Woodlands Publications, pg 47

Austria
Buchkultur Verlags GmbH Zeitschrift fuer Literatur & Kunst, pg 49
Development News Ltd, pg 50
Dr Verena Hofstaetter, pg 52
Linde Verlag Wien GmbH, pg 53
Medien & Recht, pg 54
Oesterreichischer Kunst und Kulturverlag, pg 55
Springer-Verlag Wien, pg 58
Studien Verlag Gmbh, pg 58
Edition Va Bene, pg 59
WUV/Facultas Universitaetsverlag, pg 60

Belgium
Editions De Boeck-Larcier SA, pg 66
EPO Publishers, Printers, Booksellers, pg 67
VUB Brussels University Press, pg 74

Brazil
AGIR S/A Editora, pg 77
Editora Campus Ltda, pg 79
Editora Elevacao, pg 81
Fundacao Sao Paulo, EDUC, pg 82
Editora Lidador Ltda, pg 85
Edicoes Loyola SA, pg 85
Editora Mantiqueira de Ciencia e Arte, pg 86
Paulinas Editorial, pg 88
Editora Rocco Ltda, pg 89
Summus Editorial Ltda, pg 91
Talento Publicacoes Editora e Grafica Ltda, pg 91
Vozes Editora Ltda, pg 92

Bulgaria
Sita-MB, pg 97
Todor Kableshkov University of Transport, pg 97

Chile
Arrayan Editores, pg 98

China
Chemical Industry Press, pg 101
Chengdu Maps Publishing House, pg 101
Dalian Maritime University Press, pg 104
Electronics Industry Publishing House, pg 104
Fudan University Press, pg 104
Fujian Science & Technology Publishing House, pg 104
Heilongjiang Science & Technology Press, pg 105
Language Publishing House, pg 106
The People's Communications Publishing House, pg 106
The People's Posts & Telecommunication Publishing House, pg 107
Shandong University Press, pg 108
Shanghai Far East Publishers, pg 108

Colombia
Instituto Misionerao Hijas De San Pablo, pg 112
Editorial Panamericana, pg 112
Universidad Nacional Abierta y a Distancia, pg 113
Editorial Voluntad SA, pg 113

The Democratic Republic of the Congo
Facultes Catoliques de Kinshasa, pg 114
Saint-Paul, pg 114

Cote d'Ivoire
Universite d'Abidjan, pg 117

Czech Republic
Omnipress Praha, pg 126
Portal spol sro, pg 126

Denmark
Samfundslitteratur, pg 134

Dominican Republic
Pontificia Universidad Catolica Madre y Maestra, pg 136

Ecuador
Centro De Educacion Popular, pg 136
CIESPAL (Centro Internacional de Estudios Superiores de Comunicacion para America Latina), pg 136

Finland
Yliopistopaino/Helsinki University Press, pg 145

PUBLISHERS SUBJECT INDEX

France
Academie Nationale de Reims, pg 145
Editions Breal, pg 151
CNRS Editions, pg 155
Editions La Decouverte, pg 157
Les Editions du CFPJ (Centre de Formation et de Perfectionnement des Journalistes) - Sarl Presse et Formation, pg 160
Les Editions ESF, pg 160
ELLUG (Editions Litteraires et Linguistiques de l'Universite de Grenoble III), pg 161
Editions Juris Service, pg 170
Presses Universitaires de Grenoble, pg 181
Presses Universitaires de Nancy, pg 181
TOP Editions, pg 188
UNESCO Publishing, pg 188

Germany
Art Directors Club Verlag GmbH, pg 194
Bertelsmann Lexikon Verlag GmbH, pg 200
Beuth Verlag GmbH, pg 200
Oscar Brandstetter Verlag GmbH & Co KG, pg 204
Hans Christians Druckerei und Verlag GmbH & Co KG, pg 208
Cornelsen Verlag GmbH & Co OHG, pg 210
Daedalus Verlag, pg 210
Datacom Buchverlag GmbH, pg 211
Deutscher Fachverlag GmbH, pg 212
Deutscher Wirtschaftsdienst John von Freyend GmbH, pg 214
Deutsches Bucharchiv Muenchen, Institut fur Buchwissenschaften, pg 214
Extent Verlag und Service Wolfgang M Flamm, pg 223
Fachverlag Schiele & Schoen GmbH, pg 223
Feltron-Elektronik Zeissler & Co GmbH, pg 223
Festland Verlag GmbH, pg 224
Verlag Reinhard Fischer, pg 225
Franzis-Verlag GmbH, pg 226
Herbert von Halem Verlag, pg 233
von Hase & Koehler Verlag KG, pg 234
Huthig GmbH & Co KG, pg 240
Edition ID-Archiv/ID-Verlag, pg 240
Iudicium Verlag GmbH, pg 242
kopaed verlagsgmbh, pg 249
Kriebel Verlag GmbH, pg 250
Leipziger Universitaetsverlag GmbH, pg 253
Richard Pflaum Verlag GmbH & Co KG, pg 269
Psychologie Verlags Union GmbH, pg 272
Quintessenz Verlags-GmbH, pg 273
Verlag an der Ruhr GmbH, pg 277
I H Sauer Verlag GmbH, pg 278
K G Saur Verlag GmbH, A Gale/Thomson Learning Company, pg 278
Schueren Verlag GmbH, pg 281
Spiess Volker Wissenschaftsverlag GmbH, pg 284
Stauffenburg Verlag Brigitte Narr GmbH, pg 287
Telex-Verlag Jaeger & Waldmann GmbH, pg 289
Tuduv Verlagsgesellschaft mbH, pg 292
UVK Verlagsgesellschaft mbH, pg 294
VDE-Verlag GmbH, pg 294
Verlag Moderne Industrie AG & Co KG, pg 295
Vogel Medien GmbH & Co KG, pg 296
VS Verlag fur Sozialwissenschaften, pg 297
WEKA Firmengruppe GmbH & Co KG, pg 298
Herbert Wichmann Verlag, pg 299

Ghana
Ghana Universities Press (GUP), pg 304

Greece
Hestia-I D Hestia-Kollaros & Co Corporation, pg 308

Hong Kong
Electronic Technology Publishing Co Ltd, pg 317
Hong Kong University Press, pg 317
Modern Electronic & Computing Publishing Co Ltd, pg 318
Technology Exchange Ltd, pg 319

Hungary
Kossuth Kiado RT, pg 322
Osiris Kiado, pg 323

India
Asian Trading Corporation, pg 329
BS Publications, pg 331
Concept Publishing Co, pg 332
Gyan Publishing House, pg 335
Khanna Publishers, pg 339
Reliance Publishing House, pg 346
SAGE Publications India Pvt Ltd, pg 347
Satprakashan Sanchar Kendra, pg 348
Scientific Book Agency, pg 348
Somaiya Publications Pvt Ltd, pg 349
Sterling Publishers Pvt Ltd, pg 350
Viva Books Pvt Ltd, pg 352
A H Wheeler & Co Ltd, pg 353

Indonesia
Bina Rena Pariwara, pg 354

Ireland
Irish Management Institute, pg 361

Italy
Gruppo Abele, pg 374
Editore Armando Armando SRL, pg 376
Capone Editore SRL, pg 379
Edizioni Cultura della Pace, pg 383
Editori Laterza, pg 386
Esselibri, pg 388
In Dialogo, pg 393
Itaca, pg 393
RAI-ERI, pg 405

Jamaica
Association of Development Agencies, pg 413

Japan
Chikuma Shobo Publishing Co Ltd, pg 416
Nippon Hoso Shuppan Kyokai (NHK Publishing), pg 424
Thomson Learning Japan, pg 429

Kenya
Paulines Publications-Africa, pg 435

Democratic People's Republic of Korea
Grand People's Study House, pg 436
Korea Science and Encyclopedia Publishing House, pg 436

Republic of Korea
Bum-Woo Publishing Co, pg 437
Chung Rim Publishing Co Ltd, pg 438
Nanam Publications Co, pg 441
Oruem Publishing House, pg 442

Latvia
Nordik/Tapals Publishers Ltd, pg 445

The Former Yugoslav Republic of Macedonia
Medis, Skopje, pg 452

Madagascar
Societe Malgache d'Edition, pg 454

Malaysia
Pustaka Cipta Sdn Bhd, pg 458

Malta
Media Centre, pg 460

Mexico
Editorial Edicol SA, pg 464
Fondo de Cultura Economica, pg 465
Editorial Limusa SA de CV, pg 467
Nova Grupo Editorial SA de CV, pg 469
Plaza y Valdes SA de CV, pg 470

Morocco
Access International Services, pg 474
Societe Ennewrasse Service Librairie et Imprimerie, pg 475

Netherlands
BIS Publishers, pg 479
Boom Uitgeverij, pg 479
Uitgeverij Coutinho BV, pg 481
Otto Cramwinckel Uitgever, pg 481
Educatieve Uitgeverij Edu'Actief BV, pg 481
Uitgeverij Lemma BV, pg 485
Uitgeverij H Nelissen BV, pg 486

New Zealand
Moss Associates Ltd, pg 498
Nelson Price Milburn Ltd, pg 499

Peru
Ediciones Brown SA, pg 516
Universidad de Lima-Fondo de Desarollo Editorial, pg 517

Philippines
Communication Foundation for Asia Media Group (CFAMG), pg 518
Logos (Divine Word) Publications Inc, pg 519
New Day Publishers, pg 520
Our Lady of Manaoag Publisher, pg 520
Salesiana Publishers Inc, pg 521

Poland
Wydawnictwa Komunikacji i Lacznosci Co Ltd, pg 524

Portugal
Editora Classica, pg 530
Gradiva-Publicacnoes Lda, pg 532
Vega-Publicacao e Distribuicao de Livros e Revistas, Lda, pg 536

Romania
Aion Verlag, pg 538
Editura Excelsior Art, pg 539
Polirom Verlag, pg 542
Rentrop & Straton Verlagsgruppe und Wirtschaftsconsulting, pg 542

Russian Federation
N E Bauman Moscow State Technical University Publishers, pg 544
Fizmatlit Publishing Co, pg 545
Izdatelstvo Mir, pg 546
Nauka Publishers, pg 547
Izdatelstvo Radio i Svyaz, pg 548
Teorija Verojatnostej i ee Primenenija, pg 549

Serbia and Montenegro
Savez Inzenjera i Tehnicara Jugoslavije, pg 553

Singapore
McGallen & Bolden Associates, pg 557

Slovenia
Zalozba Mihelac d o o, pg 562

South Africa
Human & Rousseau (Pty) Ltd, pg 564

Spain
Editorial Bruno, pg 575
Comunidad Autonoma de Madrid, Servicio de Documentacion y Publicaciones, pg 578
Fragua Editorial, pg 583
Editorial Gustavo Gili SA, pg 585
Grupo Comunicar, pg 585
Marcombo SA, pg 590
Ediciones Paidos Iberica SA, pg 594
Editorial Sintesis, SA, pg 600
Ediciones de la Torre, pg 602

Sri Lanka
National Library & Documentation Centre, pg 607

Sweden
Allt om Hobby AB, pg 609
Bokforlaget Nya Doxa AB, pg 614
Samsprak Forlags AB, pg 615

935

SUBJECT INDEX

Switzerland
Castle Publications SA, pg 620
Drei-D-World und Foto-World Verlag und Vertrieb, pg 622
Promoedition SA, pg 631
Verkehrshaus der Schweiz, pg 636

Syrian Arab Republic
Damascus University Press, pg 638

Taiwan, Province of China
Designer Publisher Inc, pg 639

Thailand
Unesco Regional Office, Asia & the Pacific, pg 646

Turkey
IKI Nokta Research Press & Publications Industry & Trade Ltd, pg 650

United Kingdom
Adamantine Press Ltd, pg 655
Artech House, pg 659
Bloomsbury Publishing PLC, pg 668
DMG Business Media Ltd, pg 688
Elsevier Ltd, pg 691
ERA Technology Ltd, pg 692
The Eurospan Group, pg 692
ICC United Kingdom, pg 711
Institution of Electrical Engineers, pg 713
Kluwer Academic/Plenum Publishers, pg 718
Pearson Education Europe, Mideast & Africa, pg 739
Polybooks Ltd, pg 744
Research Studies Press Ltd (RSP), pg 749
Routledge, pg 751
SAGE Publications Ltd, pg 753
TFPL, pg 764
VNU Business Publications, pg 770

Uruguay
Nordan-Comunidad, pg 778
Ediciones Trilce, pg 778

Viet Nam
Science & Technics Publishing House, pg 780

Zambia
Multimedia Zambia, pg 781

Zimbabwe
Thomson Publications Zimbabwe (Pvt) Ltd, pg 784

COMPUTER SCIENCE

Argentina
Diana Argentina SA, Editorial, pg 5
Gram Editora, pg 6
Editorial Idearium de la Universidad de Mendoza (EDIUM), pg 6
Instituto Nacional de Ciencia y Tecnica Hidrica (INCYTH), pg 7

Australia
Edward Arnold (Australia) Pty Ltd, pg 12
Blackwell Publishing Asia, pg 15
Church Archivists Press, pg 18
Emerald City Books, pg 21
Illert Publications, pg 26
McGraw-Hill Australia Pty Ltd, pg 31
OTEN (Open Training & Education Network), pg 34
Pearson Education Australia, pg 36
Prospect Media Pty Ltd, pg 37
Tertiary Press, pg 43

Austria
Bohmann Druck und Verlag GmbH & Co KG, pg 49
International Institute for Applied Systems Analysis (IIASA), pg 52
Medien & Recht, pg 54
Andreas Schnider Verlags-Atelier, pg 57
Springer-Verlag Wien, pg 58

Belarus
Publishing Center of Belarus State University, pg 62

Belgium
Campinia Media VZW, pg 64
Easy Computing NV, pg 67
Marabout, pg 71
Wolters Plantyn Educatieve Uitgevers, pg 74

Brazil
Antenna Edicoes Tecnicas Ltda, pg 77
ARTMED Editora, pg 78
Berkeley Brasil Editora Ltda, pg 78
Callis Editora Ltda, pg 79
Editora Campus Ltda, pg 79
Editora Harbra Ltda, pg 83
Livraria Editora Infobook SA, pg 85
Edicoes Loyola SA, pg 85
LTC-Livros Tecnicos e Cientificos Editora S/A, pg 85
Makron Books do Brasil Editora Ltda, pg 86
Livraria Pioneira Editora/Enio Matheus Guazzelli e Cia Ltd, pg 88
Editora Revan Ltda, pg 89
Selecoes Eletronicas Editora Ltda, pg 90

Bulgaria
Aleks Soft, pg 93
Foi-Commerce, pg 94
Makros 2000 - Plovdiv, pg 95
Regalia 6 Publishing House, pg 96
TEMTO, pg 97

Chile
Arrayan Editores, pg 98

China
Aviation Industry Press, pg 101
Beijing Publishing House, pg 101
Beijing University Press, pg 101
Chengdu Maps Publishing House, pg 101
China Machine Press (CMP), pg 102
China Ocean Press, pg 102
Dalian Maritime University Press, pg 104
East China University of Science & Technology Press, pg 104
Electronics Industry Publishing House, pg 104
Fudan University Press, pg 104
Fujian Science & Technology Publishing House, pg 104
Guangdong Science & Technology Press, pg 105
Higher Education Press, pg 105
International Academic Publishers (IAP), pg 105
Jiangsu Science & Technology Publishing House, pg 105
Jilin Science & Technology Publishing House, pg 105
Metallurgical Industry Press (MIP), pg 106
Nanjing University Press, pg 106
National Defence Industry Press, pg 106
The People's Posts & Telecommunication Publishing House, pg 107
Science Press, pg 107
Shandong University Press, pg 108
Sichuan University Press, pg 108
South China University of Science & Technology Press, pg 108
Southwest China Jiaotong University Press, pg 108
Tianjin Science & Technology Publishing House, pg 108
Tsinghua University Press, pg 109
Wuhan University Press, pg 109
Zhejiang University Press, pg 109

Colombia
Pearson Educacion de Colombia LTDA, pg 112
Universidad Nacional Abierta y a Distancia, pg 113

The Democratic Republic of the Congo
Facultes Catoliques de Kinshasa, pg 114

Costa Rica
Instituto Interamericano de Cooperacion para la Agricultura (IICA), pg 115
Editorial de la Universidad de Costa Rica, pg 116

Cuba
Apocalipis Digital, pg 120
Pueblo y Educacion Editorial (PE), pg 121

Czech Republic
Grada Publishing, pg 123
SystemConsult, pg 127
Votobia sro, pg 128

Denmark
Ingenioeren/Boger, pg 132
Systime, pg 135

Egypt (Arab Republic of Egypt)
Dar Al-Thakafia Publishing, pg 138
Dar El Shorouk, pg 138

Finland
Docendo Finland Oy, pg 141

France
Editions Bertrand-Lacoste, pg 149
Editions Breal, pg 151
Cepadues Editions SA, pg 153
Dunod Editeur, pg 159
Editions d'Organisation, pg 160
Editions Eyrolles, pg 162
Editions First, pg 163
InterEditions, pg 169
Microsoft Press France, pg 175
Pearson Education France, pg 179
Presses de l'Ecole Nationale des Ponts et Chaussees, pg 181
Editions Springer France, pg 186
Editions Technip SA, pg 187
Editions Weka, pg 189

Germany
AOL-Verlag Frohmut Menze, pg 193
Verlag Beruf und Schule Belz KG, pg 200
Oscar Brandstetter Verlag GmbH & Co KG, pg 204
Data Becker GmbH & Co KG, pg 210
Econ Taschenbuchverlag, pg 218
Verlag Europa-Lehrmittel GmbH & Co KG, pg 221
Feltron-Elektronik Zeissler & Co GmbH, pg 223
Ferd Dummler's Verlag, pg 223
Franzis-Verlag GmbH, pg 226
Friedrich Kiehl Verlag GmbH, pg 227
Carl Hanser Verlag, pg 234
Rudolf Haufe Verlag GmbH & Co KG, pg 235
Huthig GmbH & Co KG, pg 240
International Thomson Publishing (ITP), pg 242
ITpress Verlag, pg 242
Konradin-Verlagsgruppe, pg 249
Naumann & Goebel Verlagsgesellschaft mbH, pg 263
Net World Vision GmbH, pg 263
Neuer Honos Verlag GmbH, pg 264
Pearson Education Deutschland GmbH, pg 268
Rossipaul Kommunikation GmbH, pg 277
Springer Science+Business Media GmbH & Co KG, pg 284
Sybex Verlag GmbH, pg 289
Tangens Systemverlag GmbH, pg 289
Te-Wi Verlag Unternehmensbereich Buch der Ziff Verlag GmbH, pg 289
B G Teubner Verlag, pg 290
UTB fuer Wissenschaft Uni Taschenbuecher GmbH, pg 294
Verlag Moderne Industrie AG & Co KG, pg 295
Friedr Vieweg & Sohn Verlag, pg 296
Vogel Medien GmbH & Co KG, pg 296
WRS Verlag Wirtschaft, Recht und Steuern GmbH & Co KG, pg 301
Fachbuchverlag Armin W Wuth, pg 301

Ghana
Building & Road Research Institute (BRRI), pg 303

Greece
Diavlos, pg 306
Epikerotita, pg 307
Giourdas Moschos, pg 307
Govostis Publishing SA, pg 307
Kastaniotis Editions SA, pg 309
Kleidarithmos, Ekdoseis, pg 309

Hong Kong
Chung Hwa Book Co (HK) Ltd, pg 316
Electronic Technology Publishing Co Ltd, pg 317
Modern Electronic & Computing Publishing Co Ltd, pg 318

Times Publishing (Hong Kong) Ltd, pg 319
The University of Hong Kong, Department of Philosophy, pg 320

Hungary

Magyar Tudomanyos Akademia Koezponti Fizikai Kutato Intezet Koenyvtara, pg 322
Mueszaki Koenyvkiado Ltd, pg 323
Panem, pg 324
Statiqum Kiado es Nyomda Kft, pg 324

India

Addison-Wesley Pte Ltd, pg 327
Affiliated East West Press Pvt Ltd, pg 327
Allied Book Centre, pg 328
Authorspress, pg 329
Bhawan Book Service, Publishers & Distributors, pg 330
Bookionics, pg 331
BPB Publications, pg 331
BS Publications, pg 331
Frank Brothers & Co Publishers Ltd, pg 334
Galgotia Publications Pvt Ltd, pg 334
Heritage Publishers, pg 335
Khanna Publishers, pg 339
Laxmi Publications Pvt Ltd, pg 340
Mehta Publishers, pg 341
Narosa Publishing House, pg 342
Pitambar Publishing Co (P) Ltd, pg 345
Popular Prakashan Pvt Ltd, pg 345
Pustak Mahal, pg 345
Scientific Book Agency, pg 348
Shaibya Prakashan Bibhag, pg 349
Sita Books & Periodicals Pvt Ltd, pg 349
Sterling Information Technologies, pg 350
Sultan Chand & Sons Pvt Ltd, pg 350
Vidya Puri, pg 352
Vidyarthi Mithram Press, pg 352
Vikas Publishing House Pvt Ltd, pg 352
S Viswanathan (Printers & Publishers) Pvt Ltd, pg 352
A H Wheeler & Co Ltd, pg 353

Indonesia

Andi Offset, pg 353
Dinastindo, pg 354
Gramedia, pg 355
PT Indira, pg 355

Ireland

The Educational Company of Ireland, pg 359

Israel

Dalia Peled Publishers, Division of Modan, pg 366
Hod-Ami, Computer Books Ltd, pg 368
Open University of Israel, pg 371

Italy

Edizioni di Comunita SpA, pg 383
Esselibri, pg 388
Giuseppe Laterza Editore, pg 391
Herbita Editrice di Leonardo Palermo, pg 392
Marsilio Editori SpA, pg 397
Franco Muzzio Editore, pg 400
Editoriale Scienza, pg 407

Tecniche Nuove SpA, pg 410
Zanichelli Editore SpA, pg 412

Japan

Baifukan Co Ltd, pg 415
Corona Publishing Co Ltd, pg 416
Dobunshoin Publishers Co, pg 416
Gakken Co Ltd, pg 417
Keigaku Publishing Co Ltd, pg 420
Kindai Kagaku Sha Co Ltd, pg 421
Kyoritsu Shuppan Co Ltd, pg 422
Maruzen Co Ltd, pg 422
Nikkagiren Shuppan-Sha (JUSE Press Ltd), pg 424
Nippon Jitsugyo Publishing Co Ltd, pg 424
Obunsha Co Ltd, pg 424
Pearson Education Japan, pg 425
Sagano Shoin, pg 426
Sangyo-Tosho Publishing Co Ltd, pg 426
Seibido Shuppan Company Ltd, pg 426
Toppan Co Ltd, pg 430

Jordan

Jordan Book Centre Co Ltd, pg 432

Kazakstan

Al-Farabi Kazakh National University, pg 432

Republic of Korea

Ahn Graphics, pg 437
B & B, pg 437
Bo Moon Dang, pg 437
Chung Rim Publishing Co Ltd, pg 438
Hakmunsa Publishing Co, pg 439
Hongik Media Plus Ltd, pg 439
Ohmsa, pg 441
Pearson Education Korea Ltd, pg 442
Prompter Publications, pg 442

Latvia

Lielvards Ltd, pg 445

Lebanon

Arab Institute for Research & Publishing, pg 445
Arab Scientific Publishers BP, pg 445
Librairie du Liban Publishers (Sal), pg 446

Lithuania

Klaipedos Universiteto Leidykla, pg 449
TEV Leidykla, pg 450

The Former Yugoslav Republic of Macedonia

Medis, Skopje, pg 452
Seizmoloska Opservatorija, pg 453
Zumpres Publishing Firm, pg 453

Malaysia

Federal Publications Sdn Bhd, pg 455
Penerbit Universiti Sains Malaysia, pg 458
Pustaka Cipta Sdn Bhd, pg 458
Penerbit Universiti Teknologi Malaysia, pg 459

Mauritius

Editions de l'Ocean Indien Ltd, pg 461

Mexico

Alfaomega Grupo Editor SA de CV, pg 462
Editora Cientifica Medica Latinoamerican SA de CV, pg 463
Centro de Estudios Monetarios Latinoamericanos (CEMLA), pg 465
Grupo Editorial Iberoamerica, SA de CV, pg 466
Editorial Limusa SA de CV, pg 467
Organizacion Cultural LP SA de CV, pg 469
Pearson Educacion de Mexico, SA de CV, pg 470
Sayrols Editorial SA de CV, pg 471
Ventura Ediciones, SA de CV, pg 473

Netherlands

Erven J Bijleveld, pg 479
BoekWerk, pg 479
A W Bruna Uitgevers BV, pg 480
Elsevier Science BV, pg 482
Hagen & Stam Uitgeverij Ten, pg 483
IOS Press BV, pg 484
De Muiderkring BV, pg 486
Pearson Education Netherlands, pg 487
Uitgeverij Het Spectrum BV, pg 489
Sybex BV, pg 490
Tirion Uitgevers BV, pg 490
Twente University Press, pg 490
Unieboek BV, pg 490
VNU Business Press Group BV, pg 492

New Zealand

ESA Publications (NZ) Ltd, pg 496
Learning Guides (Writers & Publishers Ltd), pg 497
Nelson Price Milburn Ltd, pg 499

Norway

Vett & Viten AS, pg 511

Paraguay

Instituto de Ciencias de la Computacion (NCR), pg 516
Intercontinental Editora, pg 516

Peru

Fondo Editorial de la Pontificia Universidad Catolica del Peru, pg 517
Universidad de Lima-Fondo de Desarollo Editorial, pg 517

Philippines

Mutual Book Inc, pg 519
Salesiana Publishers Inc, pg 521

Poland

Komputerowa Oficyna Wydawnicza Help, pg 523
Wydawnictwa Naukowo-Techniczne, pg 524
Polish Scientific Publishers PWN, pg 525
Oficyna Wydawnicza Read Me, pg 526

Portugal

Edicoes Cetop, pg 529
Dinalivro, pg 530
FCA Editora de Informatica, pg 531

Gradiva-Publicacnoes Lda, pg 532
Lidel Edicoes Tecnicas, Lda, pg 533
Livraria Minerva, pg 533
Lua Viajante-Edicao e Distribuicao de Livros e Material Audiovisual, Lda, pg 533
Editora McGraw-Hill de Portugal Lda, pg 533
Editorial Presenca, pg 535
Edicoes Silabo, pg 536
Vega-Publicacao e Distribuicao de Livros e Revistas, Lda, pg 536

Romania

Editura Academiei Romane, pg 538
Editora All, pg 538
Editura Clusium, pg 539
Editura Minerva, pg 541
Pallas-Akademia Editura, pg 541
Rentrop & Straton Verlagsgruppe und Wirtschaftsconsulting, pg 542
Editura Teora, pg 542

Russian Federation

N E Bauman Moscow State Technical University Publishers, pg 544
Energoatomizdat, pg 544
FGUP Izdatelstvo Mashinostroenie, pg 544
Finansy i Statistika Publishing House, pg 544
Fizmatlit Publishing Co, pg 545
INFRA-M Izdatel'skij dom, pg 545
KUbK Publishing House, pg 546
Izdatelstvo Mir, pg 546
Nauka Publishers, pg 547
Izdatel'stvo Nizhegorodskogo Gosudarstvennogo Univ, pg 547
Izdatelstvo Prosveshchenie, pg 548
Izdatelstvo Radio i Svyaz, pg 548

Serbia and Montenegro

Tehnicka Knjiga, pg 552

Singapore

APAC Publishers Services Pte Ltd, pg 554
McGallen & Bolden Associates, pg 557
Tech Publications Pte Ltd, pg 558
World Scientific Publishing Co Pte Ltd, pg 559

Slovakia

Ustav informacii a prognoz skolstva mladeze a telovychovy, pg 561

South Africa

Educum Publishers Ltd, pg 563
Heinemann Publishers (Pty) Ltd, pg 564
Reader's Digest Southern Africa, pg 568

Spain

Centro de Estudios Adams-Ediciones Valbuena SA, pg 571
Ediciones Diaz de Santos SA, pg 579
Ediciones Gestio 2000 SA, pg 585
Marcombo SA, pg 590
Editorial Paraninfo SA, pg 595
Pulso Ediciones, SL, pg 597
RA-MA, Libreria y Editorial Microinformatica, pg 597
Servicio de Publicaciones Universidad de Cordoba, pg 599
Editorial Sintesis, SA, pg 600

SUBJECT INDEX   BOOK

Editores Tecnicos Asociados SA, pg 601
Universidad de Valladolid Secretariado de Publicaciones e Intercambio Editorial, pg 604
Edicions de la Universitat Politecnica de Catalunya SL, pg 604
Editorial Zendrera Zariquiey, SA, pg 605

Sri Lanka

Ministry of Education, pg 607
National Library & Documentation Centre, pg 607

Sweden

Pagina Forlags AB, pg 614
Bokforlaget Spektra AB, pg 615
Studentlitteratur AB, pg 616

Switzerland

Bibliographisches Institut & F A Brockhaus AG, pg 619
Verlag Harri Deutsch, pg 622
Pearson Education, pg 631
Presses Polytechniques et Universitaires Romandes, PPUR, pg 631
Vdf Hochschulverlag AG an der ETH Zurich, pg 636
Weka Informations Schriften Verlag AG, pg 637

Syrian Arab Republic

Damascus University Press, pg 638

Taiwan, Province of China

Fuh-Wen Book Co, pg 639
Chu Hai Publishing (Taiwan) Co Ltd, pg 640
Hsiao Yuan Publication Co, Ltd, pg 640
Lead Wave Publishing Company Ltd, pg 640
San Min Book Co Ltd, pg 641
Shy Mau & Shy Chaur Publishing Co Ltd, pg 641
Wu Nan Book Co Ltd, pg 642

United Republic of Tanzania

Press & Publicity Centre Ltd, pg 644

Turkey

Alkim Kitapcilik-Yayimcilik, pg 649
Arkadas Ltd, pg 649
Saray Medikal Yayin Tic Ltd Sti, pg 651
Seckin Yayinevi, pg 651
Yetkin Printing & Publishing Co Inc, pg 652
Yuce Reklam Yay Dagt AS, pg 652

Ukraine

ASK Ltd, pg 653
Naukova Dumka Publishers, pg 653

United Kingdom

Advisory Unit: Computers in Education, pg 655
Artech House, pg 659
Association for Science Education, pg 661
Bernard Babani (Publishing) Ltd, pg 662
Blackwell Publishing Ltd, pg 666
Cambridge University Press, pg 674

Dickson Price Publishers Ltd, pg 687
Eaglemoss Publications Ltd, pg 689
Edinburgh University Press Ltd, pg 689
Edition XII, pg 690
Elsevier Ltd, pg 691
ERA Technology Ltd, pg 692
The Eurospan Group, pg 692
Facet Publishing, pg 694
W H Freeman & Co Ltd, pg 697
Haynes Publishing, pg 706
Helicon Publishing Ltd, pg 707
Hodder Education, pg 709
Immediate Publishing, pg 712
Institute of Physics Publishing, pg 713
Institution of Electrical Engineers, pg 713
Intellect Ltd, pg 713
Jones & Bartlett International, pg 716
Kluwer Academic/Plenum Publishers, pg 718
Learning Matters Ltd, pg 720
Letts Educational, pg 720
McGraw-Hill Publishing Company, pg 726
MIT Press Ltd, pg 728
Open University Worldwide, pg 736
Palgrave Publishers Ltd, pg 737
PC Publishing, pg 739
Pearson Education, pg 739
Research Studies Press Ltd (RSP), pg 749
Rooster Books Ltd, pg 751
SAGE Publications Ltd, pg 753
Skoob Russell Square, pg 758
Springer-Verlag London Ltd, pg 760
Take That Ltd, pg 762
Taylor & Francis, pg 763
Taylor Graham Publishing, pg 764
TFPL, pg 764
Transworld Publishers Ltd, pg 766
TSO (The Stationery Office), pg 767
VNU Business Publications, pg 770
Ward Lock Educational Co Ltd, pg 771
Which? Ltd, pg 772
Wiley Europe Ltd, pg 773
WIT Press, pg 774

Uruguay

La Flor del Itapebi, pg 777
Editia Uruguay, pg 778

Venezuela

Vadell Hermanos Editores CA, pg 780

Viet Nam

Science & Technics Publishing House, pg 780

COOKERY

Albania

NL SH, pg 1

Argentina

Editorial Caymi SACI, pg 4
Editorial Ruy Diaz SAEIC, pg 5
Errepar SA, pg 5
Librograf Editora, pg 7
Ediciones Preescolar SA, pg 8

Australia

ACP Publishing Pty Ltd, pg 10
Allen & Unwin Pty Ltd, pg 11

Edward Arnold (Australia) Pty Ltd, pg 12
Barbara Beckett Publishing Pty Ltd, pg 14
Cookery Book, pg 18
Egan Publishing Pty Ltd, pg 21
Horan Wall & Walker, pg 26
Lansdowne Publishing Pty Ltd, pg 28
Sandra Lee Agencies, pg 28
Mayne Publishing, pg 31
Anne O'Donovan Pty Ltd, pg 34
Oriental Publications, pg 34
Parabel Place, pg 35
Penguin Group (Australia), pg 36
R & R Publications Pty Ltd, pg 38
Rams Skull Press, pg 38
Regency Publishing, pg 39
Simon & Schuster (Australia) Pty Ltd, pg 41
Social Club Books, pg 41
Wakefield Press Pty Ltd, pg 46
The Watermark Press, pg 46

Austria

Carinthia Verlag, pg 49
Czernin Verlag Ltd, pg 49
Ennsthaler GesmbH & Co KG, pg 50
Haymon-Verlag GesmbH, pg 51
Leopold Stocker Verlag, pg 53
Niederosterreichisches Pressehaus Druck- und Verlagsgesellschaft mbH, pg 54
Verlag Orac im Verlag Kremayr & Scheriau, pg 56
Verlag des Osterr Kneippbundes GmbH, pg 56
Richard Pils Publication PN°1, pg 56
Pinguin-Verlag, Pawlowski GmbH, pg 56
Verlag Anton Pustet, pg 56
Trauner Verlag, pg 58
Verlag Veritas Mediengesellschaft mbH, pg 59

Belarus

Belaruskaya Encyklapedyya, pg 62

Belgium

NV Artis-Historia, pg 63
Koepel van de Vlaamse Noord - Zuidbeweging 11.11.11, pg 69
Uitgeverij Lannoo NV, pg 69
Marabout, pg 71
Henri Proost & Co, Pvba, pg 72

Brazil

A & A & A Edicoes e Promocoes Internacionais Ltda, pg 76
Abril SA, pg 76
AGIR S/A Editora, pg 77
Editora Antroposofica Ltda, pg 77
Editora Bertrand Brasil Ltda, pg 78
Brinque Book Editora de Livros Ltda, pg 79
Callis Editora Ltda, pg 79
Editora Companhia das Letras/ Editora Schwarcz Ltda, pg 80
Conquista, Empresa de Publicacoes Ltda, pg 80
Companhia Editora Forense, pg 81
Editora Gaia Ltda, pg 82
Editora Globo SA, pg 82
LDA Editores Ltda, pg 84
Libreria Editora Ltda, pg 85
Livraria Nobel S/A, pg 85
Editora Manole Ltda, pg 86
Editora Marco Zero Ltda, pg 86
Editora Melhoramentos Ltda, pg 86

Editora Nova Alexandria Ltda, pg 87
Rede Das Artes (Boccato Editores Collector's), pg 89
Editora Rideel Ltda, pg 89
Editora Vecchi SA, pg 92

Bulgaria

Darzhavno Izdatelstvo Zemizdat, pg 93
Pejo K Javorov Publishing House, pg 95
Kibea Publishing Co, pg 95
Kralica MAB, pg 95
MATEX, pg 95
Rakla, pg 96

Chile

Editora Nueva Generacion, pg 100

China

Beijing Publishing House, pg 101
China Light Industry Press, pg 102
Foreign Languages Press, pg 104
Guangdong Science & Technology Press, pg 105
Higher Education Press, pg 105
Jilin Science & Technology Publishing House, pg 105
Jinan Publishing House, pg 105
Morning Glory Press, pg 106
Tianjin Science & Technology Publishing House, pg 108

Colombia

Editorial Santillana SA, pg 112
Villegas Editores Ltda, pg 113
Editorial Voluntad SA, pg 113

Costa Rica

Editorial de la Universidad de Costa Rica, pg 116

Croatia

ALFA dd za izdavacke, graficke i trgovacke poslove, pg 117
Vitagraf, pg 119

Cuba

Editorial Oriente, pg 120

Czech Republic

Nakladatelstvi Jan Vasut, pg 124
Pavla Momcilova, pg 125
Vitalis sro, pg 128
Votobia sro, pg 128

Denmark

Aschehoug Dansk Forlag A/S, pg 129
Christian Ejlers' Forlag aps, pg 131
Gads Forlag, pg 131
Forlaget Hjulet, pg 132
Politikens Forlag A/S, pg 133

Estonia

Perioodika, pg 140
Sinisukk, pg 140
Valgus Publishers, pg 140

Fiji

Lotu Pacifika Productions, pg 141

Finland

SV-Kauppiaskanava Oy, pg 144

PUBLISHERS SUBJECT INDEX

France

Editions de l'Armancon, pg 147
Armenia Editions, pg 147
ATP - Packager, pg 148
Editions de l'Aube, pg 148
Editions A Barthelemy, pg 149
Societe Nouvelle Rene Baudouin, pg 149
Editions Bertout, pg 149
Pierre Bordas & Fils, Editions, pg 150
Editions Casterman, pg 152
Editions du Chene, pg 154
Le Cherche Midi Editeur, pg 154
Jean-P Delville Editions, pg 157
Editions Edisud, pg 159
Editions Entente, pg 161
EPA (Editions Pratiques Automobiles), pg 161
Editions Pierre Fanlac, pg 162
Editions Filipacchi-Sonodip, pg 163
Editions Jean Paul Gisserot, pg 165
Editions Glenat, pg 165
Editions Jacques Grancher, pg 165
Hachette Pratiques, pg 167
Editions du Jaguar, pg 169
Jouvence Editions, pg 170
Editions Lacour-Olle, pg 170
Michel Lafon Publishing, pg 171
Langues & Mondes-L'Asiatheque, pg 171
Editions du Laquet, pg 171
Editions Larousse, pg 171
Editions Lavoisier, pg 171
LT Editions-Jacques Lanore, pg 173
Editions Menges, pg 175
Editions Albin Michel, pg 175
Noir Sur Blanc, pg 177
Editions Ouest-France, pg 178
Payot & Rivages, pg 179
Editions Christian Pirot, pg 180
Editions Rombaldi SA, pg 183
Editions du Rouergue, pg 183
Editions Sang de la Terre, pg 184
Editions Sud Ouest, pg 186
Taride Editions, pg 187
Terre Vivante, pg 187
La Vague a l'ame, pg 188

French Polynesia

Scoop/Au Vent des Iles, pg 189

Germany

Ars Edition GmbH, pg 194
Ars Vivendi Verlag, pg 194
Artcolor, pg 194
Aufstieg-Verlag GmbH, pg 195
Bassermann Verlag, pg 197
Buchverlage Langen-Mueller/Herbig, pg 205
Aenne Burda Verlag, pg 206
Chmielorz GmbH Verlag, pg 208
Christian Verlag GmbH, pg 208
Hans Christians Druckerei und Verlag GmbH & Co KG, pg 208
Compact Verlag GmbH, pg 209
Edition Dia, pg 214
Dreisam Ratgeber in der Rutsker Verlag GmbH, pg 216
Verlagsgruppe Droemer Knaur GmbH & Co KG, pg 216
DuMont monte Verlag GmbH & Co KG, pg 217
DuMont Reiseverlag GmbH & Co KG, pg 217
Fachbuchverlag Pfanneberg & Co, pg 223
Falken-Verlag GmbH, pg 223
Gildefachverlag GmbH & Co KG, pg 229
Graefe und Unzer Verlag GmbH, pg 230

Walter Haedecke Verlag, pg 232
Mary Hahn's Kochbuchverlag, pg 233
Heel Verlag GmbH, pg 235
F A Herbig Verlagsbuchhandlung GmbH, pg 236
Wilhelm Heyne Verlag, pg 237
Verlag Wolfgang Hoelker, pg 238
Jahreszeiten-Verlag GmbH, pg 242
Verlag Winfried Jenior, pg 243
Kochbuch Verlag Olga Leeb, pg 247
Koenemann Verlagesellschaft mbH, pg 248
Kunstverlag Weingarten GmbH, pg 251
Landbuch-Verlagsgesellschaft mbH, pg 251
Matthaes Verlag GmbH, pg 257
Medizinisch-Literarische Verlagsgesellschaft mbH, pg 258
Midena Verlag, pg 260
Mosaik Verlag GmbH, pg 262
Naumann & Goebel Verlagsgesellschaft mbH, pg 263
Nebel Verlag GmbH, pg 263
Neuer Honos Verlag GmbH, pg 264
Verlag Neues Leben GmbH, pg 264
Oertel & Sporer GmbH & Co, pg 266
Dr Oetker Verlag KG, pg 266
Orbis Verlag fur Publizistik GmbH, pg 267
Pala-Verlag GmbH, pg 268
Walter Rau Verlag GmbH & Co KG, pg 273
Regura Verlag, pg 274
Romiosini Verlag, pg 276
Schangrila Verlags und Vertriebs GmbH, pg 279
Sigloch Edition Helmut Sigloch GmbH & Co KG, pg 283
Springer Science+Business Media GmbH & Co KG, pg 284
Suedwest Verlag GmbH & Co KG, pg 289
Tipress Dienstleistungen fur das Verlagswesen GmbH, pg 291
Tomus Verlag GmbH, pg 291
Neuer Umschau Buchverlag, pg 293
Verlagsgruppe Weltbild GmbH, pg 298
Westholsteinische Verlagsanstalt und Verlagsdruckerei Boyens & Co, pg 299
Zambon Verlag, pg 302
ZS Verlag Zabert Sandmann GmbH, pg 302

Ghana

Adaex Educational Publications Ltd, pg 302
Black Mask Ltd, pg 303
World Literature Project, pg 305

Greece

Akritas, pg 305
Alamo Hellas, pg 305
Vefa Alexiadou Editions, pg 305
Chrysi Penna - Golden Pen Books, pg 306
Ekdoseis Domi AE, pg 306
Exandas Publishers, pg 307
Kalentis & Sia, pg 308
Kastaniotis Editions SA, pg 309
Orfanidis Publications, pg 311
Patakis Publishers, pg 311

Hong Kong

CFW Publications Ltd, pg 316
Chopsticks Publications Ltd, pg 316
Ming Pao Publications Ltd, pg 318
SCMP Book Publishing Ltd, pg 319

Hungary

Advent Kiado, pg 320
Aranyhal Konyvkiado Goldfish Publishing, pg 320
Corvina Books Ltd, pg 321
Novorg International Szervezo es Kiado kft, pg 323
Officina Nova Konyvek, pg 323

Iceland

Bokautgafan Orn og Orlygur ehf, pg 325
Setberg, pg 326

India

Ananda Publishers Pvt Ltd, pg 328
Bani Mandir, Book-Sellers, Publishers & Educational Suppliers, pg 329
Brijbasi Printers Pvt Ltd, pg 331
Diamond Comics (P) Ltd, pg 333
Dutta Publishing Co Ltd, pg 333
Frank Brothers & Co Publishers Ltd, pg 334
Full Circle Publishing, pg 334
Gyan Publishing House, pg 335
Jaico Publishing House, pg 338
Orient Paperbacks, pg 344
Popular Prakashan Pvt Ltd, pg 345
Prabhat Prakashan, pg 345
Pratibha Pratishthan, pg 345
Pustak Mahal, pg 345
Roli Books Pvt Ltd, pg 347
Sat Sahitya Prakashan, pg 348
Scientific Book Agency, pg 348
UBS Publishers Distributors Ltd, pg 351
Vakils Feffer & Simons Ltd, pg 352
Vidyarthi Mithram Press, pg 352
Vision Books Pvt Ltd, pg 352

Indonesia

PT Dian Rakyat, pg 354
Gramedia, pg 355

Ireland

A & A Farmar, pg 357
An Gum, pg 358
Attic Press Ltd, pg 358
Careers & Educational Publishers Ltd, pg 358
Estragon Press Ltd, pg 359
Gill & Macmillan Ltd, pg 360
The Goldsmith Press Ltd, pg 360
The O'Brien Press Ltd, pg 362
On Stream Publications Ltd, pg 362

Israel

Classikaletet, pg 366
Dekel Publishing House, pg 366
Feldheim Publishers Ltd, pg 367
Gefen Publishing House Ltd, pg 367
Massada Press Ltd, pg 370
Massada Publishers Ltd, pg 370
Modan Publishers Ltd, pg 370
Pitspopany Press, pg 371
R Sirkis Publishers Ltd, pg 372
Steimatzky Group Ltd, pg 372
Zmora-Bitan, Publishers Ltd, pg 374

Italy

Athesia Verlag Bozen, pg 377
Giuseppe Bonanno Editore, pg 378
Casa Editrice Bonechi, pg 378
Il Castello srl, pg 380
Di Baio Editore SpA, pg 385
Editoriale Domus SpA, pg 385

ERGA SNC di Carla Ottino Merli & C (Edizioni Realizzazioni Grafiche - Artigiana), pg 388
Fenice 2000, pg 389
Editoriale Fernando Folini, pg 389
Arnaldo Forni Editore SRL, pg 389
Adriano Gallina Editore sas, pg 389
Ernesto Gremese Editore srl, pg 391
Gremese International srl, pg 391
Macro Edizioni, pg 397
McRae Books, pg 398
Mundici - Zanetti, pg 400
Maria Pacini Fazzi Editore, pg 402
Pheljna Edizioni d'Arte e Suggestione, pg 403
Daniela Piazza Editore, pg 403
Edizioni Piemme SpA, pg 403
Priuli e Verlucca, Editori, pg 404
Rara Istituto Editoriale di Bibliofilia e Reprints, pg 405
Reverdito Edizioni, pg 405
Edizioni del Riccio SAS di G Bernardi, pg 405
Edizioni Scientifiche Italiane, pg 407
Tappeiner, pg 409
La Tartaruga Edizioni SAS, pg 409
TEA Tascabili degli Editori Associati SpA, pg 409
Zanfi-Logos, pg 412

Jamaica

Carib Publishing Ltd, pg 413
LMH Publishing Ltd, pg 414
Ian Randle Publishers Ltd, pg 414

Japan

Contex Corporation, pg 416
Dohosha Publishing Co Ltd, pg 417
Japan Publications Inc, pg 419
Kodansha International Ltd, pg 421
Nagaoka Shoten Co Ltd, pg 423
Nihon Vogue Co Ltd, pg 424
Nippon Hoso Shuppan Kyokai (NHK Publishing), pg 424
President Inc, pg 425
Sanyo Shuppan Boeki Co Inc, pg 426
Seibido Shuppan Company Ltd, pg 426
Shufu-to-Seikatsu Sha Ltd, pg 428
Shufunotomo Co Ltd, pg 428
Tankosha Publishing Co Ltd, pg 429
Charles E Tuttle Publishing Co Inc, pg 430

Kenya

Heinemann Kenya Ltd (EAEP), pg 434
Kenway Publications Ltd, pg 434

Democratic People's Republic of Korea

The Foreign Language Press Group, pg 436

Republic of Korea

Hak Won Publishing Co, pg 439
Hollym Corporation; Publishers, pg 439
Seoul International Publishing House, pg 443
Shinkwang Publishing Co, pg 443
Yearimdang Publishing Co, pg 443

Laos People's Democratic Republic

Lao-phanit, pg 444

SUBJECT INDEX

Latvia
Alberts XII, pg 444

Lebanon
Arab Institute for Research & Publishing, pg 445
Arab Scientific Publishers BP, pg 445
Dar El Ilm Lilmalayin, pg 446
Librairie du Liban Publishers (Sal), pg 446
Librairie Orientale sal, pg 446

Lithuania
Baltos Lankos, pg 449

Luxembourg
Guy Binsfeld & Co Sarl, pg 450
Editions Emile Borschette, pg 450

Madagascar
Foibe Filan-Kevitry NY Mpampianatra (FOFIPA), pg 453

Malaysia
S Abdul Majeed & Co, pg 454
Berita Publishing Sdn Bhd, pg 455
Times Educational Co Sdn Bhd, pg 459

Malta
Publishers' Enterprises Group (PEG) Ltd, pg 460

Mauritius
Editions de l'Ocean Indien Ltd, pg 461
Vizavi Editions, pg 461

Mexico
Ediciones Alpe, pg 462
Grupo Editorial Armonia, pg 462
Centro Editorial Mexicano Osiris SA, pg 463
Editorial Diana SA de CV, pg 464
Editorial Iztaccihuatl SA, pg 467
Editorial Jilguero, SA de CV, pg 467
Libra Editorial SA de CV, pg 467
Editorial Limusa SA de CV, pg 467
Editorial Minutiae Mexicana SA, pg 468
Naves Internacional de Ediciones SA, pg 469
Organizacion Cultural LP SA de CV, pg 469
Salvat Editores de Mexico, pg 471
Sayrols Editorial SA de CV, pg 471
Servicios Especiales Maciel SA de CV, pg 472
Sistemas Tecnicos de Edicion SA de CV, pg 472
Ediciones Suromex SA, pg 472

Myanmar
Smart & Mookerdum, pg 476

Netherlands
BZZTOH Publishers, pg 480
Uitgeverij Christofoor, pg 480
Uitgeverij De Fontein BV, pg 482
Mets & Schilt Uitgevers en Distributeurs, pg 486
Uitgeverij Terra bv, pg 490
Uitgeverij De Toorts, pg 490
Unieboek BV, pg 490
Zuid Boekprodukties BV, pg 493

New Zealand
ABA Books, pg 493
Barkfire Press, pg 494
David Bateman Ltd, pg 494
Bush Press Communications Ltd, pg 494
Concept Publishing Ltd, pg 495
Halcyon Publishing Ltd, pg 496
HarperCollins Publishers (New Zealand) Ltd, pg 497
Hazard Press Ltd, pg 497
Hodder Moa Beckett Publishers Ltd, pg 497
Reed Publishing (NZ) Ltd, pg 500
Tandem Press, pg 501

Nigeria
Fourth Dimension Publishing Co Ltd, pg 504
Riverside Communications, pg 507

Norway
Det Norske Samlaget, pg 508
Ex Libris Forlag A/S, pg 509

Pakistan
Jang Publishers, pg 513
Maqbool Academy, pg 513

Philippines
Anvil Publishing Inc, pg 518
Bookmark Inc, pg 518
Books for Pleasure Inc, pg 518
Marren Publishing House, Inc, pg 519
New Day Publishers, pg 520
Rex Bookstores & Publishers, pg 520

Poland
Iskry - Publishing House Ltd spotka zoo, pg 523
Muza SA, pg 524

Portugal
Difusao Cultural, pg 530
Editorial Estampa, Lda, pg 531
Everest Editora, pg 531
Meriberica/Liber, pg 533
Editorial Noticias, pg 534
Editorial Presenca, pg 535
Texto Editora, pg 536
Vega-Publicacao e Distribuicao de Livros e Revistas, Lda, pg 536

Romania
Editura Excelsior Art, pg 539
Editura Niculescu, pg 541

Russian Federation
Airis Press, pg 543
Dom, Izdatel'stvo sovetskogo deskkogo fonda im & I Lenina, pg 544
Izdatelstvo 'Ekonomika', pg 544
Interbook-Business AO, pg 545
KUbK Publishing House, pg 546
Permskaja Kniga, pg 548
Profizdat, pg 548
Izdatelstvo Prosveshchenie, pg 548
Raduga Publishers, pg 548
Russkaya Kniga Izdatelstvo (Publishers), pg 548

Serbia and Montenegro
Alfa-Narodna Knjiga, pg 552

Singapore
Archipelago Press, pg 555
Shing Lee Group Publishers, pg 558
Times Media Pte Ltd, pg 559

Slovakia
Vydavatepstvo Praca spol sro, pg 560

Slovenia
Cankarjeva Zalozba, pg 561
Mladinska Knjiga International, pg 561
Zalozba Obzorja d d Maribor, pg 562

South Africa
Educum Publishers Ltd, pg 563
Human & Rousseau (Pty) Ltd, pg 564
New Africa Books (Pty) Ltd, pg 567
Queillerie Publishers, pg 568
Reader's Digest Southern Africa, pg 568
Struik Publishers (Pty) Ltd, pg 569
Tafelberg Publishers Ltd, pg 569

Spain
Editorial Acanto SA, pg 570
Alta Fulla Editorial, pg 572
Ambit Serveis Editorials, SA, pg 572
Editorial Astri SA, pg 573
Editorial Cantabrica SA, pg 575
Comunidad Autonoma de Madrid, Servicio de Documentacion y Publicaciones, pg 578
Ediciones Daly S L, pg 578
Edi-Liber Irlan SA, pg 580
Ediciones l'Isard, S L, pg 580
Edilesa-Ediciones Leonesas SA, pg 581
Editorial Everest SA, pg 581
Ediciones Elfos SL, pg 582
Enciclopedia Catalana, SA, pg 582
Editorial Espasa-Calpe SA, pg 582
Icaria Editorial SA, pg 587
Ediciones Irusa, pg 588
Ediciones Libertarias/Prodhufi SA, pg 589
Libsa Editorial SA, pg 589
Lunwerg Editores, SA, pg 589
Edicions de la Magrana SA, pg 590
Mandala Ediciones, pg 590
Ediciones Medici SA, pg 591
Noguer y Caralt Editores SA, pg 593
Ediciones Norma SA, pg 593
OASIS, Producciones Generales de Comunicacion, pg 593
Instituto Provincial de Investigaciones y Estudios Toledanos (IPIET), pg 597
Editora Regional de Murcia - ERM, pg 597
Ediciones Rialp SA, pg 598
Axel Springer Publicaciones, pg 601
Ediciones Susaeta SA, pg 601
Trea Ediciones, SL, pg 602
Tursen, SA, pg 603
Ediciones Tutor SA, pg 603
Ediciones 29 - Libros Rio Nuevo, pg 603
Editorial De Vecchi SA, pg 604
Editorial Zendrera Zariquiey, SA, pg 605

Sweden
Bokforlaget Atlantis AB, pg 609
Akademiforlaget Goteborgslitteratur, pg 609
BBT Bhaktivedanta Book Trust, pg 610
Albert Bonniers Forlag AB, pg 610
BOOX, pg 610
ICA bokforlag, pg 612
Informationsfoerlaget AB, pg 612
Natur och Kultur Fakta etc, pg 614
Bokforlaget Prisma, pg 614
Bokforlaget Semic AB, pg 615
Semic Bokforlaget International AB, pg 615
Stromberg, pg 616
Wahlstrom & Widstrand, pg 616

Switzerland
AT Verlag, pg 618
Cockatoo Press (Schweiz), Thailand-Publikationen, pg 621
Duboux Editions SA, pg 622
Hallwag Kuemmerly & Frey AG, pg 625
Junod Nicolas, pg 626
Kanisius Verlag, pg 626
Verlag Rene Kramer AG, pg 627
Mueller Rueschlikon Verlags AG, pg 629
Les Editions Noir sur Blanc, pg 629

Taiwan, Province of China
Hilit Publishing Co Ltd, pg 640
Linking Publishing Company Ltd, pg 641
Wei-Chuan Publishing Company Ltd, pg 642
Youth Cultural Publishing Co, pg 642

Thailand
Sangdad Publishing Company Ltd, pg 645

Turkey
Alkim Kitapcilik-Yayimcilik, pg 649
Arkadas Ltd, pg 649
Inkilap Publishers Ltd, pg 650

Uganda
Fountain Publishers Ltd, pg 652

Ukraine
ASK Ltd, pg 653

United Arab Emirates
Motivate Publishing, pg 654

United Kingdom
Absolute Press, pg 655
Ian Allan Publishing Ltd, pg 656
Apple Press, pg 658
Appletree Press Ltd, pg 658
Ashgrove Publishing, pg 660
BBC Worldwide Publishers, pg 663
BCA - Book Club Associates, pg 663
Mitchell Beazley, pg 664
Blackstaff Press, pg 666
Bloomsbury Publishing PLC, pg 668
Bounty Books, pg 669
Breslich & Foss Ltd, pg 671
The Brown Reference Group PLC, pg 672
Jon Carpenter Publishing, pg 675
Carroll & Brown Ltd, pg 675
Cassell & Co, pg 675

PUBLISHERS   SUBJECT INDEX

Kyle Cathie Ltd, pg 676
Marshall Cavendish Partworks Ltd, pg 676
Colour Library Direct, pg 681
Compendium Publishing, pg 681
Paul H Crompton Ltd, pg 684
David & Charles Ltd, pg 686
Christopher Davies Publishers Ltd, pg 686
Dorling Kindersley Ltd, pg 688
Eaglemoss Publications Ltd, pg 689
Elliot Right Way Books, pg 690
The Erskine Press, pg 692
Express Newspapers, pg 693
Foulsham Publishers, pg 696
Fourth Estate, pg 696
Garnet Publishing Ltd, pg 698
Grange Books PLC, pg 702
The Greek Bookshop, pg 702
Grub Street, pg 703
Haldane Mason Ltd, pg 704
Robert Hale Ltd, pg 704
Hamlyn, pg 704
HarperCollins UK, pg 705
Headline Book Publishing Ltd, pg 706
Hemming Information Services, pg 707
Hendon Publishing Co Ltd, pg 708
Hodder & Stoughton General, pg 709
Angus Hudson Ltd, pg 710
Y Lolfa Cyf, pg 722
Lorenz Books, pg 722
Macmillan Audio Books, pg 723
Kenneth Mason Publications Ltd, pg 726
Mercat Press, pg 726
Metro Books, pg 727
MQ Publications, pg 729
National Trust, pg 731
Neil Wilson Publishing Ltd, pg 732
New Holland Publishers (UK) Ltd, pg 732
NMS Enterprises Ltd - Publishing, pg 733
Octopus Publishing Group, pg 734
Pavilion Books Ltd, pg 739
Piatkus Books, pg 741
PRC Publishing Ltd, pg 745
Prism Press Book Publishers Ltd, pg 745
Quadrille Publishing Ltd, pg 746
Quiller Publishing Ltd, pg 747
Ramboro Books Plc, pg 747
Random House UK Ltd, pg 747
The Reader's Digest Association Ltd, pg 748
Regency House Publishing Ltd, pg 749
Robson Books, pg 750
Rosendale Press Ltd, pg 751
Roundhouse Group, pg 751
Ryland Peters & Small Ltd, pg 752
Salamander Books Ltd, pg 753
Saqi Books, pg 754
SAWD Publications, pg 754
Serif, pg 756
Sheldrake Press, pg 757
Sidgwick & Jackson Ltd, pg 757
Charles Skilton Ltd, pg 758
Stacey International, pg 761
Telegraph Books, pg 764
Transedition Ltd, pg 766
Vallentine, Mitchell & Co Ltd, pg 769
The Vegetarian Society, pg 769
Verulam Publishing Ltd, pg 770
Viking, pg 770
Ward Lock Ltd, pg 771
Websters International Publishers Ltd, pg 772
WI Enterprises Ltd, pg 773

Wiley Europe Ltd, pg 773
Wordwright Publishing, pg 775

Uruguay

Ediciones de Juan Darien, pg 777

Zambia

Multimedia Zambia, pg 781

Zimbabwe

College Press Publishers (Pvt) Ltd, pg 783
Longman Zimbabwe (Pvt) Ltd, pg 783
Zimbabwe Publishing House (Pvt) Ltd, pg 784

CRAFTS, GAMES, HOBBIES

Albania

NL SH, pg 1

Armenia

Arevik, pg 10

Australia

Egan Publishing Pty Ltd, pg 21
David Ell Press Pty Ltd, pg 21
Graffiti Publications, pg 23
Horan Wall & Walker, pg 26
Kangaroo Press, pg 28
Little Hills Press Pty Ltd, pg 29
Tracy Marsh Publications Pty Ltd, pg 31
Mayne Publishing, pg 31
J M McGregor Pty Ltd, pg 31
Off the Shelf Publishing, pg 34
Jill Oxton Publications Pty Ltd, pg 35
R & R Publications Pty Ltd, pg 38
Rams Skull Press, pg 38
Simon & Schuster (Australia) Pty Ltd, pg 41
Skills Publishing, pg 41
Turton & Armstrong Pty Ltd Publishers, pg 44
The Watermark Press, pg 46

Belarus

Belaruskaya Encyklapedyya, pg 62

Belgium

NV Artis-Historia, pg 63
Caramel, Uitgeverij, pg 64
Editions Chanlis, pg 65
Uitgeverij Contact NV, pg 65
Glenat Benelux SA, pg 67
Editions Hemma, pg 68
Infoboek NV, pg 68
Editeurs de Litterature Biblique, pg 70
Marabout, pg 71
Stichting Kunstboek bvba, pg 73
Vita, pg 74
Zuid-Nederlandse Uitgeverij NV/Central Uitgeverij, pg 75

Brazil

Icone Editora Ltda, pg 83
Editora Manole Ltda, pg 86

Bulgaria

Darzhavno Izdatelstvo Zemizdat, pg 93
Interpres, pg 95
Regalia 6 Publishing House, pg 96
Slavena, pg 97

China

China Braille Publishing House, pg 102
China Film Press, pg 102
China Textile Press, pg 103
China Theatre Publishing House, pg 103
The People's Posts & Telecommunication Publishing House, pg 107
People's Sports Publishing House, pg 107
Sichuan Science & Technology Publishing House, pg 108

Colombia

RAM Editores, pg 112
Editorial Voluntad SA, pg 113

Croatia

Mladost d d Izdavacku graficku i informaticku djelatnost, pg 119
Vitagraf, pg 119

Cuba

Editorial Oriente, pg 120

Cyprus

James Bendon Ltd, pg 121

Czech Republic

Granit sro, pg 123
Nakladatelstvi Jan Vasut, pg 124
Nakladatelstvi Jota spol sro, pg 124

Denmark

Bogfabrikken Fakta ApS, pg 129
Borgens Forlag A/S, pg 129
Dansk Teknologisk Institut, Forlaget, pg 130
Gads Forlag, pg 131
Host & Son Publishers Ltd, pg 132
Forlaget Hovedland, pg 132
Forlaget Klematis A/S, pg 132
Politikens Forlag A/S, pg 133
Square Dance Partners Forlag, pg 135
Wisby & Wilkens, pg 135

Ecuador

CIDAP, pg 136

Estonia

Sinisukk, pg 140
Valgus Publishers, pg 140

Finland

Lasten Keskus Oy, pg 143
SV-Kauppiaskanava Oy, pg 144

France

Editions Amphora SA, pg 146
Editions Andre Bonne, pg 150
Pierre Bordas & Fils, Editions, pg 150
Bragelonne, pg 151
Editions Buchet-Chastel Pierre Zech Editeur, pg 151
Editions Didier Carpentier, pg 152
Philippe Chancerel Editeur, pg 153
Chasse Maree, pg 153
Dessain et Tolra SA, pg 158
Editions ELOR, pg 160
Editions Eyrolles, pg 162
Editions Fleurus, pg 163
Imprimerie Librairie Gardet, pg 165
Hachette Pratiques, pg 167
Librairie Leonce Laget, pg 171
Editions Lito, pg 172

Editions Mango, pg 174
Les Presses d'Ile-de-France Sarl, pg 181
Editions Rombaldi SA, pg 183
Editions Sang de la Terre, pg 184
Ulisse Editions, pg 188

Germany

Alba Fachverlag GmbH & Co KG, pg 191
ALS-Verlag GmbH, pg 192
Ars Edition GmbH, pg 194
AUE-Verlag GmbH, pg 195
Augustus Verlag, pg 195
Bassermann Verlag, pg 197
Joachim Beyer Verlag, pg 200
Eberhard Blottner Verlag GmbH, pg 202
Aenne Burda Verlag, pg 206
Verlag Georg D W Callwey GmbH & Co, pg 207
Christophorus-Verlag GmbH, pg 208
Marianne Cieslik, pg 209
Compact Verlag GmbH, pg 209
DuMont monte Verlag GmbH & Co KG, pg 217
Egmont Pestalozzi-Verlag, pg 218
Egmont vgs verlagsgesellschaft mbH, pg 218
Ehrenwirth Verlag GmbH, pg 218
Englisch Verlag GmbH, pg 220
Eulen Verlag, pg 221
Fachverlag Schiele & Schoen GmbH, pg 223
Falken-Verlag GmbH, pg 223
Ferd Dummler's Verlag, pg 223
Franckh-Kosmos Verlags-GmbH & Co, pg 226
frechverlag GmbH, pg 226
H Gietl Verlag & Publikationsservice GmbH, pg 229
Gildefachverlag GmbH & Co KG, pg 229
Verlag Gruppenpaedagogischer Literatur, pg 231
Heel Verlag GmbH, pg 235
Idea Verlag GmbH, pg 240
Jahreszeiten-Verlag GmbH, pg 242
Kallmeyer'sche Verlagsbuchhandlung GmbH, pg 244
Landbuch-Verlagsgesellschaft mbH, pg 251
Gebr Mann Verlag GmbH & Co, pg 257
Edition Maritim GmbH, pg 257
Otto Meissner Verlag, pg 259
Moby Dick Verlag, pg 261
Mosaik Verlag GmbH, pg 262
Naumann & Goebel Verlagsgesellschaft mbH, pg 263
nymphenburger, pg 266
Oekobuch Verlag & Versand GmbH, pg 266
Oertel & Sporer GmbH & Co, pg 266
Ravensburger Buchverlag Otto Maier GmbH, pg 274
Ritterbach Verlag GmbH, pg 276
Rosenheimer Verlagshaus GmbH & Co KG, pg 276
Verlag Th Schaefer im Vicentz Verlag KG, pg 278
M & H Schaper GmbH & Co KG, pg 279
Ulrich Schiefer bahn Verlag, pg 279
Schwaneberger Verlag GmbH, pg 282
Siebert Verlag GmbH, pg 283
Tipress Dienstleistungen fur das Verlagswesen GmbH, pg 291

941

Tomus Verlag GmbH, pg 291
Mario Truant Verlag, pg 292
Verlagsgruppe Weltbild GmbH, pg 298
Verlagshaus Wohlfarth, pg 301
Zweipunkt Verlag K Kaiser KG, pg 302

Greece

Dorikos Publishing House, pg 306
Ilias Kambanas Publishing Organization, SA, pg 309
Kastaniotis Editions SA, pg 309
Editions Moressopoulos, pg 310

Hong Kong

SCMP Book Publishing Ltd, pg 319
Unicorn Books Ltd, pg 320

Hungary

Aranyhal Konyvkiado Goldfish Publishing, pg 320
Ifjusagi Lap-eskonyvkiado Vallalat, pg 321

Iceland

Skjaldborg Ltd, pg 326

India

Diamond Comics (P) Ltd, pg 333
Dolphin Publications, pg 333
Gyan Publishing House, pg 335
Heritage Publishers, pg 335
Inter-India Publications, pg 338
International Book Distributors, pg 338
Mapin Publishing Pvt Ltd, pg 341
Orient Paperbacks, pg 344
Pankaj Publications, pg 344
Pustak Mahal, pg 345
Rupa & Co, pg 347
Tara Publishing, pg 351

Indonesia

Gaya Favorit Press, pg 355
Gramedia, pg 355
PT Indira, pg 355

Ireland

Careers & Educational Publishers Ltd, pg 358

Israel

Dekel Publishing House, pg 366
R Sirkis Publishers Ltd, pg 372

Italy

Mario Adda Editore SNC, pg 374
L'Airone Editrice, pg 375
Gruppo Editoriale Armenia SpA, pg 376
Il Castello srl, pg 380
La Coccinella Editrice SRL, pg 383
Giovanni De Vecchi Editore SpA, pg 384
Di Baio Editore SpA, pg 385
ETR (Editrice Trasporti su Rotaie), pg 388
Fenice 2000, pg 389
Ernesto Gremese Editore srl, pg 391
Gremese International srl, pg 391
Mucchi Editore SRL, pg 399
Franco Cosimo Panini Editore, pg 402
RCS Libri SpA, pg 405
RCS Rizzoli Libri SpA, pg 405
Editoriale Scienza, pg 407
Vaccari SRL, pg 411
Vinciana Editrice sas, pg 412

Japan

Bijutsu Shuppan-Sha, Ltd, pg 415
Hoikusha Publishing Co Ltd, pg 418
International Society for Educational Information (ISEI), pg 419
Japan Broadcast Publishing Co Ltd, pg 419
Japan Publications Inc, pg 419
Kaisei-Sha Publishing Co Ltd, pg 420
Kodansha International Ltd, pg 421
Nagaoka Shoten Co Ltd, pg 423
Nihon Vogue Co Ltd, pg 424
Nippon Hoso Shuppan Kyokai (NHK Publishing), pg 424
Ondorisha Publishers Ltd, pg 424
Seibido Shuppan Company Ltd, pg 426
Seibundo Shinkosha Publishing Co Ltd, pg 426
Shufu-to-Seikatsu Sha Ltd, pg 428
Shufunotomo Co Ltd, pg 428
Tankosha Publishing Co Ltd, pg 429
Toho Book Store, pg 429
Toho Shuppan, pg 429
Tokuma Shoten Publishing Co Ltd, pg 429
Charles E Tuttle Publishing Co Inc, pg 430

Republic of Korea

Chung Rim Publishing Co Ltd, pg 438
Dae Won Sa Co Ltd, pg 438
Prompter Publications, pg 442
Pyeong-hwa Chulpansa, pg 442
Samho Music Publishing Co Ltd, pg 442
Youlhwadang Publisher, pg 444

Latvia

Alberts XII, pg 444
Nordik/Tapals Publishers Ltd, pg 445
Preses Nams, pg 445

Lebanon

Khayat Book and Publishing Co Sarl, pg 446

Lithuania

Sviesa Publishers, pg 449
Victoria Publishers, pg 450

Malta

Gozo Press, pg 460
Publishers' Enterprises Group (PEG) Ltd, pg 460

Mexico

Editorial Jilguero, SA de CV, pg 467
Ediciones Libra, SA de CV, pg 467
Libros y Revistas SA de CV, pg 467
Editorial Limusa SA de CV, pg 467
Editorial Minutiae Mexicana SA, pg 468
Sayrols Editorial SA de CV, pg 471
Selector SA de CV, pg 471
Editorial Trillas SA de CV, pg 472

Monaco

Les Editions du Rocher, pg 474

Netherlands

BV Uitgevery NZV (Nederlandse Zondagsschool Vereniging), pg 480
Uitgeverij Cantecleer BV, pg 480
Uitgeverij Christoofor, pg 480
Gottmer Uitgevers Groep, pg 483
De Muiderkring BV, pg 486
Rebo Productions BV, pg 488
Uitgeverij Terra bv, pg 490
Tirion Uitgevers BV, pg 490
Unieboek BV, pg 490
Zuid Boekprodukties BV, pg 493

New Zealand

Bush Press Communications Ltd, pg 494
Craig Potton Publishing, pg 495
David's Marine Books, pg 495
Halcyon Publishing Ltd, pg 496
Shoal Bay Press Ltd, pg 501

Norway

Tell Forlag, pg 511

Philippines

Anvil Publishing Inc, pg 518
Bright Concepts Printing House, pg 518
Sonny A Mendoza, pg 519

Poland

Wydawnictwo Arkady, pg 522
Wydawnictwa Normalizacyjne Alfa-Wero, pg 525
Wydawnictwo Podsiedlik-Raniowski i Spolka, pg 525
Wydawn Na Sprawa' Wydawniczo-Oswiatowa Spotdzielnia Inwalidow, pg 528

Portugal

Gradiva-Publicacnoes Lda, pg 532
Editorial Presenca, pg 535

Reunion

Editions Ocean, pg 538

Romania

Alcor-Edimpex (Verlag) Ltd, pg 538
Editura Excelsior Art, pg 539

Russian Federation

Airis Press, pg 543
Dom, Izdatel'stvo sovetskogo deskkogo fonda im & I Lenina, pg 544
Druzhba Narodov, pg 544
Interbook-Business AO, pg 545
Permskaja Kniga, pg 548
Izdatelstvo Prosveshchenie, pg 548
Scorpion Publishers, pg 548

Singapore

Archipelago Press, pg 555

Slovakia

Vydavatepstvo Praca spol sro, pg 560
Smena Publishing House, pg 560

Slovenia

Mladinska Knjiga International, pg 561
Zalozba Obzorja d d Maribor, pg 562

South Africa

Human & Rousseau (Pty) Ltd, pg 564
Tafelberg Publishers Ltd, pg 569
Witwatersrand University Press, pg 570

Spain

Editorial Acanto SA, pg 570
Alta Fulla Editorial, pg 572
Editorial Astri SA, pg 573
Central Catequistica Salesiana (CCS), pg 576
Comunidad Autonoma de Madrid, Servicio de Documentacion y Publicaciones, pg 578
Ediciones Daly S L, pg 578
Editorial Everest SA, pg 581
Editorial Fundamentos, pg 584
Idea Books, SA, pg 587
LEDA (Las Ediciones de Arte), pg 589
Libsa Editorial SA, pg 589
Ediciones Martinez-Roca SA, pg 591
Editorial Noray, pg 593
Obelisco Ediciones S, pg 593
Parramon Ediciones SA, pg 595
Pleniluni Edicions, pg 596
Editora Regional de Murcia - ERM, pg 597
Equipo Sirius SA, pg 600
Axel Springer Publicaciones, pg 601
Ediciones Susaeta SA, pg 601
Tursen, SA, pg 603
Ediciones Tutor SA, pg 603
Editorial De Vecchi SA, pg 604

Sweden

Allt om Hobby AB, pg 609
Berghs, pg 610
BOOX, pg 610
ICA bokforlag, pg 612
Jannersten Forlag AB, pg 613
Johnston & Streiffert Editions, pg 613
Natur och Kultur Fakta etc, pg 614
Bokforlaget Semic AB, pg 615
Semic Bokforlaget International AB, pg 615
Bokforlaget Spektra AB, pg 615

Switzerland

Paul Haupt Bern, pg 625
Motovun Book GmbH, pg 629
Mueller Rueschlikon Verlags AG, pg 629
Office du Livre SA (Buchhaus AG), pg 630
Sinwel-Buchhandlung Verlag, pg 634
Editions du Tricorne, pg 635
Verlagsbuchhandlung AG, pg 636
Wiese Verlag AG, pg 637
Zumstein & Cie, pg 638

Taiwan, Province of China

Echo Publishing Company Ltd, pg 639
Hilit Publishing Co Ltd, pg 640
Wei-Chuan Publishing Company Ltd, pg 642
Wu Nan Book Co Ltd, pg 642
Youth Cultural Publishing Co, pg 642

Turkey

Alkim Kitapcilik-Yayimcilik, pg 649
Soez Yayin/Oyunajans, pg 651

PUBLISHERS

United Kingdom
Amber Books Ltd, pg 657
Apple Press, pg 658
Appletree Press Ltd, pg 658
Arms & Armour Press, pg 659
Art Books International Ltd, pg 659
Ashmolean Museum Publications, pg 660
Batsford Ltd, pg 663
BCA - Book Club Associates, pg 663
Ruth Bean Publishers, pg 664
Belitha Press Ltd, pg 664
Bellew Publishing Co Ltd, pg 664
Bishopsgate Press Ltd, pg 666
BLA Publishing Ltd, pg 666
A & C Black Publishers Ltd, pg 666
Blaketon Hall Ltd, pg 667
Blandford Publishing Ltd, pg 668
Bloomsbury Publishing PLC, pg 668
Books International, pg 669
Bounty Books, pg 669
Breslich & Foss Ltd, pg 671
British Museum Press, pg 672
The Brown Reference Group PLC, pg 672
Carroll & Brown Ltd, pg 675
Cassell & Co, pg 675
Marshall Cavendish Partworks Ltd, pg 676
Christian Education, pg 679
Compendium Publishing, pg 681
Conran Octopus, pg 682
Paul H Crompton Ltd, pg 684
The Crowood Press Ltd, pg 684
David & Charles Ltd, pg 686
Diagram Visual Information Ltd, pg 687
Dorling Kindersley Ltd, pg 688
Eaglemoss Publications Ltd, pg 689
Elliot Right Way Books, pg 690
Floris Books, pg 695
Foulsham Publishers, pg 696
Stanley Gibbons Publications, pg 700
GMC Publications Ltd, pg 700
Grange Books PLC, pg 702
Hamlyn, pg 704
HarperCollins UK, pg 705
Hawthorn Press, pg 706
Hodder Education, pg 709
Frances Lincoln Ltd, pg 720
Y Lolfa Cyf, pg 722
Lorenz Books, pg 722
Lund Humphries, pg 723
The Lutterworth Press, pg 723
Marshall Editions Ltd, pg 725
Merrell Publishers Ltd, pg 727
MQ Publications Ltd, pg 729
New Holland Publishers (UK) Ltd, pg 732
Newpro UK Ltd, pg 733
Nexus Special Interests, pg 733
Octopus Publishing Group, pg 734
Oldcastle Books Ltd, pg 734
Orion Publishing Group Ltd, pg 736
Osprey Publishing Ltd, pg 737
Parapress Ltd, pg 738
David Porteous Editions, pg 744
PRC Publishing Ltd, pg 745
Quadrille Publishing Ltd, pg 746
Quarto Publishing plc, pg 746
Quintet Publishing Ltd, pg 747
The Reader's Digest Association Ltd, pg 748
Regency House Publishing Ltd, pg 749
Salamander Books Ltd, pg 753
Savitri Books Ltd, pg 754
Search Press Ltd, pg 756
Shire Publications Ltd, pg 757
Sigma Press, pg 758
Silver Link Publishing Ltd, pg 758
Spon Press, pg 760
Stobart Davies Ltd, pg 761
Thames & Hudson Ltd, pg 764
Vacation Work Publications, pg 769
White Cockade Publishing, pg 772
WI Enterprises Ltd, pg 773

Viet Nam
Science & Technics Publishing House, pg 780

CRIMINOLOGY

Argentina
Abeledo-Perrot SAE e I, pg 2
Juris Editorial, pg 6

Australia
Australian Institute of Criminology, pg 13
Australian Institute of Family Studies (AIFS), pg 13
Kingsclear Books, pg 28
Law Book Co Information Services, pg 28
McGraw-Hill Australia Pty Ltd, pg 31
Pearson Education Australia, pg 36
Jurriaan Plesman, pg 37
Wileman Publications, pg 46

Austria
Edition S der OSD, pg 50
Haymon-Verlag GesmbH, pg 51

Belarus
Interdigest Publishing House, pg 62

Belgium
Uitgeverij Acco, pg 62
Leuven University Press, pg 70

Brazil
Livraria Francisco Alves Editora SA, pg 77
Centro de Estudos Juridicosdo Para (CEJUP), pg 79
Companhia Editora Forense, pg 81
Editora Revan Ltda, pg 89

Chile
Edeval (Universidad de Valparaiso), pg 99

Colombia
Universidad Externado de Colombia, pg 111

Denmark
Bonnier Publications A/S, pg 129

France
Librairie des Champs-Elysees/Le Masque, pg 153
Editions Eres, pg 162
FBT de R Editions, pg 163
Editions des Limbes d'Or FBT de R Editions, pg 172

Germany
Verlag Beleke KG, pg 198
Centaurus-Verlagsgesellschaft GmbH, pg 207
Duncker und Humblot GmbH, pg 217

SUBJECT INDEX

Europaeische Verlagsanstalt GmbH & Rotbuch Verlag GmbH & Co KG, pg 222
Wilhelm Goldmann Verlag GmbH, pg 230
Huthig GmbH & Co KG, pg 240
Juventa Verlag GmbH, pg 244
Pendragon Verlag, pg 269
Max Schmidt-Roemhild Verlag, pg 280
Springer Science+Business Media GmbH & Co KG, pg 284
Zebulon Verlag GmbH & Co KG, pg 302

Hong Kong
Hong Kong University Press, pg 317

India
Abhinav Publications, pg 326
APH Publishing Corp, pg 328
Book Circle, pg 330
Diamond Comics (P) Ltd, pg 333
Indian Council of Social Science Research (ICSSR), pg 336
Jaico Publishing House, pg 338
Law Publishers, pg 340
Reliance Publishing House, pg 346

Ireland
Emerald Publications, pg 359
The O'Brien Press Ltd, pg 362
Round Hall Sweet & Maxwell, pg 363

Israel
Dyonon/Papyrus Publishing House of the Tel-Aviv, pg 366
Schocken Publishing House Ltd, pg 371
Tcherikover Publishers Ltd, pg 372

Italy
CEDAM (Casa Editrice Dr A Milani), pg 380
Levante Editori, pg 395

Japan
Tokyo Sogensha Co Ltd, pg 430

Kazakhstan
Al-Farabi Kazakh National University, pg 432

Latvia
Nordik/Tapals Publishers Ltd, pg 445

Lithuania
Eugrimas, pg 449

Mexico
Editorial Limusa SA de CV, pg 467
Siglo XXI Editores SA de CV, pg 472

Morocco
Societe Ennewrasse Service Librairie et Imprimerie, pg 475

Netherlands
Uitgeverij de Arbeiderspers, pg 477
De Boekerij BV, pg 479
Cadans, pg 480
Koninklijke Vermande bv, pg 485
Kugler Publications, pg 485
Sjaloom Uitgeverijen, pg 489

Sociaal en Cultureel Planbureau, pg 489
Uitgeverij Het Spectrum BV, pg 489
SWP, BV Uitgeverij, pg 490

Pakistan
Sang-e-Meel Publications, pg 514

Papua New Guinea
National Research Institute of Papua New Guinea, pg 515

Philippines
Rex Bookstores & Publishers, pg 520

Poland
Wydawnictwo Prawnicze Co, pg 526

Portugal
Quid Juris - Sociedade Editora, pg 535

Russian Federation
Izdatelstvo Kazanskago Universiteta, pg 545

Serbia and Montenegro
Alfa-Narodna Knjiga, pg 552

Singapore
Taylor & Francis Asia Pacific, pg 558

Slovenia
Zalozba Obzorja d d Maribor, pg 562

South Africa
Human Sciences Research Council, pg 565

Spain
Bosch Casa Editorial SA, pg 575
Editorial M J Bosch, SL, pg 575
Instituto Vasco de Criminologia, pg 587
Tirant lo Blanch SL Libreriaa, pg 602

Switzerland
Ruegger Verlag, pg 633

Turkey
Altin Kitaplar Yayinevi, pg 649
Sabah Kitaplari, pg 651

United Kingdom
Amber Books Ltd, pg 657
Ashgate Publishing Ltd, pg 660
John Blake Publishing Ltd, pg 667
Blandford Publishing Ltd, pg 668
Breedon Books Publishing Company Ltd, pg 670
Carlton Publishing Group, pg 675
Cavendish Publishing Ltd, pg 676
Constable & Robinson Ltd, pg 682
Delectus Books, pg 687
Eaglemoss Publications Ltd, pg 689
Farsight Press, pg 694
Gembooks, pg 699
Jessica Kingsley Publishers, pg 718
Open University Press, pg 736
Pearson Education, pg 739

SUBJECT INDEX

Perpetuity Press, pg 741
Piatkus Books, pg 741
Pluto Press, pg 743
Police Review Publishing Company Ltd, pg 744
Profile Books Ltd, pg 746
Roundhouse Group, pg 751
SAGE Publications Ltd, pg 753
Scottish Executive Library & Information Services, pg 755
Serpent's Tail Ltd, pg 756
Transworld Publishers Ltd, pg 766
Virgin Publishing Ltd, pg 770
Whiting & Birch Ltd, pg 773

Uruguay
Fundacion de Cultura Universitaria, pg 777

DEVELOPING COUNTRIES

Albania
NL SH, pg 1

Australia
Ocean Press, pg 34
Spinifex Press, pg 42

Austria
Development News Ltd, pg 50
Guthmann & Peterson Liber Libri, Edition, pg 51
Verlag Jungbrunnen - Wiener Spielzeugschachtel GesellschaftmbH, pg 52
Promedia Verlagsges mbH, pg 56
Edition Va Bene, pg 59

Belgium
EPO Publishers, Printers, Booksellers, pg 67
Institut Royal des Relations Internationales, pg 68
IPIS vzw (International Peace Information Service), pg 69
Koepel van de Vlaamse Noord - Zuidbeweging 11.11.11, pg 69
Wereldwijd Mediahuis VzW, pg 74

Burundi
Editions Intore, pg 98

Chile
Ediciones Cieplan, pg 99

China
World Affairs Press, pg 109

Costa Rica
Centro Agronomico Tropical de Investigacion y Ensenanza (CATIE), pg 115
Instituto Interamericano de Cooperacion para la Agricultura (IICA), pg 115
Union Mundial para la Naturaleza (UICN), Oficina Regional para Mesoamerica, pg 116

Cote d'Ivoire
Universite d'Abidjan, pg 117
Heritage Publishing Co, pg 117

Denmark
Forlaget Hjulet, pg 132
Mellemfolkeligt Samvirke, pg 133
Samfundslitteratur, pg 134

Dominican Republic
Pontificia Universidad Catolica Madre y Maestra, pg 136

Egypt (Arab Republic of Egypt)
Al Arab Publishing House, pg 137

France
Editions La Decouverte, pg 157
Editions Entente, pg 161
Futuribles SARL, pg 164
Groupe de Recherche et d'Echanges Technologiques (GRET), pg 166
L'Harmattan, pg 167
IRD Editions, pg 169
Karthala Editions-Diffusion, pg 170

Germany
Altberliner Verlag GmbH, pg 192
ARCult Media, pg 193
Brandes & Apsel Verlag GmbH, pg 204
Claudius Verlag, pg 209
Deutscher Instituts-Verlag GmbH, pg 213
Verlag J H W Dietz Nachf GmbH, pg 214
agenda Verlag Thomas Dominikowski, pg 215
Duncker und Humblot GmbH, pg 217
Eppinger-Verlag OHG, pg 220
Erlanger Verlag Fuer Mission und Okumene, pg 220
Espresso Verlag GmbH, pg 221
Verlag des Gustav-Adolf-Werks, pg 232
Peter Hammer Verlag GmbH, pg 233
Horlemann Verlag, pg 239
Edition ID-Archiv/ID-Verlag, pg 240
IKO Verlag fur Interkulturelle Kommunikation, pg 241
Informationsstelle Suedliches Afrika eV (ISSA), pg 241
Konkret Literatur Verlag, pg 249
Lamuv Verlag GmbH, pg 251
Libertas- Europaeisches Institut GmbH, pg 254
Margraf Verlag, pg 257
Medico International eV, pg 258
Missio eV, pg 260
Verlag Neuer Weg, pg 264
Nusser Verlag, pg 266
Orlanda Frauenverlag, pg 267
Pahl-Rugenstein Verlag Nachfolger-GmbH, pg 267
PapyRossa Verlags GmbH & Co Kommanditgesellschaft KG, pg 268
Verlag an der Ruhr GmbH, pg 277
Franz Steiner Verlag Wiesbaden GmbH, pg 287
Steyler Verlag, pg 288
UNO-Verlag GmbH, pg 293
Unrast Verlag e V, pg 293
Vervuert Verlagsgesellschaft, pg 295
Weltforum Verlag GmbH, pg 299
Zambon Verlag, pg 302

Ghana
World Literature Project, pg 305

Guinea-Bissau
Instituto Nacional de Estudos e Pesquisa (INEP), pg 314

Guyana
Guyana Community Based Rehabilitation Progeamme, pg 314

India
Cosmo Publications, pg 332
Gyan Publishing House, pg 335
National Book Organization, pg 342
Navrang Booksellers & Publishers, pg 343
Oxford University Press, pg 344
Reliance Publishing House, pg 346
SAGE Publications India Pvt Ltd, pg 347
Scientific Book Agency, pg 348
South Asian Publishers Pvt Ltd, pg 350
Sterling Publishers Pvt Ltd, pg 350

Indonesia
Lembaga Demografi Fakultas Ekonomi Universitas Indonesia, pg 355
Yayasan Obor Indonesia, pg 357

Ireland
On Stream Publications Ltd, pg 362
Veritas Co Ltd, pg 364

Israel
Hanitzotz A-Sharara Publishing House, pg 367

Italy
Edizioni Cultura della Pace, pg 383
Fatatrac, pg 388

Jamaica
Association of Development Agencies, pg 413

Japan
Koyo Shobo, pg 422
Sobun-Sha, pg 428
United Nations University Press, pg 430

Kenya
Academy Science Publishers, pg 432
Action Publishers, pg 433
African Centre for Technology Studies (ACTS), pg 433
Kenya Quality & Productivity Institute, pg 435
Midi Teki Publishers, pg 435
Nairobi University Press, pg 435
Sasa Sema Publications Ltd, pg 435
Shirikon Publishers, pg 436

Madagascar
Maison d'Edition Protestante ANTSO, pg 453

Malaysia
Forum Publications, pg 456
Holograms (M) Sdn Bhd, pg 456

Mexico
El Colegio de Michoacan A C, pg 464
Fondo de Cultura Economica, pg 465
Instituto Nacional de Estadistica, Geographia e Informatica, pg 469

Morocco
Cabinet Conseil CCMLA, pg 474

Namibia
Desert Research Foundation of Namibia (DRFN), pg 476
Multi-Disciplinary Research Centre Library, pg 476

Netherlands
KIT - Royal Tropical Institute Publishers, pg 484
Mets & Schilt Uitgevers en Distributeurs, pg 486

Nigeria
International Publishing & Research Company, pg 505
JAD Publishers Ltd, pg 505
Riverside Communications, pg 507

Pakistan
Pakistan Institute of Development Economics (PIDE), pg 514

Papua New Guinea
National Research Institute of Papua New Guinea, pg 515

Peru
Instituto de Estudios Peruanos, pg 517
Sur Casa de Estudios del Socialismo, pg 517

Philippines
Our Lady of Manaoag Publisher, pg 520

Poland
Verbinum Wydawnictwo Ksiezy Werbistow, pg 527

Senegal
CODESRIA (Council for the Development of Social Science Research in Africa), pg 551

Singapore
Select Publishing Pte Ltd, pg 557

South Africa
Institute for Reformational Studies CHE, pg 565
New Africa Books (Pty) Ltd, pg 567

Spain
Editorial AEDOS SA, pg 571
Amnistia Internacional Editorial SL, pg 572
Icaria Editorial SA, pg 587
Mundo Negro Editorial, pg 592
Ediciones del Oriente y del Mediterraneo, pg 594

Suriname
Stichting Wetenschappelijke Informatie, pg 608

Switzerland
Rotpunktverlag, pg 632
Verlag im Waldgut AG, pg 636

United Republic of Tanzania
DUP (1996) Ltd, pg 643

PUBLISHERS

Togo
Editions Akpagnon, pg 646

United Kingdom
Association of Commonwealth Universities (ACU), pg 661
Business Monitor International, pg 672
Jon Carpenter Publishing, pg 675
Frank Cass Publishers, pg 675
Cassell & Co, pg 675
Catholic Institute for International Relations, pg 676
Commonwealth Secretariat, pg 681
James Currey Ltd, pg 685
Earthscan Publications Ltd, pg 689
The Economist Intelligence Unit, pg 689
Edward Elgar Publishing Ltd, pg 690
Europa Publications, pg 692
The Eurospan Group, pg 692
Institute of Development Studies, pg 712
ITDG Publishing, pg 715
Letterbox Library, pg 720
Open University Press, pg 736
Open University Worldwide, pg 736
Oxfam, pg 737
Panos Institute, pg 738
Pathfinder London, pg 739
Pluto Books Ltd, pg 743
Pluto Press, pg 743
Profile Books Ltd, pg 746
Rough Guides Ltd, pg 751
Routledge, pg 751
RoutledgeCurzon, pg 751
Royal Institute of International Affairs, pg 752
Saqi Books, pg 754
Serif, pg 756
I B Tauris & Co Ltd, pg 763
Vacation Work Publications, pg 769

Uruguay
Nordan-Comunidad, pg 778
Ediciones Trilce, pg 778

Venezuela
Biblioteca Ayacucho, pg 779
Editorial Nueva Sociedad, pg 780

Zambia
Aafzam Ltd, pg 781
MFK Management Consultants Services, pg 781

Zimbabwe
Journal on Social Change, pg 783
Sapes Trust Ltd, pg 784
Zimbabwe International Book Fair, pg 784

DISABILITY, SPECIAL NEEDS

Argentina
Alfagrama SRL ediciones, pg 3

Australia
Australian Institute of Family Studies (AIFS), pg 13
Bolinda Publishing Pty Ltd, pg 15
Ginninderra Press, pg 23
Indra Publishing, pg 27
Killara Press, pg 28
Little Red Apple Publishing, pg 29
MacLennan & Petty Pty Ltd, pg 30
McGraw-Hill Australia Pty Ltd, pg 31
OTEN (Open Training & Education Network), pg 34
Spinifex Press, pg 42
Villamonta Publishing Services Inc, pg 45

Azerbaijan
Sada, Literaturno-Izdatel'skij Centr, pg 60

Barbados
Business Tutors, pg 62

Brazil
Editora Antroposofica Ltda, pg 77
Fundacao Sao Paulo, EDUC, pg 82

China
China Braille Publishing House, pg 102
People's Education Press, pg 106

Czech Republic
Portal spol sro, pg 126

France
CTNERHI - Centre Technique National d'Etudes et de Recherches sur les Handicaps et les Inadaptations, pg 156

Germany
Catia Monser Eggcup-Verlag, pg 207
Engel & Bengel Verlag, pg 220
Harald Fischer Verlag GmbH, pg 224
Lebenshilfe-Verlag Marburg, Verlag der Bundesvereinigung Lebenshilfe fuer Menschen mit geistiger Behinderung eV, pg 253
Edition Marhold, pg 257
Meyer & Meyer Verlag, pg 260

Guyana
Guyana Community Based Rehabilitation Progeamme, pg 314

Hong Kong
Hong Kong University Press, pg 317

Iceland
Namsgagnastofnun, pg 326

India
Heritage Publishers, pg 335
Reliance Publishing House, pg 346
Somaiya Publications Pvt Ltd, pg 349

Ireland
Veritas Co Ltd, pg 364

Italy
Editore Armando Armando SRL, pg 376
Edizioni Cantagalli, pg 379
Gangemi Editore spa, pg 390
Milella di Lecce Spazio Vivo srl, pg 398

Japan
Kaisei-Sha Publishing Co Ltd, pg 420
Minerva Shobo Co Ltd, pg 422
Reimei-Shobo Co Ltd, pg 425
Tokyo Shoseki Co Ltd, pg 430

Latvia
Preses Nams, pg 445

Mexico
Maria Esther De Fleischmann, pg 464

New Zealand
Reach Publications, pg 500

Norway
Solum Forlag A/S, pg 510

Spain
Editorial Dossat SA, pg 580
Ediciones Morata SL, pg 592
Tursen, SA, pg 603

United Kingdom
Advisory Unit: Computers in Education, pg 655
Association for Science Education, pg 661
BILD Publications, pg 665
Colourpoint Books, pg 681
Drake Educational Associates Ltd, pg 688
The Eurospan Group, pg 692
David Fulton Publishers Ltd, pg 698
Institute of Employment Rights, pg 712
Jessica Kingsley Publishers, pg 718
Letterbox Library, pg 720
National Council for Voluntary Organisations (NCVO), pg 730
Open University Worldwide, pg 736
The Policy Press, pg 744
Psychological Corporation Ltd, pg 746
The Robinswood Press Ltd, pg 750
Scottish Executive Library & Information Services, pg 755
Speechmark Publishing Ltd, pg 760
Supportive Learning Publications, pg 762
Wilmington Business Information Ltd, pg 774
The Women's Press Ltd, pg 775
Anglia Young Books, pg 776

DRAMA, THEATER

Albania
NL SH, pg 1

Argentina
Ada Korn Editora SA, pg 3
Beatriz Viterbo Editora, pg 4
Bonum Editorial SACI, pg 4
Ediciones Corregidor SAICI y E, pg 4
Ediciones Don Bosco Argentina, pg 5
EUDEBA (Editorial Universitaria de Buenos Aires), pg 5
Ediciones de la Flor SRL, pg 6
Editorial Galerna SRL, pg 6
Editorial Losada SA, pg 7
Ediciones Nueva Vision SAIC, pg 8
Editorial Quetzal-Domingo Cortizo, pg 8

SUBJECT INDEX

Australia
Currency Press Pty Ltd, pg 19
Geoffrey Hamlyn-Harris, pg 24
Jika Publishing, pg 27
Magabala Books Aboriginal Corporation, pg 30
Playbox Theatre Co, pg 37
Playlab Press, pg 37
Wizard Books Pty Ltd, pg 47

Austria
Aarachne Verlag, pg 48
Literature Verlag Droschl, pg 50
Gerda Leber Buch-Kunst-und Musikverlag Proscenium Edition, pg 53
LOG-Internationale Zeitschrift fuer Literatur, pg 53
Mueller-Speiser Wissenschaftlicher Verlag, pg 54
Verlag Neues Leben, pg 54
Richard Pils Publication PN°1, pg 56
Residenz Verlag GmbH, pg 57
Salzburger Nachrichten Verlagsgesellschaft mbH & Co KG, pg 57
Wieser Verlag, pg 60

Azerbaijan
Sada, Literaturno-Izdatel'skij Centr, pg 60

Bangladesh
Bangladesh Publishers, pg 61
Gatidhara, pg 61

Belarus
Belaruskaya Encyklapedyya, pg 62

Belgium
Abimo, pg 62
Lansman Editeur, pg 69
Toneelfonds J Janssens BVBA, pg 73

Brazil
AGIR S/A Editora, pg 77
Editora Bertrand Brasil Ltda, pg 78
Centro de Estudos Juridicosdo Para (CEJUP), pg 79
Dumara Distribuidora de Publicacoes Ltda, pg 81
Edicon Editora e Consultorial Ltda, pg 81
Editora Globo SA, pg 82
Imago Editora Importacao e Exportacao Ltda, pg 84
Edicoes Loyola SA, pg 85
Editora Paz e Terra, pg 88
Editora Perspectiva, pg 88
Edicoes Tabajara, pg 91
34 Literatura S/C Ltda, pg 91

Bulgaria
Fondacija Zlatno Kljuce, pg 94
Zunica, pg 97

Cameroon
Editions CLE, pg 98
Editions Buma Kor & Co Ltd, pg 98
Editions Semences Africaines, pg 98

Chile
Arrayan Editores, pg 98

945

SUBJECT INDEX

China
Beijing Publishing House, pg 101
China Film Press, pg 102
China Theatre Publishing House, pg 103
Foreign Languages Press, pg 104
Shandong Literature & Art Publishing House, pg 107

Colombia
Editorial Panamericana, pg 112
Universidad de Antioquia, Division Publicaciones, pg 113

The Democratic Republic of the Congo
Saint-Paul, pg 114

Costa Rica
Ediciones Promesa, pg 116

Cote d'Ivoire
Akohi Editions, pg 117
Les Nouvelles Editions Ivoiriennes, pg 117

Croatia
AGM doo, pg 117
Durieux d o o, pg 118
Knjizevni Krug Split, pg 118
Matica hrvatska, pg 118

Cuba
Holguin, Ediciones, pg 120
Editorial Letras Cubanas, pg 120

Cyprus
Chrysopolitissa Publishers, pg 121

Czech Republic
Divadelni Ustav, pg 123
Lyra Pragensis Obecne Prospelna Spolecnost, pg 125
Narodni Muzeum, pg 126
PressArt Nakladatelstvi, pg 127

Denmark
Aarhus Universitetsforlag, pg 128
The Danish Literature Centre, pg 130
Teaterforlaget Drama, pg 135

Dominican Republic
Pontificia Universidad Catolica Madre y Maestra, pg 136

Finland
Yliopistopaino/Helsinki University Press, pg 145

France
Editions Actes Sud, pg 145
Editions Al Liamm, pg 146
L'Arche Editeur, pg 147
Editions Atlantica Seguier, pg 148
Editions d'Aujourd'hui (Les Introuvables), pg 148
Editions l'Avant-Scene de Prette Technique, pg 149
Editions Jacques Bremond, pg 151
Cahiers du Cinema, pg 151
Centre pour l'Innovation et la Recherche en Communication de l'Entreprise (CIRCE), pg 152
Cicero Editeurs, pg 154
Compagnie Francaise des Arts Graphiques SA, pg 155
La Delirante, pg 157

Editions Espaces 34, pg 162
Editions Des Femmes, pg 163
Association Frank, pg 164
Editions Infrarouge, pg 168
Institut International de la Marionnette, pg 169
Michel Lafon Publishing, pg 171
Editions du Laquet, pg 171
Le Livre de Poche-L G F (Librairie Generale Francaise), pg 173
Editions Medianes, pg 175
Librairie A-G Nizet Sarl, pg 177
Noir Sur Blanc, pg 177
Editions Norma, pg 177
Editions Plume, pg 180
Editions POL, pg 180
Presses de la Sorbonne Nouvelle/PSN, pg 181
Presses Universitaires de Nancy, pg 181
Publications Orientalistes de France (POF), pg 182
Editions Ramsay, pg 182
Editions Andre Silvaire Sarl, pg 185
Editions Theatrales, pg 187
Transeuropeennes/RCE, pg 188
La Vague a l'ame, pg 188
La Voix du Regard, pg 189

Germany
A Francke Verlag (Tubingen und Basel), pg 190
Alexander Verlag Berlin, pg 192
Alpha Literatur Verlag/Alpha Presse, pg 192
AOL-Verlag Frohmut Menze, pg 193
Arcadia Verlag GmbH, pg 193
ARCult Media, pg 193
Verlag der Autoren GmbH & Co KG, pg 196
Belser Wissenschaftlicher Dienst, pg 199
Betzel Verlag GmbH, pg 200
Das Arsenal, Verlag fuer Kultur und Politik GmbH, pg 210
Domino Verlag, Guenther Brinek GmbH, pg 215
Edition Aragon-Verlagsgesellschaft mbH, pg 218
Fabel-Verlag Gudrun Liebchen, pg 223
Erhard Friedrich Verlag, pg 227
Siegfried Haring Literatten-Verlag Ulm, pg 234
Edition Hentrich Druck & Verlag Gebr Hentrich und Tank GmbH & Co KG, pg 236
Anton Hiersemann, Verlag, pg 237
Impuls-Theater-Verlag, pg 241
Iudicium Verlag GmbH, pg 242
Alfred Kroner Verlag, pg 250
Verlag Antje Kunstmann GmbH, pg 251
Robert Lienau GmbH & Co KG, pg 254
Annemarie Maeger, pg 256
Merlin Verlag Andreas Meyer Verlags GmbH und Co KG, pg 259
Merz & Solitude - Akademie Schloss Solitude, pg 259
Meyer & Meyer Verlag, pg 260
Edition Octopus & Okeanos Presse, pg 266
Oekotopia Verlag, Wolfgang Hoffman GmbH & Co KG, pg 266
Georg Olms Verlag AG, pg 267
Gerhard Rautenberg Druckerei und Verlag GmbH & Co KG, pg 273
Otto Teich, pg 289

Trotzdem-Verlags Genossenschaft eG, pg 292
Vervuert Verlagsgesellschaft, pg 295
Weidler Buchverlag Berlin, pg 298

Ghana
Black Mask Ltd, pg 303
Bureau of Ghana Languages, pg 303
Woeli Publishing Services, pg 305

Greece
Dorikos Publishing House, pg 306
Ekdoseis Kazantzaki (Kazantzakis Publications), pg 307
Etaireia Spoudon Neoellinikou Politismou Kai Genikis Paideias, pg 307
Govostis Publishing SA, pg 307
Hestia-I D Hestia-Kollaros & Co Corporation, pg 308
Kastaniotis Editions SA, pg 309
Kedros Publishers, pg 309
Ed Nea Acropolis, pg 310
Patakis Publishers, pg 311
To Rodakio, pg 312
S J Zacharopoulos SA Publishing Co, pg 313

Hungary
Jelenkor Verlag, pg 322
Nemzetkozi Szinhazi Intezet Magyar Kozpontja, pg 323

India
Abhinav Publications, pg 326
Ananda Publishers Pvt Ltd, pg 328
CICC Book House, Leading Publishers & Booksellers, pg 332
Cosmo Publications, pg 332
DK Printworld (P) Ltd, pg 333
Gyan Publishing House, pg 335
Indian Council for Cultural Relations, pg 336
Kali For Women, pg 339
Kitab Ghar, pg 339
Mudgala Trust, pg 342
Munshiram Manoharlal Publishers Pvt Ltd, pg 342
Omsons Publications, pg 344
Orient Paperbacks, pg 344
Reliance Publishing House, pg 346
Sharda Prakashan, pg 349
Vidyarthi Mithram Press, pg 352

Indonesia
Dunia Pustaka Jaya PT, pg 354

Ireland
Campus Publishing Ltd, pg 358
Clo Iar-Chonnachta Teo, pg 358
The Gallery Press, pg 360

Israel
Hakibbutz Hameuchad Publishing House Ltd, pg 367
Schocken Publishing House Ltd, pg 371

Italy
Edizioni Abete, pg 374
Argalia Editore delle Arti Grafiche Editoriali SRL, pg 376
Artioli Editore, pg 377
BMG Ricordi SpA, pg 378
Bompiani-RCS Libri, pg 378
Bulzoni Editore SRL (Le Edizioni Universitarie d'Italia), pg 379
Cappelli Editore, pg 380
Colonnese Editore, pg 383

Costa e Nolan SpA, pg 383
Edistudio, pg 386
Effata Editrice, pg 387
Essegi, pg 388
Arnaldo Forni Editore SRL, pg 389
Ernesto Gremese Editore srl, pg 391
Kaos Edizioni SRL, pg 394
Lalli Editore SRL, pg 394
Levante Editori, pg 395
Editrice Liguria SNC di Norberto Sabatelli & C, pg 395
Vincenzo Lo Faro Editore, pg 395
Angelo Longo Editore, pg 396
Editrice Massimo SAS di Crespi Cesare e C, pg 397
Casa Editrice Menna di Sinisgalli Menna Giuseppina, pg 398
Mondolibro Editore SNC, pg 399
Officina Edizioni di Aldo Quinti, pg 401
Maria Pacini Fazzi Editore, pg 402
Luigi Pellegrini Editore, pg 403
Pratiche Editrice, pg 404
Rubbettino Editore, pg 406
Edizioni Scientifiche Italiane, pg 407
SEMAR Publishers SRL, pg 408
Sicania, pg 408
La Tartaruga Edizioni SAS, pg 409
Edizioni Ubulibri SAS, pg 410
Viviani Editore srl, pg 412
Edizioni Zara, pg 412

Jamaica
Carlong Publishers (Caribbean) Ltd, pg 413

Japan
Hakusui-Sha Co Ltd, pg 417
Hayakawa Publishing Inc, pg 418
Koyo Shobo, pg 422
Nippon Hoso Shuppan Kyokai (NHK Publishing), pg 424
Shakai Shiso-Sha, pg 427

Kenya
Heinemann Kenya Ltd (EAEP), pg 434
Lake Publishers & Enterprises Ltd, pg 435

Republic of Korea
Bum-Woo Publishing Co, pg 437

Latvia
Preses Nams, pg 445

Lithuania
Klaipedos Universiteto Leidykla, pg 449
Scena, pg 449

Luxembourg
Editions Emile Borschette, pg 450
Edition Objectif Lune, pg 451
Editions Phi, pg 451

The Former Yugoslav Republic of Macedonia
Ktitor, pg 452

Mauritius
De l'edition Bukie Banane, pg 461

Mexico
Editorial AGATA SA de CV, pg 462
Aguilar Altea Taurus Alfaguara SA de CV, pg 462

PUBLISHERS

Arbol Editorial SA de CV, pg 462
Editorial Avante SA de Cv, pg 462
Editorial Extemporaneos SA, pg 465
Fondo de Cultura Economica, pg 465
Editorial Limusa SA de CV, pg 467
Universidad Nacional Autonoma de Mexico (National University of Mexico), pg 472
Universidad Veracruzana Direccion General Editorial y de Publicaciones, pg 472

Monaco

Les Editions du Rocher, pg 474

Morocco

Edition Diffusion de Livre au Maroc, pg 474
Editions Le Fennec, pg 474

Netherlands

De Walburg Pers, pg 481
Uitgevery International Theatre & Film Books, pg 484
Em Querido's Uitgeverij BV, pg 488

New Zealand

Aoraki Press Ltd, pg 493
Clerestory Press, pg 495
Hazard Press Ltd, pg 497
Huia Publishers, pg 497
Nelson Price Milburn Ltd, pg 499
Victoria University Press, pg 502

Nigeria

Evans Brothers (Nigeria Publishers) Ltd, pg 504
Saros International Publishers, pg 507
Vantage Publishers International Ltd, pg 507

Pakistan

Maqbool Academy, pg 513
Sang-e-Meel Publications, pg 514

Philippines

Ateneo de Manila University Press, pg 518

Poland

Wydawnictwa Artystyczne i Filmowe, pg 522
Energeia sp zoo Wydawnictwo, pg 523
Wydawnictwo Literackie, pg 524
Panstwowy Instytut Wydawniczy (PIW), pg 525

Portugal

Atica, SA Editores e Livreiros, pg 529
Bezerr-Editorae e Distribuidora de Abel Antonio Bezerra, pg 529
Editora Classica, pg 530
Editorial Estampa, Lda, pg 531
Europress Editores e Distribuidores de Publicacoes Lda, pg 531
Guimaraes Editores, Lda, pg 532
Livraria Minerva, pg 533
Livraria Tavares Martins, pg 533
Nova Arrancada Sociedade Editora SA, pg 534
Platano Editora SA, pg 534

Quimera Editores Lda, pg 535
Vega-Publicacao e Distribuicao de Livros e Revistas, Lda, pg 536

Romania

Editura Cartea Romaneasca, pg 538
Editura Excelsior Art, pg 539
Mentor Kiado, pg 540
Editura Meridiane, pg 540
Est-Samuel Tastet Verlag, pg 542

Russian Federation

BLIC, russko-Baltijskij informaciionnyj centr, AO, pg 544
Izdatelstvo Iskusstvo, pg 545
Sovremennik Publishers Too, pg 548

Saudi Arabia

Dar Al-Shareef for Publishing & Distribution, pg 550

Senegal

Centre Africain d'Animation et d'Echanges Culturels Editions Khoudia (CAEC), pg 551

Singapore

Select Publishing Pte Ltd, pg 557

Slovakia

Slovansky Tatran, Vydavatel 'stro spoi sro, pg 560

Slovenia

Mladinska Knjiga International, pg 561
Zalozba Mihelac d o o, pg 562
Zalozba Obzorja d d Maribor, pg 562

South Africa

Human & Rousseau (Pty) Ltd, pg 564
New Africa Books (Pty) Ltd, pg 567
University of Durban-Westville Library, pg 569
Witwatersrand University Press, pg 570

Spain

Agencia Espanola de Cooperacion, pg 571
Edicios do Castro, pg 576
Central Catequistica Salesiana (CCS), pg 576
Diputacion Provincial de Malaga, pg 579
Editorial Don Quijote, pg 579
Edi-Liber Irlan SA, pg 580
Editorial Fundamentos, pg 584
Lunwerg Editores, SA, pg 589
Antonio Machado, SA, pg 590
MK Ediciones y Publicaciones, pg 591
Naque Editora, pg 592
Pages Editors, SL, pg 594
El Paisaje Editorial, pg 594
Editorial Pliegos, pg 596
Instituto Provincial de Investigaciones y Estudios Toledanos (IPIET), pg 597
Edicions 62, pg 600
Grup 62, pg 600
Ediciones de la Torre, pg 602
Editorial Verbum SL, pg 604
Vinaches Lopez, Luisa, pg 605

Sri Lanka

Dayawansa Jayakody & Co, pg 606

Sweden

Bokforlaget Axplock, pg 609

Switzerland

Editions L'Age d'Homme - La Cite, pg 617
Caux Edition SA, pg 620
Diogenes Verlag AG, pg 622
G+B Arts International, pg 623
Editions Minkoff, pg 628
Les Editions Noir sur Blanc, pg 629

Taiwan, Province of China

World Book Co Ltd, pg 642

United Republic of Tanzania

DUP (1996) Ltd, pg 643
Tanzania Publishing House, pg 644

Tunisia

Academie Tunisienne des Sciences, des Lettres et des Arts Beit El Hekma, pg 647
Maison Tunisienne de l'Edition, pg 648

Turkey

Afa Yayincilik Sanayi Tic AS, pg 648
Alkim Kitapcilik-Yayimcilik, pg 649
Inkilap Publishers Ltd, pg 650
Turkish Republic - Ministry of Culture, pg 652
Kabalci Yayinevi, pg 652

Ukraine

Mystetstvo Publishers, pg 653

United Kingdom

Amber Lane Press Ltd, pg 657
Art Books International Ltd, pg 659
Atlas Press, pg 661
Ruth Bean Publishers, pg 664
A & C Black Publishers Ltd, pg 666
Blackstaff Press, pg 666
Bloomsbury Publishing PLC, pg 668
Marion Boyars Publishers Ltd, pg 669
Brown, Son & Ferguson, Ltd, pg 672
Calder Publications Ltd, pg 673
Cambridge University Press, pg 674
Chadwyck-Healey Ltd, pg 677
Chapman, pg 677
Christian Education, pg 679
The Continuum International Publishing Group Ltd, pg 682
Cressrelles Publishing Company Ltd, pg 684
James Currey Ltd, pg 685
Dramatic Lines Publishers, pg 688
The Eurospan Group, pg 692
Faber & Faber Ltd, pg 694
Feather Books, pg 694
Samuel French Ltd, pg 697
Golden Cockerel Press Ltd, pg 701
Ian Henry Publications Ltd, pg 708
Nick Hern Books Ltd, pg 708
Intellect Ltd, pg 713
Kenyon-Deane, pg 717
The Littman Library of Jewish Civilization, pg 721
Maney Publishing, pg 725
Methuen, pg 727

SUBJECT INDEX

J Garnet Miller, pg 728
Moorley's Print & Publishing Ltd, pg 729
National Association for the Teaching of English (NATE), pg 730
New Playwrights' Network, pg 732
Northcote House Publishers Ltd, pg 733
Octopus Publishing Group, pg 734
The Oleander Press, pg 735
Peter Owen Ltd, pg 737
Parthian Books, pg 738
Pearson Education Europe, Mideast & Africa, pg 739
Phaidon Press Ltd, pg 741
The Playwrights Publishing Co, pg 743
Plexus Publishing Ltd, pg 743
Polygon, pg 744
Roundhouse Group, pg 751
SchoolPlay Productions Ltd, pg 755
Seren, pg 756
Sheffield Academic Press Ltd, pg 757
Colin Smythe Ltd, pg 759
Supportive Learning Publications, pg 762
Thomson Gale, pg 765
Time Out Group Ltd, pg 765
Trentham Books Ltd, pg 767
University of Exeter Press, pg 768
University of Hertfordshire Press, pg 768
Wilmington Business Information Ltd, pg 774
World Microfilms Publications Ltd, pg 775

Uruguay

Editorial Arca SRL, pg 776

Venezuela

Biblioteca Ayacucho, pg 779

Zambia

Zambia Educational Publishing House, pg 782
Zambia Printing Company Ltd (ZPC), pg 782

Zimbabwe

Anvil Press, pg 782
College Press Publishers (Pvt) Ltd, pg 783
The Literature Bureau, pg 783
Zimbabwe Foundation for Education with Production (ZIMFEP), pg 784

EARTH SCIENCES

Albania

NL SH, pg 1
State Textbook Publishing House, pg 1

Argentina

Instituto Nacional de Ciencia y Tecnica Hidrica (INCYTH), pg 7
Oikos, pg 8

Australia

Allen & Unwin Pty Ltd, pg 11
Aussie Books, pg 12
Australian Marine Conservation Society Inc (AMCS), pg 13
Beazer Publishing Company Pty Ltd, pg 14
Blackwell Publishing Asia, pg 15

SUBJECT INDEX — BOOK

Brookfield Press, pg 16
Department of Energy (NSW), pg 20
McGraw-Hill Australia Pty Ltd, pg 31
Queen Victoria Museum & Art Gallery Publications, pg 38
University of New South Wales Press Ltd, pg 44

Azerbaijan
Sada, Literaturno-Izdatel'skij Centr, pg 60

Belgium
Abimo, pg 62

Botswana
The Botswana Society, pg 76

Brazil
Editora Edgard Blucher Ltda, pg 79
Edicon Editora e Consultorial Ltda, pg 81
Empresa Brasileira de Pesquisa Agropecuaria, pg 81
Editora Harbra Ltda, pg 83
Edit Palavra Magica, pg 88
Thex Editora e Distribuidora Ltda, pg 91

Bulgaria
Pensoft Publishers, pg 96

Chile
Instituto Geografico Militar, pg 99

China
Chengdu Maps Publishing House, pg 101
China Cartographic Publishing House, pg 102
China Ocean Press, pg 102
Jiangsu Science & Technology Publishing House, pg 105
Metallurgical Industry Press (MIP), pg 106
Nanjing University Press, pg 106
Science Press, pg 107
Shandong Science & Technology Press, pg 107
Xi'an Cartography Publishing House, pg 109

Colombia
Editorial Libros y Libres SA, pg 112

Costa Rica
Instituto Interamericano de Cooperacion para la Agricultura (IICA), pg 115
Editorial de la Universidad de Costa Rica, pg 116

Czech Republic
Mariadan, pg 125
Mendelova zemedelska a lesnicka univerzita v Brne, pg 125
Narodni Muzeum, pg 126
Vydavatelstvi Cesky Geologicky Ustav, pg 128

Egypt (Arab Republic of Egypt)
American University in Cairo Press, pg 137

Estonia
Eesti Entsuklopeediakirjastus, pg 139

Finland
Ursa ry, pg 144

France
ATP - Packager, pg 148
Editions BRGM, pg 151
Bureau des Longitudes, pg 151
Cemagref Editions, pg 152
Corsaire Editions, pg 156
Doin Editeurs, pg 159
Elf Exploration Production, pg 161
Editions Eyrolles, pg 162
INRA Editions (Institut National de la Recherche Agronomique), pg 168
IRD Editions, pg 169
Jouvence Editions, pg 170
Librairie Scientifique et Technique Albert Blanchard, pg 172
Nanga, pg 176
Editions Ophrys, pg 177
Ouest Editions, pg 178
Editions Pedone, pg 179
Presses de l'Ecole Nationale des Ponts et Chaussees, pg 181
Service des Publications Scientifiques du Museum National d'Histoire Naturelle, pg 184
Editions Springer France, pg 186
Editions Technip SA, pg 187
Editions Vague Verte, pg 188
Librairie Vuibert, pg 189

French Polynesia
Haere Po Editions, pg 189

Germany
Aluminium-Verlag Marketing & Kommunikation GmbH, pg 192
Eberhard Blottner Verlag GmbH, pg 202
C C Buchners Verlag GmbH & Co KG, pg 205
Chmielorz GmbH Verlag, pg 208
Verlag Harri Deutsch, pg 211
Deutsche Verlags-Anstalt GmbH (DVA), pg 212
Deutscher Verlag fur Grundstoffindustrie GmbH, pg 213
Ferd Dummler's Verlag, pg 223
Fraunhofer IRB Verlag Fraunhofer Informationszentrum Raum und Bau, pg 226
Gebrueder Borntraeger Science Publishers, pg 228
Verlag Glueckauf GmbH, pg 229
Huthig GmbH & Co KG, pg 240
Ambro Lacus, Buch- und Bildverlag Walter A Kremnitz, pg 251
Verlag Natur & Wissenschaft Harro Hieronimus & Dr Jurgen Schmidt, pg 263
Palazzi Verlag GmbH, pg 268
Renate Schenk Verlag, pg 279
E Schweizerbart'sche Verlagsbuchhandlung (Naegele und Obermiller), pg 282
Springer Science+Business Media GmbH & Co KG, pg 284
Steiger Verlag, pg 287
Franz Steiner Verlag Wiesbaden GmbH, pg 287
Trans Tech Publications, pg 292
Guenter Albert Ulmer Verlag, pg 293

Weidler Buchverlag Berlin, pg 298
Herbert Wichmann Verlag, pg 299
Verlag Konrad Wittwer GmbH, pg 301

Ghana
Building & Road Research Institute (BRRI), pg 303

Greece
Michalis Sideris, pg 312

Holy See (Vatican City State)
Pontificia Academia Scientiarum, pg 314

Hong Kong
Geocarto International Centre, pg 317

Hungary
Akademiai Kiado, pg 320
Janus Pannonius Tudomanyegyetem, pg 322
Springer Hungarica Kiado Kft, pg 324
Szarvas Andras Cartographic Agency, pg 324

India
Agam Kala Prakashan, pg 327
Allied Book Centre, pg 328
Bhawan Book Service, Publishers & Distributors, pg 330
BS Publications, pg 331
BSMPS - M/s Bishen Singh Mahendra Pal Singh, pg 331
Concept Publishing Co, pg 332
Daya Publishing House, pg 333
Gyan Publishing House, pg 335
Nem Chand & Brothers, pg 343
Oxford & IBH Publishing Co Pvt Ltd, pg 344
Rahul Publishing House, pg 346
Rastogi Publications, pg 346
Reliance Publishing House, pg 346
Scientific Book Agency, pg 348
Viva Books Pvt Ltd, pg 352

Indonesia
Yayasan Obor Indonesia, pg 357

Ireland
Royal Irish Academy, pg 363

Italy
Archimede Edizioni, pg 376
BeMa, pg 377
Casa Editrice Giuseppe Principato Spa, pg 380
Damanhur Edizioni, pg 384
Arnaldo Forni Editore SRL, pg 389
Editoriale Jaca Book SpA, pg 394
Paravia Bruno Mondadori Editori, pg 402
Principato, pg 404
Red/Studio Redazionale, pg 405
SAIE Editrice SRL, pg 406
Editoriale Scienza, pg 407
Zanichelli Editore SpA, pg 412

Jamaica
The Jamaica Bauxite Institute, pg 413

Japan
Morikita Shuppan Co Ltd, pg 423
Nippon Hoso Shuppan Kyokai (NHK Publishing), pg 424
Sanseido Co Ltd, pg 426
Shogakukan Inc, pg 427
Tokai University Press, pg 429
Tsukiji Shokan Publishing Co, pg 430
Yama-Kei Publishers Co Ltd, pg 431

Kazakstan
Gylym, Izd-Vo, pg 432

Kenya
African Centre for Technology Studies (ACTS), pg 433

Republic of Korea
Korea University Press, pg 440
Seoul National University Press, pg 443

Latvia
Nordik/Tapals Publishers Ltd, pg 445

Liechtenstein
Botanisch-Zoologische Gesellschaft, pg 447

The Former Yugoslav Republic of Macedonia
Seizmoloska Opservatorija, pg 453

Mexico
Centro de Estudios Mexicanos y Centroamericanos, pg 463
Fondo de Cultura Economica, pg 465
Editorial Limusa SA de CV, pg 467
Instituto Nacional de Estadistica, Geographia e Informatica, pg 469
Sistemas Tecnicos de Edicion SA de CV, pg 472
Ediciones Suromex SA, pg 472

Namibia
Desert Research Foundation of Namibia (DRFN), pg 476

Nepal
International Standards Books & Periodicals (P) Ltd, pg 476

Netherlands
Backhuys Publishers BV, pg 478
A A Balkema Uitgevers BV, pg 478
Elsevier Science BV, pg 482
V S P International Science Publishers, pg 491

New Zealand
Bush Press Communications Ltd, pg 494
Wendy Crane Books, pg 495
Landcare Research NZ, pg 497
New House Publishers Ltd, pg 499
SIR Publishing, pg 501

Norway
Chr Schibsteds Forlag A/S, pg 510
Vett & Viten AS, pg 511

PUBLISHERS

Peru
Instituto Frances de Estudios Andinos, IFEA, pg 517

Philippines
Salesiana Publishers Inc, pg 521

Poland
Instytut Historii Nauki PAN, pg 523
Instytut Meteorologii i Gospodarki Wodnej, pg 523
Polish Scientific Publishers PWN, pg 525

Portugal
Constancia Editores, SA, pg 530
Gradiva-Publicacnoes Lda, pg 532
Instituto de Investigacao Cientifica Tropical, pg 532
Planeta Editora, LDA, pg 534

Romania
Editura Academiei Romane, pg 538
Editura Gryphon, pg 540

Russian Federation
N E Bauman Moscow State Technical University Publishers, pg 544
Gidrometeoizdat, pg 545
Izdatelstvo Metallurgiya, pg 546
Izdatelstvo Mir, pg 546
Nauka Publishers, pg 547
Izdatelstvo Nedra, pg 547
Pressa Publishing House, pg 548
Izdatelstvo Prosveshchenie, pg 548

Slovakia
VEDA (Vydavatel'stvo Slovenskej akademie vied), pg 561

Slovenia
Zalozba Obzorja d d Maribor, pg 562

Spain
Editorial AEDOS SA, pg 571
Instituto de Estudios Riojanos, pg 583
Idea Books, SA, pg 587
Loguez Ediciones, pg 589
Mandala Ediciones, pg 590
OASIS, Producciones Generales de Comunicacion, pg 593
Oikos-Tau SA Ediciones, pg 593
Rueda, SL Editorial, pg 598
Editorial Sintesis, SA, pg 600
Universidad de Malaga, pg 603

Switzerland
Association Suisse des Editeurs de Langue Francaise, pg 618
Bibliographisches Institut & F A Brockhaus AG, pg 619
Marcel Dekker AG, pg 621
Editions Delachaux et Niestle SA, pg 621
Ott Verlag Thun, pg 630
Presses Polytechniques et Universitaires Romandes, PPUR, pg 631
Schweizerische Stiftung fuer Alpine Forschungen, pg 634
Wepf & Co AG, pg 637

Syrian Arab Republic
Damascus University Press, pg 638

Taiwan, Province of China
Yi Hsien Publishing Co Ltd, pg 642

Turkey
Ruh ve Madde Yayinlari ve Saglik Hizmetleri AS, pg 651

Ukraine
Naukova Dumka Publishers, pg 653

United Kingdom
Andromeda Oxford Ltd, pg 658
Artetech Publishing Co, pg 660
Blackwell Science Ltd, pg 667
Cambridge University Press, pg 674
E W Classey Ltd, pg 680
Commonwealth Secretariat, pg 681
Dunedin Academic Press, pg 688
Elsevier Ltd, pg 691
The Eurospan Group, pg 692
W H Freeman & Co Ltd, pg 697
Gateway Books, pg 698
Geological Society Publishing House, pg 699
Harvard University Press, pg 705
Hyden House Ltd, pg 711
IWA Publishing, pg 715
Jones & Bartlett International, pg 716
Manson Publishing Ltd, pg 725
MIT Press Ltd, pg 728
Open University Worldwide, pg 736
Orpheus Books Ltd, pg 736
The Reader's Digest Association Ltd, pg 748
RICS Books, pg 750
Snowbooks Ltd, pg 759
The Society of Metaphysicians Ltd, pg 759
Thistle Press, pg 765
TSO (The Stationery Office), pg 767
Wiley Europe Ltd, pg 773
WIT Press, pg 774

Uruguay
A Monteverde y Cia SA, pg 777

Viet Nam
Science & Technics Publishing House, pg 780

ECONOMICS

Albania
NL SH, pg 1

Argentina
Editorial Abaco de Rodolfo Depalma SRL, pg 2
Aguilar Altea Taurus Alfaguara SA de Ediciones, pg 3
Editorial Albatros SACI, pg 3
Amorrortu Editores SA, pg 3
Editorial Astrea de Alfredo y Ricardo Depalma SRL, pg 3
AZ Editora SA, pg 3
Editorial Cangallo SACI, pg 4
Ediciones Corregidor SAICI y E, pg 4
Diana Argentina SA, Editorial, pg 5
Errepar SA, pg 5
EUDEBA (Editorial Universitaria de Buenos Aires), pg 5
Fundacion Editorial de Belgrano, pg 6
Editorial Idearium de la Universidad de Mendoza (EDIUM), pg 6
La Ley SA Editora e Impresora, pg 7
Marymar Ediciones SA, pg 7
Editorial Plus Ultra SA, pg 8
Instituto Torcuato Di Tella, pg 9
Editorial Universidad SRL, pg 9

Australia
Allen & Unwin Pty Ltd, pg 11
Australian Institute of Family Studies (AIFS), pg 13
Crystal Publishing, pg 19
Dabill Publications, pg 19
Emerald City Books, pg 21
Macmillan Education Australia, pg 30
McGraw-Hill Australia Pty Ltd, pg 31
Melbourne Institute of Applied Economic & Social Research, pg 31
Oxfam Community Aid Abroad, pg 35
Pearson Education Australia, pg 36
Spinifex Press, pg 42
Tertiary Press, pg 43
VCTA Publishing, pg 45

Austria
Compass-Verlag GmbH, pg 49
Verlag fuer Geschichte und Politik, pg 51
Horst Knapp Finanznachrichten, pg 53
Linde Verlag Wien GmbH, pg 53
MANZ'sche Verlags- und Universitaetsbuchhandlung GMBH, pg 54
Verlag Neues Leben, pg 54
Verlag Orac im Verlag Kremayr & Scheriau, pg 56
Passagen Verlag GmbH, pg 56
Dr A Schendl GmbH und Co KG, pg 57
Springer-Verlag Wien, pg 58
Verlag Carl Ueberreuter GmbH, pg 58
WUV/Service Fachverlag, pg 60

Azerbaijan
Sada, Literaturno-Izdatel'skij Centr, pg 60

Bangladesh
Ankur Prakashani, pg 61
Bangladesh Publishers, pg 61
The University Press Ltd, pg 61

Belarus
Belarus (The Belorussia), pg 62
Narodnaya Asveta, pg 62

Belgium
Academia Press, pg 62
Uitgeverij Acco, pg 62
Creadif, pg 65
Editions De Boeck-Larcier SA, pg 66
Documenta CV, pg 66
Garant Publishers Ltd, pg 67
Institut Royal des Relations Internationales, pg 68
Editions Juridiques Kluwer a Deurne Anvers, pg 69
King Baudouin Foundation, pg 69
Koepel van de Vlaamse Noord - Zuidbeweging 11.11.11, pg 69
Editions Labor, pg 69
Uitgeverij Lannoo NV, pg 69
Leuven University Press, pg 70
Maklu, pg 70
Nauwelaerts Edition SA, pg 71
Presses Universitaires de Bruxelles asbl, pg 72
Publications des Facultes Universitaires Saint Louis, pg 72
Roularta Books NV, pg 72
Scoop Infotex NV, pg 73
Editions de l'Universite de Bruxelles, pg 74
Vander Editions, SA, pg 74
Les Editions Vie ouvriere ASBL, pg 74
Wolters Kluwer Belgie NV, pg 74
Wolters Plantyn Educatieve Uitgevers, pg 74

Brazil
Editora Alfa Omega Ltda, pg 77
Editora Antroposofica Ltda, pg 77
ARTMED Editora, pg 78
Editora Atlas SA, pg 78
Editora Campus Ltda, pg 79
Editora Contexto (Editora Pinsky Ltda), pg 80
Empresa Brasileira de Pesquisa Agropecuaria, pg 81
Editora Forense Universitaria Ltda, pg 81
Fundacao Instituto Brasileiro de Geografia e Estatistica (IBGE - CDDI/DECOP), pg 82
Fundacao Joaquim Nabuco-Editora Massangana, pg 82
Fundacao Sao Paulo, EDUC, pg 82
Editora Globo SA, pg 82
Edicoes Graal Ltda, pg 83
IBRASA (Instituicao Brasileira de Difusao Cultural Ltda), pg 83
Iglu Editora Ltda, pg 84
Editora Lidador Ltda, pg 85
Livraria Nobel S/A, pg 85
Edicoes Loyola SA, pg 85
LTC-Livros Tecnicos e Cientificos Editora S/A, pg 85
Editora Lucre Comercio e Representacoes, pg 85
Editora Ortiz SA, pg 88
Pearson Education Do Brasil, pg 88
Editora Perspectiva, pg 88
Livraria Pioneira Editora/Enio Matheus Guazzelli e Cia Ltd, pg 88
Qualitymark Editora Ltda, pg 89
Saraiva SA, Livreiros Editores, pg 90
Thex Editora e Distribuidora Ltda, pg 91
Editora Universidade Federal do Rio de Janeiro, pg 92
Fundacao Getulio Vargas, pg 92
Jorge Zahar Editor, pg 92

Bulgaria
Agencija Za Ikonomicesko Programirane i Razvitie, pg 93
Ciela Publishing House, pg 93
Dolphin Press Group Ltd, pg 94
EA EOOD, pg 94
Galaktika Publishing House, pg 94
Gea-Libris Publishing House, pg 94
Makros 2000 - Plovdiv, pg 95
Naouka i Izkoustvo, Ltd, pg 95
Slavena, pg 97
Todor Kableshkov University of Transport, pg 97

Cameroon
Editions Buma Kor & Co Ltd, pg 98
Presses Universitaires d'Afrique, pg 98

SUBJECT INDEX

Chile
Arrayan Editores, pg 98
Ediciones Cieplan, pg 99
Edeval (Universidad de Valparaiso), pg 99
Pontificia Universidad Catolica de Chile, pg 100

China
Anhui People's Publishing House, pg 101
Aviation Industry Press, pg 101
Beijing Publishing House, pg 101
Beijing University Press, pg 101
China Braille Publishing House, pg 102
China Foreign Economic Relations & Trade Publishing House, pg 102
China Forestry Publishing House, pg 102
China Materials Management Publishing House, pg 102
China Tibetology Publishing House, pg 103
China Translation & Publishing Corp, pg 103
CITIC Publishing House, pg 103
Dalian Maritime University Press, pg 104
Foreign Languages Press, pg 104
Fudan University Press, pg 104
Guizhou Education Publishing House, pg 105
Heilongjiang Science & Technology Press, pg 105
Jinan Publishing House, pg 105
Lanzhou University Press, pg 106
Liaoning People's Publishing House, pg 106
Nanjing University Press, pg 106
SDX (Shenghuo-Dushu-Xinzhi) Joint Publishing Co, pg 107
Shandong Science & Technology Press, pg 107
Shandong University Press, pg 108
Shanghai Far East Publishers, pg 108
Sichuan University Press, pg 108
South China University of Science & Technology Press, pg 108
Universidade de Macau, Centro de Publicacoes, pg 109
Wuhan University Press, pg 109
Xinhua Publishing House, pg 109

Colombia
El Ancora Editores, pg 111
Fundacion Centro de Investigacion y Educacion Popular (CINEP), pg 111
Fundacion Universidad de la Sabana Ediciones INSE, pg 111
LEGIS - Editores SA, pg 111
McGraw-Hill Colombia, pg 112
Procultura SA, pg 112
Tercer Mundo Editores SA, pg 113
Universidad de los Andes Editorial, pg 113
Universidad Nacional Abierta y a Distancia, pg 113
Carlos Valencia Editores, pg 113

The Democratic Republic of the Congo
Facultes Catoliques de Kinshasa, pg 114
Presses Universitaires du Zaiire (PUZ), pg 114

Costa Rica
Academia de Centro America, pg 114
Asamblea Legislativa, Biblioteca Monsenor Sanabria, pg 115
Centro Agronomico Tropical de Investigacion y Ensenanza (CATIE), pg 115
Editorial DEI (Departamento Ecumenico de Investigaciones), pg 115
Editorial Porvenir, pg 116
Editorial de la Universidad de Costa Rica, pg 116
Editorial Universidad Estatal a Distancia (EUNED), pg 116

Cote d'Ivoire
Universite d'Abidjan, pg 117

Croatia
Informator dd, pg 118
Masmedia, pg 118
Naklada Ljevak doo, pg 119

Cuba
ISCAH Fructuoso Rodriguez, pg 120
Editora Politica, pg 120

Czech Republic
Academia, pg 122
Babtext Nakladatelska Spolecnost, pg 122
Barrister & Principal, pg 122
Doplnek, pg 123
Grada Publishing, pg 123
Josef Hribal, pg 124
Karolinum, nakladatelstvi, pg 124
Libri spol sro, pg 125
Mendelova zemedelska a lesnicka univerzita v Brne, pg 125
Trizonia, pg 128

Denmark
Akademisk Forlag A/S, pg 128
Djof Publishing Jurist-og Okonomforbundets Forlag, pg 130
Fremad A/S, pg 131
Gads Forlag, pg 131
Forlaget Hovedland, pg 132
Joergen Paludan Forlag ApS, pg 133
Samfundslitteratur, pg 134
Systime, pg 135

Dominican Republic
Pontificia Universidad Catolica Madre y Maestra, pg 136
Sociedad Editorial Americana, pg 136
Editora Taller, pg 136

Ecuador
Centro De Educacion Popular, pg 136
Corporacion Editora Nacional, pg 136
Pontificia Universidad Catolica del Ecuador, Centro de Publicaciones, pg 137

Egypt (Arab Republic of Egypt)
Al Arab Publishing House, pg 137
Ummah Press, pg 138

Estonia
Eesti Entsuklopeediakirjastus, pg 139
Olion Publishers, pg 140

Finland
Tietoteos Publishing Co, pg 144

France
Editions Anthropos, pg 147
Editions de l'Atelier, pg 148
Editions de l'Aube, pg 148
Editions Bertrand-Lacoste, pg 149
Editions Breal, pg 151
Les Cahiers Fiscaux Europeens Sarl, pg 151
Editions Calmann-Levy SA, pg 152
Editions Casteilla, pg 152
Centre de Librairie et d'Editions Techniques (CLET), pg 152
Chotard et Associes Editeurs, pg 154
CNRS Editions, pg 155
Editions Cujas, pg 156
DAFSA, pg 156
Editions Dalloz Sirey, pg 157
Editions La Decouverte, pg 157
Editions Delmas, pg 157
Editions Denoel, pg 157
Les Devenirs Visuels, pg 158
La Documentation Francaise, pg 158
Dunod Editeur, pg 159
Editions de l'Ecole des Hautes Etudes en Sciences Sociales (EHESS), pg 159
Les Editions ESF, pg 160
Editions rue d'Ulm, pg 160
Editions Entente, pg 161
Editions de l'Epargne, pg 161
Editions Eska, pg 162
FBT de R Editions, pg 163
Editions Foucher, pg 164
Futuribles SARL, pg 164
Editions Jacques Gabay, pg 164
Gammaprim, pg 165
Groupe Express-Expansion, pg 166
Hachette Livre, pg 167
Hachette Livre International, pg 167
Editions Hatier SA, pg 167
Editions d'Histoire Sociale (EDHIS), pg 168
INRA Editions (Institut National de la Recherche Agronomique), pg 168
Karthala Editions-Diffusion, pg 170
Editions Legislatives, pg 171
Les Editions LGDJ-Montchrestien, pg 172
Editions John Libbey Eurotext, pg 172
Editions des Limbes d'Or FBT de R Editions, pg 172
Editions de la Maison des Sciences de l'Homme, Paris, pg 173
Maxima Laurent du Mesnil Editeur, pg 174
Nouvelles Editions Fiduciaires, pg 177
Editions Odile Jacob, pg 177
Organisation for Economic Co-operation & Development OECD, pg 178
Ouest Editions, pg 178
Editions Pedone, pg 179
Presses de Sciences Politiques, pg 181
Les Presses du Management, pg 181
Presses Universitaires de Grenoble, pg 181
Presses Universitaires de Lyon, pg 181
Presses Universitaires de Nancy, pg 181
Selection du Reader's Digest SA, pg 184
Publications de la Sorbonne, pg 185
Editions Springer France, pg 186
Editions Village Mondial, pg 189
Librairie Vuibert, pg 189

Germany
A Francke Verlag (Tubingen und Basel), pg 190
Accedo Verlagsgesellschaft mbH, pg 190
Bank-Verlag GmbH, pg 197
Verlag Dr Albert Bartens KG, pg 197
Bayerische Verlagsanstalt GmbH, pg 198
Verlag C H Beck oHG, pg 198
Berliner Wissenschafts-Verlag GmbH (BWV), pg 199
Bertelsmann Lexikon Verlag GmbH, pg 200
Oscar Brandstetter Verlag GmbH & Co KG, pg 204
Buchverlage Langen-Mueller/Herbig, pg 205
Bund-Verlag GmbH, pg 206
Campus Verlag GmbH, pg 207
Chmielorz GmbH Verlag, pg 208
Cornelsen Verlag GmbH & Co OHG, pg 210
Verlag Harri Deutsch, pg 211
Deutscher Betriebswirte-Verlag GmbH, pg 212
Deutscher Instituts-Verlag GmbH, pg 213
Deutscher Universitats-Verlag, pg 213
Die Verlag H Schafer GmbH, pg 214
Dreisam Ratgeber in der Rutsker Verlag GmbH, pg 216
Droste Verlag GmbH, pg 216
DSI Data Service & Information, pg 217
Duncker und Humblot GmbH, pg 217
Econ Taschenbuchverlag, pg 218
Econ Verlag GmbH, pg 218
Eppinger-Verlag OHG, pg 220
Verlag Europa-Lehrmittel GmbH & Co KG, pg 221
Festland Verlag GmbH, pg 224
Verlag Franz Vahlen GmbH, pg 226
Friedrich Kiehl Verlag GmbH, pg 227
Verlag A Fromm im Druck- u Verlagshaus Fromm GmbH & Co KG, pg 227
Betriebswirtschaftlicher Verlag Dr Th Gabler, pg 228
Griese Ingolf Wipe Griese, pg 231
Gunter Olzog Verlag GmbH, pg 231
Carl Hanser Verlag, pg 234
Rudolf Haufe Verlag GmbH & Co KG, pg 235
Heckners Verlag, pg 235
Joh Heider Verlag GmbH, pg 235
HelfRecht Verlag und Druck, pg 236
Carl Heymanns Verlag KG, pg 237
Hofbauer, Christoph und Trojanow Ilia, Akademischer Verlag Muenchen, pg 238
Keip GmbH, pg 245
Klages-Verlag, pg 246
Verlag Fritz Knapp GmbH, pg 247
Verlag Knut Reim, Jugendpresseverlag, pg 247
Koelner Universitaets-Verlag GmbH, pg 248

PUBLISHERS SUBJECT INDEX

Verlag Koenigshausen und Neumann GmbH, pg 248
W Kohlhammer GmbH, pg 248
Leitfadenverlag Verlag Dieter Sudholt, pg 253
Libertas- Europaeisches Institut GmbH, pg 254
LIT Verlag, pg 255
Lucius & Lucius Verlagsgesellschaft mbH, pg 255
Marketing & Wirtschaft Verlagsges, Flade & Partner mbH, pg 257
Metropolis- Verlag fur Okonomie, Gesellschaft und Politik GmbH, pg 259
Metropolitan Verlag, pg 259
Mohr Siebeck, pg 261
Mosaik Verlag GmbH, pg 262
Munzinger-Archiv GmbH Archiv fuer publizistische Arbeit, pg 262
Neuer ISP Verlag GmbH, pg 264
Nomos Verlagsgesellschaft mbH und Co KG, pg 265
Nusser Verlag, pg 266
Georg Olms Verlag AG, pg 267
Philosophia Verlag GmbH, pg 270
Physica-Verlag, pg 270
Rationalisierungs-Kuratorium der Deutschen Wirtschaft eV (RKW), pg 273
Verlag Recht und Wirtschaft GmbH, pg 274
I H Sauer Verlag GmbH, pg 278
Schaeffer-Poeschel Verlag fuer Wirtschaft Steuern Recht, pg 279
Schueren Verlag GmbH, pg 281
Schulz-Kirchner Verlag GmbH, pg 282
Scientia Verlag und Antiquariat Schilling OHG, pg 282
Societaets-Verlag, pg 283
Springer Science+Business Media GmbH & Co KG, pg 284
Springer Science+Business Media GmbH & Co KG, Berlin, pg 285
Verlag H Stam GmbH, pg 286
Stollfuss Verlag Bonn GmbH & Co KG, pg 288
S Toeche-Mittler Verlag GmbH, pg 291
UNO-Verlag GmbH, pg 293
UTB fuer Wissenschaft Uni Taschenbuecher GmbH, pg 294
Verlag Moderne Industrie AG & Co KG, pg 295
Verlagsgruppe Jehle-Rehm GmbH, pg 295
Dokument und Analyse Verlag Bogislaw von Randow, pg 296
Werner Verlag GmbH & Co KG, pg 299
Wison Verlag GmbH, pg 300
Wissenschaftliche Buchgesellschaft, pg 300
WRS Verlag Wirtschaft, Recht und Steuern GmbH & Co KG, pg 301
Fachbuchverlag Armin W Wuth, pg 301

Ghana

Black Mask Ltd, pg 303
Frank Publishing Ltd, pg 304
Kwamfori Publishing Enterprise, pg 304

Greece

Ekdotikos Oikos Adelfon Kyriakidi A E, pg 307
Exandas Publishers, pg 307
Forma Edkotiki E P E, pg 307
Gutenberg Publications, pg 307
Idryma Meleton Chersonisou tou Aimou, pg 308

Irini Publishing House - Vassilis G Katsikeas SA, pg 308
Kastaniotis Editions SA, pg 309
Kritiki Publishing, pg 309
Nomiki Bibliothiki, pg 310
Papazissis Publishers SA, pg 311
Sakkoulas Publications SA, pg 312

Hong Kong

Ming Pao Publications Ltd, pg 318
Sun Mui Press, pg 319
Yazhou Zhoukan Ltd, pg 320

Hungary

Akademiai Kiado, pg 320
Central European University Press, pg 321
KJK-Kerszov, pg 322
Novorg International Szervezo es Kiado kft, pg 323
Osiris Kiado, pg 323
Panem, pg 324
Saldo Penzugyi Tanacsado es Informatikai Rt, pg 324
Statiqum Kiado es Nyomda Kft, pg 324

India

Addison-Wesley Pte Ltd, pg 327
Affiliated East West Press Pvt Ltd, pg 327
Agricole Publishing Academy, pg 327
Allied Publishers Pvt Ltd, pg 328
Amar Prakashan, pg 328
Ananda Publishers Pvt Ltd, pg 328
APH Publishing Corp, pg 328
Associated Publishing House, pg 329
Authorspress, pg 329
Avinash Reference Publications, pg 329
K P Bagchi & Co, pg 329
Bani Mandir, Book-Sellers, Publishers & Educational Suppliers, pg 329
Bhawan Book Service, Publishers & Distributors, pg 330
Big Database Publishing Pvt Ltd, pg 330
BR Publishing Corporation, pg 331
S Chand & Co Ltd, pg 331
Chowkhamba Sanskrit Series Office, pg 332
Concept Publishing Co, pg 332
Cosmo Publications, pg 332
Dastane Ramchandra & Co, pg 333
Disha Prakashan, pg 333
Ess Ess Publications, pg 334
Frank Brothers & Co Publishers Ltd, pg 334
Full Circle Publishing, pg 334
Gitanjali Publishing House, pg 335
Goel Prakashen, pg 335
Gyan Publishing House, pg 335
Heritage Publishers, pg 335
Indian Council of Social Science Research (ICSSR), pg 336
Inter-India Publications, pg 338
Jaico Publishing House, pg 338
Law Publishers, pg 340
Manohar Publishers & Distributors, pg 340
Minerva Associates (Publications) Pvt Ltd, pg 341
National Book Organization, pg 342
National Council of Applied Economic Research, Publications Division, pg 342
Omsons Publications, pg 344
Oxford University Press, pg 344

Pitambar Publishing Co (P) Ltd, pg 345
Pointer Publishers, pg 345
Popular Prakashan Pvt Ltd, pg 345
Promilla & Publishers, pg 345
Radiant Publishers, pg 346
Rajasthan Hindi Granth Academy, pg 346
Rajesh Publications, pg 346
Reliance Publishing House, pg 346
SAGE Publications India Pvt Ltd, pg 347
Sasta Sahitya Mandal, pg 348
Scientific Book Agency, pg 348
Sita Books & Periodicals Pvt Ltd, pg 349
Somaiya Publications Pvt Ltd, pg 349
South Asia Publications, pg 349
Sterling Publishers Pvt Ltd, pg 350
Sultan Chand & Sons Pvt Ltd, pg 350
Vidyarthi Mithram Press, pg 352
Vikas Publishing House Pvt Ltd, pg 352
Viva Books Pvt Ltd, pg 352
Vivek Prakashan, pg 353

Indonesia

Alumni PT, pg 353
Bhratara Karya Aksara, pg 354
Bina Rena Pariwara, pg 354
PT Bulan Bintang, pg 354
Bumi Aksara PT, pg 354
PT Dian Rakyat, pg 354
Eresco PT, pg 354
Lembaga Demografi Fakultas Ekonomi Universitas Indonesia, pg 355
Mutiara Sumber Widya PT, pg 356
Pustaka Utama Grafiti, PT, pg 356
Yayasan Obor Indonesia, pg 357

Iraq

National House for Publishing, Distributing & Advertising, pg 357

Ireland

The Economic & Social Research Institute, pg 359
Gill & Macmillan Ltd, pg 360
Institute of Public Administration, pg 361
Irish Management Institute, pg 361
New Books/Connolly Books, pg 362

Israel

Bar Ilan University Press, pg 365
Dyonon/Papyrus Publishing House of the Tel-Aviv, pg 366
Hakibbutz Hameuchad Publishing House Ltd, pg 367
Hanitzotz A-Sharara Publishing House, pg 367
The Institute for Israeli Arabs Studies, pg 368
Open University of Israel, pg 371
Schocken Publishing House Ltd, pg 371
Shalem Press, pg 372
Tcherikover Publishers Ltd, pg 372
Zmora-Bitan, Publishers Ltd, pg 374

Italy

Edizioni Abete, pg 374
Edizioni della Fondazione Giovanni Agnelli, pg 374
Franco Angeli SRL, pg 375
Apimondia, pg 375

Argalia Editore delle Arti Grafiche Editoriali SRL, pg 376
Baha'i, pg 377
Bancaria Editrice SpA, pg 377
Bollati Boringhieri Editore, pg 378
Giuseppe Bonanno Editore, pg 378
Buffetti, pg 379
Cacucci Editore, pg 379
Camera dei Deputati Ufficio Pubblicazioni Informazione Parlamentare, pg 379
CEDAM (Casa Editrice Dr A Milani), pg 380
Celuc Libri, pg 381
Centro Studi Terzo Mondo, pg 381
il Cerchio Iniziative Editoriali, pg 381
Cisalpino, pg 382
CLUEB (Cooperativa Libraria Universitaria Editrice Bologna), pg 382
Edizioni di Comunita SpA, pg 383
Costa e Nolan SpA, pg 383
La Cultura Sociologica, pg 384
Datanews, pg 384
Ediciclo Editore SRL, pg 386
EGEA (Edizioni Giuridiche Economiche Aziendali), pg 387
Edi.Ermes srl, pg 388
Esselibri, pg 388
Etas Libri, pg 388
Edizioni Europa, pg 388
Arnaldo Forni Editore SRL, pg 389
G Giappichelli Editore SRL, pg 390
A Giuffre Editore SpA, pg 390
Gius Laterza e Figli SpA, pg 391
Herbita Editrice di Leonardo Palermo, pg 392
Ila - Palma, Tea Nova, pg 393
Editoriale Jaca Book SpA, pg 394
L Japadre Editore, pg 394
Casa Editrice Dott Eugenio Jovene SpA, pg 394
Edizioni Lavoro SRL, pg 394
LED - Edizioni Universitarie di Lettere Economia Diritto, pg 395
Liguori Editore SRL, pg 395
Monduzzi Editore SpA, pg 399
Societa Editrice Il Mulino, pg 399
Nardini Editore srl, pg 400
Accademia Naz dei Lincei, pg 400
Psicologica Editrice, pg 404
RCS Rizzoli Libri SpA, pg 405
Rirea Casa Editrice della Rivista Italiana di Ragioneria e di Economia Aziendale, pg 405
Editori Riuniti, pg 405
Rubbettino Editore, pg 406
SAGEP Libri & Comunicazione Srl, pg 406
SAIE Editrice SRL, pg 406
Edizioni Scientifiche Italiane, pg 407
SIPI (Servizio Italiano Pubblicazioni Internazionali) Srl, pg 408
Il Sole 24 Ore Libri, pg 408
Il Sole 24 Ore Pirola, pg 409
Sperling e Kupfer Editori SpA, pg 409
Edizioni Studio Tesi SRL, pg 409
Zanichelli Editore SpA, pg 412

Jamaica

The Jamaica Bauxite Institute, pg 413

Japan

Aoki Shoten Co Ltd, pg 415
Chikuma Shobo Publishing Co Ltd, pg 416
Chuokoron-Shinsha Inc, pg 416
Daiichi Shuppan Co Ltd, pg 416

Diamond Inc, pg 416
Hikarinokuni Ltd, pg 418
Horitsu Bunka-Sha, pg 418
Ie-No-Hikari Association, pg 419
International Society for Educational Information (ISEI), pg 419
Iwanami Shoten, Publishers, pg 419
Keisuisha Publishing Company Ltd, pg 420
Kodansha Ltd, pg 421
Koyo Shobo, pg 422
Minerva Shobo Co Ltd, pg 422
Nihon Keizai Shimbun Inc Publications Bureau, pg 423
Nippon Hoso Shuppan Kyokai (NHK Publishing), pg 424
Nippon Jitsugyo Publishing Co Ltd, pg 424
Otsuki Shoten Publishers, pg 425
Pearson Education Japan, pg 425
President Inc, pg 425
Ryosho-Fukyu-Kai Co Ltd, pg 425
Sagano Shoin, pg 426
Sankyo Publishing Company Ltd, pg 426
Seibundo, pg 426
Seizando-Shoten Publishing Co Ltd, pg 427
Shogakukan Inc, pg 427
Shufu-to-Seikatsu Sha Ltd, pg 428
Shunjusha, pg 428
The Simul Press Inc, pg 428
Sobun-Sha, pg 428
Springer-Verlag Tokyo, pg 428
Surugadai-Shuppan Sha, pg 429
Taimeido Publishing Co Ltd, pg 429
Toho Book Store, pg 429
Tokuma Shoten Publishing Co Ltd, pg 429
Toyo Keizai Shinpo-Sha, pg 430
United Nations University Press, pg 430
Waseda University Press, pg 431
Yuhikaku Publishing Co Ltd, pg 431
Yushodo Shuppan, pg 431
Zeimukeiri-Kyokai, pg 431
Zenkoku Kyodo Shuppan, pg 431

Jordan

Jordan Book Centre Co Ltd, pg 432

Kazakstan

Gylym, Izd-Vo, pg 432
Al-Farabi Kazakh National University, pg 432
Kazakhstan, Izd-Vo, pg 432

Kenya

Heinemann Kenya Ltd (EAEP), pg 434
Kenya Quality & Productivity Institute, pg 435
Shirikon Publishers, pg 436

Democratic People's Republic of Korea

Academy of Sciences Publishing House, pg 436
Korea Science and Encyclopedia Publishing House, pg 436

Republic of Korea

Bi-bong Publishing Co, pg 437
Chung Rim Publishing Co Ltd, pg 438
Hanul Publishing Co, pg 439
Hollym Corporation; Publishers, pg 439
Hyangmunsa Publishing Co, pg 439
Koreaone Press Inc, pg 440

Maeil Gyeongje, pg 441
Oruem Publishing House, pg 442
Twenty-First Century Publishers, Inc, pg 443
YBM/Si-sa, pg 443

Laos People's Democratic Republic

Lao-phanit, pg 444

Lebanon

Arab Institute for Research & Publishing, pg 445

Liechtenstein

Verlag der Liechtensteinischen Akademischen Gesellschaft, pg 448
Megatrade AG, pg 448
Topos Verlag AG, pg 448

Lithuania

Eugrimas, pg 449
Klaipedos Universiteto Leidykla, pg 449
Margi Rastai Publishers, pg 449

Luxembourg

Editions Promoculture, pg 451
Service Central de la Statistique et des Etudes Economiques (STATEC), pg 451
Varkki Verghese, pg 452

The Former Yugoslav Republic of Macedonia

Strk Publishing House, pg 453

Madagascar

Societe Malgache d'Edition, pg 454

Malaysia

Forum Publications, pg 456
MDC Publishers Printers Sdn Bhd, pg 457
Pelanduk Publications (M) Sdn Bhd, pg 457
Penerbit Jayatinta Sdn Bhd, pg 458
Pustaka Delta Pelajaran Sdn Bhd, pg 458
University of Malaya, Department of Publications, pg 459
Utusan Publications & Distributors Sdn Bhd, pg 459

Mauritius

Editions de l'Ocean Indien Ltd, pg 461

Mexico

Editores Asociados Mexicanos SA de CV (EDAMEX), pg 462
Libreria y Ediciones Botas SA, pg 462
Ediciones el Caballito SA, pg 462
Centro de Estudios Mexicanos y Centroamericanos, pg 463
El Colegio de Mexico AC, pg 463
Colegio de Postgraduados en Ciencias Agricolas, pg 463
Publicaciones Cruz O SA, pg 463
Editorial Diana SA de CV, pg 464
Ediciones Era SA de CV, pg 465
Centro de Estudios Monetarios Latinoamericanos (CEMLA), pg 465
Editorial Extemporaneos SA, pg 465

Fondo de Cultura Economica, pg 465
Grupo Editorial Iberoamerica, SA de CV, pg 466
Editorial Jus SA de CV, pg 467
Editorial Limusa SA de CV, pg 467
Mercametrica Ediciones SA Edicion de Libros, pg 468
Instituto Nacional de Estadistica, Geographia e Informatica, pg 469
Editorial Nueva Imagen SA, pg 469
Pearson Educacion de Mexico, SA de CV, pg 470
Siglo XXI Editores SA de CV, pg 472
Editorial Turner de Mexico, pg 472
Universidad Nacional Autonoma de Mexico (National University of Mexico), pg 472

Republic of Moldova

Editura Cartea Moldovei, pg 473

Monaco

Editions EGC, pg 473

Morocco

Access International Services, pg 474
Cabinet Conseil CCMLA, pg 474
Dar Nachr Al Maarifa Pour L'Edition et La Distribution, pg 474
Editions Le Fennec, pg 474
Les Editions du Journal L' Unite Maghrebine, pg 475
Editions Okad, pg 475
Editions La Porte, pg 475

Mozambique

Centro De Estudos Africanos, pg 475

Namibia

Multi-Disciplinary Research Centre Library, pg 476

Nepal

International Standards Books & Periodicals (P) Ltd, pg 476

Netherlands

Uitgeverij Jan van Arkel, pg 478
Business Contact BV, pg 480
Uitgeverij Coutinho BV, pg 481
Educatieve Uitgeverij Edu'Actief BV, pg 481
Elsevier Science BV, pg 482
KITLV Press Royal Institute of Linguistics & Anthropology, pg 484
Kluwer Bedrijfswetenschappen, pg 485
Uitgeverij Lemma BV, pg 485
Uitgeverij H Nelissen BV, pg 486
Pearson Education Netherlands, pg 487
Tilburg University Press, pg 490
Van Gorcum & Comp BV, pg 491
VU Boekhandel/Uitgeverij BV, pg 492

New Zealand

Dunmore Press Ltd, pg 495
ESA Publications (NZ) Ltd, pg 496
Fraser Books, pg 496
Nelson Price Milburn Ltd, pg 499
New House Publishers Ltd, pg 499
Oxford University Press, pg 499
Statistics New Zealand, pg 501

Nigeria

Evans Brothers (Nigeria Publishers) Ltd, pg 504
JAD Publishers Ltd, pg 505
Nigerian Institute of International Affairs, pg 506
West African Book Publishers Ltd, pg 507

Norway

Aschehoug Forlag, pg 508
H Aschehoug & Co (W Nygaard) A/S, pg 508
Cappelen akademisk forlag, pg 508
Glydendal Akademisk, pg 509

Pakistan

Academy of Education Planning & Management (AEPAM), pg 511
Centre for South Asian Studies, pg 512
Pakistan Institute of Development Economics (PIDE), pg 514
Publishers United Pvt Ltd, pg 514
Royal Book Co, pg 514
Vanguard Books Ltd, pg 515

Papua New Guinea

IMPS Research Ltd, pg 515
National Research Institute of Papua New Guinea, pg 515

Peru

Instituto de Estudios Peruanos, pg 517
Fondo Editorial de la Pontificia Universidad Catolica del Peru, pg 517
Editorial Horizonte, pg 517
Sur Casa de Estudios del Socialismo, pg 517
Universidad de Lima-Fondo de Desarollo Editorial, pg 517

Philippines

Ateneo de Manila University Press, pg 518
Mutual Book Inc, pg 519
New Day Publishers, pg 520
Rex Bookstores & Publishers, pg 520
Saint Mary's Publishing Corp, pg 520
SIBS Publishing House Inc, pg 521
Sinag-Tala Publishers Inc, pg 521
UST Publishing House, pg 521

Poland

Polskie Wydawnictwo Ekonomiczne PWE SA, pg 522
Polish Scientific Publishers PWN, pg 525
Oficyna Wydawnicza Read Me, pg 526
Oficyna Wydawnicza Szkoly Glownej Handlowej w Warszawie Oficyna Wydawnicza SGH, pg 527
Wydawnictwa Uniwersytetu Warszawskiego, pg 527
Zaklad Wydawnictw Statystycznych, pg 528

Portugal

Livraria Civilizacao (Americo Fraga Lamares & Ca Lda), pg 529
Constancia Editores, SA, pg 530
Edicoes Cosmos, pg 530
Difusao Cultural, pg 530
Editorial Estampa, Lda, pg 531

Gradiva-Publicacnoes Lda, pg 532
Impala, pg 532
Imprensa Nacional-Casa da Moeda, pg 532
Editorial Inquerito Lda, pg 532
Livraria Luzo-Espanhola Lda, pg 533
Editora McGraw-Hill de Portugal Lda, pg 533
Nova Arrancada Sociedade Editora SA, pg 534
Quid Juris - Sociedade Editora, pg 535
Edicoes Silabo, pg 536
Almerinda Teixeira, pg 536
Teorema, pg 536
Vega-Publicacao e Distribuicao de Livros e Revistas, Lda, pg 536

Romania
Editura Aius, pg 538
Enzyklopadie Verlag, pg 539
Editura Excelsior Art, pg 539
Casa de editura Globus, pg 540
Nemira Verlag, pg 541
Editura Niculescu, pg 541
Rentrop & Straton Verlagsgruppe und Wirtschaftsconsulting, pg 542
Editura Teora, pg 542

Russian Federation
Aspect Press Ltd, pg 543
N E Bauman Moscow State Technical University Publishers, pg 544
Izdatelstvo 'Ekonomika', pg 544
FGUP Izdatelstvo Mashinostroenie, pg 544
Finansy i Statistika Publishing House, pg 544
INFRA-M Izdatel'skij dom, pg 545
Izvestia Sovetov Narodnyh Deputatov Russian Federation (RF), pg 545
Izdatelstvo Kazanskago Universiteta, pg 545
Izdatelstvo Mordovskogo gosudar stvennogo, pg 547
Izdatelstvo Mysl, pg 547
Nauka Publishers, pg 547
Izdatel'stvo Nizhegorodskogo Gosudarstvennogo Univ, pg 547
Novosti Izdatelstvo, pg 547
Progress Publishers, pg 548
Teorija Verojatnostej i ee Primenenija, pg 549
Voronezh State University Publishers, pg 549
Izdatelstvo Vysshaya Shkola, pg 549

Senegal
CODESRIA (Council for the Development of Social Science Research in Africa), pg 551
Societe Africaine d'Edition, pg 551

Serbia and Montenegro
Izdavacka Organizacija Rad, pg 553
Privredni Pregled, pg 553
Radnicka Stampa, pg 553
Savez Inzenjera i Tehnicara Jugoslavije, pg 553
Savremena Administracija, pg 553

Singapore
APAC Publishers Services Pte Ltd, pg 554
Hillview Publications Pte Ltd, pg 556

Institute of Southeast Asian Studies, pg 556
McGallen & Bolden Associates, pg 557
Singapore University Press Pte Ltd, pg 558
Taylor & Francis Asia Pacific, pg 558
World Scientific Publishing Co Pte Ltd, pg 559

Slovakia
Danubiaprint, pg 559
Sofa, pg 560
Technicka Univerzita, pg 561

Slovenia
East West Operation (EWO) Ltd, pg 561
Univerza v Ljubljani Ekonomska Fakulteta, pg 562
Zalozba Obzorja d d Maribor, pg 562

South Africa
Educum Publishers Ltd, pg 563
Heinemann Educational Publishers Southern Africa, pg 564
Human & Rousseau (Pty) Ltd, pg 564
LexisNexis Butterworths South Africa, pg 566
New Africa Books (Pty) Ltd, pg 567
Ravan Press (Pty) Ltd, pg 568
South African Institute of International Affairs, pg 569
Unisa Press, pg 569
Van Schaik Publishers, pg 569
Witwatersrand University Press, pg 570

Spain
Editorial AEDOS SA, pg 571
Agencia Espanola de Cooperacion, pg 571
Ediciones Akal SA, pg 571
Alta Fulla Editorial, pg 572
Editorial Ariel SA, pg 573
Editorial Biblioteca Nueva SL, pg 574
Antoni Bosch Editor SA, pg 574
Edicios do Castro, pg 576
Celeste Ediciones, pg 576
Civitas SA Editorial, pg 577
Ediciones de la Universidad Complutense de Madrid, pg 577
Comunidad Autonoma de Madrid, Servicio de Documentacion y Publicaciones, pg 578
Editorial Constitucion y Leyes SA - COLEX, pg 578
Ediciones Diaz de Santos SA, pg 579
Dykinson SL, pg 580
Ediciones Encuentro SA, pg 582
Esic Editorial, pg 582
Instituto de Estudios Fiscales, pg 583
Publicaciones Etea, pg 583
EUNSA (Ediciones Universidad de Navarra SA), pg 583
Fondo de Cultura Economica de Espana, SL, pg 583
Fundacion de Estudios Libertarios Anselmo Lorenzo, pg 584
Ediciones Gestio 2000 SA, pg 585
Editorial Gredos SA, pg 585
Editorial Herder SA, pg 586
Icaria Editorial SA, pg 587

Instituto de Estudios Economicos, pg 587
Ediciones Internacionales Universitarias SA, pg 588
Editorin Laiovento SL, pg 588
LID Editorial Empresarial, SL, pg 589
Marcial Pons Ediciones Juridicas SA, pg 590
Marcombo SA, pg 590
Mundi-Prensa Libros SA, pg 592
Oikos-Tau SA Ediciones, pg 593
Ediciones Piramide SA, pg 596
Publicaciones de la Universidad de Alicante, pg 597
Publicaciones de la Universidad Pontificia Comillas-Madrid, pg 597
Editora Regional de Murcia - ERM, pg 597
Ediciones Rialp SA, pg 598
Servicio de Publicaciones Universidad de Cordoba, pg 599
Editorial Sintesis, SA, pg 600
Editorial Tecnos SA, pg 601
Editorial Trivium, SA, pg 602
Universidad de Malaga, pg 603
Universidad de Valladolid Secretariado de Publicaciones e Intercambio Editorial, pg 604
Publicacions de la Universitat de Barcelona, pg 604
Universitat de Valencia Servei de Publicacions, pg 604
Xunta de Galicia, pg 605

Sri Lanka
Karunaratne & Sons Ltd, pg 606
Sunera Publishers, pg 607

Sweden
Iustus Forlag AB, pg 613
SNS Foerlag, pg 615
Stromberg, pg 616
Timbro, pg 616

Switzerland
Archivio Storico Ticinese, pg 617
Association Suisse des Editeurs de Langue Francaise, pg 618
Bibliographisches Institut & F A Brockhaus AG, pg 619
Verlag Harri Deutsch, pg 622
Gottlieb Duttweiler Institute for Trends & Futures, pg 622
Elvetica Edizioni SA, pg 623
Georg Editeur SA, pg 624
Graduate Institute of International Studies, pg 624
Paul Haupt Bern, pg 625
Helbing und Lichtenhahn Verlag AG, pg 625
Interfrom AG Editions, pg 625
Kranich-Verlag, Dres AG & H R Bosch-Gwalter, pg 627
Orell Fuessli Buchhandlungs AG, pg 630
Ott Verlag Thun, pg 630
Ruegger Verlag, pg 633
SAB Schweiz Arbeitsgemeinschaft fuer die Berggebiete, pg 633
Editions du Tricorne, pg 635
Der Universitatsverlag Freiburg, pg 636
Vdf Hochschulverlag AG an der ETH Zurich, pg 636
Versus Verlag AG, pg 636

Syrian Arab Republic
Damascus University Press, pg 638

Taiwan, Province of China
Commonwealth Publishing Company Ltd, pg 639
Fuh-Wen Book Co, pg 639
Linking Publishing Company Ltd, pg 641
San Min Book Co Ltd, pg 641

Tajikistan
Irfon, pg 642

United Republic of Tanzania
Bureau of Statistics, pg 643
Readit Books, pg 644

Trinidad & Tobago
Inprint Caribbean Ltd, pg 647

Tunisia
Dar Arabia Lil Kitab, pg 648

Turkey
Alkim Kitapcilik-Yayimcilik, pg 649
Altin Kitaplar Yayinevi, pg 649
Inkilap Publishers Ltd, pg 650
Seckin Yayinevi, pg 651

Uganda
Fountain Publishers Ltd, pg 652

Ukraine
ASK Ltd, pg 653
Naukova Dumka Publishers, pg 653
Osnovy Publishers, pg 654

United Kingdom
Advisory Unit: Computers in Education, pg 655
Aldwych Press Ltd, pg 656
Anglo-German Foundation for the Study of Industrial Society, pg 658
Ashgate Publishing Ltd, pg 660
The Athlone Press Ltd, pg 661
Berghahn Books Ltd, pg 665
Blackwell Publishing Ltd, pg 666
Bloomsbury Publishing PLC, pg 668
Bookmarks Publications, pg 668
BPP Publishing Ltd, pg 670
Dr Barry Bracewell-Milnes, pg 670
Nicholas Brealey Publishing, pg 670
Business Monitor International, pg 672
Cambridge University Press, pg 674
Capstone Publishing Ltd, pg 674
Jon Carpenter Publishing, pg 675
Frank Cass Publishers, pg 675
Catholic Institute for International Relations, pg 676
Causeway Press Ltd, pg 676
Chadwyck-Healey Ltd, pg 677
Commonwealth Secretariat, pg 681
Conservative Policy Forum, pg 682
James Currey Ltd, pg 687
Dunedin Academic Press, pg 688
The Economist Intelligence Unit, pg 689
Edinburgh University Press Ltd, pg 689
Edition XII, pg 690
Edward Elgar Publishing Ltd, pg 690
Elsevier Ltd, pg 691
Euromonitor PLC, pg 692
Europa Publications, pg 692
European Schoolbooks Ltd, pg 692
The Eurospan Group, pg 692

Fabian Society, pg 694
Forbes Publications Ltd, pg 696
Freedom Press, pg 697
W H Freeman & Co Ltd, pg 697
Green Books Ltd, pg 702
Harvard University Press, pg 705
C Hurst & Co (Publishers) Ltd, pg 711
ICC United Kingdom, pg 711
Institute for Fiscal Studies, pg 712
Institute of Development Studies, pg 712
Institute of Economic Affairs, pg 712
Institute of Employment Rights, pg 712
Islamic Foundation Publications, pg 714
JAI Press Ltd, pg 715
Lawrence & Wishart, pg 719
Letts Educational, pg 720
Macmillan Reference Ltd, pg 724
Manchester University Press, pg 724
Adam Matthew Publications, pg 726
The Merlin Press Ltd, pg 727
MIT Press Ltd, pg 728
National Assembly for Wales, pg 730
W W Norton & Company Ltd, pg 734
NTC Research, pg 734
Open Gate Press, pg 735
Open University Worldwide, pg 736
Oxfam, pg 737
Oxford University Press, pg 737
Palgrave Publishers Ltd, pg 737
Pathfinder London, pg 739
Pearson Education, pg 739
Pearson Education Europe, Mideast & Africa, pg 739
Pickering & Chatto Publishers Ltd, pg 742
Pluto Books Ltd, pg 743
Pluto Press, pg 743
The Policy Press, pg 744
Policy Studies Institute (PSI), pg 744
Profile Books Ltd, pg 746
ProQuest Information & Learning, pg 746
Rooster Books Ltd, pg 751
Routledge, pg 751
RoutledgeCurzon, pg 751
Royal Institute of International Affairs, pg 752
SAGE Publications Ltd, pg 753
Scottish Executive Library & Information Services, pg 755
Shepheard-Walwyn (Publishers) Ltd, pg 757
Sidgwick & Jackson Ltd, pg 757
Skoob Russell Square, pg 758
Spokesman, pg 760
Taylor & Francis, pg 763
TSO (The Stationery Office), pg 767
University of Wales Press, pg 769
Verso, pg 770
VNU Business Publications, pg 770
Westview Press, pg 772
WI Enterprises Ltd, pg 773
Wiley Europe Ltd, pg 773
Wimbledon Publishing Company Ltd, pg 774
Witherby & Co Ltd, pg 775
World Microfilms Publications Ltd, pg 775
World of Information, pg 776

Uruguay
Editorial Arca SRL, pg 776
Arpoador, pg 777
Ediciones de Juan Darien, pg 777
Fundacion de Cultura Universitaria, pg 777
Nordan-Comunidad, pg 778
Ediciones Trilce, pg 778
Vinten Editor, pg 778

Uzbekistan
Izdatelstvo Uzbekistan, pg 778

Venezuela
Alfadil Ediciones, pg 778
Monte Avila Editores Latinoamericana CA, pg 779
Fundacion Centro Gumilla, pg 779
Editorial Nueva Sociedad, pg 780
Vadell Hermanos Editores CA, pg 780

Viet Nam
Science & Technics Publishing House, pg 780

Zambia
MFK Management Consultants Services, pg 781

Zimbabwe
College Press Publishers (Pvt) Ltd, pg 783
Journal on Social Change, pg 783
Longman Zimbabwe (Pvt) Ltd, pg 783
Manhattan Publications, pg 784
Nehanda Publishers, pg 784
Sapes Trust Ltd, pg 784
Thomson Publications Zimbabwe (Pvt) Ltd, pg 784

EDUCATION

Albania
NL SH, pg 1
State Textbook Publishing House, pg 1

Argentina
Amorrortu Editores SA, pg 3
Bonum Editorial SACI, pg 4
Centro Editor de America Latina SA, pg 4
Editorial Ciudad Nueva de la Sefoma, pg 4
Libreria del Colegio SA, pg 4
Diana Argentina SA, Editorial, pg 5
Editorial Ruy Diaz SAEIC, pg 5
Ediciones Don Bosco Argentina, pg 5
Errepar SA, pg 5
Angel Estrada y Cia SA, pg 5
EUDEBA (Editorial Universitaria de Buenos Aires), pg 5
Gram Editora, pg 6
Editorial Guadalupe, pg 6
Editorial Idearium de la Universidad de Mendoza (EDIUM), pg 6
Kapelusz Editora SA, pg 7
Laffont Ediciones Electronicas SA, pg 7
Librograf Editora, pg 7
Editorial Losada SA, pg 7
Marymar Ediciones SA, pg 7
Editorial Norte SA, pg 8
Editorial Paidos SAICF, pg 8
Editorial Plus Ultra SA, pg 8
Ediciones Preescolar SA, pg 8
Ricordi Americana SAEC, pg 8
San Pablo, pg 9

Armenia
Arevik, pg 10

Australia
Aboriginal Studies Press, pg 10
ACER Press, pg 10
ACHPER Inc (Australian Council for Health, Physical Education & Recreation), pg 10
The Advancement Centre, pg 11
Allen & Unwin Pty Ltd, pg 11
Robert Andersen & Associates Pty Ltd, pg 11
Ansay Pty Ltd, pg 11
Auslib Press Pty Ltd, pg 12
Austed Publishing Co, pg 12
Beri Publishing, pg 14
Board of Studies, pg 15
Cambridge University Press, pg 16
Candlelight Trust T/A Candlelight Farm, pg 17
Centre Publications, pg 17
CIS Publishers, pg 18
Coolabah Publishing, pg 18
Curriculum Corporation, pg 19
Eleanor Curtain Publishing, pg 19
Dabill Publications, pg 19
Dellasta Publishing, pg 19
Educational Advantage, pg 20
Elsevier Australia, pg 21
Era Publications, pg 21
Fernfawn Publications, pg 22
Finch Publishing, pg 22
Fremantle Arts Centre Press, pg 23
Ginninderra Press, pg 23
Greater Glider Productions Australia Pty Ltd, pg 24
Kerri Hamer, pg 24
Hargreen Publishing Co, pg 24
Illert Publications, pg 26
Institute of Aboriginal Development (IAD Press), pg 27
James Nicholas Publishers Pty Ltd, pg 27
Jenelle Press, pg 27
Little Red Apple Publishing, pg 29
MacLennan & Petty Pty Ltd, pg 30
Macmillan Education Australia, pg 30
Macmillan Publishers Australia Pty Ltd, pg 30
Horwith Martin Education, pg 31
Matthias Media, pg 31
McGraw-Hill Australia Pty Ltd, pg 31
J M McGregor Pty Ltd, pg 31
Museum of Victoria, pg 33
Newman Centre Publications, pg 33
Openbook Publishers, pg 34
Oxfam Community Aid Abroad, pg 35
Pademelon Press, pg 35
Pascal Press, pg 36
Pearson Education Australia, pg 36
Price Publishing, pg 37
Priestley Consulting, pg 37
Reader's Digest (Australia) Pty Ltd, pg 39
Ready-Ed Publications, pg 39
RIC Publications Pty Ltd, pg 39
Ruskin Rowe Press, pg 40
St Clair Press, pg 40
St Joseph Publications, pg 40
St Pauls Publications, pg 40
Scholastic Australia Pty Ltd, pg 40
Science Press, pg 40
Social Science Press, pg 41
South Australian Government - Department of Education, Employment & Training, pg 41
Spectrum Publications, pg 41
Spinifex Press, pg 42
Summer Institute of Linguistics, Australian Aborigines Branch, pg 42
Tirian Publications, pg 43
Uniting Education, pg 44
Vista Publications, pg 45
Vital Publications, pg 45
Wileman Publications, pg 46
John Wiley & Sons Australia, Ltd, pg 46
Wizard Books Pty Ltd, pg 47
Woodlands Publications, pg 47

Austria
Braintrust Marketing Services Ges mbH Verlag, pg 49
Cura Verlag GmbH, pg 49
DachsVerlag GmbH, pg 49
Development News Ltd, pg 50
Doecker Verlag GmbH & Co KG, pg 50
Helbling Verlags-Gesellschaft mbH, pg 51
NOI - Verlag, pg 55
oebv & hpt Verlagsgesellschaft mbH & Co KG, pg 55
Oesterreichischer Bundesverlag Gmbh, pg 55
Andreas Schnider Verlags-Atelier, pg 57
Springer-Verlag Wien, pg 58
Studien Verlag Gmbh, pg 58
Verlag Styria, pg 58
Verband der Wissenschaftlichen Gesellschaften Oesterreichs (VWGOe), pg 59
Verlag Veritas Mediengesellschaft mbH, pg 59

Azerbaijan
Sada, Literaturno-Izdatel'skij Centr, pg 60

Bangladesh
Ankur Prakashani, pg 61
Gatidhara, pg 61
Mullick Bros, pg 61
The University Press Ltd, pg 61

Belarus
Belaruskaya Encyklapedyya, pg 62
Publishing Center of Belarus State University, pg 62

Belgium
Abimo, pg 62
Uitgeverij Acco, pg 62
Actualquarto, pg 63
NV Uitgeverij Altiora Averbode, pg 63
De Boeck et Larcier SA, pg 64
Carto BVBA, pg 64
Uitgeverij Contact NV, pg 65
Editions De Boeck-Larcier SA, pg 66
Dessain - Departement de De Boeck & Larcier SA, pg 66
Garant Publishers Ltd, pg 67
Infoboek NV, pg 68
Uitgeverij J van In, pg 69
Die Keure, pg 69
Editions Labor, pg 69
Lansman Editeur, pg 69
Leuven University Press, pg 70
Editeurs de Litterature Biblique, pg 70
Editions Lumen Vitae ASBL, pg 70
Mardaga, Pierre, Editeur, pg 71
Reader's Digest SA, pg 72
Uitgeverij De Sikkel NV, pg 73

PUBLISHERS

Sonneville Press (Uitgeverij) VTW, pg 73
Toulon Uitgeverij, pg 73
Uitgeverij Averbode NV, pg 74
Imprimeur - Editeur Vaillant-Carmanne SA, pg 74
Vlaamse Esperantobond VZW, pg 74
Wolters Plantyn Educatieve Uitgevers, pg 74

Bosnia and Herzegovina

Bemust, pg 76

Brazil

A & A & A Edicoes e Promocoes Internacionais Ltda, pg 76
AGIR S/A Editora, pg 77
Editora Antroposofica Ltda, pg 77
Ao Livro Tecnico Industria e Comercio Ltda, pg 77
ARTMED Editora, pg 78
Editora Bertrand Brasil Ltda, pg 78
Editora do Brasil SA, pg 79
Editora Brasiliense SA, pg 79
Centro de Estudos Juridicosdo Para (CEJUP), pg 79
Consultor Assessoria de Planejamento Ltda, pg 80
Editora Contexto (Editora Pinsky Ltda), pg 80
E P U Editora Pedagogica e Universitaria Ltd, pg 81
Edicon Editora e Consultorial Ltda, pg 81
Companhia Editora Forense, pg 81
EDUSC - Editora da Universidade do Sagrado Coracao, pg 81
Editora Elevacao, pg 81
Editora Expressao e Cultura-Exped Ltda, pg 81
Editora FCO Ltda, pg 81
Livraria Martins Fontes Editora Ltda, pg 81
Formato Editorial ltda, pg 82
Fundacao Cultural Avatar, pg 82
Fundacao Joaquim Nabuco-Editora Massangana, pg 82
Fundacao Sao Paulo, EDUC, pg 82
Global Editora e Distribuidora Ltda, pg 82
Editora Globo SA, pg 82
Edicoes Graal Ltda, pg 83
Grafica Editora Primor Ltda, pg 83
IBRASA (Instituicao Brasileira de Difusao Cultural Ltda), pg 83
Iglu Editora Ltda, pg 84
Editora Kuarup Ltda, pg 84
Editora Leitura Ltda, pg 84
Editora Lidador Ltda, pg 85
Waldir Lima Editora, pg 85
LISA (Livros Irradiantes SA), pg 85
Editora Logosofica, pg 85
Edicoes Loyola SA, pg 85
Editora Mercado Aberto Ltda, pg 86
MG Editores Associados Ltda, pg 86
Editora Moderna Ltda, pg 86
Modulo Editora e Desenvolvimento Educacional Ltda, pg 87
Cia Editora Nacional, pg 87
Editora Nova Alexandria Ltda, pg 87
Editora Nova Fronteira SA, pg 87
Olho D'Agua Comercio e Servicos Editoriais Ltda, pg 87
Paulinas Editorial, pg 88
Paulus Editora, pg 88
Editora Perspectiva, pg 88
Livraria Pioneira Editora/Enio Matheus Guazzelli e Cia Ltd, pg 88

Qualitymark Editora Ltda, pg 89
Editora Resenha Tributaria Ltda, pg 89
Saraiva SA, Livreiros Editores, pg 90
Editora Scipione Ltda, pg 90
Editora Sinodal, pg 90
Summus Editorial Ltda, pg 91
Edicoes Tabajara, pg 91
Thex Editora e Distribuidora Ltda, pg 91
Editora UNESP, pg 91
Editora Universidade Federal do Rio de Janeiro, pg 92
Fundacao Getulio Vargas, pg 92
Editora Verbo Ltda, pg 92
Editora Vigilia Ltda, pg 92
Jorge Zahar Editor, pg 92

Bulgaria

Abagar, Veliko Tarnovo, pg 93
Antroposfsko Izdatelstvo Dimo R Daskalov OOD, pg 93
Bulvest 2000 Ltd, pg 93
Ciela Publishing House, pg 93
Eurasia Academic Publishers, pg 94
Factor-Alias, pg 94
Fondacija Zlatno Kljuce, pg 94
Hermes Publishing House, pg 94
Interpres, pg 95
Izdatelstvo Lettera, pg 95
LIK Izdanija, pg 95
Makros 2000 - Plovdiv, pg 95
MATEX, pg 95
Musica Publishing House Ltd, pg 95
Prohazka I Kacarmazov, pg 96
Prosveta Publishers AS, pg 96
Regalia 6 Publishing House, pg 96
Sila & Zivot, pg 97
Slavena, pg 97
Sluntse Publishing House, pg 97

Cameroon

Presses Universitaires d'Afrique, pg 98

Chile

Arrayan Editores, pg 98
Editorial Andres Bello/Editorial Juridica de Chile, pg 99
Ediciones Mil Hojas Ltda, pg 99
Pontificia Universidad Catolica de Chile, pg 100
Publicaciones Lo Castillo SA, pg 100
Red Internacional Del Libro, pg 100
J.C. Saez Editor, pg 100
Ediciones Universitarias de Valparaiso, pg 100

China

Beijing Education Publishing House, pg 101
Beijing Juvenile & Children's Books Publishing House, pg 101
Beijing Publishing House, pg 101
Beijing University Press, pg 101
Chemical Industry Press, pg 101
Chengdu Maps Publishing House, pg 101
China Braille Publishing House, pg 102
China Theatre Publishing House, pg 103
China Tibetology Publishing House, pg 103
China Translation & Publishing Corp, pg 103
China Youth Publishing House, pg 103

SUBJECT INDEX

Chinese Pedagogics Publishing House, pg 103
East China University of Science & Technology Press, pg 104
Education Science Publishing House, pg 104
Encyclopedia of China Publishing House, pg 104
Fudan University Press, pg 104
Fujian Children's Publishing House, pg 104
Guizhou Education Publishing House, pg 105
Higher Education Press, pg 105
Jinan Publishing House, pg 105
Lanzhou University Press, pg 106
New Times Press, pg 106
Shandong Education Publishing House, pg 107
Shandong Science & Technology Press, pg 107
Shanghai Educational Publishing House, pg 108
Shanghai Foreign Language Education Press, pg 108
South China University of Science & Technology Press, pg 108
Tsinghua University Press, pg 109
Universidade de Macau, Centro de Publicacoes, pg 109
Zhejiang Education Publishing House, pg 109
Zhejiang University Press, pg 109

Colombia

Bedout Editores SA, pg 110
Consejo Episcopal Latinoamericano (CELAM), pg 110
Ediciones Culturales Ver Ltda, pg 110
Eurolibros Ltda, pg 111
Universidad Externado de Colombia, pg 111
Instituto Caro y Cuervo, pg 111
Kapelusz Ltda Editorial, pg 111
Editorial Libros y Libres SA, pg 112
Instituto Misionerao Hijas De San Pablo, pg 112
Pearson Educacion de Colombia LTDA, pg 112
Tercer Mundo Editores SA, pg 113
Universidad de Antioquia, Division Publicaciones, pg 113

The Democratic Republic of the Congo

Centre de Recherche, et Pedagogie Appliquee, pg 114
Presses Universitaires du Zaiire (PUZ), pg 114

Costa Rica

Asamblea Legislativa, Biblioteca Monsenor Sanabria, pg 115
Centro Agronomico Tropical de Investigacion y Ensenanza (CATIE), pg 115
Jose Alfonso Sandoval Nunez, pg 115
Ediciones Promesa, pg 116
Editorial de la Universidad de Costa Rica, pg 116
Editorial Universidad Estatal a Distancia (EUNED), pg 116
Editorial Universidad Nacional (EUNA), pg 116

Croatia

ALFA dd za izdavacke, graficke i trgovacke poslove, pg 117
Izdavacka Delatnost Hrvatske Akademije Znanosti I Umjetnosti, pg 118
Skolska Knjiga, pg 119

Cuba

ISCAH Fructuoso Rodriguez, pg 120
Editora Politica, pg 120
Pueblo y Educacion Editorial (PE), pg 121

Czech Republic

Barrister & Principal, pg 122
Doplnek, pg 123
Galaxie, vydavatelelstvi a nakladatelstvi, pg 123
Granit sro, pg 123
Karolinum, nakladatelstvi, pg 124
Pavla Momcilova, pg 125
Editio Moravia-Moravske hudebni vydavatelstvi, pg 125
Portal spol sro, pg 126
Psychoanalyticke Nakladatelstvi, pg 127

Denmark

Akademisk Forlag A/S, pg 128
Atuakkiorfik A/S Det Greenland Publishers, pg 129
Borgens Forlag A/S, pg 129
Dafolo Forlag, pg 130
Christian Ejlers' Forlag aps, pg 131
Gads Forlag, pg 131
Forlaget GMT, pg 131
Gyldendalske Boghandel - Nordisk Forlag A/S, pg 131
P Haase & Sons Forlag A/S, pg 131
Edition Wilhelm Hansen AS, pg 131
Kaleidoscope Publishers Ltd, pg 132
Mallings ApS, pg 132
Mellemfolkeligt Samvirke, pg 133
New Era Publications International ApS, pg 133
Joergen Paludan Forlag ApS, pg 133
Hans Reitzel Publishers Ltd, pg 134
Samfundslitteratur, pg 134
Scandinavia Publishing House, pg 134
Forlaget Thomson A/S, pg 135

Dominican Republic

Pontificia Universidad Catolica Madre y Maestra, pg 136

Ecuador

Centro de Planificacion y Estudios Sociales (CEPLAES), pg 136
Corporacion Editora Nacional, pg 136
Libresa S A, pg 137
SECAP, pg 137

Egypt (Arab Republic of Egypt)

Dar Al-Kitab Al-Masri, pg 137
Dar El Shorouk, pg 138
Dar Al Maaref, pg 138
Sphinx Publishing Co, pg 138

Estonia

Olion Publishers, pg 140

SUBJECT INDEX

BOOK

Fiji
Lotu Pacifika Productions, pg 141
University of the South Pacific, pg 141

Finland
AB Svenska Laromedel-Editum, pg 141
Lasten Keskus Oy, pg 143
Osuuskunta Vastapaino, pg 144
Werner Soederstrom Osakeyhtio (WSOY), pg 145
Yliopistopaino/Helsinki University Press, pg 145

France
Editions Al Liamm, pg 146
Alsatia SA, pg 146
L'Amitie par le Livre, pg 146
Editions Aubier-Montaigne SA, pg 148
Bayard Presse, pg 149
Editions Belin, pg 149
Societe d'Edition Les Belles Lettres, pg 149
Editions Bordas, pg 150
Pierre Bordas & Fils, Editions, pg 150
Presses Universitaires de Bordeaux (PUB), pg 150
Brud Nevez, pg 151
Editions Buchet-Chastel Pierre Zech Editeur, pg 151
Centre National de Documentation Pedagogique (CNDP), pg 152
Cepadues Editions SA, pg 153
Editions Circonflexe, pg 154
Cle International, pg 154
CNRS Editions, pg 155
Codes Rousseau, pg 155
Armand Colin, Editeur, pg 155
Comite National d'Evaluation (CNE), pg 155
Editions Cujas, pg 156
Editions Desvigne, pg 158
Doin Editeurs, pg 159
Dunod Editeur, pg 159
Editions de l'Ecole, pg 159
Les Editions ESF, pg 160
Editions Entente, pg 161
Editions Foucher, pg 164
Imprimerie Librairie Gardet, pg 165
Editions Jean Paul Gisserot, pg 165
Groupe Express-Expansion, pg 166
Hachette Education, pg 166
Hachette Livre, pg 167
Hachette Livre International, pg 167
Editions Hatier SA, pg 167
Jouvence Editions, pg 170
Karthala Editions-Diffusion, pg 170
Langues & Mondes-L'Asiatheque, pg 171
Editions Fernand Lanore Sarl, pg 171
Magnard, pg 173
Editions MDI (La Maison des Instituteurs), pg 175
Editions Modernes Media, pg 176
Editions Fernand Nathan, pg 176
Institut National de Recherche Pedagogique INRP, pg 176
Nouvelle Cite, pg 177
Editions Ophrys, pg 177
Pearson Education France, pg 179
Editions A et J Picard SA, pg 179
Editions Pierron, pg 180
Presses Universitaires de Nancy, pg 181
Editions Prosveta, pg 182
Editions Revue EPS, pg 183
Service Technique pour l'Education, pg 184
Editions Spratbrow, pg 186
Librairie Pierre Tequi et Editions Tequi, pg 187
UNESCO Publishing, pg 188

Germany
ALS-Verlag GmbH, pg 192
AOL-Verlag Frohmut Menze, pg 193
AUE-Verlag GmbH, pg 195
Auer Verlag GmbH, pg 195
Aussaat Verlag, pg 195
C Bange GmbH & Co KG, pg 196
Verlag Bertelsmann Stiftung, pg 200
W Bertelsmann Verlag GmbH & Co KG, pg 200
BW Bildung und Wissen Verlag und Software GmbH, pg 201
Verlag Die Blaue Eule, pg 202
Boehlau-Verlag GmbH & Cie, pg 202
Gustav Bosse GmbH & Co KG, pg 203
Brandes & Apsel Verlag GmbH, pg 204
Buchverlag Junge Welt GmbH, pg 205
Buechse der Pandora Verlags-GmbH, pg 205
Burckhardthaus-Laetare Verlag GmbH, pg 206
Calwer Verlag GmbH, pg 207
Centaurus-Verlagsgesellschaft GmbH, pg 207
Chancerel International Publishers Ltd, pg 208
Hans Christians Druckerei und Verlag GmbH & Co KG, pg 208
Compact Verlag GmbH, pg 209
Cornelsen und Oxford University Press GmbH & Co, pg 210
Cornelsen Verlag GmbH & Co OHG, pg 210
Cornelsen Verlag Scriptor GmbH & Co KG, pg 210
J G Cotta'sche Buchhandlung Nachfolger GmbH, pg 210
Verlag CSA Rosemarie Schneider, pg 210
Deutscher Taschenbuch Verlag GmbH & Co KG (dtv), pg 213
Deutsches Jugendinstitut (DJI), pg 214
Diesterweg, Moritz Verlag, pg 214
Dipa-Verlag GmbH, pg 215
Don Bosco Verlag, pg 215
Dreisam Ratgeber in der Rutsker Verlag GmbH, pg 216
Verlag Duerr & Kessler GmbH, pg 217
Ensslin und Laiblin Verlag GmbH & Co KG, pg 220
Falken-Verlag GmbH, pg 223
Festland Verlag GmbH, pg 224
Festo Didactic GmbH & Co KG, pg 224
Finken Verlag GmbH, pg 224
Flensburger Hefte Verlag GmbH, pg 225
Verlag Freies Geistesleben, pg 227
Erhard Friedrich Verlag, pg 227
Friedrich Kiehl Verlag GmbH, pg 227
Verlag A Fromm im Druck- u Verlagshaus Fromm GmbH & Co KG, pg 227
Verlag Junge Gemeinde E Schwinghammer GmbH & Co KG, pg 228
Wilhelm Goldmann Verlag GmbH, pg 230
Verlag Gruppenpaedagogischer Literatur, pg 231
Dr Curt Haefner-Verlag GmbH, pg 233
Hahnsche Buchhandlung, pg 233
Verlag Handwerk und Technik GmbH, pg 233
von Hase & Koehler Verlag KG, pg 234
Haufe Mediengruppe, pg 235
Verlag Herder GmbH & Co KG, pg 236
Holland & Josenhans GmbH & Co, pg 239
Verlagsgruppe Georg von Holtzbrinck GmbH, pg 239
Hans Holzmann Verlag GmbH und Co KG, pg 239
Horlemann Verlag, pg 239
Hans Huber, pg 239
Max Hueber Verlag GmbH & Co KG, pg 239
IKO Verlag fur Interkulturelle Kommunikation, pg 241
Iudicium Verlag GmbH, pg 242
J Ch Mellinger Verlag GmbH, pg 242
Julius Klinkhardt Verlagsbuchhandlung, pg 243
Juventa Verlag GmbH, pg 244
Kallmeyer'sche Verlagsbuchhandlung GmbH, pg 244
Katzmann Verlag KG, pg 245
Klens Verlag GmbH, pg 246
Ernst Klett Verlag GmbH, pg 247
Koelner Universitaets-Verlag GmbH, pg 248
Verlag Koenigshausen und Neumann GmbH, pg 248
Koesel-Verlag GmbH & Co, pg 248
W Kohlhammer GmbH, pg 248
Konkordia Verlag GmbH, pg 249
kopaed verlagsgmbh, pg 249
Verlag Waldemar Kramer, pg 250
Verlag Antje Kunstmann GmbH, pg 251
Peter Lang GmbH Europaeischer Verlag der Wissenschaften, pg 252
Langenscheidt-Hachette, pg 252
Anton G Leitner Verlag (AGLV), pg 253
LEU-VERLAG Wolfgang Leupelt, pg 254
Hermann Luchterhand Verlag GmbH, pg 255
Manz G J Verlag und Druckerei, pg 257
Matzker Verlag DiA, pg 258
Midena Verlag, pg 260
Naumann & Goebel Verlagsgesellschaft mbH, pg 263
Verlag Neuer Weg, pg 264
Nusser Verlag, pg 266
Oekotopia Verlag, Wolfgang Hoffman GmbH & Co KG, pg 266
R Oldenbourg Verlag GmbH, pg 267
Georg Olms Verlag AG, pg 267
Propylaeen Verlag, Zweigniederlassung Berlin der Ullstein Buchverlage GmbH, pg 272
Psychologie Verlags Union GmbH, pg 272
Quelle und Meyer Verlag GmbH & Co, pg 273
Dr Josef Raabe-Verlags GmbH, pg 273
Raethgloben Verlagsgesellschaft mbH, pg 273
Ravensburger Buchverlag Otto Maier GmbH, pg 274
Ernst Reinhardt Verlag GmbH & Co KG, pg 275
Ritterbach Verlag GmbH, pg 276
Verlag an der Ruhr GmbH, pg 277
Sax-Verlag Beucha, pg 278
Richard Scherpe Verlag GmbH, pg 279
Schott Musik International GmbH & Co KG, pg 281
Scientia Verlag und Antiquariat Schilling OHG, pg 282
Franz Steiner Verlag Wiesbaden GmbH, pg 287
Suin Buch-Verlag, pg 289
TR - Verlagsunion GmbH, pg 291
Trotzdem-Verlags Genossenschaft eG, pg 292
UNO-Verlag GmbH, pg 293
Vandenhoeck & Ruprecht, pg 294
VAS-Verlag fuer Akademische Schriften, pg 294
Verlag und Druckkontor Kamp GmbH, pg 295
Volk und Wissen Verlag GmbH & Co, pg 296
VWB-Verlag fur Wissenschaft & Bildung, Amand Aglaster, pg 297
Waxmann Verlag GmbH, pg 297
Weber Zucht & Co, pg 298
Weidler Buchverlag Berlin, pg 298
Westermann Schulbuchverlag GmbH, pg 299
Windmuehle GmbH Verlag und Vertrieb von Medien, pg 300
Dr Dieter Winkler, pg 300
Wissenschaftliche Buchgesellschaft, pg 300
Wochenschau Verlag, Dr Kurt Debus GmbH, pg 301

Ghana
Black Mask Ltd, pg 303
Ekab Business Ltd, pg 303
Quick Service Books Ltd, pg 304
Sedco Publishing Ltd, pg 305
Sub-Saharan Publishers, pg 305

Greece
Athina, Mary Mavrogiannis, pg 306
Editions Athina-Mavrogianni, pg 306
Atlantis M Pechlivanides & Co SA, pg 306
Axiotelis G, pg 306
Boukoumanis' Editions, pg 306
Chrysi Penna - Golden Pen Books, pg 306
Etaireia Spoudon Neoellinikou Politismou Kai Genikis Paideias, pg 307
Gutenberg Publications, pg 307
Hestia-I D Hestia-Kollaros & Co Corporation, pg 308
I Prooptiki, Ekdoseis, pg 308
Idryma Meleton Chersonisou tou Aimou, pg 308
Institute of Neohellenic Studies, Manolis Triantaphyllidis Foundation, pg 308
Kastaniotis Editions SA, pg 309
Panepistimio Ioanninon, pg 311
Papazissis Publishers SA, pg 311
Patakis Publishers, pg 311
Rossi, E Kdoseis Eleni Rossi-Petsiou, pg 312
Michalis Sideris, pg 312

Guyana
Guyana Community Based Rehabilitation Progeamme, pg 314

PUBLISHERS — SUBJECT INDEX

Haiti
Deschamps Imprimerie, pg 314
Editions du Soleil, pg 314

Honduras
Editorial Guaymuras, pg 315

Hong Kong
The Chinese University Press, pg 316
Commercial Press (Hong Kong) Ltd, pg 316
The Dharmasthiti Buddist Institute Ltd, pg 317
Hong Kong University Press, pg 317
Island Press, pg 317
Ling Kee Publishing Group, pg 318
Modern Electronic & Computing Publishing Co Ltd, pg 318
Vista Productions Ltd, pg 320

Hungary
Advent Kiado, pg 320
Aranyhal Konyvkiado Goldfish Publishing, pg 320
KJK-Kerszov, pg 322
Kossuth Kiado RT, pg 322
Marton Aron Kiado Publishing House, pg 323
Nemzeti Tankoenyvkiado, pg 323
Szepirodalmi Koenyvkiado Kiado, pg 324

Iceland
Bokaverslun Sigfusar Eymundssonar, pg 325
Isafoldarprentsmidja hf, pg 326
Mal og menning, pg 326
Namsgagnastofnun, pg 326
Setberg, pg 326

India
Agricole Publishing Academy, pg 327
Allied Publishers Pvt Ltd, pg 328
Ambar Prakashan, pg 328
Anmol Publications Pvt Ltd, pg 328
APH Publishing Corp, pg 328
Atma Ram & Sons, pg 329
Authorspress, pg 329
Baha'i Publishing Trust of India, pg 329
Bani Mandir, Book-Sellers, Publishers & Educational Suppliers, pg 329
Bhawan Book Service, Publishers & Distributors, pg 330
Concept Publishing Co, pg 332
Cosmo Publications, pg 332
Doaba Publications, pg 333
Era Books, pg 334
Eurasia Publishing House Private Ltd, pg 334
Frank Brothers & Co Publishers Ltd, pg 334
General Printers & Publishers, pg 335
Gyan Publishing House, pg 335
HarperCollins Publishers India Pty Ltd, pg 335
Heritage Publishers, pg 335
Indian Council of Social Science Research (ICSSR), pg 336
Manohar Publishers & Distributors, pg 340
Mehta Publishers, pg 341
Minerva Associates (Publications) Pvt Ltd, pg 341
A Mukherjee & Co Pvt Ltd, pg 342
National Book Organization, pg 342
National Council of Educational Research & Training, Publication Department, pg 343
Navrang Booksellers & Publishers, pg 343
Neeta Prakashan, pg 343
Omsons Publications, pg 344
Parimal Prakashan, pg 345
Pointer Publishers, pg 345
Radiant Publishers, pg 346
Rajasthan Hindi Granth Academy, pg 346
Rajesh Publications, pg 346
Rajkamal Prakashan Pvt Ltd, pg 346
Rastogi Publications, pg 346
Regency Publications, pg 346
Reliance Publishing House, pg 346
Rupa & Co, pg 347
SABDA, pg 347
Sasta Sahitya Mandal, pg 348
Scientific Book Agency, pg 348
Selina Publishers, pg 349
Shiksha Bharati, pg 349
Sita Books & Periodicals Pvt Ltd, pg 349
Somaiya Publications Pvt Ltd, pg 349
Sterling Publishers Pvt Ltd, pg 350
Sultan Chand & Sons Pvt Ltd, pg 350
Tara Publishing, pg 351
Vikas Publishing House Pvt Ltd, pg 352
Vision Books Pvt Ltd, pg 352
Viva Books Pvt Ltd, pg 352

Indonesia
Aurora, pg 353
Balai Pustaka, pg 353
Bhratara Karya Aksara, pg 354
Bina Rena Pariwara, pg 354
PT Bulan Bintang, pg 354
Institut Teknologi Bandung, pg 355
Karya Anda, CV, pg 355
Lembaga Demografi Fakultas Ekonomi Universitas Indonesia, pg 355
Mutiara Sumber Widya PT, pg 356
Yayasan Obor Indonesia, pg 357

Iraq
National House for Publishing, Distributing & Advertising, pg 357

Ireland
An Gum, pg 358
Campus Publishing Ltd, pg 358
Careers & Educational Publishers Ltd, pg 358
The Economic & Social Research Institute, pg 359
Fitzwilliam Publishing Co Ltd, pg 360
Folens Publishers, pg 360
Gill & Macmillan Ltd, pg 360
Institute of Public Administration, pg 361
Irish YouthWork Press, pg 361
Veritas Co Ltd, pg 364

Israel
Ach Publishing House, pg 364
Bar Ilan University Press, pg 365
Boostan Publishing House, pg 365
Breslov Research Institute, pg 365
Carta, The Israel Map & Publishing Co Ltd, pg 365
Dyonon/Papyrus Publishing House of the Tel-Aviv, pg 366
Haifa University Press, pg 367
Hakibbutz Hameuchad Publishing House Ltd, pg 367
Otzar Hamore, pg 367
Hanitzotz A-Sharara Publishing House, pg 367
Intermedia Audio, Video Book Publishing Ltd, pg 368
Kernerman Publishing Ltd, pg 369
Ma'ariv Book Guild (Sifriat Ma'ariv), pg 370
Massada Press Ltd, pg 370
Open University of Israel, pg 371
Rubin Mass Ltd, pg 371
Schocken Publishing House Ltd, pg 371
Tcherikover Publishers Ltd, pg 372
Yad Vashem - The Holocaust Martyrs' & Heroes' Remembrance Authority, pg 373

Italy
Gruppo Abele, pg 374
De Agostini Scolastica, pg 374
Alinari Fratelli SpA Istituto di Edizioni Artistiche, pg 375
Archimede Edizioni, pg 376
Argalia Editore delle Arti Grafiche Editoriali SRL, pg 376
Editore Armando Armando SRL, pg 376
Baha'i, pg 377
Belforte Editore Libraio srl, pg 377
Bonacci editore, pg 378
Edizioni Borla SRL, pg 379
Casa Musicale G Zanibon SRL, pg 380
Centro Programmazione Editoriale (CPE), pg 381
Edizioni Centro Studi Erickson, pg 381
Ciranna - Roma, pg 382
Citta Nuova Editrice, pg 382
CLUEB (Cooperativa Libraria Universitaria Editrice Bologna), pg 382
La Coccinella Editrice SRL, pg 383
Continental SRL Editrice, pg 383
Edizioni Cultura della Pace, pg 383
D'Anna, pg 384
G De Bono Editore, pg 384
Edizioni Dehoniane Bologna (EDB), pg 384
Edizioni Dehoniane, pg 384
Editrice Edisco, pg 386
Edistudio, pg 386
Effata Editrice, pg 387
Elle Di Ci - Libreria Dottrina Cristiana, pg 387
Fatatrac, pg 388
Editrice Garigliano SRL, pg 390
Giunti Gruppo Editoriale, pg 390
Piero Gribaudi Editore, pg 391
Guerra Edizioni GURU srl, pg 392
In Dialogo, pg 393
Lalli Editore SRL, pg 394
Laruffa Editore SRL, pg 394
Editrice LAS, pg 394
Libreria Editrice Fiorentina, pg 395
Vincenzo Lo Faro Editore, pg 395
Lusva Editrice, pg 396
Macro Edizioni, pg 397
Milella di Lecce Spazio Vivo srl, pg 398
Minerva Italica SpA, pg 398
Arnoldo Mondadori Editore SpA, pg 398
Edumond Le Monnier, pg 399
Mucchi Editore SRL, pg 399
Gruppo Ugo Mursia Editore SpA, pg 400
Nagard, pg 400
Nardini Editore srl, pg 400
Nuova Coletti Editore Roma, pg 401
OCTAVO Produzioni Editoriali Associale, pg 401
Franco Cosimo Panini Editore, pg 402
Edizioni Franco Cosimo Panini, pg 402
Paravia Bruno Mondadori Editori, pg 402
Il Pensiero Scientifico Editore SRL, pg 403
Psicologica Editrice, pg 404
Editori Riuniti, pg 405
SAIE Editrice SRL, pg 406
Editrice San Marco SRL, pg 407
Scala Group spa, pg 407
Editrice la Scuola SpA, pg 407
Societa Editrice Internazionale - SEI, pg 408
Le Stelle Scuola, pg 409
Nicola Teti e C Editore SRL, pg 410
Edizioni Thyrus SRL, pg 410
Zanichelli Editore SpA, pg 412

Jamaica
Carib Publishing Ltd, pg 413
Eureka Press Ltd, pg 413
Jamaica Publishing House Ltd, pg 414

Japan
Aoki Shoten Co Ltd, pg 415
AVACO - Christian Mass Communications Center, pg 415
Bunkashobo-Hakubun-Sha, pg 415
Chikuma Shobo Publishing Co Ltd, pg 416
Chikyu-sha Co Ltd, pg 416
Child Honsha Co Ltd, pg 416
Chuo-Tosho Co Ltd, pg 416
Dainippon Tosho Publishing Co, Ltd, pg 416
Froebel - kan Co Ltd, pg 417
Fukumura Shuppan Inc, pg 417
Fumaido Publishing Company Ltd, pg 417
Gakken Co Ltd, pg 417
Heibonsha Ltd, Publishers, pg 418
Hikarinokuni Ltd, pg 418
Hokuryukan Co Ltd, pg 418
Holp Book Co Ltd, pg 418
Hyoronsha Publishing Co Ltd, pg 418
Japan Broadcast Publishing Co Ltd, pg 419
Kaitakusha, pg 420
Kazamashobo Co Ltd, pg 420
Keisuisha Publishing Company Ltd, pg 420
Kin-No-Hoshi Sha Co Ltd, pg 421
Kodansha Ltd, pg 421
Kokudo-Sha Co Ltd, pg 421
Kokushokankokai Co Ltd, pg 421
Komine Shoten Co Ltd, pg 421
Kosei Publishing Co Ltd, pg 421
Koseisha-Koseikaku Co Ltd, pg 422
Koyo Shobo, pg 422
Minerva Shobo Co Ltd, pg 422
Myrtos Inc, pg 423
Nan'un-Do Co Ltd, pg 423
Nihon Bunka Kagakusha Co Ltd, pg 423
Nihon-Bunkyo Shuppan (Japan Educational Publishing Co Ltd), pg 423
Nihon Tosho Center Co Ltd, pg 423
Nikkagiren Shuppan-Sha (JUSE Press Ltd), pg 424
Nippon Hoso Shuppan Kyokai (NHK Publishing), pg 424
Nosangyoson Bunka Kyokai, pg 424

SUBJECT INDEX

Obunsha Co Ltd, pg 424
Ongaku No Tomo Sha Corporation, pg 425
Reimei-Shobo Co Ltd, pg 425
Riso-Sha, pg 425
Saela Shobo (Librairie Ca et La), pg 425
Sagano Shoin, pg 426
Sanseido Co Ltd, pg 426
Sanshusha Publishing Co, Ltd, pg 426
Sekai Bunka-Sha, pg 427
Shingakusha Co Ltd, pg 427
Shogakukan Inc, pg 427
Shokokusha Publishing Co Ltd, pg 428
Shufunotomo Co Ltd, pg 428
The Simul Press Inc, pg 428
Sobun-Sha, pg 428
Sogensha Publishing Co Ltd, pg 428
Takahashi Shoten Co Ltd, pg 429
Tamagawa University Press, pg 429
Tokyo Shoseki Co Ltd, pg 430
Waseda University Press, pg 431
Yamaguchi Shoten, pg 431
Yuhikaku Publishing Co Ltd, pg 431
Zoshindo JukenKenkyusha, pg 431

Jordan

Al-Tanwir Al Ilmi (Scientific Enlightenment Publishing House), pg 432

Kenya

Action Publishers, pg 433
African Centre for Technology Studies (ACTS), pg 433
Focus Publications Ltd, pg 433
Heinemann Kenya Ltd (EAEP), pg 434
Kenya Literature Bureau, pg 434
Lake Publishers & Enterprises Ltd, pg 435
Paulines Publications-Africa, pg 435
Phoenix Publishers Ltd, pg 435
Shirikon Publishers, pg 436
Transafrica Press, pg 436
Vipopremo Agencies, pg 436

Democratic People's Republic of Korea

Academy of Sciences Publishing House, pg 436
Educational Books Publishing House, pg 436
The Foreign Language Press Group, pg 436
Grand People's Study House, pg 436
Korea Science and Encyclopedia Publishing House, pg 436

Republic of Korea

BCM Media Inc, pg 437
Bo Ri Publishing Co Ltd, pg 437
Chung Rim Publishing Co Ltd, pg 438
Ewha Womans University Press, pg 438
Hainaim Publishing Co Ltd, pg 439
Hakmunsa Publishing Co, pg 439
Hongik Media Plus Ltd, pg 439
Hyein Publishing House, pg 439
Iljo-gag Publishers, pg 439
Korea Britannica Corp, pg 440
Korea Textbook Co Ltd, pg 440
Korea University Press, pg 440
Koreaone Press Inc, pg 440
Minjisa Publishing Co, pg 441

Oruem Publishing House, pg 442
Seogwangsa, pg 442
Woongjin.com Co Ltd, pg 443
Yearimdang Publishing Co, pg 443

Kuwait

Ministry of Information, pg 444

Laos People's Democratic Republic

Lao-phanit, pg 444

Latvia

Preses Nams, pg 445
Zvaigzne ABC Publishers Ltd, pg 445

Lebanon

Dar El Ilm Lilmalayin, pg 446
Khayat Book and Publishing Co Sarl, pg 446
Librairie du Liban Publishers (Sal), pg 446
Librairie Orientale sal, pg 446
World Book Publishing, pg 447

Liechtenstein

Rheintal Handelsgesellschaft Anstalt, pg 448
Topos Verlag AG, pg 448

Lithuania

Baltos Lankos, pg 449
Eugrimas, pg 449
Klaipedos Universiteto Leidykla, pg 449
Lietus Ltd, pg 449
Sviesa Publishers, pg 449
Svietimo ir mokslo ministerijos Leidybos centras, pg 449
TEV Leidykla, pg 450
Tyto Alba Publishers, pg 450
Vyturys Vyturio leidykla, UAB, pg 450

Luxembourg

Editions APESS ASBL, pg 450
Editions Emile Borschette, pg 450
Keyware sarl, pg 451

The Former Yugoslav Republic of Macedonia

Medis, Skopje, pg 452
Murgorski Zoze, pg 453
Prosvetno Delo Publishing House, pg 453

Madagascar

Maison d'Edition Protestante ANTSO, pg 453
Societe Malgache d'Edition, pg 454

Malawi

Dzuka Publishing Co Ltd, pg 454

Malaysia

Amiza Associate Malaysia Sdn Bhd, pg 455
Berita Publishing Sdn Bhd, pg 455
Darulfikir, pg 455
Federal Publications Sdn Bhd, pg 455
Geetha Publishers Sdn Bhd, pg 456
Mahir Publications Sdn Bhd, pg 456
Malaya Educational Supplies Sdn Bhd, pg 456
The Malaya Press Sdn Bhd, pg 456

Penerbit Universiti Sains Malaysia, pg 458
Penerbitan Tinta, pg 458
Preston Corporation Sdn Bhd, pg 458
Pustaka Cipta Sdn Bhd, pg 458
Syarikat Cultural Supplies Sdn Bhd, pg 458
Trix Corporation Sdn Bhd, pg 459
Uni-Text Book Co, pg 459
Penerbit Universiti Teknologi Malaysia, pg 459
Utusan Publications & Distributors Sdn Bhd, pg 459

Maldive Islands

Non-Formal Education Centre, pg 459

Malta

Media Centre, pg 460
Publishers' Enterprises Group (PEG) Ltd, pg 460

Martinique

George Lise-Huyghes des Etages, pg 460

Mauritania

Imprimerie Commerciale et Administrative de Mauritanie, pg 461

Mauritius

Editions Capucines, pg 461
Hemco Publications, pg 461
Editions de l'Ocean Indien Ltd, pg 461

Mexico

Aconcagua Ediciones y Publicaciones SA, pg 461
Adivinar y Multiplicar, SA de CV, pg 461
Aguilar Altea Taurus Alfaguara SA de CV, pg 462
Editorial Avante SA de Cv, pg 462
Colegio de Postgraduados en Ciencias Agricolas, pg 463
Editorial Diana SA de CV, pg 464
Editorial Edicol SA, pg 464
El Colegio de Michoacan A C, pg 464
Entretenlibro SA de CV, pg 465
Editorial Extemporaneos SA, pg 465
Fernandez Editores SA de CV, pg 465
Fondo de Cultura Economica, pg 465
Editorial Jus SA de CV, pg 467
Libra Editorial SA de CV, pg 467
Libros y Revistas SA de CV, pg 467
Editorial Limusa SA de CV, pg 467
Nova Grupo Editorial SA de CV, pg 469
Editorial Pax Mexico, pg 470
Pearson Educacion de Mexico, SA de CV, pg 470
Ediciones Cientificas La Prensa Medica Mexicana SA de CV, pg 470
Editorial Progreso SA de C V, pg 470
Ediciones Promesa, SA de CV, pg 470
Ediciones Roca, SA, pg 471
Sayrols Editorial SA de CV, pg 471
Siglo XXI Editores SA de CV, pg 472

Editorial Trillas SA de CV, pg 472
Universidad Nacional Autonoma de Mexico (National University of Mexico), pg 472
Universidad Veracruzana Direccion General Editorial y de Publicaciones, pg 472
Editorial Varazen SA, pg 473

Morocco

Dar Nachr Al Maarifa Pour L'Edition et La Distribution, pg 474
Edition Diffusion de Livre au Maroc, pg 474

Mozambique

Empresa Moderna Lda, pg 475

Myanmar

Knowledge Press & Bookhouse, pg 475

Namibia

Desert Research Foundation of Namibia (DRFN), pg 476

Nepal

International Standards Books & Periodicals (P) Ltd, pg 476

Netherlands

Ankh-Hermes BV, pg 477
John Benjamins BV, pg 479
Boekencentrum BV, pg 479
Boom Uitgeverij, pg 479
Uitgeverij Christofoor, pg 480
Uitgeverij Coutinho BV, pg 481
Uitgeversmaatschappij Ad Donker BV, pg 481
Educatieve Uitgeverij Edu'Actief BV, pg 481
Uitgeverij Vrij Geestesleven, pg 482
LCG Malmberg BV, pg 485
Uitgeverij Lemma BV, pg 485
Mirananda Publishers BV, pg 486
Uitgeverij H Nelissen BV, pg 486
Partners Training & Innovatie, pg 487
Pearson Education Netherlands, pg 487
Sociaal en Cultureel Planbureau, pg 489
Stichting IVIO, pg 489
Swets & Zeitlinger Publishers, pg 489
ThiemeMeulenhoff, pg 490
Twente University Press, pg 490
Van Gorcum & Comp BV, pg 491

New Zealand

Clerestory Press, pg 495
Commonwealth Council for Educational Administration & Management, pg 495
Dunmore Press Ltd, pg 495
Gondwanaland Press, pg 496
Huia Publishers, pg 497
Learning Media Ltd, pg 498
Magari Publishing, pg 498
Nagare Press, pg 499
Nelson Price Milburn Ltd, pg 499
New Zealand Council for Educational Research, pg 499
Reach Publications, pg 500
Resource Books Ltd, pg 500
Shearwater Associates Ltd, pg 501
Statistics New Zealand, pg 501
University of Otago Press, pg 502

PUBLISHERS SUBJECT INDEX

Nigeria

Adebara Publishers Ltd, pg 503
Ahmadu Bello University Press Ltd, pg 503
Albah Publishers, pg 503
Book Representation & Publishing Co Ltd, pg 503
ECWA Productions Ltd, pg 504
Evans Brothers (Nigeria Publishers) Ltd, pg 504
Olaiya Fagbamigbe Ltd (Publishers), pg 504
Fourth Dimension Publishing Co Ltd, pg 504
Gbabeks Publishers Ltd, pg 505
Literamed Publications Nigeria Ltd, pg 505
New Africa Publishing Company Ltd, pg 505
Nwamife Publishers Ltd, pg 506
Obafemi Awolowo University Press Ltd, pg 506
Paperback Publishers Ltd, pg 507
Spectrum Books Ltd, pg 507
University of Lagos Press, pg 507
Vantage Publishers International Ltd, pg 507

Norway

Ariel Lydbokforlag, pg 508
Aschehoug Forlag, pg 508
H Aschehoug & Co (W Nygaard) A/S, pg 508
Det Norske Samlaget, pg 508
J W Eides Forlag A/S, pg 509
Fono Forlag, pg 509
Glydendal Akademisk, pg 509
Lunde Forlag AS, pg 509
Novus Forlag, pg 510
Universitetsforlaget, pg 511

Pakistan

Academy of Education Planning & Management (AEPAM), pg 511
The Book House, pg 512
Hamdard Foundation Pakistan, pg 512
International Educational Services, pg 512
Maqbool Academy, pg 513
Nafees Academy, pg 513
Sh Ghulam Ali & Sons (Pvt) Ltd, pg 514
Urdu Academy Sind, pg 514

Panama

Editorial Universitaria, pg 515

Papua New Guinea

Kristen Press, pg 515
National Research Institute of Papua New Guinea, pg 515

Peru

Asociacion Editorial Bruno, pg 516
Instituto de Estudios Peruanos, pg 517
Fondo Editorial de la Pontificia Universidad Catolica del Peru, pg 517
Editorial Horizonte, pg 517
Tarea Asociacion de Publicaciones Educativas, pg 517
Tassorello, SA, pg 517

Philippines

Abiva Publishing House Inc, pg 518
Ateneo de Manila University Press, pg 518
Bookman Printing & Publishing House Inc, pg 518
De La Salle University, pg 519
Garotech, pg 519
Logos (Divine Word) Publications Inc, pg 519
New Day Publishers, pg 520
Our Lady of Manaoag Publisher, pg 520
Philippine Education Co Inc, pg 520
Rex Bookstores & Publishers, pg 520
Saint Mary's Publishing Corp, pg 520
SIBS Publishing House Inc, pg 521
University of the Philippines Press, pg 521
UST Publishing House, pg 521

Poland

Instytut Historii Nauki PAN, pg 523
Impuls, pg 523
Instytut Wydawniczy Pax, Inco-Veritas, pg 523
KAW Krajowa Agencja Wydawnicza, pg 523
Muza SA, pg 524
Wydawnictwo Nasza Ksiegarnia Sp zoo, pg 524
Wydawnictwo Podsiedlik-Raniowski i Spolka, pg 525
Polish Scientific Publishers PWN, pg 525
Wydawnictwa Radia i Telewizji, pg 526
Oficyna Wydawnicza Read Me, pg 526
Res Polona, pg 526
Wydawnictwo RTW, pg 526
Wydawnictwa Szkolne i Pedagogiczne, pg 527
Wydawnictwa Uniwersytetu Warszawskiego, pg 527
Videograf II Sp z o o Zaklad Poracy Chronionej, pg 527
Wydawnictwo Wilga sp zoo, pg 527

Portugal

Livraria Almedina, pg 528
Basica Editora, pg 529
Bezerr-Editorae e Distribuidora de Abel Antonio Bezerra, pg 529
Biblioteca Geral da Universidade de Coimbra, pg 529
Coimbra Editora Lda, pg 530
Constancia Editores, SA, pg 530
Dinalivro, pg 530
Edicoes ELO, pg 531
Editorial Estampa, Lda, pg 531
Publicacoes Europa-America Lda, pg 531
Gradiva-Publicacnoes Lda, pg 532
Impala, pg 532
Edicoes ITAU (Instituto Tecnico de Alimentacao Humana) Lda, pg 532
Livros Horizonte Lda, pg 533
Editora McGraw-Hill de Portugal Lda, pg 533
Palas Editores Lda, pg 534
Porto Editora Lda, pg 535
Editorial Presenca, pg 535
Publicacoes Dom Quixote Lda, pg 535
Edicoes Salesianas, pg 535
Edicoes 70 Lda, pg 535
Texto Editora, pg 536
Vega-Publicacao e Distribuicao de Livros e Revistas, Lda, pg 536
Editorial Verbo SA, pg 536
Livraria Verdade e Vida Editora, pg 536

Puerto Rico

McGraw-Hill Intermericana del Caribe, Inc, pg 537
University of Puerto Rico Press (EDUPR), pg 537

Romania

Editora All, pg 538
Corint Publishing Group, pg 539
Editura Excelsior Art, pg 539
Hasefer, pg 540
Editura Institutul European, pg 540
Editura Militara, pg 541
Editura Minerva, pg 541
Nemira Verlag, pg 541
Editura Niculescu, pg 541
Petrion Verlag, pg 542
Grupul Editorial RAO, pg 542
Realitatea Casa de Edituri Productie Audio-Video Film, pg 542
Editura Univers SA, pg 543
Universal Dalsi, pg 543
Vremea Publishers Ltd, pg 543

Russian Federation

Airis Press, pg 543
N E Bauman Moscow State Technical University Publishers, pg 544
Dom, Izdatel'stvo sovetskogo deskkogo fonda im & I Lenina, pg 544
Izdatelstvo 'Ekonomika', pg 544
INFRA-M Izdatel'skij dom, pg 545
Izdatelskii Dom Kompozitor, pg 546
Izdatelstvo Mordovskogo gosudar stvennogo, pg 547
Moscow University Press, pg 547
Izdatelstvo Muzyka, pg 547
Nauka Publishers, pg 547
Izdatel'stvo Nizhegorodskogo Gosudarstvennogo Univ, pg 547
Okoshko Ltd Publishers (Izdatelstvo), pg 547
Pedagogika Press, pg 548
Izdatelstvo Prosveshchenie, pg 548
Raduga Publishers, pg 548
St Andrew's Biblical Theological College, pg 548
Izdatelstvo Sudostroenie, pg 549

Senegal

Centre Africain d'Animation et d'Echanges Culturels Editions Khoudia (CAEC), pg 551
CODESRIA (Council for the Development of Social Science Research in Africa), pg 551
Les Nouvelles Editions Africaines du Senegal NEAS, pg 551

Serbia and Montenegro

Naucna Knjiga, pg 552
Niro Decje Novine, pg 553
Obod, pg 553
Republicki Zavod za Unapredivanje Vaspitanja i Obrazovanja, pg 553
Zavod za Izdavanje Udzbenika, pg 554
Zavod za udzbenike i nastavna sredstva, pg 554

Singapore

Cannon International, pg 555
Chopsons Pte Ltd, pg 555
EPB Publishers Pte Ltd, pg 555
Federal Publications (S) Pte Ltd, pg 556
Graham Brash Pte Ltd, pg 556
Hillview Publications Pte Ltd, pg 556
McGallen & Bolden Associates, pg 557
Pan Pacific Publications (S) Pte Ltd, pg 557
Pearson Education Asia Pte Ltd, pg 557
SNP Panpac Pacific Publishing Pte Ltd, pg 558
Stamford College Publishers/ Authors-Publishers, pg 558
Success Publications Pte Ltd, pg 558
Taylor & Francis Asia Pacific, pg 558

Slovakia

Luc vydavatelske druzstvo, pg 559
Vydavatel'stvo Osveta (Verlag Osveta), pg 560
Slovenske pedagogicke nakladateistvo, pg 560
Technicka Univerzita, pg 561
Ustav informacii a prognoz skolstva mladeze a telovychovy, pg 561

Slovenia

Cankarjeva Zalozba, pg 561
Mladinska Knjiga International, pg 561
Zalozba Obzorja d d Maribor, pg 562

South Africa

Clever Books, pg 563
Educum Publishers Ltd, pg 563
Government Printer, pg 564
HAUM - Daan Retief Publishers (Pty) Ltd, pg 564
HAUM (Hollandsch Afrikaansche Uitgevers Maatschappij), pg 564
Heinemann Educational Publishers Southern Africa, pg 564
Human Sciences Research Council, pg 565
Institute for Reformational Studies CHE, pg 565
Ivy Publications, pg 565
Jacana Education, pg 565
Johannesburg Art Gallery, pg 565
Juta & Co, pg 565
LexisNexis Butterworths South Africa, pg 566
Maskew Miller Longman, pg 566
Nasionale Boekhandel Ltd, pg 567
New Africa Books (Pty) Ltd, pg 567
Pearson Education (Prentice Hall), pg 567
Perskor Books (Pty) Ltd, pg 567
Publitoria Publishers, pg 568
Ravan Press (Pty) Ltd, pg 568
Sasavona Publishers & Booksellers, pg 568
Unisa Press, pg 569
University of KwaZulu-Natal Press, pg 569
Van Schaik Publishers, pg 569
Vivlia Publishers & Booksellers, pg 570
Witwatersrand University Press, pg 570

Spain

Agencia Espanola de Cooperacion, pg 571
Ediciones Akal SA, pg 571
Altea, Taurus, Alfaguara SA, pg 572
Amnistia Internacional Editorial SL, pg 572
Ediciones Anaya SA, pg 572
Anglo-Didactica, SL Editorial, pg 573

Sociedad de Educacion Atenas SA, pg 573
Editorial Barcanova SA, pg 574
Editorial Bruno, pg 575
Editorial Casals SA, pg 575
Editorial Castalia, pg 576
CEAC, Grupo Editorial SA, pg 576
Central Catequistica Salesiana (CCS), pg 576
Centro UNESCO de San Sebastian, pg 577
Comunidad Autonoma de Madrid, Servicio de Documentacion y Publicaciones, pg 578
CTE-Centro de Tecnologia Educativa SA, pg 578
Ediciones Daly S L, pg 578
Diseno Editorial SA, pg 579
Dykinson SL, pg 580
Edebe, pg 580
Edex, Centro de Recursos Comunitarios, pg 580
Edigol Ediciones SA, pg 581
Elkar, Euskal Liburu eta Kantuen Argitaldaria, SL, pg 582
Enciclopedia Catalana, SA, pg 582
Erein, pg 582
Editorial Esin, SA, pg 582
Eumo Editorial, pg 583
EUNSA (Ediciones Universidad de Navarra SA), pg 583
La Galera, SA Editorial, pg 584
Editorial Gedisa SA, pg 584
Generalitat de Catalunya Diari Oficial de la Generalitat vern, pg 584
Grao Editorial, pg 585
Editorial Gredos SA, pg 585
Grupo Comunicar, pg 585
Grupo Editorial CEAC SA, pg 586
Grupo Santillana de Ediciones SA, pg 586
Hercules de Ediciones, SA, pg 586
Editorial Herder SA, pg 586
Editorial Horsori SL, pg 586
Ibaizabal Edelvives SA, pg 586
Editorial Iberia, SA, pg 586
Publicaciones ICCE, pg 587
Idea Books, pg 587
Imagen y Deporte, SL, pg 587
Laertes SA de Ediciones, pg 588
Editorin Laiovento SL, pg 588
Llibres del Segle, pg 589
Loguez Ediciones, pg 589
Editorial Luis Vives (Edelvives), pg 589
Antonio Machado, SA, pg 590
Editorial Magisterio Espanol SA, pg 590
Editorial Marfil SA, pg 590
Ediciones Marova SL, pg 590
McGraw-Hill/Interamericana de Espana SAU, pg 591
Ediciones Medici SA, pg 591
Ediciones Mensajero, pg 591
Editorial Molino, pg 592
Ediciones Morata SL, pg 592
Editorial la Muralla SA, pg 592
Naque Editora, pg 592
Narcea SA de Ediciones, pg 593
Ediciones Oceano Grupo SA, pg 593
Oikos-Tau SA Ediciones, pg 593
Ediciones del Oriente y del Mediterraneo, pg 594
Oxford University Press Espana SA, pg 594
Editorial Paidotribo SL, pg 594
Pais Vasco Servicio Central de Publicaciones, pg 594
Ediciones Palabra SA, pg 595
Parramon Ediciones SA, pg 595
Pearson Educacion S A, pg 595
Editorial Perpetuo Socorro, pg 596
Pirene Editorial, sal, pg 596
Editorial Playor SA, pg 596
Editorial Popular SA, pg 596
PPC Editorial y Distribuidora, SA, pg 596
Editorial Presencia Gitana, pg 597
Editora Regional de Murcia - ERM, pg 597
Ediciones Rialp SA, pg 598
Editorial Miguel A Salvatella SA, pg 598
San Pablo Ediciones, pg 598
Ediciones San Pio X, pg 599
Universidad de Santiago de Compostela, pg 599
Editorial Sintesis, SA, pg 600
Equipo Sirius SA, pg 600
Ediciones SM, pg 600
Editorial Rudolf Steiner, pg 601
Ediciones Tarraco, pg 601
Editorial Tecnos SA, pg 601
Editorial Teide SA, pg 601
Thales Sociedad Andaluza de Educacion Matematica, pg 602
Tirant lo Blanch SL Libreriaa, pg 602
Ediciones de la Torre, pg 602
Trea Ediciones, SL, pg 602
Universidad de Granada, pg 603
Universidad de Malaga, pg 603
Ediciones Universidad de Salamanca, pg 603
Universidad de Valladolid Secretariado de Publicaciones e Intercambio Editorial, pg 604
Publicacions de la Universitat de Barcelona, pg 604
Universitat de Valencia Servei de Publicacions, pg 604
Editorial Vicens-Vives, pg 605
Visor Distribuciones, SA, pg 605
Edicions Xerais de Galicia, pg 605
Xunta de Galicia, pg 605

Sri Lanka
Colombo Book Association, pg 606
Karunaratne & Sons Ltd, pg 606
Lake House Investments Ltd, pg 606
Samayawardena Printers Publishers & Booksellers, pg 607
Swarna Hansa Foundation, pg 607

Swaziland
Macmillan Boleswa Publishers (Pty) Ltd, pg 609

Sweden
Acta Universitatis Gothoburgensis, pg 609
Akademiforlaget Corona AB, pg 609
Akademiforlaget Goteborgslitteratur, pg 609
Ekelunds Forlag AB, pg 611
Folkuniversitetets foerlag, pg 611
Foerlagshuset Gothia, pg 612
Hallgren och Fallgren Studieforlag AB, pg 612
Invandrarfoerlaget, pg 612
Hans Richter Laromedel, pg 613
Lidman Production AB, pg 613
Psykologifoerlaget AB, pg 614
Samsprak Forlags AB, pg 615
Stromberg, pg 616
Studentlitteratur AB, pg 616

Switzerland
Aare-Verlag, pg 617
Antonius-Verlag, pg 617
Bibliographisches Institut & F A Brockhaus AG, pg 619
Bugra Suisse Burchler Grafino AG, pg 620
Les Editions Camphill, pg 620
CEC-Cosmic Energy Connections, pg 620
Christiana-Verlag, pg 620
Editions Delachaux et Niestle SA, pg 621
Editions Eisele SA, pg 622
Maurice et Pierre Foetisch SA, pg 623
Paul Haupt Bern, pg 625
Interfrom AG Editions, pg 625
Jugend mit einer Mission Verlag, pg 626
Klett und Balmer & Co Verlag, pg 626
Editions H Messeiller SA, pg 628
Natura-Verlag Arlesheim, pg 629
Novalis Media AG, pg 630
Orell Fuessli Buchhandlungs AG, pg 630
Pedrazzini Tipografia, pg 631
Philosophisch-Anthroposophischer Verlag am Goetheanum, pg 631
Editions Pro Schola, pg 631
Psychosophische Gesellschaft, pg 632
Rex Verlag, pg 632
Ruegger Verlag, pg 633
Sabe AG Verlagsinstitut, pg 633
Editions Saint-Paul, pg 633
Sauerlaender AG, pg 633
Schweizer Spiegel Verlag Mit, pg 634
Editions D'Art Albert Skira SA, pg 634
Editions 24 Heures, pg 635
Verlag im Waldgut AG, pg 636
Zbinden Druck und Verlag AG, pg 637

Syrian Arab Republic
Damascus University Press, pg 638

Taiwan, Province of China
Cheng Chung Book Co, Ltd, pg 639
Chu Liu Book Company, pg 639
Chung Hwa Book Co Ltd, pg 639
Far East Book Co Ltd, pg 639
Kuang Fu Book Co Ltd, pg 640
Laureate Book Co Ltd, pg 640
San Min Book Co Ltd, pg 641
Shuttle Multimedia Inc, pg 641
Youth Cultural Publishing Co, pg 642

United Republic of Tanzania
Bureau of Statistics, pg 643
East African Publishing House, pg 643
General Publications Ltd, pg 643
Nyota Publishers Ltd, pg 644
Press & Publicity Centre Ltd, pg 644
Tema Publishers Ltd, pg 644

Thailand
Pracha Chang & Co Ltd, pg 645
Thai Watana Panich Co, Ltd, pg 646
Unesco Regional Office, Asia & the Pacific, pg 646

Togo
Editions Akpagnon, pg 646
Editogo, pg 646

Trinidad & Tobago
Inprint Caribbean Ltd, pg 647

Tunisia
Dar Arabia Lil Kitab, pg 648
Maison Tunisienne de l'Edition, pg 648

Turkey
ABC Kitabevi AS, pg 648
Arkin Kitabevi, pg 649
Bilden Bilgisayar, pg 649
Ezel Erverdi (Dergah Yayinlari AS) Muessese Muduru, pg 650
Kok Yayincilik, pg 650
Redhouse Press, pg 651
Remzi Kitabevi, pg 651

Uganda
Centenary Publishing House Ltd, pg 652
Fountain Publishers Ltd, pg 652

Ukraine
Lybid (University of Kyyiv Press), pg 653
Osvita, pg 654

United Kingdom
AP Information Services Ltd, pg 658
Apex Publishing Ltd, pg 658
Association of Commonwealth Universities (ACU), pg 661
Association for Science Education, pg 661
Bible Reading Fellowship, pg 665
A & C Black Publishers Ltd, pg 666
Books of Zimbabwe Publishing Co (Pvt) Ltd, pg 669
BPS Books (British Psychological Society), pg 670
Brewin Books Ltd, pg 671
Brilliant Publications, pg 671
British Educational Communication & Technology Agency (BECTA), pg 671
Cambridge University Press, pg 674
Capall Bann Publishing, pg 674
Cardiff Academic Press, pg 675
Cassell & Co, pg 675
The Catholic Truth Society, pg 676
Centaur Press (1954), pg 677
Centre for Information on Language Teaching & Research (CILT), pg 677
Child's World Education Ltd, pg 679
Christian Education, pg 679
Colourpoint Books, pg 681
Commonwealth Secretariat, pg 681
The Continuum International Publishing Group Ltd, pg 682
Council for British Archaeology, pg 683
Crown House Publishing Ltd, pg 684
CTBI Publications, pg 685
James Currey Ltd, pg 685
Drake Educational Associates Ltd, pg 688
Dramatic Lines Publishers, pg 688
Dunedin Academic Press, pg 688
Edinburgh University Press Ltd, pg 689
Edition XII, pg 690
Elsevier Ltd, pg 691
Europa Publications, pg 692
The Eurospan Group, pg 692

PUBLISHERS

First & Best in Education Ltd, pg 695
Flame Tree Publishing, pg 695
Folens Ltd, pg 695
Forbes Publications Ltd, pg 696
Foulsham Publishers, pg 696
David Fulton Publishers Ltd, pg 698
Ginn & Co Ltd, pg 700
Global Oriental Ltd, pg 700
Gomer Press (J D Lewis & Sons Ltd), pg 701
Graham-Cameron Publishing & Illustration, pg 701
Harvard University Press, pg 705
Harvey Map Services Ltd, pg 705
Hawthorn Press, pg 706
Heinemann Educational Publishing, pg 707
Hobsons, pg 709
Iaith Cyf, pg 711
Institute of Development Studies, pg 712
Institute of Economic Affairs, pg 712
Institute of Education, University of London, pg 712
Inter-Varsity Press, pg 713
International Bee Research Association, pg 714
Islamic Foundation Publications, pg 714
JAI Press Ltd, pg 715
Janus Publishing Co Ltd, pg 716
Karnak House, pg 717
Jessica Kingsley Publishers, pg 718
Kogan Page Ltd, pg 718
Kuperard, pg 718
Ladybird Books Ltd, pg 719
The Latchmere Press, pg 719
Lawrence & Wishart, pg 719
LDA-Living & Learning (Cambridge) Ltd, pg 719
Learning Matters Ltd, pg 720
Learning Together, pg 720
Letterland International Ltd, pg 720
Liverpool University Press, pg 722
Lucis Press Ltd, pg 723
Lucky Duck Publishing Ltd, pg 723
The Lutterworth Press, pg 723
Management Pocketbooks Ltd, pg 724
McCrimmon Publishing Co Ltd, pg 726
Monarch Books, pg 729
Motilal (UK) Books of India, pg 729
Multilingual Matters Ltd, pg 729
National Assembly for Wales, pg 730
National Association for the Teaching of English (NATE), pg 730
National Centre for Language & Literacy, pg 730
National Extension College, pg 730
National Foundation for Educational Research, pg 731
National Institute of Adult Continuing Education (NIACE), pg 731
Nelson Thornes Ltd, pg 732
New Era Publications UK Ltd, pg 732
The NFER-NELSON Publishing Co Ltd, pg 733
Nile & Mackenzie Ltd, pg 733
James Nisbet & Co Ltd, pg 733
Northcote House Publishers Ltd, pg 733
Norwood Publishers Ltd, pg 734
Octagon Press Ltd, pg 734
Oneworld Publications, pg 735
Open University Press, pg 736
Open University Worldwide, pg 736
Oxford University Press, pg 737
Pan Macmillan, pg 738
Parapress Ltd, pg 738
Pearson Education, pg 739
Pearson Education Europe, Mideast & Africa, pg 739
Peepal Tree Press Ltd, pg 740
Pergamon Flexible Learning, pg 740
Philip & Tacey Ltd, pg 741
The Policy Press, pg 744
Policy Studies Institute (PSI), pg 744
Prim-Ed Publishing UK Ltd, pg 745
Qualum Publishing, pg 746
Quartz Editions, pg 746
Ravette Publishing Ltd, pg 748
Reader's Digest Children's Books, pg 748
Reed Educational & Professional Publishing, pg 749
The Robinswood Press Ltd, pg 750
Routledge, pg 751
Royal College of General Practitioners (RCGP), pg 752
The Royal Society, pg 752
SAGE Publications Ltd, pg 753
Scottish Executive Library & Information Services, pg 755
Scripture Union, pg 756
SEDA Publications, pg 756
Sherwood Publishing, pg 757
Southgate Publishers, pg 759
Speechmark Publishing Ltd, pg 760
SRHE, pg 760
Stacey International, pg 761
Stainer & Bell Ltd, pg 761
Rudolf Steiner Press, pg 761
Supportive Learning Publications, pg 762
Tarquin Publications, pg 762
Tate Publishing Ltd, pg 763
Taylor & Francis, pg 763
Telegraph Books, pg 764
Thoemmes Press, pg 765
Thrass (UK) Ltd, pg 765
Tobin Music, pg 766
Trentham Books Ltd, pg 767
Trotman Publishing, pg 767
TSO (The Stationery Office), pg 767
Ulster Historical Foundation, pg 768
University of Exeter Press, pg 768
University of Hertfordshire Press, pg 768
University of Wales Press, pg 769
The Vegetarian Society, pg 769
Veritas Foundation Publication Centre, pg 770
Virago Press, pg 770
Whiting & Birch Ltd, pg 773
Whurr Publishers Ltd, pg 773
The Woburn Press, pg 775

Uruguay
Ediciones de Juan Darien, pg 777
EQ Opciones en Educacion, pg 777
Nordan-Comunidad, pg 778
Ediciones Trilce, pg 778
Vinten Editor, pg 778

Venezuela
Monte Avila Editores Latinoamericana CA, pg 779
Fundacion Centro Gumilla, pg 779
Teduca, Tecnicas Educativas, CA, pg 780
Vadell Hermanos Editores CA, pg 780

Viet Nam
Giao Duc Publishing House, pg 780
Science & Technics Publishing House, pg 780

Zambia
Bookworld Ltd, pg 781
Wilfred Bwalya Chilangwa Publications, pg 781
Lundula Publishing House, pg 781
University of Zambia Press (UNZA Press), pg 782
Zambia Educational Publishing House, pg 782
Zambia Printing Company Ltd (ZPC), pg 782

Zimbabwe
Academic Books (Pvt) Ltd, pg 782
HarperCollins Publishers Zimbabwe Pvt Ltd, pg 783
Longman Zimbabwe (Pvt) Ltd, pg 783
Mercury Press Pvt Ltd, pg 784
Vision Publications, pg 784
Zimbabwe Foundation for Education with Production (ZIMFEP), pg 784
Zimbabwe Publishing House (Pvt) Ltd, pg 784
Zimbabwe Women's Bureau, pg 785

SUBJECT INDEX

ELECTRONICS, ELECTRICAL ENGINEERING

Albania
NL SH, pg 1
State Textbook Publishing House, pg 1

Argentina
Editorial Albatros SACI, pg 3
Editorial Idearium de la Universidad de Mendoza (EDIUM), pg 6

Australia
EA Books, pg 20
McGraw-Hill Australia Pty Ltd, pg 31
OTEN (Open Training & Education Network), pg 34
Standards Association of Australia, pg 42

Austria
Andreas Schnider Verlags-Atelier, pg 57
Springer-Verlag Wien, pg 58

Belgium
Documenta CV, pg 66
Easy Computing NV, pg 67

Brazil
Antenna Edicoes Tecnicas Ltda, pg 77
Editora Edgard Blucher Ltda, pg 79
Editora Campus Ltda, pg 79
Hemus Editora Ltda, pg 83
Livro Ibero-Americano Ltda, pg 83
Selecoes Eletronicas Editora Ltda, pg 90

Bulgaria
Makros 2000 - Plovdiv, pg 95
MATEX, pg 95
Todor Kableshkov University of Transport, pg 97

China
Chemical Industry Press, pg 101
China Machine Press (CMP), pg 102
Dalian Maritime University Press, pg 104
Electronics Industry Publishing House, pg 104
Fudan University Press, pg 104
Fujian Science & Technology Publishing House, pg 104
Heilongjiang Science & Technology Press, pg 105
Inner Mongolia Science & Technology Publishing House, pg 105
International Academic Publishers (IAP), pg 105
Jilin Science & Technology Publishing House, pg 105
Metallurgical Industry Press (MIP), pg 106
National Defence Industry Press, pg 106
New Times Press, pg 106
The People's Posts & Telecommunication Publishing House, pg 107
Printing Industry Publishing House, pg 107
Science Press, pg 107
Shandong Science & Technology Press, pg 107
Shandong University Press, pg 108
South China University of Science & Technology Press, pg 108
Southwest China Jiaotong University Press, pg 108
Tianjin Science & Technology Publishing House, pg 108
Tsinghua University Press, pg 109
Water Resources and Electric Power Press (CWPP), pg 109

Colombia
Cekit SA, pg 110

Czech Republic
Cesky normalizacni institut, pg 126

Dominican Republic
Pontificia Universidad Catolica Madre y Maestra, pg 136

Estonia
Valgus Publishers, pg 140

France
Editions Breal, pg 151
Codes Rousseau, pg 155
Dunod Editeur, pg 159
Institute Editeur, pg 160
Editions d'Organisation, pg 160
Editions Eyrolles, pg 162
Editions Hermes Science Publications, pg 167
Editions Lavoisier, pg 171
Polytechnica SA, pg 180
Editions Springer France, pg 186
Editions Technip SA, pg 187
Editions Weka, pg 189

SUBJECT INDEX

Germany
Beuth Verlag GmbH, pg 200
Verlag Erwin Bochinsky GmbH & Co KG, pg 202
Oscar Brandstetter Verlag GmbH & Co KG, pg 204
Verlag Harri Deutsch, pg 211
Elektor-Verlag GmbH, pg 219
Verlag Europa-Lehrmittel GmbH & Co KG, pg 221
expert verlag GmbH, Fachverlag fuer Wirtschaft & Technik, pg 222
Feltron-Elektronik Zeissler & Co GmbH, pg 223
Franz Ferzak World & Space Publications, pg 224
Festo Didactic GmbH & Co KG, pg 224
Franckh-Kosmos Verlags-GmbH & Co, pg 226
Franzis-Verlag GmbH, pg 226
frechverlag GmbH, pg 226
Carl Hanser Verlag, pg 234
Huss-Medien GmbH, pg 240
Huss-Verlag GmbH, pg 240
Huthig GmbH & Co KG, pg 240
ITpress Verlag, pg 242
Konradin-Verlagsgruppe, pg 249
R Oldenbourg Verlag GmbH, pg 267
Richard Pflaum Verlag GmbH & Co KG, pg 269
Springer Science+Business Media GmbH & Co KG, pg 284
B G Teubner Verlag, pg 290
UTB fuer Wissenschaft Uni Taschenbuecher GmbH, pg 294
VDE-Verlag GmbH, pg 294
Friedr Vieweg & Sohn Verlag, pg 296
Vogel Medien GmbH & Co KG, pg 296
WEKA Firmengruppe GmbH & Co KG, pg 298

Greece
Hiotellis P, pg 308
Kleidarithmos, Ekdoseis, pg 309

Hong Kong
Electronic Technology Publishing Co Ltd, pg 317
Technology Exchange Ltd, pg 319

Hungary
Foldmuvelesugyi Miniszterium Muszaki Intezet, pg 321
Magyar Tudomanyos Akademia Koezponti Fizikai Kutato Intezet Koenyvtara, pg 322
Mueszaki Koenyvkiado Ltd, pg 323

India
Addison-Wesley Pte Ltd, pg 327
Affiliated East West Press Pvt Ltd, pg 327
B I Publications Pvt Ltd, pg 329
BPB Publications, pg 331
BS Publications, pg 331
Heritage Publishers, pg 335
Khanna Publishers, pg 339
Laxmi Publications Pvt Ltd, pg 340
Pitambar Publishing Co (P) Ltd, pg 345
Scientific Book Agency, pg 348
Shaibya Prakashan Bibhag, pg 349
Sita Books & Periodicals Pvt Ltd, pg 349
South Asian Publishers Pvt Ltd, pg 350
Sultan Chand & Sons Pvt Ltd, pg 350
Viva Books Pvt Ltd, pg 352

Indonesia
Andi Offset, pg 353
Gramedia, pg 355
Institut Teknologi Bandung, pg 355

Italy
Edizioni Cremonese SRL, pg 383
DEI Tipographia del Genio Civile, pg 384
Editrice Edisco, pg 386
Giuseppe Laterza Editore, pg 391
Franco Muzzio Editore, pg 400
Tecniche Nuove SpA, pg 410
Zanichelli Editore SpA, pg 412

Japan
Bun-ichi Sogo Shuppan, pg 415
CMC Publishing Co Ltd, pg 416
Corona Publishing Co Ltd, pg 416
Fuji Keizai Company Ltd, pg 417
Gakken Co Ltd, pg 417
Iwanami Shoten, Publishers, pg 419
Keigaku Publishing Co Ltd, pg 420
Kindai Kagaku Sha Co Ltd, pg 421
Maruzen Co Ltd, pg 422
Nippon Hoso Shuppan Kyokai (NHK Publishing), pg 424
Sangyo-Tosho Publishing Co Ltd, pg 426
Seibundo Shinkosha Publishing Co Ltd, pg 426

Jordan
Al-Tanwir Al Ilmi (Scientific Enlightenment Publishing House), pg 432

Kenya
Kenya Meteorological Department, pg 435

Democratic People's Republic of Korea
Grand People's Study House, pg 436
Korea Science and Encyclopedia Publishing House, pg 436

Republic of Korea
Bo Moon Dang, pg 437
Chung Rim Publishing Co Ltd, pg 438

The Former Yugoslav Republic of Macedonia
Medis, Skopje, pg 452
Seizmoloska Opservatorija, pg 453

Malaysia
Penerbit Universiti Sains Malaysia, pg 458
Penerbit Universiti Teknologi Malaysia, pg 459

Mexico
Alfaomega Grupo Editor SA de CV, pg 462
Editorial Limusa SA de CV, pg 467
Sistemas Universales, SA, pg 472

Netherlands
Delft University Press, pg 481
Hagen & Stam Uitgeverij Ten, pg 483
IOS Press BV, pg 484
De Muiderkring BV, pg 486
Segment BV, pg 488

New Zealand
David's Marine Books, pg 495
Nelson Price Milburn Ltd, pg 499

Nigeria
Evans Brothers (Nigeria Publishers) Ltd, pg 504

Norway
NKI Forlaget, pg 510
Vett & Viten AS, pg 511

Poland
Wydawnictwa Komunikacji i Lacznosci Co Ltd, pg 524
Wydawnictwa Naukowo-Techniczne, pg 524
Polish Scientific Publishers PWN, pg 525
Wydawnictwa Przemyslowe WEMA, pg 526

Portugal
Dinalivro, pg 530
Editora McGraw-Hill de Portugal Lda, pg 533
Almerinda Teixeira, pg 536

Romania
Editura Academiei Romane, pg 538
Editura Dacia, pg 539
Editura Militara, pg 541
Editura Teora, pg 542

Russian Federation
N E Bauman Moscow State Technical University Publishers, pg 544
Energoatomizdat, pg 544
Izdatelstvo Mir, pg 546
Nauka Publishers, pg 547
Izdatel'stvo Nizhegorodskogo Gosudarstvennogo Univ, pg 547
Izdatelstvo Radio i Svyaz, pg 548

Serbia and Montenegro
Tehnicka Knjiga, pg 552
Savez Inzenjera i Tehnicara Jugoslavije, pg 553

Singapore
Reed Elsevier, South East Asia, pg 557
Tech Publications Pte Ltd, pg 558
World Scientific Publishing Co Pte Ltd, pg 559

Spain
AMV Ediciones, pg 572
CEAC, Grupo Editorial SA, pg 576
Editorial Dossat SA, pg 580
Marcombo SA, pg 590
Progensa, pg 597
Universidad de Santiago de Compostela, pg 599
Ediciones Tecnicas Rede, SA, pg 601
Universidad de Valladolid Secretariado de Publicaciones e Intercambio Editorial, pg 604
Edicions de la Universitat Politecnica de Catalunya SL, pg 604
Ediciones A Madrid Vicente, pg 605

Sweden
Allt om Hobby AB, pg 609

Switzerland
Marcel Dekker AG, pg 621
Verlag Harri Deutsch, pg 622
Elektrowirtschaft Verlag, pg 623
Verlag Industrielle Organisation, pg 625
Presses Polytechniques et Universitaires Romandes, PPUR, pg 631
Vogt-Schild Ag, Druck und Verlag, pg 636

Syrian Arab Republic
Damascus University Press, pg 638

Taiwan, Province of China
Fuh-Wen Book Co, pg 639
Hsiao Yuan Publication Co, Ltd, pg 640

United Republic of Tanzania
DUP (1996) Ltd, pg 643

Thailand
Graphic Art (28) Co Ltd, pg 645

Trinidad & Tobago
Caribbean Telecommunications Union, pg 647

Turkey
Caglayan Kitabevi, pg 649
Inkilap Publishers Ltd, pg 650
Yuce Reklam Yay Dagt AS, pg 652

United Kingdom
Artech House, pg 659
Bernard Babani (Publishing) Ltd, pg 662
Dickson Price Publishers Ltd, pg 687
Elsevier Ltd, pg 691
ERA Technology Ltd, pg 692
W H Freeman & Co Ltd, pg 697
Imperial College Press, pg 712
Institute of Physics Publishing, pg 713
Institution of Electrical Engineers, pg 713
James & James (Science Publishers) Ltd, pg 715
Kluwer Academic/Plenum Publishers, pg 718
Open University Worldwide, pg 736
PC Publishing, pg 739
ProQuest Information & Learning, pg 746
Research Studies Press Ltd (RSP), pg 749
Shire Publications Ltd, pg 757
The Society of Metaphysicians Ltd, pg 759
WIT Press, pg 774

Viet Nam
Science & Technics Publishing House, pg 780

Zimbabwe
Standards Association of Zimbabwe (SAZ), pg 784

PUBLISHERS SUBJECT INDEX

ENERGY

Albania
NL SH, pg 1
State Textbook Publishing House, pg 1

Austria
IAEA - International Atomic Energy Agency, pg 52
International Institute for Applied Systems Analysis (IIASA), pg 52
Metrica Fachverlag u Versandbuchhandlung Ing Bartak, pg 54

Brazil
Comissao Nacional de Energia Nuclear (CNEN), pg 80

Bulgaria
EnEffect, Center for Energy Efficiency, pg 94

China
Chemical Industry Press, pg 101
China Oil & Gas Periodical Office, pg 102
Shandong Science & Technology Press, pg 107
Shandong University Press, pg 108
Water Resources and Electric Power Press (CWPP), pg 109

Costa Rica
Editorial de la Universidad de Costa Rica, pg 116

Dominican Republic
Pontificia Universidad Catolica Madre y Maestra, pg 136

France
Editions Edisud, pg 159
Editions Entente, pg 161
L'Ere Nouvelle, pg 161
Editions Paradigme, pg 178
Polytechnica SA, pg 180
PYC Edition, pg 182
Editions Technip SA, pg 187
Terre Vivante, pg 187

Germany
Aerogie-Verlag, pg 191
AOL-Verlag Frohmut Menze, pg 193
Verlag Dr Albert Bartens KG, pg 197
Bauverlag GmbH, pg 198
Beuth Verlag GmbH, pg 200
Deutscher Verlag fur Grundstoffindustrie GmbH, pg 213
Deutscher Wirtschaftsdienst John von Freyend GmbH, pg 214
expert verlag GmbH, Fachverlag fuer Wirtschaft & Technik, pg 222
Franz Ferzak World & Space Publications, pg 224
Verlag Glueckauf GmbH, pg 229
Hessisches Ministerium fuer Umwelt, Landwirtschaft und Forsten, pg 237
Huthig GmbH & Co KG, pg 240
Institut fuer Landes- und Stadtentwicklungsforschung des Landes Nordrhein-Westfalen, pg 251

Marketing & Wirtschaft Verlagsges, Flade & Partner mbH, pg 257
C F Mueller Verlag, Huethig GmbH & Co, pg 262
Oekobuch Verlag & Versand GmbH, pg 266
Schulz-Kirchner Verlag GmbH, pg 282
Adolf Sponholtz Verlag, pg 284
Springer Science+Business Media GmbH & Co KG, pg 284
TUeV-Verlag GmbH, pg 293
UNO-Verlag GmbH, pg 293
Vulkan-Verlag GmbH, pg 297
WEKA Firmengruppe GmbH & Co KG, pg 298

Greece
Hestia-I D Hestia-Kollaros & Co Corporation, pg 308
Michalis Sideris, pg 312

Hong Kong
Friends of the Earth (Charity) Ltd, pg 317

Hungary
Foldmuvelesugyi Miniszterium Muszaki Intezet, pg 321

India
Agricole Publishing Academy, pg 327
Allied Book Centre, pg 328
Allied Publishers Pvt Ltd, pg 328
APH Publishing Corp, pg 328
BS Publications, pg 331
Concept Publishing Co, pg 332
Khanna Publishers, pg 339
Reliance Publishing House, pg 346
Scientific Book Agency, pg 348
Sita Books & Periodicals Pvt Ltd, pg 349
Viva Books Pvt Ltd, pg 352

Indonesia
PT Indira, pg 355

Italy
Franco Muzzio Editore, pg 400
Editrice San Marco SRL, pg 407
Tecniche Nuove SpA, pg 410

Kenya
Kenya Energy & Environment Organisation, Kengo, pg 434

Lithuania
Academia, pg 448

Mexico
Fondo de Cultura Economica, pg 465
Editorial Limusa SA de CV, pg 467

Namibia
Desert Research Foundation of Namibia (DRFN), pg 476

Netherlands
Hagen & Stam Uitgeverij Ten, pg 483

Portugal
Constancia Editores, SA, pg 530

Romania
Editura Academiei Romane, pg 538

Russian Federation
N E Bauman Moscow State Technical University Publishers, pg 544
Nauka Publishers, pg 547
Izdatelstvo Nedra, pg 547

Singapore
Institute of Southeast Asian Studies, pg 556

Spain
Editorial AEDOS SA, pg 571
Icaria Editorial SA, pg 587
Marcombo SA, pg 590
Progensa, pg 597

Switzerland
SAB Schweiz Arbeitsgemeinschaft fuer die Berggebiete, pg 633

United Kingdom
Association for Science Education, pg 661
Business Monitor International, pg 672
Centre for Alternative Technology, pg 677
CMP Information Ltd, pg 680
Commonwealth Secretariat, pg 681
Elsevier Ltd, pg 691
The Energy Information Centre, pg 691
The Eurospan Group, pg 692
Institution of Electrical Engineers, pg 713
James & James (Science Publishers) Ltd, pg 715
Oilfield Publications Ltd, pg 734
Professional Engineering Publishing Ltd, pg 745
Research Studies Press Ltd (RSP), pg 749
Royal Institute of International Affairs, pg 752
The Royal Society, pg 752
Scottish Executive Library & Information Services, pg 755
TSO (The Stationery Office), pg 767
Woodhead Publishing Ltd, pg 775

Viet Nam
Science & Technics Publishing House, pg 780

Zimbabwe
Standards Association of Zimbabwe (SAZ), pg 784

ENGINEERING (GENERAL)

Albania
NL SH, pg 1
State Textbook Publishing House, pg 1

Argentina
Diana Argentina SA, Editorial, pg 5
Editorial Idearium de la Universidad de Mendoza (EDIUM), pg 6

Australia
Blackwell Publishing Asia, pg 15
Hayes Publishing Co, pg 25
Histec Publications, pg 25

The Images Publishing Group Pty Ltd, pg 26
Macmillan Publishers Australia Pty Ltd, pg 30
McGraw-Hill Australia Pty Ltd, pg 31
Pearson Education Australia, pg 36
Regency Publishing, pg 39
RMIT Publishing, pg 39
Standards Association of Australia, pg 42
University of New South Wales Press Ltd, pg 44

Austria
Metrica Fachverlag u Versandbuchhandlung Ing Bartak, pg 54
Oesterreichischer Kunst und Kulturverlag, pg 55
Verlag Oldenbourg, pg 56
Springer-Verlag Wien, pg 58

Belgium
Presses Universitaires de Bruxelles asbl, pg 72

Brazil
Editora Edgard Blucher Ltda, pg 79
Editora Campus Ltda, pg 79
Comissao Nacional de Energia Nuclear (CNEN), pg 80
Editora FCO Ltda, pg 81
Livraria Kosmos Editora Ltda, pg 85
LTC-Livros Tecnicos e Cientificos Editora S/A, pg 85
Pearson Education Do Brasil, pg 88

Bulgaria
Todor Kableshkov University of Transport, pg 97

Chile
Arrayan Editores, pg 98
Pontificia Universidad Catolica de Chile, pg 100
Ediciones Universitarias de Valparaiso, pg 100

China
Beijing Publishing House, pg 101
Chemical Industry Press, pg 101
East China University of Science & Technology Press, pg 104
Higher Education Press, pg 105
International Academic Publishers (IAP), pg 105
Jiangsu Science & Technology Publishing House, pg 105
Jilin Science & Technology Publishing House, pg 105
Metallurgical Industry Press (MIP), pg 106
Printing Industry Publishing House, pg 107
Shandong Science & Technology Press, pg 107
Shandong University Press, pg 108
Shanghai Scientific & Technical Publishers, pg 108
Shanghai Scientific & Technological Literature Press, pg 108
Southwest China Jiaotong University Press, pg 108
Tianjin Science & Technology Publishing House, pg 108
Tsinghua University Press, pg 109
Water Resources and Electric Power Press (CWPP), pg 109

SUBJECT INDEX — BOOK

Colombia
Escala Ltda, pg 111
McGraw-Hill Colombia, pg 112

Costa Rica
Centro Agronomico Tropical de Investigacion y Ensenanza (CATIE), pg 115
Editorial de la Universidad de Costa Rica, pg 116

Croatia
Skolska Knjiga, pg 119
Tehnicka Knjiga, pg 119

Cuba
Editorial Cientifico Tecnica, pg 120

Czech Republic
Academia, pg 122
Cesky normalizacni institut, pg 126

Denmark
Akademisk Forlag A/S, pg 128
Ingenioeren/Boger, pg 132
Polyteknisk Boghandel & Forlag, pg 133

Dominican Republic
Pontificia Universidad Catolica Madre y Maestra, pg 136

Estonia
Valgus Publishers, pg 140

Finland
Docendo Finland Oy, pg 141

France
Cemagref Editions, pg 152
Chotard et Associes Editeurs, pg 154
Editions d'Organisation, pg 160
EDP Sciences, pg 161
Editions Eska, pg 162
Hachette Livre, pg 167
Editions Hermes Science Publications, pg 167
Editions Lavoisier, pg 171
Editions Pedone, pg 179
Polytechnica SA, pg 180
Presses Universitaires de France (PUF), pg 181
Editions Springer France, pg 186
Editions Technip SA, pg 187

Germany
Aerogie-Verlag, pg 191
Beuth Verlag GmbH, pg 200
Bibliographisches Institut & F A Brockhaus AG, pg 200
Brandenburgisches Verlagshaus in der Dornier Medienholding GmbH, pg 204
Oscar Brandstetter Verlag GmbH & Co KG, pg 204
Charles Coleman Verlag GmbH & Co KG, pg 209
Verlag Harri Deutsch, pg 211
Deutscher Fachverlag GmbH, pg 212
Deutscher Verlag fur Grundstoffindustrie GmbH, pg 213
Ecomed Verlagsgesellschaft AG & Co KG, pg 218
Elektor-Verlag GmbH, pg 219
Fachverlag Schiele & Schoen GmbH, pg 223
Franz Ferzak World & Space Publications, pg 224
Festo Didactic GmbH & Co KG, pg 224
Harald Fischer Verlag GmbH, pg 224
Rita G Fischer Verlag, pg 225
Franckh-Kosmos Verlags-GmbH & Co, pg 226
Alfons W Gentner Verlag GmbH & Co KG, pg 228
Gieck-Verlag GmbH, pg 229
Gloatz, Hille GmbH & Co KG fur Mehrfarben und Zellglasdruck, pg 229
Haag und Herchen Verlag GmbH, pg 232
Carl Hanser Verlag, pg 234
Hestra-Verlag Hernichel & Dr Strauss GmbH & Co KG, pg 237
Carl Heymanns Verlag KG, pg 237
S Hirzel Verlag GmbH und Co, pg 238
Huss-Verlag GmbH, pg 240
Kallmeyer'sche Verlagsbuchhandlung GmbH, pg 244
W Kohlhammer GmbH, pg 248
Konradin-Verlagsgruppe, pg 249
C F Mueller Verlag, Huethig GmbH & Co, pg 262
R Oldenbourg Verlag GmbH, pg 267
Verlag Walter Podszun Burobedarf-Bucher Abt, pg 270
Rationalisierungs-Kuratorium der Deutschen Wirtschaft eV (RKW), pg 273
Verlag Werner Sachon GmbH & Co, pg 277
Springer Science+Business Media GmbH & Co KG, pg 284
Springer Science+Business Media GmbH & Co KG, Berlin, pg 285
Verlag Stahleisen GmbH, pg 286
UTB fuer Wissenschaft Uni Taschenbuecher GmbH, pg 294
VDI Verlag GmbH, pg 294
Verlag fur Schweissen und Verwandte Verfahren, pg 295
Vulkan-Verlag GmbH, pg 297
WEKA Firmengruppe GmbH & Co KG, pg 298
Werner Verlag GmbH & Co KG, pg 299
Wison Verlag GmbH, pg 300

Greece
Giourdas Moschos, pg 307

Hungary
Akademiai Kiado, pg 320
Foldmuvelesugyi Miniszterium Muszaki Intezet, pg 321
Panem, pg 324
Springer Hungarica Kiado Kft, pg 324

India
Agricole Publishing Academy, pg 327
Atma Ram & Sons, pg 329
B I Publications Pvt Ltd, pg 329
Book Circle, pg 330
Bookionics, pg 331
BS Publications, pg 331
Charotar Publishing House, pg 332
Eurasia Publishing House Private Ltd, pg 334
Galgotia Publications Pvt Ltd, pg 334
Arnold Heinman Publishers (India) Pvt Ltd, pg 335
Heritage Publishers, pg 335
Jaico Publishing House, pg 338
Khanna Publishers, pg 339
Law Publishers, pg 340
Multitech Publishing Co, pg 342
Narosa Publishing House, pg 342
Oxford & IBH Publishing Co Pvt Ltd, pg 344
Oxonian Press (P) Ltd, pg 344
People's Publishing House (P) Ltd, pg 345
Scientific Book Agency, pg 348
Scientific Publishers India, pg 349
Sita Books & Periodicals Pvt Ltd, pg 349
Somaiya Publications Pvt Ltd, pg 349
South Asian Publishers Pvt Ltd, pg 350
Sultan Chand & Sons Pvt Ltd, pg 350
Tata McGraw-Hill Publishing Co Ltd, pg 351
Vikas Publishing House Pvt Ltd, pg 352
Viva Books Pvt Ltd, pg 352

Indonesia
PT Bulan Bintang, pg 354
Institut Teknologi Bandung, pg 355

Israel
Freund Publishing House Ltd, pg 367

Italy
Alinea, pg 375
BeMa, pg 377
Bianco, pg 377
Editoriale Bios, pg 378
Bulzoni Editore SRL (Le Edizioni Universitarie d'Italia), pg 379
Casa Editrice Libraria Ulrico Hoepli SpA, pg 380
CELID, pg 381
CLEUP - Cooperative Libraria Editrice dell'Universita di Padova, pg 382
Edizioni Cremonese SRL, pg 383
Etas Libri, pg 388
Gruppo Editoriale Faenza Editrice SpA, pg 391
Monduzzi Editore SpA, pg 399
Patron Editore SrL, pg 402
Pitagora Editrice SRL, pg 403
Il Sole 24 Ore Pirola, pg 409
Zanichelli Editore SpA, pg 412

Japan
Baifukan Co Ltd, pg 415
Bun-ichi Sogo Shuppan, pg 415
Chijin Shokan Co Ltd, pg 416
Kaibundo Shuppan, pg 420
Kajima Institute Publishing Co Ltd, pg 420
Kogyo Chosakai Publishing Co Ltd, pg 421
Kyoritsu Shuppan Co Ltd, pg 422
The Nikkan Kogyo Shimbun Ltd, pg 424
Ohmsha Ltd, pg 424
Sangyo-Tosho Publishing Co Ltd, pg 426
Shokokusha Publishing Co Ltd, pg 428
Tokyo Kagaku Dojin Co Ltd, pg 429
Universal Academy Press, Inc, pg 430
University of Tokyo Press, pg 430
Yokendo Ltd, pg 431

Jordan
Jordan Book Centre Co Ltd, pg 432

Kazakstan
Gylym, Izd-Vo, pg 432

Democratic People's Republic of Korea
Korea Science and Encyclopedia Publishing House, pg 436

Republic of Korea
Bo Moon Dang, pg 437
Hakmunsa Publishing Co, pg 439
Hyangmunsa Publishing Co, pg 439
Iljo-gag Publishers, pg 439
Ki Moon Dang, pg 440
Korea University Press, pg 440
Mun Un Dang, pg 441
Pearson Education Korea Ltd, pg 442

Lithuania
TEV Leidykla, pg 450

Malaysia
Penerbit Universiti Teknologi Malaysia, pg 459

Mexico
Alfaomega Grupo Editor SA de CV, pg 462
Compania Editorial Continental SA de CV, pg 463
Grupo Editorial Iberoamerica, SA de CV, pg 466
Editorial Limusa SA de CV, pg 467
McGraw-Hill Interamericana Editores, SA de CV, pg 468
Universidad Nacional Autonoma de Mexico (National University of Mexico), pg 472

Nepal
International Standards Books & Periodicals (P) Ltd, pg 476

Netherlands
A A Balkema Uitgevers BV, pg 478
Delft University Press, pg 481
Elsevier Science BV, pg 482
Hagen & Stam Uitgeverij Ten, pg 483
Swets & Zeitlinger Publishers, pg 489

Norway
Teknologisk Forlag, pg 510
Vett & Viten AS, pg 511

Peru
Universidad de Lima-Fondo de Desarollo Editorial, pg 517
Universidad Nacional Mayor de San Marcos, pg 517

Poland
Polish Scientific Publishers PWN, pg 525
Oficyna Wydawnicza Politechniki Wroclawskiej, pg 525

PUBLISHERS

Portugal
Dinalivro, pg 530
Publicacoes Europa-America Lda, pg 531
Gradiva-Publicacnoes Lda, pg 532
Editora McGraw-Hill de Portugal Lda, pg 533
Monitor-Projectos e Edicoes, LDA, pg 533

Puerto Rico
McGraw-Hill Intermericana del Caribe, Inc, pg 537

Romania
Editura Clusium, pg 539
Editura Militara, pg 541
Editura Niculescu, pg 541
Pallas-Akademia Editura, pg 541
Editura Tehnica, pg 542

Russian Federation
N E Bauman Moscow State Technical University Publishers, pg 544
FGUP Izdatelstvo Mashinostroenie, pg 544
Izdatelstvo Metallurgiya, pg 546
Izdatelstvo Mir, pg 546
Izdatelstvo Mordovskogo gosudar stvennogo, pg 547
Nauka Publishers, pg 547
Izdatel'stvo Nizhegorodskogo Gosudarstvennogo Univ, pg 547
Izdatelstvo Sudostroenie, pg 549

Serbia and Montenegro
Gradevinska Knjiga, pg 552
Tehnicka Knjiga, pg 552
Naucna Knjiga, pg 552
Izdavacka Organizacija Rad, pg 553
Savez Inzenjera i Tehnicara Jugoslavije, pg 553

Singapore
APAC Publishers Services Pte Ltd, pg 554
Taylor & Francis Asia Pacific, pg 558
World Scientific Publishing Co Pte Ltd, pg 559

South Africa
Educum Publishers Ltd, pg 563

Spain
AMV Ediciones, pg 572
CEAC, Grupo Editorial SA, pg 576
Ediciones Daly S L, pg 578
Editorial Donostiarra SA, pg 579
Editorial Dossat SA, pg 580
EUNSA (Ediciones Universidad de Navarra SA), pg 583
Editorial Reverte SA, pg 598
Servicio de Publicaciones Universidad de Cadiz, pg 599
Editorial Sintesis, SA, pg 600
Editores Tecnicos Asociados SA, pg 601
Universidad de Valladolid Secretariado de Publicaciones e Intercambio Editorial, pg 604
Edicions de la Universitat Politecnica de Catalunya SL, pg 604
Urmo SA de Ediciones, pg 604

Sweden
Studentlitteratur AB, pg 616

Switzerland
Birkhauser Verlag AG, pg 619
Presses Polytechniques et Universitaires Romandes, PPUR, pg 631
Vdf Hochschulverlag AG an der ETH Zurich, pg 636

Syrian Arab Republic
Damascus University Press, pg 638

Taiwan, Province of China
Chung Hwa Book Co Ltd, pg 639
Fuh-Wen Book Co, pg 639
Chu Hai Publishing (Taiwan) Co Ltd, pg 640
Wu Nan Book Co Ltd, pg 642

Turkey
Caglayan Kitabevi, pg 649
Eren Yayincilik ve Kitapcilik Ltd Sti, pg 650
Saray Medikal Yayin Tic Ltd Sti, pg 651

United Kingdom
Artech House, pg 659
Business Monitor International, pg 672
Cambridge University Press, pg 674
Concrete Information Ltd, pg 682
DMG Business Media Ltd, pg 688
Edition XII, pg 690
The Eurospan Group, pg 692
Hodder Education, pg 709
Imperial College Press, pg 712
IOM Communications Ltd, pg 714
Maney Publishing, pg 725
McGraw-Hill Publishing Company, pg 726
Nexus Special Interests, pg 733
Oxford University Press, pg 737
Palgrave Publishers Ltd, pg 737
Pearson Education, pg 739
Professional Engineering Publishing Ltd, pg 745
Research Studies Press Ltd (RSP), pg 749
The Royal Society, pg 752
The Royal Society of Chemistry, pg 752
SAGE Publications Ltd, pg 753
Springer-Verlag London Ltd, pg 760
Sutton Publishing Ltd, pg 762
Taylor & Francis, pg 763
Training Publications Ltd, pg 766
WIT Press, pg 774
Woodhead Publishing Ltd, pg 775

Viet Nam
Science & Technics Publishing House, pg 780

Zimbabwe
Standards Association of Zimbabwe (SAZ), pg 784

ENGLISH AS A SECOND LANGUAGE

Albania
NL SH, pg 1
State Textbook Publishing House, pg 1

Armenia
Arevik, pg 10

Australia
INT Press, pg 27
McGraw-Hill Australia Pty Ltd, pg 31
Melting Pot Press, pg 32
Mimosa Publications Pty Ltd, pg 32
OTEN (Open Training & Education Network), pg 34
Wileman Publications, pg 46

Austria
Development News Ltd, pg 50
Helbling Verlags-Gesellschaft mbH, pg 51
Oesterreichischer Bundesverlag Gmbh, pg 55
Oesterreichischer Gewerbeverlag GmbH, pg 55
Verlag Mag Wanzenbock, pg 59

Azerbaijan
Sada, Literaturno-Izdatel'skij Centr, pg 60

Belarus
Kavaler Publishers, pg 62

Belgium
De Boeck et Larcier SA, pg 64
Editions De Boeck-Larcier SA, pg 66
Marabout, pg 71
Uitgeverij De Sikkel NV, pg 73
Zuid-Nederlandse Uitgeverij NV/Central Uitgeverij, pg 75

Botswana
Maskew Miller Longman, pg 76

Brazil
Livraria Martins Fontes Editora Ltda, pg 81
Fundacao Sao Paulo, EDUC, pg 82
Libreria Editora Ltda, pg 85
Waldir Lima Editora, pg 85
Editora Meca Ltda, pg 86
Editora Melhoramentos Ltda, pg 86

Bulgaria
Factor-Alias, pg 94
Izdatelstvo Lettera, pg 95
Prozoretz Ltd Publishing House, pg 96
Regalia 6 Publishing House, pg 96
Sanra Book Trust, pg 96
Seven Hills Publishers, pg 96

China
Aviation Industry Press, pg 101
Beijing Publishing House, pg 101
Beijing University Press, pg 101
China Braille Publishing House, pg 102
China Foreign Economic Relations & Trade Publishing House, pg 102
Dalian Maritime University Press, pg 104
East China University of Science & Technology Press, pg 104
Education Science Publishing House, pg 104
Foreign Language Teaching & Research Press, pg 104
Fudan University Press, pg 104
Guangdong Science & Technology Press, pg 105
Higher Education Press, pg 105

SUBJECT INDEX

Jilin Science & Technology Publishing House, pg 105
Nanjing University Press, pg 106
New Times Press, pg 106
Shandong Science & Technology Press, pg 107
Shandong University Press, pg 108
Shanghai Educational Publishing House, pg 108
Shanghai Far East Publishers, pg 108
Shanghai Foreign Language Education Press, pg 108
Tianjin Science & Technology Publishing House, pg 108
Tsinghua University Press, pg 109
Wuhan University Press, pg 109
Yunnan University Press, pg 109
Zhejiang Education Publishing House, pg 109

Colombia
Editorial Panamericana, pg 112

Costa Rica
Editorial de la Universidad de Costa Rica, pg 116

Denmark
Forlaget alokke AS, pg 129
Gads Forlag, pg 131
Kaleidoscope Publishers Ltd, pg 132
Samfundslitteratur, pg 134
Systime, pg 135

Dominican Republic
Pontificia Universidad Catolica Madre y Maestra, pg 136

Egypt (Arab Republic of Egypt)
Dar El Shorouk, pg 138

Estonia
Valgus Publishers, pg 140

France
Editions Jean Paul Gisserot, pg 165
Hachette Livre International, pg 167
Editions Hatier SA, pg 167
Editions Ophrys, pg 177
Editions Spratbrow, pg 186

Germany
AOL-Verlag Frohmut Menze, pg 193
Bayerischer Schulbuch-Verlag GmbH, pg 198
Compact Verlag GmbH, pg 209
Cornelsen Verlag GmbH & Co OHG, pg 210
Finken Verlag GmbH, pg 224
Knowledge Media International, pg 247
Logophon Verlag und Bildungsreisen GmbH, pg 255
Orbis Verlag fur Publizistik GmbH, pg 267
Verlag Sigrid Persen, pg 269
Verlag an der Ruhr GmbH, pg 277
Stauffenburg Verlag Brigitte Narr GmbH, pg 287
Stiefel Eurocart GmbH, pg 288
TR - Verlagsunion GmbH, pg 291

Ghana
Beginners Publishers, pg 303
Frank Publishing Ltd, pg 304

Ghana Institute of Linguistics Literacy & Bible Translation (GILLBT), pg 304
Kwamfori Publishing Enterprise, pg 304
Manhill Publication, pg 304
Sam Woode Ltd, pg 304
Sedco Publishing Ltd, pg 305

Greece
Alamo Hellas, pg 305
Macmillan Heinemann ELT, pg 310
Pagoulatos Bros, pg 311
Pagoulatos G-G P Publications, pg 311
Scripta Theofilus Palevratzis-Ashover, pg 312
Michalis Sideris, pg 312

Haiti
Editions Caraibes SA, pg 314

Hong Kong
Book Marketing Ltd, pg 315
Chung Hwa Book Co (HK) Ltd, pg 316
Hong Kong University Press, pg 317
Lea Publications Ltd, pg 318
Ling Kee Publishing Group, pg 318
Sesame Publication Co, pg 319

India
Addison-Wesley Pte Ltd, pg 327
Ambar Prakashan, pg 328
Bhawan Book Service, Publishers & Distributors, pg 330
Doaba Publications, pg 333
Frank Brothers & Co Publishers Ltd, pg 334
General Book Depot, pg 335
Shaibya Prakashan Bibhag, pg 349
Somaiya Publications Pvt Ltd, pg 349
Star Publications (P) Ltd, pg 350
Sterling Publishers Pvt Ltd, pg 350
Sultan Chand & Sons Pvt Ltd, pg 350
S Viswanathan (Printers & Publishers) Pvt Ltd, pg 352
Viva Books Pvt Ltd, pg 352

Indonesia
PT Indira, pg 355

Israel
Gefen Publishing House Ltd, pg 367
Intermedia Audio, Video Book Publishing Ltd, pg 368
K Dictionaries Ltd, pg 369
Kernerman Publishing Ltd, pg 369
University Publishing Projects Ltd, pg 373

Italy
Archimede Edizioni, pg 376
Arcipelago Edizioni di Chiani Marisa, pg 376
BeMa, pg 377
Casa Editrice Giuseppe Principato Spa, pg 380
Editrice Edisco, pg 386
Hora, pg 392
Loescher Editore SRL, pg 396
Macmillan Heinemann ELT, pg 396
Milella di Lecce Spazio Vivo srl, pg 398
Paravia Bruno Mondadori Editori, pg 402

Principato, pg 404
Zanichelli Editore SpA, pg 412

Japan
Eichosha Company Ltd, pg 417
Kaitakusha, pg 420
Nihon-Bunkyo Shuppan (Japan Educational Publishing Co Ltd), pg 423
Nippon Hoso Shuppan Kyokai (NHK Publishing), pg 424
Pearson Education Japan, pg 425
Sanshusha Publishing Co, Ltd, pg 426
Seibido, pg 426
Thomson Learning Japan, pg 429
Tokyo Shoseki Co Ltd, pg 430
Yamaguchi Shoten, pg 431
Yohan Shuppan, pg 431

Kenya
Danmar Publishers, pg 433
Dhillon Publishers Ltd, pg 433
Focus Publications Ltd, pg 433

Republic of Korea
Chung Rim Publishing Co Ltd, pg 438
Hakmunsa Publishing Co, pg 439
Hongik Media Plus Ltd, pg 439
Ke Mong Sa Publishing Co Ltd, pg 440
Koreaone Press Inc, pg 440
Moon Jin Media Co Ltd, pg 441
Pyeong-hwa Chulpansa, pg 442
Sohaksa, pg 443
Woongjin.com Co Ltd, pg 443
YBM/Si-sa, pg 443

Latvia
Avots, pg 444
Zvaigzne ABC Publishers Ltd, pg 445

Lebanon
Librairie Orientale sal, pg 446

Lithuania
Alma Littera, pg 448
Dargenis Publishers, pg 449
Sviesa Publishers, pg 449
Svietimo ir mokslo ministerijos Leidybos centras, pg 449

Luxembourg
Eiffes Romain, pg 451

The Former Yugoslav Republic of Macedonia
Murgorski Zoze, pg 453

Madagascar
Foibe Filan-Kevitry NY Mpampianatra (FOFIPA), pg 453

Malaysia
S Abdul Majeed & Co, pg 454
Federal Publications Sdn Bhd, pg 455
Mahir Publications Sdn Bhd, pg 456
Minerva Publications, pg 457
Penerbit Jayatinta Sdn Bhd, pg 458
Penerbitan Pelangi Sdn Bhd (Pelangi Publishing Pte Ltd), pg 458
Penerbitan Tinta, pg 458

Pustaka Cipta Sdn Bhd, pg 458
Pustaka Delta Pelajaran Sdn Bhd, pg 458

Maldive Islands
Non-Formal Education Centre, pg 459

Mexico
Ediciones Larousse SA de CV, pg 467
Selector SA de CV, pg 471
Sistemas Universales, SA, pg 472
Editorial Trillas SA de CV, pg 472

Netherlands
Uitgeverij Coutinho BV, pg 481

New Zealand
ESA Publications (NZ) Ltd, pg 496
Maori Publications Unit, pg 498
New House Publishers Ltd, pg 499
Taylor Books, pg 501

Nigeria
Vantage Publishers International Ltd, pg 507

Norway
NKI Forlaget, pg 510

Pakistan
Academy of Education Planning & Management (AEPAM), pg 511
International Educational Services, pg 512

Peru
Ediciones Brown SA, pg 516

Philippines
Bookman Printing & Publishing House Inc, pg 518
Saint Mary's Publishing Corp, pg 520
SIBS Publishing House Inc, pg 521
UST Publishing House, pg 521

Poland
Energeia sp zoo Wydawnictwo, pg 523
Polish Scientific Publishers PWN, pg 525
'Slask' Ltd, pg 526
Oficyna Wydawnicza Szkoly Glownej Handlowej w Warszawie Oficyna Wydawnicza SGH, pg 527
Wydawnictwa Uniwersytetu Warszawskiego, pg 527

Portugal
Constancia Editores, SA, pg 530
Editora Replicacao Lda, pg 535
Solivros, pg 536

Puerto Rico
McGraw-Hill Intermericana del Caribe, Inc, pg 537

Romania
Coresi SRL, pg 539
Editura Institutul European, pg 540
Editura Niculescu, pg 541

Russian Federation
Airis Press, pg 543
Izdatel'stvo Nizhegorodskogo Gosudarstvennogo Univ, pg 547
Okoshko Ltd Publishers (Izdatelstvo), pg 547
Russkij Jazyk, pg 548

Singapore
Hillview Publications Pte Ltd, pg 556
Success Publications Pte Ltd, pg 558

Slovakia
Slovenske pedagogicke nakladateistvo, pg 560

Slovenia
Zalozba Mihelac d o o, pg 562
Zalozba Obzorja d d Maribor, pg 562

South Africa
Clever Books, pg 563
Heinemann Educational Publishers Southern Africa, pg 564
Ivy Publications, pg 565
Jacana Education, pg 565
New Africa Books (Pty) Ltd, pg 567

Spain
Ediciones Akal SA, pg 571
Anglo-Didactica, SL Editorial, pg 573
Didaco Comunicacion y Didactica, SA, pg 579
Editorial Espasa-Calpe SA, pg 582
Sociedad General Espanola de Libreria SA - SGEL, pg 600

Sri Lanka
Colombo Book Association, pg 606
Samayawardena Printers Publishers & Booksellers, pg 607

Sweden
Akademiforlaget Goteborgslitteratur, pg 609
Ekelunds Forlag AB, pg 611
Hans Richter Laromedel, pg 613
Liber AB, pg 613

Switzerland
Editions Pro Schola, pg 631

Syrian Arab Republic
Damascus University Press, pg 638

Taiwan, Province of China
Farseeing Publishing Company Ltd, pg 639
Hsiao Yuan Publication Co, Ltd, pg 640
Jillion Publishing Co, pg 640
Linking Publishing Company Ltd, pg 641
Shuttle Multimedia Inc, pg 641
Sinorama Magazine Co, pg 641

United Republic of Tanzania
Ben and Company Ltd, pg 643
Nyota Publishers Ltd, pg 644
Tanzania Publishing House, pg 644

PUBLISHERS

Thailand
New Generation Publishing Co Ltd, pg 645

Turkey
Arkadas Ltd, pg 649
Pearson Education Turkey, pg 651

Ukraine
ASK Ltd, pg 653
Osvita, pg 654

United Kingdom
BBC English, pg 663
The British Council, Design, Publishing & Print Department, pg 671
Cambridge University Press, pg 674
English Teaching Professional, pg 691
EPER, pg 691
Evans Brothers Ltd, pg 693
Garnet Publishing Ltd, pg 698
Graham-Cameron Publishing & Illustration, pg 701
HarperCollins UK, pg 705
Hugo's Language Books Ltd, pg 710
Impart Books, pg 712
Ladybird Books Ltd, pg 719
Language Teaching Publications, pg 719
Letterbox Library, pg 720
Magi Publications, pg 724
National Association for the Teaching of English (NATE), pg 730
National Centre for Language & Literacy, pg 730
National Extension College, pg 730
Reed Educational & Professional Publishing, pg 749
The Robinswood Press Ltd, pg 750
Supportive Learning Publications, pg 762

Viet Nam
Science & Technics Publishing House, pg 780

Zambia
Lundula Publishing House, pg 781

Zimbabwe
College Press Publishers (Pvt) Ltd, pg 783
HarperCollins Publishers Zimbabwe Pvt Ltd, pg 783
Longman Zimbabwe (Pvt) Ltd, pg 783
Mercury Press Pvt Ltd, pg 784

ENVIRONMENTAL STUDIES

Argentina
Editorial Albatros SACI, pg 3
Cesarini Hermanos, pg 4
Editorial Idearium de la Universidad de Mendoza (EDIUM), pg 6
Marymar Ediciones SA, pg 7
Editorial Paidos SAICF, pg 8
Editorial Planeta Argentina SAIC, pg 8

Australia
Appropriate Technology Development Group (Inc) WA, pg 11
Australian Academy of Science, pg 13
Australian Marine Conservation Society Inc (AMCS), pg 13
Australian Scholarly Publishing, pg 13
Beazer Publishing Company Pty Ltd, pg 14
Robert Berthold Photography, pg 14
Candlelight Trust T/A Candlelight Farm, pg 17
Chiron Media, pg 17
CSIRO Publishing (Commonwealth Scientific & Industrial Research Organisation), pg 19
Dabill Publications, pg 19
Deakin University Press, pg 19
Dellasta Publishing, pg 19
Envirobook, pg 21
The Federation Press, pg 22
Hartys Creek Press, pg 25
Illert Publications, pg 26
Law Book Co Information Services, pg 28
McGraw-Hill Australia Pty Ltd, pg 31
Mulavon Press Pty Ltd, pg 32
Ocean Press, pg 34
Oxfam Community Aid Abroad, pg 35
Palms Press, pg 35
Pioneer Design Studio Pty Ltd, pg 37
Pluto Press Australia Pty Ltd, pg 37
Prospect Media Pty Ltd, pg 37
Rainforest Publishing, pg 38
Reed Educational Publishing Australia, pg 39
Royal Society of New South Wales, pg 40
Spinifex Press, pg 42
Terania Rainforest Publishing, pg 43
University of New South Wales Press Ltd, pg 44
Vista Publications, pg 45
Yanagang Publishing, pg 47

Austria
Abakus Verlag GmbH, pg 48
Bohmann Druck und Verlag GmbH & Co KG, pg 49
Edition Ergo Sum, pg 50
IAEA - International Atomic Energy Agency, pg 52
International Institute for Applied Systems Analysis (IIASA), pg 52
NOI - Verlag, pg 55
Oesterreichischer Agrarverlag, Druck- und Verlags- GmbH, pg 55
Verlag Orac im Verlag Kremayr & Scheriau, pg 56
Springer-Verlag Wien, pg 58

Bangladesh
The University Press Ltd, pg 61

Belarus
Narodnaya Asveta, pg 62

Belgium
Artel, pg 63
Editions De Boeck-Larcier SA, pg 66
Leuven University Press, pg 70
Presses agronomiques de Gembloux ASBL, pg 72
VUB Brussels University Press, pg 74

Botswana
The Botswana Society, pg 76

Brazil
Editora Aquariana Ltda, pg 77
Editora Campus Ltda, pg 79
Comissao Nacional de Energia Nuclear (CNEN), pg 80
Editora Gaia Ltda, pg 82
Editora Globo SA, pg 82
Editora Ground Ltda, pg 83
Editora Guanabara Koogan SA, pg 83
Editora Index Ltda, pg 84
Qualitymark Editora Ltda, pg 89
Editora Scipione Ltda, pg 90

Bulgaria
Darzhavno Izdatelstvo Zemizdat, pg 93
EnEffect, Center for Energy Efficiency, pg 94
Gea-Libris Publishing House, pg 94
Pensoft Publishers, pg 96

Chile
Arrayan Editores, pg 98
Cetal Ediciones, pg 99

China
Beijing Medical University Press, pg 101
Chemical Industry Press, pg 101
China Ocean Press, pg 102
East China University of Science & Technology Press, pg 104
Jiangsu Science & Technology Publishing House, pg 105
Jilin Science & Technology Publishing House, pg 105
Metallurgical Industry Press (MIP), pg 106
Nanjing University Press, pg 106
Science Press, pg 107
Shandong Science & Technology Press, pg 107
Shandong University Press, pg 108
Water Resources and Electric Power Press (CWPP), pg 109
Xi'an Cartography Publishing House, pg 109

Colombia
Amazonas Editores Ltda, pg 110
Tercer Mundo Editores SA, pg 113
Universidad Nacional Abierta y a Distancia, pg 113

The Democratic Republic of the Congo
Centre de Vulgarisation Agricole, pg 114

Costa Rica
Academia de Centro America, pg 114
Centro Agronomico Tropical de Investigacion y Ensenanza (CATIE), pg 115
Instituto Interamericano de Cooperacion para la Agricultura (IICA), pg 115
Union Mundial para la Naturaleza (UICN), Oficina Regional para Mesoamerica, pg 116
Editorial de la Universidad de Costa Rica, pg 116

Cote d'Ivoire
Universite d'Abidjan, pg 117

Croatia
Drzavna Uprava za Zastitu Prirode i Okolisa (State Directorate for the Protection of Nature & Environment), pg 118

Cuba
ISCAH Fructuoso Rodriguez, pg 120

Czech Republic
Doplnek, pg 123
Cesky normalizacni institut, pg 126

Denmark
Bogfabrikken Fakta ApS, pg 129
Borgens Forlag A/S, pg 129
Gads Forlag, pg 131
Host & Son Publishers Ltd, pg 132
Forlaget Hovedland, pg 132
IT-og Telestyrelsen, pg 132
Samfundslitteratur, pg 134
Schultz Information, pg 134

Dominican Republic
Pontificia Universidad Catolica Madre y Maestra, pg 136

Ecuador
Ediciones Abya-Yala, pg 136

Fiji
University of the South Pacific, pg 141

Finland
Yliopistopaino/Helsinki University Press, pg 145

France
Editions de l'Aube, pg 148
Pierre Bordas & Fils, Editions, pg 150
Presses Universitaires de Bordeaux (PUB), pg 150
Editions Bornemann, pg 150
Editions BRGM, pg 151
Cemagref Editions, pg 152
CNRS Editions, pg 155
Editions Courrier du Livre, pg 156
Editeurs Crepin-Leblond, pg 156
Editions du Demi-Cercle, pg 157
Institut pour le Developpement Forestier, pg 158
La Documentation Francaise, pg 158
Editions Edisud, pg 159
Editions Grund, pg 160
Editions Entente, pg 161
Institut Francais de Recherche pour l'Exploitation de la Mer (IFREMER), pg 164
Futuribles SARL, pg 164
Hachette Livre International, pg 167
Editions Hatier SA, pg 167
INRA Editions (Institut National de la Recherche Agronomique), pg 168
IRD Editions, pg 169
Editions Lavoisier, pg 171

Editions Legislatives, pg 171
Editions John Libbey Eurotext, pg 172
Le Livre de Poche-L G F (Librairie Generale Francaise), pg 173
Revue Espaces et Societes, pg 183
Editions Sang de la Terre, pg 184
Selection du Reader's Digest SA, pg 184
Service des Publications Scientifiques du Museum National d'Histoire Naturelle, pg 184
Societe Nouveaux Loisirs, pg 185
Editions Vague Verte, pg 188

Germany

Aerogie-Verlag, pg 191
ALS-Verlag GmbH, pg 192
AOL-Verlag Frohmut Menze, pg 193
Roland Asanger Verlag GmbH, pg 194
Baken-Verlag Walter Schnoor, pg 196
Dr Wolfgang Baur Verlag Kunst & Alltag, pg 198
Bauverlag GmbH, pg 198
Bayerischer Schulbuch-Verlag GmbH, pg 198
Berliner Wissenschafts-Verlag GmbH (BWV), pg 199
Beuth Verlag GmbH, pg 200
Blackwell Wissenschafts-Verlag GmbH, pg 201
Eberhard Blottner Verlag GmbH, pg 202
Deutscher Verlag fur Grundstoffindustrie GmbH, pg 213
Deutscher Wirtschaftsdienst John von Freyend GmbH, pg 214
Verlag J H W Dietz Nachf GmbH, pg 214
DLV Deutscher Landwirtschaftsverlag GmbH, pg 215
agenda Verlag Thomas Dominikowski, pg 215
Dreisam Ratgeber in der Rutsker Verlag GmbH, pg 216
Duncker und Humblot GmbH, pg 217
Echo Verlag, pg 217
Ecomed Verlagsgesellschaft AG & Co KG, pg 218
EinfallsReich Verlagsgesellschaft MbH, pg 219
Elektor-Verlag GmbH, pg 219
expert verlag GmbH, Fachverlag fuer Wirtschaft & Technik, pg 222
Fabel-Verlag Gudrun Liebchen, pg 223
Focus-Verlag Gesellschaft mbH, pg 225
Franckh-Kosmos Verlags-GmbH & Co, pg 226
Fraunhofer IRB Verlag Fraunhofer Informationszentrum Raum und Bau, pg 226
Verlag A Fromm im Druck- u Verlagshaus Fromm GmbH & Co KG, pg 227
Alfons W Gentner Verlag GmbH & Co KG, pg 228
Verlag Glueckauf GmbH, pg 229
Lehrmittelverlag Wilhelm Hagemann GmbH, pg 233
Carl Hanser Verlag, pg 234
Hessisches Ministerium fuer Umwelt, Landwirtschaft und Forsten, pg 237

F Hirthammer Verlag GmbH, pg 238
Horlemann Verlag, pg 239
IKO Verlag fur Interkulturelle Kommunikation, pg 241
Justus-Liebig-Universitat Giessen, pg 244
Kallmeyer'sche Verlagsbuchhandlung GmbH, pg 244
Kleiner Bachmann Verlag fur Kinder und Umwelt, pg 246
Verlag Waldemar Kramer, pg 250
Kulturbuch-Verlag GmbH, pg 250
Institut fuer Landes- und Stadtentwicklungsforschung des Landes Nordrhein-Westfalen, pg 251
Libertas- Europaeisches Institut GmbH, pg 254
Margraf Verlag, pg 257
Metropolis- Verlag fur Okonomie, Gesellschaft und Politik GmbH, pg 259
Verlag Stephanie Naglschmid, pg 263
Verlag Natur & Wissenschaft Harro Hieronimus & Dr Jurgen Schmidt, pg 263
Neue Erde Verlags GmbH, pg 264
Verlag Neuer Weg, pg 264
Neumann Verlag, pg 264
Nusser Verlag, pg 266
Oeko-Test Verlag GmbH & Co KG Betriebsgesellschaft, pg 266
Oekobuch Verlag & Versand GmbH, pg 266
Oekotopia Verlag, Wolfgang Hoffman GmbH & Co KG, pg 266
Pala-Verlag GmbH, pg 268
Palazzi Verlag GmbH, pg 268
Pollner Verlag, pg 271
Pro Natur Verlag GmbH, pg 272
Psychologie Verlags Union GmbH, pg 272
Dr Josef Raabe-Verlags GmbH, pg 273
Reed Elsevier Deutschland GmbH, pg 274
Verlag an der Ruhr GmbH, pg 277
Ryvellus Medienagentur Dopfer, pg 277
Schapen Edition, H W Louis, pg 279
Schillinger Verlag GmbH, pg 279
E Schweizerbart'sche Verlagsbuchhandlung (Naegele und Obermiller), pg 282
Seibt Verlag GmbH, pg 282
Adolf Sponholtz Verlag, pg 284
Springer Science+Business Media GmbH & Co KG, pg 284
Stiefel Eurocart GmbH, pg 288
TUeV-Verlag GmbH, pg 293
Guenter Albert Ulmer Verlag, pg 293
Verlag Eugen Ulmer GmbH & Co, pg 293
UNO-Verlag GmbH, pg 293
VAS-Verlag fuer Akademische Schriften, pg 294
Vogel Medien GmbH & Co KG, pg 296
Ellen Vogt Garbe Verlag, pg 296
Vulkan-Verlag GmbH, pg 297
Weber Zucht & Co, pg 298
WEKA Firmengruppe GmbH & Co KG, pg 298
Verlagsgruppe Weltbild GmbH, pg 298
Zebulon Verlag GmbH & Co KG, pg 302

Ghana

Ghana Institute of Linguistics Literacy & Bible Translation (GILLBT), pg 304
Sub-Saharan Publishers, pg 305
Unimax Macmillan Ltd, pg 305

Greece

Boukoumanis' Editions, pg 306
Exandas Publishers, pg 307
Papazissis Publishers SA, pg 311

Guinea-Bissau

Instituto Nacional de Estudos e Pesquisa (INEP), pg 314

Holy See (Vatican City State)

Pontificia Academia Scientiarum, pg 314

Honduras

Editorial Guaymuras, pg 315

Hong Kong

Friends of the Earth (Charity) Ltd, pg 317
Hong Kong University Press, pg 317
Island Press, pg 317
Joint Publishing (HK) Co Ltd, pg 317

Hungary

Foldmuvelesugyi Miniszterium Muszaki Intezet, pg 321
Mezogazda Kiado, pg 323

India

Affiliated East West Press Pvt Ltd, pg 327
Agricole Publishing Academy, pg 327
Allied Book Centre, pg 328
Anmol Publications Pvt Ltd, pg 328
APH Publishing Corp, pg 328
Bani Mandir, Book-Sellers, Publishers & Educational Suppliers, pg 329
BS Publications, pg 331
BSMPS - M/s Bishen Singh Mahendra Pal Singh, pg 331
Concept Publishing Co, pg 332
Daya Publishing House, pg 333
Frank Brothers & Co Publishers Ltd, pg 334
Gyan Publishing House, pg 335
IBD Publisher & Distributors, pg 336
Indus Publishing Co, pg 338
International Book Distributors, pg 338
Kali For Women, pg 339
Khanna Publishers, pg 339
Law Publishers, pg 340
Ministry of Information & Broadcasting, pg 341
Narosa Publishing House, pg 342
National Book Organization, pg 342
Naya Prokash, pg 343
Omsons Publications, pg 344
Pointer Publishers, pg 345
Radiant Publishers, pg 346
Regency Publications, pg 346
Reliance Publishing House, pg 346
SAGE Publications India Pvt Ltd, pg 347
Scientific Book Agency, pg 348
Sita Books & Periodicals Pvt Ltd, pg 349

South Asian Publishers Pvt Ltd, pg 350
Viva Books Pvt Ltd, pg 352

Indonesia

Karya Anda, CV, pg 355
Lembaga Demografi Fakultas Ekonomi Universitas Indonesia, pg 355
Yayasan Obor Indonesia, pg 357

Ireland

The Economic & Social Research Institute, pg 359
Environmental Research Unit, pg 359
Gandon Editions, pg 360
O'Brien Educational, pg 362
Roberts Rinehart Publishers, pg 363
Royal Irish Academy, pg 363
Tir Eolas, pg 363
Veritas Co Ltd, pg 364

Israel

Freund Publishing House Ltd, pg 367
The Israel Academy of Sciences & Humanities, pg 368

Italy

Gruppo Abele, pg 374
Edizioni Abete, pg 374
Arcadia Edizioni Srl, pg 375
Edizioni Cultura della Pace, pg 383
Datanews, pg 384
Ediciclo Editore SRL, pg 386
Editoriale Fernando Folini, pg 389
Edizioni Futuro SRL, pg 389
Edizioni GB, pg 390
Vincenzo Lo Faro Editore, pg 395
Macro Edizioni, pg 397
Pitagora Editrice SRL, pg 403
Priuli e Verlucca, Editori, pg 404
Red/Studio Redazionale, pg 405
SEMAR Publishers SRL, pg 408
Edizioni Zara, pg 412

Jamaica

American Chamber of Commerce of Jamaica, pg 413
University of the West Indies Press, pg 414

Japan

Bun-ichi Sogo Shuppan, pg 415
Diamond Inc, pg 416
Gakken Co Ltd, pg 417
Kaisei-Sha Publishing Co Ltd, pg 420
Koyo Shobo, pg 422
Nippon Hoso Shuppan Kyokai (NHK Publishing), pg 424
Nosangyoson Bunka Kyokai, pg 424
Toppan Co Ltd, pg 430
Tsukiji Shokan Publishing Co, pg 430
United Nations University Press, pg 430

Kazakstan

Al-Farabi Kazakh National University, pg 432

Kenya

Academy Science Publishers, pg 432
African Centre for Technology Studies (ACTS), pg 433
International Centre for Research in Agroforestry (ICRAF), pg 434

PUBLISHERS

Kenya Energy & Environment Organisation, Kengo, pg 434
Kenya Medical Research Institute (KEMRI), pg 435
Kenya Meteorological Department, pg 435
Phoenix Publishers Ltd, pg 435
Tree Shade Technical Services, pg 436

Republic of Korea

Dae Won Sa Co Ltd, pg 438
Gim-Yeong Co, pg 438
Koreaone Press Inc, pg 440

Latvia

Nordik/Tapals Publishers Ltd, pg 445
Preses Nams, pg 445

Madagascar

Tsipika Edition, pg 454

Malaysia

Penerbit Jayatinta Sdn Bhd, pg 458
Pustaka Delta Pelajaran Sdn Bhd, pg 458

Maldive Islands

Non-Formal Education Centre, pg 459

Mexico

Arbol Editorial SA de CV, pg 462
Centro de Estudios Mexicanos y Centroamericanos, pg 463
El Colegio de Mexico AC, pg 463
El Colegio de Michoacan A C, pg 464
Fernandez Editores SA de CV, pg 465
Grupo Editorial Iberoamerica, SA de CV, pg 466
Ediciones Roca, SA, pg 471

Namibia

Desert Research Foundation of Namibia (DRFN), pg 476
Multi-Disciplinary Research Centre Library, pg 476

Netherlands

Uitgeverij Jan van Arkel, pg 478
A A Balkema Uitgevers BV, pg 478
Boom Uitgeverij, pg 479
Hagen & Stam Uitgeverij Ten, pg 483
IOS Press BV, pg 484
KITLV Press Royal Institute of Linguistics & Anthropology, pg 484
Koninklijke Vermande bv, pg 485
Uitgeverij Het Spectrum BV, pg 489
Twente University Press, pg 490

New Zealand

Lincoln College Centre for Resource Management, pg 498
RSVP Publishing Co Ltd, pg 500
SIR Publishing, pg 501
University of Otago Press, pg 502

Nigeria

Ahmadu Bello University Press Ltd, pg 503
Evans Brothers (Nigeria Publishers) Ltd, pg 504

JAD Publishers Ltd, pg 505
Riverside Communications, pg 507

Norway

NKI Forlaget, pg 510
Vett & Viten AS, pg 511

Pakistan

Pakistan Institute of Development Economics (PIDE), pg 514

Papua New Guinea

National Research Institute of Papua New Guinea, pg 515

Philippines

Ateneo de Manila University Press, pg 518
Claretian Communications Inc, pg 518
Communication Foundation for Asia Media Group (CFAMG), pg 518
Rex Bookstores & Publishers, pg 520
SIBS Publishing House Inc, pg 521

Poland

Wydawnictwo Arkady, pg 522
Polskie Wydawnictwo Ekonomiczne PWE SA, pg 522
Impuls, pg 523
Instytut Meteorologii i Gospodarki Wodnej, pg 523
Ossolineum Zaklad Narodowy im Ossolinskich - Wydawnictwo, pg 525
Panstwowe Wydawnictwo Rolnicze i Lesne, pg 525
Polish Scientific Publishers PWN, pg 525
Oficyna Wydawnicza Politechniki Wroclawskiej, pg 525
Wydawnictwa Uniwersytetu Warszawskiego, pg 527

Portugal

Publicacoes Ciencia e Vida Lda, pg 529
Edicoes Colibri, pg 530
Difusao Cultural, pg 530
Gradiva-Publicacnoes Lda, pg 532
Instituto de Investigacao Cientifica Tropical, pg 532
Editora McGraw-Hill de Portugal Lda, pg 533

Romania

Editura Ceres, pg 539

Russian Federation

Izdatelstvo Ekologija, pg 544
Energoatomizdat, pg 544
FGUP Izdatelstvo Mashinostroenie, pg 544
Finansy i Statistika Publishing House, pg 544
Gidrometeoizdat, pg 545
Izdatelstvo Kazanskago Universiteta, pg 545
Izdatelstvo Mir, pg 546
Nauka Publishers, pg 547
Izdatel'stvo Nizhegorodskogo Gosudarstvennogo Univ, pg 547

Senegal

CODESRIA (Council for the Development of Social Science Research in Africa), pg 551

Singapore

APAC Publishers Services Pte Ltd, pg 554
Institute of Southeast Asian Studies, pg 556
Singapore University Press Pte Ltd, pg 558
Taylor & Francis Asia Pacific, pg 558
World Scientific Publishing Co Pte Ltd, pg 559

Slovakia

Technicka Univerzita, pg 561

Slovenia

Zalozba Obzorja d d Maribor, pg 562

South Africa

Ashanti Publishing, pg 562
Jacana Education, pg 565
National Botanical Institute, pg 567
New Africa Books (Pty) Ltd, pg 567
Oceanographic Research Institute, pg 567
Ravan Press (Pty) Ltd, pg 568
Struik Publishers (Pty) Ltd, pg 569

Spain

Editorial AEDOS SA, pg 571
Cedel, Ediciones Jose O Avila Monteso ES, pg 576
Fundacion Marcelino Botin, pg 584
Icaria Editorial SA, pg 587
Incafo Archivo Fotografico Editorial, SL, pg 587
Mandala Ediciones, pg 590
OASIS, Producciones Generales de Comunicacion, pg 593
Editorial Parthenon Communication, SL, pg 595
Editora Regional de Murcia - ERM, pg 597
Rueda, SL Editorial, pg 598
Tursen, SA, pg 603

Sri Lanka

Swarna Hansa Foundation, pg 607

Switzerland

Association Suisse des Editeurs de Langue Francaise, pg 618
Bibliographisches Institut & F A Brockhaus AG, pg 619
Birkhauser Verlag AG, pg 619
Daimon Verlag AG, pg 621
Georg Editeur SA, pg 624
Helbing und Lichtenhahn Verlag AG, pg 625
Verlag Huber & Co AG, pg 625
Interfrom AG Editions, pg 625
Editions Jouvence, pg 626
Verlag Friedrich Reinhardt AG, pg 632
Ruegger Verlag, pg 633
SAB Schweiz Arbeitsgemeinschaft fuer die Berggebiete, pg 633
Vdf Hochschulverlag AG an der ETH Zurich, pg 636
Buchverlag der Druckerei Wetzikon AG, pg 637

Syrian Arab Republic

Damascus University Press, pg 638

SUBJECT INDEX

Taiwan, Province of China

Fuh-Wen Book Co, pg 639
Chu Hai Publishing (Taiwan) Co Ltd, pg 640
Morning Star Publisher Inc, pg 641
Petroleum Information Publishing Co, pg 641
Sinorama Magazine Co, pg 641
Wu Nan Book Co Ltd, pg 642

United Republic of Tanzania

Press & Publicity Centre Ltd, pg 644
Tema Publishers Ltd, pg 644

Turkey

Arkadas Ltd, pg 649
Kubbealti Akademisi Kultur ve Sasat Vakfi, pg 650

Uganda

Centre for Basic Research, pg 652

Ukraine

Naukova Dumka Publishers, pg 653
Urozaj, pg 654

United Kingdom

Acair Ltd, pg 655
Anglo-German Foundation for the Study of Industrial Society, pg 658
Arnold, pg 659
Artetech Publishing Co, pg 660
Ashgate Publishing Ltd, pg 660
Banson, pg 662
Belitha Press Ltd, pg 664
Bellew Publishing Co Ltd, pg 664
Cambridge University Press, pg 674
Cameron & Hollis, pg 674
Capall Bann Publishing, pg 674
Jon Carpenter Publishing, pg 675
Cassell & Co, pg 675
Centaur Press (1954), pg 677
The Chartered Institute of Building, pg 678
E W Classey Ltd, pg 680
Colour Library Direct, pg 681
Commonwealth Secretariat, pg 681
CTBI Publications, pg 685
James Currey Ltd, pg 685
Terence Dalton Ltd, pg 685
Earthscan Publications Ltd, pg 689
Edinburgh University Press Ltd, pg 689
Element Books Ltd, pg 690
Edward Elgar Publishing Ltd, pg 690
Elsevier Ltd, pg 691
ERA Technology Ltd, pg 692
Ethics International Press Ltd, pg 692
European Schoolbooks Ltd, pg 692
The Eurospan Group, pg 692
Forth Naturalist & Historian, pg 696
W H Freeman & Co Ltd, pg 697
Gaia Books Ltd, pg 698
Gateway Books, pg 698
Green Books Ltd, pg 702
Harley Books, pg 705
Hyden House Ltd, pg 711
ICC United Kingdom, pg 711
Institute of Development Studies, pg 712
Intercept Ltd, pg 714
IWA Publishing, pg 715
James & James (Publishers) Ltd, pg 715
James & James (Science Publishers) Ltd, pg 715

SUBJECT INDEX

Lawrence & Wishart, pg 719
Letterbox Library, pg 720
Liverpool University Press, pg 722
MIT Press Ltd, pg 728
Multilingual Matters Ltd, pg 729
National Extension College, pg 730
Nelson Thornes Ltd, pg 732
Packard Publishing Ltd, pg 737
Panos Institute, pg 738
Pearson Education, pg 739
Pluto Press, pg 743
Policy Studies Institute (PSI), pg 744
Pomegranate Europe Ltd, pg 744
Prism Press Book Publishers Ltd, pg 745
Profile Books Ltd, pg 746
Ravette Publishing Ltd, pg 748
Regency Press CP Ltd, pg 749
The Richmond Publishing Co Ltd, pg 750
RICS Books, pg 750
Roadmaster Publishing, pg 750
Royal Institute of International Affairs, pg 752
SAGE Publications Ltd, pg 753
Science Reviews Ltd, pg 755
Scottish Cultural Press, pg 755
Scottish Executive Library & Information Services, pg 755
The Society of Metaphysicians Ltd, pg 759
Southgate Publishers, pg 759
Spokesman, pg 760
Spon Press, pg 760
Stokesby House Publications, pg 761
The Tarragon Press, pg 765
Thistle Press, pg 765
TSO (The Stationery Office), pg 767
Tuckwell Press Ltd, pg 767
UCL Press Ltd, pg 768
Westview Press, pg 772
WIT Press, pg 774
The Women's Press Ltd, pg 775
Yale University Press London, pg 776
Zed Books Ltd, pg 776

Uruguay

Nordan-Comunidad, pg 778

Venezuela

Armitano Editores CA, pg 779
Editorial Nueva Sociedad, pg 780

Viet Nam

Science & Technics Publishing House, pg 780

Zambia

Zambia Printing Company Ltd (ZPC), pg 782

Zimbabwe

Action Magazine, pg 782
Anvil Press, pg 782
College Press Publishers (Pvt) Ltd, pg 783
Longman Zimbabwe (Pvt) Ltd, pg 783
Nehanda Publishers, pg 784
Sapes Trust Ltd, pg 784

EROTICA

Brazil

Editora Lidador Ltda, pg 85

France

Editions Dominique Leroy, pg 171

Germany

Verlagsgruppe Droemer Knaur GmbH & Co KG, pg 216
Hyperion - Verlag, pg 240
TASCHEN GmbH, pg 289
Treves Editions Verein Zur Foerderung der Kuenstlerischen Taetigkeiten, pg 292
Zettner Verlag GmbH & Co KG, pg 302

Greece

Exandas Publishers, pg 307
Kalentis & Sia, pg 308

India

Roli Books Pvt Ltd, pg 347

Italy

Ernesto Gremese Editore srl, pg 391

Netherlands

Cadans, pg 480
Sjaloom Uitgeverijen, pg 489

New Zealand

Huia Publishers, pg 497

South Africa

Janssen Publishers CC, pg 565

Spain

Ediciones 29 - Libros Rio Nuevo, pg 603

Sweden

Bonnier Carlsen Bokforlag AB, pg 610

Switzerland

Verlag Die Waage, pg 636

United Kingdom

Atlas Press, pg 661
Carlton Publishing Group, pg 675
Compendium Publishing, pg 681
Constable & Robinson Ltd, pg 682
Creation Books, pg 683
Delectus Books, pg 687
Polybooks Ltd, pg 744
Roundhouse Group, pg 751
Charles Skilton Ltd, pg 758
Virgin Publishing Ltd, pg 770

ETHNICITY

Afghanistan

Government Press, pg 1

Argentina

Editorial Sopena Argentina SACI e I, pg 9
Manrique Zago Ediciones SRL, pg 9

Australia

Aboriginal Studies Press, pg 10
Allen & Unwin Pty Ltd, pg 11
Athena Press, pg 12
Ausmed Publications Pty Ltd, pg 12
Centre for Comparative Literature & Cultural Studies, pg 17
Dangaroo Press, pg 19

Indra Publishing, pg 27
INT Press, pg 27
Owl Publishing, pg 35
Papyrus Publishing, pg 35
Polliteon Publications, pg 37
State Library of NSW Press, pg 42
Tom Publications, pg 43

Austria

Aarachne Verlag, pg 48
CEEBA Publications Antenne d'Autriche, pg 49
DachsVerlag GmbH, pg 49
Development News Ltd, pg 50
NOI - Verlag, pg 55
E Perlinger Naturprodukte Handelsgesellschaft mbH, pg 56
Dr A Schendl GmbH und Co KG, pg 57
Edition Tusch, pg 58
Edition Va Bene, pg 59

Belgium

Centre Aequatoria, pg 63
Creadif, pg 65
Cremers (Schoollandkaarten) PVBA, pg 66
Sonneville Press (Uitgeverij) VTW, pg 73
Stichting Ons Erfdeel VZW, pg 73
Editions Techniques et Scientifiques SPRL, pg 73

Brazil

Pallas Editora e Distribuidora Ltda, pg 88

Bulgaria

Bilblioteka Nov den - Sajuz na Svobodnite Demokrati (Union of Free Democrats), pg 93
Hriker, pg 94

Burundi

Editions Intore, pg 98

Chile

Arrayan Editores, pg 98

China

Xinhua Publishing House, pg 109
Yunnan University Press, pg 109

The Democratic Republic of the Congo

Presses Universitaires du Zaiire (PUZ), pg 114

Croatia

Hrvatsko filozofsko drustvo, pg 118
Sveucilisna tiskara doo, pg 119

Cuba

Casa de las Americas, pg 120

Cyprus

MAM (The House of Cyprus & Cyprological Publications), pg 121
Nikoklis Publishers, pg 121

Czech Republic

Galaxie, vydavatelelstvi a nakladatelstvi, pg 123
Vysehrad spol sro, pg 128

Denmark

Arnkrone Forlaget A/S, pg 129
Dansk Historisk Handbogsforlag ApS, pg 130
Mellemfolkeligt Samvirke, pg 133
Strandbergs Forlag, pg 135
Tiderne Skifter Forlag A/S, pg 135

Estonia

Academic Library of Tallinn Pedagogical University, pg 139

Fiji

Lotu Pacifika Productions, pg 141

Finland

Kirja-Leitzinger, pg 142

France

Editions d'Amerique et d'Orient, Adrien Maisonneuve, pg 146
Editions d'Aujourd'hui (Les Introuvables), pg 148
Berger-Levrault Editions SAS, pg 149
CLD, pg 154
CNRS Editions, pg 155
Editions du Comite des Travaux Historiques et Scientifiques (CTHS), pg 155
Editions Edisud, pg 159
Editions Recherche sur les Civilisations (ERC), pg 160
Institut d'Ethnologie du Museum National d'Histoire Naturelle, pg 162
Laffitte Reprints, pg 170
Editions de la Reunion des Musees Nationaux, pg 176
Editions Parentheses, pg 179
Editions A et J Picard SA, pg 179
Editions Jean Picollec, pg 179
Sepia Editions, pg 184

French Polynesia

Haere Po Editions, pg 189

Germany

Dr Wolfgang Baur Verlag Kunst & Alltag, pg 198
BKV-Brasilienkunde Verlag GmbH, pg 201
Brandes & Apsel Verlag GmbH, pg 204
Hans Christians Druckerei und Verlag GmbH & Co KG, pg 208
Domowina Verlag GmbH, pg 215
Verlag A Fromm im Druck- u Verlagshaus Fromm GmbH & Co KG, pg 227
IKO Verlag fur Interkulturelle Kommunikation, pg 241
Insel Verlag, pg 241
Verlag Koenigshausen und Neumann GmbH, pg 248
Dr Anton Kovac Slavica Verlag, pg 249
Lettre International Kulturzeitung, pg 253
LIT Verlag, pg 255
Verlag Neue Musikzeitung GmbH, pg 264
Oekumenischer Verlag Dr R-F Edel, pg 266
Orlanda Frauenverlag, pg 267
Edition Parabolis, pg 268
Propylaeen Verlag, Zweigniederlassung Berlin der Ullstein Buchverlage GmbH, pg 272

Dr Mohan Krischke Ramaswamy Edition RE, pg 273
Konrad Reich Verlag GmbH, pg 274
Dietrich Reimer Verlag GmbH, pg 274
Wilhelm Schmitz Verlag, pg 280
Otto Schwartz Fachbochhandlung GmbH, pg 282
Tuduv Verlagsgesellschaft mbH, pg 292
Tuebinger Vereinigung fur Volkskunde eV (TVV), pg 292
Vervuert Verlagsgesellschaft, pg 295
VWB-Verlag fur Wissenschaft & Bildung, Amand Aglaster, pg 297
Waxmann Verlag GmbH, pg 297
Verlagsgruppe Weltbild GmbH, pg 298
Verlag Wissenschaft und Politik, pg 300

Ghana
Ghana Publishing Corporation, pg 304
Moxon Paperbacks, pg 304
Waterville Publishing House, pg 305

Greece
Denise Harvey, pg 308
Ianos, pg 308
Idryma Meleton Chersonisou tou Aimou, pg 308
Nea Thesis - Evrotas, pg 310
Stochastis, pg 312

Honduras
Editorial Guaymuras, pg 315

Hong Kong
Commercial Press (Hong Kong) Ltd, pg 316
The Dharmasthiti Buddist Institute Ltd, pg 317

India
Abhinav Publications, pg 326
Ajanta Publications (India), pg 327
Amar Prakashan, pg 328
APH Publishing Corp, pg 328
Asian Educational Services, pg 329
Bani Mandir, Book-Sellers, Publishers & Educational Suppliers, pg 329
Bharatiya Vidya Bhavan, pg 330
Central Tibetan Secretariat, pg 331
Chanakya Publications, pg 331
Concept Publishing Co, pg 332
Cosmo Publications, pg 332
Indian Council for Cultural Relations, pg 336
Indian Institute of World Culture, pg 337
Inter-India Publications, pg 338
Jaico Publishing House, pg 338
Lalit Kala Akademi, pg 339
Manohar Publishers & Distributors, pg 340
Minerva Associates (Publications) Pvt Ltd, pg 341
Ministry of Information & Broadcasting, pg 341
Mudgala Trust, pg 342
National Museum, pg 343
National Publishing House, pg 343
Navrang Booksellers & Publishers, pg 343
Navyug Publishers, pg 343
Pankaj Publications, pg 344
Parimal Prakashan, pg 345
Regency Publications, pg 346
Reliance Publishing House, pg 346
Sasta Sahitya Mandal, pg 348
DB Taraporevala Sons & Co Pvt Ltd, pg 351
N M Tripathi Pvt Ltd Publishers & Booksellers, pg 351
Vani Prakashan, pg 352

Indonesia
Balai Pustaka, pg 353
Dunia Pustaka Jaya PT, pg 354
Lembaga Demografi Fakultas Ekonomi Universitas Indonesia, pg 355
Yayasan Lontar, pg 357

Ireland
Dublin Institute for Advanced Studies, pg 359
The Educational Company of Ireland, pg 359
Fitzwilliam Publishing Co Ltd, pg 360
Ossian Publications, pg 363
Roberts Rinehart Publishers, pg 363
Royal Irish Academy, pg 363

Israel
Ben-Zvi Institute, pg 365
Habermann Institute for Literary Research, pg 367
The Institute for Israeli Arabs Studies, pg 368
Misgav Yerushalayim, pg 370
Urim Publications, pg 373

Italy
Gruppo Abele, pg 374
Edizioni Brenner, pg 379
Capone Editore SRL, pg 379
Centro Studi Terzo Mondo, pg 381
Edizioni Cultura della Pace, pg 383
La Cultura Sociologica, pg 384
Datanews, pg 384
Editalia (Edizioni d'Italia), pg 386
Edizioni del Centro Camuno di Studi Preistorici, pg 386
Edizioni Il Punto d'Incontro SAS, pg 386
ERGA SNC di Carla Ottino Merli & C (Edizioni Realizzazioni Grafiche - Artigiana), pg 388
Adriano Gallina Editore sas, pg 389
Galzerano Editore, pg 390
Grafica e Arte srl, pg 391
Grafo, pg 391
L Japadre Editore, pg 394
Lalli Editore SRL, pg 394
Officina Edizioni di Aldo Quinti, pg 401
Pizzicato Edizioni Musicali, pg 403
Priuli e Verlucca, Editori, pg 404
SAGEP Libri & Comunicazione Srl, pg 406
Sapere 2000 SRL, pg 407

Jamaica
Institute of Jamaica Publications, pg 413
The Press, pg 414
University of the West Indies Press, pg 414

Japan
Koyo Shobo, pg 422
Sagano Shoin, pg 426
Sobun-Sha, pg 428
Tankosha Publishing Co Ltd, pg 429
United Nations University Press, pg 430

Kenya
British Institute in Eastern Africa, pg 433

Lithuania
Vaga Ltd, pg 450

Luxembourg
Centre Culturel De Differdange, pg 451

Madagascar
Editions Ambozontany, pg 453

Malaysia
Holograms (M) Sdn Bhd, pg 456
Vinpress Sdn Bhd, pg 459

Malta
The University of Malta Publications Section, pg 460

Mexico
Centro de Estudios Mexicanos y Centroamericanos, pg 463
Ediciones Culturales Internacionales SA de CV Edicion Compra y Venta de Libros, Casetes, Videos, pg 463
Fondo de Cultura Economica, pg 465
Instituto Panamericano de Geografia e Historia, pg 469
Universidad Nacional Autonoma de Mexico (National University of Mexico), pg 472
Editorial Varazen SA, pg 473

Morocco
Les Editions du Journal L'Unite Maghrebine, pg 475

Myanmar
Sarpay Beikman Public Library, pg 476

Netherlands
De Walburg Pers, pg 481
Sociaal en Cultureel Planbureau, pg 489
Uitgeverij SUN, pg 489
Uniepers BV, pg 491
Uitgeverij Waanders BV, pg 492

New Zealand
Barkfire Press, pg 494
Dunmore Press Ltd, pg 495
Huia Publishers, pg 497
Tandem Press, pg 501
University of Otago Press, pg 502
Viking Sevenseas NZ Ltd, pg 502

Nicaragua
Editorial Nueva Nicaragua, pg 502

Nigeria
Adebara Publishers Ltd, pg 503
Alliance West African Publishers & Co, pg 503
CSS Bookshops, pg 504
Daystar Press (Publishers), pg 504
Educational Research & Study Group, pg 504
Heritage Books, pg 505
Ibadan University Press, pg 505
Institute of African Studies, Onyeka, A, pg 505
Longman Nigeria Plc, pg 505
Nwamife Publishers Ltd, pg 506
Obafemi Awolowo University Press Ltd, pg 506
Onibon-Oje Publishers, pg 506
University of Lagos Press, pg 507
University Publishing Co, pg 507

Norway
Hjemmenes Forlag, pg 509

Pakistan
Centre for South Asian Studies, pg 512
International Institute of Islamic Thought, pg 512
National Institute of Historical & Cultural Research, pg 514

Peru
Instituto de Estudios Peruanos, pg 517
Fondo Editorial de la Pontificia Universidad Catolica del Peru, pg 517
Libreria Studium SA, pg 517

Philippines
Garotech, pg 519
New Day Publishers, pg 520
Our Lady of Manaoag Publisher, pg 520
Vibal Publishing House Inc (VPHI), pg 521

Poland
KAW Krajowa Agencja Wydawnicza, pg 523
Panstwowy Instytut Wydawniczy (PIW), pg 525
Spotdzielna Anagram, pg 526
Wydawnictwa Uniwersytetu Warszawskiego, pg 527

Portugal
Bezerr-Editorae e Distribuidora de Abel Antonio Bezerra, pg 529
Imprensa Nacional-Casa da Moeda, pg 532
Instituto de Investigacao Cientifica Tropical, pg 532

Puerto Rico
Publishing Resources Inc, pg 537

Romania
Editura Excelsior Art, pg 539
Editura Kriterion SA, pg 540
Mentor Kiado, pg 540
Pallas-Akademia Editura, pg 541

Russian Federation
Kabardino-Balkarskoye knizhnoye izdatelstvo, pg 545

Senegal
Centre Africain d'Animation et d'Echanges Culturels Editions Khoudia (CAEC), pg 551
CODESRIA (Council for the Development of Social Science Research in Africa), pg 551
Les Nouvelles Editions Africaines du Senegal NEAS, pg 551

Sierra Leone
Sierra Leone University Press, pg 554

SUBJECT INDEX

Singapore
Graham Brash Pte Ltd, pg 556
Taylor & Francis Asia Pacific, pg 558

Slovakia
Slo Viet, pg 560
Slovenska Narodna Kniznica, Martin, pg 560
Slovenske pedagogicke nakladateistvo, pg 560

South Africa
HAUM (Hollandsch Afrikaansche Uitgevers Maatschappij), pg 564
Ravan Press (Pty) Ltd, pg 568
Shuter & Shooter (Pty) Ltd, pg 568
South African Institute of Race Relations, pg 569
Witwatersrand University Press, pg 570

Spain
Edicions Alfons el Magnanim, Institucio Valenciana d'Estudis i Investigacio, pg 572
Curial Edicions Catalanes SA, pg 578
Rafael Dalmau, Editor, pg 578
Dilagro SA, pg 579
Mundo Negro Editorial, pg 592
OASIS, Producciones Generales de Comunicacion, pg 593
Ediciones del Oriente y del Mediterraneo, pg 594
Pages Editors, SL, pg 594
Editorial Presencia Gitana, pg 597
Instituto Provincial de Investigaciones y Estudios Toledanos (IPIET), pg 597
Selecta-Catalonia Ed, pg 599
Editorial Txertoa, pg 603
Editorial Vicens-Vives, pg 605

Sri Lanka
International Centre for Ethnic Studies, pg 606
Karunaratne & Sons Ltd, pg 606
Ministry of Cultural Affairs, pg 607
National Library & Documentation Centre, pg 607

Sudan
Khartoum University Press, pg 608

Suriname
Stichting Wetenschappelijke Informatie, pg 608

Sweden
Alfabeta Bokforlag AB, pg 609
Industrilitteratur Vindex, Forlags AB, pg 612
Invandrarfoerlaget, pg 612
Mezopotamya Publishing & Distribution, pg 613
Bokforlaget Nya Doxa AB, pg 614

Switzerland
Bergli Books AG, pg 619
Drei-D-World und Foto-World Verlag und Vertrieb, pg 622
Georg Editeur SA, pg 624
Th Gut Verlag, pg 624
Verlag Huber & Co AG, pg 625
Interfrom AG Editions, pg 625
ISIOM Verlag fur Tondokumente, Weinreb Tonarchiv, pg 625
Librairie-Editions J Marguerat, pg 628
Editions Olizane, pg 630
Punktum AG, Buchredaktion und Bildarchiv, pg 632
Strom-Verlag Luzern, pg 635
Der Universitatsverlag Freiburg, pg 636
Verlagsbuchhandling AG, pg 636
Verlag im Waldgut AG, pg 636
Wepf & Co AG, pg 637

Taiwan, Province of China
Yee Wen Publishing Co Ltd, pg 642

Thailand
Suriyaban Publishers, pg 646
White Lotus Co Ltd, pg 646

Tunisia
Faculte des Sciences Humaines et Sociales de Tunis, pg 648

Turkey
Ataturk Kultur, Dil ve Tarih, Yusek Kurumu Baskanligi, pg 649
Ezel Erverdi (Dergah Yayinlari AS) Muessese Muduru, pg 650
Iletisim Yayinlari, pg 650
Toker Yayinlari, pg 651
Alev Yayinlari, pg 652

Uganda
Centre for Basic Research, pg 652

Ukraine
Mystetstvo Publishers, pg 653

United Kingdom
Berg Publishers, pg 664
Bridge Books, pg 671
British Museum Press, pg 672
James Currey Ltd, pg 685
The Eurospan Group, pg 692
Free Association Books Ltd, pg 697
Institute of Employment Rights, pg 712
Institute of Irish Studies, The Queens University of Belfast, pg 713
Lawrence & Wishart, pg 719
Letterbox Library, pg 720
The Littman Library of Jewish Civilization, pg 721
Adam Matthew Publications, pg 726
Old Vicarage Publications, pg 734
Pluto Press, pg 743
The Policy Press, pg 744
Pomegranate Europe Ltd, pg 744
Profile Books Ltd, pg 746
RoutledgeCurzon, pg 751
SAGE Publications Ltd, pg 753
Saqi Books, pg 754
Serpent's Tail Ltd, pg 756
Shire Publications Ltd, pg 757
Thames & Hudson Ltd, pg 764
Trentham Books Ltd, pg 767
Verso, pg 770
Whiting & Birch Ltd, pg 773
The Women's Press Ltd, pg 775

Uruguay
Rosebud Ediciones, pg 778

Venezuela
Editorial Nueva Sociedad, pg 780

Zambia
Zambia Educational Publishing House, pg 782

Zimbabwe
National Archives of Zimbabwe, pg 784

FASHION

Australia
Australasian Textiles & Fashion Publishers, pg 12
The Images Publishing Group Pty Ltd, pg 26
Little Hills Press Pty Ltd, pg 29
National Gallery of Victoria, pg 33
OTEN (Open Training & Education Network), pg 34
RMIT Publishing, pg 39
Thames & Hudson (Australia) Pty Ltd, pg 43

Austria
Thomas Mlakar Verlag, pg 54

Brazil
Global Editora e Distribuidora Ltda, pg 82

China
China Film Press, pg 102
China Light Industry Press, pg 102
Shandong Friendship Publishing House, pg 107
Shanghai Calligraphy & Painting Publishing House, pg 108
Sichuan Science & Technology Publishing House, pg 108

Colombia
Editorial Panamericana, pg 112
RAM Editores, pg 112

Costa Rica
Ediciones Promesa, pg 116

Denmark
Bogfabrikken Fakta ApS, pg 129

France
Adam Biro Editions, pg 150
Association Frank, pg 164
Hachette Pratiques, pg 167
Association Paris-Musees, pg 179
Editions Plume, pg 180
Revue Noire, pg 183
Editions Soline, pg 185
Editions Thames & Hudson, pg 187

Germany
Arnoldsche Verlagsanstalt GmbH, pg 194
Deutscher Fachverlag GmbH, pg 212
Extent Verlag und Service Wolfgang M Flamm, pg 223
Jahreszeiten-Verlag GmbH, pg 242
LIT Verlag, pg 255
mode information Heinz Kramer GmbH, pg 261
Naumann & Goebel Verlagsgesellschaft mbH, pg 263
Verlag Hans Schoener GmbH, pg 281
teNeues Verlag GmbH & Co KG, pg 290
Verlag fuer die Frau GmbH, pg 295
Verlagsgruppe Weltbild GmbH, pg 298

Hungary
Szabad Ter Kiado, pg 324

India
Nem Chand & Brothers, pg 343
Sita Books & Periodicals Pvt Ltd, pg 349

Israel
R Sirkis Publishers Ltd, pg 372

Italy
Essegi, pg 388
Ernesto Gremese Editore srl, pg 391
Idea Books, pg 392
Lybra Immagine, pg 396
Zanfi-Logos, pg 412

Japan
Bunkasha Publishing Co Ltd, pg 415
Nippon Hoso Shuppan Kyokai (NHK Publishing), pg 424
Shufu-to-Seikatsu Sha Ltd, pg 428
Shufunotomo Co Ltd, pg 428

Kenya
Heinemann Kenya Ltd (EAEP), pg 434

Republic of Korea
Suhagsa, pg 443

Mexico
Grupo Editorial Armonia, pg 462
Janibi Editores SA de CV, pg 467
Ediciones Libra, SA de CV, pg 467
Libros y Revistas SA de CV, pg 467
Ediciones Promesa, SA de CV, pg 470
Sayrols Editorial SA de CV, pg 471

Netherlands
The Pepin Press, pg 487

Pakistan
Maqbool Academy, pg 513

Portugal
Impala, pg 532
Vega-Publicacao e Distribuicao de Livros e Revistas, Lda, pg 536

Romania
Editura Meridiane, pg 540

Spain
Editorial Astri SA, pg 573

Taiwan, Province of China
Youth Cultural Publishing Co, pg 642

United Kingdom
Apple Press, pg 658
Art Books International Ltd, pg 659
Batsford Ltd, pg 663
Ruth Bean Publishers, pg 664
Berg Publishers, pg 664
Blackwell Science Ltd, pg 667
Carlton Publishing Group, pg 675

Hamlyn, pg 704
Laurence King Publishing Ltd, pg 717
Piatkus Books, pg 741
Plexus Publishing Ltd, pg 743
Quintet Publishing Ltd, pg 747
Random House UK Ltd, pg 747
Rivers Oram Press, pg 750
Taschen UK Ltd, pg 763
Thames & Hudson Ltd, pg 764
Thomson Gale, pg 765
Time Out Group Ltd, pg 765
Philip Wilson Publishers, pg 774

FICTION

Afghanistan

Book Publishing Institute, pg 1

Albania

Botimpex Publications Import-Export Agency, pg 1
Fan Noli Verlag Rexhep Hida, pg 1

Algeria

Enterprise Nationale du Livre (ENAL), pg 2

Argentina

Editorial Abril SA, pg 2
Editorial Acme SA, pg 3
Ada Korn Editora SA, pg 3
Alianza Editorial de Argentina SA, pg 3
Editorial Argentina Plaza y Janes SA, pg 3
Editorial Atlantida SA, pg 3
Beas Ediciones SRL, pg 4
Beatriz Viterbo Editora, pg 4
Critica, pg 5
Emece Editores SA, pg 5
Ediciones de la Flor SRL, pg 6
Editorial Losada SA, pg 7
Marymar Ediciones SA, pg 7
Ediciones Minotauro SA, pg 7
Editorial Planeta Argentina SAIC, pg 8
Editorial Sudamericana SA, pg 9
Editoria Universitaria de la Patagonia, pg 9
Javier Vergara Editor SA, pg 9

Armenia

Arevik, pg 10

Australia

ABC Books (Australian Broadcasting Corporation), pg 10
Allen & Unwin Pty Ltd, pg 11
Angel Publications, pg 11
Ansay Pty Ltd, pg 11
Ashling Books, pg 12
Austed Publishing Co, pg 12
Bandicoot Books, pg 14
Bolinda Publishing Pty Ltd, pg 15
Louis Braille Audio, pg 16
Egan Publishing Pty Ltd, pg 21
Fremantle Arts Centre Press, pg 23
Galley Press Publishing, pg 23
Gangan Publishing, pg 23
Garr Publishing, pg 23
Ginninderra Press, pg 23
Geoffrey Hamlyn-Harris, pg 24
HarperCollinsReligious, pg 25
Hat Box Press, pg 25
Hunter Books, pg 26
Indra Publishing, pg 27
Jarrah Publications, pg 27
Killara Press, pg 28

Levanter Publishing & Associates, pg 29
Little Red Apple Publishing, pg 29
Magabala Books Aboriginal Corporation, pg 30
Mayne Publishing, pg 31
Narkaling Inc, pg 33
New Creation Publications Ministries & Resource Centre, pg 33
New Endeavour Press, pg 33
New Era Publications Australia Pty Ltd, pg 33
Newman Centre Publications, pg 33
Ollif Publishing, pg 34
Omnibus Books, pg 34
Pan Macmillan Australia Pty Ltd, pg 35
Papyrus Publishing, pg 35
Pascoe Publishing Pty Ltd, pg 36
Pearson Education Australia, pg 36
Penguin Group (Australia), pg 36
Plantagenet Press, pg 37
Quakers Hill Press, pg 38
Random House Australia, pg 38
Spinifex Press, pg 42
The Text Publishing Company Pty Ltd, pg 43
Tom Publications, pg 43
Tomorrow Publications, pg 44
Transworld Publishers Pty Ltd, pg 44
Troll Books of Australia, pg 44
Tropicana Press, pg 44
University of Queensland Press, pg 45
University of Western Australia Press, pg 45
Wakefield Press Pty Ltd, pg 46
Weather Press, pg 46

Austria

Aarachne Verlag, pg 48
Amalthea-Verlag, pg 48
Andreas und Andreas Verlagsbuchhandel, pg 48
Astor-Verlag, Willibald Schlager, pg 48
Danubia Werbung und Verlagsservice, pg 49
Development News Ltd, pg 50
Doecker Verlag GmbH & Co KG, pg 50
Edition S der OSD, pg 50
Edition Ergo Sum, pg 50
Fremdenverkehrs Aktiengessellschaft, pg 51
Verlag Lynkeus/H Hakel Gesellschaft, pg 51
Edition Graphischer Zirkel, pg 51
Haymon-Verlag GesmbH, pg 51
Johannes Heyn GmbH & Co KG, pg 52
Verlag Jungbrunnen - Wiener Spielzeugschachtel GesellschaftmbH, pg 52
Karolinger Verlag GmbH & Co KG, pg 52
Leykam Buchverlagsges mbH, pg 53
Merbod Verlag, pg 54
Milena Verlag, pg 54
Paul Neff Verlag KG, pg 54
Oesterreichischer Agrarverlag, Druck- und Verlags- GmbH, pg 55
Richard Pils Publication PN°1, pg 56
Georg Prachner KG, pg 56
Andreas Schnider Verlags-Atelier, pg 57
Verlag Carl Ueberreuter GmbH, pg 58

Wieser Verlag, pg 60
Paul Zsolnay Verlag GmbH, pg 60

Azerbaijan

Azernesr, pg 60

Bangladesh

Ankur Prakashani, pg 61
Gatidhara, pg 61
Agamee Prakashani, pg 61

Belarus

Belaruskaya Encyklapedyya, pg 62
Interdigest Publishing House, pg 62
Kavaler Publishers, pg 62
Izdatelstvo Mastatskaya Litaratura, pg 62

Belgium

Caramel, Uitgeverij, pg 64
Editions Chantecler, pg 65
Uitgeverij Clavis, pg 65
Davidsfonds Uitgeverij NV, pg 66
Uitgeverij de Eenhoorn, pg 67
EPO Publishers, Printers, Booksellers, pg 67
Helyode Editions (SA-ADN), pg 68
Editions Hemma, pg 68
Les Editions du Lombard SA, pg 70
La Longue Vue, pg 70
Editions Memor, pg 71
Paradox Pers vzw, pg 71
Standaard Uitgeverij, pg 73
Vlaamse Esperantobond VZW, pg 74
Editions Luce Wilquin, pg 74

Bermuda

The Bermudian Publishing Co, pg 75

Bosnia and Herzegovina

Veselin Maslesa, pg 76

Botswana

Maskew Miller Longman, pg 76

Brazil

AGIR S/A Editora, pg 77
Livraria Francisco Alves Editora SA, pg 77
Artes e Oficios Editora Ltda, pg 78
Editora Bertrand Brasil Ltda, pg 78
Centro de Estudos Juridicosdo Para (CEJUP), pg 79
Editora Companhia das Letras/Editora Schwarcz Ltda, pg 80
Dumara Distribuidora de Publicacoes Ltda, pg 81
Editora Globo SA, pg 82
Editora e Grafica Carisio Ltda, Minas Editora, pg 83
Imago Editora Importacao e Exportacao Ltda, pg 84
Editora Lidador Ltda, pg 85
Editora Mantiqueira de Ciencia e Arte, pg 86
Memorias Futuras Edicoes Ltda, pg 86
Editora Mercado Aberto Ltda, pg 86
Editora Mercuryo Ltda, pg 86
Editora Moderna Ltda, pg 86
Editora Mundo Cristao, pg 87
Cia Editora Nacional, pg 87
Editora Nova Alexandria Ltda, pg 87
Editora Nova Fronteira SA, pg 87
Editora Objetiva Ltda, pg 87
Editora Primor Ltda, pg 89

Distribuidora Record de Servicos de Imprensa SA, pg 89
Editora Revan Ltda, pg 89
Editora Scipione Ltda, pg 90
Sobrindes Linha Grafica E Editora Ltda, pg 90
Thex Editora e Distribuidora Ltda, pg 91
34 Literatura S/C Ltda, pg 91

Bulgaria

Abagar Pablioing, pg 92
Abagar, Veliko Tarnovo, pg 93
Bulgarski Pissatel, pg 93
Bulvest 2000 Ltd, pg 93
Ciela Publishing House, pg 93
DA-Izdatelstvo Publishers, pg 93
Hristo G Danov State Publishing House, pg 93
EA EOOD, pg 94
Factor-Alias, pg 94
Gea-Libris Publishing House, pg 94
Hermes Publishing House, pg 94
Heron Press Publishing House, pg 94
Publishing House Hristo Botev, pg 94
Izdatelstvo Lettera, pg 95
Pejo K Javorov Publishing House, pg 95
Kibea Publishing Co, pg 95
Kolibri Publishing Group, pg 95
MATEX, pg 95
Mladezh IK, pg 95
Prozorets Ltd Publishing House, pg 96
Reporter, pg 96
Sluntse Publishing House, pg 97
Svetra Publishing House, pg 97
Trud - Izd kasta, pg 97
Ivan Vazov Publishing House, pg 97
Zunica, pg 97

Cameroon

Editions CLE, pg 98
Editions Buma Kor & Co Ltd, pg 98
Editions Semences Africaines, pg 98

Chile

Editorial Cuarto Propio, pg 99

China

Beijing Publishing House, pg 101
China Film Press, pg 102
China Theatre Publishing House, pg 103
Chinese Literature Press, pg 103
Encyclopedia of China Publishing House, pg 104
Shandong Education Publishing House, pg 107
Shandong Friendship Publishing House, pg 107
World Affairs Press, pg 109
Writers' Publishing House, pg 109
Zhong Hua Book Co, pg 110

Colombia

Siglo XXI Editores de Colombia Ltda, pg 112

The Democratic Republic of the Congo

Centre Protestant d'Editions et de Diffusion (CEDI), pg 114
Saint-Paul, pg 114

SUBJECT INDEX

BOOK

Costa Rica
Libreria Imprenta y Litografia Lehmann SA, pg 115

Cote d'Ivoire
Heritage Publishing Co, pg 117

Croatia
ALFA dd za izdavacke, graficke i trgovacke poslove, pg 117
Durieux d o o, pg 118
Faust Vrani, pg 118
Globus-Nakladni zavod, pg 118
Graficki zavod Hrvatske, pg 118
Mladost d d Izdavacku graficku i informaticku djelatnost, pg 119
Naklada Ljevak doo, pg 119
Otokar Kersovani, pg 119

Cuba
Editorial Letras Cubanas, pg 120
Editorial Oriente, pg 120

Czech Republic
AULOS sro, pg 122
Aurora, pg 122
Baronet, pg 122
Brody, pg 122
Euromedia Group-Odeon, pg 123
Galaxie, vydavatelelstvi a nakladatelstvi, pg 123
Horacek Ladislav-Paseka, pg 123
Karolinum, nakladatelstvi, pg 124
Knihovna A Tiskarna Pro Nevidome, pg 124
Labyrint, pg 125
Lidove Noviny Publishing House, pg 125
Lyra Pragensis Obecne Prospelna Spolecnost, pg 125
Mariadan, pg 125
Mlada fronta, pg 125
Nava, pg 126
Prostor, nakladatelstvi sro, pg 127
Vitalis sro, pg 128

Denmark
Alma, pg 128
Aschehoug Dansk Forlag A/S, pg 129
Atuakkiorfik A/S Det Greenland Publishers, pg 129
Bonnier Publications A/S, pg 129
Bonniers Specialmagasiner A/S Bogdivisionen, pg 129
Borgens Forlag A/S, pg 129
Carit Andersens Forlag A/S, pg 130
Forlaget Centrum, pg 130
Cicero-Chr Erichsens, pg 130
The Danish Literature Centre, pg 130
Forlaget Forum, pg 131
Fremad A/S, pg 131
J Frimodt Forlag, pg 131
Forlaget GMT, pg 131
Grevas Forlag, pg 131
Gyldendalske Boghandel - Nordisk Forlag A/S, pg 131
P Haase & Sons Forlag A/S, pg 131
Hekla Forlag, pg 131
Hernovs Forlag, pg 132
Forlaget Hjulet, pg 132
Host & Son Publishers Ltd, pg 132
Forlaget Hovedland, pg 132
Interpresse A/S, pg 132
Forlaget Klematis A/S, pg 132
Lindhardt og Ringhof Forlag A/S, pg 132
Lohse Forlag, pg 132
Forlaget Modtryk AMBA, pg 133

Nyt Nordisk Forlag Arnold Busck A/S, pg 133
Politisk Revy, pg 133
Samlerens Forlag A/S, pg 134
Det Schonbergske Forlag A/S, pg 134
Sommer & Sorensen, pg 134
Syddansk Universitetsforlag, pg 135
Tiderne Skifter Forlag A/S, pg 135
Unitas Forlag, pg 135
Forlaget Vindrose A/S, pg 135
Wisby & Wilkens, pg 135
Forlaget Woldike K/S, pg 135

Egypt (Arab Republic of Egypt)
Al Arab Publishing House, pg 137
Dar El Shorouk, pg 138
Dar Al Hilal Publishing Institution, pg 138
Middle East Book Centre, pg 138

Estonia
Ilmamaa, pg 139
Kirjastus Kunst, pg 139
Kupar Publishers, pg 139
Olion Publishers, pg 140
Oue Eesti Raamat, pg 140
Sinisukk, pg 140

Finland
AB Svenska Laromedel-Editum, pg 141
Basam Books Oy, pg 141
Gummerus Publishers, pg 142
Kaantopiiri Oy, pg 142
Karisto Oy, pg 142
Kirjayhtyma Oy, pg 142
Kustannus Oy Uusi Tie, pg 143
Kustannusosakeyhtio Tammi, pg 143
Oy LIKE Kustannus, pg 143
Otava Publishing Co Ltd, pg 143
Schildts Forlags AB, pg 144
Scriptum Forlags AB, pg 144
Soderstroms Forlag, pg 144
Werner Soederstrom Osakeyhtio (WSOY), pg 145

France
Editions Al Liamm, pg 146
Editions de l'Archipel, pg 147
Publications Aredit, pg 147
Editions Atlantica Seguier, pg 148
Aubanel Editions, pg 148
Editions d'Aujourd'hui (Les Introuvables), pg 148
Autrement Editions, pg 148
Editions Balland, pg 149
Societe d'Edition Les Belles Lettres, pg 149
Christian Bourgois Editeur, pg 151
Bragelonne, pg 151
Brud Nevez, pg 151
Editions Calmann-Levy SA, pg 152
Editions Casterman, pg 152
Centre pour l'Innovation et la Recherche en Communication de l'Entreprise (CIRCE), pg 152
Editions Champ Vallon, pg 153
Le Cherche Midi Editeur, pg 154
Editions Circonflexe, pg 154
Editions Jose Corti, pg 156
Culture et Bibliotheque pour Tous, pg 156
Dargaud, pg 157
Editions du Dauphin, pg 157
Nouvelles Editions Debresse, pg 157
Editions La Decouverte, pg 157
Editions Denoel, pg 157

Les Editions des Deux Coqs d'Or, pg 158
Editions Dis Voir, pg 158
Les Editions de Minuit SA, pg 160
Librairie Artheme Fayard, pg 163
FBT de R Editions, pg 163
Editions Des Femmes, pg 163
Flammarion SA, pg 163
Editions Fleurus, pg 163
Association Frank, pg 164
Editions Gallimard, pg 164
Editions Gerard de Villiers, pg 165
Editions Glenat, pg 165
Editions Grandir, pg 166
Hachette Livre, pg 167
Editions de l'Herne, pg 167
Editions Hoebeke, pg 168
Pierre Horay Editeur, pg 168
Editions Infrarouge, pg 168
Editions J'ai Lu, pg 169
Editions Jean-Claude Lattes, pg 169
Editions Robert Laffont, pg 170
Michel Lafon Publishing, pg 171
Editions du Laquet, pg 171
Editions Dominique Leroy, pg 171
Liana Levi Editions, pg 172
Editions des Limbes d'Or FBT de R Editions, pg 172
Le Livre de Poche-L G F (Librairie Generale Francaise), pg 173
Editions Marie-Noelle, pg 174
Mercure de France SA, pg 175
Editions A M Metailie, pg 175
Editions Albin Michel, pg 175
Nil Editions, pg 177
Noir Sur Blanc, pg 177
Nouvelles Editions Latines, pg 177
Editions Odile Jacob, pg 177
Payot & Rivages, pg 179
Editions Jean Picollec, pg 179
Editions Christian Pirot, pg 180
Editions POL, pg 180
Le Pre-aux-clercs, pg 180
Presence Africaine Editions, pg 180
Presses de la Cite, pg 180
Editions Pygmalion, pg 182
Editions Ramsay, pg 182
Editions Roudil SA, pg 183
Editions du Rouergue, pg 183
Editions Sand et Tchou SA, pg 184
Selection du Reader's Digest SA, pg 184
Sepia Editions, pg 184
Editions de Septembre, pg 184
Editions Le Serpent a Plumes, pg 184
Service Technique pour l'Education, pg 184
Editions du Seuil, pg 184
Editions Andre Silvaire Sarl, pg 185
Societe des Editions Grasset et Fasquelle, pg 185
Association d'Editions Sorg, pg 186
Spengler Editeur, pg 186
Editions Stock, pg 186
Les Editions de la Table Ronde, pg 186
Editions Tallandier, pg 187
10/18, pg 187
La Voix du Regard, pg 189

French Polynesia
Scoop/Au Vent des Iles, pg 189
Simone Sanchez, pg 190

Germany
Altberliner Verlag GmbH, pg 192
AOL-Verlag Frohmut Menze, pg 193
Arena Verlag GmbH, pg 193
Argon Verlag GmbH, pg 194
Argument-Verlag, pg 194

Ars Edition GmbH, pg 194
Verlag Atelier im Bauernhaus Fischerhude Wolf-Dietmar Stock, pg 195
Aufbau Taschenbuch Verlag GmbH, pg 195
Aufbau-Verlag GmbH, pg 195
Aufstieg-Verlag GmbH, pg 195
Aussaat Verlag, pg 195
C Bange GmbH & Co KG, pg 196
Bastei Luebbe Taschenbuecher, pg 197
Bastei Verlag, pg 197
Beerenverlag, pg 198
Berliner Handpresse Wolfgang Joerg und Erich Schonig, pg 199
C Bertelsmann Verlag GmbH, pg 199
Bertelsmann Lexikon Verlag GmbH, pg 200
Betzel Verlag GmbH, pg 200
Bleicher Verlag GmbH, pg 202
Brandes & Apsel Verlag GmbH, pg 204
R Brockhaus Verlag, pg 204
BRUEN-Verlag, Gorenflo, pg 205
Buchverlage Langen-Mueller/Herbig, pg 205
Bund-Verlag GmbH, pg 206
Fachverlag Hans Carl GmbH, pg 207
Carlsen Verlag GmbH, pg 207
Chmielorz GmbH Verlag, pg 208
Claassen Verlag GmbH, pg 209
ComMedia & Arte Verlag Bernd Mayer, pg 209
J G Cotta'sche Buchhandlung Nachfolger GmbH, pg 210
Das Arsenal, Verlag fuer Kultur und Politik GmbH, pg 210
Deutsche Verlags-Anstalt GmbH (DVA), pg 212
Deutscher Taschenbuch Verlag GmbH & Co KG (dtv), pg 213
Dipa-Verlag GmbH, pg 215
Cecilie Dressler Verlag GmbH & Co KG, pg 216
Verlagsgruppe Droemer Knaur GmbH & Co KG, pg 216
Karl Elser Druck GmbH, pg 216
Echter Wurzburg Frankische Gesellschaftsdruckerei und Verlag GmbH, pg 217
Econ Verlag GmbH, pg 218
Egmont Franz Schneider Verlag GmbH, pg 218
Egmont vgs verlagsgesellschaft mbH, pg 218
Ehrenwirth Verlag, pg 218
Ehrenwirth Verlag GmbH, pg 218
Eichborn AG, pg 219
EinfallsReich Verlagsgesellschaft MbH, pg 219
Engel & Bengel Verlag, pg 220
Verlag Peter Engstler, pg 220
Ensslin und Laiblin Verlag GmbH & Co KG, pg 220
EOS Verlag der Benefiktiner der Erzabtei St. Ottilien, pg 220
Eremiten-Presse und Verlag GmbH, pg 220
Ernst Kabel Verlag GmbH, pg 221
Europa Verlag GmbH, pg 222
Evangelische Verlagsanstalt GmbH, pg 222
Fahrner & Fahrner, pg 223
Karin Fischer Verlag GmbH, pg 225
Rita G Fischer Verlag, pg 225
S Fischer Verlag GmbH, pg 225
Franckh-Kosmos Verlags-GmbH & Co, pg 226

PUBLISHERS

SUBJECT INDEX

Margarethe Freudenberger - selbstverlag fur jedermann, pg 227
Gerth Medien GmbH, pg 229
Gilles und Francke Verlag, pg 229
Gmelin Verlag GmbH, pg 230
Wilhelm Goldmann Verlag GmbH, pg 230
Grafit Verlag GmbH, pg 231
Guenther Butkus, pg 231
Carl Hanser Verlag, pg 234
Heinz-Theo Gremme Verlag, pg 236
Hellerau-Verlag Dresden GmbH, pg 236
Wilhelm Heyne Verlag, pg 237
Hoffmann und Campe Verlag GmbH, pg 238
Hohenrain-Verlag GmbH, pg 239
Holos Verlag, pg 239
Verlagsgruppe Georg von Holtzbrinck GmbH, pg 239
Horlemann Verlag, pg 239
Hyperion - Verlag, pg 240
Klaus Isele, pg 242
Iudicium Verlag GmbH, pg 242
J Ch Mellinger Verlag GmbH, pg 242
Karl-May-Verlag Lothar Schmid GmbH, pg 244
KBV Verlags-und Medien - GmbH, pg 245
Verlag Kiepenheuer & Witsch, pg 245
Verlag Kleine Schritte Ursula Dahm & Co, pg 246
Kleiner Bachmann Verlag fur Kinder und Umwelt, pg 246
Albrecht Knaus Verlag GmbH, pg 247
Verlag Knut Reim, Jugendpresseverlag, pg 247
Koehlers Verlagsgesellschaft mbH, pg 248
Lucy Koerner Verlag, pg 248
Dr Anton Kovac Slavica Verlag, pg 249
Krueger Verlag GmbH, pg 250
Krug & Schadenberg, pg 250
Verlag Antje Kunstmann GmbH, pg 251
Lambda Edition GmbH, pg 251
Ingrid Langner, pg 252
Lentz Verlag, pg 253
Dr Gisela Lermann, pg 253
Libertas- Europaeisches Institut GmbH, pg 254
Liebenzeller Mission, GmbH, Abt. Verlag, pg 254
Logos-Verlag Literatur & Layout GmbH, pg 255
Luchterhand Literaturverlag GmbH/ Verlag Volk & Welt GmbH, pg 255
Gustav Luebbe Verlag, pg 256
Verlagsgruppe Luebbe GmbH & Co KG, pg 256
Lusatia Verlag-Dr Stuebner & Co KG, pg 256
Edition Maritim GmbH, pg 257
Maro Verlag und Druck, Benno Kasmayr, pg 257
Matthes und Seitz Verlag GmbH, pg 258
Matzker Verlag DiA, pg 258
Merlin Verlag Andreas Meyer Verlags GmbH und Co KG, pg 259
Merz & Solitude - Akademie Schloss Solitude, pg 259
Mitteldeutscher Verlag GmbH, pg 261
Monia Verlag, pg 261

Naumann & Goebel Verlagsgesellschaft mbH, pg 263
Verlag Neue Kritik KG, pg 264
Verlag Neue Stadt GmbH, pg 264
Neuer Honos Verlag GmbH, pg 264
Verlag Neues Leben GmbH, pg 264
Neuthor - Verlag, pg 265
C W Niemeyer Buchverlage GmbH, pg 265
nymphenburger, pg 266
Oekotopia Verlag, Wolfgang Hoffman GmbH & Co KG, pg 266
Verlag Friedrich Oetinger GmbH, pg 266
Oncken Verlag KG, pg 267
Ostfalia-Verlag Jurgen Schierer, pg 267
Pandion-Verlag, Ulrike Schmoll, pg 268
Passavia Druckerei GmbH, Verlag, pg 268
Pelikan Vertriebsgesellschaft mbH & Co KG, pg 269
Pendragon Verlag, pg 269
Pfalzische Verlagsanstalt GmbH, pg 269
Philipp Reclam Jun Verlag GmbH, pg 269
Piper Verlag GmbH, pg 270
Projektion J Buch- und Musikverlag GmbH, pg 272
Propylaeen Verlag, Zweigniederlassung Berlin der Ullstein Buchverlage GmbH, pg 272
Pulp Master Frank Nowatzki Verlag, pg 272
Quell Verlag, pg 273
Querverlag GmbH, pg 273
Quintessenz Verlags-GmbH, pg 273
Radius-Verlag GmbH, pg 273
Rake Verlag GmbH, pg 273
Gerhard Rautenberg Druckerei und Verlag GmbH & Co KG, pg 273
Ravensburger Buchverlag Otto Maier GmbH, pg 274
Regura Verlag, pg 274
Konrad Reich Verlag GmbH, pg 274
Rogner und Bernhard GmbH & Co Verlags KG, pg 276
Romiosini Verlag, pg 276
Rosenheimer Verlagshaus GmbH & Co KG, pg 276
Rowohlt Berlin Verlag GmbH, pg 277
Rowohlt Verlag GmbH, pg 277
Ruetten & Loening Berlin GmbH, pg 277
Eugen Salzer-Verlag GmbH & Co KG, pg 278
Verlag der Sankt-Johannis-Druckerei C Schweickhardt, pg 278
Verlag Sauerlaender GmbH, pg 278
Richard Scherpe Verlag GmbH, pg 279
Schillinger Verlag GmbH, pg 279
Agora Verlag Manfred Schlosser, pg 280
Schoeffling & Co, pg 281
Verlag R S Schulz GmbH, pg 282
H O Schulze KG, pg 282
Theodor Schuster, pg 282
Buchkonzept Simon KG, pg 283
Adolf Sponholtz Verlag, pg 284
L Staackmann Verlag KG, pg 286
Steidl Verlag, pg 287
Verlag Stendel, pg 287
Suhrkamp Verlag, pg 289
Svato Zapletal, pg 289
Tangens Systemverlag GmbH, pg 289
Thienemann Verlag GmbH, pg 291

Titania-Verlag Ferdinand Schroll, pg 291
Treves Editions Verein Zur Foerderung der Kuenstlerischen Taetigkeiten, pg 292
Mario Truant Verlag, pg 292
Ullstein Heyne List GmbH & Co KG, pg 293
Ulrike Helmer Verlag, pg 293
Unrast Verlag e V, pg 293
Edition Vincent Klink, pg 296
Verlag Volk & Welt, pg 296
W Ludwig Verlag GmbH, pg 297
Verlag Klaus Wagenbach, pg 297
A Weichert Verlag GmbH & Co KG, pg 298
Weidler Buchverlag Berlin, pg 298
Verlagsgruppe Weltbild GmbH, pg 298
Wolf's-Verlag Berlin, pg 301
Das Wunderhorn Verlag GmbH, pg 301
Wunderlich Verlag, pg 301
Zettner Verlag GmbH & Co KG, pg 302

Ghana
Adaex Educational Publications Ltd, pg 302
Afram Publications (Ghana) Ltd, pg 303
Africa Christian Press, pg 303
Anowuo Educational Publications, pg 303
Asempa Publishers, pg 303
Beginners Publishers, pg 303
Bureau of Ghana Languages, pg 303
Educational Press & Manufacturers Ltd, pg 303
Ghana Publishing Corporation, pg 304
Manhill Publication, pg 304
Moxon Paperbacks, pg 304
Sedco Publishing Ltd, pg 305
Waterville Publishing House, pg 305
Woeli Publishing Services, pg 305

Greece
Atlantis M Pechlivanides & Co SA, pg 306
Chrysi Penna - Golden Pen Books, pg 306
Dodoni Publications, pg 306
Dorikos Publishing House, pg 306
Ekdoseis Kazantzaki (Kazantzakis Publications), pg 307
Eleftheroudakis, GCSA International Bookstore, pg 307
Elliniki Leschi Tou Vivliou, pg 307
Exandas Publishers, pg 307
Govostis Publishing SA, pg 307
Harlenic Hellas Publishing SA, pg 308
Hestia-I D Hestia-Kollaros & Co Corporation, pg 308
Irini Publishing House - Vassilis G Katsikeas SA, pg 308
Kalentis & Sia, pg 308
Kastaniotis Editions SA, pg 309
Kedros Publishers, pg 309
Kritiki Publishing, pg 309
Medusa/Selas Publishers, pg 310
Minoas SA, pg 310
Kyr I Papadopoulos E E, pg 311
Patakis Publishers, pg 311
M Psaropoulos & Co EE, pg 311
Psichogios Publications SA, pg 311
Siamantas VA A Ouvas, pg 312
Sigma, pg 312
To Rodakio, pg 312

J Vassiliou Bibliopolein, pg 313
Vlassis, pg 313

Guatemala
Grupo Editorial RIN-78, pg 313

Guyana
Roraima Publishers Ltd, pg 314

Haiti
Deschamps Imprimerie, pg 314
Theodor (Imprimerie), pg 314

Hong Kong
Asia 2000 Ltd, pg 315
Breakthrough Ltd - Breakthrough Publishers, pg 315
Hong Kong Publishing Co Ltd, pg 317
Lea Publications Ltd, pg 318
Ming Pao Publications Ltd, pg 318
Research Centre for Translation, pg 319
SCMP Book Publishing Ltd, pg 319
Sesame Publication Co, pg 319
Sun Ya Publications (HK) Ltd, pg 319
Witman Publishing Co (HK) Ltd, pg 320

Hungary
Europa Konyvkiado, pg 321
Ifjusagi Lap-eskonyvkiado Vallalat, pg 321
Jelenkor Verlag, pg 322
Magveto Koenyvkiado, pg 322
Szepirodalmi Koenyvkiado Kiado, pg 324
Tevan Kiado Vallalat, pg 324

Iceland
Almenna Bokafelagid, pg 325
Fjolvi, pg 325
Frjals fjolmiolun hf-Urvalsbaekur, pg 325
Idunn, pg 325
Isafoldarprentsmidja hf, pg 326
Mal og menning, pg 326
Setberg, pg 326
Skjaldborg Ltd, pg 326
Skuggsja bokaforlag, pg 326

India
Ananda Publishers Pvt Ltd, pg 328
APH Publishing Corp, pg 328
The Bangalore Printing & Publishing Co Ltd, pg 329
Bharatiya Vidya Bhavan, pg 330
Chanakya Publications, pg 331
CICC Book House, Leading Publishers & Booksellers, pg 332
Current Books, pg 332
DC Books, pg 333
Diamond Comics (P) Ltd, pg 333
Frank Brothers & Co Publishers Ltd, pg 334
Hans Prakashan, pg 335
HarperCollins Publishers India Pty Ltd, pg 335
Arnold Heinman Publishers (India) Pvt Ltd, pg 335
Hind Pocket Books Private Ltd, pg 336
Hindi Pracharak Sansthan, pg 336
Kairali Children's Book Trust, pg 339
Kairalee Mudralayam, pg 339
Kali For Women, pg 339
Kitab Ghar, pg 339

975

M/S Gulshan Nanda Publications, pg 342
Natraj Prakashan, Publishers & Exporters, pg 343
Omsons Publications, pg 344
Orient Paperbacks, pg 344
Paico Publishing House, pg 344
Panchasheel Prakashan, pg 344
Pitambar Publishing Co (P) Ltd, pg 345
Prabhat Prakashan, pg 345
Pratibha Pratishthan, pg 345
Rajpal & Sons, pg 346
Regency Publications, pg 346
Reliance Publishing House, pg 346
Roli Books Pvt Ltd, pg 347
Rupa & Co, pg 347
M C Sarkar & Sons (P) Ltd, pg 348
Sat Sahitya Prakashan, pg 348
Scientific Book Agency, pg 348
Sharda Prakashan, pg 349
R R Sheth & Co, pg 349
Somaiya Publications Pvt Ltd, pg 349
Sterling Publishers Pvt Ltd, pg 350
Tara Publishing, pg 351
UBS Publishers Distributors Ltd, pg 351
Vani Prakashan, pg 352
Vision Books Pvt Ltd, pg 352
Vivek Prakashan, pg 353

Indonesia

Angkasa CV, pg 353
Bina Aksara Parta, pg 354
PT Bulan Bintang, pg 354
Dunia Pustaka Jaya PT, pg 354
Gaya Favorit Press, pg 355
Gramedia, pg 355
Karya Anda, CV, pg 355

Ireland

Brandon Book Publishers Ltd, pg 358
The Children's Press, pg 358
Clo Iar-Chonnachta Teo, pg 358
Gill & Macmillan Ltd, pg 360
The Goldsmith Press Ltd, pg 360
Irish Times Ltd, pg 361
The Lilliput Press Ltd, pg 361
Mercier Press Ltd, pg 362
Mount Eagle Publications Ltd, pg 362
The O'Brien Press Ltd, pg 362
Poolbeg Press Ltd, pg 363
Publishers Group South West (Ireland), pg 363
Roberts Rinehart Publishers, pg 363
Town House & Country House, pg 364
Wolfhound Press Ltd, pg 364

Israel

Achiasaf Publishing House Ltd, pg 364
Am Oved Publishers Ltd, pg 365
Amichai Publishing House Ltd, pg 365
Bitan Publishers Ltd, pg 365
Boostan Publishing House, pg 365
DAT Publications, pg 366
Gefen Publishing House Ltd, pg 367
Gvanim Publishing House, pg 367
Hakibbutz Hameuchad Publishing House Ltd, pg 367
Karni Publishers Ltd, pg 369
Keter Publishing House Ltd, pg 369
Kiryat Sefer, pg 369
Ma'ariv Book Guild (Sifriat Ma'ariv), pg 370
Machbarot Lesifrut, pg 370
Massada Publishers Ltd, pg 370
M Mizrahi Publishers, pg 370
Pitspopany Press, pg 371
Saar Publishing House, pg 371
Schocken Publishing House Ltd, pg 371
Sifriat Poalim Ltd, pg 372
Steimatzky Group Ltd, pg 372
Urim Publications, pg 373
Yavneh Publishing House Ltd, pg 373
Yedioth Ahronoth Books, pg 373
Zmora-Bitan, Publishers Ltd, pg 374

Italy

Adelphi Edizioni SpA, pg 374
Archimede Edizioni, pg 376
Argalia Editore delle Arti Grafiche Editoriali SRL, pg 376
Gruppo Editoriale Armenia SpA, pg 376
Belforte Editore Libraio srl, pg 377
Bompiani-RCS Libri, pg 378
Giuseppe Bonanno Editore, pg 378
Bulzoni Editore SRL (Le Edizioni Universitarie d'Italia), pg 379
Campanotto, pg 379
Cappelli Editore, pg 380
Casa Editrice Castalia, pg 380
Editrice Il Castoro, pg 380
Colonnese Editore, pg 383
Costa e Nolan SpA, pg 383
Dami Editore SRL, pg 384
G De Bono Editore, pg 384
Organizzazione Didattica Editoriale Ape, pg 385
Edizioni E/O, pg 385
Edistudio, pg 386
Edizioni l'Arciere SRL, pg 387
Effata Editrice, pg 387
Giulio Einaudi Editore SpA, pg 387
Giangiacomo Feltrinelli SpA, pg 389
Fogola Editore in Torino, pg 389
Edizioni Frassinelli SRL, pg 389
Fratelli Conte Editori SRL, pg 389
Galzerano Editore, pg 390
Gamberetti Editrice SRL, pg 390
Garzanti Libri, pg 390
Giunti Gruppo Editoriale, pg 390
Ernesto Gremese Editore srl, pg 391
Ibis, pg 392
Editoriale Jaca Book SpA, pg 394
L Japadre Editore, pg 394
Lalli Editore SRL, pg 394
Editrice Liguria SNC di Norberto Sabatelli & C, pg 395
Lindau, pg 395
Vincenzo Lo Faro Editore, pg 395
Longanesi & C, pg 396
Angelo Longo Editore, pg 396
Lorenzo Editore, pg 396
La Luna, pg 396
Lusva Editrice, pg 396
Tommaso Marotta Editore Srl, pg 397
Marsilio Editori SpA, pg 397
Editrice Massimo SAS di Crespi Cesare e C, pg 397
Milano Libri, pg 398
Minerva Italica SpA, pg 398
Il Minotauro, pg 398
Arnoldo Mondadori Editore SpA, pg 398
Mondolibro Editore SNC, pg 399
Gruppo Ugo Mursia Editore SpA, pg 400
Newton & Compton Editori, pg 400
Il Nuovo Melangolo, pg 401
OCTAVO Produzioni Editoriali Associate, pg 401
Luigi Pellegrini Editore, pg 403
Edizioni Piemme SpA, pg 403
La Pilotta Editrice Coop RL, pg 403
Il Quadrante SRL, pg 404
RAI-ERI, pg 405
RCS Rizzoli Libri SpA, pg 405
Editori Riuniti, pg 405
Il Saggiatore, pg 406
Adriano Salani Editore srl, pg 406
Salerno Editrice SRL, pg 406
Edizioni San Paolo SRL, pg 407
Sansoni-RCS Libri, pg 407
Sardini Editrice, pg 407
Edizioni Segno SRL, pg 407
Sonzogno, pg 409
Sperling e Kupfer Editori SpA, pg 409
Le Stelle Scuola, pg 409
Edizioni Studio Tesi SRL, pg 409
Sugarco Edizioni SRL, pg 409
TEA Tascabili degli Editori Associati SpA, pg 409
Edizioni Thyrus SRL, pg 410
Todariana Editrice, pg 410
Giovanni Tranchida Editore, pg 410
Transeuropa, pg 410
Marco Tropea Editore, pg 410
Edizioni La Vita Felice, pg 412

Jamaica

Carib Publishing Ltd, pg 413
Institute of Jamaica Publications, pg 413
LMH Publishing Ltd, pg 414

Japan

Akita Shoten Publishing Co Ltd, pg 415
Bunkasha Publishing Co Ltd, pg 415
Chikuma Shobo Publishing Co Ltd, pg 416
Dainippon Tosho Publishing Co, Ltd, pg 416
Fukuinkan Shoten Publishers Inc, pg 417
Hakusui-Sha Co Ltd, pg 417
Hayakawa Publishing Inc, pg 418
Japan Broadcast Publishing Co Ltd, pg 419
Kadokawa Shoten Publishing Co Ltd, pg 420
Kawade Shobo Shinsha Publishers, pg 420
Kodansha International Ltd, pg 421
Kodansha Ltd, pg 421
Kokushokankokai Co Ltd, pg 421
Nippon Hoso Shuppan Kyokai (NHK Publishing), pg 424
Poplar Publishing Co Ltd, pg 425
Saela Shobo (Librairie Ca et La), pg 425
Seibu Time Co Ltd, pg 426
Shakai Shiso-Sha, pg 427
Shincho-Sha Co Ltd, pg 427
Akane Shobo Co Ltd, pg 427
Shueisha Inc, pg 428
Shufu-to-Seikatsu Sha Ltd, pg 428
Shufunotomo Co Ltd, pg 428
Tokuma Shoten Publishing Co Ltd, pg 429
Tokyo Shoseki Co Ltd, pg 430
Charles E Tuttle Publishing Co Inc, pg 430

Jordan

Jordan Book Centre Co Ltd, pg 432

Kenya

Focus Publications Ltd, pg 433
Heinemann Kenya Ltd (EAEP), pg 434
Jacaranda Designs Ltd, pg 434
Lake Publishers & Enterprises Ltd, pg 435
Sasa Sema Publications Ltd, pg 435
Transafrica Press, pg 436
Uzima Press Ltd, pg 436

Democratic People's Republic of Korea

Literature and Art Publishing House, pg 436
Working People's Organization Publishing House, pg 437

Republic of Korea

Big Tree Publishing, pg 437
Borim Publishing Co, pg 437
Bum-Woo Publishing Co, pg 437
Chung Rim Publishing Co Ltd, pg 438
Gim-Yeong Co, pg 438
Hainaim Publishing Co Ltd, pg 439
Hollym Corporation; Publishers, pg 439
Hw Moon Publishing Co, pg 439
Iljisa Publishing House, pg 439
Jeong-eum Munhwasa, pg 439
Jigyungsa Ltd, pg 440
Ke Mong Sa Publishing Co Ltd, pg 440
Koreaone Press Inc, pg 440
Kumsung Publishing Co Ltd, pg 440
Min-eumsa Publishing Co Ltd, pg 441
Munye Publishing Co, pg 441
O Neul Publishing Co, pg 441
St Pauls, pg 442
Woongjin Media Corporation, pg 443
Yearimdang Publishing Co, pg 443

Laos People's Democratic Republic

Lao-phanit, pg 444

Latvia

Artava Ltd, pg 444
Egmont Latvia SIA, pg 444
Madris, pg 445
Nordik/Tapals Publishers Ltd, pg 445
Preses Nams, pg 445
Spriditis Publishers, pg 445
Vaidelote, SIA, pg 445
Zvaigzne ABC Publishers Ltd, pg 445

Lebanon

Khayat Book and Publishing Co Sarl, pg 446
Librairie du Liban Publishers (Sal), pg 446
Naufal Group Sarl, pg 447

Lithuania

Algarve, pg 448
Alma Littera, pg 448
Baltos Lankos, pg 449
Egmont Lietuva, pg 449
Lietus Ltd, pg 449
Lietuvos Rasytoju Sajungos Leidykla, pg 449
Margi Rastai Publishers, pg 449
Tyto Alba Publishers, pg 450
Vaga Ltd, pg 450
Vyturys Vyturio leidykla, UAB, pg 450

PUBLISHERS

Luxembourg
Guy Binsfeld & Co Sarl, pg 450

The Former Yugoslav Republic of Macedonia
Detska radost, pg 452
Makedonska kniga (Knigoizdatelstvo), pg 452
Zumpres Publishing Firm, pg 453

Madagascar
Imprimerie Takariva, pg 454
Trano Printy Fiangonana Loterana Malagasy (TPFLM)-(Imprimerie Lutherienne), pg 454

Malawi
Christian Literature Association in Malawi, pg 454
Dzuka Publishing Co Ltd, pg 454
Popular Publications, pg 454

Malaysia
Associated Educational Distributors (M) Sdn Bhd, pg 455
Berita Publishing Sdn Bhd, pg 455
Holograms (M) Sdn Bhd, pg 456
K Publishing & Distributors Sdn Bhd, pg 456
Pustaka Cipta Sdn Bhd, pg 458
Tempo Publishing (M) Sdn Bhd, pg 458
University of Malaya, Department of Publications, pg 459

Mali
EDIM SA, pg 460

Mauritius
Editions de l'Ocean Indien Ltd, pg 461

Mexico
Aguilar Altea Taurus Alfaguara SA de CV, pg 462
Ediciones Alpe, pg 462
Libreria y Ediciones Botas SA, pg 462
Editorial Diana SA de CV, pg 464
Empresas Editoriales SA, pg 465
Ediciones Era SA de CV, pg 465
Fondo de Cultura Economica, pg 465
Editorial Grijalbo SA de CV, pg 466
Editorial Hermes SA, pg 466
Hoja Casa Editorial SA de CV, pg 466
Editorial Joaquin Mortiz SA de CV, pg 467
Editores Mexicanos Unidos SA, pg 468
Editorial Nueva Imagen SA, pg 469
Editorial Planeta Mexicana SA, pg 470
Ediciones Promesa, SA de CV, pg 470
Ediciones Roca, SA, pg 471
Salvat Editores de Mexico, pg 471
Universidad Veracruzana Direccion General Editorial y de Publicaciones, pg 472
Universo Editorial SA de CV Edicion de Libros Revistas y Periodicos, pg 473
Editorial Universo SA de CV, pg 473
Javier Vergara Editor SA de CV, pg 473

Republic of Moldova
Editura Cartea Moldovei, pg 473
Editura Hyperion, pg 473

Monaco
Les Editions du Rocher, pg 474
Rondeau Giannipiero a Monaco, pg 474
Editions Andre Sauret SA, pg 474

Morocco
Edition Diffusion de Livre au Maroc, pg 474
Editions Le Fennec, pg 474

Mozambique
Empresa Moderna Lda, pg 475

Netherlands
Uitgeverij Ambo BV, pg 477
Uitgeverij Anthos, pg 477
Uitgeverij de Arbeiderspers, pg 477
Uitgeverij Arena BV, pg 478
Uitgevirj Aristos, pg 478
Uitgeverij Balans, pg 478
De Bezige Bij B V Uitgeverij, pg 479
De Boekerij BV, pg 479
A W Bruna Uitgevers BV, pg 480
BZZTOH Publishers, pg 480
Cadans, pg 480
Callenbach BV, pg 480
Uitgeverij Christofoor, pg 480
Uitgeverij Conserve, pg 481
Uitgeversmaatschappij Ad Donker BV, pg 481
ECI voor Boeken en platen BV, pg 481
Uitgeverij Elzenga, pg 482
Uitgeverij De Fontein BV, pg 482
Uitgeverij en boekhandel Van Gennep BV, pg 482
Uitgeverij De Geus BV, pg 482
Gottmer Uitgevers Groep, pg 483
De Harmonie Uitgeverij, pg 483
Heuff Amsterdam Uitgever, pg 483
Uitgeverij Holland, pg 483
Uitgeverij Hollandia BV, pg 483
Uitgeverij J H Kok BV, pg 485
Uitgeverij Leopold BV, pg 485
J M Meulenhoff bv, pg 486
Uitgeverij Mingus, pg 486
Uitgeverij Maarten Muntinga, pg 486
Nederlands Literair Produktie-en Vertalingen Fonds (NLPVF), pg 486
Nijgh & Van Ditmar Amsterdam, pg 487
Omega Boek BV, pg 487
Uitgeverij Ploegsma BV, pg 487
Podium Uitgeverij, pg 487
Em Querido's Uitgeverij BV, pg 488
Sjaloom Uitgeverijen, pg 489
Uniboek BV, pg 490
Van Buuren Uitgeverij BV, pg 491
Uitgeverij Vassallucci bv, pg 491
Wereldbibliotheek, pg 492
Uitgeverij Westers, pg 492

New Zealand
Brick Row Publishing Co Ltd, pg 494
Cape Catley Ltd, pg 495
Church Mouse Press, pg 495
Cicada Press, pg 495
David's Marine Books, pg 495
HarperCollins Publishers (New Zealand) Ltd, pg 497
Hazard Press Ltd, pg 497

Hodder Moa Beckett Publishers Ltd, pg 497
Huia Publishers, pg 497
Lincoln University Press, pg 498
David Ling Publishing, pg 498
Nagare Press, pg 499
Orca Publishing Services Ltd, pg 499
Reed Publishing (NZ) Ltd, pg 500
RSVP Publishing Co Ltd, pg 500
Shearwater Associates Ltd, pg 501
Tandem Press, pg 501
University of Otago Press, pg 502
Words Work, pg 502

Nicaragua
Editorial Nueva Nicaragua, pg 502

Nigeria
Adebara Publishers Ltd, pg 503
Cross Continent Press Ltd, pg 504
Delta Publications (Nigeria) Ltd, pg 504
Ethiope Publishing Corporation, pg 504
Evans Brothers (Nigeria Publishers) Ltd, pg 504
Fourth Dimension Publishing Co Ltd, pg 504
Heritage Books, pg 505
Longman Nigeria Plc, pg 505
Thomas Nelson (Nigeria) Ltd, pg 505
New Era Publishers, pg 506
New Horn Press Ltd, pg 506
Nwamife Publishers Ltd, pg 506
Obobo Books, pg 506
Onibon-Oje Publishers, pg 506
Paperback Publishers Ltd, pg 507
Saros International Publishers, pg 507
Spectrum Books Ltd, pg 507
Tana Press Ltd & Flora Nwapa Books Ltd, pg 507
Vantage Publishers International Ltd, pg 507

Norway
Ariel Lydbokforlag, pg 508
Aschehoug Forlag, pg 508
H Aschehoug & Co (W Nygaard) A/S, pg 508
Atheneum Forlag A/S, pg 508
Bladkompaniet A/S, pg 508
J W Cappelens Forlag A/S, pg 508
N W Damm og Son A/S, pg 508
Det Norske Samlaget, pg 508
Fonna Forlag L/L, pg 509
Fono Forlag, pg 509
John Grieg Forlag AS, pg 509
Gyldendal Norsk Forlag A/S, pg 509
Lunde Forlag AS, pg 509
Luther Forlag A/S, pg 509
Norsk Bokreidingslag L/L, pg 510
Pax Forlag A/S, pg 510
Erik Sandberg, pg 510
Snofugl Forlag, pg 510
Solum Forlag A/S, pg 510
Stabenfeldt A/S, pg 510
Tiden Norsk Forlag, pg 511

Pakistan
Classic, pg 512
Malik Sirajuddin & Sons, pg 513
Maqbool Academy, pg 513
Sang-e-Meel Publications, pg 514

Papua New Guinea
Kristen Press, pg 515

SUBJECT INDEX

Philippines
Anvil Publishing Inc, pg 518
Ateneo de Manila University Press, pg 518
De La Salle University, pg 519
Estrella Publishing, pg 519
Kadena Press, pg 519
Marren Publishing House, Inc, pg 519
National Book Store Inc, pg 519
New Day Publishers, pg 520
Philippine Education Co Inc, pg 520
Solidaridad Publishing House, pg 521
University of the Philippines Press, pg 521

Poland
Albatros, pg 522
Spoldzielnia Wydawnicza 'Czytelnik', pg 522
Wydawnictwo Dolnoslaskie, pg 522
Ksiaznica Publishing Ltd, pg 524
Muza SA, pg 524
Wydawnictwo Nasza Ksiegarnia Sp zoo, pg 524
Norbertinum, pg 524
Wydawnictwa Normalizacyjne Alfa-Wero, pg 525
Panstwowy Instytut Wydawniczy (PIW), pg 525
Wydawnictwa Radia i Telewizji, pg 526
Videograf II Sp z o o Zaklad Poracy Chronionej, pg 526
Wydawnictwo WAB, pg 527
Wydawnictwo Wilga sp zoo, pg 527

Portugal
Edicoes Antigona, pg 528
Bezerr-Editorae e Distribuidora de Abel Antonio Bezerra, pg 529
Brasilia Editora (J Carvalho Branco), pg 529
Editorial Caminho SARL, pg 529
Livraria Civilizacao (Americo Fraga Lamares & Ca Lda), pg 529
Editora Classica, pg 530
Contexto Editora, pg 530
DIFEL - Difusao Editorial SA, pg 530
Difusao Cultural, pg 530
Editorial Estampa, Lda, pg 531
Publicacoes Europa-America Lda, pg 531
Europress Editores e Distribuidores de Publicacoes Lda, pg 531
Gradiva-Publicacnoes Lda, pg 532
Guimaraes Editores, Lda, pg 532
Editorial Minerva, pg 533
Editorial Noticias, pg 534
Planeta Editora, LDA, pg 534
Editorial Presenca, pg 535
Publicacoes Dom Quixote Lda, pg 535
Puma Editora Lda, pg 535
Quatro Elementos Editores, pg 535
Quimera Editores Lda, pg 535
Almerinda Teixeira, pg 536
Teorema, pg 536
Texto Editora, pg 536
Vega-Publicacao e Distribuicao de Livros e Revistas, Lda, pg 536
Livraria Verdade e Vida Editora, pg 536

Puerto Rico
Modern Guides Company, pg 537

977

SUBJECT INDEX

Romania
Editora All, pg 538
Ars Longa Publishing House, pg 538
Editura Cartea Romaneasca, pg 538
Editura Clusium, pg 539
Corint Publishing Group, pg 539
Editure Ion Creanga, pg 539
Editura Dacia, pg 539
Editura Excelsior Art, pg 539
Humanitas Publishing House, pg 540
Editura Kriterion SA, pg 540
Editura Niculescu, pg 541
Pallas-Akademia Editura, pg 541
Pandora Publishing House, pg 541
Grupul Editorial RAO, pg 542
RAO International Publishing Co, pg 542
Saeculum IO, pg 542
Est-Samuel Tastet Verlag, pg 542
Editura Univers SA, pg 543
Universal Dalsi, pg 543
Editura de Vest, pg 543
Vremea Publishers Ltd, pg 543

Russian Federation
Armada Publishing House, pg 543
BLIC, russko-Baltijskij informaciionnyj centr, AO, pg 544
CentrePolygraph Traders & Publishers Co, pg 544
Izdatelstvo Detskaya Literatura, pg 544
Dom, Izdatel'stvo sovetskogo deskkogo fonda im & I Lenina, pg 544
Glas New Russian Writing, pg 545
Kavkazskaya Biblioteka Publishing House, pg 545
Izdatelstvo Khudozhestvennaya Literatura, pg 545
Izdatelstvo Knizhnaya Palata, pg 546
Ladomir Publishing House, pg 546
Izdatelstvo Lenizdat, pg 546
Publishing House Limbus Press, pg 546
Izdatelstvo Mir, pg 546
Mir Knigi Ltd, pg 546
Izdatelstvo Moskovskii Rabochii, pg 547
Novosti Izdatelstvo, pg 547
Obdeestro Znanie, pg 547
Panorama Publishing House, pg 547
Permskaja Kniga, pg 548
Pressa Publishing House, pg 548
Profizdat, pg 548
Progress Publishers, pg 548
Raduga Publishers, pg 548
Russkaya Kniga Izdatelstvo (Publishers), pg 548
Sovremennik Publishers Too, pg 548
Sredne-Uralskoye knizhnoye izatelstve (Middle Urals Publishing House), pg 549
Top Secret Collection Publishers, pg 549
Voyenizdat, pg 549
Vsesoyuznii Molodejnii Knizhnii Centre, pg 549

Senegal
Centre Africain d'Animation et d'Echanges Culturels Editions Khoudia (CAEC), pg 551
Les Nouvelles Editions Africaines du Senegal NEAS, pg 551

Serbia and Montenegro
Alfa-Narodna Knjiga, pg 552
Forum, pg 552
Nolit Publishing House, pg 553
Obod, pg 553
Partenon MAM Sistem, pg 553
Svetovi, pg 554

Singapore
Chopsons Pte Ltd, pg 555
McGallen & Bolden Associates, pg 557
Select Publishing Pte Ltd, pg 557

Slovakia
Danubiaprint, pg 559
Kalligram spol sro, pg 559
Vydavatel'stvo Osveta (Verlag Osveta), pg 560
Slovensky Spisovatel Ltd as, pg 560
Smena Publishing House, pg 560
Sport Publishing House Ltd, pg 561
Vydavatelstvo Wist sro, pg 561

Slovenia
Cankarjeva Zalozba, pg 561
Franc-Franc podjetje za promocijo kulture Murska Sobota d o o, pg 561
Mladinska Knjiga International, pg 561
Pomurska zalozba, pg 561
Zalozba Mihelac d o o, pg 562
Zalozba Obzorja d d Maribor, pg 562

South Africa
HAUM (Hollandsch Afrikaansche Uitgevers Maatschappij), pg 564
The Hippogriff Press CC, pg 564
Human & Rousseau (Pty) Ltd, pg 564
Ithemba! Publishing, pg 565
Jacklin Enterprises (Pty) Ltd, pg 565
Juventus/Femina Publishers, pg 565
LAPA Publishers (Pty) Ltd, pg 566
Nasou Via Afrika, pg 567
New Africa Books (Pty) Ltd, pg 567
Queillerie Publishers, pg 568
Ravan Press (Pty) Ltd, pg 568
Struik Publishers (Pty) Ltd, pg 569
Tafelberg Publishers Ltd, pg 569

Spain
Publicacions de l'Abadia de Montserrat, pg 570
Acento Editorial, pg 570
Editorial Aguaclara, pg 571
Aguilar SA de Ediciones, pg 571
Alfaguara Ediciones SA - Grupo Santillana, pg 572
Ediciones Alfar SA, pg 572
Alianza Editorial SA, pg 572
Ediciones B, SA, pg 574
Calambur Editorial, SL, pg 575
Calamo Editorial, pg 575
CEAC, Grupo Editorial SA, pg 576
Circe Ediciones, SA, pg 577
Columna Edicions, Libres i Comunicacio, pg 577
Ediciones Destino SA, pg 579
Editorial Don Quijote, pg 579
Edebe, pg 580
EDHASA (Editora y Distribuidora Hispano-Americana SA), pg 580
Edi-Liber Irlan SA, pg 580
Enciclopedia Catalana, SA, pg 582
Editorial Esin, SA, pg 582
Editorial Espasa-Calpe SA, pg 582
Editorial Fundamentos, pg 584
Grijalbo Mondadori SA, pg 585
Editorial Iberia, SA, pg 586
Ediciones Jucar, pg 588
Editorial Juventud SA, pg 588
Laertes SA de Ediciones, pg 588
Edicions de l'Eixample, SA, pg 589
Loguez Ediciones, pg 589
Editorial Lumen SA, pg 589
Editorial Magisterio Espanol SA, pg 590
Edicions de la Magrana SA, pg 590
Ediciones Martinez-Roca SA, pg 591
Ediciones Minotauro, pg 591
Editorial Molino, pg 592
Editorial Moll SL, pg 592
Noguer y Caralt Editores SA, pg 593
Editorial Noray, pg 593
Ediciones Oceano Grupo SA, pg 593
Ediciones Olimpic, SL, pg 594
Ediciones del Oriente y del Mediterraneo, pg 594
Pages Editors, SL, pg 594
El Paisaje Editorial, pg 594
Pirene Editorial, sal, pg 596
Editorial Planeta SA, pg 596
Plaza y Janes Editores SA, pg 596
Editorial Pliegos, pg 596
Pre-Textos, pg 596
Editorial Prensa Espanola, pg 597
Edicions Proa, SA, pg 597
Publicaciones y Ediciones Salamandra, pg 597
Editorial Seix Barral SA, pg 599
Sirmio, pg 600
Ediciones Siruela SA, pg 600
Edicions 62, pg 600
Grup 62, pg 600
Anna Soler-Pont Literary Agecy, pg 600
Ediciones Susaeta SA, pg 601
Editorial Thassalia, pg 602
Gregorio del Toro Editor, pg 602
Trea Ediciones, SL, pg 602
Tusquets Editores, pg 603
Ultramar Editores SA, pg 603
Ediciones Urano, SA, pg 604
Editorial Verbum SL, pg 604
Javier Vergara Editor SA, pg 604
Editorial Vicens-Vives, pg 605
Vinaches Lopez, Luisa, pg 605
Edicions Xerais de Galicia, pg 605
Xunta de Galicia, pg 605

Sri Lanka
Dayawansa Jayakody & Co, pg 606
Lake House Investments Ltd, pg 606
Pradeepa Publishers, pg 607
Saman Saha Madara Publishers, pg 607

Sudan
Al-Ayam Press Co Ltd, pg 608
Khartoum University Press, pg 608

Suriname
Lutchman, Drs LFS, pg 608

Sweden
Bokforlaget Atlantis AB, pg 609
Akademiforlaget Corona AB, pg 609
Albert Bonniers Forlag, pg 609
Alfabeta Bokforlag AB, pg 609
Bokforlaget Axplock, pg 609
Bonnier Audio, pg 610
Bonnier Carlsen Bokforlag AB, pg 610
Albert Bonniers Forlag AB, pg 610
Bokforlaget Bra Bocker AB, pg 610
Brombergs Bokforlag AB, pg 610
Rene Coeckelberghs Bokfoerlag AB, pg 610
Delta Forlags AB, pg 611
Egmont Serieforlaget, pg 611
Ekonomibok Forlag AB, pg 611
Ellerstroms, pg 611
Bokforlaget Fingraf AB, pg 611
Fischer & Co, pg 611
Bokforlaget Forum AB, pg 611
Gedins Forlag, pg 611
Lars Hoekerbergs Bokfoerlag, pg 612
Interculture, pg 612
Libris Bokforlaget, pg 613
Bokfoerlaget Natur och Kultur, pg 613
Norstedts Forlag, pg 614
Bokforlaget Opal AB, pg 614
Ordfront Foerlag AB, pg 614
Bokforlaget Plus AB, pg 614
Bokforlaget Prisma, pg 614
Richters Egmont, pg 615
Sjoestrands Foerlag, pg 615
Bokforlaget Spektra AB, pg 615
AB Wahlstroem & Widstrand, pg 616
Wahlstrom & Widstrand, pg 616
B Wahlstroms, pg 616
Zindermans AB, pg 617

Switzerland
Editions L'Age d'Homme - La Cite, pg 617
Ammann Verlag & Co, pg 617
Arche Verlag AG, Raabe und Vitali, pg 617
Association Suisse des Editeurs de Langue Francaise, pg 618
Atrium Verlag AG, pg 618
Bohem Press Kinderbuchverlag, pg 619
Brunnen-Verlag Basel, pg 620
Verlag Bo Cavefors, pg 620
Chronos Verlag, pg 621
Cosmos-Verlag AG, pg 621
Diogenes Verlag AG, pg 622
Verlag ED Emmentaler Druck AG, pg 622
Edition Epoca, pg 622
eFeF-Verlag/Edition Ebersbach, pg 622
Haffmans Verlag AG, pg 624
Limmat Verlag, pg 628
Manesse Verlag GmbH, pg 628
Les Editions la Matze, pg 628
Mueller Rueschlikon Verlags AG, pg 629
Verlag Nagel & Kimche AG, Zurich, pg 629
Les Editions Noir sur Blanc, pg 629
Oesch Verlag AG, pg 630
Editions du Panorama, pg 630
Editions Patino, pg 631
Robert Raeber, Buchhandlung am Schweizerhof, pg 632
Verlag Friedrich Reinhardt AG, pg 632
Rex Verlag, pg 632
Rotpunktverlag, pg 632
Verlag fuer Schoene Wissenschaften, pg 633
Speer -Verlag, pg 634
Sphinx Verlag AG, pg 634
Strom-Verlag Luzern, pg 635
Theseus Verlag AG, pg 635
Istituto Editoriale Ticinese (IET) SA, pg 635
Verlag Die Waage, pg 636

PUBLISHERS

SUBJECT INDEX

Taiwan, Province of China
Asian Culture Co Ltd, pg 638
Chung Hwa Book Co Ltd, pg 639
Commonwealth Publishing Company Ltd, pg 639
Grimm Press Ltd, pg 640
Hilit Publishing Co Ltd, pg 640
Kuang Fu Book Co Ltd, pg 640
Lin Pai Press Company Ltd, pg 641
Linking Publishing Company Ltd, pg 641
Morning Star Publisher Inc, pg 641
UNITAS Publishing Co Ltd, pg 642
Yuan Liou Publishing Co, Ltd, pg 642

Tajikistan
Irfon, pg 642

United Republic of Tanzania
Akajase Enterprises, pg 643
East African Publishing House, pg 643
Ndanda Mission Press, pg 644
Nyota Publishers Ltd, pg 644
Press & Publicity Centre Ltd, pg 644
Readit Books, pg 644
Tanzania Publishing House, pg 644
Tema Publishers Ltd, pg 644

Thailand
Bannakit Trading, pg 645
Chokechai Theues Shop, pg 645
New Generation Publishing Co Ltd, pg 645
Ruamsarn (1977) Co Ltd, pg 645

Togo
Les Nouvelles Editions Africaines du TOGO (NEA-TOGO), pg 646

Tunisia
Alyssa Editions, pg 647

Turkey
Altin Kitaplar Yayinevi, pg 649
Cep Kitaplari AS, pg 649
Iletisim Yayinlari, pg 650
Inkilap Publishers Ltd, pg 650
Kiyi Yayinlari, pg 650
Pan Yayincilik, pg 651
Parantez Yayinlari Ltd, pg 651
Remzi Kitabevi, pg 651
Soez Yayin/Oyunajans, pg 651
Varlik Yayinlari AS, pg 652
Kabalci Yayinevi, pg 652

Turkmenistan
Izdatelstvo Turkmenistan, pg 652

Uganda
Fountain Publishers Ltd, pg 652

Ukraine
ASK Ltd, pg 653
Dnipro, pg 653
Veselka Publishers, pg 654

United Kingdom
Acair Ltd, pg 655
Act 3 Publishing, pg 655
AK Press & Distribution, pg 656
Allied Mouse Ltd, pg 656
Alun Books, pg 657
Andersen Press Ltd, pg 657
Apex Publishing Ltd, pg 658
Arcadia Books, pg 659
Atlas Press, pg 661
BBC Audiobooks, pg 663
BCA - Book Club Associates, pg 663
Bellew Publishing Co Ltd, pg 664
Birlinn Ltd, pg 666
Black Ace Books, pg 666
Black Spring Press Ltd, pg 666
Blackstaff Press, pg 666
John Blake Publishing Ltd, pg 667
Bloomsbury Publishing PLC, pg 668
Blorenge Books, pg 668
The Book Guild Ltd, pg 668
Books of Zimbabwe Publishing Co (Pvt) Ltd, pg 669
Boulevard Books UK/The Babel Guides, pg 669
Bounty Books, pg 669
Marion Boyars Publishers Ltd, pg 669
Breese Books Ltd, pg 670
Brewin Books Ltd, pg 671
Brimax Books, pg 671
Calder Publications Ltd, pg 673
Canongate Books Ltd, pg 674
Carcanet Press Ltd, pg 674
Cassell & Co, pg 675
Chorion IP, pg 679
Christian Focus Publications Ltd, pg 679
The Chrysalis Press, pg 679
Creation Books, pg 683
Dedalus Ltd, pg 687
Delancey Press Ltd, pg 687
Denor Press, pg 687
Gerald Duckworth & Co Ltd, pg 688
Eland Publishing Ltd, pg 690
Faber & Faber Ltd, pg 694
Feather Books, pg 694
Flambard Press, pg 695
Fourth Estate, pg 696
Gairm Publications, pg 698
Geiser Productions, pg 699
Gembooks, pg 699
George Mann Publications, pg 699
GMP Publishers Ltd, pg 700
Gollancz/Witherby, pg 701
Gomer Press (J D Lewis & Sons Ltd), pg 701
Grandreams Ltd, pg 702
Granta Books, pg 702
Peter Halban Publishers Ltd, pg 703
Robert Hale Ltd, pg 704
Hamish Hamilton Ltd, pg 704
Patrick Hardy Books, pg 705
HarperCollins UK, pg 705
The Harvill Press, pg 705
Headline Book Publishing Ltd, pg 706
Heinemann Educational Publishing, pg 707
William Heinemann Ltd, pg 707
Ian Henry Publications Ltd, pg 708
Hodder & Stoughton General, pg 709
Hodder Children's Books, pg 709
Honeyglen Publishing Ltd, pg 710
Honno Welsh Women's Press, pg 710
Independent Writers Publications Ltd, pg 712
Isis Publishing Ltd, pg 714
Janus Publishing Co Ltd, pg 716
Michael Joseph Ltd, pg 716
Ladybird Books Ltd, pg 719
Letterbox Library, pg 720
Libris Ltd, pg 720
Y Lolfa Cyf, pg 722
Luath Press Ltd, pg 722
Macmillan Audio Books, pg 723
Macmillan Children's Books, pg 723
Macmillan Ltd, pg 723
Magi Publications, pg 724
Mandrake of Oxford, pg 725
The Mansk Svenska Publishing Co Ltd, pg 725
Methuen, pg 727
Monarch Books, pg 729
John Murray (Publishers) Ltd, pg 730
Neil Wilson Publishing Ltd, pg 732
New Era Publications UK Ltd, pg 732
Octopus Publishing Group, pg 734
Oldcastle Books Ltd, pg 734
Onlywomen Press Ltd, pg 735
Orion Publishing Group Ltd, pg 736
Peter Owen Ltd, pg 737
Oyster Books Ltd, pg 737
Parthian Books, pg 738
Peepal Tree Press Ltd, pg 740
Piatkus Books, pg 741
Piccadilly Press, pg 742
Plough Publishing House of Bruderhof Communities in the UK, pg 743
Polybooks Ltd, pg 744
Polygon, pg 744
Pookie Productions Ltd, pg 744
Mathew Price Ltd, pg 745
Quartet Books Ltd, pg 746
Quartz Editions, pg 746
Ramsay Head Press, pg 747
Random House UK Ltd, pg 747
Ravette Publishing Ltd, pg 748
The Reader's Digest Association Ltd, pg 748
The Robinswood Press Ltd, pg 750
The Rubicon Press, pg 752
St George's Press, pg 753
The Salariya Book Co Ltd, pg 753
Sangam Books Ltd, pg 754
Saqi Books, pg 754
Steve Savage Publishers Ltd, pg 754
Scholastic Ltd, pg 754
Scottish Cultural Press, pg 755
Martin Secker & Warburg, pg 756
Seren, pg 756
Serpent's Tail Ltd, pg 756
Severn House Publishers Inc, pg 756
Shearwater Press Ltd, pg 757
Sidgwick & Jackson Ltd, pg 757
Simon & Schuster Ltd, pg 758
Skoob Russell Square, pg 758
Snowbooks Ltd, pg 759
Souvenir Press Ltd, pg 759
Sutton Publishing Ltd, pg 762
Tabb House, pg 762
Tiger Books International PLC, pg 765
Time Warner Book Group UK, pg 766
Transworld Publishers Ltd, pg 766
Tuba Press, pg 767
Ulverscroft Large Print Books Ltd, pg 768
United Writers Publications Ltd, pg 768
Van Molle Publishing, pg 769
Viking, pg 770
Virago Press, pg 770
Walker Books Ltd, pg 771
The Watts Publishing Group Ltd, pg 771
Wilmington Business Information Ltd, pg 774
The Women's Press Ltd, pg 775
Anglia Young Books, pg 776

Uruguay
La Flor del Itapebi, pg 777
Rosebud Ediciones, pg 778
Ediciones Trilce, pg 778

Venezuela
Alfadil Ediciones, pg 778
Monte Avila Editores Latinoamericana CA, pg 779
Biblioteca Ayacucho, pg 779
Ediciones Ekare, pg 779

Zambia
Apple Books, pg 781
Multimedia Zambia, pg 781
Zambia Educational Publishing House, pg 782

Zimbabwe
Academic Books (Pvt) Ltd, pg 782
College Press Publishers (Pvt) Ltd, pg 783
The Graham Publishing Company (Pvt) Ltd, pg 783
Mambo Press, pg 783
Vision Publications, pg 784

FILM, VIDEO

Argentina
Marymar Ediciones SA, pg 7

Australia
Australian Film Television & Radio School, pg 13
R J Cleary Publishing, pg 18
Currency Press Pty Ltd, pg 19
McGraw-Hill Australia Pty Ltd, pg 31
Power Publications, pg 37

Austria
Czernin Verlag Ltd, pg 49
Doecker Verlag GmbH & Co KG, pg 50
Edition S der OSD, pg 50
Dr Verena Hofstaetter, pg 52
Residenz Verlag GmbH, pg 57

Belgium
Graton Editeur NV, pg 68
Claude Lefrancq Editeur, pg 70

Brazil
Editora Brasil-America (EBAL) SA, pg 79
Imago Editora Importacao e Exportacao Ltda, pg 84
Summus Editorial Ltda, pg 91

China
China Film Press, pg 102
China Light Industry Press, pg 102
The People's Communications Publishing House, pg 106
Shanghai Far East Publishers, pg 108

Colombia
Universidad Nacional Abierta y a Distancia, pg 113

Costa Rica
Ediciones Promesa, pg 116

Cuba
Casa Editora Abril, pg 120

SUBJECT INDEX

BOOK

Czech Republic
Cinema, pg 123
Narodni filmovy archiv, pg 126

Denmark
Interpresse A/S, pg 132
Kaleidoscope Publishers Ltd, pg 132
Systime, pg 135

Estonia
Sinisukk, pg 140

Finland
Koala-Kustannus Oy, pg 143

France
Editions d'Aujourd'hui (Les Introuvables), pg 148
Editions l'Avant-Scene de Prette Technique, pg 149
Editions Balland, pg 149
Bragelonne, pg 151
Editions Climats, pg 154
Editions Copernic, pg 155
Editions Dis Voir, pg 158
Dreamland Editeur, pg 159
Dunod Editeur, pg 159
Editions du Jeu de Paume, pg 169
Michel Lafon Publishing, pg 171
Lettres Modernes Minard, pg 172
Macula, pg 173
Librairie Minard, pg 176
Editions Paul Montel, pg 176
Editions Plume, pg 180
Editions du Centre Pompidou, pg 180
Editions Stock, pg 186
La Voix du Regard, pg 189

Germany
Alba Fachverlag GmbH & Co KG, pg 191
Alexander Verlag Berlin, pg 192
AOL-Verlag Frohmut Menze, pg 193
Aufbau Taschenbuch Verlag GmbH, pg 195
Aufbau-Verlag GmbH, pg 195
Verlag der Autoren GmbH & Co KG, pg 196
Bertelsmann Lexikon Verlag GmbH, pg 200
F Bruckmann Munchen Verlag & Druck GmbH & Co Produkt KG, pg 204
Corian-Verlag Heinrich Wimmer, pg 209
Klaus D Dutz, pg 217
Egmont Franz Schneider Verlag GmbH, pg 218
Egmont vgs verlagsgesellschaft mbH, pg 218
EK-Verlag GmbH, pg 219
Emons Verlag, pg 219
FN-Verlag der Deutschen Reiterlichen Vereinigung GmbH, pg 225
Wilhelm Goldmann Verlag GmbH, pg 230
Gunter Olzog Verlag GmbH, pg 231
Haenssler Verlag GmbH, pg 233
Litteraturverlag Karlheinz Hartmann, pg 234
Heel Verlag GmbH, pg 235
Wilhelm Heyne Verlag, pg 237
Felicitas Huebner Verlag, pg 239
Huthig GmbH & Co KG, pg 240
Impuls-Theater-Verlag, pg 241
Jovis Verlag GmbH, pg 243
Verlagsgruppe Koehler/Mittler, pg 248
kopaed verlagsgmbh, pg 249
Edition Axel Menges, pg 259
J B Metzlersche Verlagsbuchhandlung, pg 260
Mosaik Verlag GmbH, pg 262
Verlag Stephanie Naglschmid, pg 263
Philipp Reclam Jun Verlag GmbH, pg 269
Polyband Gesellschaft fur Bild Tontraeger mbH & Co Betriebs KG, pg 271
Propylaeen Verlag, Zweigniederlassung Berlin der Ullstein Buchverlage GmbH, pg 272
Quintessenz Verlags-GmbH, pg 273
Ulrich Schiefer bahn Verlag, pg 279
Schueren Verlag GmbH, pg 281
Spiess Volker Wissenschaftsverlag GmbH, pg 284
edition Text & Kritik im Richard Boorberg Verlag GmbH & Co, pg 290
TR - Verlagsunion GmbH, pg 291
Trescher Verlag GmbH, pg 292
Tuebinger Vereinigung fur Volkskunde eV (TVV), pg 292
UVK Verlagsgesellschaft mbH, pg 294
Das Wunderhorn Verlag GmbH, pg 301

Ghana
World Literature Project, pg 305

Greece
Apostoliki Diakonia tis Ekklisias tis Hellados, pg 305
Kastaniotis Editions SA, pg 309
Medusa/Selas Publishers, pg 310

Hong Kong
Benefit Publishing Co, pg 315
Hong Kong University Press, pg 317
Joint Publishing (HK) Co Ltd, pg 317

Hungary
Jelenkor Verlag, pg 322
Osiris Kiado, pg 323

Indonesia
PT Indira, pg 355

Israel
Hanitzotz A-Sharara Publishing House, pg 367
The Harry Karren Institute for the Analysis of Propaganda, Yad Labanim, pg 369
Rolnik Publishers, pg 371

Italy
Arcipelago Edizioni di Chiani Marisa, pg 376
Bulzoni Editore SRL (Le Edizioni Universitarie d'Italia), pg 379
Cappelli Editore, pg 380
Editrice Il Castoro, pg 380
Edizioni Dedalo SRL, pg 384
Ernesto Gremese Editore srl, pg 391
Gremese International srl, pg 391
IHT Gruppo Editoriale SRL, pg 393
Kaos Edizioni SRL, pg 394
Lalli Editore SRL, pg 394
Lindau, pg 395
Angelo Longo Editore, pg 396
Giuseppe Maimone Editore, pg 397
Marsilio Editori SpA, pg 397
Edizioni Gabriele Mazzotta SRL, pg 397
Mondolibro Editore SNC, pg 399
Officina Edizioni di Aldo Quinti, pg 401
RAI-ERI, pg 405
SAIE Editrice SRL, pg 406
Scala Group spa, pg 407
Transeuropa, pg 410
Edizioni Ubulibri SAS, pg 410

Japan
Bunkasha Publishing Co Ltd, pg 415
Genko-Sha, pg 417
Shincho-Sha Co Ltd, pg 427
Waseda University Press, pg 431

Republic of Korea
Youlhwadang Publisher, pg 444

Latvia
Egmont Latvia SIA, pg 444
Preses Nams, pg 445

Luxembourg
Edition Objectif Lune, pg 451

Mexico
Ediciones Promesa, SA de CV, pg 470
SCRIPTA - Distribucion y Servicios Editoriales, SA de CV, pg 471

Netherlands
Uitgeverij Cantecleer BV, pg 480
Frank Fehmers Productions, pg 482
Uitgevery International Theatre & Film Books, pg 484
Tirion Uitgevers BV, pg 490

Norway
J W Eides Forlag A/S, pg 509
Vett & Viten AS, pg 511

Peru
Universidad de Lima-Fondo de Desarollo Editorial, pg 517

Philippines
Communication Foundation for Asia Media Group (CFAMG), pg 518
Our Lady of Manaoag Publisher, pg 520

Poland
Wydawnictwa Artystyczne i Filmowe, pg 522
Wydawnictwo Literackie, pg 524
Videograf II Sp z o o Zaklad Poracy Chronionej, pg 527

Portugal
Edicoes Afrontamento, pg 528

Romania
Editura Meridiane, pg 540
Editura Minerva, pg 541
Editura Niculescu, pg 541

Russian Federation
INFRA-M Izdatel'skij dom, pg 545
Izdatelstvo Iskusstvo, pg 545

Spain
Ediciones Akal SA, pg 571
Editorial Astri SA, pg 573
Ediciones Catedra SA, pg 576
Comunidad Autonoma de Madrid, Servicio de Documentacion y Publicaciones, pg 578
Editorial Donostiarra SA, pg 579
Ediciones Ebenezer, pg 580
Editorial Fundamentos, pg 584
Laertes SA de Ediciones, pg 588
Mandala Ediciones, pg 590
Ediciones Omega SA, pg 594
Ultramar Editores SA, pg 603

Sweden
Alfabeta Bokforlag AB, pg 609
Interculture, pg 612
Schultz Forlag AB, pg 615

Switzerland
Editions L'Age d'Homme - La Cite, pg 617
Chronos Verlag, pg 621
Editions Esprit Ouvert, pg 623
Editions Foma SA, pg 623
Lehrmittelverlag des Kantons Zurich, pg 627
Edition Olms AG, pg 630
Promoedition SA, pg 631
Hans Rohr Verlag, pg 632
3 Dimension World (3-D-World), pg 635
Vexer Verlag, pg 636

Turkey
Afa Yayincilik Sanayi Tic AS, pg 648
Parantez Yayinlari Ltd, pg 651
Payel Yayinevi, pg 651
Soez Yayin/Oyunajans, pg 651

Ukraine
Mystetstvo Publishers, pg 653

United Kingdom
Act 3 Publishing, pg 655
The Athlone Press Ltd, pg 661
Aurum Press Ltd, pg 661
Batsford Ltd, pg 663
BCA - Book Club Associates, pg 663
Berg Publishers, pg 664
BFI Publishing, pg 665
Bishopsgate Press Ltd, pg 666
Boxtree Ltd, pg 669
Marion Boyars Publishers Ltd, pg 669
Boydell & Brewer Ltd, pg 669
Cameron & Hollis, pg 674
Carlton Publishing Group, pg 675
Cassell & Co, pg 675
Chadwyck-Healey Ltd, pg 677
Chorion IP, pg 679
CMP Information Ltd, pg 680
Creation Books, pg 683
Edinburgh University Press Ltd, pg 689
Ethics International Press Ltd, pg 692
The Eurospan Group, pg 692
Faber & Faber Ltd, pg 694
Flicks Books, pg 695
Foulsham Publishers, pg 696
Furco Ltd, pg 698
Golden Cockerel Press Ltd, pg 701
Hamlyn, pg 704
HarperCollins UK, pg 705
Harvard University Press, pg 705

PUBLISHERS

Institute of Irish Studies, The Queens University of Belfast, pg 713
Intellect Ltd, pg 713
Janus Publishing Co Ltd, pg 716
Laurence King Publishing Ltd, pg 717
Lawrence & Wishart, pg 719
John Libbey & Co Ltd, pg 720
Manchester University Press, pg 724
National Association for the Teaching of English (NATE), pg 730
Octopus Publishing Group, pg 734
Old Vicarage Publications, pg 734
Orion Publishing Group Ltd, pg 736
Pavilion Books Ltd, pg 739
Plexus Publishing Ltd, pg 743
Polygon, pg 744
The Reader's Digest Association Ltd, pg 748
Reaktion Books Ltd, pg 748
Roundhouse Group, pg 751
Routledge, pg 751
I B Tauris & Co Ltd, pg 763
Time Out Group Ltd, pg 765
Titan Books Ltd, pg 766
Transworld Publishers Ltd, pg 766
University of Exeter Press, pg 768
Verso, pg 770
Virgin Publishing Ltd, pg 770
World Microfilms Publications Ltd, pg 775
Zwemmer Holdings Co Ltd, pg 776

FINANCE

Albania
NL SH, pg 1

Australia
D&B Marketing Pty Ltd, pg 19
Horan Wall & Walker, pg 26
Law Book Co Information Services, pg 28
Life Planning Foundation of Australia, Inc, pg 29
Anne O'Donovan Pty Ltd, pg 34
OTEN (Open Training & Education Network), pg 34
Prospect Media Pty Ltd, pg 37
The Real Estate Institute of Australia, pg 39
The Useful Publishing Co, pg 45
VCTA Publishing, pg 45
Woodlands Publications, pg 47
Wrightbooks Pty Ltd, pg 47

Austria
Compass-Verlag GmbH, pg 49
Horst Knapp Finanznachrichten, pg 53
WUV/Service Fachverlag, pg 60

Azerbaijan
Sada, Literaturno-Izdatel'skij Centr, pg 60

Bangladesh
The University Press Ltd, pg 61

Belarus
Belaruskaya Encyklapedyya, pg 62

Belgium
Editions De Boeck-Larcier SA, pg 66
Intersentia Uitgevers NV, pg 68

Brazil
Editora Atlas SA, pg 78
Editora Lucre Comercio e Representacoes, pg 85
Editora Ortiz SA, pg 88
Qualitymark Editora Ltda, pg 89
Saraiva SA, Livreiros Editores, pg 90
Jorge Zahar Editor, pg 92

Bulgaria
Ciela Publishing House, pg 93
Dolphin Press Group Ltd, pg 94
Pensoft Publishers, pg 96

Cameroon
Presses Universitaires d'Afrique, pg 98

China
Beijing Publishing House, pg 101
Beijing University Press, pg 101
China Foreign Economic Relations & Trade Publishing House, pg 102
CITIC Publishing House, pg 103
East China University of Science & Technology Press, pg 104
Fudan University Press, pg 104
Higher Education Press, pg 105
Shandong University Press, pg 108

Colombia
Universidad Externado de Colombia, pg 111
Universidad Nacional Abierta y a Distancia, pg 113

Costa Rica
Academia de Centro America, pg 114
Confederacion de Cooperativas del Caribe y Centro America (CCCCA), pg 115

Croatia
Informator dd, pg 118
Masmedia, pg 118

Czech Republic
NS Svoboda spol sro, pg 127

Denmark
Djof Publishing Jurist-og Okonomforbundets Forlag, pg 130
Samfundslitteratur, pg 134

France
Bottin SA, pg 151
Centre de Librairie et d'Editions Techniques (CLET), pg 152
DAFSA, pg 156
Editions Dalloz Sirey, pg 157
Les Editions ESF, pg 160
Editions de l'Epargne, pg 161
Groupe de Recherche et d'Echanges Technologiques (GRET), pg 166
Maxima Laurent du Mesnil Editeur, pg 174
Pearson Education France, pg 179
TOP Editions, pg 188
Editions Village Mondial, pg 189

Germany
Bank-Verlag GmbH, pg 197
Bund-Verlag GmbH, pg 206
Deutscher Wirtschaftsdienst John von Freyend GmbH, pg 214

SUBJECT INDEX

Duncker und Humblot GmbH, pg 217
Verlag Franz Vahlen GmbH, pg 226
Friedrich Kiehl Verlag GmbH, pg 227
Betriebswirtschaftlicher Verlag Dr Th Gabler, pg 228
von Hase & Koehler Verlag KG, pg 234
Rudolf Haufe Verlag GmbH & Co KG, pg 235
Hoppenstedt GmbH & Co KG, pg 239
IDW-Verlag GmbH, pg 241
Verlag Fritz Knapp GmbH, pg 247
Libertas- Europaeisches Institut GmbH, pg 254
Mosaik Verlag GmbH, pg 262
Verlag Norbert Mueller AG & Co KG, pg 262
Physica-Verlag, pg 270
pmi Verlag, pg 270
Verlag Norman Rentrop, pg 275
Richardi Helmut Verlag GmbH, pg 276
Rossipaul Kommunikation GmbH, pg 277
Schaeffer-Poeschel Verlag fuer Wirtschaft Steuern Recht, pg 279
Verlag Dr Otto Schmidt KG, pg 280
Erich Schmidt Verlag GmbH & Co, pg 280
Schulz-Kirchner Verlag GmbH, pg 282
Springer Science+Business Media GmbH & Co KG, pg 284
Stollfuss Verlag Bonn GmbH & Co KG, pg 288
UNO-Verlag GmbH, pg 293

Greece
Kritiki Publishing, pg 309
Vivliothiki Eftychia Galeou, pg 313

Hong Kong
Asia Pacific Communications Ltd, pg 315
Joint Publishing (HK) Co Ltd, pg 317
SCMP Book Publishing Ltd, pg 319
Thomson Corporation, pg 319
Yazhou Zhoukan Ltd, pg 320

Hungary
Kossuth Kiado RT, pg 322
Novorg International Szervezo es Kiado kft, pg 323
Saldo Penzugyi Tanacsado es Informatikai Rt, pg 324

India
Ananda Publishers Pvt Ltd, pg 328
Authorspress, pg 329
Reliance Publishing House, pg 346
Scientific Book Agency, pg 348
Sita Books & Periodicals Pvt Ltd, pg 349
South Asia Publications, pg 349
Sultan Chand & Sons Pvt Ltd, pg 350

Indonesia
Bina Rena Pariwara, pg 354
PT Bulan Bintang, pg 354

Ireland
The Economic & Social Research Institute, pg 359
Irish Management Institute, pg 361

Oak Tree Press, pg 362
Round Hall Sweet & Maxwell, pg 363

Israel
Dyonon/Papyrus Publishing House of the Tel-Aviv, pg 366

Italy
Bancaria Editrice SpA, pg 377
CEDAM (Casa Editrice Dr A Milani), pg 380
EGEA (Edizioni Giuridiche Economiche Aziendali), pg 387

Japan
Institute for Financial Affairs Inc-KINZAI, pg 419
KINZAI Corporation, pg 421
Nikkagiren Shuppan-Sha (JUSE Press Ltd), pg 424
President Inc, pg 425
Sobun-Sha, pg 428
Toyo Keizai Shinpo-Sha, pg 430
Waseda University Press, pg 431

Kenya
Focus Publications Ltd, pg 433
Heinemann Kenya Ltd (EAEP), pg 434

Republic of Korea
Chung Rim Publishing Co Ltd, pg 438

Liechtenstein
Bonafides Verlags-Anstalt, pg 447
Liechtenstein Verlag AG, pg 448

Luxembourg
Editions Promoculture, pg 451
Service Central de la Statistique et des Etudes Economiques (STATEC), pg 451

Madagascar
Societe Malgache d'Edition, pg 454

Mexico
Centro de Estudios Monetarios Latinoamericanos (CEMLA), pg 465
Grupo Editorial Iberoamerica, SA de CV, pg 466
Editorial Limusa SA de CV, pg 467
Editorial Turner de Mexico, pg 472

Netherlands
Business Contact BV, pg 480
BZZTOH Publishers, pg 480
Samsom BedrijfsInformatie BV, pg 488
SDU Juridische & Fiscale Uitgeverij, pg 488

New Zealand
Business Bureau Christchurch Ltd, pg 494
Legislation Direct, pg 498
Nelson Price Milburn Ltd, pg 499
Shoal Bay Press Ltd, pg 501
Statistics New Zealand, pg 501

Nigeria
Goldland Business Co Ltd, pg 505
New Africa Publishing Company Ltd, pg 505

981

Norway
Glydendal Akademisk, pg 509

Pakistan
Royal Book Co, pg 514

Peru
Universidad de Lima-Fondo de Desarollo Editorial, pg 517

Philippines
Rex Bookstores & Publishers, pg 520

Poland
Polskie Wydawnictwo Ekonomiczne PWE SA, pg 522
Polish Scientific Publishers PWN, pg 525
Oficyna Wydawnicza Szkoly Glownej Handlowej w Warszawie Oficyna Wydawnicza SGH, pg 527

Portugal
Edicoes Cetop, pg 529
Livraria Minerva, pg 533

Romania
Editura Dacia, pg 539
FF Press, pg 540
Editura Minerva, pg 541
Rentrop & Straton Verlagsgruppe und Wirtschaftsconsulting, pg 542

Russian Federation
Izdatelstvo 'Ekonomika', pg 544
Finansy i Statistika Publishing House, pg 544
INFRA-M Izdatel 'skij dom, pg 545

Singapore
Institute of Southeast Asian Studies, pg 556
Singapore University Press Pte Ltd, pg 558
World Scientific Publishing Co Pte Ltd, pg 559

Slovakia
Dom Techniky Zvazu Slovenskych Vedeckotechnickych Spolocnosti Ltd, pg 559
Vydavatepstvo Praca spol sro, pg 560

Slovenia
Univerza v Ljubljani Ekonomska Fakulteta, pg 562

South Africa
Witwatersrand University Press, pg 570

Spain
Editorial Aranzadi SA, pg 573
Editorial Donostiarra SA, pg 579
Ediciones Deusto SA, pg 580
Ediciones Gestio 2000 SA, pg 585
LID Editorial Empresarial, SL, pg 589
Marcombo SA, pg 590
Xunta de Galicia, pg 605

Sweden
Ekonomibok Forlag AB, pg 611
Iustus Forlag AB, pg 613

Switzerland
Cosmos-Verlag AG, pg 621
Fortuna Finanz-Verlag AG, pg 623
Promoedition SA, pg 631
Versus Verlag AG, pg 636

Syrian Arab Republic
Damascus University Press, pg 638

Taiwan, Province of China
Fuh-Wen Book Co, pg 639
Wu Nan Book Co Ltd, pg 642

Turkey
Alkim Kitapcilik-Yayimcilik, pg 649
Soez Yayin/Oyunajans, pg 651

Ukraine
Osnovy Publishers, pg 654

United Kingdom
ABG Professional Information, pg 655
Age Concern Books, pg 656
AP Information Services Ltd, pg 658
Ashton & Denton Publishing Co (CI) Ltd, pg 660
Bishopsgate Press Ltd, pg 666
Blackwell Publishing Ltd, pg 666
Bloomsbury Publishing PLC, pg 668
Dr Barry Bracewell-Milnes, pg 670
Nicholas Brealey Publishing, pg 670
Business Monitor International, pg 672
Butterworths Tolley, pg 673
The Chartered Institute of Public Finance & Accountancy, pg 678
Chorion IP, pg 679
Commonwealth Secretariat, pg 681
Croner CCH Group Ltd, pg 684
The Economist Intelligence Unit, pg 689
Edward Elgar Publishing Ltd, pg 690
Elliot Right Way Books, pg 690
The Eurospan Group, pg 692
Foulsham Publishers, pg 696
HarperCollins UK, pg 705
HB Publications, pg 706
ICC United Kingdom, pg 711
Institute for Fiscal Studies, pg 712
Institute of Financial Services, pg 712
ITDG Publishing, pg 715
Kogan Page Ltd, pg 718
Letts Educational, pg 720
LLP Ltd, pg 722
London Chamber of Commerce & Industry Examinations Board (LCCIEB), pg 722
Macmillan Reference Ltd, pg 724
Mars Business Associates Ltd, pg 725
MIT Press Ltd, pg 728
National Council for Voluntary Organisations (NCVO), pg 730
Profile Books Ltd, pg 746
SAGE Publications Ltd, pg 753
Scottish Executive Library & Information Services, pg 755
Take That Ltd, pg 762
Taylor & Francis, pg 763
TSO (The Stationery Office), pg 767
VNU Business Publications, pg 770
Which? Ltd, pg 772
Wiley Europe Ltd, pg 773
Wilmington Business Information Ltd, pg 774
Woodhead Publishing Ltd, pg 775

Uruguay
Fundacion de Cultura Universitaria, pg 777

Viet Nam
Science & Technics Publishing House, pg 780

Zambia
MFK Management Consultants Services, pg 781

Zimbabwe
Zimbabwe Women's Bureau, pg 785

FOREIGN COUNTRIES

Albania
NL SH, pg 1

Australia
AHB Publications, pg 11
Bandicoot Books, pg 14
Emperor Publishing, pg 21
Indra Publishing, pg 27
Oxfam Community Aid Abroad, pg 35
Polliteon Publications, pg 37
Thames & Hudson (Australia) Pty Ltd, pg 43

Austria
Pinguin-Verlag, Pawlowski GmbH, pg 56
Promedia Verlagsges mbH, pg 56
Verlag Josef Otto Slezak, pg 57
Edition Va Bene, pg 59

Belgium
Abimo, pg 62
Institut Royal des Relations Internationales, pg 68
IPIS vzw (International Peace Information Service), pg 69

Bulgaria
Kibea Publishing Co, pg 95
Sluntse Publishing House, pg 97

China
Chengdu Maps Publishing House, pg 101
Foreign Language Teaching & Research Press, pg 104
World Affairs Press, pg 109

The Democratic Republic of the Congo
Presses Universitaires du Zaiire (PUZ), pg 114

Czech Republic
Karolinum, nakladatelstvi, pg 124
Libri spol sro, pg 125
Mariadan, pg 125
Vitalis sro, pg 128

Denmark
Dafolo Forlag, pg 130
Mellemfolkeligt Samvirke, pg 133
Museum Tusculanum Press, pg 133

Finland
Kaantopiiri Oy, pg 142
Kirja-Leitzinger, pg 142

France
Editions de l'Aube, pg 148
Autrement Editions, pg 148
Blondel La Rougery SARL, pg 150
Editions La Decouverte, pg 157
FBT de R Editions, pg 163
Paul Geuthner Librairie Orientaliste, pg 165
Editions Jean Paul Gisserot, pg 165
L'Harmattan, pg 167
Editions d'Histoire Sociale (EDHIS), pg 168
Editions Juridiques Africaines, pg 170
Langues & Mondes-L'Asiatheque, pg 171
Editions des Limbes d'Or FBT de R Editions, pg 172
Editions Norma, pg 177
Sepia Editions, pg 184
Editions Le Serpent a Plumes, pg 184
Transeuropeennes/RCE, pg 188

Germany
AOL-Verlag Frohmut Menze, pg 193
Aufstieg-Verlag GmbH, pg 195
Bertelsmann Lexikon Verlag GmbH, pg 200
W Bertelsmann Verlag GmbH & Co KG, pg 200
BKV-Brasilienkunde Verlag GmbH, pg 201
Verlag Hermann Boehlaus Nachfolger Weimar GmbH & Co, pg 203
Brandenburgisches Verlagshaus in der Dornier Medienholding GmbH, pg 204
Egmont vgs verlagsgesellschaft mbH, pg 218
Ellert & Richter Verlag GmbH, pg 219
Eppinger-Verlag OHG, pg 220
Frederking & Thaler Verlag GmbH, pg 226
Gunter Olzog Verlag GmbH, pg 231
Peter Hammer Verlag GmbH, pg 233
Horlemann Verlag, pg 239
Iudicium Verlag GmbH, pg 242
Jahreszeiten-Verlag GmbH, pg 242
Jan Thorbecke Verlag GmbH & Co, pg 243
Knowledge Media International, pg 247
Dr Anton Kovac Slavica Verlag, pg 249
Adam Kraft Verlag, pg 250
Idime Verlag Inge Melzer, pg 259
Munzinger-Archiv GmbH Archiv fuer publizistische Arbeit, pg 262
Neuthor - Verlag, pg 265
Nusser Verlag, pg 266
Palazzi Verlag GmbH, pg 268
Palmyra Verlag, pg 268
Pfalzische Verlagsanstalt GmbH, pg 269
Reise Know-How Verlag Peter Rump GmbH, pg 275
Schillinger Verlag GmbH, pg 279
Wilhelm Schmitz Verlag, pg 280
Buchkonzept Simon KG, pg 283
Steiger Verlag, pg 287
Franz Steiner Verlag Wiesbaden GmbH, pg 287
Vervuert Verlagsgesellschaft, pg 295

PUBLISHERS

Weidlich Verlag, pg 298
Ziethen-Panorama Verlag GmbH, pg 302

Hong Kong
Macmillan Publishers (China) Ltd, pg 318

India
Kairali Children's Book Trust, pg 339
National Book Trust India, pg 342
Omsons Publications, pg 344
Scientific Book Agency, pg 348

Israel
Ben-Zvi Institute, pg 365
Hakibbutz Hameuchad Publishing House Ltd, pg 367
Hanitzotz A-Sharara Publishing House, pg 367
Ministry of Defence Publishing House, pg 370
Tel Aviv University, pg 372
The Van Leer Jerusalem Institute, pg 373

Italy
Giuseppe Bonanno Editore, pg 378
Edizioni Cultura della Pace, pg 383
Giorgio Mondadori & Associati, pg 399

Jamaica
Carlong Publishers (Caribbean) Ltd, pg 413

Japan
The American Chamber of Commerce in Japan, pg 415
Kaisei-Sha Publishing Co Ltd, pg 420
Nippon Hoso Shuppan Kyokai (NHK Publishing), pg 424
Sobun-Sha, pg 428

Kazakhstan
Al-Farabi Kazakh National University, pg 432

Kenya
Sasa Sema Publications Ltd, pg 435

Republic of Korea
Hakgojae Publishing Inc, pg 439

Malaysia
University of Malaya, Department of Publications, pg 459

Maldive Islands
Novelty Printers & Publishers, pg 459

Mexico
Centro de Estudios Mexicanos y Centroamericanos, pg 463

Mozambique
Centro De Estudos Africanos, pg 475

Namibia
Agrivet Publishers, pg 476

Netherlands
Educatieve Uitgeverij Edu'Actief BV, pg 481
Uitgeverij en boekhandel Van Gennep BV, pg 482
Mets & Schilt Uitgevers en Distributeurs, pg 486

Netherlands Antilles
Bredero, pg 493

New Zealand
Aoraki Press Ltd, pg 493
Millwood Press Ltd, pg 498

Nigeria
Adebara Publishers Ltd, pg 503
Alliance West African Publishers & Co, pg 503
CSS Bookshops, pg 504
Daily Times of Nigeria Ltd (Publication Division), pg 504
Educational Research & Study Group, pg 504
Ethiope Publishing Corporation, pg 504
Ibadan University Press, pg 505
Onibon-Oje Publishers, pg 506
University of Lagos Press, pg 507
University Publishing Co, pg 507

Peru
Ediciones Peisa (Promocion Editorial Inca SA), pg 517

Philippines
Garotech, pg 519
Vibal Publishing House Inc (VPHI), pg 521

Poland
Instytut Meteorologii i Gospodarki Wodnej, pg 523

Romania
Editura Academiei Romane, pg 538
The Center for Romanian Studies, pg 539

Senegal
Societe Africaine d'Edition, pg 551
Societe d'Edition d'Afrique Nouvelle, pg 551

Singapore
Institute of Southeast Asian Studies, pg 556
Masagung Books Pte Ltd, pg 557
Pustaka Nasional Pte Ltd, pg 557

Slovakia
Serafin, pg 560

Slovenia
Zalozba Mihelac d o o, pg 562

South Africa
Ashanti Publishing, pg 562
Galago Publishing Pty Ltd, pg 564
South African Institute of International Affairs, pg 569

Spain
Editorial AEDOS SA, pg 571
Amnistia Internacional Editorial SL, pg 572
Ediciones Maeva, pg 590
Mundo Negro Editorial, pg 592
Ediciones del Oriente y del Mediterraneo, pg 594

Switzerland
Bergli Books AG, pg 619
Cockatoo Press (Schweiz), Thailand-Publikationen, pg 621
Drei-D-World und Foto-World Verlag und Vertrieb, pg 622
Verlag im Waldgut AG, pg 636

United Arab Emirates
Motivate Publishing, pg 654

United Kingdom
ABC-CLIO, pg 654
Belitha Press Ltd, pg 664
Books of Zimbabwe Publishing Co (Pvt) Ltd, pg 669
Nicholas Brealey Publishing, pg 670
Business Monitor International, pg 672
James Currey Ltd, pg 685
Ernst & Young, pg 692
Europa Publications, pg 692
European Schoolbooks Ltd, pg 692
The Eurospan Group, pg 692
Garnet Publishing Ltd, pg 698
Grant & Cutler Ltd, pg 702
Gwasg Gwenffrwd, pg 703
Harden's Ltd, pg 704
HarperCollins UK, pg 705
Icon Press, pg 711
Jane's Information Group, pg 715
Letterbox Library, pg 720
Ravette Publishing Ltd, pg 748
Reardon Publishing, pg 748
Rough Guides Ltd, pg 751
RoutledgeCurzon, pg 751
Royal Institute of International Affairs, pg 752
The Salariya Book Co Ltd, pg 753
Saqi Books, pg 754
Serif, pg 756
Sheffield Academic Press Ltd, pg 757
Stacey International, pg 761
Vacation Work Publications, pg 769
Vacher Dod Publishing Ltd, pg 769

Uruguay
Nordan-Comunidad, pg 778

Zimbabwe
Bold ADS, pg 782
Nehanda Publishers, pg 784

GARDENING, PLANTS

Albania
NL SH, pg 1

Argentina
Editorial Albatros SACI, pg 3
Editorial Caymi SACI, pg 4
Editorial Hemisferio Sur SA, pg 6

Armenia
Arevik, pg 10

Australia
Bloomings Books, pg 15
Candlelight Trust T/A Candlelight Farm, pg 17
Cornucopia Press, pg 18
Department of Primary Industries, Queensland, pg 20
Egan Publishing Pty Ltd, pg 21
Flora Publications International Pty Ltd, pg 22
Florilegium, pg 22
Freshet Press, pg 23
Hyland House Publishing Pty Ltd, pg 26
Kangaroo Press, pg 28
Landarc Publications, pg 28
Lansdowne Publishing Pty Ltd, pg 28
Mulini Press, pg 32
Pioneer Design Studio Pty Ltd, pg 37
R & R Publications Pty Ltd, pg 38
Social Club Books, pg 41
Terania Rainforest Publishing, pg 43
Three Sisters Publications Pty Ltd, pg 43
University of New South Wales Press Ltd, pg 44
The Watermark Press, pg 46

Austria
Leopold Stocker Verlag, pg 53

Belgium
Uitgeverij Lannoo NV, pg 69
Marabout, pg 71
Henri Proost & Co, Pvba, pg 72
Roularta Books NV, pg 72
Stichting Kunstboek bvba, pg 73
Zuid-Nederlandse Uitgeverij NV/Central Uitgeverij, pg 75

Brazil
Livraria Nobel S/A, pg 85
Rede Das Artes (Boccato Editores Collector's), pg 89

Bulgaria
Gea-Libris Publishing House, pg 94
Rakla, pg 96
Sluntse Publishing House, pg 97

Chile
Editorial Texido Ltda, pg 100

China
China Agriculture Press, pg 102
China Forestry Publishing House, pg 102
Guangdong Science & Technology Press, pg 105
Guizhou Education Publishing House, pg 105
Henan Science & Technology Publishing House, pg 105
Higher Education Press, pg 105
Science Press, pg 107
Tianjin Science & Technology Publishing House, pg 108

The Democratic Republic of the Congo
Centre de Vulgarisation Agricole, pg 114

Costa Rica
Centro Agronomico Tropical de Investigacion y Ensenanza (CATIE), pg 115

Croatia
ALFA dd za izdavacke, graficke i trgovacke poslove, pg 117

SUBJECT INDEX

BOOK

Czech Republic
Aventinum Nakladatelstvi spol sro, pg 122
Granit sro, pg 123

Denmark
Gads Forlag, pg 131

El Salvador
Editorial Universitaria de la Universidad de El Salvador, pg 139

Estonia
Sinisukk, pg 140
Valgus Publishers, pg 140

France
ATP - Packager, pg 148
Editions Belin, pg 149
Bookmaker, pg 150
Editions Courrier du Livre, pg 156
Editions Edisud, pg 159
Flammarion SA, pg 163
Editions Jean Paul Gisserot, pg 165
Hachette Pratiques, pg 167
Editions Larousse, pg 171
Editions Mango, pg 174
Editions Menges, pg 175
Editions du Rouergue, pg 183
Editions Sang de la Terre, pg 184
Editions Soline, pg 185
Terre Vivante, pg 187

Germany
August Guese Verlag GmbH, pg 195
Augustus Verlag, pg 195
Bassermann Verlag, pg 197
Blackwell Wissenschafts-Verlag GmbH, pg 201
BLV Verlagsgesellschaft mbH, pg 202
Bonsai-Centrum, pg 203
F Bruckmann Munchen Verlag & Druck GmbH & Co Produkt KG, pg 204
Verlag Georg D W Callwey GmbH & Co, pg 207
Christian Verlag GmbH, pg 208
Hans Christians Druckerei und Verlag GmbH & Co KG, pg 208
Compact Verlag GmbH, pg 209
DLV Deutscher Landwirtschaftsverlag GmbH, pg 215
DuMont monte Verlag GmbH & Co KG, pg 217
DuMont Reiseverlag GmbH & Co KG, pg 217
Ecomed Verlagsgesellschaft AG & Co KG, pg 218
Egmont vgs verlagsgesellschaft mbH, pg 218
Ellert & Richter Verlag GmbH, pg 219
Falken-Verlag GmbH, pg 223
Franckh-Kosmos Verlags-GmbH & Co, pg 226
Gerstenberg Verlag, pg 228
GLB Parkland Verlags-und Vertriebs GmbH, pg 229
Graefe und Unzer Verlag GmbH, pg 230
Heel Verlag GmbH, pg 235
Jahreszeiten-Verlag GmbH, pg 242
Knowledge Media International, pg 247
Ambro Lacus, Buch- und Bildverlag Walter A Kremnitz, pg 251
Mosaik Verlag GmbH, pg 262

Verlag Natur & Wissenschaft Harro Hieronimus & Dr Jurgen Schmidt, pg 263
Naumann & Goebel Verlagsgesellschaft mbH, pg 263
Nebel Verlag GmbH, pg 263
Neumann Verlag, pg 264
Georg Olms Verlag AG, pg 267
Orbis Verlag fur Publizistik GmbH, pg 267
Pala-Verlag GmbH, pg 268
Thalacker Medien GmbH Co KG, pg 290
Guenter Albert Ulmer Verlag, pg 293
Verlag Eugen Ulmer GmbH & Co, pg 293
Verlagsgruppe Weltbild GmbH, pg 298

Greece
Alamo Hellas, pg 305
Orfanidis Publications, pg 311

Hong Kong
SCMP Book Publishing Ltd, pg 319
Unicorn Books Ltd, pg 320

Hungary
Mezogazda Kiado, pg 323
Officina Nova Konyvek, pg 323
Park Konyvkiado Kft (Park Publisher), pg 324

Iceland
Bokautgafan Orn og Orlygur ehf, pg 325
Skjaldborg Ltd, pg 326

India
Allied Book Centre, pg 328
Ananda Publishers Pvt Ltd, pg 328
Full Circle Publishing, pg 334
International Book Distributors, pg 338
Naya Prokash, pg 343
Nem Chand & Brothers, pg 343
Sterling Publishers Pvt Ltd, pg 350
Vakils Feffer & Simons Ltd, pg 352

Indonesia
Gramedia, pg 355

Israel
R Sirkis Publishers Ltd, pg 372

Italy
L'Archivolto, pg 376
Giovanni De Vecchi Editore SpA, pg 384
Di Baio Editore SpA, pg 385
Edagricole - Edizioni Agricole, pg 385
Fenice 2000, pg 389
Arnaldo Forni Editore SRL, pg 389
Istituto Geografico de Agostini SpA, pg 390
Edizioni Mediterranee SRL, pg 398
Giorgio Mondadori & Associati, pg 399
Edizioni Piemme SpA, pg 403
Zanfi-Logos, pg 412

Japan
Gakken Co Ltd, pg 417
Nagaoka Shoten Co Ltd, pg 423
Nihon Vogue Co Ltd, pg 424
Nippon Hoso Shuppan Kyokai (NHK Publishing), pg 424

Seibido Shuppan Company Ltd, pg 426
Seibundo Shinkosha Publishing Co Ltd, pg 426
Shufunotomo Co Ltd, pg 428
Tankosha Publishing Co Ltd, pg 429

Kenya
Space Sellers Ltd, pg 436

Republic of Korea
Pyeong-hwa Chulpansa, pg 442

Latvia
Avots, pg 444
Preses Nams, pg 445

Liechtenstein
Botanisch-Zoologische Gesellschaft, pg 447

Luxembourg
Guy Binsfeld & Co Sarl, pg 450
Editions Emile Borschette, pg 450

Malaysia
Federal Publications Sdn Bhd, pg 455

Martinique
Editions Gondwana, pg 460

Mexico
Ediciones Suromex SA, pg 472

Nepal
International Standards Books & Periodicals (P) Ltd, pg 476

Netherlands
Ankh-Hermes BV, pg 477
Hotei Publishing, pg 484
Rebo Productions BV, pg 488
Uitgeverij Terra bv, pg 490
Zuid Boekprodukties BV, pg 493

Netherlands Antilles
De Wit Stores NV, pg 493

New Zealand
David Bateman Ltd, pg 494
Bush Press Communications Ltd, pg 494
Business Bureau Christchurch Ltd, pg 494
The Caxton Press, pg 495
Godwit Publishing Ltd, pg 496
HarperCollins Publishers (New Zealand) Ltd, pg 497
Hazard Press Ltd, pg 497
Longacre Press, pg 498
Shoal Bay Press Ltd, pg 501

Norway
Aschehoug Forlag, pg 508
H Aschehoug & Co (W Nygaard) A/S, pg 508
Forlaget Fag og Kultur, pg 509

Oman
Apex Press & Publishing, pg 511

Pakistan
Maqbool Academy, pg 513

Philippines
Anvil Publishing Inc, pg 518
Bookmark Inc, pg 518

Poland
Wydawnictwo Baturo, pg 522
Videograf II Sp z o o Zaklad Poracy Chronionej, pg 527

Portugal
Dinalivro, pg 530
Impala, pg 532
Editorial Presenca, pg 535

Romania
MAST Verlag, pg 540
Editura Niculescu, pg 541
Vox Editura, pg 543

Russian Federation
Airis Press, pg 543
Interbook-Business AO, pg 545
Permskaja Kniga, pg 548
Profizdat, pg 548

Singapore
Times Media Pte Ltd, pg 559

Slovakia
Priroda Publishing, pg 560

Slovenia
East West Operation (EWO) Ltd, pg 561
Mladinska Knjiga International, pg 561
Zalozba Obzorja d d Maribor, pg 562

South Africa
Human & Rousseau (Pty) Ltd, pg 564
Jacana Education, pg 565
National Botanical Institute, pg 567
Reader's Digest Southern Africa, pg 568
Southern Book Publishers (Pty) Ltd, pg 569
Struik Publishers (Pty) Ltd, pg 569
Tafelberg Publishers Ltd, pg 569

Spain
Editorial Acanto SA, pg 570
AMV Ediciones, pg 572
Editorial Astri SA, pg 573
Comunidad Autonoma de Madrid, Servicio de Documentacion y Publicaciones, pg 578
Ediciones Daly S L, pg 578
Editorial Everest SA, pg 581
Vicent Garcia Editores, SA, pg 584
Grijalbo Mondadori SA, pg 585
Editorial Hispano Europea SA, pg 586
Libsa Editorial SA, pg 589
Mundi-Prensa Libros SA, pg 592
Pronaos, SA Ediciones, pg 597
Editora Regional de Murcia - ERM, pg 597
Ediciones Rialp SA, pg 598
Rueda, SL Editorial, pg 598
Axel Springer Publicaciones, pg 601
Ediciones Susaeta SA, pg 601
Tursen, SA, pg 603
Ediciones Tutor SA, pg 603

PUBLISHERS

Sweden
Bokforlaget Axplock, pg 609
BOOX, pg 610
Hagaberg AB, pg 612
ICA bokforlag, pg 612
Natur och Kultur Fakta etc, pg 614
Bokforlaget Prisma, pg 614
Bokforlaget Semic AB, pg 615

Switzerland
Ott Verlag Thun, pg 630

Taiwan, Province of China
Chu Hai Publishing (Taiwan) Co Ltd, pg 640
Hilit Publishing Co Ltd, pg 640
Shy Mau & Shy Chaur Publishing Co Ltd, pg 641

United Republic of Tanzania
Tanzania Publishing House, pg 644

Tunisia
Les Editions de l'Arbre, pg 647

Turkey
Inkilap Publishers Ltd, pg 650

Ukraine
ASK Ltd, pg 653
Urozaj, pg 654

United Kingdom
Ian Allan Publishing Ltd, pg 656
Umberto Allemandi & Co Publishing, pg 656
Andromeda Oxford Ltd, pg 658
Antique Collectors' Club Ltd, pg 658
Batsford Ltd, pg 663
BBC Worldwide Publishers, pg 663
BCA - Book Club Associates, pg 663
Mitchell Beazley, pg 664
Bounty Books, pg 669
Breslich & Foss Ltd, pg 671
Burall Floraprint Ltd, pg 672
Capall Bann Publishing, pg 674
Carroll & Brown Ltd, pg 675
Cassell & Co, pg 675
Kyle Cathie Ltd, pg 676
Marshall Cavendish Partworks Ltd, pg 676
Centre for Alternative Technology, pg 677
Conran Octopus, pg 682
The Crowood Press Ltd, pg 684
David & Charles Ltd, pg 686
Discovery Walking Guides Ltd, pg 687
Dorling Kindersley Ltd, pg 688
Aidan Ellis Publishing, pg 690
Eurobook Ltd, pg 692
The Factory Shop Guide, pg 694
Foulsham Publishers, pg 696
Gaia Books Ltd, pg 698
Garden Art Press Ltd, pg 698
GMC Publications Ltd, pg 700
Grange Books PLC, pg 702
Hamlyn, pg 704
HarperCollins UK, pg 705
The Harvill Press, pg 705
Headline Book Publishing Ltd, pg 706
Hyden House Ltd, pg 711
Intercept Ltd, pg 714
Interpet Publishing, pg 714
Knockabout Comics, pg 718
Frances Lincoln Ltd, pg 720
Lorenz Books, pg 722
Marshall Editions Ltd, pg 725
Marston House, pg 725
Mercat Press, pg 726
Metro Books, pg 727
National Trust, pg 731
Nexus Special Interests, pg 733
Octopus Publishing Group, pg 734
Open Books Publishing Ltd, pg 735
Packard Publishing Ltd, pg 737
Pavilion Books Ltd, pg 739
PRC Publishing Ltd, pg 745
Primrose Hill Press Ltd, pg 745
Quadrille Publishing Ltd, pg 746
Quarto Publishing plc, pg 746
Quintet Publishing Ltd, pg 747
The Reader's Digest Association Ltd, pg 748
Ryland Peters & Small Ltd, pg 752
Salamander Books Ltd, pg 753
SAWD Publications, pg 754
Search Press Ltd, pg 756
Shire Publications Ltd, pg 757
Stacey International, pg 761
Telegraph Books, pg 764
Timber Press Inc, pg 765
Transedition Ltd, pg 766
Ward Lock Ltd, pg 771
Which? Ltd, pg 772
WI Enterprises Ltd, pg 773
Wordwright Publishing, pg 775

Viet Nam
Science & Technics Publishing House, pg 780

Zambia
Zambia Printing Company Ltd (ZPC), pg 782

GAY & LESBIAN

Argentina
Alfagrama SRL ediciones, pg 3

Australia
Allen & Unwin Pty Ltd, pg 11
Extraordinary People Press, pg 22
Spectrum Publications, pg 41
Spinifex Press, pg 42

Austria
Milena Verlag, pg 54

Brazil
Edicon Editora e Consultorial Ltda, pg 81

Finland
Yliopistopaino/Helsinki University Press, pg 145

France
Editions du Centre Pompidou, pg 180

Germany
Argument-Verlag, pg 194
ComMedia & Arte Verlag Bernd Mayer, pg 209
Edition Dia, pg 214
Gatzanis Verlags GmbH, pg 228
Bruno Gmuender Verlag GmbH, pg 230
Himmelsturmer Verlag, pg 237
Holos Verlag, pg 239
KBV Verlags-und Medien - GmbH, pg 245
Verlag Kleine Schritte Ursula Dahm & Co, pg 246
Krug & Schadenberg, pg 250
Mannerschwarm Skript Verlag GmbH, pg 257
Merlin Verlag Andreas Meyer Verlags GmbH und Co KG, pg 259
Verlag Neues Leben GmbH, pg 264
Orlanda Frauenverlag, pg 267
Querverlag GmbH, pg 273
Verlag Anke Schaefer, pg 278
Ulrike Helmer Verlag, pg 293
Rosa Winkel Verlag GmbH, pg 300

Mexico
Libra Editorial SA de CV, pg 467

Netherlands
Prometheus, pg 488

New Zealand
Lincoln University Press, pg 498
Longacre Press, pg 498

Portugal
Vega-Publicacao e Distribuicao de Livros e Revistas, Lda, pg 536

Russian Federation
ARGO-RISK Publisher, pg 543

Slovenia
Zalozba Obzorja d d Maribor, pg 562

South Africa
Janssen Publishers CC, pg 565
Queillerie Publishers, pg 568

Spain
Egales (Editorial Gai y Lesbiana), pg 581
Laertes SA de Ediciones, pg 588
Loguez Ediciones, pg 589

Turkey
Parantez Yayinlari Ltd, pg 651

United Kingdom
Absolute Press, pg 655
Arcadia Books Ltd, pg 659
Cassell & Co, pg 675
Constable & Robinson Ltd, pg 682
Delectus Books, pg 687
The Eurospan Group, pg 692
Fourth Estate, pg 696
GMP Publishers Ltd, pg 700
HarperCollins UK, pg 705
Lawrence & Wishart, pg 719
Letterbox Library, pg 720
Monarch Books, pg 729
Onlywomen Press Ltd, pg 735
Peter Owen Ltd, pg 737
Rivers Oram Press, pg 750
Serpent's Tail Ltd, pg 756
Time Out Group Ltd, pg 765
The Women's Press Ltd, pg 775

GENEALOGY

Argentina
Theoria SRL Distribuidora y Editora, pg 9

Australia
Access Press, pg 10
Church Archivists Press, pg 18
Gould Genealogy, pg 23
Hale & Iremonger Pty Ltd, pg 24
Illert Publications, pg 26
Library of Australian History, pg 29
Lucasville Press, pg 30
Navarine Publishing, pg 33
Oxfam Community Aid Abroad, pg 35
Seanachas Press, pg 40
State Library of NSW Press, pg 42

Belgium
Dexia Bank, pg 66
Marabout, pg 71

China
Fudan University Press, pg 104

Costa Rica
Museo Historico Cultural Juan Santamaria, pg 115

Denmark
Dansk Historisk Handbogsforlag ApS, pg 130

Finland
Kirja-Leitzinger, pg 142

France
Editions Bertout, pg 149
Editions Jean Paul Gisserot, pg 165
Librairie Guenegaud, pg 166
Editions Herault, pg 167
Editions Lyonnaises d'Art et d'Histoire, pg 173
Editions Ophrys, pg 177
References cf, pg 183

Germany
Verlag Ekkehard & Ulrich Brockhaus GmbH & Co KG, pg 204
Degener & Co, Manfred Dreiss Verlag, pg 211
Anton Hiersemann, Verlag, pg 237
Vittorio Klostermann GmbH, pg 247
C A Starke Verlag, pg 287
Verlag Wissenschaft und Politik, pg 300

Ireland
Ballinakella Press, pg 358
Dee-Jay Publications, pg 359
Flyleaf Press, pg 360
Herodotus Press, pg 361
History House Publishing, pg 361
Irish Times Ltd, pg 361
Sean Ros Press, pg 363

Israel
Agudat Sabah, pg 364
Dyonon/Papyrus Publishing House of the Tel-Aviv, pg 366

Italy
Arnaldo Forni Editore SRL, pg 389
Palatina Editrice, pg 402

Netherlands
Uitgeverij Verloren, pg 492

New Zealand

Bush Press Communications Ltd, pg 494
Clerestory Press, pg 495
Evagean Publishing, pg 496
Godwit Publishing Ltd, pg 496
Graphic Educational Publications, pg 496
Heritage Press Ltd, pg 497

Poland

Wydawnictwo DiG, pg 522
Wydawnictwa Uniwersytetu Warszawskiego, pg 527

Russian Federation

Ministerstvo Kul 'tury RF, pg 546

South Africa

University of KwaZulu-Natal Press, pg 569

Sri Lanka

Waruni Publishers, pg 607

United Kingdom

Borthwick Institute Publications, pg 669
Breedon Books Publishing Company Ltd, pg 670
Brewin Books Ltd, pg 671
Bridge Books, pg 671
Countryside Books, pg 683
Debrett's Ltd, pg 687
Elliot Right Way Books, pg 690
The Eurospan Group, pg 692
Gwasg Gwenffrwd, pg 703
Ian Henry Publications Ltd, pg 708
Heraldry Today, pg 708
Luath Press Ltd, pg 722
National Library of Wales, pg 731
Scottish Text Society, pg 755
Shire Publications Ltd, pg 757
Stacey International, pg 761
Sutton Publishing Ltd, pg 762
Thomson Gale, pg 765
Twelveheads Press, pg 767
Ulster Historical Foundation, pg 768

Zimbabwe

National Archives of Zimbabwe, pg 784

GEOGRAPHY, GEOLOGY

Albania

NL SH, pg 1

Argentina

EUDEBA (Editorial Universitaria de Buenos Aires), pg 5
Laffont Ediciones Electronicas SA, pg 7
Instituto Nacional de Ciencia y Tecnica Hidrica (INCYTH), pg 7
Oikos, pg 8
Editoria Universitaria de la Patagonia, pg 9

Armenia

Arevik, pg 10

Australia

Edward Arnold (Australia) Pty Ltd, pg 12
Aussie Books, pg 12
Australian Academy of Science, pg 13
Australian Marine Conservation Society Inc (AMCS), pg 13
Australian Scholarly Publishing, pg 13
Brookfield Press, pg 16
Dabill Publications, pg 19
Dellasta Publishing, pg 19
Encyclopaedia Britannica (Australia) Inc, pg 21
Hartys Creek Press, pg 25
Macmillan Education Australia, pg 30
McGraw-Hill Australia Pty Ltd, pg 31
Reed Educational Publishing Australia, pg 39
Royal Society of New South Wales, pg 40
Tabletop Press, pg 42
Three Sisters Publications Pty Ltd, pg 43
Tudor Australia Press, pg 44

Austria

Verlag Harald Denzel, Auto- und Freizeitfuehrer, pg 50
Freytag-Berndt und Artaria, Kartographische Anstalt, pg 51
IAEA - International Atomic Energy Agency, pg 52
Pinguin-Verlag, Pawlowski GmbH, pg 56
Dr A Schendl GmbH und Co KG, pg 57
Vorarlberger Verlagsanstalt Aktiengesellschaft, pg 59
Universitaetsverlag Wagner GmbH, pg 59

Bangladesh

The University Press Ltd, pg 61

Belarus

Narodnaya Asveta, pg 62

Belgium

NV Artis-Historia, pg 63
Carto BVBA, pg 64
Creadif, pg 65
Cremers (Schoollandkaarten) PVBA, pg 66
Editions De Boeck-Larcier SA, pg 66
Dessain - Departement de De Boeck & Larcier SA, pg 66
Dexia Bank, pg 66
Georeto-Geogidsen, pg 67
Koepel van de Vlaamse Noord - Zuidbeweging 11.11.11, pg 69
Leuven University Press, pg 70
Pelckmans NV, De Nederlandsche Boekhandel, pg 72
Reader's Digest SA, pg 72
Sonneville Press (Uitgeverij) VTW, pg 73
Editions Techniques et Scientifiques SPRL, pg 73

Bosnia and Herzegovina

Bemust, pg 76

Botswana

Maskew Miller Longman, pg 76

Brazil

Editora Bertrand Brasil Ltda, pg 78
Fundacao Instituto Brasileiro de Geografia e Estatistica (IBGE - CDDI/DECOP), pg 82
Fundacao Sao Paulo, EDUC, pg 82
Libreria Editora Ltda, pg 85
Modulo Editora e Desenvolvimento Educacional Ltda, pg 87
Editora Scipione Ltda, pg 90
Editora Verbo Ltda, pg 92

Bulgaria

Gea-Libris Publishing House, pg 94
Heron Press Publishing House, pg 94
Makros 2000 - Plovdiv, pg 95
Medicina i Fizkultura EOOD, pg 95

Chile

Arrayan Editores, pg 98
Instituto Geografico Militar, pg 99

China

Chengdu Maps Publishing House, pg 101
China Cartographic Publishing House, pg 102
China Ocean Press, pg 102
Foreign Languages Press, pg 104
Fudan University Press, pg 104
Geological Publishing House, pg 105
Higher Education Press, pg 105
Jiangsu Science & Technology Publishing House, pg 105
Metallurgical Industry Press (MIP), pg 106
Shandong University Press, pg 108
Xi'an Cartography Publishing House, pg 109

The Democratic Republic of the Congo

Centre de Recherche, et Pedagogie Appliquee, pg 114

Czech Republic

Academia, pg 122
Columbus, pg 123
Granit sro, pg 123
Libri spol sro, pg 125
Vydavatelstvi Cesky Geologicky Ustav, pg 128

Denmark

Scan-Globe A/S, pg 134
Systime, pg 135

Dominican Republic

Pontificia Universidad Catolica Madre y Maestra, pg 136

Ecuador

Corporacion Editora Nacional, pg 136

Estonia

Academic Library of Tallinn Pedagogical University, pg 139
Eesti Entsuklopeediakirjastus, pg 139
Valgus Publishers, pg 140

Ethiopia

Addis Ababa University Press, pg 140

France

Actes-Graphiques, pg 145
Atelier National de Reproduction des Theses, pg 148
Blondel La Rougery SARL, pg 150
Presses Universitaires de Bordeaux (PUB), pg 150
Editions BRGM, pg 151
Brud Nevez, pg 151
CNRS Editions, pg 155
Armand Colin, Editeur, pg 155
Editions du Comite des Travaux Historiques et Scientifiques (CTHS), pg 155
Les Devenirs Visuels, pg 158
Editions Edisud, pg 159
Elf Exploration Production, pg 161
Gammaprim, pg 165
Paul Geuthner Librairie Orientaliste, pg 165
Editions Hermes Science Publications, pg 167
INRA Editions (Institut National de la Recherche Agronomique), pg 168
IRD Editions, pg 169
Editions du Jaguar, pg 169
Karthala Editions-Diffusion, pg 170
Editions Lavoisier, pg 171
Editions Loubatieres, pg 173
Editions MDI (La Maison des Instituteurs), pg 175
Editions Franck Mercier, pg 175
Presses Universitaires du Mirail, pg 176
Editions Ophrys, pg 177
Ouest Editions, pg 178
Editions Paradigme, pg 178
Presses Universitaires de Caen, pg 181
Presses Universitaires de France (PUF), pg 181
Presses Universitaires de Nancy, pg 181
PRODIG, pg 182
Publications de l'Universite de Rouen, pg 182
Siloe - Kerdore, pg 185
Societe Nouveaux Loisirs, pg 185
Publications de la Sorbonne, pg 185
Editions Tallandier, pg 187
Taride Editions, pg 187
Publications de l'Universite de Pau, pg 188

French Polynesia

Scoop/Au Vent des Iles, pg 189

Germany

Accedo Verlagsgesellschaft mbH, pg 190
Antiqua-Verlag GmbH, pg 193
Ardey-Verlag GmbH, pg 193
Aulis Verlag Deubner & Co KG, pg 195
Bayerischer Schulbuch-Verlag GmbH, pg 198
Berndtson & Berndtson GmbH Verlag-Publishing, pg 199
Bibliographisches Institut & F A Brockhaus AG, pg 200
Brockhaus/Kommission GmbH, pg 204
Chmielorz GmbH Verlag, pg 208
Hans Christians Druckerei und Verlag GmbH & Co KG, pg 208
Columbus Verlag Paul Oestergaard GmbH, pg 209
Cornelsen Verlag GmbH & Co OHG, pg 210

Deutscher Verlag fur Grundstoffindustrie GmbH, pg 213
Verlag Europa-Lehrmittel GmbH & Co KG, pg 221
Ferdinand Enke Verlag, pg 224
Franckh-Kosmos Verlags-GmbH & Co, pg 226
Gebrueder Borntraeger Science Publishers, pg 228
GeoCenter Touristik Medienservice GmbH, pg 228
Gloatz, Hille GmbH & Co KG fur Mehrfarben und Zellglasdruck, pg 229
Goldschneck Verlag, pg 230
Holos Verlag, pg 239
Kartographischer Verlag Reinhard Ryborsch, pg 244
Kirschbaum Verlag GmbH, pg 246
Ernst Klett Verlag GmbH, pg 247
Knowledge Media International, pg 247
K F Koehler Verlag GmbH, pg 248
Anton H Konrad Verlag, pg 249
Verlag Waldemar Kramer, pg 250
Michael Lassleben Verlag und Druckerei, pg 252
Siegbert Linnemann Verlag, pg 254
Logos-Verlag Literatur & Layout GmbH, pg 255
Margraf Verlag, pg 257
Verlag Natur & Wissenschaft Harro Hieronimus & Dr Jurgen Schmidt, pg 263
Nusser Verlag, pg 266
Georg Olms Verlag AG, pg 267
Palazzi Verlag GmbH, pg 268
Justus Perthes Verlag Gotha GmbH, pg 269
Propylaeen Verlag, Zweigniederlassung Berlin der Ullstein Buchverlage GmbH, pg 272
Raethgloben Verlagsgesellschaft mbH, pg 273
Konrad Reich Verlag GmbH, pg 274
Dr Ludwig Reichert Verlag, pg 274
Reise Know-How Verlag Peter Rump GmbH, pg 275
Verlag an der Ruhr GmbH, pg 277
H O Schulze KG, pg 282
E Schweizerbart'sche Verlagsbuchhandlung (Naegele und Obermiller), pg 282
Springer Science+Business Media GmbH & Co KG, pg 284
Stadler Verlagsgesellschaft mbH, pg 286
Staedte-Verlag, E v Wagner und J Mitterhuber GmbH, pg 286
Stapp Verlag Wolfgang Stapp, pg 286
Steiger Verlag, pg 287
Franz Steiner Verlag Wiesbaden GmbH, pg 287
Stiefel Eurocart GmbH, pg 288
Verlag Dr Alfons Uhl, pg 293
Volk und Wissen Verlag GmbH & Co, pg 296
VWB-Verlag fur Wissenschaft & Bildung, Amand Aglaster, pg 297
Weidler Buchverlag Berlin, pg 298
Herbert Wichmann Verlag, pg 299
Wochenschau Verlag, Dr Kurt Debus GmbH, pg 301

Greece
Anixis Publications, pg 305
Ekdoseis Domi AE, pg 306
Giovanis Publications, Pangosmios Ekdotikos Organismos, pg 307
Hestia-I D Hestia-Kollaros & Co Corporation, pg 308
Orfanidis Publications, pg 311
D Papadimas, pg 311

Hong Kong
The Chinese University Press, pg 316
Geocarto International Centre, pg 317
Hong Kong University Press, pg 317
Times Publishing (Hong Kong) Ltd, pg 319

Hungary
Kossuth Kiado RT, pg 322
Nemzeti Tankoenyvkiado, pg 323
Szarvas Andras Cartographic Agency, pg 324

India
Affiliated East West Press Pvt Ltd, pg 327
Allied Book Centre, pg 328
Anmol Publications Pvt Ltd, pg 328
APH Publishing Corp, pg 328
Bharat Publishing House, pg 330
Bhawan Book Service, Publishers & Distributors, pg 330
BS Publications, pg 331
BSMPS - M/s Bishen Singh Mahendra Pal Singh, pg 331
Chowkhamba Sanskrit Series Office, pg 332
Concept Publishing Co, pg 332
Daya Publishing House, pg 333
Frank Brothers & Co Publishers Ltd, pg 334
Gyan Publishing House, pg 335
Indian Council of Social Science Research (ICSSR), pg 336
Indian Museum, pg 337
Inter-India Publications, pg 338
National Book Organization, pg 342
Omsons Publications, pg 344
Pointer Publishers, pg 345
Rajendra Publishing House Pvt Ltd, pg 346
Rajesh Publications, pg 346
Regency Publications, pg 346
Reliance Publishing House, pg 346
Scientific Book Agency, pg 348
Sultan Chand & Sons Pvt Ltd, pg 350

Ireland
An Gum, pg 358
Ballinakella Press, pg 358
Cork University Press, pg 359
The Educational Company of Ireland, pg 359
Royal Irish Academy, pg 363

Israel
Ariel Publishing House, pg 365
Bar Ilan University Press, pg 365
Hakibbutz Hameuchad Publishing House Ltd, pg 367
The Israel Academy of Sciences & Humanities, pg 368
Israel Exploration Society, pg 368
Ma'ariv Book Guild (Sifriat Ma'ariv), pg 370
Tcherikover Publishers Ltd, pg 372
Yad Izhak Ben-Zvi Press, pg 373

Italy
Edizioni della Fondazione Giovanni Agnelli, pg 374
De Agostini Scolastica, pg 374
Athesia Verlag Bozen, pg 377
BeMa, pg 377
Edizioni Cartografiche Milanesi, pg 380
Casa Editrice Giuseppe Principato Spa, pg 380
Centro Documentazione Alpina, pg 381
Centro Studi Terzo Mondo, pg 381
Ciranna - Roma, pg 382
Edizioni Della Torre di Salvatore Fozzi & C SAS, pg 385
Edistudio, pg 386
Edizioni l'Arciere SRL, pg 387
EuroGeoGrafiche Mencattini, pg 388
Arnaldo Forni Editore SRL, pg 389
Istituto Geografico de Agostini SpA, pg 390
Bruno Ghigi Editore, pg 390
Herbita Editrice di Leonardo Palermo, pg 392
Editoriale Jaca Book SpA, pg 394
Kompass Fleischmann, pg 394
LAC - Litografia Artistica Cartografica Srl, pg 394
Loescher Editore SRL, pg 396
Marzorati Editore SRL, pg 397
McRae Books, pg 398
Leo S Olschki, pg 401
Paravia Bruno Mondadori Editori, pg 402
Pitagora Editrice SRL, pg 403
Principato, pg 404
Edizioni Scientifiche Italiane, pg 407
Editoriale Scienza, pg 407
Societa Editrice Internazionale - SEI, pg 408
Le Stelle Scuola, pg 409
Tappeiner, pg 409
Editrice Tirrenia Stampatori SAS, pg 410
Zanichelli Editore SpA, pg 412
Edizioni Zara, pg 412

Jamaica
Carib Publishing Ltd, pg 413
Carlong Publishers (Caribbean) Ltd, pg 413
Jamaica Publishing House Ltd, pg 414

Japan
Fuzambo Publishing Co, pg 417
GakuseiSha Publishing Co Ltd, pg 417
Hoikusha Publishing Co Ltd, pg 418
Holp Book Co Ltd, pg 418
International Society for Educational Information (ISEI), pg 419
Japan Broadcast Publishing Co Ltd, pg 419
Japan Travel Bureau Inc, pg 420
Kodansha Ltd, pg 421
Morikita Shuppan Co Ltd, pg 423
Nippon Hoso Shuppan Kyokai (NHK Publishing), pg 424
Poplar Publishing Co Ltd, pg 425
Sekai Bunka-Sha, pg 427
Shogakukan Inc, pg 427
Taimeido Publishing Co Ltd, pg 429
Teikoku-Shoin Co Ltd, pg 429
Toho Book Store, pg 429
United Nations University Press, pg 430
Yama-Kei Publishers Co Ltd, pg 431

Kazakstan
Al-Farabi Kazakh National University, pg 432

Kenya
Heinemann Kenya Ltd (EAEP), pg 434
Nairobi University Press, pg 435
Phoenix Publishers Ltd, pg 435

Democratic People's Republic of Korea
Academy of Sciences Publishing House, pg 436
Korea Science and Encyclopedia Publishing House, pg 436

Republic of Korea
Hanul Publishing Co, pg 439
Ke Mong Sa Publishing Co Ltd, pg 440

Kuwait
Ministry of Information, pg 444

Laos People's Democratic Republic
Lao-phanit, pg 444

Latvia
Lielvards Ltd, pg 445

Lithuania
Academia, pg 448
Klaipedos Universiteto Leidykla, pg 449
Victoria Publishers, pg 450

The Former Yugoslav Republic of Macedonia
Seizmoloska Opservatorija, pg 453

Malawi
Dzuka Publishing Co Ltd, pg 454

Malaysia
Penerbit Jayatinta Sdn Bhd, pg 458
Pustaka Delta Pelajaran Sdn Bhd, pg 458

Mauritius
Editions de l'Ocean Indien Ltd, pg 461

Mexico
Editorial Esfinge SA de CV, pg 465
Editorial Limusa SA de CV, pg 467
Instituto Nacional de Estadistica, Geographia e Informatica, pg 469
Instituto Panamericano de Geografia e Historia, pg 469
Salvat Editores de Mexico, pg 471
Universidad Nacional Autonoma de Mexico (National University of Mexico), pg 472

Republic of Moldova
Editura Lumina, pg 473

Mongolia
State Press, pg 474

SUBJECT INDEX — BOOK

Namibia

Desert Research Foundation of Namibia (DRFN), pg 476
Multi-Disciplinary Research Centre Library, pg 476

Nepal

International Standards Books & Periodicals (P) Ltd, pg 476

Netherlands

Uitgeverij Jan van Arkel, pg 478
Backhuys Publishers BV, pg 478
A A Balkema Uitgevers BV, pg 478
Educatieve Uitgeverij Edu'Actief BV, pg 481
Van Gorcum & Comp BV, pg 491

New Zealand

Barkfire Press, pg 494
Bush Press Communications Ltd, pg 494
Wendy Crane Books, pg 495
ESA Publications (NZ) Ltd, pg 496
Nelson Price Milburn Ltd, pg 499
New House Publishers Ltd, pg 499

Nigeria

Evans Brothers (Nigeria Publishers) Ltd, pg 504
Ogunsanya Press, Publishers and Bookstores Ltd, pg 506
West African Book Publishers Ltd, pg 507

Norway

Vett & Viten AS, pg 511

Pakistan

Sheikh Muhammad Ashraf Publishers, pg 511
Publishers United Pvt Ltd, pg 514

Panama

Editorial Universitaria, pg 515

Peru

Instituto Frances de Estudios Andinos, IFEA, pg 517

Philippines

National Museum of the Philippines, pg 520
Saint Mary's Publishing Corp, pg 520

Poland

Wydawnictwa Geologiczne, pg 523
Instytut Historii Nauki PAN, pg 523
Instytut Meteorologii i Gospodarki Wodnej, pg 523
Polish Scientific Publishers PWN, pg 525
Wydawnictwo RTW, pg 526
Towarzystwo Naukowe w Toruniu, pg 527
Wydawnictwa Uniwersytetu Warszawskiego, pg 527

Portugal

Centro Estudos Geograficos, pg 529
Edicoes Colibri, pg 530
Constancia Editores, SA, pg 530
Edicoes Cosmos, pg 530
Editorial Estampa, Lda, pg 531
Gradiva-Publicacnoes Lda, pg 532
Impala, pg 532
Instituto de Investigacao Cientifica Tropical, pg 532

Romania

Corint Publishing Group, pg 539
Editura Dacia, pg 539
Editura Niculescu, pg 541
Editura Stiintifica SA, pg 542

Russian Federation

Gidrometeoizdat, pg 545
Izdatelstvo Mir, pg 546
Izdatelstvo Mordovskogo gosudar stvennogo, pg 547
Izdatelstvo Mysl, pg 547
Nauka Publishers, pg 547
Izdatelstvo Nedra, pg 547
Izdatelstvo Prosveshchenie, pg 548
Stroyizdat Publishing House, pg 549
Voronezh State University Publishers, pg 549

Saudi Arabia

King Saud University, pg 550

Singapore

Daiichi Media Pte Ltd, pg 555
Hillview Publications Pte Ltd, pg 556
McGallen & Bolden Associates, pg 557

South Africa

Educum Publishers Ltd, pg 563
Government Printer, pg 564

Spain

Aguilar SA de Ediciones, pg 571
Ambit Serveis Editorials, SA, pg 572
Editorial Ariel SA, pg 573
Cabildo Insular de Gran Canaria Departamento de Ediciones, pg 575
Casa de Velazquez, pg 575
Edicios do Castro, pg 576
Curial Edicions Catalanes SA, pg 578
Rafael Dalmau, Editor, pg 578
Editorial Diagonal del grup 62, pg 579
Ediciones Diputacion de Salamanca, pg 579
Diputacion Provincial de Malaga, pg 579
Edigol Ediciones SA, pg 581
Enciclopedia Catalana, SA, pg 582
Instituto de Estudios Riojanos, pg 583
Idea Books, SA, pg 587
Institucion Fernando el Catolico de la Excma Diputacion de Zaragoza, pg 587
Editorial la Muralla SA, pg 592
Noguer y Caralt Editores SA, pg 593
Ediciones Oceano Grupo SA, pg 593
Oikos-Tau SA Ediciones, pg 593
Ediciones Omega SA, pg 594
Instituto Provincial de Investigaciones y Estudios Toledanos (IPIET), pg 597
Editora Regional de Murcia - ERM, pg 597
Rueda, SL Editorial, pg 598
Universidad de Santiago de Compostela, pg 599
Servicio de Publicaciones Universidad de Cordoba, pg 599
Editorial Sintesis, SA, pg 600
Ediciones de la Torre, pg 602
Trea Ediciones, SL, pg 602
Editorial Txertoa, pg 603
Universidad de Granada, pg 603
Universidad de Valladolid Secretariado de Publicaciones e Intercambio Editorial, pg 604
Xunta de Galicia, pg 605

Sri Lanka

Ministry of Education, pg 607

Sweden

Bokforlaget Bra Bocker AB, pg 610
Liber AB, pg 613
Bokforlaget Rediviva, Facsimileforlaget, pg 615

Switzerland

Atlantis-Verlag AG, pg 618
Augustin-Verlag, pg 618
Bibliographisches Institut & F A Brockhaus AG, pg 619
Kuemmerly & Frey (Geographischer Verlag), pg 627
Librairie-Editions J Marguerat, pg 628
Motovun Book GmbH, pg 629
Orell Fuessli Buchhandlungs AG, pg 630
Ott Verlag Thun, pg 630
Sabe AG Verlagsinstitut, pg 633
Schweizerische Stiftung fuer Alpine Forschungen, pg 634
Terra Grischuna Verlag Buch-und Zeitschriftenverlag, pg 635
3 Dimension World (3-D-World), pg 635
Wepf & Co AG, pg 637

Syrian Arab Republic

Damascus University Press, pg 638
Institut Francais d'Etudes Arabes de Damas, pg 638

Taiwan, Province of China

Yee Wen Publishing Co Ltd, pg 642

United Republic of Tanzania

Eastern Africa Publications Ltd, pg 643
Press & Publicity Centre Ltd, pg 644
Tanzania Publishing House, pg 644

Tunisia

Academie Tunisienne des Sciences, des Lettres et des Arts Beit El Hekma, pg 647
Faculte des Sciences Humaines et Sociales de Tunis, pg 648

Turkey

IKI Nokta Research Press & Publications Industry & Trade Ltd, pg 650

Uganda

Centre for Basic Research, pg 652

Ukraine

Derzhavne Naukovo-Vyrobnyche Pidpryemstro Kartografia, pg 653
Naukova Dumka Publishers, pg 653

United Kingdom

Advisory Unit: Computers in Education, pg 655
Andromeda Oxford Ltd, pg 658
Arnold, pg 659
BCA - Book Club Associates, pg 663
Belitha Press Ltd, pg 664
Blackwell Publishing Ltd, pg 666
Blackwell Science Ltd, pg 667
Cambridge University Press, pg 674
Cassell & Co, pg 675
Causeway Press Ltd, pg 676
G L Crowther, pg 684
Dunedin Academic Press, pg 688
European Schoolbooks Ltd, pg 692
The Eurospan Group, pg 692
Evans Brothers Ltd, pg 693
Ex Libris Press, pg 693
W H Freeman & Co Ltd, pg 697
The Geographical Association, pg 699
Geological Society Publishing House, pg 699
Global Oriental Ltd, pg 700
Hakluyt Society, pg 703
Robert Hale Ltd, pg 704
Hodder Education, pg 709
Institute of Irish Studies, The Queens University of Belfast, pg 713
Intercept Ltd, pg 714
Jones & Bartlett International, pg 716
Hilda King Educational, pg 717
Letterbox Library, pg 720
Liverpool University Press, pg 722
Marshall Editions Ltd, pg 725
Multilingual Matters Ltd, pg 729
Nelson Thornes Ltd, pg 732
NMS Enterprises Ltd - Publishing, pg 733
North York Moors National Park, pg 733
Octopus Publishing Group, pg 734
Orpheus Books Ltd, pg 736
Packard Publishing Ltd, pg 737
Pearson Education, pg 739
Philip's, pg 741
Pion Ltd, pg 742
The Policy Press, pg 744
Quentin Books Ltd, pg 747
Quintet Publishing Ltd, pg 747
Ransom Publishing Ltd, pg 748
Reaktion Books Ltd, pg 748
Roadmaster Publishing, pg 750
Rough Guides Ltd, pg 751
Routledge, pg 751
The Royal Society, pg 752
The Salariya Book Co Ltd, pg 753
Shearwater Press Ltd, pg 757
Stacey International, pg 761
Supportive Learning Publications, pg 762
Thoemmes Press, pg 765
Two-Can Publishing Ltd, pg 768
UCL Press Ltd, pg 768
University of Wales Press, pg 769
Ward Lock Educational Co Ltd, pg 771
Wordwright Publishing, pg 775

Uruguay

Editorial Arca SRL, pg 776
A Monteverde y Cia SA, pg 777

Venezuela

Alfadil Ediciones, pg 778
Monte Avila Editores Latinoamericana CA, pg 779
Vadell Hermanos Editores CA, pg 780

Viet Nam
Science & Technics Publishing House, pg 780

Zimbabwe
Academic Books (Pvt) Ltd, pg 782
College Press Publishers (Pvt) Ltd, pg 783
Geological Survey Department, pg 783
Zimbabwe Publishing House (Pvt) Ltd, pg 784

GOVERNMENT, POLITICAL SCIENCE

Albania
NL SH, pg 1
State Textbook Publishing House, pg 1

Argentina
Editorial Astrea de Alfredo y Ricardo Depalma SRL, pg 3
Editorial Claridad SA, pg 4
Fundacion Editorial de Belgrano, pg 6
Marymar Ediciones SA, pg 7
Editorial Paidos SAICF, pg 8
Editorial Pleamar, pg 8
Editorial Plus Ultra SA, pg 8
Editorial Sopena Argentina SACI e I, pg 9
Theoria SRL Distribuidora y Editora, pg 9
Instituto Torcuato Di Tella, pg 9

Armenia
Ajstan Publishers, pg 10

Australia
Allen & Unwin Pty Ltd, pg 11
Edward Arnold (Australia) Pty Ltd, pg 12
Australian Scholarly Publishing, pg 13
Chiron Media, pg 17
Crawford House Publishing Pty Ltd, pg 18
Crystal Publishing, pg 19
Hale & Iremonger Pty Ltd, pg 24
James Nicholas Publishers Pty Ltd, pg 27
Macmillan Education Australia, pg 30
Mayne Publishing, pg 31
Ocean Press, pg 34
Oxfam Community Aid Abroad, pg 35
Pearson Education Australia, pg 36
Pluto Press Australia Pty Ltd, pg 37
University of New South Wales Press Ltd, pg 44
Vista Publications, pg 45

Austria
Boehlau Verlag GmbH & Co KG, pg 48
Development News Ltd, pg 50
Verlag fuer Geschichte und Politik, pg 51
Globus Buchvertrieb, pg 51
Guthmann & Peterson Liber Libri, Edition, pg 51
Karolinger Verlag GmbH & Co KG, pg 52
Horst Knapp Finanznachrichten, pg 53
Leopold Stocker Verlag, pg 53

Verlag des Oesterreichischen Gewerkschaftsbundes GmbH, pg 55
Verlag Orac im Verlag Kremayr & Scheriau, pg 56
Passagen Verlag GmbH, pg 56
Promedia Verlagsges mbH, pg 56
Andreas Schnider Verlags-Atelier, pg 57
Suedwind - Buchwelt GmbH, pg 58
Verlag Carl Ueberreuter GmbH, pg 58
Wieser Verlag, pg 60

Azerbaijan
Azernesr, pg 60

Bangladesh
Ankur Prakashani, pg 61
Agamee Prakashani, pg 61
The University Press Ltd, pg 61

Belarus
Belarus (The Belorussia), pg 62

Belgium
Artel, pg 63
Vanden Broele NV, pg 64
Etablessements Emile Bruylant SA, pg 64
La Charte Editions juridiques, pg 65
Editions De Boeck-Larcier SA, pg 66
Espace de Libertes, pg 67
Institut Royal des Relations Internationales, pg 68
IPIS vzw (International Peace Information Service), pg 69
Koepel van de Vlaamse Noord - Zuidbeweging 11.11.11, pg 69
Uitgeverij Lannoo NV, pg 69
Leuven University Press, pg 70
Maklu, pg 70
Presses Universitaires de Liege, pg 72
Scoop Infotex NV, pg 73
Sonneville Press (Uitgeverij) VTW, pg 73
Uitgeverij De Garve, pg 74
Editions de l'Universite de Bruxelles, pg 74
Imprimeur - Editeur Vaillant-Carmanne SA, pg 74
Vander Editions, SA, pg 74
VUB Brussels University Press, pg 74

Bosnia and Herzegovina
Veselin Maslesa, pg 76

Botswana
The Botswana Society, pg 76

Brazil
Editora Bertrand Brasil Ltda, pg 78
Camara Dos Deputados Coordenacao De Publicacoes, pg 79
Editora Campus Ltda, pg 79
Editora Forense Universitaria Ltda, pg 81
Fundacao Sao Paulo, EDUC, pg 82
IBRASA (Instituicao Brasileira de Difusao Cultural Ltda), pg 83
Editora Paz e Terra, pg 88
Editora UNESP, pg 91
Editora Universidade de Brasilia, pg 91

Bulgaria
Publishing House Hristo Botev, pg 94
Mladezh IK, pg 95
Ivan Vazov Publishing House, pg 97

Chile
Edeval (Universidad de Valparaiso), pg 99
Ediciones y Publicidad Melquiades, pg 99

China
Anhui People's Publishing House, pg 101
China Foreign Economic Relations & Trade Publishing House, pg 102
Foreign Languages Press, pg 104
Fudan University Press, pg 104
Lanzhou University Press, pg 106
SDX (Shenghuo-Dushu-Xinzhi) Joint Publishing Co, pg 107
Universidade de Macau, Centro de Publicacoes, pg 109
World Affairs Press, pg 109
Wuhan University Press, pg 109
Xinhua Publishing House, pg 109

Colombia
Amazonas Editores Ltda, pg 110
Universidad Externado de Colombia, pg 111
Siglo XXI Editores de Colombia Ltda, pg 112
Tercer Mundo Editores SA, pg 113
Carlos Valencia Editores, pg 113

The Democratic Republic of the Congo
Facultes Catoliques de Kinshasa, pg 114

Costa Rica
Editorial DEI (Departamento Ecumenico de Investigaciones), pg 115
Editorial de la Universidad de Costa Rica, pg 116
Editorial Universidad Estatal a Distancia (EUNED), pg 116

Cote d'Ivoire
Heritage Publishing Co, pg 117

Croatia
ALFA dd za izdavacke, graficke i trgovacke poslove, pg 117
Globus-Nakladni zavod, pg 118
Izdavacka Delatnost Hrvatske Akademije Znanosti I Umjetnosti, pg 118
Informator dd, pg 118
Naklada Ljevak doo, pg 119

Cuba
Editorial Capitan San Luis, pg 120
Editora Politica, pg 120

Czech Republic
Barrister & Principal, pg 122
Iuventus, pg 124
Konsultace spol sro, pg 125
Prostor, nakladatelstvi sro, pg 127
Slon Sociologicke Nakladatelstvi, pg 127

Denmark
Forlaget GMT, pg 131
IT-og Telestyrelsen, pg 132
Joergen Paludan Forlag ApS, pg 133
Politisk Revy, pg 133
Samlerens Forlag A/S, pg 134

Dominican Republic
Pontificia Universidad Catolica Madre y Maestra, pg 136

Ecuador
Corporacion Editora Nacional, pg 136
Pontificia Universidad Catolica del Ecuador, Centro de Publicaciones, pg 137

Egypt (Arab Republic of Egypt)
Al Arab Publishing House, pg 137
Ummah Press, pg 138

El Salvador
Editorial Universitaria de la Universidad de El Salvador, pg 139

Finland
Ekenas Tryckeri AB, pg 142
Kirja-Leitzinger, pg 142
Kuva ja Sana, pg 143

France
Actes-Graphiques, pg 145
Editions Anthropos, pg 147
Editions de l'Atelier, pg 148
Beauchesne Editeur, pg 149
Editions Cujas, pg 156
Editions Denoel, pg 157
La Documentation Francaise, pg 158
FBT de R Editions, pg 163
Futuribles SARL, pg 164
Groupe Express-Expansion, pg 166
Hachette Livre, pg 167
Editions de l'Herne, pg 167
Editions du Jaguar, pg 169
Les Editions LGDJ-Montchrestien, pg 172
Editions des Limbes d'Or FBT de R Editions, pg 172
LiTec (Librairies Techniques SA), pg 172
Le Livre de Poche-L G F (Librairie Generale Francaise), pg 173
Editions Odile Jacob, pg 177
Editions Jean Picollec, pg 179
Presses de Sciences Politiques, pg 181
Presses Universitaires de France (PUF), pg 181
Presses Universitaires de Lyon, pg 181
Presses Universitaires de Nancy, pg 181
Editions du Seuil, pg 184
Publications de la Sorbonne, pg 185
10/18, pg 187

Georgia
Sakartvelo Publishing House, pg 190

Germany
A Francke Verlag (Tubingen und Basel), pg 190
Accedo Verlagsgesellschaft mbH, pg 190

SUBJECT INDEX — BOOK

Ahriman-Verlag GmbH, pg 191
Verlag und Antiquariat Frank Albrecht, pg 192
AOL-Verlag Frohmut Menze, pg 193
Arbeiterpresse Verlags- und Vertriebsgesellschaft mbH, pg 193
Argument-Verlag, pg 194
Asgard-Verlag Dr Werner Hippe GmbH, pg 194
Aufbau Taschenbuch Verlag GmbH, pg 195
Aufbau-Verlag GmbH, pg 195
BasisDruck Verlag GmbH, pg 197
be.bra verlag GmbH, pg 198
Berliner Debatte Wissenschafts Verlag, GSFP-Gesellschaft fur Sozialwissen-schaftliche Forschung und Publizistik mbH & Co KG, pg 199
Berliner Wissenschafts-Verlag GmbH (BWV), pg 199
C Bertelsmann Verlag GmbH, pg 199
Verlag Bertelsmann Stiftung, pg 200
Bleicher Verlag GmbH, pg 202
Bouvier Verlag, pg 203
Verlag Brandenburger Tor GmbH, pg 203
Brandes & Apsel Verlag GmbH, pg 204
C C Buchners Verlag GmbH & Co KG, pg 205
Buchergilde Gutenberg Verlagsgesellschaft mbH, pg 205
Bund demokratischer Wissenschaftlerinnen und Wissenschafler eV (BdWi), pg 205
Bund-Verlag GmbH, pg 206
Bundesanzeiger Verlagsgesellschaft, pg 206
Campus Verlag GmbH, pg 207
Daedalus Verlag, pg 210
Deutsche Verlags-Anstalt GmbH (DVA), pg 212
Deutscher Gemeindeverlag GmbH, pg 212
Deutscher Taschenbuch Verlag GmbH & Co KG (dtv), pg 213
Die Verlag H Schafer GmbH, pg 214
Dietrich zu Klampen Verlag, pg 214
Verlag J H W Dietz Nachf GmbH, pg 214
Dietz Verlag Berlin GmbH, pg 215
Dipa-Verlag GmbH, pg 215
agenda Verlag Thomas Dominikowski, pg 215
Donat Verlag, pg 215
Droste Verlag GmbH, pg 216
Druffel-Verlag, pg 216
Duncker und Humblot GmbH, pg 217
DVG-Deutsche Verlagsgesellschaft mbH, pg 217
Verlag Peter Engstler, pg 220
Espresso Verlag GmbH, pg 221
Europa Union Verlag GmbH, pg 222
Europa Verlag GmbH, pg 222
Europaeische Verlagsanstalt GmbH & Rotbuch Verlag GmbH & Co KG, pg 222
Ferd Dummler's Verlag, pg 223
Festland Verlag GmbH, pg 224
Rita G Fischer Verlag, pg 225
Forum Verlag Leipzig Buch-Gesellschaft mbH, pg 225
Verlag A Fromm im Druck- u Verlagshaus Fromm GmbH & Co KG, pg 227

Verlagsbuchhandlung Megapress, Franz-J Gaber, pg 228
Goll Bruno Verlag fur Aussergewoehnliche Perspektiven (VAP), pg 230
Gunter Olzog Verlag GmbH, pg 231
Guetersloher Verlagshaus, pg 232
Verlag Klaus Guhl, pg 232
Haag und Herchen Verlag GmbH, pg 232
Edition Hentrich Druck & Verlag Gebr Hentrich und Tank GmbH & Co KG, pg 236
Hans-Alfred Herchen & Co Verlag KG, pg 236
Verlag Herder GmbH & Co KG, pg 236
Carl Heymanns Verlag KG, pg 237
Hohenrain-Verlag GmbH, pg 239
Horlemann Verlag, pg 239
Heinrich Hugendubel Verlag GmbH, pg 240
Edition ID-Archiv/ID-Verlag, pg 240
Verlag fuer Internationale Politik GmbH, pg 242
Junius Verlag GmbH, pg 244
KBV Verlags-und Medien - GmbH, pg 245
SachBuchVerlag Kellner, pg 245
Klartext Verlagsgesellschaft mbH, pg 246
K F Koehler Verlag GmbH, pg 248
Koelner Universitaets-Verlag GmbH, pg 248
W Kohlhammer GmbH, pg 248
Konkret Literatur Verlag, pg 249
KONTEXTverlag, pg 249
Dr Anton Kovac Slavica Verlag, pg 249
Karin Kramer Verlag, pg 250
Kulturstiftung der deutschen Vertriebenen, pg 250
Verlag Antje Kunstmann GmbH, pg 251
Lamuv Verlag GmbH, pg 251
Peter Lang GmbH Europaeischer Verlag der Wissenschaften, pg 252
Dr Gisela Lermann, pg 253
Lettre International Kulturzeitung, pg 253
Libertas- Europaeisches Institut GmbH, pg 254
Christoph Links Verlag - LinksDruck GmbH, pg 254
Merlin Verlag Andreas Meyer Verlags GmbH und Co KG, pg 259
Metropolis- Verlag fur Okonomie, Gesellschaft und Politik GmbH, pg 259
Militzke Verlag, pg 260
E S Mittler und Sohn GmbH, pg 261
Munzinger-Archiv GmbH Archiv fuer publizistische Arbeit, pg 262
MUT Verlag, pg 263
Edition Nautilus Verlag, pg 263
NDV Neue Darmstadter Verlagsanstalt, pg 263
Neuer ISP Verlag GmbH, pg 264
Verlag Neuer Weg, pg 264
Nomos Verlagsgesellschaft mbH und Co KG, pg 265
Nusser Verlag, pg 266
Oberbaum Verlag GmbH, pg 266
Verlag Offene Worte, pg 266
Georg Olms Verlag AG, pg 267
Pahl-Rugenstein Verlag Nachfolger-GmbH, pg 267
Palmyra Verlag, pg 268

PapyRossa Verlags GmbH & Co Kommanditgesellschaft KG, pg 268
Propylaeen Verlag, Zweigniederlassung Berlin der Ullstein Buchverlage GmbH, pg 272
Roehrig Universitaets Verlag Gmbh, pg 276
Rombach GmbH Druck und Verlagshaus & Co, pg 276
Ruetten & Loening Berlin GmbH, pg 277
Dieter Ruggeberg Verlagsbuchhandlung, pg 277
Richard Scherpe Verlag GmbH, pg 279
Ferdinand Schoeningh Verlag GmbH, pg 281
Schueren Verlag GmbH, pg 281
Siedler Verlag, pg 283
Siegler & Co Verlag fuer Zeitarchive GmbH, pg 283
Springer Science+Business Media GmbH & Co KG, pg 284
Edition Temmen, pg 290
Toleranz Verlag, Nielsen Frederic W, pg 291
Trotzdem-Verlags Genossenschaft eG, pg 292
Tuduv Verlagsgesellschaft mbH, pg 292
UNO-Verlag GmbH, pg 293
Unrast Verlag e V, pg 293
UTB fuer Wissenschaft Uni Taschenbuecher GmbH, pg 294
VAS-Verlag fuer Akademische Schriften, pg 294
Dokument und Analyse Verlag Bogislaw von Randow, pg 296
VVF Verlag V Florentz GmbH, pg 297
Verlag Klaus Wagenbach, pg 297
Weber Zucht & Co, pg 298
Verlag Wissenschaft und Politik, pg 300
Wochenschau Verlag, Dr Kurt Debus GmbH, pg 301
Zambon Verlag, pg 302
Zebulon Verlag GmbH & Co KG, pg 302

Ghana

Frank Publishing Ltd, pg 304
Ghana Universities Press (GUP), pg 304

Greece

Axiotelis G, pg 306
Boukoumanis' Editions, pg 306
Dorikos Publishing House, pg 306
Exandas Publishers, pg 307
Govostis Publishing SA, pg 307
Gutenberg Publications, pg 307
Irini Publishing House - Vassilis G Katsikeas SA, pg 308
Kastaniotis Editions SA, pg 309
Kritiki Publishing, pg 309
Nea Thesis - Evrotas, pg 310
Papazissis Publishers SA, pg 311
Pontiki Publications SA, pg 311
Proskinio Spyros Ch Marinis, pg 311

Honduras

Editorial Guaymuras, pg 315

Hong Kong

Asia 2000 Ltd, pg 315
Celeluck Co Ltd, pg 316
The Chinese University Press, pg 316
Friends of the Earth (Charity) Ltd, pg 317
Hong Kong University Press, pg 317
Sun Mui Press, pg 319

Hungary

Central European University Press, pg 321
Joszoveg Muhely Kiado, pg 322
KJK-Kerszov, pg 322
Osiris Kiado, pg 323
Szabad Ter Kiado, pg 324

Iceland

Hid Islenzka Bokmenntafelag, pg 325

India

Abhinav Publications, pg 326
Abhishek Publications, pg 327
Ajanta Publications (India), pg 327
Allied Publishers Pvt Ltd, pg 328
Amar Prakashan, pg 328
Ankur Publishing Co, pg 328
APH Publishing Corp, pg 328
K P Bagchi & Co, pg 329
BR Publishing Corporation, pg 331
S Chand & Co Ltd, pg 331
Cosmo Publications, pg 332
Eastern Law House Pvt Ltd, pg 334
Frank Brothers & Co Publishers Ltd, pg 334
Gitanjali Publishing House, pg 335
Goel Prakashen, pg 335
Gyan Publishing House, pg 335
Arnold Heinman Publishers (India) Pvt Ltd, pg 335
Indian Society for Promoting Christian Knowledge (ISPCK), pg 337
Intellectual Publishing House, pg 338
Inter-India Publications, pg 338
Islamic Publishing House, pg 338
Jaico Publishing House, pg 338
Konark Publishers Pvt Ltd, pg 339
Law Publishers, pg 340
Manohar Publishers & Distributors, pg 340
Minerva Associates (Publications) Pvt Ltd, pg 341
A Mukherjee & Co Pvt Ltd, pg 342
National Book Organization, pg 342
Naya Prokash, pg 343
Omsons Publications, pg 344
Pointer Publishers, pg 345
Popular Prakashan Pvt Ltd, pg 345
Promilla & Publishers, pg 345
Radiant Publishers, pg 346
Rastogi Publications, pg 346
Regency Publications, pg 346
Reliance Publishing House, pg 346
Roli Books Pvt Ltd, pg 347
SABDA, pg 347
SAGE Publications India Pvt Ltd, pg 347
Scientific Book Agency, pg 348
Somaiya Publications Pvt Ltd, pg 349
South Asian Publishers Pvt Ltd, pg 350
Sterling Publishers Pvt Ltd, pg 350
Sultan Chand & Sons Pvt Ltd, pg 350
UBS Publishers Distributors Ltd, pg 351

Indonesia

Bina Rena Pariwara, pg 354
PT Bulan Bintang, pg 354

PUBLISHERS SUBJECT INDEX

Pustaka Utama Grafiti, PT, pg 356
Yayasan Obor Indonesia, pg 357

Iraq

National House for Publishing, Distributing & Advertising, pg 357

Ireland

Attic Press Ltd, pg 358
Emerald Publications, pg 359
Gill & Macmillan Ltd, pg 360
Government Publications Ireland, pg 360
Institute of Public Administration, pg 361
New Books/Connolly Books, pg 362
Royal Irish Academy, pg 363

Israel

Gefen Publishing House Ltd, pg 367
Hakibbutz Hameuchad Publishing House Ltd, pg 367
The Institute for Israeli Arabs Studies, pg 368
Israel Universities Press, pg 368
Jabotinsky Institute in Israel, pg 368
Ma'ariv Book Guild (Sifriat Ma'ariv), pg 370
Machbarot Lesifrut, pg 370
Open University of Israel, pg 371
Rubin Mass Ltd, pg 371
Shalem Press, pg 372
Tel Aviv University, pg 372
The Van Leer Jerusalem Institute, pg 373
Zmora-Bitan, Publishers Ltd, pg 374

Italy

Edizioni della Fondazione Giovanni Agnelli, pg 374
Arnaud Editore SRL, pg 376
Giuseppe Bonanno Editore, pg 378
Edizioni Borla SRL, pg 379
Cappelli Editore, pg 380
CEDAM (Casa Editrice Dr A Milani), pg 380
Celuc Libri, pg 381
Centro Studi Terzo Mondo, pg 381
il Cerchio Iniziative Editoriali, pg 381
CLEUP - Cooperative Libraria Editrice dell 'Universita di Padova, pg 382
Edizioni di Comunita SpA, pg 383
Edizioni Cultura della Pace, pg 383
La Cultura Sociologica, pg 384
Datanews, pg 384
Edizioni Dedalo SRL, pg 384
Edizioni EBE, pg 385
Edizioni Associate/Editrice Internazionale Srl, pg 386
Esselibri, pg 388
Edizioni Europa, pg 388
Galzerano Editore, pg 390
Garzanti Libri, pg 390
Edizioni GB, pg 390
G Giappichelli Editore SRL, pg 390
A Giuffre Editore SpA, pg 390
Giuseppe Laterza Editore, pg 391
Herbita Editrice di Leonardo Palermo, pg 392
In Dialogo, pg 393
Editoriale Jaca Book SpA, pg 394
Kaos Edizioni SRL, pg 394
Lalli Editore SRL, pg 394
Edizioni Lavoro SRL, pg 394
Manifestolibri, pg 397
Edizioni Medicea SRL, pg 398
Il Minotauro, pg 398

Societa Editrice Il Mulino, pg 399
Newton & Compton Editori, pg 400
Leo S Olschki, pg 401
Istituto Poligrafico e Zecca dello Stato, pg 403
Edition Raetia Srl-GmbH, pg 405
Editori Riuniti, pg 405
Rubbettino Editore, pg 406
Editrice San Marco SRL, pg 407
Sapere 2000 SRL, pg 407
SIPI (Servizio Italiano Pubblicazioni Internazionali) Srl, pg 408
Nicola Teti e C Editore SRL, pg 410

Jamaica

The Press, pg 414

Japan

Chuokoron-Shinsha Inc, pg 416
Hayakawa Publishing Inc, pg 418
Koyo Shobo, pg 422
Minerva Shobo Co Ltd, pg 422
Nippon Hoso Shuppan Kyokai (NHK Publishing), pg 424
President Inc, pg 425
Ryosho-Fukyu-Kai Co Ltd, pg 425
Teikoku-Shoin Co Ltd, pg 429
Waseda University Press, pg 431

Kazakhstan

Al-Farabi Kazakh National University, pg 432
Kazakhstan, Izd-Vo, pg 432

Kenya

Cosmopolitan Publishers Ltd, pg 433
Heinemann Kenya Ltd (EAEP), pg 434
Kenway Publications Ltd, pg 434
Lake Publishers & Enterprises Ltd, pg 435
Midi Teki Publishers, pg 435
Nairobi University Press, pg 435
Gideon S Were Press, pg 436

Democratic People's Republic of Korea

Korea Science and Encyclopedia Publishing House, pg 436
Working People's Organization Publishing House, pg 437

Republic of Korea

Korea Textbook Co Ltd, pg 440
Kyobo Book Centre Co Ltd, pg 440
Oruem Publishing House, pg 442

Lebanon

Institute for Palestine Studies, Publishing & Research Organization (IPS), pg 446

Liechtenstein

Bonafides Verlags-Anstalt, pg 447
Liechtenstein Verlag AG, pg 448
Verlag der Liechtensteinischen Akademischen Gesellschaft, pg 448

Lithuania

Eugrimas, pg 449
Vaga Ltd, pg 450

Luxembourg

Varkki Verghese, pg 452

Malaysia

Forum Publications, pg 456
University of Malaya, Department of Publications, pg 459

Mauritius

Vizavi Editions, pg 461

Mexico

Editores Asociados Mexicanos SA de CV (EDAMEX), pg 462
Centro de Estudios Mexicanos y Centroamericanos, pg 463
El Colegio de Mexico AC, pg 463
Comision Nacional Forestal, pg 463
El Colegio de Michoacan A C, pg 464
Ediciones Era SA de CV, pg 465
Editorial Extemporaneos SA, pg 465
Fondo de Cultura Economica, pg 465
Ibcon SA, pg 466
Editorial Jus SA de CV, pg 467
Editorial Limusa SA de CV, pg 467
Siglo XXI Editores SA de CV, pg 472

Republic of Moldova

Editura Cartea Moldovei, pg 473

Mongolia

State Press, pg 474

Morocco

Editions Al-Fourkane, pg 474
Les Editions du Journal L' Unite Maghrebine, pg 475
Editions La Porte, pg 475

Mozambique

Centro De Estudos Africanos, pg 475

Myanmar

Knowledge Press & Bookhouse, pg 475
Shwepyidan Printing & Publishing House, pg 476

Namibia

Multi-Disciplinary Research Centre Library, pg 476

Nepal

International Standards Books & Periodicals (P) Ltd, pg 476

Netherlands

Uitgeverij Jan van Arkel, pg 478
Boom Uitgeverij, pg 479
Uitgeverij en boekhandel Van Gennep BV, pg 482
Uitgeverij H Nelissen BV, pg 486
Sdu Uitgevers bv, pg 488
Sociaal en Cultureel Planbureau, pg 489
Uitgeverij Van Wijnen, pg 491

New Zealand

Auckland University Press, pg 493
Fraser Books, pg 496
Gondwanaland Press, pg 496
Hazard Press Ltd, pg 497
Legislation Direct, pg 498
University of Otago Press, pg 502
Victoria University Press, pg 502
Bridget Williams Books Ltd, pg 502

Nicaragua

Editorial Nueva Nicaragua, pg 502

Nigeria

Ahmadu Bello University Press Ltd, pg 503
Evans Brothers (Nigeria Publishers) Ltd, pg 504
Fourth Dimension Publishing Co Ltd, pg 504
Goldland Business Co Ltd, pg 505
International Publishing & Research Company, pg 505
JAD Publishers Ltd, pg 505
Literamed Publications Nigeria Ltd, pg 505
Tabansi Press Ltd, pg 507
Vantage Publishers International Ltd, pg 507
West African Book Publishers Ltd, pg 507

Norway

Glydendal Akademisk, pg 509
Gyldendal Norsk Forlag A/S, pg 509
Snofugl Forlag, pg 510

Pakistan

Sheikh Muhammad Ashraf Publishers, pg 511
Centre for South Asian Studies, pg 512
Jang Publishers, pg 513
Maqbool Academy, pg 513
Pak American Commercial (Pvt) Ltd, pg 514
Royal Book Co, pg 514
Shibil Publications (Pvt) Ltd, pg 514

Papua New Guinea

IMPS Research Ltd, pg 515
National Research Institute of Papua New Guinea, pg 515

Paraguay

Intercontinental Editora, pg 516

Peru

Centro de la Mujer Peruana Flora Tristan, pg 516
Instituto de Estudios Peruanos, pg 517

Philippines

Ateneo de Manila University Press, pg 518
Garotech, pg 519
Heritage Publishing House, pg 519
University of the Philippines Press, pg 521

Poland

KAW Krajowa Agencja Wydawnicza, pg 523
'Ksiazka i Wiedza' Spotdzielnia Wydawniczo-Handlowa, pg 524
Wydawnictwo Lubelskie, pg 524
Magnum Publishing House Ltd, pg 524
Spotdzielnia Anagram, pg 526
Wydawnictwo TPPR Wspolpraca, pg 527
Wydawnictwa Uniwersytetu Warszawskiego, pg 527

SUBJECT INDEX

Portugal
Edicoes Afrontamento, pg 528
Armenio Amado Editora de Simoes, Beirao & Ca Lda, pg 528
Edicoes Antigona, pg 528
Brasilia Editora (J Carvalho Branco), pg 529
Editorial Caminho SARL, pg 529
Livraria Civilizacao (Americo Fraga Lamares & Ca Lda), pg 529
Gradiva-Publicacnoes Lda, pg 532
Imprensa Nacional-Casa da Moeda, pg 532
Editora Livros do Brasil Sarl, pg 533
Editora McGraw-Hill de Portugal Lda, pg 533
Nova Arrancada Sociedade Editora SA, pg 534
Perspectivas e Realidades, Artes Graficas, Lda, pg 534
Editorial Presenca, pg 535
Edicoes Rolim Lda, pg 535

Puerto Rico
Libros-Ediciones Homines, pg 537

Romania
Casa de editura Globus, pg 540
Humanitas Publishing House, pg 540
Editura Institutul European, pg 540
Nemira Verlag, pg 541
Editura Niculescu, pg 541
Realitatea Casa de Edituri Productie Audio-Video Film, pg 542
Editura 'Scrisul Romanesc', pg 542

Russian Federation
Aspect Press Ltd, pg 543
INFRA-M Izdatel 'skij dom, pg 545
Izvestia Sovetov Narodnyh Deputatov Russian Federation (RF), pg 545
Ladomir Publishing House, pg 546
Izdatelstvo Lenizdat, pg 546
Izdatelstvo Mezdunarodnye Otnoshenia, pg 546
Izdatelstvo Molodaya Gvardia, pg 546
Nauka Publishers, pg 547
Izdatel'stvo Nizhegorodskogo Gosudarstvennogo Univ, pg 547
Novosti Izdatelstvo, pg 547
Progress Publishers, pg 548
Respublika, pg 548
Russkaya Kniga Izdatelstvo (Publishers), pg 548
Voyenizdat, pg 549

Saudi Arabia
Al Jazirah Organization for Press, Printing, Publishing, pg 550

Senegal
CODESRIA (Council for the Development of Social Science Research in Africa), pg 551
Societe Africaine d'Edition, pg 551

Serbia and Montenegro
Alfa-Narodna Knjiga, pg 552
Forum, pg 552
Izdavacka Organizacija Rad, pg 553
Panorama NIJP/ID Grigorije Bozovic, pg 553
Radnicka Stampa, pg 553

Singapore
Chopsons Pte Ltd, pg 555
Graham Brash Pte Ltd, pg 556
Institute of Southeast Asian Studies, pg 556
Singapore University Press Pte Ltd, pg 558
Taylor & Francis Asia Pacific, pg 558
Times Media Pte Ltd, pg 559

Slovakia
ARCHA sro Vydavatel'stro, pg 559
Danubiaprint, pg 559

Slovenia
Univerza v Ljubljani Ekonomska Fakulteta, pg 562
Zalozba Mihelac d o o, pg 562

South Africa
Ashanti Publishing, pg 562
Jonathan Ball Publishers, pg 562
Educum Publishers Ltd, pg 563
Human Sciences Research Council, pg 565
Institute for Reformational Studies CHE, pg 565
New Africa Books (Pty) Ltd, pg 567
Ravan Press (Pty) Ltd, pg 568
South African Institute of International Affairs, pg 569
South African Institute of Race Relations, pg 569
University of KwaZulu-Natal Press, pg 569
Van Schaik Publishers, pg 569
Witwatersrand University Press, pg 570

Spain
Edicions Alfons el Magnanim, Institucio Valenciana d'Estudis i Investigacio, pg 572
Alianza Editorial SA, pg 572
Altea, Taurus, Alfaguara SA, pg 572
Amnistia Internacional Editorial SL, pg 572
Centro de Estudios Politicos Y Constitucionales, pg 576
Editorial Constitucion y Leyes SA - COLEX, pg 578
Fondo de Cultura Economica de Espana, SL, pg 583
Editorial Fundamentos, pg 584
Ediciones Jucar, pg 588
Ediciones Libertarias/Prodhufi SA, pg 589
Antonio Machado, SA, pg 590
Editorial Popular SA, pg 596
Siglo XXI de Espana Editores SA, pg 599
Universidad de Valladolid Secretariado de Publicaciones e Intercambio Editorial, pg 604
VOSA, SL Ediciones, pg 605

Sri Lanka
Warna Publishers, pg 607

Suriname
Stichting Wetenschappelijke Informatie, pg 608

Sweden
Forlaget By och Bygd, pg 610
Carlsson Bokfoerlag AB, pg 610
Iustus Forlag AB, pg 613

Timbro, pg 616
Zindermans AB, pg 617

Switzerland
Athenaeum Verlag AG, pg 618
Cahiers de la Renaissance Vaudoise, pg 620
Europa Verlag AG, pg 623
Georg Editeur SA, pg 624
Editions Francois Grounauer, pg 624
Th Gut Verlag, pg 624
Helbing und Lichtenhahn Verlag AG, pg 625
Verlag Huber & Co AG, pg 625
Interfrom AG Editions, pg 625
Junod Nicolas, pg 626
Klett und Balmer & Co Verlag, pg 626
Lenos Verlag, pg 627
Limmat Verlag, pg 628
Peter Meili & Co, Buchhandlung, pg 628
Les Editions Nagel SA (Paris), pg 629
Verlag Organisator AG, pg 630
Pendo Verlag GmbH, pg 631
Rotpunktverlag, pg 632
Ruegger Verlag, pg 633
Verlag SOI (Schweizerisches Ost-Institut), pg 634
Staempfli Verlag AG, pg 634
Editions des Trois Collines Francois Lachenal, pg 635
Der Universitatsverlag Freiburg, pg 636
Weltrundschau Verlag AG, pg 637

Syrian Arab Republic
Damascus University Press, pg 638

Taiwan, Province of China
Laureate Book Co Ltd, pg 640
San Min Book Co Ltd, pg 641

Tajikistan
Irfon, pg 642

United Republic of Tanzania
Eastern Africa Publications Ltd, pg 643
Kajura Publications, pg 643
Tanzania Publishing House, pg 644

Thailand
Suksit Siam Co Ltd, pg 646
Thai Watana Panich Co, Ltd, pg 646

Trinidad & Tobago
Inprint Caribbean Ltd, pg 647

Tunisia
Dar El Afaq, pg 648

Turkey
Afa Yayincilik Sanayi Tic AS, pg 648
Ezel Erverdi (Dergah Yayinlari AS) Muessese Muduru, pg 650
Iletisim Yayinlari, pg 650
Alev Yayinlari, pg 652

Turkmenistan
Izdatelstvo Turkmenistan, pg 652

Uganda
Centre for Basic Research, pg 652
Fountain Publishers Ltd, pg 652

Ukraine
Osnovy Publishers, pg 654

United Kingdom
Aldwych Press Ltd, pg 656
Anglo-German Foundation for the Study of Industrial Society, pg 658
Arms & Armour Press, pg 659
Ashgate Publishing Ltd, pg 660
Baha'i Publishing Trust, pg 662
Berg Publishers, pg 664
Berghahn Books Ltd, pg 665
Blackwell Publishing Ltd, pg 666
Bookmarks Publications, pg 668
British Educational Communication & Technology Agency (BECTA), pg 671
Business Monitor International, pg 672
Cambridge University Press, pg 674
Jon Carpenter Publishing, pg 675
Catholic Institute for International Relations, pg 676
Causeway Press Ltd, pg 676
Colourpoint Books, pg 681
Commonwealth Secretariat, pg 681
Conservative Policy Forum, pg 682
The Continuum International Publishing Group Ltd, pg 682
James Currey Ltd, pg 685
Andre Deutsch Ltd, pg 687
Edinburgh University Press Ltd, pg 689
Edward Elgar Publishing Ltd, pg 690
Ethics International Press Ltd, pg 692
Europa Publications, pg 692
The Eurospan Group, pg 692
Fabian Society, pg 694
Francis Balsom Associates, pg 696
Freedom Press, pg 697
Geiser Productions, pg 699
Golden Cockerel Press Ltd, pg 701
HarperCollins UK, pg 705
Harvard University Press, pg 705
William Heinemann Ltd, pg 707
Helicon Publishing Ltd, pg 707
Hemming Information Services, pg 707
C Hurst & Co (Publishers) Ltd, pg 711
ICC United Kingdom, pg 711
Institute of Development Studies, pg 712
Institute of Employment Rights, pg 712
Institute of Governance, pg 713
Institute of Irish Studies, The Queens University of Belfast, pg 713
International Institute for Strategic Studies, pg 714
Islamic Foundation Publications, pg 714
JAI Press Ltd, pg 715
Macmillan Reference Ltd, pg 724
Mainstream Publishing Co (Edinburgh) Ltd, pg 724
Manchester University Press, pg 724
The Merlin Press Ltd, pg 727
Microform Academic Publishers, pg 728
National Assembly for Wales, pg 730
National Library of Wales, pg 731

New European Publications Ltd, pg 732
W W Norton & Company Ltd, pg 734
NTC Research, pg 734
Open Gate Press, pg 735
Open University Press, pg 736
Oxfam, pg 737
Oxford University Press, pg 737
Pathfinder London, pg 739
Pearson Education, pg 739
Pearson Education Europe, Mideast & Africa, pg 739
Pluto Books Ltd, pg 743
Pluto Press, pg 743
The Policy Press, pg 744
Policy Studies Institute (PSI), pg 744
Prism Press Book Publishers Ltd, pg 745
Random House UK Ltd, pg 747
Reaktion Books Ltd, pg 748
Rivers Oram Press, pg 750
Robson Books, pg 750
Routledge, pg 751
Royal Institute of International Affairs, pg 752
SAGE Publications Ltd, pg 753
Saqi Books, pg 754
Scottish Executive Library & Information Services, pg 755
Seren, pg 756
Serif, pg 756
Shaw & Sons Ltd, pg 756
Shepheard-Walwyn (Publishers) Ltd, pg 757
Sidgwick & Jackson Ltd, pg 757
Skoob Russell Square, pg 758
Snowbooks Ltd, pg 759
The Society of Metaphysicians Ltd, pg 759
Spokesman, pg 760
I B Tauris & Co Ltd, pg 763
Taylor & Francis, pg 763
Transworld Publishers Ltd, pg 766
TSO (The Stationery Office), pg 767
UCL Press Ltd, pg 768
Vacher Dod Publishing Ltd, pg 769
Verso, pg 770
Virago Press, pg 770
Welsh Academic Press, pg 772
Westview Press, pg 772
Wild Goose Publications, pg 773
Wimbledon Publishing Company Ltd, pg 774
The Women's Press Ltd, pg 775
World of Information, pg 776
Yale University Press London, pg 776

Uruguay

Fundacion de Cultura Universitaria, pg 777
Linardi y Risso Libreria, pg 777
Nordan-Comunidad, pg 778
Ediciones Trilce, pg 778

Uzbekistan

Izdatelstvo Uzbekistan, pg 778

Venezuela

Editorial Ateneo de Caracas, pg 779
Monte Avila Editores Latinoamericana CA, pg 779
Fundacion Centro Gumilla, pg 779
Editorial Nueva Sociedad, pg 780

Viet Nam

Su Hoc (Historical) Publishing House, pg 781
Su That (Truth) Publishing House, pg 781

Zambia

Aafzam Ltd, pg 781
MFK Management Consultants Services, pg 781
Movement for Multi-Party Democracy, pg 781
Zambia Association for Research & Development (ZARD), pg 782
Zambia Educational Publishing House, pg 782

Zimbabwe

Journal on Social Change, pg 783
Nehanda Publishers, pg 784
Sapes Trust Ltd, pg 784

HEALTH, NUTRITION

Argentina

Libreria Akadia Editorial, pg 3
Editorial Albatros SACI, pg 3
Editorial Kier SACIFI, pg 7
Ediciones Lidiun, pg 7
Editorial Planeta Argentina SAIC, pg 8
Ediciones Preescolar SA, pg 8
San Pablo, pg 9
Editorial Sopena Argentina SACI e I, pg 9

Australia

Allen & Unwin Pty Ltd, pg 11
Michelle Anderson Publishing, pg 11
Edward Arnold (Australia) Pty Ltd, pg 12
Ausmed Publications Pty Ltd, pg 12
Bio Concepts Publishing, pg 14
Centre Publications, pg 17
CHOICE Magazine, pg 17
Dynamo House P/L, pg 20
Extraordinary People Press, pg 22
Family Health Publications, pg 22
Fraser Publications, pg 22
Ginninderra Press, pg 23
Greater Glider Productions Australia Pty Ltd, pg 24
Hale & Iremonger Pty Ltd, pg 24
James Nicholas Publishers Pty Ltd, pg 27
Kingsclear Books, pg 28
Lansdowne Publishing Pty Ltd, pg 28
Life Planning Foundation of Australia, Inc, pg 29
Thomas C Lothian Pty Ltd, pg 29
MacLennan & Petty Pty Ltd, pg 30
Mayne Publishing, pg 31
McGraw-Hill Australia Pty Ltd, pg 31
Moon-Ta-Gu Books, pg 32
Mouse House Press, pg 32
Anne O'Donovan Pty Ltd, pg 34
Oidium Books, pg 34
Oxfam Community Aid Abroad, pg 35
Pan Macmillan Australia Pty Ltd, pg 35
Pearson Education Australia, pg 36
Jurriaan Plesman, pg 37
R & R Publications Pty Ltd, pg 38
Reed Educational Publishing Australia, pg 39
Regency Publishing, pg 39
Simon & Schuster (Australia) Pty Ltd, pg 41
Spinifex Press, pg 42
Stirling Press, pg 42
Tomorrow Publications, pg 44
Transworld Publishers Pty Ltd, pg 44
Unity Press, pg 44
Veritas Press, pg 45
Vista Publications, pg 45
Wellness Australia, pg 46
Women's Health Advisory Service, pg 47
Zoe Publishing Pty Ltd, pg 47

Austria

CEEBA Publications Antenne d'Autriche, pg 49
Ennsthaler GesmbH & Co KG, pg 50
Alois Goschl & Co, pg 51
IAEA - International Atomic Energy Agency, pg 52
Niederosterreichisches Pressehaus Druck- und Verlagsgesellschaft mbH, pg 54
NOI - Verlag, pg 55
Verlag Orac im Verlag Kremayr & Scherien, pg 56
Verlag des Osterr Kneippbundes GmbH, pg 56
Verlag Carl Ueberreuter GmbH, pg 58
Edition Va Bene, pg 59
Verlag Veritas Mediengesellschaft mbH, pg 59
Dr Otfried Weise Verlag Tabula Smaragdina, pg 59

Bangladesh

Gatidhara, pg 61
Gono Prakashani, Gono Shasthya Kendra, pg 61

Belarus

Belaruskaya Encyklapedyya, pg 62
Interdigest Publishing House, pg 62

Belgium

Altina, pg 63
Editions De Boeck-Larcier SA, pg 66
Koepel van de Vlaamse Noord - Zuidbeweging 11.11.11, pg 69
Uitgeverij Lannoo NV, pg 69
Marabout, pg 71
Vita, pg 74

Brazil

Editora Agora Ltda, pg 77
Editora Antroposofica Ltda, pg 77
ARTMED Editora, pg 78
Editora Campus Ltda, pg 79
Editora Contexto (Editora Pinsky Ltda), pg 80
Companhia Editora Forense, pg 81
EDUSC - Editora da Universidade do Sagrado Coracao, pg 81
Editora Elevacao, pg 81
Editora Gaia Ltda, pg 82
Global Editora e Distribuidora Ltda, pg 82
Editora Ground Ltda, pg 83
IBRASA (Instituicao Brasileira de Difusao Cultural Ltda), pg 83
Iglu Editora Ltda, pg 84
Imago Editora Importacao e Exportacao Ltda, pg 84
Interlivros Edicoes Ltda, pg 84
Livraria Nobel S/A, pg 85
Editora Manole Ltda, pg 86
Editora Mercado Aberto Ltda, pg 86
Editora Moderna Ltda, pg 86
Editora Nova Fronteira SA, pg 87
Rede Das Artes (Boccato Editores Collector's), pg 89

Bulgaria

Abagar, Veliko Tarnovo, pg 93
Aratron, IK, pg 93
Gea-Libris Publishing House, pg 94
Hermes Publishing House, pg 94
Kibea Publishing Co, pg 95
LIK Izdanija, pg 95
MATEX, pg 95
Medicina i Fizkultura EOOD, pg 95
Prozoretz Ltd Publishing House, pg 96
Reporter, pg 96
Sluntse Publishing House, pg 97
TEMTO, pg 97

China

Beijing Medical University Press, pg 101
Chemical Industry Press, pg 101
Fudan University Press, pg 104
Fujian Science & Technology Publishing House, pg 104
Heilongjiang Science & Technology Press, pg 105
Jiangsu Science & Technology Publishing House, pg 105
Jilin Science & Technology Publishing House, pg 105
Knowledge Press, pg 106
People's Medical Publishing House (PMPH), pg 107
Shanghai College of Traditional Chinese Medicine Press, pg 108
Shanghai Far East Publishers, pg 108
Sichuan Science & Technology Publishing House, pg 108
Tianjin Science & Technology Publishing House, pg 108

Colombia

RAM Editores, pg 112

The Democratic Republic of the Congo

Centre de Vulgarisation Agricole, pg 114

Costa Rica

Academia de Centro America, pg 114
Editorial Nacional de Salud y Seguridad Social Ednass, pg 116
Editorial de la Universidad de Costa Rica, pg 116

Croatia

Znaci Vremena, Institut Za Istrazivanje Biblije, pg 119

Cuba

Editorial Oriente, pg 120
Editora Politica, pg 120

Czech Republic

Dimenze 2 Plus 2 Praha, pg 123
Erika spol sro, pg 123
Granit sro, pg 123
Nakladatelstvi Jota spol sro, pg 124
Luxpress VOS, pg 125
Maxdorf Ltd, pg 125
Pavla Momcilova, pg 125
Pragma 4, pg 126

SUBJECT INDEX

BOOK

Denmark
Aschehoug Dansk Forlag A/S, pg 129
Bogan's Forlag, pg 129
Borgens Forlag A/S, pg 129
Fremad A/S, pg 131
P Haase & Sons Forlag A/S, pg 131
Politikens Forlag A/S, pg 133

Dominican Republic
Pontificia Universidad Catolica Madre y Maestra, pg 136

Ecuador
Centro de Planificacion y Estudios Sociales (CEPLAES), pg 136

Estonia
Valgus Publishers, pg 140

Ethiopia
Addis Ababa University Press, pg 140

Finland
Kirjatoimi, pg 142
Weilin & Goos Oy, pg 144
Yliopistopaino/Helsinki University Press, pg 145

France
Adverbum SARL, pg 146
Editions ALTESS, pg 146
Editions Amrita SA, pg 146
ATP - Packager, pg 148
Editions A Barthelemy, pg 149
Alain Brethes Editions, pg 151
Editions Chiron, pg 154
Editions Courrier du Livre, pg 156
De Vecchi Editions SA, pg 157
Doin Editeurs, pg 159
Ellebore Editions, pg 161
L'Ere Nouvelle, pg 161
Editions First, pg 163
Editions Jacques Grancher, pg 165
Hachette Pratiques, pg 167
Editions Hermes Science Publications, pg 167
INRA Editions (Institut National de la Recherche Agronomique), pg 168
Editions INSERM, pg 168
IRD Editions, pg 169
Editions du Jaguar, pg 169
Le Jour, Editeur, pg 169
Jouvence Editions, pg 170
Editions Universitaires LCF, pg 171
LT Editions-Jacques Lanore, pg 173
Editions Josette Lyon, pg 173
Maisonneuve Editeur, pg 174
Editions Mango, pg 174
Editions Menges, pg 175
Editions Pardes, pg 179
Polytechnica SA, pg 180
Le Pre-aux-clercs, pg 180
Guide Rosenwald, pg 183
Editions du Rouergue, pg 183
Editions Sand et Tchou SA, pg 184
Editions Sang de la Terre, pg 184
Terre Vivante, pg 187

Germany
AOL-Verlag Frohmut Menze, pg 193
Roland Asanger Verlag GmbH, pg 194
Asgard-Verlag Dr Werner Hippe GmbH, pg 194
Verlag Hermann Bauer Gmbh & Co KG, pg 197
Beuth Verlag GmbH, pg 200
Blaukreuz-Verlag Wuppertal, pg 202
Buchverlage Langen-Mueller/Herbig, pg 205
Catia Monser Eggcup-Verlag, pg 207
Chmielorz GmbH Verlag, pg 208
Compact Verlag GmbH, pg 209
Copress Verlag, pg 209
Deutsche Landwirtschafts-Gesellschaft VerlagsgesGmbH, pg 212
Deutscher Taschenbuch Verlag GmbH & Co KG (dtv), pg 213
Dreisam Ratgeber in der Rutsker Verlag GmbH, pg 216
Econ Taschenbuchverlag, pg 218
Egmont vgs verlagsgesellschaft mbH, pg 218
Elsevier GmbH/Urban & Fischer Verlag, pg 219
Ergebnisse Verlag GmbH, pg 220
Esogetics GmbH, pg 221
Fachbuchverlag Pfanneberg & Co, pg 223
Falken-Verlag GmbH, pg 223
Verlagsgruppe J Fink GmbH & Co KG, pg 224
Flensburger Hefte Verlag GmbH, pg 225
Gesundheits-Dialog Verlag GmbH, pg 229
Gildefachverlag GmbH & Co KG, pg 229
Gmelin Verlag GmbH, pg 230
Graefe und Unzer Verlag GmbH, pg 230
Verlag der Stiftung Gralsbotschaft GmbH, pg 231
Walter Haedecke Verlag, pg 232
Dr Curt Haefner-Verlag GmbH, pg 233
Lehrmittelverlag Wilhelm Hagemann GmbH, pg 233
Happy Mental Buch- und Musik Verlag, pg 234
Karl F Haug Verlag GmbH & Co, pg 235
F A Herbig Verlagsbuchhandlung GmbH, pg 236
F Hirthammer Verlag GmbH, pg 238
Felicitas Huebner Verlag, pg 239
Heinrich Hugendubel Verlag GmbH, pg 240
Huthig GmbH & Co KG, pg 240
Jahreszeiten-Verlag GmbH, pg 242
Dr Werner Jopp Verlag, pg 243
Joy Verlag GmbH, pg 243
Jutta Pohl Verlag, pg 244
Juventa Verlag GmbH, pg 244
J Kamphausen Verlag & Distribution GmbH, pg 244
Verlag im Kilian GmbH, pg 246
Knowledge Media International, pg 247
Kolibri-Verlag GmbH, pg 249
Konkret Literatur Verlag, pg 249
Kunstverlag Weingarten GmbH, pg 251
Lebenshilfe-Verlag Marburg, Verlag der Bundesvereinigung Lebenshilfe fuer Menschen mit geistiger Behinderung eV, pg 253
Medico International eV, pg 258
Medizinisch-Literarische Verlagsgesellschaft mbH, pg 258
Meyer & Meyer Verlag, pg 260
Midena Verlag, pg 260
Mosaik Verlag GmbH, pg 262
NaturaViva Verlags GmbH, pg 263
Naumann & Goebel Verlagsgesellschaft mbH, pg 263
Neue Dimension Buch und Musikverlag, pg 264
Neuer Honos Verlag GmbH, pg 264
Verlag Neuer Weg, pg 264
Neuland-Verlagsgesellschaft mbH, pg 264
nymphenburger, pg 266
Oeko-Test Verlag GmbH & Co KG Betriebsgesellschaft, pg 266
Orbis Verlag fur Publizistik GmbH, pg 267
Orlanda Frauenverlag, pg 267
Pala-Verlag GmbH, pg 268
pmi Verlag, pg 270
Propylaeen Verlag, Zweigniederlassung Berlin der Ullstein Buchverlage GmbH, pg 272
Psychiatrie-Verlag GmbH, pg 272
Quintessenz Verlags-GmbH, pg 273
Rossipaul Kommunikation GmbH, pg 277
Ryvellus Medienagentur Dopfer, pg 277
Saatkorn-Verlag GmbH, pg 277
Verlag Werner Sachon GmbH & Co, pg 277
Schnitzer GmbH & Co KG, pg 281
Schulz-Kirchner Verlag GmbH, pg 282
Verlag R S Schulz GmbH, pg 282
Spiridon-Verlags GmbH, pg 284
Springer Science+Business Media GmbH & Co KG, pg 284
Dr Dietrich Steinkopff Verlag GmbH & Co, pg 287
Suedwest Verlag GmbH & Co KG, pg 289
Synthesis Verlag, pg 289
Georg Thieme Verlag KG, pg 291
Tipress Dienstleistungen fur das Verlagswesen GmbH, pg 291
TR - Verlagsunion GmbH, pg 291
Treves Editions Verein Zur Foerderung der Kuenstlerischen Taetigkeiten, pg 292
Trias Verlag in MVS Medizinverlage Stuttgart GmbH & Co KG, pg 292
Guenter Albert Ulmer Verlag, pg 293
Neuer Umschau Buchverlag, pg 293
UNO-Verlag GmbH, pg 293
UTB fuer Wissenschaft Uni Taschenbuecher GmbH, pg 294
WDV Wirtschaftsdienst Gesellschaft fur Medien & Kommunikation mbH & Co OHG, pg 298
Verlagsgruppe Weltbild GmbH, pg 298
Verlag DAS WORT GmbH, pg 301
Zebulon Verlag GmbH & Co KG, pg 302
ZS Verlag Zabert Sandmann GmbH, pg 302

Ghana
Adaex Educational Publications Ltd, pg 302
Ghana Institute of Linguistics Literacy & Bible Translation (GILLBT), pg 304
World Literature Project, pg 305

Greece
Chrysi Penna - Golden Pen Books, pg 306
Kalentis & Sia, pg 308
Kastaniotis Editions SA, pg 309
Medusa/Selas Publishers, pg 310
Patakis Publishers, pg 311

Guinea-Bissau
Instituto Nacional de Estudos e Pesquisa (INEP), pg 314

Hong Kong
Friends of the Earth (Charity) Ltd, pg 317
Joint Publishing (HK) Co Ltd, pg 317
Ming Pao Publications Ltd, pg 318
Peace Book Co Ltd, pg 318
SCMP Book Publishing Ltd, pg 319
Times Publishing (Hong Kong) Ltd, pg 319

Hungary
Advent Kiado, pg 320
Vince Kiado Kft, pg 322
Kossuth Kiado RT, pg 322
Officina Nova Konyvek, pg 323

Iceland
Bokaforlag Birtingur, pg 325
Bokautgafan Orn og Orlygur ehf, pg 325

India
Agricole Publishing Academy, pg 327
APH Publishing Corp, pg 328
B I Publications Pvt Ltd, pg 329
The Bangalore Printing & Publishing Co Ltd, pg 329
BR Publishing Corporation, pg 331
Chowkhamba Sanskrit Series Office, pg 332
Diamond Comics (P) Ltd, pg 333
Frank Brothers & Co Publishers Ltd, pg 334
Full Circle Publishing, pg 334
Heritage Publishers, pg 335
Islamic Publishing House, pg 338
Jaico Publishing House, pg 338
B Jain Publishers Overseas, pg 338
B Jain Publishers (P) Ltd, pg 339
Kali For Women, pg 339
Orient Paperbacks, pg 344
Popular Prakashan Pvt Ltd, pg 345
Pustak Mahal, pg 345
Rajendra Publishing House Pvt Ltd, pg 346
Scientific Book Agency, pg 348
Sultan Chand & Sons Pvt Ltd, pg 350
Vision Books Pvt Ltd, pg 352

Indonesia
Advent Indonesia Publishing, pg 353
Bhratara Karya Aksara, pg 354
Institut Teknologi Bandung, pg 355
Lembaga Demografi Fakultas Ekonomi Universitas Indonesia, pg 355

Ireland
Attic Press Ltd, pg 358
The Economic & Social Research Institute, pg 359
Emerald Publications, pg 359
Gill & Macmillan Ltd, pg 360
Institute of Public Administration, pg 361
On Stream Publications Ltd, pg 362
Tivenan Publications, pg 364

Israel
Books in the Attic Publishers Ltd, pg 365
Breslov Research Institute, pg 365

Carta, The Israel Map & Publishing Co Ltd, pg 365
Feldheim Publishers Ltd, pg 367
Gefen Publishing House Ltd, pg 367
Hakibbutz Hameuchad Publishing House Ltd, pg 367
Intermedia Audio, Video Book Publishing Ltd, pg 368
(JDC) Brookdale Institute of Gerontology & Adult Human Development in Israel, pg 369
Pitspopany Press, pg 371
Schocken Publishing House Ltd, pg 371
R Sirkis Publishers Ltd, pg 372
Yedioth Ahronoth Books, pg 373

Italy

Gruppo Abele, pg 374
Arcanta Aries Gruppo Editoriale, pg 375
Editore Armando Armando SRL, pg 376
Gruppo Editoriale Armenia SpA, pg 376
Centro Scientifico Torinese, pg 381
CIC Edizioni Internazionali, pg 381
Giovanni De Vecchi Editore SpA, pg 384
Demetra SRL, pg 385
Edagricole - Edizioni Agricole, pg 385
Edizioni Il Punto d'Incontro SAS, pg 386
Editoriale Fernando Folini, pg 389
Ernesto Gremese Editore srl, pg 391
Hermes Edizioni SRL, pg 392
Lyra Libri, pg 396
Macro Edizioni, pg 397
Edizioni Mediterranee SRL, pg 398
Il Pensiero Scientifico Editore SRL, pg 403
Il Punto D Incontro, pg 404
Red/Studio Redazionale, pg 405
Reverdito Edizioni, pg 405
Samaya SRL, pg 406
Editoriale Scienza, pg 407
Sperling e Kupfer Editori SpA, pg 409
Stampa Alternativa - Nuovi Equilibri, pg 409
TEA Tascabili degli Editori Associati SpA, pg 409
Tecniche Nuove SpA, pg 410
Voce della Bibbia, pg 412
Zanfi-Logos, pg 412

Japan

Daiichi Shuppan Co Ltd, pg 416
Fumaido Publishing Company Ltd, pg 417
Hakutei-Sha, pg 418
Ishiyaku Publishers Inc, pg 419
Japan Publications Inc, pg 419
Mejikaru Furendo-sha, pg 422
Nagaoka Shoten Co Ltd, pg 423
Nihon Vogue Co Ltd, pg 424
Nippon Hoso Shuppan Kyokai (NHK Publishing), pg 424
Nosangyoson Bunka Kyokai, pg 424
Seibido Shuppan Company Ltd, pg 426
Shufunotomo Co Ltd, pg 428
United Nations University Press, pg 430

Kenya

African Centre for Technology Studies (ACTS), pg 433
Kenya Literature Bureau, pg 434
Kenya Medical Research Institute (KEMRI), pg 435
Sudan Literature Centre, pg 436

Republic of Korea

Hanul Publishing Co, pg 439
Hyein Publishing House, pg 439
Minjisa Publishing Co, pg 441
Suhagsa, pg 443

Latvia

Alberts XII, pg 444
Lielvards Ltd, pg 445
Patmos, izdevnieciba, pg 445
Preses Nams, pg 445

Lebanon

Arab Institute for Research & Publishing, pg 445
Librairie du Liban Publishers (Sal), pg 446

Lithuania

Algarve, pg 448

Malaysia

S Abdul Majeed & Co, pg 454
Vinpress Sdn Bhd, pg 459

Maldive Islands

Non-Formal Education Centre, pg 459

Mauritius

Editions de l'Ocean Indien Ltd, pg 461

Mexico

Ediciones Alpe, pg 462
Arbol Editorial SA de CV, pg 462
Grupo Editorial Armonia, pg 462
Editorial Diana SA de CV, pg 464
Editorial El Manual Moderno SA de CV, pg 464
Ediciones Exclusivas SA, pg 465
Ibcon SA, pg 466
Libros y Revistas SA de CV, pg 467
Editorial Limusa SA de CV, pg 467
Nova Grupo Editorial SA de CV, pg 469
Editorial Nueva Imagen SA, pg 469
Panorama Editorial, SA, pg 470
Editorial Pax Mexico, pg 470
Selector SA de CV, pg 471
Siglo XXI Editores SA de CV, pg 472

Monaco

Les Editions du Rocher, pg 474

Morocco

Editions Le Fennec, pg 474

Netherlands

Ankh-Hermes BV, pg 477
De Boekerij BV, pg 479
BZZTOH Publishers, pg 480
De Driehoek BV, Uitgeverij, pg 481
Elmar BV, pg 482
Uitgeverij Vrij Geestesleven, pg 482
Uitgeverij Homeovisie BV, pg 483
IOS Press BV, pg 484
KIT - Royal Tropical Institute Publishers, pg 484
Uitgeverij Lemma BV, pg 485
Servire BV Uitgevers, pg 489
Sjaloom Uitgeverijen, pg 489
Sociaal en Cultureel Planbureau, pg 489
A J G Strengholt's Boeken, Anno 1928, BV, pg 489
Swets & Zeitlinger Publishers, pg 489
Uitgeverij Terra bv, pg 490
Uitgeverij de Tijdstroom BV, pg 490
Tirion Uitgevers BV, pg 490
Uitgeverij De Toorts, pg 490
Uniepers BV, pg 491

Netherlands Antilles

De Wit Stores NV, pg 493

New Zealand

Barkfire Press, pg 494
ESA Publications (NZ) Ltd, pg 496
Nelson Price Milburn Ltd, pg 499
Spinal Publications New Zealand Ltd, pg 501
Tandem Press, pg 501

Nigeria

Daystar Press (Publishers), pg 504

Norway

Ascheoug Forlag, pg 508
H Ascheoug & Co (W Nygaard) A/S, pg 508
Ex Libris Forlag A/S, pg 509
Genesis Forlag, pg 509
Glydendal Akademisk, pg 509
Hilt & Hansteen A/S, pg 509
Sandviks Bokforlag, pg 510

Pakistan

Hamdard Foundation Pakistan, pg 512
HMR Publishing Co, pg 512
Sang-e-Meel Publications, pg 514

Papua New Guinea

Kristen Press, pg 515

Peru

Centro de la Mujer Peruana Flora Tristan, pg 516
Instituto de Estudios Peruanos, pg 517

Philippines

Anvil Publishing Inc, pg 518
UST Publishing House, pg 521

Poland

Ksiaznica Publishing Ltd, pg 524
Panstwowe Wydawnictwo Rolnicze i Lesne, pg 525
PZWL Wydawnictwo Lekarskie Ltd, pg 526
Oficyna Wydawnicza Read Me, pg 526
Wydawnictwo WAB, pg 527

Portugal

Brasilia Editora (J Carvalho Branco), pg 529
Dinalivro, pg 530
Editorial Estampa, Lda, pg 531
Europress Editores e Distribuidores de Publicacoes Lda, pg 531
Edicoes ITAU (Instituto Tecnico de Alimentacao Humana) Lda, pg 532
Edicoes Manuel Lencastre, pg 532
Editora McGraw-Hill de Portugal Lda, pg 533
Paz-Editora de Multimedia, LDA, pg 534
Editorial Presenca, pg 535
Editora Replicacao Lda, pg 535
Texto Editora, pg 536

Romania

Editura Excelsior Art, pg 539
Editura Gryphon, pg 540
Editura Niculescu, pg 541
Vremea Publishers Ltd, pg 543

Russian Federation

Airis Press, pg 543
Interbook-Business AO, pg 545
Izdatelstvo Medicina, pg 546
Izdatelstvo Mir, pg 546
Nauka Publishers, pg 547
Panorama Publishing House, pg 547
Russkaya Kniga Izdatelstvo (Publishers), pg 548
Scorpion Publishers, pg 548

Serbia and Montenegro

Alfa-Narodna Knjiga, pg 552

Singapore

Daiichi Media Pte Ltd, pg 555
Times Media Pte Ltd, pg 559

Slovakia

AV Studio Reklamno-vydavatel'ska agentura, pg 559
Sofa, pg 560

Slovenia

East West Operation (EWO) Ltd, pg 561
Mladinska Knjiga International, pg 561
Zalozba Obzorja d d Maribor, pg 562

South Africa

Jacana Education, pg 565
Reader's Digest Southern Africa, pg 568
Southern Book Publishers (Pty) Ltd, pg 569
University of KwaZulu-Natal Press, pg 569

Spain

Editorial Acanto SA, pg 570
Editorial 'Alas', pg 571
AMV Ediciones, pg 572
Editorial Astri SA, pg 573
Ediciones Atril, pg 574
CEAC, Grupo Editorial SA, pg 576
Cedel, Ediciones Jose O Avila Monteso ES, pg 576
Didaco Comunicacion y Didactica, SA, pg 579
Ediciones Doce Calles SL, pg 579
Editorial Donostiarra SA, pg 579
Editorial EDAF SA, pg 580
Ediciones l'Isard, S L, pg 580
Editorial Editex SA, pg 581
Ediciones Elfos SL, pg 582
Enciclopedia Catalana, SA, pg 582
Eumo Editorial, pg 583
Generalitat de Catalunya Diari Oficial de la Generalitat vern, pg 584
Editorial Hispano Europea SA, pg 586
Editorial Iberia, SA, pg 586
Instituto Nacional de la Salud, pg 587

Ediciones Libertarias/Prodhufi SA, pg 589
Libsa Editorial SA, pg 589
Mandala Ediciones, pg 590
Ediciones Martinez-Roca SA, pg 591
McGraw-Hill/Interamericana de Espana SAU, pg 591
Ediciones Medici SA, pg 591
Editorial Mediterrania SL, pg 591
OASIS, Producciones Generales de Comunicacion, pg 593
Obelisco Ediciones S, pg 593
Editorial Paidotribo SL, pg 594
Pais Vasco Servicio Central de Publicaciones, pg 594
Parramon Ediciones SA, pg 595
Pulso Ediciones, SL, pg 597
Ediciones Rialp SA, pg 598
Ediciones ROL SA, pg 598
Editorial Sintes SA, pg 600
Ediciones Tutor SA, pg 603
Ediciones Urano, SA, pg 604
Xunta de Galicia, pg 605

Sri Lanka

Swarna Hansa Foundation, pg 607

Sweden

Bokforlaget Atlantis AB, pg 609
Energica Foerlags AB/Halsabocker, pg 611
Foerlagshuset Gothia, pg 612
ICA bokforlag, pg 612
Liber AB, pg 613
Natur och Kultur Fakta etc, pg 614
Bokforlaget Prisma, pg 614
Sober Foerlags AB, pg 615
AB Wahlstroem & Widstrand, pg 616

Switzerland

AT Verlag, pg 618
Bibliographisches Institut & F A Brockhaus AG, pg 619
Blaukreuz-Verlag Bern, pg 619
Eular Verlag, pg 623
Editions Jouvence, pg 626
Junod Nicolas, pg 626
Oesch Verlag AG, pg 630
Editions du Parvis, pg 631
Editiones Roche, pg 632
Sphinx Verlag AG, pg 634
Tobler Verlag, pg 635
Editions Vivez Soleil SA, pg 636
Weber SA d'Editions, pg 637

Syrian Arab Republic

Damascus University Press, pg 638

Taiwan, Province of China

Asian Culture Co Ltd, pg 638
Commonwealth Publishing Company Ltd, pg 639
Farseeing Publishing Company Ltd, pg 639
Chu Hai Publishing (Taiwan) Co Ltd, pg 640
Ho-Chi Book Publishing Co, pg 640
Kuang Fu Book Co Ltd, pg 640
Linking Publishing Company Ltd, pg 641
Morning Star Publisher Inc, pg 641
Shy Mau & Shy Chaur Publishing Co Ltd, pg 641
Torch of Wisdom, pg 642
Yi Hsien Publishing Co Ltd, pg 642
Yuan Liou Publishing Co, Ltd, pg 642

United Republic of Tanzania

Press & Publicity Centre Ltd, pg 644
Tanzania Publishing House, pg 644

Thailand

Thai Watana Panich Co, Ltd, pg 646

Turkey

Kok Yayincilik, pg 650
Soez Yayin/Oyunajans, pg 651

Uganda

Fountain Publishers Ltd, pg 652

Ukraine

Naukova Dumka Publishers, pg 653

United Kingdom

Age Concern Books, pg 656
Amberwood Publishing Ltd, pg 657
Anglo-German Foundation for the Study of Industrial Society, pg 658
Apex Publishing Ltd, pg 658
Apple Press, pg 658
Ashgrove Publishing, pg 660
Beaconsfield Publishers Ltd, pg 664
BILD Publications, pg 665
Blackwell Science Ltd, pg 667
Breslich & Foss Ltd, pg 671
Brewin Books Ltd, pg 671
Camden Press Ltd, pg 674
Carlton Publishing Group, pg 675
Jon Carpenter Publishing, pg 675
Carroll & Brown Ltd, pg 675
Kyle Cathie Ltd, pg 676
Causeway Press Ltd, pg 676
Marshall Cavendish Partworks Ltd, pg 676
Class Publishing, pg 680
CMP Information Ltd, pg 680
Coachwise Ltd, pg 680
Constable & Robinson Ltd, pg 682
Paul H Crompton Ltd, pg 684
Croner CCH Group Ltd, pg 684
The C W Daniel Co Ltd, pg 686
David & Charles Ltd, pg 686
Christopher Davies Publishers Ltd, pg 686
Denor Press, pg 687
Dobro Publishing, pg 688
Dorling Kindersley Ltd, pg 688
Element Books Ltd, pg 690
Elliot Right Way Books, pg 690
Elsevier Ltd, pg 691
The Eurospan Group, pg 692
Forbes Publications Ltd, pg 696
Foulsham Publishers, pg 696
Francis Balsom Associates, pg 696
Gaia Books Ltd, pg 698
Gateway Books, pg 698
Global Oriental Ltd, pg 700
Godsfield Press Ltd, pg 701
Grub Street, pg 703
Haldane Mason Ltd, pg 704
Hamlyn, pg 704
HarperCollins UK, pg 705
Health Development Agency, pg 706
Isis Publishing Ltd, pg 714
Janus Publishing Co Ltd, pg 716
Jones & Bartlett International, pg 716
King's Fund Publishing, pg 718
Knockabout Comics, pg 718
Learning Development Aids, pg 719
Letterbox Library, pg 720
Frances Lincoln Ltd, pg 720
Lorenz Books, pg 722
Mandrake of Oxford, pg 725
Marshall Editions Ltd, pg 725
Kenneth Mason Publications Ltd, pg 726
Metro Books, pg 727
Micelle Press, pg 727
MQ Publications Ltd, pg 729
National Assembly for Wales, pg 730
New Era Publications UK Ltd, pg 732
The NFER-NELSON Publishing Co Ltd, pg 733
Norwood Publishers Ltd, pg 734
Octopus Publishing Group, pg 734
Open University Press, pg 736
Parapress Ltd, pg 738
Pearson Education, pg 739
Pharmaceutical Press, pg 741
Piatkus Books, pg 741
The Policy Press, pg 744
Portland Press Ltd, pg 745
Quadrille Publishing Ltd, pg 746
Quarto Publishing plc, pg 746
Quintet Publishing Ltd, pg 747
Random House UK Ltd, pg 747
The Reader's Digest Association Ltd, pg 748
Rosendale Press Ltd, pg 751
Roundhouse Group, pg 751
Royal College of General Practitioners (RCGP), pg 752
The Royal Society of Chemistry, pg 752
Ryland Peters & Small Ltd, pg 752
SAGE Publications Ltd, pg 753
Salamander Books Ltd, pg 753
Scottish Executive Library & Information Services, pg 755
Sheldon Press, pg 757
Silver Link Publishing Ltd, pg 758
Smith-Gordon & Co Ltd, pg 758
Speechmark Publishing Ltd, pg 760
Rudolf Steiner Press, pg 761
Stott's Correspondence College, pg 761
Telegraph Books, pg 764
The Tarragon Press, pg 765
Transworld Publishers Ltd, pg 766
TSO (The Stationery Office), pg 767
Virago Press, pg 770
Ward Lock Ltd, pg 771
Websters International Publishers Ltd, pg 772
Which? Ltd, pg 772
Wimbledon Publishing Company Ltd, pg 774
The Women's Press Ltd, pg 775
Woodhead Publishing Ltd, pg 775

Uruguay

Editorial Arca SRL, pg 776
Nordan-Comunidad, pg 778
Prensa Medica Latinoamericana, pg 778

Viet Nam

Science & Technics Publishing House, pg 780

Zambia

Zambia Association for Research & Development (ZARD), pg 782

Zimbabwe

Action Magazine, pg 782
Zimbabwe Women's Bureau, pg 785

HISTORY

Afghanistan

Book Publishing Institute, pg 1
Government Press, pg 1

Albania

Botimpex Publications Import-Export Agency, pg 1
NL SH, pg 1
State Textbook Publishing House, pg 1

Algeria

Les Editions Algeriennes En-Nahdha, pg 2
Enterprise Nationale du Livre (ENAL), pg 2

Argentina

Editorial Abaco de Rodolfo Depalma SRL, pg 2
Alianza Editorial de Argentina SA, pg 3
Editorial Astrea de Alfredo y Ricardo Depalma SRL, pg 3
AZ Editora SA, pg 3
Centro Editor de America Latina SA, pg 4
Editorial Claridad SA, pg 4
Club de Lectores, pg 4
Depalma SRL, pg 5
Diana Argentina SA, Editorial, pg 5
Ediciones Don Bosco Argentina, pg 5
Emece Editores SA, pg 5
EUDEBA (Editorial Universitaria de Buenos Aires), pg 5
Ediciones de la Flor SRL, pg 6
Editorial Galerna SRL, pg 6
Editorial Guadalupe, pg 6
Editorial Idearium de la Universidad de Mendoza (EDIUM), pg 6
Laffont Ediciones Electronicas SA, pg 7
La Ley SA Editora e Impresora, pg 7
Editorial Losada SA, pg 7
Marymar Ediciones SA, pg 7
Editorial Planeta Argentina SAIC, pg 8
Editorial Plus Ultra SA, pg 8
Editorial Sopena Argentina SACI e I, pg 9
Editorial Sudamericana SA, pg 9
Theoria SRL Distribuidora y Editora, pg 9
Tipografica Editora Argentina, pg 9
Instituto Torcuato Di Tella, pg 9
Editoria Universitaria de la Patagonia, pg 9
Javier Vergara Editor SA, pg 9

Armenia

Arevik, pg 10

Australia

Aboriginal Studies Press, pg 10
Access Press, pg 10
Aletheia Publishing, pg 11
Allen & Unwin Pty Ltd, pg 11
Artmoves Inc, pg 12
Athena Press, pg 12
Aussie Books, pg 12
Australasian Medical Publishing Company Ltd (AMPCO), pg 12
Australian Scholarly Publishing, pg 13
Bandicoot Books, pg 14
Joycelyn Bayne, pg 14

PUBLISHERS SUBJECT INDEX

Bernal Publishing, pg 14
Blubber Head Press, pg 15
Boolarong Press, pg 15
Louis Braille Audio, pg 16
Bridge To Peace Publications, pg 16
Casket Publications, pg 17
Catholic Institute of Sydney, pg 17
Centenary of Technical Education in Bairnsdale Group, pg 17
Church Archivists Press, pg 18
Covenanter Press, pg 18
Crawford House Publishing Pty Ltd, pg 18
Dagraja Press, pg 19
Dryden Press, pg 20
Elton Publications, pg 21
Enterprise Publications, pg 21
Fremantle Arts Centre Press, pg 23
Ginninderra Press, pg 23
Gould Genealogy, pg 23
Hale & Iremonger Pty Ltd, pg 24
F H Halpern, pg 24
Hargreen Publishing Co, pg 24
Hat Box Press, pg 25
Histec Publications, pg 25
Hunter House Publications, pg 26
Illert Publications, pg 26
Institute of Aboriginal Development (IAD Press), pg 27
Joval Publications, pg 28
Kangaroo Press, pg 28
Kingsclear Books, pg 28
Lansdowne Publishing Pty Ltd, pg 28
Library of Australian History, pg 29
Little Red Apple Publishing, pg 29
Lowden Publishing Co, pg 30
Lucasville Press, pg 30
Macmillan Education Australia, pg 30
Yvonne McBurney, pg 31
Melbourne University Press, pg 32
Mostly Unsung, pg 32
Mulini Press, pg 32
Museum of Victoria, pg 33
Navarine Publishing, pg 33
Ocean Press, pg 34
Oceans Enterprises, pg 34
Ollif Publishing, pg 34
Outback Books - CQU Press, pg 34
Palms Press, pg 35
Pascoe Publishing Pty Ltd, pg 36
Kevin J Passey, pg 36
Pearson Education Australia, pg 36
Pinevale Publications, pg 36
Pioneer Design Studio Pty Ltd, pg 37
Plantagenet Press, pg 37
Playlab Press, pg 37
Pluto Press Australia Pty Ltd, pg 37
The Polding Press, pg 37
Polliteon Publications, pg 37
Protestant Publications, pg 38
Quakers Hill Press, pg 38
Queen Victoria Museum & Art Gallery Publications, pg 38
Rainforest Publishing, pg 38
Reed Educational Publishing Australia, pg 39
Ruskin Rowe Press, pg 40
St Joseph Publications, pg 40
Seanachas Press, pg 40
The Sheringa Book Committee, pg 41
Simon & Schuster (Australia) Pty Ltd, pg 41
Slouch Hat Publications, pg 41
Spectrum Publications, pg 41
State Library of NSW Press, pg 42
State Publishing Unit of State Print SA, pg 42
Tabletop Press, pg 42
Tarka Publishing, pg 42

The Text Publishing Company Pty Ltd, pg 43
Thames & Hudson (Australia) Pty Ltd, pg 43
Caroline Thornton, pg 43
Three Sisters Publications Pty Ltd, pg 43
Transpareon Press, pg 44
Tudor Australia Press, pg 44
Turton & Armstrong Pty Ltd Publishers, pg 44
University of New South Wales Press Ltd, pg 44
University of Queensland Press, pg 45
University of Western Australia Press, pg 45
Vista Publications, pg 45
Wakefield Press Pty Ltd, pg 46

Austria
Alekto Verlag GmbH, pg 48
Verlag Der Apfel, pg 48
Boehlau Verlag GmbH & Co KG, pg 48
BSE Verlag Dr Bernhard Schuttengruber, pg 49
Carinthia Verlag, pg 49
CEEBA Publications Antenne d'Autriche, pg 49
Czernin Verlag Ltd, pg 49
Development News Ltd, pg 50
Doecker Verlag GmbH & Co KG, pg 50
Edition S der OSD, pg 50
Ennsthaler GesmbH & Co KG, pg 50
Fassbaender Verlag, pg 50
Fremdenverkehrs Aktiengesellschaft, pg 51
Verlag fuer Geschichte und Politik, pg 51
Graz Stadtmuseum, pg 51
Haymon-Verlag GesmbH, pg 51
Herold Druck-und Verlagsgesellschaft mbH, pg 52
Johannes Heyn GmbH & Co KG, pg 52
Innverlag + Gatt, pg 52
Karolinger Verlag GmbH & Co KG, pg 52
Kremayr & Scheriau Verlag, pg 53
Leopold Stocker Verlag, pg 53
Loecker Verlag, pg 53
Merbod Verlag, pg 54
Milena Verlag, pg 54
Thomas Mlakar Verlag, pg 54
Verlag Monte Verita, pg 54
Otto Mueller Verlag, pg 54
Wolfgang Neugebauer Verlag GmbH, pg 54
Niederosterreichisches Pressehaus Druck- und Verlagsgesellschaft mbH, pg 54
NOI - Verlag, pg 55
Verlag der Oesterreichischen Akademie der Wissenschaften (OEAW), pg 55
Verlag des Oesterreichischen Gewerkschaftsbundes GmbH, pg 55
Oesterreichischer Bundesverlag Gmbh, pg 55
Oesterreichischer Kunst und Kulturverlag, pg 55
Verlag Oldenbourg, pg 56
Georg Prachner KG, pg 56
Promedia Verlagsges mbH, pg 56
Verlag Anton Pustet, pg 56
Salzburger Nachrichten Verlagsgesellschaft mbH & Co KG, pg 57
Verlag fuer Sammler, pg 57

Dr A Schendl GmbH und Co KG, pg 57
Andreas Schnider Verlags-Atelier, pg 57
Verlag Josef Otto Slezak, pg 57
Studien Verlag Gmbh, pg 58
Verlag Styria, pg 58
Verlag Carl Ueberreuter GmbH, pg 58
Verband der Wissenschaftlichen Gesellschaften Oesterreichs (VWGOe), pg 59
Verlag Anton Schroll & Co, pg 59
Vorarlberger Verlagsanstalt Aktiengesellschaft, pg 59
Universitaetsverlag Wagner GmbH, pg 59
WUV/Facultas Universitaetsverlag, pg 60
Paul Zsolnay Verlag GmbH, pg 60

Azerbaijan
Sada, Literaturno-Izdatel'skij Centr, pg 60

Bangladesh
The University Press Ltd, pg 61

Belarus
Belaruskaya Encyklapedyya, pg 62
Kavaler Publishers, pg 62
Narodnaya Asveta, pg 62

Belgium
Uitgeverij Acco, pg 62
Centre Aequatoria, pg 63
Artel, pg 63
NV Artis-Historia, pg 63
Maison d'Editions Baha'ies ASBL, pg 63
Brepols Publishers NV, pg 64
Carto BVBA, pg 64
Editions Chanlis, pg 65
Editions Complexe SPRL, pg 65
Creadif, pg 65
Cremers (Schoollandkaarten) PVBA, pg 66
Le Cri Editions, pg 66
Davidsfonds Uitgeverij NV, pg 66
Dexia Bank, pg 66
EPO Publishers, Printers, Booksellers, pg 67
Espace de Libertes, pg 67
Georeto-Geogidsen, pg 67
Groeninghe NV, pg 68
Imprimerie Hayez SPRL, pg 68
Helyode Editions (SA-ADN), pg 68
Editions Labor, pg 69
Uitgeverij Lannoo NV, pg 69
Leuven University Press, pg 70
Les Editions du Lombard SA, pg 70
Marabout, pg 71
Mercatorfonds NV, pg 71
Nauwelaerts Edition SA, pg 71
Uitgeverij Peeters Leuven (Belgie), pg 71
Pelckmans NV, De Nederlandsche Boekhandel, pg 72
Uitgeverij Pelckmans NV, pg 72
Le Pole Nord ASBL, pg 72
Henri Proost & Co, Pvba, pg 72
Publications des Facultes Universitaires Saint Louis, pg 72
Editions Racine, pg 72
Reader's Digest SA, pg 72
La Renaissance du Livre, pg 72
Scaillet, SA, pg 73
Scoop Infotex NV, pg 73
Sonneville Press (Uitgeverij) VTW, pg 73
Stichting Kunstboek bvba, pg 73

Editions Techniques et Scientifiques SPRL, pg 73
UGA Editions (Uitgeverij), pg 73
Editions de l'Universite de Bruxelles, pg 74
Imprimeur - Editeur Vaillant-Carmanne SA, pg 74
Marc Van de Wiele bvba, pg 74
Les Editions Vie ouvriere ASBL, pg 74
C De Vries Brouwers BVBA, pg 74
VUB Brussels University Press, pg 74
Editions Luce Wilquin, pg 74

Bolivia
Editorial Don Bosco, pg 75
Gisbert y Cia SA, pg 75
Universidad Autonoma Tomas Frias, Div de Extension Universitaria, pg 75

Bosnia and Herzegovina
Bemust, pg 76

Botswana
The Botswana Society, pg 76
Maskew Miller Longman, pg 76

Brazil
Action Editora Ltda, pg 76
AGIR S/A Editora, pg 77
Editora Alfa Omega Ltda, pg 77
Editora do Brasil SA, pg 79
Editora Campus Ltda, pg 79
Editora Companhia das Letras/Editora Schwarcz Ltda, pg 80
Editora Contexto (Editora Pinsky Ltda), pg 80
Companhia Editora Forense, pg 81
EDUSC - Editora da Universidade do Sagrado Coracao, pg 81
Livraria Martins Fontes Editora Ltda, pg 81
Fundacao Joaquim Nabuco-Editora Massangana, pg 82
Fundacao Sao Paulo, EDUC, pg 82
Global Editora e Distribuidora Ltda, pg 82
Editora Globo SA, pg 82
Edicoes Graal Ltda, pg 83
Livro Ibero-Americano Ltda, pg 83
IBRASA (Instituicao Brasileira de Difusao Cultural Ltda), pg 83
Imago Editora Importacao e Exportacao Ltda, pg 84
Editora Index Ltda, pg 84
LDA Editores Ltda, pg 84
Livraria Kosmos Editora Ltda, pg 85
Edicoes Loyola SA, pg 85
Editora Mantiqueira de Ciencia e Arte, pg 86
Editora Melhoramentos Ltda, pg 86
Editora Mercado Aberto Ltda, pg 86
Editora Mercuryo Ltda, pg 86
Editora Moderna Ltda, pg 86
Modulo Editora e Desenvolvimento Educacional Ltda, pg 87
Cia Editora Nacional, pg 87
Editora Nova Alexandria Ltda, pg 87
Editora Nova Fronteira SA, pg 87
Editora Perspectiva, pg 88
Livraria Pioneira Editora/Enio Matheus Guazzelli e Cia Ltd, pg 88
Casa Editora Presbiteriana SC, pg 88
Distribuidora Record de Servicos de Imprensa SA, pg 89

SUBJECT INDEX

Editora Rideel Ltda, pg 89
Editora Scipione Ltda, pg 90
Sobrindes Linha Grafica E Editora Ltda, pg 90
Editora UNESP, pg 91
Editora Universidade Federal do Rio de Janeiro, pg 92
Editora Verbo Ltda, pg 92
Jorge Zahar Editor, pg 92

Bulgaria

Abagar Pablioing, pg 92
Abagar, Veliko Tarnovo, pg 93
Bilblioteka Nov den - Sajuz na Svobodnite Demokrati (Union of Free Democrats), pg 93
DA-Izdatelstvo Publishers, pg 93
Eurasia Academic Publishers, pg 94
Heron Press Publishing House, pg 94
Publishing House Hristo Botev, pg 94
Pejo K Javorov Publishing House, pg 95
Kibea Publishing Co, pg 95
LIK Izdanija, pg 95
Makros 2000 - Plovdiv, pg 95
Naouka i Izkoustvo, Ltd, pg 95
Nov Covek Publishing House, pg 96
Pensoft Publishers, pg 96
Rakla, pg 96
Slavena, pg 97
Trud - Izd kasta, pg 97
Ivan Vazov Publishing House, pg 97
Voenno Izdatelstvo, pg 97

Burundi

Editions Intore, pg 98

Cameroon

Centre d'Edition et de Production pour l'Enseignement et la Recherche (CEPER), pg 98
Editions Semences Africaines, pg 98

Chile

Arrayan Editores, pg 98
Ediciones Bat, pg 99
Editorial Andres Bello/Editorial Juridica de Chile, pg 99
Edeval (Universidad de Valparaiso), pg 99
Pontificia Universidad Catolica de Chile, pg 100
Ediciones Universitarias de Valparaiso, pg 100

China

Anhui People's Publishing House, pg 101
Beijing Publishing House, pg 101
China Film Press, pg 102
China Theatre Publishing House, pg 103
Cultural Relics Publishing House, pg 103
Foreign Language Teaching & Research Press, pg 104
Foreign Languages Press, pg 104
Fudan University Press, pg 104
Guizhou Education Publishing House, pg 105
Higher Education Press, pg 105
Lanzhou University Press, pg 106
Liaoning People's Publishing House, pg 106
Morning Glory Press, pg 106
People's Fine Arts Publishing House, pg 106

SDX (Shenghuo-Dushu-Xinzhi) Joint Publishing Co, pg 107
Shandong University Press, pg 108
Shanghai Educational Publishing House, pg 108
Sichuan University Press, pg 108
Universidade de Macau, Centro de Publicacoes, pg 109
World Affairs Press, pg 109
Wuhan University Press, pg 109
Zhejiang University Press, pg 109
Zhong Hua Book Co, pg 110

Colombia

Amazonas Editores Ltda, pg 110
El Ancora Editores, pg 111
Lerner Ediciones, pg 111
Editorial Panamericana, pg 112
Procultura SA, pg 112
Siglo XXI Editores de Colombia Ltda, pg 112
Tercer Mundo Editores SA, pg 113
Universidad de Antioquia, Division Publicaciones, pg 113

The Democratic Republic of the Congo

Facultes Catoliques de Kinshasa, pg 114
Presses Universitaires du Zaiire (PUZ), pg 114

Costa Rica

Editorial DEI (Departamento Ecumenico de Investigaciones), pg 115
Museo Historico Cultural Juan Santamaria, pg 115
Editorial Porvenir, pg 116
Ediciones Promesa, pg 116
Editorial de la Universidad de Costa Rica, pg 116
Editorial Universidad Estatal a Distancia (EUNED), pg 116
Editorial Universidad Nacional (EUNA), pg 116
Editorial Universitaria Centroamericana (EDUCA), pg 117

Cote d'Ivoire

Centre d'Edition et de Diffusion Africaines, pg 117
Les Nouvelles Editions Ivoiriennes, pg 117

Croatia

AGM doo, pg 117
ArTresor naklada, pg 117
Durieux d o o, pg 118
Filozofski Fakultet Sveucilista u Zagrebu, pg 118
Globus-Nakladni zavod, pg 118
Izdavacka Delatnost Hrvatske Akademije Znanosti I Umjetnosti, pg 118
Knjizevni Krug Split, pg 118
Matica hrvatska, pg 118
Mladost d d Izdavacku graficku i informaticku djelatnost, pg 119
Naklada Ljevak doo, pg 119
Skolska Knjiga, pg 119
Vitagraf, pg 119

Cuba

Casa Editora Abril, pg 120
Holguin, Ediciones, pg 120
Editorial Oriente, pg 120
Editora Politica, pg 120

Cyprus

Andreou Chr Publishers, pg 121
James Bendon Ltd, pg 121

Czech Republic

Academia, pg 122
Atlantis sro, pg 122
AVCR Historicky ustav, pg 122
Barrister & Principal, pg 122
Ceska Expedice, pg 123
Chvojkova nakladatelstvi, pg 123
Columbus, pg 123
Doplnek, pg 123
Horacek Ladislav-Paseka, pg 123
Nakladatelstvi Jota spol sro, pg 124
Kalich SRO, pg 124
Karmelitanske Nakladatelstvi, pg 124
Karolinum, nakladatelstvi, pg 124
Konsultace spol sro, pg 125
Libri spol sro, pg 125
Lidove Noviny Publishing House, pg 125
Mariadan, pg 125
Maxdorf Ltd, pg 125
Mlada fronta, pg 125
Narodni Muzeum, pg 126
Nase vojsko, nakladatelstvi a knizni obchod, pg 126
Nava, pg 126
Prazske nakladatelstvi Pluto, pg 127
Pressfoto Vydavatelstvi Ceske Tiskove Kancelare, pg 127
Prostor, nakladatelstvi sro, pg 127
Slon Sociologicke Nakladatelstvi, pg 127
NS Svoboda spol sro, pg 127
SystemConsult, pg 127
Votobia sro, pg 128

Denmark

Akademisk Forlag A/S, pg 128
Dafolo Forlag, pg 130
Dansk Historisk Handbogsforlag ApS, pg 130
Christian Ejlers' Forlag aps, pg 131
Forlaget Forum, pg 131
Fremad A/S, pg 131
Gads Forlag, pg 131
Forlaget GMT, pg 131
Gyldendalske Boghandel - Nordisk Forlag A/S, pg 131
Host & Son Publishers Ltd, pg 132
Forlaget Hovedland, pg 132
Museum Tusculanum Press, pg 133
Nyt Nordisk Forlag Arnold Busck A/S, pg 133
Joergen Paludan Forlag ApS, pg 133
Samfundslitteratur, pg 134
Samlerens Forlag A/S, pg 134
Det Schonbergske Forlag A/S, pg 134
Syddansk Universitetsforlag, pg 135
Systime, pg 135

Dominican Republic

Pontificia Universidad Catolica Madre y Maestra, pg 136
Sociedad Editorial Americana, pg 136
Editora Taller, pg 136

Ecuador

Corporacion Editora Nacional, pg 136
Pontificia Universidad Catolica del Ecuador, Centro de Publicaciones, pg 137

Egypt (Arab Republic of Egypt)

American University in Cairo Press, pg 137
Al Arab Publishing House, pg 137
Dar Al-Thakafia Publishing, pg 138
Dar El Shorouk, pg 138
Lehnert & Landrock Bookshop, pg 138
Middle East Book Centre, pg 138
Senouhy Publishers, pg 138

Estonia

Academic Library of Tallinn Pedagogical University, pg 139
Eesti Entsuklopeediakirjastus, pg 139
Eesti Piibliselts, pg 139
Eesti Rahvusraamatukogu, pg 139
Ilmamaa, pg 139
Kirjastus Kunst, pg 139
Mats Publishers Ltd, pg 140
Olion Publishers, pg 140

Ethiopia

Addis Ababa University Press, pg 140

Finland

Akateeminen Kustannusliike Oy, pg 141
Atena Kustannus Oy, pg 141
Ekenas Tryckeri AB, pg 142
Herattaja-yhdistys Ry, pg 142
Kirja-Leitzinger, pg 142
Koala-Kustannus Oy, pg 143
Kustannuskiila Oy, pg 143
Otava Publishing Co Ltd, pg 143
Schildts Forlags AB, pg 144
Soderstroms Forlag, pg 144
Suomalaisen Kirjallisuuden Seura, pg 144
Osuuskunta Vastapaino, pg 144
Weilin & Goos Oy, pg 144
Yliopistopaino/Helsinki University Press, pg 145

France

Academie Nationale de Reims, pg 145
Action Artistique de la Ville de Paris, pg 145
Alsatia SA, pg 146
Editions d'Amerique et d'Orient, Adrien Maisonneuve, pg 146
Editions l'Ancre de Marine, pg 147
Editions Anthropos, pg 147
Editions de l'Armancon, pg 147
Armenia Editions, pg 147
Editions de l'Atelier, pg 148
Atelier National de Reproduction des Theses, pg 148
ATP - Packager, pg 148
Editions Aubier-Montaigne SA, pg 148
Autrement Editions, pg 148
Beauchesne Editeur, pg 149
Societe d'Edition Les Belles Lettres, pg 149
Berg International Editeur, pg 149
Berger-Levrault Editions SAS, pg 149
Editions Bertout, pg 149
Bibliotheque Nationale de France, pg 150
De Boccard Edition-Diffusion, pg 150
Editions Andre Bonne, pg 150
Presses Universitaires de Bordeaux (PUB), pg 150
Bragelonne, pg 151
Editions Breal, pg 151

Editions du Cadratin, pg 151
Editions des Cahiers Bourbonnais, pg 151
Editions Calmann-Levy SA, pg 152
Editions Canope, pg 152
Editions Casterman, pg 152
Editions Cenomane, pg 152
CERDIC-Publications, pg 153
Editions du Cerf, pg 153
Editions Champ Vallon, pg 153
Chasse Maree, pg 153
Le Cherche Midi Editeur, pg 154
Editions Circonflexe, pg 154
CLD, pg 154
CNRS Editions, pg 155
Armand Colin, Editeur, pg 155
Editions du Comite des Travaux Historiques et Scientifiques (CTHS), pg 155
Communication Par Livre (CPL), pg 155
Editions Copernic, pg 155
Editions Coprur, pg 155
Corsaire Editions, pg 156
Editions Criterion, pg 156
Editions Cujas, pg 156
Culture et Bibliotheque pour Tous, pg 156
Nouvelles Editions Debresse, pg 157
Editions La Decouverte, pg 157
Jean-P Delville Editions, pg 157
Editions Denoel, pg 157
Dervy Editions, pg 158
Desclee de Brouwer SA, pg 158
Les Editions des Deux Coqs d'Or, pg 158
Les Dossiers d'Aquitaine, pg 159
Editions de l'Ecole des Hautes Etudes en Sciences Sociales (EHESS), pg 159
Editions Edisud, pg 159
Institute Editeur, pg 160
Editions Recherche sur les Civilisations (ERC), pg 160
Editions rue d'Ulm, pg 160
EPA (Editions Pratiques Automobiles), pg 161
Editions de l'Epargne, pg 161
Editions Errance, pg 162
Institut d'Etudes Augustiniennes, pg 162
Institut d'Etudes Slaves IES, pg 162
Librairie Artheme Fayard, pg 163
Editions Des Femmes, pg 163
Librairie Fischbacher, International Art Book Distribution (import-export), pg 163
Folklore Comtois, pg 164
Editions Galilee, pg 164
Editions Gallimard, pg 164
Gammaprim, pg 165
Imprimerie Librairie Gardet, pg 165
Paul Geuthner Librairie Orientaliste, pg 165
Editions Jean Paul Gisserot, pg 165
Sarl Editions Jean Grassin, pg 166
Librairie Guenegaud, pg 166
Hachette Livre, pg 167
Editions Herault, pg 167
Editions d'Histoire Sociale (EDHIS), pg 168
Editions Honore Champion, pg 168
Pierre Horay Editeur, pg 168
Editions Imago, pg 168
IRD Editions, pg 169
Isoete, pg 169
Ivrea, pg 169
Editions du Jaguar, pg 169
Editions Jannink, SARL, pg 169
Kailash Editions, pg 170
Editions Klincksieck, pg 170
L'Adret editions, pg 170

Laffitte Reprints, pg 170
Michel Lafon Publishing, pg 171
Librairie Leonce Laget, pg 171
Editions Fernand Lanore Sarl, pg 171
Editions Larousse, pg 171
Editions Universitaires LCF, pg 171
Letouzey et Ane Editeurs, pg 171
Liana Levi Editions, pg 172
Les Editions LGDJ-Montchrestien, pg 172
Le Livre de Poche-L G F (Librairie Generale Francaise), pg 173
Editions Loubatieres, pg 173
Editions Lyonnaises d'Art et d'Histoire, pg 173
Macula, pg 173
Editions de la Maison des Sciences de l'Homme, Paris, pg 174
Editions MDI (La Maison des Instituteurs), pg 175
Editions Medianes, pg 175
Mercure de France SA, pg 175
Editions Albin Michel, pg 175
Presses Universitaires du Mirail, pg 176
Gerard Monfort Editeur Sarl, pg 176
Muller Edition, pg 176
Editions de la Reunion des Musees Nationaux, pg 176
Editions Fernand Nathan, pg 176
Editions Norma, pg 177
Nouvelles Editions Francaises, pg 177
Nouvelles Editions Latines, pg 177
Editions Odile Jacob, pg 177
Editions Ophrys, pg 177
Editions de l'Orante, pg 178
Ouest Editions, pg 178
Editions Ouest-France, pg 178
Editions Paradigme, pg 178
Editions Pardes, pg 179
Association Paris-Musees, pg 179
Payot & Rivages, pg 179
Peeters-France, pg 179
Editions A et J Picard SA, pg 179
Editions Jean Picollec, pg 179
Editions Pierron, pg 180
Le Pre-aux-clercs, pg 180
Presence Africaine Editions, pg 180
Presses de la Cite, pg 180
Presses de la Sorbonne Nouvelle/PSN, pg 181
Presses de Sciences Politiques, pg 181
Presses Universitaires de Caen, pg 181
Presses Universitaires de France (PUF), pg 181
Presses Universitaires de Grenoble, pg 181
Presses Universitaires de Lyon, pg 181
Presses Universitaires de Nancy, pg 181
Presses Universitaires de Strasbourg, pg 182
Presses Universitaires du Septentrion, pg 182
Publications de l'Universite de Rouen, pg 182
Publications Orientalistes de France (POF), pg 182
Editions Pygmalion, pg 182
Editions Ramsay, pg 182
References cf, pg 183
Editions Roudil SA, pg 183
Selection du Reader's Digest SA, pg 184
Service Technique pour l'Education, pg 184
Editions du Seuil, pg 184

Siloe - Kerdore, pg 185
Societe Nouveaux Loisirs, pg 185
Publications de la Sorbonne, pg 185
Association d'Editions Sorg, pg 186
Editions SOS (Editions du Secours Catholique), pg 186
Editions Sud Ouest, pg 186
Les Editions de la Table Ronde, pg 186
Editions Tallandier, pg 187
Editions Tiresias Michel Reynaud, pg 187
Transeuropeennes/RCE, pg 188
Universitas, pg 188
Editions Vague Verte, pg 188
Editions Vilo SA, pg 189
Librairie Philosophique J Vrin, pg 189

French Polynesia

Scoop/Au Vent des Iles, pg 189
Haere Po Editions, pg 189
Simone Sanchez, pg 190

Germany

Accedo Verlagsgesellschaft mbH, pg 190
Ahriman-Verlag GmbH, pg 191
Aisthesis Verlag, pg 191
Akademie Verlag GmbH, pg 191
akg-images gmbh, pg 191
Verlag Karl Alber GmbH, pg 191
Verlag und Antiquariat Frank Albrecht, pg 192
Anabas-Verlag Guenter Kaempf GmbH & Co KG, pg 192
AOL-Verlag Frohmut Menze, pg 193
arani-Verlag GmbH, pg 193
Arbeiterpresse Verlags- und Vertriebsgesellschaft mbH, pg 193
Ardey-Verlag GmbH, pg 193
Arkana Verlag Tete Boettger Rainer Wunderlich GmbH, pg 194
Aschendorffsche Verlagsbuchhandlung GmbH & Co KG, pg 194
Auer Verlag GmbH, pg 195
Aufstieg-Verlag GmbH, pg 195
Aulis Verlag Deubner & Co KG, pg 195
Dr Bachmaier Verlag GmbH, pg 196
Baken-Verlag Walter Schnoor, pg 196
Basilisken-Presse, pg 197
BasisDruck Verlag GmbH, pg 197
Bayerischer Schulbuch-Verlag GmbH, pg 198
Verlag C H Beck oHG, pg 198
Bergstadtverlag Wilhelm Gottlieb Korn GmbH Wuerzburg, pg 199
Berliner Debatte Wissenschafts Verlag, GSFP-Gesellschaft fur Sozialwissen-schaftliche Forschung und Publizistik mbH & Co KG, pg 199
Berliner Wissenschafts-Verlag GmbH (BWV), pg 199
Bertelsmann Lexikon Verlag GmbH, pg 200
Biblio Verlag, pg 200
Verlag Die Blaue Eule, pg 202
Bleicher Verlag GmbH, pg 202
Boehlau-Verlag GmbH & Cie, pg 202
Verlag Hermann Boehlaus Nachfolger Weimar GmbH & Co, pg 203
Klaus Boer Verlag, pg 203

Brandenburgisches Verlagshaus in der Dornier Medienholding GmbH, pg 204
F Bruckmann Munchen Verlag & Druck GmbH & Co Produkt KG, pg 204
BRUEN-Verlag, Gorenflo, pg 205
C C Buchners Verlag GmbH & Co KG, pg 205
Buchergilde Gutenberg Verlagsgesellschaft mbH, pg 205
Bundesanzeiger Verlagsgesellschaft, pg 206
Campus Verlag GmbH, pg 207
Fachverlag Hans Carl GmbH, pg 207
Centaurus-Verlagsgesellschaft GmbH, pg 207
Chr Belser AG fur Verlagsgeschaefte und Co KG, pg 208
Hans Christians Druckerei und Verlag GmbH & Co KG, pg 208
Compact Verlag GmbH, pg 209
Copress Verlag, pg 209
Cornelsen Verlag GmbH & Co OHG, pg 210
J G Cotta'sche Buchhandlung Nachfolger GmbH, pg 210
Das Arsenal, Verlag fuer Kultur und Politik GmbH, pg 210
Degener & Co, Manfred Dreiss Verlag, pg 211
Deutsche Verlags-Anstalt GmbH (DVA), pg 212
Deutscher Taschenbuch Verlag GmbH & Co KG (dtv), pg 213
Dieterichsche Verlagsbuchhandlung Mainz, pg 214
Verlag J H W Dietz Nachf GmbH, pg 214
Dietz Verlag Berlin GmbH, pg 215
Dipa-Verlag GmbH, pg 215
Edition Diskord, pg 215
Dolling und Galitz Verlag GmbH, pg 215
agenda Verlag Thomas Dominikowski, pg 215
Donat Verlag, pg 215
Droste Verlag GmbH, pg 216
Druffel-Verlag, pg 216
Duncker und Humblot GmbH, pg 217
DVG-Deutsche Verlagsgesellschaft mbH, pg 217
Echter Wurzburg Frankische Gesellschaftsdruckerei und Verlag GmbH, pg 217
Egmont Franz Schneider Verlag GmbH, pg 218
Egmont vgs verlagsgesellschaft mbH, pg 218
Ehrenwirth Verlag GmbH, pg 218
Eichborn AG, pg 219
Eironeia-Verlag, pg 219
Ellert & Richter Verlag GmbH, pg 219
N G Elwert Verlag, pg 219
EOS Verlag der Benefiktiner der Erzabtei St. Ottilien, pg 220
Ergebnisse Verlag GmbH, pg 220
Espresso Verlag GmbH, pg 221
Europaeische Verlagsanstalt GmbH & Rotbuch Verlag GmbH & Co KG, pg 222
Fackeltrager-Verlag GmbH, pg 223
Falken-Verlag GmbH, pg 223
Ferd Dummler's Verlag, pg 223
Wilhelm Fink GmbH & Co Verlags-KG, pg 224
Harald Fischer Verlag GmbH, pg 224

Fischer Taschenbuch Verlag GmbH, pg 225
Fleischhauer & Spohn GmbH & Co, pg 225
Flensburger Hefte Verlag GmbH, pg 225
Flugzeug Publikations GmbH, pg 225
Focus-Verlag Gesellschaft mbH, pg 225
Forum Verlag Leipzig Buch-Gesellschaft mbH, pg 225
Verlag Freies Geistesleben, pg 227
Verlag A Fromm im Druck- u Verlagshaus Fromm GmbH & Co KG, pg 227
Friedrich Frommann Verlag, pg 227
G Braun (vormals G Braun'sche Hofbuchdruckerei und Verlag) Gmbh, pg 227
Georgi GmbH, pg 228
Germanisches Nationalmuseum, pg 228
Verlag fuer Geschichte der Naturwissenschaften und der Technik, pg 229
H Gietl Verlag & Publikationsservice GmbH, pg 229
Wilhelm Goldmann Verlag GmbH, pg 230
Gondrom Verlag GmbH & Co KG, pg 230
Grabert-Verlag, pg 230
Grote'sche Verlagsbuchhandlung GmbH & Co KG, pg 231
Walter de Gruyter GmbH & Co KG, pg 231
Gunter Olzog Verlag GmbH, pg 231
Dr Rudolf Habelt GmbH, pg 232
Hahnsche Buchhandlung, pg 233
Liselotte Hamecher, pg 233
Harenberg Kommunikation Verlags- und Medien-GmbH & Co KG, pg 234
Haude und Spenersche Verlagsbuchhandlung, pg 235
Hellerau-Verlag Dresden GmbH, pg 236
Edition Hentrich Druck & Verlag Gebr Hentrich und Tank GmbH & Co KG, pg 236
F A Herbig Verlagsbuchhandlung GmbH, pg 236
Verlag Herder GmbH & Co KG, pg 236
Wilhelm Heyne Verlag, pg 237
Anton Hiersemann, Verlag, pg 237
Verlag Hinder und Deelmann, pg 237
Dieter Hoffmann Verlag, pg 238
Hoffmann und Campe Verlag GmbH, pg 238
Hohenrain-Verlag GmbH, pg 239
Holos Verlag, pg 239
Edition ID-Archiv/ID-Verlag, pg 240
Ikarus - Buchverlag, pg 241
Inno Vatio Verlags AG, pg 241
Iudicium Verlag GmbH, pg 242
Jan Thorbecke Verlag GmbH & Co, pg 243
Janus Verlagsgesellschaft, Dr Norbert Meder & Co, pg 243
JKL Publikationen GmbH, pg 243
Jonas Verlag fuer Kunst und Literatur GmbH, pg 243
Jovis Verlag GmbH, pg 243
Juventa Verlag GmbH, pg 244
Kastell Verlag GmbH, pg 244
Keip GmbH, pg 245
Kerber Verlag, pg 245

Verlag Kiepenheuer & Witsch, pg 245
Klartext Verlagsgesellschaft mbH, pg 246
Klosterhaus-Verlagsbuchhandlung Dr Grimm KG, pg 247
Vittorio Klostermann GmbH, pg 247
Albrecht Knaus Verlag GmbH, pg 247
Knowledge Media International, pg 247
Koehler & Amelang Verlagsgesellschaft, pg 248
K F Koehler Verlag GmbH, pg 248
Verlagsgruppe Koehler/Mittler, pg 248
Koenemann Verlagesgesellschaft mbH, pg 248
Verlag Valentin Koerner GmbH, pg 248
W Kohlhammer GmbH, pg 248
Konkret Literatur Verlag, pg 249
Anton H Konrad Verlag, pg 249
Dr Anton Kovac Slavica Verlag, pg 249
Karin Kramer Verlag, pg 250
Verlag Waldemar Kramer, pg 250
Hubert Kretschmar Leipziger Verlagsgesellschaft, pg 250
Alfred Kroner Verlag, pg 250
Verlag Ernst Kuhn, pg 250
Kulturstiftung der deutschen Vertriebenen, pg 250
Peter Lang GmbH Europaeischer Verlag der Wissenschaften, pg 252
Karl Robert Langewiesche Nachfolger Hans Koester KG, pg 252
Michael Lassleben Verlag und Druckerei, pg 252
J Latka Verlag GmbH, pg 253
Leipziger Universitaetsverlag GmbH, pg 253
Libertas- Europaeisches Institut GmbH, pg 254
Edition Libri Illustri GmbH, pg 254
Christoph Links Verlag - LinksDruck GmbH, pg 254
Logos Verlag GmbH, pg 255
Gustav Luebbe Verlag, pg 256
Lukas Verlag fur Kunst- und Geistesgeschichte, pg 256
Annemarie Maeger, pg 256
Gebr Mann Verlag GmbH & Co, pg 257
Manutius Verlag, pg 257
Matthes und Seitz Verlag GmbH, pg 258
Karl-Heinz Metz, pg 259
J B Metzlersche Verlagsbuchhandlung, pg 260
Preubmpassling Verlag Gisela Meussling, pg 260
Mitteldeutscher Verlag GmbH, pg 261
Mohr Siebeck, pg 261
Motorbuch-Verlag, pg 262
Mueller & Schindler Verlag ek, pg 262
Munzinger-Archiv GmbH Archiv fuer publizistische Arbeit, pg 262
Musikantiquariat und Dr Hans Schneider Verlag GmbH, pg 262
Muster-Schmidt Verlag, pg 263
MUT Verlag, pg 263
Naumann & Goebel Verlagsgesellschaft mbH, pg 263
Nebel Verlag GmbH, pg 263
Net World Vision GmbH, pg 263
Neuer ISP Verlag GmbH, pg 264
Verlag Neuer Weg, pg 264

Verlag Neues Leben GmbH, pg 264
Neuthor - Verlag, pg 265
Niederland-Verlag Helmut Michel, pg 265
C W Niemeyer Buchverlage GmbH, pg 265
Max Niemeyer Verlag GmbH, pg 265
Nusser Verlag, pg 266
Oberbaum Verlag GmbH, pg 266
Oekotopia Verlag, Wolfgang Hoffman GmbH & Co KG, pg 266
Oekumenischer Verlag Dr R-F Edel, pg 266
R Oldenbourg Verlag GmbH, pg 267
Georg Olms Verlag AG, pg 267
Orbis Verlag fur Publizistik GmbH, pg 267
Pahl-Rugenstein Verlag Nachfolger-GmbH, pg 267
PapyRossa Verlags GmbH & Co Kommanditgesellschaft KG, pg 268
Patmos Verlag GmbH & Co KG, pg 268
Pendragon Verlag, pg 269
Justus Perthes Verlag Gotha GmbH, pg 269
Philipp Reclam Jun Verlag GmbH, pg 269
Philipps-Universitaet Marburg, pg 270
Piper Verlag GmbH, pg 270
Guido Pressler Verlag, pg 271
Propylaeen Verlag, Zweigniederlassung Berlin der Ullstein Buchverlage GmbH, pg 272
Psychosozial-Verlag, pg 272
Verlag Friedrich Pustet GmbH & Co Kg, pg 272
edition q Berlin Edition in der Quintessenz Verlags-GmbH, pg 272
Quell Verlag, pg 273
Quelle und Meyer Verlag GmbH & Co, pg 273
Reclam Verlag Leipzig, pg 274
Verlag fur Regionalgeschichte, pg 274
Dr Ludwig Reichert Verlag, pg 274
E Reinhold Verlag, pg 275
RVBG Rheinland-Verlag-und Betriebsgesellschaft des Landschaftsverbandes Rheinland mbH, pg 276
Ritzau KG Verlag Zeit und Eisenbahn, pg 276
Roehrig Universitaets Verlag GmbH, pg 276
Rombach GmbH Druck und Verlagshaus & Co, pg 276
Romiosini Verlag, pg 276
Rosenheimer Verlagshaus GmbH & Co KG, pg 276
Ruetten & Loening Berlin GmbH, pg 277
Verlag an der Ruhr GmbH, pg 277
Saarbrucker Druckerei und Verlag GmbH (SDV), pg 277
K G Saur Verlag GmbH, A Gale/Thomson Learning Company, pg 278
Sax-Verlag Beucha, pg 278
scaneg Verlag, pg 278
Schild-Verlag GmbH, pg 279
Schillinger Verlag GmbH, pg 279
Max Schmidt-Roemhild Verlag, pg 280
Verlag Schnell und Steiner GmbH, pg 281

Ferdinand Schoeningh Verlag GmbH, pg 281
Verlag Karl Waldemar Schuetz, pg 281
Schulz-Kirchner Verlag GmbH, pg 282
H O Schulze KG, pg 282
Scientia Verlag und Antiquariat Schilling OHG, pg 282
Siedler Verlag, pg 283
Siegler & Co Verlag fuer Zeitarchive GmbH, pg 283
Societaets-Verlag, pg 283
Spee Buchverlag GmbH, pg 284
Spiess Volker Wissenschaftsverlag GmbH, pg 284
Adolf Sponholtz Verlag, pg 284
Springer Science+Business Media GmbH & Co KG, pg 284
Staatliche Museen Kassel, pg 286
Stadler Verlagsgesellschaft mbH, pg 286
Stapp Verlag Wolfgang Stapp, pg 286
C A Starke Verlag, pg 287
Steidl Verlag, pg 287
Franz Steiner Verlag Wiesbaden GmbH, pg 287
J F Steinkopf Verlag GmbH, pg 287
Steinweg-Verlag, Jurgen vomHoff, pg 287
Stern-Verlag Janssen & Co, pg 288
Sternberg-Verlag bei Ernst Franz, pg 288
Stiefel Eurocart GmbH, pg 288
Sueddeutsche Verlagsgesellschaft mbH, pg 288
Suin Buch-Verlag, pg 289
Edition Temmen, pg 290
Konrad Theiss Verlag GmbH, pg 290
Toleranz Verlag, Nielsen Frederic W, pg 291
Traditionell Bogenschiessen Verlag Angelika Hornig, pg 292
Trautvetter & Fischer Nachf, pg 292
Trees Wolfgang Triangel Verlag, pg 292
Treves Editions Verein Zur Foerderung der Kuenstlerischen Taetigkeiten, pg 292
Trotzdem-Verlags Genossenschaft eG, pg 292
Tuduv Verlagsgesellschaft mbH, pg 292
Tuebinger Vereinigung fur Volkskunde eV (TVV), pg 292
Ullstein Heyne List GmbH & Co KG, pg 293
Ulrike Helmer Verlag, pg 293
UTB fuer Wissenschaft Uni Taschenbuecher GmbH, pg 294
UVK Universitatsverlag Konstanz GmbH, pg 294
UVK Verlagsgesellschaft mbH, pg 294
Vandenhoeck & Ruprecht, pg 294
VAS-Verlag fuer Akademische Schriften, pg 294
Verlag Volk & Welt GmbH, pg 296
W Ludwig Verlag GmbH, pg 297
Wachholtz Verlag GmbH, pg 297
Verlag Klaus Wagenbach, pg 297
Waxmann Verlag GmbH, pg 297
Weber Zucht & Co, pg 298
Wehr & Wissen Verlagsgesellschaft mbH, pg 298
Weidmannsche Verlagsbuchhandlung GmbH, pg 298
Verlagsgruppe Weltbild GmbH, pg 298

PUBLISHERS

Westermann Schulbuchverlag GmbH, pg 299
Wichern Verlag GmbH, pg 299
Wichern-Verlag GmbH, pg 299
Dr Dieter Winkler, pg 300
Verlag Wissenschaft und Politik, pg 300
Wissenschaftliche Buchgesellschaft, pg 300
Friedrich Wittig Verlag GmbH, pg 301
Wochenschau Verlag, Dr Kurt Debus GmbH, pg 301
Das Wunderhorn Verlag GmbH, pg 301
Wunderlich Verlag, pg 301
Verlag Philipp von Zabern, pg 302
Zambon Verlag, pg 302
Verlag Clemens Zerling, pg 302
Verlag im Ziegelhaus Ulrich Gohl, pg 302

Ghana

Adaex Educational Publications Ltd, pg 302
Anowuo Educational Publications, pg 303
Ghana Publishing Corporation, pg 304
Ghana Universities Press (GUP), pg 304
Moxon Paperbacks, pg 304
Sedco Publishing Ltd, pg 305
Waterville Publishing House, pg 305

Greece

Akritas, pg 305
Anixis Publications, pg 305
Apostoliki Diakonia tis Ekklisias tis Hellados, pg 305
D I Arsenidis Publications, pg 306
Bergadis, pg 306
Boukoumanis' Editions, pg 306
Chryssos Typos AE Ekodeis, pg 306
Dodoni Publications, pg 306
Dorikos Publishing House, pg 306
Ecole francaise d'Athenes, pg 307
Ekdoseis Thetili, pg 307
Ekdotike Athenon SA, pg 307
Ekdotikos Oikos Adelfon Kyriakidi A E, pg 307
Elliniki Leschi Tou Vivliou, pg 307
Etaireia Spoudon Neoellinikou Politismou Kai Genikis Paideias, pg 307
Evrodiastasi, pg 307
Exandas Publishers, pg 307
Forma Edkotiki E P E, pg 307
Giovanis Publications, Pangosmios Ekdotikos Organismos, pg 307
Govostis Publishing SA, pg 307
Gutenberg Publications, pg 307
Hestia-I D Hestia-Kollaros & Co Corporation, pg 308
Hiotellis P, pg 308
Ianos, pg 308
Idmon Publications, pg 308
Idryma Meleton Chersonisou tou Aimou, pg 308
Irini Publishing House - Vassilis G Katsikeas SA, pg 308
Kalentis & Sia, pg 308
Dionysuis P Karavias Ekdoseis, pg 309
Kardamitsa A, pg 309
Kastaniotis Editions SA, pg 309
Kedros Publishers, pg 309
Knossos Publications, pg 309
Kritiki Publishing, pg 309
Kyriakidis Vasileios, pg 309
A G Leventis Foundation, pg 309
Melissa Publishing House, pg 310

Minoas SA, pg 310
Morfotiko Idryma Ethnikis Trapezas, pg 310
Ed Nea Acropolis, pg 310
Nea Thesis - Evrotas, pg 310
Oceanida, pg 310
Odysseas Publications Ltd, pg 311
Panepistimio Ioanninon, pg 311
D Papadimas, pg 311
Kyr I Papadopoulos E E, pg 311
Papazissis Publishers SA, pg 311
Patakis Publishers, pg 311
Pontiki Publications SA, pg 311
Proskinio Spyros Ch Marinis, pg 311
Siamantas VA A Ouvas, pg 312
Society for Macedonian Studies, pg 312
Stochastis, pg 312
J Vassiliou Bibliopolein, pg 313
S J Zacharopoulos SA Publishing Co, pg 313
Har Zolindakis, pg 313

Guatemala

Fundacion para la Cultura y el Desarrollo, pg 313
Grupo Editorial RIN-78, pg 313

Guinea-Bissau

Instituto Nacional de Estudos e Pesquisa (INEP), pg 314

Haiti

Editions Caraibes SA, pg 314
Theodor (Imprimerie), pg 314

Holy See (Vatican City State)

Biblioteca Apostolica Vaticana, pg 314
Libreria Editrice Vaticana, pg 315

Honduras

Editorial Guaymuras, pg 315

Hong Kong

Celeluck Co Ltd, pg 316
The Chinese University Press, pg 316
Chung Hwa Book Co (HK) Ltd, pg 316
FormAsia Books Ltd, pg 317
Hong Kong University Press, pg 317
Joint Publishing (HK) Co Ltd, pg 317
Ling Kee Publishing Group, pg 318
Sun Mui Press, pg 319
Witman Publishing Co (HK) Ltd, pg 320

Hungary

Akademiai Kiado, pg 320
Atlantisz Kiado, pg 320
Balassi Kiado Kft, pg 321
Central European University Press, pg 321
Corvina Books Ltd, pg 321
Helikon Kiado, pg 321
Janus Pannonius Tudomanyegyetem, pg 322
Jelenkor Verlag, pg 322
Magveto Koenyvkiado, pg 322
Mult es Jovo Kiado, pg 323
Nemzeti Tankoenyvkiado, pg 323
Officina Nova Konyvek, pg 323
Osiris Kiado, pg 323

Park Konyvkiado Kft (Park Publisher), pg 324
Tajak Korok Muzeumok Egyesuelet, pg 324

Iceland

Almenna Bokafelagid, pg 325
Haskolautgafan - University of Iceland Press, pg 325
Hid Islenzka Bokmenntafelag, pg 325
Idunn, pg 325
Stofnun Arna Magnussonar a Islandi, pg 326

India

Abhinav Publications, pg 326
Abhishek Publications, pg 327
The Academic Press, pg 327
Agam Kala Prakashan, pg 327
Amar Prakashan, pg 328
Ananda Publishers Pvt Ltd, pg 328
APH Publishing Corp, pg 328
Asian Educational Services, pg 329
Associated Publishing House, pg 329
Atma Ram & Sons, pg 329
Authorspress, pg 329
K P Bagchi & Co, pg 329
Bharatiya Vidya Bhavan, pg 330
Books & Books, pg 331
BR Publishing Corporation, pg 331
Chowkhamba Sanskrit Series Office, pg 332
Concept Publishing Co, pg 332
Cosmo Publications, pg 332
Dastane Ramchandra & Co, pg 333
Disha Prakashan, pg 333
DK Printworld (P) Ltd, pg 333
Dolphin Publications, pg 333
Enkay Publishers Pvt Ltd, pg 334
Ess Ess Publications, pg 334
Frank Brothers & Co Publishers Ltd, pg 334
Geeta Prakashan, pg 335
Gitanjali Publishing House, pg 335
Goel Prakashen, pg 335
Gyan Publishing House, pg 335
Heritage Publishers, pg 335
Indian Council of Social Science Research (ICSSR), pg 336
Indus Publishing Co, pg 338
Intellectual Publishing House, pg 338
Inter-India Publications, pg 338
Intertrade Publications Pvt Ltd, pg 338
Islamic Publishing House, pg 338
Jaico Publishing House, pg 338
Kali For Women, pg 339
Law Publishers, pg 340
Manohar Publishers & Distributors, pg 340
Minerva Associates (Publications) Pvt Ltd, pg 341
Ministry of Information & Broadcasting, pg 341
Motilal Banarsidass Publishers Pvt Ltd, pg 341
Munshiram Manoharlal Publishers Pvt Ltd, pg 342
National Book Organization, pg 342
Navajivan Trust, pg 343
Navrang Booksellers & Publishers, pg 343
Naya Prakash, pg 343
Omsons Publications, pg 344
Oxford University Press, pg 344
Paico Publishing House, pg 344
Panjab University Publication Bureau, pg 344

SUBJECT INDEX

People's Publishing House (P) Ltd, pg 345
Pitambar Publishing Co (P) Ltd, pg 345
Pointer Publishers, pg 345
Popular Prakashan Pvt Ltd, pg 345
Promilla & Publishers, pg 345
Pustak Mahal, pg 345
Rahul Publishing House, pg 346
Rajendra Publishing House Pvt Ltd, pg 346
Rajesh Publications, pg 346
Regency Publications, pg 346
Reliance Publishing House, pg 346
Roli Books Pvt Ltd, pg 347
Rupa & Co, pg 347
Sasta Sahitya Mandal, pg 348
Sri Satguru Publications, pg 348
Scientific Book Agency, pg 348
Somaiya Publications Pvt Ltd, pg 349
South Asia Publications, pg 349
Star Publications (P) Ltd, pg 350
Sterling Publishers Pvt Ltd, pg 350
Sultan Chand & Sons Pvt Ltd, pg 350
Suman Prakashan Pvt Ltd, pg 351
Tara Publishing, pg 351
DB Taraporevala Sons & Co Pvt Ltd, pg 351
Theosophical Publishing House, pg 351
Vani Prakashan, pg 352
Vision Books Pvt Ltd, pg 352
S Viswanathan (Printers & Publishers) Pvt Ltd, pg 352

Indonesia

Bhratara Karya Aksara, pg 354
PT Bulan Bintang, pg 354
Pustaka Utama Grafiti, PT, pg 356
Tintamas Indonesia PT, pg 356
Yayasan Obor Indonesia, pg 357

Islamic Republic of Iran

Scientific and Cultural Publications, pg 357

Ireland

Attic Press Ltd, pg 358
Ballinakella Press, pg 358
Edmund Burke Publisher, pg 358
The Children's Press, pg 358
Clo Iar-Chonnachta Teo, pg 358
The Collins Press, pg 358
The Columba Press, pg 359
Cork University Press, pg 359
Dee-Jay Publications, pg 359
Dominican Publications, pg 359
The Educational Company of Ireland, pg 359
Four Courts Press Ltd, pg 360
Gandon Editions, pg 360
Gill & Macmillan Ltd, pg 360
The Goldsmith Press Ltd, pg 360
Herodotus Press, pg 361
History House Publishing, pg 361
Institute of Public Administration, pg 361
Irish Academic Press, pg 361
Irish Texts Society (Cumann Na Scribeann nGaedhilge), pg 361
Kerryman Ltd, pg 361
The Lilliput Press Ltd, pg 361
Mercier Press Ltd, pg 362
Mount Eagle Publications Ltd, pg 362
New Books/Connolly Books, pg 362
O'Brien Educational, pg 362
The O'Brien Press Ltd, pg 362
On Stream Publications Ltd, pg 362
Poolbeg Press Ltd, pg 363

1001

SUBJECT INDEX — BOOK

Relay Books, pg 363
Roberts Rinehart Publishers, pg 363
Sean Ros Press, pg 363
Royal Irish Academy, pg 363
Tir Eolas, pg 363
Tomar Publishing Ltd, pg 364

Israel

Agudat Sabah, pg 364
Am Oved Publishers Ltd, pg 365
Ariel Publishing House, pg 365
Bar Ilan University Press, pg 365
Ben-Zvi Institute, pg 365
The Bialik Institute, pg 365
Boostan Publishing House, pg 365
Breslov Research Institute, pg 365
Carta, The Israel Map & Publishing Co Ltd, pg 365
DAT Publications, pg 366
Dyonon/Papyrus Publishing House of the Tel-Aviv, pg 366
Edanim Publishers Ltd, pg 366
Feldheim Publishers Ltd, pg 367
The Arnold & Leona Finkler Institute of Holocaust Research, pg 367
Gefen Publishing House Ltd, pg 367
Hadar Publishing House Ltd, pg 367
Haifa University Press, pg 367
Hakibbutz Hameuchad Publishing House Ltd, pg 367
The Israel Academy of Sciences & Humanities, pg 368
Israel Exploration Society, pg 368
Jabotinsky Institute in Israel, pg 368
The Jerusalem Publishing House Ltd, pg 369
Ma'ariv Book Guild (Sifriat Ma'ariv), pg 370
Machbarot Lesifrut, pg 370
The Magnes Press, pg 370
MAP-Mapping & Publishing Ltd, pg 370
Massada Press Ltd, pg 370
Massada Publishers Ltd, pg 370
Ministry of Defence Publishing House, pg 370
Misgav Yerushalayim, pg 370
M Mizrahi Publishers, pg 370
The Moshe Dayan Center for Middle Eastern & African Studies, pg 371
Open University of Israel, pg 371
Schocken Publishing House Ltd, pg 371
Shalem Press, pg 372
Sifriat Poalim Ltd, pg 372
Tcherikover Publishers Ltd, pg 372
Tel Aviv University, pg 372
Yad Izhak Ben-Zvi Press, pg 373
Yad Vashem - The Holocaust Martyrs' & Heroes' Remembrance Authority, pg 373
Y L Peretz Publishing Co, pg 373
The Zalman Shazar Center, pg 374
Zmora-Bitan, Publishers Ltd, pg 374

Italy

Mario Adda Editore SNC, pg 374
Adelphi Edizioni SpA, pg 374
De Agostini Scolastica, pg 374
Alberti Libraio Editore, pg 375
All'Insegna del Giglio, pg 375
Franco Angeli SRL, pg 375
Archimede Edizioni, pg 376
Archivio Guido Izzi Edizioni, pg 376
Argalia Editore delle Arti Grafiche Editoriali SRL, pg 376
Arnaud Editore SRL, pg 376
Athesia Verlag Bozen, pg 377
Bardi Editore srl, pg 377
Bastogi, pg 377
Bianco, pg 377
Bollati Boringhieri Editore, pg 378
Giuseppe Bonanno Editore, pg 378
Bonsignori Editore SRL, pg 378
Bookservice, pg 378
Edizioni Borla SRL, pg 379
Bovolenta, pg 379
Edizioni Brenner, pg 379
Editore Giorgio Bretschneider, pg 379
Edizioni Cadmo SRL, pg 379
Calosci, pg 379
Camera dei Deputati Ufficio Pubblicazioni Informazione Parlamentare, pg 379
Campanotto, pg 379
Canova SRL, pg 379
Edizioni Cantagalli, pg 379
Capone Editore SRL, pg 379
Cappelli Editore, pg 380
Edizioni Carmelitane, pg 380
Casa Editrice Giuseppe Principato Spa, pg 380
CELID, pg 381
Celuc Libri, pg 381
Centro Ambrosiano di Documentazione e Studi Religiosi, pg 381
Centro Italiano Studi Alto Medioevo, pg 381
Centro Studi Terzo Mondo, pg 381
il Cerchio Iniziative Editoriali, pg 381
Ciranna - Roma, pg 382
Cisalpino, pg 382
Claudiana Editrice, pg 382
CLUEB (Cooperativa Libraria Universitaria Editrice Bologna), pg 382
Colonnese Editore, pg 383
Edizioni di Comunita SpA, pg 383
Edizioni Cultura della Pace, pg 383
La Cultura Sociologica, pg 384
D'Anna, pg 384
Datanews, pg 384
M d'Auria Editore SAS, pg 384
Edizioni Dedalo SRL, pg 384
Edizioni Della Torre di Salvatore Fozzi & C SAS, pg 385
Edizioni dell'Orso, pg 385
Direzione Generale Archivi, pg 385
Edizioni EBE, pg 385
Ecole Francaise de Rome, pg 385
EDAS, pg 385
Ediciclo Editore SRL, pg 386
EDIFIR SRL, pg 386
Edipuglia, pg 386
Editalia (Edizioni d'Italia), pg 386
Editori Laterza, pg 386
Edizioni del Centro Camuno di Studi Preistorici, pg 386
Edizioni di Storia e Letteratura, pg 386
Edizioni l'Arciere SRL, pg 387
EGEA (Edizioni Giuridiche Economiche Aziendali), pg 387
Giulio Einaudi Editore SpA, pg 387
ERGA SNC di Carla Ottino Merli & C (Edizioni Realizzazioni Grafiche - Artigiana), pg 388
L'Erma di Bretschneider SRL, pg 388
Essegi, pg 388
Edizioni Europa, pg 388
Giangiacomo Feltrinelli SpA, pg 389
Festina Lente Edizioni, pg 389
Flaccovio Editore, pg 389
Fogola Editore in Torino, pg 389
Arnaldo Forni Editore SRL, pg 389
Biblioteca Francescana, pg 389
Frati Editori di Quaracchi, pg 389
Galzerano Editore, pg 390
Gangemi Editore spa, pg 390
Garzanti Libri, pg 390
Istituto Geografico de Agostini SpA, pg 390
Bruno Ghigi Editore, pg 390
Edizioni del Girasole srl, pg 390
A Giuffre Editore SpA, pg 390
Giunti Gruppo Editoriale, pg 390
Gius Laterza e Figli SpA, pg 391
Grafica e Arte srl, pg 391
Grafo, pg 391
Gremese International srl, pg 391
Herder Editrice e Libreria, pg 392
Institutum Historicum Societatis Iesu, pg 392
Hopeful Monster Editore, pg 392
Ibis, pg 392
Ila - Palma, Tea Nova, pg 393
Instituti Editoriali E Poligrafici Internazionali SRL, pg 393
Edizioni Internazionali di Letteratura e Scienze, pg 393
Editoriale Jaca Book SpA, pg 394
L Japadre Editore, pg 394
Jouvence, pg 394
Kaos Edizioni SRL, pg 394
Laruffa Editore SRL, pg 394
Edizioni Lavoro SRL, pg 394
Il Lavoro Editoriale, pg 395
LED - Edizioni Universitarie di Lettere Economia Diritto, pg 395
Casa Editrice Le Lettere SRL, pg 395
Liguori Editore SRL, pg 395
Editrice Liguria SNC di Norberto Sabatelli & C, pg 395
Editrice la Locusta, pg 395
Loescher Editore SRL, pg 396
Loffredo Editore Napoli SpA®, pg 396
Longanesi & C, pg 396
Angelo Longo Editore, pg 396
Edizioni di Luca SRL, pg 396
Giuseppe Maimone Editore, pg 397
Manfrini Editori, pg 397
Casa Editrice Marietti SpA, pg 397
Tommaso Marotta Editore Srl, pg 397
Marzorati Editore SRL, pg 397
Editrice Massimo SAS di Crespi Cesare e C, pg 397
McRae Books, pg 398
Memorie Domenicane, pg 398
Casa Editrice Menna di Sinisgalli Menna Giuseppina, pg 398
Messaggero di San Antonio, pg 398
Milella di Lecce Spazio Vivo srl, pg 398
Arnoldo Mondadori Editore SpA, pg 398
Edumond Le Monnier, pg 399
Editrice Morcelliana SpA, pg 399
Mucchi Editore SRL, pg 399
Societa Editrice Il Mulino, pg 399
Gruppo Ugo Mursia Editore SpA, pg 400
Museo storico in Trento, pg 400
Giorgio Nada Editore SRL, pg 400
Accademia Naz dei Lincei, pg 400
Istituto Nazionale di Studi Romani, pg 400
Newton & Compton Editori, pg 400
NodoLibri, pg 400
Nuova Coletti Editore Roma, pg 401
La Nuova Italia Editrice SpA, pg 401
Editrice Nuovi Autori, pg 401
Nuovi Sentieri Editore, pg 401
OCTAVO Produzioni Editoriali Associale, pg 401
Leo S Olschki, pg 401
Osanna Venosa, pg 402
Maria Pacini Fazzi Editore, pg 402
Pagano Editore, pg 402
Palatina Editrice, pg 402
Fratelli Palombi SRL, pg 402
Paravia Bruno Mondadori Editori, pg 402
Passigli Editori, pg 402
Patron Editore SrL, pg 402
Luigi Pellegrini Editore, pg 403
Daniela Piazza Editore, pg 403
Piero Lacaita Editore, pg 403
Il Poligrafo, pg 404
Il Pomerio, pg 404
Pontificio Istituto di Archeologia Cristiana, pg 404
Neri Pozza Editore, pg 404
Pratiche Editrice, pg 404
Principato, pg 404
Edizioni Quasar di Severino Tognon SRL, pg 404
Edizioni Quattroventi SNC, pg 404
Edition Raetia Srl-GmbH, pg 405
Rara Istituto Editoriale di Bibliofilia e Reprints, pg 405
RCS Libri SpA, pg 405
RCS Rizzoli Libri SpA, pg 405
Reverdito Edizioni, pg 405
Riccardo Ricciardi Editore SpA, pg 405
Edizioni Ripostes, pg 405
Editori Riuniti, pg 405
Rossato, pg 406
Rubbettino Editore, pg 406
Rusconi Libri Srl, pg 406
SAGEP Libri & Comunicazione Srl, pg 406
Il Saggiatore, pg 406
Salerno Editrice SRL, pg 406
Edizioni San Paolo SRL, pg 407
Sardini Editrice, pg 407
Salvatore Sciascia Editore, pg 407
Edizioni Scientifiche Italiane, pg 407
Sellerio Editore, pg 408
Sicania, pg 408
Edizioni Librarie Siciliane, pg 408
Societa Editrice Internazionale - SEI, pg 408
Societa Napoletana Storia Patria Napoli, pg 408
Societa Storica Catanese, pg 408
Le Stelle Scuola, pg 409
Istituto Storico Italiano per l'Eta Moderna e Contemporanea, pg 409
Studio Bibliografico Adelmo Polla, pg 409
Studio Editoriale Programma, pg 409
Edizioni Studio Tesi SRL, pg 409
Edizioni Studium SRL, pg 409
Sugarco Edizioni SRL, pg 409
Tappeiner, pg 409
Tassotti Editore, pg 409
TEA Tascabili degli Editori Associati SpA, pg 409
Edizioni del Teresianum, pg 410
Nicola Teti e C Editore SRL, pg 410
Edizioni Thyrus SRL, pg 410
Editrice Tirrenia Stampatori SAS, pg 410
Trainer International Editore-I Libri del Bargello, pg 410
Transeuropa, pg 410
Editoriale Umbra SAS di Carnevali e, pg 411
UTET (Unione Tipografico-Editrice Torinese), pg 411

Vita e Pensiero, pg 412
Zanichelli Editore SpA, pg 412

Jamaica

Carib Publishing Ltd, pg 413
Carlong Publishers (Caribbean) Ltd, pg 413
Institute of Jamaica Publications, pg 413
Jamaica Publishing House Ltd, pg 414
The Press, pg 414
Ian Randle Publishers Ltd, pg 414
University of the West Indies Press, pg 414

Japan

Akita Shoten Publishing Co Ltd, pg 415
Aoki Shoten Co Ltd, pg 415
Baseball Magazine-Sha Co Ltd, pg 415
Bunkasha Publishing Co Ltd, pg 415
Bunkashobo-Hakubun-Sha, pg 415
Chikuma Shobo Publishing Co Ltd, pg 416
Chuokoron-Shinsha Inc, pg 416
Dohosha Publishing Co Ltd, pg 417
Fukumura Shuppan Inc, pg 417
Fuzambo Publishing Co, pg 417
GakuseiSha Publishing Co Ltd, pg 417
Hakusui-Sha Co Ltd, pg 417
Hayakawa Publishing Inc, pg 418
Heibonsha Ltd, Publishers, pg 418
Hoikusha Publishing Co Ltd, pg 418
Hyoronsha Publishing Co Ltd, pg 418
International Society for Educational Information (ISEI), pg 419
Iwanami Shoten, Publishers, pg 419
Japan Broadcast Publishing Co Ltd, pg 419
Japan Travel Bureau Inc, pg 420
Kadokawa Shoten Publishing Co Ltd, pg 420
Kaisei-Sha Publishing Co Ltd, pg 420
Kawade Shobo Shinsha Publishers, pg 420
Kazamashobo Co Ltd, pg 420
Keisuisha Publishing Company Ltd, pg 420
Kinokuniya Co Ltd (Publishing Department), pg 421
Kodansha International Ltd, pg 421
Kodansha Ltd, pg 421
Kokushokankokai Co Ltd, pg 421
Kosei Publishing Co Ltd, pg 421
Koyo Shobo, pg 422
Meiji Shoin Co Ltd, pg 422
Minerva Shobo Co Ltd, pg 422
Mirai-Sha, pg 422
Myrtos Inc, pg 423
Nensho-Sha, pg 423
Nigensha Publishing Co Ltd, pg 423
Nihon Tosho Center Co Ltd, pg 423
Nippon Hoso Shuppan Kyokai (NHK Publishing), pg 424
Obunsha Co Ltd, pg 424
Otsuki Shoten Publishers, pg 425
Poplar Publishing Co Ltd, pg 425
Rinsen Book Co Ltd, pg 425
Sanseido Co Ltd, pg 426
Seibundo Shuppan, pg 426
Sekai Bunka-Sha, pg 427
Shakai Shiso-Sha, pg 427
Shibun-Do, pg 427
Shimizu-Shoin, pg 427
Shogakukan Inc, pg 427

Shufu-to-Seikatsu Sha Ltd, pg 428
Shunjusha, pg 428
The Simul Press Inc, pg 428
Sobun-Sha, pg 428
Sogensha Publishing Co Ltd, pg 428
Taimeido Publishing Co Ltd, pg 429
Tankosha Publishing Co Ltd, pg 429
Teikoku-Shoin Co Ltd, pg 429
Toho Book Store, pg 429
Toho Shuppan, pg 429
Tokai University Press, pg 429
Tokuma Shoten Publishing Co Ltd, pg 429
Tokyo Shoseki Co Ltd, pg 430
Tokyo Sogensha Co Ltd, pg 430
Tosui Shobo Publishers, pg 430
University of Tokyo Press, pg 430
Waseda University Press, pg 431
Yuhikaku Publishing Co Ltd, pg 431

Jordan

Jordan Distribution Agency Co Ltd, pg 432

Kazakstan

Al-Farabi Kazakh National University, pg 432

Kenya

British Institute in Eastern Africa, pg 433
Heinemann Kenya Ltd (EAEP), pg 434
Kenway Publications Ltd, pg 434
Nairobi University Press, pg 435
Paulines Publications-Africa, pg 435
Phoenix Publishers Ltd, pg 435
Sasa Sema Publications Ltd, pg 435
Shirikon Publishers, pg 436
Transafrica Press, pg 436
Gideon S Were Press, pg 436

Democratic People's Republic of Korea

Academy of Sciences Publishing House, pg 436
The Foreign Language Press Group, pg 436
Korea Science and Encyclopedia Publishing House, pg 436

Republic of Korea

Ba-reunsa Publishing Co, pg 437
Borim Publishing Co, pg 437
Bum-Woo Publishing Co, pg 437
Chang-josa Publishing Co, pg 438
Chong No Books Publishing Co Ltd, pg 438
Chung Rim Publishing Co Ltd, pg 438
DanKook University Press, pg 438
Dong Hwa Publishing Co, pg 438
Eulyu Publishing Co Ltd, pg 438
Hainain Publishing Co Ltd, pg 439
Hakgojae Publishing Inc, pg 439
Hangil Art Vision, pg 439
Hanul Publishing Co, pg 439
Hollym Corporation; Publishers, pg 439
Hw Moon Publishing Co, pg 439
Hyangmunsa Publishing Co, pg 439
Iljisa Publishing House, pg 439
Iljo-gag Publishers, pg 439
Korea University Press, pg 440
Min-eumsa Publishing Co Ltd, pg 441
Minjisa Publishing Co, pg 441
Munhag-gwan, pg 441
Munye Publishing Co, pg 441

O Neul Publishing Co, pg 441
PoChinChai Printing Co Ltd, pg 442
Samseong Publishing Co Ltd, pg 442
Sejong Daewang Kinyom Saophoe, pg 442
Seoul International Publishing House, pg 443
Seoul National University Press, pg 443
Sogang University Press, pg 443
Sohaksa, pg 443
Woongjin Media Corporation, pg 443
Yonsei University Press, pg 444

Kuwait

Ministry of Information, pg 444

Laos People's Democratic Republic

Lao-phanit, pg 444

Latvia

Lielvards Ltd, pg 445
Nordik/Tapals Publishers Ltd, pg 445
Preses Nams, pg 445
Spriditis Publishers, pg 445
Vieda, SIA, pg 445

Lebanon

Dar-El-Machreq Sarl, pg 446
Khayat Book and Publishing Co Sarl, pg 446
Librairie Orientale sal, pg 446
Naufal Group Sarl, pg 447

Lesotho

Mazenod Book Centre, pg 447
Saint Michael's Mission Social Centre, pg 447

Liechtenstein

Verlag HP Gassner AG, pg 447
Historischer Verein fur das Furstentum Liechtenstein, pg 448
Liechtenstein Verlag AG, pg 448
Saendig Reprint Verlag, Hans-Rainer Wohlwend, pg 448

Lithuania

Baltos Lankos, pg 449
Eugrimas, pg 449
Klaipedos Universiteto Leidykla, pg 449
Lithuanian National Museum Publishing House, pg 449
Mokslo ir enciklopediju leidybos institutas, pg 449
Margi Rastai Publishers, pg 449
Svietimo ir mokslo ministerijos Leidybos centras, pg 449

Luxembourg

Editions APESS ASBL, pg 450
Editions Emile Borschette, pg 450
Cahiers Luxembourgeois, pg 451
Editions Saint-Paul, pg 451
Editions Tousch, pg 452

Macau

Museu Maritimo, pg 452
Instituto Portugues Oriente, pg 452

The Former Yugoslav Republic of Macedonia

Macedonia Prima Publishing House, pg 452
Strk Publishing House, pg 453
Zumpres Publishing Firm, pg 453

Madagascar

Editions Ambozontany, pg 453
Madagascar Print & Press Company, pg 453
Tsipika Edition, pg 454

Malawi

Central Africana Ltd, pg 454
Christian Literature Association in Malawi, pg 454
Dzuka Publishing Co Ltd, pg 454

Malaysia

Forum Publications, pg 456
Geetha Publishers Sdn Bhd, pg 456
Penerbit Jayatinta Sdn Bhd, pg 458
Pustaka Delta Pelajaran Sdn Bhd, pg 458
Uni-Text Book Co, pg 459
University of Malaya, Department of Publications, pg 459

Mali

EDIM SA, pg 460

Malta

Gaulitana, pg 460
Gozo Press, pg 460

Mauritius

Editions Capucines, pg 461
Vizavi Editions, pg 461

Mexico

Aconcagua Ediciones y Publicaciones SA, pg 461
Libreria y Ediciones Botas SA, pg 462
Ediciones el Caballito SA, pg 462
Centro de Estudios Mexicanos y Centroamericanos, pg 463
El Colegio de Mexico AC, pg 463
Comision Nacional Forestal, pg 463
Editorial Diana SA de CV, pg 464
Editorial Edicol SA, pg 464
El Colegio de Michoacan A C, pg 464
Ediciones Era SA de CV, pg 465
Editorial Esfinge SA de CV, pg 465
Ediciones Euroamericanas, pg 465
Fernandez Editores SA de CV, pg 465
Fondo de Cultura Economica, pg 465
Editorial Hermes SA, pg 466
Instituto Indigenista Interamericano, pg 466
Editorial Jilguero, SA de CV, pg 467
Editorial Joaquin Mortiz SA de CV, pg 467
Editorial Jus SA de CV, pg 467
Phillip Richard Conover Lazo, pg 467
Editorial Minutiae Mexicana SA, pg 468
Instituto Nacional de Antropologia e Historia, pg 469
Editorial Nueva Imagen SA, pg 469
Instituto Panamericano de Geografia e Historia, pg 469
Panorama Editorial, SA, pg 470
Editorial Patria SA de CV, pg 470

Pearson Educacion de Mexico, SA de CV, pg 470
Editorial Planeta Mexicana SA, pg 470
Ediciones Roca, SA, pg 471
Salvat Editores de Mexico, pg 471
SCRIPTA - Distribucion y Servicios Editoriales, SA de CV, pg 471
Siglo XXI Editores SA de CV, pg 472
Sistemas Tecnicos de Edicion SA de CV, pg 472
Universidad Nacional Autonoma de Mexico (National University of Mexico), pg 472
Universidad Veracruzana Direccion General Editorial y de Publicaciones, pg 472
Javier Vergara Editor SA de CV, pg 473

Republic of Moldova

Editura Lumina, pg 473

Monaco

Editions EGC, pg 473
Les Editions du Rocher, pg 474
Rondeau Giannipiero a Monaco, pg 474

Morocco

Association de la Recherche Historique et Sociale, pg 474
Dar El Kitab, pg 474
Dar Nachr Al Maarifa Pour L'Edition et La Distribution, pg 474
Edition Diffusion de Livre au Maroc, pg 474
Editions Okad, pg 475
Societe Ennewrasse Service Librairie et Imprimerie, pg 475

Mozambique

Empresa Moderna Lda, pg 475
Centro De Estudos Africanos, pg 475

Myanmar

Sarpay Beikman Public Library, pg 476

Nepal

International Standards Books & Periodicals (P) Ltd, pg 476
Royal Nepal Academy, pg 477

Netherlands

Uitgeversmaatschappij Agon B V, pg 477
Uitgeverij Ambo BV, pg 477
APA (Academic Publishers Associated), pg 477
Uitgeverij de Arbeiderspers, pg 477
Uitgeverij Balans, pg 478
Erven J Bijleveld, pg 479
De Boekerij BV, pg 479
Boom Uitgeverij, pg 479
Brill Academic Publishers, pg 479
A W Bruna Uitgevers BV, pg 480
Cadans, pg 480
Callenbach BV, pg 480
Uitgeverij Christofoor, pg 480
Uitgeverij Conserve, pg 481
Uitgeverij Coutinho BV, pg 481
De Walburg Pers, pg 481
Uitgeversmaatschappij Ad Donker BV, pg 481
Elmar BV, pg 482
Uitgeverij De Fontein BV, pg 482

Uitgeverij en boekhandel Van Gennep BV, pg 482
HES & De Graaf Publishers BV, pg 483
Heuff Amsterdam Uitgever, pg 483
Uitgeverij Heureka, pg 483
Historische Uitgeverij, pg 483
Holland University Press BV (APA), pg 483
Hotei Publishing, pg 484
KITLV Press Royal Institute of Linguistics & Anthropology, pg 484
Uitgeverij J H Kok BV, pg 485
Uitgeverij Leopold BV, pg 485
Mets & Schilt Uitgevers en Distributeurs, pg 486
J M Meulenhoff bv, pg 486
Uitgeverij Maarten Muntinga, pg 486
Narratio Theologische Uitgeverij, pg 486
The Pepin Press, pg 487
Philo Press (APA), pg 487
Podium Uitgeverij, pg 487
De Prom, pg 488
Prometheus, pg 488
Em Querido's Uitgeverij BV, pg 488
Sjaloom Uitgeverijen, pg 489
Uitgeverij Het Spectrum BV, pg 489
A J G Strengholt's Boeken, Anno 1928, BV, pg 489
Uitgeverij SUN, pg 489
Tirion Uitgevers BV, pg 490
Unieboek BV, pg 490
Uniepers BV, pg 491
Van Buuren Uitgeverij BV, pg 491
Van Gorcum & Comp BV, pg 491
Uitgeverij Van Wijnen, pg 491
Uitgeverij Verloren, pg 492
VU Boekhandel/Uitgeverij BV, pg 492
Uitgeverij Waanders BV, pg 492
Wereldbibliotheek, pg 492
Uitgeverij 010, pg 493

Netherlands Antilles

Bredero, pg 493

New Caledonia

Editions du Santal, pg 493

New Zealand

Aoraki Press Ltd, pg 493
Aspect Press, pg 493
Auckland University Press, pg 493
Bush Press Communications Ltd, pg 494
C&S Publications, pg 494
Canterbury University Press, pg 494
Cape Catley Ltd, pg 495
Clerestory Press, pg 495
Craig Printing Co Ltd, pg 495
Dunmore Press Ltd, pg 495
ESA Publications (NZ) Ltd, pg 496
Fraser Books, pg 496
Gondwanaland Press, pg 496
Grantham House Publishing, pg 496
HarperCollins Publishers (New Zealand) Ltd, pg 497
Hazard Press Ltd, pg 497
Heritage Press Ltd, pg 497
Huia Publishers, pg 497
IPL Publishing Group, pg 497
David Ling Publishing, pg 498
Nelson Price Milburn Ltd, pg 499
Nestegg Books, pg 499
Northland Historical Publications Society, pg 499
Otago Heritage Books, pg 499

Outrigger Publishers, pg 499
Oxford University Press, pg 499
Reed Publishing (NZ) Ltd, pg 500
River Press, pg 500
Shearwater Associates Ltd, pg 501
Shoal Bay Press Ltd, pg 501
Te Waihora Press, pg 501
University of Otago Press, pg 502
Victoria University Press, pg 502
Bridget Williams Books Ltd, pg 502

Nigeria

ABIC Books & Equipment Ltd, pg 503
Ahmadu Bello University Press Ltd, pg 503
Alliance West African Publishers & Co, pg 503
Black Academy Press, pg 503
CSS Bookshops, pg 504
Educational Research & Study Group, pg 504
Ethiope Publishing Corporation, pg 504
Evans Brothers (Nigeria Publishers) Ltd, pg 504
Ibadan University Press, pg 505
JAD Publishers Ltd, pg 505
Longman Nigeria Plc, pg 505
Nwamife Publishers Ltd, pg 506
Obafemi Awolowo University Press Ltd, pg 506
Obobo Books, pg 506
Ogunsanya Press, Publishers and Bookstores Ltd, pg 506
Onibon-Oje Publishers, pg 506
Riverside Communications, pg 507
University Publishing Co, pg 507

Norway

Andresen & Butenschon AS, pg 508
Aschehoug Forlag, pg 508
Det Norske Samlaget, pg 508
J W Eides Forlag A/S, pg 509
Gyldendal Norsk Forlag A/S, pg 509
Hjemmenes Forlag, pg 509
Norsk Bokreidingslag L/L, pg 510
Snofugl Forlag, pg 510

Oman

Apex Press & Publishing, pg 511

Pakistan

Sheikh Muhammad Ashraf Publishers, pg 511
Hamdard Foundation Pakistan, pg 512
Islamic Research Institute, pg 513
H I Jaffari & Co Publishers, pg 513
Jang Publishers, pg 513
Maqbool Academy, pg 513
Nafees Academy, pg 513
National Institute of Historical & Cultural Research, pg 514
Pak American Commercial (Pvt) Ltd, pg 514
Pakistan Publishing House, pg 514
Publishers United Pvt Ltd, pg 514
Royal Book Co, pg 514
Sang-e-Meel Publications, pg 514

Panama

Editorial Universitaria, pg 515

Paraguay

Intercontinental Editora, pg 516

Peru

Librerias ABC SA, pg 516
Centro de la Mujer Peruana Flora Tristan, pg 516
Instituto de Estudios Peruanos, pg 517
Fondo Editorial de la Pontificia Universidad Catolica del Peru, pg 517
Instituto Frances de Estudios Andinos, IFEA, pg 517
Editorial Horizonte, pg 517
Sur Casa de Estudios del Socialismo, pg 517

Philippines

Abiva Publishing House Inc, pg 518
Ateneo de Manila University Press, pg 518
Bookmark Inc, pg 518
Galleon Publications, pg 519
Garotech, pg 519
Heritage Publishing House, pg 519
J C Palabay Enterprises, pg 519
New Day Publishers, pg 520
Our Lady of Manaoag Publisher, pg 520
Philippine Baptist Mission SBC FMB Church Growth International, pg 520
Rex Bookstores & Publishers, pg 520
Saint Mary's Publishing Corp, pg 520
San Carlos Publications, pg 521
SIBS Publishing House Inc, pg 521
Solidaridad Publishing House, pg 521
UST Publishing House, pg 521
Vera-Reyes Inc, pg 521

Poland

Aritbus et Historiae, Rivista Internationale di arti visive ecinema, Institut IRSA - Verlagsanstatt, pg 522
Wydawnictwo DiG, pg 522
Wydawnictwo Dolnoslaskie, pg 522
Instytut Historii Nauki PAN, pg 523
Instytut Wydawniczy Pax, Inco-Veritas, pg 523
Interpress, pg 523
Iskry - Publishing House Ltd spotka zoo, pg 523
Katolicki Uniwersytet Wydawniczo -Redakcja, pg 523
'Ksiazka i Wiedza' Spotdzielnia Wydawniczo-Handlowa, pg 524
Wydawnictwo Literackie, pg 524
Ludowa Spoldzielnia Wydawnicza, pg 524
Magnum Publishing House Ltd, pg 524
Norbertinum, pg 524
Ossolineum Zaklad Narodowy im Ossolinskich - Wydawnictwo, pg 525
Panstwowy Instytut Wydawniczy (PIW), pg 525
Wydawnictwo Podsiedlik-Raniowski i Spolka, pg 525
Polish Scientific Publishers PWN, pg 525
Rosikon Press, pg 526
Wydawnictwo RTW, pg 526
'Slask' Ltd, pg 526
Spoleczny Instytut Wydawniczy Znak, pg 526
Oficyna Wydawnicza Szkoly Glownej Handlowej w Warszawie Oficyna Wydawnicza SGH, pg 527

PUBLISHERS SUBJECT INDEX

Towarzystwo Naukowe w Toruniu, pg 527
Wydawnictwa Uniwersytetu Warszawskiego, pg 527

Portugal

Publicacoes Alfa SA, pg 528
Armenio Amado Editora de Simoes, Beirao & Ca Lda, pg 528
Edicoes Antigona, pg 528
Assirio & Alvim, pg 528
Bezerr-Editorae e Distribuidora de Abel Antonio Bezerra, pg 529
Biblioteca Geral da Universidade de Coimbra, pg 529
Camara Municipal de Castelo, pg 529
Livraria Civilizacao (Americo Fraga Lamares & Ca Lda), pg 529
Editora Classica, pg 530
Edicoes Colibri, pg 530
Constancia Editores, SA, pg 530
Edicoes Cosmos, pg 530
Dinalivro, pg 530
Edicoes ELO, pg 531
Editorial Estampa, Lda, pg 531
Publicacoes Europa-America Lda, pg 531
Europress Editores e Distribuidores de Publicacoes Lda, pg 531
Chaves Ferreira Publicacoes SA, pg 531
Editorial Franciscana, pg 531
Gradiva-Publicacnoes Lda, pg 532
Guimaraes Editores, Lda, pg 532
Imprensa Nacional-Casa da Moeda, pg 532
Editorial Inquerito Lda, pg 532
Instituto de Investigacao Cientifica Tropical, pg 532
Latina Livraria Editora, pg 532
Editora Livros do Brasil Sarl, pg 533
Livros Horizonte Lda, pg 533
Livraria Tavares Martins, pg 533
Editorial Noticias, pg 534
Internationale Nouvelle Acropole, pg 534
Nova Arrancada Sociedade Editora SA, pg 534
Palas Editores Lda, pg 534
Editorial Presenca, pg 535
Publicacoes Dom Quixote Lda, pg 535
Quimera Editores Lda, pg 535
Edicoes Rolim Lda, pg 535
Sa da Costa Livraria, pg 535
Edicoes 70 Lda, pg 535
Almerinda Teixeira, pg 536
Teorema, pg 536
Vega-Publicacao e Distribuicao de Livros e Revistas, Lda, pg 536
Editorial Verbo SA, pg 536
Livraria Verdade e Vida Editora, pg 536

Puerto Rico

Instituto de Cultura Puertorriquena, pg 537
Editorial Cultural Inc, pg 537
Ediciones Huracan Inc, pg 537
University of Puerto Rico Press (EDUPR), pg 537

Reunion

Editions Ocean, pg 538

Romania

Editura Academiei Romane, pg 538
Editura Aius, pg 538
Editura Albatros, pg 538
Alcor-Edimpex (Verlag) Ltd, pg 538

Editora All, pg 538
Ararat -Tiped, Editura, pg 538
Ars Longa Publishing House, pg 538
Artemis Verlag, pg 538
Casa Editoriala Independenta Europa, pg 538
The Center for Romanian Studies, pg 539
Editura Clusium, pg 539
Corint Publishing Group, pg 539
Editure Ion Creanga, pg 539
Editura Eminescu, pg 539
Enzyklopadie Verlag, pg 539
Editura Excelsior Art, pg 539
FF Press, pg 540
Casa de editura Globus, pg 540
Hasefer, pg 540
Humanitas Publishing House, pg 540
Editura Institutul European, pg 540
Editura Kriterion SA, pg 540
Lider Verlag, pg 540
Mentor Kiado, pg 540
Editura Meridiane, pg 540
Editura Militara, pg 541
Editura Niculescu, pg 541
Polirom Publishing House, pg 542
Grupul Editorial RAO, pg 542
Saeculum IO, pg 542
Editura Stiintifica SA, pg 542
Vestala Verlag, pg 543
Vremea Publishers Ltd, pg 543

Russian Federation

Agni Publishing House, pg 543
Aspect Press Ltd, pg 543
BLIC, russko-Baltijskij informaciionnyj centr, AO, pg 544
Izdatelstvo Detskaya Literatura, pg 544
Interbook-Business AO, pg 545
Izdatelstvo Iskusstvo, pg 545
Ladomir Publishing House, pg 546
Ministerstvo Kul 'tury RF, pg 546
Izdatelstvo Molodaya Gvardia, pg 546
Izdatelstvo Mordovskogo gosudar stvennogo, pg 547
Izdatelstvo Mysl, pg 547
Nauka Publishers, pg 547
Izdatel'stvo Nizhegorodskogo Gosudarstvennogo Univ, pg 547
Novosti Izdatelstvo, pg 547
Panorama Publishing House, pg 547
Progress Publishers, pg 548
Izdatelstvo Prosveshchenie, pg 548
Raduga Publishers, pg 548
Respublika, pg 548
Russkaya Kniga Izdatelstvo (Publishers), pg 548
St Andrew's Biblical Theological College, pg 548
Izdatelstvo Sudostroenie, pg 549
Voyenizdat, pg 549
Izdatelstvo Vysshaya Shkola, pg 549

Saudi Arabia

Dar Al-Shareeff for Publishing & Distribution, pg 550

Senegal

CODESRIA (Council for the Development of Social Science Research in Africa), pg 551
Les Nouvelles Editions Africaines du Senegal NEAS, pg 551

Serbia and Montenegro

Alfa-Narodna Knjiga, pg 552
Jugoslavijapublik, pg 552
Narodna Biblioteka Srbije, pg 552
Nolit Publishing House, pg 553
Panorama NIJP/ID Grigorije Bozovic, pg 553
Izdavacko Preduzece Matice Srpske, pg 553
Srpska Knjizevna Zadruga, pg 553
Vuk Karadzic, pg 554

Sierra Leone

Sierra Leone University Press, pg 554

Singapore

Archipelago Press, pg 555
Asiapac Books Pte Ltd, pg 555
Daiichi Media Pte Ltd, pg 555
McGallen & Bolden Associates, pg 557
Singapore University Press Pte Ltd, pg 558
Taylor & Francis Asia Pacific, pg 558

Slovakia

ARCHA sro Vydavatel'stro, pg 559
Danubiaprint, pg 559
Luc vydavatelske druzstvo, pg 559
Slo Viet, pg 560
Slovenske pedagogicke nakladateistvo, pg 560
Smena Publishing House, pg 560
VEDA (Vydavatel'stvo Slovenskej akademie vied), pg 561

Slovenia

Cankarjeva Zalozba, pg 561
East West Operation (EWO) Ltd, pg 561
Mladinska Knjiga International, pg 561
Zalozba Mihelac d o o, pg 562
Zalozba Obzorja d d Maribor, pg 562

South Africa

Jonathan Ball Publishers, pg 562
The Brenthurst Press (Pty) Ltd, pg 563
Educum Publishers Ltd, pg 563
Fernwood Press (Pty) Ltd, pg 563
Galago Publishing Pty Ltd, pg 564
HAUM (Hollandsch Afrikaansche Uitgevers Maatschappij), pg 564
Human & Rousseau (Pty) Ltd, pg 564
Mayibuye Books, pg 566
New Africa Books (Pty) Ltd, pg 567
Ravan Press (Pty) Ltd, pg 568
Shuter & Shooter (Pty) Ltd, pg 568
Unisa Press, pg 569
University of KwaZulu-Natal Press, pg 569
Van Schaik Publishers, pg 569
Witwatersrand University Press, pg 570

Spain

Publicacions de l'Abadia de Montserrat, pg 570
Acantilado, pg 570
Editorial Acervo SL, pg 570
Editorial Afers, SL, pg 571
Agencia Espanola de Cooperacion, pg 571
Aguilar SA de Ediciones, pg 571

Ediciones Alfar SA, pg 572
Edicions Alfons el Magnanim, Institucio Valenciana d'Estudis i Investigacio, pg 572
Editorial Algazara, pg 572
Alianza Editorial SA, pg 572
Altea, Taurus, Alfaguara SA, pg 572
Arco Libros SL, pg 573
Editorial Ariel SA, pg 573
Biblioteca de Autores Cristianos, pg 574
Baile del Sol, Colectivo Cultural, pg 574
Editorial Biblioteca Nueva SL, pg 574
Cabildo Insular de Gran Canaria Departamento de Ediciones, pg 575
Edicions Camacuc, pg 575
Carroggio SA de Ediciones, pg 575
Casa de Velazquez, pg 575
Edicios do Castro, pg 576
Biblioteca de Catalunya, pg 576
Ediciones Catedra SA, pg 576
Celeste Ediciones, pg 576
Centro de Estudios Politicos Y Constitucionales, pg 576
Editora Comercial de Publicaciones, pg 577
Compania Literaria, pg 577
Ediciones de la Universidad Complutense de Madrid, pg 577
Complutense, SA Editorial, pg 577
Comunidad Autonoma de Madrid, Servicio de Documentacion y Publicaciones, pg 578
Ediciones Cristiandad, pg 578
Curial Edicions Catalanes SA, pg 578
Rafael Dalmau, Editor, pg 578
Editorial Deimos, SL, pg 578
Ediciones Destino SA, pg 579
Editorial Diagonal del grup 62, pg 579
Dilagro SA, pg 579
Ediciones Diputacion de Salamanca, pg 579
Diputacion Provincial de Malaga, pg 579
Diputacion Provincial de Sevilla, Servicio de Publicaciones, pg 579
Ediciones Doce Calles SL, pg 579
Editorial Don Quijote, pg 579
Editorial EDAF SA, pg 580
EDERSA (Editoriales de Derecho Reunidas SA), pg 580
EDHASA (Editora y Distribuidora Hispano-Americana SA), pg 580
Editorial Everest SA, pg 581
Enciclopedia Catalana, SA, pg 582
Ediciones Encuentro SA, pg 582
Editorial Espasa-Calpe SA, pg 582
Instituto de Estudios Riojanos, pg 583
Eumo Editorial, pg 583
EUNSA (Ediciones Universidad de Navarra SA), pg 583
Fondo de Cultura Economica de Espana, SL, pg 583
Fundacion de Estudios Libertarios Anselmo Lorenzo, pg 584
Fundacion Marcelino Botin, pg 584
Galaxia SA Editorial, pg 584
Vicent Garcia Editores, SA, pg 584
Generalitat de Catalunya Diari Oficial de la Generalitat vern, pg 584
Editorial Gredos SA, pg 585
Guadalquivir SL Ediciones, pg 586
Publicaciones ICCE, pg 587
Institucion Fernando el Catolico de la Excma Diputacion de Zaragoza, pg 587

1005

Ediciones Istmo SA, pg 588
Joyas Bibliograficas SA, pg 588
Junta de Castilla y Leon Consejeria de Educacion y Cultura, pg 588
Editorial Juventud SA, pg 588
Editorin Laiovento SL, pg 588
Ediciones Libertarias/Prodhufi SA, pg 589
Llibres del Segle, pg 589
Lunwerg Editores, SA, pg 589
Antonio Machado, SA, pg 590
Ediciones Maeva, pg 590
Editorial Mediterrania SL, pg 591
Editorial Moll SL, pg 592
Mundo Negro Editorial, pg 592
Munoz Moya Editor, pg 592
Editorial la Muralla SA, pg 592
Editorial Nerea SL, pg 593
Noguer y Caralt Editores SA, pg 593
Nueva Acropolis, pg 593
Ediciones Oceano Grupo SA, pg 593
Oikos-Tau SA Ediciones, pg 593
Ediciones del Oriente y del Mediterraneo, pg 594
Pages Editors, SL, pg 594
Pais Vasco Servicio Central de Publicaciones, pg 594
Ediciones Palabra SA, pg 595
Parlamento Vasco, pg 595
Pearson Educacion S A, pg 595
Editorial Playor SA, pg 596
Plaza y Janes Editores SA, pg 596
Polifemo, Ediciones, pg 596
Prensas Universitarias de Zaragoza, pg 597
Editorial Presencia Gitana, pg 597
Instituto Provincial de Investigaciones y Estudios Toledanos (IPIET), pg 597
Publicaciones de la Universidad Pontificia Comillas-Madrid, pg 597
Publicaciones y Ediciones Salamandra SA, pg 597
Quaderns Crema SA, pg 597
Editora Regional de Murcia - ERM, pg 597
Ediciones Rialp SA, pg 598
Riquelme y Vargas Ediciones SL, pg 598
Editorial Roasa SL, pg 598
Editorial San Martin, pg 598
Universidad de Santiago de Compostela, pg 599
Servicio de Publicaciones Universidad de Cadiz, pg 599
Siglo XXI de Espana Editores SA, pg 599
Signament I Comunicacio, SL Signament Edicions, pg 599
Ediciones Sigueme SA, pg 600
Silex Ediciones, pg 600
Editorial Sintesis, SA, pg 600
Sirmio, pg 600
Edicions 62, pg 600
Grup 62, pg 600
Anna Soler-Pont Literary Agecy, pg 600
Ramon Sopena SA, pg 600
Axel Springer Publicaciones, pg 601
Stanley Editorial, pg 601
Ediciones Tabapress, SA, pg 601
Editorial Tecnos SA, pg 601
Ediciones Temas de Hoy, SA, pg 601
Editorial Sal Terrae, pg 602
Editorial Thassalia, SA, pg 602
Ediciones de la Torre, pg 602
Trea Ediciones, SL, pg 602
Trotta SA Editorial, pg 602
Turner Publicaciones, pg 602
Tusquets Editores, pg 603
Universidad de Granada, pg 603
Universidad de Malaga, pg 603
Ediciones Universidad de Salamanca, pg 603
Universidad de Valladolid Secretariado de Publicaciones e Intercambio Editorial, pg 604
Publicacions de la Universitat de Barcelona, pg 604
Universitat de Valencia Servei de Publicacions, pg 604
Javier Vergara Editor SA, pg 604
Editorial Vicens-Vives, pg 605
VOSA, SL Ediciones, pg 605
Edicions Xerais de Galicia, pg 605
Xunta de Galicia, pg 605

Sri Lanka

Karunaratne & Sons Ltd, pg 606
KVG de Silva & Sons, pg 606
Lake House Investments Ltd, pg 606
Swarna Hansa Foundation, pg 607

Sudan

Khartoum University Press, pg 608

Suriname

Stichting Wetenschappelijke Informatie, pg 608
Vaco NV Uitgeversmij, pg 608

Sweden

Bokforlaget Atlantis AB, pg 609
Allt om Hobby AB, pg 609
Bokforlaget Axplock, pg 609
Bonnier Carlsen Bokforlag AB, pg 610
Bokforlaget Bra Bocker AB, pg 610
Carlsson Bokfoerlag AB, pg 610
Bokforlaget Cordia AB, pg 610
Fischer & Co, pg 611
Bengt Forsbergs Foerlag AB, pg 611
Gidlunds Bokforlag, pg 612
Liber AB, pg 613
Mezopotamya Publishing & Distribution, pg 613
Bokfoerlaget Natur och Kultur, pg 613
Bokforlaget Nya Doxa AB, pg 614
Ordfront Foerlag AB, pg 614
Bokforlaget Prisma, pg 614
Stroemberg B&T Forlag AB, pg 616
Svenska Foerlaget liv & ledarskap ab, pg 616
Wahlstrom & Widstrand, pg 616
Zindermans AB, pg 617

Switzerland

Ammann Verlag & Co, pg 617
Archivio Storico Ticinese, pg 617
Association Suisse des Editeurs de Langue Francaise, pg 618
Athenaeum Verlag AG, pg 618
Augustin-Verlag, pg 618
Editions de la Baconniere SA, pg 618
H R Balmer AG Verlag, pg 618
Berichthaus Verlag, Dr Conrad Ulrich, pg 619
Bibliographisches Institut & F A Brockhaus AG, pg 619
Cahiers de la Renaissance Vaudoise, pg 620
Edizioni Casagrande SA, pg 620
Christoph Merian Verlag, pg 620
Chronos Verlag, pg 621
Edizioni Armando Dado, Tipografia Stazione, pg 621
Daimon Verlag AG, pg 621
Librairie Droz SA, pg 622
Eboris-Coda-Bompiani, pg 622
Editions Edita, pg 622
Editions Eisele SA, pg 622
Europa Verlag AG, pg 623
Edition Exodus, pg 623
Faksimile Verlag AG, pg 623
Fondation de l'Encyclopedie de Geneve, pg 623
Frobenius AG, pg 623
G+B Arts International, pg 623
Georg Editeur SA, pg 624
Giampiero Casagrande Editore, pg 624
Graduate Institute of International Studies, pg 624
Editions Francois Grounauer, pg 624
Hallwag Kuemmerly & Frey AG, pg 625
Helbing und Lichtenhahn Verlag AG, pg 625
Verlag Huber & Co AG, pg 625
Interfrom AG Editions, pg 625
Junod Nicolas, pg 626
Juris Druck & Verlag AG, pg 626
Editions Ketty & Alexandre, pg 626
Kranich-Verlag, Dres AG & H R Bosch-Gwalter, pg 627
Peter Lang AG, pg 627
Lia rumantscha, pg 627
E Lopfe-Benz AG Rorschach, Graphische Anstalt und Verlag, pg 628
Maihof Verlag, pg 628
Manesse Verlag GmbH, pg 628
Librairie-Editions J Marguerat, pg 628
Les Editions la Matze, pg 628
Peter Meili & Co, Buchhandlung, pg 628
Editions Minkoff, pg 628
Motovun Book GmbH, pg 629
Neptun-Verlag, pg 629
Les Editions Noir sur Blanc, pg 629
Novalis Media AG, pg 630
Orell Fuessli Buchhandlungs AG, pg 630
Ostschweiz Druck und Verlag, pg 630
Editions Payot Lausanne, pg 631
Pedrazzini Tipografia, pg 631
Pendo Verlag GmbH, pg 631
Punktum AG, Buchredaktion und Bildarchiv, pg 632
Verlag Friedrich Reinhardt AG, pg 632
Rodera-Verlag der Cardun AG, pg 632
Rotpunktverlag, pg 632
Sabe AG Verlagsinstitut, pg 633
Scherz Verlag AG, pg 633
Schwabe & Co AG, pg 633
Verlag SOI (Schweizerisches Ost-Institut), pg 634
Theologischer Verlag und Buchhandlungen AG, pg 635
Editions 24 Heures, pg 635
Der Universitatsverlag Freiburg, pg 636
Verlag Die Waage, pg 636
Wyss Verlag AG Bern, pg 637
Editions Zoe, pg 638

Syrian Arab Republic

Damascus University Press, pg 638
Institut Francais d'Etudes Arabes de Damas, pg 638

Taiwan, Province of China

Art Book Co Ltd, pg 638
Asian Culture Co Ltd, pg 638
Cheng Wen Publishing Company, pg 639
Chu Liu Book Company, pg 639
Chung Hwa Book Co Ltd, pg 639
Far East Book Co Ltd, pg 639
Grimm Press Ltd, pg 640
Kuang Fu Book Co Ltd, pg 640
Laureate Book Co Ltd, pg 640
Linking Publishing Company Ltd, pg 641
National Museum of History, pg 641
National Palace Museum, pg 641
Shy Mau & Shy Chaur Publishing Co Ltd, pg 641
Sinorama Magazine Co, pg 641
SMC Publishing Inc, pg 642
World Book Co Ltd, pg 642
Wu Nan Book Co Ltd, pg 642
Yee Wen Publishing Co Ltd, pg 642
Yuan Liou Publishing Co, Ltd, pg 642

United Republic of Tanzania

DUP (1996) Ltd, pg 643
Eastern Africa Publications Ltd, pg 643
Ndanda Mission Press, pg 644
Tanzania Publishing House, pg 644

Thailand

New Generation Publishing Co Ltd, pg 645
Ruamsarn (1977) Co Ltd, pg 645
Sangdad Publishing Company Ltd, pg 645
Thai Watana Panich Co, Ltd, pg 646

Trinidad & Tobago

Joan Bacchus-Xavier, pg 646
Inprint Caribbean Ltd, pg 647

Tunisia

Academie Tunisienne des Sciences, des Lettres et des Arts Beit El Hekma, pg 647
Alyssa Editions, pg 647
Les Editions de l'Arbre, pg 647
Arcs Editions, pg 647
Editions Bouslama, pg 647
Dar Arabia Lil Kitab, pg 648
Faculte des Sciences Humaines et Sociales de Tunis, pg 648
Maison d'Edition Mohamed Ali Hammi, pg 648
Maison Tunisienne de l'Edition, pg 648
Publications de la Fondation Temimi pour la Recherche Scientifique et L'Information, pg 648

Turkey

Altin Kitaplar Yayinevi, pg 649
Arkeoloji Ve Sanat Yayinlari, pg 649
Ataturk Kultur, Dil ve Tarih, Yusek Kurumu Baskanligi, pg 649
Dost Kitabevi Yayinlari, pg 649
Ezel Erverdi (Dergah Yayinlari AS) Muessese Muduru, pg 650
IKI Nokta Research Press & Publications Industry & Trade Ltd, pg 650
Iletisim Yayinlari, pg 650
Isis Yayin Tic ve San Ltd, pg 650

PUBLISHERS — SUBJECT INDEX

Kubbealti Akademisi Kultur ve Sasat Vakfi, pg 650
Payel Yayinevi, pg 651
Remzi Kitabevi, pg 651
Sabah Kitaplari, pg 651
Toker Yayinlari, pg 651
Turkish Republic - Ministry of Culture, pg 652
Kabalci Yayinevi, pg 652

Uganda
Centre for Basic Research, pg 652
Fountain Publishers Ltd, pg 652

Ukraine
Mystetstvo Publishers, pg 653
Naukova Dumka Publishers, pg 653
Osnovy Publishers, pg 654
Osvita, pg 654

United Arab Emirates
Motivate Publishing, pg 654

United Kingdom
Abbotsford Publishing, pg 654
ABC-CLIO, pg 654
Acair Ltd, pg 655
Acumen Publishing Ltd, pg 655
Alun Books, pg 657
Andromeda Oxford Ltd, pg 658
Anvil Books Ltd, pg 658
Appletree Press Ltd, pg 658
Argyll Publishing, pg 659
Arms & Armour Press, pg 659
Arnold, pg 659
Ashgate Publishing Ltd, pg 660
Ashmolean Museum Publications, pg 660
The Athlone Press Ltd, pg 661
Atlantic Transport Publishers, pg 661
Aulis Publishers, pg 661
Avero Publications Ltd, pg 662
The Banton Press, pg 662
Batsford Ltd, pg 663
BBC Worldwide Publishers, pg 663
BCA - Book Club Associates, pg 663
Bellew Publishing Co Ltd, pg 664
Berg Publishers, pg 664
Berghahn Books Ltd, pg 665
Birlinn Ltd, pg 666
Black Ace Books, pg 666
Blackstaff Press, pg 666
Blackwell Publishing Ltd, pg 666
Blandford Publishing Ltd, pg 668
Bloomsbury Publishing PLC, pg 668
Blorenge Books, pg 668
The Book Guild Ltd, pg 668
Book Packaging & Marketing, pg 668
Bookmarks Publications, pg 668
Books International, pg 669
Books of Zimbabwe Publishing Co (Pvt) Ltd, pg 669
Borthwick Institute Publications, pg 669
Bounty Books, pg 669
Boydell & Brewer Ltd, pg 669
Brassey's UK Ltd, pg 670
Breedon Books Publishing Company Ltd, pg 670
Brewin Books Ltd, pg 671
Bridge Books, pg 671
The British Academy, pg 671
British Library Publications, pg 672
The Brown Reference Group PLC, pg 672
Bryntirion Press, pg 672
Cambridge University Press, pg 674
Canongate Books Ltd, pg 674
Carlton Publishing Group, pg 675
Jon Carpenter Publishing, pg 675
Frank Cass Publishers, pg 675
Cassell & Co, pg 675
Kyle Cathie Ltd, pg 676
Causeway Press Ltd, pg 676
Chadwyck-Healey Ltd, pg 677
Chartered Institute of Library & Information Professionals in Scotland, pg 678
James Clarke & Co Ltd, pg 680
Cockbird Press, pg 680
Colourpoint Books, pg 681
Compendium Publishing, pg 681
Constable & Robinson Ltd, pg 682
The Continuum International Publishing Group Ltd, pg 682
Leo Cooper, pg 683
Cottage Publications, pg 683
Countryside Books, pg 683
Countyvise Ltd, pg 683
CTBI Publications, pg 685
James Currey Ltd, pg 685
Darf Publishers Ltd, pg 686
Christopher Davies Publishers Ltd, pg 686
Andre Deutsch Ltd, pg 687
John Donald Publishers Ltd, pg 688
Dorling Kindersley Ltd, pg 688
Dunedin Academic Press, pg 688
Edinburgh University Press Ltd, pg 689
Elm Publications, pg 691
The Erskine Press, pg 692
The Eurospan Group, pg 692
Evans Brothers Ltd, pg 693
Ex Libris Press, pg 693
Faber & Faber Ltd, pg 694
Firebird Books Ltd, pg 695
Flame Tree Publishing, pg 695
Forth Naturalist & Historian, pg 696
Fourth Estate, pg 696
Freedom Press, pg 697
Frontier Publishing Ltd, pg 697
Garnet Publishing Ltd, pg 698
Genesis Publications Ltd, pg 699
E J W Gibb Memorial Trust, pg 700
Glasgow City Libraries Publications, pg 700
Global Oriental Ltd, pg 700
GMP Publishers Ltd, pg 700
Golden Cockerel Press Ltd, pg 701
Gollancz/Witherby, pg 701
Granta Books, pg 702
The Greek Bookshop, pg 702
Greenhill Books/Lionel Leventhal Ltd, pg 703
Gresham Books Ltd, pg 703
Gwasg Gwenffrwd, pg 703
Hakluyt Society, pg 703
Peter Halban Publishers Ltd, pg 703
Robert Hale Ltd, pg 704
Hambledon & London Ltd, pg 704
Hamish Hamilton Ltd, pg 704
Hamlyn, pg 704
HarperCollins UK, pg 705
Harvard University Press, pg 705
The Harvill Press, pg 705
Haynes Publishing, pg 706
Headline Book Publishing Ltd, pg 706
William Heinemann Ltd, pg 707
Helicon Publishing Ltd, pg 707
Helion & Co, pg 707
Helm Information Ltd, pg 707
Hendon Publishing Co Ltd, pg 708
Ian Henry Publications Ltd, pg 708
Heraldry Today, pg 708
Hodder & Stoughton General, pg 709
Honeyglen Publishing Ltd, pg 710
C Hurst & Co (Publishers) Ltd, pg 711
Hutton Press Ltd, pg 711
Icon Press, pg 711
Institute of Irish Studies, The Queens University of Belfast, pg 713
Institution of Electrical Engineers, pg 713
Islamic Foundation Publications, pg 714
The Islamic Texts Society, pg 715
James & James (Publishers) Ltd, pg 715
Jarrold Publishing, pg 716
John Jones Publishing Ltd, pg 716
Michael Joseph Ltd, pg 716
Karnak House, pg 717
Hilda King Educational, pg 717
Ladybird Books Ltd, pg 719
Landy Publishing, pg 719
Lang Syne Publishers Ltd, pg 719
Letterbox Library, pg 720
Libris Ltd, pg 720
Linen Hall Library, pg 721
The Littman Library of Jewish Civilization, pg 721
Liverpool University Press, pg 722
Luath Press Ltd, pg 722
The Lutterworth Press, pg 723
Macmillan Audio Books, pg 723
Macmillan Reference Ltd, pg 724
Mainstream Publishing Co (Edinburgh) Ltd, pg 724
Manchester University Press, pg 724
Maney Publishing, pg 725
The Mansk Svenska Publishing Co Ltd, pg 725
Peter Marcan Publications, pg 725
Marcham Manor Press, pg 725
Marshall Editions Ltd, pg 725
Adam Matthew Publications, pg 726
Willem A Meeuws Publisher, pg 726
The Merlin Press Ltd, pg 727
Methuen, pg 727
Microform Academic Publishers, pg 728
Harvey Miller Publishers, pg 728
E J Morten (Publishers), pg 729
Motilal (UK) Books of India, pg 729
MQ Publications Ltd, pg 729
Murchison's Pantheon Ltd, pg 730
National Archives of Scotland, pg 730
National Library of Scotland, pg 731
National Portrait Gallery Publications, pg 731
National Trust, pg 731
Neil Wilson Publishing Ltd, pg 732
Nelson Thornes Ltd, pg 732
Newpro UK Ltd, pg 733
NMS Enterprises Ltd - Publishing, pg 733
W W Norton & Company Ltd, pg 734
Oakwood Press, pg 734
The Oleander Press, pg 735
Michael O'Mara Books Ltd, pg 735
Oneworld Publications, pg 735
Onlywomen Press Ltd, pg 735
Orion Publishing Group Ltd, pg 736
The Orkney Press Ltd, pg 736
Orpheus Books Ltd, pg 736
Osborne Books Ltd, pg 736
Osprey Publishing Ltd, pg 737
Oxford University Press, pg 737
Palgrave Publishers Ltd, pg 737
Parapress Ltd, pg 738
Paternoster Publishing, pg 738
Pathfinder London, pg 739
Pearson Education, pg 739
Pearson Education Europe, Mideast & Africa, pg 739
Peepal Tree Press Ltd, pg 740
Pen & Sword Books Ltd, pg 740
Phaidon Press Ltd, pg 741
Phillimore & Co Ltd, pg 741
Pickering & Chatto Publishers Ltd, pg 742
Pitkin Unichrome Ltd, pg 743
Pluto Books Ltd, pg 743
Pluto Press, pg 743
Polo Publishing, pg 744
Polybooks Ltd, pg 744
Polygon, pg 744
Porthill Publishers, pg 744
Prim-Ed Publishing UK Ltd, pg 745
Profile Books Ltd, pg 746
Quartet Books Ltd, pg 746
Quentin Books Ltd, pg 747
Quiller Publishing Ltd, pg 747
Quintet Publishing Ltd, pg 747
Ramboro Books Plc, pg 747
Ramsay Head Press, pg 747
Reaktion Books Ltd, pg 748
Rivers Oram Press, pg 750
Roadmaster Publishing, pg 750
Rough Guides Ltd, pg 751
Roundhouse Group, pg 751
Routledge, pg 751
RoutledgeCurzon, pg 751
The Rubicon Press, pg 752
SAGE Publications Ltd, pg 753
Saint Andrew Press, pg 753
Salamander Books Ltd, pg 753
The Salariya Book Co Ltd, pg 753
The Saltire Society, pg 753
Saqi Books, pg 754
SB Publications, pg 754
Scarthin Books, pg 754
School of Oriental & African Studies, pg 755
Scottish Cultural Press, pg 755
Scottish Text Society, pg 755
Seren, pg 756
Serif, pg 756
Shearwater Press Ltd, pg 757
Sheed & Ward UK, pg 757
Sheldrake Press, pg 757
Shelfmark Books, pg 757
Shepheard-Walwyn (Publishers) Ltd, pg 757
Shire Publications Ltd, pg 757
Sidgwick & Jackson Ltd, pg 757
Silver Link Publishing Ltd, pg 758
Charles Skilton Ltd, pg 758
Skoob Russell Square, pg 758
Smith Settle Ltd, pg 758
Souvenir Press Ltd, pg 759
SPA Books Ltd, pg 759
Spellmount Ltd Publishers, pg 760
Stacey International, pg 761
Stenlake Publishing Ltd, pg 761
Supportive Learning Publications, pg 762
Sussex Publications, pg 762
Sutton Publishing Ltd, pg 762
Sydney Jary Ltd, pg 762
I B Tauris & Co Ltd, pg 763
Taylor & Francis, pg 763
Thames & Hudson Ltd, pg 764
Thistle Press, pg 765
Thoemmes Press, pg 765
Thomson Gale, pg 765
Toucan Press, pg 766
Transedition Ltd, pg 766
TSO (The Stationery Office), pg 766
Tuckwell Press Ltd, pg 767
Twelveheads Press, pg 767
Two-Can Publishing Ltd, pg 768
UCL Press Ltd, pg 768
Ulster Historical Foundation, pg 768

University of Exeter Press, pg 768
University of Hertfordshire Press, pg 768
University of Wales Press, pg 769
Vallentine, Mitchell & Co Ltd, pg 769
Verso, pg 770
Viking, pg 770
Virago Press, pg 770
Virgin Publishing Ltd, pg 770
Voltaire Foundation Ltd, pg 771
The Warburg Institute, pg 771
Ward Lock Educational Co Ltd, pg 771
Welsh Academic Press, pg 772
Westview Press, pg 772
Wharncliffe Publishing Ltd, pg 772
White Cockade Publishing, pg 772
Wimbledon Publishing Company Ltd, pg 774
The Windrush Press Ltd, pg 774
Wordsworth Editions Ltd, pg 775
Wordwright Publishing, pg 775
World Microfilms Publications Ltd, pg 775
Yale University Press London, pg 776
Anglia Young Books, pg 776

Uruguay
Editorial Arca SRL, pg 776
Arpoador, pg 777
Ediciones de Juan Darien, pg 777
Fundacion de Cultura Universitaria, pg 777
Linardi y Risso Libreria, pg 777
A Monteverde y Cia SA, pg 777
Luis A Retta Libros, pg 778
Rosebud Ediciones, pg 778
Ediciones Sol del Sur, pg 778
Ediciones Trilce, pg 778

Uzbekistan
Izdatelstvo Uzbekistan, pg 778

Venezuela
Alfadil Ediciones, pg 778
Armitano Editores CA, pg 779
Editorial Ateneo de Caracas, pg 779
Monte Avila Editores Latinoamericana CA, pg 779
Biblioteca Ayacucho, pg 779

Zambia
Apple Books, pg 781
Historical Association of Zambia, pg 781
Zambia Educational Publishing House, pg 782
Zambia Printing Company Ltd (ZPC), pg 782

Zimbabwe
Academic Books (Pvt) Ltd, pg 782
College Press Publishers (Pvt) Ltd, pg 783
The Graham Publishing Company (Pvt) Ltd, pg 783
Longman Zimbabwe (Pvt) Ltd, pg 783
Mambo Press, pg 783
National Archives of Zimbabwe, pg 784
University of Zimbabwe Publications, pg 784
Zimbabwe Publishing House (Pvt) Ltd, pg 784
ZRD Trust, pg 785

HOUSE & HOME

Australia
CHOICE Magazine, pg 17
Simon & Schuster (Australia) Pty Ltd, pg 41
Skills Publishing, pg 41

Belarus
Belaruskaya Encyklapedyya, pg 62

Belgium
Uitgeverij Lannoo NV, pg 69

Brazil
Livraria Nobel S/A, pg 85

Bulgaria
Sluntse Publishing House, pg 97

Chile
Publicaciones Lo Castillo SA, pg 100

China
China Light Industry Press, pg 102
Jilin Science & Technology Publishing House, pg 105

Cuba
Editorial Oriente, pg 120

Estonia
Mats Publishers Ltd, pg 140
Sinisukk, pg 140

Finland
SV-Kauppiaskanava Oy, pg 144

France
Editions Alternatives, pg 146
ATP - Packager, pg 148
Editions Didier Carpentier, pg 152
Editions d'Organisation, pg 160
Editions Filipacchi-Sonodip, pg 163
Flammarion SA, pg 163
Folklore Comtois, pg 164
LT Editions-Jacques Lanore, pg 173
Editions Mango, pg 174
Editions Charles Massin et Cie, pg 174
Editions Norma, pg 177
Nouvelles Editions Francaises, pg 177
Editions Soline, pg 185
Terre Vivante, pg 187
Ulisse Editions, pg 188

Germany
Ars Edition GmbH, pg 194
Eberhard Blottner Verlag GmbH, pg 202
Verlag Georg D W Callwey GmbH & Co, pg 207
Columbus Verlag Paul Oestergaard GmbH, pg 209
Compact Verlag GmbH, pg 209
DuMont monte Verlag GmbH & Co KG, pg 217
Egmont vgs verlagsgesellschaft mbH, pg 218
Franckh-Kosmos Verlags-GmbH & Co, pg 226
Fraunhofer IRB Verlag Fraunhofer Informationszentrum Raum und Bau, pg 226
Mary Hahn's Kochbuchverlag, pg 233
Hammonia-Verlag GmbH Fachverlag der Wohnungswirtschaft, pg 233
Jahreszeiten-Verlag GmbH, pg 242
Landbuch-Verlagsgesellschaft mbH, pg 251
Mosaik Verlag GmbH, pg 262
Naumann & Goebel Verlagsgesellschaft mbH, pg 263
Neumann Verlag, pg 264
Oekobuch Verlag & Versand GmbH, pg 266
Passavia Druckerei GmbH, Verlag, pg 268
Verlag Th Schaefer im Vicentz Verlag KG, pg 278
Dr Wolfgang Schwarze Verlag, pg 282
Verlag Deutsches Volksheimstaettenwerk GmbH, pg 296
Verlagshaus Wohlfarth, pg 301
WRS Verlag Wirtschaft, Recht und Steuern GmbH & Co KG, pg 301

Hong Kong
Press Mark Media Ltd, pg 318

Hungary
Ifjusagi Lap-eskonyvkiado Vallalat, pg 321
Park Konyvkiado Kft (Park Publisher), pg 324

India
Nem Chand & Brothers, pg 343
Pustak Mahal, pg 345

Israel
Classikaletet, pg 366

Italy
Umberto Allemandi & C SRL, pg 375
Di Baio Editore SpA, pg 385
Ernesto Gremese Editore srl, pg 391
Macro Edizioni, pg 397
Giorgio Mondadori & Associati, pg 399
Mundici - Zanetti, pg 400

Jamaica
Association of Development Agencies, pg 413
Jamaica Publishing House Ltd, pg 414

Japan
Daiichi Shuppan Co Ltd, pg 416
Gakken Co Ltd, pg 417
Hikarinokuni Ltd, pg 418
Ie-No-Hikari Association, pg 419
Kodansha Ltd, pg 421
Nagaoka Shoten Co Ltd, pg 423
Sankyo Publishing Company Ltd, pg 426
Seibido Shuppan Company Ltd, pg 426
Shufu-to-Seikatsu Sha Ltd, pg 428
Shufunotomo Co Ltd, pg 428
Tokuma Shoten Publishing Co Ltd, pg 429

Republic of Korea
O Neul Publishing Co, pg 441
Suhagsa, pg 443

Latvia
Avots, pg 444
Preses Nams, pg 445

Lithuania
Sviesa Publishers, pg 449

Mexico
Grupo Editorial Armonia, pg 462
Editorial Limusa SA de CV, pg 467
Ediciones Suromex SA, pg 472
Editorial Trillas SA de CV, pg 472

Netherlands
Uitgeverij Cantecleer BV, pg 480
Gottmer Uitgevers Groep, pg 483

New Zealand
Barkfire Press, pg 494

Nigeria
Daystar Press (Publishers), pg 504

Poland
Muza SA, pg 524

Portugal
Edicoes ELO, pg 531
Latina Livraria Editora, pg 532

Romania
Editura Niculescu, pg 541

Russian Federation
Dom, Izdatel'stvo sovetskogo deskkogo fonda im & I Lenina, pg 544
Panorama Publishing House, pg 547
Permskaja Kniga, pg 548

Slovakia
Priroda Publishing, pg 560

Slovenia
Mladinska Knjiga International, pg 561

South Africa
Human & Rousseau (Pty) Ltd, pg 564

Spain
Editorial Astri SA, pg 573
Libsa Editorial SA, pg 589

Sweden
ICA bokforlag, pg 612
Natur och Kultur Fakta etc, pg 614
Bokforlaget Prisma, pg 614
Bokforlaget Semic AB, pg 615

Tunisia
Les Editions de l'Arbre, pg 647

Turkey
Kok Yayincilik, pg 650

Ukraine
Urozaj, pg 654

United Kingdom
Apple Press, pg 658
Batsford Ltd, pg 663
Mitchell Beazley, pg 664
Cassell & Co, pg 675

PUBLISHERS SUBJECT INDEX

Dorling Kindersley Ltd, pg 688
Elliot Right Way Books, pg 690
Foulsham Publishers, pg 696
HarperCollins UK, pg 705
Haynes Publishing, pg 706
Laurence King Publishing Ltd, pg 717
Frances Lincoln Ltd, pg 720
Kenneth Mason Publications Ltd, pg 726
New Holland Publishers (UK) Ltd, pg 732
Pavilion Books Ltd, pg 739
Quarto Publishing plc, pg 746
Quiller Publishing Ltd, pg 747
Quintet Publishing Ltd, pg 747
The Reader's Digest Association Ltd, pg 748
Ryland Peters & Small Ltd, pg 752
Salamander Books Ltd, pg 753
Sheldrake Press, pg 757
Shire Publications Ltd, pg 757
Sutton Publishing Ltd, pg 762
Ward Lock Ltd, pg 771

HOW-TO

Argentina

Editorial Acme SA, pg 3
Centro Editor de America Latina SA, pg 4
Angel Estrada y Cia SA, pg 5
Editorial Planeta Argentina SAIC, pg 8
Editorial Sopena Argentina SACI e I, pg 9

Australia

Ashling Books, pg 12
Bridge To Peace Publications, pg 16
Crista International, pg 18
Elephas Books Pty Ltd, pg 21
Great Western Press Pty Ltd, pg 24
Kerri Hamer, pg 24
Hospitality Books, pg 26
Hyland House Publishing Pty Ltd, pg 26
Mayne Publishing, pg 31
Palms Press, pg 35
Jurriaan Plesman, pg 37
Press for Success, pg 37
R & R Publications Pty Ltd, pg 38
Simon & Schuster (Australia) Pty Ltd, pg 41
Skills Publishing, pg 41
Tomorrow Publications, pg 44
Vista Publications, pg 45
Wileman Publications, pg 46
Worsley Press, pg 47

Austria

Johannes Heyn GmbH & Co KG, pg 52
Linde Verlag Wien GmbH, pg 53

Brazil

Editora Globo SA, pg 82
Imago Editora Importacao e Exportacao Ltda, pg 84
Editora Marco Zero Ltda, pg 86
Paulus Editora, pg 88
Ediouro Publicacoes, SA, pg 89

Bulgaria

Aratron, IK, pg 93
Kibea Publishing Co, pg 95

Cameroon

Editions CLE, pg 98

China

Beijing Publishing House, pg 101
CITIC Publishing House, pg 103
Fudan University Press, pg 104
Heilongjiang Science & Technology Press, pg 105
Jilin Science & Technology Publishing House, pg 105
Zhejiang University Press, pg 109

Costa Rica

Centro Agronomico Tropical de Investigacion y Ensenanza (CATIE), pg 115

Croatia

Mladost d d Izdavacku graficku i informaticku djelatnost, pg 119
Skolska Knjiga, pg 119

Denmark

Aschehoug Dansk Forlag A/S, pg 129
Borgens Forlag A/S, pg 129
Gyldendalske Boghandel - Nordisk Forlag A/S, pg 131
Nyt Nordisk Forlag Arnold Busck A/S, pg 133
Square Dance Partners Forlag, pg 135

Estonia

Sinisukk, pg 140

Finland

Rakentajain Kustannus Oy (Building Publications Ltd), pg 143
Otava Publishing Co Ltd, pg 143
Soderstroms Forlag, pg 144

France

Adverbum SARL, pg 146
Alsatia SA, pg 146
Editions Alternatives, pg 146
Editions Amrita SA, pg 146
Blay Foldex, pg 150
Blondel La Rougery SARL, pg 150
Editions Bornemann, pg 150
Editions Casterman, pg 152
Chasse Maree, pg 153
Editions Chiron, pg 154
Editions du Dauphin, pg 157
De Vecchi Editions SA, pg 157
Jean-P Delville Editions, pg 157
Dessain et Tolra SA, pg 158
Doin Editeurs, pg 159
Les Dossiers d'Aquitaine, pg 159
Editions Edisud, pg 159
Editions d'Organisation, pg 160
Editions Grund, pg 160
Editions de l'Epargne, pg 161
Editions Fivedit, pg 163
Association Frank, pg 164
Editions Jean Paul Gisserot, pg 165
Editions Jacques Grancher, pg 165
Pierre Horay Editeur, pg 168
Editions du Jaguar, pg 169
Le Jour, Editeur, pg 169
Jouvence Editions, pg 170
Le Livre de Paris, pg 173
LLB France (Ligue pour la Lecture de la Bible), pg 173
Editions Lyonnaises d'Art et d'Histoire, pg 173
Editions Mango, pg 174
Editions Franck Mercier, pg 175
Editions Albin Michel, pg 175
Muller Edition, pg 176
Editions Odile Jacob, pg 177
Le Pre-aux-clercs, pg 180
Les Presses du Management, pg 181
Editions du Puits Fleuri, pg 182
Editions du Rouergue, pg 183
Editions Sand et Tchou SA, pg 184
Editions Sang de la Terre, pg 184
Selection du Reader's Digest SA, pg 184
Editions Selection J Jacobs SA, pg 184
Editions du Seuil, pg 184
Siloe - Kerdore, pg 185
Societe Nouveaux Loisirs, pg 185
Editions Sud Ouest, pg 186
TOP Editions, pg 188
Editions de Vergeures, pg 188

French Polynesia

Scoop/Au Vent des Iles, pg 189

Germany

ALS-Verlag GmbH, pg 192
Bertelsmann Lexikon Verlag GmbH, pg 200
Bielefelder Verlagsanstalt GmbH & Co KG Richard Kaselowsky, pg 201
Verlag Georg D W Callwey GmbH & Co, pg 207
Christophorus-Verlag GmbH, pg 208
Compact Verlag GmbH, pg 209
Verlag Werner Dausien, pg 211
Verlagsgruppe Droemer Knaur GmbH & Co KG, pg 216
DuMont monte Verlag GmbH & Co KG, pg 217
Ehrenwirth Verlag, pg 218
Ehrenwirth Verlag GmbH, pg 218
Engel & Bengel Verlag, pg 220
Englisch Verlag GmbH, pg 220
Falken-Verlag GmbH, pg 223
Rita G Fischer Verlag, pg 225
Verlag Freies Geistesleben, pg 227
Margarethe Freudenberger - selbstverlag fur jedermann, pg 227
Gabal-Verlag GmbH, pg 227
Georgi GmbH, pg 228
Wilhelm Goldmann Verlag GmbH, pg 230
Haag und Herchen Verlag GmbH, pg 232
Wilhelm Heyne Verlag, pg 237
Jahreszeiten-Verlag GmbH, pg 242
Ingrid Klein Verlag GmbH, pg 246
Karl Robert Langewiesche Nachfolger Hans Koester KG, pg 252
Verlag Gerald Leue, pg 254
Gustav Luebbe Verlag, pg 256
Naumann & Goebel Verlagsgesellschaft mbH, pg 263
Verlag Neue Stadt GmbH, pg 264
Neuer Honos Verlag GmbH, pg 264
Paul Pietsch Verlage GmbH & Co, pg 270
Projektion J Buch- und Musikverlag GmbH, pg 272
Propylaeen Verlag, Zweigniederlassung Berlin der Ullstein Buchverlage GmbH, pg 272
Eugen Salzer-Verlag GmbH & Co KG, pg 278
Sportverlag Berlin GmbH SVB, pg 284
J F Steinkopf Verlag GmbH, pg 287
Traditionell Bogenschiessen Verlag Angelika Hornig, pg 292
Verlag Eugen Ulmer GmbH & Co, pg 293
Vier Tuerme GmbH Verlag Klosterbetriebe, pg 295
Wehr & Wissen Verlagsgesellschaft mbH, pg 298
WEKA Firmengruppe GmbH & Co KG, pg 298

Ghana

Adaex Educational Publications Ltd, pg 302
Anowuo Educational Publications, pg 303
World Literature Project, pg 305

Greece

Diavlos, pg 306
Editions Moressopoulos, pg 310

Hong Kong

Breakthrough Ltd - Breakthrough Publishers, pg 315
Commercial Press (Hong Kong) Ltd, pg 316
Electronic Technology Publishing Co Ltd, pg 317
Ling Kee Publishing Group, pg 318
Modern Electronic & Computing Publishing Co Ltd, pg 318
SCMP Book Publishing Ltd, pg 319
Unicorn Books Ltd, pg 320

Hungary

Vince Kiado Kft, pg 322
Novorg International Szervezo es Kiado kft, pg 323

Iceland

Bokautgafan Orn og Orlygur ehf, pg 325
Skjaldborg Ltd, pg 326

India

Atma Ram & Sons, pg 329
Diamond Comics (P) Ltd, pg 333
Full Circle Publishing, pg 334
General Book Depot, pg 335
Hind Pocket Books Private Ltd, pg 336
Orient Paperbacks, pg 344
Rajendra Publishing House Pvt Ltd, pg 346
Sultan Chand & Sons Pvt Ltd, pg 350
Tara Publishing, pg 351
Vision Books Pvt Ltd, pg 352

Indonesia

Gramedia, pg 355
Katalis PT Bina Mitra Plaosan, pg 355

Ireland

The Hannon Press, pg 361
On Stream Publications Ltd, pg 362
Ossian Publications, pg 363

Israel

Bitan Publishers Ltd, pg 365
Boostan Publishing House, pg 365
Classikaletet, pg 366
Dekel Publishing House, pg 366
Gefen Publishing House Ltd, pg 367
Karni Publishers Ltd, pg 369
Keter Publishing House Ltd, pg 369
Massada Press Ltd, pg 370
Massada Publishers Ltd, pg 370
Prolog Publishing House, pg 371
R Sirkis Publishers Ltd, pg 372
Yedioth Ahronoth Books, pg 373

1009

SUBJECT INDEX

Italy
Franco Angeli SRL, pg 375
Gruppo Editoriale Armenia SpA, pg 376
Athesia Verlag Bozen, pg 377
Casa Editrice Libraria Ulrico Hoepli SpA, pg 380
Giovanni De Vecchi Editore SpA, pg 384
Edizioni Futuro SRL, pg 389
Giunti Gruppo Editoriale, pg 390
Ernesto Gremese Editore srl, pg 391
Hermes Edizioni SRL, pg 392
Longanesi & C, pg 396
Macro Edizioni, pg 397
Edizioni Mediterranee SRL, pg 398
Arnoldo Mondadori Editore SpA, pg 398
Newton & Compton Editori, pg 400
Edizioni San Paolo SRL, pg 407
Sperling e Kupfer Editori SpA, pg 409
Sugarco Edizioni SRL, pg 409
TEA Tascabili degli Editori Associati SpA, pg 409
Vinciana Editrice sas, pg 412

Japan
Bijutsu Shuppan-Sha, Ltd, pg 415
Dobunshoin Publishers Co, pg 416
Dohosha Publishing Co Ltd, pg 417
Genko-Sha, pg 417
Hoikusha Publishing Co Ltd, pg 418
Japan Broadcast Publishing Co Ltd, pg 419
Kodansha International Ltd, pg 421
Nagaoka Shoten Co Ltd, pg 423
Seibido Shuppan Company Ltd, pg 426
Shufunotomo Co Ltd, pg 428
Soryusha, pg 428
Tokuma Shoten Publishing Co Ltd, pg 429

Kenya
Action Publishers, pg 433
Space Sellers Ltd, pg 436
Transafrica Press, pg 436
Vipopremo Agencies, pg 436

Republic of Korea
Chung Rim Publishing Co Ltd, pg 438
Gim-Yeong Co, pg 438
Pyeong-hwa Chulpansa, pg 442
Woongjin.com Co Ltd, pg 443

Latvia
Artava Ltd, pg 444
Avots, pg 444

Lebanon
Librairie Orientale sal, pg 446

Lithuania
Tyto Alba Publishers, pg 450

Luxembourg
Guy Binsfeld & Co Sarl, pg 450
Editions Emile Borschette, pg 450

Malaysia
Geetha Publishers Sdn Bhd, pg 456

Mexico
Aconcagua Ediciones y Publicaciones SA, pg 461
Libra Editorial SA de CV, pg 467
Editorial Patria SA de CV, pg 470
Editorial Pax Mexico, pg 470

Monaco
Les Editions du Rocher, pg 474

Morocco
Access International Services, pg 474
Edition Diffusion de Livre au Maroc, pg 474
Editions Oum, pg 475
Editions Services et Informations pour Etudiants, pg 475

Netherlands
Business Contact BV, pg 480
Uitgeverij Christofoor, pg 480
Elmar BV, pg 482
Uitgeverij Ploegsma BV, pg 487
A J G Strengholt's Boeken, Anno 1928, BV, pg 489
Unieboek BV, pg 490

New Caledonia
Savannah Editions SARL, pg 493

New Zealand
Barkfire Press, pg 494
Bush Press Communications Ltd, pg 494
David's Marine Books, pg 495
Learning Guides (Writers & Publishers Ltd), pg 497
Words Work, pg 502

Nigeria
Africana-FEP Publishers Ltd, pg 503
Alliance West African Publishers & Co, pg 503
Aromolaran Publishing Co Ltd, pg 503
Cross Continent Press Ltd, pg 504
Educational Research & Study Group, pg 504
Goldland Business Co Ltd, pg 505
Kola Sanya Publishing Enterprise, pg 505
New Horn Press Ltd, pg 506
Nwamife Publishers Ltd, pg 506
Onibon-Oje Publishers, pg 506
John West Publications Co Ltd, pg 507

Norway
Andresen & Butenschon AS, pg 508
Aschehoug Forlag, pg 508
H Aschehoug & Co (W Nygaard) A/S, pg 508
Gyldendal Norsk Forlag A/S, pg 509
Chr Schibsteds Forlag A/S, pg 510
Teknologisk Forlag, pg 510

Pakistan
Malik Sirajuddin & Sons, pg 513

Peru
Ediciones Brown SA, pg 516

Philippines
Anvil Publishing Inc, pg 518
National Book Store Inc, pg 519
New Day Publishers, pg 520
University of the Philippines Press, pg 521

Poland
Wydawnictwo Baturo, pg 522
Wydawnictwo Podsiedlik-Raniowski i Spolka, pg 525

Portugal
Brasilia Editora (J Carvalho Branco), pg 529
Publicacoes Europa-America Lda, pg 531
Impala, pg 532
Editorial Presenca, pg 535

Puerto Rico
Piedras Press, Inc, pg 537

Romania
Aion Verlag, pg 538
Rentrop & Straton Verlagsgruppe und Wirtschaftsconsulting, pg 542

Russian Federation
Airis Press, pg 543
Dom, Izdatel'stvo sovetskogo deskkogo fonda im & I Lenina, pg 544

Serbia and Montenegro
Alfa-Narodna Knjiga, pg 552
Tehnicka Knjiga, pg 552

Singapore
Aquanut Agencies Pte Ltd, pg 555

Slovakia
Priroda Publishing, pg 560

Slovenia
Cankarjeva Zalozba, pg 561
Mladinska Knjiga International, pg 561

South Africa
Human & Rousseau (Pty) Ltd, pg 564
Kima Global Publishers, pg 566
Southern Book Publishers (Pty) Ltd, pg 569

Spain
Acento Editorial, pg 570
Aguilar SA de Ediciones, pg 571
Editorial Astri SA, pg 573
Iberico Europea de Ediciones SA, pg 586
Ediciones Martinez-Roca SA, pg 591
Ediciones Mensajero, pg 591
Ediciones Norma SA, pg 593
Obelisco Ediciones S, pg 593
Ediciones El Pais SA, pg 594
Editorial Paraninfo SA, pg 595
Parramon Ediciones SA, pg 595
Progensa, pg 597
Editores Tecnicos Asociados SA, pg 601
Ediciones Temas de Hoy, SA, pg 601
Ediciones Urano, SA, pg 604

Sweden
Bokforlaget Axplock, pg 609
ICA bokforlag, pg 612
Informationsfoerlaget AB, pg 612
Johnston & Streiffert Editions, pg 613
Bokforlaget Spektra AB, pg 615
Zindermans AB, pg 617

Switzerland
Ariston Editions, pg 617
Association Suisse des Editeurs de Langue Francaise, pg 618
AT Verlag, pg 618
Brunnen-Verlag Basel, pg 620
Drei-D-World und Foto-World Verlag und Vertrieb, pg 622
Hallwag Kuemmerly & Frey AG, pg 625
Paul Haupt Bern, pg 625
Leonis Verlag, pg 627
Mueller Rueschlikon Verlags AG, pg 629
Orell Fuessli Buchhandlungs AG, pg 630
Verlag Friedrich Reinhardt AG, pg 632

Taiwan, Province of China
Art Book Co Ltd, pg 638
Hilit Publishing Co Ltd, pg 640
Jillion Publishing Co, pg 640
Morning Star Publisher Inc, pg 641
Shy Mau & Shy Chaur Publishing Co Ltd, pg 641
Wei-Chuan Publishing Company Ltd, pg 642
Yuan Liou Publishing Co, Ltd, pg 642

United Republic of Tanzania
East African Publishing House, pg 643

Turkey
Alkim Kitapcilik-Yayimcilik, pg 649
Soez Yayin/Oyunajans, pg 651

United Kingdom
Amber Books Ltd, pg 657
BCA - Book Club Associates, pg 663
Blaketon Hall Ltd, pg 667
Bloomsbury Publishing PLC, pg 668
Carroll & Brown Ltd, pg 675
Cassell & Co, pg 675
Compendium Publishing, pg 681
Computer Step, pg 681
David & Charles Ltd, pg 686
Elliot Right Way Books, pg 690
Faber & Faber Ltd, pg 694
Foulsham Publishers, pg 696
GMC Publications Ltd, pg 700
Green Books Ltd, pg 702
Robert Hale Ltd, pg 704
HarperCollins UK, pg 705
Haynes Publishing, pg 706
How To Books Ltd, pg 710
Hugo's Language Books Ltd, pg 710
Lawpack Publishing Ltd, pg 719
Lorenz Books, pg 722
New Holland Publishers (UK) Ltd, pg 732
Parapress Ltd, pg 738
David Porteous Editions, pg 744
PRC Publishing Ltd, pg 745
Quadrille Publishing Ltd, pg 746
Quarto Publishing plc, pg 746
Quintet Publishing Ltd, pg 747
The Reader's Digest Association Ltd, pg 748
Savitri Books Ltd, pg 754
Search Press Ltd, pg 756
Souvenir Press Ltd, pg 759
Stobart Davies Ltd, pg 761
Telegraph Books, pg 764
Ward Lock Ltd, pg 771

PUBLISHERS   SUBJECT INDEX

Viet Nam
Science & Technics Publishing House, pg 780

HUMAN RELATIONS

Argentina
San Pablo, pg 9

Australia
ACER Press, pg 10
Australian Institute of Family Studies (AIFS), pg 13
Joan Blair, pg 15
Bridge To Peace Publications, pg 16
Crossroad Distributors Pty Ltd, pg 18
Deva Wings Publications, pg 20
Extraordinary People Press, pg 22
Finch Publishing, pg 22
Gnostic Editions, pg 23
Kerri Hamer, pg 24
Hawker Brownlow, pg 25
Jarrah Publications, pg 27
Killara Press, pg 28
Life Planning Foundation of Australia, Inc, pg 29
Little Red Apple Publishing, pg 29
Magabala Books Aboriginal Corporation, pg 30
New Creation Publications Ministries & Resource Centre, pg 33
St Pauls Publications, pg 40
Tertiary Press, pg 43
Thin Rich Press, pg 43
Uniting Education, pg 44
Wileman Publications, pg 46
Windhorse Books, pg 47

Austria
Aarachne Verlag, pg 48
Edition S der OSD, pg 50
Verlag Jungbrunnen - Wiener Spielzeugschachtel GesellschaftmbH, pg 52
Niederosterreichisches Pressehaus Druck- und Verlagsgesellschaft mbH, pg 54

Belgium
Editions De Boeck-Larcier SA, pg 66
Marabout, pg 71
Mardaga, Pierre, Editeur, pg 71

Brazil
Artes e Oficios Editora Ltda, pg 78
Editora Crescer Ltda, pg 80
Editora Elevacao, pg 81
Editora Lidador Ltda, pg 85
Editora Mercuryo Ltda, pg 86
Editora Objetiva Ltda, pg 87
Edit Palavra Magica, pg 88
Pallas Editora e Distribuidora Ltda, pg 88
Paulinas Editorial, pg 88
Editora Perspectiva, pg 88
Summus Editorial Ltda, pg 91
Thex Editora e Distribuidora Ltda, pg 91
Editora Universidade de Brasilia, pg 91
Jorge Zahar Editor, pg 92

Bulgaria
Interpres, pg 95
Kibea Publishing Co, pg 95
Nov Covek Publishing House, pg 96

Sita-MB, pg 97
Sluntse Publishing House, pg 97

Chile
Edeval (Universidad de Valparaiso), pg 99
Editora Nueva Generacion, pg 100
Editorial Texido Ltda, pg 100

China
Beijing Publishing House, pg 101
China Materials Management Publishing House, pg 102
Education Science Publishing House, pg 104
Fudan University Press, pg 104
Guizhou Education Publishing House, pg 105
Knowledge Press, pg 106
Shandong University Press, pg 108

Costa Rica
Ediciones Promesa, pg 116

Cote d'Ivoire
Akohi Editions, pg 117

Croatia
Znaci Vremena, Institut Za Istrazivanje Biblije, pg 119

Cuba
Editora Politica, pg 120

Czech Republic
Luxpress VOS, pg 125
Portal spol sro, pg 126

Denmark
Borgens Forlag A/S, pg 129
C A Reitzel Boghandel & Forlag A/S, pg 134

Egypt (Arab Republic of Egypt)
Al Ahram Establishment, pg 137

Estonia
Kupar Publishers, pg 139
Tuum, pg 140

Finland
Karas-Sana Oy, pg 142
Lasten Keskus Oy, pg 143

France
Editions d'Aujourd'hui (Les Introuvables), pg 148
Beauchesne Editeur, pg 149
Bottin SA, pg 151
Alain Brethes Editions, pg 151
Chronique Sociale, pg 154
Editions de Compostelle, pg 155
Culture et Bibliotheque pour Tous, pg 156
Dervy Editions, pg 158
Editions Entente, pg 161
FBT de R Editions, pg 163
Editions du Jaguar, pg 169
Jouvence Editions, pg 170
Editions des Limbes d'Or FBT de R Editions, pg 172
Matrice, pg 174
Maxima Laurent du Mesnil Editeur, pg 174
Le Pre-aux-clercs, pg 180
Presses Universitaires de France (PUF), pg 181

Presses Universitaires de Lyon, pg 181
Editions Salvator Sarl, pg 183
Editeurs Tacor International, pg 186
UNESCO Publishing, pg 188
Editions Village Mondial, pg 189

Germany
Blaukreuz-Verlag Wuppertal, pg 202
Brandes & Apsel Verlag GmbH, pg 204
Carl-Auer-Systeme Verlag, pg 207
Catia Monser Eggcup-Verlag, pg 207
Connection Medien GmbH, pg 209
J G Cotta'sche Buchhandlung Nachfolger GmbH, pg 210
Maximilian Dietrich Verlag, pg 214
Dreisam Ratgeber in der Rutsker Verlag GmbH, pg 216
Eironeia-Verlag, pg 219
Engel & Bengel Verlag, pg 220
Extent Verlag und Service Wolfgang M Flamm, pg 223
Flensburger Hefte Verlag GmbH, pg 225
Margarethe Freudenberger - selbstverlag fur jedermann, pg 227
Gatzanis Verlags GmbH, pg 228
Genius Verlag, pg 228
Verlag der Stiftung Gralsbotschaft GmbH, pg 231
Gruner + Jahr AG & Co, pg 231
Dr Curt Haefner-Verlag GmbH, pg 233
Heinz-Theo Gremme Verlag, pg 236
Verlag Peter Hoell, pg 238
Heinrich Hugendubel Verlag GmbH, pg 240
Edition Humanistische Psychologie (EHP), pg 240
Verlag Kleine Schritte Ursula Dahm & Co, pg 246
Kleiner Bachmann Verlag fur Kinder und Umwelt, pg 246
Krug & Schadenberg, pg 250
Leibniz Verlag, pg 253
Dr Gisela Lermann, pg 253
Logophon Verlag und Bildungsreisen GmbH, pg 255
Otto Meissner Verlag, pg 259
Midena-Verlag, pg 260
Mosaik Verlag GmbH, pg 262
Verlag Neues Leben GmbH, pg 264
Oekotopia Verlag, Wolfgang Hoffmann GmbH & Co KG, pg 266
Osho Verlag GmbH, pg 267
PapyRossa Verlags GmbH & Co Kommanditgesellschaft KG, pg 268
Projektion J Buch- und Musikverlag GmbH, pg 272
Verlag an der Ruhr GmbH, pg 277
Suin Buch-Verlag, pg 289
Guenter Albert Ulmer Verlag, pg 293
VAS-Verlag fuer Akademische Schriften, pg 294
Verlag DAS WORT GmbH, pg 301
Zeitgeist Media GmbH, pg 302

Ghana
World Literature Project, pg 305

Greece
Akritas, pg 305
Elliniki Leschi Tou Vivliou, pg 307
Hestia-I D Hestia-Kollaros & Co Corporation, pg 308

Odysseas Publications Ltd, pg 311
Thymari Publications, pg 312

Holy See (Vatican City State)
Scuola Vaticana Paleografia - Scuola Vaticana di Paleografia Diplomatica e Archivistica, pg 315

Hong Kong
Breakthrough Ltd - Breakthrough Publishers, pg 315

Hungary
Marton Aron Kiado Publishing House, pg 323

India
Abhinav Publications, pg 326
The Academic Press, pg 327
Arihant Publishers, pg 328
Bihar Hindi Granth Akademi, pg 330
Chanakya Publications, pg 331
Chugh Publications, pg 332
Ess Ess Publications, pg 334
Firma KLM Privatee Ltd, Publishers & International Booksellers, pg 334
Gitanjali Publishing House, pg 335
Gyan Publishing House, pg 335
Islamic Publishing House, pg 338
Konark Publishers Pvt Ltd, pg 339
Lokvangmaya Griha Pvt Ltd, pg 340
National Book Organization, pg 342
National Book Trust India, pg 342
National Publishing House, pg 343
Parimal Prakashan, pg 345
Rajasthan Hindi Granth Academy, pg 346
Rajpal & Sons, pg 346
Reliance Publishing House, pg 346
Scientific Book Agency, pg 348
Sultan Chand & Sons Pvt Ltd, pg 350
Theosophical Publishing House, pg 351

Indonesia
Advent Indonesia Publishing, pg 353
Nusa Indah, pg 356

Ireland
The Collins Press, pg 358

Israel
Bitan Publishers Ltd, pg 365
Hakibbutz Hameuchad Publishing House Ltd, pg 367
Urim Publications, pg 373

Italy
Gruppo Abele, pg 374
Adea Edizioni, pg 374
Belforte Editore Libraio srl, pg 377
Centro Scientifico Torinese, pg 381
CLUEB (Cooperativa Libraria Universitaria Editrice Bologna), pg 382
CLUT Editrice, pg 383
Edizioni Cultura della Pace, pg 383
Effata Editrice, pg 387
Piero Gribaudi Editore, pg 391
In Dialogo, pg 393
Editoriale Jaca Book SpA, pg 394
Il Lavoro Editoriale, pg 395

1011

Milella di Lecce Spazio Vivo srl, pg 398
Moretti & Vitali Editori srl, pg 399
Piero Manni srl, pg 403
Edizioni Universitarie Romane, pg 406
Edizioni Librarie Siciliane, pg 408
Editrice Uomini Nuovi, pg 411

Jamaica

Carlong Publishers (Caribbean) Ltd, pg 413

Japan

Chikuma Shobo Publishing Co Ltd, pg 416
Kosei Publishing Co Ltd, pg 421
Mirai-Sha, pg 422
Misuzu Shobo Ltd, pg 422
Nikkagiren Shuppan-Sha (JUSE Press Ltd), pg 424
Zeimukeiri-Kyokai, pg 431

Republic of Korea

Chung Rim Publishing Co Ltd, pg 438
Ewha Womans University Press, pg 438
St Pauls, pg 442

Latvia

Nordik/Tapals Publishers Ltd, pg 445
Preses Nams, pg 445

Lithuania

Dargenis Publishers, pg 449
Tyto Alba Publishers, pg 450

The Former Yugoslav Republic of Macedonia

Zumpres Publishing Firm, pg 453

Martinique

George Lise-Huyghes des Etages, pg 460

Mexico

Del Verbo Emprender SA de CV, pg 464
Editorial Diana SA de CV, pg 464
Ediciones Exclusivas SA, pg 465
Editorial Limusa SA de CV, pg 467
Panorama Editorial, SA, pg 470
Ediciones Promesa, SA de CV, pg 470
Selector SA de CV, pg 471

Republic of Moldova

Editura Cartea Moldovei, pg 473

Morocco

Access International Services, pg 474
Societe Ennewrasse Service Librairie et Imprimerie, pg 475

Nepal

International Standards Books & Periodicals (P) Ltd, pg 476

Netherlands

APA (Academic Publishers Associated), pg 477
Uitgeverij Bohn Stafleu Van Loghum BV, pg 479
Buijten en Schipperheijn BV Drukkerij en Uitgeversmaatschappij, pg 480
Uitgeverij Coutinho BV, pg 481
Holland University Press BV (APA), pg 483
Philo Press (APA), pg 487
Rodopi, pg 488
Servire BV Uitgevers, pg 489
Telos Boeken, pg 490
Uitgeverij De Toorts, pg 490
Unieboek BV, pg 490

New Zealand

Moss Associates Ltd, pg 498
Nagare Press, pg 499

Nigeria

New Africa Publishing Company Ltd, pg 505
University of Lagos Press, pg 507
West African Book Publishers Ltd, pg 507

Norway

Ex Libris Forlag A/S, pg 509
Genesis Forlag, pg 509
Hilt & Hansteen A/S, pg 509

Peru

Tassorello, SA, pg 517

Philippines

New Day Publishers, pg 520
Rex Bookstores & Publishers, pg 520
Salesiana Publishers Inc, pg 521

Poland

Wydawnictwo Lodzkie, pg 524
Wydawnictwo Lubelskie, pg 524
Wydawnictwo SIC, pg 526
Wydawnictwo WAB, pg 527

Portugal

Gradiva-Publicacnoes Lda, pg 532
Editora McGraw-Hill de Portugal Lda, pg 533
Monitor-Projectos e Edicoes, LDA, pg 533
Paulinas, pg 534
Editorial Presenca, pg 535

Romania

Aion Verlag, pg 538
Editura Excelsior Art, pg 539

Russian Federation

Izdatel'stovo Dal'nevostonogo Gosudarstvennogo Universite, pg 544
Finansy i Statistika Publishing House, pg 544
Kavkazskaya Biblioteka Publishing House, pg 545

Serbia and Montenegro

Izdavacko Preduzece Matice Srpske, pg 553
Prosveta, pg 553

Singapore

Aquanut Agencies Pte Ltd, pg 555

Slovakia

Sofa, pg 560

South Africa

Centre for Conflict Resolution, pg 563
Human Sciences Research Council, pg 565
Kima Global Publishers, pg 566
Queillerie Publishers, pg 568
South African Institute of Race Relations, pg 569

Spain

Editorial AEDOS SA, pg 571
Editorial Barath SA, pg 574
Calamo Editorial, pg 575
Ediciones Catedra SA, pg 576
Fundacion Marcelino Botin, pg 584
Editorial Gedisa SA, pg 584
Ediciones Gestio 2000 SA, pg 585
Grijalbo Mondadori SA, pg 585
Editorial Gulaab, pg 586
Idea Books, SA, pg 587
Ediciones Medici SA, pg 591
Ediciones Morata SL, pg 592
Obelisco Ediciones S, pg 593
Ediciones ROL SA, pg 598
Ediciones de la Torre, pg 602

Sri Lanka

National Library & Documentation Centre, pg 607

Sweden

Akademiforlaget Goteborgslitteratur, pg 609
Bokforlaget Cordia AB, pg 610
Egmont Serieforlaget, pg 611
Svenska Foerlaget liv & ledarskap ab, pg 616

Switzerland

Bergli Books AG, pg 619
CEC-Cosmic Energy Connections, pg 620
Verlag Industrielle Organisation, pg 625
La Maison de la Bible, pg 628
Editions Du Signal Rene Gaillard, pg 634
Versus Verlag AG, pg 636
Editions Vivez Soleil SA, pg 636

Taiwan, Province of China

Campus Evangelical Fellowship, Literature Department, pg 639
Chu Liu Book Company, pg 639
Linking Publishing Company Ltd, pg 641
Morning Star Publisher Inc, pg 641

Thailand

Unesco Regional Office, Asia & the Pacific, pg 646

Turkey

Kok Yayincilik, pg 650

United Kingdom

Act 3 Publishing, pg 655
Andromeda Oxford Ltd, pg 658
Arnold, pg 659
Baha'i Publishing Trust, pg 662
The British Council, Design, Publishing & Print Department, pg 671
Chartered Institute of Personnel & Development, pg 678
Commission for Racial Equality, pg 681
Emerald, pg 691
The Eurospan Group, pg 692
Helen Exley Giftbooks, pg 693
Forbes Publications Ltd, pg 696
Free Association Books Ltd, pg 697
George Mann Publications, pg 699
HarperCollins UK, pg 705
Hodder & Stoughton Religious, pg 709
Holyoake Books, pg 710
Lawrence & Wishart, pg 719
Letterbox Library, pg 720
Macmillan Reference Ltd, pg 724
Palgrave Publishers Ltd, pg 737
RELATE, pg 749
Rosendale Press Ltd, pg 751
SAGE Publications Ltd, pg 753
St Pauls Publishing, pg 753
Sherwood Publishing, pg 757
The Society of Metaphysicians Ltd, pg 759
Sutton Publishing Ltd, pg 762
Taylor & Francis, pg 763
TFPL, pg 764
UCL Press Ltd, pg 768

Uruguay

Instituto del Tercer Mundo, pg 777

Zambia

Wilfred Bwalya Chilangwa Publications, pg 781
M & M Management & Labour Consultants Ltd, pg 781

Zimbabwe

Zimbabwe Women's Bureau, pg 785

HUMOR

Albania

NL SH, pg 1

Argentina

Beas Ediciones SRL, pg 4
Ediciones de la Flor SRL, pg 6
Editorial Galerna SRL, pg 6

Armenia

Arevik, pg 10

Australia

Aussies Afire Publishing, pg 12
Cole Publications, pg 18
Dynamo House P/L, pg 20
Emperor Publishing, pg 21
Fernfawn Publications, pg 22
Hartys Creek Press, pg 25
Little Red Apple Publishing, pg 29
New Endeavour Press, pg 33
Orin Books, pg 34
Palms Press, pg 35
Pan Macmillan Australia Pty Ltd, pg 35
Penguin Group (Australia), pg 36
Plantagenet Press, pg 37
Playlab Press, pg 37
The Text Publishing Company Pty Ltd, pg 43
Thin Rich Press, pg 43
Transworld Publishers Pty Ltd, pg 44
The Watermark Press, pg 46

Austria

Astor-Verlag, Willibald Schlager, pg 48
Verlag Lynkeus/H Hakel Gesellschaft, pg 51

PUBLISHERS SUBJECT INDEX

Merbod Verlag, pg 54
Niederosterreichisches Pressehaus Druck- und Verlagsgesellschaft mbH, pg 54

Azerbaijan

Sada, Literaturno-Izdatel'skij Centr, pg 60

Bangladesh

Gatidhara, pg 61

Belgium

Editions Dupuis SA, pg 66
Glenat Benelux SA, pg 67
Helyode Editions (SA-ADN), pg 68
Claude Lefrancq Editeur, pg 70
Les Editions du Lombard SA, pg 70
Marabout, pg 71
Standaard Uitgeverij, pg 73
Zuid-Nederlandse Uitgeverij NV/Central Uitgeverij, pg 75

Brazil

Artes e Oficios Editora Ltda, pg 78
Editora Companhia das Letras/ Editora Schwarcz Ltda, pg 80
Fundacao Sao Paulo, EDUC, pg 82
Editora Globo SA, pg 82
Editora Objetiva Ltda, pg 87
Editora Primor Ltda, pg 89

Bulgaria

Interpres, pg 95
Izdatelstvo Lettera, pg 95
Pejo K Javorov Publishing House, pg 95
Trud - Izd kasta, pg 97
Ivan Vazov Publishing House, pg 97
Zunica, pg 97

Chile

Editora Nueva Generacion, pg 100

China

Fujian Children's Publishing House, pg 104
Shanghai Far East Publishers, pg 108

Colombia

El Ancora Editores, pg 111
Editorial Oveja Negra Ltda, pg 112

Cuba

Casa Editora Abril, pg 120

Czech Republic

Aurora, pg 122
Doplnek, pg 123
Nakladatelstvi Jan Vasut, pg 124
Knihovna A Tiskarna Pro Nevidome, pg 124
Konsultace spol sro, pg 125
Josef Lukasik A Spol sro, pg 125
Nase vojsko, nakladatelstvi a knizni obchod, pg 126
Nava, pg 126

Denmark

Bogan's Forlag, pg 129
Borgens Forlag A/S, pg 129
Forlaget Carlsen A/S, pg 130
Forlaget Forum, pg 131
P Haase & Sons Forlag A/S, pg 131
Forlaget Hovedland, pg 132
Interpresse A/S, pg 132

Det Schonbergske Forlag A/S, pg 134
Strandbergs Forlag, pg 135
Wisby & Wilkens, pg 135

France

Actes-Graphiques, pg 145
L'Amitie par le Livre, pg 146
Editions Balland, pg 149
Bragelonne, pg 151
Editions Calmann-Levy SA, pg 152
Editions Canal, pg 152
Philippe Chancerel Editeur, pg 153
Le Cherche Midi Editeur, pg 154
Editions Circonflexe, pg 154
Corsaire Editions, pg 156
Dargaud, pg 157
Editions J Dupuis, pg 159
Editions First, pg 163
Editions Jean Paul Gisserot, pg 165
Editions Glenat, pg 165
Editions Jacques Grancher, pg 165
Editions Hoebeke, pg 168
Editions Infrarouge, pg 168
Editions Dominique Leroy, pg 171
Editions Albin Michel, pg 175
Editions Omnibus, pg 177
Payot & Rivages, pg 179
Les Editions Albert Rene, pg 183
Editions Rombaldi SA, pg 183
Editions de Septembre, pg 184
Association d'Editions Sorg, pg 186
Editions Tarmeye, pg 187
La Vague a l'ame, pg 188
Les Editions Vaillant-Miroir-Sprint Publications, pg 188
Vents d'Ouest, pg 188

Germany

Achterbahn AG Buch, pg 190
Aufstieg-Verlag GmbH, pg 195
Dr Wolfgang Baur Verlag Kunst & Alltag, pg 198
Beerenverlag, pg 198
Verlag Beruf und Schule Belz KG, pg 200
F Bruckmann Munchen Verlag & Druck GmbH & Co Produkt KG, pg 204
Carlsen Verlag GmbH, pg 207
Claudius Verlag, pg 209
Deutscher Taschenbuch Verlag GmbH & Co KG (dtv), pg 213
Verlagsgruppe Droemer Knaur GmbH & Co KG, pg 216
Droste Verlag GmbH, pg 216
Egmont EHAPA Verlag GmbH, pg 218
Eichborn AG, pg 219
EinfallsReich Verlagsgesellschaft MbH, pg 219
Espresso Verlag GmbH, pg 221
Fackeltrager-Verlag GmbH, pg 223
Falken-Verlag GmbH, pg 223
Forum Verlag Leipzig Buch- Gesellschaft mbH, pg 225
Margarethe Freudenberger - selbstverlag fur jedermann, pg 227
Gatzanis Verlags GmbH, pg 228
Heel Verlag GmbH, pg 235
Wilhelm Heyne Verlag, pg 237
Krueger Verlag GmbH, pg 250
Verlag Antje Kunstmann GmbH, pg 251
Landbuch-Verlagsgesellschaft mbH, pg 251
Verlag Gerald Leue, pg 254
C W Niemeyer Buchverlage GmbH, pg 265

Oekotopia Verlag, Wolfgang Hoffman GmbH & Co KG, pg 266
Passavia Druckerei GmbH, Verlag, pg 268
Verlag Walter Podszun Burobedarf- Bucher Abt, pg 270
Pollner Verlag, pg 271
Propylaeen Verlag, Zweigniederlassung Berlin der Ullstein Buchverlage GmbH, pg 272
Rake Verlag GmbH, pg 273
Gerhard Rautenberg Druckerei und Verlag GmbH & Co KG, pg 273
Theodor Schuster, pg 282
Suedverlag GmbH, pg 288
Otto Teich, pg 289
Tomus Verlag GmbH, pg 291
Verein der Benediktiner zu Beuron- Beuroner Kunstverlag, pg 294
Ellen Vogt Garbe Verlag, pg 296
Verlag W Weinmann, pg 298
Zeitgeist Media GmbH, pg 302

Ghana

Kwamfori Publishing Enterprise, pg 304
World Literature Project, pg 305

Greece

Diavlos, pg 306
Kastaniotis Editions SA, pg 309
Kedros Publishers, pg 309
Mamuth Comix EPE, pg 310

Hong Kong

Breakthrough Ltd - Breakthrough Publishers, pg 315

Hungary

Aranyhal Konyvkiado Goldfish Publishing, pg 320
Officina Nova Konyvek, pg 323

Iceland

Skjaldborg Ltd, pg 326

India

Full Circle Publishing, pg 334
Jaico Publishing House, pg 338
Kairalee Mudralayam, pg 339
Omsons Publications, pg 344
Orient Paperbacks, pg 344
Prabhat Prakashan, pg 345
Pratibha Pratishthan, pg 345
Reliance Publishing House, pg 346
Sat Sahitya Prakashan, pg 348
Scientific Book Agency, pg 348
Vision Books Pvt Ltd, pg 352

Indonesia

Karya Anda, CV, pg 355
Pustaka Utama Grafiti, PT, pg 356

Ireland

Attic Press Ltd, pg 358
Mercier Press Ltd, pg 362
The O'Brien Press Ltd, pg 362

Israel

Classikaletet, pg 366
Dalia Peled Publishers, Division of Modan, pg 366
DAT Publications, pg 366
Kivunim-Arsan Publishing House, pg 369
Pitspopany Press, pg 371
Saar Publishing House, pg 371

Italy

L'Airone Editrice, pg 375
Gruppo Editoriale Armenia SpA, pg 376
Athesia Verlag Bozen, pg 377
Colonnese Editore, pg 383
Giovanni De Vecchi Editore SpA, pg 384
Piero Gribaudi Editore, pg 391
Lalli Editore SRL, pg 394
Mundici - Zanetti, pg 400
Edition Raetia Srl-GmbH, pg 405
TEA Tascabili degli Editori Associati SpA, pg 409

Japan

Bunkasha Publishing Co Ltd, pg 415
Kodansha Ltd, pg 421

Kenya

Kenway Publications Ltd, pg 434
Sasa Sema Publications Ltd, pg 435

Republic of Korea

Chung Rim Publishing Co Ltd, pg 438

Latvia

Preses Nams, pg 445

Lithuania

AS Narbuto Leidykla (AS Narbutas' Publishers), pg 448

Luxembourg

Editions Emile Borschette, pg 450
Hubsch, pg 451
Editions Tousch, pg 452

Mexico

Ediciones Alpe, pg 462
Editores Asociados Mexicanos SA de CV (EDAMEX), pg 462
Editorial Extemporaneos SA, pg 465
Libra Editorial SA de CV, pg 467
Editorial Nueva Imagen SA, pg 469
Panorama Editorial, SA, pg 470
Selector SA de CV, pg 471

Monaco

Les Editions du Rocher, pg 474
Rondeau Giannipiero a Monaco, pg 474

Morocco

Edition Diffusion de Livre au Maroc, pg 474

Netherlands

BZZTOH Publishers, pg 480
Elmar BV, pg 482
Uitgeverij De Fontein BV, pg 482
De Harmonie Uitgeverij, pg 483
Kartoen, pg 484
Mondria Publishers, pg 486
Uitgeverij Maarten Muntinga, pg 486
Nijgh & Van Ditmar Amsterdam, pg 487
Tirion Uitgevers BV, pg 490

New Zealand

HarperCollins Publishers (New Zealand) Ltd, pg 497
Hazard Press Ltd, pg 497

1013

SUBJECT INDEX

BOOK

Hodder Moa Beckett Publishers Ltd, pg 497
Magari Publishing, pg 498
Saint Publishing, pg 501

Nigeria
New Africa Publishing Company Ltd, pg 505
Joe-Tolalu & Associates, pg 507

Norway
Det Norske Samlaget, pg 508
Ex Libris Forlag A/S, pg 509
Fono Forlag, pg 509

Pakistan
Jang Publishers, pg 513
Maqbool Academy, pg 513

Philippines
Anvil Publishing Inc, pg 518
Sonny A Mendoza, pg 519
New Day Publishers, pg 520
Our Lady of Manaoag Publisher, pg 520

Portugal
Europress Editores e Distribuidores de Publicacoes Lda, pg 531
Editorial Futura, pg 531
Gradiva-Publicacnoes Lda, pg 532
Impala, pg 532
Meriberica/Liber, pg 533
Editora Replicacao Lda, pg 535
Edicoes Salesianas, pg 535
Vega-Publicacao e Distribuicao de Livros e Revistas, Lda, pg 536

Romania
Editura Clusium, pg 539
Editura Excelsior Art, pg 539
Editura Niculescu, pg 541
Pandora Publishing House, pg 541

Saudi Arabia
Dar Al-Shareff for Publishing & Distribution, pg 550

Singapore
Aquanut Agencies Pte Ltd, pg 555
Asiapac Books Pte Ltd, pg 555

Slovakia
Egmont Neografia spol sro, pg 559

South Africa
Media House Publications, pg 566
New Africa Books (Pty) Ltd, pg 567
Struik Publishers (Pty) Ltd, pg 569

Spain
Aguilar SA de Ediciones, pg 571
Ediciones B, SA, pg 574
Calambur Editorial, SL, pg 575
Editorial Cantabrica SA, pg 575
Casset Ediciones SL, pg 576
Ediciones la Cupula SL, pg 578
Edicomunicacion SA, pg 581
Ediciones Elfos SL, pg 582
Grijalbo Mondadon SA Junior, pg 585
Grijalbo Mondadori SA, pg 585
Ediciones Irusa, pg 588
Editorial Lumen SA, pg 589
Pirene Editorial, sal, pg 596
Editorial Presencia Gitana, pg 597
Ediciones Siruela SA, pg 600
Ediciones SM, pg 600
Ediciones Temas de Hoy, SA, pg 601
Ediciones Tutor SA, pg 603

Sweden
Bokforlaget Axplock, pg 609
Bokforlaget Fingraf AB, pg 611
Bokforlaget Opal AB, pg 614
Semic Bokforlaget International AB, pg 615

Switzerland
Werner Classen Verlag, pg 621
Edition Hans Erpf Edition, pg 623
Globi Verlag AG, pg 624
Haffmans Verlag AG, pg 624
Junod Nicolas, pg 626
E Lopfe-Benz AG Rorschach, Graphische Anstalt und Verlag, pg 628
Nebelspalter-Verlag, pg 629
Les Editions Noir sur Blanc, pg 629
Edition Olms AG, pg 630
Rhein-Trio, Edition/Editions du Fou, pg 632
Satyr-Verlag Dr Humbel, pg 633
Viktoria-Verlag Peter Marti, pg 636

Taiwan, Province of China
Grimm Press Ltd, pg 640

Tunisia
Les Editions de l'Arbre, pg 647

Turkey
Dost Yayinlari, pg 650
Inkilap Publishers Ltd, pg 650
Parantez Yayinlari Ltd, pg 651

Uganda
Fountain Publishers Ltd, pg 652

United Kingdom
Act 3 Publishing, pg 655
BCA - Book Club Associates, pg 663
Blackstaff Press, pg 666
Bloomsbury Publishing PLC, pg 668
Boxtree Ltd, pg 669
Carlton Publishing Group, pg 675
Cassell & Co, pg 675
Constable & Robinson Ltd, pg 682
Defiant Publications, pg 687
Delancey Press Ltd, pg 687
Andre Deutsch Ltd, pg 687
Elliot Right Way Books, pg 690
Helen Exley Giftbooks, pg 693
Express Newspapers, pg 693
Foulsham Publishers, pg 696
Fourth Estate, pg 696
Hawk Books, pg 706
Hodder & Stoughton General, pg 709
Hodder & Stoughton Religious, pg 709
Icon Press, pg 711
Knockabout Comics, pg 718
Jay Landesman, pg 719
Lang Syne Publishers Ltd, pg 719
Methuen, pg 727
Monarch Books, pg 729
Neil Wilson Publishing Ltd, pg 732
Michael O'Mara Books Ltd, pg 735
Parapress Ltd, pg 738
Piatkus Books, pg 741
Piccadilly Press, pg 742
Polygon, pg 744
Quiller Publishing Ltd, pg 747
Random House UK Ltd, pg 747
Ravette Publishing Ltd, pg 748
Robson Books, pg 750
Sainsbury Publishing Ltd, pg 753
St Pauls Publishing, pg 753
Saqi Books, pg 754
Steve Savage Publishers Ltd, pg 754
SAWD Publications, pg 754
Silver Link Publishing Ltd, pg 758
Smith Settle Ltd, pg 758
The Sportsman's Press, pg 760
Supportive Learning Publications, pg 762
Telegraph Books, pg 764
Transworld Publishers Ltd, pg 766
Trentham Books Ltd, pg 767
Verulam Publishing Ltd, pg 770
Virgin Publishing Ltd, pg 770
Wimbledon Publishing Company Ltd, pg 774
The Windrush Press Ltd, pg 774
Wordwright Publishing, pg 775

Uruguay
Editorial Arca SRL, pg 776
Rosebud Ediciones, pg 778
Ediciones Trilce, pg 778

Zambia
Apple Books, pg 781

JOURNALISM

Argentina
Editorial Abaco de Rodolfo Depalma SRL, pg 2
Diana Argentina SA, Editorial, pg 5
Ediciones Don Bosco Argentina, pg 5

Australia
McGraw-Hill Australia Pty Ltd, pg 31
New Endeavour Press, pg 33
Pearson Education Australia, pg 36
Plantagenet Press, pg 37

Austria
Aarachne Verlag, pg 48
Buchkultur Verlags GmbH Zeitschrift fuer Literatur & Kunst, pg 49
Development News Ltd, pg 50
Doecker Verlag GmbH & Co KG, pg 50
Verlag Lafite, pg 53
Medien & Recht, pg 54
Studien Verlag Gmbh, pg 58
Verlag Styria, pg 58

Bangladesh
Agamee Prakashani, pg 61

Belgium
Academia-Bruylant, pg 62
Academia Press, pg 62
EPO Publishers, Printers, Booksellers, pg 67
Graton Editeur NV, pg 68
Koepel van de Vlaamse Noord - Zuidbeweging 11.11.11, pg 69
Scoop Infotex NV, pg 73

Brazil
Artes e Oficios Editora Ltda, pg 78
EDUSC - Editora da Universidade do Sagrado Coracao, pg 81
Empresa Brasileira de Pesquisa Agropecuaria, pg 81
Editora Globo SA, pg 82
LDA Editores Ltda, pg 84
Editora Mantiqueira de Ciencia e Arte, pg 86
Olho D'Agua Comercio e Servicos Editoriais Ltda, pg 87
Ediouro Publicacoes, SA, pg 89
Sobrindes Linha Grafica E Editora Ltda, pg 90
Summus Editorial Ltda, pg 91

Burundi
Editions Intore, pg 98

Chile
Arrayan Editores, pg 98
Publicaciones Lo Castillo SA, pg 100

China
World Affairs Press, pg 109
Xinhua Publishing House, pg 109

Colombia
El Ancora Editores, pg 111
Universidad de Antioquia, Division Publicaciones, pg 113
Editorial Voluntad SA, pg 113

Croatia
Faust Vrani, pg 118
Prosvjeta, pg 119

Cuba
Casa Editora Abril, pg 120

Czech Republic
Barrister & Principal, pg 122
Doplnek, pg 123

Denmark
Samfundslitteratur, pg 134

Ecuador
CIESPAL (Centro Internacional de Estudios Superiores de Comunicacion para America Latina), pg 136

Egypt (Arab Republic of Egypt)
Al Arab Publishing House, pg 137
Ummah Press, pg 138

Finland
Osuuskunta Vastapaino, pg 144
Yliopistopaino/Helsinki University Press, pg 145

France
Beauchesne Editeur, pg 149
Le Cherche Midi Editeur, pg 154
Les Editions du CFPJ (Centre de Formation et de Perfectionnement des Journalistes) - Sarl Presse et Formation, pg 160
Groupe de Recherche et d'Echanges Technologiques (GRET), pg 166
Editions de Septembre, pg 184

Germany
ARCult Media, pg 193
Boehlau-Verlag GmbH & Cie, pg 202
Deutsches Bucharchiv Muenchen, Institut fur Buchwissenschaften, pg 214
agenda Verlag Thomas Dominikowski, pg 215

PUBLISHERS

Verlag Reinhard Fischer, pg 225
Gunter Olzog Verlag GmbH, pg 231
Herbert von Halem Verlag, pg 233
Jahreszeiten-Verlag GmbH, pg 242
Siedler Verlag, pg 283
Spiess Volker Wissenschaftsverlag GmbH, pg 284
UVK Verlagsgesellschaft mbH, pg 294

Greece

Hestia-I D Hestia-Kollaros & Co Corporation, pg 308

Hong Kong

Celeluck Co Ltd, pg 316
The Chinese University Press, pg 316
Island Press, pg 317

Hungary

KJK-Kerszov, pg 322

India

Authorspress, pg 329
Central Tibetan Secretariat, pg 331
Concept Publishing Co, pg 332
Gyan Publishing House, pg 335
Minerva Associates (Publications) Pvt Ltd, pg 341
Reliance Publishing House, pg 346
Scientific Book Agency, pg 348
Somaiya Publications Pvt Ltd, pg 349
Sterling Publishers Pvt Ltd, pg 350

Israel

Intermedia Audio, Video Book Publishing Ltd, pg 368
The Harry Karren Institute for the Analysis of Propaganda, Yad Labanim, pg 369
Open University of Israel, pg 371

Italy

Editore Armando Armando SRL, pg 376
La Luna, pg 396
Messaggero di San Antonio, pg 398
RAI-ERI, pg 405

Kazakstan

Al-Farabi Kazakh National University, pg 432

Republic of Korea

Chung Rim Publishing Co Ltd, pg 438
Hanul Publishing Co, pg 439
Nanam Publications Co, pg 441

The Former Yugoslav Republic of Macedonia

Mi-An Knigoizdatelstvo, pg 452
Nov svet (New World), pg 453

Madagascar

Maison d'Edition Protestante ANTSO, pg 453
Societe Malgache d'Edition, pg 454

Malaysia

Pustaka Cipta Sdn Bhd, pg 458

Mexico

Editorial AGATA SA de CV, pg 462
Editorial Diana SA de CV, pg 464
Edamex SA de CV, pg 464
Editorial Limusa SA de CV, pg 467
Universidad Nacional Autonoma de Mexico (National University of Mexico), pg 472
Universo Editorial SA de CV Edicion de Libros Revistas y Periodicos, pg 473

Netherlands

Uitgeverij Balans, pg 478
Historische Uitgeverij, pg 483
Mets & Schilt Uitgevers en Distributeurs, pg 486

New Zealand

Barkfire Press, pg 494

Nigeria

Evans Brothers (Nigeria Publishers) Ltd, pg 504

Pakistan

Sang-e-Meel Publications, pg 514

Peru

Universidad de Lima-Fondo de Desarollo Editorial, pg 517

Philippines

SIBS Publishing House Inc, pg 521

Poland

Spoldzielnia Wydawnicza 'Czytelnik', pg 522

Portugal

Gradiva-Publicacnoes Lda, pg 532
Editorial Noticias, pg 534
Quid Juris - Sociedade Editora, pg 535

Romania

Aion Verlag, pg 538
Editura Excelsior Art, pg 539
Pallas-Akademia Editura, pg 541
Polirom Verlag, pg 542

Serbia and Montenegro

Alfa-Narodna Knjiga, pg 552

Slovenia

Franc-Franc podjetje za promocijo kulture Murska Sobota d o o, pg 561
Zalozba Mihelac d o o, pg 562
Zalozba Obzorja d d Maribor, pg 562

South Africa

Ivy Publications, pg 565

Spain

Aguilar SA de Ediciones, pg 571
Bosch Casa Editorial SA, pg 575
Compania Literaria, pg 577
Consello da Cultura Galega - CCG, pg 578
Editorial Dossat SA, pg 580
EUNSA (Ediciones Universidad de Navarra SA), pg 583
Fragua Editorial, pg 583
Ediciones Internacionales Universitarias SA, pg 588
Ediciones El Pais SA, pg 594
Editorial Pliegos, pg 596
Editorial Portic SA, pg 596
Editorial Sintesis, SA, pg 600
Ediciones de la Torre, pg 602

Sri Lanka

Swarna Hansa Foundation, pg 607

Sweden

Carlsson Bokfoerlag AB, pg 610
Ordfront Foerlag AB, pg 614

Switzerland

Lenos Verlag, pg 627

Syrian Arab Republic

Damascus University Press, pg 638

Taiwan, Province of China

Lin Pai Press Company Ltd, pg 641
Shy Mau & Shy Chaur Publishing Co Ltd, pg 641
UNITAS Publishing Co Ltd, pg 642

United Republic of Tanzania

Tanzania Publishing House, pg 644

Tunisia

Academie Tunisienne des Sciences, des Lettres et des Arts Beit El Hekma, pg 647

United Kingdom

Business Monitor International, pg 672
The Eurospan Group, pg 692
Geiser Productions, pg 699
Pluto Press, pg 743
Telegraph Books, pg 764

Uruguay

Cotidiano Mujer, pg 777
Editorial Dismar, pg 777

Venezuela

Alfadil Ediciones, pg 778

SUBJECT INDEX

LABOR, INDUSTRIAL RELATIONS

Albania

NL SH, pg 1
Shtepia Botuese Enciklopedike, pg 1

Australia

Allen & Unwin Pty Ltd, pg 11
Histec Publications, pg 25
Law Book Co Information Services, pg 28
McGraw-Hill Australia Pty Ltd, pg 31
Pearson Education Australia, pg 36
Pluto Press Australia Pty Ltd, pg 37

Austria

Doecker Verlag GmbH & Co KG, pg 50
Linde Verlag Wien GmbH, pg 53
Verlag des Oesterreichischen Gewerkschaftsbundes GmbH, pg 55

Belgium

King Baudouin Foundation, pg 69
Koepel van de Vlaamse Noord - Zuidbeweging 11.11.11, pg 69
Wolters Kluwer Belgie NV, pg 74

Brazil

Qualitymark Editora Ltda, pg 89

Bulgaria

Sibi, pg 97
Sita-MB, pg 97

Chile

Edeval (Universidad de Valparaiso), pg 99

China

China Labour Publishing House, pg 102

Costa Rica

Academia de Centro America, pg 114

Denmark

Dansk Teknologisk Institut, Forlaget, pg 130

France

Editions J B Bailliere, pg 149
Editions Eska, pg 162
Association Frank, pg 164
Futuribles SARL, pg 164
Editions Lavoisier, pg 171
Editions Legislatives, pg 171
LiTec (Libraries Techniques SA), pg 172
Editions Weka, pg 189

Germany

Arbeiterpresse Verlags- und Vertriebsgesellschaft mbH, pg 193
Asso Verlag, pg 195
Belser Wissenschaftlicher Dienst, pg 199
W Bertelsmann Verlag GmbH & Co KG, pg 200
Deutscher Instituts-Verlag GmbH, pg 213
Ecomed Verlagsgesellschaft AG & Co KG, pg 218
Verlag Handwerk und Technik GmbH, pg 233
IKO Verlag fur Interkulturelle Kommunikation, pg 241
SachBuchVerlag Kellner, pg 245
Nusser Verlag, pg 266
Rationalisierungs-Kuratorium der Deutschen Wirtschaft eV (RKW), pg 273
I H Sauer Verlag GmbH, pg 278
Schueren Verlag GmbH, pg 281
Schulz-Kirchner Verlag GmbH, pg 282
UNO-Verlag GmbH, pg 293
VVF Verlag V Florentz GmbH, pg 297
Verlag Westfaelisches Dampfboot, pg 299

Greece

Nomiki Bibliothiki, pg 310
Sakkoulas Publications SA, pg 312

Hong Kong

Hong Kong University Press, pg 317

1015

India
Agricole Publishing Academy, pg 327
APH Publishing Corp, pg 328
Konark Publishers Pvt Ltd, pg 339
Minerva Associates (Publications) Pvt Ltd, pg 341
National Book Organization, pg 342
Reliance Publishing House, pg 346
Scientific Book Agency, pg 348
Sita Books & Periodicals Pvt Ltd, pg 349
Somaiya Publications Pvt Ltd, pg 349
South Asian Publishers Pvt Ltd, pg 350
Sultan Chand & Sons Pvt Ltd, pg 350

Indonesia
Lembaga Demografi Fakultas Ekonomi Universitas Indonesia, pg 355

Ireland
Irish Management Institute, pg 361
Libra House Ltd, pg 361
Oak Tree Press, pg 362
Round Hall Sweet & Maxwell, pg 363

Israel
Hanitzotz A-Sharara Publishing House, pg 367
The Institute for Israeli Arabs Studies, pg 368
Sifriat Poalim Ltd, pg 372

Italy
Esselibri, pg 388
Edizioni Lavoro SRL, pg 394
Editrice San Marco SRL, pg 407
SIPI (Servizio Italiano Pubblicazioni Internazionali) Srl, pg 408

Japan
Hakuyu-Sha, pg 418
Koseisha-Koseikaku Co Ltd, pg 422
Nihon Rodo Kenkyu Kiko, pg 423
Toyo Keizai Shinpo-Sha, pg 430

Kenya
Lake Publishers & Enterprises Ltd, pg 435

Republic of Korea
Bo Ri Publishing Co Ltd, pg 437
Chung Rim Publishing Co Ltd, pg 438

Luxembourg
Service Central de la Statistique et des Etudes Economiques (STATEC), pg 451

Malaysia
Forum Publications, pg 456

Mexico
Editorial Limusa SA de CV, pg 467

Netherlands
Hagen & Stam Uitgeverij Ten, pg 483
Uitgeverij Lemma BV, pg 485
Uitgeverij H Nelissen BV, pg 486

Samsom BedrijfsInformatie BV, pg 488
Swets & Zeitlinger Publishers, pg 489

Pakistan
Pakistan Institute of Development Economics (PIDE), pg 514

Philippines
New Day Publishers, pg 520
Rex Bookstores & Publishers, pg 520

Poland
Instytut Wydawniczy Zwiazkow Zawodowych, pg 528

Portugal
Lidel Edicoes Tecnicas, Lda, pg 533

Russian Federation
Legprombytizdat, pg 546
Profizdat, pg 548

Senegal
CODESRIA (Council for the Development of Social Science Research in Africa), pg 551

Slovakia
Ustav informacii a prognoz skolstva mladeze a telovychovy, pg 561

South Africa
Queillerie Publishers, pg 568
Ravan Press (Pty) Ltd, pg 568
Van Schaik Publishers, pg 569

Spain
Centro de Estudios Adams-Ediciones Valbuena SA, pg 571
Editorial AEDOS SA, pg 571
Publicaciones Etea, pg 583
Fundacion de Estudios Libertarios Anselmo Lorenzo, pg 584
Tirant lo Blanch SL Libreriaa, pg 602

Suriname
Stichting Wetenschappelijke Informatie, pg 608

Switzerland
Verlag Organisator AG, pg 630
SAB Schweiz Arbeitsgemeinschaft fuer die Berggebiete, pg 633
Versus Verlag AG, pg 636

United Republic of Tanzania
Tanzania Publishing House, pg 644

Uganda
Centre for Basic Research, pg 652

United Kingdom
Anglo-German Foundation for the Study of Industrial Society, pg 658
Barmarick Publications, pg 663
Blackwell Publishing Ltd, pg 666
Bookmarks Publications, pg 668
Cassell & Co, pg 675
Croner CCH Group Ltd, pg 684
Edward Elgar Publishing Ltd, pg 690

The Eurospan Group, pg 692
Lawrence & Wishart, pg 719
Letts Educational, pg 720
The Merlin Press Ltd, pg 727
Pathfinder London, pg 739
Pluto Press, pg 743
The Policy Press, pg 744
Policy Studies Institute (PSI), pg 744
Shire Publications Ltd, pg 757
Spokesman, pg 760
Sutton Publishing Ltd, pg 762

Venezuela
Fundacion Centro Gumilla, pg 779

Zambia
M & M Management & Labour Consultants Ltd, pg 781

Zimbabwe
Journal on Social Change, pg 783

LANGUAGE ARTS, LINGUISTICS

Albania
NL SH, pg 1

Argentina
Academia Argentina de Letras, pg 2
Diana Argentina SA, Editorial, pg 5
Edicial SA, pg 5
Editorial Guadalupe, pg 6
Editorial Idearium de la Universidad de Mendoza (EDIUM), pg 6
San Pablo, pg 9
Editorial Sopena Argentina SACI e I, pg 9

Armenia
Arevik, pg 10

Australia
Aboriginal Studies Press, pg 10
Bandicoot Books, pg 14
Boombana Publications, pg 16
China Books, pg 17
Dellasta Publishing, pg 19
Illert Publications, pg 26
Institute of Aboriginal Development (IAD Press), pg 27
McGraw-Hill Australia Pty Ltd, pg 31
Mimosa Publications Pty Ltd, pg 32
New Endeavour Press, pg 33
Nimrod Publications, pg 33
Oriental Publications, pg 34
Pearson Education Australia, pg 36
Phoenix Education Pty Ltd, pg 36
RMIT Publishing, pg 39
Summer Institute of Linguistics, Australian Aborigines Branch, pg 42
Wileman Publications, pg 46

Austria
Abakus Verlag GmbH, pg 48
Akademische Druck-u Verlagsanstalt Dr Paul Struzl GmbH, pg 48
Boehlau Verlag GmbH & Co KG, pg 48
CEEBA Publications Antenne d'Autriche, pg 49
Fassbaender Verlag, pg 50
Gerold & Co, pg 51
LOG-Internationale Zeitschrift fuer Literatur, pg 53

Wolfgang Neugebauer Verlag GmbH, pg 54
Verlag der Oesterreichischen Akademie der Wissenschaften (OEAW), pg 55
Oesterreichischer Bundesverlag Gmbh, pg 55
Studien Verlag Gmbh, pg 58
Universitaetsverlag Wagner GmbH, pg 59
WUV/Facultas Universitaetsverlag, pg 60

Azerbaijan
Sada, Literaturno-Izdatel'skij Centr, pg 60

Belarus
Belaruskaya Encyklapedyya, pg 62

Belgium
Uitgeverij Acco, pg 62
Centre Aequatoria, pg 63
Assimil NV, pg 63
De Boeck et Larcier SA, pg 64
Bourdeaux-Capelle SA, pg 64
Brepols Publishers NV, pg 64
Campinia Media VZW, pg 64
La Charte Editions juridiques, pg 65
Editions De Boeck-Larcier SA, pg 66
Infoboek NV, pg 68
Uitgeverij J van In, pg 69
Editions Lessius ASBL, pg 70
Leuven University Press, pg 70
Mardaga, Pierre, Editeur, pg 71
La Part de L'Oeil, pg 71
Uitgeverij Peeters Leuven (Belgie), pg 71
Pelckmans NV, De Nederlandsche Boekhandel, pg 72
Sonneville Press (Uitgeverij) VTW, pg 73
Stichting Ons Erfdeel VZW, pg 73
UGA Editions (Uitgeverij), pg 73
Uitgeverij De Garve, pg 74
Vlaamse Esperantobond VZW, pg 74
Wolters Plantyn Educatieve Uitgevers, pg 74

Botswana
The Botswana Society, pg 76
Maskew Miller Longman, pg 76

Brazil
Ao Livro Tecnico Industria e Comercio Ltda, pg 77
Ars Poetica Editora Ltda, pg 78
Editora Forense Universitaria Ltda, pg 81
Fundacao Sao Paulo, EDUC, pg 82
Editora Globo SA, pg 82
Livro Ibero-Americano Ltda, pg 83
Imago Editora Importacao e Exportacao Ltda, pg 84
Libreria Editora Ltda, pg 85
Waldir Lima Editora, pg 85
Livraria Kosmos Editora Ltda, pg 85
Editora Nova Fronteira SA, pg 87
Livraria Pioneira Editora/Enio Matheus Guazzelli e Cia Ltd, pg 88
Editora Rideel Ltda, pg 89
Edicoes Tabajara, pg 91
Editora Universidade Federal do Rio de Janeiro, pg 92
Vozes Editora Ltda, pg 92

PUBLISHERS SUBJECT INDEX

Bulgaria

Interpres, pg 95
Izdatelstvo Lettera, pg 95
Naouka i Izkoustvo, Ltd, pg 95
Pensoft Publishers, pg 96
Prohazka I Kacarmazov, pg 96
Seven Hills Publishers, pg 96

Chile

Arrayan Editores, pg 98

China

Beijing Publishing House, pg 101
China Light Industry Press, pg 102
China Youth Publishing House, pg 103
Chinese Pedagogics Publishing House, pg 103
Chongqing University Press, pg 103
Foreign Language Teaching & Research Press, pg 104
Fudan University Press, pg 104
Higher Education Press, pg 105
Shanghai Foreign Language Education Press, pg 108
Zhong Hua Book Co, pg 110

Colombia

Asociacion Instituto Linguistico de Verano, pg 110
Instituto Caro y Cuervo, pg 111
Siglo XXI Editores de Colombia Ltda, pg 112
Editorial Voluntad SA, pg 113

The Democratic Republic of the Congo

Centre de Recherche, et Pedagogie Appliquee, pg 114

Costa Rica

Ediciones Promesa, pg 116
Editorial de la Universidad de Costa Rica, pg 116

Cote d'Ivoire

Heritage Publishing Co, pg 117

Croatia

ArTresor naklada, pg 117
Filozofski Fakultet Sveucilista u Zagrebu, pg 118
Knjizevni Krug Split, pg 118
Matica hrvatska, pg 118
Sveucilisna tiskara doo, pg 119

Czech Republic

Academia, pg 122
Barrister & Principal, pg 122
Jan Kanzelsberger Praha, pg 124
Karolinum, nakladatelstvi, pg 124
Lidove Noviny Publishing House, pg 125
P & R Centrum Vydavateistvi a Nakladateistvi, pg 126
Verlag Harry Putz, pg 127

Denmark

Aarhus Universitetsforlag, pg 128
Akademisk Forlag A/S, pg 128
Fremad A/S, pg 131
Kaleidoscope Publishers Ltd, pg 132
Museum Tusculanum Press, pg 133
Samfundslitteratur, pg 134

Dominican Republic

Pontificia Universidad Catolica Madre y Maestra, pg 136

Ecuador

Ediciones Abya-Yala, pg 136

Egypt (Arab Republic of Egypt)

American University in Cairo Press, pg 137
Al Arab Publishing House, pg 137
Elias Modern Publishing House, pg 138
Middle East Book Centre, pg 138

Ethiopia

Addis Ababa University Press, pg 140

Finland

Akateeminen Kustannusliike Oy, pg 141
Suomalaisen Kirjallisuuden Seura, pg 144
Yliopistopaino/Helsinki University Press, pg 145

France

Adverbum SARL, pg 146
Armenia Editions, pg 147
Editions Assimil SA, pg 148
Atelier National de Reproduction des Theses, pg 148
Editions Aubier-Montaigne SA, pg 148
Societe d'Edition Les Belles Lettres, pg 149
Editions Breal, pg 151
Brud Nevez, pg 151
Editions Circonflexe, pg 154
Cle International, pg 154
CNRS Editions, pg 155
Counseil International de la Langue Francaise, pg 156
Dunod Editeur, pg 159
ELLUG (Editions Litteraires et Linguistiques de l'Universite de Grenoble III), pg 161
Institut d'Ethnologie du Museum National d'Histoire Naturelle, pg 162
Institut d'Etudes Slaves IES, pg 162
Hachette Livre, pg 167
L'Harmattan, pg 167
Editions Hermes Science Publications, pg 167
Editions Klincksieck, pg 170
Langues & Mondes-L'Asiatheque, pg 171
Editions Fernand Lanore Sarl, pg 171
Editions Larousse, pg 171
Le Livre de Poche-L G F (Librairie Generale Francaise), pg 173
Maisonneuve et Larose, pg 174
Presses Universitaires du Mirail, pg 176
Editions Modernes Media, pg 176
Editions Ophrys, pg 177
Payot & Rivages, pg 179
Peeters-France, pg 179
Editions A et J Picard SA, pg 179
Presses de la Sorbonne Nouvelle/PSN, pg 181
Presses Universitaires de Caen, pg 181
Presses Universitaires de Grenoble, pg 181
Presses Universitaires de Lyon, pg 181
Presses Universitaires de Nancy, pg 181
Presses Universitaires du Septentrion, pg 182
Publications Orientalistes de France (POF), pg 182
Editions Spratbrow, pg 186
Universitas, pg 188
Publications de l'Universite de Pau, pg 188
Editions Vilo SA, pg 189

French Polynesia

Haere Po Editions, pg 189

Germany

Akademie Verlag GmbH, pg 191
Aschendorffsche Verlagsbuchhandlung GmbH & Co KG, pg 194
Assimil GmbH, pg 195
Beacon Verlag Koerber OHG, pg 198
Verlag C H Beck oHG, pg 198
Biblio Verlag, pg 200
Bibliographisches Institut & F A Brockhaus AG, pg 200
Verlag Die Blaue Eule, pg 202
Boehlau-Verlag GmbH & Cie, pg 202
Oscar Brandstetter Verlag GmbH & Co KG, pg 204
Buchhandlung Holl & Knoll KG, Verlag Alte Uni, pg 205
Helmut Buske Verlag GmbH, pg 206
Chancerel International Publishers Ltd, pg 208
Verlag Darmstaedter Blaetter Schwarz und Co, pg 210
Diesterweg, Moritz Verlag, pg 214
Verlag Duerr & Kessler GmbH, pg 217
Klaus D Dutz, pg 217
Ferd Dummler's Verlag, pg 223
Wilhelm Fink GmbH & Co Verlags-KG, pg 224
Harald Fischer Verlag GmbH, pg 224
Friedrich Frommann Verlag, pg 227
Graf Editions, pg 231
Verlag Grundlagen und Praxis GmbH & Co, pg 231
Walter de Gruyter GmbH & Co KG, pg 231
Harrassowitz Verlag, pg 234
S Hirzel Verlag GmbH und Co, pg 238
Holos Verlag, pg 239
Max Hueber Verlag GmbH & Co KG, pg 239
Intertrans-Verlag GmbH, pg 242
Iudicium Verlag GmbH, pg 242
Janus Verlagsgesellschaft, Dr Norbert Meder & Co, pg 243
W Kohlhammer GmbH, pg 248
Dr Anton Kovac Slavica Verlag, pg 249
Alfred Kroner Verlag, pg 250
Peter Lang GmbH Europaeischer Verlag der Wissenschaften, pg 252
Langenscheidt-Hachette, pg 252
Ingrid Langner, pg 252
Leibniz Verlag, pg 253
Logophon Verlag und Bildungsreisen GmbH, pg 255
mentis Verlag GmbH, pg 259
J B Metzlersche Verlagsbuchhandlung, pg 260
Peter Meyer Verlag (pmv), pg 260
Ursala Meyer und Dr Manfred Duker Ein-Fach-Verlag, pg 260
Net World Vision GmbH, pg 263
Neuer Honos Verlag GmbH, pg 264
Max Niemeyer Verlag GmbH, pg 265
Oekumenischer Verlag Dr R-F Edel, pg 266
Georg Olms Verlag AG, pg 267
Orbis Verlag fur Publizistik GmbH, pg 267
Verlag Sigrid Persen, pg 269
Quelle und Meyer Verlag GmbH & Co, pg 273
Dr Ludwig Reichert Verlag, pg 274
Reise Know-How Verlag Peter Rump GmbH, pg 275
Verlagsgruppe Reise Know-How, pg 275
Roehrig Universitaets Verlag Gmbh, pg 276
Rossipaul Kommunikation GmbH, pg 277
Saarbrucker Druckerei und Verlag GmbH (SDV), pg 277
Verlag Otto Sagner, pg 278
J D Sauerlaender's Verlag, pg 278
Wilhelm Schmitz Verlag, pg 280
Ferdinand Schoeningh Verlag GmbH, pg 281
Schulz-Kirchner Verlag GmbH, pg 282
Spiess Volker Wissenschaftsverlag GmbH, pg 284
Stauffenburg Verlag Brigitte Narr GmbH, pg 287
Franz Steiner Verlag Wiesbaden GmbH, pg 287
Stern-Verlag Janssen & Co, pg 288
Steyler Verlag, pg 288
Stiefel Eurocart GmbH, pg 288
Tuduv Verlagsgesellschaft mbH, pg 292
Tuebinger Vereinigung fur Volkskunde eV (TVV), pg 292
Universitaetsverlag Winter GmbH Heidelberg, pg 293
UTB fuer Wissenschaft Uni Taschenbuecher GmbH, pg 294
Vandenhoeck & Ruprecht, pg 294
VAS-Verlag fuer Akademische Schriften, pg 294
Vervuert Verlagsgesellschaft, pg 295
Wachholtz Verlag GmbH, pg 297
Weidler Buchverlag Berlin, pg 298
Weidmannsche Verlagsbuchhandlung GmbH, pg 298
Verlag Wissenschaft und Politik, pg 300
Wissenschaftliche Buchgesellschaft, pg 300

Ghana

Beginners Publishers, pg 303
Ghana Institute of Linguistics Literacy & Bible Translation (GILLBT), pg 304
Ghana Publishing Corporation, pg 304
Ghana Universities Press (GUP), pg 304

Greece

Editions Athina-Mavrogianni, pg 306
Hestia-I D Hestia-Kollaros & Co Corporation, pg 308
Institute of Neohellenic Studies, Manolis Triantaphyllidis Foundation, pg 308
Morfotiko Idryma Ethnikis Trapezas, pg 310
Patakis Publishers, pg 311
J Sideris OE Ekdoseis, pg 312

1017

Guadeloupe
JASOR, pg 313

Holy See (Vatican City State)
Biblioteca Apostolica Vaticana, pg 314
Scuola Vaticana Paleografia - Scuola Vaticana di Paleografia Diplomatica e Archivistica, pg 315

Honduras
Editorial Guaymuras, pg 315

Hong Kong
The Chinese University Press, pg 316
Chung Hwa Book Co (HK) Ltd, pg 316
Commercial Press (Hong Kong) Ltd, pg 316
Hong Kong University Press, pg 317
Joint Publishing (HK) Co Ltd, pg 317
Witman Publishing Co (HK) Ltd, pg 320

Hungary
Akademiai Kiado, pg 320
Aranyhal Konyvkiado Goldfish Publishing, pg 320
Balassi Kiado Kft, pg 321
Corvina Books Ltd, pg 321
Nemzeti Tankoenyvkiado, pg 323
Osiris Kiado, pg 323

Iceland
Hid Islenzka Bokmenntafelag, pg 325
Stofnun Arna Magnussonar a Islandi, pg 326

India
Agam Kala Prakashan, pg 327
Ajanta Publications (India), pg 327
Asian Educational Services, pg 329
K P Bagchi & Co, pg 329
Bharat Publishing House, pg 330
Cosmo Publications, pg 332
Disha Prakashan, pg 333
Dutta Publishing Co Ltd, pg 333
Full Circle Publishing, pg 334
General Book Depot, pg 335
Gyan Publishing House, pg 335
Heritage Publishers, pg 335
Jaico Publishing House, pg 338
Motilal Banarsidass Publishers Pvt Ltd, pg 341
Munshiram Manoharlal Publishers Pvt Ltd, pg 342
Naya Prokash, pg 343
New Light Publishers, pg 343
Paramount Sales (India) Pvt Ltd, pg 344
Pustak Mahal, pg 345
Rahul Publishing House, pg 346
Rajasthan Hindi Granth Academy, pg 346
Regency Publications, pg 346
Samkaleen Prakashan, pg 348
Sri Satguru Publications, pg 348
Somaiya Publications Pvt Ltd, pg 349
Star Publications (P) Ltd, pg 350

Indonesia
Bhratara Karya Aksara, pg 354
Nusa Indah, pg 356

Israel
Agudat Sabah, pg 364
Amichai Publishing House Ltd, pg 365
Bar Ilan University Press, pg 365
Ben-Zvi Institute, pg 365
Dekel Publishing House, pg 366
Gefen Publishing House Ltd, pg 367
Haifa University Press, pg 367
K Dictionaries Ltd, pg 369
Machbarot Lesifrut, pg 370
Misgav Yerushalayim, pg 370
Prolog Publishing House, pg 371
Tcherikover Publishers Ltd, pg 372

Italy
Arcipelago Edizioni di Chiani Marisa, pg 376
Editore Armando Armando SRL, pg 376
Atlantica Editrice SARL, pg 377
Book Editore, pg 378
Bulzoni Editore SRL (Le Edizioni Universitarie d'Italia), pg 379
Edizioni Cadmo SRL, pg 379
Ciranna - Roma, pg 382
Cisalpino, pg 382
CLEUP - Cooperative Libraria Editrice dell 'Universita di Padova, pg 382
CLUEB (Cooperativa Libraria Universitaria Editrice Bologna), pg 382
Colonnese Editore, pg 383
Edizioni Della Torre di Salvatore Fozzi & C SAS, pg 385
Edizioni dell'Orso, pg 385
Edistudio, pg 386
L'Erma di Bretschneider SRL, pg 388
Essegi, pg 388
Arnaldo Forni Editore SRL, pg 389
Giunti Gruppo Editoriale, pg 390
Guerra Edizioni GURU srl, pg 392
Herder Editrice e Libreria, pg 392
Editrice Innocenti SNC, pg 393
Istituti Editoriali E Poligrafici Internazionali SRL, pg 393
Edizioni Internazionali di Letteratura e Scienze, pg 393
L Japadre Editore, pg 394
Casa Editrice Le Lettere SRL, pg 395
Liguori Editore SRL, pg 395
Loescher Editore SRL, pg 396
Loffredo Editore Napoli SpA®, pg 396
Angelo Longo Editore, pg 396
Macmillan Heinemann ELT, pg 396
Edumond Le Monnier, pg 399
Mucchi Editore SRL, pg 399
Societa Editrice Il Mulino, pg 399
Officina Edizioni di Aldo Quinti, pg 401
Leo S Olschki, pg 401
Palatina Editrice, pg 402
G B Palumbo & C Editore SpA, pg 402
Patron Editore SrL, pg 402
Pitagora Editrice SRL, pg 403
Istituto Poligrafico e Zecca dello Stato, pg 403
Riccardo Ricciardi Editore SpA, pg 405
Editori Riuniti, pg 405
Rosenberg e Sellier Editori in Torino, pg 406
SAIE Editrice SRL, pg 406
Salerno Editrice SRL, pg 406
Schena Editore, pg 407
Sicania, pg 408
Studio Bibliografico Adelmo Polla, pg 409
Editrice Tirrenia Stampatori SAS, pg 410
Todariana Editrice, pg 410
Unipress, pg 411
Valmartina Editore SRL, pg 411
Zanichelli Editore SpA, pg 412
Edizioni Zara, pg 412

Jamaica
Carlong Publishers (Caribbean) Ltd, pg 413
Jamaica Publishing House Ltd, pg 414

Japan
Eichosha Company Ltd, pg 417
Fuzambo Publishing Co, pg 417
GakuseiSha Publishing Co Ltd, pg 417
Hakusui-Sha Co Ltd, pg 417
Hakutei-Sha, pg 418
Hyoronsha Publishing Co Ltd, pg 418
Japan Broadcast Publishing Co Ltd, pg 419
Japan Travel Bureau Inc, pg 420
Kaitakusha, pg 420
Keisuisha Publishing Company Ltd, pg 420
Kenkyusha Ltd, pg 421
Kodansha International Ltd, pg 421
Kodansha Ltd, pg 421
Kokushokankokai Co Ltd, pg 421
Nankodo Co Ltd, pg 423
Nan'un-Do Co Ltd, pg 423
Nippon Hoso Shuppan Kyokai (NHK Publishing), pg 424
Obunsha Co Ltd, pg 424
Saela Shobo (Librairie Ca et La), pg 425
Sanseido Co Ltd, pg 426
Sanshusha Publishing Co, Ltd, pg 426
Seibido, pg 426
Seibundo Shuppan, pg 426
Seiwa Shoten Co Ltd, pg 427
Shueisha Inc, pg 428
The Simul Press Inc, pg 428
Takahashi Shoten Co Ltd, pg 429
Thomson Learning Japan, pg 429
3A Corporation, pg 429
Toho Book Store, pg 429
Tokai University Press, pg 429
Charles E Tuttle Publishing Co Inc, pg 430
Yamaguchi Shoten, pg 431
Yohan Shuppan, pg 431

Kenya
British Institute in Eastern Africa, pg 433
Kenway Publications Ltd, pg 434

Republic of Korea
Bakyoung Publishing Co, pg 437
BCM Media Inc, pg 437
Chang-josa Publishing Co, pg 438
Chong No Books Publishing Co Ltd, pg 438
Eulyu Publishing Co Ltd, pg 438
Ewha Womans University Press, pg 438
Iljisa Publishing House, pg 439
Korea University Press, pg 440
Koreaone Press Inc, pg 440
Literature Academy Publishing, pg 441
Pan Korea Book Corporation, pg 442
Samhwa Publishing Co Ltd, pg 442
Seoul International Publishing House, pg 443
Seoul National University Press, pg 443
Sogang University Press, pg 443

Kuwait
Ministry of Information, pg 444

Latvia
Avots, pg 444

Lebanon
Arab Institute for Research & Publishing, pg 445
Dar-El-Machreq Sarl, pg 446
Librairie du Liban Publishers (Sal), pg 446
Librairie Orientale sal, pg 446

Liechtenstein
Saendig Reprint Verlag, Hans-Rainer Wohlwend, pg 448

Lithuania
Academia, pg 448
AS Narbuto Leidykla (AS Narbutas' Publishers), pg 448
Baltos Lankos, pg 449
Mokslo ir enciklopediju leidybos institutas, pg 449

Luxembourg
Editions Emile Borschette, pg 450

Macau
Instituto Portugues Oriente, pg 452

The Former Yugoslav Republic of Macedonia
Murgorski Zoze, pg 453
Zumpres Publishing Firm, pg 453

Malaysia
Darulfikir, pg 455
Oscar Book International, pg 457
Pelanduk Publications (M) Sdn Bhd, pg 457

Malta
The University of Malta Publications Section, pg 460

Mexico
Aguilar Altea Taurus Alfaguara SA de CV, pg 462
Editorial Avante SA de Cv, pg 462
El Colegio de Mexico AC, pg 463
Editorial Edicol SA, pg 464
El Colegio de Michoacan A C, pg 464
Libra Editorial SA de CV, pg 467
Instituto Nacional de Antropologia e Historia, pg 469
Nova Grupo Editorial SA de CV, pg 469
Editorial Nueva Imagen SA, pg 469
Pearson Educacion de Mexico, SA de CV, pg 470
Ediciones Promesa, SA de CV, pg 470
Siglo XXI Editores SA de CV, pg 472
Sistemas Tecnicos de Edicion SA de CV, pg 472
Universidad Nacional Autonoma de Mexico (National University of Mexico), pg 472

PUBLISHERS

Republic of Moldova
Editura Lumina, pg 473

Morocco
Editions Le Fennec, pg 474
Editions Okad, pg 475
Editions La Porte, pg 475

Nepal
International Standards Books & Periodicals (P) Ltd, pg 476

Netherlands
APA (Academic Publishers Associated), pg 477
John Benjamins BV, pg 479
Boom Uitgeverij, pg 479
Uitgeverij Coutinho BV, pg 481
HES & De Graaf Publishers BV, pg 483
Holland University Press BV (APA), pg 483
ICG Publications BV, pg 484
Uitgeverij Intertaal BV, pg 484
IOS Press BV, pg 484
KITLV Press Royal Institute of Linguistics & Anthropology, pg 484
Mirananda Publishers BV, pg 486
Prometheus, pg 488
Swets & Zeitlinger Publishers, pg 489
Tilburg University Press, pg 490
Van Gorcum & Comp BV, pg 491
VU Boekhandel/Uitgeverij BV, pg 492

New Zealand
ABA Books, pg 493
Nelson Price Milburn Ltd, pg 499
New House Publishers Ltd, pg 499
Outrigger Publishers, pg 499
Victoria University Press, pg 502

Nicaragua
Academia Nicaraguense de la Lengua, pg 502

Nigeria
Gbabeks Publishers Ltd, pg 505
Ogunsanya Press, Publishers and Bookstores Ltd, pg 506
Riverside Communications, pg 507
Vantage Publishers International Ltd, pg 507

Norway
Aschehoug Forlag, pg 508
H Aschehoug & Co (W Nygaard) A/S, pg 508
Forlaget Fag og Kultur, pg 509
Norsk Bokreidingslag L/L, pg 510
Universitetsforlaget, pg 511

Pakistan
International Educational Services, pg 512

Papua New Guinea
Summer Institute of Linguistics, pg 516

Peru
Ediciones Brown SA, pg 516
Fondo Editorial de la Pontificia Universidad Catolica del Peru, pg 517
Instituto Frances de Estudios Andinos, IFEA, pg 517
Editorial Horizonte, pg 517

Philippines
Anvil Publishing Inc, pg 518
Saint Mary's Publishing Corp, pg 520
Salesiana Publishers Inc, pg 521
SIBS Publishing House Inc, pg 521
Vibal Publishing House Inc (VPHI), pg 521

Poland
Wydawnictwo DiG, pg 522
Energeia sp zoo Wydawnictwo, pg 523
Ossolineum Zaklad Narodowy im Ossolinskich - Wydawnictwo, pg 525
Polish Scientific Publishers PWN, pg 525
Towarzystwo Naukowe w Toruniu, pg 527
'Wiedza Powszechna' Panstwowe Wydawnictwo, pg 527

Portugal
Armenio Amado Editora de Simoes, Beirao & Ca Lda, pg 528
Coimbra Editora Lda, pg 530
Constancia Editores, SA, pg 530
Edicoes Cosmos, pg 530
Imprensa Nacional-Casa da Moeda, pg 532
Lidel Edicoes Tecnicas, Lda, pg 533
Porto Editora Lda, pg 535
Editorial Presenca, pg 535
Edicoes Rolim Lda, pg 535
Edicoes 70 Lda, pg 535
Almerinda Teixeira, pg 536

Puerto Rico
Piedras Press, Inc, pg 537

Romania
Editura Academiei Romane, pg 538
Ars Longa Publishing House, pg 538
The Center for Romanian Studies, pg 539
Coresi SRL, pg 539
Editura Excelsior Art, pg 539
Lider Verlag, pg 540
Editura Meridiane, pg 540
Editura Niculescu, pg 541
Editura Stiintifica si Enciclopedica, pg 542

Russian Federation
Airis Press, pg 543
INFRA-M Izdatel 'skij dom, pg 545
Izdatelstvo Mordovskogo gosudar stvennogo, pg 547
Nauka Publishers, pg 547
Okoshko Ltd Publishers (Izdatelstvo), pg 547
Progress Publishers, pg 548
Voronezh State University Publishers, pg 549
Izdatelstvo Vysshaya Shkola, pg 549

Saudi Arabia
King Saud University, pg 550

Senegal
Centre de Linguistique Appliquee, pg 551

Serbia and Montenegro
Alfa-Narodna Knjiga, pg 552
Obod, pg 553

Singapore
Cannon International, pg 555
Celebrity Educational Publishers, pg 555
Global Educational Services Pte Ltd, pg 556
Intellectual Publishing Co, pg 556
McGallen & Bolden Associates, pg 557
Singapore University Press Pte Ltd, pg 558

Slovakia
Slo Viet, pg 560
Slovenske pedagogicke nakladateistvo, pg 560
VEDA (Vydavatel'stvo Slovenskej akademie vied), pg 561

Slovenia
Franc-Franc podjetje za promocijo kulture Murska Sobota d o o, pg 561
Mladinska Knjiga International, pg 561
Univerza v Ljubljani Ekonomska Fakulteta, pg 562
Zalozba Mihelac d o o, pg 562
Zalozba Obzorja d d Maribor, pg 562

South Africa
Clever Books, pg 563
Human & Rousseau (Pty) Ltd, pg 564
Ivy Publications, pg 565
Maskew Miller Longman, pg 566
Unisa Press, pg 569
Van Schaik Publishers, pg 569
Witwatersrand University Press, pg 570

Spain
Publicacions de l'Abadia de Montserrat, pg 570
Academia de la Llingua Asturiana, pg 570
Aguilar SA de Ediciones, pg 571
Altea, Taurus, Alfaguara SA, pg 572
Anglo-Didactica, SL Editorial, pg 573
Arco Libros SL, pg 573
Bosch Casa Editorial SA, pg 575
Calesa SA Editorial La, pg 575
Editorial Cantabrica SA, pg 575
Casa de Velazquez, pg 575
Ediciones Catedra SA, pg 576
Ediciones Colegio De Espana (ECE), pg 577
Didaco Comunicacion y Didactica, SA, pg 579
Editorial Ediseis SA, pg 581
Instituto de Estudios Riojanos, pg 583
EUNSA (Ediciones Universidad de Navarra SA), pg 583
Fondo de Cultura Economica de Espana, SL, pg 583
Fragua Editorial, pg 583
Vicent Garcia Editores, SA, pg 584
Editorial Herder SA, pg 586
Ediciones Hiperion SL, pg 586
Ediciones Istmo SA, pg 588
Editorial Juventud SA, pg 588
Libsa Editorial SA, pg 589

SUBJECT INDEX

LID Editorial Empresarial, SL, pg 589
Antonio Machado, SA, pg 590
Editorial Moll SL, pg 592
Editorial la Muralla SA, pg 592
Oikos-Tau SA Ediciones, pg 593
Oxford University Press Espana SA, pg 594
Ediciones El Pais SA, pg 594
Ediciones Partenon, pg 595
Pearson Educacion S A, pg 595
Editorial Playor SA, pg 596
Pre-Textos, pg 596
Josep Ruaix Editor, pg 598
Universidad de Santiago de Compostela, pg 599
Editorial Sintesis, SA, pg 600
Grup 62, pg 600
Ramon Sopena SA, pg 600
SPES Editorial SL, pg 600
Axel Springer Publicaciones, pg 601
Stanley Editorial, pg 601
Tres Torres Ediciones SA, pg 602
Editorial Txertoa, pg 603
Universidad de Oviedo Servicio de Publicaciones, pg 603
Editorial Verbum SL, pg 604
Visor Libros, pg 605
Edicions Xerais de Galicia, pg 605

Sri Lanka
Inter-Cultural Book Promoters, pg 606

Sweden
Acta Universitatis Gothoburgensis, pg 609
Akademiforlaget Goteborgslitteratur, pg 609
Bokforlaget Axplock, pg 609
Folkuniversitetets foerlag, pg 611
Hans Richter Laromedel, pg 613
Liber AB, pg 613
Mezopotamya Publishing & Distribution, pg 613
Studentlitteratur AB, pg 616

Switzerland
Bibliographisches Institut & F A Brockhaus AG, pg 619
Les Editions de la Fondation Martin Bodmer, pg 619
Castle Publications SA, pg 620
Cockatoo Press (Schweiz), Thailand-Publikationen, pg 621
Georg Editeur SA, pg 624
Helbing und Lichtenhahn Verlag AG, pg 625
Verlag Huber & Co AG, pg 625
Kolumbus-Verlag, pg 626
Kranich-Verlag, Dres AG & H R Bosch-Gwalter, pg 627
Peter Lang AG, pg 627
Langenscheidt AG Zuerich-Zug, pg 627
Lia rumantscha, pg 627
Peter Meili & Co, Buchhandlung, pg 628
Novalis Media AG, pg 630
Editions Pro Schola, pg 631
Hans Rohr Verlag, pg 632
Sabe AG Verlagsinstitut, pg 633

Syrian Arab Republic
Damascus University Press, pg 638
Institut Francais d'Etudes Arabes de Damas, pg 638

Taiwan, Province of China
Jillion Publishing Co, pg 640
World Book Co Ltd, pg 642

SUBJECT INDEX

Wu Nan Book Co Ltd, pg 642
Youth Cultural Publishing Co, pg 642

United Republic of Tanzania

DUP (1996) Ltd, pg 643
Institute of Kiswahili Research, pg 643
Northwestern Publishers, pg 644
Press & Publicity Centre Ltd, pg 644
Tanzania Publishing House, pg 644

Thailand

Graphic Art (28) Co Ltd, pg 645
Thai Watana Panich Co, Ltd, pg 646

Tunisia

Academie Tunisienne des Sciences, des Lettres et des Arts Beit El Hekma, pg 647
Les Editions de l'Arbre, pg 647
Dar Arabia Lil Kitab, pg 648
Faculte des Sciences Humaines et Sociales de Tunis, pg 648
Maison d'Edition Mohamed Ali Hammi, pg 648

Turkey

Ataturk Kultur, Dil ve Tarih, Yusek Kurumu Baskanligi, pg 649
Bilden Bilgisayar, pg 649

Uganda

Fountain Publishers Ltd, pg 652

Ukraine

Naukova Dumka Publishers, pg 653

United Kingdom

Arnold, pg 659
Audio-Forum - The Language Source, pg 661
BBC Worldwide Publishers, pg 663
Joseph Biddulph Publisher, pg 665
Blackwell Publishing Ltd, pg 666
Cambridge University Press, pg 674
Centre for Information on Language Teaching & Research (CILT), pg 677
Chapter Two, pg 678
Gerald Duckworth & Co Ltd, pg 688
Educational Explorers (Publishers) Ltd, pg 690
EPER, pg 691
European Schoolbooks Ltd, pg 692
The Eurospan Group, pg 692
Global Oriental Ltd, pg 700
Gomer Press (J D Lewis & Sons Ltd), pg 701
Graham-Cameron Publishing & Illustration, pg 701
Gwasg Gwenffrwd, pg 703
Helicon Publishing Ltd, pg 707
Hodder Education, pg 709
Hugo's Language Books Ltd, pg 710
Institute of Irish Studies, The Queens University of Belfast, pg 713
Intellect Ltd, pg 713
Karnak House, pg 717
Letterland International Ltd, pg 720
Linguaphone Institute Ltd, pg 721
Y Lolfa Cyf, pg 722
Maney Publishing, pg 725
MIT Press Ltd, pg 728

Motilal (UK) Books of India, pg 729
Multilingual Matters Ltd, pg 729
National Centre for Language & Literacy, pg 730
Nelson Thornes Ltd, pg 732
The Oleander Press, pg 735
Peter Owen Ltd, pg 737
Oxford University Press, pg 737
Packard Publishing Ltd, pg 737
Pearson Education, pg 739
Pearson Education Europe, Mideast & Africa, pg 739
Prim-Ed Publishing UK Ltd, pg 745
Psychological Corporation Ltd, pg 746
Ransom Publishing Ltd, pg 748
Reaktion Books Ltd, pg 748
Roundhouse Group, pg 751
Routledge, pg 751
RoutledgeCurzon, pg 751
SAGE Publications Ltd, pg 753
St Jerome Publishing, pg 753
Saqi Books, pg 754
School of Oriental & African Studies, pg 755
Sheffield Academic Press Ltd, pg 757
Speechmark Publishing Ltd, pg 760
Taylor & Francis, pg 763
Thoemmes Press, pg 765
University of Exeter Press, pg 768
University of Wales Press, pg 769
Verbatim, pg 769
Voltaire Foundation Ltd, pg 771
Whiting & Birch Ltd, pg 773
Wimbledon Publishing Company Ltd, pg 774
Yale University Press London, pg 776

Uruguay

Nordan-Comunidad, pg 778

Venezuela

Editorial Biosfera CA, pg 779

Zambia

Lundula Publishing House, pg 781
Zambia Educational Publishing House, pg 782

Zimbabwe

Mercury Press Pvt Ltd, pg 784
University of Zimbabwe Publications, pg 784
Vision Publications, pg 784

LAW

Albania

NL SH, pg 1

Argentina

Editorial Abaco de Rodolfo Depalma SRL, pg 2
Abeledo-Perrot SAE e I, pg 2
Editorial Astrea de Alfredo y Ricardo Depalma SRL, pg 3
AZ Editora SA, pg 3
Editorial Cangallo SACI, pg 4
Editorial Claridad SA, pg 4
Depalma SRL, pg 5
Editorial Ruy Diaz SAEIC, pg 5
EUDEBA (Editorial Universitaria de Buenos Aires), pg 5
Fundacion Editorial de Belgrano, pg 6
Editorial Idearium de la Universidad de Mendoza (EDIUM), pg 6

Juris Editorial, pg 6
La Ley SA Editora e Impresora, pg 7
Editorial Losada SA, pg 7
Instituto Nacional de Ciencia y Tecnica Hidrica (INCYTH), pg 7
Editorial Plus Ultra SA, pg 8
Ediciones La Rocca, pg 8
Tipografica Editora Argentina, pg 9
Editorial Universidad SRL, pg 9
Victor P de Zavalia SA, pg 10
Editorial Zeus SRL, pg 10

Armenia

Ajstan Publishers, pg 10

Australia

Edward Arnold (Australia) Pty Ltd, pg 12
Beazer Publishing Company Pty Ltd, pg 14
Blackstone Press Pty Ltd, pg 14
Butterworths Australia Ltd, pg 16
Cavendish Publishing Pty Ltd, pg 17
The Federation Press, pg 22
Fernfawn Publications, pg 22
Law Book Co Information Services, pg 28
Pearson Education Australia, pg 36
Prospect Media Pty Ltd, pg 37
Thornbill Press, pg 43
VCTA Publishing, pg 45
Villamonta Publishing Services Inc, pg 45
Wileman Publications, pg 46

Austria

Boehlau Verlag GmbH & Co KG, pg 48
Czernin Verlag Ltd, pg 49
Hollinek Bruder & Co mbH Gesellschaftsdruckerei & Verlagsbuchhandring, pg 52
IAEA - International Atomic Energy Agency, pg 52
Linde Verlag Wien GmbH, pg 53
MANZ'sche Verlags- und Universitaetsbuchhandlung GMBH, pg 54
Medien & Recht, pg 54
Verlag der Oesterreichischen Akademie der Wissenschaften (OEAW), pg 55
Verlag des Oesterreichischen Gewerkschaftsbundes GmbH, pg 55
Andreas Schnider Verlags-Atelier, pg 57
Springer-Verlag Wien, pg 58
WUV/Facultas Universitaetsverlag, pg 60
WUV/Service Fachverlag, pg 60

Belarus

Belaruskaya Encyklapedyya, pg 62
Publishing Center of Belarus State University, pg 62

Belgium

Academia-Bruylant, pg 62
Uitgeverij Acco, pg 62
Maison d'Editions Baha'ies ASBL, pg 63
Vanden Broele NV, pg 64
Etablissements Emile Bruylant SA, pg 64
Editions de la Chambre de Commerce et d'Industrie SA (ECCI), pg 65
La Charte Editions juridiques, pg 65

Creadif, pg 65
Editions De Boeck-Larcier SA, pg 66
Institut Royal des Relations Internationales, pg 68
Intersentia Uitgevers NV, pg 68
Uitgeverij J van In, pg 69
Editions Juridiques Kluwer a Deurne Anvers, pg 69
Larcier-Department of De Boeck & Larcier SA, pg 70
Editions Lessius ASBL, pg 70
Leuven University Press, pg 70
Maklu, pg 70
Presses Universitaires de Liege, pg 72
Publications des Facultes Universitaires Saint Louis, pg 72
Sonneville Press (Uitgeverij) VTW, pg 73
Editions Techniques et Scientifiques SPRL, pg 73
UGA Editions (Uitgeverij), pg 73
Uitgeverij De Garve, pg 74
Editions de l'Universite de Bruxelles, pg 74
Imprimeur - Editeur Vaillant-Carmanne SA, pg 74
Vander Editions, SA, pg 74
Wolters Kluwer Belgie NV, pg 74

Bolivia

Gisbert y Cia SA, pg 75

Bosnia and Herzegovina

Bemust, pg 76

Botswana

The Botswana Society, pg 76
Morula Press, Business School of Botswana, pg 76

Brazil

Aide Editora e Comercio de Livros Ltda, pg 77
Editora Alfa Omega Ltda, pg 77
Editora Atlas SA, pg 78
Centro de Estudos Juridicosdo Para (CEJUP), pg 79
Editorial Dimensao Ltda, pg 80
Edipro-Edicoes Profissionais Ltda, pg 81
Companhia Editora Forense, pg 81
EDUSC - Editora da Universidade do Sagrado Coracao, pg 81
Livraria Martins Fontes Editora Ltda, pg 81
Editora Forense Universitaria Ltda, pg 81
Livraria Freitas Bastos Editora SA, pg 82
Fundacao Sao Paulo, EDUC, pg 82
Editora Globo SA, pg 82
Hemus Editora Ltda, pg 83
Icone Editora Ltda, pg 83
Iglu Editora Ltda, pg 84
Livraria Dos Advogados Editora Ltda, pg 85
Edicoes Loyola SA, pg 85
LTR Editora Ltda, pg 85
Oliveira Rocha-Comercio e Servics Ltda, pg 87
Editora Resenha Tributaria Ltda, pg 89
Saraiva SA, Livreiros Editores, pg 90
Livraria Sulina Editora, pg 91
Tempus Editores, pg 91
Livraria e Editora Universitaria de Direito Ltda, pg 92

PUBLISHERS   SUBJECT INDEX

Bulgaria
Ciela Publishing House, pg 93
Dolphin Press Group Ltd, pg 94
Naouka i Izkoustvo, Ltd, pg 95
Seven Hills Publishers, pg 96
Sibi, pg 97
Slavena, pg 97

Cameroon
Presses Universitaires d'Afrique, pg 98

Chile
Editorial Andres Bello/Editorial Juridica de Chile, pg 99
Edeval (Universidad de Valparaiso), pg 99
Ediciones Universitarias de Valparaiso, pg 100

China
Anhui People's Publishing House, pg 101
Beijing Publishing House, pg 101
China Film Press, pg 102
CITIC Publishing House, pg 103
Foreign Languages Press, pg 104
Fudan University Press, pg 104
Lanzhou University Press, pg 106
The Law Publishing House, pg 106
Patent Documentation Publishing House, pg 106
Science Press, pg 107
Wuhan University Press, pg 109

Colombia
Centro Regional para el Fomento del Libro en America Latina y el Caribe, pg 110
Universidad Externado de Colombia, pg 111
LEGIS - Editores SA, pg 111
Ediciones Monserrate, pg 112

The Democratic Republic of the Congo
Connaissance et Pratique du Droit Zairos (CDPZ), pg 114
Presses Universitaires du Zaiire (PUZ), pg 114

Costa Rica
Juricom, pg 115
Editorial Porvenir, pg 116
Editorial de la Universidad de Costa Rica, pg 116

Cote d'Ivoire
Universite d'Abidjan, pg 117
Centre d'Edition et de Diffusion Africaines, pg 117

Croatia
Informator dd, pg 118
Knjizevni Krug Split, pg 118
Narodne Novine, pg 119

Cuba
Editora Politica, pg 120

Czech Republic
Babtext Nakladatelska Spolecnost, pg 122
Doplnek, pg 123
Grada Publishing, pg 123
Josef Hribal, pg 124
Karolinum, nakladatelstvi, pg 124
Trizonia, pg 128

Denmark
Akademisk Forlag A/S, pg 128
Dansk Historisk Handbogsforlag ApS, pg 130
Djof Publishing Jurist-og Okonomforbundets Forlag, pg 130
Christian Ejlers' Forlag aps, pg 131
Schultz Information, pg 134
Forlaget Thomson A/S, pg 135

Dominican Republic
Pontificia Universidad Catolica Madre y Maestra, pg 136
Sociedad Editorial Americana, pg 136

Ecuador
Corporacion de Estudios y Publicaciones, pg 136
Corporacion Editora Nacional, pg 136
Ediciones Legales SA, pg 136
Pontificia Universidad Catolica del Ecuador, Centro de Publicaciones, pg 137

Egypt (Arab Republic of Egypt)
Al Arab Publishing House, pg 137
Dar al-Nahda al Arabia, pg 138
Dar El Shorouk, pg 138

Estonia
Eesti Rahvusraamatukogu, pg 139
Olion Publishers, pg 140

Finland
Kauppakaari Oyj, pg 142

France
Atelier National de Reproduction des Theses, pg 148
Editions Bertrand-Lacoste, pg 149
Presses Universitaires de Bordeaux (PUB), pg 150
Editions Breal, pg 151
Editions Casteilla, pg 152
Centre de Librairie et d'Editions Techniques (CLET), pg 152
CERDIC-Publications, pg 153
Editions Charles-Lavauzelle SA, pg 153
CNRS Editions, pg 155
Codes Rousseau, pg 155
Council of Europe Publishing, pg 156
Editions Cujas, pg 156
Editions Dalloz Sirey, pg 157
Editions Delmas, pg 157
La Documentation Francaise, pg 158
Editions d'Organisation, pg 160
Les Editions ESF, pg 160
Editions de l'Epargne, pg 161
Editions Eres, pg 162
Editions Eska, pg 162
Paul Geuthner Librairie Orientaliste, pg 165
Groupe Express-Expansion, pg 166
Hachette Livre International, pg 167
Editions Hermes Science Publications, pg 167
Joly Editions, pg 169
Editions Juridiques Africaines, pg 170
Editions Juridiques et Techniques Lamy SA, pg 170
Editions du Juris-Classeur, pg 170
Editions Juris Service, pg 170
Editions Universitaires LCF, pg 171
Editions Francis Lefebvre, pg 171
Editions Legislatives, pg 171
Les Editions LGDJ-Montchrestien, pg 172
LiTec (Librairies Techniques SA), pg 172
LT Editions-Jacques Lanore, pg 173
Maxima Laurent du Mesnil Editeur, pg 174
Editions du Moniteur, pg 176
Nouvelles Editions Fiduciaires, pg 177
Editions Odile Jacob, pg 177
Editions du Papyrus, pg 178
Editions Paradigme, pg 178
Editions Pedone, pg 179
Presses Universitaires de France (PUF), pg 181
Presses Universitaires de Grenoble, pg 181
Presses Universitaires de Lyon, pg 181
Presses Universitaires de Nancy, pg 181
Presses Universitaires du Septentrion, pg 182
Publications de l'Universite de Rouen, pg 182
Editions du Puits Fleuri, pg 182
Sofiac (Societe Francaise des Imprimeries Administratives Centrales), pg 185
Publications de la Sorbonne, pg 185
Publications de l'Universite de Pau, pg 188
Librairie Vuibert, pg 189
Editions Weka, pg 189

Germany
Bank-Verlag GmbH, pg 197
Verlag C H Beck oHG, pg 198
Berliner Wissenschafts-Verlag GmbH (BWV), pg 199
Bertelsmann Lexikon Verlag GmbH, pg 200
W Bertelsmann Verlag GmbH & Co KG, pg 200
Biblio Verlag, pg 200
Verlag Hermann Boehlaus Nachfolger Weimar GmbH & Co, pg 203
CB-Verlag Carl Boldt, pg 203
Richard Boorberg Verlag GmbH & Co, pg 203
Oscar Brandstetter Verlag GmbH & Co KG, pg 204
Bund-Verlag GmbH, pg 206
Bundesanzeiger Verlagsgesellschaft, pg 206
Carl Link Verlag-Gesellschaft mbH Fachverlag fur Verwaltungsrecht, pg 207
Centaurus-Verlagsgesellschaft GmbH, pg 207
Chmielorz GmbH Verlag, pg 208
Compact Verlag GmbH, pg 209
Deutscher Taschenbuch Verlag GmbH & Co KG (dtv), pg 213
Die Verlag H Schafer GmbH, pg 214
Dreisam Ratgeber in der Rutsker Verlag GmbH, pg 216
Duncker und Humblot GmbH, pg 217
N G Elwert Verlag, pg 219
Erich Fleischer Verlag, pg 225
Verlag Franz Vahlen GmbH, pg 226
Friedrich Kiehl Verlag GmbH, pg 227
Friedrich Frommann Verlag, pg 227
Verlag Ernst und Werner Gieseking GmbH, pg 229
Wilhelm Goldmann Verlag GmbH, pg 230
Walter de Gruyter GmbH & Co KG, pg 231
Alfred Hammer, pg 233
Haufe Mediengruppe, pg 235
Rudolf Haufe Verlag GmbH & Co KG, pg 235
Joh Heider Verlag GmbH, pg 235
Hestra-Verlag Hernichel & Dr Strauss GmbH & Co KG, pg 237
Carl Heymanns Verlag KG, pg 237
Hans Holzmann Verlag GmbH und Co KG, pg 239
Huthig GmbH & Co KG, pg 240
Industria-Verlagsbuchhandlung GmbH, pg 241
Keip GmbH, pg 245
SachBuchVerlag Kellner, pg 245
Kirschbaum Verlag GmbH, pg 246
Klages-Verlag, pg 246
Vittorio Klostermann GmbH, pg 247
Verlag Knut Reim, Jugendpresseverlag, pg 247
K F Koehler Verlag GmbH, pg 248
Verlagsgruppe Koehler/Mittler, pg 248
Verlag Koenigshausen und Neumann GmbH, pg 248
W Kohlhammer GmbH, pg 248
Kulturbuch-Verlag GmbH, pg 250
Kulturstiftung der deutschen Vertriebenen, pg 250
Ambro Lacus, Buch- und Bildverlag Walter A Kremnitz, pg 251
Institut fuer Landes- und Stadtentwicklungsforschung des Landes Nordrhein-Westfalen, pg 251
Peter Lang GmbH Europaeischer Verlag der Wissenschaften, pg 252
Lebenshilfe-Verlag Marburg, Verlag der Bundesvereinigung Lebenshilfe fuer Menschen mit geistiger Behinderung eV, pg 253
Leipziger Universitaetsverlag GmbH, pg 253
Leitfadenverlag Verlag Dieter Sudholt, pg 253
Libertas- Europaeisches Institut GmbH, pg 254
Hermann Luchterhand Verlag GmbH, pg 255
Mohr Siebeck, pg 261
Verlag Neue Wirtschafts-Briefe GmbH & Co, pg 264
Nomos Verlagsgesellschaft mbH und Co KG, pg 265
Georg Olms Verlag AG, pg 267
pmi Verlag, pg 270
PIAG Presse Informations AG, pg 271
Verlag Recht und Wirtschaft GmbH, pg 274
Rossipaul Kommunikation GmbH, pg 277
Schapen Edition, H W Louis, pg 279
Verlag Dr Otto Schmidt KG, pg 280
Erich Schmidt Verlag GmbH & Co, pg 280
Max Schmidt-Roemhild Verlag, pg 280
Verlag R S Schulz GmbH, pg 282
Otto Schwartz Fachbochhandlung GmbH, pg 282
Scientia Verlag und Antiquariat Schilling OHG, pg 282
Dr Arthur L Sellier & Co KG-Walter de Gruyter GmbH & Co KG OHG, pg 283

SUBJECT INDEX

BOOK

Springer Science+Business Media GmbH & Co KG, pg 284
Verlag fuer Standesamtswesen GmbH, pg 286
Franz Steiner Verlag Wiesbaden GmbH, pg 287
Stollfuss Verlag Bonn GmbH & Co KG, pg 288
S Toeche-Mittler Verlag GmbH, pg 291
Wirtschaftsverlag Carl Ueberreuter, pg 293
Verlag fur die Rechts- und Anwaltspraxis GmbH & Co, pg 295
Verlagsgruppe Jehle-Rehm GmbH, pg 295
Verlag Deutsches Volksheimstaettenwerk GmbH, pg 296
Dokument und Analyse Verlag Bogislaw von Randow, pg 296
Votum Verlag GmbH, pg 297
VVF Verlag V Florentz GmbH, pg 297
Walhalla Fachverlag GmbH & Co KG Praetoria, pg 297
WEKA Firmengruppe GmbH & Co KG, pg 298
Werner Verlag GmbH & Co KG, pg 299
Verlag Westfaelisches Dampfboot, pg 299
Wiley-VCH Verlag GmbH, pg 300
Verlag fuer Wirtschaft & Verwaltung Hubert Wingen GmbH & Co KG, pg 300
Verlag Wissenschaft und Politik, pg 300
Wissenschaftliche Buchgesellschaft, pg 300
WRS Verlag Wirtschaft, Recht und Steuern GmbH & Co KG, pg 301

Ghana
Sedco Publishing Ltd, pg 305

Greece
Alamo Hellas, pg 305
Hestia-I D Hestia-Kollaros & Co Corporation, pg 308
Nomiki Bibliothiki, pg 310
Papazissis Publishers SA, pg 311
Sakkoulas Publications SA, pg 312

Holy See (Vatican City State)
Biblioteca Apostolica Vaticana, pg 314

Hong Kong
Butterworths Hong Kong, pg 316
The Chinese University Press, pg 316
Hong Kong University Press, pg 317
Joint Publishing (HK) Co Ltd, pg 317

Hungary
Akademiai Kiado, pg 320
Janus Pannonius Tudomanyegyetem, pg 322
KJK-Kerszov, pg 322
Nemzeti Tankoenyvkiado, pg 323
Novorg International Szervezo es Kiado kft, pg 323
Osiris Kiado, pg 323
Saldo Penzugyi Tanacsado es Informatikai Rt, pg 324

India
Academic Book Corporation, pg 327
APH Publishing Corp, pg 328
Bharat Law House Pvt Ltd, pg 330
Eastern Book Co, pg 333
Eastern Law House Pvt Ltd, pg 334
Full Circle Publishing, pg 334
Gyan Publishing House, pg 335
Himalaya Publishing House, pg 335
Indian Council of Social Science Research (ICSSR), pg 336
Islamic Publishing House, pg 338
Jaico Publishing House, pg 338
Kali For Women, pg 339
Law Publishers, pg 340
National Book Organization, pg 342
Rajasthan Hindi Granth Academy, pg 346
Regency Publications, pg 346
Samkaleen Prakashan, pg 348
Scientific Book Agency, pg 348
Sultan Chand & Sons Pvt Ltd, pg 350
Vidhi, pg 352

Indonesia
Alumni PT, pg 353
PT Bulan Bintang, pg 354
Bumi Aksara PT, pg 354
Eresco PT, pg 354
Tintamas Indonesia PT, pg 356

Ireland
Emerald Publications, pg 359
Four Courts Press Ltd, pg 360
Gill & Macmillan Ltd, pg 360
Institute of Public Administration, pg 361
Oak Tree Press, pg 362
Round Hall Sweet & Maxwell, pg 363
Topaz Publications, pg 364

Israel
Bar Ilan University Press, pg 365
Eretz Hemdah Institute for Advanced Jewish Studies, pg 366
Gefen Publishing House Ltd, pg 367
The Magnes Press, pg 370
Sadan Publishing Ltd, pg 371
Schlesinger Institute, pg 371
Schocken Publishing House Ltd, pg 371

Italy
Athesia Verlag Bozen, pg 377
Bancaria Editrice SpA, pg 377
Giuseppe Bonanno Editore, pg 378
Edizioni Bucalo SNC, pg 379
Buffetti, pg 379
Bulzoni Editore SRL (Le Edizioni Universitarie d'Italia), pg 379
Cacucci Editore, pg 379
Camera dei Deputati Ufficio Pubblicazioni Informazione Parlamentare, pg 379
Casa Editrice Libraria Ulrico Hoepli SpA, pg 380
CEDAM (Casa Editrice Dr A Milani), pg 380
Celuc Libri, pg 381
Il Cigno Galileo Galilei-Edizioni di Arte e Scienza, pg 382
Ciranna - Roma, pg 382
Cisalpino, pg 382
Edizioni di Comunita SpA, pg 383
Giovanni De Vecchi Editore SpA, pg 384
DEI Tipographia del Genio Civile, pg 384
Direzione Generale Archivi, pg 385
Ecole Francaise de Rome, pg 385
Editori Laterza, pg 386
EGEA (Edizioni Giuridiche Economiche Aziendali), pg 387
ERGA SNC di Carla Ottino Merli & C (Edizioni Realizzazioni Grafiche - Artigiana), pg 388
Esselibri, pg 388
Arnaldo Forni Editore SRL, pg 389
G Giappichelli Editore SRL, pg 390
A Giuffre Editore SpA, pg 390
Giuseppe Laterza Editore, pg 391
Herbita Editrice di Leonardo Palermo, pg 392
Jandi-Sapi Editori, pg 394
Casa Editrice Dott Eugenio Jovene SpA, pg 394
LED - Edizioni Universitarie di Lettere Economia Diritto, pg 395
Liguori Editore SRL, pg 395
Vincenzo Lo Faro Editore, pg 395
Casa Editrice Menna di Sinisgalli Menna Giuseppina, pg 398
Edizioni del Mondo Giudiziario, pg 399
Monduzzi Editore SpA, pg 399
Mucchi Editore SRL, pg 399
Societa Editrice Il Mulino, pg 399
Patron Editore SrL, pg 402
Piccin Nuova Libraria SpA, pg 403
Istituto Poligrafico e Zecca dello Stato, pg 403
Editori Riuniti, pg 405
Laurus Robuffo Edizioni, pg 405
Rubbettino Editore, pg 406
Edizioni Scientifiche Italiane, pg 407
Societa Storica Catanese, pg 408
Il Sole 24 Ore Libri, pg 408
Il Sole 24 Ore Pirola, pg 409
Spirali Edizioni, pg 409
Urbaniana University Press, pg 411
UTET (Unione Tipografico-Editrice Torinese), pg 411
Zanichelli Editore SpA, pg 412

Jamaica
Jamaica Printing Services, pg 414
Ian Randle Publishers Ltd, pg 414

Japan
Fuzambo Publishing Co, pg 417
GakuseiSha Publishing Co Ltd, pg 417
Horitsu Bunka-Sha, pg 418
Hyoronsha Publishing Co Ltd, pg 418
Ichiryu-Sha, pg 418
Koyo Shobo, pg 422
Nagaoka Shoten Co Ltd, pg 423
Nippon Hoso Shuppan Kyokai (NHK Publishing), pg 424
Ryosho-Fukyu-Kai Co Ltd, pg 425
Sagano Shoin, pg 426
Sanseido Co Ltd, pg 426
Seibundo, pg 426
Seizando-Shoten Publishing Co Ltd, pg 427
Sobun-Sha, pg 428
Surugadai-Shuppan Sha, pg 429
Takahashi Shoten Co Ltd, pg 429
Waseda University Press, pg 431
Yuhikaku Publishing Co Ltd, pg 431
Zeimukeiri-Kyokai, pg 431
Zenkoku Kyodo Shuppan, pg 431

Kazakstan
Al-Farabi Kazakh National University, pg 432

Kenya
African Centre for Technology Studies (ACTS), pg 433
Focus Publications Ltd, pg 433
Kenya Literature Bureau, pg 434
Nairobi University Press, pg 435

Democratic People's Republic of Korea
Korea Science and Encyclopedia Publishing House, pg 436

Republic of Korea
Chung Rim Publishing Co Ltd, pg 438
Hanul Publishing Co, pg 439
Iljo-gag Publishers, pg 439
Kyobo Book Centre Co Ltd, pg 440

Latvia
Nordik/Tapals Publishers Ltd, pg 445
S/A Tiesiskas informacijas cerfus, pg 445

Lebanon
Arab Institute for Research & Publishing, pg 445
Naufal Group Sarl, pg 447

Liechtenstein
Liechtenstein Verlag AG, pg 448
Verlag der Liechtensteinischen Akademischen Gesellschaft, pg 448
Megatrade AG, pg 448
Topos Verlag AG, pg 448

Lithuania
Centre of Legal Information, pg 449
Eugrimas, pg 449

Luxembourg
Guy Binsfeld & Co Sarl, pg 450
Editions Promoculture, pg 451
Service Central des Imprimes et des Fournitures de Bureau de l'Etat, pg 451

Madagascar
Societe Malgache d'Edition, pg 454

Malaysia
International Law Book Services, pg 456
Malayan Law Journal Sdn Bhd, pg 456
The Malaysian Current Law Journal Sdn Bhd, pg 457
MDC Publishers Printers Sdn Bhd, pg 457

Malta
The University of Malta Publications Section, pg 460

Mexico
Editorial Banca y Comercio SA de CV, pg 462
Libreria y Ediciones Botas SA, pg 462
Publicaciones Cruz O SA, pg 463
Editorial Esfinge SA de CV, pg 465

PUBLISHERS   SUBJECT INDEX

Ibcon SA, pg 466
Editorial Jus SA de CV, pg 467
Editorial Limusa SA de CV, pg 467
Siglo XXI Editores SA de CV, pg 472
Editorial Trillas SA de CV, pg 472
Universidad Nacional Autonoma de Mexico (National University of Mexico), pg 472

Mongolia

State Press, pg 474

Morocco

Access International Services, pg 474
Dar Nachr Al Maarifa Pour L'Edition et La Distribution, pg 474
Edition Diffusion de Livre au Maroc, pg 474
Editions La Porte, pg 475
Societe Ennewrasse Service Librairie et Imprimerie, pg 475

Myanmar

Sarpay Beikman Public Library, pg 476
Shwepyidan Printing & Publishing House, pg 476

Nepal

International Standards Books & Periodicals (P) Ltd, pg 476

Netherlands

APA (Academic Publishers Associated), pg 477
Boom Uitgeverij, pg 479
Holland University Press BV (APA), pg 483
Kluwer Academic Publishers, pg 484
Kluwer Law International, pg 485
Koninklijke Vermande bv, pg 485
Uitgeverij Lemma BV, pg 485
SDU Juridische & Fiscale Uitgeverij, pg 488
Van Gorcum & Comp BV, pg 491
VU Boekhandel/Uitgeverij BV, pg 492
Wolters Kluwer B.V. Juridische Boekenen Tijschriften, pg 492

Netherlands Antilles

Drukkerij Scherpenheuvel Haseth, pg 493

New Zealand

Aoraki Press Ltd, pg 493
Brookers Ltd, pg 494
Butterworths New Zealand Ltd, pg 494
CCH New Zealand Ltd, pg 495
Clerestory Press, pg 495
Legislation Direct, pg 498
Nelson Price Milburn Ltd, pg 499
Oxford University Press, pg 499
RSVP Publishing Co Ltd, pg 500
Victoria University Press, pg 502

Nigeria

Ahmadu Bello University Press Ltd, pg 503
CSS Bookshops, pg 504
Ethiope Publishing Corporation, pg 504
Evans Brothers (Nigeria Publishers) Ltd, pg 504
Fourth Dimension Publishing Co Ltd, pg 504
Ibadan University Press, pg 505
JAD Publishers Ltd, pg 505
New Africa Publishing Company Ltd, pg 505
Nigerian Institute of Advanced Legal Studies, pg 506
Nigerian Institute of International Affairs, pg 506
Nwamife Publishers Ltd, pg 506
Obafemi Awolowo University Press Ltd, pg 506
University of Lagos Press, pg 507

Norway

Aschehoug Forlag, pg 508
H Aschehoug & Co (W Nygaard) A/S, pg 508
Elanders Publishing AS, pg 509
Glydendal Akademisk, pg 509
Universitetsforlaget, pg 511

Pakistan

Sheikh Muhammad Ashraf Publishers, pg 511
Islamic Research Institute, pg 513
Pakistan Publishing House, pg 514

Panama

Editorial Universitaria, pg 515

Paraguay

Intercontinental Editora, pg 516

Peru

Fondo Editorial de la Pontificia Universidad Catolica del Peru, pg 517
Universidad de Lima-Fondo de Desarollo Editorial, pg 517
Universidad Nacional Mayor de San Marcos, pg 517

Philippines

Claretian Communications Inc, pg 518
Rex Bookstores & Publishers, pg 520
University of the Philippines Press, pg 521

Poland

Katolicki Uniwersytet Wydawniczo -Redakcja, pg 523
Wydawnictwo Prawnicze Co, pg 526
Oficyna Wydawnicza Szkoly Glownej Handlowej w Warszawie Oficyna Wydawnicza SGH, pg 527
Towarzystwo Naukowe w Toruniu, pg 527

Portugal

Livraria Almedina, pg 528
Armenio Amado Editora de Simoes, Beirao & Ca Lda, pg 528
Livraria Arnado Lda, pg 528
Coimbra Editora Lda, pg 530
Edicoes Cosmos, pg 530
Editorial Estampa, Lda, pg 531
Europress Editores e Distribuidores de Publicacoes Lda, pg 531
Imprensa Nacional-Casa da Moeda, pg 532
Editorial Inquerito Lda, pg 532
Livraria Tavares Martins, pg 533
Editora McGraw-Hill de Portugal Lda, pg 533
Editorial Noticias, pg 534
Petrony Livraria, pg 534
Portugalmundo, pg 535
Quid Juris - Sociedade Editora, pg 535
Usus Editora, pg 536
Vega-Publicacao e Distribuicao de Livros e Revistas, Lda, pg 536

Romania

Editura Academiei Romane, pg 538
Monitorul Oficial, Editura, pg 541
Editura Niculescu, pg 541
Rentrop & Straton Verlagsgruppe und Wirtschaftsconsulting, pg 542
Editura Teora, pg 542

Russian Federation

N E Bauman Moscow State Technical University Publishers, pg 544
Izdatelstvo 'Ekonomika', pg 544
Finansy i Statistika Publishing House, pg 544
INFRA-M Izdatel'skij dom, pg 545
Izvestia Sovetov Narodnyh Deputatov Russian Federation (RF), pg 545
Nauka Publishers, pg 547
Izdatel'stvo Nizhegorodskogo Gosudarstvennogo Univ, pg 547
Progress Publishers, pg 548
Izdatelstvo Standartov, pg 549

Saudi Arabia

Al Jazirah Organization for Press, Printing, Publishing, pg 550

Serbia and Montenegro

Privredni Pregled, pg 553
Savremena Administracija, pg 553
Sluzbeni List, pg 553

Singapore

LexisNexis, pg 557
Reed Elsevier, South East Asia, pg 557
Singapore University Press Pte Ltd, pg 558

Slovakia

ARCHA sro Vydavatel'stro, pg 559
Danubiaprint, pg 559
Vydavatelstvo Obzor, pg 560
Vydavatepstvo Praca spol sro, pg 560

Slovenia

Cankarjeva Zalozba, pg 561
Casopisni zavod Uradni list Republike Slovenije, pg 561
Univerza v Ljubljani Ekonomska Fakulteta, pg 562
Zalozba Obzorja d d Maribor, pg 562

South Africa

Digma Publications, pg 563
Juta & Co, pg 565
LAPA Publishers (Pty) Ltd, pg 566
LexisNexis Butterworths South Africa, pg 566
Perskor Books (Pty) Ltd, pg 567
South African Institute of Race Relations, pg 569
Unisa Press, pg 569
Witwatersrand University Press, pg 570

Spain

Editorial Acervo SL, pg 570
Agencia Espanola de Cooperacion, pg 571
Ediciones Akal SA, pg 571
Amnistia Internacional Editorial SL, pg 572
Editorial Aranzadi SA, pg 573
Boletin Oficial del Estado, pg 574
Bosch Casa Editorial SA, pg 575
J M Bosch Editor, pg 575
Editorial M J Bosch, SL, pg 575
Centro de Estudios Politicos Y Constitucionales, pg 576
Civitas SA Editorial, pg 577
Editora Comercial de Publicaciones, pg 577
Comunidad Autonoma de Madrid, Servicio de Documentacion y Publicaciones, pg 578
Consello da Cultura Galega - CCG, pg 578
Editorial Constitucion y Leyes SA - COLEX, pg 578
Dykinson SL, pg 580
EDERSA (Editoriales de Derecho Reunidas SA), pg 580
Instituto de Estudios Fiscales, pg 583
EUNSA (Ediciones Universidad de Navarra SA), pg 583
Fondo de Cultura Economica de Espana, SL, pg 583
Vicent Garcia Editores, SA, pg 584
Generalitat de Catalunya Diari Oficial de la Generalitat vern, pg 584
Impredisur, SL, pg 587
Institucion Fernando el Catolico de la Excma Diputacion de Zaragoza, pg 587
Mad SL Editorial, pg 590
Marcial Pons Ediciones Juridicas SA, pg 590
Ministerio de Justicia e Interior, Centro de Publicaciones, pg 591
Pais Vasco Servicio Central de Publicaciones, pg 594
Parlamento Vasco, pg 595
Ediciones Piramide SA, pg 596
Publicaciones de la Universidad Pontificia Comillas-Madrid, pg 597
Editorial Reus SA, pg 598
Riquelme y Vargas Ediciones SL, pg 598
Universidad de Santiago de Compostela, pg 599
Servicio de Publicaciones Universidad de Cadiz, pg 599
Servicio de Publicaciones Universidad de Cordoba, pg 599
Editorial Tecnos SA, pg 601
Tirant lo Blanch SL Libreriaa, pg 602
Editorial Trivium, SA, pg 602
Trotta SA Editorial, pg 602
Universidad de Granada, pg 603
Universidad de Malaga, pg 603
Universidad de Valladolid Secretariado de Publicaciones e Intercambio Editorial, pg 604
Publicacions de la Universitat de Barcelona, pg 604
Xunta de Galicia, pg 605

Sri Lanka

Lake House Investments Ltd, pg 606
Law Publishers Association, pg 607
Sunera Publishers, pg 607

SUBJECT INDEX — BOOK

Sweden
Iustus Forlag AB, pg 613
Norstedts Juridik, pg 614
Stromberg, pg 616
Studentlitteratur AB, pg 616

Switzerland
Association Suisse des Editeurs de Langue Francaise, pg 618
Comite international de la Croix-Rouge, pg 621
Editions Francois Feij, pg 623
Frobenius AG, pg 623
Georg Editeur SA, pg 624
Graduate Institute of International Studies, pg 624
Helbing und Lichtenhahn Verlag AG, pg 625
Editions Ides et Calendes SA, pg 625
Juris Druck & Verlag AG, pg 626
Kranich-Verlag, Dres AG & H R Bosch-Gwalter, pg 627
Peter Lang AG, pg 627
Editions H Messeiller SA, pg 628
Orell Fuessli Buchhandlungs AG, pg 630
Editions Payot Lausanne, pg 631
Verlag fuer Recht und Gesellschaft AG, pg 632
Schulthess Polygraphischer Verlag AG, pg 633
Staempfli Verlag AG, pg 634
Tobler Verlag, pg 635
Der Universitatsverlag Freiburg, pg 636
Versus Verlag AG, pg 636
Weka Informations Schriften Verlag AG, pg 637
Wyss Verlag AG Bern, pg 637

Syrian Arab Republic
Damascus University Press, pg 638

Taiwan, Province of China
Asian Culture Co Ltd, pg 638
San Min Book Co Ltd, pg 641
Senate Books Co Ltd, pg 641
Shy Mau & Shy Chaur Publishing Co Ltd, pg 641
Wu Nan Book Co Ltd, pg 642

United Republic of Tanzania
Tanzania Publishing House, pg 644

Thailand
Sut Phaisan, pg 646

Tunisia
Academie Tunisienne des Sciences, des Lettres et des Arts Beit El Hekma, pg 647

Turkey
Alkim Kitapcilik-Yayimcilik, pg 649
Seckin Yayinevi, pg 651
Yetkin Printing & Publishing Co Inc, pg 652

Uganda
Centre for Basic Research, pg 652

Ukraine
ASK Ltd, pg 653
Naukova Dumka Publishers, pg 653
Osnovy Publishers, pg 654

United Kingdom
Aldwych Press Ltd, pg 656
Ashgate Publishing Ltd, pg 660
Aslib, The Association for Information Management, pg 660
The Athlone Press Ltd, pg 661
Blackwell Publishing Ltd, pg 666
Blackwell Science Ltd, pg 667
Butterworths Tolley, pg 673
Cambridge University Press, pg 674
Frank Cass Publishers, pg 675
Cavendish Publishing Ltd, pg 676
CCH Editions Ltd, pg 677
Chancellor Publications, pg 677
Deborah Charles Publications, pg 678
The Chartered Institute of Building, pg 678
Class Publishing, pg 680
Commonwealth Secretariat, pg 681
Croner CCH Group Ltd, pg 684
James Currey Ltd, pg 685
CyberClub, pg 685
Dunedin Academic Press, pg 688
Edition XII, pg 690
Elm Publications, pg 691
Ethics International Press Ltd, pg 692
The Eurospan Group, pg 692
W Green The Scottish Law Publisher, pg 702
Hart Publishing, pg 705
Harvard University Press, pg 705
HLT Publications, pg 709
ICC United Kingdom, pg 711
ICSA Publishing Ltd, pg 711
Institute of Employment Rights, pg 712
Institute of Financial Services, pg 712
The Islamic Texts Society, pg 715
Jordan Publishing Ltd, pg 716
Lawpack Publishing Ltd, pg 719
Legal Action Group, pg 720
Lemos & Crane, pg 720
Letts Educational, pg 720
Liberty, pg 720
LLP Ltd, pg 722
Kenneth Mason Publications Ltd, pg 726
Oxford University Press, pg 737
Pearson Education, pg 739
Perpetuity Press, pg 741
Pharmaceutical Press, pg 741
Pluto Press, pg 743
Police Review Publishing Company Ltd, pg 744
Professional Book Supplies Ltd, pg 745
Routledge, pg 751
Shaw & Sons Ltd, pg 756
SLS Legal Publications (NI), pg 758
Sweet & Maxwell Ltd, pg 762
Telegraph Books, pg 764
Trentham Books Ltd, pg 767
TSO (The Stationery Office), pg 767
Which? Ltd, pg 772
Wilmington Business Information Ltd, pg 774
Yale University Press London, pg 776

Uruguay
Editorial Libreria Amalio M Fernandez, pg 777
Fundacion de Cultura Universitaria, pg 777

Uzbekistan
Izdatelstvo Uzbekistan, pg 778

Zimbabwe
HarperCollins Publishers Zimbabwe Pvt Ltd, pg 783
Legal Resources Foundation Publications Unit, pg 783

LIBRARY & INFORMATION SCIENCES

Albania
NL SH, pg 1

Argentina
Alfagrama SRL ediciones, pg 3
Marymar Ediciones SA, pg 7
Instituto Nacional de Ciencia y Tecnica Hidrica (INCYTH), pg 7

Australia
Auslib Press Pty Ltd, pg 12
Elephas Books Pty Ltd, pg 21
Ginninderra Press, pg 23
Magpies Magazine Pty Ltd, pg 30
Online Information Resources, pg 34
Pearson Education Australia, pg 36
Thorpe-Bowker, pg 43

Austria
Milena Verlag, pg 54

Belgium
Alamire vzw, Music Publishers, pg 63
Editions du CEFAL, pg 65

Brazil
A & A & A Edicoes e Promocoes Internacionais Ltda, pg 76
Editora Universidade Federal do Rio de Janeiro, pg 92

Bulgaria
Foi-Commerce, pg 94

China
Fudan University Press, pg 104
Shandong University Press, pg 108
Wuhan University Press, pg 109

Cuba
Instituto de Informacion Cientifica y Tecnologica (IDICT), pg 120

Czech Republic
Labyrint, pg 125
Narodni Knihovna CR, pg 126
Statni Vedecka Knihovna Usti Nad Labem, pg 127

Denmark
Dansk Biblioteks Center, pg 130
IT-og Telestyrelsen, pg 132

Dominican Republic
Pontificia Universidad Catolica Madre y Maestra, pg 136

Ecuador
SECAP, pg 137

Egypt (Arab Republic of Egypt)
Dar Al-Matbo at Al-Gadidah, pg 138

Estonia
Academic Library of Tallinn Pedagogical University, pg 139
Eesti Rahvusraamatukogu, pg 139

France
Agence Bibliographique de l'Enseignement Superieur, pg 146
Bibliotheque Nationale de France, pg 150
Editions Unes, pg 160
Electre, pg 161
Editions Legislatives, pg 171
OGC Michele Broutta Editeur, pg 177
Opsys Operating System, pg 178
PRODIG, pg 182
References cf, pg 183

Germany
Belser Wissenschaftlicher Dienst, pg 199
Berliner Wissenschafts-Verlag GmbH (BWV), pg 199
Bock und Herchen Verlag, pg 202
Deutsches Bucharchiv Muenchen, Institut fur Buchwissenschaften, pg 214
Eulenhof-Verlag Wolfgang Ehrhardt Heinold, pg 221
Harald Fischer Verlag GmbH, pg 224
Herbert von Halem Verlag, pg 233
Harrassowitz Verlag, pg 234
Dr Ernst Hauswedell & Co, pg 235
Anton Hiersemann, Verlag, pg 237
Iudicium Verlag GmbH, pg 242
Vittorio Klostermann GmbH, pg 247
Roman Kovar Verlag, pg 249
C W Niemeyer Buchverlage GmbH, pg 265
Georg Olms Verlag AG, pg 267
Philipps-Universitaet Marburg, pg 270
Dr Ludwig Reichert Verlag, pg 274
K G Saur Verlag GmbH, A Gale/Thomson Learning Company, pg 278
Staatsbibliothek zu Berlin - Preussischer Kulturbesitz, pg 286
UTB fuer Wissenschaft Uni Taschenbuecher GmbH, pg 294

Greece
Hestia-I D Hestia-Kollaros & Co Corporation, pg 308

Holy See (Vatican City State)
Scuola Vaticana Paleografia - Scuola Vaticana di Paleografia Diplomatica e Archivistica, pg 315

Hong Kong
Hong Kong University Press, pg 317

Hungary
Osiris Kiado, pg 323

India
Anmol Publications Pvt Ltd, pg 328
APH Publishing Corp, pg 328
Authorspress, pg 329
Concept Publishing Co, pg 332
Cosmo Publications, pg 332
Dastane Ramchandra & Co, pg 333
Ess Ess Publications, pg 334
Gyan Publishing House, pg 335

PUBLISHERS

Law Publishers, pg 340
Omsons Publications, pg 344
Pointer Publishers, pg 345
Prabhat Prakashan, pg 345
Pratibha Pratishthan, pg 345
Rajasthan Hindi Granth Academy, pg 346
Reliance Publishing House, pg 346
Sat Sahitya Prakashan, pg 348
Sita Books & Periodicals Pvt Ltd, pg 349
Sterling Publishers Pvt Ltd, pg 350

Indonesia
Lembaga Demografi Fakultas Ekonomi Universitas Indonesia, pg 355

Israel
University of Haifa Library, pg 373

Italy
AIB Associazione Italiana Bibliotheche, pg 374
Belforte Editore Libraio srl, pg 377
Editrice Bibliografica SpA, pg 378
Istituto Centrale per il Catalogo Unico delle Biblioteche Italiane e per le Informazioni Bibliografiche, pg 381
Direzione Generale Archivi, pg 385
Edizioni GB, pg 390
Leo S Olschki, pg 401

Japan
Nikkagiren Shuppan-Sha (JUSE Press Ltd), pg 424
Riso-Sha, pg 425
Toppan Co Ltd, pg 430

Kenya
Africa Book Services (EA) Ltd, pg 433

Republic of Korea
Prompter Publications, pg 442

Lithuania
Klaipedos Universiteto Leidykla, pg 449
Martynas Mazvydas National Library of Lithuania, pg 449

Luxembourg
Service Central de la Statistique et des Etudes Economiques (STATEC), pg 451

The Former Yugoslav Republic of Macedonia
St Clement of Ohrid National & University Library, pg 453

Mexico
El Colegio de Mexico AC, pg 463
Ibcon SA, pg 466

Monaco
Editions Andre Sauret SA, pg 474

Netherlands
APA (Academic Publishers Associated), pg 477
Stedelijk Van Abbemuseum, pg 489
Tilburg University Press, pg 490
VNU Business Press Group BV, pg 492

Pakistan
Academy of Education Planning & Management (AEPAM), pg 511
Library Promotion Bureau, pg 513
Pakistan Institute of Development Economics (PIDE), pg 514
Publishers United Pvt Ltd, pg 514

Poland
Biblioteka Narodowa, pg 522
Wydawnictwo DiG, pg 522
Instytut Meteorologii i Gospodarki Wodnej, pg 523

Portugal
Biblioteca Geral da Universidade de Coimbra, pg 529

Romania
Editura Excelsior Art, pg 539
Editura Minerva, pg 541

Russian Federation
Finansy i Statistika Publishing House, pg 544
Izdatelstvo Kniga, pg 545
Ministerstvo Kul'tury RF, pg 546
Nauka Publishers, pg 547

Singapore
Taylor & Francis Asia Pacific, pg 558

Slovakia
Sofa, pg 560
Ustav informacii a prognoz skolstva mladeze a telovychovy, pg 561

South Africa
Cape Provincial Library Service, pg 563

Spain
Arco Libros SL, pg 573
Biblioteca de Catalunya, pg 576
Eumo Editorial, pg 583
EUNSA (Ediciones Universidad de Navarra SA), pg 583
Fragua Editorial, pg 583
Editorial Sintesis, SA, pg 600
Trea Ediciones, SL, pg 602

Sri Lanka
National Library & Documentation Centre, pg 607

Sweden
Bibliotekstjaenst AB, pg 610

Switzerland
Verlag Stocker-Schmid AG, pg 635
Weber SA d'Editions, pg 637

Syrian Arab Republic
Damascus University Press, pg 638

United Republic of Tanzania
Tanzania Library Services Board, pg 644

Tunisia
Publications de la Fondation Temimi pour la Recherche Scientifique et L'Information, pg 648

United Kingdom
Aldwych Press Ltd, pg 656
Anderson Rand Ltd, pg 657
Ashgate Publishing Ltd, pg 660
Aslib, The Association for Information Management, pg 660
Cassell & Co, pg 675
Chartered Institute of Library & Information Professionals in Scotland, pg 678
James Clarke & Co Ltd, pg 680
CSA (Cambridge Scientific Abstracts), pg 684
Electronic Publishing Services Ltd (EPS), pg 690
Elm Publications, pg 691
Elsevier Ltd, pg 691
Emerald, pg 691
The Eurospan Group, pg 692
Evans Brothers Ltd, pg 693
Facet Publishing, pg 694
JAI Press Ltd, pg 715
Letts Educational, pg 720
Linen Hall Library, pg 721
LISU, pg 721
Maney Publishing, pg 725
National Library of Wales, pg 731
Taylor Graham Publishing, pg 764
TFPL, pg 764
Trigon Press, pg 767
TSO (The Stationery Office), pg 767

SUBJECT INDEX

LITERATURE, LITERARY CRITICISM, ESSAYS

Albania
Botimpex Publications Import-Export Agency, pg 1
NL SH, pg 1
State Textbook Publishing House, pg 1

Argentina
Academia Argentina de Letras, pg 2
Aguilar Altea Taurus Alfaguara SA de Ediciones, pg 3
Alianza Editorial de Argentina SA, pg 3
Beatriz Viterbo Editora, pg 4
Bonum Editorial SACI, pg 4
Centro Editor de America Latina SA, pg 4
Colmegna SA, pg 4
Ediciones Corregidor SAICI y E, pg 4
Diana Argentina SA, Editorial, pg 5
Ediciones del Eclipse, pg 5
Edicial SA, pg 5
Emece Editores SA, pg 5
EUDEBA (Editorial Universitaria de Buenos Aires), pg 5
Ediciones de la Flor SRL, pg 6
Fundacion Editorial de Belgrano, pg 6
Editorial Galerna SRL, pg 6
Editorial Guadalupe, pg 6
Editorial Planeta Argentina SAIC, pg 8
Editorial Plus Ultra SA, pg 8
Editorial Quetzal-Domingo Cortizo, pg 8
Editorial Santiago Rueda, pg 9
Seix Barral, pg 9
Editorial Sopena Argentina SACI e I, pg 9
Editorial Sudamericana SA, pg 9
Theoria SRL Distribuidora y Editora, pg 9
Editorial Troquel SA, pg 9

Armenia
Ajstan Publishers, pg 10

Australia
Access Press, pg 10
Allen & Unwin Pty Ltd, pg 11
Boombana Publications, pg 16
Centre for Comparative Literature & Cultural Studies, pg 17
Eleanor Curtain Publishing, pg 19
Dangaroo Press, pg 19
Dragon Press, pg 20
Experimental Art Foundation, pg 22
Fremantle Arts Centre Press, pg 23
Freshet Press, pg 23
Gangan Publishing, pg 23
Hat Box Press, pg 25
Hudson Publishing, pg 26
Indra Publishing, pg 27
Institute of Aboriginal Development (IAD Press), pg 27
Macmillan Publishers Australia Pty Ltd, pg 30
Magabala Books Aboriginal Corporation, pg 30
Horwitz Martin Education, pg 31
Melbourne University Press, pg 32
Mulini Press, pg 32
Nimrod Publications, pg 33
NMA Publications, pg 33
Owl Publishing, pg 35
Pan Macmillan Australia Pty Ltd, pg 35
Papyrus Publishing, pg 35
Pascoe Publishing Pty Ltd, pg 36
Penguin Group (Australia), pg 36
Playlab Press, pg 37
Pollitecon Publications, pg 37
Spaniel Books, pg 41
Spinifex Press, pg 42
State Library of NSW Press, pg 42
The Text Publishing Company Pty Ltd, pg 43
Thames & Hudson (Australia) Pty Ltd, pg 43
Thornbill Press, pg 43
University of Queensland Press, pg 45
University of Western Australia Press, pg 45
Wakefield Press Pty Ltd, pg 46
Wizard Books Pty Ltd, pg 47

Austria
Aarachne Verlag, pg 48
Verlag Der Apfel, pg 48
Astor-Verlag, Willibald Schlager, pg 48
Der Baum Wolfgang Biedermann Verlag, pg 48
Buchkultur Verlags GmbH Zeitschrift fuer Literatur & Kunst, pg 49
CEEBA Publications Antenne d'Autriche, pg 49
Czernin Verlag Ltd, pg 49
DachsVerlag GmbH, pg 49
Franz Deuticke Verlagsgesmbh, pg 50
Development News Ltd, pg 50
Literature Verlag Droschl, pg 50
Edition S der OSD, pg 50
Gangan Verlag, pg 51
Verlag Lynkeus/H Hakel Gesellschaft, pg 51
Edition Graphischer Zirkel, pg 51
Guthmann & Peterson Liber Libri, Edition, pg 51

SUBJECT INDEX

Haymon-Verlag GesmbH, pg 51
Karolinger Verlag GmbH & Co KG, pg 52
Loecker Verlag, pg 53
LOG-Internationale Zeitschrift fuer Literatur, pg 53
Merbod Verlag, pg 54
Milena Verlag, pg 54
Thomas Mlakar Verlag, pg 54
Verlag Monte Verita, pg 54
Otto Mueller Verlag, pg 54
Wolfgang Neugebauer Verlag GmbH, pg 54
Passagen Verlag GmbH, pg 56
Richard Pils Publication PN°1, pg 56
Rhombus Verlag, pg 57
Ritter Druck und Verlags KEG, pg 57
Dr A Schendl GmbH und Co KG, pg 57
Andreas Schnider Verlags-Atelier, pg 57
Studien Verlag Gmbh, pg 58
Edition Va Bene, pg 59
Wespennest - Zeitschrift fuer brauchbare Texte und Bilder, pg 59
Wieser Verlag, pg 60
Zirkular - Verlag der Dokumentationsstelle fuer neuere oesterreichische Literatur, pg 60

Bangladesh

Ankur Prakashani, pg 61
Gatidhara, pg 61
Agamee Prakashani, pg 61

Belarus

Belaruskaya Encyklapedyya, pg 62
Izdatelstvo Mastatskaya Litaratura, pg 62

Belgium

Bartleby & Co, pg 63
De Boeck et Larcier SA, pg 64
Brepols Publishers NV, pg 64
Editions Complexe SPRL, pg 65
Conservart SA, pg 65
Uitgeverij Contact NV, pg 65
Le Cri Editions, pg 66
Le Daily-Bul, pg 66
Maison d'Editions Claude Dejaie, pg 66
Editions les Eperonniers, pg 67
EPO Publishers, Printers, Booksellers, pg 67
Huis Van Het Boek, pg 68
Infoboek NV, pg 68
Koepel van de Vlaamse Noord - Zuidbeweging 11.11.11, pg 69
Lansman Editeur, pg 69
Claude Lefrancq Editeur, pg 70
Editions Lessius ASBL, pg 70
Leuven University Press, pg 70
La Longue Vue, pg 70
Editions Memor, pg 71
Nauwelaerts Edition SA, pg 71
La Part de L'Oeil, pg 71
Uitgeverij Peeters Leuven (Belgie), pg 71
Pelckmans NV, De Nederlandsche Boekhandel, pg 72
Roularta Books NV, pg 72
Scoop Infotex NV, pg 73
Snoeck-Ducaju en Zoon NV, pg 73
Sonneville Press (Uitgeverij) VTW, pg 73
Stichting Ons Erfdeel VZW, pg 73
Vita, pg 74
Editions Luce Wilquin, pg 74
Zuid En Noord VZW, pg 75

Bolivia

Editorial Don Bosco, pg 75
Universidad Autonoma Tomas Frias, Div de Extension Universitaria, pg 75

Botswana

Maskew Miller Longman, pg 76

Brazil

AGIR S/A Editora, pg 77
Livraria Francisco Alves Editora SA, pg 77
Editora Atica SA, pg 78
Editora Bertrand Brasil Ltda, pg 78
Editora Brasiliense SA, pg 79
Alzira Chagas Carpigiani, pg 79
Editora Companhia das Letras/ Editora Schwarcz Ltda, pg 80
Conquista, Empresa de Publicacoes Ltda, pg 80
Consultor Assessoria de Planejamento Ltda, pg 80
Livraria Duas Cidades Ltda, pg 80
EDUSC - Editora da Universidade do Sagrado Coracao, pg 81
Editora Expressao e Cultura-Exped Ltda, pg 81
Formato Editorial ltda, pg 82
Fundacao Sao Paulo, EDUC, pg 82
Editora Globo SA, pg 82
IBRASA (Instituicao Brasileira de Difusao Cultural Ltda), pg 83
Imago Editora Importacao e Exportacao Ltda, pg 84
LDA Editores Ltda, pg 84
Oficina de Livros Ltda, pg 85
Edicoes Loyola SA, pg 85
Editora Marco Zero Ltda, pg 86
Editora Melhoramentos Ltda, pg 86
Editora Mercado Aberto Ltda, pg 86
Editora Mercuryo Ltda, pg 86
Editora Moderna Ltda, pg 86
Editora Nova Alexandria Ltda, pg 87
Editora Nova Fronteira SA, pg 87
Olho D'Agua Comercio e Servicos Editoriais Ltda, pg 87
Editora Paz e Terra, pg 88
Ediouro Publicacoes, SA, pg 89
RHJ Livros Ltda, pg 89
Editora Santuario, pg 90
Editora Scipione Ltda, pg 90
Selinunte Editora Ltda, pg 90
Siciliano SA, pg 90
Tempus Editores, pg 91
Thex Editora e Distribuidora Ltda, pg 91
34 Literatura S/C Ltda, pg 91
Editora da Universidade de Sao Paulo, pg 91
Jorge Zahar Editor, pg 92

Bulgaria

EA EOOD, pg 94
Fama, pg 94
Galaktika Publishing House, pg 94
Hriker, pg 94
Publishing House Hristo Botev, pg 94
Interpres, pg 95
Kolibri Publishing Group, pg 95
Kralica MAB, pg 95
LIK Izdanija, pg 95
Makros 2000 - Plovdiv, pg 95
Narodna Kultura, pg 96
Pet Plus, pg 96
Prohazka I Kacarmazov, pg 96
Slavena, pg 97
Srebaren lav, pg 97

Svetra Publishing House, pg 97
Ivan Vazov Publishing House, pg 97

Burundi

Editions Intore, pg 98

Cameroon

Editions CLE, pg 98
Presses Universitaires d'Afrique, pg 98

Chile

Arrayan Editores, pg 98
Ediciones Bat, pg 99
Editorial Andres Bello/Editorial Juridica de Chile, pg 99
Ediciones y Publicidad Melquiades, pg 99
Norma de Chile, pg 99
Pehuen Editores Ltda, pg 100
Pontificia Universidad Catolica de Chile, pg 100
Red Internacional Del Libro, pg 100
J.C. Saez Editor, pg 100
Editorial Universitaria SA, pg 100
Ediciones Universitarias de Valparaiso, pg 100
Zig-Zag SA, pg 101

China

Beijing Publishing House, pg 101
China Film Press, pg 102
China Theatre Publishing House, pg 103
China Youth Publishing House, pg 103
Foreign Language Teaching & Research Press, pg 104
Foreign Languages Press, pg 104
Fudan University Press, pg 104
Fujian Children's Publishing House, pg 104
Kunlun Publishing House, pg 106
People's Literature Publishing House, pg 106
SDX (Shenghuo-Dushu-Xinzhi) Joint Publishing Co, pg 107
Shandong Literature & Art Publishing House, pg 107
Shanghai Far East Publishers, pg 108
Shanghai Foreign Language Education Press, pg 108
Universidade de Macau, Centro de Publicacoes, pg 109
Zhong Hua Book Co, pg 110

Colombia

Bedout Editores SA, pg 110
Centro Regional para el Fomento del Libro en America Latina y el Caribe, pg 110
Dosmil Editora, pg 110
El Ancora Editores, pg 111
Editora Guadalupe Ltda, pg 111
Lerner Ediciones, pg 111
Editorial Oveja Negra Ltda, pg 112
Editorial Panamericana, pg 112
Procultura SA, pg 112
Tercer Mundo Editores SA, pg 113
Universidad de Antioquia, Division Publicaciones, pg 113

The Democratic Republic of the Congo

Presses Universitaires du Zaiire (PUZ), pg 114
Saint-Paul, pg 114

Costa Rica

Ediciones Promesa, pg 116
Editorial Universidad Nacional (EUNA), pg 116

Cote d'Ivoire

Akohi Editions, pg 117
Les Nouvelles Editions Ivoiriennes, pg 117
Les Nouvelles Editions Ivoiriennes (NEI), pg 117

Croatia

AGM doo, pg 117
ALFA dd za izdavacke, graficke i trgovacke poslove, pg 117
ArTresor naklada, pg 117
Durieux d o o, pg 118
Faust Vrani, pg 118
Filozofski Fakultet Sveucilista u Zagrebu, pg 118
Knjizevni Krug Split, pg 118
Matica hrvatska, pg 118
Nasa Djeca Publishing, pg 119
Sveucilisna tiskara doo, pg 119
Tehnicka Knjiga, pg 119

Cuba

Editorial Capitan San Luis, pg 120
Casa Editora Abril, pg 120
Holguin, Ediciones, pg 120
Editorial Letras Cubanas, pg 120
Editorial Oriente, pg 120
Pueblo y Educacion Editorial (PE), pg 121
Union de Escritores y Artistas de Cuba, pg 121

Cyprus

Andreou Chr Publishers, pg 121
Chrysopolitissa Publishers, pg 121
Omilos Pnevmatikis Ananeoseos, pg 121

Czech Republic

Atlantis sro, pg 122
AULOS sro, pg 122
Brody, pg 122
Ceska Expedice, pg 123
Concordia, pg 123
Doplnek, pg 123
Galaxie, vydavatelelstvi a nakladatelstvi, pg 123
Horacek Ladislav-Paseka, pg 123
Libri spol sro, pg 125
P & R Centrum Vydavateistvi a Nakladateistvi, pg 126
Votobia sro, pg 128

Denmark

Aarhus Universitetsforlag, pg 128
Borgens Forlag A/S, pg 129
The Danish Literature Centre, pg 130
Forlaget Hjulet, pg 132
Forlaget Hovedland, pg 132
Kaleidoscope Publishers Ltd, pg 132
Museum Tusculanum Press, pg 133
Politisk Revy, pg 133
C A Reitzel Boghandel & Forlag A/S, pg 134
Samlerens Forlag A/S, pg 134
Syddansk Universitetsforlag, pg 135
Tiderne Skifter Forlag A/S, pg 135
Wisby & Wilkens, pg 135

PUBLISHERS

Dominican Republic

Pontificia Universidad Catolica Madre y Maestra, pg 136
Sociedad Editorial Americana, pg 136
Editora Taller, pg 136

Ecuador

Corporacion Editora Nacional, pg 136
Libresa S A, pg 137
Pontificia Universidad Catolica del Ecuador, Centro de Publicaciones, pg 137

Egypt (Arab Republic of Egypt)

American University in Cairo Press, pg 137
Al Arab Publishing House, pg 137
Dar al-Nahda al Arabia, pg 138
Dar El Shorouk, pg 138
Elias Modern Publishing House, pg 138
Middle East Book Centre, pg 138

El Salvador

Clasicos Roxsil Editorial SA de CV, pg 138
Editorial Universitaria de la Universidad de El Salvador, pg 139

Estonia

Ilmamaa, pg 139
Tuum, pg 140

Ethiopia

Addis Ababa University Press, pg 140

Finland

Basam Books Oy, pg 141
Herattaja-yhdistys Ry, pg 142
Kaantopiiri Oy, pg 142
Suomalaisen Kirjallisuuden Seura, pg 144
Osuuskunta Vastapaino, pg 144
Yliopistopaino/Helsinki University Press, pg 145

France

Actes-Graphiques, pg 145
Editions Actes Sud, pg 145
ADPF Publications, pg 145
Editions Al Liamm, pg 146
L'Amitie par le Livre, pg 146
L'Anabase, pg 146
L'Arbalete, pg 147
L'Arche Editeur, pg 147
Editions de l'Archipel, pg 147
Editions de l'Armancon, pg 147
Armenia Editions, pg 147
Atelier National de Reproduction des Theses, pg 148
Editions Atlantica Seguier, pg 148
Editions de l'Aube, pg 148
Editions d'Aujourd'hui (Les Introuvables), pg 148
Autrement Editions, pg 148
Autres Temps, pg 148
La Bartavelle, pg 149
Beauchesne Editeur, pg 149
Editions Belin, pg 149
Societe d'Edition Les Belles Lettres, pg 149
Berg International Editeur, pg 149
La Bibliotheque des Arts, pg 150
Bibliotheque Nationale de France, pg 150
William Blake & Co, pg 150
Editions Andre Bonne, pg 150
Pierre Bordas & Fils, Editions, pg 150
Presses Universitaires de Bordeaux (PUB), pg 150
Bragelonne, pg 151
Editions Jacques Bremond, pg 151
Brud Nevez, pg 151
Editions du Cadratin, pg 151
Editions des Cahiers Bourbonnais, pg 151
Le Castor Astral, pg 152
Editions Cenomane, pg 152
Centre pour l'Innovation et la Recherche en Communication de l'Entreprise (CIRCE), pg 152
Editions Jacqueline Chambon, pg 153
Editions Champ Vallon, pg 153
Le Cherche Midi Editeur, pg 154
Cicero Editeurs, pg 154
Editions Climats, pg 154
CNRS Editions, pg 155
Armand Colin, Editeur, pg 155
Editions Comp'Act, pg 155
Corsaire Editions, pg 156
Editions Jose Corti, pg 156
Editions Criterion, pg 156
Culture et Bibliotheque pour Tous, pg 156
La Delirante, pg 157
Desclee de Brouwer SA, pg 158
Desclee Editions, pg 158
Editions de la Difference, pg 158
Le Dilettante, pg 158
Editions Dis Voir, pg 158
Les Dossiers d'Aquitaine, pg 159
Dunod Editeur, pg 159
Les Editeurs Reunis, pg 160
Edition1, pg 160
Les Editions de Minuit SA, pg 160
Editions rue d'Ulm, pg 160
Editions Unes, pg 160
ELLUG (Editions Litteraires et Linguistiques de l'Universite de Grenoble III), pg 161
Editions Entente, pg 161
Editions Espaces 34, pg 162
L'Esprit Du Temps, pg 162
Institut d'Etudes Slaves IES, pg 162
Editions Fallois, pg 162
Editions Pierre Fanlac, pg 162
Editions Fata Morgana, pg 162
FBT de R Editions, pg 163
Editions Des Femmes, pg 163
Editions du Feu Nouveau, pg 163
Flammarion SA, pg 163
France-Loisirs, pg 164
Association Frank, pg 164
Editions Galilee, pg 164
Gammaprim, pg 165
Sarl Editions Jean Grassin, pg 166
Groupe Express-Expansion, pg 166
Groupement d'Information Promotion Presse Edition (GIPPE), pg 166
Hachette Livre International, pg 167
Editions Viviane Hamy, pg 167
L'Harmattan, pg 167
Ici et Ailleurs-Vents d'Ailleurs, pg 168
Editions Imago, pg 168
Indigo & Cote-Femmes Editions, pg 168
Editions Infrarouge, pg 168
Les Editions Interferences, pg 169
Isoete, pg 169
Ivrea, pg 169
Kailash Editions, pg 170
Karthala Editions-Diffusion, pg 170
Editions Klincksieck, pg 170
Langues & Mondes-L'Asiatheque, pg 171
Editions du Laquet, pg 171
Editions Dominique Leroy, pg 171
Lettres Modernes Minard, pg 172
Lettres Vives Editions, pg 172
Editions des Limbes d'Or FBT de R Editions, pg 172
Le Livre de Poche-L G F (Librairie Generale Francaise), pg 173
Editions Lyonnaises d'Art et d'Histoire, pg 173
Macula, pg 173
Editions Marie-Noelle, pg 174
Editions Medianes, pg 175
Mercure de France SA, pg 175
Editions A M Metailie, pg 175
Editions Albin Michel, pg 175
Mille et Une Nuits, pg 175
Librairie Minard, pg 176
Presses Universitaires du Mirail, pg 176
Editions Modernes Media, pg 176
Gerard Monfort Editeur Sarl, pg 176
Editions Maurice Nadeau, Les Lettres Nouvelles, pg 176
Nanga, pg 176
Nil Editions, pg 177
Librairie A-G Nizet Sarl, pg 177
Noir Sur Blanc, pg 177
Editions Mare Nostrum, pg 177
Nouvelle Cite, pg 177
Editions Obsidiane, pg 177
Editions J H Paillet et B Drouaud, pg 178
Editions Paradigme, pg 178
Payot & Rivages, pg 179
Peeters-France, pg 179
Editions Phebus, pg 179
Editions A et J Picard SA, pg 179
Editions Jean Picollec, pg 179
Editions Philippe Picquier, pg 180
Editions Christian Pirot, pg 180
Jean-Michel Place, pg 180
Editions POL, pg 180
Le Pre-aux-clercs, pg 180
Presses de la Sorbonne Nouvelle/PSN, pg 181
Presses Universitaires de Caen, pg 181
Presses Universitaires de Grenoble, pg 181
Presses Universitaires de Lyon, pg 181
Presses Universitaires de Nancy, pg 181
Presses Universitaires de Strasbourg, pg 182
Presses Universitaires du Septentrion, pg 182
Publi-Fusion, pg 182
Publications de l'Universite de Rouen, pg 182
Publications Orientalistes de France (POF), pg 182
Editions Pygmalion, pg 182
Editions Ramsay, pg 182
Revue Noire, pg 183
Salvy Editeur, pg 183
Editions de Septembre, pg 184
Editions Le Serpent a Plumes, pg 184
Editions du Seuil, pg 184
Siloe - Kerdore, pg 185
Editions Andre Silvaire Sarl, pg 185
Societe des Editions Grasset et Fasquelle, pg 185
Publications de la Sorbonne, pg 185
Souffles, pg 186
Spectres Familiers, pg 186
Spengler Editeur, pg 186
Editions Stil, pg 186
Editions Stock, pg 186
SUD, pg 186

SUBJECT INDEX

10/18, pg 187
Editions Tiresias Michel Reynaud, pg 187
Transedition ASBL, pg 188
Transeuropeennes/RCE, pg 188
Universitas, pg 188
Publications de l'Universite de Pau, pg 188
Editions Vague Verte, pg 188
Editions Verdier, pg 188
Editions Vilo SA, pg 189
La Voix du Regard, pg 189
YMCA-Press, pg 189

French Polynesia

Scoop/Au Vent des Iles, pg 189

Germany

A Francke Verlag (Tubingen und Basel), pg 190
Aisthesis Verlag, pg 191
Akademie Verlag GmbH, pg 191
M Akselrad, pg 191
Verlag und Antiquariat Frank Albrecht, pg 192
Alexander Verlag Berlin, pg 192
Alibaba Verlag GmbH, pg 192
Altberliner Verlag GmbH, pg 192
AOL-Verlag Frohmut Menze, pg 193
Verlag APHAIA Svea Haske, Sonja Schumann GbR, pg 193
Ardey-Verlag GmbH, pg 193
Asclepios Edition Lothar Baus, pg 194
Aufbau Taschenbuch Verlag GmbH, pg 195
Aufbau-Verlag GmbH, pg 195
J J Augustin Verlag GmbH, pg 195
AvivA Britta Jurgs GmbH, pg 196
Dr Bachmaier Verlag GmbH, pg 196
Bayerische Verlagsanstalt GmbH, pg 198
Bayerischer Schulbuch-Verlag GmbH, pg 198
Verlag C H Beck oHG, pg 198
Bergstadtverlag Wilhelm Gottlieb Korn GmbH Wuerzburg, pg 199
Edition Klaus Blahak Dr Fredric Kroll, pg 202
Blaukreuz-Verlag Wuppertal, pg 202
Verlag Hermann Boehlaus Nachfolger Weimar GmbH & Co, pg 203
Klaus Boer Verlag, pg 203
Bonifatius GmbH Druck-Buch-Verlag, pg 203
Brandes & Apsel Verlag GmbH, pg 204
Verlag Das Brennglas, pg 204
Buch- und Kunstverlag Kleinheinrich, pg 205
Buchergilde Gutenberg Verlagsgesellschaft mbH, pg 205
Buechse der Pandora Verlags-GmbH, pg 205
Christliches Verlagshaus GmbH, pg 208
Claassen Verlag GmbH, pg 209
J G Cotta'sche Buchhandlung Nachfolger GmbH, pg 210
Verlag Horst Deike KG, pg 211
Die Deutsche Bibliothek/Deutsche Buecherei Leipzig, pg 211
Deutsche Verlags-Anstalt GmbH (DVA), pg 212
Deutscher Taschenbuch Verlag GmbH & Co KG (dtv), pg 213
Diagonal-Verlag GbR Rink-Schweer, pg 214
Sammlung Dieterich Verlagsgesellschaft mbH, pg 214

1027

Dieterichsche Verlagsbuchhandlung Mainz, pg 214
Dolling und Galitz Verlag GmbH, pg 215
Drei Ulmen Verlag GmbH, pg 216
Duncker und Humblot GmbH, pg 217
Eichborn AG, pg 219
EinfallsReich Verlagsgesellschaft MbH, pg 219
Eironeia-Verlag, pg 219
N G Elwert Verlag, pg 219
Verlag Peter Engstler, pg 220
Ensslin und Laiblin Verlag GmbH & Co KG, pg 220
Espresso Verlag GmbH, pg 221
Europa Verlag GmbH, pg 222
Europaeische Verlagsanstalt GmbH & Rotbuch Verlag GmbH & Co KG, pg 222
Evangelische Haupt-Bibelgesellschaft und von Cansteinsche Bibelanstalt, pg 222
Extent Verlag und Service Wolfgang M Flamm, pg 223
Fabel-Verlag Gudrun Liebchen, pg 223
Fahrner & Fahrner, pg 223
Wilhelm Fink GmbH & Co Verlags-KG, pg 224
Karin Fischer Verlag GmbH, pg 225
S Fischer Verlag GmbH, pg 225
Fischer Taschenbuch Verlag GmbH, pg 225
Friedrich Frommann Verlag, pg 227
Gabal-Verlag GmbH, pg 227
Konkursbuch Verlag Claudia Gehrke, pg 228
Gilles und Francke Verlag, pg 229
Gmelin Verlag GmbH, pg 230
Gondrom Verlag GmbH & Co KG, pg 230
Walter de Gruyter GmbH & Co KG, pg 231
Verlag Klaus Guhl, pg 232
Haenssler Verlag GmbH, pg 233
Heinz-Jurgen Hausser, pg 233
Peter Hammer Verlag GmbH, pg 233
Hannibal-Verlag, pg 234
Hansa Verlag Ingwert Paulsen Jr, pg 234
Litteraturverlag Karlheinz Hartmann, pg 234
von Hase & Koehler Verlag KG, pg 234
Anton Hiersemann, Verlag, pg 237
Hinstorff Verlag GmbH, pg 237
Verlag Peter Hoell, pg 238
Hofbauer, Christoph und Trojanow Ilia, Akademischer Verlag Muenchen, pg 238
Horlemann Verlag, pg 239
Edition Humanistische Psychologie (EHP), pg 240
Edition Hundertmark, pg 240
Hyperion - Verlag, pg 240
Edition ID-Archiv/ID-Verlag, pg 240
Idea Verlag GmbH, pg 240
Ikarus - Buchverlag, pg 241
Informationsstelle Suedliches Afrika eV (ISSA), pg 241
Insel Verlag, pg 241
Klaus Isele, pg 242
Iudicium Verlag GmbH, pg 242
Jan Thorbecke Verlag GmbH & Co, pg 243
Peter Kirchheim Verlag, pg 246
Vittorio Klostermann GmbH, pg 247
Koenemann Verlagesellschaft mbH, pg 248

Verlag Koenigshausen und Neumann GmbH, pg 248
KONTEXTverlag, pg 249
Dr Anton Kovac Slavica Verlag, pg 249
Roman Kovar Verlag, pg 249
Karin Kramer Verlag, pg 250
Hubert Kretschmar Leipziger Verlagsgesellschaft, pg 250
Alfred Kroner Verlag, pg 250
Krug & Schadenberg, pg 250
Kulturstiftung der deutschen Vertriebenen, pg 250
Verlag Antje Kunstmann GmbH, pg 251
Kunstverlag Weingarten GmbH, pg 251
Kupfergraben Verlagsgesellschaft mbH, pg 251
Lamuv Verlag GmbH, pg 251
Peter Lang GmbH Europaeischer Verlag der Wissenschaften, pg 252
Ingrid Langner, pg 252
Michael Lassleben Verlag und Druckerei, pg 252
Leibniz-Buecherwarte, pg 253
Anton G Leitner Verlag (AGLV), pg 253
Dr Gisela Lermann, pg 253
Lettre International Kulturzeitung, pg 253
Lienhard Pallast Verlag, pg 254
Logos-Verlag Literatur & Layout GmbH, pg 255
Luchterhand Literaturverlag GmbH/Verlag Volk & Welt GmbH, pg 255
Verlag Waldemar Lutz, pg 256
Manutius Verlag, pg 257
Mattes Verlag GmbH, pg 257
Matthes und Seitz Verlag GmbH, pg 258
mentis Verlag GmbH, pg 259
Merlin Verlag Andreas Meyer Verlags GmbH und Co KG, pg 259
J B Metzlersche Verlagsbuchhandlung, pg 260
Miranda-Verlag Stefan Ehlert, pg 260
Mitteldeutscher Verlag GmbH, pg 261
Monia Verlag, pg 261
Multi Media Kunst Verlag Dresden, pg 262
Edition Nautilus Verlag, pg 263
Nebel Verlag GmbH, pg 263
Neckar Verlag GmbH, pg 263
Nie/Nie/Sagen-Verlag, pg 265
C W Niemeyer Buchverlage GmbH, pg 265
Max Niemeyer Verlag GmbH, pg 265
Oberbaum Verlag GmbH, pg 266
Edition Octopus & Okeanos Presse, pg 266
Georg Olms Verlag AG, pg 267
Orlanda Frauenverlag, pg 267
Oros Verlag, pg 267
Paranus Verlag - Bruecke Neumuenster GmbH, pg 268
Patmos Verlag GmbH & Co KG, pg 268
Pawel Panpresse, pg 268
Pendragon Verlag, pg 269
Guido Pressler Verlag, pg 271
Propylaeen Verlag, Zweigniederlassung Berlin der Ullstein Buchverlage GmbH, pg 272

edition q Berlin Edition in der Quintessenz Verlags-GmbH, pg 272
Quelle und Meyer Verlag GmbH & Co, pg 273
Quintessenz Verlags-GmbH, pg 273
Reclam Verlag Leipzig, pg 274
Rigodon-Verlag Norbert Wehr, pg 276
Rimbaud Verlagsgesellschaft mbH, pg 276
Roehrig Universitaets Verlag Gmbh, pg 276
Rombach GmbH Druck und Verlagshaus & Co, pg 276
Romiosini Verlag, pg 276
Ruetten & Loening Berlin GmbH, pg 277
Verlag an der Ruhr GmbH, pg 277
Verlag Otto Sagner, pg 278
Sassafras Verlag, pg 278
K G Saur Verlag GmbH, A Gale/Thomson Learning Company, pg 278
scaneg Verlag, pg 278
Schild-Verlag GmbH, pg 279
Agora Verlag Manfred Schlosser, pg 280
Wilhelm Schmitz Verlag, pg 280
Schoeffling & Co, pg 281
Ferdinand Schoeningh Verlag GmbH, pg 281
Verlag und Schriftenmission der Evangelischen Gesellschaft Wuppertal, pg 281
Societaets-Verlag, pg 283
Adolf Sponholtz Verlag, pg 284
Stapp Verlag Wolfgang Stapp, pg 286
Stattbuch Verlag GmbH, pg 287
Stauffenburg Verlag Brigitte Narr GmbH, pg 287
Steidl Verlag, pg 287
J F Steinkopf Verlag GmbH, pg 287
Verlag Stendel, pg 287
Edition Gunter Stoberlein, pg 288
Straelener Manuskripte Verlag GmbH, pg 288
Stroemfeld Verlag, pg 288
Edition Temmen, pg 290
edition Text & Kritik im Richard Boorberg Verlag GmbH & Co, pg 290
Treves Editions Verein Zur Foerderung der Kuenstlerischen Taetigkeiten, pg 292
Tuduv Verlagsgesellschaft mbH, pg 292
Ullstein Heyne List GmbH & Co KG, pg 293
Ulrike Helmer Verlag, pg 293
Universitaetsverlag Winter GmbH Heidelberg GmbH, pg 293
UTB fuer Wissenschaft Uni Taschenbuecher GmbH, pg 294
UVK Universitatsverlag Konstanz GmbH, pg 294
Vervuert Verlagsgesellschaft, pg 295
Verlag Klaus Wagenbach, pg 297
Friedenauer Presse Katharina Wagenbach-Wolff, pg 297
Uwe Warnke Verlag, pg 297
Wartburg Verlag GmbH, pg 297
Waxmann Verlag GmbH, pg 297
Weidler Buchverlag Berlin, pg 298
Westholsteinische Verlagsanstalt und Verlagsdruckerei Boyens & Co, pg 299
Wissenschaftliche Buchgesellschaft, pg 300
Wolf's-Verlag Berlin, pg 301

Wolgang Fietkau, pg 301
Das Wunderhorn Verlag GmbH, pg 301

Ghana
Ghana Academy of Arts & Sciences, pg 304
Manhill Publication, pg 304

Greece
Difros Publications, pg 306
Dioptra Publishing, pg 306
Dorikos Publishing House, pg 306
Ekdoseis Kazantzaki (Kazantzakis Publications), pg 307
Etaireia Spoudon Neoellinikou Politismou Kai Genikis Paideias, pg 307
Exandas Publishers, pg 307
Ekdoseis Filon, pg 307
Forma Edkotiki E P E, pg 307
Gutenberg Publications, pg 307
Harlenic Hellas Publishing SA, pg 308
Denise Harvey, pg 308
Hestia-I D Hestia-Kollaros & Co Corporation, pg 308
Hiotellis P, pg 308
Ianos, pg 308
Idmon Publications, pg 308
Ikaros Ekdotiki, pg 308
Kardamitsa A, pg 309
Kastaniotis Editions SA, pg 309
Kedros Publishers, pg 309
Knossos Publications, pg 309
Kritiki Publishing, pg 309
Kyriakidis Vasileios, pg 309
Morfotiko Idryma Ethnikis Trapezas, pg 310
Oceanida, pg 310
Kyr I Papadopoulos E E, pg 311
Patakis Publishers, pg 311
J Sideris OE Ekdoseis, pg 312
Stochastis, pg 312
To Rodakio, pg 312
Vlassis, pg 313
Zyrichidi Bros, pg 313

Guadeloupe
JASOR, pg 313

Guatemala
Grupo Editorial RIN-78, pg 313

Haiti
Deschamps Imprimerie, pg 314
Theodor (Imprimerie), pg 314

Holy See (Vatican City State)
Libreria Editrice Vaticana, pg 315

Hong Kong
Breakthrough Ltd - Breakthrough Publishers, pg 315
Chinese Christian Literature Council Ltd, pg 316
The Chinese University Press, pg 316
Chung Hwa Book Co (HK) Ltd, pg 316
Island Press, pg 317
Joint Publishing (HK) Co Ltd, pg 317
Research Centre for Translation, pg 319

Hungary
Akademiai Kiado, pg 320
Aranyhal Konyvkiado Goldfish Publishing, pg 320

PUBLISHERS — SUBJECT INDEX

Balassi Kiado Kft, pg 321
Central European University Press, pg 321
Jelenkor Verlag, pg 322
Kiiarat Konyvdiado, pg 322
Lang Kiado, pg 322
Mult es Jovo Kiado, pg 323
Nemzeti Tankoenyvkiado, pg 323
Nemzetkozi Szinhazi Intezet Magyar Kozpontja, pg 323
Osiris Kiado, pg 323
Polgar Kiado Kft, pg 324
Szabad Ter Kiado, pg 324

Iceland

Hid Islenzka Bokmenntafelag, pg 325
Iceland Review, pg 325
Mal og menning, pg 326
Stofnun Arna Magnussonar a Islandi, pg 326

India

Abhinav Publications, pg 326
Ajanta Publications (India), pg 327
Ankur Publishing Co, pg 328
K P Bagchi & Co, pg 329
Bharatiya Vidya Bhavan, pg 330
BR Publishing Corporation, pg 331
CICC Book House, Leading Publishers & Booksellers, pg 332
Cosmo Publications, pg 332
Dastane Ramchandra & Co, pg 333
DC Books, pg 333
Disha Prakashan, pg 333
Doaba Publications, pg 333
Dutta Publishing Co Ltd, pg 333
Geeta Prakashan, pg 335
Arnold Heinman Publishers (India) Pvt Ltd, pg 335
Heritage Publishers, pg 335
Indian Council for Cultural Relations, pg 336
Intellectual Publishing House, pg 338
Manohar Publishers & Distributors, pg 340
Minerva Associates (Publications) Pvt Ltd, pg 341
Motilal Banarsidass Publishers Pvt Ltd, pg 341
Natraj Prakashan, Publishers & Exporters, pg 343
Omsons Publications, pg 344
Oxford University Press, pg 344
Parimal Prakashan, pg 345
Pointer Publishers, pg 345
Rajpal & Sons, pg 346
Reliance Publishing House, pg 346
Rupa & Co, pg 347
SABDA, pg 347
Sahitya Akademi, pg 348
Sahitya Pravarthaka Co-operative Society Ltd, pg 348
Sasta Sahitya Mandal, pg 348
Sri Satguru Publications, pg 348
Sharda Prakashan, pg 349
R R Sheth & Co, pg 349
Sita Books & Periodicals Pvt Ltd, pg 349
Star Publications (P) Ltd, pg 350
Sterling Publishers Pvt Ltd, pg 350
Surjeet Publications, pg 351
Vani Prakashan, pg 352
Vidya Puri, pg 352
Vivek Prakashan, pg 353

Indonesia

PT Bulan Bintang, pg 354
PT Dian Rakyat, pg 354
Djambatan PT, pg 354
Dunia Pustaka Jaya PT, pg 354

Katalis PT Bina Mitra Plaosan, pg 355
Nusa Indah, pg 356
Pustaka Utama Grafiti, PT, pg 356
Yayasan Lontar, pg 357
Yayasan Obor Indonesia, pg 357

Ireland

A & A Farmar, pg 357
Attic Press Ltd, pg 358
Brandon Book Publishers Ltd, pg 358
Campus Publishing Ltd, pg 358
Four Courts Press Ltd, pg 360
Gill & Macmillan Ltd, pg 360
The Goldsmith Press Ltd, pg 360
Irish Academic Press, pg 361
Irish Times Ltd, pg 361
The Lilliput Press Ltd, pg 361
Mount Eagle Publications Ltd, pg 362
New Writers' Press, pg 362
Relay Books, pg 363

Israel

Bar Ilan University Press, pg 365
Ben-Zvi Institute, pg 365
The Bialik Institute, pg 365
Bitan Publishers Ltd, pg 365
Breslov Research Institute, pg 365
DAT Publications, pg 366
Dvir Publishing Ltd, pg 366
Habermann Institute for Literary Research, pg 367
Hadar Publishing House Ltd, pg 367
Haifa University Press, pg 367
Hakibbutz Hameuchad Publishing House Ltd, pg 367
The Institute for the Translation of Hebrew Literature, pg 368
Machbarot Lesifrut, pg 370
Misgav Yerushalayim, pg 370
Open University of Israel, pg 371
Schocken Publishing House Ltd, pg 371
Y Sreberk, pg 372
Tcherikover Publishers Ltd, pg 372
Urim Publications, pg 373
Y L Peretz Publishing Co, pg 373

Italy

Edizioni Abete, pg 374
Accademia (Milano), pg 374
Mario Adda Editore SNC, pg 374
Adea Edizioni, pg 374
Adelphi Edizioni SpA, pg 374
Alba, pg 375
Rosellina Archinto Editore, pg 376
Archivio Guido Izzi Edizioni, pg 376
Arcipelago Edizioni di Chiani Marisa, pg 376
Argalia Editore delle Arti Grafiche Editoriali SRL, pg 376
Bastogi, pg 377
Casa Editrice Luigi Battei, pg 377
Belforte Editore Libraio srl, pg 377
Bibliopolis - Edizioni di Filosofia e Scienze Srl, pg 378
Bollati Boringhieri Editore, pg 378
Giuseppe Bonanno Editore, pg 378
Book Editore, pg 378
Bookservice, pg 378
Bovolenta, pg 379
Bulzoni Editore SRL (Le Edizioni Universitarie d'Italia), pg 379
Calosci, pg 379
Campanotto, pg 379
Capone Editore SRL, pg 379
Casa Editrice Giuseppe Principato Spa, pg 380

Celuc Libri, pg 381
Centro Italiano Studi Alto Medioevo, pg 381
Centro Studi Terzo Mondo, pg 381
il Cerchio Iniziative Editoriali, pg 381
Cideb Editrice SRL, pg 382
Ciranna - Roma, pg 382
Cisalpino, pg 382
CLUEB (Cooperativa Libraria Universitaria Editrice Bologna), pg 382
Colonnese Editore, pg 383
Costa e Nolan SpA, pg 383
D'Anna, pg 384
M d'Auria Editore SAS, pg 384
Demetra SRL, pg 385
ECIG, pg 385
Editrice Edisco, pg 386
Edistudio, pg 386
Edizioni Associate/Editrice Internazionale Srl, pg 386
Edizioni di Storia e Letteratura, pg 386
Edizioni l'Arciere SRL, pg 387
ERGA SNC di Carla Ottino Merli & C (Edizioni Realizzazioni Grafiche - Artigiana), pg 388
Essegi, pg 388
Fatatrac, pg 388
Feguagiskia' Studios, pg 389
Festina Lente Edizioni, pg 389
Fogola Editore in Torino, pg 389
Arnaldo Forni Editore, pg 389
Gamberetti Editrice SRL, pg 390
Gangemi Editore spa, pg 390
Editrice Garigliano SRL, pg 390
Garzanti Libri, pg 390
Istituto Geografico de Agostini SpA, pg 390
Giunti Gruppo Editoriale, pg 390
Giuseppe Laterza Editore, pg 391
Ernesto Gremese Editore srl, pg 391
Herbita Editrice di Leonardo Palermo, pg 392
Ibis, pg 392
Ila - Palma, Tea Nova, pg 393
Edizioni Internazionali di Letteratura e Scienze, pg 393
Iperborea, pg 393
Ist Patristico Augustinianum, pg 393
Editoriale Jaca Book SpA, pg 394
Editrice Janus SpA, pg 394
L Japadre Editore, pg 394
Jouvence, pg 394
Il Lavoro Editoriale, pg 395
LED - Edizioni Universitarie di Lettere Economia Diritto, pg 395
Casa Editrice Le Lettere SRL, pg 395
Liguori Editore SRL, pg 395
Editrice Liguria SNC di Norberto Sabatelli & C, pg 395
Editrice la Locusta, pg 395
Loescher Editore SRL, pg 396
Loffredo Editore Napoli SpA®, pg 396
Angelo Longo Editore, pg 396
Lorenzo Editore, pg 396
Lubrina, pg 396
La Luna, pg 396
Luni, pg 396
Casa Editrice Maccari (CEM), pg 396
Giuseppe Maimone Editore, pg 397
Manfrini Editori, pg 397
Casa Editrice Marietti SpA, pg 397
Aldo Marino Editore, pg 397
Marsilio Editori SpA, pg 397
Marzorati Editore SRL, pg 397
Editrice Massimo SAS di Crespi Cesare e C, pg 397

Casa Editrice Menna di Sinisgalli Menna Giuseppina, pg 398
Milano Libri, pg 398
Milella di Lecce Spazio Vivo srl, pg 398
Il Minotauro, pg 398
Mondolibro Editore SNC, pg 399
Monduzzi Editore SpA, pg 399
Moretti & Vitali Editori srl, pg 399
Mucchi Editore SRL, pg 399
Museo storico in Trento, pg 400
Nardini Editore srl, pg 400
Istituto Nazionale di Studi Romani, pg 400
New Magazine Edizioni, pg 400
Nistri - Lischi Editori, pg 400
Novecento Editrice Srl, pg 401
Nuova Alfa Editoriale, pg 401
Nuova Coletti Editore Roma, pg 401
Editrice Nuovi Autori, pg 401
Nuovi Sentieri Editore, pg 401
Il Nuovo Melangolo, pg 401
Leo S Olschki, pg 401
Osanna Venosa, pg 402
Maria Pacini Fazzi Editore, pg 402
Pagano Editore, pg 402
Palatina Editrice, pg 402
G B Palumbo & C Editore SpA, pg 402
Franco Cosimo Panini Editore SpA, pg 402
Paravia Bruno Mondadori Editori, pg 402
Passigli Editori, pg 402
Patron Editore SrL, pg 402
Luigi Pellegrini Editore, pg 403
Piccin Nuova Libraria SpA, pg 403
Piero Lacaita Editore, pg 403
Piero Manni srl, pg 403
La Pilotta Editrice Coop RL, pg 403
Istituto Poligrafico e Zecca dello Stato, pg 403
Il Poligrafo, pg 404
Neri Pozza Editore, pg 404
Principato, pg 404
Il Quadrante SRL, pg 404
Edizioni Quattroventi SNC, pg 404
Rara Istituto Editoriale di Bibliofilia e Reprints, pg 405
Reverdito Edizioni, pg 405
Riccardo Ricciardi Editore SpA, pg 405
Edizioni Ripostes, pg 405
Editori Riuniti, pg 405
Rubbettino Editore, pg 406
Rusconi Libri Srl, pg 406
Il Saggiatore, pg 406
SAIE Editrice SRL, pg 406
Salerno Editrice SRL, pg 406
Editoriale San Giusto SRL Edizioni Parnaso, pg 406
Schena Editore, pg 407
Salvatore Sciascia Editore, pg 407
Edizioni Scientifiche Italiane, pg 407
Sellerio Editore, pg 408
SEMAR Publishers SRL, pg 408
Sicania, pg 408
Societa Editrice Internazionale - SEI, pg 408
Societa Storica Catanese, pg 408
Spirali Edizioni, pg 409
Stampa Alternativa - Nuovi Equilibri, pg 409
Studio Bibliografico Adelmo Polla, pg 409
Studio Editoriale Programma, pg 409
Edizioni Studio Tesi SRL, pg 409
Edizioni Studium SRL, pg 409
La Tartaruga Edizioni SAS, pg 409
Edizioni Thyrus SRL, pg 410
Tilgher-Genova sas, pg 410

1029

Editrice Tirrenia Stampatori SAS, pg 410
Todariana Editrice, pg 410
Giovanni Tranchida Editore, pg 410
Transeuropa, pg 410
Editoriale Umbra SAS di Carnevale, pg 411
Edizioni Unicopli SpA, pg 411
Unipress, pg 411
Vita e Pensiero, pg 412
Edizioni La Vita Felice, pg 412
Viviani Editore srl, pg 412
Zanichelli Editore SpA, pg 412
Edizioni Zara, pg 412

Jamaica

Carlong Publishers (Caribbean) Ltd, pg 413
Jamaica Publishing House Ltd, pg 414
Ian Randle Publishers Ltd, pg 414
University of the West Indies Press, pg 414
UWI Publishers' Association, pg 414

Japan

Akita Shoten Publishing Co Ltd, pg 415
Bunkasha Publishing Co Ltd, pg 415
Bunkashobo-Hakubun-Sha, pg 415
Chuokoron-Shinsha Inc, pg 416
Eichosha Company Ltd, pg 417
The Eihosha Ltd, pg 417
Fukuinkan Shoten Publishers Inc, pg 417
Fuzambo Publishing Co, pg 417
GakuseiSha Publishing Co Ltd, pg 417
Hakusui-Sha Co Ltd, pg 417
Hakutei-Sha, pg 418
Hayakawa Publishing Inc, pg 418
Holp Book Co Ltd, pg 418
Iwanami Shoten, Publishers, pg 419
Japan Broadcast Publishing Co Ltd, pg 419
Kadokawa Shoten Publishing Co Ltd, pg 420
Kaitakusha, pg 420
Kazamashobo Co Ltd, pg 420
Keisuisha Publishing Company Ltd, pg 420
Kinokuniya Co Ltd (Publishing Department), pg 421
Kodansha Ltd, pg 421
Kokudo-Sha Co Ltd, pg 421
Kokushokankokai Co Ltd, pg 421
Kosei Publishing Co Ltd, pg 421
Meiji Shoin Co Ltd, pg 422
Mirai-Sha, pg 422
Misuzu Shobo Ltd, pg 422
Myrtos Inc, pg 423
Nan'un-Do Co Ltd, pg 423
Nihon Tosho Center Co Ltd, pg 423
Nippon Hoso Shuppan Kyokai (NHK Publishing), pg 424
Otsuki Shoten Publishers, pg 425
Rinsen Book Co Ltd, pg 425
Sagano Shoin, pg 426
Sanseido Co Ltd, pg 426
Sanshusha Publishing Co, Ltd, pg 426
Seibido, pg 426
Seibundo Shuppan, pg 426
Shibun-Do, pg 427
Shincho-Sha Co Ltd, pg 427
Akane Shobo Co Ltd, pg 427
Shueisha Inc, pg 428
Shufu-to-Seikatsu Sha Ltd, pg 428
Shunjusha, pg 428
The Simul Press Inc, pg 428

Sony Magazines Inc, pg 428
Soshisha Co Ltd, pg 428
Surugadai-Shuppan Sha, pg 429
TBS-Britannica Co Ltd, pg 429
Toho Book Store, pg 429
Tokai University Press, pg 429
Tokuma Shoten Publishing Co Ltd, pg 429
Tokyo Sogensha Co Ltd, pg 430
Charles E Tuttle Publishing Co Inc, pg 430
Waseda University Press, pg 431
Yamaguchi Shoten, pg 431

Kazakstan

Zazusy, Izd-Vo, pg 432

Kenya

Heinemann Kenya Ltd (EAEP), pg 434
Lake Publishers & Enterprises Ltd, pg 435
Shirikon Publishers, pg 436

Democratic People's Republic of Korea

Korea Science and Encyclopedia Publishing House, pg 436

Republic of Korea

Bakyoung Publishing Co, pg 437
Bo Ri Publishing Co Ltd, pg 437
Bum-Woo Publishing Co, pg 437
Chang-josa Publishing Co, pg 438
Chong No Books Publishing Co Ltd, pg 438
Chung Rim Publishing Co Ltd, pg 438
DanKook University Press, pg 438
Dong Hwa Publishing Co, pg 438
Eulyu Publishing Co Ltd, pg 438
Hak Won Publishing Co, pg 439
Hakgojae Publishing Inc, pg 439
Hanjin Publishing Co, pg 439
Hangil Art Vision, pg 439
Hanul Publishing Co, pg 439
Haseo Publishing Co, pg 439
Hyun Am Publishing Co, pg 439
Korea University Press, pg 440
Koreaone Press Inc, pg 440
Kyobo Book Centre Co Ltd, pg 440
Literature Academy Publishing, pg 441
Min-eumsa Publishing Co Ltd, pg 441
Minjisa Publishing Co, pg 441
Mirinae, pg 441
Munhag-gwan, pg 441
Munye Publishing Co, pg 441
Nanam Publications Co, pg 441
Omun Gak, pg 441
Pan Korea Book Corporation, pg 442
Pyeong-hwa Chulpansa, pg 442
Samseong Publishing Co Ltd, pg 442
Seoul National University Press, pg 443
Sogang University Press, pg 443
Woongjin.com Co Ltd, pg 443
YBM/Si-sa, pg 443
Yeha Publishing Co, pg 443

Kuwait

Ministry of Information, pg 444

Latvia

Preses Nams, pg 445
Zvaigzne ABC Publishers Ltd, pg 445

Lebanon

Dar El Ilm Lilmalayin, pg 446
Dar-El-Machreq Sarl, pg 446
Librairie du Liban Publishers (Sal), pg 446
Librairie Orientale sal, pg 446
Naufal Group Sarl, pg 447
World Book Publishing, pg 447

Lesotho

Mazenod Book Centre, pg 447

Liechtenstein

Verlag HP Gassner AG, pg 447

Lithuania

AS Narbuto Leidykla (AS Narbutas' Publishers), pg 448
Baltos Lankos, pg 449
Klaipedos Universiteto Leidykla, pg 449
Lietuvos Rasytoju Sajungos Leidykla, pg 449
Mokslo ir enciklopediju leidybos institutas, pg 449
Vaga Ltd, pg 450
Vyturys Vyturio leidykla, UAB, pg 450

Luxembourg

Editions APESS ASBL, pg 450
Editions Emile Borschette, pg 450
Cahiers Luxembourgeois, pg 451
Centre Culturel De Differdange, pg 451
Essay und Zeitgeist Verlag, pg 451
Editions Phi, pg 451
Editions Saint-Paul, pg 451

Macau

Instituto Portugues Oriente, pg 452

The Former Yugoslav Republic of Macedonia

Detska radost, pg 452
Ktitor, pg 452
Macedonia Prima Publishing House, pg 452
Mi-An Knigoizdatelstvo, pg 452
Nov svet (New World), pg 453
Strk Publishing House, pg 453
Zumpres Publishing Firm, pg 453

Madagascar

Maison d'Edition Protestante ANTSO, pg 453
Madagascar Print & Press Company, pg 453

Malaysia

Pearson Education Malaysia Sdn Bhd, pg 457
Pustaka Cipta Sdn Bhd, pg 458
Tempo Publishing (M) Sdn Bhd, pg 458
Uni-Text Book Co, pg 459

Malta

Gozo Press, pg 460
Progress Press Co Ltd, pg 460

Mauritius

Editions de l'Ocean Indien Ltd, pg 461
Vizavi Editions, pg 461

Mexico

Aconcagua Ediciones y Publicaciones SA, pg 461
Editorial AGATA SA de CV, pg 462
Aguilar Altea Taurus Alfaguara SA de CV, pg 462
Editores Asociados Mexicanos SA de CV (EDAMEX), pg 462
Editorial Azteca SA, pg 462
Centro Editorial Mexicano Osiris SA, pg 463
El Colegio de Mexico AC, pg 463
Ediciones Corunda SA de CV, pg 463
Editorial Diana SA de CV, pg 464
Ediciones Era SA de CV, pg 465
Editorial Esfinge SA de CV, pg 465
Editorial Extemporaneos SA, pg 465
Fernandez Editores SA de CV, pg 465
Fondo de Cultura Economica, pg 465
Hoja Casa Editorial SA de CV, pg 466
Editorial Iztaccihuatl SA, pg 467
Editorial Joaquin Mortiz SA de CV, pg 467
Editorial Jus SA de CV, pg 467
Lasser Press Mexicana SA de CV, pg 467
Phillip Richard Conover Lazo, pg 467
Editorial Orion, pg 469
Editorial Patria SA de CV, pg 470
Editorial Porrua SA, pg 470
Ediciones Roca, SA, pg 471
Siglo XXI Editores SA de CV, pg 472
Editorial Turner de Mexico, pg 472
Universidad Nacional Autonoma de Mexico (National University of Mexico), pg 472
Universo Editorial SA de CV Edicion de Libros Revistas y Periodicos, pg 473

Republic of Moldova

Editura Cartea Moldovei, pg 473
Editura Hyperion, pg 473
Editura Lumina, pg 473

Monaco

Editions EGC, pg 473
Les Editions du Rocher, pg 474
Rondeau Giannipiero a Monaco, pg 474

Morocco

Dar Nachr Al Maarifa Pour L'Edition et La Distribution, pg 474
Edition Diffusion de Livre au Maroc, pg 474
Editions Le Fennec, pg 474
Societe Ennewrasse Service Librairie et Imprimerie, pg 475

Myanmar

Sarpay Beikman Public Library, pg 476

Namibia

Gamsberg Macmillan Publishers (Pty) Ltd, pg 476

PUBLISHERS

Nepal

International Standards Books & Periodicals (P) Ltd, pg 476
Royal Nepal Academy, pg 477
Sajha Prakashan, Co-operative Publishing Organization, pg 477

Netherlands

Uitgeverij Ambo BV, pg 477
Uitgeverij de Arbeiderspers, pg 477
Uitgeverij Arena BV, pg 478
Uitgeverij Aristos, pg 478
Uitgeverij Balans, pg 478
John Benjamins BV, pg 479
De Bezige Bij B V Uitgeverij, pg 479
BZZTOH Publishers, pg 480
Cadans, pg 480
Castrum Peregrini Presse, pg 480
Uitgeverij Conserve, pg 481
Uitgeverij Coutinho BV, pg 481
Gaberbocchus Press, pg 482
Uitgeverij Vrij Geestesleven, pg 482
Uitgeverij en boekhandel Van Gennep BV, pg 482
Uitgeverij CJ Goossens BV, pg 483
De Harmonie Uitgeverij, pg 483
HES & De Graaf Publishers BV, pg 483
Historische Uitgeverij, pg 483
J M Meulenhoff bv, pg 486
Uitgeverij Maarten Muntinga, pg 486
Nijgh & Van Ditmar Amsterdam, pg 487
Podium Uitgeverij, pg 487
De Prom, pg 488
Prometheus, pg 488
Sjaloom Uitgeverijen, pg 489
Uitgeverij Het Spectrum BV, pg 489
Thoth Publishers, pg 490
Uitgeverij Altamira-Becht BV, pg 490
Unieboek BV, pg 490
Van Gorcum & Comp BV, pg 491
Uitgeverij G A van Oorschot bv, pg 491
Uitgeverij Vassallucci bv, pg 491
West-Friesland/Boekproject-ontwikkeling, pg 492

New Zealand

Auckland University Press, pg 493
Brick Row Publishing Co Ltd, pg 494
Cape Catley Ltd, pg 495
Clerestory Press, pg 495
Hazard Press Ltd, pg 497
Kahurangi Cooperative, pg 497
Lincoln University Press, pg 498
Outrigger Publishers, pg 499
Oxford University Press, pg 499
University of Otago Press, pg 502
Victoria University Press, pg 502

Nicaragua

Editorial Nueva Nicaragua, pg 502

Nigeria

Ahmadu Bello University Press Ltd, pg 503
Evans Brothers (Nigeria Publishers) Ltd, pg 504
Hudanuda Publishing Co Ltd, pg 505
Saros International Publishers, pg 507
Vantage Publishers International Ltd, pg 507

Norway

Det Norske Samlaget, pg 508
Fono Forlag, pg 509
Snofugl Forlag, pg 510
Tiden Norsk Forlag, pg 511

Pakistan

Fazlee Sons (Pvt) Ltd, pg 512
Hamdard Foundation Pakistan, pg 512
Jang Publishers, pg 513
Maqbool Academy, pg 513
Nashiran-e-Quran Pvt Ltd, pg 513
Pakistan Publishing House, pg 514
Sang-e-Meel Publications, pg 514
Urdu Academy Sind, pg 514

Panama

Editorial Universitaria, pg 515

Papua New Guinea

The Christian Book Centre, pg 515

Paraguay

Intercontinental Editora, pg 516

Peru

Centro de la Mujer Peruana Flora Tristan, pg 516
Fondo Editorial de la Pontificia Universidad Catolica del Peru, pg 517
Editorial Horizonte, pg 517
Lluvia Editores Srl, pg 517
Sur Casa de Estudios del Socialismo, pg 517
Universidad Nacional Mayor de San Marcos, pg 517

Philippines

Anvil Publishing Inc, pg 518
Ateneo de Manila University Press, pg 518
De La Salle University, pg 519
New Day Publishers, pg 520
Salesiana Publishers Inc, pg 521
SIBS Publishing House Inc, pg 521
UST Publishing House, pg 521

Poland

Wydawnictwo DiG, pg 522
Wydawnictwo Dolnoslaskie, pg 522
Energeia sp zoo Wydawnictwo, pg 523
Impuls, pg 523
Instytut Wydawniczy Pax, Inco-Veritas, pg 523
Iskry - Publishing House Ltd spotka zoo, pg 523
Wydawnictwo Literackie, pg 524
Ludowa Spoldzielnia Wydawnicza, pg 524
Norbertinum, pg 524
Ossolineum Zaklad Narodowy im Ossolinskich - Wydawnictwo, pg 525
Panstwowy Instytut Wydawniczy (PIW), pg 525
'Slask' Ltd, pg 526
Wydawnictwo TPPR Wspolpraca, pg 527

Portugal

Edicoes Afrontamento, pg 528
Edicoes Antigona, pg 528
Apaginastantas - Cooperativa de Servicos Culturais, pg 528
Livraria Arnado Lda, pg 528
Assirio & Alvim, pg 528

SUBJECT INDEX

Atica, SA Editores e Livreiros, pg 529
Bertrand Editora Lda, pg 529
Biblioteca Geral da Universidade de Coimbra, pg 529
Coimbra Editora Lda, pg 530
Edicoes Colibri, pg 530
Edicoes Cosmos, pg 530
Dinalivro, pg 530
Editorial Estampa, Lda, pg 531
Europress Editores e Distribuidores de Publicacoes Lda, pg 531
Fenda Edicoes, pg 531
Livraria Editora Figueirinhas Lda, pg 531
Editorial Futura, pg 531
Gradiva-Publicacnoes Lda, pg 532
Impala, pg 532
Imprensa Nacional-Casa da Moeda, pg 532
Edicoes ITAU (Instituto Tecnico de Alimentacao Humana) Lda, pg 532
Latina Livraria Editora, pg 532
Livraria Minerva, pg 533
Melhoramentos de Portugal Editora, Lda, pg 533
Nova Arrancada Sociedade Editora SA, pg 534
Paulinas, pg 534
Perspectivas e Realidades, Artes Graficas, Lda, pg 534
Quatro Elementos Editores, pg 535
Quetzal Editores, pg 535
Edicoes Rolim Lda, pg 535
Sa da Costa Livraria, pg 535
Edicoes 70 Lda, pg 535
Solivros, pg 536
Teorema, pg 536
Editora Ulisseia Lda, pg 536
Usus Editora, pg 536
Vega-Publicacao e Distribuicao de Livros e Revistas, Lda, pg 536

Puerto Rico

Editorial Cordillera Inc, pg 537
Instituto de Cultura Puertorriquena, pg 537
Editorial Cultural Inc, pg 537
Ediciones Huracan Inc, pg 537

Romania

Editura Aius, pg 538
Editura Albatros, pg 538
Ararat -Tiped, Editura, pg 538
Ars Longa Publishing House, pg 538
Editura Cartea Romaneasca, pg 538
Casa Editoriala Independenta Europa, pg 538
The Center for Romanian Studies, pg 539
Editura Clusium, pg 539
Editure Ion Creanga, pg 539
Editura DOINA SRL, pg 539
Editura Excelsior Art, pg 539
FF Press, pg 540
Hasefer, pg 540
Humanitas Publishing House, pg 540
Editura Institutul European, pg 540
Editura Junimea, pg 540
Editura Kriterion SA, pg 540
Lider Verlag, pg 540
Litera Publishing House, pg 540
Mentor Kiado, pg 540
Editura Meridiane, pg 540
Nemira Verlag, pg 541
Editura Paideia, pg 541
Pallas-Akademia Editura, pg 541
Pandora Publishing House, pg 541
Polirom Verlag, pg 542

RAO International Publishing Co, pg 542
Realitatea Casa de Edituri Productie Audio-Video Film, pg 542
Saeculum IO, pg 542
Editura 'Scrisul Romanesc', pg 542
Editura Stiintifica si Enciclopedica, pg 542
Est-Samuel Tastet Verlag, pg 542
Editura Univers SA, pg 543
Universal Dalsi, pg 543
Vestala Verlag, pg 543
Vremea Publishers Ltd, pg 543

Russian Federation

ARGO-RISK Publisher, pg 543
Izdatelstvo Detskaya Literatura, pg 544
Izdatelstvo 'Ekonomika', pg 544
Energoatomizdat, pg 544
Glas New Russian Writing, pg 545
Kavkazskaya Biblioteka Publishing House, pg 545
Izdatelstvo Khudozhestvennaya Literatura, pg 545
Izdatelstvo Molodaya Gvardia, pg 546
Izdatelstvo Mordovskogo gosudar stvennogo, pg 547
Nauka Publishers, pg 547
Pressa Publishing House, pg 548
Progress Publishers, pg 548
Izdatelstvo Prosveshchenie, pg 548
Raduga Publishers, pg 548
Izdatelstvo Sovetskii Pisatel, pg 548
Sovremennik Publishers Too, pg 548
Sredne-Uralskoye knizhnoye izatelstve (Middle Urals Publishing House), pg 549
Izdatelstvo Ural' skogo, pg 549
Voronezh State University Publishers, pg 549
Vsesoyuznii Molodejnii Knizhnii Centre, pg 549
Izdatelstvo Vysshaya Shkola, pg 549

Rwanda

INADES (Institut Africain pour le Developpment Economique et Social), pg 550

Saudi Arabia

Dar Al-Shareff for Publishing & Distribution, pg 550
Saudi Publishing & Distributing House, pg 550

Senegal

Nouvelles Editions Africaines du Senegal (NEAS), pg 551
Centre Africain d'Animation et d'Echanges Culturels Editions Khoudia (CAEC), pg 551
Centre de Linguistique Appliquee, pg 551

Serbia and Montenegro

Alfa-Narodna Knjiga, pg 552
Izdavacko Preduzece Matice Srpske, pg 553

Singapore

Cannon International, pg 555
Singapore University Press Pte Ltd, pg 558
Times Media Pte Ltd, pg 559

1031

SUBJECT INDEX — BOOK

Slovakia
Vydavatelstvo Obzor, pg 560
Vydavatel'stvo SFVU Pallas, pg 560
Slovansky Tatran, Vydavatel 'stro spoi sro, pg 560
Slovenske pedagogicke nakladateistvo, pg 560
Slovensky Spisovatel Ltd as, pg 560
VEDA (Vydavatel'stvo Slovenskej akademie vied), pg 561

Slovenia
Franc-Franc podjetje za promocijo kulture Murska Sobota d o o, pg 561
Mladinska Knjiga International, pg 561
Pomurska zalozba, pg 561
Slovenska matica, pg 561
Zalozba Mihelac d o o, pg 562
Zalozba Obzorja d d Maribor, pg 562

South Africa
Jonathan Ball Publishers, pg 562
Educum Publishers Ltd, pg 563
HAUM - De Jager Publishers, pg 564
Human & Rousseau (Pty) Ltd, pg 564
Ivy Publications, pg 565
Maskew Miller Longman, pg 566
Mayibuye Books, pg 566
New Africa Books (Pty) Ltd, pg 567
Sasavona Publishers & Booksellers, pg 568
Tafelberg Publishers Ltd, pg 569
University of KwaZulu-Natal Press, pg 569
Vivlia Publishers & Booksellers, pg 570
Witwatersrand University Press, pg 570

Spain
Publicacions de l'Abadia de Montserrat, pg 570
Academia de la Llingua Asturiana, pg 570
Acantilado, pg 570
Editorial Acervo SL, pg 570
Agencia Espanola de Cooperacion, pg 571
Agora Editorial, pg 571
Editorial Aguaclara, pg 571
Alberdania SL, pg 571
Alfaguara Ediciones SA - Grupo Santillana, pg 572
Ediciones Alfar SA, pg 572
Editorial Algazara, pg 572
Altea, Taurus, Alfaguara SA, pg 572
Ediciones Altera SL, pg 572
Editorial Anagrama, pg 572
Arco Libros SL, pg 573
Editorial Ariel SA, pg 573
Editorial Barcino SA, pg 574
Bosch Casa Editorial SA, pg 575
Edicions Bromera SL, pg 575
Calamo Editorial, pg 575
Edicions Camacuc, pg 575
Carroggio SA de Ediciones, pg 575
Casa de Velazquez, pg 575
Editorial Casals SA, pg 575
Editorial Castalia, pg 576
Edicios do Castro, pg 576
Biblioteca de Catalunya, pg 576
Ediciones Catedra SA, pg 576
Circe Ediciones, SA, pg 577
Ediciones Colegio De Espana (ECE), pg 577
Compania Literaria, pg 577
Curial Edicions Catalanes SA, pg 578
Ediciones Destino SA, pg 579
Diputacion Provincial de Malaga, pg 579
Diputacion Provincial de Sevilla, Servicio de Publicaciones, pg 579
Diseno Editorial SA, pg 579
Editorial Don Quijote, pg 579
Editorial EDAF SA, pg 580
Edebe, pg 580
EDHASA (Editora y Distribuidora Hispano-Americana SA), pg 580
Edi-Liber Irlan SA, pg 580
Edilesa-Ediciones Leonesas SA, pg 581
Enciclopedia Catalana, SA, pg 582
Ediciones Encuentro SA, pg 582
Erein, pg 582
Editorial Espasa-Calpe SA, pg 582
Instituto de Estudios Riojanos, pg 583
Eumo Editorial, pg 583
EUNSA (Ediciones Universidad de Navarra SA), pg 583
Fondo de Cultura Economica de Espana, SL, pg 583
Fundacion de Estudios Libertarios Anselmo Lorenzo, pg 584
Fundacion Rosacruz, pg 584
Editorial Fundamentos, pg 584
Galaxia SA Editorial, pg 584
Editorial Gredos SA, pg 585
Grijalbo Mondadori SA, pg 585
Editorial Grupo Cero, pg 585
Guadalquivir SL Ediciones, pg 586
Ediciones Hiperion SL, pg 586
Ibaizabal Edelvives SA, pg 586
Editorial Iberia, SA, pg 586
Icaria Editorial SA, pg 587
Institucion Fernando el Catolico de la Excma Diputacion de Zaragoza, pg 587
Iralka Editorial SL, pg 588
Ediciones Istmo SA, pg 588
Joyas Bibliograficas SA, pg 588
Ediciones Jucar, pg 588
Junta de Castilla y Leon Consejeria de Educacion y Cultura, pg 588
Laertes SA de Ediciones, pg 588
Editorin Laiovento SL, pg 588
Ediciones Libertarias/Prodhufi SA, pg 589
Libsa Editorial SA, pg 589
Llibres del Segle, pg 589
Loguez Ediciones, pg 589
Editorial Lumen SA, pg 589
Antonio Machado, SA, pg 590
Ediciones Maeva, pg 590
Editorial Magisterio Espanol SA, pg 590
Edicions de la Magrana SA, pg 590
Editorial Marfil SA, pg 590
Ediciones Martinez-Roca SA, pg 591
Editorial Mediterrania SL, pg 591
Ediciones Minotauro, pg 591
Editorial Moll SL, pg 592
Anaya & Mario Muchnik, pg 592
Munoz Moya Editor, pg 592
Editorial la Muralla SA, pg 592
Naque Editora, pg 592
Noguer y Caralt Editores SA, pg 593
Ediciones Oceano Grupo SA, pg 593
Oikos-Tau SA Ediciones, pg 593
Ediciones del Oriente y del Mediterraneo, pg 594
El Paisaje Editorial, pg 594
Ediciones Partenon, pg 595
Centre de Pastoral Liturgica, pg 595
Perea Ediciones, pg 595
Editorial Playor SA, pg 596
Editorial Pliegos, pg 596
Editorial Popular SA, pg 596
Editorial Portic SA, pg 596
Pre-Textos, pg 596
Prensas Universitarias de Zaragoza, pg 597
Edicions Proa, SA, pg 597
Publicaciones de la Universidad de Alicante, pg 597
Quaderns Crema SA, pg 597
Editora Regional de Murcia - ERM, pg 597
Ediciones Rialp SA, pg 598
Riquelme y Vargas Ediciones SL, pg 598
Selecta-Catalonia Ed, pg 599
Servicio de Publicaciones Universidad de Cadiz, pg 599
Ediciones Seyer, pg 599
Siglo XXI de Espana Editores SA, pg 599
Editorial Sintesis, SA, pg 600
Sirmio, pg 600
Ediciones Siruela SA, pg 600
Edicions 62, pg 600
Grup 62, pg 600
Ediciones SM, pg 600
Anna Soler-Pont Literary Agecy, pg 600
Editorial Tecnos SA, pg 601
Ediciones Temas de Hoy, SA, pg 601
Editorial Sal Terrae, pg 602
Tf Editores, pg 602
Ediciones de la Torre, pg 602
Torremozas SL Ediciones, pg 602
Trea Ediciones, SL, pg 602
Trotta SA Editorial, pg 602
Turner Publicaciones, pg 602
Tusquets Editores, pg 603
Ediciones 29 - Libros Rio Nuevo, pg 603
Editorial Txertoa, pg 603
Ultramar Editores SA, pg 603
Universidad de Granada, pg 603
Ediciones Universidad de Salamanca, pg 603
Universidad de Valladolid Secretariado de Publicaciones e Intercambio Editorial, pg 604
Universitat de Valencia Servei de Publicacions, pg 604
Editorial Verbum SL, pg 604
Veron Editor, pg 604
Ediciones Versal SA, pg 604
Vinaches Lopez, Luisa, pg 605
Visor Distribuciones, SA, pg 605
Visor Libros, pg 605
Ediciones Vulcano, pg 605
Xunta de Galicia, pg 605

Sri Lanka
Danuma Prakashakayo, pg 606
Dayawansa Jayakody & Co, pg 606
Ministry of Cultural Affairs, pg 607
National Library & Documentation Centre, pg 607
Pradeepa Publishers, pg 607
Saman Saha Madara Publishers, pg 607
Swarna Hansa Foundation, pg 607

Suriname
Stichting Wetenschappelijke Informatie, pg 608

Sweden
Acta Universitatis Gothoburgensis, pg 609
Carlsson Bokfoerlag AB, pg 610
Ellerstroms, pg 611
Klassikerforlaget, pg 613
Bokforlaget Nya Doxa AB, pg 614
Bokforlaget Opal AB, pg 614
Schultz Forlag AB, pg 615

Switzerland
Editions L'Age d'Homme - La Cite, pg 617
Ammann Verlag & Co, pg 617
Arche Verlag AG, Raabe und Vitali, pg 617
Archivio Storico Ticinese, pg 617
Athenaeum Verlag AG, pg 618
Atrium Verlag AG, pg 618
H R Balmer AG Verlag, pg 618
Bargezzi-Verlag AG, pg 618
Bartschi Publishing, pg 618
Bergli Books AG, pg 619
Edizioni Casagrande SA, pg 620
Christoph Merian Verlag, pg 620
Edizioni Armando Dado, Tipografia Stazione, pg 621
Editions Andre Delcourt & Cie, pg 621
Diogenes Verlag AG, pg 622
Librairie Droz SA, pg 622
Eboris-Coda-Bompiani, pg 622
Eco Verlags AG, pg 622
Edition Epoca, pg 622
Erker-Verlag, pg 623
Edition Hans Erpf Edition, pg 623
Editions Esprit Ouvert, pg 623
Editions Foma SA, pg 623
Frobenius, pg 623
Haffmans Verlag AG, pg 624
Kranich-Verlag, Dres AG & H R Bosch-Gwalter, pg 627
Peter Lang AG, pg 627
Lia rumantscha, pg 627
Limmat Verlag, pg 628
Manesse Verlag GmbH, pg 628
Memory/Cage Editions, pg 628
Les Editions Noir sur Blanc, pg 629
Editions Payot Lausanne, pg 631
Pedrazzini Tipografia, pg 631
Philosophisch-Anthroposophischer Verlag am Goetheanum, pg 631
Editions Pourquoi Pas, pg 631
Raphael, Editions, pg 632
Rauhreif Verlag, pg 632
Rodera-Verlag der Cardun AG, pg 632
Satyr-Verlag Dr Humbel, pg 633
Verlag fuer Schoene Wissenschaften, pg 633
Schwabe & Co AG, pg 633
Istituto Editoriale Ticinese (IET) SA, pg 635
Der Universitatsverlag Freiburg, pg 636
Vexer Verlag, pg 636
Verlag Die Waage, pg 636
Verlag Alexander Wild, pg 637
Editions Zoe, pg 638

Syrian Arab Republic
Institut Francais d'Etudes Arabes de Damas, pg 638

Taiwan, Province of China
Ai Chih Book Co Ltd, pg 638
Asian Culture Co Ltd, pg 638
Bookman Books Ltd, pg 639
Cheng Wen Publishing Company, pg 639
Chu Liu Book Company, pg 639
Chung Hwa Book Co Ltd, pg 639
Far East Book Co Ltd, pg 639
Hsiao Yuan Publication Co, Ltd, pg 640

PUBLISHERS

Kuang Fu Book Co Ltd, pg 640
Laureate Book Co Ltd, pg 640
Lin Pai Press Company Ltd, pg 641
Linking Publishing Company Ltd, pg 641
San Min Book Co Ltd, pg 641
UNITAS Publishing Co Ltd, pg 642
World Book Co Ltd, pg 642
Wu Nan Book Co Ltd, pg 642
Yee Wen Publishing Co Ltd, pg 642
Youth Cultural Publishing Co, pg 642

United Republic of Tanzania

Bilal Muslim Mission of Tanzania, pg 643
Institute of Kiswahili Research, pg 643
Oxford University Press, pg 644
Press & Publicity Centre Ltd, pg 644

Thailand

Suriyaban Publishers, pg 646

Togo

Editions Akpagnon, pg 646

Tunisia

Academie Tunisienne des Sciences, des Lettres et des Arts Beit El Hekma, pg 647
Les Editions de l'Arbre, pg 647
Dar Arabia Lil Kitab, pg 648
Dar El Afaq, pg 648
Faculte des Sciences Humaines et Sociales de Tunis, pg 648
Maison d'Edition Mohamed Ali Hammi, pg 648
Maison Tunisienne de l'Edition, pg 648
Sud Editions, pg 648

Turkey

Dost Yayinlari, pg 650
Ezel Erverdi (Dergah Yayinlari AS) Muessese Muduru, pg 650
Iletisim Yayinlari, pg 650
Kiyi Yayinlari, pg 650
Kubbealti Akademisi Kultur ve Sasat Vakfi, pg 650
Metis Yayinlari, pg 650
Payel Yayinevi, pg 651
Toker Yayinlari, pg 651
Toros Yayinlari Ltd Co, pg 652
Turkish Republic - Ministry of Culture, pg 652
Kabalci Yayinevi, pg 652
Alev Yayinlari, pg 652

Ukraine

Dnipro, pg 653
Lybid (University of Kyyiv Press), pg 653
Mystetstvo Publishers, pg 653
Naukova Dumka Publishers, pg 653
Osvita, pg 654
Veselka Publishers, pg 654

United Kingdom

ABC-CLIO, pg 654
Appletree Press Ltd, pg 658
Arnold, pg 659
Ashgate Publishing Ltd, pg 660
Association for Scottish Literary Studies, pg 661
BCA - Book Club Associates, pg 663
Berghahn Books Ltd, pg 665
Joseph Biddulph Publisher, pg 665
Blackstaff Press, pg 666
Blackwell Publishing Ltd, pg 666
Bloomsbury Publishing PLC, pg 668
The Book Guild Ltd, pg 668
Boulevard Books UK/The Babel Guides, pg 669
Marion Boyars Publishers Ltd, pg 669
Boydell & Brewer Ltd, pg 669
The British Academy, pg 671
Calder Publications Ltd, pg 673
Cambridge University Press, pg 674
Canongate Books Ltd, pg 674
Carcanet Press Ltd, pg 674
Cardiff Academic Press, pg 675
Frank Cass Publishers, pg 675
Chadwyck-Healey Ltd, pg 677
Chapman, pg 677
The Chrysalis Press, pg 679
James Clarke & Co Ltd, pg 680
Constable & Robinson Ltd, pg 682
The Continuum International Publishing Group Ltd, pg 682
Cyhoeddiadau Barddas, pg 685
Dedalus Ltd, pg 687
Gerald Duckworth & Co Ltd, pg 688
Dunedin Academic Press, pg 688
Edinburgh University Press Ltd, pg 689
Element Books Ltd, pg 690
Aidan Ellis Publishing, pg 690
The Eurospan Group, pg 692
Ex Libris Press, pg 693
Faber & Faber Ltd, pg 694
Fourth Estate, pg 696
Garnet Publishing Ltd, pg 698
Genesis Publications Ltd, pg 699
E J W Gibb Memorial Trust, pg 700
Global Oriental Ltd, pg 700
Golden Cockerel Press Ltd, pg 701
Grant & Cutler Ltd, pg 702
Granta Books, pg 702
The Greek Bookshop, pg 702
HarperCollins UK, pg 705
Harvard University Press, pg 705
The Harvill Press, pg 705
Helm Information Ltd, pg 707
Hippopotamus Press, pg 709
Hodder Education, pg 709
Libris Ltd, pg 720
Linen Hall Library, pg 721
The Littman Library of Jewish Civilization, pg 721
Liverpool University Press, pg 722
Luath Press Ltd, pg 722
Mainstream Publishing Co (Edinburgh) Ltd, pg 724
Manchester University Press, pg 724
Maney Publishing, pg 725
Mango Publishing, pg 725
Mercat Press, pg 726
Merrion Press, pg 727
Microform Academic Publishers, pg 728
Motilal (UK) Books of India, pg 729
National Association for the Teaching of English (NATE), pg 730
National Library of Wales, pg 731
Northcote House Publishers Ltd, pg 733
W W Norton & Company Ltd, pg 734
Octopus Publishing Group, pg 734
The Oleander Press, pg 735
Osborne Books Ltd, pg 736
Peter Owen Ltd, pg 737
Oxford University Press, pg 737
Parapress Ltd, pg 738
Pearson Education, pg 739
Peepal Tree Press Ltd, pg 740
Pickering & Chatto Publishers Ltd, pg 742
Planet, pg 743
Plantin Publishers, pg 743
Polybooks Ltd, pg 744
Polygon, pg 744
Ramsay Head Press, pg 747
Rationalist Press Association, pg 748
Reaktion Books Ltd, pg 748
Redcliffe Press Ltd, pg 749
Roundhouse Group, pg 751
Routledge, pg 751
The Rubicon Press, pg 752
St George's Press, pg 753
The Saltire Society, pg 753
Saqi Books, pg 754
Steve Savage Publishers Ltd, pg 754
School of Oriental & African Studies, pg 755
Scottish Cultural Press, pg 755
Scottish Text Society, pg 755
Seren, pg 756
Serpent's Tail Ltd, pg 756
Sheffield Academic Press Ltd, pg 757
Shelfmark Books, pg 757
Skoob Russell Square, pg 758
Colin Smythe Ltd, pg 759
Sutton Publishing Ltd, pg 762
Tabb House, pg 762
Tern Press, pg 764
Thomson Gale, pg 765
Toucan Press, pg 766
Trigon Press, pg 767
Tuckwell Press Ltd, pg 767
Ulverscroft Large Print Books Ltd, pg 768
University of Exeter Press, pg 768
University of Hertfordshire Press, pg 768
University of Wales Press, pg 769
Vallentine, Mitchell & Co Ltd, pg 769
Verso, pg 770
Voltaire Foundation Ltd, pg 771
Welsh Academic Press, pg 772
Whiting & Birch Ltd, pg 773
Wimbledon Publishing Company Ltd, pg 774
The Women's Press Ltd, pg 775
Wordsworth Editions Ltd, pg 775
Yale University Press London, pg 776

Uruguay

Arpoador, pg 777
Barreiro y Ramos SA, pg 777
Ediciones de Juan Darien, pg 777
Linardi y Risso Libreria, pg 777
A Monteverde y Cia SA, pg 777
Mosca Hermanos, pg 777
Nordan-Comunidad, pg 778
Punto de Encuentro Ediciones, pg 778
Luis A Retta Libros, pg 778
Ediciones Sol del Sur, pg 778
Ediciones Trilce, pg 778
La Urpila Editores, pg 778
Vinten Editor, pg 778

Uzbekistan

Izdatelstvo Literatury i isskustva, pg 778

Venezuela

Alfadil Ediciones, pg 778
Editorial Ateneo de Caracas, pg 779
Monte Avila Editores Latinoamericana CA, pg 779
Biblioteca Ayacucho, pg 779

Zambia

Zambia Educational Publishing House, pg 782

Zimbabwe

Academic Books (Pvt) Ltd, pg 782
Anvil Press, pg 782
The Literature Bureau, pg 783
Nehanda Publishers, pg 784
University of Zimbabwe Publications, pg 784
Vision Publications, pg 784
Zimbabwe Publishing House (Pvt) Ltd, pg 784

MANAGEMENT

Albania

NL SH, pg 1

Australia

Boolarong Press, pg 15
Fernfawn Publications, pg 22
Hale & Iremonger Pty Ltd, pg 24
James Nicholas Publishers Pty Ltd, pg 27
Macmillan Education Australia, pg 30
McGraw-Hill Australia Pty Ltd, pg 31
OTEN (Open Training & Education Network), pg 34
Pearson Education Australia, pg 36
Plum Press, pg 37
The Real Estate Institute of Australia, pg 39
RMIT Publishing, pg 39
Simon & Schuster (Australia) Pty Ltd, pg 41
Tertiary Press, pg 43
Wellness Australia, pg 46
Wrightbooks Pty Ltd, pg 47

Austria

Braintrust Marketing Services Ges mbH Verlag, pg 49
International Institute for Applied Systems Analysis (IIASA), pg 52
Linde Verlag Wien GmbH, pg 53
Verlag Orac im Verlag Kremayr & Scheriau, pg 56
WUV/Service Fachverlag, pg 60

Azerbaijan

Sada, Literaturno-Izdatel'skij Centr, pg 60

Bangladesh

The University Press Ltd, pg 61

Barbados

Business Tutors, pg 62

Belgium

Editions De Boeck-Larcier SA, pg 66
Documenta CV, pg 66
Uitgeverij Lannoo NV, pg 69
Maklu, pg 70
Roularta Books NV, pg 72
Scoop Infotex NV, pg 73

Brazil

Editora Alfa Omega Ltda, pg 77
Editora Aquariana Ltda, pg 77
ARTMED Editora, pg 78
Editora Atlas SA, pg 78
Editora Edgard Blucher Ltda, pg 79

Editora FCO Ltda, pg 81
Editora Harbra Ltda, pg 83
Livraria Editora Infobook SA, pg 85
Edicoes Loyola SA, pg 85
LTC-Livros Tecnicos e Cientificos Editora S/A, pg 85
Editora Lucre Comercio e Representacoes, pg 85
Editora Ortiz SA, pg 88
Livraria Pioneira Editora/Enio Matheus Guazzelli e Cia Ltd, pg 88
Qualitymark Editora Ltda, pg 89
Editora Rocco Ltda, pg 89
Saraiva SA, Livreiros Editores, pg 90
Editora Universidade Federal do Rio de Janeiro, pg 92
Jorge Zahar Editor, pg 92

Bulgaria
Dolphin Press Group Ltd, pg 94
Makros 2000 - Plovdiv, pg 95
Sita-MB, pg 97

Chile
Norma de Chile, pg 99

China
Beijing Publishing House, pg 101
China Foreign Economic Relations & Trade Publishing House, pg 102
China Machine Press (CMP), pg 102
China Materials Management Publishing House, pg 102
China Ocean Press, pg 102
China Textile Press, pg 103
China Translation & Publishing Corp, pg 103
Chongqing University Press, pg 103
CITIC Publishing House, pg 103
Dalian Maritime University Press, pg 104
Fudan University Press, pg 104
Heilongjiang Science & Technology Press, pg 105
Higher Education Press, pg 105
Jilin Science & Technology Publishing House, pg 105
Metallurgical Industry Press (MIP), pg 106
Printing Industry Publishing House, pg 107
SDX (Shenghuo-Dushu-Xinzhi) Joint Publishing Co, pg 107
Shandong University Press, pg 108
Shanghai Far East Publishers, pg 108
Southwest China Jiaotong University Press, pg 108
Universidade de Macau, Centro de Publicacoes, pg 109
Yunnan University Press, pg 109

Colombia
Universidad Externado de Colombia, pg 111
Fundacion Universidad de la Sabana Ediciones INSE, pg 111
LEGIS - Editores SA, pg 111
Editorial Santillana SA, pg 112
Universidad Nacional Abierta y a Distancia, pg 113

Costa Rica
Editorial de la Universidad de Costa Rica, pg 116

Croatia
Masmedia, pg 118

Cuba
ISCAH Fructuoso Rodriguez, pg 120

Czech Republic
NS Svoboda spol sro, pg 127
Svoboda Servis GmbH, pg 127

Denmark
Bierman og Bierman I/S, pg 129
Borsen Forlag, pg 129
New Era Publications International ApS, pg 133
Samfundslitteratur, pg 134

Dominican Republic
Pontificia Universidad Catolica Madre y Maestra, pg 136

Egypt (Arab Republic of Egypt)
Dar El Shorouk, pg 138

France
Editions Breal, pg 151
Centre de Librairie et d'Editions Techniques (CLET), pg 152
Chotard et Associes Editeurs, pg 154
La Documentation Francaise, pg 158
Dunod Editeur, pg 159
Institute Editeur, pg 160
Editions d'Organisation, pg 160
Les Editions ESF, pg 160
Editions Eska, pg 162
Editions Eyrolles, pg 162
Association Francaise de Normalisation, pg 164
Futuribles SARL, pg 164
Hachette Pratiques, pg 167
InterEditions, pg 169
Editions Juris Service, pg 170
Maxima Laurent du Mesnil Editeur, pg 174
Nouvelles Editions Fiduciaires, pg 177
Editions Pedone, pg 179
Les Presses du Management, pg 181
Presses Universitaires de Grenoble, pg 181
Presses Universitaires de Lyon, pg 181
TOP Editions, pg 188
Editions Village Mondial, pg 189
Editions Weka, pg 189

Germany
Accedo Verlagsgesellschaft mbH, pg 190
AOL-Verlag Frohmut Menze, pg 193
ARCult Media, pg 193
Bank-Verlag GmbH, pg 197
Verlag C H Beck oHG, pg 198
Berliner Wissenschafts-Verlag GmbH (BWV), pg 199
Bertelsmann Lexikon Verlag GmbH, pg 200
W Bertelsmann Verlag GmbH & Co KG, pg 200
Beuth Verlag GmbH, pg 200
Brandenburgisches Verlagshaus in der Dornier Medienholding GmbH, pg 204
Campus Verlag GmbH, pg 207
Carl-Auer-Systeme Verlag, pg 207
Cornelsen Verlag GmbH & Co OHG, pg 210
J G Cotta'sche Buchhandlung Nachfolger GmbH, pg 210
Deutscher Wirtschaftsdienst John von Freyend GmbH, pg 214
Die Verlag H Schafer GmbH, pg 214
Eppinger-Verlag OHG, pg 220
expert verlag GmbH, Fachverlag fuer Wirtschaft & Technik, pg 222
Verlag Franz Vahlen GmbH, pg 226
Gabal-Verlag GmbH, pg 227
Betriebswirtschaftlicher Verlag Dr Th Gabler, pg 228
Walter de Gruyter GmbH & Co KG, pg 231
Gunter Olzog Verlag GmbH, pg 231
Alfred Hammer, pg 233
Carl Hanser Verlag, pg 234
Rudolf Haufe Verlag GmbH & Co KG, pg 235
Carl Heymanns Verlag KG, pg 237
Heinrich Hugendubel Verlag GmbH, pg 240
Edition Humanistische Psychologie (EHP), pg 240
Junfermann-Verlag, pg 243
W Kohlhammer GmbH, pg 248
Libertas- Europaeisches Institut GmbH, pg 254
Hermann Luchterhand Verlag GmbH, pg 255
mode information Heinz Kramer GmbH, pg 261
Verlag Norbert Mueller AG & Co KG, pg 262
Projektion J Buch- und Musikverlag GmbH, pg 272
Quintessenz Verlags-GmbH, pg 273
Dr Josef Raabe-Verlags GmbH, pg 273
Rationalisierungs-Kuratorium der Deutschen Wirtschaft eV (RKW), pg 273
Ernst Reinhardt Verlag GmbH & Co KG, pg 275
Rossipaul Kommunikation GmbH, pg 277
Ruhland Verlag Gimblt, pg 277
Verlag Werner Sachon GmbH & Co, pg 277
I H Sauer Verlag GmbH, pg 278
Schaeffer-Poeschel Verlag fuer Wirtschaft Steuern Recht, pg 279
Springer Science+Business Media GmbH & Co KG, pg 284
Wirtschaftsverlag Carl Ueberreuter, pg 293
Verlag Moderne Industrie AG & Co KG, pg 295
Verlag und Studio fuer Hoerbuchproduktionen, pg 295
Vogel Medien GmbH & Co KG, pg 296
Weidler Buchverlag Berlin, pg 298
WEKA Firmengruppe GmbH & Co KG, pg 298
Windmuehle GmbH Verlag und Vertrieb von Medien, pg 300
WRS Verlag Wirtschaft, Recht und Steuern GmbH & Co KG, pg 301

Greece
Hestia-I D Hestia-Kollaros & Co Corporation, pg 308
Kleidarithmos, Ekdoseis, pg 309
Kritiki Publishing, pg 309
Patakis Publishers, pg 311
Sakkoulas Publications SA, pg 312
Vivliothiki Eftychia Galeou, pg 313

Hong Kong
Chung Hwa Book Co (HK) Ltd, pg 316
Design Human Resources Training & Development, pg 317
Joint Publishing (HK) Co Ltd, pg 317
Ming Pao Publications Ltd, pg 318
SCMP Book Publishing Ltd, pg 319

Hungary
Janus Pannonius Tudomanyegyetem, pg 322
Kossuth Kiado RT, pg 322
Mueszaki Koenyvkiado Ltd, pg 323
Novorg International Szervezo es Kiado kft, pg 323
Park Konyvkiado Kft (Park Publisher), pg 324

India
Academic Book Corporation, pg 327
Academic Publishers, pg 327
Addison-Wesley Pte Ltd, pg 327
Affiliated East West Press Pvt Ltd, pg 327
Ajanta Publications (India), pg 327
Allied Publishers Pvt Ltd, pg 328
Amar Prakashan, pg 328
Anmol Publications Pvt Ltd, pg 328
APH Publishing Corp, pg 328
Bookionics, pg 331
BS Publications, pg 331
Concept Publishing Co, pg 332
Ess Ess Publications, pg 334
Frank Brothers & Co Publishers Ltd, pg 334
Full Circle Publishing, pg 334
Galgotia Publications Pvt Ltd, pg 334
Gyan Publishing House, pg 335
Himalaya Publishing House, pg 335
Indian Council of Social Science Research (ICSSR), pg 336
Jaico Publishing House, pg 338
Khanna Publishers, pg 339
Law Publishers, pg 340
Multitech Publishing Co, pg 342
National Book Organization, pg 342
Naya Prokash, pg 343
Omsons Publications, pg 344
Pointer Publishers, pg 345
Popular Prakashan Pvt Ltd, pg 345
Rajendra Publishing House Pvt Ltd, pg 346
Rajesh Publications, pg 346
Reliance Publishing House, pg 346
Roli Books Pvt Ltd, pg 347
SAGE Publications India Pvt Ltd, pg 347
Scientific Book Agency, pg 348
Sita Books & Periodicals Pvt Ltd, pg 349
Somaiya Publications Pvt Ltd, pg 349
South Asia Publications, pg 349
Sterling Information Technologies, pg 350
Sterling Publishers Pvt Ltd, pg 350
Sultan Chand & Sons Pvt Ltd, pg 350
Tata McGraw-Hill Publishing Co Ltd, pg 351
UBS Publishers Distributors Ltd, pg 351
Vakils Feffer & Simons Ltd, pg 352
Vikas Publishing House Pvt Ltd, pg 352
Vision Books Pvt Ltd, pg 352
Viva Books Pvt Ltd, pg 352

PUBLISHERS

SUBJECT INDEX

Indonesia
Andi Offset, pg 353
Bumi Aksara PT, pg 354
Dinastindo, pg 354
Gramedia, pg 355

Ireland
Irish Management Institute, pg 361
Oak Tree Press, pg 362

Israel
Agudat Sabah, pg 364
Kivunim-Arsan Publishing House, pg 369
Open University of Israel, pg 371
Tcherikover Publishers Ltd, pg 372

Italy
Franco Angeli SRL, pg 375
Arcipelago Edizioni di Chiani Marisa, pg 376
Bancaria Editrice SpA, pg 377
Buffetti, pg 379
CEDAM (Casa Editrice Dr A Milani), pg 380
Cisalpino, pg 382
EGEA (Edizioni Giuridiche Economiche Aziendali), pg 387
Etas Libri, pg 388
Edizioni Guerini e Associati SpA, pg 392
Ila - Palma, Tea Nova, pg 393
Isper SRL, pg 393
Itaca, pg 393
Accademia Naz dei Lincei, pg 400
Edizioni Olivares, pg 401
Rirea Casa Editrice della Rivista Italiana di Ragioneria e di Economia Aziendale, pg 405
Il Sole 24 Ore Libri, pg 408
Il Sole 24 Ore Pirola, pg 409
Sperling e Kupfer Editori SpA, pg 409
Who's Who In Italy srl, pg 412

Jamaica
American Chamber of Commerce of Jamaica, pg 413
CFM Publications, pg 413

Japan
Diamond Inc, pg 416
Hayakawa Publishing Inc, pg 418
Koyo Shobo, pg 422
Nikkagiren Shuppan-Sha (JUSE Press Ltd), pg 424
Nippon Hoso Shuppan Kyokai (NHK Publishing), pg 424
Nippon Jitsugyo Publishing Co Ltd, pg 424
President Inc, pg 425
Seibundo Shinkosha Publishing Co Ltd, pg 426
3A Corporation, pg 429
Yuhikaku Publishing Co Ltd, pg 431
Zeimukeiri-Kyokai, pg 431
Zenkoku Kyodo Shuppan, pg 431

Kazakhstan
Al-Farabi Kazakh National University, pg 432

Kenya
Cosmopolitan Publishers Ltd, pg 433
Heinemann Kenya Ltd (EAEP), pg 434
Kenya Quality & Productivity Institute, pg 435
Shirikon Publishers, pg 436

Republic of Korea
Bi-bong Publishing Co, pg 437
Chung Rim Publishing Co Ltd, pg 438
Gim-Yeong Co, pg 438
Koreaone Press Inc, pg 440
Sohaksa, pg 443
Twenty-First Century Publishers, Inc, pg 443

Lithuania
Klaipedos Universiteto Leidykla, pg 449

Malaysia
S Abdul Majeed & Co, pg 454
Glad Sounds Sdn Bhd, pg 456
MDC Publishers Printers Sdn Bhd, pg 457
Pelanduk Publications (M) Sdn Bhd, pg 457
Penerbit Universiti Sains Malaysia, pg 458
Penerbitan Tinta, pg 458
Utusan Publications & Distributors Sdn Bhd, pg 459

Mauritius
Editions de l'Ocean Indien Ltd, pg 461

Mexico
Alfaomega Grupo Editor SA de CV, pg 462
Compania Editorial Continental SA de CV, pg 463
Del Verbo Emprender SA de CV, pg 464
Editorial Diana SA de CV, pg 464
Edamex SA de CV, pg 464
Grupo Editorial Iberoamerica, SA de CV, pg 466
Editorial Limusa SA de CV, pg 467
Mercametrica Ediciones SA Edicion de Libros, pg 468
Organizacion Cultural LP SA de CV, pg 469
Panorama Editorial, SA, pg 470
Pearson Educacion de Mexico, SA de CV, pg 470
Sistemas Tecnicos de Edicion SA de CV, pg 472

Netherlands
Ankh-Hermes BV, pg 477
Uitgevirj Aristos, pg 478
BoekWerk, pg 479
Business Contact BV, pg 480
Educatieve Uitgeverij Edu'Actief BV, pg 481
Hagen & Stam Uitgeverij Ten, pg 483
IOS Press BV, pg 484
Kluwer Technische Boeken BV, pg 485
Koninklijke Vermande bv, pg 485
Uitgeverij Lemma BV, pg 485
Uitgeverij H Nelissen BV, pg 486
Omega Boek BV, pg 487
Pearson Education Netherlands, pg 487
Samsom BedrijfsInformatie BV, pg 488
Scriptum, pg 488
Uitgeverij Het Spectrum BV, pg 489
SWP, BV Uitgeverij, pg 490
Uitgeverij de Tijdstroom BV, pg 490
Twente University Press, pg 490

New Zealand
Commonwealth Council for Educational Administration & Management, pg 495
Learning Guides (Writers & Publishers Ltd), pg 497
Moss Associates Ltd, pg 498
Nelson Price Milburn Ltd, pg 499
Shoal Bay Press Ltd, pg 501

Nigeria
Evans Brothers (Nigeria Publishers) Ltd, pg 504
Goldland Business Co Ltd, pg 505
New Africa Publishing Company Ltd, pg 505

Norway
Cappelen akademisk forlag, pg 508
Tiden Norsk Forlag, pg 511

Pakistan
Academy of Education Planning & Management (AEPAM), pg 511
International Educational Services, pg 512

Peru
Universidad de Lima-Fondo de Desarollo Editorial, pg 517

Philippines
Mutual Book Inc, pg 519
New Day Publishers, pg 520
Our Lady of Manaoag Publisher, pg 520

Poland
Polskie Wydawnictwo Ekonomiczne PWE SA, pg 522
Polish Scientific Publishers PWN, pg 525

Portugal
Edicoes Cetop, pg 529
Editora Classica, pg 530
Difusao Cultural, pg 530
Gradiva-Publicacnoes Lda, pg 532
Editora McGraw-Hill de Portugal Lda, pg 533
Monitor-Projectos e Edicoes, LDA, pg 533
Editorial Presenca, pg 535
Edicoes Silabo, pg 536
Almerinda Teixeira, pg 536
Texto Editora, pg 536

Romania
Editura Niculescu, pg 541
Polirom Verlag, pg 542
Rentrop & Straton Verlagsgruppe und Wirtschaftsconsulting, pg 542

Russian Federation
N E Bauman Moscow State Technical University Publishers, pg 544
Izdatelstvo 'Ekonomika', pg 544
Finansy i Statistika Publishing House, pg 544
INFRA-M Izdatel'skij dom, pg 545
Nauka Publishers, pg 547

Serbia and Montenegro
Privredni Pregled, pg 553

Singapore
APAC Publishers Services Pte Ltd, pg 554
Singapore University Press Pte Ltd, pg 558
Taylor & Francis Asia Pacific, pg 558
World Scientific Publishing Co Pte Ltd, pg 559

Slovakia
Dom Techniky Zvazu Slovenskych Vedeckotechnickych Spolocnosti Ltd, pg 559
Priroda Publishing, pg 560
Ustav informacii a prognoz skolstva mladeze a telovychovy, pg 561

Slovenia
Univerza v Ljubljani Ekonomska Fakulteta, pg 562
Zalozba Obzorja d d Maribor, pg 562

South Africa
Human & Rousseau (Pty) Ltd, pg 564
Ivy Publications, pg 565
Ravan Press (Pty) Ltd, pg 568
Van Schaik Publishers, pg 569

Spain
Editorial AEDOS SA, pg 571
Editorial Aranzadi SA, pg 573
Comunidad Autonoma de Madrid, Servicio de Documentacion y Publicaciones, pg 578
Editorial Constitucion y Leyes SA - COLEX, pg 578
Espanola Desclee De Brouwer SA, pg 578
Ediciones Diaz de Santos SA, pg 579
Ediciones Deusto SA, pg 580
Editorial Editex SA, pg 581
Ediciones Gestio 2000 SA, pg 585
Marcombo SA, pg 590
Ediciones Oceano Grupo SA, pg 593
Editorial Paraninfo SA, pg 595
Editorial Sintesis, SA, pg 600
Tirant lo Blanch SL Libreriaa, pg 602
Ediciones Urano, SA, pg 604
Xunta de Galicia, pg 605

Sri Lanka
Sunera Publishers, pg 607

Sweden
Iustus Forlag AB, pg 613
Kungl Ingenjoersvetenskapsakademien (IVA), pg 613
Studentlitteratur AB, pg 616
Svenska Foerlaget liv & ledarskap ab, pg 616

Switzerland
Cosmos-Verlag AG, pg 621
Gottlieb Duttweiler Institute for Trends & Futures, pg 622
Helbing und Lichtenhahn Verlag AG, pg 625
Verlag Industrielle Organisation, pg 625

1035

SUBJECT INDEX

Oesch Verlag AG, pg 630
Ott Verlag Thun, pg 630
Presses Polytechniques et Universitaires Romandes, PPUR, pg 631
Ruegger Verlag, pg 633
Tobler Verlag, pg 635
Editions du Tricorne, pg 635
Vdf Hochschulverlag AG an der ETH Zurich, pg 636
Versus Verlag AG, pg 636
Weka Informations Schriften Verlag AG, pg 637

Taiwan, Province of China

Commonwealth Publishing Company Ltd, pg 639
Laureate Book Co Ltd, pg 640
Linking Publishing Company Ltd, pg 641
Morning Star Publisher Inc, pg 641
Newton Publishing Company Ltd, pg 641
Shy Mau & Shy Chaur Publishing Co Ltd, pg 641

United Republic of Tanzania

Tanzania Publishing House, pg 644

Thailand

Thai Watana Panich Co, Ltd, pg 646

Turkey

Alkim Kitapcilik-Yayimcilik, pg 649
Caglayan Kitabevi, pg 649
Inkilap Publishers Ltd, pg 650
Sabah Kitaplari, pg 651
Soez Yayin/Oyunajans, pg 651
Yetkin Printing & Publishing Co Inc, pg 652

Uganda

Roce (Consultants) Ltd, pg 653

Ukraine

Osnovy Publishers, pg 654

United Kingdom

ABG Professional Information, pg 655
Anglo-German Foundation for the Study of Industrial Society, pg 658
Artech House, pg 659
Ashgate Publishing Ltd, pg 660
Aslib, The Association for Information Management, pg 660
Barmarick Publications, pg 663
Bloomsbury Publishing PLC, pg 668
Bowerdean Publishing Co Ltd, pg 669
BPS Books (British Psychological Society), pg 670
Nicholas Brealey Publishing, pg 670
Capstone Publishing Ltd, pg 674
Cassell & Co, pg 675
The Chartered Institute of Building, pg 678
Chartered Institute of Personnel & Development, pg 678
Christian Research Association, pg 679
Commonwealth Secretariat, pg 681
The Economist Intelligence Unit, pg 689
Element Books Ltd, pg 690
Elm Publications, pg 691
Emerald, pg 691

Ernst & Young, pg 692
Ethics International Press Ltd, pg 692
The Eurospan Group, pg 692
Express Newspapers, pg 693
Facet Publishing, pg 694
Gower Publishing Ltd, pg 701
HarperCollins UK, pg 705
HB Publications, pg 706
How To Books Ltd, pg 710
ICSA Publishing Ltd, pg 711
Institute of Financial Services, pg 712
Institution of Electrical Engineers, pg 713
JAI Press Ltd, pg 715
Kogan Page Ltd, pg 718
Lawpack Publishing Ltd, pg 719
Lemos & Crane, pg 720
Letts Educational, pg 720
LISU, pg 721
Management Books 2000 Ltd, pg 724
Management Pocketbooks Ltd, pg 724
Marshall Editions Ltd, pg 725
McGraw-Hill Publishing Company, pg 726
National Council for Voluntary Organisations (NCVO), pg 730
New Era Publications UK Ltd, pg 732
Open University Press, pg 736
Orion Publishing Group Ltd, pg 736
Palgrave Publishers Ltd, pg 737
Pearson Education, pg 739
Pergamon Flexible Learning, pg 740
Perpetuity Press, pg 741
Piatkus Books, pg 741
The Policy Press, pg 744
Professional Engineering Publishing Ltd, pg 745
Profile Books Ltd, pg 746
ProQuest Information & Learning, pg 746
SAGE Publications Ltd, pg 753
Sherwood Publishing, pg 757
Snowbooks Ltd, pg 759
Sydney Jary Ltd, pg 762
Taylor & Francis, pg 763
Taylor Graham Publishing, pg 764
Thoemmes Press, pg 765
VNU Business Publications, pg 770
Wiley Europe Ltd, pg 773
Witherby & Co Ltd, pg 775

Viet Nam

Science & Technics Publishing House, pg 780

Zambia

M & M Management & Labour Consultants Ltd, pg 781
MFK Management Consultants Services, pg 781

MARITIME

Argentina

Instituto de Publicaciones Navales, pg 8

Australia

Australian Marine Conservation Society Inc (AMCS), pg 13
Robert Berthold Photography, pg 14
Crawford House Publishing Pty Ltd, pg 18
Dragon Press, pg 20
Enterprise Publications, pg 21
Kingfisher Books, pg 28

McGraw-Hill Australia Pty Ltd, pg 31
Navarine Publishing, pg 33
Oceans Enterprises, pg 34
OTEN (Open Training & Education Network), pg 34
Saltwater Publications, pg 40
Ian Stewart Marine Publications, pg 42
Turton & Armstrong Pty Ltd Publishers, pg 44
Windward Publications, pg 47

Austria

Edition S der OSD, pg 50
Herbert Weishaupt Verlag, pg 59

Bulgaria

Publishing House Narodno delo OOD, pg 96

Chile

Edeval (Universidad de Valparaiso), pg 99

China

China Ocean Press, pg 102
Dalian Maritime University Press, pg 104

Croatia

Knjizevni Krug Split, pg 118

Czech Republic

Nase vojsko, nakladatelstvi a knizni obchod, pg 126

Denmark

Ascheoug Dansk Forlag A/S, pg 129
P Haase & Sons Forlag A/S, pg 131

Finland

Koala-Kustannus Oy, pg 143

France

Editions l'Ancre de Marine, pg 147
Brud Nevez, pg 151
Chasse Maree, pg 153
EPA (Editions Pratiques Automobiles), pg 161
Institut Francais de Recherche pour l'Exploitation de la Mer (IFREMER), pg 164
Editions Jean Paul Gisserot, pg 165
Editions Lavoisier, pg 171
Librarie Maritime Outremer, pg 172
Editions Pedone, pg 179

Germany

Brandenburgisches Verlagshaus in der Dornier Medienholding GmbH, pg 204
Verlag Busse und Seewald GmbH, pg 206
Delius, Klasing und Co, pg 211
Delius Klasing Verlag, pg 211
Gebrueder Borntraeger Science Publishers, pg 228
Liselotte Hamecher, pg 233
Heel Verlag GmbH, pg 235
Verlagsgruppe Koehler/Mittler, pg 248
Koehlers Verlagsgesellschaft mbH, pg 248
Edition Maritim GmbH, pg 257
E S Mittler und Sohn GmbH, pg 261

Paul Pietsch Verlage GmbH & Co, pg 270
Propylaeen Verlag, Zweigniederlassung Berlin der Ullstein Buchverlage GmbH, pg 272
E Schweizerbart'sche Verlagsbuchhandlung (Naegele und Obermiller), pg 282
Stadler Verlagsgesellschaft mbH, pg 286
Edition Temmen, pg 290
Tetra Verlag Gmbh, pg 290

Greece

Melissa Publishing House, pg 310
Sakkoulas Publications SA, pg 312

India

Sita Books & Periodicals Pvt Ltd, pg 349

Ireland

Dee-Jay Publications, pg 359
Herodotus Press, pg 361

Italy

Automobilia srl, pg 377
Istituto Idrografico della Marina, pg 393
Gruppo Ugo Mursia Editore SpA, pg 400

Japan

Kaibundo Shuppan, pg 420
Seizando-Shoten Publishing Co Ltd, pg 427

Lithuania

Klaipedos Universiteto Leidykla, pg 449

Macau

Museu Maritimo, pg 452

Netherlands

BV Uitgeversbedrijf Het Goede Boek, pg 482
Uitgeverij Hollandia BV, pg 483

Netherlands Antilles

Bredero, pg 493

New Caledonia

Savannah Editions SARL, pg 493

New Zealand

Exisle Publishing Ltd, pg 496
Halcyon Publishing Ltd, pg 496
David Ling Publishing, pg 498
Publishing Solutions Ltd, pg 500
River Press, pg 500
Southern Press Ltd, pg 501

Norway

Elanders Publishing AS, pg 509
Sandviks Bokforlag, pg 510

Philippines

Rex Bookstores & Publishers, pg 520

Poland

Iskry - Publishing House Ltd spotka zoo, pg 523

PUBLISHERS

Russian Federation

BLIC, russko-Baltijskij informaciionnyj centr, AO, pg 544
Izdatelstvo Sudostroenie, pg 549
Izdatelstvo Transport, pg 549

Singapore

Singapore University Press Pte Ltd, pg 558

South Africa

Flesch Financial Publications (Pty) Ltd, pg 563

Spain

Lunwerg Editores, SA, pg 589
Editorial Noray, pg 593
Ediciones Seyer, pg 599
Silex Ediciones, pg 600
Xunta de Galicia, pg 605

Sweden

Allt om Hobby AB, pg 609
Johnston & Streiffert Editions, pg 613
Nautiska Foerlaget AB, pg 614
Frank Stenvalls Forlag, pg 615

Switzerland

Maihof Verlag, pg 628

United Kingdom

Abbotsford Publishing, pg 654
Ian Allan Publishing Ltd, pg 656
Amber Books Ltd, pg 657
Arms & Armour Press, pg 659
BLA Publishing Ltd, pg 666
A & C Black Publishers Ltd, pg 666
Books International, pg 669
Brassey's UK Ltd, pg 670
Brown, Son & Ferguson, Ltd, pg 672
Capall Bann Publishing, pg 674
Chatham Publishing, pg 678
Colourpoint Books, pg 681
Compendium Publishing, pg 681
Conway Maritime Press, pg 683
Leo Cooper, pg 683
Countyvise Ltd, pg 683
The Crowood Press Ltd, pg 684
Terence Dalton Ltd, pg 685
David & Charles Ltd, pg 686
DMG Business Media Ltd, pg 688
Gerald Duckworth & Co Ltd, pg 688
Aidan Ellis Publishing, pg 690
The Eurospan Group, pg 692
Fernhurst Books, pg 694
Fishing News Books Ltd, pg 695
Greenhill Books/Lionel Leventhal Ltd, pg 703
Halldale Publishing & Media Ltd, pg 704
Haynes Publishing, pg 706
Hutton Press Ltd, pg 711
Jane's Information Group, pg 715
LLP Ltd, pg 722
Maritime Books, pg 725
Kenneth Mason Publications Ltd, pg 726
James Munro & Co, pg 729
W W Norton & Company Ltd, pg 734
Oilfield Publications Ltd, pg 734
Opus Book Publishing Ltd, pg 736
The Orkney Press Ltd, pg 736
Parapress Ltd, pg 738
Pen & Sword Books Ltd, pg 740
Perpetuity Press, pg 741
Quintet Publishing Ltd, pg 747
SB Publications, pg 754
Shire Publications Ltd, pg 757
Silver Link Publishing Ltd, pg 758
Stenlake Publishing Ltd, pg 761
Sutton Publishing Ltd, pg 762
Twelveheads Press, pg 767
University of Exeter Press, pg 768
Whittles Publishing, pg 773
WIT Press, pg 774
Witherby & Co Ltd, pg 775

Viet Nam

Science & Technics Publishing House, pg 780

MARKETING

Albania

NL SH, pg 1

Argentina

Diana Argentina SA, Editorial, pg 5

Australia

Art on the Move, pg 12
Crista International, pg 18
James Nicholas Publishers Pty Ltd, pg 27
Marketing Focus, pg 30
McGraw-Hill Australia Pty Ltd, pg 31
OTEN (Open Training & Education Network), pg 34
Priestley Consulting, pg 37
The Real Estate Institute of Australia, pg 39
Tertiary Press, pg 43

Austria

Herold Business Data AG, pg 52
Dr Verena Hofstaetter, pg 52
Linde Verlag Wien GmbH, pg 53
Modulverlag, pg 54
WUV/Service Fachverlag, pg 60

Azerbaijan

Sada, Literaturno-Izdatel'skij Centr, pg 60

Belgium

Editions De Boeck-Larcier SA, pg 66
Roularta Books NV, pg 72
Scoop Infotex NV, pg 73

Brazil

Editora Aquariana Ltda, pg 77
ARTMED Editora, pg 78
Editora Atlas SA, pg 78
Editora Ortiz SA, pg 88
Pearson Education Do Brasil, pg 88
Saraiva SA, Livreiros Editores, pg 90
Summus Editorial Ltda, pg 91
Thex Editora e Distribuidora Ltda, pg 91
Fundacao Getulio Vargas, pg 92
Jorge Zahar Editor, pg 92

Bulgaria

Dolphin Press Group Ltd, pg 94
Sluntse Publishing House, pg 97

Chile

Arrayan Editores, pg 98
Norma de Chile, pg 99

SUBJECT INDEX

China

Beijing Publishing House, pg 101
China Film Press, pg 102
China Foreign Economic Relations & Trade Publishing House, pg 102
China Materials Management Publishing House, pg 102
CITIC Publishing House, pg 103
Fudan University Press, pg 104
Heilongjiang Science & Technology Press, pg 105
Jilin Science & Technology Publishing House, pg 105
Sichuan University Press, pg 108
Yunnan University Press, pg 109

Colombia

LEGIS - Editores SA, pg 111

Costa Rica

Instituto Interamericano de Cooperacion para la Agricultura (IICA), pg 115

Croatia

Informator dd, pg 118
Masmedia, pg 118

Czech Republic

NS Svoboda spol sro, pg 127

Denmark

Samfundslitteratur, pg 134

Dominican Republic

Pontificia Universidad Catolica Madre y Maestra, pg 136

France

Editions Breal, pg 151
Chotard et Associes Editeurs, pg 154
Editions Dalloz Sirey, pg 157
Les Editions ESF, pg 160
Editions First, pg 163
Maxima Laurent du Mesnil Editeur, pg 174
Les Presses du Management, pg 181
Presses Universitaires de Grenoble, pg 181
TOP Editions, pg 188
Editions Village Mondial, pg 189

Germany

AZ Bertelsmann Direct GmbH, pg 196
Berliner Wissenschafts-Verlag GmbH (BWV), pg 199
Bertelsmann Lexikon Verlag GmbH, pg 200
Cornelsen Verlag GmbH & Co OHG, pg 210
Deutscher Fachverlag GmbH, pg 212
Duncker und Humblot GmbH, pg 217
Verlag Reinhard Fischer, pg 225
Verlag Franz Vahlen GmbH, pg 226
Friedrich Kiehl Verlag GmbH, pg 227
Betriebswirtschaftlicher Verlag Dr Th Gabler, pg 228
Walter de Gruyter GmbH & Co KG, pg 231
Gunter Olzog Verlag GmbH, pg 231
Rudolf Haufe Verlag GmbH & Co KG, pg 235
Hans Holzmann Verlag GmbH und Co KG, pg 239
Hoppenstedt GmbH & Co KG, pg 239
W Kohlhammer GmbH, pg 248
Max Schimmel Verlag, pg 258
mode information Heinz Kramer GmbH, pg 261
Verlag Norbert Mueller AG & Co KG, pg 262
Verlag Werner Sachon GmbH & Co, pg 277
I H Sauer Verlag GmbH, pg 278
Schaeffer-Poeschel Verlag fuer Wirtschaft Steuern Recht, pg 279
Schulz-Kirchner Verlag GmbH, pg 282
Springer Science+Business Media GmbH & Co KG, pg 284
Steidl Verlag, pg 287
Tangens Systemverlag GmbH, pg 289
Verlag Moderne Industrie AG & Co KG, pg 295
Verlag und Studio fuer Hoerbuchproduktionen, pg 295
Weidler Buchverlag Berlin, pg 298
Wer liefert was? GmbH, pg 299
WRS Verlag Wirtschaft, Recht und Steuern GmbH & Co KG, pg 301

Ghana

World Literature Project, pg 305

Greece

Kleidarithmos, Ekdoseis, pg 309
Kritiki Publishing, pg 309
Vivliothiki Eftychia Galeou, pg 313

Haiti

Editions Caraibes SA, pg 314

Hong Kong

Chung Hwa Book Co (HK) Ltd, pg 316
Electronic Technology Publishing Co Ltd, pg 317
Joint Publishing (HK) Co Ltd, pg 317
SCMP Book Publishing Ltd, pg 319

Hungary

Janus Pannonius Tudomanyegyetem, pg 322
KJK-Kerszov, pg 322
Nemzeti Tankoenyvkiado, pg 323
Novorg International Szervezo es Kiado kft, pg 323

India

APH Publishing Corp, pg 328
Full Circle Publishing, pg 334
Omsons Publications, pg 344
Reliance Publishing House, pg 346
Scientific Book Agency, pg 348
Sita Books & Periodicals Pvt Ltd, pg 349
Somaiya Publications Pvt Ltd, pg 349
Sterling Information Technologies, pg 350
Sultan Chand & Sons Pvt Ltd, pg 350
Viva Books Pvt Ltd, pg 352

Indonesia

Andi Offset, pg 353
Bumi Aksara PT, pg 354

Ireland

Oak Tree Press, pg 362

SUBJECT INDEX — BOOK

Italy
Franco Angeli SRL, pg 375
Apimondia, pg 375
Arcipelago Edizioni di Chiani Marisa, pg 376
Bancaria Editrice SpA, pg 377
CEDAM (Casa Editrice Dr A Milani), pg 380
EGEA (Edizioni Giuridiche Economiche Aziendali), pg 387
Itaca, pg 393
Lybra Immagine, pg 396
Editrice San Marco SRL, pg 407

Jamaica
American Chamber of Commerce of Jamaica, pg 413

Japan
The American Chamber of Commerce in Japan, pg 415
Diamond Inc, pg 416
Koyo Shobo, pg 422
Nippon Jitsugyo Publishing Co Ltd, pg 424
President Inc, pg 425
Sagano Shoin, pg 426
Zeimukeiri-Kyokai, pg 431

Republic of Korea
Chung Rim Publishing Co Ltd, pg 438
Gim-Yeong Co, pg 438

Lithuania
Klaipedos Universiteto Leidykla, pg 449

Malaysia
S Abdul Majeed & Co, pg 454
Penerbitan Tinta, pg 458

Mauritius
Editions de l'Ocean Indien Ltd, pg 461

Mexico
Ibcon SA, pg 466
Editorial Limusa SA de CV, pg 467
Mercametrica Ediciones SA Edicion de Libros, pg 468

Netherlands
BoekWerk, pg 479
Business Contact BV, pg 480
Educatieve Uitgeverij Edu'Actief BV, pg 481
Uitgeverij Lemma BV, pg 485
Samsom BedrijfsInformatie BV, pg 488
Scriptum, pg 488
VNU Business Press Group BV, pg 492

New Zealand
Nelson Price Milburn Ltd, pg 499
Shoal Bay Press Ltd, pg 501

Nigeria
Goldland Business Co Ltd, pg 505

Pakistan
International Educational Services, pg 512

Panama
Focus Publications International SA, pg 515

Peru
Universidad de Lima-Fondo de Desarollo Editorial, pg 517

Philippines
New Day Publishers, pg 520
Rex Bookstores & Publishers, pg 520

Poland
Polskie Wydawnictwo Ekonomiczne PWE SA, pg 522
Polish Scientific Publishers PWN, pg 525
Wydawnictwo Prawnicze Co, pg 526

Portugal
GECTI (Gabinete de Especializacao e Cooperacao Tecnica Internacional L), pg 531
Editora McGraw-Hill de Portugal Lda, pg 533
Editorial Presenca, pg 535

Romania
Nemira Verlag, pg 541
Editura Niculescu, pg 541
Polirom Verlag, pg 542
Rentrop & Straton Verlagsgruppe und Wirtschaftsconsulting, pg 542

Russian Federation
Finansy i Statistika Publishing House, pg 544
INFRA-M Izdatel'skij dom, pg 545
Nauka Publishers, pg 547
Izdatel'stvo Nizhegorodskogo Gosudarstvennogo Univ, pg 547

Slovakia
Dom Techniky Zvazu Slovenskych Vedeckotechnickych Spolocnosti Ltd, pg 559

Slovenia
Univerza v Ljubljani Ekonomska Fakulteta, pg 562
Zalozba Obzorja d d Maribor, pg 562

South Africa
Human & Rousseau (Pty) Ltd, pg 564

Spain
Ediciones Gestio 2000 SA, pg 585
LID Editorial Empresarial, SL, pg 589
Marcombo SA, pg 590
Oikos-Tau SA Ediciones, pg 593
Tres Torres Ediciones SA, pg 602
Xunta de Galicia, pg 605

Sweden
Industrilitteratur Vindex, Forlags AB, pg 612

Switzerland
Drei-D-World und Foto-World Verlag und Vertrieb, pg 622
Gottlieb Duttweiler Institute for Trends & Futures, pg 622
Verlag Industrielle Organisation, pg 625
Oesch Verlag AG, pg 630
3 Dimension World (3-D-World), pg 635
Tobler Verlag, pg 635
Versus Verlag AG, pg 636

Syrian Arab Republic
Damascus University Press, pg 638

Taiwan, Province of China
Fuh-Wen Book Co, pg 639
Newton Publishing Company Ltd, pg 641

Thailand
Thai Watana Panich Co, Ltd, pg 646

Turkey
Alkim Kitapcilik-Yayimcilik, pg 649

Uganda
Roce (Consultants) Ltd, pg 653

Ukraine
ASK Ltd, pg 653

United Kingdom
Ashgate Publishing Ltd, pg 660
Bloomsbury Publishing PLC, pg 668
BPP Publishing Ltd, pg 670
Cassell & Co, pg 675
Emerald, pg 691
Euromonitor PLC, pg 692
The Eurospan Group, pg 692
HB Publications, pg 706
Hemming Information Services, pg 707
Hollis Publishing Ltd, pg 709
ICC United Kingdom, pg 711
Johnson Publications Ltd, pg 716
Kogan Page Ltd, pg 718
Letts Educational, pg 720
Management Books 2000 Ltd, pg 724
NTC Research, pg 734
Pergamon Flexible Learning, pg 740
Profile Books Ltd, pg 746
ProQuest Information & Learning, pg 746
SAGE Publications Ltd, pg 753
Verulam Publishing Ltd, pg 770
Wiley Europe Ltd, pg 773

Viet Nam
Science & Technics Publishing House, pg 780

MATHEMATICS

Albania
NL SH, pg 1
State Textbook Publishing House, pg 1

Argentina
EUDEBA (Editorial Universitaria de Buenos Aires), pg 5
Editorial Idearium de la Universidad de Mendoza (EDIUM), pg 6
Juegos & Co SRL, pg 6
Instituto Nacional de Ciencia y Tecnica Hidrica (INCYTH), pg 7

Armenia
Arevik, pg 10

Australia
Edward Arnold (Australia) Pty Ltd, pg 12
Austed Publishing Co, pg 12
Australian Academy of Science, pg 13
Blackwell Publishing Asia, pg 15
Deakin University Press, pg 19
Dellasta Publishing, pg 19
Dubois Publishing, pg 20
Educational Advantage, pg 20
Elsevier Australia, pg 21
Emerald City Books, pg 21
Hawker Brownlow, pg 25
Illert Publications, pg 26
Macmillan Education Australia, pg 30
McGraw-Hill Australia Pty Ltd, pg 31
Mimosa Publications Pty Ltd, pg 32
K & Z Mostafanejad, pg 32
Pearson Education Australia, pg 36
Phoenix Education Pty Ltd, pg 36
Quakers Hill Press, pg 38
Reed Educational Publishing Australia, pg 39
Royal Society of New South Wales, pg 40
Rumsby Scientific Publishing, pg 40

Austria
Abakus Verlag GmbH, pg 48
Verlag Hoelder-Pichler-Tempsky, pg 52
International Institute for Applied Systems Analysis (IIASA), pg 52
Springer-Verlag Wien, pg 58
Verband der Wissenschaftlichen Gesellschaften Oesterreichs (VWGOe), pg 59

Belarus
Belaruskaya Encyklapedyya, pg 62
Narodnaya Asveta, pg 62
Publishing Center of Belarus State University, pg 62

Belgium
Uitgeverij Acco, pg 62
Artel, pg 63
Editions De Boeck-Larcier SA, pg 66
Dessain - Departement de De Boeck & Larcier SA, pg 66
Leuven University Press, pg 70
Pelckmans NV, De Nederlandsche Boekhandel, pg 72
Presses agronomiques de Gembloux ASBL, pg 72
Editions Techniques et Scientifiques SPRL, pg 73
Uitgeverij De Garve, pg 74
Editions de l'Universite de Bruxelles, pg 74
Wolters Plantyn Educatieve Uitgevers, pg 74

Bolivia
Editorial Don Bosco, pg 75

Brazil
Editora Edgard Blucher Ltda, pg 79
Edicon Editora e Consultorial Ltda, pg 81
Fundacao Instituto Brasileiro de Geografia e Estatistica (IBGE - CDDI/DECOP), pg 82
Fundacao Sao Paulo, EDUC, pg 82
LTC-Livros Tecnicos e Cientificos Editora S/A, pg 85
Editora Moderna Ltda, pg 86

PUBLISHERS

Modulo Editora e Desenvolvimento Educacional Ltda, pg 87
Saraiva SA, Livreiros Editores, pg 90
Editora Scipione Ltda, pg 90
Edicoes Tabajara, pg 91

Bulgaria

Abagar Pablioing, pg 92
Foi-Commerce, pg 94
Gea-Libris Publishing House, pg 94
Heron Press Publishing House, pg 94
Izdatelstvo Lettera, pg 95
LIK Izdanija, pg 95
Makros 2000 - Plovdiv, pg 95
MATEX, pg 95
Naouka i Izkoustvo, Ltd, pg 95
Pensoft Publishers, pg 96
Regalia 6 Publishing House, pg 96
TEMTO, pg 97

Cameroon

Editions Buma Kor & Co Ltd, pg 98

Chile

Arrayan Editores, pg 98

China

Fudan University Press, pg 104
Guangdong Science & Technology Press, pg 105
Inner Mongolia Science & Technology Publishing House, pg 105
Jilin Science & Technology Publishing House, pg 105
Metallurgical Industry Press (MIP), pg 106
Science Press, pg 107
Shandong University Press, pg 108
Sichuan University Press, pg 108
Southwest China Jiaotong University Press, pg 108
Tianjin Science & Technology Publishing House, pg 108
Tsinghua University Press, pg 109
Wuhan University Press, pg 109

Colombia

Universidad Externado de Colombia, pg 111
Universidad Nacional Abierta y a Distancia, pg 113

The Democratic Republic of the Congo

Centre de Recherche, et Pedagogie Appliquee, pg 114

Costa Rica

Jose Alfonso Sandoval Nunez, pg 115

Czech Republic

Academia, pg 122
Karolinum, nakladatelstvi, pg 124

Denmark

Fremad A/S, pg 131
Gads Forlag, pg 131
Systime, pg 135

Dominican Republic

Pontificia Universidad Catolica Madre y Maestra, pg 136

Finland

Yliopistopaino/Helsinki University Press, pg 145

France

Editions Breal, pg 151
Cepadues Editions SA, pg 153
CNRS Editions, pg 155
EDP Sciences, pg 161
Elsevier SAS (Editions Scientifiques et Medicales Elsevier), pg 161
Editions Espaces 34, pg 162
Editions Jacques Gabay, pg 164
Gammaprim, pg 165
Hachette Livre International, pg 167
Hermann editeurs des Sciences et des Arts SA, pg 167
InterEditions, pg 169
Librairie Scientifique et Technique Albert Blanchard, pg 172
Presses Universitaires de Grenoble, pg 181
Societe Mathematique de France - Institut Henri Poincare, pg 185
Editions Springer France, pg 186
Editions Technip SA, pg 187
Librairie Vuibert, pg 189

Germany

AOL-Verlag Frohmut Menze, pg 193
Auer Verlag GmbH, pg 195
Aulis Verlag Deubner & Co KG, pg 195
Bayerischer Schulbuch-Verlag GmbH, pg 198
Berliner Wissenschafts-Verlag GmbH (BWV), pg 199
Verlag Beruf und Schule Belz KG, pg 200
Beuth Verlag GmbH, pg 200
Cornelsen Verlag GmbH & Co OHG, pg 210
Verlag Harri Deutsch, pg 211
Ferd Dummler's Verlag, pg 223
Finken Verlag GmbH, pg 224
Friedrich Frommann Verlag, pg 227
Walter de Gruyter GmbH & Co KG, pg 231
Carl Hanser Verlag, pg 234
Konkordia Verlag GmbH, pg 249
Anton G Leitner Verlag (AGLV), pg 253
Annemarie Maeger, pg 256
Naumann & Goebel Verlagsgesellschaft mbH, pg 263
Verlag Sigrid Persen, pg 269
Verlag an der Ruhr GmbH, pg 277
Springer Science+Business Media GmbH & Co KG, pg 284
Stiefel Eurocart GmbH, pg 288
B G Teubner Verlag, pg 290
Friedr Vieweg & Sohn Verlag, pg 296
Volk und Wissen Verlag GmbH & Co, pg 296
Wissenschaftliche Buchgesellschaft, pg 300
Verlag Konrad Wittwer GmbH, pg 301

Ghana

Beginners Publishers, pg 303
EPP Books Services, pg 304
Sam Woode Ltd, pg 304
Sedco Publishing Ltd, pg 305
Unimax Macmillan Ltd, pg 305

Greece

Athina, Mary Mavrogiannis, pg 306
Editions Athina-Mavrogianni, pg 306
Diavlos, pg 306
Ekdotikos Oikos Adelfon Kyriakidi A E, pg 307
Katoptro Publications, pg 309
Pagoulatos Bros, pg 311
Michalis Sideris, pg 312

Holy See (Vatican City State)

Pontificia Academia Scientiarum, pg 314

Hong Kong

Times Publishing (Hong Kong) Ltd, pg 319
Vision Pub Co Ltd, pg 320
Witman Publishing Co (HK) Ltd, pg 320

Hungary

Magyar Tudomanyos Akademia Koezponti Fizikai Kutato Intezet Koenyvtara, pg 322
Mueszaki Koenyvkiado Ltd, pg 323
Nemzeti Tankoenyvkiado, pg 323
Statiqum Kiado es Nyomda Kft, pg 324
Typotex Kft Elektronikus Kiado, pg 324

India

Addison-Wesley Pte Ltd, pg 327
Affiliated East West Press Pvt Ltd, pg 327
Ambar Prakashan, pg 328
Bharat Publishing House, pg 330
Book Circle, pg 330
Dolphin Publications, pg 333
Era Books, pg 334
Frank Brothers & Co Publishers Ltd, pg 334
Goel Prakashen, pg 335
Indian Book Depot, pg 336
Khanna Publishers, pg 339
Laxmi Publications Pvt Ltd, pg 340
Narosa Publishing House, pg 342
Pitambar Publishing Co (P) Ltd, pg 345
Scientific Book Agency, pg 348
Sita Books & Periodicals Pvt Ltd, pg 349
South Asian Publishers Pvt Ltd, pg 350
Sultan Chand & Sons Pvt Ltd, pg 350
Suman Prakashan Pvt Ltd, pg 351
Vikas Publishing House Pvt Ltd, pg 352
S Viswanathan (Printers & Publishers) Pvt Ltd, pg 352

Indonesia

Institut Teknologi Bandung, pg 355
Mutiara Sumber Widya PT, pg 356

Ireland

An Gum, pg 358
The Educational Company of Ireland, pg 359
Royal Irish Academy, pg 363

Israel

Dekel Publishing House, pg 366
Freund Publishing House Ltd, pg 367
Otzar Hamore, pg 367

Intermedia Audio, Video Book Publishing Ltd, pg 368
Open University of Israel, pg 371

Italy

Adelphi Edizioni SpA, pg 374
Archimede Edizioni, pg 376
Bibliopolis - Edizioni di Filosofia e Scienze Srl, pg 378
Cacucci Editore, pg 379
Casa Editrice Giuseppe Principato Spa, pg 380
CEDAM (Casa Editrice Dr A Milani), pg 380
Celuc Libri, pg 381
Centro Programmazione Editoriale (CPE), pg 381
Il Cigno Galileo Galilei-Edizioni di Arte e Scienza, pg 382
Ciranna - Roma, pg 382
CLEUP - Cooperative Libraria Editrice dell 'Universita di Padova, pg 382
Edizioni Cremonese SRL, pg 383
Etas Libri, pg 388
Arnaldo Forni Editore SRL, pg 389
Giunti Gruppo Editoriale, pg 390
Herbita Editrice di Leonardo Palermo, pg 392
Liguori Editore SRL, pg 395
Accademia Naz dei Lincei, pg 400
Newton & Compton Editori, pg 400
Paravia Bruno Mondadori Editori, pg 402
Pitagora Editrice SRL, pg 403
Principato, pg 404
Edizioni Universitarie Romane, pg 406
Editoriale Scienza, pg 407
Societa Editrice Internazionale - SEI, pg 408
Editrice Tirrenia Stampatori SAS, pg 410
Vita e Pensiero, pg 412

Jamaica

Carib Publishing Ltd, pg 413
Carlong Publishers (Caribbean) Ltd, pg 413
Jamaica Publishing House Ltd, pg 414
Packer-Evans & Associates Ltd, pg 414

Japan

Baifukan Co Ltd, pg 415
Holp Book Co Ltd, pg 418
Kindai Kagaku Sha Co Ltd, pg 421
Kyoritsu Shuppan Co Ltd, pg 422
Morikita Shuppan Co Ltd, pg 423
Nikkagiren Shuppan-Sha (JUSE Press Ltd), pg 424
Nippon Hoso Shuppan Kyokai (NHK Publishing), pg 424
Saela Shobo (Librairie Ca et La), pg 425
Sangyo-Tosho Publishing Co Ltd, pg 426
Shokabo Publishing Co Ltd, pg 428
Soryusha, pg 428
Springer-Verlag Tokyo, pg 428
Tokyo Shoseki Co Ltd, pg 430
Tokyo Tosho Co Ltd, pg 430

Kazakstan

Gylym, Izd-Vo, pg 432
Al-Farabi Kazakh National University, pg 432

SUBJECT INDEX

Kenya
Cosmopolitan Publishers Ltd, pg 433
Guru Publishers Ltd, pg 434
Kenya Literature Bureau, pg 434
Kenya Quality & Productivity Institute, pg 435
Lake Publishers & Enterprises Ltd, pg 435
Nairobi University Press, pg 435
Phoenix Publishers Ltd, pg 435

Democratic People's Republic of Korea
Korea Science and Encyclopedia Publishing House, pg 436

Republic of Korea
Prompter Publications, pg 442

Kuwait
Ministry of Information, pg 444

Liechtenstein
Saendig Reprint Verlag, Hans-Rainer Wohlwend, pg 448

Lithuania
Klaipedos Universiteto Leidykla, pg 449
Mokslo ir enciklopediju leidybos institutas, pg 449
Svietimo ir mokslo ministerijos Leidybos centras, pg 449
TEV Leidykla, pg 450

Luxembourg
Editions Emile Borschette, pg 450

The Former Yugoslav Republic of Macedonia
Medis, Skopje, pg 452

Malawi
Dzuka Publishing Co Ltd, pg 454

Malaysia
Federal Publications Sdn Bhd, pg 455
Pearson Education Malaysia Sdn Bhd, pg 457
Penerbit Universiti Sains Malaysia, pg 458
Pustaka Delta Pelajaran Sdn Bhd, pg 458
Tropical Press Sdn Bhd, pg 459
Penerbit Universiti Teknologi Malaysia, pg 459

Mexico
Adivinar y Multiplicar, SA de CV, pg 461
Editorial Banca y Comercio SA de CV, pg 462
Colegio de Postgraduados en Ciencias Agricolas, pg 463
Compania Editorial Continental SA de CV, pg 463
Editorial Esfinge SA de CV, pg 465
Fernandez Editores SA de CV, pg 465
Grupo Editorial Iberoamerica, SA de CV, pg 466
Editorial Limusa SA de CV, pg 467
McGraw-Hill Interamericana Editores, SA de CV, pg 468
Nova Grupo Editorial SA de CV, pg 469

Pearson Educacion de Mexico, SA de CV, pg 470
Sistemas Tecnicos de Edicion SA de CV, pg 472
Editorial Trillas SA de CV, pg 472
Universidad Nacional Autonoma de Mexico (National University of Mexico), pg 472

Republic of Moldova
Editura Lumina, pg 473

Morocco
Dar Nachr Al Maarifa Pour L'Edition et La Distribution, pg 474

Nepal
International Standards Books & Periodicals (P) Ltd, pg 476

Netherlands
Elsevier Science BV, pg 482
IOS Press BV, pg 484
Em Querido's Uitgeverij BV, pg 488
A J G Strengholt's Boeken, Anno 1928, BV, pg 489
V S P International Science Publishers, pg 491

New Zealand
ABA Books, pg 493
ESA Publications (NZ) Ltd, pg 496
Eton Press (Auckland) Ltd, pg 496
Nelson Price Milburn Ltd, pg 499
New House Publishers Ltd, pg 499
Statistics New Zealand, pg 501

Nigeria
Evans Brothers (Nigeria Publishers) Ltd, pg 504
JAD Publishers Ltd, pg 505
NPS Educational Publishers Ltd (Nigeria Publishers Services), pg 506
Ogunsanya Press, Publishers and Bookstores Ltd, pg 506
Riverside Communications, pg 507
West African Book Publishers Ltd, pg 507

Norway
Aschehoug Forlag, pg 508
H Aschehoug & Co (W Nygaard) A/S, pg 508
NKI Forlaget, pg 510
Universitetsforlaget, pg 511

Pakistan
Publishers United Pvt Ltd, pg 514

Philippines
Bookman Printing & Publishing House Inc, pg 518
Mutual Book Inc, pg 519
Rex Bookstores & Publishers, pg 520
Saint Mary's Publishing Corp, pg 520
Salesiana Publishers Inc, pg 521
SIBS Publishing House Inc, pg 521
Vibal Publishing House Inc (VPHI), pg 521

Poland
Wydawnictwa Geologiczne, pg 523
Wydawnictwa Naukowo-Techniczne, pg 524

Polish Scientific Publishers PWN, pg 525
Oficyna Wydawnicza Szkoly Glownej Handlowej w Warszawie Oficyna Wydawnicza SGH, pg 527
Zaklad Wydawnictw Statystycznych, pg 528

Portugal
Livraria Arnado Lda, pg 528
Constancia Editores, SA, pg 530
Didactica Editora, pg 530
Gradiva-Publicacnoes Lda, pg 532
Editora McGraw-Hill de Portugal Lda, pg 533
Editora Replicacao Lda, pg 535
Edicoes Silabo, pg 536

Romania
Editura Academiei Romane, pg 538
Corint Publishing Group, pg 539
Editura Niculescu, pg 541
Petrion Verlag, pg 542
Editura Stiintifica SA, pg 542

Russian Federation
N E Bauman Moscow State Technical University Publishers, pg 544
Izdatel'stovo Dal'nevostongo Gosudarstvennogo Universite, pg 544
FGUP Izdatelstvo Mashinostroenie, pg 544
Finansy i Statistika Publishing House, pg 544
Fizmatlit Publishing Co, pg 545
Izdatelstvo Kazanskago Universiteta, pg 545
Izdatelstvo Mir, pg 546
Izdatelstvo Mordovskogo gosudar stvennogo, pg 547
Moscow University Press, pg 547
Nauka Publishers, pg 547
Izdatel'stvo Nizhegorodskogo Gosudarstvennogo Univ, pg 547
Izdatelstvo Prosveshchenie, pg 548
Teorija Verojatnostej i ee Primenenija, pg 549
Izdatelstvo Ural' skogo, pg 549
Voronezh State University Publishers, pg 549

Saudi Arabia
King Saud University, pg 550

Singapore
Daiichi Media Pte Ltd, pg 555
Global Educational Services Pte Ltd, pg 556
Hillview Publications Pte Ltd, pg 556
Success Publications Pte Ltd, pg 558
World Scientific Publishing Co Pte Ltd, pg 559

Slovakia
Slovenske pedagogicke nakladateistvo, pg 560

Slovenia
Mladinska Knjiga International, pg 561
Univerza v Ljubljani Ekonomska Fakulteta, pg 562
Zalozba Obzorja d d Maribor, pg 562

South Africa
Clever Books, pg 563
Educum Publishers Ltd, pg 563
Heinemann Educational Publishers Southern Africa, pg 564
Vivlia Publishers & Booksellers, pg 570

Spain
Agora Editorial, pg 571
Ediciones Alfar SA, pg 572
Alianza Editorial SA, pg 572
Calesa SA Editorial La, pg 575
Editorial Casals SA, pg 575
Celeste Ediciones, pg 576
Editorial Deimos, SL, pg 578
Instituto de Estudios Riojanos, pg 583
Instituto Nacional de Estadistica, pg 587
Marcombo SA, pg 590
Editorial la Muralla SA, pg 592
Editorial Playor SA, pg 596
Editorial Sintesis, SA, pg 600
Thales Sociedad Andaluza de Educacion Matematica, pg 602
Tres Torres Ediciones SA, pg 602
Publicacions de la Universitat de Barcelona, pg 604
Editorial Vicens-Vives, pg 605

Sri Lanka
Gihan Book Shop, pg 606
Ministry of Education, pg 607
Warna Publishers, pg 607

Sweden
Akademiforlaget Goteborgslitteratur, pg 609
Liber AB, pg 613
Studentlitteratur AB, pg 616

Switzerland
Bibliographisches Institut & F A Brockhaus AG, pg 619
Birkhauser Verlag AG, pg 619
Marcel Dekker AG, pg 621
Verlag Harri Deutsch, pg 622
Philosophisch-Anthroposophischer Verlag am Goetheanum, pg 631
Presses Polytechniques et Universitaires Romandes, PPUR, pg 631
Sabe AG Verlagsinstitut, pg 633
Editions du Tricorne, pg 635
Vdf Hochschulverlag AG an der ETH Zurich, pg 636

Syrian Arab Republic
Damascus University Press, pg 638

Taiwan, Province of China
Fuh-Wen Book Co, pg 639
Hsiao Yuan Publication Co, Ltd, pg 640
Newton Publishing Company Ltd, pg 641
San Min Book Co Ltd, pg 641

United Republic of Tanzania
Ben and Company Ltd, pg 643
DUP (1996) Ltd, pg 643
Tanzania Publishing House, pg 644

Thailand
Thai Watana Panich Co, Ltd, pg 646

PUBLISHERS

Tunisia
Academie Tunisienne des Sciences, des Lettres et des Arts Beit El Hekma, pg 647
Maison d'Edition Mohamed Ali Hammi, pg 648

Turkey
Arkadas Ltd, pg 649
Aydin Yayincilik, pg 649
Bilden Bilgisayar, pg 649
Caglayan Kitabevi, pg 649
Inkilap Publishers Ltd, pg 650
Kok Yayincilik, pg 650

Uganda
Fountain Publishers Ltd, pg 652

Ukraine
Naukova Dumka Publishers, pg 653
Osvita, pg 654

United Kingdom
Advisory Unit: Computers in Education, pg 655
Belitha Press Ltd, pg 664
Cambridge University Press, pg 674
Causeway Press Ltd, pg 676
Educational Explorers (Publishers) Ltd, pg 690
The Eurospan Group, pg 692
Evans Brothers Ltd, pg 693
W H Freeman & Co Ltd, pg 697
The Harvill Press, pg 705
Hodder Education, pg 709
Impart Books, pg 712
Imperial College Press, pg 712
Institute of Physics Publishing, pg 713
Jones & Bartlett International, pg 716
Hilda King Educational, pg 717
Kluwer Academic/Plenum Publishers, pg 718
Learning Together, pg 720
Letts Educational, pg 720
McGraw-Hill Publishing Company, pg 726
Nelson Thornes Ltd, pg 732
Oxford University Press, pg 737
Pearson Education, pg 739
Pion Ltd, pg 742
Prim-Ed Publishing UK Ltd, pg 745
Research Studies Press Ltd (RSP), pg 749
The Royal Society, pg 752
Skoob Russell Square, pg 758
Southgate Publishers, pg 759
Springer-Verlag London Ltd, pg 760
Supportive Learning Publications, pg 762
Tarquin Publications, pg 762
Taylor & Francis, pg 763
University of Hertfordshire Press, pg 768
Ward Lock Educational Co Ltd, pg 771
Wiley Europe Ltd, pg 773
WIT Press, pg 774

Uruguay
La Flor del Itapebi, pg 777
A Monteverde y Cia SA, pg 777

Venezuela
Editorial Biosfera CA, pg 779
Sociedad Fondo Editorial Cenamec, pg 779

Viet Nam
Science & Technics Publishing House, pg 780

Zimbabwe
College Press Publishers (Pvt) Ltd, pg 783
Longman Zimbabwe (Pvt) Ltd, pg 783
Zimbabwe Publishing House (Pvt) Ltd, pg 784

MECHANICAL ENGINEERING

Albania
NL SH, pg 1

Australia
EA Books, pg 20
H&H Publishing, pg 24
McGraw-Hill Australia Pty Ltd, pg 31
Standards Association of Australia, pg 42

Austria
Springer-Verlag Wien, pg 58

Bulgaria
Todor Kableshkov University of Transport, pg 97

China
Aviation Industry Press, pg 101
Chemical Industry Press, pg 101
China Machine Press (CMP), pg 102
China Ocean Press, pg 102
Henan Science & Technology Publishing House, pg 105
Jilin Science & Technology Publishing House, pg 105
Metallurgical Industry Press (MIP), pg 106
Printing Industry Publishing House, pg 107
Shandong Science & Technology Press, pg 107
Shandong University Press, pg 108
Southwest China Jiaotong University Press, pg 108

Czech Republic
Cesky normalizacni institut, pg 126

Dominican Republic
Pontificia Universidad Catolica Madre y Maestra, pg 136

France
Cemagref Editions, pg 152
Cepadues Editions SA, pg 153
EDP Sciences, pg 161
Editions Eyrolles, pg 162
Polytechnica SA, pg 180
PYC Edition, pg 182
Editions Springer France, pg 186

Germany
Beuth Verlag GmbH, pg 200
Charles Coleman Verlag GmbH & Co KG, pg 209
Deutscher Verlag fur Grundstoffindustrie GmbH, pg 213

SUBJECT INDEX

expert verlag GmbH, Fachverlag fuer Wirtschaft & Technik, pg 222
Ferd Dummler's Verlag, pg 223
Gieck-Verlag GmbH, pg 229
Carl Hanser Verlag, pg 234
Huss-Medien GmbH, pg 240
Verlag Werner Sachon GmbH & Co, pg 277
Seibt Verlag GmbH, pg 282
Springer Science+Business Media GmbH & Co KG, pg 284
Verlag Stahleisen GmbH, pg 286
B G Teubner Verlag, pg 290
Trans Tech Publications, pg 292
Verlag fur Schweissen und Verwandte Verfahren, pg 295
Friedr Vieweg & Sohn Verlag, pg 296
Vogel Medien GmbH & Co KG, pg 296
Vulkan-Verlag GmbH, pg 297
WEKA Firmengruppe GmbH & Co KG, pg 298

Greece
Kleidarithmos, Ekdoseis, pg 309

Hong Kong
Business & Industrial Publication Co Ltd, pg 315

Hungary
Foldmuvelesugyi Miniszterium Muszaki Intezet, pg 321
Nemzeti Tankoenyvkiado, pg 323

India
Affiliated East West Press Pvt Ltd, pg 327
B I Publications Pvt Ltd, pg 329
Book Circle, pg 330
BS Publications, pg 331
Khanna Publishers, pg 339
Law Publishers, pg 340
Laxmi Publications Pvt Ltd, pg 340
Multitech Publishing Co, pg 342
Oxford & IBH Publishing Co Pvt Ltd, pg 344
Scientific Book Agency, pg 348
Sita Books & Periodicals Pvt Ltd, pg 349
Somaiya Publications Pvt Ltd, pg 349
Viva Books Pvt Ltd, pg 352

Israel
Freund Publishing House Ltd, pg 367

Italy
Edizioni Cremonese SRL, pg 383
Editrice Edisco, pg 386
Zanichelli Editore SpA, pg 412

Japan
Corona Publishing Co Ltd, pg 416
Maruzen Co Ltd, pg 422
Nippon Hoso Shuppan Kyokai (NHK Publishing), pg 424
Sangyo-Tosho Publishing Co Ltd, pg 426

Kazakstan
Al-Farabi Kazakh National University, pg 432

Democratic People's Republic of Korea
Korea Science and Encyclopedia Publishing House, pg 436

Republic of Korea
Bo Moon Dang, pg 437

Lithuania
Klaipedos Universiteto Leidykla, pg 449

Malaysia
Penerbit Universiti Teknologi Malaysia, pg 459

Mexico
Grupo Editorial Iberoamerica, SA de CV, pg 466
Editorial Limusa SA de CV, pg 467

Myanmar
Shumawa Publishing House, pg 476

Netherlands
A A Balkema Uitgevers BV, pg 478
Delft University Press, pg 481
Hagen & Stam Uitgeverij Ten, pg 483
IOS Press BV, pg 484
Kluwer Technische Boeken BV, pg 485
Twente University Press, pg 490

New Zealand
Southern Press Ltd, pg 501

Norway
NKI Forlaget, pg 510
Universitetsforlaget, pg 511

Poland
Wydawnictwa Komunikacji i Lacznosci Co Ltd, pg 524
Wydawnictwa Naukowo-Techniczne, pg 524
Polish Scientific Publishers PWN, pg 525
Wydawnictwa Przemyslowe WEMA, pg 526

Portugal
Editora McGraw-Hill de Portugal Lda, pg 533

Romania
Editura Excelsior Art, pg 539

Russian Federation
N E Bauman Moscow State Technical University Publishers, pg 544
FGUP Izdatelstvo Mashinostroenie, pg 544
Fizmatlit Publishing Co, pg 545
Izdatelstvo Mir, pg 546
Nauka Publishers, pg 547
Izdatel'stvo Nizhegorodskogo Gosudarstvennogo Univ, pg 547
Stroyizdat Publishing House, pg 549
Izdatelstvo Sudostroenie, pg 549

Serbia and Montenegro
Savez Inzenjera i Tehnicara Jugoslavije, pg 553

1041

SUBJECT INDEX

Singapore
World Scientific Publishing Co Pte Ltd, pg 559

Slovakia
Dom Techniky Zvazu Slovenskych Vedeckotechnickych Spolocnosti Ltd, pg 559

South Africa
Heinemann Educational Publishers Southern Africa, pg 564

Spain
Mundi-Prensa Libros SA, pg 592
Editorial Sintesis, SA, pg 600

Switzerland
Presses Polytechniques et Universitaires Romandes, PPUR, pg 631
Trans Tech Publications SA, pg 635

Syrian Arab Republic
Damascus University Press, pg 638

Taiwan, Province of China
Fuh-Wen Book Co, pg 639

United Republic of Tanzania
DUP (1996) Ltd, pg 643

Turkey
Caglayan Kitabevi, pg 649

Ukraine
Naukova Dumka Publishers, pg 653

United Kingdom
Atlantic Transport Publishers, pg 661
Elsevier Ltd, pg 691
Merrow Publishing Co Ltd, pg 727
Professional Engineering Publishing Ltd, pg 745
Research Studies Press Ltd (RSP), pg 749
The Royal Society, pg 752
The Royal Society of Chemistry, pg 752
Veloce Publishing Ltd, pg 769
Wiley Europe Ltd, pg 773
WIT Press, pg 774

Viet Nam
Science & Technics Publishing House, pg 780

Zimbabwe
Standards Association of Zimbabwe (SAZ), pg 784

MEDICINE, NURSING, DENTISTRY

Albania
NL SH, pg 1
State Textbook Publishing House, pg 1

Argentina
Libreria Akadia Editorial, pg 3
Editorial Albatros SACI, pg 3
Editorial Caymi SACI, pg 4
Diana Argentina SA, Editorial, pg 5

EUDEBA (Editorial Universitaria de Buenos Aires), pg 5
Editorial Idearium de la Universidad de Mendoza (EDIUM), pg 6
Lopez Libreros Editores S R L, pg 7
Editorial Medica Panamericana SA, pg 7
Editorial Polemos SA, pg 8

Australia
Ausmed Publications Pty Ltd, pg 12
Australasian Medical Publishing Company Ltd (AMPCO), pg 12
Blackwell Publishing Asia, pg 15
Cavendish Publishing Pty Ltd, pg 17
Deakin University Press, pg 19
Elsevier Australia, pg 21
Fraser Publications, pg 22
Hampden Press, pg 24
James Nicholas Publishers Pty Ltd, pg 27
Law Book Co Information Services, pg 28
MacLennan & Petty Pty Ltd, pg 30
McGraw-Hill Australia Pty Ltd, pg 31
Pearson Education Australia, pg 36
Jurriaan Plesman, pg 37
Royal Society of New South Wales, pg 40
Veritas Press, pg 45

Austria
Ennsthaler GesmbH & Co KG, pg 50
Wilhelm Maudrich KG, pg 54
Verlag Neues Leben, pg 54
Verlag des Osterr Kneippbundes GmbH, pg 56
E Perlinger Naturprodukte Handelsgesellschaft mbH, pg 56
Springer-Verlag Wien, pg 58
Trauner Verlag, pg 58
Urban und Schwarzenberg GmbH, pg 59
WUV/Facultas Universitaetsverlag, pg 60

Bangladesh
Gono Prakashani, Gono Shasthya Kendra, pg 61

Belarus
Belarus (The Belorussia), pg 62
Belaruskaya Encyklapedyya, pg 62

Belgium
Uitgeverij Acco, pg 62
Aurelia Books PVBA, pg 63
Editions De Boeck-Larcier SA, pg 66
Imprimerie Hayez SPRL, pg 68
Leuven University Press, pg 70
Marabout, pg 71
Nauwelaerts Edition SA, pg 71
Presses Universitaires de Bruxelles asbl, pg 72
Presses Universitaires de Liege, pg 72
Prodim SPRL, pg 72
Paul Schiltz, pg 73
Editions de l'Universite de Bruxelles, pg 74
Imprimeur - Editeur Vaillant-Carmanne SA, pg 74

Brazil
Editora Antroposofica Ltda, pg 77
Editora Artes Medicas Ltda, pg 78

ARTMED Editora, pg 78
Editora Atheneu Ltda, pg 78
Editora Cultura Medica Ltda, pg 80
E P U Editora Pedagogica e Universitaria Ltd, pg 81
Fundacao Sao Paulo, EDUC, pg 82
Editora Globo SA, pg 82
Edicoes Graal Ltda, pg 83
Editora Guanabara Koogan SA, pg 83
IBRASA (Instituicao Brasileira de Difusao Cultural Ltda), pg 83
Icone Editora Ltda, pg 83
Interlivros Edicoes Ltda, pg 84
Editora Manole Ltda, pg 86
Medicina Panamericana Editora Do Brasil Ltda, pg 86
Medsi - Editora Medica e Cientifica Ltda, pg 86
Organizacao Andrei Editora Ltda, pg 87
Proton Editora Ltda, pg 89
Editora de Publicacoes Medicas Ltda, pg 89
Qualitymark Editora Ltda, pg 89
Livraria Editora Revinter Ltda, pg 89
Editora Rideel Ltda, pg 89
Livraria Roca Ltda, pg 89
Livraria Santos Editora Comercio e Importacao Ltda, pg 90
Sarvier - Editora de Livros Medicos Ltda, pg 90
Editora da Universidade de Sao Paulo, pg 91

Bulgaria
Ciela Publishing House, pg 93
DA-Izdatelstvo Publishers, pg 93
Heron Press Publishing House, pg 94
Makros 2000 - Plovdiv, pg 95
Medicina i Fizkultura EOOD, pg 95
Seven Hills Publishers, pg 96

Chile
Arrayan Editores, pg 98
Editorial Andres Bello/Editorial Juridica de Chile, pg 99
Publicaciones Tecnicas Mediterraneo, pg 100

China
Beijing Medical University Press, pg 101
Beijing Publishing House, pg 101
Chemical Industry Press, pg 101
Foreign Languages Press, pg 104
Fujian Science & Technology Publishing House, pg 104
Guangdong Science & Technology Press, pg 105
Heilongjiang Science & Technology Press, pg 105
Henan Science & Technology Publishing House, pg 105
International Academic Publishers (IAP), pg 105
Jilin Science & Technology Publishing House, pg 105
Jinan Publishing House, pg 105
People's Medical Publishing House (PMPH), pg 107
Science Press, pg 107
Shandong Science & Technology Press, pg 107
Shanghai Scientific & Technical Publishers, pg 108
Shanghai Scientific & Technological Literature Press, pg 108

Sichuan Science & Technology Publishing House, pg 108
Tianjin Science & Technology Publishing House, pg 108

Colombia
Lerner Ediciones, pg 111
Universidad de Antioquia, Division Publicaciones, pg 113

The Democratic Republic of the Congo
Centre de Recherche, et Pedagogie Appliquee, pg 114
Presses Universitaires du Zaiire (PUZ), pg 114

Costa Rica
Litografia Artex, SA, pg 115
Editorial Nacional de Salud y Seguridad Social Ednass, pg 116
Editorial Universidad Estatal a Distancia (EUNED), pg 116

Croatia
Izdavacka Delatnost Hrvatske Akademije Znanosti I Umjetnosti, pg 118
Matica hrvatska, pg 118
Skolska Knjiga, pg 119

Czech Republic
Karolinum, nakladatelstvi, pg 124
Mariadan, pg 125
Maxdorf Ltd, pg 125
Pavla Momcilova, pg 125
Cesky normalizacni institut, pg 126
Omnipress Praha, pg 126
Psychoanalyticke Nakladatelstvi, pg 127

Denmark
Akademisk Forlag A/S, pg 128
Arnkrone Forlaget A/S, pg 129
FADL's Forlag A/S, pg 131
Forlaget for Faglitteratur A/S, pg 131
Gyldendalske Boghandel - Nordisk Forlag A/S, pg 131
Nyt Nordisk Forlag Arnold Busck A/S, pg 133
Syddansk Universitetsforlag, pg 135

Dominican Republic
Pontificia Universidad Catolica Madre y Maestra, pg 136

Estonia
AS Medicina, pg 140
Valgus Publishers, pg 140

Finland
Kustannus Oy Duodecim, pg 141
Recallmed Oy, pg 144
Sairaanhoitajien Koulutussaatio, pg 144
Yliopistopaino/Helsinki University Press, pg 145

France
Adverbum SARL, pg 146
Alsatia SA, pg 146
Arnette, pg 147
Editions J B Bailliere, pg 149
Bottin SA, pg 151
Council of Europe Publishing, pg 156
Counseil International de la Langue Francaise, pg 156

Les Editions Roger Dacosta, pg 156
Editions Dangles SA-Edilarge SA, pg 157
Doin Editeurs, pg 159
Ellipses - Edition Marketing SA, pg 161
Elsevier SAS (Editions Scientifiques et Medicales Elsevier), pg 161
Editions Eska, pg 162
Editions Espaces 34, pg 162
L'Esprit Du Temps, pg 162
L'Expansion Scientifique Francaise, pg 162
Flammarion SA, pg 163
Editions Foucher, pg 164
Hermann editeurs des Sciences et des Arts SA, pg 167
Editions INSERM, pg 168
InterEditions, pg 169
Le Jour, Editeur, pg 169
Jouvence Editions, pg 170
Editions Lamarre SA, pg 171
Editions Larousse, pg 171
Editions Lavoisier, pg 171
Editions Legislatives, pg 171
Editions John Libbey Eurotext, pg 172
Librairie Luginbuhl, pg 172
Maisonneuve Editeur, pg 174
Editions Maloine, pg 174
Masson Editeur, pg 174
Masson-Williams et Wilkins, pg 174
Presses Universitaires de France (PUF), pg 181
Guide Rosenwald, pg 183
Editions Saint-Michel SA, pg 183
Sauramps Medical, pg 184
Selection du Reader's Digest SA, pg 184
Editions Springer France, pg 186
Editions Vigot Universitaire, pg 188

Germany

Accedo Verlagsgesellschaft mbH, pg 190
Antiqua-Verlag GmbH, pg 193
Asgard-Verlag Dr Werner Hippe GmbH, pg 194
Basilisken-Presse, pg 197
Verlag Beleke KG, pg 198
Berliner Wissenschafts-Verlag GmbH (BWV), pg 199
Bertelsmann Lexikon Verlag GmbH, pg 200
Bibliographisches Institut & F A Brockhaus AG, pg 200
Bibliomed - Medizinische Verlagsgesellschaft mbH, pg 201
Biermann Verlag GmbH, pg 201
Blackwell Wissenschafts-Verlag GmbH, pg 201
CB-Verlag Carl Boldt, pg 203
Oscar Brandstetter Verlag GmbH & Co KG, pg 204
Catia Monser Eggcup-Verlag, pg 207
Chmielorz GmbH Verlag, pg 208
Darescht Consulting und Handels GmbH, pg 210
Deutscher Aerzte-Verlag GmbH, pg 212
Deutscher Apotheker Verlag Dr Roland Schmiedel GmbH & Co, pg 212
Dreisam Ratgeber in der Rutsker Verlag GmbH, pg 216
Dustri-Verlag Dr Karl Feistle, pg 217
Ecomed Verlagsgesellschaft AG & Co KG, pg 218
Elsevier GmbH/Urban & Fischer Verlag, pg 219
Ergebnisse Verlag GmbH, pg 220
Esogetics GmbH, pg 221
EVT Energy Video Training & Verlag GmbH, pg 222
Fachverlag Schiele & Schoen GmbH, pg 223
Ferdinand Enke Verlag, pg 224
Harald Fischer Verlag GmbH, pg 224
Rita G Fischer Verlag, pg 225
Verlag Freies Geistesleben, pg 227
Friedrich Kiehl Verlag GmbH, pg 227
Alfons W Gentner Verlag GmbH & Co KG, pg 228
Gesundheits-Dialog Verlag GmbH, pg 229
Gloatz, Hille GmbH & Co KG fur Mehrfarben und Zellglasdruck, pg 229
Gmelin Verlag GmbH, pg 230
Wilhelm Goldmann Verlag GmbH, pg 230
Verlag Grundlagen und Praxis GmbH & Co, pg 231
Walter de Gruyter GmbH & Co KG, pg 231
Haag und Herchen Verlag GmbH, pg 232
Dr Curt Haefner-Verlag GmbH, pg 233
Karl F Haug Verlag GmbH & Co, pg 235
Hippokrates-Verlag GmbH, pg 238
F Hirthammer Verlag GmbH, pg 238
Hogrefe Verlag GmbH & Co Kg, pg 238
Hans Huber, pg 239
Huthig GmbH & Co KG, pg 240
Mediteg-Gesellschaft fuer Informatik Technik und Systeme Verlag, pg 241
J Kamphausen Verlag & Distribution GmbH, pg 244
S Karger GmbH Verlag fuer Medizin und Naturwissenschaften, pg 244
Verlag im Kilian GmbH, pg 246
W Kohlhammer GmbH, pg 248
Konkret Literatur Verlag, pg 249
Lebenshilfe-Verlag Marburg, Verlag der Bundesvereinigung Lebenshilfe fuer Menschen mit geistiger Behinderung eV, pg 253
Leipziger Universitaetsverlag GmbH, pg 253
Mattes Verlag GmbH, pg 257
Medizinisch-Literarische Verlagsgesellschaft mbH, pg 258
Medpharm Scientific Publishers, pg 258
Midena Verlag, pg 260
Mueller und Steinicke Verlag, pg 262
Naumann & Goebel Verlagsgesellschaft mbH, pg 263
Neuland-Verlagsgesellschaft mbH, pg 264
Nusser Verlag, pg 266
Pala-Verlag GmbH, pg 268
Richard Pflaum Verlag GmbH & Co KG, pg 269
pmi Verlag, pg 270
Quintessenz Verlags-GmbH, pg 273
Reed Elsevier Deutschland GmbH, pg 274
Reichl Verlag Der Leuchter, pg 274
Ernst Reinhardt Verlag GmbH & Co KG, pg 275
Schangrila Verlags und Vertriebs GmbH, pg 279
Schattauer GmbH Verlag fuer Medizin und Naturwissenschaften, pg 279
Max Schmidt-Roemhild Verlag, pg 280
Wilhelm Schmitz Verlag, pg 280
Schulz-Kirchner Verlag GmbH, pg 282
Seibt Verlag GmbH, pg 282
Springer Science+Business Media GmbH & Co KG, pg 284
Springer Science+Business Media GmbH & Co KG, Berlin, pg 285
Dr Dietrich Steinkopff Verlag GmbH & Co, pg 287
Georg Thieme Verlag KG, pg 291
Tuduv Verlagsgesellschaft mbH, pg 292
Universitatsverlag Ulm GmbH, pg 293
Urban & Vogel Medien und Medizin Verlagsgesellschaft mbH & Co KG, pg 294
UTB fuer Wissenschaft Uni Taschenbuecher GmbH, pg 294
Curt R Vincentz Verlag, pg 296
VWB-Verlag fur Wissenschaft & Bildung, Amand Aglaster, pg 297
WEKA Firmengruppe GmbH & Co KG, pg 298
Wissenschaftliche Buchgesellschaft, pg 300
Wissenschaftliche Verlagsgesellschaft mbH, pg 300
Fachbuchverlag Armin W Wuth, pg 301

Ghana

Ghana Universities Press (GUP), pg 304
World Literature Project, pg 305

Greece

Beta Medical Publishers, pg 306
Chryssos Typos AE Ekodeis, pg 306
Giovanis Publications, Pangosmios Ekdotikos Organismos, pg 307
Kalentis & Sia, pg 308
M Psaropoulos & Co EE, pg 311
Alex Siokis & Co, pg 312

Holy See (Vatican City State)

Pontificia Academia Scientiarum, pg 314

Hong Kong

Commercial Press (Hong Kong) Ltd, pg 316
Hong Kong University Press, pg 317
Joint Publishing (HK) Co Ltd, pg 317

Hungary

Advent Kiado, pg 320
Akademiai Kiado, pg 320
Medicina Koenyvkiado, pg 323
Springer Hungarica Kiado Kft, pg 324

India

Academic Publishers, pg 327
AL Publishers, pg 327
Atma Ram & Sons, pg 329
B I Publications Pvt Ltd, pg 329
Book Circle, pg 330
BS Publications, pg 331
S Chand & Co Ltd, pg 331
Galgotia Publications Pvt Ltd, pg 334
Arnold Heinman Publishers (India) Pvt Ltd, pg 335
Heritage Publishers, pg 335
Intertrade Publications Pvt Ltd, pg 338
B Jain Publishers Overseas, pg 338
B Jain Publishers (P) Ltd, pg 339
Jaypee Brothers Medical Publishers Pvt Ltd, pg 339
Mehta Publishers, pg 341
Motilal Banarsidass Publishers Pvt Ltd, pg 341
Narosa Publishing House, pg 342
Parimal Prakashan, pg 345
Popular Prakashan Pvt Ltd, pg 345
Pustak Mahal, pg 345
Rajasthan Hindi Granth Academy, pg 346
Reliance Publishing House, pg 346
Research Signpost, pg 347
Sri Satguru Publications, pg 348
Scientific Book Agency, pg 348
Sterling Publishers Pvt Ltd, pg 350
Transworld Research Network, pg 351
Vision Books Pvt Ltd, pg 352
S Viswanathan (Printers & Publishers) Pvt Ltd, pg 352

Indonesia

Alumni PT, pg 353
PT Dian Rakyat, pg 354

Ireland

On Stream Publications Ltd, pg 362

Israel

Books in the Attic Publishers Ltd, pg 365
Boostan Publishing House, pg 365
Dyonon/Papyrus Publishing House of the Tel-Aviv, pg 366
Freund Publishing House Ltd, pg 367
Gefen Publishing House Ltd, pg 367
Intermedia Audio, Video Book Publishing Ltd, pg 368
Medcom Ltd, pg 370
M Mizrahi Publishers, pg 370
Rubin Mass Ltd, pg 371
Schlesinger Institute, pg 371

Italy

Editore Armando Armando SRL, pg 376
Editoriale Bios, pg 378
Edizioni Brenner, pg 379
Calosci, pg 379
Cappelli Editore, pg 380
CEDAM (Casa Editrice Dr A Milani), pg 380
Centro Scientifico Torinese, pg 381
CG Ediz Medico-Scientifiche, pg 381
CIC Edizioni Internazionali, pg 381
CLEUP - Cooperativa Libraria Editrice dell 'Universita di Padova, pg 382
Libreria Cortina Editrice SRL, pg 383
Giovanni De Vecchi Editore SpA, pg 384
Edi.Ermes srl, pg 388
Festina Lente Edizioni, pg 389
Editoriale Fernando Folini, pg 389
Arnaldo Forni Editore SRL, pg 389
Gangemi Editore spa, pg 390
Edizioni GB, pg 390
Gruppo Editoriale Faenza Editrice SpA, pg 391
Hermes Edizioni SRL, pg 392

SUBJECT INDEX

Casa Editrice Libraria Idelson di G Gnocchi, pg 392
Idelson-Gnocchi Edizioni Scientifiche, pg 393
International University Press Srl, pg 393
Liguori Editore SRL, pg 395
Vincenzo Lo Faro Editore, pg 395
Longanesi & C, pg 396
Casa Editrice Maccari (CEM), pg 396
Masson SpA, pg 397
Mediserve SRL, pg 398
Edizioni Mediterranee SRL, pg 398
Arnoldo Mondadori Editore SpA, pg 398
Monduzzi Editore SpA, pg 399
Nardini Editore srl, pg 400
New Magazine Edizioni, pg 400
OEMF srl International, pg 401
Patron Editore SrL, pg 402
Piccin Nuova Libraria SpA, pg 403
Edizioni Luigi Pozzi SRL, pg 404
Rara Istituto Editoriale di Bibliofilia e Reprints, pg 405
RCS Libri SpA, pg 405
RCS Rizzoli Libri SpA, pg 405
Red/Studio Redazionale, pg 405
Edizioni del Riccio SAS di G Bernardi, pg 405
Edizioni Universitarie Romane, pg 406
SAIE Editrice SRL, pg 406
Edizioni San Paolo SRL, pg 407
Edizioni Scientifiche Italiane, pg 407
Società Editrice la Goliardica Pavese SRL, pg 408
Sorbona, pg 409
Stampa Alternativa - Nuovi Equilibri, pg 409
Transeuropa, pg 410
UTET Periodici Scientifici, pg 411
Vita e Pensiero, pg 412
Zanichelli Editore SpA, pg 412

Japan

Chijin Shokan Co Ltd, pg 416
Daiichi Shuppan Co Ltd, pg 416
Dobunshoin Publishers Co, pg 416
Dohosha Publishing Co Ltd, pg 417
Hirokawa Publishing Co, pg 418
Hokuryukan Co Ltd, pg 418
Igaku-Shoin Ltd, pg 419
Ishiyaku Publishers Inc, pg 419
Kanehara & Co Ltd, pg 420
Kinpodo, pg 421
Kodansha Ltd, pg 421
Kyodo-Isho Shuppan Co Ltd, pg 422
Kyoritsu Shuppan Co Ltd, pg 422
Medical Sciences International Ltd, pg 422
Mejikaru Furendo-sha, pg 422
Minerva Shobo Co Ltd, pg 422
Mita Press, Mita Industrial Co Ltd, pg 422
Nagai Shoten Co Ltd, pg 423
Nakayama Shoten Co Ltd, pg 423
Nankodo Co Ltd, pg 423
Nanzando Co Ltd, pg 423
Nihon Bunka Kagakusha Co Ltd, pg 423
Nishimura Co Ltd, pg 424
Nosangyoson Bunka Kyokai, pg 424
Pearson Education Japan, pg 425
Seibido Shuppan Company Ltd, pg 426
Seiwa Shoten Co Ltd, pg 427
Shorin-Sha Co ltd, pg 428
Shufu-to-Seikatsu Sha Ltd, pg 428
Shufunotomo Co Ltd, pg 428
Sogensha Publishing Co Ltd, pg 428
Springer-Verlag Tokyo, pg 428
Takahashi Shoten Co Ltd, pg 429
Toho Book Store, pg 429
Tokyo Kagaku Dojin Co Ltd, pg 429
Universal Academy Press, Inc, pg 430
University of Tokyo Press, pg 430
Yakuji Nippo Ltd, pg 431

Jordan

Jordan Book Centre Co Ltd, pg 432
Jordan House for Publication, pg 432

Kazakstan

Kazakhstan, Izd-Vo, pg 432

Kenya

Kenya Literature Bureau, pg 434
Kenya Medical Research Institute (KEMRI), pg 435

Democratic People's Republic of Korea

Korea Science and Encyclopedia Publishing House, pg 436

Republic of Korea

Hanul Publishing Co, pg 439
Iljo-gag Publishers, pg 439
Panmun Book Co Ltd, pg 442
Seoul National University Press, pg 443
Shinkwang Publishing Co, pg 443
Yonsei University Press, pg 444

Lebanon

Arab Institute for Research & Publishing, pg 445
Khayat Book and Publishing Co Sarl, pg 446

Lithuania

Academia, pg 448
AS Narbuto Leidykla (AS Narbutas' Publishers), pg 448
Mokslo ir enciklopediju leidybos institutas, pg 449

The Former Yugoslav Republic of Macedonia

Medis, Skopje, pg 452

Malaysia

University of Malaya, Department of Publications, pg 459

Mauritius

Hemco Publications, pg 461

Mexico

Libreria y Ediciones Botas SA, pg 462
Editora Cientifica Medica Latinoamerican SA de CV, pg 463
Comision Nacional Forestal, pg 463
Editorial El Manual Moderno SA de CV, pg 464
Ediciones Exclusivas SA, pg 465
Intersistemas SA de CV, pg 467
Editorial Limusa SA de CV, pg 467
Mundo Medico SA de CV Edicion y Distribucion de Revistas Medicas, pg 469
Ediciones Cientificas La Prensa Medica Mexicana SA de CV, pg 470
Salvat Editores de Mexico, pg 471
Editorial Trillas SA de CV, pg 472
Universidad Nacional Autonoma de Mexico (National University of Mexico), pg 472
Universo Editorial SA de CV Edicion de Libros Revistas y Periodicos, pg 473

Republic of Moldova

Editura Lumina, pg 473

Morocco

Edition Diffusion de Livre au Maroc, pg 474
Editions Oum, pg 475

Mozambique

Editora Minerva Central, pg 475

Nepal

International Standards Books & Periodicals (P) Ltd, pg 476

Netherlands

B M Israel BV, pg 478
Uitgeverij Bohn Stafleu Van Loghum BV, pg 479
De Driehoek BV, Uitgeverij, pg 481
Elsevier Science BV, pg 482
Uitgeverij Homeovisie BV, pg 483
ICG Publications BV, pg 484
IOS Press BV, pg 484
Kluwer Academic Publishers, pg 484
Kugler Publications, pg 485
Swets & Zeitlinger Publishers, pg 489
Uitgeverij de Tijdstroom BV, pg 490
Tirion Uitgevers BV, pg 490
Twente University Press, pg 490
V S P International Science Publishers, pg 491
Van Gorcum & Comp BV, pg 491
VU Boekhandel/Uitgeverij BV, pg 492

New Zealand

Resource Books Ltd, pg 500

Nigeria

CSS Bookshops, pg 504
Evans Brothers (Nigeria Publishers) Ltd, pg 504
Ibadan University Press, pg 505
Obafemi Awolowo University Press Ltd, pg 506
Riverside Communications, pg 507
University of Lagos Press, pg 507

Norway

Elanders Publishing AS, pg 509
Glydendal Akademisk, pg 509
Sandviks Bokforlag, pg 510
Universitetsforlaget, pg 511
Vett & Viten AS, pg 511

Pakistan

HMR Publishing Co, pg 512

Papua New Guinea

Papua New Guinea Institute of Medical Research, pg 516

Peru

Universidad Nacional Mayor de San Marcos, pg 517

Philippines

University of the Philippines Press, pg 521
UST Publishing House, pg 521
Vera-Reyes Inc, pg 521

Poland

Wydawnictwo Medyczne Urban & Partner, pg 524
Ossolineum Zaklad Narodowy im Ossolinskich - Wydawnictwo, pg 525
PZWL Wydawnictwo Lekarskie Ltd, pg 526
Towarzystwo Naukowe w Toruniu, pg 527

Portugal

Publicacoes Ciencia e Vida Lda, pg 529
Dinalivro, pg 530
Editorial Estampa, Lda, pg 531
Publicacoes Europa-America Lda, pg 531
Europress Editores e Distribuidores de Publicacoes Lda, pg 531
Imprensa Nacional-Casa da Moeda, pg 532
Livraria Luzo-Espanhola Lda, pg 533
Livraria Minerva, pg 533
Livraria Lopes Da Silva-Editora de M Moreira Soares Rocha Lda, pg 533
Editora McGraw-Hill de Portugal Lda, pg 533

Puerto Rico

McGraw-Hill Intermericana del Caribe, Inc, pg 537

Romania

Editura Academiei Romane, pg 538
Editura Aius, pg 538
Editora All, pg 538
Editura Clusium, pg 539
Editura Excelsior Art, pg 539
Editura Gryphon, pg 540
Editura Institutul European, pg 540
Lider Verlag, pg 540
MAST Verlag, pg 540
Editura Medicala, pg 540
Editura Meridiane, pg 540
Polirom Verlag, pg 542
Editura Teora, pg 542
Vremea Publishers Ltd, pg 543

Russian Federation

Airis Press, pg 543
Izdatelstvo Medicina, pg 546
Izdatelstvo Mordovskogo gosudar stvennogo, pg 547
Moscow University Press, pg 547
Nauka Publishers, pg 547

Saudi Arabia

Dar Al-Shareef for Publishing & Distribution, pg 550
King Saud University, pg 550

Serbia and Montenegro

Alfa-Narodna Knjiga, pg 552
Naucna Knjiga, pg 552
Panorama NIJP/ID Grigorije Bozovic, pg 553

PUBLISHERS

Singapore
APAC Publishers Services Pte Ltd, pg 554
Maruzen Asia (Pte) Ltd, pg 557
McGallen & Bolden Associates, pg 557
PG Medical Books, pg 557
Taylor & Francis Asia Pacific, pg 558
World Scientific Publishing Co Pte Ltd, pg 559

Slovakia
Vydavatel'stvo Osveta (Verlag Osveta), pg 560

Slovenia
Zalozba Mihelac d o o, pg 562
Zalozba Obzorja d d Maribor, pg 562

South Africa
Heinemann Publishers (Pty) Ltd, pg 564
Jacana Education, pg 565
Juta & Co, pg 565
Nasionale Boekhandel Ltd, pg 567
Reader's Digest Southern Africa, pg 568
Van Schaik Publishers, pg 569
Witwatersrand University Press, pg 570

Spain
Editorial Acribia SA, pg 571
Aguilar SA de Ediciones, pg 571
Ediciones Alfar SA, pg 572
AMV Ediciones, pg 572
Ediciones Atril, pg 574
Comunidad Autonoma de Madrid, Servicio de Documentacion y Publicaciones, pg 578
Ediciones Diaz de Santos SA, pg 579
Ediciones Doce Calles SL, pg 579
Editorial Dossat SA, pg 580
Ediciones Doyma SA, pg 580
Edika-Med, SA, pg 581
Editorial Espaxs SA, pg 582
EUNSA (Ediciones Universidad de Navarra SA), pg 583
Editorial Grupo Cero, pg 585
Editorial Herder SA, pg 586
Mandala Ediciones, pg 590
Editorial Marin SA, pg 590
McGraw-Hill/Interamericana de Espana SAU, pg 591
Editorial Medica JIMS, SL, pg 591
Ediciones Medici SA, pg 591
M Moleiro Editor, SA, pg 592
Ediciones Norma SA, pg 593
Obelisco Ediciones S, pg 593
Oikos-Tau SA Ediciones, pg 593
Pearson Educacion S A, pg 595
Permanyer Publications, pg 596
Publicaciones de la Universidad de Alicante, pg 597
Publicaciones de la Universidad Pontificia Comillas-Madrid, pg 597
Pulso Ediciones, SL, pg 597
Ediciones ROL SA, pg 598
Ediciones Scriba SA, pg 599
Servicio de Publicaciones Universidad de Cadiz, pg 599
Signament I Comunicacio, SL Signament Edicions, pg 599
Axel Springer Publicaciones, pg 601
Universidad de Granada, pg 603
Universidad de Malaga, pg 603
Universidad de Valladolid Secretariado de Publicaciones e Intercambio Editorial, pg 604
Universitat de Valencia Servei de Publicacions, pg 604

Sri Lanka
Lake House Investments Ltd, pg 606

Sweden
Akademiforlaget Goteborgslitteratur, pg 609
AB Arcanum, pg 609
Bokforlaget Fingraf AB, pg 611
Bengt Forsbergs Foerlag AB, pg 611
Foerlagshuset Gothia, pg 612
Liber AB, pg 613
Studentlitteratur AB, pg 616

Switzerland
Antonius-Verlag, pg 617
Ariston Editions, pg 617
Association Suisse des Editeurs de Langue Francaise, pg 618
Marcel Dekker AG, pg 621
Editions Delachaux et Niestle SA, pg 621
Editions Andre Delcourt & Cie, pg 621
Eular Verlag, pg 623
S Karger AG, Medical & Scientific Publishers, pg 626
Medecine et Hygiene, pg 628
Editions Payot Lausanne, pg 631
Philosophisch-Anthroposophischer Verlag am Goetheanum, pg 631
RECOM Verlag, pg 632
Schwabe & Co AG, pg 633
Sciamed Verlag AG, pg 634
Der Universitatsverlag Freiburg, pg 636

Syrian Arab Republic
Damascus University Press, pg 638

Taiwan, Province of China
Chung Hwa Book Co Ltd, pg 639
Farseeing Publishing Company Ltd, pg 639
Chu Hai Publishing (Taiwan) Co Ltd, pg 640
Ho-Chi Book Publishing Co, pg 640
Kuang Fu Book Co Ltd, pg 640
Newton Publishing Company Ltd, pg 641
Sinorama Magazine Co, pg 641
SMC Publishing Inc, pg 642
World Book Co Ltd, pg 642
Yi Hsien Publishing Co Ltd, pg 642

Tajikistan
Irfon, pg 642

United Republic of Tanzania
DUP (1996) Ltd, pg 643
Ndanda Mission Press, pg 644
Nyota Publishers Ltd, pg 644

Togo
Presses de l'Universite du Benin, pg 646

Tunisia
Academie Tunisienne des Sciences, des Lettres et des Arts Beit El Hekma, pg 647

Turkey
Saray Medikal Yayin Tic Ltd Sti, pg 651
Yuce Reklam Yay Dagt AS, pg 652

Ukraine
Naukova Dumka Publishers, pg 653

United Kingdom
Ai Interactive Ltd, pg 656
Arnold, pg 659
Beaconsfield Publishers Ltd, pg 664
Biocommerce Data Ltd, pg 665
BIOS Scientific Publishers Ltd, pg 665
Blackwell Science Ltd, pg 667
Bloomsbury Publishing PLC, pg 668
BMJ Publishing Group, pg 668
Cambridge University Press, pg 674
Castlemead Publications, pg 676
Cavendish Publishing Ltd, pg 676
Class Publishing, pg 680
Current Science Group, pg 685
Denor Press, pg 687
Dobro Publishing, pg 688
Elsevier Ltd, pg 691
The Eurospan Group, pg 692
W H Freeman & Co Ltd, pg 697
Harvard University Press, pg 705
Hawker Publications Ltd, pg 706
Health Development Agency, pg 706
Horizon Scientific Press, pg 710
Imperial College Press, pg 712
Intercept Ltd, pg 714
Jones & Bartlett International, pg 716
Jessica Kingsley Publishers, pg 718
John Libbey & Co Ltd, pg 720
Lippincott Williams & Wilkins, pg 721
Liverpool University Press, pg 722
Manson Publishing Ltd, pg 725
McGraw-Hill Publishing Company, pg 726
Nelson Thornes Ltd, pg 732
Oxford University Press, pg 737
PasTest, pg 738
Pearson Education Europe, Mideast & Africa, pg 739
Pharmaceutical Press, pg 741
Portland Press Ltd, pg 745
Quintessence Publishing Co Ltd, pg 747
Radcliffe Medical Press Ltd, pg 747
Roundhouse Group, pg 751
Royal College of General Practitioners (RCGP), pg 752
Royal Society of Medicine Press Ltd, pg 752
SAGE Publications Ltd, pg 753
Sangam Books Ltd, pg 754
Science Reviews Ltd, pg 755
Sheffield Academic Press Ltd, pg 757
Smith-Gordon & Co Ltd, pg 758
Souvenir Press Ltd, pg 759
Speechmark Publishing Ltd, pg 760
Springer-Verlag London Ltd, pg 760
Harold Starke Publishers Ltd, pg 761
Taylor & Francis, pg 763
Taylor & Francis Medical Books, pg 763
The Tarragon Press, pg 765
TSO (The Stationery Office), pg 767
University of Hertfordshire Press, pg 768
Whurr Publishers Ltd, pg 773
Wiley Europe Ltd, pg 773

Uruguay
Editorial Dismar, pg 777
Prensa Medica Latinoamericana, pg 778

Venezuela
Universidad de los Andes, Consejo de Publicaciones, pg 780

Viet Nam
Science & Technics Publishing House, pg 780
Y Hoc Publishing House, pg 781

Zimbabwe
University of Zimbabwe Publications, pg 784

MICROCOMPUTERS

Albania
NL SH, pg 1

Australia
OTEN (Open Training & Education Network), pg 34
Price Publishing, pg 37
Tertiary Press, pg 43

Barbados
Business Tutors, pg 62

Belgium
Easy Computing NV, pg 67

Brazil
Antenna Edicoes Tecnicas Ltda, pg 77
Berkeley Brasil Editora Ltda, pg 78
Callis Editora Ltda, pg 79
Editora Campus Ltda, pg 79
Selecoes Eletronicas Editora Ltda, pg 90

Bulgaria
Aleks Soft, pg 93
Makros 2000 - Plovdiv, pg 95
TEMTO, pg 97

China
China Machine Press (CMP), pg 102
Electronics Industry Publishing House, pg 104
Fudan University Press, pg 104
Inner Mongolia Science & Technology Publishing House, pg 105
Jilin Science & Technology Publishing House, pg 105
National Defence Industry Press, pg 106
Shandong University Press, pg 108
Shanghai Educational Publishing House, pg 108
Tianjin Science & Technology Publishing House, pg 108

Cote d'Ivoire
Universite d'Abidjan, pg 117

Cuba
Apocalipis Digital, pg 120
Casa Editora Abril, pg 120

Finland
Docendo Finland Oy, pg 141

SUBJECT INDEX

France
Dunod Editeur, pg 159
Les Editions ESF, pg 160
Editions Mango, pg 174
Pearson Education France, pg 179
Sybex, pg 186

Germany
Data Becker GmbH & Co KG, pg 210
Elektor-Verlag GmbH, pg 219
Feltron-Elektronik Zeissler & Co GmbH, pg 223
Carl Hanser Verlag, pg 234
ITpress Verlag, pg 242

Greece
Kleidarithmos, Ekdoseis, pg 309

Hong Kong
Modern Electronic & Computing Publishing Co Ltd, pg 318

Hungary
Magyar Tudomanyos Akademia Koezponti Fizikai Kutato Intezet Koenyvtara, pg 322

India
Affiliated East West Press Pvt Ltd, pg 327
BS Publications, pg 331
Pitambar Publishing Co (P) Ltd, pg 345
Scientific Book Agency, pg 348
Sita Books & Periodicals Pvt Ltd, pg 349
Sterling Information Technologies, pg 350

Indonesia
Gramedia, pg 355

Italy
IHT Gruppo Editoriale SRL, pg 393

Japan
Dobunshoin Publishers Co, pg 416
Kaibundo Shuppan, pg 420
Pearson Education Japan, pg 425

Republic of Korea
Ohmsa, pg 441

The Former Yugoslav Republic of Macedonia
Medis, Skopje, pg 452

Mexico
Alfaomega Grupo Editor SA de CV, pg 462
Ibcon SA, pg 466
Editorial Limusa SA de CV, pg 467
Pearson Educacion de Mexico, SA de CV, pg 470
Sistemas Universales, SA, pg 472
Ventura Ediciones, SA de CV, pg 473

Netherlands
Erven J Bijleveld, pg 479
BoekWerk, pg 479
Hagen & Stam Uitgeverij Ten, pg 483

Pakistan
Academy of Education Planning & Management (AEPAM), pg 511

Paraguay
Instituto de Ciencias de la Computacion (NCR), pg 516

Poland
Wydawnictwa Naukowo-Techniczne, pg 524
Oficyna Wydawnicza Politechniki Wroclawskiej, pg 525
Oficyna Wydawnicza Read Me, pg 526

Portugal
Edicoes Cetop, pg 529
Impala, pg 532

Romania
Petrion Verlag, pg 542

Russian Federation
N E Bauman Moscow State Technical University Publishers, pg 544
Finansy i Statistika Publishing House, pg 544
Fizmatlit Publishing Co, pg 545
Izdatelstvo Mir, pg 546
Nauka Publishers, pg 547
Izdatel'stvo Nizhegorodskogo Gosudarstvennogo Univ, pg 547

Slovakia
Ustav informacii a prognoz skolstva mladeze a telovychovy, pg 561

Spain
Marcombo SA, pg 590
RA-MA, Libreria y Editorial Microinformatica, pg 597
Urmo SA de Ediciones, pg 604

Taiwan, Province of China
Lead Wave Publishing Company Ltd, pg 640

Turkey
Alkim Kitapcilik-Yayimcilik, pg 649

Ukraine
ASK Ltd, pg 653

United Kingdom
Advisory Unit: Computers in Education, pg 655
BCA - Book Club Associates, pg 663
CTBI Publications, pg 685
The Eurospan Group, pg 692
Research Studies Press Ltd (RSP), pg 749

Viet Nam
Science & Technics Publishing House, pg 780

MILITARY SCIENCE

Albania
NL SH, pg 1

Argentina
Instituto de Publicaciones Navales, pg 8
Theoria SRL Distribuidora y Editora, pg 9

Armenia
Ajstan Publishers, pg 10

Australia
Macmillan Publishers Australia Pty Ltd, pg 30
Mostly Unsung, pg 32
Oceans Enterprises, pg 34
Slouch Hat Publications, pg 41
The Watermark Press, pg 46

Austria
Akademische Druck-u Verlagsanstalt Dr Paul Struzl GmbH, pg 48
Leopold Stocker Verlag, pg 53
Herbert Weishaupt Verlag, pg 59

Bangladesh
The University Press Ltd, pg 61

Belgium
Editions Chanlis, pg 65
IPIS vzw (International Peace Information Service), pg 69
De Krijger, pg 69

Brazil
Action Editora Ltda, pg 76
Callis Editora Ltda, pg 79
Editora Revan Ltda, pg 89

Bulgaria
Voenno Izdatelstvo, pg 97

China
Education Science Publishing House, pg 104
Kunlun Publishing House, pg 106
National Defence Industry Press, pg 106

Czech Republic
Aurora, pg 122
Baronet, pg 122
Nakladatelstvi Jota spol sro, pg 124
Nase vojsko, nakladatelstvi a knizni obchod, pg 126

Denmark
Bonnier Publications A/S, pg 129

Estonia
Eesti Entsuklopeediakirjastus, pg 139

Finland
Koala-Kustannus Oy, pg 143

France
Editions Anthropos, pg 147
Publications Aredit, pg 147
Editions Cenomane, pg 152
Editions Charles-Lavauzelle SA, pg 153
EPA (Editions Pratiques Automobiles), pg 161
Editions Jacques Grancher, pg 165
Ivrea, pg 169
Muller Edition, pg 176

Germany
Bernard und Graefe Verlag, pg 199
Biblio Verlag, pg 200
Brandenburgisches Verlagshaus in der Dornier Medienholding GmbH, pg 204
Degener & Co, Manfred Dreiss Verlag, pg 211
Duncker und Humblot GmbH, pg 217
DVG-Deutsche Verlagsgesellschaft mbH, pg 217
Liselotte Hamecher, pg 233
Verlagsgruppe Koehler/Mittler, pg 248
E S Mittler und Sohn GmbH, pg 261
Motorbuch-Verlag, pg 262
Nusser Verlag, pg 266
Verlag Offene Worte, pg 266
Paul Pietsch Verlage GmbH & Co, pg 270
Podzun-Pallas Verlag GmbH, pg 270
Propylaeen Verlag, Zweigniederlassung Berlin der Ullstein Buchverlage GmbH, pg 272
Schild-Verlag GmbH, pg 279
Verlag Karl Waldemar Schuetz, pg 281
Edition Temmen, pg 290
Trees Wolfgang Triangel Verlag, pg 292
Weber Zucht & Co, pg 298

Guatemala
Grupo Editorial RIN-78, pg 313

Hungary
Zrinyi Kiado, pg 325

India
Asian Educational Services, pg 329
Heritage Publishers, pg 335
Himalayan Books, pg 336
Lancer Publisher's & Distributors, pg 340
National Book Organization, pg 342
Naya Prokash, pg 343
Reliance Publishing House, pg 346
Scientific Book Agency, pg 348
Vision Books Pvt Ltd, pg 352
Viva Books Pvt Ltd, pg 352

Indonesia
Yayasan Obor Indonesia, pg 357

Ireland
Irish Academic Press, pg 361

Israel
Dekel Publishing House, pg 366
Gefen Publishing House Ltd, pg 367
Ministry of Defence Publishing House, pg 370
Tel Aviv University, pg 372

Italy
Gruppo Abele, pg 374
Ermanno Albertelli Editore, pg 375
Athesia Verlag Bozen, pg 377
Edizioni l'Arciere SRL, pg 387
IHT Gruppo Editoriale SRL, pg 393
Edizioni Mediterranee SRL, pg 398
Rossato, pg 406

PUBLISHERS

Japan
Kokushokankokai Co Ltd, pg 421

Lebanon
Arab Institute for Research & Publishing, pg 445

Monaco
Les Editions du Rocher, pg 474

Namibia
McGregor Publishers, pg 476

Netherlands
Omega Boek BV, pg 487

Romania
Editura Militara, pg 541

Russian Federation
Izdatel'stvo Patriot, pg 548
Izdatelstvo Sudostroenie, pg 549
Teorija Verojatnostej i ee Primenenija, pg 549
Voyenizdat, pg 549

Serbia and Montenegro
Vojnoizdavacki i novinski centar, pg 554

Slovenia
Mladinska Knjiga International, pg 561

South Africa
Ashanti Publishing, pg 562
Galago Publishing Pty Ltd, pg 564
South African Institute of International Affairs, pg 569

Spain
Ediciones Rialp SA, pg 598
Editorial San Martin, pg 598
Axel Springer Publicaciones, pg 601
Xunta de Galicia, pg 605

Sweden
Allt om Hobby AB, pg 609

Switzerland
Les Editions la Matze, pg 628
Ott Verlag Thun, pg 630
Verlag Stocker-Schmid AG, pg 635
Editions 24 Heures, pg 635

Taiwan, Province of China
Asian Culture Co Ltd, pg 638
Wu Nan Book Co Ltd, pg 642

United Kingdom
Airlife Publishing Ltd, pg 656
Aldwych Press Ltd, pg 656
Amber Books Ltd, pg 657
Arms & Armour Press, pg 659
Aurum Press Ltd, pg 661
BCA - Book Club Associates, pg 663
Berghahn Books Ltd, pg 665
The Book Guild Ltd, pg 668
Book Packaging & Marketing, pg 668
Books International, pg 669
Brassey's UK Ltd, pg 670
Brewin Books Ltd, pg 671
Bridge Books, pg 671
Frank Cass Publishers, pg 675
Cassell & Co, pg 675
Compendium Publishing, pg 681
Constable & Robinson Ltd, pg 682
Leo Cooper, pg 683
The Eurospan Group, pg 692
Firebird Books Ltd, pg 695
Greenhill Books/Lionel Leventhal Ltd, pg 703
Guinness World Records Ltd, pg 703
Hodder & Stoughton General, pg 709
International Institute for Strategic Studies, pg 714
Jane's Information Group, pg 715
Macmillan Audio Books, pg 723
Marshall Editions Ltd, pg 725
Middleton Press, pg 728
Midland Publishing, pg 728
Osprey Publishing Ltd, pg 737
Oxford University Press, pg 737
Parapress Ltd, pg 738
Pen & Sword Books Ltd, pg 740
PRC Publishing Ltd, pg 745
Quintet Publishing Ltd, pg 747
Research Studies Press Ltd (RSP), pg 749
Robson Books, pg 750
Shire Publications Ltd, pg 757
Sidgwick & Jackson Ltd, pg 757
SPA Books Ltd, pg 759
Spellmount Ltd Publishers, pg 760
Sutton Publishing Ltd, pg 762
Sydney Jary Ltd, pg 762
Telegraph Books, pg 764
Unicorn Books, pg 768

Viet Nam
Popular Army Publishing House, pg 780

MUSIC, DANCE

Albania
NL SH, pg 1

Argentina
Bonum Editorial SACI, pg 4
Cesarini Hermanos, pg 4
Ediciones Corregidor SAICI y E, pg 4
Diana Argentina SA, Editorial, pg 5
EUDEBA (Editorial Universitaria de Buenos Aires), pg 5
Ediciones de Arte Gaglianone, pg 6
Editorial Guadalupe, pg 6
Marymar Ediciones SA, pg 7
Editorial Quetzal-Domingo Cortizo, pg 8
Ricordi Americana SAEC, pg 8
Javier Vergara Editor SA, pg 9

Australia
Aboriginal Studies Press, pg 10
Currency Press Pty Ltd, pg 19
Ginninderra Press, pg 23
Grainger Museum, pg 24
Moonlight Publishing, pg 32
NMA Publications, pg 33
Anne O'Donovan Pty Ltd, pg 34
Playlab Press, pg 37
St Joseph Publications, pg 40
Spectrum Publications, pg 41
Thames & Hudson (Australia) Pty Ltd, pg 43
Turton & Armstrong Pty Ltd Publishers, pg 44
Unity Press, pg 44
Yanagang Publishing, pg 47

SUBJECT INDEX

Austria
Akademische Druck-u Verlagsanstalt Dr Paul Struzl GmbH, pg 48
Amalthea-Verlag, pg 48
Verlag Der Apfel, pg 48
DachsVerlag GmbH, pg 49
Ludwig Doblinger (Bernhard Herzmansky) Musikverlag KG, pg 50
Helbling Verlags-Gesellschaft mbH, pg 51
Johannes Heyn GmbH & Co KG, pg 52
Kremayr & Scheriau Verlag, pg 53
Verlag Lafite, pg 53
Gerda Leber Buch-Kunst-und Musikverlag Proscenium Edition, pg 53
Mueller-Speiser Wissenschaftlicher Verlag, pg 54
Paul Neff Verlag KG, pg 54
Oesterreichischer Bundesverlag Gmbh, pg 55
Residenz Verlag GmbH, pg 57
Ritter Druck und Verlags KEG, pg 57
Salzburger Kulturvereinigung, pg 57
Salzburger Nachrichten Verlagsgesellschaft mbH & Co KG, pg 57
Dr A Schendl GmbH und Co KG, pg 57
Studien Verlag Gmbh, pg 58
Verlag Carl Ueberreuter GmbH, pg 58
Universal Edition AG, pg 58
Verband der Wissenschaftlichen Gesellschaften Oesterreichs (VWGOe), pg 59

Azerbaijan
Sada, Literaturno-Izdatel'skij Centr, pg 60

Bangladesh
Agamee Prakashani, pg 61

Belarus
Belarus (The Belorussia), pg 62
Interdigest Publishing House, pg 62

Belgium
Alamire vzw, Music Publishers, pg 63
Altina, pg 63
NV Artis-Historia, pg 63
Dexia Bank, pg 66
Infoboek NV, pg 68
Koninklijke Vlaamse Academie van Belgie voor Wetenschappen en Kunsten, pg 69
Leuven University Press, pg 70
Editeurs de Litterature Biblique, pg 70
Mardaga, Pierre, Editeur, pg 71
Schott Freres SA (Editeurs de Musique), pg 73
Sonneville Press (Uitgeverij) VTW, pg 73
Stichting Kunstboek bvba, pg 73
Uitgeverij De Garve, pg 74

Botswana
The Botswana Society, pg 76

Brazil
Brinque Book Editora de Livros Ltda, pg 79
Concordia Editora Ltda, pg 80
Companhia Editora Forense, pg 81
Fundacao Sao Paulo, EDUC, pg 82
Global Editora e Distribuidora Ltda, pg 82
Editora Globo SA, pg 82
Horus Editora Ltda, pg 83
Editora Lidador Ltda, pg 85
Livraria Kosmos Editora Ltda, pg 85
Musimed Edicoes Musicais Importacao E Exportacao Ltda, pg 87
Pallas Editora e Distribuidora Ltda, pg 88
Paulus Editora, pg 88
Editora Perspectiva, pg 88
Editora Sinodal, pg 90
Summus Editorial Ltda, pg 91
34 Literatura S/C Ltda, pg 91
Triom Centro de Estudos Marina e Martin Hawey Editorial e Comercial Ltda, pg 91
Jorge Zahar Editor, pg 92

Bulgaria
Makros 2000 - Plovdiv, pg 95
Musica Publishing House Ltd, pg 95
Sila & Zivot, pg 97

Chile
Arrayan Editores, pg 98
Ediciones Universitarias de Valparaiso, pg 100

China
Shandong Literature & Art Publishing House, pg 107

Colombia
Universidad de Antioquia, Division Publicaciones, pg 113
Editorial Voluntad SA, pg 113

Costa Rica
Ediciones Promesa, pg 116

Cote d'Ivoire
Akohi Editions, pg 117

Croatia
Faust Vrani, pg 118
Mladost d d Izdavacku graficku i informaticku djelatnost, pg 119
Muzicka Naklada, pg 119
Skolska Knjiga, pg 119

Czech Republic
Lyra Pragensis Obecne Prospelna Spolecnost, pg 125
Editio Moravia-Moravske hudebni vydavatelstvi, pg 125
Narodni Muzeum, pg 126
P & R Centrum Vydavateistvi a Nakladateistvi, pg 126
Evzen Uher, Musikverlag UHER, pg 128
Votobia sro, pg 128

Denmark
Borgens Forlag A/S, pg 129
Gyldendalske Boghandel - Nordisk Forlag A/S, pg 131
Edition Wilhelm Hansen AS, pg 131
Nyt Nordisk Forlag Arnold Busck A/S, pg 133
Square Dance Partners Forlag, pg 135

SUBJECT INDEX

Estonia

Eesti Entsuklopeediakirjastus, pg 139
Eesti Rahvusraamatukogu, pg 139

Finland

Kirja-Leitzinger, pg 142
Koala-Kustannus Oy, pg 143
Recallmed Oy, pg 144
Schildts Forlags AB, pg 144
Yliopistopaino/Helsinki University Press, pg 145

France

Editions Alternatives, pg 146
L'Arche Editeur, pg 147
Armenia Editions, pg 147
Editions d'Aujourd'hui (Les Introuvables), pg 148
Editions l'Avant-Scene de Prette Technique, pg 149
Chasse Maree, pg 153
Editions Chiron, pg 154
Cicero Editeurs, pg 154
Editions Climats, pg 154
CNRS Editions, pg 155
Compagnie Francaise des Arts Graphiques SA, pg 155
Editions Dis Voir, pg 158
Editions Edisud, pg 159
Librairie Artheme Fayard, pg 163
Librairie Fischbacher, International Art Book Distribution (import-export), pg 163
Editions Gallimard, pg 164
Paul Geuthner Librairie Orientaliste, pg 165
Editions Jean Paul Gisserot, pg 165
Pierre Horay Editeur, pg 168
Editions Klincksieck, pg 170
Editions Larousse, pg 171
Editions de la Maison des Sciences de l'Homme, Paris, pg 173
Editions Albin Michel, pg 175
Editions Parentheses, pg 179
Editions A et J Picard SA, pg 179
Editions Christian Pirot, pg 180
Editions Plume, pg 180
Le Pre-aux-clercs, pg 180
Les Presses d'Ile-de-France Sarl, pg 181
Presses Universitaires de France (PUF), pg 181
Publications Orientalistes de France (POF), pg 182
Revue Noire, pg 183
Editions Sand et Tchou SA, pg 184
Service Technique pour l'Education, pg 184
Editions du Seuil, pg 184
Editions Stil, pg 186
Editions Van de Velde, pg 188

Germany

Abakus Musik Barbara Fietz, pg 190
Alexander Verlag Berlin, pg 192
Alkor-Edition Kassel GmbH, pg 192
Angelika und Lothar Binding, pg 192
Verlag APHAIA Svea Haske, Sonja Schumann GbR, pg 193
Apollo-Verlag Paul Lincke GmbH, pg 193
Arcadia Verlag GmbH, pg 193
ARCult Media, pg 193
Auer Verlag GmbH, pg 195
Barenreiter-Verlag Karl-Votterle GmbH & Co KG, pg 197
Bayerischer Schulbuch-Verlag GmbH, pg 198
Verlag C H Beck oHG, pg 198
Berliner Wissenschafts-Verlag GmbH (BWV), pg 199
Verlag Die Blaue Eule, pg 202
Verlag Erwin Bochinsky GmbH & Co KG, pg 202
Bonifatius GmbH Druck-Buch-Verlag, pg 203
Boosey & Hawkes Music Publishers LTD, London, pg 203
Gustav Bosse GmbH & Co KG, pg 203
Bote & Bock Musikalienhandelsgesellschaft mbH, pg 203
Breitkopf & Hartel, pg 204
R Brockhaus Verlag, pg 204
Chr Belser AG fur Verlagsgeschaefte und Co KG, pg 208
Hans Christians Druckerei und Verlag GmbH & Co KG, pg 208
Corona Verlag, pg 210
Verlag Werner Dausien, pg 211
Verlag Horst Deike KG, pg 211
Deutsche Verlags-Anstalt GmbH (DVA), pg 212
Deutscher Taschenbuch Verlag GmbH & Co KG (dtv), pg 213
Christoph Dohr, pg 215
Dolling und Galitz Verlag GmbH, pg 215
Egmont vgs verlagsgesellschaft mbH, pg 218
EinfallsReich Verlagsgesellschaft MbH, pg 219
Eres Editions-Horst Schubert Musikverlag, pg 220
ERF-Verlag GmbH, pg 220
EVT Energy Video Training & Verlag GmbH, pg 222
Extent Verlag und Service Wolfgang M Flamm, pg 223
Wilhelm Fink GmbH & Co Verlags-KG, pg 224
Verlag Freies Geistesleben, pg 227
Genius Verlag, pg 228
Georgi Verlag, pg 228
Klaus Gerth Musikverlag, pg 229
Verlag Ernst und Werner Gieseking GmbH, pg 229
Verlag Gruppenpaedagogischer Literatur, pg 231
Wolfgang G Haas - Musikverlag Koeln ek, pg 232
Haenssler Verlag GmbH, pg 233
Happy Mental Buch- und Musik Verlag, pg 234
Harenberg Kommunikation Verlags- und Medien-GmbH & Co KG, pg 234
Harth Musik Verlag-Pro musica Verlag GmbH, pg 234
Heel Verlag GmbH, pg 235
G Henle Verlag, pg 236
Max Hieber KG, pg 237
Hoffmann und Campe Verlag GmbH, pg 238
Friedrich Hofmeister Musikverlag, pg 238
Impuls-Theater-Verlag, pg 241
Iudicium Verlag GmbH, pg 242
Jutta Pohl Verlag, pg 244
Kallmeyer'sche Verlagsbuchhandlung GmbH, pg 244
Kastell Verlag GmbH, pg 244
Koenemann Verlagesellschaft mbH, pg 248
Verlag Valentin Koerner GmbH, pg 248
Alfred Kroner Verlag, pg 250
Verlag Ernst Kuhn, pg 250
Kunstverlag Weingarten GmbH, pg 251
Laaber-Verlag, pg 251
LEU-VERLAG Wolfgang Leupelt, pg 254
Robert Lienau GmbH & Co KG, pg 254
Martha Lindner Verlags-GmbH, pg 254
Manutius Verlag, pg 257
Matthes und Seitz Verlag GmbH, pg 258
Medium-Buchmarkt, pg 258
Menschenkinder Verlag und Vertrieb GmbH, pg 259
Merz & Solitude - Akademie Schloss Solitude, pg 259
J B Metzlersche Verlagsbuchhandlung, pg 260
Meyer & Meyer Verlag, pg 260
Karl Heinrich Moeseler Verlag, pg 261
Munzinger-Archiv GmbH Archiv fuer publizistische Arbeit, pg 262
Musikantiquariat und Dr Hans Schneider Verlag GmbH, pg 262
Musikverlag Zimmermann, pg 262
Neue Dimension Buch und Musikverlag, pg 264
Verlag Neue Musik GmbH, pg 264
Verlag Neue Musikzeitung GmbH, pg 264
Verlag Neue Stadt GmbH, pg 264
Nieswand-Verlag, pg 265
Florian Noetzel Verlag, pg 265
Oekotopia Verlag, Wolfgang Hoffman GmbH & Co KG, pg 266
Georg Olms Verlag AG, pg 267
Oreos Verlag GmbH, pg 267
Palmyra Verlag, pg 268
Verlag Sigrid Persen, pg 269
C F Peters Musikverlag GmbH & Co KG, pg 269
Philipp Reclam Jun Verlag GmbH, pg 269
Piper Verlag GmbH, pg 270
Premop Verlag GmbH, pg 271
Projektion J Buch- und Musikverlag GmbH, pg 272
Propylaeen Verlag, Zweigniederlassung Berlin der Ullstein Buchverlage GmbH, pg 272
Dr Mohan Krischke Ramaswamy Edition RE, pg 273
Dr Ludwig Reichert Verlag, pg 274
Ernst Reinhardt Verlag GmbH & Co KG, pg 275
Respublica Verlag, pg 275
Rimbaud Verlagsgesellschaft mbH, pg 276
Erich Roeth-Verlag, pg 276
Romiosini Verlag, pg 276
Sattva Kunst Verlag, pg 278
K G Saur Verlag GmbH, A Gale/Thomson Learning Company, pg 278
Agora Verlag Manfred Schlosser, pg 280
Verlag Schnell und Steiner GmbH, pg 281
Verlag Hans Schoener GmbH, pg 281
Schott Musik International GmbH & Co KG, pg 281
Sonnentanz-Verlag Roland Kron, pg 284
Stadler Verlagsgesellschaft mbH, pg 286
Stapp Verlag Wolfgang Stapp, pg 286
Franz Steiner Verlag Wiesbaden GmbH, pg 287
edition Text & Kritik im Richard Boorberg Verlag GmbH & Co, pg 290
Treves Editions Verein Zur Foerderung der Kuenstlerischen Taetigkeiten, pg 292
Edition Vincent Klink, pg 296
Voggenreiter-Verlag, pg 296
VWB-Verlag fur Wissenschaft & Bildung, Amand Aglaster, pg 297
Wissenschaftliche Buchgesellschaft, pg 300
Wolke Verlags GmbH, pg 301

Ghana

Asempa Publishers, pg 303
Ghana Academy of Arts & Sciences, pg 304

Greece

Apostoliki Diakonia tis Ekklisias tis Hellados, pg 305
Hestia-I D Hestia-Kollaros & Co Corporation, pg 308
Medusa/Selas Publishers, pg 310
Minoas SA, pg 310
Editions Moressopoulos, pg 310
Nakas Music House, pg 310
Ed Nea Acropolis, pg 310

Hong Kong

Benefit Publishing Co, pg 315
Chinese Christian Literature Council Ltd, pg 316
Shanghai Book Co Ltd, pg 319

Hungary

Akademiai Kiado, pg 320
Magveto Koenyvkiado, pg 322
Nemzeti Tankoenyvkiado, pg 323
Planetas Kiadoi es Kereskedelmi Kft, pg 324
Zenemukiado Vallalat, pg 325

Iceland

Stofnun Arna Magnussonar a Islandi, pg 326

India

Abhinav Publications, pg 326
Ananda Publishers Pvt Ltd, pg 328
Asian Educational Services, pg 329
Chowkhamba Sanskrit Series Office, pg 332
Cosmo Publications, pg 332
DK Printworld (P) Ltd, pg 333
Gyan Publishing House, pg 335
Marg Publications, pg 341
Mudgala Trust, pg 342
Munshiram Manoharlal Publishers Pvt Ltd, pg 342
Oxonian Press (P) Ltd, pg 344
Pankaj Publications, pg 344
Popular Prakashan Pvt Ltd, pg 345
Pustak Mahal, pg 345
Reliance Publishing House, pg 346
Roli Books Pvt Ltd, pg 347
Sri Satguru Publications, pg 348
Somaiya Publications Pvt Ltd, pg 349
Sri Satguru Publications, pg 350

Indonesia

Bina Aksara Parta, pg 354
Mutiara Sumber Widya PT, pg 356

PUBLISHERS

Ireland
Clo Iar-Chonnachta Teo, pg 358
The O'Brien Press Ltd, pg 362
Ossian Publications, pg 363

Israel
Classikaletet, pg 366
Doko Video Ltd, pg 366
Hakibbutz Hameuchad Publishing House Ltd, pg 367
Israel Music Institute (IMI), pg 368
Israeli Music Publications Ltd, pg 368
The Magnes Press, pg 370
Massada Press Ltd, pg 370
Y Sreberk, pg 372
Yavneh Publishing House Ltd, pg 373
Yedioth Ahronoth Books, pg 373

Italy
Mario Adda Editore SNC, pg 374
Bardi Editore srl, pg 377
BMG Ricordi SpA, pg 378
Edizioni Cadmo SRL, pg 379
Calosci, pg 379
Campanotto, pg 379
Edizioni Cantagalli, pg 379
Cappelli Editore, pg 380
Casa Musicale Edizioni Carrara SRL, pg 380
Casa Musicale G Zanibon SRL, pg 380
CLUEB (Cooperativa Libraria Universitaria Editrice Bologna), pg 382
Edizioni Curci SRL, pg 384
Edistudio, pg 386
Edizioni la Scala, pg 387
EDT Edizioni di Torino, pg 387
Giulio Einaudi Editore SpA, pg 387
Elle Di Ci - Libreria Dottrina Cristiana, pg 387
ERGA SNC di Carla Ottino Merli & C (Edizioni Realizzazioni Grafiche - Artigiana), pg 388
Edizioni Europa, pg 388
Arnaldo Forni Editore SRL, pg 389
Adriano Gallina Editore sas, pg 389
Ernesto Gremese Editore srl, pg 391
Gremese International srl, pg 391
Editoriale Jaca Book SpA, pg 394
Kaos Edizioni SRL, pg 394
LIM Editrice SRL, pg 395
Longanesi & C, pg 396
Angelo Longo Editore, pg 396
Tommaso Marotta Editore Srl, pg 397
mnemes - Alfieri & Ranieri Publishing, pg 398
Arnaldo Mondadori Editore SpA, pg 398
Franco Muzzio Editore, pg 400
Leo S Olschki, pg 401
Pagano Editore, pg 402
Paideia Editrice, pg 402
Palatina Editrice, pg 402
Passigli Editori, pg 402
Pizzicato Edizioni Musicali, pg 403
RCS Libri SpA, pg 405
RCS Rizzoli Libri SpA, pg 405
Rugginenti Editore, pg 406
Rusconi Libri Srl, pg 406
Il Saggiatore, pg 406
Edizioni San Paolo SRL, pg 407
Edizioni Scientifiche Italiane, pg 407
SEMAR Publishers SRL, pg 408
Spirali Edizioni, pg 409
Stampa Alternativa - Nuovi Equilibri, pg 409
Le Stelle Scuola, pg 409
Edizioni Studio Tesi SRL, pg 409
Turris, pg 410
Edizioni Ubulibri SAS, pg 410
UT Orpheus Edizioni Srl, pg 411
UTET (Unione Tipografico-Editrice Torinese), pg 411
Voce della Bibbia, pg 412

Jamaica
LMH Publishing Ltd, pg 414
Ian Randle Publishers Ltd, pg 414

Japan
Hakusui-Sha Co Ltd, pg 417
Hoikusha Publishing Co Ltd, pg 418
Kosei Publishing Co Ltd, pg 421
Nippon Hoso Shuppan Kyokai (NHK Publishing), pg 424
Ongaku No Tomo Sha Corporation, pg 425
Seibido Shuppan Company Ltd, pg 426
Shakai Shiso-Sha, pg 427
Shunjusha, pg 428
Sony Magazines Inc, pg 428
Tokyo Sogensha Co Ltd, pg 430

Kenya
Action Publishers, pg 433
Heinemann Kenya Ltd (EAEP), pg 434
Kenway Publications Ltd, pg 434
Lake Publishers & Enterprises Ltd, pg 435

Republic of Korea
Chung Rim Publishing Co Ltd, pg 438
Ewha Womans University Press, pg 438
Samho Music Publishing Co Ltd, pg 442
Se-Kwang Music Publishing Co, pg 442
Yeha Publishing Co, pg 443
Youlhwadang Publisher, pg 444

Laos People's Democratic Republic
Lao-phanit, pg 444

Latvia
Preses Nams, pg 445

Liechtenstein
Saendig Reprint Verlag, Hans-Rainer Wohlwend, pg 448

Lithuania
Klaipedos Universiteto Leidykla, pg 449
Svietimo ir mokslo ministerijos Leidybos centras, pg 449

Luxembourg
Editions Emile Borschette, pg 450
Eiffes Romain, pg 451
Op der Lay, pg 451
Varkki Verghese, pg 452

The Former Yugoslav Republic of Macedonia
Ktitor, pg 452

Mexico
Aguilar Altea Taurus Alfaguara SA de CV, pg 462
Centro de Estudios Mexicanos y Centroamericanos, pg 463
Janibi Editores SA de CV, pg 467
Editorial Jilguero, SA de CV, pg 467
Ediciones Libra, SA de CV, pg 467
Instituto Nacional de Antropologia e Historia, pg 469
Ediciones Promesa, SA de CV, pg 470
Universidad Nacional Autonoma de Mexico (National University of Mexico), pg 472
Universidad Veracruzana Direccion General Editorial y de Publicaciones, pg 472
Javier Vergara Editor SA de CV, pg 473

Republic of Moldova
Editura Hyperion, pg 473

Monaco
Editions de l'Oiseau-Lyre SAM, pg 473

Morocco
Edition Diffusion de Livre au Maroc, pg 474

Nepal
International Standards Books & Periodicals (P) Ltd, pg 476

Netherlands
Uitgeverij Ambo BV, pg 477
BZZTOH Publishers, pg 480
East-West Publications Fonds BV, pg 481
Heuff Amsterdam Uitgever, pg 483
Uitgevery International Theatre & Film Books, pg 484
De Prom, pg 488
Swets & Zeitlinger Publishers, pg 489
Tirion Uitgevers BV, pg 490
Uitgeverij De Toorts, pg 490
Uniepers BV, pg 491

New Zealand
Aoraki Press Ltd, pg 493
Barkfire Press, pg 494

Norway
J W Eides Forlag A/S, pg 509
Gyldendal Norsk Forlag A/S, pg 509

Philippines
National Book Store Inc, pg 519
University of the Philippines Press, pg 521

Poland
Polskie Wydawnictwo Muzyczne, pg 524

Portugal
Biblioteca Geral da Universidade de Coimbra, pg 529
Constancia Editores, SA, pg 530
Edicoes Cosmos, pg 530
Publicacoes Europa-America Lda, pg 531
Editorial Franciscana, pg 531

SUBJECT INDEX

Impala, pg 532
Latina Livraria Editora, pg 532
Musicoteca Lda, pg 534
Editora Pergaminho Lda, pg 534
Edicoes 70 Lda, pg 535
Edicoes Talento, pg 536

Puerto Rico
Instituto de Cultura Puertoriquena, pg 537
Publicaciones Voz de Gracia, pg 537

Romania
Editure Ion Creanga, pg 539
Editura Meridiane, pg 540
Editura Muzicala, pg 541

Russian Federation
Izdatelstvo Khudozhestvennaya Literatura, pg 545
Izdatelskii Dom Kompozitor, pg 546
Izdatelstvo Muzyka, pg 547
Izdatelstvo Prosveshchenie, pg 548

Slovakia
Opus Records & Publishing House, pg 560
Slovenske pedagogicke nakladateistvo, pg 560

Slovenia
Zalozba Obzorja d d Maribor, pg 562

South Africa
Educum Publishers Ltd, pg 563
Human & Rousseau (Pty) Ltd, pg 564
Ravan Press (Pty) Ltd, pg 568
University of Durban-Westville Library, pg 569

Spain
Publicacions de l'Abadia de Montserrat, pg 570
Acento Editorial, pg 570
Alianza Editorial SA, pg 572
Altea, Taurus, Alfaguara SA, pg 572
Arambol, SL, pg 573
Antoni Bosch Editor SA, pg 574
Editorial Casals SA, pg 575
Biblioteca de Catalunya, pg 576
Ediciones Catedra SA, pg 576
Celeste Ediciones, pg 576
Comunidad Autonoma de Madrid, Servicio de Documentacion y Publicaciones, pg 578
Dinsic Publicacions Musicals, pg 579
Ediciones Ebenezer, pg 580
Editorial Fundamentos, pg 584
Iberico Europea de Ediciones SA, pg 586
Idea Books, SA, pg 587
Institucion Fernando el Catolico de la Excma Diputacion de Zaragoza, pg 587
Ediciones Jucar, pg 588
Loguez Ediciones, pg 589
Antonio Machado, SA, pg 590
Mandala Ediciones, pg 590
La Mascara, SL Editorial, pg 591
Editorial la Muralla SA, pg 592
Editorial Musica Moderna, pg 592
Opera Tres Ediciones Musicales, pg 594
El Paisaje Editorial, pg 594
Editorial El Perpetuo Socorro, pg 596

SUBJECT INDEX

Pre-Textos, pg 596
Editora Regional de Murcia - ERM, pg 597
Ediciones Rialp SA, pg 598
Ediciones Seyer, pg 599
Edicions 62, pg 600
Axel Springer Publicaciones, pg 601
Trito Edicions, SL, pg 602
Universidad de Granada, pg 603
Editorial Verbum SL, pg 604
Javier Vergara Editor SA, pg 604

Sri Lanka
J K Publications, pg 606
Lake House Investments Ltd, pg 606

Sweden
Akademiforlaget Goteborgslitteratur, pg 609
Alfabeta Bokforlag AB, pg 609
Bokforlaget Axplock, pg 609
BBT Bhaktivedanta Book Trust, pg 610
SK-Gehrmans Musikforlag AB, pg 611
Hans Richter Laromedel, pg 613
Verbum Foerlag AB, pg 616

Switzerland
Editions L'Age d'Homme - La Cite, pg 617
Arche Verlag AG, Raabe und Vitali, pg 617
Atlantis Musikbuch, pg 618
Editions de la Baconniere SA, pg 618
Barenreiter Verlag Basel AG, pg 618
Benziger Verlag AG, pg 619
Bibliographisches Institut & F A Brockhaus AG, pg 619
Werner Classen Verlag, pg 621
Maurice et Pierre Foetisch SA, pg 623
Georg Editeur SA, pg 624
Hug & Co, pg 625
Edition Kunzelmann GmbH, pg 627
Lia rumantscha, pg 627
Librairie-Editions J Marguerat, pg 628
Editions Minkoff, pg 628
Editions Musicales De La Schola Cantorum, pg 629
Edition Olms AG, pg 630
Ostschweiz Druck und Verlag, pg 630
Editions Payot Lausanne, pg 631
Editions 24 Heures, pg 635
Der Universitatsverlag Freiburg, pg 636
Verlagsbuchhandlung AG, pg 636

Taiwan, Province of China
Chung Hwa Book Co Ltd, pg 639
San Min Book Co Ltd, pg 641

Thailand
Thai Watana Panich Co, Ltd, pg 646

Trinidad & Tobago
Jett Samm Publishing Ltd, pg 647

Tunisia
Academie Tunisienne des Sciences, des Lettres et des Arts Beit El Hekma, pg 647

Turkey
Arkadas Ltd, pg 649
Inkilap Publishers Ltd, pg 650
Kok Yayincilik, pg 650
Kubbealti Akademisi Kultur ve Sasat Vakfi, pg 650
Pan Yayincilik, pg 651

Ukraine
Osvita, pg 654

United Kingdom
Amber Lane Press Ltd, pg 657
Appletree Press Ltd, pg 658
Art Books International Ltd, pg 659
Ashgate Publishing Ltd, pg 660
Barn Dance Publications Ltd, pg 663
BCA - Book Club Associates, pg 663
Belitha Press Ltd, pg 664
A & C Black Publishers Ltd, pg 666
Black Spring Press Ltd, pg 666
Blackstaff Press, pg 666
Blandford Publishing Ltd, pg 668
Boosey & Hawkes Music Publishers Ltd, pg 669
Marion Boyars Publishers Ltd, pg 669
Boydell & Brewer Ltd, pg 669
The Brown Reference Group PLC, pg 672
Calder Publications Ltd, pg 673
Cambridge University Press, pg 674
Canongate Books Ltd, pg 674
Capall Bann Publishing, pg 674
Carlton Publishing Group, pg 675
Cassell & Co, pg 675
Chadwyck-Healey Ltd, pg 677
Coachwise Ltd, pg 680
Curiad, pg 685
Dance Books Ltd, pg 686
Denor Press, pg 687
Andre Deutsch Ltd, pg 687
Dorling Kindersley Ltd, pg 688
East-West Publications (UK) Ltd, pg 689
Edinburgh University Press Ltd, pg 689
Element Books Ltd, pg 690
The Eurospan Group, pg 692
Evans Brothers Ltd, pg 693
Faber & Faber Ltd, pg 694
Feather Books, pg 694
Flame Tree Publishing, pg 695
Gairm Publications, pg 698
Golden Cockerel Press Ltd, pg 701
Gollancz/Witherby, pg 701
Gresham Books Ltd, pg 703
Guinness World Records Ltd, pg 703
Robert Hale Ltd, pg 704
Hamish Hamilton Ltd, pg 704
Hamlyn, pg 704
Heartland Publishing Ltd, pg 707
Helicon Publishing Ltd, pg 707
Kahn & Averill, pg 716
Lang Syne Publishers Ltd, pg 719
Y Lolfa Cyf, pg 722
Macmillan Reference Ltd, pg 724
Peter Marcan Publications, pg 725
Marcham Manor Press, pg 725
Adam Matthew Publications, pg 726
McCrimmon Publishing Co Ltd, pg 726
Media Research Publishing Ltd, pg 726
Mercat Press, pg 726
Methuen, pg 727
Moorley's Print & Publishing Ltd, pg 729
Muze UK Ltd, pg 730
Neil Wilson Publishing Ltd, pg 732
Nelson Thornes Ltd, pg 732
Northcote House Publishers Ltd, pg 733
W W Norton & Company Ltd, pg 734
Novello & Co Ltd, pg 734
Octopus Publishing Group, pg 734
Omnibus Press, pg 735
Peter Owen Ltd, pg 737
Oxford University Press, pg 737
Parapress Ltd, pg 738
PC Publishing, pg 739
Pearson Education, pg 739
Pearson Education Europe, Mideast & Africa, pg 739
Peartree Publications, pg 740
Plexus Publishing Ltd, pg 743
Polygon, pg 744
PRC Publishing Ltd, pg 745
ProQuest Information & Learning, pg 746
Quartet Books Ltd, pg 746
Quintet Publishing Ltd, pg 747
Retail Entertainment Data Publishing Ltd, pg 750
Rough Guides Ltd, pg 751
Roundhouse Group, pg 751
Salvationist Publishing & Supplies Ltd, pg 754
Saqi Books, pg 754
SchoolPlay Productions Ltd, pg 755
Seren, pg 756
Serpent's Tail Ltd, pg 756
Sheldrake Press, pg 757
Shire Publications Ltd, pg 757
Sidgwick & Jackson Ltd, pg 757
Sigma Press, pg 758
Southgate Publishers, pg 759
Souvenir Press Ltd, pg 759
Stainer & Bell Ltd, pg 761
Rudolf Steiner Press, pg 761
Sussex Publications, pg 762
Taigh Na Teud Music Publishers, pg 762
Thames & Hudson Ltd, pg 764
Thomson Gale, pg 765
Timber Press Inc, pg 765
Tobin Music, pg 766
Unicorn Books, pg 768
Virgin Publishing Ltd, pg 770
Ward Lock Educational Co Ltd, pg 771
Wild Goose Publications, pg 773
Wilmington Business Information Ltd, pg 774
Windsor Books International, pg 774
The Women's Press Ltd, pg 775
World Microfilms Publications Ltd, pg 775
Yale University Press London, pg 776

Uruguay
Editorial Arca SRL, pg 776
A Monteverde y Cia SA, pg 777
Ediciones Trilce, pg 778

Venezuela
Alfadil Ediciones, pg 778
Monte Avila Editores Latinoamericana CA, pg 779

Zambia
Aafzam Ltd, pg 781

BOOK

MYSTERIES

Albania
NL SH, pg 1

Argentina
Emece Editores SA, pg 5

Australia
Bandicoot Books, pg 14
Gnostic Editions, pg 23
Spacevision Publishing, pg 41
Unity Press, pg 44
Wakefield Press Pty Ltd, pg 46

Austria
Aarachne Verlag, pg 48
Franz Deuticke Verlagsgesmbh, pg 50
Haymon-Verlag GesmbH, pg 51
oebv & hpt Verlagsgesellschaft mbH & Co KG, pg 55

Azerbaijan
Sada, Literaturno-Izdatel'skij Centr, pg 60

Belgium
Editions Hemma, pg 68
Claude Lefrancq Editeur, pg 70

Brazil
Editora Globo SA, pg 82
Imago Editora Importacao e Exportacao Ltda, pg 84
Editora Marco Zero Ltda, pg 86
Editora Mercuryo Ltda, pg 86
Editora Nova Fronteira SA, pg 87
Livraria Pioneira Editora/Enio Matheus Guazzelli e Cia Ltd, pg 88
Ediouro Publicacoes, SA, pg 89
Editora Scipione Ltda, pg 90
Thex Editora e Distribuidora Ltda, pg 91

Bulgaria
Abagar Pablioing, pg 92
Kralica MAB, pg 95
Litera Prima, pg 95
Trud - Izd kasta, pg 97
Zunica, pg 97

Czech Republic
Knihovna A Tiskarna Pro Nevidome, pg 124
Josef Lukasik A Spol sro, pg 125
Nase vojsko, nakladatelstvi a knizni obchod, pg 126
NS Svoboda spol sro, pg 127
Svoboda Servis GmbH, pg 127

Denmark
Cicero-Chr Erichsens, pg 130
Forlaget Forum, pg 131
Forlaget Hovedland, pg 132
Forlaget Modtryk AMBA, pg 133

Egypt (Arab Republic of Egypt)
Dar El Shorouk, pg 138

France
Actes-Graphiques, pg 145
Editions de l'Aube, pg 148
Bragelonne, pg 151
Librairie des Champs-Elysees/Le Masque, pg 153

PUBLISHERS

Editions Climats, pg 154
Culture et Bibliotheque pour Tous, pg 156
Dargaud, pg 157
Editions Gerard de Villiers, pg 165
Editions A M Metailie, pg 175
Payot & Rivages, pg 179
Le Pre-aux-clercs, pg 180
Presses de la Cite, pg 180
10/18, pg 187
Editions Vague Verte, pg 188

French Polynesia
Scoop/Au Vent des Iles, pg 189

Germany
Altberliner Verlag GmbH, pg 192
Aufbau-Verlag GmbH, pg 195
Catia Monser Eggcup-Verlag, pg 207
Dagmar Dreves Verlag, pg 210
Verlagsgruppe Droemer Knaur GmbH & Co KG, pg 216
Econ Taschenbuchverlag, pg 218
Egmont vgs verlagsgesellschaft mbH, pg 218
Eichborn AG, pg 219
Emons Verlag, pg 219
Espresso Verlag GmbH, pg 221
Europa Verlag GmbH, pg 222
Fabylon-Verlag, pg 223
Grafit Verlag GmbH, pg 231
Wilhelm Heyne Verlag, pg 237
Iudicium Verlag GmbH, pg 242
KBV Verlags-und Medien - GmbH, pg 245
Knowledge Media International, pg 247
Dr Gisela Lermann, pg 253
Logos-Verlag Literatur & Layout GmbH, pg 255
Karl-Heinz Metz, pg 259
Moby Dick Verlag, pg 261
Neuthor - Verlag, pg 265
C W Niemeyer Buchverlage GmbH, pg 265
Propylaeen Verlag, Zweigniederlassung Berlin der Ullstein Buchverlage GmbH, pg 272
Pulp Master Frank Nowatzki Verlag, pg 272
Quintessenz Verlags-GmbH, pg 273
Ruetten & Loening Berlin GmbH, pg 277
Treves Editions Verein Zur Foerderung der Kuenstlerischen Taetigkeiten, pg 292
Verlag und Studio fuer Hoerbuchproduktionen, pg 295

Ghana
World Literature Project, pg 305

Greece
Exandas Publishers, pg 307
Hestia-I D Hestia-Kollaros & Co Corporation, pg 308
Ed Nea Acropolis, pg 310
Orfanidis Publications, pg 311

Hong Kong
SCMP Book Publishing Ltd, pg 319

Hungary
Ifjusagi Lap-eskonyvkiado Vallalat, pg 321
Szabad Ter Kiado, pg 324

Iceland
Bokaforlag Birtingur, pg 325
Frjals fjolmiolun hf-Urvalsbaekur, pg 325

India
Ananda Publishers Pvt Ltd, pg 328
Reliance Publishing House, pg 346
Scientific Book Agency, pg 348
Theosophical Publishing House, pg 351

Indonesia
Gramedia, pg 355

Israel
Bitan Publishers Ltd, pg 365
Pitspopany Press, pg 371

Italy
Adelphi Edizioni SpA, pg 374
L'Airone Editrice, pg 375
Damanhur Edizioni, pg 384
Levante Editori, pg 395
Arnoldo Mondadori Editore SpA, pg 398
Edizioni Segno SRL, pg 407
Sonzogno, pg 409

Japan
Hayakawa Publishing Inc, pg 418
Nippon Hoso Shuppan Kyokai (NHK Publishing), pg 424
Shincho-Sha Co Ltd, pg 427
Tokyo Sogensha Co Ltd, pg 430

Republic of Korea
Gim-Yeong Co, pg 438
Koreaone Press Inc, pg 440
O Neul Publishing Co, pg 441
Woongjin.com Co Ltd, pg 443

Lebanon
Librairie du Liban Publishers (Sal), pg 446

Lithuania
Baltos Lankos, pg 449

The Former Yugoslav Republic of Macedonia
Zumpres Publishing Firm, pg 453

Monaco
Les Editions du Rocher, pg 474

Morocco
Editions Le Fennec, pg 474

Netherlands
De Boekerij BV, pg 479
A W Bruna Uitgevers BV, pg 480
BZZTOH Publishers, pg 480
Cadans, pg 480
Callenbach BV, pg 480
Uitgeverij Conserve, pg 481
Uitgeverij Elzenga, pg 482
Uitgeverij De Fontein BV, pg 482
Nijgh & Van Ditmar Amsterdam, pg 487
Sjaloom Uitgeverijen, pg 489
Uitgeverij Het Spectrum BV, pg 489
Unieboek BV, pg 490
Van Buuren Uitgeverij BV, pg 491

New Zealand
Cape Catley Ltd, pg 495
River Press, pg 500

Norway
Fono Forlag, pg 509
Hilt & Hansteen A/S, pg 509

Pakistan
Jang Publishers, pg 513

Philippines
Anvil Publishing Inc, pg 518
Books for Pleasure Inc, pg 518

Poland
Wydawnictwo Dolnoslaskie, pg 522
Iskry - Publishing House Ltd spotka zoo, pg 523
Videograf II Sp z o o Zaklad Poracy Chronionej, pg 527

Portugal
Planeta Editora, LDA, pg 534
Editorial Presenca, pg 535

Romania
Editura Excelsior Art, pg 539
Editura Militara, pg 541
Editura Niculescu, pg 541
RAO International Publishing Co, pg 542
Saeculum IO, pg 542
Vestala Verlag, pg 543

Russian Federation
Armada Publishing House, pg 543
CentrePolygraph Traders & Publishers Co, pg 544

Serbia and Montenegro
Alfa-Narodna Knjiga, pg 552

Slovakia
Vydavatelstvo Obzor, pg 560

Slovenia
Mladinska Knjiga International, pg 561

Spain
Fundacion Rosacruz, pg 584
Editorial Molino, pg 592
Munoz Moya Editor, pg 592
Ediciones Siruela SA, pg 600
Ediciones Urano, SA, pg 604

Sweden
Bokforlaget Axplock, pg 609
Bonnier Carlsen Bokforlag AB, pg 610

Switzerland
AT Verlag, pg 618
Cockatoo Press (Schweiz), Thailand-Publikationen, pg 621
Diogenes Verlag AG, pg 622
Govinda-Verlag, pg 624
Haffmans Verlag AG, pg 624
Origo Verlag, pg 630
Rhein-Trio, Edition/Editions du Fou, pg 632
Speer -Verlag, pg 634
Verlag Die Waage, pg 636

Taiwan, Province of China
Lin Pai Press Company Ltd, pg 641

SUBJECT INDEX

Tunisia
Alyssa Editions, pg 647

United Kingdom
Ashgrove Publishing, pg 660
The Banton Press, pg 662
BBC Audiobooks, pg 663
BCA - Book Club Associates, pg 663
Blorenge Books, pg 668
Capall Bann Publishing, pg 674
Gateway Books, pg 698
Gembooks, pg 699
Gollancz/Witherby, pg 701
HarperCollins UK, pg 705
Hodder & Stoughton General, pg 709
Isis Publishing Ltd, pg 714
Lang Syne Publishers Ltd, pg 719
Macmillan Audio Books, pg 723
Octopus Publishing Group, pg 734
Oldcastle Books Ltd, pg 734
Orion Publishing Group Ltd, pg 736
Quintet Publishing Ltd, pg 747
The Reader's Digest Association Ltd, pg 748
Serpent's Tail Ltd, pg 756
Severn House Publishers Inc, pg 756
Time Warner Book Group UK, pg 766
Ulverscroft Large Print Books Ltd, pg 768
The Windrush Press Ltd, pg 774

MYTHOLOGY

Chile
Arrayan Editores, pg 98

Germany
Verlag Die Blaue Eule, pg 202

Greece
Sigma, pg 312

India
Reliance Publishing House, pg 346

Italy
il Cerchio Iniziative Editoriali, pg 381

Mexico
Editorial Grijalbo SA de CV, pg 466

Spain
Alta Fulla Editorial, pg 572

United Kingdom
The Harvill Press, pg 705

NATIVE AMERICAN STUDIES

Albania
NL SH, pg 1

Belgium
Brepols Publishers NV, pg 64

Bulgaria
Sluntse Publishing House, pg 97

SUBJECT INDEX — BOOK

Germany
Arun-Verlag, pg 194

Italy
Editoriale Jaca Book SpA, pg 394

Mexico
El Colegio de Michoacan A C, pg 464
Instituto Nacional de Antropologia e Historia, pg 469

New Zealand
Barkfire Press, pg 494

United Kingdom
Salamander Books Ltd, pg 753

NATURAL HISTORY

Armenia
Arevik, pg 10

Australia
Australian Marine Conservation Society Inc (AMCS), pg 13
Robert Berthold Photography, pg 14
Bloomings Books, pg 15
E J Brill, Robert Brown & Associates, pg 16
Crawford House Publishing Pty Ltd, pg 18
CSIRO Publishing (Commonwealth Scientific & Industrial Research Organisation), pg 19
Enterprise Publications, pg 21
Envirobook, pg 21
Greater Glider Productions Australia Pty Ltd, pg 24
Illert Publications, pg 26
Institute of Aboriginal Development (IAD Press), pg 27
Kangaroo Press, pg 28
Laurel Press, pg 28
Magabala Books Aboriginal Corporation, pg 30
Melbourne University Press, pg 32
Mulavon Press Pty Ltd, pg 32
Pandani Press, pg 35
Queen Victoria Museum & Art Gallery Publications, pg 38
Simon & Schuster (Australia) Pty Ltd, pg 41
State Library of NSW Press, pg 42
Terania Rainforest Publishing, pg 43
Thames & Hudson (Australia) Pty Ltd, pg 43
Three Sisters Publications Pty Ltd, pg 43
University of New South Wales Press Ltd, pg 44
University of Western Australia Press, pg 45

Austria
Ferdinand Berger und Sohne, pg 50
Thomas Mlakar Verlag, pg 54
Verlag fuer Sammler, pg 57
Dr A Schendl GmbH und Co KG, pg 57
Herbert Weishaupt Verlag, pg 59

Azerbaijan
Sada, Literaturno-Izdatel'skij Centr, pg 60

Belarus
Belaruskaya Encyklapedyya, pg 62

Belgium
NV Artis-Historia, pg 63
Dessain - Departement de De Boeck & Larcier SA, pg 66

Botswana
The Botswana Society, pg 76

Brazil
Libreria Editora Ltda, pg 85
Editora Nova Fronteira SA, pg 87

Bulgaria
Eurasia Academic Publishers, pg 94
Heron Press Publishing House, pg 94
Litera Prima, pg 95
Pensoft Publishers, pg 96

China
Education Science Publishing House, pg 104
Fudan University Press, pg 104
Science Press, pg 107

Costa Rica
Centro Agronomico Tropical de Investigacion y Ensenanza (CATIE), pg 115
Editorial de la Universidad de Costa Rica, pg 116

Croatia
Matica hrvatska, pg 118

Czech Republic
Aventinum Nakladatelstvi spol sro, pg 122
Granit sro, pg 123
Narodni Muzeum, pg 126

Denmark
Gads Forlag, pg 131

Estonia
Eesti Entsuklopeediakirjastus, pg 139
Tuum, pg 140

Fiji
University of the South Pacific, pg 141

France
L'Amitie par le Livre, pg 146
ATP - Packager, pg 148
Autrement Editions, pg 148
Editions Coprur, pg 155
Editions Jean Paul Gisserot, pg 165
Librairie Scientifique et Technique Albert Blanchard, pg 172
Service des Publications Scientifiques du Museum National d'Histoire Naturelle, pg 184
Editions Vague Verte, pg 188

French Polynesia
Haere Po Editions, pg 189

Germany
Alouette Verlag, pg 192
AOL-Verlag Frohmut Menze, pg 193
Blackwell Wissenschafts-Verlag GmbH, pg 201
BLV Verlagsgesellschaft mbH, pg 202
Hans Christians Druckerei und Verlag GmbH & Co KG, pg 208
Verlag Harri Deutsch, pg 211
Egmont vgs verlagsgesellschaft mbH, pg 218
Finken Verlag GmbH, pg 224
Franckh-Kosmos Verlags-GmbH & Co, pg 226
Graefe und Unzer Verlag GmbH, pg 230
S Hirzel Verlag GmbH und Co, pg 238
Knowledge Media International, pg 247
Verlag Waldemar Kramer, pg 250
Johannes Loriz Verlag der Kooperative Duernau, pg 255
Mergus Verlag GmbH Hans A Baensch, pg 259
Verlag Stephanie Naglschmid, pg 263
Verlag Natur & Wissenschaft Harro Hieronimus & Dr Jurgen Schmidt, pg 263
Net World Vision GmbH, pg 263
Neumann Verlag, pg 264
Palazzi Verlag GmbH, pg 268
Renate Schenk Verlag, pg 279
Stapp Verlag Wolfgang Stapp, pg 286
Guenter Albert Ulmer Verlag, pg 293

Greece
Hestia-I D Hestia-Kollaros & Co Corporation, pg 308

Hong Kong
Hong Kong University Press, pg 317
Steve Lu Publishing Ltd, pg 318

Hungary
Kossuth Kiado RT, pg 322
Tajak Korok Muzeumok Egyesuelet, pg 324

Iceland
Hid Islenzka Bokmenntafelag, pg 325

India
Allied Book Centre, pg 328
APH Publishing Corp, pg 328
Asian Educational Services, pg 329
Brijbasi Printers Pvt Ltd, pg 331
BSMPS - M/s Bishen Singh Mahendra Pal Singh, pg 331
Cosmo Publications, pg 332
Daya Publishing House, pg 333
Dolphin Publications, pg 333
Gyan Publishing House, pg 335
Indus Publishing Co, pg 338
International Book Distributors, pg 338
Minerva Associates (Publications) Pvt Ltd, pg 341
Oxford & IBH Publishing Co Pvt Ltd, pg 344
Oxford University Press, pg 344
Scientific Book Agency, pg 348
Scientific Publishers India, pg 349
Today & Tomorrow's Printers & Publishers, pg 351

Indonesia
Yayasan Obor Indonesia, pg 357

Ireland
The Collins Press, pg 358
Flyleaf Press, pg 360
The Lilliput Press Ltd, pg 361
Roberts Rinehart Publishers, pg 363
Sean Ros Press, pg 363
Tir Eolas, pg 363

Israel
Hakibbutz Hameuchad Publishing House Ltd, pg 367

Italy
Alberti Libraio Editore, pg 375
Edizioni Della Torre di Salvatore Fozzi & C SAS, pg 385
Editoriale Jaca Book SpA, pg 394
Kompass Fleischmann, pg 394
Leo S Olschki, pg 401
Edizioni Librarie Siciliane, pg 408
Nicola Teti e C Editore SRL, pg 410
Edizioni Zara, pg 412

Jamaica
Institute of Jamaica Publications, pg 413
University of the West Indies Press, pg 414

Japan
Bun-ichi Sogo Shuppan, pg 415
Hoikusha Publishing Co Ltd, pg 418
Kyoritsu Shuppan Co Ltd, pg 422

Kenya
Kenway Publications Ltd, pg 434

Democratic People's Republic of Korea
Korea Science and Encyclopedia Publishing House, pg 436

Luxembourg
Service Central des Imprimes et des Fournitures de Bureau de l'Etat, pg 451

Malaysia
Tropical Press Sdn Bhd, pg 459

Malta
The University of Malta Publications Section, pg 460

Mexico
Editorial Minutiae Mexicana SA, pg 468

Morocco
Association de la Recherche Historique et Sociale, pg 474

Namibia
Desert Research Foundation of Namibia (DRFN), pg 476

Nepal
International Standards Books & Periodicals (P) Ltd, pg 476

Netherlands
Backhuys Publishers BV, pg 478
A A Balkema Uitgevers BV, pg 478
Uniepers BV, pg 491

PUBLISHERS

New Zealand
Barkfire Press, pg 494
David Bateman Ltd, pg 494
Bush Press Communications Ltd, pg 494
Canterbury University Press, pg 494
Craig Potton Publishing, pg 495
Exisle Publishing Ltd, pg 496
Godwit Publishing Ltd, pg 496
HarperCollins Publishers (New Zealand) Ltd, pg 497
Landcare Research NZ, pg 497
Longacre Press, pg 498
Nestegg Books, pg 499
Otago Heritage Books, pg 499
Oxford University Press, pg 499
Reed Publishing (NZ) Ltd, pg 500
Shearwater Associates Ltd, pg 501
Shoal Bay Press Ltd, pg 501
University of Otago Press, pg 502
Viking Sevenseas NZ Ltd, pg 502

Philippines
National Museum of the Philippines, pg 520

Portugal
Constancia Editores, SA, pg 530
Gradiva-Publicacnoes Lda, pg 532

Romania
Editura Niculescu, pg 541

Russian Federation
Izdatelstvo 'Ekonomika', pg 544
Nauka Publishers, pg 547

Singapore
Archipelago Press, pg 555

South Africa
Acorn Books, pg 562
The Brenthurst Press (Pty) Ltd, pg 563
Educum Publishers Ltd, pg 563
Fernwood Press (Pty) Ltd, pg 563
Russel Friedman Books, pg 564
Human & Rousseau (Pty) Ltd, pg 564
National Botanical Institute, pg 567
New Africa Books (Pty) Ltd, pg 567
Oceanographic Research Institute, pg 567
Southern Book Publishers (Pty) Ltd, pg 569
Struik Publishers (Pty) Ltd, pg 569
Witwatersrand University Press, pg 570

Spain
Editorial Acribia SA, pg 571
Cabildo Insular de Gran Canaria Departamento de Ediciones, pg 575
Carroggio SA de Ediciones, pg 575
Comunidad Autonoma de Madrid, Servicio de Documentacion y Publicaciones, pg 578
Ediciones Doce Calles SL, pg 579
Incafo Archivo Fotografico Editorial, SL, pg 587
Lynx Edicions, pg 590
Editorial Moll SL, pg 592
Ediciones Omega SA, pg 594

Sri Lanka
Department of National Museums, pg 607

Switzerland
Kinderbuchverlag Luzern, pg 626
Editiones Roche, pg 632
Sabe AG Verlagsinstitut, pg 633
Strom-Verlag Luzern, pg 635
Terra Grischuna Verlag Buch-und Zeitschriftenverlag, pg 635

Syrian Arab Republic
Damascus University Press, pg 638

Thailand
New Generation Publishing Co Ltd, pg 645
White Lotus Co Ltd, pg 646

Tunisia
Les Editions de l'Arbre, pg 647

Uganda
T & E Publishers, pg 653

Ukraine
Naukova Dumka Publishers, pg 653

United Arab Emirates
Motivate Publishing, pg 654

United Kingdom
Abbotsford Publishing, pg 654
Andromeda Oxford Ltd, pg 658
Colin Baxter Photography Ltd, pg 663
BBC Worldwide Publishers, pg 663
BCA - Book Club Associates, pg 663
Belitha Press Ltd, pg 664
A & C Black Publishers Ltd, pg 666
Blackstaff Press, pg 666
Blandford Publishing Ltd, pg 668
Bounty Books, pg 669
The Brown Reference Group PLC, pg 672
Cameron & Hollis, pg 674
Carlton Publishing Group, pg 675
Cassell & Co, pg 675
Castlemead Publications, pg 676
Kyle Cathie Ltd, pg 676
E W Classey Ltd, pg 680
The Crowood Press Ltd, pg 684
Christopher Davies Publishers Ltd, pg 686
Edinburgh University Press Ltd, pg 689
Aidan Ellis Publishing, pg 690
Eurobook Ltd, pg 692
The Eurospan Group, pg 692
Forth Naturalist & Historian, pg 696
Genesis Publications Ltd, pg 699
Gollancz/Witherby, pg 701
Grange Books PLC, pg 702
Hamlyn, pg 704
Harley Books, pg 705
HarperCollins UK, pg 705
Harvard University Press, pg 705
The Harvill Press, pg 705
Christopher Helm (Publishers) Ltd, pg 707
Helm Information Ltd, pg 707
Hodder Education, pg 709
Intercept Ltd, pg 714
International Bee Research Association, pg 714
The Islamic Texts Society, pg 715
The Kenilworth Press Ltd, pg 717
Ladybird Books Ltd, pg 719
Luath Press Ltd, pg 722
The Lutterworth Press, pg 723
Macmillan Audio Books, pg 723
Maney Publishing, pg 725
Marshall Editions Ltd, pg 725
Mercat Press, pg 726
Micelle Press, pg 727
New Holland Publishers (UK) Ltd, pg 732
Newpro UK Ltd, pg 733
NMS Enterprises Ltd - Publishing, pg 733
North York Moors National Park, pg 733
Octopus Publishing Group, pg 734
The Orkney Press Ltd, pg 736
Orpheus Books Ltd, pg 736
Packard Publishing Ltd, pg 737
Pearson Education, pg 739
PRC Publishing Ltd, pg 745
Quarto Publishing plc, pg 746
Quintet Publishing Ltd, pg 747
The Richmond Publishing Co Ltd, pg 750
Roadmaster Publishing, pg 750
Roundhouse Group, pg 751
Sainsbury Publishing Ltd, pg 753
Salamander Books Ltd, pg 753
The Salariya Book Co Ltd, pg 753
Savitri Books Ltd, pg 754
Shire Publications Ltd, pg 757
Stacey International, pg 761
Stobart Davies Ltd, pg 761
Tern Press, pg 764
Two-Can Publishing Ltd, pg 768
Whittet Books Ltd, pg 773
Whittles Publishing, pg 773
Wordwright Publishing, pg 775
Yale University Press London, pg 776

Uruguay
Hemisferio Sur Edicion Agropecuaria, pg 777
A Monteverde y Cia SA, pg 777

Viet Nam
Science & Technics Publishing House, pg 780

Zambia
Zambian Ornithological Society (ZOS), pg 782

Zimbabwe
Longman Zimbabwe (Pvt) Ltd, pg 783
Mambo Press, pg 783
Zimbabwe Publishing House (Pvt) Ltd, pg 784

SUBJECT INDEX

NONFICTION (GENERAL)

Albania
Fan Noli Verlag Rexhep Hida, pg 1
NL SH, pg 1

Algeria
Enterprise Nationale du Livre (ENAL), pg 2

Argentina
Editorial Abril SA, pg 2
Ada Korn Editora SA, pg 3
Editorial Argentina Plaza y Janes SA, pg 3
Editorial Atlantida SA, pg 3
Beas Ediciones SRL, pg 4
Beatriz Viterbo Editora, pg 4
Bonum Editorial SACI, pg 4
Cesarini Hermanos, pg 4
Critica, pg 5
Emece Editores SA, pg 5
Editorial Planeta Argentina SAIC, pg 8
Editorial Stella, pg 9
Editorial Sudamericana SA, pg 9
Javier Vergara Editor SA, pg 9

Australia
ABC Books (Australian Broadcasting Corporation), pg 10
Access Press, pg 10
Allen & Unwin Pty Ltd, pg 11
Edward Arnold (Australia) Pty Ltd, pg 12
Australian Scholarly Publishing, pg 13
Bernal Publishing, pg 14
Bolinda Publishing Pty Ltd, pg 15
Boolarong Press, pg 15
Boombana Publications, pg 16
Bridge To Peace Publications, pg 16
Dangaroo Press, pg 19
Deva Wings Publications, pg 20
Emperor Publishing, pg 21
Era Publications, pg 21
Extraordinary People Press, pg 22
Finch Publishing, pg 22
Hale & Iremonger Pty Ltd, pg 24
Geoffrey Hamlyn-Harris, pg 24
Hargreen Publishing Co, pg 24
HarperCollinsReligious, pg 25
Hudson Publishing, pg 26
Hyland House Publishing Pty Ltd, pg 26
Institute of Aboriginal Development (IAD Press), pg 27
Kangaroo Press, pg 28
Life Planning Foundation of Australia, Inc, pg 29
Little Hills Press Pty Ltd, pg 29
Little Red Apple Publishing, pg 29
Thomas C Lothian Pty Ltd, pg 29
Magabala Books Aboriginal Corporation, pg 30
Media East Press, pg 31
Melbourne University Press, pg 32
Mulavon Press Pty Ltd, pg 32
Narkaling Inc, pg 33
Navarine Publishing, pg 33
Anne O'Donovan Pty Ltd, pg 34
Omnibus Books, pg 34
Outback Books - CQU Press, pg 34
Pan Macmillan Australia Pty Ltd, pg 35
Penguin Group (Australia), pg 36
Plantagenet Press, pg 37
Quakers Hill Press, pg 38
Random House Australia, pg 38
Ruskin Rowe Press, pg 40
St George Books, pg 40
St Pauls Publications, pg 40
Simon & Schuster (Australia) Pty Ltd, pg 41
Spectrum Publications, pg 41
Spinifex Press, pg 42
State Library of NSW Press, pg 42
The Text Publishing Company Pty Ltd, pg 43
Tom Publications, pg 43
Transworld Publishers Pty Ltd, pg 44
Troll Books of Australia, pg 44
Turton & Armstrong Pty Ltd Publishers, pg 44
University of New South Wales Press Ltd, pg 44
University of Queensland Press, pg 45
University of Western Australia Press, pg 45
The Useful Publishing Co, pg 45
Vista Publications, pg 45

SUBJECT INDEX

The Watermark Press, pg 46
John Wiley & Sons Australia, Ltd, pg 46

Austria
Franz Deuticke Verlagsgesmbh, pg 50
Development News Ltd, pg 50
Edition Ergo Sum, pg 50
Ibera VerlagsgesmbH, pg 52
Kremayr & Scheriau Verlag, pg 53
Merbod Verlag, pg 54
Milena Verlag, pg 54
Niederosterreichisches Pressehaus Druck- und Verlagsgesellschaft mbH, pg 54
oebv & hpt Verlagsgesellschaft mbH & Co KG, pg 55
Oesterreichischer Bundesverlag Gmbh, pg 55
Oesterreichischer Kunst und Kulturverlag, pg 55
Verlag Orac im Verlag Kremayr & Scheriau, pg 56
Pinguin-Verlag, Pawlowski GmbH, pg 56
Promedia Verlagsges mbH, pg 56
Suedwind - Buchwelt GmbH, pg 58
Edition Tau u Tau Type Druck Verlags-und Handels GmbH, pg 58
Tyrolia Verlagsanstalt GmbH, pg 58
Verlag Carl Ueberreuter GmbH, pg 58
Dr Otfried Weise Verlag Tabula Smaragdina, pg 59
Herbert Weishaupt Verlag, pg 59
WUV/Facultas Universitaetsverlag, pg 60
Paul Zsolnay Verlag GmbH, pg 60

Bangladesh
Ankur Prakashani, pg 61

Belarus
Interdigest Publishing House, pg 62
Kavaler Publishers, pg 62

Belgium
Altina, pg 63
Editions Chantecler, pg 65
Uitgeverij Clavis, pg 65
EPO Publishers, Printers, Booksellers, pg 67
IPIS vzw (International Peace Information Service), pg 69
Uitgeverij Lannoo NV, pg 69
Editions Racine, pg 72
Roularta Books NV, pg 72

Brazil
Agalma Psicanalise Editora Ltda, pg 77
Livraria Francisco Alves Editora SA, pg 77
Editora Bertrand Brasil Ltda, pg 78
Callis Editora Ltda, pg 79
Editora Campus Ltda, pg 79
Companhia Editora Forense, pg 81
Livraria Martins Fontes Editora Ltda, pg 81
Imago Editora Importacao e Exportacao Ltda, pg 84
Editora Marco Zero Ltda, pg 86
Editora Mercuryo Ltda, pg 86
Editora Nova Fronteira SA, pg 87
Editora Objetiva Ltda, pg 87
Editora Primor Ltda, pg 89
Qualitymark Editora Ltda, pg 89
Distribuidora Record de Servicos de Imprensa SA, pg 89
Editora Scipione Ltda, pg 90

Bulgaria
Aratron, IK, pg 93
Ciela Publishing House, pg 93
Darzhavno Izdatelstvo Zemizdat, pg 93
Hermes Publishing House, pg 94
Heron Press Publishing House, pg 94
Pejo K Javorov Publishing House, pg 95
Kibea Publishing Co, pg 95
Kolibri Publishing Group, pg 95
MATEX, pg 95
Reporter, pg 96
Sluntse Publishing House, pg 97
Ivan Vazov Publishing House, pg 97

Cameroon
Centre d'Edition et de Production pour l'Enseignement et la Recherche (CEPER), pg 98
Editions Buma Kor & Co Ltd, pg 98

Chile
Editorial Cuarto Propio, pg 99
Editorial Cuatro Vientos, pg 99
Editorial Texido Ltda, pg 100

China
Beijing Publishing House, pg 101
China Theatre Publishing House, pg 103
CITIC Publishing House, pg 103
Jinan Publishing House, pg 105
Kunlun Publishing House, pg 106
People's Literature Publishing House, pg 106
Shanghai Far East Publishers, pg 108
Xi'an Cartography Publishing House, pg 109

Colombia
Consejo Episcopal Latinoamericano (CELAM), pg 110

Costa Rica
Libreria Imprenta y Litografia Lehmann SA, pg 115

Cote d'Ivoire
Centre de Publications Evangeliques, pg 117
Centre d'Edition et de Diffusion Africaines, pg 117
Heritage Publishing Co, pg 117

Croatia
AGM doo, pg 117
Matica hrvatska, pg 118

Czech Republic
Aurora, pg 122
Baronet, pg 122
Brody, pg 122
Erika spol sro, pg 123
Josef Hribal, pg 124
Lidove Noviny Publishing House, pg 125
Josef Lukasik A Spol sro, pg 125
Mlada fronta, pg 125
Nase vojsko, nakladatelstvi a knizni obchod, pg 126
Prostor, nakladatelstvi sro, pg 127
NS Svoboda spol sro, pg 127

Denmark
Atuakkiorfik A/S Det Greenland Publishers, pg 129
Bogan's Forlag, pg 129
Bogfabrikken Fakta ApS, pg 129
Bonniers Specialmagasiner A/S Bogdivisionen, pg 129
Borgens Forlag A/S, pg 129
Carit Andersens Forlag A/S, pg 130
Forlaget Centrum, pg 130
Christian Ejlers' Forlag aps, pg 131
Gads Forlag, pg 131
P Haase & Sons Forlag A/S, pg 131
Hekla Forlag, pg 131
Hernovs Forlag, pg 132
Holkenfeldt 3, pg 132
Forlaget Hovedland, pg 132
Forlaget Klematis A/S, pg 132
Lindhardt og Ringhof Forlag A/S, pg 132
Forlaget Modtryk AMBA, pg 133
Joergen Paludan Forlag ApS, pg 133
Politisk Revy, pg 133
C A Reitzel Boghandel & Forlag A/S, pg 134
Schultz Information, pg 134
Spektrum Forlagsaktieselskab, pg 134
Wisby & Wilkens, pg 135
Forlaget Woldike K/S, pg 135

Egypt (Arab Republic of Egypt)
Dar El Shorouk, pg 138
Dar Al Hilal Publishing Institution, pg 138
Senouhy Publishers, pg 138

Estonia
Eesti Entsuklopeediakirjastus, pg 139
Ilmamaa, pg 139
Olion Publishers, pg 140
Sinisukk, pg 140

Finland
AB Svenska Laromedel-Editum, pg 141
Atena Kustannus Oy, pg 141
Fenix-Kustannus Oy, pg 142
Gummerus Publishers, pg 142
Kaantopiiri Oy, pg 142
Karisto Oy, pg 142
Kirjayhtyma Oy, pg 142
Koala-Kustannus Oy, pg 143
Kustannus Oy Kolibri, pg 143
Kustannusosakeyhtio Tammi, pg 143
Oy LIKE Kustannus, pg 143
Otava Publishing Co Ltd, pg 143
Weilin & Goos Oy, pg 144
Werner Soederstrom Osakeyhtio (WSOY), pg 145

France
Autrement Editions, pg 148
Editions Bordas, pg 150
Editions Canal, pg 152
Centre pour l'Innovation et la Recherche en Communication de l'Entreprise (CIRCE), pg 152
Le Cherche Midi Editeur, pg 154
Edition1, pg 160
Flammarion SA, pg 163
Editions Jacques Grancher, pg 165
Hachette Jeunesse Image, pg 166
Hachette Livre, pg 167
Editions Jean-Claude Lattes, pg 169
Liana Levi Editions, pg 172
Editions Lito, pg 172
Editions Albin Michel, pg 175
Payot & Rivages, pg 179
Editions Jean Picollec, pg 179
Le Pre-aux-clercs, pg 180
Presses de la Cite, pg 180
Editions Ramsay, pg 182
Societe des Editions Grasset et Fasquelle, pg 185
Editions Stock, pg 186
Les Editions de la Table Ronde, pg 186
Editions Vilo SA, pg 189

Germany
M Akselrad, pg 191
AOL-Verlag Frohmut Menze, pg 193
Ardey-Verlag GmbH, pg 193
Arena Verlag GmbH, pg 193
Argon Verlag GmbH, pg 194
Ars Edition GmbH, pg 194
Ars Vivendi Verlag, pg 194
Aulis Verlag Deubner & Co KG, pg 195
Bassermann Verlag, pg 197
Bastei Luebbe Taschenbuecher, pg 197
Verlag C H Beck oHG, pg 198
Verlag Beleke KG, pg 198
Bergverlag Rother GmbH, pg 199
C Bertelsmann Verlag GmbH, pg 199
Blackwell Wissenschafts-Verlag GmbH, pg 201
Verlag Erwin Bochinsky GmbH & Co KG, pg 202
Brandenburgisches Verlagshaus in der Dornier Medienholding GmbH, pg 204
BRUEN-Verlag, Gorenflo, pg 205
Verlag C J Bucher GmbH, pg 205
Verlag Busse und Seewald GmbH, pg 206
Caann Verlag, Klaus Wagner, pg 206
Chr Belser AG fur Verlagsgeschaefte und Co KG, pg 208
Christian Verlag GmbH, pg 208
Hans Christians Druckerei und Verlag GmbH & Co KG, pg 208
Claassen Verlag GmbH, pg 209
Compact Verlag GmbH, pg 209
Coppenrath Verlag, pg 209
J G Cotta'sche Buchhandlung Nachfolger GmbH, pg 210
Daedalus Verlag, pg 210
Dagmar Dreves Verlag, pg 210
Deutscher Fachverlag GmbH, pg 212
Deutscher Taschenbuch Verlag GmbH & Co KG (dtv), pg 213
Deutscher Verlag fur Grundstoffindustrie GmbH, pg 213
Edition Dia, pg 214
Verlag J H W Dietz Nachf GmbH, pg 214
Dipa-Verlag GmbH, pg 215
Verlagsgruppe Droemer Knaur GmbH & Co KG, pg 216
DRW-Verlag Weinbrenner-GmbH & Co, pg 216
Econ Taschenbuchverlag, pg 218
Econ Verlag GmbH, pg 218
Egmont Franz Schneider Verlag GmbH, pg 218
Egmont vgs verlagsgesellschaft mbH, pg 218
Ehrenwirth Verlag, pg 218
Eichborn AG, pg 219
EinfallsReich Verlagsgesellschaft MbH, pg 219
Elektor-Verlag GmbH, pg 219

Ellert & Richter Verlag GmbH, pg 219
Ensslin und Laiblin Verlag GmbH & Co KG, pg 220
Ernst Kabel Verlag GmbH, pg 221
Europa Verlag GmbH, pg 222
Fabel-Verlag Gudrun Liebchen, pg 223
Verlagsgruppe J Fink GmbH & Co KG, pg 224
Karin Fischer Verlag GmbH, pg 225
S Fischer Verlag GmbH, pg 225
Fischer Taschenbuch Verlag GmbH, pg 225
Forum Verlag Leipzig Buch-Gesellschaft mbH, pg 225
Franckh-Kosmos Verlags-GmbH & Co, pg 226
Gerstenberg Verlag, pg 228
Gerth Medien GmbH, pg 229
Gmelin Verlag GmbH, pg 230
Gondrom Verlag GmbH & Co KG, pg 230
Verlag der Stiftung Gralsbotschaft GmbH, pg 231
Carl Hanser Verlag, pg 234
Haude und Spenersche Verlagsbuchhandlung, pg 235
Heel Verlag GmbH, pg 235
Edition Hentrich Druck & Verlag Gebr Hentrich und Tank GmbH & Co KG, pg 236
F A Herbig Verlagsbuchhandlung GmbH, pg 236
Verlag Herder GmbH & Co KG, pg 236
Hoffmann und Campe Verlag GmbH, pg 238
Verlagsgruppe Georg von Holtzbrinck GmbH, pg 239
Horlemann Verlag, pg 239
Heinrich Hugendubel Verlag GmbH, pg 240
Edition Humanistische Psychologie (EHP), pg 240
Humboldt-Taschenbuch Verlag Jacobi KG, pg 240
Verlag der Islam, pg 242
ITpress Verlag, pg 242
Jovis Verlag GmbH, pg 243
Kallmeyer'sche Verlagsbuchhandlung GmbH, pg 244
KBV Verlags-und Medien - GmbH, pg 245
SachBuchVerlag Kellner, pg 245
Verlag Kiepenheuer & Witsch, pg 245
Gustav Kiepenheuer Verlag GmbH, pg 245
Kinderbuchverlag, pg 246
Klartext Verlagsgesellschaft mbH, pg 246
Verlag Kleine Schritte Ursula Dahm & Co, pg 246
Albrecht Knaus Verlag GmbH, pg 247
Knowledge Media International, pg 247
Koehlers Verlagsgesellschaft mbH, pg 248
Koenigsfurt Verlag, Evelin Buerger et Johannes Fiebig, pg 248
Koesler Verlag GmbH, pg 248
Kolibri-Verlag GmbH, pg 249
Konkret Literatur Verlag, pg 249
kopaed verlagsgmbh, pg 249
Koptisch-Orthodoxes Zentrum, pg 249
Karin Kramer Verlag, pg 250
Krueger Verlag GmbH, pg 250
Verlag Antje Kunstmann GmbH, pg 251

Ambro Lacus, Buch- und Bildverlag Walter A Kremnitz, pg 251
Landbuch-Verlagsgesellschaft mbH, pg 251
Lebenshilfe-Verlag Marburg, Verlag der Bundesvereinigung Lebenshilfe fuer Menschen mit geistiger Behinderung eV, pg 253
Lentz Verlag, pg 253
Dr Gisela Lermann, pg 253
Libertas- Europaeisches Institut GmbH, pg 254
Logos-Verlag Literatur & Layout GmbH, pg 255
Luchterhand Literaturverlag GmbH/ Verlag Volk & Welt GmbH, pg 255
Gustav Luebbe Verlag, pg 256
Verlagsgruppe Luebbe GmbH & Co KG, pg 256
Otto Meissner Verlag, pg 259
Meyer & Meyer Verlag, pg 260
Mitteldeutscher Verlag GmbH, pg 261
Motorbuch-Verlag, pg 262
Neuer Honos Verlag GmbH, pg 264
Verlag Neues Leben GmbH, pg 264
nymphenburger, pg 266
Oekotopia Verlag, Wolfgang Hoffman GmbH & Co KG, pg 266
Oertel & Sporer GmbH & Co, pg 266
Palmyra Verlag, pg 268
Edition Parabolis, pg 268
Pattloch Verlag GmbH & Co, pg 268
Projektion J Buch- und Musikverlag GmbH, pg 272
Propylaeen Verlag, Zweigniederlassung Berlin der Ullstein Buchverlage GmbH, pg 272
Querverlag GmbH, pg 273
Ravensburger Buchverlag Otto Maier GmbH, pg 274
Rossipaul Kommunikation GmbH, pg 277
Rowohlt Berlin Verlag GmbH, pg 277
Rowohlt Verlag GmbH, pg 277
Ryvellus Medienagentur Dopfer, pg 277
Sax-Verlag Beucha, pg 278
Schueren Verlag GmbH, pg 281
H O Schulze KG, pg 282
Theodor Schuster, pg 282
Siedler Verlag, pg 283
Adolf Sponholtz Verlag, pg 284
Springer Science+Business Media GmbH & Co KG, pg 284
Stadler Verlagsgesellschaft mbH, pg 286
Stapp Verlag Wolfgang Stapp, pg 286
C A Starke Verlag, pg 287
Steidl Verlag, pg 287
Stern-Verlag Janssen & Co, pg 288
Sueddeutsche Verlagsgesellschaft mbH, pg 288
Suedwest Verlag GmbH & Co KG, pg 289
Tangens Systemverlag GmbH, pg 289
Edition Temmen, pg 290
Konrad Theiss Verlag GmbH, pg 290
S Toeche-Mittler Verlag GmbH, pg 291
Trescher Verlag GmbH, pg 292
Treves Editions Verein Zur Foerderung der Kuenstlerischen Taetigkeiten, pg 292

Trias Verlag in MVS Medizinverlage Stuttgart GmbH & Co KG, pg 292
Guenter Albert Ulmer Verlag, pg 293
Neuer Umschau Buchverlag, pg 293
Urania Verlag mit Ravensburger Ratgebern, pg 294
Verlag Volk & Welt GmbH, pg 296
W Ludwig Verlag GmbH, pg 297
Verlag Klaus Wagenbach, pg 297
Weber Zucht & Co, pg 298
Weidler Buchverlag Berlin, pg 298
Verlagsgruppe Weltbild GmbH, pg 298
Georg Westermann Verlag GmbH, pg 299
Rosa Winkel Verlag GmbH, pg 300
Dr Dieter Winkler, pg 300
Verlag Konrad Wittwer GmbH, pg 301
WRS Verlag Wirtschaft, Recht und Steuern GmbH & Co KG, pg 301
Wunderlich Verlag, pg 301
Xenos Verlagsgesellschaft mbH, pg 301
Zebulon Verlag GmbH & Co KG, pg 302

Ghana
Afram Publications (Ghana) Ltd, pg 303
Africa Christian Press, pg 303
Asempa Publishers, pg 303
Ghana Publishing Corporation, pg 304
Moxon Paperbacks, pg 304
Waterville Publishing House, pg 305

Greece
Atlantis M Pechlivanides & Co SA, pg 306
Chrysi Penna - Golden Pen Books, pg 306
Diavlos, pg 306
Dodoni Publications, pg 306
Elliniki Leschi Tou Vivliou, pg 307
Govostis Publishing SA, pg 307
Denise Harvey, pg 308
Katoptro Publications, pg 309
Kritiki Publishing, pg 309
Medusa/Selas Publishers, pg 310
Minoas SA, pg 310
Morfotiko Idryma Ethnikis Trapezas, pg 310
Kyr I Papadopoulos E E, pg 311
Patakis Publishers, pg 311
Siamantas VA A Ouvas, pg 312

Guyana
Roraima Publishers Ltd, pg 314

Hong Kong
Ling Kee Publishing Group, pg 318
Ming Pao Publications Ltd, pg 318
SCMP Book Publishing Ltd, pg 319
Sun Ya Publications (HK) Ltd, pg 319

Hungary
Aranyhal Konyvkiado Goldfish Publishing, pg 320
Balassi Kiado Kft, pg 321
Gondolat Kiado, pg 321
Park Konyvkiado Kft (Park Publisher), pg 324
Szabvanykiado, pg 324

Iceland
Almenna Bokafelagid, pg 325
Fjolvi, pg 325
Idunn, pg 325
Mal og menning, pg 326
Setberg, pg 326
Skjaldborg Ltd, pg 326

India
Cosmo Publications, pg 332
Current Books, pg 332
Dolphin Publications, pg 333
Frank Brothers & Co Publishers Ltd, pg 334
Full Circle Publishing, pg 334
General Book Depot, pg 335
Hind Pocket Books Private Ltd, pg 336
Kali For Women, pg 339
A Mukherjee & Co Pvt Ltd, pg 342
Orient Paperbacks, pg 344
Prabhat Prakashan, pg 345
Pratibha Pratishthan, pg 345
Reliance Publishing House, pg 346
M C Sarkar & Sons (P) Ltd, pg 348
Sat Sahitya Prakashan, pg 348
Somaiya Publications Pvt Ltd, pg 349
Vision Books Pvt Ltd, pg 352

Indonesia
Angkasa CV, pg 353
Bina Rena Pariwara, pg 354
PT Bulan Bintang, pg 354
Gaya Favorit Press, pg 355
Katalis PT Bina Mitra Plaosan, pg 355
Yayasan Obor Indonesia, pg 357

Ireland
Brandon Book Publishers Ltd, pg 358
Dee-Jay Publications, pg 359
Gandon Editions, pg 360
Mercier Press Ltd, pg 362
Mount Eagle Publications Ltd, pg 362
The O'Brien Press Ltd, pg 362
On Stream Publications Ltd, pg 362
Poolbeg Press Ltd, pg 363
Veritas Co Ltd, pg 364

Israel
Achiasaf Publishing House Ltd, pg 364
Astrolog Publishing House, pg 365
Bitan Publishers Ltd, pg 365
Breslov Research Institute, pg 365
Classikaletet, pg 366
DAT Publications, pg 366
Dyonon/Papyrus Publishing House of the Tel-Aviv, pg 366
Gefen Publishing House Ltd, pg 367
Hakibbutz Hameuchad Publishing House Ltd, pg 367
MAP-Mapping & Publishing Ltd, pg 370
Schocken Publishing House Ltd, pg 371
Tcherikover Publishers Ltd, pg 372
Yad Vashem - The Holocaust Martyrs' & Heroes' Remembrance Authority, pg 373
Yedioth Ahronoth Books, pg 373
Zmora-Bitan, Publishers Ltd, pg 374

Italy
L'Airone Editrice, pg 375
Rosellina Archinto Editore, pg 376

Gruppo Editoriale Armenia SpA, pg 376
Belforte Editore Libraio srl, pg 377
Bompiani-RCS Libri, pg 378
Edizioni Cantagalli, pg 379
Edizioni Centro Studi Erickson, pg 381
il Cerchio Iniziative Editoriali, pg 381
l'Eta dell'Acquario, pg 388
Edizioni Frassinelli SRL, pg 389
Gremese International srl, pg 391
Editoriale Jaca Book SpA, pg 394
Kaos Edizioni SRL, pg 394
La Luna, pg 396
Manfrini Editori, pg 397
Marsilio Editori SpA, pg 397
McRae Books, pg 398
Mondolibro Editore SNC, pg 399
Franco Muzzio Editore, pg 400
Edizioni Piemme SpA, pg 403
RAI-ERI, pg 405
Rusconi Libri Srl, pg 406
Il Saggiatore, pg 406
Editoriale Scienza, pg 407
Edizioni Segno SRL, pg 407
Sonzogno, pg 409
Sperling e Kupfer Editori SpA, pg 409
TEA Tascabili degli Editori Associati SpA, pg 409
Marco Tropea Editore, pg 410

Jamaica

Institute of Jamaica Publications, pg 413
LMH Publishing Ltd, pg 414

Japan

Chikuma Shobo Publishing Co Ltd, pg 416
Diamond Inc, pg 416
Dobunshoin Publishers Co, pg 416
Fukuinkan Shoten Publishers Inc, pg 417
Gakken Co Ltd, pg 417
Hakusui-Sha Co Ltd, pg 417
Hakuyo-Sha, pg 418
Hayakawa Publishing Inc, pg 418
Heibonsha Ltd, Publishers, pg 418
Japan Broadcast Publishing Co Ltd, pg 419
The Japan Times Ltd, pg 420
Kawade Shobo Shinsha Publishers, pg 420
Kodansha Ltd, pg 421
Kosei Publishing Co Ltd, pg 421
Mita Press, Mita Industrial Co Ltd, pg 422
Nippon Hoso Shuppan Kyokai (NHK Publishing), pg 424
Seibu Time Co Ltd, pg 426
Shimizu-Shoin, pg 427
Shincho-Sha Co Ltd, pg 427
Akane Shobo Co Ltd, pg 427
Shueisha Inc, pg 428
Shufunotomo Co Ltd, pg 428
Soshisha Co Ltd, pg 428
Toho Book Store, pg 429
Tokuma Shoten Publishing Co Ltd, pg 429
Toyo Keizai Shinpo-Sha, pg 430

Jordan

Jordan Book Centre Co Ltd, pg 432

Kenya

Africa Book Services (EA) Ltd, pg 433
Heinemann Kenya Ltd (EAEP), pg 434
Jacaranda Designs Ltd, pg 434
Kenway Publications Ltd, pg 434
Paulines Publications-Africa, pg 435
Transafrica Press, pg 436
Uzima Press Ltd, pg 436

Republic of Korea

Big Tree Publishing, pg 437
Borim Publishing Co, pg 437
Chung Rim Publishing Co Ltd, pg 438
Hainaim Publishing Co Ltd, pg 439
Jigyungsa Ltd, pg 440
Ke Mong Sa Publishing Co Ltd, pg 440
Koreaone Press Inc, pg 440
Kumsung Publishing Co Ltd, pg 440
Kyohaksa Publishing Co Ltd, pg 440
Min-eumsa Publishing Co Ltd, pg 441
Munye Publishing Co, pg 441
O Neul Publishing Co, pg 441
Woongjin Media Corporation, pg 443
Woongjin.com Co Ltd, pg 443
Yearimdang Publishing Co, pg 443

Latvia

Alberts XII, pg 444
Avots, pg 444
Egmont Latvia SIA, pg 444
Nordik/Tapals Publishers Ltd, pg 445
Zvaigzne ABC Publishers Ltd, pg 445

Lebanon

Librairie Orientale sal, pg 446

Liechtenstein

Bonafides Verlags-Anstalt, pg 447

Lithuania

Baltos Lankos, pg 449
Egmont Lietuva, pg 449
Lietus Ltd, pg 449
Tyto Alba Publishers, pg 450
Vaga Ltd, pg 450

Luxembourg

Guy Binsfeld & Co Sarl, pg 450

The Former Yugoslav Republic of Macedonia

Detska radost, pg 452

Malaysia

Pustaka Cipta Sdn Bhd, pg 458
Tempo Publishing (M) Sdn Bhd, pg 458

Mali

EDIM SA, pg 460

Mauritius

Vizavi Editions, pg 461

Mexico

Ediciones el Caballito SA, pg 462
El Colegio de Mexico AC, pg 463
Editorial Diana SA de CV, pg 464
Fernandez Editores SA de CV, pg 465
Fondo de Cultura Economica, pg 465
Editorial Grijalbo SA de CV, pg 466
Editorial Joaquin Mortiz SA de CV, pg 467
Lasser Press Mexicana SA de CV, pg 467
Libra Editorial SA de CV, pg 467
Editores Mexicanos Unidos SA, pg 468
Nova Grupo Editorial SA de CV, pg 469
Editorial Planeta Mexicana SA, pg 470
Selector SA de CV, pg 471
Time-Life Internacional de Mexico, pg 472
Editorial Universo SA de CV, pg 473
Javier Vergara Editor SA de CV, pg 473

Netherlands

Uitgeverij Ambo BV, 477
Uitgeverij de Arbeiderspers, 477
Uitgeverij Arena BV, 478
Uitgeverij Aristos, pg 478
Uitgeverij Balans, pg 478
De Bezige Bij B V Uitgeverij, pg 479
De Boekerij BV, pg 479
A W Bruna Uitgevers BV, pg 480
BZZTOH Publishers, pg 480
Cadans, pg 480
Uitgeverij Cantecleer BV, pg 480
ECI voor Boeken en platen BV, pg 481
Educatieve Uitgeverij Edu'Actief BV, pg 481
Elmar BV, pg 482
Uitgeverij De Fontein BV, pg 482
Uitgeverij De Geus BV, pg 482
Gottmer Uitgevers Groep, pg 483
Historische Uitgeverij, pg 483
Mets & Schilt Uitgevers en Distributeurs, pg 486
J M Meulenhoff bv, pg 486
Uitgeverij Mingus, pg 486
Uitgeverij Maarten Muntinga, pg 486
Nederlands Literair Produktie-en Vertalingen Fonds (NLPVF), pg 486
Nijgh & Van Ditmar Amsterdam, pg 487
Omega Boek BV, pg 487
Uitgeverij Ploegsma BV, pg 487
Podium Uitgeverij, pg 487
Prometheus, pg 488
Sjaloom Uitgeverijen, pg 489
Uitgeverij Het Spectrum BV, pg 489
A J G Strengholt's Boeken, Anno 1928, BV, pg 489
Thoth Publishers, pg 490
Unieboek BV, pg 490
Van Buuren Uitgeverij BV, pg 491
Uitgeverij G A van Oorschot bv, pg 491
Uitgeverij Vassallucci bv, pg 491
Wereldbibliotheek, pg 492
West-Friesland/Boekproject-ontwikkeling, pg 492

Netherlands Antilles

Bredero, pg 493

New Zealand

Brick Row Publishing Co Ltd, pg 494
Bush Press Communications Ltd, pg 494
Canterbury University Press, pg 494
Cape Catley Ltd, pg 495
The Caxton Press, pg 495
Craig Potton Publishing, pg 495
Craig Printing Co Ltd, pg 495
Dunmore Press Ltd, pg 495
Exisle Publishing Ltd, pg 496
Godwit Publishing Ltd, pg 496
Hazard Press Ltd, pg 497
Hodder Moa Beckett Publishers Ltd, pg 497
Legislation Direct, pg 498
Longacre Press, pg 498
Mills Group, pg 498
Orca Publishing Services Ltd, pg 499
Reed Publishing (NZ) Ltd, pg 500
RIMU Publishing Co Ltd, pg 500
River Press, pg 500
RSVP Publishing Co Ltd, pg 500
Shearwater Associates Ltd, pg 501
Shoal Bay Press Ltd, pg 501
Tandem Press, pg 501
Bridget Williams Books Ltd, pg 502

Nicaragua

Editorial Nueva Nicaragua, pg 502

Nigeria

Black Academy Press, pg 503
Cross Continent Press Ltd, pg 504
CSS Bookshops, pg 504
Educational Research & Study Group, pg 504
Heritage Books, pg 505
Kola Sanya Publishing Enterprise, pg 505
Longman Nigeria Plc, pg 505
Thomas Nelson (Nigeria) Ltd, pg 505
New Horn Press Ltd, pg 506
Northern Nigerian Publishing Co Ltd, pg 506
Nwamife Publishers Ltd, pg 506
Onibon-Oje Publishers, pg 506
Riverside Communications, pg 507
University Publishing Co, pg 507
Vantage Publishers International Ltd, pg 507
John West Publications Co Ltd, pg 507

Norway

Cappelen akademisk forlag, pg 508
J W Cappelens Forlag A/S, pg 508
N W Damm og Son A/S, pg 508
Det Norske Samlaget, pg 508
Fono Forlag, pg 509
Genesis Forlag, pg 509
John Grieg Forlag AS, pg 509
Pax Forlag A/S, pg 510
Erik Sandberg, pg 510
Chr Schibsteds Forlag A/S, pg 510
Snofugl Forlag, pg 510
Stabenfeldt A/S, pg 510
Tiden Norsk Forlag, pg 511

Pakistan

Jang Publishers, pg 513

Peru

Ediciones Brown SA, pg 516

Philippines

Bookman Printing & Publishing House Inc, pg 518
National Book Store Inc, pg 519
New Day Publishers, pg 520
SIBS Publishing House Inc, pg 521

PUBLISHERS

Poland
Albatros, pg 522
Ksiaznica Publishing Ltd, pg 524
Muza SA, pg 524
'Slask' Ltd, pg 526
Wydawnictwo WAB, pg 527

Portugal
DIFEL - Difusao Editorial SA, pg 530
Distri Cultural Lda, pg 530
Editorial Estampa, Lda, pg 531
Europress Editores e Distribuidores de Publicacoes Lda, pg 531
Gradiva-Publicacnoes Lda, pg 532
Porto Editora Lda, pg 535
Editorial Presenca, pg 535
Puma Editora Lda, pg 535
Edicoes 70 Lda, pg 535
Teorema, pg 536

Puerto Rico
McGraw-Hill Intermericana del Caribe, Inc, pg 537
University of Puerto Rico Press (EDUPR), pg 537

Romania
Editora All, pg 538
Artemis Verlag, pg 538
Editura Clusium, pg 539
Editura Excelsior Art, pg 539
Editura Meridiane, pg 540
Editura Niculescu, pg 541
Pandora Publishing House, pg 541
Grupul Editorial RAO, pg 542
RAO International Publishing Co, pg 542
Realitatea Casa de Edituri Productie Audio-Video Film, pg 542
Rentrop & Straton Verlagsgruppe und Wirtschaftsconsulting, pg 542
Editura Stiintifica SA, pg 542

Russian Federation
BLIC, russko-Baltijskij informaciionnyj centr, AO, pg 544
Publishing House Limbus Press, pg 546
Mir Knigi Ltd, pg 546
Izdatelstvo Moskovskii Rabochii, pg 547
Novosti Izdatelstvo, pg 547
Profizdat, pg 548
Top Secret Collection Publishers, pg 549

Saudi Arabia
Dar Al-Shareff for Publishing & Distribution, pg 550

Senegal
Les Nouvelles Editions Africaines du Senegal NEAS, pg 551

Serbia and Montenegro
Alfa-Narodna Knjiga, pg 552
Obod, pg 553

Sierra Leone
Sierra Leone University Press, pg 554

Singapore
Aquanut Agencies Pte Ltd, pg 555

Slovakia
Vydavatel'stvo Osveta (Verlag Osveta), pg 560
Slovansky Tatran, Vydavatel 'stro spoi sro, pg 560
VEDA (Vydavatel'stvo Slovenskej akademie vied), pg 561

Slovenia
Mladinska Knjiga International, pg 561
Zalozba Obzorja d d Maribor, pg 562

South Africa
Ad Donker (Pty) Ltd, pg 563
Fernwood Press (Pty) Ltd, pg 563
Galago Publishing Pty Ltd, pg 564
HAUM (Hollandsch Afrikaansche Uitgevers Maatschappij), pg 564
Heinemann Publishers (Pty) Ltd, pg 564
Human & Rousseau (Pty) Ltd, pg 564
Ivy Publications, pg 565
Juventus/Femina Publishers, pg 565
LAPA Publishers (Pty) Ltd, pg 566
Media House Publications, pg 566
New Africa Books (Pty) Ltd, pg 567
Queillerie Publishers, pg 568
Ravan Press (Pty) Ltd, pg 568
Reader's Digest Southern Africa, pg 568
Shuter & Shooter (Pty) Ltd, pg 568
Southern Book Publishers (Pty) Ltd, pg 569
Struik Publishers (Pty) Ltd, pg 569
Tafelberg Publishers Ltd, pg 569
Unisa Press, pg 569

Spain
Acento Editorial, pg 570
Aguilar SA de Ediciones, pg 571
Amnistia Internacional Editorial SL, pg 572
Editorial Astri SA, pg 573
Ediciones B, SA, pg 574
Circe Ediciones, SA, pg 577
Compania Literaria, pg 577
Ediciones Destino SA, pg 579
Didaco Comunicacion y Didactica, SA, pg 579
Edicomunicacion SA, pg 581
Editorial Espasa-Calpe SA, pg 582
Eumo Editorial, pg 583
Editorial Gedisa SA, pg 584
Grijalbo Mondadori SA, pg 585
Ediciones Internacionales Universitarias SA, pg 588
Libsa Editorial SA, pg 589
Llibres del Segle, pg 589
Ediciones Maeva, pg 590
Editorial Marin SA, pg 590
Ediciones Martinez-Roca SA, pg 591
Ediciones Medici SA, pg 591
Ediciones Nauta Credito SA, pg 593
Noguer y Caralt Editores SA, pg 593
Obelisco Ediciones S, pg 593
Ediciones del Oriente y del Mediterraneo, pg 594
Pages Editors, SL, pg 594
Ediciones El Pais SA, pg 594
Editorial Planeta SA, pg 596
Plaza y Janes Editores SA, pg 596
Pre-Textos, pg 596
Editorial Prensa Espanola, pg 597
Editorial Sintesis, SA, pg 600
Ediciones Siruela SA, pg 600

SUBJECT INDEX

Edicions 62, pg 600
Grup 62, pg 600
Tesitex, SL, pg 602
Editorial Thassalia, SA, pg 602
Gregorio del Toro Editor, pg 602
Ediciones de la Torre, pg 602
Trea Ediciones, SL, pg 602
Turner Publicaciones, pg 602
Javier Vergara Editor SA, pg 604
Veron Editor, pg 604
Ediciones Versal SA, pg 604
Vinaches Lopez, Luisa, pg 605

Sri Lanka
Samayawardena Printers Publishers & Booksellers, pg 607

Sudan
Al-Ayam Press Co Ltd, pg 608
Khartoum University Press, pg 608

Sweden
Bokforlaget Atlantis AB, pg 609
Akademiforlaget Corona AB, pg 609
Albert Bonniers Forlag, pg 609
Alfabeta Bokforlag AB, pg 609
Bokforlaget Axplock, pg 609
Berghs, pg 610
Albert Bonniers Forlag AB, pg 610
BOOX, pg 610
Brombergs Bokforlag AB, pg 610
Rene Coeckelberghs Bokfoerlag AB, pg 610
Bokforlaget Cordia AB, pg 610
Delta Forlags AB, pg 611
Fischer & Co, pg 611
Bokforlaget Forum AB, pg 611
Gedins Forlag, pg 611
Lars Hoekerbergs Bokfoerlag, pg 612
Bokforlaget Robert Larson AB, pg 613
Bokfoerlaget Natur och Kultur, pg 613
Norstedts Forlag, pg 614
Bokforlaget Nya Doxa AB, pg 614
Bokforlaget Plus AB, pg 614
Raben och Sjoegren Bokforlag, pg 614
Richters Egmont, pg 615
Bokforlaget Settern AB, pg 615
Sjoestrands Foerlag, pg 615
Stromberg, pg 616
Svenska Foerlaget liv & ledarskap ab, pg 616
Timbro, pg 616
Var Skola Foerlag AB, pg 616
AB Wahlstroem & Widstrand, pg 616
Wahlstrom & Widstrand, pg 616
B Wahlstroms, pg 616
Zindermans AB, pg 617

Switzerland
Ammann Verlag & Co, pg 617
Ariston Editions, pg 617
Athenaeum Verlag AG, pg 618
Basilius Presse AG, pg 618
Bergli Books AG, pg 619
Bibliographisches Institut & F A Brockhaus AG, pg 619
Chronos Verlag, pg 621
Rene Coeckelberghs Editions, pg 621
Eco Verlags AG, pg 622
Hallwag Kuemmerly & Frey AG, pg 625
Kinderbuchverlag Luzern, pg 626
Lenos Verlag, pg 627
Oesch Verlag AG, pg 630
Ott Verlag Thun, pg 630

Editions Payot Lausanne, pg 631
Rotpunktverlag, pg 632
Sauerlaender AG, pg 633
Tobler Verlag, pg 635
Uranium Verlag Zug, pg 636
Verbandsdruckerei AG, pg 636
Weltwoche ABC-Verlag, pg 637

Taiwan, Province of China
Commonwealth Publishing Company Ltd, pg 639
Linking Publishing Company Ltd, pg 641
Newton Publishing Company Ltd, pg 641
UNITAS Publishing Co Ltd, pg 642

United Republic of Tanzania
East African Publishing House, pg 643
Eastern Africa Publications Ltd, pg 643
Inland Publishers, pg 643
Tanzania Publishing House, pg 644
Tema Publishers Ltd, pg 644

Thailand
Odeon Store LP, pg 645

Turkey
Afa Yayincilik Sanayi Tic AS, pg 648
Alkim Kitapcilik-Yayimcilik, pg 649
Altin Kitaplar Yayinevi, pg 649
Cep Kitaplari AS, pg 649
Iletisim Yayinlari, pg 650
Kiyi Yayinlari, pg 650
Metis Yayinlari, pg 650
Remzi Kitabevi, pg 650
Ruh ve Madde Yayinlari ve Saglik Hizmetleri AS, pg 651
Sabah Kitaplari, pg 651
Varlik Yayinlari AS, pg 652
Kabalci Yayinevi, pg 652

Uganda
Fountain Publishers Ltd, pg 652

Ukraine
ASK Ltd, pg 653

United Kingdom
Act 3 Publishing, pg 655
Aladdin Books Ltd, pg 656
Amber Books Ltd, pg 657
Apex Publishing Ltd, pg 658
Apple Press, pg 658
Argo Spoken Word, pg 659
Aurum Press Ltd, pg 661
Batsford Ltd, pg 663
BBC Audiobooks, pg 663
BCA - Book Club Associates, pg 663
Belitha Press Ltd, pg 664
A & C Black Publishers Ltd, pg 666
Blackstaff Press, pg 666
John Blake Publishing Ltd, pg 667
Blaketon Hall Ltd, pg 667
Bloomsbury Publishing PLC, pg 668
Books of Zimbabwe Publishing Co (Pvt) Ltd, pg 669
Brewin Books Ltd, pg 671
Brimax Books, pg 671
Brown Wells & Jacobs Ltd, pg 672
Calder Publications Ltd, pg 673
Canongate Books Ltd, pg 674
Carroll & Brown Ltd, pg 675

Cassell & Co, pg 675
Centre for Alternative Technology, pg 677
Chatham Publishing, pg 678
James Clarke & Co Ltd, pg 680
Compass Equestrian Ltd, pg 681
Compendium Publishing, pg 681
Constable & Robinson Ltd, pg 682
The Continuum International Publishing Group Ltd, pg 682
Leo Cooper, pg 683
Creation Books, pg 683
Delta Books (Pty) Ltd, pg 687
Denor Press, pg 687
Dorling Kindersley Ltd, pg 688
Gerald Duckworth & Co Ltd, pg 688
Gwasg Dwyfor, pg 688
Eddison Sadd Editions Ltd, pg 689
Aidan Ellis Publishing, pg 690
Eurobook Ltd, pg 692
The Eurospan Group, pg 692
Helen Exley Giftbooks, pg 693
Frontier Publishing Ltd, pg 697
George Mann Publications, pg 699
GMP Publishers Ltd, pg 700
Gollancz/Witherby, pg 701
Gomer Press (J D Lewis & Sons Ltd), pg 701
Grandreams Ltd, pg 702
Grange Books PLC, pg 702
Granta Books, pg 702
Grub Street, pg 703
Hamlyn, pg 704
Patrick Hardy Books, pg 705
HarperCollins UK, pg 705
Harvard University Press, pg 705
The Harvill Press, pg 705
Headline Book Publishing Ltd, pg 706
Heinemann Educational Publishing, pg 707
William Heinemann Ltd, pg 707
Helion & Co, pg 707
Heritage Press, pg 708
Hodder Children's Books, pg 709
Honno Welsh Women's Press, pg 710
Isis Publishing Ltd, pg 714
The Islamic Texts Society, pg 715
Janus Publishing Co Ltd, pg 716
Karnak House, pg 717
Ladybird Books Ltd, pg 719
Letterbox Library, pg 720
Lion Hudson PLC, pg 721
Luath Press Ltd, pg 722
The Lutterworth Press, pg 723
Macmillan Children's Books, pg 723
Macmillan Ltd, pg 723
Marston House, pg 725
Mercat Press, pg 726
Metro Books, pg 727
Moonlight Publishing Ltd, pg 729
John Murray (Publishers) Ltd, pg 730
New Cavendish Books, pg 732
New Era Publications UK Ltd, pg 732
NMS Enterprises Ltd - Publishing, pg 733
Octopus Publishing Group, pg 734
Michael O'Mara Books Ltd, pg 735
Open Books Publishing Ltd, pg 735
Orion Publishing Group Ltd, pg 736
Oyster Books Ltd, pg 737
Pan Macmillan, pg 738
Parapress Ltd, pg 738
Piatkus Books, pg 741
Piccadilly Press, pg 742
Polybooks Ltd, pg 744
Polygon, pg 744
PRC Publishing Ltd, pg 745

Mathew Price Ltd, pg 745
Profile Books Ltd, pg 746
Quarto Publishing plc, pg 746
Quartz Editions, pg 746
Quiller Publishing Ltd, pg 747
Random House UK Ltd, pg 747
Ravette Publishing Ltd, pg 748
The Reader's Digest Association Ltd, pg 748
Reaktion Books Ltd, pg 748
Regency House Publishing Ltd, pg 749
Rivers Oram Press, pg 750
The Robinswood Press Ltd, pg 750
Michael Russell Publishing Ltd, pg 752
Sangam Books Ltd, pg 754
Saqi Books, pg 754
Steve Savage Publishers Ltd, pg 754
SAWD Publications, pg 754
Scholastic Ltd, pg 754
Scottish Cultural Press, pg 755
Martin Secker & Warburg, pg 756
Serpent's Tail Ltd, pg 756
Shaw & Sons Ltd, pg 756
Sheldrake Press, pg 757
Shepheard-Walwyn (Publishers) Ltd, pg 757
Silver Link Publishing Ltd, pg 758
Simon & Schuster Ltd, pg 758
Smith Settle Ltd, pg 758
Snowbooks Ltd, pg 759
SPA Books Ltd, pg 759
Spellmount Ltd Publishers, pg 760
Sutton Publishing Ltd, pg 762
Tabb House, pg 762
I B Tauris & Co Ltd, pg 763
Tiger Books International PLC, pg 765
Time Warner Book Group UK, pg 766
Tobin Music, pg 766
Transworld Publishers Ltd, pg 766
Ulverscroft Large Print Books Ltd, pg 768
Verso, pg 770
Viking, pg 770
Virgin Publishing Ltd, pg 770
John Waite Ltd, pg 771
Walker Books Ltd, pg 771
Ward Lock Ltd, pg 771
The Watts Publishing Group Ltd, pg 771
Webb & Bower (Publishers) Ltd, pg 772
The Windrush Press Ltd, pg 774
The Women's Press Ltd, pg 775
Wordwright Publishing, pg 775
Yale University Press London, pg 776

Uruguay

Ediciones de Juan Darien, pg 777
Rosebud Ediciones, pg 778
Vinten Editor, pg 778

Venezuela

Alfadil Ediciones, pg 778
Editorial Biosfera CA, pg 779

Zimbabwe

Academic Books (Pvt) Ltd, pg 782
The Graham Publishing Company (Pvt) Ltd, pg 783
Mambo Press, pg 783
National Archives of Zimbabwe, pg 784
Vision Publications, pg 784
Zimbabwe Women Writers, pg 785

OUTDOOR RECREATION

Argentina

Ediciones Lidiun, pg 7

Australia

Robert Berthold Photography, pg 14
Enterprise Publications, pg 21
Envirobook, pg 21
Flora Publications International Pty Ltd, pg 22
Mulavon Press Pty Ltd, pg 32
Rankin Publishers, pg 39
Saltwater Publications, pg 40
Simon & Schuster (Australia) Pty Ltd, pg 41

Austria

Verlag Harald Denzel, Auto- und Freizeitfuehrer, pg 50
Doecker Verlag GmbH & Co KG, pg 50
Niederosterreichisches Pressehaus Druck- und Verlagsgesellschaft mbH, pg 54
Verlag des Osterr Kneippbundes GmbH, pg 56
Verlag Veritas Mediengesellschaft mbH, pg 59

Belgium

Georeto-Geogidsen, pg 67

China

China Film Press, pg 102
Jilin Science & Technology Publishing House, pg 105
Yunnan University Press, pg 109

Colombia

Eurolibros Ltda, pg 111

Czech Republic

Aurora, pg 122
Nakladatelstvi Jota spol sro, pg 124

Denmark

Wisby & Wilkens, pg 135

France

ATP - Packager, pg 148
Editions Chiron, pg 154
De Vecchi Editions SA, pg 157
Editions Edisud, pg 159
Federation Francaise de la Randonnee Pedestre, pg 163
Institut Francais de Recherche pour l'Exploitation de la Mer (IFREMER), pg 164
Librairie Guenegaud, pg 166
Editions Fernand Lanore Sarl, pg 171
Editions Mango, pg 174
Editions Franck Mercier, pg 175
Les Presses d'Ile-de-France Sarl, pg 181
Editions Sud Ouest, pg 186

Germany

Alba Fachverlag GmbH & Co KG, pg 191
ALS-Verlag GmbH, pg 192
AOL-Verlag Frohmut Menze, pg 193
ARCult Media, pg 193
Bassermann Verlag, pg 197
Bergverlag Rother GmbH, pg 199
Bielefelder Verlagsanstalt GmbH & Co KG Richard Kaselowsky, pg 201
BLV Verlagsgesellschaft mbH, pg 202
F Bruckmann Munchen Verlag & Druck GmbH & Co Produkt KG, pg 204
Verlag Busse und Seewald GmbH, pg 206
Fachverlag Hans Carl GmbH, pg 207
Hans Christians Druckerei und Verlag GmbH & Co KG, pg 208
Christophorus-Verlag GmbH, pg 208
Copress Verlag, pg 209
Delius, Klasing und Co, pg 211
Deutscher Wanderverlag Dr Mair & Schnabel & Co, pg 214
Drei Brunnen Verlag GmbH & Co, pg 216
Egmont vgs verlagsgesellschaft mbH, pg 218
Eulen Verlag, pg 221
Verlagsgruppe J Fink GmbH & Co KG, pg 224
Franckh-Kosmos Verlags-GmbH & Co, pg 226
Fraunhofer IRB Verlag Fraunhofer Informationszentrum Raum und Bau, pg 226
Verlag Gruppenpaedagogischer Literatur, pg 231
Heel Verlag GmbH, pg 235
Dieter Hoffmann Verlag, pg 238
Jutta Pohl Verlag, pg 244
SachBuchVerlag Kellner, pg 245
Landbuch-Verlagsgesellschaft mbH, pg 251
Institut fuer Landes- und Stadtentwicklungsforschung des Landes Nordrhein-Westfalen, pg 251
Moby Dick Verlag, pg 261
Verlag Stephanie Naglschmid, pg 263
Verlag J Neumann-Neudamm GmbH & Co KG, pg 264
nymphenburger, pg 266
Oekotopia Verlag, Wolfgang Hoffman GmbH & Co KG, pg 266
Pollner Verlag, pg 271
Rossipaul Kommunikation GmbH, pg 277
Adolf Sponholtz Verlag, pg 284
Stadler Verlagsgesellschaft mbH, pg 286
Staedte-Verlag, E v Wagner und J Mitterhuber GmbH, pg 286
Stapp Verlag Wolfgang Stapp, pg 286
Steiger Verlag, pg 287
Conrad Stein Verlag GmbH, pg 287
Stoeppel Verlag-Buchvertrieb KG, pg 288
Traditionell Bogenschiessen Verlag Angelika Hornig, pg 292
Trescher Verlag GmbH, pg 292
WEKA Firmengruppe GmbH & Co KG, pg 298
Zeitgeist Media GmbH, pg 302

Ghana

World Literature Project, pg 305

Hungary

Aranyhal Konyvkiado Goldfish Publishing, pg 320

PUBLISHERS

Ireland
Tir Eolas, pg 363

Israel
Bitan Publishers Ltd, pg 365

Italy
Athesia Verlag Bozen, pg 377
Il Castello srl, pg 380
Giovanni De Vecchi Editore SpA, pg 384
Ediciclo Editore SRL, pg 386
Editoriale Olimpia SpA, pg 401
RCS Libri SpA, pg 405
Tappeiner, pg 409
Zanfi-Logos, pg 412

Japan
Gakken Co Ltd, pg 417
Seibido Shuppan Company Ltd, pg 426

Republic of Korea
Pyeong-hwa Chulpansa, pg 442
Samho Music Publishing Co Ltd, pg 442

Malta
Publishers' Enterprises Group (PEG) Ltd, pg 460

Mexico
Editorial Jilguero, SA de CV, pg 467

New Caledonia
Savannah Editions SARL, pg 493

New Zealand
Barkfire Press, pg 494
Bush Press Communications Ltd, pg 494
Craig Potton Publishing, pg 495
Exisle Publishing Ltd, pg 496
Halcyon Publishing Ltd, pg 496
Nelson Price Milburn Ltd, pg 499
Reed Publishing (NZ) Ltd, pg 500
Shoal Bay Press Ltd, pg 501
Tandem Press, pg 501

Oman
Apex Press & Publishing, pg 511

Poland
Oficyna Wydawnicza Read Me, pg 526

Romania
Corint Publishing Group, pg 539
Editura Niculescu, pg 541

Russian Federation
Izdatelstvo Fizkultura i Sport, pg 545

Slovakia
Vydavatepstvo Praca spol sro, pg 560
Priroda Publishing, pg 560
Ustav informacii a prognoz skolstva mladeze a telovychovy, pg 561

Spain
Editorial Mediterrania SL, pg 591
Noguer y Caralt Editores SA, pg 593

OASIS, Producciones Generales de Comunicacion, pg 593
Editora Regional de Murcia - ERM, pg 597
Tursen, SA, pg 603
Ediciones Tutor SA, pg 603

Switzerland
Mueller Rueschlikon Verlags AG, pg 629
Rotpunktverlag, pg 632
Sinwel-Buchhandlung Verlag, pg 634

Trinidad & Tobago
Joan Bacchus-Xavier, pg 646

Tunisia
Les Editions de l'Arbre, pg 647

United Kingdom
Adlard Coles Nautical, pg 655
Batsford Ltd, pg 663
BCA - Book Club Associates, pg 663
Blandford Publishing Ltd, pg 668
Blorenge Books, pg 668
Bradt Travel Guides Ltd, pg 670
Cassell & Co, pg 675
Cicerone Press, pg 680
Coachwise Ltd, pg 680
Cordee Ltd, pg 683
The Crowood Press Ltd, pg 684
David & Charles Ltd, pg 686
Eaglemoss Publications Ltd, pg 689
Geiser Productions, pg 699
Gollancz/Witherby, pg 701
HarperCollins UK, pg 705
Haynes Publishing, pg 706
Luath Press Ltd, pg 722
Mercat Press, pg 726
Neil Wilson Publishing Ltd, pg 732
Parapress Ltd, pg 738
Quarto Publishing plc, pg 746
Quiller Publishing Ltd, pg 747
Quintet Publishing Ltd, pg 747
Rough Guides Ltd, pg 751
Scarthin Books, pg 754
Sheldrake Press, pg 757
Sigma Press, pg 758
Thistle Press, pg 765
Vacation Work Publications, pg 769
Veloce Publishing Ltd, pg 769
Ward Lock Ltd, pg 771
Wharncliffe Publishing Ltd, pg 772

PARAPSYCHOLOGY

Argentina
Editorial Kier SACIFI, pg 7
Editorial Planeta Argentina SAIC, pg 8

Australia
Angel Publications, pg 11
Gnostic Editions, pg 23
Hihorse Publishing Pty Ltd, pg 25
Unity Press, pg 44
Wileman Publications, pg 46

Austria
Edition S der OSD, pg 50
Resch Verlag, pg 56

Belarus
Belaruskaya Encyklapedyya, pg 62

Belgium
Parsifal BVBA, pg 71

Brazil
Editora Elevacao, pg 81
IBRASA (Instituicao Brasileira de Difusao Cultural Ltda), pg 83
Editora Lidador Ltda, pg 85
Editora Meca Ltda, pg 86
Editora Mercuryo Ltda, pg 86

Bulgaria
Aratron, IK, pg 93
Kibea Publishing Co, pg 95
Kralica MAB, pg 95
Litera Prima, pg 95
Sila & Zivot, pg 97

Czech Republic
Chvojkova nakladatelstvi, pg 123
Columbus, pg 123

Estonia
Kupar Publishers, pg 139

France
Editions Amrita SA, pg 146
Editions du Chariot, pg 153
Editions de Compostelle, pg 155
Editions Dangles SA-Edilarge SA, pg 157
De Vecchi Editions SA, pg 157
Editions Jacques Grancher, pg 165
Editions Lacour-Olle, pg 170
Editions Pygmalion, pg 182
Editions Saint-Michel SA, pg 183

Germany
Aquamarin Verlag, pg 193
Verlag Hermann Bauer Gmbh & Co KG, pg 197
Buchverlage Langen-Mueller/ Herbig, pg 205
Connection Medien GmbH, pg 209
Dagmar Dreves Verlag, pg 210
Divyanand Verlags GmbH, pg 215
Verlag Esoterische Philosophie GmbH, pg 221
EVT Energy Video Training & Verlag GmbH, pg 222
Verlag der Stiftung Gralsbotschaft GmbH, pg 231
AIG I Hilbinger Verlag GmbH, pg 237
F Hirthammer Verlag GmbH, pg 238
Lorber-Verlag & Turm-Verlag Otto Zluhan, pg 255
Merlin Verlag Andreas Meyer Verlags GmbH und Co KG, pg 259
Neue Erde Verlags GmbH, pg 264
Reichl Verlag Der Leuchter, pg 274
Heinrich Schwab Verlag KG, pg 282
Die Silberschnur Verlag GmbH, pg 283
Spieth-Verlag Verlag fuer Symbolforschung, pg 284
Mario Truant Verlag, pg 292

Greece
Ed Nea Acropolis, pg 310

Iceland
Bokaforlag Birtingur, pg 325

India
Pustak Mahal, pg 345
Scientific Book Agency, pg 348
Somaiya Publications Pvt Ltd, pg 349
Theosophical Publishing House, pg 351

Italy
L'Airone Editrice, pg 375
Gruppo Editoriale Armenia SpA, pg 376
Crisalide, pg 383
l'Eta dell'Acquario, pg 388
Hermes Edizioni SRL, pg 392
Edizioni Mediterranee SRL, pg 398
Reverdito Edizioni, pg 405

Latvia
Vieda, SIA, pg 445

Lithuania
AS Narbuto Leidykla (AS Narbutas' Publishers), pg 448

The Former Yugoslav Republic of Macedonia
Zumpres Publishing Firm, pg 453

Mexico
Centro Editorial Mexicano Osiris SA, pg 463
Editorial Diana SA de CV, pg 464
Edamex SA de CV, pg 464
Editorial Orion, pg 469

Netherlands
Ankh-Hermes BV, pg 477

Norway
Hilt & Hansteen A/S, pg 509

Paraguay
Intercontinental Editora, pg 516

Philippines
Rex Bookstores & Publishers, pg 520

Poland
Iskry - Publishing House Ltd spotka zoo, pg 523

Portugal
Editorial Estampa, Lda, pg 531
Edicoes 70 Lda, pg 535

Romania
Editura Excelsior Art, pg 539
Saeculum IO, pg 542
Vestala Verlag, pg 543
Vremea Publishers Ltd, pg 543

Slovakia
Vydavatelstvo Obzor, pg 560

Slovenia
Zalozba Mihelac d o o, pg 562

Spain
Editorial 'Alas', pg 571
Casset Ediciones SL, pg 576
Edicomunicacion SA, pg 581
Nueva Acropolis, pg 593
Obelisco Ediciones S, pg 593
Grup 62, pg 600

SUBJECT INDEX

Switzerland
Ariston Editions, pg 617
Govinda-Verlag, pg 624
Origo Verlag, pg 630
Scherz Verlag AG, pg 633
Tobler Verlag, pg 635
Editions Vivez Soleil SA, pg 636

Togo
Editions Akpagnon, pg 646

Turkey
Ruh ve Madde Yayinlari ve Saglik Hizmetleri AS, pg 651

Ukraine
ASK Ltd, pg 653

United Kingdom
Amber Books Ltd, pg 657
Capall Bann Publishing, pg 674
Mandrake of Oxford, pg 725
The Society of Metaphysicians Ltd, pg 759
University of Hertfordshire Press, pg 768

PHILOSOPHY

Albania
NL SH, pg 1

Algeria
Enterprise Nationale du Livre (ENAL), pg 2

Argentina
Editorial Abaco de Rodolfo Depalma SRL, pg 2
Abeledo-Perrot SAE e I, pg 2
Aguilar Altea Taurus Alfaguara SA de Ediciones, pg 3
Alianza Editorial de Argentina SA, pg 3
Amorrortu Editores SA, pg 3
Editorial Astrea de Alfredo y Ricardo Depalma SRL, pg 3
Bonum Editorial SACI, pg 4
Editorial Claridad SA, pg 4
Club de Lectores, pg 4
Diana Argentina SA, Editorial, pg 5
Edicial SA, pg 5
EUDEBA (Editorial Universitaria de Buenos Aires), pg 5
Ediciones de la Flor SRL, pg 6
Editorial Guadalupe, pg 6
Editorial Idearium de la Universidad de Mendoza (EDIUM), pg 6
La Ley SA Editora e Impresora, pg 7
Editorial Losada SA, pg 7
Marymar Ediciones SA, pg 7
Editorial Paidos SAICF, pg 8
Editorial Plus Ultra SA, pg 8
Editorial Sudamericana SA, pg 9
Editoria Universitaria de la Patagonia, pg 9

Australia
Michelle Anderson Publishing, pg 11
Angel Publications, pg 11
Bridge To Peace Publications, pg 16
Catholic Institute of Sydney, pg 17
Crystal Publishing, pg 19
Experimental Art Foundation, pg 22
Freshet Press, pg 23
Gnostic Editions, pg 23

Hale & Iremonger Pty Ltd, pg 24
In-Tune Books, pg 26
Inwardpath Publishers, pg 27
Magabala Books Aboriginal Corporation, pg 30
McGraw-Hill Australia Pty Ltd, pg 31
Newman Centre Publications, pg 33
Quakers Hill Press, pg 38
Tamarind Publications, pg 42
Thin Rich Press, pg 43
Unity Press, pg 44

Austria
Verlag Alexander Bernhardt, pg 48
Bethania Verlag, pg 48
Franz Deuticke Verlagsgesmbh, pg 50
Diotima Presse, pg 50
Edition Ergo Sum, pg 50
Gerold & Co, pg 51
Haymon-Verlag GesmbH, pg 51
Verlag Hoelder-Pichler-Tempsky, pg 52
Milena Verlag, pg 54
Verlag Monte Verita, pg 54
Mueller-Speiser Wissenschaftlicher Verlag, pg 54
Oesterreichischer Bundesverlag Gmbh, pg 55
Verlag Oldenbourg, pg 56
Verlag des Osterr Kneippbundes GmbH, pg 56
Passagen Verlag GmbH, pg 56
Verlag Anton Pustet, pg 56
Springer-Verlag Wien, pg 58
Studien Verlag Gmbh, pg 58
Verlag Styria, pg 58
Edition Va Bene, pg 59
Verband der Wissenschaftlichen Gesellschaften Oesterreichs (VWGOe), pg 59
WUV/Facultas Universitaetsverlag, pg 60

Bangladesh
Agamee Prakashani, pg 61

Belgium
Uitgeverij Acco, pg 62
Altina, pg 63
Maison d'Editions Baha'ies ASBL, pg 63
Brepols Publishers NV, pg 64
Editions De Boeck-Larcier SA, pg 66
Maison d'Editions Claude Dejaie, pg 66
Editions les Eperonniers, pg 67
Espace de Libertes, pg 67
Imprimerie Hayez SPRL, pg 68
Infoboek NV, pg 68
Koninklijke Vlaamse Academie van Belgie voor Wetenschappen en Kunsten, pg 69
Editions Labor, pg 69
Editions Lessius ASBL, pg 70
Leuven University Press, pg 70
Editeurs de Litterature Biblique, pg 70
La Longue Vue, pg 70
Mardaga, Pierre, Editeur, pg 71
Nauwelaerts Edition SA, pg 71
Paradox Pers vzw, pg 71
Parsifal BVBA, pg 71
La Part de L'Oeil, pg 71
Uitgeverij Peeters Leuven (Belgie), pg 72
Pelckmans NV, De Nederlandsche Boekhandel, pg 72
Uitgeverij Pelckmans NV, pg 72

Presses Universitaires de Bruxelles asbl, pg 72
Publications des Facultes Universitaires Saint Louis, pg 72
Sonneville Press (Uitgeverij) VTW, pg 73
Editions de l'Universite de Bruxelles, pg 74
Vita, pg 74
VUB Brussels University Press, pg 74

Bolivia
Editorial Don Bosco, pg 75

Bosnia and Herzegovina
Bemust, pg 76
Veselin Maslesa, pg 76

Brazil
Agalma Psicanalise Editora Ltda, pg 77
AGIR S/A Editora, pg 77
Editora Alfa Omega Ltda, pg 77
Editora Antroposofica Ltda, pg 77
Associacao Palas Athena do Brasil, pg 78
Editora Companhia das Letras/Editora Schwarcz Ltda, pg 80
Livraria Duas Cidades Ltda, pg 80
E P U Editora Pedagogica e Universitaria Ltd, pg 81
Edicon Editora e Consultorial Ltda, pg 81
Companhia Editora Forense, pg 81
EDUSC - Editora da Universidade do Sagrado Coracao, pg 81
Editora Elevacao, pg 81
Livraria Martins Fontes Editora Ltda, pg 81
Editora Forense Universitaria Ltda, pg 81
Fundacao Cultural Avatar, pg 82
Fundacao Sao Paulo, EDUC, pg 82
Editora Gente Livraria e Editora Ltda, pg 82
Edicoes Graal Ltda, pg 83
Ordem do Graal na Terra, pg 83
Editora Ground Ltda, pg 83
Hemus Editora Ltda, pg 83
Livro Ibero-Americano Ltda, pg 83
IBRASA (Instituicao Brasileira de Difusao Cultural Ltda), pg 83
Imago Editora Importacao e Exportacao Ltda, pg 84
LDA Editores Ltda, pg 84
Editora Logosofica, pg 85
Edicoes Loyola SA, pg 85
Cia Editora Nacional, pg 87
Editora Nova Alexandria Ltda, pg 87
Editora Nova Fronteira SA, pg 87
Pallas Editora e Distribuidora Ltda, pg 88
Paulus Editora, pg 88
Editora Paz e Terra, pg 88
Editora Perspectiva, pg 88
Distribuidora Record de Servicos de Imprensa SA, pg 89
Saraiva SA, Livreiros Editores, pg 90
34 Literatura S/C Ltda, pg 91
Editora UNESP, pg 91
Editora da Universidade de Sao Paulo, pg 91
Editora Vecchi SA, pg 92
Editora Vigilia Ltda, pg 92
Vozes Editora Ltda, pg 92
Jorge Zahar Editor, pg 92

Bulgaria
Antroposofsko Izdatelstvo Dimo R Daskalov OOD, pg 93
Bilblioteka Nov den - Sajuz na Svobodnite Demokrati (Union of Free Democrats), pg 93
EA EOOD, pg 94
Eurasia Academic Publishers, pg 94
Hriker, pg 94
Publishing House Hristo Botev, pg 94
Kibea Publishing Co, pg 95
Kralica MAB, pg 95
LIK Izdanija, pg 95
Makros 2000 - Plovdiv, pg 95
Mladezh IK, pg 95
Naouka i Izkoustvo, Ltd, pg 95
Nov Covek Publishing House, pg 96
Prozoretz Ltd Publishing House, pg 96
Sila & Zivot, pg 97

Burundi
Editions Intore, pg 98

Chile
Arrayan Editores, pg 98
Edeval (Universidad de Valparaiso), pg 99
Pehuen Editores Ltda, pg 100
Pontificia Universidad Catolica de Chile, pg 100
Ediciones Universitarias de Valparaiso, pg 100

China
Anhui People's Publishing House, pg 101
Beijing Publishing House, pg 101
China Social Sciences Publishing House, pg 103
Foreign Languages Press, pg 104
Fudan University Press, pg 104
Lanzhou University Press, pg 106
SDX (Shenghuo-Dushu-Xinzhi) Joint Publishing Co, pg 107
Shandong University Press, pg 108

Colombia
Consejo Episcopal Latinoamericano (CELAM), pg 110
Fundacion Universidad de la Sabana Ediciones INSE, pg 111
Instituto Misionerao Hijas De San Pablo, pg 111
Siglo XXI Editores de Colombia Ltda, pg 112
Universidad de Antioquia, Division Publicaciones, pg 113
Universidad Nacional Abierta y a Distancia, pg 113

The Democratic Republic of the Congo
Presses Universitaires du Zaiire (PUZ), pg 114

Costa Rica
Ediciones Promesa, pg 116
Editorial Universidad Estatal a Distancia (EUNED), pg 116

Cote d'Ivoire
Centre d'Edition et de Diffusion Africaines, pg 117

Croatia
AGM doo, pg 117
ArTresor naklada, pg 117
Durieux d o o, pg 118

PUBLISHERS SUBJECT INDEX

Faust Vrani, pg 118
Globus-Nakladni zavod, pg 118
Izdavacka Delatnost Hrvatske Akademije Znanosti I Umjetnosti, pg 118
Hrvatsko filozofsko drustvo, pg 118
Matica hrvatska, pg 118
Mladost d d Izdavacku grafiku i informaticku djelatnost, pg 119
Naklada Ljevak doo, pg 119
Skolska Knjiga, pg 119

Cuba

Casa Editora Abril, pg 120
Editora Politica, pg 120

Czech Republic

Academia, pg 122
AULOS sro, pg 122
Aurora, pg 122
Barrister & Principal, pg 122
Brody, pg 122
Dimenze 2 Plus 2 Praha, pg 123
Inspirace, pg 124
Kalich SRO, pg 124
Karolinum, nakladatelstvi, pg 124
Konsultace spol sro, pg 125
Lyra Pragensis Obecne Prospelna Spolecnost, pg 125
Melantrich, akc spol, pg 125
Mlada fronta, pg 125
Nase vojsko, nakladatelstvi a knizni obchod, pg 126
Omnipress Praha, pg 126
Pragma 4, pg 126
Prostor, nakladatelstvi sro, pg 127
Slon Sociologicke Nakladatelstvi, pg 127
Svoboda Servis GmbH, pg 127
Vodnar, pg 128
Votobia sro, pg 128
Vysehrad spol sro, pg 128

Denmark

Aarhus Universitetsforlag, pg 128
Akademisk Forlag A/S, pg 128
Borgens Forlag A/S, pg 129
Forlaget GMT, pg 131
Gyldendalske Boghandel - Nordisk Forlag A/S, pg 131
Forlaget Hovedland, pg 132
Museum Tusculanum Press, pg 133
New Era Publications International ApS, pg 133
Nyt Nordisk Forlag Arnold Busck A/S, pg 133
Politisk Revy, pg 133
C A Reitzel Boghandel & Forlag A/S, pg 134
Hans Reitzel Publishers Ltd, pg 134
Det Schonbergske Forlag A/S, pg 134
Syddansk Universitetsforlag, pg 135
Systime, pg 135

Dominican Republic

Pontificia Universidad Catolica Madre y Maestra, pg 136
Sociedad Editorial Americana, pg 136

Ecuador

Corporacion Editora Nacional, pg 136
Libresa S A, pg 137
Pontificia Universidad Catolica del Ecuador, Centro de Publicaciones, pg 137

Egypt (Arab Republic of Egypt)

Al Arab Publishing House, pg 137
Middle East Book Centre, pg 138

El Salvador

UCA Editores, pg 138
Editorial Universitaria de la Universidad de El Salvador, pg 139

Estonia

Eesti Entsuklopeediakirjastus, pg 139
Ilmamaa, pg 139
Olion Publishers, pg 140
Tuum, pg 140

Finland

Basam Books Oy, pg 141
Schildts Forlags AB, pg 144
Soderstroms Forlag, pg 144
Osuuskunta Vastapaino, pg 144

France

ADPF Publications, pg 145
Editions d'Amerique et d'Orient, Adrien Maisonneuve, pg 146
Editions Amrita SA, pg 146
L'Anabase, pg 146
Editions Anthropos, pg 147
L'Arche Editeur, pg 147
Atelier National de Reproduction des Theses, pg 148
Editions de l'Aube, pg 148
Editions Aubier-Montaigne SA, pg 148
Autrement Editions, pg 148
Societe d'Edition Les Belles Lettres, pg 149
Berg International Editeur, pg 149
William Blake & Co, pg 150
Presses Universitaires de Bordeaux (PUB), pg 150
Editions Breal, pg 151
Alain Brethes Editions, pg 151
Editions Calmann-Levy SA, pg 152
Editions Caracteres, pg 152
Centre pour l'Innovation et la Recherche en Communication de l'Entreprise (CIRCE), pg 152
Editions du Cerf, pg 153
Editions Jacqueline Chambon, pg 153
Editions Champ Vallon, pg 153
Chronique Sociale, pg 154
CNRS Editions, pg 155
Armand Colin, Editeur, pg 155
Editions de Compostelle, pg 155
Editions Copernic, pg 155
Editions Courrier du Livre, pg 156
Editions La Decouverte, pg 157
Editions Denoel, pg 157
Desclee Editions, pg 158
Editions Dis Voir, pg 158
Editions de l'Eclat, pg 159
Editions et Publications de l'Ecole Lacanienne (EPEL), pg 159
Les Editions de Minuit SA, pg 160
Editions rue d'Ulm, pg 160
L'Ere Nouvelle, pg 161
Editions Eres, pg 162
Institut d'Etudes Augustiniennes, pg 162
Editions Fata Morgana, pg 162
Librairie Artheme Fayard, pg 163
Federation d'Activities Culturelles, Fac Editions, pg 163
Librairie Fischbacher, International Art Book Distribution (import-export), pg 163
Editions Jacques Gabay, pg 164

Editions Galilee, pg 164
Editions Gallimard, pg 164
Gammaprim, pg 165
Editions Ganymede, pg 165
Paul Geuthner Librairie Orientaliste, pg 165
Hachette Livre, pg 167
Editions de l'Herne, pg 167
Editions Imago, pg 168
Jouvence Editions, pg 170
Editions Fernand Lanore Sarl, pg 171
Librairie Scientifique et Technique Albert Blanchard, pg 172
Le Livre de Poche-L G F (Librairie Generale Francaise), pg 173
Maison de la Revelation, pg 173
Mercure de France SA, pg 175
Editions Albin Michel, pg 175
Presses Universitaires du Mirail, pg 176
Editions Modernes Media, pg 176
Editions Fernand Nathan, pg 176
Nil Editions, pg 177
Editions Mare Nostrum, pg 177
Editions Odile Jacob, pg 177
Editions de l'Orante, pg 178
L'Originel - Editions Accarias, pg 178
Editions Paradigme, pg 178
Payot & Rivages, pg 179
Peeters-France, pg 179
Jean-Michel Place, pg 180
Presence Africaine Editions, pg 180
Presses de la Renaissance, pg 181
Presses Universitaires de Caen, pg 181
Presses Universitaires de France (PUF), pg 181
Presses Universitaires de Nancy, pg 181
Presses Universitaires de Strasbourg, pg 182
Presses Universitaires du Septentrion, pg 182
Editions Prosveta, pg 182
Editions Roudil SA, pg 183
Editions Saint-Paul SA, pg 183
Service Technique pour l'Education, pg 184
Editions du Seuil, pg 184
Editions Andre Silvaire Sarl, pg 185
Societe des Editions Grasset et Fasquelle, pg 185
Publications de la Sorbonne, pg 185
Association d'Editions Sorg, pg 186
Editions SOS (Editions du Secours Catholique), pg 186
Librairie Pierre Tequi et Editions Tequi, pg 187
Transeuropeennes/RCE, pg 188
Universitas, pg 188
Editions Verdier, pg 188
Librairie Philosophique J Vrin, pg 189

Germany

A Francke Verlag (Tubingen und Basel), pg 190
Accedo Verlagsgesellschaft mbH, pg 190
AGIS Verlag GmbH, pg 191
Aisthesis Verlag, pg 191
Akademie Verlag GmbH, pg 191
Verlag Karl Alber GmbH, pg 191
Aquamarin Verlag, pg 193
Argument-Verlag, pg 194
Arun-Verlag, pg 194
Aschendorffsche Verlagsbuchhandlung GmbH & Co KG, pg 194
Asclepios Edition Lothar Baus, pg 194

Otto Wilhelm Barth-Verlag KG, pg 197
Verlag Hermann Bauer GmbH & Co KG, pg 197
Dr Wolfgang Baur Verlag Kunst & Alltag, pg 198
Bayerischer Schulbuch-Verlag GmbH, pg 198
Verlag C H Beck oHG, pg 198
Berliner Debatte Wissenschafts Verlag, GSFP-Gesellschaft fur Sozialwissen-schaftliche Forschung und Publizistik mbH & Co KG, pg 199
Berliner Wissenschafts-Verlag GmbH (BWV), pg 199
Betzel Verlag GmbH, pg 200
Biblio Verlag, pg 200
Verlag Die Blaue Eule, pg 202
Klaus Boer Verlag, pg 203
Buechse der Pandora Verlags-GmbH, pg 205
Ulrich Burgdorf/Homeopathic Publishing House, pg 206
Caann Verlag, Klaus Wagner, pg 206
Campus Verlag GmbH, pg 207
Carl-Auer-Systeme Verlag, pg 207
Fachverlag Hans Carl GmbH, pg 207
J G Cotta'sche Buchhandlung Nachfolger GmbH, pg 210
Verlag Darmstaedter Blaetter Schwarz und Co, pg 210
Das Arsenal, Verlag fuer Kultur und Politik GmbH, pg 210
Verlag Deutsche Unitarier, pg 212
Deutsche Verlags-Anstalt GmbH (DVA), pg 212
Deutscher Taschenbuch Verlag GmbH & Co KG (dtv), pg 213
Sammlung Dieterich Verlagsgesellschaft mbH, pg 214
Dieterichsche Verlagsbuchhandlung Mainz, pg 214
Dietrich zu Klampen Verlag, pg 214
Edition Diskord, pg 215
Divyanand Verlags GmbH, pg 215
Drei Eichen Verlag Manuel Kissener, pg 216
Duncker und Humblot GmbH, pg 217
Klaus D Dutz, pg 217
Eironeia-Verlag, pg 219
Elpis Verlag GmbH, pg 219
Verlag Esoterische Philosophie GmbH, pg 221
Europa Verlag GmbH, pg 222
Europaeische Verlagsanstalt GmbH & Rotbuch Verlag GmbH & Co KG, pg 222
Evangelischer Presseverband fuer Bayern eV, pg 222
Wilhelm Fink GmbH & Co Verlags-KG, pg 224
Harald Fischer Verlag GmbH, pg 224
Karin Fischer Verlag GmbH, pg 225
Flensburger Hefte Verlag GmbH, pg 225
Verlag Freies Geistesleben, pg 227
Friedrich Frommann Verlag, pg 227
Genius Verlag, pg 228
Gmelin Verlag GmbH, pg 230
Verlag der Stiftung Gralsbotschaft GmbH, pg 231
Walter de Gruyter GmbH & Co KG, pg 231
Guetersloher Verlagshaus, pg 232
Herbert von Halem Verlag, pg 233
Carl Hanser Verlag, pg 234
Verlag Hinder und Deelmann, pg 237

SUBJECT INDEX

F Hirthammer Verlag GmbH, pg 238
S Hirzel Verlag GmbH und Co, pg 238
Hoffmann und Campe Verlag GmbH, pg 238
Holos Verlag, pg 239
Horlemann Verlag, pg 239
Hyperion - Verlag, pg 240
Iudicium Verlag GmbH, pg 242
Johannes Verlag Einsiedeln, Freiburg, pg 243
Junius Verlag GmbH, pg 244
Vittorio Klostermann GmbH, pg 247
Verlagsgruppe Koehler/Mittler, pg 248
Verlag Koenigshausen und Neumann GmbH, pg 248
Koesel-Verlag GmbH & Co, pg 248
W Kohlhammer GmbH, pg 248
Kolibri-Verlag GmbH, pg 249
Anton H Konrad Verlag, pg 249
KONTEXTverlag, pg 249
Dr Anton Kovac Slavica Verlag, pg 249
Karin Kramer Verlag, pg 250
Alfred Kroner Verlag, pg 250
Peter Lang GmbH Europaeischer Verlag der Wissenschaften, pg 252
Leibniz Verlag, pg 253
Leibniz-Buecherwarte, pg 253
Leipziger Universitaetsverlag GmbH, pg 253
Dr Gisela Lermann, pg 253
Libertas- Europaeisches Institut GmbH, pg 254
Lukas Verlag fur Kunst- und Geistesgeschichte, pg 256
Maeander Verlag GmbH, pg 256
Annemarie Maeger, pg 256
Manutius Verlag, pg 257
Matthes und Seitz Verlag GmbH, pg 258
Felix Meiner Verlag GmbH, pg 258
mentis Verlag GmbH, pg 259
Merlin Verlag Andreas Meyer Verlags GmbH und Co KG, pg 259
Metropolis- Verlag fur Okonomie, Gesellschaft und Politik GmbH, pg 259
J B Metzlersche Verlagsbuchhandlung, pg 260
Preubmpassling Verlag Gisela Meussling, pg 260
Ursala Meyer und Dr Manfred Duker Ein-Fach-Verlag, pg 260
Mohr Siebeck, pg 261
Verlag Neue Kritik KG, pg 264
Neuer ISP Verlag GmbH, pg 264
Max Niemeyer Verlag GmbH, pg 265
nymphenburger, pg 266
Oekumenischer Verlag Dr R-F Edel, pg 266
Georg Olms Verlag AG, pg 267
Oros Verlag, pg 267
Osho Verlag GmbH, pg 267
Pahl-Rugenstein Verlag Nachfolger-GmbH, pg 267
Verlag Dr Friedrich Pfeil, pg 269
Philipp Reclam Jun Verlag GmbH, pg 269
Philosophia Verlag GmbH, pg 270
Piper Verlag GmbH, pg 270
Guido Pressler Verlag, pg 271
Quell Verlag, pg 273
Quelle und Meyer Verlag GmbH & Co, pg 273
Radius-Verlag GmbH, pg 273
Reclam Verlag Leipzig, pg 274

Ernst Reinhardt Verlag GmbH & Co KG, pg 275
Verlag an der Ruhr GmbH, pg 277
K G Saur Verlag GmbH, A Gale/Thomson Learning Company, pg 278
Schangrila Verlags und Vertriebs GmbH, pg 279
Ferdinand Schoeningh Verlag GmbH, pg 281
Schulz-Kirchner Verlag GmbH, pg 282
Heinrich Schwab Verlag KG, pg 282
Scientia Verlag und Antiquariat Schilling OHG, pg 282
Spieth-Verlag Verlag fuer Symbolforschung, pg 284
Springer Science+Business Media GmbH & Co KG, pg 284
Steidl Verlag, pg 287
Franz Steiner Verlag Wiesbaden GmbH, pg 287
Stern-Verlag Janssen & Co, pg 288
Suhrkamp Verlag, pg 289
Suin Buch-Verlag, pg 289
Ullstein Heyne List GmbH & Co KG, pg 293
Ulrike Helmer Verlag, pg 293
UTB fuer Wissenschaft Uni Taschenbuecher GmbH, pg 294
UVK Universitatsverlag Konstanz GmbH, pg 294
Vandenhoeck & Ruprecht, pg 294
VJK Verlag Josef Knecht Carolusdruckerei GmbH, pg 296
Ellen Vogt Garbe Verlag, pg 296
Weber Zucht & Co, pg 298
Weidler Buchverlag Berlin, pg 298
Weidmannsche Verlagsbuchhandlung GmbH, pg 298
Verlagsgruppe Weltbild GmbH, pg 298
Erich Wewel Verlag GmbH, pg 299
Wissenschaftliche Buchgesellschaft, pg 300
Verlag DAS WORT GmbH, pg 301

Greece

Alamo Hellas, pg 305
D I Arsenidis Publications, pg 306
Boukoumanis' Editions, pg 306
Dorikos Publishing House, pg 306
Ekdoseis Kazantzaki (Kazantzakis Publications), pg 307
Elliniki Leschi Tou Vivliou, pg 307
Ekdoseis Filon, pg 307
Gutenberg Publications, pg 307
Denise Harvey, pg 308
Hestia-I D Hestia-Kollaros & Co Corporation, pg 308
Ianos, pg 308
Kalentis & Sia, pg 308
Kardamitsa A, pg 309
Kastaniotis Editions SA, pg 309
Katoptro Publications, pg 309
Kedros Publishers, pg 309
Kritiki Publishing, pg 309
Morfotiko Idryma Ethnikis Trapezas, pg 310
Ed Nea Acropolis, pg 310
Nea Thesis - Evrotas, pg 310
Odysseas Publications Ltd, pg 311
Orfanidis Publications, pg 311
Patakis Publishers, pg 311
Psichogios Publications SA, pg 311
Society for Macedonian Studies, pg 312
Stochastis, pg 312
J Vassiliou Bibliopolein, pg 313

Guatemala

Grupo Editorial RIN-78, pg 313

Holy See (Vatican City State)

Biblioteca Apostolica Vaticana, pg 314
Libreria Editrice Vaticana, pg 315

Hong Kong

The Chinese University Press, pg 316
Chung Hwa Book Co (HK) Ltd, pg 316
The Dharmasthiti Buddist Institute Ltd, pg 317
Hong Kong University Press, pg 317
Ming Pao Publications Ltd, pg 318
Philopsychy Press, pg 318
The University of Hong Kong, Department of Philosophy, pg 320

Hungary

Akademiai Kiado, pg 320
Atlantisz Kiado, pg 320
Balassi Kiado Kft, pg 321
Europa Konyvkiado, pg 321
Janus Pannonius Tudomanyegyetem, pg 322
Jelenkor Verlag, pg 322
Joszoveg Muhely Kiado, pg 322
Kiiarat Konyvdiado, pg 322
Kossuth Kiado RT, pg 322
Magveto Koenyvkiado, pg 322
Nemzeti Tankoenyvkiado, pg 323
Osiris Kiado, pg 323
Typotex Kft Elektronikus Kiado, pg 324

Iceland

Bokaforlag Birtingur, pg 325
Haskolautgafan - University of Iceland Press, pg 325

India

Abhinav Publications, pg 326
Abhishek Publications, pg 327
The Academic Press, pg 327
Ajanta Publications (India), pg 327
Ananda Publishers Pvt Ltd, pg 328
APH Publishing Corp, pg 328
Asian Educational Services, pg 329
Asian Trading Corporation, pg 329
Associated Publishing House, pg 329
Atma Ram & Sons, pg 329
Authorspress, pg 329
The Bangalore Printing & Publishing Co Ltd, pg 329
Bharatiya Vidya Bhavan, pg 330
Book Circle, pg 330
Books & Books, pg 331
S Chand & Co Ltd, pg 331
Chetana Private Ltd Publishers & International Booksellers, pg 332
Chowkhamba Sanskrit Series Office, pg 332
The Christian Literature Society, pg 332
Concept Publishing Co, pg 332
Cosmo Publications, pg 332
Disha Prakashan, pg 333
DK Printworld (P) Ltd, pg 333
Ess Ess Publications, pg 334
Ganesh & Co, pg 334
Geeta Prakashan, pg 335
Gyan Publishing House, pg 335
Arnold Heinman Publishers (India) Pvt Ltd, pg 335

Heritage Publishers, pg 335
Himalayan Books, pg 336
Intellectual Publishing House, pg 338
Inter-India Publications, pg 338
Intertrade Publications Pvt Ltd, pg 338
Islamic Publishing House, pg 338
Jaico Publishing House, pg 338
Manohar Publishers & Distributors, pg 340
Sri Ramakrishna Math, pg 341
Minerva Associates (Publications) Pvt Ltd, pg 341
Motilal Banarsidass Publishers Pvt Ltd, pg 341
Mudgala Trust, pg 342
Munshiram Manoharlal Publishers Pvt Ltd, pg 342
Narosa Publishing House, pg 342
Navajivan Trust, pg 343
Navrang Booksellers & Publishers, pg 343
Omsons Publications, pg 344
Oxford University Press, pg 344
Panjab University Publication Bureau, pg 344
People's Publishing House (P) Ltd, pg 345
Rajasthan Hindi Granth Academy, pg 346
Rajesh Publications, pg 346
Rebel Publishing House Pvt Ltd, pg 346
Regency Publications, pg 346
Reliance Publishing House, pg 346
Rupa & Co, pg 347
SABDA, pg 347
Sasta Sahitya Mandal, pg 348
Sri Satguru Publications, pg 348
SBW Publishers, pg 348
Scientific Book Agency, pg 348
Somaiya Publications Pvt Ltd, pg 349
Sterling Publishers Pvt Ltd, pg 350
Theosophical Publishing House, pg 351

Indonesia

PT Bulan Bintang, pg 354
Djambatan PT, pg 354
Dunia Pustaka Jaya PT, pg 354
Eresco PT, pg 354
Pustaka Utama Grafiti, PT, pg 356
Tintamas Indonesia PT, pg 356
Yayasan Obor Indonesia, pg 357

Islamic Republic of Iran

Scientific and Cultural Publications, pg 357

Ireland

Cathedral Books Ltd, pg 358
Four Courts Press Ltd, pg 360
New Books/Connolly Books, pg 362
Publishers Group South West (Ireland), pg 363
Runa Press, pg 363
Veritas Co Ltd, pg 364

Israel

Am Oved Publishers Ltd, pg 365
Bar Ilan University Press, pg 365
The Bialik Institute, pg 365
Breslov Research Institute, pg 365
DAT Publications, pg 366
Dyonon/Papyrus Publishing House of the Tel-Aviv, pg 366
Feldheim Publishers Ltd, pg 367
Haifa University Press, pg 367

PUBLISHERS — SUBJECT INDEX

Hakibbutz Hameuchad Publishing House Ltd, pg 367
Intermedia Audio, Video Book Publishing Ltd, pg 368
The Israel Academy of Sciences & Humanities, pg 368
Keter Publishing House Ltd, pg 369
The Magnes Press, pg 370
Massada Press Ltd, pg 370
Misgav Yerushalayim, pg 370
Nehora Press, pg 371
Rav Kook Institute, pg 371
Rubin Mass Ltd, pg 371
Schocken Publishing House Ltd, pg 371
Shalem Press, pg 372
Sifriat Poalim Ltd, pg 372
Yachdav, United Publishers Co Ltd, pg 373
Y L Peretz Publishing Co, pg 373

Italy

Edizioni Abete, pg 374
Mario Adda Editore SNC, pg 374
Adea Edizioni, pg 374
Adelphi Edizioni SpA, pg 374
Aesthetica, pg 374
Edizioni ARES, pg 376
Argalia Editore delle Arti Grafiche Editoriali SRL, pg 376
Arktos, pg 376
Editore Armando Armando SRL, pg 376
Casa Editrice Astrolabio-Ubaldini Editore, pg 377
Belforte Editore Libraio srl, pg 377
Bibliopolis - Edizioni di Filosofia e Scienze Srl, pg 378
Bollati Boringhieri Editore, pg 378
Book Editore, pg 378
Bookservice, pg 378
Edizioni Borla SRL, pg 379
Bovolenta, pg 379
Bulzoni Editore SRL (Le Edizioni Universitarie d'Italia), pg 379
Edizioni Cadmo SRL, pg 379
Campanotto, pg 379
Edizioni Cantagalli, pg 379
Capone Editore SRL, pg 379
Cappelli Editore, pg 380
Casa Editrice Giuseppe Principato Spa, pg 380
CEDAM (Casa Editrice Dr A Milani), pg 380
Celuc Libri, pg 381
Centro Italiano Studi Alto Medioevo, pg 381
il Cerchio Iniziative Editoriali, pg 381
Ciranna - Roma, pg 382
Citta Nuova Editrice, pg 382
CLUEB (Cooperativa Libraria Universitaria Editrice Bologna), pg 382
Edizioni Cultura della Pace, pg 383
La Cultura Sociologica, pg 384
G De Bono Editore, pg 384
Edizioni Dedalo SRL, pg 384
Edizioni Dehoniane, pg 384
ECIG, pg 385
Editori Laterza, pg 386
Edizioni di Storia e Letteratura, pg 386
Edizioni Il Punto d'Incontro SAS, pg 386
Edizioni la Scala, pg 387
Edizioni Studio Domenicano (ESD), pg 387
EGEA (Edizioni Giuridiche Economiche Aziendali), pg 387
Giulio Einaudi Editore SpA, pg 387
Giangiacomo Feltrinelli SpA, pg 389

Arnaldo Forni Editore SRL, pg 389
Gangemi Editore spa, pg 390
Editrice Garigliano SRL, pg 390
Edizioni GB, pg 390
G Giappichelli Editore SRL, pg 390
Gius Laterza e Figli SpA, pg 391
Libreria Editrice Gregoriana, pg 391
Edizioni Guerini e Associati SpA, pg 392
Herbita Editrice di Leonardo Palermo, pg 392
Herder Editrice e Libreria, pg 392
Hopeful Monster Editore, pg 392
Ibis, pg 392
Ila - Palma, Tea Nova, pg 393
Instituti Editoriali E Poligrafici Internazionali SRL, pg 393
Editoriale Jaca Book SpA, pg 394
L Japadre Editore, pg 394
Jouvence, pg 394
Lalli Editore SRL, pg 394
Editrice LAS, pg 394
Edizioni Lavoro SRL, pg 394
LED - Edizioni Universitarie di Lettere Economia Diritto, pg 395
Casa Editrice Le Lettere SRL, pg 395
Levante Editori, pg 395
Liguori Editore SRL, pg 395
Vincenzo Lo Faro Editore, pg 395
Loescher Editore SRL, pg 396
Loffredo Editore Napoli SpA®, pg 396
Longanesi & C, pg 396
Angelo Longo Editore, pg 396
Lubrina, pg 396
Luni, pg 396
Macro Edizioni, pg 397
Manifestolibri, pg 397
Casa Editrice Marietti SpA, pg 397
Marzorati Editore SRL, pg 397
Editrice Massimo SAS di Crespi Cesare e C, pg 397
Edizioni Mediterranee SRL, pg 398
Milella di Lecce Spazio Vivo srl, pg 398
Il Minotauro, pg 398
Arnoldo Mondadori Editore SpA, pg 398
Edumond Le Monnier, pg 399
Editrice Morcelliana SpA, pg 399
Mucchi Editore SRL, pg 399
Societa Editrice Il Mulino, pg 399
Gruppo Ugo Mursia Editore SpA, pg 400
Nardini Editore srl, pg 400
Newton & Compton Editori, pg 400
Nuova Coletti Editore Roma, pg 401
La Nuova Italia Editrice SpA, pg 401
Il Nuovo Melangolo, pg 401
Leo S Olschki, pg 401
Maria Pacini Fazzi Editore, pg 402
Paideia Editrice, pg 402
Paravia Bruno Mondadori Editori, pg 402
Patron Editore SrL, pg 402
Il Poligrafo, pg 404
Pratiche Editrice, pg 404
Psicologica Editrice, pg 404
Il Punto D Incontro, pg 404
Edizioni Quattroventi SNC, pg 404
Editrice Queriniana, pg 404
Riccardo Ricciardi Editore SpA, pg 405
Edizioni Ripostes, pg 405
Editori Riuniti, pg 405
Rosenberg e Sellier Editori in Torino, pg 405
Rubbettino Editore, pg 406
Rusconi Libri Srl, pg 406
Il Saggiatore, pg 406

SAIE Editrice SRL, pg 406
Editoriale San Giusto SRL Edizioni Parnaso, pg 406
Edizioni San Paolo SRL, pg 407
Edizioni Scientifiche Italiane, pg 407
Editrice la Scuola SpA, pg 407
SEMAR Publishers SRL, pg 408
Sicania, pg 408
Edizioni Librarie Siciliane, pg 408
Societa Editrice Internazionale - SEI, pg 408
Edizioni Rosminiane Sodalitas, pg 408
Spirali Edizioni, pg 409
Edizioni Studium SRL, pg 409
Sugarco Edizioni SRL, pg 409
TEA Tascabili degli Editori Associati SpA, pg 409
Tilgher-Genova sas, pg 410
Editrice Tirrenia Stampatori SAS, pg 410
Giovanni Tranchida Editore, pg 410
Transeuropa, pg 410
Unipress, pg 411
Urbaniana University Press, pg 411
UTET (Unione Tipografico-Editrice Torinese), pg 411
Vita e Pensiero, pg 412
Vivere In SRL, pg 412
Zanichelli Editore SpA, pg 412
Edizioni Zara, pg 412

Japan

Aoki Shoten Co Ltd, pg 415
Chikuma Shobo Publishing Co Ltd, pg 416
Chuokoron-Shinsha Inc, pg 416
Fukumura Shuppan Inc, pg 417
Fuzambo Publishing Co, pg 417
GakuseiSha Publishing Co Ltd, pg 417
Hakusui-Sha Co Ltd, pg 417
Hayakawa Publishing Inc, pg 418
Heibonsha Ltd, Publishers, pg 418
The Hokuseido Press, pg 418
Horitsu Bunka-Sha, pg 418
Hyoronsha Publishing Co Ltd, pg 418
Iwanami Shoten, Publishers, pg 419
Kawade Shobo Shinsha Publishers, pg 420
Kazamashobo Co Ltd, pg 420
Keisuisha Publishing Company Ltd, pg 420
Kinokuniya Co Ltd (Publishing Department), pg 421
Kodansha International Ltd, pg 421
Kodansha Ltd, pg 421
Kosei Publishing Co Ltd, pg 421
Koseisha-Koseikaku Co Ltd, pg 422
Koyo Shobo, pg 422
Meiji Shoin Co Ltd, pg 422
Minerva Shobo Co Ltd, pg 422
Mirai-Sha, pg 422
Myrtos Inc, pg 423
Otsuki Shoten Publishers, pg 425
President Inc, pg 425
Riso-Sha, pg 425
Sangyo-Tosho Publishing Co Ltd, pg 426
Sanshusha Publishing Co, Ltd, pg 426
Shibun-Do, pg 427
Shimizu-Shoin, pg 427
Mitsumura Suiko Shoin, pg 428
Shufu-to-Seikatsu Sha Ltd, pg 428
The Simul Press Inc, pg 428
Sobun-Sha, pg 428
Sogensha Publishing Co, Ltd, pg 428
Surugadai-Shuppan Sha, pg 429
Taimeido Publishing Co Ltd, pg 429

Tamagawa University Press, pg 429
Tankosha Publishing Co Ltd, pg 429
Toho Book Store, pg 429
Toho Shuppan, pg 429
Tokai University Press, pg 429
Tokyo Sogensha Co Ltd, pg 430
University of Tokyo Press, pg 430
Waseda University Press, pg 431

Jordan

Al-Tanwir Al Ilmi (Scientific Enlightenment Publishing House), pg 432

Kazakstan

Al-Farabi Kazakh National University, pg 432

Kenya

Action Publishers, pg 433
Heinemann Kenya Ltd (EAEP), pg 434
Nairobi University Press, pg 435
Shirikon Publishers, pg 436

Democratic People's Republic of Korea

Academy of Sciences Publishing House, pg 436
The Foreign Language Press Group, pg 436
Korea Science and Encyclopedia Publishing House, pg 436

Republic of Korea

Bakyoung Publishing Co, pg 437
Bum-Woo Publishing Co, pg 437
Chong No Books Publishing Co Ltd, pg 438
Chung Rim Publishing Co Ltd, pg 438
Dae Won Sa Co Ltd, pg 438
Dong Hwa Publishing Co, pg 438
Eulyu Publishing Co Ltd, pg 438
Ewha Womans University Press, pg 438
Gim-Yeong Co, pg 438
Hangil Art Vision, pg 439
Hanul Publishing Co, pg 439
Hw Moon Publishing Co, pg 439
Hyun Am Publishing Co, pg 439
Iljisa Publishing House, pg 439
Jeong-eum Munhwasa, pg 439
Korea University Press, pg 440
Koreaone Press Inc, pg 440
Kyungnam University Press, pg 441
Min-eumsa Publishing Co Ltd, pg 441
Munhag-gwan, pg 441
Munye Publishing Co, pg 441
Prompter Publications, pg 442
St Pauls, pg 442
Seogwangsa, pg 442
Seoul National University Press, pg 443
Sohaksa, pg 443
Yonsei University Press, pg 444

Latvia

Preses Nams, pg 445
Vieda, SIA, pg 445

Lebanon

Arab Institute for Research & Publishing, pg 445
Dar-El-Machreq Sarl, pg 446
Librairie Orientale sal, pg 446
World Book Publishing, pg 447

Lithuania
Academia, pg 448
Baltos Lankos, pg 449
Eugrimas, pg 449
Klaipedos Universiteto Leidykla, pg 449
Tyto Alba Publishers, pg 450
Vaga Ltd, pg 450

Luxembourg
Editions APESS ASBL, pg 450
Essay und Zeitgeist Verlag, pg 451

The Former Yugoslav Republic of Macedonia
Ktitor, pg 452
Nov svet (New World), pg 453
Zumpres Publishing Firm, pg 453

Malaysia
Penerbit Jayatinta Sdn Bhd, pg 458
Vinpress Sdn Bhd, pg 459

Mauritius
Editions de l'Ocean Indien Ltd, pg 461

Mexico
Aguilar Altea Taurus Alfaguara SA de CV, pg 462
Libreria y Ediciones Botas SA, pg 462
El Colegio de Mexico AC, pg 463
Publicaciones Cruz O SA, pg 463
Editorial Diana SA de CV, pg 464
El Colegio de Michoacan A C, pg 464
Editorial Extemporaneos SA, pg 465
Fondo de Cultura Economica, pg 465
Editorial Joaquin Mortiz SA de CV, pg 467
Editorial Jus SA de CV, pg 467
Phillip Richard Conover Lazo, pg 467
Editorial Orion, pg 469
Editorial Patria SA de CV, pg 470
Ediciones Promesa, SA de CV, pg 470
Siglo XXI Editores SA de CV, pg 472
Universidad Nacional Autonoma de Mexico (National University of Mexico), pg 472
Universidad Veracruzana Direccion General Editorial y de Publicaciones, pg 472

Monaco
Les Editions du Rocher, pg 474

Morocco
Dar El Kitab, pg 474
Edition Diffusion de Livre au Maroc, pg 474

Nepal
International Standards Books & Periodicals (P) Ltd, pg 476

Netherlands
Uitgeverij Ambo BV, pg 477
Ankh-Hermes BV, pg 477
APA (Academic Publishers Associated), pg 477
Uitgeverij de Arbeiderspers, pg 477
John Benjamins BV, pg 479
Erven J Bijleveld, pg 479
Boom Uitgeverij, pg 479
A W Bruna Uitgevers BV, pg 480
Buijten en Schipperheijn BV Drukkerij en Uitgeversmaatschappij, pg 480
BZZTOH Publishers, pg 480
Uitgeverij Christofoor, pg 480
Uitgeverij Coutinho BV, pg 481
Uitgeverij en boekhandel Van Gennep BV, pg 482
Uitgeverij Ten Have, pg 483
HES & De Graaf Publishers BV, pg 483
Historische Uitgeverij, pg 483
Mirananda Publishers BV, pg 486
Uitgeverij H Nelissen BV, pg 486
Picaron Editions, pg 487
Prometheus, pg 488
Segment BV, pg 488
Uitgeverij SUN, pg 489
Telos Boeken, pg 490
Tilburg University Press, pg 490
Tirion Uitgevers BV, pg 490
Van Gorcum & Comp BV, pg 491
Uitgeverij Van Wijnen, pg 491
VU Boekhandel/Uitgeverij BV, pg 492
Wereldbibliotheek, pg 492

New Zealand
Brookfield Press, pg 494
Gnostic Press Ltd, pg 496

Nigeria
Evans Brothers (Nigeria Publishers) Ltd, pg 504
Ibadan University Press, pg 505
International Publishing & Research Company, pg 505
Obafemi Awolowo University Press Ltd, pg 506
University Publishing Co, pg 507

Norway
Aschehoug Forlag, pg 508
H Aschehoug & Co (W Nygaard) A/S, pg 508
Det Norske Samlaget, pg 508
Glydendal Akademisk, pg 509
Gyldendal Norsk Forlag A/S, pg 509
Pax Forlag A/S, pg 510
Teknologisk Forlag, pg 510
Universitetsforlaget, pg 511

Pakistan
Publishers United Pvt Ltd, pg 514

Panama
Editorial Universitaria, pg 515

Peru
Fondo Editorial de la Pontificia Universidad Catolica del Peru, pg 517
Editorial Horizonte, pg 517
Sur Casa de Estudios del Socialismo, pg 517

Philippines
Communication Foundation for Asia Media Group (CFAMG), pg 518
De La Salle University, pg 519
New Day Publishers, pg 520
Our Lady of Manaoag Publisher, pg 520
University of the Philippines Press, pg 521
UST Publishing House, pg 521
Vera-Reyes Inc, pg 521

Poland
Impuls, pg 523
Instytut Wydawniczy Pax, Inco-Veritas, pg 523
Iskry - Publishing House Ltd spotka zoo, pg 523
Katolicki Uniwersytet Wydawniczo-Redakcja, pg 523
'Ksiazka i Wiedza' Spotdzielnia Wydawniczo-Handlowa, pg 524
Ossolineum Zaklad Narodowy im Ossolinskich - Wydawnictwo, pg 525
Pallottinum Wydawnictwo Stowarzyszenia Apostolstwa Katolickiego, pg 525
Polish Scientific Publishers PWN, pg 525
Przedsiebiorstwo Wydawniczo-Handlowe Wydawnictwo Siedmiorog, pg 526
Spoleczny Instytut Wydawniczy Znak, pg 526
Oficyna Wydawnicza Szkoly Glownej Handlowej w Warszawie Oficyna Wydawnicza SGH, pg 527

Portugal
Armenio Amado Editora de Simoes, Beirao & Ca Lda, pg 528
Brasilia Editora (J Carvalho Branco), pg 529
Edicoes Colibri, pg 530
Constancia Editores, SA, pg 530
Edicoes Cosmos, pg 530
Editorial Estampa, Lda, pg 531
Publicacoes Europa-America Lda, pg 531
Editorial Franciscana, pg 531
Gradiva-Publicacnoes Lda, pg 532
Guimaraes Editores, Lda, pg 532
Imprensa Nacional-Casa da Moeda, pg 532
Editorial Inquerito Lda, pg 532
Edicoes Manuel Lencastre, pg 532
Livraria Apostolado da Imprensa, pg 533
Livraria Minerva, pg 533
Editora Livros do Brasil Sarl, pg 533
Livraria Tavares Martins, pg 533
Internationale Nouvelle Acropole, pg 534
Editorial Presenca, pg 535
Publicacoes Dom Quixote Lda, pg 535
Sa da Costa Livraria, pg 535
Edicoes 70 Lda, pg 535
Edicoes Silabo, pg 536
Teorema, pg 536
Usus Editora, pg 536
Vega-Publicacao e Distribuicao de Livros e Revistas, Lda, pg 536
Livraria Verdade e Vida Editora, pg 536

Puerto Rico
University of Puerto Rico Press (EDUPR), pg 537

Romania
Editura Academiei Romane, pg 538
Aion Verlag, pg 538
Ararat -Tiped, Editura, pg 538
Ars Longa Publishing House, pg 538
Editura Clusium, pg 539
Editura Excelsior Art, pg 539
Humanitas Publishing House, pg 540
Editura Institutul European, pg 540
Lider Verlag, pg 540
Mentor Kiado, pg 540
Editura Niculescu, pg 541
Editura Paideia, pg 541
Polirom Verlag, pg 542
Realitatea Casa de Edituri Productie Audio-Video Film, pg 542
Saeculum IO, pg 542
Editura Stiintifica SA, pg 542
Editura Teora, pg 542
Editura Univers SA, pg 543
Universal Dalsi, pg 543
Vestala Verlag, pg 543
Vremea Publishers Ltd, pg 543

Russian Federation
Agni Publishing House, pg 543
Aspect Press Ltd, pg 543
Izdatelstvo Iskusstvo, pg 545
Ladomir Publishing House, pg 546
Izdatelstvo Mordovskogo gosudar stvennogo, pg 547
Izdatelstvo Mysl, pg 547
Izdatel'stvo Nizhegorodskogo Gosudarstvennogo Univ, pg 547
Novosti Izdatelstvo, pg 547
Progress Publishers, pg 548
Raduga Publishers, pg 548
St Andrew's Biblical Theological College, pg 548
Scorpion Publishers, pg 548
Izdatelstvo Ural' skogo, pg 549
Izdatelstvo Vysshaya Shkola, pg 549

Saudi Arabia
Dar Al-Shareff for Publishing & Distribution, pg 550

Senegal
Les Nouvelles Editions Africaines du Senegal NEAS, pg 551

Serbia and Montenegro
Alfa-Narodna Knjiga, pg 552
Beogradski Izdavacko-Graficki Zavod, pg 552
Jugoslavijapublik, pg 552
Nolit Publishing House, pg 553
Izdavacka Organizacija Rad, pg 553
Panorama NIJP/ID Grigorije Bozovic, pg 553
Svetovi, pg 554
Vuk Karadzic, pg 554

Singapore
Asiapac Books Pte Ltd, pg 555
McGallen & Bolden Associates, pg 557
Taylor & Francis Asia Pacific, pg 558

Slovakia
ARCHA sro Vydavatel'stro, pg 559
Danubiaprint, pg 559
Kalligram spol sro, pg 559
Luc vydavatelske druzstvo, pg 559
Smena Publishing House, pg 560
Sofa, pg 560
VEDA (Vydavatel'stvo Slovenskej akademie vied), pg 561

Slovenia
Cankarjeva Zalozba, pg 561
Slovenska matica, pg 561
Zalozba Mihelac d o o, pg 562
Zalozba Obzorja d d Maribor, pg 562

PUBLISHERS — SUBJECT INDEX

South Africa

Human & Rousseau (Pty) Ltd, pg 564
Human Sciences Research Council, pg 565
LAPA Publishers (Pty) Ltd, pg 566

Spain

Publicacions de l'Abadia de Montserrat, pg 570
Aguilar SA de Ediciones, pg 571
Ediciones Akal SA, pg 571
Ediciones Alfar SA, pg 572
Alianza Editorial SA, pg 572
Altea, Taurus, Alfaguara SA, pg 572
Editorial Anagrama, pg 572
Editorial Ariel SA, pg 573
Biblioteca de Autores Cristianos, pg 574
Editorial Casals SA, pg 575
Ediciones Catedra SA, pg 576
Centro de Estudios Politicos Y Constitucionales, pg 576
Editora Comercial de Publicaciones, pg 577
Complutense, SA Editorial, pg 577
Ediciones Cristiandad, pg 578
EDERSA (Editoriales de Derecho Reunidas SA), pg 580
Ediciones Encuentro SA, pg 582
EUNSA (Ediciones Universidad de Navarra SA), pg 583
Fondo de Cultura Economica de Espana, SL, pg 583
Fragua Editorial, pg 583
Fundacion Rosacruz, pg 584
Editorial Fundamentos, pg 584
Galaxia SA Editorial, pg 584
Editorial Gedisa SA, pg 584
Editorial Gredos SA, pg 585
Editorial Gulaab, pg 586
Editorial Herder SA, pg 586
Editorial Horsori SL, pg 586
Idea Books, SA, pg 587
Ediciones Internacionales Universitarias SA, pg 588
Iralka Editorial SL, pg 588
Ediciones Istmo SA, pg 588
Editorial Kairos SA, pg 588
Laertes SA de Ediciones, pg 588
Antonio Machado, SA, pg 590
Editorial Magisterio Espanol SA, pg 590
Edicions de la Magrana SA, pg 590
Ediciones Mensajero, pg 591
Ediciones Morata SL, pg 592
Nueva Acropolis, pg 593
Ediciones del Oriente y del Mediterraneo, pg 594
Pages Editors, SL, pg 594
Pearson Educacion S A, pg 595
Pentalfa Ediciones, pg 595
PPC Editorial y Distribuidora, SA, pg 596
Pre-Textos, pg 596
Publicaciones de la Universidad Pontificia Comillas-Madrid, pg 597
Editora Regional de Murcia - ERM, pg 597
Editorial Revista Agustiniana, pg 598
Ediciones Rialp SA, pg 598
Ediciones San Pio X, pg 599
Universidad de Santiago de Compostela, pg 599
Siglo XXI de Espana Editores SA, pg 599
Ediciones Sigueme SA, pg 600
Editorial Sintesis, SA, pg 600
Sirmio, pg 600
Ediciones Siruela SA, pg 600
Edicions 62, pg 600
Grup 62, pg 600
Ediciones SM, pg 600
Editorial Rudolf Steiner, pg 601
Editorial Tecnos SA, pg 601
Editorial Sal Terrae, pg 602
Ediciones de la Torre, pg 602
Trotta SA Editorial, pg 602
Turner Publicaciones, pg 602
Universidad de Granada, pg 603
Universidad de Malaga, pg 603
Ediciones Universidad de Salamanca, pg 603
Universidad de Valladolid Secretariado de Publicaciones e Intercambio Editorial, pg 604
Universitat de Valencia Servei de Publicacions, pg 604
Editorial Verbum SL, pg 604
Visor Distribuciones, SA, pg 605

Sri Lanka

Inter-Cultural Book Promoters, pg 606
Karunaratne & Sons Ltd, pg 606
Samayawardena Printers Publishers & Booksellers, pg 607

Sudan

Khartoum University Press, pg 608

Sweden

Akademiforlaget Goteborgslitteratur, pg 609
BBT Bhaktivedanta Book Trust, pg 610
Gidlunds Bokforlag, pg 612
Hagaberg AB, pg 612
Bokforlaget Nya Doxa AB, pg 614
Studentlitteratur AB, pg 616
Svenska Foerlaget liv & ledarskap ab, pg 616

Switzerland

ADIRA, pg 617
Editions L'Age d'Homme - La Cite, pg 617
Editions de la Baconniere SA, pg 618
Bibliographisches Institut & F A Brockhaus AG, pg 619
CEC-Cosmic Energy Connections, pg 620
Christiana-Verlag, pg 620
Diogenes Verlag AG, pg 622
Edition Epoca, pg 622
Erker-Verlag, pg 623
Europa Verlag AG, pg 623
Edition Exodus, pg 623
Verlag Gachnang & Springer, Bern-Berlin, pg 623
Georg Editeur SA, pg 624
Govinda-Verlag, pg 624
Haffmans Verlag AG, pg 624
Herder AG Basel, pg 625
ISIOM Verlag fur Tondokumente, Weinreb Tonarchiv, pg 625
Klett und Balmer & Co Verlag, pg 626
Kober Verlag Bern AG, pg 626
Kolumbus-Verlag, pg 626
Kranich-Verlag, Dres AG & H R Bosch-Gwalter, pg 627
Peter Lang AG, pg 627
Manesse Verlag GmbH, pg 628
Les Editions Nagel SA (Paris), pg 629
Natura-Verlag Arlesheim, pg 629
Novalis Media AG, pg 630
Origo Verlag, pg 630
Editions Patino, pg 631
Editions Payot Lausanne, pg 631
Verlag Die Pforte im Rudolf Steiner Verlag, pg 631
Philosophisch-Anthroposophischer Verlag am Goetheanum, pg 631
Psychosophische Gesellschaft, pg 632
Editions Saint-Paul, pg 633
Scherz Verlag AG, pg 633
Schwabe & Co AG, pg 633
Speer -Verlag, pg 634
Sphinx Verlag AG, pg 634
Rudolf Steiner Verlag, pg 634
Theseus - Verlag AG, pg 635
Tobler Verlag, pg 635
Editions du Tricorne, pg 635
Editions des Trois Collines Francois Lachenal, pg 635
Der Universitatsverlag Freiburg, pg 636
Verlag Die Waage, pg 636

Syrian Arab Republic

Damascus University Press, pg 638
Institut Francais d'Etudes Arabes de Damas, pg 638

Taiwan, Province of China

Asian Culture Co Ltd, pg 638
Cheng Wen Publishing Company, pg 639
Chu Liu Book Company, pg 639
Chung Hwa Book Co Ltd, pg 639
Laureate Book Co Ltd, pg 640
San Min Book Co Ltd, pg 641
World Book Co Ltd, pg 642
Yee Wen Publishing Co Ltd, pg 642

Tajikistan

Irfon, pg 642

Thailand

Graphic Art (28) Co Ltd, pg 645
Thai Watana Panich Co, Ltd, pg 646
White Lotus Co Ltd, pg 646

Togo

Editions Akpagnon, pg 646

Tunisia

Academie Tunisienne des Sciences, des Lettres et des Arts Beit El Hekma, pg 647
Faculte des Sciences Humaines et Sociales de Tunis, pg 648
Maison d'Edition Mohamed Ali Hammi, pg 648
Maison Tunisienne de l'Edition, pg 648

Turkey

Altin Kitaplar Yayinevi, pg 649
Ezel Erverdi (Dergah Yayinlari AS) Muessese Muduru, pg 650
Iletisim Yayinlari, pg 650
Inkilap Publishers Ltd, pg 650
Metis Yayinlari, pg 650
Remzi Kitabevi, pg 651
Ruh ve Madde Yayinlari ve Saglik Hizmetleri AS, pg 651
Saray Medikal Yayin Tic Ltd Sti, pg 651
Kabalci Yayinevi, pg 652

Ukraine

Naukova Dumka Publishers, pg 653
Osnovy Publishers, pg 654

United Kingdom

Acumen Publishing Ltd, pg 655
AK Press & Distribution, pg 656
Aldwych Press Ltd, pg 656
Apex Publishing Ltd, pg 658
Arthur James Ltd, pg 660
Ashgate Publishing Ltd, pg 660
The Athlone Press Ltd, pg 661
Baha'i Publishing Trust, pg 662
Black Ace Books, pg 666
Blackwell Publishing Ltd, pg 666
Marion Boyars Publishers Ltd, pg 669
Boydell & Brewer Ltd, pg 669
The British Academy, pg 671
Calder Publications Ltd, pg 673
Cambridge University Press, pg 674
Capall Bann Publishing, pg 674
Kyle Cathie Ltd, pg 676
Deborah Charles Publications, pg 678
James Clarke & Co Ltd, pg 680
James Currey Ltd, pg 685
Gerald Duckworth & Co Ltd, pg 688
Dunedin Academic Press, pg 688
Edinburgh University Press Ltd, pg 689
Element Books Ltd, pg 690
Ethics International Press Ltd, pg 692
The Europsan Group, pg 692
Faber & Faber Ltd, pg 694
Free Association Books Ltd, pg 697
Freedom Press, pg 697
Gateway Books, pg 698
George Mann Publications, pg 699
E J W Gibb Memorial Trust, pg 700
Golden Cockerel Press Ltd, pg 701
The Greek Bookshop, pg 702
Green Books Ltd, pg 702
Peter Halban Publishers Ltd, pg 703
Robert Hale Ltd, pg 704
HarperCollins UK, pg 705
Harvard University Press, pg 705
The Harvill Press, pg 705
The Islamic Texts Society, pg 715
Janus Publishing Co Ltd, pg 716
Karnak House, pg 717
The Littman Library of Jewish Civilization, pg 721
Lucis Press Ltd, pg 723
Marcham Manor Press, pg 725
The Merlin Press Ltd, pg 727
MIT Press Ltd, pg 728
Motilal (UK) Books of India, pg 729
New Era Publications UK Ltd, pg 732
Octagon Press Ltd, pg 734
Oneworld Publications, pg 735
Open Gate Press, pg 735
The Orkney Press Ltd, pg 736
Oxford University Press, pg 737
Paternoster Publishing, pg 738
Pearson Education, pg 739
Pearson Education Europe, Mideast & Africa, pg 739
Pickering & Chatto Publishers Ltd, pg 742
Pluto Press, pg 743
Polygon, pg 744
Prism Press Book Publishers Ltd, pg 745
Quartet Books Ltd, pg 746
Ramakrishna Vedanta Centre, pg 747
Random House UK Ltd, pg 747
Rationalist Press Association, pg 748
Roundhouse Group, pg 751
Routledge, pg 751
RoutledgeCurzon, pg 751

SUBJECT INDEX BOOK

SAGE Publications Ltd, pg 753
St Pauls Publishing, pg 753
Sheed & Ward UK, pg 757
Shepheard-Walwyn (Publishers) Ltd, pg 757
Skoob Russell Square, pg 758
Snowbooks Ltd, pg 759
The Society of Metaphysicians Ltd, pg 759
Souvenir Press Ltd, pg 759
Rudolf Steiner Press, pg 761
Thames & Hudson Ltd, pg 764
Thoemmes Press, pg 765
UCL Press Ltd, pg 768
University of Exeter Press, pg 768
University of Wales Press, pg 769
Verso, pg 770
Virago Press, pg 770
Voltaire Foundation Ltd, pg 771
The Warburg Institute, pg 771
Yale University Press London, pg 776

Uruguay
A Monteverde y Cia SA, pg 777
Nordan-Comunidad, pg 778

Venezuela
Alfadil Ediciones, pg 778
Monte Avila Editores Latinoamericana CA, pg 779
Biblioteca Ayacucho, pg 779

Viet Nam
Su Hoc (Historical) Publishing House, pg 781
Su That (Truth) Publishing House, pg 781

Zambia
MFK Management Consultants Services, pg 781

Zimbabwe
University of Zimbabwe Publications, pg 784

PHOTOGRAPHY

Albania
NL SH, pg 1

Argentina
Diana Argentina SA, Editorial, pg 5

Australia
Robert Berthold Photography, pg 14
Emperor Publishing, pg 21
Enterprise Publications, pg 21
Joval Publications, pg 28
Laurel Press, pg 28
McGraw-Hill Australia Pty Ltd, pg 31
J M McGregor Pty Ltd, pg 31
Mountain House Press, pg 32
Raincloud Productions, pg 38
Rankin Publishers, pg 39
Tabletop Press, pg 42
Thames & Hudson (Australia) Pty Ltd, pg 43
Wellington Lane Press Pty Ltd, pg 46

Austria
Christian Brandstaetter Verlagsgesellschaft mbH, pg 49
Camera Austria, pg 49
Loecker Verlag, pg 53

Richard Pils Publication PN°1, pg 56
Andreas Schnider Verlags-Atelier, pg 57

Belarus
Belaruskaya Encyklapedyya, pg 62

Belgium
Editions Gerard Blanchart & Cie SA, pg 63
Conservart SA, pg 65
Dexia Bank, pg 66
Graton Editeur NV, pg 68
Uitgeverij Lannoo NV, pg 69
Les Editions Vie ouvriere ASBL, pg 74

Brazil
Editora Companhia das Letras/ Editora Schwarcz Ltda, pg 80
Livro Ibero-Americano Ltda, pg 83
Livraria Pioneira Editora/Enio Matheus Guazzelli e Cia Ltd, pg 88
Rede Das Artes (Boccato Editores Collector's), pg 89

China
China Film Press, pg 102
Fudan University Press, pg 104
Heilongjiang Science & Technology Press, pg 105
Jilin Science & Technology Publishing House, pg 105
Morning Glory Press, pg 106
People's Fine Arts Publishing House, pg 106
Printing Industry Publishing House, pg 107
Shanghai Calligraphy & Painting Publishing House, pg 108
Shanghai People's Fine Arts Publishing House, pg 108
Yunnan University Press, pg 109

Colombia
Villegas Editores Ltda, pg 113

Czech Republic
Moravska Galerie v Brno, pg 126
Prostor, nakladatelstvi sro, pg 127

Denmark
Politisk Revy, pg 133
Tiderne Skifter Forlag A/S, pg 135

France
Actes-Graphiques, pg 145
ADPF Publications, pg 145
Editions Alternatives, pg 146
L'Amitie par le Livre, pg 146
Anako Editions, pg 146
Editions de l'Armancon, pg 147
La Bartavelle, pg 149
Adam Biro Editions, pg 150
William Blake & Co, pg 150
Editions Buchet-Chastel Pierre Zech Editeur, pg 151
Editions Jacqueline Chambon, pg 153
Editions Comp'Act, pg 155
Dunod Editeur, pg 159
Editions Pierre Fanlac, pg 162
Editions Des Femmes, pg 163
Editions Filipacchi-Sonodip, pg 163
Editions Fragments, pg 164
Editions Hoebeke, pg 168
Image/Magie, pg 168
Isoete, pg 169

Editions du Jeu de Paume, pg 169
Eric Koehler, pg 170
Macula, pg 173
Editions Marval, pg 174
Editions Medianes, pg 175
Editions Paul Montel, pg 176
Centre National de la Photographie, pg 176
Association Paris-Musees, pg 179
Jean-Michel Place, pg 180
Editions Plume, pg 180
Revue Noire, pg 183
Editions du Seuil, pg 184
Siloe - Kerdore, pg 185
Somogy editions d'art, pg 185
Editions Thames & Hudson, pg 187
Alain Thomas Editeur, pg 187
Transeuropeennes/RCE, pg 188
Publications de l'Universite de Pau, pg 188
La Vague a l'ame, pg 188
Editions VM, pg 189
La Voix du Regard, pg 189

Germany
F A Ackermanns Kunstverlag GmbH, pg 190
Arnoldsche Verlagsanstalt GmbH, pg 194
Artcolor, pg 194
Augustus Verlag, pg 195
Bildarchiv Preussischer Kulturbesitz bpk, pg 201
Verlag C J Bucher GmbH, pg 205
Ulrich Burgdorf/Homeopathic Publishing House, pg 206
Dr Cantz'sche Druckerei GmbH & Co, pg 207
Christian Verlag GmbH, pg 208
Hans Christians Druckerei und Verlag GmbH & Co KG, pg 208
CTL-Presse Clemens-Tobias Lange, pg 210
Dolling und Galitz Verlag GmbH, pg 215
Espresso Verlag GmbH, pg 221
Eulen Verlag, pg 221
Falken-Verlag GmbH, pg 223
Frederking & Thaler Verlag GmbH, pg 226
Gruner + Jahr AG & Co, pg 231
Haschemi Edition Cologne Kunstverlag fuer Fotografie, pg 234
Hatje Cantz Verlag, pg 234
Heel Verlag GmbH, pg 235
Johannis, pg 243
Jovis Verlag GmbH, pg 243
Kilda Verlag, pg 246
Knesebeck Verlag, pg 247
Koenemann Verlagesellschaft mbH, pg 248
Verlag Hubert Kretschmer, pg 250
Verlag der Kunst/G+B Fine Arts Verlag GmbH, pg 251
Kunstverlag Weingarten GmbH, pg 251
Karl Robert Langewiesche Nachfolger Hans Koester KG, pg 252
Edition Axel Menges, pg 259
Merz & Solitude - Akademie Schloss Solitude, pg 259
Mitteldeutscher Verlag GmbH, pg 261
Verlag Stephanie Naglschmid, pg 263
Nicolaische Verlagsbuchhandlung Beuermann GmbH, pg 265
Nieswand-Verlag GmbH, pg 265
nymphenburger, pg 266
Edition Octopus & Okeanos Presse, pg 266

Prestel Verlag, pg 271
E Reinhold Verlag, pg 275
Reise Know-How Verlag Helmut Hermann, pg 275
Rimbaud Verlagsgesellschaft mbH, pg 276
Rogner und Bernhard GmbH & Co Verlags KG, pg 276
Schirmer/Mosel Verlag GmbH, pg 279
Verlag Hans Schoener GmbH, pg 281
Steidl Verlag, pg 287
Steinweg-Verlag, Jurgen vomHoff, pg 287
TASCHEN GmbH, pg 289
teNeues Verlag GmbH & Co KG, pg 290
Trotzdem-Verlags Genossenschaft eG, pg 292
Uwe Warnke Verlag, pg 297

Greece
Chryssos Typos AE Ekodeis, pg 306
Giovanis Publications, Pangosmios Ekdotikos Organismos, pg 307
Hestia-I D Hestia-Kollaros & Co Corporation, pg 308
Editions Moressopoulos, pg 310

Hong Kong
Asia 2000 Ltd, pg 315
Steve Lu Publishing Ltd, pg 318
Photoart Ltd, pg 318

Iceland
Forlagid, pg 325

India
Ananda Publishers Pvt Ltd, pg 328
Mapin Publishing Pvt Ltd, pg 341

Ireland
The Collins Press, pg 358
Real Ireland Design, pg 363
Roberts Rinehart Publishers, pg 363
Wolfhound Press Ltd, pg 364

Israel
Bezalel Academy of Arts & Design, pg 365
Gefen Publishing House Ltd, pg 367

Italy
A & A, pg 374
Mario Adda Editore SNC, pg 374
L'Airone Editrice, pg 375
Alinari Fratelli SpA Istituto di Edizioni Artistiche, pg 375
Umberto Allemandi & C SRL, pg 375
L'Archivolto, pg 376
Artioli Editore, pg 377
Campanotto, pg 379
Edizioni del Capricorno, pg 380
Il Castello srl, pg 380
Colonnese Editore, pg 383
Electa, pg 387
Essegi, pg 388
Fatatrac, pg 388
Federico Motta Editore SpA, pg 389
Fenice 2000, pg 389
Edizioni del Girasole srl, pg 390
Grafica e Arte srl, pg 391
Gremese International srl, pg 391
Hopeful Monster Editore, pg 392
Idea Books, pg 392
Editoriale Jaca Book SpA, pg 394
Linea d'Ombra Libri, pg 395

PUBLISHERS

Angelo Longo Editore, pg 396
Lybra Immagine, pg 396
Magnus Edizioni SpA, pg 397
Edizioni Gabriele Mazzotta SRL, pg 397
NodoLibri, pg 400
Novecento Editrice Srl, pg 401
Nuovi Sentieri Editore, pg 401
OCTAVO Produzioni Editoriali Associale, pg 401
Pheljna Edizioni d'Arte e Suggestione, pg 403
Priuli e Verlucca, Editori, pg 404
Edition Raetia Srl-GmbH, pg 405
Edizioni Ripostes, pg 405
Scala Group spa, pg 407
Sellerio Editore, pg 408
SEMAR Publishers SRL, pg 408
Sicania, pg 408
Silvana Editoriale SpA, pg 408
Tomo Edizioni srl, pg 410
Vianello Libri, pg 411
Zanichelli Editore SpA, pg 412

Japan

Bun-ichi Sogo Shuppan, pg 415
Genko-Sha, pg 417
Iwanami Shoten, Publishers, pg 419
Seibido Shuppan Company Ltd, pg 426
Shincho-Sha Co Ltd, pg 427
Shufunotomo Co Ltd, pg 428
Tankosha Publishing Co Ltd, pg 429
Toho Shuppan, pg 429

Kazakstan

Kramds-reklama Publishing & Advertising, pg 432

Republic of Korea

Hakgojae Publishing Inc, pg 439
Seoul International Publishing House, pg 443
YBM/Si-sa, pg 443
Youlhwadang Publisher, pg 444

Latvia

Preses Nams, pg 445

Lithuania

Baltos Lankos, pg 449
Lithuanian National Museum Publishing House, pg 449
Vaga Ltd, pg 450

Luxembourg

Guy Binsfeld & Co Sarl, pg 450
Editions Emile Borschette, pg 450
Galerie Editions Kutter, pg 451
Edition Objectif Lune, pg 451
Editions Tousch, pg 452

Macau

Livros Do Oriente, pg 452

The Former Yugoslav Republic of Macedonia

Macedonia Prima Publishing House, pg 452

Malaysia

Penerbitan Pelangi Sdn Bhd (Pelangi Publishing Pte Ltd), pg 458

Mexico

Aguilar Altea Taurus Alfaguara SA de CV, pg 462
Fondo de Cultura Economica, pg 465
Instituto Nacional de Antropologia e Historia, pg 469
Naves Internacional de Ediciones SA, pg 469
Servicios Especiales Maciel SA de CV, pg 472
Editorial Turner de Mexico, pg 472

Morocco

Editions Oum, pg 475

Netherlands

Uitgeverij Ambo BV, pg 477
Uitgeverij Cantecleer BV, pg 480
Hotei Publishing, pg 484
De Prom, pg 488
Tirion Uitgevers BV, pg 490
Unieboek BV, pg 490
Uniepers BV, pg 491
Uitgeverij 010, pg 493

New Zealand

Barkfire Press, pg 494
Bush Press Communications Ltd, pg 494
Craig Potton Publishing, pg 495
RSVP Publishing Co Ltd, pg 500
Shoal Bay Press Ltd, pg 501
Tandem Press, pg 501
University of Otago Press, pg 502

Peru

Universidad de Lima-Fondo de Desarollo Editorial, pg 517

Poland

Wydawnictwo Arkady, pg 522
Wydawnictwa Artystyczne i Filmowe, pg 522
Wydawnictwo Baturo, pg 522
BOSZ scp, pg 522
Rosikon Press, pg 526
Videograf II Sp z o o Zaklad Poracy Chronionej, pg 527

Portugal

Assirio & Alvim, pg 528
Dinalivro, pg 530
Impala, pg 532
Latina Livraria Editora, pg 532
Quatro Elementos Editores, pg 535
Edicoes 70 Lda, pg 535
Vega-Publicacao e Distribuicao de Livros e Revistas, Lda, pg 536

Singapore

Archipelago Press, pg 555

Slovenia

Zalozba Mihelac d o o, pg 562
Zalozba Obzorja d d Maribor, pg 562

South Africa

Janssen Publishers CC, pg 565
Johannesburg Art Gallery, pg 565
New Africa Books (Pty) Ltd, pg 567

Spain

Ambit Serveis Editorials, SA, pg 572
CEAC, Grupo Editorial SA, pg 576
Celeste Ediciones, pg 576
Consello da Cultura Galega - CCG, pg 578
Edilesa-Ediciones Leonesas SA, pg 581
Edilux, pg 581
El Viso, SA Ediciones, pg 582
Fragua Editorial, pg 583
Editorial Gustavo Gili SA, pg 585
Lunwerg Editores, SA, pg 589
Editorial Mediterrania SL, pg 591
Ediciones Omega SA, pg 594
Omnicon, SA, pg 594
Silex Ediciones, pg 600
Equipo Sirius SA, pg 600
Tf Editores, pg 602
Trea Ediciones, SL, pg 602
Turner Publicaciones, pg 602
Tursen, SA, pg 603

Sweden

Allt om Hobby AB, pg 609
BOOX, pg 610
Bengt Forsbergs Foerlag AB, pg 611
Natur och Kultur Fakta etc, pg 614
Schultz Forlag AB, pg 615

Switzerland

U Baer Verlag, pg 618
Benteli Verlag, pg 618
Christoph Merian Verlag, pg 620
Edizioni Armando Dado, Tipografia Stazione, pg 621
Editions Andre Delcourt & Cie, pg 621
Drei-D-World und Foto-World Verlag und Vertrieb, pg 622
Eboris-Coda-Bompiani, pg 622
Verlag ED Emmentaler Druck AG, pg 622
FEDA SA, pg 623
Editions Foma SA, pg 623
G+B Arts International, pg 623
Giampiero Casagrande Editore, pg 624
Bernard Letu Editeur, pg 627
Memory/Cage Editions, pg 628
Lars Mueller Publishers, pg 629
Editions Olizane, pg 630
Edition Olms AG, pg 630
Perret Edition, pg 631
Reich Verlag AG, pg 632
Schwabe & Co AG, pg 633
Edition Stemmle AG, pg 635
Strom-Verlag Luzern, pg 635
Tobler Verlag, pg 635
Weber SA d'Editions, pg 637

Taiwan, Province of China

Asian Culture Co Ltd, pg 638
Hilit Publishing Co Ltd, pg 640

United Republic of Tanzania

Tanzania Publishing House, pg 644

Thailand

Graphic Art (28) Co Ltd, pg 645

Turkey

Arkeoloji Ve Sanat Yayinlari, pg 649
Inkilap Publishers Ltd, pg 650

Ukraine

Naukova Dumka Publishers, pg 653

SUBJECT INDEX

United Kingdom

Ian Allan Publishing Ltd, pg 656
Apple Press, pg 658
Appletree Press Ltd, pg 658
Art Books International Ltd, pg 659
Arts Council of England, pg 660
Aurum Press Ltd, pg 661
Batsford Ltd, pg 663
Colin Baxter Photography Ltd, pg 663
BCA - Book Club Associates, pg 663
Blackstaff Press, pg 666
Blueprint, pg 668
Book Packaging & Marketing, pg 668
Cassell & Co, pg 675
Colour Library Direct, pg 681
Constable & Robinson Ltd, pg 682
Creation Books, pg 683
Creative Monochrome Ltd, pg 684
David & Charles Ltd, pg 686
Andre Deutsch Ltd, pg 687
Dorling Kindersley Ltd, pg 688
Eaglemoss Publications Ltd, pg 689
Elfande Ltd, pg 690
Frontier Publishing Ltd, pg 697
Garnet Publishing Ltd, pg 698
GMC Publications Ltd, pg 700
The Harvill Press, pg 705
Hayward Gallery Publishing, pg 706
Hilmarton Manor Press, pg 708
Hodder Education, pg 709
Kegan Paul International Ltd, pg 717
Frances Lincoln Ltd, pg 720
Lund Humphries, pg 723
Mainstream Publishing Co (Edinburgh) Ltd, pg 724
Merrell Publishers Ltd, pg 727
National Galleries of Scotland, pg 731
National Library of Wales, pg 731
National Portrait Gallery Publications, pg 731
National Trust, pg 731
Newpro UK Ltd, pg 733
W W Norton & Company Ltd, pg 734
Octopus Publishing Group, pg 734
Osborne Books Ltd, pg 736
Pavilion Books Ltd, pg 739
Phaidon Press Ltd, pg 741
Plexus Publishing Ltd, pg 743
Pomegranate Europe Ltd, pg 744
Quintet Publishing Ltd, pg 747
Reaktion Books Ltd, pg 748
Regency House Publishing Ltd, pg 749
RotoVision SA, pg 751
Roundhouse Group, pg 751
Saqi Books, pg 754
Seren, pg 756
Shire Publications Ltd, pg 757
Sutton Publishing Ltd, pg 762
Taschen UK Ltd, pg 763
Thames & Hudson Ltd, pg 764
Verulam Publishing Ltd, pg 770
Yale University Press London, pg 776
Zwemmer Holdings Co Ltd, pg 776

Venezuela

Biblioteca Ayacucho, pg 779

PHYSICAL SCIENCES

Albania

NL SH, pg 1

SUBJECT INDEX

BOOK

Australia
Blackwell Publishing Asia, pg 15
CSIRO Publishing (Commonwealth Scientific & Industrial Research Organisation), pg 19
McGraw-Hill Australia Pty Ltd, pg 31
Queen Victoria Museum & Art Gallery Publications, pg 38

Austria
Bethania Verlag, pg 48
IAEA - International Atomic Energy Agency, pg 52
Verlag der Oesterreichischen Akademie der Wissenschaften (OEAW), pg 55
Pinguin-Verlag, Pawlowski GmbH, pg 56
Edition Va Bene, pg 59
Verband der Wissenschaftlichen Gesellschaften Oesterreichs (VWGOe), pg 59

Belgium
Academia-Bruylant, pg 62
Editions De Boeck-Larcier SA, pg 66
Leuven University Press, pg 70

Brazil
Editora Harbra Ltda, pg 83
Editora Universidade de Brasilia, pg 91
Editora Universidade Federal do Rio de Janeiro, pg 92

Bulgaria
Abagar Pablioing, pg 92
Gea-Libris Publishing House, pg 94
Heron Press Publishing House, pg 94
Litera Prima, pg 95
Makros 2000 - Plovdiv, pg 95

Chile
Arrayan Editores, pg 98

China
China Ocean Press, pg 102
Fudan University Press, pg 104
Heilongjiang Science & Technology Press, pg 105
Henan Science & Technology Publishing House, pg 105
Jiangsu Science & Technology Publishing House, pg 105
Jilin Science & Technology Publishing House, pg 105
Shandong University Press, pg 108
Tianjin Science & Technology Publishing House, pg 108

The Democratic Republic of the Congo
Centre de Recherche, et Pedagogie Appliquee, pg 114

Costa Rica
Editorial de la Universidad de Costa Rica, pg 116

Czech Republic
Karolinum, nakladatelstvi, pg 124
Mendelova zemedelska a lesnicka univerzita v Brne, pg 125
Vydavatelstvi Cesky Geologicky Ustav, pg 128

Dominican Republic
Pontificia Universidad Catolica Madre y Maestra, pg 136

Estonia
Eesti Entsuklopeediakirjastus, pg 139

Finland
Ursa ry, pg 144

France
Editions Breal, pg 151
Les Devenirs Visuels, pg 158
Editions Eyrolles, pg 162
Editions Jacques Gabay, pg 164
Editions Grandir, pg 166
Polytechnica SA, pg 180

Germany
AOL-Verlag Frohmut Menze, pg 193
Blackwell Wissenschafts-Verlag GmbH, pg 201
Oscar Brandstetter Verlag GmbH & Co KG, pg 204
Cornelsen Verlag GmbH & Co OHG, pg 210
Verlag Harri Deutsch, pg 211
DRW-Verlag Weinbrenner-GmbH & Co, pg 216
Elektor-Verlag GmbH, pg 219
Ferd Dummler's Verlag, pg 223
Franz Ferzak World & Space Publications, pg 224
Gmelin Verlag GmbH, pg 230
Walter de Gruyter GmbH & Co KG, pg 231
Lehrmittelverlag Wilhelm Hagemann GmbH, pg 233
Heigl Verlag, Horst Edition, pg 235
F A Herbig Verlagsbuchhandlung GmbH, pg 236
Hofbauer, Christoph und Trojanow Ilia, Akademischer Verlag Muenchen, pg 238
Institut fuer Landes- und Stadtentwicklungsforschung des Landes Nordrhein-Westfalen, pg 251
Preubmpassling Verlag Gisela Meussling, pg 260
Verlag Stephanie Naglschmid, pg 263
Verlag Neuer Weg, pg 264
Palazzi Verlag GmbH, pg 268
Verlag an der Ruhr GmbH, pg 277
Springer Science+Business Media GmbH & Co KG, pg 284
Universitatsverlag Ulm GmbH, pg 293
Volk und Wissen Verlag GmbH & Co, pg 296
Wiley-VCH Verlag GmbH, pg 300
Verlag Zeitschrift fur Naturforschung, pg 302

Ghana
Sam Woode Ltd, pg 304

Greece
Diavlos, pg 306

Hungary
Janus Pannonius Tudomanyegyetem, pg 322
Vince Kiado Kft, pg 322
Magyar Tudomanyos Akademia Koezponti Fizikai Kutato Intezet Koenyvtara, pg 322

India
Affiliated East West Press Pvt Ltd, pg 327
BS Publications, pg 331
Chowkhamba Sanskrit Series Office, pg 332
Law Publishers, pg 340
Scientific Book Agency, pg 348

Ireland
Royal Irish Academy, pg 363

Italy
Adea Edizioni, pg 374
Bibliopolis - Edizioni di Filosofia e Scienze Srl, pg 378
Edizioni Dedalo SRL, pg 384
Edizioni GB, pg 390
Leo S Olschki, pg 401
Editoriale Scienza, pg 407
Societa Editrice la Goliardica Pavese SRL, pg 408
Societa Stampa Sportiva, pg 408

Japan
Chijin Shokan Co Ltd, pg 416
Mita Press, Mita Industrial Co Ltd, pg 422
Sangyo-Tosho Publishing Co Ltd, pg 426
Yokendo Ltd, pg 431

Kazakstan
Gylym, Izd-Vo, pg 432

Kenya
Heinemann Kenya Ltd (EAEP), pg 434
Nairobi University Press, pg 435
Phoenix Publishers Ltd, pg 435

Democratic People's Republic of Korea
Korea Science and Encyclopedia Publishing House, pg 436

Liechtenstein
Botanisch-Zoologische Gesellschaft, pg 447
Saendig Reprint Verlag, Hans-Rainer Wohlwend, pg 448

Lithuania
Klaipedos Universiteto Leidykla, pg 449

Malaysia
Tropical Press Sdn Bhd, pg 459
Penerbit Universiti Teknologi Malaysia, pg 459

Mexico
Editorial Limusa SA de CV, pg 467

Namibia
Desert Research Foundation of Namibia (DRFN), pg 476

Netherlands
Uitgeverij Lemma BV, pg 485

New Zealand
ABA Books, pg 493
Wendy Crane Books, pg 495
Nelson Price Milburn Ltd, pg 499

Peru
Fondo Editorial de la Pontificia Universidad Catolica del Peru, pg 517

Poland
Instytut Meteorologii i Gospodarki Wodnej, pg 523
Polish Scientific Publishers PWN, pg 525
Oficyna Wydawnicza Politechniki Wroclawskiej, pg 525
Towarzystwo Naukowe w Toruniu, pg 527

Portugal
Constancia Editores, SA, pg 530
Didactica Editora, pg 530

Romania
Editura Academiei Romane, pg 538

Russian Federation
N E Bauman Moscow State Technical University Publishers, pg 544
Fizmatlit Publishing Co, pg 545
Izdatelstvo Mir, pg 546
Izdatel'stvo Nizhegorodskogo Gosudarstvennogo Univ, pg 547
Izdatelstvo Prosveshchenie, pg 548

Singapore
Reed Elsevier, South East Asia, pg 557
Taylor & Francis Asia Pacific, pg 558

South Africa
Clever Books, pg 563
Educum Publishers Ltd, pg 563

Spain
Instituto de Estudios Riojanos, pg 583
Editorial la Muralla SA, pg 592
Editorial Paraninfo SA, pg 595
Editorial Sintesis, SA, pg 600
Equipo Sirius SA, pg 600
Universidad de Oviedo Servicio de Publicaciones, pg 603

Sweden
Studentlitteratur AB, pg 616

Taiwan, Province of China
Fuh-Wen Book Co, pg 639
Hsiao Yuan Publication Co, Ltd, pg 640
Newton Publishing Company Ltd, pg 641

United Republic of Tanzania
DUP (1996) Ltd, pg 643

Uganda
Fountain Publishers Ltd, pg 652

Ukraine
Naukova Dumka Publishers, pg 653
Osvita, pg 654

United Kingdom
Aulis Publishers, pg 661
Cambridge University Press, pg 674
W H Freeman & Co Ltd, pg 697
Imperial College Press, pg 712

PUBLISHERS

Institute of Physics Publishing, pg 713
Institution of Electrical Engineers, pg 713
Kluwer Academic/Plenum Publishers, pg 718
Micelle Press, pg 727
Pion Ltd, pg 742
Portland Press Ltd, pg 745
The Royal Society, pg 752
The Society of Metaphysicians Ltd, pg 759
The Tarragon Press, pg 765
Yale University Press London, pg 776

Uruguay

A Monteverde y Cia SA, pg 777

Viet Nam

Science & Technics Publishing House, pg 780

PHYSICS

Albania

NL SH, pg 1

Argentina

EUDEBA (Editorial Universitaria de Buenos Aires), pg 5
Editorial Idearium de la Universidad de Mendoza (EDIUM), pg 6

Australia

Robert Berthold Photography, pg 14
Blackwell Publishing Asia, pg 15
Brookfield Press, pg 16
CSIRO Publishing (Commonwealth Scientific & Industrial Research Organisation), pg 19
Emerald City Books, pg 21
Illert Publications, pg 26
Macmillan Education Australia, pg 30
McGraw-Hill Australia Pty Ltd, pg 31
Rankin Publishers, pg 39
Reed Educational Publishing Australia, pg 39
Royal Society of New South Wales, pg 40

Austria

Verlag Hoelder-Pichler-Tempsky, pg 52
IAEA - International Atomic Energy Agency, pg 52
Resch Verlag, pg 56
Roetzer Druck GmbH & Co KG, pg 57
Springer-Verlag Wien, pg 58
Urban und Schwarzenberg GmbH, pg 59

Bangladesh

Bangladesh Publishers, pg 61

Belarus

Belaruskaya Encyklapedyya, pg 62
Publishing Center of Belarus State University, pg 62

Belgium

Campinia Media VZW, pg 64
Dessain - Departement de De Boeck & Larcier SA, pg 66
Leuven University Press, pg 70

Uitgeverij De Garve, pg 74
Wolters Plantyn Educatieve Uitgevers, pg 74

Bolivia

Editorial Don Bosco, pg 75

Brazil

Editora Edgard Blucher Ltda, pg 79
Editora Campus Ltda, pg 79
Edicon Editora e Consultorial Ltda, pg 81
LTC-Livros Tecnicos e Cientificos Editora S/A, pg 85
Editora Scipione Ltda, pg 90

Bulgaria

Heron Press Publishing House, pg 94
Makros 2000 - Plovdiv, pg 95
Naouka i Izkoustvo, Ltd, pg 95
Pensoft Publishers, pg 96

China

Beijing Publishing House, pg 101
China Ocean Press, pg 102
Fudan University Press, pg 104
Inner Mongolia Science & Technology Publishing House, pg 105
Jilin Science & Technology Publishing House, pg 105
Lanzhou University Press, pg 106
Science Press, pg 107
Shandong University Press, pg 108
Shanghai Educational Publishing House, pg 108

Colombia

Kapelusz Ltda Editorial, pg 111
McGraw-Hill Colombia, pg 112
Universidad Nacional Abierta y a Distancia, pg 113

Czech Republic

Academia, pg 122

Denmark

Gads Forlag, pg 131
Systime, pg 135

Dominican Republic

Pontificia Universidad Catolica Madre y Maestra, pg 136

France

Editions Breal, pg 151
CNRS Editions, pg 155
EDP Sciences, pg 161
Elsevier SAS (Editions Scientifiques et Medicales Elsevier), pg 161
Editions Jacques Gabay, pg 164
Gammaprim, pg 165
Editions Ganymede, pg 165
Hachette Livre International, pg 167
Hermann editeurs des Sciences et des Arts SA, pg 167
InterEditions, pg 169
Librairie Scientifique et Technique Albert Blanchard, pg 172
Polytechnica SA, pg 180
Editions Springer France, pg 186
Librairie Vuibert, pg 189

Germany

AOL-Verlag Frohmut Menze, pg 193
Aulis Verlag Deubner & Co KG, pg 195

Bayerischer Schulbuch-Verlag GmbH, pg 198
Beuth Verlag GmbH, pg 200
Cornelsen Verlag GmbH & Co OHG, pg 210
Verlag Harri Deutsch, pg 211
Verlag Europa-Lehrmittel GmbH & Co KG, pg 221
Ferd Dummler's Verlag, pg 223
Franz Ferzak World & Space Publications, pg 224
Franckh-Kosmos Verlags-GmbH & Co, pg 226
Walter de Gruyter GmbH & Co KG, pg 231
Carl Hanser Verlag, pg 234
Hildegard Liebaug-Dartmann, pg 254
Springer Science+Business Media GmbH & Co KG, pg 284
B G Teubner Verlag, pg 290
UTB fuer Wissenschaft Uni Taschenbuecher GmbH, pg 294
Volk und Wissen Verlag GmbH & Co, pg 296
Wiley-VCH Verlag GmbH, pg 300

Ghana

Sedco Publishing Ltd, pg 305

Greece

Editions Athina-Mavrogianni, pg 306
Diavlos, pg 306
Govostis Publishing SA, pg 307
Panepistimio Ioanninon, pg 311
Michalis Sideris, pg 312

Haiti

Editions Caraibes SA, pg 314

Holy See (Vatican City State)

Pontificia Academia Scientiarum, pg 314

Hungary

Aranyhal Konyvkiado Goldfish Publishing, pg 320
Magyar Tudomanyos Akademia Koezponti Fizikai Kutato Intezet Koenyvtara, pg 322
Mueszaki Koenyvkiado Ltd, pg 323
Nemzeti Tankoenyvkiado, pg 323
Typotex Kft Elektronikus Kiado, pg 324

India

Addison-Wesley Pte Ltd, pg 327
Affiliated East West Press Pvt Ltd, pg 327
B I Publications Pvt Ltd, pg 329
Bharat Publishing House, pg 330
BS Publications, pg 331
Frank Brothers & Co Publishers Ltd, pg 334
Heritage Publishers, pg 335
Narosa Publishing House, pg 342
Publications & Information Directorate, CSIR, pg 345
Rajasthan Hindi Granth Academy, pg 346
Scientific Book Agency, pg 348
Sita Books & Periodicals Pvt Ltd, pg 349
South Asian Publishers Pvt Ltd, pg 350
Sultan Chand & Sons Pvt Ltd, pg 350

SUBJECT INDEX

Vikas Publishing House Pvt Ltd, pg 352
S Viswanathan (Printers & Publishers) Pvt Ltd, pg 352

Indonesia

Mutiara Sumber Widya PT, pg 356

Ireland

Dublin Institute for Advanced Studies, pg 359

Israel

Open University of Israel, pg 371

Italy

Adelphi Edizioni SpA, pg 374
Bibliopolis - Edizioni di Filosofia e Scienze Srl, pg 378
Casa Editrice Giuseppe Principato Spa, pg 380
Edizioni Dedalo SRL, pg 384
Editrice Edisco, pg 386
Editoriale Jaca Book SpA, pg 394
Masson SpA, pg 397
Monduzzi Editore SpA, pg 399
Principato, pg 404
Societa Editrice Internazionale - SEI, pg 408
Societa Editrice la Goliardica Pavese SRL, pg 408
Sorbona, pg 409
Zanichelli Editore SpA, pg 412

Japan

Baifukan Co Ltd, pg 415
Kindai Kagaku Sha Co Ltd, pg 421
Kyoritsu Shuppan Co Ltd, pg 422
Maruzen Co Ltd, pg 422
Mita Press, Mita Industrial Co Ltd, pg 422
Morikita Shuppan Co Ltd, pg 423
Sangyo-Tosho Publishing Co Ltd, pg 426
Sankyo Publishing Company Ltd, pg 426
Tokyo Tosho Co Ltd, pg 430

Kazakhstan

Al-Farabi Kazakh National University, pg 432

Kenya

Heinemann Kenya Ltd (EAEP), pg 434
Nairobi University Press, pg 435

Democratic People's Republic of Korea

Academy of Sciences Publishing House, pg 436
Korea Science and Encyclopedia Publishing House, pg 436

Republic of Korea

Prompter Publications, pg 442

Kuwait

Ministry of Information, pg 444

Laos People's Democratic Republic

Lao-phanit, pg 444

Latvia

Lielvards Ltd, pg 445

SUBJECT INDEX   BOOK

Lebanon
Librairie du Liban Publishers (Sal), pg 446

Lithuania
Mokslo ir enciklopediju leidybos institutas, pg 449
TEV Leidykla, pg 450

Malaysia
Pearson Education Malaysia Sdn Bhd, pg 457
Penerbit Universiti Teknologi Malaysia, pg 459

Mexico
Editorial Esfinge SA de CV, pg 465
Fernandez Editores SA de CV, pg 465
Editorial Limusa SA de CV, pg 467
Pearson Educacion de Mexico, SA de CV, pg 470
Universidad Nacional Autonoma de Mexico (National University of Mexico), pg 472

Republic of Moldova
Editura Lumina, pg 473

Nepal
International Standards Books & Periodicals (P) Ltd, pg 476

Netherlands
A A Balkema Uitgevers BV, pg 478
Delft University Press, pg 481
Elsevier Science BV, pg 482
IOS Press BV, pg 484
LCG Malmberg BV, pg 485
Uitgeverij de Tijdstroom BV, pg 490
V S P International Science Publishers, pg 491

New Zealand
ABA Books, pg 493
ESA Publications (NZ) Ltd, pg 496
Nelson Price Milburn Ltd, pg 499
New House Publishers Ltd, pg 499

Norway
NKI Forlaget, pg 510

Pakistan
Publishers United Pvt Ltd, pg 514

Philippines
Rex Bookstores & Publishers, pg 520
Salesiana Publishers Inc, pg 521

Poland
Wydawnictwa Naukowo-Techniczne, pg 524
Polish Scientific Publishers PWN, pg 525
Oficyna Wydawnicza Politechniki Wroclawskiej, pg 525

Portugal
Dinalivro, pg 530
Gradiva-Publicacnoes Lda, pg 532
Editora McGraw-Hill de Portugal Lda, pg 533
Edicoes Silabo, pg 536

Romania
Editura Academiei Romane, pg 538
Corint Publishing Group, pg 539
Editura Niculescu, pg 541
Petrion Verlag, pg 542

Russian Federation
Energoatomizdat, pg 544
Fizmatlit Publishing Co, pg 545
Izdatelstvo Mir, pg 546
Nauka Publishers, pg 547
Izdatel'stvo Nizhegorodskogo Gosudarstvennogo Univ, pg 547
Izdatelstvo Prosveshchenie, pg 548
Teorija Verojatnostej i ee Primenenija, pg 549
Izdatelstvo Vysshaya Shkola, pg 549

Singapore
Hillview Publications Pte Ltd, pg 556
Reed Elsevier, South East Asia, pg 557
World Scientific Publishing Co Pte Ltd, pg 559

Slovakia
Slovenske pedagogicke nakladateistvo, pg 560
Sofa, pg 560

Slovenia
Mladinska Knjiga International, pg 561
Zalozba Obzorja d d Maribor, pg 562

South Africa
Educum Publishers Ltd, pg 563

Spain
Editorial Everest SA, pg 581
Editorial Iberia, SA, pg 586
Idea Books, SA, pg 587
Editorial la Muralla SA, pg 592
Universidad de Santiago de Compostela, pg 599
Ediciones de la Torre, pg 602
Universidad de Valladolid Secretariado de Publicaciones e Intercambio Editorial, pg 604

Sri Lanka
Ministry of Education, pg 607

Switzerland
Association Suisse des Editeurs de Langue Francaise, pg 618
Bibliographisches Institut & F A Brockhaus AG, pg 619
Birkhauser Verlag AG, pg 619
Verlag Harri Deutsch, pg 622
Presses Polytechniques et Universitaires Romandes, PPUR, pg 631
Trans Tech Publications SA, pg 635
Vdf Hochschulverlag AG an der ETH Zurich, pg 636

Syrian Arab Republic
Damascus University Press, pg 638

Taiwan, Province of China
Far East Book Co Ltd, pg 639
Fuh-Wen Book Co, pg 639

United Republic of Tanzania
DUP (1996) Ltd, pg 643
Tanzania Publishing House, pg 644

Thailand
Graphic Art (28) Co Ltd, pg 645

Tunisia
Academie Tunisienne des Sciences, des Lettres et des Arts Beit El Hekma, pg 647

Turkey
Arkadas Ltd, pg 649
Caglayan Kitabevi, pg 649
Inkilap Publishers Ltd, pg 650

Ukraine
Osvita, pg 654

United Kingdom
Association for Science Education, pg 661
The Eurospan Group, pg 692
Hodder Education, pg 709
Institute of Physics Publishing, pg 713
James & James (Science Publishers) Ltd, pg 715
Kluwer Academic/Plenum Publishers, pg 718
Nelson Thornes Ltd, pg 732
Pearson Education, pg 739
Pion Ltd, pg 742
ProQuest Information & Learning, pg 746
The Royal Society, pg 752
Snowbooks Ltd, pg 759
The Society of Metaphysicians Ltd, pg 759
Taylor & Francis, pg 763
Two-Can Publishing Ltd, pg 768
Wiley Europe Ltd, pg 773

Uruguay
A Monteverde y Cia SA, pg 777

Venezuela
Sociedad Fondo Editorial Cenamec, pg 779

Viet Nam
Science & Technics Publishing House, pg 780

Zimbabwe
College Press Publishers (Pvt) Ltd, pg 783

POETRY

Albania
Botimpex Publications Import-Export Agency, pg 1
NL SH, pg 1

Algeria
Enterprise Nationale du Livre (ENAL), pg 2

Argentina
Beatriz Viterbo Editora, pg 4
Editorial Claridad SA, pg 4
Colmegna SA, pg 4
Ediciones Corregidor SAICI y E, pg 4
Editorial Galerna SRL, pg 6
Editorial Losada SA, pg 7
Editora Patria Grande, pg 8
Editorial Quetzal-Domingo Cortizo, pg 8

Armenia
Arevik, pg 10

Australia
Access Press, pg 10
Aeolian Press, pg 11
Ashling Books, pg 12
Bandicoot Books, pg 14
Church Archivists Press, pg 18
Cornford Press, pg 18
Eleanor Curtain Publishing, pg 19
Dangaroo Press, pg 19
Dragon Press, pg 20
Feakle Press, pg 22
Fremantle Arts Centre Press, pg 23
Freshet Press, pg 23
Galley Press Publishing, pg 23
Gangan Publishing, pg 23
Ginninderra Press, pg 23
Geoffrey Hamlyn-Harris, pg 24
Incunabula Press, pg 26
Island Press Co-operative, pg 27
Jesuit Publications, pg 27
Jika Publishing, pg 27
Joval Publications, pg 28
Little Red Apple Publishing, pg 29
Mimosa Publications Pty Ltd, pg 32
Mountain House Press, pg 32
Mulini Press, pg 32
New Endeavour Press, pg 33
Nimrod Publications, pg 33
Omnibus Books, pg 34
Owl Publishing, pg 35
Papyrus Publishing, pg 35
Pinchgut Press, pg 36
Raincloud Productions, pg 38
South Head Press, pg 41
Spinifex Press, pg 42
Tamarind Publications, pg 42
Tarka Publishing, pg 42
Thin Rich Press, pg 43
Tom Publications, pg 43
Unity Press, pg 44
University of Queensland Press, pg 45
Veritas Press, pg 45
Vista Publications, pg 45
Windhorse Books, pg 47
Yanagang Publishing, pg 47

Austria
Alekto Verlag GmbH, pg 48
BSE Verlag Dr Bernhard Schuttengruber, pg 49
Czernin Verlag Ltd, pg 49
Denkmayr GmbH Druck & Verlag, pg 50
Development News Ltd, pg 50
Diotima Presse, pg 50
Literature Verlag Droschl, pg 50
Ennsthaler GesmbH & Co KG, pg 50
Edition Ergo Sum, pg 50
Verlag Lynkeus/H Hakel Gesellschaft, pg 51
Edition Graphischer Zirkel, pg 51
Johannes Heyn GmbH & Co KG, pg 52
Edition Koenigstein, pg 53
LOG-Internationale Zeitschrift fuer Literatur, pg 53
Merbod Verlag, pg 54
Otto Mueller Verlag, pg 54
Edition Neues Marchen, pg 54
Richard Pils Publication PN°1, pg 56
Residenz Verlag GmbH, pg 57

PUBLISHERS SUBJECT INDEX

Verlag Roeschnar, pg 57
Andreas Schnider Verlags-Atelier, pg 57
Thanhaeuser Edition, pg 58
Edition Thurnhof KEG, pg 58
Edition Va Bene, pg 59
Weilburg Verlag, pg 59
Wieser Verlag, pg 60
Paul Zsolnay Verlag GmbH, pg 60

Bangladesh

Gatidhara, pg 61
Agamee Prakashani, pg 61

Belarus

Belaruskaya Encyklapedyya, pg 62
Kavaler Publishers, pg 62

Belgium

Libraire Ancienne Noel Anselot, pg 63
Le Daily-Bul, pg 66
Imprimerie Hayez SPRL, pg 68
Editions Labor, pg 69
Uitgeverij Lannoo NV, pg 69
La Longue Vue, pg 70
Paradox Pers vzw, pg 71
La Part de L'Oeil, pg 71
Poeziecentrum, pg 72
Standaard Uitgeverij, pg 73
Vita, pg 74
Vlaamse Esperantobond VZW, pg 74
Zuid En Noord VZW, pg 75

Bosnia and Herzegovina

Bemust, pg 76

Botswana

Maskew Miller Longman, pg 76

Brazil

Ars Poetica Editora Ltda, pg 78
Editora Bertrand Brasil Ltda, pg 78
Editora Companhia das Letras/ Editora Schwarcz Ltda, pg 80
Edicon Editora e Consultorial Ltda, pg 81
Editora Elevacao, pg 81
Global Editora e Distribuidora Ltda, pg 82
Editora Globo SA, pg 82
Editora Mantiqueira de Ciencia e Arte, pg 86
Editora Nova Alexandria Ltda, pg 87
Editora Nova Fronteira SA, pg 87
Thex Editora e Distribuidora Ltda, pg 91
34 Literatura S/C Ltda, pg 91

Bulgaria

Hristo G Danov State Publishing House, pg 93
EA EOOD, pg 94
Hriker, pg 94
Pejo K Javorov Publishing House, pg 95
Kibea Publishing Co, pg 95
Musica Publishing House Ltd, pg 95
Narodna Kultura, pg 96
Pet Plus, pg 96
Prohazka I Kacarmazov, pg 96
Prozoretz Ltd Publishing House, pg 96
Svetra Publishing House, pg 97
TEMTO, pg 97
Ivan Vazov Publishing House, pg 97
Zunica, pg 97

Cameroon

Editions CLE, pg 98
Editions Buma Kor & Co Ltd, pg 98
Editions Semences Africaines, pg 98

Chile

Editorial Cuarto Propio, pg 99
Pehuen Editores Ltda, pg 100
Red Internacional Del Libro, pg 100

China

Beijing Publishing House, pg 101
Chinese Literature Press, pg 103
Fudan University Press, pg 104
People's Literature Publishing House, pg 106
Writers' Publishing House, pg 109
Zhong Hua Book Co, pg 110

Colombia

Amazonas Editores Ltda, pg 110
El Ancora Editores, pg 111
Editorial Oveja Negra Ltda, pg 112
Editorial Panamericana, pg 112
Procultura SA, pg 112
Universidad de Antioquia, Division Publicaciones, pg 113

The Democratic Republic of the Congo

Centre Protestant d'Editions et de Diffusion (CEDI), pg 114
Presses Universitaires du Zaiire (PUZ), pg 114

Costa Rica

Litografia Artex, SA, pg 115
Ediciones Promesa, pg 116
Editorial de la Universidad de Costa Rica, pg 116
Editorial Universidad Nacional (EUNA), pg 116
Editorial Universitaria Centroamericana (EDUCA), pg 117

Cote d'Ivoire

Akohi Editions, pg 117
Les Nouvelles Editions Ivoiriennes (NEI), pg 117

Croatia

ALFA dd za izdavacke, graficke i trgovacke poslove, pg 117
ArTresor naklada, pg 117
Durieux d o o, pg 118
Faust Vrani, pg 118
Knjizevni Krug Split, pg 118
Matica hrvatska, pg 118
Mladost d d Izdavacku graficku i informaticku djelatnost, pg 119
Nasa Djeca Publishing, pg 119
Skolska Knjiga, pg 119

Cuba

Casa Editora Abril, pg 120
Holguin, Ediciones, pg 120
Editorial Letras Cubanas, pg 120
Editorial Oriente, pg 120
Editora Politica, pg 120

Czech Republic

AULOS sro, pg 122
Aurora, pg 122
Barrister & Principal, pg 122
Ceska Expedice, pg 123
Euromedia Group-Odeon, pg 123

Horacek Ladislav-Paseka, pg 123
Karmelitanske Nakladatelstvi, pg 124
Knihovna A Tiskarna Pro Nevidome, pg 124
Konsultace spol sro, pg 125
Labyrint, pg 125
Lidove Noviny Publishing House, pg 125
Lyra Pragensis Obecne Prospelna Spolecnost, pg 125
Melantrich, akc spol, pg 125
Mlada fronta, pg 125
Pavla Momcilova, pg 125
Ladislav Vasicek, pg 128
Vitalis sro, pg 128
Votobia sro, pg 128
Vysehrad spol sro, pg 128

Denmark

Borgens Forlag A/S, pg 129
The Danish Literature Centre, pg 130
Grevas Forlag, pg 131
Gyldendalske Boghandel - Nordisk Forlag A/S, pg 131
Politisk Revy, pg 133
Det Schonbergske Forlag A/S, pg 134
Forlaget Vindrose A/S, pg 135

Dominican Republic

Pontificia Universidad Catolica Madre y Maestra, pg 136

Egypt (Arab Republic of Egypt)

Al Arab Publishing House, pg 137
Dar El Shorouk, pg 138
Elias Modern Publishing House, pg 138
Middle East Book Centre, pg 138
Senouhy Publishers, pg 138

El Salvador

Clasicos Roxsil Editorial SA de CV, pg 138
Editorial Universitaria de la Universidad de El Salvador, pg 139

Estonia

Ilmamaa, pg 139
Oue Eesti Raamat, pg 140
Tuum, pg 140

Fiji

Lotu Pacifika Productions, pg 141

Finland

Basam Books Oy, pg 141
Herattaja-yhdistys Ry, pg 142
Schildts Forlags AB, pg 144
Scriptum Forlags AB, pg 144
Soderstroms Forlag, pg 144
Svenska Oesterbottens Litteraturfoerening, pg 144

France

Editions Actes Sud, pg 145
ADPF Publications, pg 145
Editions Al Liamm, pg 146
Alsatia SA, pg 146
Editions ALTESS, pg 146
L'Amitie par le Livre, pg 146
Editions Arcam, pg 147
Armenia Editions, pg 147
Editions Aubier-Montaigne SA, pg 148
Editions d'Aujourd'hui (Les Introuvables), pg 148

Editions Belin, pg 149
La Bibliotheque des Arts, pg 150
William Blake & Co, pg 150
Editions Andre Bonne, pg 150
Pierre Bordas & Fils, Editions, pg 150
Editions Jacques Bremond, pg 151
Brud Nevez, pg 151
Editions des Cahiers Bourbonnais, pg 151
Editions Caracteres, pg 152
Centre pour l'Innovation et la Recherche en Communication de l'Entreprise (CIRCE), pg 152
Editions Champ Vallon, pg 153
Le Cherche Midi Editeur, pg 154
Editions Comp'Act, pg 155
Corsaire Editions, pg 156
Editions Jose Corti, pg 156
Nouvelles Editions Debresse, pg 157
La Delirante, pg 157
Editions de la Difference, pg 158
Les Dossiers d'Aquitaine, pg 159
Editions Unes, pg 160
Encres Vives, pg 161
Editions Entente, pg 161
Editions Pierre Fanlac, pg 162
Editions Des Femmes, pg 163
Association Frank, pg 164
Editions Galilee, pg 164
Editions Gallimard, pg 164
Sarl Editions Jean Grassin, pg 166
Editions de l'Herne, pg 167
Ivrea, pg 169
Lettres Vives Editions, pg 172
Editions Librairie-Galerie Racine, pg 172
Le Livre de Poche-L G F (Librairie Generale Francaise), pg 173
Mercure de France SA, pg 175
Nanga, pg 176
Editions Mare Nostrum, pg 177
Nouvelles Editions Latines, pg 177
Editions Obsidiane, pg 177
Editions de l'Orante, pg 178
Editions Christian Pirot, pg 180
Editions POL, pg 180
Le Pre-aux-clercs, pg 180
Presence Africaine Editions, pg 180
Propos de Campagne, pg 182
Publications Orientalistes de France (POF), pg 182
Revue Noire, pg 183
Editions Seghers, pg 184
Service Technique pour l'Education, pg 184
Editions du Seuil, pg 184
Editions Andre Silvaire Sarl, pg 185
Spectres Familiers, pg 186
Editions Stock, pg 186
SUD, pg 186
Publications de l'Universite de Pau, pg 188
La Vague a l'ame, pg 188
Editions Vague Verte, pg 188
La Voix du Regard, pg 189

Germany

Alpha Literatur Verlag/Alpha Presse, pg 192
Anabas-Verlag Guenter Kaempf GmbH & Co KG, pg 192
Verlag APHAIA Svea Haske, Sonja Schumann GbR, pg 193
Asso Verlag, pg 195
Atelier Verlag Andernach (AVA), pg 195
Aufbau Taschenbuch Verlag GmbH, pg 195
Aufbau-Verlag GmbH, pg 195

1071

SUBJECT INDEX — BOOK

Babel Verlag Kevin Perryman, pg 196
Dr Bachmaier Verlag GmbH, pg 196
Dr Wolfgang Baur Verlag Kunst & Alltag, pg 198
Beerenverlag, pg 198
Belser Wissenschaftlicher Dienst, pg 199
Bergstadtverlag Wilhelm Gottlieb Korn GmbH Wuerzburg, pg 199
Verlag Beruf und Schule Belz KG, pg 200
Betzel Verlag GmbH, pg 200
Verlag Hermann Boehlaus Nachfolger Weimar GmbH & Co, pg 203
Brandes & Apsel Verlag GmbH, pg 204
Brigg Verlag Franz-Josef Buchler KG, pg 204
BRUEN-Verlag, Gorenflo, pg 205
Bund-Verlag GmbH, pg 206
Fachverlag Hans Carl GmbH, pg 207
Christusbruderschaft Selbitz ev, Abt Verlag, pg 209
CMA Edition, pg 209
J G Cotta'sche Buchhandlung Nachfolger GmbH, pg 210
CTL-Presse Clemens-Tobias Lange, pg 210
Deutsche Verlags-Anstalt GmbH (DVA), pg 212
Deutscher Taschenbuch Verlag GmbH & Co KG (dtv), pg 213
Diagonal-Verlag GbR Rink-Schweer, pg 214
Dieterichsche Verlagsbuchhandlung Mainz, pg 214
Dietrich zu Klampen Verlag, pg 214
Ehrenwirth Verlag GmbH, pg 218
Elpis Verlag GmbH, pg 219
Verlag Peter Engstler, pg 220
Eremiten-Presse und Verlag GmbH, pg 220
Fabel-Verlag Gudrun Liebchen, pg 223
Wolfgang Fietkau Verlag, pg 224
Karin Fischer Verlag GmbH, pg 225
Rita G Fischer Verlag, pg 225
Margarethe Freudenberger - selbstverlag fur jedermann, pg 227
Galrev Druck-und Verlagsgesellschaft Hesse & Partner OHG, pg 228
Gilles und Francke Verlag, pg 229
GLB Parkland Verlags-und Vertriebs GmbH, pg 229
Guenther Butkus, pg 231
Carl Hanser Verlag, pg 234
Litteraturverlag Karlheinz Hartmann, pg 234
von Hase & Koehler Verlag KG, pg 234
Heinz-Theo Gremme Verlag, pg 236
Axel Hertenstein, Hertenstein-Presse, pg 237
Hoffmann und Campe Verlag GmbH, pg 238
Horlemann Verlag, pg 239
Klaus Isele, pg 242
Iudicium Verlag GmbH, pg 242
Verlag J P Peter, Gebr Holstein GmbH & Co KG, pg 242
Peter Kirchheim Verlag, pg 246
Verlag Kleine Schritte Ursula Dahm & Co, pg 246
Konkret Literatur Verlag, pg 249
Dr Anton Kovac Slavica Verlag, pg 249
Karin Kramer Verlag, pg 250
Lahn-Verlag GmbH, pg 251
Verlag Langewiesche-Brandt KG, pg 252
Anton G Leitner Verlag (AGLV), pg 253
Dr Gisela Lermann, pg 253
Lienhard Pallast Verlag, pg 254
Logos-Verlag Literatur & Layout GmbH, pg 255
Maro Verlag und Druck, Benno Kasmayr, pg 257
Matthes und Seitz Verlag GmbH, pg 258
Matzker Verlag DiA, pg 258
Merlin Verlag Andreas Meyer Verlags GmbH und Co KG, pg 259
Mitteldeutscher Verlag GmbH, pg 261
Monia Verlag, pg 261
Verlag Neue Kritik KG, pg 264
Neues Literaturkontor, pg 264
Nie/Nie/Sagen-Verlag, pg 265
Edition Octopus & Okeanos Presse, pg 266
Ostfalia-Verlag Jurgen Schierer, pg 267
Pandion-Verlag, Ulrike Schmoll, pg 268
Pawel Panpresse, pg 268
Pendragon Verlag, pg 269
Philipp Reclam Jun Verlag GmbH, pg 269
Prasenz Verlag der Jesus Bruderschaft eV, pg 271
Propylaeen Verlag, Zweigniederlassung Berlin der Ullstein Buchverlage GmbH, pg 272
Rimbaud Verlagsgesellschaft mbH, pg 276
Romiosini Verlag, pg 276
Ruetten & Loening Berlin GmbH, pg 277
Sassafras Verlag, pg 278
scaneg Verlag, pg 278
Agora Verlag Manfred Schlosser, pg 280
Theodor Schuster, pg 282
Siebenberg-Verlag, pg 283
Steidl Verlag, pg 287
Edition Gunter Stoberlein, pg 288
Straelener Manuskripte Verlag GmbH, pg 288
Suhrkamp Verlag, pg 289
Svato Zapletal, pg 289
Tangens Systemverlag GmbH, pg 289
Toleranz Verlag, Nielsen Frederic W, pg 291
Treves Editions Verein Zur Foerderung der Kuenstlerischen Taetigkeiten, pg 292
Guenter Albert Ulmer Verlag, pg 293
Verlag und Studio fuer Hoerbuchproduktionen, pg 295
Edition Vincent Klink, pg 296
Ellen Vogt Garbe Verlag, pg 296
Verlag Klaus Wagenbach, pg 297
Uwe Warnke Verlag, pg 297
Weidler Buchverlag Berlin, pg 298
Wolgang Fietkau Verlag, pg 301
Das Wunderhorn Verlag GmbH, pg 301
Zambon Verlag, pg 302

Ghana

Anowuo Educational Publications, pg 303
Asempa Publishers, pg 303
Bureau of Ghana Languages, pg 303
Ghana Publishing Corporation, pg 304
Moxon Paperbacks, pg 304
Waterville Publishing House, pg 305
Woeli Publishing Services, pg 305

Greece

Athina, Mary Mavrogiannis, pg 306
Dorikos Publishing House, pg 306
Ekdoseis Kazantzaki (Kazantzakis Publications), pg 307
Elliniki Leschi Tou Vivliou, pg 307
Etaireia Spoudon Neoellinikou Politismou Kai Genikis Paideias, pg 307
Ekdoseis Filon, pg 307
Forma Edkotiki E P E, pg 307
Govostis Publishing SA, pg 307
Denise Harvey, pg 308
Hestia-I D Hestia-Kollaros & Co Corporation, pg 308
Hiotellis P, pg 308
Idmon Publications, pg 308
Irini Publishing House - Vassilis G Katsikeas SA, pg 308
Kalentis & Sia, pg 308
Kastaniotis Editions SA, pg 309
Kedros Publishers, pg 309
Knossos Publications, pg 309
Patakis Publishers, pg 311
To Rodakio, pg 312
S J Zacharopoulos SA Publishing Co, pg 313

Guatemala

Grupo Editorial RIN-78, pg 313

Hong Kong

Breakthrough Ltd - Breakthrough Publishers, pg 315
Research Centre for Translation, pg 319

Hungary

Advent Kiado, pg 320
Europa Konyvkiado, pg 321
Jelenkor Verlag, pg 322
Magveto Koenyvkiado, pg 322
Szepirodalmi Koenyvkiado Kiado, pg 324
Tevan Kiado Vallalat, pg 324

Iceland

Almenna Bokafelagid, pg 325
Godord, pg 325
Idunn, pg 325
Mal og menning, pg 326
Stofnun Arna Magnussonar a Islandi, pg 326

India

Affiliated East West Press Pvt Ltd, pg 327
Ananda Publishers Pvt Ltd, pg 328
Associated Publishing House, pg 329
Chanakya Publications, pg 331
Chowkhamba Sanskrit Series Office, pg 332
DC Books, pg 333
Dutta Publishing Co Ltd, pg 333
Full Circle Publishing, pg 334
Geeta Prakashan, pg 335
HarperCollins Publishers India Pty Ltd, pg 335
Arnold Heinman Publishers (India) Pvt Ltd, pg 335
Intertrade Publications Pvt Ltd, pg 338
Kitab Ghar, pg 339
Natraj Prakashan, Publishers & Exporters, pg 343
Orient Paperbacks, pg 344
Panjab University Publication Bureau, pg 344
People's Publishing House (P) Ltd, pg 345
Prabhat Prakashan, pg 345
Pratibha Pratishthan, pg 345
Reliance Publishing House, pg 346
SABDA, pg 347
Samkaleen Prakashan, pg 348
Sat Sahitya Prakashan, pg 348
Vani Prakashan, pg 352

Indonesia

Dunia Pustaka Jaya PT, pg 354
Nusa Indah, pg 356

Ireland

Clo Iar-Chonnachta Teo, pg 358
The Gallery Press, pg 360
The Goldsmith Press Ltd, pg 360
Irish Texts Society (Cumann Na Scribeann nGaedhilge), pg 361
The Lilliput Press Ltd, pg 361
New Writers' Press, pg 362
Publishers Group South West (Ireland), pg 363
Runa Press, pg 363
Salmon Publishing, pg 363

Israel

Am Oved Publishers Ltd, pg 365
The Bialik Institute, pg 365
Bitan Publishers Ltd, pg 365
Boostan Publishing House, pg 365
Dvir Publishing Ltd, pg 366
Gefen Publishing House Ltd, pg 367
Gvanim Publishing House, pg 367
Habermann Institute for Literary Research, pg 367
Hakibbutz Hameuchad Publishing House Ltd, pg 367
The Institute for the Translation of Hebrew Literature, pg 368
Karni Publishers Ltd, pg 369
Kiryat Sefer, pg 369
Schocken Publishing House Ltd, pg 371
Y L Peretz Publishing Co, pg 373

Italy

Mario Adda Editore SNC, pg 374
Adelphi Edizioni SpA, pg 374
Alba, pg 375
Rosellina Archinto Editore, pg 376
Argalia Editore delle Arti Grafiche Editoriali SRL, pg 376
Athesia Verlag Bozen, pg 377
Belforte Editore Libraio srl, pg 377
Book Editore, pg 378
Bookservice, pg 378
Campanotto, pg 379
Cappelli Editore, pg 380
Centro Studi Terzo Mondo, pg 381
Colonnese Editore, pg 383
Edizioni Della Torre di Salvatore Fozzi & C SAS, pg 385
Edizioni dell'Orso, pg 385
Edistudio, pg 386
Edizioni l'Arciere SRL, pg 387
Giulio Einaudi Editore SpA, pg 387
ERGA SNC di Carla Ottino Merli & C (Edizioni Realizzazioni Grafiche - Artigiana), pg 388
Giangiacomo Feltrinelli SpA, pg 389
Adriano Gallina Editore sas, pg 389
Galzerano Editore, pg 390

PUBLISHERS — SUBJECT INDEX

Garzanti Libri, pg 390
Edizioni del Girasole srl, pg 390
Giuseppe Laterza Editore, pg 391
Ugo Guanda Editore, pg 392
Editoriale Jaca Book SpA, pg 394
L Japadre Editore, pg 394
Lalli Editore SRL, pg 394
Editrice Liguria SNC di Norberto Sabatelli & C, pg 395
Linea d'Ombra Libri, pg 395
Vincenzo Lo Faro Editore, pg 395
Editrice la Locusta, pg 395
Angelo Longo Editore, pg 396
Lorenzo Editore, pg 396
Lusva Editrice, pg 396
Tommaso Marotta Editore Srl, pg 397
Casa Editrice Menna di Sinisgalli Menna Giuseppina, pg 398
Arnoldo Mondadori Editore SpA, pg 398
Gruppo Ugo Mursia Editore SpA, pg 400
Nardini Editore srl, pg 400
Newton & Compton Editori, pg 400
Editrice Nuovi Autori, pg 401
Nuovi Sentieri Editore, pg 401
Il Nuovo Melangolo, pg 401
Paideia Editrice, pg 402
Franco Cosimo Panini Editore SpA, pg 402
Passigli Editori, pg 402
Luigi Pellegrini Editore, pg 403
Daniela Piazza Editore, pg 403
Piero Manni srl, pg 403
La Pilotta Editrice Coop RL, pg 403
Edizioni Quasar di Severino Tognon SRL, pg 404
Reverdito Edizioni, pg 405
Riccardo Ricciardi Editore SpA, pg 405
Edizioni Ripostes, pg 405
Rubbettino Editore, pg 406
Il Saggiatore, pg 406
Sardini Editrice, pg 407
Salvatore Sciascia Editore, pg 407
Edizioni Segno SRL, pg 407
SEMAR Publishers SRL, pg 408
Societa Storica Catanese, pg 408
Spirali Edizioni, pg 409
TEA Tascabili degli Editori Associati SpA, pg 409
Todariana Editrice, pg 410
Edizioni La Vita Felice, pg 412
Vivere In SRL, pg 412

Jamaica
Ian Randle Publishers Ltd, pg 414

Japan
Hoikusha Publishing Co Ltd, pg 418
The Hokuseido Press, pg 418
Meiji Shoin Co Ltd, pg 422
Shakai Shiso-Sha, pg 427
Charles E Tuttle Publishing Co Inc, pg 430

Kazakstan
Zazusy, Izd-Vo, pg 432

Kenya
Foundation Books Ltd, pg 434
Heinemann Kenya Ltd (EAEP), pg 434
Lake Publishers & Enterprises Ltd, pg 435
Phoenix Publishers Ltd, pg 435
Sasa Sema Publications Ltd, pg 435
Transafrica Press, pg 436

Republic of Korea
Ba-reunsa Publishing Co, pg 437
Haedong, pg 438
Hollym Corporation; Publishers, pg 439
Hw Moon Publishing Co, pg 439
Iljisa Publishing House, pg 439
Literature Academy Publishing, pg 441
Mirinae, pg 441
Nanam Publications Co, pg 441
O Neul Publishing Co, pg 441
St Pauls, pg 442

Latvia
Artava Ltd, pg 444
Madris, pg 445
Nordik/Tapals Publishers Ltd, pg 445
Preses Nams, pg 445

Lebanon
World Book Publishing, pg 447

Liechtenstein
Kliemand Verlag, pg 448

Lithuania
Andrena Publishers, pg 448
Baltos Lankos, pg 449
Klaipedos Universiteto Leidykla, pg 449
Lietuvos Rasytoju Sajungos Leidykla, pg 449
Vaga Ltd, pg 450
Vyturys Vyturio leidykla, UAB, pg 450

Luxembourg
Editions APESS ASBL, pg 450
Editions Emile Borschette, pg 450
Cahiers Luxembourgeois, pg 451
Eiffes Romain, pg 451
Op der Lay, pg 451
Editions Tousch, pg 452
Varkki Verghese, pg 452

The Former Yugoslav Republic of Macedonia
Detska radost, pg 452
Ktitor, pg 452
Macedonia Prima Publishing House, pg 452
Mi-An Knigoizdatelstvo, pg 452
Nov svet (New World), pg 453
Strk Publishing House, pg 453
Zumpres Publishing Firm, pg 453

Malawi
Christian Literature Association in Malawi, pg 454

Malaysia
Pustaka Cipta Sdn Bhd, pg 458
University of Malaya, Department of Publications, pg 459

Mali
EDIM SA, pg 460

Mauritius
De l'edition Bukie Banane, pg 461
Editions de l'Ocean Indien Ltd, pg 461

Mexico
Editorial AGATA SA de CV, pg 462
Aguilar Altea Taurus Alfaguara SA de CV, pg 462
Ediciones Alpe, pg 462
Artes de Mexico y del Mundo SA de CV, pg 462
Editorial Avante SA de Cv, pg 462
Centro Editorial Mexicano Osiris SA, pg 463
Ediciones CUPSA, Centro de Comunicacion Cultural CUPSA, AC, pg 463
Fondo de Cultura Economica, pg 465
Editorial Grijalbo SA de CV, pg 466
Editorial Joaquin Mortiz SA de CV, pg 467
Phillip Richard Conover Lazo, pg 467
Ediciones Promesa, SA de CV, pg 470
Universo Editorial SA de CV Edicion de Libros Revistas y Periodicos, pg 473

Morocco
Association de la Recherche Historique et Sociale, pg 474
Editions Le Fennec, pg 474
Editions Okad, pg 475

Netherlands
Uitgeverij de Arbeiderspers, pg 477
De Bezige Bij B V Uitgeverij, pg 479
Buijten en Schipperheijn BV Drukkerij en Uitgeversmaatschappij, pg 480
Cadans, pg 480
Callenbach BV, pg 480
Castrum Peregrini Presse, pg 480
De Harmonie Uitgeverij, pg 483
Historische Uitgeverij, pg 483
Uitgeverij Holland, pg 483
Uitgeverij J H Kok BV, pg 485
J M Meulenhoff bv, pg 486
Nederlands Literair Produktie-en Vertalingen Fonds (NLPVF), pg 486
Nijgh & Van Ditmar Amsterdam, pg 487
Prometheus, pg 488
Em Querido's Uitgeverij BV, pg 488
Uitgeverij G A van Oorschot bv, pg 491

New Zealand
Auckland University Press, pg 493
Brick Row Publishing Co Ltd, pg 494
Cape Catley Ltd, pg 495
Cicada Press, pg 495
Hazard Press Ltd, pg 497
Nagare Press, pg 499
Nelson Price Milburn Ltd, pg 499
Orca Publishing Services Ltd, pg 499
Oxford University Press, pg 499
Seagull Press, pg 501
University of Otago Press, pg 502
Victoria University Press, pg 502
Words Work, pg 502

Nicaragua
Editorial Nueva Nicaragua, pg 502

Nigeria
ABIC Books & Equipment Ltd, pg 503
Aromolaran Publishing Co Ltd, pg 503
Black Academy Press, pg 503
Cross Continent Press Ltd, pg 504
Heritage Books, pg 505
Longman Nigeria Plc, pg 505
New Horn Press Ltd, pg 506
Northern Nigerian Publishing Co Ltd, pg 506
Nwamife Publishers Ltd, pg 506
Onibon-Oje Publishers, pg 506
Saros International Publishers, pg 507
University Publishing Co, pg 507
Vantage Publishers International Ltd, pg 507

Norway
Ariel Lydbokforlag, pg 508
Aschehoug Forlag, pg 508
H Aschehoug & Co (W Nygaard) A/S, pg 508
Atheneum Forlag A/S, pg 508
Det Norske Samlaget, pg 508
Fonna Forlag L/L, pg 509
Gyldendal Norsk Forlag A/S, pg 509
Lunde Forlag AS, pg 509
Norsk Bokreidingslag L/L, pg 510
Snofugl Forlag, pg 510
Solum Forlag A/S, pg 510

Pakistan
Sheikh Shaukat Ali & Sons, pg 511
H I Jaffari & Co Publishers, pg 513
Jang Publishers, pg 513
Maqbool Academy, pg 513
Sang-e-Meel Publications, pg 514

Paraguay
Intercontinental Editora, pg 516

Peru
Centro de la Mujer Peruana Flora Tristan, pg 516

Philippines
Ateneo de Manila University Press, pg 518
De La Salle University, pg 519
New Day Publishers, pg 520
UST Publishing House, pg 521

Poland
Spoldzielnia Wydawnicza 'Czytelnik', pg 522
Wydawnictwo Dolnoslaskie, pg 522
Instytut Wydawniczy Pax, Inco-Veritas, pg 523
Wydawnictwo Lubelskie, pg 524
Ludowa Spoldzielnia Wydawnicza, pg 524
Norbertinum, pg 524
Ossolineum Zaklad Narodowy im Ossolinskich - Wydawnictwo, pg 525
Panstwowy Instytut Wydawniczy (PIW), pg 525
Wydawnictwo Podsiedlik-Raniowski i Spolka, pg 525
'Slask' Ltd, pg 526

Portugal
Apostolado da Oracao Secretariado Nacional, pg 528
Atica, SA Editores e Livreiros, pg 529

SUBJECT INDEX

Bezerr-Editorae e Distribuidora de Abel Antonio Bezerra, pg 529
Brasilia Editora (J Carvalho Branco), pg 529
Camara Municipal de Castelo, pg 529
Contexto Editora, pg 530
Publicacoes Europa-America Lda, pg 531
Europress Editores e Distribuidores de Publicacoes Lda, pg 531
Fenda Edicoes, pg 531
Guimaraes Editores, Lda, pg 532
Imprensa Nacional-Casa da Moeda, pg 532
Edicoes ITAU (Instituto Tecnico de Alimentacao Humana) Lda, pg 532
Livraria Minerva, pg 533
Livraria Tavares Martins, pg 533
Perspectivas e Realidades, Artes Graficas, Lda, pg 534
Platano Editora SA, pg 534
Editorial Presenca, pg 535
Publicacoes Dom Quixote Lda, pg 535
Quatro Elementos Editores, pg 535
Quetzal Editores, pg 535
Realizacoes Artis, pg 535
Solivros, pg 536
Almerinda Teixeira, pg 536
Usus Editora, pg 536
Vega-Publicacao e Distribuicao de Livros e Revistas, Lda, pg 536

Puerto Rico

Instituto de Cultura Puertorriquena, pg 537
Ediciones Puerto, pg 537
University of Puerto Rico Press (EDUPR), pg 537

Romania

Ars Longa Publishing House, pg 538
Editura Cartea Romaneasca, pg 538
The Center for Romanian Studies, pg 539
Editura Clusium, pg 539
Editure Ion Creanga, pg 539
Editura Eminescu, pg 539
Editura Excelsior Art, pg 539
FF Press, pg 540
Editura Kriterion SA, pg 540
Mentor Kiado, pg 540
Pandora Publishing House, pg 541
Saeculum IO, pg 542
Est-Samuel Tastet Verlag, pg 542
Editura Univers SA, pg 543
Universal Dalsi, pg 543
Vremea Publishers Ltd, pg 543

Russian Federation

ARGO-RISK Publisher, pg 543
BLIC, russko-Baltijskij informaciionnyj centr, AO, pg 544
Izdatelstvo Detskaya Literatura, pg 544
Kavkazskaya Biblioteka Publishing House, pg 545
Izdatelstvo Khudozhestvennaya Literatura, pg 545
Izdatelstvo Molodaya Gvardia, pg 546
Permskaja Kniga, pg 548
Profizdat, pg 548
Izdatelstvo Prosveshchenie, pg 548
Raduga Publishers, pg 548
Izdatelstvo Sovetskii Pisatel, pg 548

Senegal

Centre Africain d'Animation et d'Echanges Culturels Editions Khoudia (CAEC), pg 551
Les Nouvelles Editions Africaines du Senegal NEAS, pg 551

Serbia and Montenegro

Alfa-Narodna Knjiga, pg 552
Beogradski Izdavacko-Graficki Zavod, pg 552
Obod, pg 553
Izdavacka Organizacija Rad, pg 553
Svetovi, pg 554

Singapore

Chopsons Pte Ltd, pg 555

Slovakia

Luc vydavatelske druzstvo, pg 559
Serafin, pg 560
Slo Viet, pg 560
Slovansky Tatran, Vydavatel 'stro spoi sro, pg 560
Slovensky Spisovatel Ltd as, pg 560
Smena Publishing House, pg 560

Slovenia

Cankarjeva Zalozba, pg 561
Franc-Franc podjetje za promocijo kulture Murska Sobota d o o, pg 561
Mladinska Knjiga International, pg 561
Pomurska zalozba, pg 561
Zalozba Obzorja d d Maribor, pg 562

South Africa

Educum Publishers Ltd, pg 563
HAUM (Hollandsch Afrikaansche Uitgevers Maatschappij), pg 564
The Hippogriff Press CC, pg 564
Human & Rousseau (Pty) Ltd, pg 564
Nasou Via Afrika, pg 567
New Africa Books (Pty) Ltd, pg 567
Publitoria Publishers, pg 568
University of KwaZulu-Natal Press, pg 569

Spain

Acantilado, pg 570
Agencia Espanola de Cooperacion, pg 571
Editorial Aguaclara, pg 571
Alianza Editorial SA, pg 572
Baile del Sol, Colectivo Cultural, pg 574
Editorial Biblioteca Nueva SL, pg 574
Calambur Editorial, SL, pg 575
Edicios do Castro, pg 576
Ediciones Catedra SA, pg 576
Columna Edicions, Libres i Comunicacio, SA, pg 577
Comunidad Autonoma de Madrid, Servicio de Documentacion y Publicaciones, pg 578
Diputacion Provincial de Malaga, pg 579
Editorial Don Quijote, pg 579
Edi-Liber Irlan SA, pg 580
Edicomunicacion SA, pg 581
Enciclopedia Catalana, SA, pg 582
Ediciones Endymion, pg 582
Erein, pg 582
Eumo Editorial, pg 583
Galaxia SA Editorial, pg 584
Instituto de Cultura Juan Gil-Albert, pg 585
Grijalbo Mondadori SA, pg 585
Editorial Grupo Cero, pg 585
Ediciones Hiperion SL, pg 586
Icaria Editorial SA, pg 587
Iralka Editorial SL, pg 588
Joyas Bibliograficas SA, pg 588
Ediciones Jucar, pg 588
Junta de Castilla y Leon Consejeria de Educacion y Cultura, pg 588
Editorin Laiovento SL, pg 588
Ediciones Libertarias/Prodhufi SA, pg 589
Llibres del Segle, pg 589
Editorial Lumen SA, pg 589
La Mascara, SL Editorial, pg 591
Editorial Moll SL, pg 592
Munoz Moya Editor, pg 592
Oikos-Tau SA Ediciones, pg 593
Ediciones del Oriente y del Mediterraneo, pg 594
El Paisaje Editorial, pg 594
Editorial Pliegos, pg 596
Pre-Textos, pg 596
Edicions Proa, SA, pg 597
Instituto Provincial de Investigaciones y Estudios Toledanos (IPIET), pg 597
Quaderns Crema SA, pg 597
Editora Regional de Murcia - ERM, pg 597
Ediciones Rialp SA, pg 598
Editorial Seix Barral SA, pg 599
Ediciones Seyer, pg 599
Sirmio, pg 600
Ediciones Siruela SA, pg 600
Edicions 62, pg 600
Grup 62, pg 600
Suaver, Javier Presa Suarez, pg 601
Ediciones de la Torre, pg 602
Torremozas SL Ediciones, pg 602
Trea Ediciones, SL, pg 602
Turner Publicaciones, pg 602
Ediciones 29 - Libros Rio Nuevo, pg 603
Editorial Verbum SL, pg 604
Vinaches Lopez, Luisa, pg 605
Visor Libros, pg 605
Ediciones Vulcano, pg 605
Edicions Xerais de Galicia, pg 605

Sri Lanka

Danuma Prakashakayo, pg 606
Dayawansa Jayakody & Co, pg 606
Swarna Hansa Foundation, pg 607

Sudan

Al-Ayam Press Co Ltd, pg 608
Khartoum University Press, pg 608

Suriname

Lutchman, Drs LFS, pg 608

Sweden

Bokforlaget Axplock, pg 609
Rene Coeckelberghs Bokfoerlag AB, pg 610
Ellerstroms, pg 611
Schultz Forlag AB, pg 615
AB Wahlstroem & Widstrand, pg 616

Switzerland

Adonia-Verlag, pg 617
Editions L'Age d'Homme - La Cite, pg 617
Ammann Verlag & Co, pg 617
Arche Verlag AG, Raabe und Vitali, pg 617
Editions de la Baconniere SA, pg 618
Bartschi Publishing, pg 618
Verlag Bibliophile Drucke von Josef Stocker AG, pg 619
Verlag Bo Cavefors, pg 620
Werner Classen Verlag, pg 621
Daimon Verlag AG, pg 621
Daphnis-Verlag, pg 621
Erker-Verlag, pg 623
Govinda-Verlag, pg 624
Haffmans Verlag AG, pg 624
Kranich-Verlag, Dres AG & H R Bosch-Gwalter, pg 627
Lia rumantscha, pg 627
E Lopfe-Benz AG Rorschach, Graphische Anstalt und Verlag, pg 628
Manesse Verlag GmbH, pg 628
Orte-Verlag, pg 630
Ostschweiz Druck und Verlag, pg 630
Pendo Verlag GmbH, pg 631
Rhein-Trio, Edition/Editions du Fou, pg 632
Verlag fuer Schoene Wissenschaften, pg 633
Speer -Verlag, pg 634
Istituto Editoriale Ticinese (IET) SA, pg 635
Editions du Tricorne, pg 635
Editions Eliane Vernay, pg 636
Verlag Die Waage, pg 636
Verlag im Waldgut AG, pg 636
Zbinden Druck und Verlag AG, pg 637

Syrian Arab Republic

Damascus University Press, pg 638

Taiwan, Province of China

Chung Hwa Book Co Ltd, pg 639
Far East Book Co Ltd, pg 639
UNITAS Publishing Co Ltd, pg 642
World Book Co Ltd, pg 642

United Republic of Tanzania

East African Publishing House, pg 643
Eastern Africa Publications Ltd, pg 643
Oxford University Press, pg 644
Tanzania Publishing House, pg 644

Togo

Editions Akpagnon, pg 646
Les Nouvelles Editions Africaines du TOGO (NEA-TOGO), pg 646

Tunisia

Academie Tunisienne des Sciences, des Lettres et des Arts Beit El Hekma, pg 647
Les Editions de l'Arbre, pg 647
Maison Tunisienne de l'Edition, pg 648

Turkey

Inkilap Publishers Ltd, pg 650
Kiyi Yayinlari, pg 650
Metis Yayinlari, pg 650
Varlik Yayinlari AS, pg 652
Kabalci Yayinevi, pg 652

Uganda

Fountain Publishers Ltd, pg 652
Roce (Consultants) Ltd, pg 653

PUBLISHERS

Ukraine
Osnovy Publishers, pg 654

United Arab Emirates
Department of Culture & Information Government of Sharjah, pg 654

United Kingdom
Abbotsford Publishing, pg 654
Acair Ltd, pg 655
Act 3 Publishing, pg 655
AK Press & Distribution, pg 656
Alun Books, pg 657
Anvil Press Poetry Ltd, pg 658
Apex Publishing Ltd, pg 658
Argo Spoken Word, pg 659
Argyll Publishing, pg 659
BCA - Book Club Associates, pg 663
Blackstaff Press, pg 666
Bloodaxe Books Ltd, pg 668
Calder Publications Ltd, pg 673
Canongate Books Ltd, pg 674
Carcanet Press Ltd, pg 674
Cassell & Co, pg 675
Chapman, pg 677
Cyhoeddiadau Barddas, pg 685
The Eurospan Group, pg 692
Faber & Faber Ltd, pg 694
Famedram Publishers Ltd, pg 694
Feather Books, pg 694
Flambard Press, pg 695
Frontier Publishing Ltd, pg 697
Gairm Publications, pg 698
Genesis Publications Ltd, pg 699
Gomer Press (J D Lewis & Sons Ltd), pg 701
The Greek Bookshop, pg 702
Gwasg Gwenffrwd, pg 703
Robert Hale Ltd, pg 704
The Harvill Press, pg 705
Heartland Publishing Ltd, pg 707
Hippopotamus Press, pg 709
Honno Welsh Women's Press, pg 710
Icon Press, pg 711
The Islamic Texts Society, pg 715
Janus Publishing Co Ltd, pg 716
Jay Landesman, pg 719
Libris Ltd, pg 720
The Littman Library of Jewish Civilization, pg 721
Y Lolfa Cyf, pg 722
Luath Press Ltd, pg 722
Macmillan Audio Books, pg 723
Macmillan Children's Books, pg 723
Mango Publishing, pg 725
The Medici Society Ltd, pg 726
MGM, pg 727
Moorley's Print & Publishing Ltd, pg 729
National Association for the Teaching of English (NATE), pg 730
NMS Enterprises Ltd - Publishing, pg 733
Octagon Press Ltd, pg 734
Octopus Publishing Group, pg 734
The Oleander Press, pg 735
Onlywomen Press Ltd, pg 735
Orion Publishing Group Ltd, pg 736
Oxford University Press, pg 737
PARAS, pg 738
Pearson Education, pg 739
Peepal Tree Press Ltd, pg 740
Pentathol Publishing, pg 740
Planet, pg 743
Plough Publishing House of Bruderhof Communities in the UK, pg 743
Polygon, pg 744
Primrose Hill Press Ltd, pg 745
Ramsay Head Press, pg 747
Random House UK Ltd, pg 747
Regency House Publishing Ltd, pg 749
Scottish Cultural Press, pg 755
Scottish Text Society, pg 755
Seren, pg 756
Sherbourne Publications, pg 757
Charles Skilton Ltd, pg 758
Skoob Russell Square, pg 758
Souvenir Press Ltd, pg 759
Supportive Learning Publications, pg 762
Tabb House, pg 762
Tern Press, pg 764
Time Out Group Ltd, pg 765
Triumph House, pg 767
Tuba Press, pg 767
University of Exeter Press, pg 768
Ward Lock Educational Co Ltd, pg 771
Wordsworth Editions Ltd, pg 775

Uruguay
Editorial Arca SRL, pg 776
Ediciones de Juan Darien, pg 777
Nordan-Comunidad, pg 778
Luis A Retta Libros, pg 778
Rosebud Ediciones, pg 778
Ediciones Trilce, pg 778
La Urpila Editores, pg 778
Vinten Editor, pg 778

Venezuela
Alfadil Ediciones, pg 778
Editorial Ateneo de Caracas, pg 779
Monte Avila Editores Latinoamericana CA, pg 779
Biblioteca Ayacucho, pg 779

Zambia
Zambia Educational Publishing House, pg 782

Zimbabwe
College Press Publishers (Pvt) Ltd, pg 783
The Literature Bureau, pg 783
Longman Zimbabwe (Pvt) Ltd, pg 783
Mambo Press, pg 783
Mercury Press Pvt Ltd, pg 784
Phantom Publishers, pg 784
Vision Publications, pg 784
Zimbabwe Women Writers, pg 785

SUBJECT INDEX

PSYCHOLOGY, PSYCHIATRY

Albania
NL SH, pg 1
State Textbook Publishing House, pg 1

Argentina
Editorial Abaco de Rodolfo Depalma SRL, pg 2
Alianza Editorial de Argentina SA, pg 3
Amorrortu Editores SA, pg 3
AZ Editora SA, pg 3
Bonum Editorial SACI, pg 4
Centro Editor de America Latina SA, pg 4
Club de Lectores, pg 4
Ediciones del Eclipse, pg 5
EUDEBA (Editorial Universitaria de Buenos Aires), pg 5
Ediciones de la Flor SRL, pg 6
Fundacion Editorial de Belgrano, pg 6
Editorial Guadalupe, pg 6
Kapelusz Editora SA, pg 7
Ediciones Lidiun, pg 7
Editorial Losada SA, pg 7
Marymar Ediciones SA, pg 7
Editorial Medica Panamericana SA, pg 7
Ediciones Nueva Vision SAIC, pg 8
Editorial Paidos SAICF, pg 8
Editorial Planeta Argentina SAIC, pg 8
Editorial Plus Ultra SA, pg 8
Editorial Polemos SA, pg 8
San Pablo, pg 9
Editorial Sudamericana SA, pg 9
Editorial Troquel SA, pg 9
Javier Vergara Editor SA, pg 9

Australia
ACER Press, pg 10
The Advancement Centre, pg 11
Michelle Anderson Publishing, pg 11
Edward Arnold (Australia) Pty Ltd, pg 12
Australian Academic Press Pty Ltd, pg 13
Blackwell Publishing Asia, pg 15
Bridge To Peace Publications, pg 16
Deva Wings Publications, pg 20
Elsevier Australia, pg 21
Extraordinary People Press, pg 22
Finch Publishing, pg 22
Freshet Press, pg 23
Gnostic Editions, pg 23
Hale & Iremonger Pty Ltd, pg 24
Kerri Hamer, pg 24
Hampden Press, pg 24
Kurlana Publishing, pg 28
Linking-Up Publishing, pg 29
Macmillan Publishers Australia Pty Ltd, pg 30
McGraw-Hill Australia Pty Ltd, pg 31
Melbourne University Press, pg 32
Jurriaan Plesman, pg 37
Spectrum Publications, pg 41
Unity Press, pg 44
Wellness Australia, pg 46
Wileman Publications, pg 46
Windhorse Books, pg 47

Austria
CEEBA Publications Antenne d'Autriche, pg 49
DachsVerlag GmbH, pg 49
Alois Goschl & Co, pg 51
Literas-Verlag GmbH, pg 53
Wilhelm Maudrich KG, pg 54
Otto Mueller Verlag, pg 54
Verlag des Osterr Kneippbundes GmbH, pg 56
Verlag Anton Pustet, pg 56
Andreas Schnider Verlags-Atelier, pg 57
Springer-Verlag Wien, pg 58
Urban und Schwarzenberg GmbH, pg 59
WUV/Facultas Universitaetsverlag, pg 60

Belgium
Academia Press, pg 62
Uitgeverij Acco, pg 62
Altina, pg 63
Editions De Boeck-Larcier SA, pg 66
Editest, SPRL, pg 67
EPO Publishers, Printers, Booksellers, pg 67
Editions Labor, pg 69
Leuven University Press, pg 70
Mardaga, Pierre, Editeur, pg 71
Nauwelaerts Edition SA, pg 71
La Part de L'Oeil, pg 71
Publications des Facultes Universitaires Saint Louis, pg 72
Vander Editions, SA, pg 74
Les Editions Vie ouvriere ASBL, pg 74
Wolters Plantyn Educatieve Uitgevers, pg 74

Brazil
Agalma Psicanalise Editora Ltda, pg 77
Editora Agora Ltda, pg 77
Editora Antroposofica Ltda, pg 77
Ars Poetica Editora Ltda, pg 78
Artes e Oficios Editora Ltda, pg 78
ARTMED Editora, pg 78
Associacao Palas Athena do Brasil, pg 78
Editora Atheneu Ltda, pg 78
Editora do Brasil SA, pg 79
Editora Campus Ltda, pg 79
CEPA - Centro Editor de Psicologia Aplicada Ltda, pg 80
Editorial Dimensao Ltda, pg 80
Livraria Duas Cidades Ltda, pg 80
E P U Editora Pedagogica e Universitaria Ltd, pg 81
Companhia Editora Forense, pg 81
EDUSC - Editora da Universidade do Sagrado Coracao, pg 81
Livraria Martins Fontes Editora Ltda, pg 81
Editora Forense Universitaria Ltda, pg 81
Fundacao Cultural Avatar, pg 82
Fundacao Sao Paulo, EDUC, pg 82
Editora Gente Livraria e Editora Ltda, pg 82
Edicoes Graal Ltda, pg 83
Horus Editora Ltda, pg 83
Livro Ibero-Americano Ltda, pg 83
IBRASA (Instituicao Brasileira de Difusao Cultural Ltda), pg 83
Imago Editora Importacao e Exportacao Ltda, pg 84
Interlivros Edicoes Ltda, pg 84
Edicoes Loyola SA, pg 85
Editora Mercuryo Ltda, pg 86
Cia Editora Nacional, pg 87
Editora Nova Fronteira SA, pg 87
Olho D'Agua Comercio e Servicos Editoriais Ltda, pg 87
Paulinas Editorial, pg 88
Paulus Editora, pg 88
Editora Perspectiva, pg 88
Livraria Pioneira Editora/Enio Matheus Guazzelli e Cia Ltd, pg 88
Proton Editora Ltda, pg 89
Saraiva SA, Livreiros Editores, pg 90
Livraria Sulina Editora, pg 91
Summus Editorial Ltda, pg 91
Totalidade Editora Ltda, pg 91
Editora UNESP, pg 91
Fundacao Getulio Vargas, pg 92
Editora Verbo Ltda, pg 92
Vozes Editora Ltda, pg 92
Jorge Zahar Editor, pg 92

Bulgaria
Aratron, IK, pg 93
Ciela Publishing House, pg 93
DA-Izdatelstvo Publishers, pg 93

SUBJECT INDEX

EA EOOD, pg 94
Eurasia Academic Publishers, pg 94
Kibea Publishing Co, pg 95
Kralica MAB, pg 95
LIK Izdanija, pg 95
Makros 2000 - Plovdiv, pg 95
Naouka i Izkoustvo, Ltd, pg 95
Nov Covek Publishing House, pg 96
Seven Hills Publishers, pg 96
TEMTO, pg 97

Chile
Arrayan Editores, pg 98
Editorial Cuatro Vientos, pg 99
Pontificia Universidad Catolica de Chile, pg 100

China
Beijing Medical University Press, pg 101
Fudan University Press, pg 104
Higher Education Press, pg 105
Lanzhou University Press, pg 106
SDX (Shenghuo-Dushu-Xinzhi) Joint Publishing Co, pg 107
Shanghai Far East Publishers, pg 108

Colombia
Kapelusz Ltda Editorial, pg 111
McGraw-Hill Colombia, pg 112
Siglo XXI Editores de Colombia Ltda, pg 112
Tercer Mundo Editores SA, pg 113

The Democratic Republic of the Congo
Presses Universitaires du Zaiire (PUZ), pg 114

Costa Rica
Editorial Porvenir, pg 116
Ediciones Promesa, pg 116

Croatia
Hrvatsko filozofsko drustvo, pg 118
Naklada Ljevak doo, pg 119
Skolska Knjiga, pg 119

Cuba
Editora Politica, pg 120
Pueblo y Educacion Editorial (PE), pg 121

Czech Republic
Barrister & Principal, pg 122
Chvojkova nakladatelstvi, pg 123
Doplnek, pg 123
Knihovna A Tiskarna Pro Nevidome, pg 124
Portal spol sro, pg 126
Psychoanalyticke Nakladatelstvi, pg 127
Slon Sociologicke Nakladatelstvi, pg 127

Denmark
Aarhus Universitetsforlag, pg 128
Akademisk Forlag A/S, pg 128
Forlaget Apostrof ApS, pg 129
Borgens Forlag A/S, pg 129
Dansk Psykologisk Forlag, pg 130
Forlaget GMT, pg 131
Gyldendalske Boghandel - Nordisk Forlag A/S, pg 131
Nyt Nordisk Forlag Arnold Busck A/S, pg 133
Joergen Paludan Forlag ApS, pg 133
Politikens Forlag A/S, pg 133
Politisk Revy, pg 133
Hans Reitzel Publishers Ltd, pg 134
Det Schonbergske Forlag A/S, pg 134

Egypt (Arab Republic of Egypt)
Al Arab Publishing House, pg 137
Dar El Shorouk, pg 138

Estonia
Sinisukk, pg 140
Tuum, pg 140

Finland
Basam Books Oy, pg 141
Kustannus Oy Duodecim, pg 141
Forsamlingsforbundets Forlags AB, pg 142
Soderstroms Forlag, pg 144
Yliopistopaino/Helsinki University Press, pg 145

France
Editions ALTESS, pg 146
L'Anabase, pg 146
L'Arche Editeur, pg 147
Atelier National de Reproduction des Theses, pg 148
Aubanel Editions, pg 148
Editions Aubier-Montaigne SA, pg 148
Autrement Editions, pg 148
Alain Brethes Editions, pg 151
Editions Calmann-Levy SA, pg 152
Editions Champ Vallon, pg 153
Editions Chiron, pg 154
Chotard et Associes Editeurs, pg 154
Chronique Sociale, pg 154
CNRS Editions, pg 155
Armand Colin, Editeur, pg 155
CTNERHI - Centre Technique National d'Etudes et de Recherches sur les Handicaps et les Inadaptations, pg 156
Editions Dangles SA-Edilarge SA, pg 157
Editions du Dauphin, pg 157
Editions Denoel, pg 157
Dervy Editions, pg 158
Doin Editeurs, pg 159
Dunod Editeur, pg 159
Editions et Publications de l'Ecole Lacanienne (EPEL), pg 159
Les Editions ESF, pg 160
Ellebore Editions, pg 161
L'Ere Nouvelle, pg 161
Editions Eres, pg 162
L'Esprit Du Temps, pg 162
Editions Fleurus, pg 163
Editions Galilee, pg 164
Editions Ganymede, pg 165
Editions Jacques Grancher, pg 165
Editions Imago, pg 168
InterEditions, pg 169
Le Jour, Editeur, pg 169
Jouvence Editions, pg 170
Editions Larousse, pg 171
Macula, pg 173
Editions de la Maison des Sciences de l'Homme, Paris, pg 173
Masson Editeur, pg 174
Medius Editions, pg 175
Presses Universitaires du Mirail, pg 176
Editions Fernand Nathan, pg 176
Editions Odile Jacob, pg 177
Point Hors Ligne Editions, pg 180
Les Presses du Management, pg 181
Presses Universitaires de France (PUF), pg 181
Presses Universitaires de Grenoble, pg 181
Presses Universitaires de Nancy, pg 181
Presses Universitaires du Septentrion, pg 182
Publications de l'Universite de Rouen, pg 182
Editions Sand et Tchou SA, pg 184
Editions du Seuil, pg 184
Editions Springer France, pg 186
Les Editions de la Table Ronde, pg 186
Librairie Philosophique J Vrin, pg 189

Germany
A Francke Verlag (Tubingen und Basel), pg 190
Ahriman-Verlag GmbH, pg 191
Roland Asanger Verlag GmbH, pg 194
Aschendorffsche Verlagsbuchhandlung GmbH & Co KG, pg 194
Auer Verlag GmbH, pg 195
Belser Wissenschaftlicher Dienst, pg 199
Beust Verlag GmbH, pg 200
Verlag Die Blaue Eule, pg 202
Brandes & Apsel Verlag GmbH, pg 204
R Brockhaus Verlag, pg 204
Bund demokratischer Wissenschaftlerinnen und Wissenschafler eV (BdWi), pg 205
Burckhardthaus-Laetare Verlag GmbH, pg 206
Ulrich Burgdorf/Homeopathic Publishing House, pg 206
Carl-Auer-Systeme Verlag, pg 207
Centaurus-Verlagsgesellschaft GmbH, pg 207
Corona Verlag, pg 210
J G Cotta'sche Buchhandlung Nachfolger GmbH, pg 210
Verlag CSA Rosemarie Schneider, pg 210
Daedalus Verlag, pg 210
Dareschta Consulting und Handels GmbH, pg 210
Verlag Darmstaedter Blaetter Schwarz und Co, pg 210
Deutsche Verlags-Anstalt GmbH (DVA), pg 212
Deutscher Psychologen Verlag GmbH (DPV), pg 213
Deutscher Studien Verlag, pg 213
Deutscher Taschenbuch Verlag GmbH & Co KG (dtv), pg 213
Dietrich zu Klampen Verlag, pg 214
Edition Diskord, pg 215
Dreisam Ratgeber in der Rutsker Verlag GmbH, pg 216
Ehrenwirth Verlag GmbH, pg 218
Ergebnisse Verlag GmbH, pg 220
Ernst Kabel Verlag GmbH, pg 221
EVT Energy Video Training & Verlag GmbH, pg 222
Ferdinand Enke Verlag, pg 224
Wilhelm Fink GmbH & Co Verlags-KG, pg 224
Rita G Fischer Verlag, pg 225
Fischer Taschenbuch Verlag GmbH, pg 225
Focus-Verlag Gesellschaft mbH, pg 225
Verlag Freies Geistesleben, pg 227
Friedrich Frommann Verlag, pg 227
Wilhelm Goldmann Verlag GmbH, pg 230
Haag und Herchen Verlag GmbH, pg 232
Wilhelm Heyne Verlag, pg 237
S Hirzel Verlag GmbH und Co, pg 238
Hoffmann und Campe Verlag GmbH, pg 238
Hogrefe Verlag GmbH & Co Kg, pg 238
Holos Verlag, pg 239
Hans Huber, pg 239
Heinrich Hugendubel Verlag GmbH, pg 240
Edition Humanistische Psychologie (EHP), pg 240
Iudicium Verlag GmbH, pg 242
Julius Klinkhardt Verlagsbuchhandlung, pg 243
Junfermann-Verlag, pg 243
Juventa Verlag GmbH, pg 244
S Karger GmbH Verlag fuer Medizin und Naturwissenschaften, pg 244
Ingrid Klein Verlag GmbH, pg 246
Verlag Kleine Schritte Ursula Dahm & Co, pg 246
Koenigsfurt Verlag, Evelin Buerger et Johannes Fiebig, pg 248
Verlag Koenigshausen und Neumann GmbH, pg 248
Koesel-Verlag GmbH & Co, pg 248
W Kohlhammer GmbH, pg 248
Dr Gisela Lermann, pg 253
Mattes Verlag GmbH, pg 257
Matthias-Gruenewald-Verlag GmbH, pg 258
Midena Verlag, pg 260
Neuland-Verlagsgesellschaft mbH, pg 264
Oekotopia Verlag, Wolfgang Hoffman GmbH & Co KG, pg 266
R Oldenbourg Verlag GmbH, pg 267
Orlanda Frauenverlag, pg 267
Osho Verlag GmbH, pg 267
Pal Verlagsgesellschaft mbH, pg 267
Paranus Verlag - Bruecke Neumuenster GmbH, pg 268
J Pfeiffer Verlag, pg 269
Philipps-Universitaet Marburg, pg 270
Piper Verlag GmbH, pg 270
Guido Pressler Verlag, pg 271
Psychiatrie-Verlag GmbH, pg 272
Psychologie Verlags Union GmbH, pg 272
Psychosozial-Verlag, pg 272
Quelle und Meyer Verlag GmbH & Co, pg 273
Radius-Verlag GmbH, pg 273
Ernst Reinhardt Verlag GmbH & Co KG, pg 275
Ryvellus Medienagentur Dopfer, pg 277
I H Sauer Verlag GmbH, pg 278
Heinrich Schwab Verlag KG, pg 282
Spieth-Verlag Verlag fuer Symbolforschung, pg 284
Springer Science+Business Media GmbH & Co KG, pg 284
Steidl Verlag, pg 287
Dr Dietrich Steinkopff Verlag GmbH & Co, pg 287
Verlag Stendel, pg 288
Stroemfeld Verlag, pg 288
Suhrkamp Verlag, pg 289
Georg Thieme Verlag KG, pg 291
Trias Verlag in MVS Medizinverlage Stuttgart GmbH & Co KG, pg 292

PUBLISHERS SUBJECT INDEX

Ullstein Heyne List GmbH & Co KG, pg 293
UTB fuer Wissenschaft Uni Taschenbuecher GmbH, pg 294
Vandenhoeck & Ruprecht, pg 294
VAS-Verlag fuer Akademische Schriften, pg 294
Votum Verlag GmbH, pg 297
VWB-Verlag fur Wissenschaft & Bildung, Amand Aglaster, pg 297
Waxmann Verlag GmbH, pg 297
Weidler Buchverlag Berlin, pg 298
Windpferd Verlagsgesellschaft mbH, pg 300
Wissenschaftliche Buchgesellschaft, pg 300

Ghana
World Literature Project, pg 305

Greece
Akritas, pg 305
Boukoumanis' Editions, pg 306
Dioptra Publishing, pg 306
Dorikos Publishing House, pg 306
Ekdoseis Thetili, pg 307
Exandas Publishers, pg 307
Gutenberg Publications, pg 307
Hestia-I D Hestia-Kollaros & Co Corporation, pg 308
Kastaniotis Editions SA, pg 309
Kedros Publishers, pg 309
Kyriakidis Vasileios, pg 309
Odysseas Publications Ltd, pg 311
Panepistimio Ioanninon, pg 311
Patakis Publishers, pg 311
Thymari Publications, pg 312

Hong Kong
The Chinese University Press, pg 316
Ming Pao Publications Ltd, pg 318
Philopsychy Press, pg 318
SCMP Book Publishing Ltd, pg 319

Hungary
Joszoveg Muhely Kiado, pg 322
KJK-Kerszov, pg 322
Kossuth Kiado RT, pg 322
Nemzeti Tankoenyvkiado, pg 323
Osiris Kiado, pg 323

Iceland
Bokaforlag Birtingur, pg 325
Hid Islenzka Bokmenntafelag, pg 325

India
Affiliated East West Press Pvt Ltd, pg 327
Ananda Publishers Pvt Ltd, pg 328
The Bangalore Printing & Publishing Co Ltd, pg 329
Concept Publishing Co, pg 332
Eurasia Publishing House Private Ltd, pg 334
Gyan Publishing House, pg 335
Himalaya Publishing House, pg 335
Indian Council of Social Science Research (ICSSR), pg 336
Jaico Publishing House, pg 338
Law Publishers, pg 340
Minerva Associates (Publications) Pvt Ltd, pg 341
Narosa Publishing House, pg 342
Omsons Publications, pg 344
Oxford & IBH Publishing Co Pvt Ltd, pg 345
Reliance Publishing House, pg 346
SABDA, pg 347

SAGE Publications India Pvt Ltd, pg 347
Scientific Book Agency, pg 348
Sita Books & Periodicals Pvt Ltd, pg 349
Somaiya Publications Pvt Ltd, pg 349
Viva Books Pvt Ltd, pg 352

Indonesia
Alumni PT, pg 353
PT Bulan Bintang, pg 354
Eresco PT, pg 354

Ireland
Cathedral Books Ltd, pg 358
Gill & Macmillan Ltd, pg 360

Israel
Am Oved Publishers Ltd, pg 365
Bar Ilan University Press, pg 365
Boostan Publishing House, pg 365
Breslov Research Institute, pg 365
Classikaletet, pg 366
Gefen Publishing House Ltd, pg 367
Hakibbutz Hameuchad Publishing House Ltd, pg 367
Otzar Hamore, pg 367
Keter Publishing House Ltd, pg 369
The Magnes Press, pg 370
Massada Press Ltd, pg 370
Open University of Israel, pg 371
Rubin Mass Ltd, pg 371
Schocken Publishing House Ltd, pg 371
R Sirkis Publishers Ltd, pg 372
Tcherikover Publishers Ltd, pg 372
The Van Leer Jerusalem Institute, pg 373
Yachdav, United Publishers Co Ltd, pg 373

Italy
Franco Angeli SRL, pg 375
Apostolato della Preghiera, pg 375
Arcanta Aries Gruppo Editoriale, pg 375
Edizioni ARES, pg 376
Editore Armando Armando SRL, pg 376
Casa Editrice Astrolabio-Ubaldini Editore, pg 377
Belforte Editore Libraio srl, pg 377
Edizioni Borla SRL, pg 379
Cappelli Editore, pg 380
CEDAM (Casa Editrice Dr A Milani), pg 380
Centro Programmazione Editoriale (CPE), pg 381
Centro Scientifico Torinese, pg 381
Edizioni Centro Studi Erickson, pg 381
CIC Edizioni Internazionali, pg 381
Ciranna - Roma, pg 382
Citta Nuova Editrice, pg 382
Cittadella Editrice, pg 382
CLEUP - Cooperativa Libraria Editrice dell 'Universita di Padova, pg 382
CLUEB (Cooperativa Libraria Universitaria Editrice Bologna), pg 382
Crisalide, pg 383
Edizioni Dedalo SRL, pg 384
Edizioni Dehoniane, pg 384
ECIG, pg 385
Effata Editrice, pg 387
Giulio Einaudi Editore SpA, pg 387
Esselibri, pg 388
Festina Lente Edizioni, pg 389

Arnaldo Forni Editore SRL, pg 389
Editrice Garigliano SRL, pg 390
Giunti Gruppo Editoriale, pg 390
Gius Laterza e Figli SpA, pg 391
Giuseppe Laterza Editore, pg 391
Libreria Editrice Gregoriana, pg 391
Edizioni Guerini e Associati SpA, pg 392
Hermes Edizioni SRL, pg 392
L Japadre Editore, pg 394
Editrice LAS, pg 394
LED - Edizioni Universitarie di Lettere Economia Diritto, pg 395
Levante Editori, pg 395
Longanesi & C, pg 396
Lubrina, pg 396
Lyra Libri, pg 396
Macro Edizioni, pg 397
Marsilio Editori SpA, pg 397
Editrice Massimo SAS di Crespi Cesare e C, pg 397
Edizioni Mediterranee SRL, pg 398
Milella di Lecce Spazio Vivo srl, pg 398
Arnoldo Mondadori Editore SpA, pg 398
Monduzzi Editore SpA, pg 399
Moretti & Vitali Editori srl, pg 399
Societa Editrice Il Mulino, pg 399
Newton & Compton Editori, pg 400
La Nuova Italia Editrice SpA, pg 401
OS (Organizzazioni Speciali SRL), pg 401
Patron Editore SrL, pg 402
Il Pensiero Scientifico Editore SRL, pg 403
Il Poligrafo, pg 404
Psicologica Editrice, pg 404
Red/Studio Redazionale, pg 405
Edizioni del Riccio SAS di G Bernardi, pg 405
Edizioni Ripostes, pg 405
Editori Riuniti, pg 405
Edizioni Universitarie Romane, pg 406
Rusconi Libri Srl, pg 406
Edizioni San Paolo SRL, pg 407
Edizioni Scientifiche Italiane, pg 407
Editrice la Scuola SpA, pg 407
Societa Editrice Internazionale - SEI, pg 408
Spirali Edizioni, pg 409
TEA Tascabili degli Editori Associati SpA, pg 409
Edizioni Thyrus SRL, pg 410
Editrice Tirrenia Stampatori SAS, pg 410
Todariana Editrice, pg 410
Giovanni Tranchida Editore, pg 410
Unipress, pg 411
Editrice Uomini Nuovi, pg 411
Urbaniana University Press, pg 411
UTET (Unione Tipografico-Editrice Torinese), pg 411
Vita e Pensiero, pg 412
Zanichelli Editore SpA, pg 412

Jamaica
Jamaica Publishing House Ltd, pg 414

Japan
Baifukan Co Ltd, pg 415
Baseball Magazine-Sha Co Ltd, pg 415
Dainippon Tosho Publishing Co, Ltd, pg 416
Diamond Inc, pg 416
Fukumura Shuppan Inc, pg 417
Hakuyo-Sha, pg 418

Iwanami Shoten, Publishers, pg 419
Kazamashobo Co Ltd, pg 420
Kinokuniya Co Ltd (Publishing Department), pg 421
Kokudo-Sha Co Ltd, pg 421
Kosei Publishing Co Ltd, pg 421
Koyo Shobo, pg 422
Minerva Shobo Co Ltd, pg 422
Misuzu Shobo Ltd, pg 422
Mita Press, Mita Industrial Co Ltd, pg 422
Nippon Jitsugyo Publishing Co Ltd, pg 424
Reimei-Shobo Co Ltd, pg 425
Riso-Sha, pg 425
Sangyo-Tosho Publishing Co Ltd, pg 426
Seishin Shobo, pg 427
Seiwa Shoten Co Ltd, pg 427
Shunjusha, pg 428
Sogensha Publishing Co Ltd, pg 428
University of Tokyo Press, pg 430
Waseda University Press, pg 431
Yuhikaku Publishing Co Ltd, pg 431

Kazakstan
Al-Farabi Kazakh National University, pg 432

Kenya
Cosmopolitan Publishers Ltd, pg 433
Paulines Publications-Africa, pg 435

Republic of Korea
Chung Rim Publishing Co Ltd, pg 438
Iljo-gag Publishers, pg 439
Korea Psychological Testing Institute, pg 440
Korea University Press, pg 440
Minjisa Publishing Co, pg 441
Sohaksa, pg 443

Latvia
Preses Nams, pg 445
Zvaigzne ABC Publishers Ltd, pg 445

Lebanon
Arab Institute for Research & Publishing, pg 445

Lithuania
Andrena Publishers, pg 448
Dargenis Publishers, pg 449
Klaipedos Universiteto Leidykla, pg 449

The Former Yugoslav Republic of Macedonia
Zumpres Publishing Firm, pg 453

Martinique
George Lise-Huyghes des Etages, pg 460

Mexico
Aguilar Altea Taurus Alfaguara SA de CV, pg 462
Publicaciones Cruz O SA, pg 463
Editorial El Manual Moderno SA de CV, pg 464
Ediciones Exclusivas SA, pg 465
Editorial Fata Morgana SA de CV, pg 465

SUBJECT INDEX

Fondo de Cultura Economica, pg 465
Editorial Joaquin Mortiz SA de CV, pg 467
Editorial Limusa SA de CV, pg 467
Editorial Orion, pg 469
Editorial Pax Mexico, pg 470
Pearson Educacion de Mexico, SA de CV, pg 470
Editorial Planeta Mexicana SA, pg 470
Ediciones Promesa, SA de CV, pg 470
Siglo XXI Editores SA de CV, pg 472
Editorial Trillas SA de CV, pg 472
Universidad Nacional Autonoma de Mexico (National University of Mexico), pg 472
Universidad Veracruzana Direccion General Editorial y de Publicaciones, pg 472
Javier Vergara Editor SA de CV, pg 473

Republic of Moldova
Editura Lumina, pg 473

Monaco
Les Editions du Rocher, pg 474

Morocco
Edition Diffusion de Livre au Maroc, pg 474
Editions Le Fennec, pg 474

Nepal
International Standards Books & Periodicals (P) Ltd, pg 476

Netherlands
Uitgeverij Ambo BV, pg 477
John Benjamins BV, pg 479
Erven J Bijleveld, pg 479
Boom Uitgeverij, pg 479
A W Bruna Uitgevers BV, pg 480
Buijten en Schipperheijn BV Drukkerij en Uitgeversmaatschappij, pg 480
Uitgeverij Christofoor, pg 480
Uitgeversmaatschappij Ad Donker BV, pg 481
Uitgeverij Vrij Geestesleven, pg 482
Uitgeverij en boekhandel Van Gennep BV, pg 482
Historische Uitgeverij, pg 483
Uitgeverij Lemma BV, pg 485
Lemniscaat, pg 485
Mirananda Publishers BV, pg 486
Uitgeverij H Nelissen BV, pg 486
Prometheus, pg 488
Servire BV Uitgevers, pg 489
Swets & Zeitlinger Publishers, pg 489
SWP, BV Uitgeverij, pg 490
Uitgeverij de Tijdstroom BV, pg 490
Tilburg University Press, pg 490
Tirion Uitgevers BV, pg 490
Uitgeverij De Toorts, pg 490
V S P International Science Publishers, pg 491
Van Gorcum & Comp BV, pg 491
VU Boekhandel/Uitgeverij BV, pg 492

New Zealand
Outrigger Publishers, pg 499
Tandem Press, pg 501
University of Otago Press, pg 502

Nigeria
Ibadan University Press, pg 505
Longman Nigeria Plc, pg 505

Norway
Atheneum Forlag A/S, pg 508
Genesis Forlag, pg 509
Glydendal Akademisk, pg 509
Gyldendal Norsk Forlag A/S, pg 509
Pax Forlag A/S, pg 510

Pakistan
Malik Sirajuddin & Sons, pg 513
Publishers United Pvt Ltd, pg 514

Peru
Fondo Editorial de la Pontificia Universidad Catolica del Peru, pg 517
Universidad de Lima-Fondo de Desarollo Editorial, pg 517

Philippines
Ateneo de Manila University Press, pg 518
Rex Bookstores & Publishers, pg 520
University of the Philippines Press, pg 521

Poland
Gdanskie Wydawnictwo Psychologiczne SC, pg 523
Katolicki Uniwersytet Wydawniczo-Redakcja, pg 523
Polish Scientific Publishers PWN, pg 525
PZWL Wydawnictwo Lekarskie Ltd, pg 526
Wydawnictwa Szkolne i Pedagogiczne, pg 527

Portugal
Armenio Amado Editora de Simoes, Beirao & Ca Lda, pg 528
Brasilia Editora (J Carvalho Branco), pg 529
Coimbra Editora Lda, pg 530
Dinalivro, pg 530
Editorial Estampa, Lda, pg 531
Publicacoes Europa-America Lda, pg 531
Fenda Edicoes, pg 531
Gradiva-Publicacnoes Lda, pg 532
Livros Horizonte Lda, pg 533
Editora McGraw-Hill de Portugal Lda, pg 533
Editorial Presenca, pg 535
Edicoes Salesianas, pg 535
Almerinda Teixeira, pg 536
Teorema, pg 536
Livraria Verdade e Vida Editora, pg 536

Puerto Rico
University of Puerto Rico Press (EDUPR), pg 537

Romania
Editura Academiei Romane, pg 538
Aion Verlag, pg 538
Editura Excelsior Art, pg 539
Humanitas Publishing House, pg 540
Polirom Verlag, pg 542
Editura Stiintifica SA, pg 542
Editura Teora, pg 542

Russian Federation
Izdatelstvo Medicina, pg 546
Izdatelstvo Mir, pg 546
Nauka Publishers, pg 547
Izdatel'stvo Nizhegorodskogo Gosudarstvennogo Univ, pg 547

Senegal
Les Nouvelles Editions Africaines du Senegal NEAS, pg 551

Serbia and Montenegro
Alfa-Narodna Knjiga, pg 552
Nolit Publishing House, pg 553
Vuk Karadzic, pg 554

Singapore
McGallen & Bolden Associates, pg 557
Singapore University Press Pte Ltd, pg 558
Taylor & Francis Asia Pacific, pg 558

Slovakia
Slovenske pedagogicke nakladateistvo, pg 560
Smena Publishing House, pg 560
Sofa, pg 560
Ustav informacii a prognoz skolstva mladeze a telovychovy, pg 561
VEDA (Vydavatel'stvo Slovenskej akademie vied), pg 561

Slovenia
Cankarjeva Zalozba, pg 561
Mladinska Knjiga International, pg 561
Zalozba Mihelac d o o, pg 562
Zalozba Obzorja d d Maribor, pg 562

South Africa
Human Sciences Research Council, pg 565
Kima Global Publishers, pg 566
Unisa Press, pg 569
University of KwaZulu-Natal Press, pg 569

Spain
Centro de Estudios Adams-Ediciones Valbuena SA, pg 571
Ediciones Akal SA, pg 571
Editorial Anagrama, pg 572
Editorial Ariel SA, pg 573
Sociedad de Educacion Atenas SA, pg 573
Editorial Biblioteca Nueva SL, pg 574
Ediciones de la Universidad Complutense de Madrid, pg 577
Espanola Desclee De Brouwer SA, pg 578
Dykinson SL, pg 580
Edika-Med, SA, pg 581
EOS Gabinete de Orientacion Psicologica, pg 582
Estudio de Bioinformacion, S L, pg 583
Fondo de Cultura Economica de Espana, SL, pg 583
Editorial Fundamentos, pg 584
Editorial Gedisa SA, pg 584
Editorial Gredos SA, pg 585
Editorial Grupo Cero, pg 585
Editorial Herder SA, pg 586
Editorial Iberia, SA, pg 586
Publicaciones ICCE, pg 587
Editorial Kairos SA, pg 588
Ediciones Libertarias/Prodhufi SA, pg 589
Antonio Machado, SA, pg 590
Mandala Ediciones, pg 590
Editorial Marfil SA, pg 590
Ediciones Marova SL, pg 590
Ediciones Martinez-Roca SA, pg 591
Ediciones Mensajero, pg 591
Ediciones Morata SL, pg 592
Narcea SA de Ediciones, pg 593
OASIS, Producciones Generales de Comunicacion, pg 593
Obelisco Ediciones S, pg 593
Oikos-Tau SA Ediciones, pg 593
Pages Editors, SL, pg 594
Ediciones Paidos Iberica SA, pg 594
Pearson Educacion S A, pg 595
Ediciones Piramide SA, pg 596
Pulso Ediciones, SL, pg 597
Ediciones ROL SA, pg 598
Siglo XXI de Espana Editores SA, pg 599
Editorial Sintesis, SA, pg 600
Grup 62, pg 600
Editorial Rudolf Steiner, pg 601
TEA Ediciones SA, pg 601
Editorial Tecnos SA, pg 601
Editorial Sal Terrae, pg 602
Trotta SA Editorial, pg 602
Universidad de Valladolid Secretariado de Publicaciones e Intercambio Editorial, pg 604
Ediciones Urano, SA, pg 604
Javier Vergara Editor SA, pg 604
Visor Distribuciones, SA, pg 605
Ediciones Xandro, pg 605

Sweden
Alfabeta Bokforlag AB, pg 609
Energica Foerlags AB/Halsabocker, pg 611
Hagaberg AB, pg 612
Bokfoerlaget Natur och Kultur, pg 613
Psykologifoerlaget AB, pg 614
Studentlitteratur AB, pg 616
Svenska Foerlaget liv & ledarskap ab, pg 616
AB Wahlstroem & Widstrand, pg 616
Zindermans AB, pg 617

Switzerland
Editions L'Age d'Homme - La Cite, pg 617
Antonius-Verlag, pg 617
Ariston Editions, pg 617
Astrodata AG, pg 618
H R Balmer AG Verlag, pg 618
Bartschi Publishing, pg 618
CEC-Cosmic Energy Connections, pg 620
Werner Classen Verlag, pg 621
Daimon Verlag AG, pg 621
Editions Delachaux et Niestle SA, pg 621
Editions Foma SA, pg 623
Georg Editeur SA, pg 624
Editions Jouvence, pg 626
S Karger AG, Medical & Scientific Publishers, pg 626
Kindler Verlag AG, pg 626
Kranich-Verlag, Dres AG & H R Bosch-Gwalter, pg 627
Medecine et Hygiene, pg 628
Editions H Messeiller SA, pg 628
Novalis Media AG, pg 630
Origo Verlag, pg 630

PUBLISHERS

Psychosophische Gesellschaft, pg 632
Raphael, Editions, pg 632
Ruegger Verlag, pg 633
Editions Saint-Paul, pg 633
Scherz Verlag AG, pg 633
Schwabe & Co AG, pg 633
Schweizer Spiegel Verlag Mit, pg 634
Sphinx Verlag AG, pg 634
Tobler Verlag, pg 635
Editions du Tricorne, pg 635
Editions des Trois Collines Francois Lachenal, pg 635
Der Universitatsverlag Freiburg, pg 636
Editions Vivez Soleil SA, pg 636
Walter Verlag AG, pg 637

Syrian Arab Republic
Damascus University Press, pg 638

Taiwan, Province of China
Chu Liu Book Company, pg 639
Chung Hwa Book Co Ltd, pg 639
Ho-Chi Book Publishing Co, pg 640
Laureate Book Co Ltd, pg 640
Shy Mau & Shy Chaur Publishing Co Ltd, pg 641
Yi Hsien Publishing Co Ltd, pg 642
Youth Cultural Publishing Co, pg 642
Yuan Liou Publishing Co, Ltd, pg 642

Thailand
Thai Watana Panich Co, Ltd, pg 646

Tunisia
Faculte des Sciences Humaines et Sociales de Tunis, pg 648

Turkey
Alkim Kitapcilik-Yayimcilik, pg 649
Altin Kitaplar Yayinevi, pg 649
Inkilap Publishers Ltd, pg 650
Metis Yayinlari, pg 650
Payel Yayinevi, pg 651
Remzi Kitabevi, pg 651
Soez Yayin/Oyunajans, pg 651

Uganda
Fountain Publishers Ltd, pg 652

Ukraine
Naukova Dumka Publishers, pg 653

United Kingdom
Act 3 Publishing, pg 655
Arnold, pg 659
Arthur James Ltd, pg 660
BAAF Adoption & Fostering, pg 662
Blackwell Publishing Ltd, pg 666
Blackwell Science Ltd, pg 667
Cambridge University Press, pg 674
Capall Bann Publishing, pg 674
Causeway Press Ltd, pg 676
Constable & Robinson Ltd, pg 682
The Continuum International Publishing Group Ltd, pg 682
Crown House Publishing Ltd, pg 684
Delectus Books, pg 687
Dobro Publishing, pg 688
Gerald Duckworth & Co Ltd, pg 688
Educational Explorers (Publishers) Ltd, pg 690
Element Books Ltd, pg 690
The Eurospan Group, pg 692
Faber & Faber Ltd, pg 694
Free Association Books Ltd, pg 697
W H Freeman & Co Ltd, pg 697
Gateway Books, pg 698
HarperCollins UK, pg 705
Harvard University Press, pg 705
Hawthorn Press, pg 706
JAI Press Ltd, pg 715
Karnac Books Ltd, pg 716
Jessica Kingsley Publishers, pg 718
Learning Matters Ltd, pg 720
McGraw-Hill Publishing Company, pg 726
Metro Books, pg 727
MGM, pg 727
MIND Publications, pg 728
MIT Press Ltd, pg 728
Monarch Books, pg 729
The NFER-NELSON Publishing Co Ltd, pg 733
W W Norton & Company Ltd, pg 734
Octagon Press Ltd, pg 734
Oneworld Publications, pg 735
Open Gate Press, pg 735
Open University Press, pg 736
Oxford University Press, pg 737
Pearson Education, pg 739
Pearson Education Europe, Mideast & Africa, pg 739
Piatkus Books, pg 741
Pion Ltd, pg 742
Profile Books Ltd, pg 746
Psychological Corporation Ltd, pg 746
Rationalist Press Association, pg 748
RELATE, pg 749
Rivers Oram Press, pg 750
Roundhouse Group, pg 751
Routledge, pg 751
Royal College of General Practitioners (RCGP), pg 752
The Royal Society, pg 752
SAGE Publications Ltd, pg 753
Sheldon Press, pg 757
Sherwood Publishing, pg 757
Snowbooks Ltd, pg 759
The Society of Metaphysicians Ltd, pg 759
Souvenir Press Ltd, pg 759
Speechmark Publishing Ltd, pg 760
Taylor & Francis, pg 763
Taylor & Francis Medical Books, pg 763
Thames & Hudson Ltd, pg 764
Trentham Books Ltd, pg 767
Verso, pg 770
Whurr Publishers Ltd, pg 773
Wiley Europe Ltd, pg 773
The Women's Press Ltd, pg 775
Yale University Press London, pg 776

Uruguay
Editorial Dismar, pg 777
Nordan-Comunidad, pg 778
Prensa Medica Latinoamericana, pg 778
Ediciones Trilce, pg 778

Venezuela
Editorial Ateneo de Caracas, pg 779
Monte Avila Editores Latinoamericana CA, pg 779
Vadell Hermanos Editores CA, pg 780

SUBJECT INDEX

PUBLIC ADMINISTRATION

Albania
NL SH, pg 1

Argentina
Editorial Abaco de Rodolfo Depalma SRL, pg 2
Abeledo-Perrot SAE e I, pg 2

Australia
Chiron Media, pg 17
Hale & Iremonger Pty Ltd, pg 24
Palms Press, pg 35
University of New South Wales Press Ltd, pg 44

Austria
Fachverlag fur Burgerinformation, Eigenvelag, pg 49
Innverlag + Gatt, pg 52

Bangladesh
Bangladesh Publishers, pg 61
The University Press Ltd, pg 61

Belgium
Vanden Broele NV, pg 64
Editions Delta SA, pg 66
UGA Editions (Uitgeverij), pg 73

Brazil
A & A & A Edicoes e Promocoes Internacionais Ltda, pg 76
Camara Dos Deputados Coordenacao De Publicacoes, pg 79
Editora Ortiz SA, pg 88
Qualitymark Editora Ltda, pg 89
Fundacao Getulio Vargas, pg 92
Vozes Editora Ltda, pg 92

Bulgaria
Dolphin Press Group Ltd, pg 94

Cameroon
Presses Universitaires d'Afrique, pg 98

Chile
Ediciones Cieplan, pg 99

China
Fudan University Press, pg 104
Shandong University Press, pg 108
Universidade de Macau, Centro de Publicacoes, pg 109
Yunnan University Press, pg 109

Costa Rica
Confederacion de Cooperativas del Caribe y Centro America (CCCCA), pg 115
Editorial Nacional de Salud y Seguridad Social Ednass, pg 116
Editorial de la Universidad de Costa Rica, pg 116

Cote d'Ivoire
Universite d'Abidjan, pg 117

Czech Republic
Vysehrad spol sro, pg 128

Denmark
IT-og Telestyrelsen, pg 132
Samfundslitteratur, pg 134
A/S Skattekartoteket, pg 134

Ecuador
Corporacion de Estudios y Publicaciones, pg 136
SECAP, pg 137

France
Blondel La Rougery SARL, pg 150
Counseil International de la Langue Francaise, pg 156
Editions Delmas, pg 157
Editions Foucher, pg 164
Les Editions LGDJ-Montchrestien, pg 172
Sofiac (Societe Francaise des Imprimeries Administratives Centrales), pg 185

Germany
Asgard-Verlag Dr Werner Hippe GmbH, pg 194
Berliner Wissenschafts-Verlag GmbH (BWV), pg 199
W Bertelsmann Verlag GmbH & Co KG, pg 200
Chmielorz GmbH Verlag, pg 208
Deutscher Betriebswirte-Verlag GmbH, pg 212
Dr Curt Haefner-Verlag GmbH, pg 233
Carl Heymanns Verlag KG, pg 237
ITpress Verlag, pg 242
SachBuchVerlag Kellner, pg 245
Klages-Verlag, pg 246
Verlagsgruppe Koehler/Mittler, pg 248
W Kohlhammer GmbH, pg 248
Institut fuer Landes- und Stadtentwicklungsforschung des Landes Nordrhein-Westfalen, pg 251
LIT Verlag, pg 255
Dr Josef Raabe-Verlags GmbH, pg 273
Verlag Norman Rentrop, pg 275
Otto Schwartz Fachbochhandlung GmbH, pg 282
Stadt Duisburg - Amt Fuer Statistik, Stadtforschung und Europaangelegenheiten, pg 286
Stollfuss Verlag Bonn GmbH & Co KG, pg 288
Walhalla Fachverlag GmbH & Co KG Praetoria, pg 297
Verlag fuer Wirtschaft & Verwaltung Hubert Wingen GmbH & Co KG, pg 300

Greece
Exandas Publishers, pg 307
Hestia-I D Hestia-Kollaros & Co Corporation, pg 308
Sakkoulas Publications SA, pg 312

Hong Kong
Hong Kong University Press, pg 317

Hungary
Lang Kiado, pg 322
Novorg International Szervezo es Kiado kft, pg 323
Saldo Penzugyi Tanacsado es Informatikai Rt, pg 324

1079

SUBJECT INDEX — BOOK

India
Ajanta Publications (India), pg 327
APH Publishing Corp, pg 328
Associated Publishing House, pg 329
Concept Publishing Co, pg 332
Gyan Publishing House, pg 335
Indian Council of Social Science Research (ICSSR), pg 336
Minerva Associates (Publications) Pvt Ltd, pg 341
Reliance Publishing House, pg 346
SAGE Publications India Pvt Ltd, pg 347
Scientific Book Agency, pg 348
Sterling Publishers Pvt Ltd, pg 350
Sultan Chand & Sons Pvt Ltd, pg 350
Viva Books Pvt Ltd, pg 352

Ireland
Institute of Public Administration, pg 361

Israel
Haifa University Press, pg 367
Yachdav, United Publishers Co Ltd, pg 373

Italy
Cacucci Editore, pg 379
CEDAM (Casa Editrice Dr A Milani), pg 380
Ciranna - Roma, pg 382
Direzione Generale Archivi, pg 385
EGEA (Edizioni Giuridiche Economiche Aziendali), pg 387
Esselibri, pg 388
Rubbettino Editore, pg 406

Japan
Horitsu Bunka-Sha, pg 418
Ryosho-Fukyu-Kai Co Ltd, pg 425
Charles E Tuttle Publishing Co Inc, pg 430

Kenya
Heinemann Kenya Ltd (EAEP), pg 434
Midi Teki Publishers, pg 435

Republic of Korea
Daeyoung Munhwasa, pg 438
Korea Local Authorities Foundation for International Relations, pg 440
Oruem Publishing House, pg 442

Lithuania
Klaipedos Universiteto Leidykla, pg 449

Luxembourg
Service Central de la Statistique et des Etudes Economiques (STATEC), pg 451
Service Central des Imprimes et des Fournitures de Bureau de l'Etat, pg 451

Mexico
Edamex SA de CV, pg 464
Fondo de Cultura Economica, pg 465
Editorial Limusa SA de CV, pg 467
McGraw-Hill Interamericana Editores, SA de CV, pg 468
Plaza y Valdes SA de CV, pg 470

Netherlands
Samsom BedrijfsInformatie BV, pg 488
Twente University Press, pg 490
VU Boekhandel/Uitgeverij BV, pg 492
Wereldbibliotheek, pg 492

New Zealand
Gondwanaland Press, pg 496

Nigeria
Vantage Publishers International Ltd, pg 507

Poland
Wydawnictwo Prawnicze Co, pg 526
Oficyna Wydawnicza Szkoly Glownej Handlowej w Warszawie Oficyna Wydawnicza SGH, pg 527

Portugal
Edicoes Cosmos, pg 530
GECTI (Gabinete de Especializacao e Cooperacao Tecnica Internacional L), pg 531
Imprensa Nacional-Casa da Moeda, pg 532

Russian Federation
Finansy i Statistika Publishing House, pg 544
Izvestia Sovetov Narodnyh Deputatov Russian Federation (RF), pg 545

South Africa
South African Institute of Race Relations, pg 569
Van Schaik Publishers, pg 569

Spain
Centro de Estudios Adams-Ediciones Valbuena SA, pg 571
Boletin Oficial del Estado, pg 574
Bosch Casa Editorial SA, pg 575
Civitas SA Editorial, pg 577
Instituto de Estudios Fiscales, pg 583
Generalitat de Catalunya Diari Oficial de la Generalitat vern, pg 584
Marcial Pons Ediciones Juridicas SA, pg 590
Pais Vasco Servicio Central de Publicaciones, pg 594
Trea Ediciones, SL, pg 602
Xunta de Galicia, pg 605

Sweden
Industrilitteratur Vindex, Forlags AB, pg 612
Iustus Forlag AB, pg 613

Switzerland
Editions H Messeiller SA, pg 628
Versus Verlag AG, pg 636

Syrian Arab Republic
Damascus University Press, pg 638

United Republic of Tanzania
Tanzania Publishing House, pg 644

Trinidad & Tobago
Caribbean Telecommunications Union, pg 647

Tunisia
Maison Tunisienne de l'Edition, pg 648

Ukraine
Osnovy Publishers, pg 654

United Kingdom
Anglo-German Foundation for the Study of Industrial Society, pg 658
Ashgate Publishing Ltd, pg 660
Commonwealth Secretariat, pg 681
Edinburgh University Press Ltd, pg 689
Ethics International Press Ltd, pg 692
The Eurospan Group, pg 692
ICSA Publishing Ltd, pg 711
Institute for Fiscal Studies, pg 712
Institute of Development Studies, pg 712
LISU, pg 721
National Assembly for Wales, pg 730
National Council for Voluntary Organisations (NCVO), pg 730
Open University Press, pg 736
The Policy Press, pg 744
Policy Studies Institute (PSI), pg 744
Virago Press, pg 770

Zambia
Movement for Multi-Party Democracy, pg 781

Zimbabwe
Sapes Trust Ltd, pg 784

PUBLISHING & BOOK TRADE REFERENCE

Albania
NL SH, pg 1

Argentina
Alfagrama SRL ediciones, pg 3

Australia
Australian Scholarly Publishing, pg 13
Magpie Books, pg 30
Melway Publishing Pty Ltd, pg 32
Thorpe-Bowker, pg 43
Worsley Press, pg 47

Austria
Autorensolidaritat - Verlag der Interessengemeinschaft osterreichischer Autorinnen und Autoren, pg 48
Buchkultur Verlags GmbH Zeitschrift fuer Literatur & Kunst, pg 49
IG Autorinnen Autoren, pg 52

Bangladesh
The University Press Ltd, pg 61

Belgium
Huis Van Het Boek, pg 68

Brazil
Editora Nova Fronteira SA, pg 87

Bulgaria
Abagar Pablioing, pg 92
Ciela Publishing House, pg 93
Musica Publishing House Ltd, pg 95
Sluntse Publishing House, pg 97

Chile
Edeval (Universidad de Valparaiso), pg 99

China
Inner Mongolia Science & Technology Publishing House, pg 105
Southwest China Jiaotong University Press, pg 108

Denmark
Mellemfolkeligt Samvirke, pg 133

Ecuador
CIESPAL (Centro Internacional de Estudios Superiores de Comunicacion para America Latina), pg 136

France
Editions des Cahiers Bourbonnais, pg 151
Culture et Bibliotheque pour Tous, pg 156
Les Dossiers d'Aquitaine, pg 159
Jean-Michel Place, pg 180

Germany
ARCult Media, pg 193
Berliner Wissenschafts-Verlag GmbH (BWV), pg 199
Verlag Beruf und Schule Belz KG, pg 200
BuchMarkt Verlag K Werner GmbH, pg 205
Chmielorz GmbH Verlag, pg 208
Deutsches Bucharchiv Muenchen, Institut fur Buchwissenschaften, pg 214
Dumjahn Verlag, pg 217
Harald Fischer Verlag GmbH, pg 224
Gunter Olzog Verlag GmbH, pg 231
Gutenberg-Gesellschaft eV, pg 232
Hardt und Worner Marketing fur das Buch, pg 234
Dr Ernst Hauswedell & Co, pg 235
Edition ID-Archiv/ID-Verlag, pg 240
Vittorio Klostermann GmbH, pg 247
K F Koehler Verlag GmbH, pg 248
MVB Marketing- und Verlagsservice des Buchhandels GmbH, pg 263
Polygraph Verlag GmbH, pg 271
K G Saur Verlag GmbH, A Gale/Thomson Learning Company, pg 278

Ghana
World Literature Project, pg 305

Greece
Nomiki Bibliothiki, pg 310

PUBLISHERS

Hong Kong
Benefit Publishing Co, pg 315
Island Press, pg 317
Photoart Ltd, pg 318
Press Mark Media Ltd, pg 318

India
Reliance Publishing House, pg 346
Shaibya Prakashan Bibhag, pg 349
Sita Books & Periodicals Pvt Ltd, pg 349

Indonesia
Yayasan Obor Indonesia, pg 357

Israel
Rubin Mass Ltd, pg 371

Kenya
Bookman Consultants Ltd, pg 433

Republic of Korea
Bum-Woo Publishing Co, pg 437
Korean Publishers Association, pg 440
Samho Music Publishing Co Ltd, pg 442

Latvia
Bibliography Institute of the National Library of Latvia, pg 444

The Former Yugoslav Republic of Macedonia
Mi-An Knigoizdatelstvo, pg 452

Malaysia
Geetha Publishers Sdn Bhd, pg 456
Pustaka Cipta Sdn Bhd, pg 458

Morocco
Access International Services, pg 474

Netherlands
Frank Fehmers Productions, pg 482

Nigeria
International Publishing & Research Company, pg 505

Norway
Ex Libris Forlag A/S, pg 509

Pakistan
International Educational Services, pg 512

Romania
Editura Excelsior Art, pg 539

Russian Federation
Izdatelstvo Kniga, pg 545
Izdatelstvo Knizhnaya Palata, pg 546
St Andrew's Biblical Theological College, pg 548

Singapore
Newscom Pte Ltd, pg 557

Slovakia
Sofa, pg 560

South Africa
New Africa Books (Pty) Ltd, pg 567

Spain
Enciclopedia Catalana, SA, pg 582
Antonio Machado, SA, pg 590
Tesitex, SL, pg 602

Sweden
Ordfront Foerlag AB, pg 614
Bokforlaget Spektra AB, pg 615

Switzerland
Pedrazzini Tipografia, pg 631

Taiwan, Province of China
Yi Hsien Publishing Co Ltd, pg 642

Tunisia
Les Editions de l'Arbre, pg 647

United Kingdom
Anderson Rand Ltd, pg 657
Blueprint, pg 668
Book Marketing Ltd, pg 668
Books International, pg 669
Cassell & Co, pg 675
James Clarke & Co Ltd, pg 680
CMP Information Ltd, pg 680
CSA (Cambridge Scientific Abstracts), pg 684
DMG Business Media Ltd, pg 688
Electronic Publishing Services Ltd (EPS), pg 690
Euromonitor PLC, pg 692
Europa Publications, pg 692
Hollis Publishing Ltd, pg 709
Merchiston Publishing, pg 727
National Library of Wales, pg 731
Nielsen BookData, pg 733
Peter Owen Ltd, pg 737
Oxford University Press, pg 737
PIRA Intl, pg 742
Publishing Training Centre at BookHouse, pg 746
Skoob Russell Square, pg 758

RADIO, TV

Albania
NL SH, pg 1
State Textbook Publishing House, pg 1

Argentina
Ediciones Don Bosco Argentina, pg 5
Fundacion Editorial de Belgrano, pg 6

Australia
Australian Film Television & Radio School, pg 13

Brazil
Summus Editorial Ltda, pg 91

Chile
Arrayan Editores, pg 98

China
Electronics Industry Publishing House, pg 104

Croatia
Vitagraf, pg 119

Czech Republic
AMA nakladatelstvi, pg 122

Ecuador
CIESPAL (Centro Internacional de Estudios Superiores de Comunicacion para America Latina), pg 136

France
Bragelonne, pg 151
Dreamland Editeur, pg 159
La Voix du Regard, pg 189

Germany
ARCult Media, pg 193
Bertelsmann Lexikon Verlag GmbH, pg 200
Die Verlag H Schafer GmbH, pg 214
Egmont vgs verlagsgesellschaft mbH, pg 218
Verlag Reinhard Fischer, pg 225
Herbert von Halem Verlag, pg 233
von Hase & Koehler Verlag KG, pg 234
Huss-Medien GmbH, pg 240
kopaed verlagsgmbh, pg 249
Schueren Verlag GmbH, pg 281
TR - Verlagsunion GmbH, pg 291
UVK Verlagsgesellschaft mbH, pg 294

Hong Kong
Electronic Technology Publishing Co Ltd, pg 317
South China Morning Post Ltd, pg 319
Technology Exchange Ltd, pg 319

Italy
Editore Armando Armando SRL, pg 376
Campanotto, pg 379
Ernesto Gremese Editore srl, pg 391
Edizioni Medicea SRL, pg 398
RAI-ERI, pg 405
SAIE Editrice SRL, pg 406

Japan
Gakken Co Ltd, pg 417

Mexico
Ediciones Alpe, pg 462
Editorial Limusa SA de CV, pg 467
Medios y Medios, Sa de CV, pg 468

Netherlands
Otto Cramwinckel Uitgever, pg 481
Frank Fehmers Productions, pg 482
Sociaal en Cultureel Planbureau, pg 489

Norway
J W Eides Forlag A/S, pg 509
Vett & Viten AS, pg 511

Peru
Universidad de Lima-Fondo de Desarrollo Editorial, pg 517

Poland
Wydawnictwa Komunikacji i Lacznosci Co Ltd, pg 524
Wydawnictwa Radia i Telewizji, pg 526

Portugal
Impala, pg 532
Editora Pergaminho Lda, pg 534

Russian Federation
Nauka Publishers, pg 547
Izdatelstvo Radio i Svyaz, pg 548

Spain
Bosch Casa Editorial SA, pg 575
Fragua Editorial, pg 583
Ediciones JLA, pg 588
Marcombo SA, pg 590
Ediciones de la Torre, pg 602

Switzerland
Maurice et Pierre Foetisch SA, pg 623
Junod Nicolas, pg 626
Lehrmittelverlag des Kantons Zurich, pg 627

United Kingdom
Artech House, pg 659
Bernard Babani (Publishing) Ltd, pg 662
BFI Publishing, pg 665
John Blake Publishing Ltd, pg 667
Boxtree Ltd, pg 669
Carlton Publishing Group, pg 675
Chadwyck-Healey Ltd, pg 677
DMG Business Media Ltd, pg 688
The Eurospan Group, pg 692
Faber & Faber Ltd, pg 694
Fourth Estate, pg 696
Furco Ltd, pg 698
Manchester University Press, pg 724
NTC Research, pg 734
Plexus Publishing Ltd, pg 743
Roundhouse Group, pg 751
Time Out Group Ltd, pg 765
Titan Books Ltd, pg 766
Virgin Publishing Ltd, pg 770
Windsor Books International, pg 774

Uruguay
Nordan-Comunidad, pg 778

Viet Nam
Science & Technics Publishing House, pg 780

REAL ESTATE

Australia
Horan Wall & Walker, pg 26
Law Book Co Information Services, pg 28
OTEN (Open Training & Education Network), pg 34
The Real Estate Institute of Australia, pg 39
Wrightbooks Pty Ltd, pg 47

China
China Ocean Press, pg 102

Costa Rica
Editorial Texto Ltda, pg 116

SUBJECT INDEX

France
Communication Par Livre (CPL), pg 155
Editions Delmas, pg 157
Editions Juris Service, pg 170
Editions Legislatives, pg 171
Presses de l'Ecole Nationale des Ponts et Chaussees, pg 181

Germany
Berliner Wissenschafts-Verlag GmbH (BWV), pg 199
Compact Verlag GmbH, pg 209
Rudolf Haufe Verlag GmbH & Co KG, pg 235
Verlag Norbert Mueller AG & Co KG, pg 262
Verlag Norman Rentrop, pg 275
Richardi Helmut Verlag GmbH, pg 276
WEKA Firmengruppe GmbH & Co KG, pg 298
Verlag fuer Wirtschaft & Verwaltung Hubert Wingen GmbH & Co KG, pg 300

Ghana
Building & Road Research Institute (BRRI), pg 303

Hong Kong
Hong Kong University Press, pg 317

Hungary
Novorg International Szervezo es Kiado kft, pg 323

India
Agricole Publishing Academy, pg 327

Kenya
Nairobi University Press, pg 435

Republic of Korea
Chung Rim Publishing Co Ltd, pg 438

Mexico
Editorial Limusa SA de CV, pg 467

Netherlands
BZZTOH Publishers, pg 480
Hagen & Stam Uitgeverij Ten, pg 483
Sociaal en Cultureel Planbureau, pg 489

Russian Federation
Finansy i Statistika Publishing House, pg 544

Switzerland
Drei-D-World und Foto-World Verlag und Vertrieb, pg 622

Taiwan, Province of China
Shy Mau & Shy Chaur Publishing Co Ltd, pg 641

United Kingdom
Management Books 2000 Ltd, pg 724
RICS Books, pg 750
Spon Press, pg 760

REGIONAL INTERESTS

Afghanistan
Government Press, pg 1

Albania
Shtepia Botuese Enciklopedike, pg 1

Algeria
Enterprise Nationale du Livre (ENAL), pg 2

Argentina
Amorrortu Editores SA, pg 3
Edicial SA, pg 5

Australia
Aboriginal Studies Press, pg 10
Aussies Afire Publishing, pg 12
Blubber Head Press, pg 15
Book Agencies of Tasmania, pg 15
R J Cleary Publishing, pg 18
Enterprise Publications, pg 21
The Five Mile Press Pty Ltd, pg 22
Gangan Publishing, pg 23
Histec Publications, pg 25
Institute of Aboriginal Development (IAD Press), pg 27
Kangaroo Press, pg 28
Library of Australian History, pg 29
Yvonne McBurney, pg 31
Mostly Unsung, pg 32
Navarine Publishing, pg 33
On The Stone, pg 34
Outback Books - CQU Press, pg 34
Pacific Publications (Australia) Pty Ltd, pg 35
Kevin J Passey, pg 36
Peter Pan Publications, pg 36
Pollitecon Publications, pg 37
Ruskin Rowe Press, pg 40
St George Books, pg 40
State Publishing Unit of State Print SA, pg 42
Tabletop Press, pg 42
Transpareon Press, pg 44
University of Western Australia Press, pg 45
VCTA Publishing, pg 45
Wellington Lane Press Pty Ltd, pg 46

Austria
Akademische Druck-u Verlagsanstalt Dr Paul Struzl GmbH, pg 48
Astor-Verlag, Willibald Schlager, pg 48
Christian Brandstaetter Verlagsgesellschaft mbH, pg 49
Buchkultur Verlags GmbH Zeitschrift fuer Literatur & Kunst, pg 49
Cura Verlag GmbH, pg 49
Denkmayr GmbH Druck & Verlag, pg 50
Franz Deuticke Verlagsgesmbh, pg 50
Development News Ltd, pg 50
Ennsthaler GesmbH & Co KG, pg 50
Fremdenverkehrs Aktiengesellschaft, pg 51
Graz Stadtmuseum, pg 51
Oesterreichischer Kunst und Kulturverlag, pg 55
Verlag Sankt Peter, pg 56
Salzburger Nachrichten Verlagsgesellschaft mbH & Co KG, pg 57
Verlag Veritas Mediengesellschaft mbH, pg 59
Vorarlberger Verlagsanstalt Aktiengesellschaft, pg 59
Herbert Weishaupt Verlag, pg 59

Barbados
Carib Research & Publications Inc, pg 62

Belgium
Centre Aequatoria, pg 63
Aurelia Books PVBA, pg 63
Glenat Benelux SA, pg 67
Stichting Ons Erfdeel VZW, pg 73

Bolivia
Los Amigos del Libro Ediciones, pg 75

Bosnia and Herzegovina
Bemust, pg 76

Botswana
The Botswana Society, pg 76

Brazil
Editora Atica SA, pg 78
Editora Nova Fronteira SA, pg 87
Edit Palavra Magica, pg 88
Editora Paz e Terra, pg 88

Bulgaria
Publishing House Narodno delo OOD, pg 96

Cameroon
Editions Semences Africaines, pg 98

Chile
Arrayan Editores, pg 98

China
Fudan University Press, pg 104

Colombia
Consejo Episcopal Latinoamericano (CELAM), pg 110
Dosmil Editora, pg 110
Fundacion Centro de Investigacion y Educacion Popular (CINEP), pg 111
RAM Editores, pg 112
Carlos Valencia Editores, pg 113

Costa Rica
Editorial Costa Rica, pg 115
Editorial Texto Ltda, pg 116
Editorial Universitaria Centroamericana (EDUCA), pg 117

Cote d'Ivoire
Centre d'Edition et de Diffusion Africaines, pg 117

Croatia
Matica hrvatska, pg 118

Cuba
Union de Escritores y Artistas de Cuba, pg 121

Cyprus
Andreou Chr Publishers, pg 121

Czech Republic
Pressfoto Vydavatelstvi Ceske Tiskove Kancelare, pg 127

Denmark
Borgens Forlag A/S, pg 129
Dansk Historisk Handbogsforlag ApS, pg 130
Host & Son Publishers Ltd, pg 132
Kraks Forlag AS, pg 132

Dominican Republic
Pontificia Universidad Catolica Madre y Maestra, pg 136

Egypt (Arab Republic of Egypt)
Dar Al-Kitab Al-Masri, pg 137
Dar Al Maaref, pg 138
Middle East Book Centre, pg 138
Senouhy Publishers, pg 138
Ummah Press, pg 138

El Salvador
Editorial Universitaria de la Universidad de El Salvador, pg 139

Fiji
University of the South Pacific, pg 141

France
Actes-Graphiques, pg 145
Editions l'Ancre de Marine, pg 147
Editions de l'Armancon, pg 147
Armenia Editions, pg 147
Aubanel Editions, pg 148
Autrement Editions, pg 148
Editions A Barthelemy, pg 149
Editions Bertout, pg 149
Editions Canope, pg 152
Editions Cenomane, pg 152
CLD, pg 154
Editions Coprur, pg 155
Editions Edisud, pg 159
Editions Pierre Fanlac, pg 162
Imprimerie Librairie Gardet, pg 165
Editions Jean Paul Gisserot, pg 165
Librairie Guenegaud, pg 166
Editions Herault, pg 167
Isoete, pg 169
Editions du Jaguar, pg 169
Editions Lacour-Olle, pg 170
L'Adret editions, pg 170
Laffitte Reprints, pg 170
Editions Larousse, pg 171
Editions Loubatieres, pg 173
Maisonneuve et Larose, pg 174
Martelle, pg 174
Editions Medianes, pg 175
Editions Norma, pg 177
Editions Ophrys, pg 177
Ouest Editions, pg 178
Editions Jean Picollec, pg 179
Siloe - Kerdore, pg 185
Societe des Editions Privat SA, pg 185
Societe Nouveaux Loisirs, pg 185
Editions Sud Ouest, pg 186
Editions Vague Verte, pg 188

French Polynesia
Simone Sanchez, pg 190

Georgia
Merani Publishing House, pg 190

PUBLISHERS SUBJECT INDEX

Germany

Joh van Acken GmbH & Co KG, pg 190
arani-Verlag GmbH, pg 193
Ardey-Verlag GmbH, pg 193
Artcolor, pg 194
Aschendorffsche Verlagsbuchhandlung GmbH & Co KG, pg 194
Asso Verlag, pg 195
Verlag Atelier im Bauernhaus Fischerhude Wolf-Dietmar Stock, pg 195
J P Bachem Verlag GmbH, pg 196
Badenia Verlag und Druckerei GmbH, pg 196
Baken-Verlag Walter Schnoor, pg 196
Bautz Traugott, pg 198
Bayerische Verlagsanstalt GmbH, pg 198
be.bra verlag GmbH, pg 198
Verlag Beleke KG, pg 198
Bergstadtverlag Wilhelm Gottlieb Korn GmbH Wuerzburg, pg 199
Bindernagelsche Buchhandlung, pg 201
BKV-Brasilienkunde Verlag GmbH, pg 201
Bouvier Verlag, pg 203
Brandenburgisches Verlagshaus in der Dornier Medienholding GmbH, pg 204
Brigg Verlag Franz-Joset Buchler KG, pg 204
F Bruckmann Munchen Verlag & Druck GmbH & Co Produkt KG, pg 204
BRUEN-Verlag, Gorenflo, pg 205
Buchhandlung Holl & Knoll KG, Verlag Alte Uni, pg 205
C C Buchners Verlag GmbH & Co KG, pg 205
Bundesanzeiger Verlagsgesellschaft, pg 206
Verlag Busse und Seewald GmbH, pg 206
Fachverlag Hans Carl GmbH, pg 207
Hans Christians Druckerei und Verlag GmbH & Co KG, pg 208
Degener & Co, Manfred Dreiss Verlag, pg 211
Delp'sche Verlagsbuchhandlung, pg 211
Dialog-Verlag GmbH, pg 214
Maximilian Dietrich Verlag, pg 214
agenda Verlag Thomas Dominikowski, pg 215
Donat Verlag, pg 215
Karl Elser Druck GmbH, pg 216
DRW-Verlag Weinbrenner-GmbH & Co, pg 216
Echter Wurzburg Frankische Gesellschaftsdruckerei und Verlag GmbH, pg 217
Eppinger-Verlag OHG, pg 220
Ergebnisse Verlag GmbH, pg 220
Eulen Verlag, pg 221
Fleischhauer & Spohn GmbH & Co, pg 225
Forum Verlag Leipzig Buch-Gesellschaft mbH, pg 225
Fraunhofer IRB Verlag Fraunhofer Informationszentrum Raum und Bau, pg 226
Verlag Walter Frey, pg 227
G Braun (vormals G Braun'sche Hofbuchdruckerei und Verlag) Gmbh, pg 227
Greven Verlag Koeln GmbH, pg 231
H L Schlapp Buch- und Antiquariatshandlung GmbH und Co KG Abt Verlag, pg 232
Verlag H M Hauschild GmbH, pg 232
Dr Rudolf Habelt GmbH, pg 232
Hahnsche Buchhandlung, pg 233
Haude und Spenersche Verlagsbuchhandlung, pg 235
Hellerau-Verlag Dresden GmbH, pg 236
Harro V Hirschheydt, pg 238
S Hirzel Verlag GmbH und Co, pg 238
Husum Druck- und Verlagsgesellschaft mbH Co KG, pg 240
Jan Thorbecke Verlag GmbH & Co, pg 243
Verlag Winfried Jenior, pg 243
Gustav Kiepenheuer Verlag GmbH, pg 245
Peter Kirchheim Verlag, pg 246
Klartext Verlagsgesellschaft mbH, pg 246
Koehler & Amelang Verlagsgesellschaft, pg 248
Konkordia Verlag GmbH, pg 249
Anton H Konrad Verlag, pg 249
Adam Kraft Verlag, pg 250
Hubert Kretschmar Leipziger Verlagsgesellschaft, pg 250
Kulturbuch-Verlag GmbH, pg 250
Verlag der Kunst/G+B Fine Arts Verlag GmbH, pg 251
Lamuv Verlag, pg 251
Landbuch-Verlagsgesellschaft mbH, pg 251
Institut fuer Landes- und Stadtentwicklungsforschung des Landes Nordrhein-Westfalen, pg 251
Libertas- Europaeisches Institut GmbH, pg 254
Logos-Verlag Literatur & Layout GmbH, pg 255
Lusatia Verlag-Dr Stuebner & Co KG, pg 256
Lutherische Verlagsgesellschaft mbH, pg 256
Verlag Waldemar Lutz, pg 256
Mairs Geographischer Verlag, pg 256
J A Mayersche Buchhandlung GmbH & Co KG Abt Verlag, pg 258
Peter Meyer Verlag (pmv), pg 260
Missionshandlung, pg 261
Mitteldeutscher Verlag, pg 261
Morsak Verlag, pg 261
Nicolaische Verlagsbuchhandlung Beuermann GmbH, pg 265
Niederland-Verlag Helmut Michel, pg 265
Oberbaum Verlag GmbH, pg 266
Oreos Verlag GmbH, pg 267
Ostfalia-Verlag Jurgen Schierer, pg 267
Pandion-Verlag, Ulrike Schmoll, pg 268
Verlag Parzeller GmbH & Co KG, pg 268
Physica-Verlag, pg 270
Presse Verlagsgesellschaft mbH, pg 271
Gerhard Rautenberg Druckerei und Verlag GmbH & Co KG, pg 273
REGENSBERG Druck & Verlag GmbH & Co, pg 274
Verlag fur Regionalgeschichte, pg 274
E Reinhold Verlag, pg 275
Respublica Verlag, pg 275
RVBG Rheinland-Verlag-und Betriebsgesellschaft des Landschaftsverbandes Rheinland mbH, pg 276
Rombach GmbH Druck und Verlagshaus & Co, pg 276
Rosenheimer Verlagshaus GmbH & Co KG, pg 276
Sachsenbuch Verlagsgesellschaft Mbh, pg 277
Sax-Verlag Beucha, pg 278
Schelzky & Jeep, Verlag fuer Reisen und Wissen, pg 279
Schillinger Verlag GmbH, pg 279
Max Schmidt-Roemhild Verlag, pg 280
Carl Ed Schuenemann KG, pg 281
Schueren Verlag GmbH, pg 281
Schwabenverlag Aktiengesellschaft, pg 282
Silberburg-Verlag Titus Haeussermann GmbH, pg 283
Stadler Verlagsgesellschaft mbH, pg 286
Stapp Verlag Wolfgang Stapp, pg 286
Steiger Verlag, pg 287
Steinweg-Verlag, Jurgen vomHoff, pg 287
Sueddeutsche Verlagsgesellschaft mbH, pg 288
Suedverlag GmbH, pg 288
Verlag Theodor Thoben, pg 291
Trautvetter & Fischer Nachf, pg 292
Trees Wolfgang Triangel Verlag, pg 292
Tuebinger Vereinigung fur Volkskunde eV (TVV), pg 292
TUeV-Verlag GmbH, pg 293
Guenter Albert Ulmer Verlag, pg 293
VJK Verlag Josef Knecht Carolusdruckerei GmbH, pg 296
VVF Verlag V Florentz GmbH, pg 297
Wartburg Verlag GmbH, pg 297
Weidler Buchverlag Berlin, pg 298
Westholsteinische Verlagsanstalt und Verlagsdruckerei Boyens & Co, pg 299
Dr Dieter Winkler, pg 300
Verlagshaus Wohlfarth, pg 301
Verlag Philipp von Zabern, pg 302
Zambon Verlag, pg 302
Ziethen-Panorama Verlag GmbH, pg 302

Ghana

Anowuo Educational Publications, pg 303

Greece

D Papadimas, pg 311
Papazissis Publishers SA, pg 311
Vivliofilia K Ch Spanos, pg 312

Hong Kong

Asia 2000 Ltd, pg 315
The Dharmasthiti Buddist Institute Ltd, pg 317
Ming Pao Publications Ltd, pg 318
Press Mark Media Ltd, pg 318
Yazhou Zhoukan Ltd, pg 320

Hungary

Szarvas Andras Cartographic Agency, pg 324

Iceland

Iceland Review, pg 325
Stofnun Arna Magnussonar a Islandi, pg 326

India

Himalayan Books, pg 336
Rahul Publishing House, pg 346
Regency Publications, pg 346
Rekha Prakashan, pg 346
Reliance Publishing House, pg 346
Sahasrara Publications, pg 348
SBW Publishers, pg 348
Sri Satguru Publications, pg 350

Indonesia

PATCO, pg 356

Ireland

Ballinakella Press, pg 358
Clo Iar-Chonnachta Teo, pg 358
Eason & Son Ltd, pg 359
Gill & Macmillan Ltd, pg 360
The Goldsmith Press Ltd, pg 360
The Lilliput Press Ltd, pg 361
Mercier Press Ltd, pg 362
National Library of Ireland, pg 362
Relay Books, pg 363
Roberts Rinehart Publishers, pg 363

Israel

Agudat Sabah, pg 364
Ariel Publishing House, pg 365
Ben-Zvi Institute, pg 365
Edanim Publishers Ltd, pg 366
Hakibbutz Hameuchad Publishing House Ltd, pg 367
The Institute for Israeli Arabs Studies, pg 368
Israel Universities Press, pg 368
L B Publishing Co, pg 369
Tel Aviv University, pg 372
Yad Izhak Ben-Zvi Press, pg 373

Italy

Mario Adda Editore SNC, pg 374
Alberti Libraio Editore, pg 375
Artioli Editore, pg 376
Atlantica Editrice SARL, pg 377
Casa Editrice Luigi Battei, pg 377
Belforte Editore Libraio srl, pg 377
Edizioni Brenner, pg 379
Calosci, pg 379
Edizioni Cantagalli, pg 379
Capone Editore SRL, pg 379
Edizioni Della Torre di Salvatore Fozzi & C SAS, pg 385
Edizioni dell'Orso, pg 385
Organizzazione Didattica Editoriale Ape, pg 385
Edizioni l'Arciere SRL, pg 387
ERGA SNC di Carla Ottino Merli & C (Edizioni Realizzazioni Grafiche - Artigiana), pg 388
Flaccovio Editore, pg 389
Arnaldo Forni Editore SRL, pg 389
Adriano Gallina Editore sas, pg 389
Istituto Geografico de Agostini SpA, pg 390
Grafo, pg 391
Lalli Editore SRL, pg 394
Libreria Editrice Fiorentina, pg 395
Giuseppe Maimone Editore, pg 397
Tommaso Marotta Editore Srl, pg 397
NodoLibri, pg 400
Nuovi Sentieri Editore, pg 401
Palatina Editrice, pg 402
Fratelli Palombi SRL, pg 402
Daniela Piazza Editore, pg 403
Il Poligrafo, pg 404

SUBJECT INDEX

Priuli e Verlucca, Editori, pg 404
Edition Raetia Srl-GmbH, pg 405
Sardini Editrice, pg 407
Sicania, pg 408
SIPI (Servizio Italiano Pubblicazioni Internazionali) Srl, pg 408
Societa Storica Catanese, pg 408
Edizioni Thyrus SRL, pg 410
Editoriale Umbra SAS di Carnevali e, pg 411
Vivere In SRL, pg 412

Jamaica
Association of Development Agencies, pg 413

Japan
Nippon Hoso Shuppan Kyokai (NHK Publishing), pg 424
Seibundo Shuppan, pg 426
Shibun-Do, pg 427
The Simul Press Inc, pg 428
Tamagawa University Press, pg 429
Toho Book Store, pg 429
Yushodo Shuppan, pg 431

Kenya
Camerapix Publishers International Ltd, pg 433
Kenway Publications Ltd, pg 434
Transafrica Press, pg 436

Republic of Korea
Kwangmyong Publishing Co, pg 440
Seoul International Publishing House, pg 443

Lebanon
GEOprojects Sarl, pg 446
Librairie Orientale sal, pg 446

Lesotho
Mazenod Book Centre, pg 447
Saint Michael's Mission Social Centre, pg 447

Luxembourg
Editions Emile Borschette, pg 450
Cahiers Luxembourgeois, pg 451
Galerie Editions Kutter, pg 451

Malawi
Christian Literature Association in Malawi, pg 454

Malaysia
Forum Publications, pg 456
Uni-Text Book Co, pg 459
Penerbit Universiti Teknologi Malaysia, pg 459
Vinpress Sdn Bhd, pg 459

Maldive Islands
Novelty Printers & Publishers, pg 459

Malta
The University of Malta Publications Section, pg 460

Mauritius
De l'edition Bukie Banane, pg 461

Mexico
Editorial AGATA SA de CV, pg 462
Ediciones el Caballito SA, pg 462

Ediciones Euroamericanas, pg 465
Fondo Editorial de la Plastica Mexicana, pg 466
Editorial Nueva Imagen SA, pg 469
Instituto Panamericano de Geografia e Historia, pg 469
Panorama Editorial, SA, pg 470
Siglo XXI Editores SA de CV, pg 472

Morocco
Dar El Kitab, pg 474

Mozambique
Empresa Moderna Lda, pg 475
Centro De Estudos Africanos, pg 475

Namibia
Desert Research Foundation of Namibia (DRFN), pg 476

Netherlands
Uitgeversmaatschappij Agon B V, pg 477
Uitgeverij Balans, pg 478
Cadans, pg 480
East-West Publications Fonds BV, pg 481
Sjaloom Uitgeverijen, pg 489
Twente University Press, pg 490
Uniepers BV, pg 491
West-Friesland/Boekproject-ontwikkeling, pg 492

Netherlands Antilles
De Wit Stores NV, pg 493

New Zealand
Aoraki Press Ltd, pg 493
Bush Press Communications Ltd, pg 494
Clerestory Press, pg 495
Craig Printing Co Ltd, pg 495
Fraser Books, pg 496
Grantham House Publishing, pg 496
HarperCollins Publishers (New Zealand) Ltd, pg 497
Heritage Press Ltd, pg 497
Kahurangi Cooperative, pg 497
Kotuku Media Ltd, pg 497
Nestegg Books, pg 499
Otago Heritage Books, pg 499
Paerangi Books, pg 500
Reed Publishing (NZ) Ltd, pg 500

Nigeria
Northern Nigerian Publishing Co Ltd, pg 506

Pakistan
East & West Publishing Co, pg 512
Ferozsons (Pvt) Ltd, pg 512
Jang Publishers, pg 513
National Institute of Historical & Cultural Research, pg 514
Vanguard Books Ltd, pg 515

Poland
Interpress, pg 523
Iskry - Publishing House Ltd spotka zoo, pg 523
Laumann-Polska, pg 524
'Slask' Ltd, pg 526
Towarzystwo Naukowe w Toruniu, pg 527

Portugal
Solivros, pg 536

Puerto Rico
Libros-Ediciones Homines, pg 537
Publishing Resources Inc, pg 537

Romania
Editura Excelsior Art, pg 539
Pallas-Akademia Editura, pg 541

Russian Federation
Interbook-Business AO, pg 545

Rwanda
INADES (Institut Africain pour le Developpment Economique et Social), pg 550

Saudi Arabia
International Publications Agency (IPA), pg 550

Slovakia
Slovansky Tatran, Vydavatel 'stro spoi sro, pg 560
VEDA (Vydavatel'stvo Slovenskej akademie vied), pg 561

Slovenia
Franc-Franc podjetje za promocijo kulture Murska Sobota d o o, pg 561
Mladinska Knjiga International, pg 561
Zalozba Mihelac d o o, pg 562
Zalozba Obzorja d d Maribor, pg 562

South Africa
The Brenthurst Press (Pty) Ltd, pg 563
Fernwood Press (Pty) Ltd, pg 563
HAUM - Daan Retief Publishers (Pty) Ltd, pg 564
Human Sciences Research Council, pg 565
Ithemba! Publishing, pg 565
New Africa Books (Pty) Ltd, pg 567
University of KwaZulu-Natal Press, pg 569

Spain
Editorial Afers, SL, pg 571
Amnistia Internacional Editorial SL, pg 572
Ayalga Ediciones SA, pg 574
Cabildo Insular de Gran Canaria Departamento de Ediciones, pg 575
Dilagro SA, pg 579
Ediciones Diputacion de Salamanca, pg 579
Instituto de Estudios Riojanos, pg 583
Generalitat de Catalunya Diari Oficial de la Generalitat vern, pg 584
Gran Enciclopedia-Asturiana Silverio Canada, pg 585
Impredisur, SL, pg 587
Junta de Castilla y Leon Consejeria de Educacion y Cultura, pg 588
Antonio Machado, SA, pg 590
Ediciones Maeva, pg 590
Editorial Moll SL, pg 592
Publicaciones de la Universidad de Alicante, pg 597

Editora Regional de Murcia - ERM, pg 597
Selecta-Catalonia Ed, pg 599
Turner Publicaciones, pg 602
Editorial Txertoa, pg 603

Sri Lanka
KVG de Silva & Sons, pg 606
National Library & Documentation Centre, pg 607

Suriname
Vaco NV Uitgeversmij, pg 608
Drs F H R Oedayrajsingh Varma, pg 608

Sweden
Foerlagshuset Gothia, pg 612
Hanseproduktion AB, pg 612
Hillelforlaget, pg 612
Stromberg, pg 616

Switzerland
Editions L'Age d'Homme - La Cite, pg 617
AT Verlag, pg 618
Bugra Suisse Burchler Grafino AG, pg 620
Christoph Merian Verlag, pg 620
Cosmos-Verlag AG, pg 621
Verlag ED Emmentaler Druck AG, pg 622
Frobenius AG, pg 623
Th Gut Verlag, pg 624
Verlag Huber & Co AG, pg 625
Lia rumantscha, pg 627
Peter Meili & Co, Buchhandlung, pg 628
Editions Payot Lausanne, pg 631
Hans Rohr Verlag, pg 632
SAB Schweiz Arbeitsgemeinschaft fuer die Berggebiete, pg 633
Verlag Stocker-Schmid AG, pg 635
Terra Grischuna Verlag Buch-und Zeitschriftenverlag, pg 635
Editions du Tricorne, pg 635
Verbandsdruckerei AG, pg 636
Verlagsbuchhandlung AG, pg 636
Viktoria-Verlag Peter Marti, pg 636
Walter Verlag AG, pg 637

Taiwan, Province of China
Morning Star Publisher Inc, pg 641
Yee Wen Publishing Co Ltd, pg 642

United Republic of Tanzania
East African Publishing House, pg 643

Thailand
Graphic Art (28) Co Ltd, pg 645
White Lotus Co Ltd, pg 646

Tunisia
Alyssa Editions, pg 647

Turkey
Altin Kitaplar Yayinevi, pg 649
Nurdan YayinlariSanayi ve Ticaret Ltd Sti, pg 651

United Arab Emirates
Department of Culture & Information Government of Sharjah, pg 654

PUBLISHERS   SUBJECT INDEX

United Kingdom

Abbotsford Publishing, pg 654
Appletree Press Ltd, pg 658
Ashmolean Museum Publications, pg 660
Ashton & Denton Publishing Co (CI) Ltd, pg 660
Birlinn Ltd, pg 666
Blackstaff Press, pg 666
Brewin Books Ltd, pg 671
Bridge Books, pg 671
The British Council, Design, Publishing & Print Department, pg 671
Canongate Books Ltd, pg 674
Cardiff Academic Press, pg 675
Castlemead Publications, pg 676
Paul Cave Publications Ltd, pg 676
The Chartered Institute of Building, pg 678
Chartered Institute of Library & Information Professionals in Scotland, pg 678
Cottage Publications, pg 683
Countryside Books, pg 683
Countyvise Ltd, pg 683
Terence Dalton Ltd, pg 685
John Donald Publishers Ltd, pg 688
The Eurospan Group, pg 692
Gairm Publications, pg 698
Glasgow City Libraries Publications, pg 700
Gomer Press (J D Lewis & Sons Ltd), pg 701
Gwasg Gwenffrwd, pg 703
Ian Henry Publications Ltd, pg 708
C Hurst & Co (Publishers) Ltd, pg 711
Hutton Press Ltd, pg 711
Icon Press, pg 711
Institute of Irish Studies, The Queens University of Belfast, pg 713
Intellect Ltd, pg 713
Jarrold Publishing, pg 716
Kingfisher Publications Plc, pg 717
Landy Publishing, pg 719
Liverpool University Press, pg 722
Lodenek Press, pg 722
Y Lolfa Cyf, pg 722
Luath Press Ltd, pg 722
Mercat Press, pg 726
Merchiston Publishing, pg 727
Meresborough Books Ltd, pg 727
Middleton Press, pg 728
E J Morten (Publishers), pg 729
MWH London Publishers, pg 730
National Library of Scotland, pg 731
Neil Wilson Publishing Ltd, pg 732
North York Moors National Park, pg 733
Old Vicarage Publications, pg 734
The Oleander Press, pg 735
Phillimore & Co Ltd, pg 741
Quentin Books Ltd, pg 747
Redcliffe Press Ltd, pg 749
Regency House Publishing Ltd, pg 749
Roadmaster Publishing, pg 750
RoutledgeCurzon, pg 751
Saint Andrew Press, pg 753
SB Publications, pg 754
Scottish Cultural Press, pg 755
Shearwater Press Ltd, pg 757
Sigma Press, pg 758
Smith Settle Ltd, pg 758
SPA Books Ltd, pg 759
Stenlake Publishing Ltd, pg 761
Sutton Publishing Ltd, pg 762
Thistle Press, pg 765
Twelveheads Press, pg 767
Ulster Historical Foundation, pg 768
University of Exeter Press, pg 768
Wharncliffe Publishing Ltd, pg 772
White Cockade Publishing, pg 772
Whittles Publishing, pg 773

Uruguay

Editorial Arca SRL, pg 776
Fundacion de Cultura Universitaria, pg 777
Ediciones Sol del Sur, pg 778
Ediciones Trilce, pg 778

Venezuela

Monte Avila Editores Latinoamericana CA, pg 779
Universidad de los Andes, Consejo de Publicaciones, pg 780

Zimbabwe

Nehanda Publishers, pg 784

RELIGION - BUDDHIST

Argentina

Editorial Kier SACIFI, pg 7

Australia

Oriental Publications, pg 34
Spectrum Publications, pg 41
Tamarind Publications, pg 42
Thin Rich Press, pg 43
Unity Press, pg 44
Windhorse Books, pg 47

Brazil

Editora Bertrand Brasil Ltda, pg 78
Companhia Editora Forense, pg 81
Horus Editora Ltda, pg 83
Francisco J Laissue Livraria, pg 84

Bulgaria

Eurasia Academic Publishers, pg 94
Kibea Publishing Co, pg 95

China

China Ocean Press, pg 102
China Tibetology Publishing House, pg 103
Fudan University Press, pg 104

Czech Republic

Lyra Pragensis Obecne Prospelna Spolecnost, pg 125
Votobia sro, pg 128

France

Paul Geuthner Librairie Orientaliste, pg 165
Langues & Mondes-L'Asiatheque, pg 171
L'Originel - Editions Accarias, pg 178
Editions Pardes, pg 179

Germany

Aquamarin Verlag, pg 193
Connection Medien GmbH, pg 209
Dharma Edition, Tibetisches Zentrum, pg 214
Verlag Esoterische Philosophie GmbH, pg 221
Happy Mental Buch- und Musik Verlag, pg 234
Verlag Herder GmbH & Co KG, pg 236
Anton Hiersemann, Verlag, pg 237
F Hirthammer Verlag GmbH, pg 238
Klaus Isele, pg 242
Joy Verlag GmbH, pg 243
Kolibri-Verlag GmbH, pg 249
Nie/Nie/Sagen-Verlag, pg 265
Nusser Verlag, pg 266
nymphenburger, pg 266
Osho Verlag GmbH, pg 267
Franz Steiner Verlag Wiesbaden GmbH, pg 287
Edition Vincent Klink, pg 296

Hong Kong

Chung Hwa Book Co (HK) Ltd, pg 316
The Dharmasthiti Buddist Institute Ltd, pg 317
Hong Kong University Press, pg 317

India

Asian Educational Services, pg 329
Book Circle, pg 330
Book Faith India, pg 330
Books & Books, pg 331
Cosmo Publications, pg 332
DK Printworld (P) Ltd, pg 333
Gyan Publishing House, pg 335
Indus Publishing Co, pg 338
B Jain Publishers (P) Ltd, pg 339
Law Publishers, pg 340
Minerva Associates (Publications) Pvt Ltd, pg 341
Munshiram Manoharlal Publishers Pvt Ltd, pg 342
Navrang Booksellers & Publishers, pg 343
Pitambar Publishing Co (P) Ltd, pg 345
Reliance Publishing House, pg 346
Roli Books Pvt Ltd, pg 347
Sri Satguru Publications, pg 348
Somaiya Publications Pvt Ltd, pg 349
South Asian Publishers Pvt Ltd, pg 350
Sri Satguru Publications, pg 350
Tara Publishing, pg 351

Italy

Adea Edizioni, pg 374
Adelphi Edizioni SpA, pg 374
Crisalide, pg 383
Edizioni Cultura della Pace, pg 383
Edizioni Il Punto d'Incontro SAS, pg 386
Hermes Edizioni SRL, pg 392
Luni, pg 396
Il Nuovo Melangolo, pg 401
Il Punto D Incontro, pg 404
Zanfi-Logos, pg 412

Japan

Chikuma Shobo Publishing Co Ltd, pg 416
Dohosha Publishing Co Ltd, pg 417
Hakutei-Sha, pg 418
Hyoronsha Publishing Co Ltd, pg 418
Kokushokankokai Co Ltd, pg 421
Kosei Publishing Co Ltd, pg 421
Nippon Hoso Shuppan Kyokai (NHK Publishing), pg 424
Rinsen Book Co Ltd, pg 425
Riso-Sha, pg 425
Sanshusha Publishing Co, Ltd, pg 426
Mitsumura Suiko Shoin, pg 428
Shufunotomo Co Ltd, pg 428
Toho Shuppan, pg 429
Tokyo Shoseki Co Ltd, pg 430

Republic of Korea

Koreaone Press Inc, pg 440
Seogwangsa, pg 442

Mauritius

Hemco Publications, pg 461

Mexico

Publicaciones Cruz O SA, pg 463
Phillip Richard Conover Lazo, pg 467
Plaza y Valdes SA de CV, pg 470

Netherlands

Ankh-Hermes BV, pg 477
BZZTOH Publishers, pg 480
De Driehoek BV, Uitgeverij, pg 481
Uitgeverij en boekhandel Van Gennep BV, pg 482
Hotei Publishing, pg 484
Servire BV Uitgevers, pg 489

New Zealand

Aspect Press, pg 493
Gnostic Press Ltd, pg 496

Portugal

Edicoes Manuel Lencastre, pg 532
Editorial Presenca, pg 535
Vega-Publicacao e Distribuicao de Livros e Revistas, Lda, pg 536

Romania

Humanitas Publishing House, pg 540

Russian Federation

Ladomir Publishing House, pg 546

Slovenia

Zalozba Mihelac d o o, pg 562

Spain

Editorial 'Alas', pg 571
Editorial Gulaab, pg 586
Mandala Ediciones, pg 590
Munoz Moya Editor, pg 592
Obelisco Ediciones S, pg 593
Ediciones Siruela SA, pg 600
Editorial Thassalia, SA, pg 602

Sri Lanka

Buddhist Publication Society Inc, pg 605
Inter-Cultural Book Promoters, pg 606
Karunaratne & Sons Ltd, pg 606
Pradeepa Publishers, pg 607
Samayawardena Printers Publishers & Booksellers, pg 607
Somawathi Hewavitharana Fund, pg 607
Swarna Hansa Foundation, pg 607

Switzerland

Cockatoo Press (Schweiz), Thailand-Publikationen, pg 621
Garuda-Verlag, pg 624
Origo Verlag, pg 630
Theseus - Verlag AG, pg 635

Taiwan, Province of China

Heavenly Lotus Publishing Co, Ltd, pg 640
San Min Book Co Ltd, pg 641

1085

SUBJECT INDEX — BOOK

SMC Publishing Inc, pg 642
Torch of Wisdom, pg 642
Zen Now Press, pg 642

Thailand

Thai Watana Panich Co, Ltd, pg 646

United Kingdom

Arthur James Ltd, pg 660
Blackstaff Press, pg 666
The Eurospan Group, pg 692
Janus Publishing Co Ltd, pg 716
Motilal (UK) Books of India, pg 729
Oneworld Publications, pg 735
RoutledgeCurzon, pg 751
Textile & Art Publications Ltd, pg 764
Tharpa Publications, pg 764
Windhorse Publications, pg 774

RELIGION - CATHOLIC

Argentina

Bonum Editorial SACI, pg 4
Editorial Ciudad Nueva de la Sefoma, pg 4
Editorial Claretiana, pg 4
Ediciones Don Bosco Argentina, pg 5
Errepar SA, pg 5
Gram Editora, pg 6
Editorial Guadalupe, pg 6
San Pablo, pg 9
Theoria SRL Distribuidora y Editora, pg 9

Australia

Ashling Books, pg 12
Bible Society in Australia National Headquarters, pg 14
Catholic Institute of Sydney, pg 17
Instauratio Press, pg 27
Jesuit Publications, pg 27
Little Red Apple Publishing, pg 29
Newman Centre Publications, pg 33
Protestant Publications, pg 38
St Joseph Publications, pg 40
St Pauls Publications, pg 40
Spectrum Publications, pg 41

Austria

Ennsthaler GesmbH & Co KG, pg 50
Herold Druck-und Verlagsgesellschaft mbH, pg 52
Verlag St Gabriel, pg 57
Andreas Schnider Verlags-Atelier, pg 57
Edition Va Bene, pg 59
Wiener Dom-Verlag GmbH, pg 59

Belgium

Artel, pg 63
Editions Gerard Blanchart & Cie SA, pg 63
Dessain - Departement de De Boeck & Larcier SA, pg 66
Uitgeverij Lannoo NV, pg 69
Editions Lessius ASBL, pg 70
Editions Lumen Vitae ASBL, pg 70
Pelckmans NV, De Nederlandsche Boekhandel, pg 72
Uitgeverij Averbode NV, pg 74

Bolivia

Editorial Don Bosco, pg 75

Brazil

Editora Cidade Nova, pg 80
EDUSC - Editora da Universidade do Sagrado Coracao, pg 81
Horus Editora Ltda, pg 83
Edit Palavra Magica, pg 88
Pallas Editora e Distribuidora Ltda, pg 88
Paulinas Editorial, pg 88
Paulus Editora, pg 88
Raboni Editora Ltda, pg 89
Editora Santuario, pg 90

Chile

Congregacion Paulinas - Hijas de San Pablo, pg 99

Colombia

Consejo Episcopal Latinoamericano (CELAM), pg 110
Eurolibros Ltda, pg 111
Fundacion Universidad de la Sabana Ediciones INSE, pg 111

Costa Rica

Litografia Artex, SA, pg 115
Ediciones Promesa, pg 116

Croatia

ALFA dd za izdavacke, graficke i trgovacke poslove, pg 117

Cuba

Editora Politica, pg 120

Czech Republic

Barrister & Principal, pg 122
Kalich SRO, pg 124
Karmelitanske Nakladatelstvi, pg 124
Portal spol sro, pg 126

Dominican Republic

Pontificia Universidad Catolica Madre y Maestra, pg 136

France

Actes-Graphiques, pg 145
Adverbum SARL, pg 146
Editions de l'Atelier, pg 148
Ateliers et Presses de Taize, pg 148
Editions des Beatitudes, Pneumatheque, pg 149
Societe Biblique Francaise, pg 150
Editions Buchet-Chastel Pierre Zech Editeur, pg 151
CERDIC-Publications, pg 153
Editions du Chalet, pg 153
Decanord, pg 157
Les Editions des Deux Coqs d'Or, pg 158
Editions Droguet et Ardant, pg 159
Editions ELOR, pg 160
Institut d'Etudes Augustiniennes, pg 162
Editions Fata Morgana, pg 162
Federation d'Activities Culturelles, Fac Editions, pg 163
Editions du Feu Nouveau, pg 163
Les Editions Franciscaines SA, pg 164
Paul Geuthner Librairie Orientaliste, pg 165
Editions Jean Paul Gisserot, pg 165
Editions Jacques Grancher, pg 165
Karthala Editions-Diffusion, pg 170
Editions Lacour-Olle, pg 170
Editions Le Laurier, pg 171
P Lethielleux Editions, pg 171
Letouzey et Ane Editeurs, pg 171
Editions Mediaspaul, pg 175
Les Presses d'Ile-de-France Sarl, pg 181
Editions Le Sarment, pg 184
Siloe - Kerdore, pg 185
Editions Tardy SA, pg 187
Librairie Pierre Tequi et Editions Tequi, pg 187
La Vague a l'ame, pg 188

Germany

Auer Verlag GmbH, pg 195
Belser Wissenschaftlicher Dienst, pg 199
Born-Verlag, pg 203
Bundes-Verlag GmbH, pg 206
Butzon & Bercker GmbH, pg 206
Dareschta Consulting und Handels GmbH, pg 210
Deutscher EC-Verband, pg 212
Echter Wurzburg Frankische Gesellschaftsdruckerei und Verlag GmbH, pg 217
Verlag am Eschbach GmbH, pg 221
Franz-Sales-Verlag, pg 226
Verlag Herder GmbH & Co KG, pg 236
Anton Hiersemann, Verlag, pg 237
Iudicium Verlag GmbH, pg 242
Johannes Verlag Einsiedeln, Freiburg, pg 243
Verlag Katholisches Bibelwerk GmbH, pg 245
W Kohlhammer GmbH, pg 248
Lahn-Verlag GmbH, pg 251
Medien-Verlag Bernhard Gregor GmbH, pg 258
Missio eV, pg 260
Nusser Verlag, pg 266
Osho Verlag GmbH, pg 267
Verlag Parzeller GmbH & Co KG, pg 268
Verlag Friedrich Pustet GmbH & Co Kg, pg 272
Verlag Schnell und Steiner GmbH, pg 281
Ferdinand Schoeningh Verlag GmbH, pg 281
Schwabenverlag Aktiengesellschaft, pg 282
Steyler Verlag, pg 288
Sueddeutsche Verlagsgesellschaft mbH, pg 288
Suin Buch-Verlag, pg 289
Verein der Benediktiner zu Beuron-Beuroner Kunstverlag, pg 294
Vier Tuerme GmbH Verlag Klosterbetriebe, pg 295
Verlag fuer Wirtschaft & Verwaltung Hubert Wingen GmbH & Co KG, pg 300

Ghana

Frank Publishing Ltd, pg 304

Greece

Alamo Hellas, pg 305

Hungary

Agape Ferences Nyomda es Konyvkiado Kft, pg 320
Kossuth Kiado RT, pg 322
Marton Aron Kiado Publishing House, pg 323
Osiris Kiado, pg 323

Iceland

Katholska kirkjan a Islandi - Landakot Publishers Thorlakssjodur, pg 326

India

Asian Trading Corporation, pg 329
Satprakashan Sanchar Kendra, pg 348

Indonesia

Aurora, pg 353
Nusa Indah, pg 356

Ireland

Campus Publishing Ltd, pg 358
Cathedral Books Ltd, pg 358
The Columba Book Service, pg 359
The Columba Press, pg 359
Dominican Publications, pg 359
Four Courts Press Ltd, pg 360
Mercier Press Ltd, pg 362
Veritas Co Ltd, pg 364

Italy

Athesia Verlag Bozen, pg 377
Campanotto, pg 379
Edizioni Cantagalli, pg 379
Edizioni Carmelitane, pg 380
Edizioni Carroccio, pg 380
Casa Musicale Edizioni Carrara SRL, pg 380
Centro Editoriale Valtortiano SRL, pg 381
Cittadella Editrice, pg 382
Edizioni Cultura della Pace, pg 383
Edizioni Dehoniane Bologna (EDB), pg 384
Edizioni Il Punto d'Incontro SAS, pg 386
Edizioni la Scala, pg 387
Edizioni Qiqajon, pg 387
Edizioni Studio Domenicano (ESD), pg 387
Effata Editrice, pg 387
EFR-Editrici Francescane, pg 387
Elle Di Ci - Libreria Dottrina Cristiana, pg 387
Arnaldo Forni Editore SRL, pg 389
Biblioteca Francescana, pg 389
Piero Gribaudi Editore, pg 391
Herbita Editrice di Leonardo Palermo, pg 392
In Dialogo, pg 393
Ist Patristico Augustinianum, pg 393
Editoriale Jaca Book SpA, pg 394
Laruffa Editore SRL, pg 394
Editrice LAS, pg 394
Casa Editrice Marietti SpA, pg 397
Editrice Massimo SAS di Crespi Cesare e C, pg 397
Edumond Le Monnier, pg 399
Nuova Coletti Editore Roma, pg 401
Il Nuovo Melangolo, pg 401
Leo S Olschki, pg 401
Paideia Editrice, pg 402
Edizioni Piemme SpA, pg 403
Pontifico Istituto Orientale, pg 404
Editrice Queriniana, pg 404
Reverdito Edizioni, pg 405
Sardini Editrice, pg 407
Edizioni Segno SRL, pg 407
Segretariato Nazionale Apostolato della Preghiera, pg 408
Servitium, pg 408
Societa Editrice Internazionale - SEI, pg 408
Edizioni del Teresianum, pg 410
Urbaniana University Press, pg 411
Vivere In SRL, pg 412
Edizioni Zara, pg 412

Japan

Nippon Hoso Shuppan Kyokai (NHK Publishing), pg 424
Riso-Sha, pg 425

PUBLISHERS

Salesian Press/Don Bosco Sha, pg 426
Shiko-Sha Co Ltd, pg 427

Kenya
Focus Publications Ltd, pg 433
Gaba Publications Amecea, Pastoral Institute, pg 434
Paulines Publications-Africa, pg 435
Shirikon Publishers, pg 436

Republic of Korea
St Pauls, pg 442
Seogwangsa, pg 442

Latvia
Spriditis Publishers, pg 445

Lebanon
Dar-El-Machreq Sarl, pg 446
Librairie Orientale sal, pg 446

Lithuania
Andrena Publishers, pg 448
Klaipedos Universiteto Leidykla, pg 449
Vaga Ltd, pg 450

Malta
Gaulitana, pg 460
Media Centre, pg 460

Mauritius
Hemco Publications, pg 461

Mexico
Publicaciones Cruz O SA, pg 463
Editorial Diana SA de CV, pg 464
El Colegio de Michoacan A C, pg 464
Fernandez Editores SA de CV, pg 465
Editorial Jus SA de CV, pg 467
Editorial Limusa SA de CV, pg 467
Editorial Minutiae Mexicana SA, pg 468
Palabra Ediciones S A de C V, pg 469
Editorial Progreso SA de C V, pg 470
Ediciones Promesa, SA de CV, pg 470

Netherlands
Uitgeverij en boekhandel Van Gennep BV, pg 482
Katholieke Bijbelstichting, pg 484
Uitgeverij Meinema, pg 485
Narratio Theologische Uitgeverij, pg 486
De Prom, pg 488

Nigeria
Riverside Communications, pg 507

Papua New Guinea
Melanesian Institute, pg 515

Peru
Asociacion Editorial Bruno, pg 516

Philippines
Anvil Publishing Inc, pg 518
Ateneo de Manila University Press, pg 518
De La Salle University, pg 519
New Day Publishers, pg 520

Our Lady of Manaoag Publisher, pg 520
Salesiana Publishers Inc, pg 521
Sinag-Tala Publishers Inc, pg 521
UST Publishing House, pg 521

Poland
Drukarnia I Ksiegarnia Swietego Wojciecha, Dziat Wydawniczy, pg 522
Impuls, pg 523
Instytut Wydawniczy Pax, Inco-Veritas, pg 523
Katolicki Uniwersytet Wydawniczo-Redakcja, pg 523
Norbertinum, pg 524
Pallottinum Wydawnictwo Stowarzyszenia Apostolstwa Katolickiego, pg 525
Rosikon Press, pg 526
Vocatio Publishing House, pg 527

Portugal
Biblioteca Geral da Universidade de Coimbra, pg 529
Edicoes Manuel Lencastre, pg 532
Nova Arrancada Sociedade Editora SA, pg 534
Edicoes Ora & Labora, pg 534
Paulinas, pg 534
Solivros, pg 536

Romania
Ars Longa Publishing House, pg 538
Humanitas Publishing House, pg 540
Pallas-Akademia Editura, pg 541

Serbia and Montenegro
AGAPE, pg 552

Slovakia
Luc vydavatelske druzstvo, pg 559
Serafin, pg 560

Slovenia
Zalozba Mihelac d o o, pg 562

Spain
Publicacions de l'Abadia de Montserrat, pg 570
Editorial Aguaclara, pg 571
Editorial Bruno, pg 575
Editorial Casals SA, pg 575
Central Catequistica Salesiana (CCS), pg 576
Editora Comercial de Publicaciones, pg 577
Ediciones Cristiandad, pg 578
Editorial Deimos, SL, pg 578
Ediciones El Almendro de Cordoba, pg 580
Editorial Everest SA, pg 581
Enciclopedia Catalana, SA, pg 582
Editorial Esin, SA, pg 582
Vicent Garcia Editores, SA, pg 584
Ibaizabal Edelvives SA, pg 586
Loguez Ediciones, pg 589
Editorial Magisterio Espanol SA, pg 590
Editorial Mediterrania SL, pg 591
Editorial Monte Carmelo, pg 592
Mundo Negro Editorial, pg 592
Munoz Moya Editor, pg 592
Obelisco Ediciones S, pg 593
Pages Editors, SL, pg 594
Editorial El Perpetuo Socorro, pg 596

Editorial Revista Agustiniana, pg 598
Ediciones San Pio X, pg 599
Secretariado Trinitario, pg 599
Ediciones Sigueme SA, pg 600
Ediciones Siruela SA, pg 600
Trotta SA Editorial, pg 602
Ediciones 29 - Libros Rio Nuevo, pg 603
Editorial Verbo Divino, pg 604

Sri Lanka
Inter-Cultural Book Promoters, pg 606

Switzerland
Benziger Verlag AG, pg 619
Verlag Bo Cavefors, pg 620
Christiana-Verlag, pg 620
Edition Exodus, pg 623
Jordanverlag AG, pg 625
Kanisius Verlag, pg 626
Kranich-Verlag, Dres AG & H R Bosch-Gwalter, pg 627
NZN Buchverlag AG, pg 630
Editions du Parvis, pg 631
Rex Verlag, pg 632
Editions Saint-Augustin, pg 633
Verlag Schweizerisches Katholisches Bibelwerk, pg 634

United Republic of Tanzania
Ndanda Mission Press, pg 644

United Kingdom
Arthur James Ltd, pg 660
Blackstaff Press, pg 666
Cassell & Co, pg 675
The Catholic Truth Society, pg 676
Christian Research Association, pg 679
Church Union, pg 680
James Clarke & Co Ltd, pg 680
CTBI Publications, pg 685
Darton, Longman & Todd Ltd, pg 686
Eagle/Inter Publishing Service (IPS) Ltd, pg 689
The Eurospan Group, pg 692
Gresham Books Ltd, pg 703
Hodder & Stoughton Religious, pg 709
Institute of Irish Studies, The Queens University of Belfast, pg 713
Lion Hudson PLC, pg 721
Marcham Manor Press, pg 725
McCrimmon Publishing Co Ltd, pg 726
Oneworld Publications, pg 735
St Pauls Publishing, pg 753
SCM-Canterbury Press Ltd, pg 755
Colin Smythe Ltd, pg 759
The Society for Promoting Christian Knowledge (SPCK), pg 759
Wild Goose Publications, pg 773

Venezuela
Fundacion Centro Gumilla, pg 779
Ediciones Tripode, pg 780

RELIGION - HINDU

Argentina
Errepar SA, pg 5
Editorial Kier SACIFI, pg 7

SUBJECT INDEX

Australia
Oriental Publications, pg 34
Spectrum Publications, pg 41

Bangladesh
Bangladesh Publishers, pg 61

Belgium
Editions Lessius ASBL, pg 70

Brazil
Editora Bertrand Brasil Ltda, pg 78
Horus Editora Ltda, pg 83
Francisco J Laissue Livraria, pg 84

Bulgaria
Eurasia Academic Publishers, pg 94

France
Editions Fata Morgana, pg 162
Paul Geuthner Librairie Orientaliste, pg 165
Langues & Mondes-L'Asiatheque, pg 171
L'Originel - Editions Accarias, pg 178
Editions Pardes, pg 179

Germany
Aquamarin Verlag, pg 193
Happy Mental Buch- und Musik Verlag, pg 234
Anton Hiersemann, Verlag, pg 237
F Hirthammer Verlag GmbH, pg 238
Ursala Meyer und Dr Manfred Duker Ein-Fach-Verlag, pg 260
Nusser Verlag, pg 266
Osho Verlag GmbH, pg 267
Franz Steiner Verlag Wiesbaden GmbH, pg 287

India
Advaita Ashrama, pg 327
APH Publishing Corp, pg 328
Asian Educational Services, pg 329
Book Faith India, pg 330
Books & Books, pg 331
Brijbasi Printers Pvt Ltd, pg 331
Cosmo Publications, pg 332
Diamond Comics (P) Ltd, pg 333
DK Printworld (P) Ltd, pg 333
Dutta Publishing Co Ltd, pg 333
Ess Ess Publications, pg 334
Gyan Publishing House, pg 335
Indus Publishing Co, pg 338
B Jain Publishers (P) Ltd, pg 339
Law Publishers, pg 340
Mapin Publishing Pvt Ltd, pg 341
Sri Ramakrishna Math, pg 341
Minerva Associates (Publications) Pvt Ltd, pg 341
Munshiram Manoharlal Publishers Pvt Ltd, pg 342
Natraj Prakashan, Publishers & Exporters, pg 343
Navrang Booksellers & Publishers, pg 343
Oxford University Press, pg 344
Pitambar Publishing Co (P) Ltd, pg 345
Reliance Publishing House, pg 346
Roli Books Pvt Ltd, pg 347
SABDA, pg 347
Sasta Sahitya Mandal, pg 348
Shaibya Prakashan Bibhag, pg 349
Somaiya Publications Pvt Ltd, pg 349

South Asian Publishers Pvt Ltd, pg 350
Star Publications (P) Ltd, pg 350
Sterling Publishers Pvt Ltd, pg 350
Tara Publishing, pg 351
N M Tripathi Pvt Ltd Publishers & Booksellers, pg 351
Vakils Feffer & Simons Ltd, pg 352
S Viswanathan (Printers & Publishers) Pvt Ltd, pg 352

Indonesia
Bina Aksara Parta, pg 354

Italy
Adelphi Edizioni SpA, pg 374
Edizioni Cultura della Pace, pg 383
Edizioni Il Punto d'Incontro SAS, pg 386
Hermes Edizioni SRL, pg 392
Il Punto D Incontro, pg 404

Japan
Nippon Hoso Shuppan Kyokai (NHK Publishing), pg 424

Republic of Korea
Seogwangsa, pg 442

Mauritius
Editions Capucines, pg 461
Hemco Publications, pg 461

Mexico
Ediciones Alpe, pg 462
Phillip Richard Conover Lazo, pg 467

Netherlands
BZZTOH Publishers, pg 480
Uitgeverij en boekhandel Van Gennep BV, pg 482
Servire BV Uitgevers, pg 489

New Zealand
Gnostic Press Ltd, pg 496

Portugal
Edicoes Manuel Lencastre, pg 532

Romania
Humanitas Publishing House, pg 540

Russian Federation
Ladomir Publishing House, pg 546

Spain
Editorial Gulaab, pg 586
Mandala Ediciones, pg 590
Obelisco Ediciones S, pg 593
Ediciones Siruela SA, pg 600
Editorial Thassalia, SA, pg 602

Sri Lanka
Inter-Cultural Book Promoters, pg 606

Sweden
BBT Bhaktivedanta Book Trust, pg 610

Switzerland
Govinda-Verlag, pg 624

United Kingdom
Arthur James Ltd, pg 660
Blackstaff Press, pg 666
The Eurospan Group, pg 692
Letterbox Library, pg 720
Mandrake of Oxford, pg 725
Motilal (UK) Books of India, pg 729
Oneworld Publications, pg 735
Ramakrishna Vedanta Centre, pg 747
RoutledgeCurzon, pg 751

RELIGION - ISLAMIC

Argentina
Editorial Kier SACIFI, pg 7

Australia
Oriental Publications, pg 34
Spectrum Publications, pg 41

Bangladesh
Gatidhara, pg 61
The University Press Ltd, pg 61

Belgium
Academia-Bruylant, pg 62

Bosnia and Herzegovina
Bemust, pg 76

Brazil
Horus Editora Ltda, pg 83
Francisco J Laissue Livraria, pg 84

China
China Ocean Press, pg 102

Egypt (Arab Republic of Egypt)
Al Arab Publishing House, pg 137
Dar El Shorouk, pg 138
Ummah Press, pg 138

France
Berg International Editeur, pg 149
CERDIC-Publications, pg 153
Editions de l'Eclat, pg 159
Editions Fata Morgana, pg 162
Paul Geuthner Librairie Orientaliste, pg 165
Editions Jacques Grancher, pg 165
Editions du Jaguar, pg 169
Karthala Editions-Diffusion, pg 170
Letouzey et Ane Editeurs, pg 171
Editions Verdier, pg 188

Germany
J J Augustin Verlag GmbH, pg 195
Dreisam Ratgeber in der Rutsker Verlag GmbH, pg 216
Elpis Verlag GmbH, pg 219
Erlanger Verlag Fuer Mission und Okumene, pg 220
Verlag Herder GmbH & Co KG, pg 236
Anton Hiersemann, Verlag, pg 237
Horlemann Verlag, pg 239
Verlag der Islam, pg 242
W Kohlhammer GmbH, pg 248
Nusser Verlag, pg 266
Georg Olms Verlag AG, pg 267
Osho Verlag GmbH, pg 267
Franz Steiner Verlag Wiesbaden GmbH, pg 287

Greece
Alamo Hellas, pg 305

India
APH Publishing Corp, pg 328
Asian Educational Services, pg 329
Authorspress, pg 329
Books & Books, pg 331
Cosmo Publications, pg 332
DK Printworld (P) Ltd, pg 333
Gyan Publishing House, pg 335
Islamic Publishing House, pg 338
Law Publishers, pg 340
Mapin Publishing Pvt Ltd, pg 341
Munshiram Manoharlal Publishers Pvt Ltd, pg 342
Roli Books Pvt Ltd, pg 347
Sterling Publishers Pvt Ltd, pg 350
Vakils Feffer & Simons Ltd, pg 352

Indonesia
PT Pustaka Antara Publishing & Printing, pg 353
Bina Rena Pariwara, pg 354
PT Bulan Bintang, pg 354
Bumi Aksara PT, pg 354
Mizan, pg 355

Israel
The Institute for Israeli Arabs Studies, pg 368

Italy
Arktos, pg 376
il Cerchio Iniziative Editoriali, pg 381
Edizioni Cultura della Pace, pg 383
Edizioni Il Punto d'Incontro SAS, pg 386
Jouvence, pg 394
Edizioni Lavoro SRL, pg 394
Luni, pg 396
Casa Editrice Marietti SpA, pg 397
SEMAR Publishers SRL, pg 408

Japan
Nippon Hoso Shuppan Kyokai (NHK Publishing), pg 424

Kenya
Life Challenge AFRICA, pg 435
Sasa Sema Publications Ltd, pg 435

Lebanon
Dar-El-Machreq Sarl, pg 446
World Book Publishing, pg 447

Malaysia
S Abdul Majeed & Co, pg 454
Darulfikir, pg 455
Dewan Pustaka Islam, pg 455
Forum Publications, pg 456
Minerva Publications, pg 457
Pelanduk Publications (M) Sdn Bhd, pg 457
Penerbit Jayatinta Sdn Bhd, pg 458
Pustaka Cipta Sdn Bhd, pg 458
Pustaka Delta Pelajaran Sdn Bhd, pg 458
Penerbit Universiti Teknologi Malaysia, pg 459

Maldive Islands
Non-Formal Education Centre, pg 459

Mauritius
Hemco Publications, pg 461

Morocco
Access International Services, pg 474
Editions Al-Fourkane, pg 474
Editions Le Fennec, pg 474
Editions La Porte, pg 475
Societe Ennewrasse Service Librairie et Imprimerie, pg 475

Netherlands
Brill Academic Publishers, pg 479
Uitgeverij en boekhandel Van Gennep BV, pg 482
Oriental Press BV (APA), pg 487
Philo Press (APA), pg 487
Servire BV Uitgevers, pg 489

New Zealand
Gnostic Press Ltd, pg 496

Pakistan
Sheikh Shaukat Ali & Sons, pg 511
Ferozsons (Pvt) Ltd, pg 512
Hamdard Foundation Pakistan, pg 512
HMR Publishing Co, pg 512
Institute of Islamic Culture, pg 512
International Institute of Islamic Thought, pg 512
Islamic Publications (Pvt) Ltd, pg 513
H I Jaffari & Co Publishers, pg 513
Jang Publishers, pg 513
Malik Sirajuddin & Sons, pg 513
Maqbool Academy, pg 513
Nashiran-e-Quran Pvt Ltd, pg 513
National Book Foundation, pg 513
Pakistan Institute of Development Economics (PIDE), pg 514
Publishers United Pvt Ltd, pg 514
Sh Ghulam Ali & Sons (Pvt) Ltd, pg 514
Vanguard Books Ltd, pg 515
West-Pakistan Publishing Co (Pvt) Ltd, pg 515

Portugal
Edicoes Manuel Lencastre, pg 532

Romania
Humanitas Publishing House, pg 540

Russian Federation
Ladomir Publishing House, pg 546

Saudi Arabia
Asam Establishment for Publishing & Distribution, pg 550
Dar Al-Shareff for Publishing & Distribution, pg 550

Singapore
Pustaka Nasional Pte Ltd, pg 557

Spain
Calamo Editorial, pg 575
Ediciones Hiperion SL, pg 586
Mandala Ediciones, pg 590
Obelisco Ediciones S, pg 593
Ediciones del Oriente y del Mediterraneo, pg 594
Editora Regional de Murcia - ERM, pg 597
Ediciones Siruela SA, pg 600
Editorial Thassalia, SA, pg 602
Trotta SA Editorial, pg 602

PUBLISHERS / SUBJECT INDEX

Sri Lanka
Inter-Cultural Book Promoters, pg 606

Switzerland
Ammann Verlag & Co, pg 617

Syrian Arab Republic
Damascus University Press, pg 638
Institut Francais d'Etudes Arabes de Damas, pg 638

Tunisia
Academie Tunisienne des Sciences, des Lettres et des Arts Beit El Hekma, pg 647
Dar El Afaq, pg 648
Maison Tunisienne de l'Edition, pg 648

Turkey
Cep Kitaplari AS, pg 649
Inkilap Publishers Ltd, pg 650
Kubbealti Akademisi Kultur ve Sasat Vakfi, pg 650
Oguz Yayinlari, pg 651
Ruh ve Madde Yayinlari ve Saglik Hizmetleri AS, pg 651

United Kingdom
Andromeda Oxford Ltd, pg 658
Blackstaff Press, pg 666
Darf Publishers Ltd, pg 686
Edinburgh University Press Ltd, pg 689
The Eurospan Group, pg 692
Garnet Publishing Ltd, pg 698
Islam International Publications Ltd, pg 714
Islamic Foundation Publications, pg 714
The Islamic Texts Society, pg 715
Letterbox Library, pg 720
Motilal (UK) Books of India, pg 729
Octagon Press Ltd, pg 734
Oneworld Publications, pg 735
RoutledgeCurzon, pg 751
Stacey International, pg 761
Ta Ha Publishers Ltd, pg 762
I B Tauris & Co Ltd, pg 763
World of Islam Altajir Trust, pg 776

RELIGION - JEWISH

Argentina
Editorial Kier SACIFI, pg 7

Australia
Spectrum Publications, pg 41

Belgium
Editions Lessius ASBL, pg 70

Brazil
Editora Bertrand Brasil Ltda, pg 78
Horus Editora Ltda, pg 83
Francisco J Laissue Livraria, pg 84

China
China Ocean Press, pg 102

Czech Republic
Kalich SRO, pg 124

France
Berg International Editeur, pg 149
CERDIC-Publications, pg 153
Editions de l'Eclat, pg 159
Editions Fata Morgana, pg 162
Paul Geuthner Librairie Orientaliste, pg 165
Editions Jacques Grancher, pg 165
Maisonneuve et Larose, pg 174
Editions Mare Nostrum, pg 177
Service Technique pour l'Education, pg 184
Editions Thames & Hudson, pg 187
Editions Verdier, pg 188

Germany
arani-Verlag GmbH, pg 193
Hans Christians Druckerei und Verlag GmbH & Co KG, pg 208
Verlag Darmstaedter Blaetter Schwarz und Co, pg 210
Dolling und Galitz Verlag GmbH, pg 215
Donat Verlag, pg 215
Harald Fischer Verlag GmbH, pg 224
Haude und Spenersche Verlagsbuchhandlung, pg 235
Edition Hentrich Druck & Verlag Gebr Hentrich und Tank GmbH & Co KG, pg 236
Anton Hiersemann, Verlag, pg 237
Juedischer Verlag GmbH, pg 243
W Kohlhammer GmbH, pg 248
Roman Kovar Verlag, pg 249
Verlag Neues Leben GmbH, pg 264
Nusser Verlag, pg 266
Georg Olms Verlag AG, pg 267
Osho Verlag GmbH, pg 267
Prasenz Verlag der Jesus Bruderschaft eV, pg 271
Dr Ludwig Reichert Verlag, pg 274
Agora Verlag Manfred Schlosser, pg 280
Thauros Verlag GmbH, pg 290
Verlag Wissenschaft und Politik, pg 300

Greece
Alamo Hellas, pg 305

India
Roli Books Pvt Ltd, pg 347

Israel
Agudat Sabah, pg 364
Bar Ilan University Press, pg 365
Ben-Zvi Institute, pg 365
The Bialik Institute, pg 365
Breslov Research Institute, pg 365
Dvir Publishing Ltd, pg 366
Eretz Hemdah Institute for Advanced Jewish Studies, pg 366
Eshkol Books Publishers & Printing Ltd, pg 367
Feldheim Publishers Ltd, pg 367
The Arnold & Leona Finkler Institute of Holocaust Research, pg 367
Gefen Publishing House Ltd, pg 367
Habermann Institute for Literary Research, pg 367
Hakibbutz Hameuchad Publishing House Ltd, pg 367
The Israel Academy of Sciences & Humanities, pg 368
The Jerusalem Publishing House Ltd, pg 369
Koren Publishers Jerusalem Ltd, pg 369

L B Publishing Co, pg 369
Maaliyot-Institute for Research Publications, pg 370
Massada Press Ltd, pg 370
Misgav Yerushalayim, pg 370
Modan Publishers Ltd, pg 370
Nehora Press, pg 371
Open University of Israel, pg 371
Pitspopany Press, pg 371
Rav Kook Institute, pg 371
Rubin Mass Ltd, pg 371
Schlesinger Institute, pg 371
Schocken Publishing House Ltd, pg 371
Sinai Publishing Co, pg 372
Steimatzky Group Ltd, pg 372
Talmudic Encyclopedia Publications, pg 372
University Publishing Projects Ltd, pg 373
Urim Publications, pg 373
Yad Eliahu Kitov, pg 373
Yad Izhak Ben-Zvi Press, pg 373
Yavneh Publishing House Ltd, pg 373
Yedioth Ahronoth Books, pg 373
Y L Peretz Publishing Co, pg 373
The Zalman Shazar Center, pg 374

Italy
Belforte Editore Libraio srl, pg 377
Edizioni Cultura della Pace, pg 383
Edizioni Qiqajon, pg 387
Editrice la Giuntina, pg 391
Piero Gribaudi Editore, pg 391
Casa Editrice Marietti SpA, pg 397
Il Nuovo Melangolo, pg 401
Leo S Olschki, pg 401
Paideia Editrice, pg 402

Japan
Myrtos Inc, pg 423
Nippon Hoso Shuppan Kyokai (NHK Publishing), pg 424

Lithuania
Vaga Ltd, pg 450

Mexico
Publicaciones Cruz O SA, pg 463

Netherlands
Erven J Bijleveld, pg 479
Brill Academic Publishers, pg 479
BZZTOH Publishers, pg 480
Uitgeverij en boekhandel Van Gennep BV, pg 482
Uitgeverij Ten Have, pg 483
Philo Press (APA), pg 487
Servire BV Uitgevers, pg 489

New Zealand
Barkfire Press, pg 494
Outrigger Publishers, pg 499

Romania
Humanitas Publishing House, pg 540

South Africa
Witwatersrand University Press, pg 570

Spain
Ediciones El Almendro de Cordoba, pg 580
Ediciones Hiperion SL, pg 586
Munoz Moya Editor, pg 592
Obelisco Ediciones S, pg 593

Ediciones Siruela SA, pg 600
Trotta SA Editorial, pg 602

Sri Lanka
Inter-Cultural Book Promoters, pg 606

Sweden
Hillelforlaget, pg 612

Switzerland
Victor Goldschmidt Verlagsbuchhandlung, pg 624
ISIOM Verlag fur Tondokumente, Weinreb Tonarchiv, pg 625
Origo Verlag, pg 630
Verlag Die Waage, pg 636

United Kingdom
Andromeda Oxford Ltd, pg 658
Arthur James Ltd, pg 660
Berghahn Books Ltd, pg 665
Blackstaff Press, pg 666
The Eurospan Group, pg 692
Harvard University Press, pg 705
Janus Publishing Co Ltd, pg 716
Letterbox Library, pg 720
The Littman Library of Jewish Civilization, pg 721
Oneworld Publications, pg 735
Polo Publishing, pg 744
RoutledgeCurzon, pg 751
SCM-Canterbury Press Ltd, pg 755
Sheffield Academic Press Ltd, pg 757
Vallentine, Mitchell & Co Ltd, pg 769
Yale University Press London, pg 776

RELIGION - PROTESTANT

Australia
Aletheia Publishing, pg 11
Aquila Press, pg 11
Aussies Afire Publishing, pg 12
Bible Society in Australia National Headquarters, pg 14
Bridgeway Publications, pg 16
Covenanter Press, pg 18
Crossroad Distributors Pty Ltd, pg 18
Jesuit Publications, pg 27
Matthias Media, pg 31
Openbook Publishers, pg 34
PCE Press, pg 36
Protestant Publications, pg 38
Spectrum Publications, pg 41
Uniting Education, pg 44

Belgium
Editions Gerard Blanchart & Cie SA, pg 63

Brazil
Ars Poetica Editora Ltda, pg 78
Alzira Chagas Carpigiani, pg 79
Koinonia Comunidade Edicoes Ltda (Editora Koinonia Ltda), pg 84
Editora Mundo Cristao, pg 87
Editora Vida Crista Ltda, pg 92

Cameroon
Editions CLE, pg 98
Editions Buma Kor & Co Ltd, pg 98

1089

SUBJECT INDEX — BOOK

Cote d'Ivoire
Centre de Publications Evangeliques, pg 117

Croatia
Znaci Vremena, Institut Za Istrazivanje Biblije, pg 119

Czech Republic
Kalich SRO, pg 124

Denmark
J Frimodt Forlag, pg 131
Samfundslitteratur, pg 134
Unitas Forlag, pg 135

Finland
Akateeminen Kustannusliike Oy, pg 141
Forsamlingsforbundets Forlags AB, pg 142
Herattaja-yhdistys Ry, pg 142
Karas-Sana Oy, pg 142
Kirjatoimi, pg 142
Lasten Keskus Oy, pg 143
Paiva Osakeyhtio, pg 143

France
Ateliers et Presses de Taize, pg 148
Societe Biblique Francaise, pg 150
CERDIC-Publications, pg 153
Editions Farel, pg 162
Librairie Fischbacher, International Art Book Distribution (import-export), pg 163
Paul Geuthner Librairie Orientaliste, pg 165
Editions Jean Paul Gisserot, pg 165
Editions Jacques Grancher, pg 165
Karthala Editions-Diffusion, pg 170
Editions Lacour-Olle, pg 170
LLB France (Ligue pour la Lecture de la Bible), pg 173

Germany
Agentur des Rauhen Hauses Hamburg GmbH, pg 191
AUE-Verlag GmbH, pg 195
Aussaat Verlag, pg 195
Born-Verlag, pg 203
Christusbruderschaft Selbitz ev, Abt Verlag, pg 209
Claudius Verlag, pg 209
Dareschta Consulting und Handels GmbH, pg 210
Deutscher EC-Verband, pg 212
Verlagsgesellschaft des Erziehungsvereins GmbH, pg 221
Verlag am Eschbach GmbH, pg 221
Evangelische Verlagsanstalt GmbH, pg 222
Evangelischer Presseverband fuer Baden eV, pg 222
Friedrich Frommann Verlag, pg 227
Verlag Junge Gemeinde E Schwinghammer GmbH & Co KG, pg 228
Grass-Verlag, pg 231
Guetersloher Verlagshaus, pg 232
Verlag des Gustav-Adolf-Werks, pg 232
Anton Hiersemann, Verlag, pg 237
Johannis, pg 243
Verlag Ernst Kaufmann GmbH, pg 245
W Kohlhammer GmbH, pg 248
Verlag Otto Lembeck, pg 253
Logos Verlag GmbH, pg 255
Luther-Verlag GmbH, pg 256
Mohr Siebeck, pg 261

Nusser Verlag, pg 266
Georg Olms Verlag AG, pg 267
Osho Verlag GmbH, pg 267
Pahl-Rugenstein Verlag Nachfolger-GmbH, pg 267
Verlag Parzeller GmbH & Co KG, pg 268
Verlag der Sankt-Johannis-Druckerei C Schweickhardt, pg 278
Verlag Schnell und Steiner GmbH, pg 281
Sternberg-Verlag bei Ernst Franz, pg 288
Suin Buch-Verlag, pg 289
Guenter Albert Ulmer Verlag, pg 293
Verein der Benediktiner zu Beuron-Beuroner Kunstverlag, pg 294
Wartburg Verlag GmbH, pg 297

Ghana
Asempa Publishers, pg 303
Frank Publishing Ltd, pg 304
Ghana Institute of Linguistics Literacy & Bible Translation (GILLBT), pg 304

Greece
Alamo Hellas, pg 305
Logos, pg 309

Hong Kong
Chinese Christian Literature Council Ltd, pg 316
Christian Communications Ltd, pg 316
Philopsychy Press, pg 318
Times Publishing (Hong Kong) Ltd, pg 319

Hungary
Advent Kiado, pg 320
Osiris Kiado, pg 323

India
The Christian Literature Society, pg 332

Indonesia
Advent Indonesia Publishing, pg 353
Aurora, pg 353

Ireland
Campus Publishing Ltd, pg 358
The Columba Book Service, pg 359
The Columba Press, pg 359
Veritas Co Ltd, pg 364

Italy
Centro Biblico, pg 381
Claudiana Editrice, pg 382
Edizioni Cultura della Pace, pg 383
Edizioni Qiqajon, pg 387
Paideia Editrice, pg 402

Japan
AVACO - Christian Mass Communications Center, pg 415
Myrtos Inc, pg 423
Nippon Hoso Shuppan Kyokai (NHK Publishing), pg 424
Shiko-Sha Co Ltd, pg 427

Kenya
Evangel Publishing House, pg 433
Lake Publishers & Enterprises Ltd, pg 435
Nairobi University Press, pg 435

Sasa Sema Publications Ltd, pg 435
Shirikon Publishers, pg 436
Sudan Literature Centre, pg 436
Uzima Press Ltd, pg 436

Republic of Korea
Chung Rim Publishing Co Ltd, pg 438
Kukmin Doseo Publishing Co Ltd, pg 440
Word of Life Press, pg 443

Latvia
Patmos, izdevnieciba, pg 445
Spriditis Publishers, pg 445

Lithuania
Klaipedos Universiteto Leidykla, pg 449
Svietimo ir mokslo ministerijos Leidybos centras, pg 449

Madagascar
Maison d'Edition Protestante ANTSO, pg 453

Mexico
Ediciones CUPSA, Centro de Comunicacion Cultural CUPSA, AC, pg 463

Netherlands
Ankh-Hermes BV, pg 477
Ark Boeken, pg 478
Boekencentrum BV, pg 479
Callenbach BV, pg 480
Uitgeverij en boekhandel Van Gennep BV, pg 482
Uitgeverij Ten Have, pg 483
Uitgeverij Meinema, pg 485
Narratio Theologische Uitgeverij, pg 486
De Prom, pg 488
Servire BV Uitgevers, pg 489
Telos Boeken, pg 490
Tirion Uitgevers BV, pg 490
Uitgeverij De Vuurbaak BV, pg 492

New Zealand
Words Work, pg 502

Nigeria
Riverside Communications, pg 507
Vantage Publishers International Ltd, pg 507

Norway
Genesis Forlag, pg 509
Luther Forlag A/S, pg 509

Papua New Guinea
Kristen Press, pg 515
Melanesian Institute, pg 515
Victory Books, pg 516

Philippines
New Day Publishers, pg 520
Philippine Baptist Mission SBC FMB Church Growth International, pg 520

Poland
Vocatio Publishing House, pg 527

Singapore
Tecman Bible House, pg 558

South Africa
Educum Publishers Ltd, pg 563
Human & Rousseau (Pty) Ltd, pg 564
Institute for Reformational Studies CHE, pg 565
The Methodist Publishing House, pg 566

Spain
Editorial Clie, pg 577
Obelisco Ediciones S, pg 593
Editorial Peregrino SL, pg 595
Ediciones Sigueme SA, pg 600

Sri Lanka
Calvary Press, pg 606
Inter-Cultural Book Promoters, pg 606

Sweden
Forlaget Sanctus (Metodistkyrkans Forlag), pg 615

Switzerland
Benziger Verlag AG, pg 619
Berchtold Haller Verlag, pg 619
Bibellesbund Verlag, pg 619
Blaukreuz-Verlag Bern, pg 619
Edition Exodus, pg 623
Jordanverlag AG, pg 625
Jugend mit einer Mission Verlag, pg 626
Kranich-Verlag, Dres AG & H R Bosch-Gwalter, pg 627
La Maison de la Bible, pg 628
Raphael, Editions, pg 632

Taiwan, Province of China
Campus Evangelical Fellowship, Literature Department, pg 639

United Republic of Tanzania
Central Tanganyika Press, pg 643
Kanisa la Biblia Publishers (KLB), pg 643
Northwestern Publishers, pg 644

United Kingdom
Arthur James Ltd, pg 660
The Banner of Truth Trust, pg 662
McCall Barbour, pg 663
Bible Reading Fellowship, pg 665
Blackstaff Press, pg 666
Bryntirion Press, pg 672
Cassell & Co, pg 675
Chapter Two, pg 678
Christian Education, pg 679
Christian Focus Publications Ltd, pg 679
Christian Research Association, pg 679
Church Society, pg 679
Church Union, pg 680
James Clarke & Co Ltd, pg 680
Crossbridge Books, pg 684
CTBI Publications, pg 685
Cyhoeddiadau'r Gair, pg 685
Darton, Longman & Todd Ltd, pg 686
Eagle/Inter Publishing Service (IPS) Ltd, pg 689
Epworth Press, pg 691
The Europsan Group, pg 692
Evangelical Press & Services Ltd, pg 693
Gresham Books Ltd, pg 703
Highland Books Ltd, pg 708
Hodder & Stoughton Religious, pg 709

Angus Hudson Ltd, pg 710
Institute of Irish Studies, The Queens University of Belfast, pg 713
Kingsway Publications, pg 718
Letterbox Library, pg 720
Lion Hudson PLC, pg 721
The Lutterworth Press, pg 723
Marcham Manor Press, pg 725
Methodist Publishing House, pg 727
Monarch Books, pg 729
Moorley's Print & Publishing Ltd, pg 729
Oneworld Publications, pg 735
SAGE Publications Ltd, pg 753
Saint Andrew Press, pg 753
SCM-Canterbury Press Ltd, pg 755
Scottish Text Society, pg 755
Scripture Union, pg 756
The Society for Promoting Christian Knowledge (SPCK), pg 759
Sovereign World Ltd, pg 759
Sutton Publishing Ltd, pg 762
Tuckwell Press Ltd, pg 767
Wild Goose Publications, pg 773

Zimbabwe

Vision Publications, pg 784

RELIGION - OTHER

Afghanistan

Book Publishing Institute, pg 1

Algeria

Enterprise Nationale du Livre (ENAL), pg 2

Argentina

Amorrortu Editores SA, pg 3
Asociacion Bautista Argentina de Publicaciones, pg 3
Bonum Editorial SACI, pg 4
Club de Lectores, pg 4
Diana Argentina SA, Editorial, pg 5
Errepar SA, pg 5
Gram Editora, pg 6
Editorial Kier SACIFI, pg 7
Ediciones Lidiun, pg 7
Editora Patria Grande, pg 8
Editorial Planeta Argentina SAIC, pg 8
Editorial Troquel SA, pg 9

Australia

Aletheia Publishing, pg 11
Anzea Publishers Ltd, pg 11
Desbooks Pty Ltd, pg 20
Freshet Press, pg 23
John Garratt Publishing, pg 23
Gnostic Editions, pg 23
Jesuit Publications, pg 27
Little Red Apple Publishing, pg 29
Barry Long Books, pg 29
Lowden Publishing Co, pg 30
Magabala Books Aboriginal Corporation, pg 30
Mission Publications of Australia, pg 32
Openbook Publishers, pg 34
Peter Pan Publications, pg 36
The Polding Press, pg 37
Rainbow Book Agencies Pty Ltd, pg 38
Spectrum Publications, pg 41
Unity Press, pg 44
Vital Publications, pg 45

Austria

Carinthia Verlag, pg 49
CEEBA Publications Antenne d'Autriche, pg 49
Cura Verlag GmbH, pg 49
Development News Ltd, pg 50
Otto Mueller Verlag, pg 54
Mueller-Speiser Wissenschaftlicher Verlag, pg 54
Oesterreichisches Katholisches Bibelwerk, pg 55
Verlag Sankt Peter, pg 56
Andreas Schnider Verlags-Atelier, pg 57
J Steinbrener OHG, pg 58
Verlag Styria, pg 58
Edition Tau u Tau Type Druck Verlags-und Handels GmbH, pg 58
Tyrolia Verlagsanstalt GmbH, pg 58

Belarus

Belaruskaya Encyklapedyya, pg 62

Belgium

Uitgeverij Acco, pg 62
Aurelia Books PVBA, pg 63
NV Uitgeverij Altiora Averbode, pg 63
Maison d'Editions Baha'ies ASBL, pg 63
Editions Gerard Blanchart & Cie SA, pg 63
Brepols Publishers NV, pg 64
Carmelitana VZW, pg 64
Espace de Libertes, pg 67
Imprimerie Hayez SPRL, pg 68
Infoboek NV, pg 68
Ligue pour la lecture de la Bible, pg 70
Editeurs de Litterature Biblique, pg 70
Uitgeverij Peeters Leuven (Belgie), pg 71
Uitgeverij Pelckmans NV, pg 72
Henri Proost & Co, Pvba, pg 72
Sonneville Press (Uitgeverij) VTW, pg 73
Unistad Verspreiding CV, pg 74
Imprimeur - Editeur Vaillant-Carmanne SA, pg 74
Les Editions Vie ouvriere ASBL, pg 74

Brazil

Associacao Palas Athena do Brasil, pg 78
Editora Betania S/C, pg 79
Concordia Editora Ltda, pg 80
Livraria Duas Cidades Ltda, pg 80
Editora Elevacao, pg 81
Fundacao Cultural Avatar, pg 82
Ordem do Graal na Terra, pg 83
Editora e Grafica Carisio Ltda, Minas Editora, pg 83
Horus Editora Ltda, pg 83
Livro Ibero-Americano Ltda, pg 83
Imago Editora Importacao e Exportacao Ltda, pg 84
Junta de Educacao Religiosa e Publicacoes da Convencao Batista Brasileira (JUERP), pg 84
Editora Kuarup Ltda, pg 84
Edicoes Loyola SA, pg 85
Editora Mercuryo Ltda, pg 86
Edit Palavra Magica, pg 88
Pallas Editora e Distribuidora Ltda, pg 88
Paulus Editora, pg 88
Editora Perspectiva, pg 88
Petit Editora e Distribuidora Ltda, pg 88
Casa Editora Presbiteriana SC, pg 88
Editora Rideel Ltda, pg 89
Editora Scipione Ltda, pg 90
Editora Sinodal, pg 90
Sobrindes Linha Grafica E Editora Ltda, pg 90
Editora Vecchi SA, pg 92
Editora Verbo Ltda, pg 92
Vozes Editora Ltda, pg 92

Bulgaria

Bilblioteka Nov den - Sajuz na Svobodnite Demokrati (Union of Free Democrats), pg 93
Kibea Publishing Co, pg 95
Pensoft Publishers, pg 96
Pet Plus, pg 96
Prozoretz Ltd Publishing House, pg 96
Sinodalno Izdatelstvo na Balgarskata pravoslavna carkva, pg 97

Cameroon

Editions Semences Africaines, pg 98

Chile

Editorial Patris SA, pg 100
Pontificia Universidad Catolica de Chile, pg 100

Colombia

Editorial Panamericana, pg 112

The Democratic Republic of the Congo

Centre Protestant d'Editions et de Diffusion (CEDI), pg 114
Presses Universitaires du Zaiire (PUZ), pg 114

Cote d'Ivoire

Centre de Publications Evangeliques, pg 117
Les Nouvelles Editions Ivoiriennes, pg 117

Croatia

Krscanska sadasnjost, pg 118

Cuba

Editora Politica, pg 120

Czech Republic

Inspirace, pg 124
Kalich SRO, pg 124
Karolinum, nakladatelstvi, pg 124
Knihovna A Tiskarna Pro Nevidome, pg 124
Luxpress VOS, pg 125
Vysehrad spol sro, pg 128

Denmark

Aarhus Universitetsforlag, pg 128
Borgens Forlag A/S, pg 129
Lohse Forlag, pg 132
Museum Tusculanum Press, pg 133
Nyt Nordisk Forlag Arnold Busck A/S, pg 133
Systime, pg 135

Egypt (Arab Republic of Egypt)

Al Arab Publishing House, pg 137
Middle East Book Centre, pg 138
Senouhy Publishers, pg 138

El Salvador

UCA Editores, pg 138

Fiji

Lotu Pacifika Productions, pg 141

Finland

Kustannus Oy Uusi Tie, pg 143
Kuva ja Sana, pg 143
Paiva Osakeyhtio, pg 143
Soderstroms Forlag, pg 144

France

Actes-Graphiques, pg 145
Alsatia SA, pg 146
Editions ALTESS, pg 146
Editions d'Amerique et d'Orient, Adrien Maisonneuve, pg 146
Editions Amrita SA, pg 146
Armenia Editions, pg 147
Editions Aubier-Montaigne SA, pg 148
Bayard Presse, pg 149
Beauchesne Editeur, pg 149
Societe d'Edition Les Belles Lettres, pg 149
Berg International Editeur, pg 149
De Boccard Edition-Diffusion, pg 150
CERDIC-Publications, pg 153
Editions du Cerf, pg 153
Editions du Chalet, pg 153
Chronique Sociale, pg 154
CLD, pg 154
CNRS Editions, pg 155
Editions de Compostelle, pg 155
Cooperative Regionale de l'Enseignement Religieux (CRER), pg 155
Editions Copernic, pg 155
Editions Courrier du Livre, pg 156
Nouvelles Editions Debresse, pg 157
Dervy Editions, pg 158
Desclee de Brouwer SA, pg 158
Desclee Editions, pg 158
Les Editions des Deux Coqs d'Or, pg 158
Les Editeurs Reunis, pg 160
Editions Fata Morgana, pg 162
Librairie Artheme Fayard, pg 163
Editions du Feu Nouveau, pg 163
Editions Fleurus, pg 163
Les Editions Gabalda et Cie, pg 164
Editions Jacques Grancher, pg 165
Editions Infrarouge, pg 168
Editions Lacour-Olle, pg 170
Editions Fernand Lanore Sarl, pg 171
Letouzey et Ane Editeurs, pg 171
Maison de la Revelation, pg 173
Editions Albin Michel, pg 175
Nouvelle Cite, pg 177
Nouvelles Editions Latines, pg 177
Editions de l'Orante, pg 178
L'Originel - Editions Accarias, pg 178
Payot & Rivages, pg 179
Editions A et J Picard SA, pg 179
Presence Africaine Editions, pg 180
Presses Universitaires de France (PUF), pg 181
Presses Universitaires de Nancy, pg 181
Editions Prosveta, pg 182
Editions Saint-Paul SA, pg 183
Editions Salvator Sarl, pg 183
Service Technique pour l'Education, pg 184
Editions du Seuil, pg 184
Editions SOS (Editions du Secours Catholique), pg 186

Les Editions de la Source Sarl, pg 186
Les Editions de la Table Ronde, pg 186
Editeurs Tacor International, pg 186
Editions Tardy SA, pg 187
Editions Vilo SA, pg 189
Librairie Philosophique J Vrin, pg 189
YMCA-Press, pg 189

Germany

Abakus Musik Barbara Fietz, pg 190
Agentur des Rauhen Hauses Hamburg GmbH, pg 191
Ahriman-Verlag GmbH, pg 191
Ardey-Verlag GmbH, pg 193
Arun-Verlag, pg 194
Aschendorffsche Verlagsbuchhandlung GmbH & Co KG, pg 194
AUE-Verlag GmbH, pg 195
Augustinus-Verlag Wurzburg Inh Augustinerprovinz, pg 195
Aussaat Verlag, pg 195
Baha'i Verlag GmbH, pg 196
Otto Wilhelm Barth-Verlag KG, pg 197
Biblio Verlag, pg 200
BKV-Brasilienkunde Verlag GmbH, pg 201
Breklumer Buchhandlung und Verlag, pg 204
Joh & Sohn Brendow Verlag GmbH, pg 204
R Brockhaus Verlag, pg 204
Brunnen-Verlag GmbH, pg 205
Burckhardthaus-Laetare Verlag GmbH, pg 206
Calwer Verlag GmbH, pg 207
Centaurus-Verlagsgesellschaft GmbH, pg 207
Chr Belser AG fur Verlagsgeschaefte und Co KG, pg 208
Christliche Verlagsgesellschaft mbH, pg 208
Christliches Verlagshaus GmbH, pg 208
Claudius Verlag, pg 209
Concordia-Buchhandlung & Verlag, pg 209
Connection Medien GmbH, pg 209
Verlag CSA Rosemarie Schneider, pg 210
Verlag Deutsche Unitarier, pg 212
Deutscher Taschenbuch Verlag GmbH & Co KG (dtv), pg 213
Diagonal-Verlag GbR Rink-Schweer, pg 214
Dieterichsche Verlagsbuchhandlung Mainz, pg 214
Divyanand Verlags GmbH, pg 215
Dolling und Galitz Verlag GmbH, pg 215
Don Bosco Verlag, pg 215
Echter Wurzburg Frankische Gesellschaftsdruckerei und Verlag GmbH, pg 217
N G Elwert Verlag, pg 219
EOS Verlag der Benefiktiner der Erzabtei St. Ottilien, pg 220
ERF-Verlag GmbH, pg 220
Erlanger Verlag Fuer Mission und Okumene, pg 220
Verlag Esoterische Philosophie GmbH, pg 221
Evangelische Verlagsanstalt GmbH, pg 222
Flensburger Hefte Verlag GmbH, pg 225
Verlag Freies Geistesleben, pg 227

Freimund-Verlag der Gesellschaft fur Innere und Aeussere Mission im Sinne der Lutherischen Kirche eV, pg 227
Klaus Gerth Musikverlag, pg 229
Gerth Medien GmbH, pg 229
Verlag der Stiftung Gralsbotschaft GmbH, pg 231
Guetersloher Verlagshaus, pg 232
Gutersloher Verlaghaus GmbH /Chr Kaiser/Kiefel/Quell, pg 232
Haenssler Verlag GmbH, pg 233
Harmonie Verlag, pg 234
Heigl Verlag, Horst Edition, pg 235
Verlag Herder GmbH & Co KG, pg 236
Anton Hiersemann, Verlag, pg 237
Verlag Hinder und Deelmann, pg 237
F Hirthammer Verlag GmbH, pg 238
Heinrich Hugendubel Verlag GmbH, pg 240
Verlag J P Peter, Gebr Holstein GmbH & Co KG, pg 242
Katzmann Verlag KG, pg 245
Verlag Ernst Kaufmann GmbH, pg 245
Klens Verlag GmbH, pg 246
Koesel-Verlag GmbH & Co, pg 248
W Kohlhammer GmbH, pg 248
Koptisches-Orthodoxes Zentrum, pg 249
Dr Anton Kovac Slavica Verlag, pg 249
Alfred Kroner Verlag, pg 250
Leibniz-Buecherwarte, pg 253
Verlag Otto Lembeck, pg 253
Leuchter-Verlag EG, pg 254
Edition Libri Illustri GmbH, pg 254
Lorber-Verlag & Turm-Verlag Otto Zluhan, pg 255
Lutherisches Verlagshaus GmbH, pg 256
Matthias-Gruenewald-Verlag GmbH, pg 258
Missio eV, pg 260
Mohr Siebeck, pg 261
Morus-Verlag GmbH, pg 262
Mueller & Schindler Verlag ek, pg 262
Neue Dimension Buch und Musikverlag, pg 264
Verlag Neue Stadt GmbH, pg 264
New Era Publications Deutschland GmbH, pg 265
Nie/Nie/Sagen-Verlag, pg 265
Hans-Nietsch-Verlag, pg 265
Edition Octopus & Okeanos Presse, pg 266
Oekumenischer Verlag Dr R-F Edel, pg 266
Oncken Verlag KG, pg 267
Osho Verlag GmbH, pg 267
Pandion-Verlag, Ulrike Schmoll, pg 268
Verlag Parzeller GmbH & Co KG, pg 268
Patmos Verlag GmbH & Co KG, pg 268
Paulinus Verlag GmbH, pg 268
J Pfeiffer Verlag, pg 269
Philipp Reclam Jun Verlag GmbH, pg 269
Projektion J Buch- und Musikverlag GmbH, pg 272
Quell Verlag, pg 273
Quelle und Meyer Verlag GmbH & Co, pg 273
Radius-Verlag GmbH, pg 273
Reichl Verlag Der Leuchter, pg 274
Ernst Reinhardt Verlag GmbH & Co KG, pg 275

Dieter Ruggeberg Verlagsbuchhandlung, pg 277
Verlag an der Ruhr GmbH, pg 277
Verlag und Schriftenmission der Evangelischen Gesellschaft Wuppertal, pg 281
Heinrich Schwab Verlag KG, pg 282
Schwabenverlag Aktiengesellschaft, pg 282
Scientia Verlag und Antiquariat Schilling OHG, pg 282
Spieth-Verlag Verlag fuer Symbolforschung, pg 284
J F Steinkopf Verlag GmbH, pg 287
Stephanus Edition Verlags GmbH, pg 287
Stiefel Eurocart GmbH, pg 288
Suin Buch-Verlag, pg 289
Thauros Verlag GmbH, pg 290
TR - Verlagsunion GmbH, pg 291
Ullstein Heyne List GmbH & Co KG, pg 293
UTB fuer Wissenschaft Uni Taschenbuecher GmbH, pg 294
Vandenhoeck & Ruprecht, pg 294
Verein der Benediktiner zu Beuron-Beuroner Kunstverlag, pg 294
VJK Verlag Josef Knecht Carolusdruckerei GmbH, pg 296
Erich Wewel Verlag GmbH, pg 299
Wichern Verlag GmbH, pg 299
Wichern Verlag GmbH, pg 299
Wissenschaftliche Buchgesellschaft, pg 300
Friedrich Wittig Verlag GmbH, pg 301
Verlag DAS WORT GmbH, pg 301
Verlag Clemens Zerling, pg 302

Ghana

The Advent Press, pg 303
Africa Christian Press, pg 303
Asempa Publishers, pg 303
Frank Publishing Ltd, pg 304
Waterville Publishing House, pg 305
World Literature Project, pg 305

Greece

Akritas, pg 305
Apostoliki Diakonia tis Ekklisias tis Hellados, pg 305
Giovanis Publications, Pangosmios Ekdotikos Organismos, pg 307
ZOI, pg 313

Haiti

Deschamps Imprimerie, pg 314

Holy See (Vatican City State)

Libreria Editrice Vaticana, pg 315

Hungary

Atlantisz Kiado, pg 320

Iceland

Bokaforlag Birtingur, pg 325

India

Abhinav Publications, pg 326
The Academic Press, pg 327
Ajanta Publications (India), pg 327
APH Publishing Corp, pg 328
Asian Educational Services, pg 329
Asian Trading Corporation, pg 329
Associated Publishing House, pg 329
Baha'i Publishing Trust of India, pg 329

The Bangalore Printing & Publishing Co Ltd, pg 329
Bharatiya Vidya Bhavan, pg 330
Central Tibetan Secretariat, pg 331
Chetana Private Ltd Publishers & International Booksellers, pg 332
Chowkhamba Sanskrit Series Office, pg 332
Disha Prakashan, pg 333
Dutta Publishing Co Ltd, pg 333
Enkay Publishers Pvt Ltd, pg 334
Full Circle Publishing, pg 334
Ganesh & Co, pg 334
Geeta Prakashan, pg 335
Arnold Heinman Publishers (India) Pvt Ltd, pg 335
Heritage Publishers, pg 335
Himalayan Books, pg 336
Indian Society for Promoting Christian Knowledge (ISPCK), pg 337
Intellectual Publishing House, pg 338
Inter-India Publications, pg 338
Intertrade Publications Pvt Ltd, pg 338
Jaico Publishing House, pg 338
Manohar Publishers & Distributors, pg 340
Motilal Banarsidass Publishers Pvt Ltd, pg 341
Mudgala Trust, pg 342
A Mukherjee & Co Pvt Ltd, pg 342
Munshiram Manoharlal Publishers Pvt Ltd, pg 342
Narosa Publishing House, pg 342
National Book Organization, pg 342
Navajivan Trust, pg 343
Panjab University Publication Bureau, pg 344
Promilla & Publishers, pg 345
Radiant Publishers, pg 346
Rajesh Publications, pg 346
Rebel Publishing House Pvt Ltd, pg 346
Regency Publications, pg 346
Rupa & Co, pg 347
SABDA, pg 347
Samkaleen Prakashan, pg 348
Sri Satguru Publications, pg 348
Sawan Kirpal Publications, pg 348
SBW Publishers, pg 348
South Asia Publications, pg 349
Sterling Publishers Pvt Ltd, pg 350
Theosophical Publishing House, pg 351
UBS Publishers Distributors Ltd, pg 351
Vakils Feffer & Simons Ltd, pg 352
Vision Books Pvt Ltd, pg 352

Indonesia

Advent Indonesia Publishing, pg 353
Angkasa CV, pg 353
Diponegoro CV, pg 354
Djambatan PT, pg 354
PT BPK Gunung Mulia, pg 355
Mutiara Sumber Widya PT, pg 356
PT Bhakti Baru, pg 356
Pustaka Utama Grafiti, PT, pg 356
Tintamas Indonesia PT, pg 356

Islamic Republic of Iran

Scientific and Cultural Publications, pg 357

Ireland

Campus Publishing Ltd, pg 358
The Columba Book Service, pg 359
The Educational Company of Ireland, pg 359

PUBLISHERS

Kerryman Ltd, pg 361
Veritas Co Ltd, pg 364

Israel

Ariel Publishing House, pg 365
Astrolog Publishing House, pg 365
DAT Publications, pg 366
Doko Video Ltd, pg 366
Kiryat Sefer, pg 369
Ma'ariv Book Guild (Sifriat Ma'ariv), pg 370
Massada Press Ltd, pg 370
Rav Kook Institute, pg 371
Rubin Mass Ltd, pg 371
Terra Sancta Arts, pg 372
Yavneh Publishing House Ltd, pg 373

Italy

Editrice Ancora, pg 375
Editrice Antroposofica SRL, pg 375
Apostolato della Preghiera, pg 375
Baha'i, pg 377
Bastogi, pg 377
Edizioni Borla SRL, pg 379
Campanotto, pg 379
Cappelli Editore, pg 380
Edizioni Carroccio, pg 380
Celuc Libri, pg 381
Centro Ambrosiano di Documentazione e Studi Religiosi, pg 381
il Cerchio Iniziative Editoriali, pg 381
Citta Nuova Editrice, pg 382
Cittadella Editrice, pg 382
Edizioni Cultura della Pace, pg 383
M d'Auria Editore SAS, pg 384
Edizioni Dehoniane Bologna (EDB), pg 384
Edizioni Dehoniane, pg 384
Editori Laterza, pg 386
Edizioni del Centro Camuno di Studi Preistorici, pg 386
Edizioni Il Punto d'Incontro SAS, pg 386
ERGA SNC di Carla Ottino Merli & C (Edizioni Realizzazioni Grafiche - Artigiana), pg 388
L'Erma di Bretschneider SRL, pg 388
l'Eta dell'Acquario, pg 388
Arnaldo Forni Editore SRL, pg 389
Frati Editori di Quaracchi, pg 389
Istituto Geografico de Agostini SpA, pg 390
Gius Laterza e Figli SpA, pg 391
Libreria Editrice Gregoriana, pg 391
Herder Editrice e Libreria, pg 392
Hermes Edizioni SRL, pg 392
Editoriale Jaca Book SpA, pg 394
L Japadre Editore, pg 394
Lalli Editore SRL, pg 394
Libreria Editrice Fiorentina, pg 395
Vincenzo Lo Faro Editore, pg 395
Loffredo Editore Napoli SpA®, pg 396
Longanesi & C, pg 396
Luni, pg 396
Macro Edizioni, pg 397
Editrice Massimo SAS di Crespi Cesare e C, pg 397
McRae Books, pg 398
Edizioni Mediterranee SRL, pg 398
Messaggero di San Antonio, pg 398
Editrice Missionaria Italiana (EMI), pg 398
Arnoldo Mondadori Editore SpA, pg 398
Editrice Morcelliana SpA, pg 399
Gruppo Ugo Mursia Editore SpA, pg 400

Nardini Editore srl, pg 400
Il Nuovo Melangolo, pg 401
Paideia Editrice, pg 402
Palatina Editrice, pg 402
Pontificio Istituto di Archeologia Cristiana, pg 404
Pontifico Istituto Orientale, pg 404
Editrice Queriniana, pg 404
RCS Rizzoli Libri SpA, pg 405
Libreria Editrice Rogate (LER), pg 406
Rubbettino Editore, pg 406
Rusconi Libri Srl, pg 406
SAIE Editrice SRL, pg 406
Edizioni San Paolo SRL, pg 407
Sapere 2000 SRL, pg 407
Editrice la Scuola SpA, pg 407
Le Stelle Scuola, pg 409
Edizioni Studium SRL, pg 409
Editrice Uomini Nuovi, pg 411
UTET (Unione Tipografico-Editrice Torinese), pg 411
Vita e Pensiero, pg 412

Jamaica

Eureka Press Ltd, pg 413

Japan

Chuokoron-Shinsha Inc, pg 416
Fuzambo Publishing Co, pg 417
GakuseiSha Publishing Co Ltd, pg 417
Hayakawa Publishing Inc, pg 418
The Hokuseido Press, pg 418
Hyoronsha Publishing Co Ltd, pg 418
Kadokawa Shoten Publishing Co Ltd, pg 420
Kodansha Ltd, pg 421
Mirai-Sha, pg 422
Nippon Hoso Shuppan Kyokai (NHK Publishing), pg 424
Sangyo-Tosho Publishing Co Ltd, pg 426
Shufu-to-Seikatsu Sha Ltd, pg 428
Shunjusha, pg 428
The Simul Press Inc, pg 428
Sobun-Sha, pg 428
Sogensha Publishing Co Ltd, pg 428
Taimeido Publishing Co Ltd, pg 429
Tamagawa University Press, pg 429
Tankosha Publishing Co Ltd, pg 429
Toho Book Store, pg 429
Tokai University Press, pg 429
University of Tokyo Press, pg 430

Kenya

Action Publishers, pg 433
Evangel Publishing House, pg 433
Gaba Publications Amecea, Pastoral Institute, pg 434
Heinemann Kenya Ltd (EAEP), pg 434
Life Challenge AFRICA, pg 435
Paulines Publications-Africa, pg 435
Transafrica Press, pg 436
Uzima Press Ltd, pg 436

Republic of Korea

Chong No Books Publishing Co Ltd, pg 438
Ewha Womans University Press, pg 438
Gim-Yeong Co, pg 438
Hanjin Publishing Co, pg 439
Hw Moon Publishing Co, pg 439
Hyun Am Publishing Co, pg 439
Sejong Daewang Kinyom Saophoe, pg 442

Seogwangsa, pg 442
Yonsei University Press, pg 444

Lebanon

Khayat Book and Publishing Co Sarl, pg 446

Lesotho

Mazenod Book Centre, pg 447
Saint Michael's Mission Social Centre, pg 447

Liechtenstein

Saendig Reprint Verlag, Hans-Rainer Wohlwend, pg 448

The Former Yugoslav Republic of Macedonia

Ktitor, pg 452

Madagascar

Editions Ambozontany, pg 453
Trano Printy Fiangonana Loterana Malagasy (TPFLM)-(Imprimerie Lutherienne), pg 454

Malawi

Christian Literature Association in Malawi, pg 454

Malaysia

Glad Sounds Sdn Bhd, pg 456
Uni-Text Book Co, pg 459
Utusan Publications & Distributors Sdn Bhd, pg 459
Vinpress Sdn Bhd, pg 459

Mali

EDIM SA, pg 460

Malta

Gozo Press, pg 460

Mauritius

Editions Capucines, pg 461
Hemco Publications, pg 461

Mexico

Aconcagua Ediciones y Publicaciones SA, pg 461
Arbol Editorial SA de CV, pg 462
Ediciones CUPSA, Centro de Comunicacion Cultural CUPSA, AC, pg 463
Ediciones Dabar, SA de CV, pg 464
Ediciones Don Bosco SA de C, pg 464
Editorial Orion, pg 469
Ediciones Roca, SA, pg 471
Ediciones Suromex SA, pg 472

Monaco

Les Editions du Rocher, pg 474

Morocco

Edition Diffusion de Livre au Maroc, pg 474
Editions La Porte, pg 475

Myanmar

Knowledge Press & Bookhouse, pg 475
Kyi-Pwar-Ye Book House, pg 475
Shwepyidan Printing & Publishing House, pg 476
Thudhammawaddy Press, pg 476

SUBJECT INDEX

Netherlands

Uitgeverij Ambo BV, pg 477
APA (Academic Publishers Associated), pg 477
Uitgeverij Arbor, pg 477
Uitgeverij Balans, pg 478
Erven J Bijleveld, pg 479
Brill Academic Publishers, pg 479
Buijten en Schipperheijn BV Drukkerij en Uitgeversmaatschappij, pg 480
BV Uitgevery NZV (Nederlandse Zondagsschool Vereniging), pg 480
Callenbach BV, pg 480
De Graaf Publishers, pg 481
East-West Publications Fonds BV, pg 481
Uitgeverij en boekhandel Van Gennep BV, pg 482
Gottmer Uitgevers Groep, pg 483
Uitgeverij Ten Have, pg 483
Uitgeverij J H Kok BV, pg 485
Mirananda Publishers BV, pg 486
Uitgeverij H Nelissen BV, pg 486
Servire BV Uitgevers, pg 489
Van Gorcum & Comp BV, pg 491
Uitgeverij Van Wijnen, pg 491

New Zealand

Cicada Press, pg 495
Gnostic Press Ltd, pg 496

Nicaragua

Editorial Nueva Nicaragua, pg 502

Nigeria

Adebara Publishers Ltd, pg 503
Aromolaran Publishing Co Ltd, pg 503
CSS Bookshops, pg 504
Daystar Press (Publishers), pg 504
ECWA Productions Ltd, pg 504
Educational Research & Study Group, pg 504
Longman Nigeria Plc, pg 505
Northern Nigerian Publishing Co Ltd, pg 506
Obafemi Awolowo University Press Ltd, pg 506
Onibon-Oje Publishers, pg 506
Tabansi Press Ltd, pg 507
Joe-Tolalu & Associates, pg 507
University Publishing Co, pg 507

Norway

Atheneum Forlag A/S, pg 508
J W Cappelens Forlag A/S, pg 508
Det Norske Samlaget, pg 508
Gyldendal Norsk Forlag A/S, pg 509
Lunde Forlag AS, pg 509
Luther Forlag A/S, pg 509
Sambandet Forlag, pg 510

Pakistan

Sheikh Muhammad Ashraf Publishers, pg 511
Fazlee Sons (Pvt) Ltd, pg 512
Islamic Book Centre, pg 512
Islamic Research Institute, pg 513
Maqbool Academy, pg 513

Papua New Guinea

Assemblies of God Mission, pg 515
The Christian Book Centre, pg 515
Melanesian Institute, pg 515

1093

Philippines
Abiva Publishing House Inc, pg 518
Bookmark Inc, pg 518
Communication Foundation for Asia Media Group (CFAMG), pg 518
Logos (Divine Word) Publications Inc, pg 519
SIBS Publishing House Inc, pg 521
University of the Philippines Press, pg 521
Vera-Reyes Inc, pg 521
Vibal Publishing House Inc (VPHI), pg 521

Poland
Spoleczny Instytut Wydawniczy Znak, pg 526
Verbinum Wydawnictwo Ksiezy Werbistow, pg 527

Portugal
Armenio Amado Editora de Simoes, Beirao & Ca Lda, pg 528
Apostolado da Oracao Secretariado Nacional, pg 528
Biblioteca Geral da Universidade de Coimbra, pg 529
Brasilia Editora (J Carvalho Branco), pg 529
Editorial Estampa, Lda, pg 531
Europress Editores e Distribuidores de Publicacoes Lda, pg 531
Editorial Franciscana, pg 531
Edicoes Manuel Lencastre, pg 532
Livraria Tavares Martins, pg 533
Editorial Noticias, pg 534
Edicoes Salesianas, pg 535
Almerinda Teixeira, pg 536
Vega-Publicacao e Distribuicao de Livros e Revistas, Lda, pg 536
Livraria Verdade e Vida Editora, pg 536

Romania
Aion Verlag, pg 538
Editura Albatros, pg 538
Alcor-Edimpex (Verlag) Ltd, pg 538
Artemis Verlag, pg 538
Editura Clusium, pg 539
Enzyklopadie Verlag, pg 539
Editura Excelsior Art, pg 539
Hasefer, pg 540
Editura Institutul European, pg 540
Editura Meridiane, pg 540
Editura Paideia, pg 541
RAO International Publishing Co, pg 542
Vremea Publishers Ltd, pg 543

Russian Federation
BLIC, russko-Baltijskij informaciionnyj centr, AO, pg 544
St Andrew's Biblical Theological College, pg 548

Rwanda
INADES (Institut Africain pour le Developpment Economique et Social), pg 550

Saudi Arabia
Saudi Publishing & Distributing House, pg 550

Senegal
Les Nouvelles Editions Africaines du Senegal NEAS, pg 551
Societe d'Edition d'Afrique Nouvelle, pg 551

Serbia and Montenegro
Alfa-Narodna Knjiga, pg 552
Jugoslavijapublik, pg 552

Sierra Leone
Sierra Leone University Press, pg 554

Singapore
Chopsons Pte Ltd, pg 555
Graham Brash Pte Ltd, pg 556
McGallen & Bolden Associates, pg 557
Taylor & Francis Asia Pacific, pg 558

Slovakia
AV Studio Reklamno-vydavatel'ska agentura, pg 559

Slovenia
Zalozba Obzorja d d Maribor, pg 562

South Africa
Bible Society of South Africa, pg 562
Digma Publications, pg 563
HAUM - De Jager Publishers, pg 564
Kima Global Publishers, pg 566
LAPA Publishers (Pty) Ltd, pg 566
Lux Verbi (Pty) Ltd, pg 566
Sasavona Publishers & Booksellers, pg 568
Waterkant-Uitgewers (Edms) Bpk, pg 570

Spain
Aguilar SA de Ediciones, pg 571
Sociedad de Educacion Atenas SA, pg 573
Biblioteca de Autores Cristianos, pg 574
Editorial Ciudad Nueva, pg 577
Editorial Claret SA, pg 577
Espanola Desclee De Brouwer SA, pg 578
Ediciones Ega, pg 581
Etu Ediciones SL, pg 583
EUNSA (Ediciones Universidad de Navarra SA), pg 583
Fundacion Rosacruz, pg 584
Editorial Gulaab, pg 586
Editorial Herder SA, pg 586
Publicaciones ICCE, pg 587
Idea Books, SA, pg 587
Editorial Kairos SA, pg 588
Loguez Ediciones, pg 589
Ediciones Marova SL, pg 590
Ediciones Mensajero, pg 591
Mundo Negro Editorial, pg 592
Narcea SA de Ediciones, pg 593
Nueva Acropolis, pg 593
Obelisco Ediciones S, pg 593
Ediciones Palabra SA, pg 595
Centre de Pastoral Liturgica, pg 595
Editorial Perpetuo Socorro, pg 596
PPC Editorial y Distribuidora, SA, pg 596
Ediciones Rialp SA, pg 598
San Pablo Ediciones, pg 598
Secretariado Trinitario, pg 599
Ediciones Siruela SA, pg 600
Ediciones SM, pg 600
Editorial Rudolf Steiner, pg 601
Editorial Sal Terrae, pg 602
Trotta SA Editorial, pg 602
Editorial Txertoa, pg 603

Sri Lanka
Inter-Cultural Book Promoters, pg 606
KVG de Silva & Sons, pg 606
Ministry of Cultural Affairs, pg 607

Sudan
Khartoum University Press, pg 608

Sweden
BBT Bhaktivedanta Book Trust, pg 610
Stroemberg B&T Forlag AB, pg 616
Svenska alliansmissionens (SAM) foerlage, pg 616
Verbum Foerlag AB, pg 616

Switzerland
ADIRA, pg 617
Editions L'Age d'Homme - La Cite, pg 617
Bargezzi-Verlag AG, pg 618
Basileia Verlag und Basler Missionsbuchhandlung, pg 618
Bibliographisches Institut & F A Brockhaus AG, pg 619
Blaukreuz-Verlag Bern, pg 619
Brunnen-Verlag Basel, pg 620
Caux Books, pg 620
Caux Edition SA, pg 620
Editions l'Eau Vive, pg 622
Georg Editeur SA, pg 624
Gotthelf-Verlag, pg 624
Govinda-Verlag, pg 624
Herder AG Basel, pg 625
Kober Verlag Bern AG, pg 626
Labor et Fides SA, pg 627
Leonis Verlag, pg 627
Lia rumantscha, pg 627
Editions H Messeiller SA, pg 628
Motovun Book GmbH, pg 629
Novalis Media AG, pg 630
Origo Verlag, pg 630
Pedrazzini Tipografia, pg 631
Pendo Verlag GmbH, pg 631
Philosophisch-Anthroposophischer Verlag am Goetheanum, pg 631
Verlag Friedrich Reinhardt AG, pg 632
Theologischer Verlag und Buchhandlungen AG, pg 635
Trachsel - Verlag AG, pg 635
Editions du Tricorne, pg 635
Der Universitatsverlag Freiburg, pg 636
Verlag Die Waage, pg 636
Walter Verlag AG, pg 637
World Council of Churches (WCC Publications), pg 637

Taiwan, Province of China
Chung Hwa Book Co Ltd, pg 639
San Min Book Co Ltd, pg 641
Wu Nan Book Co Ltd, pg 642
Yee Wen Publishing Co Ltd, pg 642

United Republic of Tanzania
East African Publishing House, pg 643
Inland Publishers, pg 643
Ndanda Mission Press, pg 644
Peramiho Publications, pg 644

Thailand
Suriyaban Publishers, pg 646
White Lotus Co Ltd, pg 646

Tunisia
Dar Arabia Lil Kitab, pg 648

Turkey
Ruh ve Madde Yayinlari ve Saglik Hizmetleri AS, pg 651

Uganda
Centenary Publishing House Ltd, pg 652

United Kingdom
Apex Publishing Ltd, pg 658
Ashgrove Publishing, pg 660
Baha'i Publishing Trust, pg 662
The Banton Press, pg 662
Bishopsgate Press Ltd, pg 666
BLA Publishing Ltd, pg 666
Blackstaff Press, pg 666
Blackwell Publishing Ltd, pg 666
Bounty Books, pg 669
Capall Bann Publishing, pg 674
Cardiff Academic Press, pg 675
Carroll & Brown Ltd, pg 675
Church House Publishing, pg 679
Church Union, pg 680
Colourpoint Books, pg 681
Covenant Publishing Co Ltd, pg 683
CTBI Publications, pg 685
Darton, Longman & Todd Ltd, pg 686
Gerald Duckworth & Co Ltd, pg 688
Eagle/Inter Publishing Service (IPS) Ltd, pg 689
East-West Publications (UK) Ltd, pg 689
Element Books Ltd, pg 690
Epworth Press, pg 691
The Eurospan Group, pg 692
Evans Brothers Ltd, pg 693
Faber & Faber Ltd, pg 694
Flame Tree Publishing, pg 695
Floris Books, pg 695
The Foundational Book Company for the John W Doorly Trust, pg 696
Gateway Books, pg 698
E J W Gibb Memorial Trust, pg 700
Global Oriental Ltd, pg 700
Gracewing Publishing, pg 701
Peter Halban Publishers Ltd, pg 703
Patrick Hardy Books, pg 705
Hodder & Stoughton Religious, pg 709
Home Health Education Service, pg 710
John Hunt Publishing Ltd, pg 710
C Hurst & Co (Publishers) Ltd, pg 711
Hymns Ancient & Modern Ltd, pg 711
Inter-Varsity Press, pg 713
Karnak House, pg 717
Laurence King Publishing Ltd, pg 717
Kingsway Publications, pg 718
Letterbox Library, pg 720
Lucis Press Ltd, pg 723
Mandrake of Oxford, pg 725
Marshall Editions Ltd, pg 725
Adam Matthew Publications, pg 726
McCrimmon Publishing Co Ltd, pg 726
Nelson Thornes Ltd, pg 732
New Era Publications UK Ltd, pg 732
Octagon Press Ltd, pg 734
Oneworld Publications, pg 735
Orion Publishing Group Ltd, pg 736
Oxford University Press, pg 737
Paternoster Publishing, pg 738
Pearson Education, pg 739

PUBLISHERS

Pearson Education Europe, Mideast & Africa, pg 739
Plough Publishing House of Bruderhof Communities in the UK, pg 743
Prim-Ed Publishing UK Ltd, pg 745
Quaker Books, pg 746
Rationalist Press Association, pg 748
George Ronald Publisher Ltd, pg 750
Roundhouse Group, pg 751
Routledge, pg 751
RoutledgeCurzon, pg 751
Saint Andrew Press, pg 753
St Pauls Publishing, pg 753
Salvationist Publishing & Supplies Ltd, pg 754
School of Oriental & African Studies, pg 755
SCM-Canterbury Press Ltd, pg 755
Sheed & Ward UK, pg 757
Shepheard-Walwyn (Publishers) Ltd, pg 757
SLG Press, pg 758
Souvenir Press Ltd, pg 759
Stainer & Bell Ltd, pg 761
Taylor & Francis, pg 763
Thames & Hudson Ltd, pg 764
Transedition Ltd, pg 766
Triumph House, pg 767
Veritas Foundation Publication Centre, pg 770
Ward Lock Educational Co Ltd, pg 771
White Eagle Publishing Trust, pg 772
Wiley Europe Ltd, pg 773
World Microfilms Publications Ltd, pg 775
Anglia Young Books, pg 776

Uruguay
Editorial Arca SRL, pg 776
Barreiro y Ramos SA, pg 777
Mosca Hermanos, pg 777
Ediciones Trilce, pg 778

Venezuela
Ediciones Tripode, pg 780

Zambia
Multimedia Zambia, pg 781

Zimbabwe
Longman Zimbabwe (Pvt) Ltd, pg 783
Mambo Press, pg 783
University of Zimbabwe Publications, pg 784

ROMANCE

Australia
D'Artagnan Publishing, pg 19
Great Western Press Pty Ltd, pg 24
Indra Publishing, pg 27
Jarrah Publications, pg 27
Levanter Publishing & Associates, pg 29
Little Red Apple Publishing, pg 29
Tom Publications, pg 43
Transworld Publishers Pty Ltd, pg 44

Austria
oebv & hpt Verlagsgesellschaft mbH & Co KG, pg 55
Edition Va Bene, pg 59

Belgium
Claude Lefrancq Editeur, pg 70
Editions Luce Wilquin, pg 74
Zuid En Noord VZW, pg 75

Brazil
Agalma Psicanalise Editora Ltda, pg 77
Artes e Oficios Editora Ltda, pg 78
Editora Bertrand Brasil Ltda, pg 78
Alzira Chagas Carpigiani, pg 79
Edicon Editora e Consultorial Ltda, pg 81
Companhia Editora Forense, pg 81
Editora Elevacao, pg 81
Global Editora e Distribuidora Ltda, pg 82
Imago Editora Importacao e Exportacao Ltda, pg 84
Livraria Nobel S/A, pg 85
Editora Mercado Aberto Ltda, pg 86
Editora Nova Alexandria Ltda, pg 87
Editora Nova Fronteira SA, pg 87
Edit Palavra Magica, pg 88
Editora Scipione Ltda, pg 90
Tempus Editores, pg 91
34 Literatura S/C Ltda, pg 91

Bulgaria
Aleks Print Publishing House, pg 93
EA EOOD, pg 94
Hermes Publishing House, pg 94
Sluntse Publishing House, pg 97
Zunica, pg 97

China
Writers' Publishing House, pg 109

Costa Rica
Editorial Universitaria Centroamericana (EDUCA), pg 117

Cuba
Editorial Letras Cubanas, pg 120

Czech Republic
Baronet, pg 122
Josef Lukasik A Spol sro, pg 125

Estonia
Perioodika, pg 140

France
Publications Aredit, pg 147
Armenia Editions, pg 147
Le Cherche Midi Editeur, pg 154
Culture et Bibliotheque pour Tous, pg 156
Librairie Guenegaud, pg 166
Harlequin SA, pg 167
Le Pre-aux-clercs, pg 180
Presses de la Cite, pg 180
Editions du Rouergue, pg 183

Germany
Ars Edition GmbH, pg 194
Aufbau Taschenbuch Verlag GmbH, pg 195
Aufbau-Verlag GmbH, pg 195
Wilhelm Heyne Verlag, pg 237
Dr Gisela Lermann, pg 253
Verlagsgruppe Luebbe GmbH & Co KG, pg 256
Nebel Verlag GmbH, pg 263
Georg Olms Verlag AG, pg 267

Propylaeen Verlag, Zweigniederlassung Berlin der Ullstein Buchverlage GmbH, pg 272
Ruetten & Loening Berlin GmbH, pg 277
Weidmannsche Verlagsbuchhandlung GmbH, pg 298

Ghana
Beginners Publishers, pg 303

Greece
Elliniki Leschi Tou Vivliou, pg 307
Exandas Publishers, pg 307
Harlenic Hellas Publishing SA, pg 308
Hestia-I D Hestia-Kollaros & Co Corporation, pg 308
Kedros Publishers, pg 309
Odysseas Publications Ltd, pg 311

Hungary
Ifjusagi Lap-eskonyvkiado Vallalat, pg 321

Iceland
Frjals fjolmiolun hf-Urvalsbaekur, pg 325

India
Pustak Mahal, pg 345

Ireland
Town House & Country House, pg 364

Italy
ERGA SNC di Carla Ottino Merli & C (Edizioni Realizzazioni Grafiche - Artigiana), pg 388
Gangemi Editore spa, pg 390
Edizioni del Girasole srl, pg 390
Edizioni Internazionali di Letteratura e Scienze, pg 393
Edizioni Lavoro SRL, pg 394
La Luna, pg 396
Editrice Massimo SAS di Crespi Cesare e C, pg 397
Arnoldo Mondadori Editore SpA, pg 398
Edizioni Piemme SpA, pg 403
Rubbettino Editore, pg 406
Il Saggiatore, pg 406
Servitium, pg 408

Jamaica
LMH Publishing Ltd, pg 414

Japan
Shincho-Sha Co Ltd, pg 427

Republic of Korea
Big Tree Publishing, pg 437
Chung Rim Publishing Co Ltd, pg 438
Koreaone Press Inc, pg 440
Woongjin.com Co Ltd, pg 443

Latvia
Alberts XII, pg 444
Artava Ltd, pg 444
Zvaigzne ABC Publishers Ltd, pg 445

SUBJECT INDEX

Lithuania
Andrena Publishers, pg 448
Baltos Lankos, pg 449
Victoria Publishers, pg 450
Vyturys Vyturio leidykla, UAB, pg 450

Luxembourg
Hubsch, pg 451

Macau
Livros Do Oriente, pg 452

The Former Yugoslav Republic of Macedonia
Strk Publishing House, pg 453

Mexico
Ediciones Alpe, pg 462

Monaco
Les Editions du Rocher, pg 474

Netherlands
Uitgeverij de Arbeiderspers, pg 477
De Boekerij BV, pg 479
BZZTOH Publishers, pg 480
Em Querido's Uitgeverij BV, pg 488
Unieboek BV, pg 490

New Zealand
River Press, pg 500

Nigeria
Evans Brothers (Nigeria Publishers) Ltd, pg 504

Pakistan
Maqbool Academy, pg 513

Philippines
Anvil Publishing Inc, pg 518
Books for Pleasure Inc, pg 518
Estrella Publishing, pg 519
Sonny A Mendoza, pg 519
New Day Publishers, pg 520

Poland
Arlekin-Wydawnictwo Harlequin Enterprises sp zoo, pg 522
Ksiaznica Publishing Ltd, pg 524

Portugal
Editorial Estampa, Lda, pg 531
Europress Editores e Distribuidores de Publicacoes Lda, pg 531
Gradiva-Publicacnoes Lda, pg 532
Latina Livraria Editora, pg 532
Livraria Minerva, pg 533
Paulinas, pg 534
Quetzal Editores, pg 535
Teorema, pg 536
Vega-Publicacao e Distribuicao de Livros e Revistas, Lda, pg 536

Romania
Lider Verlag, pg 540
Mentor Kiado, pg 540
RAO International Publishing Co, pg 542
Realitatea Casa de Edituri Productie Audio-Video Film, pg 542
Saeculum IO, pg 542
Editura Univers SA, pg 543

1095

SUBJECT INDEX

Russian Federation
Armada Publishing House, pg 543
BLIC, russko-Baltijskij informaciionnyj centr, AO, pg 544
KUbK Publishing House, pg 546
Permskaja Kniga, pg 548
Raduga Publishers, pg 548

Saudi Arabia
Dar Al-Shareff for Publishing & Distribution, pg 550

Slovakia
Vydavatepstvo Praca spol sro, pg 560
Vydavatelstvo Wist sro, pg 561

Slovenia
Mladinska Knjiga International, pg 561

South Africa
Human & Rousseau (Pty) Ltd, pg 564
Ivy Publications, pg 565
Jacklin Enterprises (Pty) Ltd, pg 565
Tafelberg Publishers Ltd, pg 569

Spain
Enciclopedia Catalana, SA, pg 582
Harlequin Iberica SA, pg 586
Ediciones Martinez-Roca SA, pg 591
Publicaciones y Ediciones Salamandra SA, pg 597
Ediciones Urano, SA, pg 604

Sweden
Bonnier Carlsen Bokforlag AB, pg 610

Switzerland
Berchtold Haller Verlag, pg 619
Terra Grischuna Verlag Buch-und Zeitschriftenverlag, pg 635
Verlag Die Waage, pg 636

Taiwan, Province of China
Asian Culture Co Ltd, pg 638
Lin Pai Press Company Ltd, pg 641
Morning Star Publisher Inc, pg 641
UNITAS Publishing Co Ltd, pg 642

Thailand
Chokechai Theues Shop, pg 645

United Kingdom
BBC Audiobooks, pg 663
BCA - Book Club Associates, pg 663
The Greek Bookshop, pg 702
HarperCollins UK, pg 705
Motilal (UK) Books of India, pg 729
Orion Publishing Group Ltd, pg 736
Pan Macmillan, pg 738
Severn House Publishers Inc, pg 756
Time Warner Book Group UK, pg 766
Ulverscroft Large Print Books Ltd, pg 768

Uruguay
Fundacion de Cultura Universitaria, pg 777

SCIENCE (GENERAL)

Albania
NL SH, pg 1
State Textbook Publishing House, pg 1

Algeria
Enterprise Nationale du Livre (ENAL), pg 2

Argentina
Ada Korn Editora SA, pg 3
Alfagrama SRL ediciones, pg 3
Centro Editor de America Latina SA, pg 4
EUDEBA (Editorial Universitaria de Buenos Aires), pg 5
Editorial Hemisferio Sur SA, pg 6
Laffont Ediciones Electronicas SA, pg 7
Marymar Ediciones SA, pg 7
Editorial Polemos SA, pg 8

Armenia
Ajstan Publishers, pg 10

Australia
Allen & Unwin Pty Ltd, pg 11
Beazer Publishing Company Pty Ltd, pg 14
Robert Berthold Photography, pg 14
Blackwell Publishing Asia, pg 15
Bureau of Resource Sciences, pg 16
CSIRO Publishing (Commonwealth Scientific & Industrial Research Organisation), pg 19
Dellasta Publishing, pg 19
Elsevier Australia, pg 21
Emerald City Books, pg 21
Encyclopaedia Britannica (Australia) Inc, pg 21
Great Western Press Pty Ltd, pg 24
Greater Glider Productions Australia Pty Ltd, pg 24
Illert Publications, pg 26
Macmillan Education Australia, pg 30
Macmillan Publishers Australia Pty Ltd, pg 30
Mimosa Publications Pty Ltd, pg 32
K & Z Mostafanejad, pg 32
Nimaroo Publishers, pg 33
Pearson Education Australia, pg 36
Rankin Publishers, pg 39
Royal Society of New South Wales, pg 40
Royal Society of Victoria Inc, pg 40
Transpareon Press, pg 44
Troll Books of Australia, pg 44
University of New South Wales Press Ltd, pg 44
Veritas Press, pg 45
Wizard Books Pty Ltd, pg 47

Austria
Bethania Verlag, pg 48
Boehlau Verlag GmbH & Co KG, pg 48
Danubia Werbung und Verlagsservice, pg 49
Franz Deuticke Verlagsgesmbh, pg 50
Fassbaender Verlag, pg 50
Fremdenverkehrs Aktiengessellschaft, pg 51
Georg Fromme und Co, pg 51
Guthmann & Peterson Liber Libri, Edition, pg 51
Johannes Heyn GmbH & Co KG, pg 52
International Institute for Applied Systems Analysis (IIASA), pg 52
Verlag der Oesterreichischen Akademie der Wissenschaften (OEAW), pg 55
Verlag Oldenbourg, pg 56
Resch Verlag, pg 56
Springer-Verlag Wien, pg 58
Studien Verlag Gmbh, pg 58
Trauner Verlag, pg 58
Verlag Carl Ueberreuter GmbH, pg 58
Edition Va Bene, pg 59
Universitaetsverlag Wagner GmbH, pg 59
WUV/Facultas Universitaetsverlag, pg 60

Azerbaijan
Azernesr, pg 60

Bangladesh
Agamee Prakashani, pg 61

Belarus
Belaruskaya Encyklapedyya, pg 62
Publishing Center of Belarus State University, pg 62

Belgium
Academia Press, pg 62
Uitgeverij Acco, pg 62
Campinia Media VZW, pg 64
Editions Complexe SPRL, pg 65
Editions De Boeck-Larcier SA, pg 66
Dessain - Departement de De Boeck & Larcier SA, pg 66
Editions les Eperonniers, pg 67
Imprimerie Hayez SPRL, pg 68
Koninklijke Vlaamse Academie van Belgie voor Wetenschappen en Kunsten, pg 69
Editions Labor, pg 69
Leuven University Press, pg 70
Presses Universitaires de Bruxelles asbl, pg 72
Editions Techniques et Scientifiques SPRL, pg 73
Presses Universitaires de Louvain-UCL, pg 74
Imprimeur - Editeur Vaillant-Carmanne SA, pg 74
Vander Editions, SA, pg 74
VUB Brussels University Press, pg 74
Wolters Plantyn Educatieve Uitgevers, pg 74

Bolivia
Editorial Don Bosco, pg 75

Bosnia and Herzegovina
Veselin Maslesa, pg 76
Svjetlost, pg 76

Brazil
Abril SA, pg 76
Livraria Francisco Alves Editora SA, pg 77
ARTMED Editora, pg 78
Editora Edgard Blucher Ltda, pg 79
Cadence Publicacoes Internacionais Ltda, pg 79
Editora Campus Ltda, pg 79
EDUSC - Editora da Universidade do Sagrado Coracao, pg 81
Editora Globo SA, pg 82
Editora Harbra Ltda, pg 83
IBRASA (Instituicao Brasileira de Difusao Cultural Ltda), pg 83
Icone Editora Ltda, pg 83
Editora Interciencia Ltda, pg 84
Modulo Editora e Desenvolvimento Educacional Ltda, pg 87
Cia Editora Nacional, pg 87
Editora Nova Fronteira SA, pg 87
Editora Objetiva Ltda, pg 87
Proton Editora Ltda, pg 89
Editora Revan Ltda, pg 89
Editora Rocco Ltda, pg 89
Editora Scipione Ltda, pg 90
Livraria Sulina Editora, pg 91
Edicoes Tabajara, pg 91
Editora da Universidade de Sao Paulo, pg 91
Jorge Zahar Editor, pg 92

Bulgaria
Abagar Pablioing, pg 92
Abagar, Veliko Tarnovo, pg 93
Aleks Print Publishing House, pg 93
Antroposofsko Izdatelstvo Dimo R Daskalov OOD, pg 93
Izdatelstvo na Balgarskata Akademija na Naukite, pg 93
Bulvest 2000 Ltd, pg 93
Darzhavno Izdatelstvo Zemizdat, pg 93
Foi-Commerce, pg 94
Gea-Libris Publishing House, pg 94
Heron Press Publishing House, pg 94
Litera Prima, pg 95
Makros 2000 - Plovdiv, pg 95
Naouka i Izkoustvo, Ltd, pg 95
Universitetsko Izdatelstvo 'Kliment Ochridski', pg 96
Pensoft Publishers, pg 96
Regalia 6 Publishing House, pg 96
Slavena, pg 97
Technica, pg 97
Ivan Vazov Publishing House, pg 97

Cameroon
Centre d'Edition et de Production pour l'Enseignement et la Recherche (CEPER), pg 98

Chile
Editorial Universitaria SA, pg 100
Ediciones Universitarias de Valparaiso, pg 100

China
Beijing Publishing House, pg 101
China Ocean Press, pg 102
China Youth Publishing House, pg 103
Chongqing University Press, pg 103
Dalian Maritime University Press, pg 104
Foreign Languages Press, pg 104
Fudan University Press, pg 104
Fujian Science & Technology Publishing House, pg 104
Heilongjiang Science & Technology Press, pg 105
Higher Education Press, pg 105
Inner Mongolia Science & Technology Publishing House, pg 105
Jiangsu Science & Technology Publishing House, pg 105
Jilin Science & Technology Publishing House, pg 105
Knowledge Press, pg 106
National Defence Industry Press, pg 106
New Times Press, pg 106

Patent Documentation Publishing House, pg 106
Science Press, pg 107
Shandong University Press, pg 108
Shanghai College of Traditional Chinese Medicine Press, pg 108
Shanghai Educational Publishing House, pg 108
Shanghai Scientific & Technical Publishers, pg 108
Shanghai Scientific & Technological Literature Press, pg 108
Sichuan Science & Technology Publishing House, pg 108
Southwest China Jiaotong University Press, pg 108
Tianjin Science & Technology Publishing House, pg 108
Zhejiang University Press, pg 109

Colombia
Editora Guadalupe Ltda, pg 111
Editorial Libros y Libres SA, pg 112
Universidad Nacional Abierta y a Distancia, pg 113

The Democratic Republic of the Congo
Presses Universitaires du Zaiire (PUZ), pg 114

Costa Rica
Editorial Tecnologica de Costa Rica, pg 116
Editorial de la Universidad de Costa Rica, pg 116

Cote d'Ivoire
Centre d'Edition et de Diffusion Africaines, pg 117

Croatia
Izdavacka Delatnost Hrvatske Akademije Znanosti I Umjetnosti, pg 118
Matica hrvatska, pg 118
Mladost d d Izdavacku graficku i informaticku djelatnost, pg 119
Naklada Ljevak doo, pg 119
Narodne Novine, pg 119
Skolska Knjiga, pg 119
Sveucilisna tiskara doo, pg 119
Tehnicka Knjiga, pg 119

Cuba
Editorial Cientifico Tecnica, pg 120
Editora Politica, pg 120
Pueblo y Educacion Editorial (PE), pg 121

Czech Republic
Granit sro, pg 123
Karolinum, nakladatelstvi, pg 124
Lidove Noviny Publishing House, pg 125
Maxdorf Ltd, pg 125
Mlada fronta, pg 125
Narodni Muzeum, pg 126
Omnipress Praha, pg 126
Vysehrad spol sro, pg 128

Denmark
Akademisk Forlag A/S, pg 128
Bogan's Forlag, pg 129
Bogfabrikken Fakta ApS, pg 129
Fremad A/S, pg 131
Gyldendalske Boghandel - Nordisk Forlag A/S, pg 131
Nyt Nordisk Forlag Arnold Busck A/S, pg 133
Polyteknisk Boghandel & Forlag, pg 133
C A Reitzel Boghandel & Forlag A/S, pg 134
Rosenkilde & Bagger, pg 134
Forlaget Vindrose A/S, pg 135

Ecuador
Pontificia Universidad Catolica del Ecuador, Centro de Publicaciones, pg 137

Egypt (Arab Republic of Egypt)
Al Ahram Establishment, pg 137
Dar Al Maaref, pg 138
Middle East Book Centre, pg 138

Estonia
Eesti Entsuklopeediakirjastus, pg 139
Estonian Academy Publishers, pg 139
Valgus Publishers, pg 140

Ethiopia
Addis Ababa University Press, pg 140

Finland
Abo Akademis forlag - Abo Akademi University Press, pg 141
Soderstroms Forlag, pg 144
Ursa ry, pg 144

France
Editions Belin, pg 149
Bureau des Longitudes, pg 151
Cepadues Editions SA, pg 153
Le Cherche Midi Editeur, pg 154
CNRS Editions, pg 155
Le Dilettante, pg 158
Doin Editeurs, pg 159
Dunod Editeur, pg 159
Editions rue d'Ulm, pg 160
EDP Sciences, pg 161
Ellipses - Edition Marketing SA, pg 161
Editions Entente, pg 161
Librairie Artheme Fayard, pg 163
Editions Jacques Gabay, pg 164
Editions Ganymede, pg 165
Groupe Express-Expansion, pg 166
Hachette Livre, pg 167
L'Harmattan, pg 167
Hermann editeurs des Sciences et des Arts SA, pg 167
IRD Editions, pg 169
Editions Klincksieck, pg 170
Editions Larousse, pg 171
Librairie Scientifique et Technique Albert Blanchard, pg 172
Le Livre de Poche-L G F (Librairie Generale Francaise), pg 173
Editions MDI (La Maison des Instituteurs), pg 175
Editions Fernand Nathan, pg 176
Editions Odile Jacob, pg 177
Editions Ouest-France, pg 178
Polytechnica SA, pg 180
Selection du Reader's Digest SA, pg 184
Editions de Septembre, pg 184
Editions du Seuil, pg 184
UNESCO Publishing, pg 188

Georgia
Sakartvelo Publishing House, pg 190

Germany
Accedo Verlagsgesellschaft mbH, pg 190
Aerogie-Verlag, pg 191
AGIS Verlag GmbH, pg 191
Ahriman-Verlag GmbH, pg 191
Aisthesis Verlag, pg 191
AOL-Verlag Frohmut Menze, pg 193
Aquamarin Verlag, pg 193
Arkana Verlag Tete Boettger Rainer Wunderlich Verlag, pg 194
Auer Verlag GmbH, pg 195
J J Augustin Verlag GmbH, pg 195
Aulis Verlag Deubner & Co KG, pg 195
Dr Bachmaier Verlag GmbH, pg 196
Dr Wolfgang Baur Verlag Kunst & Alltag, pg 198
Bayerische Akademie der Wissenschaften, pg 198
Julius Beltz GmbH & Co KG, pg 199
W Bertelsmann Verlag GmbH & Co KG, pg 200
Bibliographisches Institut & F A Brockhaus AG, pg 200
Verlag Die Blaue Eule, pg 202
Bock und Herchen Verlag, pg 202
Verlag Hermann Boehlaus Nachfolger Weimar GmbH & Co, pg 203
Bouvier Verlag, pg 203
F Bruckmann Munchen Verlag & Druck GmbH & Co Produkt KG, pg 204
Buchverlag Junge Welt GmbH, pg 205
Fachverlag Hans Carl GmbH, pg 207
J G Cotta'sche Buchhandlung Nachfolger GmbH, pg 210
Deutsche Verlags-Anstalt GmbH (DVA), pg 212
Deutscher Taschenbuch Verlag GmbH & Co KG (dtv), pg 213
Deutscher Universitats-Verlag, pg 213
Diagonal-Verlag GbR Rink-Schweer, pg 214
Dietrich zu Klampen Verlag, pg 214
Verlagsgruppe Droemer Knaur GmbH & Co KG, pg 216
Duncker und Humblot GmbH, pg 217
Klaus D Dutz, pg 217
Econ Verlag GmbH, pg 218
Elsevier GmbH/Urban & Fischer Verlag, pg 219
Esogetics GmbH, pg 221
Verlag Esoterische Philosophie GmbH, pg 221
Ferdinand Enke Verlag, pg 224
Franz Ferzak World & Space Publications, pg 224
Harald Fischer Verlag GmbH, pg 224
Franckh-Kosmos Verlags-GmbH & Co, pg 226
Verlag Freies Geistesleben, pg 227
Verlag A Fromm im Druck- u Verlagshaus Fromm GmbH & Co KG, pg 227
Genius Verlag, pg 228
Georgi GmbH, pg 228
Germanisches Nationalmuseum, pg 228
Gmelin Verlag GmbH, pg 230
Wilhelm Goldmann Verlag GmbH, pg 230
Walter de Gruyter GmbH & Co KG, pg 231
Haag und Herchen Verlag GmbH, pg 232
Dr Curt Haefner-Verlag GmbH, pg 233
Hahner Verlagsgesellschaft mbH, pg 233
Dr Ernst Hauswedell & Co, pg 235
Anton Hiersemann, Verlag, pg 237
S Hirzel Verlag GmbH und Co, pg 238
Hoffmann und Campe Verlag GmbH, pg 238
Verlagsgruppe Georg von Holtzbrinck GmbH, pg 239
Edition Humanistische Psychologie (EHP), pg 240
Huthig GmbH & Co KG, pg 240
Idea Verlag GmbH, pg 240
IKO Verlag fur Interkulturelle Kommunikation, pg 241
Janus Verlagsgesellschaft, Dr Norbert Meder & Co, pg 243
Johann Wolfgang Goethe Universitat, pg 243
S Karger GmbH Verlag fuer Medizin und Naturwissenschaften, pg 244
Keysersche Verlagsbuchhandlung GmbH, pg 245
Vittorio Klostermann GmbH, pg 247
Reinhold Kraemer Verlag, pg 249
Verlag Waldemar Kramer, pg 250
Ambro Lacus, Buch- und Bildverlag Walter A Kremnitz, pg 251
Peter Lang GmbH Europaeischer Verlag der Wissenschaften, pg 252
Leibniz Verlag, pg 253
Leipziger Universitaetsverlag GmbH, pg 253
Martha Lindner Verlags-GmbH, pg 254
LIT Verlag, pg 255
Verlag an der Lottbek, pg 255
Annemarie Maeger, pg 256
Matthiesen Verlag Ingwert Paulsen Jr, pg 258
Ursala Meyer und Dr Manfred Duker Ein-Fach-Verlag, pg 260
Musikantiquariat und Dr Hans Schneider Verlag GmbH, pg 262
Naumann & Goebel Verlagsgesellschaft mbH, pg 263
Verlag J Neumann-Neudamm GmbH & Co KG, pg 264
Neumann Verlag, pg 264
Nusser Verlag, pg 266
R Oldenbourg Verlag GmbH, pg 267
Georg Olms Verlag AG, pg 267
Passavia Universitaetsverlag und -Druck GmbH, pg 268
Philipps-Universitaet Marburg, pg 270
Physica-Verlag, pg 270
Piper Verlag GmbH, pg 270
Propylaeen Verlag, Zweigniederlassung Berlin der Ullstein Buchverlage GmbH, pg 272
Dr Josef Raabe-Verlags GmbH, pg 273
Raethgloben Verlagsgesellschaft mbH, pg 273
Dr Ludwig Reichert Verlag, pg 274
Ernst Reinhardt Verlag GmbH & Co KG, pg 275
Roehrig Universitaets Verlag Gmbh, pg 276
Verlag Sauerlaender GmbH, pg 278
Sax-Verlag Beucha, pg 278

SUBJECT INDEX

Schattauer GmbH Verlag fuer Medizin und Naturwissenschaften, pg 279
Schmidt Periodicals GmbH, pg 280
Schueren Verlag GmbH, pg 281
Schulz-Kirchner Verlag GmbH, pg 282
E Schweizerbart'sche Verlagsbuchhandlung (Naegele und Obermiller), pg 282
Spektrum der Wissenschaft Verlagsgesellschaft mbH, pg 284
Springer Science+Business Media GmbH & Co KG, pg 284
Springer Science+Business Media GmbH & Co KG, Berlin, pg 285
Steyler Verlag, pg 288
Suhrkamp Verlag, pg 289
Synthesis Verlag, pg 289
Tomus Verlag GmbH, pg 291
Ullstein Heyne List GmbH & Co KG, pg 293
Verlag Eugen Ulmer GmbH & Co, pg 293
Neuer Umschau Buchverlag, pg 293
UVK Universitatsverlag Konstanz GmbH, pg 294
Dorothea van der Koelen, pg 294
VDI Verlag GmbH, pg 294
Verlag fuer die Frau GmbH, pg 295
Dokument und Analyse Verlag Bogislaw von Randow, pg 296
VWB-Verlag fur Wissenschaft & Bildung, Amand Aglaster, pg 297
Waxmann Verlag GmbH, pg 297
Weber Zucht & Co, pg 298
Weidler Buchverlag Berlin, pg 298
Wiley-VCH Verlag GmbH, pg 300
Dr Dieter Winkler, pg 300
Verlag Wissenschaft und Politik, pg 300
Wissenschaftliche Buchgesellschaft, pg 300
Wissenschaftliche Verlagsgesellschaft mbH, pg 300
Verlag Konrad Wittwer GmbH, pg 301
Das Wunderhorn Verlag GmbH, pg 301
Zettner Verlag GmbH & Co KG, pg 302

Ghana
Anowuo Educational Publications, pg 303
Bureau of Ghana Languages, pg 303
Ghana Academy of Arts & Sciences, pg 304
Ghana Publishing Corporation, pg 304
Sam Woode Ltd, pg 304
Sedco Publishing Ltd, pg 305
Unimax Macmillan Ltd, pg 305
Waterville Publishing House, pg 305

Greece
Chryssos Typos AE Ekodeis, pg 306
Diavlos, pg 306
Giovanis Publications, Pangosmios Ekdotikos Organismos, pg 307
Katoptro Publications, pg 309
Kedros Publishers, pg 309
Morfotiko Idryma Ethnikis Trapezas, pg 310
J Sideris OE Ekdoseis, pg 312
Technical Chamber of Greece, pg 312
S J Zacharopoulos SA Publishing Co, pg 313

Holy See (Vatican City State)
Pontificia Academia Scientiarum, pg 314

Hong Kong
The Chinese University Press, pg 316
Times Publishing (Hong Kong) Ltd, pg 319

Hungary
Akademiai Kiado, pg 320
Foldmuvelesugyi Miniszterium Muszaki Intezet, pg 321
Hatter Lap- es Konyvkiado Kft, pg 321
Idegenforgalmi Propaganda es Kiado Vallalat, pg 321
Mezogazda Kiado, pg 323
Mueszaki Koenyvkiado Ltd, pg 323
Panem, pg 324
Polgar Kiado Kft, pg 324
Pro Natura, pg 324
Zrinyi Kiado, pg 325

India
Addison-Wesley Pte Ltd, pg 327
Affiliated East West Press Pvt Ltd, pg 327
Allied Book Centre, pg 328
Ambar Prakashan, pg 328
Ananda Publishers Pvt Ltd, pg 328
Ankur Publishing Co, pg 328
Anmol Publications Pvt Ltd, pg 328
APH Publishing Corp, pg 328
Arya Medi Publishing House, pg 328
Asia Pacific Business Press Inc, pg 328
Atma Ram & Sons, pg 329
Bharat Publishing House, pg 330
Bihar Hindi Granth Akademi, pg 330
S Chand & Co Ltd, pg 331
Dastane Ramchandra & Co, pg 333
Eurasia Publishing House Private Ltd, pg 334
Frank Brothers & Co Publishers Ltd, pg 334
Geeta Prakashan, pg 335
Himalaya Publishing House, pg 335
IBD Publisher & Distributors, pg 336
Indian Museum, pg 337
International Book Distributors, pg 338
Kalyani Publishers, pg 339
Kitab Ghar, pg 339
Law Publishers, pg 340
Manohar Publishers & Distributors, pg 340
Ministry of Information & Broadcasting, pg 341
National Institute of Industrial Research (NIIR), pg 343
Naya Prokash, pg 343
Oxford & IBH Publishing Co Pvt Ltd, pg 344
Oxonian Press (P) Ltd, pg 344
Paico Publishing House, pg 344
Publications & Information Directorate, CSIR, pg 345
Pustak Mahal, pg 345
Rajasthan Hindi Granth Academy, pg 346
Rajendra Publishing House Pvt Ltd, pg 346
Rajpal & Sons, pg 346
Rastogi Publications, pg 346
Research Signpost, pg 347
Researchco Reprints, pg 347
Scientific Book Agency, pg 348
Shaibya Prakashan Bibhag, pg 349
South Asian Publishers Pvt Ltd, pg 350
Sterling Publishers Pvt Ltd, pg 350
Suman Prakashan Pvt Ltd, pg 351
Tata McGraw-Hill Publishing Co Ltd, pg 351
Theosophical Publishing House, pg 351
Today & Tomorrow's Printers & Publishers, pg 351
Transworld Research Network, pg 351
Vikas Publishing House Pvt Ltd, pg 352
Vision Books Pvt Ltd, pg 352
S Viswanathan (Printers & Publishers) Pvt Ltd, pg 352
Viva Books Pvt Ltd, pg 352

Indonesia
Andi Offset, pg 353
Bhratara Karya Aksara, pg 354
PT Bulan Bintang, pg 354
Institut Teknologi Bandung, pg 355
Katalis PT Bina Mitra Plaosan, pg 355
PT Pustaka LP3ES Indonesia, pg 356
Yayasan Obor Indonesia, pg 357

Islamic Republic of Iran
Scientific and Cultural Publications, pg 357

Iraq
National House for Publishing, Distributing & Advertising, pg 357

Ireland
An Gum, pg 358
The Educational Company of Ireland, pg 359
O'Brien Educational, pg 362
Royal Dublin Society, pg 363

Israel
Achiasaf Publishing House Ltd, pg 364
Amichai Publishing House Ltd, pg 365
Freund Publishing House Ltd, pg 367
Ma'ariv Book Guild (Sifriat Ma'ariv), pg 370
The Magnes Press, pg 370
Massada Press Ltd, pg 370
M Mizrahi Publishers, pg 370
The Van Leer Jerusalem Institute, pg 373
Yavneh Publishing House Ltd, pg 373

Italy
Adelphi Edizioni SpA, pg 374
De Agostini Scolastica, pg 374
Umberto Allemandi & C SRL, pg 375
Argalia Editore delle Arti Grafiche Editoriali SRL, pg 376
Editrice Atanor SRL, pg 377
Atlantica Editrice SARL, pg 377
Bianco, pg 377
Bibliopolis - Edizioni di Filosofia e Scienze Srl, pg 378
Bollati Boringhieri Editore, pg 378
Bompiani-RCS Libri, pg 378
Bulzoni Editore SRL (Le Edizioni Universitarie d'Italia), pg 379
Edizioni Cantagalli, pg 379
Cappelli Editore, pg 380
Casa Editrice Lint Srl, pg 380
Celuc Libri, pg 381
il Cerchio Iniziative Editoriali, pg 381
Il Cigno Galileo Galilei-Edizioni di Arte e Scienza, pg 382
Ciranna - Roma, pg 382
CLEUP - Cooperative Libraria Editrice dell 'Universita di Padova, pg 382
CLUEB (Cooperativa Libraria Universitaria Editrice Bologna), pg 382
CLUT Editrice, pg 383
Edizioni di Comunita SpA, pg 383
Libreria Cortina Editrice SRL, pg 383
Edizioni Cremonese SRL, pg 383
Edizioni Dedalo SRL, pg 384
Edagricole - Edizioni Agricole, pg 385
EDAS, pg 385
Ediciclo Editore SRL, pg 386
Editrice Edisco, pg 386
Edistudio, pg 386
ERGA SNC di Carla Ottino Merli & C (Edizioni Realizzazioni Grafiche - Artigiana), pg 388
Giangiacomo Feltrinelli SpA, pg 389
Flaccovio Editore, pg 389
Edizioni GB, pg 390
Giunti Gruppo Editoriale, pg 390
Gius Laterza e Figli SpA, pg 391
Gruppo Editoriale Faenza Editrice SpA, pg 391
Hopeful Monster Editore, pg 392
IHT Gruppo Editoriale SRL, pg 393
Editoriale Jaca Book SpA, pg 394
L Japadre Editore, pg 394
Lalli Editore SRL, pg 394
Levrotto e Bella Libreria Editrice Universitaria SAS, pg 395
Liguori Editore SRL, pg 395
Loffredo Editore Napoli SpA®, pg 396
Longanesi & C, pg 396
Macro Edizioni, pg 397
Manfrini Editori, pg 397
Aldo Marino Editore, pg 397
Editrice Massimo SAS di Crespi Cesare e C, pg 397
Masson SpA, pg 397
McRae Books, pg 398
Edizioni Medicea SRL, pg 398
Mediserve SRL, pg 398
Arnoldo Mondadori Editore SpA, pg 398
Mucchi Editore SRL, pg 399
Gruppo Ugo Mursia Editore SpA, pg 400
Franco Muzzio Editore, pg 400
Newton & Compton Editori, pg 400
Leo S Olschki, pg 401
Piccin Nuova Libraria SpA, pg 403
Il Poligrafo, pg 404
Psicologica Editrice, pg 404
RCS Libri SpA, pg 405
Editori Riuniti, pg 405
Edizioni Universitarie Romane, pg 406
SAGEP Libri & Comunicazione Srl, pg 406
Il Saggiatore, pg 406
Sardini Editrice, pg 407
Edizioni Scientifiche Italiane, pg 407
Editoriale Scienza, pg 407

Societa Editrice la Goliardica Pavese SRL, pg 408
Sorbona, pg 409
Sperling e Kupfer Editori SpA, pg 409
Le Stelle Scuola, pg 409
Edizioni Studio Tesi SRL, pg 409
Edizioni Studium SRL, pg 409
UTET (Unione Tipografico-Editrice Torinese), pg 411
Zanichelli Editore SpA, pg 412

Jamaica

Carib Publishing Ltd, pg 413
Carlong Publishers (Caribbean) Ltd, pg 413
Institute of Jamaica Publications, pg 413

Japan

Bun-ichi Sogo Shuppan, pg 415
Business Center for Academic Societies Japan, pg 416
Chijin Shokan Co Ltd, pg 416
Chuokoron-Shinsha Inc, pg 416
CMC Publishing Co Ltd, pg 416
Corona Publishing Co Ltd, pg 416
Dainippon Tosho Publishing Co, Ltd, pg 416
Diamond Inc, pg 416
Dobunshoin Publishers Co, pg 416
Fukuinkan Shoten Publishers Inc, pg 417
Hakuyo-Sha, pg 418
Hakuyu-Sha, pg 418
Hayakawa Publishing Inc, pg 418
Heibonsha Ltd, Publishers, pg 418
Hirokawa Publishing Co, pg 418
Hoikusha Publishing Co Ltd, pg 418
Hokkaido University Press, pg 418
Hokuryukan Co Ltd, pg 418
Holp Book Co Ltd, pg 418
Iwanami Shoten, Publishers, pg 419
Japan Broadcast Publishing Co Ltd, pg 419
Kawade Shobo Shinsha Publishers, pg 420
Keigaku Publishing Co Ltd, pg 420
Kinokuniya Co Ltd (Publishing Department), pg 421
Kodansha Scientific Ltd, pg 421
Kogyo Chosakai Publishing Co Ltd, pg 421
Komine Shoten Co Ltd, pg 421
Koseisha-Koseikaku Co Ltd, pg 422
Maruzen Co Ltd, pg 422
Misuzu Shobo Ltd, pg 422
Mita Press, Mita Industrial Co Ltd, pg 422
Morikita Shuppan Co Ltd, pg 423
Nakayama Shoten Co Ltd, pg 423
Nankodo Co Ltd, pg 423
Nensho-Sha, pg 423
Nihon Keizai Shimbun Inc Publications Bureau, pg 423
Nikkagiren Shuppan-Sha (JUSE Press Ltd), pg 424
Nippon Hoso Shuppan Kyokai (NHK Publishing), pg 424
Nippon Jitsugyo Publishing Co Ltd, pg 424
Obunsha Co Ltd, pg 424
Ohmsha Co Ltd, pg 424
Poplar Publishing Co Ltd, pg 425
Saela Shobo (Librairie Ca et La), pg 425
Sangyo-Tosho Publishing Co Ltd, pg 426
Sankyo Publishing Company Ltd, pg 426
Sanseido Co Ltd, pg 426
Sanshusha Publishing Co, Ltd, pg 426
Sanyo Shuppan Boeki Co Inc, pg 426
Seibundo Shinkosha Publishing Co Ltd, pg 426
Shincho-Sha Co Ltd, pg 427
Akane Shobo Co Ltd, pg 427
Shokabo Publishing Co Ltd, pg 428
Shokokusha Publishing Co Ltd, pg 428
Soshisha Co Ltd, pg 428
Springer-Verlag Tokyo, pg 428
Tokyo Kagaku Dojin Co Ltd, pg 429
Tokyo Shoseki Co Ltd, pg 430
Tokyo Tosho Co Ltd, pg 430
Universal Academy Press, Inc, pg 430
University of Tokyo Press, pg 430
Yokendo Ltd, pg 431
Yoshioka Shoten, pg 431

Jordan

Al-Tanwir Al Ilmi (Scientific Enlightenment Publishing House), pg 432

Kazakstan

Gylym, Izd-Vo, pg 432
Kazakhstan, Izd-Vo, pg 432

Kenya

Academy Science Publishers, pg 432
African Centre for Technology Studies (ACTS), pg 433
Kenya Literature Bureau, pg 434

Democratic People's Republic of Korea

Academy of Sciences Publishing House, pg 436
Korea Science and Encyclopedia Publishing House, pg 436

Republic of Korea

Ba-reunsa Publishing Co, pg 437
Bakyoung Publishing Co, pg 437
Bo Moon Dang, pg 437
Borim Publishing Co, pg 437
Cheong-mun-gag Publishing Co, pg 438
Chung Rim Publishing Co, pg 438
Dae Won Sa Co Ltd, pg 438
Ewha Womans University Press, pg 438
Gim-Yeong Co, pg 438
Gyeom-jisa, pg 438
Hainaim Publishing Co Ltd, pg 439
Hakmunsa Publishing Co, pg 439
Hyangmunsa Publishing Co, pg 439
Hyein Publishing House, pg 439
Iljo-gag Publishers, pg 439
Ke Mong Sa Publishing Co Ltd, pg 440
Koreaone Press Inc, pg 440
Min-eumsa Publishing Co Ltd, pg 441
Mun Un Dang, pg 441
Panmun Book Co Ltd, pg 442
Prompter Publications, pg 442
Seoul National University Press, pg 443
Shinkwang Publishing Co, pg 443
Sogang University Press, pg 443
Woongjin Media Corporation, pg 443
Yonsei University Press, pg 444

Latvia

Madris, pg 445

Lebanon

Dar El Ilm Lilmalayin, pg 446
Librairie du Liban Publishers (Sal), pg 446

Liechtenstein

Saendig Reprint Verlag, Hans-Rainer Wohlwend, pg 448

Lithuania

Algarve, pg 448
Klaipedos Universiteto Leidykla, pg 449
Mokslo ir enciklopediju leidybos institutas, pg 449
TEV Leidykla, pg 450

Luxembourg

Editions APESS ASBL, pg 450

The Former Yugoslav Republic of Macedonia

Ktitor, pg 452
Menora Publishing House, pg 452
Nov svet (New World), pg 453

Malaysia

Federal Publications Sdn Bhd, pg 455
Pearson Education Malaysia Sdn Bhd, pg 457
Penerbit Jayatinta Sdn Bhd, pg 458
Pustaka Cipta Sdn Bhd, pg 458
Pustaka Delta Pelajaran Sdn Bhd, pg 458
Tropical Press Sdn Bhd, pg 459
Penerbit Universiti Teknologi Malaysia, pg 459
University of Malaya, Department of Publications, pg 459

Maldive Islands

Non-Formal Education Centre, pg 459

Mauritius

Editions de l'Ocean Indien Ltd, pg 461

Mexico

Editorial Azteca SA, pg 462
Libreria y Ediciones Botas SA, pg 462
Centro de Estudios Mexicanos y Centroamericanos, pg 463
El Colegio de Mexico AC, pg 463
Colegio de Postgraduados en Ciencias Agricolas, pg 463
Compania Editorial Continental SA de CV, pg 463
Fernandez Editores SA de CV, pg 465
Fondo de Cultura Economica, pg 465
Editorial Limusa SA de CV, pg 467
Nova Grupo Editorial SA de CV, pg 469
Editorial Nueva Imagen SA, pg 469
Pearson Educacion de Mexico, SA de CV, pg 470
Plaza y Valdes SA de CV, pg 470
Siglo XXI Editores SA de CV, pg 472
Editorial Trillas SA de CV, pg 472
Universidad Nacional Autonoma de Mexico (National University of Mexico), pg 472

Morocco

Dar El Kitab, pg 474
Dar Nachr Al Maarifa Pour L'Edition et La Distribution, pg 474
Les Editions du Journal L' Unite Maghrebine, pg 475

Mozambique

Editora Minerva Central, pg 475

Myanmar

Sarpay Beikman Public Library, pg 476
Smart & Mookerdum, pg 476

Namibia

Desert Research Foundation of Namibia (DRFN), pg 476
Multi-Disciplinary Research Centre Library, pg 476

Nepal

Royal Nepal Academy, pg 477

Netherlands

Uitgeverij Anthos, pg 477
APA (Academic Publishers Associated), pg 477
B M Israel BV, pg 478
Brill Academic Publishers, pg 479
A W Bruna Uitgevers BV, pg 480
Delft University Press, pg 481
Educatieve Partners Nederland bv, pg 481
Elsevier Science BV, pg 482
Uitgeverij De Fontein BV, pg 482
Gottmer Uitgevers Groep, pg 483
Hagen & Stam Uitgeverij Ten, pg 483
Uitgeverij Holland, pg 483
Kluwer Academic Publishers, pg 484
Kluwer Technische Boeken BV, pg 485
Uitgeverij J H Kok BV, pg 485
Koninklijke Vermande bv, pg 485
Mirananda Publishers BV, pg 486
Philo Press (APA), pg 487
Uitgeverij Ploegsma BV, pg 487
Prometheus, pg 488
Reed Elsevier Nederland BV, pg 488
Segment BV, pg 488
Swets & Zeitlinger Publishers, pg 489
V S P International Science Publishers, pg 491
VU Boekhandel/Uitgeverij BV, pg 492

New Zealand

ABA Books, pg 493
Brick Row Publishing Co Ltd, pg 494
ESA Publications (NZ) Ltd, pg 496
Landcare Research NZ, pg 497
Learning Guides (Writers & Publishers Ltd), pg 497
Nelson Price Milburn Ltd, pg 499
New House Publishers Ltd, pg 499
SIR Publishing, pg 501

Nigeria

Africana-FEP Publishers Ltd, pg 503
Ahmadu Bello University Press Ltd, pg 503
Alliance West African Publishers & Co, pg 503
Aromolaran Publishing Co Ltd, pg 503
CSS Bookshops, pg 504
Educational Research & Study Group, pg 504
Evans Brothers (Nigeria Publishers) Ltd, pg 504
Gbabeks Publishers Ltd, pg 505
Ibadan University Press, pg 505
Kola Sanya Publishing Enterprise, pg 505
Longman Nigeria Plc, pg 505
Thomas Nelson (Nigeria) Ltd, pg 505
New Era Publishers, pg 506
NPS Educational Publishers Ltd (Nigeria Publishers Services), pg 506
Nwamife Publishers Ltd, pg 506
Ogunsanya Press, Publishers and Bookstores Ltd, pg 506
Onibon-Oje Publishers, pg 506
Riverside Communications, pg 507
Tabansi Press Ltd, pg 507
West African Book Publishers Ltd, pg 507

Norway

Aschehoug Forlag, pg 508
H Aschehoug & Co (W Nygaard) A/S, pg 508
F Bruns Bokhandel og Forlag A/S, pg 508
Forlaget Fag og Kultur, pg 509
Novus Forlag, pg 510
Solum Forlag A/S, pg 510
Teknologisk Forlag, pg 510
Universitetsforlaget, pg 511

Pakistan

HMR Publishing Co, pg 512
Maqbool Academy, pg 513
Urdu Academy Sind, pg 514

Panama

Editorial Universitaria, pg 515

Peru

Centro de la Mujer Peruana Flora Tristan, pg 516
Fondo Editorial de la Pontificia Universidad Catolica del Peru, pg 517
Universidad de Lima-Fondo de Desarollo Editorial, pg 517
Universidad Nacional Mayor de San Marcos, pg 517

Philippines

Abiva Publishing House Inc, pg 518
Bookman Printing & Publishing House Inc, pg 518
Rex Bookstores & Publishers, pg 520
Saint Mary's Publishing Corp, pg 520
Salesiana Publishers Inc, pg 521
SIBS Publishing House Inc, pg 521
University of the Philippines Press, pg 521
Vibal Publishing House Inc (VPHI), pg 521

Poland

Interpress, pg 523
KAW Krajowa Agencja Wydawnicza, pg 523
Wydawnictwo Lubelskie, pg 524
Wydawnictwo Nasza Ksiegarnia Sp zoo, pg 524
Norbertinum, pg 524
Wydawnictwa Normalizacyjne Alfa-Wero, pg 525
Ossolineum Zaklad Narodowy im Ossolinskich - Wydawnictwo, pg 525
Panstwowy Instytut Wydawniczy (PIW), pg 525
Polish Scientific Publishers PWN, pg 525
Oficyna Wydawnicza Politechniki Wroclawskiej, pg 525
Wydawnictwa Radia i Telewizji, pg 526
Wydawnictwo RTW, pg 526
'Slask' Ltd, pg 526
Spotdzielna Anagram, pg 526
'Wiedza Powszechna' Panstwowe Wydawnictwo, pg 527

Portugal

Didactica Editora, pg 530
Dinalivro, pg 530
Publicacoes Europa-America Lda, pg 531
Europress Editores e Distribuidores de Publicacoes Lda, pg 531
Gradiva-Publicacnoes Lda, pg 532
Editora Livros do Brasil Sarl, pg 533
Livraria Lopes Da Silva-Editora de M Moreira Soares Rocha Lda, pg 533
Editora McGraw-Hill de Portugal Lda, pg 533
Editorial Presenca, pg 535
Publicacoes Dom Quixote Lda, pg 535
Editora Replicacao Lda, pg 535
Edicoes Silabo, pg 536
Almerinda Teixeira, pg 536
Teorema, pg 536
Editorial Verbo SA, pg 536

Puerto Rico

Publishing Resources Inc, pg 537

Romania

Editora All, pg 538
Casa Editoriala Independenta Europa, pg 538
Editura Clusium, pg 539
Editura Excelsior Art, pg 539
FF Press, pg 540
Editura Gryphon, pg 540
Humanitas Publishing House, pg 540
Editura Niculescu, pg 541
Pallas-Akademia Editura, pg 541
Pandora Publishing House, pg 541
Editura Stiintifica SA, pg 542
Editura Stiintifica si Enciclopedica, pg 542
Editura Tehnica, pg 542
Universal Dalsi, pg 543
Editura de Vest, pg 543

Russian Federation

N E Bauman Moscow State Technical University Publishers, pg 544
BLIC, russko-Baltijskij informaciionnyj centr, AO, pg 544
Izdatelstvo 'Ekonomika', pg 544
Energoatomizdat, pg 544
Gidrometeoizdat, pg 545
Izdatelstvo Lenizdat, pg 546
Izdatelstvo Medicina, pg 546
Izdatelstvo Mir, pg 546
Moscow University Press, pg 547
Izdatelstvo Mysl, pg 547
Nauka Publishers, pg 547
Obdeestro Znanie, pg 547
Pedagogika Press, pg 548
Izdatelstvo Sudostroenie, pg 549
Vsesoyuznii Molodejnii Knizhnii Centre, pg 549

Saudi Arabia

Saudi Publishing & Distributing House, pg 550

Senegal

Les Nouvelles Editions Africaines du Senegal NEAS, pg 551

Serbia and Montenegro

Alfa-Narodna Knjiga, pg 552
Izdavacka preduzece Gradina, pg 552
Tehnicka Knjiga, pg 552
Minerva, pg 552
Naucna Knjiga, pg 552
Nio Pobjeda - Oour Izdavacko-Publicisticka Djelatnost, pg 552
Obod, pg 553
Partenon MAM Sistem, pg 553
Savez Inzenjera i Tehnicara Jugoslavije, pg 553
Vuk Karadzic, pg 554

Singapore

APAC Publishers Services Pte Ltd, pg 554
Celebrity Educational Publishers, pg 555
Chopsons Pte Ltd, pg 555
Daiichi Media Pte Ltd, pg 555
Global Educational Services Pte Ltd, pg 556
Reed Elsevier, South East Asia, pg 557
Singapore University Press Pte Ltd, pg 558
Success Publications Pte Ltd, pg 558
Taylor & Francis Asia Pacific, pg 558

Slovakia

ARCHA sro Vydavatel'stro, pg 559
Vydavatel'stvo Osveta (Verlag Osveta), pg 560
Technicka Univerzita, pg 561

Slovenia

Mladinska Knjiga International, pg 561
Zalozba Obzorja d d Maribor, pg 562

South Africa

Clever Books, pg 563
Educum Publishers Ltd, pg 563
Heinemann Publishers (Pty) Ltd, pg 564
Nasou Via Afrika, pg 567
National Botanical Institute, pg 567
Oceanographic Research Institute, pg 567
Shuter & Shooter (Pty) Ltd, pg 568
Vivlia Publishers & Booksellers, pg 570
Witwatersrand University Press, pg 570

Spain

Acento Editorial, pg 570
Editorial Acribia SA, pg 571
Aguilar SA de Ediciones, pg 571
Alianza Editorial SA, pg 572
AMV Ediciones, pg 572
Editorial Ariel SA, pg 573
Ediciones Bellaterra SA, pg 574
Antoni Bosch Editor SA, pg 574
Editorial Casals SA, pg 575
Edicios do Castro, pg 576
Celeste Ediciones, pg 576
Complutense, SA Editorial, pg 577
Comunidad Autonoma de Madrid, Servicio de Documentacion y Publicaciones, pg 578
Consejo Superior de Investigaciones Cientificas, pg 578
Ediciones Diaz de Santos SA, pg 579
Editorial Dossat SA, pg 580
Fondo de Cultura Economica de Espana, SL, pg 583
Fundacion Marcelino Botin, pg 584
Editorial Iberia, SA, pg 586
Idea Books, SA, pg 587
Junta de Castilla y Leon Consejeria de Educacion y Cultura, pg 588
Editorin Laiovento SL, pg 588
Edicions de la Magrana SA, pg 590
McGraw-Hill/Interamericana de Espana SAU, pg 591
Ediciones Oceano Grupo SA, pg 593
Ediciones Omega SA, pg 594
Editorial Paraninfo SA, pg 595
Pearson Educacion S A, pg 595
Ediciones Piramide SA, pg 596
Editorial Playor SA, pg 596
Prensas Universitarias de Zaragoza, pg 597
Publicaciones de la Universidad de Alicante, pg 597
Pulso Ediciones, SL, pg 597
Editorial Reverte SA, pg 598
Ediciones Rialp SA, pg 598
Ediciones ROL SA, pg 598
Universidad de Santiago de Compostela, pg 599
Ediciones Scriba SA, pg 599
Servicio de Publicaciones Universidad de Cadiz, pg 599
Editorial Sintesis, SA, pg 600
Equipo Sirius SA, pg 600
Grup 62, pg 600
Ramon Sopena SA, pg 600
Axel Springer Publicaciones, pg 601
Editorial Tecnos SA, pg 601
Ediciones de la Torre, pg 602
Tusquets Editores, pg 603
Editorial Txertoa, pg 603
Universidad de Granada, pg 603
Universidad de Oviedo Servicio de Publicaciones, pg 603
Ediciones Universidad de Salamanca, pg 603
Universidad de Valladolid Secretariado de Publicaciones e Intercambio Editorial, pg 604
Publicacions de la Universitat de Barcelona, pg 604
Edicions de la Universitat Politecnica de Catalunya SL, pg 604
Urmo SA de Ediciones, pg 604
Editorial Vicens-Vives, pg 605
Xunta de Galicia, pg 605

PUBLISHERS

Sri Lanka
Lake House Investments Ltd, pg 606
Ministry of Education, pg 607
Vidura Science Publishers, pg 607
Warna Publishers, pg 607

Sudan
Khartoum University Press, pg 608

Suriname
Stichting Wetenschappelijke Informatie, pg 608

Sweden
Almqvist och Wiksell International, pg 609
Delta Forlags AB, pg 611
Hallgren och Fallgren Studieforlag AB, pg 612
Ingenjoersforlaget AB, pg 612
ITK Laromedel AB, pg 612
Kungl Ingenjoersvetenskapsakademien (IVA), pg 613
Liber AB, pg 613
Bokfoerlaget Natur och Kultur, pg 613
Natur och Kultur Fakta etc, pg 614
Bokforlaget Nya Doxa AB, pg 614
Bokforlaget Spektra AB, pg 615

Switzerland
Ammann Verlag & Co, pg 617
Association Suisse des Editeurs de Langue Francaise, pg 618
Athenaeum Verlag AG, pg 618
Basilius Presse AG, pg 618
Bibliographisches Institut & F A Brockhaus AG, pg 619
Editions Delachaux et Niestle SA, pg 621
Verlag Harri Deutsch, pg 622
Editions Eisele SA, pg 622
Georg Editeur SA, pg 624
Hallwag Kuemmerly & Frey AG, pg 625
Paul Haupt Bern, pg 625
Interfrom AG Editions, pg 625
Klett und Balmer & Co Verlag, pg 626
Herbert Lang & Cie AG, Buchhandlung, Antiquariat, pg 627
Medecine et Hygiene, pg 628
Editions Payot Lausanne, pg 631
Philosophisch-Anthroposophischer Verlag am Goetheanum, pg 631
Presses Polytechniques et Universitaires Romandes, PPUR, pg 631
Editiones Roche, pg 632
Sphinx Verlag AG, pg 634
Strom-Verlag Luzern, pg 635
Vdf Hochschulverlag AG an der ETH Zurich, pg 636
World Meteorological Organization, pg 637

Syrian Arab Republic
Damascus University Press, pg 638

Taiwan, Province of China
Chung Hwa Book Co Ltd, pg 639
Commonwealth Publishing Company Ltd, pg 639
Fuh-Wen Book Co, pg 639
Grimm Press Ltd, pg 640
Kuang Fu Book Co Ltd, pg 640
Newton Publishing Company Ltd, pg 641
Petroleum Information Publishing Co, pg 641
San Min Book Co Ltd, pg 641
Shy Mau & Shy Chaur Publishing Co Ltd, pg 641
Wu Nan Book Co Ltd, pg 642
Yee Wen Publishing Co Ltd, pg 642
Yi Hsien Publishing Co Ltd, pg 642
Youth Cultural Publishing Co, pg 642

United Republic of Tanzania
Ben and Company Ltd, pg 643
East African Publishing House, pg 643
Eastern Africa Publications Ltd, pg 643
Press & Publicity Centre Ltd, pg 644
Readit Books, pg 644
Tanzania Publishing House, pg 644

Thailand
New Generation Publishing Co Ltd, pg 645
Thai Watana Panich Co, Ltd, pg 646

Togo
Presses de l'Universite du Benin, pg 646

Turkey
Arkin Kitabevi, pg 649
Aydin Yayincilik, pg 649
Bilden Bilgisayar, pg 649
Cep Kitaplari AS, pg 649
Pan Yayincilik, pg 651
Payel Yayinevi, pg 651
Remzi Kitabevi, pg 651
Varlik Yayinlari AS, pg 652
Kabalci Yayinevi, pg 652

Turkmenistan
Izdatelstvo Turkmenistan, pg 652

Uganda
Fountain Publishers Ltd, pg 652

Ukraine
Lybid (University of Kyyiv Press), pg 653

United Kingdom
Andromeda Oxford Ltd, pg 658
Artech House, pg 659
Association for Science Education, pg 661
The Athlone Press Ltd, pg 661
BCA - Book Club Associates, pg 663
Blackwell Science Ltd, pg 667
The Brown Reference Group PLC, pg 672
Cassell & Co, pg 675
Chadwyck-Healey Ltd, pg 677
E W Classey Ltd, pg 680
Current Science Group, pg 685
Gerald Duckworth & Co Ltd, pg 688
Edinburgh University Press Ltd, pg 689
Element Books Ltd, pg 690
Eurobook Ltd, pg 692
The Eurospan Group, pg 692
Evans Brothers Ltd, pg 693
Floris Books, pg 695
Forbes Publications Ltd, pg 696
W H Freeman & Co Ltd, pg 697
Genesis Publications Ltd, pg 699
Geological Society Publishing House, pg 699
Gollancz/Witherby, pg 701
Harvard University Press, pg 705
Helicon Publishing Ltd, pg 707
Hobsons, pg 709
Hodder Education, pg 709
Horizon Scientific Press, pg 710
Imperial College Press, pg 712
Institute of Food Science & Technology, pg 713
Institute of Physics Publishing, pg 713
Intercept Ltd, pg 714
Karnak House, pg 717
Learning Together, pg 720
Liverpool University Press, pg 722
Macmillan Reference Ltd, pg 724
Mandrake of Oxford, pg 725
Marshall Editions Ltd, pg 725
Adam Matthew Publications, pg 726
McGraw-Hill Publishing Company, pg 726
Merrow Publishing Co Ltd, pg 727
Micelle Press, pg 727
MIT Press Ltd, pg 728
Nelson Thornes Ltd, pg 732
NMS Enterprises Ltd - Publishing, pg 733
Orion Publishing Group Ltd, pg 736
The Orkney Press Ltd, pg 736
Orpheus Books Ltd, pg 736
Oxford University Press, pg 737
Palgrave Publishers Ltd, pg 737
Pearson Education, pg 739
Pearson Education Europe, Mideast & Africa, pg 739
Portland Press Ltd, pg 745
Prim-Ed Publishing UK Ltd, pg 745
ProQuest Information & Learning, pg 746
Rapra Technology Ltd, pg 748
Rationalist Press Association, pg 748
The Reader's Digest Association Ltd, pg 748
The Royal Society, pg 752
The Salariya Book Co Ltd, pg 753
Sangam Books Ltd, pg 754
Science Reviews Ltd, pg 755
Sheffield Academic Press Ltd, pg 757
Simon & Schuster Ltd, pg 758
Skoob Russell Square, pg 758
Smith-Gordon & Co Ltd, pg 758
Snowbooks Ltd, pg 759
The Society of Metaphysicians Ltd, pg 759
Southgate Publishers, pg 759
Supportive Learning Publications, pg 762
Tarquin Publications, pg 762
Thames & Hudson Ltd, pg 764
The Tarragon Press, pg 765
Thoemmes Press, pg 765
Two-Can Publishing Ltd, pg 768
The Warburg Institute, pg 771
Ward Lock Educational Co Ltd, pg 771
World Microfilms Publications Ltd, pg 775

Uruguay
Ediciones Trilce, pg 778

Venezuela
Editorial Ateneo de Caracas, pg 779
Monte Avila Editores Latinoamericana CA, pg 779

SUBJECT INDEX

Editorial Biosfera CA, pg 779
Universidad de los Andes, Consejo de Publicaciones, pg 780
Vadell Hermanos Editores CA, pg 780

Viet Nam
Science & Technics Publishing House, pg 780

Zimbabwe
Academic Books (Pvt) Ltd, pg 782
College Press Publishers (Pvt) Ltd, pg 783
Longman Zimbabwe (Pvt) Ltd, pg 783
University of Zimbabwe Publications, pg 784
Zimbabwe Publishing House (Pvt) Ltd, pg 784

SCIENCE FICTION, FANTASY

Albania
NL SH, pg 1

Argentina
Editorial Caymi SACI, pg 4
Ediciones Minotauro SA, pg 7

Armenia
Arevik, pg 10

Australia
Crawford House Publishing Pty Ltd, pg 18
Geoffrey Hamlyn-Harris, pg 24
Jarrah Publications, pg 27
K & Z Mostafanejad, pg 32
Nimrod Publications, pg 33
Penguin Group (Australia), pg 36
Tomorrow Publications, pg 44
Transworld Publishers Pty Ltd, pg 44
University of Western Australia Press, pg 45

Austria
Aarachne Verlag, pg 48
Verlag Carl Ueberreuter GmbH, pg 58

Belgium
Editions Hemma, pg 68
Les Editions du Lombard SA, pg 70

Brazil
A & A & A Edicoes e Promocoes Internacionais Ltda, pg 76
Livraria Francisco Alves Editora SA, pg 77
Centro de Estudos Juridicosdo Para (CEJUP), pg 79
Edicon Editora e Consultorial Ltda, pg 81
Imago Editora Importacao e Exportacao Ltda, pg 84
Editora Mercuryo Ltda, pg 86
Ediouro Publicacoes, SA, pg 89
34 Literatura S/C Ltda, pg 91

Bulgaria
Abagar Pablioing, pg 92
Aleks Print Publishing House, pg 93
Galaktika Publishing House, pg 94
MATEX, pg 95

1101

SUBJECT INDEX

Svetra Publishing House, pg 97
Zunica, pg 97

Chile
Norma de Chile, pg 99

China
Education Science Publishing House, pg 104
Jilin Science & Technology Publishing House, pg 105

Colombia
Editorial Santillana SA, pg 112
Tercer Mundo Editores SA, pg 113

Croatia
Faust Vrani, pg 118

Cuba
Casa Editora Abril, pg 120
Editorial Letras Cubanas, pg 120

Czech Republic
Baronet, pg 122
Doplnek, pg 123
Nakladatelstvi Jota spol sro, pg 124
Knihovna A Tiskarna Pro Nevidome, pg 124
Mariadan, pg 125
Mlada fronta, pg 125
Svoboda Servis GmbH, pg 127
Touzimsky & Moravec, pg 127

Denmark
New Era Publications International ApS, pg 133
Wisby & Wilkens, pg 135

Estonia
Tuum, pg 140

Finland
Oy LIKE Kustannus, pg 143

France
Publications Aredit, pg 147
Bragelonne, pg 151
Editions Calmann-Levy SA, pg 152
Editions Copernic, pg 155
Dargaud, pg 157
Editions Denoel, pg 157
Editions Glenat, pg 165
Editions Infrarouge, pg 168
Editions J'ai Lu, pg 169
Le Livre de Poche-L G F (Librairie Generale Francaise), pg 173
Editions Marie-Noelle, pg 174
Payot & Rivages, pg 179
Presses de la Cite, pg 180
Vents d'Ouest, pg 188

Germany
Argument-Verlag, pg 194
Dr Bachmaier Verlag GmbH, pg 196
Bastei Verlag, pg 197
Corian-Verlag Heinrich Wimmer, pg 209
Dana Verlag, pg 210
Deutscher Taschenbuch Verlag GmbH & Co KG (dtv), pg 213
Drei Eichen Verlag Manuel Kissener, pg 216
Egmont Franz Schneider Verlag GmbH, pg 218
Egmont vgs verlagsgesellschaft mbH, pg 218
Ensslin und Laiblin Verlag GmbH & Co KG, pg 220
Fabylon-Verlag, pg 223
Wilhelm Goldmann Verlag GmbH, pg 230
Heel Verlag GmbH, pg 235
Heinz-Theo Gremme Verlag, pg 236
Wilhelm Heyne Verlag, pg 237
Karin Kramer Verlag, pg 250
Logos-Verlag Literatur & Layout GmbH, pg 255
New Era Publications Deutschland GmbH, pg 265
Rainar Nitzsche Verlag, pg 265
Verlag Stendel, pg 287
Mario Truant Verlag, pg 292

Greece
Diavlos, pg 306
Elliniki Leschi Tou Vivliou, pg 307
Exandas Publishers, pg 307
Hestia-I D Hestia-Kollaros & Co Corporation, pg 308
Medusa/Selas Publishers, pg 310

Guatemala
Grupo Editorial RIN-78, pg 313

Hungary
Ifjusagi Lap-eskonyvkiado Vallalat, pg 321
Mora Ferenc Ifjusagi Koenyvkiado Rt, pg 323

India
Ananda Publishers Pvt Ltd, pg 328
Dastane Ramchandra & Co, pg 333
Reliance Publishing House, pg 346
Shaibya Prakashan Bibhag, pg 349

Israel
Pitspopany Press, pg 371

Italy
Gruppo Editoriale Armenia SpA, pg 376
Fanucci, pg 388
Fatatrac, pg 388
Edizioni Internazionali di Letteratura e Scienze, pg 393
Casa Editrice Nord SRL, pg 400
Editoriale Scienza, pg 407
TEA Tascabili degli Editori Associati SpA, pg 409
Todariana Editrice, pg 410

Japan
Fukuinkan Shoten Publishers Inc, pg 417
Hayakawa Publishing Inc, pg 418
Shincho-Sha Co Ltd, pg 427
Tokyo Sogensha Co Ltd, pg 430

Kenya
Kenya Literature Bureau, pg 434
Sasa Sema Publications Ltd, pg 435

Republic of Korea
Chung Rim Publishing Co Ltd, pg 438
Koreaone Press Inc, pg 440

Latvia
Alberts XII, pg 444
Artava Ltd, pg 444
Hermess Ltd, pg 444
Zvaigzne ABC Publishers Ltd, pg 445

Lebanon
Librairie du Liban Publishers (Sal), pg 446

Luxembourg
Hubsch, pg 451

The Former Yugoslav Republic of Macedonia
Detska radost, pg 452
Macedonia Prima Publishing House, pg 452

Malaysia
Pustaka Cipta Sdn Bhd, pg 458

Mexico
Ediciones Corunda SA de CV, pg 463
Fernandez Editores SA de CV, pg 465
Fondo de Cultura Economica, pg 465
Pangea Editores, Sa de CV, pg 470
Plaza y Valdes SA de CV, pg 470
Selector SA de CV, pg 471

Monaco
Les Editions du Rocher, pg 474

Netherlands
De Boekerij BV, pg 479
Uitgeverij Christofoor, pg 480
Uitgeverij Het Spectrum BV, pg 489

Norway
H Aschehoug & Co (W Nygaard) A/S, pg 508
Gyldendal Norsk Forlag A/S, pg 509
Tiden Norsk Forlag, pg 511

Philippines
Anvil Publishing Inc, pg 518
New Day Publishers, pg 520

Poland
Iskry - Publishing House Ltd spotka zoo, pg 523
Wydawnictwa Normalizacyjne Alfa-Wero, pg 525
Przedsiebiorstwo Wydawniczo-Handlowe Wydawnictwo Siedmiorog, pg 526

Portugal
Editora Classica, pg 530
Gradiva-Publicacnoes Lda, pg 532
Editora Livros do Brasil Sarl, pg 533
Paulinas, pg 534
Planeta Editora, LDA, pg 534
Vega-Publicacao e Distribuicao de Livros e Revistas, Lda, pg 536

Romania
Editura Excelsior Art, pg 539
Nemira Verlag, pg 541
Pandora Publishing House, pg 541
Grupul Editorial RAO, pg 542
RAO International Publishing Co, pg 542
Editura Teora, pg 542
Editura Univers SA, pg 543
Vremea Publishers Ltd, pg 543

Russian Federation
Armada Publishing House, pg 543
BLIC, russko-Baltijskij informaciionnyj centr, AO, pg 544
CentrePolygraph Traders & Publishers Co, pg 544
Kavkazskaya Biblioteka Publishing House, pg 545
Ladomir Publishing House, pg 546
Izdatelstvo Lenizdat, pg 546
Izdatelstvo Mir, pg 546
Obdeestvo Znanie, pg 547
Raduga Publishers, pg 548

Slovakia
Sport Publishing House Ltd, pg 561

Slovenia
Mladinska Knjiga International, pg 561

Spain
Editorial Acervo SL, pg 570
Editorial Astri SA, pg 573
Edicions Camacuc, pg 575
CEAC, Grupo Editorial SA, pg 576
Editorial Espasa-Calpe SA, pg 582
Grupo Editorial CEAC SA, pg 586
Editorin Laiovento SL, pg 588
Ediciones Libertarias/Prodhufi SA, pg 589
Ediciones Martinez-Roca SA, pg 591
Ediciones Minotauro, pg 591
Ediciones Olimpic, SL, pg 594
Pleniluni Ediciones, pg 596
Ediciones Seyer, pg 599
Ultramar Editores SA, pg 603

Sri Lanka
Danuma Prakashakayo, pg 606
Warna Publishers, pg 607

Sweden
Bonnier Carlsen Bokforlag AB, pg 610
Sjoestrands Foerlag, pg 615

Switzerland
Editions L'Age d'Homme - La Cite, pg 617
Haffmans Verlag AG, pg 624

United Republic of Tanzania
Kajura Publications, pg 643

Thailand
Chokechai Theues Shop, pg 645
Graphic Art (28) Co Ltd, pg 645

Turkey
Altin Kitaplar Yayinevi, pg 649
Cep Kitaplari AS, pg 649
Iletisim Yayinlari, pg 650
Metis Yayinlari, pg 650

Ukraine
ASK Ltd, pg 653

United Kingdom
Apex Publishing Ltd, pg 658
BCA - Book Club Associates, pg 663
Boxtree Ltd, pg 669
Cassell & Co, pg 675
Constable & Robinson Ltd, pg 682
The Eurospan Group, pg 692

PUBLISHERS

Feather Books, pg 694
Gollancz/Witherby, pg 701
HarperCollins UK, pg 705
Hodder Children's Books, pg 709
Janus Publishing Co Ltd, pg 716
Liverpool University Press, pg 722
Y Lolfa Cyf, pg 722
Luath Press Ltd, pg 722
Mandrake of Oxford, pg 725
New Era Publications UK Ltd, pg 732
Octopus Publishing Group, pg 734
Orion Publishing Group Ltd, pg 736
Severn House Publishers Inc, pg 756
Snowbooks Ltd, pg 759
Time Warner Book Group UK, pg 766
Titan Books Ltd, pg 766
Transworld Publishers Ltd, pg 766
Trigon Press, pg 767
Virgin Publishing Ltd, pg 770

SECURITIES

Albania
NL SH, pg 1

Argentina
Bonum Editorial SACI, pg 4
Editorial Ciudad Nueva de la Sefoma, pg 4

Brazil
Editora Manuais Tecnicos de Seguros Ltda, pg 86
Saraiva SA, Livreiros Editores, pg 90

China
Fudan University Press, pg 104

France
Editions Delmas, pg 157
Joly Editions, pg 169
TOP Editions, pg 188

Germany
Bank-Verlag GmbH, pg 197
Beuth Verlag GmbH, pg 200
Hoppenstedt GmbH & Co KG, pg 239

Ghana
World Literature Project, pg 305

Israel
Dekel Publishing House, pg 366

Italy
Esselibri, pg 388

Malaysia
Trix Corporation Sdn Bhd, pg 459

Mexico
Pearson Educacion de Mexico, SA de CV, pg 470

Poland
Wydawnictwo Prawnicze Co, pg 526

Portugal
Paulinas, pg 534

Russian Federation
Finansy i Statistika Publishing House, pg 544
Teorija Verojatnostej i ee Primenenija, pg 549

Slovenia
Univerza v Ljubljani Ekonomska Fakulteta, pg 562

United Kingdom
Business Monitor International, pg 672
Cavendish Publishing Ltd, pg 676
DMG Business Media Ltd, pg 688

Viet Nam
Science & Technics Publishing House, pg 780

SELF-HELP

Albania
NL SH, pg 1

Argentina
Beas Ediciones SRL, pg 4
Bonum Editorial SACI, pg 4
Editorial Caymi SACI, pg 4
Diana Argentina SA, Editorial, pg 5
Errepar SA, pg 5
Editorial Kier SACIFI, pg 7
Editorial Paidos SAICF, pg 8
San Pablo, pg 9
Javier Vergara Editor SA, pg 9

Australia
Angel Publications, pg 11
Ashling Books, pg 12
Bio Concepts Publishing, pg 14
Joan Blair, pg 15
Bridge To Peace Publications, pg 16
CHOICE Magazine, pg 17
Crawford House Publishing Pty Ltd, pg 18
Crista International, pg 18
Crossroad Distributors Pty Ltd, pg 18
Deva Wings Publications, pg 20
Extraordinary People Press, pg 22
Finch Publishing, pg 22
Fraser Publications, pg 22
Gnostic Editions, pg 23
Hale & Iremonger Pty Ltd, pg 24
Kerri Hamer, pg 24
Hihorse Publishing Pty Ltd, pg 25
In-Tune Books, pg 26
Life Planning Foundation of Australia, Inc, pg 29
Barry Long Books, pg 29
Thomas C Lothian Pty Ltd, pg 29
Mayne Publishing, pg 31
Moon-Ta-Gu Books, pg 32
New Era Publications Australia Pty Ltd, pg 33
Anne O'Donovan Pty Ltd, pg 34
Pan Macmillan Australia Pty Ltd, pg 35
Penguin Group (Australia), pg 36
Pinchgut Press, pg 36
Jurriaan Plesman, pg 37
Priestley Consulting, pg 37
The Real Estate Institute of Australia, pg 39
Simon & Schuster (Australia) Pty Ltd, pg 41
Single X Publications, pg 41
Spectrum Publications, pg 41
Stirling Press, pg 42
Thin Rich Press, pg 43

Tomorrow Publications, pg 44
Transworld Publishers Pty Ltd, pg 44
Unity Press, pg 44
Wileman Publications, pg 46
Windhorse Books, pg 47
Wrightbooks Pty Ltd, pg 47

Austria
Denkmayr GmbH Druck & Verlag, pg 50

Bangladesh
Gono Prakashani, Gono Shasthya Kendra, pg 61

Barbados
Business Tutors, pg 62

Belgium
Altina, pg 63
Uitgeverij Lannoo NV, pg 69
Marabout, pg 71

Brazil
Editora Agora Ltda, pg 77
Editora Aquariana Ltda, pg 77
Editora Bertrand Brasil Ltda, pg 78
Editora Crescer Ltda, pg 80
Companhia Editora Forense, pg 81
Editora Elevacao, pg 81
Editora Gaia Ltda, pg 82
Editora Globo SA, pg 82
Ordem do Graal na Terra, pg 83
Editora e Grafica Carisio Ltda, Minas Editora, pg 83
Editora Harbra Ltda, pg 83
Imago Editora Importacao e Exportacao Ltda, pg 84
Livraria Nobel S/A, pg 85
Edicoes Loyola SA, pg 85
Madras Editora, pg 86
Editora Mercuryo Ltda, pg 86
Editora Nova Fronteira SA, pg 87
Editora Objetiva Ltda, pg 87
Pallas Editora e Distribuidora Ltda, pg 88
Paulinas Editorial, pg 88
Paulus Editora, pg 88
Qualitymark Editora Ltda, pg 89
Editora Revan Ltda, pg 89
Editora Rocco Ltda, pg 89
Summus Editorial Ltda, pg 91
Thex Editora e Distribuidora Ltda, pg 91
Totalidade Editora Ltda, pg 91

Bulgaria
Aratron, IK, pg 93
Kibea Publishing Co, pg 95
Prozoretz Ltd Publishing House, pg 96
Sila & Zivot, pg 97

Cameroon
Editions Buma Kor & Co Ltd, pg 98

Chile
Arrayan Editores, pg 98
Ediciones Mil Hojas Ltda, pg 99
Norma de Chile, pg 99

China
Beijing Juvenile & Children's Books Publishing House, pg 101
Beijing Publishing House, pg 101
Yunnan University Press, pg 109

SUBJECT INDEX

Colombia
Editorial Panamericana, pg 112
RAM Editores, pg 112
Editorial Santillana SA, pg 112
Tercer Mundo Editores SA, pg 113

Costa Rica
Ediciones Promesa, pg 116

Cuba
Editorial Oriente, pg 120

Czech Republic
Pavla Momcilova, pg 125
Pragma 4, pg 126

Denmark
Borgens Forlag A/S, pg 129
Forlaget Hovedland, pg 132
New Era Publications International ApS, pg 133
Joergen Paludan Forlag ApS, pg 133
Politikens Forlag A/S, pg 133

Estonia
Sinisukk, pg 140

Finland
Karas-Sana Oy, pg 142

France
Chronique Sociale, pg 154
Edition1, pg 160
Hachette Livre, pg 167
Editions Hatier SA, pg 167
Jouvence Editions, pg 170
Langues & Mondes-L'Asiatheque, pg 171
Editions Larousse, pg 171
Editions Ophrys, pg 177
Les Presses du Management, pg 181
Editions Spratbrow, pg 186

Germany
Blaukreuz-Verlag Wuppertal, pg 202
Buchverlage Langen-Mueller/Herbig, pg 205
Claudius Verlag, pg 209
Connection Medien GmbH, pg 209
Verlag CSA Rosemarie Schneider, pg 210
Deutscher Taschenbuch Verlag GmbH & Co KG (dtv), pg 213
Divyanand Verlags GmbH, pg 215
Drei Eichen Verlag Manuel Kissener, pg 216
Verlagsgruppe Droemer Knaur GmbH & Co KG, pg 216
Econ Taschenbuchverlag, pg 218
Ernst Kabel Verlag GmbH, pg 221
EVT Energy Video Training & Verlag GmbH, pg 222
Gatzanis Verlags GmbH, pg 228
Genius Verlag, pg 228
Gerth Medien GmbH, pg 229
Graefe und Unzer Verlag GmbH, pg 230
Verlag der Stiftung Gralsbotschaft GmbH, pg 231
Walter Haedecke Verlag, pg 232
Heinz-Theo Gremme Verlag, pg 236
Verlag Herder GmbH & Co KG, pg 236
AIG I Hilbinger Verlag GmbH, pg 237
Heinrich Hugendubel Verlag GmbH, pg 240
Joy Verlag GmbH, pg 243
Junfermann-Verlag, pg 243

1103

SUBJECT INDEX

BOOK

Peter Kirchheim Verlag, pg 246
Klartext Verlagsgesellschaft mbH, pg 246
Ingrid Klein Verlag GmbH, pg 246
Verlag Kleine Schritte Ursula Dahm & Co, pg 246
Koenigsfurt Verlag, Evelin Buerger et Johannes Fiebig, pg 248
Krug & Schadenberg, pg 250
Lebenshilfe-Verlag Marburg, Verlag der Bundesvereinigung Lebenshilfe fuer Menschen mit geistiger Behinderung eV, pg 253
Midena Verlag, pg 260
Mosaik Verlag GmbH, pg 262
Neue Erde Verlags GmbH, pg 264
Neuland-Verlagsgesellschaft mbH, pg 264
New Era Publications Deutschland GmbH, pg 265
Nie/Nie/Sagen-Verlag, pg 265
nymphenburger, pg 266
Orlanda Frauenverlag, pg 267
Osho Verlag GmbH, pg 267
Projektion J Buch- und Musikverlag GmbH, pg 272
Rake Verlag GmbH, pg 273
Reichl Verlag Der Leuchter, pg 274
Schueren Verlag GmbH, pg 281
Spieth-Verlag Verlag fuer Symbolforschung, pg 284
Suin Buch-Verlag, pg 289
Weber Zucht & Co, pg 298
Verlag DAS WORT GmbH, pg 301

Ghana
World Literature Project, pg 305

Greece
Kedros Publishers, pg 309
Kritiki Publishing, pg 309

Hong Kong
Book Marketing Ltd, pg 315
Chung Hwa Book Co (HK) Ltd, pg 316
Design Human Resources Training & Development, pg 317
Philopsychy Press, pg 318
Unicorn Books Ltd, pg 320

Hungary
Park Konyvkiado Kft (Park Publisher), pg 324

India
Concept Publishing Co, pg 332
Dastane Ramchandra & Co, pg 333
Full Circle Publishing, pg 334
General Book Depot, pg 335
Gyan Publishing House, pg 335
Hind Pocket Books Private Ltd, pg 336
Jaico Publishing House, pg 338
B Jain Publishers Overseas, pg 338
Lancer Publisher's & Distributors, pg 340
New Light Publishers, pg 343
Orient Paperbacks, pg 344
Rajendra Publishing House Pvt Ltd, pg 346
Sultan Chand & Sons Pvt Ltd, pg 350

Indonesia
Dinastindo, pg 354

Ireland
Campus Publishing Ltd, pg 358
Cathedral Books Ltd, pg 358
The Columba Book Service, pg 359
The Columba Press, pg 359
Gill & Macmillan Ltd, pg 360
The O'Brien Press Ltd, pg 362
Tivenan Publications, pg 364

Israel
Bitan Publishers Ltd, pg 365
Breslov Research Institute, pg 365
DAT Publications, pg 366
Dekel Publishing House, pg 366
Intermedia Audio, Video Book Publishing Ltd, pg 368
Pitspopany Press, pg 371
R Sirkis Publishers Ltd, pg 372
Zmora-Bitan, Publishers Ltd, pg 374

Italy
Editore Armando Armando SRL, pg 376
Gruppo Editoriale Armenia SpA, pg 376
Edizioni Centro Studi Erickson, pg 381
Effata Editrice, pg 387
ERGA SNC di Carla Ottino Merli & C (Edizioni Realizzazioni Grafiche - Artigiana), pg 388
Editoriale Fernando Folini, pg 389
Piero Gribaudi Editore, pg 391
Lyra Libri, pg 396
Edizioni Piemme SpA, pg 403
Il Punto D Incontro, pg 404
TEA Tascabili degli Editori Associati SpA, pg 409
Editrice Uomini Nuovi, pg 411

Jamaica
Association of Development Agencies, pg 413

Japan
Diamond Inc, pg 416
Kosei Publishing Co Ltd, pg 421
Nikkagiren Shuppan-Sha (JUSE Press Ltd), pg 424

Kenya
Action Publishers, pg 433
Kenya Quality & Productivity Institute, pg 435
Space Sellers Ltd, pg 436

Republic of Korea
Gim-Yeong Co, pg 438

Latvia
Artava Ltd, pg 444

Lithuania
Dargenis Publishers, pg 449
Tyto Alba Publishers, pg 450
Vaga Ltd, pg 450

Malaysia
Federal Publications Sdn Bhd, pg 455
Glad Sounds Sdn Bhd, pg 456
Minerva Publications, pg 457

Mexico
Aguilar Altea Taurus Alfaguara SA de CV, pg 462
Ediciones Alpe, pg 462
Del Verbo Emprender SA de CV, pg 464
Editorial Diana SA de CV, pg 464
Edamex SA de CV, pg 464
Editorial El Manual Moderno SA de CV, pg 464
Editorial Grijalbo SA de CV, pg 466
Hoja Casa Editorial SA de CV, pg 466
Editorial Jus SA de CV, pg 467
Libra Editorial SA de CV, pg 467
Nova Grupo Editorial SA de CV, pg 469
Pangea Editores, Sa de CV, pg 470
Panorama Editorial, SA, pg 470
Selector SA de CV, pg 471
Sistemas Tecnicos de Edicion SA de CV, pg 472
Ediciones Suromex SA, pg 472
Javier Vergara Editor SA de CV, pg 473

Monaco
Les Editions du Rocher, pg 474

Netherlands
BZZTOH Publishers, pg 480
Kartoen, pg 484
Uitgeverij Maarten Muntinga, pg 486
Servire BV Uitgevers, pg 489
Uitgeverij De Toorts, pg 490
Unieboek BV, pg 490

Netherlands Antilles
De Wit Stores NV, pg 493

New Zealand
Gnostic Press Ltd, pg 496
HarperCollins Publishers (New Zealand) Ltd, pg 497
Magari Publishing, pg 498
Spinal Publications New Zealand Ltd, pg 501
Tandem Press, pg 501
Taylor Books, pg 501

Nigeria
Evans Brothers (Nigeria Publishers) Ltd, pg 504

Norway
Aschehoug Forlag, pg 508
H Aschehoug & Co (W Nygaard) A/S, pg 508
Hilt & Hansteen A/S, pg 509

Paraguay
Intercontinental Editora, pg 516

Philippines
New Day Publishers, pg 520

Poland
Gdanskie Wydawnictwo Psychologiczne SC, pg 523
Iskry - Publishing House Ltd spotka zoo, pg 523
Oficyna Wydawnicza Read Me, pg 526
Wydawnictwo SIC, pg 526

Portugal
Gradiva-Publicacnoes Lda, pg 532
Monitor-Projectos e Edicoes, LDA, pg 533
Editorial Noticias, pg 534
Editorial Presenca, pg 535

Puerto Rico
Piedras Press, Inc, pg 537

Romania
Editura Niculescu, pg 541
Grupul Editorial RAO, pg 542
Rentrop & Straton Verlagsgruppe und Wirtschaftsconsulting, pg 542

Russian Federation
Finansy i Statistika Publishing House, pg 544
Izdatelstvo Mir, pg 546
Obdeestro Znanie, pg 547

Serbia and Montenegro
Alfa-Narodna Knjiga, pg 552

Singapore
Aquanut Agencies Pte Ltd, pg 555
Graham Brash Pte Ltd, pg 556

Slovakia
Priroda Publishing, pg 560

Slovenia
Mladinska Knjiga International, pg 561
Zalozba Mihelac d o o, pg 562
Zalozba Obzorja d d Maribor, pg 562

South Africa
Human & Rousseau (Pty) Ltd, pg 564
Kima Global Publishers, pg 566

Spain
Acento Editorial, pg 570
Aguilar SA de Ediciones, pg 571
Editorial Astri SA, pg 573
Baile del Sol, Colectivo Cultural, pg 574
Los Libros del Comienzo, pg 577
Editorial EDAF SA, pg 580
Editorial Espasa-Calpe SA, pg 582
Editorial Iberia, SA, pg 586
Libsa Editorial SA, pg 589
LID Editorial Empresarial, SL, pg 589
Loguez Ediciones, pg 589
Antonio Machado, SA, pg 590
Ediciones Martinez-Roca SA, pg 591
Ediciones Morata SL, pg 592
Ediciones Norma SA, pg 593
OASIS, Producciones Generales de Comunicacion, pg 593
Obelisco Ediciones S, pg 593
Ediciones Paidos Iberica SA, pg 594
Ediciones El Pais SA, pg 594
Ediciones Temas de Hoy, SA, pg 601
Tursen, SA, pg 603
Ediciones 29 - Libros Rio Nuevo, pg 603
Ediciones Urano, SA, pg 604
Javier Vergara Editor SA, pg 604

Sweden
Bokforlaget Axplock, pg 609
ICA bokforlag, pg 612
Svenska Foerlaget liv & ledarskap ab, pg 616

Switzerland
Ariston Editions, pg 617
Association Suisse des Editeurs de Langue Francaise, pg 618
Brunnen-Verlag Basel, pg 620

CEC-Cosmic Energy Connections, pg 620
Editions Jouvence, pg 626
Kanisius Verlag, pg 626
Leonis Verlag, pg 627
Oesch Verlag AG, pg 630

Taiwan, Province of China

Asian Culture Co Ltd, pg 638
Commonwealth Publishing Company Ltd, pg 639
Linking Publishing Company Ltd, pg 641
Morning Star Publisher Inc, pg 641
Shy Mau & Shy Chaur Publishing Co Ltd, pg 641
Yuan Liou Publishing Co, Ltd, pg 642

Togo

Editions Akpagnon, pg 646

Tunisia

Les Editions de l'Arbre, pg 647

Turkey

Ruh ve Madde Yayinlari ve Saglik Hizmetleri AS, pg 651
Saray Medikal Yayin Tic Ltd Sti, pg 651
Soez Yayin/Oyunajans, pg 651
Varlik Yayinlari AS, pg 652

United Kingdom

Act 3 Publishing, pg 655
Apex Publishing Ltd, pg 658
Ashgrove Publishing, pg 660
BCA - Book Club Associates, pg 663
Bloomsbury Publishing PLC, pg 668
Nicholas Brealey Publishing, pg 670
Capall Bann Publishing, pg 674
Crossbridge Books, pg 684
The C W Daniel Co Ltd, pg 686
Dorling Kindersley Ltd, pg 688
Element Books Ltd, pg 690
Elliot Right Way Books, pg 690
Findhorn Press Inc, pg 695
Foulsham Publishers, pg 696
Gateway Books, pg 698
Green Books Ltd, pg 702
HarperCollins UK, pg 705
The Harvill Press, pg 705
Hawthorn Press, pg 706
Highland Books Ltd, pg 708
Hodder & Stoughton General, pg 709
Hodder & Stoughton Religious, pg 709
How To Books Ltd, pg 710
Isis Publishing Ltd, pg 714
Kogan Page Ltd, pg 718
Lawpack Publishing Ltd, pg 719
Lion Hudson PLC, pg 721
Kenneth Mason Publications Ltd, pg 726
MIND Publications, pg 728
Monarch Books, pg 729
National Extension College, pg 730
New Era Publications UK Ltd, pg 732
Oneworld Publications, pg 735
Orion Publishing Group Ltd, pg 736
Pan Macmillan, pg 738
Parapress Ltd, pg 738
Piatkus Books, pg 741
Plough Publishing House of Bruderhof Communities in the UK, pg 743
Prism Press Book Publishers Ltd, pg 745
Quarto Publishing plc, pg 746
Ravette Publishing Ltd, pg 748
Rosendale Press Ltd, pg 751
Roundhouse Group, pg 751
Ryland Peters & Small Ltd, pg 752
Sheldon Press, pg 757
Sherwood Publishing, pg 757
The Society for Promoting Christian Knowledge (SPCK), pg 759
Rudolf Steiner Press, pg 761
Telegraph Books, pg 764
Ward Lock Ltd, pg 771
Which? Ltd, pg 772
Wimbledon Publishing Company Ltd, pg 774
The Women's Press Ltd, pg 775
World Microfilms Publications Ltd, pg 775

Uruguay

Rosebud Ediciones, pg 778

Venezuela

Alfadil Ediciones, pg 778

SOCIAL SCIENCES, SOCIOLOGY

Albania

NL SH, pg 1
State Textbook Publishing House, pg 1

Algeria

Enterprise Nationale du Livre (ENAL), pg 2

Argentina

Editorial Abaco de Rodolfo Depalma SRL, pg 2
Editorial Albatros SACI, pg 3
Alianza Editorial de Argentina SA, pg 3
Amorrortu Editores SA, pg 3
Editorial Astrea de Alfredo y Ricardo Depalma SRL, pg 3
Centro Editor de America Latina SA, pg 4
Club de Lectores, pg 4
Depalma SRL, pg 5
Ediciones de la Flor SRL, pg 6
Fundacion Editorial de Belgrano, pg 6
Editorial Galerna SRL, pg 6
Editorial Guadalupe, pg 6
Editorial Idearium de la Universidad de Mendoza (EDIUM), pg 6
Marymar Ediciones SA, pg 7
Ediciones Nueva Vision SAIC, pg 8
Oikos, pg 8
Editorial Paidos SAICF, pg 8
Editorial Pleamar, pg 8
Editorial Plus Ultra SA, pg 8
Editorial Polemos SA, pg 8
Instituto Torcuato Di Tella, pg 9
Editorial Universidad SRL, pg 9

Australia

Ausmed Publications Pty Ltd, pg 12
Australian Institute of Family Studies (AIFS), pg 13
Australian Scholarly Publishing, pg 13
Crawford House Publishing Pty Ltd, pg 18
Crystal Publishing, pg 19
Dabill Publications, pg 19
Dangaroo Press, pg 19
Elsevier Australia, pg 21
Extraordinary People Press, pg 22
Finch Publishing, pg 22
Freshet Press, pg 23
Kerri Hamer, pg 24
Histec Publications, pg 25
James Nicholas Publishers Pty Ltd, pg 27
Macmillan Education Australia, pg 30
Macmillan Publishers Australia Pty Ltd, pg 30
McGraw-Hill Australia Pty Ltd, pg 31
Melbourne Institute of Applied Economic & Social Research, pg 31
Ocean Press, pg 34
Pascoe Publishing Pty Ltd, pg 36
Pearson Education Australia, pg 36
Jurriaan Plesman, pg 37
Pluto Press Australia Pty Ltd, pg 37
Pollitecon Publications, pg 37
Priestley Consulting, pg 37
St Pauls Publications, pg 40
Spinifex Press, pg 42
State Library of NSW Press, pg 42
University of New South Wales Press Ltd, pg 44
University of Western Australia Press, pg 45
Vista Publications, pg 45
Wileman Publications, pg 46

Austria

Boehlau Verlag GmbH & Co KG, pg 48
CEEBA Publications Antenne d'Autriche, pg 49
DachsVerlag GmbH, pg 49
Development News Ltd, pg 50
Verlag fuer Geschichte und Politik, pg 51
Guthmann & Peterson Liber Libri, Edition, pg 51
Haymon-Verlag GesmbH, pg 51
Dr Verena Hofstaetter, pg 52
Milena Verlag, pg 54
NOI - Verlag, pg 55
Verlag der Oesterreichischen Akademie der Wissenschaften (OEAW), pg 55
Oesterreichischer Kunst und Kulturverlag, pg 55
Verlag Oldenbourg, pg 56
Verlag fuer Sammler, pg 57
WUV/Facultas Universitaetsverlag, pg 60

Bangladesh

Academic Publishers, pg 61
Gono Prakashani, Gono Shasthya Kendra, pg 61
Agamee Prakashani, pg 61

Belgium

Academia-Bruylant, pg 62
Academia Press, pg 62
Uitgeverij Acco, pg 62
Centre Aequatoria, pg 63
Artel, pg 63
Vanden Broele NV, pg 64
Campinia Media VZW, pg 64
La Charte Editions juridiques, pg 65
Editions De Boeck-Larcier SA, pg 66
EPO Publishers, Printers, Booksellers, pg 67
Espace de Libertes, pg 67
Garant Publishers Ltd, pg 67
King Baudouin Foundation, pg 69
Editions Labor, pg 69
Editions Lessius ASBL, pg 70
Leuven University Press, pg 70
Maklu, pg 70
Nauwelaerts Edition SA, pg 71
Uitgeverij Pelckmans NV, pg 72
Presses Universitaires de Liege, pg 72
Publications des Facultes Universitaires Saint Louis, pg 72
Sonneville Press (Uitgeverij) VTW, pg 73
UGA Editions (Uitgeverij), pg 73
Uitgeverij De Garve, pg 74
Editions de l'Universite de Bruxelles, pg 74
Vander Editions, SA, pg 74
Les Editions Vie ouvriere ASBL, pg 74
VUB Brussels University Press, pg 74
Wolters Kluwer Belgie NV, pg 74

Bermuda

The Bermudian Publishing Co, pg 75

Brazil

AGIR S/A Editora, pg 77
Editora Alfa Omega Ltda, pg 77
Editora do Brasil SA, pg 79
Editora Brasiliense SA, pg 79
Editora Campus Ltda, pg 79
Centro de Estudos Juridicosdo Para (CEJUP), pg 79
Editora Cidade Nova, pg 80
Livraria Duas Cidades Ltda, pg 80
Dumara Distribuidora de Publicacoes Ltda, pg 81
Companhia Editora Forense, pg 81
EDUSC - Editora da Universidade do Sagrado Coracao, pg 81
Empresa Brasileira de Pesquisa Agropecuaria, pg 81
Livraria Martins Fontes Editora Ltda, pg 81
Editora Forense Universitaria Ltda, pg 81
Fundacao Joaquim Nabuco-Editora Massangana, pg 82
Fundacao Sao Paulo, EDUC, pg 82
Global Editora e Distribuidora Ltda, pg 82
Edicoes Graal Ltda, pg 83
Editora Harbra Ltda, pg 83
IBRASA (Instituicao Brasileira de Difusao Cultural Ltda), pg 83
Editora Lidador Ltda, pg 85
Oficina de Livros Ltda, pg 85
Edicoes Loyola SA, pg 85
Editora Moderna Ltda, pg 86
Cia Editora Nacional, pg 87
Editora Nova Fronteira SA, pg 87
Olho D'Agua Comercio e Servicos Editoriais Ltda, pg 87
Edit Palavra Magica, pg 88
Pallas Editora e Distribuidora Ltda, pg 88
Paulinas Editorial, pg 88
Paulus Editora, pg 88
Editora Paz e Terra, pg 88
Editora Perspectiva, pg 88
Livraria Pioneira Editora/Enio Matheus Guazzelli e Cia Ltd, pg 88
Editora Revan Ltda, pg 89
Editora Rocco Ltda, pg 89
Editora Sinodal, pg 90
Edicoes Tabajara, pg 91
Thex Editora e Distribuidora Ltda, pg 91
Editora UNESP, pg 91

SUBJECT INDEX

Editora Universidade de Brasilia, pg 91
Editora da Universidade de Sao Paulo, pg 91
Editora Universidade Federal do Rio de Janeiro, pg 92
Fundacao Getulio Vargas, pg 92
Editora Verbo Ltda, pg 92
Vozes Editora Ltda, pg 92
Jorge Zahar Editor, pg 92

Bulgaria
Antroposofsko Izdatelstvo Dimo R Daskalov OOD, pg 93
Publishing House Hristo Botev, pg 94
LIK Izdanija, pg 95
Makros 2000 - Plovdiv, pg 95
Mladezh IK, pg 95
Naouka i Izkoustvo, Ltd, pg 95
Narodna Kultura, pg 96
Nov Covek Publishing House, pg 96
Prohazka I Kacarmazov, pg 96
Voenno Izdatelstvo, pg 97

Burundi
Editions Intore, pg 98

Cameroon
Centre d'Edition et de Production pour l'Enseignement et la Recherche (CEPER), pg 98
Editions CLE, pg 98
Presses Universitaires d'Afrique, pg 98

Chile
Arrayan Editores, pg 98
Edeval (Universidad de Valparaiso), pg 99
Ediciones y Publicidad Melquiades, pg 99
Editora Nueva Generacion, pg 100
Pehuen Editores Ltda, pg 100
Editorial Universitaria SA, pg 100
Ediciones Universitarias de Valparaiso, pg 100

China
Anhui People's Publishing House, pg 101
Beijing Publishing House, pg 101
China Ocean Press, pg 102
China Social Sciences Publishing House, pg 103
China Tibetology Publishing House, pg 103
China Youth Publishing House, pg 103
Chongqing University Press, pg 103
Foreign Language Teaching & Research Press, pg 104
Fudan University Press, pg 104
Higher Education Press, pg 105
Jinan Publishing House, pg 105
Knowledge Press, pg 106
Kunlun Publishing House, pg 106
Lanzhou University Press, pg 106
SDX (Shenghuo-Dushu-Xinzhi) Joint Publishing Co, pg 107
Shanghai Educational Publishing House, pg 108
Shanghai Far East Publishers, pg 108
Universidade de Macau, Centro de Publicacoes, pg 109
World Affairs Press, pg 109
Wuhan University Press, pg 109
Xinhua Publishing House, pg 109
Yunnan University Press, pg 109

Colombia
Bedout Editores SA, pg 110
Dosmil Editora, pg 110
El Ancora Editores, pg 111
Universidad Externado de Colombia, pg 111
Fundacion Centro de Investigacion y Educacion Popular (CINEP), pg 111
Editorial Libros y Libres SA, pg 112
McGraw-Hill Colombia, pg 112
Editorial Oveja Negra Ltda, pg 112
Siglo XXI Editores de Colombia Ltda, pg 112
Tercer Mundo Editores SA, pg 113
Universidad de Antioquia, Division Publicaciones, pg 113
Universidad Nacional Abierta y a Distancia, pg 113
Carlos Valencia Editores, pg 113

The Democratic Republic of the Congo
Presses Universitaires du Zaiire (PUZ), pg 114

Costa Rica
Asamblea Legislativa, Biblioteca Monsenor Sanabria, pg 115
Centro Agronomico Tropical de Investigacion y Ensenanza (CATIE), pg 115
Editorial Nacional de Salud y Seguridad Social Ednass, pg 116
Editorial Porvenir, pg 116
Ediciones Promesa, pg 116
Editorial de la Universidad de Costa Rica, pg 116
Editorial Universitaria Centroamericana (EDUCA), pg 117

Cote d'Ivoire
Universite d'Abidjan, pg 117
Centre d'Edition et de Diffusion Africaines, pg 117

Croatia
AGM doo, pg 117
Filozofski Fakultet Sveucilista u Zagrebu, pg 118
Globus-Nakladni zavod, pg 118
Hrvatsko filozofsko drustvo, pg 118
Informator dd, pg 118
Matica hrvatska, pg 118
Mladost d d Izdavacku graficku i informaticku djelatnost, pg 119
Naklada Ljevak doo, pg 119
Skolska Knjiga, pg 119

Cuba
Casa de las Americas, pg 120
Editorial de Ciencias Sociales, pg 120
Editora Politica, pg 120
Pueblo y Educacion Editorial (PE), pg 121

Czech Republic
Barrister & Principal, pg 122
Doplnek, pg 123
Kalich SRO, pg 124
Karolinum, nakladatelstvi, pg 124
Libri spol sro, pg 125
Lidove Noviny Publishing House, pg 125
Slon Sociologicke Nakladatelstvi, pg 127

Denmark
Aarhus Universitetsforlag, pg 128
Akademisk Forlag A/S, pg 128
Djof Publishing Jurist-og Okonomforbundets Forlag, pg 130
Fremad A/S, pg 131
Forlaget GMT, pg 131
Gyldendalske Boghandel - Nordisk Forlag A/S, pg 131
Forlaget Hovedland, pg 132
Museum Tusculanum Press, pg 133
Nyt Nordisk Forlag Arnold Busck A/S, pg 133
Politisk Revy, pg 133
Hans Reitzel Publishers Ltd, pg 134
Samfundslitteratur, pg 134
Forlaget Vindrose A/S, pg 135

Dominican Republic
Pontificia Universidad Catolica Madre y Maestra, pg 136
Sociedad Editorial Americana, pg 136

Ecuador
Centro de Planificacion y Estudios Sociales (CEPLAES), pg 136
Corporacion Editora Nacional, pg 136
Pontificia Universidad Catolica del Ecuador, Centro de Publicaciones, pg 137

Egypt (Arab Republic of Egypt)
American University in Cairo Press, pg 137
Al Arab Publishing House, pg 137
Dar Al-Matbo at Al-Gadidah, pg 138
Middle East Book Centre, pg 138

El Salvador
UCA Editores, pg 138
Editorial Universitaria de la Universidad de El Salvador, pg 139

Estonia
Eesti Entsuklopeediakirjastus, pg 139
Kupar Publishers, pg 139
Olion Publishers, pg 140

Finland
Kuva ja Sana, pg 143
Osuuskunta Vastapaino, pg 144
Yliopistopaino/Helsinki University Press, pg 145

France
Editions d'Amerique et d'Orient, Adrien Maisonneuve, pg 146
L'Anabase, pg 146
Editions Anthropos, pg 147
L'Arche Editeur, pg 147
Association pour la Recherche et l'Information demographiques (APRD), pg 148
Editions de l'Atelier, pg 148
Atelier National de Reproduction des Theses, pg 148
Editions de l'Aube, pg 148
Editions Aubier-Montaigne SA, pg 148
Autrement Editions, pg 148
Beauchesne Editeur, pg 149
Berger-Levrault Editions SAS, pg 149
Editions Calmann-Levy SA, pg 152

CERDIC-Publications, pg 153
Editions du Cerf, pg 153
Editions Champ Vallon, pg 153
Le Cherche Midi Editeur, pg 154
Chotard et Associes Editeurs, pg 154
Chronique Sociale, pg 154
CNRS Editions, pg 155
Armand Colin, Editeur, pg 155
Corsaire Editions, pg 156
Council of Europe Publishing, pg 156
Editions Criterion, pg 156
CTNERHI - Centre Technique National d'Etudes et de Recherches sur les Handicaps et les Inadaptations, pg 156
Editions Cujas, pg 156
Nouvelles Editions Debresse, pg 157
Editions La Decouverte, pg 157
Dervy Editions, pg 158
Desclee de Brouwer SA, pg 158
Doin Editeurs, pg 159
Editions de l'Ecole des Hautes Etudes en Sciences Sociales (EHESS), pg 159
Les Editions de Minuit SA, pg 160
Editions d'Organisation, pg 160
Editions Recherche sur les Civilisations (ERC), pg 160
Editions rue d'Ulm, pg 160
L'Ere Nouvelle, pg 161
Editions Eres, pg 162
Editions Espaces 34, pg 162
Librairie Artheme Fayard, pg 163
Librairie Fischbacher, International Art Book Distribution (import-export), pg 163
Editions Fleurus, pg 163
Futuribles SARL, pg 164
Editions Galilee, pg 164
Editions Gamma, pg 165
Paul Geuthner Librairie Orientaliste, pg 165
Groupe Express-Expansion, pg 166
Hachette Livre, pg 167
L'Harmattan, pg 167
Editions de l'Herne, pg 167
Editions d'Histoire Sociale (EDHIS), pg 168
Editions Imago, pg 168
Editions Infrarouge, pg 168
INRA Editions (Institut National de la Recherche Agronomique), pg 168
Editions INSERM, pg 168
IRD Editions, pg 169
Ivrea, pg 169
Editions du Jaguar, pg 169
Jouvence Editions, pg 170
Editions Juridiques et Techniques Lamy SA, pg 170
Karthala Editions-Diffusion, pg 170
Editions Klincksieck, pg 170
Editions Larousse, pg 171
Les Editions LGDJ-Montchrestien, pg 172
Le Livre de Poche-L G F (Librairie Generale Francaise), pg 173
Editions de la Maison des Sciences de l'Homme, Paris, pg 173
Editions A M Metailie, pg 175
Editions Albin Michel, pg 175
Presses Universitaires du Mirail, pg 176
Editions Fernand Nathan, pg 176
Editions Odile Jacob, pg 177
Editions Ophrys, pg 177
L'Originel - Editions Accarias, pg 178
Editions Pardes, pg 179
Payot & Rivages, pg 179

PUBLISHERS SUBJECT INDEX

Presses de Sciences Politiques, pg 181
Presses Universitaires de Caen, pg 181
Presses Universitaires de France (PUF), pg 181
Presses Universitaires de Grenoble, pg 181
Presses Universitaires de Nancy, pg 181
Presses Universitaires de Strasbourg, pg 182
Presses Universitaires du Septentrion, pg 182
Publications Orientalistes de France (POF), pg 182
Revue Espaces et Societes, pg 183
Editions Sand et Tchou SA, pg 184
Selection du Reader's Digest SA, pg 184
Sepia Editions, pg 184
Editions de Septembre, pg 184
Editions du Seuil, pg 184
Editions Andre Silvaire Sarl, pg 185
Publications de la Sorbonne, pg 185
Editions SOS (Editions du Secours Catholique), pg 186
Editions Stock, pg 186
Editeurs Tacor International, pg 186
Librairie Pierre Tequi et Editions Tequi, pg 187
Transeuropeennes/RCE, pg 188
UNESCO Publishing, pg 188
Publications de l'Universite de Pau, pg 188
Editions Weka, pg 189

Georgia

Sakartvelo Publishing House, pg 190

Germany

A Francke Verlag (Tubingen und Basel), pg 190
Accedo Verlagsgesellschaft mbH, pg 190
Akademie Verlag GmbH, pg 191
Arbeiterpresse Verlags- und Vertriebsgesellschaft mbH, pg 193
ARCult Media, pg 193
Argument-Verlag, pg 194
Roland Asanger Verlag GmbH, pg 194
Asgard-Verlag Dr Werner Hippe GmbH, pg 194
Asso Verlag, pg 195
Verlag C H Beck oHG, pg 198
Belser Wissenschaftlicher Dienst, pg 199
Berliner Debatte Wissenschafts Verlag, GSFP-Gesellschaft fur Sozialwissen-schaftliche Forschung und Publizistik mbH & Co KG, pg 199
W Bertelsmann Verlag GmbH & Co KG, pg 200
BKV-Brasilienkunde Verlag GmbH, pg 201
Verlag Die Blaue Eule, pg 202
Bleicher Verlag GmbH, pg 202
Boehlau-Verlag GmbH & Cie, pg 202
Brandes & Apsel Verlag GmbH, pg 204
Bund demokratischer Wissenschaftlerinnen und Wissenschafler eV (BdWi), pg 205
Caann Verlag, Klaus Wagner, pg 206
Campus Verlag GmbH, pg 207

Centaurus-Verlagsgesellschaft GmbH, pg 207
Chmielorz GmbH Verlag, pg 208
Hans Christians Druckerei und Verlag GmbH & Co KG, pg 208
Daedalus Verlag, pg 210
Darescha Consulting und Handels GmbH, pg 210
Verlag Darmstaedter Blaetter Schwarz und Co, pg 210
Deutscher Studien Verlag, pg 213
Deutscher Taschenbuch Verlag GmbH & Co KG (dtv), pg 213
Deutscher Universitats-Verlag, pg 213
Deutsches Jugendinstitut (DJI), pg 214
Diesterweg, Moritz Verlag, pg 214
Dietrich zu Klampen Verlag, pg 214
Verlag J H W Dietz Nachf GmbH, pg 214
Dietz Verlag Berlin GmbH, pg 215
Edition Diskord, pg 215
agenda Verlag Thomas Dominikowski, pg 215
Droste Verlag GmbH, pg 216
DSI Data Service & Information, pg 217
Duncker und Humblot GmbH, pg 217
Ehrenwirth Verlag GmbH, pg 218
N G Elwert Verlag, pg 219
Espresso Verlag GmbH, pg 221
Ferdinand Enke Verlag, pg 224
Festland Verlag GmbH, pg 224
Wilhelm Fink GmbH & Co Verlags-KG, pg 224
Karin Fischer Verlag GmbH, pg 225
Rita G Fischer Verlag, pg 225
Flensburger Hefte Verlag GmbH, pg 225
Focus-Verlag Gesellschaft mbH, pg 225
Verlag Freies Geistesleben, pg 227
Verlag A Fromm im Druck- u Verlagshaus Fromm GmbH & Co KG, pg 227
Friedrich Frommann Verlag, pg 227
Gesellschaft fuer Organisationswissenschaft e V, pg 229
Wilhelm Goldmann Verlag GmbH, pg 230
Walter de Gruyter GmbH & Co KG, pg 231
Gunter Olzog Verlag GmbH, pg 231
Haag und Herchen Verlag GmbH, pg 232
Dr Curt Haefner-Verlag GmbH, pg 233
Herbert von Halem Verlag, pg 233
Joh Heider Verlag GmbH, pg 235
Edition Hentrich Druck & Verlag Gebr Hentrich und Tank GmbH & Co KG, pg 236
Hans-Alfred Herchen & Co Verlag KG, pg 236
Verlag Hinder und Deelmann, pg 237
Hoffmann und Campe Verlag GmbH, pg 238
Holos Verlag, pg 239
Horlemann Verlag, pg 239
Edition Humanistische Psychologie (EHP), pg 240
Iudicium Verlag GmbH, pg 242
Janus Verlagsgesellschaft, Dr Norbert Meder & Co, pg 243
Junius Verlag GmbH, pg 244
Juventa Verlag GmbH, pg 244
Katzmann Verlag KG, pg 245
Keip GmbH, pg 245

Verlag Kiepenheuer & Witsch, pg 245
Klartext Verlagsgesellschaft mbH, pg 246
K F Koehler Verlag GmbH, pg 248
Verlagsgruppe Koehler/Mittler, pg 248
Koelner Universitaets-Verlag GmbH, pg 248
Verlag Koenigshausen und Neumann GmbH, pg 248
W Kohlhammer GmbH, pg 248
Konkret Literatur Verlag, pg 249
Karin Kramer Verlag, pg 250
Institut fuer Landes- und Stadtentwicklungsforschung des Landes Nordrhein-Westfalen, pg 251
Lebenshilfe-Verlag Marburg, Verlag der Bundesvereinigung Lebenshilfe fuer Menschen mit geistiger Behinderung eV, pg 253
Libertas- Europaeisches Institut GmbH, pg 254
LIT Verlag, pg 255
Logos-Verlag Literatur & Layout GmbH, pg 255
Lucius & Lucius Verlagsgesellschaft mbH, pg 255
Lukas Verlag fur Kunst- und Geistesgeschichte, pg 256
Metropolis- Verlag fur Okonomie, Gesellschaft und Politik GmbH, pg 259
Karl-Heinz Metz, pg 259
Mohr Siebeck, pg 261
Neuer ISP Verlag GmbH, pg 264
Neuland-Verlagsgesellschaft mbH, pg 264
Nomos Verlagsgesellschaft mbH und Co KG, pg 265
R Oldenbourg Verlag GmbH, pg 267
Georg Olms Verlag AG, pg 267
Orlanda Frauenverlag, pg 267
Pahl-Rugenstein Verlag Nachfolger-GmbH, pg 267
PapyRossa Verlags GmbH & Co Kommanditgesellschaft KG, pg 268
Edition Parabolis, pg 268
Propylaeen Verlag, Zweigniederlassung Berlin der Ullstein Buchverlage GmbH, pg 272
Psychologie Verlags Union GmbH, pg 272
Psychosozial-Verlag, pg 272
Quelle und Meyer Verlag GmbH & Co, pg 273
Dr Mohan Krischke Ramaswamy Edition RE, pg 273
Verlag Recht und Wirtschaft GmbH, pg 274
Verlag fur Regionalgeschichte, pg 274
Ernst Reinhardt Verlag GmbH & Co KG, pg 275
Rombach GmbH Druck und Verlagshaus & Co, pg 276
K G Saur Verlag GmbH, A Gale/Thomson Learning Company, pg 278
Sax-Verlag Beucha, pg 278
Schelzky & Jeep, Verlag fuer Reisen und Wissen, pg 279
Max Schmidt-Roemhild Verlag, pg 280
Schueren Verlag GmbH, pg 281
Schulz-Kirchner Verlag GmbH, pg 282
Verlag R S Schulz GmbH, pg 282

Otto Schwartz Fachbochhandlung GmbH, pg 282
Scientia Verlag und Antiquariat Schilling OHG, pg 282
Edition Sigma e.Kfm, pg 283
Spiess Volker Wissenschaftsverlag GmbH, pg 284
Springer Science+Business Media GmbH & Co KG, pg 284
J F Steinkopf Verlag GmbH, pg 287
Steinweg-Verlag, Jurgen vomHoff, pg 287
Suin Buch-Verlag, pg 289
Edition Temmen, pg 290
Trotzdem-Verlags Genossenschaft eG, pg 292
Tuduv Verlagsgesellschaft mbH, pg 292
Tuebinger Vereinigung fur Volkskunde eV (TVV), pg 292
Ullstein Heyne List GmbH & Co KG, pg 293
Ulrike Helmer Verlag, pg 293
UNO-Verlag GmbH, pg 293
UTB fuer Wissenschaft Uni Taschenbuecher GmbH, pg 294
UVK Verlagsgesellschaft mbH, pg 294
VAS-Verlag fuer Akademische Schriften, pg 294
Vervuert Verlagsgesellschaft, pg 295
VJK Verlag Josef Knecht Carolusdruckerei GmbH, pg 296
Dokument und Analyse Verlag Bogislaw von Randow, pg 296
Votum Verlag GmbH, pg 297
VS Verlag fur Sozialwissenschaften, pg 297
VWB-Verlag fur Wissenschaft & Bildung, Amand Aglaster, pg 297
Wachholtz Verlag GmbH, pg 297
Verlag Klaus Wagenbach, pg 297
Waxmann Verlag GmbH, pg 297
Weber Zucht & Co, pg 298
Weidler Buchverlag Berlin, pg 298
Verlag Westfaelisches Dampfboot, pg 299
Dr Dieter Winkler, pg 300
Verlag Wissenschaft und Politik, pg 300
Wissenschaftliche Buchgesellschaft, pg 300

Ghana

Asempa Publishers, pg 303
Black Mask Ltd, pg 303
EPP Books Services, pg 304
Ghana Publishing Corporation, pg 304
Ghana Universities Press (GUP), pg 304
Waterville Publishing House, pg 305

Greece

Apostoliki Diakonia tis Ekklisias tis Hellados, pg 305
D I Arsenidis Publications, pg 306
Bergadis, pg 306
Boukoumanis' Editions, pg 306
Ecole francaise d'Athenes, pg 307
Etaireia Spoudon Neoellinikou Politismou Kai Genikis Paideias, pg 307
Exandas Publishers, pg 307
Gutenberg Publications, pg 307
Hestia-I D Hestia-Kollaros & Co Corporation, pg 308
Idryma Meleton Chersonisou tou Aimou, pg 308
Irini Publishing House - Vassilis G Katsikeas SA, pg 308
Kedros Publishers, pg 309

Kritiki Publishing, pg 309
Kyriakidis Vasileios, pg 309
Panepistimio Ioanninon, pg 311
Papazissis Publishers SA, pg 311
Patakis Publishers, pg 311
Sakkoulas Publications SA, pg 312
Stochastis, pg 312
Thymari Publications, pg 312

Guatemala

Grupo Editorial RIN-78, pg 313

Guinea-Bissau

Instituto Nacional de Estudos e Pesquisa (INEP), pg 314

Honduras

Editorial Guaymuras, pg 315

Hong Kong

The Chinese University Press, pg 316
Chung Hwa Book Co (HK) Ltd, pg 316
Hong Kong University Press, pg 317

Hungary

Akademiai Kiado, pg 320
Atlantisz Kiado, pg 320
Balassi Kiado Kft, pg 321
Central European University Press, pg 321
Corvina Books Ltd, pg 321
Janus Pannonius Tudomanyegyetem, pg 322
Joszoveg Muhely Kiado, pg 322
KJK-Kerszov, pg 322
Mult es Jovo Kiado, pg 323
Osiris Kiado, pg 323
Statiqum Kiado es Nyomda Kft, pg 324

Iceland

Hid Islenzka Bokmenntafelag, pg 325

India

Abhinav Publications, pg 326
The Academic Press, pg 327
Addison-Wesley Pte Ltd, pg 327
Agricole Publishing Academy, pg 327
Ajanta Publications (India), pg 327
Amar Prakashan, pg 328
Ananda Publishers Pvt Ltd, pg 328
Anmol Publications Pvt Ltd, pg 328
APH Publishing Corp, pg 328
Arihant Publishers, pg 328
Arya Medi Publishing House, pg 328
Asian Educational Services, pg 329
Asian Trading Corporation, pg 329
Associated Publishing House, pg 329
Atma Ram & Sons, pg 329
Authorspress, pg 329
Avinash Reference Publications, pg 329
K P Bagchi & Co, pg 329
Baha'i Publishing Trust of India, pg 329
The Bangalore Printing & Publishing Co Ltd, pg 329
Bharatiya Vidya Bhavan, pg 330
Book Circle, pg 330
Booklinks Corporation, pg 331
BR Publishing Corporation, pg 331
Chanakya Publications, pg 331
S Chand & Co Ltd, pg 331
Chugh Publications, pg 332
Classical Publishing Co, pg 332
Concept Publishing Co, pg 332
Cosmo Publications, pg 332
Dastane Ramchandra & Co, pg 333
Disha Prakashan, pg 333
Eastern Book Centre, pg 333
Eastern Law House Pvt Ltd, pg 334
Enkay Publishers Pvt Ltd, pg 334
Ess Ess Publications, pg 334
Eurasia Publishing House Private Ltd, pg 334
Firma KLM Privatee Ltd, Publishers & International Booksellers, pg 334
Geeta Prakashan, pg 335
Gitanjali Publishing House, pg 335
Gyan Publishing House, pg 335
Arnold Heinman Publishers (India) Pvt Ltd, pg 335
Heritage Publishers, pg 335
Himalaya Publishing House, pg 335
Indian Council of Social Science Research (ICSSR), pg 336
Indian Institute of Advanced Study, pg 337
Indian Society for Promoting Christian Knowledge (ISPCK), pg 337
Indus Publishing Co, pg 338
Intellectual Publishing House, pg 338
Inter-India Publications, pg 338
Kali For Women, pg 339
Kitab Ghar, pg 339
Konark Publishers Pvt Ltd, pg 339
Lokvangmaya Griha Pvt Ltd, pg 340
Manohar Publishers & Distributors, pg 340
Minerva Associates (Publications) Pvt Ltd, pg 341
Ministry of Information & Broadcasting, pg 341
Mittal Publications, pg 341
National Book Organization, pg 342
National Publishing House, pg 343
Naya Prokash, pg 343
Omsons Publications, pg 344
Panjab University Publication Bureau, pg 344
Parimal Prakashan, pg 345
People's Publishing House (P) Ltd, pg 345
Pointer Publishers, pg 345
Popular Prakashan Pvt Ltd, pg 345
Promilla & Publishers, pg 345
Radiant Publishers, pg 346
Rajasthan Hindi Granth Academy, pg 346
Rajendra Publishing House Pvt Ltd, pg 346
Regency Publications, pg 346
Reliance Publishing House, pg 346
SABDA, pg 347
SAGE Publications India Pvt Ltd, pg 347
SBW Publishers, pg 348
Scientific Book Agency, pg 348
Scientific Publishers India, pg 349
Somaiya Publications Pvt Ltd, pg 349
South Asian Publishers Pvt Ltd, pg 350
Spectrum Publications, pg 350
Sterling Publishers Pvt Ltd, pg 350
Sultan Chand & Sons Pvt Ltd, pg 350
Surjeet Publications, pg 351
DB Taraporevala Sons & Co Pvt Ltd, pg 351
Tata McGraw-Hill Publishing Co Ltd, pg 351
Viva Books Pvt Ltd, pg 352
Vivek Prakashan, pg 353

Indonesia

Alumni PT, pg 353
Bhratara Karya Aksara, pg 354
PT Bulan Bintang, pg 354
Djambatan PT, pg 354
Lembaga Demografi Fakultas Ekonomi Universitas Indonesia, pg 355
Pustaka Utama Grafiti, PT, pg 356
Yayasan Obor Indonesia, pg 357

Iraq

National House for Publishing, Distributing & Advertising, pg 357

Ireland

Attic Press Ltd, pg 358
Campus Publishing Ltd, pg 358
Cork University Press, pg 359
The Economic & Social Research Institute, pg 359
Institute of Public Administration, pg 361
Irish YouthWork Press, pg 361

Israel

Am Oved Publishers Ltd, pg 365
Bar Ilan University Press, pg 365
Dyonon/Papyrus Publishing House of the Tel-Aviv, pg 366
Freund Publishing House Ltd, pg 367
Hakibbutz Hameuchad Publishing House Ltd, pg 367
Hanitzotz A-Sharara Publishing House, pg 367
The Institute for Israeli Arabs Studies, pg 368
Israel Universities Press, pg 368
(JDC) Brookdale Institute of Gerontology & Adult Human Development in Israel, pg 369
Keter Publishing House Ltd, pg 369
Massada Press Ltd, pg 370
Open University of Israel, pg 371
Sifriat Poalim Ltd, pg 372
Tel Aviv University, pg 372
The Van Leer Jerusalem Institute, pg 373
Yachdav, United Publishers Co Ltd, pg 373
Y L Peretz Publishing Co, pg 373

Italy

Mario Adda Editore SNC, pg 374
Edizioni della Fondazione Giovanni Agnelli, pg 374
Editrice Ancora, pg 375
Franco Angeli SRL, pg 375
Arcipelago Edizioni di Chiani Marisa, pg 376
Editore Armando Armando SRL, pg 376
Casa Editrice Astrolabio-Ubaldini Editore, pg 377
Baha'i, pg 377
Bollati Boringhieri Editore, pg 378
Bookservice, pg 378
Edizioni Borla SRL, pg 379
Bulzoni Editore SRL (Le Edizioni Universitarie d'Italia), pg 379
Edizioni Cadmo SRL, pg 379
Cappelli Editore, pg 380
Casa Editrice Libraria Ulrico Hoepli SpA, pg 380
CEDAM (Casa Editrice Dr A Milani), pg 380
Celuc Libri, pg 381
Edizioni Centro Studi Erickson, pg 381
Centro Studi Terzo Mondo, pg 381
il Cerchio Iniziative Editoriali, pg 381
Citta Nuova Editrice, pg 382
Cittadella Editrice, pg 382
Edizioni di Comunita SpA, pg 383
Edizioni Cultura della Pace, pg 383
La Cultura Sociologica, pg 384
Damanhur Edizioni, pg 384
Edizioni Dedalo SRL, pg 384
Edizioni Dehoniane, pg 384
Ediciclo Editore SRL, pg 386
Edizioni Studio Domenicano (ESD), pg 387
Giulio Einaudi Editore SpA, pg 387
Gangemi Editore spa, pg 390
Edizioni GB, pg 390
G Giappichelli Editore SRL, pg 390
A Giuffre Editore SpA, pg 390
Gius Laterza e Figli SpA, pg 391
Libreria Editrice Gregoriana, pg 391
Edizioni Guerini e Associati SpA, pg 392
Ibis, pg 392
Instituti Editoriali E Poligrafici Internazionali SRL, pg 393
Edizioni Internazionali di Letteratura e Scienze, pg 393
Editoriale Jaca Book SpA, pg 394
L Japadre Editore, pg 394
Kaos Edizioni SRL, pg 394
Lalli Editore SRL, pg 394
Laruffa Editore SRL, pg 394
Editrice LAS, pg 394
Edizioni Lavoro SRL, pg 394
LED - Edizioni Universitarie di Lettere Economia Diritto, pg 395
Libreria Editrice Fiorentina, pg 395
Liguori Editore SRL, pg 395
Vincenzo Lo Faro Editore, pg 395
Longanesi & C, pg 396
Manifestolibri, pg 397
Marsilio Editori SpA, pg 397
Editrice Massimo SAS di Crespi Cesare e C, pg 397
Edizioni Medicea SRL, pg 398
Milella di Lecce Spazio Vivo srl, pg 398
Editrice Missionaria Italiana (EMI), pg 398
Monduzzi Editore SpA, pg 399
Editrice Morcelliana SpA, pg 399
Societa Editrice Il Mulino, pg 399
Gruppo Ugo Mursia Editore SpA, pg 400
Museo storico in Trento, pg 400
Newton & Compton Editori, pg 400
La Nuova Italia Editrice SpA, pg 401
Officina Edizioni di Aldo Quinti, pg 401
Leo S Olschki, pg 401
Maria Pacini Fazzi Editore, pg 402
Patron Editore SrL, pg 402
Piero Manni srl, pg 403
RAI-ERI, pg 405
RCS Rizzoli Libri SpA, pg 405
Editori Riuniti, pg 405
Edizioni Universitarie Romane, pg 406
Rosenberg e Sellier Editori in Torino, pg 406
Rubbettino Editore, pg 406
Il Saggiatore, pg 406
Salerno Editrice SRL, pg 406
Sapere 2000 SRL, pg 407
Edizioni Scientifiche Italiane, pg 407
Sellerio Editore, pg 408
Societa Storica Catanese, pg 408

PUBLISHERS

Il Sole 24 Ore Pirola, pg 409
Edizioni Studium SRL, pg 409
Nicola Teti e C Editore SRL, pg 410
Edizioni Thyrus SRL, pg 410
Editrice Tirrenia Stampatori SAS, pg 410
Todariana Editrice, pg 410
UTET (Unione Tipografico-Editrice Torinese), pg 411
Vivere In SRL, pg 412
Zanichelli Editore SpA, pg 412

Jamaica

Carlong Publishers (Caribbean) Ltd, pg 413
Institute of Jamaica Publications, pg 413
Jamaica Publishing House Ltd, pg 414
University of the West Indies Press, pg 414

Japan

Akita Shoten Publishing Co Ltd, pg 415
Aoki Shoten Co Ltd, pg 415
Baifukan Co Ltd, pg 415
Bunkasha Publishing Co Ltd, pg 415
Bunkashobo-Hakubun-Sha, pg 415
Chikuma Shobo Publishing Co Ltd, pg 416
Chuokoron-Shinsha Inc, pg 416
Dobunshoin Publishers Co, pg 416
Fukumura Shuppan Inc, pg 417
Fuzambo Publishing Co, pg 417
GakuseiSha Publishing Co Ltd, pg 417
Hayakawa Publishing Inc, pg 418
Heibonsha Ltd, Publishers, pg 418
Hokkaido University Press, pg 418
Horitsu Bunka-Sha, pg 418
Hyoronsha Publishing Co Ltd, pg 418
Ichiryu-Sha, pg 418
Ie-No-Hikari Association, pg 419
Iwanami Shoten, Publishers, pg 419
Japan Broadcast Publishing Co Ltd, pg 419
Kajima Institute Publishing Co Ltd, pg 420
Kansai University Press, pg 420
Kawade Shobo Shinsha Publishers, pg 420
Kazamashobo Co Ltd, pg 420
Keisuisha Publishing Company Ltd, pg 420
Kinokuniya Co Ltd (Publishing Department), pg 421
Kodansha Ltd, pg 421
Kokudo-Sha Co Ltd, pg 421
Koseisha-Koseikaku Co Ltd, pg 422
Koyo Shobo, pg 422
Minerva Shobo Co Ltd, pg 422
Mirai-Sha, pg 422
Misuzu Shobo Ltd, pg 422
Nihon Bunka Kagakusha Co Ltd, pg 423
Nihon-Bunkyo Shuppan (Japan Educational Publishing Co Ltd), pg 423
Nihon Keizai Shimbun Inc Publications Bureau, pg 423
Nihon Tosho Center Co Ltd, pg 423
Nippon Hoso Shuppan Kyokai (NHK Publishing), pg 424
Otsuki Shoten Publishers, pg 425
PHP Institute Inc, pg 425
Riso-Sha, pg 425
Ryosho-Fukyu-Kai Co Ltd, pg 425
Sanseido Co Ltd, pg 426

Sanshusha Publishing Co, Ltd, pg 426
Seibundo, pg 426
Seishin Shobo, pg 427
Shakai Shiso-Sha, pg 427
Shunjusha, pg 428
The Simul Press Inc, pg 428
Tamagawa University Press, pg 429
TBS-Britannica Co Ltd, pg 429
Tokai University Press, pg 429
Tokuma Shoten Publishing Co Ltd, pg 429
Tokyo Sogensha Co Ltd, pg 430
Toyo Keizai Shinpo-Sha, pg 430
Tsukiji Shokan Publishing Co, pg 430
Charles E Tuttle Publishing Co Inc, pg 430
United Nations University Press, pg 430
University of Tokyo Press, pg 430
Waseda University Press, pg 431
Yuhikaku Publishing Co Ltd, pg 431
Yuki Shobo, pg 431
Zenkoku Kyodo Shuppan, pg 431

Jordan

Al-Tanwir Al Ilmi (Scientific Enlightenment Publishing House), pg 432

Kazakstan

Gylym, Izd-Vo, pg 432
Al-Farabi Kazakh National University, pg 432
Kazakhstan, Izd-Vo, pg 432

Kenya

African Centre for Technology Studies (ACTS), pg 433
Heinemann Kenya Ltd (EAEP), pg 434
Midi Teki Publishers, pg 435
Nairobi University Press, pg 435
Phoenix Publishers Ltd, pg 435
Shirikon Publishers, pg 436
Transafrica Press, pg 436
Uzima Press Ltd, pg 436
Gideon S Were Press, pg 436

Democratic People's Republic of Korea

Korea Science and Encyclopedia Publishing House, pg 436

Republic of Korea

Bakyoung Publishing Co, pg 437
Bum-Woo Publishing Co, pg 437
Chung Rim Publishing Co Ltd, pg 438
Ewha Womans University Press, pg 438
Hak Won Publishing Co, pg 439
Hakmunsa Publishing Co, pg 439
Hangil Art Vision, pg 439
Hanul Publishing Co, pg 439
Haseo Publishing Co, pg 439
Iljisa Publishing House, pg 439
Iljo-gag Publishers, pg 439
Jeong-eum Munhwasa, pg 439
Korea University Press, pg 440
Koreaone Press Inc, pg 440
Kukminseokwan Publishing Co Ltd, pg 440
Kyungnam University Press, pg 441
Min-eumsa Publishing Co Ltd, pg 441
Munhag-gwan, pg 441
Munye Publishing Co, pg 441
Nanam Publications Co, pg 441

Omun Gak, pg 441
Oruem Publishing House, pg 442
Panmun Book Co Ltd, pg 442
PoChinChai Printing Co Ltd, pg 442
Samhwa Publishing Co Ltd, pg 442
Samkwang Publishing Co, pg 442
Seoul National University Press, pg 443
Sogang University Press, pg 443
Sohaksa, pg 443
Yonsei University Press, pg 444

Kuwait

Ministry of Information, pg 444

Laos People's Democratic Republic

Lao-phanit, pg 444

Latvia

Lielvards Ltd, pg 445

Lebanon

Institute for Palestine Studies, Publishing & Research Organization (IPS), pg 446
Khayat Book and Publishing Co Sarl, pg 446

Lesotho

Saint Michael's Mission Social Centre, pg 447

Liechtenstein

Topos Verlag AG, pg 448

Lithuania

Academia, pg 448
Baltos Lankos, pg 449
Klaipedos Universiteto Leidykla, pg 449
Vaga Ltd, pg 450

Luxembourg

Essay und Zeitgeist Verlag, pg 451
Service Central de la Statistique et des Etudes Economiques (STATEC), pg 451

Macau

Livros Do Oriente, pg 452

The Former Yugoslav Republic of Macedonia

Macedonia Prima Publishing House, pg 452

Madagascar

Editions Ambozontany, pg 453

Malaysia

Pelanduk Publications (M) Sdn Bhd, pg 457
Penerbit Universiti Sains Malaysia, pg 458
Penerbit Universiti Teknologi Malaysia, pg 459
University of Malaya, Department of Publications, pg 459

Maldive Islands

Non-Formal Education Centre, pg 459

Mali

EDIM SA, pg 460

SUBJECT INDEX

Malta

Media Centre, pg 460

Mexico

Aguilar Altea Taurus Alfaguara SA de CV, pg 462
Editores Asociados Mexicanos SA de CV (EDAMEX), pg 462
Editorial Avante SA de Cv, pg 462
Ediciones el Caballito SA, pg 462
Centro de Estudios Mexicanos y Centroamericanos, pg 463
El Colegio de Mexico AC, pg 463
Colegio de Postgraduados en Ciencias Agricolas, pg 463
Comision Nacional Forestal, pg 463
Publicaciones Cruz O SA, pg 463
Edamex SA de CV, pg 464
Editorial Edicol SA, pg 464
El Colegio de Michoacan A C, pg 464
Ediciones Era SA de CV, pg 465
Editorial Extemporaneos SA, pg 465
Fernandez Editores SA de CV, pg 465
Fondo de Cultura Economica, pg 465
Editorial Joaquin Mortiz SA de CV, pg 467
Editorial Jus SA de CV, pg 467
Editorial Limusa SA de CV, pg 467
McGraw-Hill Interamericana Editores, SA de CV, pg 468
Instituto Nacional de Antropologia e Historia, pg 469
Instituto Nacional de Estadistica, Geografia e Informatica, pg 469
Editorial Nuestro Tiempo SA, pg 469
Editorial Nueva Imagen SA, pg 469
Editorial Planeta Mexicana SA, pg 470
Plaza y Valdes SA de CV, pg 470
Ediciones Cientificas La Prensa Medica Mexicana SA de CV, pg 470
Siglo XXI Editores SA de CV, pg 472
Editorial Trillas SA de CV, pg 472
Universidad Nacional Autonoma de Mexico (National University of Mexico), pg 472
Universidad Veracruzana Direccion General Editorial y de Publicaciones, pg 472

Republic of Moldova

Editura Cartea Moldovei, pg 473

Morocco

Editions Al-Fourkane, pg 474
Dar El Kitab, pg 474
Dar Nachr Al Maarifa Pour L'Edition et La Distribution, pg 474
Edition Diffusion de Livre au Maroc, pg 474
Editions Le Fennec, pg 474

Myanmar

Knowledge Press & Bookhouse, pg 475

Namibia

Multi-Disciplinary Research Centre Library, pg 476

SUBJECT INDEX

Nepal
International Standards Books & Periodicals (P) Ltd, pg 476
Royal Nepal Academy, pg 477

Netherlands
Uitgeverij Ambo BV, pg 477
APA (Academic Publishers Associated), pg 477
Uitgeverij Jan van Arkel, pg 478
John Benjamins BV, pg 479
Erven J Bijleveld, pg 479
Uitgeverij Bohn Stafleu Van Loghum BV, pg 479
Boom Uitgeverij, pg 479
Brill Academic Publishers, pg 479
A W Bruna Uitgevers BV, pg 480
Uitgeversmaatschappij Ad Donker BV, pg 481
Uitgeverij en boekhandel Van Gennep BV, pg 482
KITLV Press Royal Institute of Linguistics & Anthropology, pg 484
Kluwer Academic Publishers, pg 484
Uitgeverij J H Kok BV, pg 485
Uitgeverij Lemma BV, pg 485
Lemniscaat, pg 485
Mets & Schilt Uitgevers en Distributeurs, pg 486
Uitgeverij H Nelissen BV, pg 486
Nijgh & Van Ditmar Amsterdam, pg 487
Podium Uitgeverij, pg 487
Samsom BedrijfsInformatie BV, pg 488
Sociaal en Cultureel Planbureau, pg 489
Uitgeverij de Tijdstroom BV, pg 490
Tirion Uitgevers BV, pg 490
Twente University Press, pg 490
Van Gorcum & Comp BV, pg 491
VU Boekhandel/Uitgeverij BV, pg 492

New Zealand
Aoraki Press Ltd, pg 493
Auckland University Press, pg 493
ESA Publications (NZ) Ltd, pg 496
Fraser Books, pg 496
Nelson Price Milburn Ltd, pg 499
RSVP Publishing Co Ltd, pg 500
University of Otago Press, pg 502
Victoria University Press, pg 502

Nicaragua
Editorial Nueva Nicaragua, pg 502

Nigeria
Ahmadu Bello University Press Ltd, pg 503
Educational Research & Study Group, pg 504
Ethiope Publishing Corporation, pg 504
Evans Brothers (Nigeria Publishers) Ltd, pg 504
Fourth Dimension Publishing Co Ltd, pg 504
Gbabeks Publishers Ltd, pg 505
Ibadan University Press, pg 505
International Publishing & Research Company, pg 505
JAD Publishers Ltd, pg 505
Literamed Publications Nigeria Ltd, pg 505
Longman Nigeria Plc, pg 505
Thomas Nelson (Nigeria) Ltd, pg 505
Obafemi Awolowo University Press Ltd, pg 506
Ogunsanya Press, Publishers and Bookstores Ltd, pg 506
Onibon-Oje Publishers, pg 506
Tabansi Press Ltd, pg 507
University of Lagos Press, pg 507
Vantage Publishers International Ltd, pg 507

Norway
Aschehoug Forlag, pg 508
H Aschehoug & Co (W Nygaard) A/S, pg 508
Glydendal Akademisk, pg 509
Gyldendal Norsk Forlag A/S, pg 509
Pax Forlag A/S, pg 510

Pakistan
Centre for South Asian Studies, pg 512
Pakistan Institute of Development Economics (PIDE), pg 514
Quaid-i-Azam University Department of Biological Sciences, pg 514

Panama
Editorial Universitaria, pg 515

Papua New Guinea
Melanesian Institute, pg 515
National Research Institute of Papua New Guinea, pg 515
Papua New Guinea Institute of Medical Research, pg 516

Peru
Centro de la Mujer Peruana Flora Tristan, pg 516
Instituto de Estudios Peruanos, pg 517
Fondo Editorial de la Pontificia Universidad Catolica del Peru, pg 517
Instituto Frances de Estudios Andinos, IFEA, pg 517
Editorial Horizonte, pg 517
Sur Casa de Estudios del Socialismo, pg 517
Editorial Universo SA, pg 517

Philippines
Ateneo de Manila University Press, pg 518
Philippine Education Co Inc, pg 520
Rex Bookstores & Publishers, pg 520
Saint Mary's Publishing Corp, pg 520
Salesiana Publishers Inc, pg 521
San Carlos Publications, pg 521
SIBS Publishing House Inc, pg 521
University of the Philippines Press, pg 521
UST Publishing House, pg 521
Vibal Publishing House Inc (VPHI), pg 521

Poland
Spoldzielnia Wydawnicza 'Czytelnik', pg 522
Impuls, pg 523
Katolicki Uniwersytet Wydawniczo-Redakcja, pg 523
'Ksiazka i Wiedza' Spotdzielnia Wydawniczo-Handlowa, pg 524
Wydawnictwo Lubelskie, pg 524
Muza SA, pg 524
Norbertinum, pg 524
Ossolineum Zaklad Narodowy im Ossolinskich - Wydawnictwo, pg 525
Polish Scientific Publishers PWN, pg 525
Spotdzielna Anagram, pg 526
Oficyna Wydawnicza Szkoly Glownej Handlowej w Warszawie Oficyna Wydawnicza SGH, pg 527
Wydawnictwa Uniwersytetu Warszawskiego, pg 527
Zaklad Wydawnictw Statystycznych, pg 528

Portugal
Edicoes Afrontamento, pg 528
Armenio Amado Editora de Simoes, Beirao & Ca Lda, pg 528
Edicoes Antigona, pg 528
Apaginastantas - Cooperativa de Servicos Culturais, pg 528
Atica, SA Editores e Livreiros, pg 529
Bertrand Editora Lda, pg 529
Brasilia Editora (J Carvalho Branco), pg 529
Centro Estudos Geograficos, pg 529
Livraria Civilizacao (Americo Fraga Lamares & Ca Lda), pg 529
Editora Classica, pg 530
Edicoes Colibri, pg 530
Constancia Editores, SA, pg 530
Edicoes Cosmos, pg 530
Dinalivro, pg 530
Direccao Geral Familia, pg 530
Editorial Estampa, Lda, pg 531
Publicacoes Europa-America Lda, pg 531
Gradiva-Publicacnoes Lda, pg 532
Guimaraes Editores, Lda, pg 532
Imprensa Nacional-Casa da Moeda, pg 532
Editorial Inquerito Lda, pg 532
Instituto de Investigacao Cientifica Tropical, pg 532
Edicoes ITAU (Instituto Tecnico de Alimentacao Humana) Lda, pg 532
Livros Horizonte Lda, pg 533
Editora McGraw-Hill de Portugal Lda, pg 533
Nova Arrancada Sociedade Editora SA, pg 534
Editorial Presenca, pg 535
Publicacoes Dom Quixote Lda, pg 535
Quid Juris - Sociedade Editora, pg 535
Edicoes Rolim Lda, pg 535
Edicoes 70 Lda, pg 535
Almerinda Teixeira, pg 536
Teorema, pg 536
Vega-Publicacao e Distribuicao de Livros e Revistas, Lda, pg 536

Puerto Rico
Editorial Cordillera Inc, pg 537
Libros-Ediciones Homines, pg 537
Ediciones Huracan Inc, pg 537
Ediciones Puerto, pg 537
University of Puerto Rico Press (EDUPR), pg 537

Reunion
Editions Ocean, pg 538

Romania
Editura Academiei Romane, pg 538
Aion Verlag, pg 538
Ararat -Tiped, Editura, pg 538
Editura Clusium, pg 539
Corint Publishing Group, pg 539
Editura Excelsior Art, pg 539
Humanitas Publishing House, pg 540
Mentor Kiado, pg 540
Editura Meridiane, pg 540
Editura Militara, pg 541
Editura Niculescu, pg 541
Editura Paideia, pg 541
Pallas-Akademia Editura, pg 541
Polirom Verlag, pg 542
Editura 'Scrisul Romanesc', pg 542
Editura Stiintifica si Enciclopedica, pg 542
Universal Dalsi, pg 543
Vremea Publishers Ltd, pg 543

Russian Federation
Aspect Press Ltd, pg 543
Izvestia Sovetov Narodnyh Deputatov Russian Federation (RF), pg 545
Legprombytizdat, pg 546
Ministerstvo Kul'tury RF, pg 546
Izdatelstvo Molodaya Gvardia, pg 546
Izdatelstvo Mordovskogo gosudarstvennogo, pg 547
Nauka Publishers, pg 547
Izdatel'stvo Nizhegorodskogo Gosudarstvennogo Univ, pg 547
Novosti Izdatelstvo, pg 547
Progress Publishers, pg 548
Stroyizdat Publishing House, pg 549
Voronezh State University Publishers, pg 549

Rwanda
INADES (Institut Africain pour le Developpment Economique et Social), pg 550

Senegal
Nouvelles Editions Africaines du Senegal (NEAS), pg 551
CODESRIA (Council for the Development of Social Science Research in Africa), pg 551
Les Nouvelles Editions Africaines du Senegal NEAS, pg 551

Serbia and Montenegro
Beogradski Izdavacko-Graficki Zavod, pg 552
Nolit Publishing House, pg 553
Izdavacka Organizacija Rad, pg 553
Panorama NIJP/ID Grigorije Bozovic, pg 553
Radnicka Stampa, pg 553
Vuk Karadzic, pg 554

Sierra Leone
Sierra Leone University Press, pg 554

Singapore
APAC Publishers Services Pte Ltd, pg 554
Aquanut Agencies Pte Ltd, pg 555
Chopsons Pte Ltd, pg 555
Hillview Publications Pte Ltd, pg 556
Institute of Southeast Asian Studies, pg 556
Maruzen Asia (Pte) Ltd, pg 557
McGallen & Bolden Associates, pg 557
Reed Elsevier, South East Asia, pg 557

PUBLISHERS

Singapore University Press Pte Ltd, pg 558
Taylor & Francis Asia Pacific, pg 558

Slovakia

ARCHA sro Vydavatel'stro, pg 559
Danubiaprint, pg 559
Kalligram spol sro, pg 559
Slovenske pedagogicke nakladateistvo, pg 560
Smena Publishing House, pg 560
Sofa, pg 560
Ustav informacii a prognoz skolstva mladeze a telovychovy, pg 561
VEDA (Vydavatel'stvo Slovenskej akademie vied), pg 561

Slovenia

Cankarjeva Zalozba, pg 561
Zalozba Mihelac d o o, pg 562
Zalozba Obzorja d d Maribor, pg 562

South Africa

Centre for Conflict Resolution, pg 563
Educum Publishers Ltd, pg 563
Human Sciences Research Council, pg 565
Juventus/Femina Publishers, pg 565
Nasou Via Afrika, pg 567
Ravan Press (Pty) Ltd, pg 568
Shuter & Shooter (Pty) Ltd, pg 568
South African Institute of Race Relations, pg 569
University of KwaZulu-Natal Press, pg 569
Van Schaik Publishers, pg 569

Spain

Editorial Afers, SL, pg 571
Agencia Espanola de Cooperacion, pg 571
Ediciones Akal SA, pg 571
Ediciones Alfar SA, pg 572
Edicions Alfons el Magnanim, Institucio Valenciana d'Estudis i Investigacio, pg 572
Alianza Editorial SA, pg 572
Alta Fulla Editorial, pg 572
Amnistia Internacional Editorial SL, pg 572
Editorial Anagrama, pg 572
Editorial Ariel SA, pg 573
Editorial Ayuso, pg 574
Ediciones Bellaterra SA, pg 574
Casa de Velazquez, pg 575
Editorial Casals SA, pg 575
Edicios do Castro, pg 576
Centro de Estudios Politicos Y Constitucionales, pg 576
Compania Literaria, pg 577
Ediciones de la Universidad Complutense de Madrid, pg 577
Complutense, SA Editorial, pg 577
Ediciones Cristiandad, pg 578
Diputacion Provincial de Sevilla, Servicio de Publicaciones, pg 579
EDERSA (Editoriales de Derecho Reunidas SA), pg 580
Ediciones Encuentro SA, pg 582
Editorial Espasa-Calpe SA, pg 582
Instituto de Estudios Riojanos, pg 583
Fondo de Cultura Economica de Espana, SL, pg 583
Fundacion de Estudios Libertarios Anselmo Lorenzo, pg 584
Editorial Fundamentos, pg 584
Galaxia SA Editorial, pg 584

Editorial Gedisa SA, pg 584
Instituto de Cultura Juan Gil-Albert, pg 585
Editorial Grupo Cero, pg 585
Editorial Herder SA, pg 586
Iberico Europea de Ediciones SA, pg 586
Icaria Editorial SA, pg 587
Publicaciones ICCE, pg 587
Instituto de Estudios Economicos, pg 587
Iralka Editorial SL, pg 588
Ediciones Istmo SA, pg 588
Editorial Kairos SA, pg 588
Editorin Laiovento SL, pg 588
Ediciones Libertarias/Prodhufi SA, pg 589
Llibres del Segle, pg 589
Editorial Lumen SA, pg 589
Antonio Machado, SA, pg 590
Edicions de la Magrana SA, pg 590
Ediciones Marova SL, pg 590
Ediciones Mensajero, pg 591
Editorial Moll SL, pg 592
Ediciones Morata SL, pg 592
Narcea SA de Ediciones, pg 593
Oikos-Tau SA Ediciones, pg 593
Ediciones Olimpic, SL, pg 594
Ediciones del Oriente y del Mediterraneo, pg 594
Pages Editors, SL, pg 594
Ediciones Paidos Iberica SA, pg 594
Pais Vasco Servicio Central de Publicaciones, pg 594
Parlamento Vasco, pg 595
Ediciones Partenon, pg 595
Editorial Popular SA, pg 596
Prensas Universitarias de Zaragoza, pg 597
Editorial Presencia Gitana, pg 597
Edicions Proa, SA, pg 597
Instituto Provincial de Investigaciones y Estudios Toledanos (IPIET), pg 597
Publicaciones de la Universidad de Alicante, pg 597
Publicaciones de la Universidad Pontificia Comillas-Madrid, pg 597
Ediciones ROL SA, pg 598
Ediciones San Pio X, pg 599
Universidad de Santiago de Compostela, pg 599
Siglo XXI de Espana Editores SA, pg 599
Editorial Sintesis, SA, pg 600
Ediciones Siruela SA, pg 600
Edicions 62, pg 600
Ediciones SM, pg 600
Editorial Tecnos SA, pg 601
Tirant lo Blanch SL Libreriaa, pg 602
Ediciones de la Torre, pg 602
Trotta SA Editorial, pg 602
Editorial Txertoa, pg 603
Universidad de Granada, pg 603
Universidad de Malaga, pg 603
Universidad de Oviedo Servicio de Publicaciones, pg 603
Universidad de Valladolid Secretariado de Publicaciones e Intercambio Editorial, pg 604
Publicacions de la Universitat de Barcelona, pg 604
Editorial Verbo Divino, pg 604
Edicions Xerais de Galicia, pg 605

Sri Lanka

Karunaratne & Sons Ltd, pg 606
National Library & Documentation Centre, pg 607
Swarna Hansa Foundation, pg 607

SUBJECT INDEX

Sudan

Khartoum University Press, pg 608

Suriname

Stichting Wetenschappelijke Informatie, pg 608

Sweden

Acta Universitatis Gothoburgensis, pg 609
Bonnier Carlsen Bokforlag AB, pg 610
Forlaget By och Bygd, pg 610
Gidlunds Bokforlag, pg 612
Liber AB, pg 613
Bokfoerlaget Natur och Kultur, pg 613
Bokforlaget Nya Doxa AB, pg 614
Bokforlaget Opal AB, pg 614
Ordfront Foerlag AB, pg 614
SNS Foerlag, pg 615
Sober Foerlags AB, pg 615
Studentlitteratur AB, pg 616
Timbro, pg 616
Zindermans AB, pg 617

Switzerland

Editions L'Age d'Homme - La Cite, pg 617
Editions de la Baconniere SA, pg 618
Basileia Verlag und Basler Missionsbuchhandlung, pg 618
Les Editions Camphill, pg 620
Caux Books, pg 620
Caux Edition SA, pg 620
Chronos Verlag, pg 621
Cockatoo Press (Schweiz), Thailand-Publikationen, pg 621
Cultur Prospectiv, Edition, pg 621
Editions Delachaux et Niestle SA, pg 621
Librairie Droz SA, pg 622
Gottlieb Duttweiler Institute for Trends & Futures, pg 622
Edition Epoca, pg 622
Edition Exodus, pg 623
Georg Editeur SA, pg 624
Editions Francois Grounauer, pg 624
Paul Haupt Bern, pg 625
Interfrom AG Editions, pg 625
Editions Jouvence, pg 626
Labor et Fides SA, pg 627
Peter Lang AG, pg 627
Limmat Verlag, pg 628
Novalis Media AG, pg 630
Ostschweiz Druck und Verlag, pg 630
Editions Payot Lausanne, pg 631
Ruegger Verlag, pg 633
SAB Schweiz Arbeitsgemeinschaft fuer die Berggebiete, pg 633
Schulthess Polygraphischer Verlag AG, pg 633
Verlag SOI (Schweizerisches Ost-Institut), pg 634
Editions du Tricorne, pg 635
Verlag Die Waage, pg 636
Editions Zoe, pg 638

Syrian Arab Republic

Damascus University Press, pg 638
Institut Francais d'Etudes Arabes de Damas, pg 638

Taiwan, Province of China

Bookman Books Ltd, pg 639
Chu Liu Book Company, pg 639
Chung Hwa Book Co Ltd, pg 639

Chu Hai Publishing (Taiwan) Co Ltd, pg 640
Laureate Book Co Ltd, pg 640
Newton Publishing Company Ltd, pg 641
Shy Mau & Shy Chaur Publishing Co Ltd, pg 641
World Book Co Ltd, pg 642

Tajikistan

Irfon, pg 642

United Republic of Tanzania

East African Publishing House, pg 643
Kisambo Publishers Ltd, pg 643
Ndanda Mission Press, pg 644

Thailand

Suksit Siam Co Ltd, pg 646
Thai Watana Panich Co, Ltd, pg 646
Unesco Regional Office, Asia & the Pacific, pg 646

Togo

Editions Akpagnon, pg 646

Trinidad & Tobago

Inprint Caribbean Ltd, pg 647

Tunisia

Academie Tunisienne des Sciences, des Lettres et des Arts Beit El Hekma, pg 647
Faculte des Sciences Humaines et Sociales de Tunis, pg 648
Publications de la Fondation Temimi pour la Recherche Scientifique et L'Information, pg 648

Turkey

Bilden Bilgisayar, pg 649
Dost Kitabevi Yayinlari, pg 649
Iletisim Yayinlari, pg 650
Isis Yayin Tic ve San Ltd, pg 650
Metis Yayinlari, pg 650
Payel Yayinevi, pg 651
Remzi Kitabevi, pg 651
Saray Medikal Yayin Tic Ltd Sti, pg 651
Varlik Yayinlari AS, pg 652
Kabalci Yayinevi, pg 652

Turkmenistan

Izdatelstvo Turkmenistan, pg 652

Uganda

Centre for Basic Research, pg 652
Fountain Publishers Ltd, pg 652

Ukraine

ASK Ltd, pg 653
Osnovy Publishers, pg 654

United Kingdom

AK Press & Distribution, pg 656
Aldwych Press Ltd, pg 656
Anglo-German Foundation for the Study of Industrial Society, pg 658
Appletree Press Ltd, pg 658
Arnold, pg 659
Arthur James Ltd, pg 660
Ashgate Publishing Ltd, pg 660
The Athlone Press Ltd, pg 661

BAAF Adoption & Fostering, pg 662
Baha'i Publishing Trust, pg 662
Barmarick Publications, pg 663
Batsford Ltd, pg 663
Berg Publishers, pg 664
Berghahn Books Ltd, pg 665
BFI Publishing, pg 665
Blackwell Publishing Ltd, pg 666
Bowerdean Publishing Co Ltd, pg 669
The British Academy, pg 671
The Brown Reference Group PLC, pg 672
Business Monitor International, pg 672
Cambridge University Press, pg 674
Camden Press Ltd, pg 674
Cardiff Academic Press, pg 675
Jon Carpenter Publishing, pg 675
Cassell & Co, pg 675
Causeway Press Ltd, pg 676
Cavendish Publishing Ltd, pg 676
Chadwyck-Healey Ltd, pg 677
Deborah Charles Publications, pg 678
Commonwealth Secretariat, pg 681
James Currey Ltd, pg 685
Dunedin Academic Press, pg 688
Edinburgh University Press Ltd, pg 689
Edition XII, pg 690
Ethics International Press Ltd, pg 692
European Schoolbooks Ltd, pg 692
The Eurospan Group, pg 692
Faber & Faber Ltd, pg 694
Free Association Books Ltd, pg 697
Freedom Press, pg 697
Golden Cockerel Press Ltd, pg 701
Gregg Publishing Co, pg 703
Harvard University Press, pg 705
Holyoake Books, pg 710
ITDG Publishing, pg 715
JAI Press Ltd, pg 715
Karnac Books Ltd, pg 716
King's Fund Publishing, pg 718
Jessica Kingsley Publishers, pg 718
Kluwer Academic/Plenum Publishers, pg 718
Knockabout Comics, pg 718
Lawrence & Wishart, pg 719
Learning Matters Ltd, pg 720
Liverpool University Press, pg 722
Lucis Press Ltd, pg 723
Macmillan Reference Ltd, pg 724
Manchester University Press, pg 724
Adam Matthew Publications, pg 726
McGraw-Hill Publishing Company, pg 726
The Merlin Press Ltd, pg 727
Microform Academic Publishers, pg 728
MIT Press Ltd, pg 728
Motilal (UK) Books of India, pg 729
Multilingual Matters Ltd, pg 729
National Assembly for Wales, pg 730
National Trust, pg 731
Nelson Thornes Ltd, pg 732
Norwood Publishers Ltd, pg 734
Open Gate Press, pg 735
Open University Press, pg 736
Peter Owen Ltd, pg 737
Oxfam, pg 737
Oxford University Press, pg 737
Palgrave Publishers Ltd, pg 737
Pathfinder London, pg 739
Pavilion Publishing (Brighton) Ltd, pg 739
Pearson Education, pg 739

Pearson Education Europe, Mideast & Africa, pg 739
Peepal Tree Press Ltd, pg 740
Pluto Books Ltd, pg 743
Pluto Press, pg 743
The Policy Press, pg 744
Policy Studies Institute (PSI), pg 744
Profile Books Ltd, pg 746
ProQuest Information & Learning, pg 746
Rationalist Press Association, pg 748
RELATE, pg 749
Roundhouse Group, pg 751
Routledge, pg 751
RoutledgeCurzon, pg 751
SAGE Publications Ltd, pg 753
St Pauls Publishing, pg 753
Sangam Books Ltd, pg 754
Saqi Books, pg 754
Scottish Cultural Press, pg 755
Scottish Executive Library & Information Services, pg 755
Shire Publications Ltd, pg 757
The Society of Metaphysicians Ltd, pg 759
Souvenir Press Ltd, pg 759
Speechmark Publishing Ltd, pg 760
Spokesman, pg 760
Sutton Publishing Ltd, pg 762
Taylor & Francis, pg 763
Thoemmes Press, pg 765
Trentham Books Ltd, pg 767
TSO (The Stationery Office), pg 767
UCL Press Ltd, pg 768
University of Wales Press, pg 769
University Presses of California, Columbia & Princeton Ltd, pg 769
Verso, pg 770
Viking, pg 770
Virago Press, pg 770
Westview Press, pg 772
White Cockade Publishing, pg 772
Whiting & Birch Ltd, pg 773
Wordwright Publishing, pg 775
Yale University Press London, pg 776
Zed Books Ltd, pg 776

Uruguay
Ediciones de Juan Darien, pg 777
Editorial Libreria Amalio M Fernandez, pg 777
Fundacion de Cultura Universitaria, pg 777
Nordan-Comunidad, pg 778
Ediciones Trilce, pg 778
Vinten Editor, pg 778

Venezuela
Alfadil Ediciones, pg 778
Monte Avila Editores Latinoamericana CA, pg 779
Fundacion Centro Gumilla, pg 779
Editorial Nueva Sociedad, pg 780
Universidad de los Andes, Consejo de Publicaciones, pg 780
Vadell Hermanos Editores CA, pg 780

Viet Nam
Su That (Truth) Publishing House, pg 781

Zambia
Lundula Publishing House, pg 781
MFK Management Consultants Services, pg 781

Multimedia Zambia, pg 781
University of Zambia Press (UNZA Press), pg 782
Zambia Association for Research & Development (ZARD), pg 782
Zambia Educational Publishing House, pg 782

Zimbabwe
Anvil Press, pg 782
Journal on Social Change, pg 783
National Archives of Zimbabwe, pg 784
Sapes Trust Ltd, pg 784
University of Zimbabwe Publications, pg 784

SPORTS, ATHLETICS

Albania
NL SH, pg 1
State Textbook Publishing House, pg 1

Algeria
Enterprise Nationale du Livre (ENAL), pg 2

Argentina
Editorial Albatros SACI, pg 3
Editorial Caymi SACI, pg 4
Diana Argentina SA, Editorial, pg 5
Ediciones Lidiun, pg 7
Instituto de Publicaciones Navales, pg 8
Ediciones Preescolar SA, pg 8

Australia
ACHPER Inc (Australian Council for Health, Physical Education & Recreation), pg 10
Robert Berthold Photography, pg 14
Bio Concepts Publishing, pg 14
Boobook Publications, pg 15
Galley Press Publishing, pg 23
Kangaroo Press, pg 28
Thomas C Lothian Pty Ltd, pg 29
McGraw-Hill Australia Pty Ltd, pg 31
Oceans Enterprises, pg 34
R & R Publications Pty Ltd, pg 38
Single X Publications, pg 41
University of Queensland Press, pg 45
Wild Publications Pty Ltd, pg 46

Austria
Innverlag + Gatt, pg 52
Oesterreichischer Bundesverlag Gmbh, pg 55
Verlag des Osterr Kneippbundes GmbH, pg 56

Belarus
Belaruskaya Encyklapedyya, pg 62

Belgium
Uitgeverij Contact NV, pg 65
Graton Editeur NV, pg 68
Imprimerie Hayez SPRL, pg 68
Infoboek NV, pg 68
Editeurs de Litterature Biblique, pg 70
Reader's Digest SA, pg 72
Roularta Books NV, pg 72
Sonneville Press (Uitgeverij) VTW, pg 73

Bermuda
The Bermudian Publishing Co, pg 75

Brazil
Action Editora Ltda, pg 76
Ao Livro Tecnico Industria e Comercio Ltda, pg 77
Ars Poetica Editora Ltda, pg 78
ARTMED Editora, pg 78
Companhia Editora Forense, pg 81
Editora Elevacao, pg 81
Editora Globo SA, pg 82
IBRASA (Instituicao Brasileira de Difusao Cultural Ltda), pg 83
Icone Editora Ltda, pg 83
Livraria Nobel S/A, pg 85
Editora Manole Ltda, pg 86
Modulo Editora e Desenvolvimento Educacional Ltda, pg 87
Editora Nova Alexandria Ltda, pg 87
Rede Das Artes (Boccato Editores Collector's), pg 89
Summus Editorial Ltda, pg 91

Bulgaria
Medicina i Fizkultura EOOD, pg 95

Chile
Arrayan Editores, pg 98
Ediciones Mil Hojas Ltda, pg 99

China
Foreign Languages Press, pg 104
Jilin Science & Technology Publishing House, pg 105
People's Sports Publishing House, pg 107

Colombia
Editorial Panamericana, pg 112
Editorial Voluntad SA, pg 113

Costa Rica
Editorial de la Universidad de Costa Rica, pg 116

Croatia
Mladost d d Izdavacku grafiku i informaticku djelatnost, pg 119

Cuba
ISCAH Fructuoso Rodriguez, pg 120
Editorial Oriente, pg 120
Pueblo y Educacion Editorial (PE), pg 121

Czech Republic
Nakladatelstvi Jan Vasut, pg 124
Narodni Muzeum, pg 126
Nakladatelstvi Olympia AS, pg 126

Denmark
Forlaget Hovedland, pg 132

Estonia
Eesti Entsuklopeediakirjastus, pg 139

Finland
Koala-Kustannus Oy, pg 143
Recallmed Oy, pg 144

France
Editions ACLA, pg 145
Editions Amphora SA, pg 146

PUBLISHERS SUBJECT INDEX

Editions Bornemann, pg 150
Bottin SA, pg 151
Editions Calmann-Levy SA, pg 152
Editions Canal, pg 152
Philippe Chancerel Editeur, pg 153
Editions Charles-Lavauzelle SA, pg 153
Le Cherche Midi Editeur, pg 154
Editions Chiron, pg 154
Editions Courrier du Livre, pg 156
Editeurs Crepin-Leblond, pg 156
De Vecchi Editions SA, pg 157
Editions Edisud, pg 159
Edition1, pg 160
EPA (Editions Pratiques Automobiles), pg 161
Federation Francaise de la Randonnee Pedestre, pg 163
Editions Glenat, pg 165
Hachette Livre, pg 167
Hachette Pratiques, pg 167
Jouvence Editions, pg 170
Michel Lafon Publishing, pg 171
Editions Larousse, pg 171
Librarie Maritime Outremer, pg 172
Editions Mango, pg 174
Editions Menges, pg 175
Editions Franck Mercier, pg 175
Presses Universitaires de Grenoble, pg 181
Editions Revue EPS, pg 183
Ulisse Editions, pg 188
Les Editions Vaillant-Miroir-Sprint Publications, pg 188
Editions Vigot Universitaire, pg 188
Editions Vilo SA, pg 189
Editions Philateliques Yvert et Tellier, pg 189

Germany

E Albrecht Verlags-KG, pg 192
AOL-Verlag Frohmut Menze, pg 193
Auer Verlag GmbH, pg 195
Bergverlag Rother GmbH, pg 199
BLV Verlagsgesellschaft mbH, pg 202
Chmielorz GmbH Verlag, pg 208
Copress Verlag, pg 209
Verlag Harri Deutsch, pg 211
Falken-Verlag GmbH, pg 223
Ferd Dummler's Verlag, pg 223
Verlagsgruppe J Fink GmbH & Co KG, pg 224
Gesundheits-Dialog Verlag GmbH, pg 229
Griese Ingolf Wipe Griese, pg 231
Verlag Gruppenpaedagogischer Literatur, pg 231
Heel Verlag GmbH, pg 235
Verlag Karl Hofmann GmbH & Co, pg 238
Felicitas Huebner Verlag, pg 239
Idea Verlag GmbH, pg 240
Jutta Pohl Verlag, pg 244
Kallmeyer'sche Verlagsbuchhandlung GmbH, pg 244
Klartext Verlagsgesellschaft mbH, pg 246
Knowledge Media International, pg 247
Koesler Verlag GmbH, pg 248
Kolibri-Verlag GmbH, pg 249
Limpert Verlag, pg 254
Edition Maritim GmbH, pg 257
Medizinisch-Literarische Verlagsgesellschaft mbH, pg 258
Meyer & Meyer Verlag, pg 260
Moby Dick Verlag, pg 261
Mosaik Verlag GmbH, pg 262
Munzinger-Archiv GmbH Archiv fuer publizistische Arbeit, pg 262

Verlag Stephanie Naglschmid, pg 263
Verlag J Neumann-Neudamm GmbH & Co KG, pg 264
nymphenburger, pg 266
Pala-Verlag GmbH, pg 268
Philippka-Sportverlag, pg 269
Walter Rau Verlag GmbH & Co KG, pg 273
Max Schmidt-Roemhild Verlag, pg 280
Spiridon-Verlags GmbH, pg 284
Sportverlag Berlin GmbH SVB, pg 284
Steiger Verlag, pg 287
Stiebner Verlag GmbH, pg 288
S Toeche-Mittler Verlag GmbH, pg 291
Traditionell Bogenschiessen Verlag Angelika Hornig, pg 292
Verlag W Weinmann, pg 298

Greece

Editions Moressopoulos, pg 310

Hong Kong

Courseguides International Ltd, pg 317
Press Mark Media Ltd, pg 318

Hungary

Medicina Koenyvkiado, pg 323

India

Ananda Publishers Pvt Ltd, pg 328
Dastane Ramchandra & Co, pg 333
Dutta Publishing Co Ltd, pg 333
Gyan Publishing House, pg 335
Orient Paperbacks, pg 344
Regency Publications, pg 346
Reliance Publishing House, pg 346
Rupa & Co, pg 347

Indonesia

PT Bulan Bintang, pg 354

Ireland

The O'Brien Press Ltd, pg 362

Israel

Dekel Publishing House, pg 366

Italy

L'Airone Editrice, pg 375
Arcadia Edizioni Srl, pg 375
Arcanta Aries Gruppo Editoriale, pg 375
Giovanni De Vecchi Editore SpA, pg 384
Ediciclo Editore SRL, pg 386
Edistudio, pg 386
ERGA SNC di Carla Ottino Merli & C (Edizioni Realizzazioni Grafiche - Artigiana), pg 388
Edi.Ermes srl, pg 388
Edizioni GB, pg 390
Ernesto Gremese Editore srl, pg 391
Hermes Edizioni SRL, pg 392
Luni, pg 396
Edizioni Mediterranee SRL, pg 398
Gruppo Ugo Mursia Editore SpA, pg 400
Editoriale Olimpia SpA, pg 401
Edizioni Franco Cosimo Panini, pg 402
Edizioni Quattroventi SNC, pg 404
Societa Stampa Sportiva, pg 408
Sperling e Kupfer Editori SpA, pg 409
Vivalda Editori SRL, pg 412

Jamaica

Ian Randle Publishers Ltd, pg 414

Japan

Aiki News, pg 415
Baseball Magazine-Sha Co Ltd, pg 415
Bunkasha Publishing Co Ltd, pg 415
Dobunshoin Publishers Co, pg 416
Fumaido Publishing Company Ltd, pg 417
Hakutei-Sha, pg 418
Kodansha International Ltd, pg 421
Nagaoka Shoten Co Ltd, pg 423
Nihon-Bunkyo Shuppan (Japan Educational Publishing Co Ltd), pg 423
Nihon Vogue Co Ltd, pg 424
Nippon Hoso Shuppan Kyokai (NHK Publishing), pg 424
Obunsha Co Ltd, pg 424
Sagano Shoin, pg 426
Seibido Shuppan Company Ltd, pg 426
Tokuma Shoten Publishing Co Ltd, pg 429
Tsukiji Shokan Publishing Co, pg 430
Charles E Tuttle Publishing Co Inc, pg 430
Waseda University Press, pg 431
Yama-Kei Publishers Co Ltd, pg 431
Yuki Shobo, pg 431

Kenya

Kenway Publications Ltd, pg 434

Republic of Korea

Pyeong-hwa Chulpansa, pg 442
Samho Music Publishing Co Ltd, pg 442

Latvia

Egmont Latvia SIA, pg 444
Preses Nams, pg 445

Lebanon

Khayat Book and Publishing Co Sarl, pg 446

Liechtenstein

Frank P van Eck Publishers, pg 448

Lithuania

Margi Rastai Publishers, pg 449
Sviesa Publishers, pg 449

Malaysia

Federal Publications Sdn Bhd, pg 455

Maldive Islands

Non-Formal Education Centre, pg 459

Mexico

Editorial Diana SA de CV, pg 464
Edamex SA de CV, pg 464
Editorial Limusa SA de CV, pg 467
Organizacion Cultural LP SA de CV, pg 469
Pearson Educacion de Mexico, SA de CV, pg 470
Sayrols Editorial SA de CV, pg 471
Ediciones Suromex SA, pg 472

Monaco

Les Editions du Rocher, pg 474

Morocco

Les Editions du Journal L' Unite Maghrebine, pg 475

Netherlands

BZZTOH Publishers, pg 480
Elmar BV, pg 482
BV Uitgeversbedrijf Het Goede Boek, pg 482
Uitgeverij Hollandia BV, pg 483
Tirion Uitgevers BV, pg 490

New Caledonia

Savannah Editions SARL, pg 493

New Zealand

David's Marine Books, pg 495
Halcyon Publishing Ltd, pg 496
HarperCollins Publishers (New Zealand) Ltd, pg 497
Hodder Moa Beckett Publishers Ltd, pg 497
Longacre Press, pg 498
Nelson Price Milburn Ltd, pg 499
R P L Books, pg 500
Saint Publishing, pg 501
Shoal Bay Press Ltd, pg 501
Shortland Publications Ltd, pg 501

Nigeria

Ahmadu Bello University Press Ltd, pg 503
Evans Brothers (Nigeria Publishers) Ltd, pg 504

Norway

John Grieg Forlag AS, pg 509

Pakistan

H I Jaffari & Co Publishers, pg 513
Jang Publishers, pg 513

Portugal

Editorial Estampa, Lda, pg 531
Europress Editores e Distribuidores de Publicacoes Lda, pg 531
Impala, pg 532
Editorial Presenca, pg 535
Editora Replicacao Lda, pg 535
Edicoes Talento, pg 536

Romania

The Center for Romanian Studies, pg 539
Editura Teora, pg 542

Russian Federation

BLIC, russko-Baltijskij informaciionnyj centr, AO, pg 544
Izdatelstvo Fizkultura i Sport, pg 545
Interbook-Business AO, pg 545
Izvestia Sovetov Narodnyh Deputatov Russian Federation (RF), pg 545
Ladomir Publishing House, pg 546
Izdatelstvo Molodaya Gvardia, pg 546
Moscow University Press, pg 547
Profizdat, pg 548

Saudi Arabia

Dar Al-Shareff for Publishing & Distribution, pg 550

1113

SUBJECT INDEX — BOOK

Serbia and Montenegro
MiS Sport IGP, pg 552

Slovakia
Slovenske pedagogicke nakladateistvo, pg 560
Sport Publishing House Ltd, pg 561

South Africa
Ashanti Publishing, pg 562
Jonathan Ball Publishers, pg 562
Human & Rousseau (Pty) Ltd, pg 564

Spain
Editorial Acanto SA, pg 570
Editorial 'Alas', pg 571
Editorial Cantabrica SA, pg 575
Comunidad Autonoma de Madrid, Servicio de Documentacion y Publicaciones, pg 578
Dorleta SA, pg 579
Editorial Gedisa SA, pg 584
Editorial Hispano Europea SA, pg 586
Imagen y Deporte, SL, pg 587
Editorial Juventud SA, pg 588
Ediciones Martinez-Roca SA, pg 591
Editorial Mediterrania SL, pg 591
Editorial Molino, pg 592
Editorial Noray, pg 593
OASIS, Producciones Generales de Comunicacion, pg 593
Editorial Paidotribo SL, pg 594
Pleniluni Edicions, pg 596
Ediciones Seyer, pg 599
Editorial Sintes SA, pg 600
Axel Springer Publicaciones, pg 601
Editorial Augusto E Pila Telena SL, pg 601
Tursen, SA, pg 603
Ediciones Tutor SA, pg 603
Editorial De Vecchi SA, pg 604
Xunta de Galicia, pg 605

Sri Lanka
Lake House Investments Ltd, pg 606

Sweden
Bonnier Carlsen Bokforlag AB, pg 610
Johnston & Streiffert Editions, pg 613
Bokforlaget Opal AB, pg 614
Bokforlaget Semic AB, pg 615
Semic Bokforlaget International AB, pg 615
Stroemberg B&T Forlag AB, pg 616

Switzerland
CEC-Cosmic Energy Connections, pg 620
Verlag Harri Deutsch, pg 622
Editions Foma SA, pg 623
Office du Livre SA (Buchhaus AG), pg 630
Ott Verlag Thun, pg 630
Weltrundschau Verlag AG, pg 637

United Republic of Tanzania
Tanzania Publishing House, pg 644

Turkey
Alkim Kitapcilik-Yayimcilik, pg 649

United Kingdom
ABC-CLIO, pg 654
Adlard Coles Nautical, pg 655
Amber Books Ltd, pg 657
Aurum Press Ltd, pg 661
BCA - Book Club Associates, pg 663
A & C Black Publishers Ltd, pg 666
Blackwell Science Ltd, pg 667
Blandford Publishing Ltd, pg 668
Bounty Books, pg 669
Breedon Books Publishing Company Ltd, pg 670
Carlton Publishing Group, pg 675
Cassell & Co, pg 675
Coachwise Ltd, pg 680
Compendium Publishing, pg 681
Countyvise Ltd, pg 683
The Crowood Press Ltd, pg 684
Andre Deutsch Ltd, pg 687
John Donald Publishers Ltd, pg 688
Dorling Kindersley Ltd, pg 688
Eaglemoss Publications Ltd, pg 689
Elliot Right Way Books, pg 690
Express Newspapers, pg 693
Francis Balsom Associates, pg 696
Geiser Productions, pg 699
Gollancz/Witherby, pg 701
Guinness World Records Ltd, pg 703
Haldane Mason Ltd, pg 704
Robert Hale Ltd, pg 704
Hamlyn, pg 704
HarperCollins UK, pg 705
Harvey Map Services Ltd, pg 705
Headline Book Publishing Ltd, pg 706
Health Development Agency, pg 706
Hodder & Stoughton General, pg 709
Hodder Education, pg 709
International Communications, pg 714
The Kenilworth Press Ltd, pg 717
Luath Press Ltd, pg 722
Mainstream Publishing Co (Edinburgh) Ltd, pg 724
Neil Wilson Publishing Ltd, pg 732
Octopus Publishing Group, pg 734
Orion Publishing Group Ltd, pg 736
Parapress Ltd, pg 738
Queen Anne Press, pg 747
Quintet Publishing Ltd, pg 747
Robson Books, pg 750
Roundhouse Group, pg 751
Salamander Books Ltd, pg 753
Seren, pg 756
Shire Publications Ltd, pg 757
Sidgwick & Jackson Ltd, pg 757
Sigma Press, pg 758
Souvenir Press Ltd, pg 759
Spon Press, pg 760
The Sportsman's Press, pg 760
Sutton Publishing Ltd, pg 762
Telegraph Books, pg 764
Transworld Publishers Ltd, pg 766
United Writers Publications Ltd, pg 768
Verulam Publishing Ltd, pg 770
Virgin Publishing Ltd, pg 770
Ward Lock Ltd, pg 771
Weatherbys Allen Ltd, pg 772
Wordwright Publishing, pg 775

TECHNOLOGY

Albania
NL SH, pg 1
State Textbook Publishing House, pg 1

Argentina
Alfagrama SRL ediciones, pg 3
Cesarini Hermanos, pg 4
Editorial Idearium de la Universidad de Mendoza (EDIUM), pg 6
Marymar Ediciones SA, pg 7
Instituto Nacional de Ciencia y Tecnica Hidrica (INCYTH), pg 7
Editorial Troquel SA, pg 9

Australia
Appropriate Technology Development Group (Inc) WA, pg 11
Edward Arnold (Australia) Pty Ltd, pg 12
David Boyce Publishing, pg 16
CSIRO Publishing (Commonwealth Scientific & Industrial Research Organisation), pg 19
Hawker Brownlow, pg 25
Illert Publications, pg 26
Spinifex Press, pg 42
Standards Association of Australia, pg 42
Tertiary Press, pg 43
University of New South Wales Press Ltd, pg 44

Austria
IAEA - International Atomic Energy Agency, pg 52
Metrica Fachverlag u Versandbuchhandlung Ing Bartak, pg 54
Springer-Verlag Wien, pg 58

Azerbaijan
Azernesr, pg 60

Bangladesh
The University Press Ltd, pg 61

Belgium
Documenta CV, pg 66
Presses agronomiques de Gembloux ASBL, pg 72
Editions Techniques et Scientifiques SPRL, pg 73

Bosnia and Herzegovina
Bemust, pg 76

Brazil
Antenna Edicoes Tecnicas Ltda, pg 77
ARTMED Editora, pg 78
Berkeley Brasil Editora Ltda, pg 78
Editora Edgard Blucher Ltda, pg 79
Cadence Publicacoes Internacionais Ltda, pg 79
Empresa Brasileira de Pesquisa Agropecuaria, pg 81
Icone Editora Ltda, pg 83
Livraria Nobel S/A, pg 85
LTC-Livros Tecnicos e Cientificos Editora S/A, pg 85
Cia Editora Nacional, pg 87
Pearson Education Do Brasil, pg 88
Selecoes Eletronicas Editora Ltda, pg 90
34 Literatura S/C Ltda, pg 91

Bulgaria
Ciela Publishing House, pg 93

Cameroon
Centre d'Edition et de Production pour l'Enseignement et la Recherche (CEPER), pg 98

Chile
Arrayan Editores, pg 98
Ediciones Cieplan, pg 99
Ediciones Universitarias de Valparaiso, pg 100

China
Chemical Industry Press, pg 101
China Agriculture Press, pg 102
China Machine Press (CMP), pg 102
China Ocean Press, pg 102
Chongqing University Press, pg 103
East China University of Science & Technology Press, pg 104
Encyclopedia of China Publishing House, pg 104
Fudan University Press, pg 104
Fujian Science & Technology Publishing House, pg 104
Heilongjiang Science & Technology Press, pg 105
Higher Education Press, pg 105
International Academic Publishers (IAP), pg 105
Jiangsu Science & Technology Publishing House, pg 105
Jilin Science & Technology Publishing House, pg 105
Metallurgical Industry Press (MIP), pg 106
National Defence Industry Press, pg 106
New Times Press, pg 106
Patent Documentation Publishing House, pg 106
Printing Industry Publishing House, pg 107
Science Press, pg 107
Shandong Science & Technology Press, pg 107
Shandong University Press, pg 108
Shanghai Scientific & Technical Publishers, pg 108
Sichuan Science & Technology Publishing House, pg 108
Tianjin Science & Technology Publishing House, pg 108
Tsinghua University Press, pg 109
Zhejiang University Press, pg 109

Colombia
Editora Guadalupe Ltda, pg 111
McGraw-Hill Colombia, pg 112
Tercer Mundo Editores SA, pg 113

The Democratic Republic of the Congo
Presses Universitaires du Zaiire (PUZ), pg 114

Costa Rica
Centro Agronomico Tropical de Investigacion y Ensenanza (CATIE), pg 115
Instituto Interamericano de Cooperacion para la Agricultura (IICA), pg 115
Editorial Tecnologica de Costa Rica, pg 116

Cuba
Instituto de Informacion Cientifica y Tecnologica (IDICT), pg 120
Pueblo y Educacion Editorial (PE), pg 121

PUBLISHERS SUBJECT INDEX

Czech Republic
Grada Publishing, pg 123

Denmark
Forlaget for Faglitteratur A/S, pg 131
Syddansk Universitetsforlag, pg 135
Systime, pg 135

Dominican Republic
Pontificia Universidad Catolica Madre y Maestra, pg 136

Ecuador
CIESPAL (Centro Internacional de Estudios Superiores de Comunicacion para America Latina), pg 136

Estonia
Eesti Entsuklopeediakirjastus, pg 139

Ethiopia
Addis Ababa University Press, pg 140

France
Editions J B Bailliere, pg 149
CEP Editions, pg 153
Cepadues Editions SA, pg 153
CTIF (Center Technique Industriel de la Fonderie), pg 156
La Documentation Francaise, pg 158
Les Editions ESF, pg 160
EDP Sciences, pg 161
Editions Entente, pg 161
Librairie Artheme Fayard, pg 163
Institut Francais de Recherche pour l'Exploitation de la Mer (IFREMER), pg 164
Futuribles SARL, pg 164
Groupe de Recherche et d'Echanges Technologiques (GRET), pg 166
Groupe Express-Expansion, pg 166
Hermann editeurs des Sciences et des Arts SA, pg 167
IRD Editions, pg 169
Editions Larousse, pg 171
Editions Lavoisier, pg 171
LT Editions-Jacques Lanore, pg 173
Editions du Moniteur, pg 176
Payot & Rivages, pg 179
Polytechnica SA, pg 180
Selection du Reader's Digest SA, pg 184
Editions Selection J Jacobs SA, pg 184
Editions Technip SA, pg 187
Terre Vivante, pg 187

Germany
Autovision Verlag Guenther & Co, pg 196
Verlag Dr Albert Bartens KG, pg 197
Bertelsmann Lexikon Verlag GmbH, pg 200
Beuth Verlag GmbH, pg 200
Oscar Brandstetter Verlag GmbH & Co KG, pg 204
Buchverlag Junge Welt GmbH, pg 205
Cornelsen Verlag GmbH & Co OHG, pg 210
Deutscher Verlag fur Grundstoffindustrie GmbH, pg 213
Deutscher Wirtschaftsdienst John von Freyend GmbH, pg 214
Ecomed Verlagsgesellschaft AG & Co KG, pg 218
Elektor-Verlag GmbH, pg 219
Eppinger-Verlag OHG, pg 220
Ernst, Wilhelm & Sohn, Verlag Architektur und technische Wissenschaft GmbH & Co, pg 221
Fachverlag Schiele & Schoen GmbH, pg 223
Franz Ferzak World & Space Publications, pg 224
Franckh-Kosmos Verlags-GmbH & Co, pg 226
Huss-Medien GmbH, pg 240
Huthig GmbH & Co KG, pg 240
Idea Verlag GmbH, pg 240
Konradin-Verlagsgruppe, pg 249
Institut fuer Landes- und Stadtentwicklungsforschung des Landes Nordrhein-Westfalen, pg 251
Meisenbach Verlag GmbH, pg 258
Moby Dick Verlag, pg 261
C F Mueller Verlag, Huethig Gmb H & Co, pg 262
R Oldenbourg Verlag GmbH, pg 267
Polygraph Verlag GmbH, pg 271
Rationalisierungs-Kuratorium der Deutschen Wirtschaft eV (RKW), pg 273
Sigloch Edition Helmut Sigloch GmbH & Co KG, pg 283
Spektrum der Wissenschaft Verlagsgesellschaft mbH, pg 284
Springer Science+Business Media GmbH & Co KG, pg 284
Verlag Stahleisen GmbH, pg 286
Verlag H Stam GmbH, pg 286
B G Teubner Verlag, pg 290
Tuduv Verlagsgesellschaft mbH, pg 292
TUeV-Verlag GmbH, pg 293
VDI Verlag GmbH, pg 294
Verlag fur Schweissen und Verwandte Verfahren, pg 295
Verlag Moderne Industrie AG & Co KG, pg 295
Friedr Vieweg & Sohn Verlag, pg 296
WEKA Firmengruppe GmbH & Co KG, pg 298

Ghana
Building & Road Research Institute (BRRI), pg 303
Ghana Publishing Corporation, pg 304

Greece
Chrysi Penna - Golden Pen Books, pg 306
Technical Chamber of Greece, pg 312

Guinea-Bissau
Instituto Nacional de Estudos e Pesquisa (INEP), pg 314

Hong Kong
Business & Industrial Publication Co Ltd, pg 315
Electronic Technology Publishing Co Ltd, pg 317
Modern Electronic & Computing Publishing Co Ltd, pg 318
Vision Pub Co Ltd, pg 320

Hungary
Foldmuvelesugyi Miniszterium Muszaki Intezet, pg 321
Mueszaki Koenyvkiado Ltd, pg 323

India
Agricole Publishing Academy, pg 327
Allied Book Centre, pg 328
Asia Pacific Business Press Inc, pg 328
Atma Ram & Sons, pg 329
Authorspress, pg 329
S Chand & Co Ltd, pg 331
The Christian Literature Society, pg 332
IBD Publisher & Distributors, pg 336
International Book Distributors, pg 338
Khanna Publishers, pg 339
Law Publishers, pg 340
Multitech Publishing Co, pg 342
National Institute of Industrial Research (NIIR), pg 343
Publications & Information Directorate, CSIR, pg 345
Reliance Publishing House, pg 346
Researchco Reprints, pg 347
Samkaleen Prakashan, pg 348
Scientific Book Agency, pg 348
Sita Books & Periodicals Pvt Ltd, pg 349
Small Industry Research Institute (SIRI), pg 349
Somaiya Publications Pvt Ltd, pg 349
South Asian Publishers Pvt Ltd, pg 350
Sterling Information Technologies, pg 350
Sterling Publishers Pvt Ltd, pg 350
Sultan Chand & Sons Pvt Ltd, pg 350
Vikas Publishing House Pvt Ltd, pg 352
Viva Books Pvt Ltd, pg 352

Indonesia
Andi Offset, pg 353
Bhratara Karya Aksara, pg 354
PT Bulan Bintang, pg 354
Gramedia, pg 355
Institut Teknologi Bandung, pg 355
Yayasan Obor Indonesia, pg 357

Italy
Apimondia, pg 375
BeMa, pg 377
Casa Editrice Libraria Ulrico Hoepli SpA, pg 380
Ciranna - Roma, pg 382
CLUT Editrice, pg 383
Edizioni Cremonese SRL, pg 383
DEI Tipographia del Genio Civile, pg 384
Di Baio Editore SpA, pg 385
Esselibri, pg 388
IHT Gruppo Editoriale SRL, pg 393
L Japadre Editore, pg 394
Levrotto e Bella Libreria Editrice Universitaria SAS, pg 395
Editrice Liguria SNC di Norberto Sabatelli & C, pg 395
Masson SpA, pg 397
Editoriale Olimpia SpA, pg 401
Pitagora Editrice SRL, pg 403
Rara Istituto Editoriale di Bibliofilia e Reprints, pg 405
Red/Studio Redazionale, pg 405
Editrice San Marco SRL, pg 407
Edizioni Scientifiche Italiane, pg 407
Editoriale Scienza, pg 407
Tecniche Nuove SpA, pg 410

Japan
Chijin Shokan Co Ltd, pg 416
CMC Publishing Co Ltd, pg 416
Corona Publishing Co Ltd, pg 416
Hokkaido University Press, pg 418
Kaibundo Shuppan, pg 420
Kogyo Chosakai Publishing Co Ltd, pg 421
Koseisha-Koseikaku Co Ltd, pg 422
Kyoritsu Shuppan Co Ltd, pg 422
Mita Press, Mita Industrial Co Ltd, pg 422
Morikita Shuppan Co Ltd, pg 423
Nankodo Co Ltd, pg 423
Nensho-Sha, pg 423
Nikkagiren Shuppan-Sha (JUSE Press Ltd), pg 424
The Nikkan Kogyo Shimbun Ltd, pg 424
Nippon Hoso Shuppan Kyokai (NHK Publishing), pg 424
Saela Shobo (Librairie Ca et La), pg 425
Sangyo-Tosho Publishing Co Ltd, pg 426
Seibundo Shinkosha Publishing Co Ltd, pg 426
Seizando-Shoten Publishing Co Ltd, pg 427
Shokabo Publishing Co Ltd, pg 428
Shufu-to-Seikatsu Sha Ltd, pg 428
Takahashi Shoten Co Ltd, pg 429
Tokai University Press, pg 429
Universal Academy Press, Inc, pg 430

Kenya
Academy Science Publishers, pg 432
African Centre for Technology Studies (ACTS), pg 433

Democratic People's Republic of Korea
Korea Science and Encyclopedia Publishing House, pg 436

Republic of Korea
Cheong-mun-gag Publishing Co, pg 438
Chung Rim Publishing Co Ltd, pg 438
Dai Hak Publishing Co, pg 438
Pan Korea Book Corporation, pg 442
PoChinChai Printing Co Ltd, pg 442
Yonsei University Press, pg 444

Lebanon
Librairie du Liban Publishers (Sal), pg 446

Lithuania
Klaipedos Universiteto Leidykla, pg 449

Macau
Museu Maritimo, pg 452

Malaysia
Pustaka Cipta Sdn Bhd, pg 458
Tropical Press Sdn Bhd, pg 459

SUBJECT INDEX   BOOK

Penerbit Universiti Teknologi Malaysia, pg 459
Utusan Publications & Distributors Sdn Bhd, pg 459

Mexico

Aconcagua Ediciones y Publicaciones SA, pg 461
Alfaomega Grupo Editor SA de CV, pg 462
Colegio de Postgraduados en Ciencias Agricolas, pg 463
Compania Editorial Continental SA de CV, pg 463
Editorial Limusa SA de CV, pg 467
Pearson Educacion de Mexico, SA de CV, pg 470
Universidad Nacional Autonoma de Mexico (National University of Mexico), pg 472

Netherlands

B M Israel BV, pg 478
Delft University Press, pg 481
Elsevier Science BV, pg 482
Uitgeverij De Fontein BV, pg 482
Hagen & Stam Uitgeverij Ten, pg 483
IOS Press BV, pg 484
Kluwer Academic Publishers, pg 484
Kluwer Bedrijfswetenschappen, pg 485
Kluwer Technische Boeken BV, pg 485
Uitgeverij Lemma BV, pg 485
Pearson Education Netherlands, pg 487
Samsom BedrijfsInformatie BV, pg 488
Swets & Zeitlinger Publishers, pg 489
Twente University Press, pg 490
V S P International Science Publishers, pg 491

New Zealand

Nelson Price Milburn Ltd, pg 499
New House Publishers Ltd, pg 499
Southern Press Ltd, pg 501

Nigeria

Ahmadu Bello University Press Ltd, pg 503
Evans Brothers (Nigeria Publishers) Ltd, pg 504
Goldland Business Co Ltd, pg 505
Ibadan University Press, pg 505
Longman Nigeria Plc, pg 505

Norway

F Bruns Bokhandel og Forlag A/S, pg 508
Forlaget Fag og Kultur, pg 509
Vett & Viten AS, pg 511

Paraguay

Instituto de Ciencias de la Computacion (NCR), pg 516

Peru

Instituto de Estudios Peruanos, pg 517

Philippines

Salesiana Publishers Inc, pg 521
University of the Philippines Press, pg 521

Poland

Wydawnictwa Naukowo-Techniczne, pg 524
Polish Scientific Publishers PWN, pg 525
Oficyna Wydawnicza Politechniki Wroclawskiej, pg 525

Portugal

Edicoes Cetop, pg 529
Constancia Editores, SA, pg 530
Publicacoes Europa-America Lda, pg 531
Chaves Ferreira Publicacoes SA, pg 531
Livraria Lopes Da Silva-Editora de M Moreira Soares Rocha Lda, pg 533

Puerto Rico

McGraw-Hill Intermericana del Caribe, Inc, pg 537

Romania

Editura Clusium, pg 539
Editura Excelsior Art, pg 539
Editura Gryphon, pg 540
Editura Junimea, pg 540
Pallas-Akademia Editura, pg 541
Editura Signata, pg 542
Editura Tehnica, pg 542
Editura Teora, pg 542
Editura de Vest, pg 543

Russian Federation

N E Bauman Moscow State Technical University Publishers, pg 544
Energoatomizdat, pg 544
FGUP Izdatelstvo Mashinostroenie, pg 544
INFRA-M Izdatel'skij dom, pg 545
Izdatelstvo Lenizdat, pg 546
Izdatelstvo Metallurgiya, pg 546
Izdatelstvo Mir, pg 546
Nauka Publishers, pg 547
Izdatelstvo Sudostroenie, pg 549
Izdatelstvo Vysshaya Shkola, pg 549

Saudi Arabia

King Saud University, pg 550

Serbia and Montenegro

Savez Inzenjera i Tehnicara Jugoslavije, pg 553

Singapore

APAC Publishers Services Pte Ltd, pg 554
Maruzen Asia (Pte) Ltd, pg 557
Newscom Pte Ltd, pg 557
Reed Elsevier, South East Asia, pg 557
World Scientific Publishing Co Pte Ltd, pg 559

Slovakia

Technicka Univerzita, pg 561
VEDA (Vydavatel'stvo Slovenskej akademie vied), pg 561

South Africa

Educum Publishers Ltd, pg 563
Heinemann Publishers (Pty) Ltd, pg 564
Jacklin Enterprises (Pty) Ltd, pg 565

Nasou Via Afrika, pg 567
Shuter & Shooter (Pty) Ltd, pg 568

Spain

AMV Ediciones, pg 572
Ediciones Bellaterra SA, pg 574
Ediciones Daly S L, pg 578
Editorial Donostiarra SA, pg 579
Edebe, pg 580
Fondo de Cultura Economica de Espana, SL, pg 583
Fragua Editorial, pg 583
Ediciones Gestio 2000 SA, pg 585
Editorial Gustavo Gili SA, pg 585
Grupo Editorial CEAC SA, pg 586
Editorin Laiovento SL, pg 588
McGraw-Hill/Interamericana de Espana SAU, pg 591
Mundi-Prensa Libros SA, pg 592
Editorial la Muralla SA, pg 592
Ediciones Omega SA, pg 594
Editorial Paraninfo SA, pg 595
Ediciones Piramide SA, pg 596
Progensa, pg 597
Editorial Tecnos SA, pg 601
Ediciones A Madrid Vicente, pg 605
Ediciones Vulcano, pg 605

Sudan

Khartoum University Press, pg 608

Sweden

Akademiforlaget Goteborgslitteratur, pg 609
ITK Laromedel AB, pg 612
Kungl Ingenjoersvetenskapsakademien (IVA), pg 613
Liber AB, pg 613
Studentlitteratur AB, pg 616

Switzerland

Verlag Harri Deutsch, pg 622
Presses Polytechniques et Universitaires Romandes, PPUR, pg 631
Vogt-Schild Ag, Druck und Verlag, pg 636
World Meteorological Organization, pg 637

Taiwan, Province of China

Grimm Press Ltd, pg 640
Ho-Chi Book Publishing Co, pg 640
Hsiao Yuan Publication Co, Ltd, pg 640
Petroleum Information Publishing Co, pg 641
San Min Book Co Ltd, pg 641
Wu Nan Book Co Ltd, pg 642

Tajikistan

Irfon, pg 642

Trinidad & Tobago

Caribbean Telecommunications Union, pg 647

Turkey

Caglayan Kitabevi, pg 649

Ukraine

Urozaj, pg 654

United Kingdom

Advisory Unit: Computers in Education, pg 655
Artech House, pg 659
Aslib, The Association for Information Management, pg 660
British Educational Communication & Technology Agency (BECTA), pg 671
Causeway Press Ltd, pg 676
Centre for Alternative Technology, pg 677
Commonwealth Secretariat, pg 681
Computer Step, pg 681
Elsevier Ltd, pg 691
ERA Technology Ltd, pg 692
The Eurospan Group, pg 692
Facet Publishing, pg 694
Forbes Publications Ltd, pg 696
Foulsham Publishers, pg 696
Haynes Publishing, pg 706
Hobsons, pg 709
Institute of Food Science & Technology, pg 713
Institute of Physics Publishing, pg 713
Institution of Electrical Engineers, pg 713
Intercept Ltd, pg 714
ITDG Publishing, pg 715
Adam Matthew Publications, pg 726
Merrow Publishing Co Ltd, pg 727
Micelle Press, pg 727
MIT Press Ltd, pg 728
Motor Racing Publications Ltd, pg 729
Nelson Thornes Ltd, pg 732
New Cavendish Books, pg 732
NMS Enterprises Ltd - Publishing, pg 733
Palgrave Publishers Ltd, pg 737
Pearson Education Europe, Mideast & Africa, pg 739
PIRA Intl, pg 742
Prism Press Book Publishers Ltd, pg 745
Professional Engineering Publishing Ltd, pg 745
Qualum Publishing, pg 746
Quintet Publishing Ltd, pg 747
Rapra Technology Ltd, pg 748
Research Studies Press Ltd (RSP), pg 749
The Salariya Book Co Ltd, pg 753
Sangam Books Ltd, pg 754
Sheffield Academic Press Ltd, pg 757
Skoob Russell Square, pg 758
Smith-Gordon & Co Ltd, pg 758
Sutton Publishing Ltd, pg 762
Taylor Graham Publishing, pg 764
Thames & Hudson Ltd, pg 764
Trentham Books Ltd, pg 767
TSO (The Stationery Office), pg 767
Two-Can Publishing Ltd, pg 768
UCL Press Ltd, pg 768
VNU Business Publications, pg 770
Wiley Europe Ltd, pg 773
WIT Press, pg 774
Witherby & Co Ltd, pg 775
Woodhead Publishing Ltd, pg 775

Uruguay

Editorial Arca SRL, pg 776
Ediciones Trilce, pg 778

PUBLISHERS

Venezuela
Editorial Nueva Sociedad, pg 780
Universidad de los Andes, Consejo de Publicaciones, pg 780
Vadell Hermanos Editores CA, pg 780

Viet Nam
Science & Technics Publishing House, pg 780

Zimbabwe
University of Zimbabwe Publications, pg 784

THEOLOGY

Albania
NL SH, pg 1

Argentina
Bonum Editorial SACI, pg 4
Editorial Ciudad Nueva de la Sefoma, pg 4
Editorial Claretiana, pg 4
EUDEBA (Editorial Universitaria de Buenos Aires), pg 5
Editorial Galerna SRL, pg 6
Editorial Guadalupe, pg 6
San Pablo, pg 9

Australia
Aletheia Publishing, pg 11
Bible Society in Australia National Headquarters, pg 14
Bridgeway Publications, pg 16
Catholic Institute of Sydney, pg 17
Church Archivists Press, pg 18
Covenanter Press, pg 18
Crossroad Distributors Pty Ltd, pg 18
Desbooks Pty Ltd, pg 20
Gnostic Editions, pg 23
Granrott Press, pg 24
Jesuit Publications, pg 27
New Creation Publications Ministries & Resource Centre, pg 33
St Pauls Publications, pg 40
Spaniel Books, pg 41
Spectrum Publications, pg 41
Uniting Education, pg 44

Austria
Ennsthaler GesmbH & Co KG, pg 50
Otto Mueller Verlag, pg 54
Mueller-Speiser Wissenschaftlicher Verlag, pg 54
Wolfgang Neugebauer Verlag GmbH, pg 54
Passagen Verlag GmbH, pg 56
Verlag Anton Pustet, pg 56
Resch Verlag, pg 56
Verlag St Gabriel, pg 57
Andreas Schnider Verlags-Atelier, pg 57
Edition Va Bene, pg 59

Belgium
Artel, pg 63
Editions Lessius ASBL, pg 70
Leuven University Press, pg 70
Editions Lumen Vitae ASBL, pg 70
Nauwelaerts Edition SA, pg 71
Uitgeverij Peeters Leuven (Belgie), pg 71
Publications des Facultes Universitaires Saint Louis, pg 72
Vita, pg 74

Brazil
Ars Poetica Editora Ltda, pg 78
Editora Cidade Nova, pg 80
Concordia Editora Ltda, pg 80
Editora Elevacao, pg 81
Fundacao Sao Paulo, EDUC, pg 82
Horus Editora Ltda, pg 83
Editora Mundo Cristao, pg 87
Editora Nova Fronteira SA, pg 87
Olho D'Agua Comercio e Servicos Editoriais Ltda, pg 87
Pallas Editora e Distribuidora Ltda, pg 88
Paulinas Editorial, pg 88
Paulus Editora, pg 88
Editora Sinodal, pg 90

Bulgaria
Kralica MAB, pg 95
Nov Covek Publishing House, pg 96
Sila & Zivot, pg 97

Cameroon
Presses Universitaires d'Afrique, pg 98

Chile
Congregacion Paulinas - Hijas de San Pablo, pg 99

Colombia
Consejo Episcopal Latinoamericano (CELAM), pg 110

Costa Rica
Editorial DEI (Departamento Ecumenico de Investigaciones), pg 115
Ediciones Promesa, pg 116

Croatia
Krscanska sadasnjost, pg 118
Znaci Vremena, Institut Za Istrazivanje Biblije, pg 119

Czech Republic
Barrister & Principal, pg 122
Ceska Biblicka Spolecnost, pg 123
Kalich SRO, pg 124
Karmelitanske Nakladatelstvi, pg 124

Denmark
Aarhus Universitetsforlag, pg 128
Forlaget Hovedland, pg 132
Scandinavia Publishing House, pg 134
Unitas Forlag, pg 135

Dominican Republic
Pontificia Universidad Catolica Madre y Maestra, pg 136

Ecuador
Ediciones Abya-Yala, pg 136
Pontificia Universidad Catolica del Ecuador, Centro de Publicaciones, pg 137

Egypt (Arab Republic of Egypt)
Dar Al-Thakafia Publishing, pg 138

El Salvador
UCA Editores, pg 138

Finland
Herattaja-yhditsys Ry, pg 142
Kustannus Oy Uusi Tie, pg 143
Yliopistopaino/Helsinki University Press, pg 145

France
Armenia Editions, pg 147
Beauchesne Editeur, pg 149
Editions Buchet-Chastel Pierre Zech Editeur, pg 151
Editions du Chalet, pg 153
Editions de Compostelle, pg 155
Desclee de Brouwer SA, pg 158
Institut d'Etudes Augustiniennes, pg 162
Federation d'Activities Culturelles, Fac Editions, pg 163
Librairie Fischbacher, International Art Book Distribution (import-export), pg 163
Les Editions Franciscaines SA, pg 164
Les Editions Gabalda et Cie, pg 164
P Lethielleux Editions, pg 171
LLB France (Ligue pour la Lecture de la Bible), pg 173
Editions Mediaspaul, pg 175
Peeters-France, pg 179
Editions Saint-Paul SA, pg 183
Les Editions de la Source Sarl, pg 186
Librairie Pierre Tequi et Editions Tequi, pg 187

Germany
A Francke Verlag (Tubingen und Basel), pg 190
Agentur des Rauhen Hauses Hamburg GmbH, pg 191
Aschendorffsche Verlagsbuchhandlung GmbH & Co KG, pg 194
Auer Verlag GmbH, pg 195
Aussaat Verlag, pg 195
Bautz Traugott, pg 198
Ludwig Bechauf Verlag, pg 198
Verlag C H Beck oHG, pg 198
Berliner Wissenschafts-Verlag GmbH (BWV), pg 199
Beuth Verlag GmbH, pg 200
Verlag Die Blaue Eule, pg 202
Verlag Hermann Boehlaus Nachfolger Weimar GmbH & Co, pg 203
Bonifatius GmbH Druck-Buch-Verlag, pg 203
R Brockhaus Verlag, pg 204
Brunnen-Verlag GmbH, pg 205
Butzon & Bercker GmbH, pg 206
Calwer Verlag GmbH, pg 207
Chr Belser AG fur Verlagsgeschaefte und Co KG, pg 208
Christusbruderschaft Selbitz ev, Abt Verlag, pg 209
Claudius Verlag, pg 209
Concordia-Buchhandlung & Verlag, pg 209
Duncker und Humblot GmbH, pg 217
Echter Wurzburg Frankische Gesellschaftsdruckerei und Verlag GmbH, pg 217
Elpis Verlag GmbH, pg 219
EOS Verlag der Benefiktiner der Erzabtei St. Ottilien, pg 220
Erlanger Verlag Fuer Mission und Okumene, pg 220
Verlagsgesellschaft des Erziehungsvereins GmbH, pg 221
Evangelische Verlagsanstalt GmbH, pg 222
Evangelischer Presseverband fuer Bayern eV, pg 222
Verlag der Francke Buchhandlung GmbH, pg 226
Franz-Sales-Verlag, pg 226
Friedrich Frommann Verlag, pg 227
Genius Verlag, pg 228
Klaus Gerth Musikverlag, pg 229
Walter de Gruyter GmbH & Co KG, pg 231
Guetersloher Verlagshaus, pg 232
Verlag des Gustav-Adolf-Werks, pg 232
Gutersloher Verlaghaus GmbH /Chr Kaiser/Kiefel/Quell, pg 232
Verlag Herder GmbH & Co KG, pg 236
Anton Hiersemann, Verlag, pg 237
Iudicium Verlag GmbH, pg 242
Jan Thorbecke Verlag GmbH & Co, pg 243
Johannes Verlag Einsiedeln, Freiburg, pg 243
Johannis, pg 243
Katzmann Verlag KG, pg 245
Verlag Valentin Koerner GmbH, pg 248
W Kohlhammer GmbH, pg 248
Lahn-Verlag GmbH, pg 251
Peter Lang GmbH Europaeischer Verlag der Wissenschaften, pg 252
Liebenzeller Mission, GmbH, Abt. Verlag, pg 254
Martha Lindner Verlags-GmbH, pg 254
Logos Verlag GmbH, pg 255
Lutherische Verlagsgesellschaft mbH, pg 256
Lutherisches Verlagshaus GmbH, pg 256
Annemarie Maeger, pg 256
Matthes und Seitz Verlag GmbH, pg 258
Matthias-Gruenewald-Verlag GmbH, pg 258
Medien-Verlag Bernhard Gregor GmbH, pg 258
Mohr Siebeck, pg 261
Verlag Neue Stadt GmbH, pg 264
Oekumenischer Verlag Dr R-F Edel, pg 266
Georg Olms Verlag AG, pg 267
Oros Verlag, pg 267
Pahl-Rugenstein Verlag Nachfolger-GmbH, pg 267
Patmos Verlag GmbH & Co KG, pg 268
Paulinus Verlag GmbH, pg 268
Piper Verlag GmbH, pg 270
Projektion J Buch- und Musikverlag GmbH, pg 272
Verlag Friedrich Pustet GmbH & Co Kg, pg 272
Saatkorn-Verlag GmbH, pg 277
Verlag Schnell und Steiner GmbH, pg 281
Ferdinand Schoeningh Verlag GmbH, pg 281
Schwabenverlag Aktiengesellschaft, pg 282
Scientia Verlag und Antiquariat Schilling OHG, pg 282
Sternberg-Verlag bei Ernst Franz, pg 288
Suin Buch-Verlag, pg 289
Guenter Albert Ulmer Verlag, pg 293
Vandenhoeck & Ruprecht, pg 294
Vereinte Evangelische Mission, Abt Verlag, pg 295

Vier Tuerme GmbH Verlag Klosterbetriebe, pg 295
VJK Verlag Josef Knecht Carolusdruckerei GmbH, pg 296
Waxmann Verlag GmbH, pg 297
Erich Wewel Verlag GmbH, pg 299
Wichern Verlag GmbH, pg 299
Wolgang Fietkau, pg 301

Ghana
Asempa Publishers, pg 303

Greece
Akritas, pg 305
Alamo Hellas, pg 305
Apostoliki Diakonia tis Ekklisias tis Hellados, pg 305
Ekdotikos Oikos Adelfon Kyriakidi A E, pg 307
Denise Harvey, pg 308
D Papadimas, pg 311

Holy See (Vatican City State)
Biblioteca Apostolica Vaticana, pg 314
Libreria Editrice Vaticana, pg 315

Hong Kong
Chinese Christian Literature Council Ltd, pg 316
Philopsychy Press, pg 318

Hungary
Atlantisz Kiado, pg 320
Marton Aron Kiado Publishing House, pg 323
Osiris Kiado, pg 323

India
Asian Educational Services, pg 329
Asian Trading Corporation, pg 329
Indian Society for Promoting Christian Knowledge (ISPCK), pg 337
Rebel Publishing House Pvt Ltd, pg 346
Sree Rama Publishers, pg 350
Theosophical Publishing House, pg 351

Indonesia
Nusa Indah, pg 356

Ireland
Cathedral Books Ltd, pg 358
The Columba Book Service, pg 359
The Columba Press, pg 359
Dominican Publications, pg 359
Emerald Publications, pg 359
Four Courts Press Ltd, pg 360
Veritas Co Ltd, pg 364

Israel
Breslov Research Institute, pg 365
DAT Publications, pg 366
Gefen Publishing House Ltd, pg 367
Hakibbutz Hameuchad Publishing House Ltd, pg 367
Rav Kook Institute, pg 371

Italy
Adea Edizioni, pg 374
Edizioni ARES, pg 376
Edizioni Cantagalli, pg 379
Edizioni Carmelitane, pg 380
Centro Biblico, pg 381
Centro Editoriale Valtortiano SRL, pg 381

Citta Nuova Editrice, pg 382
Cittadella Editrice, pg 382
Claudiana Editrice, pg 382
Edizioni Cultura della Pace, pg 383
Edizioni Dehoniane Bologna (EDB), pg 384
Edizioni Dehoniane, pg 384
Edizioni Qiqajon, pg 387
Edizioni Studio Domenicano (ESD), pg 387
Elle Di Ci - Libreria Dottrina Cristiana, pg 387
Biblioteca Francescana, pg 389
Frati Editori di Quaracchi, pg 389
Glossa, pg 391
Piero Gribaudi Editore, pg 391
Herder Editrice e Libreria, pg 392
In Dialogo, pg 393
Editoriale Jaca Book SpA, pg 394
Editrice LAS, pg 394
Liguori Editore SRL, pg 395
Casa Editrice Marietti SpA, pg 397
Editrice Massimo SAS di Crespi Cesare e C, pg 397
Memorie Domenicane, pg 398
Nuova Coletti Editore Roma, pg 401
Il Nuovo Melangolo, pg 401
Leo S Olschki, pg 401
Edizioni Piemme SpA, pg 403
Editrice Queriniana, pg 404
Libreria Editrice Rogate (LER), pg 406
Rubbettino Editore, pg 406
Sardini Editrice, pg 407
Edizioni Segno SRL, pg 407
SEMAR Publishers SRL, pg 408
Servitium, pg 408
Edizioni Rosminiane Sodalitas, pg 408
Edizioni del Teresianum, pg 410
Edizioni Thyrus SRL, pg 410
Urbaniana University Press, pg 411
Vivere In SRL, pg 412

Jamaica
Eureka Press Ltd, pg 413

Kenya
Action Publishers, pg 433
Evangel Publishing House, pg 433
Gaba Publications Amecea, Pastoral Institute, pg 434
Heinemann Kenya Ltd (EAEP), pg 434
Paulines Publications-Africa, pg 435
Shirikon Publishers, pg 436
Uzima Press Ltd, pg 436

Republic of Korea
Hanul Publishing Co, pg 439
Kukmin Doseo Publishing Co Ltd, pg 440
St Pauls, pg 442

Latvia
Patmos, izdevnieciba, pg 445

Lebanon
Dar-El-Machreq Sarl, pg 446
Librairie Orientale sal, pg 446

Lithuania
Klaipedos Universiteto Leidykla, pg 449
Vaga Ltd, pg 450

Luxembourg
Varkki Verghese, pg 452

Mexico
Ediciones CUPSA, Centro de Comunicacion Cultural CUPSA, AC, pg 463
El Colegio de Michoacan A C, pg 464
Editorial Jus SA de CV, pg 467
Phillip Richard Conover Lazo, pg 467
Ediciones Promesa, SA de CV, pg 470

Netherlands
Uitgeverij Ambo BV, pg 477
APA (Academic Publishers Associated), pg 477
Erven J Bijleveld, pg 479
Boekencentrum BV, pg 479
Brill Academic Publishers, pg 479
Buijten en Schipperheijn BV Drukkerij en Uitgeversmaatschappij, pg 480
Callenbach BV, pg 480
Uitgeverij Ten Have, pg 483
HES & De Graaf Publishers BV, pg 483
Holland University Press BV (APA), pg 483
Uitgeverij Meinema, pg 485
Narratio Theologische Uitgeverij, pg 486
Philo Press (APA), pg 487
De Prom, pg 488
Servire BV Uitgevers, pg 489
Telos Boeken, pg 490
Tilburg University Press, pg 490
Tirion Uitgevers BV, pg 490
Uitgeverij Van Wijnen, pg 491
VU Boekhandel/Uitgeverij BV, pg 492
Uitgeverij De Vuurbaak BV, pg 492

New Zealand
Church Mouse Press, pg 495

Norway
Genesis Forlag, pg 509
Lunde Forlag AS, pg 509

Pakistan
Publishers United Pvt Ltd, pg 514

Papua New Guinea
Kristen Press, pg 515
Melanesian Institute, pg 515
Victory Books, pg 516

Peru
Fondo Editorial de la Pontificia Universidad Catolica del Peru, pg 517

Philippines
Ateneo de Manila University Press, pg 518
Claretian Communications Inc, pg 518
Communication Foundation for Asia Media Group (CFAMG), pg 518
New Day Publishers, pg 520
Philippine Baptist Mission SBC FMB Church Growth International, pg 520
Rex Bookstores & Publishers, pg 520
UST Publishing House, pg 521

Poland
Drukarnia I Ksiegarnia Swietego Wojciecha, Dziat Wydawniczy, pg 522
Instytut Wydawniczy Pax, Inco-Veritas, pg 523
Katolicki Uniwersytet Wydawniczo-Redakcja, pg 523
Norbertinum, pg 524
Pallottinum Pydawnictwo Stowarzyszenia Apostolstwa Katolickiego, pg 525
Vocatio Publishing House, pg 527

Portugal
Apostolado da Oracao Secretariado Nacional, pg 528
Editorial Franciscana, pg 531
Edicoes Ora & Labora, pg 534
Usus Editora, pg 536
Livraria Verdade e Vida Editora, pg 536

Romania
Ars Longa Publishing House, pg 538
Humanitas Publishing House, pg 540
Editura Institutul European, pg 540
Saeculum IO, pg 542
Universal Dalsi, pg 543

Russian Federation
Druzhba Narodov, pg 544
St Andrew's Biblical Theological College, pg 548
Scorpion Publishers, pg 548

Serbia and Montenegro
AGAPE, pg 552

Singapore
Tecman Bible House, pg 558

Slovakia
Luc vydavatelske druzstvo, pg 559

Slovenia
Zalozba Mihelac d o o, pg 562

South Africa
Institute for Reformational Studies CHE, pg 565
Lux Verbi (Pty) Ltd, pg 566
Unisa Press, pg 569

Spain
Publicacions de l'Abadia de Montserrat, pg 570
Biblioteca de Autores Cristianos, pg 574
Avgvstinvs, pg 574
Ediciones Encuentro SA, pg 582
EUNSA (Ediciones Universidad de Navarra SA), pg 583
Editorial Herder SA, pg 586
Ediciones Internacionales Universitarias SA, pg 588
Loguez Ediciones, pg 589
Ediciones Marova SL, pg 590
Mundo Negro Editorial, pg 592
Centre de Pastoral Liturgica, pg 595
Editorial El Perpetuo Socorro, pg 596
Editorial Perpetuo Socorro, pg 596
Publicaciones de la Universidad Pontificia Comillas-Madrid, pg 597
San Pablo Ediciones, pg 598

PUBLISHERS

Ediciones San Pio X, pg 599
Secretariado Trinitario, pg 599
Ediciones Sigueme SA, pg 600
Ediciones Siruela SA, pg 600
Ediciones SM, pg 600
Editorial Sal Terrae, pg 602
Trotta SA Editorial, pg 602
Editorial Verbo Divino, pg 604

Sweden

Hagaberg AB, pg 612
Libris Bokforlaget, pg 613
Bokforlaget Nya Doxa AB, pg 614
Forlaget Sanctus (Metodistkyrkans Forlag), pg 615
Verbum Foerlag AB, pg 616

Switzerland

Benziger Verlag AG, pg 619
Edition Exodus, pg 623
Herder AG Basel, pg 625
ISIOM Verlag fur Tondokumente, Weinreb Tonarchiv, pg 625
Jugend mit einer Mission Verlag, pg 626
Kanisius Verlag, pg 626
Kober Verlag Bern AG, pg 626
Kranich-Verlag, Dres AG & H R Bosch-Gwalter, pg 627
Labor et Fides SA, pg 627
Peter Lang AG, pg 627
La Maison de la Bible, pg 628
Novalis Media AG, pg 630
Origo Verlag, pg 630
Philosophisch-Anthroposophischer Verlag am Goetheanum, pg 631
Psychosophische Gesellschaft, pg 632
Verlag Friedrich Reinhardt AG, pg 632
Rodera-Verlag der Cardun AG, pg 632
Editions Saint-Augustin, pg 633
Schwabe & Co AG, pg 633
Swedenborg - Verlag, pg 635
Theologischer Verlag und Buchhandlungen AG, pg 635
Der Universitatsverlag Freiburg, pg 636
Verlag Die Waage, pg 636
World Council of Churches (WCC Publications), pg 637

United Republic of Tanzania

Kanisa la Biblia Publishers (KLB), pg 643
Kisambo Publishers Ltd, pg 643
Ndanda Mission Press, pg 644
Northwestern Publishers, pg 644

Turkey

Oguz Yayinlari, pg 651

United Kingdom

Arthur James Ltd, pg 660
Ashgate Publishing Ltd, pg 660
Bible Reading Fellowship, pg 665
Bryntirion Press, pg 672
Cambridge University Press, pg 674
Cassell & Co, pg 675
Catholic Institute for International Relations, pg 676
Chapter Two, pg 678
Christian Focus Publications Ltd, pg 679
Church Society, pg 679
James Clarke & Co Ltd, pg 680
CTBI Publications, pg 685
Darton, Longman & Todd Ltd, pg 686
Dunedin Academic Press, pg 688
Edinburgh University Press Ltd, pg 689
Epworth Press, pg 691
The Eurospan Group, pg 692
Evangelical Press & Services Ltd, pg 693
Golden Cockerel Press Ltd, pg 701
Gracewing Publishing, pg 701
The Handsel Press, pg 704
HarperCollins UK, pg 705
Hodder & Stoughton Religious, pg 709
Hodder Education, pg 709
Angus Hudson Ltd, pg 710
Islam International Publications Ltd, pg 714
Janus Publishing Co Ltd, pg 716
Kingsway Publications, pg 718
Lion Hudson PLC, pg 721
The Littman Library of Jewish Civilization, pg 721
The Lutterworth Press, pg 723
Marcham Manor Press, pg 725
Methodist Publishing House, pg 727
Monarch Books, pg 729
Moorley's Print & Publishing Ltd, pg 729
Plough Publishing House of Bruderhof Communities in the UK, pg 743
Saint Andrew Press, pg 753
St Pauls Publishing, pg 753
SCM-Canterbury Press Ltd, pg 755
Scottish Text Society, pg 755
Scripture Union, pg 756
Sheffield Academic Press Ltd, pg 757
SLG Press, pg 758
The Society for Promoting Christian Knowledge (SPCK), pg 759
Thoemmes Press, pg 765
Transedition Ltd, pg 766
University of Wales Press, pg 769
Vallentine, Mitchell & Co Ltd, pg 769
Wild Goose Publications, pg 773
World of Islam Altajir Trust, pg 776
Yale University Press London, pg 776

Venezuela

Fundacion Centro Gumilla, pg 779

Zimbabwe

Christian Audio-Visual Action (CAVA), pg 783
Vision Publications, pg 784

SUBJECT INDEX

TRANSPORTATION

Australia

Kangaroo Press, pg 28
Lowden Publishing Co, pg 30
Marque Publishing Co Pty Ltd, pg 30
Navarine Publishing, pg 33
Turton & Armstrong Pty Ltd Publishers, pg 44

Austria

Bohmann Druck und Verlag GmbH & Co KG, pg 49
Verlag Josef Otto Slezak, pg 57

Belgium

Editions Gerard Blanchart & Cie SA, pg 63
Ediblanchart sprl, pg 67

Bulgaria

DA-Izdatelstvo Publishers, pg 93
Todor Kableshkov University of Transport, pg 97

China

Chemical Industry Press, pg 101
China Cartographic Publishing House, pg 102
Fujian Science & Technology Publishing House, pg 104
Heilongjiang Science & Technology Press, pg 105
The People's Communications Publishing House, pg 106
Southwest China Jiaotong University Press, pg 108

Czech Republic

SystemConsult, pg 127

Denmark

Bogfabrikken Fakta ApS, pg 129
Mercantila Publishers A/S, pg 133

Estonia

Mats Publishers Ltd, pg 140

France

Blondel La Rougery SARL, pg 150
Editions Cenomane, pg 152
Cepadues Editions SA, pg 153
Le Cherche Midi Editeur, pg 154
Codes Rousseau, pg 155
Compagnie d'Editions Libres, Sociales et Economiques (CELSE), pg 155
EPA (Editions Pratiques Automobiles), pg 161
Institut Francais de Recherche pour l'Exploitation de la Mer (IFREMER), pg 164
Payot & Rivages, pg 179
Presses de l'Ecole Nationale des Ponts et Chaussees, pg 181

Germany

Aerogie-Verlag, pg 191
AOL-Verlag Frohmut Menze, pg 193
Arbeitsgruppe LOK Report eV, pg 193
Beuth Verlag GmbH, pg 200
Deutsche Gesellschaft fuer Eisenbahngeschichte eV, pg 212
Dumjahn Verlag, pg 217
Ecomed Verlagsgesellschaft AG & Co KG, pg 218
EK-Verlag GmbH, pg 219
Verkehrs-Verlag J Fischer GmbH & Co KG, pg 224
Heel Verlag GmbH, pg 235
Hestra-Verlag Hernichel & Dr Strauss GmbH & Co KG, pg 237
Huss-Verlag GmbH, pg 240
Kirschbaum Verlag GmbH, pg 246
Koenemann Verlagesellschaft mbH, pg 248
Institut fuer Landes- und Stadtentwicklungsforschung des Landes Nordrhein-Westfalen, pg 251
Libertas- Europaeisches Institut GmbH, pg 254
Edition Maritim GmbH, pg 257
Moby Dick Verlag, pg 261
Verlag Walter Podszun Burobedarf-Bucher Abt, pg 270
Ritzau KG Verlag Zeit und Eisenbahn, pg 276
Ulrich Schiefer bahn Verlag, pg 279
Verlag Schweers + Wall GmbH, pg 282
Springer Science+Business Media GmbH & Co KG, Berlin, pg 285
Tetzlaff Verlag, pg 290
Transpress Verlagsgesellschaft mbH, pg 292
TUeV-Verlag GmbH, pg 293

Ghana

Building & Road Research Institute (BRRI), pg 303

Hungary

Hatter Lap- es Konyvkiado Kft, pg 321
Szarvas Andras Cartographic Agency, pg 324

India

BS Publications, pg 331
Inter-India Publications, pg 338

Ireland

Libra House Ltd, pg 361

Italy

Ermanno Albertelli Editore, pg 375
Automobilia srl, pg 377
Calosci, pg 379
Editoriale Domus SpA, pg 385
ETR (Editrice Trasporti su Rotaie), pg 388
Instituti Editoriali E Poligrafici Internazionali SRL, pg 393
Giorgio Nada Editore SRL, pg 400

Japan

Seizando-Shoten Publishing Co Ltd, pg 427

Macau

Museu Maritimo, pg 452

Mexico

Editorial Limusa SA de CV, pg 467

Netherlands

Hagen & Stam Uitgeverij Ten, pg 483
Uitgeverij Hollandia BV, pg 483
Ministerie van Verkeer en Waterstaat, pg 486
V S P International Science Publishers, pg 491

New Zealand

Grantham House Publishing, pg 496
Hodder Moa Beckett Publishers Ltd, pg 497
IPL Publishing Group, pg 497
Southern Press Ltd, pg 501

Norway

Elanders Publishing AS, pg 509
NKI Forlaget, pg 510

Poland

Wydawnictwa Komunikacji i Lacznosci Co Ltd, pg 524

Russian Federation

Izdatelstvo Sudostroenie, pg 549
Izdatelstvo Transport, pg 549

SUBJECT INDEX

BOOK

South Africa
Jacklin Enterprises (Pty) Ltd, pg 565

Spain
Centro de Estudios Adams-Ediciones Valbuena SA, pg 571
Comunidad Autonoma de Madrid, Servicio de Documentacion y Publicaciones, pg 578
Lunwerg Editores, SA, pg 589
Axel Springer Publicaciones, pg 601

Sweden
Allt om Hobby AB, pg 609
Frank Stenvalls Forlag, pg 615

Switzerland
Pharos-Verlag, Hansrudolf Schwabe AG, pg 631
Editions 24 Heures, pg 635
Verkehrshaus der Schweiz, pg 636
Vogt-Schild Ag, Druck und Verlag, pg 636

Syrian Arab Republic
Damascus University Press, pg 638

United Kingdom
Airlife Publishing Ltd, pg 656
Ian Allan Publishing Ltd, pg 656
Amber Books Ltd, pg 657
Apple Press, pg 658
Arms & Armour Press, pg 659
Artech House, pg 659
Ashgate Publishing Ltd, pg 660
Atlantic Transport Publishers, pg 661
Books International, pg 669
Bounty Books, pg 669
Brewin Books Ltd, pg 671
Castlemead Publications, pg 676
Colourpoint Books, pg 681
Compendium Publishing, pg 681
Countyvise Ltd, pg 683
Croner CCH Group Ltd, pg 684
G L Crowther, pg 684
David & Charles Ltd, pg 686
Defiant Publications, pg 687
DMG Business Media Ltd, pg 688
Eaglemoss Publications, pg 689
Elliot Right Way Books, pg 690
Global Oriental Ltd, pg 700
A H Gordon, pg 701
Grange Books PLC, pg 702
Greenhill Books/Lionel Leventhal Ltd, pg 703
Haynes Publishing, pg 706
Jane's Information Group, pg 715
Kogan Page Ltd, pg 718
Middleton Press, pg 728
Midland Publishing, pg 728
Motor Racing Publications Ltd, pg 729
Oakwood Press, pg 734
Old Pond Publishing, pg 734
Orpheus Books Ltd, pg 736
Platform 5 Publishing Ltd, pg 743
PRC Publishing Ltd, pg 745
Professional Engineering Publishing Ltd, pg 745
Quintet Publishing Ltd, pg 747
Ramboro Books Plc, pg 747
Regency House Publishing Ltd, pg 749
Research Studies Press Ltd (RSP), pg 749
Roadmaster Publishing, pg 750
Salamander Books Ltd, pg 753
SB Publications, pg 754
Scottish Executive Library & Information Services, pg 755
Sheldrake Press, pg 757
Shire Publications Ltd, pg 757
Sigma Press, pg 758
Silver Link Publishing Ltd, pg 758
Spon Press, pg 760
Sutton Publishing Ltd, pg 762
Taylor & Francis, pg 763
Transport Bookman Publications Ltd, pg 766
TSO (The Stationery Office), pg 767
Twelveheads Press, pg 767
Unicorn Books, pg 768
Veloce Publishing Ltd, pg 769
WIT Press, pg 774
Witherby & Co Ltd, pg 775

Viet Nam
Science & Technics Publishing House, pg 780

TRAVEL

Algeria
Enterprise Nationale du Livre (ENAL), pg 2

Argentina
Diana Argentina SA, Editorial, pg 5

Australia
Blubber Head Press, pg 15
Louis Braille Audio, pg 16
E J Brill, Robert Brown & Associates, pg 16
CHOICE Magazine, pg 17
Companion Travel Guide Books, pg 18
Cornford Press, pg 18
Crawford House Publishing Pty Ltd, pg 18
Dryden Press, pg 20
Emperor Publishing, pg 21
Garradunga Press, pg 23
F H Halpern, pg 24
Hartys Creek Press, pg 25
Hema Maps Pty Ltd, pg 25
Horan Wall & Walker, pg 26
Kangaroo Press, pg 28
Kingsclear Books, pg 28
Little Hills Press Pty Ltd, pg 29
Lonely Planet Publications Pty Ltd, pg 29
Tracy Marsh Publications Pty Ltd, pg 31
Media East Press, pg 31
Melbourne University Press, pg 32
Oceans Enterprises, pg 34
Off the Shelf Publishing, pg 34
Pan Macmillan Australia Pty Ltd, pg 35
Penguin Group (Australia), pg 36
Pinevale Publications, pg 36
RMIT Publishing, pg 39
See Australia Guides P/L, pg 40
Single X Publications, pg 41
Spinifex Press, pg 42
Thames & Hudson (Australia) Pty Ltd, pg 43
Universal Press Pty Ltd, pg 44
University of Queensland Press, pg 45
Wakefield Press Pty Ltd, pg 46
The Watermark Press, pg 46
Windward Publications, pg 47
Woodlands Publications, pg 47

Austria
Bohmann Druck und Verlag GmbH & Co KG, pg 49
Verlag Harald Denzel, Auto- und Freizeitfuehrer, pg 50
Edition Graphischer Zirkel, pg 51
Kuemmerly und Frey Verlags GmbH, pg 53
Niederosterreichisches Pressehaus Druck- und Verlagsgesellschaft mbH, pg 54
Pinguin-Verlag, Pawlowski GmbH, pg 56
Promedia Verlagsges mbH, pg 56
Verlag Anton Pustet, pg 56
Tyrolia Verlagsanstalt GmbH, pg 58
Edition Va Bene, pg 59
Verlag Anton Schroll & Co, pg 59
Herbert Weishaupt Verlag, pg 59
Wienerland Zeitung & Verlag, pg 60

Bangladesh
The University Press Ltd, pg 61

Belgium
NV Artis-Historia, pg 63
Carto BVBA, pg 64
Cartoeristiek (Federatie van Belgische Autobus- en Autocarondernemers) (BAAV), pg 64
Creadif, pg 65
Cremers (Schoollandkaarten) PVBA, pg 66
Daphne Diffusion SA, pg 66
DEF (De Blauwe Vogel) NV/SA, pg 66
Uitgevery Gelbis NV, pg 67
Koepel van de Vlaamse Noord - Zuidbeweging 11.11.11, pg 69
Uitgeverij Lannoo NV, pg 69
Michelin Editions des Voyages, pg 71
Henri Proost & Co, Pvba, pg 72
Reader's Digest SA, pg 72
Roularta Books NV, pg 72
Scoop Infotex NV, pg 73
Sonneville Press (Uitgeverij) VTW, pg 73
Editions Techniques et Scientifiques SPRL, pg 73

Botswana
Maskew Miller Longman, pg 76

Brazil
Artes e Oficios Editora Ltda, pg 78
Editora Campus Ltda, pg 79
Companhia Editora Forense, pg 81
Editora Globo SA, pg 82
LDA Editores Ltda, pg 84
Livraria Kosmos Editora Ltda, pg 85
Livraria Nobel S/A, pg 85
Editora Mantiqueira de Ciencia e Arte, pg 86
Editora Marco Zero Ltda, pg 86
Rede Das Artes (Boccato Editores Collector's), pg 89

Bulgaria
Aleks Print Publishing House, pg 93
Publishing House Narodno delo OOD, pg 96

Chile
Arrayan Editores, pg 98
Ediciones Mil Hojas Ltda, pg 99
Publicaciones Lo Castillo SA, pg 100

China
Chengdu Maps Publishing House, pg 101
China Cartographic Publishing House, pg 102
Foreign Languages Press, pg 104
Higher Education Press, pg 105
Jilin Science & Technology Publishing House, pg 105
Shandong Friendship Publishing House, pg 107
Shanghai Far East Publishers, pg 108
Yunnan University Press, pg 109
Zhong Hua Book Co, pg 110

Colombia
Ediciones Gamma, pg 111

Cyprus
Action Publications, pg 121
Nikoklis Publishers, pg 121

Czech Republic
Konias, pg 124
Lidove Noviny Publishing House, pg 125
Mlada fronta, pg 125
Nakladatelstvi Olympia AS, pg 126
Prazske nakladatelstvi Pluto, pg 127
SystemConsult, pg 127

Denmark
Gads Forlag, pg 131
Forlaget Hjulet, pg 132
Mellemfolkeligt Samvirke, pg 133
Det Schonbergske Forlag A/S, pg 134

Egypt (Arab Republic of Egypt)
Lehnert & Landrock Bookshop, pg 138

Finland
Kirja-Leitzinger, pg 142
Suomen Matkailuliitto ry, pg 144
Tietoteos Publishing Co, pg 144
Yliopistopaino/Helsinki University Press, pg 145

France
Anako Editions, pg 146
Armenia Editions, pg 147
Aubanel Editions, pg 148
Autrement Editions, pg 148
Editions A Barthelemy, pg 149
La Bibliotheque des Arts, pg 150
Editions Andre Bonne, pg 150
Pierre Bordas & Fils, Editions, pg 150
Brud Nevez, pg 151
Editions du Buot, pg 151
Editions du Chene, pg 154
CLD, pg 154
Editions Grund, pg 160
Editions Pierre Fanlac, pg 162
FBT de R Editions, pg 163
Editions Filipacchi-Sonodip, pg 163
Editions Fivedit, pg 163
Editions du Garde-Temps, pg 165
Editions Jean Paul Gisserot, pg 165
Editions Glenat, pg 165
Editions Jacques Grancher, pg 165
Hachette Livre, pg 167
Image/Magie, pg 168
Editions du Jaguar, pg 169
Kailash Editions, pg 170
Karthala Editions-Diffusion, pg 170
Editions Fernand Lanore Sarl, pg 171

PUBLISHERS

Editions du Laquet, pg 171
Editions des Limbes d'Or FBT de R Editions, pg 172
Lonely Planet, pg 173
Editions Loubatieres, pg 173
LT Editions-Jacques Lanore, pg 173
Editions Marcus, pg 174
Editions Franck Mercier, pg 175
Michelin Editions des Voyages, pg 175
Nouvelles Editions Latines, pg 177
Editions Ophrys, pg 177
Editions Ouest-France, pg 178
Payot & Rivages, pg 179
Editions Jean Picollec, pg 179
Editions Christian Pirot, pg 180
Selection du Reader's Digest SA, pg 184
Siloe - Kerdore, pg 185
Taride Editions, pg 187
Alain Thomas Editeur, pg 187
Ulisse Editions, pg 188
La Vague a l'ame, pg 188
Editions Vague Verte, pg 188
Editions Vilo SA, pg 189

French Polynesia

Haere Po Editions, pg 189

Germany

Alouette Verlag, pg 192
Anabas-Verlag Guenter Kaempf GmbH & Co KG, pg 192
Ars Vivendi Verlag, pg 194
Artcolor, pg 194
Badenia Verlag und Druckerei GmbH, pg 196
Beerenverlag, pg 198
Bergstadtverlag Wilhelm Gottlieb Korn GmbH Wuerzburg, pg 199
Bergverlag Rother GmbH, pg 199
Berndtson & Berndtson GmbH Verlag-Publishing, pg 199
Bertelsmann Lexikon Verlag GmbH, pg 200
Bielefelder Verlagsanstalt GmbH & Co KG Richard Kaselowsky, pg 201
BLV Verlagsgesellschaft mbH, pg 202
Brandenburgisches Verlagshaus in der Dornier Medienholding GmbH, pg 204
F Bruckmann Munchen Verlag & Druck GmbH & Co Produkt KG, pg 204
Verlag C J Bucher GmbH, pg 205
Kartographischer Verlag Busche GmbH, pg 206
Verlag Busse und Seewald GmbH, pg 206
CartoTravel Verlag GmbH & Co KG, pg 207
Chr Belser AG fur Verlagsgeschaefte und Co KG, pg 208
Hans Christians Druckerei und Verlag GmbH & Co KG, pg 208
Compact Verlag GmbH, pg 209
Deutsche Landwirtschafts-Gesellschaft VerlagsgesGmbH, pg 212
Deutscher Wanderverlag Dr Mair & Schnabel & Co, pg 214
Dialog-Verlag GmbH, pg 214
Drei Brunnen Verlag GmbH & Co, pg 216
Drei Ulmen Verlag GmbH, pg 216
Dumjahn Verlag, pg 217
DuMont Reiseverlag GmbH & Co KG, pg 217

Edition Aragon-Verlagsgesellschaft mbH, pg 218
Egmont vgs verlagsgesellschaft mbH, pg 218
EinfallsReich Verlagsgesellschaft MbH, pg 219
Elektor-Verlag GmbH, pg 219
Ellert & Richter Verlag GmbH, pg 219
Eulen Verlag, pg 221
Flechsig Buchvertrieb, pg 225
Fleischhauer & Spohn GmbH & Co, pg 225
Frederking & Thaler Verlag GmbH, pg 226
G Braun (vormals G Braun'sche Hofbuchdruckerei und Verlag) Gmbh, pg 227
Konkursbuch Verlag Claudia Gehrke, pg 228
GLB Parkland Verlags-und Vertriebs GmbH, pg 229
Graefe und Unzer Verlag GmbH, pg 230
Graf Editions, pg 231
Harenberg Kommunikation Verlags- und Medien-GmbH & Co KG, pg 234
Haschemi Edition Cologne Kunstverlag fuer Fotografie, pg 234
Haude und Spenersche Verlagsbuchhandlung, pg 235
Hayit Reisefuhrer in der Rutsker Verlag GmbH, pg 235
Heel Verlag GmbH, pg 235
F A Herbig Verlagsbuchhandlung GmbH, pg 236
Humboldt-Taschenbuch Verlag Jacobi KG, pg 240
Ikarus - Buchverlag, pg 241
Interconnections Reisen und Arbeiten Georg Beckmann, pg 242
Klaus Isele, pg 242
Reisebuchverlag Iwanowski GmbH, pg 242
Jahreszeiten-Verlag GmbH, pg 242
Jan Thorbecke Verlag GmbH & Co, pg 243
Verlag Winfried Jenior, pg 243
KaJo Verlag, pg 244
Verlag Karl Baedeker GmbH, pg 244
Karto + Grafik Verlagsgesellschaft (K & G Verlagsgesellschaft), pg 244
Kartographischer Verlag Reinhard Ryborsch, pg 244
SachBuchVerlag Kellner, pg 245
Kleiner Bachmann Verlag fur Kinder und Umwelt, pg 246
Doris Knop-Verlag, pg 247
Knowledge Media International, pg 247
Adam Kraft Verlag, pg 250
Ambro Lacus, Buch- und Bildverlag Walter A Kremnitz, pg 251
Landbuch-Verlagsgesellschaft mbH, pg 251
J Latka Verlag GmbH, pg 253
Siegbert Linnemann Verlag, pg 254
Stefan Loose Verlag, pg 255
Lusatia Verlag-Dr Stuebner & Co KG, pg 256
Karin Mader, pg 256
Mairs Geographischer Verlag, pg 256
Edition Maritim GmbH, pg 257
Edition Axel Menges, pg 259
Meyer & Meyer Verlag, pg 260
Peter Meyer Verlag (pmv), pg 260

Mitteldeutscher Verlag GmbH, pg 261
Moby Dick Verlag, pg 261
Mundo Verlag GmbH, pg 262
Verlag Stephanie Naglschmid, pg 263
Naumann & Goebel Verlagsgesellschaft mbH, pg 263
Nebel Verlag GmbH, pg 263
Nelles Verlag GmbH, pg 263
Neuer Honos Verlag GmbH, pg 264
Neumann Verlag, pg 264
Neuthor - Verlag, pg 265
Georg Olms Verlag AG, pg 267
Palazzi Verlag GmbH, pg 268
Passavia Druckerei GmbH, Verlag, pg 268
Jens Peters Publikationen, pg 269
Paul Pietsch Verlage GmbH & Co, pg 270
Pollner Verlag, pg 271
Polyglott-Verlag, pg 271
Propylaeen Verlag, Zweigniederlassung Berlin der Ullstein Buchverlage GmbH, pg 272
Werner Rau Verlag, pg 273
Konrad Reich Verlag GmbH, pg 274
E Reinhold Verlag, pg 275
Reise Know-How, pg 275
Reise Know-How Verlag-Daerr GmbH, pg 275
Reise Know-How Verlag Helmut Hermann, pg 275
Reise Know-How Verlag Peter Rump GmbH, pg 275
Reise Know-How Verlag Tondok, pg 275
Verlagsgruppe Reise Know-How, pg 275
Romiosini Verlag, pg 276
Schelzky & Jeep, Verlag fuer Reisen und Wissen, pg 279
Renate Schenk Verlag, pg 279
Schillinger Verlag GmbH, pg 279
Schmid Verlag GmbH, pg 280
Verlag Schnell und Steiner GmbH, pg 281
Schoeffling & Co, pg 281
H O Schulze KG, pg 282
Verlag Schweers + Wall GmbH, pg 282
Buchkonzept Simon KG, pg 283
Stapp Verlag Wolfgang Stapp, pg 286
Stattbuch Verlag GmbH, pg 287
Steiger Verlag, pg 287
Conrad Stein Verlag GmbH, pg 287
Stoeppel Verlag-Buchvertrieb KG, pg 288
Sturtz Verlag GmbH, pg 288
Suedwest Verlag GmbH & Co KG, pg 289
Edition Temmen, pg 290
teNeues Verlag GmbH & Co KG, pg 290
Tomus Verlag GmbH, pg 291
TR - Verlagsunion GmbH, pg 291
Trees Wolfgang Triangel Verlag, pg 292
Trescher Verlag GmbH, pg 292
Treves Editions Verein Zur Foerderung der Kuenstlerischen Taetigkeiten, pg 292
Turkischer Schulbuchverlag Onel Cengiz, pg 293
Vista Point Verlag GmbH, pg 296
VJK Verlag Josef Knecht Carolusdruckerei GmbH, pg 296
W Ludwig Verlag GmbH, pg 297
WDV Wirtschaftsdienst Gesellschaft fur Medien & Kommunikation mbH & Co OHG, pg 298

SUBJECT INDEX

Weidlich Verlag, pg 298
Wolf's-Verlag Berlin, pg 301
Zambon Verlag, pg 302
Zeitgeist Media GmbH, pg 302
Ziethen-Panorama Verlag GmbH, pg 302

Ghana

Moxon Paperbacks, pg 304

Greece

Alamo Hellas, pg 305
Ekdoseis Kazantzaki (Kazantzakis Publications), pg 307
Ekdotike Athenon SA, pg 307
Evrodiastasi, pg 307
Hestia-I D Hestia-Kollaros & Co Corporation, pg 308
Kedros Publishers, pg 309
Knossos Publications, pg 309
Editions Moressopoulos, pg 310
Patakis Publishers, pg 311
Stochastis, pg 312

Hong Kong

CFW Publications Ltd, pg 316
Hong Kong China Tourism Press, pg 317
Hong Kong Publishing Co Ltd, pg 317
Island Press, pg 317
Steve Lu Publishing Ltd, pg 318
Press Mark Media Ltd, pg 318
SCMP Book Publishing Ltd, pg 319

Hungary

Idegenforgalmi Propaganda es Kiado Vallalat, pg 321
Kossuth Kiado RT, pg 322
Magyar Kemikusok Egyesulete, pg 323
Medicina Koenyvkiado, pg 323
Officina Nova Konyvek, pg 323
Szarvas Andras Cartographic Agency, pg 324

Iceland

Forlagid, pg 325
Mal og menning, pg 326

India

APH Publishing Corp, pg 328
Asian Educational Services, pg 329
Associated Publishing House, pg 329
Brijbasi Printers Pvt Ltd, pg 331
General Book Depot, pg 335
Gyan Publishing House, pg 335
Himalayan Books, pg 336
Indian Book Depot, pg 336
Indus Publishing Co, pg 338
Islamic Publishing House, pg 338
A Mukherjee & Co Pvt Ltd, pg 342
Omsons Publications, pg 344
Reliance Publishing House, pg 346
Roli Books Pvt Ltd, pg 347
Spectrum Publications, pg 350
Vakils Feffer & Simons Ltd, pg 352
Vision Books Pvt Ltd, pg 352
Viva Books Pvt Ltd, pg 352

Indonesia

Bina Aksara Parta, pg 354
Bina Rena Pariwara, pg 354

Ireland

Ballinakella Press, pg 358
Dee-Jay Publications, pg 359
Estragon Press Ltd, pg 359
Gill & Macmillan Ltd, pg 360

SUBJECT INDEX

Libra House Ltd, pg 361
The O'Brien Press Ltd, pg 362
On Stream Publications Ltd, pg 362
Real Ireland Design, pg 363
Roberts Rinehart Publishers, pg 363

Israel

Bitan Publishers Ltd, pg 365
Classikaletet, pg 366
Gefen Publishing House Ltd, pg 367
Hakibbutz Hameuchad Publishing House Ltd, pg 367
Inbal Travel Information, pg 368
Ma'ariv Book Guild (Sifriat Ma'ariv), pg 370
MAP-Mapping & Publishing Ltd, pg 370
Saar Publishing House, pg 371
Schocken Publishing House Ltd, pg 371
R Sirkis Publishers Ltd, pg 372
Steimatzky Group Ltd, pg 372
Steinhart-Katzir Publishers, pg 372

Italy

L'Airone Editrice, pg 375
Arcadia Edizioni Srl, pg 375
Athesia Verlag Bozen, pg 377
Casa Editrice Bonechi, pg 378
Bonechi-Edizioni Il Turismo Srl, pg 378
Editoriale Domus SpA, pg 385
Ediciclo Editore SRL, pg 386
Edizioni l'Arciere SRL, pg 387
EDT Edizioni di Torino, pg 387
ETR (Editrice Trasporti su Rotaie), pg 388
EuroGeoGrafiche Mencattini, pg 388
Adriano Gallina Editore sas, pg 389
Edizioni GB, pg 390
Ernesto Gremese Editore srl, pg 391
Gremese International srl, pg 391
Hopeful Monster Editore, pg 392
Ibis, pg 392
Kompass Fleischmann, pg 394
LAC - Litografia Artistica Cartografica Srl, pg 394
Laruffa Editore SRL, pg 394
Levante Editori, pg 395
Editrice Liguria SNC di Norberto Sabatelli & C, pg 395
Manfrini Editori, pg 397
Il Minotauro, pg 398
Mondolibro Editore SNC, pg 399
Palatina Editrice, pg 402
Passigli Editori, pg 402
Daniela Piazza Editore, pg 403
Plurigraf SPA, pg 403
Edizioni Primavera SRL, pg 404
Priuli e Verlucca, Editori, pg 404
Edizioni Quasar di Severino Tognon SRL, pg 404
Edizioni del Riccio SAS di G Bernardi, pg 405
Rossato, pg 406
SAGEP Libri & Comunicazione Srl, pg 406
Scala Group spa, pg 407
Sperling e Kupfer Editori SpA, pg 409
Studio Bibliografico Adelmo Polla, pg 409
Studio Editoriale Programma, pg 409
Tassotti Editore, pg 409
Todariana Editrice, pg 410
Trainer International Editore-I Libri del Bargello, pg 410
Valmartina Editore SRL, pg 411
Zanfi-Logos, pg 412

Jamaica

LMH Publishing Ltd, pg 414

Japan

The American Chamber of Commerce in Japan, pg 415
Baseball Magazine-Sha Co Ltd, pg 415
Contex Corporation, pg 416
Japan Travel Bureau Inc, pg 420
Kosei Publishing Co Ltd, pg 421
Nagaoka Shoten Co Ltd, pg 423
Nippon Hoso Shuppan Kyokai (NHK Publishing), pg 424
Sanshusha Publishing Co, Ltd, pg 426
Seibido Shuppan Company Ltd, pg 426
Shakai Shiso-Sha, pg 427
Shobunsha Publications Inc, pg 427
Shufunotomo Co Ltd, pg 428
Tokyo Shoseki Co Ltd, pg 430
Charles E Tuttle Publishing Co Inc, pg 430
Yama-Kei Publishers Co Ltd, pg 431

Kenya

Camerapix Publishers International Ltd, pg 433
Kenway Publications Ltd, pg 434
Space Sellers Ltd, pg 436

Democratic People's Republic of Korea

Transportation Publishing House, pg 436

Republic of Korea

Chung Rim Publishing Co Ltd, pg 438
Dae Won Sa Co Ltd, pg 438
Hollym Corporation; Publishers, pg 439
Hyein Publishing House, pg 439
Pyeong-hwa Chulpansa, pg 442
Seoul International Publishing House, pg 443
Woongjin.com Co Ltd, pg 443
YBM/Si-sa, pg 443

Latvia

Madris, pg 445
Preses Nams, pg 445
Spriditis Publishers, pg 445
Zvaigzne ABC Publishers Ltd, pg 445

Lebanon

Arab Scientific Publishers BP, pg 445
GEOprojects Sarl, pg 446
Librairie du Liban Publishers (Sal), pg 446

Lithuania

Sviesa Publishers, pg 449

Luxembourg

Op der Lay, pg 451

Macau

Livros Do Oriente, pg 452

Madagascar

Musee d'Art et d'Archaeologie, pg 454

Malawi

Central Africana Ltd, pg 454

Malaysia

S Abdul Majeed & Co, pg 454
Panther Publishing, pg 457
Pustaka Cipta Sdn Bhd, pg 458

Maldive Islands

Novelty Printers & Publishers, pg 459

Malta

Gaulitana, pg 460
Publishers' Enterprises Group (PEG) Ltd, pg 460

Mauritius

Editions de l'Ocean Indien Ltd, pg 461

Mexico

Editorial AGATA SA de CV, pg 462
Editorial Jilguero, SA de CV, pg 467
Editorial Minutiae Mexicana SA, pg 468
Panorama Editorial, SA, pg 470
Promociones de Mercados Turisticos SA de CV, pg 471

Morocco

Edition Diffusion de Livre au Maroc, pg 474
Editions La Porte, pg 475

Myanmar

Kyi-Pwar-Ye Book House, pg 475

Namibia

Agrivet Publishers, pg 476

Netherlands

Uitgeversmaatschappij Agon B V, pg 477
Uitgeverij de Arbeiderspers, pg 477
Uitgeverij Arena BV, pg 478
B M Israel BV, pg 478
Buijten en Schipperheijn BV Drukkerij en Uitgeversmaatschappij, pg 480
BZZTOH Publishers, pg 480
Cadans, pg 480
Elmar BV, pg 482
Gottmer Uitgevers Groep, pg 483
Uitgeverij Hollandia BV, pg 483
Mets & Schilt Uitgevers en Distributeurs, pg 486
J M Meulenhoff bv, pg 486
Uitgeverij Het Spectrum BV, pg 489
Telos Boeken, pg 490
Tirion Uitgevers BV, pg 490
Unieboek BV, pg 490

Netherlands Antilles

Bredero, pg 493
De Wit Stores NV, pg 493

New Caledonia

Editions du Santal, pg 493
Savannah Editions SARL, pg 493

New Zealand

Barkfire Press, pg 494
David Bateman Ltd, pg 494
Craig Printing Co Ltd, pg 495
David's Marine Books, pg 495
HarperCollins Publishers (New Zealand) Ltd, pg 497
Hazard Press Ltd, pg 497
Kowhai Publishing Ltd, pg 497
Reed Publishing (NZ) Ltd, pg 500
River Press, pg 500
RSVP Publishing Co Ltd, pg 500
Shoal Bay Press Ltd, pg 501
Tandem Press, pg 501

Nigeria

Joe-Tolalu & Associates, pg 507

Norway

Aschehoug Forlag, pg 508
H Aschehoug & Co (W Nygaard) A/S, pg 508
Chr Schibsteds Forlag A/S, pg 510

Oman

Apex Press & Publishing, pg 511

Pakistan

Jang Publishers, pg 513
Sang-e-Meel Publications, pg 514

Panama

Focus Publications International SA, pg 515

Philippines

Bookmark Inc, pg 518
Galleon Publications, pg 519
Rex Bookstores & Publishers, pg 520

Poland

BOSZ scp, pg 522
Iskry - Publishing House Ltd spotka zoo, pg 523
KAW Krajowa Agencja Wydawnicza, pg 523
'Ksiazka i Wiedza' Spotdzielnia Wydawniczo-Handlowa, pg 524
Laumann-Polska, pg 524
Muza SA, pg 524
Oficyna Wydawnicza Read Me, pg 526

Portugal

Bezerr-Editorae e Distribuidora de Abel Antonio Bezerra, pg 529
Edicoes Cetop, pg 529
Distri Cultural Lda, pg 530
Edicoes ELO, pg 531
Everest Editora, pg 531
Latina Livraria Editora, pg 532
Editorial Presenca, pg 535
Quetzal Editores, pg 535

Puerto Rico

Modern Guides Company, pg 537
Publishing Resources Inc, pg 537

Romania

Alcor-Edimpex (Verlag) Ltd, pg 538
Corint Publishing Group, pg 539
Editura Cronos SRL, pg 539
Editura Meridiane, pg 540
Rentrop & Straton Verlagsgruppe und Wirtschaftsconsulting, pg 542

Russian Federation

Top Secret Collection Publishers, pg 549

PUBLISHERS

Serbia and Montenegro
Jugoslovenska Revija, pg 552

Singapore
APA Production Pte Ltd, pg 554
Archipelago Press, pg 555
Reed Elsevier, South East Asia, pg 557
Times Media Pte Ltd, pg 559

Slovakia
Vydavatel'stvo Osveta (Verlag Osveta), pg 560
Priroda Publishing, pg 560
Slovenske pedagogicke nakladateistvo, pg 560
Sport Publishing House Ltd, pg 561

Slovenia
Mladinska Knjiga International, pg 561
Zalozba Mihelac d o o, pg 562
Zalozba Obzorja d d Maribor, pg 562

South Africa
Acorn Books, pg 562
Fernwood Press (Pty) Ltd, pg 563
Jacana Education, pg 565
Reader's Digest Southern Africa, pg 568
Southern Book Publishers (Pty) Ltd, pg 569
Struik Publishers (Pty) Ltd, pg 569

Spain
Acento Editorial, pg 570
Aguilar SA de Ediciones, pg 571
Alfaguara Ediciones SA - Grupo Santillana, pg 572
Anaya-Touring Club, pg 573
Calamo Editorial, pg 575
Celeste Ediciones, pg 576
Compania Literaria, pg 577
Comunidad Autonoma de Madrid, Servicio de Documentacion y Publicaciones, pg 578
Edilesa-Ediciones Leonesas SA, pg 581
Edilux, pg 581
Enciclopedia Catalana, SA, pg 582
Galaxia SA Editorial, pg 584
Vicent Garcia Editores, SA, pg 584
Editorial Gustavo Gili SA, pg 585
Editorial Iberia, SA, pg 586
Junta de Castilla y Leon Consejeria de Educacion y Cultura, pg 588
Editorial Juventud SA, pg 588
Laertes SA de Ediciones, pg 588
Lunwerg Editores, SA, pg 589
Ediciones Maeva, pg 590
Editorial Mediterrania SL, pg 591
Editorial Moll SL, pg 592
Ediciones El Pais SA, pg 594
Polifemo, Ediciones, pg 596
Silex Ediciones, pg 600
Editorial Sintesis, SA, pg 600
Edicions 62, pg 600
Grup 62, pg 600
Ediciones Susaeta SA, pg 601
Trea Ediciones, SL, pg 602
Tursen, SA, pg 603
Ediciones Vulcano, pg 605
Editorial Zendrera Zariquiey, SA, pg 605

Sweden
Alfabeta Bokforlag AB, pg 609
Carlsson Bokforlag AB, pg 610
Streiffert Forlag AB, pg 615

Switzerland
Ammann Verlag & Co, pg 617
Arche Verlag AG, Raabe und Vitali, pg 617
Bergli Books AG, pg 619
Cockatoo Press (Schweiz), Thailand-Publikationen, pg 621
Drei-D-World und Foto-World Verlag und Vertrieb, pg 622
Duboux Editions SA, pg 622
GVA Publishers Ltd, pg 624
Hallwag Kuemmerly & Frey AG, pg 625
JPM Publications SA, pg 626
Kranich-Verlag, Dres AG & H R Bosch-Gwalter, pg 627
Kuemmerly & Frey (Geographischer Verlag), pg 627
Librairie-Editions J Marguerat, pg 628
Motovun Book GmbH, pg 629
Les Editions Nagel SA (Paris), pg 629
Neptun-Verlag, pg 629
Editions Olizane, pg 630
Punktum AG, Buchredaktion und Bildarchiv, pg 632
Robert Raeber, Buchhandlung am Schweizerhof, pg 632
Regenbogen Verlag, pg 632
Hans Rohr Verlag, pg 632
Rotpunktverlag, pg 632
Strom-Verlag Luzern, pg 635
Terra Grischuna Verlag Buch-und Zeitschriftenverlag, pg 635
3 Dimension World (3-D-World), pg 635

Taiwan, Province of China
Chu Hai Publishing (Taiwan) Co Ltd, pg 640
Hilit Publishing Co Ltd, pg 640
Linking Publishing Company Ltd, pg 641
Shy Mau & Shy Chaur Publishing Co Ltd, pg 641
Youth Cultural Publishing Co, pg 642

Thailand
Sangdad Publishing Company Ltd, pg 645

Trinidad & Tobago
Joan Bacchus-Xavier, pg 646
Jett Samm Publishing Ltd, pg 647

Turkey
Arkeoloji Ve Sanat Yayinlari, pg 649
Dost Kitabevi Yayinlari, pg 649

Uganda
Fountain Publishers Ltd, pg 652

Ukraine
Mystetstvo Publishers, pg 653

United Arab Emirates
Motivate Publishing, pg 654

United Kingdom
A A Publishing, pg 654
Abbotsford Publishing, pg 654
Absolute Press, pg 655
Alun Books, pg 657
Chris Andrews Publications, pg 657
Arcadia Books, pg 659
Ashmolean Museum Publications, pg 660
Aurum Press Ltd, pg 661
Colin Baxter Photography Ltd, pg 663
BCA - Book Club Associates, pg 663
Bellew Publishing Co Ltd, pg 664
Blackstaff Press, pg 666
Blorenge Books, pg 668
The Book Guild Ltd, pg 668
Book Packaging & Marketing, pg 668
Boydell & Brewer Ltd, pg 669
Bradt Travel Guides Ltd, pg 670
Brewin Books Ltd, pg 671
British Tourist Authority, pg 672
Bwrdd Croeso Cymru, pg 673
Cadogan Guides, pg 673
Camerapix Publishers International Ltd, pg 674
Canongate Books Ltd, pg 674
Cicerone Press, pg 680
Cockbird Press, pg 680
Colour Library Direct, pg 681
Compendium Publishing, pg 681
Constable & Robinson Ltd, pg 682
Leo Cooper, pg 683
Cordee Ltd, pg 683
Darf Publishers Ltd, pg 686
David & Charles Ltd, pg 686
Andre Deutsch Ltd, pg 687
Discovery Walking Guides Ltd, pg 687
John Donald Publishers Ltd, pg 688
The Economist Intelligence Unit, pg 689
Eland Publishing Ltd, pg 690
Element Books Ltd, pg 690
Elm Publications, pg 691
The Erskine Press, pg 692
The Factory Shop Guide, pg 694
Famedram Publishers Ltd, pg 694
FHG Publications Ltd, pg 694
Foulsham Publishers, pg 696
Frontier Publishing Ltd, pg 697
Garnet Publishing Ltd, pg 698
Global Oriental Ltd, pg 700
Gollancz/Witherby, pg 701
Grange Books PLC, pg 702
Granta Books, pg 702
The Greek Bookshop, pg 702
Hakluyt Society, pg 703
Harden's Ltd, pg 704
HarperCollins UK, pg 705
The Harvill Press, pg 705
Heartland Publishing Ltd, pg 707
William Heinemann Ltd, pg 707
Hodder & Stoughton General, pg 709
Angus Hudson Ltd, pg 710
Icon Press, pg 711
Jarrold Publishing, pg 716
John Jones Publishing Ltd, pg 716
Kegan Paul International Ltd, pg 717
Kuperard, pg 718
Roger Lascelles, pg 719
Lonely Planet, UK, pg 722
Luath Press Ltd, pg 722
Mainstream Publishing Co (Edinburgh) Ltd, pg 724
Marshall Editions Ltd, pg 725
Meridian Books, pg 727
Methuen, pg 727
Metro Books, pg 727
Michelin Tyre PLC, Tourism Dept, Maps & Guides Division, pg 728
Multilingual Matters Ltd, pg 729
Murchison's Pantheon Ltd, pg 730
National Trust, pg 731
New European Publications Ltd, pg 732
New Holland Publishers (UK) Ltd, pg 732
Octagon Press Ltd, pg 734
Octopus Publishing Group, pg 734
Old Vicarage Publications, pg 734
The Oleander Press, pg 735
Pallas Athene, pg 738
Pavilion Books Ltd, pg 739
Pitkin Unichrome Ltd, pg 743
Profile Books Ltd, pg 746
Quiller Publishing Ltd, pg 747
Quintet Publishing Ltd, pg 747
Random House UK Ltd, pg 747
The Reader's Digest Association Ltd, pg 748
Reaktion Books Ltd, pg 748
Robson Books, pg 750
Rooster Books Ltd, pg 751
Rough Guides Ltd, pg 751
Roundhouse Group, pg 751
RoutledgeCurzon, pg 751
The Rubicon Press, pg 752
The Rutland Press, pg 752
Saqi Books, pg 754
SB Publications, pg 754
Sheldrake Press, pg 757
Sidgwick & Jackson Ltd, pg 757
SPA Books Ltd, pg 759
Stacey International, pg 761
Sunflower Books, pg 761
Sutton Publishing Ltd, pg 762
Thames & Hudson Ltd, pg 764
Thistle Press, pg 765
Time Out Group Ltd, pg 765
Time Warner Book Group UK, pg 766
Ulverscroft Large Print Books Ltd, pg 768
United Writers Publications Ltd, pg 768
Vacation Work Publications, pg 769
Viking, pg 770
Virago Press, pg 770
Virgin Publishing Ltd, pg 770
Websters International Publishers Ltd, pg 772
Which? Ltd, pg 772
The Windrush Press Ltd, pg 774
Windsor Books International, pg 774

Zimbabwe
The Graham Publishing Company (Pvt) Ltd, pg 783

VETERINARY SCIENCE

Albania
NL SH, pg 1

Argentina
Editorial Albatros SACI, pg 3
EUDEBA (Editorial Universitaria de Buenos Aires), pg 5
Editorial Hemisferio Sur SA, pg 6
Inter-Medica, pg 6

Australia
Bureau of Resource Sciences, pg 16
Chiron Media, pg 17
Elsevier Australia, pg 21

Austria
Alois Goschl & Co, pg 51
IAEA - International Atomic Energy Agency, pg 52
Andreas Schnider Verlags-Atelier, pg 57

SUBJECT INDEX   BOOK

Brazil
ARTMED Editora, pg 78
Empresa Brasileira de Pesquisa Agropecuaria, pg 81
Editora Guanabara Koogan SA, pg 83
Editora Manole Ltda, pg 86
Organizacao Andrei Editora Ltda, pg 87
Livraria Roca Ltda, pg 89
Livraria Santos Editora Comercio e Importacao Ltda, pg 90

Chile
Arrayan Editores, pg 98

China
China Agriculture Press, pg 102
Heilongjiang Science & Technology Press, pg 105
Inner Mongolia Science & Technology Publishing House, pg 105
Jilin Science & Technology Publishing House, pg 105

Costa Rica
Instituto Interamericano de Cooperacion para la Agricultura (IICA), pg 115

Cuba
ISCAH Fructuoso Rodriguez, pg 120

France
Cirad, pg 154
INRA Editions (Institut National de la Recherche Agronomique), pg 168
Editions Maloine, pg 174
Masson Editeur, pg 174
Les Editions du Point Veterinaire, pg 180
Editions Vigot Universitaire, pg 188

Germany
Blackwell Wissenschafts-Verlag GmbH, pg 201
Ferdinand Enke Verlag, pg 224
M & H Schaper GmbH & Co KG, pg 279
Verlag R S Schulz GmbH, pg 282
Verlag Eugen Ulmer GmbH & Co, pg 293
UTB fuer Wissenschaft Uni Taschenbuecher GmbH, pg 294

Greece
Beta Medical Publishers, pg 306
Gartaganis D, pg 307
Hestia-I D Hestia-Kollaros & Co Corporation, pg 308

Hungary
Akademiai Kiado, pg 320
Mezogazda Kiado, pg 323

India
Affiliated East West Press Pvt Ltd, pg 327
Allied Book Centre, pg 328
Book Circle, pg 330
Cosmo Publications, pg 332
Daya Publishing House, pg 333
International Book Distributors, pg 338
Omsons Publications, pg 344
Scientific Book Agency, pg 348

Italy
Apimondia, pg 375
CG Ediz Medico-Scientifiche, pg 381
Edagricole - Edizioni Agricole, pg 385
Edi.Ermes srl, pg 388
Giuseppe Laterza Editore, pg 391
OEMF srl International, pg 401
UTET (Unione Tipografico-Editrice Torinese), pg 411
Vinciana Editrice sas, pg 412

Japan
Ishiyaku Publishers Inc, pg 419
Nishimura Co Ltd, pg 424

Kenya
Kenya Literature Bureau, pg 434
Nairobi University Press, pg 435

Democratic People's Republic of Korea
Korea Science and Encyclopedia Publishing House, pg 436

Mexico
AGT Editor SA, pg 462
Colegio de Postgraduados en Ciencias Agricolas, pg 463
Editorial El Manual Moderno SA de CV, pg 464
Editorial Limusa SA de CV, pg 467
Ediciones Cientificas La Prensa Medica Mexicana SA de CV, pg 470
Editorial Trillas SA de CV, pg 472
Universidad Nacional Autonoma de Mexico (National University of Mexico), pg 472

Namibia
Agrivet Publishers, pg 476

Netherlands
Tirion Uitgevers BV, pg 490

New Zealand
Publishing Solutions Ltd, pg 500

Nigeria
Ahmadu Bello University Press Ltd, pg 503
Riverside Communications, pg 507

Poland
Panstwowe Wydawnictwo Rolnicze i Lesne, pg 525
PZWL Wydawnictwo Lekarskie Ltd, pg 526

Portugal
Instituto de Investigacao Cientifica Tropical, pg 532

Romania
Editura Ceres, pg 539
Editura Gryphon, pg 540
MAST Verlag, pg 540

Russian Federation
Scorpion Publishers, pg 548

Saudi Arabia
Dar Al-Shareff for Publishing & Distribution, pg 550

Slovakia
Priroda Publishing, pg 560

Spain
Editorial Acribia SA, pg 571
Editorial AEDOS SA, pg 571
Mundi-Prensa Libros SA, pg 592
Permanyer Publications, pg 596
Pulso Ediciones, SL, pg 597
Servicio de Publicaciones Universidad de Cordoba, pg 599

Switzerland
S Karger AG, Medical & Scientific Publishers, pg 626

Taiwan, Province of China
Ho-Chi Book Publishing Co, pg 640
Yi Hsien Publishing Co Ltd, pg 642

Tunisia
Academie Tunisienne des Sciences, des Lettres et des Arts Beit El Hekma, pg 647

Ukraine
Urozaj, pg 654

United Kingdom
Blackwell Science Ltd, pg 667
The Eurospan Group, pg 692
Interpet Publishing, pg 714
The Kenilworth Press Ltd, pg 717
Lippincott Williams & Wilkins, pg 721
Liverpool University Press, pg 722
Manson Publishing Ltd, pg 725
Old Pond Publishing, pg 734
Pearson Education, pg 739
Pharmaceutical Press, pg 741

Viet Nam
Science & Technics Publishing House, pg 780

WESTERN FICTION

Bulgaria
Factor-Alias, pg 94
Trud - Izd kasta, pg 97

China
Beijing Publishing House, pg 101
Foreign Language Teaching & Research Press, pg 104

Czech Republic
Touzimsky & Moravec, pg 127

Denmark
Bonnier Publications A/S, pg 129

Estonia
Kupar Publishers, pg 139
Olion Publishers, pg 140

France
Publications Aredit, pg 147
Dargaud, pg 157
Alain Thomas Editeur, pg 187

Germany
Bastei Verlag, pg 197
Karl-May-Verlag Lothar Schmid GmbH, pg 244
Projektion J Buch- und Musikverlag GmbH, pg 272

Japan
Kokushokankokai Co Ltd, pg 421
Nippon Hoso Shuppan Kyokai (NHK Publishing), pg 424

Republic of Korea
Koreaone Press Inc, pg 440

Latvia
Egmont Latvia SIA, pg 444

Monaco
Les Editions du Rocher, pg 474

Philippines
Anvil Publishing Inc, pg 518

Portugal
Europress Editores e Distribuidores de Publicacoes Lda, pg 531

Romania
Editura Excelsior Art, pg 539

Russian Federation
CentrePolygraph Traders & Publishers Co, pg 544

Slovakia
Sport Publishing House Ltd, pg 561

Spain
Editorial Astri SA, pg 573
Ediciones Olimpic, SL, pg 594

Turkey
Metis Yayinlari, pg 650

Ukraine
ASK Ltd, pg 653

United Kingdom
BBC Audiobooks, pg 663
Isis Publishing Ltd, pg 714
New Era Publications UK Ltd, pg 732
Orion Publishing Group Ltd, pg 736
Ulverscroft Large Print Books Ltd, pg 768

WINE & SPIRITS

Argentina
Editorial Hemisferio Sur SA, pg 6

Australia
Australian Scholarly Publishing, pg 13
Cookery Book, pg 18
Crawford House Publishing Pty Ltd, pg 18
Hospitality Books, pg 26
R & R Publications Pty Ltd, pg 38
Regency Publishing, pg 39
The Watermark Press, pg 46
Winetitles, pg 47

PUBLISHERS

Austria
Leopold Stocker Verlag, pg 53
Niederosterreichisches Pressehaus Druck- und Verlagsgesellschaft mbH, pg 54

Belarus
Kavaler Publishers, pg 62

Belgium
Glenat Benelux SA, pg 67

Brazil
Rede Das Artes (Boccato Editores Collector's), pg 89

China
China Light Industry Press, pg 102

Croatia
Vitagraf, pg 119

Finland
Kustannus Oy Kolibri, pg 143

France
Editions de l'Armancon, pg 147
ATP - Packager, pg 148
Presses Universitaires de Bordeaux (PUB), pg 150
Editions Edisud, pg 159
EPA (Editions Pratiques Automobiles), pg 161
Flammarion SA, pg 163
Editions Jean Paul Gisserot, pg 165
Hachette Pratiques, pg 167
Editions Universitaires LCF, pg 171
Editions Mango, pg 174
Editions du Rouergue, pg 183
Siloe - Kerdore, pg 185
Editions Soline, pg 185

Germany
Verlag Busse und Seewald GmbH, pg 206
Fachverlag Hans Carl GmbH, pg 207
Christian Verlag GmbH, pg 208
Verlagsgruppe Droemer Knaur GmbH & Co KG, pg 216
Echter Wurzburg Frankische Gesellschaftsdruckerei und Verlag GmbH, pg 217
Walter Haedecke Verlag, pg 232
Jahreszeiten-Verlag GmbH, pg 242
Mosaik Verlag GmbH, pg 262
Munich, Edition, Verlag, Handels- und Dienstleistungskontar GmbH, pg 262
Pfalzische Verlagsanstalt GmbH, pg 269
Verlag Werner Sachon GmbH & Co, pg 277
ZS Verlag Zabert Sandmann GmbH, pg 302

Greece
Editions Moressopoulos, pg 310

Hong Kong
Press Mark Media Ltd, pg 318

Hungary
Kossuth Kiado RT, pg 322
Mezogazda Kiado, pg 323

Ireland
A & A Farmar, pg 357
Estragon Press Ltd, pg 359
The O'Brien Press Ltd, pg 362
On Stream Publications Ltd, pg 362

Israel
Gefen Publishing House Ltd, pg 367

Italy
Belforte Editore Libraio srl, pg 377
Ernesto Gremese Editore srl, pg 391
Trainer International Editore-I Libri del Bargello, pg 410

Mexico
Editorial Iztaccihuatl SA, pg 467

Netherlands
Uitgeverij Cantecleer BV, pg 480
Uitgeverij De Toorts, pg 490

New Zealand
Barkfire Press, pg 494
Nagare Press, pg 499

Portugal
Editora Classica, pg 530
Latina Livraria Editora, pg 532

Romania
Editura Niculescu, pg 541

Slovenia
East West Operation (EWO) Ltd, pg 561

South Africa
Fernwood Press (Pty) Ltd, pg 563

Spain
AMV Ediciones, pg 572
Comunidad Autonoma de Madrid, Servicio de Documentacion y Publicaciones, pg 578
Ediciones l'Isard, S L, pg 580
Lunwerg Editores, SA, pg 589

Sweden
BOOX, pg 610
Informationsfoerlaget AB, pg 612
Tryckeriforlaget AB, pg 616

Switzerland
Mueller Rueschlikon Verlags AG, pg 629
Pharos-Verlag, Hansrudolf Schwabe AG, pg 631

Taiwan, Province of China
Linking Publishing Company Ltd, pg 641

United Kingdom
Absolute Press, pg 655
BCA - Book Club Associates, pg 663
Mitchell Beazley, pg 664
Breslich & Foss Ltd, pg 671
Carlton Publishing Group, pg 675
Dorling Kindersley Ltd, pg 688
Faber & Faber Ltd, pg 694
Famedram Publishers Ltd, pg 694
Foulsham Publishers, pg 696
Grange Books PLC, pg 702
Grub Street, pg 703
HarperCollins UK, pg 705
Headline Book Publishing Ltd, pg 706
Hilmarton Manor Press, pg 708
Luath Press Ltd, pg 722
Marshall Editions Ltd, pg 725
Neil Wilson Publishing Ltd, pg 732
Nexus Special Interests, pg 733
Octopus Publishing Group, pg 734
Polybooks Ltd, pg 744
PRC Publishing Ltd, pg 745
Prism Press Book Publishers Ltd, pg 745
Quadrille Publishing Ltd, pg 746
Quintet Publishing Ltd, pg 747
Ryland Peters & Small Ltd, pg 752
Saqi Books, pg 754
Websters International Publishers Ltd, pg 772

Zambia
Aafzam Ltd, pg 781

WOMEN'S STUDIES

Albania
NL SH, pg 1

Argentina
Alfagrama SRL ediciones, pg 3
Editorial Paidos SAICF, pg 8

Australia
Artmoves Inc, pg 12
Australian Institute of Family Studies (AIFS), pg 13
Dangaroo Press, pg 19
Deakin University Press, pg 19
Finch Publishing, pg 22
Granrott Press, pg 24
Hale & Iremonger Pty Ltd, pg 24
Indra Publishing, pg 27
Ocean Press, pg 34
Oxfam Community Aid Abroad, pg 35
Parabel Place, pg 35
Playlab Press, pg 37
Pluto Press Australia Pty Ltd, pg 37
Ruskin Rowe Press, pg 40
Spinifex Press, pg 42
State Library of NSW Press, pg 42
Tarka Publishing, pg 42
Transpareon Press, pg 44
Unity Press, pg 44
University of New South Wales Press Ltd, pg 44
University of Western Australia Press, pg 45
Windhorse Books, pg 47
Women's Health Advisory Service, pg 47

Austria
Boehlau Verlag GmbH & Co KG, pg 48
Development News Ltd, pg 50
Doecker Verlag GmbH & Co KG, pg 50
Milena Verlag, pg 54
Promedia Verlagsges mbH, pg 56
Studien Verlag Gmbh, pg 58
WUV/Facultas Universitaetsverlag, pg 60

Bangladesh
Agamee Prakashani, pg 61
The University Press Ltd, pg 61

Belarus
Interdigest Publishing House, pg 62

SUBJECT INDEX

Belgium
VUB Brussels University Press, pg 74

Brazil
Editora Bertrand Brasil Ltda, pg 78
Companhia Editora Forense, pg 81
Editora Moderna Ltda, pg 86
Editora Rocco Ltda, pg 89
Summus Editorial Ltda, pg 91
Triom Centro de Estudos Marina e Martin Hawey Editorial e Comercial Ltda, pg 91

Chile
Editorial Cuarto Propio, pg 99

China
Beijing Publishing House, pg 101
Fudan University Press, pg 104
Higher Education Press, pg 105
Shanghai Far East Publishers, pg 108

Colombia
Instituto Misionerao Hijas De San Pablo, pg 112
Tercer Mundo Editores SA, pg 113

Costa Rica
Editorial DEI (Departamento Ecumenico de Investigaciones), pg 115
Instituto Interamericano de Cooperacion para la Agricultura (IICA), pg 115
Ediciones Promesa, pg 116

Denmark
Museum Tusculanum Press, pg 133

Ecuador
Centro de Planificacion y Estudios Sociales (CEPLAES), pg 136

Estonia
Perioodika, pg 140

Finland
Kaantopiiri Oy, pg 142
Osuuskunta Vastapaino, pg 144
Yliopistopaino/Helsinki University Press, pg 145

France
CERDIC-Publications, pg 153
Indigo & Cote-Femmes Editions, pg 168
Le Jour, Editeur, pg 169
Presses Universitaires du Mirail, pg 176

Germany
ARCult Media, pg 193
Argument-Verlag, pg 194
AvivA Britta Jurgs GmbH, pg 196
Belser Wissenschaftlicher Dienst, pg 199
Boehlau-Verlag GmbH & Cie, pg 202
Bund demokratischer Wissenschaftlerinnen und Wissenschafler eV (BdWi), pg 205
Campus Verlag GmbH, pg 207
Centaurus-Verlagsgesellschaft GmbH, pg 207
Dareschta Consulting und Handels GmbH, pg 210

1125

Edition Diskord, pg 215
agenda Verlag Thomas Dominikowski, pg 215
Espresso Verlag GmbH, pg 221
Harald Fischer Verlag GmbH, pg 224
Fischer Taschenbuch Verlag GmbH, pg 225
Frauenoffensive Verlagsgesellschaft MbH, pg 226
Konkursbuch Verlag Claudia Gehrke, pg 228
IKO Verlag fur Interkulturelle Kommunikation, pg 241
Iudicium Verlag GmbH, pg 242
Jahreszeiten-Verlag GmbH, pg 242
Verlag Kleine Schritte Ursula Dahm & Co, pg 246
Konkret Literatur Verlag, pg 249
Krug & Schadenberg, pg 250
Institut fuer Landes- und Stadtentwicklungsforschung des Landes Nordrhein-Westfalen, pg 251
Leipziger Universitaetsverlag GmbH, pg 253
Dr Gisela Lermann, pg 253
Annemarie Maeger, pg 256
Preubmpassling Verlag Gisela Meussling, pg 260
Ursala Meyer und Dr Manfred Duker Ein-Fach-Verlag, pg 260
Mosaik Verlag GmbH, pg 262
Verlag Neue Kritik KG, pg 264
Verlag Neuer Weg, pg 264
PapyRossa Verlags GmbH & Co Kommanditgesellschaft KG, pg 268
Verlag Anke Schaefer, pg 278
Stauffenburg Verlag Brigitte Narr GmbH, pg 287
Tuebinger Vereinigung fur Volkskunde eV (TVV), pg 292
Ulrike Helmer Verlag, pg 293
Unrast Verlag e V, pg 293
VAS-Verlag fuer Akademische Schriften, pg 294
Votum Verlag GmbH, pg 297
VWB-Verlag fur Wissenschaft & Bildung, Amand Aglaster, pg 297
Waxmann Verlag GmbH, pg 297
Verlag Westfaelisches Dampfboot, pg 299
Das Wunderhorn Verlag GmbH, pg 301
Zebulon Verlag GmbH & Co KG, pg 302

Ghana
Ghana Institute of Linguistics Literacy & Bible Translation (GILLBT), pg 304
Woeli Publishing Services, pg 305
World Literature Project, pg 305

Greece
Ekdoseis Thetili, pg 307
Hestia-I D Hestia-Kollaros & Co Corporation, pg 308
Odysseas Publications Ltd, pg 311

Hong Kong
Hong Kong University Press, pg 317

India
Affiliated East West Press Pvt Ltd, pg 327
Anmol Publications Pvt Ltd, pg 328
APH Publishing Corp, pg 328
Authorspress, pg 329
Book Circle, pg 330
The Christian Literature Society, pg 332
Concept Publishing Co, pg 332
Dastane Ramchandra & Co, pg 333
Gyan Publishing House, pg 335
Inter-India Publications, pg 338
Kali For Women, pg 339
Law Publishers, pg 340
National Book Organization, pg 342
Nem Chand & Brothers, pg 343
Omsons Publications, pg 344
Pointer Publishers, pg 345
Popular Prakashan Pvt Ltd, pg 345
Promilla & Publishers, pg 345
Radiant Publishers, pg 346
Regency Publications, pg 346
Reliance Publishing House, pg 346
SAGE Publications India Pvt Ltd, pg 347
Somaiya Publications Pvt Ltd, pg 349
Sterling Publishers Pvt Ltd, pg 350
Stree, pg 350

Indonesia
Lembaga Demografi Fakultas Ekonomi Universitas Indonesia, pg 355

Ireland
Attic Press Ltd, pg 358
Cathedral Books Ltd, pg 358
Cork University Press, pg 359
The O'Brien Press Ltd, pg 362

Israel
Bitan Publishers Ltd, pg 365
Hakibbutz Hameuchad Publishing House Ltd, pg 367
The Institute for Israeli Arabs Studies, pg 368
Schocken Publishing House Ltd, pg 371
Urim Publications, pg 373

Italy
Belforte Editore Libraio srl, pg 377
Colonnese Editore, pg 383
Edizioni Cultura della Pace, pg 383
Angelo Longo Editore, pg 396
La Luna, pg 396
Lyra Libri, pg 396
Edizioni Olivares, pg 401
Psicologica Editrice, pg 404
Rosenberg e Sellier Editori in Torino, pg 406
Rubbettino Editore, pg 406
La Tartaruga Edizioni SAS, pg 409
Transeuropa, pg 410

Jamaica
Association of Development Agencies, pg 413
University of the West Indies Press, pg 414

Japan
Chikuma Shobo Publishing Co Ltd, pg 416
Sagano Shoin, pg 426

Kenya
Paulines Publications-Africa, pg 435
Phoenix Publishers Ltd, pg 435
Shirikon Publishers, pg 436
Gideon S Were Press, pg 436

Republic of Korea
Chung Rim Publishing Co Ltd, pg 438
Hanul Publishing Co, pg 439
Munye Publishing Co, pg 441
O Neul Publishing Co, pg 441
Samseong Publishing Co Ltd, pg 442

Latvia
Preses Nams, pg 445

Lithuania
Victoria Publishers, pg 450

Luxembourg
Varkki Verghese, pg 452

Malaysia
Pustaka Cipta Sdn Bhd, pg 458

Mexico
El Colegio de Mexico AC, pg 463
Fondo de Cultura Economica, pg 465
Ibcon SA, pg 466
Libra Editorial SA de CV, pg 467
Ediciones Promesa, SA de CV, pg 470
Sayrols Editorial SA de CV, pg 471

Morocco
Edition Diffusion de Livre au Maroc, pg 474
Editions Le Fennec, pg 474
Societe Ennewrasse Service Librairie et Imprimerie, pg 475

Netherlands
Uitgeverij Jan van Arkel, pg 478
BZZTOH Publishers, pg 480
Uitgeverij De Fontein BV, pg 482
KITLV Press Royal Institute of Linguistics & Anthropology, pg 484
Narratio Theologische Uitgeverij, pg 486
Servire BV Uitgevers, pg 489
Sociaal en Cultureel Planbureau, pg 489
Unieboek BV, pg 490

Netherlands Antilles
De Wit Stores NV, pg 493

New Zealand
Auckland University Press, pg 493
Barkfire Press, pg 494
Clerestory Press, pg 495
Lincoln University Press, pg 498
New Women's Press Ltd, pg 499
Statistics New Zealand, pg 501
Tandem Press, pg 501
Bridget Williams Books Ltd, pg 502

Nigeria
International Publishing & Research Company, pg 505

Norway
Pax Forlag A/S, pg 510

Pakistan
ASR Publications, pg 512
Pakistan Institute of Development Economics (PIDE), pg 514

Papua New Guinea
Kristen Press, pg 515

Peru
Instituto de Estudios Peruanos, pg 517

Philippines
Anvil Publishing Inc, pg 518
Ateneo de Manila University Press, pg 518
Claretian Communications Inc, pg 518

Portugal
Comissao para a Igualdade e Direitos das Mulheres, pg 530
Impala, pg 532

Puerto Rico
Libros-Ediciones Homines, pg 537

Russian Federation
Dom, Izdatel'stvo sovetskogo deskkogo fonda im & I Lenina, pg 544

Saudi Arabia
Dar Al-Shareff for Publishing & Distribution, pg 550

Senegal
CODESRIA (Council for the Development of Social Science Research in Africa), pg 551

Slovenia
Mladinska Knjiga International, pg 561

South Africa
Human Sciences Research Council, pg 565
Institute for Reformational Studies CHE, pg 565
Juventus/Femina Publishers, pg 565
New Africa Books (Pty) Ltd, pg 567
Ravan Press (Pty) Ltd, pg 568
University of KwaZulu-Natal Press, pg 569

Spain
Ediciones Catedra SA, pg 576
Complutense, SA Editorial, pg 577
El Hogar y la Moda SA, pg 581
Eumo Editorial, pg 583
Editorial Gulaab, pg 586
Icaria Editorial SA, pg 587
Ediciones Morata SL, pg 592
Editorial Nerea SA, pg 593
Ediciones del Oriente y del Mediterraneo, pg 594
Publicaciones de la Universidad Pontificia Comillas-Madrid, pg 597
Anna Soler-Pont Literary Agecy, pg 600
Torremozas SL Ediciones, pg 602
Vinaches Lopez, Luisa, pg 605

Sri Lanka
International Centre for Ethnic Studies, pg 606
Karunaratne & Sons Ltd, pg 606
Swarna Hansa Foundation, pg 607

PUBLISHERS

Suriname
Stichting Wetenschappelijke Informatie, pg 608

Sweden
Acta Universitatis Gothoburgensis, pg 609
Carlsson Bokfoerlag AB, pg 610
Bokforlaget Nya Doxa AB, pg 614

Switzerland
Adonia-Verlag, pg 617
Bergli Books AG, pg 619
eFeF-Verlag/Edition Ebersbach, pg 622
Limmat Verlag, pg 628
Ruegger Verlag, pg 633
Verlag Die Waage, pg 636

Taiwan, Province of China
Asian Culture Co Ltd, pg 638
Laureate Book Co Ltd, pg 640
Linking Publishing Company Ltd, pg 641
UNITAS Publishing Co Ltd, pg 642

United Republic of Tanzania
DUP (1996) Ltd, pg 643
Tema Publishers Ltd, pg 644

Turkey
Cep Kitaplari AS, pg 649
Metis Yayinlari, pg 650
Payel Yayinevi, pg 651
Varlik Yayinlari AS, pg 652

Uganda
Centre for Basic Research, pg 652
Fountain Publishers Ltd, pg 652

Ukraine
Osnovy Publishers, pg 654

United Kingdom
Berg Publishers, pg 664
Berghahn Books Ltd, pg 665
BFI Publishing, pg 665
Blackwell Publishing Ltd, pg 666
Camden Press Ltd, pg 674
Capall Bann Publishing, pg 674
Cardiff Academic Press, pg 675
Chapman, pg 677
Commonwealth Secretariat, pg 681
The Continuum International Publishing Group Ltd, pg 682
CTBI Publications, pg 685
Edinburgh University Press Ltd, pg 689
Element Books Ltd, pg 690
The Eurospan Group, pg 692
Robert Hale Ltd, pg 704

HarperCollins UK, pg 705
Harvard University Press, pg 705
Hawthorn Press, pg 706
Health Development Agency, pg 706
Institute of Development Studies, pg 712
Institute of Employment Rights, pg 712
Intellect Ltd, pg 713
Adam Matthew Publications, pg 726
MIND Publications, pg 728
Motilal (UK) Books of India, pg 729
Onlywomen Press Ltd, pg 735
Open University Press, pg 736
Peter Owen Ltd, pg 737
Oxfam, pg 737
Parapress Ltd, pg 738
Pathfinder London, pg 739
Pearson Education, pg 739
Pickering & Chatto Publishers Ltd, pg 742
Pluto Press, pg 743
The Policy Press, pg 744
Polygon, pg 744
Pomegranate Europe Ltd, pg 744
Rivers Oram Press, pg 750
Routledge, pg 751
RoutledgeCurzon, pg 751
The Rubicon Press, pg 752
SAGE Publications Ltd, pg 753
Seren, pg 756

Serpent's Tail Ltd, pg 756
Thomson Gale, pg 765
Trentham Books Ltd, pg 767
University of Wales Press, pg 769
Verso, pg 770
Virago Press, pg 770
White Cockade Publishing, pg 772
WI Enterprises Ltd, pg 773
Wimbledon Publishing Company Ltd, pg 774
The Women's Press Ltd, pg 775
Wordwright Publishing, pg 775
Yale University Press London, pg 776
Zed Books Ltd, pg 776

Uruguay
Cotidiano Mujer, pg 777
Nordan-Comunidad, pg 778
Luis A Retta Libros, pg 778
Ediciones Trilce, pg 778

Venezuela
Editorial Nueva Sociedad, pg 780

Zambia
Zambia Association for Research & Development (ZARD), pg 782
Zambia Printing Company Ltd (ZPC), pg 782

Literary Agents

Argentina

International Editors' Co
Ave Cabildo 1156 - 1 A, 1426 Buenos Aires
Tel: (011) 4788-2992; (011) 4786-0888
   Fax: (011) 4786-0888
E-mail: costa@lvd.com.ar
Founded: 1939
Agencia Literaria; Subsidiaries in Spain & Brazil.

Guillermo Schavelzon
Rodriguez Pena 2067, 3A, 1021 Buenos Aires
Tel: (011) 48 13 84 20 *Fax:* (011) 48 13 28 76
E-mail: info@schavelzon.com
Key Personnel
Main Agent: Guillermo Schavelzon
Foreign Rights: Monica Herrero
   E-mail: monicaherrero@schavelzon.com
Licensing: Hugo Princ
Founded: 1998
No unsolicited mss, query first; submit a brief author's biblio-biography (2-3 pgs), a summary of the work that the author intends to submit (2-3 pgs), a sample reading of the work consisting of 2-3 chapters; no reading fees, online content providers.
Specializes in Latin American writers (fiction & nonfiction).

Australia

Australian Licensing Corp
Affiliate of Little Hare Books Pty Ltd
Unit 4/21 Mary St, Surry Hills, NSW 2010
Tel: (02) 9280 2220 *Fax:* (02) 9280 2223
E-mail: rodhare@alc-online.com
Web Site: www.alc-online.com
Founded: 1999
Membership(s): Australian Publishers Association.
Specializes in childrens' books.

Curtis Brown (Australia) Pty Ltd
27 Union St, Paddington, Sydney, NSW 2021
Mailing Address: PO Box 19, Paddington, NSW 2021
Tel: (02) 9331 5301 *Fax:* (02) 9360 3935
E-mail: info@curtisbrown.com.au
Key Personnel
Man Dir: Fiona Inglis
Dir: Tim Curnow *E-mail:* tim@curtisbrown.com.au
Contact: Garth Nix
Founded: 1967

Bryson Agency Australia Pty Ltd
313-315 Flinders Lane, 1st floor, Melbourne 3000
Mailing Address: PO Box 226, Flinders Lane PO, Melbourne 8009
Tel: (03) 9620 9100 *Fax:* (03) 9621 2788
E-mail: agency@bryson.com.au
Web Site: www.bryson.com.au
Key Personnel
Contact: Fran Bryson
Book manuscrips only, in hard copy. Must send a sample of first chapters (5000 words maximum), a synopsis (1-2 pages), CV & return postage.

The Mary Cunnane Agency Pty Ltd
28 Milina Rd, Matcham, NSW 2250
Mailing Address: PO Box 781, Terrigal, NSW 2260
Tel: (02) 438599922 *Fax:* (02) 43651093
E-mail: info@cunnaneagency.com
Web Site: www.cunnaneagency.com
Key Personnel
Dir: Mary Cunnane
Founded: 1999
Entire mss & sample chapters in hard copy only after query which may be by mail, phone or email. Adult fiction & nonfiction.

Diversity Management
PO Box 1449, Darlinghurst, NSW 1300
Tel: (02) 9130 4305 *Fax:* (02) 9365 1426
Key Personnel
Agent: Bill Tikos *E-mail:* bill@diversitym.com.au
Specialize in adult nonfiction. Contact via e-mail.

The Drummond Agency
PO Box 572, Woodend, Victoria 3442
Tel: (03) 5427 3644 *Fax:* (03) 5427 3655
Key Personnel
Dir: Sheila Drummond *E-mail:* sheilad@ozemail.com.au
Founded: 1995
Also offers international rights consultancy to publishers.

Austria

Literaturagentur Andreas Brunner
Formerly Literarische Agentur Diana Voigt
Schaeffergasse 22/4, 1040 Vienna
Tel: (01) 5333191 *Fax:* (01) 5333191-15
E-mail: brunner@literaturagentur.at
Web Site: www.literaturagentur.at
Key Personnel
Dir & Owner: Andreas Brunner
Founded: 1996 (as Literary Agency Diana Voigt)
Covering the German language market for US, UK & Canadian publishers & international authors.
Specializes in high quality fiction, psychology, self help, history, politics, theatre, film.

Literarische Agentur Diana Voigt, see Literaturagentur Andreas Brunner

Barbados

The Barbados National Trust
Wildey Great House, Wildey St, St Michael
Tel: 246-426-2421 *Fax:* 246-429-9055
E-mail: natrust@sunbeach.net
Web Site: trust.funbarbados.com
Key Personnel
President: John Cole
Executive Dir: Penelope Hynam Roach
Founded: 1961
Specializes in heritage & environmental conservation.

Belgium

Toneelfonds J Janssens BVBA
Te Boelaerlei 107, 2140 Borgerhout, Antwerp
Tel: (03) 366 44 00 *Fax:* (03) 366 45 01
E-mail: info@toneelfonds.be
Web Site: www.toneelfonds.be
Key Personnel
Dir: Jessica Janssens *E-mail:* jessica.janssens@toneelfonds.be
Founded: 1880
Publisher of plays & literary agent for playwrights.
Specializes in plays.

Brazil

Agencia Literaria Balcells Mello e Souza Riff S/C Ltda (Balcells Mello & Souza Riff Literary Agency)
Rua Visconde de Piraja, 414/1108, 22410-002 Rio de Janeiro-RJ
Tel: (021) 2287-6299 *Fax:* (021) 2287-6393
E-mail: bmsr@bmsr.com.br
Web Site: www.bmsr.com.br
Key Personnel
Literary Agent & Executive: Lucia Riff
   E-mail: lucia@bmsr.com.br
Founded: 1991
Co-agent of foreign publishers & literary agencies.
Specializes in foreign authors for the Brazilian/Portuguese language market & Brazilian authors for Brazil & abroad.

BMSR Literary Agency, see Agencia Literaria Balcells Mello e Souza Riff S/C Ltda

Pagina da Cultura Agencia Literaria Ideias sobre Linhas Ltda (Pagina da Cultura Literary Agency Ideas over Liens Ltda)
Affiliate of Camara Brasileira do Livro
R Coronel Jose Eusebio, 95, Vila Dona Paula Casa 2, 01239-030 Sao Paulo
Tel: (011) 31293900
E-mail: paginadacultura@pobox.com
Web Site: www.pagina-da-cultura.com.br
Key Personnel
Contact: Marisa Moura *E-mail:* marisa.moura@paginadacultura.com.br
Founded: 1994
Specializes in business, essays, fiction, history, religions, self-help, children & juvenile books.

Karin Schindler
CP 19051, 04505-970 Sao Paulo
Tel: (011) 5041-9177 *Fax:* (011) 5041-9077
E-mail: kschind@terra.com.br
Key Personnel
Contact: Karin Schindler

Czech Republic

A R T Dialog
Michelska 81, 141 00 Prague 4
Tel: (0420) 24148 2808 *Fax:* (0420) 24148 1442
E-mail: artdialog@mybox.cz
Web Site: www.artdialog-literary.wz.cz
Key Personnel
Contact: Rene J Tesar *E-mail:* rene.tesar@worldonline.cz; Daniela Vranovska
Founded: 1990
Specializes in import of English & German language literature translation rights to Czech book market.

Agency Rene Tesar Dialog, see A R T Dialog

DILIA
Kratkeho 1, 19003 Prague 9
Tel: (02) 83891587 *Fax:* (02) 826348; (02) 83893599; (02) 83890598; (02) 83890597
E-mail: chabr@dilia.cz
Web Site: www.dilia.cz *Cable:* DILIA PRAG
Key Personnel
Man Dir: Ladislav Simon
Contact: Dr Vera Stranska
Theatrical & literary agency.
Membership(s): Society for Protection of Authors' Rights.

Denmark

Bookman Literary Agency
Bastager 3, 2950 Vedbaek, Copenhagen
Tel: 45892520 *Fax:* 45892501
Web Site: www.bookman.dk *Cable:* BOOKMAN; COPENHAGEN
Key Personnel
Agent: Ib H Lauritzen *E-mail:* ihl@bookman.dk; Mrs Bebbe Lauritzen
Founded: 1912
Also acts as a literary agent in Denmark, Sweden, Norway, Finland & Iceland for foreign authors.
Specializes in business, general fiction, quality novels, sales to magazines, sports (golf, tennis).

ICBS, see ICBS/IBIS ApS

ICBS/IBIS ApS
Kvaesthusgade 3F, 1251 Copenhagen
Tel: 33114255 *Fax:* 33911167
E-mail: icbs@get2net.dk
Web Site: www.icbs-ibis.dk
Key Personnel
Contact: Virginia Allen Jensen; Johan Broensted
Founded: 1962
Specializes in children's books, co-productions, adult fiction & nonfiction.

Leonhardt & Hoier Literary Agency ApS
Studiestr 35, 1455 Copenhagen
Tel: 33132523 *Fax:* 33134992
Web Site: www.leonhardt-hoier.dk
Key Personnel
Dir: Anneli Hoier *E-mail:* anneli@leonhardt-hoier.dk
Contact: Monica Gram *E-mail:* monica@leonhardt-hoier.dk
Representing international publishers & agents in Scandinavia & Scandinavian authors worldwide.
Specializes in modern fiction.

Licht & Licht Literary Agency
Maglemosevej 46, DK-2920 Charlottenlund
Tel: 39610908 *Fax:* 39611105
Key Personnel
Chief Executive: Ole Licht; Agnes Licht
Representing American, Australian, British & Canadian agents & publishers in Denmark, Finland, Iceland, Norway & Sweden & representing Scandanavian authors worldwide.

Ulla Lohren Literary Agency
Vaerebrovej 89, 2880 Bagsvaerd
Tel: 44494515 *Fax:* 44493515
E-mail: ulla.litag@get2net.dk

Scanvik Books Import ApS
Esplanaden 8 B, 1263 Copenhagen
Tel: 3312 7766 *Fax:* 3391 2882
E-mail: mail@scanvik.dk; scanvik@bog.dk
Web Site: www.scanvik.dk
Key Personnel
Dir: John Roberts; Uwe Schultheiss
Founded: 1980
Wholesaler, distributor & agent.
Specializes in maps & travel guides.

Egypt (Arab Republic of Egypt)

The Egyptian Society for the Dissemination of Universal Culture and Knowledge (ESDUCK)
1081 Corniche El Nil, Garden City, Cairo
Mailing Address: PO Box 21, Cairo
Tel: (02) 3542 0295 *Fax:* (02) 3540295 *Cable:* ESDUCK
Key Personnel
Executive Manager: Dr Amin El-Gamal

ESDUCK, see The Egyptian Society for the Dissemination of Universal Culture and Knowledge (ESDUCK)

Finland

Werner Soederstrom Osakeyhtio (WSOY)
Bulevardi 12, 00120 Helsinki
Mailing Address: PO Box 222, 00121 Helsinki
Tel: (00) 61681 *Fax:* (90) 61683566
Telex: 122644 Wsoy *Cable:* WSOY HELSINKI
Key Personnel
Rights & Permissions: Sirkku Klemola
Founded: 1878
Also Publisher.
Parent Company: Sanoma WSOY

WSOY, see Werner Soederstrom Osakeyhtio (WSOY)

France

Agence de l'Est
11, rue Git-le-Coeur, 75006 Paris
Tel: (01) 46334816; (06) 6546 7928 *Fax:* (01) 46334816
E-mail: agencedelest1@wanadoo.fr
Founded: 1999
Represents French authors in central & eastern Europe.
Specializes in negotiating between France & Eastern Europe (from Estonia to Albania & from the Czech Republic to Russia) for non-illustrated & illustrated books.

Eliane Benisti Literary Agency
80 rue des Sts-Peres, 75007 Paris
Tel: (01) 42228533 *Fax:* (01) 45441817
E-mail: benisti@compuserve.com
Key Personnel
Dir: Eliane Benisti

EAIS Literary Agents
8/12 rue de l'Abreuvoir, 92400 Courbevoie
Tel: (01) 47 88 08 40 *Fax:* (01) 47 88 08 40
Key Personnel
Vice President: Vera le Marie *E-mail:* vera.le.marie@wanadoo.fr
Founded: 1983
Representation of American publishers & writers in France, & French publishers & writers in the USA & Russia. Specialize in foreign languages: English, German, French, Dutch, & Polish.
Ultimate Parent Company: EAIS - France
U.S. Office(s): European American Information Services Inc, Sarasota, FL 34236, United States, Contact: Dr Allan M Chyrtowski
Tel: 941-955-3472 *Fax:* 941-955-5365

European American Information Services Inc, see EAIS Literary Agents

Lora Fountain & Associates Literary Agency
(Agence Litteraire Lora Fountain & Associates)
7 rue de Belfort, 75011 Paris
Tel: (01) 43562196 *Fax:* (01) 43482272
E-mail: lora@fountlit.com
Key Personnel
Man Dir: Lora Fountain
Associate Agent: Alexandre Civico
E-mail: alexandre@fountlit.com; Svetlana Ramon *E-mail:* svetlana@fountlit.com
Founded: 1985
No unsol mss.
Specializes in French rights sales for English-language publishers (UK, Ireland, USA, Canada, Australia & New Zealand). Also sale of rights to Italy, Netherlands, Spain & Russia. Quality adult fiction & nonfiction, children's literature.

Agence Hoffman
77 Blvd St-Michel, 75005 Paris
Tel: (01) 43265694 *Fax:* (01) 43263407
E-mail: info@agence-hoffman.com
Telex: 203605 F *Cable:* AGHOFF PARIS
Key Personnel
Contact: Boris Hoffman; Ursula Veit; Georges Hoffman
Branch Office(s)
Munich, Germany

Michelle Lapautre
6 rue Jean Carries, 75007 Paris
Tel: (01) 47348241 *Fax:* (01) 47340090
E-mail: lapautre@club-internet.fr
Parent Company: Agence Michelle Lapautre

Montreal-Contacts/The Rights Agency
70 bd de Picpus, 75012 Paris
Tel: (01) 43 40 06 10 *Fax:* (01) 43 40 02 12
Key Personnel
Owner: Luc Jutras *Tel:* 450-461-1575 (Canada)
E-mail: ljutras@montreal-contacts.com

Dir: Anne Confuron *E-mail:* aconfuron@montreal-contacts.com
Represents American, Canadian & other foreign publishers &/or literary exclusively. No author representation.

La Nouvelle Agence
7 rue Corneille, 75006 Paris
Tel: (01) 43258560 *Fax:* (01) 43254798
E-mail: lnaparis@aol.com
Telex: 250303 F (Paris Bourse)
Key Personnel
Contact: Mary Kling

Frederique Porretta
70 rue d'Assas, 75006 Paris
Tel: (01) 45448868 *Fax:* (01) 45446936
E-mail: frederique.porretta@wanadoo.fr
Key Personnel
Rights Dir: Frederique Poretta
Founded: 1992

Shelley Power Literary Agency Ltd
13 rue du Pre Saint Gervais, 75019 Paris
Tel: (01) 42383649 *Fax:* (01) 40407008
Key Personnel
Dir: Shelley Power *E-mail:* shelley.power@wanadoo.fr
Founded: 1976
Handles general commercial fiction, quality fiction, business, self-help, health, true crime, investigative exposes, film & entertainment. No scripts, short stories, children's or poetry. Preliminary letter with brief outline of project plus return postage. No reading fee.

Promotion Litteraire
12 rue Pergolese, F-75116 Paris
Tel: (01) 45004210 *Fax:* (01) 45001018
E-mail: promolit@club-internet.fr
Key Personnel
Dir: Mariella Giannetti
Specializes in literary translations, book & article translations.

Germany

Asien und Lateinamerika eV, see Society for the Promotion of African, Asian & Latin American Literature

Agence Hoffman
Bechsteinstr 2, 80804 Munich
Tel: (089) 3084807; (089) 3087469 *Fax:* (089) 3082108
E-mail: info@agencehoffman.de
Web Site: www.agencehoffman.de *Cable:* AGHOFF MUNICH
Key Personnel
Contact: Ursula Bender *E-mail:* u.bender@agencehoffman.de
Literary agents & publishers from UK & USA.
Branch Office(s)
Blvd St Michel, 77, 75005 Paris, France

Autoren- und Verlags-Agentur GmbH (AVA)
Seeblickstr 46, 82211 Herrsching-Breitbrunn, Bavaria
Tel: (08152) 925883 *Fax:* (08152) 3076
E-mail: avagmbh@aol.com
Founded: 1989
Specializes in fiction & nonfiction.

AVA, see Autoren- und Verlags-Agentur GmbH (AVA)

Dr Ivanka Beil, Internationale Handelsvermittlung im Medien- und Verlagswesen
Schollstr 1, 69469 Weinheim
Tel: (06201) 14611 *Fax:* (06201) 16883
Founded: 1984
Specializes in copyright intervention, co-productions, representation of publishing houses, authors, illustrators, children's & young readers' books (also on film & television productions), marketing.
Branch Office(s)
Theodor Heuss Str 14, 69469 Weinheim

The Berlin Agency (Jung-Lindemann & Olechnowitz)
Niebuhrstr 74, 10629 Berlin
Tel: (030) 88702888 *Fax:* (030) 88702889
E-mail: junglindemann@berlinagency.de
Web Site: www.berlinagency.de
Key Personnel
Contact: Ms Frauke Jung-Lindemann
Founded: 1999
Specializes in fiction & nonfiction.

Cartoon-Caricature-Contor (CCC)
Rosmarinstr 4, 80939 Munich
Tel: (089) 3233669 *Fax:* (089) 3226859
E-mail: ccc@c5.net
Web Site: www.c5.net
Key Personnel
Dir: Arno Koch
Founded: 1977
Acts as agents for cartoons, caricatures & illustrations.
Specializes in cartoons, with stock of about 100,000.

CCC, see Cartoon-Caricature-Contor (CCC)

Copyright International Agency Corina GmbH
Beerenstr 22A, 14163 Berlin
Tel: (030) 80902386 *Fax:* (030) 80902388
E-mail: info@corina.com
Web Site: www.corina.com
Key Personnel
President: Werner B Thiele
Founded: 1998
Internet literary agency. Offers translation rights.
Specializes in literature from & for Middle & Eastern European countries.

DMK-Verlag
Hutergasse 4, 90403 Nurnberg
Tel: (0911) 203946; (0911) 227698 *Fax:* (0911) 208897 *Cable:* KLINGERKUNST
Key Personnel
Contact: D M Klinger
Specializes in art, photography, the arts.

Gesellschaft zur Foerderung der Literatur aus Afrika, see Society for the Promotion of African, Asian & Latin American Literature

Gina Schlenz Literatur-Agentur Koln
Gruenenborn 49, 53797 Lohmar
Tel: (02206) 81125 *Fax:* (02206) 81125
E-mail: litschlenz@aol.com
Founded: 1989
Specializes in children & young adults.

Agentur Literatur Gudrun Hebel
Behaimstr 20, 10585 Berlin
Tel: (030) 34 70 77 67 *Fax:* (030) 34 70 77 68
E-mail: info@agentur-literatur.de; gudrun.hebel@agentur-literatur.de
Web Site: www.agentur-literatur.de
Key Personnel
Contact: Gudrun Hebel
Representing foreign publishers, agencies & authors in German-language-countries as well as German authors & publishers worldwide.
Specializes in Scandinavian literature.

IBA International Media & Book Agency
Heinrich Roller-Str 16 - 17 2 Hof, 10405 Berlin
Mailing Address: Postfach 550 142, 10371 Berlin
Tel: (030) 4437 9155 *Fax:* (030) 4437 9199
E-mail: office@iba-berlin.de
Web Site: www.iba-berlin.de
Key Personnel
President & Executive Dir: Ingo-Eric M Schmidt-Braul
Founded: 1991
Also acts as representative of authors & publishing houses.
Specializes in fiction, nonfiction, economics.

Keil & Keil Literary Agency
Schulterblatt 58, 20357 Hamburg
Tel: (040) 27166892 *Fax:* (040) 27166896
E-mail: anfragen@keil-keil.com
Web Site: www.keil-keil.com
Key Personnel
Agent: Anja Keil *Tel:* (040) 27166894
  E-mail: ak@keil-keil.com; Bettina Keil
  Tel: (040) 27166893 *E-mail:* bk@keil-keil.com
Founded: 1995
Email queries preferred (no attachments).
Specializes in general trade fiction & nonfiction. No fantasy, sci-fi & children's & young adult. Have representatives in all major international markets. No unsol mss, query first; provide outline with SASE.

Ingrid Anna Kleihues Verlags und Autorenagentur
Weinbergweg 62A, 70569 Stuttgart
Tel: (0711) 6788800 *Fax:* (0711) 6788801
E-mail: info@agentur-kleihues.de
Founded: 1990
Specializes in non-fiction.

LITkom Elisabeth Falk Agentur fur Literatur und Kommunikation (LITkom Elisabeth Falk Agency for Literature & Communication)
Auf Erden 2, 54610 Buedesheim, Rheinland-Pfalz
E-mail: falk@litkom.de
Web Site: www.litkom.de *Cable:* LITKOM E.FALK
Key Personnel
Agent: Elisabeth Falk
Founded: 1993
Represents authors & handles their manuscripts; exhibits international book art objects; organizes literary events.
Specializes in art books, exhibitions & literary functions.

MBMS-Bibliography & Management Service
Postfach 1206, 57271 Hilchenbach
Tel: (02733) 7657 *Fax:* (02733) 8492
Key Personnel
Contact: Christiane Urlea-Schoen *E-mail:* urlea@cheerful.com
Founded: 1989
Specializes in literature, medicine, management, business.

Medienbuero Muenchen (Media Agency Munich)
Division of Philosophia Verlag GmbH
Gundelindenstr 4, 80805 Munich
Mailing Address: Postfach 221362, 80503 Munich
Tel: (089) 299975 *Fax:* (089) 299975
E-mail: info@medienbuero-muenchen.com
Web Site: www.medienbuero-muenchen.com
Key Personnel
Publisher: Ulrich Staudinger *E-mail:* ulrich.staudinger@philosophiaverlag.com

GERMANY

Founded: 2000
Agency for authors & publishers in print, TV, film & new media.
Specializes in nonfiction, science, fiction.

Merchandising Muenchen KG
Reichenbachstr 2, 85737 Ismaning
Mailing Address: Postfach 1339, 85767 Unterfohring
Tel: (089) 95078600 *Fax:* (089) 95078700
E-mail: info.line@merchandising-muenchen.de
Web Site: www.merchandisingmedia.com
Key Personnel
Contact: Bettina Koeckler *E-mail:* bettina.koeckler@merchandisingmedia.com
Specializes in sales, marketing, business licenses.
Branch Office(s)
Hausvogteiplatz 1, 10117 Berlin *Tel:* (030) 20902658 *Fax:* (030) 20902643

Dr Ray-Gude Mertin Literarische Agentur
Friedrichstr 1, 61348 Bad Homburg
Tel: (06172) 29842 *Fax:* (06172) 29771
E-mail: mertin@em.uni-frankfurt.de
Key Personnel
Contact: Mrs Ray-Guede Mertin
Worldwide representation of authors from Brazil, Portugal, Africa, Latin America & Spain.
Specializes in fiction & nonfiction.

Literaturbetreuung Klaus Middendorf (LKM)
Auerbergweg 8, 86836 Graben
Tel: (08232) 78463 *Fax:* (08232) 78468
E-mail: lkmcorp@t-online.de
Web Site: www.lkmcorp.com
Key Personnel
Contact: Klaus Middendorf
Founded: 1986
Author & Publisher Representation.

Martina M Oepping Literary Agency
Wolfsgangstr 34, 60322 Frankfurt am Main
Tel: (069) 59790011 *Fax:* (069) 59790012
E-mail: litag@oepping.de
Web Site: www.oepping.de
Key Personnel
Literary Agent: Martina M Oepping
Founded: 1996
Specializes in children's & juvenile books, authors & illustrators.

Literatur-Agentur Axel Poldner
Ostpreussentr 27, 81927 Munich
Mailing Address: Raduhner Str 11, 12355 Berlin
Tel: (089) 909 558 92 *Fax:* (089) 909 558 91
E-mail: info@poldner.de
Web Site: www.poldner.de
Key Personnel
Contact: Axel Poldner *E-mail:* axel.poldner@poldner.de
Founded: 1970
Specializes in multimedia projects.

Quelle Press
Schoenbergerstr 49, 79227 Schallstadt
Mailing Address: Postfach 1314, 79013 Freiburg/Br
Tel: (07664) 7016 *Fax:* (07664) 60979
E-mail: quellepress.germany@gmx.net *Cable:* QUELLEPRESS -SHALLSTADT
Key Personnel
President: Friedrich-Wilhelm Koenig
Founded: 1948
Services include editing advice, reading, translation & international activities; global licensing for 50 years; 18,900 copyrights sold.
Specializes in mass market, business books, esoteric, holistic, new age, romances, anthologies, newspaper (serials), books for young readers, trade books, alternative medicine, basic business books, self counsel books, self improvement books, life style books, psychology, religion, human science, sports, self help books for young readers.
Branch Office(s)
Australia
Bulgaria
China
Croatia
Czech Republic
France
Hungary
India
Indonesia
Italy
Japan
Republic of Korea
Poland
Portugal
Russian Federation (East European Market)
Slovakia
Spain
Taiwan, Province of China

Thomas Schlueck GmbH
Hinter der Worth 12, 30827 Garbsen
Tel: (05131) 497560 *Fax:* (05131) 497589
E-mail: mail@schlueckagent.com
Web Site: www.schlueckagent.com
Key Personnel
Contact: Joachim Jessen; Bastian Schlueck; Thomas Schlueck
Founded: 1970
Full representation of Anglo-American authors, agents & publishers in German language areas, as well as representation of German authors. Handle second rights of cover illustrations, Europe wide.

Skandinavia Verlag
Ithweg 31, 14163 Berlin
Tel: (030) 8137006 *Fax:* (030) 8141029
Key Personnel
Contact: Marianne Weno
Founded: 1969
Specializes in Scandinavian stage, radio & TV plays.

Society for the Promotion of African, Asian & Latin American Literature
Reineckstr 3, 60313 Frankfurt am Main
Mailing Address: Postfach 10 01 16, 60001 Frankfurt am Main
Tel: (069) 2102247 *Fax:* (069) 2102227
E-mail: litprom@book-fair.com
Web Site: www.litprom.de
Key Personnel
President: Peter Weidhaas
Dir: Peter Ripken
Founded: 1980
The Society seeks to promote German translations of creative writing from Africa, Asia & Latin America. It works as a non-profit agency & as a consultant for German language publishers & for "Third World" publishers & authors who have German translation rights to offer. Publishes *LiteraturNachrichten* (Literary News).

Tipress Deutschland GmbH, see Tipress Dienstleistungen fur das Verlagswesen GmbH

Tipress Dienstleistungen fur das Verlagswesen GmbH
Johannes-Fecht-Str 2, 79295 Sulzburg
Tel: (07634) 591193 *Fax:* (07634) 591192
E-mail: tipress@tipress.com
Web Site: www.tipress.com *Cable:* TIPRESS
Key Personnel
Chief Executive: Roberto Toso
Assistant: Claudia Robert
Founded: 1980
Specializes in co-editions, illustrated books, handbooks, encyclopedias, children's books.
Branch Office(s)
Tipress Deutschland GmbH, via Cernaia 34, 10122 Turino, Italy, Contact: Ms Claudia Robert *Tel:* (011) 533487 *Fax:* (011) 535283

Hungary

Artisjus
Meszaros utca 15-17, 1016 Budapest
Tel: (01) 488 2600 *Fax:* (01) 212 1544
E-mail: info@artisjus.com
Web Site: www.artisjus.hu *Cable:* ARTISJUS
Key Personnel
Contact: Anita Kenedi
Agency for Theater & Literature of the Hungarian Bureau for Copyright Protection.

Katai & Bolza Irodalmi Ugynokseg (Katai & Bolza Literary Agents)
Vamhaz Krt 15, 1st floor, No 8, 1093 Budapest
Mailing Address: PO Box 1666, 1465 Budapest
Tel: (01) 456-0313 *Fax:* (01) 215-4420
Web Site: www.kataibolza.hu
Key Personnel
Agent: Peter Bolza *E-mail:* peter@kataibolza.hu; Katalin Katai *E-mail:* katalin@kataibolza.hu
Founded: 1995
Represents mainly US & British publishers & agents in the Hungarian market.

India

Ajanta Books International
One U B Jawahar Nagar, Bangalow Rd, Delhi 110007
Tel: (011) 3926182 *Fax:* (011) 7415016
E-mail: ajantabi@ndf.vsnl.net.in; ajantabi@id.erh.net
Key Personnel
Proprietor: Mr S Balwant
Founded: 1975
Specializes in social sciences & humanities, children, paperbook.

Dipak Kumar Guha
PO Box 3205, New Delhi 110013
Tel: (011) 2-553-1842 *Fax:* (011) 2-550-0998
E-mail: dkguha@eth.net; anybody@bol.net.in
Founded: 1986
Activities also include market evaluation, promotion & public relations, special sales, excess inventory sales.
Specializes in east/west rights, co-editions, English & regional languages, wire services syndication/hook-ups, magazine syndication & reprint consulting, seek multi-media rights on CDs, multimedia OEM & distribution marketing consulting service.

Ireland

The Office of Public Works, Publications Branch (OPW)
51 St Stephen's Green, Dublin 2
Tel: (01) 6476000 *Fax:* (01) 6610747
E-mail: info@opw.ie
Web Site: www.opw.ie

Key Personnel
Minister of State, Department of Finance: Tom Pardon
Irish Government Publications.
Specializes in government publications.

OPW, see The Office of Public Works, Publications Branch (OPW)

Jonathan Williams Literary Agency
Ferrybank House, 6 Park Rd, Dun Laoghaire, County Dublin
Tel: (01) 2803482 *Fax:* (01) 2803482
Key Personnel
Dir: Jonathan Williams
Founded: 1981
International coupons, return postage appreciated.
Specializes in works by Irish writers or of Irish interest.
Branch Office(s)
Loecher & Lawrence, Munich, Germany
Lora Fountain, Paris, France
Jan Michael, Amsterdam, Netherlands
Piergiorgio Nicolazzini Literary Agency, Milan, Italy

Israel

The Book Publishers' Association of Israel, International Promotion & Literary Rights Department
29 Carlebach St, Tel Aviv 67132
Mailing Address: PO Box 20123, Tel Aviv 61201
Tel: (03) 5614121 *Fax:* (03) 5611996
E-mail: hamol@tbpai.co.il
Web Site: www.tbpai.co.il
Key Personnel
Chairman: Shay Hausman
Man Dir: Amnon Ben-Shmuel
Founded: 1939

Harris-Elon Agency
9 Yael St, Jerusalem
Mailing Address: PO Box 8528, Jerusalem 91083
Tel: (02) 563-3237 *Fax:* (02) 561-8711
E-mail: litagent@netvision.net.il
Key Personnel
Dir: Deborah Harris *E-mail:* d_harris@netvision.net.il; Beth Elon *E-mail:* b_elon@netvision.net.il
Foreign Rights Dir: Efrat Lev *E-mail:* litagent@netvision.net.il
Managing Editor: Ines Austern *E-mail:* iaustern@netvision.net.il
Founded: 1991
Branch Office(s)
43 Emek Refa'im St, Jerusalem *Tel:* (02) 563 3237 *Fax:* (02) 561 8711 (foreign rights)

The Institute for the Translation of Hebrew Literature
23 Baruch Hirsch St, Bnei Brak
Mailing Address: PO Box 1005 1, 52001 Ramat Gan
Tel: (03) 579 6830 *Fax:* (03) 579 6832
E-mail: hamachon@inter.net.il; litscene@ithl.org.il
Web Site: www.ithl.org.il
Key Personnel
Dir: Mrs Nilli Cohen
Founded: 1962
Main activities include promotion of modern Hebrew literature & children's literature in translation; general literary agency services; subsidies to authors & publishers for translation of Hebrew literary works & their publication abroad; assistance in the preparation of anthologies of Hebrew literature.
Specializes in Hebrew literature in translation.

Italy

Agenzia Letteraria Internazionale
Via Valpetrosa 1, 20123 Milan
Tel: (02) 865445; (02) 861572 *Fax:* (02) 876222
E-mail: alidmb@tin.it
Key Personnel
President: Dr Donatella Barbieri
Founded: 1898
Right's Representative.

Luigi Bernabo Associates SRL
Via Cernaia, 4, 20121 Milan
Tel: (02) 45473700 *Fax:* (02) 45473577
E-mail: bernabo.luigi@tin.it
Key Personnel
Contact: Luigi Bernabo; Daniela Bernabo

Daniel Doglioli
Via Lomonaco 15/B, 27100 Pavia
Tel: (0382) 529317 *Fax:* (0382) 529317
Web Site: www.filastrocche.it/contempo/daniele/daniele.asp
Key Personnel
Contact: Daniel Doglioli *E-mail:* daniel.doglioli@iol.it
Founded: 1994

Eulama Literary Agencies
Via Guido de Ruggiero 28/2, Int 6, 00142 Rome
Tel: (06) 5407309 *Fax:* (06) 5408772
E-mail: eulama@tiscalinet.it *Cable:* EULAROM
Key Personnel
President: Harald Kahnemann
Founded: 1967
Also translation agency.
Specializes in architecture, books for young readers, computer science, education, linguistics & literature, mass-media, philosophy, politics, psychology, quality fiction, religion, social sciences, Spanish & Latin-American literature, technology, urban studies.
Branch Office(s)
Eulama SA, Germany

Grandi & Associati SRL
Via Caradosso 12, 20123 Milan
Tel: (02) 4695541; (02) 4818962 *Fax:* (02) 48195108
E-mail: agenzia@grandieassociati.it
Key Personnel
Contact: Laura Grandi; Stefano Tettamanti; Viviana Vuscovich *E-mail:* viviana.vuscovich@grandieassociati.it
Represents writers & acts as a subagent for selected publishing houses & agencies outside Italy. Sells foreign rights & acts as a consultant for various Italian publishing houses.

ILA (International Literary Agency) USA
18010 Terzorio (IM)
Tel: (0184) 484048; (0347) 9334966 *Fax:* (0184) 487292
E-mail: books@librigg.com
Key Personnel
Contact: Tomas D W Friedmann
Founded: 1970
An American agency headquartered in Europe. Specialize in handling of foreign language translation rights to multi-volume book & magazine projects, children's books, encyclopedias, bestsellers, illustrated books on antiques & collectibles (in all European languages).
Specializes in mass market, antiques & collectibles, nonfiction, fiction.

International Literary Agency, see ILA (International Literary Agency) USA

Living Literary Agency
Via Poliziano 8, 20154 Milan
Tel: (02) 33100584 *Fax:* (02) 33100618
E-mail: living@galactica.it
Key Personnel
Contact: Elfriede Pexa
Founded: 1976
Specializes in Italian translation rights in books in English & German.

Pietro Missorini & Co - Libreria Commissionaria
Via Abbeveratoia 63, 43100 Parma PR
Mailing Address: PO Box 326, 43100 Parma PR
Tel: (0521) 993919 *Fax:* (0521) 993929
E-mail: info@missorini.it
Web Site: www.rsadvnet.it/missorini/
Key Personnel
Administration: Pietro Missorini
 E-mail: missorini@rsadvnet.it
Contact: Lucia Missorini
Founded: 1972
Vat nr IT01514140340.
Specializes in food service & technology.

Natoli Stefan & Oliva Literary Agency
Corso Plebiscito 12, 20129 Milan
Tel: (02) 70 00 16 45 *Fax:* (02) 741277
E-mail: natoli.oliva@tiscalinet.it
Key Personnel
Partner: Roberta Oliva
Founded: 1962
Handles foreign publishers, agents authors in Italy & Italian authors in Italy & worldwide.

Piergiorgio Nicolazzini Literary Agency
Via G B Moroni 22, 20146 Milan
Tel: (02) 48713365 *Fax:* (02) 48713365
E-mail: info@pnla.it
Web Site: www.pnla.it
Key Personnel
Owner: Piergiorgio Nicolazzini
 E-mail: piergiorgio.nicolazzini@tin.it
Founded: 1998
Represents foreign publishers, agents & authors in Italy.
Specializes in fiction & nonfiction.

RCS Rizzoli Libri SpA
Via Mecenate 91, 20138 Milan
Tel: (02) 50951 *Fax:* (02) 5065361
Web Site: www.rcs.it
Telex: 333543
Key Personnel
President: Giorgio Fattori
Dir General: Giovanni Ungarelli
Editorial Dirs: Rosaria Carpinelli; Evaldo Violo
Also Publisher & Major Bookseller.
Specializes in literature, fiction, essays, art, history.

Susanna Zevi Agenzia Letteraria
Via Appiani, 19, 20121 Milan
Tel: (02) 6570863; (02) 6570867 *Fax:* (02) 6570915
E-mail: susiz@tin.it

Japan

The Asano Agency, Inc
Tokuda Bldg 302, 4-44-8 Sengoku, Bunkyo-ku, Tokyo 112-0011
Tel: (03) 39434171 *Fax:* (03) 39437637
Telex: 272-2436 ASANO K
Key Personnel
President: Kiyoshi Asano
Founded: 1988

The English Agency (Japan) Ltd
Sakuragi Bldg 4F, 6-7-3 Minami Aoyama, Minto-ku, Tokyo 107-0062
Tel: (03) 3406 5385 *Fax:* (03) 3406 5387
E-mail: info@eaj.co.jp
Key Personnel
Executive Dir: Junzo Sawa
Man Dir: Hamish Macaskill
Dir: William Miller *E-mail:* willmill@eaj.co.jp; Peter Thompson
Agent, Adult Books: Yoshinori Kaba; Kaori Shibayama
Agent, Academic Books: Tsutomu Yawata
Agent, Children's Books: Noriko Hasegawa
Agent, Business Books: Yukako Higuchi
London Representative: Louise Allen-Jones
Tel: (020) 7720-2453
Founded: 1979
Sales of book & ancillary rights for translation mainly into Japanese; author's agent for books with international appeal by writers living in or frequently visiting Japan.

Japan Foreign-Rights Centre (JFC)
27-18-804 Naka-Ochiai 2-chome, Shinjuku-ku, Tokyo 161-0032
Tel: (03) 59960321 *Fax:* (03) 59960323
Key Personnel
Man Dir: Akiko Kurita
Manager, General Books: Harumi Sakai
Manager, Children's Books: Yurika Yokota Yoshida
Founded: 1981 (as Kurita-Bando Literary Agency)
Specializes in foreign rights to Japanese books, co-production, packaging.

Japan UNI Agency Inc
Tokyodo-Jinbocho Dai, No 2 Bldg, 1-27 Kanda Jinbocho, Chiyoda-ku, Tokyo 101-0051
Tel: (03) 32950301 *Fax:* (03) 32945173
E-mail: info@japanuni.co.jp
Telex: J27260 Unilit *Cable:* UNILITERARY
Key Personnel
Chairman: Noboru Miyata
President: Yoshio Taketomi
Dir: Tatsuko Nagasawa; Okimitsu Ohishi
Founded: 1967

JFC, see Japan Foreign-Rights Centre (JFC)

Motovun Co Ltd, Tokyo
Coop Nomura Ichibancho, No 103, 15-6 Ichiban-cho, Chiyoda-ku, Tokyo 102-0082
Tel: (03) 32614002 *Fax:* (03) 32641443
Key Personnel
President: Mari Koga *E-mail:* koga_motovun@mbd.ocn.ne.jp
Dir: Norio Irie *E-mail:* irie_motovun@mbd.ocn.ne.jp
Founded: 1983
Firm sells rights & co-production between foreign publishers & Japanese publishers.

The Sakai Agency Inc
Ganshodo Bldg, 1-7-12 Kanda-Jinbocho, Chiyoda-ku, Tokyo 101-0051
Tel: (03) 32951405 *Fax:* (03) 32954366
E-mail: sakai@sakaiagency.com
Key Personnel
Contact: Tatemi Sakai
Founded: 1952
Specializes in book rights, serial rights, co-editions, theatrical performing rights, motion picture rights, TV & radio broadcasting rights, video rights, merchandising rights; both rights for export/import market, representing Japanese authors.

Tuttle-Mori Agency Inc
Dai ichi Fuji Bldg, 2-15 Kanda-Jinbocho, Chiyoda-ku, Tokyo 101-0051
Tel: (03) 3230-4081 *Fax:* (03) 3234-5249
Key Personnel
President: Ken Mori
Man Dir: Yuji Takeda *E-mail:* yuji@tuttlemori.com
Executive Dir: Yoshikazu Iwasaki
Financial Dir: Sakae Mino
Specializes in book rights, serial rights, co-productions, motion picture, TV, radio & stage rights, merchandising rights.
Branch Office(s)
5F, No 8, Wu-Chuan Third Rd, Shin-Juang, Taipei County 242, Taiwan, Province of China *Tel:* (02) 3234-4255 *Fax:* (02) 3234-4244
Siam Inter Comics Bldg, 6th floor 459 Soi Pi-boonopathum Ladprao 48, Samsen Nok, Huay Kwang, Bangkok 10310, Thailand *Tel:* (02) 694-3026 *Fax:* (02) 694-3027 (Affiliate)
58 Clifton Gardens, London W9 1AU, United Kingdom, Contact: Anne Martyn *Tel:* (020) 7286-8701 *Fax:* (020) 7286-8629
U.S. Office(s): Sanford J Greenburger Associates Inc, 55 Fifth Ave, New York, NY 10003, United States, Contact: Carol Frederick *Tel:* 212-206-5610 *Fax:* 212-627-9281
Foreign Rep(s): Anne Martyn & Nina Martyn; Carol Frederick

Republic of Korea

Imprima Korea Agency
Mijin Bldg, 3rd floor, 464-41 Seokyo-Dong, Mapo-ku, Seoul 121-210
Tel: (02) 325-9155 *Fax:* (02) 334-9160
E-mail: imprima@chollian.net
Web Site: www.imprima.co.kr
Key Personnel
President: Hong Sung-Il
Dir: Duram Kim *E-mail:* duramkim@hnc.net
Founded: 1993
Specializes in publishing newspaper.

International Publications Service, see IPS Copyright Agency (International Publications Service)

IPS Copyright Agency (International Publications Service)
YBM/Si-sa Bldg 9F, 48-1, Chongro 2-ga, Chongro-gu, Seoul 110-772
Tel: (02) 21158800 *Fax:* (02) 22646936
E-mail: copyright@ips-korea.com
Web Site: www.ipsbook.com
Founded: 1986
Promoting foreign rights to Korean publishers.

Mediabank
Kwanghwamoon, Seoul 110-605
Mailing Address: PO Box 530, Seoul 110-605
Tel: (02) 7420425 *Fax:* (02) 7452174
E-mail: sales@mediabank.biz
Web Site: www.mediabank.pe.kr
Key Personnel
President: Jay Sung Rhee *E-mail:* jaysrhee@nownuri.net
Founded: 1985
Also deals in video rights for home & educational markets.
Specializes in children's books, el-hi reference books & instructional multi-media.

Shin Won Agency Co
513-12 Paju Book City, Munbal-ri, Gyoha-eup, Paju-si, Gyeonggi-do
Tel: (031) 955-2255; (031) 955-2265; (031) 955-2266
E-mail: main@shinwonagency.co.kr
Web Site: www.shinwonagency.co.kr
Key Personnel
Man Dir: Soon Eung Kim
Dir: Jaechul Choi; Jong Hoon Kang; Gi Seok Lee
Founded: 1986
Literary Agency & Editorial Production.
Branch Office(s)
PT Infozone Ina Shinwon, Jl Kemang Gisan Utama II, No 54, Palmerah, Jakarta Barat 11480, Indonesia *Tel:* (021) 530-0454 *Fax:* (021) 548-2515 *E-mail:* main@infozone.co.id
Sunshine Mansion 2018, No 1, Xiao Li, Chaoyang District, Beijing, China *Tel:* (010) 6463-9562 *Fax:* (010) 6463-3730 *Web Site:* www.shinwonagency.com

Time-Space Inc
Hanyoung Bldg, 57-8 Chungmuro 3 Ga, Jung-gu, Seoul 100-013
Tel: (02) 2272 2381 *Fax:* (02) 2273 8900
E-mail: tspace@timespace.co.kr
Web Site: www.fotato.com
Key Personnel
Contact: Hyang-Ja Yim
Founded: 1984
Specialize in stock photography & royalty free CD-ROM.
Specializes in photography, arts.

Universal Publications Agency Press
UPA Bldg, No 2, Suite 1001, 20 Hyoje-dong, Chongno-ku, Seoul 110-850
Tel: (02) 3672 0044 *Fax:* (02) 3672 1222
E-mail: upa@upa.co.kr
Web Site: www.upa.co.kr
Telex: K 22702 *Cable:* CHANGHOSHIN SEOUL
Key Personnel
Chairman: Chang-Ho Shin
President: Kwang-Hoon Cow
Founded: 1958
Also publisher & distributor.
Specializes in advertising, media representation.
Branch Office(s)
Will Academia, No 1, Jangkyo-dong, Suite 2613, Chung-ku, Seoul 100-760

Eric Yang Agency
3rd floor, E Bldg, 54-7 Banpo-dong, Seocho-ku, Seoul 137-803
Tel: (02) 5923356 *Fax:* (02) 5923359
E-mail: info@ericyangagency.co.kr
Web Site: www.ericyangagency.co.kr
Key Personnel
President: Eric Yang *E-mail:* ericyang@ericyangagency.co.kr
Founded: 1994

Liechtenstein

Liechtenstein Verlag AG
Herrengasse 21, 9490 Vaduz
Mailing Address: PO Box 339, 9490 Vaduz

Tel: (0423) 2322414 *Fax:* (0423) 2324340
E-mail: flbooks@verlag-ag.lol.li
Key Personnel
Man Dir: Albart Piet Schiks
Founded: 1945
Firm is also a publisher.

Lithuania

Penki Kontinentai
Stulginskio-5, 2001 Vilnius
Fax: (05) 2664501
E-mail: info@5ci.lt
Web Site: www.5ci.lt
Key Personnel
Contact: Irena Juskauskaite
Founded: 1992
Represents Nordic Council of Ministers, Oxford University Press & Cambridge University Press.

Netherlands

Auteursbureau Greta Baars-Jelgersma
Maasstaete 40, 6585 CB Mook
Tel: (024) 6963336 *Fax:* (024) 6963293
E-mail: 6963336@hetnet.nl
Web Site: home.hetnet.nl/~jelgersma696
Founded: 1951
Literary agent & sworn translator-interpreter.
Specializes in international co-printing of illustrated books, mediation of copyrights, translations from Scandinavian & German languages into Dutch, sworn interpreter/translator Danish, Norwegian, Swedish.

Foundation for the Production & Translation of Dutch Literature
Singel 464, 1017 AW Amsterdam
Tel: (020) 6206261 *Fax:* (020) 6207179
E-mail: office@nlpvf.nl
Web Site: www.nlpvf.nl
Key Personnel
Man Dir: Henk Propper
Founded: 1991

Caroline van Gelderen Literary Agency
Kerkstr 301, 1017 GZ Amsterdam
Tel: (020) 6126475 *Fax:* (020) 6180843
Key Personnel
Dir: Caroline van Gelderen
  E-mail: cvangelderen@carvang.nl
Founded: 1979
Representative of American & English publishers & agents for the Dutch territories.
Specializes in translation rights.

International Literatuur Bureau BV
Koninginneweg 2A, 1217 KW Hilversum
Mailing Address: Postbus 10014, 1201 DA Hilversum
Tel: (035) 6213500 *Fax:* (035) 6215771
E-mail: info@ilb.nu
Web Site: www.ilb.nu *Cable:* ILB
Key Personnel
Chief Executive: Linda Kohn *E-mail:* lkohn@planet.nl

Lijnkamp Literary Agents
Johannes Verhulststr 153-B, 1075 GW Amsterdam
Tel: (020) 6207742 *Fax:* (020) 6385298
E-mail: info@lijnkamp.nl

Web Site: www.lijnkamp.nl
Key Personnel
Dir: Marijke Lijnkamp
Assistant Literary Agent: Liz Waters
Founded: 1989
Represents foreign literary agencies & publishing houses in Netherlands. Represents Dutch authors worldwide.
Specializes in The Netherlands & Flemish Belgium as representative areas.

De Lindenboom/INOR Publikaties
M A de Ruyterstr 20A, 7482 BZ Haaksbergen
Mailing Address: Postbus 202, 7480 AE Haaksbergen
Tel: (053) 5740004 *Fax:* (053) 5729296
E-mail: lindeboo@worldonline.nl
Telex: 49642 UDOL
Represents Nordic Council of Ministers Publications. Also book distributor.

Servire BV Uitgevers
Maliebaan 74, 3581 CV Utrecht
Mailing Address: Postbus 13288, 3507 LG Utrecht
Tel: (030) 2349211 *Fax:* (030) 2349247
E-mail: info@kosmoszk.nl
Web Site: www.servire.nl; www.boekenwereld.com
Key Personnel
Chief Executive: Felix Erkelens
Founded: 1921
Also publisher.
Specializes in psychology, health, spirituality.

Alice Toledo, see Toledo Creative Management

Toledo Creative Management
Binnenkant 20, 1011 BH Amsterdam
Tel: (020) 6226873 *Fax:* (020) 6276720
E-mail: agency@toledo-cm.nl
Founded: 1991
Literary, TV & film agency. Represents Dutch authors & directors.

New Zealand

John Bentley Book Agencies
Milford, Auckland 9
Mailing Address: PO Box 31-328, Auckland 9
Tel: (09) 4736920 *Fax:* (09) 4736920
E-mail: sjsb@connected.net.nzed
Key Personnel
Contact: John Bentley
Founded: 1982
Commission agent acting for publishers on a representation only basis.

Michael Gifkins & Associates
PO Box 6496, Auckland 1
Tel: (09) 5235032 *Fax:* (09) 5235033
E-mail: michael.gifkins@xtra.co.nz
Key Personnel
Principal: Michael Gifkins
Founded: 1983
Specializes in general, adult fiction, juvenile, film, television, co-publications.

Playmarket
Level 2, 16 Cambridge Terrace, Wellington
Mailing Address: PO Box 9767, Te Aro, Wellington
Tel: (04) 3828462 *Fax:* (04) 3828461
E-mail: info@playmarket.org.nz
Web Site: www.playmarket.org.nz
Key Personnel
President: Andrew Caisley

Secretary: Emma Carter
Founded: 1973
Playwrights Agency & Script Advisory Service.

Richards Literary Agency
11 Channel View Rd, Campbells Bay, Auckland 1311
Mailing Address: PO Box 31240, Milford, Auckland 9
Tel: (09) 479 5681 *Fax:* (09) 479 5681
Key Personnel
Partner: Ray Richards *E-mail:* rla.richards@clear.net.nz; Nicki Richards Wallace
Founded: 1977
Specializes in fiction, nonfiction, educational, academic, juvenile, young adult, films, television, stage, radio.

Norway

June Heggenhougen
Brannpostveien 5, 3014 Drammen
Tel: 32832125 *Fax:* 32832125
Key Personnel
International Consultant: Gudbrand Heggenhougen *E-mail:* gudbrand@online.no
Publishing Consultant: June Heggenhougen

Pakistan

Mirza Book Agency
65 Shahrah-e-Quaid-e-Azam, 54000 Lahore
Mailing Address: PO Box 729, 54000 Lahore
Tel: (042) 7353601 *Fax:* (042) 5763714
E-mail: merchant@brain.net.pk *Cable:* KNOWLEDGE
Key Personnel
Proprietor: Mirza Mahmud
Founded: 1949
Deals with foreign publication & government publication; Subscription Agent.
Specializes in educational & professional books, developing countries, dictionaries, reference, social science, scientific, medical.
Branch Office(s)
Mirza Book Corporation, 247/A-3, Gulberg-3, Lahore 54660 *Tel:* (042) 5714653 *Fax:* (042) 5763714 *E-mail:* merchant@brain.net.pk

Romania

Simona Kessler International Copyright Agency Ltd
Str Banul Antonache 37, 70 000 Bucharest 1
Tel: (021) 231 81 50 *Fax:* (021) 231 45 22
Key Personnel
President: Simona Kessler *E-mail:* simona@kessler-agency.ro
Founded: 1995
Specializes in subsidiary rights.

Russian Federation

RAO, see Rossijskoye avtorskoye obshestvo

RUSSIAN FEDERATION

Rossijskoye avtorskoye obshestvo (Russian Author's Society)
6-A Bolshaya Bronnaya, K-104, Moscow 103670
Tel: (095) 2033777; (095) 2033260
E-mail: rao@rao.ru
Web Site: www.rao.ru
Telex: 411327 Avtor SU *Cable:* Moscow Avtor
Key Personnel
Chairman: V Tverdovsky
Vice Chairman & Dir,Legal Dept: Arkady Tourkine
Dir, Rights & Permissions Dept: G Zareev
 Tel: (095) 203-06-95
Literary & big rights, internet, mechanical & musical rights; licensing of TV & radio stations.

Slovakia

LITA Ochranna Autorska Spolocnost' Agentura
Mozartova 9, 81530 Bratislava
Tel: (07) 62 80 22 48 *Fax:* (07) 62 80 22 46
E-mail: lita@lita.sk
Key Personnel
Contact: Yvona Vlasata
Slovak Literary Agency: the copyright organization representing Slovak authors in foreign transactions & foreign authors in the territory of Slovakia; Member of CISAC.

South Africa

Frances Bond Literary Services
14 Grays Inn Crescent, Westville, Kwazulu Natal 3630
Mailing Address: PO Box 223, Westville, Kwazulu Natal 3630
Tel: (031) 2662007 *Fax:* (031) 2662007
E-mail: fbond@mweb.com.za
Key Personnel
Chief Executive: Frances Bond
Chief Editor: Eileen Molver
Founded: 1983
Specializes in adult fiction & nonfiction, children's books.

Cherokee Literary Agency
3 Blythwood Rd, Rondebosch, Cape Province 7700
Tel: (021) 671-4508 *Fax:* (021) 761-4329
Key Personnel
Dir: DonnaKay Lee *E-mail:* dklee@mweb.co.za
Founded: 1988
Specializes in children's picture books.

The International Press Agency (Pty) Ltd
Sunrise House, 56 Morningside, Ndabeni, Cape Town 7405
Tel: (021) 5311926; (021) 5318197 *Fax:* (021) 5318789
E-mail: inpra@iafrica.com
Web Site: www.inpra.co.za
Key Personnel
Manager & Dir: Terry Temple
Founded: 1934
Specializes in literary agents & press.
Branch Office(s)
London, United Kingdom, Contact: Ursula A Bennett *Tel:* (020) 8767-4828

Spain

ACER Agencia Literaria
Amor de Dios, 1, 28014 Madrid
Tel: (091) 3692061 *Fax:* (091) 3692052
Key Personnel
Contact: Elizbeth Atkins *E-mail:* eatkins@acerliteraria.com; Laure Merle d'Aubigne
 E-mail: lma@acerliteraria.com
Founded: 1959

Carmen Balcells Agencia Literaria SA (The Balcells Agency)
Diagonal 580, 08021 Barcelona
Tel: (093) 2008565; (093) 2008933 *Fax:* (093) 2007041
E-mail: ag-balcells@mx2.redestb.es *Cable:* COPYRIGHT BARCELONA
Key Personnel
President: Carmen Balcells
Contact: Gloria Gutierrez

Bookbank SA
San Martin de Porres, 14, 28035 Madrid
Tel: (091) 3733539 *Fax:* (091) 3165591
E-mail: bookbank@nexo.es
Key Personnel
Contact: Alicia Gonzalez Sterling
Correspondence in Spanish & English.

International Editors' Co SL
Rambla de Cataluna 63 - 3 1a, 08007 Barcelona
Tel: (093) 2158812 *Fax:* (093) 4873583
E-mail: ieco@es.inter.net
Key Personnel
Manager: Isabel Monteagudo
Branch Office(s)
Buenos Aires, Argentina

Ute Koerner Literary Agent
Ronda Guinardo 40-3, 08025 Barcelona
Tel: (093) 4550414; (093) 4502588 *Fax:* (093) 4365548
E-mail: office@uklitag.com
Web Site: www.uklitag.com
Key Personnel
Founder & Agent: Ute Koerner
Agent: Guenter G Rodewald
Founded: 1984
Representing foreign publishers, authors & agents in Spanish & Portuguese-speaking countries.

Marcombo SA
Gran Via de les Corts Catalanes 594, Barcelona 08007
Tel: (093) 3180079 *Fax:* (093) 3189339
E-mail: marcombo.boixareu@marcombo.es
Web Site: www.marcombo.es
Key Personnel
Man Dir: Josep M Boixareu Vilaplana
Founded: 1945
Specializes in technical books.

Les Muriers Editions
Division of Les Muriers Estates SL
Ave Constitucion 8, Apdo 925, Ciutadella de Menorca, Islas Baleares 07760
Tel: (0971) 484 423 *Fax:* (0971) 484 423
Web Site: www.lmeditions.com
Key Personnel
Dir: Janet Greco *E-mail:* janet@lesmuriers.com
Founded: 2003
Work with a small & select group of promising new writers & accomplished authors, writing in English only. Also represent feature-length screenplays.
No unsol mss - query first (in English) by e-mail with sample chapters.
Specializes in children's/young readers, commercial fiction (mysteries, political thrillers, thrillers), literary fiction, nonfiction (biography, comedy, cooking, history, how-to, humor, ghosts & graveyards, New Jerseyana, offbeat cooking, popular culture, self development & improvement, writing).
U.S. Office(s): 281 Terhune Drive, Wayne, NJ 07470, United States *Tel:* (609) 361-8696

RDC Agencia Literaria
Plaza de Las Salesas 9, 1 izq, 28004 Madrid
Tel: (091) 3085585 *Fax:* (091) 3085600
E-mail: rdc@idecnet.com
Key Personnel
Contact: Raquel de la Concha
Representing Spanish writers & foreign publishers, fiction & nonfiction.

Mercedes Ros Literary Agency
Castell 38, 08329 Teia, Barcelona
Tel: (093) 5401353 *Fax:* (093) 5401346
E-mail: info@mercedesros.com
Web Site: www.mercedesros.com
Key Personnel
Dir: Mercedes Ros *E-mail:* mercedes@mercedesros.com
Founded: 1996
Represents publishers, packagers & authors all over the world.
Specializes in children: fiction & nonfiction, albums, board books, games & crafts; adults: crafts, hobbies, parenting, self-help & sports.

Lennart Sane Agency AB
Paseo de Mejico 65, Las Cumbres-Elviria, 29600 Marbella, Malaga
Tel: (0952) 834180 *Fax:* (0952) 833196
E-mail: lennart.sane@telia.com
Key Personnel
Dir: Elisabeth Sane; Lennart Sane
Branch Office(s)
Hollandareplan 9, 374 34 Karlshamn, Sweden
Tel: (0454) 123 56 *Fax:* (0454) 149 20

Sant Jordi Asociados Agencia
Arquitecte Sert nº 31 5º - 1a, 08005 Barcelona
Tel: (093) 2240107 *Fax:* (093) 2254539
E-mail: info@santjordi-asociados.com
Web Site: www.santjordi-asociados.com
Key Personnel
Contact: Monica Antunes
Founded: 1994
Specializes in Latin America authors & Spanish.

Cristina Vizcaino Literary Agency
Juan de Austria 31 1B, 28010 Madrid
Tel: (091) 5944992
E-mail: vizcaino@infornet.es
Key Personnel
Manager: Cristina Vizcaino
Associate: Paula Serraller
Founded: 1997
Specializes in children & juvenile titles, education, gay & lesbian, literature & reference.

Julio F Yanez, Agencia Literaria S L
Via Augusta 139 - 6º 2a, 08021 Barcelona
Tel: (093) 2007107; (093) 2005443 *Fax:* (093) 2094865
E-mail: yanezag@retemail.es *Cable:* AGENLITER
Key Personnel
Dir: Julio F Yanez; Montse F Yanez
Founded: 1960
Covering all Spanish & Portuguese-speaking countries.
Specializes in modern literature, documents & memoirs; educational: history, art, sociology; topical books on modern facts; co-productions.

Sweden

Ann-Christine Danielsson Agency
Haeggstigen 17, 24013 Genarpe
Tel: (040) 482380 *Fax:* (040) 482190
E-mail: acd.agency@swipnet.se

Monica Heyum Agency
Vendelsoe, Box 3300, S-136 03 Haninge
Tel: (08) 7451934 *Fax:* (08) 7771470
Key Personnel
Dir & Literary Agent: Monica Heyum
 E-mail: monica@heum-agency.a.se
Founded: 1985

Kerstin Kvint Literary & Co-Production Agency
PO Box 45164, 104 30 Stockholm
Tel: (08) 107014 *Fax:* (08) 107606
Handles foreign rights' sales for individual writers & Scandinavian publishers. Co-productions arranged for children's picture books.

Bengt Nordin Agency
Triewaldsgrand 2, 111 29 Stockholm
Mailing Address: PO Box 2101, 103 13 Stockholm
Tel: (08) 57168525 *Fax:* (08) 57168524
E-mail: info@nordinagency.se
Web Site: www.nordinagency.se
Key Personnel
President: Bengt Nordin *E-mail:* bengt.nordin@nordinagency.se
Founded: 1990
Specializes in film, TV & literary agency.

Pan Agency
Division of P A Norstedt & Soner AB
Birger Jarls Torg 5, 111 28 Stockholm
Mailing Address: PO Box 2052, 103 12 Stockholm
Tel: (08) 769 87 00 *Fax:* (08) 769 88 04
Web Site: www.panagency.se
Key Personnel
Rights Dir: Linda Altrov-Berg *E-mail:* linda.altrovberg@panagency.com; Lillevi Cederin *E-mail:* lillevi.cederin@panagency.se
Rights Director: Magdalena Hedlund *E-mail:* magdalena.hedlund@panagency.se
Rights Dir: Agneta Markas *E-mail:* agneta.markas@panagency.se; Kerstin Oberg *E-mail:* kerstin.oberg@panagency.se
Foreign rights division of P A Norstedt & Sonder, representing Norstedts; Prisma Raben & Sjogren; Tiden.

Lennart Sane Agency AB
Hollandareplan 9, 374 34 Karlshamn
Tel: (0454) 123 56 *Fax:* (0454) 149 20
E-mail: lennart.sane@telia.com
Key Personnel
Dir: Lennart Sane
Assistant Dir: Lina Lindau; Elisabeth Sane; Ann-Mari Selander
Founded: 1969
Branch Office(s)
Paseo de Mejico 65, Las Cumbres-Elviria, 29600 Marbella, Malaga, Spain *Tel:* (0952) 83 41 80 *Fax:* (0952) 83 31 96

Sane Toregard Agency
Hollaendareplan 9, 374 34 Karlshamn
Tel: (0454) 123 56 *Fax:* (0454) 149 20
Key Personnel
Dir: Ulf Toregard *E-mail:* ulf.toregard@sanetoregard.se
Founded: 1995
Representing publishers & agents in Scandinavia & Holland for rights in fiction & nonfiction.

Switzerland

Paul und Peter Fritz AG Literary Agency
Jupiterstr 1, 8032 Zurich
Mailing Address: Postfach 1773, 8032 Zurich
Tel: (01) 44 388 41 40 *Fax:* (01) 44 388 41 30
E-mail: info@fritzagency.com
Web Site: www.fritzagency.com
Key Personnel
Man Dir: Peter S Fritz *E-mail:* pfritz@fritzagency.com
Founded: 1962
Representation of American & English authors, agents & publishers in German-language areas, German-language authors worldwide.

Gaia Media AG/Literary & Media Agency
Spalenvorstadt 13, CH-4003 Basel
Tel: (061) 2619119 *Fax:* (061) 2619117
E-mail: gaiamediaag@access.ch
Key Personnel
President: Dieter A Hagenbach
Founded: 1990

Liepman Agency AG
Maienburgweg 23, 8044 Zurich
Tel: (044) 2617660 *Fax:* (044) 2610124
E-mail: info@liepmanagency.com
Key Personnel
Dir: Eva Koralnik; Ruth Weibel *E-mail:* ruth.weibel@liepmanagency.com
Contact: A G Liepman
Founded: 1949
Represent authors, publishers & agents for the German language publication rights, & authors from manuscript on throughout the world.

MOHRBOOKS AG, Literary Agency
Klosbachstr 110, 8032 Zurich
Tel: (043) 2448626 *Fax:* (043) 2448627
E-mail: info@mohrbooks.com
Web Site: www.mohrbooks.de
Key Personnel
Agent: Sabine Ibach *E-mail:* sabine.ibach@mohrbooks.com; Sebastian Ritscher *E-mail:* sebastian.ritscher@mohrbooks.com
Agent, Children's Books: Sabina Sciarrone *E-mail:* sabina.sciarrone@mohrbooks.com
Contracts & Permissions: Barbara Brachwitz *E-mail:* barbara.brachwitz@mohrbooks.com; Bettina Kaufmann *E-mail:* bettina.kaufmann@mohrbooks.com
Branch Office(s)
Am Zirkus 5, 10117 Berlin, Germany *Tel:* (030) 28879474 *Fax:* (030) 28879475 *E-mail:* mohrberlin@mohrbooks.com

Neue Presse Agentur, see NPA (Neue Presse Agentur)

Niedieck Linder AG
Zollikerstr 87, 8034 Zurich
Tel: (01) 3816592 *Fax:* (01) 3816513
E-mail: info@nlagency.ch
Web Site: www.nlagency.ch
Key Personnel
Contact: Antoinette Matejka
Agent: Leonardo LaRosa *E-mail:* larosa@nlagency.ch
Founded: 1975
Representation of German-language authors (including major authors' estates) as well as Italian publishers & agencies on the German language market. Commission: 10-15% of author's gross income.
Specializes in Giulio Einaudi, Bollati Boringhieri, Rusconi Libri, Edizioni EL, Sellerio Editore, Avagliano Editore, Agenzia Letteraria Internazionale, Agenzia Letteraria Agnese Incisa for German speaking countries.

NPA (Neue Presse Agentur)
Haldenstr 5, Haus am Herterberg, 8500 Frauenfeld-Herten
Tel: (052) 7214374 *Cable:* NPA, CH-8500 FRAUENFELD
Key Personnel
Contact: Rene Marti
Founded: 1950
Specializes in serialization in newspapers & magazines, especially women's & educational interest, fiction, exclusives.

Syrian Arab Republic

Nour E-Sham Book Centre
Omar Al-Mukhtar St, Opp to the Ministry of Education, Damascus
Mailing Address: PO Box 249, Damascus
Tel: (011) 4440575 *Fax:* (011) 3324913
E-mail: nouresham@mail.sy
Key Personnel
Manager: Mr Maher Abul-Zahab
Founded: 1983
Represents the following publishers in Syria: Oxford University Press UK, Cambridge University Press UK, BBC UK, Macmillan UK, Wiley USA, McGraw-Hill USA, McGraw-Hill UK, Penguin UK, Didaco Spain.
Specializes in English language teaching (ELT).
Branch Office(s)
Aleppo

Taiwan, Province of China

Bardon-Chinese Media Agency
4F, No 230, Hsin-Yi Rd, Sec 2, Taipei
Tel: (02) 33932585 *Fax:* (02) 23929577
Web Site: www.bardonchinese.com
Key Personnel
President: Phillip C Chen *E-mail:* phillip@bardon.com.tw
Contact: Yiwen Chen; Mingming Lu; Jianmei Wang
Founded: 1988
Literary & Rights agency covering Taiwan, Hong Kong, Singapore & China.
Specializes in Chinese language, simplified & complex.

Big Apple Tuttle-Mori Agency Inc
7F, No 38, Wugong 5th Rd, Wu-Ku Industrial Area, Wugu Township, Taipei County 248
Mailing Address: c/o Anne Martyn, 55 Earl's Court Sq, Flat 17, London SW5 9DG, United Kingdom
Tel: (02) 8990-1238 *Fax:* (02) 8990-1129
E-mail: bigapple1@worldnet.att.net
Web Site: www.bigapple1.info
Key Personnel
President: Lily Chen
Executive Vice President: Dr Luc Kwanten
US Representative: Chandler Crawford *Tel:* 212-206-5600

European Representative: Anne Martyn *Tel:* (071) 2868701
Affiliates in all major countries. Rights & authors agent.
Branch Office(s)
Chinan, China
Nanking, China
Shanghai, China *Tel:* (021) 6273 4184
Big Apple Tuttle-Mori, 10F No 801, Jeng-Cheng Rd, Jeng-He City, Taipei 235 *Tel:* (02) 506 7828 *Fax:* (02) 506 5827
Big Apple Tuttle-Mori Beijing, Beijing, China *Tel:* (010) 6591 8528
Tuttle-Mori Agency, Fuji Bldg 8F, 2-15 Kanda Jimbocho, Chiyoda-ku, Tokyo, Japan *Tel:* (03) 3230 40181 *Fax:* (03) 3234 5249
Tuttle-Mori Big Apple, Siam Inter Comics Bldg, 6th floor, 459 Soi Piboonupathum Ladprao 48, Samsen Nok, Huay Kwang, Bangkok 10310, Thailand *Tel:* (02) 694 3026 *Fax:* (02) 694 3027

Thailand

Silkroad Publishers Agency, Ltd
32/3 Sukhumvit 31 Rd, Bangkok 10110
Tel: (02) 2584798; (02) 2588266 *Fax:* (02) 6620553
E-mail: silkroad@ji-net.com
Key Personnel
Man Dir: Jane Ngarmpun Vejjajiva
Founded: 1994
Specializes in general trade fiction & nonfiction, juvenile.

Turkey

Akcali Copyright Agency
Bahariye Caddesi No 8/6, 81300 Kadikoy, Istanbul
Tel: (0216) 3388771; (0216) 3485160 *Fax:* (0216) 3490778
E-mail: akcali@attglobal.net
Key Personnel
President & Dir: Ms Kezban Akcali
Handles fiction & nonfiction adult, young adult & children's books.

Gamma Medya Agency
Eceler Sok, No 6/1, Florya, 34810 Istanbul
Tel: (0212) 663 96 80 *Fax:* (0212) 663 96 81
E-mail: web@gammamedya.net
Web Site: www.gammamedya.net
Key Personnel
Man Dir: Zeynep Ataman *E-mail:* zeynep@gammamedya.net
Founded: 1991
Publishing, press & licensing agency.

Nurcihan Kesim Literary Agency, Inc
Gazeteciler Cemiyeti Basin, Saray, No 1 Kat 2, Turkocagi cd, Istanbul
Mailing Address: PO Box 868, 34410 Istanbul
Tel: (0212) 5285797; (0212) 5111317; (0212) 5111078 *Fax:* (0212) 5285791
E-mail: kesim@superonline.com; contact@nurcihankesim.com
Web Site: www.nurcihankesim.com
Key Personnel
Man Dir & Executive President: Nurcihan Kesim
Rights & Permissions: Karasuil Asli
Founded: 1971
Specializes in fiction, nonfiction, art works, serials, encyclopedias, licensing, merchandising, music rights, children's books.

ONK Agency Ltd
Inonu Caddesi, 31/7 Taksim, 34437 Istanbul
Mailing Address: PO Box 983, Sirkeci, 34115 Istanbul
Tel: (0212) 2498602; (0212) 2498603 *Fax:* (0212) 2525153
E-mail: karaca@onkagency.com
Web Site: www.onkagency.com *Cable:* COPYRIGHT ISTANBUL
Key Personnel
President: Osman N Karaca *E-mail:* karaca@onkagency.com
Vice President: Mehmet N Karaca
Man Dir: Orsan K Oymen
Rights: Ms Hatice Gok *E-mail:* hatice@onkagency.com
Founded: 1959
Representing Turkish writers, illustrators, playwriters, SACD, many major foreign publishers & agents. Syndicated materials, Sipa press. Literary, dramatic & TV rights.
Specializes in books, (adult/young adult & children books), serials, encyclopedias, comics & cartoons, plays, Dia Positive.

United Kingdom

A & B Personal Management Ltd
Paurelle House, 91 Regent St, London W1B 4EL
Tel: (020) 7734 6047; (020) 7734 6048 *Fax:* (020) 7734 6318
E-mail: admin@writewords.org.uk
Key Personnel
Dir: R W Ellis
Founded: 1982
Full-length mss for TV, theatre, cinema; also fiction, nonfiction & performance rights. No unsol mss. Send letter first with return postage. No reading fee for synopsis, plays or screenplays, but fee charged for full-length mss.

The Agency (London) Ltd
24 Pottery Lane, Holland Park, London W11 4LZ
Tel: (020) 7727 1346 *Fax:* (020) 7727 9037
E-mail: info@theagency.co.uk
Web Site: www.writersservices.com/wrhandbook/agency_london.htm
Key Personnel
Dir: Stephen Durbridge
Contact: Sebastian Born; Julia Kreitman; Leah Schmidt
Founded: 1995
Works in conjunction with agents in USA & all foreign countries. No adult fiction or nonfiction. Send letter with self-addressed envelope; no reading fee. Commission: Home 10%; USA varies.
Specializes in theater, film, TV, radio, novels, children's fiction.

Gillon Aitken Associates Ltd
18-21 Cavaye Pl, London SW10 9PT
Tel: (020) 7373 8672 *Fax:* (020) 7373 6002
E-mail: reception@gillonaitken.co.uk
Key Personnel
Dir & Chairman: Gillon Aitken
Contact: Clare Alexander
Founded: 1977
Handles fiction & nonfiction. No plays or scripts. Send preliminary letter with half page synopsis, first 30 pages & return postage. No reading fee. Commission: Home 10%; US 15%; Translation 20%.

Darley Anderson Literary TV & Film Agency
Estelle House, 11 Eustace Rd, London SW6 1JB
Tel: (020) 7385 6652 *Fax:* (020) 7386 5571; (020) 7386 9689
E-mail: enquiries@darleyanderson.com
Web Site: www.darleyanderson.com
Key Personnel
President & Contact, Thrillers: Darley Anderson
Foreign Rights Associate & Contact: Lucie Whitehouse
Contact, TV Film & Children's: Julia Churchill
Contact, Women's & Fiction: Elizabeth Wright
Founded: 1988
Handles commercial fiction & nonfiction, children's fiction & selected scripts for film & TV. Send letter & outline of first three chapters, self-addressed envelope & return postage. Commission: Home 15%; USA 20%; Translation 20-25%; TV/Film/Radio 20%.
Specializes in fiction: American & Irish novels, crime/mystery, humor, thrillers, women's & male fiction; nonfiction: animals, beauty, biographies, celebrity autobiographies, cookery, diet, fashions, gardening, health, history, humor/cartoons, inspirational, popular psychology, religion, science, self-improvement.
Branch Office(s)
Darley Anderson Books

Book Production Consultants PLC
25-27 High St, Chesterton, Cambridge CB4 1ND
Tel: (01223) 352790 *Fax:* (01223) 460718
E-mail: tl@bpccam.co.uk
Web Site: www.bpccam.co.uk
Key Personnel
Joint Dir: Tony Littlechild
Dir: Colin Walsh *E-mail:* cw@bpccam.co.uk
Editorial, Rights: Roz Williams
Founded: 1974
Organization includes international publishing, production & involvement in all media. Joint ventures with London Tourist Board, & National Childbirth Trust.
Specializes in book & magazine publishing services.
Branch Office(s)
c/o Bank of Bermuda, London Representative Office, Austin Friars House, 2-6 Austin Friars, London EC2N 2HE, Corporate Publisher: Stephanie Zarach *E-mail:* bpc@bpcion.co.uk

Booklink
43 Maycock Grove, Northwood, Middlesex HA6 3PU
Tel: (01923) 828612 *Fax:* (01923) 828455
E-mail: info@booklink.co.uk
Web Site: www.booklink.co.uk
Key Personnel
President: Evelyne Duval
Founded: 1978
International Rights Agency.
Specializes in foreign rights, co-editions.

Felicity Bryan
2A N Parade, Banbury Rd, Oxford OX2 6LX
Tel: (01865) 513816 *Fax:* (01865) 310055
Key Personnel
Dir: Felicity Bryan *E-mail:* agency@felicitybryan.com
Associate, Europe: Andrew Nurnberg
Handles fiction & nonfiction with emphasis on history, biography, science & current affairs. No scripts for TV, radio or theatre; no crafts, how-to, science fiction or light romance. No unsol mss or reading fee. Commission: Home 10%; USA & Translation 20%.

AGENTS UNITED KINGDOM

The Buckman Agency
Ryman's Cottage, Little Tew, Oxford OX7 4JJ
Tel: (01608) 683677 *Fax:* (01608) 683449
Key Personnel
Contact: Rosemarie Buckman *E-mail:* r.buckman@talk21.com; Jessica Buckman
Tel: (020) 7385 3135 *Fax:* (020) 7385 3137
E-mail: j.buckman@talk21.com
Representing American & UK publishers & agents for the handling of all translation rights. Specializes in translation rights.

Bycornute Books
76a Ashford Rd, Eastbourne BN21 3TE
Tel: (01323) 649053
Key Personnel
Contact: Asia Haleem *E-mail:* asia@layish.co.uk
Founded: 1986
Specializes in illustrated books on art history, religion, cosmology, ancient history, mythology, archaeology, card novelties.

Campbell Thomson & McLaughlin Ltd
One King's Mews, London WC1N 2JA
Tel: (020) 7242 0958 *Fax:* (020) 7242 2408
Key Personnel
Man Dir: John McLaughlin
Contact: Charlotte Bruton
Founded: 1931
No plays, film/TV scripts, articles, short stories or poetry. No unsolicited mss or synopses. Preliminary letter with self-addressed envelope essential. No reading fee.
Specializes in fiction & general nonfiction, excluding children's.
Foreign Rep(s): Fox Chase Agency; Raines & Raines

Carnell Literary Agency
Danescroft, Goose Lane, Little Hallingbury, Herts CM22 7RG
Tel: (01279) 723626 *Fax:* (01279) 600308
Key Personnel
Contact: Pamela Buckmaster
Send letter with outline, two chapters & return postage.
Specializes in science fiction, fantasy, horror, fiction, nonfiction.

Casarotto Ramsay & Associates Ltd
National House, 60-66 Wardour St, London W1V 4ND
Tel: (020) 7287 4450 *Fax:* (020) 7287 9128
E-mail: agents@casarotto.uk.com
Web Site: www.casarotto.uk.com
Key Personnel
Man Dir: Giorgio Casarotto
Dir (Film & TV): Jenne Casarotto
Dir (Theatre): Tom Erhardt; Mel Kenyon
Also represent writers, producers, directors & key technical staff in film, TV & theater.

Jonathan Clowes Ltd
10 Iron Bridge House, Bridge Approach, London NW1 8BD
Tel: (020) 7722 7674 *Fax:* (020) 7722 7677
Key Personnel
Dir: Ann Evans
Contact: Isobel Creed; Lisa Whadcock
Founded: 1960
Handles fiction, nonfiction & scripts. No textbooks or children's. No unsol mss, authors come by recommendation or by successful follow-ups to preliminary letters. Commission: Home & US 15%; Translation 19%.
Specializes in film & TV rights, situation comedy.

Elspeth Cochrane Agency
Southbank Commercial Centre, 14/2 2nd floor, 140 Battersea Park Rd, London SW11 4NB
Tel: (020) 7622 0314 *Fax:* (020) 7622 5815
E-mail: info@elspethcochrane.co.uk
Key Personnel
Manager: Elspeth Cochrane
Founded: 1960
Handles fiction, nonfiction, biographies & screenplays. Commission: 12 1/2% (negotiable).

Rosica Colin Ltd
One Clareville Grove Mews, London SW7 5AH
Tel: (020) 7370 1080 *Fax:* (020) 7244 6441
Key Personnel
Contact: Johanna Marston
Handles full-length mss, plus theatre, film, TV & radio. Preliminary letter with return postage essential. No reading fee. Commission: Home 10%; USA 15%; Translation 20%.

Jane Conway-Gordon
One Old Compton St, London W1D 5JA
Tel: (020) 7494 0148 *Fax:* (020) 7287 9264
Key Personnel
Contact: Jane Conway-Gordon
Founded: 1982
Works in association with Andrew Mann Ltd. No poetry or science fiction. Unsol mss welcome; preliminary letter & return postage essential. No reading fee. Commission: Home 15%; US & Translation 20%.
Specializes in fiction, general nonfiction.
Foreign Rep(s): McIntosh & Otis, Inc

Copytrain
Pitts, Lower End, Great Milton, Oxford, Oxon OX44 7NF
Tel: (01844) 279345 *Fax:* (01844) 279345
Key Personnel
Proprietor: Richard Balkwill *E-mail:* rbalkwill@aol.com
Founded: 1992
Copyrighting & training consultancy.
Specializes in co-publishing, contract review, supplier agreements.

Rupert Crew Ltd
One A King's Mews, London WC1N 2JA
Tel: (020) 7242 8586 *Fax:* (020) 7831 7914
E-mail: rupertcrew@compuserve.com
Key Personnel
Chairman & Joint Man Dir: Doreen Montgomery
Joint Man Dir: Caroline Montgomery
Founded: 1927
International representation, handling volume & subsidiary rights in fiction & nonfiction. No plays, poetry, journalism or short stories. Preliminary letter & return postage required. Commission: Home 15%; Elsewhere 20%.
Specializes in fiction, nonfiction, major book projects with international appeal.

Curtis Brown Group Ltd
Haymarket House, 28-29 Haymarket, London SW1Y 4SP
Tel: (020) 7393 4400 *Fax:* (020) 7393 4401
E-mail: cb@curtisbrown.co.uk
Key Personnel
Group Man Dir: Jonathan Lloyd *E-mail:* jlloyd@curtisbrown.co.uk
Dir: Mark Collingbourne; Jacquie Drewe; Jonny Geller; Ben Hall; Nick Marston; Peter Robinson
Dir (CB Australia): Fiona Inglis
Founded: 1899
Representation of directors, writers, designers, presenters & actors in theater, film & television & a wide range of authors of fiction & nonfiction. Commission: Home 15%; US & Translation 20%.

David Godwin Associates
55 Monmouth St, London WC2H 9DG
Tel: (020) 7240 9992 *Fax:* (020) 7395 6110
E-mail: assistant@davidgodwinassociates.co.uk
Founded: 1995
Specializes in fiction & general nonfiction.

Diagram Visual Information Ltd
195 Kentish Town Rd, London NW5 2JU
Tel: (020) 7482 3633 *Fax:* (020) 7482 4932
E-mail: diagramvis@aol.com
Key Personnel
Dir: Bruce Robertson
Secretary: Carole A Dease
Founded: 1967

Drake Educational Associates Ltd
Saint Fagans Rd, Fairwater, Cardiff CF5 3AE
Tel: (029) 2056 0333 *Fax:* (029) 2055 4909
E-mail: info@drakeav.com
Web Site: www.drakegroup.co.uk; www.drakeed.com
Key Personnel
Man Dir: Mr R G Drake
Specializes in education, children's.

Toby Eady Associates Ltd
9 Orme Court, 3rd floor, London W2 4RL
Tel: (020) 7792 0092 *Fax:* (020) 7792 0879
E-mail: toby@tobyeady.demon.co.uk
Web Site: www.tobyeadyassociates.co.uk
Key Personnel
Dir: Toby Eady *E-mail:* toby@tobyeady.demon.co.uk; Jessica Woollard *E-mail:* jessica@tobyeady.demon.co.uk
Founded: 1968
Commission: UK: 15%; elsewhere 20%.
Specializes in China, Middle East, Africa, India. handle fiction, nonfiction.
Foreign Rep(s): Ed Breslin; Buckman Agency; JLM Literary Agency; Katai & Bolza; La Nouvelle Agence; Jan Michael; Mohrbooks; Kristen Olson; Prava i Prevodi; Joanne Wang

Faith Evans Associates
27 Park Ave North, London N8 7RU
Tel: (020) 8340 9920 *Fax:* (020) 8340 9910
Key Personnel
Contact: Faith Evans
Founded: 1987
Only accept calls or submissions by recommendations. Commission: Home 15%; US & Translation 20%.

Anne Louise Fisher & Suzy Lucas
29 D'Arblay St, London W1F 8EP
Tel: (020) 7494 4609 *Fax:* (020) 7494 4611
Key Personnel
Publisher's Scout: Anne-Louise Fisher *E-mail:* annelouise@alfisher.co.uk; Suzy Lucas *E-mail:* suzy@alfisher.co.uk
Literary scout representing Doubleday, Nan Talese & Broadway Books in US; Librarie Plon & Poruet in France; Karl Blessing Verlag, Berlin Verlag & Siedler Verlag in Germany; Arnoldo Mondadori Editore in Italy; Albert Bonniers Bokforlag in Sweden; Octava in Finland; Gyldendal Norsk Forlag in Norway; De Boekerij & M Publishers in the Netherlands; Plaza y Janes, Editorial Debate, Lumen & Mondatori Iberica in Spain; Patakis Publications in Greece.

French's
78 Loudoun Rd, London NW8 0NA
Tel: (020) 7483 4269 *Fax:* (020) 7722 0574
Key Personnel
Contact: Mark Taylor
Founded: 1973
Handles fiction, nonfiction & scripts for all media, especially novels & screenplays. No religious or medical books. No unsol mss. For unpublished authors we offer a reading service

for a fee per ms, exclusive of postage. Interested authors should write in the first instance. Commission: Home 10%.

Blake Friedmann Literary Agency Ltd
122 Arlington Rd, London NW1 7HP
Tel: (020) 7284 0408 *Fax:* (020) 7284 0442
Web Site: www.blakefriedmann.co.uk
Key Personnel
Joint Man Dir: Carole Blake *E-mail:* carole@blakefriedmann.co.uk; Julian Friedmann
Finance Dir: Barbara Jones
Dir: Isobel Dixon; Conrad William
Founded: 1977
Handles fiction & nonfiction, scripts for TV, radio & film. No poetry, juvenile, science fiction or short stories. Send initial letter with synopsis & first two chapters. No reading fee. Commission: Home 15%; US & Translation 20%; Radio/TV/Film 15%.
Specializes in commercial women's fiction, literary fiction, up-market nonfiction.

Vernon Futerman Associates
17 Deanhill Rd, London SW14 7DQ
Tel: (020) 76292414 *Fax:* (020) 76297181
Key Personnel
Man Dir: Vernon Futerman
Dir: Guy Rose *E-mail:* grose@aol.com; Alexandra Groom
Founded: 1984
Specializes in fiction & academic nonfiction, TV film & theatre scripts.

Eric Glass Ltd
25 Ladbroke Crescent, Notting Hill, London W11 1PS
Tel: (020) 7229 9500 *Fax:* (020) 7229 6220
Key Personnel
Dir: Janet Glass; Sissi Liechtenstein
Founded: 1934
Handles fiction, nonfiction & scripts for publication or production in all media. No poetry, short stories, or children's works. No unsol mss. No reading fee. Commission: Home 10%; US & Translation 20%.
Represents Societe des Auteurs et Compositeurs Dramatiques (SACD), Paris & Societe Civil des Auteurs Multimedia (SCAM) (formerly Societe des Gens de Lettres).

Christine Green Authors' Agent
6 Whitehorse Mews, Westminster Bridge, London SE1 7QD
Tel: (020) 7041 8844 *Fax:* (020) 7686 8860
E-mail: info@christinegreen.co.uk
Web Site: www.christinegreen.co.uk
Key Personnel
Contact: Christine Green
Founded: 1984
No scripts, poetry or children's. No unsol mss; initial letter & synopsis preferred. No reading fee but return postage essential. Commission: Home 10 percent; US & Translation 20 percent.
Specializes in general fiction, general nonfiction, literary fiction.

Greene & Heaton Ltd
37 Goldhawk Rd, London W12 8QQ
Tel: (020) 8749 0315 *Fax:* (020) 8749 0318
Web Site: www.greeneheaton.co.uk
Key Personnel
Contact: Carol Heaton; Judith Murray; Antony Topping
Contact, Children's: Linda Davis
Handles all types of fiction & nonfiction. No original scripts for theatre, film or TV. Commission: Home 15%; US & Translation 20%.

Gregory & Company Authors' Agents
3 Barb Mews, London W6 7PA
Tel: (020) 7610 4676 *Fax:* (020) 7610 4686
E-mail: info@gregoryandcompany.co.uk
Web Site: www.gregoryandcompany.co.uk
Key Personnel
Partner: Jane Gregory *E-mail:* jane@gregoryandcompany.co.uk
Rights: Jane Barlow *E-mail:* janeb@gregoryandcompany.co.uk; Claire Morris
Founded: 1987
No original plays, film or TV scripts, no science fiction, fantasy, poetry, academic or children's books. No reading fee. Editorial advice given to own authors. No unsol mss; send a preliminary letter with cv, synopsis, first three chapters & future writing plans (plus return postage). Short submission by fax or e-mail. Commission: Home 15%; US, Translation, Radio/TV/Film 20%. Represented throughout Europe, Asia & US.
Specializes in fiction, general non-fiction, special interest fiction-literary, commercial, crime, suspense & thrillers.

David Grossman Literary Agency Ltd
118B Holland Park Ave, London W11 4UA
Tel: (020) 7221 2770 *Fax:* (020) 7221 1445
Founded: 1976
Handles full-length fiction & general nonfiction. No verse or technical books for students. No original screenplays or teleplays. Approach by preliminary letter giving full description of the work &, in the case of fiction, with the first 50 pages. All material must by accompanied by return postage. No approaches or submissions by fax or e-mail. No unsol mss. No reading fee. Material should be addressed to the Submissions Dept. Commission Rates vary for different markets. Overseas associates throughout Europe, Asia, Brazil & the USA.

Gundhild Lenz-Mulligan
15 Sandbourne Ave, Merton Park, London SW19 3EW
Tel: (020) 8543 7846 *Fax:* (020) 8543 8909
E-mail: glenz-mulligan@dial.pipex.com
Key Personnel
Contact: Gundhild Lenz-Mulligan
Founded: 1998
Specializes in children's books.

Gunnar Lie & Associates Ltd
Roebuck House, 3rd floor, 288 Upper Richmond Rd W, London SW14 7JG
Tel: (020) 8487 9020 *Fax:* (020) 8878 2832
E-mail: gunnarlie@compuserve.com
Key Personnel
Man Dir: Gunnar Lie
Export Manager: John Edgeler *Tel:* (020) 8487 9021 *E-mail:* johnedgeler@compuserve.com
Founded: 1995
Specializes in international sales & marketing.

A M Heath & Co Ltd
79 St Martin's Lane, London WC2N 4RE
Tel: (020) 7836 4271 *Fax:* (020) 7497 2561
E-mail: amheath@demon.co.uk *Cable:* SCRIPT LONDON WC2
Key Personnel
Chairman: Michael Thomas
Dir: Sara Fisher; William Hamilton; Victoria Hobbs; Sarah Molloy
Founded: 1919
No dramatic scripts, poetry or short stories. Preliminary letter & synopsis essential. No reading fee. Commission: Home 10-15%; US & Translation 20%; Film & TV 15%. Overseas associates in the US, Europe, South America, Japan & the Far East.
Specializes in fiction, general nonfiction & children's.

David Higham Associates Ltd
5-8 Lower John St, Golden Sq, London W1F 9HA
Tel: (020) 7434 5900 *Fax:* (020) 7437 1072
E-mail: dha@davidhigham.co.uk
Web Site: www.davidhigham.co.uk
Key Personnel
Contact, Books: Veronique Baxter; Anthony Goff; Bruce Hunter; Jacqueline Korn; Lizzy Kremer; Caroline Walsh
Contact, Scripts: Gemma Hirst; Nicky Lund; Georgina Ruffhead
Founded: 1935
Handles fiction, nonfiction (biography, history, current affairs), children's books & scripts. Preliminary letter with synopsis required. No reading fee. Commission: Home 15%; US & Translation 20%.

Vanessa Holt Ltd
59 Crescent Rd, Leigh-on-Sea, Essex SS9 2PF
Tel: (01702) 473787 *Fax:* (01702) 471890
E-mail: vanessa@holtlimited.freeserve.co.uk
Key Personnel
Contact: Vanessa Holt
Founded: 1989
No unsolicited material. Handles general fiction, nonfiction & non-illustrated children's books. Commission: Home 15%; US & Translation 20%; Radio/TV/Film 15%.
Specializes in commercial & literary fiction, crime fiction & books with potential for international sales.

Kate Hordern
18 Mortimer Rd, Clifton, Bristol BS8 4EY
Tel: (0117) 923 9368 *Fax:* (0117) 973 1941
E-mail: katehorden@blueyonder.co.uk
Handles quality literary & commercial fiction, including women's, suspense & genre fictions. Also general nonfiction. No children's books. Commission: Home 15%; US & Translation 20%.

Tanja Howarth Literary Agency
19 New Row, London WC2N 4LA
Tel: (020) 7240 5553 *Fax:* (020) 7379 0969
E-mail: tanja.howarth@btinternet.com
Founded: 1970
No children's books, plays or poetry. No unsol mss. Preliminary letter preferred. No reading fee. Established agent for foreign literature, particularly from the German language. Commission: Home 15%; Translation 20%.
Specializes in fiction & nonfiction from British authors.

Hutton-Williams Agency
58 Melbury Gardens, London SW20 0DJ
Tel: (020) 8879 0237 *Fax:* (020) 8879 3831
Key Personnel
Contact: Mr C Hutton Williams *E-mail:* hwagency@email.com
Founded: 1988
Syndication & foreign rights of newspapers, magazines & books throughout the world.
Specializes in annuals, special issues, supplements & partworks.

Imrie & Dervis Literary Agency
7 Carlton Mansions, Holmleigh Rd, London N16 5PX
Tel: (020) 8809 3282 *Fax:* (020) 8880 2086
E-mail: info@imriedervis.com
Key Personnel
Agent: Martina Dervis *E-mail:* martina@imriedervis.com; Malcolm Imrie *E-mail:* malcolm@imriedervis.com

Information Agents Ltd
26 Rosebery Ave, London EC1R 4SX

Tel: (020) 7837 3345 *Fax:* (020) 7837 8901
E-mail: eps@epsltd.com
Web Site: www.epsltd.com
Key Personnel
Chairman: David Worlock
Dir: D J Powell
Founded: 1985
Specializes in negotiating electronic rights.

Intercontinental Literary Agency, see PFD

Intercontinental Literary Agency
33 Bedford St, London WC2E 9ED
Tel: (020) 7379 6611 *Fax:* (020) 7379 6790
E-mail: ila@ila-agency.co.uk
Key Personnel
Dir: Nicki Kennedy *E-mail:* nicki-kennedy@ila-agency.co.uk
Founded: 1965
Translation rights only.

International Scripts Ltd
IA Kidbrooke Park Rd, Blackheath, London SE3 0LR
Tel: (020) 8319 8666 *Fax:* (020) 8319 0801
Key Personnel
Man Dir: Bob Tanner
Dir: Jill Lawson
Founded: 1979
Involved in selling UK & Commonwealth, translation & US rights & subsidiary rights. Also involved in film & TV scripts. Preliminary letter & self-addressed envelope required. Commission: Home 15%; US & Translation 20%.
Specializes in fiction: commerical, women's (contemporary, sagas, romance), mystery & detective, Irish (women's contemporary & sagas), horror; nonfiction: mind, body & spirit, health & fitness, biographies, popular business.

Jane Judd Literary Agency
18 Belitha Villas, London N1 1PD
Tel: (020) 7607 0273 *Fax:* (020) 7607 0623
Key Personnel
Contact: Jane Judd
Founded: 1986
Handles general fiction & nonfiction. Also represents US companies Avon Books & Mercury House & US agents Marian Young & Penguin Canada. No scripts, academic, gardenig or DIY. Approach with letter, including synopsis, first chapter & return postage. Initial telephone call helpful in the case of nonfiction. Commission: Home 10%, US & Translation 20%.
Specializes in biography, crime, health, humor, investigative journalism, literary, thrillers, travel, women's interests.

The Frances Kelly Agency
111 Clifton Rd, Kingston-upon-Thames, Surrey KT2 6PL
Tel: (020) 8549 7830 *Fax:* (020) 8547 0051
Founded: 1978
No unsol mss. Send letter with brief synopsis, CV & return postage. Commission: Home 10%; US & Translation 20%.
Specializes in nonfiction, including illustrated biography, history, art, self-help, food & wine, complementary medicine & therapies, finance & business; trade, reference, academic.

Knight Features
20 Crescent Grove, London SW4 7AH
Tel: (020) 7622 1467 *Fax:* (020) 7622 1522
E-mail: gaby@knightfeatures.co.uk
Key Personnel
Dir, Proprietor: Peter Knight *E-mail:* peter@knightfeatures.co.uk
Founded: 1985
No poetry, science fiction or cookery. No unsol mss. Send cover letter, self-addressed envelope & synopsis of proposed work. Commission dependent upon authors & territories.
Specializes in strip cartoons, major features, serializations, autobiography/memoirs/letters, biography, astrology, business & economics, history, humour, formula one racing, puzzles.
Branch Office(s)
Peter Knight Literary Agency
Foreign Rep(s): United Media

LAW Ltd (Lucas Alexander Whitley)
14 Vernon St, London W14 0RJ
Tel: (020) 7471 7900 *Fax:* (020) 7471 7910
E-mail: law@lawagency.co.uk
Key Personnel
Contact: Julian Alexander *E-mail:* julian@lawagency.co.uk; Lucinda Cook *E-mail:* lucinda@lawagency.co.uk; Celia Hayley *E-mail:* celia@lawagency.co.uk; Mark Lucas *E-mail:* mark@lawagency.co.uk; Helen Mulligan *E-mail:* helen@lawagency.co.uk; Peta Nightingale *E-mail:* peta@lawagency.co.uk; Alice Saunders *E-mail:* alice@lawagency.co.uk; Araminta Whitley *E-mail:* araminta@lawagency.co.uk
Contact, Children's: Philippa Milnes-Smith *E-mail:* philippa@lawagency.co.uk
Founded: 1996
Handles full-length commercial & literary fiction, nonfiction & children's books. No plays, poetry, textbooks or fantasy. Film & TV scripts handled for established clients only. Unsol mss considered; send brief covering letter, short synopsis & two sample chapters. Self-addressed envelope required. No e-mailed submissions. Commission: Home 15%; US & Translation 20%. Overseas associates worldwide.

Barbara Levy Literary Agency
64 Greenhill, Hampstead High St, London NW3 5TZ
Tel: (020) 7435 9046 *Fax:* (020) 7431 2063
Key Personnel
Dir: Barbara Levy *E-mail:* blevy@dircon.co.uk
Associate: John F Selby
Founded: 1986
Handles fiction, nonfiction & film & TV rights. No unsol mss. Send detailed preliminary letter. Commission: Home 10%; US 20%.

Litopia Corp Ltd
186 Bickenhall Mansions, Bickenhall St, London W1H 3DE
Tel: (020) 7224 1748 *Fax:* (020) 7224 1802
E-mail: enquiries@litopia.com
Web Site: www.litopia.com
Key Personnel
Chief Executive Officer: Peter Cox *E-mail:* peter@litopia.com
Contact: Peggy Brusseau *E-mail:* peggy@litopia.com; Jane Mountbatten *E-mail:* jane@litopia.com
Founded: 1993
Require all submissions to follow the guidelines on website. Commission by negotiation.
Specializes in general, no children's or poetry.

Christopher Little Literary Agency
10 Eel Brook Studios, 125 Moore Park Rd, London SW6 4PS
Tel: (020) 7736 4455 *Fax:* (020) 7736 4490
Key Personnel
Proprietor: Christopher J Little *E-mail:* christopher@christopherlittle.net
Contact: Kellee Nunley *E-mail:* kellee@christopherlittle.net
Founded: 1979
Handles commercial & literary full-length fiction & nonfiction. Send detailed letter, synopsis &/or first two chapters & self-addressed envelope. Commission: Home 15%; US, Canada, Translation, Audio & Motion Picture 20%.
Specializes in crime, thriller, popular science & investigative nonfiction.

London Independent Books
26 Chalcot Crescent, London NW1 8YD
Tel: (020) 7706 0486 *Fax:* (020) 7724 3122
Key Personnel
Literary Agent: Carolyn Whitaker
Founded: 1971
All subjects considered except young children's & computer books. Commission: Home 15%; US & Translation 20%.
Specializes in crime fiction, fantasy fiction, travel, young adult fiction.

Andrew Lownie Literary Agency Ltd
17 Sutherland St, London SW1V 4JU
Tel: (020) 7828 1274 *Fax:* (020) 7828 7608
E-mail: lownie@globalnet.co.uk
Web Site: www.andrewlownie.co.uk
Key Personnel
Chief Executive: Andrew Lownie *E-mail:* lownie@globalnet.co.uk
Founded: 1988
Specializes in nonfiction, history, biography, current affairs.

Lucas Alexander Whitley, see LAW Ltd (Lucas Alexander Whitley)

Lutyens & Rubinstein
231 Westbourne Park Rd, London W11 1EB
Tel: (020) 7792 4855 *Fax:* (020) 7792 4833
Key Personnel
Partner: Sarah Lutyens *E-mail:* sarah@lutyensrubinstein.co.uk; Felicity Rubinstein *E-mail:* felicity@lutyensrubinstein.co.uk
Submissions: Susannah Godman *E-mail:* susannah@lutyensrubinstein.co.uk
Founded: 1993
Membership(s): Association of Authors' Agents.
No TV, film radio or theatre scripts. Unsol mss accepted; send introductory letter, CV, two chapters & return postage for all material submitted. No reading fee. Commission: Home 15%; US & Translation 20%.
Specializes in adult fiction & non-fiction.

MacLean Dubois Ltd (Writers & Agents)
Hillend House, Hillend, Edinburgh EH10 7DX
Tel: (0131) 445 5885 *Fax:* (0131) 445 5898
E-mail: info@whiskymax.co.uk
Key Personnel
Dir: Charles MacLean
Founded: 1976
Copywriter, brochures, annual reports & promotional material.
Specializes in Scottish fiction & nonfiction, journalism, writing & related services.

The Marsh Agency
11 Dover St, London W1S 4LJ
Tel: (020) 7399 2800 *Fax:* (020) 7399 2801
E-mail: enquiries@marsh-agency.co.uk
Web Site: www.marsh-agency.co.uk
Key Personnel
Partner: Paul Marsh; Susanna Nicklin
Rights Manager: Camilla Ferrier
Founded: 1994
Specializes in international rights.

Blanche Marvin Agency
21A St Johns Wood High St, London NW8 7NG
Tel: (020) 7722 2313 *Fax:* (020) 7722 2313
Key Personnel
Editor & Publisher: Blanche Marvin *E-mail:* blanchemarvin@madasafish.com
Founded: 1968
Established work only.
Specializes in theater & drama.

UNITED KINGDOM

MBA Literary Agents Ltd
62 Grafton Way, London W1T 5DW
Tel: (020) 7387 2076 *Fax:* (020) 7387 2042
Key Personnel
Man Dir: Diana Tyler *E-mail:* diana@mbalit.co.uk
Dir: Meg Davis *E-mail:* meg@mbalit.co.uk; John Richard Parker *E-mail:* john@mbalit.co.uk
Contact: Laura Longrigg *E-mail:* laura@@mbalit.co.uk; David Riding *E-mail:* david@mbalit.co.uk
Founded: 1971
Handles fiction & nonfiction, TV, film radio & theatre scripts. No poetry. Works in conjunction with agents in most countries. No unsol mss. Commission: Home 15%, Overseas 20%; Theatre/TV Radio 10%; Film 10-20%.
Foreign Rep(s): JABberwocky Agency; Donald Maass Agency; Writers House, Inc

Cathy Miller Foreign Rights Agency
18 The Quadrangle, 49 Atalanta St, London SW6 6TU
Tel: (020) 7386 5473 *Fax:* (020) 7385 1774
Key Personnel
Managing Dir: Cathy Miller *E-mail:* cathy@millerrightsagency.com
Founded: 1981
Consultants to publishers worldwide in the field of translation rights, worldwide market research for publishers interested in European potential, help with negotiating rights contracts & representation.
Specializes in foreign rights.

William Morris Agency (UK) Ltd
52/53 Poland St, London W1F 7LX
Tel: (020) 7534 6800 *Fax:* (020) 7534 6900
Web Site: www.wma.com
Key Personnel
Man Dir: Stephanie Cabot
Literary Agent, Books: Eugenie Furniss
Literary Agent, TV: Holly Pie; Hans Schiff
Contact: Holly Pye
Founded: 1965
Worldwide theatrical & literary agency with offices in New York, Beverly Hills & Nashville & associates in Sydney. Handles TV scripts, fiction & general nonfiction. No unsol film, TV or stage material at all. Mss for books with preliminary letter. No reading fee. Commission: TV 10%; UK Books 15%; US Books & Translation 20%.

Michael Motley Ltd
The Old Vicarage Tredington, Tewkesbury, Glos GL20 7BP
Tel: (01684) 276390 *Fax:* (01684) 297355
E-mail: michael.motley@amserve.com
Key Personnel
Contact: Michael Motley
Founded: 1973
Handles full-length fiction & nonfiction only. No unsolicited work considered. New clients by referral only. Commission: Home 10%; US 15%; Translation 20%.

Negotiate Ltd
99 Caiyside, Edinburgh EH10 7HR
Tel: (0131) 445 7571; (0131) 477 7858
Fax: (0131) 445 7572
E-mail: gavin@negotiate.demon.co.uk
Web Site: www.negotiate.co.uk
Key Personnel
Man Dir: Gavin Kennedy *E-mail:* gavin@negweb.com
Founded: 1986
Negotiation of authors, publishers, agents & contracts.
Specializes in contract negotiation.

The Maggie Noach Literary Agency
22 Dorville Crescent, London W6 0HJ
Tel: (020) 8748 2926 *Fax:* (020) 8748 8057
E-mail: m-noach@dircon.co.uk
Key Personnel
Contact: Maggie Noach
Founded: 1982
No scientific, academic or specialist nonfiction. No poetry, plays, short stories or books for the very young. No unsol mss. Approach by letter (not by telephone or e-mail), giving a brief description of the book & enclosing a few sample pages. Return postage essential. No reading fee. Commission: Home 15%; US & Translation 20%.
Specializes in general nonfiction, biography, commercial fiction & non-illustrated children's books for ages 7-12.

Andrew Nurnberg Associates Ltd
Clerkenwell House, 45-47 Clerkenwell Green, London EC1R 0QX
Tel: (020) 7417 8800 *Fax:* (020) 7417 8812
E-mail: all@nurnberg.co.uk
Telex: 23353 *Cable:* NURNBOOKS LONDON
Key Personnel
Man Dir: Andrew Nurnberg
Dir: Sarah Nundy
Contact: Vicky Mark; D Roger Seaton
Commission: Home 15%; US & Translation 20%.
Specializes in foreign rights.
Branch Office(s)
Andrew Nurnberg Associates Baltic, PO Box 77, Riga LV-1011, Latvia, Contact: Tatjana Zoldnere *Tel:* 7289759; 7506495 *Fax:* 7821241; 7506494 *E-mail:* zoldnere@anab.apollo.lv
Andrew Nurnberg Associates Beijing, Room 3404 FLTP, Bldg 19, Xi San Huan Builu, Beijing 100089, China, Contact: Jackie Huang *Tel:* (010) 684-20958 *Fax:* (010) 689-17896 *E-mail:* jhuang@nurnberg.com.cn
Andrew Nurnberg Associates Bucharest, Casa Presei Libere Nr 1, Intrarea A, Etaj 4, Camera 457, Sector 1, Bucharest, Romania *Tel:* (01) 224-0479 *Fax:* (01) 224-0479 *E-mail:* andrew@fx.ro
Andrew Nurnberg Associates Budapest, Hold u 29, 1054 Budapest, Hungary, Contact: Judit Hermann *Tel:* (01) 3026451 *Fax:* (01) 1113948 *E-mail:* jhermann@matavnet.hu
Andrew Nurnberg Associates Prague, Seifertova 81, Prague 3, Czech Republic, Contact: Petra Tobiskova *Tel:* (02) 227 82041 *Fax:* (02) 227 82308 *E-mail:* nurnprg@mbox.vol.cz
Andrew Nurnberg Associates Sofia, 11 Slaveikov Sq, PO Box 453, 1000 Sofia, Bulgaria, Contact: Anna Droumeva *Tel:* (02) 9862819 *Fax:* (02) 9862819 *E-mail:* anas@tea.bg
Andrew Nurnberg Associates Warsaw, UL Milobedzka 10/2, 02-634 Warsaw, Poland, Contact: Aleksandra Matuszak *Tel:* (022) 6465860 *Fax:* (022) 6465860 *E-mail:* aleksandra@literatura.com.pl
Andrew Nurnberg Literary Agency (Moscow), Voprosy Literatury, Bolshoi Gnezdnikovsky 10, Moscow 103009, Russian Federation, Contact: Ludmilla Sushkova *Tel:* (095) 229-5281 *Fax:* (095) 883-6403 *E-mail:* sushkova@adonis.iasnet.ru

David O'Leary Literary Agents
10 Lansdowne Court, Lansdowne Rise, London W11 2NR
Tel: (020) 7229 1623 *Fax:* (020) 7727 9624
E-mail: d.o'leary@virgin.net
Key Personnel
Contact: David O'Leary
Founded: 1988
Include brief synopsis of subject of novel with initial correspondence. Include self-addressed envelope if return requested. Commission: Home 10%; US 10%.
Specializes in fiction & nonfiction (both literary & commercial), history, popular science & Irish subjects.

Deborah Owen Ltd
78 Narrow St, Limehouse, London E14 8BP
Tel: (020) 7987 5119; (020) 7987 5441
Fax: (020) 7538 4004
E-mail: do@deborahowen.co.uk
Founded: 1971
Represents only two authors. No new authors. Commission: Home 10%; US & Translation 15%.

Paterson Marsh Ltd
Affiliate of Marsh Agency
11 Dover St, London W1S 4LJ
Tel: (0207) 399 2800 *Fax:* (0207) 399 2801
E-mail: info@markpaterson.co.uk
Web Site: www.patersonmarsh.co.uk
Key Personnel
Dir: Paul Marsh *E-mail:* paul@patersonmarsh.co.uk; Mark Paterson *E-mail:* mark@patersonmarsh.co.uk
Foreign Rights Manager: Stephanie Ebdon *E-mail:* steph@patersonmarsh.co.uk
Founded: 1961
World rights representatives of authors & publishers.
Specializes in psychology, psychotherapy, psychoanalysis, history.

John Pawsey
60 High St, Tarring, Worthing, West Sussex BN14 7NR
Tel: (01903) 205167 *Fax:* (01903) 205167
Key Personnel
Proprietor: John Pawsey
Founded: 1981
Represents American publishers & literary agencies in the UK. Handles nonfiction: biography, politics, current affairs, popular culture, travel, sport, business & music. Also fiction: crime, thrillers & suspense. No children's, science fiction, horror, drama scripts, poetry, academic, short stories or journalism. Send preliminary letter with self-addressed envelope. No reading fee. Commission: Home 10-15%; US & Translation 19-25%.

Peake Associates Tony Peake
14 Grafton Crescent, London NW1 8SL
Tel: (020) 7267 8033 *Fax:* (020) 7284 1876
E-mail: peakeassoc@aol.com
Web Site: www.tonypeake.com
Specializes in fiction & non-fiction.

Maggie Pearlstine Associates Ltd
31 Ashley Gardens, Ambrosden Ave, London SW1P 1QE
Tel: (020) 7828 4212 *Fax:* (020) 7834 5546
E-mail: post@pearlstine.co.uk
Key Personnel
Dir: Maggie Pearlstine
Associate: John Oates *E-mail:* john@pearlstine.co.uk
Founded: 1989
Small, selective agency. UK based authors only. Handles general nonfiction & fiction. No children's poetry, horror, science fiction short stories or scripts. Commission: Home 12 1/2% (fiction), 10% (nonfiction); US & Translation 20%; TV, Film & Journalism 20%.
Specializes in biography, current affairs, health & history.

A D Peters & Co, see PFD

AGENTS — UNITED KINGDOM

PFD
Drury House, 34-43 Russell St, London WC2B 5HA
Tel: (020) 7344 1000 *Fax:* (020) 7836 9539
E-mail: postmaster@pfd.co.uk
Web Site: www.pfd.co.uk
Key Personnel
Joint Chair: Tim Corrie; Anthony Jones
Man Dir: Anthony Baring
Agent: Annabel Hardman *Tel:* (020) 7344 1054
  E-mail: ahardman@pfd.co.uk
Founded: 1988
Handles fiction & children's, plus scripts for film, theatre, radio & TV material. Send letter with a detailed outline & sample chapters. Screenplays & TV scripts should be addressed to the Film & Script Dept, enclose self-addressed envelope. No reading fee. Commission: Home 10%; US & Translation 20%.
Specializes in literary, film & actors agency.
Parent Company: CSS Stellar

Pollinger Ltd
9 Staple Inn, Holborn, London WC1V 7QH
Tel: (020) 7404 0342 *Fax:* (020) 7242 5737
E-mail: info@pollingerltd.com
Web Site: www.pollingerltd.com
Key Personnel
Dir: Leigh Pollinger
Man Dir: Lesley Hadcroft Pollinger
  E-mail: lesleypollinger@pollingerltd.com
Secretary: John Furzer *E-mail:* johnfurzer@pollingerltd.com
Authors' Agent: Joanna Devereux
  E-mail: jdevereux@pollingerltd.com
Founded: 2002
Authors' agents.
Specializes in adult fiction & nonfiction, children's, literary estates.

Rogers, Coleridge & White Ltd
20 Powis Mews, London W11 1JN
Tel: (020) 7221 3717 *Fax:* (020) 7229 9084
E-mail: rcwlitagency@rcwlitagency.co.uk *Cable:* DEBROGERS LONDON W11
Key Personnel
Dir: Gill Coleridge; David Miller; Deborah Rogers; Peter Straus
Dir, USA: Patricia White
Consultant: Ann Warnford-Davis
Foreign Rights: Stephen Edwards; Laurence Laluyaux
Founded: 1967
No poetry, plays or technical books. No unsol mss, no submissions by fax or e-mail. Commission: Home 10%; US 15%; Translation 20%.
Specializes in fiction, non-fiction & children's.
Foreign Rep(s): ICM

Elizabeth Roy Literary Agency
White Cottage, Greatford, Near Stamford, Lincs PE9 4PR
Tel: (01778) 560672 *Fax:* (01778) 560672
Key Personnel
Contact: Elizabeth Roy
Founded: 1990
Send preliminary letter, synopsis, sample chapters, names of previous publishers & agents & return postage. No reading fee. Commission: Home 10-15%; Overseas 20%.
Specializes in children's books (fiction & nonfiction), children's books illustrators.

The Sayle Literary Agency
Bickerton House, 25-27 Bickerton Rd, London N19 5JT
Tel: (020) 7263 8681 *Fax:* (020) 7561 0529
Key Personnel
Contact: Rachel Calder
Preliminary letter & return postage required. No reading fee.
Specializes in full-length fiction, nonfiction.

Sheil Land Associates Ltd
43 Doughty St, London WC1N 2LH
Tel: (020) 7405 9351 *Fax:* (020) 7831 2127
E-mail: info@sheilland.co.uk
Key Personnel
Chairman: Anthony Sheil
Chief Executive: Sonia Land
Rights Dir: Laura Susijn
Contact: Luigi Bonomi; Sam Boyce; Vivien Green; Amanda Preston
Founded: 1962
Literary, Theatre & Film Agents. Preliminary letter with self-addressed envelope essential, no reading fee. Commission: Home 15%; US & Translation 20%.
Specializes in commercial & literary fiction & nonfiction, including politics, business, history, military history, gardening, thrillers, crime, romance, fantasy, drama, biography, travel, cookery & humor.
U.S. Office(s): Sheil Land Associates in association with George Borchart Inc, 136 E 57 St, New York, NY 10022, United States *Tel:* 212-753-5785
Foreign Rep(s): APA; Georges Borchardt, Inc; CAA; Farrar, Straus & Giroux, Inc

Caroline Sheldon Literary Agency
Thorley Manor Farm, Thorley, Yarmouth PO41 0S1
Tel: (01938) 760205
Key Personnel
Literary Agent & Proprietor: Caroline Sheldon
Founded: 1985
Handles adult fiction, including women's, commercial & literary novels. Send letter with synopsis of four chapters & large self-addressed envelope. No reading fee. Commission: Home 10%; US & Translation 20%.

Dorie Simmonds Agency
67 Upper Berkeley St, London W1H 7QX
Tel: (020) 7486 9228 *Fax:* (020) 7486 8228
Key Personnel
Proprietor: Dorie Simmonds
  E-mail: dhsimmonds@aol.com
Agent: Jennifer Callaghan
Rights: Almarie de Lange
Handles a wide range of subjects including general nonfiction & commercial fiction, children's books & associated rights.
Outline required for nonfiction, short synopsis for fiction with 2-3 sample chapters, writing experience & publishing history explained. Include SASE if return requested.
Specializes in contemporary personalities, historical biographies, self-help & women's fiction.

Jeffrey Simmons
15 Penn House, Mallory St, London NW8 8SX
Tel: (020) 7224 8917 *Fax:* (020) 7224 8918
E-mail: jas@london-inc.com
Key Personnel
Contact: Jeffrey Simmons
Founded: 1978
No science fiction/fantasy, children's books, cookery, crafts, hobbies or gardening. Film scripts handled only if by book-writing clients. Commission: Home 10-15%; US & Foreign 15%.
Specializes in biography & autobiography, cinema & theatre, fiction (both quality & commercial), history, law & crime, politics & world affairs, parapsychology & sport.

The Stationery Office, see TSO (The Stationery Office)

Abner Stein
10 Roland Gardens, London SW7 3PH
Tel: (020) 7373 0456 *Fax:* (020) 7370 6316
E-mail: abnerstein@compuserve.com
Key Personnel
Contact: Abner Stein
Founded: 1971
No scientific, technical. Commission: Home 10%; US & Translation 20%.
Specializes in children's books, fiction, nonfiction.

Micheline Steinberg Associates
104 Great Portland St, London W1W 6PE
Tel: (020) 7631 1310 *Fax:* (020) 7631 1146
E-mail: info@steinplays.com
Key Personnel
Contact: Ginny Sennett; Micheline Steinberg
Founded: 1988
Preliminary letter with self-addressed envelope. Dramatic associate for Laurence Pollinger Limited. Commission: Home 10%; Elsewhere 15%.
Specializes in plays for stage, TV, radio & film.

J M Thurley Management
30 Cambridge Rd, Teddington, Middlesex TW11 8DR
Tel: (020) 8977 3176 *Fax:* (020) 8943 2678
Key Personnel
Proprietor: J M Thurley *E-mail:* jmthurley@aol.com
Founded: 1976
Specialize in literary & commercial fiction & nonfiction.

Lavinia Trevor Literary Agency
The Glasshouse, 49A Goldhawk Rd, London W12 8QP
Tel: (020) 8749 8481 *Fax:* (020) 8749 7377
Key Personnel
Contact: Lavinia Trevor
Founded: 1993
No poetry, academic, technical or children's books. No TV, film, radio, theatre scripts. Preliminary letter, a brief autobiography & first 50-100 typewritten pages. Send self-addressed envelope. No reading fee. Commission rate by agreement with author.
Specializes in general fiction & nonfiction, including popular science.

TSO (The Stationery Office)
51 Nine Elms Lane, London SW8 5DR
Tel: (020) 7873 8787 *Fax:* (0870) 600 5533 (orders)
E-mail: customer.services@tso.co.uk
Web Site: www.tso.co.uk
Key Personnel
Chief Executive Officer: Tim Hailstone
Man Dir: Keith Burbage
Founded: 1996
Provider of information management services.
Branch Office(s)
The Parliamentary Press - London, Mandela Way, London SE1 5SS *Tel:* (020) 7394 4200
TSO Wales, G50, Phase Two, Government Bldgs, Ty-Glas, Llanishen, Cardiff CF14 5ST *Tel:* (02920) 765892
TSO Brussels, Martens International Consulting, 70, rue Philippe le Bon, 1000 Brussels, Belgium, Contact: Roger Lecocq *Tel:* (02) 235 0857; (02) 235 0850 *Fax:* (02) 235 0855
TSO Content Solutions, 84-90 East St, Epsom, Surrey KT17 1HF *Tel:* (01372) 845700
TSO Ireland, 16 Arthur St, Belfast BT1 4GD, Ireland *Tel:* (02890) 238451
TSO - Norwich, St Crispins, Duke St, Norwich NR3 1PD *Tel:* (01603) 622211
TSO Scotland, 71-73 Lothian Rd, Edinburgh EH3 9AZ *Tel:* (0870) 6065566
Bookshop(s): 16 Arthur St, Belfast BT1 4GD, Ireland *Tel:* (02890) 238451

Turnaround Publisher Services Ltd
Unit 3, Olympia Trading Estate, Coburg Rd, Wood Green, London N22 6TZ

UNITED KINGDOM

Tel: (020) 8829 3000 *Fax:* (020) 8881 5088
E-mail: enquiries@turnaround-uk.com; orders@turnaround-uk.com
Key Personnel
President & Man Dir: Bill Godber *Tel:* (020) 8829 3008 *E-mail:* bill@turnaround-uk.com
Marketing Manager: Claire Thompson *Tel:* (020) 8829 3009 *E-mail:* claire@turnaround-uk.com
Promotions Manager: Mollie Godfrey *Tel:* (020) 8829 3010 *E-mail:* mollie@turnaround-uk.com
Order Processing Manager: Julie Thelot *Tel:* (020) 8829 3002 *E-mail:* julie@turnaround-uk.com
Finance Dir: Sue Gregg *Tel:* (020) 8829 3006 *E-mail:* sue@turnaround-uk.com
Founded: 1984
Sales agent & distributor to the UK & continental European booktrade for a wide variety of quality US & UK publishers.
Specializes in black interest, gay interest, American imports, fiction, music, social & political issues, arts.

Jane Turnbull
13 Wendell Rd, London W12 9RS
Tel: (020) 8743 9580 *Fax:* (020) 8749 6079
E-mail: agents@cwcom.net
Key Personnel
Contact: Jane Turnbull *E-mail:* jane.turnbull@btintenet.com
Founded: 1986
No science fiction, sagas or romantic fiction. No unsol mss or reading fee. Approach with letter in the first instance. Translation rights handled by Gillon Aitken Associates Ltd. Commission: Home 10%; US & Foreign 20%.
Specializes in biography, history, current affairs, health & diet, fiction & nonfiction.

Kelvin van Hasselt Publishing Services
Willow House, The Street, Briningham, Norfolk NR24 2PY
Tel: (01263) 862724 *Fax:* (01263) 862803
E-mail: kvhbooks@aol.com
Key Personnel
Man Dir: Kevin van Hasselt
Order Processing: Gill Hinds
Representing Book Publishers in Africa, Asia & the Caribbean.
Specializes in academic & professional.

Van Lear Ltd
50 Kilmaine Rd, Fulham, London SW6 7JX
Mailing Address: PO Box 21816, Fulham, London SW6 5ZU
Tel: (020) 7385 1199 *Fax:* (020) 7385 6262
E-mail: evl@vanlear.co.uk

Key Personnel
Contact: Anne-Marie Doulton; Elizabeth Van Lear
International publishers representative literary scout.

Ed Victor Ltd
6 Bayley St, Bedford Square, London WC1B 3HB
Tel: (020) 7304 4100 *Fax:* (020) 7304 4111
Key Personnel
Man Dir: Ed Victor
Dir: Graham Greene; Maggie Phillips; Sophie Hicks; Carol Ryan; Leon Morgan
Contact: Lizzy Kremer
Founded: 1976
No scripts, academic, poetry. Commission: Home 15%; US 15%; Translation 20%.
Specializes in commercial fiction & nonfiction.

S Walker Literary Agency
96 Church Lane, Goldington, Bedford MK41 0AS
Tel: (01234) 216229
Key Personnel
Partner: Alan Oldfield; Cora-Louise Oldfield
Founded: 1939
No reading fee.
Specializes in full-length fiction.

Peter Ward Book Exports
Taylors Yard, Unit 3, 67 Alderbrook Rd, London SW12 8AD
Tel: (020) 8772 3300 *Fax:* (020) 8772 3309
E-mail: peter@pwbookex.dircon.co.uk
Key Personnel
Partner: Peter Ward; Richard Ward *E-mail:* richard@pwbookex.dircon.co.uk
Founded: 1974
Freelance representatives of UK & US publishers.
Specializes in Middle East, Cyprus, Turkey, Iran, Greece & Malta.

Watson, Little Ltd
Capo Di Monte, Windmill Hill, London NW3 6RJ
Tel: (020) 7431 0770 *Fax:* (020) 7431 7225
Key Personnel
Dir: Sheila Watson; Amanda Little; Sugra Zaman *E-mail:* sz@watsonlittle.com
Handles fiction & nonfiction. No scripts. Send preliminary letter with synopsis. Commission: Home 15%; US 24%; Translation 19%.
Specializes in business, history, popular science, psychology & self-help.

A P Watt Ltd
20 John St, London WC1N 2DR

Tel: (020) 7405 6774 *Fax:* (020) 7831 2154
E-mail: apw@apwatt.co.uk
Web Site: www.apwatt.co.uk
Key Personnel
Man Dir: Caradoc King
Foreign Rights Dir: Linda Shaughnessy
Joint Manager: Derek Johns
Founded: 1875
Literary, film & television agents. No unsol mss. Commission: Home 10%; US & Translation 20%.

Josef Weinberger Plays
12-14 Mortimer St, London W1T 3JJ
Tel: (020) 7580 2827 *Fax:* (020) 7436 9616
E-mail: general.info@jwmail.co.uk
Web Site: www.josef-weinberger.com
Key Personnel
Manager: Michael Callahan
Founded: 1885
No unsol mss; introductory letter essential. No reading fee.
Agent & publisher of scripts for the theatre.

Dinah Wiener Ltd
12 Cornwall Grove, Chiswick, London W4 2LB
Tel: (020) 8994 6011 *Fax:* (020) 8994 6044
E-mail: dinahwiener@enterprise.net
Key Personnel
Contact: Dinah Wiener
Founded: 1985
Handles fiction & general nonfiction. No scripts, children's or poetry. Mss submitted must include self-addressed envelope & be typed in double-spacing. Commission: Home 15%; US & Translation 20%.
Specializes in autobiography, cookery, popular science.

Zebra Agency
Broadlands House, One Broadlands, Shevington, Lancs WN6 8DH
Tel: (077193) 75575
E-mail: admin@zebraagency.co.uk
Web Site: www.zebraagency.co.uk
Key Personnel
Contact: Dee Jones; Cara Wooi
Nonfiction & general fiction including crime, suspense & drama, murder, mysteries, adventure, thrillers, horror & science fiction, plus scripts for TV/radio/film/theatre. No reading fee. Editorial advice given to authors. No unsolicited mss; send preliminary letter giving publishing history & brief cv, with synopsis (plus SASE). No phone calls or submissions by fax or e-mail. Commission: home 10%, US & translation 15%.

International Publishing Services

Listed within this section are U.S. and Canadian companies offering services to the book publishing industry internationally.

MapQuest
Subsidiary of Time Warner
3710 Hempland Rd, Mountville, PA 17554
Mailing Address: PO Box 601, Mountville, PA 17554-0601
Tel: 717-285-8500 *Fax:* 717-285-8456
E-mail: infomapquest@aol.com
Web Site: www.mapquest.com; www.oneworldmapping.com
Key Personnel
VP: Jim Hilliard *Tel:* 717-285-8412
 E-mail: jhilliardmqst@aol.com
Sales Dir: Bennett Moe *Tel:* 443-367-3046
 E-mail: bmoemapquest@aol.com
Mktg Mgr: Ed Kladky *Tel:* 717-285-8480
 E-mail: ekladkymapquest@aol..com
Founded: 1967
Serves the world's leading publishers with creative maps & mapping solutions in any media. Develop exciting map products & custom cartography for reference books, travel guides, directories & textbooks.
ISBN Prefix(es): 1-57262; 1-879856
Branch Office(s)
6470-D Dobbin Rd, Columbia, MD 21045
 Tel: 443-367-3042
Membership(s): Association of Directory Publishers; International Map Trade Association

Translation Agencies & Associations

Austria

Oesterreichischer Uebersetzer- und Dolmetscherverband Universitas
Gymnasiumstr 50, 1190 Vienna
Tel: (01) 368 60 60 *Fax:* (01) 368 60 08
E-mail: info@universitas.org
Web Site: www.universitas.org
Key Personnel
President: Florika Griessner
Austrian Association of Interpreters & Translators.

Uebersetzergemeinschaft Interessengemeinschaft von Uebersetzerinnen und Uebersetzern literarischer und wissenschaftlicher Werke
Seidengasse 13, 1070 Vienna
Tel: (01) 526 20 44-18 *Fax:* (01) 524 64 35
E-mail: ueg@literaturhaus.at
Web Site: www.translators.at
Key Personnel
Chairman: Werner Richter
Secretary General: Brigitte Rapp *E-mail:* br@literaturhaus.at
Austrian Association of Literary & Scientific Translators.
Publication(s): *Literature Infonet* (handbook); *The Translators' Companion*; *Uebersetzerverzeichnis* (directory)

Bulgaria

Union of Translators of Bulgaria, Magazin Panorama
ul Graf Ignatiev 16, Sofia
Tel: (02) 65 51 90; (02) 65 61 87
Key Personnel
Editor: Gancho Savov
Publication(s): *Panorama* (magazine)
Branch Office(s)
Magazine & Publishing House

China

CIPG Editorial & Translation Research Center
Wa Wen Bldg, 24 Baiwanzhuang St, Beijing 100037
Tel: (010) 68326681
E-mail: ftrchina@public3.bta.net.cn
Web Site: www.tac-online.org.cn
Key Personnel
Dir: Sun Chengtang
Publication(s): *Chinese Translators Journal*

Polyglot Translation
New World Times Center, 904 S Tower, 2191 Guangyuan Rd E, Guangzhou 510500
Tel: (020) 8764-1878 *Fax:* (020) 8764-2003
E-mail: info@polyglot.com.cn
Web Site: www.polyglot.com.cn
A professional translation organization that provides translation, interpretation & simultaneous meeting interpretation in all fields. In addition, we provide localization of websites into Chinese, writing articles in multi-languages, foreign languages recording, proofreading, interpreters/translators recommending, website designing & making & so on. We can provide a large variety of languages translating services such as English, Japanese, French, German, Russian, Korean, Italian, Spanish, Dutch, Swedish, Finnish, Portuguese, Czech, Slovak, Romanian, Polish, Hungarian, Bulgarian, Arabic, Turkish, Cambodian, Malay, Indonesian, Thai, Vietnamese, Nepali, Laotian, Burmese, Mongolian, Indic, Bengalese, Tamil etc. Altogether, we can provide more than 30-languages translation service fast & accurately. For details please visit our website.

Translator's Association of China (TAC), see CIPG Editorial & Translation Research Center

Cuba

Centro de Traducciones y Terminologia Especializada (CTTE) (Translation & Specialized Terminology Center)
Dept Comercial y de Marketing, Capitola de la Habana, Prado entre Dragones y San Jose, 10200 La Habana
Tel: (07) 862-6531; (07) 860-3411 *Fax:* (07) 862-6531
E-mail: comercial@idict.cu
Web Site: www.cubaciencia.cu/
Key Personnel
Dir: Luis Alberto Gonzalez Moreno
Publication(s): *Catalogo de Cubalingua*

Czech Republic

Jednota Tlumocniku a Prekladatelu (JTP - Union of Interpreters and Translators)
Senovazne Namesti 23, 110 00 Prague 1
Tel: (02) 24 142 517 *Fax:* (02) 24 142 312
E-mail: info@jtpunion.org
Web Site: www.jtpunion.org
Key Personnel
President: Dr Andrej Ra'dy
Dir: Peter Kautsky
Press Officer: Jiri Eichler
Glossaries, dictionaries, terminology, proceedings of specialised conferences.
Publication(s): *ToP* (quarterly, bulletin)

Translators Guild (Obec Prekladatelu)
Pod nuselskymi schody 3, 120 00 Prague 2
Tel: 222 564 082
E-mail: info@obecprekladatelu.cz
Web Site: www.obecprekladatelu.cz
Key Personnel
President: Hana Linhartova

Egypt (Arab Republic of Egypt)

Al Ahram Establishment
6 Al-Galaa' St, Cairo
Tel: (02) 5786200; (02) 5786300; (02) 5786400; (02) 5786500 *Fax:* (02) 5786126; (02) 5786833
E-mail: ahram@ahram.org.eg
Web Site: www.extra.ahram.org.eg
Telex: 20185-92544

The Egyptian Society for the Dissemination of Universal Culture and Knowledge (ESDUCK)
1081 Corniche el Nil St, Garden City, Cairo
Mailing Address: PO Box 21, Garden City, Cairo
Tel: (02) 3542 0295; (02) 35425079
Telex: 92548

ESDUCK, see The Egyptian Society for the Dissemination of Universal Culture and Knowledge (ESDUCK)

France

Societe Francaise des Traducteurs
Affiliate of Federation Internationale der Traducteurs (FIT)
22 rue des Martyrs, 75009 Paris
Tel: (01) 48 78 43 32 *Fax:* (01) 44 53 01 14
E-mail: sft@tiscali.fr
Web Site: www.sft.fr
Key Personnel
President: Maria Lebret-Sanchez
Vice President: Marie-Christine Garcin
Secretary General: Rupert Swyer
Editor-in-Chief: Muriel Valenta *Tel:* (05) 45 36 02 81 *E-mail:* muriel.valenta@wanadoo.fr
Founded: 1947
French Union of Translators.
Publication(s): *Traduire* (quarterly)

Germany

BDU, see Bundesverband der Dolmetscher und Ubersetzer eV (BDU)

Bundesverband der Dolmetscher und Ubersetzer eV (BDU) (German Association of Interpreters & Translators)
Kurfuerstendamm 170, 10707 Berlin
Tel: (030) 88712830 *Fax:* (030) 88712840
E-mail: bgs@bdue.de
Web Site: www.bdue.de
Key Personnel
President: Barbara Boeer Alves
Publication(s): *Mitteilungsblatt fuer Dolmetscher und Uebersetzer - MDU*

GERMANY

VDU, see Verband deutschsprachiger Uebersetzer literarischer und wissenschaftlicher Werke eV (VDUe)

Verband deutschsprachiger Uebersetzer literarischer und wissenschaftlicher Werke eV (VDUe) (Association of German-speaking Translators of Literary & Scientific Works)
c/o Sabine Herholz, Verband Deutscher Schriftseller, FB8, Potsdamer Platz 10, 10785 Berlin
Tel: (030) 6956-2331 *Fax:* (030) 6956-3655
Web Site: www.literaturuebersetzer.de
Key Personnel
Secretary: Friedrich Griese

Ghana

Bureau of Ghana Languages
PO Box 1851, Accra
Tel: (021) 665461
Also Publisher.
Branch Office(s)
PO Box 177, Tamale, Northern Region

Greece

EEML, see Elliniki Etaireia Metafraston Logotechnias

Elliniki Etaireia Metafraston Logotechnias
 (Hellenic Society of Translators of Literature)
7 E Tsakona St, Paleo Psychiko, 15452 Athens
Tel: (01) 6717466 *Fax:* (01) 6717466
Key Personnel
President: Dr Vassilis Vitsaxis
General Secretary: Costas Assimekopoulos
Founded: 1983
Also publish Greek Letters Yearbook containing translations in English, French, German, Italian & Spanish of contemporary Greek literature.
Membership(s): Federation of International Translators (FIT); EWG.
Publication(s): *Greek Letters Yearly* (in English, French, Spanish, Italian & German)

Hong Kong

KAMS Information & Publishing Ltd
PO Box 72050, Kowloon Central Post Office, Kowloon
Tel: 23889172 *Fax:* 27716403
E-mail: kamsinfo@hkstar.com
Web Site: kamsinfo.com
Key Personnel
Project Dir: Kam-sun Yiu
Founded: 1989
Specialize in editing, translation & publishing services in more than 20 languages.

KCL Language Consultancy Ltd
Shop 1, G/F, 46 Lyndhurst Terrace, Central Hong Kong
Tel: (02) 8811368 *Fax:* (02) 8080389
E-mail: kcl@iohk.com
Web Site: www.iohk.com/userpages/kcl
Key Personnel
Dir: Karen Chan

Hungary

Magyar Iroszovetseg Konyvtara
Bajza u 18, 1062 Budapest
Tel: (01) 322-8840; (01) 322-0631 *Fax:* (01) 321-3419
Key Personnel
President: Marton Kalasz
Library of Hungarian Writers' Union.

India

National Institute of Science Communication & Information Resources (NISCAIR)
14 Satsang Vihar Marg, New Delhi 110 067
Tel: (011) 2650141 *Fax:* (011) 26862228
E-mail: webmaster@niscair.res.in
Web Site: www.niscom.res.in
Telex: 031-73099
Key Personnel
Dir: Mr V K Gupta *E-mail:* vkgupta@niscair.res.in
Translating European & Asian languages into English; specializes in library automation, computer networking & database design; national member of FID.
Publication(s): *Annals of Library Science & Documentation; Database on Indian Patents (INPAT); Databases - Current Contents of Indian Journals; Directory of Indian Scientific Periodicals; Directory of Scientific Research Institutions in India; Indian Science Abstracts; Medical & Aromatic Plants Abstracts (MAPA); Metallurgy Index; National Union Catalogue of Scientific Serials in India (NUCSSI); Polymer Science Database*
Branch Office(s)
Bangalore
Chennai
Kolkata

Ireland

Cumann Aistritheoiri nahEireann, see Irish Translators' & Interpreters' Association

Ireland Literature Exchange (Idirmhalartan Litriocht Eireann)
Irish Writers Centre, 19 Parnell Sq, Dublin 1
Tel: (01) 8727900 *Fax:* (01) 8727875
E-mail: info@irelandliterature.com
Web Site: www.irelandliterature.com
Key Personnel
Dir: Sinead MacAodha *E-mail:* sinead@irelandliterature.com
Administrator: Maire N Dhonnchadha *E-mail:* maire@irelandliterature.com
Founded: 1994
Not-for-profit organization founded to fund translations of literature from Ireland into foreign languages & foreign literature into English & Irish.

Irish Translators' & Interpreters' Association
The Irish Writers' Centre, 19 Parnell Sq, Dublin 1
Tel: (01) 8721302 *Fax:* (01) 8726282
E-mail: translation@eircom.net
Web Site: www.translatorsassociation.ie
Key Personnel
FIT Literary Translation Committee Representative: Miriam Lee *Tel:* (01) 2859137

TRANSLATION AGENCIES

Membership(s): International Federation of Translators (FIT); European Board of Literary Translators Associations (CEATL).
Publication(s): *Transverse; Transverse II*

Israel

Freund Publishing House Ltd
PO Box 35010, 61350 Tel Aviv
Tel: (03) 562-8540 *Fax:* (03) 562-8538
E-mail: h_freund@netvision.net.il
Web Site: www.freundpublishing.com
Key Personnel
Man Dir & Publisher: Edmund Freund
Founded: 1968

The Institute for the Translation of Hebrew Literature
23 Baruch Hirsch St, Bnei Brak
Mailing Address: PO Box 1005 1, 52001 Ramat Gan
Tel: (03) 579 6830 *Fax:* (03) 579 6832
E-mail: hamachon@inter.net.il
Web Site: www.ithl.org.il
Key Personnel
Chairman: Prof Ory Bernstein
Man Dir: Nilli Cohen
Office Manager: Debbie Dagan
Founded: 1962
Main activities include promotion of modern Hebrew literature & children's literature in translation & serves as literary agent for a large number of Israeli writers & assists in the preparation of anthologies of Hebrew literature. Specializes in Hebrew Literature in Translation.

Israel Translators' Association
PO Box 13184, 61131 Tel Aviv
Tel: (09) 741 5279 *Fax:* (09) 760 2369
Web Site: www.ita.org.il
Key Personnel
Chairperson: Ms Sarah Yarkoni *E-mail:* sarahy@netvision.net.il
Association of some 500 translators, mostly freelance. Detailed database of members, with languages & specialties.
Publication(s): *Targima*

Italy

AITI (Associazione Italiana Traduttori e Interpreti) (Association of Italian Translators & Interpreters)
Via dei Prati Fiscali 158, 00141 Rome
Tel: (081) 7645362 *Fax:* (081) 7645362
E-mail: segreteria@aiti.org
Web Site: www.aiti.org
Key Personnel
President: Vittoria Lo Faro
Vice President: Rose-Marie Olivier
Secretary: Grazia Di Bartolomeo
Founded: 1950
Membership(s): Federation Internationale des Traducteurs (FIT).
Publication(s): *Il traduttore nuovo* (biannually, periodical)

Associazione Italiana Traduttori e Interpreti, see AITI (Associazione Italiana Traduttori e Interpreti)

Lebanon

Ecole de Traducteurs et d'Interpretes de Beyrouth-Universite Saint-Joseph (ETIB)
Campus des Sciences Humaines, Rue de Damas, BP 17-5208 - Mar Mikhael, Beirut 1104 2020
Tel: (01) 611 456 (ext 5512) *Fax:* (01) 611 360
E-mail: etib@usj.edu.lb
Web Site: www.usj.edu.lb
Key Personnel
Dir: Henri Awaiss

Norway

The Norwegian Association of Literary Translators
Postboks 579 Sentrum, 0150 Oslo
Tel: 22478090 *Fax:* 22420356
E-mail: post@translators.no
Web Site: skrift.no/no/english/index.asp; skrift.no/no/index.asp
Key Personnel
Contact: Hilde Sveinsson *E-mail:* hilde@translators.no
Founded: 1948

Poland

Stowarzyszenie Tlumaczy Polskich (Association of Polish Translators & Interpreters)
ul Jaworzynska 3 m 22, 00-634 Warsaw
Tel: (022) 621 56 78; (022) 825 09 04 *Fax:* (022) 621 56 78
E-mail: stp-waw@interkom.pl
Web Site: www.stp.org.pl
Key Personnel
President: Ryszard Dulinicz
Vice President: Danuta Kierzkowska; Wojciech Dawiec
Branch Office(s)
Oddzial Gdanski, ul Gdynskich Kosynierow 11, 80-866 Gdansk *Tel:* (058) 305-30-65 *Fax:* (058) 305-30-65 *E-mail:* stpgdansk@gd.home.pl
Oddzial Katowicki, ul Mlynska 21/23, 40-098 Katowice *Tel:* (032) 253-80-87 *Fax:* (032) 253-80-87 *Toll Free Fax:* stp_ok@poczta.onet.pl
Oddzial Krakowski, ul Dunin-Wasowicza 26/16, 31-112 Krakow *Tel:* (012) 429-26-56 *Fax:* (012) 429-26-56
Oddzial Lodzki, ul Piotrkowska 67, 90-422 Lodz *Tel:* (042) 633-65-80 *Fax:* (042) 633-65-80 *E-mail:* granicki@dawid.com.pl
Oddzial Poznanski, ul Przybyszewskiego 62/1, 60-357 Poznan *Tel:* (061) 867-96-00 *Fax:* (061) 867-96-00 *E-mail:* tomzeb@amu.edu.pl
Oddzial Szczecinski, ul Jagiellonska 8/4, 70-436 Szczecin *Tel:* (091) 43-43-556 *Fax:* (091) 43-43-556 *E-mail:* zespol@biurotlumaczen.pl
Oddzial Warszawski *Tel:* (022) 621-73-76; (022) 629-50-47 *Fax:* (022) 621-73-76 *E-mail:* stpata@medianet.com.pl

STP, see Stowarzyszenie Tlumaczy Polskich

Spain

Tek Translation International SA
OneWorld Localization Center, Centro Empresarial El Plantio Ochandiano, 10, 28023 Madrid
Tel: (091) 4141111 *Fax:* (091) 4144444
E-mail: sales@tektrans.com
Web Site: www.tektrans.com
Key Personnel
Group Head: Alba Guix
Account Manager: Veit Gunther
Founded: 1961
Technical specialists in over 100 languages, including Chinese, Arabic, Japanese, Russian.

Sweden

Exportradet Spraktjanst AB
Storgatan 19, 114 85 Stockholm
Mailing Address: Box 5513, 114 85 Stockholm
Tel: (08) 783 85 00 *Fax:* (08) 662 90 93
E-mail: infocenter@swedishtrade.se
Web Site: www.swedishtrade.se
Telex: 15679
Key Personnel
President: Gunnar Lindberg
Translating & Interpreting Service of the Swedish Trade Council (See Sveriges Exportrad under Publishers).

Foereningen Auktoriserade Translatorer (The Federation of Authorized Translator in Sweden)
Norra Parkvagen 15, 756 45 Uppsala
E-mail: info@eurofat.se
Web Site: www.eurofat.se
Key Personnel
Chairman: Kerstin E Wallin *Tel:* (018) 301658
Secretary: Nadezjda Chekhov *Tel:* (08) 6426124
Founded: 1932
Publication(s): *FATaburen* (in Swedish, 4 issues annually)

Switzerland

Association Suisse des Traducteurs Terminologues et Interpretes (ASTTI) (Swiss Association of Translators & Interpreters)
Postgasse 17, 3011 Berne
Tel: (031) 313 88 10 *Fax:* (031) 313 88 99
E-mail: astti@astti.ch
Web Site: www.astti.ch
Key Personnel
President: Doris Schmidt
Vice President: Henry Braun; David Fuhruann
Contact: Marianne Hofmann *E-mail:* m.i.hofmann@bluewin.ch
Branch Office(s)
Susenbergstr 111, 8044 Zurich, Ekaterina Ovsiannikova-Keymer *E-mail:* o-key@swissonline.ch

Taiwan, Province of China

National Institute for Compilation & Translation
179 He-ping E Rd, Sec 1, Da-an District, Taipei
Tel: (02) 33225558 *Fax:* (02) 33225559
Key Personnel
Dir: Shun-Te Lan
Publication(s): *Counter Attack*

United Republic of Tanzania

Baraza la Kiswahili la Taifa
PO Box 4766, Dar Es Salaam
Tel: (051) 23452; (051) 24139
Key Personnel
Chief Editor: Mastidia Kailembo Mbeo
Translations in English, Kiswahili, Arabic, French, Portuguese & Spanish.

United Kingdom

Ad-Ex Translations Ltd, see RWS Translations Ltd

Deborah Adlam
Member of Edinburgh University & Oxford University
41 W Savile Terrace, Edinburgh EH9 3DP
Tel: (0131) 6676048
Key Personnel
Contact: Deborah Adlam *E-mail:* deborahadlam@hotmail.com
Founded: 1982
Translation into English carried out from Latin, Russian, French & Classical Greek. Academic, literary, medical, legal & theological texts. Research work also carried out.
Specializes in 12th-19th century Latin legal documents, Classical Greek & Latin texts.

AE Technical Translation Services
Ty Coch, Betws Garmon, Caernarfon, Gwynedd LL54 7AQ
Tel: (01286) 650667; (01286) 650555 *Fax:* (01286) 650500
Key Personnel
Contact: Debra Lockett
Services include interpreting, laser printing, typesetting, color printing, & translations in over 100 language combinations, specializing in rare languages.

Alpnet UK, see SDL Agency

ARADCO VSI Ltd
132 Cleveland St, London W1T 6AB
Tel: (020) 7692 7700 *Fax:* (020) 7692 7711

Web Site: www.aradco.com
Key Personnel
Contact: R Dawood

Asgard Publishing Services
One Gledhow Park Grove, Leeds LS7 4JW
Tel: (0113) 262 8373 *Fax:* (0113) 262 8373
Web Site: www.asgardpublishing.co.uk
Key Personnel
Partner: Philip Gardner *E-mail:* philip.gardner@asgardpublishing.co.uk; Michael Scott Rohan *Tel:* (01223) 842185 *Fax:* (01223) 842185 *E-mail:* mike.scott.rohan@asgardpublishing.co.uk; Allan Scott *Tel:* (01449) 741747 *Fax:* (01449) 740118 *E-mail:* allan.scott@asgardpublishing.co.uk; Andrew Shackleton *Tel:* (0113) 2741037 *Fax:* (0113) 2741037 *E-mail:* andrew.shackleton@asgardpublishing.co.uk
Services include editorial, translation, audio-visual & multimedia.

Associated Translation & Typesetting
Alexander House, 64 Robin Hood Lane, Hall Green, Birmingham B28 0JT
Tel: (0121) 603 6344 *Fax:* (0121) 603 6399
E-mail: ATTEuro@aol.com (European translation); ATTAsia@aol.com (Eastern/Asian translation); ATTgraphic@jaure.demon.com (web design/graphics)
Web Site: www.jaure.demon.co.uk
Key Personnel
Dir: Mr S Ahmed
Specializes in translation & typesetting into most European languages (& vice versa), plus Arabic, Bengali, Chinese (Cantonese, Hakka & Mandarin) Farsi (Persian), Greek, Hindi, Punjabi, Polish, Russian, Somali, Turkish, Urdu, Vietnamese & Welsh. Also typesetting of European, Russian, Vietnamese, Chinese & other Indian languages. Provide translation services of multilingual technical translation, documentation, computer manuals, reports, promotional literature, brochures, packaging & books.

The Big Word
Formerly Link Up Mitaka Ltd
59 Charlotte St, London W1T 4PE
Tel: (0870) 7488000 *Fax:* (0870) 7488001
E-mail: production@thebigword.com
Web Site: www.thebigword.com
Key Personnel
Chief Executive Officer: Laurence J Gould *E-mail:* larry.gould@thebigword.com
Chief Financial Officer: Chris Ball *E-mail:* chris.ball@thebigword.com
Chief Operations Officer: Diane Miller *E-mail:* diane.miller@thebigword.com
Chief Technical Officer: Ian Harris *E-mail:* ian.harris@thebigword.com
Non-Executive Dir: John Westwood *E-mail:* john.westwood@thebigword.com
Group Sales Manager: Adam Barnett *E-mail:* adam.barnett@thebigword.com
Scandinavian Manager: Per Severinsen *E-mail:* per.severinsen@thebigword.com
Belgium Manager: Rachel Wild *E-mail:* rachel.wild@thebigword.com
Specialists in Far Eastern Languages.
Branch Office(s)
The Big Word Scandinavia, Larsbjrnsstrde 3, 1454 Copenhagen K, Denmark *Tel:* 33 37 71 71 *Fax:* 33 32 43 70
Global Service Center, Belmont House, 20 Wood Lane, Headingley, Leeds LS6 2AE
Mitaka-The Big Word, 30F Shinjuku Park Tower, 3-7-1 Nishi Shinjuku, Shinjuku Ku, Tokyo 163-1030, Japan *Tel:* (03) 5326 3144 *Fax:* (03) 5326-3001

Park Atrium, 11, Rue des Colonies, 1000 Brussels, Belgium *Tel:* (02) 517 7113 *Fax:* (02) 517 65
U.S. Office(s): The Big Word US, 48 Wall St, Suite 1100, New York, NY 10005-2902, United States *Tel:* 212-918-4557 *Fax:* 212-918-4561

Castle Translations
11 Castle Hill, Lancaster LA1 1YS
Tel: (01524) 841169 *Fax:* (01524) 381721
E-mail: info@castletranslations.co.uk
Web Site: ukpetsearch.freeuk.com/castletrans
Key Personnel
Owner: Lynda Burke *E-mail:* lyndaburke@castletrans.free-online.co.uk
Founded: 1986
Translating & interpreting of all languages; language training.

CBA Translations
Straightway Head, Whimple Nr, Exeter EX5 2QT
Tel: (01404) 822284 *Fax:* (01404) 823136
E-mail: info@cbatranslations.co.uk
Web Site: www.cbatranslations.co.uk
Key Personnel
Proprietor: Gerd Ziemer

Chinese Marketing & Communications
Wuhan House, 5th floor, 16 Nicholas St, Manchester M1 4EJ
Tel: (0161) 237 3821 *Fax:* (0161) 236 7558
E-mail: support@chinese-marketing.com
Web Site: www.chinese-marketing.com
Key Personnel
Editor: Jamie Kenny; Shen Yan
Project Manager: David Starway
Marketing materials in Chinese language, market research & advertising agency.
Publication(s): Chinese Business Impact (English, monthly); *Siyu Chinese Times* (Chinese, monthly)
Branch Office(s)
First Floor West, 90-98 Shaftesbury Ave, London W1V 7DM

Conference Interpreters Group
10 Barley Mow Passage, Chiswick, London W4 4PH
Tel: (0208) 9950801 *Fax:* (0208) 7421066
E-mail: ciglondon@aol.com
Key Personnel
Executive Secretary: Andrew Brock *E-mail:* abrock3650@aol.com

Dutch Connection
196 Prestbury Rd, Macclesfield SK10 3BS
Tel: (01625) 610613 *Fax:* (01625) 610613
E-mail: dutchconnection@aol.com
Key Personnel
Contact: M Kuik
Founded: 1982

East Word
170a Kennington Park Rd, London SE11 4BT
Tel: (020) 7582 9349 *Fax:* (020) 7793 0474
E-mail: info@eastword.uk.com
Key Personnel
Dir: Gladys Ko
Oriental language translation including Chinese, Japanese, Korean, Thai & Vietnamese.

Esperanto Translating Service
Kebbell House, Delta Gain, Watford WD19 5BE
Mailing Address: 137 Penrose Ave, Watford WD1 5AA
Tel: (020) 84282829 *Fax:* (020) 84282829
E-mail: espero@moose.co.uk
Key Personnel
Owner & Manager: Peter W Miles
Also provides guide lecturers in approximately 35 languages.

Euro Translations
6 Field End, Coulsdon, Surrey CR5 2AY
Tel: (0208) 6686133 *Fax:* (0208) 6686133
E-mail: info@euro-translations.net
Web Site: www.euro-translations.net
Key Personnel
Owner: Mrs P Kain
Founded: 1983

First Edition Translations Ltd
6 Wellington Ct, Wellington St, Cambridge CB1 1HZ
Tel: (01223) 356733 *Fax:* (01223) 321488
E-mail: info@firstedit.co.uk
Web Site: www.firstedit.co.uk
Key Personnel
Dir: Sheila Waller *E-mail:* sheila@firstedit.co.uk
Founded: 1981
Services include copy-editing, proof-reading, indexing, interpreting, voice-overs, typesetting. Specializes in translations of all material for publication.

Michael Fulton Partners
The Chase, Behoes Lane, Woodcote, Reading, Berks RG8 0PP
Tel: (01491) 680042 *Fax:* (01491) 680085
Web Site: www.foreignword.biz/cv/410.htm
Key Personnel
Senior Partner: Dr Michael Fulton *E-mail:* mike@fultonm.fsnet.co.uk
Founded: 1968
Translations from Spanish & Portuguese (technical, scientific, commercial & patents subject matter); Spanish interpreting.

GLS Language Services
250 Crow Rd, Glasgow G11 7LA
Tel: (0141) 357 6611 *Fax:* (0141) 357 6605
E-mail: info@glslanguages.demon.co.uk
Web Site: www.glslanguageservices.co.uk
Key Personnel
Partner: Dagmar Fortsch
Founded: 1983

Greek Institute
34 Bush Hill Rd, London N21 2DS
Tel: (020) 8360 7968 *Fax:* (020) 8360 7968
Key Personnel
Dir: Dr Kypros Tofallis
Publication(s): Greek Institute Review (quarterly, journal)

Hook & Hatton Ltd
34 Central Ave, Northampton NN2 8DZ
Tel: (01604) 847278 *Fax:* (01604) 821486
E-mail: hook_hatton@compuserve.com
Key Personnel
Chief Executive: Terence Lewis
Specializes in Specialize in translation of Scientific & Technical Texts.

Indo Lingua Services Ltd
125 Poplar High St, London E14 0AE
Tel: (020) 7515 3987
E-mail: indolingua@compuserve.com
Key Personnel
Man Dir: Prithvi Raj
Consultant: Pyare Shivpuri
Branch Office(s)
17B Ramesh Nagar, New Delhi 110 015 *Tel:* (011) 5461055 *Fax:* (011) 5461055

Institute of Linguists
Saxon House, 48 Southwark St, London SE1 1UN
Tel: (020) 7940 3100 *Fax:* (020) 7940 3101
E-mail: info@iol.org.uk
Web Site: www.iol.org.uk
Key Personnel
Chief Executive & Dir: Henry Pavlovich

Membership organization for professional translators, interpreters, language educationalists & those using languages in industry & commerce.
Publication(s): *Basic Handbook for the Training of Public Service Interpreters*; *Bilingual in Britain*; *Careers Using Languages*; *Glossary of Educational Terms*; *Glossary of Social Services Terms*; *Languages & Your Career*; *The Linguist* (bimonthly, journal); *Non-English Speakers & the English Legal System*; *Talk It Through*

Institute of Translation & Interpreting
Fortuna House, South Fifth Street, Milton Keynes MK9 2EU
Tel: (01908) 325250 *Fax:* (01908) 325259
E-mail: info@iti.org.uk
Web Site: www.iti.org.uk
Key Personnel
General Secretary: Alan Wheatley *Tel:* (01908) 325256 *E-mail:* alan@iti.org.uk

Intercultural Networking Ltd (ICN)
133 John Trundle Court, London EC2Y 8DJ
Tel: (0171) 628 5876 *Fax:* (0171) 628 9147
E-mail: icn@dircon.co.uk
Web Site: www.users.dircon.co.uk/~icn/
Key Personnel
Man Dir: Atsuko Takenaka
Dir: Chieko Takanaka
Specializes in nonfiction book translation Japanese-English through to camera-ready copy.

International Language & Translation School
216 Great Portland St, London W1N 5HG
Tel: (020) 8882 3362 *Fax:* (020) 8882 3362
Key Personnel
Principal: Mr Li Ke-Mo
Tuition in 80 languages by correspondence, oral, telephone, fax & cassette courses. Translation, interpreting in 80 Oriental, European & African languages.

International Translations Ltd
Lloyds House, 1st floor, 18-22 Lloyd St, Manchester M2 5WA
Tel: (0161) 834 7431 *Fax:* (0161) 832 4717
E-mail: admin@ititranslations.co.uk; inttrans@compuserve.com
Key Personnel
Dir: Christine Wood
Founded: 1919
Translations in over 30 languages; literary, commercial, technical & legal topics.
Specializes in Translation, Interpreting, Proofreading, Typewetting, Voice Overs.

Key Language Services
32 Rockingham Dr, Linford Wood, Milton Keynes MK14 6LY
Tel: (01908) 232101 *Fax:* (01908) 232815
E-mail: sales@keylanguageservices.co.uk
Web Site: www.keylanguageservices.co.uk
Key Personnel
Partner: Sarah Clutton; Gail Farrell
Founded: 1988
Branch Office(s)
Business Development Centre, Suite C, Stafford Park 4, Telford TF3 3BA *Tel:* (01952) 293 450 *Fax:* (01952) 290 552

Language Consultancy Services
138 Melrose Ave, London NW2 4JX
Tel: (020) 8450 5344 *Fax:* (020) 8452 9005
E-mail: lucifer@ladet.demon.co.uk
Key Personnel
Contact: Lucia Alvarez de Toledo

Legal & Technical Translation Services
13 Earl St, Maidstone, Kent ME14 1PL
Tel: (01622) 751537; (01622) 751189 *Fax:* (01622) 754431
E-mail: translation@ltts.co.uk
Web Site: www.ltts.co.uk
Key Personnel
Dir: J M Sallares

Lexus Ltd
60 Brook St, Glasgow G402AB
Tel: (0141) 2215266 *Fax:* (0141) 2263139
Web Site: www.lexusforlanguages.co.uk
Telex: 9312134404
Key Personnel
Man Dir: Peter Terrell *E-mail:* peterterrell@lexusforlanguages.co.uk
Founded: 1980
Also publisher & packager.
Specializes in Bilingual Dictionaries.

Link Up Mitaka Ltd, see The Big Word

Peak Translations
Shepherd's Bank, Kettleshulme SK23 7QU
Tel: (01663) 732074 *Fax:* (01663) 735499
E-mail: info@peak-translations.co.uk
Web Site: www.peak-translations.co.uk
Key Personnel
Contact: Ian Gordon *E-mail:* ian@peak-translations.co.uk
Founded: 1978
Also supply software translation tools for professional translators.

Marilyn Potts International Language Consultants
Saint Thomas St, Newcastle-upon-Tyne NE1 4LE
Tel: (0191) 222 1775 *Fax:* (0191) 261 6426
E-mail: info@marilyn-potts.co.uk
Web Site: www.marilyn-potts.co.uk
Key Personnel
Contact: Marilyn Potts
Founded: 1987
Services include translations & interpreting.
Membership(s): Institute of Translation & Interpreting.

Rosie O'Hara German Translations
PO Box 6064, Nairn IV12 4YH
Tel: (01667) 456 222 *Fax:* (01667) 456 222
Web Site: www.rosieohara.co.uk/index1.htm
Key Personnel
Contact: Rosie O'Hara
Provide translation, interpreting & tuition into & out of German only.

RWS Translations Ltd
Formerly Ad-Ex Translations Ltd
Marsham Way, Gerrards Cross, Bucks SL9 8BQ
Tel: (01753) 480200 *Fax:* (01753) 480280
E-mail: rwstrans@rws.com
Web Site: www.rws.com
Key Personnel
Man Dir: Mr Wojtek Brodnicki
Chief Editor: Ian Watson
Head Foreign Language Operations: George M Dudzinski
Production Manager: Patrick Sutton
Business Development Executive: Nicola Richards
Office Manager: Diane Dye
Service includes medical & pharmaceutical translations in English, German, French, Spanish & Italian.
Branch Office(s)
RWS Information Ltd, Tavistock House, Tavistock Sq, London WC1H 9LG *Tel:* (020) 7554 5400 *Fax:* (020) 7554 5454 *E-mail:* rwsinfo@rws.com

Satrap Publishing & Translation
271 King St, London W6 9LZ
Tel: (020) 8748 9397 *Fax:* (020) 8748 9394
E-mail: satrap@btconnect.com
Web Site: www.satrap.co.uk
Key Personnel
Man Dir: Alex Vahdat
Founded: 1989
A single source for translation, typesetting, publishing, marketing & advertising literature in major languages of the world.
Specializes in Middle & Far Eastern, East & West European languages.

SDL Agency
Formerly Alpnet UK
Aspect Court, Pond Hill, Sheffield, South Yorks S1 2BG
Tel: (0114) 253 5353 *Toll Free Tel:* 800 917 0044 *Fax:* (0114) 253 5200
Web Site: www.sdl.com
Key Personnel
Dir: Ray King
Services include foreign language publishing, translating & interpreting.
U.S. Office(s): 5700 Granite Parkway, Suite 410, Plano, TX 75024, United States *Tel:* 214-387-9124

SEL, see Services for Export & Language (SEL)

SELTA, see Swedish-English Literary Translators' Association (SELTA)

Services for Export & Language (SEL)
Maxwell Bldg, University of Salford, Manchester M5 4WT
Tel: (0161) 7457480 *Fax:* (0161) 2955110
E-mail: sales@sel-uk.com
Web Site: www.sel-uk.com
Key Personnel
Translations Manager: Patrick Murphy *E-mail:* p.m.murphy@salford.ac.uk
Founded: 1986
Service includes translation, foreign language training & interpreting.

Swedish-English Literary Translators' Association (SELTA)
14 Grennell Close, Sutton, Surrey SM1 3LU
Tel: (020) 8641 8176 *Fax:* (020) 8641 8176
Web Site: www.swedishbookreview.com
Key Personnel
Honorary Secretary: Tom Geddes
Founded: 1982
SELTA aims to promote the publication of Swedish literature in English & to represent the interests of those involved in its translation.
Publication(s): *Swedish Book Review* (twice a year)

TransAction Translators Ltd
Redlands, 3/5 Tapton House Rd, Sheffield S10 5BY
Tel: (0114) 2661103 *Fax:* (0114) 2631959
E-mail: transaction@transaction.co.uk
Web Site: www.transaction.co.uk
Key Personnel
Contact: Maryline Tergella
Founded: 1983

Translators Association
84 Drayton Gardens, London SW10 9SB
Tel: (020) 7373 6642 *Fax:* (020) 7373 5768
E-mail: info@societyofauthors.org
Web Site: www.societyofauthors.org/translators
Key Personnel
Awards Secretary: Dorothy Sym *E-mail:* dsym@societyofauthors.org
The Translators Association is a specialist group within The Society of Authors.
Publication(s): *In Other Words*

UNITED KINGDOM

UPS Translations
111 Baker St, London W1U 6RR
Tel: (020) 7837 8300 *Fax:* (020) 7486 3272
E-mail: production@upstranslations.com
Web Site: www.upstranslations.com
Key Personnel
Chairman & Man Dir: Bernard Silver
  E-mail: bernard@upstranslations.com
Head of Translation: Sarah Parkhurst
Founded: 1947
Translation company
Membership(s): ATC; ITI; ISO: 9001.
Specializes in Translation for publishing, film, video & the media.
Parent Company: United Publicity Services PLC

Sally Walker Language Services
43 St Nicholas St, Bristol BS1 1TP
Tel: (0117) 929 1594 *Fax:* (0117) 929 6033
E-mail: translations@sallywalker.co.uk; languages@sallywalker.co.uk
Web Site: www.sallywalker.co.uk
Key Personnel
Man Dir: Sally Walker
Dir: Joseph Walker Cousins
Sales & Marketing Dir: David J Poole
Translations Manager: Loys Heyworth; Gwen Parrott
Translations & Marketing Manager: Elizabeth Niklewska
Founded: 1969
Translation & Interpreting Service.
Specializes in 70 languages, all subjects.
Publication(s): *Sallylang* (journal)
Branch Office(s)
Perch Bldgs, 9 Mount Stuart Sq, Cardiff CF10 5EE *Tel:* (029) 204 807 47 *Fax:* (029) 204 887 36

Wessex Translations
Unit A1, The Premier Centre, Abbey Park Industrial Estate, Romsey, Hampshire SO51 9AQ
Tel: (0870) 1669 300 *Toll Free Tel:* 800 975 5900 *Fax:* (0870) 1669 299
E-mail: sales@wt-lm.com; info@wt-lm.com
Web Site: www.wt-languagemanagement.com
Key Personnel
Dir: Jonathan Nater *E-mail:* jonathan@wt-lm.com
Contact: Robin Weber
Translations & interpreting software localisation, language training, transcription, typesetting, telemarketing, editing & proofreading, voice-overs, copywriting, web page translation.
Membership(s): Association of Translation Companies & Institute of Translations & Interpreters.

WT Language Management, see Wessex Translations

Manufacturing

Complete Book Manufacturing

This section includes companies throughout the world that offer complete book manufacturing services. Those U.S. and Canadian companies with 10% or more of their business done outside North America are also included.

Australia

ACI International Ltd
390 St Kilda Rd, 15th floor, Melbourne 3004
Tel: (03) 6058555
Key Personnel
Chairman: Brian W Scott
Man Dir, Security Printing & Computer Services Group: I D Reid

Austria

ADEVA (Akademische Druck-u Verlagsanstalt)
Auersperggasse 12, 8010 Graz
Tel: (0316) 3644 *Fax:* (0316) 364424
E-mail: info@adeva.com
Web Site: www.adeva.com *Cable:* ADEVA-GRAZ
Key Personnel
Dir: Dr Ursula Struzl
Founded: 1949
Print Runs: 300 min - 10,000 max
Business from Other Countries: 80%
Branch Office(s)
Purgleitnergasse 10, Ecke Marburgerstr, 8042 Graz

Akademische Druck- u Verlagsanstalt, see ADEVA (Akademische Druck-u Verlagsanstalt)

Dr Paul Struzl GmbH, see ADEVA (Akademische Druck-u Verlagsanstalt)

Belgium

Drukkerij Lannoo NV (Lannoo Printers)
Kasteelstr 97, 8700 Tielt
Tel: (051) 42 42 11 *Fax:* (051) 40 70 70
E-mail: lannoo@lannooprint.be
Web Site: www.lannooprint.be
Key Personnel
General Manager & Marketing Dir: Stefaan Lannoo *E-mail:* stefaan.lannoo@lannooprint.be
Founded: 1909
Turnaround: 10 Workdays
Print Runs: 100 min - 1,000,000 max
Business from Other Countries: 30%

Canada

Aardvark Enterprises
Division of Speers Investments Ltd
204 Millbank Dr SW, Calgary, AB T2Y 2H9
Tel: 403-256-4639
Key Personnel
Pres: J Alvin Speers
Founded: 1970 (Small Press Pioneers)
Turnaround: 30 Workdays
Print Runs: 10 min - 1,000 max
Business from Other Countries: 25%

Friesens Corp
One Printers Way, Altona, MB R0G 0B0
Tel: 204-324-6401 *Fax:* 204-324-1333
E-mail: friesens@friesens.com
Key Personnel
Pres & CEO: David Friesen *E-mail:* davidf@friesens.com
Sales Mgr: Frank Friesen *E-mail:* frankf@friesens.com
Founded: 1907
Turnaround: 20-25 Workdays
Business from Other Countries: 30%
Branch Office(s)
Spectrum Book, 2300 Bethards Dr, Suite C, Santa Rosa, CA 95405-8568, United States, Duncan McCallum *Tel:* 707-542-6044 *Fax:* 707-542-6045 *E-mail:* specbooks@aol.com
528 S Ardmore Ave, Chicago, IL 60181, United States *Tel:* 630-834-9954 *Fax:* 815-653-9486 *E-mail:* dawn@friesens.com
Four Colour Imports, 2843 Brownboro Rd, No 102, Louisville, KY 40206, United States, George Dick *Tel:* 502-896-9644 *Fax:* 502-896-9594 *E-mail:* georged@friesens.com
10011 167 Court W, Lakeville, MN 55044, United States, Renee Craft *Tel:* 612-435-1997 *Fax:* 612-898-0227 *E-mail:* reneecraft@earthlink.net
Membership(s): BMI; Canadian Book Manufacturers Association

Mad Dog Design Connection Inc
22 Saint Leonards Ave, Toronto, ON M4N 1J9
Tel: 416-467-0090 *Fax:* 416-484-1140
E-mail: maddogs9@rogers.com
Key Personnel
Owner & Designer: Linda Pellowe
Designer & Digital Artist: David Szolcsanyi
Founded: 1998
Turnaround: As needed/to deadline
Business from Other Countries: 10%

Maracle Press Ltd
1156 King St E, Oshawa, ON L1H 7N4
Tel: 905-723-3438 *Toll Free Tel:* 800-558-8604
Fax: 905-428-6024
E-mail: maracle@maraclepress.com
Web Site: www.maraclepress.com
Key Personnel
Pres & Gen Mgr: Bruce A Fenton *E-mail:* bfenton@maraclepress.com
VP, Busn Devt: Ronald G Taylor *E-mail:* rtaylor@maraclepress.com
Founded: 1920
Turnaround: 10 Workdays
Print Runs: 500 min - 500,000 max
Business from Other Countries: 20%
Membership(s): BMI; Canadian Book Manufacturers Association; CPIA; GATF; Ontario Printing & Imaging Association; Printing Industries of America

McLaren Morris & Todd Co
Subsidiary of Mail-Well
3270 American Dr, Mississauga, ON L4V 1B5
Tel: 905-677-3592 *Fax:* 905-677-3675; 905-677-7766
Web Site: www.mmt.ca
Key Personnel
VP, Fin: Tom Englehart
Pres & CEO: Tony Sgro
Contact: Anthony Sgro
Founded: 1956
Turnaround: 15 Workdays
Print Runs: 5,000 min - 1,000,000 max
Business from Other Countries: 10%

PrintWest
1150 Eighth Ave, Regina, SK S4R 1C9
Tel: 306-525-2304 *Toll Free Tel:* 800-236-6438 *Fax:* 306-757-2439
E-mail: general@printwest.com
Web Site: www.printwest.com
Key Personnel
CEO: Wayne UnRuh
VP, Sales: Ken Benson
Founded: 1992
Turnaround: 15 Workdays
Print Runs: 1,000 min - 100,000 max
Business from Other Countries: 15%
Branch Office(s)
Box 2500, 2310 Millar Ave, Saskatoon, SK S7K 2C4 *Tel:* 306-665-3560 *Fax:* 306-653-1255

Transcontinental Printing Book Group
Division of Transcontinental Group
395 Lebeau Blvd, St-Laurent, PQ H4N 1S2
Tel: 514-337-8560 *Toll Free Tel:* 800-361-3599 *Fax:* 514-339-5230
Web Site: www.transcontinental.com; www.transcontinental-printing.com
Key Personnel
Sr VP, Book Group: Jacques Gregoire
US Sales Mgr: Denis Beaudin *Tel:* 514-339-2220 ext 4101 *E-mail:* beaudind@transcontinental.ca
Founded: 1976

CANADA

Turnaround: 10 working days casebound; 7-10 working days softcover
Print Runs: 500 min
Business from Other Countries: 30%
Branch Office(s)
614 Yates Ave, Calumet City, IL 60409, United States, Contact: Kristopher D Levy *Tel:* 708-832-1528 *Fax:* 708-832-9510 *E-mail:* kris.levy@transcontinental.ca (Midwest)
3653 W Leland Ave, Suite One W, Chicago, IL 60625, United States, Contact: Tim Taylor *Tel:* 773-583-8155 *Fax:* 773-583-8162 *E-mail:* tim.taylor@transcontinental.com (Midwest)
19 Crown St, Milton, MA 02186-1419, United States, Contact: Mike Gazzola *Tel:* 617-696-1435 *Fax:* 617-696-1025 *E-mail:* mikebook@attbi.com (East Coast)
37 Herman Blvd, Franklin Square, NY 11010, United States, Contact: Tom Malloy *Tel:* 516-775-2980 *Fax:* 516-488-0253 *E-mail:* tmmalloy@aol.com (NY)
245 Eliot St, Ashland, MA 01721, United States, Contact: Ed Catania *Tel:* 508-881-1119 *Fax:* 508-881-7739 *E-mail:* ecatania@attbi.com (East Coast)
3175 Summit Square Dr, Suite C9, Oakton, VA 22124, United States, Contact: David Avesian *Tel:* 703-255-1332 *Fax:* 703-255-1343 *E-mail:* davesian@cox.rr.com (Southeast)
559 Lowrys Rd, Parksville, BC V9P 2R8, Contact: Mike Davies *Tel:* 250-248-9700 *Fax:* 250-248-2353 *E-mail:* bookguys@shaw.ca (West Coast)
15373 Victoria Ave, White Rock, BC V4B 1H1, Contact: Wade Davies *Tel:* 604-535-8800 *Fax:* 604-535-8802 *E-mail:* daviesw@shaw.ca (West Coast)
490 Wilfred Dr, Peterborough, ON K9K 2H1, Contact: Tom Lang *Tel:* 705-760-9594 *Fax:* 705-760-9485 *E-mail:* langt@transcontinental.ca (NY)
395 Lebeau Blvd, St-Laurent, PQ H4N 1S2, Contact: Stephane Lavoie *Tel:* 514-337-8560 *Fax:* 514-339-2252 *E-mail:* lavoies@transcontinental.ca
Membership(s): BMI; National Association for Printing Leadership; Printing Industries of America

Tri-Graphic Printing (Ottawa) Ltd
485 Industrial Ave, Ottawa, ON K1G 0Z1
Tel: 613-731-7441 *Toll Free Tel:* 800-267-9750 *Fax:* 613-731-3741
Web Site: www.tri-graphic.com
Key Personnel
VP & Gen Mgr: Doug K Doane
 E-mail: ddoane@tri-graphic.com
VP, Prodn & Servs: Fred Malleau *Tel:* 905-665-8500 *E-mail:* fmalleau@tri-graphic.com
Founded: 1968
Turnaround: 10-15 Workdays
Print Runs: 1,000 min - 100,000 max
Business from Other Countries: 10%
Branch Office(s)
213 Byron St S, Suite 201, Whitby, ON L1N 4P7 *Tel:* 905-665-8500 *Fax:* 905-665-8501

University of Toronto Press Inc
Printing Division, 5201 Dufferin St, North York, ON M3H 5T8
Tel: 416-667-7767 *Fax:* 416-667-7803
E-mail: printing@utpress.utoronto.ca
Web Site: www.utpress.utoronto.ca
Key Personnel
Pres & Publr: George Meadows
Founded: 1901
Turnaround: 10-15 Workdays
Print Runs: 10 min - 200,000 max
Business from Other Countries: 15%
Membership(s): BMI

Webcom Ltd
3480 Pharmacy Ave, Toronto, ON M1W 2S7
Tel: 416-496-1000 *Toll Free Tel:* 800-665-9322 *Fax:* 416-496-1537
E-mail: webcom@webcomlink.com
Web Site: www.webcomlink.com
Key Personnel
VP, Sales & Mktg: Mike Collinge
Mktg Mgr: Charlie Scime
Founded: 1976
Turnaround: 15 Workdays
Print Runs: 50 min - 100,000 max
Business from Other Countries: 40%

China

Jardine Wenwu Printing Co
No 21 Bei St, Xihuangchenggen, Hicheng District, Beijing
Tel: 6617 5748
Web Site: www.cypdirect.com

Croatia

Mehanograf
Kovinska 12, 10090 Zagreb
Tel: (01) 3498-411 *Fax:* (01) 3498-414
E-mail: mehanograf@zg.hinet.hr
Web Site: www.cursor.hr/pa.nsf
Key Personnel
Dir: Zeljko Vincetic

Radin-Repro I Roto
Zagrebacka 194, 10000 Zagreb
Tel: (01) 3869 200 *Fax:* (01) 3862 673
E-mail: radin-repro-i-roto@zg.tel.hr
Web Site: www.odisej.hr
Key Personnel
Dir: Marijan Arambasin
Contact: Sanja Pusec

Vjesnik dd (Croatian Printing Plant)
Slavonska Avenija 4, 10 000 Zagreb
Tel: (01) 61 66 666; (01) 36 41 111 *Fax:* (01) 61 61 602; (01) 61 61 650
E-mail: vjesnik@vjesnik.hr; vjesnik@vjesnik.com
Web Site: www.vjesnik.hr; www.vjesnik.com
Key Personnel
General Manager: Ivan Bozicevic
Sales Manager: Irena Gnjidic
Technical Manager: Zeljko Bajs; Mijo Paradzik; Ivan Srsen
Purchasing Manager: Renata Bozickovic
Finance Manager: Koraljka Kokotovic
Founded: 1999 (In 1999 Vjesnik Publishing Company & Hrvatska tishava dd joined together to create Vjesnik dd)
Print Runs: 25,000 min - 55,000 max
Business from Other Countries: 1%

Denmark

Ingenioeren/Boger (Engineering Books Danish Technical Press)
Ingerslevsgade 44, 1503 Copenhagen V
Tel: 63 15 17 00 *Fax:* 63 15 17 33
Web Site: www.bog.ing.dk
Key Personnel
Marketing: Soren Bertelsen

Finland

Enso Oy, see Stora Enso Oyj

Stora Enso Oyj
Formerly Enso Oy
Kanavaranta 1, 00101 Helsinki
Mailing Address: PO Box 309, 00101 Helsinki
Tel: (09) 2046 131 *Fax:* (09) 2046 214 71
Web Site: www.storaenso.com
Key Personnel
Sales Manager: Ove Backlund; Aarno Yrjo-Koskinen

UPM-Kymmene Ltd
Subsidiary of UPM-Kymmene Group
PO Box 380, Helsinki
Tel: 358 204 15111 *Fax:* 358 204 150500
E-mail: info@upm-kymmene.com
Web Site: www.upm-kymmene.com
Key Personnel
Marketing: Miss C E Burgess; S P Daykin

WS Bookwell Ltd
Teollisuustie 4, 06100 Porvoo
Tel: (019) 21 941 *Fax:* (019) 2194 802
Web Site: www.bookwell.fi
Key Personnel
Sales Manager: Rainer Poysa *Tel:* (019) 219 4664 *E-mail:* rainer.poysa@bookwell.fi
Founded: 1878
Parent Company: Werner Soderstrom Corp
Ultimate Parent Company: SanomaWSOY
Branch Office(s)
Messdorferstr 127, 53123 Bonn, Germany, Contact: Markku Rapeli *Tel:* (0228) 986 4006 *Fax:* (0228) 986 4008
WS Bookwell AB, Borgveien 2, Ytre Enebakk 1914, Norway, Contact: Kristen Sande *Tel:* (064) 925 840 *Fax:* (064) 925 841 *E-mail:* k.sande.wsoy@oslo.online.no
PO Box 3, Lowestoft, Suffolk NR33 8EY, United Kingdom, Contact: David Sowter *Tel:* (1502) 742 038 *Fax:* (1502) 742 039 *E-mail:* ds@bookwell.co.uk

France

Imprimerie Bene
12 rue Pradier, F-30000 Nimes
Tel: (04) 66294897 *Fax:* (04) 66382146
Key Personnel
President: Jacques Enfer
Print Runs: 100 min - 10,000 max
Business from Other Countries: 20%

Imprimerie Carlo Descamps SA
36 place Pierre Delcourt, 59163 Conde sur l'Escaut
Tel: (03) 27400208 *Fax:* (03) 27405683
Key Personnel
Contact: Carlo Bertin
Founded: 1830
Turnaround: 2-5 Workdays
Print Runs: 800 min - 20,000 max
Business from Other Countries: 12%

Plein Chant
16120 Bassac
Tel: (05) 45 81 93 26 *Fax:* (05) 45 81 92 83
Web Site: www.nanga.fr
Key Personnel
Contact: Edmond Thomas
Founded: 1971

Print Runs: 600 min - 1,000 max
Business from Other Countries: 5%

Germany

Adobe Systems GmbH
Ohmstr 1, 85716 Unterschleistraheim
Tel: (089) 31 70 50 *Fax:* (089) 31 70 5705
Web Site: www.adobe.de

Ludwig Auer GmbH
Heilig-Kreuz-Str 16, 86609 Donauwoerth
Mailing Address: Postfach 1152, 86601 Donauwoerth
Tel: (0906) 73-0 *Fax:* (0906) 73-130 (management); (0906) 73-184 (sales)
E-mail: org@auer-medien.de
Web Site: www.auer-medien.de
Key Personnel
Manager: Wolfgang Meier *Tel:* (0906) 73-230
Sales Manager: Eduard Steinle *Tel:* (0906) 73-250

Bertelsmann AG
Carl-Bertelsmannstr 270, 33311 Gutersloh
Mailing Address: Postfach 111, 33311 Gutersloh
Tel: (05241) 80-0 *Fax:* (05241) 80-9662
E-mail: info@bertelsmann.de
Web Site: www.bertelsmann.de
Key Personnel
Division President: Frank Woessner
Founded: 1835

C L Baader Buch & Offsetdruckere GmbH & Co KG
Gutenbergstr 1, 72525 Muensingen
Tel: (07381) 791 *Fax:* (07381) 411412 *Cable:* BAADER-MUNSINGEN
Founded: 1835
Turnaround: 1 Workday
Print Runs: 1,000 min - 15,000 max

Druck & Verlagshaus Fromm GmbH & Co KG
Subsidiary of Neue Osnabruecker Zeitung, Druckzentrum Osnabrueck; Verlag A Fromm; Fromm International Publ Corp; Edition Interfrom AG
Breiter Gang 10-16, 49074 Osnabrueck
Tel: (0541) 310-0 *Fax:* (0541) 310315
E-mail: druckhaus@fromm-os.de
Web Site: www.fromm-os.de
Key Personnel
Publisher: Leo V Fromm
Chief Executive Officer: A Harms-Hunold
Founded: 1868

Media-Print Informationstechnologie GmbH
Schwarzenraben 7, 59558 Lippstadt
Tel: (02941) 2 72-300 *Fax:* (02941) 2 72-540
E-mail: kg@mediaprint.de
Web Site: www.mediaprint.de
Key Personnel
Man Dir: Dr Otto W Drosihn *E-mail:* drdrosihn@kg.mediaprint.de
Founded: 1993
Turnaround: 5-10 Workdays
Print Runs: 100 min - 30,000 max
Business from Other Countries: 10%

MOHN Media
Subsidiary of Bertelsmann AG
Carl-Bertelsmann-Str 161M, 33311 Gueterslsoh
Tel: (05241) 80-4 04 10 *Fax:* (05241) 2 42 82
E-mail: mohnmedia@bertelsmann.de
Web Site: www.mohnmedia.de

Key Personnel
Man Dir: Markus Dohle
Founded: 1824
Business from Other Countries: 25%

Priese GmbH & Co
Auerbacher Str 9, 14193 Berlin
Tel: (030) 8263024 *Fax:* (030) 3249630
Key Personnel
Contact: Elma Priese; Hans Joachim Priese

Sankt-Johannis-Druckerei
Heiligenstr 24, 77933 Lahr
Tel: (07821) 581-0 *Fax:* (07821) 581-26
Web Site: www.medienverbaende.de
Telex: 782122

Papierfabrik Scheufelen GmbH & Co KG
Adolf-Scheufelen-Str 26, 73250 Lenningen
Tel: (07026) 66-779 *Fax:* (07026) 66-719
Web Site: 213.174.48.47/scheufelen/

Strobel Druck & Verlag - A Strobel GmbH & Co KG
Zur Feldmuehle 11, 59821 Arnsberg
Mailing Address: PO Box 5654, 59806 Arnsberg
Tel: (02931) 89 00 0 *Fax:* (02931) 89 00 38
E-mail: info@a-strobel.de
Web Site: www.ikz.de
Key Personnel
Project Manager: Guenther Klauke *E-mail:* g.klauke@myshk.com
Print Runs: 2,500 min - 90,000 max

Topic Verlag GmbH
Birkenstr 10, 85757 Karlsfeld B Munich
Tel: (08131) 97038 *Fax:* (08131) 98404
Founded: 1982
Business from Other Countries: 50%

Wissenschaftliche Verlagsgesellschaft mbH
Birkenwaldstr 44, 70191 Stuttgart
Tel: (0711) 2582-0 *Fax:* (0711) 2582-290
E-mail: service@wissenschaftliche-verlagsgesellschaft.de
Web Site: www.dav-buchhandlung.de
Key Personnel
Man Dir: Dr Christian Rotta

Hong Kong

The American Chamber of Commerce in Hong Kong
1904 Bank of America Tower, 12 Harcourt Rd, Central Hong Kong
Tel: 2526-0165 *Fax:* 2810-1289
E-mail: amcham@amcham.org.hk
Web Site: www.amcham.org.hk
Key Personnel
Publications Manager: Fred Armentrout *E-mail:* farmen@amcham.org.hk

Bright Future Printing Co Ltd
Sunview Industrial Building, Block D, 5/F, 3 On Yip St, Chai Wan
Tel: 2515 1776 *Fax:* 2897 2799; 2558 1717
Key Personnel
Chairman: Richard Ng
Turnaround: 60 Workdays (including shipping)
Print Runs: 3,000 min - 30,000 max
Business from Other Countries: 30%

C A Design, see Communication Art Design & Printing Ltd

C & C Offset Printing Co Ltd
Subsidiary of C & C Joint Printing Co (HK) Ltd under Sino United (Holdings) Hong Kong Ltd
C&C Bldg, floors 1-9, 36 Ting Lai Rd, Tai Po, New Territories
Tel: 2666-4988 *Fax:* 2666-4938
E-mail: offsetprinting@candcprinting.com
Web Site: www.ccoffset.com
Key Personnel
Dir & General Manager: Jackson Leung
Deputy Man Dir: Kee Lee
Deputy General Manager: Ivy Lam
Assistant General Manager: Kit Wong
Senior Sales Manager (Special Project): Francis Ho
Dir & Executive Vice President, C & C Offset Printing Co (USA) Inc, Portland OR, USA: Charles H Clark, IV *E-mail:* cclark@ccoffset.com
Development Manager, C & C Offset Printing Co (USA) Inc, Portland, OR, USA: Jenny Whittier *E-mail:* jwhittier@ccoffset.com
Customer Service Manager, C & C Offset Printing Co (USA) Inc, Portland, OR, USA: Ernest Li *E-mail:* ernestli@ccoffset.com
Dir & Executive Vice President, C & C Offset Printing Co (NY) Inc, New York, NY, USA: Simon Chan *E-mail:* schan@ccoffset.com
Assistant General Manager-China Sales, C & C Joint Printing Co (Ghuangdong) Ltd, Shenzhen, China: Simon Zhang
President, C & C Printing Japan Co Ltd, Tokyo, Japan: Yamamoto Masaaki
Customer Service Manager, C & C Offset Printing Co (NYC), Inc, New York, NY: Frances Harkness *E-mail:* fharkness@ccoffset.com
Man Dir, C & C Joint Printing Co (Beijing), Ltd, Beijing, China: Zhang Lin Gui
Dir, C & C Offset Printing Co (UK), Ltd: Tracy Broderick
Account Manager, C & C Offset Printing Co (UK) Ltd: Fia Fornari
Founded: 1980
Turnaround: 30-42 Workdays for printing, binding & book finishing
Print Runs: 2,000 min - 1,000,000 max
Business from Other Countries: 60%
Branch Office(s)
C & C Joint Printing Co (Guangdong) Ltd, Chunhu Industrial Estate, Pinghu, Long Gang, Shenzhen 518111, China *Tel:* (0755) 2845-8333 *Fax:* (0755) 2845-9911 *E-mail:* guangdong@candcprinting.com *Web Site:* www.candcprinting.com (Plant)
C & C Printing Japan Co Ltd, 2-6-12 Hitotsubashi, Tozaido Bldg 3F, Chiyoda-ku, Tokyo 101-0003, Japan *Tel:* (03) 5216-4580 *Fax:* (03) 5216-4610 *E-mail:* mail@candcprinting.co.jp *Web Site:* www.candcprinting.co.jp
C & C Joint Printing Co (Guangdong) Ltd, 7/F, Flat H, Green View Apartment, No 38, Hou Guang Ping Hu Tong, Xi Cheng Qu, Beijing 100035, China *Tel:* (010) 6650-3176 *Fax:* (010) 6650-3175 *E-mail:* beijing@candcprinting.com
C & C Joint Printing Co (Guangdong) Ltd, Room 304, Fang Fa Bldg, No 29, 165 Ave, Dongzhuanbin Rd, Shanghai 200050, China *Tel:* (021) 6240-1305 *Fax:* (021) 6240-2090 *E-mail:* shanghaioffice@candcprinting.com
C & C Joint Printing Co (Guangdong) Ltd, Room 1511, Hua Xin Bldg, East Block, 2 Shuiyin Rd, Huanshi East, Guangzhou 510075, China *Tel:* (020) 3760-0979 *Fax:* (020) 3760-0977 *E-mail:* guangzhou@candcprinting.com
C & C Offset Printing Co (UK) Ltd, 2 New Burlington St, 4th floor, London W1S 2JE, United Kingdom, Director: Tracy Broderick *Tel:* (020) 7287 7787 *Fax:* (020) 7287 7187 *E-mail:* tracy@candcoffset.co.uk
U.S. Office(s): C & C Offset Printing Co (USA) Inc, 2632 SE 25th Ave, Suite E, PO Box 82037, Portland, OR 97282-0037, United States, Dir: Charlie Clark *Tel:* 503-233-1834

Fax: 503-233-7815 E-mail: portlandinfo@ccoffset.com
C & C Offset Printing Co (NY) Inc, 401 Broadway, Suite 2015, New York, NY 10013-3004, United States, Dir: Simon M K Chan *Tel:* 212-431-4210 *Fax:* 212-431-3960 *E-mail:* nyinfo@ccoffset.com

Caritas Printing Training Centre
Caritas House, 3rd floor, Block D, 2 Caine Rd, Hong Kong
Tel: 2526 1148 *Fax:* 2537 1231
E-mail: info@caritas.org.hk
Web Site: www.caritas.org.hk
Key Personnel
General Manager: Isaac Mak
Founded: 1953
Print Runs: 1,000 min - 100,000 max
Business from Other Countries: 50%

Colorprint Offset
Unit 1808-9, 18/F, 8 Commercial Tower, 8 Sun Yip St, Chai Wan
Tel: 2896-7777 *Fax:* 2889-6606
E-mail: info@cpo.com.hk
Web Site: www.cpo.com.hk
Key Personnel
Sales Manager: Jennifer Weston *Tel:* 2903-5062
Contact: Eva Lav; Ian Lee
Turnaround: Standard turnaround of 2 weeks
Print Runs: 3,000 min - 100,000 max
Business from Other Countries: 80%
Branch Office(s)
Gainsborough House, 81 Oxford St, London W1R 1RB, United Kingdom *Tel:* (020) 7903-5060 *Fax:* (020) 7903-5063 *E-mail:* uk@cpo.com.hk
U.S. Office(s): 80 Park Ave, Suite 10N, New York, NY 10016, United States, Lee Moncho *Tel:* 212-681-9400 *Fax:* 212-681-9362 *E-mail:* ny@cpo.com.hk

Communication Art Design & Printing Ltd
19th floor, China Hong Kong Tower, 8-12 Hennessy Rd, Wan Chai
Tel: 2865 6787 *Fax:* 2866 3429
E-mail: cadesign@pacific.net.hk
Key Personnel
Man Dir: Rosanne Chan
Founded: 1984
Print Runs: 500 min
Business from Other Countries: 50%

Dai Nippon Printing Co (Hong Kong) Ltd
Division of Dai Nippon Printing Co Ltd
Tsuen Wan Industrial Centre, 2-5/F, 220-248 Texaco Rd, Tsuen Wan, New Territories
Tel: 2408-0188 *Fax:* 2408-8479
Web Site: www.dnp.co.jp *Cable:* DNPICO
Key Personnel
Administration & Finance Dir: Mr K Miya
Print Runs: 5,000 min - 200,000 max
Business from Other Countries: 85%
Branch Office(s)
Dai Nippon Printing Co (Australia) Pty Ltd, St Martins Tower, Level 10, Suite 1002, 31 Market St, Sydney, NSW 2000, Australia *Tel:* (02) 9267-8166 *Fax:* (02) 9267-9533
DNP America LLC, Los Angeles Office, 3858 Carson St, Suite 300, Torrance, CA 90503, United States *Tel:* 310-540-5123 *Fax:* 310-543-3260
DNP America LLC, New York Office, 335 Madison Ave, 3rd floor, New York, NY 10017, United States *Tel:* 212-503-1060 *Fax:* 212-286-1501
DNP America LLC, Silicon Valley Office, 3235 Kifer Rd, Suite 100, Santa Clara, CA 95051, United States *Tel:* 408-735-8880 *Fax:* 408-735-0453
DNP Corporation USA, New York Office, 335 Madison Ave, 3rd floor, New York, NY 10017, United States *Tel:* 212-503-1850 *Fax:* 212-286-1490
DNP Corporation USA, San Francisco Office, 577 Airport Blvd, Suite 620, Burlingame, CA 94010, United States *Tel:* 650-558-4050 *Fax:* 650-340-6095
DNP Denmark A/S, Skrueganger 2, 2690 Karlslunde, Denmark *Tel:* 4616-5100 *Fax:* 4616-5200
DNP Electronics America LLC, 2391 Fenton St, Chula Vista 91914, United States *Tel:* 619-397-6700 *Fax:* 619-397-6729
DNP Europa GmbH, Berliner Allee 26, 40212 Dusseldorf, Germany *Tel:* (0211) 8620-180 *Fax:* (0211) 8620-1895
DNP IMS America Corporation, 4524 Enterprise Dr NW, Concord, NC 28027, United States *Tel:* 704-784-8100 *Fax:* 704-784-2777
DNP IMS France SAS, 14, rue da la Violette, 22100 Dinan, France
DNP Korea Co Ltd, Hae sung 2 Bldg 8F, Doechi Dong, Kangnam-ku, Seoul 942-10, Republic of Korea *Tel:* (02) 408-0188 *Fax:* (02) 408-8479
DNP Photomask Europe SpA, Via Olivatti 2/A, 20041 Agrate Brianza, Italy *Tel:* (039) 65493-3000 *Fax:* (039) 65493-215
DNP Singapore Pte Ltd, 896 Dunearn Rd, No 04-09, Sime Darby Centre, Singapore 589472, Singapore *Tel:* 469-7611 *Fax:* 466-8486
DNP Taiwan Co Ltd, Rm D, 6 fl, 44 Chung-Shan N Rd Sec 2, Taipei 104, Taiwan, Province of China *Tel:* (02) 2327-8311 *Fax:* (02) 2327-8283
DNP UK Co Ltd, 27 Throgmorton St, 4th floor, London EC2N 2AQ, United Kingdom *Tel:* (020) 7588 2088 *Fax:* (020) 7588 2089
PT DNP Indonesia, Kawasan Industri Pulogadung, Jalan Pulogadung Kaveling II, Blok H, No 2-3, Jakarta Timur, Indonesia *Tel:* (021) 4610313 *Fax:* (021) 4605795
Tien Wah Press (Pte) Ltd, 4 Pandan Crescent, Singapore 128475, Singapore *Tel:* 466-6222 *Fax:* 469-3894
TWP Sdn Bhd, 89, Jalan Tampoi, Kawasan Perindustrian Tampoi, 80350 Johor Bahru, Johor, Malaysia *Tel:* (07) 2369899 *Fax:* (07) 2363148

Elgin Consultants Ltd
Crawford Tower, 99 Jervois St, Sheung Wan
Tel: 2815 1680
Founded: 1983
Turnaround: 21 Workdays
Business from Other Countries: 10%

Elite Printing Co Ltd
Hong Man Industrial Center, Room 1401-08, 1413 & 1414, 2 Hong Man St, Chai Wan
Tel: 2558 0119 *Fax:* 2897 2675
E-mail: sales@elite.com.hk
Web Site: www.elite.com.hk
Key Personnel
Man Dir: Mak Tong Kee
Sales & Marketing Manager: Fred Chu
Founded: 1979
Turnaround: 7-15 Workdays
Print Runs: 2,000 min - 50,000 max
Business from Other Countries: 30%

Empire Printing Ltd
3 Dai Shun St, Tai Po Ind Estate, Tai Po, New Territories
Tel: 2665 5193 *Fax:* 2661 7722
Key Personnel
Sales Manager: Lok-Tsang Li
Founded: 1978
Turnaround: 2 Workdays
Print Runs: 2,500 min - 500,000 max
Business from Other Countries: 15%

Everbest Printing Co Ltd
Ko Fai Industrial Bldg, Block C5, 10th floor, 7 Ko Fai Rd, Yau Tong, Kowloon
Tel: 2727 4433 *Fax:* 2772 7687
E-mail: sales@everbest.com.hk
Web Site: www.everbest.com
Key Personnel
Man Dir: Kenneth Chung
Customer Account Executive: Frankie Lee; Ronny Ng
Founded: 1954
Turnaround: 28 Workdays
Print Runs: 1,000 min - 1,000,000 max
Business from Other Countries: 90%
Branch Office(s)
100 Macaulay Rd, Stanmore, NSW 2048, Australia, Contact: Lionel Marz *Tel:* 612-9568-5879 *Fax:* 612-9568-5902 *E-mail:* lmarz@onaustralia.com.au (Australian & New Zealand Office)
Everbest Canada, 50 Emblem Court, Scarborough, ON M1S 1B1, Canada, Contact: Connie Chung *Tel:* 416-286-2525 *Fax:* 416-286-2526 *E-mail:* everbestcan@aprinco.com
U.S. Office(s): Spectrum Books Inc, 2300 Bethards Dr, Suite C, Santa Rosa, CA 95405-8658, United States, Duncan McCallum *Tel:* 707-542-6044 *Fax:* 707-542-6045 *E-mail:* specbooks@aol.com
Four Colour Imports, 2843 Brownsboro Rd, Suite 102, Louisville, KY 40206, United States, Contact: George Dick *Tel:* 502-896-9644 *Fax:* 502-896-9594 *E-mail:* sales@fourcolour.com *Web Site:* www.fourcolour.com
Everbest Midwest, 6428 Margaret's Lane, Edina, MN 55439, United States, Contact: Dr Josie Lo *Tel:* 612-944-0854 *Fax:* 912-829-7670 *E-mail:* sklo@aol.com

Golden Cup Printing Co Ltd
Seapower Industrial Centre, 6/F, 177 Hoi Bun Rd, Kwun Tong, Kowloon
Tel: 23434254 *Fax:* 23415426
E-mail: info@goldencup.com.hk
Web Site: www.goldencup.com.hk
Key Personnel
Man Dir: Yeung Kam Kai
General Manager: W K Ngan
Sales Manager: Mary Yeung *E-mail:* mary@goldencup.com.hk
Founded: 1971
Turnaround: 25 Workdays
Print Runs: 5,000 min - 200,000 max
Business from Other Countries: 80%
Branch Office(s)
Dongguan, China
Guangdong, China
Kunming, China
Yunan, China

Great Wall Graphics Ltd
2/F, 13 Wyndhan St, Hong Kong
Tel: 2524 0014 *Fax:* 2845 3588
Key Personnel
Dir: Paul Zimmerman
Founded: 1982
Turnaround: 3-28 Workdays
Print Runs: 2,000 min - 500,000 max
Business from Other Countries: 50%

H & Y Printing Ltd
Blk C, 2/F Shing Tak Industrial Bldg, 44 Wong Chuk Hang Rd, Aberdeen
Tel: 2870 2379 *Fax:* 2555 0028
E-mail: hyphk@netvigator.com
Key Personnel
Contact: Jason Ma
Founded: 1996
Print Runs: 1,000 min - 100,000 max

Hill & Knowlton Asia Ltd
Subsidiary of WPP

MANUFACTURING HONG KONG

PCCW Tower, 36th floor, Taikoo Pl, 979 King's Rd, Quarry Bay
Tel: 2894 6321 *Fax:* 2576 3551
Web Site: www.hillandknowlton.com
Telex: 25763551
Key Personnel
Man Dir: Denise Maguire
Founded: 1927
Branch Office(s)
Hill & Knowlton Melbourne, 484 St Kilda Rd, Level 15, Melbourne, Victoria 3004, Australia, General Manager: Rod Nockles *Tel:* (03) 9868 9370 *Fax:* (03) 9868 9369
Hill & Knowlton (NZ) Ltd, PriceWaterhouseCoopers Centre, Level 15, 66 Wyndham St, Auckland, New Zealand *Tel:* (09) 367 6370 *Fax:* (09) 367 6371
Hill & Knowlton (SEA) Pte Ltd, 100 Beach Rd, 25-11 Shaw Tower, Singapore, Singapore
Hill & Knowlton (SEA) Sdn Bhd, UBN Tower, Lot 6E, 6th floor, 10 Jalan P Ramlee, 50250 Kuala Lumpur, Malaysia, Man Dir: Julia Ahmad *Tel:* (03) 2026 0899 *Fax:* (03) 2026 0699
Hill & Knowlton Thailand, Q House, Ploenjit Bldg, Unit 14C, 14th floor, 598 Ploenchit Rd, Lumpini Pathumwan, Bangkok 10330, Thailand, Man Dir: Kanpirom Ungpakorn *Tel:* (02) 627 3501-6 *Fax:* (02) 627 3510
Hill & Knowlton Zhonglian, Scitech Tower, Suite 1901, Beijing 100004, China, Man Dir: Annabelle Warren *Tel:* (010) 6512 8811 *Fax:* (010) 6512 3712
Hill & Knowlton Zhonglian PR Consulting Ltd, Westgate Tower, 26th floor, Suite 2606, 1038 Nanjing West Rd, Shanghai 200041, China, General Manager: Carol Yang *Tel:* (021) 6218 6150 *Fax:* (021) 6218 6125

Hoi Kwong Printing Co Ltd
Wah Ha Industry Bldg, 5/F, Block C-D, 8 Shipyard Lane, Quarry Bay
Tel: 2562-1641 *Fax:* 2564-2142
E-mail: sales@hoikwong.com
Web Site: www.hoikwong.com
Key Personnel
Man Dir: David Chan *E-mail:* dchan@hoikwong.com
Founded: 1960

Hong Kong Christian Service
33 Granville Rd, Tsimshatsui, Kowloon, Hong Kong SAR
Tel: 2731-6316 *Fax:* 2731-6333
E-mail: info@hkcs.org
Web Site: www.hkcs.org
Key Personnel
Dir: Mr Ng Shui Lai
Founded: 1952
Turnaround: 40 Workdays
Business from Other Countries: 1%
Parent Company: Hong Kong Christian Council

Hung Hing Off-set Printing Co Ltd
Subsidiary of Hung Hing Printing Group Ltd
Tai Po Industrial Estate, 17-19 Dai Hei St, New Territories
Tel: 2664 8682 *Fax:* 2664 2070
E-mail: info@hhop.com.hk
Web Site: www.hhop.com.hk
Key Personnel
Executive Dir: Alvin Chan Siu Man
Founded: 1950
Turnaround: 20-30 Workdays
Print Runs: 5,000 min - 1,000,000 max
Business from Other Countries: 15%

Image Printing Company Ltd
Unit 4, 4/F Cornell Centre, 50 Wing Tai Rd, Chai Wan
Tel: 2873 2633 *Fax:* 2558 3044
E-mail: imageprt@pop3.hknet.com
Key Personnel
Man Dir: Philip Chow Sung Ming
Founded: 1992
Print Runs: 1,000 min - 50,000 max
Business from Other Countries: 50%

Imago Services (HK) Ltd
Tung Chong Factory Bldg, 6th floor, Flat B, 653-659 Kings Rd, North Point
Tel: 2811 3316 *Fax:* 2597 5256
E-mail: enquiries@imago.com.hk
Web Site: www.imago.co.uk
Key Personnel
Man Dir: Kendrick Cheung
Branch Office(s)
Macpherson Industrial Complex, No 5 Lorong Bakar Batu, Hex 05-01, Singapore 348742, Singapore *Tel:* 748 4433 *Fax:* 748 6082
Albury Court, Albury, Thame, Oxon 0X9 2LP, United Kingdom *Tel:* (01844) 337000 *Fax:* (01844) 339935
U.S. Office(s): 1431 Broadway-Penthouse, New York, NY 10018, United States *Tel:* 212-921-4411 *Fax:* 212-921-8226
17 N Loomis St, No 4A, Chicago, IL 60607, United States *Tel:* 312-829-4051 *Fax:* 312-829-4059
31952 Camino Capistrano, Suite C22, San Juan Capistrano, CA 92675, United States *Tel:* 949-661-5998 *Fax:* 949-661-8013

Leo Paper Products Ltd
7/F, Kader Bldg, 22 Kai Cheung Rd, Kowloon Bay, Kowloon
Tel: 28841374 *Fax:* 25130698
E-mail: lpp@leo.com.hk
Web Site: www.leo.com.hk
Key Personnel
Man Dir: Johnny Fung *E-mail:* johnny@leo.com.hk; Michael Leung *E-mail:* michael@leo.com.hk
Marketing Dir: Kelly Fok *E-mail:* kelly@leo.com.uk
Founded: 1991
Turnaround: 15-30 Workdays
Print Runs: 5,000 min
Parent Company: Leo Paper Bags Manufacturing Ltd
Sales Office(s): Leo Paper Products (Europe) BVBA, Keizerstr 5, 200 Antwerpen, Belgium, Contact: Jan Van Gijsel *Tel:* (03) 203-0912 *Fax:* (03) 255-1303 *E-mail:* leo@leo-europe.com
Leo Paper USA, 27 W 24 St, Suite 701, New York, NY 10010-3204, United States *Tel:* 917-305-0708 *Fax:* 917-305-0709 *E-mail:* leo@leousanewyork.com
Leo Paper USA, 1180 NW Maple St, Suite 102, Issaquah, WA 98027, United States, Contact: Bijan Pakzad *Tel:* 425-646-8801 *Fax:* 425-646-8805 *E-mail:* leousa@leousa.com
Leo Paper Products (UK) Ltd, St Michaels House, 94 High St, Wallingford, Oxon OX10 0BW, United Kingdom *Tel:* (01844) 274-244 *Fax:* (01844) 275-105 *E-mail:* tim.leo@btinternet.com

Literature Ministry Department
5/F, 128 Castle Peak Rd, Shamshuipo, Kowloon
Tel: 2725 8558 *Fax:* 2386 2304
E-mail: hkccllmd@hkstar.com
Founded: 1971
Print Runs: 2,000 min - 200,000 max
Business from Other Countries: 50%

Mei Ka Printing & Publishing Enterprise Ltd
Cheung Ka Industrial Bldg, Block B, 9th floor, 179-180 Connaught Rd W, Hong Kong
Tel: 2540 1131 *Fax:* 2559 8718; 2559 7137
E-mail: mkpp@netvigator.com
Web Site: www.meika-printing.com
Key Personnel
Dir: Hong Chin Huo
Founded: 1995

Midas Printing Ltd
1/F, 100 Texaco Rd, Tsuen Wan, New Territories
Tel: 2407 6888 *Fax:* 2408 0611
E-mail: info@midasprinting.com
Web Site: www.midasprinting.com
Key Personnel
Chairman: Sheung Chiu Chan
Man Dir: Tin Lap Kwong; Ann Li Mee Sum
Deputy Man Dir: Chi Fai Kwok
Sales & Marketing: Paul Tang Chow Ming *E-mail:* paul@midasprinting.com
Contact: Annie Wong *E-mail:* annie@midasprinting.com
Founded: 1990
Turnaround: 14-21 Workdays
Print Runs: 5,000 min - 100,000 max
Business from Other Countries: 25%

Morris Press Ltd
Wah Ha Industrial Bldg, 15/F, Block C, 8 Shipyard Lane, Quarry Bay
Tel: 2563 2187; 2563 2188 *Fax:* 2565 9069
E-mail: crprint@netvigator.com
Web Site: www.cgan.net/enterprise/crprint
Key Personnel
Dir: Raymond Shing
Sales Dir: William Shue *E-mail:* william@creativeprinting.com.hk
Turnaround: 15 Workdays
Print Runs: 5,000 min - 100,000 max
Business from Other Countries: 50%

New Island Printing Co Ltd
New Island Printing Centre, Yuen Long Industrial Estate, 38 Wang Lee St, Yuen Long, New Territories
Tel: 2442 8282 *Fax:* 2443 9882
E-mail: info@newisland.com
Web Site: www.newisland.com
Key Personnel
Dir, Business Development: John Currie
Group Dir, Sales & Marketing: Karen Fung

Palace Press International
Wah Ha Factory Bldg, 10th floor, Block 10, 8 Shipyard Lane, Quarry Bay
Tel: 2357 9019 *Fax:* 415-532-3007
E-mail: palacehk@palacepress.ocm; ppihk@palacepress.com; info@palacepress.com
Web Site: www.palacepress.com
Key Personnel
Dir: Lesley Sun *E-mail:* lesley@palacepress.com
Project Manager: Maria Ramos *Tel:* 415-626-1080 (ext 208) *E-mail:* maria@palacepress.com
Founded: 1980
Branch Office(s)
239C Joo Chiat Rd, Singapore 427496, Singapore, Contact: Lesley Sun *Tel:* (0342) 3117 *Fax:* (0342) 3115 *E-mail:* ppispore@palacepress.com *Web Site:* www.palacepress.com
U.S. Office(s): 1585-A Folsom St, San Francisco, CA 94103, United States *Tel:* 415-626-1080 *Fax:* 415-626-1510 *E-mail:* ppisfo@palacepress.com *Web Site:* www.palacepress.com
180 Varick St, 10th floor, New York, NY 10014, United States *Tel:* 212-462-2622 *Fax:* 212-463-9130 *E-mail:* nyoffice@palacepress.com *Web Site:* www.palacepress.com
Palace Press Marin, 17 Paul Dr, San Rafael, CA 94903, United States *Tel:* 415-526-1370 *Fax:* 415-532-3259 *E-mail:* ppimarin@palacepress.com *Web Site:* www.palacepress.com

Paper Art Product Ltd
Sung Fung Centre, Unit 816, 88 Kwok Shui Rd, Kwai Chung
Tel: 2481 2929 *Fax:* 2489 2255
E-mail: paperart@netvigator.com
Key Personnel
Dir: Ho Hok Cheung
Turnaround: 2-4 weeks
Print Runs: 2,000 min - 100,000 max
Business from Other Countries: 80%

Paper Communication Printing Express Ltd
4A Dragon Industrial Bldg, 93 King Lam St, Cheung Sha Wan, Kowloon
Tel: 27864191 *Fax:* 27864498
E-mail: pcpe@papercom.com.hk
Key Personnel
Marketing Dir: Alam Ng
Contact: Wayne Lui
Founded: 1981
Turnaround: 28 to 56 Workdays
Print Runs: 1,000 min - 200,000 max
Business from Other Countries: 100%

Paramount Printing Co Ltd
Member of Paramount Publishing Group Ltd
3 Chun Kwong St, Tseung Kwan O Industrial Estate, Kowloon
Tel: 2896-8688 *Fax:* 2897-8942
E-mail: paraprin@netvigator.com
Web Site: www.paramount.com.hk
Key Personnel
President: Victor Oh
Account Dir: Kelvin Lai
Founded: 1968
Turnaround: 30-45 Workdays
Print Runs: 1,000 min - 1,000,000 max
Business from Other Countries: 60%
U.S. Office(s): Paramount Printing USA Inc, 111 Chestnut St, Suite 508, San Francisco, CA 94111, United States, Vice President, Sales: Bobby Tan *Tel:* 415-391-9111 *Fax:* 415-398-9333 *E-mail:* bobbytan@aol.com
Paramount Printing USA Inc, 386 Park Ave S, Room 315, New York, NY 10016, United States, President: Jason Cheng *Tel:* 212-696-5821 *Fax:* 212-696-5428 *E-mail:* jason3@ix.netcom.com

Pearl River Printing Co Ltd
Flat A, Evergreen Bldg, 13th Floor, 12 Yip Fat St, Aberdeen
Tel: 2540-6114 *Fax:* 2559-7042
E-mail: pearlriv@sage.net
Web Site: www.pearlriv.com
Key Personnel
Man Dir: Alan Scott Jordan
Founded: 1984
Turnaround: 5-40 Workdays
Print Runs: 500 min - 50,000 max
Business from Other Countries: 50%

Professional Publishing Co
2/F, 65, Wyndham St, Central Hong Kong
Tel: 25254623 *Fax:* 28453681
Key Personnel
Business Dir: Michael Pak
Founded: 1970
Turnaround: 20-40 Workdays
Print Runs: 5,000 min - 50,000 max
Business from Other Countries: 20%

Prontaprint Asia Ltd
1/F, Gaylord Commercial Bldg, 114 Lockhart Rd, Wanchai
Tel: 28657525 *Fax:* 28661064
E-mail: postmaster@pronta.com.hk
Key Personnel
Man Dir: Clive Howard
Founded: 1986
Business from Other Countries: 40%

Review Publishing Co Ltd
Subsidiary of Dow Jones & Co Inc
GPO Box 160, Hong Kong
Tel: 2573 7121 *Fax:* 2503 1530
E-mail: review@feer.com
Web Site: www.feer.com
Telex: 75297 *Cable:* REVIEW
Key Personnel
Editor: David Plott *E-mail:* david.plott@feer.com
Chief Correspondent: Michael Vatikiotis *E-mail:* michael.vatikiotis@feer.com
Founded: 1946

Sing Cheong Printing Co Ltd
G/F, 655 Kings Rd, North Point
Tel: 25618801; 25626317 *Fax:* 25659467
E-mail: info@singcheong.com.hk
Key Personnel
Dir & Manager: Karen Shen Fishel
Founded: 1965
Business from Other Countries: 96%

Sino Publishing House Ltd
Valley Centre Room 301-302, 80-82 Morrison Hill Rd, Wanchai
Tel: 2884 9963 *Fax:* 2884 9321
E-mail: info@sinophl.com
Web Site: www.sinophl.com
Key Personnel
Dir: Stephen Stringer
Contact: Debbie Lindsay *E-mail:* debbie@sinophl.com
Founded: 1993
Print Runs: 500 min - 500,000 max
Business from Other Countries: 75%

SNP Leefung Holdings Ltd
Rm 1001-1003, Wing On House, 10th floor, 71 Des Voeux Rd, Central Hong Kong
Tel: 2810 6801 *Fax:* 2810 5612
Web Site: www.leefung-asco.com
Key Personnel
Chairman: Peter Yang
General Manager: Mr Jin Ling
Founded: 1960

South China Printing Co (1988) Ltd
Subsidiary of Sing Tao Group
6/F Block B, Shatin Industrial Center, 5-7 Yuen Chun Circuit, Shatin, New Territories
Tel: 26373611 *Fax:* 26374221
Web Site: www.nysingtao.com
Key Personnel
General Manager & Dir: Raymond Ching
Senior Division Manager: Ivan Cheung
Assistant to General Manager: Athena Yuen *E-mail:* ayuen@scpc.com.hk
Founded: 1988
Turnaround: 20 Workdays
Print Runs: 2,000 min - 150,000 max
Business from Other Countries: 98%
Branch Office(s)
Sydney, Australia, Contact: Mr Anders Hagberg *E-mail:* anders@bigpond.com
Bedfordshire, United Kingdom, Contact: Mr Alan Lynch *Tel:* (0152) 523-7455 *Fax:* (0152) 523-7756 *E-mail:* alan.lynch@LineOne.net
U.S. Office(s): Los Angeles, CA, United States, Contact: Mr Moon Chuen Lo *Tel:* (626) 291-7398 *Fax:* (626) 285-2870 *E-mail:* moonclo@earthlink.com
New York, NY, United States, Contact: Mr Peter Lawrence *Tel:* (212) 570-9010 *Fax:* (212) 628-0137 *E-mail:* scpco@aol.com

South Sea International Press Ltd
3/F, Yip Cheung Centre, 10 Fung Yip St, Chai Wan
Tel: 2897 1083 *Fax:* 2558 1473
E-mail: books@ssip.com.hk
Web Site: www.ssip.com.hk

Key Personnel
Man Dir: Franky Ho
Founded: 1984
Print Runs: 3,000 min - 500,000 max
Business from Other Countries: 80%

Speedflex Asia Ltd
3/F Tianjin Bldg, 167 Connaught Rd W, Hong Kong
Tel: 2542 2780 *Fax:* 2542 3733
E-mail: info@speedflex.com.hk
Web Site: www.speedflex.com.hk
Founded: 1981
Turnaround: 1 Workday
Print Runs: 1 min
Business from Other Countries: 20%

Sunshine Press Ltd
21/F Fullager Ind Bldg, 234 Aberdeen Main Rd, Hong Kong
Tel: 25532386 *Fax:* 28732930
E-mail: spl@sunshinepress.com.hk
Key Personnel
Administrative Assistant: Trevin Tong
Contact: Joney Chan
Founded: 1976
Turnaround: 21-28 Workdays
Print Runs: 3,000 min - 500,000 max
Business from Other Countries: 25%

Unicorn International Printing Co Ltd
Block C & A, 13/F, Shing King Bldg, 45 Kut Shing St, Chai Wan
Mailing Address: Block G, 2/F, Phase 1, Kwun Tong Ind Center, 472 Kwun Tong Rd, Kowloon
Tel: 2515-9810 *Fax:* 2515-9992
E-mail: unicorn7@netvigator.com; unicornhk@netvigator.com
Web Site: www.unicorn88.com
Key Personnel
General Manager: Paul chi-sing Choi
Founded: 1994
Turnaround: 7 Workdays
Print Runs: 1,000 min - 100,000 max
Business from Other Countries: 20%
Branch Office(s)
Shenzhen, China

Wing King Tong Group
Leader Industrial Centre, Block I, 3/F, 188-202 Texaco Rd, Tsuen Wan, New Territories
Tel: 24073287; 24073309; 24074547 *Fax:* 24074130
E-mail: humanre@wkt-group.com
Web Site: www.cgan.com
Key Personnel
Man Dir: Alex Yan Tak Chung *E-mail:* ayan@hk.super.net
Marketing Dir: Jeremy Kuo
Founded: 1944
Turnaround: 15 Workdays
Print Runs: 1,000 min - 100,000 max
Business from Other Countries: 95%

Ying Tat Co
Division of Quality Printing & Paper Products
Wing Wah Industrial Bldg, 8th floor, 677 Kings Rd, North Point
Tel: 25645980; 25645963; 25639981 *Fax:* 28111280
Web Site: www.cgan.com
Key Personnel
Sales Manager: Kan Chan
Founded: 1968
Turnaround: 7-10 Workdays
Print Runs: 1,000 min - 1,000,000 max
Business from Other Countries: 30%

Hungary

Interpress Aussenhandels GmbH
Bajcsy-Zsilinszky ut 21, 1065 Budapest
Tel: (01) 302-7525; (01) 2508267 *Fax:* (01) 302-7530
Key Personnel
Manager: Miklos Pollak; Sandor Kovacs; Julia Kovacs
Founded: 1991

India

Hiralal Printing Works Ltd
Subsidiary of Conway Printers Pvt Ltd
D-41/1 TTC Industrial Area MIDC, opp Turbhe tel exchange, Mumbai 400613
Tel: (022) 7672726; (022) 7683012 *Fax:* (022) 7631191
Key Personnel
Chairman: G P Agrawal
Man Dir: Mr Rakesh Kumar Agrawal
Founded: 1981
Turnaround: 40-45 Workdays
Print Runs: 5,000 min - 100,000 max
Business from Other Countries: 75%

Indonesia

Victory Offset Prima PT
Jalan Raya Pegangsaan, Dua No 17, Jakarta 14250
Tel: (021) 460-2742; (021) 460-8968; (021) 4682-0555 *Fax:* (021) 460-2740; (021) 4682-0551
E-mail: info@victoryoffset.com
Web Site: www.victoryoffset.com
Key Personnel
President: Zainal F Stanley *E-mail:* zainal@victoryoffset.com
General Manager: S Wilson Pinady *E-mail:* wilson@victoryoffset.com
Founded: 1971
Turnaround: 14 days
Print Runs: 5,000 min
Business from Other Countries: 10%

Ireland

Tower Books
13 Hawthorn Ave, Inniscarra View Estate, Ballincollig, County Cork
Tel: (021) 4872294 *Fax:* (021) 4872294
Key Personnel
Contact: Patricia Daly
Founded: 1970
Turnaround: 7-30 Workdays
Print Runs: 300 min - 2,000 max

Israel

Chronicles Publishers Ltd
24 Haarbaah St, Tel Aviv 61200
Mailing Address: PO Box 20774, Tel Aviv 61200
Tel: (03) 5615052 *Fax:* (03) 5624104
E-mail: chronicl@inter.net.il
Key Personnel
Man Dir: Dr Yehuda Atac
Manager: Farida Yashkuner *Tel:* (03) 5613614
Founded: 1993

The Government Printer
One Miriam Ha'hashmonait St, Jerusalem 91007
Mailing Address: PO Box 765, Jerusalem 91007
Tel: (02) 5685111; (02) 5685200 *Fax:* (02) 5685226
Key Personnel
Comptroller: Shimon Hochster
Founded: 1948

Har-El Printers & Publishers
Jaffa Port, Jaffa 61081
Mailing Address: Jaffa Port, PO Box 8053, Jaffa 61081
Tel: (03) 681 6834 *Fax:* (03) 681 3563
Web Site: www.harelart.com
Key Personnel
Manager: Jaacov Har-El
Export Dir: Monique L Harel *E-mail:* mharel@harelart.co.il
Founded: 1974
Turnaround: 60-90 Workdays
Print Runs: 30 min - 5,000 max
Business from Other Countries: 70%

Keterpress Enterprises Jerusalem
PO Box 7145, 91071 Jerusalem
Mailing Address: PO Box 7145, Jerusalem 91071
Tel: (02) 6557822 *Fax:* (02) 6528962
E-mail: info@keter-books.co.il
Web Site: www.keter-books.co.il
Key Personnel
Plant Manager: Peter Tomkins *E-mail:* peter@keter-books.co.il
Sales Manager: Zvi Weller
Print Runs: 500 min - 500,000 max
Business from Other Countries: 10%
Parent Company: Keter Publishing House Ltd

Technosdar Ltd
5 Levontine St, Tel Aviv 61316
Tel: (03) 560-7418; (03) 5605951 *Fax:* (03) 5605951
E-mail: technos@internet-zahav.net
Key Personnel
General Manager: Avraham Weiss
Founded: 1972
Turnaround: 7-16 Workdays
Business from Other Countries: 10%

Youval Tal Ltd
PO Box 61009, Jerusalem 91610
Tel: (02) 6248897 *Fax:* (02) 6245434
Key Personnel
Dir: Youval Tal

Italy

Calderini SRL
Subsidiary of Edagricole-Edizioni Agricole
Via Emilia Levante 31/2, 40139 Bologna
Tel: (051) 6226822 *Fax:* (051) 549329
E-mail: comm@calderini.agriline.it
Web Site: www.calderini.it; www.gce.it
Key Personnel
Editorial Dir: Alberto Perdisa
Founded: 1960

Canale G e C SpA
Via Liguria 24, 10071 Borgaro Turin
Tel: (011) 40 78 511 *Fax:* (011) 40 78 527
E-mail: info@canale.it
Web Site: www.canale.it
Key Personnel
Dir General: Canale Giacomo *E-mail:* canale@canale.it
Founded: 1915
Turnaround: 30 Workdays
Print Runs: 3,000 min
Business from Other Countries: 65%

Dedalo Litostampa SRL
Viale Luigi Jacobini 5, 70123 Bari
Mailing Address: Casella Postale BA/19, 70123 Bari
Tel: (080) 531 14 13; (080) 531 14 00; (080) 531 14 01 *Fax:* (080) 531 14 14
E-mail: info@edizionidedalo.it
Web Site: www.edizionidedalo.it
Key Personnel
Man Dir: Raimondo Coga
General Manager: Sergio Coga *E-mail:* s.coga@edizionidedalo.it
Founded: 1965
Print Runs: 2,000 min - 10,000 max

Minerva Medica
Corso Bramante 83/85, 10126 Turin
Tel: (011) 67-82-82 *Fax:* (011) 67-45-02
E-mail: minervamedica@minervamedica.it
Web Site: www.minervamedica.it
Key Personnel
President: Dr Alberto Oliaro
Founded: 1937
Print Runs: 1,000 min - 10,000 max
Business from Other Countries: 8%
Branch Office(s)
Via Lamarmora 3, 20122 Milano *Tel:* (02) 551-843-79, 599-000-41 *Fax:* (02) 551-809-54 *E-mail:* guerrini.minmed.milan@minervamedica.it
Via Spallanzani 9, 00161 Rome *Tel:* (06) 442-512-10 *Fax:* (06) 442-915-00 *E-mail:* lucentini.minmed.rome@minervamedica.it

Istituto Poligrafico e Zecca Dello Stato
Piazza Verdi 10, 00198 Rome
Tel: (06) 85081 *Toll Free Tel:* 800 864035 *Fax:* (06) 8508-2517
E-mail: infoipzs@ipzs.it
Web Site: www.ipzs.it
Telex: 611008 IPZSRO
Key Personnel
Legal Representative: Giovanni Ruggeri
Founded: 1928

Valdonega SRL
via Genova 17, 37020 Arbizzano (Verona)
Tel: (045) 6020444 *Fax:* (045) 6020334
E-mail: valdonega@valdonega.it
Web Site: www.valdonega.it
Key Personnel
General Manager: Martino Mardersteig
Founded: 1948
Print Runs: 1,000 min
Business from Other Countries: 70%

Republic of Korea

Daehan Printing & Publishing Co Ltd
344-12, Sangdaewon 1-dong, Jungwon-gu, Seongnam-si, Gyeonggi-do, Seoul
Tel: (031) 730-3850 *Fax:* (031) 735-8104
E-mail: mschung@daehane.com
Web Site: www.daehane.com
Key Personnel
President: Sungshick Kim
Manager: Jongjun Yu
Founded: 1948

Lithuania

Spindulys Printing House
Gedimino 10, 3000 Kaunas
Tel: (037) 226243 *Fax:* (037) 204970
E-mail: spaustuve@spindulys.lt
Web Site: www.spindulys.lt
Key Personnel
Contact: Elena Kapustinskiene
Founded: 1928
Print Runs: 500 min - 100,000 max
Business from Other Countries: 6%

Madagascar

Imprimerie Catholique
127 Rue Lenine-Antanimena, Tananrive 101
Tel: (02) 22304

Societe Malgache d'Edition
Route des Hydrocarbures, Ankorondrano, BP 659, Antananarivo/Tananrive 101
Tel: (020) 2222635 *Fax:* (020) 2222254
E-mail: tribune@bow.dts.mg
Web Site: www.madagascar-tribune.com
Telex: (020) 223-40
Key Personnel
Dir of Publication: Rahaga Ramaholimihaso
Founded: 1943
Print Runs: 7,000 min - 15,000 max

Malawi

Likuni Press
Division of Odini Bookshop
PO Box 133, Lilongwe
Tel: 721135; 721388 *Fax:* 72114133
Key Personnel
Chief Executive: S P Kalilombe
Managing Editor: P I Akomenji
Bookshop Manager: D H Bvalamwendo
Founded: 1949
Print Runs: 12,000 min - 15,000 max
Business from Other Countries: 5%

Malta

Interprint Ltd - Malta
Subsidiary of Malta Government Investment Ltd
Industrial Estate, Marsa LQA 06
Tel: (021) 240169; (021) 222720 *Fax:* (021) 243780; (021) 238115
Web Site: www.interprintmalta.com
Key Personnel
General Manager: Alfred Azzopardi
Commercial Manager: Joseph Bonnici
 E-mail: jbonnici@interprintmalta.com
Founded: 1963
Turnaround: 15 Workdays
Print Runs: 500 min - 200,000 max
Business from Other Countries: 80%

Netherlands

Bosch en Keuning grafische bedrijven
Ericastr 1, 3742 SG Baarn
Mailing Address: Postbus 1, 3740 AA Baarn
Tel: (035) 5412050 *Fax:* (035) 2202446
Key Personnel
Contact: P P E Rings

Collectieve Propaganda van het Nederlandse Boek (CPNB) (Foundation for the Collective Promotion of the Dutch Book)
Keizersgracht 391, 1016 EJ Amsterdam
Tel: (020) 626 49 71 *Fax:* (020) 623 16 96
E-mail: info@cpnb.nl
Web Site: www.cpnb.nl
Key Personnel
Man Dir: Henk Kraima
Founded: 1983

CPNB, see Collectieve Propaganda van het Nederlandse Boek (CPNB)

Foundation of Marginal Printers, see Stichting Drukwerk in de Marge

Stichting Drukwerk in de Marge (Foundation of Marginal Printers)
Sint Antoniesbreestr 3d, 1001 HB Amsterdam
Mailing Address: Postbus 16477, 1001 RN Amsterdam
Tel: (020) 6227748 *Fax:* (020) 6227748
Web Site: www.drukwerkindemarge.nl
Key Personnel
Contact: A A Sanders
Founded: 1975

New Zealand

Bookprint Consultants Ltd
Division of Grantham House Publishing
9 Wilkinson St, Apt 6, Oriental Bay, Wellington 6001
Tel: (04) 381 3071 *Fax:* (04) 381 3067
E-mail: gstewart@iconz.co.nz
Key Personnel
Chief Executive: Graham C Stewart
Founded: 1982
Print Runs: 2,000 min - 7,500 max
Business from Other Countries: 10%

The Caxton Press
113 Victoria St, Christchurch
Toll Free Tel: 800 229 866 *Fax:* (03) 365 7840
E-mail: print.design@caxton.co.nz
Web Site: www.caxton.co.nz
Key Personnel
Man Dir: Bruce Bascand *Tel:* (03) 353 0731
General Manager: Peter Watson *Tel:* (03) 353 0734
Customer Services: Lorene Soli
Founded: 1935

PPP Printers Ltd
PO Box 22785, Christchurch
Tel: (03) 3662727 *Fax:* (03) 3654606
Web Site: www.scoop.co.nz
Key Personnel
Man Dir: D C Richardson
Founded: 1958
Turnaround: 10 Workdays
Print Runs: 100 min - 100,000 max
Business from Other Countries: 10%

Rogan McIndoe Print Ltd
51 Crawford St, Dunedin
Mailing Address: PO Box 1361, Dunedin
Tel: (03) 474 0111 *Toll Free Tel:* 800-477-0355
 Fax: (03) 477 0116
Web Site: www.rogan.co.nz
Key Personnel
Man Dir: Brendan A Murphy
Advertising: Amanda Cushen *E-mail:* amanda@mcindoes.co.nz
Founded: 1893
Print Runs: 21 min - 30 max
Business from Other Countries: 1%

Norway

ISSN Norway
National Library of Norway, Oslo Division, PO Box 2674, N-0203 Oslo
Tel: (023) 27 61 79; (023) 27 61 81 *Fax:* (023) 27 60 50
E-mail: nbo@nb.no
Web Site: www.nb.no
Key Personnel
Dir: Vigdis Moe Skarstein

Philippines

Cacho Hermanos Inc, see Cacho Publishing inc

Cacho Publishing inc
Formerly Cacho Hermanos Inc
Pines Cor, Union St, Mandaluyong, Metro Manila
Tel: (02) 6318362; (02) 6318363; (02) 6318364; (02) 6318365 *Fax:* (02) 6315244
E-mail: cacho@mozcom.com
Key Personnel
President: Herbert T Veloso
Founded: 1880
Turnaround: 7-120 Workdays
Print Runs: 500 min - 50,000 max
Parent Company: National Book Store

Polygraphics Trading
2619 Rockefeller St, Sn Isidro, 1234 Makati City
Tel: (02) 817-9556 *Fax:* (02) 817-9564
Web Site: www.piap.org.ph
Key Personnel
Proprietor & General Manager: Carlito B Bacurin
Founded: 1977
Branch Office(s)
6 Molave St, Phase II, Dona Justa Village, Angono, Rizal

Ready Press
246 Katipunan Ave, 1109 Blueridge, Quezon City
Tel: (02) 6471163; (02) 6471227 *Fax:* (02) 6471158
E-mail: casper@pworld.net.ph
Web Site: www.metro.com.sg
Key Personnel
General Manager: Alda Sylianteng
Turnaround: 15 Workdays
Print Runs: 5,000 min
Business from Other Countries: 10%
Parent Company: Metro Holdings Corp
Branch Office(s)
37 Balagtas St, Marikina City
Sales Office(s): 777 Burgos St, Mandaue City, Cebu

Reyes Publishing Inc
Mariwasa Bldg, 717 Aurora Blvd, 1112 Quezon City
Tel: (02) 721-8792 *Fax:* (02) 721-8782
E-mail: reyesbub@skyinet.net
Key Personnel
Operations Manager: Roman Paolo Reyes, V
Founded: 1964
Business from Other Countries: 90%

Portugal

Edicoes Silabo
Rua Passos Manuel, 99-5º E, 1100 Lisbon
Tel: (021) 8130345 *Fax:* (021) 8166719
E-mail: silabo@silabo.pt
Web Site: www.silabo.pt
Key Personnel
Marketing Dir: Manuel Robalo
    E-mail: manuelrobalo@silabo.pt
Founded: 1983
Turnaround: 5 Workdays

Romania

Editura si Atelierele Tipografice Metropol SRL
Str Stefan cel Mare, nr 2, Bucharest
Tel: (01) 2104593; (01) 2108433 *Fax:* (01) 2106987
Key Personnel
President: Dr Bansoiu Ion
Founded: 1990
Turnaround: 3-20 Workdays
Print Runs: 500 min - 50,000 max
Business from Other Countries: 10%

Editura Paideia
2, Sos.Stefan cel Mare, 71216 Bucharest, Sector 1
Tel: (01) 2104593 *Fax:* (01) 2106987
E-mail: paideia@fx.ro
Web Site: www.paideia.ro
Key Personnel
President: Ion Bansoiu
Founded: 1990
Turnaround: 3-20 Workdays
Business from Other Countries: 10%

Singapore

Alkem Company Pte Ltd
Division of Toppan Printing Co Ltd
No 1 Penjuru Close, Jurong Town, Singapore 608617
Tel: 62656666 *Fax:* 62617875
E-mail: microsoft@alkem.com.sq
Telex: RS 21596 *Cable:* TOPPAN
Key Personnel
Contact: Mr Takayuki Seki
Man Dir: Chu Bong *E-mail:* chubong@alkem.com.sg
General Manager: M Sonoda
Founded: 1968
Turnaround: 3 - 4 Weeks
Print Runs: 3,000 min - 500,000 max
Business from Other Countries: 70%

Chong Moh Offset Printing Ltd
Subsidiary of Chassis Graphic Art Pte Ltd
19 Joo Koon Rd, Jurong Town 628978
Tel: 8622701 *Fax:* 8624335
E-mail: chongmoh@singnet.com.sg
Key Personnel
Chairman: James Ng
Founded: 1946
Turnaround: 10-14 Workdays
Print Runs: 1,000 min
Business from Other Countries: 35%

CS Graphics Pte Ltd
10 Tuas Ave 20, Singapore 638822
Tel: 861-0100 *Fax:* 861-0190
Key Personnel
Man Dir: Mr Lee Sian Tee *E-mail:* stlee@csgraphics-world.com
Founded: 1987
Turnaround: 80 Workdays (with pre-press); 20-60 Workdays (without pre-press)
Print Runs: 1,000 min - 200,000 max
Business from Other Countries: 100%
Sales Office(s): 8969 Lake Court, Granite Bay, CA 95746, United States, Contact: Rick Marment *Tel:* 916-791-9066 *Fax:* 916-791-9112
    E-mail: csgraphics@csi.com

Eurasia Press Pte Ltd
10/14 Kampong Ampat-1336, Singapore 368320
Tel: 2805522 *Fax:* 2800593; 3825458
E-mail: eurasia@mbox3.singnet.com.sg
Key Personnel
Marketing Dir: Allan Fong
Founded: 1937
Turnaround: 14 Workdays
Print Runs: 500 min - 100,000 max
Business from Other Countries: 65%

HB Media Holdings Pte Ltd
Division of International Printing Division
Subsidiary of HBM Print Ltd
745 Lor 5 TOA Payoh, HBM Bldg, Singapore 319455
Tel: 62591919 *Fax:* 67443895
Key Personnel
Chief Operating Officer: Mr Wong Wai Mong
Founded: 1980
Turnaround: 5 Workdays
Business from Other Countries: 97%
Branch Office(s)
50 Kallang Bahru No 02-14/23, Kallang Basin Industrial Estate, Singapore 339334

Ho Printing Singapore Pte Ltd
31 Changi South St One, Changi South Industrial Estate, Singapore 486769
Tel: 5429322 *Fax:* 5428322
Telex: RS 39685 HOFSET
Key Personnel
Sales Executive: Ho Wah Yuen
Founded: 1951
Turnaround: 35-50 Workdays
Print Runs: 5,000 min - 50,000 max
Business from Other Countries: 30%

International Press Co Pte Ltd
26 Kallang Ave, Singapore 339417
Tel: 2983800; 2952437 *Fax:* 2971668
Key Personnel
Marketing Manager: Kok Leong Koo
Founded: 1972
Print Runs: 3,000 min - 50,000 max
Business from Other Countries: 60%

Khai Wah-Ferco Pte Ltd
No 61 Yishun Industrial Park A, No 02-00, Singapore 768767
Tel: 67583313
E-mail: kwfppi@pacific.net.sg
Key Personnel
General Manager: Sim Huat Hoe

Kim Hup Lee Printing Co Pte Ltd
22 Lim Teck Boo Rd, Singapore 1953
Tel: 2833306 *Fax:* 2889222
Key Personnel
Dir: Mr Lim Geok Khoon

Magenta Lithographic Consultants
1093 Lower Delta Rd, No 04-01, Singapore
Tel: 2746288
E-mail: magenta@singaporebusinessguide.com
Telex: RS39478Mlcols
Key Personnel
Managing Proprietor: Mr Lim Choon Kiat
Founded: 1975
Turnaround: 2-3 Workdays
Business from Other Countries: 30%

Markono Print Media Pte Ltd
Subsidiary of Markono Holdings Pte Ltd
21 Neythal Rd, Singapore 628586
Tel: 6281-1118 *Fax:* 6286-6663
E-mail: saleslead@markono.sg
Web Site: www.markono.com.sg
Key Personnel
Executive Dir: Mr Ho Tian Lam *Tel:* 393 2338
Associate Dir: Mr Shaun Poh *Tel:* 393 2384
Corporate Affairs: Cindy Gui *Tel:* 393 2359; 393 2392
Turnaround: 14 Workdays
Print Runs: 1,000 min - 100,000 max
Business from Other Countries: 20%
Branch Office(s)
Kin Keong Colour Printing (M) Sdn Bhd, Port Klang 539538

Saik Wah Press (Pte) Ltd
52 Kallang Bahru, No 07-19/20, Singapore 339335
Tel: 6292 8759 *Fax:* 6296 0638
E-mail: sales@saikwah.com.sg
Web Site: www.saikwah.com.sg
Telex: RS38564
Key Personnel
Man Dir: Mr Chin San Hwa
Founded: 1973
Turnaround: 20 Workdays
Print Runs: 1,000 min - 100,000 max
Business from Other Countries: 70%

SNP SPrint Pte Ltd
97 Ubi Ave 4, Singapore 408754
Tel: 6741-2500 *Fax:* 6744-7098; 6743-9661
E-mail: enquiries@snpcorp.com
Web Site: www.snpcorp.com
Telex: SNPRS14462
Key Personnel
Man Dir: Foong Kee Loon
Sales & Operations Dir: Tung Chee Seng
Turnaround: 30 Workdays
Print Runs: 2,000 min - 200,000 max
Business from Other Countries: 40%
Parent Company: SNP Corporation Ltd

Stamford Press Pte Ltd
209, Kallang Bahru, Singapore 339344
Tel: 6294 7227 *Fax:* 6294 4396; 6294 3319
E-mail: lynn@stamford.com.sg
Web Site: www.stamford.com.sg
Telex: RS56414 STAMFO
Key Personnel
Dir Sales & Marketing: Mr V Balu *Tel:* 6294 7227 (ext 228) *E-mail:* balu@stamford.com.sg
Man Dir: Mr R Theyvendran
Founded: 1963
Turnaround: 3-4 Workdays for small jobs; 3-4 weeks for big jobs
Print Runs: 1,500 min - 50,000 max
Business from Other Countries: 20%

Times Printers Pte Ltd
Subsidiary of Times Publishing Group

16 Tuas Ave 5, Singapore 639340
Tel: 6311-2888 *Fax:* 682-1313
E-mail: tp@timesprinters.com
Web Site: www.tpl.com.sg; www.timesprinters.
 com *Cable:* TIMESPRINT
Key Personnel
Head of Sales & Customer Service: Patsy Tan
General Manager, International Sales & Marketing: Howard Wang *E-mail:* howardwang@
 timesprinters.com
Founded: 1968
Turnaround: 5-25 Workdays
Print Runs: 3,000 min - 300,000 max
Business from Other Countries: 75%

Viva Lithographers Pte Ltd
Blk 3 Pasir Panjang Rd, No 06-22/23 Alexandra
 Distripark, Singapore 118483
Tel: 2721880 *Fax:* 2735425
E-mail: vivasing@singnet.com.sg
Web Site: ifc.tp.edu.sg/Project_2000July/Viva
Key Personnel
Man Dir: Michael Oh

Slovenia

Gorenjski Tisk Printing House
Mirka Vadnova 6, 4000 Kranj
Tel: (04) 2016300 *Fax:* (04) 2016301
E-mail: info@go-tisk.si
Web Site: www.go-tisk.si
Telex: 34560 YU GOTISK
Key Personnel
Dir: Kristina Kobal
Commercial Manager: Boris Krist
Founded: 1888
Turnaround: 30 Workdays
Print Runs: 3,000 min - 15,000 max
Business from Other Countries: 50%

Spain

Offo SL
Los Mesejos 23, 28007 Madrid
Tel: (01) 5514214 *Fax:* (01) 5010699
Key Personnel
Export Manager: Jose A Martinez Minuesa

Graficas Santamaria SA
Division of Fotomecanica
Bekolarra, 4 Pol Ali Gobeo, 01010 Vitoria
 Gasteiz
Tel: (0945) 229100 *Fax:* (0945) 246393
E-mail: grsantamaria@sea.es; grsantamaria@
 graficassantamaria
Web Site: www.graficassantamaria.com
Key Personnel
Contact: Jesus Alzola Aguinaco
Founded: 1963
Turnaround: 1 Workday
Print Runs: 500 min - 150,000 max
Business from Other Countries: 15%

Luis Vives (Edelvives)
Xaudaro, 25, 28034 Madrid
Tel: (091) 334 48 83; (091) 334 48 82 *Fax:* (091)
 334 48 92
E-mail: dediciones@edelvives.es
Web Site: www.grupoeditorialluisvives.com
Key Personnel
Production Dir: Jesus Agudo Perez
Founded: 1890

Turnaround: 1 Workday
Business from Other Countries: 25%

Sri Lanka

Sarvodaya Vishva Lekha
41 Lumbini Ave, Ratmalana
Tel: (01) 714820; (01) 714829; (01) 731601
 Fax: (01) 738932
E-mail: sarvs101@sri.lanka.net
Key Personnel
Man Dir: Mr Sausiri de Silva
Founded: 1984
Print Runs: 500 min
Business from Other Countries: 5%

Sumathi Book Printing (Pvt) Ltd
Division of Sumathi Group
445, Sirimovo Bandaranaike Mawatha, Colombo
 14
Tel: (0941) 330-673-5 *Fax:* (0941) 449-593
E-mail: lakbima@isplanka.lk
Web Site: www.sumathi.lk
Telex: 22104 SUMATHI CE SUMATISONS
Key Personnel
General Manager: Nawas A Rahim
Business from Other Countries: 75%

Switzerland

Autorinnen und Autoren der Schweiz AdS
 (Association of Swiss Authors)
Nordstr 9, 8035 Zurich
Tel: (01) 350 04 60 *Fax:* (01) 350 04 61
E-mail: sekretariat@a-d-s.ch
Web Site: www.a-d-s.ch
Key Personnel
Secretary: Peter A Schmid
Founded: 2002

Hallwag Kuemmerly & Frey AG
Nordring 4, Postfach, CH-3001 Bern
Tel: (031) 335 55 55 *Fax:* (031) 414133
Telex: 912-661 HAWA CH
Key Personnel
President: Dr Juergen Schad

IBBY, see International Board on Books for
 Young People (IBBY)

**International Board on Books for Young
 People (IBBY)**
Nonnenweg 12, 4003 Basel
Tel: (061) 272 29 17 *Fax:* (061) 272 27 57
E-mail: ibby@ibby.org
Web Site: www.ibby.org
Key Personnel
President: Peter Schneck
Administrative Dir: Elizabeth Page
Founded: 1953

Ott Verlag Thun (Ott Publishers, Inc)
Laenggasse 57, Postfach 802, 3607 Thun 7
Tel: (033) 225 39 39 *Fax:* (033) 225 39 33
E-mail: info@ott-verlag.ch
Web Site: www.ott-verlag.ch
Key Personnel
Man Dir: Hans M Ott

United Republic of Tanzania

Peramiho Publications
PO Box 41, Peramiho
Tel: (054) 2730 *Fax:* (054) 2917
Key Personnel
Chief Executive: Fr Gerold Rupper
Founded: 1937
Print Runs: 4,000 min - 6,000 max

Thailand

J Film Process Co Ltd
440/7 Soi Rajchawitee 3, Rajathevee Rd,
 Bangkok 10400
Tel: (02) 247-4042; (02) 248 6888 *Fax:* (02) 247-
 4719
Key Personnel
President: Peer Prayukvong
Vice President: Siriporn Prayukvong
Man Dir: Pira Prayookwongse
Founded: 1970
Turnaround: 6 Workdays
Print Runs: 25,000 min - 65,000 max
Business from Other Countries: 45%

Phongwarin Printing Company Ltd
299 Mu 10, Sukhumvit 107, Sumrongnue, Ampur
 Muang, Samutprakarn 10260
Tel: (02) 7498934-45; (02) 3994525-31; (02)
 7498275-9 *Fax:* (02) 3994524; (02) 3994255
E-mail: somphong@phongwarin.com
Web Site: www.phongwarin.com
Key Personnel
Man Dir: Mr Somphong Charnsirisaksakul
Founded: 1983
Turnaround: 7 Workdays
Print Runs: 1,000 min - 500,000 max
Business from Other Countries: 5%

Thai Watana Panich Press Co Ltd
891 Rama 1 Rd, Bangkok 10330
Tel: (02) 2150060-3 *Fax:* (02) 2152360
E-mail: twpp@loxinfo.co.th
Web Site: www.twppress.com
Telex: 72303 Thaiwat th
Key Personnel
Man Dir: Thira T Suwan
Founded: 1935
Print Runs: 5,000 min

United Kingdom

J W Arrowsmith Ltd
Winterstoke Rd, Bristol BS3 2NT
Tel: (0117) 966 7545 *Fax:* (0117) 963 7829
E-mail: jw@arrowsmith.co.uk
Web Site: www.arrowsmith.co.uk
Key Personnel
Sales Dir: David J Hooper *E-mail:* dhooper@
 arrowsmith.co.uk
Founded: 1854
Turnaround: 15 Workdays

MANUFACTURING — UNITED KINGDOM

Print Runs: 500 min - 15,000 max
Business from Other Countries: 25%

BAS Printers Ltd
115 Tollgate Rd, Salisbury, Wilts SP1 2JG
Tel: (01722) 411711 *Fax:* (01722) 411727
E-mail: sales@basprint.co.uk
Web Site: www.basprint.co.uk
Key Personnel
Man Dir: David Gumn
Sales Dir: Paul G Gumn *E-mail:* paul@basprint.co.uk
Founded: 1948
Print Runs: 350 min - 40,000 max
Business from Other Countries: 10%

The Bath Press
Subsidiary of Bath Press Group PLC
Lower Bristol Rd, Bath BA2 3BL
Tel: (01225) 428101 *Fax:* (01225) 312418
E-mail: bath@cpi-group.co.uk
Web Site: www.cpi-group.net/bathbas.htm
Key Personnel
Sales & Marketing Dir: Harry Elson
 Tel: (020) 7637 9700 *Fax:* (020) 7637 0183
 E-mail: helson@cpi-group.co.uk
Sales Manager: Gordon Reade *Tel:* (020) 7637 9700 *Fax:* (020) 7637 0183 *E-mail:* greade@cpi-group.co.uk
Founded: 1846
Turnaround: 10-15 Workdays
Print Runs: 3,000 min - 300,000 max
Business from Other Countries: 5%

BCS Publishing Ltd
1 Bignell Park Barns, Kirtlington Rd, Bicester, Oxford OX6 8TD
Tel: (01869) 324423 *Fax:* (01869) 324385
Key Personnel
Man Dir: Steve McCurdy
Founded: 1993
Business from Other Countries: 40%

Bell & Bain Ltd
303 Burnfield Rd, Thornliebank, Glasgow G46 7UQ
Tel: (0141) 649 5697 *Fax:* (0141) 632 8733
E-mail: info@bell-bain.demon.co.uk
Web Site: www.bell-bain.co.uk
Key Personnel
Man Dir: I Walker
Sales Dir: D Stewart
Founded: 1831
Turnaround: 7-10 Workdays
Print Runs: 100 min - 100,000 max
Business from Other Countries: 25%

Biddles Ltd
Division of W & G Baird Ltd
Hardwick Industrial Estate, 24 Rollesby Rd, King's Lynn, Norfolk PE30 4LS
Tel: (01553) 764 728 *Fax:* (01553) 764 633
E-mail: enquiries@biddles.co.uk
Web Site: www.biddles.co.uk
Key Personnel
Man Dir: Rod Willett *E-mail:* rwillett@biddles.co.uk
Founded: 1885
Turnaround: 20 Workdays
Print Runs: 250 min - 50,000 max
Business from Other Countries: 8%

Roy Bloom Ltd
Fanshaw House, 3/9 Fanshaw St, London N1 6HX
Tel: (0207) 7295373 *Fax:* (0207) 7292375
E-mail: info@roybloom.com
Web Site: www.remainder-books.com
Key Personnel
Chairman: Roy Bloom *E-mail:* roybloom@roybloom.com
Man Dir: Adam Bloom
Sales Dir: Paul White *E-mail:* paul.white@roybloom.com
Founded: 1969
Business from Other Countries: 40%

Book Creation
20 Lochaline St, London W6 9SH
Tel: (020) 7583 0553 *Fax:* (020) 7583 9439
Key Personnel
Chairman: Hal Robinson *E-mail:* hal@librios.com
Founded: 1991
Business from Other Countries: 30%

Book Production Consultants PLC
25-27 High St, Chesterton, Cambridge CB4 1ND
Tel: (01223) 352790 *Fax:* (01223) 460718
Web Site: www.bpccam.co.uk
Key Personnel
Dir: Tony Littlechild *E-mail:* tl@bpccam.co.uk;
 Colin Walsh *E-mail:* cw@bpccam.co.uk
Founded: 1973
Turnaround: 50 Workdays
Print Runs: 500 min
Business from Other Countries: 25%

British Sisalkraft Ltd
Subsidiary of David S Smith (Holdings)
Commissioners Rd, Rochester, Strood, Kent ME2 4ED
Tel: (01634) 292700 *Fax:* (01634) 291029
E-mail: sales@bsk-laminating.com
Web Site: www.bsk-laminating.com
Key Personnel
Sales & Marketing Dir: Keith Travis
Brand Products Manager: Lawrence Kuhn
Founded: 1937
Business from Other Countries: 27%

D Brown & Sons Ltd
14 High St, 2nd floor, Cambridge CF71 7AG
Tel: (01446) 771475 *Fax:* (01446) 771476
Key Personnel
Dir: J M Whitaker *Tel:* (01446) 774213
Finance Dir: Jane C Brown
Founded: 1895
Business from Other Countries: 5%

Center Print Ltd
Colwick Business Park, Private Rd No 2, Colwick, Nottingham NG4 2JR
Tel: (0115) 961 2277 *Fax:* (0115) 938 1424
Key Personnel
General Manager: Nicola Lesley
Print Runs: 1,000 min - 250,000 max

Chase Publishing Services
Mead, Fortescue Rd, Sidmouth, Devon EX10 9QG
Tel: (01395) 514709 *Fax:* (01395) 514709
E-mail: r.addicott@btinternet.com
Key Personnel
President: Ray Addicott *E-mail:* r.addicott@btinternet.com
Founded: 1989

Clays Ltd
Subsidiary of St Ives Plc
Popson St, Bungay, Suffolk NR35 1ED
Tel: (01986) 893211 *Fax:* (01986) 895293
E-mail: sales@clays.co.uk
Web Site: www.clays.co.uk
Key Personnel
Contact: Sarah Orell
Founded: 1817
Turnaround: 15 Workdays
Print Runs: 1,000 min - 1,000,000 max
Business from Other Countries: 15%

William Clowes Ltd
Beccles, Suffolk NR34 9QE
Tel: (01502) 712884 *Fax:* (01502) 717003
E-mail: william@clowes.co.uk
Web Site: www.clowes.co.uk
Key Personnel
Man Dir: Alex Evans
Sales Dir: David C Browne *Tel:* (07768) 658820
 E-mail: dbrowne@clowes.co.uk
Founded: 1803
Turnaround: 10 Workdays
Print Runs: 2,000 min
Business from Other Countries: 1%
Sales Office(s): 2 Fore St, London EC2Y 5DA
 Tel: (020) 7588 0754 *Fax:* (020) 7588 0550
 E-mail: londonoffice@clowes.co.uk

Cox & Wyman Ltd
Cardiff Rd, Reading, Berks RG1 8EX
Tel: (0118) 953 0500 *Fax:* (0118) 950 7222
E-mail: enquiries@coxandwyman.co.uk;
 coxandwyman@cpi-group.net
Web Site: www.cpi-group.net
Key Personnel
General Manager: Tom Roberts
Sales Manager: Ruth Smith
Contact: Jack McCabe *Tel:* (01225) 428 101 *Fax:* (01225) 483 632 *E-mail:* jmccabe@bathpress.co.uk
Founded: 1777
Turnaround: 10 workdays
Print Runs: 2,000 min - 2,000,000 max
Business from Other Countries: 12%

Dorriston Publishers Ltd
59 Stroud Green Rd, London N4 3EG
Tel: (020) 7272 2722 *Fax:* (020) 7272 7274
Key Personnel
Man Dir: A G Dicomites

Edition
Subsidiary of Cameron Books
PO Box 1, Moffat DG10 9SU
Tel: (01683) 220808 *Fax:* (01683) 220012
E-mail: sales@cameronbooks.co.uk
Web Site: www.cameronbooks.co.uk
Key Personnel
Dir: Ian Cameron; Jill Hollis
Founded: 1976

Export Booksellers Group
Division of Booksellers Association of the United Kingdom & Ireland Ltd
272 Vauxhall Bridge Rd, London SW1V 1BA
Tel: (020) 7834 5477 *Fax:* (020) 7834 8812
E-mail: mail@booksellers.org.uk
Web Site: www.booksellers.org.uk
Key Personnel
Meetings Executive: John Parke *E-mail:* john.parke@booksellers.org.uk

Gardenhouse Editions
15 Grafton Sq, London SW4 0DQ
Tel: (020) 76221720 *Fax:* (020) 7720 9114
Key Personnel
Man Dir: L Johnson

Gee & Son (Denbigh) Ltd-Gwasg Gee-Gee's Press
Chapel St, Denbigh, Denbighshire LL16 35W
Tel: (01745) 812020 *Fax:* (01745) 812825
Key Personnel
Man Dir: Emlyn Evans
Founded: 1808

The Guernsey Press Co Ltd
Braye Rd, Vale, Guernsey GY1 3BW
Mailing Address: PO Box 57, Vale, Guernsey GY1 3BW
Tel: (01481) 240240; (01481) 243657 (ISDN)
 Fax: (01481) 240275

UNITED KINGDOM

E-mail: books@guernsey-press.com
Web Site: www.guernsey-press.com
Key Personnel
Manager: Karen Taylor
Founded: 1897
Turnaround: 10 Workdays
Print Runs: 2,000 min - 50,000 max
Business from Other Countries: 80%

Robert Hale Ltd
45-47 Clerkenwell Green, London EC1R 0HT
Tel: (020) 7251 2661 *Fax:* (020) 7490 4958
E-mail: english@halebooks.com
Web Site: www.halebooks.com
Key Personnel
Chairman: John Hare
Marketing Dir: Martin Kendall
Founded: 1936

Hammond Packaging Ltd
Division of Hammond Bindery Ltd
Flanshaw Way, Flanshaw Lane, Wakefield WF2 9LP
Tel: (01924) 369598 *Fax:* (01924) 298075; (01924) 364108
E-mail: hammpack@dial.pipex.com
Web Site: www.hammpack.co.uk; www.charlesworth.com
Key Personnel
Man Dir: Steve Allan *E-mail:* s_allan@hammond-bindery.co.uk
Regional Sales Executive: Kirk Allan
  E-mail: kallan@hammond-bindery.co.uk
Founded: 1991
Turnaround: 5-15 Workdays
Print Runs: 100 min - 500,000 max

Ikon Document Management Services
Subsidiary of Microgen Holdings Plc
19 The Business Centre, Molly Millars Lane, Wokingham, Berks RG41 2QY
Tel: (0118) 9770510 *Fax:* (0118) 9770513
Key Personnel
Man Dir: Dave Weller
Business Development Dir: Aaron Biggs
Founded: 1972
Turnaround: 2-5 Workdays
Print Runs: 1 min - 5,000 max
Business from Other Countries: 40%
Branch Office(s)
Microgen City Park Watchmead, Welwyn Garden City, Herts AL7 1LT

Intype Libra Ltd
Units 3 & 4, Elm Grove Industrial Estate, Elm Grove, Wimbledon SW19 4HE
Tel: (020) 8947 7863 *Fax:* (020) 8947 3652
E-mail: intype@btconnect.com
Web Site: www.intype.co.uk
Key Personnel
Man Dir: Tony Chapman *E-mail:* tony.chapman@intypelibra.co.uk
Production: Jane Rogers
Founded: 1976
Turnaround: 10-15 Workdays for proofs; 5-10 Workdays for books
Print Runs: 5 min - 2,500 max
Business from Other Countries: 5%

ITD
Rabans Lane Industrial Estate, Faraday Rd, Aylesbury, Bucks HP19 3RY
Tel: (01296) 27211 *Fax:* (01296) 392019
Key Personnel
Man Dir: Roy Jackson-Moore
Founded: 1976
Turnaround: 7-10 Workdays
Business from Other Countries: 10%

Gerald Judd Sales Ltd
Paper House, 47-51 Gillingham St, London SW1V 1HS
Tel: (020) 7828 8821 *Fax:* (020) 7828 0840
Key Personnel
Man Dir: Simon Perks
Sales Dir: Jonathan Addy
Founded: 1936

The Lavenham Press Ltd
47 Water St, Lavenham, Suffolk CO10 9RN
Tel: (01787) 247436; (01787) 248267 (ISDN)
  Fax: (01787) 248267
E-mail: lpl@lavenhamgroup.co.uk
Web Site: www.lavenhampress.co.uk
Key Personnel
Man Dir: Terence Dalton *E-mail:* terence@lavenhamgroup.co.uk
Sales Dir: Nic Waller *E-mail:* nic@lavenhamgroup.co.uk
Production Dir: Ken Hampton *E-mail:* ken@lavenhamgroup.co.uk
Publishing Dir: Lis Whitehair *E-mail:* lis@lavenhamgroup.co.uk
Founded: 1953
Business from Other Countries: 1%

Charles Letts & Co Ltd
Thorneybank Industrial Estate, Dalkeith, Midlothian EH22 2NE
Tel: (0131) 663 1971 *Fax:* (0131) 660 3225
E-mail: sales@letts.co.uk; diaries@letts.co.uk
Web Site: www.letts.co.uk
Key Personnel
Man Dir: Gordon Presly
Founded: 1796

Masons Design & Print
Viscount House, River Lane, Saltney, Chester CH4 8RH
Tel: (01244) 674433 *Fax:* (01244) 674274
E-mail: sales@masonsprint.com
Web Site: www.masonsprint.com
Key Personnel
Man Dir: Timothy Leaman
Founded: 1908
Turnaround: 5-10 Workdays
Print Runs: 500 min - 500,000 max

MPG Books Ltd
Division of MPG Ltd
Victoria Sq, Bodmin, Cornwall PL31 1EB
Tel: (01208) 73266; (01208) 72008 (ISDN)
  Fax: (01208) 73603
E-mail: print@mpg-books.co.uk
Web Site: www.mpg-books.com
Key Personnel
Man Dir: Tony Chard
Deputy Managing Dir: Jeff Swift *Tel:* (01869) 324 992 *Fax:* (01869) 324 992 *E-mail:* jswift@mpg-books.co.uk
Sales Executive: Roy Skinner *Tel:* (01843) 231 029 *E-mail:* rskinner@mpg-books.co.uk
Sales & Marketing Development Manager: Colin Porter *Tel:* (0117) 968 8838 *Fax:* (0117) 968 8838 *E-mail:* cporter@mpg-books.co.uk
Founded: 1967
Turnaround: 10-15 days
Print Runs: 400 min - 10,000 max
Business from Other Countries: 5%
Ultimate Parent Company: Martins Printing Group

NES Arnold Ltd
Subsidiary of Group Holdings PLC
Findel House, Excelsior Rd, Ashby Park, Ashby de la Zouch, Leics LE65 1NG
Tel: (0845) 120 4525 *Fax:* (0800) 328 0001
E-mail: enquiries@nesarnold.co.uk
Web Site: www.nesarnold.co.uk

Telex: (0602) 377082
Key Personnel
Marketing Manager: Anita Ladva
  E-mail: aladva@novara.co.uk

Page Bros Ltd (Norwich)
Subsidiary of Milex Ltd
Mile Cross Lane, Norwich, Norfolk NR6 6SA
Tel: (01603) 429141 *Fax:* (01603) 485126
Key Personnel
Sales Dir: Steve Commons
Founded: 1750
Turnaround: 10 Workdays
Print Runs: 100 min - 30,000 max
Business from Other Countries: 20%
Branch Office(s)
105-A Euston St, London NW1 2ET *Tel:* (020) 7383 2212 *Fax:* (020) 7383 4145

Paternoster Publishing
Subsidiary of STL Ltd
Kingstown Broadway, Carlisle, Cumbria CA3 0QS
Mailing Address: PO Box 300, Carlisle, Cumbria CA3 0QS
Tel: (01228) 512512 *Fax:* (01228) 514949
E-mail: info@Paternoster-Publishing.com
Web Site: www.paternoster-publishing.com
Key Personnel
Man Dir: Pieter Kwant
Founded: 1935
Print Runs: 3,000 min - 10,000 max

Pensord Press Ltd
Tram Rd, Pontllanfraith, Blackwood NP12 2YA
Tel: (01495) 223721; (01495) 222020 (customer service) *Fax:* (01495) 220672
E-mail: sales@pensord.co.uk
Web Site: www.pensord.co.uk
Key Personnel
International Sales, Coordinator: Louise Williams
  E-mail: louise.williams@pensord.co.uk

Polestar Purnell Ltd
Subsidiary of BPC Ltd
Paulton, Bristol BS39 7LQ
Tel: (01761) 404142 *Fax:* (01761) 404191
Web Site: www.polestar-group.com/purnell
Key Personnel
Man Dir: Tony Hall
Production Manager: Andy Casling
Manufacturing Dir: Tony Kington
Finance Dir: Gerald Richardson
Founded: 1839

Precision Publishing Papers Ltd
Subsidiary of Ekman Cleave Group Ltd
Court Ash House, Court Ash, Yeovil, Somerset BA20 1HG
Tel: (01935) 431800; (732) 563-9292 (USA & other) *Fax:* (01935) 431805
E-mail: precisionpub@pppl.co.uk
Web Site: www.hspg.com/precision
Key Personnel
Man Dir: David Darwood

The Q Group Plc
Calverley House, 45 Dane St, Bishop's Stortford, Herts CM23 3BT
Tel: (01279) 719070 *Fax:* (01279) 757409
E-mail: marketing@qgroupplc.com; support@qgroupplc.com
Web Site: www.qgroupplc.com
Key Personnel
Man Dir: P F Poulter *E-mail:* ppoulter@qgroupplc.com
Founded: 1993

F J Ratchford Ltd
Subsidiary of Bookcraft Supplies Ltd

Kennedy Way, Green Lane, Stockport, Cheshire SK4 2JX
Tel: (0161) 4808484 *Fax:* (0161) 4803679
E-mail: info@fjratchford.co.uk
Web Site: www.fjratchford.co.uk
Key Personnel
Dir: J P Ratchford
Founded: 1889

Antony Rowe Ltd
Bumper's Farm Industrial Estate, Chippenham, Wilts SN14 6LH
Tel: (01249) 659 705 *Fax:* (01249) 448 900
E-mail: sales@antonyrowe.co.uk
Web Site: www.antonyrowe.co.uk
Key Personnel
Chief Executive: Ralph Bell
Production Dir: Mike Bando
Technical Dir: Andy Burns
Founded: 1983
Turnaround: 20 Workdays
Print Runs: 50 min - 2,000 max
Business from Other Countries: 2%

Scottish Braille Press
Craigmillar Park, Edinburgh EH16 5NB
Tel: (0131) 662 4445 *Fax:* (0131) 662 1968
E-mail: enquiries@scottish-braille.press.org
Web Site: www.scottish-braille-press.org
Key Personnel
Manager: John Donaldson *E-mail:* john.donaldson@scottish-braille-press.org
Sales & Marketing Manager: Stewart Connell
   E-mail: stewart.connell@dial.pipex.com
Founded: 1891
Turnaround: 15-20 Workdays
Parent Company: Royal Blind Asylum & School

Society of Authors
84 Drayton Gardens, London SW10 9SB
Tel: (020) 7373 6642 *Fax:* (020) 7373 5768
E-mail: info@societyofauthors.org
Web Site: www.societyofauthors.org/prizes.htm
Key Personnel
General Secretary: Mark Le Fanu
Founded: 1884

M & A Thomson Litho Ltd
Kelvin Industrial Estate, 2-16 Colvilles Pl, East Kilbride, Glasgow G75 0SN
Tel: (01355) 233081 *Fax:* (01355) 245 039
E-mail: enquiries@thomsonlitho.com
Web Site: www.thomsonlitho.com
Key Personnel
Contact: Ken Thomson
Deputy Chairman: Gary Thomson

TJ International Ltd
Subsidiary of Ulverscroft Large Print Books
Trecerus Industrial Estate, Padstow, Cornwall PL28 8RW
Tel: (01841) 532691 *Fax:* (01841) 532862
E-mail: sales@tjinternational.ltd.uk
Web Site: www.tjinternational.ltd.uk
Key Personnel
Chief Executive Officer: Angus Clark
   E-mail: angus@tjinternational.ltd.uk
Founded: 1970
Turnaround: 15 Workdays
Business from Other Countries: 5%

Toppan Printing Co (UK) Ltd
Subsidiary of Toppan Printing Co Ltd
Gillingham House, 38-44 Gillingham St, London SW1V 1HU
Tel: (020) 7828 7292; (020) 7828 7296
   Fax: (020) 7828 5210
E-mail: kawamura@toppan.co.uk; info.e@toppan.co.jp
Web Site: www.toppan.co.jp

Key Personnel
President: Mr K Jo
Manager: Mr P Harty
Founded: 1983

UK Serials Group-UKSG
The Old Brewery, Priory Lane, Burford, Oxon OX18 4SG
Tel: (01635) 254292 *Fax:* (01635) 253826
E-mail: uksg.admin@dial.pipex.com
Web Site: www.uksg.org
Key Personnel
Business Manager: Alison Whitehorn
Founded: 1978

UKSG, see UK Serials Group-UKSG

United Kingdom Serials Group, see UK Serials Group-UKSG

Vista Computer Services Ltd
Link House, 19 Colonial Way, Watford, Herts WD24 4JL
Tel: (01923) 830200 *Fax:* (01923) 238789
E-mail: solutions@vistacomp.com
Web Site: www.vistacomp.com
Key Personnel
Chairman: Denis Bennett
Man Dir: Colin Bottle
Marketing Manager: Marlyn Daniels
Founded: 1977
Business from Other Countries: 50%
Associate Companies: Vista Computer Services Inc, 80 Cottontail Lane, 4th floor, Somerset, NJ 08873, United States *Tel:* 732-563-9292 *Fax:* 732-563-9044; Vista Computer Services Pty, 5 Alexander St, Crows Nest, Sydney, NSW 2065, Australia *Tel:* (02) 9906 1222 *Fax:* (02) 9906 1441

Watkiss Automation Ltd
Subsidiary of The Watkiss Group
Watkiss House, Blaydon Rd, Middlefield Industrial Estate, Sandy, Beds SG19 1RZ
Tel: (01767) 682177 *Fax:* (01767) 691769
E-mail: info@watkiss.com; contact@watkiss.com
Web Site: www.watkiss.com
Key Personnel
Technical Dir: M Watkiss
Contact: Jo Watkiss
Founded: 1959
Print Runs: 200 min - 10,000 max
Business from Other Countries: 5%

The Word Factory
Syntax House, PO Box 186, Nottingham NG11 6DU
Tel: (0115) 914 5654 *Fax:* (0115) 914 5675
E-mail: info@thewordfactory.co.uk
Web Site: www.thewordfactory.co.uk
Key Personnel
Contact: Rory Baxter *E-mail:* roryb@thewordfactory.co.uk

Zoe Books Ltd
15 Worthy Lane, Winchester, Hants SO23 7AB
Tel: (01962) 851318 *Fax:* (01962) 843015
E-mail: enquiries@zoebooks.co.uk
Web Site: www.zoebooks.co.uk
Key Personnel
Man Dir: Imogen Dawson *E-mail:* imogen@easynet.co.uk
Founded: 1990
Business from Other Countries: 75%

United States

A-R Editions Inc
8551 Research Way, Suite 180, Middleton, WI 53562
Tel: 608-836-9000 *Toll Free Tel:* 800-736-0070 (US book orders only) *Fax:* 608-831-8200
E-mail: info@areditions.com
Web Site: www.areditions.com
Key Personnel
Pres & CEO: Patrick Wall
Dir, Sales & Mktg: James L Zychowicz
   E-mail: james.zychowicz@areditions.com
Founded: 1962
Business from Other Countries: 10%

ADR/BookPrint Inc
2012 Northern Ave E, Wichita, KS 67216
Tel: 316-522-5599 *Toll Free Tel:* 800-767-6066
   Fax: 316-522-5445
E-mail: info@adrbookprint.com
Web Site: www.adrbookprint.com
Key Personnel
Pres: James E Rishel; Grace M Rishel
   E-mail: grace@adrbookprint.com
Prodn Mgr: Marc Seiwert
Founded: 1978
Print Runs: 50 min - 25,000 max
Business from Other Countries: 10%
Membership(s): DMIA; Printing Industries of America

American Pizzi Offset Corp
Subsidiary of Arti Grafiche Amilcare Pizzi (Milan)
370 Lexington Ave, Suite 1505, New York, NY 10017
Tel: 212-986-1658 *Fax:* 212-286-1887
E-mail: info@americanpizzi.com
Key Personnel
Pres: Massimo Pizzi
Sales Mgr, New York: Barbara Sadick
Sales Mgr, Italy: Elena Gaiardelli
Founded: 1914
Business from Other Countries: 50%

Asia Pacific Offset Inc
1332 Corcoran St NW, Suite 6, Washington, DC 20009
Tel: 202-462-5436 *Toll Free Tel:* 800-756-4344
   Fax: 202-986-4030
Web Site: www.asiapacificoffset.com
Key Personnel
Pres: Andrew Clarke *E-mail:* andrew@asiapacificoffset.com
Dir, Sales (NY Office): Timothy Linn
   Tel: 212-941-8300 *Fax:* 212-941-9810
   E-mail: timothy@asiapacificoffset.com
Founded: 1997
Turnaround: 104 Workdays including color separation & shipping
Print Runs: 2,000 min
Business from Other Countries: 100%
Branch Office(s)
Phoenix Offset, Unit F1-2 2nd fl, Yeung Yiu Chung No 8 Industrial Bldg, 20 Wang Hoi Rd, Kowloon Bay, Hong Kong, Contact: Edmond Chan *Tel:* 2751-9962 *Fax:* 2755-8408 *E-mail:* edmond.chan@phoenixoffset.com
Sales Office(s): 270 Lafayette St, Suite 502, New York, NY 10012, Timothy Linn *Tel:* 212-941-8300 *Fax:* 212-941-9810 *E-mail:* timothy@asiapacificoffset.com *Web Site:* www.asiapacificoffset.com
870 Market St, Suite 801, San Francisco, CA 94102, Dir, Sales: Amy Armstrong *Tel:* 415-433-3488 *Fax:* 415-433-3489 *E-mail:* amy@asiapacificoffset.com *Web Site:* www.asiapacificoffset.com

UNITED STATES

BookBuilders New York Inc
353 Strawtown Rd, New City, NY 10956
Tel: 845-639-5316 *Fax:* 845-639-5318
Web Site: www.mcabooks.com
Key Personnel
Pres: Martin Cook *E-mail:* martin@mcabooks.com
Founded: 1977
Turnaround: 30-45 Workdays
Print Runs: 2,000 min - 500,000 max
Business from Other Countries: 60%

C & C Offset Printing Co Ltd
Subsidiary of C & C Joint Printing Co (HK) Ltd under Sino United Publishing (Holdings) Ltd
2632 SE 25 Ave, Suite E, Portland, OR 97202
Mailing Address: PO Box 82037, Portland, OR 97282-0037
Tel: 503-233-1834 *Fax:* 503-233-7815
E-mail: portlandinfo@ccoffset.com
Web Site: www.ccoffset.com
Key Personnel
Dir & Gen Mgr, Hong Kong Head Off: Jackson Leung
Deputy Man Dir, Hong Kong Head Office: Ken Lee
Deputy Gen Mgr, Hong Kong Head Office: Ivy Lam
Sr Sales Mgr, Hong Kong Head Office: Francis Ho
Dir, C & C Offset Printing Co (USA) Inc, Portland, OR, USA: Charles H Clark, IV *E-mail:* cclark@ccoffset.com
Devt Mgr, C & C Offset Printing Co (USA) Inc, Portland, OR, USA: Jenny Whittier *E-mail:* jwhittier@ccoffset.com
Cust Serv Mgr, C & C Offset Printing Co (USA) Inc, Portland, OR, USA: Ernest Li *E-mail:* ernestli@ccoffset.com
Dir & Exec VP, C & C Offset Printing Co (NYC) Inc, New York, NY, USA: Simon Chan *E-mail:* schan@ccoffset.com
Cust Serv Mgr, C & C Offset Printing Co (NY): Frances Harkness *E-mail:* fharkness@ccoffset.com
Pres, C & C Offset Japan Printing Co Ltd, Tokyo, Japan: Yamamoto Masaaki
Man Dir, C & C Joint Printing Co (Beijing) Ltd, Beijing, China: Zhang Lin Gui
Dir, C & C Offset Printing Co (UK) Ltd: Tracy Broderick
Acct Mgr, C & C Offset Printing Co (UK), Ltd: Fia Fornari
Founded: 1980
Turnaround: varies
Print Runs: 2,000 min - 1,000,000 max
Business from Other Countries: 70%
Branch Office(s)
C & C Printing Co (NY) Inc, 401 Broadway, Suite 2015, New York, NY 10013-3005 *Tel:* 212-431-4210 *Fax:* 212-431-3960 *E-mail:* newyorkinfo@ccoffset.com (New York City office)
C & C Joint Printing Co (Guangdong) Ltd, Intercontinental Bldg, Rm 706, 16 An Wai An De Rd, DongCheng District, Beijing 100011, China, Contact: Mr Xiao Mungshen *Tel:* (010) 6650 3175 *Fax:* (010) 6650 3175 *E-mail:* beijing@candcprinting.com (regional office)
C & C Joint Printing Co (Beijing) Ltd, Beijing Economic & Technological Developent Area (BDA), No 3, Donghuan North Rd, Beijing 100176, China, Contact: Mr Zhang Lin Gui *Tel:* (010) 678 6655 *Fax:* (010) 678 8255 *E-mail:* ccbj@candcprinting.com
C & C Bldg, 36 Ting Lai Rd, Tai Po, New Territories, Hong Kong *Tel:* 2666-4988 *Fax:* 2666-4938 *E-mail:* offsetprinting@candcprinting.com (corporate headquarters)
C & C Joint Printing Co (Guangdong) Ltd (Changsha Office), The Building of Changsha City, Commercial Bank, No 1, Frong Middle Rd, Rm 1218, Changsha, Hunan 41005, China, Contact: Ms Chen Jian *Tel:* (0731) 225 0288 *Fax:* (0731) 225 0178 *E-mail:* changsha@candcprinting.com (regional office)
C & C Offset Printing Co (Guangdong) Ltd, Fang Fa Bldg, No 29, Rm 304, 165 Dongzhu Anbin Rd, Shanghai 200050, China, Contact: Ms Wu Xiaohung *Tel:* (021) 6240 1305 *Fax:* (021) 6240 2090 *E-mail:* shanghai@candcprinting.com (regional office)
C & C Joint Printing Co (Guangdong) Ltd, Chunhu Industrial Estate, Pinghu, Long Gang, Shenzhen 518111, China *Tel:* (0755) 845 8333 *Fax:* (0755) 845 9111 *E-mail:* guangdong@candcprinting.com (plant)
C & C Printing Japan Co Ltd, Tozaido Bldg, 3F, 2-6-12 Hitotsubashi, Chiyoda-ku, Tokyo 101-0003, Japan, Contact: Mr Yamamoto Masaaki *Tel:* (03) 5216 4580 *Fax:* (03) 5216-4610 *E-mail:* mail@candcprinting.co.jp *Web Site:* www.candcprinting.co.jp (regional office)
C & C Joint Printing Co (Guangdong) Ltd (Xian Office), 10 Xuanfengquiao, Jianguo Rd, Xian 710001, China *Tel:* (029) 741 8407 *Fax:* (029) 743 5730 *E-mail:* xian@candcprinting.co (regional office)
C & C Joint Printing Co (Guangdong) Ltd, Hua Xin Bldg E Block, Rm 1511, 2 Shuiyin Rd, Huanshi East, Guangzhou 510075, China, Contact: Mr Peng Ji Shan *Tel:* (020) 3760 0979; (020) 3760 0980 *Fax:* (020) 3760 0977 *E-mail:* guangzhou@candcprinting.com (regional office)
C & C Offset Printing Co (UK) Ltd, 2 New Burlington St, 4th fl, London W1S 2JE, United Kingdom *Tel:* (020) 7287-7787 *Fax:* (020) 7287-7187 *E-mail:* tracy@candcoffset.co.uk

Codra Enterprises Inc
5912 Bolsa Ave, Suite 200, Huntington Beach, CA 92649
Tel: 714-891-5652 *Fax:* 714-891-5642
E-mail: codra@codra.com; sales@codra.com
Web Site: www.codra.com
Key Personnel
Gen Mgr: Jay Kim *E-mail:* jaykim@codra.com
Sales: Chris Sanatar *E-mail:* chriss@codra.com
Founded: 1985
Turnaround: 4-6 Weeks
Print Runs: 5,000 min
Business from Other Countries: 10%
Membership(s): Independent Publishers Association; Pacific Northwest Booksellers Association; Publishers Association of the West

Colorprint Offset Inc
Division of Colorprint Offset (Hong Kong)
80 Park Ave, Suite 10N, New York, NY 10016
Tel: 212-681-9400 *Fax:* 212-681-9362
Key Personnel
Pres: Lee Moncho *E-mail:* lee@colorprintoffset.com
Prod Dir & Cust Serv Mgr: Kate Brady *E-mail:* kate@colorprintoffset.com
Founded: 1986
Turnaround: 15 Workdays
Print Runs: 100 min - 50,000 max
Business from Other Countries: 65%

Coneco Litho Graphics
Division of NET 2 PRESS Inc
58 Dix Ave, Glens Falls, NY 12801
Mailing Address: PO Box 3255, Glen Falls, NY 12801-7255
Tel: 518-793-3823 *Fax:* 518-793-5823
Web Site: www.conecolithographics.com
Key Personnel
Gen Mgr: Steve Webber *E-mail:* swebber@conecolithographics.com
Client Servs Mgr: George Moses *E-mail:* gmoses@conecolithographics.com
Founded: 1984
Turnaround: 15 Workdays
Print Runs: 250 min - 25,000 max
Business from Other Countries: 27%

Consolidated Printers Inc
2630 Eighth St, Berkeley, CA 94710
Tel: 510-843-8524; 510-843-8565 *Fax:* 510-486-0580
E-mail: cpi@consoprinters.com
Web Site: www.consoprinters.com
Key Personnel
CEO: Lawrence A Hawkins
Founded: 1952
Turnaround: 2-20 Workdays
Print Runs: 2,000 min - 500,000 max
Business from Other Countries: 15%

Martin Cook Associates Ltd
353 Strawtown Rd, New City, NY 10956
Tel: 845-639-5316 *Fax:* 845-639-5318
E-mail: mcanewcity@aol.com
Web Site: www.mcabooks.com
Key Personnel
Pres: Martin Cook *E-mail:* mcanewcity@aol.com
Founded: 1977
Turnaround: 30-45 Workdays
Print Runs: 2,000 min - 500,000 max
Business from Other Countries: 15%

CS Graphics USA Inc
Subsidiary of CS Graphics Pte Ltd Singapore
8969 Lake Ct, Granite Bay, CA 95746
Tel: 916-791-9066 *Fax:* 916-791-9112
Key Personnel
Mgr, Sales & Mktg: Rick Marment *E-mail:* r.marment@csgraphics-world.com
Founded: 1980
Turnaround: 80 Workdays
Print Runs: 1,000 min - 75,000 max
Business from Other Countries: 30%

DNP America LLC
Subsidiary of Dai Nippon Printing Co Ltd
335 Madison Ave, 3rd fl, New York, NY 10017
Tel: 212-687-2746; 212-503-1060 *Fax:* 212-286-1505
Web Site: www.dnp.co.jp/ *Cable:* DAIPRINTS NY
Key Personnel
Pres: Yoji Yamakawa
VP & Gen Mgr, Graphic Printing: Kohei Tsumori *E-mail:* tsumori-k@mail.dnp.co.jp
Founded: 1974
Print Runs: 1,000 min
Business from Other Countries: 54%

Elegance Printing & Book Binding (USA)
Member of The Elegance Printing Group
708 Glen Cove Ave, Glen Head, NY 11545
Tel: 516-676-5941 *Fax:* 516-676-5973
Web Site: www.elegancebooks.com
Key Personnel
Man Dir: Frank DeLuca *E-mail:* frank@elegancebooks.com
Founded: 1977
Turnaround: Reprints ship within 14 days. New bks artwork to press within 2 wks-ship within 30 days
Print Runs: 1,000 min - 1,000,000 max
Business from Other Countries: 40%

Express Media Corp
1419 Donelson Pike, Nashville, TN 37217
Tel: 615-360-6400 *Toll Free Tel:* 888-EXPMEDIA (397-6342) *Fax:* 615-360-3140
E-mail: info@expressmedia.com
Web Site: www.expressmedia.com
Key Personnel
Pres: Andrew Cameron
Exec VP: Andrew S Cameron *E-mail:* ascameron@expressmedia.com

MANUFACTURING
UNITED STATES

Founded: 1996
Turnaround: 3 Workdays
Print Runs: 1 min - 10,000 max
Business from Other Countries: 10%

Hamilton Printing Co
22 Hamilton Way, Castleton-on-Hudson, NY 12033
Tel: 518-732-4491 *Toll Free Tel:* 800-242-4222 *Fax:* 518-732-7714
Key Personnel
Pres: Brian F Payne
VP, Fin: Michael H Hart
VP, Mfg: Rick Dunn
Prod Mgr: Judy Rappold
Sales Rep: Stephen H Feuer; Scott Payne; Larry Ritchie; Michael C Rosenhack *E-mail:* miker@hpcbook.com
Founded: 1912
Turnaround: Flexible, time-sensitive scheduling
Business from Other Countries: 10%
Membership(s): BMI

Hindy's Enterprise
Division of Jinno International
3 Christine Dr, Chestnut Ridge, NY 10977-6802
Tel: 845-735-4666 *Fax:* 617-344-5905
Key Personnel
Pres: Yoh Jinno *E-mail:* jinno@hotmail.com
Founded: 1989
Turnaround: 40 Workdays
Print Runs: 500 min - 2,000,000 max
Business from Other Countries: 70%
Branch Office(s)
Melbourne Industrial Bldg, Block A, 20th fl, 16 Westlands Rd, Quarry Bay, Hong Kong *Tel:* 25166318 *Fax:* 25165161

IBT Global Ltd, see Integrated Book Technology Inc

Imago
1431 Broadway, Penthouse, New York, NY 10018
Tel: 212-921-4411 *Fax:* 212-921-8226
E-mail: sales@imagousa.com
Web Site: www.imagousa.com
Key Personnel
Pres: Joseph E Braff *E-mail:* jbraff@imagousa.com
Northeast Sales: Linda Readerman *E-mail:* lreaderman@imagousa.com
USA Prodn Dir: Howard R Musk *E-mail:* hmusk@imagousa.com
Founded: 1985
Turnaround: 14 Workdays for color separations; 6 Weeks for printing & binding
Print Runs: 5,000 min
Business from Other Countries: 100%
Branch Office(s)
Imago West Coast, 31952 Camino Capistrano, Suite C22, San Juan Capistrano, CA 92675, West Coast Sales: Greg Lee *Tel:* 949-661-5998 *Fax:* 949-661-8013 *E-mail:* glee@imagousa.com
Imago Midwest, 17 N Loomis St, Unit 4A, Chicago, IL 60607, Midwest Sales: Ma Yan *Tel:* 312-829-4051 *Fax:* 312-829-4059 *E-mail:* myan@imagousa.com
Imago Australia, 14 Brown St, Suite 241, Chatswood, Sydney 2067, Australia, Contact: Emma Bell *Tel:* (02) 9415 2713 *Fax:* (02) 9415 2714 *E-mail:* sales@imagoaus.com
Imago France, 6 eme Etage, 42, rue le Peletier, 75009 Paris, France, Contact: Matt Critchlow *Tel:* (1) 42 81 41 24 *Fax:* (1) 42 81 41 24 *E-mail:* sales@imagogroup.com
Imago Services (HKG) Ltd, 653-659 Kings Rd, 6th fl, Flat B, North Point, Hong Kong, Contact: Kendrick Cheung *Tel:* 2811 3316 *Fax:* 2597 5256 *E-mail:* enquiries@imago.com.hk

Imago Productions (FE) Pte Ltd, MacPherson Industrial Complex, Suite 05-01, 5 Lorong Bakar Batu, Singapore 348742, Singapore, Contact: K C Ng *Tel:* 6748 4433 *Fax:* 6748 6082 *E-mail:* enquiries@imago.com.sg
Imago (UK/Europe) Publishing Ltd, Albury Ct, Albury Thame, Oxfordshire OX9 2LP, United Kingdom, Contact: Colin Risk *Tel:* (01844) 337000 *Fax:* (01844) 339935 *E-mail:* sales@imago.co.uk *Web Site:* www.imago.co.uk

Integrated Book Technology Inc
Subsidiary of The IBT Group
18 Industrial Park Rd, Troy, NY 12180
Tel: 518-271-5117 *Fax:* 518-266-9422
E-mail: mail@integratedbook.com
Web Site: www.integratedbook.com
Key Personnel
CEO & Pres: John R Paeglow *E-mail:* johnp@integratedbook.com
VP & Chief Technol Officer: William Clockel *E-mail:* billc@integratedbook.com
VP, Sales & Mktg: Robert Lindberg *E-mail:* bobl@integratedbook.com
Dir, Sales & Cust Serv: Karen Lombardo
Dir, Info Technol: Michael Whalen *E-mail:* mikew@integratedbook.com
Regl Sales: Tim Knickerbocker *E-mail:* timk@integratedbook.com
Founded: 1991
Turnaround: 1-15 Workdays
Print Runs: 10 min - 2,500 max
Business from Other Countries: 20%
Branch Office(s)
The IBT Global Ltd, 2 Finsbury Park Rd, London N4-2JZ, United Kingdom, Intl Strategist: Peter Kenyon *Tel:* (020) 7354 3332 *Fax:* (020) 73543332
Membership(s): BMI

Jinno International Group
3 Christine Dr, Chestnut Ridge, NY 10977-6802
Tel: 845-735-4666 *Fax:* 617-344-5905
E-mail: jinno@hotmail.com
Key Personnel
Pres: Yoh Jinno
VP: Sharon Jinno
Founded: 1989
Turnaround: 21-30 Workdays US, 45-75 Workdays overseas
Print Runs: 500 min - 3,000,000 max
Business from Other Countries: 98%
Branch Office(s)
Hindy's Enterprise, Melbourne Industrial Bldg, 16 Westlands Rd, Block A, 20th fl, Quarry Bay, Hong Kong *Tel:* 516-6318 *Fax:* 516-5161
Wing Yiu Printing Co, Melbourne Industrial Bldg, 6th fl, Block A, 16 Westlands Rd, Quarry Bay, Hong Kong, Contact: Law Ming Wah *Tel:* 561 0283 *Fax:* 565 8233
c/o Eurasia Press Pte Ltd, 10/14 Kampong Ampat, Singapore 1336, Singapore, Contact: Allan Fong *Tel:* 280 5522 *Fax:* 280 0593
Jinno International Singapore, 710 Ang Mo Kio, Ave 8, Suite 07-2615, Singapore 2056, Singapore *Tel:* 458 0778

KNI Inc
1261 S State College Pkwy, Anaheim, CA 92806
Tel: 714-956-7300 *Toll Free Tel:* 800-886-7301 *Fax:* 714-635-1744
E-mail: kni@kniinc.com
Web Site: www.kniinc.com
Key Personnel
Pres: Jeremy R Bernstein
VP, Sales: Peggy Bryant
VP & Cont: Dan Jacintho
Founded: 1970
Print Runs: 50 min - 100,000 max
Business from Other Countries: 17%

Leo Paper USA
1180 NW Maple St, Suite 102, Issaquah, WA 98027
Tel: 425-646-8801 *Fax:* 425-646-8805
E-mail: leo@leousa.com; sales@leousa.com
Web Site: www.leousa.com
Key Personnel
VP: Peter R Gillies *E-mail:* peter@leousa.com
Sales: Tom Leach *E-mail:* tom@leousa.com; Greg Witt *E-mail:* greg@leousa.com
Founded: 1982
Turnaround: 90 Workdays
Print Runs: 3,500 min - 2,000,000 max
Business from Other Countries: 20%
Branch Office(s)
27 W 24 St, Suite 701, New York, NY 10010-3204, Contact: Jeanine Laborne *Tel:* 917-305-0708 *Fax:* 917-305-0709 *E-mail:* sales@leoausanewyork.com

LK Litho
Division of The Linick Group Inc
Linick Bldg, 7 Putter Lane, Middle Island, NY 11953
Mailing Address: PO Box 102, Middle Island, NY 11953-0102
Tel: 631-924-3888
E-mail: linickgrp@att.net
Web Site: www.lgroup.addr.com
Key Personnel
VP: Roger Dextor
Founded: 1968
Turnaround: 10 Workdays
Print Runs: 2,500 min - 2,000,000 max
Business from Other Countries: 20%

Marrakech Express Inc
720 Wesley Ave, No 10, Tarpon Springs, FL 34689
Tel: 727-942-2218 *Toll Free Tel:* 800-940-6566 *Fax:* 727-937-4758
E-mail: print@marrak.com
Web Site: www.marrak.com
Key Personnel
CEO: Peter Henzell
Prodn Mgr: Steen Sigmund
Sales/Estimator: Shirley Copperman
Founded: 1976
Turnaround: 10 days
Print Runs: 500 min - 25,000 max
Business from Other Countries: 12%

Mazer Publishing Services
Division of The Mazer Corporation
6680 Poe Ave, Dayton, OH 45414
Tel: 937-264-2600 *Fax:* 937-264-2624
E-mail: info@mazer.com
Web Site: www.mazer.com
Key Personnel
Pres: William Franklin *E-mail:* bill_franklin@mazer.com
Exec VP: Ken Fultz *E-mail:* ken_fultz@mazer.com
VP & Gen Mgr, Creative Servs: Bill Scroggie
Exec Dir, Sales: Bill Faber *Fax:* 937-264-2622 *E-mail:* bill_faber@mazer.com
Founded: 1964
Print Runs: 50 min - 25,000 max
Business from Other Countries: 10%
Branch Office(s)
2460 Sand Lake Rd, Orlando, FL 32809, Contact: Brian Blakley *Tel:* 407-859-5552 *Fax:* 407-859-0643 *E-mail:* brian_blakley@mazer.com
224 Lexington Ave, Fox River Grove, IL 60021, Contact: Dennis Bowman *Tel:* 847-639-1555 *Fax:* 847-639-1562 *E-mail:* dennis_bowman@mazer.com
22 Lehigh Rd, Wellesley, MA 02181, Contact: Ken Leahy *Tel:* 781-237-4112 *Fax:* 781-431-6184 *E-mail:* ken_leahy@mazer.com
22 Laurel Place, Upper Montclair, NJ 07043 *Tel:* 973-744-4320 *Fax:* 973-746-5608 *E-mail:* john_martel@mazer.com

URUGUAY

3081 Glenmere Ct, Kettering, OH 45440, Contact: Mark Brewer *Tel:* 937-299-5746 *Fax:* 937-299-5761 *E-mail:* mark_brewer@mazer.com
363 Porter Rd, Bishop, TX 78602,
  Contact: Deborah VanLandingham
  Tel: 512-303-9758 *Fax:* 513-303-9791
  E-mail: deborah_vanlandingham@mazer.com
Membership(s): BMI

Milanostampa/New Interlitho USA Inc
Subsidiary of Milanostampa New Interlitho Italia SpA
299 Broadway, Suite 901, New York, NY 10007
Tel: 212-964-2430 *Fax:* 212-964-2497
Web Site: www.milanostampa.com
Key Personnel
Chmn & Sales Rep: Rino Varrasso *Tel:* 917-225-9460 *E-mail:* rvarrasso@milanostampa-usa.com
Founded: 1998
Turnaround: 30 Workdays
Print Runs: 1,000 min - 3,000,000 max
Business from Other Countries: 75%

Overseas Printing Corporation
99 The Embarcadero, San Francisco, CA 94105
Tel: 415-835-9999 *Fax:* 415-835-9899
Web Site: www.overseasprinting.com
Key Personnel
Pres: Hal Belmont *E-mail:* hal@overseasprinting.com
VP: Vito Badalamenti *E-mail:* vito@overseasprinting.com
Founded: 1972
Turnaround: 8 - 12 Weeks, or shorter depending on job requirements
Business from Other Countries: 10%

Palace Press International - Corporate Headquarters
17 Paul Dr, San Rafael, CA 94903
Tel: 415-526-1370 *Fax:* 415-526-1394
E-mail: info@palacepress.com
Web Site: www.palacepress.com
Key Personnel
CEO: Raoul Goff *E-mail:* raoul@palacepress.com
Dir, Intl Sales & Mktg: Gordon Goff
  E-mail: gordon@palacepress.com
Gen Mgr: Steve Schneiderman
  E-mail: sschneiderman@palacepress.com
Founded: 1984
Turnaround: 90 Workdays
Print Runs: 3,000 min - 1,000,000 max
Business from Other Countries: 20%
Branch Office(s)
Palace Press International Los Angeles, 303 W Newby Ave, Suite C, San Gabriel, CA 91777, Contact: Roger Ma *Tel:* 626-282-8877 *Fax:* 626-282-6880 *E-mail:* roger@palacepress.com
Palace Press International New York, 180 Varick St, 10th fl, New York, NY 10014, Contact: Jessica Jones *Tel:* 212-462-2622 *Fax:* 212-463-9130 *E-mail:* jessica@palacepress.com

Pioneer Graphic Scanning
Division of Jinno International
3 Christine Dr, Chestnut Ridge, NY 10977-6802
Tel: 845-735-4666 *Fax:* 617-344-5905
Key Personnel
Pres: Yoh Jinno *E-mail:* jinno@hotmail.com
Mktg Dir: Stewart Sum
Founded: 1989
Turnaround: 10-60 Workdays
Print Runs: 500 min - 3,000,000 max
Business from Other Countries: 95%

Printing Corp of the Americas Inc
620 SW 12 Ave, Fort Lauderdale, FL 33312
Tel: 954-781-8100 *Fax:* 954-781-8421
E-mail: pcaprint@bellsouth.net
Web Site: www.pcaprint.bellsouth.net
Key Personnel
Pres: Jan Tuchman
Founded: 1979
Turnaround: 5-10 Workdays
Print Runs: 500 min - 100,000 max
Business from Other Countries: 10%

Regent Publishing Services
9327 Rambler Dr, St Louis, MO 63123
Tel: 314-631-7581 *Fax:* 314-638-5113
E-mail: regentstl@aol.com
Key Personnel
Sales Dir: Carol Davis-Tierney
Mktg Dir: James J Tierney
Founded: 1985
Turnaround: 3-4 Months
Print Runs: 2,000 min - 100,000 max
Business from Other Countries: 100%

Taylor Publishing Company
1550 W Mockingbird Lane, Dallas, TX 75235
Tel: 214-819-8226 *Toll Free Tel:* 800-677-2800
  Fax: 214-630-1852
E-mail: info@taylorpub.com
Web Site: www.taylorpub.com
Key Personnel
CEO: Dave Fiore
Commercial Printing/Fine Books Div: Jay Love
Dir, Mktg: Mike Taylor
Founded: 1939
Turnaround: 45 Workdays
Print Runs: 300 min - 25,000 max
Business from Other Countries: 10%

Times Publishing Group
Division of Times Publishing Ltd/Singapore
99 White Plains Rd, Tarrytown, NY 10591
Tel: 914-366-9888 *Fax:* 914-366-9898
Web Site: www.tpl.com.sg
Key Personnel
Cust Serv Exec: Bonnie Stone *E-mail:* bstone@marshallcavendish.com
Sales Mgr: Suresh Kumar *E-mail:* skumar@marshallcavendish.com
Founded: 1965
Print Runs: 2,000 min - 500,000 max
Business from Other Countries: 90%

Toppan Printing Co America Inc
Subsidiary of Toppan Printing Co Ltd
650 Fifth Ave, 12th fl, New York, NY 10019
Tel: 212-489-7740 *Fax:* 212-246-3067
Web Site: www.ta.toppan.com
Key Personnel
Sr VP: John Lee
Gen Sales Mgr: Shinichi Ito
Founded: 1965
Turnaround: 3-5 Months
Business from Other Countries: 10%
Branch Office(s)
4551 Glencoe Ave, Suite 230, Marina del Rey, CA 90292, Sales Mgr: Yoshihei Okamoto *Tel:* 310-823-0050 *Fax:* 310-823-0777 *Web Site:* www.ta.toppan.com

Vicks Lithograph & Printing Corp
5166 Commercial Dr, Yorkville, NY 13495
Mailing Address: PO Box 270, Yorkville, NY 13495-0270
Tel: 315-736-9344 *Fax:* 315-736-1901
Web Site: www.vickslitho.com
Key Personnel
Chmn: Dwight E "Duke" Vicks, Jr
Pres: Dwight E Vicks, III
Sales: Mike Tracy *Tel:* 315-527-2059
  E-mail: mtracy@vickslitho.com; Brian Engle *Tel:* 315-527-8844 *E-mail:* bengle@vickslitho.com
Founded: 1918
Turnaround: 10-20 Workdays
Print Runs: 1,000 min - 100,000 max
Business from Other Countries: 10%
Membership(s): BMI; Printing Industries of America

Uruguay

Barreiro y Ramos SA
Juan Carlos Gomez, Montevideo 1430
Tel: (02) 986621 *Fax:* (02) 962358
Telex: 23901PB.CVJA.UY *Cable:* BAREIRAMOS
Key Personnel
President: Gaston Barreiro
Vice President: Guzman Barreiro
Founded: 1837
Print Runs: 1,000 min - 50,000 max
Business from Other Countries: 10%

Prepress Services Index

ART & DESIGN

Belgium
IMPF bvba, pg 1175
Drukkerij Lannoo NV, pg 1175

Canada
David Berman Developments Inc, pg 1175
Coach House Printing, pg 1175
Leanne Franson, pg 1175
Celia Godkin, pg 1175
Maracle Press Ltd, pg 1175
Preney Print & Litho Inc, pg 1175
PrintWest, pg 1175
David Shaw & Associates Ltd, pg 1176
Barbara Spurll Illustration, pg 1176
University of Toronto Press Inc, pg 1176

Germany
C L Baader Buch & Offsetdruckere GmbH & Co KG, pg 1176
Priese GmbH & Co, pg 1177
Topic Verlag GmbH, pg 1177

Hong Kong
Cristy's Atelier, pg 1177
Elegance Finance Printing Services Ltd, pg 1178
Golden Cup Printing Co Ltd, pg 1178
Mei Ka Printing & Publishing Enterprise Ltd, pg 1178
Prontaprint Asia Ltd, pg 1179
Sota Graphic Arts Co Ltd, pg 1179
Ying Tat Co, pg 1179

India
Paragon Prepress Inc, pg 1179

Indonesia
Ichtiar Baru I Van Hoeve, pg 1179
Victory Offset Prima PT, pg 1179

Ireland
ICPC Ltd, pg 1180
Smurfit Print, pg 1180
Ultragraphics, pg 1180

Israel
Har-El Printers & Publishers, pg 1180

Italy
Canale G e C SpA, pg 1180

Lithuania
Spindulys Printing House, pg 1180

New Zealand
Egan-Reid Ltd, pg 1181
PPP Printers Ltd, pg 1181
Rogan McIndoe Print Ltd, pg 1181

Puerto Rico
Publishing Resources Inc, pg 1181

Singapore
Craft Print Pte Ltd, pg 1181
SNP SPrint Pte Ltd, pg 1182
Stamford Press Pte Ltd, pg 1182
Times Graphics, pg 1182

Slovenia
Gorenjski Tisk Printing House, pg 1182

Spain
Graficas Santamaria SA, pg 1182

Sri Lanka
Sumathi Book Printing (Pvt) Ltd, pg 1182

United Republic of Tanzania
Peramiho Publications, pg 1182

Thailand
Phongwarin Printing Company Ltd, pg 1182

United Kingdom
BAS Printers Ltd, pg 1183
Baseline Creative Ltd, pg 1183
BCS Publishing Ltd, pg 1183
Black Bear Press Ltd, pg 1183
Book Creation, pg 1183
Book Production Consultants PLC, pg 1183
D Brown & Sons Ltd, pg 1183
Chase Publishing Services, pg 1184
Cooper Dale, pg 1184
Cradley Print Ltd, pg 1184
The Diagram Group, pg 1184
Edition, pg 1184
Fern House, pg 1184
Goldshield Communications Ltd, pg 1184
The Guernsey Press Co Ltd, pg 1184
Hammond Packaging Ltd, pg 1184
Holbrook Design, pg 1184
Ikon Document Management Services, pg 1184
Linden Artists Ltd, pg 1185
Multiplex Medway Ltd, pg 1185
Page Bros Ltd (Norwich), pg 1185
Severnside Printers Ltd, pg 1185
Watkiss Automation Ltd, pg 1185

United States
Alpina Color Graphics Inc, pg 1186
BookBuilders New York Inc, pg 1186
Coneco Litho Graphics, pg 1187
Martin Cook Associates Ltd, pg 1187
Custom Services, pg 1187
Desktop Miracles Inc, pg 1187
DNP America LLC, pg 1187
Editoriale Bortolazzi-Stei srl, pg 1187
The Font Bureau Inc, pg 1187
High Resolution Inc, pg 1187
Hindy's Enterprise, pg 1187
Integrated Book Technology Inc, pg 1188
ITC, pg 1188
Leo Paper USA, pg 1188
LK Litho, pg 1188
Mazer Publishing Services, pg 1188
Palace Press International - Corporate Headquarters, pg 1188
Photoengraving Inc, pg 1189
Pioneer Graphic Scanning, pg 1189
PrePress Imaging Inc, pg 1189
Quantum Colorgraphics, pg 1189
Sencor, pg 1189
SNP Best-Set Typesetter Ltd, pg 1189
SpectraComp, pg 1189
Square Two Design Inc, pg 1189
Studio 31, pg 1189
Fred Weidner & Daughter Printers, pg 1189

Uruguay
Barreiro y Ramos SA, pg 1189

COLOR SEPARATIONS

Austria
ADEVA (Akademische Druck-u Verlagsanstalt), pg 1175

Belgium
IMPF bvba, pg 1175
Drukkerij Lannoo NV, pg 1175

Canada
Coach House Printing, pg 1175
Maracle Press Ltd, pg 1175
Preney Print & Litho Inc, pg 1175
Printcrafters Inc, pg 1175
Schawk, pg 1175
Transcontinental Printing Book Group, pg 1176

Denmark
Bianco Lunos Bogtrykkeri AS, pg 1176

Finland
Gummerus Printing, pg 1176

Germany
Media-Print Informationstechnologie GmbH, pg 1176
MOHN Media, pg 1176
Priese GmbH & Co, pg 1177
Topic Verlag GmbH, pg 1177
Vier-Tuerme GmbH Benedikt Press, pg 1177

Hong Kong
Bookbuilders Ltd, pg 1177
Bright Arts Hong Kong Ltd, pg 1177
Bright Future Printing Co Ltd, pg 1177
C & C Offset Printing Co Ltd, pg 1177
Colorprint Offset, pg 1177
Dai Nippon Printing Co (Hong Kong) Ltd, pg 1177
Everbest Printing Co Ltd, pg 1178
Golden Cup Printing Co Ltd, pg 1178
The Green Pagoda Press Ltd, pg 1178
H K Scanner Arts International Ltd, pg 1178
Hindy's Enterprise Co Ltd, pg 1178
Hung Hing Off-set Printing Co Ltd, pg 1178
Image Printing Company Ltd, pg 1178
Leo Paper Products Ltd, pg 1178
Leo Reprographic Ltd, pg 1178
Midas Printing Ltd, pg 1178
New Arts Graphic Reproduction Co Ltd, pg 1178
Prontaprint Asia Ltd, pg 1179
Rainbow Graphic & Printing Co Ltd, pg 1179
SNP Best-Set Typesetter Ltd, pg 1179
Sota Graphic Arts Co Ltd, pg 1179
South Sea International Press Ltd, pg 1179
Sunshine Press Ltd, pg 1179
Toppan Printing Co (HK) Ltd, pg 1179
Wing King Tong Group, pg 1179
Ying Tat Co, pg 1179

India
Hiralal Printing Works Ltd, pg 1179

Indonesia
Victory Offset Prima PT, pg 1179

Ireland
Graphic Reproductions Ltd, pg 1179
Kilkenny People/Wellbrook Press, pg 1180
Ultragraphics, pg 1180

Israel
Har-El Printers & Publishers, pg 1180
Keterpress Enterprises Jerusalem, pg 1180
Monoline Ltd, pg 1180
Technosdar Ltd, pg 1180

Italy
Canale G e C SpA, pg 1180
Dedalo Litostampa SRL, pg 1180
Nuovo Instituto Italiano d'Arti Grafiche, pg 1180
Amilcare Pizzi SpA, pg 1180

Republic of Korea
Daehan Printing & Publishing Co Ltd, pg 1180
Pyunghwa Dang Printing Co Ltd, pg 1180

Lithuania
Spindulys Printing House, pg 1180

Netherlands
Bosch en Keuning grafische bedrijven, pg 1181

New Zealand
Rogan McIndoe Print Ltd, pg 1181

Portugal
Edicoes Silabo, pg 1181

Singapore

Chong Moh Offset Printing Ltd, pg 1181
Chroma Graphics (Overseas) Pte Ltd, pg 1181
Craft Print Pte Ltd, pg 1181
CS Graphics Pte Ltd, pg 1181
Eurasia Press Pte Ltd, pg 1181
Ho Printing Singapore Pte Ltd, pg 1181
Markono Print Media Pte Ltd, pg 1181
Pica Digital Pte Ltd, pg 1182
Sang Choy International Pte Ltd, pg 1182
SNP SPrint Pte Ltd, pg 1182
Stamford Press Pte Ltd, pg 1182
Times Graphics, pg 1182
Times Printers Pte Ltd, pg 1182

Slovenia

Gorenjski Tisk Printing House, pg 1182

Spain

Graficas Santamaria SA, pg 1182

Switzerland

Photolitho AG, pg 1182

United Republic of Tanzania

Peramiho Publications, pg 1182

United Kingdom

Adroit Birmingham Ltd, pg 1182
BAS Printers Ltd, pg 1183
The Bath Press, pg 1183
Book Creation, pg 1183
Book Production Consultants PLC, pg 1183
D Brown & Sons Ltd, pg 1183
Butler & Tanner Ltd, pg 1183
Chase Publishing Services, pg 1184
William Clowes Ltd, pg 1184
Cradley Print Ltd, pg 1184
Goldshield Communications Ltd, pg 1184
The Guernsey Press Co Ltd, pg 1184
Holbrook Design, pg 1184
Lowfield Printing Co Ltd, pg 1185

United States

Alpina Color Graphics Inc, pg 1186
Asia Pacific Offset Inc, pg 1186
Bang Printing Co Inc, pg 1186
Blaze International Productions Inc, pg 1186
BookBuilders New York Inc, pg 1186
C & C Offset Printing Co Ltd, pg 1186
Colorprint Offset Inc, pg 1187
Coneco Litho Graphics, pg 1187
Martin Cook Associates Ltd, pg 1187
CS Graphics USA Inc, pg 1187
Custom Services, pg 1187
DNP America LLC, pg 1187
Editoriale Bortolazzi-Stei srl, pg 1187
Elegance Printing & Book Binding (USA), pg 1187
High Resolution Inc, pg 1187
Hindy's Enterprise, pg 1187
Leo Paper USA, pg 1188
Linick International Inc, pg 1188
LK Litho, pg 1188
Milanostampa/New Interlitho USA Inc, pg 1188

Palace Press International - Corporate Headquarters, pg 1188
Photoengraving Inc, pg 1189
Pioneer Graphic Scanning, pg 1189
Prepare Inc, pg 1189
PrePress Imaging Inc, pg 1189
Printing Corp of the Americas Inc, pg 1189
Quantum Colorgraphics, pg 1189
Regent Publishing Services, pg 1189
SNP Best-Set Typesetter Ltd, pg 1189
SpectraComp, pg 1189
Times Publishing Group, pg 1189
Fred Weidner & Daughter Printers, pg 1189

Uruguay

Barreiro y Ramos SA, pg 1189

COMPUTERIZED TYPESETTING

Belgium

IMPF bvba, pg 1175
Drukkerij Lannoo NV, pg 1175

Canada

David Berman Developments Inc, pg 1175
Coach House Printing, pg 1175
Girol Books Inc, pg 1175
Maracle Press Ltd, pg 1175
Preney Print & Litho Inc, pg 1175
Transcontinental Printing Book Group, pg 1176
Tri-Graphic Printing (Ottawa) Ltd, pg 1176
University of Toronto Press Inc, pg 1176

Denmark

Bianco Lunos Bogtrykkeri AS, pg 1176

Finland

Gummerus Printing, pg 1176

France

Signes du Monde, pg 1176

Germany

C L Baader Buch & Offsetdruckere GmbH & Co KG, pg 1176
Fachhochschule Fur Druk, Studiengang Verlagswirtschaft und Verlagsherstellung, pg 1176
Hallwag Kuemmerly & Frey AG, pg 1176
C Maurer Druck und Verlag, pg 1176
Media-Print Informationstechnologie GmbH, pg 1176
MOHN Media, pg 1176
Oertel & Sporer GmbH & Co, pg 1176
Priese GmbH & Co, pg 1177
Vier-Tuerme GmbH Benedikt Press, pg 1177

Hong Kong

Bookbuilders Ltd, pg 1177
Caritas Printing Training Centre, pg 1177
Elegance Finance Printing Services Ltd, pg 1178
Golden Cup Printing Co Ltd, pg 1178

The Green Pagoda Press Ltd, pg 1178
Prontaprint Asia Ltd, pg 1179
SNP Best-Set Typesetter Ltd, pg 1179
Sota Graphic Arts Co Ltd, pg 1179
Sunshine Press Ltd, pg 1179
Ying Tat Co, pg 1179

India

Paragon Prepress Inc, pg 1179

Indonesia

Ichtiar Baru I Van Hoeve, pg 1179
Victory Offset Prima PT, pg 1179

Ireland

Doyle Graphics, pg 1179
ICPC Ltd, pg 1180
Smurfit Print, pg 1180

Israel

Keterpress Enterprises Jerusalem, pg 1180
Technosdar Ltd, pg 1180

Italy

Canale G e C SpA, pg 1180
Dedalo Litostampa SRL, pg 1180

Republic of Korea

Daehan Printing & Publishing Co Ltd, pg 1180

Lithuania

Spindulys Printing House, pg 1180

Madagascar

Societe Malgache d'Edition, pg 1181

New Zealand

Egan-Reid Ltd, pg 1181
Rogan McIndoe Print Ltd, pg 1181

Philippines

Naldoza Printers, pg 1181
Reyes Publishing Inc, pg 1181

Portugal

Edicoes Silabo, pg 1181

Puerto Rico

Publishing Resources Inc, pg 1181

Singapore

Chong Moh Offset Printing Ltd, pg 1181
Eurasia Press Pte Ltd, pg 1181
Markono Print Media Pte Ltd, pg 1181
SNP SPrint Pte Ltd, pg 1182
Stamford Press Pte Ltd, pg 1182
Times Graphics, pg 1182
Times Printers Pte Ltd, pg 1182

Slovenia

Gorenjski Tisk Printing House, pg 1182

United Republic of Tanzania

Peramiho Publications, pg 1182

Thailand

Phongwarin Printing Company Ltd, pg 1182

United Kingdom

The Alden Group Ltd, pg 1182
AlpnetCompuType Ltd, pg 1183
J W Arrowsmith Ltd, pg 1183
Associated Translation & Typesetting, pg 1183
W & G Baird Ltd, pg 1183
BAS Printers Ltd, pg 1183
Baseline Creative Ltd, pg 1183
Black Bear Press Ltd, pg 1183
Blackmore Ltd, pg 1183
Book Creation, pg 1183
Book Production Consultants PLC, pg 1183
Butler & Tanner Ltd, pg 1183
Cambridge University Press - Printing Division, pg 1183
Center Print Ltd, pg 1183
The Charlesworth Group, pg 1184
Chase Publishing Services, pg 1184
William Clowes Ltd, pg 1184
Edition, pg 1184
Goldshield Communications Ltd, pg 1184
Heyden & Son, pg 1184
Hobbs The Printers Ltd, pg 1184
Holbrook Design, pg 1184
Ikon Document Management Services, pg 1184
Intype Libra Ltd, pg 1185
Keytec Typesetting Ltd, pg 1185
Lowfield Printing Co Ltd, pg 1185
Maney Publishing, pg 1185
MPG Ltd, pg 1185
Page Bros Ltd (Norwich), pg 1185
Redwood Books Ltd, pg 1185
J R Reid Printing Group Ltd, pg 1185
Antony Rowe Ltd, pg 1185
Santype International Ltd, pg 1185
Severnside Printers Ltd, pg 1185
Thomas Technology Solutions (UK) Ltd, pg 1185
M & A Thomson Litho Ltd, pg 1185
Tradespools Ltd, pg 1185

United States

A-R Editions Inc, pg 1185
Alpina Color Graphics Inc, pg 1186
Any Photo Type, pg 1186
Bang Printing Co Inc, pg 1186
BookBuilders New York Inc, pg 1186
Coneco Litho Graphics, pg 1187
Martin Cook Associates Ltd, pg 1187
Custom Services, pg 1187
Datapage Technologies International Inc, pg 1187
Desktop Miracles Inc, pg 1187
Elegance Printing & Book Binding (USA), pg 1187
Fairfield Marketing Group Inc, pg 1187
Huron Valley Graphics Inc, pg 1187
ICSI Corp, pg 1188
Innodata Isogen Inc, pg 1188
ITC, pg 1188
Leo Paper USA, pg 1188
Linick International Inc, pg 1188
LK Litho, pg 1188
Mazer Publishing Services, pg 1188
Pageworks, pg 1188
Photoengraving Inc, pg 1189
Prepare Inc, pg 1189
PrePress Imaging Inc, pg 1189
Sencor, pg 1189
SNP Best-Set Typesetter Ltd, pg 1189
SpectraComp, pg 1189
Studio 31, pg 1189

MANUFACTURING

Taylor Publishing Company, pg 1189
Fred Weidner & Daughter Printers, pg 1189

Uruguay
Barreiro y Ramos SA, pg 1189

DATA PROCESSING SERVICES

Belgium
Drukkerij Lannoo NV, pg 1175

Canada
Maracle Press Ltd, pg 1175

Hong Kong
The Green Pagoda Press Ltd, pg 1178
SNP Best-Set Typesetter Ltd, pg 1179
Sota Graphic Arts Co Ltd, pg 1179

Italy
Canale G e C SpA, pg 1180

New Zealand
Egan-Reid Ltd, pg 1181

United States
Alpina Color Graphics Inc, pg 1186
Datapage Technologies International Inc, pg 1187
Express Media Corp, pg 1187
Fairfield Marketing Group Inc, pg 1187
Huron Valley Graphics Inc, pg 1187
Innodata Isogen Inc, pg 1188
ITC, pg 1188
Sencor, pg 1189
SNP Best-Set Typesetter Ltd, pg 1189

FOREIGN LANGUAGE COMPOSITION

Belgium
Drukkerij Lannoo NV, pg 1175

Canada
David Berman Developments Inc, pg 1175
Girol Books Inc, pg 1175
Maracle Press Ltd, pg 1175
University of Toronto Press Inc, pg 1176

Denmark
Bianco Lunos Bogtrykkeri AS, pg 1176

Finland
Gummerus Printing, pg 1176

Germany
C L Baader Buch & Offsetdruckere GmbH & Co KG, pg 1176
MOHN Media, pg 1176
Priese GmbH & Co, pg 1177

Hong Kong
The Green Pagoda Press Ltd, pg 1178
Prontaprint Asia Ltd, pg 1179
SNP Best-Set Typesetter Ltd, pg 1179
Sota Graphic Arts Co Ltd, pg 1179
Sunshine Press Ltd, pg 1179

Ireland
ICPC Ltd, pg 1180

Israel
Keterpress Enterprises Jerusalem, pg 1180
Technosdar Ltd, pg 1180

Italy
Canale G e C SpA, pg 1180
Dedalo Litostampa SRL, pg 1180

Republic of Korea
Daehan Printing & Publishing Co Ltd, pg 1180

Lithuania
Spindulys Printing House, pg 1180

New Zealand
Egan-Reid Ltd, pg 1181

Puerto Rico
Publishing Resources Inc, pg 1181

Singapore
Eurasia Press Pte Ltd, pg 1181
SNP SPrint Pte Ltd, pg 1182
Times Graphics, pg 1182

Slovenia
Gorenjski Tisk Printing House, pg 1182

South Africa
CTP Book Printers (Pty) Ltd, pg 1182

Spain
Graficas Santamaria SA, pg 1182

United Republic of Tanzania
Peramiho Publications, pg 1182

United Kingdom
AlpnetCompuType Ltd, pg 1183
ARADCO VSI Ltd, pg 1183
J W Arrowsmith Ltd, pg 1183
Associated Translation & Typesetting, pg 1183
Baseline Creative Ltd, pg 1183
Book Creation, pg 1183
Book Production Consultants PLC, pg 1183
D Brown & Sons Ltd, pg 1183
Cambridge University Press - Printing Division, pg 1183
The Charlesworth Group, pg 1184
Goldshield Communications Ltd, pg 1184
Ikon Document Management Services, pg 1184
Intype Libra Ltd, pg 1185
Maney Publishing, pg 1185
Multiplex Medway Ltd, pg 1185
Antony Rowe Ltd, pg 1185
Tradespools Ltd, pg 1185

United States
A-R Editions Inc, pg 1185
Alpina Color Graphics Inc, pg 1186
Any Photo Type, pg 1186

PREPRESS SERVICES INDEX

BookBuilders New York Inc, pg 1186
Custom Services, pg 1187
Datapage Technologies International Inc, pg 1187
Huron Valley Graphics Inc, pg 1187
ICSI Corp, pg 1188
Innodata Isogen Inc, pg 1188
Leo Paper USA, pg 1188
Palace Press International - Corporate Headquarters, pg 1188
Prepare Inc, pg 1189
PrePress Imaging Inc, pg 1189
Sencor, pg 1189
SNP Best-Set Typesetter Ltd, pg 1189
SpectraComp, pg 1189

Uruguay
Barreiro y Ramos SA, pg 1189

INDEXING

Belgium
Drukkerij Lannoo NV, pg 1175

Denmark
Bianco Lunos Bogtrykkeri AS, pg 1176

Germany
C L Baader Buch & Offsetdruckere GmbH & Co KG, pg 1176
Priese GmbH & Co, pg 1177
Topic Verlag GmbH, pg 1177

Hong Kong
Golden Cup Printing Co Ltd, pg 1178
Midas Printing Ltd, pg 1178
SNP Best-Set Typesetter Ltd, pg 1179
South Sea International Press Ltd, pg 1179

India
Paragon Prepress Inc, pg 1179

Indonesia
Ichtiar Baru I Van Hoeve, pg 1179

Ireland
ICPC Ltd, pg 1180

Italy
Canale G e C SpA, pg 1180

Republic of Korea
Daehan Printing & Publishing Co Ltd, pg 1180

New Zealand
Egan-Reid Ltd, pg 1181
Rogan McIndoe Print Ltd, pg 1181

Portugal
Edicoes Silabo, pg 1181

Singapore
SNP SPrint Pte Ltd, pg 1182

United Republic of Tanzania
Peramiho Publications, pg 1182

United Kingdom
Book Creation, pg 1183
Book Production Consultants PLC, pg 1183
Chase Publishing Services, pg 1184
William Clowes Ltd, pg 1184
Fern House, pg 1184
Goldshield Communications Ltd, pg 1184
Hobbs The Printers Ltd, pg 1184
Ikon Document Management Services, pg 1184

United States
A-R Editions Inc, pg 1185
BookBuilders New York Inc, pg 1186
Martin Cook Associates Ltd, pg 1187
Datapage Technologies International Inc, pg 1187
Desktop Miracles Inc, pg 1187
Elegance Printing & Book Binding (USA), pg 1187
Innodata Isogen Inc, pg 1188
Leo Paper USA, pg 1188
Linick International Inc, pg 1188
LK Litho, pg 1188
Sencor, pg 1189
SNP Best-Set Typesetter Ltd, pg 1189
SpectraComp, pg 1189
Fred Weidner & Daughter Printers, pg 1189

MATHEMATICS & CHEMISTRY COMPOSITION

Canada
University of Toronto Press Inc, pg 1176

Finland
Gummerus Printing, pg 1176

Hong Kong
Golden Cup Printing Co Ltd, pg 1178
SNP Best-Set Typesetter Ltd, pg 1179

Indonesia
Ichtiar Baru I Van Hoeve, pg 1179

Ireland
ICPC Ltd, pg 1180
SciPrint Ltd, pg 1180
Smurfit Print, pg 1180

Israel
Monoline Ltd, pg 1180
Technosdar Ltd, pg 1180

Italy
Canale G e C SpA, pg 1180

Republic of Korea
Daehan Printing & Publishing Co Ltd, pg 1180

Lithuania
Spindulys Printing House, pg 1180

New Zealand
Egan-Reid Ltd, pg 1181

1171

PREPRESS SERVICES INDEX — BOOK

Portugal
Edicoes Silabo, pg 1181

Singapore
Times Graphics, pg 1182

Slovenia
Gorenjski Tisk Printing House, pg 1182

United Kingdom
J W Arrowsmith Ltd, pg 1183
Baseline Creative Ltd, pg 1183
Book Production Consultants PLC, pg 1183
Cambridge University Press - Printing Division, pg 1183
The Charlesworth Group, pg 1184
Goldshield Communications Ltd, pg 1184
Hobbs The Printers Ltd, pg 1184
Keytec Typesetting Ltd, pg 1185
Antony Rowe Ltd, pg 1185
Santype International Ltd, pg 1185
Thomas Technology Solutions (UK) Ltd, pg 1185

United States
Datapage Technologies International Inc, pg 1187
Elegance Printing & Book Binding (USA), pg 1187
Huron Valley Graphics Inc, pg 1187
ICSI Corp, pg 1188
ITC, pg 1188
Leo Paper USA, pg 1188
Prepare Inc, pg 1189
Sencor, pg 1189
SNP Best-Set Typesetter Ltd, pg 1189

MUSIC COMPOSITION

Canada
University of Toronto Press Inc, pg 1176

Germany
C L Baader Buch & Offsetdruckere GmbH & Co KG, pg 1176

Hong Kong
Golden Cup Printing Co Ltd, pg 1178
Ying Tat Co, pg 1179

Lithuania
Spindulys Printing House, pg 1180

New Zealand
Egan-Reid Ltd, pg 1181

United Republic of Tanzania
Peramiho Publications, pg 1182

United Kingdom
Holbrook Design, pg 1184

United States
A-R Editions Inc, pg 1185
Better Music Type, pg 1186
Leo Paper USA, pg 1188
Prepare Inc, pg 1189

NON-ROMAN ALPHABETS

Belgium
Drukkerij Lannoo NV, pg 1175

Canada
University of Toronto Press Inc, pg 1176

Denmark
Bianco Lunos Bogtrykkeri AS, pg 1176

Germany
Priese GmbH & Co, pg 1177

Hong Kong
Prontaprint Asia Ltd, pg 1179
Sunshine Press Ltd, pg 1179

Indonesia
Ichtiar Baru I Van Hoeve, pg 1179

Israel
Technosdar Ltd, pg 1180

Italy
Canale G e C SpA, pg 1180

Lithuania
Spindulys Printing House, pg 1180

New Zealand
Egan-Reid Ltd, pg 1181
Rogan McIndoe Print Ltd, pg 1181

Singapore
Markono Print Media Pte Ltd, pg 1181
Times Graphics, pg 1182

Slovenia
Gorenjski Tisk Printing House, pg 1182

United Kingdom
J W Arrowsmith Ltd, pg 1183
Book Creation, pg 1183
Book Production Consultants PLC, pg 1183
Goldshield Communications Ltd, pg 1184
Antony Rowe Ltd, pg 1185

United States
A-R Editions Inc, pg 1185
BookBuilders New York Inc, pg 1186
Martin Cook Associates Ltd, pg 1187
Custom Services, pg 1187
Elegance Printing & Book Binding (USA), pg 1187
Huron Valley Graphics Inc, pg 1187
ICSI Corp, pg 1188
Leo Paper USA, pg 1188
Prepare Inc, pg 1189

PRODUCTION SERVICES

Austria
ADEVA (Akademische Druck-u Verlagsanstalt), pg 1175

Belgium
Drukkerij Lannoo NV, pg 1175

Canada
Aardvark Enterprises, pg 1175
David Berman Developments Inc, pg 1175
Maracle Press Ltd, pg 1175
University of Toronto Press Inc, pg 1176

Denmark
Bianco Lunos Bogtrykkeri AS, pg 1176

France
Signes du Monde, pg 1176

Germany
C L Baader Buch & Offsetdruckere GmbH & Co KG, pg 1176
Fachhochschule Fur Druk, Studiengang Verlagswirtschaft und Verlagsherstellung, pg 1176
C Maurer Druck und Verlag, pg 1176
Media-Print Informationstechnologie GmbH, pg 1176
Priese GmbH & Co, pg 1177
Topic Verlag GmbH, pg 1177

Hong Kong
Caritas Printing Training Centre, pg 1177
Colorprint Offset, pg 1177
Cristy's Atelier, pg 1177
Dai Nippon Printing Co (Hong Kong) Ltd, pg 1177
Everbest Printing Co Ltd, pg 1178
Golden Cup Printing Co Ltd, pg 1178
The Green Pagoda Press Ltd, pg 1178
Image Printing Company Ltd, pg 1178
Mei Ka Printing & Publishing Enterprise Ltd, pg 1178
New Arts Graphic Reproduction Co Ltd, pg 1178
Prontaprint Asia Ltd, pg 1179
Sota Graphic Arts Co Ltd, pg 1179
Ying Tat Co, pg 1179

Indonesia
Ichtiar Baru I Van Hoeve, pg 1179
Victory Offset Prima PT, pg 1179

Ireland
ICPC Ltd, pg 1180
Kilkenny People/Wellbrook Press, pg 1180
Ultragraphics, pg 1180

Israel
Keterpress Enterprises Jerusalem, pg 1180
Technosdar Ltd, pg 1180

Italy
Canale G e C SpA, pg 1180
Milanostampa SpA, pg 1180

Republic of Korea
Daehan Printing & Publishing Co Ltd, pg 1180

Lithuania
Spindulys Printing House, pg 1180

New Zealand
Egan-Reid Ltd, pg 1181

Puerto Rico
Publishing Resources Inc, pg 1181

Singapore
Eurasia Press Pte Ltd, pg 1181
Markono Print Media Pte Ltd, pg 1181
SNP SPrint Pte Ltd, pg 1182
Stamford Press Pte Ltd, pg 1182
Times Graphics, pg 1182
Times Printers Pte Ltd, pg 1182

Slovenia
Gorenjski Tisk Printing House, pg 1182

Spain
Graficas Santamaria SA, pg 1182

Sri Lanka
Sumathi Book Printing (Pvt) Ltd, pg 1182

Switzerland
Photolitho AG, pg 1182

Thailand
Phongwarin Printing Company Ltd, pg 1182

United Kingdom
BAS Printers Ltd, pg 1183
Baseline Creative Ltd, pg 1183
Book Creation, pg 1183
Book Production Consultants PLC, pg 1183
D Brown & Sons Ltd, pg 1183
Caledonian International Book Manufacturing, pg 1183
Chase Publishing Services, pg 1184
William Clowes Ltd, pg 1184
Cox & Wyman Ltd, pg 1184
Fern House, pg 1184
Goldshield Communications Ltd, pg 1184
Hobbs The Printers Ltd, pg 1184
Holbrook Design, pg 1184
Ikon Document Management Services, pg 1184
Intype Libra Ltd, pg 1185
Page Bros Ltd (Norwich), pg 1185
Santype International Ltd, pg 1185
Thomas Technology Solutions (UK) Ltd, pg 1185

United States
A-R Editions Inc, pg 1185
ADR/BookPrint Inc, pg 1186
Alpina Color Graphics Inc, pg 1186
Blaze International Productions Inc, pg 1186
BookBuilders New York Inc, pg 1186
C & C Offset Printing Co Ltd, pg 1186
Coneco Litho Graphics, pg 1187
Martin Cook Associates Ltd, pg 1187
Custom Services, pg 1187
Datapage Technologies International Inc, pg 1187
Desktop Miracles Inc, pg 1187
DNP America LLC, pg 1187
Editoriale Bortolazzi-Stei srl, pg 1187

MANUFACTURING

Elegance Printing & Book Binding
  (USA), pg 1187
Express Media Corp, pg 1187
High Resolution Inc, pg 1187
Hindy's Enterprise, pg 1187
Huron Valley Graphics Inc, pg 1187
Ikon Document Services, pg 1188
Innodata Isogen Inc, pg 1188
Leo Paper USA, pg 1188
Linick International Inc, pg 1188
LK Litho, pg 1188
Pageworks, pg 1188
Palace Press International -
  Corporate Headquarters, pg 1188
Photoengraving Inc, pg 1189
Pioneer Graphic Scanning, pg 1189
Prepare Inc, pg 1189
PrePress Imaging Inc, pg 1189
Printing Corp of the Americas Inc,
  pg 1189
Regent Publishing Services,
  pg 1189
Sencor, pg 1189
SpectraComp, pg 1189
Studio 31, pg 1189
Fred Weidner & Daughter Printers,
  pg 1189

Uruguay

Barreiro y Ramos SA, pg 1189

PROOFING

Belgium

Drukkerij Lannoo NV, pg 1175

Canada

Coach House Printing, pg 1175
Maracle Press Ltd, pg 1175
Schawk, pg 1175
University of Toronto Press Inc,
  pg 1176

Denmark

Bianco Lunos Bogtrykkeri AS,
  pg 1176

Finland

Gummerus Printing, pg 1176

Germany

C L Baader Buch & Offsetdruckere
  GmbH & Co KG, pg 1176
C Maurer Druck und Verlag,
  pg 1176
Priese GmbH & Co, pg 1177
Topic Verlag GmbH, pg 1177

Hong Kong

Bright Arts Hong Kong Ltd,
  pg 1177
Colorprint Offset, pg 1177
Dai Nippon Printing Co (Hong
  Kong) Ltd, pg 1177
Golden Cup Printing Co Ltd,
  pg 1178
The Green Pagoda Press Ltd,
  pg 1178
Hindy's Enterprise Co Ltd, pg 1178
Hung Hing Off-set Printing Co Ltd,
  pg 1178
Leo Paper Products Ltd, pg 1178
Leo Reprographic Ltd, pg 1178
Midas Printing Ltd, pg 1178
New Arts Graphic Reproduction Co
  Ltd, pg 1179
Prontaprint Asia Ltd, pg 1179
SNP Best-Set Typesetter Ltd,
  pg 1179

Sota Graphic Arts Co Ltd, pg 1179
South Sea International Press Ltd,
  pg 1179
Toppan Printing Co (HK) Ltd,
  pg 1179

India

Hiralal Printing Works Ltd, pg 1179
Paragon Prepress Inc, pg 1179

Indonesia

Victory Offset Prima PT, pg 1179

Ireland

ICPC Ltd, pg 1180
Smurfit Print, pg 1180
Ultragraphics, pg 1180

Italy

Canale G e C SpA, pg 1180

Republic of Korea

Daehan Printing & Publishing Co
  Ltd, pg 1180
Pyunghwa Dang Printing Co Ltd,
  pg 1180

Lithuania

Spindulys Printing House, pg 1180

New Zealand

Egan-Reid Ltd, pg 1181
Rogan McIndoe Print Ltd, pg 1181

Portugal

Edicoes Silabo, pg 1181

Singapore

CS Graphics Pte Ltd, pg 1181
Eurasia Press Pte Ltd, pg 1181
Ho Printing Singapore Pte Ltd,
  pg 1181
Markono Print Media Pte Ltd,
  pg 1181
Sang Choy International Pte Ltd,
  pg 1182
SNP SPrint Pte Ltd, pg 1182
Stamford Press Pte Ltd, pg 1182
Times Graphics, pg 1182
Times Printers Pte Ltd, pg 1182

Slovenia

Gorenjski Tisk Printing House,
  pg 1182

Switzerland

Photolitho AG, pg 1182

United Republic of Tanzania

Peramiho Publications, pg 1182

United Kingdom

Book Creation, pg 1183
Book Production Consultants PLC,
  pg 1183
Chase Publishing Services, pg 1184
William Clowes Ltd, pg 1184
Fern House, pg 1184
Goldshield Communications Ltd,
  pg 1184
The Guernsey Press Co Ltd,
  pg 1184
Hobbs The Printers Ltd, pg 1184
Holbrook Design, pg 1184
Ikon Document Management
  Services, pg 1184

Image & Print Group Ltd, pg 1184
Watkiss Automation Ltd, pg 1185

United States

Alpina Color Graphics Inc, pg 1186
Asia Pacific Offset Inc, pg 1186
Bang Printing Co Inc, pg 1186
BookBuilders New York Inc,
  pg 1186
C & C Offset Printing Co Ltd,
  pg 1186
Coneco Litho Graphics, pg 1187
Martin Cook Associates Ltd,
  pg 1187
CS Graphics USA Inc, pg 1187
Datapage Technologies International
  Inc, pg 1187
Desktop Miracles Inc, pg 1187
Elegance Printing & Book Binding
  (USA), pg 1187
High Resolution Inc, pg 1187
Huron Valley Graphics Inc, pg 1187
Ikon Document Services, pg 1188
Innodata Isogen Inc, pg 1188
ITC, pg 1188
Leo Paper USA, pg 1188
Linick International Inc, pg 1188
LK Litho, pg 1188
Milanostampa/New Interlitho USA
  Inc, pg 1188
Palace Press International -
  Corporate Headquarters, pg 1188
Photoengraving Inc, pg 1189
PrePress Imaging Inc, pg 1189
Regent Publishing Services,
  pg 1189
SpectraComp, pg 1189
Times Publishing Group, pg 1189
Fred Weidner & Daughter Printers,
  pg 1189

Uruguay

Barreiro y Ramos SA, pg 1189

SCIENTIFIC COMPOSITION

Canada

University of Toronto Press Inc,
  pg 1176

Denmark

Bianco Lunos Bogtrykkeri AS,
  pg 1176

Germany

C L Baader Buch & Offsetdruckere
  GmbH & Co KG, pg 1176
Priese GmbH & Co, pg 1177

Hong Kong

Golden Cup Printing Co Ltd,
  pg 1178
SNP Best-Set Typesetter Ltd,
  pg 1179

Ireland

ICPC Ltd, pg 1180
SciPrint Ltd, pg 1180
Smurfit Print, pg 1180

Israel

Monoline Ltd, pg 1180
Technosdar Ltd, pg 1180

Italy

Canale G e C SpA, pg 1180

PREPRESS SERVICES INDEX

Republic of Korea

Daehan Printing & Publishing Co
  Ltd, pg 1180

Lithuania

Spindulys Printing House, pg 1180

New Zealand

Egan-Reid Ltd, pg 1181

Singapore

Times Graphics, pg 1182

Slovenia

Gorenjski Tisk Printing House,
  pg 1182

United Kingdom

J W Arrowsmith Ltd, pg 1183
Book Production Consultants PLC,
  pg 1183
Cambridge University Press -
  Printing Division, pg 1183
The Charlesworth Group, pg 1184
Goldshield Communications Ltd,
  pg 1184
Hobbs The Printers Ltd, pg 1184
Keytec Typesetting Ltd, pg 1185
Page Bros Ltd (Norwich), pg 1185
Antony Rowe Ltd, pg 1185
Santype International Ltd, pg 1185
Thomas Technology Solutions (UK)
  Ltd, pg 1185

United States

Datapage Technologies International
  Inc, pg 1187
Elegance Printing & Book Binding
  (USA), pg 1187
Huron Valley Graphics Inc, pg 1187
ICSI Corp, pg 1188
Innodata Isogen Inc, pg 1188
ITC, pg 1188
Leo Paper USA, pg 1188
Prepare Inc, pg 1189
Sencor, pg 1189
SNP Best-Set Typesetter Ltd,
  pg 1189

UPC & BAR CODE SERVICES

Belgium

Drukkerij Lannoo NV, pg 1175

Canada

Barcode Graphics Inc, pg 1175

Hong Kong

The Green Pagoda Press Ltd,
  pg 1178

United Kingdom

Axicon Auto ID Ltd, pg 1183
Holbrook Design, pg 1184

United States

C & C Offset Printing Co Ltd,
  pg 1186
Datapage Technologies International
  Inc, pg 1187
Desktop Miracles Inc, pg 1187
Elegance Printing & Book Binding
  (USA), pg 1187
PrePress Imaging Inc, pg 1189
SpectraComp, pg 1189

PREPRESS SERVICES INDEX

WORD PROCESSING INTERFACE

Belgium
Drukkerij Lannoo NV, pg 1175

Canada
David Berman Developments Inc, pg 1175
Coach House Printing, pg 1175
Maracle Press Ltd, pg 1175
Tri-Graphic Printing (Ottawa) Ltd, pg 1176
University of Toronto Press Inc, pg 1176

Denmark
Bianco Lunos Bogtrykkeri AS, pg 1176

Germany
C L Baader Buch & Offsetdruckere GmbH & Co KG, pg 1176
C Maurer Druck und Verlag, pg 1176
Media-Print Informationstechnologie GmbH, pg 1176
Oertel & Sporer GmbH & Co, pg 1176
Priese GmbH & Co, pg 1177
Topic Verlag GmbH, pg 1177
Vier-Tuerme GmbH Benedikt Press, pg 1177

Hong Kong
Golden Cup Printing Co Ltd, pg 1178
The Green Pagoda Press Ltd, pg 1178
Prontaprint Asia Ltd, pg 1179
Sota Graphic Arts Co Ltd, pg 1179

Indonesia
Ichtiar Baru I Van Hoeve, pg 1179

Ireland
ICPC Ltd, pg 1180
Smurfit Print, pg 1180
Ultragraphics, pg 1180

Israel
Keterpress Enterprises Jerusalem, pg 1180
Monoline Ltd, pg 1180
Technosdar Ltd, pg 1180

Italy
Canale G e C SpA, pg 1180
Dedalo Litostampa SRL, pg 1180

Republic of Korea
Daehan Printing & Publishing Co Ltd, pg 1180

New Zealand
Egan-Reid Ltd, pg 1181
Rogan McIndoe Print Ltd, pg 1181

Philippines
Naldoza Printers, pg 1181

Portugal
Edicoes Silabo, pg 1181

Singapore
Eurasia Press Pte Ltd, pg 1181
Markono Print Media Pte Ltd, pg 1181
SNP SPrint Pte Ltd, pg 1182
Stamford Press Pte Ltd, pg 1182
Times Graphics, pg 1182

Slovenia
Gorenjski Tisk Printing House, pg 1182

United Republic of Tanzania
Peramiho Publications, pg 1182

United Kingdom
J W Arrowsmith Ltd, pg 1183
W & G Baird Ltd, pg 1183
BAS Printers Ltd, pg 1183
Baseline Creative Ltd, pg 1183
The Bath Press, pg 1183
Bell & Bain Ltd, pg 1183
Blackmore Ltd, pg 1183
Book Creation, pg 1183
D Brown & Sons Ltd, pg 1183
Chase Publishing Services, pg 1184
William Clowes Ltd, pg 1184
Goldshield Communications Ltd, pg 1184
The Guernsey Press Co Ltd, pg 1184
Hobbs The Printers Ltd, pg 1184
Holbrook Design, pg 1184
Ikon Document Management Services, pg 1184
Image & Print Group Ltd, pg 1184
Intype Libra Ltd, pg 1185
J R Reid Printing Group Ltd, pg 1185
Antony Rowe Ltd, pg 1185
Severnside Printers Ltd, pg 1185
Watkiss Automation Ltd, pg 1185

United States
A-R Editions Inc, pg 1185
Alpina Color Graphics Inc, pg 1186
American Pizzi Offset Corp, pg 1186
Bang Printing Co Inc, pg 1186
BookBuilders New York Inc, pg 1186
Coneco Litho Graphics, pg 1187
Martin Cook Associates Ltd, pg 1187
Custom Services, pg 1187
Datapage Technologies International Inc, pg 1187
Huron Valley Graphics Inc, pg 1187
ICSI Corp, pg 1188
Innodata Isogen Inc, pg 1188
ITC, pg 1188
Linick International Inc, pg 1188
LK Litho, pg 1188
Pageworks, pg 1188
Prepare Inc, pg 1189
PrePress Imaging Inc, pg 1189
SpectraComp, pg 1189

Prepress Services

This section includes companies throughout the world that offer a variety of prepress services. Those U.S. and Canadian companies with 10% or more of their business done outside North America are also included. Immediately preceding this section is an index classifying companies by services offered.

Austria

ADEVA (Akademische Druck-u Verlagsanstalt)
Auersperggasse 12, 8010 Graz
Mailing Address: Postfach 598, 8011 Graz
Tel: (0316) 3644 *Fax:* (0316) 364424
E-mail: info@adeva.com
Web Site: www.adeva.com *Cable:* ADEVA-GRAZ
Key Personnel
Editor: Dr Michael Struzl *E-mail:* struzl@adeva.com
General Manager: Dr Ursula Struzl
    E-mail: struzl@adeva.com
Founded: 1949
Print Runs: 300 min - 10,000 max
Business from Other Countries: 80%
Branch Office(s)
Purgleitnergasse 10, Ecke Marburgerstr, 8042 Graz

Akademische Druck- u Verlagsanstalt, see ADEVA (Akademische Druck-u Verlagsanstalt)

Dr Paul Struzl GmbH, see ADEVA (Akademische Druck-u Verlagsanstalt)

Belgium

IMPF bvba
Sint-Amandstr 18, 9000 Gent
Tel: (09) 225 44 29 *Fax:* 058 315 77
E-mail: maarten@fotobeurs.com
Web Site: www.fotobeurs.com
Key Personnel
Manager: Xavier Dewulf
Founded: 1958
Business from Other Countries: 10%

Drukkerij Lannoo NV (Lannoo Printers)
Kasteelstr 97, 8700 Tielt
Tel: (051) 42 42 11 *Fax:* (051) 40 70 70
E-mail: lannoo@lannooprint.be
Web Site: www.lannooprint.be
Key Personnel
General Manager & Marketing Dir: Stefaan Lannoo *E-mail:* stefaan.lannoo@lannooprint.be
Founded: 1909
Turnaround: 10 Workdays
Print Runs: 100 min - 1,000,000 max
Business from Other Countries: 30%

Canada

Aardvark Enterprises
Division of Speers Investments Ltd
204 Millbank Dr SW, Calgary, AB T2Y 2H9
Tel: 403-256-4639
Key Personnel
Pres: J Alvin Speers
Founded: 1970 (Small Press Pioneers)
Turnaround: 30 Workdays
Print Runs: 10 min - 1,000 max
Business from Other Countries: 25%

Barcode Graphics Inc
25 Brodie Dr, Unit 5, Richmond Hill, ON L4B 3K7
Tel: 416-751-1474 *Toll Free Tel:* 800-263-3669
    Fax: 416-751-1575
E-mail: info@barcodegraphics.com
Web Site: www.barcodegraphics.com
Key Personnel
Pres: John Herzig *E-mail:* jherzig@barcodegraphics.com
Founded: 1981
Turnaround: 1-2 Workdays
Print Runs: 2,000,000 max
Business from Other Countries: 10%

David Berman Developments Inc
239 Atlantis Ave, Ottawa, ON K2A 1X9
Tel: 613-728-6777 *Fax:* 613-728-2867
E-mail: info@timewise.net
Web Site: www.timewise.net
Key Personnel
Pres: David Berman
Founded: 1987
Business from Other Countries: 50%

Coach House Printing
401 Huron St, Rear, Toronto, ON M5S 2G5
Tel: 416-979-2217 *Fax:* 416-977-1158
E-mail: mail@chbooks.com
Web Site: www.chbooks.com
Key Personnel
Publr: Stan Bevington
Edit Consultant: Darren Wershler-Henry
Founded: 1965
Turnaround: 14 Workdays
Print Runs: 200 min - 2,000 max
Business from Other Countries: 10%

Leanne Franson
4323 Parthenais, Montreal, PQ H2H 2G2
Tel: 514-526-4236 *Fax:* 514-526-0972
E-mail: inksports@videotron.ca
Web Site: www.theispot.com/artist/LFranson
Founded: 1991
Turnaround: 3-7 plus Workdays
Business from Other Countries: 50%
Membership(s): Association des Illustrateurs et d'Illustratries du Quebec

Girol Books Inc
120 Somerset St W, Ottawa, ON K2P 0H8
Mailing Address: Box 5473, Sta F, Ottawa, ON K2C 3M1
Tel: 613-233-9044 *Fax:* 613-233-9044
E-mail: info@girol.com
Web Site: www.girol.com
Key Personnel
Owner: Miguel Angel Giella; Peter Roster
Mgr: Leslie Roster *E-mail:* lroster@girol.com
Founded: 1975
Business from Other Countries: 30%

Celia Godkin
Mod 6, Comp 12, 10 James St, Frankville, ON K0E 1H0
Tel: 613-275-7204 *Fax:* 613-275-7204
E-mail: celia.godkin@utoronto.ca
Founded: 1983
Business from Other Countries: 10%
Membership(s): CANSCAIP; The Writers' Union of Canada

Maracle Press Ltd
1156 King St E, Oshawa, ON L1H 7N4
Mailing Address: Box 606, Oshawa, ON L1H 7N4
Tel: 905-723-3438 *Toll Free Tel:* 800-558-8604
    Fax: 905-428-6024
E-mail: maracle@maraclepress.com
Web Site: www.maraclepress.com
Key Personnel
Pres & Gen Mgr: Bruce A Fenton
    E-mail: bfenton@maraclepress.com
VP, Busn Devt: Ronald G Taylor
    E-mail: rtaylor@maraclepress.com
Founded: 1920
Turnaround: 10 Workdays
Print Runs: 500 min - 500,000 max
Business from Other Countries: 25%
Membership(s): BMI

Preney Print & Litho Inc
1457 Lauzon Rd, Windsor, ON N8F 3N2
Tel: 519-966-3412 *Toll Free Tel:* 877-870-4164
    Fax: 519-966-4996
E-mail: contactus@preneyprint.com
Founded: 1972
Turnaround: 15 Workdays
Print Runs: 2,000 min
Business from Other Countries: 20%

Printcrafters Inc
78 Hutchings St, Winnipeg, MB R2X 3B1
Tel: 204-633-7117 *Fax:* 204-694-1519
E-mail: info@printcraftersinc.com
Web Site: www.printcraftersinc.com
Key Personnel
Pres: Bob Payne *Tel:* 204-633-7117 ext 223
    Fax: 204-694-1594 *E-mail:* bpayne@printcraftersinc.com
Founded: 1996 (Employee owned)
Turnaround: 5-20 Workdays
Print Runs: 200,000 min - 500,000 max
Business from Other Countries: 30%
Membership(s): CPIA

PrintWest
1150 Eighth Ave, Regina, SK S4R 1C9
Tel: 306-525-2304 *Toll Free Tel:* 800-236-6438
    Fax: 306-757-2439
E-mail: general@printwest.com
Web Site: www.printwest.com
Key Personnel
CEO: Wayne UnRuh
VP, Sales: Ken Benson
Founded: 1992
Turnaround: 15 Workdays
Print Runs: 1,000 min - 100,000 max
Business from Other Countries: 15%
Branch Office(s)
Box 2500, 2310 Millar Ave, Saskatoon, SK S7K 2C4 *Tel:* 306-665-3560 *Fax:* 306-653-1255

Schawk
543 Richmond St W, Suite 125, Toronto, ON M5V 1Y6

CANADA

Tel: 416-703-1445 *Fax:* 416-703-1494
Web Site: www.schawk.com
Key Personnel
Pres: Mark Quesnelle
Founded: 1965
Business from Other Countries: 10%

David Shaw & Associates Ltd
108 Ranleigh Ave, Toronto, ON M4N 1W9
Tel: 416-487-2019 *Fax:* 416-486-1744
E-mail: djshaw@simpatico.ca
Key Personnel
Pres: David Shaw
Founded: 1977
Business from Other Countries: 25%

Barbara Spurll Illustration
1180 Danforth Ave, Toronto, ON M4J 1M3
Tel: 416-594-6594
E-mail: bspurll@yahoo.com
Web Site: www.barbaraspurll.com
Founded: 1975
Business from Other Countries: 70%

Transcontinental Printing Book Group
Division of Transcontinental Group
395 Lebeau Blvd, St-Laurent, PQ H4N 1S2
Tel: 514-337-8560 *Toll Free Tel:* 800-361-3599
Fax: 514-339-5230
Web Site: www.transcontinental.com; www.transcontinental-printing.com
Key Personnel
VP, Book Group: Jacques Gregoire
US Sales Mgr: Denis Beaudin *Tel:* 514-339-2220 ext 4101 *E-mail:* beaudind@transcontinental.ca
Founded: 1976
Turnaround: 4 weeks casebound; 3 weeks softcover
Print Runs: 1,000 min
Business from Other Countries: 15%
Branch Office(s)
614 Yates Ave, Calumet City, IL 60409, United States, Contact: Kristopher D Levy *Tel:* 708-832-1528 *Fax:* 708-832-9510 *E-mail:* kris.levy@transcontinental.ca (Midwest)
3653 W Leland Ave, Suite One W, Chicago, IL 60625, United States, Contact: Tim Taylor *Tel:* 773-583-8155 *Fax:* 773-583-8162 *E-mail:* tim.taylor@transcontinental.ca (Midwest)
245 Eliot St, Ashland, MA 01721, United States, Contact: Ed Catania *Tel:* 508-881-1119 *E-mail:* ecatania@attbi.com (East Coast)
19 Crown St, Milton, MA 02186-1419, United States, Contact: Mike Gazzola *Tel:* 617-696-1435 *Fax:* 617-696-1025 *E-mail:* mikebook@attbi.com (East Coast)
37 Herman Blvd, Franklin Square, NY 11010, United States, Contact: Tom Malloy *Tel:* 516-775-2980 *Fax:* 516-488-0253 *E-mail:* tmmalloy@aol.com
3175 Summit Square Dr, Suite C9, Oakton, VA 22124, United States, Contact: David Avesian *Tel:* 703-255-1332 *Fax:* 703-255-1343 *E-mail:* davesian@cox.rr.com (Southeast)
559 Lowrys Rd, Parksville, BC V9P 2R8, Contact: Mike Davies *Tel:* 250-248-9700 *Fax:* 250-248-2353 *E-mail:* bookguys@shaw.ca (West Coast)
15373 Victoria Ave, White Rock, BC V4B 1H1, Contact: Wade Davies *Tel:* 604-535-8800 *Fax:* 604-535-8802 *E-mail:* daviesw@shaw.ca (West Coast)
490 Wilfred Dr, Peterborough, ON K9K 2H1, Contact: Tom Lang *Tel:* 705-760-9594 *Fax:* 705-760-9485 *E-mail:* langt@transcontinental.ca (NY)

Tri-Graphic Printing (Ottawa) Ltd
485 Industrial Ave, Ottawa, ON K1G 0Z1
Tel: 613-731-7441 *Toll Free Tel:* 800-267-9750
Fax: 613-731-3741
Web Site: www.tri-graphic.com
Key Personnel
VP & Gen Mgr: Doug K Doane
  E-mail: ddoane@tri-graphic.com
VP, Prodn & Servs: Fred Malleau *Tel:* 905-665-8500 *E-mail:* fmalleau@tri-graphic.com
Founded: 1968
Turnaround: 10-15 Workdays
Print Runs: 1,000 min - 100,000 max
Business from Other Countries: 10%
Sales Office(s): 213 Byron St S, Suite 201, Whitby, ON L1N 4P7, VP Prod Devt: Fred Malleau *Tel:* 905-665-8500 *Fax:* 905-665-8501 *E-mail:* fmalleau@tri-graphic.com
Membership(s): BMI

University of Toronto Press Inc
Printing Division, 5201 Dufferin St, North York, ON M3H 5T8
Tel: 416-667-7767 *Fax:* 416-667-7803
E-mail: printing@utpress.utoronto.ca
Web Site: www.utpress.utoronto.ca
Key Personnel
Pres & Publr: George Meadows
Founded: 1901
Turnaround: 10-15 Workdays
Print Runs: 10 min - 200,000 max
Business from Other Countries: 15%
Membership(s): BMI

Denmark

Bianco Lunos Bogtrykkeri AS
Subsidiary of Carl Allers Etablissement AS
Otto Monsteds Gade 3, 1571 Copenhagen V
Tel: (03) 615 3300 *Fax:* (03) 615 3301
Web Site: www.aller.dk
Key Personnel
General Manager: J Heede Sorensen
Founded: 1871

Finland

Gummerus Printing
Division of Gummerus Kirjapaino Oy
Subsidiary of Gummerus Oy
Alasinkatu 1-3, 40351 Jyvaskyla
Mailing Address: PL 444, 40351 Jyvaskyla
Tel: (014) 683 500 *Fax:* (014) 676 770
E-mail: etunimi.sukunimi@gummerus.fi
Web Site: www.gummerus.fi
Key Personnel
Marketing Dir: Mr Martti Aaltonen
Man Dir: Mr Jarmo Porkka
Founded: 1872
Turnaround: 20-60 Workdays
Print Runs: 1,000 min - 100,000 max
Business from Other Countries: 15%

France

Signes du Monde
1424 ch du Dupere Hubert Saint-Genez, 40380 Povartin
Tel: (06) 12 99 73 37 *Fax:* (0561) 575717
Key Personnel
Production: Hubert Saint-Genez

Germany

C L Baader Buch & Offsetdruckere GmbH & Co KG
Gutenbergstr 1, 72525 Muensingen
Tel: (07381) 791 *Fax:* (07381) 411412 *Cable:* BAADER-MUNSINGEN
Founded: 1835
Turnaround: 1 Workday
Print Runs: 1,000 min - 15,000 max

Fachhochschule Fur Druk, Studiengang Verlagswirtschaft und Verlagsherstellung
Nobelstr 10, 70569 Stuttgart
Tel: (0711) 685 2807 *Fax:* (0711) 685 6650
E-mail: info@hdm-stuttgart.de
Web Site: www.hdm-stuttgart.de
Telex: 725 185 fhd d
Key Personnel
Contact: Prof Eduard H Schoenstedt

Hallwag Kuemmerly & Frey AG
Grubenstr 109, CH-3322 Schoenbuehl-Bern
Tel: (031) 850 31 31 *Fax:* (031) 850 31 00
E-mail: info@swisstravelcenter.ch
Web Site: www.swisstravelcenter.ch; www.hallwag.com
Telex: 912-661 HAWA CH
Key Personnel
Chief Executive Officer: Peter Niederhauser
Marketing, Public Relations: Danielle Zingg
Sales: Juerg Burri; Benro Paul Meyerhans

C Maurer Druck und Verlag
Schubartstr 21, 73312 Geislingen/Steige
Tel: (07331) 930-0 *Fax:* (07331) 93 0-190
Web Site: www.maurer-online.de
Key Personnel
Management: Carl-Otto Maurer *Tel:* 930-112
  E-mail: c.maurer@maurer-online.de
Sales: Christoph Traub *Tel:* 930-120
  E-mail: traub@maurer-online.de
Founded: 1856

Media-Print Informationstechnologie GmbH
Eggertstr 28, 33100 Paderborn
Tel: (051) 522-300 *Fax:* (051) 522-480
E-mail: contact@mediaprintpb.de
Web Site: www.mediaprint.de
Key Personnel
Man Dir: Rainer Rings *Tel:* (05251) 522-460
  E-mail: rings@mediaprint.de
Contact: Udo Sengstock *E-mail:* sengst@mediaprint.de
Founded: 1993
Turnaround: 5-10 Workdays
Print Runs: 100 min - 30,000 max
Business from Other Countries: 10%

MOHN Media
Subsidiary of Bertelsmann AG
Carl-Bertelsmann-Str 161M, 33311 Guetersloh
Tel: (05241) 80 56 29 *Fax:* (05241) 1 66 92
Key Personnel
Contact: Alfred Hahn
Founded: 1824
Business from Other Countries: 25%

Oertel & Sporer GmbH & Co
Burgstr 1-7, 72764 Reutlingen
Mailing Address: Postfach 1642, 72706 Reutlingen
Tel: (07121) 302555 *Fax:* (07121) 302558
Key Personnel
Publisher: Valdo Lehari
Manager & Printer: Ermo Lehari
Print Runs: 500 min - 50,000 max

Priese GmbH & Co
Auerbacher Str 9, 14193 Berlin
Tel: (030) 8263024 *Fax:* (030) 3249630
Key Personnel
Contact: Elma Priese; Hans Joachim Priese

Topic Verlag GmbH
Birkenstr 10, 85757 Karlsfeld B Munich
Tel: (08131) 97038 *Fax:* (08131) 98404
Founded: 1982
Business from Other Countries: 50%

Vier-Tuerme GmbH Benedikt Press
Schweinfurter Str 40, 97359 Muensterschwarzach Abtei
Tel: (09324) 20292 *Fax:* (09324) 20495
E-mail: info@vier-tuerme.de
Web Site: www.vier-tuerme.de
Key Personnel
Contact: Josef Stoecklein
Founded: 1951
Turnaround: 8-16 Workdays
Print Runs: 300 min - 20,000 max
Business from Other Countries: 5%

Hong Kong

Bookbuilders Ltd
Unit J 13/F Yeung Yiu Chung No 8 Industrial Bldg, 20 Wang Hoi Rd, Kowloon Bay, Kowloon
Tel: 27968123 *Fax:* 27968267; 27968690
E-mail: lph@netvigator.com
Key Personnel
Man Dir: Leslie Henman
General Manager: Edward Chan

Bright Arts Hong Kong Ltd
Tung Chong Factory Bldg, 11/F, Block D, 659 Kings Rd, North Point
Tel: 25620119 *Fax:* 25657031
E-mail: william@brightartshk.com
Web Site: www.brightartshk.com
Key Personnel
Man Dir: Sunny Shum
Dir, China Operations: Jimmy Wong
Customer Service Manager, China: Tino Kwok
Customer Service Manager, Hong Kong: William Yue

Bright Future Printing Co Ltd
Sunview Industrial Building, Block D, 5/F, 3 On Yip St, Chai Wan
Tel: 2515 1776 *Fax:* 2897 2799; 2558 1717
Key Personnel
Chairman: Richard Ng
Turnaround: 60 Workdays (including shipping)
Print Runs: 3,000 min - 30,000 max
Business from Other Countries: 30%

C & C Offset Printing Co Ltd
Subsidiary of C & C Joint Printing Co (HK) Ltd under Sino United (Holdings) Hong Kong Ltd
C&C Bldg, floor 14, 36 Ting Lai Rd, Tai Po, New Territories
Tel: 2666-4988 *Fax:* 2666-4938
E-mail: offsetprinting@candcprinting.com
Web Site: www.ccoffset.com
Key Personnel
Dir & General Manager: Jackson Leung
Deputy Man Dir: Kee Lee
Deputy General Manager: Ivy Lam
Assistant General Manager: Kit Wong
Senior Sales Manager (Special Project): Francis Ho
Dir & Executive Vice President, C & C Offset Printing Co (USA) Inc, Portland OR, USA: Charles H Clark, IV *E-mail:* cclark@ccoffset.com
Development Manager, C & C Offset Printing Co (USA) Inc, Portland, OR, USA: Jenny Whittier *E-mail:* jwhittier@ccoffset.com
Customer Service Manager, C & C Offset Printing Co (USA) Inc, Portland, OR, USA: Ernest Li *E-mail:* ernestli@ccoffset.com
Dir & Executive Vice President, C & C Offset Printing Co (NY) Inc, New York, NY, USA: Simon Chan *E-mail:* schan@ccoffset.com
Assistant General Manager-China Sales, C & C Joint Printing Co (Ghuangdong) Ltd, Shenzhen, China: Simon Zhang
President, C & C Printing Japan Co Ltd, Tokyo, Japan: Yamamoto Masaaki
Customer Service Manager, C & C Offset Printing Co (NYC), Inc, New York, NY: Frances Harkness *E-mail:* fharkness@ccoffset.com
Man Dir, C & C Joint Printing Co (Beijing), Ltd, Beijing, China: Zhang Lin Gui
Dir, C & C Offset Printing Co (UK), Ltd: Tracy Broderick
Account Manager, C & C Offset Printing Co (UK) Ltd: Fia Fornari
Founded: 1980
Turnaround: 30-42 Workdays for printing, binding & book finishing
Print Runs: 2,000 min - 1,000,000 max
Business from Other Countries: 60%
Branch Office(s)
C & C Joint Printing Co (Guangdong) Ltd, Chunhu Industrial Estate, Pinghu, Long Gang, Shenzhen 518111, China *Tel:* (0755) 2845-8333 *Fax:* (0755) 2845-9911 *E-mail:* guangdong@candcprinting.com *Web Site:* www.candcprinting.com (Plant)
C & C Printing Japan Co Ltd, 2-6-12 Hitotsubashi, Tozaido Bldg 3F, Chiyoda-ku, Tokyo 101-0003, Japan *Tel:* (03) 5216-4580 *Fax:* (03) 5216-4610 *E-mail:* mail@candcprinting.co.jp *Web Site:* www.candcprinting.co.jp
C & C Joint Printing Co (Guangdong) Ltd, 7/F, Flat H, Green View Apartment, No 38, Hou Guang Ping Hu Tong, Xi Cheng Qu, Beijing 100035, China *Tel:* (010) 6650-3176 *Fax:* (010) 6650-3175 *E-mail:* beijing@candcprinting.com
C & C Joint Printing Co (Guangdong) Ltd, Room 304, Fang Fa Bldg, No 29, 165 Ave, Dongzhuanbin Rd, Shanghai 200050, China *Tel:* (021) 6240-1305 *Fax:* (021) 6240-2090 *E-mail:* shanghaioffice@candcprinting.com
C & C Joint Printing Co (Guangdong) Ltd, Room 1511, Hua Xin Bldg, East Block, 2 Shuiyin Rd, Huanshi East, Guangzhou 510075, China *Tel:* (020) 3760 0979 *Fax:* (020) 3760 0977 *E-mail:* guangzhou@candcprinting.com
C & C Offset Printing Co (UK) Ltd, 2 New Burlington St, 4th floor, London W1S 2JE, United Kingdom *Tel:* (0207) 2877787 *Fax:* (0207) 2877187 *E-mail:* tracy@candcoffset.co.uk
U.S. Office(s): C & C Offset Printing Co (USA) Inc, 2632 SE 25th Ave, Suite D, Portland, OR 97202, United States *Tel:* 503-233-1834 *Fax:* 503-233-7815 *E-mail:* portlandinfo@ccoffset.com (shipping)
C & C Offset Printing Co (NY) Inc, 401 Broadway, Suite 2015, New York, NY 10013-3004, United States *Tel:* 212-431-4210 *Fax:* 212-431-3960 *E-mail:* newyorkinfo@ccoffset.com

Caritas Printing Training Centre
Caritas House, 3rd floor, Block D, 2 Caine Rd, Hong Kong
Tel: 25261148 *Fax:* 25371231
Key Personnel
General Manager: Isaac Mak
Print Runs: 1,000 min - 100,000 max
Business from Other Countries: 50%

Colorprint Offset
Unit 1808-9, 18/F, 8 Commercial Tower, 8 Sun Yip St, Chai Wan
Tel: 2896-7777 *Fax:* 2889-6606
E-mail: info@cpo.com.hk
Web Site: www.cpo.com.hk
Key Personnel
Sales Manager: Jennifer Weston *Tel:* 2903-5062
Contact: Eva Lav; Ian Lee
Turnaround: 30-40 Workdays
Print Runs: 3,000 min - 100,000 max
Business from Other Countries: 80%
Sales Office(s): Gainsborough House, 81 Oxford St, London W1R 1RB, United Kingdom *Tel:* (02) 7903-5060 *Fax:* (02) 7903-5063 *E-mail:* uk@cpo.com.hk
80 Park Ave, Suite 10N, New York, NY 10016, United States *Tel:* 212-681-9400 *Fax:* 212-681-9362 *E-mail:* ny@cpo.com.hk

Cristy's Atelier
37-39 Jervois St, Sheung Wan
Tel: 25418609 *Fax:* 28540995
E-mail: cristys@intercon.net
Founded: 1982

Dai Nippon Printing Co (Hong Kong) Ltd
Division of Dai Nippon Printing Co Ltd
Tsuen Wan Industrial Centre, 2-5/F, 220-248 Texaco Rd, Tsuen Wan, New Territories
Tel: 2408-0188 *Fax:* 2408-8479
E-mail: info@mail.dnp.co.jp
Web Site: www.dnp.co.jp *Cable:* DNPICO
Key Personnel
Administration & Finance Dir: Mr K Miya
Print Runs: 5,000 min - 200,000 max
Business from Other Countries: 85%
Branch Office(s)
DAI Nippon IMS (America) Corp, 4524 Enterprise Dr NW, Concord, NC 28027, United States *Tel:* 704-784-8100 *Fax:* 704-784-2777
Dai Nippon Printing Co (Australia) Pty Ltd, 45 Clarence St, Suite 904, Level 9, KPMG Centre, Sydney NSW 2000, Australia *Tel:* (02) 9299-3155
Dai Nippon Printing Co Ltd, 1-1-1, Ichigaya-Kagacho, Shinjuku-ku, Tokyo, Japan
Dai Nippon Printing Co (Australia) Pty Ltd, St Martins Tower, Level 10, Suite 1002, 31 Market St, Sydney, NSW 2000, Australia *Tel:* (02) 9267-8166 *Fax:* (02) 9267-9533
Dai Nippon Printing Co (Singapore) Pte Ltd, 896 Dunearn Rd, No 04-09, Sime Darby Centre, Singapore 589472, Singapore *Tel:* 469-7611 *Fax:* 469-8486
Dai Nippon Printing Co (UK) Ltd, 27 Throgmorton St, 4th floor, London EC2N 2AQ, United Kingdom *Tel:* (020) 7588-2088 *Fax:* (020) 7588-2089
DAI Nippon Printing (Europe) GmbH, Berliner Allee 26, 40212 Dusseldorf, Germany *Tel:* (0211) 8620-180 *Fax:* (0211) 8620-1895
DAI Nippon Printing (Taiwan) Co, LTD, 85 Chung Hsiao East Rd, Sec 1 Taipei, Taiwan, China *Tel:* (02) 2327-8311 *Fax:* (02) 2327-8283
DNP Denmark A/S, Skruegangen 2, DK-2690 Karlslunde, Denmark *Tel:* 4616-5100 *Fax:* 4616-5200
P T Dai Nippon Printing Indonesia, Kawasan Industri Pulogadung, Jalan Pulogadung Kaveling II, Blok H No 2-3, Jakarta Timur, Indonesia *Tel:* (021) 4610313 *Fax:* (021) 4605795
PT Tien Wah Press Indonesia, Janlan Tenaru, Desa Cangkir, Kec Driyorejo, Gresik 61177, Indonesia *Tel:* (031) 7507403
TEP Sdn Bhd, 89, Jalan Tampoi, Kawasan Perindustrian Tampoi, 80350 Johor Bahru, Johor, Malaysia *Tel:* (07) 2369899 *Fax:* (07) 2363148
Tien Wah Press Pte Ltd, 4 Pandan Crescent, Singapore 128475, Singapore *Tel:* 466-6222 *Fax:* 469-3894

Sales Office(s): DNP America Inc, 7425 Mission Valley Rd, Suite 201, San Diego, CA 92108, United States *Tel:* 619-295-8111 *Fax:* 619-295-7809

DNP America LLC, Los Angeles Office, 3858 Carson St, Suite 300, Torrance, CA 90503, United States *Tel:* 310-540-5123 *Fax:* 310-543-3260

DNP America LLC, Silicon Valley Office, 3235 Kifer Rd, Suite 100, Santa Clara, CA 95051, United States *Tel:* 408-735-8880 *Fax:* 408-735-0453

U.S. Office(s): DNP Corporation USA, San Francisco Office, 577 Airport Blvd, Suite 620, Burlingame, CA 94010, United States

DNP Corporation USA, New York Office, 335 Madison Ave, 3rd floor, New York, NY 10017, United States *Tel:* 212-503-1850 *Fax:* 212-286-1490

Elegance Finance Printing Services Ltd
Subsidiary of Elegance Printing Company Limited
2401 Alexandra House, 16-20 Chater Rd, Central Hong Kong
Tel: 2283 2222 *Fax:* 2521 3616
E-mail: saledept@elegancefinptg.com
Print Runs: 500 min - 7,200 max
Business from Other Countries: 2%

Everbest Printing Co Ltd
Ko Fai Industrial Bldg, Block C5, 10th floor, 7 Ko Fai Rd, Yau Tong, Kowloon
Tel: 2727 4433 *Fax:* 2772 7687
E-mail: sales@everbest.com.hk
Web Site: www.everbest.com
Key Personnel
Man Dir: Kenneth Chung
Customer Account Executive: Frankie Lee; Ronny Ng
Founded: 1954
Turnaround: 28 Workdays
Print Runs: 1,000 min - 1,000,000 max
Business from Other Countries: 90%
Branch Office(s)
Everbest Printing, 100 Macauley Rd, Stanmore, NSW 2048, Australia, Contact: Lionel Marz *Tel:* (02) 9568-5879 *Fax:* (02) 9568-8694 *E-mail:* lmarz@onaustralia.com.au (Australia & New Zealand office)
Everbest Canada, 50 Emblem Court, Scarborough, ON M1S 1B1, Canada, Connie Chung *Tel:* 416-286-2525 *Fax:* 416-286-2526 *E-mail:* everbestcan@aprinco.com
U.S. Office(s): Spectrum Books Inc, 2300 Bethards Dr, Suite C, Santa Rosa, CA 95405-8658, United States, Contact: Duncan McCallum *Tel:* 707-542-6044 *Fax:* 707-542-6045 *E-mail:* specbooks@aol.com
Four Colour Imports, 2843 Brownsboro Rd, Suite 102, Louisville, KY 40206, United States, George Dick *Tel:* 502-896-9644 *Fax:* 502-896-9594 *E-mail:* sales@fourcolor.com *Web Site:* www.fourcolor.com
Everbest Midwest, 6428 Margaret's Lane, Edina, MN 55439, United States, Dr Josie Lo *Tel:* 612-944-0854 *Fax:* 912-829-7670 *E-mail:* sklo@aol.com

Golden Cup Printing Co Ltd
Seapower Industrial Centre, 6/F, 177 Hoi Bun Rd, Kwun Tong, Kowloon
Tel: 23434254; 23434255 *Fax:* 23415426
E-mail: sales@goldencup.com.hk
Web Site: www.goldencup.com.hk
Key Personnel
Man Dir: Yeung Kam Kai
General Manager: W K Ngan
Sales Manager: Mary Yeung *E-mail:* mary@goldencup.com.hk
Founded: 1971
Turnaround: 25 Workdays

Print Runs: 5,000 min - 200,000 max
Business from Other Countries: 80%
Branch Office(s)
Dongguan, China
Guangdong, China
Kunming, China
Yunan, China

The Green Pagoda Press Ltd
9/F, Block B, Tung Chong Factory Bldg, 653-655 King's Rd, North Point
Tel: 2561 1924 *Fax:* 2811 0946
E-mail: gpinfo@gpp.com.hk
Web Site: www.greenpagoda.com
Key Personnel
Man Dir: Derek Yip
Founded: 1957
Turnaround: 1-14 days
Print Runs: 10 min - 500,000 max
Business from Other Countries: 30%

H K Scanner Arts International Ltd
Block B1, 6/F Fortune Factory Bldg, 40 Lee Chung St, Chai Wan
Tel: 29760302 *Fax:* 29760292
Key Personnel
Dir, Sales & Marketing: Wayne C Ling
Man Dir: Y C Luk

Hindy's Enterprise Co Ltd
Flat A 20/F, Melbourne Industrial Bldg, 16 Wetlands Rd, Quarry Bay
Tel: 25166318 *Fax:* 25165161
Key Personnel
General Manager: Cecilia Chung

Hung Hing Off-set Printing Co Ltd
Subsidiary of Hung Hing Printing Group Ltd
Tai Po Industrial Estate, 17-19 Dai Hei St, New Territories
Tel: 2664 8682 *Fax:* 2664 2070
E-mail: info@hhop.com.hk
Web Site: www.hhop.com.hk
Key Personnel
Man Dir: Matthew Yum *E-mail:* matthew@hhop.com.hk
Contact: Yam Cheong Hung
Founded: 1950
Turnaround: 20-30 Workdays
Print Runs: 5,000 min - 1,000,000 max
Business from Other Countries: 15%

Image Printing Company Ltd
Unit 4, 4/F Cornell Centre, 50 Wing Tai Rd, Chai Wan
Tel: 2873 2633 *Fax:* 2558 3044
E-mail: imageprt@pop3.hknet.com
Key Personnel
Man Dir: Philip Chow Sung Ming
Founded: 1992
Print Runs: 1,000 min - 50,000 max
Business from Other Countries: 50%

Leo Paper Products Ltd
7/F, Kader Bldg, 22 Kai Cheung Rd, Kowloon Bay, Kowloon
Tel: 28841374 *Fax:* 25130698
E-mail: lpp@leo.com.hk
Web Site: www.leo.com.hk
Key Personnel
Deputy Man Dir: Burman Tam *E-mail:* burman@leo.com.hk
Founded: 1991
Turnaround: 15-30 Workdays
Print Runs: 5,000 min
Parent Company: Leo Paper Bags Manufacturing Ltd
Branch Office(s)
Leo Paper USA, 1180 NW Maple St, Suite 102, Issaquah, WA 98027, United States, Contact: Bijan Pakzad *Tel:* 425-646-8801 *Fax:* 425-646-8805 *E-mail:* sales@leousa.com
Leo Paper USA - New York, 27 W 24 St, Suite 701, New York, NY 10010-3204, United States *Tel:* 917-305-0708 *Fax:* 917-305-0709 *E-mail:* sales@leousanewyork.com
Sales Office(s): Leo Paper Products (Europe) BVBA, Keizerstr 5, 200 Antwerpen, Belgium, Sales Dir: Jan Van Gijsel *Tel:* (03) 203-0912 *Fax:* (03) 255-1303 *E-mail:* leo@leo-europe.com
Leo Paper Products (UK) Ltd, St Michaels House, 94 High St, Wallingford, Oxon OX10 0BW *Tel:* (01491) 827827 *Fax:* (01491) 837127 *E-mail:* info@leouk.com

Leo Reprographic Ltd
7/F Kader Bldg, 22 Kai Cheung Rd, Kowloon Bay, Kowloon
Tel: (02) 25696293 *Fax:* (02) 25138400
E-mail: lrg@leo.com.hk
Web Site: www.leo.com.hk
Key Personnel
Managing Deputy Dir: Burman Tam
 E-mail: burman@leo.com.hk
Founded: 1991
Turnaround: 7 Workdays for 128pp A4 size
Parent Company: Leo Paper Bags Manufacturing Ltd
Sales Office(s): Leo Marketing Ltd, The Malthouse, Malthouse Sq, Princes Risborough, Bucks HP27 9AB, United Kingdom, Director: Sally Wood *Tel:* (018) 274-244 *Fax:* (018) 275-105 *E-mail:* sallywood.leo@btinternet.com
Leo Paper Products (Europe) BVBA, De Wilde Zee, Wiegstraat 19, 2000 Antwerp, Belgium, Sales Director: Jan Van Gijsel *Tel:* (03) 203-0912 *Fax:* (03) 255-1303 *E-mail:* leo@leo-europe.com
U.S. Office(s): Leo Paper USA, 1180 NW Maple St, Suite 102, Issaquah, WA 98027, United States, Contact: Bijan Pakzad *Tel:* 425-646-8801 *Fax:* 425-646-8805 *E-mail:* sales@leousa.com

Mei Ka Printing & Publishing Enterprise Ltd
Cheung Ka Industrial Bldg, 9/F Block B, 180 Connaught Rd W, West Hong Kong
Tel: 2540 1131 *Fax:* 2559 8718; 2559 7137
E-mail: mkpp@netvigator.com
Web Site: www.meika-printing.com; www.meika-printing.b2s.com
Key Personnel
Dir: Hong Chin Huo

Midas Printing Ltd
1/F, 100 Texaco Rd, Tsuen Wan, New Territories
Tel: 2407 6888 *Fax:* 2408 0611
E-mail: info@midasprinting.com
Web Site: www.midasprinting.com
Key Personnel
Project Manager: Raymond Chan
Executive Dir: Gloria Y P Kan
Contact: Annie Wong *E-mail:* annie@midasprinting.com
Founded: 1990
Turnaround: 14-21 Workdays
Print Runs: 5,000 min - 100,000 max
Business from Other Countries: 25%

New Arts Graphic Reproduction Co Ltd
Loks Industrial Bldg, 4/F, 204 Tsat Tse Mui Rd, North Point
Tel: 25641323; 25618161 *Fax:* 25658262
E-mail: newarts@writeme.com
Key Personnel
Man Dir: Paul Sik-Kwong Choy
Manager: Andrew Choy *E-mail:* andchoy@netvigator.com
Founded: 1970
Business from Other Countries: 50%

Paper Communication Printing Express Ltd
4A Dragon Industrial Bldg, 93 King Lam St, Cheung Sha Wan, Kowloon
Tel: 27864191 *Fax:* 27864498
E-mail: pcpc@papercom.com.hk
Key Personnel
Marketing Dir: Alam Ng
Founded: 1981
BISAC compatible software
Turnaround: 28 to 56 Workdays
Print Runs: 1,000 min - 3,000,000 max
Business from Other Countries: 90%

Prontaprint Asia Ltd
1/F, Gaylord Commercial Bldg, 114 Lockhart Rd, Wanchai
Tel: 28657525 *Fax:* 28661064
E-mail: postmaster@pronta.com.hk
Key Personnel
Man Dir: Clive Howard
Founded: 1986
Business from Other Countries: 40%

Rainbow Graphic & Printing Co Ltd
Tseung Kwan O Industrial Estate, 8 Chun Ying St, 4/F, Kowloon
Tel: 27523423 *Fax:* 28974890
E-mail: rgarts@netvigator.com
Telex: 61310 RBART HX
Key Personnel
General Manager: Willie Lim *E-mail:* willylim@netvigator.com
Business from Other Countries: 90%

SNP Best-Set Typesetter Ltd
6 Sun Yip St, Honour Industrial Centre, Room 304, 3rd floor, Chai Wan
Tel: 2897 6033 *Fax:* 2897 5170
E-mail: bestset@snpcorp.com
Web Site: www.bestset-typesetter.com
Key Personnel
Dir (Hong Kong): Johnson Yeung *Tel:* 852-289-6033 *E-mail:* johnson@bestset-typesetter.com
Manager: Cynthia Hui *E-mail:* cynthiahui@snpcorp.com
Sales Rep: Wai Man Yeung
   E-mail: waimanyeung@snpcorp.com
Founded: 1986
Turnaround: 5 workdays
Print Runs: 100 min - 200,000 max
Business from Other Countries: 98%
Branch Office(s)
3 Da Song Jiang nan Main Ave C, 3rd floor, Guangzhou, Patrick Au *Tel:* (020) 8441 5873 *Fax:* (020) 8441 5874 *E-mail:* gzbestset@snpcorp.com
Sales Office(s): 157 Fisher Ave, Suite 6, Eastchester, NY 10709, United States, Contact: Wai Man Yeung *Tel:* 914-961-6223 *Fax:* 914-961-8212 *E-mail:* waimanyeung@snpcorp.com
33 Alpin Way, TW7 4RJ Isleworth, Middlesex, United Kingdom, Contact: Keith Harrocks *Tel:* (0208) 847-4947 *Fax:* (0208) 847-4947 *E-mail:* keithharrocks@snpcorp.com

Sota Graphic Arts Co Ltd
Seapower Industrial Centre, 6/F, 177 Hoi Bun Rd, Kwun Tong
Tel: 23421083 *Fax:* 23415426
E-mail: sales@goldencup.com.hk
Key Personnel
Man Dir: K K Yeung
General Manager: Wai Kwong Ngan
Assistant Manager: Mary Yeung *E-mail:* mary@goldencup.com.hk
Founded: 1985
Turnaround: 10 Workdays
Print Runs: 2,000 min
Business from Other Countries: 90%

South Sea International Press Ltd
3/F, Yip Cheung Centre, 10 Fung Yip St, Chai Wan
Tel: 2897 1083 *Fax:* 2558 1473
E-mail: books@ssip.com.hk
Web Site: www.ssip.com.hk
Key Personnel
Man Dir: P Y Lee; Franky Ho
Founded: 1984
Print Runs: 3,000 min - 500,000 max
Business from Other Countries: 80%
Branch Office(s)
Haverdreef 39, 7006 LH, Doetinchem, Netherlands, Contact: Buro Doral *Tel:* (0314) 35 40 40 *Fax:* (0314) 35 46 00 *E-mail:* info@ssip-holland.nl *Web Site:* www.ssip-holland.nl
The High Barn, Snailing Lane, Hawkley GU33 6NJ, United Kingdom, Contact: Myles Wells *Tel:* (01) 730 827 326 *Fax:* (01) 730 827 537 *E-mail:* mwells@eastwest.fsworld.co.uk

Sunshine Press Ltd
21/F Fullager Ind Bldg, 234 Aberdeen Main Rd, Hong Kong
Tel: 25532386 *Fax:* 28732930
E-mail: spl@sunshinepress.com.hk
Key Personnel
Administrative Assistant: Trevin Tong
Contact: Joney Chan
Founded: 1976
Turnaround: 21-28 Workdays
Print Runs: 3,000 min - 500,000 max
Business from Other Countries: 25%

Toppan Printing Co (HK) Ltd
Division of Toppan Printing Co Ltd
Yuen Long Industrial Estate, One Fuk Wang St, Yuen Long, New Territories
Tel: 2475-5666; 2561-0101 *Fax:* 2475-4321
E-mail: info@toppan.co.jp
Web Site: www.toppan.co.jp
Key Personnel
Man Dir: James Lee Lee
Sales Manager: Yukata Ito
Founded: 1963
Turnaround: 30 Workdays
Business from Other Countries: 25%

Wing King Tong Group
Leader Industrial Centre, Block I, 3/F, 188-202 Texaco Rd, Tsuen Wan, New Territories
Tel: 24073287; 24073309; 24074547 *Fax:* 24074130
Key Personnel
Man Dir: Alex Yan Tak Chung *E-mail:* ayan@hk.super.net
Marketing Dir: Jeremy Kuo
Founded: 1944
Turnaround: 15 Workdays
Print Runs: 1,000 min - 100,000 max
Business from Other Countries: 95%

Ying Tat Co
Division of Quality Printing & Paper Products
Wing Wah Industrial Bldg, 8/F, 677 Kings Rd, North Point
Tel: 25645980; 25645963; 25639981 *Fax:* 28111280
Key Personnel
Sales Manager: Kan Chan
Contact: Chan Dun Yin
Founded: 1968
Turnaround: 7-10 Workdays
Print Runs: 1,000 min - 1,000,000 max
Business from Other Countries: 30%

India

Hiralal Printing Works Ltd
Subsidiary of Conway Printers Pvt Ltd
D-41/1 TTC Industrial Area MIDC, opp Turbhe tel exchange, Mumbai 400613
Tel: (022) 7672726; (022) 7683012 *Fax:* (022) 7631191
Key Personnel
Chairman: G P Agrawal
Man Dir: Mr Rakesh Kumar Agrawal
Founded: 1981
Turnaround: 40-45 Workdays
Print Runs: 5,000 min - 100,000 max
Business from Other Countries: 75%

Paragon Prepress Inc
N-31, Kalkaji, New Delhi 110019
Tel: (011) 2622 44 51; (011) 5160 1485
   Fax: (011) 2622 44 51
E-mail: information@paragonpress.com
Web Site: www.paragonprepress.com
Key Personnel
Chief Executive Officer: Shailander Malhotra
   E-mail: shailander@paragonpress.com
Production Manager: T Malhotra *E-mail:* tarun@paragonprepress.com
Founded: 1991

Indonesia

Ichtiar Baru I Van Hoeve
Jln Cideng Barat 62/Jl Raya Pasar Jumat No 38 D-E Pondok Pinang, POB 1376/jks, Jakarta Pusat 12013
Tel: (021) 7511856
Founded: 1972
Turnaround: 6 Workdays
Print Runs: 500 min - 18,000 max

Victory Offset Prima PT
Jalan Raya Pegangsaan, Dua No 17, Jakarta 14250
Tel: (021) 460-2742; (021) 460-8968; (021) 4682-0555 *Fax:* (021) 460-2740; (021) 4682-0551
E-mail: info@victoryoffset.com
Web Site: www.victoryoffset.com
Key Personnel
President: Zainal F Stanley *E-mail:* zainal@victoryoffset.com
General Manager: S Wilson Pinady
   E-mail: wilson@victoryoffset.com
Founded: 1971
Turnaround: 14 days
Print Runs: 5,000 min
Business from Other Countries: 10%

Ireland

Doyle Graphics
Esker House, Patrick St, Tullamore, Co Offaly
Tel: (0506) 21970 *Fax:* (0506) 51323
Key Personnel
Contact: Desmond Doyle
Production Manager: Tom Clarke

Graphic Reproductions Ltd
Westlink House, Old Lucan Rd, Palmerstown, Dublin 20
Tel: (01) 6230101 *Fax:* (01) 6166598; (01) 6166599

IRELAND

Key Personnel
Contact: David Malone; Tim Hurley
Branch Office(s)
Graphic Reproductions, 475 Park Ave S, New York, NY 10016, United States *Tel:* 212-679-4351 *Fax:* 212-679-4352

ICPC Ltd
Subsidiary of The Irish Times
Greencastle Parade, Coolock, Dublin 17
Tel: (01) 8474711 *Fax:* (01) 8474546
Web Site: www.icpc.ie
Key Personnel
Man Dir: Seamus McCague *E-mail:* seamus@icpc.ie
Production Manager: Wayne Nial *E-mail:* wayne@icpc.ie
Founded: 1976
Turnaround: 10 Workdays
Business from Other Countries: 95%

Kilkenny People/Wellbrook Press
34 High St, Kilkenny
Tel: (056) 63366 *Fax:* (056) 63388
Web Site: www.srhplc.com; www.kilkennypeople.ie
Key Personnel
Man Dir: Joe Hayes *E-mail:* jhayes@kilkennypeople.ie
Sales Manager: Martin Brett
Founded: 1892
Business from Other Countries: 10%
Ultimate Parent Company: Scottish Radio Holdings

SciPrint Ltd
Bay 93, Shannon Industrial Estate, Shannon, Co Clare
Tel: (061) 472114; (061) 472520 *Fax:* (061) 472021
Key Personnel
Man Dir, Sales: M K Parsons
Chairman: B Lane
Founded: 1974
Turnaround: 15-20 Workdays
Print Runs: 300 min - 10,000 max
Business from Other Countries: 95%

Smurfit Print
Beech Hill, Clonskeagh, Dublin 4
Tel: (01) 202-7000 *Fax:* (01) 269-4481
Web Site: www.smurfit.ie
Key Personnel
Sales Manager: Donal Greene *E-mail:* dgreene@smurfitprint.ie
Print Runs: 200 min - 5,000,000 max
Business from Other Countries: 20%
Parent Company: Jefferson Smurfit Group plc

Ultragraphics
Unit 78A, Cookstown Industrial Estate, Tallaght, Dublin 24
Tel: (01) 4599133 *Fax:* (01) 4512368
Key Personnel
President: Tony Lovett
Turnaround: 4-5 Workdays
Business from Other Countries: 80%

Israel

Har-El Printers & Publishers
Jaffa Port, Jaffa 61081
Mailing Address: Jaffa Port, PO Box 8053, Jaffa 61081
Tel: (03) 681 6834 *Fax:* (03) 681 3563
E-mail: mharel@harelart.co.il
Web Site: www.harelart.com

Key Personnel
Manager: Jaacov Har-El
Founded: 1974
Turnaround: 60-90 Workdays
Print Runs: 30 min - 5,000 max
Business from Other Countries: 70%

Keterpress Enterprises Jerusalem
PO Box 7145, 91071 Jerusalem
Mailing Address: PO Box 7145, Jerusalem 91071
Tel: (02) 6521201 *Fax:* (02) 6527956
E-mail: info@keter-books.co.il
Web Site: www.keter-books.co.il
Key Personnel
Plant Manager: Peter Tomkins *E-mail:* peter@keter-books.co.il
Sales Manager: Zvi Weller
Print Runs: 500 min - 500,000 max
Business from Other Countries: 10%
Parent Company: Keter Publishing House Ltd

Monoline Ltd
3 Avnei Nezer, Kiryat Sefer
Tel: (08) 9741456 *Fax:* (08) 9741454
Key Personnel
Dir: S J Colthof
Founded: 1959
Business from Other Countries: 30%

Technosdar Ltd
5 Levontine St, Tel Aviv 61316
Tel: (03) 560-7418; (03) 5605951 *Fax:* (03) 5605951
Key Personnel
General Manager: Avraham Weiss
Founded: 1972
Turnaround: 7-16 Workdays
Business from Other Countries: 10%

Italy

Canale G e C SpA
Subsidiary of Istituto Grafico Bertello SpA
Via Liguria 24, 10071 Borgaro Turin
Tel: (011) 40 78 511 *Fax:* (011) 40 78 527
E-mail: info@canale.it
Key Personnel
Dir General: Canale Giacomo *E-mail:* canale@canale.it
Founded: 1915
Turnaround: 30 Workdays
Print Runs: 3,000 min
Business from Other Countries: 65%
Parent Company: Ledi Srl; PPG Srl

Dedalo Litostampa SRL
Viale Luigi Jacobini 5, Bari 70123
Mailing Address: Casella Postale BA/19, 70123 Bari
Tel: (080) 531 14 13; (080) 531 1400 *Fax:* (080) 531 14 14
E-mail: info@edizionidedalo.it
Web Site: www.edizionidedalo.it
Key Personnel
Man Dir: Raimondo Coga
General Manager: Sergio Coga *E-mail:* s.coga@edizionidedalo.it
Founded: 1965
Print Runs: 2,000 min - 15,000 max

Milanostampa SpA
Corso Ferrero, 5, 12060 Farigliano
Tel: (0173) 746111 *Fax:* (0173) 746248; (0173) 746249
E-mail: info@milanostampa.com; sales@milanostampa.com
Web Site: www.milanostampa.com

Telex: 212428
Key Personnel
Commercial Dir: Riccardo Sardo
Man Dir: Fuad Lahham
Founded: 1965
Turnaround: 15 Workdays
Print Runs: 3,000 min - 80,000 max
Business from Other Countries: 65%
Branch Office(s)
Via Statuto, 4, 20121 Milan *Tel:* (02) 6200 1311 *Fax:* (02) 6200 1313

Nuovo Instituto Italiano d'Arti Grafiche
Via Zanica 92, 24126 Bergamo
Tel: (035) 329111 *Fax:* (035) 329346
E-mail: artigraf@bertelsmann.de
Telex: (035) 300114
Founded: 1871
Turnaround: 10 Workdays
Business from Other Countries: 30%

Amilcare Pizzi SpA
Via A Pizzi, 14, 20092 Cinisello Balsamo
Tel: (02) 618361 *Fax:* (02) 61 83 62 83
E-mail: info@amilcarepizzi.it
Key Personnel
Chief Executive Officer: Massimo Pizzi
Founded: 1914
Business from Other Countries: 45%
Branch Office(s)
American Pizzi Offset Corp, 370 Lexington Ave, Suite 505, New York, NY 10017, United States *Tel:* 212-986-1658 *Fax:* 212-286-1887

Republic of Korea

Daehan Printing & Publishing Co Ltd
344-12, Sangdaewon 1-dong, Jungwon-gu, Seongnam-si, Gyeonggi-do, Seoul
Tel: (031) 730-3850 *Fax:* (031) 735-8104
E-mail: mschung@daehane.com
Web Site: www.daehane.com
Key Personnel
Manager: Jongjun Yu
President & Chief Executive Officer: Tae-Rang Hwang
Founded: 1948
U.S. Office(s): 3271 Sawtelle Blvd No 104, Los Angeles, CA 90066, United States *Tel:* 310-737-0058 *Fax:* 310-737-9213 (sales)

Pyunghwa Dang Printing Co Ltd
60 Kyunji-Dong, Chongro-ku, Seoul 110-170
Tel: (02) 735-4011 *Fax:* (02) 734-5201
E-mail: comuser@hitel.kol.co.kr *Cable:* PHDPRINTCO SEOUL
Key Personnel
President: Mr Il Soo Lee
Vice President: Mr Hae Kun Oh
Executive Dir: Mr Sang Woo Lee
Founded: 1923
Turnaround: 10 Workdays
Print Runs: 2,000 min - 500,000 max
Business from Other Countries: 7%

Lithuania

Spindulys Printing House
Gedimino g 10, 3000 Kaunas
Tel: (037) 226243 *Fax:* (037) 204970
E-mail: spindul@kaunas.aiva.lt
Key Personnel
Contact: Elena Kapustinskiene

Founded: 1928
Print Runs: 500 min - 100,000 max
Business from Other Countries: 6%

Madagascar

Societe Malgache d'Edition
Route des Hydrocarbures, Ankorondrano, BP 659,
 Antananarivo/Tananrive 101
Tel: (020) 2222635 *Fax:* (020) 2222254
E-mail: tribune@bow.dts.mg
Web Site: www.madagascar-tribune.com
Telex: (020) 223-40
Key Personnel
Dir of Publication: Rahaga Ramaholimihaso
Founded: 1943
Print Runs: 7,000 min - 15,000 max

Netherlands

Bosch en Keuning grafische bedrijven
Ericastr 1, 3742 SG Baarn
Tel: (035) 5412050 *Fax:* (035) 2202446
Key Personnel
Contact: P P E Rings

New Zealand

Egan-Reid Ltd
Level 2, 38 Ireland St, Freemans Bay, Auckland 1001
Tel: (09) 3784100 *Fax:* (09) 3784300
E-mail: publishing@eganreid.com
Web Site: www.egan-reid.com
Key Personnel
Man Dir: Gerard Reid *E-mail:* gerard@eganreid.co.nz
Contact: Mary Egan *E-mail:* mary@eganreid.co.nz
Founded: 1988
Turnaround: 2 Workdays
Business from Other Countries: 75%

PPP Printers Ltd
339 St Asaph St, Christchurch
Tel: (03) 3662727 *Fax:* (03) 3654606
Key Personnel
Man Dir: D C Richardson
Founded: 1958
Turnaround: 10 Workdays
Print Runs: 100 min - 100,000 max
Business from Other Countries: 10%

Rogan McIndoe Print Ltd
51 Crawford St, Dunedin
Mailing Address: PO Box 1361, Dunedin
Tel: (03) 474 0111 *Toll Free Tel:* 800-477-0355 *Fax:* (03) 474 0116
E-mail: quality@rogan.co.nz
Web Site: www.rogan.co.nz
Key Personnel
Man Dir: Brendan A Murphy
Founded: 1893
Print Runs: 21 min - 30 max
Business from Other Countries: 1%
Branch Office(s)
73 Durham St, Sydenham, Christchurch *Tel:* (03) 377 4637 *Fax:* (03) 377 4639

Philippines

Naldoza Printers
362 Tupaz St, 6000 Cebu City
Tel: (032) 261-7326 *Fax:* (032) 261-7326
E-mail: naldoza@ebu.skyinet.net
Key Personnel
Chief Executive Officer: John R Naldoza
Founded: 1989
Parent Company: Business Developers Inc
Membership(s): Philippine Printing Technical Foundation

Reyes Publishing Inc
Mariwasa Bldg, 717 Aurora Blvd, 1112 Quezon City
Tel: (02) 721-7492 *Fax:* (02) 721-8782
E-mail: reyesbub@skyinet.net
Key Personnel
Operations Manager: Roman Paolo Reyes, V
Founded: 1964
Business from Other Countries: 90%

Portugal

Edicoes Silabo
Rua Cidade de Manchester 2, 1170 100 Lisbon
Tel: (021) 316 12 81 *Fax:* (021) 314 58 80
E-mail: silabo@mail.telepac.pt
Key Personnel
Marketing Dir: Manuel Robalo
 E-mail: manuelrobalo@silabo.pt
Founded: 1983
Turnaround: 5 Workdays

Puerto Rico

Publishing Resources Inc
373 San Jorge St, 2nd floor, Santurce 00912
Mailing Address: PO Box 41307, Minillas Station, Santurce 00940
Tel: 787-268-8080 *Fax:* (787) 774-5781
E-mail: pri@tld.net
Key Personnel
Owner & President: Ronald J Chevako
Editorial Dir: Anne W Chevako
Founded: 1976
Print Runs: 500 min - 10,000 max
Business from Other Countries: 5%

Singapore

Alkem Company Pte Ltd
No 1 Penjuru Close, Jurong Town, Singapore 608617
Tel: 6265 6666 *Fax:* 6261-7875
E-mail: enquiry@alkem.com.sg
Key Personnel
Man Dir: Chu Bong *E-mail:* chubong@alkem.com.sg
Founded: 1998
Turnaround: 15 Workdays
Print Runs: 1,000 min - 1,000,000 max
Business from Other Countries: 90%

Chong Moh Offset Printing Ltd
Subsidiary of Chassis Graphic Art Pte Ltd
19 Joo Koon Rd, Jurong Town 628978
Tel: 8622701 *Fax:* 8624335
E-mail: chongmoh@singnet.com.sg
Key Personnel
Chairman: James Ng
Founded: 1946
Turnaround: 10-14 Workdays
Print Runs: 1,000 min
Business from Other Countries: 35%

Chroma Graphics (Overseas) Pte Ltd
Blk 12, Lorong Bakar Batu, No 05-08, Singapore 348745
Tel: 67423706 *Fax:* 67486712
Telex: 55962 CG SEP
Key Personnel
Man Dir: Thomas K P Chan
 E-mail: thomaschan@chromographics.com.sg
Founded: 1978
Turnaround: 7-10 Workdays
Business from Other Countries: 85%

Craft Print Pte Ltd
9 Joo Koon Circle, Jurong, Singapore 629041
Tel: 861 4040 *Fax:* 861 0530
E-mail: craftprt@singet.com.sg
Key Personnel
Man Dir: Charlie Chan

CS Graphics Pte Ltd
10 Tuas Ave 20, Singapore 638822
Tel: 6865 2010 *Fax:* 6861 0190
Web Site: ourworld.compuserve.com/homepages/csgraphics
Key Personnel
Man Dir: Mr Lee Sian Tee *E-mail:* stlee@csgraphics-world.com
Founded: 1980
Turnaround: 80 Workdays
Print Runs: 1,000 min - 100,000 max
Business from Other Countries: 100%

Eurasia Press Pte Ltd
10/14 Kampong Ampat-1336, Singapore 368320
Tel: 2805522 *Fax:* 2800593; 3825458
E-mail: eurasia@mbox3.singnet.com.sg
Key Personnel
Marketing Dir: Allan Fong
Founded: 1937
Turnaround: 14 Workdays
Print Runs: 500 min - 100,000 max
Business from Other Countries: 65%

Ho Printing Singapore Pte Ltd
31 Changi South St One, Changi South Industrial Estate, Singapore 486769
Tel: 5429322 *Fax:* 5428322
Telex: RS 39685 HOFSET
Key Personnel
Man Dir: Ho Wai Hoi
Founded: 1951
Turnaround: 35-50 Workdays
Print Runs: 5,000 min - 50,000 max
Business from Other Countries: 30%

Markono Print Media Pte Ltd
Subsidiary of Markono Holdings Pte Ltd
21 Neythal Rd, Singapore 628586
Tel: 6281-1118 *Fax:* 6286-6663
E-mail: kinkeong@pacific.net.sg
Key Personnel
Dir: Bob Lee Song Tioh *E-mail:* blee@markono.com.sg
Turnaround: 14 Workdays
Print Runs: 1,000 min - 100,000 max
Business from Other Countries: 20%
Branch Office(s)
Kin Keong Colour Printing (M) Sdn Bhd, Port Klang 539538

SINGAPORE

Pica Digital Pte Ltd
Formerly Pica Overseas Color Separation Ltd
Block 55, 2nd floor, 11-22 Ayer Rajah Crescent, Singapore 139949
Tel: 67761311 *Fax:* 67793055
E-mail: picaosea@singnet.com.sg
Key Personnel
Dir: Thomas Ling
Founded: 1977
Turnaround: 4 Workdays
Business from Other Countries: 60%

Pica Overseas Color Separation Ltd, see Pica Digital Pte Ltd

Sang Choy International Pte Ltd
Harrison Ind Bldg, 05-01, 9 Harrison Rd, Singapore 369651
Tel: (065) 6289 0829 *Fax:* (065) 6282 7673
E-mail: marketing@sc-international.com.sg
Web Site: www.sc-international.com.sg
Key Personnel
Dir of Operations: Almond Ko
Founded: 1992
Business from Other Countries: 90%

SNP SPrint Pte Ltd
97 Ubi Ave 4, Singapore 408754
Tel: 6826-9600 *Fax:* 6820-3341
E-mail: enquiries@snpcorp.com
Web Site: www.snp-corp.com
Telex: SNPRS14462
Key Personnel
Chief Executive Officer & President: Yeo Chee Tong
Executive Vice President Security Printing: Paul Wong Pao Lu *E-mail:* paulwong@snp.com.sg
US Sales Manager: Patrick Chung
Turnaround: 30 Workdays
Print Runs: 2,000 min - 200,000 max
Business from Other Countries: 40%
Parent Company: SNP Corporation Ltd

Stamford Press Pte Ltd
209, Kallang Bahru, Singapore 339344
Tel: 6294 7227 *Fax:* 6294 4396; 6294 3319
E-mail: stamfad@singnet.com.sg
Web Site: www.stamford.com.sg
Telex: RS56414 STAMFO
Key Personnel
Dir: Mr L Rajesh *Tel:* 6294 7227 (ext 233)
  E-mail: rajesh@stamford.com.sg
Founded: 1963
Turnaround: 3-4 Workdays for small jobs; 3-4 weeks for big jobs
Print Runs: 1,500 min - 50,000 max
Business from Other Countries: 20%

Times Graphics
Division of Times Printers Pte Ltd
Subsidiary of Times Publishing Ltd
Times Centre, One New Industrial Rd, Singapore 536196
Tel: 6213-9288 *Fax:* 6284 4733; 6288 1186
E-mail: tpl@tpl.com.sg
Web Site: www.tpl.com.sg
Telex: RS 25713
Key Personnel
Manager: Andrew Wong Weng Fook
Founded: 1986
Turnaround: 15 Workdays
Business from Other Countries: 40%

Times Printers Pte Ltd
Subsidiary of Times Publishing Group
16 Tuas Ave 5, Singapore 639340
Tel: 6311-2888 *Fax:* 6862-1313
E-mail: tp@timesprinters.com; enquiry@timesprinters.com
Web Site: www.timesprinters.com; www.tpl.com.sg *Cable:* TIMESPRINT

Key Personnel
Corporate General Manager: Ronald Pereira
  E-mail: ronaldpereira@tpl.com.sg
Head of Sales: Patsy Tan *Tel:* 63112 763
  E-mail: patsytan@timesprinters.com
Sales Manager: Koo Kok Leong
Founded: 1968
Turnaround: 5-25 Workdays
Print Runs: 3,000 min - 300,000 max
Business from Other Countries: 75%

Slovenia

Gorenjski Tisk Printing House
Mirka Vadnova 6, 4000 Kranj
Tel: (04) 2016300 *Fax:* (04) 2016301
E-mail: info@go-tisk.si
Web Site: www.go-tisk.si
Telex: 34560 YU GOTISK
Key Personnel
Dir: Kristina Kobal
Commercial Manager: Boris Krist
Founded: 1888
Turnaround: 30 Workdays
Print Runs: 3,000 min - 15,000 max
Business from Other Countries: 50%

South Africa

CTP Book Printers (Pty) Ltd
PO Box 1610, Parklands
Tel: (011) 8890600 *Fax:* (011) 8890922
E-mail: ctpjhb@iafrica.com

Spain

Graficas Santamaria SA
Division of Fotomecanica
Bekolarra, 4 Pol Ali Gobeo, 01010 Vitoria Gasteiz
Tel: (0945) 229100 *Fax:* (0945) 246393
E-mail: grsantamaria@sea.es; grsantamaria@graficassantamaria.com
Web Site: www.graficassantamaria.com
Key Personnel
Contact: Jesus Alzola Aguinaco
Founded: 1963
Turnaround: 1 Workday
Print Runs: 500 min - 150,000 max
Business from Other Countries: 15%

Sri Lanka

Sumathi Book Printing (Pvt) Ltd
Division of Sumathi Group
445, Sirimovo Bandaranaike Mawatha, Colombo 14
Tel: (0941) 330-673-5 *Fax:* (0941) 449-593
E-mail: lakbima@isplanka.lk
Web Site: www.sumathi.lk
Telex: 22104 SUMATHI CE SUMATISONS
Key Personnel
General Manager: Nawas A Rahim
Business from Other Countries: 75%

Switzerland

Photolitho AG
Industriestr 12, 8625 Gossau ZH
Tel: (043) 833 70 20 *Fax:* (043) 833 70 30
E-mail: info@photolitho.ch
Web Site: www.photolitho.ch
Key Personnel
President: Dietmar von Eicke *Tel:* (043) 833 70 24 *E-mail:* dve@photolitho.ch
Administrator: Werner Holliger *Tel:* (043) 833 70 23 *E-mail:* w.holliger@photolitho.ch
Founded: 1965
Business from Other Countries: 50%

United Republic of Tanzania

Peramiho Publications
PO Box 41, Peramiho
Tel: (054) 2730 *Fax:* (054) 2917
Key Personnel
Chief Executive: Fr Gerold Rupper
Founded: 1937
Print Runs: 4,000 min - 6,000 max

Thailand

Phongwarin Printing Company Ltd
299 Mu 10, Sukhumvit 107, Sumrongnue, Ampur Muang, Samutprakarn 10260
Tel: (02) 7498934-45; (02) 3994525-31; (02) 7498275-9 *Fax:* (02) 3994524; (02) 3994255
E-mail: somphong@phongwarin.com
Web Site: www.phongwarin.com
Key Personnel
Man Dir: Mr Somphong Charnsirisaksakul
Founded: 1983
Turnaround: 7 Workdays
Print Runs: 1,000 min - 500,000 max
Business from Other Countries: 5%

United Kingdom

Adroit Birmingham Ltd
Cecil St, Birmingham B19 3ST
Tel: (0121) 3596831 *Fax:* (0121) 3593974
Key Personnel
Sales Manager: Jackie Robotham

The Alden Group Ltd
Osney Mead, Oxford OX2 0EF
Tel: (01865) 253 200 *Fax:* (01865) 249 070
E-mail: alden.press@alden.co.uk
Web Site: www.alden.co.uk
Key Personnel
Group Technical/Development Dir: Robert Hay
Sales Dir: Michael Angless
Marketing Administrator: Gemma Webb
  E-mail: gwebb@alden.co.uk

SERVICES UNITED KINGDOM

AlpnetCompuType Ltd
Horton Parade Horton Rd, West Drayton UB7 8EP
Tel: (01895) 440791 *Fax:* (01895) 441500
E-mail: computype@computype.co.uk
Key Personnel
Business Manager: Brian Trowse
Founded: 1976

ARADCO VSI Ltd
Aradco House, 132 Cleveland St, London W1T 6AB
Tel: (020) 7692 7700 *Fax:* (020) 7692 7711
E-mail: aradco@compuserve.com
Web Site: www.aradco.com
Key Personnel
Contact: R Dawood
Founded: 1958
Business from Other Countries: 20%

J W Arrowsmith Ltd
Winterstoke Rd, Bristol BS3 2NT
Tel: (0117) 966 7545 *Fax:* (0117) 963 7829
E-mail: jw@arrowsmith.co.uk
Web Site: www.arrowsmith.co.uk
Key Personnel
Sales Dir: David J Hooper *E-mail:* dhooper@arrowsmith.co.uk
Founded: 1854
Turnaround: 15 Workdays
Print Runs: 500 min - 15,000 max
Business from Other Countries: 40%

Associated Translation & Typesetting
Alexander House, 64 Robin Hood Lane, Hall Green, Birmingham B28 0JT
Tel: (0121) 603 6344 *Fax:* (0121) 603 6399
E-mail: ATTEuro@aol.com (European translation); ATTAsia@aol.com (Eastern/Asian translation)
Web Site: www.jaure.demon.co.uk
Key Personnel
Dir: Mr S Ahmed
Founded: 1971
Business from Other Countries: 50%

Axicon Auto ID Ltd
Weston on the Green, Bicester, Church Rd, Oxon OX25 3QP
Tel: (01869) 351155 *Fax:* (01869) 351205
E-mail: sales@axicon.com
Web Site: www.axicon.com
Key Personnel
Dir: Jenny Hicks *E-mail:* jmh@axicon.com
Founded: 1981
Turnaround: 1-2 Workdays
Business from Other Countries: 30%

W & G Baird Ltd
Subsidiary of The Baird Group
Greystone Press, Caulside Dr, Antrim BT41 2RS
Tel: (028) 9446 3911 *Fax:* (028) 9446 6250
E-mail: wgbaird@wgbaird.com
Web Site: www.wgbaird.org
Key Personnel
Man Dir: Dairmuid McGarry *E-mail:* dairmuid.mcgarry@wgbaird.com
Founded: 1863
Print Runs: 500 min - 100,000 max
Business from Other Countries: 45%
Branch Office(s)
Textflow, Belfast, Ireland
MSO, Belfast, Ireland
Biddles Ltd, Woodbridge Park, Woodbridge Rd, Guildford, Surrey GU1 1DA

BAS Printers Ltd
115 Tollgate Rd, Salisbury, Wilts SP1 2JG
Tel: (01722) 411711 *Fax:* (01722) 411727
E-mail: sales@basprint.co.uk
Web Site: www.basprint.co.uk
Key Personnel
Man Dir: David Gumn
Sales Dir: Paul G Gumn *E-mail:* paul@basprint.co.uk
Founded: 1948
Print Runs: 350 min - 40,000 max
Business from Other Countries: 10%

Baseline Creative Ltd
60A Northumbria Dr, Henleaze, Bristol BS9 4HW
Tel: (0117) 962 0006 *Fax:* (0117) 962 5006
E-mail: contact@base.co.uk
Web Site: www.base.co.uk
Key Personnel
Man Dir & Creative Dir: John Buchmueller *E-mail:* john@base.co.uk
Account Manager: Nicholas J Wood *E-mail:* nick@base.co.uk
Senior Designer: David Sheppard *E-mail:* david@base.co.uk; Rob Wilkins *E-mail:* rob@base.co.uk
Founded: 1985
Turnaround: 30 Workdays

The Bath Press
Subsidiary of Bath Press Group PLC
Lower Bristol Rd, Bath BA2 3BL
Tel: (01225) 428101 *Fax:* (01225) 312418
E-mail: bath@cpi-group.co.uk
Web Site: www.cpi-group.net
Key Personnel
Man Dir: Peter Palframan
Marketing Dir: Keith Johnson
Contact: Jack McCabe *E-mail:* jmccabe@bathpress.co.uk
Founded: 1846
Turnaround: 10-15 Workdays
Print Runs: 3,000 min - 300,000 max
Business from Other Countries: 5%

BCS Publishing Ltd
One Bignell Park Barns, Kirtlington Rd, Oxon OX6 8TD
Tel: (01869) 324423 *Fax:* (01869) 324385
Key Personnel
Man Dir: Steve McCurdy
Founded: 1993
Business from Other Countries: 40%

Bell & Bain Ltd
303 Burnfield Rd, Thornliebank, Glasgow G46 7UQ
Tel: (0141) 649 5697 *Fax:* (0141) 632 8733
E-mail: info@bell-bain.demon.co.uk
Web Site: www.bell-bain.co.uk
Key Personnel
Man Dir: I Walker
Sales Dir: D Stewart
Turnaround: 7-10 Workdays
Print Runs: 100 min - 100,000 max
Business from Other Countries: 25%

Black Bear Press Ltd
King's Hedges Rd, Cambridge CB4 2PQ
Tel: (01223) 424571 *Fax:* (01223) 426877
E-mail: black_bear_pres@msn.com
Key Personnel
Man Dir: K Fentiman
Sales Manager: Mike Hallam
Contact: Mary Simpson

Blackmore Ltd
Longmead Industrial Estate, Shaftesbury, Dorset SP7 8PX
Tel: (01747) 853034 *Fax:* (01747) 854500
E-mail: sales@blackmore.co.uk
Web Site: www.blackmore.co.uk
Key Personnel
Group Chief Executive: Chris Brickell
Man Dir: Peter Smith
Sales Dir: Aubrey Aviss

Book Creation
20 Lochaline St, London W6 9SH
Tel: (020) 7583 0553 *Fax:* (020) 7583 9439
E-mail: info@librios.com
Key Personnel
Chairman: Hal Robinson *E-mail:* hal@librios.com
Founded: 1991
Business from Other Countries: 30%

Book Production Consultants PLC
25-27 High St, Chesterton, Cambridge CB4 1ND
Tel: (01223) 352790 *Fax:* (01223) 460718
E-mail: bpc@bpccam.co.uk
Web Site: www.bpccam.co.uk
Key Personnel
Dir: Tony Littlechild *E-mail:* tl@bpccam.co.uk; Colin Walsh
Founded: 1973
Print Runs: 500 min
Business from Other Countries: 25%

D Brown & Sons Ltd
North Rd, Bridgend Industrial Estate, Bridgend CF31 3TP
Tel: (01446) 771475 *Fax:* (01446) 771476
Key Personnel
Dir: J M Whitaker *Tel:* (01446) 774213
Finance Dir: Jane C Brown
Founded: 1895
Print Runs: 1 min - 1,000,000 max
Business from Other Countries: 20%
Branch Office(s)
Eastgate Press, 62 Eastgate, Cowbridge, S Glam CF7 7AB

Butler & Tanner Ltd
Selwood Printing Works, Caxton Rd, Frome, Somerset BA11 1NF
Tel: (01373) 451500 *Fax:* (01373) 451333
E-mail: manufacturing@butlerandtanner.com
Web Site: www.butlerandtanner.com
Key Personnel
President: John Clare *Tel:* (01373) 463366
Joint Man Dir: A Huett
Sales Dir: N White

Caledonian International Book Manufacturing
Westerhill Rd, Bishopbriggs, Glasgow G64 2QR
Tel: (0141) 7623000 *Fax:* (0141) 7620922
E-mail: 101622.235@compuserve.com
Key Personnel
Man Dir: Kevin McKenna
Commercial Dir: G Morrison
Group Sales Manager: Martin Platt *E-mail:* martin@platt44.freeserve.co.uk
Founded: 1819

Cambridge University Press - Printing Division
Division of Cambridge University Press
University Printing House, Edinburgh Bldg, Shaftesbury Rd, Cambridge CB2 2RU
Tel: (01223) 358331 *Fax:* (01223) 325672
E-mail: info@cup.cam.ac.uk
Web Site: printing.cambridge.org
Key Personnel
Executive Dir: Sandra Ward *Tel:* (01223) 325608 *E-mail:* sward@cambridge.org
Founded: 1534
Print Runs: 1 min

Center Print Ltd
Subsidiary of Beshara Press
Private Rd 2, Colwich Business Park, Colwich, Nottingham NG4 2JR
Tel: (0115) 961 2277 *Fax:* (0115) 938 1424
E-mail: cprint@besharapress.co.uk
Web Site: www.besharapress.com

UNITED KINGDOM

Key Personnel
General Manager: Nicola Lesley
Print Runs: 1,000 min - 250,000 max

The Charlesworth Group
254 Deighton Rd, Huddersfield, West Yorks HD2 1JJ
Tel: (01484) 517077 *Fax:* (01484) 517068
E-mail: sales@charlesworth.com
Web Site: www.charlesworth.com
Key Personnel
Marketing Manager: Sarah Philp
 E-mail: s_philp@charlesworth.com
Founded: 1928
Turnaround: 1 to 10 Workdays
Print Runs: 1 min - 10,000 max
Business from Other Countries: 30%

Chase Publishing Services
Mead, Fortescue Rd, Sidmouth, Devon EX10 9QG
Tel: (01395) 514709 *Fax:* (01395) 514709
Key Personnel
President: Ray Addicott *E-mail:* r.addicott@btinternet.com
Founded: 1989

William Clowes Ltd
Beccles, Suffolk NR34 9QE
Tel: (01502) 712884 *Fax:* (01502) 717003
E-mail: william@clowes.co.uk
Web Site: www.clowes.co.uk
Key Personnel
Chief Executive Dir: Alex Evans
Sales Dir: David C Browne *Tel:* (07768) 658820
 E-mail: dbrowne@clowes.co.uk
Contact: Tracy Humphrey
Founded: 1803
Turnaround: 10 Workdays
Print Runs: 2,000 min
Business from Other Countries: 1%

Cooper Dale
1a Dalling Rd, London W6 0RA
Tel: (020) 8748 6824 *Fax:* (020) 8748 5689
Key Personnel
Design Dir: Roger Pring
Founded: 1985
Print Runs: 1 min - 1,000,000 max
Business from Other Countries: 10%

Cox & Wyman Ltd
Cardiff Rd, Reading, Berks RG1 8EX
Tel: (0118) 953 0500 *Fax:* (0118) 950 7222
Key Personnel
General Manager: Tom Roberts
Sales Manager: Paul Hicks
Sales Executive: Ruth Goodman
Founded: 1777
Turnaround: 10 Workdays reprints/15 workdays new books
Print Runs: 2,000 min - 2,000,000 max
Business from Other Countries: 5%
Parent Company: Chevrillon Philippe Industrie

Cradley Print Ltd
Chester Rd, Cradley Heath, West Midlands B64 6AB
Tel: (01384) 414100; (01384) 414102 (sales)
 Fax: (01384) 414102
E-mail: sales@cradleygp.co.uk
Web Site: www.cradleygp.co.uk
Key Personnel
Man Dir: Chris Jordan
Turnaround: 5 Workdays
Print Runs: 1,000 min - 500,000 max
Business from Other Countries: 7%
Branch Office(s)
Quadcolor Repro

The Diagram Group
195 Kentish Town Rd, London NW5 2JU
Tel: (020) 7482 3633 *Fax:* (020) 7482 4932
E-mail: diagramuis@aol.com
Key Personnel
Contact: Bruce Robertson
Secretary: C A Dease
Founded: 1967
Business from Other Countries: 80%

Edition
Subsidiary of Cameron Books
PO Box 1, Moffat DG10 9SU
Tel: (01683) 220808 *Fax:* (01683) 220012
E-mail: editorial@cameronbooks.co.uk; sales@cameronbooks.co.uk
Web Site: www.cameronbooks.co.uk
Key Personnel
Dir: Ian Cameron; Jill Hollis
Founded: 1976

Fern House
19 High St, Haddenham, Ely, Cambs CB6 3XA
Tel: (01353) 740222 *Fax:* (01353) 741987
E-mail: info@fernhouse.com
Web Site: www.fernhouse.com
Key Personnel
Contact: Rodney Dale
Founded: 1976

Goldshield Communications Ltd
Banners Bldg, Attercliffe Rd, Sheffield S9 3QS
Tel: (0114) 2431000 *Fax:* (0114) 2433000
Key Personnel
Man Dir & Overseas-Special Projects: Sandra Potesta *E-mail:* sandra@goldcom.co.uk
Technical & Production: Stefano Potesta
Founded: 1984
Business from Other Countries: 40%

The Guernsey Press Co Ltd
Braye Rd, Vale, Guernsey GY1 3BW
Mailing Address: PO Box 57, Vale, Guernsey GY1 3BW
Tel: (01481) 240240; (01481) 243657 (ISDN)
 Fax: (01481) 240290; (01481) 240275
E-mail: books@guernsey-press.com
Web Site: www.guernsey-press.com
Key Personnel
Editor: Richard Digard
Contact: Mr T A R Duquemin
Founded: 1897
Turnaround: 10 Workdays
Print Runs: 2,000 min - 50,000 max
Business from Other Countries: 80%

Hammond Packaging Ltd
Division of Hammond Bindery Ltd
Flanshaw Way, Flanshaw Lane, Wakefield WF2 9LP
Tel: (01924) 369598 *Fax:* (01924) 298075
E-mail: hammpack@dial.pipex.com
Web Site: www.hammpack.co.uk
Key Personnel
Man Dir: Steve Allan *E-mail:* s_allan@hammond-bindery.co.uk
Sales Manager: Susan Sheldon
 E-mail: s_sheldon@hammond-bindery.co.uk
Founded: 1991
Turnaround: 5-15 Workdays
Print Runs: 100 min - 500,000 max

Headley Brothers Ltd
Invicta Press, Queens Rd, Ashford, Kent TN24 8HH
Tel: (01233) 623131 *Fax:* (01233) 612345
E-mail: printing@headley.co.uk
Web Site: www.headley.co.uk
Key Personnel
Sales Manager: Bruce Finn *E-mail:* bruce.finn@headley.co.uk
Commercial Dir: Jon Pitt *E-mail:* jon.pitt@headley.co.uk
European Sales: Ingrid Eissfeldt
Man Dir: Roger Pitt *E-mail:* roger.pitt@headley.co.uk
Founded: 1881
Print Runs: 1,000 min - 200,000 max
Business from Other Countries: 5%

Heyden & Son
Spectrum House, Hillview Gardens, London NW4 2JQ
Tel: (020) 8203 5171 *Fax:* (020) 8203 1027
E-mail: sales@heyden.com
Key Personnel
Dir: Edward Heyden

Hobbs The Printers Ltd
Brunel Rd, Totton, Hants SO40 3WX
Tel: (023) 8066 4800 *Fax:* (023) 8066 4801
E-mail: info@hobbs.uk.com
Web Site: www.hobbstheprinters.co.uk; www.hobbs.uk.com
Key Personnel
Man Dir: David Hobbs *E-mail:* d.a.hobbs@hobbs.uk.com
Commercial Dir: Terry Ozanne *E-mail:* t.ozanne@hobbs.uk.com
Sales Manager: Sajid Ali *E-mail:* s.ali@hobbs.uk.com
Founded: 1884
Turnaround: 5-10 days litho; up to 5 days digital
Print Runs: 10 min - 50,000 max
Business from Other Countries: 4%

Holbrook Design
Holbrook House, 105 Rose Hill, Oxford OX4 4HT
Tel: (01865) 459000 *Fax:* (01865) 459006
E-mail: info@holbrook-design.co.uk
Web Site: www.holbrook-design.co.uk
Key Personnel
Design Dir: Peter Tucker *E-mail:* pgt@holbrook-design.co.uk
Founded: 1974
Business from Other Countries: 20%

Ikon Document Management Services
Subsidiary of Microgen Holdings Plc
19 The Business Centre, Molly Millars Lane, Wokingham, Berks RG41 2QY
Tel: (0118) 9770510 *Fax:* (0118) 9770513
E-mail: pamh@ikonds.co.uk
Web Site: www.ikon.com
Key Personnel
Man Dir: Dave Weller
Business Development Dir: Aaron Biggs
Founded: 1972
Turnaround: 2-5 Workdays
Print Runs: 1 min - 5,000 max
Business from Other Countries: 40%
Branch Office(s)
Microgen City Park Watchmead, Welwyn Garden City, Herts AL7 1LT

Image & Print Group Ltd
Unit 9, Oakbank Industrial Estate, Glasgow G20 7LU
Tel: (0141) 353 1900 *Fax:* (0141) 353 8611
E-mail: info@imageandprint.co.uk
Web Site: www.imageandprint.co.uk
Key Personnel
Man Dir: Ken Roberts
Production: Stephen McPhee *E-mail:* stephen@imageandprint.co.uk
Founded: 1975
Turnaround: 5 Workdays
Print Runs: 1,000 min - 250,000 max

SERVICES

Intype Libra Ltd
Units 3 & 4, Elm Grove Industrial Estate, Elm Grove, Wimbledon SW19 4HE
Tel: (020) 8947 7863 *Fax:* (020) 8947 3652
E-mail: intype@btconnect.com
Key Personnel
Man Dir: Tony Chapman *E-mail:* tony.chapman@intypelibra.co.uk
Production: Richard Mayne
Dir: Alan Johnson
Founded: 1976
Turnaround: 10-15 Workdays for proofs; 5-10 Workdays for books
Print Runs: 25 min - 1,000 max
Business from Other Countries: 5%

Keytec Typesetting Ltd
Unit 2-5, Hounsell Bldgs, North Mills Trading Estate, Bridport, Dorset DT6 3BE
Tel: (01308) 427580 *Fax:* (01308) 421961
E-mail: all@keytectype.co.uk
Web Site: www.keytectype.co.uk
Key Personnel
Man Dir: Mark Riddington
Founded: 1983

Linden Artists Ltd
41 Battersea Business Centre, 103 Lavender Hill, London SW11 5QL
Tel: (020) 7738 2505 *Fax:* (020) 7738 2513
E-mail: martyr@btinternet.com
Key Personnel
Dir: Dennis J Bosdet; Martin J Gibbs; Sheila Wall
Founded: 1962
Business from Other Countries: 30%

Lowfield Printing Co Ltd
9 Kennet Rd, Dartford, Kent DA1 4QT
Tel: (01322) 522216 *Fax:* (01322) 555362
E-mail: lowfield@compuserve.com
Key Personnel
Dir: Ian J Starkey
Founded: 1964
Print Runs: 500 min - 20,000 max

Maney Publishing
Subsidiary of The Charlesworth Group of Companies
Hudson Rd, Leeds LS9 7DL
Tel: (0113) 249 7481 *Fax:* (0113) 248 6983
E-mail: maney@maney.co.uk
Web Site: www.maney.co.uk
Key Personnel
Man Dir: Michael Gallico *E-mail:* m.gallico@maney.co.uk
Founded: 1900
Print Runs: 350 min - 100,000 max
Business from Other Countries: 2%

MPG Ltd
Division of Martins Printing Group
The Gresham Press, Old Woking, Surrey GU22 9LH
Tel: (01483) 757501 *Fax:* (01483) 724629
E-mail: print@mpgltd.co.uk
Key Personnel
Man Dir: Simon Moore
Founded: 1945
Turnaround: 5 Workdays
Print Runs: 3,000 min - 75,000 max
Divisions: MPG Books Ltd; Unwin Brothers Ltd
Branch Office(s)
Bodmin
Peterborough
Rochester
St Albans
Wimbledon
Woking

Multiplex Medway Ltd
Lordswood Industrial Estate, Gleaming Wood Dr, Walderslade, Kent ME5 8XT
Tel: (01634) 684371 *Fax:* (01634) 683840
E-mail: enquiries@multiplex-medway.co.uk
Web Site: www.multiplex-medway.co.uk
Key Personnel
Dir: Jon Chandler
Sales Manager: Paul Abson

Page Bros Ltd (Norwich)
Subsidiary of Milex Ltd
Mile Cross Lane, Norwich NR6 6SA
Tel: (01603) 429141 *Fax:* (01603) 485126
Key Personnel
Sales Dir: Steve Commons
Founded: 1750
Turnaround: 10 Workdays
Print Runs: 100 min - 30,000 max
Business from Other Countries: 20%
Branch Office(s)
105-A Euston St, London NW1 2ET *Tel:* (020) 7383 2212 *Fax:* (020) 7383 4145

Redwood Books Ltd
Division of CPI (UK) Ltd
Kennet Way, Trowbridge, Wilts BA14 8RN
Tel: (01225) 769979 *Fax:* (01225) 769050
E-mail: enquiries@redwood-books.co.uk
Web Site: www.cpi-group.net
Key Personnel
General Manager: Trevor Gee
Commercial Manager: Tony Warner
  E-mail: tony@redwood-books.co.uk
Production Manager: Peter Grant
Founded: 1993
Turnaround: 10 Workdays
Print Runs: 10 min - 20,000 max
Business from Other Countries: 8%
Parent Company: CPI France
Branch Office(s)
London Sales Office, 22 Bloomsbury Sq, London WC1A 2NS *Tel:* (020) 7580 9328 *Fax:* (020) 7580 9337

J R Reid Print & Media Group, see J R Reid Printing Group Ltd

J R Reid Printing Group Ltd
79-99 Glasgow Rd, Blantyre, Glasgow G72 0YL
Tel: (01698) 826000 *Fax:* (01698) 824944
E-mail: office@reid-print-group.co.uk
Web Site: www.reid-print-group.co.uk
Key Personnel
Joint Man Dir: John R Reid *E-mail:* johnreid@reid-print-group.co.uk

Antony Rowe Ltd
Division of Rexam Plc
Bumper's Farm Industrial Estate, Chippenham, Wilts SN14 6LH
Tel: (01249) 659 705 *Fax:* (01249) 448 900
E-mail: sales@antonyrowe.co.uk
Web Site: www.antonyrowe.co.uk
Key Personnel
Chief Executive: Ralph Bell
Sales Manager: Andrew Copley
Founded: 1897
Turnaround: 10 Workdays
Print Runs: 50 min - 100,000 max
Business from Other Countries: 10%

Santype International Ltd
Netherhampton Rd, Salisbury, Wilts SP2 8PS
Tel: (01722) 334261 *Fax:* (01722) 333171
E-mail: info@santype.com
Web Site: www.santype.com
Key Personnel
Sales Dir: John Roost *Fax:* (0870) 1372738
  E-mail: jroost@santype.co.uk
Business from Other Countries: 35%

UNITED STATES

Severnside Printers Ltd
Bridge House, Upton-upon-Severn, Worcs WR8 0HG
Tel: (0684) 594521 *Fax:* (0684) 594344
Key Personnel
President & Chief Executive: Norman H Beechey
Turnaround: 14-20 Workdays
Print Runs: 500 min - 5,000 max
Business from Other Countries: 10%

Thomas Technology Solutions (UK) Ltd
Lee House, 1st floor, 109 Hammersmith Rd, London W14 0QH
Tel: (020) 7070 7550 *Fax:* (020) 7070 7551
E-mail: marketing@thomastechsolutions.com
Web Site: www.thomastechsolutions.com
Key Personnel
Man Dir: Peter Camilleri
Founded: 1964
Parent Company: Thomas Publishing Co, LLC, New York, NY, United States
U.S. Office(s): Thomas Technology Solutions Inc, One Progress Drive, Horsham, PA 15044, United States *Tel:* 215-682-5000

M & A Thomson Litho Ltd
Kelvin Industrial Estate, 2-16 Colvilles Pl, East Kilbride, Glasgow G75 0SN
Tel: (01355) 233 081 *Fax:* (01355) 245 039
Web Site: www.thomsonlitho.com
Key Personnel
Contact: Ken Thomson
Environment Quality Dir: Angela Hart
  E-mail: ahart@tlitho.co.uk

Tradespools Ltd
Vallis House, Robins Lane, Frome, Somerset BA11 3EG
Tel: (01373) 461475 *Fax:* (01373) 474112
E-mail: sales@tradespools.co.uk
Web Site: www.tradespools.co.uk
Key Personnel
Sales Dir: Roger Carraher
Founded: 1967
Print Runs: 1 min - 10,000 max
Business from Other Countries: 30%
Ultimate Parent Company: Antony Rowe Group

Watkiss Automation Ltd
Subsidiary of The Watkiss Group
Watkiss House, Blaydon Rd, Middlefield Industrial Estate, Sandy, Beds SG19 1RZ
Tel: (01767) 682177 *Fax:* (01767) 691769
E-mail: contact@watkiss.com
Web Site: www.watkiss.com
Key Personnel
Technical Dir: M Watkiss
Founded: 1959
Print Runs: 200 min - 10,000 max
Business from Other Countries: 5%

United States

A-R Editions Inc
8551 Research Way, Suite 180, Middleton, WI 53562
Tel: 608-836-9000 *Toll Free Tel:* 800-736-0070 (US book orders only) *Fax:* 608-831-8200
E-mail: info@areditions.com
Web Site: www.areditions.com
Key Personnel
Pres & CEO: Patrick Wall
Dir, Sales & Mktg: James L Zychowicz
  E-mail: james.zychowicz@areditions.com
Founded: 1962
Business from Other Countries: 10%

UNITED STATES

PREPRESS

ADR/BookPrint Inc
2012 Northern Ave E, Wichita, KS 67216
Tel: 316-522-5599 *Toll Free Tel:* 800-767-6066
  Fax: 316-522-5445
E-mail: info@adrbookprint.com
Web Site: www.adrbookprint.com
Key Personnel
Pres: Grace M Rishel *E-mail:* grace@
  adrbookprint.com
VP: James E Rishel
Founded: 1978
Print Runs: 50 min - 20,000 max
Business from Other Countries: 10%
Membership(s): DMIA; Printing Industries of
  America

Alpina Color Graphics Inc
Subsidiary of Alpina International Inc
102 Madison Ave, New York, NY 10016
Tel: 212-683-2535 *Toll Free Tel:* 866-338-1214
  Fax: 212-683-3965
E-mail: info@alpina.net
Web Site: www.alpina.net
Key Personnel
Contact: Raj Sawhney *E-mail:* raj@alpinanyc.com
Founded: 1980
Turnaround: 2-3 Workdays
Print Runs: 1,000 min - 200,000 max
Business from Other Countries: 20%
Branch Office(s)
Alpina Graphics, 27 Cliff St, New York, NY
  10038

American Pizzi Offset Corp
Subsidiary of Arti Grafiche Amilcare Pizzi (Milan)
370 Lexington Ave, Suite 1505, New York, NY
  10017
Tel: 212-986-1658 *Fax:* 212-286-1887
E-mail: apocnyusa@aol.com
Key Personnel
Pres: Massimo Pizzi
Sales Mgr, New York: Barbara Sadick
Founded: 1914
Business from Other Countries: 50%

Any Photo Type
210 W 29 St, New York, NY 10001
Tel: 212-244-1130 *Fax:* 212-594-4697
Key Personnel
Pres: Harold Katzman
Founded: 1977
Turnaround: 1-2 Workdays
Business from Other Countries: 15%

Asia Pacific Offset Inc
1332 Corcoran St NW, Suite 6, Washington, DC
  20009
Tel: 202-462-5436 *Toll Free Tel:* 800-756-4344
  Fax: 202-986-4030
Web Site: www.asiapacificoffset.com
Key Personnel
Pres: Andrew Clarke *E-mail:* andrew@
  asiapacificoffset.com
Dir, Sales (NY Office): Timothy Linn
  Tel: 212-941-8300 *Fax:* 212-941-9810
  E-mail: timothy@asiapacificoffset.com
Founded: 1997
Turnaround: 105 Workdays including color separation & shipping
Print Runs: 2,000 min
Business from Other Countries: 100%
Branch Office(s)
Phoenix Offset, Unit F1-2 2nd fl, Yeung Yiu
  Chung No 8 Industrial Bldg, 20 Wang Hoi Rd,
  Kowloon Bay, Hong Kong, Contact: Edmond
  Chan *Tel:* 852-2751-9962 *Fax:* 852-2755-8408
  E-mail: Phoffset@netvigator.com
Sales Office(s): 270 Lafayette St, Suite 502, New
  York, NY 10012 *Tel:* 212-941-8300 *Fax:* 212-
  941-9810 *E-mail:* Timothy@asiapacificoffset.
  com

870 Market St, Suite 801, San Francisco, CA
  94102, Dir of Sales: Rick Conant *Tel:* 415-
  433-3488 *Fax:* 415-433-3489 *E-mail:* Rick@
  asiapacificoffset.com

Bang Printing Co Inc
3323 Oak St, Brainerd, MN 56401
Mailing Address: PO Box 587, Brainerd, MN
  56401-0587
Tel: 218-829-2877 *Toll Free Tel:* 800-328-0450
  Fax: 218-829-7145
Web Site: www.bangprinting.com
Key Personnel
VP, Sales: Todd Vanek *Tel:* 218-822-2124
  E-mail: toddv@bangprinting.com
Founded: 1899
Turnaround: 10-25 Workdays
Print Runs: 500 min - 100,000 max
Business from Other Countries: 50%

Better Music Type
324 Timberdale Ct, Nashville, TN 37211
Tel: 615-833-0800
Key Personnel
Contact: Laurens A Blankers
Founded: 1977
Business from Other Countries: 30%
Membership(s): BMI

Blaze International Productions Inc
225 W 35 St, Suite 1100, New York, NY 10001
Tel: 212-967-7501 *Fax:* 212-967-7551
Key Personnel
Pres: Eugene Sanchez *Tel:* 212-967-7501 ext 222
  E-mail: e.sanchez@blazeint.com
Founded: 1990
Turnaround: 10-15 Workdays
Print Runs: 500 min - 1,000,000 max
Business from Other Countries: 80%
Branch Office(s)
Flat 12 18/F, Kodak House, Phase 2, No 39
  Healthy Street, North Point, Hong Kong
  Tel: 2967 9360 *Fax:* 2967 1800
Membership(s): Bookbinders Guild of New York

BookBuilders New York Inc
353 Strawtown Rd, New City, NY 10956
Tel: 845-639-5316 *Fax:* 845-639-5318
Web Site: www.mcabooks.com
Key Personnel
Pres: Martin Cook *E-mail:* martin@mcabooks.
  com
Founded: 1977
Turnaround: 30-45 Workdays
Print Runs: 2,000 min - 500,000 max
Business from Other Countries: 60%

C & C Offset Printing Co Ltd
Subsidiary of C & C Joint Printing Co (HK) Ltd
  under Sino United Publishing (Holdings) Ltd
2632 SE 25 Ave, Suite E, Portland, OR 97202
Mailing Address: PO Box 82037, Portland, OR
  97282-0037
Tel: 503-233-1834 *Fax:* 503-233-7815
E-mail: portlandinfo@ccoffset.com
Web Site: www.ccoffset.com
Key Personnel
Dir & Gen Mgr, Hong Kong Head Off: Jackson
  Leung
Deputy Man Dir, Hong Kong Head Office: Ken
  Lee
Deputy Gen Mgr, Hong Kong Head Office: Ivy
  Lam
Sr Sales Mgr, Hong Kong Head Office: Francis
  Ho
Dir, C & C Offset Printing Co (USA) Inc,
  Portland, OR, USA: Charles H Clark, IV
  E-mail: cclark@ccoffset.com
Devt Mgr, C & C Offset Printing Co (USA)
  Inc, Portland, OR, USA: Jenny Whittier
  E-mail: jwhittier@ccoffset.com

Cust Serv Mgr, C & C Offset Printing Co
  (USA) Inc, Portland, OR, USA: Ernest Li
  E-mail: ernestli@ccoffset.com
Dir & Exec VP, C & C Offset Printing Co
  (NYC) Inc, New York, NY, USA: Simon Chan
  E-mail: schan@ccoffset.com
Cust Serv Mgr, C & C Offset Printing Co (NY):
  Frances Harkness *E-mail:* fharkness@ccoffset.
  com
Dir & Gen Mgr, C & C Joint Printing Co
  (Guangdong) Ltd, Shenzhen, China: Jackson
  Leung
Pres, C & C Printing Japan Co Ltd, Tokyo,
  Japan: Yamamoto Masaaki
Man Dir, C & C Joint Printing Co (Beijing) Ltd,
  Beijing, China: Zhang Lin Gui
Dir, C & C Offset Printing Co (UK) Ltd: Tracy
  Broderick
Acct Mgr, C & C Offset Printing Co (UK), Ltd:
  Fia Fornari
Founded: 1980
Turnaround: 21 Workdays for printing, binding &
  book finishing
Print Runs: 2,000 min - 1,000,000 max
Business from Other Countries: 70%
Branch Office(s)
C & C Printing Co (NY) Inc, 401 Broadway, Suite 2015, New York, NY 10013-
  3005 *Tel:* 212-431-4210 *Fax:* 212-431-3960
  E-mail: newyorkinfo@ccoffset.com (New York
  City office)
C & C Joint Printing Co (Beijing) Ltd, Beijing
  Economic & Technological Developent Area
  (BDA), No 3, Donghuan North Rd, Beijing
  100176, China, Dir & Gen Mgr: Mr Zhang
  Lin Gui *Tel:* (010) 6787 6655 *Fax:* (010) 6787
  8255 *E-mail:* ccbj@cancprinting.com
C & C Joint Printing Co (Guangdong) Ltd, Intercontinental Bldg, Rm 706, 16 An Wai
  An De Rd, DongCheng District, Beijing
  100011, China, Contact: Mr Xiao Mungshen *Tel:* (010) 6650 3176 *Fax:* (010) 6650
  3175 *E-mail:* beijing@cancprinting.com *Web
  Site:* www.candcprinting.com (regional office)
C & C Joint Printing Co (Guangdong) Ltd, Hua
  Xin Bldg E Block, Rm 1511, 2 Shuiyin Rd,
  Huanshi East, Guangzhou 510075, China,
  Contact: Mr Peng Ji Shan *Tel:* (020) 3760
  0979; (020) 3760 0980 *Fax:* (020) 3760 0977
  E-mail: guangzhou@candcprinting.com (regional office)
C & C Joint Printing Co (Guangdong) Ltd
  (Changsha Office), The Building of Changsha City, Commercial Bank, No 1, Frong
  Middle Rd, Rm 1218, Changsha, Hunan 41005, China, Contact: Ms Chen Jian
  Tel: (0731) 225 0288 *Fax:* (0731) 225 0178
  E-mail: changsha@candcprinting.com *Web
  Site:* www.candcprinting.com (regional office)
C & C Joint Printing Co (Guangdong) Ltd,
  Chunhu Industrial Estate, Pinghu, Long Gang,
  Shenzhen 518111, China *Tel:* 755-845-8333
  Fax: 755-885-9911 *E-mail:* guangdong@
  candcprinting.com (plant)
C & C Offset Printing Co (Guangdong)
  Ltd, Fang Fa Bldg, No 29, Rm 304, 165
  Dongzhu Anbin Rd, Shanghai 200050, China
  Tel: (021) 6240-1305 *Fax:* (021) 6240-2090
  E-mail: shanghai@candcprinting.com *Web
  Site:* www.candcprinting.com (regional office)
C & C Joint Printing Co (Guangdong) Ltd (Xian
  Office), 10 Xuanfengquiao, Jianguo Rd, Xian
  710001, China *Tel:* (029) 741 8407 *Fax:* (029)
  743 5730 *E-mail:* xian@candcprinting.co *Web
  Site:* www.candcprinting.com (regional office)
C & C Bldg, 36 Ting Lai Rd, Tai Po, New Territories, Hong Kong *Tel:* 2666-4988 *Fax:* 2666-
  4938 *E-mail:* offsetprinting@candcprinting.com
  Web Site: www.candcprinting.com (corporate
  headquarters)
C & C Printing Japan Co Ltd, Tozaido Bldg, 3F,
  2-6-12 Hitotsubashi, Chiyoda-ku, Tokyo 101-
  0003, Japan, Contact: Mr Yamamoto Masaaki
  Tel: (03) 5216-4580 *Fax:* (03) 5216-4610

SERVICES UNITED STATES

E-mail: mail@candcprinting.co.jp (regional office)
C & C Offset Printing Co (UK) Ltd, 2 New Burlington St, 4th fl, London W1S 2JE, United Kingdom *Tel:* (020) 7287 7787 *Fax:* (020) 7287 7187 *E-mail:* tracy@candcoffset.co.uk

Colorprint Offset Inc
80 Park Ave, Suite 10N, New York, NY 10016
Tel: 212-681-9400 *Fax:* 212-681-9362
Web Site: www.cpo.hk
Key Personnel
Pres: Justin Wakefield *E-mail:* justin@colorprintoffset.com; Lee Moncho *E-mail:* lee@colorprintoffset.com
Prod Dir & Cust Serv Mgr: Kate Brady *E-mail:* kate@colorprintoffset.com
Founded: 1986
Turnaround: 15 Workdays
Print Runs: 100 min - 50,000 max
Business from Other Countries: 65%

Coneco Litho Graphics
Division of NET 2 PRESS Inc
58 Dix Ave, Glens Falls, NY 12801
Mailing Address: PO Box 3255, Glen Falls, NY 12801-7255
Tel: 518-793-3823 *Fax:* 518-793-5823
Web Site: www.conecolithographics.com
Key Personnel
Gen Mgr: Steve Webber *E-mail:* swebber@conecolithographics.com
Client Servs Mgr: George Moses *E-mail:* gmoses@conecolithographics.com
Pres & CEO: Garth E Grandchamp *E-mail:* garth@conecolithographics.com
Founded: 1984
Turnaround: 15 Workdays
Print Runs: 250 min - 25,000 max
Business from Other Countries: 27%

Martin Cook Associates Ltd
353 Strawtown Rd, New City, NY 10956
Tel: 845-639-5316 *Fax:* 845-639-5318
E-mail: mcanewcity@aol.com
Web Site: www.mcabooks.com
Key Personnel
Pres: Martin Cook
Founded: 1977
Turnaround: 30-45 Workdays
Print Runs: 2,000 min - 300,000 max
Business from Other Countries: 15%
Membership(s): Bookbinders Guild of New York

CS Graphics USA Inc
Subsidiary of CS Graphics Pte Ltd Singapore
8969 Lake Ct, Granite Bay, CA 95746
Tel: 916-791-9066 *Fax:* 916-791-9112
Key Personnel
Mgr, Sales & Mktg: Rick Marment *E-mail:* r.marment@csgraphics-world.com
Founded: 1980
Turnaround: 80 Workdays
Print Runs: 1,000 min - 75,000 max
Business from Other Countries: 30%

Custom Services
Subsidiary of Nationwide Custom Services Inc
77 Main St, Tappan, NY 10983
Mailing Address: PO Box 76, Tappan, NY 10983
Tel: 845-365-0414 *Fax:* 845-365-0864
Key Personnel
Owner & Pres: Norman Shaifer
VP & Mgr: Helen Newman
VP: Harry Title
Founded: 1960
Print Runs: 500 min - 10,000 max
Business from Other Countries: 30%

Datapage Technologies International Inc
222 Turner Blvd, St Peters, MO 63376-1079
Tel: 636-278-8888 *Toll Free Tel:* 800-876-3844
Fax: 636-278-2180
Web Site: www.datapage.com
Key Personnel
Pres: Jack M Delo
VP, Sales: John E Ingerslew
VP, Publg: Linda S Blevins *E-mail:* lindab@datapage.com
VP, Info Systems: Ron McCafferty
Founded: 1969
Turnaround: 1-15 Workdays
Business from Other Countries: 10%

Desktop Miracles Inc
112 S Main, PMB 294, Stowe, VT 05672
Tel: 802-253-7900 *Fax:* 802-253-1900
Web Site: www.desktopmiracles.com
Key Personnel
Pres & CEO: Barry T Kerrigan *E-mail:* barry@desktopmiracles.com
Founded: 1994
Turnaround: 10-15 Workdays
Print Runs: 2,500 min
Business from Other Countries: 10%

DNP America LLC
Subsidiary of Dai Nippon Printing Co Ltd
335 Madison Ave, 3rd fl, New York, NY 10017
Tel: 212-687-2746; 212-503-1060 *Fax:* 212-286-1505
Web Site: www.dnp.co.jp/ *Cable:* DAIPRINTS NY
Key Personnel
Pres: Yoji Yamakawa
VP & Gen Mgr, Graphic Printing: Kohei Tsumori *E-mail:* tsumori-k@mail.dnp.co.jp
Founded: 1974
Turnaround: 30-60 Workdays
Print Runs: 1,000 min - 1,000,000 max
Business from Other Countries: 54%
Branch Office(s)
577 Airport Blvd, Suite 620, Burlingame, CA 94010, Gen Mgr: Kosuke Tago *Tel:* 650-340-6061 *Fax:* 650-340-6090

Editoriale Bortolazzi-Stei srl
39 Kane Ave, Larchmont, NY 10538
Tel: 914-834-9594 *Fax:* 914-833-9106
E-mail: fulvioforcellini@ebs-bortolazzi.com
Key Personnel
US Rep: Umberto Paolucci *E-mail:* pbert30@aol.com
Founded: 1952
Print Runs: 2,000 min - 90,000 max
Business from Other Countries: 20%
Branch Office(s)
Via Monte Comun, 40, San Giovanni Lupatoto, Verona 37057, Italy

Elegance Printing & Book Binding (USA)
Member of The Elegance Printing Group
708 Glen Cove Ave, Glen Head, NY 11545
Tel: 516-676-5941 *Fax:* 516-676-5973
Web Site: www.elegancebooks.com
Key Personnel
Man Dir: Frank DeLuca *E-mail:* frank@elegancebooks.com
Founded: 1977
Turnaround: CTP projects, disk to proof 5 days. Reprints ship within 14 days. Proof to board books, ready to ship 3 weeks
Print Runs: 1,000 min - 1,000,000 max
Business from Other Countries: 40%

Express Media Corp
1419 Donelson Pike, Nashville, TN 37217
Tel: 615-360-6400 *Toll Free Tel:* 888-EXPMEDIA (397-6342) *Fax:* 615-360-3140
E-mail: info@expressmedia.com
Web Site: www.expressmedia.com
Key Personnel
Pres: Andrew Cameron
Founded: 1996
Turnaround: 3 Workdays
Print Runs: 1 min - 10,000 max
Business from Other Countries: 10%

Fairfield Marketing Group Inc
Subsidiary of FMG Inc
830 Sport Hill Rd, Easton, CT 06612-1250
Tel: 203-261-5585; 203-261-5568 *Fax:* 203-261-0884
E-mail: ffldmktgrp@aol.com
Web Site: www.fairfieldmarketing.com
Key Personnel
CEO & Pres: Edward P Washchilla *E-mail:* fmg.inc@aol.com
VP, Fin: Pamela L Johnson
VP, Fulfillment: Jason Paul Miller *Tel:* 203-261-5585 ext 203
Cust Servs Rep: Mike Lozada *Tel:* 203-261-5585 ext 204
Founded: 1987
Turnaround: 5-10 Workdays
Print Runs: 2,500 min - 1,000,000 max
Business from Other Countries: 10%
Membership(s): ABA; Association of Educational Publishers; DMA; Direct Marketing Club of New York (DMCNY); DMA; Hudson Valley Direct Marketing Association; International Reading Association; National School Supply & Equipment Association; United States Chamber of Congress

The Font Bureau Inc
326 "A" St, Suite 6C, Boston, MA 02210
Tel: 617-423-8770 *Fax:* 617-423-8771
E-mail: info@fontbureau.com
Web Site: www.fontbureau.com
Key Personnel
Retail Sales Mgr: Harry Parker
Founded: 1989
Turnaround: 1 Workday
Business from Other Countries: 20%

High Resolution Inc
30 Belmont Ave, Camden, ME 04843
Tel: 207-236-3777 *Fax:* 207-236-2500
Web Site: www.highres.com
Key Personnel
Pres & Owner: Peter Koons *E-mail:* pdk@highres.com
Owner & Mktg Dir: Sandra Soards *E-mail:* sandy@high.res.com
Founded: 1986
Turnaround: 2 Workdays
Business from Other Countries: 10%

Hindy's Enterprise
Division of Jinno International
3 Christine Dr, Chestnut Ridge, NY 10977-6802
Tel: 845-735-4666 *Fax:* 617-344-5905; 530-324-8964
Key Personnel
Pres: Yoh Jinno *E-mail:* jinno@hotmail.com
Founded: 1989
Turnaround: 40 Workdays
Print Runs: 500 min - 2,000,000 max
Business from Other Countries: 70%
Branch Office(s)
Melbourne Industrial Bldg, Block A, 20th fl, 16 Westlands Rd, Quarry Bay, Hong Kong *Tel:* 2516 6318 *Fax:* 2516 5161

Huron Valley Graphics Inc
4597 Platt Rd, Ann Arbor, MI 48108
Tel: 734-477-0448 *Toll Free Tel:* 800-362-9655 *Fax:* 734-477-0393
E-mail: custserv@hvg.com
Web Site: www.hvg.com

Key Personnel
Pres: Claudia Lybrink
Cust Serv Mgr, Sales & Mktg: Yvonne Robinson
Data Servs Mgr: Francis O'Donnell
Founded: 1971
Turnaround: 15 Workdays
Business from Other Countries: 10%

IBT Global Ltd, see Integrated Book Technology Inc

ICSI Corp
2274 S Arlington Rd, Akron, OH 44319-1900
Tel: 330-645-0004; 330-786-0002
  Toll Free Tel: 800-860-0709; 800-965-0004
  Fax: 330-786-0056
Web Site: www.icsidata.com
Key Personnel
Reg Mktg Dir: Arthur Williams
  E-mail: artwilliam@worldnet.att.net
Founded: 1985
Turnaround: 1 Workday
Business from Other Countries: 30%

Ikon Document Services
399 River Rd, Hudson, MA 01749-2627
Tel: 978-562-9131 *Fax:* 978-562-4304
Key Personnel
VP: David Trombino *E-mail:* dtrombino@ikon.com
Founded: 1973
Turnaround: 3 Workdays
Print Runs: 10 min - 5,000 max
Business from Other Countries: 10%

Innodata Isogen Inc
Three University Plaza, Hackensack, NJ 07601
Tel: 201-488-1200 *Toll Free Tel:* 800-567-4784
  Fax: 201-488-9099
E-mail: solutions@innodata-isogen.com
Web Site: www.innodata-isogen.com
Key Personnel
CEO: Jack Abuhoff
Exec VP: George Kondrach
VP, Sales: Martin Korsin
VP: Jan Palmen
VP, Mktg & Communs: Al Girardi
VP, Fin: Steven Agress
Founded: 1989
Turnaround: As little as 12 hours
Business from Other Countries: 25%
Membership(s): AAP; ALA; Center for Information Development & Content Management Strategies; International Digital Enterprise Alliance; Localization Industry Standards Association; National Initiative for a Networked Cultural Heritage; Organization of Advancement of Structured Information Standards; Society for Scholarly Publishing; Software & Information Industry Association; World Wide Web Consortium

Integrated Book Technology Inc
Division of The IBT Group
18 Industrial Park Rd, Troy, NY 12180
Tel: 518-271-5117 *Fax:* 518-266-9422
E-mail: mail@integratedbook.com
Web Site: www.integratedbook.com
Key Personnel
CEO & Pres: John R Paeglow *E-mail:* johnp@integratedbook.com
VP & Chief Technol Officer: William Clockel
  E-mail: billc@integratedbook.com
VP, Sales & Mktg: Robert Lindberg
  E-mail: bobl@integratedbook.com
Dir, Sales & Cust Serv: Karen Lombardo
Dir, Info Technol: Michael Whalen
  E-mail: mikew@integratedbook.com
Regl Sales: Tim Knickerbocker *E-mail:* timk@integratedbook.com
Founded: 1991

Turnaround: 1-15 Workdays
Print Runs: 10 min - 3,000 max
Business from Other Countries: 20%
Branch Office(s)
Rollesby Rd, King's Lynn, Norfolk PE3 3NR, United Kingdom *Tel:* (015) 5376 9072
Membership(s): BMI

ITC
Division of Software Services
2921 W Cypress Creek Rd, Fort Lauderdale, FL 33309
Tel: 954-623-3101 *Fax:* 954-623-3122
E-mail: team@inttype.com
Web Site: www.inttype.com
Key Personnel
Pres: Mukesh Narang
Dir, Sales & Mktg: Jane Stark *E-mail:* janes@inttype.com
Founded: 1995
BISAC compatible software
Turnaround: 10-20 workdays - rush service available (48 hr turnaround)
Business from Other Countries: 10%

Leo Paper USA
1180 NW Maple St, Suite 102, Issaquah, WA 98027
Tel: 425-646-8801 *Fax:* 425-646-8805
E-mail: leo@leousa.com
Web Site: www.leousa.com
Key Personnel
VP: Peter R Gillies *E-mail:* peter@leousa.com
Sales: Tom Leach *E-mail:* tom@leousa.com; Greg Witt *E-mail:* greg@leousa.com
Founded: 1983
Turnaround: 90 Workdays
Print Runs: 3,500 min - 2,000,000 max
Business from Other Countries: 20%
Branch Office(s)
27 W 24 St, Suite 701, New York, NY 10010-3204, Contact: Janine Laborne *Tel:* 917-305-0708 *Fax:* 917-305-0709
Leo Paper Products Ltd, 7/F Kader Bldg, 22 Kai Cheung Rd, Kowloon Bay, Hong Kong, Man Dir: Johnny Fung *Tel:* 8841374 *Fax:* 28853520 *E-mail:* lpp@leo.com.hk *Web Site:* www.leo.com.hk
Sales Office(s): Leo Paper Products (Europe) BVBA, De Wilde Zee Wiegstraat 19, 2000 Antwerp, Belgium, Contact: Jan Van Gijsel *Tel:* (03) 203 0912 *Fax:* (03) 225-1303 *E-mail:* leo@leo-europe.com
Leo Marketing, The Malthouse, Malthouse Sq, Princes Risborough, Bucks HP27 9AB, United Kingdom, Contact: Sally Wood *Tel:* (1844) 274-244 *Fax:* (1844) 275-105 *E-mail:* sallywood.leo@btinternet.com

Linick International Inc
Division of The Linick Group Inc
Linick Bldg, 7 Putter Lane, Middle Island, NY 11953
Mailing Address: PO Box 102, Middle Island, NY 11953-0102
Tel: 631-924-3888 *Fax:* 631-924-3890
E-mail: linickgrp@att.net
Web Site: www.lgroup.addr.com
Key Personnel
Chmn & CEO: Andrew S Linick, PhD
Treas: Marvin Glickman
Exec VP: Roger Dextor
Founded: 1972
Turnaround: 21-30 Workdays
Print Runs: 3,000 min - 50,000 max
Business from Other Countries: 30%

LK Litho
Division of The Linick Group Inc
Linick Bldg, 7 Putter Lane, Middle Island, NY 11953

Mailing Address: PO Box 102, Middle Island, NY 11953-0102
Tel: 631-924-3888
E-mail: linickgrp@att.net
Web Site: www.lgroup.addr.com
Key Personnel
VP: Roger Dextor
Founded: 1968
Turnaround: 10 Workdays
Print Runs: 5,000 min - 2,000,000 max
Business from Other Countries: 20%
Membership(s): Copywriters Council of America; DMA; LIAC

Mazer Publishing Services
Division of The Mazer Corporation
6680 Poe Ave, Dayton, OH 45414
Tel: 937-264-2600 *Fax:* 937-264-2624
E-mail: info@mazer.com
Web Site: www.mazer.com
Key Personnel
Pres: William Franklin *E-mail:* bill_franklin@mazer.com
Exec VP: Ken Fultz *E-mail:* ken_fultz@mazer.com
Exec Dir, Sales: Bill Faber *Fax:* 937-264-2622
  E-mail: bill_faber@mazer.com
Founded: 1964
Print Runs: 50 min - 25,000 max
Business from Other Countries: 10%
Branch Office(s)
2460 Sand Lake Rd, Orlando, FL 32809, Contact: Bryan Blakley *Tel:* 407-859-5552 *Fax:* 407-859-0643 *E-mail:* bryan_blakley@mazer.com
224 Lexington Ave, Fox River Grove, IL 60021, Contact: Dennis Bowman *Tel:* 847-639-1555 *Fax:* 847-639-1562 *E-mail:* dennis_bowman@mazer.com
22 Lehigh Rd, Wellesley, MA 02181, Contact: Ken Leahy *Tel:* 781-237-4112 *Fax:* 781-431-6184 *E-mail:* ken_leahy@mazer.com
22 Laurel Place, Upper Montclair, NJ 07043, Contact: John Martel *Tel:* 973-744-4320 *Fax:* 973-746-5608 *E-mail:* john_martel@mazer.com
3081 Glenmere Ct, Kettering, OH 45440, Contact: Mark Brewer *Tel:* 937-299-5746 *Fax:* 937-299-5761 *E-mail:* mark_brewer@mazer.com
363 Porter Rd, Bishop, TX 78602, Contact: Deborah VanLandingham *Tel:* 512-303-9758 *Fax:* 512-303-9791
Membership(s): BMI

Milanostampa/New Interlitho USA Inc
Unit of Milanostampa New Interlitho AGG Printing Stars SRL
299 Broadway, Suite 901, New York, NY 10007
Tel: 212-964-2430 *Fax:* 212-964-2497
Web Site: www.milanostampa.com
Key Personnel
Chmn: Maria Rosa Filippino
Chmn & Sales Rep: Rino Varrasso *Tel:* 917-225-9460 *E-mail:* rvarrasso@milanostampa-usa.com
Founded: 1974
Turnaround: 30 Workdays
Print Runs: 1,000 min - 3,000,000 max
Business from Other Countries: 75%

Pageworks
4 Gibbons Circle, Old Saybrook, CT 06475
Tel: 860-395-2022; 860-434-3605 *Fax:* 860-388-4353
Key Personnel
Owner: Maggie Dana *E-mail:* maggiedana@aol.com; Jamie Temple *E-mail:* j23hc@sbcglobal.net
Founded: 1987
Business from Other Countries: 10%

Palace Press International - Corporate Headquarters
17 Paul Dr, San Rafael, CA 94903

SERVICES

Tel: 415-526-1370 *Toll Free Tel:* 800-809-3792
Fax: 415-526-1394
E-mail: info@palacepress.com
Web Site: www.palacepress.com
Key Personnel
CEO: Raoul Goff *E-mail:* raoul@palacepress.com
Dir, Intl Sales & Mktg: Gordon Goff
  E-mail: gordon@palacepress.com
Dir: Steven Goff *E-mail:* steven@palacepress.com
Founded: 1984
Turnaround: 90 Workdays
Print Runs: 3,000 min - 1,000,000 max
Business from Other Countries: 20%
Branch Office(s)
Palace Press International Los Angeles, 303 W Newby Ave, Suite C, San Gabriel, CA 91777, Contact: Roger Ma *Tel:* 626-282-8877 *Fax:* 626-282-6880 *E-mail:* roger@palacepress.com
4308 Fence Place, Louisville, KY 40241, Contact: Joe Rackowski *Tel:* 502-429-9276 *Fax:* 502-423-0760 *E-mail:* joe@palacepress.com
Palace Press International New York, 180 Varick St, 10th fl, New York, NY 10014 *Tel:* 212-462-2622 *Fax:* 212-463-9130 *E-mail:* jessica@palacepress.com

Photoengraving Inc
502 N Willow Ave, Tampa, FL 33606
Tel: 813-253-3427 *Fax:* 813-253-5491
Web Site: www.photoengravinginc.com
Key Personnel
Owner: Ed Dalton, Jr *E-mail:* eddalton@photoengravinginc.com
Founded: 1953
Turnaround: 3 Workdays
Business from Other Countries: 25%

Pioneer Graphic Scanning
Division of Jinno International
3 Christine Dr, Chestnut Ridge, NY 10977-6802
Tel: 845-735-4666 *Fax:* 617-344-5905
Key Personnel
Pres: Yoh Jinno *E-mail:* jinno@hotmail.com
Mktg Dir: Stewart Sum
Founded: 1989
Turnaround: 10-60 Workdays
Print Runs: 500 min - 3,000,000 max
Business from Other Countries: 95%

Prepare Inc
Affiliate of Emilcomp srl
36 Woodcliff Lake Rd, Saddle River, NJ 07458
Tel: 201-934-8451 *Fax:* 201-934-2992
E-mail: csr@emilcomp.it; prepare@optonline.net
Key Personnel
Pres: Fran Daniele
VP: Rose Mello
Founded: 1987
Business from Other Countries: 50%

PrePress Imaging Inc
1864 Scherer Pkwy, St Charles, MO 63303
Tel: 636-940-9146 *Toll Free Tel:* 800-886-6122
  Fax: 636-896-8107
E-mail: mail@ppi-stl.com
Web Site: www.ppi-stl.com
Key Personnel
Pres & Owner: Wayne Kissel *E-mail:* wkissel@ppi-stl.com
Account Mgr: Christine Merrick
  E-mail: cmerrick@ppi-stl.com; Ron Zyk
  E-mail: rzyk@ppi-stl.com
Founded: 1989
Turnaround: 1-2
Business from Other Countries: 20%

Printing Corp of the Americas Inc
620 SW 12 Ave, Fort Lauderdale, FL 33312
Tel: 954-781-8100 *Fax:* 954-781-8421
E-mail: pcaprint@bellsouth.net
Web Site: www.pcaprint.bellsouth.net
Key Personnel
Pres: Jan Tuchman
Founded: 1979
Turnaround: 5-10 Workdays
Print Runs: 500 min - 100,000 max
Business from Other Countries: 15%

Quantum Colorgraphics
166 Midland Ave, Montclair, NJ 07042
Tel: 973-783-0462 *Fax:* 973-783-0637
Key Personnel
Sr Acct Exec: Jeffrey Sestilio *E-mail:* jeff.cgi@verizon.net
Print Runs: 1,000 min - 300,000 max
Business from Other Countries: 30%

Regent Publishing Services
9327 Rambler Dr, St Louis, MO 63123
Tel: 314-631-7581 *Fax:* 314-638-5113
E-mail: regentstl@aol.com
Key Personnel
Sales Dir: Carol Davis-Tierney
Mktg Dir: James J Tierney
Founded: 1985
Turnaround: 3-4 Months
Print Runs: 2,000 min - 100,000 max
Business from Other Countries: 100%

Sencor
One W 34 St, Suite 1104, New York, NY 10001
Tel: 212-947-5601 *Fax:* 212-947-5604
E-mail: sales@sencor.net
Web Site: www.sencor.net
Key Personnel
Pres & CEO: George Martel *E-mail:* gmartel@sencor.net
VP: Michael Martel *E-mail:* mvmartel@sencor.net
Founded: 1984
BISAC compatible software
Turnaround: 5 Workdays
Business from Other Countries: 10%
Branch Office(s)
1991 Taft Ave, Pasay City, Manila 1306, Philippines

SNP Best-Set Typesetter Ltd
Subsidiary of SNP Corp Ltd
157 Fisher Ave, Suite 6, Eastchester, NY 10709
Toll Free Tel: 866-888-8767 *Fax:* 914-961-8212
Web Site: www.bestset-typesetter.com
Key Personnel
Dir (Hong Kong): Johnson Yeung *Tel:* 852-289-6033 *E-mail:* johnson@bestset-typesetter.com
Sales Rep: Wai Man Yeung
  E-mail: waimanyeung@snpcorp.com
Founded: 1986
Turnaround: 5 Workdays
Print Runs: 100 min - 200,000 max
Business from Other Countries: 98%
Branch Office(s)
3 Jiang nan Main Ave C, 3rd fl, Guangzhou, China
6 Sun Yip St, Honour Industrial Centre, Room 304, 3rd floor, Chai Wan, Hong Kong
33 Alpin Way, TW7 4RJ Isleworth, Middlesex, United Kingdom

SpectraComp
1609 Main St, Mechanicsburg, PA 17055
Tel: 717-697-8600 *Toll Free Tel:* 800-666-2662
  Fax: 717-691-0433
E-mail: info@spectracomp.com
Web Site: www.spectracomp.com
Key Personnel
Pres: Terry Fackler *E-mail:* tfackler@spectracomp.com
VP, Opers: Jeffrey Fackler
Founded: 1966

URUGUAY

Turnaround: 1-10 Workdays
Business from Other Countries: 10%

Square Two Design Inc
2325 Third St, Suite 401, San Francisco, CA 94107
Tel: 415-437-3888 *Fax:* 415-437-3880
E-mail: sq2d@square2.com
Web Site: www.square2.com
Key Personnel
Pres: Eddie Lee
Founded: 1992
Business from Other Countries: 10%

Studio 31
2740 SW Martha Downs Blvd, No 358, Palm City, FL 34990
Tel: 772-781-7195 *Fax:* 772-781-6044
E-mail: studio31@mindspring.com
Web Site: www.studio31.com
Key Personnel
Pres: Jim Wasserman
Founded: 1977
Business from Other Countries: 15%

Taylor Publishing Company
1550 W Mockingbird Lane, Dallas, TX 75235
Tel: 214-819-8226 *Toll Free Tel:* 800-677-2800
  Fax: 214-630-1852
E-mail: info@taylorpub.com
Web Site: www.taylorpub.com
Key Personnel
CEO: Dave Fiore
Dir, Fine Books & Div Sales Mgr: W Jay Love
Dir, Mktg: Mike Taylor
Founded: 1939
Turnaround: 45 Workdays
Print Runs: 300 min - 25,000 max
Business from Other Countries: 10%

Times Publishing Group
Division of Times Publishing Ltd/Singapore
99 White Plains Rd, Tarrytown, NY 10591
Tel: 914-366-9888 *Fax:* 914-366-9898
Web Site: www.tpl.com.sg
Key Personnel
Cust Serv Exec: Bonnie Stone *E-mail:* bstone@marshallcavendish.com
Sales Mgr: Suresh Kumar *E-mail:* skumar@marshallcavendish.com
Founded: 1965
Print Runs: 2,000 min - 500,000 max
Business from Other Countries: 90%

Fred Weidner & Daughter Printers
15 Maiden Lane, Suite 1505, New York, NY 10038
Tel: 212-964-8676 *Fax:* 212-964-8677
E-mail: info@fwdprinters.com
Web Site: www.fwdprinters.com
Key Personnel
Exec VP: Cynthia Weidner *E-mail:* cynthia@fwdprinters.com
Creative Dir: Carol Mittelsdorf
Founded: 1860
Turnaround: 5-10 Workdays
Print Runs: 1,000 min - 500,000 max
Business from Other Countries: 25%

Uruguay

Barreiro y Ramos SA
Juan Carlos Gomez, Montevideo 1430
Tel: (02) 986621 *Fax:* (02) 962358
Telex: 23901PB.CVJA.UY *Cable:* BAREIRAMOS

URUGUAY

Key Personnel
President: Gaston Barreiro
Vice President: Guzman Barreiro
Founded: 1837
Print Runs: 1,000 min - 50,000 max
Business from Other Countries: 10%

Printing, Binding & Book Finishing Index

ADHESIVE BINDING - HARD

Australia
Southwood Press Pty Ltd, pg 1215

Belgium
Drukkerij Lannoo NV, pg 1215

Canada
Appleby's Bindery Ltd, pg 1215
Printcrafters Inc, pg 1215
Transcontinental Printing Book Group, pg 1216
Tri-Graphic Printing (Ottawa) Ltd, pg 1216
University of Toronto Press Inc, pg 1216
Webcom Ltd, pg 1216

Czech Republic
GRASPO CZ AS - Druckerei und Buchbinderei, pg 1216

Denmark
Bianco Lunos Bogtrykkeri AS, pg 1216

Finland
Gummerus Printing, pg 1216
WS Bookwell Ltd, pg 1216

Germany
C L Baader Buch & Offsetdruckere GmbH & Co KG, pg 1216
C Maurer Druck und Verlag, pg 1217
Media-Print Informationstechnologie GmbH, pg 1217
MOHN Media, pg 1217
Oertel & Sporer GmbH & Co, pg 1217
Priese GmbH & Co, pg 1217
Vier-Tuerme GmbH Benedikt Press, pg 1217

Hong Kong
C & C Offset Printing Co Ltd, pg 1217
Dai Nippon Printing Co (Hong Kong) Ltd, pg 1217
Everbest Printing Co Ltd, pg 1218
Golden Cup Printing Co Ltd, pg 1218
Hung Hing Off-set Printing Co Ltd, pg 1218
Midas Printing Ltd, pg 1219
Morris Press Ltd, pg 1219
Paramount Printing Co Ltd, pg 1219
Prontaprint Asia Ltd, pg 1219
Sing Cheong Printing Co Ltd, pg 1219
Sino Publishing House Ltd, pg 1219
SNP Best-Set Typesetter Ltd, pg 1219
Speedflex Asia Ltd, pg 1219
Unicorn International Printing Co Ltd, pg 1219
Wing King Tong Group, pg 1220

Indonesia
Ichtiar Baru I Van Hoeve, pg 1220
Victory Offset Prima PT, pg 1220

Italy
Canale G e C SpA, pg 1220
Milanostampa SpA, pg 1220

Republic of Korea
Pyunghwa Dang Printing Co Ltd, pg 1221

Lithuania
Spindulys Printing House, pg 1221

New Zealand
Bookprint Consultants Ltd, pg 1221

Philippines
Cacho Publishing inc, pg 1222
Philippine Graphic Arts Inc, pg 1222

Singapore
Eurasia Press Pte Ltd, pg 1222
Ho Printing Singapore Pte Ltd, pg 1222
Markono Print Media Pte Ltd, pg 1222
SNP SPrint Pte Ltd, pg 1223
World Publications Printers Pte Ltd, pg 1223

Slovenia
Gorenjski Tisk Printing House, pg 1223

Spain
Luis Vives (Edelvives), pg 1223

United Republic of Tanzania
Peramiho Publications, pg 1224

Thailand
J Film Process Co Ltd, pg 1224
Mavisu International Co Ltd, pg 1224

United Kingdom
Biddles Ltd, pg 1225
Caledonian International Book Manufacturing, pg 1225
Center Print Ltd, pg 1225
Clays Ltd, pg 1225
William Clowes Ltd, pg 1225
Cradley Print Ltd, pg 1225
Hammond Packaging Ltd, pg 1226
Intype Libra Ltd, pg 1226
Charles Letts & Co Ltd, pg 1226
MPG Books Ltd, pg 1227
Redwood Books Ltd, pg 1227
Antony Rowe Ltd, pg 1227
TJ International Ltd, pg 1227
Watkiss Automation Ltd, pg 1227

United States
Bind-It Corp, pg 1228
Blaze International Productions Inc, pg 1228
BookBuilders New York Inc, pg 1228
Colorprint Offset Inc, pg 1229
Martin Cook Associates Ltd, pg 1229
CS Graphics USA Inc, pg 1229
DNP America LLC, pg 1229
Elegance Printing & Book Binding (USA), pg 1229
Express Media Corp, pg 1229
Hamilton Printing Co, pg 1229
Hindy's Enterprise, pg 1229
Imago, pg 1229
Integrated Book Technology Inc, pg 1230
Jinno International Group, pg 1230
KNI Inc, pg 1230
Leo Paper USA, pg 1230
Linick International Inc, pg 1230
LK Litho, pg 1230
Milanostampa/New Interlitho USA Inc, pg 1231
Palace Press International - Corporate Headquarters, pg 1231
Regent Publishing Services, pg 1231
Spraymation Inc, pg 1231
Fred Weidner & Daughter Printers, pg 1231

Uruguay
Barreiro y Ramos SA, pg 1231

ADHESIVE BINDING - SOFT

Australia
Southwood Press Pty Ltd, pg 1215

Belgium
Drukkerij Lannoo NV, pg 1215

Canada
Appleby's Bindery Ltd, pg 1215
Blitzprint Inc, pg 1215
Coach House Printing, pg 1215
Maracle Press Ltd, pg 1215
Preney Print & Litho Inc, pg 1215
Printcrafters Inc, pg 1215
Transcontinental Printing Book Group, pg 1216
Tri-Graphic Printing (Ottawa) Ltd, pg 1216
University of Toronto Press Inc, pg 1216
Webcom Ltd, pg 1216

Denmark
Bianco Lunos Bogtrykkeri AS, pg 1216

Finland
Gummerus Printing, pg 1216
WS Bookwell Ltd, pg 1216

Germany
C L Baader Buch & Offsetdruckere GmbH & Co KG, pg 1216
C Maurer Druck und Verlag, pg 1217
Media-Print Informationstechnologie GmbH, pg 1217
MOHN Media, pg 1217
Priese GmbH & Co, pg 1217
Vier-Tuerme GmbH Benedikt Press, pg 1217

Hong Kong
C & C Offset Printing Co Ltd, pg 1217
Colorprint Offset, pg 1217
Dai Nippon Printing Co (Hong Kong) Ltd, pg 1217
Everbest Printing Co Ltd, pg 1218
Golden Cup Printing Co Ltd, pg 1218
Hung Hing Off-set Printing Co Ltd, pg 1218
Liang Yu Printing Factory Ltd, pg 1218
Midas Printing Ltd, pg 1219
Morris Press Ltd, pg 1219
Paramount Printing Co Ltd, pg 1219
Prontaprint Asia Ltd, pg 1219
Sheck Wah Tong Printing Press Ltd, pg 1219
Sing Cheong Printing Co Ltd, pg 1219
Sino Publishing House Ltd, pg 1219
SNP Best-Set Typesetter Ltd, pg 1219
Speedflex Asia Ltd, pg 1219
Toppan Printing Co (HK) Ltd, pg 1219
Unicorn International Printing Co Ltd, pg 1219
Wing King Tong Group, pg 1220

Indonesia
Ichtiar Baru I Van Hoeve, pg 1220
Victory Offset Prima PT, pg 1220

Ireland
Kilkenny People/Wellbrook Press, pg 1220
Smurfit Print, pg 1220

Israel
Keterpress Enterprises Jerusalem, pg 1220
Technosdar Ltd, pg 1220

Italy
Canale G e C SpA, pg 1220
Milanostampa SpA, pg 1220
Minerva Medica, pg 1221

Republic of Korea
Daehan Printing & Publishing Co Ltd, pg 1221
Pyunghwa Dang Printing Co Ltd, pg 1221

Lithuania
Spindulys Printing House, pg 1221

New Zealand
Bookprint Consultants Ltd, pg 1221

PRINTING, BINDING & BOOK FINISHING INDEX

Philippines
Cacho Publishing inc, pg 1222
Philippine Graphic Arts Inc, pg 1222

Singapore
Chong Moh Offset Printing Ltd, pg 1222
CS Graphics Pte Ltd, pg 1222
Eurasia Press Pte Ltd, pg 1222
Ho Printing Singapore Pte Ltd, pg 1222
Markono Print Media Pte Ltd, pg 1222
SNP SPrint Pte Ltd, pg 1223
Times Printers Pte Ltd, pg 1223
World Publications Printers Pte Ltd, pg 1223

Slovenia
Gorenjski Tisk Printing House, pg 1223

Spain
Grafos SA Arte Sobre Papel, pg 1223
Rotedic SA, pg 1223
Luis Vives (Edelvives), pg 1223

United Republic of Tanzania
Peramiho Publications, pg 1224

Thailand
J Film Process Co Ltd, pg 1224
Mavisu International Co Ltd, pg 1224

United Kingdom
J W Arrowsmith Ltd, pg 1224
BAS Printers Ltd, pg 1224
Biddles Ltd, pg 1225
J W Braithwaite & Son Ltd, pg 1225
Caledonian International Book Manufacturing, pg 1225
Center Print Ltd, pg 1225
Clays Ltd, pg 1225
The Guernsey Press Co Ltd, pg 1226
Hammond Packaging Ltd, pg 1226
Intype Libra Ltd, pg 1226
Charles Letts & Co Ltd, pg 1226
Lowfield Printing Co Ltd, pg 1226
MPG Books Ltd, pg 1227
Page Bros Ltd (Norwich), pg 1227
Redwood Books Ltd, pg 1227
Antony Rowe Ltd, pg 1227
Severnside Printers Ltd, pg 1227
TJ International Ltd, pg 1227
Watkiss Automation Ltd, pg 1227
WH Trade Binders Ltd, pg 1227

United States
ADR/BookPrint Inc, pg 1228
Bind-It Corp, pg 1228
Blaze International Productions Inc, pg 1228
BookBuilders New York Inc, pg 1228
C & C Offset Printing Co Ltd, pg 1228
Colorprint Offset Inc, pg 1229
Coneco Litho Graphics, pg 1229
Martin Cook Associates Ltd, pg 1229
CS Graphics USA Inc, pg 1229
DNP America LLC, pg 1229
Elegance Printing & Book Binding (USA), pg 1229

Express Media Corp, pg 1229
Hamilton Printing Co, pg 1229
Hindy's Enterprise, pg 1229
Imago, pg 1229
Integrated Book Technology Inc, pg 1230
Jinno International Group, pg 1230
Leo Paper USA, pg 1230
Linick International Inc, pg 1230
LK Litho, pg 1230
Milanostampa/New Interlitho USA Inc, pg 1231
Palace Press International - Corporate Headquarters, pg 1231
Printing Corp of the Americas Inc, pg 1231
Regent Publishing Services, pg 1231
Spraymation Inc, pg 1231
Vicks Lithograph & Printing Corp, pg 1231
Fred Weidner & Daughter Printers, pg 1231

Uruguay
Barreiro y Ramos SA, pg 1231

BOOK PRINTING - HARDBOUND

Australia
Southwood Press Pty Ltd, pg 1215

Austria
ADEVA (Akademische Druck-u Verlagsanstalt), pg 1215

Belgium
Drukkerij Lannoo NV, pg 1215

Canada
Aardvark Enterprises, pg 1215
Coach House Printing, pg 1215
McLaren Morris & Todd Co, pg 1215
Printcrafters Inc, pg 1215
Transcontinental Printing Book Group, pg 1216
Tri-Graphic Printing (Ottawa) Ltd, pg 1216
University of Toronto Press Inc, pg 1216

Denmark
Bianco Lunos Bogtrykkeri AS, pg 1216

Finland
Gummerus Printing, pg 1216
WS Bookwell Ltd, pg 1216

France
Imprimerie Gaignault, pg 1216
Signes du Monde, pg 1216

Germany
G Braun (vormals G Braun'sche Hofbuchdruckerei und Verlag), pg 1217
C Maurer Druck und Verlag, pg 1217
Media-Print Informationstechnologie GmbH, pg 1217
MOHN Media, pg 1217
Priese GmbH & Co, pg 1217
Vier-Tuerme GmbH Benedikt Press, pg 1217

Hong Kong
Bookbuilders Ltd, pg 1217
C & C Offset Printing Co Ltd, pg 1217
Caritas Printing Training Centre, pg 1217
Colorprint Offset, 1217
Dai Nippon Printing Co (Hong Kong) Ltd, pg 1217
Everbest Printing Co Ltd, pg 1218
Excel United Company Ltd, pg 1218
Golden Cup Printing Co Ltd, pg 1218
Hoi Kwong Printing Co Ltd, pg 1218
Hung Hing Off-set Printing Co Ltd, pg 1218
Image Printing Company Ltd, pg 1218
Lammar Offset Printing Co, pg 1218
Leo Paper Products Ltd, pg 1218
Liang Yu Printing Factory Ltd, pg 1218
Midas Printing Ltd, pg 1219
Morris Press Ltd, pg 1219
Paper Art Product Ltd, pg 1219
Paper Communication Printing Express Ltd, pg 1219
Paramount Printing Co Ltd, pg 1219
Prontaprint Asia Ltd, pg 1219
Sing Cheong Printing Co Ltd, pg 1219
Sino Publishing House Ltd, pg 1219
SNP Best-Set Typesetter Ltd, pg 1219
South Sea International Press Ltd, pg 1219
Speedflex Asia Ltd, pg 1219
Sun Fung Offset Binding Co Ltd, pg 1219
Sunny Printing (Hong Kong) Co Ltd, pg 1219
Sunshine Press Ltd, pg 1219
Toppan Printing Co (HK) Ltd, pg 1219
Unicorn International Printing Co Ltd, pg 1219
Wing King Tong Group, pg 1220

Hungary
Interpress Aussenhandels GmbH, pg 1220
Kultura, pg 1220

Indonesia
Ichtiar Baru I Van Hoeve, pg 1220
Victory Offset Prima PT, pg 1220

Israel
Keterpress Enterprises Jerusalem, pg 1220
Monoline Ltd, pg 1220
Technosdar Ltd, pg 1220

Italy
Canale G e C SpA, pg 1220
Dedalo Litostampa SRL, pg 1220
Milanostampa SpA, pg 1220
Amilcare Pizzi SpA, pg 1221

Japan
Dai Nippon Printing Co Ltd, pg 1221

Republic of Korea
Daehan Printing & Publishing Co Ltd, pg 1221
Pyunghwa Dang Printing Co Ltd, pg 1221

Lithuania
Spindulys Printing House, pg 1221

Madagascar
Societe Malgache d'Edition, pg 1221

Malta
Interprint Ltd - Malta, pg 1221

Netherlands
Koninklijke Wohrmann Bv, pg 1221

New Zealand
Bookprint Consultants Ltd, pg 1221
PPP Printers Ltd, pg 1221
Rogan McIndoe Print Ltd, pg 1221

Philippines
Cacho Publishing inc, pg 1222
Philippine Graphic Arts Inc, pg 1222

Portugal
Printer Portuguesa Industria Grafica Lda, pg 1222

Singapore
CS Graphics Pte Ltd, pg 1222
Eurasia Press Pte Ltd, pg 1222
Fong & Sons Printers Pte Ltd, pg 1222
Ho Printing Singapore Pte Ltd, pg 1222
International Press Co Pte Ltd, pg 1222
SNP SPrint Pte Ltd, pg 1223
Tien Wah Press Pte Ltd, pg 1223
World Publications Printers Pte Ltd, pg 1223

Slovenia
Gorenjski Tisk Printing House, pg 1223

South Africa
CTP Book Printers (Pty) Ltd, pg 1223

Spain
Grafos SA Arte Sobre Papel, pg 1223
Printer Industria Grafica SA, pg 1223
Graficas Santamaria SA, pg 1223
Luis Vives (Edelvives), pg 1223

Sri Lanka
Sumathi Book Printing (Pvt) Ltd, pg 1224

Switzerland
Hallwag Kuemmerly & Frey AG, pg 1224

Taiwan, Province of China
Taipei Yung Chang Printing, pg 1224

MANUFACTURING

PRINTING, BINDING & BOOK FINISHING INDEX

United Republic of Tanzania
Peramiho Publications, pg 1224

Thailand
J Film Process Co Ltd, pg 1224
Phongwarin Printing Company Ltd, pg 1224

United Arab Emirates
Emirates Printing Press (LLC), pg 1224

United Kingdom
The Alden Group Ltd, pg 1224
W & G Baird Ltd, pg 1224
BAS Printers Ltd, pg 1224
Ebenezer Baylis & Son Ltd, pg 1224
Biddles Ltd, pg 1225
Book Creation, pg 1225
Butler & Tanner Ltd, pg 1225
Caledonian International Book Manufacturing, pg 1225
Center Print Ltd, pg 1225
The Charlesworth Group, pg 1225
Clays Ltd, pg 1225
William Clowes Ltd, pg 1225
Cradley Print Ltd, pg 1225
Eagle Press, pg 1225
Goldshield Communications Ltd, pg 1226
Hammond Packaging Ltd, pg 1226
Headley Brothers Ltd, pg 1226
Intype Libra Ltd, pg 1226
Charles Letts & Co Ltd, pg 1226
MPG Books Ltd, pg 1227
Multiplex Medway Ltd, pg 1227
George Over Ltd, pg 1227
Redwood Books Ltd, pg 1227
Antony Rowe Ltd, pg 1227
Severnside Printers Ltd, pg 1227
Stott Brothers Ltd, pg 1227
TJ International Ltd, pg 1227

United States
Asia Pacific Offset Inc, pg 1228
Blaze International Productions Inc, pg 1228
BookBuilders New York Inc, pg 1228
Butler & Tanner Inc, pg 1228
C & C Offset Printing Co Ltd, pg 1228
Carvajal International Inc, pg 1228
Colorprint Offset Inc, pg 1229
Coneco Litho Graphics, pg 1229
Martin Cook Associates Ltd, pg 1229
CS Graphics USA Inc, pg 1229
DNP America LLC, pg 1229
Elegance Printing & Book Binding (USA), pg 1229
Express Media Corp, pg 1229
Hamilton Printing Co, pg 1229
Hindy's Enterprise, pg 1229
Imago, pg 1229
Integrated Book Technology Inc, pg 1230
Jinno International Group, pg 1230
Leo Paper USA, pg 1230
Linick International Inc, pg 1230
LK Litho, pg 1230
Milanostampa/New Interlitho USA Inc, pg 1231
Outskirts Press, pg 1231
Palace Press International - Corporate Headquarters, pg 1231
Printing Corp of the Americas Inc, pg 1231
Regent Publishing Services, pg 1231

Taylor Publishing Company, pg 1231
Times Publishing Group, pg 1231
Fred Weidner & Daughter Printers, pg 1231

Uruguay
Barreiro y Ramos SA, pg 1231

BOOK PRINTING - MASS MARKET

Belgium
Drukkerij Lannoo NV, pg 1215

Canada
Webcom Ltd, pg 1216

Czech Republic
GRASPO CZ AS - Druckerei und Buchbinderei, pg 1216

Germany
MOHN Media, pg 1217
Priese GmbH & Co, pg 1217

Hong Kong
Dai Nippon Printing Co (Hong Kong) Ltd, pg 1217
Golden Cup Printing Co Ltd, pg 1218
The Green Pagoda Press Ltd, pg 1218
Hoi Kwong Printing Co Ltd, pg 1218
Midas Printing Ltd, pg 1219
Paramount Printing Co Ltd, pg 1219
Sheck Wah Tong Printing Press Ltd, pg 1219
Sing Cheong Printing Co Ltd, pg 1219
Sino Publishing House Ltd, pg 1219
Unicorn International Printing Co Ltd, pg 1219

Hungary
Interpress Aussenhandels GmbH, pg 1220

India
Hiralal Printing Works Ltd, pg 1220

Indonesia
Victory Offset Prima PT, pg 1220

Ireland
Ultragraphics, pg 1220

Israel
Keterpress Enterprises Jerusalem, pg 1220

Italy
Canale G e C SpA, pg 1220
Milanostampa SpA, pg 1220
Amilcare Pizzi SpA, pg 1221

Republic of Korea
Daehan Printing & Publishing Co Ltd, pg 1221
Pyunghwa Dang Printing Co Ltd, pg 1221

Lithuania
Spindulys Printing House, pg 1221

Netherlands
Koninklijke Wohrmann Bv, pg 1221

New Zealand
Bookprint Consultants Ltd, pg 1221
Rogan McIndoe Print Ltd, pg 1221

Philippines
Cacho Publishing inc, pg 1222

Singapore
Markono Print Media Pte Ltd, pg 1222
Times Printers Pte Ltd, pg 1223

Slovenia
Gorenjski Tisk Printing House, pg 1223

Spain
Graficas Santamaria SA, pg 1223
Luis Vives (Edelvives), pg 1223

United Republic of Tanzania
Peramiho Publications, pg 1224

Thailand
J Film Process Co Ltd, pg 1224
Mavisu International Co Ltd, pg 1224
Phongwarin Printing Company Ltd, pg 1224

United Kingdom
Caledonian International Book Manufacturing, pg 1225
Clays Ltd, pg 1225
Goldshield Communications Ltd, pg 1226
The Guernsey Press Co Ltd, pg 1226
The Lavenham Press Ltd, pg 1226
Charles Letts & Co Ltd, pg 1226
Redwood Books Ltd, pg 1227

United States
Asia Pacific Offset Inc, pg 1228
Blaze International Productions Inc, pg 1228
BookBuilders New York Inc, pg 1228
C & C Offset Printing Co Ltd, pg 1228
Carvajal International Inc, pg 1228
Colorprint Offset Inc, pg 1229
Martin Cook Associates Ltd, pg 1229
DNP America LLC, pg 1229
Elegance Printing & Book Binding (USA), pg 1229
Express Media Corp, pg 1229
Hamilton Printing Co, pg 1229
Hindy's Enterprise, pg 1229
Jinno International Group, pg 1230
Leo Paper USA, pg 1230
Linick International Inc, pg 1230
LK Litho, pg 1230
Outskirts Press, pg 1231
Printing Corp of the Americas Inc, pg 1231
Times Publishing Group, pg 1231
Fred Weidner & Daughter Printers, pg 1231

BOOK PRINTING - PROFESSIONAL

Australia
Southwood Press Pty Ltd, pg 1215

Belgium
Drukkerij Lannoo NV, pg 1215

Canada
Blitzprint Inc, pg 1215
Maracle Press Ltd, pg 1215
Printcrafters Inc, pg 1215
Transcontinental Printing Book Group, pg 1216
Tri-Graphic Printing (Ottawa) Ltd, pg 1216
University of Toronto Press Inc, pg 1216
Webcom Ltd, pg 1216

Czech Republic
GRASPO CZ AS - Druckerei und Buchbinderei, pg 1216

Denmark
Bianco Lunos Bogtrykkeri AS, pg 1216

Finland
Gummerus Printing, pg 1216

Germany
C L Baader Buch & Offsetdruckerei GmbH & Co KG, pg 1216
Fachhochschule Fur Druk, Studiengang Verlagswirtschaft und Verlagsherstellung, pg 1217
G Braun (vormals G Braun'sche Hofbuchdruckerei und Verlag), pg 1217
Media-Print Informationstechnologie GmbH, pg 1217
MOHN Media, pg 1217
Priese GmbH & Co, pg 1217

Hong Kong
Dai Nippon Printing Co (Hong Kong) Ltd, pg 1217
Everbest Printing Co Ltd, pg 1218
Golden Cup Printing Co Ltd, pg 1218
The Green Pagoda Press Ltd, pg 1218
Hoi Kwong Printing Co Ltd, pg 1218
Image Printing Company Ltd, pg 1218
Midas Printing Ltd, pg 1219
Paper Art Product Ltd, pg 1219
Paramount Printing Co Ltd, pg 1219
Prontaprint Asia Ltd, pg 1219
Sheck Wah Tong Printing Press Ltd, pg 1219
Sing Cheong Printing Co Ltd, pg 1219
Sino Publishing House Ltd, pg 1219
South Sea International Press Ltd, pg 1219
Speedflex Asia Ltd, pg 1219
Sunshine Press Ltd, pg 1219
Unicorn International Printing Co Ltd, pg 1219
Wing King Tong Group, pg 1220

Hungary
Interpress Aussenhandels GmbH, pg 1220

1193

PRINTING, BINDING & BOOK FINISHING INDEX

Indonesia
Victory Offset Prima PT, pg 1220

Ireland
Ultragraphics, pg 1220

Israel
Keterpress Enterprises Jerusalem, pg 1220
Monoline Ltd, pg 1220
Technosdar Ltd, pg 1220

Italy
Canale G e C SpA, pg 1220
Dedalo Litostampa SRL, pg 1220
Milanostampa SpA, pg 1220

Republic of Korea
Daehan Printing & Publishing Co Ltd, pg 1221
Pyunghwa Dang Printing Co Ltd, pg 1221

Madagascar
Societe Malgache d'Edition, pg 1221

New Zealand
Bookprint Consultants Ltd, pg 1221
PPP Printers Ltd, pg 1221

Philippines
Cacho Publishing inc, pg 1222

Portugal
Edicoes Silabo, pg 1222

Singapore
Chong Moh Offset Printing Ltd, pg 1222
CS Graphics Pte Ltd, pg 1222
Eurasia Press Pte Ltd, pg 1222
Ho Printing Singapore Pte Ltd, pg 1222
PacPress Media Pte Ltd, pg 1223
SNP SPrint Pte Ltd, pg 1223
Times Printers Pte Ltd, pg 1223
World Publications Printers Pte Ltd, pg 1223

Slovenia
Gorenjski Tisk Printing House, pg 1223

Spain
Grafos SA Arte Sobre Papel, pg 1223
Graficas Santamaria SA, pg 1223
Luis Vives (Edelvives), pg 1223

United Republic of Tanzania
Peramiho Publications, pg 1224

Thailand
Phongwarin Printing Company Ltd, pg 1224

United Kingdom
BAS Printers Ltd, pg 1224
Ebenezer Baylis & Son Ltd, pg 1224
Bemrose Booth, pg 1225
Biddles Ltd, pg 1225
Blackmore Ltd, pg 1225
Book Creation, pg 1225
Butler & Tanner Ltd, pg 1225
Caledonian International Book Manufacturing, pg 1225
Cambridge University Press - Printing Division, pg 1225
The Charlesworth Group, pg 1225
Clays Ltd, pg 1225
William Clowes Ltd, pg 1225
Cradley Print Ltd, pg 1225
Goldshield Communications Ltd, pg 1226
Hammond Packaging Ltd, pg 1226
Hobbs The Printers Ltd, pg 1226
Ikon Document Management Services, pg 1226
Charles Letts & Co Ltd, pg 1226
MPG Books Ltd, pg 1227
Multiplex Medway Ltd, pg 1227
Redwood Books Ltd, pg 1227
Antony Rowe Ltd, pg 1227
Selwood Printing, pg 1227
Severnside Printers Ltd, pg 1227

United States
ADR/BookPrint Inc, pg 1228
Asia Pacific Offset Inc, pg 1228
Blaze International Productions Inc, pg 1228
BookBuilders New York Inc, pg 1228
Carvajal International Inc, pg 1228
Colorprint Offset Inc, pg 1229
Coneco Litho Graphics, pg 1229
Martin Cook Associates Ltd, pg 1229
DNP America LLC, pg 1229
Elegance Printing & Book Binding (USA), pg 1229
Express Media Corp, pg 1229
Hamilton Printing Co, pg 1229
Hindy's Enterprise, pg 1229
Imago, pg 1229
KNI Inc, pg 1230
Linick International Inc, pg 1230
LK Litho, pg 1230
Marrakech Express Inc, pg 1230
Outskirts Press, pg 1231
Palace Press International - Corporate Headquarters, pg 1231
Printing Corp of the Americas Inc, pg 1231
Times Publishing Group, pg 1231
Vicks Lithograph & Printing Corp, pg 1231
Fred Weidner & Daughter Printers, pg 1231

BOOK PRINTING - SOFTBOUND

Australia
Southwood Press Pty Ltd, pg 1215

Belgium
Drukkerij Lannoo NV, pg 1215

Canada
Blitzprint Inc, pg 1215
Coach House Printing, pg 1215
Maracle Press Ltd, pg 1215
Preney Print & Litho Inc, pg 1215
Printcrafters Inc, pg 1215
Transcontinental Printing Book Group, pg 1216
Tri-Graphic Printing (Ottawa) Ltd, pg 1216
University of Toronto Press Inc, pg 1216
Webcom Ltd, pg 1216

Czech Republic
GRASPO CZ AS - Druckerei und Buchbinderei, pg 1216

Denmark
Bianco Lunos Bogtrykkeri AS, pg 1216

Finland
Gummerus Printing, pg 1216
WS Bookwell Ltd, pg 1216

France
Imprimerie Bene, pg 1216
Plein Chant, pg 1216
Signes du Monde, pg 1216

Germany
C Maurer Druck und Verlag, pg 1217
MOHN Media, pg 1217
Priese GmbH & Co, pg 1217
Vier-Tuerme GmbH Benedikt Press, pg 1217

Hong Kong
Bookbuilders Ltd, pg 1217
C & C Offset Printing Co Ltd, pg 1217
Caritas Printing Training Centre, pg 1217
Colorprint Offset, pg 1217
Dai Nippon Printing Co (Hong Kong) Ltd, pg 1217
Golden Cup Printing Co Ltd, pg 1218
The Green Pagoda Press Ltd, pg 1218
Hoi Kwong Printing Co Ltd, pg 1218
Hung Hing Off-set Printing Co Ltd, pg 1218
Image Printing Company Ltd, pg 1218
Leo Paper Products Ltd, pg 1218
Midas Printing Ltd, pg 1219
Morris Press Ltd, pg 1219
Paper Art Product Ltd, pg 1219
Paper Communication Printing Express Ltd, pg 1219
Paramount Printing Co Ltd, pg 1219
Prontaprint Asia Ltd, pg 1219
Sheck Wah Tong Printing Press Ltd, pg 1219
Sing Cheong Printing Co Ltd, pg 1219
Sino Publishing House Ltd, pg 1219
SNP Best-Set Typesetter Ltd, pg 1219
South Sea International Press Ltd, pg 1219
Speedflex Asia Ltd, pg 1219
Sunshine Press Ltd, pg 1219
Toppan Printing Co (HK) Ltd, pg 1219
Unicorn International Printing Co Ltd, pg 1219

Hungary
Interpress Aussenhandels GmbH, pg 1220
Kultura, pg 1220

Indonesia
Ichtiar Baru I Van Hoeve, pg 1220
Victory Offset Prima PT, pg 1220

Israel
Keterpress Enterprises Jerusalem, pg 1220
Monoline Ltd, pg 1220
Technosdar Ltd, pg 1220

Italy
Canale G e C SpA, pg 1220
Dedalo Litostampa SRL, pg 1220
Milanostampa SpA, pg 1220
Amilcare Pizzi SpA, pg 1221

Republic of Korea
Daehan Printing & Publishing Co Ltd, pg 1221
Pyunghwa Dang Printing Co Ltd, pg 1221

Lithuania
Spindulys Printing House, pg 1221

Madagascar
Societe Malgache d'Edition, pg 1221

Malaysia
Web Printers Sdn Bhd, pg 1221

Malta
Interprint Ltd - Malta, pg 1221

Netherlands
Koninklijke Wohrmann Bv, pg 1221

New Zealand
Bookprint Consultants Ltd, pg 1221
PPP Printers Ltd, pg 1221
Rogan McIndoe Print Ltd, pg 1221

Philippines
Cacho Publishing inc, pg 1222
Philippine Graphic Arts Inc, pg 1222

Portugal
Printer Portuguesa Industria Grafica Lda, pg 1222

Singapore
Chong Moh Offset Printing Ltd, pg 1222
Craft Print Pte Ltd, pg 1222
CS Graphics Pte Ltd, pg 1222
Eurasia Press Pte Ltd, pg 1222
Ho Printing Singapore Pte Ltd, pg 1222
International Press Co Pte Ltd, pg 1222
Markono Print Media Pte Ltd, pg 1222
SNP SPrint Pte Ltd, pg 1223
Stamford Press Pte Ltd, pg 1223
Tien Wah Press Pte Ltd, pg 1223
Times Printers Pte Ltd, pg 1223
World Publications Printers Pte Ltd, pg 1223

Slovenia
Gorenjski Tisk Printing House, pg 1223

Spain
Grafos SA Arte Sobre Papel, pg 1223
Printer Industria Grafica SA, pg 1223
Rotedic SA, pg 1223

MANUFACTURING

Graficas Santamaria SA, pg 1223
Luis Vives (Edelvives), pg 1223

Sri Lanka

Sumathi Book Printing (Pvt) Ltd, pg 1224

Switzerland

Hallwag Kuemmerly & Frey AG, pg 1224
Photolitho AG, pg 1224

United Republic of Tanzania

Peramiho Publications, pg 1224

Thailand

Mavisu International Co Ltd, pg 1224
Phongwarin Printing Company Ltd, pg 1224

United Arab Emirates

Emirates Printing Press (LLC), pg 1224

United Kingdom

J W Arrowsmith Ltd, pg 1224
BAS Printers Ltd, pg 1224
Bell & Bain Ltd, pg 1224
Biddles Ltd, pg 1225
Book Creation, pg 1225
Caledonian International Book Manufacturing, pg 1225
Clays Ltd, pg 1225
William Clowes Ltd, pg 1225
Cox & Wyman Ltd, pg 1225
Cradley Print Ltd, pg 1225
Goldshield Communications Ltd, pg 1226
The Guernsey Press Co Ltd, pg 1226
Headley Brothers Ltd, pg 1226
Hobbs The Printers Ltd, pg 1226
Intype Libra Ltd, pg 1226
Charles Letts & Co Ltd, pg 1226
Lowfield Printing Co Ltd, pg 1226
MacKays of Chatham PLC, pg 1226
MPG Books Ltd, pg 1227
George Over Ltd, pg 1227
Page Bros Ltd (Norwich), pg 1227
Redwood Books Ltd, pg 1227
Antony Rowe Ltd, pg 1227
Severnside Printers Ltd, pg 1227
TJ International Ltd, pg 1227
Watkiss Automation Ltd, pg 1227

United States

ADR/BookPrint Inc, pg 1228
Asia Pacific Offset Inc, pg 1228
Blaze International Productions Inc, pg 1228
BookBuilders New York Inc, pg 1228
Butler & Tanner Inc, pg 1228
C & C Offset Printing Co Ltd, pg 1228
Carvajal International Inc, pg 1228
Colorprint Offset Inc, pg 1229
Coneco Litho Graphics, pg 1229
Consolidated Printers Inc, pg 1229
Martin Cook Associates Ltd, pg 1229
CS Graphics USA Inc, pg 1229
DNP America LLC, pg 1229
Elegance Printing & Book Binding (USA), pg 1229
Express Media Corp, pg 1229
Hamilton Printing Co, pg 1229
Hindy's Enterprise, pg 1229
Imago, pg 1229

Integrated Book Technology Inc, pg 1230
Jinno International Group, pg 1230
KNI Inc, pg 1230
Leo Paper USA, pg 1230
LK Litho, pg 1230
Marrakech Express Inc, pg 1230
Milanostampa/New Interlitho USA Inc, pg 1231
Outskirts Press, pg 1231
Palace Press International - Corporate Headquarters, pg 1231
Printing Corp of the Americas Inc, pg 1231
Regent Publishing Services, pg 1231
Times Publishing Group, pg 1231
Vicks Lithograph & Printing Corp, pg 1231
Fred Weidner & Daughter Printers, pg 1231

Uruguay

Barreiro y Ramos SA, pg 1231

BOUND GALLEYS

Canada

Blitzprint Inc, pg 1215

Germany

Priese GmbH & Co, pg 1217

Hong Kong

Caritas Printing Training Centre, pg 1217
Morris Press Ltd, pg 1219
Paramount Printing Co Ltd, pg 1219
Prontaprint Asia Ltd, pg 1219
Unicorn International Printing Co Ltd, pg 1219

New Zealand

Bookprint Consultants Ltd, pg 1221

Singapore

Markono Print Media Pte Ltd, pg 1222
SNP SPrint Pte Ltd, pg 1223
World Publications Printers Pte Ltd, pg 1223

United Republic of Tanzania

Peramiho Publications, pg 1224

United Kingdom

Redwood Books Ltd, pg 1227

United States

Asia Pacific Offset Inc, pg 1228
Coneco Litho Graphics, pg 1229
Express Media Corp, pg 1229
Integrated Book Technology Inc, pg 1230
Jinno International Group, pg 1230
Leo Paper USA, pg 1230
Linick International Inc, pg 1230
LK Litho, pg 1230
Outskirts Press, pg 1231
Fred Weidner & Daughter Printers, pg 1231

BURST BINDING

Australia

Southwood Press Pty Ltd, pg 1215

PRINTING, BINDING & BOOK FINISHING INDEX

Canada

Tri-Graphic Printing (Ottawa) Ltd, pg 1216
Webcom Ltd, pg 1216

Germany

Priese GmbH & Co, pg 1217

Hong Kong

Caritas Printing Training Centre, pg 1217
Everbest Printing Co Ltd, pg 1218
Golden Cup Printing Co Ltd, pg 1218
Midas Printing Ltd, pg 1219
Morris Press Ltd, pg 1219
Sheck Wah Tong Printing Press Ltd, pg 1219
Sing Cheong Printing Co Ltd, pg 1219
Unicorn International Printing Co Ltd, pg 1219

Italy

Canale G e C SpA, pg 1220

New Zealand

Bookprint Consultants Ltd, pg 1221
Rogan McIndoe Print Ltd, pg 1221

Singapore

Chong Moh Offset Printing Ltd, pg 1222
World Publications Printers Pte Ltd, pg 1223

United Republic of Tanzania

Peramiho Publications, pg 1224

United Kingdom

Bell & Bain Ltd, pg 1224
Caledonian International Book Manufacturing, pg 1225
Center Print Ltd, pg 1225
Hammond Bindery Ltd, pg 1226
Hobbs The Printers Ltd, pg 1226
Lowfield Printing Co Ltd, pg 1226
MPG Books Ltd, pg 1227
Page Bros Ltd (Norwich), pg 1227
Redwood Books Ltd, pg 1227
TJ International Ltd, pg 1227
WH Trade Binders Ltd, pg 1227

United States

Asia Pacific Offset Inc, pg 1228
Blaze International Productions Inc, pg 1228
BookBuilders New York Inc, pg 1228
Martin Cook Associates Ltd, pg 1229
Hamilton Printing Co, pg 1229
Integrated Book Technology Inc, pg 1230
Jinno International Group, pg 1230
Linick International Inc, pg 1230
Regent Publishing Services, pg 1231
Fred Weidner & Daughter Printers, pg 1231

CALENDAR PRINTING

Belgium

Drukkerij Lannoo NV, pg 1215

Canada

McLaren Morris & Todd Co, pg 1215
Printcrafters Inc, pg 1215
Schawk, pg 1216
Transcontinental Printing Book Group, pg 1216
University of Toronto Press Inc, pg 1216
Webcom Ltd, pg 1216

Czech Republic

GRASPO CZ AS - Druckerei und Buchbinderei, pg 1216

Germany

Fachhochschule Fur Druk, Studiengang Verlagswirtschaft und Verlagsherstellung, pg 1217
C Maurer Druck und Verlag, pg 1217
MOHN Media, pg 1217
Priese GmbH & Co, pg 1217
Vier-Tuerme GmbH Benedikt Press, pg 1217

Hong Kong

C & C Offset Printing Co Ltd, pg 1217
Colorprint Offset, pg 1217
Dai Nippon Printing Co (Hong Kong) Ltd, pg 1217
Everbest Printing Co Ltd, pg 1218
Golden Cup Printing Co Ltd, pg 1218
The Green Pagoda Press Ltd, pg 1218
Hindy's Enterprise Co Ltd, pg 1218
Hoi Kwong Printing Co Ltd, pg 1218
Hung Hing Off-set Printing Co Ltd, pg 1218
Image Printing Company Ltd, pg 1218
Midas Printing Ltd, pg 1219
Morris Press Ltd, pg 1219
Paper Art Product Ltd, pg 1219
Paper Communication Printing Express Ltd, pg 1219
Paramount Printing Co Ltd, pg 1219
Prontaprint Asia Ltd, pg 1219
Sheck Wah Tong Printing Press Ltd, pg 1219
Sing Cheong Printing Co Ltd, pg 1219
Sino Publishing House Ltd, pg 1219
SNP Best-Set Typesetter Ltd, pg 1219
South Sea International Press Ltd, pg 1219
Speedflex Asia Ltd, pg 1219
Sunshine Press Ltd, pg 1219
Toppan Printing Co (HK) Ltd, pg 1219
Unicorn International Printing Co Ltd, pg 1219
Wing King Tong Group, pg 1220

Hungary

Interpress Aussenhandels GmbH, pg 1220

Indonesia

Victory Offset Prima PT, pg 1220

Ireland

Ultragraphics, pg 1220

Israel

Technosdar Ltd, pg 1220

1195

PRINTING, BINDING & BOOK FINISHING INDEX

BOOK

Italy
Canale G e C SpA, pg 1220
Mariani Ritti Grafiche SRL, pg 1220
Amilcare Pizzi SpA, pg 1221

Republic of Korea
Daehan Printing & Publishing Co Ltd, pg 1221
Pyunghwa Dang Printing Co Ltd, pg 1221

Lithuania
Spindulys Printing House, pg 1221

New Zealand
Bookprint Consultants Ltd, pg 1221
PPP Printers Ltd, pg 1221
Rogan McIndoe Print Ltd, pg 1221

Peru
Industrias del Envase SA, pg 1222

Philippines
Cacho Publishing inc, pg 1222

Singapore
Columbia Overseas Marketing Pte Ltd, pg 1222
CS Graphics Pte Ltd, pg 1222
Eurasia Press Pte Ltd, pg 1222
Ho Printing Singapore Pte Ltd, pg 1222
International Press Co Pte Ltd, pg 1222
SNP SPrint Pte Ltd, pg 1223
World Publications Printers Pte Ltd, pg 1223

Slovenia
Gorenjski Tisk Printing House, pg 1223

Spain
Grafos SA Arte Sobre Papel, pg 1223
Graficas Santamaria SA, pg 1223
Luis Vives (Edelvives), pg 1223

Sri Lanka
Sumathi Book Printing (Pvt) Ltd, pg 1224

United Republic of Tanzania
Peramiho Publications, pg 1224

Thailand
J Film Process Co Ltd, pg 1224
Mavisu International Co Ltd, pg 1224
Phongwarin Printing Company Ltd, pg 1224

United Arab Emirates
Emirates Printing Press (LLC), pg 1224

United Kingdom
Center Print Ltd, pg 1225
William Clowes Ltd, pg 1225
Cradley Print Ltd, pg 1225
The Guernsey Press Co Ltd, pg 1226
Headley Brothers Ltd, pg 1226
Image & Print Group Ltd, pg 1226
The Malvern Press Ltd, pg 1227
Redwood Books Ltd, pg 1227

J R Reid Printing Group Ltd, pg 1227
Severnside Printers Ltd, pg 1227

United States
Asia Pacific Offset Inc, pg 1228
Blaze International Productions Inc, pg 1228
BookBuilders New York Inc, pg 1228
C & C Offset Printing Co Ltd, pg 1228
Carvajal International Inc, pg 1228
Colorprint Offset Inc, pg 1229
Coneco Litho Graphics, pg 1229
Martin Cook Associates Ltd, pg 1229
CS Graphics USA Inc, pg 1229
DNP America LLC, pg 1229
Elegance Printing & Book Binding (USA), pg 1229
Hindy's Enterprise, pg 1229
Imago, pg 1229
Jinno International Group, pg 1230
KNI Inc, pg 1230
Leo Paper USA, pg 1230
Linick International Inc, pg 1230
Milanostampa/New Interlitho USA Inc, pg 1231
Palace Press International - Corporate Headquarters, pg 1231
Printing Corp of the Americas Inc, pg 1231
Regent Publishing Services, pg 1231
Times Publishing Group, pg 1231
Fred Weidner & Daughter Printers, pg 1231

Uruguay
Barreiro y Ramos SA, pg 1231

CASEBINDING

Belgium
Drukkerij Lannoo NV, pg 1215

Canada
Appleby's Bindery Ltd, pg 1215
Coach House Printing, pg 1215
Printcrafters Inc, pg 1215
Transcontinental Printing Book Group, pg 1216
Tri-Graphic Printing (Ottawa) Ltd, pg 1216
University of Toronto Press Inc, pg 1216

Czech Republic
GRASPO CZ AS - Druckerei und Buchbinderei, pg 1216

Denmark
Bianco Lunos Bogtrykkeri AS, pg 1216

Finland
Gummerus Printing, pg 1216

Germany
MOHN Media, pg 1217
Priese GmbH & Co, pg 1217

Hong Kong
C & C Offset Printing Co Ltd, pg 1217
Caritas Printing Training Centre, pg 1217

Colorprint Offset, pg 1217
Dai Nippon Printing Co (Hong Kong) Ltd, pg 1217
Golden Cup Printing Co Ltd, pg 1218
Hung Hing Off-set Printing Co Ltd, pg 1218
Image Printing Company Ltd, pg 1218
Leo Paper Products Ltd, pg 1218
Liang Yu Printing Factory Ltd, pg 1218
Midas Printing Ltd, pg 1219
Morris Press Ltd, pg 1219
Paper Communication Printing Express Ltd, pg 1219
Paramount Printing Co Ltd, pg 1219
Prontaprint Asia Ltd, pg 1219
Sing Cheong Printing Co Ltd, pg 1219
Sino Publishing House Ltd, pg 1219
Toppan Printing Co (HK) Ltd, pg 1219
Unicorn International Printing Co Ltd, pg 1219
Wing King Tong Group, pg 1220

India
Hiralal Printing Works Ltd, pg 1220

Indonesia
Ichtiar Baru I Van Hoeve, pg 1220
Victory Offset Prima PT, pg 1220

Ireland
Smurfit Print, pg 1220

Israel
Keterpress Enterprises Jerusalem, pg 1220

Italy
Canale G e C SpA, pg 1220
Milanostampa SpA, pg 1220

Republic of Korea
Pyunghwa Dang Printing Co Ltd, pg 1221

Malta
Interprint Ltd - Malta, pg 1221

New Zealand
Bookprint Consultants Ltd, pg 1221
Rogan McIndoe Print Ltd, pg 1221

Philippines
Cacho Publishing inc, pg 1222

Singapore
CS Graphics Pte Ltd, pg 1222
Eurasia Press Pte Ltd, pg 1222
Fong & Sons Printers Pte Ltd, pg 1222
Ho Printing Singapore Pte Ltd, pg 1222
International Press Co Pte Ltd, pg 1222
Kyodo Printing Co (S'pore) Pte Ltd, pg 1222
Markono Print Media Pte Ltd, pg 1222
SNP SPrint Pte Ltd, pg 1223
Tien Wah Press Pte Ltd, pg 1223
World Publications Printers Pte Ltd, pg 1223

Slovenia
Gorenjski Tisk Printing House, pg 1223

Spain
Grafos SA Arte Sobre Papel, pg 1223
Graficas Santamaria SA, pg 1223

United Republic of Tanzania
Peramiho Publications, pg 1224

United Arab Emirates
Emirates Printing Press (LLC), pg 1224

United Kingdom
The Alden Group Ltd, pg 1224
BAS Printers Ltd, pg 1224
Biddles Ltd, pg 1225
Book Creation, pg 1225
J W Braithwaite & Son Ltd, pg 1225
Butler & Tanner Ltd, pg 1225
Caledonian International Book Manufacturing, pg 1225
Cambridge University Press - Printing Division, pg 1225
CB Print Finishers Ltd, pg 1225
Center Print Ltd, pg 1225
The Charlesworth Group, pg 1225
Cedric Chivers Ltd, pg 1225
Clays Ltd, pg 1225
William Clowes Ltd, pg 1225
Eagle Press, pg 1225
Goldshield Communications Ltd, pg 1226
Green Street Bindery, pg 1226
Hammond Bindery Ltd, pg 1226
Hammond Packaging Ltd, pg 1226
Headley Brothers Ltd, pg 1226
Hunter & Foulis Ltd, pg 1226
Ikon Document Management Services, pg 1226
Intype Libra Ltd, pg 1226
Charles Letts & Co Ltd, pg 1226
MacKays of Chatham PLC, pg 1226
MPG Books Ltd, pg 1227
Page Bros Ltd (Norwich), pg 1227
Redwood Books Ltd, pg 1227
Antony Rowe Ltd, pg 1227
TJ International Ltd, pg 1227

United States
Asia Pacific Offset Inc, pg 1228
Blaze International Productions Inc, pg 1228
BookBuilders New York Inc, pg 1228
Butler & Tanner Inc, pg 1228
C & C Offset Printing Co Ltd, pg 1228
Colorprint Offset Inc, pg 1229
Coneco Litho Graphics, pg 1229
Martin Cook Associates Ltd, pg 1229
CS Graphics USA Inc, pg 1229
DNP America LLC, pg 1229
Elegance Printing & Book Binding (USA), pg 1229
Express Media Corp, pg 1229
Hamilton Printing Co, pg 1229
Imago, pg 1229
Integrated Book Technology Inc, pg 1230
Jinno International Group, pg 1230
Leo Paper USA, pg 1230
Linick International Inc, pg 1230
Milanostampa/New Interlitho USA Inc, pg 1231

MANUFACTURING

PRINTING, BINDING & BOOK FINISHING INDEX

Palace Press International - Corporate Headquarters, pg 1231
Printing Corp of the Americas Inc, pg 1231
Regent Publishing Services, pg 1231
Taylor Publishing Company, pg 1231
Times Publishing Group, pg 1231
Fred Weidner & Daughter Printers, pg 1231

Uruguay

Barreiro y Ramos SA, pg 1231

CATALOG PRINTING

Belgium

IMPF bvba, pg 1215
Drukkerij Lannoo NV, pg 1215

Canada

Blitzprint Inc, pg 1215
Maracle Press Ltd, pg 1215
McLaren Morris & Todd Co, pg 1215
Preney Print & Litho Inc, pg 1215
Printcrafters Inc, pg 1215
Schawk, pg 1216
Transcontinental Printing Book Group, pg 1216
University of Toronto Press Inc, pg 1216
Webcom Ltd, pg 1216

Czech Republic

GRASPO CZ AS - Druckerei und Buchbinderei, pg 1216

Denmark

Bianco Lunos Bogtrykkeri AS, pg 1216

Finland

WS Bookwell Ltd, pg 1216

France

Imprimerie Gaignault, pg 1216

Germany

C L Baader Buch & Offsetdruckere GmbH & Co KG, pg 1216
Fachhochschule Fur Druk, Studiengang Verlagsherstellung, pg 1217
C Maurer Druck und Verlag, pg 1217
Media-Print Informationstechnologie GmbH, pg 1217
MOHN Media, pg 1217
Priese GmbH & Co, pg 1217
Vier-Tuerme GmbH Benedikt Press, pg 1217

Hong Kong

C & C Offset Printing Co Ltd, pg 1217
Colorprint Offset, pg 1217
Dai Nippon Printing Co (Hong Kong) Ltd, pg 1217
Golden Cup Printing Co Ltd, pg 1218
The Green Pagoda Press Ltd, pg 1218
Hoi Kwong Printing Co Ltd, pg 1218
Hung Hing Off-set Printing Co Ltd, pg 1218
Image Printing Company Ltd, pg 1218
Midas Printing Ltd, pg 1219
Morris Press Ltd, pg 1219
Paper Art Product Ltd, pg 1219
Paper Communication Printing Express Ltd, pg 1219
Paramount Printing Co Ltd, pg 1219
Prontaprint Asia Ltd, pg 1219
Sheck Wah Tong Printing Press Ltd, pg 1219
Sing Cheong Printing Co Ltd, pg 1219
Sino Publishing House Ltd, pg 1219
South Sea International Press Ltd, pg 1219
Speedflex Asia Ltd, pg 1219
Sunshine Press Ltd, pg 1219
Toppan Printing Co (HK) Ltd, pg 1219
Unicorn International Printing Co Ltd, pg 1219
Wing King Tong Group, pg 1220

Hungary

Interpress Aussenhandels GmbH, pg 1220

India

Hiralal Printing Works Ltd, pg 1220

Indonesia

Victory Offset Prima PT, pg 1220

Ireland

Kilkenny People/Wellbrook Press, pg 1220
Smurfit Print, pg 1220
Ultragraphics, pg 1220

Israel

Keterpress Enterprises Jerusalem, pg 1220
Technosdar Ltd, pg 1220

Italy

Canale G e C SpA, pg 1220
Dedalo Litostampa SRL, pg 1220
Mariani Ritti Grafiche SRL, pg 1220
Milanostampa SpA, pg 1220
Amilcare Pizzi SpA, pg 1221

Republic of Korea

Daehan Printing & Publishing Co Ltd, pg 1221
Pyunghwa Dang Printing Co Ltd, pg 1221

Lithuania

Spindulys Printing House, pg 1221

New Zealand

Bookprint Consultants Ltd, pg 1221
PPP Printers Ltd, pg 1221
Rogan McIndoe Print Ltd, pg 1221

Peru

Industrias del Envase SA, pg 1222

Singapore

Chong Moh Offset Printing Ltd, pg 1222
Columbia Overseas Marketing Pte Ltd, pg 1222
CS Graphics Pte Ltd, pg 1222
Eurasia Press Pte Ltd, pg 1222
Ho Printing Singapore Pte Ltd, pg 1222
International Press Co Pte Ltd, pg 1222
PacPress Media Pte Ltd, pg 1223
SNP SPrint Pte Ltd, pg 1223
Times Printers Pte Ltd, pg 1223
World Publications Printers Pte Ltd, pg 1223

Slovenia

Gorenjski Tisk Printing House, pg 1223

Spain

Eurohueco SA, pg 1223
Grafos SA Arte Sobre Papel, pg 1223
Printer Industria Grafica SA, pg 1223
Graficas Santamaria SA, pg 1223
Luis Vives (Edelvives), pg 1223

Switzerland

Hallwag Kuemmerly & Frey AG, pg 1224

Thailand

J Film Process Co Ltd, pg 1224
Mavisu International Co Ltd, pg 1224
Phongwarin Printing Company Ltd, pg 1224

United Kingdom

J W Arrowsmith Ltd, pg 1224
BAS Printers Ltd, pg 1224
Bemrose Booth, pg 1225
Biddles Ltd, pg 1225
Black Bear Press Ltd, pg 1225
Blackmore Ltd, pg 1225
William Clowes Ltd, pg 1225
Cradley Print Ltd, pg 1225
Goldshield Communications Ltd, pg 1226
The Guernsey Press Co Ltd, pg 1226
Headley Brothers Ltd, pg 1226
Hobbs The Printers Ltd, pg 1226
Ikon Document Management Services, pg 1226
Image & Print Group Ltd, pg 1226
The Lavenham Press Ltd, pg 1226
The Malvern Press Ltd, pg 1227
Multiplex Medway Ltd, pg 1227
Redwood Books Ltd, pg 1227
J R Reid Printing Group Ltd, pg 1227
Stott Brothers Ltd, pg 1227
Watkiss Automation Ltd, pg 1227
The Wolsey Press, pg 1227

United States

ADR/BookPrint Inc, pg 1228
Asia Pacific Offset Inc, pg 1228
BookBuilders New York Inc, pg 1228
Butler & Tanner Inc, pg 1228
C & C Offset Printing Co Ltd, pg 1228
Carvajal International Inc, pg 1228
Colorprint Offset Inc, pg 1229
Coneco Litho Graphics, pg 1229
Consolidated Printers Inc, pg 1229
Martin Cook Associates Ltd, pg 1229
CS Graphics USA Inc, pg 1229
DNP America LLC, pg 1229
Elegance Printing & Book Binding (USA), pg 1229
Express Media Corp, pg 1229
Fairfield Marketing Group Inc, pg 1229
Hamilton Printing Co, pg 1229
Hindy's Enterprise, pg 1229
Imago, pg 1229
Jinno International Group, pg 1230
KNI Inc, pg 1230
Leo Paper USA, pg 1230
Linick International Inc, pg 1230
LK Litho, pg 1230
Marrakech Express Inc, pg 1230
Palace Press International - Corporate Headquarters, pg 1231
Printing Corp of the Americas Inc, pg 1231
Regent Publishing Services, pg 1231
Times Publishing Group, pg 1231
Fred Weidner & Daughter Printers, pg 1231

Uruguay

Barreiro y Ramos SA, pg 1231

COMIC BOOK PRINTING

Belgium

Drukkerij Lannoo NV, pg 1215

Canada

Preney Print & Litho Inc, pg 1215
Transcontinental Printing Book Group, pg 1216

Czech Republic

GRASPO CZ AS - Druckerei und Buchbinderei, pg 1216

Germany

MOHN Media, pg 1217
Priese GmbH & Co, pg 1217

Hong Kong

Dai Nippon Printing Co (Hong Kong) Ltd, pg 1217
Hoi Kwong Printing Co Ltd, pg 1218
Image Printing Company Ltd, pg 1218
Midas Printing Ltd, pg 1219
Paramount Printing Co Ltd, pg 1219
Sing Cheong Printing Co Ltd, pg 1219
Sino Publishing House Ltd, pg 1219
Toppan Printing Co (HK) Ltd, pg 1219
Unicorn International Printing Co Ltd, pg 1219

Hungary

Interpress Aussenhandels GmbH, pg 1220

Italy

Canale G e C SpA, pg 1220

Republic of Korea

Daehan Printing & Publishing Co Ltd, pg 1221
Pyunghwa Dang Printing Co Ltd, pg 1221

New Zealand

Bookprint Consultants Ltd, pg 1221

PRINTING, BINDING & BOOK FINISHING INDEX

Philippines
Cacho Publishing inc, pg 1222

Singapore
CS Graphics Pte Ltd, pg 1222
SNP SPrint Pte Ltd, pg 1223
Times Printers Pte Ltd, pg 1223

Slovenia
Gorenjski Tisk Printing House, pg 1223

Spain
Graficas Santamaria SA, pg 1223
Luis Vives (Edelvives), pg 1223

United Republic of Tanzania
Peramiho Publications, pg 1224

Thailand
J Film Process Co Ltd, pg 1224
Mavisu International Co Ltd, pg 1224

United Kingdom
The Guernsey Press Co Ltd, pg 1226
Redwood Books Ltd, pg 1227
Severnside Printers Ltd, pg 1227

United States
Asia Pacific Offset Inc, pg 1228
C & C Offset Printing Co Ltd, pg 1228
DNP America LLC, pg 1229
Elegance Printing & Book Binding (USA), pg 1229
Jinno International Group, pg 1230
Linick International Inc, pg 1230
Marrakech Express Inc, pg 1230
Palace Press International - Corporate Headquarters, pg 1231
Fred Weidner & Daughter Printers, pg 1231

Uruguay
Barreiro y Ramos SA, pg 1231

DIE-CUTTING

Belgium
Drukkerij Lannoo NV, pg 1215

Canada
Transcontinental Printing Book Group, pg 1216
University of Toronto Press Inc, pg 1216

France
Signes du Monde, pg 1216

Germany
Priese GmbH & Co, pg 1217

Hong Kong
Caritas Printing Training Centre, pg 1217
Colorprint Offset, pg 1217
Dai Nippon Printing Co (Hong Kong) Ltd, pg 1217
Everbest Printing Co Ltd, pg 1218
Golden Cup Printing Co Ltd, pg 1218
The Green Pagoda Press Ltd, pg 1218

Hung Hing Off-set Printing Co Ltd, pg 1218
Image Printing Company Ltd, pg 1218
Leo Paper Products Ltd, pg 1218
Midas Printing Ltd, pg 1219
Paper Art Product Ltd, pg 1219
Paramount Printing Co Ltd, pg 1219
Prontaprint Asia Ltd, pg 1219
Sing Cheong Printing Co Ltd, pg 1219
Sino Publishing House Ltd, pg 1219
South Sea International Press Ltd, pg 1219
Speedflex Asia Ltd, pg 1219
Unicorn International Printing Co Ltd, pg 1219
Wing King Tong Group, pg 1220

Indonesia
Victory Offset Prima PT, pg 1220

Ireland
Smurfit Print, pg 1220

Israel
Technosdar Ltd, pg 1220

Italy
Canale G e C SpA, pg 1220
Dedalo Litostampa SRL, pg 1220

Republic of Korea
Daehan Printing & Publishing Co Ltd, pg 1221
Pyunghwa Dang Printing Co Ltd, pg 1221

Lithuania
Spindulys Printing House, pg 1221

New Zealand
Bookprint Consultants Ltd, pg 1221
Rogan McIndoe Print Ltd, pg 1221

Singapore
Columbia Overseas Marketing Pte Ltd, pg 1222
CS Graphics Pte Ltd, pg 1222
Eurasia Press Pte Ltd, pg 1222
Ho Printing Singapore Pte Ltd, pg 1222
International Press Co Pte Ltd, pg 1222
Markono Print Media Pte Ltd, pg 1222
SNP SPrint Pte Ltd, pg 1223
Stamford Press Pte Ltd, pg 1223
World Publications Printers Pte Ltd, pg 1223

Spain
Grafos SA Arte Sobre Papel, pg 1223

United Republic of Tanzania
Peramiho Publications, pg 1224

Thailand
J Film Process Co Ltd, pg 1224
Mavisu International Co Ltd, pg 1224

United Arab Emirates
Emirates Printing Press (LLC), pg 1224

United Kingdom
J W Braithwaite & Son Ltd, pg 1225
Center Print Ltd, pg 1225
The Guernsey Press Co Ltd, pg 1226
Harveys Ltd, pg 1226
Image & Print Group Ltd, pg 1226
The Malvern Press Ltd, pg 1227

United States
Asia Pacific Offset Inc, pg 1228
BookBuilders New York Inc, pg 1228
C & C Offset Printing Co Ltd, pg 1228
Colorprint Offset Inc, pg 1229
Coneco Litho Graphics, pg 1229
Martin Cook Associates Ltd, pg 1229
DNP America LLC, pg 1229
Elegance Printing & Book Binding (USA), pg 1229
Fairfield Marketing Group Inc, pg 1229
Hindy's Enterprise, pg 1229
Imago, pg 1229
Jinno International Group, pg 1230
Leo Paper USA, pg 1230
Linick International Inc, pg 1230
LK Litho, pg 1230
Milanostampa/New Interlitho USA Inc, pg 1231
Palace Press International - Corporate Headquarters, pg 1231
Regent Publishing Services, pg 1231
Fred Weidner & Daughter Printers, pg 1231

EDITION (HARDCOVER) BINDING

Belgium
Drukkerij Lannoo NV, pg 1215

Canada
Aardvark Enterprises, pg 1215
Appleby's Bindery Ltd, pg 1215
Transcontinental Printing Book Group, pg 1216

Czech Republic
GRASPO CZ AS - Druckerei und Buchbinderei, pg 1216

Denmark
Bianco Lunos Bogtrykkeri AS, pg 1216

France
Signes du Monde, pg 1216

Germany
MOHN Media, pg 1217
Priese GmbH & Co, pg 1217

Hong Kong
Colorprint Offset, pg 1217
Dai Nippon Printing Co (Hong Kong) Ltd, pg 1217
Everbest Printing Co Ltd, pg 1218
Golden Cup Printing Co Ltd, pg 1218
Image Printing Company Ltd, pg 1218
Midas Printing Ltd, pg 1219
Paramount Printing Co Ltd, pg 1219

Prontaprint Asia Ltd, pg 1219
Sing Cheong Printing Co Ltd, pg 1219
Sino Publishing House Ltd, pg 1219
SNP Best-Set Typesetter Ltd, pg 1219
South Sea International Press Ltd, pg 1219
Unicorn International Printing Co Ltd, pg 1219

Indonesia
Victory Offset Prima PT, pg 1220

Israel
Har-El Printers & Publishers, pg 1220
Keterpress Enterprises Jerusalem, pg 1220
Technosdar Ltd, pg 1220

Italy
Canale G e C SpA, pg 1220
Milanostampa SpA, pg 1220
Minerva Medica, pg 1221

Republic of Korea
Pyunghwa Dang Printing Co Ltd, pg 1221

Lithuania
Spindulys Printing House, pg 1221

New Zealand
Bookprint Consultants Ltd, pg 1221
Rogan McIndoe Print Ltd, pg 1221

Philippines
Cacho Publishing inc, pg 1222

Singapore
CS Graphics Pte Ltd, pg 1222
Eurasia Press Pte Ltd, pg 1222
Ho Printing Singapore Pte Ltd, pg 1222
International Press Co Pte Ltd, pg 1222
Markono Print Media Pte Ltd, pg 1222
SNP SPrint Pte Ltd, pg 1223
World Publications Printers Pte Ltd, pg 1223

Slovenia
Gorenjski Tisk Printing House, pg 1223

Spain
Grafos SA Arte Sobre Papel, pg 1223
Luis Vives (Edelvives), pg 1223

United Republic of Tanzania
Peramiho Publications, pg 1224

Thailand
J Film Process Co Ltd, pg 1224

United Kingdom
Book Creation, pg 1225
Caledonian International Book Manufacturing, pg 1225
Center Print Ltd, pg 1225
Cedric Chivers Ltd, pg 1225
Clays Ltd, pg 1225
William Clowes Ltd, pg 1225
Charles Letts & Co Ltd, pg 1226

MANUFACTURING

PRINTING, BINDING & BOOK FINISHING INDEX

MPG Books Ltd, pg 1227
Redwood Books Ltd, pg 1227
TJ International Ltd, pg 1227

United States

Asia Pacific Offset Inc, pg 1228
Blaze International Productions Inc, pg 1228
BookBuilders New York Inc, pg 1228
Butler & Tanner Inc, pg 1228
C & C Offset Printing Co Ltd, pg 1228
Colorprint Offset Inc, pg 1229
Martin Cook Associates Ltd, pg 1229
CS Graphics USA Inc, pg 1229
DNP America LLC, pg 1229
Elegance Printing & Book Binding (USA), pg 1229
Express Media Corp, pg 1229
Hamilton Printing Co, pg 1229
Hindy's Enterprise, pg 1229
Imago, pg 1229
Integrated Book Technology Inc, pg 1230
Jinno International Group, pg 1230
Leo Paper USA, pg 1230
Linick International Inc, pg 1230
LK Litho, pg 1230
Milanostampa/New Interlitho USA Inc, pg 1231
Outskirts Press, pg 1231
Palace Press International - Corporate Headquarters, pg 1231
Printing Corp of the Americas Inc, pg 1231
Taylor Publishing Company, pg 1231
Times Publishing Group, pg 1231
Fred Weidner & Daughter Printers, pg 1231

Uruguay

Barreiro y Ramos SA, pg 1231

EMBOSSING

Belgium

Drukkerij Lannoo NV, pg 1215

Canada

Appleby's Bindery Ltd, pg 1215
Transcontinental Printing Book Group, pg 1216
Tri-Graphic Printing (Ottawa) Ltd, pg 1216
University of Toronto Press Inc, pg 1216

Czech Republic

GRASPO CZ AS - Druckerei und Buchbinderei, pg 1216

Denmark

Bianco Lunos Bogtrykkeri AS, pg 1216

Finland

Gummerus Printing, pg 1216

France

Signes du Monde, pg 1216

Germany

MOHN Media, pg 1217
Priese GmbH & Co, pg 1217

Hong Kong

Caritas Printing Training Centre, pg 1217
Colorprint Offset, pg 1217
Dai Nippon Printing Co (Hong Kong) Ltd, pg 1217
Everbest Printing Co Ltd, pg 1218
Golden Cup Printing Co Ltd, pg 1218
The Green Pagoda Press Ltd, pg 1218
Hung Hing Off-set Printing Co Ltd, pg 1218
Image Printing Company Ltd, pg 1218
Leo Paper Products Ltd, pg 1218
Midas Printing Ltd, pg 1219
Morris Press Ltd, pg 1219
Paper Art Product Ltd, pg 1219
Paramount Printing Co Ltd, pg 1219
Prontaprint Asia Ltd, pg 1219
Sing Cheong Printing Co Ltd, pg 1219
Sino Publishing House Ltd, pg 1219
SNP Best-Set Typesetter Ltd, pg 1219
South Sea International Press Ltd, pg 1219
Speedflex Asia Ltd, pg 1219
Toppan Printing Co (HK) Ltd, pg 1219
Unicorn International Printing Co Ltd, pg 1219
Wing King Tong Group, pg 1220

Hungary

Interpress Aussenhandels GmbH, pg 1220

Indonesia

Ichtiar Baru I Van Hoeve, pg 1220
Victory Offset Prima PT, pg 1220

Ireland

Smurfit Print, pg 1220

Israel

Keterpress Enterprises Jerusalem, pg 1220

Italy

Canale G e C SpA, pg 1220
Milanostampa SpA, pg 1220

Republic of Korea

Daehan Printing & Publishing Co Ltd, pg 1221
Pyunghwa Dang Printing Co Ltd, pg 1221

Lithuania

Spindulys Printing House, pg 1221

New Zealand

Bookprint Consultants Ltd, pg 1221
Rogan McIndoe Print Ltd, pg 1221

Philippines

Cacho Publishing inc, pg 1222

Singapore

Columbia Overseas Marketing Pte Ltd, pg 1222
CS Graphics Pte Ltd, pg 1222
Eurasia Press Pte Ltd, pg 1222
Ho Printing Singapore Pte Ltd, pg 1222

International Press Co Pte Ltd, pg 1222
Markono Print Media Pte Ltd, pg 1222
SNP SPrint Pte Ltd, pg 1223
Stamford Press Pte Ltd, pg 1223
Times Printers Pte Ltd, pg 1223
World Publications Printers Pte Ltd, pg 1223

Slovenia

Gorenjski Tisk Printing House, pg 1223

Sri Lanka

Sumathi Book Printing (Pvt) Ltd, pg 1224

Thailand

Mavisu International Co Ltd, pg 1224

United Arab Emirates

Emirates Printing Press (LLC), pg 1224

United Kingdom

Blockfoil Ltd, pg 1225
D Brown & Sons Ltd, pg 1225
Caledonian International Book Manufacturing, pg 1225
Clays Ltd, pg 1225
Cox & Wyman Ltd, pg 1225
The Guernsey Press Co Ltd, pg 1226
Hammond Packaging Ltd, pg 1226
Harveys Ltd, pg 1226
Image & Print Group Ltd, pg 1226
The Malvern Press Ltd, pg 1227
Page Bros Ltd (Norwich), pg 1227
Printafoil Ltd, pg 1227

United States

Asia Pacific Offset Inc, pg 1228
BookBuilders New York Inc, pg 1228
C & C Offset Printing Co Ltd, pg 1228
Colorprint Offset Inc, pg 1229
Coneco Litho Graphics, pg 1229
Martin Cook Associates Ltd, pg 1229
CS Graphics USA Inc, pg 1229
D & K Group, pg 1229
DNP America LLC, pg 1229
Elegance Printing & Book Binding (USA), pg 1229
Hindy's Enterprise, pg 1229
Imago, pg 1229
Jinno International Group, pg 1230
Leo Paper USA, pg 1230
Linick International Inc, pg 1230
LK Litho, pg 1230
Milanostampa/New Interlitho USA Inc, pg 1231
Palace Press International - Corporate Headquarters, pg 1231
Printing Corp of the Americas Inc, pg 1231
Regent Publishing Services, pg 1231
Taylor Publishing Company, pg 1231
Times Publishing Group, pg 1231
Fred Weidner & Daughter Printers, pg 1231

Uruguay

Barreiro y Ramos SA, pg 1231

ENGRAVING

Belgium

Drukkerij Lannoo NV, pg 1215

Canada

Transcontinental Printing Book Group, pg 1216

Czech Republic

GRASPO CZ AS - Druckerei und Buchbinderei, pg 1216

Denmark

Bianco Lunos Bogtrykkeri AS, pg 1216

France

Signes du Monde, pg 1216

Germany

Priese GmbH & Co, pg 1217

Hong Kong

Midas Printing Ltd, pg 1219
Paramount Printing Co Ltd, pg 1219
Prontaprint Asia Ltd, pg 1219
Speedflex Asia Ltd, pg 1219

Italy

Canale G e C SpA, pg 1220

Republic of Korea

Daehan Printing & Publishing Co Ltd, pg 1221

New Zealand

Bookprint Consultants Ltd, pg 1221

Philippines

Cacho Publishing inc, pg 1222

Singapore

CS Graphics Pte Ltd, pg 1222
SNP SPrint Pte Ltd, pg 1223
Stamford Press Pte Ltd, pg 1223
World Publications Printers Pte Ltd, pg 1223

Spain

Grafos SA Arte Sobre Papel, pg 1223
Graficas Santamaria SA, pg 1223

United Republic of Tanzania

Peramiho Publications, pg 1224

United Kingdom

Cox & Wyman Ltd, pg 1225
The Malvern Press Ltd, pg 1227

United States

Asia Pacific Offset Inc, pg 1228
BookBuilders New York Inc, pg 1228
Martin Cook Associates Ltd, pg 1229
DNP America LLC, pg 1229
Elegance Printing & Book Binding (USA), pg 1229
Jinno International Group, pg 1230
Leo Paper USA, pg 1230
Linick International Inc, pg 1230
LK Litho, pg 1230

1199

PRINTING, BINDING & BOOK FINISHING INDEX

Palace Press International - Corporate Headquarters, pg 1231
Regent Publishing Services, pg 1231
Fred Weidner & Daughter Printers, pg 1231

FILM LAMINATING

Canada
Blitzprint Inc, pg 1215
Coach House Printing, pg 1215
Maracle Press Ltd, pg 1215
Printcrafters Inc, pg 1215
Transcontinental Printing Book Group, pg 1216
Tri-Graphic Printing (Ottawa) Ltd, pg 1216
University of Toronto Press Inc, pg 1216
Webcom Ltd, pg 1216

Czech Republic
GRASPO CZ AS - Druckerei und Buchbinderei, pg 1216

Denmark
Bianco Lunos Bogtrykkeri AS, pg 1216

Finland
Gummerus Printing, pg 1216
WS Bookwell Ltd, pg 1216

Germany
Priese GmbH & Co, pg 1217

Hong Kong
Caritas Printing Training Centre, pg 1217
Colorprint Offset, pg 1217
Dai Nippon Printing Co (Hong Kong) Ltd, pg 1217
Everbest Printing Co Ltd, pg 1218
Golden Cup Printing Co Ltd, pg 1218
Hung Hing Off-set Printing Co Ltd, pg 1218
Image Printing Company Ltd, pg 1218
Leo Paper Products Ltd, pg 1218
Midas Printing Ltd, pg 1219
Morris Press Ltd, pg 1219
Paper Communication Printing Express Ltd, pg 1219
Paramount Printing Co Ltd, pg 1219
Prontaprint Asia Ltd, pg 1219
Sing Cheong Printing Co Ltd, pg 1219
Sino Publishing House Ltd, pg 1219
SNP Best-Set Typesetter Ltd, pg 1219
South Sea International Press Ltd, pg 1219
Speedflex Asia Ltd, pg 1219
Toppan Printing Co (HK) Ltd, pg 1219
Unicorn International Printing Co Ltd, pg 1219
Wing King Tong Group, pg 1220

India
Hiralal Printing Works Ltd, pg 1220

Indonesia
Ichtiar Baru I Van Hoeve, pg 1220
Victory Offset Prima PT, pg 1220

Israel
Keterpress Enterprises Jerusalem, pg 1220
Technosdar Ltd, pg 1220

Italy
Canale G e C SpA, pg 1220
Milanostampa SpA, pg 1220

Republic of Korea
Daehan Printing & Publishing Co Ltd, pg 1221
Pyunghwa Dang Printing Co Ltd, pg 1221

Lithuania
Spindulys Printing House, pg 1221

Malta
Interprint Ltd - Malta, pg 1221

New Zealand
Bookprint Consultants Ltd, pg 1221
Rogan McIndoe Print Ltd, pg 1221

Philippines
Cacho Publishing inc, pg 1222

Singapore
Columbia Overseas Marketing Pte Ltd, pg 1222
CS Graphics Pte Ltd, pg 1222
Eurasia Press Pte Ltd, pg 1222
Ho Printing Singapore Pte Ltd, pg 1222
International Press Co Pte Ltd, pg 1222
Markono Print Media Pte Ltd, pg 1222
SNP SPrint Pte Ltd, pg 1223
Stamford Press Pte Ltd, pg 1223
Tien Wah Press Pte Ltd, pg 1223
Times Printers Pte Ltd, pg 1223
World Publications Printers Pte Ltd, pg 1223

Slovenia
Gorenjski Tisk Printing House, pg 1223

Spain
Grafos SA Arte Sobre Papel, pg 1223
Rotedic SA, pg 1223
Luis Vives (Edelvives), pg 1223

Thailand
J Film Process Co Ltd, pg 1224
Mavisu International Co Ltd, pg 1224

United Arab Emirates
Emirates Printing Press (LLC), pg 1224

United Kingdom
Ebenezer Baylis & Son Ltd, pg 1224
Biddles Ltd, pg 1225
Clays Ltd, pg 1225
Cox & Wyman Ltd, pg 1225
Furnival Press, pg 1226
The Guernsey Press Co Ltd, pg 1226
Hammond Bindery Ltd, pg 1226
Hobbs The Printers Ltd, pg 1226
Hunter & Foulis Ltd, pg 1226
Intype Libra Ltd, pg 1226
Page Bros Ltd (Norwich), pg 1227
Peak Technologies UK Ltd, pg 1227
Redwood Books Ltd, pg 1227
Watkiss Automation Ltd, pg 1227
The Wolsey Press, pg 1227

United States
Asia Pacific Offset Inc, pg 1228
Blaze International Productions Inc, pg 1228
BookBuilders New York Inc, pg 1228
C & C Offset Printing Co Ltd, pg 1228
Colorprint Offset Inc, pg 1229
Coneco Litho Graphics, pg 1229
Martin Cook Associates Ltd, pg 1229
CS Graphics USA Inc, pg 1229
D & K Group, pg 1229
DNP America LLC, pg 1229
Elegance Printing & Book Binding (USA), pg 1229
Express Media Corp, pg 1229
Fairfield Marketing Group Inc, pg 1229
Hindy's Enterprise, pg 1229
Imago, pg 1229
Jinno International Group, pg 1230
Leo Paper USA, pg 1230
Linick International Inc, pg 1230
LK Litho, pg 1230
Milanostampa/New Interlitho USA Inc, pg 1231
Palace Press International - Corporate Headquarters, pg 1231
Printing Corp of the Americas Inc, pg 1231
Regent Publishing Services, pg 1231
Times Publishing Group, pg 1231
Vicks Lithograph & Printing Corp, pg 1231
Fred Weidner & Daughter Printers, pg 1231

Uruguay
Barreiro y Ramos SA, pg 1231

FOILING

Belgium
Drukkerij Lannoo NV, pg 1215

Canada
Appleby's Bindery Ltd, pg 1215
Printcrafters Inc, pg 1215
Transcontinental Printing Book Group, pg 1216
Tri-Graphic Printing (Ottawa) Ltd, pg 1216
University of Toronto Press Inc, pg 1216

Czech Republic
GRASPO CZ AS - Druckerei und Buchbinderei, pg 1216

Denmark
Bianco Lunos Bogtrykkeri AS, pg 1216

Finland
Gummerus Printing, pg 1216

Germany
Priese GmbH & Co, pg 1217

Hong Kong
Dai Nippon Printing Co (Hong Kong) Ltd, pg 1217
Everbest Printing Co Ltd, pg 1218
Golden Cup Printing Co Ltd, pg 1218
Hung Hing Off-set Printing Co Ltd, pg 1218
Image Printing Company Ltd, pg 1218
Leo Paper Products Ltd, pg 1218
Midas Printing Ltd, pg 1219
Morris Press Ltd, pg 1219
Paper Art Product Ltd, pg 1219
Paper Communication Printing Express Ltd, pg 1219
Paramount Printing Co Ltd, pg 1219
Prontaprint Asia Ltd, pg 1219
Sing Cheong Printing Co Ltd, pg 1219
Sino Publishing House Ltd, pg 1219
SNP Best-Set Typesetter Ltd, pg 1219
South Sea International Press Ltd, pg 1219
Speedflex Asia Ltd, pg 1219
Wing King Tong Group, pg 1220

Hungary
Interpress Aussenhandels GmbH, pg 1220

Indonesia
Ichtiar Baru I Van Hoeve, pg 1220
Victory Offset Prima PT, pg 1220

Ireland
Smurfit Print, pg 1220

Israel
Keterpress Enterprises Jerusalem, pg 1220
Technosdar Ltd, pg 1220

Italy
Canale G e C SpA, pg 1220

Malta
Interprint Ltd - Malta, pg 1221

New Zealand
Bookprint Consultants Ltd, pg 1221
Rogan McIndoe Print Ltd, pg 1221

Singapore
CS Graphics Pte Ltd, pg 1222
Eurasia Press Pte Ltd, pg 1222
Ho Printing Singapore Pte Ltd, pg 1222
International Press Co Pte Ltd, pg 1222
SNP SPrint Pte Ltd, pg 1223
Stamford Press Pte Ltd, pg 1223
Times Printers Pte Ltd, pg 1223
World Publications Printers Pte Ltd, pg 1223

Slovenia
Gorenjski Tisk Printing House, pg 1223

Sri Lanka
Sumathi Book Printing (Pvt) Ltd, pg 1224

Thailand
J Film Process Co Ltd, pg 1224

MANUFACTURING

PRINTING, BINDING & BOOK FINISHING INDEX

United Arab Emirates
Emirates Printing Press (LLC), pg 1224

United Kingdom
Biddles Ltd, pg 1225
Blockfoil Ltd, pg 1225
J W Braithwaite & Son Ltd, pg 1225
Caledonian International Book Manufacturing, pg 1225
Clays Ltd, pg 1225
Cox & Wyman Ltd, pg 1225
The Guernsey Press Co Ltd, pg 1226
Hammond Packaging Ltd, pg 1226
Harveys Ltd, pg 1226
Image & Print Group Ltd, pg 1226
Charles Letts & Co Ltd, pg 1226
The Malvern Press Ltd, pg 1227
Printafoil Ltd, pg 1227

United States
Asia Pacific Offset Inc, pg 1228
BookBuilders New York Inc, pg 1228
C & C Offset Printing Co Ltd, pg 1228
Colorprint Offset Inc, pg 1229
Coneco Litho Graphics, pg 1229
Martin Cook Associates Ltd, pg 1229
CS Graphics USA Inc, pg 1229
DNP America LLC, pg 1229
Elegance Printing & Book Binding (USA), pg 1229
Fairfield Marketing Group Inc, pg 1229
Hindy's Enterprise, pg 1229
Imago, pg 1229
Jinno International Group, pg 1230
Leo Paper USA, pg 1230
Linick International Inc, pg 1230
LK Litho, pg 1230
Palace Press International - Corporate Headquarters, pg 1231
Regent Publishing Services, pg 1231
Taylor Publishing Company, pg 1231
Times Publishing Group, pg 1231
Fred Weidner & Daughter Printers, pg 1231

Uruguay
Barreiro y Ramos SA, pg 1231

GILDING

Canada
Appleby's Bindery Ltd, pg 1215
University of Toronto Press Inc, pg 1216

Czech Republic
GRASPO CZ AS - Druckerei und Buchbinderei, pg 1216

Germany
Priese GmbH & Co, pg 1217

Hong Kong
Dai Nippon Printing Co (Hong Kong) Ltd, pg 1217
Everbest Printing Co Ltd, pg 1218
Leo Paper Products Ltd, pg 1218
Morris Press Ltd, pg 1219
Sing Cheong Printing Co Ltd, pg 1219
Sino Publishing House Ltd, pg 1219
South Sea International Press Ltd, pg 1219
Speedflex Asia Ltd, pg 1219
Unicorn International Printing Co Ltd, pg 1219
Wing King Tong Group, pg 1220

Hungary
Interpress Aussenhandels GmbH, pg 1220

Indonesia
Victory Offset Prima PT, pg 1220

Israel
Technosdar Ltd, pg 1220

Italy
Milanostampa SpA, pg 1220

Republic of Korea
Pyunghwa Dang Printing Co Ltd, pg 1221

New Zealand
Bookprint Consultants Ltd, pg 1221

Singapore
CS Graphics Pte Ltd, pg 1222
Eurasia Press Pte Ltd, pg 1222
SNP SPrint Pte Ltd, pg 1223

Slovenia
Gorenjski Tisk Printing House, pg 1223

Spain
Grafos SA Arte Sobre Papel, pg 1223
Graficas Santamaria SA, pg 1223
Luis Vives (Edelvives), pg 1223

United Kingdom
Biddles Ltd, pg 1225
Caledonian International Book Manufacturing, pg 1225
Center Print Ltd, pg 1225
Clays Ltd, pg 1225
Cox & Wyman Ltd, pg 1225
Hammond Packaging Ltd, pg 1226
Charles Letts & Co Ltd, pg 1226
MPG Books Ltd, pg 1227

United States
Asia Pacific Offset Inc, pg 1228
BookBuilders New York Inc, pg 1228
C & C Offset Printing Co Ltd, pg 1228
Martin Cook Associates Ltd, pg 1229
DNP America LLC, pg 1229
Elegance Printing & Book Binding (USA), pg 1229
Imago, pg 1229
Jinno International Group, pg 1230
Leo Paper USA, pg 1230
Linick International Inc, pg 1230
LK Litho, pg 1230
Palace Press International - Corporate Headquarters, pg 1231
Regent Publishing Services, pg 1231
Times Publishing Group, pg 1231
Fred Weidner & Daughter Printers, pg 1231

GLUE OR PASTE BINDING

Belgium
Drukkerij Lannoo NV, pg 1215

Canada
Appleby's Bindery Ltd, pg 1215
Blitzprint Inc, pg 1215
Printcrafters Inc, pg 1215
Transcontinental Printing Book Group, pg 1216

Czech Republic
GRASPO CZ AS - Druckerei und Buchbinderei, pg 1216

Denmark
Bianco Lunos Bogtrykkeri AS, pg 1216

Germany
C L Baader Buch & Offsetdruckerei GmbH & Co KG, pg 1216
Priese GmbH & Co, pg 1217
Vier-Tuerme GmbH Benedikt Press, pg 1217

Hong Kong
Dai Nippon Printing Co (Hong Kong) Ltd, pg 1217
Hung Hing Off-set Printing Co Ltd, pg 1218
Image Printing Company Ltd, pg 1218
Midas Printing Ltd, pg 1219
Morris Press Ltd, pg 1219
Paramount Printing Co Ltd, pg 1219
Prontaprint Asia Ltd, pg 1219
Sing Cheong Printing Co Ltd, pg 1219
Speedflex Asia Ltd, pg 1219
Toppan Printing Co (HK) Ltd, pg 1219
Unicorn International Printing Co Ltd, pg 1219

Indonesia
Victory Offset Prima PT, pg 1220

Ireland
Kilkenny People/Wellbrook Press, pg 1220

Italy
Canale G e C SpA, pg 1220
Milanostampa SpA, pg 1220
Minerva Medica, pg 1221

Republic of Korea
Daehan Printing & Publishing Co Ltd, pg 1221
Pyunghwa Dang Printing Co Ltd, pg 1221

New Zealand
Bookprint Consultants Ltd, pg 1221

Singapore
CS Graphics Pte Ltd, pg 1222
Eurasia Press Pte Ltd, pg 1222
International Press Co Pte Ltd, pg 1222
Markono Print Media Pte Ltd, pg 1222

SNP SPrint Pte Ltd, pg 1223
World Publications Printers Pte Ltd, pg 1223

Spain
Luis Vives (Edelvives), pg 1223

United Republic of Tanzania
Peramiho Publications, pg 1224

Thailand
J Film Process Co Ltd, pg 1224
Mavisu International Co Ltd, pg 1224

United Kingdom
Clays Ltd, pg 1225
Hunter & Foulis Ltd, pg 1226
Severnside Printers Ltd, pg 1227
Watkiss Automation Ltd, pg 1227

United States
ADR/BookPrint Inc, pg 1228
Asia Pacific Offset Inc, pg 1228
Bind-It Corp, pg 1228
BookBuilders New York Inc, pg 1228
C & C Offset Printing Co Ltd, pg 1228
DNP America LLC, pg 1229
Elegance Printing & Book Binding (USA), pg 1229
Hindy's Enterprise, pg 1229
Imago, pg 1229
Jinno International Group, pg 1230
Leo Paper USA, pg 1230
Linick International Inc, pg 1230
Milanostampa/New Interlitho USA Inc, pg 1231
Spraymation Inc, pg 1231
Fred Weidner & Daughter Printers, pg 1231

Uruguay
Barreiro y Ramos SA, pg 1231

GRAVURE

Belgium
Drukkerij Lannoo NV, pg 1215

Germany
Priese GmbH & Co, pg 1217

Hong Kong
Speedflex Asia Ltd, pg 1219

Israel
Har-El Printers & Publishers, pg 1220
Technosdar Ltd, pg 1220

Spain
Eurohueco SA, pg 1223

United Kingdom
Cox & Wyman Ltd, pg 1225

United States
BookBuilders New York Inc, pg 1228
DNP America LLC, pg 1229
Jinno International Group, pg 1230
Leo Paper USA, pg 1230
Linick International Inc, pg 1230
LK Litho, pg 1230

PRINTING, BINDING & BOOK FINISHING INDEX

Palace Press International - Corporate Headquarters, pg 1231
Fred Weidner & Daughter Printers, pg 1231

HAND BOOKBINDING

Austria
ADEVA (Akademische Druck-u Verlagsanstalt), pg 1215

Canada
Aardvark Enterprises, pg 1215
Printcrafters Inc, pg 1215
University of Toronto Press Inc, pg 1216

Finland
Gummerus Printing, pg 1216

Germany
C L Baader Buch & Offsetdruckerei GmbH & Co KG, pg 1216
Fachhochschule Fur Druk, Studiengang Verlagswirtschaft und Verlagsherstellung, pg 1217
Priese GmbH & Co, pg 1217

Hong Kong
Dai Nippon Printing Co (Hong Kong) Ltd, pg 1217
Everbest Printing Co Ltd, pg 1218
Hua Yang Printing Holding Co Ltd, pg 1218
Hung Hing Off-set Printing Co Ltd, pg 1218
Image Printing Company Ltd, pg 1218
Midas Printing Ltd, pg 1219
Nordica Printing Co Ltd, pg 1219
Paramount Printing Co Ltd, pg 1219
Prontaprint Asia Ltd, pg 1219
Sing Cheong Printing Co Ltd, pg 1219
South Sea International Press Ltd, pg 1219
Speedflex Asia Ltd, pg 1219
Sun Fung Offset Binding Co Ltd, pg 1219
Sunshine Press Ltd, pg 1219
Toppan Printing Co (HK) Ltd, pg 1219
Unicorn International Printing Co Ltd, pg 1219

Indonesia
Victory Offset Prima PT, pg 1220

Republic of Korea
Daehan Printing & Publishing Co Ltd, pg 1221

Lithuania
Spindulys Printing House, pg 1221

Singapore
CS Graphics Pte Ltd, pg 1222
Markono Print Media Pte Ltd, pg 1222
World Publications Printers Pte Ltd, pg 1223

United Republic of Tanzania
Peramiho Publications, pg 1224

Thailand
J Film Process Co Ltd, pg 1224
Mavisu International Co Ltd, pg 1224

United Kingdom
Cedric Chivers Ltd, pg 1225
Green Street Bindery, pg 1226
Hammond Packaging Ltd, pg 1226
Ikon Document Management Services, pg 1226
MPG Books Ltd, pg 1227

United States
BookBuilders New York Inc, pg 1228
C & C Offset Printing Co Ltd, pg 1228
Colorprint Offset Inc, pg 1229
CS Graphics USA Inc, pg 1229
Elegance Printing & Book Binding (USA), pg 1229
Hindy's Enterprise, pg 1229
Imago, pg 1229
Integrated Book Technology Inc, pg 1230
Leo Paper USA, pg 1230
Linick International Inc, pg 1230
Palace Press International - Corporate Headquarters, pg 1231
Regent Publishing Services, pg 1231
Fred Weidner & Daughter Printers, pg 1231

HOLOGRAMS

Belgium
Drukkerij Lannoo NV, pg 1215

Germany
MOHN Media, pg 1217
Priese GmbH & Co, pg 1217

Hong Kong
Sing Cheong Printing Co Ltd, pg 1219
Speedflex Asia Ltd, pg 1219
Unicorn International Printing Co Ltd, pg 1219

Ireland
Smurfit Print, pg 1220

Singapore
CS Graphics Pte Ltd, pg 1222

United Kingdom
Cox & Wyman Ltd, pg 1225
The Malvern Press Ltd, pg 1227
Printafoil Ltd, pg 1227

United States
BookBuilders New York Inc, pg 1228
DNP America LLC, pg 1229
Elegance Printing & Book Binding (USA), pg 1229
Imago, pg 1229
Linick International Inc, pg 1230
LK Litho, pg 1230
Palace Press International - Corporate Headquarters, pg 1231
Fred Weidner & Daughter Printers, pg 1231

JOURNAL PRINTING

Austria
ADEVA (Akademische Druck-u Verlagsanstalt), pg 1215

Canada
Coach House Printing, pg 1215
Maracle Press Ltd, pg 1215
Printcrafters Inc, pg 1215
Transcontinental Printing Book Group, pg 1216
University of Toronto Press Inc, pg 1216
Webcom Ltd, pg 1216

Czech Republic
GRASPO CZ AS - Druckerei und Buchbinderei, pg 1216

Germany
C L Baader Buch & Offsetdruckerei GmbH & Co KG, pg 1216
Fachhochschule Fur Druk, Studiengang Verlagswirtschaft und Verlagsherstellung, pg 1217
G Braun (vormals G Braun'sche Hofbuchdruckerei und Verlag), pg 1217
C Maurer Druck und Verlag, pg 1217
Media-Print Informationstechnologie GmbH, pg 1217
MOHN Media, pg 1217
Priese GmbH & Co, pg 1217

Hong Kong
Image Printing Company Ltd, pg 1218
Liang Yu Printing Factory Ltd, pg 1218
Midas Printing Ltd, pg 1219
Paramount Printing Co Ltd, pg 1219
Sing Cheong Printing Co Ltd, pg 1219
Sino Publishing House Ltd, pg 1219
SNP Best-Set Typesetter Ltd, pg 1219
South Sea International Press Ltd, pg 1219
Speedflex Asia Ltd, pg 1219
Toppan Printing Co (HK) Ltd, pg 1219
Unicorn International Printing Co Ltd, pg 1219

Hungary
Interpress Aussenhandels GmbH, pg 1220

Ireland
Smurfit Print, pg 1220

Israel
Keterpress Enterprises Jerusalem, pg 1220
Monoline Ltd, pg 1220
Technosdar Ltd, pg 1220

Italy
Canale G e C SpA, pg 1220

Japan
Dai Nippon Printing Co Ltd, pg 1221

Republic of Korea
Daehan Printing & Publishing Co Ltd, pg 1221
Pyunghwa Dang Printing Co Ltd, pg 1221

Lithuania
Spindulys Printing House, pg 1221

New Zealand
Bookprint Consultants Ltd, pg 1221
PPP Printers Ltd, pg 1221

Philippines
JF Printhaus, pg 1222

Singapore
Chong Moh Offset Printing Ltd, pg 1222
Columbia Overseas Marketing Pte Ltd, pg 1222
CS Graphics Pte Ltd, pg 1222
Eurasia Press Pte Ltd, pg 1222
Markono Print Media Pte Ltd, pg 1222
PacPress Media Pte Ltd, pg 1223
SNP SPrint Pte Ltd, pg 1223
Stamford Press Pte Ltd, pg 1223
Times Printers Pte Ltd, pg 1223
World Publications Printers Pte Ltd, pg 1223

South Africa
CTP Book Printers (Pty) Ltd, pg 1223

Spain
Graficas Santamaria SA, pg 1223
Luis Vives (Edelvives), pg 1223

Sri Lanka
Sumathi Book Printing (Pvt) Ltd, pg 1224

Switzerland
Hallwag Kuemmerly & Frey AG, pg 1224

United Republic of Tanzania
Peramiho Publications, pg 1224

Thailand
J Film Process Co Ltd, pg 1224

United Arab Emirates
Emirates Printing Press (LLC), pg 1224

United Kingdom
The Alden Group Ltd, pg 1224
J W Arrowsmith Ltd, pg 1224
W & G Baird Ltd, pg 1224
Bell & Bain Ltd, pg 1224
Biddles Ltd, pg 1225
Cambridge University Press - Printing Division, pg 1225
The Charlesworth Group, pg 1225
Clays Ltd, pg 1225
Cradley Print Ltd, pg 1225
R R Donnelley, pg 1225
Goldshield Communications Ltd, pg 1226
Norman Hardy Printing Group, pg 1226
Headley Brothers Ltd, pg 1226
Hobbs The Printers Ltd, pg 1226

MANUFACTURING

Ikon Document Management Services, pg 1226
Intype Libra Ltd, pg 1226
The Lavenham Press Ltd, pg 1226
Lowfield Printing Co Ltd, pg 1226
Multiplex Medway Ltd, pg 1227
Page Bros Ltd (Norwich), pg 1227
Redwood Books Ltd, pg 1227
J R Reid Printing Group Ltd, pg 1227
Antony Rowe Ltd, pg 1227
Severnside Printers Ltd, pg 1227
Watkiss Automation Ltd, pg 1227

United States

Asia Pacific Offset Inc, pg 1228
C & C Offset Printing Co Ltd, pg 1228
Carvajal International Inc, pg 1228
Coneco Litho Graphics, pg 1229
DNP America LLC, pg 1229
Elegance Printing & Book Binding (USA), pg 1229
EP Graphics, pg 1229
Express Media Corp, pg 1229
Fairfield Marketing Group Inc, pg 1229
Hamilton Printing Co, pg 1229
Ikon Document Services, pg 1229
Imago, pg 1229
Integrated Book Technology Inc, pg 1230
Jinno International Group, pg 1230
KNI Inc, pg 1230
Leo Paper USA, pg 1230
Linick International Inc, pg 1230
LK Litho, pg 1230
Marrakech Express Inc, pg 1230
Palace Press International - Corporate Headquarters, pg 1231
Printing Corp of the Americas Inc, pg 1231
Regent Publishing Services, pg 1231
Times Publishing Group, pg 1231
Vicks Lithograph & Printing Corp, pg 1231
Fred Weidner & Daughter Printers, pg 1231

LETTERPRESS

Canada

Blitzprint Inc, pg 1215
Printcrafters Inc, pg 1215

Germany

C L Baader Buch & Offsetdruckere GmbH & Co KG, pg 1216
Fachhochschule Fur Druk, Studiengang Verlagswirtschaft und Verlagsherstellung, pg 1217
MOHN Media, pg 1217
Priese GmbH & Co, pg 1217

Hong Kong

The Green Pagoda Press Ltd, pg 1218
Unicorn International Printing Co Ltd, pg 1219

Hungary

Interpress Aussenhandels GmbH, pg 1220

Ireland

Ultragraphics, pg 1220

Israel

Monoline Ltd, pg 1220

Republic of Korea

Daehan Printing & Publishing Co Ltd, pg 1221

New Zealand

Rogan McIndoe Print Ltd, pg 1221

Philippines

Philippine Graphic Arts Inc, pg 1222

Portugal

Edicoes Silabo, pg 1222

Spain

Graficas Santamaria SA, pg 1223

Sri Lanka

Sumathi Book Printing (Pvt) Ltd, pg 1224

United Republic of Tanzania

Peramiho Publications, pg 1224

United Kingdom

Caledonian International Book Manufacturing, pg 1225
J R Reid Printing Group Ltd, pg 1227
Selwood Printing, pg 1227

United States

Elegance Printing & Book Binding (USA), pg 1229
Fairfield Marketing Group Inc, pg 1229
Jinno International Group, pg 1230
Leo Paper USA, pg 1230
LK Litho, pg 1230
Palace Press International - Corporate Headquarters, pg 1231
Fred Weidner & Daughter Printers, pg 1231

Uruguay

Barreiro y Ramos SA, pg 1231

LOOSELEAF BINDING

Belgium

Drukkerij Lannoo NV, pg 1215

Canada

Maracle Press Ltd, pg 1215
Printcrafters Inc, pg 1215
Tri-Graphic Printing (Ottawa) Ltd, pg 1216
University of Toronto Press Inc, pg 1216

Germany

Priese GmbH & Co, pg 1217

Hong Kong

Dai Nippon Printing Co (Hong Kong) Ltd, pg 1217
Hung Hing Off-set Printing Co Ltd, pg 1218
Image Printing Company Ltd, pg 1218
Midas Printing Ltd, pg 1219
Prontaprint Asia Ltd, pg 1219
Sing Cheong Printing Co Ltd, pg 1219
Sino Publishing House Ltd, pg 1219
Speedflex Asia Ltd, pg 1219
Unicorn International Printing Co Ltd, pg 1219

Indonesia

Victory Offset Prima PT, pg 1220

Ireland

Smurfit Print, pg 1220

Israel

Technosdar Ltd, pg 1220

Italy

Canale G e C SpA, pg 1220

Netherlands

Koninklijke Wohrmann Bv, pg 1221

New Zealand

Bookprint Consultants Ltd, pg 1221

Singapore

CS Graphics Pte Ltd, pg 1222
Eurasia Press Pte Ltd, pg 1222
International Press Co Pte Ltd, pg 1222
Markono Print Media Pte Ltd, pg 1222
Stamford Press Pte Ltd, pg 1223
World Publications Printers Pte Ltd, pg 1223

United Republic of Tanzania

Peramiho Publications, pg 1224

United Kingdom

J W Braithwaite & Son Ltd, pg 1225
Butler & Tanner Ltd, pg 1225
William Clowes Ltd, pg 1225
Goldshield Communications Ltd, pg 1226
Hammond Bindery Ltd, pg 1226
Harveys Ltd, pg 1226
Hobbs The Printers Ltd, pg 1226
Ikon Document Management Services, pg 1226
Intype Libra Ltd, pg 1226
Charles Letts & Co Ltd, pg 1226
Lowfield Printing Co Ltd, pg 1226
MacKays of Chatham PLC, pg 1226
Multiplex Medway Ltd, pg 1227
Page Bros Ltd (Norwich), pg 1227
Redwood Books Ltd, pg 1227
Antony Rowe Ltd, pg 1227
M & A Thomson Litho Ltd, pg 1227
Watkiss Automation Ltd, pg 1227

United States

ADR/BookPrint Inc, pg 1228
Asia Pacific Offset Inc, pg 1228
Bind-It Corp, pg 1228
BookBuilders New York Inc, pg 1228
Coneco Litho Graphics, pg 1229
Martin Cook Associates Ltd, pg 1229
DNP America LLC, pg 1229
Elegance Printing & Book Binding (USA), pg 1229
Express Media Corp, pg 1229
Hamilton Printing Co, pg 1229
Hindy's Enterprise, pg 1229
Ikon Document Services, pg 1229
Imago, pg 1229
Integrated Book Technology Inc, pg 1230
Jinno International Group, pg 1230
KNI Inc, pg 1230
Leo Paper USA, pg 1230
Linick International Inc, pg 1230
LK Litho, pg 1230
Palace Press International - Corporate Headquarters, pg 1231
Printing Corp of the Americas Inc, pg 1231
Fred Weidner & Daughter Printers, pg 1231

MANUAL PRINTING

Belgium

Drukkerij Lannoo NV, pg 1215

Canada

Aardvark Enterprises, pg 1215
Blitzprint Inc, pg 1215
Coach House Printing, pg 1215
Maracle Press Ltd, pg 1215
Preney Print & Litho Inc, pg 1215
Printcrafters Inc, pg 1215
Transcontinental Printing Book Group, pg 1216
Tri-Graphic Printing (Ottawa) Ltd, pg 1216
University of Toronto Press Inc, pg 1216
Webcom Ltd, pg 1216

Czech Republic

GRASPO CZ AS - Druckerei und Buchbinderei, pg 1216

Denmark

Bianco Lunos Bogtrykkeri AS, pg 1216

Finland

Gummerus Printing, pg 1216

Germany

C L Baader Buch & Offsetdruckere GmbH & Co KG, pg 1216
MOHN Media, pg 1217
Priese GmbH & Co, pg 1217

Hong Kong

Image Printing Company Ltd, pg 1218
Midas Printing Ltd, pg 1219
Paper Communication Printing Express Ltd, pg 1219
Paramount Printing Co Ltd, pg 1219
Prontaprint Asia Ltd, pg 1219
Sing Cheong Printing Co Ltd, pg 1219
Speedflex Asia Ltd, pg 1219
Unicorn International Printing Co Ltd, pg 1219

Hungary

Interpress Aussenhandels GmbH, pg 1220

Indonesia

Victory Offset Prima PT, pg 1220

Ireland

Smurfit Print, pg 1220

PRINTING, BINDING & BOOK FINISHING INDEX

BOOK

Israel
Keterpress Enterprises Jerusalem, pg 1220
Monoline Ltd, pg 1220

Italy
Canale G e C SpA, pg 1220

Republic of Korea
Daehan Printing & Publishing Co Ltd, pg 1221
Pyunghwa Dang Printing Co Ltd, pg 1221

Lithuania
Spindulys Printing House, pg 1221

New Zealand
Bookprint Consultants Ltd, pg 1221
PPP Printers Ltd, pg 1221

Portugal
Edicoes Silabo, pg 1222

Singapore
Chong Moh Offset Printing Ltd, pg 1222
CS Graphics Pte Ltd, pg 1222
Ho Printing Singapore Pte Ltd, pg 1222
International Press Co Pte Ltd, pg 1222
Markono Print Media Pte Ltd, pg 1222
SNP SPrint Pte Ltd, pg 1223
Times Printers Pte Ltd, pg 1223
World Publications Printers Pte Ltd, pg 1223

Slovenia
Gorenjski Tisk Printing House, pg 1223

Spain
Graficas Santamaria SA, pg 1223
Luis Vives (Edelvives), pg 1223

Sri Lanka
Sumathi Book Printing (Pvt) Ltd, pg 1224

Thailand
J Film Process Co Ltd, pg 1224
Phongwarin Printing Company Ltd, pg 1224

United Kingdom
W & G Baird Ltd, pg 1224
Bell & Bain Ltd, pg 1224
Biddles Ltd, pg 1225
The Charlesworth Group, pg 1225
Clays Ltd, pg 1225
William Clowes Ltd, pg 1225
Goldshield Communications Ltd, pg 1226
Hobbs The Printers Ltd, pg 1226
Ikon Document Management Services, pg 1226
Image & Print Group Ltd, pg 1226
Intype Libra Ltd, pg 1226
The Malvern Press Ltd, pg 1227
Page Bros Ltd (Norwich), pg 1227
Redwood Books Ltd, pg 1227
J R Reid Printing Group Ltd, pg 1227
Antony Rowe Ltd, pg 1227
Watkiss Automation Ltd, pg 1227

United States
ADR/BookPrint Inc, pg 1228
Asia Pacific Offset Inc, pg 1228
C & C Offset Printing Co Ltd, pg 1228
Carvajal International Inc, pg 1228
Coneco Litho Graphics, pg 1229
Consolidated Printers Inc, pg 1229
Martin Cook Associates Ltd, pg 1229
DNP America LLC, pg 1229
Elegance Printing & Book Binding (USA), pg 1229
Express Media Corp, pg 1229
Fairfield Marketing Group Inc, pg 1229
Hamilton Printing Co, pg 1229
Integrated Book Technology Inc, pg 1230
Jinno International Group, pg 1230
KNI Inc, pg 1230
Linick International Inc, pg 1230
LK Litho, pg 1230
Marrakech Express Inc, pg 1230
Printing Corp of the Americas Inc, pg 1231
Regent Publishing Services, pg 1231
Times Publishing Group, pg 1231
Fred Weidner & Daughter Printers, pg 1231

Uruguay
Barreiro y Ramos SA, pg 1231

MAP PRINTING

Canada
Maracle Press Ltd, pg 1215
Printcrafters Inc, pg 1215
Schawk, pg 1216
Transcontinental Printing Book Group, pg 1216
University of Toronto Press Inc, pg 1216

Czech Republic
GRASPO CZ AS - Druckerei und Buchbinderei, pg 1216

Germany
Priese GmbH & Co, pg 1217

Hong Kong
Dai Nippon Printing Co (Hong Kong) Ltd, pg 1217
Everbest Printing Co Ltd, pg 1218
Golden Cup Printing Co Ltd, pg 1218
Sing Cheong Printing Co Ltd, pg 1219
Unicorn International Printing Co Ltd, pg 1219

Indonesia
Ichtiar Baru I Van Hoeve, pg 1220
Victory Offset Prima PT, pg 1220

Italy
Canale G e C SpA, pg 1220

Republic of Korea
Daehan Printing & Publishing Co Ltd, pg 1221
Pyunghwa Dang Printing Co Ltd, pg 1221

New Zealand
Bookprint Consultants Ltd, pg 1221
PPP Printers Ltd, pg 1221

Philippines
Cacho Publishing inc, pg 1222

Singapore
CS Graphics Pte Ltd, pg 1222
SNP SPrint Pte Ltd, pg 1223

Spain
Graficas Santamaria SA, pg 1223

Switzerland
Hallwag Kuemmerly & Frey AG, pg 1224

Thailand
Phongwarin Printing Company Ltd, pg 1224

United Arab Emirates
Emirates Printing Press (LLC), pg 1224

United Kingdom
Goldshield Communications Ltd, pg 1226
Headley Brothers Ltd, pg 1226

United States
Asia Pacific Offset Inc, pg 1228
BookBuilders New York Inc, pg 1228
C & C Offset Printing Co Ltd, pg 1228
Martin Cook Associates Ltd, pg 1229
DNP America LLC, pg 1229
Elegance Printing & Book Binding (USA), pg 1229
Jinno International Group, pg 1230
KNI Inc, pg 1230
Leo Paper USA, pg 1230
Maps.com, pg 1230
Printing Corp of the Americas Inc, pg 1231
Regent Publishing Services, pg 1231
Fred Weidner & Daughter Printers, pg 1231

Uruguay
Barreiro y Ramos SA, pg 1231

MCCAIN SEWN BINDING

Denmark
Bianco Lunos Bogtrykkeri AS, pg 1216

Germany
Priese GmbH & Co, pg 1217

Hong Kong
Dai Nippon Printing Co (Hong Kong) Ltd, pg 1217
Speedflex Asia Ltd, pg 1219
Toppan Printing Co (HK) Ltd, pg 1219
Unicorn International Printing Co Ltd, pg 1219
Wing King Tong Group, pg 1220

Lithuania
Spindulys Printing House, pg 1221

Philippines
Cacho Publishing inc, pg 1222

Singapore
Markono Print Media Pte Ltd, pg 1222
SNP SPrint Pte Ltd, pg 1223
World Publications Printers Pte Ltd, pg 1223

Spain
Grafos SA Arte Sobre Papel, pg 1223
Graficas Santamaria SA, pg 1223
Luis Vives (Edelvives), pg 1223

United Republic of Tanzania
Peramiho Publications, pg 1224

United Kingdom
J W Arrowsmith Ltd, pg 1224
BAS Printers Ltd, pg 1224
Goldshield Communications Ltd, pg 1226
Hobbs The Printers Ltd, pg 1226

United States
Asia Pacific Offset Inc, pg 1228
BookBuilders New York Inc, pg 1228
Martin Cook Associates Ltd, pg 1229
DNP America LLC, pg 1229
Elegance Printing & Book Binding (USA), pg 1229
Express Media Corp, pg 1229
Hindy's Enterprise, pg 1229
Jinno International Group, pg 1230
Linick International Inc, pg 1230
Regent Publishing Services, pg 1231
Fred Weidner & Daughter Printers, pg 1231

METAL COMPOSITION

Germany
Priese GmbH & Co, pg 1217

Hong Kong
Unicorn International Printing Co Ltd, pg 1219

Lithuania
Spindulys Printing House, pg 1221

New Zealand
Rogan McIndoe Print Ltd, pg 1221

Spain
Graficas Santamaria SA, pg 1223

United Republic of Tanzania
Peramiho Publications, pg 1224

United Kingdom
J R Reid Printing Group Ltd, pg 1227
Watkiss Automation Ltd, pg 1227

MANUFACTURING

PRINTING, BINDING & BOOK FINISHING INDEX

United States
Elegance Printing & Book Binding (USA), pg 1229
Fred Weidner & Daughter Printers, pg 1231

Uruguay
Barreiro y Ramos SA, pg 1231

NOTCH BINDING

Canada
Blitzprint Inc, pg 1215
Maracle Press Ltd, pg 1215
Printcrafters Inc, pg 1215
Transcontinental Printing Book Group, pg 1216
Tri-Graphic Printing (Ottawa) Ltd, pg 1216
University of Toronto Press Inc, pg 1216

Germany
Priese GmbH & Co, pg 1217

Hong Kong
C & C Offset Printing Co Ltd, pg 1217
Caritas Printing Training Centre, pg 1217
Dai Nippon Printing Co (Hong Kong) Ltd, pg 1217
Everbest Printing Co Ltd, pg 1218
Golden Cup Printing Co Ltd, pg 1218
Leo Paper Products Ltd, pg 1218
Midas Printing Ltd, pg 1219
Morris Press Ltd, pg 1219
Paramount Printing Co Ltd, pg 1219
South Sea International Press Ltd, pg 1219
Unicorn International Printing Co Ltd, pg 1219

Indonesia
Victory Offset Prima PT, pg 1220

Italy
Canale G e C SpA, pg 1220

New Zealand
Bookprint Consultants Ltd, pg 1221

Singapore
Chong Moh Offset Printing Ltd, pg 1222
CS Graphics Pte Ltd, pg 1222
Eurasia Press Pte Ltd, pg 1222
SNP SPrint Pte Ltd, pg 1223

United Republic of Tanzania
Peramiho Publications, pg 1224

United Arab Emirates
Emirates Printing Press (LLC), pg 1224

United Kingdom
Biddles Ltd, pg 1225
Caledonian International Book Manufacturing, pg 1225
Goldshield Communications Ltd, pg 1226
MPG Books Ltd, pg 1227
Page Bros Ltd (Norwich), pg 1227
Redwood Books Ltd, pg 1227
TJ International Ltd, pg 1227
Watkiss Automation Ltd, pg 1227

United States
Asia Pacific Offset Inc, pg 1228
Blaze International Productions Inc, pg 1228
BookBuilders New York Inc, pg 1228
C & C Offset Printing Co Ltd, pg 1228
Martin Cook Associates Ltd, pg 1229
CS Graphics USA Inc, pg 1229
DNP America LLC, pg 1229
Express Media Corp, pg 1229
Hamilton Printing Co, pg 1229
Hindy's Enterprise, pg 1229
Imago, pg 1229
Jinno International Group, pg 1230
Leo Paper USA, pg 1230
Linick International Inc, pg 1230
Regent Publishing Services, pg 1231
Fred Weidner & Daughter Printers, pg 1231

OFFSET PRINTING - SHEETFED

Australia
Southwood Press Pty Ltd, pg 1215

Austria
ADEVA (Akademische Druck-u Verlagsanstalt), pg 1215

Belgium
Delabie Europrint SA, pg 1215
IMPF bvba, pg 1215

Canada
Blitzprint Inc, pg 1215
Coach House Printing, pg 1215
Maracle Press Ltd, pg 1215
Preney Print & Litho Inc, pg 1215
Printcrafters Inc, pg 1215
Schawk, pg 1216
Transcontinental Printing Book Group, pg 1216
Tri-Graphic Printing (Ottawa) Ltd, pg 1216
University of Toronto Press Inc, pg 1216
Webcom Ltd, pg 1216

Czech Republic
GRASPO CZ AS - Druckerei und Buchbinderei, pg 1216

Denmark
Bianco Lunos Bogtrykkeri AS, pg 1216

Finland
Gummerus Printing, pg 1216
WS Bookwell Ltd, pg 1216

France
Imprimerie Gaignault, pg 1216
Plein Chant, pg 1216
Signes du Monde, pg 1216

Germany
C L Baader Buch & Offsetdruckere GmbH & Co KG, pg 1216
C Maurer Druck und Verlag, pg 1217
MOHN Media, pg 1217
Oertel & Sporer GmbH & Co, pg 1217
Priese GmbH & Co, pg 1217
Vier-Tuerme GmbH Benedikt Press, pg 1217

Hong Kong
C & C Offset Printing Co Ltd, pg 1217
Caritas Printing Training Centre, pg 1217
Dai Nippon Printing Co (Hong Kong) Ltd, pg 1217
Everbest Printing Co Ltd, pg 1218
Golden Cup Printing Co Ltd, pg 1218
The Green Pagoda Press Ltd, pg 1218
Hoi Kwong Printing Co Ltd, pg 1218
Hung Hing Off-set Printing Co Ltd, pg 1218
Image Printing Company Ltd, pg 1218
Leo Paper Products Ltd, pg 1218
Liang Yu Printing Factory Ltd, pg 1218
Midas Printing Ltd, pg 1219
Morris Press Ltd, pg 1219
Paper Art Product Ltd, pg 1219
Paper Communication Printing Express Ltd, pg 1219
Paramount Printing Co Ltd, pg 1219
Prontaprint Asia Ltd, pg 1219
Sheck Wah Tong Printing Press Ltd, pg 1219
Sing Cheong Printing Co Ltd, pg 1219
Sino Publishing House Ltd, pg 1219
SNP Best-Set Typesetter Ltd, pg 1219
South Sea International Press Ltd, pg 1219
Sunshine Press Ltd, pg 1219
Toppan Printing Co (HK) Ltd, pg 1219
Unicorn International Printing Co Ltd, pg 1219
Wing King Tong Group, pg 1220

Hungary
Interpress Aussenhandels GmbH, pg 1220

India
Hiralal Printing Works Ltd, pg 1220

Indonesia
Ichtiar Baru I Van Hoeve, pg 1220
Victory Offset Prima PT, pg 1220

Ireland
Kilkenny People/Wellbrook Press, pg 1220
Smurfit Print, pg 1220
Ultragraphics, pg 1220

Israel
Keterpress Enterprises Jerusalem, pg 1220
Technosdar Ltd, pg 1220

Italy
Canale G e C SpA, pg 1220
Dedalo Litostampa SRL, pg 1220
Mariani Ritti Grafiche SRL, pg 1220
Milanostampa SpA, pg 1220
Nuovo Instituto Italiano d'Arti Grafiche, pg 1221
Amilcare Pizzi SpA, pg 1221

Japan
Nissha Printing Co Ltd, pg 1221

Republic of Korea
Daehan Printing & Publishing Co Ltd, pg 1221
Pyunghwa Dang Printing Co Ltd, pg 1221

Lithuania
Spindulys Printing House, pg 1221

Malaysia
Web Printers Sdn Bhd, pg 1221

Malta
Interprint Ltd - Malta, pg 1221

Netherlands
Bosch en Keuning grafische bedrijven, pg 1221

New Zealand
Bookprint Consultants Ltd, pg 1221
PPP Printers Ltd, pg 1221
Rogan McIndoe Print Ltd, pg 1221

Peru
Industrias del Envase SA, pg 1222

Philippines
Cacho Publishing inc, pg 1222
JF Printhaus, pg 1222
Naldoza Printers, pg 1222
Philippine Graphic Arts Inc, pg 1222

Singapore
Chong Moh Offset Printing Ltd, pg 1222
Columbia Overseas Marketing Pte Ltd, pg 1222
CS Graphics Pte Ltd, pg 1222
Eurasia Press Pte Ltd, pg 1222
Ho Printing Singapore Pte Ltd, pg 1222
International Press Co Pte Ltd, pg 1222
Markono Print Media Pte Ltd, pg 1222
PacPress Media Pte Ltd, pg 1223
SNP SPrint Pte Ltd, pg 1223
Stamford Press Pte Ltd, pg 1223
Tien Wah Press Pte Ltd, pg 1223
World Publications Printers Pte Ltd, pg 1223

Slovenia
Gorenjski Tisk Printing House, pg 1223

Spain
Grafos SA Arte Sobre Papel, pg 1223
Printer Industria Grafica SA, pg 1223
Rotedic SA, pg 1223
Graficas Santamaria SA, pg 1223
Luis Vives (Edelvives), pg 1223

Sri Lanka
Sumathi Book Printing (Pvt) Ltd, pg 1224

PRINTING, BINDING & BOOK FINISHING INDEX

United Republic of Tanzania
Peramiho Publications, pg 1224

Thailand
J Film Process Co Ltd, pg 1224
Mavisu International Co Ltd, pg 1224
Phongwarin Printing Company Ltd, pg 1224

United Arab Emirates
Emirates Printing Press (LLC), pg 1224

United Kingdom
The Alden Group Ltd, pg 1224
J W Arrowsmith Ltd, pg 1224
BAS Printers Ltd, pg 1224
Ebenezer Baylis & Son Ltd, pg 1224
Biddles Ltd, pg 1225
Black Bear Press Ltd, pg 1225
Blackmore Ltd, pg 1225
Butler & Tanner Ltd, pg 1225
Caledonian International Book Manufacturing, pg 1225
Cambridge University Press - Printing Division, pg 1225
The Charlesworth Group, pg 1225
Clays Ltd, pg 1225
William Clowes Ltd, pg 1225
Cox & Wyman Ltd, pg 1225
Cradley Print Ltd, pg 1225
Furnival Press, pg 1226
Goldshield Communications Ltd, pg 1226
The Guernsey Press Co Ltd, pg 1226
Headley Brothers Ltd, pg 1226
The Lavenham Press Ltd, pg 1226
Charles Letts & Co Ltd, pg 1226
Lowfield Printing Co Ltd, pg 1226
MacKays of Chatham PLC, pg 1226
The Malvern Press Ltd, pg 1227
MPG Books Ltd, pg 1227
Multiplex Medway Ltd, pg 1227
Redwood Books Ltd, pg 1227
J R Reid Printing Group Ltd, pg 1227
Antony Rowe Ltd, pg 1227
Selwood Printing, pg 1227
Severnside Printers Ltd, pg 1227
TJ International Ltd, pg 1227
Watkiss Automation Ltd, pg 1227

United States
ADR/BookPrint Inc, pg 1228
Asia Pacific Offset Inc, pg 1228
Blaze International Productions Inc, pg 1228
BookBuilders New York Inc, pg 1228
Butler & Tanner Inc, pg 1228
C & C Offset Printing Co Ltd, pg 1228
Colorprint Offset Inc, pg 1229
Coneco Litho Graphics, pg 1229
Martin Cook Associates Ltd, pg 1229
CS Graphics USA Inc, pg 1229
DNP America LLC, pg 1229
Elegance Printing & Book Binding (USA), pg 1229
Fairfield Marketing Group Inc, pg 1229
Hamilton Printing Co, pg 1229
Hindy's Enterprise, pg 1229
Ikon Document Services, pg 1229
Imago, pg 1229
Integrated Book Technology Inc, pg 1230
Jinno International Group, pg 1230
KNI Inc, pg 1230
Leo Paper USA, pg 1230
Linick International Inc, pg 1230
LK Litho, pg 1230
Marrakech Express Inc, pg 1230
Mazer Publishing Services, pg 1230
Milanostampa/New Interlitho USA Inc, pg 1231
Naturegraph Publishers Inc, pg 1231
Palace Press International - Corporate Headquarters, pg 1231
Printing Corp of the Americas Inc, pg 1231
Regent Publishing Services, pg 1231
Taylor Publishing Company, pg 1231
Times Publishing Group, pg 1231
Vicks Lithograph & Printing Corp, pg 1231
Fred Weidner & Daughter Printers, pg 1231

Uruguay
Barreiro y Ramos SA, pg 1231

OFFSET PRINTING - WEB

Belgium
Delabie Europrint SA, pg 1215

Canada
Arpeco Engineering, pg 1215
Maracle Press Ltd, pg 1215
Preney Print & Litho Inc, pg 1215
Transcontinental Printing Book Group, pg 1216
Tri-Graphic Printing (Ottawa) Ltd, pg 1216
Webcom Ltd, pg 1216

Czech Republic
GRASPO CZ AS - Druckerei und Buchbinderei, pg 1216

Finland
Gummerus Printing, pg 1216
WS Bookwell Ltd, pg 1216

Germany
MOHN Media, pg 1217
Priese GmbH & Co, pg 1217

Hong Kong
C & C Offset Printing Co Ltd, pg 1217
Dai Nippon Printing Co (Hong Kong) Ltd, pg 1217
Paramount Printing Co Ltd, pg 1219
Speedflex Asia Ltd, pg 1219
Toppan Printing Co (HK) Ltd, pg 1219

Hungary
Interpress Aussenhandels GmbH, pg 1220

Ireland
Kilkenny People/Wellbrook Press, pg 1220
Ultragraphics, pg 1220

Italy
Canale G e C SpA, pg 1220
Milanostampa SpA, pg 1220
Nuovo Instituto Italiano d'Arti Grafiche, pg 1221
Amilcare Pizzi SpA, pg 1221

Japan
Nissha Printing Co Ltd, pg 1221

Republic of Korea
Daehan Printing & Publishing Co Ltd, pg 1221
Pyunghwa Dang Printing Co Ltd, pg 1221

Lithuania
Spindulys Printing House, pg 1221

Malaysia
Web Printers Sdn Bhd, pg 1221

Netherlands
Bosch en Keuning grafische bedrijven, pg 1221

Philippines
Cacho Publishing inc, pg 1222

Singapore
Huntsmen Offset Printing Pte Ltd, pg 1222
Markono Print Media Pte Ltd, pg 1222
Times Printers Pte Ltd, pg 1223

South Africa
CTP Book Printers (Pty) Ltd, pg 1223

Spain
Printer Industria Grafica SA, pg 1223
Rotedic SA, pg 1223

Sri Lanka
Sumathi Book Printing (Pvt) Ltd, pg 1224

United Republic of Tanzania
Peramiho Publications, pg 1224

Thailand
J Film Process Co Ltd, pg 1224

United Kingdom
Biddles Ltd, pg 1225
Blackmore Ltd, pg 1225
Caledonian International Book Manufacturing, pg 1225
Clays Ltd, pg 1225
William Clowes Ltd, pg 1225
Cox & Wyman Ltd, pg 1225
Cradley Print Ltd, pg 1225
Goldshield Communications Ltd, pg 1226
The Guernsey Press Co Ltd, pg 1226
Headley Brothers Ltd, pg 1226
Charles Letts & Co Ltd, pg 1226
MacKays of Chatham PLC, pg 1226
MPG Books Ltd, pg 1227
J R Reid Printing Group Ltd, pg 1227

United States
ADR/BookPrint Inc, pg 1228
Asia Pacific Offset Inc, pg 1228
Blaze International Productions Inc, pg 1228
BookBuilders New York Inc, pg 1228
Consolidated Printers Inc, pg 1229
Martin Cook Associates Ltd, pg 1229
DNP America LLC, pg 1229
Fairfield Marketing Group Inc, pg 1229
Hamilton Printing Co, pg 1229
Imago, pg 1229
Jinno International Group, pg 1230
KNI Inc, pg 1230
Linick International Inc, pg 1230
LK Litho, pg 1230
Mazer Publishing Services, pg 1230
Palace Press International - Corporate Headquarters, pg 1231
Printing Corp of the Americas Inc, pg 1231
Times Publishing Group, pg 1231
Vicks Lithograph & Printing Corp, pg 1231
Fred Weidner & Daughter Printers, pg 1231

ON DEMAND PRINTING

Canada
Blitzprint Inc, pg 1215

Germany
C Maurer Druck und Verlag, pg 1217

Philippines
JF Printhaus, pg 1222

United Kingdom
The Charlesworth Group, pg 1225
Redwood Books Ltd, pg 1227

United States
ADR/BookPrint Inc, pg 1228
Asia Pacific Offset Inc, pg 1228
Elegance Printing & Book Binding (USA), pg 1229
Outskirts Press, pg 1231

PERFECT (ADHESIVE) BINDING

Australia
Southwood Press Pty Ltd, pg 1215

Belgium
Drukkerij Lannoo NV, pg 1215

Canada
Appleby's Bindery Ltd, pg 1215
Blitzprint Inc, pg 1215
Coach House Printing, pg 1215
Maracle Press Ltd, pg 1215
Preney Print & Litho Inc, pg 1215
Printcrafters Inc, pg 1215
Transcontinental Printing Book Group, pg 1216
Tri-Graphic Printing (Ottawa) Ltd, pg 1216
University of Toronto Press Inc, pg 1216
Webcom Ltd, pg 1216

Czech Republic
GRASPO CZ AS - Druckerei und Buchbinderei, pg 1216

MANUFACTURING

PRINTING, BINDING & BOOK FINISHING INDEX

Denmark
Bianco Lunos Bogtrykkeri AS, pg 1216

Finland
Gummerus Printing, pg 1216

Germany
Media-Print Informationstechnologie GmbH, pg 1217
MOHN Media, pg 1217
Priese GmbH & Co, pg 1217
Vier-Tuerme GmbH Benedikt Press, pg 1217

Hong Kong
C & C Offset Printing Co Ltd, pg 1217
Caritas Printing Training Centre, pg 1217
Colorprint Offset, pg 1217
Dai Nippon Printing Co (Hong Kong) Ltd, pg 1217
Everbest Printing Co Ltd, pg 1218
Golden Cup Printing Co Ltd, pg 1218
The Green Pagoda Press Ltd, pg 1218
Hung Hing Off-set Printing Co Ltd, pg 1218
Image Printing Company Ltd, pg 1218
Leo Paper Products Ltd, pg 1218
Liang Yu Printing Factory Ltd, pg 1218
Midas Printing Ltd, pg 1219
Paper Art Product Ltd, pg 1219
Paper Communication Printing Express Ltd, pg 1219
Paramount Printing Co Ltd, pg 1219
Prontaprint Asia Ltd, pg 1219
Sing Cheong Printing Co Ltd, pg 1219
Sino Publishing House Ltd, pg 1219
South Sea International Press Ltd, pg 1219
Speedflex Asia Ltd, pg 1219
Sunshine Press Ltd, pg 1219
Toppan Printing Co (HK) Ltd, pg 1219
Unicorn International Printing Co Ltd, pg 1219
Wing King Tong Group, pg 1220

Hungary
Interpress Aussenhandels GmbH, pg 1220

India
Hiralal Printing Works Ltd, pg 1220

Indonesia
Victory Offset Prima PT, pg 1220

Ireland
Kilkenny People/Wellbrook Press, pg 1220
Smurfit Print, pg 1220

Israel
Keterpress Enterprises Jerusalem, pg 1220

Italy
Canale G e C SpA, pg 1220
Milanostampa SpA, pg 1220
Nuovo Instituto Italiano d'Arti Grafiche, pg 1221
Amilcare Pizzi SpA, pg 1221

Republic of Korea
Daehan Printing & Publishing Co Ltd, pg 1221
Pyunghwa Dang Printing Co Ltd, pg 1221

Lithuania
Spindulys Printing House, pg 1221

New Zealand
Bookprint Consultants Ltd, pg 1221
Rogan McIndoe Print Ltd, pg 1221

Philippines
Cacho Publishing inc, pg 1222
Philippine Graphic Arts Inc, pg 1222

Singapore
Chong Moh Offset Printing Ltd, pg 1222
Columbia Overseas Marketing Pte Ltd, pg 1222
Craft Print Pte Ltd, pg 1222
CS Graphics Pte Ltd, pg 1222
Eurasia Press Pte Ltd, pg 1222
Ho Printing Singapore Pte Ltd, pg 1222
Huntsmen Offset Printing Pte Ltd, pg 1222
International Press Co Pte Ltd, pg 1222
Markono Print Media Pte Ltd, pg 1222
SNP SPrint Pte Ltd, pg 1223
Stamford Press Pte Ltd, pg 1223
Times Printers Pte Ltd, pg 1223
World Publications Printers Pte Ltd, pg 1223

Slovenia
Gorenjski Tisk Printing House, pg 1223

Spain
Grafos SA Arte Sobre Papel, pg 1223
Printer Industria Grafica SA, pg 1223
Rotedic SA, pg 1223

Sri Lanka
Sumathi Book Printing (Pvt) Ltd, pg 1224

United Republic of Tanzania
Peramiho Publications, pg 1224

Thailand
J Film Process Co Ltd, pg 1224

United Arab Emirates
Emirates Printing Press (LLC), pg 1224

United Kingdom
J W Arrowsmith Ltd, pg 1224
BAS Printers Ltd, pg 1224
Biddles Ltd, pg 1225
Black Bear Press Ltd, pg 1225
Book Creation, pg 1225
J W Braithwaite & Son Ltd, pg 1225
Caledonian International Book Manufacturing, pg 1225
CB Print Finishers Ltd, pg 1225
The Charlesworth Group, pg 1225
Clays Ltd, pg 1225
William Clowes Ltd, pg 1225
Cox & Wyman Ltd, pg 1225
Cradley Print Ltd, pg 1225
Goldshield Communications Ltd, pg 1226
The Guernsey Press Co Ltd, pg 1226
Hammond Bindery Ltd, pg 1226
Headley Brothers Ltd, pg 1226
Hobbs The Printers Ltd, pg 1226
Ikon Document Management Services, pg 1226
Intype Libra Ltd, pg 1226
Lowfield Printing Co Ltd, pg 1226
MPG Books Ltd, pg 1227
Page Bros Ltd (Norwich), pg 1227
Redwood Books Ltd, pg 1227
Antony Rowe Ltd, pg 1227
Selwood Printing, pg 1227
Severnside Printers Ltd, pg 1227
TJ International Ltd, pg 1227
Watkiss Automation Ltd, pg 1227
WH Trade Binders Ltd, pg 1227

United States
ADR/BookPrint Inc, pg 1228
Asia Pacific Offset Inc, pg 1228
Blaze International Productions Inc, pg 1228
BookBuilders New York Inc, pg 1228
Colorprint Offset Inc, pg 1229
Coneco Litho Graphics, pg 1229
Consolidated Printers Inc, pg 1229
Martin Cook Associates Ltd, pg 1229
CS Graphics USA Inc, pg 1229
DNP America LLC, pg 1229
Elegance Printing & Book Binding (USA), pg 1229
Express Media Corp, pg 1229
Hamilton Printing Co, pg 1229
Hindy's Enterprise, pg 1229
Ikon Document Services, pg 1229
Imago, pg 1229
Integrated Book Technology Inc, pg 1230
Jinno International Group, pg 1230
KNI Inc, pg 1230
Leo Paper USA, pg 1230
Linick International Inc, pg 1230
LK Litho, pg 1230
Milanostampa/New Interlitho USA Inc, pg 1231
Naturegraph Publishers Inc, pg 1231
Printing Corp of the Americas Inc, pg 1231
Regent Publishing Services, pg 1231
Times Publishing Group, pg 1231
Vicks Lithograph & Printing Corp, pg 1231
Fred Weidner & Daughter Printers, pg 1231

Uruguay
Barreiro y Ramos SA, pg 1231

PHOTOCOMPOSITION

Canada
Coach House Printing, pg 1215
Maracle Press Ltd, pg 1215
Transcontinental Printing Book Group, pg 1216
Tri-Graphic Printing (Ottawa) Ltd, pg 1216
University of Toronto Press Inc, pg 1216
Webcom Ltd, pg 1216

Czech Republic
GRASPO CZ AS - Druckerei und Buchbinderei, pg 1216

Denmark
Bianco Lunos Bogtrykkeri AS, pg 1216

France
Imprimerie Gaignault, pg 1216

Germany
C L Baader Buch & Offsetdruckerei GmbH & Co KG, pg 1216
Priese GmbH & Co, pg 1217

Hong Kong
Commercial Colorlab Ltd, pg 1217
Unicorn International Printing Co Ltd, pg 1219

Hungary
Interpress Aussenhandels GmbH, pg 1220

Ireland
Kilkenny People/Wellbrook Press, pg 1220
Smurfit Print, pg 1220

Israel
Keterpress Enterprises Jerusalem, pg 1220
Monoline Ltd, pg 1220
Technosdar Ltd, pg 1220

Italy
Canale G e C SpA, pg 1220
Dedalo Litostampa SRL, pg 1220
Minerva Medica, pg 1221
Nuovo Instituto Italiano d'Arti Grafiche, pg 1221

Republic of Korea
Daehan Printing & Publishing Co Ltd, pg 1221

Lithuania
Spindulys Printing House, pg 1221

Malta
Interprint Ltd - Malta, pg 1221

New Zealand
Rogan McIndoe Print Ltd, pg 1221

Philippines
Cacho Publishing inc, pg 1222

Portugal
Edicoes Silabo, pg 1222

Puerto Rico
Publishing Resources Inc, pg 1222

Singapore
Stamford Press Pte Ltd, pg 1223

Slovenia
Gorenjski Tisk Printing House, pg 1223

Spain
Graficas Santamaria SA, pg 1223

1207

PRINTING, BINDING & BOOK FINISHING INDEX

Switzerland
Photolitho AG, pg 1224

United Republic of Tanzania
Peramiho Publications, pg 1224

Thailand
Mavisu International Co Ltd, pg 1224

United Kingdom
J W Arrowsmith Ltd, pg 1224
Cambridge University Press - Printing Division, pg 1225
The Charlesworth Group, pg 1225
Ikon Document Management Services, pg 1226
Image & Print Group Ltd, pg 1226
Intype Libra Ltd, pg 1226
J R Reid Printing Group Ltd, pg 1227
Stott Brothers Ltd, pg 1227
Watkiss Automation Ltd, pg 1227

United States
Coneco Litho Graphics, pg 1229
Martin Cook Associates Ltd, pg 1229
Dix, pg 1229
Elegance Printing & Book Binding (USA), pg 1229
Ikon Document Services, pg 1229
Jinno International Group, pg 1230
Leo Paper USA, pg 1230
Linick International Inc, pg 1230
LK Litho, pg 1230
Fred Weidner & Daughter Printers, pg 1231

Uruguay
Barreiro y Ramos SA, pg 1231

PLASTIC COMB BINDING

Canada
Blitzprint Inc, pg 1215
Maracle Press Ltd, pg 1215
University of Toronto Press Inc, pg 1216

Germany
Priese GmbH & Co, pg 1217

Hong Kong
C & C Offset Printing Co Ltd, pg 1217
Dai Nippon Printing Co (Hong Kong) Ltd, pg 1217
The Green Pagoda Press Ltd, pg 1218
Hung Hing Off-set Printing Co Ltd, pg 1218
Image Printing Company Ltd, pg 1218
Leo Paper Products Ltd, pg 1218
Midas Printing Ltd, pg 1219
Prontaprint Asia Ltd, pg 1219
Sing Cheong Printing Co Ltd, pg 1219
Sino Publishing House Ltd, pg 1219
South Sea International Press Ltd, pg 1219
Speedflex Asia Ltd, pg 1219
Unicorn International Printing Co Ltd, pg 1219

Italy
Canale G e C SpA, pg 1220

New Zealand
Bookprint Consultants Ltd, pg 1221

Singapore
CS Graphics Pte Ltd, pg 1222
Eurasia Press Pte Ltd, pg 1222
Ho Printing Singapore Pte Ltd, pg 1222
Markono Print Media Pte Ltd, pg 1222
SNP SPrint Pte Ltd, pg 1223

Slovenia
Gorenjski Tisk Printing House, pg 1223

United Republic of Tanzania
Peramiho Publications, pg 1224

United Kingdom
Biddles Ltd, pg 1225
J W Braithwaite & Son Ltd, pg 1225
Center Print Ltd, pg 1225
Ikon Document Management Services, pg 1226
Redwood Books Ltd, pg 1227
J R Reid Printing Group Ltd, pg 1227
Watkiss Automation Ltd, pg 1227

United States
ADR/BookPrint Inc, pg 1228
Asia Pacific Offset Inc, pg 1228
Bind-It Corp, pg 1228
Blaze International Productions Inc, pg 1228
BookBuilders New York Inc, pg 1228
C & C Offset Printing Co Ltd, pg 1228
Coneco Litho Graphics, pg 1229
Martin Cook Associates Ltd, pg 1229
DNP America LLC, pg 1229
Elegance Printing & Book Binding (USA), pg 1229
Express Media Corp, pg 1229
Hamilton Printing Co, pg 1229
Hindy's Enterprise, pg 1229
Ikon Document Services, pg 1229
Imago, pg 1229
Integrated Book Technology Inc, pg 1230
Jinno International Group, pg 1230
KNI Inc, pg 1230
Leo Paper USA, pg 1230
Linick International Inc, pg 1230
LK Litho, pg 1230
Printing Corp of the Americas Inc, pg 1231
Regent Publishing Services, pg 1231
Vicks Lithograph & Printing Corp, pg 1231
Fred Weidner & Daughter Printers, pg 1231

SADDLE STITCH BINDING

Belgium
Drukkerij Lannoo NV, pg 1215

Canada
Aardvark Enterprises, pg 1215
Blitzprint Inc, pg 1215
Maracle Press Ltd, pg 1215
Preney Print & Litho Inc, pg 1215
Printcrafters Inc, pg 1215
Transcontinental Printing Book Group, pg 1216
Tri-Graphic Printing (Ottawa) Ltd, pg 1216
University of Toronto Press Inc, pg 1216
Webcom Ltd, pg 1216

Czech Republic
GRASPO CZ AS - Druckerei und Buchbinderei, pg 1216

Denmark
Bianco Lunos Bogtrykkeri AS, pg 1216

Germany
C Maurer Druck und Verlag, pg 1217
Priese GmbH & Co, pg 1217

Hong Kong
C & C Offset Printing Co Ltd, pg 1217
Colorprint Offset, pg 1217
Dai Nippon Printing Co (Hong Kong) Ltd, pg 1217
Everbest Printing Co Ltd, pg 1218
Golden Cup Printing Co Ltd, pg 1218
The Green Pagoda Press Ltd, pg 1218
Hing Yip Printing Co Ltd, pg 1218
Hung Hing Off-set Printing Co Ltd, pg 1218
Image Printing Company Ltd, pg 1218
Leo Paper Products Ltd, pg 1218
Midas Printing Ltd, pg 1219
Morris Press Ltd, pg 1219
Paper Art Product Ltd, pg 1219
Paper Communication Printing Express Ltd, pg 1219
Paramount Printing Co Ltd, pg 1219
Prontaprint Asia Ltd, pg 1219
Sing Cheong Printing Co Ltd, pg 1219
Sino Publishing House Ltd, pg 1219
SNP Best-Set Typesetter Ltd, pg 1219
South Sea International Press Ltd, pg 1219
Speedflex Asia Ltd, pg 1219
Sunshine Press Ltd, pg 1219
Toppan Printing Co (HK) Ltd, pg 1219
Unicorn International Printing Co Ltd, pg 1219
Wing King Tong Group, pg 1220

India
Hiralal Printing Works Ltd, pg 1220

Indonesia
Victory Offset Prima PT, pg 1220

Ireland
Smurfit Print, pg 1220

Israel
Keterpress Enterprises Jerusalem, pg 1220

Italy
Canale G e C SpA, pg 1220
Milanostampa SpA, pg 1220

Republic of Korea
Daehan Printing & Publishing Co Ltd, pg 1221
Pyunghwa Dang Printing Co Ltd, pg 1221

Malta
Interprint Ltd - Malta, pg 1221

New Zealand
Bookprint Consultants Ltd, pg 1221
PPP Printers Ltd, pg 1221
Rogan McIndoe Print Ltd, pg 1221

Philippines
Cacho Publishing inc, pg 1222
Philippine Graphic Arts Inc, pg 1222

Singapore
Chong Moh Offset Printing Ltd, pg 1222
Columbia Overseas Marketing Pte Ltd, pg 1222
CS Graphics Pte Ltd, pg 1222
Eurasia Press Pte Ltd, pg 1222
Ho Printing Singapore Pte Ltd, pg 1222
Huntsmen Offset Printing Pte Ltd, pg 1222
International Press Co Pte Ltd, pg 1222
Markono Print Media Pte Ltd, pg 1222
SNP SPrint Pte Ltd, pg 1223
Stamford Press Pte Ltd, pg 1223
Times Printers Pte Ltd, pg 1223
World Publications Printers Pte Ltd, pg 1223

Slovenia
Gorenjski Tisk Printing House, pg 1223

Spain
Printer Industria Grafica SA, pg 1223
Rotedic SA, pg 1223

United Republic of Tanzania
Peramiho Publications, pg 1224

Thailand
J Film Process Co Ltd, pg 1224

United Arab Emirates
Emirates Printing Press (LLC), pg 1224

United Kingdom
The Alden Group Ltd, pg 1224
J W Arrowsmith Ltd, pg 1224
BAS Printers Ltd, pg 1224
Bell & Bain Ltd, pg 1224
Biddles Ltd, pg 1225
Black Bear Press Ltd, pg 1225
Blackmore Ltd, pg 1225
Book Creation, pg 1225
Caledonian International Book Manufacturing, pg 1225
Cambridge University Press - Printing Division, pg 1225
Center Print Ltd, pg 1225

MANUFACTURING

The Charlesworth Group, pg 1225
William Clowes Ltd, pg 1225
Cradley Print Ltd, pg 1225
Furnival Press, pg 1226
The Guernsey Press Co Ltd, pg 1226
Headley Brothers Ltd, pg 1226
Hobbs The Printers Ltd, pg 1226
Ikon Document Management Services, pg 1226
Intype Libra Ltd, pg 1226
Lowfield Printing Co Ltd, pg 1226
Redwood Books Ltd, pg 1227
J R Reid Printing Group Ltd, pg 1227
M & A Thomson Litho Ltd, pg 1227
Watkiss Automation Ltd, pg 1227

United States
ADR/BookPrint Inc, pg 1228
Asia Pacific Offset Inc, pg 1228
Blaze International Productions Inc, pg 1228
BookBuilders New York Inc, pg 1228
Butler & Tanner Inc, pg 1228
C & C Offset Printing Co Ltd, pg 1228
Colorprint Offset Inc, pg 1229
Coneco Litho Graphics, pg 1229
Consolidated Printers Inc, pg 1229
Martin Cook Associates Ltd, pg 1229
DNP America LLC, pg 1229
Elegance Printing & Book Binding (USA), pg 1229
Express Media Corp, pg 1229
Fairfield Marketing Group Inc, pg 1229
Hamilton Printing Co, pg 1229
Hindy's Enterprise, pg 1229
Ikon Document Services, pg 1229
Imago, pg 1229
Integrated Book Technology Inc, pg 1230
Jinno International Group, pg 1230
KNI Inc, pg 1230
Leo Paper USA, pg 1230
Linick International Inc, pg 1230
LK Litho, pg 1230
Milanostampa/New Interlitho USA Inc, pg 1231
Palace Press International - Corporate Headquarters, pg 1231
Printing Corp of the Americas Inc, pg 1231
Regent Publishing Services, pg 1231
Times Publishing Group, pg 1231
Vicks Lithograph & Printing Corp, pg 1231
Fred Weidner & Daughter Printers, pg 1231

SHORT RUN PRINTING

Austria
ADEVA (Akademische Druck-u Verlagsanstalt), pg 1215

Canada
Aardvark Enterprises, pg 1215
Blitzprint Inc, pg 1215
Coach House Printing, pg 1215
Maracle Press Ltd, pg 1215
Preney Print & Litho Inc, pg 1215
Printcrafters Inc, pg 1215
Transcontinental Printing Book Group, pg 1216

Tri-Graphic Printing (Ottawa) Ltd, pg 1216
University of Toronto Press Inc, pg 1216
Webcom Ltd, pg 1216

Denmark
Bianco Lunos Bogtrykkeri AS, pg 1216

Finland
Gummerus Printing, pg 1216

Germany
C L Baader Buch & Offsetdruckere GmbH & Co KG, pg 1216
C Maurer Druck und Verlag, pg 1217
Media-Print Informationstechnologie GmbH, pg 1217
Priese GmbH & Co, pg 1217

Hong Kong
The Green Pagoda Press Ltd, pg 1218
Image Printing Company Ltd, pg 1218
Morris Press Ltd, pg 1219
Paper Communication Printing Express Ltd, pg 1219
Prontaprint Asia Ltd, pg 1219
Sing Cheong Printing Co Ltd, pg 1219
SNP Best-Set Typesetter Ltd, pg 1219
Speedflex Asia Ltd, pg 1219
Unicorn International Printing Co Ltd, pg 1219

Hungary
Interpress Aussenhandels GmbH, pg 1220

Ireland
Kilkenny People/Wellbrook Press, pg 1220
Smurfit Print, pg 1220
Ultragraphics, pg 1220

Israel
Har-El Printers & Publishers, pg 1220
Keterpress Enterprises Jerusalem, pg 1220
Technosdar Ltd, pg 1220

Italy
Canale G e C SpA, pg 1220

Republic of Korea
Daehan Printing & Publishing Co Ltd, pg 1221

Lithuania
Spindulys Printing House, pg 1221

Malta
Interprint Ltd - Malta, pg 1221

New Zealand
Bookprint Consultants Ltd, pg 1221
PPP Printers Ltd, pg 1221
Rogan McIndoe Print Ltd, pg 1221

Philippines
Cacho Publishing inc, pg 1222
JF Printhaus, pg 1222

PRINTING, BINDING & BOOK FINISHING INDEX

Singapore
CS Graphics Pte Ltd, pg 1222
Eurasia Press Pte Ltd, pg 1222
Fong & Sons Printers Pte Ltd, pg 1222
Ho Printing Singapore Pte Ltd, pg 1222
Kyodo Printing Co (S'pore) Pte Ltd, pg 1222
Markono Print Media Pte Ltd, pg 1222
SNP SPrint Pte Ltd, pg 1223
Stamford Press Pte Ltd, pg 1223

Slovenia
Gorenjski Tisk Printing House, pg 1223

Spain
Graficas Santamaria SA, pg 1223

United Republic of Tanzania
Peramiho Publications, pg 1224

Thailand
Mavisu International Co Ltd, pg 1224
Phongwarin Printing Company Ltd, pg 1224

United Kingdom
J W Arrowsmith Ltd, pg 1224
BAS Printers Ltd, pg 1224
Bell & Bain Ltd, pg 1224
Biddles Ltd, pg 1225
Cambridge University Press - Printing Division, pg 1225
The Charlesworth Group, pg 1225
Cedric Chivers Ltd, pg 1225
Furnival Press, pg 1226
Goldshield Communications Ltd, pg 1226
Hammond Bindery Ltd, pg 1226
Headley Brothers Ltd, pg 1226
Hobbs The Printers Ltd, pg 1226
Ikon Document Management Services, pg 1226
Intype Libra Ltd, pg 1226
The Malvern Press Ltd, pg 1227
MPG Books Ltd, pg 1227
MPG Ltd, pg 1227
Page Bros Ltd (Norwich), pg 1227
Redwood Books Ltd, pg 1227
J R Reid Printing Group Ltd, pg 1227
Antony Rowe Ltd, pg 1227
Selwood Printing, pg 1227
Severnside Printers Ltd, pg 1227
Watkiss Automation Ltd, pg 1227

United States
ADR/BookPrint Inc, pg 1228
Asia Pacific Offset Inc, pg 1228
Blaze International Productions Inc, pg 1228
Colorprint Offset Inc, pg 1229
Coneco Litho Graphics, pg 1229
CS Graphics USA Inc, pg 1229
DNP America LLC, pg 1229
Elegance Printing & Book Binding (USA), pg 1229
Express Media Corp, pg 1229
Fairfield Marketing Group Inc, pg 1229
Hamilton Printing Co, pg 1229
Hindy's Enterprise, pg 1229
Ikon Document Services, pg 1229
Integrated Book Technology Inc, pg 1230
Jinno International Group, pg 1230

KNI Inc, pg 1230
Linick International Inc, pg 1230
LK Litho, pg 1230
Marrakech Express Inc, pg 1230
Mazer Publishing Services, pg 1230
Naturegraph Publishers Inc, pg 1231
Outskirts Press, pg 1231
Palace Press International - Corporate Headquarters, pg 1231
Printing Corp of the Americas Inc, pg 1231
Taylor Publishing Company, pg 1231
Times Publishing Group, pg 1231
Fred Weidner & Daughter Printers, pg 1231

SIDE STITCH BINDING

Canada
Appleby's Bindery Ltd, pg 1215
Printcrafters Inc, pg 1215
University of Toronto Press Inc, pg 1216

Czech Republic
GRASPO CZ AS - Druckerei und Buchbinderei, pg 1216

Germany
Media-Print Informationstechnologie GmbH, pg 1217
Priese GmbH & Co, pg 1217

Hong Kong
Dai Nippon Printing Co (Hong Kong) Ltd, pg 1217
Everbest Printing Co Ltd, pg 1218
Golden Cup Printing Co Ltd, pg 1218
The Green Pagoda Press Ltd, pg 1218
Hung Hing Off-set Printing Co Ltd, pg 1218
Image Printing Company Ltd, pg 1218
Leo Paper Products Ltd, pg 1218
Midas Printing Ltd, pg 1219
Morris Press Ltd, pg 1219
Prontaprint Asia Ltd, pg 1219
Sing Cheong Printing Co Ltd, pg 1219
Sino Publishing House Ltd, pg 1219
South Sea International Press Ltd, pg 1219
Speedflex Asia Ltd, pg 1219
Toppan Printing Co (HK) Ltd, pg 1219
Unicorn International Printing Co Ltd, pg 1219
Wing King Tong Group, pg 1220

India
Hiralal Printing Works Ltd, pg 1220

Indonesia
Victory Offset Prima PT, pg 1220

Ireland
Smurfit Print, pg 1220

Italy
Canale G e C SpA, pg 1220

Republic of Korea
Daehan Printing & Publishing Co Ltd, pg 1221

PRINTING, BINDING & BOOK FINISHING INDEX

BOOK

New Zealand
Bookprint Consultants Ltd, pg 1221
Rogan McIndoe Print Ltd, pg 1221

Philippines
Philippine Graphic Arts Inc, pg 1222

Singapore
CS Graphics Pte Ltd, pg 1222
Eurasia Press Pte Ltd, pg 1222
Ho Printing Singapore Pte Ltd, pg 1222
Markono Print Media Pte Ltd, pg 1222

United Republic of Tanzania
Peramiho Publications, pg 1224

Thailand
J Film Process Co Ltd, pg 1224
Mavisu International Co Ltd, pg 1224

United Kingdom
J W Arrowsmith Ltd, pg 1224
J W Braithwaite & Son Ltd, pg 1225
Goldshield Communications Ltd, pg 1226
Hobbs The Printers Ltd, pg 1226
Ikon Document Management Services, pg 1226
Intype Libra Ltd, pg 1226
J R Reid Printing Group Ltd, pg 1227
Watkiss Automation Ltd, pg 1227

United States
ADR/BookPrint Inc, pg 1228
Asia Pacific Offset Inc, pg 1228
BookBuilders New York Inc, pg 1228
C & C Offset Printing Co Ltd, pg 1228
Coneco Litho Graphics, pg 1229
Martin Cook Associates Ltd, pg 1229
DNP America LLC, pg 1229
Elegance Printing & Book Binding (USA), pg 1229
Express Media Corp, pg 1229
Hindy's Enterprise, pg 1229
Ikon Document Services, pg 1229
Imago, pg 1229
Integrated Book Technology Inc, pg 1230
Jinno International Group, pg 1230
KNI Inc, pg 1230
Leo Paper USA, pg 1230
Linick International Inc, pg 1230
LK Litho, pg 1230
Milanostampa/New Interlitho USA Inc, pg 1231
Palace Press International - Corporate Headquarters, pg 1231
Printing Corp of the Americas Inc, pg 1231
Regent Publishing Services, pg 1231
Fred Weidner & Daughter Printers, pg 1231

SMYTH-TYPE SEWN BINDING

Australia
Southwood Press Pty Ltd, pg 1215

Canada
Maracle Press Ltd, pg 1215
Printcrafters Inc, pg 1215
Transcontinental Printing Book Group, pg 1216
Tri-Graphic Printing (Ottawa) Ltd, pg 1216
University of Toronto Press Inc, pg 1216

Denmark
Bianco Lunos Bogtrykkeri AS, pg 1216

Germany
MOHN Media, pg 1217
Priese GmbH & Co, pg 1217

Hong Kong
C & C Offset Printing Co Ltd, pg 1217
Caritas Printing Training Centre, pg 1217
Colorprint Offset, pg 1217
Everbest Printing Co Ltd, pg 1218
Golden Cup Printing Co Ltd, pg 1218
Hing Yip Printing Co Ltd, pg 1218
Hung Hing Off-set Printing Co Ltd, pg 1218
Image Printing Company Ltd, pg 1218
Leo Paper Products Ltd, pg 1218
Midas Printing Ltd, pg 1219
Morris Press Ltd, pg 1219
Paper Communication Printing Express Ltd, pg 1219
Paramount Printing Co Ltd, pg 1219
Sheck Wah Tong Printing Press Ltd, pg 1219
Sing Cheong Printing Co Ltd, pg 1219
Sino Publishing House Ltd, pg 1219
SNP Best-Set Typesetter Ltd, pg 1219
South Sea International Press Ltd, pg 1219
Speedflex Asia Ltd, pg 1219
Sunshine Press Ltd, pg 1219
Toppan Printing Co (HK) Ltd, pg 1219
Unicorn International Printing Co Ltd, pg 1219
Wing King Tong Group, pg 1220

Israel
Keterpress Enterprises Jerusalem, pg 1220

Italy
Canale G e C SpA, pg 1220
Dedalo Litostampa SRL, pg 1220
Milanostampa SpA, pg 1220
Amilcare Pizzi SpA, pg 1221

Republic of Korea
Pyunghwa Dang Printing Co Ltd, pg 1221

Malta
Interprint Ltd - Malta, pg 1221

Netherlands
Koninklijke Wohrmann Bv, pg 1221

Philippines
Cacho Publishing inc, pg 1222
Philippine Graphic Arts Inc, pg 1222

Singapore
Chong Moh Offset Printing Ltd, pg 1222
CS Graphics Pte Ltd, pg 1222
Eurasia Press Pte Ltd, pg 1222
Ho Printing Singapore Pte Ltd, pg 1222
International Press Co Pte Ltd, pg 1222
SNP SPrint Pte Ltd, pg 1223

Slovenia
Gorenjski Tisk Printing House, pg 1223

Spain
Grafos SA Arte Sobre Papel, pg 1223

United Republic of Tanzania
Peramiho Publications, pg 1224

Thailand
Mavisu International Co Ltd, pg 1224

United Arab Emirates
Emirates Printing Press (LLC), pg 1224

United Kingdom
J W Arrowsmith Ltd, pg 1224
BAS Printers Ltd, pg 1224
J W Braithwaite & Son Ltd, pg 1225
Clays Ltd, pg 1225
William Clowes Ltd, pg 1225
Goldshield Communications Ltd, pg 1226
Intype Libra Ltd, pg 1226
Charles Letts & Co Ltd, pg 1226
Redwood Books Ltd, pg 1227

United States
Asia Pacific Offset Inc, pg 1228
Blaze International Productions Inc, pg 1228
BookBuilders New York Inc, pg 1228
Butler & Tanner Inc, pg 1228
C & C Offset Printing Co Ltd, pg 1228
Colorprint Offset Inc, pg 1229
Martin Cook Associates Ltd, pg 1229
CS Graphics USA Inc, pg 1229
DNP America LLC, pg 1229
Elegance Printing & Book Binding (USA), pg 1229
Express Media Corp, pg 1229
Hamilton Printing Co, pg 1229
Hindy's Enterprise, pg 1229
Imago, pg 1229
Integrated Book Technology Inc, pg 1230
Jinno International Group, pg 1230
Leo Paper USA, pg 1230
Linick International Inc, pg 1230
Milanostampa/New Interlitho USA Inc, pg 1231
Palace Press International - Corporate Headquarters, pg 1231
Printing Corp of the Americas Inc, pg 1231
Regent Publishing Services, pg 1231
Times Publishing Group, pg 1231
Fred Weidner & Daughter Printers, pg 1231

SPECIALTY BINDING

Belgium
Drukkerij Lannoo NV, pg 1215

Canada
Aardvark Enterprises, pg 1215
Appleby's Bindery Ltd, pg 1215
Printcrafters Inc, pg 1215

Germany
Priese GmbH & Co, pg 1217

Hong Kong
Hung Hing Off-set Printing Co Ltd, pg 1218
Image Printing Company Ltd, pg 1218
Leo Paper Products Ltd, pg 1218
Morris Press Ltd, pg 1219
Prontaprint Asia Ltd, pg 1219
Sing Cheong Printing Co Ltd, pg 1219
Speedflex Asia Ltd, pg 1219

Indonesia
Victory Offset Prima PT, pg 1220

New Zealand
Bookprint Consultants Ltd, pg 1221

Singapore
CS Graphics Pte Ltd, pg 1222
SNP SPrint Pte Ltd, pg 1223

United Republic of Tanzania
Peramiho Publications, pg 1224

United Kingdom
Cedric Chivers Ltd, pg 1225
Hammond Packaging Ltd, pg 1226
Redwood Books Ltd, pg 1227

United States
Asia Pacific Offset Inc, pg 1228
Blaze International Productions Inc, pg 1228
BookBuilders New York Inc, pg 1228
C & C Offset Printing Co Ltd, pg 1228
Martin Cook Associates Ltd, pg 1229
Elegance Printing & Book Binding (USA), pg 1229
Hindy's Enterprise, pg 1229
Imago, pg 1229
Jinno International Group, pg 1230
KNI Inc, pg 1230
Leo Paper USA, pg 1230
Linick International Inc, pg 1230
LK Litho, pg 1230
Palace Press International - Corporate Headquarters, pg 1231
Printing Corp of the Americas Inc, pg 1231
Regent Publishing Services, pg 1231
Fred Weidner & Daughter Printers, pg 1231

SPIRAL BINDING

Belgium
Drukkerij Lannoo NV, pg 1215

MANUFACTURING — PRINTING, BINDING & BOOK FINISHING INDEX

Canada
Blitzprint Inc, pg 1215
Maracle Press Ltd, pg 1215
Printcrafters Inc, pg 1215
Transcontinental Printing Book Group, pg 1216
University of Toronto Press Inc, pg 1216
Webcom Ltd, pg 1216

Germany
Priese GmbH & Co, pg 1217
Vier-Tuerme GmbH Benedikt Press, pg 1217

Hong Kong
C & C Offset Printing Co Ltd, pg 1217
Caritas Printing Training Centre, pg 1217
Dai Nippon Printing Co (Hong Kong) Ltd, pg 1217
Everbest Printing Co Ltd, pg 1218
Hung Hing Off-set Printing Co Ltd, pg 1218
Image Printing Company Ltd, pg 1218
Leo Paper Products Ltd, pg 1218
Midas Printing Ltd, pg 1219
Morris Press Ltd, pg 1219
Paper Art Product Ltd, pg 1219
Paramount Printing Co Ltd, pg 1219
Prontaprint Asia Ltd, pg 1219
Sing Cheong Printing Co Ltd, pg 1219
Sino Publishing House Ltd, pg 1219
SNP Best-Set Typesetter Ltd, pg 1219
South Sea International Press Ltd, pg 1219
Speedflex Asia Ltd, pg 1219
Unicorn International Printing Co Ltd, pg 1219
Wing King Tong Group, pg 1220

Hungary
Interpress Aussenhandels GmbH, pg 1220

India
Hiralal Printing Works Ltd, pg 1220

Indonesia
Victory Offset Prima PT, pg 1220

Israel
Technosdar Ltd, pg 1220

Italy
Canale G e C SpA, pg 1220
Amilcare Pizzi SpA, pg 1221

Lithuania
Spindulys Printing House, pg 1221

New Zealand
Bookprint Consultants Ltd, pg 1221
Rogan McIndoe Print Ltd, pg 1221

Singapore
CS Graphics Pte Ltd, pg 1222
Ho Printing Singapore Pte Ltd, pg 1222
SNP SPrint Pte Ltd, pg 1223
Tien Wah Press Pte Ltd, pg 1223

Slovenia
Gorenjski Tisk Printing House, pg 1223

Spain
Graficas Santamaria SA, pg 1223

United Republic of Tanzania
Peramiho Publications, pg 1224

Thailand
Mavisu International Co Ltd, pg 1224

United Kingdom
CB Print Finishers Ltd, pg 1225
Goldshield Communications Ltd, pg 1226
Ikon Document Management Services, pg 1226
Antony Rowe Ltd, pg 1227
Watkiss Automation Ltd, pg 1227

United States
ADR/BookPrint Inc, pg 1228
Asia Pacific Offset Inc, pg 1228
BookBuilders New York Inc, pg 1228
C & C Offset Printing Co Ltd, pg 1228
Colorprint Offset Inc, pg 1229
Coneco Litho Graphics, pg 1229
Martin Cook Associates Ltd, pg 1229
DNP America LLC, pg 1229
Elegance Printing & Book Binding (USA), pg 1229
Express Media Corp, pg 1229
Fairfield Marketing Group Inc, pg 1229
Hindy's Enterprise, pg 1229
Imago, pg 1229
Integrated Book Technology Inc, pg 1230
Jinno International Group, pg 1230
KNI Inc, pg 1230
Leo Paper USA, pg 1230
Linick International Inc, pg 1230
LK Litho, pg 1230
Palace Press International - Corporate Headquarters, pg 1231
Printing Corp of the Americas Inc, pg 1231
Regent Publishing Services, pg 1231
Vicks Lithograph & Printing Corp, pg 1231
Fred Weidner & Daughter Printers, pg 1231

Uruguay
Barreiro y Ramos SA, pg 1231

STRUCK-IMAGE COMPOSITION

Germany
C L Baader Buch & Offsetdruckerei GmbH & Co KG, pg 1216
Priese GmbH & Co, pg 1217

Hong Kong
Commercial Colorlab Ltd, pg 1217

New Zealand
Bookprint Consultants Ltd, pg 1221
Rogan McIndoe Print Ltd, pg 1221

Spain
Graficas Santamaria SA, pg 1223

United Republic of Tanzania
Peramiho Publications, pg 1224

United States
Fred Weidner & Daughter Printers, pg 1231

TEXTBOOK PRINTING - COLLEGE

Belgium
Drukkerij Lannoo NV, pg 1215

Canada
Blitzprint Inc, pg 1215
Maracle Press Ltd, pg 1215
McLaren Morris & Todd Co, pg 1215
Printcrafters Inc, pg 1215
Transcontinental Printing Book Group, pg 1216
Tri-Graphic Printing (Ottawa) Ltd, pg 1216
Webcom Ltd, pg 1216

Czech Republic
GRASPO CZ AS - Druckerei und Buchbinderei, pg 1216

Finland
Gummerus Printing, pg 1216

Germany
Priese GmbH & Co, pg 1217

Hong Kong
Dai Nippon Printing Co (Hong Kong) Ltd, pg 1217
Golden Cup Printing Co Ltd, pg 1218
Hoi Kwong Printing Co Ltd, pg 1218
Image Printing Company Ltd, pg 1218
Midas Printing Ltd, pg 1219
Nordica Printing Co Ltd, pg 1219
Paramount Printing Co Ltd, pg 1219
Sing Cheong Printing Co Ltd, pg 1219
Sino Publishing House Ltd, pg 1219
SNP Best-Set Typesetter Ltd, pg 1219
South Sea International Press Ltd, pg 1219
Unicorn International Printing Co Ltd, pg 1219

Hungary
Interpress Aussenhandels GmbH, pg 1220

Indonesia
Victory Offset Prima PT, pg 1220

Ireland
Kilkenny People/Wellbrook Press, pg 1220
Smurfit Print, pg 1220

Israel
Monoline Ltd, pg 1220
Technosdar Ltd, pg 1220

Italy
Canale G e C SpA, pg 1220
Milanostampa SpA, pg 1220

Republic of Korea
Daehan Printing & Publishing Co Ltd, pg 1221
Pyunghwa Dang Printing Co Ltd, pg 1221

Lithuania
Spindulys Printing House, pg 1221

Malta
Interprint Ltd - Malta, pg 1221

New Zealand
Bookprint Consultants Ltd, pg 1221
PPP Printers Ltd, pg 1221

Philippines
Cacho Publishing inc, pg 1222

Portugal
Edicoes Silabo, pg 1222

Singapore
Chong Moh Offset Printing Ltd, pg 1222
CS Graphics Pte Ltd, pg 1222
Eurasia Press Pte Ltd, pg 1222
Huntsmen Offset Printing Pte Ltd, pg 1222
Markono Print Media Pte Ltd, pg 1222
SNP SPrint Pte Ltd, pg 1223
Stamford Press Pte Ltd, pg 1223

Slovenia
Gorenjski Tisk Printing House, pg 1223

Spain
Graficas Santamaria SA, pg 1223
Luis Vives (Edelvives), pg 1223

Sri Lanka
Sumathi Book Printing (Pvt) Ltd, pg 1224

United Republic of Tanzania
Peramiho Publications, pg 1224

United Kingdom
J W Arrowsmith Ltd, pg 1224
Biddles Ltd, pg 1225
Cambridge University Press - Printing Division, pg 1225
Clays Ltd, pg 1225
Goldshield Communications Ltd, pg 1226
Hobbs The Printers Ltd, pg 1226
The Lavenham Press Ltd, pg 1226
Charles Letts & Co Ltd, pg 1226
MPG Books Ltd, pg 1226
Page Bros Ltd (Norwich), pg 1227
Redwood Books Ltd, pg 1227
J R Reid Printing Group Ltd, pg 1227
Antony Rowe Ltd, pg 1227
Severnside Printers Ltd, pg 1227
Watkiss Automation Ltd, pg 1227

United States
ADR/BookPrint Inc, pg 1228
Asia Pacific Offset Inc, pg 1228

PRINTING, BINDING & BOOK FINISHING INDEX

Blaze International Productions Inc, pg 1228
DNP America LLC, pg 1229
Elegance Printing & Book Binding (USA), pg 1229
Express Media Corp, pg 1229
Fairfield Marketing Group Inc, pg 1229
Hamilton Printing Co, pg 1229
Integrated Book Technology Inc, pg 1230
Jinno International Group, pg 1230
Linick International Inc, pg 1230
LK Litho, pg 1230
Marrakech Express Inc, pg 1230
Times Publishing Group, pg 1231
Fred Weidner & Daughter Printers, pg 1231

Uruguay
Barreiro y Ramos SA, pg 1231

TEXTBOOK PRINTING - EL-HI

Belgium
Drukkerij Lannoo NV, pg 1215

Canada
Blitzprint Inc, pg 1215
Maracle Press Ltd, pg 1215
Printcrafters Inc, pg 1215
Transcontinental Printing Book Group, pg 1216
Tri-Graphic Printing (Ottawa) Ltd, pg 1216
Webcom Ltd, pg 1216

Finland
Gummerus Printing, pg 1216

Germany
MOHN Media, pg 1217
Priese GmbH & Co, pg 1217

Hong Kong
Golden Cup Printing Co Ltd, pg 1218
Hoi Kwong Printing Co Ltd, pg 1218
Image Printing Company Ltd, pg 1218
Midas Printing Ltd, pg 1219
Nordica Printing Co Ltd, pg 1219
Paramount Printing Co Ltd, pg 1219
Sing Cheong Printing Co Ltd, pg 1219
Sino Publishing House Ltd, pg 1219

Hungary
Interpress Aussenhandels GmbH, pg 1220

Ireland
Ultragraphics, pg 1220

Israel
Monoline Ltd, pg 1220
Technosdar Ltd, pg 1220

Italy
Canale G e C SpA, pg 1220
Milanostampa SpA, pg 1220

Republic of Korea
Daehan Printing & Publishing Co Ltd, pg 1221
Pyunghwa Dang Printing Co Ltd, pg 1221

New Zealand
Bookprint Consultants Ltd, pg 1221

Philippines
Cacho Publishing inc, pg 1222

Singapore
Chong Moh Offset Printing Ltd, pg 1222
CS Graphics Pte Ltd, pg 1222
Markono Print Media Pte Ltd, pg 1222
SNP SPrint Pte Ltd, pg 1223

Slovenia
Gorenjski Tisk Printing House, pg 1223

Spain
Graficas Santamaria SA, pg 1223
Luis Vives (Edelvives), pg 1223

United Kingdom
J W Arrowsmith Ltd, pg 1224
Biddles Ltd, pg 1225
Goldshield Communications Ltd, pg 1226
Hobbs The Printers Ltd, pg 1226
The Lavenham Press Ltd, pg 1226
Charles Letts & Co Ltd, pg 1226
Page Bros Ltd (Norwich), pg 1227
Antony Rowe Ltd, pg 1227
Watkiss Automation Ltd, pg 1227

United States
Asia Pacific Offset Inc, pg 1228
Blaze International Productions Inc, pg 1228
Carvajal International Inc, pg 1228
DNP America LLC, pg 1229
Elegance Printing & Book Binding (USA), pg 1229
Express Media Corp, pg 1229
Fairfield Marketing Group Inc, pg 1229
Hamilton Printing Co, pg 1229
Imago, pg 1229
Jinno International Group, pg 1230
Regent Publishing Services, pg 1231
Times Publishing Group, pg 1231
Fred Weidner & Daughter Printers, pg 1231

WIRE-O BINDING

Belgium
Drukkerij Lannoo NV, pg 1215

Canada
Blitzprint Inc, pg 1215
Coach House Printing, pg 1215
Maracle Press Ltd, pg 1215
Printcrafters Inc, pg 1215
Transcontinental Printing Book Group, pg 1216
University of Toronto Press Inc, pg 1216
Webcom Ltd, pg 1216

Denmark
Bianco Lunos Bogtrykkeri AS, pg 1216

Germany
MOHN Media, pg 1217
Oertel & Sporer GmbH & Co, pg 1217
Priese GmbH & Co, pg 1217
Vier-Tuerme GmbH Benedikt Press, pg 1217

Hong Kong
C & C Offset Printing Co Ltd, pg 1217
Caritas Printing Training Centre, pg 1217
Colorprint Offset, pg 1217
Dai Nippon Printing Co (Hong Kong) Ltd, pg 1217
Golden Cup Printing Co Ltd, pg 1218
The Green Pagoda Press Ltd, pg 1218
Hing Yip Printing Co Ltd, pg 1218
Hung Hing Off-set Printing Co Ltd, pg 1218
Image Printing Company Ltd, pg 1218
Leo Paper Products Ltd, pg 1218
Liang Yu Printing Factory Ltd, pg 1218
Midas Printing Ltd, pg 1219
Morris Press Ltd, pg 1219
Paper Art Product Ltd, pg 1219
Paramount Printing Co Ltd, pg 1219
Prontaprint Asia Ltd, pg 1219
Sheck Wah Tong Printing Press Ltd, pg 1219
Sing Cheong Printing Co Ltd, pg 1219
Sino Publishing House Ltd, pg 1219
SNP Best-Set Typesetter Ltd, pg 1219
South Sea International Press Ltd, pg 1219
Speedflex Asia Ltd, pg 1219
Sunshine Press Ltd, pg 1219
Unicorn International Printing Co Ltd, pg 1219
Wing King Tong Group, pg 1220

Hungary
Interpress Aussenhandels GmbH, pg 1220

Indonesia
Victory Offset Prima PT, pg 1220

Italy
Canale G e C SpA, pg 1220
Amilcare Pizzi SpA, pg 1221

New Zealand
Bookprint Consultants Ltd, pg 1221
Rogan McIndoe Print Ltd, pg 1221

Singapore
Columbia Overseas Marketing Pte Ltd, pg 1222
CS Graphics Pte Ltd, pg 1222
Eurasia Press Pte Ltd, pg 1222
Ho Printing Singapore Pte Ltd, pg 1222
International Press Co Pte Ltd, pg 1222
Markono Print Media Pte Ltd, pg 1222
SNP SPrint Pte Ltd, pg 1223
Stamford Press Pte Ltd, pg 1223

Slovenia
Gorenjski Tisk Printing House, pg 1223

Spain
Graficas Santamaria SA, pg 1223

United Republic of Tanzania
Peramiho Publications, pg 1224

Thailand
Mavisu International Co Ltd, pg 1224

United Arab Emirates
Emirates Printing Press (LLC), pg 1224

United Kingdom
J W Braithwaite & Son Ltd, pg 1225
CB Print Finishers Ltd, pg 1225
Center Print Ltd, pg 1225
Hammond Packaging Ltd, pg 1226
Hobbs The Printers Ltd, pg 1226
Hunter & Foulis Ltd, pg 1226
Ikon Document Management Services, pg 1226
Charles Letts & Co Ltd, pg 1226
Page Bros Ltd (Norwich), pg 1227
Redwood Books Ltd, pg 1227
J R Reid Printing Group Ltd, pg 1227
Antony Rowe Ltd, pg 1227
Watkiss Automation Ltd, pg 1227

United States
ADR/BookPrint Inc, pg 1228
Asia Pacific Offset Inc, pg 1228
Blaze International Productions Inc, pg 1228
BookBuilders New York Inc, pg 1228
C & C Offset Printing Co Ltd, pg 1228
Colorprint Offset Inc, pg 1229
Coneco Litho Graphics, pg 1229
Martin Cook Associates Ltd, pg 1229
CS Graphics USA Inc, pg 1229
DNP America LLC, pg 1229
Elegance Printing & Book Binding (USA), pg 1229
Express Media Corp, pg 1229
Hamilton Printing Co, pg 1229
Hindy's Enterprise, pg 1229
Ikon Document Services, pg 1229
Imago, pg 1229
Integrated Book Technology Inc, pg 1230
Jinno International Group, pg 1230
KNI Inc, pg 1230
Leo Paper USA, pg 1230
Linick International Inc, pg 1230
LK Litho, pg 1230
Milanostampa/New Interlitho USA Inc, pg 1231
Palace Press International - Corporate Headquarters, pg 1231
Printing Corp of the Americas Inc, pg 1231
Regent Publishing Services, pg 1231
Fred Weidner & Daughter Printers, pg 1231

WORKBOOK PRINTING

Belgium
Drukkerij Lannoo NV, pg 1215

Canada
Blitzprint Inc, pg 1215
Maracle Press Ltd, pg 1215
Printcrafters Inc, pg 1215
Transcontinental Printing Book Group, pg 1216
Tri-Graphic Printing (Ottawa) Ltd, pg 1216
University of Toronto Press Inc, pg 1216
Webcom Ltd, pg 1216

Finland
Gummerus Printing, pg 1216

Germany
C L Baader Buch & Offsetdruckere GmbH & Co KG, pg 1216
Priese GmbH & Co, pg 1217

Hong Kong
Dai Nippon Printing Co (Hong Kong) Ltd, pg 1217
Golden Cup Printing Co Ltd, pg 1218
Hoi Kwong Printing Co Ltd, pg 1218
Image Printing Company Ltd, pg 1218
Midas Printing Ltd, pg 1219
Paper Communication Printing Express Ltd, pg 1219
Paramount Printing Co Ltd, pg 1219
Prontaprint Asia Ltd, pg 1219
Sing Cheong Printing Co Ltd, pg 1219
Sino Publishing House Ltd, pg 1219
SNP Best-Set Typesetter Ltd, pg 1219
Unicorn International Printing Co Ltd, pg 1219

Hungary
Interpress Aussenhandels GmbH, pg 1220

India
Hiralal Printing Works Ltd, pg 1220

Ireland
Smurfit Print, pg 1220
Ultragraphics, pg 1220

Israel
Monoline Ltd, pg 1220
Technosdar Ltd, pg 1220

Italy
Canale G e C SpA, pg 1220
Milanostampa SpA, pg 1220

Republic of Korea
Daehan Printing & Publishing Co Ltd, pg 1221
Pyunghwa Dang Printing Co Ltd, pg 1221

New Zealand
Bookprint Consultants Ltd, pg 1221
PPP Printers Ltd, pg 1221

Philippines
Cacho Publishing inc, pg 1222
Philippine Graphic Arts Inc, pg 1222

Portugal
Edicoes Silabo, pg 1222

Singapore
Chong Moh Offset Printing Ltd, pg 1222
CS Graphics Pte Ltd, pg 1222
Eurasia Press Pte Ltd, pg 1222
Markono Print Media Pte Ltd, pg 1222
SNP SPrint Pte Ltd, pg 1223

Slovenia
Gorenjski Tisk Printing House, pg 1223

Spain
Graficas Santamaria SA, pg 1223
Luis Vives (Edelvives), pg 1223

Thailand
Mavisu International Co Ltd, pg 1224

United Kingdom
J W Arrowsmith Ltd, pg 1224
Biddles Ltd, pg 1225
Goldshield Communications Ltd, pg 1226
The Guernsey Press Co Ltd, pg 1226
Hobbs The Printers Ltd, pg 1226
Charles Letts & Co Ltd, pg 1226
Page Bros Ltd (Norwich), pg 1227
J R Reid Printing Group Ltd, pg 1227
Antony Rowe Ltd, pg 1227
Severnside Printers Ltd, pg 1227
Watkiss Automation Ltd, pg 1227

United States
ADR/BookPrint Inc, pg 1228
Asia Pacific Offset Inc, pg 1228
Blaze International Productions Inc, pg 1228
Butler & Tanner Inc, pg 1228
Consolidated Printers Inc, pg 1229
DNP America LLC, pg 1229
Elegance Printing & Book Binding (USA), pg 1229
Express Media Corp, pg 1229
Fairfield Marketing Group Inc, pg 1229
Hamilton Printing Co, pg 1229
Ikon Document Services, pg 1229
Integrated Book Technology Inc, pg 1230
Jinno International Group, pg 1230
KNI Inc, pg 1230
Linick International Inc, pg 1230
LK Litho, pg 1230
Marrakech Express Inc, pg 1230
Printing Corp of the Americas Inc, pg 1231
Vicks Lithograph & Printing Corp, pg 1231
Fred Weidner & Daughter Printers, pg 1231

Printing, Binding & Book Finishing

This section includes companies throughout the world that offer printing, binding and/or book finishing services. Those U.S. and Canadian companies with 10% or more of their business done outside North America are also included here. Immediately preceding this section is an index classifying companies by services offered.

Australia

Southwood Press Pty Ltd
76-82 Chapel St, Marrickville, NSW 2204
Tel: (02) 9560 5100 *Fax:* (02) 9550 0097
E-mail: info@southwoodpress.com.au
Web Site: www.southwoodpress.com.au
Key Personnel
Production Manager: Patrick Jayatilake
Sales Manager: Elizabeth Finniecome
Special Projects: Bruce Welch
Founded: 1966
Turnaround: 15-20 workdays
Print Runs: 500 min - 20,000 max
Business from Other Countries: 1%

Austria

ADEVA (Akademische Druck-u Verlagsanstalt)
Auersperggasse 12, 8010 Graz
Mailing Address: Postfach 598, 8011 Graz
Tel: (0316) 3644 *Fax:* (0316) 364424
E-mail: info@adeva.com
Web Site: www.adeva.com *Cable:* ADEVA-GRAZ
Key Personnel
Dir: Dr Ursula Struzl
Founded: 1949
Print Runs: 300 min - 10,000 max
Business from Other Countries: 80%
Branch Office(s)
Purgleitnergasse 10, Ecke Marburgerstr, 8042 Graz

Akademische Druck- u Verlagsanstalt, see ADEVA (Akademische Druck-u Verlagsanstalt)

Dr Paul Struzl GmbH, see ADEVA (Akademische Druck-u Verlagsanstalt)

Belgium

Delabie Europrint SA
Blvd de l'Eurozone 8, 7700 Mouscron
Tel: (056) 84 10 00
Key Personnel
PDG: D M Delabie
Sales Manager: Willem Mandeville
Finance: Luc Haspeslagh
Production: Debie Bertrand
Founded: 1964
Turnaround: 8 Workdays
Print Runs: 100,000 min - 1,000,000 max
Business from Other Countries: 60%

IMPF bvba
Sint-Amandstr 18, 9000 Gent
Tel: (09) 225 44 29
Key Personnel
Manager: Xavier Dewulf
Founded: 1958
Business from Other Countries: 10%

Drukkerij Lannoo NV (Lannoo Printers)
Kasteelstr 97, 8700 Tielt
Tel: (051) 42 42 11 *Fax:* (051) 40 70 70
E-mail: lannoo@lannooprint.be
Web Site: www.lannooprint.be
Key Personnel
General Manager & Marketing Dir: Stefaan Lannoo *E-mail:* stefaan.lannoo@lannooprint.be
Founded: 1909
Turnaround: 10 Workdays
Print Runs: 100 min - 1,000,000 max
Business from Other Countries: 30%

Canada

Aardvark Enterprises
Division of Speers Investments Ltd
204 Millbank Dr SW, Calgary, AB T2Y 2H9
Tel: 403-256-4639
Key Personnel
Pres: J Alvin Speers
Founded: 1970 (Small Press Pioneers)
Turnaround: 30 Workdays
Print Runs: 10 min - 1,000 max
Business from Other Countries: 25%

Appleby's Bindery Ltd
1303 Route 102, Upper Gagetown, NB E5M 1R5
Tel: 506-488-2086 *Toll Free Tel:* 800-561-2005 (Canada only) *Fax:* 506-488-2086
E-mail: applbind@nbnet.nb.ca
Key Personnel
Pres & Owner: David E Appleby
Mgr: John Appleby
Founded: 1976
Turnaround: 30 Workdays
Business from Other Countries: 10%

Arpeco Engineering
7095 Ordan Dr, Mississauga, ON L5T 1K6
Tel: 905-564-5150 *Toll Free Tel:* 800-387-4806 *Fax:* 905-564-2943
E-mail: sales@arpeco.com
Web Site: www.arpeco.com
Key Personnel
Dir, Mktg: Jim Wright
Founded: 1965
Business from Other Countries: 70%

Blitzprint Inc
1235 64 Ave SE, Calgary, AB T2H 2J7
Tel: 403-253-5151 *Toll Free Tel:* 866-479-3248 *Fax:* 403-253-5642
E-mail: blitzprint@blitzprint.com
Web Site: www.blitzprint.com
Key Personnel
Pres: Kevin Lanuke *Tel:* 866-479-3248 *E-mail:* klanuke@blitzprint.com
COO: Peter Friebel *Tel:* 866-479-3248 *E-mail:* pfriebel@blitzprint.com
VP: Gwen Gates *Tel:* 866-479-3248 *E-mail:* ggades@blitzprint.com
Turnaround: 10
Print Runs: 1 min - 10,000 max
Business from Other Countries: 50%
Membership(s): Association of Book Publishers of British Columbia; Canadian Booksellers Association

Coach House Printing
401 Huron St, Rear, Toronto, ON M5S 2G5
Tel: 416-979-2217 *Fax:* 416-977-1158
E-mail: mail@chbooks.com
Web Site: www.chbooks.com
Key Personnel
Publr: Stan Bevington
Founded: 1965
Turnaround: 14 Workdays
Print Runs: 200 min - 2,000 max
Business from Other Countries: 10%

Maracle Press Ltd
1156 King St E, Oshawa, ON L1H 7N4
Tel: 905-723-3438 *Toll Free Tel:* 800-558-8604 *Fax:* 905-428-6024
E-mail: maracle@maraclepress.com
Web Site: www.maraclepress.com
Key Personnel
Pres & Gen Mgr: Bruce A Fenton *E-mail:* bfenton@maraclepress.com
VP, Busn Devt: Ronald G Taylor *E-mail:* rtaylor@maraclepress.com
Founded: 1920
Turnaround: 10 Workdays
Print Runs: 500 min - 500,000 max
Business from Other Countries: 25%
Membership(s): BMI; CPIA; Ontario Printing & Imaging Association; Printing Industries of America

McLaren Morris & Todd Co
3270 American Dr, Mississauga, ON L4V 1B5
Tel: 905-677-3592 *Fax:* 905-677-3675; 905-677-7766
Web Site: www.mmt.ca
Key Personnel
Pres: Alan George
Cont: Nancy Marquis *Tel:* 905-677-3592 ext 247
Founded: 1956
Turnaround: 15 Workdays
Print Runs: 5,000 min - 1,000,000 max
Business from Other Countries: 10%

Preney Print & Litho Inc
1457 Lauzon Rd, Windsor, ON N8F 3N2
Tel: 519-966-3412 *Toll Free Tel:* 877-870-4164 *Fax:* 519-966-4996
E-mail: contacts@preneyprint.com
Web Site: www.preneyprint.com
Key Personnel
Pres: John Preney
Founded: 1972
Turnaround: 15 Workdays
Print Runs: 2,000 min
Business from Other Countries: 20%

Printcrafters Inc
78 Hutchings St, Winnipeg, MB R2X 3B1
Tel: 204-633-7117 *Fax:* 204-694-1519
E-mail: info@printcraftersinc.com
Key Personnel
Pres: Bob Payne *Tel:* 204-633-7117 ext 223

Fax: 204-694-1594 E-mail: bpayne@printcraftersinc.com
Founded: 1996 (Employee owned)
Turnaround: 5-20 Workdays
Print Runs: 500,000 min
Business from Other Countries: 30%
Membership(s): CPIA

Schawk
543 Richmond St W, Suite 125, Toronto, ON M5V 1Y6
Tel: 416-703-1445 Fax: 416-703-1494
Web Site: www.schawk.com
Key Personnel
Pres: Bob Cockerill
Founded: 1965
Business from Other Countries: 10%

Transcontinental Printing Book Group
Division of Transcontinental Group
395 Lebeau Blvd, St-Laurent, PQ H4N 1S2
Tel: 514-337-8560 Toll Free Tel: 800-361-3599 Fax: 514-339-5230
Web Site: www.transcontinental.com; www.transcontinental-printing.com
Key Personnel
Sr VP, Book Group: Jacques Gregoire
US Sales Mgr: Denis Beaudin Tel: 514-339-2220 ext 4101 E-mail: beaudind@transcontinental.ca
Founded: 1976
Turnaround: 15-20 workdays casebound; 10-15 workdays softcover
Print Runs: 1,000 min
Business from Other Countries: 30%
Branch Office(s)
614 Yates Ave, Calumet City, IL 60409, United States, Contact: Kristopher D Levy Tel: 708-832-1528 Fax: 708-832-9510 (Midwest)
3653 W Leland Ave, Suite One W, Chicago, IL 60625, United States, Contact: Tim Taylor Tel: 773-583-8155 Fax: 773-583-8162 E-mail: tim.taylor@transcontinental.ca (Midwest)
245 Eliot St, Ashland, MA 01721, United States, Contact: Ed Catania Tel: 508-881-1119 Fax: 508-881-7739 E-mail: ecatania@attbi.com (East Coast)
19 Crown St, Milton, MA 02186-1419, United States, Contact: Mike Gazzola Tel: 617-696-1435 Fax: 617-696-1025 E-mail: mikebook@attbi.com (East Coast)
37 Herman Blvd, Franklin Square, NY 11010, United States, Contact: Tom Malloy Tel: 516-775-2980 Fax: 516-488-0253 E-mail: tmmalloy@aol.com (NY)
3175 Summit Square Dr, Suite C9, Oakton, VA 22124, United States, Contact: David Avesian Tel: 703-255-1332 Fax: 703-255-1343 E-mail: davesian@cox.rr.com (Southeast)
559 Lowrys Rd, Parksville, BC V9P 2R8, Contact: Mike Davies Tel: 250-248-9700 Fax: 250-248-2353 E-mail: bookguys@shaw.ca (West Coast)
15373 Victoria Ave, White Rock, BC V4B 1H1, Contact: Wade Davies Tel: 604-535-8800 Fax: 604-535-8802 E-mail: davies@shaw.ca (West Coast)
490 Wilfred Dr, Peterborough, ON K9K 2H1, Contact: Tom Lang Tel: 705-760-9594 Fax: 705-760-9485 E-mail: langt@transcontinental.ca (NY)
Membership(s): BMI; National Association for Printing Leadership; Printing Industries of America

Tri-Graphic Printing (Ottawa) Ltd
485 Industrial Ave, Ottawa, ON K1G 0Z1
Tel: 613-731-7441 Toll Free Tel: 800-267-9750 Fax: 613-731-3741
Web Site: www.tri-graphic.com

Key Personnel
VP & Gen Mgr: Doug K Doane E-mail: ddoane@tri-graphic.com
VP, Prodn & Servs: Fred Malleau Tel: 905-665-8500 E-mail: fmalleau@tri-graphic.com
Founded: 1968
Turnaround: 10-15 Workdays
Print Runs: 1,000 min - 100,000 max
Business from Other Countries: 10%
Branch Office(s)
213 Byron St S, Suite 201, Whitby, ON L1N 4P7 Tel: 905-665-8500 Fax: 905-665-8501

University of Toronto Press Inc
Printing Division, 5201 Dufferin St, North York, ON M3H 5T8
Tel: 416-667-7767 Fax: 416-667-7803
E-mail: printing@utpress.utoronto.ca
Web Site: www.utpress.utoronto.ca
Key Personnel
Pres & Publr: George Meadows
Founded: 1901
Turnaround: 10-15 Workdays
Print Runs: 10 min - 200,000 max
Business from Other Countries: 15%
Membership(s): BMI

Webcom Ltd
3480 Pharmacy Ave, Toronto, ON M1W 2S7
Tel: 416-496-1000 Toll Free Tel: 800-665-9322 Fax: 416-496-1537
E-mail: webcom@webcomlink.com
Web Site: www.webcomlink.com
Key Personnel
VP, Sales & Mktg: Mike Collinge
Mktg Mgr: Charlie Scime
Founded: 1976
Turnaround: 15 Workdays
Print Runs: 50 min - 100,000 max
Business from Other Countries: 40%

Czech Republic

GRASPO CZ AS - Druckerei und Buchbinderei
Pod Sternberkem 324, 76302 Zlin
Tel: (0577) 606111 Fax: (0577) 104052
E-mail: graspo@graspo.com; mp@graspo.com
Web Site: www.graspo.com
Founded: 1995
Print Runs: 1,000 min
Business from Other Countries: 50%
Branch Office(s)
Racianska 109/c, 83102 Bratislava
Sinkulova 48, 14000 Prague 4

Denmark

Bianco Lunos Bogtrykkeri AS
Subsidiary of Carl Allers Etablissement AS
Otto Monsteds Gade 3, 1571 Copenhagen V
Tel: 33140781 Fax: 33913808
Key Personnel
General Manager: J Heede Sorensen
Founded: 1871

Finland

Gummerus Printing
Subsidiary of Gummerus Oy

Alasinkatu 1-3, 40351 Jyvaskyla
Mailing Address: PO Box 444, 40351 Jyvaskyla
Tel: (014) 683 500 Fax: (014) 676 770
E-mail: etunimi.sukunimi@gummerus.fi
Web Site: www.gummerus.fi
Key Personnel
Marketing Dir: Mr Martti Aaltonen
Man Dir: Mr Jarmo Porkka
Founded: 1872
Turnaround: 20-60 Workdays
Print Runs: 1,000 min - 100,000 max
Business from Other Countries: 15%

WS Bookwell Ltd
Teollisuustie 4, 06100 Porvoo
Tel: (019) 21 941 Fax: (019) 219 4800
E-mail: pekka.tykkylainen@bookwell.fi
Web Site: www.bookwell.fi
Key Personnel
Man Dir: Magnus Breitenstein Tel: (019) 2194 608 E-mail: magnus.breitenstein@bookwell.fi
Marketing Manager: Pekka Tykkyloinen Tel: (019) 219 4663 E-mail: pekka.tykkylainen@bookwell.fi
Founded: 1878
Business from Other Countries: 50%
Parent Company: WSOY
Ultimate Parent Company: Sanoma WSOY
Branch Office(s)
Messdorferstr 127, 53123 Bonn, Germany, Contact: Markku Rapeli Tel: (0228) 986 4006 Fax: (0228) 986 4008
PO Box 3, Lowestoft, Suffolk NR33 8EY, United Kingdom Tel: (502) 742 038 Fax: (502) 742 039

France

Imprimerie Bene
12 rue Pradier, F-30000 Nimes
Tel: (04) 66294897 Fax: (04) 66382146
Key Personnel
President: Jacques Enfer
Print Runs: 100 min - 10,000 max
Business from Other Countries: 20%

Imprimerie Gaignault
Route De Levroux, 36100 Issoudun

Plein Chant
16120 Bassac
Tel: (05) 45 81 93 26 Fax: (05) 45 81 92 83
Key Personnel
Contact: Edmond Thomas
Founded: 1971
Print Runs: 600 min - 1,000 max
Business from Other Countries: 5%

Signes du Monde
1424 ch du Dupere Hubert Saint-Genez, 40380 Povartin
Tel: (06) 12 99 73 37 Fax: (0561) 575717
Key Personnel
Production: Hubert Saint-Genez

Germany

C L Baader Buch & Offsetdruckere GmbH & Co KG
Gutenbergstr 1, 72525 Muensingen
Tel: (07381) 791 Cable: BAADER-MUNSINGEN
Founded: 1835
Turnaround: 1 Workday
Print Runs: 1,000 min - 15,000 max

Fachhochschule Fur Druk, Studiengang Verlagswirtschaft und Verlagsherstellung
Nobelstr 10, 70569 Stuttgart
Tel: (0711) 6852807 *Fax:* (0711) 6852834
E-mail: info@fhd-stuttgart.de
Web Site: www.fhd-stuttgart.de
Telex: 725 185 fhd d
Key Personnel
Contact: Prof Eduard H Schoenstedt

G Braun (vormals G Braun'sche Hofbuchdruckerei und Verlag)
Karl-Friedrichstr 14-18, 76 133 Karlsruhe
Tel: (0721) 1607320 *Fax:* (0721) 1607321
E-mail: info@gbraun-immo.de
Web Site: www.gbraun.de
Telex: 7 826 904
Key Personnel
Contact: Michael Schimmele

C Maurer Druck und Verlag
Schubartstr 21, 73312 Geislingen/Steige
Tel: (07331) 9300
Web Site: www.maurer-online.de
Key Personnel
Contact: Carl Otto Maurer *Tel:* (07331) 930-112
Founded: 1856

Media-Print Informationstechnologie GmbH
Unit of Media-Print GmbH & Co KG
Schwarzenraben 7, 59558 Lippstadt
Tel: (02941) 2 72-300 *Fax:* (02941) 2 72-540
E-mail: kg@mediaprint.de
Web Site: www.mediaprint.de
Key Personnel
Man Dir: Dr Otto W Drosihn *E-mail:* drdrosihn@kg.mediaprint.de
Founded: 1993
Turnaround: 5-10 Workdays
Print Runs: 100 min - 300,000 max
Business from Other Countries: 10%

MOHN Media
Subsidiary of Bertelsmann AG
Carl-Bertelsmann-Str 161M, 33311 Guetersloh
Tel: (05241) 80-4 04 10 *Fax:* (05241) 2 42 82
E-mail: mohnmedia@bertelsmann.de
Web Site: www.mohnmedia.de
Key Personnel
Man Dir: Markus Dohle
Founded: 1824
Business from Other Countries: 25%

Oertel & Sporer GmbH & Co
Burgstr 1-7, 72764 Reutlingen
Mailing Address: Postfach 1642, D-72706 Reutlingen
Tel: (07121) 302555 *Fax:* (07121) 302558
Key Personnel
Publisher: Valdo Lehari
Manager & Printer: Ermo Lehari
Print Runs: 500 min - 50,000 max

Priese GmbH & Co
Auerbacher Str 9, 14193 Berlin
Tel: (030) 8263024 *Fax:* (030) 8266024
Key Personnel
Contact: Elma Priese; Hans Joachim Priese

Vier-Tuerme GmbH Benedikt Press
Schweinfurter Str 40, 97359 Muensterschwarzach Abtei
Tel: (09324) 20214 *Fax:* (09324) 20444
Web Site: www.vier-tuerme.de/benedictpress
Key Personnel
Contact: Josef Stoecklein
Founded: 1951
Turnaround: 8-16 Workdays
Print Runs: 300 min - 20,000 max
Business from Other Countries: 5%

Hong Kong

Bookbuilders Ltd
Unit J 13/F Yeung Yiu Chung No 8 Industrial Bldg, 20 Wang Hoi Rd, Kowloon Bay, Kowloon
Tel: 27968123 *Fax:* 27968267; 27968690
E-mail: lph@netvigator.com
Key Personnel
Man Dir: Leslie Henman
General Manager: Edward Chan

C & C Offset Printing Co Ltd
Subsidiary of C & C Joint Printing Co (HK) Ltd under Sino United (Holdings) Hong Kong Ltd
C&C Bldg, floor 14, 36 Ting Lai Rd, Tai Po, New Territories
Tel: 2666-4988 *Fax:* 2666-4938
E-mail: offsetprinting@candcprinting.com
Web Site: www.ccoffset.com
Key Personnel
Dir & General Manager: Jackson Leung
Deputy Man Dir: Kee Lee
Deputy General Manager: Ivy Lam
Assistant General Manager: Kit Wong
Senior Sales Manager (Special Project): Francis Ho
Dir & Executive Vice President, C & C Offset Printing Co (USA) Inc, Portland OR, USA: Charles H Clark, IV *E-mail:* cclark@ccoffset.com
Development Manager, C & C Offset Printing Co (USA) Inc, Portland, OR, USA: Jenny Whittier *E-mail:* jwhittier@ccoffset.com
Customer Service Manager, C & C Offset Printing Co (USA) Inc, Portland, OR, USA: Ernest Li *E-mail:* ernestli@ccoffset.com
Dir & Executive Vice President, C & C Offset Printing Co (NY) Inc, New York, NY, USA: Simon Chan *E-mail:* schan@ccoffset.com
Assistant General Manager-China Sales, C & C Joint Printing Co (Ghuangdong) Ltd, Shenzhen, China: Simon Zhang
President, C & C Printing Japan Co Ltd, Tokyo, Japan: Yamamoto Masaaki
Customer Service Manager, C & C Offset Printing Co (NYC), Inc, New York, NY: Frances Harkness *E-mail:* fharkness@ccoffset.com
Man Dir, C & C Joint Printing Co (Beijing), Ltd, Beijing, China: Zhang Lin Gui
Dir, C & C Offset Printing Co (UK), Ltd: Tracy Broderick
Account Manager, C & C Offset Printing Co (UK) Ltd: Fia Fornari
Founded: 1980
Turnaround: 30-42 Workdays
Print Runs: 2,000 min - 1,000,000 max
Business from Other Countries: 60%
Branch Office(s)
C & C Offset Printing Co (USA) Inc, 2632 SE 25th Ave, Suite D, Portland, OR 97202, United States *Tel:* 503-233-1834 *Fax:* 503-233-7815 *E-mail:* portlandinfo@ccoffset.com (shipping)
C & C Offset Printing Co (NY) Inc, 401 Broadway, Suite 2015, New York, NY 10013-3004, United States *Tel:* 212-431-4210 *Fax:* 212-431-3960 *E-mail:* newyorkinfo@ccoffset.com
C & C Joint Printing Co (Guangdong) Ltd, Chunhu Industrial Estate, Pinghu, Long Gang, Shenzhen 518111, China *Tel:* (0755) 2845-8333 *Fax:* (0755) 2845-9911 *E-mail:* guangdong@candcprinting.com *Web Site:* www.candcprinting.com (Plant)
C & C Printing Japan Co Ltd, 2-6-12 Hitotsubashi, Tozaido Bldg 3F, Chiyoda-ku, Tokyo 101-0003, Japan *Tel:* (03) 5216-4580 *Fax:* (03) 5216-4610 *E-mail:* mail@candcprinting.co.jp *Web Site:* www.candcprinting.com
C & C Joint Printing Co (Guangdong) Ltd, 7/F, Flat H, Green View Apartment, No 38, Hou Guang Ping Hu Tong, Xi Cheng Qu, Beijing 100035, China *Tel:* (010) 6650-3176 *Fax:* (010) 6650-3175 *E-mail:* beijing@candcprinting.com
C & C Joint Printing Co (Guangdong) Ltd, Room 304, Fang Fa Bldg, No 29, 165 Ave, Dongzhuanbin Rd, Shanghai 200050, China *Tel:* (021) 6240-1305 *Fax:* (021) 6240-2090 *E-mail:* shanghaioffice@candcprinting.com
C & C Joint Printing Co (Guangdong) Ltd, Room 1511, Hua Xin Bldg, East Block, 2 Shuiyin Rd, Huanshi East, Guangzhou 510075, China *Tel:* (020) 3760-0979 *Fax:* (020) 3760-0977 *E-mail:* quangzhou@candcprinting.com
C & C Offset Printing Co (UK) Ltd, 2 New Burlington St, 4th floor, London W1S 2JE, United Kingdom, Dir: Tracy Broderick *Tel:* (020) 7287 7787 *Fax:* (020) 7287 7187 *E-mail:* tracy@candcoffset.co.uk

Caritas Printing Training Centre
Caritas House, 3rd floor, Block D, 2 Caine Rd, Hong Kong
Tel: 2526 1148 *Fax:* 2537 1231
Key Personnel
General Manager: Isaac Mak
Print Runs: 1,000 min - 100,000 max
Business from Other Countries: 50%

Colorprint Offset
Unit 1808-9, 18/F, 8 Commercial Tower, 8 Sun Yip St, Chai Wan
Tel: 2896-7777 *Fax:* 2889-6606
E-mail: info@cpo.com.hk
Web Site: www.cpo.com.hk
Key Personnel
Sales Manager: Jennifer Weston *Tel:* 2903-5062
Contact: Eva Lav; Ian Lee
Turnaround: Standard 2 week turnaround
Print Runs: 3,000 min - 100,000 max
Business from Other Countries: 80%
Sales Office(s): Gainsborough House, 81 Oxford St, London W1R 1RB, United Kingdom
80 Park Ave, Suite 10N, New York, NY 10016, United States

Commercial Colorlab Ltd
Block A 7/F, Aik San Factory Bldg, 14 Westland Rd, Quarry Bay
Tel: 2880 5128
Key Personnel
Dir: Simon Wong; Fong Lee Yong
Turnaround: 10 Workdays
Business from Other Countries: 30%
Branch Office(s)
5/F, Block E, Finance Bldg, 254-256 Des Voeux Rd, Central

Dai Nippon Printing Co (Hong Kong) Ltd
Division of Dai Nippon Printing Co Ltd
Tsuen Wan Industrial Centre, 2-5/F, 220-248 Texaco Rd, Tsuen Wan, New Territories
Tel: 2408-0188 *Fax:* 2614-7585; 2407-6201
Web Site: www.dnp.co.jp *Cable:* DNPICO
Key Personnel
Administration & Finance Dir: Mr K Miya
Print Runs: 5,000 min - 200,000 max
Business from Other Countries: 85%
Branch Office(s)
Dai Nippon Printing Co (Australia) Pty Ltd, St Martins Tower, Suite 1002, Level 10, 31 Market St, Sydney, NSW 2000, Australia *Tel:* (02) 9267-8166 *Fax:* (02) 9267-9533
DNP America LLC, Los Angeles Office, 3858 Carson St, Suite 300, Torrance, CA 90503, United States *Tel:* 310-540-5123 *Fax:* 310-543-3260
DNP America LLC, New York Office, 335 Madison Ave, 3rd floor, New York, NY 10017, United States *Tel:* 212-503-1060 *Fax:* 212-286-1501

DNP America LLC, Silicon Valley Office, 3235 Kifer Rd, Suite 100, Santa Clara, CA 95051, United States *Tel:* 408-735-8880 *Fax:* 408-735-0453

DNP Corporation USA, New York Office, 335 Madison Ave, 3rd floor, New York, NY 10017, United States *Tel:* 212-503-1850 *Fax:* 212-286-1490

DNP Corporation USA, San Francisco Office, 577 Airport Blvd, Suite 620, Burlingame, CA 94010, United States *Tel:* 650-558-4050 *Fax:* 650-340-6095

DNP Denmark A/S, Skruegangen 2, 2690 Karlslunde, Denmark *Tel:* 4616-5100 *Fax:* 4616-5200

DNP Electronics America LLC, 2391 Fenton St, Chula Vista 91914, United States *Tel:* 619-397-6700 *Fax:* 619-397-6729

DNP Europa GmbH, Berliner Allee 26, 40212 Dusseldorf, Germany *Tel:* (0211) 8620-180 *Fax:* (0211) 8620-1895

DNP IMS America Corporation, 4524 Enterprise Dr NW, Concord, NC 28027, United States *Tel:* 704-784-8100 *Fax:* 704-784-2777

DNP IMS France SAS, 14, rue da la Violette, 22100 Dinan, France

DNP Photomask Europe SpA, Via Olivatti 2/A, 20041 Agrate Brianza, Italy *Tel:* (039) 65493-3000 *Fax:* (039) 65493-215

DNP Singapore Pte Ltd, 896 Dunearn Rd, No 04-09, Sime Darby Centre, Singapore 589472, Singapore *Tel:* 469-7611 *Fax:* 466-8486

DNP Taiwan Co Ltd, Rm D, 6 fl, 44 Chung-Shan N Rd Sec 2, Taipei 104, Taiwan, Province of China *Tel:* (02) 2327-8311 *Fax:* (02) 2327-8283

DNP UK Co Ltd, 27 Throgmorton St, 4th floor, London EC2N 2AQ, United Kingdom *Tel:* (020) 7588 2088 *Fax:* (020) 7588 2089

PT DNP Indonesia, Kawasan Industri Pulogadung, Jalan Pulogadung Kaveling II, Blok H, No 2-3, Jakarta Timur, Indonesia *Tel:* (021) 4610313 *Fax:* (021) 4605795

Tien Wah Press (Pte) Ltd, 4 Pandan Crescent, Singapore 128475, Singapore *Tel:* 466-6222 *Fax:* 469-3894

TWP Sdn Bhd, 89, Jalan Tampoi, Kawasan Perindustrian Tampoi, 80350 Johor Bahru, Johor, Malaysia *Tel:* (07) 2369899 *Fax:* (07) 2363148

Everbest Printing Co Ltd
Ko Fai Industrial Bldg, Block C5, 10th floor, 7 Ko Fai Rd, Yau Tong, Kowloon
Tel: 2727 4433 *Fax:* 2772 7687
E-mail: sales@everbest.com.hk
Web Site: www.everbest.com
Key Personnel
Man Dir: Kenneth Chung
Customer Account Executive: Frankie Lee; Ronny Ng
Founded: 1954
Turnaround: 28 Workdays
Print Runs: 1,000 min - 1,000,000 max
Business from Other Countries: 90%
Branch Office(s)
Everbest Printing (Australian & New Zealand Office), 100 Macaulay Rd, Stanmore, NSW 2048, Australia, Lionel Marz *Tel:* 612-9568-5879 *Fax:* 612-9568-5902 *E-mail:* lmarz@onaustralia.com.au
Everbest Canada, 50 Emblem Court, Scarborough, ON M1S 1B1, Canada, Connie Chung *Tel:* 416-286-2525 *Fax:* 416-286-2526 *E-mail:* everbest@aprinco.com
U.S. Office(s): Spectrum Books Inc, 2300 Bethards Dr, Suite C, Santa Rosa, CA 95405-8658, United States, Duncan McCallum *Tel:* 707-542-6044 *Fax:* 707-542-6045 *E-mail:* specbooks@aol.com
Four Colour Imports, 2843 Brownsboro Rd, Suite 102, Louisville, KY 40206, United States, George Dick *Tel:* 502-896-9644 *Fax:* 502-896-9594 *E-mail:* sales@fourcolour.com *Web Site:* www.fourcolour.com
Everbest Midwest, 6428 Margaret's Lane, Edina, MN 55439, United States, Dr Josie Lo *Tel:* 612-944-0854 *Fax:* 912-829-7670 *E-mail:* sklo@aol.com

Excel United Company Ltd
Sino Favour Centre, 25th floor, One On Yip St, Chai Wan
Tel: 2889 1078 *Fax:* 2889 1721
E-mail: info@excelunited.com
Web Site: www.excelunited.com
Key Personnel
Dir: Samuel Chung

Golden Cup Printing Co Ltd
Seapower Industrial Centre, 6/F, 177 Hoi Bun Rd, Kwun Tong, Kowloon
Tel: 23434254; 23434255 *Fax:* 23415426
E-mail: sales@goldencup.com.hk
Web Site: www.goldencup.com.hk
Key Personnel
Man Dir: Yeung Kam Kai
General Manager: W K Ngan
Sales Manager: Mary Yeung *E-mail:* mary@goldencup.com.hk
Founded: 1971
Turnaround: 25 Workdays
Print Runs: 5,000 min - 200,000 max
Business from Other Countries: 80%
Branch Office(s)
Dongguan, China
Guangdong, China
Kunming, China
Yunan, China

The Green Pagoda Press Ltd
9/F, Block B, Tung Chong Factory Bldg, 653-655 King's Rd, North Point
Tel: 2561 1924 *Fax:* 2811 0946
E-mail: gpinfo@gpp.com.hk
Web Site: www.gpp.com.hk
Key Personnel
Man Dir: Derek Yip
Founded: 1957
Turnaround: 1-14 days
Print Runs: 10 min - 500,000 max
Business from Other Countries: 30%

Hindy's Enterprise Co Ltd
Flat A 20/F, Melbourne Industrial Bldg, 16 Wetlands Rd, Quarry Bay
Tel: 25166318 *Fax:* 25165161
Key Personnel
General Manager: Cecilia Chung

Hing Yip Printing Co Ltd
Shing Tak Ind Bldg, 6/F, Block C & D, 44 Wong Chuk Hang Rd, Aberdeen
Tel: 25532432; 25532828 *Fax:* 28147887
Key Personnel
General Manager: Louis Ma
Contact: Ma Kai Chiu
Founded: 1963
Print Runs: 1,000 min - 100,000 max
Business from Other Countries: 95%

Hoi Kwong Printing Co Ltd
Wah Ha Industry Bldg, 5/F, Block C-D, 8 Shipyard Lane, Quarry Bay
Tel: 2562-1641; 2562-1096 *Fax:* 2564-2142
E-mail: sales@hoikwong.com
Web Site: www.hoikwong.com
Key Personnel
Man Dir: David Chan *E-mail:* dchan@hoikwong.com

Hua Yang Printing Holding Co Ltd
Tai Ping Industrial Centre, Unit B, 25/F, Block 1, 57 Ting Kok Rd, Tai Po, New Territories
Tel: 24167591 *Fax:* 24110235
Key Personnel
Man Dir: Mr Chan Kok Wai
Sales & Marketing: Carl Chan
Contact: Ng Kwok Cheong

Hung Hing Off-set Printing Co Ltd
Subsidiary of Hung Hing Printing Group Ltd
Tai Po Industrial Estate, 17-19 Dai Hei St, New Territories
Tel: 2664 8682 *Fax:* 2664 2070
E-mail: info@hhop.com.hk
Web Site: www.hhop.com.hk
Key Personnel
Man Dir: Matthew Yum *E-mail:* matthew@hhop.com.hk
Founded: 1950
Turnaround: 20-30 Workdays
Print Runs: 5,000 min - 1,000,000 max
Business from Other Countries: 15%

Image Printing Company Ltd
Unit 4, 4/F Cornell Centre, 50 Wing Tai Rd, Chai Wan
Tel: 2873 2633 *Fax:* 2558 3044
E-mail: imageprt@pop3.hknet.com
Key Personnel
Man Dir: Philip Chow Sung Ming
Founded: 1992
Print Runs: 1,000 min - 50,000 max
Business from Other Countries: 50%

Lammar Offset Printing Co
Flat C, 16/F Aik Sun Factory Bldg, 14 Westlands Rd, Quarry Bay
Tel: 25631068 *Fax:* 28113375
Key Personnel
Man Dir: Mr Wu Yuk Ting

Leo Paper Products Ltd
7/F, Kader Bldg, 22 Kai Cheung Rd, Kowloon Bay, Kowloon
Tel: 28841374 *Fax:* 25130698
E-mail: lpp@leo.com.hk
Web Site: www.leo.com.hk
Key Personnel
Man Dir: Johnny Fung *E-mail:* johnny@leo.com.hk; Michael Leung *E-mail:* michael@leo.com.hk
Marketing Dir: Kelly Fok *E-mail:* kelly@leo.com.uk
Founded: 1991
Turnaround: 15-30 Workdays
Print Runs: 5,000 min
Parent Company: Leo Paper Bags Manufacturing Ltd
Branch Office(s)
Leo Paper USA, 1180 NW Maple St, Suite 102, Issaquah, WA 98027, United States, Contact: Bijan Pakzad *Tel:* 425-646-8801 *Fax:* 425-646-8805 *E-mail:* bijan@pacificpier.com
Sales Office(s): Leo Paper Products (Europe) BVBA, Keizerstr 5, 200 Antwerpen, Belgium, Contact: Jan Van Gijsel *Tel:* (03) 203-0912 *Fax:* (03) 255-1303 *E-mail:* leo@leo-europe.com
Leo Paper Products (UK) Ltd, St Michaels House, 94 High St, Wallingford, Oxon OX10 0BW, United Kingdom *Tel:* (01491) 827827 *Fax:* (01491) 837127 *E-mail:* infoleouk@btconnect.com

Liang Yu Printing Factory Ltd (Good Friend's Printing Factory Ltd)
1/F, 9-11 Sai Wan Ho St, Shaukiwan
Tel: 25604453; 25677563 *Fax:* 28858099
E-mail: liangyup@netvigator.com
Key Personnel
Man Dir: Eric Yat-Sum Hui
Print Runs: 5,000 min - 100,000 max

Business from Other Countries: 40%
U.S. Office(s): 3616 167th Pl SW, Lynnwood, WI 98037, United States, Contact: Alvin Hui

Midas Printing Ltd
1/F, 100 Texaco Rd, Tsuen Wan, New Territories
Tel: 24084024 *Fax:* 24065897
Web Site: www.midasprinting.com
Key Personnel
Project Manager: Raymond Chan
Executive Dir: Gloria Y P Kan
Contact: Annie Wong *E-mail:* annie@midasprinting.com
Founded: 1990
Turnaround: 14-21 Workdays
Print Runs: 5,000 min - 100,000 max
Business from Other Countries: 25%

Morris Press Ltd
Wah Ha Industrial Bldg, 12/F, Block B, 8 Shipyard Lane, Quarry Bay
Tel: 25632187; 2563 2188 *Fax:* 25659069
Key Personnel
President & Contact: Suzy P Morris
  Tel: 732-572-5185 *Fax:* 732-572-5150
  E-mail: spmorris@ix.netcom.com
Dir: Raymond Shing; Raynond Shing
Contact: William M F Shui
Turnaround: 20 Workdays
Print Runs: 5,000 min - 100,000 max
Business from Other Countries: 50%

Nordica Printing Co Ltd
Melbourne Industrial Bldg, 1-2/F, Block C, 16 Westlands Rd, Quarry Bay
Tel: 25648444; 25648446 *Fax:* 25656445
Key Personnel
Executive Officer, Nordica Group: Benny Kwan
Dir: Alan Wong
Manager: K P Chow
Contact: Ng Tsai On

Paper Art Product Ltd
Sung Fung Centre, Unit 816, 88 Kwok Shui Rd, Kwai Chung
Tel: 2481 2929 *Fax:* 2489 2255
E-mail: paperart@netvigator.com
Turnaround: 4-8 weeks
Print Runs: 3,000 min - 1,000,000 max
Business from Other Countries: 80%

Paper Communication Printing Express Ltd
4A Dragon Industrial Bldg, 93 King Lam St, Cheung Sha Wan, Kowloon
Tel: 27864191 *Fax:* 27864498
Key Personnel
Marketing Dir: Alam Ng
Contact: Wayne Lui
Founded: 1981
Turnaround: 28 to 56 Workdays
Print Runs: 1,000 min - 100,000 max
Business from Other Countries: 10%

Paramount Printing Co Ltd
3 Chun Kwong St, Tseung Kwan O Industrial Estate, Kowloon
Tel: 2896-8688 *Fax:* 2897-8942
E-mail: paraprin@netvigator.com
Web Site: www.paramount.com.hk
Key Personnel
President: Victor Oh
Account Dir: Kelvin Lai
Founded: 1968
Turnaround: 30-45 Workdays
Print Runs: 1,000 min - 1,000,000 max
Business from Other Countries: 60%
Branch Office(s)
Paramount Printing USA Inc, 386 Park Ave S, Room 315, New York, NY 10016, United States, President: Jason Cheng *Tel:* 212-696-5821 *Fax:* 212-696-5428 *E-mail:* jason3@ix.netcom.com

Prontaprint Asia Ltd
1/F, Gaylord Commercial Bldg, 114 Lockhart Rd, Wanchai
Tel: 28657525 *Fax:* 28661064
E-mail: postmaster@pronta.com.hk
Key Personnel
Man Dir: Clive Howard
Founded: 1986
Business from Other Countries: 40%

Sheck Wah Tong Printing Press Ltd
653-659 Kings Rd, 1/F, North Point
Tel: 25628293 *Fax:* 25655431
Web Site: www.sheckwahtong.com
Key Personnel
Deputy Man Dir: K C Chiu *E-mail:* kcchiu@swt.com.hk
Founded: 1911
Turnaround: 20 Workdays
Print Runs: 3,000 min - 200,000 max

Sing Cheong Printing Co Ltd
G/F, 655 Kings Rd, North Point
Tel: 25618801; 25626317 *Fax:* 25659467
E-mail: info@singcheong.com.hk
Key Personnel
Dir & Manager: Karen Shen Fishel
Founded: 1965
Business from Other Countries: 96%

Sino Publishing House Ltd
Valley Center, Room 301 & 302, 80-82 Morrison Hill Rd, Wanchai
Tel: 2884 9963 *Fax:* 2884 9321
Web Site: www.sinophl.com
Key Personnel
Contact: Ben Yan *E-mail:* benyan@sinophl.com
Founded: 1993
Print Runs: 500 min - 500,000 max
Business from Other Countries: 75%

SNP Best-Set Typesetter Ltd
Rm 304, 3/F, Honour Industrial Centre, 6 Sun Yip St, Chai Wan
Tel: 2897 6033 *Fax:* 2897 5170
E-mail: best-set-usa@email.msn.com; bestset@snpcorp.com
Web Site: www.bestset-typesetter.com
Key Personnel
Manager: Cynthia Hui *E-mail:* cynthiahui@snpcorp.com
Dir: Johnson Yeung *Tel:* 2975 1012
Sales Representative: Wai Man Yeung *Tel:* 914 961 6223 *Fax:* 914 961 8212
Founded: 1986
Turnaround: 14 workdays
Print Runs: 500 min - 5,000,000 max
Business from Other Countries: 99%
Branch Office(s)
3rd floor, No 3 Da Song Jiang Nan Main Ave C, Guangzhou, China, Contact: Patrick Au *Tel:* (020) 8441 5873 *Fax:* (020) 8441 5874 *E-mail:* gzbestset@snpcorp.com
Sales Office(s): 157 Fisher Ave, Suite 6, Eastchester, NY 10709, United States, Contact: Wai Man Yeung *Fax:* 914-961-8212 *E-mail:* waimanyeung@snpcorp.com

Sota Graphic Arts Co Ltd
Seapower Industrial Centre, 6/F, 177 Hoi Bun Rd, Kwun Tong
Tel: 23421083 *Fax:* 23415426
E-mail: sales@goldencup.com.hk
Web Site: www.goldencup.com.hk
Key Personnel
Man Dir: K K Yeung
General Manager: Wai Kwong Ngan
Assistant Manager: Mary Yeung *E-mail:* mary@goldencup.com.hk
Founded: 1985
Turnaround: 10 Workdays
Print Runs: 2,000 min
Business from Other Countries: 90%

South Sea International Press Ltd
3/F, Yip Cheung Centre, 10 Fung Yip St, Chai Wan
Tel: 2897 1083 *Fax:* 2558 1473
E-mail: ssiphk@hk.super.net
Key Personnel
Man Dir: P Y Lee; Franky Ho
Founded: 1984
Print Runs: 3,000 min - 500,000 max
Business from Other Countries: 80%

Speedflex Asia Ltd
3/F Tianjin Bldg, 167 Connaught Rd W, Hong Kong
Tel: 2542 2780 *Fax:* 2542 3733
E-mail: info@speedflex.com.hk
Web Site: www.speedflex.com.hk
Founded: 1981
Turnaround: 1 Workday
Print Runs: 1 min
Business from Other Countries: 20%

Sun Fung Offset Binding Co Ltd
Westlands Centre, Suites 801-803, 8/F, 20 Westlands Rd, Quarry Bay
Tel: 25618109; 25623381; 25621925
Fax: 28110638
E-mail: sunfung@sunfung.com.hk
Web Site: www.sunfung.com.hk
Key Personnel
Marketing Manager: Raymond Chau
Marketing Executive: Maria Tsang

Sunny Printing (Hong Kong) Co Ltd
Ming Pao Industrial Centre, Room 12, 2/F, Block A, 18 Ka Yip St, Chai Wan
Tel: 25578663 *Fax:* 28898070
E-mail: enquiry@sunnyprinting.com.hk
Web Site: www.sunnyprinting.com.hk
Key Personnel
Man Dir: Albert T W Chan
Founded: 1991

Sunshine Press Ltd
21/F Fullager Ind Bldg, 234 Aberdeen Main Rd, Hong Kong
Tel: 25530228; 25532303 *Fax:* 28732930
E-mail: spl@sunshinepress.com.hk
Key Personnel
Administrative Assistant: Trevin Tong
Contact: Joney Chan
Founded: 1976
Turnaround: 21-28 Workdays
Print Runs: 3,000 min - 500,000 max
Business from Other Countries: 25%

Toppan Printing Co (HK) Ltd
Division of Toppan Printing Co Ltd
Yuen Long Industrial Estate, One Fuk Wang St, Yuen Long, New Territories
Tel: 2561-0101 *Fax:* 24754321
E-mail: info@toppan.co.jp
Web Site: www.toppan.co.jp
Key Personnel
Man Dir: James Lee Lee
Sales Manager: Yukata Ito
Founded: 1963
Turnaround: 30 Workdays
Business from Other Countries: 25%

Unicorn International Printing Co Ltd
Block C & A, 13/F, Shing King Bldg, 45 Kut Shing St, Chai Wan

HONG KONG

Mailing Address: Block G, 2/F, Phase 1, Kwun Tong Ind Center, 472 Kwun Tong Rd, Kowloon
Tel: 2515-9810 *Fax:* 2515-9992
E-mail: unicorn7@netvigator.com; unicornhk@netvigator.com
Web Site: www.unicorn88.com
Key Personnel
General Manager: Paul chi-sing Choi
Founded: 1994
Turnaround: 2 weeks-1 month
Print Runs: 1,000 min - 50,000 max
Business from Other Countries: 20%

Wing King Tong Group
Leader Industrial Centre, Block I, 3/F, 188-202 Texaco Rd, Tsuen Wan, New Territories
Tel: 24073287 *Fax:* 24074130; 24087939
E-mail: printing@wkt.cc; books@wkt.cc
Web Site: www.wkt.cc
Key Personnel
Man Dir: Alex Yan Tak Chung *E-mail:* ayan@hk.super.net
Marketing Dir: Jeremy Kuo
Founded: 1944
Turnaround: 15 Workdays
Print Runs: 1,000 min - 100,000 max
Business from Other Countries: 95%

Hungary

Interpress Aussenhandels GmbH
Subsidiary of ADWEST
Bajcsy-Zsilinszky ut 21, 1065 Budapest
Mailing Address: PF 290, 1364 Budapest
Tel: (01) 302-7525 *Fax:* (01) 302-7530
E-mail: office@interpress.hu
Web Site: www.interpress.hu
Key Personnel
Manager: Julia Kovacs; Sandor Kovacs; Miklos Pollak
Founded: 1991

Kultura
PO Box 149, 1389 Budapest
Tel: (01) 2501194 *Fax:* (01) 2500233
Key Personnel
Manager: Katalin Multas

India

Hiralal Printing Works Ltd
Subsidiary of Conway Printers Pvt Ltd
D-41/1 TTC Industrial Area MIDC, opp Turbhe tel exchange, Mumbai 400613
Tel: (022) 7672726; (022) 7683012
Key Personnel
Chairman: G P Agrawal
Man Dir: Mr Rakesh Kumar Agrawal
Founded: 1981
Turnaround: 40-45 Workdays
Print Runs: 5,000 min - 100,000 max
Business from Other Countries: 75%

Indonesia

Ichtiar Baru I Van Hoeve
Jln Cideng Barat 62/Jl Raya Pasar Jumat No 38 D-E Pondok Pinang, POB 1376/jks, Jakarta Pusat 12013
Tel: (021) 7511856; (021) 7511901 *Fax:* (021) 7511855
Founded: 1972
Turnaround: 6 Workdays
Print Runs: 500 min - 18,000 max

Victory Offset Prima PT
Jalan Raya Pegangsaan, Dua No 17, Jakarta 14250
Tel: (021) 460-8968; (021) 460-2742; (021) 4682-0555 *Fax:* (021) 460-2740; (021) 4682-0551
E-mail: info@victoryoffset.com
Web Site: www.victoryoffset.com
Key Personnel
President: Zainal F Stanley *E-mail:* zainal@victoryoffset.com
General Manager: S Wilson Pinady *E-mail:* wilson@victoryoffset.com
Founded: 1971
Turnaround: 14 days
Print Runs: 5,000 min
Business from Other Countries: 20%

Ireland

Kilkenny People/Wellbrook Press
34 High St, Kilkenny
Tel: (056) 77 21015 *Fax:* (056) 77 21414
E-mail: info@kilkenny-people.ie
Web Site: www.medialive.ie/press/provincial/kilkenny.html
Key Personnel
Advertising Manager: Peter Seaver
Founded: 1892
Business from Other Countries: 10%

Smurfit Print
Beech Hill, Clonskeagh, Dublin 4
Tel: (01) 202 7000 *Fax:* (01) 269 4481
Web Site: www.smurfit.ie
Key Personnel
Chief Executive: Niamh McGowan *Tel:* (01) 882 0501 *E-mail:* nmcgowan@smurfitprint.ie
Sales Dir: Doual Greene
Print Runs: 200 min - 5,000,000 max
Business from Other Countries: 20%
Parent Company: Jefferson Smurfit Group plc

Ultragraphics
Unit 78A, Cookstown Industrial Estate, Tallaght, Dublin 24
Tel: (01) 4599133 *Fax:* (01) 4512368
Key Personnel
President: Tony Lovett
Turnaround: 4-5 Workdays
Business from Other Countries: 80%

Israel

Har-El Printers & Publishers
Jaffa Port, PO Box 8053, Jaffa 61081
Tel: (03) 681 6834 *Fax:* (03) 681 3563
E-mail: mharel@harelart.co.il
Web Site: www.harelart.com
Key Personnel
Contact: Monique L Har-El
Founded: 1974
Turnaround: 60-90 Workdays
Print Runs: 30 min - 5,000 max
Business from Other Countries: 70%

Keterpress Enterprises Jerusalem
PO Box 7145, 91071 Jerusalem
Tel: (02) 6521201 *Fax:* (02) 6536811
E-mail: info@keter-books.co.il
Web Site: www.keter-books.co.il
Key Personnel
Plant Manager: Peter Tomkins *E-mail:* peter@keter-books.co.il
Sales Manager: Zvi Weller
Print Runs: 500 min - 500,000 max
Business from Other Countries: 10%
Parent Company: Keter Publishing House Ltd

Monoline Ltd
3 Avnei Nezer, Kiryat Sefer
Tel: (08) 9741456 *Fax:* (08) 9741454
Key Personnel
Dir: S J Colthof
Founded: 1959
Business from Other Countries: 30%

Technosdar Ltd
PO Box 31684, Tel Aviv 61316
Tel: (03) 560-7418 *Fax:* (03) 560-4932
E-mail: technos@zahav.net.il
Key Personnel
General Manager: Avraham Weiss
Founded: 1972
Turnaround: 7-16 Workdays
Business from Other Countries: 10%

Italy

Canale G e C SpA
Subsidiary of Istituto Grafico Bertello SpA
Via Liguria 24, 10071 Borgaro Turin
Tel: (011) 40 78 511 *Fax:* (011) 40 78 527
E-mail: info@canale.it
Web Site: www.canale.it
Key Personnel
Dir General: Canale Giacomo *E-mail:* canale@canale.it
Founded: 1915
Turnaround: 30 Workdays
Print Runs: 3,000 min
Business from Other Countries: 65%

Dedalo Litostampa SRL
V le Luigi Jacobini 5, 70123 Bari
Mailing Address: Casella Postale BA/19, 70123 Bari
Tel: (080) 531 14 13; (080) 531 14 00; (080) 531 14 01 *Fax:* (080) 531 14 14
E-mail: info@edizionidedalo.it
Web Site: www.edizionidedalo.it
Key Personnel
Man Dir: Raimondo Coga
General Manager: Sergio Coga *E-mail:* s.coga@edizionidedalo.it
Founded: 1965
Print Runs: 2,000 min - 15,000 max

Mariani Ritti Grafiche SRL
Via Rontgen 16, 20136 Milan
Tel: (02) 58310004 *Fax:* (02) 58310408
E-mail: ritti@tiw.it
Key Personnel
Manager: Giorgio Ritti
Founded: 1959
Business from Other Countries: 25%

Milanostampa SpA
Corso Ferrero 5, 12060 Farigliano (Cuneo)
Tel: (0173) 746111 *Fax:* (0173) 746248; (0173) 746249
E-mail: milanostampa@areacom.it
Web Site: www.milanostampa.com
Telex: 212428
Key Personnel
Commercial Dir: Riccardo Sardo
Man Dir: Fuad Lahham

Founded: 1965
Turnaround: 15 Workdays
Print Runs: 3,000 min - 80,000 max
Business from Other Countries: 65%

Minerva Medica
Corso Bramante 83/85, 10126 Turin
Tel: (011) 67-82-82 *Fax:* (011) 67-45-02
E-mail: minervamedica@minervamedica.it
Web Site: www.minervamedica.it
Key Personnel
President: Dr Alberto Oliaro
Founded: 1937
Print Runs: 1,000 min - 10,000 max
Business from Other Countries: 8%
Branch Office(s)
Via Spallanzani 9, 00161 Rome *Tel:* (06) 44251210 *Fax:* (06) 44291500
  E-mail: lucentini.minmed.rome@minervamedica.it

Nuovo Instituto Italiano d'Arti Grafiche
Via Zanica 92, 24126 Bergamo
Tel: (035) 329111 *Fax:* (035) 329322
E-mail: info.niiag@arvato.it
Web Site: artigrafiche.bergamo.it; www.arvato.it
Telex: (035) 300114
Founded: 1873
Turnaround: 10 Workdays
Business from Other Countries: 30%

Amilcare Pizzi SpA
Via A Pizzi, 14, 20092 Cinisello Balsamo
Tel: (02) 618361 *Fax:* (02) 61836283
E-mail: info@amilcarepizzi.it
Key Personnel
Chief Executive Officer: Massimo Pizzi
Founded: 1914
Business from Other Countries: 45%
U.S. Office(s): American Pizzi Offset Corp, 370 Lexington Ave, Suite 505, New York, NY 10017, United States *Tel:* 212-986-1658 *Fax:* 212-286-1887

Japan

Dai Nippon Printing Co Ltd
1-1, Ichigaya Kagacho 1-chome, Shinjuku-ku, Tokyo 162-8001
Tel: (03) 3266 2111
E-mail: info@mail.dnp.co.jp
Web Site: www.dnp.co.jp *Cable:* DNPRINT TOKYO
Key Personnel
President: Kitajima Yoshitoshi
Dir, International Operations: Satoshi Saruwatari
Founded: 1876
Print Runs: 5,000 min - 200,000 max
Business from Other Countries: 85%
Branch Office(s)
DNP America LLC, 3858 Carson St, Suite 300, Torrance, CA 90503, United States *Tel:* 310-540-5123 *Fax:* 310-543-3260
DNP Europa GmbH, Berliner Allee 26, 40212 Duesseldorf, Germany *Tel:* (0211) 8620-180 *Fax:* (0211) 8620-1892
DNP UK Co Ltd, 27 Throgmorton St, 4th floor, London EC2N 2AN, United Kingdom *Tel:* (020) 7588 2088 *Fax:* (020) 7588 2089
Sales Office(s): Sydney, Australia
San Francisco, CA, United States
Santa Clara, CA, United States
New York, NY, United States

Nissha Printing Co Ltd
3 Mibu Hanai-cho, Nakagyo-ku, Kyoto 604-8551
Tel: (075) 811-8111 *Fax:* (075) 801-8250
E-mail: print-info@nissha.co.jp
Web Site: www.nissha.co.jp
Key Personnel
Chairman: Mr Shozo Suzuki
President: Mr Hiroshi Furukawa
International Div: Ms Yuri Miura
Founded: 1929

Republic of Korea

Daehan Printing & Publishing Co Ltd
344-12, Sangdaewon 1-dong, Jungwon-gu, Seongnam-si, Gyeonggi-do, Seoul
Tel: (031) 730-3850; (031) 730-3813 *Fax:* (031) 735-8104
Web Site: www.dhpop.com; www.daehane.com
Key Personnel
President: Sungshick Kim
Manager: Jongjun Yu
Founded: 1948

Pyunghwa Dang Printing Co Ltd
60 Kyunji-Dong, Chongro-Ku, Seoul 110-170
Tel: (02) 735 4011 *Fax:* (02) 734 5201
E-mail: comuser@hitel.kol.co.kr
Key Personnel
President: Mr Il Soo Lee
Vice President: Mr Hae Kun Oh
Executive Dir: Mr Sang Woo Lee
Founded: 1923
Turnaround: 10 Workdays
Print Runs: 2,000 min - 500,000 max
Business from Other Countries: 7%

Lithuania

Spindulys Printing House
Gedimino g 10, 3000 Kaunas
Tel: (037) 226243 *Fax:* (037) 204970
E-mail: spaustuve@spindulys.lt
Web Site: www.spindulys.lt
Key Personnel
Contact: Elena Kapustinskiene
Founded: 1928
Print Runs: 500 min - 100,000 max
Business from Other Countries: 6%

Madagascar

Societe Malgache d'Edition
Route des Hydrocarbures, Ankorondrano, BP 659, Antananarivo/Tananrive 101
Tel: (020) 2222635 *Fax:* (020) 2222254
E-mail: tribune@bow.dts.mg; tribune@blanbir.mg
Web Site: www.madagascar-tribune.com
Telex: (020) 223-40
Key Personnel
Dir of Publication: Rahaga Ramaholimihaso
Founded: 1943
Print Runs: 7,000 min - 15,000 max

Malaysia

Web Printers Sdn Bhd
42 Jln 13/4 Sekn 13, 46200 Petaling Jaya
Tel: (03) 7956 3577 *Fax:* (03) 7726 3563
Key Personnel
General Manager: Hashim Natt
Marketing Manager: Ashraf Ali

Malta

Interprint Ltd - Malta
Subsidiary of Malta Government Investment Ltd
Industrial Estate, Marsa LQA 06
Tel: (021) 240169; (021) 222720 *Fax:* (021) 243780; (021) 238115
Web Site: www.interprintmalta.com
Key Personnel
General Manager: Alfred Azzopardi
Commercial Manager: Joseph Bonnici
  E-mail: jbonnici@interprintmalta.com
Founded: 1963
Turnaround: 15 Workdays
Print Runs: 500 min - 20,000 max
Business from Other Countries: 80%

Netherlands

Bosch en Keuning grafische bedrijven
Ericstr 1, 3742 SG Baarn
Mailing Address: Postbus 1, 3740 AA Baarn
Tel: (035) 5412050 *Fax:* (035) 2202446
Key Personnel
Contact: P P E Rings

Koninklijke Wohrmann Bv
Estlandsestr 1, 7202 CP Zutphen
Tel: (0575) 582121 *Fax:* (0575) 582128
E-mail: secretariaat@wohrmann.nl
Web Site: www.wohrmann.nl

New Zealand

Bookprint Consultants Ltd
Division of Grantham House Publishing
9 Wilkinson St, Apt 6, Oriental Bay, Wellington 6001
Tel: (04) 381 3071 *Fax:* (04) 381 3067
E-mail: gstewart@iconz.co.nz
Key Personnel
Chief Executive: Graham C Stewart
Founded: 1982
Print Runs: 2,000 min - 7,500 max
Business from Other Countries: 10%

PPP Printers Ltd
PO Box 22785, Christchurch
Tel: (03) 3662727 *Fax:* (03) 3654606
Key Personnel
Man Dir: D C Richardson
Founded: 1958
Turnaround: 10 Workdays
Print Runs: 100 min - 100,000 max
Business from Other Countries: 10%

Rogan McIndoe Print Ltd
51 Crawford St, Dunedin

Tel: (03) 477 0355 Fax: (03) 474 0116
E-mail: quality@rogan.co.nz
Web Site: www.rogan.co.nz
Key Personnel
Man Dir: Brendan A Murphy
Founded: 1893
Print Runs: 21 min - 30 max
Business from Other Countries: 1%

Peru

Industrias del Envase SA
Subsidiary of Cerveceria Backus & Johnson SA
Av Elmer Faucett 4766, Callao
Tel: (01) 574-1150 Fax: (01) 574-1287
E-mail: webmast@envase.com.pe
Web Site: www.envase.com.pe
Key Personnel
General Manager: Jose Santa Maria Zuniga
    E-mail: jsanta@envase.com.pe
Administrative & Finance Manager: Gustavo
    Domecq E-mail: gdomecq@envase.com.pe
Marketing & Sales Manager: Adolfo Vasquez
    Quijada E-mail: avasquez@envase.com.pe
Manufacturing & Project Manager: Gustavo Mancilla Mundaca E-mail: gman@envase.com.pe
Founded: 1971
Turnaround: 2 Workdays
Print Runs: 15,000 min - 1,200,000 max
Business from Other Countries: 5%

Philippines

Cacho Hermanos Inc, see Cacho Publishing inc

Cacho Publishing inc
Formerly Cacho Hermanos Inc
Pines Cor, Union St, Mandaluyong, Metro Manila
Tel: (02) 783011-13 Fax: (02) 6315244
E-mail: cacho@mozcom.com
Key Personnel
President: Herbert T Veloso
Founded: 1880
Turnaround: 7-120 Workdays
Print Runs: 500 min - 50,000 max
Ultimate Parent Company: National Book Store

JF Printhaus
Km 83.38 Maharlika Hi-way, Brgy San Francisco,
    4000 San Pablo City
Tel: (049) 800-3961 Fax: (049) 562-0916
Key Personnel
President: Victorino F Javier, Jr
Founded: 1982
Parent Company: JF Corporation
Membership(s): Philippine Printing Technical
    Foundation; Printing Industries Association of
    the Philippines

Naldoza Printers
362 Tupaz St, 6000 Cebu City
Tel: (032) 261-7326 Fax: (032) 261-7326
E-mail: naldoza@ebu.skyinet.net
Key Personnel
Chief Executive Officer: John R Naldoza
Founded: 1989
Parent Company: Business Developers Inc
Membership(s): Philippine Printing Technical
    Foundation

Philippine Graphic Arts Inc
163 Tandang Sora St, 1400 Caloocan City
Tel: (02) 364-4591 Fax: (02) 631-9733
E-mail: philippinegraphicarts@yahoo.com
Key Personnel
Pres & Gen Mgr: Igmedio R Silverio

Portugal

Printer Portuguesa Industria Grafica Lda
Sao Carlos, 2725 Mem Martins
Tel: (01) 9216025 Fax: (01) 9218363
E-mail: lissabon.printerportuguesa@bertelsmann.de
Key Personnel
Contact: Albert Lutz

Edicoes Silabo
Rua Cidade de Manchester 2, 1170 100 Lisbon
Tel: (021) 8130345 Fax: (021) 8166719
E-mail: silabo@silabo.pt
Web Site: www.silabo.pt
Key Personnel
Marketing Dir: Manuel Robalo
    E-mail: manuelrobalo@silabo.pt
Founded: 1983
Turnaround: 5 Workdays

Puerto Rico

Publishing Resources Inc
373 San Jorge St, 2nd floor, Santurce 00912
Tel: 787-268-8080 Fax: 787-774-5781
E-mail: publishingresources@worldnet.att.net
Key Personnel
Owner & President: Ronald J Chevako
Editorial Dir: Anne W Chevako
Founded: 1976
Print Runs: 500 min - 10,000 max
Business from Other Countries: 5%

Singapore

Chong Moh Offset Printing Ltd
Subsidiary of Chassis Graphic Art Pte Ltd
19 Joo Koon Rd, Jurong Town 628978
Tel: 8622701 Fax: 8624335
E-mail: chongmoh@singnet.com.sg
Key Personnel
Chairman: James Ng
Founded: 1946
Turnaround: 10-14 Workdays
Print Runs: 1,000 min
Business from Other Countries: 35%

Columbia Overseas Marketing Pte Ltd
Subsidiary of Columbia Offset Platemaking Co
77 Lorong 19 Geylang, No 02-00/05 Wing Yip
    Bldg, Singapore 388513
Tel: 7478607 Fax: 7458668
Key Personnel
Man Dir: Mr Eujin Chua
Founded: 1969
Print Runs: 1,000 min - 20,000 max
Business from Other Countries: 40%
Branch Office(s)
Columbia Binding Pte Ltd (Binding)
Columbia Laserart Pte Ltd (Printing)
Columbia Lasermould Pte Ltd (Die-cutting)

Craft Print Pte Ltd
9 Joo Koon Circle, Jurong, Singapore 629041
Tel: 861 4040 Fax: 861 0530
E-mail: info@craftprint.com
Web Site: www.craftprint.com
Key Personnel
Man Dir: Charlie Chan
Marketing Manager: Desmond Chan

CS Graphics Pte Ltd
10 Tuas Ave 20, Singapore 638822
Tel: 6865 2010 Fax: 6861 0190
Web Site: www.csgraphics.us
Key Personnel
Man Dir: Mr Lee Sian Tee E-mail: stlee@
    csgraphics-world.com
Founded: 1987
Turnaround: 20-30 Workdays
Print Runs: 1,000 min - 200,000 max
Business from Other Countries: 100%

Eurasia Press Pte Ltd
10/14 Kg Ampat, Singapore 368318
Tel: 90012349 Fax: 62931269
Key Personnel
Man Dir: Peter Ho Tel: hopeter@singapore.com
Founded: 1937
Turnaround: 14 Workdays
Print Runs: 500 min - 100,000 max
Business from Other Countries: 65%

Fong & Sons Printers Pte Ltd
40 Pandan Rd, Singapore 609282
Tel: 2663688 Fax: 2664988
Key Personnel
Man Dir: Tony Fong

Ho Printing Singapore Pte Ltd
31 Changi South St One, Changi South Industrial
    Estate, Singapore 486769
Tel: 5429322 Fax: 5428322
Telex: RS 39685 HOFSET
Key Personnel
Man Dir: Mr Ho Wai Hoi
Founded: 1951
Turnaround: 35-50 Workdays
Print Runs: 5,000 min - 50,000 max
Business from Other Countries: 30%

Huntsmen Offset Printing Pte Ltd
2 Fan Yoong Rd, Jurong Town, Singapore 629780
Tel: 2650600 Fax: 2658575
Key Personnel
General Manager: Heung Yam Yuen
Founded: 1970
Turnaround: 30 Workdays
Business from Other Countries: 60%

International Press Co Pte Ltd
26 Kallang Ave, Singapore 339417
Tel: 2983800; 2952437 Fax: 2971668
Key Personnel
Marketing Manager: Kok Leong Koo
Founded: 1972
Print Runs: 3,000 min - 50,000 max
Business from Other Countries: 60%

Kyodo Printing Co (S'pore) Pte Ltd
112 Neythal Rd, Jurong Town, Singapore 628599
Tel: 6265 2955 Fax: 6264 4939
E-mail: cschong@kyodoprinting.com.sg
Web Site: kyodosing.com
Telex: KSPRINT RS22144 Cable: SHINGPRESS
Key Personnel
Executive Secretary: Mr Ng Soo Siah

Markono Print Media Pte Ltd
Subsidiary of Markono Holdings Pte Ltd
21 Neythal Rd, Singapore 628586
Tel: 6281-1118 Fax: 6286-6663
E-mail: saleslead@markono.com.sg
Web Site: www.markono.com.sg

Key Personnel
Founder & Chairman: Ng Siow How
Dir: Bob Lee Song Tioh *E-mail:* blee@markono.com.sg
Turnaround: 7 Workdays
Print Runs: 500 min - 150,000 max
Business from Other Countries: 20%
Branch Office(s)
Kin Keong Colour Printing (M) Sdn Bhd, Port Klang 539538

PacPress Media Pte Ltd
Blk 1200 Depot Close, No 01-21/27 (off Depot Rd), Telok Blangah Industrial Estate, Singapore 0410 109675
Tel: 2768090; 2730756 *Fax:* 2730060
Key Personnel
Man Dir: Mr T H Oh

SNP SPrint Pte Ltd
97 Ubi Ave 4, Singapore 408754
Tel: 6741 2500 *Fax:* 6744 3770
E-mail: paulwong@snpcorp.com
Web Site: www.snpcorp.com
Telex: rs56289epb
Key Personnel
Chief Executive Officer & President: Yeo Chee Tong
Chief Operating Officer: Tan Jin Yan
US Sales Manager: Patrick Chung
Turnaround: 30 Workdays
Print Runs: 2,000 min - 200,000 max
Business from Other Countries: 40%
Parent Company: SNP Corporation Ltd

Stamford Press Pte Ltd
209, Kallang Bahru, Singapore 339344
Tel: 6294 7227 *Fax:* 6294 4396; 6294 3319
E-mail: lynn@stamford.com.sg
Web Site: www.stamford.com.sg
Telex: RS56414 STAMFO
Key Personnel
Dir: Mr L Rajesh *Tel:* 6294 7227 (ext 233)
  E-mail: rajesh@stamford.com.sg
Founded: 1963
Turnaround: 3-4 Workdays for small jobs; 3-4 weeks for big jobs
Print Runs: 1,500 min - 50,000 max
Business from Other Countries: 20%

Tien Wah Press Pte Ltd
977 Bt Timan Rd, Singapore 589626
Tel: 64666222 *Fax:* 64689710
Key Personnel
Man Dir: Makoto Takakura
Marketing Dir: Mrs Campos-Chia Chiu Leng
Founded: 1935
Business from Other Countries: 80%
Ultimate Parent Company: Dai Nippon Printing Co Ltd
Branch Office(s)
Tien Wah Press Aust Pty Ltd, Unit 10, 130 Pacific Highway, St Leonards, 2085 Sydney, NSW, Australia *Tel:* (02) 9436-0255 *Fax:* (02) 9438-5381
Tien Wah Press France, 62 Rue Ducourdic, 75014 Paris, France *Tel:* (01) 4279-0700 *Fax:* (01) 4279-8090
Tien Wah Press, 84 Wooster St, Suite 505, New York, NY 10012, United States *Tel:* 212-274-8090 *Fax:* 212-274-0771
TWP America Inc, 2550 Ninth St, Suite 111, Berkeley, CA 94710, United States *Tel:* 510-845-9532 *Fax:* 510-845-8580
Tien Wah Press (UK) Ltd, Unit 23, The Ivories, 6-8 Northampton St, London N1 2HY, United Kingdom *Tel:* (020) 7354-3323 *Fax:* (020) 7359-8777

Times Printers Pte Ltd
Subsidiary of Times Publishing Group
16 Tuas Ave 5, Singapore 639340
Tel: 862 3333 *Fax:* 862 1313
E-mail: tp@timesprinters.com
Web Site: www.tpl.com.sg *Cable:* TIMESPRINT
Key Personnel
Senior Vice President & Head of Printing Division: Mr Leong Kwok Sun
Head of Sales: Patsy Tan *Tel:* 63112 763
  E-mail: patsytan@timesprinters.com
Founded: 1968
Turnaround: 5-25 Workdays
Print Runs: 3,000 min - 300,000 max
Business from Other Countries: 75%

World Publications Printers Pte Ltd
Subsidiary of World Publications Distributors, Pte Ltd
39 Ubi Rd 1, World Publications Bldg, Singapore 408695
Tel: 7449888 *Fax:* 8406118
E-mail: wphsin@singnet.com.sg
Web Site: web.singnet.com.sg
Telex: RS 39283 WPD
Key Personnel
Chief Executive Officer & President: Mr S K Ng
Finance Dir: Mrs S K Ng
Vice President, Sales & Marketing: Ms Chan Sew Chu
Vice President, Corporate Affairs, Human Resources & Administration: Ms Dot Loh
Founded: 1982
Turnaround: 7-14 Workdays
Print Runs: 1 min - 70,000 max
Business from Other Countries: 80%

Slovenia

Gorenjski Tisk Printing House
Mirka Vadnova 6, 4000 Kranj
Tel: (04) 2016300 *Fax:* (04) 2016301
E-mail: info@go-tisk.si
Web Site: www.go-tisk.si
Telex: 34560 YU GOTISK
Key Personnel
Dir: Kristina Kobal
Commercial Manager: Boris Krist
Founded: 1888
Turnaround: 30 Workdays
Print Runs: 3,000 min - 15,000 max
Business from Other Countries: 50%

South Africa

CTP Book Printers (Pty) Ltd
Caxton St, Parow, 7500 Cape Town
Mailing Address: PO Box 6060, Parow East, 7501 Cape Town
Tel: (021) 930 8820 *Fax:* (021) 939 1559
E-mail: ctp@ctpbooks.co.za
Key Personnel
Managing Director: Caroline Sturgeon
  E-mail: carolines@ctpbooks.co.za
Operations Director: Colin Sturgeon
  E-mail: colins@ctpbooks.co.za
Founded: 1947

Spain

Eurohueco SA
Subsidiary of Arvato AG (Bertelsmann)
Apdo 30099, 08080 Barcelona
Tel: (093) 7730700 *Fax:* (093) 7730708
Web Site: www.eurohueco.es
Key Personnel
Vice President, Sales: Clemens Brauer *Tel:* (093) 7730703 *E-mail:* c.brauer@eurohueco.es
Founded: 1985
Print Runs: 200,000 min - 15,000,000 max
Business from Other Countries: 17%

Grafos SA Arte Sobre Papel
Zona Franca, Sector C, calle D 36, 08040 Barcelona
Tel: (093) 261 87 50 *Fax:* (093) 263 10 04
E-mail: info@grafos-barcelona.com
Web Site: www.grafos-barcelona.com
Key Personnel
Man Dir: Bernardo G Masana
  E-mail: bgmasana@compuserve.com
Domestic Sales Dir: Alberto Monclus
Packaging Sales Dir: Alejandro Hijar
Founded: 1934
Turnaround: 30 Workdays
Print Runs: 3,000 min - 60,000 max
Business from Other Countries: 45%

Printer Industria Grafica SA
Ctra N-II, Km 600, 08620 Sant Vicenc dels Horts, Barcelona
Tel: (093) 631 01 23 *Fax:* (093) 631 02 05; (093) 631 02 06
E-mail: info.printer@arvato-print.es
Web Site: www.printer-spain.com
Key Personnel
President: Joaquin Roca Ferrer
Business from Other Countries: 30%
Branch Office(s)
Cobrhi SA, Madrid
Rotedic SA, Madrid

Mercedes Ros Literary Agency
Castell 38, 08329 Teia, Barcelona
Tel: (093) 540 13 53 *Fax:* (093) 540 13 46
E-mail: info@mercedesros.com
Web Site: www.mercedesros.com
Key Personnel
Owner: Mercedes Ros *E-mail:* mercedes@mercedesros.com

Rotedic SA
Subsidiary of Novo Sistema
Ronda de Valdecarrizo, 13, 28760 Tres Cantos, Madrid
Tel: (091) 8031676 *Fax:* (091) 8038316
Web Site: www.rotedic.com
Key Personnel
Chief Executive Officer: Antonio de Haro
  E-mail: antonio@rotedic.com
President: Gregorio Juarez de Haro
Sales Manager & Commercial Dir: Francisco J de Haro *E-mail:* paco@rotedic.com
Founded: 1974
Print Runs: 50,000 min
Business from Other Countries: 7%

Graficas Santamaria SA
Division of Fotomecanica
Bekolarra, 4 Pol Ali Gobeo, 01010 Vitoria Gasteiz
Tel: (0945) 229100 *Fax:* (0945) 246393
E-mail: grsantamaria@sea.es; grsantamaria@graficassantamaria.com
Web Site: www.graficassantamaria.com
Key Personnel
Contact: Jesus Alzola Aguinaco
Founded: 1963
Turnaround: 1 Workday
Print Runs: 500 min - 150,000 max
Business from Other Countries: 15%

Luis Vives (Edelvives)
Xaudaro, 25, 28034 Madrid

SPAIN

Tel: (091) 334 48 83 *Fax:* (091) 334 48 92
E-mail: dediciones@edelvives.es
Web Site: www.grupoeditorialluisvives.com
Key Personnel
Production Dir: Jesus Agudo Perez
Founded: 1890
Turnaround: 1 Workday
Business from Other Countries: 25%

Sri Lanka

Sumathi Book Printing (Pvt) Ltd
Division of Sumathi Group
445, Sirimovo Bandaranaike Mawatha, Colombo 14
Tel: (0941) 330-673-5 *Fax:* (0941) 449-593
E-mail: lakbima@isplanka.lk
Web Site: www.sumathi.lk
Telex: 22104 SUMATHI CE SUMATISONS
Key Personnel
General Manager: Nawas A Rahim
Business from Other Countries: 75%

Switzerland

Hallwag Kuemmerly & Frey AG
Grubenstr 109, 3322 Schoenbuehl, Bern
Tel: (031) 850 31 31 *Fax:* (031) 850 31 00
E-mail: info@swisstravelcenter.com
Web Site: www.swisstravelcenter.ch
Telex: 912-661 HAWA CH
Key Personnel
President: Dr Juergen Schad

Photolitho AG
Industriestr 12, 8625 Gossau ZH
Tel: (043) 833 70 20 *Fax:* (043) 833 70 30
E-mail: info@photolitho.ch
Web Site: www.photolitho.ch
Key Personnel
President: Dietmar von Eicke *Tel:* (043) 833 70 24 *E-mail:* dve@photolitho.ch
Administrator: Werner Holliger *Tel:* (043) 833 70 23 *E-mail:* w.holliger@photolitho.ch
Founded: 1965
Business from Other Countries: 50%

Taiwan, Province of China

Taipei Yung Chang Printing
No 9, Lane 252, Sec 3, Chung Ching N Rd, Taipei 10318
Tel: (02) 5932392 *Fax:* (02) 5932763

United Republic of Tanzania

Peramiho Publications
PO Box 41, Peramiho
Tel: (054) 2730 *Fax:* (054) 2917
Key Personnel
Chief Executive: Fr Gerold Rupper
Founded: 1937
Print Runs: 4,000 min - 6,000 max

Thailand

J Film Process Co Ltd
440/7 Chaismonrapume, Ratchawithi Rd, Phayathai bangkok 10400
Tel: (02) 248 6888 *Fax:* (02) 247-4719
Key Personnel
President: Peer Prayukvong
Vice President: Siriporn Prayukvong
Man Dir: Pira Prayookwongse
Founded: 1980
Turnaround: 6 Workdays
Print Runs: 25,000 min - 65,000 max
Business from Other Countries: 45%

Mavisu International Co Ltd
11 Soi Prachanimit, Pradpatrd Phayathai, Bangkok 10400
Tel: (02) 2711148 *Fax:* (02) 2711168
Key Personnel
Man Dir: Vipavee Charoensidhi
Chairman: Marshall French
Founded: 1986
Print Runs: 15 min - 40 max
Business from Other Countries: 100%

Phongwarin Printing Company Ltd
299 Mu 10, Sukhumvit 107, Sumrongnue, Ampur Muang, Samutprakarn 10260
Tel: (02) 7498934-45; (02) 3994525-31; (02) 7498275-9 *Fax:* (02) 3994524; (02) 3994255
E-mail: somphong@phongwarin.com
Web Site: www.phongwarin.com
Key Personnel
Man Dir: Mr Somphong Charnsirisaksakul
Founded: 1983
Turnaround: 7 Workdays
Print Runs: 1,000 min - 500,000 max
Business from Other Countries: 5%

United Arab Emirates

Emirates Printing Press (LLC)
Member of Al Shirawi Group
PO Box 5106, Al Quoz, Dubai
Tel: (04) 347 5550; (04) 347 5544 *Fax:* (04) 347 5959
E-mail: eppdubai@emirates.net.ae
Web Site: www.eppdubai.com
Founded: 1974
Sales Office(s): Emirates Printing Press (UK) Ltd, Baylis House, Stoke Poges Lane, Slough, Berkshire SL1 3PB, United Kingdom, Sales Manager, UK & USA: Ron Nunn
Tel: (01753) 505612 *Fax:* (01753) 505613
E-mail: eppeurope@aol.com (Europe & USA)

United Kingdom

The Alden Group Ltd
Osney Mead, Oxford OX2 0EF
Tel: (01865) 253 200 *Fax:* (01865) 249 070
E-mail: information@alden.co.uk
Web Site: www.alden.co.uk
Key Personnel
Man Dir: William Alden
Founded: 1832

J W Arrowsmith Ltd
Winterstoke Rd, Bristol BS3 2NT
Tel: (0117) 966 7545 *Fax:* (0117) 963 7829
E-mail: jw@arrowsmith.co.uk
Web Site: www.arrowsmith.co.uk
Key Personnel
Sales Dir: David J Hooper *E-mail:* dhooper@arrowsmith.co.uk
Founded: 1854
Turnaround: 15 Workdays
Print Runs: 500 min - 15,000 max
Business from Other Countries: 40%

W & G Baird Ltd
Subsidiary of The Baird Group
Caulside Dr, Antrim BT41 2RS
Tel: (028) 9446 3911 *Fax:* (028) 9446 6250
E-mail: wgbaird@wgbaird.com
Web Site: www.wgbaird.org
Key Personnel
Man Dir: Dairmuid McGarry *E-mail:* dairmuid.mcgarry@wgbaird.com
Founded: 1863
Print Runs: 500 min - 100,000 max
Business from Other Countries: 45%
Divisions: Biddles Ltd
Branch Office(s)
MSO, Belfast, Ireland

BAS Printers Ltd
115 Tollgate Rd, Salisbury, Wilts SP1 2JG
Tel: (01722) 411711 *Fax:* (01722) 411727
E-mail: sales@basprint.co.uk
Web Site: www.basprint.co.uk
Key Personnel
Man Dir: David Gumn
Sales Dir: Paul G Gumn *E-mail:* paul@basprint.co.uk
Founded: 1948
Print Runs: 350 min - 40,000 max
Business from Other Countries: 10%

Ebenezer Baylis & Son Ltd
The Trinity Press, London Rd, Worcester, Worcs WR5 2JH
Tel: (01905) 357979 *Fax:* (01905) 354919
E-mail: theworks@ebaylis.demon.co.uk
Key Personnel
Man Dir: Ian Cranston

Bell & Bain Ltd
303 Burnfield Rd, Thornliebank, Glasgow G46 7UQ
Tel: (0141) 649 5697 *Fax:* (0141) 632 8733
E-mail: info@bell-bain.co.uk
Web Site: www.bell-bain.co.uk
Key Personnel
Man Dir: I Walker
Sales Dir: D Stewart
Founded: 1831

& BOOK FINISHING

Turnaround: 5-10 Workdays
Print Runs: 100 min - 100,000 max
Business from Other Countries: 25%

Bemrose Booth
Wayzgoose Dr, Derby DE21 6XG
Mailing Address: PO Box 18, Derby DE21 6XG
Tel: (01332) 294242; (01332) 267245
Fax: (01332) 295848; (01332) 290367
Web Site: www.bemrose.co.uk
Key Personnel
Sales Manager: Rodger Heathcote
 E-mail: rheathcote@bemrosebook.com

Biddles Ltd
Division of W & G Baird Ltd
Hardwick Industrial Estate, 24 Rollesby Rd,
 King's Lynn, Norfolk PE30 4LS
Tel: (01553) 764 728 *Fax:* (01553) 764 633
E-mail: enquiries@biddles.co.uk
Web Site: www.biddlesbooks.co.uk
Key Personnel
Customer Service Manager: Nick Faux
Founded: 1885
Turnaround: 20 Workdays
Print Runs: 250 min - 50,000 max
Business from Other Countries: 8%

Black Bear Press Ltd
King's Hedges Rd, Cambridge CB4 2PQ
Tel: (01223) 424571 *Fax:* (01223) 426877
E-mail: black_bear_press@msn.com
Key Personnel
Man Dir: K Fentiman
Sales Manager: Mike Hallam

Blackmore Ltd
Longmead Industrial Estate, Shaftesbury, Dorset
 SP7 8PX
Tel: (01747) 853034 *Fax:* (01747) 854500
E-mail: sales@blackmore.co.uk
Web Site: www.blackmore.co.uk
Key Personnel
Group Chief Executive: Chris Brickell
Man Dir: Peter Smith
Sales Dir: Aubrey Aviss

Blockfoil Ltd
Foxtail Rd, Ransomes Park, Ipswich IP3 9RT
Tel: (01473) 721701 *Fax:* (01473) 270705
E-mail: info@blockfoil.com
Web Site: www.blockfoil.com
Key Personnel
Man Dir: Barry Corbett *E-mail:* barrycorbett@
 blockfoil.com

Book Creation
20 Lochaline St, London W6 9SH
Tel: (020) 7583 0553 *Fax:* (020) 7583 9439
Key Personnel
Chairman: Hal Robinson *E-mail:* hal@librios.com
Founded: 1991
Business from Other Countries: 30%

J W Braithwaite & Son Ltd
Pountney St, Wolverhampton WV2 4HY
Tel: (01902) 452209 *Fax:* (01902) 352918
Key Personnel
Man Dir: Bruce Kidson *E-mail:* brucekidson@
 jwbraithwaite.co.uk
Founded: 1901

D Brown & Sons Ltd
14 High St, 2nd floor, Cambridge CF71 7AG
Tel: (01446) 771475 *Fax:* (01446) 771476
Key Personnel
Dir: J M Whitaker *Tel:* (01446) 774213
Finance Dir: Jane C Brown
Founded: 1895
Print Runs: 1 min - 1,000,000 max

Business from Other Countries: 20%
Branch Office(s)
Eastgate Press, 62 Eastgate, Cowbridge, S Glam
 CF7 7AB

Butler & Tanner Ltd
Caxton Rd, Frome, Somerset BA11 1NF
Tel: (01373) 451500 *Fax:* (01373) 451333
E-mail: manufacturing@butlerandtanner.com
Web Site: www.butlerandtanner.com
Key Personnel
Joint Man Dir: A Huett
Sales Dir: N White
Founded: 1850

Caledonian International Book Manufacturing
Westerhill Rd, Bishopbriggs, Glasgow G64 2QR
Tel: (0141) 7623000 *Fax:* (0141) 7620922
E-mail: 101622.235@compuserve.com
Key Personnel
Man Dir: Kevin McKenna
Commercial Dir: G Morrison
Group Sales Manager: Martin Platt
 E-mail: martin@platt44.freeserve.co.uk
Founded: 1819

Cambridge University Press - Printing Division
Division of Cambridge University Press
University Printing House, Edinburgh Bldg,
 Shaftesbury Rd, Cambridge CB2 2RU
Tel: (01223) 358331 *Fax:* (01223) 325672
Web Site: uk.cambridge.org
Key Personnel
Executive Dir: Sandra Ward *Tel:* (01223) 325608
 E-mail: sward@cambridge.org
Marketing Manager: Helen Bradbury
Founded: 1534
Print Runs: 1 min

CB Print Finishers Ltd
North Tyne Industrial Estate, Whitley Rd, Long-
 benton, Newcastle upon Tyne NE12 9TG
Tel: (0191) 2150101 *Fax:* (0191) 2701651
E-mail: sales@cbprint.co.uk
Web Site: www.cbprint.co.uk
Key Personnel
Man Dir: Paul Laidler *E-mail:* paul@cbprint.co.
 uk
Founded: 1921

Center Print Ltd
Subsidiary of The Boots Co PLC
Private Rd 2, Colwich Business Park, Colwich,
 Nottingham NG4 2JR
Tel: (0115) 961 2277 *Fax:* (0115) 938 1424
E-mail: cprint@besharapress.co.uk
Key Personnel
General Manager: Nicola Lesley
Print Runs: 1,000 min - 250,000 max

The Charlesworth Group
254 Deighton Rd, Huddersfield, West Yorks HD2
 1JJ
Tel: (01484) 517077 *Fax:* (01484) 517068
E-mail: sales@charlesworth.com
Web Site: www.charlesworth.com
Key Personnel
Chief Executive Officer: Graham Lawley
Marketing Manager: Sarah Philp
 E-mail: s_philp@charlesworth.com
Founded: 1928
Turnaround: 1-10 Workdays
Print Runs: 1 min - 10,000 max
Business from Other Countries: 30%

Cedric Chivers Ltd
Subsidiary of Information Preservation Ltd
One Beaufort Trade Park, Pucklechurch, Bristol
 BS16 9QH
Tel: (0117) 9371910 *Fax:* (0117) 9371920
E-mail: info@cedricchivers.co.uk

Web Site: www.cedricchivers.co.uk
Key Personnel
Sales & Marketing Dir: Russell Pocock
Founded: 1878
Turnaround: 15 Workdays
Print Runs: 1 min - 100 max

Clays Ltd
Subsidiary of St Ives Plc
Popson St, Bungay, Suffolk NR35 1ED
Tel: (01986) 893211 *Fax:* (01986) 895293
E-mail: sales@clays.co.uk
Web Site: www.clays.co.uk
Key Personnel
Sales Dir: Andrew Clay
Vice President, Sales-Clays USA: Andrew Copley
Founded: 1817
Turnaround: 15 Workdays
Print Runs: 1,000 min - 1,000,000 max
Business from Other Countries: 15%
U.S. Office(s): Clays, St Ives Burrups, 75 Ninth
 Ave, New York, NY 10011, United States
 Tel: 212-414-7520

William Clowes Ltd
Copland Way, Ellough, Beccles NR34 7TL
Tel: (01502) 712884 *Fax:* (01502) 717003
E-mail: william@clowes.co.uk
Web Site: www.clowes.co.uk
Key Personnel
Man Dir: Ian Foyster *E-mail:* ifoyster@clowes.co.
 uk
Founded: 1803
Turnaround: 10 Workdays
Print Runs: 2,000 min
Business from Other Countries: 1%

Cox & Wyman Ltd
Subsidiary of Rexam Plc
Cardiff Rd, Reading, Berks RG1 8EX
Tel: (0118) 953 0500 *Fax:* (0118) 950 7222
E-mail: coxandwyman@cpi-group.net
Web Site: www.cpi-group.net
Key Personnel
General Manager: Tom Roberts
Commercial Contact: Dave Watkins
 E-mail: dwatkins@cpi-group.co.uk
Founded: 1777
Turnaround: 10 Workdays
Print Runs: 2,000 min - 2,000,000 max
Business from Other Countries: 12%

Cradley Print Ltd
Chester Rd, Cradley Heath, West Midlands B64
 6AB
Tel: (01384) 414100 *Fax:* (01384) 414102
E-mail: sales@cradleygp.co.uk
Web Site: www.cradleygp.co.uk
Key Personnel
Man Dir: Chris Jordan
Turnaround: 5 Workdays
Print Runs: 1,000 min - 500,000 max
Business from Other Countries: 7%
Branch Office(s)
Quadcolor Repro

R R Donnelley
Global Media Solutions, High Barn, Midgeley
 Lane, Goldsborough, Knaresborough HG5 8NN
Tel: (01423) 796100; (01423) 866132 (ISDN)
 Fax: (01423) 796101
E-mail: gms.sales@rrd.com
Web Site: www.rrdonnelley.co.uk
Key Personnel
Man Dir: Roy Houston

Eagle Press
Riverside Way, Nottingham NG2 1DP
Tel: (0115) 9552335 *Fax:* (0115) 9552336
Key Personnel
Man Dir: S Keilpinski

UNITED KINGDOM

Furnival Press
61 Lilford Rd, London SE5 9HY
Tel: (020) 7274 2067 *Fax:* (020) 7274 6984
E-mail: furnprint@aol.com
Key Personnel
Dir: Johnny Gumb

Goldshield Communications Ltd
Banners Bldg, Attercliffe Rd, Sheffield S9 3QS
Tel: (0114) 2431000 *Fax:* (0114) 2433000
Key Personnel
Man Dir & Overseas-Special Projects: Sandra Potesta *E-mail:* sandra@goldcom.co.uk
Technical & Production: Stefano Potesta
Founded: 1984
Business from Other Countries: 40%

Green Street Bindery
9 Green St, Oxford, Oxon OX4 1YB
Tel: (01865) 243297 *Fax:* (01865) 791329
Key Personnel
Contact: Garry Phipps
Turnaround: 10-15 Workdays
Print Runs: 1 min - 10,000 max
Business from Other Countries: 5%

The Guernsey Press Co Ltd
Braye Rd, Vale, Guernsey GY1 3BW
Mailing Address: PO Box 91, Vale, Guernsey GY1 3BW
Tel: (01481) 240256; (01481) 243657 (ISDN) *Fax:* (01481) 240282
E-mail: books@guernsey-press.com
Web Site: www.guernsey-press.com
Key Personnel
Manager: Karen Taylor
Founded: 1897
Turnaround: 10 Workdays
Print Runs: 2,000 min - 50,000 max
Business from Other Countries: 80%

Hammond Bindery Ltd
Subsidiary of The Charlesworth Group
Flanshaw Way, Flanshaw Lane, Wakefield WF2 9LP
Tel: (01924) 369598 *Fax:* (01924) 298075; (01924) 364108
E-mail: sales@hammond-bindery.co.uk
Web Site: www.hammpack.co.uk
Key Personnel
Man Dir: Steve Allan *E-mail:* s_allan@hammond-bindery.co.uk
Technical Sales Dir: Brian Quarmby *E-mail:* b_quarmby@hammond-bindery.co.uk
Founded: 1974
Turnaround: 3-10 Workdays
Print Runs: 100 min - 250,000 max
Divisions: Hammond Packaging Ltd

Hammond Packaging Ltd
Division of Hammond Bindery Ltd
Flanshaw Way, Flanshaw Lane, Wakefield WF2 9LP
Tel: (01924) 369598 *Fax:* (01924) 298075; (01924) 364108
E-mail: sales@hammond-bindery.co.uk
Web Site: www.hammpack.co.uk
Key Personnel
Man Dir: Steve Allan *E-mail:* s_allan@hammond-bindery.co.uk
Sales Manager: Kirk Allan *E-mail:* k_allan@hammond-bindery.co.uk
Founded: 1991
Turnaround: 5-15 Workdays
Print Runs: 100 min - 500,000 max

Norman Hardy Printing Group
Granville House, 112 Bermondsey St, London SE1 3TX
Tel: (020) 7378 1579 *Fax:* (020) 7378 6422
E-mail: info@thehardygroup.co.uk
Web Site: www.thehardygroup.co.uk
Key Personnel
Man Dir: Stuart Hardy
Contact: Ken Stanger *E-mail:* ken@hardyprinting.co.uk
Founded: 1946

Harveys Ltd
Edgefield Road Industrial Estate, Loanhead Midlothian EH20 9SX
Tel: (0131) 440 0074 *Fax:* (0131) 440 3478
E-mail: sales@harveys.ltd.uk
Web Site: www.harveys.ltd.uk
Telex: 727985
Key Personnel
Chairman: Tom Domke *E-mail:* tom@harveys.ltd.uk
Joint Man Dir: Tom Dalgleish *E-mail:* tom.dalgleish@harveys.ltd.uk; Peter McCraw *E-mail:* peter@harveys.ltd.uk
Sales Dir: Ross Porter *E-mail:* ross@harveys.ltd.uk
Dir Customer Service: Craig Linton *E-mail:* craig@harveys.ltd.uk
Founded: 1856
Print Runs: 100 min - 250,000 max
Business from Other Countries: 10%

Headley Brothers Ltd
Invicta Press, Queens Rd, Ashford, Kent TN24 8HH
Tel: (01233) 623131 *Fax:* (01233) 612345
E-mail: printing@headley.co.uk
Web Site: www.headley.co.uk
Key Personnel
Sales Manager: Bruce Finn *E-mail:* bruce.finn@headley.co.uk
Commercial Dir: Jon Pitt *E-mail:* jon.pitt@headley.co.uk
Man Dir: Roger Pitt *E-mail:* roger.pitt@headley.co.uk
Editor: Richard Rice
Founded: 1881
Print Runs: 1,000 min - 200,000 max
Business from Other Countries: 5%

Hobbs The Printers Ltd
Brunel Rd, Totton, Hants SO40 3WX
Tel: (023) 8066 4800 *Fax:* (023) 8066 4801
E-mail: info@hobbs.uk.com
Web Site: www.hobbs.uk.com
Key Personnel
Man Dir: David Hobbs *E-mail:* d.a.hobbs@hobbs.uk.com
Commercial Dir: Terry Ozanne *E-mail:* t.ozanne@hobbs.uk.com
Founded: 1884
Turnaround: 5-10 days litho; up to 5 days digital
Print Runs: 10 min - 50,000 max
Business from Other Countries: 4%

Hunter & Foulis Ltd
Unit 3, Gateside Commerce Park, Haddington, East Lothian EH441 3ST
Tel: (01620) 826379 *Fax:* (01620) 829485
E-mail: mail@hunterfoulis.co.uk
Web Site: www.hunterfoulis.co.uk
Key Personnel
Man Dir: Richard Beese
Founded: 1857

Ikon Document Management Services
Subsidiary of Microgen Holdings Plc
19 The Business Centre, Molly Millars Lane, Wokingham, Berks RG41 2QY
Tel: (0118) 9770510 *Fax:* (0118) 9770513
Web Site: www.ikon.com
Key Personnel
Chief Executive Officer: Matthew J Espe
Vice President: Kathleen Burns
Founded: 1972
Turnaround: 2-5 Workdays
Print Runs: 1 min - 5,000 max
Business from Other Countries: 40%
Branch Office(s)
Microgen City Park Watchmead, Welwyn Garden City, Herts AL7 1LT

Image & Print Group Ltd
Unit 9, Oakbank Industrial Estate, Glasgow G20 7LU
Tel: (0141) 353 1900; (0141) 353 8620 (ISDN) *Fax:* (0141) 353 8611
E-mail: info@imageandprint.co.uk
Web Site: www.imageandprint.co.uk
Key Personnel
Man Dir: Ken Roberts
Production: Stephen McPhee *E-mail:* stephen@imageandprint.co.uk
Founded: 1975
Turnaround: 5 Workdays
Print Runs: 1,000 min - 250,000 max

Intype Libra Ltd
Units 3 & 4, Elm Grove Industrial Estate, Elm Grove, Wimbledon SW19 4HE
Tel: (020) 8947 7863 *Fax:* (020) 8947 3652
E-mail: intype@btconnect.com
Key Personnel
Man Dir: Tony Chapman *E-mail:* tony.chapman@intypelibra.co.uk
Production: Richard Mayne
Dir: Alan Johnson
Founded: 1976
Turnaround: 10-15 Workdays for proofs; 5-10 Workdays for books
Print Runs: 25 min - 1,000 max
Business from Other Countries: 5%

The Lavenham Press Ltd
Affiliate of Terence Dalton Ltd
47 Water St, Lavenham, Suffolk CO10 9RN
Tel: (01787) 247436; (01787) 248267 (ISDN) *Fax:* (01787) 248267
E-mail: lpl@lavenhamgroup.co.uk
Web Site: www.lavenhampress.co.uk
Key Personnel
Man Dir: Terence Dalton *E-mail:* terence@lavenhamgroup.co.uk
Founded: 1953
Business from Other Countries: 1%
Parent Company: The Lavenham Group PLC

Charles Letts & Co Ltd
Thorneybank Industrial Estate, Dalkeith, Midlothian EH22 2NE
Tel: (0131) 663 1971 *Fax:* (0131) 660 3225
E-mail: diaries@letts.co.uk
Web Site: www.letts.co.uk
Key Personnel
Man Dir: Gordon Presly
Founded: 1796

Lowfield Printing Co Ltd
9 Kennet Rd, Thames Rd, Dartford, Kent DA1 4QT
Tel: (01322) 522216
E-mail: lowfield@compuserve.com
Web Site: www.applegate.com
Key Personnel
Sales Manager: James Dow
Founded: 1964
Print Runs: 500 min - 20,000 max

MacKays of Chatham PLC
Badger Rd, Lordswood, Chatham, Kent ME5 8TD
Tel: (01634) 864 381 *Fax:* (01634) 867 742
E-mail: mackays@cpi-group.co.uk
Web Site: www.cpi-group.net
Key Personnel
Sales Dir: Paul Hicks

& BOOK FINISHING UNITED KINGDOM

The Malvern Press Ltd
71 Dalston Lane, London E8 2NG
Tel: (020) 7249 2991 *Fax:* (020) 7254 1720
E-mail: admin@malvernpress.com
Web Site: www.malvernpress.com
Key Personnel
Man Dir: Leslie Wynn
Marketing Dir: Peter Wynn
Founded: 1953
Turnaround: 10-15 Workdays
Print Runs: 100 min
Business from Other Countries: 15%

MPG Books Ltd
Division of MPG Ltd
Victoria Sq, Bodmin, Cornwall PL31 1EB
Tel: (01208) 73266 *Fax:* (01208) 76515
E-mail: print@mpg-books.co.uk
Web Site: www.mpg-books.com
Key Personnel
Man Dir: Tony Chard
Deputy Managing Dir: Jeff Swift *Tel:* (01869) 324 992 *Fax:* (01869) 324 992 *E-mail:* jswift@mpg-books.co.uk
Sales Executive: Roy Skinner *Tel:* (01843) 231 029 *E-mail:* rskinner@mpg-books.co.uk
Sales & Marketing Development Manager: Colin Porter *Tel:* (0117) 968 8838 *Fax:* (0117) 968 8838 *E-mail:* cporter@mpg-books.co.uk
Founded: 1967
Turnaround: 10-15 days
Print Runs: 400 min - 10,000 max
Business from Other Countries: 5%
Ultimate Parent Company: Martins Printing Group

MPG Ltd
Division of Martins Printing Group
The Gresham Press, Old Woking, Surrey GU22 9LH
Tel: (01483) 757501 *Fax:* (01483) 724629
E-mail: print@mpgltd.co.uk
Web Site: www.mpgltd.co.uk
Key Personnel
Chairman: Sir Clive Martin
Chief Executive: Mike Milton
Founded: 1945
Turnaround: 5 Workdays
Print Runs: 3,000 min - 75,000 max
Divisions: MPG Books Ltd; Unwin Brothers Ltd
Branch Office(s)
Woking
Rochester
St Albans
Wimbledon
Bodmin
Peterborough

Multiplex Medway Ltd
Lordswood Industrial Estate, Gleaming Wood Dr, Walderslade, Kent ME5 8XT
Tel: (01634) 684371; (01634) 671687 (ISDN) *Fax:* (01634) 683840
E-mail: enquiries@multiplex-medway.co.uk
Web Site: www.multiplex-medway.co.uk
Key Personnel
Dir: Jon Chandler
Sales Manager: Paul Abson

George Over Ltd
20 Somers Rd, Rugby, Warwicks CV22 7DH
Tel: (01788) 573621 *Fax:* (01788) 578738
E-mail: xuz23@dial.pinex.com
Key Personnel
Man Dir: A E H Gilbert
Sales Dir: Richard Gilbert

Page Bros Ltd (Norwich)
Subsidiary of Milex Ltd
Mile Cross Lane, Norwich NR6 6SA
Tel: (01603) 429141 *Fax:* (01603) 485126

Key Personnel
Sales Dir: Steve Commons
Founded: 1750
Turnaround: 10 Workdays
Print Runs: 100 min - 30,000 max
Business from Other Countries: 20%
Branch Office(s)
105-A Euston St, London NW1 2ET *Tel:* (020) 7383 2212 *Fax:* (020) 7383 4145

Peak Technologies UK Ltd
Silwood Park, Buckhurst Rd, Ascot, Berks SL5 7PW
Tel: (01344) 290000 *Fax:* (01344) 290001
E-mail: info@peakeurope.com
Web Site: www.peakeurope.com/uk
Key Personnel
Man Dir: Paul O'Donnell
Parent Company: Moore Corp Ltd

Printafoil Ltd
85 Mitcham Industrial Estate, Streatham Rd, Mitcham, Surrey CR4 2AP
Tel: (0181) 6403074 *Fax:* (020) 8640 2136
Key Personnel
Dir: Simon Flower

Redwood Books Ltd
Division of CPI (UK) Ltd
Kennet Way, Trowbridge, Wilts BA14 8RN
Tel: (01225) 769979 *Fax:* (01225) 769050
E-mail: enquiries@redwood-books.co.uk
Key Personnel
General Manager: Trevor Gee
Commercial Manager: Tony Warner
 E-mail: tony@redwood-books.co.uk
Production Manager: Peter Grant
Founded: 1993
Turnaround: 10 Workdays
Print Runs: 10 min - 20,000 max
Business from Other Countries: 8%
Branch Office(s)
London Sales Office, 22 Bloomsbury Sq, London WC1A 2NS *Tel:* (020) 7580-9328 *Fax:* (020) 7580-9337

J R Reid Print & Media Group, see J R Reid Printing Group Ltd

J R Reid Printing Group Ltd
79-99 Glasgow Rd, Blantyre, Glasgow G72 0YL
Tel: (01698) 826000 *Fax:* (01698) 824944
E-mail: clindsay@reid-print-group.co.uk
Web Site: www.reid-print-group.co.uk
Key Personnel
Joint Man Dir: Ian Johnstone; John R Reid
 E-mail: johnreid@reid-print-group.co.uk
Founded: 1972
Business from Other Countries: 1%

Antony Rowe Ltd
Bumper's Farm Industrial Estate, Chippenham, Wilts SN14 6LH
Tel: (01249) 659 705 *Fax:* (01249) 448 900
E-mail: sales@antonyrowe.co.uk
Web Site: www.antonyrowe.co.uk
Key Personnel
Chief Executive: Ralph Bell
Production Dir: Mike Bando
Technical Dir: Andy Burns
Founded: 1983
Turnaround: 20 Workdays
Print Runs: 50 min - 2,000 max
Business from Other Countries: 2%

Selwood Printing
Subsidiary of Lloyd's Register of Shipping
Edward Way, Burgess Hill, West Sussex RH15 9UA
Tel: (01444) 236060 *Fax:* (01444) 245043

E-mail: sales@selwood.com
Key Personnel
Man Dir: Andrew Lowden

Severnside Printers Ltd
Bridge House, Upton-on-Severn, Worcs WR8 0HG
Tel: (01684) 594521 *Fax:* (01684) 594344
Key Personnel
President & Chief Executive: Norman H Beechey
Turnaround: 14-20 Workdays
Print Runs: 500 min - 5,000 max
Business from Other Countries: 10%

Stott Brothers Ltd
Lister Lane, Halifax, W Yorks HX1 5AJ
Tel: (01422) 362184 *Fax:* (01422) 353707
E-mail: stottbros@aol.com
Key Personnel
Man Dir: Ian Bullough

M & A Thomson Litho Ltd
Kelvin Industrial Estate, 2-16 Colvilles Pl, East Kilbride, Glasgow G75 0SN
Tel: (01355) 233081 *Fax:* (01355) 245 039
Web Site: www.thomsonlitho.com
Key Personnel
Deputy Chairman: Gary Thomson
Contact: Ken Thomson
Environment Quality Dir: Angela Hart
 E-mail: ahart@tlitho.co.uk

TJ International Ltd
Subsidiary of Ulverscroft Large Print Books
Trecerus Industrial Estate, Padstow, Cornwall PL28 8RW
Tel: (01841) 532691 *Fax:* (01841) 532862
E-mail: sales@tjinternational.ltd.uk
Web Site: www.tjinternational.ltd.uk
Key Personnel
Chief Executive Officer: Angus Clark
 E-mail: angus@tjinternational.ltd.uk
Founded: 1970
Turnaround: 15 Workdays
Business from Other Countries: 5%

Watkiss Automation Ltd
Subsidiary of The Watkiss Group
Watkiss House, Blaydon Rd, Middlefield Industrial Estate, Sandy, Beds SG19 1RZ
Tel: (01767) 682177 *Fax:* (01767) 691769
E-mail: contact@watkiss.com
Web Site: www.watkiss.com
Key Personnel
Technical Dir: M Watkiss
Founded: 1959
Print Runs: 200 min - 10,000 max
Business from Other Countries: 5%

WH Trade Binders Ltd
Units 1-4, South March, Long March Idustrial Estate, Daventry, Northants NN11 4PH
Tel: (01327) 704911 *Fax:* (01327) 872588
E-mail: wh@whtradebinders.demon.co.uk
Key Personnel
Man Dir: Roger Westrop
Financial Manager: Adrian Johnson
 E-mail: adrian@whtradebinders.demon.co.uk
Founded: 1981
Print Runs: 10,000 min
Business from Other Countries: 1%

The Wolsey Press
The Drift, Nacton Rd, Ipswich, Suffolk IP3 9QR
Tel: (01473) 719377; (01473) 272616 (ISDN) *Fax:* (01473) 272115
E-mail: studio@wolseypress.co.uk
Web Site: www.wolseypress.co.uk
Key Personnel
Dir: John Robinson; Colin Jennings

United States

ADR/BookPrint Inc
2012 Northern Ave E, Wichita, KS 67216
Tel: 316-522-5599 *Toll Free Tel:* 800-767-6066
Fax: 316-522-5445
E-mail: info@adrbookprint.com
Web Site: www.adrbookprint.com
Key Personnel
Pres: James E Rishel; Grace M Rishel
   E-mail: grace@adrbookprint.com
Prodn Mgr: Marc Seiwert
Founded: 1978
Print Runs: 250 min - 5,000 max
Business from Other Countries: 10%
Membership(s): Printing Industries of America

Asia Pacific Offset Inc
1332 Corcoran St NW, Suite 6, Washington, DC 20009
Tel: 202-462-5436 *Toll Free Tel:* 800-756-4344
Fax: 202-986-4030
Web Site: www.asiapacificoffset.com
Key Personnel
Pres: Andrew Clarke *E-mail:* andrew@asiapacificoffset.com
Dir, Sales (NY Office): Timothy Linn
   Tel: 212-941-8300 *Fax:* 212-941-9810
   E-mail: timothy@asiapacificoffset.com
Founded: 1997
Turnaround: 105 Workdays including color separation & shipping
Print Runs: 2,000 min
Business from Other Countries: 100%
Branch Office(s)
Phoenix Offset, Unit F1-2 2nd fl, Yeung Yiu Chung No 8 Industrial Bldg, 20 Wang Hoi Rd, Kowloon Bay, Hong Kong, Contact: Edmond Chan *Tel:* 852-2751-9962 *Fax:* 852-2755-8408 *E-mail:* Phoffset@netvigator.com
Sales Office(s): 870 Market St, Suite 801, San Francisco, CA 94102, Dir, Sales: Amy Armstrong *Tel:* 415-433-3488 *Fax:* 415-433-3489 *E-mail:* Amy@asiapacificoffset.com
270 Lafayette St, Suite 502, New York, NY 10012, Dir, Sales: Timothy Linn *Tel:* 212-941-8300 *Fax:* 212-941-9810 *E-mail:* Timothy@asiapacificoffset.com

Bind-It Corp
150 Commerce Dr, Hauppauge, NY 11788
Tel: 631-234-2500 *Toll Free Tel:* 800-645-5110
Web Site: www.bindit.com
Key Personnel
Contact: Matt Caleca *E-mail:* m.caleca@bindit.com
Founded: 1973
Turnaround: 14 Workdays
Business from Other Countries: 20%
Branch Office(s)
5601 W Slauson Ave, Suite 101, Los Angeles, CA 90230, Contact: Theresa LaVerne *Tel:* 310-342-6767 *Fax:* 310-342-6760 *E-mail:* t.scheer@bindit.com
760 Market St, Suite 337, San Francisco, CA 94104, Contact: Mike Rose *Tel:* 415-981-9392 *Fax:* 415-981-0321 *E-mail:* m.rose@bindit.com
275 Carpenter Dr, Atlanta, GA 30328, Contact: Jeff Driscoll *Tel:* 404-851-9720 *Fax:* 404-851-9722 *E-mail:* jeffstern@bindit.com
1820 Ridge Rd, Suite 205, Homewood, IL 60430, Br Mgr: Leo Corrigan *Tel:* 708-798-6600 *Fax:* 708-798-3502 *E-mail:* l.corrigan@bindit.com
165 "M" New Boston St, Suite 248, Woburn, MA 01801, Contact: Jeff Stern *Tel:* 781-938-9296 *Fax:* 781-938-9310 *E-mail:* jeffstern@bindit.com
9 Gaylord Lane, Marlton, NJ 08053, Br Mgr: Mark O'Dea *Tel:* 856-983-1010 *Fax:* 856-983-0986 *E-mail:* m.odea@bindit.com
7 Penn Plaza, 4th fl, New York, NY 10001, Contact: Jeff Stern *Tel:* 212-629-6500 *Fax:* 212-629-5043 *E-mail:* jeffstern@bindit.com

Blaze International Productions Inc
225 W 35 St, Suite 1100, New York, NY 10001
Tel: 212-967-7501 *Fax:* 212-967-7551
Key Personnel
Pres: Eugene Sanchez *Tel:* 212-967-7501 ext 222
   E-mail: e.sanchez@blazeint.com
Founded: 1990
Turnaround: 10-15 Workdays
Print Runs: 500 min - 1,000,000 max
Business from Other Countries: 80%
Membership(s): Bookbinders Guild of New York

BookBuilders New York Inc
353 Strawtown Rd, New City, NY 10956
Tel: 845-639-5316 *Fax:* 845-639-5318
E-mail: mcanewcity@aol.com
Web Site: www.mcabooks.com
Key Personnel
Pres: Martin Cook *E-mail:* martin@mcabooks.com
Founded: 1977
Turnaround: 30-45 Workdays
Print Runs: 2,000 min - 500,000 max
Business from Other Countries: 60%

Butler & Tanner Inc
1776 Broadway, Suite 1710, New York, NY 10019
Tel: 212-262-4753 *Fax:* 212-262-4779
E-mail: sales@nyc.butlerandtanner.com
Web Site: www.butlerandtanner.com
Key Personnel
Dir, US Sales: Jeremy Snell
Founded: 1850
Turnaround: 10 days
Print Runs: 1,000 min - 200,000 max
Business from Other Countries: 10%
Parent Company: Butler & Tanner Ltd (UK)

C & C Offset Printing Co Ltd
Subsidiary of C & C Joint Printing Co (HK) Ltd under Sino United Publishing (Holdings) Ltd
2632 SE 25 Ave, Suite E, Portland, OR 97202
Mailing Address: PO Box 82037, Portland, OR 97282-0037
Tel: 503-233-1834 *Fax:* 503-233-7815
E-mail: portlandinfo@ccoffset.com
Web Site: www.ccoffset.com
Key Personnel
Dir & Gen Mgr, Hong Kong Head Off: Jackson Leung
Deputy Man Dir, Hong Kong Head Office: Ken Lee
Deputy Gen Mgr, Hong Kong Head Office: Ivy Lam
Sr Sales Mgr, Hong Kong Head Office: Francis Ho
Dir, C & C Offset Printing Co (USA) Inc, Portland, OR, USA: Charles H Clark, IV
   E-mail: cclark@ccoffset.com
Devt Mgr, C & C Offset Printing Co (USA) Inc, Portland, OR, USA: Jenny Whittier
   E-mail: jwhittier@ccoffset.com
Cust Serv Mgr, C & C Offset Printing Co (USA) Inc, Portland, OR, USA: Ernest Li
   E-mail: ernestli@ccoffset.com
Dir & Exec VP, C & C Offset Printing Co (NYC) Inc, New York, NY, USA: Simon Chan
   E-mail: schan@ccoffset.com
Cust Serv Mgr, C & C Offset Printing Co (NYC) Inc, New York, NY, USA: Frances Harkness
   E-mail: fharkness@ccoffset.com
Pres, C & C Offset Japan Printing Co Ltd, Tokyo, Japan: Yamamoto Masaaki
Man Dir, C & C Joint Printing Co (Beijing) Ltd, Beijing, China: Zhang Lin Gui
Dir, C & C Offset Printing Co (UK) Ltd: Tracy Broderick
Acct Mgr, C & C Offset Printing Co (UK) Ltd: Fia Fornari
Founded: 1980
Turnaround: varies
Print Runs: 2,000 min - 1,000,000 max
Business from Other Countries: 60%
Branch Office(s)
C & C Joint Printing Co (Beijing) Ltd, Beijing Economic & Technological Developent Area (BDA), No 3, Donghuan North Rd, Beijing 100176, China, Dir & Gen Mgr: Mr Zhang Lin Gui *Tel:* (10) 6787 6655 *Fax:* (10) 6787 8255 *E-mail:* ccbj@candcprinting.com
C & C Joint Printing Co (Guangdong) Ltd, Intercontinental Bldg, Rm 706, 16 An Wai An De Rd, DongCheng District, Beijing 100011, China, Contact: Mr Xiao Mung-shen *Tel:* (10) 6650 3176 *Fax:* (10) 6650 3175 *E-mail:* beijing@cancprinting.com *Web Site:* www.candcprinting.com (regional office)
C & C Joint Printing Co (Guangdong) Ltd, Hua Xin Bldg E Block, Rm 1511, 2 Shuiyin Rd, Huanshi East, Guangzhou 510075, China, Contact: Mr Peng Ji Shan *Tel:* (20) 3760 0979; (20) 3760 0980 *Fax:* (20) 3760 0977 *E-mail:* guangzhou@candcprinting.com *Web Site:* www.candcprinting.com (regional office)
C & C Joint Printing Co (Guangdong) Ltd (Changsha Office), The Building of Changsha City, Commercial Bank, No 1, Frong Middle Rd, Rm 1218, Changsha, Hunan 41005, China, Contact: Ms Chen Jian *Tel:* (731) 225 0288 *Fax:* (731) 225 0178 *E-mail:* changsha@candcprinting.com *Web Site:* www.candcprinting.com (regional office)
C & C Joint Printing (Guangdong) Ltd, Fang Fa Bldg, No 29 Land, 169 Dongzhu Anbin Rd, Shanghai 200050, China, Contact: Ms Wu Xiaohung *Tel:* (21) 6240 1305 *Fax:* (21) 6240 2090 *E-mail:* shanghai@candcprinting.com *Web Site:* www.candcprinting.com (regional office)
C & C Joint Printing Co (Guangdong) Ltd, Chunhu Industrial Estate, Pinghu, Long Gang, Shenzhen 518111, China *Tel:* (755) 845 8333 *Fax:* (755) 845 9111 *E-mail:* guangdong@candcprinting.com *Web Site:* www.candcprinting.com (plant)
C & C Joint Printing Co (Guangdong) Ltd (Xian Office), 10 Xuanfengquiao, Jianguo Rd, Xian 710001, China *Tel:* (29) 741 8407 *Fax:* (29) 743 5730 *E-mail:* xian@candcprinting.co (regional office)
C & C Printing Japan Co Ltd, Tozaido Bldg, 3F, 2-6-12 Hitotsubashi, Chiyoda-ku, Tokyo 101-0003, Japan, Contact: Mr Yamamoto Masaaki *Tel:* (3) 5216 4580 *Fax:* (3) 5216 4610 *E-mail:* mail@candcprinting.co.jp (regional office)
C & C Offset Printing Co (UK) Ltd, 2 New Burlington St, 4th fl, London W1S 2JE, United Kingdom *Tel:* (020) 7287-7787 *Fax:* (020) 7287-7187 *E-mail:* tracy@candcoffset.co.uk

Carvajal International Inc
Division of Carvajal Inversiones
Subsidiary of Carvajal S A
901 Ponce de Leon Blvd, 6th fl, Suite 601, Coral Gables, FL 33134
Tel: 305-448-6875 *Toll Free Tel:* 800-622-6657
Fax: 305-448-9942
E-mail: info@cargraphics.com
Web Site: www.carvajal.com.co
Key Personnel
Gen Mgr: David Ashe
Founded: 1904
Print Runs: 3,000 min - 250,000 max

Business from Other Countries: 30%
Branch Office(s)
Carvajal S A, Calle 29 N 1, 6A-40 Cali, Colombia, Alvaro Lopez Tel: 572-661-8150

Colorprint Offset Inc
Division of Colorprint Offset (Hong Kong)
80 Park Ave, Suite 10N, New York, NY 10016
Tel: 212-681-9400 *Fax:* 212-681-9362
E-mail: info@colorprintoffset.com
Key Personnel
Pres: Lee Moncho E-mail: lee@colorprintoffset.com
Prod Dir & Cust Serv Mgr: Kate Brady
 E-mail: kate@colorprintoffset.com
Founded: 1986
Turnaround: 15 Workdays
Print Runs: 100 min - 50,000 max
Business from Other Countries: 65%

Coneco Litho Graphics
Division of NET 2 PRESS Inc
58 Dix Ave, Glens Falls, NY 12801
Mailing Address: PO Box 3255, Glen Falls, NY 12801-7255
Tel: 518-793-3823 *Fax:* 518-793-5823
E-mail: support@conecolithographics.com
Web Site: www.conecolithographics.com
Key Personnel
Gen Mgr: Steve Webber E-mail: swebber@conecolithographics.com
Client Servs Mgr: George Moses
 E-mail: gmoses@conecolithographics.com
Founded: 1984
Turnaround: 15 Workdays
Print Runs: 250 min - 25,000 max
Business from Other Countries: 27%

Consolidated Printers Inc
2630 Eighth St, Berkeley, CA 94710
Tel: 510-843-8524 *Fax:* 510-486-0580
E-mail: cpi@consoprinters.com
Web Site: www.consoprinters.com
Key Personnel
CEO: Lawrence A Hawkins
Founded: 1952
Turnaround: 2-20 Workdays
Print Runs: 2,000 min
Business from Other Countries: 15%

Martin Cook Associates Ltd
353 Strawtown Rd, New City, NY 10956
Tel: 845-639-5316 *Fax:* 845-639-5318
E-mail: mcanewcity@aol.com
Web Site: www.mcabooks.com
Key Personnel
Pres: Martin Cook
Founded: 1977
Turnaround: 30-45 Workdays
Print Runs: 2,000 min - 500,000 max
Business from Other Countries: 15%
Membership(s): Bookbinders Guild of New York

CS Graphics USA Inc
Subsidiary of CS Graphics Pte Ltd Singapore
8969 Lake Ct, Granite Bay, CA 95746
Tel: 916-791-9066 *Fax:* 916-791-9112
Key Personnel
Mgr, Sales & Mktg: Rick Marment E-mail: r.marment@csgraphics-world.com
Founded: 1980
Turnaround: 80 Workdays
Print Runs: 1,000 min - 75,000 max
Business from Other Countries: 30%

D & K Group
1795 Commerce Dr, Elk Grove Village, IL 60007
Tel: 847-956-0160 *Toll Free Tel:* 800-632-2314
 Fax: 847-956-8214
E-mail: info@dkgroup.net
Web Site: www.dkgroup.com

Key Personnel
Pres: Karl Singer
VP, Sales & Mktg: Marge Hayes
Mktg Communs Coord: Holli Hagene
 E-mail: holli.hagene@dkgroup.net
Founded: 1979
Business from Other Countries: 15%

Dix
200-B Gateway Park Dr, North Syracuse, NY 13212
Tel: 315-478-4700 *Fax:* 315-703-0119
Web Site: www.dixtype.com
Key Personnel
Pres: Scott Wenger E-mail: swenger@dixtype.com
Acct Exec, Sales & Mktg: Kelly Farley
 E-mail: kfarley@dixtype.com
Founded: 1923
Turnaround: 2-10 Workdays
Business from Other Countries: 30%

DNP America LLC
Subsidiary of Dai Nippon Printing Co Ltd
335 Madison Ave, 3rd fl, New York, NY 10017
Tel: 212-503-1074 *Fax:* 212-286-1505
Web Site: www.dnp.co.jp/ *Cable:* DAIPRINTS NY
Key Personnel
Pres: Yoji Yamakawa
VP & Gen Mgr, Graphic Printing: Kohei Tsumori
 E-mail: tsumori-k@mail.dnp.co.jp
Founded: 1974
Turnaround: 30-60 Workdays
Business from Other Countries: 54%

Elegance Printing & Book Binding (USA)
Member of The Elegance Printing Group
708 Glen Cove Ave, Glen Head, NY 11545
Tel: 516-676-5941 *Fax:* 516-676-5973
Web Site: www.elegancebooks.com
Key Personnel
Man Dir: Frank DeLuca E-mail: frank@elegancebooks.com
Founded: 1977
Turnaround: 3-4 weeks for CTP projects. Reprints ship within 14 days
Print Runs: 1,000 min - 1,000,000 max
Business from Other Countries: 40%

EP Graphics
169 S Jefferson St, Berne, IN 46711
Tel: 260-589-2145 *Toll Free Tel:* 877-589-2145
 Fax: 260-589-2810
Web Site: www.epgraphics.com
Key Personnel
Pres: Thomas Muselman
Founded: 1925
Turnaround: 15 Workdays
Print Runs: 25,000 min - 500,000 max
Business from Other Countries: 80%

Express Media Corp
1419 Donelson Pike, Nashville, TN 37217
Tel: 615-360-6400 *Fax:* 615-360-3140
E-mail: info@expressmedia.com
Web Site: www.expressmedia.com
Key Personnel
Pres: Andrew Cameron
Founded: 1996
Turnaround: 3 Workdays
Print Runs: 1 min - 10,000 max
Business from Other Countries: 10%

Fairfield Marketing Group Inc
Subsidiary of FMG Inc
830 Sport Hill Rd, Easton, CT 06612-1250
Tel: 203-261-5585; 203-261-5568 *Fax:* 203-261-0884
E-mail: ffldmktgrp@aol.com
Web Site: www.fairfieldmarketing.com

Key Personnel
CEO & Pres: Edward P Washchilla E-mail: fmg.inc@aol.com
VP, Fin: Pamela L Johnson
VP, Fulfillment: Jason Paul Miller Tel: 203-261-5585 ext 203
Cust Servs Rep: Mike Lozada Tel: 203-261-5585 ext 204
Founded: 1987
Turnaround: 1-7 Workdays
Print Runs: 2,500 min - 10,000,000 max
Business from Other Countries: 10%
Membership(s): ABA; Association of Educational Publishers; DMA; Direct Marketing Club of New York (DMCNY); DMA; Hudson Valley Direct Marketing Association; International Reading Association; National School Supply & Equipment Association; United States Chamber of Congress

Hamilton Printing Co
22 Hamilton Way, Castleton-on-Hudson, NY 12033
Tel: 518-732-4491 *Toll Free Tel:* 800-242-4222
 Fax: 518-732-7714
Key Personnel
Pres: Brian F Payne
VP, Fin: Michael H Hart
VP, Mfg: Rick Dunn
Prod Mgr: Judy Rappold
Sales Rep: Stephen H Feuer; Scott Payne; Larry Ritchie; Michael C Rosenhack E-mail: miker@hpcbook.com
Founded: 1912
Turnaround: Flexible, time sensitive scheduling
Business from Other Countries: 10%
Membership(s): BMI

Hindy's Enterprise
Division of Jinno International
3 Christine Dr, Chestnut Ridge, NY 10977-6802
Tel: 845-735-4666 *Fax:* 617-344-5905
Key Personnel
Pres: Yoh Jinno E-mail: jinno@hotmail.com
Founded: 1989
Turnaround: 40 Workdays
Print Runs: 500 min - 2,000,000 max
Business from Other Countries: 70%
Branch Office(s)
Melbourne Industrial Bldg, Block A, 20th fl, 16 Westlands Rd, Quarry Bay, Hong Kong
 Tel: 25166318 Fax: 25165161

IBT Global Ltd, see Integrated Book Technology Inc

Ikon Document Services
Division of Ikon Office Solutions
399 River Rd, Hudson, MA 01749-2627
Tel: 978-562-9131 *Fax:* 978-562-4304
Web Site: www.ikon.com
Key Personnel
Sales Mgr: Jim Figler E-mail: jfigler@ikon.com
Founded: 1973
Turnaround: 3 Workdays
Print Runs: 5 min - 5,000 max
Business from Other Countries: 10%

Imago
1431 Broadway, Penthouse, New York, NY 10018
Tel: 212-921-4411 *Fax:* 212-921-8226
E-mail: sales@imagousa.com
Web Site: www.imagousa.com
Key Personnel
Pres: Joseph E Braff E-mail: jbraff@imagousa.com
Northeast Sales: Linda Readerman
 E-mail: lreaderman@imagousa.com
USA Prodn Dir: Howard R Musk
 E-mail: hmusk@imagousa.com
Founded: 1985

UNITED STATES

Turnaround: 14 Workdays for color separations; 6 Weeks for printing & binding
Print Runs: 5,000 min
Business from Other Countries: 100%
Branch Office(s)
Imago West Coast, 31952 Camino Capistrano, Suite C22, San Juan Capistrano, CA 92675, West Coast Sales: Greg Lee *Tel:* 949-661-5998 *Fax:* 949-661-8013 *E-mail:* glee@imagousa.com
Imago Midwest, 17 N Loomis St, Unit 4A, Chicago, IL 60607, Midwest Sales: Ma Yan *Tel:* 312-829-4051 *Fax:* 312-829-4059 *E-mail:* myan@imagousa.com
Imago Australia, 14 Brown St, Suite 241, Chatswood, Sydney 2067, Australia, Contact: Emma Bell *Tel:* (02) 9415 2713 *Fax:* (02) 9415 2714 *E-mail:* sales@imagoaus.com
Imago France, 6 eme Etage, 42, rue le Peletier, 75009 Paris, France, Contact: Matt Critchlow *Tel:* (1) 42 81 41 24 *Fax:* (1) 42 81 41 24 *E-mail:* sales@imagogroup.com
Imago Services (HKG) Ltd, 653-659 Kings Rd, 6th fl, Flat B, North Point, Hong Kong, Contact: Kendrick Cheung *Tel:* 2811 3316 *Fax:* 2597 5256 *E-mail:* enquiries@imago.com.hk
Imago Productions (FE) Pte Ltd, MacPherson Industrial Complex, Suite 05-01, 5 Lorong Bakar Batu, Singapore 348742, Singapore, Contact: K C Ng *Tel:* 6748 4433 *Fax:* 6748 6082 *E-mail:* enquiries@imago.com.sg
Imago (UK/Europe) Publishing Ltd, Albury Ct, Albury Thame, Oxfordshire OX9 2LP, United Kingdom, Contact: Colin Risk *Tel:* (01844) 337000 *Fax:* (01844) 339935 *E-mail:* sales@imago.co.uk *Web Site:* www.imago.co.uk

Integrated Book Technology Inc
Division of The IBT Group
18 Industrial Park Rd, Troy, NY 12180
Tel: 518-271-5117 *Fax:* 518-266-9422
E-mail: mail@integratedbook.com
Web Site: www.integratedbook.com
Key Personnel
CEO & Pres: John R Paeglow *E-mail:* johnp@integratedbook.com
VP & Chief Technol Officer: William Clockel *E-mail:* billc@integratedbook.com
VP, Sales & Mktg: Robert Lindberg *E-mail:* bobl@integratedbook.com
Dir, Sales & Cust Serv: Karen Lombardo
Dir, Info Technol: Michael Whalen *E-mail:* mikew@integratedbook.com
Regl Sales: Tim Knickerbocker *E-mail:* timk@integratedbook.com
Founded: 1991
Turnaround: 1-15 Workdays
Print Runs: 10 min - 2,000 max
Business from Other Countries: 20%
Branch Office(s)
The IBT Global Ltd, 2 Finsbury Park Rd, London N4-2JZ, United Kingdom, Intl Strategist: Peter Kenyon *Tel:* (020) 7354 3332 *Fax:* (020) 7354 3332 *E-mail:* peterk@integratedbook.com
Membership(s): BMI

Jinno International Group
3 Christine Dr, Chestnut Ridge, NY 10977-6802
Tel: 845-735-4666 *Fax:* 617-344-5905
E-mail: jinno@hotmail.com
Key Personnel
Pres: Yoh Jinno
VP: Sharon Jinno
Founded: 1989
Turnaround: 21-30 Workdays US, 45-75 Workdays overseas
Print Runs: 500 min - 3,000,000 max
Business from Other Countries: 98%
Branch Office(s)
Hindy's Enterprise, Melbourne Industrial Bldg, 16 Westlands Rd, Block A, 20th fl, Quarry Bay, Hong Kong *Tel:* 516-6318 *Fax:* 516-5161

Wing Yiu Printing Co, Melbourne Industrial Bldg, 6th fl, Block A, 16 Westlands Rd, Quarry Bay, Hong Kong, Contact: Law Ming Wah *Tel:* 561 0283 *Fax:* 565 8233
Jinno International Singapore, 710 Ang Mo Kio, Ave 8, Suite 07-2615, Singapore 2056, Singapore *Tel:* 458 0778

KNI Inc
1261 S State College Pkwy, Anaheim, CA 92806
Tel: 714-956-7300 *Toll Free Tel:* 800-886-7301 *Fax:* 714-635-1744
E-mail: kni@kniinc.com
Web Site: www.kniinc.com
Key Personnel
Pres: Jeremy R Bernstein
VP, Admin: Judith Bernstein
VP, Sales: Peggy Bryant
VP & Cont: Dan Jacintho
Founded: 1970
Print Runs: 50 min - 100,000 max
Business from Other Countries: 17%

Leo Paper USA
1180 NW Maple St, Suite 102, Issaquah, WA 98027
Tel: 425-646-8801 *Fax:* 425-646-8805
E-mail: leo@leousa.com
Web Site: www.leousa.com
Key Personnel
VP: Peter R Gillies *E-mail:* peter@leousa.com
Sales: Tom Leach *E-mail:* tom@leousa.com; Greg Witt *E-mail:* greg@leousa.com
Founded: 1983
Turnaround: 90 Workdays
Print Runs: 3,500 min - 2,000,000 max
Business from Other Countries: 20%
Branch Office(s)
Leo Paper Products Ltd, 7/F Kader Bldg, 22 Kai Cheung Rd, Kowloon Bay, Hong Kong, Man Dir: Johnny Fung *Tel:* 2884-1374 *Fax:* 2885-3520 *E-mail:* lpp@leo.com.hk *Web Site:* www.leo.com.hk
Leo Paper USA, 27 W 24 St, Suite 701, New York, NY 10010, Contact: Janine Laborne *Tel:* 917-305-0708 *Fax:* 917-305-3709 *E-mail:* leo@leousa.com
Sales Office(s): Leo Paper Products (Europe) BVBA, De Wilde Zee Wiegstraat 19, 2000 Antwerp, Belgium, Contact: Jan Van Gijsel *Tel:* (03) 203-0912 *Fax:* (03) 225-1303 *E-mail:* leo@leo-europe.com
Leo Marketing, The Malthouse, Malthouse Sq, Princes Risborough, Bucks HP27 9AB, United Kingdom, Contact: Sally Wood *Tel:* (1844) 274-244 *Fax:* (1844) 275-105 *E-mail:* sallywood.leo@btinternet.com

Linick International Inc
Division of The Linick Group Inc
Linick Bldg, 7 Putter Lane, Middle Island, NY 11953
Mailing Address: PO Box 102, Middle Island, NY 11953-0102
Tel: 631-924-3888 *Fax:* 631-924-3890
E-mail: linickgrp@att.net
Web Site: www.lgroup.addr.com
Key Personnel
Chmn & CEO: Andrew S Linick, PhD
Treas: Marvin Glickman
Exec VP: Roger Dextor
Founded: 1972
Turnaround: 21-30 Workdays
Print Runs: 3,000 min - 50,000 max
Business from Other Countries: 30%

LK Litho
Division of The Linick Group Inc
Linick Bldg, 7 Putter Lane, Middle Island, NY 11953
Mailing Address: PO Box 102, Middle Island, NY 11953-0102

Tel: 631-924-3888
E-mail: linickgrp@att.net
Web Site: www.lgroup.addr.com/lklitho.htm
Key Personnel
VP: Roger Dextor
Founded: 1968
Turnaround: 10 Workdays
Print Runs: 2,500 min - 2,000,000 max
Business from Other Countries: 20%

Maps.com
6464 Hollister Ave, Santa Barbara, CA 93117
Tel: 805-685-3100 *Toll Free Tel:* 800-929-4MAP (sales) *Fax:* 805-685-3330
E-mail: publishing@maps.com
Web Site: www.maps.com
Key Personnel
CEO & Chmn: Robert Tempkin *E-mail:* tempkinr@maps.com
Exec VP, Sales & Custom Mapping: Charlie Regan *Tel:* 805-685-3100 ext 124 *E-mail:* reganc@maps.com
Dir, Mktg: Bruce Kurtz *Tel:* 805-685-3100 ext 136 *E-mail:* kurtzb@maps.com
Founded: 1991
Print Runs: 1,000 min
Business from Other Countries: 10%
Membership(s): Association of Directory Publishers; International Map Trade Association; Yellow Pages Publishers Association

Marrakech Express Inc
720 Wesley Ave, No 10, Tarpon Springs, FL 34689
Tel: 727-942-2218 *Toll Free Tel:* 800-940-6566 *Fax:* 727-937-4758
E-mail: print@marrak.com
Web Site: www.marrak.com
Key Personnel
CEO: Peter Henzell
Prodn Mgr: Steen Sigmund
Sales/Estimator: Shirley Copperman
Founded: 1976
Turnaround: 7-10 Workdays
Print Runs: 500 min - 25,000 max
Business from Other Countries: 10%

Mazer Publishing Services
Division of The Mazer Corporation
6680 Poe Ave, Dayton, OH 45414
Tel: 937-264-2600 *Fax:* 937-264-2624
E-mail: info@mazer.com
Web Site: www.mazer.com
Key Personnel
Pres: William Franklin *E-mail:* bill_franklin@mazer.com
Exec VP: Ken Fultz *E-mail:* ken_fultz@mazer.com
Exec Dir, Sales: Bill Faber *Fax:* 937-264-2622 *E-mail:* bill_faber@mazer.com
Founded: 1964
Print Runs: 50 min - 25,000 max
Business from Other Countries: 10%
Branch Office(s)
2460 Sand Lake Rd, Orlando, FL 32809, Contact: Bryan Blakley *Tel:* 407-859-5552 *Fax:* 407-859-0643 *E-mail:* bryan_blakley@mazer.com
224 Lexington Ave, Fox River Grove, IL 60021, Contact: Dennis Bowman *Tel:* 847-639-1555 *Fax:* 847-639-1562 *E-mail:* dennis_bowman@mazer.com
22 Lehigh Rd, Wellesley, MA 02181, Contact: Ken Leahy *Tel:* 781-237-4112 *Fax:* 781-431-6184 *E-mail:* ken_leahy@mazer.com
22 Laurel Place, Upper Montclair, NJ 07043, Contact: John Martel *Tel:* 973-744-4320 *Fax:* 973-746-5608 *E-mail:* john_martel@mazer.com
3081 Glenmere Ct, Kettering, OH 45440, Contact: Mark Brewer *Tel:* 937-299-5746 *Fax:* 937-299-5761 *E-mail:* mark_brewer@mazer.com

363 Porter Rd, Bishop, TX 78602, Contact: Deborah VanLandingham *Tel:* 512-303-9758 *Fax:* 512-303-9791
Membership(s): BMI

Milanostampa/New Interlitho USA Inc
Subsidiary of Milanostampa New Interlitho Italia SpA
299 Broadway, Suite 901, New York, NY 10007
Tel: 212-964-2430 *Fax:* 212-964-2497
Web Site: www.milanostampa.com
Key Personnel
Chmn: Riccardo Sardo
Chmn & Sales Rep: Rino Varrasso *Tel:* 917-225-9460 *E-mail:* rvarrasso@milanostampa-usa.com
Founded: 1974
Turnaround: 30 Workdays
Print Runs: 1,000 min - 3,000,000 max
Business from Other Countries: 75%

Naturegraph Publishers Inc
3543 Indian Creek Rd, Happy Camp, CA 96039
Mailing Address: PO Box 1047, Happy Camp, CA 96039
Tel: 530-493-5353 *Toll Free Tel:* 800-390-5353 *Fax:* 530-493-5240
E-mail: nature@sisqtel.net
Web Site: www.naturegraph.com
Key Personnel
Owner & Mgr: Barbara Brown
Founded: 1946
Turnaround: 20-30 Workdays
Print Runs: 500 min - 10,000 max
Business from Other Countries: 10%

Outskirts Press
10940 S Parker Rd, Suite 515, Parker, CO 80134
E-mail: info@outskirtspress.com
Web Site: www.outskirtspress.com
Key Personnel
Pres: Brent Sampson
Acqs: Jeanine Laiza
Ed: Mindy Pellegrino
Founded: 1999
Turnaround: 21 Workdays
Print Runs: 1 min
Business from Other Countries: 20%

Palace Press International - Corporate Headquarters
17 Paul Dr, San Rafael, CA 94903
Tel: 415-526-1370 *Toll Free Tel:* 800-809-3792 *Fax:* 415-526-1394
E-mail: info@palacepress.com
Web Site: www.palacepress.com
Key Personnel
CEO: Raoul Goff *E-mail:* raoul@palacepress.com
Dir, Intl Sales & Mktg: Gordon Goff *E-mail:* gordon@palacepress.com
Dir: Steven Goff *E-mail:* steven@palacepress.com
Founded: 1984
Turnaround: 90 Workdays
Print Runs: 3,000 min - 1,000,000 max
Business from Other Countries: 20%
Branch Office(s)
Palace Press International Los Angeles, 303 W Newby Ave, Suite C, San Gabriel, CA 91777, Contact: Roger Ma *Tel:* 626-282-8877 *Fax:* 626-282-6880 *E-mail:* roger@palacepress.com
Palace Press International New York, 180 Varick St, 10th fl, New York, NY 10014, Contact: Paolo Cornacchia *Tel:* 212-462-2622 *Fax:* 212-463-9130 *E-mail:* paolo@palacepress.com

Printing Corp of the Americas Inc
620 SW 12 Ave, Fort Lauderdale, FL 33312
Tel: 954-781-8100 *Fax:* 954-781-8421
E-mail: pcaprint@bellsouth.net
Web Site: www.pcaprint.bellsouth.net
Key Personnel
Pres: Jan Tuchman
Founded: 1979
Turnaround: 5-10 Workdays
Print Runs: 500 min - 100,000 max
Business from Other Countries: 15%

Regent Publishing Services
9327 Rambler Dr, St Louis, MO 63123
Tel: 314-631-7581 *Fax:* 314-638-5113
E-mail: regentstl@aol.com
Key Personnel
Sales Dir: Carol Davis-Tierney
Mktg Dir: James J Tierney
Founded: 1985
Turnaround: 3-4 Months
Print Runs: 2,000 min - 100,000 max
Business from Other Countries: 100%

Spraymation Inc
5320 NW 35 Ave, Fort Lauderdale, FL 33309-6314
Tel: 954-484-9700 *Toll Free Tel:* 800-327-4985 *Fax:* 954-484-9778
E-mail: sales@spraymation.com
Web Site: www.spraymation.com
Key Personnel
Natl Sales Mgr: Anthony J Diaz
Founded: 1958
Business from Other Countries: 20%

Taylor Publishing Company
1550 W Mockingbird Lane, Dallas, TX 75235
Tel: 214-819-8226 *Toll Free Tel:* 800-677-2800 *Fax:* 214-630-1852
E-mail: info@taylorpub.com
Web Site: www.taylorpub.com
Key Personnel
CEO: Dave Fiore
Cust Serv Rep: Jay Love
Dir, Mktg: Mike Taylor
Founded: 1939
Turnaround: 45 Workdays
Print Runs: 300 min - 25,000 max
Business from Other Countries: 10%

Times Publishing Group
Division of Times Publishing Ltd/Singapore
99 White Plains Rd, Tarrytown, NY 10591
Tel: 914-366-9888 *Fax:* 914-366-9898
Web Site: www.tpl.com.sg
Key Personnel
Cust Serv Exec: Bonnie Stone *E-mail:* bstone@marshallcavendish.com
Sales Mgr: Suresh Kumar *E-mail:* skumar@marshallcavendish.com
Founded: 1965
Print Runs: 2,000 min - 500,000 max
Business from Other Countries: 90%

Tobias Associates Inc
50 Industrial Dr, Ivyland, PA 18974-0347
Tel: 215-322-1500 *Toll Free Tel:* 800-877-3367 *Fax:* 215-322-1504
E-mail: sales@tobiasinc.com
Web Site: www.densitometer.com
Key Personnel
Pres: Philip Tobias
Founded: 1960
Business from Other Countries: 10%

Vicks Lithograph & Printing Corp
5166 Commercial Dr, Yorkville, NY 13495
Mailing Address: PO Box 270, Yorkville, NY 13495-0270
Tel: 315-736-9344 *Fax:* 315-736-1901
Web Site: www.vickslitho.com
Key Personnel
Chmn: Dwight E "Duke" Vicks, Jr
Pres: Dwight E Vicks, III
Sales: Brian Engle *Tel:* 315-527-8844 *E-mail:* bengle@vickslitho.com; Mike Tracy *Tel:* 315-527-2059 *E-mail:* mtracy@vickslitho.com
Founded: 1918
Turnaround: 10-20 Workdays
Print Runs: 1,000 min - 100,000 max
Business from Other Countries: 10%
Membership(s): BMI; Printing Industries of America

Fred Weidner & Daughter Printers
15 Maiden Lane, Suite 1505, New York, NY 10038
Tel: 212-964-8676 *Fax:* 212-964-8677
E-mail: info@fwdprinters.com
Web Site: www.fwdprinters.com
Key Personnel
Exec VP: Cynthia Weidner *E-mail:* cynthia@fwdprinters.com
Creative Dir: Carol Mittelsdorf
Founded: 1860
Turnaround: 5-10 Workdays
Print Runs: 1,000 min - 500,000 max
Business from Other Countries: 25%

Uruguay

Barreiro y Ramos SA
Juan Carlos Gomez, Montevideo 1430
Tel: (02) 986621 *Fax:* (02) 962358
Telex: 23901PB.CVJA.UY *Cable:* BAREIRAMOS
Key Personnel
President: Gaston Barreiro
Vice President: Guzman Barreiro
Founded: 1837
Print Runs: 1,000 min - 50,000 max
Business from Other Countries: 10%

Manufacturing Materials Index

BINDING SUPPLIES

Hong Kong
Golden Cup Printing Co Ltd, pg 1236

Singapore
CS Graphics Pte Ltd, pg 1237

Spain
Guarro Casas SA, pg 1238

United Kingdom
Harveys Ltd, pg 1238

United States
Blaze International Productions Inc, pg 1239
Conservation Resources International Inc, pg 1240
Fibre Leather Manufacturing Corp, pg 1240
ICG/Holliston, pg 1240
Palace Press International - Corporate Headquarters, pg 1241

BOOK COVERS

Belgium
Imprimerie Bietlot Freres SA, pg 1235

Canada
Appleby's Bindery Ltd, pg 1235
McLaren Morris & Todd Co, pg 1235
Printcrafters Inc, pg 1235
PrintWest, pg 1235
Transcontinental Printing Book Group, pg 1235
University of Toronto Press Inc, pg 1235

Denmark
Bianco Lunos Bogtrykkeri AS, pg 1235

Finland
WS Bookwell Ltd, pg 1235

Germany
C L Baader Buch & Offsetdruckere GmbH & Co KG, pg 1235
MOHN Media, pg 1236
Priese GmbH & Co, pg 1236

Hong Kong
Dai Nippon Printing Co (Hong Kong) Ltd, pg 1236
Everbest Printing Co Ltd, pg 1236
Golden Cup Printing Co Ltd, pg 1236
The Green Pagoda Press Ltd, pg 1236
Image Printing Company Ltd, pg 1236
Mei Ka Printing & Publishing Enterprise Ltd, pg 1236
Prontaprint Asia Ltd, pg 1236
Sino Publishing House Ltd, pg 1236
Speedflex Asia Ltd, pg 1236
Wing King Tong Group, pg 1236
Ying Tat Co, pg 1236

Indonesia
Ichtiar Baru I Van Hoeve, pg 1237
Victory Offset Prima PT, pg 1237

Ireland
SciPrint Ltd, pg 1237

Israel
Keterpress Enterprises Jerusalem, pg 1237

Italy
Dedalo Litostampa SRL, pg 1237
Milanostampa SpA, pg 1237

Republic of Korea
Daehan Printing & Publishing Co Ltd, pg 1237

Netherlands
BN International BV, pg 1237

New Zealand
Bookprint Consultants Ltd, pg 1237
Rogan McIndoe Print Ltd, pg 1237

Singapore
Alkem Company Pte Ltd, pg 1237
Eurasia Press Pte Ltd, pg 1237
Ho Printing Singapore Pte Ltd, pg 1237
International Press Co Pte Ltd, pg 1237
Markono Print Media Pte Ltd, pg 1238
SNP SPrint Pte Ltd, pg 1238

Slovenia
Gorenjski Tisk Printing House, pg 1238

Spain
Guarro Casas SA, pg 1238

United Kingdom
Bell & Bain Ltd, pg 1238
Biddles Ltd, pg 1238
Book Creation, pg 1238
Clays Ltd, pg 1238
William Clowes Ltd, pg 1238
Cox & Wyman Ltd, pg 1238
FiberMark Red Bridge International Ltd, pg 1238
Furnival Press, pg 1238
The Guernsey Press Co Ltd, pg 1238
Hammond Bindery Ltd, pg 1238
Harveys Ltd, pg 1238
Hobbs The Printers Ltd, pg 1239
Hunter & Foulis Ltd, pg 1239
Image & Print Group Ltd, pg 1239
Intype Libra Ltd, pg 1239
The Malvern Press Ltd, pg 1239
Page Bros Ltd (Norwich), pg 1239
Printafoil Ltd, pg 1239
J R Reid Printing Group Ltd, pg 1239
Antony Rowe Ltd, pg 1239
Stott Brothers Ltd, pg 1239
M & A Thomson Litho Ltd, pg 1239
Watkiss Automation Ltd, pg 1239
Winter & Co UK Ltd, pg 1239

United States
Bang Printing Co Inc, pg 1239
Blaze International Productions Inc, pg 1239
BookBuilders New York Inc, pg 1239
Martin Cook Associates Ltd, pg 1240
CS Graphics USA Inc, pg 1240
D & K Group, pg 1240
Desktop Miracles Inc, pg 1240
DNP America LLC, pg 1240
Elegance Printing & Book Binding (USA), pg 1240
Fibre Leather Manufacturing Corp, pg 1240
ICG/Holliston, pg 1240
Imago, pg 1240
Integrated Book Technology Inc, pg 1240
Jinno International Group, pg 1240
Linick International Inc, pg 1241
LK Litho, pg 1241
Mazer Publishing Services, pg 1241
Milanostampa/New Interlitho USA Inc, pg 1241
Palace Press International - Corporate Headquarters, pg 1241
Printing Corp of the Americas Inc, pg 1241
Regent Publishing Services, pg 1241
Taylor Publishing Company, pg 1241
Times Publishing Group, pg 1241

Uruguay
Barreiro y Ramos SA, pg 1241

BOOK JACKETS

Belgium
Imprimerie Bietlot Freres SA, pg 1235

Canada
Appleby's Bindery Ltd, pg 1235
McLaren Morris & Todd Co, pg 1235
Printcrafters Inc, pg 1235
Transcontinental Printing Book Group, pg 1235
University of Toronto Press Inc, pg 1235

Denmark
Bianco Lunos Bogtrykkeri AS, pg 1235

Finland
WS Bookwell Ltd, pg 1235

Germany
C L Baader Buch & Offsetdruckere GmbH & Co KG, pg 1235
MOHN Media, pg 1236
Priese GmbH & Co, pg 1236

Hong Kong
Caritas Printing Training Centre, pg 1236
Dai Nippon Printing Co (Hong Kong) Ltd, pg 1236
Everbest Printing Co Ltd, pg 1236
Golden Cup Printing Co Ltd, pg 1236
The Green Pagoda Press Ltd, pg 1236
Image Printing Company Ltd, pg 1236
Mei Ka Printing & Publishing Enterprise Ltd, pg 1236
Prontaprint Asia Ltd, pg 1236
Sino Publishing House Ltd, pg 1236
Speedflex Asia Ltd, pg 1236
Wing King Tong Group, pg 1236
Ying Tat Co, pg 1236

Hungary
Interpress Aussenhandels GmbH, pg 1237

Indonesia
Ichtiar Baru I Van Hoeve, pg 1237

Ireland
SciPrint Ltd, pg 1237

Israel
Keterpress Enterprises Jerusalem, pg 1237

Italy
Dedalo Litostampa SRL, pg 1237
Milanostampa SpA, pg 1237

Republic of Korea
Daehan Printing & Publishing Co Ltd, pg 1237

New Zealand
Bookprint Consultants Ltd, pg 1237
Rogan McIndoe Print Ltd, pg 1237

Singapore
Alkem Company Pte Ltd, pg 1237
Eurasia Press Pte Ltd, pg 1237
Ho Printing Singapore Pte Ltd, pg 1237
International Press Co Pte Ltd, pg 1237
Markono Print Media Pte Ltd, pg 1238
SNP SPrint Pte Ltd, pg 1238

Slovenia
Gorenjski Tisk Printing House, pg 1238

Spain
Guarro Casas SA, pg 1238

MANUFACTURING MATERIALS INDEX

United Kingdom
Bell & Bain Ltd, pg 1238
Biddles Ltd, pg 1238
Book Creation, pg 1238
Clays Ltd, pg 1238
William Clowes Ltd, pg 1238
Furnival Press, pg 1238
The Guernsey Press Co Ltd, pg 1238
Harveys Ltd, pg 1238
Hunter & Foulis Ltd, pg 1239
Image & Print Group Ltd, pg 1239
Intype Libra Ltd, pg 1239
The Malvern Press Ltd, pg 1239
Page Bros Ltd (Norwich), pg 1239
Printafoil Ltd, pg 1239
J R Reid Printing Group Ltd, pg 1239
Antony Rowe Ltd, pg 1239
Watkiss Automation Ltd, pg 1239

United States
Bang Printing Co Inc, pg 1239
Blaze International Productions Inc, pg 1239
BookBuilders New York Inc, pg 1239
Coneco Litho Graphics, pg 1239
Martin Cook Associates Ltd, pg 1240
CS Graphics USA Inc, pg 1240
D & K Group, pg 1240
Desktop Miracles Inc, pg 1240
DNP America LLC, pg 1240
Elegance Printing & Book Binding (USA), pg 1240
Hindy's Enterprise, pg 1240
Imago, pg 1240
Jinno International Group, pg 1240
Linick International Inc, pg 1241
LK Litho, pg 1241
Milanostampa/New Interlitho USA Inc, pg 1241
Palace Press International - Corporate Headquarters, pg 1241
Printing Corp of the Americas Inc, pg 1241
Regent Publishing Services, pg 1241
Times Publishing Group, pg 1241

Uruguay
Barreiro y Ramos SA, pg 1241

PAPER MERCHANTS

United Kingdom
Harveys Ltd, pg 1238

United States
Palace Press International - Corporate Headquarters, pg 1241

PAPER MILLS

Canada
Tembec Paperboard Group, pg 1235

Spain
Guarro Casas SA, pg 1238

United States
Palace Press International - Corporate Headquarters, pg 1241

Manufacturing Materials

This section includes companies throughout the world involved in the production of book manufacturing materials such as paper and book cover material. Those U.S. and Canadian companies with 10% or more of their business done outside North America are also included here. Immediately preceding this section is an index classifying companies by materials manufactured.

Belgium

Imprimerie Bietlot Freres SA
rue du Rond Point 185, 6060 Gilly
Tel: (071) 283611 *Fax:* (071) 283620
E-mail: info@bietlot.be
Web Site: www.bietlot.be
Key Personnel
Man Dir: A Franquin
Founded: 1988
Business from Other Countries: 35%

Canada

Appleby's Bindery Ltd
1303 Route 102, Upper Gagetown, NB E5M 1R5
Tel: 506-488-2086 *Toll Free Tel:* 800-561-2005 (Canada only) *Fax:* 506-488-2086
E-mail: applbind@nbnet.nb.ca
Key Personnel
Pres & Owner: David E Appleby
Mgr: John Appleby
Founded: 1976
Business from Other Countries: 10%

McLaren Morris & Todd Co
3270 American Dr, Mississauga, ON L4V 1B5
Tel: 905-677-3592 *Fax:* 905-677-3675; 905-677-7766
Web Site: www.mmt.ca
Key Personnel
Pres & CEO: Tony Sgro
VP, Fin: Tom Englehart
Founded: 1956
Business from Other Countries: 10%

Printcrafters Inc
78 Hutchings St, Winnipeg, MB R2X 3B1
Tel: 204-633-7117 *Fax:* 204-694-1519
E-mail: info@printcraftersinc.com
Key Personnel
Pres: Bob Payne *Tel:* 204-633-7117 ext 223 *Fax:* 204-694-1594 *E-mail:* bpayne@printcraftersinc.com
Founded: 1996 (Employee owned)
Business from Other Countries: 30%
Membership(s): CPIA

PrintWest
1150 Eighth Ave, Regina, SK S4R 1C9
Tel: 306-525-2304 *Toll Free Tel:* 800-236-6438 *Fax:* 306-757-2439
E-mail: general@printwest.com
Web Site: www.printwest.com
Key Personnel
CEO: Wayne UnRuh
VP, Sales: Ken Benson
Founded: 1992
Business from Other Countries: 15%
Branch Office(s)
Box 2500, 2310 Millar Ave, Saskatoon, SK S7K 2C4 *Tel:* 306-665-3560 *Fax:* 306-653-1255

Tembec Paperboard Group
Division of Tembec
800 Rene Levesque blvd W, Suite 1050, Montreal, PQ H3B 1X9
Tel: 514-871-0137 *Toll Free Tel:* 800-411-7011 *Fax:* 514-397-0896
Web Site: www.tembec.com
Key Personnel
Pres: Mel Zangwill *Tel:* 514-871-2311 *E-mail:* mel.zangwill@tembec.com
VP, Sales: Phil Glatfelter *Tel:* 717-817-0300 *Fax:* 309-405-6195 *E-mail:* philip.glatfelter@tembec.com
Mktg Dir: Renee Yardley *Tel:* 514-397-3926 *E-mail:* renee.yardley@tembec.com
Founded: 1990
Business from Other Countries: 90%
Cover Line(s) Milled: Kallima® Coated Cover C1S Plus; Kallima® Web Coated Cover C1S Plus
Cover Line(s) Sold: Kallima® Coated Cover C1S Plus; Kallima® Web Coated Cover C1S Plus

Transcontinental Printing Book Group
395 Lebeau Blvd, St-Laurent, PQ H4N 1S2
Tel: 514-337-8560 *Toll Free Tel:* 800-361-3599 *Fax:* 514-339-5230
Web Site: www.transcontinental.com; www.transcontinental-printing.com
Key Personnel
VP, Book Group: Jacques Gregoire
US Sales Mgr: Denis Beaudin *Tel:* 514-339-2220 ext 4101 *E-mail:* beaudind@transcontinental.ca
Founded: 1976
Business from Other Countries: 15%
Branch Office(s)
614 Yates Ave, Calumet City, IL 60409, United States, Contact: Kristopher D Levy *Tel:* 708-832-1528 *Fax:* 708-832-9510 *E-mail:* kris.levy@transcontinental.ca (Midwest)
3653 W Leland Ave, Suite One W, Chicago, IL 60625, United States, Contact: Tim Taylor *Tel:* 773-583-8155 *Fax:* 773-583-8162 *E-mail:* tim.taylor@transcontinental.ca (Midwest)
245 Eliot St, Ashland, MA 01721, United States, Contact: Ed Catania *Tel:* 508-881-1119 *Fax:* 508-881-7739 *E-mail:* ecatania@attbi.com (East Coast)
19 Crown St, Milton, MA 02186-1419, United States, Contact: Mike Gazzola *Tel:* 617-696-1435 *Fax:* 617-696-1025 *E-mail:* mikebook@attbi.com (East Coast)
37 Herman Blvd, Franklin Square, NY 11010, United States, Contact: Tim Malloy *Tel:* 516-775-2980 *Fax:* 516-488-0253 *E-mail:* tmmalloy@aol.com (NY)
3175 Summit Square Dr, Suite C9, Oakton, VA 22124, United States, Contact: David Avesian *Tel:* 703-255-1332 *Fax:* 703-255-1343 *E-mail:* davesian@cox.rr.com (Southeast)
559 Lowrys Rd, Parksville, BC V9P 2R8, Contact: Mike Davies *Tel:* 250-248-9700 *Fax:* 250-248-2353 *E-mail:* bookguys@shaw.ca (West Coast)
15373 Victoria Ave, White Rock, BC V4B 1H1, Contact: Wade Davies *Tel:* 604-535-8800 *Fax:* 604-535-8802 *E-mail:* davies@shaw.ca (West Coast)

490 Wilfred Dr, Peterborough, ON K9K 2H1, Contact: Tom Lang *Tel:* 705-760-9594 *Fax:* 705-760-9485 *E-mail:* langt@transcontinental.ca (NY)

University of Toronto Press Inc
Printing Division, 5201 Dufferin St, North York, ON M3H 5T8
Tel: 416-667-7767 *Fax:* 416-667-7803
E-mail: printing@utpress.utoronto.ca
Web Site: www.utpress.utoronto.ca
Key Personnel
Pres & Publr: George Meadows
Founded: 1901
Business from Other Countries: 15%
Membership(s): BMI

Denmark

Bianco Lunos Bogtrykkeri AS
Subsidiary of Carl Allers Etablissement AS
Otto Monsteds Gade 3, 1571 Copenhagen V
Tel: 36 15 33 00 *Fax:* 36 15 33 01
Key Personnel
General Manager: J Heede Sorensen
Founded: 1871

Finland

WS Bookwell Ltd
Subsidiary of Werner Soderstrom Corp
Teollisuustie 4, 06100 Porvoo
Tel: (019) 21 941 *Fax:* (019) 219 4800
Web Site: www.bookwell.fi
Key Personnel
Sales Manager: Rainer Poysa *Tel:* (019) 219 4664 *E-mail:* rainer.poysa@bookwell.fi
Founded: 1999
Business from Other Countries: 70%
Branch Office(s)
Messdorferstr 127, 53123 Bonn, Germany, Contact: Markku Rapeli *Tel:* (0228) 986 4006 *Fax:* (0228) 986 4008
WS Bookwell AB, Borgveien 2, Ytre Enebakk 1914, Norway, Kristen Sande *Tel:* (064) 925840 *Fax:* (064) 925841 *E-mail:* k.sande.wsoy@oslo.online.no
PO Box 3, Lowestoft, Suffolk NR33 8EY, United Kingdom, David Sowter *Tel:* (01502) 742 038 *Fax:* (01502) 742 039 *E-mail:* ds@bookwell.co.uk

Germany

C L Baader Buch & Offsetdruckere GmbH & Co KG
Gutenbergstr 1, 72525 Muensingen

GERMANY

Tel: (07381) 791 *Fax:* (07381) 411412 *Cable:* BAADER-MUNSINGEN
Founded: 1835

MOHN Media
Subsidiary of Bertelsmann AG
Carl-Bertelsmann-Str 161M, 33311 Guetersloh
Tel: (05241) 80-4 04 10 *Fax:* (05241) 2 42 82
E-mail: mohnmedia@bertelsmann.de
Web Site: www.mohnmedia.de
Key Personnel
Man Dir: Markus Dohle
Founded: 1824
Business from Other Countries: 25%

Priese GmbH & Co
Auerbacher Str 9, 14193 Berlin
Tel: (030) 8263024 *Fax:* (030) 3249630
Key Personnel
Contact: Elma Priese; Hans Joachim Priese

Hong Kong

Caritas Printing Training Centre
Caritas House, 3rd floor, Block D, 2 Caine Rd, Hong Kong
Tel: 2524 2701 (ext 239) *Fax:* 2537 1231
Web Site: vtes.caritas.org.hk
Key Personnel
General Manager: Isaac Mak
Business from Other Countries: 50%

Dai Nippon Printing Co (Hong Kong) Ltd
Division of Dai Nippon Printing Co Ltd
Tsuen Wan Industrial Centre, 2-5/F, 220-248 Texaco Rd, Tsuen Wan, New Territories
Tel: 2408-0188 *Fax:* 2614-7585; 2407-6201
Web Site: www.dnp.co.jp *Cable:* DNPICO
Key Personnel
Administration & Finance Dir: Mr K Miya
Business from Other Countries: 85%
Branch Office(s)
Dai Nippon Printing Co (Australia) Pty Ltd, St Martins Tower, Suite 1002, Level 10, 31 Market St, Sydney, NSW 2000, Australia *Tel:* (02) 9267-8166 *Fax:* (02) 9267-9533
DNP America LLC, Los Angeles Office, 3858 Carson St, Suite 300, Torrance, CA 90503, United States *Tel:* 310-540-5123 *Fax:* 310-543-3260
DNP America LLC, New York Office, 335 Madison Ave, 3rd floor, New York, NY 10017, United States *Tel:* 212-503-1060 *Fax:* 212-286-1501
DNP America LLC, Silicon Valley Office, 3235 Kifer Rd, Suite 100, Santa Clara, CA 95051, United States *Tel:* 408-735-8880 *Fax:* 408-735-0453
DNP Corporation USA, New York Office, 335 Madison Ave, 3rd floor, New York, NY 10017, United States *Tel:* 212-503-1850 *Fax:* 212-286-1490
DNP Corporation USA, San Francisco Office, 577 Airport Blvd, Suite 620, Burlingame, CA 94010, United States *Tel:* 650-558-4050 *Fax:* 650-340-6095
DNP Denmark A/S, Skruegangen 2, 2690 Karlslunde, Denmark *Tel:* 4616-5100 *Fax:* 4616-5200
DNP Electronics America LLC, 2391 Fenton St, Chula Vista 91914, United States *Tel:* 619-397-6700 *Fax:* 613-397-6729
DNP Europa GmbH, Berliner Allee 26, 40212 Dusseldorf, Germany *Tel:* (0211) 8620-180 *Fax:* (0211) 8620-1895
DNP IMS America Corporation, 4524 Enterprise Dr NW, Concord, NC 28027, United States *Tel:* 704-784-8100 *Fax:* 704-784-2777
DNP IMS France SAS, 14, rue da la Violette, 22100 Dinan, France
DNP Photomask Europe SpA, Via Olivatti 2/A, 20041 Agrate Brianza, Italy *Tel:* (039) 65493-3000 *Fax:* (039) 65493-215
DNP Singapore Pte Ltd, 896 Dunearn Rd, No 04-09, Sime Darby Centre, Singapore 589472, Singapore *Tel:* 469-7611 *Fax:* 466-8486
DNP Taiwan Co Ltd, Rm D, 6 fl, 44 Chung-Shan N Rd Sec 2, Taipei 104, Taiwan, Province of China *Tel:* (02) 2327-8311 *Fax:* (02) 2327-8283
DNP UK Co Ltd, 27 Throgmorton St, 4th floor, London EC2N 2AQ, United Kingdom *Tel:* (020) 7588 2088 *Fax:* (020) 7588 2089
PT DNP Indonesia, Kawasan Industri Pulogadung, Jalan Pulogadung Kaveling II, Blok H, No 2-3, Jakarta Timur, Indonesia *Tel:* (021) 4610313 *Fax:* (021) 4605795
Tien Wah Press (Pte) Ltd, 4 Pandan Crescent, Singapore 128475, Singapore *Tel:* 466-6222 *Fax:* 469-3894
TWP Sdn Bhd, 89, Jalan Tampoi, Kawasan Perindustrian Tampoi, 80350 Johor Bahru, Johor, Malaysia *Tel:* (07) 2369899 *Fax:* (07) 2363148

Everbest Printing Co Ltd
Ko Fai Industrial Bldg, Block C5, 10th floor, 7 Ko Fai Rd, Yau Tong, Kowloon
Tel: 2727 4433 *Fax:* 2772 7687
E-mail: sales@everbest.com.hk
Web Site: www.everbest.com
Key Personnel
Founder: James Chung
Man Dir: Kenneth Chung
Customer Account Executive: Ronny Ng; Frankie Lee
Founded: 1954
Business from Other Countries: 90%
Branch Office(s)
Everbest Canada, 50 Emblem Court, Scarborough, ON M1S 1B1, Canada, Contact: Ms Connie Chung *Tel:* 416-286-2525 *Fax:* 416-286-2526 *E-mail:* everbestcan@aprinco.com
Everbest Printing (Australian & New Zealand Office), 100 Macaulay Rd, Stanmore, NSW 2048, Australia, Contact: Lionel Marz *Tel:* (02) 9568-5879 *Fax:* (02) 9568-5902 *E-mail:* lmarz@onaustralia.com.au
U.S. Office(s): Everbest Midwest, 6428 Margaret's Lane, Edina, MN 55439, United States, Contact: Dr Josie Lo *Tel:* 612-944-0854 *Fax:* 612-829-7670 *E-mail:* sklo@aol.com
Four Colour Imports, 2843 Brownsboro Rd, Suite 102, Louisville, KY 40206, United States, Contact: George Dick *Tel:* 502-896-9644 *Fax:* 502-896-9594 *E-mail:* sales@fourcolour.com *Web Site:* www.fourcolour.com
Spectrum Books Inc, 2300 Bethards Drive, Suite C, Santa Rosa, CA 95405-8658, United States, Contact: Duncan McCallum *Tel:* 707-542-6044 *Fax:* 707-542-6045 *E-mail:* specbooks@aol.com

Golden Cup Printing Co Ltd
Seapower Industrial Centre, 6/F, 177 Hoi Bun Rd, Kwun Tong, Kowloon
Tel: 23434254 *Fax:* 23415426
E-mail: sales@goldencup.com.hk
Web Site: www.goldencup.com.hk
Key Personnel
Man Dir: Yeung Kam Kai
General Manager: W K Ngan
Sales Manager: Mary Yeung *E-mail:* mary@goldencup.com.hk
Founded: 1969
Business from Other Countries: 80%
Branch Office(s)
Dongguan, China
Guangdong, China
Kunming, China
Yunan, China

MANUFACTURING

The Green Pagoda Press Ltd
9/F, Block B, Tung Chong Factory Bldg, 653-655 King's Rd, North Point
Tel: 2561 1924 *Fax:* 2811 0946
E-mail: gpinfo@gpp.com.hk
Web Site: www.greenpagoda.com
Key Personnel
Man Dir: Derek Yip
Founded: 1957
Business from Other Countries: 30%

Image Printing Company Ltd
Unit 4, 4/F Cornell Centre, 50 Wing Tai Rd, Chai Wan
Tel: 2873 2633 *Fax:* 2558 3044
E-mail: imageprt@pop3.hknet.com
Key Personnel
Man Dir: Philip Chow Sung Ming
Founded: 1992
Business from Other Countries: 50%

Mei Ka Printing & Publishing Enterprise Ltd
Cheung Ka Industrial Bldg, Block B, 9th floor, 179-180 Connaught Rd W, Hong Kong
Tel: 2540 1131 *Fax:* 2559 8718; 2559 7137
E-mail: mkpp@netvigator.com
Web Site: www.meika-printing.com
Key Personnel
Dir: Hong Chin Huo

Prontaprint Asia Ltd
1/F, Gaylord Commercial Bldg, 114 Lockhart Rd, Wanchai
Tel: 28657525 *Fax:* 28661064
Key Personnel
Man Dir: Clive Howard
Founded: 1986
Business from Other Countries: 40%

Sino Publishing House Ltd
Valley Centre, Room 301-302, 80-82 Morrison Hill Rd, Wanchai
Tel: 2884 9963 *Fax:* 2884 9321
Web Site: www.sinophl.com
Key Personnel
Contact: Ben Yan *E-mail:* benyan@sinophl.com
Founded: 1993
Business from Other Countries: 75%

Speedflex Asia Ltd
3/F Tianjin Bldg, 167 Connaught Rd W, Hong Kong
Tel: 2542 2780 *Fax:* 2542 3733
E-mail: info@speedflex.com.hk
Web Site: www.speedflex.com.hk
Key Personnel
Founded: 1981
Business from Other Countries: 20%

Wing King Tong Group
Leader Industrial Centre, Block I, 3/F, 188-202 Texaco Rd, Tsuen Wan, New Territories
Tel: 24073287 *Fax:* 24074130; 24087939
E-mail: printing@wkt.cc; books@wkt.cc
Web Site: www.wkt.cc
Key Personnel
Man Dir: Alex Yan Tak Chung *E-mail:* ayan@hk.super.net
Marketing Dir: Jeremy Kuo
Founded: 1944
Business from Other Countries: 95%

Ying Tat Co
Division of Quality Printing & Paper Products
Wing Wah Industrial Bldg, 8th floor, 677 Kings Rd, North Point
Tel: 25645980; 25645963; 25639981 *Fax:* 28111280
Key Personnel
Contact: Chan Dun Yin

Founded: 1968
Business from Other Countries: 30%

Hungary

Interpress Aussenhandels GmbH
Subsidiary of ADWEST
Bajcsy-Zsilinszky ut 21, 1065 Budapest
Tel: (01) 302-7525 *Fax:* (01) 302-7530
E-mail: office@interpress.hu
Web Site: www.interpress.hu
Key Personnel
Manager: Julia Kovacs; Sandor Kovacs; Miklos Pollak
Founded: 1991

Indonesia

Ichtiar Baru I Van Hoeve
Jln Cideng Barat 62/Jl Raya Pasar Jumat No 38 D-E Pondok Pinang, POB 1376/jks, Jakarta Pusat 12013
Tel: (021) 7511856
Founded: 1972

Victory Offset Prima PT
Jalan Raya Pegangsaan, Dua No 17, Jakarta 14250
Tel: (021) 460-2742; (021) 460-8968; (021) 4682-0555 *Fax:* (021) 460-2740; (021) 4682-0551
E-mail: info@victoryoffset.com
Web Site: www.victoryoffset.com
Key Personnel
President: Zainal F Stanley *E-mail:* zainal@victoryoffset.com
General Manager: S Wilson Pinady *E-mail:* wilson@victoryoffset.com
Founded: 1971
Business from Other Countries: 10%

Ireland

SciPrint Ltd
Bay 93, Shannon Industrial Estate, Shannon, Co Clare
Tel: (061) 472114; (061) 472520 *Fax:* (061) 472021
Key Personnel
Man Dir, Sales: M K Parsons
Chairman: B Lane
Founded: 1974
Business from Other Countries: 95%

Israel

Keterpress Enterprises Jerusalem
PO Box 7145, 91071 Jerusalem
Tel: (02) 655 7822 *Fax:* (02) 6536811
E-mail: info@keter-books.co.il
Web Site: www.keter-books.co.il
Key Personnel
Plant Manager: Peter Tomkins *E-mail:* peter@keter-books.co.il
Sales Manager: Zvi Weller
Business from Other Countries: 10%
Parent Company: Keter Publishing House Ltd

Italy

Dedalo Litostampa SRL
Viale Luigi Jacobini 5, Zona Ind, 70123 Bari
Mailing Address: Casella Postale BA/19, 70123 Bari
Tel: (080) 531 14 13; (080) 531 14 01; (080) 531 14 00 *Fax:* (080) 531 14 14
E-mail: info@edizionidedalo.it
Web Site: www.edizionidedalo.it
Key Personnel
Man Dir: Raimondo Coga
General Manager: Sergio Coga *E-mail:* s.coga@edizionidedalo.it
Founded: 1965

Milanostampa SpA
Corso Ferrero 5, 12060 Farigliano (Cuneo)
Tel: (0173) 746111 *Fax:* (0173) 746248; (0173) 746249
E-mail: info@milanostampa.com
Web Site: www.milanostampa.com
Telex: 212428
Key Personnel
Commercial Dir: Riccardo Sardo
Man Dir: Fuad Lahham
Founded: 1965
Business from Other Countries: 65%

Republic of Korea

Daehan Printing & Publishing Co Ltd
344-12, Sangdaewon-dong, Jungwon-gu, Sungnam-City, Kyunggi-do
Tel: (031) 730-3850 *Fax:* (031) 735-8104
Web Site: www.daehane.com; www.dhpop.com
Key Personnel
President: Sungshick Kim
Manager: Jongjun Yu
Founded: 1948
U.S. Office(s): 3271 Sawtelle Blvd, No 104, Los Angeles, CA 90066, United States *Tel:* 310-737-0058 *Fax:* 310-737-9213

Netherlands

BN International BV
Rokerijweg 5, 1271 AH Huizen
Mailing Address: PO Box 2, 1270 AA Huizen
Tel: (035) 524 84 00 *Fax:* (035) 525 60 04
Web Site: www.bninternational.com
Key Personnel
Sales & Marketing Manager: Henk Bunschoten
Founded: 1938
Business from Other Countries: 95%
Branch Office(s)
BN International UK, Unit 38, The Metro Centre, Tolpits Lane, Watford, Herts WD1 8SB, United Kingdom *Tel:* (01923) 219132 *Fax:* (01923) 219134

New Zealand

Bookprint Consultants Ltd
Division of Grantham House Publishing
9 Wilkinson St, Apt 6, Oriental Bay, Wellington 6001
Tel: (04) 381 3071 *Fax:* (04) 381 3067
E-mail: gstewart@iconz.co.nz
Key Personnel
Chief Executive: Graham C Stewart
Founded: 1982
Business from Other Countries: 10%

Rogan McIndoe Print Ltd
51 Crawford St, Dunedin
Mailing Address: 76 Vogel St, Dunedin
Tel: (03) 474 0111 *Toll Free Tel:* 800 477 0355 *Fax:* (03) 474 0116
E-mail: quality@rogan.co.nz
Web Site: www.rogan.co.nz
Key Personnel
Man Dir: Brendan A Murphy
Founded: 1893
Business from Other Countries: 1%

Singapore

Alkem Company Pte Ltd
No 1 Penjuru Close, Jurong Town, Singapore 608617
Tel: 6265 6666 *Fax:* 6261 7875
E-mail: enquiry@alkem.com.sg
Web Site: www.alkem.com.sg
Telex: RS 21596 *Cable:* TOPPAN
Key Personnel
Man Dir: Chu Bong *E-mail:* chubong@alkem.com.sg
Dir: Mr Ee Long Tear
Business Manager: Eugene Koh
Founded: 1973
Business from Other Countries: 70%

CS Graphics Pte Ltd
10 Tuas Ave 20, Singapore 638822
Tel: 6865 2010 *Fax:* 6861 0190
E-mail: rick@csgraphics.us
Web Site: www.csgraphics.us
Key Personnel
Man Dir: Mr Lee Sian Tee *E-mail:* stlee@csgraphics-world.com
Founded: 1981
Business from Other Countries: 100%

Eurasia Press Pte Ltd
10/14 Kg Ampat, Singapore 368318
Tel: 2805522 *Fax:* 2800593
E-mail: eurasia@mbox3.singnet.com.sg
Key Personnel
Marketing Dir: Allan Fong
Founded: 1937
Business from Other Countries: 65%

Ho Printing Singapore Pte Ltd
31 Changi South St One, Changi South Industrial Estate, Singapore 486769
Tel: 5429322 *Fax:* 5428322
Telex: RS 39685 HOFSET
Key Personnel
Man Dir: Ho Wai Hoi
Sales Executive: Ho Wah Yuen
Founded: 1951
Business from Other Countries: 30%

International Press Co Pte Ltd
26 Kallang Ave, Singapore 339417
Tel: 2983800 *Fax:* 2971668
Key Personnel
Marketing Manager: Kok Leong Koo

SINGAPORE

Founded: 1972
Business from Other Countries: 60%

Markono Print Media Pte Ltd
Subsidiary of Markono Holdings Pte Ltd
21 Neythal Rd, Singapore 628586
Tel: 6281-1118 *Fax:* 6286-6663
E-mail: saleslead@markono.com.sg
Web Site: www.markono.com.sg
Key Personnel
Founder & Chairman: Ng Siow How
Dir: Bob Lee Song Tioh *E-mail:* blee@markono.com.sg
Founded: 1967
Business from Other Countries: 20%
Branch Office(s)
Kin Keong Colour Printing (M) Sdn Bhd, Port Klang 539538

SNP SPrint Pte Ltd
97 Ubi Ave 4, Singapore 408754
Tel: 6741-2500 *Fax:* 6744-7098
E-mail: enquiries@snpcorp.com
Web Site: www.snpcorp.com
Telex: SNPRS14462
Key Personnel
Chief Executive Officer & President: Yeo Chee Tong
US Sales Manager: Patrick Chung
Business from Other Countries: 40%
Parent Company: SNP Corporation Ltd

Times Printers Pte Ltd
Subsidiary of Times Publishing Group
16 Tuas Ave 5, Singapore 639340
Tel: 6311-2888 *Fax:* 6862-1313
E-mail: enquiry@timesprinters.com
Web Site: www.timesprinters.com *Cable:* TIMESPRINT
Key Personnel
Man Dir: Leong Kwok Sun *Tel:* 6311-2701
  E-mail: ksleong@timesprinters.com
Head of Sales: Patsy Tan *Tel:* 6311-2763
  E-mail: patsytan@timesprinters.com
Assistant General Manager, Manufacturing: G G Krishnan *Tel:* 6311-2720 *E-mail:* ggkrishnan@timesprinters.com
Founded: 1968
Business from Other Countries: 75%

Slovenia

Gorenjski Tisk Printing House
Mirka Vadnova 6, 4000 Kranj
Tel: (064) 263 0 *Fax:* (064) 241 323
E-mail: info@go-tisk.si
Web Site: www.go-tisk.si
Telex: 34560 YU GOTISK
Key Personnel
Dir: Kristina Kobal
Commercial Manager: Boris Krist
Founded: 1888
Business from Other Countries: 50%

Spain

Grafos SA Arte Sobre Papel
Zona Franca, Sector C, calle D 36, 08040 Barcelona
Tel: (093) 261 87 50 *Fax:* (093) 263 10 04
E-mail: info@grafos-barcelona.com
Web Site: www.grafos-barcelona.com

Key Personnel
Man Dir: Bernardo G Masana
  E-mail: bgmasana@compuserve.com
Domestic Sales Dir: Alberto Monclus
Packaging Sales Dir: Alejandro Hijar
Founded: 1934
Business from Other Countries: 45%

Guarro Casas SA
Subsidiary of ArjoWiggins Appleton
Can Guarro s/n, 08790 Gelida (Barcelona)
Tel: (093) 7767676 *Fax:* (093) 7767677
E-mail: guarro@guarro.com
Web Site: www.guarro.com
Key Personnel
Export Executive Dir: Manuel Freijomil
  E-mail: mfreijomil@guarro.com
Founded: 1698
Business from Other Countries: 60%

United Kingdom

Bell & Bain Ltd
303 Burnfield Rd, Thornliebank, Glasgow G46 7UQ
Tel: (0141) 649 5697 *Fax:* (0141) 632 8733
E-mail: info@bell-bain.demon.co.uk
Web Site: www.bell-bain.co.uk
Key Personnel
Man Dir: I Walker
Sales Dir: D Stewart
Founded: 1831
Business from Other Countries: 25%

Biddles Ltd
Division of W & G Baird Ltd
Hardwick Industrial Estate, 24 Rollesby Rd, King's Lynn, Norfolk PE30 4LS
Tel: (01553) 764 728 *Fax:* (01553) 764 633
E-mail: sales@biddles.co.uk; enquiries@biddles.co.uk
Web Site: www.biddles.co.uk
Key Personnel
Man Dir: Rod Willett *E-mail:* rwillett@biddles.co.uk
Founded: 1885
Business from Other Countries: 8%

Book Creation
20 Lochaline St, London W6 9SH
Tel: (020) 7583 0553 *Fax:* (020) 7583 9439
E-mail: info@librios.com
Web Site: www.librios.com
Key Personnel
Chairman: Hal Robinson *E-mail:* hal@librios.com
Founded: 1991
Business from Other Countries: 30%

Clays Ltd
Subsidiary of St Ives Plc
Popson St, Bungay, Suffolk NR35 1ED
Tel: (01986) 893211 *Fax:* (01986) 89529
E-mail: sales@clays.co.uk
Web Site: www.st-ives.co.uk; www.clays.co.uk
Key Personnel
Contact: Sarah Orell
Founded: 1817
Business from Other Countries: 15%

William Clowes Ltd
Beccles, Suffolk NR34 9QE
Tel: (01502) 712884 *Fax:* (01502) 717003
E-mail: william@clowes.co.uk
Web Site: www.clowes.co.uk

Key Personnel
Man Dir: Ian Foyster *E-mail:* ifoyster@clowes.co.uk
Sales Dir: David C Browne *Tel:* (07768) 658820
  E-mail: dbrowne@clowes.co.uk
Founded: 1803
Business from Other Countries: 1%

Cox & Wyman Ltd
Cardiff Rd, Reading, Berks RG1 8EX
Tel: (0118) 953 0500 *Fax:* (0118) 950 7222
E-mail: coxandwyman@cpi-group.net
Web Site: www.cpi-group.net
Key Personnel
Commercial Contact: Paul Hicks
  E-mail: phicks@cpi-group.co.uk; Dave Watkins
  E-mail: dwatkins@cpi-group.co.uk
Founded: 1777
Business from Other Countries: 12%
Parent Company: Chevrillon Philippe Industrie of France

FiberMark Red Bridge International Ltd
Ainsworth, Bolton BL2 5PD
Tel: (01204) 556900 *Fax:* (01204) 384754
E-mail: sales@redbridge.co.uk
Web Site: www.redbridge.co.uk
Key Personnel
Man Dir: Denis Wolstenholme
Sales & Marketing Dir: Derek Ives
  E-mail: dives@redbridge.co.uk
Business from Other Countries: 35%
Parent Company: Rexam
U.S. Office(s): FiberMark, 161 Wellington Rd, PO Box 498, Brattleboro, VT 05302, United States *Tel:* 802-257-0365 *Fax:* 802-257-5900
E-mail: info@fibermark.com

Furnival Press
61 Lilford Rd, London SE5 9HY
Tel: (020) 7274 2067 *Fax:* (020) 7274 6984
E-mail: furnprint@aol.com
Key Personnel
Man Dir: Keith Herbert

The Guernsey Press Co Ltd
Braye Rd, Vale, Guernsey GY1 3BW
Mailing Address: PO Box 57, Vale, Guernsey GY1 3BW
Tel: (01481) 240240; (01481) 243657 (ISDN) *Fax:* (01481) 240275
E-mail: books@guernsey-press.com
Web Site: www.guernsey-press.com
Key Personnel
Contact: Mr T A R Duquemin
Founded: 1897
Business from Other Countries: 80%

Hammond Bindery Ltd
Subsidiary of The Charlesworth Group
Unit 2, Flanshaw Way, Flanshaw Lane, Wakefield, West Yorks WF2 9LP
Tel: (01924) 369598 *Fax:* (01924) 364108; (01924) 298075
Web Site: www.hammpack.co.uk
Key Personnel
Man Dir: Steve Allan *E-mail:* s_allan@hammond-bindery.co.uk
Sales Manager: Kirk Allan *E-mail:* k_allan@hammond-bindery.co.uk
Technical Sales Dir: Brian Quarmby
  E-mail: b_quarmby@hammond-bindery.co.uk
Founded: 1972

Harveys Ltd
Edgefield Road Industrial Estate, Loanhead Midlothian EH20 9SX
Tel: (0131) 440 0074; (0131) 440 0014 *Fax:* (0131) 440 3478
E-mail: sales@harveys.ltd.uk
Web Site: www.harveys.ltd.uk

MATERIALS

Key Personnel
Chairman: Tom Domke *E-mail:* tom@harveys.ltd.uk
Joint Man Dir: Tom Dalgleish *E-mail:* tom.dalgleish@harveys.ltd.uk; Peter McCraw *E-mail:* peter@harveys.ltd.uk
Dir Customer Service: Craig Linton *E-mail:* craig@harveys.ltd.uk
Sales Dir: Ross Porter *E-mail:* ross@harveys.ltd.uk
Sales Manager: Gavin Lowe *E-mail:* sales@harveys.ltd.uk
Sales Executive: Frank Johnstone *E-mail:* sales@harveys.ltd.uk; Alasdair Ponton *E-mail:* sales@harveys.ltd.uk; Chris Seaton *E-mail:* chris@harveys.ltd.uk
Founded: 1856
Business from Other Countries: 10%

Hobbs The Printers Ltd
Brunel Rd, Totton, Hants SO40 3WX
Tel: (023) 8066 4800 *Fax:* (023) 8066 4801
E-mail: info@hobbs.uk.com
Web Site: www.hobbs.uk.com; www.hobbstheprinters.co.uk
Key Personnel
Man Dir: David Hobbs *E-mail:* d.a.hobbs@hobbs.uk.com
Commercial Dir: Terry Ozanne *E-mail:* t.ozanne@hobbs.uk.com
Founded: 1884
Business from Other Countries: 4%

Hunter & Foulis Ltd
Unit 3, Gateside Commerce Park, Haddington, East Lothian EH41 3ST
Tel: (01620) 826 379 *Fax:* (01620) 829 485
E-mail: mail@hunterfoulis.co.uk
Web Site: www.hunterfoulis.co.uk
Key Personnel
Man Dir: Richard Beese
Production Dir: David Bisset
Founded: 1857

Image & Print Group Ltd
Unit 9, Oakbank Industrial Estate, Glasgow G20 7LU
Tel: (0141) 353 1900; (0141) 353 8620 (ISDN) *Fax:* (0141) 353 8611
E-mail: info@imageandprint.co.uk
Web Site: www.imageandprint.co.uk
Key Personnel
Man Dir: Ken Roberts
Production: Stephen McPhee *E-mail:* stephen@imageandprint.co.uk
Founded: 1975

Intype Libra Ltd
Units 3 & 4, Elm Grove Industrial Estate, Elm Grove, Wimbledon SW19 4HE
Tel: (020) 8947 7863 *Fax:* (020) 8947 3652
E-mail: intype@btconnect.com
Key Personnel
Man Dir: Tony Chapman *E-mail:* tony.chapman@intypelibra.co.uk
Production: Moya Birchell; Richard Mayne
Founded: 1976
Business from Other Countries: 5%

The Malvern Press Ltd
71 Dalston Lane, London E8 2NG
Tel: (020) 7249 2991 *Fax:* (020) 7254 1720
E-mail: admin@malvernpress.com
Web Site: www.malvernpress.com
Key Personnel
Man Dir: Leslie Wynn
Marketing Dir: Peter Wynn
Founded: 1953
Business from Other Countries: 15%

Page Bros Ltd (Norwich)
Subsidiary of Milex Ltd
Mile Cross Lane, Norwich, Norfolk NR6 6SA
Tel: (01603) 429141 *Fax:* (01603) 485126
E-mail: info@pagebros.co.uk
Web Site: www.milex.co.uk
Key Personnel
Sales Dir: Steve Commons
Founded: 1750
Business from Other Countries: 20%
Branch Office(s)
105-A Euston St, London NW1 2ET *Tel:* (020) 7383 2212 *Fax:* (020) 1383 4145

Printafoil Ltd
Foxtail Rd, Ransomes Park, Ipswich IP3 9RT
Tel: (01473) 721701 *Fax:* (01473) 270705
E-mail: printafoil@blockfoil.com
Web Site: www.blockfoil.com
Key Personnel
Dir: Simon Flower
General Manager: Jonathan Higgs *E-mail:* jonhiggs@blockfoil.com
Sales Executive: Barry Fairservice
Production: Norman Eyles *E-mail:* normaneyles@blockfoil.com; Simon Piddock *E-mail:* simonpiddock@blockfoil.com
Estimator: Carl Thomas

J R Reid Print & Media Group, see J R Reid Printing Group Ltd

J R Reid Printing Group Ltd
79-99 Glasgow Rd, Blantyre, Glasgow G72 0YL
Tel: (01698) 826000 *Fax:* (01698) 824944
E-mail: info@reid-print-group.co.uk
Web Site: www.reid-print-group.co.uk
Key Personnel
Joint Man Dir: John R Reid *E-mail:* johnreid@reid-print-group.co.uk
Founded: 1972

Antony Rowe Ltd
Bumper's Farm Industrial Estate, Chippenham, Wilts SN14 6LH
Tel: (01249) 659 705; (01249) 445 535 (ISDN) *Fax:* (01249) 448 900
E-mail: sales@antonyrowe.co.uk
Web Site: www.antonyrowe.co.uk
Key Personnel
Chief Executive: Ralph Bell
Production Dir: Mike Bando
Technical Dir: Andy Burns
Founded: 1983
Business from Other Countries: 2%
Branch Office(s)
Highfield Industrial Estate, 2 Whittle Dr, Eastbourne, East Sussex BN23 6QH *Tel:* (01323) 500040 *Fax:* (01323) 521117 *E-mail:* bob.hunt@antonyrowe.co.uk

Stott Brothers Ltd
Lister Lane, Halifax, W Yorks HX1 5AJ
Tel: (01422) 362184 *Fax:* (01422) 353707
E-mail: stottbros@aol.com
Key Personnel
Man Dir: Ian Bullough

M & A Thomson Litho Ltd
Kelvin Industrial Estate, 2-16 Colvilles Pl, East Kilbride, Glasgow G75 0SN
Tel: (01355) 233081 *Fax:* (01355) 245 039
Web Site: www.thomsonlitho.com
Key Personnel
Man Dir: John Williamson
Sales: Rona Chrisholm

Sales Office(s): Obrechtstr 35A, Clobe 2nd floor, 5344 AT Oss, Netherlands *Tel:* (0412) 465190 *Fax:* (0412) 465 191
Gibbs House, Kennel Ride, Ascot Berks SL5 7NT *Tel:* (01344) 893 885 *Fax:* (01344) 893 887

Watkiss Automation Ltd
Subsidiary of The Watkiss Group
Watkiss House, Blaydon Rd, Middlefield Industrial Estate, Sandy, Beds SG19 1RZ
Tel: (01767) 682177 *Fax:* (01767) 691769
E-mail: contact@watkiss.com
Web Site: www.watkiss.com
Key Personnel
Technical Dir: M Watkiss
Founded: 1959
Business from Other Countries: 5%

Winter & Co UK Ltd
Stonehill, Huntingdon, Cambs PE29 6ED
Tel: (01480) 377177 *Fax:* (01480) 377166
E-mail: sales@winteruk.com
Web Site: www.winteruk.com
Key Personnel
Man Dir: Richard Higgins *E-mail:* richardh@winteruk.com
Sales Dir: Steve Burdett *E-mail:* steveb@winteruk.com
Founded: 1892

United States

Bang Printing Co Inc
3323 Oak St, Brainerd, MN 56401
Mailing Address: PO Box 587, Brainerd, MN 56401-0587
Tel: 218-829-2877 *Toll Free Tel:* 800-328-0450 *Fax:* 218-829-7145
Web Site: www.bangprinting.com
Key Personnel
VP, Sales: Todd Vanek *Tel:* 218-822-2124 *E-mail:* toddv@bangprinting.com
Founded: 1899
Business from Other Countries: 50%

Blaze International Productions Inc
225 W 35 St, Suite 1100, New York, NY 10001
Tel: 212-967-7501 *Fax:* 212-967-7551
Key Personnel
Pres: Eugene Sanchez *Tel:* 212-967-7501 ext 222 *E-mail:* e.sanchez@blazeint.com
Founded: 1990
Business from Other Countries: 80%

BookBuilders New York Inc
353 Strawtown Rd, New City, NY 10956
Tel: 845-639-5316 *Fax:* 845-639-5318
Web Site: www.mcabooks.com
Key Personnel
Pres: Martin Cook *E-mail:* martin@mcabooks.com
Founded: 1977
Business from Other Countries: 60%

Coneco Litho Graphics
Division of NET 2 PRESS Inc
58 Dix Ave, Glens Falls, NY 12801
Mailing Address: PO Box 3255, Glen Falls, NY 12801-7255
Tel: 518-793-3823 *Fax:* 518-793-5823
Web Site: www.conecolithographics.com
Key Personnel
Gen Mgr: Steve Webber *E-mail:* swebber@conecolithographics.com
Founded: 1984
Business from Other Countries: 27%

UNITED STATES — MANUFACTURING

Conservation Resources International Inc
5532 Port Royal Rd, Springfield, VA 22151
Tel: 703-321-7730 *Toll Free Tel:* 800-634-6932
Fax: 703-321-0629
E-mail: criusa@conservationresources.com
Web Site: www.conservationresources.com
Key Personnel
Pres: William K Hollinger, Jr
VP: Lavonia Hollinger
Dir, Mktg: Abby A Shaw *Tel:* 215-625-8422
  E-mail: crisales@aol.com
Business from Other Countries: 30%
Membership(s): AIC

Martin Cook Associates Ltd
353 Strawtown Rd, New City, NY 10956
Tel: 845-639-5316 *Fax:* 845-639-5318
E-mail: mcanewcity@aol.com
Web Site: www.mcabooks.com
Key Personnel
Pres: Martin Cook *E-mail:* mcanewcity@aol.com
Founded: 1977
Business from Other Countries: 15%
Membership(s): Bookbinders Guild of New York

CS Graphics USA Inc
Subsidiary of CS Graphics Pte Ltd Singapore
8969 Lake Ct, Granite Bay, CA 95746
Tel: 916-791-9066 *Fax:* 916-791-9112
E-mail: csgraphics@mindspring.com
Key Personnel
Mgr, Sales & Mktg: Rick Marment *E-mail:* r.marment@csgraphics-world.com
Founded: 1980
Business from Other Countries: 30%

D & K Group
1795 Commerce Dr, Elk Grove Village, IL 60007
Tel: 847-956-0160 *Toll Free Tel:* 800-632-2314
  Fax: 847-956-8214
E-mail: info@dkgroup.net
Web Site: www.dkgroup.com
Key Personnel
Pres: Karl Singer
VP, Sales & Mktg: Marge Hayes
Mktg Communs Coord: Holli Hagene
  E-mail: holli.hagene@dkgroup.net
Founded: 1979
Business from Other Countries: 15%

Desktop Miracles Inc
112 S Main, PMB 294, Stowe, VT 05672
Tel: 802-253-7900 *Fax:* 802-253-1900
Web Site: www.desktopmiracles.com
Key Personnel
Pres & CEO: Barry T Kerrigan *E-mail:* barry@desktopmiracles.com
VP: Virginia Kerrigan *E-mail:* virginia@desktopmiracles.com
Founded: 1994
Business from Other Countries: 10%

DNP America LLC
Subsidiary of Dai Nippon Printing Co Ltd
335 Madison Ave, 3rd fl, New York, NY 10017
Tel: 212-687-2746; 212-503-1060 *Fax:* 212-286-1505
Web Site: www.dnp.co.jp/ *Cable:* DAIPRINTS NY
Key Personnel
Pres: Yoji Yamakawa
VP & Gen Mgr, Graphic Printing: Kohei Tsumori
  E-mail: tsumori-k@mail.dnp.co.jp
Founded: 1974
Business from Other Countries: 54%
Branch Office(s)
577 Airport Blvd, Suite 620, Burlingame, CA 94010, Gen Mgr: Kosuke Tago *Tel:* 650-340-6061 *Fax:* 650-340-6090

Elegance Printing & Book Binding (USA)
Member of The Elegance Printing Group
708 Glen Cove Ave, Glen Head, NY 11545
Tel: 516-676-5941 *Fax:* 516-676-5973
Web Site: www.elegancebooks.com
Key Personnel
Man Dir: Frank DeLuca *E-mail:* frank@elegancebooks.com
Founded: 1977
Business from Other Countries: 40%

Fibre Leather Manufacturing Corp
686 Belleville Ave, New Bedford, MA 02745
Tel: 508-997-4557 *Toll Free Tel:* 800-358-6012
  Fax: 508-997-7268
E-mail: fibreleather@earthlink.net
Key Personnel
Pres: Daniel E Finger
VP: Louis Finger
Sec: Carol Gutowski
Founded: 1927
Business from Other Countries: 20%

Graphic Services Corp
153 S Main St, Newtown, CT 06470
Tel: 203-270-7578 *Fax:* 203-270-1578
Web Site: www.independentcartongroup.com
Key Personnel
Pres: Andrew Willie *E-mail:* awillie633@aol.com
Off Mgr: Kathy Renzulli *E-mail:* krenzulli@independentcartongroup.com
Founded: 1990
Business from Other Countries: 10%
Membership(s): Independent Carton Group

Hindy's Enterprise
Division of Jinno International
3 Christine Dr, Chestnut Ridge, NY 10977-6802
Tel: 845-735-4666 *Fax:* 617-344-5905
Key Personnel
Pres: Yoh Jinno *E-mail:* jinno@hotmail.com
Founded: 1989
Business from Other Countries: 70%
Branch Office(s)
Melbourne Industrial Bldg, Block A, 20th fl, 16 Westlands Rd, Quarry Bay, Hong Kong *Tel:* 25166318 *Fax:* 25165161

IBT Global Ltd, see Integrated Book Technology Inc

ICG/Holliston
Subsidiary of Industrial Coatings Group
Hwy 11-W, Holliston Mills Rd, Church Hill, TN 37642
Mailing Address: PO Box 478, Kingsport, TN 37662-0478
Tel: 423-357-6141 *Toll Free Tel:* 800-251-0451
  Fax: 423-357-8840 *Toll Free Fax:* 800-325-0351
E-mail: custserv@icgholliston.com
Web Site: www.icgholliston.com
Key Personnel
Pres: Robert Dwyer
Exec VP, Sales: William Waldron, III
VP, Mktg: Joann Scherf *E-mail:* jscherf@holliston.com
Founded: 1897
Business from Other Countries: 10%
Cover Line(s) Milled: Arrestox/Roxite B; Imperium; Kennett; Pearl Linen; Sturdite

Imago
1431 Broadway, Penthouse, New York, NY 10018
Tel: 212-921-4411 *Fax:* 212-921-8226
E-mail: sales@imagousa.com
Web Site: www.imagousa.com
Key Personnel
Pres: Joseph E Braff *E-mail:* jbraff@imagousa.com
Northeast Sales: Linda Readerman
  E-mail: lreaderman@imagousa.com
USA Prodn Dir: Howard R Musk
  E-mail: hmusk@imagousa.com
Founded: 1985
Business from Other Countries: 100%
Branch Office(s)
Imago West Coast, 31952 Camino Capistrano, Suite C22, San Juan Capistrano, CA 92675, West Coast Sales: Greg Lee *Tel:* 949-661-5998 *Fax:* 949-661-8013 *E-mail:* glee@imagousa.com
Imago Midwest, 17 N Loomis St, Unit 4A, Chicago, IL 60607, Midwest Sales: Ma Yan *Tel:* 312-829-4051 *Fax:* 312-829-4059 *E-mail:* myan@imagousa.com
Imago Australia, 14 Brown St, Suite 241, Chatswood, Sydney 2067, Australia, Contact: Emma Bell *Tel:* (02) 9415 2713 *Fax:* (02) 9415 2714 *E-mail:* sales@imagoaus.com
Imago France, 6 eme Etage, 42, rue le Peletier, 75009 Paris, France, Contact: Matt Critchlow *Tel:* (1) 42 81 41 24 *Fax:* (1) 42 81 41 24 *E-mail:* sales@imagogroup.com
Imago Services (HKG) Ltd, 653-659 Kings Rd, 6th fl, Flat B, North Point, Hong Kong, Contact: Kendrick Cheung *Tel:* 2811 3316 *Fax:* 2597 5256 *E-mail:* enquiries@imago.com.hk
Imago Productions (FE) Pte Ltd, MacPherson Industrial Complex, Suite 05-01, 5 Lorong Bakar Batu, Singapore 348742, Singapore, Contact: K C Ng *Tel:* 6748 4433 *Fax:* 6748 6082 *E-mail:* enquiries@imago.com.sg
Imago (UK/Europe) Publishing Ltd, Albury Ct, Albury Thame, Oxfordshire OX9 2LP, United Kingdom, Contact: Colin Risk *Tel:* (01844) 337000 *Fax:* (01844) 339935 *E-mail:* sales@imago.co.uk *Web Site:* www.imago.co.uk

Integrated Book Technology Inc
Division of The IBT Group
18 Industrial Park Rd, Troy, NY 12180
Tel: 518-271-5117 *Fax:* 518-266-9422
E-mail: mail@integratedbook.com
Web Site: www.integratedbook.com
Key Personnel
CEO & Pres: John R Paeglow *E-mail:* johnp@integratedbook.com
VP & Chief Technol Officer: William Clockel
  E-mail: billc@integratedbook.com
VP, Sales & Mktg: Robert Lindberg
  E-mail: bobl@integratedbook.com
Dir, Sales & Cust Serv: Karen Lombardo
Dir, Info Technol: Michael Whalen
  E-mail: mikew@integratedbook.com
Regl Sales: Tim Knickerbocker *E-mail:* timk@integratedbook.com
Founded: 1991
Business from Other Countries: 20%
Branch Office(s)
The IBT Global Ltd, 2 Finsbury Park Rd, London N4-2JZ, United Kingdom, Intl Strategist: Peter Kenyon *Tel:* (020) 7351 3332 *Fax:* (020) 7351 3332 *E-mail:* bobl@integratedbook.com
Membership(s): BMI

Jinno International Group
3 Christine Dr, Chestnut Ridge, NY 10977-6802
Tel: 845-735-4666 *Fax:* 617-344-5905
E-mail: jinno@hotmail.com
Key Personnel
Pres: Yoh Jinno
VP: Sharon Jinno
Founded: 1989
Business from Other Countries: 98%
Branch Office(s)
Hindy's Enterprise, Melbourne Industrial Bldg, 16 Westlands Rd, Block A, 20th fl, Quarry Bay, Hong Kong *Tel:* 516-6318 *Fax:* 516-5161
Wing Yiu Printing Co, Melbourne Industrial Bldg, 6th fl, Block A, 16 Westlands Rd, Quarry

Bay, Hong Kong, Contact: Law Ming Wah *Tel:* 561 0283 *Fax:* 565 8233
c/o Eurasia Press Pte Ltd, 10/14 Kampong Ampat, Singapore 1336, Singapore, Contact: Allan Fong *Tel:* 280 5522 *Fax:* 280 0593
Jinno International Singapore, 710 Ang Mo Kio, Ave 8, Suite 07-2615, Singapore 2056, Singapore *Tel:* 458 0778

Linick International Inc
Division of The Linick Group Inc
Linick Bldg, 7 Putter Lane, Middle Island, NY 11953
Mailing Address: PO Box 102, Middle Island, NY 11953-0102
Tel: 631-924-3888 *Fax:* 631-924-3890
E-mail: linickgrp@att.net
Web Site: www.lgroup.addr.com
Key Personnel
Chmn & CEO: Andrew S Linick, PhD
Treas: Marvin Glickman
Exec VP: Roger Dextor
Founded: 1972
Business from Other Countries: 30%

LK Litho
Division of The Linick Group Inc
Linick Bldg, 7 Putter Lane, Middle Island, NY 11953
Mailing Address: PO Box 102, Middle Island, NY 11953-0102
Tel: 631-924-3888
E-mail: linickgrp@att.net
Web Site: www.lgroup.addr.com
Key Personnel
VP: Roger Dextor
Founded: 1968
Business from Other Countries: 20%

Mazer Publishing Services
Division of The Mazer Corporation
6680 Poe Ave, Dayton, OH 45414
Tel: 937-264-2600 *Fax:* 937-264-2624
E-mail: info@mazer.com
Web Site: www.mazer.com
Key Personnel
Pres: William Franklin *E-mail:* bill_franklin@mazer.com
Exec VP: Ken Fultz *E-mail:* ken_fultz@mazer.com
Exec Dir, Sales: Bill Faber *Fax:* 937-264-2622 *E-mail:* bill_faber@mazer.com
Founded: 1964
Business from Other Countries: 10%
Branch Office(s)
2460 Sand Lake Rd, Orlando, FL 32809, Contact: Bryan Blakley *Tel:* 407-859-5552 *Fax:* 407-859-0643 *E-mail:* bryan_blakley@mazer.com
224 Lexington Ave, Fox River Grove, IL 60021, Contact: Dennis Bowman *Tel:* 847-639-1555 *Fax:* 847-639-1562 *E-mail:* dennis_bowman@mazer.com
22 Lehigh Rd, Wellesley, MA 02181, Contact: Ken Leahy *Tel:* 781-237-4112 *Fax:* 781-431-6184 *E-mail:* ken_leahy@mazer.com
22 Laurel Place, Upper Montclair, NJ 07043, Contact: John Martel *Tel:* 973-744-4320 *Fax:* 973-746-5608 *E-mail:* john_martel@mazer.com
3081 Glenmere Ct, Kettering, OH 45440, Contact: Mark Brewer *Tel:* 937-299-5746 *Fax:* 937-299-5761 *E-mail:* mark_brewer@mazer.com
363 Porter Rd, Bishop, TX 78602, Contact: Steve Absher *Tel:* 512-303-9758 *Fax:* 512-303-9791 *E-mail:* steve_absher@mazer.com
Membership(s): BMI

Milanostampa/New Interlitho USA Inc
Subsidiary of Milanostampa New Interlitho Italia SpA
299 Broadway, Suite 901, New York, NY 10007
Tel: 212-964-2430 *Fax:* 212-964-2497
Web Site: www.milanostampa.com
Key Personnel
Chmn & Sales Rep: Rino Varrasso *Tel:* 917-225-9460 *E-mail:* rvarrasso@milanostampa-usa.com
Founded: 1974
Business from Other Countries: 75%

Palace Press International - Corporate Headquarters
17 Paul Dr, San Rafael, CA 94903
Tel: 415-526-1370 *Toll Free Tel:* 800-809-3792 *Fax:* 415-526-1394
E-mail: info@palacepress.com
Web Site: www.palacepress.com
Key Personnel
CEO: Raoul Goff *E-mail:* raoul@palacepress.com
Dir, Intl Sales & Mktg: Gordon Goff *E-mail:* gordon@palacepress.com
Dir: Steven Goff *E-mail:* steven@palacepress.com
Founded: 1984
Business from Other Countries: 20%
Branch Office(s)
Palace Press International Los Angeles, 303 W Newby Ave, Suite C, San Gabriel, CA 91777, Contact: Roger Ma *Tel:* 626-282-8877 *Fax:* 626-282-6880 *E-mail:* roger@palacepress.com
4308 Fence Place, Louisville, KY 40241, Contact: Joe Rackowski *Tel:* 502-429-9276 *Fax:* 502-423-0760 *E-mail:* joe@palacepress.com
Palace Press International New York, 180 Varick St, 10th fl, New York, NY 10014, Contact: Jessica Cornacchia *Tel:* 212-462-2622 *Fax:* 212-463-9130 *E-mail:* jessica@palacepress.com

Printing Corp of the Americas Inc
620 SW 12 Ave, Fort Lauderdale, FL 33312
Tel: 954-781-8100 *Fax:* 954-781-8421
E-mail: pcaprint@bellsouth.net
Web Site: www.pcaprint.bellsouth.net
Key Personnel
Pres: Jan Tuchman
Founded: 1979
Business from Other Countries: 15%

Regent Publishing Services
9327 Rambler Dr, St Louis, MO 63123
Tel: 314-631-7581 *Fax:* 314-638-5113
E-mail: regentstl@aol.com
Key Personnel
Sales Dir: Carol Davis-Tierney
Mktg Dir: James J Tierney
Founded: 1985
Business from Other Countries: 100%

Taylor Publishing Company
1550 W Mockingbird Lane, Dallas, TX 75235
Tel: 214-819-8226 *Toll Free Tel:* 800-677-2800 *Fax:* 214-630-1852
E-mail: info@taylorpub.com
Web Site: www.taylorpub.com
Key Personnel
CEO: Dave Fiore
Dir, Fine Books & Div Sales Mgr: W Jay Love
Dir, Mktg: Mike Taylor
Founded: 1939
Business from Other Countries: 10%

Times Publishing Group
Division of Times Publishing Ltd/Singapore
99 White Plains Rd, Tarrytown, NY 10591
Tel: 914-366-9888 *Fax:* 914-366-9898
Web Site: www.tpl.com.sg
Key Personnel
Cust Serv Exec: Bonnie Stone *E-mail:* bstone@marshallcavendish.com
Sales Mgr: Suresh Kumar *E-mail:* skumar@marshallcavendish.com
Founded: 1965
Business from Other Countries: 90%

Uruguay

Barreiro y Ramos SA
25 de Mayo, Esq J C Gomez, Casilla Correos, 15, Montevideo
Tel: (02) 96 23 58 *Fax:* (02) 96 23 58
Telex: 23901PB.CVJA.UY *Cable:* BAREIRAMOS
Key Personnel
President: Gaston Barreiro
Vice President: Guzman Barreiro
Founded: 1837
Business from Other Countries: 10%

Manufacturing Services & Equipment Index

BOOK MANUFACTURING EQUIPMENT

United States
AWT World Trade, pg 1248
Challenge Machinery Co, pg 1248
The Cleveland Vibrator Co, pg 1248
D & K Group, pg 1248

DISTRIBUTION & MAILING

Canada
Appleby's Bindery Ltd, pg 1245
Printcrafters Inc, pg 1245
PrintWest, pg 1245
Transcontinental Printing Book Group, pg 1245

Germany
C L Baader Buch & Offsetdruckere GmbH & Co KG, pg 1245
Priese GmbH & Co, pg 1245

Hong Kong
Elegance Finance Printing Services Ltd, pg 1245
Golden Cup Printing Co Ltd, pg 1246
Hong Kong Christian Service, pg 1246
Prontaprint Asia Ltd, pg 1246
Sino Publishing House Ltd, pg 1246

New Zealand
Bookprint Consultants Ltd, pg 1246
Rogan McIndoe Print Ltd, pg 1246

Portugal
Edicoes Silabo, pg 1246

Singapore
Craft Print Pte Ltd, pg 1246
Eurasia Press Pte Ltd, pg 1246
Ho Printing Singapore Pte Ltd, pg 1246
Markono Print Media Pte Ltd, pg 1246
Times Printers Pte Ltd, pg 1246

Slovenia
Gorenjski Tisk Printing House, pg 1246

Spain
Luis Vives (Edelvives), pg 1247

Switzerland
Schweizer Buchzentrum, pg 1247

United Republic of Tanzania
Peramiho Publications, pg 1247

Thailand
J Film Process Co Ltd, pg 1247

United Kingdom
J W Arrowsmith Ltd, pg 1247
The Bath Press, pg 1247
Book Production Consultants PLC, pg 1247
Butler & Tanner Ltd, pg 1247
Cambridge University Press - Printing Division, pg 1247
Clays Ltd, pg 1247
William Clowes Ltd, pg 1247
Cradley Print Ltd, pg 1247
Hammond Bindery Ltd, pg 1247
Headley Brothers Ltd, pg 1247
Hobbs The Printers Ltd, pg 1247
Ikon Document Management Services, pg 1248
Multiplex Medway Ltd, pg 1248
Page Bros Ltd (Norwich), pg 1248
Pillar Publications Ltd, pg 1248
Antony Rowe Ltd, pg 1248
TMS Development International Ltd, pg 1248
Turnaround Publisher Services Ltd, pg 1248
Watkiss Automation Ltd, pg 1248
John Wilson Booksales, pg 1248

United States
A-R Editions Inc, pg 1248
Express Media Corp, pg 1249
Fairfield Marketing Group Inc, pg 1249
Hamilton Printing Co, pg 1249
Integrated Book Technology Inc, pg 1249
LK Litho, pg 1249
Marrakech Express Inc, pg 1249
Mazer Publishing Services, pg 1249
Times Publishing Group, pg 1249
Fred Weidner & Daughter Printers, pg 1249

Uruguay
Barreiro y Ramos SA, pg 1250

MANUFACTURING BROKERS OR BROKERING

Belgium
IMPF bvba, pg 1245

Germany
Priese GmbH & Co, pg 1245

Hong Kong
Co-Fine Promotions, pg 1245
Colorcraft Ltd, pg 1245

Israel
Monoline Ltd, pg 1246

New Zealand
Bookprint Consultants Ltd, pg 1246
Egan-Reid Ltd, pg 1246

Puerto Rico
Publishing Resources Inc, pg 1246

Singapore
Imago Productions (Far East) Pte Ltd, pg 1246
SNP SPrint Pte Ltd, pg 1246

United Republic of Tanzania
Peramiho Publications, pg 1247

United Kingdom
Book Production Consultants PLC, pg 1247
Chase Publishing Services, pg 1247

United States
A-R Editions Inc, pg 1248
Blaze International Productions Inc, pg 1248
BookBuilders New York Inc, pg 1248
Martin Cook Associates Ltd, pg 1248
Desktop Miracles Inc, pg 1249
Linick International Inc, pg 1249
Regent Publishing Services, pg 1249
Fred Weidner & Daughter Printers, pg 1249

Manufacturing Services & Equipment

This section includes companies throughout the world that offer manufacturing services & equipment. Those U.S. and Canadian companies with 10% or more of their business done outside North America are also included here. Immediately preceding this section is an index classifying companies by services offered.

Belgium

IMPF bvba
Sint-Amandstr 18, 9000 Gent
Tel: (09) 225 44 29; (09) 265 99 00 *Fax:* (09) 233 13 38
E-mail: impf@xs4all.be
Key Personnel
Manager: Xavier Dewulf
Founded: 1958
Business from Other Countries: 10%

Canada

Appleby's Bindery Ltd
1303 Route 102, Upper Gagetown, NB E5M 1R5
Tel: 506-488-2086 *Toll Free Tel:* 800-561-2005 (Canada only) *Fax:* 506-488-2086
E-mail: applbind@nbnet.nb.ca
Key Personnel
Pres & Owner: David E Appleby
Mgr: John Appleby
Founded: 1976
Business from Other Countries: 10%

Master Flo Technology Inc
1233 Tessier St, Hawkesbury, ON K6A 3R1
Tel: 613-636-0539 *Fax:* 613-636-0762
E-mail: info@mflo.com
Web Site: www.mflo.com
Key Personnel
VP, Opers: Tim Duffy
Founded: 1984
Business from Other Countries: 75%

Printcrafters Inc
78 Hutchings St, Winnipeg, MB R2X 3B1
Tel: 204-633-7117 *Fax:* 204-694-1519
E-mail: info@printcraftersinc.com
Web Site: www.printcraftersinc.com
Key Personnel
Pres: Bob Payne *Tel:* 204-633-7117 ext 223 *Fax:* 204-694-1594 *E-mail:* bpayne@printcraftersinc.com
Founded: 1996 (Employee owned)
Business from Other Countries: 30%

PrintWest
1150 Eighth Ave, Regina, SK S4R 1C9
Tel: 306-525-2304 *Toll Free Tel:* 800-236-6438 *Fax:* 306-757-2439
E-mail: general@printwest.com
Web Site: www.printwest.com
Key Personnel
CEO: Wayne UnRuh
VP, Sales: Ken Benson
Founded: 1992
Business from Other Countries: 15%
Branch Office(s)
Box 2500, 2310 Millar Ave, Saskatoon, SK S7K 2C4 *Tel:* 306-665-3560 *Fax:* 306-653-1255

Transcontinental Printing Book Group
Division of Transcontinental Group
395 Lebeau Blvd, St-Laurent, PQ H4N 1S2
Tel: 514-337-8560 *Toll Free Tel:* 800-361-3599 *Fax:* 514-339-5230
Web Site: www.transcontinental.com
Key Personnel
VP, Book Group: Jacques Gregoire
US Sales Mgr: Denis Beaudin *Tel:* 514-339-2220 ext 4101 *E-mail:* beaudind@transcontinental.ca
Founded: 1976
Business from Other Countries: 15%
Branch Office(s)
614 Yates Ave, Calumet City, IL 60409, United States, Contact: Kristopher D Levy *Tel:* 708-832-1528 *Fax:* 708-832-9510 *E-mail:* kris.levy@transcontinental.ca (Midwest)
3653 W Leland Ave, Suite One W, Chicago, IL 60625, United States, Contact: Tim Taylor *Tel:* 773-583-8155 *Fax:* 773-583-8162 *E-mail:* tim.taylor@transcontinental.ca (Midwest)
245 Eliot St, Ashland, MA 01721, United States, Contact: Ed Catania *Tel:* 508-881-1119 *Fax:* 508-881-7739 *E-mail:* ecatania@attnbi.com (East Coast)
19 Crown St, Milton, MA 02186-1419, United States, Contact: Michael Gazzola *Tel:* 617-696-1435 *Fax:* 617-696-1025 *E-mail:* mikebook@attbi.com (East Coast)
37 Herman Blvd, Franklin Square, NY 11010, United States, Contact: Tom Malloy *Tel:* 516-775-2980 *Fax:* 516-488-0253 *E-mail:* tmmalloy@aol.com (NY)
3175 Summit Square Dr, Suite C9, Oakton, VA 22124, United States, Contact: David Avesian *Tel:* 703-255-1332 *Fax:* 703-255-1343 *E-mail:* davesian@cox.rr.com (Southeast)
559 Lowrys Rd, Parksville, BC V9P 2R8, Contact: Mike Davies *Tel:* 250-248-9700 *Fax:* 250-248-2353 *E-mail:* bookguys@shaw.ca (West Coast)
15373 Victoria Ave, White Rock, BC V4B 1H1, Contact: Wade Davies *Tel:* 604-535-8800 *Fax:* 604-535-8802 *E-mail:* daviesw@shaw.ca (West Coast)
490 Wilfred Dr, Peterborough, ON K9K 2H1, Contact: Tom Lang *Tel:* 705-760-9594 *Fax:* 705-760-9485 *E-mail:* langt@transcontinental.ca (New York)

Webcom Ltd
3480 Pharmacy Ave, Toronto, ON M1W 2S7
Tel: 416-496-1000 *Toll Free Tel:* 800-665-9322 *Fax:* 416-496-1537
E-mail: webcom@webcomlink.com
Web Site: www.webcomlink.com
Key Personnel
VP, Sales & Mktg: Mike Collinge
Mktg Mgr: Charlie Scime
Founded: 1976
Business from Other Countries: 40%
Membership(s): BMI; Canadian Book & Periodical Council; Canadian Book Manufacturers Association; CPIA; Printing Industries of America

France

Critiques Livres Distribution SAS
24 Rue Malmaison, BP 93, 93172 Bagnolet Cedex
Tel: (014) 360-3910 *Fax:* (014) 897-3706
E-mail: critiques.livres@wanadoo.fr
Key Personnel
President: Rosalind Fay-Boehlinger
Founded: 1976
Business from Other Countries: 100%

Germany

C L Baader Buch & Offsetdruckere GmbH & Co KG
Gutenbergstr 1, 72525 Muensingen
Tel: (07381) 791 *Fax:* (07381) 411412 *Cable:* BAADER-MUNSINGEN
Founded: 1835

Priese GmbH & Co
Auerbacher Str 9, 14193 Berlin
Tel: (030) 8263024 *Fax:* (030) 3249630
Key Personnel
Contact: Elma Priese; Hans Joachim Priese

Hong Kong

Co-Fine Promotions
1407 & Mezz floor, Shiu Fat Bldg, 139-141 Wai Yip St Kwun Tong, Kowloon
Tel: 25180383 *Fax:* 25180361
E-mail: cofine@netvigator.com
Key Personnel
Contact: Kenneth Derek Kan
Founded: 1988
Business from Other Countries: 30%

Colorcraft Ltd
Unit 8-9, 16/F Kodak House Phase II, 321 Java Rd, North Point
Tel: 25909033 *Fax:* 25909005; 25909271
E-mail: info.cc@colorcraft.com.hk
Web Site: www.colorcraft.com.hk
Key Personnel
Chairman & Dir: Anne Mary Walker
Business from Other Countries: 100%

Elegance Finance Printing Services Ltd
Subsidiary of Elegance Printing Company Limited
2401 Alexandra House, 16-20 Chater Rd, Central Hong Kong
Tel: 2283 2222 *Fax:* 2283 2283; 2521 3616
Web Site: www.eleganceholdings.com
Business from Other Countries: 2%

HONG KONG

Golden Cup Printing Co Ltd
Seapower Industrial Centre, 6/F, 177 Hoi Bun Rd, Kwun Tong, Kowloon
Tel: 23434254 *Fax:* 223415426
E-mail: info@goldencup.com.hk; sales@goldencup.com.hk
Web Site: www.goldencup.com.hk
Key Personnel
Man Dir: Yeung Kam Kai
General Manager: W K Ngan
Sales Manager: Mary Yeung *E-mail:* mary@goldencup.com.hk
Founded: 1969
Business from Other Countries: 80%
Branch Office(s)
Dongguan, China
Guangdong, China
Kunming, China
Yunan, China

Hong Kong Christian Service
33 Granville Rd, Tsimshatsui, Kowloon, Hong Kong SAR
Tel: 2731-6316; 2731-6360 *Fax:* 2731-6333; 2731-6363
E-mail: info@hkcs.org
Web Site: www.hkcs.org
Founded: 1952
Business from Other Countries: 1%

Prontaprint Asia Ltd
1/F, Gaylord Commercial Bldg, 114 Lockhart Rd, Wanchai
Tel: 28657525 *Fax:* 28661064
Key Personnel
Man Dir: Clive Howard
Founded: 1986
Business from Other Countries: 40%

Sino Publishing House Ltd
Room 301-302 Valley Centre, 80-82 Morrison Hill Rd, Wanchai, Hong Kong
Tel: 2884 9963 *Fax:* 2884 9321
E-mail: benyan@sinophl.com
Web Site: www.sinophl.com
Key Personnel
Dir: Stephen Stringer
Founded: 1993
Business from Other Countries: 75%

Israel

Monoline Ltd
3 Avnei Nezer, Kiryat Sefer
Tel: (08) 9741456 *Fax:* (08) 9741454
Key Personnel
Dir: S J Colthof
Founded: 1959
Business from Other Countries: 30%

New Zealand

Bookprint Consultants Ltd
Division of Grantham House Publishing
9 Wilkinson St, Apt 6, Oriental Bay, Wellington 6001
Tel: (04) 381 3071 *Fax:* (04) 381 3067
E-mail: gstewart@iconz.co.nz
Key Personnel
Chief Executive: Graham C Stewart
Founded: 1982
Business from Other Countries: 10%

Egan-Reid Ltd
Level 2, 38 Ireland St, Freemans Bay, Auckland 1001
Tel: (09) 3784100 *Fax:* (09) 3784300
E-mail: publishing@eganreid.co.nz
Web Site: www.egan-reid.com
Key Personnel
Man Dir: Gerard Reid *E-mail:* gerard@eganreid.co.nz
Contact: Mary Egan *E-mail:* mary@eganreid.co.nz
Founded: 1988
Business from Other Countries: 75%
Membership(s): Book Publishers Association of New Zealand

Rogan McIndoe Print Ltd
51 Crawford St, Dunedin
Mailing Address: PO Box 1361, Dunedin
Tel: (03) 474 0111 *Toll Free Tel:* (0800) 477 0355 *Fax:* (03) 474 0116
E-mail: production@rogan.co.nz
Web Site: www.rogan.co.nz
Key Personnel
Man Dir: Brendan A Murphy
Founded: 1893
Business from Other Countries: 1%

Portugal

Edicoes Silabo
Rua Cidade de Manchester 2, 1170 100 Lisbon
Tel: (021) 8130345 *Fax:* (021) 8166719
E-mail: silabo@silabo.pt
Web Site: www.silabo.pt
Key Personnel
Marketing Dir: Manuel Robalo *E-mail:* manuelrobalo@silabo.pt
Founded: 1983

Puerto Rico

Publishing Resources Inc
373 San Jorge St, 2nd floor, Santurce 00912
Tel: (787) 727-1800 *Fax:* (0787) 727-1823
E-mail: pri@chevako.net
Key Personnel
Owner & President: Ronald J Chevako
Editorial Dir: Anne W Chevako
Founded: 1976
Business from Other Countries: 5%

Singapore

Craft Print Pte Ltd
9 Joo Koon Circle, Jurong, Singapore 629041
Tel: 861 4040 *Fax:* 861 0530
E-mail: info@craftprint.com
Web Site: www.craftprint.com
Key Personnel
Man Dir: Charlie Chan
Marketing Manager: Desmond Chan

Eurasia Press Pte Ltd
10/14 Kg Ampat, Singapore 368318
Tel: 2805522 *Fax:* 2800593
Key Personnel
Marketing Dir: Allan Fong

MANUFACTURING SERVICES

Founded: 1937
Business from Other Countries: 65%

Ho Printing Singapore Pte Ltd
Changi South Industrial Estate, 31 Changi South St 1, Singapore 486769
Tel: 65429322 *Fax:* 65428322
Telex: RS 39685 HOFSET
Key Personnel
Man Dir: Ho Wai Hoi
Sales Executive: Ho Wah Yuen
Founded: 1951
Business from Other Countries: 30%

Imago Productions (Far East) Pte Ltd
5 Lorong Bakar Batu, Hex 05-01, MacPherson Industrial Complex, Singapore 348742
Tel: 67484433 *Fax:* 67486082
Web Site: www.imago.co.uk
Key Personnel
Man Dir: K C Ng
Branch Office(s)
Imago Sales USA Inc, 310 Madison Ave, Suite 2103, New York, NY 10017, United States
Tel: 212-921-4411 *Fax:* 212-370-4542

Markono Print Media Pte Ltd
Subsidiary of Markono Holdings Pte Ltd
21 Neythal Rd, Singapore 628586
Tel: 6281-1118 *Fax:* 6286-6663
E-mail: saleslead@markono.com.sg
Web Site: www.markono.com.sg
Key Personnel
Founder & Chairman: Ng Siow How
Dir: Bob Lee Song Tioh *E-mail:* blee@markono.com.sg
Founded: 1967
Business from Other Countries: 20%
Branch Office(s)
Kin Keong Colour Printing (M) Sdn Bhd, Port Klang 539538

SNP SPrint Pte Ltd
97 Ubi Ave 4, Singapore 408754
Tel: 6741-2500 *Fax:* 6744-3770
E-mail: enquiries@snpcorp.com
Web Site: www.snpcorp.com
Telex: SNPRS14462
Key Personnel
President & Chief Executive Officer: Yeo Chee Tong
Group Chief Financial Officer: Koo Tse Chia
Chief Operating Officer: Tan Jin Yan
US Sales Manager: Patrick Chung
Business from Other Countries: 40%
Parent Company: SNP Corporation Ltd

Times Printers Pte Ltd
Subsidiary of Times Publishing Group
16 Tuas Ave 5, Singapore 639340
Tel: 6311-2888 *Fax:* 6862-1313
E-mail: enquiry@timesprinters.com
Web Site: www.timesprinters.com *Cable:* TIMESPRINT
Key Personnel
Man Dir: Leong Kwok Sun
Corporate General Manager: Howard Wang
Sales Manager: Wendy Woo
Head of Sales & Customer Service: Patsy Tan
Founded: 1968
Business from Other Countries: 75%

Slovenia

Gorenjski Tisk Printing House
Mirka Vadnova 6, 4000 Kranj
Tel: (064) 263 0 *Fax:* (064) 241 323

E-mail: info@go-tisk.si
Web Site: www.go-tisk.si
Telex: 34560 YU GOTISK
Key Personnel
Dir: Kristina Kobal
Commercial Manager: Boris Krist
Founded: 1888
Business from Other Countries: 50%

Spain

Luis Vives (Edelvives)
Xaudaro, 25, 28034 Madrid
Tel: (091) 334 48 83 *Fax:* (091) 334 48 82
E-mail: dediciones@edelvives.es
Web Site: www.grupoeditorialluisvives.com
Key Personnel
Production Dir: Jesus Agudo Perez
Founded: 1890
Business from Other Countries: 25%

Switzerland

Schweizer Buchzentrum (Swiss Book Centre)
Buchzentrum AG (BZ), Domizil Industriestr Ost 10, 4614 Haegendorf
Tel: (062) 2092525; (062) 2092644 *Fax:* (062) 2092627; (062) 2092760
E-mail: info@sbz.ch
Web Site: www.sbz.ch
Key Personnel
Dept Manager: Michael Taylor
Founded: 1882

Centre Suisse du Livre, see Schweizer Buchzentrum

Centro Svizzero del Libro, see Schweizer Buchzentrum

Swiss Book Centre, see Schweizer Buchzentrum

United Republic of Tanzania

Peramiho Publications
PO Box 41, Peramiho
Tel: (054) 2730 *Fax:* (054) 2917
Key Personnel
Chief Executive: Fr Gerold Rupper
Founded: 1937

Thailand

J Film Process Co Ltd
440/7 Soi Rajchawitee 3, Rajathevee Rd, Bangkok 10400
Tel: (02) 248 6888 *Fax:* (0662) 247 4072; (0662) 246 4620
Key Personnel
President: Peer Prayukvong
Vice President: Siriporn Prayukvong
Man Dir: Pira Prayookwongse
Founded: 1970
Business from Other Countries: 45%

United Kingdom

J W Arrowsmith Ltd
Winterstoke Rd, Bristol BS3 2NT
Tel: (0117) 966 7545 *Fax:* (0117) 963 7829
E-mail: jw@arrowsmith.co.uk
Web Site: www.arrowsmith.co.uk
Key Personnel
Sales Dir: David J Hooper *E-mail:* dhooper@arrowsmith.co.uk
Founded: 1854
Business from Other Countries: 40%

The Bath Press
Subsidiary of Bath Press Group PLC
Lower Bristol Rd, Bath BA2 3BL
Tel: (01225) 428101 *Fax:* (01225) 312418
E-mail: bath@cpi-group.co.uk
Web Site: www.cpi-group.net
Key Personnel
Contact, Commercial: Jonathan Pickering *E-mail:* jpickering@cpi-group.co.uk
Founded: 1846
Business from Other Countries: 5%

Book Production Consultants PLC
25-27 High St, Chesterton, Cambridge CB4 1ND
Tel: (01223) 352790; (01223) 323092 (ISDN) *Fax:* (01223) 460718
E-mail: tl@bpccam.co.uk
Web Site: www.bpccam.co.uk
Key Personnel
Dir: Tony Littlechild *E-mail:* tl@bpccam.co.uk; Colin Walsh *E-mail:* cw@bpccam.co.uk
Founded: 1973
Business from Other Countries: 25%

Butler & Tanner Ltd
Caxton Rd, Frome, Somerset BA11 1NF
Tel: (01373) 451500 *Fax:* (01373) 451333
E-mail: manufacturing@butlerandtanner.com
Web Site: www.butlerandtanner.com
Key Personnel
Joint Man Dir: A Huett
Sales Dir: N White

Cambridge University Press - Printing Division
Division of Cambridge University Press
University Printing House, Edinburgh Bldg, Shaftesbury Rd, Cambridge CB2 2RU
Tel: (01223) 312393 *Fax:* (01223) 315052
Web Site: uk.cambridge.org
Key Personnel
Executive Dir: Sandra Ward *Tel:* (01223) 325608 *E-mail:* sward@cambridge.org
Marketing Manager: Helen Bradbury
Founded: 1534

Chase Publishing Services
Mead, Fortescue Rd, Sidmouth, Devon EX10 9QG
Tel: (01395) 514709 *Fax:* (01395) 514709
Key Personnel
President: Ray Addicott *E-mail:* r.addicott@btinternet.com
Founded: 1989

Clays Ltd
Subsidiary of St Ives Plc
Popson St, Bungay, Suffolk NR35 1ED
Tel: (01986) 893211 *Fax:* (01986) 895293
E-mail: sales@clays.co.uk
Web Site: www.clays.co.uk
Key Personnel
Contact: Sarah Orell
Founded: 1817
Business from Other Countries: 15%

William Clowes Ltd
Customer Service & Manufacturing Centre, Goal Lane, Beccles, Suffolk NR34 9QE
Tel: (01502) 712884 *Fax:* (01502) 717003
E-mail: william@clowes.co.uk
Web Site: www.clowes.co.uk
Key Personnel
Man Dir: Ian Foyster *E-mail:* ifoyster@clowes.co.uk
Sales Dir: David C Browne *Tel:* (07768) 658820 *E-mail:* dbrowne@clowes.co.uk
Founded: 1803
Business from Other Countries: 1%

Cradley Print Ltd
Chester Rd, Cradley Heath, Warley, West Midlands B64 6AB
Tel: (01384) 414100 *Fax:* (01384) 414102
Web Site: www.cradleygp.co.uk
Key Personnel
Man Dir: Chris Jordan
Founded: 1873
Business from Other Countries: 7%
Branch Office(s)
Quadcolor Repro

Hammond Bindery Ltd
Subsidiary of The Charlesworth Group
Unit 2, Flanshaw Way, Flanshaw Lane, Wakefield, West Yorks WF2 9LP
Tel: (01924) 369598 *Fax:* (01924) 298075
E-mail: sales@hammond-bindery.co.uk
Web Site: www.hammpack.co.uk
Key Personnel
Man Dir: Steve Allan *E-mail:* s_allan@hammond-bindery.co.uk
Sales Manager: Kirk Allan *E-mail:* k_allan@hammond-bindery.co.uk
Technical Sales Dir: Brian Quarmby *E-mail:* b_quarmby@hammond-bindery.co.uk
Founded: 1972

Headley Brothers Ltd
Invicta Press, Queens Rd, Ashford, Kent TN24 8HH
Tel: (01233) 623131 *Fax:* (01233) 612345
E-mail: printing@headley.co.uk
Web Site: www.headley.co.uk
Key Personnel
Man Dir: Roger Pitt *E-mail:* roger.pitt@headley.co.uk
Commercial Dir: Jon Pitt *E-mail:* jon.pitt@headley.co.uk
Sales Manager: Bruce Finn *E-mail:* bruce.finn@headley.co.uk
Founded: 1881
Business from Other Countries: 5%
Branch Office(s)
3rd Floor West, High Holborn House, 52-54 High Holborn, London WC1V 6LR

Hobbs The Printers Ltd
Brunel Rd, Totton, Hants SO40 3WX
Tel: (023) 8066 4800 *Fax:* (023) 8066 4801
E-mail: info@hobbs.uk.com
Web Site: www.hobbs.uk.com; www.hobbstheprinters.co.uk
Key Personnel
Man Dir: David Hobbs *E-mail:* d.a.hobbs@hobbs.uk.com
Commercial Dir: Terry Ozanne *E-mail:* t.ozanne@hobbs.uk.com

UNITED KINGDOM / MANUFACTURING SERVICES

Operations Dir: Graham Bromley *E-mail:* g.bromley@hobbs.uk.com
Operations Manager: Russell Hack *E-mail:* r.hack@hobbs.uk.com
Production Manager: Dave Smith *E-mail:* d.smith@hobbs.uk.com
Sales Representative: Sajid Ali *E-mail:* s.ali@hobbs.uk.com
Founded: 1884
Business from Other Countries: 4%

Ikon Document Management Services
Subsidiary of Microgen Holdings Plc
Telephone House, 69-77 Paul St, London EC2A 4NW
Tel: (020) 7336 6509 *Fax:* (020) 7336 7840
Web Site: www.uk.ikon.com
Key Personnel
Man Dir: Dave Weller
Business Development Dir: Aaron Biggs
Founded: 1972
Business from Other Countries: 40%
Branch Office(s)
Microgen City Park Watchmead, Welwyn Garden City, Herts AL7 1LT *Tel:* (01707) 355 555 *Fax:* (01707) 338 970

Multiplex Medway Ltd
Lordswood Industrial Estate, Gleaming Wood Dr, Walderslade, Kent ME5 8XT
Tel: (01634) 684371 *Fax:* (01634) 683840
E-mail: enquiries@multiplex-medway.co.uk
Web Site: www.multiplex-medway.co.uk
Key Personnel
Dir: Jon Chandler
Sales Manager: Paul Abson

Page Bros Ltd (Norwich)
Subsidiary of Milex Ltd
Mile Cross Lane, Norwich, Norfolk NR6 6SA
Tel: (01603) 429141 *Fax:* (01603) 485126
E-mail: info@pagebros.co.uk
Web Site: www.milex.co.uk
Key Personnel
Sales Dir: Steve Commons
Founded: 1750
Business from Other Countries: 20%
Branch Office(s)
105-A Euston St, London NW1 2ET *Tel:* (020) 7383 2212 *Fax:* (020) 7383 4145

Pillar Publications Ltd
Division of Pillar Publications Ltd
45 Woodland Grove, Weybridge, Surrey KT13 9EQ
Tel: (01932) 820282 *Fax:* (01932) 858035
E-mail: hu@bjhc.demon.co.uk
Key Personnel
Owner: Dr H de Glanville
Founded: 1981
Business from Other Countries: 10%

Antony Rowe Ltd
Division of Rexam Plc
Bumper's Farm Industrial Estate, Chippenham, Wilts SN14 6LH
Tel: (01249) 659 705; (01249) 445 535 (ISDN) *Fax:* (01249) 448 900
E-mail: sales@antonyrowe.co.uk
Web Site: www.antonyrowe.co.uk
Key Personnel
Chief Executive: Ralph Bell
Sales Manager: Andrew Copley
Founded: 1897
Business from Other Countries: 10%

TMS Development International Ltd
128 Holgate Rd, York YO24 4FL
Tel: (01904) 641640 *Fax:* (01904) 640076
E-mail: enquiry@tmsdi.com
Web Site: www.tmsdi.com

Key Personnel
Man Dir: Catherine Hick
Marketing Manager: Pat Anslow
Founded: 1989
Business from Other Countries: 30%

Turnaround Publisher Services Ltd
Unit 3, Olympia Trading Estate, Coburg Rd, Wood Green, London N22 6TZ
Tel: (020) 8829 3000 *Fax:* (020) 8881 5088
E-mail: enquires@turnaround-uk.com
Web Site: www.turnaround-uk.com
Key Personnel
Man Dir: Bill Godber *Tel:* (020) 8829 3008 *E-mail:* bill@turnaround-uk.com
Marketing Manager: Claire Thompson *Tel:* (020) 8829 3009 *E-mail:* claire@turnaround-uk.com
Finance Dir: Sue Gregg *Tel:* (020) 8829 3006 *E-mail:* sue@turnaround-uk.com
Founded: 1984
Business from Other Countries: 50%

Watkiss Automation Ltd
Subsidiary of The Watkiss Group
Watkiss House, Blaydon Rd, Middlefield Industrial Estate, Sandy, Beds SG19 1RZ
Tel: (01767) 682177 *Fax:* (01767) 691769
E-mail: contact@watkiss.com
Web Site: www.watkiss.com
Key Personnel
Technical Dir: M Watkiss
Founded: 1959
Business from Other Countries: 5%

John Wilson Booksales
One High St, Princes Risborough, Bucks HP27 0AG
Tel: (01844) 275927 *Fax:* (01844) 274402
E-mail: jw@jwbs.co.uk
Key Personnel
Contact: John S Wilson
Founded: 1982

United States

A-R Editions Inc
8551 Research Way, Suite 180, Middleton, WI 53562
Tel: 608-836-9000 *Toll Free Tel:* 800-736-0070 (US book orders only) *Fax:* 608-831-8200
E-mail: info@areditions.com
Web Site: www.areditions.com
Key Personnel
Pres & CEO: Patrick Wall
Dir, Sales & Mktg: James L Zychowicz *E-mail:* james.zychowicz@areditions.com
Founded: 1962
Business from Other Countries: 10%

AWT World Trade
4321 N Knox, Chicago, IL 60641
Tel: 773-777-7100 *Fax:* 773-777-0909
E-mail: sale@awt-gpi.com
Web Site: www.awt-gpi.com
Key Personnel
Pres: Michael Green
Business from Other Countries: 25%
Sales Office(s): AWT World Trade Europe BV, Antennstr 86, 1322 AS Almere, Netherlands *Tel:* (036) 5463070 *Fax:* (036) 5463071 *E-mail:* info@awt-europe.com
8984 NW 105 Way, Medley, FL *Tel:* 305-887-7500 *Fax:* 305-887-2300
Warehouse: AWT World Trade Europe BV, Antennstr 86, 1322 AS, Almere, Netherlands *Tel:* (036) 5463070 *Fax:* (036 5463071 *E-mail:* info@awt-europe.com

Blaze International Productions Inc
225 W 35 St, Suite 1100, New York, NY 10001
Tel: 212-967-7501 *Fax:* 212-967-7551
Key Personnel
Pres: Eugene Sanchez *Tel:* 212-967-7501 ext 222 *E-mail:* e.sanchez@blazeint.com
Founded: 1990
Business from Other Countries: 80%
Branch Office(s)
Flat 12 18/F, Kodak House, Phase 2, No 39 Healthy Street, North Point, Hong Kong *Tel:* 2967 9360 *Fax:* 2967 1800

BookBuilders New York Inc
353 Strawtown Rd, New City, NY 10956
Tel: 845-639-5316 *Fax:* 845-639-5318
Web Site: www.mcabooks.com
Key Personnel
Pres: Martin Cook *E-mail:* martin@mcabooks.com
Founded: 1977
Business from Other Countries: 60%

Challenge Machinery Co
6125 Norton Center Dr, Norton Shores, MI 49441
Tel: 231-799-8484 *Fax:* 231-798-1275
E-mail: info@challengemachinery.com
Web Site: www.challengemachinery.com
Key Personnel
Dir, Sales & Mktg: Britt Cary *E-mail:* bcary@challengemachinery.com
Founded: 1870
Business from Other Countries: 10%

The Cleveland Vibrator Co
2828 Clinton Ave, Cleveland, OH 44113
Tel: 216-241-7157 *Toll Free Tel:* 800-221-3298 *Fax:* 216-241-3480
E-mail: cvc@clevelandvibrator.com
Web Site: www.clevelandvibrator.com
Key Personnel
Gen Sales Mgr: Jack Steinbuch
Mktg Spec: Sue Kobylski
Founded: 1923
Business from Other Countries: 12%

Martin Cook Associates Ltd
353 Strawtown Rd, New City, NY 10956
Tel: 845-639-5316 *Fax:* 845-639-5318
E-mail: mcanewcity@aol.com
Web Site: www.mcabooks.com
Key Personnel
Pres: Martin Cook *E-mail:* mcanewcity@aol.com
Founded: 1977
Business from Other Countries: 15%
Membership(s): Bookbinders Guild of New York

Crathern Machinery Group Inc
879 Maple St, Contoocook, NH 03229-3319
Mailing Address: PO Box 187, Contoocook, NH 03229-0187
Tel: 603-746-4111 *Fax:* 603-746-4172
E-mail: info@crathern.com
Web Site: www.crathern.com
Business from Other Countries: 40%

D & K Group
1795 Commerce Dr, Elk Grove Village, IL 60007
Tel: 847-956-0160 *Toll Free Tel:* 800-632-2314 *Fax:* 847-956-8214
E-mail: info@dkgroup.net
Web Site: www.dkgroup.com
Key Personnel
Pres: Karl Singer
VP, Sales & Mktg: Marge Hayes
Mktg Communs Coord: Holli Hagene *E-mail:* holli.hagene@dkgroup.net
Founded: 1979
Business from Other Countries: 15%

& EQUIPMENT

Desktop Miracles Inc
112 S Main, PMB 294, Stowe, VT 05672
Tel: 802-253-7900 *Fax:* 802-253-1900
Web Site: www.desktopmiracles.com
Key Personnel
Pres & CEO: Barry T Kerrigan *E-mail:* barry@desktopmiracles.com
Founded: 1994
Business from Other Countries: 10%

Express Media Corp
1419 Donelson Pike, Nashville, TN 37217
Tel: 615-360-6400 *Toll Free Tel:* 888-EXPMEDIA (397-6342) *Fax:* 615-360-3140
E-mail: info@expressmedia.com
Web Site: www.expressmedia.com
Key Personnel
Pres: Andrew Cameron
Founded: 1996
Business from Other Countries: 10%

Fairfield Marketing Group Inc
Subsidiary of FMG Inc
830 Sport Hill Rd, Easton, CT 06612-1250
Tel: 203-261-5585; 203-261-5568 *Fax:* 203-261-0884
E-mail: ffijmktgrp@aol.com
Web Site: www.fairfieldmarketing.com
Key Personnel
CEO & Pres: Edward P Washchilla *E-mail:* fmg.inc@aol.com
VP, Fin: Pamela L Johnson
VP, Fulfillment: Jason Paul Miller *Tel:* 203-261-5585 ext 203
Cust Servs Rep: Mike Lozada *Tel:* 203-261-5585 ext 204
Founded: 1987
Business from Other Countries: 10%
Membership(s): ABA; Association of Educational Publishers; DMA; Direct Marketing Club of New York (DMCNY); DMA; Hudson Valley Direct Marketing Association; International Reading Association; National School Supply & Equipment Association; United States Chamber of Congress

Hamilton Printing Co
22 Hamilton Way, Castleton-on-Hudson, NY 12033
Tel: 518-732-4491 *Toll Free Tel:* 800-242-4222 *Fax:* 518-732-7714
Key Personnel
Pres: Brian F Payne
VP, Mfg: Rick Dunn
VP, Fin: Michael H Hart
Prod Mgr: Judy Rappold
Sales Rep: Stephen H Feuer; Scott Payne; Larry Ritchie; Michael C Rosenhack *E-mail:* miker@hpcbook.com
Founded: 1912
Business from Other Countries: 10%
Membership(s): BMI

IBT Global Ltd, see Integrated Book Technology Inc

Integrated Book Technology Inc
Division of The IBT Group
18 Industrial Park Rd, Troy, NY 12180
Tel: 518-271-5117 *Fax:* 518-266-9422
Web Site: www.integratedbook.com
Key Personnel
CEO & Pres: John R Paeglow *E-mail:* johnp@integratedbook.com
VP & Chief Technol Officer: William Clockel *E-mail:* billc@integratedbook.com
VP, Sales & Mktg: Robert Lindberg *E-mail:* bobl@integratedbook.com
Dir, Sales & Cust Serv: Karen Lombardo
Dir, Info Technol: Michael Whalen *E-mail:* mikew@integratedbook.com
Regl Sales: Tim Knickerbocker *E-mail:* timk@integratedbook.com
Founded: 1991
Business from Other Countries: 20%
Branch Office(s)
The IBT Global Ltd, 2 Finsbury Park Rd, London N4-2JZ, United Kingdom, Intl Strategist: Peter Kenyon *Tel:* (020) 7354 3332 *Fax:* (020) 7354 3332 *E-mail:* peterk@integratedbook.com
Membership(s): BMI

Linick International Inc
Division of The Linick Group Inc
Linick Bldg, 7 Putter Lane, Middle Island, NY 11953
Mailing Address: PO Box 102, Middle Island, NY 11953-0102
Tel: 631-924-3888
E-mail: linickgrp@att.net
Web Site: www.lgroup.addr.com
Key Personnel
Chmn & CEO: Andrew S Linick, PhD
Treas: Marvin Glickman
Exec VP: Roger Dextor
Founded: 1972
Business from Other Countries: 30%

LK Litho
Division of The Linick Group Inc
Linick Bldg, 7 Putter Lane, Middle Island, NY 11953
Mailing Address: PO Box 102, Middle Island, NY 11953-0102
Tel: 631-924-3888
E-mail: linickgrp@att.net
Web Site: www.lgroup.addr.com
Key Personnel
VP: Roger Dextor
Founded: 1968
Business from Other Countries: 20%

Marrakech Express Inc
720 Wesley Ave, No 10, Tarpon Springs, FL 34689
Tel: 727-942-2218 *Toll Free Tel:* 800-940-6566 *Fax:* 727-937-4758
E-mail: print@marrak.com
Web Site: www.marrak.com
Key Personnel
CEO: Peter Henzell
Prodn Mgr: Steen Sigmund
Sales/Estimator: Shirley Copperman
Founded: 1976
Business from Other Countries: 10%

Mazer Publishing Services
Division of The Mazer Corporation
6680 Poe Ave, Dayton, OH 45414
Tel: 937-264-2600 *Fax:* 937-264-2624
E-mail: info@mazer.com
Web Site: www.mazer.com
Key Personnel
Pres: William Franklin *E-mail:* bill_franklin@mazer.com
Exec VP: Ken Fultz *E-mail:* ken_fultz@mazer.com
Founded: 1964
Business from Other Countries: 10%
Branch Office(s)
2460 Sand Lake Rd, Orlando, FL 32809, Contact: Bryan Blakley *Tel:* 407-859-5552 *Fax:* 407-859-0643 *E-mail:* bryan_blakley@mazer.com
224 Lexington Ave, Fox River Grove, IL 60021, Contact: Dennis Bowman *Tel:* 847-639-1555 *Fax:* 847-639-1562 *E-mail:* dennis_bowman@mazer.com
22 Lehigh Rd, Wellesley, MA 02181, Contact: Ken Leahy *Tel:* 781-237-4112 *Fax:* 781-431-6184 *E-mail:* ken_leahy@mazer.com
22 Laurel Place, Upper Montclair, NJ 07043, Contact: John Martel *Tel:* 973-744-4320 *Fax:* 973-745-5608 *E-mail:* john_martel@mazer.com
3081 Glenmere Ct, Kettering, OH 45440, Contact: Mark Brewer *Tel:* 937-299-5746 *Fax:* 937-299-5761 *E-mail:* mark_brewer@mazer.com
363 Porter Rd, Bishop, TX 78602, Contact: Deborah VanLandingham *Tel:* 512-303-9758 *Fax:* 512-303-9791
Membership(s): BMI

Palace Press International - Corporate Headquarters
17 Paul Dr, San Rafael, CA 94903
Tel: 415-526-1370 *Toll Free Tel:* 800-809-3792 *Fax:* 415-526-1394
E-mail: info@palacepress.com
Web Site: www.palacepress.com
Key Personnel
CEO: Raoul Goff *E-mail:* raoul@palacepress.com
Dir, Intl Sales & Mktg: Gordon Goff *E-mail:* gordon@palacepress.com
Dir: Steven Goff *E-mail:* steven@palacepress.com
Founded: 1984
Business from Other Countries: 20%
Branch Office(s)
Palace Press International Los Angeles, 303 W Newby Ave, Suite C, San Gabriel, CA 91777, Contact: Roger Ma *Tel:* 626-282-8877 *Fax:* 626-282-6880 *E-mail:* roger@palacepress.com
4308 Fence Place, Louisville, KY 40241, Joe Rackowski *Tel:* 502-429-9276 *Fax:* 502-423-0760 *E-mail:* joe@palacepress.com
Palace Press International New York, 180 Varick St, 10th fl, New York, NY 10014 *Tel:* 212-462-2622 *Fax:* 212-463-9130 *E-mail:* jessica@palacepress.com

Regent Publishing Services
9327 Rambler Dr, St Louis, MO 63123
Tel: 314-631-7581 *Fax:* 314-638-5113
E-mail: regentstl@aol.com
Key Personnel
Sales Dir: Carol Davis-Tierney
Mktg Dir: James J Tierney
Founded: 1985
Business from Other Countries: 100%

Times Publishing Group
Division of Times Publishing Ltd/Singapore
99 White Plains Rd, Tarrytown, NY 10591
Tel: 914-366-9888 *Fax:* 914-366-9898
Web Site: www.tpl.com.sg
Key Personnel
Cust Serv Exec: Bonnie Stone *E-mail:* bstone@marshallcavendish.com
Sales Mgr: Suresh Kumar *E-mail:* skumar@marshallcavendish.com
Founded: 1965
Business from Other Countries: 90%

Tobias Associates Inc
50 Industrial Dr, Ivyland, PA 18974-0347
Tel: 215-322-1500 *Toll Free Tel:* 800-877-3367 *Fax:* 215-322-1504
E-mail: sales@tobiasinc.com
Web Site: www.densitometer.com
Key Personnel
Pres: Philip Tobias
VP: Eric Tobias
Founded: 1960
Business from Other Countries: 10%

Fred Weidner & Daughter Printers
15 Maiden Lane, Suite 1505, New York, NY 10038
Tel: 212-964-8676 *Fax:* 212-964-8677
E-mail: info@fwdprinters.com
Web Site: www.fwdprinters.com
Key Personnel
Exec VP: Cynthia Weidner *E-mail:* cynthia@fwdprinters.com
Creative Dir: Carol Mittelsdorf

Uruguay

Barreiro y Ramos SA
25 de Mayo, Esq J C Gomez, Casilla Correos, 15, Montevideo
Tel: (02) 96 23 58 *Fax:* (02) 96 23 58
Telex: 23901PB.CVJA.UY *Cable:* BAREIRAMOS
Key Personnel
President: Gaston Barreiro
Vice President: Guzman Barreiro
Founded: 1837
Business from Other Countries: 10%

Founded: 1860
Business from Other Countries: 25%

Book Trade Information

Book Clubs

Austria

Deutsche Buch-Gemeinschaft C A Koch's Verlag Nachfolger
Vivenotgasse 2, 1120 Vienna
Tel: (01) 8123730 *Fax:* (01) 811024
Telex: 31405
Branch Office(s)
Deutsche Buch-Gemeinschaft C A Koch's Verlag Nachfolge, Germany

Buchgemeinschaft Donauland Kremayr & Scheriau
Niederhofstr 37, 1121 Vienna
Tel: (01) 811 02 348 *Fax:* (01) 811 02 680
E-mail: donauland@donauland.at
Web Site: www.donauland.at
Telex: 131405

Buchgemeinschaft Donauland Kremayr & Scheriau, see Buchgemeinschaft Donauland Kremayr & Scheriau

Brazil

Circulo do Livro SA
Alameda Ministro Rocha de Azeredo 346, 01410 Sao Paulo
Tel: (011) 8513644 *Fax:* (011) 2827273
Telex: 31747 *Cable:* Cirlivro
Key Personnel
Man Dir: Rene Cesar Xavier dos Santos
Editorial Dir: Esnider Pizzo
Owned by: Bertelsmann AG, Germany; Abril SA Cultural e Industrial

Editora Universidade De Brasilia (J)
SCS Qd 02, Bloco C N°78, 2° andar-Ed OK, 70300-500 Brasilia-DF
Tel: (061) 226-6874 *Fax:* (061) 323-1017
E-mail: editora@unb.br
Web Site: www.editora.unb.br *Cable:* UNIVERBRASILIA EDITORA
Owned by: Fundacao Universidade de Brasilia

Chile

Clubs de Lectores Andres Bello
Ave Ricardo Lyon 946, Casilla de Correo, Providencia, Santiago
Tel: (02) 2049900; (02) 2049901 *Fax:* (02) 2253600
Telex: 240901 Edjur

Key Personnel
General Manager: Julio Serrano Lamas
Commercial Manager: Marta Mallea Araya
Established: 1947
There are two clubs: one for children (membership 20,000), the other for adults (membership 25,000).
Owned by: Editorial Andres Bello/Editorial Juridica de Chile

Colombia

Circulo de Lectores SA
Calle 57 No 6-35, Apdo Aereo 52111, Santafe de Bogota
Tel: 2173211; 2177720 *Fax:* 2178157
Telex: 41255 *Cable:* CIRLEC
Key Personnel
Dir: Eduardo Polo, Sr
Marketing: Rafael Vargas
Established: 1970
Number of Members: 650,000
Owned by: Casa Editorial El Tiempo

Czech Republic

ERB
Vaclavske nam 17, 11258 Prague 1
Tel: (02) 24009111 *Fax:* (02) 2320989
Telex: 121442 *Cable:* 1106
Established: 1968
Number of Members: 67,835
Owned by: Prace

Friends of Antiquity
Na Florenci 3, 11303 Prague 1
Tel: (02) 24811549; (02) 24225143 *Fax:* (02) 24226026
Key Personnel
Manager: Stefan Szerynski
Established: 1969
Number of Members: 6,000
Owned by: Nakladatelstvi Svoboda

KM C
c/o Albatros, Truhlarska 9, 11000 Prague 1
Tel: (02) 24810704; (02) 2311156; (02) 2314289 *Fax:* (02) 24810850
Young Readers' Club.
Owned by: Albatros

Odeon Buch- und Phonoclub
Narodni tr 36, 11000 Prague 1
Tel: (02) 264100 *Fax:* (02) 24225254
E-mail: odeon@comp.cz

Key Personnel
Editorial Dir: Dr Jiri Nasinec
Established: 1953
Subjects: Fiction, Art
Number of Members: 250,000
Owned by: Odeon; nakladatelstvi krasne literatury a umeni

Denmark

Egmont Lademann A/S (J)
Gerdasgade 37, 1795 Copenhagen V
Tel: 3615 6600 *Fax:* 3644 1162
Web Site: www.egmontbogklub.dk
Subjects: Management, Children's Books, Commercial Fiction, True Stories
Book Club(s): Bogsamleren; Bolig Og Livsstil; DisneyKlubben; Disney's Borneleksikon; Egmont Bogklubben; Girls Only; Hobbyklubben; Livsenergi Klubben; Paperback Bogklubben; Virkelighedens Verden; Bogsamleren; Bolig Og Livsstil; DisneyKlubben; Disney's Borneleksikon; Egmont Bogklubben; Girls Only; Hobbyklubben; Livsenergi Klubben; Paperback Bogklubben; Virkelighedens Verden

Fiction Factory International Ltd
Klareboderne 3, 1001 Copenhagen K
Tel: (043) 33 75 55 09 *Fax:* (043) 33 75 55 44
Key Personnel
Publisher: Jens Bendtsen *E-mail:* jens_bendtsen@gyldendal.dk
Established: 1987
Subjects: Children's, Adolescent, Adult (in English)
Publication(s): Fiction Factory (materials for teaching of modern languages)
Owned by: Kaleidoscope Publishers Ltd

Gyldendals Babybogklubben (J)
Postboks 176, 1005 Copenhagen K
Tel: 70 11 00 33 *Fax:* 70 11 01 33
E-mail: boernebogklub@gyldendal.dk
Web Site: www.gyldendal.dk
Owned by: Gyldendalske Boghandel - Nordisk Forlag A/S

Gyldendals Bogklubben (J)
Postboks 176, 1005 Copenhagen K
Tel: 70 11 00 33 *Fax:* 70 11 01 33
E-mail: gyldendals-bogklub@gyldendal.dk
Web Site: www.gyldendal.dk
Telex: 15887 gyldal dk *Cable:* GYLDENDALSKE
Subjects: Fiction, Nonfiction (General)
Owned by: Gyldendalske Boghandel - Nordisk Forlag A/S

DENMARK

Gyldendals Borne Bogklubben (J)
Postboks 176, 1005 Copenhagen K
Tel: 70 11 00 33 *Fax:* 70 11 01 33
E-mail: boernebogklub@gyldendal.dk
Web Site: www.gyldendal.dk
Telex: 15887 gyldal dk *Cable:* GYLDENDALSKE
Owned by: Gyldendalske Boghandel - Nordisk Forlag A/S

Gyldendals Junior Bogklubben (J)
Postboks 176, 1005 Copenhagen K
Tel: 70 11 00 33 *Fax:* 70 11 01 33
E-mail: boernebogklub@gyldendal.dk
Web Site: www.gyldendal.dk
Owned by: Gyldendalske Boghandel - Nordisk Forlag A/S

Samlerens Bogklub (J)
Postboks 176, 1005 Copenhagen K
Tel: 70 11 00 33 *Fax:* 70 11 01 33
E-mail: samlerens-bogklub@gyldendal.dk
Web Site: www.samlerens-bogklub.dk
Telex: 15887 gyldal dk *Cable:* GYLDENDALSKE
Subjects: Fiction, Government, Political Science, Nonfiction (General)
Owned by: Gyldendalske Boghandel - Nordisk Forlag A/S

Bogklubben 12 Boget A/S
Frederiksborggade 1, 1360 Copenhagen K
Tel: 33695050 *Fax:* 33695051
E-mail: b12b@bogklubben-12-boget.dk
Key Personnel
Man Dir: Jette Juliusson
Established: 1988
Subjects: General nonfiction
Owned by: Lindhardt & Ringhof I/S, Munksgaard

Egypt (Arab Republic of Egypt)

Al Ahram Book Club (J)
Al-Galaa St, Cairo
Tel: (02) 5786069 *Fax:* (02) 5786833
E-mail: ahram@ahram.org.eg
Web Site: www.extra.ahram.org.eg
Telex: 20185-92544
Key Personnel
General Manager: Hany Tolba
Owned by: Al Ahram Establishment

Finland

Aikamedia Oy (Aikamedia Ltd)
Heikkilantie 177, 42700 Keuruu
Mailing Address: PL 99, 42701 Keuruu
Tel: (014) 7514751 *Fax:* (014) 7514757
E-mail: asiakaspalvelu@aikamedia.fi
Web Site: www.aikamedia.fi
Key Personnel
President & Marketing Dir: Asko Kinnunen *Tel:* (09) 5660 0497 *E-mail:* asko.kinnunen@aikamedia.fi
Publishing Manager: Outi Katto *Tel:* (014) 7514731 *E-mail:* outi.katto@aikamedia.fi
Established: 1995
Christian books, music & periodicals.
Owned by: Ristin Voitto ry
Imprints: Hengellinen Laulukirja; Raamatun Tietosarja

Hengellinen Laulukirja, *imprint of* Aikamedia Oy

Raamatun Tietosarja, *imprint of* Aikamedia Oy

Suuri Suomalainen Kirjakerho Oy (Great Finnish Book Club Ltd)
PL 120, 00241 Helsinki
Tel: (09) 2705 0077; (09) 1566 830 *Fax:* (09) 145 510
E-mail: sskk.palaute@sskk.fi
Web Site: www.sskk.fi
Key Personnel
President: Pauli A Leimio *Tel:* (09) 1566 316 *E-mail:* pauli.leimio@kuvalehdet.fi
Number of Members: 280,000
Owned by: Otava Kustannusosakeyhtioe, Uudenmaankatu 10, Helsinki 00120
Parent Company: Yhtyneet Kuvalehdet Oy (United Magazines Ltd)
Ultimate Parent Company: Otava-Kuvalehdet Oy

Uudet Kirjat
Bulevardi 12, 00120 Helsinki
Mailing Address: PL 15, 00121 Helsinki
Tel: (09) 6168 3370
E-mail: uudetkirjat@wsoy.fi
Web Site: www.uudetkirjat.fi
Telex: 122644 Wsoy
Key Personnel
Contact: Raija Hynynen
The New Books.
Number of Members: 110,000
Owned by: Werner Soederstroem Osakeyhtio (WSOY)

France

L'Amitie par le Livre
BP 1031, 25001 Besancon Cedex
Tel: (03) 81820894 *Fax:* (03) 81820894
First book club founded in France in 1930, by teaching profession. It is non-profitmaking & run by voluntary effort.
Owned by: L'Amitie par le Livre

Club du Livre SA
28 rue Fortuny, 75017 Paris
Tel: (01) 47638055 *Fax:* (01) 44404865
Key Personnel
Man Dir: Philippe Lebaud
Subjects: Art, De Luxe Editions

Jean Grassin Editeur, *imprint of* Poetes Presents

Nouveau Cercle Parisien du Livre
6 rue Bonaparte, 75006 Paris
Tel: (01) 43547195 *Fax:* (01) 40518288
Key Personnel
President: Alain de Ricou
Club is associated with publisher Galerie Lucie Weill.
Subjects: Olivier Debre Illustrations, Edmond Jabese Texts
Owned by: Au Pont des Arts; Galerie Lucie Weill

PEMF, see Publications de l'Ecole Moderne Francaise (PEMF)

Poetes Presents
Pl de Port-en-Dro, 56342 Carnac Cedex
Mailing Address: BP 75, 56342 Carnac Cedex
Tel: (02) 97529363 *Fax:* (02) 97528390
Key Personnel
President: Jean Grassin
Established: 1957
Subjects: Poetry
Book Club(s): Club de Selection des Meilleurs Livre de Poesie; Club de Selection des Meilleurs Livre de Poesie
Number of Members: 1,500
Owned by: Jean Grassin Editeur
Imprints: Jean Grassin Editeur

Publications de l'Ecole Moderne Francaise (PEMF)
06376 Mouans Sartoux Cedex
Tel: (04) 92921757 *Fax:* (016) 92921804
Web Site: ceos.cnes.fr/1800 *Cable:* PEMF
This company runs five book clubs supplying series of books for children: aged 8-12 (BTJ), aged 10-15 (BT), aged over 15 (BT2); for teachers (L'Educateur) & for audiovisual supplies (BT Son).

Gerard Varin, see L'Amitie par le Livre

Germany

Bertelsmann Club
PO Box 7777, 33300 Gutersloh
Tel: (05) 415 233 *Fax:* (05) 415 744
E-mail: service@derclub.de
Web Site: www.bertelsmann-club.de
Telex: 931149
Key Personnel
Contact: Dr Stephan Kruemmer
Number of Members: 5,600,000
Owned by: Bertelsmann AG
Branch Office(s)
290 Club-Filialen/Bertelsmann Club

Buechergilde Gutenberg
Stuttgarter Str 25-29, 60329 Frankfurt am Main
Tel: (069) 27 39 08-0 *Fax:* (069) 27 39 08-25; (069) 27 39 08-26
E-mail: service@buechergilde.de
Web Site: www.buechergilde.de
Owned by: Buechergilde Gutenberg Verlagsgesellschaft mbH

Deutscher Buchkreis
Am Apfelberg 18, 72076 Tuebingen
Mailing Address: Postfach 1629, 72006 Tuebingen
Tel: (07071) 96590 *Fax:* (07071) 965965
Owned by: Grabert-Verlag Wigbert Grabert

EBG Verlags GmbH
Wolframstr 36, 70191 Stuttgart
Tel: (07154) 1340
Telex: 17715410 ebege d
Established: 1950
Number of Members: 1,300,000
Owned by: Bertelsmann AG

Europaeische Bildungsgemeinschaft Verlags GmbH, see EBG Verlags GmbH

Herder-Buchgemeinde
Hermann-Herder-Str 4, 79104 Freiburg
Tel: (0761) 27170 *Fax:* (0761) 2717520
Established: 1952
Subjects: Fiction & poetry, picture books
Owned by: Verlag Herder GmbH & Co KG

Wissenschaftliche Buchgesellschaft
Postfach 100110, 64201 Darmstadt

Tel: (06151) 3308-161 Fax: (06151) 3308208
E-mail: service@wbg-darmstadt.de
Established: 1949
Scientific Book Society.
Subjects: 25 Scientific Fields, 2500 titles available
Number of Members: 140,000

Greece

Sport & Hobby Book Club
19 Iperidou, GR-10558 Athens
Mailing Address: PO Box 30564, GR-10033 Athens
Tel: (01) 3234217 Fax: (01) 3232082
E-mail: hcp@photography.gr
Key Personnel
President: Stavros Moressopoulos E-mail: mores.s@altavista.net
Established: 1986
Subjects: Photography, Sports, Hobbies, How-to, Music, Travel, Wine & Spirits, Animals
Number of Members: 780
Owned by: Moressopoulos SA Organizing, Publishing, Advertising, Education

Iceland

The AB Book Club (BAB)
Nybylavegur 16, 200 Kopavogur
Tel: 5643170 Fax: 5643190
Key Personnel
President: Fridrik Fridriksson
Editor: Bjarni Thorsfeinsson
Established: 1974
Number of Members: 8,500
Owned by: AB Almenna bokafelagid

BAB, see The AB Book Club (BAB)

Gulur Raudur Grenn og Blar Childrens Bookclub
Sidumula 7-9, 108 Reykjavik
Tel: 5102525 Fax: 5102525
E-mail: klubbar@mm.is
Key Personnel
Contact: Thorhildur Gardosdottir
Number of Members: 10,000
Owned by: MM Mal og menning

Heima er Bezt Book Club
Armuli 23, 108 Reykjavik
Mailing Address: Postholf 8427, 128 Reykjavik
Tel: 5531599; 5882400 Fax: 5888994
Key Personnel
Editor: G Baldvinsson
Owned by: Skjaldborg Ltd

The MAB Cookery Book Club
Nybylavegur 16, 200 Kopavogur
Tel: 5643170 Fax: 5643190
Established: 1984
Number of Members: 11,500
Owned by: AB Almenna bokafelagid

MM Mal og menning
Sudurlandsbraut 12, 108 Reykjavik
Tel: 522 2000 Fax: 522 2022; 522 2026
E-mail: malogmenning@edda.is
Web Site: www.malogmenning.is
Key Personnel
Contact: Pall Valsson
Number of Members: 24,000
Publication(s): *Booksellers*

Uglan Islenski Kiljuklubburinn
Sudurlandsbraut 12, 108 Reykjavik
Tel: 522 2020 Fax: 522 2022
E-mail: bokaklubbar@edda.is
Web Site: www.edda.is
Paperback Book Club.
Number of Members: 10,000
Owned by: Edda Utgafa hf

Particip Verold
Njoervasundisa 15a, 104 Reykjavik
Tel: 5688433 Fax: 5688142
Owned by: Fjolvi; bokautgafa

India

Anand Book Club
c/o Vision Books Pvt Ltd, 24 Feroze Gandhi Rd, Lajpat Nagar-III, New Delhi 110024
Key Personnel
Dir: Sudhir Malhotra
Number of Members: 22,000
Owned by: Vision Books Pvt Ltd

Book Lovers Club
A-59 Okhla Industrial Area, Phase II, New Delhi 110020
Tel: (011) 6910050; (011) 6916209 Fax: (011) 6331241
E-mail: ghai@nde.vsnl.net.in Cable: PAPERBACKS
Established: 1986
Number of Members: 1,076
Owned by: Sterling Publishers Pvt Ltd

DC Book Club
Good Shepherd St, Kottayam, Kerala 686001
Mailing Address: PO Box 212, Kottayam, Kerala 686001
Tel: (0481) 2563114; (0481) 2563226; (0481) 2578214 Fax: (0481) 2564758
E-mail: ceo@dcbooks.com
Web Site: www.dcbooks.com
Key Personnel
Chief Executive Officer: Ravi Deecee Tel: (0481) 2301614
Established: 1975
Number of Members: 2,500
Owned by: D C Books, Printers, Publishers & Booksellers

Orient Book Club (J)
c/o Vision Books Pvt Ltd, 1590 Madarsa Rd, Kashmere Gate, Delhi 110 006
Tel: (011) 2386-2267
E-mail: orientpbk@vsnl.com
Key Personnel
Dir: Sidharth Malhotra
Established: 1979
Subjects: Cookery, How-to, Fiction, Health & Fitness, Self Help, Children's Books, Investment Personal Finance
Number of Members: 40,000
Parent Company: Vision Books Pvt Ltd

Star Publishers' Distributors
4/5 B Asaf Ali Rd, New Delhi 110002
Tel: (011) 23286757; (011) 23268651; (011) 23261696; (011) 23258993 Fax: (011) 23273335; (011) 26481565
E-mail: starpub@satyam.net.in
Web Site: www.starpublic.com Cable: STAR PUBLIS
Key Personnel
President: Mr Amar Nath Varma
Subjects: Books in English, Hindi & other Indian Languages Linguistics, Social Sciences, Children's Books
Number of Members: 15,000
Branch Office(s)
55 Warren St, London W1T 5NW, United Kingdom Tel: (020) 7380 0622; (020) 7419 9169 Fax: (020) 7419 9169 E-mail: indbooks@aol.com

Indonesia

Himpunan Masyarakat Pencinta Buku
Jin Hasanuddin 9, Bandung, Jawa Barat
Tel: (022) 470821; (022) 470287
Established: 1979
The Association of Bibliophiles.
Number of Members: 14,300
Owned by: Eresco PT

KPI
Jln Dr Wahidin 1, Jakarta
Mailing Address: PO Box 29, Jakarta
Tel: (021) 361701; (021) 41701
Telex: 45905 Prumbp Ia
Established: 1982
Klub Perpustakaan Indonesia.
Number of Members: 4,500

Israel

Ma'ariv Book Guild (Sifriat Ma'ariv)
3a Yoni Netanyahu St, Or-Yehuda 60376
Tel: (03) 5383313 Fax: (03) 6343205
Telex: 033735 Cable: MA'ARIV TELAVIV
Key Personnel
Man Dir: Eli Shimoni E-mail: shimoni@hed-arzi.co.il
Owned by: Ma'ariv Book Guild

Italy

Isper Club (J)
Corso Dante 122, 10126 Turin
Tel: (011) 66 47 803 Fax: (011) 66 79 768
E-mail: segreteria.servizi@isper.org
Web Site: www.isper.org
Key Personnel
Contact: Marco Actis Grosso E-mail: marco.actisgrosso@isper.org
Owned by: ISPER

Edi Thule Club
Via Gravina 95, I-90139 Palermo
Tel: (091) 323699
Owned by: Edizioni Thule
Imprints: Thule Spiritualita E Letteratura

Thule Spiritualita E Letteratura, *imprint of* Edi Thule Club

Japan

Fukuinkan Ehon Library
c/o Fukuinkan Shoten Publishers Inc, 6-3 Hon-Komagome 6 chome, Bunkyo-ku, Tokyo 113

Tel: (03) 39421226 *Fax:* (03) 39429691
Telex: J33597 Aab Forchild *Cable:*
  FUKUINKANSHOTEN TOKYO
Subjects: Children's Books
Owned by: Fukuinkan Shoten Publishers Inc

Kodansha Disney Children's Book Club
2-12-21 Otowa, Bunkyo-ku, Tokyo 112-8001
Tel: (03) 3946-6201 *Fax:* (03) 3944-9915
Web Site: www.kodansha.co.jp; www.kodanclub.com
Owned by: Kodan-Sha International
Branch Office(s)
  Paris Liaison Office, 4, place de l'Opera, 75002 Paris, France *Tel:* (01) 42 66 55 73 *Fax:* (01) 42 66 55 91
U.S. Office(s): 575 Lexington Ave, New York, NY 10022, United States *Tel:* 917-322-6223 *Fax:* 212-935-6529

Bookclub Psyche
2-5 Kami-Takaido 1 chome, Suginami-ku, Tokyo 168
Tel: (03) 33290031 *Fax:* (03) 33043822
Subjects: Psychiatry
Owned by: Seiwa Shoten

Mexico

Bertelsmann de Mexico SA
Ave de la Paz No 26, Col San Angel, 01000 Mexico, DF
Tel: (05) 5501620; (05) 5489048
Telex: 1761195 Cileme
Number of Members: 200,000
Owned by: Bertelsmann AG, Germany

Club de Lectores Extemporaneos
Poniente 126-A-400, No 400, Colonia Nueva Vallejo, 07750 Mexico, DF
Tel: (05) 5875424; (05) 5878785
Owned by: Editorial Extemporaneos SA

Myanmar

Sarpay Beikman Book Club
529 Merchant St, Rangoon
Tel: (01) 83611
Owned by: Sarpay Beikman Board

Netherlands

ECI voor Boeken en platen BV
Laanakkerweg 14-16, 4131 PB Vianen
Tel: (0347) 379214 *Fax:* (0347) 379380
Telex: 47449
Book Club(s): Nederlandse Boekenclub; Nederlandse Lezerskring Boek en Plaat BV; Nederlandse Boekenclub; Nederlandse Lezerskring Boek en Plaat BV

Nederlandse Boekenclub (Netherlands Book Club) (J)
Postbus 28900, 2502 KX Den Haag
Tel: (03473) 6 11 22 *Fax:* (03473) 79380
E-mail: service@nbc-club.nl
Web Site: www.nbc-club.nl
Key Personnel
Manager: A L P Bongaards

Established: 1967
Subjects: Fiction, Nonfiction (General)
Number of Members: 350,000
Owned by: ECI voor Boeken en Platen BV

Nederlandse Lezerskring Boek en Plaat BV
Laanakkerweg 14-18, 413 1EB Vianen Zh
Mailing Address: PO Box 400, 4130 EK Vianen Zh
Tel: (03473) 79214 *Fax:* (03473) 79380
Established: 1966
Number of Members: 500,000
Owned by: ECI voor Boeken en Platen BV

VCL
POB 5018, 8260 GA Kampen
Tel: (038) 3328912 *Fax:* (038) 3327331
Key Personnel
Contact: Mrs M Boltje *Tel:* (038) 3392524
  E-mail: mboltje@kok.nl
Owned by: Uitgeefmaatschappij J H Kok BV

New Zealand

Doubleday New Zealand Ltd, Book Club Division
One Parkway Dr, Mairangi Bay Industrial Estate, Auckland 10
Mailing Address: Private Bag 102947, North Shore Mail Centre, Auckland 1333
Tel: (09) 4782846 *Fax:* (09) 4781609
Telex: NZ60589
Operated by Doubleday Australia Pty Ltd, Australia. Ultimate Parent Company: Bertelsmann AG, Germany.
Book Club(s): Book New Zealand; Book of the Month Club; Doubleday Book Club; Doubleday History Book Club; Doubleday Military Book Club; The Literary Guild; Doubleday Children's Book Club; Book New Zealand; Book of the Month Club; Doubleday Book Club; Doubleday History Book Club; Doubleday Military Book Club; The Literary Guild; Doubleday Children's Book Club

Nigeria

Amebo Book Club
PO Box 1970, Ibadan
Owned by: Adebara Publishing House

Onibon-Oje Book Club
Felele Layout, Molete, Ibadan
Mailing Address: PO Box 3109, Ibadan
Tel: (022) 313956
Subjects: Fiction, Drama
Owned by: Onibon-Oje Publishers

Varsity Book Club
11 Central School Rd, Onitsha
Mailing Address: PO Box 386, Onitsha
Tel: (046) 210013
Key Personnel
President: F C Ogbalu
Vice President: S U Ogbalu
Established: 1960
Subjects: Igbo, English including primary, secondary & tertiary subjects
Owned by: Varsity Industrial Press
Branch Office(s)
14 Owerri-Orlu Rd, Owerri, Imo State

Norway

Absolutt Krim (J)
Fridtjof Nansens vei 14, 0055 Oslo
Tel: 24051000 *Fax:* 24051099
E-mail: post@damm.no
Web Site: www.dammbokklubb.no
Key Personnel
Man Dir: Cato Praner
Established: 1978
Subjects: Crime Fiction
Owned by: N W Damm & Son A/S

Peter Asschenfeldts Bokklubb
Postboks 1755 Vika, 0122 Oslo
Tel: 22429165 *Fax:* 22471098
Telex: 77074
Key Personnel
Manager: Willy Fordet
Established: 1978
Fiction.
Owned by: Hjemmets Bokforlag A/S

Barnas Hobbyklubb (J)
Fridtjof Nansens vei 14, 0055 Oslo
Tel: 24051000 *Fax:* 24051099
E-mail: post@damm.no
Web Site: www.dammbokklubb.no
Owned by: N W Damm & Son A/S

Bokklubben Bedre Ledelse (J)
Fridtjof Nansens vei 14, 0055 Oslo
Tel: 24051000 *Fax:* 24051099
E-mail: post@damm.no
Web Site: www.dammbokklubb.no
Key Personnel
Publishing Manager: Gerhard Anthun
Established: 1978
Subjects: Literature, Literary Criticism, Essays, Management
Owned by: N W Damm & Son A/S

De norske Bokklubbene A/S (J)
Gullhaug Torg 1, 0040 Oslo
Tel: 02299 *Fax:* 02212
Web Site: www.bokklubbene.no
Telex: 74213 Bokkl n
Key Personnel
Vice President: Jon Oestboe
Contact: Aud Norlin
Subjects: Fiction, Nonfiction (General)
Book Club(s): Bokklubben Krim og Spenning; Bokklubben Kunst & Interior; Bokklubben Kursiv; Bokklubben Mat- og Vinglede; Bokklubben Nye Boker; Bokklubbens Barn; Bokklubben Villmarksliv; Dagens Boker; Den Norske Bokklubben; Den Norske Lyrikklubben; Lydbokklubben; Ungdomsbokklubben; Bokklubben Krim og Spenning; Bokklubben Kunst & Interior; Bokklubben Kursiv; Bokklubben Mat- og Vinglede; Bokklubben Nye Boker; Bokklubbens Barn; Bokklubben Villmarksliv; Dagens Boker; Den Norske Bokklubben; Den Norske Lyrikklubben; Lydbokklubben; Ungdomsbokklubben
Number of Members: 550,000
Owned by: H Ascheoug & Co (W Nygaard) A/S; Gyldendal Norsk Forlag A/S; Tiden Norsk Forlag A/S

Boksamleren
Fridtjof Nansens vei 14, 0055 Oslo
Tel: 24051000 *Fax:* 24051099
E-mail: post@damm.no
Web Site: www.dammbokklubb.no
Owned by: N W Damm & Son A/S

Donald Duck's Bokklubb (J)
Fridtjof Nansens vei 14, 0055 Oslo
Tel: 24051000 *Fax:* 24051099
E-mail: post@damm.no
Web Site: www.dammbokklubb.no
Key Personnel
Publishing Manager: Gerhard Anthun
Established: 1978
Subjects: Fiction
Owned by: N W Damm & Son A/S

Hobbyglede
Fridtjof Nansens vei 14, 0055 Oslo
Tel: 24051000 *Fax:* 24051099
E-mail: post@damm.no
Web Site: www.dammbokklubb.no
Owned by: N W Damm & Son A/S

Bokklubben Natur og Kultur
Drammensvn 20C, N-0255 Oslo
Mailing Address: PO Box 465 Sentrum, 0105 Oslo
Tel: 22985600 *Fax:* 22985630
Key Personnel
Editor: Hans Tarjei Skaare
Owned by: Grondahl OG Dreyers Forlag AS

Ole Brumm (J)
Fridtjof Nansens vei 14, 0055 Oslo
Tel: 24051000 *Fax:* 24051099
E-mail: post@damm.no
Web Site: www.dammbokklubb.no
Owned by: N W Damm & Son A/S

Philippines

Alemar's Best Sellers Club
Northmall Bldg, Makati Commercial Center, Makati, Metro Manila
Tel: (02) 592617
Established: 1977
Number of Members: 2,400
Owned by: Alemar's (Sibal & Son's Inc)

Portugal

Circulo de Leitores
Rua Prof Jorge da Silva Horta, 1, 1500-499 Lisbon
Tel: (021) 762 6100 *Fax:* (021) 760 7149
E-mail: correio@circuloleitores.pt
Web Site: www.circuloleitores.pt
Telex: 18343 cilecl p
Key Personnel
Man Dir: Dr Rui Beja
Editor: Guilhermina Gomes
Subjects: Fiction, Biography, Juvenile, Encyclopedias, Scientific, Historical, General Nonfiction, Special Editions, Magazines
Number of Members: 500,000
Owned by: Bertelsmann AG, Germany
Branch Office(s)
Lexicultural

Serbia and Montenegro

Book Lovers' Club
Bulevar Vojvode Misica 17, 11000 Belgrade
Tel: (011) 651666; (011) 650399
Owned by: Beogradski Izdavacko-Graficki Zavod

Prosveta-Izdavako preduzece
Cika Ljubina 1, 11000 Belgrade
Tel: (011) 629 843; (011) 631 566; (011) 625760 *Fax:* (011) 627465

Slovakia

Tatran Publishing House
Michalska 9, 81582 Bratislava
Tel: (07) 54435849 *Fax:* (07) 54435777
   Cable: TATRAN
Key Personnel
Dir: Eva Mladekova
Established: 1947
Subjects: Classical & Modern Fiction & Nonfiction, Children's Books, Books on Art
Owned by: Tatran

Club of Young Readers
Sasinkova 5, 815 19 Bratislava 1
Tel: (02) 502 272 25 *Fax:* (02) 555 718 94
E-mail: spn@spn.sk
Web Site: www.mlade-leta.sk
Telex: 093 421
Key Personnel
Dir: Ing Oldrich Polak
Established: 1963
Subjects: Fairy Tales, Original Slovak Literature, Prose, Poetry, Anthologies, Translations of World Literature, Scientific Literature, Critiques
Number of Members: 55,000
Owned by: Mlade leta

South Africa

Klub-Dagbreek
127 Mirn Rd, Newlands, Johannesburg 2092
Tel: (011) 6736725 *Fax:* (011) 6736719
Subjects: Fiction
Owned by: Perskor-uitgewery

Eike-Boekklub
380 Bosman St, Pretoria 0002
Mailing Address: PO Box 123, Pretoria 0001
Tel: (012) 401 0700 *Fax:* (012) 3255498
E-mail: lapa@atkv.org.za
Key Personnel
Publication & Administrative Officer: Esme Smith *E-mail:* esmes@atkv.org.za
Subjects: Fiction Novels
Parent Company: LAPA Publishers (Pty) Ltd
Ultimate Parent Company: ATKV, Dover St, Randburg 2194

Keurbiblioteek
380 Bosman St, Pretoria 0002
Mailing Address: PO Box 123, Pretoria 0001
Tel: (012) 401 0700 *Fax:* (012) 3255498
E-mail: lapa@atkv.org.za
Key Personnel
Publication & Administrative Officer: Esme Smith
   E-mail: esmes@atkv.org.za
Subjects: Fiction
Parent Company: LAPA Publishers (Pty) Ltd
Ultimate Parent Company: ATKV, Dover St, Randburg 2194

New Day Readers Circle
33 Waterkant St, Cape Town 8000
Mailing Address: PO Box 1822, Cape Town 8000
Tel: (021) 421 5540 *Fax:* (021) 419 1865
E-mail: luxverbi.publ@kingsley.co.za
Telex: 526922
Owned by: Lux Verbi

President Boekklub
380 Bosman St, Pretoria 0002
Mailing Address: PO Box 123, Pretoria 0001
Tel: (012) 401 0700 *Fax:* (012) 3255498
E-mail: lapa@atkv.org.za
Web Site: www.lapauitgewers.org.za
Key Personnel
Publications & Administrative Officer: Esme Smith *E-mail:* esmes@atkv.org.za
Parent Company: LAPA Publishers (Pty) Ltd
Ultimate Parent Company: ATKV, Dover St, Randburg 2194

Klub Saffier
127 Mirn Rd, Newlands, Johannesburg 2092
Tel: (011) 6736725 *Fax:* (011) 6736719
Subjects: Fiction
Owned by: Perskor-uitgewery

Klub 707
127 Mirn Rd, Newlands, Johannesburg 2092
Tel: (011) 6736725 *Fax:* (011) 6736719
Subjects: Fiction: especially Suspense, Espionage, Detective, Thrillers (in Afrikaans)
Owned by: Perskor-uitgewery

Treffer-Boekklub
380 Bosman St, Pretoria 0002
Mailing Address: PO Box 123, Pretoria 0001
Tel: (012) 401 0700 *Fax:* (012) 3255498
E-mail: lapa@atkv.org.za
Key Personnel
Publications & Administrative Officer: Esme Smith *E-mail:* esmes@atkv.org.za
Subjects: Fiction
Parent Company: LAPA Publishers (Pty) Ltd
Ultimate Parent Company: ATKV, Dover St, Randburg 2194

Spain

Circulo de Lectores SA
Travessera de Gracia, 47-49, 08021 Barcelona
Tel: (0902) 22 33 55
E-mail: atencion-socios@circulo.es
Web Site: www.circulo.es
Key Personnel
Dir General: Hans Meinke
Literary Dir: Jordi Nadal
Marketing Dir: Bengt Johansson
Financial Dir: Pedro Piella
Number of Members: 1,540,000
Owned by: Bertelsmann AG, Germany

Sri Lanka

Book Club of the Dept of Cultural Affairs of Sri Lanka
8th floor, Sethsiripaya, Battaramulla 1
Tel: (01) 872035 *Fax:* (01) 872035
E-mail: pltm1950@sltnet.lk; gsk@sltnet.lk
Web Site: www.mca.gov.lk
Key Personnel
Dir: Mr Laxman Perera
Owned by: Department of Cultural Affairs

Sweden

Allt om Hobbys Publishing Co
Box 90133, 120 21 Stockholm
Tel: (08) 99 93 33 *Fax:* (08) 99 88 66
E-mail: order@hobby.se
Web Site: www.hobby.se
Key Personnel
President: Freddy Stenbom *E-mail:* freddy.stenbom@hobby.se
Publication(s): Allt om Hobby
Owned by: Allt om Hobby AB

Barnens Bokklubb
Box 3486, 10369 Stockholm
Tel: (08) 506 304 00 *Fax:* (08) 506 304 01
E-mail: redaktionen@barnensbokklubb.se
Web Site: www.barnensbokklubb.se
Key Personnel
Contact: Gunilla Halkjaer Olofsson
Subjects: Children's books
Number of Members: 150,000
Publication(s): Barn Posten; Laese Posten
Owned by: AB Raben och Sjoegren Bokfoerlag; Bokfoerlaget Opal AB; Astrid Lindgren; Marianne von Baumgarten-Lindberg

Battre Ledarskap (J)
c/o Liber Ekonomi, 205 10 Malmo
Tel: (040) 25 86 76 *Fax:* (040) 97 05 50
E-mail: export@liber.se
Web Site: www.battreledarskap.net
Telex: 12801 S
Key Personnel
Contact: Ann-Marie Petersson *E-mail:* ann-marie.petersson@liber.se
Subjects: Business, Economics, Management
Number of Members: 3,500
Owned by: Liber AB

Bokklubb Bra Bockesr
Soedra Vaegen, 263 80 Hoeganaes
Tel: (042) 339000 *Fax:* (042) 330504 *Cable:* BEBE BOOKS
Owned by: Bokfoerlaget Bra Boecker AB

Bonniers Bokklubb (J)
PO Box 3159, 103 63 Stockholm
Tel: (08) 696 87 80 *Fax:* (08) 696 83 51; (08) 696 83 64
E-mail: medlemsservice@bbk.bonnier.se; best@bbk.bonnier.se; avbest@bbk.bonnier.se
Web Site: www.bonniersbokklubb.se
Telex: 14546 Bonbook S *Cable:* BONNIERS
Key Personnel
Editor-in-Chief: Ingrid Carroll
Book Club Manager: Richard Ekstroem
Publication(s): Bokspegeln (The Book Mirror)
Owned by: Albert Bonniers Forlag AB

Delta Science Fiction Bok Klubb
Box 15123, 161 15 Bromma
Tel: (08) 254781
Owned by: Delta Foerlags AB

Manadens Bok (J)
Sankt Eriksgatan 63, 104 20 Stockholm
Mailing Address: Box 8090, 104 20 Stockholm
Tel: (08) 696 85 50 *Fax:* (08) 696 83 53
E-mail: info@manadensbok.se
Web Site: www.manadensbok.se
Key Personnel
Vice-Dir: Gabriella Hedlund

Reader's Digest AB
Fack 25, Kista 16493
Tel: (08) 6334800 *Fax:* (08) 7528701
E-mail: kundtjanst@readersdigest.se
Web Site: www.readersdigest.se

Richters Forlag
c/o Richter Egmont, Sallerupsvaegen 9, 205 75 Malmo
Tel: (040) 38 06 80 *Fax:* (040) 93 08 20
Web Site: www.egmontrichter.com
Telex: 33180 richt s
Key Personnel
Contact: Sara Hemmel
Book Club(s): Girls Only; Hem & Livsstil; Livsenergi; Livsutveckling; Richters Bokklubb; Bokklubben Skaparglaedje; Girls Only; Hem & Livsstil; Livsenergi; Livsutveckling; Richters Bokklubb; Bokklubben Skaparglaedje

Serie-pocket-klubben
Landsvaegen 57, S-172 22 Sundbyberg
Mailing Address: PO Box 1074, Sundbyberg
Tel: (08) 7993110 *Fax:* (08) 7645764
Telex: 17370 semic s *Cable:* SEMICPRESS SUNDBYBERG
Owned by: Semic Press AB

Stora Familjebokklubben (J)
Sveavaegen 56, 103 63 Stockholm
Mailing Address: Box 3159, 103 63 Stockholm
Tel: (08) 696 88 30 *Fax:* (08) 696 83 50
E-mail: medlemsservice@sfbk.bonnier.se; info@sfbk.bonnier.se
Web Site: www.storafamiljebokklubben.se
Telex: 14546 Bonbook s *Cable:* BONNIERS
Owned by: Albert Bonniers Forlag AB

Stora Romanklubben (J)
Sveavaegen 56, 103 63 Stockholm
Mailing Address: Box 3159, 103 63 Stockholm
Tel: (08) 696 88 40 *Fax:* (08) 696 88 41
E-mail: info@srk.bonnier.se
Web Site: www.storaromanklubben.se
Owned by: Albert Bonniers Forlag AB

Bokklubben Svalan (J)
Sveavaegen 56, 103 63 Stockholm
Mailing Address: Box 3159, 103 63 Stockholm
Tel: (08) 696 88 00 *Fax:* (08) 696 83 76
E-mail: medlemsservice@svalan.bonnier.se
Web Site: www.bokklubbensvalan.se
Telex: 14546 Bonbook S *Cable:* BONNIERS
Owned by: Albert Bonniers Forlag AB

Switzerland

Buchergilde Gutenberg AG
4601 Olten
Owned by: Edition Gutenberg

Europaring der Buch- und Schallplattenfreunde
Worblentalstr 33, 3063 Ittigen, Bern
Tel: (031) 584466
Owned by: Bertelsmann AG

NSB Buch- und Phonoclub
Schweizer Verlagshaus AG, Klausstr 10, 8008 Zurich
Tel: (01) 3833622
Key Personnel
General Manager: F Rothacher
Affiliated with Schweizer Verlagshaus AG.

Punktum AG
Klusstr, 508032 Zurich
Tel: (01) 422 45 40
This club deals exclusively with children's books, intended as gifts.
Owned by: Rada Matija AG

Thailand

Science Fiction Magazine Club
105/19-2 Naret Rd, Bangkok 10500
Tel: (02) 2330302; (02) 2356931
Telex: 20657 Graphic Th
Owned by: Graphic Art Publications

United Kingdom

BCA, see Book Club Associates

Bibliophile Books (J)
5 Thomas Rd, London E14 7BN
Tel: (020) 7515 9222 *Fax:* (020) 7538 4115
E-mail: customercare@bibliophilebooks.com
Web Site: www.bibliophilebooks.com
Key Personnel
General Manager: Anne Quigley
Established: 1978

Book Club Associates
Guild House, Farnsby St, Swindon Wilts SN1 5DD
Mailing Address: Greater London House, Hampstead Rd, London NW1 7TZ
Tel: (0870) 165 0292; (044) 1793 512100
Fax: (0870) 165 0222; (044) 1793 567711
Web Site: www.bca.co.uk
Telex: 24359 B CALON *Cable:* Booklub
Key Personnel
Chief Executive: Christian Friege
Book Club(s): Ancient & Medieval History Book Club; Arts Guild; Children's Book of the Month Club; Classical Selection Club (Audio); EBC (Netherlands); Encounters; English Book Club (France); English Book Club (Germany); English Book Club (Norway); English Book Club (Sweden); Executive World; History Guild; Home Computer - Amiga; Home Computer - Amstrad; Home Computer - Commodore 64; Home Computer - PC; Home Computer - Spectrum Sinclair; Home Computer Atari St; Irish Book Club; Leisure Circle; Literary Guild (F); Literary Guild (M); Literary Guild Gold; Military and Aviation Book Society; Music Direct (Cass); Music Direct (R/CD); Music Direct Gold; Mystery and Thriller Guild; On the Road; Paperbacks; Plate Series; Railway Book Club; Video Direct; World Books (F); World Books (M); Ancient & Medieval History Book Club; Arts Guild; Children's Book of the Month Club; Classical Selection Club (Audio); EBC (Netherlands); Encounters; English Book Club (France); English Book

Club (Germany); English Book Club (Norway); English Book Club (Sweden); Executive World; History Guild; Home Computer - Amiga; Home Computer - Amstrad; Home Computer - Commodore 64; Home Computer - PC; Home Computer - Spectrum Sinclair; Home Computer Atari St; Irish Book Club; Leisure Circle; Literary Guild (F); Literary Guild (M); Literary Guild Gold; Military and Aviation Book Society; Music Direct (Cass); Music Direct (R/CD); Music Direct Gold; Mystery and Thriller Guild; On the Road; Paperbacks; Plate Series; Railway Book Club; Video Direct; World Books (F); World Books (M)
Owned by: Reed International Books Ltd (parent company Reed Elsevier Plc); Doubleday & Company Inc, USA (parent company Bertelsmann AG, Germany)
Imprints: Guild Publishing

Bookmarks Club
265 Seven Sisters Rd, Finsbury Park, London N4 2DE
Tel: (020) 7536 9696 *Fax:* (020) 7538 0018
E-mail: bookmarks@internationalsocialist.org
Web Site: www.internationalsocialist.org
Subjects: Politics, Socialism
Owned by: IS Books Ltd
Branch Office(s)
PO Box 16085, Chicago, IL 60616, United States
Tel: (773) 665 9601 *Fax:* (773) 665 9651

Books Exports
137 Hale Lane, Edgware, Middlesex HA8 9QP
Tel: (020) 8931 2359; (020) 8959 2137
Fax: (0181) 9592137
E-mail: roshanbp@aol.com
Key Personnel
Partner & Man Dir: Mr B P Lakhani
Established: 1978
Remainders at competitive prices.

Books for Children
68 Willow Walk, London SE1 5SF
Tel: (020) 8606 3090 *Fax:* (020) 8606 3099
Established: 1977
Owned by: Time-Warner

The Bookworm Club
Rustat House, 60 Clifton Rd, Cambridge CB2 4GZ
Tel: (01223) 568650 *Fax:* (01223) 568591
E-mail: clubs@heffers.co.uk
Key Personnel
Contact: Fran Whiting
Subjects: Paperbacks for children age 8 up to the age of 13 (children's club in schools)
Owned by: W Heffer & Sons Ltd, 20 Trinity St, Cambridge CB2 3NG

English Book Club, see Book Club Associates

The Folio Society
44 Eagle St, London WC1R 4FS
Tel: (020) 7400 4200 *Fax:* (020) 7400 4242
E-mail: enquiries@foliosoc.co.uk
Web Site: www.foliosoc.co.uk
Key Personnel
Editor: Sue Bradbury
Rights & Permissions: Gilly Vincent
Contact: Kerry Davidson
Subjects: Fiction, Poetry, Biography, History

Godfrey Cave Associates
27 Wrights Lane, London W8 5TZ
Tel: (020) 7416 3000 *Fax:* (020) 7416 3289
Key Personnel
Man Dir: Kevin Binston

Guild Publishing, *imprint of* Book Club Associates

Letterbox Library
71-73 Allen Rd, Stoke Newington, London N16 8RY
Tel: (020) 7503 4801 *Fax:* (020) 7503 4800
E-mail: info@letterboxlibrary.com
Web Site: www.letterboxlibrary.com
Key Personnel
Dir: Maikim Stern
Publicity & Marketing: Kerry Mason
Children's Bookclub producing quarterly catalogue & newsletter. Once-off joining fee L5.
Subjects: Non-Sexist & Multi-Cultural Children's Books

9-12 Club
Red House School Book Club, Windough Pk, Witney, Oxon OX8 5YZ
Tel: (01993) 893456 *Fax:* (0845) 6039092
Key Personnel
Managing Dir: D M R Kewley
Subjects: Books for school children (9-12 years)
Owned by: Scholastic Publications Ltd

The Poetry Book Society Ltd
Book House, 45 East Hill, London SW18 2QZ
Tel: (020) 8870 8403 *Fax:* (020) 8870 0865
E-mail: info@poetrybooks.co.uk
Web Site: www.poetrybooks.co.uk
Key Personnel
Dir: Chris Holifield *E-mail:* chris@poetrybooks.co.uk
Membership organization which promotes selected poetry at discounted prices.
Subjects: Poetry
Number of Members: 2,200
Publication(s): *The Bulletin* (quarterly)

Puffin Book Clubs
c/o Penguin Books Ltd, 80 Strand, London WC2R 0RL
Tel: (020) 7416 3000 *Toll Free Tel:* (0500) 454 444 *Fax:* (020) 7416 3099
Web Site: www.penguin.co.uk
Key Personnel
Contact: Joan Alleyne *E-mail:* joan.alleyne@penguin.co.uk
Incorporating Fledgling (for up to 6-year-olds), Kite (for 6 to 9-year-olds) & Post (for 9 to 13-year-olds) book clubs.
Owned by: Penguin Books Ltd

Readers Union
Berkeley Square House, Berkeley Sq, London W1X 6AB
Tel: (020) 7629 8144 *Fax:* (020) 7499 9751
Telex: 264631 *Cable:* BOOKS NABBOT
Key Personnel
Marketing Dir: Lesley Godwin
Established: 1937
Book Club(s): Anglers Book Society; Belief the Religious Book Society; Birds and Natural History Book Society; Country Book Society; Country Book Society Incorporating Arena; Craft & Country Style Book Society; Craft Book Society; Craftsman Book Society; Design Book Club; Equestrian Book Society; Fieldsports Book Society; Gardeners Book Society; Golf Book Club; Maritime Book Society; Music Book Society; Nationwide & Phoenix Book Service; Needlecraft Book Society; Photographic Book Society; Ramblers & Climbers Book Society; World of Nature Book Club; World of Nature Incorporating Travel & Exploration Book Society; Anglers Book Society; Belief the Religious Book Society; Birds and Natural History Book Society; Country Book Society; Country Book Society Incorporating Arena; Craft & Country Style Book Society; Craft Book Society; Craftsman Book Society; Design Book Club; Equestrian Book Society; Fieldsports Book Society; Gardeners Book Society; Golf Book Club; Maritime Book Society; Music Book Society; Nationwide & Phoenix Book Service; Needlecraft Book Society; Photographic Book Society; Ramblers & Climbers Book Society; World of Nature Book Club; World of Nature Incorporating Travel & Exploration Book Society
Owned by: Reader's Digest Associates Ltd

The Red House Books Ltd
PO Box 142, Bangor LL57 4ZP
Tel: (0870) 191 99 80 *Fax:* (0870) 6077720
E-mail: enquiries@redhouse.co.uk
Web Site: www.redhouse.co.uk
Key Personnel
Man Dir: David Teale
Subjects: Children's
Number of Members: 350,000
Owned by: Red House Books Ltd

Scholastic Publications Ltd (J)
Windrush Park, Range Rd, Witney, Oxon OX29 0YZ
Tel: (0845) 6039091; (01993) 893475 (outside UK) *Fax:* (0845) 6039092; (01993) 893424 (outside UK)
E-mail: sbcenquiries@scholastic.co.uk
Web Site: www.scholastic.co.uk/schoolbookclub
Key Personnel
Man Dir: D M R Kewley
Publishing Dir, Education Division: Ann Peel
Editorial Dir, Scholastic Children's Books: Richard Scrivener
Finance Dir: Ian Bloodworth
Trade Sales & Marketing: Gavin Lang
Operations & Distribution Dir: Philip Owen
Office Manager: Deborah Shrives
E-mail: dshrives@scholastic.co.uk
Subjects: Education
Book Club(s): Arrow (children aged 9 to 11); Cover2Cover (children aged 11 to 14 at secondary schools); Firefly (children aged 5 to 7); Lucky (children aged 7 to 9); Seesaw (children aged 3 to 5); Arrow (children aged 9 to 11); Cover2Cover (children aged 11 to 14 at secondary schools); Firefly (children aged 5 to 7); Lucky (children aged 7 to 9); Seesaw (children aged 3 to 5)
Owned by: Scholastic Inc, 557 Broadway, New York, NY 10012, United States

6-9 Club
Red House School Book Club, Windough Pk, Witney, Oxon OX8 5YZ
Tel: (01993) 893456 *Fax:* (01993) 6039092
Key Personnel
Man Editor: D M R Kewley
Subjects: Books for school children (6-9 years)
Owned by: Scholastic Publications Ltd

Teachers Book Club (J)
Westfield Rd, Southam, Leamington Spa CV33 0JH
Tel: (01926) 813910 *Fax:* (01926) 817727
E-mail: enquiries@scholastic.co.uk
Web Site: www.scholastic.co.uk/teach_index.html
Key Personnel
Man Dir: D M R Kewley
Office Manager: Deborah Shrives
E-mail: dshrives@scholastic.co.uk
Books & resource materials for primary teachers.
Owned by: Scholastic Ltd

The Women's Press Book Club
27 Goodge St, London W1T 2LD
Tel: (020) 7636 3992 *Fax:* (020) 7637 1866
E-mail: sales@the-womens-press.com
Web Site: www.the-womens-press.com
Key Personnel
Manager: Kay Stirling *Tel:* (0207) 5539273

UNITED KINGDOM

Subjects: Books by & about women, with emphasis on fiction, women's studies, art, politics, health, biography
Number of Members: 7,000
Owned by: The Women's Press Ltd

Zambia

Read-a-Book Club
Chishango Rd, Lusaka 10101
Mailing Address: PO Box 32708, 10101 Lusaka
Tel: (01) 222324; (01) 236629 *Fax:* (01) 225073
Telex: 40056 *Cable:* HOUSE
Key Personnel
Man Dir: Beniko Mulota
Publishing Manager: Ray Munamwimbu
 E-mail: raymuna2@yahoo.co.uk
Established: 1966
Publishing, printing & distribution.
Owned by: Zambia Educational Publishing House

Book Trade Organizations

The organizations listed below include publisher and bookseller associations and ISBN agencies as well as book trade and allied organizations. Listings appear under the country in which they are physically located. Some of the organizations are specific to a particular country; others are international in nature.

† indicates those organizations that are international in scope.

‡ indicates United Nations agencies with publishing activities.

◇ indicates other international organizations with publishing activities.

Additional book trade associations can be found in the sections **Literary Associations & Societies** and **Library Associations**.

Albania

◇**Lidhja e Shkrimtareve dhe e Artisteve toe Shqiperise** (Union of Writers & Artists of Albania)
Baboci 37 z, Tirana
Tel: (042) 23843 *Fax:* (042) 23843
E-mail: bashan@natlib.tirana.al
Key Personnel
President: Dritero Agolli
Publication(s): *Albanaises* (quarterly, in French); *Drita* (weekly); *International Literatur* (quarterly); *Kultur Popullore* (annually, in Albanian & French); *Nentori* (monthly)

Algeria

Agence ISBN, see Bibliotheque Nationale

Bibliotheque Nationale
BP 127 El Hamma Les Anasser, 16000 Algiers
Tel: (021) 671967; (021) 675781; (021) 671867 *Fax:* (021) 672999
Key Personnel
Dir: Mahamed Aissamoussa
Founded: 1835

Andorra

Andorran Standard Book Numbering Agency
Placeta Sant Esteve s/n, Andorra la Vella
Tel: 826445 *Fax:* 829445
E-mail: bncultura.gov@andorra.ad
Web Site: bibnac.andorra.ad
Key Personnel
Dir: Pilar Burgues

Angola

UEA, see Uniao dos Escritores Angolanos (UEA)

Uniao dos Escritores Angolanos (UEA) (Union of Angolan Writers)
Rua Ho Chi Min (Zona Escolar), CP 2767-C, Luanda
Tel: (02) 323205; (02) 322421 *Fax:* (02) 323205
E-mail: uea@uea-angola.org
Web Site: www.uea-angola.org
Telex: 3056
Key Personnel
Secretary General: Luandino Vieira

Argentina

Agencia Argentina ISBN, see Camara Argentina del Libro

Argentine Society of Authors, see Sociedad General de Autores de la Argentina (SGAA)

Camara Argentina del Libro (Argentine Book Association)
Ave Belgrano 1580 - Piso 4°, 1093 Buenos Aires
Tel: (011) 4381-8383 *Fax:* (011) 4381-9253
E-mail: cal@editores.com
Web Site: www.editores.com *Cable:* 381-9253
Key Personnel
Dir: Noberto J Pou
Founded: 1938
Publication(s): *LEA*

Fundacion El Libro
Hipolito Yrigoyen 1628, 5° Piso, 1089 Buenos Aires
Tel: (011) 43743288 *Fax:* (011) 43750268
E-mail: fundacion@el-libro.com.ar
Web Site: www.el-libro.com.ar
Key Personnel
President: Carlos Alberto Pazos
Dir: Marta V Diaz

SGAA, see Sociedad General de Autores de la Argentina (SGAA)

Sociedad General de Autores de la Argentina (SGAA)
Pacheco de Melo 1820, 1126 Buenos Aires
Tel: (011) 4811-2582; (011) 4812-9996 *Fax:* (011) 4812-6954
E-mail: info@argentores.org.ar
Web Site: www.argentores.org.ar
Key Personnel
President: Agustin Perez Pardella
Vice President: Ricardo Halac

Standard Book Numbering Agency
Camara Argentina del Libro, Ave Belgrano 1580 - 4° Piso, 1093 Buenos Aires
Tel: (011) 4381-8383 *Fax:* (011) 4381-9253
E-mail: registrolibros@editores.com
Web Site: www.editores.com
Key Personnel
ISBN Administrator: Norberto Pou, Sr
Publication(s): *ISBN Directory*

Armenia

Gosudarstvenny Komitet Armjanskoj SSR po delam izdatel'stv, poligrafii, kniznoj targovli
Terjan 89, 375009 Erevan 9
Tel: (02) 528660
E-mail: grapalat@arminco.com
Telex: 411871 Kniga
Key Personnel
Chairman: M F Nenashev
The USSR State Committee for Publishing, Printing & the Book Trade.

Australia

ANZAAB, see The Australian & New Zealand Association of Antiquarian Booksellers

Australia Council Literature Board
372 Elizabeth St, Surry Hills NSW 2010
Mailing Address: PO Box 788, Strawberry Hills NSW 2012
Tel: (02) 9215 9000 *Toll Free Tel:* 800 226 912 *Fax:* (02) 9215 9111
E-mail: mail@ozco.gov.au
Web Site: www.ozco.gov.au
Key Personnel
Manager: Gail Cork *Tel:* (02) 9215 9058
  E-mail: g.cork@ozco.gov.au
The Literature Board supports the writing of all forms of creative literature, including novels, short stories, poetry, publishing & promotion, plays & nonfiction (especially biography, autobiography, essays, histories, literary criticism or other expository or analytical prose). All applicants must use the Literature Board's application forms.
Publication(s): *Australia Council Support for the Arts Handbook* (1997)

The Australian & New Zealand Association of Antiquarian Booksellers
Affiliate of International League of Antiquarian Booksellers (ILAB)
604 High St, Prahran, Victoria 3181
Tel: (03) 9525 1649 *Fax:* (03) 9529 1298
E-mail: admin@anzaab.com; bookshop@hincebooks.com.au
Web Site: www.anzaab.com

AUSTRALIA

Key Personnel
President: Barbara Hince
Vice President: Lovella Kerr
Founded: 1977

Australian Booksellers Association Inc
828 High St, Unit 9, Kew East, Victoria 3102
Tel: (03) 9859 7322 *Fax:* (03) 9859 7344
E-mail: mail@aba.org.au
Web Site: www.aba.org.au
Key Personnel
President: Tim Peach
Executive Dir: Celia Pollock
The ABA is a Federal Association with branches in every state & represents booksellers' interests to government bodies, publishers & other organizations.
Publication(s): Economic Survey (annually)

◇**Australian Copyright Council**
245 Chalmers St, Suite 3, Redfern, NSW 2016
Mailing Address: PO Box 1986, Strawberry Hills, NSW 2012
Tel: (02) 9318 1788 (copyright); (02) 9699 3247 (sales) *Fax:* (02) 9698 3536
E-mail: info@copyright.org.au
Web Site: www.copyright.org.au
Key Personnel
Chairman: Peter Banki
Executive Officer: Libby Baulch
Office Manager & Events Coordinator: Vickie James
Publication(s): Copyright Reporter; *Practical Guide* (Discussion paper)
ISBN Prefix(es): 0-9595513

Australian Press Council
117 York St, Suite 10-02, Sydney, NSW 2000
Tel: (02) 9261 1930 *Toll Free Tel:* 800-02-5712 *Fax:* (02) 9267 6826
E-mail: info@presscouncil.org.au
Web Site: www.presscouncil.org.au
Key Personnel
Executive Secretary: Jack R Herman
Office Manager: Deborah Kirkman

Australian Publishers Association Ltd
60/89 Jones St, Ultimo, NSW 2007
Tel: (02) 9281 9788 *Fax:* (02) 9281 1073
E-mail: apa@publishers.asn.au
Web Site: www.publishers.asn.au
Key Personnel
Chief Executive: Susan Bridge
Information Officer: Michaela Purcell
  E-mail: michaela.purcell@publishers.asn.au
Founded: 1948
Trade association representing Australian book publishers.
Publication(s): Directory of Members; *Introduction to Book Publishing*

The Australian Society of Authors Ltd
PO Box 1566, Strawberry Hills NSW 2012
Tel: (02) 93180877 *Fax:* (02) 93180530
E-mail: office@asauthors.org
Web Site: www.asauthors.org/cgi-bin/asa/information.cgi
Key Personnel
Executive Dir: Jose Borghino *E-mail:* jose@asauthors.org
Founded: 1963
Publication(s): Australian Author (trianually, magazine, magazine for writers, readers & people who love books); *Australian Book Contracts* (step-by-step guide to publishing contracts for authors)

Australian Society of Indexers
GPO Box 2069, Canberra, ACT 2601
Tel: (02) 4268-5335
Web Site: www.aussi.org

Key Personnel
President: Lynn Farkas *Tel:* (02) 6286 4818
  Fax: (02) 6286 6570 *E-mail:* president@aussi.org
Vice President: Clodagh Jones *Tel:* (03) 6225 3848 *E-mail:* vicepres@aussi.org
Secretary: Shirley Campbell *Tel:* (02) 6285 1006
  E-mail: secretary@aussi.org
Treasurer: Penelope Whitten *Tel:* (02) 6241 4289
  E-mail: treasurer@aussi.org
President, ACT Branch: Geraldine Triffitt
  Tel: (02) 6231 4975 *E-mail:* geraldine.triffitt@alianet.alia.org.au
Affiliated with indexing societies in Britain, Canada, China, South Africa & USA.
Publication(s): Australian Society of Indexers' Newsletter (10 times/yr); *Indexers Available*
Associate Companies: American Society of Indexers; Association of Southern African Indexers & Bibliographers (ASAIB); China Society of Indexers; Indexing & Abstracting Society of Canada; Society of Indexers, United Kingdom
Branch Office(s)
PO Box R598, Royal Exchange, NSW 1225, Branch President: Caroline Colton
  Tel: (02) 9568 4880 *Fax:* (02) 4285 7199
  E-mail: nswbranch@aussi.org
GPO Box 1251, Melbourne, Victoria 3000, Branch President: Ann Philpott *Tel:* (03) 9830 0494 *Fax:* (03) 9830 0494 *E-mail:* vicbranch@aussi.org

†◇**Bibliographical Society of Australia & New Zealand (BSANZ)**
PO Box 1463, Wagga Wagga, NSW 2650
Tel: (02) 6931 8669 *Fax:* (02) 6931 8669
E-mail: rsalmond@pobox.com
Web Site: www.csu.edu.au/community/BSANZ
Key Personnel
President: D H R Spennemann
  E-mail: dspennemann@csu.edu.au
Founded: 1969
Publication(s): Broadsheet (newsletter); *Bulletin* (quarterly, journal)
ISBN Prefix(es): 0-9598271

BSANZ, see Bibliographical Society of Australia & New Zealand (BSANZ)

Christian Bookselling Association of Australia Inc
Suite 2, 7-9 President Ave, Caringbah NSW 2229
Mailing Address: PO Box 576, Caringbah NSW 2229
Tel: (02) 9524 3347 *Fax:* (02) 9540 3001
E-mail: info@cbaa.com.au
Web Site: www.cbaa.com.au
Key Personnel
Executive Secretary: Jan Holt
Founded: (In existence for 28 years)
Membership: Christian Booksellers Association (USA).
Publication(s): CBAA News

Copyright Agency Ltd
157 Liverpool St, Level 19, Sydney, NSW 2000
Tel: (02) 93947600 *Fax:* (02) 93947601
E-mail: info@copyright.com.au
Web Site: www.copyright.com.au
Key Personnel
Chief Executive: Michael Fraser
Manager, Member Services: Jenny Longland
  E-mail: jlongland@copyright.com.au
Acts as a Copyright Collecting Society.

†◇**International Association of School Librarianship**
IASL Secretariat, PO Box 587, Carlton North 3054
Fax: (03) 9428 7612
E-mail: iasl@rockland.com

Web Site: www.iasl-slo.org
Key Personnel
Executive Dir: Dr Penny Moore
President: Peter Genco *Fax:* 814-474-1115
  E-mail: iaslpres@hotmail.com
Vice President, Association Operations: Dr Diljit Singh *E-mail:* diljit@um.edu.my
Administrative Manager: Mary Manning
Founded: 1971
Publication(s): Annual Conference Proceedings; *Newsletter of the International Association of School Librarianship* (quarterly); *School Libraries Worldwide* (biannually, journal)

International Standard Book Numbering Agency, see ISBN Agency Australia

ISBN Agency Australia
18 Salmon St, Locked Bag 20, Port Melbourne, Victoria 3207
Tel: (03) 9245 7385 *Fax:* (03) 9245 7393
E-mail: isbn.agency@thorpe.com.au
Web Site: www.thorpe.com.au
Key Personnel
ISBN Coordinator: Maria Watt
Publication(s): Australian Books In Print
Parent Company: D W Thorpe

Mardev
Tower 2, 475 Victoria Ave, Chatswood, NSW 2067
Tel: (02) 9422 2644 *Fax:* (02) 9422 2633
E-mail: mardevlists@reedbusiness.com.au
Web Site: www.mardevlists.com
Key Personnel
Gen Manager, UK: Nick Martin
List Manager: Maureen Ryan *E-mail:* maureen.ryan@reedbusiness.com.au
Parent Company: Reed Elsevier plc
Branch Office(s)
No 1 Temasek Ave, 17-01 Millenia Tower, Singapore 039192, Singapore *Tel:* 338 3398 *Fax:* 338 1409
Quadrant House, Sutton, Surrey SM2 5AS, United Kingdom *Tel:* (020) 8643 0955 *Fax:* (020) 8652 4580 *E-mail:* mardevlists@rbo.co.uk
2 Rector St, 26th floor, New York, NY 10006, United States *Tel:* 212-584-9370 *Fax:* 212-584-9371 *E-mail:* sales@mardevlists.com

Public Lending Right Scheme
GPO Box 3241, Canberra, ACT 2601
Tel: (02) 6271 1650 *Toll Free Tel:* 800 672 842 (Australia only) *Fax:* (02) 6271 1651
E-mail: plr.mail@dcita.gov.au
Web Site: www.dcita.gov.au
Key Personnel
PLR Administrator: Paul Bootes *Tel:* (02) 6271 1635 *E-mail:* paul.bootes@dcita.gov.au
Parent Company: Department of Communications, Information Technology & the Arts

◇**Society of Women Writers NSW Inc**
GPO Box 1388, Sydney, NSW 2001
Tel: (03) 63310267
Web Site: www.womenwritersnsw.org
Key Personnel
Federal President: Jennifer Rumsey
Editor: Marilyn Arnold
Founded: 1925
Publication(s): The Woman Writer (bi-monthly, newsletter)
ISBN Prefix(es): 0-9587871; 0-9591144; 0-9598432
Associate Companies: Society of Women Writers & Journalists London

◇**UNILINC**
Level 9, 210 Clarence St, Sydney, NSW 2000
Tel: (02) 9283 1488 *Fax:* (02) 9267 9247
E-mail: info@unilinc.edu.au

Web Site: www.unilinc.edu.au
Key Personnel
Executive Dir & Chief Executive Officer: Rona Wade *E-mail:* rona@unilinc.edu.au
Founded: 1978

Austria

†**CIE (International Commission on Illumination Central Bureau)**
Kegelgasse 27, 1030 Vienna
Tel: (01) 714 31 87 0 *Fax:* (01) 713 08 38 18
E-mail: ciecb@ping.at
Web Site: www.cie.co.at/cie
Key Personnel
President: Wout van Bommel
General Secretary: Christine Hermann
Founded: 1913
Subjects: Lighting

Fachverband der Buch und Medienwirtschaft
Wiedner-Hauptstr 63, Postfach 440, A-1045 Vienna
Tel: (01) 50105 DW 3331; (01) 50105 DW 3333 *Fax:* (01) 50105 DW 3043
E-mail: buchwirtschaft@wko.at
Web Site: www.buchwirtschaft.at
Key Personnel
President: Bernhard Weis
Vice President: Gustav Glockler
Man Dir: Johann Varga

†◇**Federation Internationale des Traducteurs (FIT)**
Dr Heinrich Maierstrasse 9, A-1180 Vienna
Tel: (01) 4403607; (01) 4709819 *Fax:* (01) 4403756; (01) 4708194
E-mail: info@fit.org
Web Site: www.fit-ift.org/
Key Personnel
President: F Herbulot
Vice President: L Sivesind
Secretary General: Liese Katschinka
  E-mail: liese.katschinka@eunet.at
International Federation of Translators.
Publication(s): *Babel* (International journal of translation); *Translatio* (FIT Newsletter)

FIT, see Federation Internationale des Traducteurs (FIT)

◇**Hauptverband des Oesterreichischen Buchhandels** (Austrian Publishers' & Booksellers' Association)
Grunangergasse 4, 1010 Vienna
Tel: (01) 512 15 35 *Fax:* (01) 512 84 82
E-mail: hvb@buecher.at
Web Site: www.buecher.at
Key Personnel
President: Dr Anton C Hilscher
Publication(s): *Adressbuch des oesterreichischen Buchhandels* (Directory of Austrian Book Trade); *Anzeiger des oesterreichischen Buchhandels* (Austrian Book Trade Gazette, bimonthly)
Associate Companies: Verband der Antiquare Oesterreichs; Verband der oesterreichischen Buch- und Presse-Grossisten und der Werbenden Zeitschriftenhaendler; Oesterreichischer Verlegerverband; Oesterreichischer Buchhaendlerverband; Verband von selbstaendigen Verlagsvertretern Oesterreichs; Standard Book Numbering Agency

IAEA, see International Atomic Energy Agency (IAEA)

†‡**International Atomic Energy Agency (IAEA)**
Wagramer Str 5, 1400 Vienna
Mailing Address: PO Box 100, 1400 Vienna
Tel: (0222) 2600-0 *Fax:* (0222) 2600-7
E-mail: official.mail@iaea.org; info@iaea.org
Web Site: www.iaea.org
Key Personnel
Editorial: M F Boemeke
Dir, Public Information: Mark Gwozdecky
  Tel: (01) 2600-21270
Senior Information Officer: Melissa Fleming
  Tel: (01) 2600-21275 *Fax:* (01) 2600-29610
  E-mail: m.fleming@iaea.org
Sales, Publicity: A Bugno; G Cazier
Founded: 1957
The International Atomic Energy Agency is an international organization within the United Nations family, having the general purpose of seeking to accelerate & enlarge the contribution of atomic energy to peace, health & prosperity throughout the world. The Agency's publications result, almost exclusively, from its own activities; published material is of intense interest only to a relatively small group of scientists & technicians
Membership: Intergovernmental Organization in Family of United Nations.
Subjects: Life Sciences, Nuclear Safety & Environmental Protection, Physics, Chemistry, Geology & Raw Materials, Reactors & Nuclear Power, Industrial Applications, Miscellaneous
Publication(s): *Meetings in Atomic Energy* (quarterly); *Nuclear Fusion* (monthly)
ISBN Prefix(es): 92-0

International Commission on Illumination Central Bureau, see CIE (International Commission on Illumination Central Bureau)

†◇**International Federation for Information Processing (IFIP)**
c/o Plamen Nedkov, Hofstr 3, 2361 Laxenburg
Tel: (02236) 73616 *Fax:* (02236) 736169
E-mail: ifip@ifip.or.at
Web Site: www.ifip.or.at

†‡**International Institute for Children's Literature & Reading Research (UNESCO category C)**
Mayerhofgasse 6, 1040 Vienna
Tel: (01) 505 03 59; (01) 505 28 31 *Fax:* (01) 505 03 59-17; (01) 505 28 31-17
E-mail: office@jugendliteratur.net
Web Site: www.jugendliteratur.net
Key Personnel
President: Dr Hilde Hawlicek
Vice President: Alois Almer
Dir: Mag Karin Haller *E-mail:* karin.haller@jugendliteratur.net
Secretary: Barbara Mladek *E-mail:* barbara.mladek@jugendliteratur.net
Founded: 1965
Internationales Institut for Jugendliteratur und Leseforschung.
Subjects: Children & Youth Literature, Research
Publication(s): *1000 und 1 Buch* (4 times/yr)

†**International Union of Geological Sciences (IUGS)** (Union internationale des Sciences Geologiques)
Rasumofskygasse 23, 1031 Vienna
Mailing Address: PO Box 127, 1031 Vienna
Tel: (01) 712 56 74 (ext 180) *Fax:* (01) 712 56 74 56
Web Site: www.iugs.org
Telex: 55417 NGU N
Key Personnel
President: Dr E F J de Mulder *E-mail:* e.demulder@nitg.tnanl
Secretary General: Dr Werner R Janoschek
  E-mail: wjanoschek@cc.geolba.ac.at
Founded: 1961
Subjects: Earth Sciences
Publication(s): *Episodes* (quarterly)

IUGS, see International Union of Geological Sciences (IUGS)

Literar-Mechana, Wahrnehmungsgesellschaft fuer Urheberrechte GmbH
Linke Wienzeile 18, 1060 Vienna
Tel: (01) 5872161-0 *Fax:* (01) 5872161-9
E-mail: literar.mechana@netway.at
Key Personnel
Man Dir: Franz Leo Popp
Organization for Copyright Protection.

Standard Book Numbering Agency
Grunangergasse 4, 1010 Vienna
Tel: (01) 512 15 35 *Fax:* (01) 512 84 82
E-mail: isbn@hvb.at
Web Site: www.buecher.at
Key Personnel
Contact: Herma Papovschek
ISBN Prefix(es): 3-85103

◇**Verband der Antiquare Oesterreichs** (Antiquarian Booksellers Association of Austria)
Grunangergasse 4, 1010 Vienna
Tel: (01) 512 15 35 *Fax:* (01) 512 84 82
E-mail: sekretariat@hvb.at
Web Site: www.antiquare.at
Key Personnel
President: Norbert Donhofer *E-mail:* donhofer@oebv.co.at
Vice President: Michael Sulzmann
  E-mail: antiquariat.ms@chello.at
Publication(s): *Anzeiger des Verbandes der Antiquare Oesterreichs* (Austrian Antiquarian Booksellers' Association Gazette)

Verband der Oesterreichischen Buch-und Presse- Grossisten und der Werbenden Zeitschriftenhaendler
Grunangergasse 4, 1010 Vienna
Tel: (01) 512 15 35 *Fax:* (01) 512 84 82
E-mail: hvb@buecher.at
Web Site: www.buecher.at
Key Personnel
President: Dr Emmerich Selch

Verband von selbstaendigen Verlagsvertreten Oesterreichs (Association of Independent Publishers Representing Austria)
Grunangergasse 4, 1010 Vienna
Tel: (01) 512 15 35 *Fax:* (01) 512 84 82
E-mail: hvb@buecher.at
Web Site: www.buecher.at
Key Personnel
President: Hans Jobst

Bangladesh

National Library
32 Justice S M Morshed Sarani, Sher-e-Bangla Nagar Agargaon, Dhaka 1207
Tel: (02) 9129992; (02) 9112733 *Fax:* (02) 9118704
Key Personnel
Contact: Mr Shahabuddin Khan
Publication(s): *Boi* (text in Bengali)

Standard Book Numbering Agency, see National Library

Belarus

National Book Chamber of Belarus
11 Masherow Ave, 220600 Minsk
Tel: (172) 235839 *Fax:* (172) 235825
E-mail: palata@palata.belpak.minsk.by
Key Personnel
Contact: Anatoli Voronko
Parent Company: Republic of Belarus

Standard Book Numbering Agency, see National Book Chamber of Belarus

Belgium

Association des Editeurs Belges (Belgian Publishers' Association)
140 Blvd Lambermont, bte 1, 1030 Brussels
Tel: (02) 241 65 80 *Fax:* (02) 216 71 31
E-mail: adeb@adeb.be
Web Site: www.adeb.irisnet.be
Key Personnel
President: Jean Vandeveld
Dir: Bernard Gerard
Publication(s): *Annuaire des Editeurs belges de Langue francaise* (Belgian Publishers in French Language Annual); *Catalogue des Editeurs scientifiques*; *Donnees statistiques sur le livre belge de langue francaise*

Boek.be
Hof ter Schrieckaan 17, 2600 Berchem, Antwerp
Tel: (03) 230 89 23 *Fax:* (03) 281 22 40
E-mail: info@boek.be
Web Site: www.boek.be
Key Personnel
President: Andre Van Halewyck
Dir: Rene Van Loon *E-mail:* rene.van.loon@boek.be
Association for the Promotion of Dutch Language Books/Books from Flanders.
Publication(s): *Adresgids voor het Boekenvan* (list of publishers & booksellers); *De Boekentrommel* (list of new children's books); *Het Boek in Vlaanderen* (list of new books); *Lijstenboek* (list of publishers & booksellers); *Tijdingen* (news)

†‡**Centre for European Policy Studies**
One Place du Congres, 1000 Brussels
Tel: (02) 2293911 *Fax:* (02) 2194151; (02) 2293971
E-mail: info@ceps.be
Web Site: www.ceps.be
Key Personnel
President: Peter Ludlow
General Manager: Catherine Chanut
Corporate Relations Manager: Staffan Jerneck
Finances & Administration Dir: Willem Roekens
Editor: Anne Harrington
Founded: 1983
Subjects: Politics, Economics, Business

EBF, see European Booksellers Federation (EBF)

†◇**European Association of Directory & Database Publishers** (Association Europeenne des Editeurs d'Annuaires/Europaeischer Adressbuchverleger-Verband)
127 Ave Franklin Roosevelt, 1050 Brussels
Tel: (02) 6463060 *Fax:* (02) 6463637
E-mail: mailbox@eadp.org
Web Site: www.eadp.be
Key Personnel
President: Frank-Peter Oppenborn
Secretary-General: Anne Lerat
Public Relations: Annie Komaromi
  E-mail: anniekomaromi@eadp.org
Founded: 1966
Publication(s): *Directories in Europe* (annually, list of members)

†◇**European Booksellers Federation (EBF)**
Chaussee de Charleroi, 51b Boite 1, 1060 Brussels
Tel: (02) 223 49 40 *Fax:* (02) 223 49 38
E-mail: eurobooks@skynet.be
Web Site: www.ebf-eu.org
Key Personnel
President: John Hitchin *Tel:* (0181) 9484932 *Fax:* (0181) 3320379
Vice President & Treasurer: Klaus Vorpahl
  Tel: (069) 314032-11 *Fax:* (069) 314969
Secretary General: Christiane Vuidar

†◇**Federation of European Publishers (FEP)**
Av de Tervueren 204, 1150 Brussels
Tel: (02) 7701110 *Fax:* (02) 7712071
Web Site: www.fep-fee.be
Key Personnel
President: Dr Anten C Hilscher
Dir General: Mechthild von Alemann
  E-mail: malemann@fep-fee.be
Deputy Dir: Anne Bergman-Tahon
  E-mail: abergman@fep-fee.be
Founded: 1967
The Federation consists of the book associations of the European Communities & European Econo mic Area (EEA) & aims at representing jointly the interests of the European publishers for all matters arising from the Treaty of Rome, Maastricht & Amsterdam & Nice (or the Treaties).

FEP, see Federation of European Publishers (FEP)

†◇**FIAF (International Federation of Film Archives)** (Federation internationale des archives du film)
One Rue Defacqz, 1000 Brussels
Tel: (02) 538 3065 *Fax:* (02) 534 4774
E-mail: info@fiafnet.org
Web Site: www.fiafnet.org
Key Personnel
Executive Secretary: Brigitte van der Elst
Founded: 1938
Dedicated to the rescue, collection, preservation & screening of moving images.
Publication(s): *Bibliography of National Filmographies*; *Cataloguing Rules for Film Archives*; *Glossary of Filmographic Terms, Version II*; *Handbook for Film Archives*; *Handling, Storage & Transport of Cellulose Nitrate Film*; *International Directory of Film & TV Documentation Collections*; *International Film Archive CD-ROM*; *Journal of Film Preservation*; *Preservation & Restoration of Moving Images & Sound*; *Technical Manual of the FIAF Preservation Commission*; *The International Index to Film & Television Periodicals*

IBF, see International Booksellers Federation (IBF)

IFRRO, see International Federation of Reproduction Rights Organisations (IFRRO)

†◇**International Booksellers Federation (IBF)**
Chaussee de Charleroi 51b, Boite 1, 1060 Brussels
Tel: (02) 223 49 40 *Fax:* (02) 223 49 38
E-mail: ibf.booksellers@skynet.be
Web Site: www.ibf-booksellers.org
Key Personnel
President: Yvonne Steinberger *E-mail:* yvonne.steinberger@ping.be
Vice President: Eric Hardin *E-mail:* hardin@club-internet.fr
Dir: Francoise Dubruille
Founded: 1955
International, non-governmental organization of booksellers associations & booksellers from around the world. Its purpose is to enable booksellers associations & individual booksellers to connect.
Publication(s): *Booksellers International* (different country reports); *The IBF* (IBF list of members)

†‡**International Catholic Organization for Cinema & Audiovisual (OCIC)**
8, rue de l'Orme, 1040 Brussels
Tel: (02) 7344294 *Fax:* (02) 7343207
E-mail: sg@ocic.org
Web Site: www.ocic.org *Cable:* OCIC.BRUXELLES
Key Personnel
President: Henk Hoegstra
Secretary General: Robert Molhant
Founded: 1928
Subjects: African Cinema, Cinema & Religion, Video & Religion, World Cinema
Publication(s): *Cineamedia* (bimonthly, magazine)
ISBN Prefix(es): 92-9080

International Federation of Film Archives, see FIAF (International Federation of Film Archives)

†◇**International Federation of Reproduction Rights Organisations (IFRRO)**
Rue de Prince Royal 87, 1050 Brussels
Tel: (02) 551 08 99 *Fax:* (02) 551 08 95
E-mail: iffro@skynet.be; secretariat@ifrro.be
Web Site: www.ifrro.org
Key Personnel
President: Peter F Shepherd
Vice President: Michael Fraser
General Secretary: Veronica Williams
  E-mail: veronica.williams@ifrro.be
Information Officer: Marie-Agnes Lenoir
  E-mail: marie.agnes.lenoir@ifrro.be
Office Manager: Avra Navez
IFRRO links together all national Reproduction Rights Organizations (RROs) & national & international associations of rightsholders. RROs are organizations engaged in the conveyance of photocopying authorizations & royalties between rightsholders & users. IFRRO's purposes are to foster the creation of RROs worldwide; to facilitate the development of formal agreements & informal relationships between, among & on behalf of its members; & to increase public awareness of copyright & the need for effective mechanisms for conveying rights & royalties between rightsholders & users.

OCIC, see International Catholic Organization for Cinema & Audiovisual (OCIC)

†‡**Tantalum-Niobium International Study Center**
40 Rue Washington, 1050 Brussels
Tel: (02) 6495158 *Fax:* (02) 6496447
E-mail: info@tanb.org
Web Site: www.tanb.org
Key Personnel
Secretary General: Judith Wickens
Subjects: Metals
ISBN Prefix(es): 92-9093

TIC, see Tantalum-Niobium International Study Center

VBB, see Vlaamse Boekverkopersbond (VBB)

◇**Vlaamse Boekverkopersbond (VBB)** (Flemish Booksellers' Association)
Hof ter Schrieklaan 17, 2600 Berchem, Antwerp
Tel: (03) 230 89 23 *Fax:* (03) 281 22 40
E-mail: info@boek.be
Web Site: www.boek.be
Key Personnel
General Secretary: Luc Tessens *E-mail:* luc.tessens@vbvb.be

Vlaamse Uitgevers Vereniging (VUV) (Publishers From Flanders)
Hof ter Schrieklaan 17, 2600 Antwerp
Tel: (03) 2308923 *Fax:* (03) 2812240
E-mail: info@boek.be
Web Site: www.vbvb.be
Key Personnel
Secretary: Jan Vanderheyden *E-mail:* jan.vanderheyden@vbvb.be
Association of Publishers of Dutch Language Books.

VUV, see Vlaamse Uitgevers Vereniging (VUV)

Bolivia

Camara Boliviana del Libro (Bolivian Booksellers' Association)
Calle Capitan Ravelo 2116, 682 La Paz
Tel: (02) 44 4239; (02) 44 4077 *Fax:* (02) 44 1523
E-mail: cabolib@ceibo.entelnet.bo
Key Personnel
President & Dir: Rolando Condori Salinas
Vice President: Nancy C de Montoya
Secretary: Teresa G de Alvarez
Distributions: Miguel Martinez
Sales: Jose Carlos Ciappesoni
Editorial: Nestor Castillo
Retail Sales: Walter Mercado

Botswana

Standard Book Numbering Agency (Botswana)
Botswana National Library Service, Pvt Bag 0036, Gaborone
Tel: 3952 397; 3952 288 *Fax:* 3957 108; 3901 149
Telex: 2414 pula bd *Cable:* BONALIBS
Key Personnel
ISBN Administrator: G K Mulindwa

Brazil

ABEU, see Associacao Brasileira dar Editoras Universitarias (ABEU)

Agencia Brasileira do ISBN
c/o Biblioteca Nacional, Av Rio Branco, 219-1°, 20040-008 Rio de Janeiro-RJ
Tel: (021) 2220-9367 *Fax:* (021) 2220-4173
E-mail: isbn@bn.br
Web Site: www.bn.br
Telex: 2122941bnrjbr
Key Personnel
Contact: Sueli Ferreira Aleixo

Associacao Brasileira dar Editoras Universitarias (ABEU)
Praca da Se 108 5° andar, 01001-900 Centro, Sao Paulo
Tel: (011) 32427171 *Fax:* (011) 32427172
E-mail: feu@editora.unesp.br
Telex: (0482) 240
Key Personnel
President: Alcides Buss
Brazilian Association of Academic Publishers.

Brazilian National Library, see Departamento Nacional do Livro

Camara Brasileira do Livro (Brazilian Book Association)
Cristiano Viana, 91, 05411-000 Sao Paulo-SP
Tel: (011) 3069-1300 *Fax:* (011) 3069-1300
E-mail: cbl@cbl.org.br
Web Site: www.cbl.org.br
Telex: 24788 Vrli
Key Personnel
President: Oswaldo Siciliano
Dir: H Carlos Dias
General Manager: Aloysio T Costa

Departamento Nacional do Livro (National Books Department)
Affiliate of Ministerio da Cultura Republica Federativa do Brazil
c/o Fundacao Biblioteca Nacional, Avenida Rio Branco, 219-1 andar, 20040-008 Rio de Janeiro-RJ
Tel: (021) 2220-1707; (021) 2220-1683 *Fax:* (021) 2220-1702
E-mail: dnl@bn.br
Web Site: www.bn.br
Key Personnel
Dir: Elmer Correa Barbosa *E-mail:* elmer@bn.br

Livraria Kosmos Editora Ltda
Rua do Rosario 135-137, Centro, CP 3481, 20041-005 Rio de Janeiro-RJ
Tel: (021) 224-8616 *Fax:* (021) 221-4582
Brazilian Association of Antiquarian Booksellers.
ISBN Prefix(es): 85-7096

Sindicato Nacional dos Editores de Livros (SNEL) (Brazilian Publishers' Association)
Av Rio Branco 37, Sala 1.504, 20090-003 Rio de Janeiro-RJ
Tel: (021) 2233-6481 *Fax:* (021) 2253-8502
E-mail: snel@snel.org.br
Web Site: www.snel.org.br
Key Personnel
President: Paulo Roberto Rocco
Dir Secretary: Francisco Bilac Pinto
Manager: Nilson Lopes da Silva
Publication(s): *Informativo Bibliografico* (annually); *Jornal do SNEL* (bimonthly); *Producao Editorial Brasileira* (Brazilian Publishing Output, annually)

SNEL, see Sindicato Nacional dos Editores de Livros (SNEL)

Standard Book Numbering Agency, see Agencia Brasileira do ISBN

Brunei Darussalam

Standard Book Numbering Agency
Bandar Seri Begawan 2064, Negara
Tel: (02) 382511 *Fax:* (02) 381817
Telex: bu 2774
Key Personnel
Contact: Ms Nellie Dato Paduka Haji Sunny

Bulgaria

Bulgarian National ISSN Centre
c/o St Cyril & Methodius National Library, Vassil Levski 88, 1037 Sophia
Tel: (02) 9461165; (02) 9882811 *Fax:* (02) 435495
E-mail: issn@nationallibary.bg
Web Site: www.nationallibrary.bg
Telex: 22432
Key Personnel
Dir: Antoaneta Totomanova *E-mail:* nbkm@nl.otel.net
Parent Company: St St Cyril & Methodius

◇**National ISBN Agency**
St Cyril & St Methodius National Library, Boul Vasil Leveski 88, 1037 Sofia
Tel: (02) 9882811; (02) 9882362 *Fax:* (02) 435495
E-mail: nl@nationallibrary.bg
Web Site: www.nationallibrary.bg
Telex: 22432 natlib
Key Personnel
ISBN Administrator: Tatjana Dermendzieva
Publication(s): *Novini ISBN i ISSN* (monthly); *Spravocnik na izdatelstva, redakcii i pecatnici v Baelgarija* (annually, directory)

Standard Book Numbering Agency, see National ISBN Agency

Cameroon

†◇**Centre Regional pour la Promotion du Livre en Afrique (CREPLA)**
POB 1646, Yaounde
Tel: 224782; 2936
Key Personnel
Secretary: William Moutchia
Founded: 1962
Regional Centre for Book Promotion in Africa (co-sponsored by UNESCO).
Publication(s): *CREPLA Bulletin*

CREPLA, see Centre Regional pour la Promotion du Livre en Afrique (CREPLA)

IFORD, see Institut de Formation et de Recherche Demographiques (IFORD)

†‡**Institut de Formation et de Recherche Demographiques (IFORD)**
BP 1556, Yaounde
Tel: (023) 222471; (023) 231917 *Fax:* (023) 226793
E-mail: wyaounde@un.cm; jtsoyenk@un.cm
Web Site: www.un.cm/iford
Telex: S/C PNUD 8304 KN
Key Personnel
Dir: Dr Eliwo Mandjale Akoto
Founded: 1972
Subjects: Demography, Population Studies
ISBN Prefix(es): 2-905327

PAID, see Pan African Institute for Development (PAID)

CAMEROON

†**Pan African Institute for Development (PAID)**
BP 4056, Douala
Mailing Address: PO Box 133, Buea
Tel: 332 28 06 *Fax:* 332 28 06
E-mail: info@paid-wa.org
Web Site: www.paid-wa.org
Telex: 6048
Key Personnel
Pres, Governing Council: Dr Mbuki V T MWamufiya
Dir: Rosetta B Thompson
Founded: 1964
Subjects: Rural Development
Publication(s): *An Integrated Approach to Rural Development* (IRD); *Community Health & Nutrition* (CHN); *Drought & Famine Preparedness & Response* (DFPR); *Food Self Sufficiency & Agricultural Development* (FSS); *Informal Sector & Small Scale Enterprises* (ISSE); *Popular Participation & the Promotion & Management of NGOs* (NGO); *Promoting Active Training Methods* (ATM); *Strengthening African Training & Research Institutions*; *Towards a Support Methodology* (SM); *Women & Health Programme* (W/H); *Women in Development* (WiD)

Canada

†◊**International Fiction Review**
University of New Brunswick, Dept of Culture & Language Studies, PO Box 4400, Fredericton, NB E3B 5A3
Tel: 506-453-4636 *Fax:* 506-447-3166
E-mail: ifr@unb.ca
Web Site: www.lib.unb.ca/Texts/IFR
Key Personnel
Editor: Chris Lorey *E-mail:* lorey@unb.ca
Founded: 1974
Publication(s): *The International Fiction Review* (annually)

Chile

Camara Chilena del Libro AG
Av Libertador Bernardo O'Higgins 1370 Oficina 501, Santiago
Tel: (02) 6989519; (02) 6724088 *Fax:* (02) 6989226
E-mail: camlibro@terra.cl; prolibro@ctcreuna.cl
Web Site: www.camlibro.cl
Key Personnel
President: Eduardo Castillo Garcia
Chilean association of publishers, distributors & booksellers. Also acts as Standard Book Numbering Agency.

CELADE, see Centro Latinoamericano de Demografia (CELADE)

†‡**Centro Latinoamericano de Demografia (CELADE)**
Edeficio Naciones Unidas, Avda Dag Hammarskjoeld 3477, Vitacura, Santiago
Mailing Address: Casilla 179-D, Santiago
Tel: (02) 4712000; (02) 2102000; (02) 2085051 *Fax:* (02) 2080252; (02) 2081946
E-mail: secepal@eclac.cl
Web Site: www.eclac.org
Telex: 340295 UNSTGOCK *Cable:* UNATIONS
Key Personnel
Dir: Reynaldo F Bajraj

Subjects: Demography, Statistics, Sociology, Population Information & Data Processing, Periodicals
Publication(s): *Boletin Demografico* (biennially); *Notas de Poblacion* (biennially); *Revista Docpal* (annually)

PROLIBRO, see Camara Chilena del Libro AG

Standard Book Numbering Agency
c/o Camara Chilena del Libro A G, Av Libertador Bernardo O'Higgins 1370 Oficina 501, Santiago
Tel: (02) 6989519; (02) 6724088 *Fax:* (02) 6989226
E-mail: camlibro@terra.cl; prolibro@ctcreuna.cl
Web Site: www.camlibro.cl
Key Personnel
President: Eduardo Castillo Garcia
Publication(s): *Catalogo ISBN Libros Chilenos (Ultima Publicacion 1996)*

China

China ISBN Agency
85 Dongsi Nan Dajie, 100703 Beijing
Tel: (010) 65127806; (010) 65212832 *Fax:* (010) 65127875
Telex: 22024 cpmcp cn
Key Personnel
ISBN Contact: Yang Muzhi

Press & Publication Administration of the People's Republic of China
85 Dongsi Nandajie, Beijing 100703
Tel: (010) 5127809 *Fax:* (010) 5127875
Key Personnel
President: Song Muwen
Chief Foreign Affairs Dept: Wei Hong

Standard Book Numbering Agency, see China ISBN Agency

Colombia

Agencia Colombiana del ISBN, Camara Columbiana del Libro
Carrera 17 A No 37-27, Bogota DC
Tel: (01) 288-6188 *Fax:* (01) 287-3320
E-mail: agenciaisbn@camlibro.com.co
Web Site: www.camlibro.com.co
Key Personnel
Contact: Sr Jaime Bravo Navarrete
Also acts as Standard Book Numbering Agency.

◊**Camara Colombiana del Libro**
Carrera 17A, No 37-27, Bogota DC
Tel: (01) 288 6188 *Fax:* (01) 287 3320
E-mail: camlibro@camlibro.com.co
Web Site: www.camlibro.com.co
Colombian Book Association.
Publication(s): *Correo Editorial - Boletin Bibliografico ISBN*
Associate Companies: Agencia Colombiana Del ISBN
Branch Office(s)
Camara Colombiana Del Libro Seccional Occidente

†◊**Centro Regional para el Fomento del Libro en America Latina y el Caribe** (Regional Center for the Promotion of Books in Latin America & the Caribbean)

Calle 70 No 9-52, Bogota DC
Mailing Address: Apdo Aereo 57348, Bogota 2
Tel: (01) 212-6056; (01) 249-5141 *Fax:* (01) 255-4614; (01) 321-7503
E-mail: libro@cerlalc.org
Web Site: www.cerlalc.org
Key Personnel
Dir: Carmen Barvo
Founded: 1971
ISBN Prefix(es): 92-9057; 958-671

CERLALC, see Centro Regional para el Fomento del Libro en America Latina y el Caribe

Standard Book Numbering Agency
Camara Colombiana del Libro, Carrera 17A, No 37-27, Apdo Aereo 8998, Santafe de Bogota
Tel: (01) 2886188 *Fax:* (01) 2873320
E-mail: agenciaisbn@camlibro.com.co
Web Site: www.camlibro.com.co
Key Personnel
Dir: Sandra Del Mar Sacanamboy Franco
Publication(s): *Libros Registrados En Colombia*; *Periodico Tinta Fresca*

Costa Rica

†◊**AIBDA**
Apdo 55, 2200 Coronado
Tel: (0506) 2160222 *Fax:* (0506) 2294741; (0506) 2160233
E-mail: iicahq@iica.ac.cr
Web Site: www.iica.int/servicios/aibda
Telex: 2144 IICACR *Cable:* IICASANJOSE
Key Personnel
Executive Secretary: Aura Mata
Founded: 1965
Publication(s): *AIBDA Actualidades* (irregularly); *Boletin Informativo* (triannually); *Boletin Tecnico* (irregularly); *Guia para Bibliotecas Agricolas*; *Quienes Quien en AIBDA*

Asociacion Interamericana de Bibliotecarios y Documentalistas Agricolas, see AIBDA

†‡**Instituto Interamericano de Cooperacion para la Agricultura (IICA)**
Apdo 55, 2200 Coronado, San Jose
Tel: (0506) 2160222 *Fax:* (0506) 2160233
E-mail: iicahq@iica.ac.cr
Web Site: www.iica.int
Telex: 2144 Iica *Cable:* IICASANJOSE
Key Personnel
Editor, General Publishing: Susana Raine
Founded: 1942
In every Latin American & Caribbean country, Canada & USA.
ISBN Prefix(es): 92-9039

Standard Book Numbering Agency
Biblioteca Nacional, San Jose 1000
Mailing Address: Apdo Postal 10008, San Jose 1000
Tel: (0506) 2212436; (0506) 2212479 *Fax:* (0506) 2235510
E-mail: proctec@racsa.co.cr
Key Personnel
General Manager: Isidro Serrano Rodriguez
Publication(s): *Catalogo Nacional ISBN*

Croatia

†**Croatian ISBN Agency**
Member of International ISBN Agency
Hrvatske bratske zajednice 4, 10000 Zagreb
Tel: (01) 6164087; (01) 6164288 *Fax:* (01) 6164371
E-mail: isbn@nsk.hr
Web Site: www.nsk.hr
Key Personnel
Contact: Ms Jasenka Zajec
Founded: 1992
Registers publishers in Croatia in the ISBN System; maintains the Croatian Publishers Database; holds statistics on book publishing in Croatia.
Subjects: National ISBN Agency
Publication(s): *Book & Music Publishers in Croatia: Directory*
Parent Company: National & University Library in Zagreb

Croatian ISMN Agency, see Croatian ISBN Agency

Cuba

Agencia Cubana del ISBN
Camara Cubana del Libro, Calle 15 No 602 esq C, Vedado, Ciudad Havana
Tel: (07) 36034 *Fax:* (07) 333441
E-mail: cclfilh@ceniai.cu
Telex: 511881 feria cu
Key Personnel
Contact: Jose A Robert Gasset

Standard Book Numbering Agency, see Agencia Cubana del ISBN

◇**Union de Escritores y Artistas de Cuba**
(Union of Writers & Artists of Cuba)
Calle 17 No 354, Plaza de la Revolucion, Havana
Tel: (07) 553113 *Fax:* (07) 333158
E-mail: informatica@uneac.co.cu
Web Site: www.uneac.com
Telex: 051156364
Key Personnel
Secretary: Armando Cristobal
Publication(s): *Union, La Gaceta de Cuba, Revista de Literatura Cubana*

Cyprus

Standard Book Numbering Agency
c/o Cyprus Centre for Registration of Books & Serials, The Cyprus Library, Byron Ave 20, Nicosia 1437
Tel: (022) 303337 *Fax:* (022) 443565
E-mail: antonism@ucy.ac.cy
Key Personnel
Dir: Dr Antonis Maratheftis
 E-mail: amaratheftis@hotmail.com
Founded: 1987
National library; Member of IFLA.
Subjects: Cyprus bibliography
ISBN Prefix(es): 9963-0

Czech Republic

ACBP, see Svaz ceskych knihkupcu a nakladatelu (SCKN)

Ceske Narodni Stredisko ISSN (Czech National ISSN Center)
Division of Statni Technicka Knihovna
Marianske nam 5, 110 01 Prague 1
Mailing Address: PO Box 206, 110 01 Prague 1
Tel: (02) 21 663 440 *Fax:* (02) 2222 1340
E-mail: issn@stk.cz
Web Site: www.stk.cz/en/issn/index.htm
Key Personnel
Dir: Dr Jan Bayer, PhD *Tel:* (02) 21 663 480
 E-mail: j.bayer@stk.cz

◇**Ministerstvo Kultury C R, Oddeleni Tisku Oddeleni Knizi Kultury** (Czech Ministry of Culture, Production Department, Publishing & Trade Book)
Milady Horakove 139, 160 41 Prague 6
Tel: (02) 57 085 111 *Fax:* (02) 24 318 155
E-mail: minkult@mkcr.cz
Web Site: www.mkcr.cz
Publication(s): *Books in Czech Republic*

Narodni agentura ISBN v CR
Klementinum 190, 11001 Prague 1
Tel: (02) 21663262 *Fax:* (02) 21663261
E-mail: isbn@nkp.cz
Web Site: www.nkp.cz
Key Personnel
ISBN Administrator: Mr Antonin Jerabek
Publication(s): *Soupis ucastniku systemu mezinarodniho standardniho cislovani knih - ISBN - v Ceske republice* (annually, directory of Czech publishers)
Parent Company: Narodni Knihovna Ceske republiky
Associate Companies: Narodna agentura ISBN v SR

SCKN, see Svaz ceskych knihkupcu a nakladatelu (SCKN)

Standard Book Numbering Agency, see Narodni agentura ISBN v CR

Svaz Antikvaru CR
Karlova 2, 110 00 Prague 1
Tel: (02) 22220286 *Fax:* (02) 22220286
E-mail: info@meissner.cz
Web Site: www.meissner.cz
Key Personnel
President: Petr Meissner
Contact: Vaclav Prosek
Member of ILAB (International League of Antiquarian Booksellers).

◇**Svaz ceskych knihkupcu a nakladatelu (SCKN)** (Association of Czech Booksellers & Publishers (ACBP))
Jana Masaryka 56, 120 00 Prague 2
Tel: (02) 24 219 944 *Fax:* (02) 24 219 942
E-mail: sckn@sckn.cz
Web Site: www.sckn.cz
Key Personnel
Chairman: Jitka Undeova
Chairman of Booksellers Section, 1st Vice Chairman: Jiri Seidl
Founded: 1879 (renewed 1990)
Membership(s): IPA.
Publication(s): *Bookseller & Publisher* (Knihkupec a nakladatel, monthly); *Czech Books In Print (Katalog kladovanych Knih)* (annually)
ISBN Prefix(es): 80-902495
Associate Companies: Svet knihy S R O (Book World Ltd)

Denmark

Dansk ISBN - Kontor (the Danish ISBN Agency)
Dansk Biblioteks Center, Tempovej 7-11, 2750 Ballerup
Tel: 44867725 *Fax:* 44867853
E-mail: isbn@dbc.dk
Web Site: www.isbn-kontoret.dk
Key Personnel
ISBN Administrator: Mrs Lone Olsen
 E-mail: lo@dbc.dk

Den Danske Boghandlerforening (The Danish Booksellers Association)
Siljangade 6 3, DK 2300 Copenhagen S
Tel: 32542255 *Fax:* 32540041
E-mail: ddb@bogpost.dk
Web Site: www.bogguide.dk
Key Personnel
President: Jesper Moller
Dir: Olaf Winslow
Memberships: European Booksellers Federation (EBF); International Booksellers Federation (IBF).
Publication(s): *Bogmarkedet* (The Booktrade, The Danish Book Market with Den Danske Forlaeggerforening)

◇**Den Danske Forlaeggerforening** (Danish Publishers' Association)
18/1 Kompagnistr, 1208 Copenhagen K
Tel: 33 15 66 88 *Fax:* 33 15 65 88
E-mail: publassn@webpartner.dk; jh@carlsen.dk
Key Personnel
President: Mr Jesper Holm *E-mail:* jh@carlsen.dk
Dir: Ib Tune Olsen
Publication(s): *Det Danske Bogmarked* (The Danish Book Market with Den Danske Boghandlerforening); *Fortegnelse over Samhandelsberettigede Boghandlere MV* (Register of Licensed Booksellers, etc)

◇**Forening for Boghaandvaerk, Nordjysk afdeling** (Association of Book Crafts, North Jutland Branch)
c/o Riget Consult, Thorshavnsgade 22, kld, 2300 Copenhagen
Tel: 32 95 85 15
Web Site: www.boghaandvaerk.dk
Key Personnel
President: Bent Joergensen *E-mail:* bj@kb.dk
Treasurer & Secretary: Lilli Riget
Founded: 1888
Danish Bookcraft Association.
Publication(s): *Arets bogarbejde* (Selected Books of the Year, yearbook); *Bogvennen* (The Book Lover, yearbook)
Parent Company: Forening for Boghaandvoerk

†◇**International Association for Mass Communication Research**
Aalborg Universitet, Fredrik Bajers Vej 5, 9100 Aalborg
Mailing Address: Postboks 159, 9100 Aalborg
Tel: (045) 9635 8080 *Fax:* (045) 9815 6864
E-mail: prehn@hum.auc.dk
Web Site: www.auc.dk/fak-hum
Key Personnel
President: Prof Cees Hamelink
Administrative Secretary: Peggy Gray
Secretary General: Ole Prehn *E-mail:* prehn@hum.auc.dk

Association internationale des etudes et recherches sur l'information.
Publication(s): *Communication & Democracy; Directions in Research; Mass Media & Man's View of Society; Mass Media & National Cultures; Mass Media & Socialization; New Structures of International Communication; The Role of Research; Social Communication & Global Problems*

†‡**Nordic Council of Ministers Publications**
Store Strandstraede 18, DK-1255 Copenhagen K
Tel: 33960200 *Fax:* 33960202
E-mail: nmr@nmr.dk
Web Site: www.norden.org
Telex: 15544 nordmr dk
Key Personnel
Secretary General: Soren Christensen
Head, Publishing Department: Agneta Sverkel-Osterberg *Tel:* 33960410 *E-mail:* aso@nmr.dk
Founded: 1971
ISBN Prefix(es): 92-893
Number of titles published annually: 200 Print

Standard Book Numbering Agency, see Dansk ISBN - Kontor (the Danish ISBN Agency)

Ecuador

Camara Ecuatoriana del Libro
Nucleo de Pichincha, Avda Eloy Alfaro, N29-61 e Inglaterra piso N 9, Quito
Tel: (02) 553311; (02) 553314 *Fax:* (02) 222150
E-mail: celnp@hoy.net
Web Site: www.celibro.org.ec
Key Personnel
Presidenta Ledo: Luis Mora Ortega

Standard Book Numbering Agency, see Camara Ecuatoriana del Libro

Egypt (Arab Republic of Egypt)

General Egyptian Book Organization
Corniche el-Nil - Ramlet Boulac, Cairo 11221
Tel: (02) 5775228; (02) 5775367; (02) 5775109; (02) 5799635; (02) 5775436; (02) 5775545; (02) 5775000 *Fax:* (02) 5765058; (02) 5799635
E-mail: info@egyptianbook.org
Web Site: www.egyptianbook.org
Telex: 93932 Book *Cable:* GEBO
Key Personnel
Chairman: Dr Mohamed Samir Gaber Sarhan
Also Publisher.
ISBN Prefix(es): 977-01

†**National Information & Documentation Centre (NIDOC)**
Al Tahrir St, Dokki, Cairo
Tel: (02) 3371696
Telex: 92111 Alsun
Key Personnel
Dir: Dr Mostago Esmat El Sarha

NIDOC, see National Information & Documentation Centre (NIDOC)

Standard Book Numbering Agency
National Library & Archives, Corniche El Nil, Ramlet Boulac, Cairo
Tel: (02) 5751078; (02) 5750886; (02) 5752883 *Fax:* (02) 5765634
E-mail: libmang@darelkotob.org
Telex: 93932

Estonia

Estonian Publishers Association
Roosikrantsi 6, 10119 Tallinn
Tel: (02) 6449866 *Fax:* (02) 6411443
E-mail: astat@eki.ee
Key Personnel
Dir: Ms A Trummal
Affiliate member of International Publishers Association.

Standard Book Numbering Agency
Eesti Rahvusraamatukogu, National Library, Tonismagi 2, 15189 Tallinn
Tel: (02) 630 7372 *Fax:* (02) 631 1200
E-mail: eraamat@nlib.ee; nlib@nlib.ee
Web Site: www.nlib.ee
Key Personnel
Contact: Ms Mai Valtna

Ethiopia

†‡**United Nations Economic Commission for Africa, ECA**
PO Box 3001, Addis Ababa
Tel: (01) 51 72 00 *Fax:* (01) 51 03 65
E-mail: ecaweb@uneca.org
Web Site: www.uneca.org
Telex: 21029 *Cable:* ECA ADDIS ABABA
Key Personnel
Librarian: Abdel-Rahman M Tahir

Faroe Islands

Foroya Landsbokasavn (National Library of the Faroe Islands)
J C Svabosgotu 16, FO-110 Torshavn
Mailing Address: PO Box 61, FO-110 Torshavn
Tel: (031) 311626 *Fax:* (031) 318895
E-mail: utlan@flb.fo
Web Site: www.flb.fo
Key Personnel
Contact: Mr Arnbjoern O Dalsgard *E-mail:* arndal@flb.fo

Standard Book Numbering Agency, see Foroya Landsbokasavn

Fiji

Regional ISBN Centre The ISBN Officer
The University of the South Pacific Library, PO Box 1168, Suva
Tel: 3313 900 *Fax:* 3300 830
E-mail: mamtora_j@usp.ac.fj; library@usp.ac.fj
Web Site: www.usp.ac.fj
Telex: fj 2276

Finland

The Finnish Book Publishers' Association, see Suomen Kustannusyhdistys

◇**Finnish ISBN Agency**
Helsinki University Library, Teollisuuskatu 23, 00014 Helsinki
Mailing Address: PO Box 26, University of Helsinki, 00014 Helsinki
Tel: (09) 19144327 *Fax:* (09) 19144341
E-mail: isbn-keskus@helsinki.fi
Web Site: www.lib.helsinki.fi
Key Personnel
ISBN Administrator: Maarit Huttunen
The Finnish ISSN Center is located at the same address.

Kirjakauppaliitto Ry (The Booksellers' Association of Finland)
Eerikinkatu 15-17 D 43-44, 00100 Helsinki
Tel: (09) 6859 9110; (050) 540 6451 *Fax:* (09) 6859 9119
E-mail: toimisto@kirjakauppaliitto.fi
Web Site: www.kirjakauppaliitto.fi
Key Personnel
President: Stig-Bjorn Nyberg *E-mail:* SBN@stockmann.fi
Vice President: Arto Lahdenpera *E-mail:* arto.lahdenpera@suomalainenkk.fi; Antti Ojajarvi *E-mail:* antti.ojajarvi@info.fi
Dir: Olli Erakivi *E-mail:* olli.erakivi@kirjakauppaliitto.fi
Publication(s): *Kirja-ja Paperialan kalenteri* (Book & Paperbranch register); *Kirjakauppaliitto* (magazine)
Parent Company: Kirjakauppalehden Julkaisu Oy
Associate Companies: Suomen Kirjakaupan Saatio

Standard Book Numbering Agency, see Finnish ISBN Agency

Suomen Kirjailijaliitto (Association of Finnish Authors)
Runeberginkatu 32 C 28, 00100 Helsinki
Tel: (09) 445392 *Fax:* (09) 492278
E-mail: info@suomenkirjailijaliitto.fi
Web Site: www.suomenkirjailijaliitto.fi
Key Personnel
President: Jarkko Laine
Executive Secretary: Ms Paeivi Liedes
Publication(s): *Suomen Runotar*

Suomen Kustannusyhdistys
PO Box 177, 00121 Helsinki
Tel: (09) 22877250 *Fax:* (09) 6121226
Web Site: www.skyry.net
Key Personnel
Dir: Veikko Sonninen *E-mail:* veikko.sonninen@skyry.net
Membership(s): International Publishers Association; Federation of European Publishers.
Publication(s): *Vuoden Kirjat* (List of books published in Finland)

France

◇**ADAGP (Societe des Auteurs dans les Arts Graphiques et Plastiques)**
11 rue Berryer, 75008 Paris
Tel: (01) 43590979 *Fax:* (01) 45634489
E-mail: adagp@adagp.fr

ORGANIZATIONS — FRANCE

Web Site: www.adagp.fr
Key Personnel
Dir: Jean-Marc Gutton
Founded: 1953
To administer & protect the rights of visual artists (painters, sculptors, engravers, architechts, graphists, photographers, illustrators) in matters of copyright in France.

ADELF, see Association des Ecrivains de Langue Francaise (ADELF)

ADMICAL (Association pour le Developpement du Mecenat Industriel et Commercial)
16 Rue Girardon, 75018 Paris
Tel: (01) 42552001 *Fax:* (01) 42557132
E-mail: contact@admical.org
Web Site: www.admical.org
Key Personnel
Dir: Marianne Eshet
Contact: Anne-Gaele Duriez *E-mail:* agduriez@admical.org
Association for the Development of business sponsorship.
Publication(s): Cultural Sponsorship in Europe (1999); Le Guide Juridique et Fiscal du Mecenat; L'Actualite du Mecenat (4 times a year); Le Repertoire du Mecenat 2001/2002 (biennially)
ISBN Prefix(es): 2-907507

AFEM, see Association Francaise du Multimedia

AFNIL, see Agence Francophone pour la Numerotation Internationale du Livre (AFNIL)

Agence Francophone pour la Numerotation Internationale du Livre (AFNIL)
35 rue Gregoire de Tour, 75279 Paris Cedex 06
Tel: (01) 44 41 29 19 *Fax:* (01) 44 41 29 03
E-mail: afnil@electre.fr
Web Site: www.afnil.org; www.afnil.com
Key Personnel
Contact: Joelle Aernoudt

AIEF, see Association Internationale des Etudes Francaises (AIEF)

ASFORED (Association Nationale pour la Formation et le Perfectionnement Professionnels dans les Metiers de l'Edition)
21 rue Charles-Fourier, 75013 Paris
Tel: (01) 45883981 *Fax:* (01) 45815492
E-mail: info@asfored.org
Web Site: www.asfored.org
Key Personnel
President: Francois (de) Waresquiel
Dir General: Pierre Tabourdeau

Association des Auteurs Autoedites (Association of Self-Published Authors)
21/23 rue Lalande, 75014 Paris
Tel: (01) 43 27 20 35 *Fax:* (01) 43 27 20 35
Web Site: www.auteurs-autoedites.com
Key Personnel
President: Robert Hentsch *Tel:* (01) 47 45 19 73
E-mail: rhentsch@club-internet.fr
Founded: 1975
500 authors members. Publications include poetry, art, novels, philosophy, science, teaching health.
Number of titles published annually: 130 Print

◇**Association Francaise du Multimedia**
8 rue Jean Gaijon, 75008 Paris
Tel: (01) 48242991 *Fax:* (01) 45231337
E-mail: info@afee.org
Web Site: www.afee.org

Key Personnel
President: Regis Poubelle
General Secretary: Pacale Ohl
French Multimedia Association.

†◇**Association Internationale de Bibliophilie** (International Association of Bibliophiles)
c/o Electre-Editions du Cercle de la Librairie, 35 rue Gregoire de Tours, 75006 Paris
Tel: (01) 44412800 *Fax:* (01) 43296895
Key Personnel
Secretary-General: Jean-Marc Chatelain
Founded: 1834
Publication(s): Le Bulletin du Bibliophile (biannually)

Association internationale des Critiques litteraires (NGO), see International Association of Literary Critics

†◇**Association Internationale des Etudes Francaises (AIEF)** (International Association of French Studies)
One rue Victor-Cousin, 75230 Paris Cedex 05
Fax: (01) 40462588
Web Site: www.aief.eu.org
Key Personnel
Contact: Prof Antoine Compagnon
E-mail: compagnon@aief.eu.org
Founded: 1949
Publication(s): Cahiers de l'AIEF (annually)
ISBN Prefix(es): 2-913718
Number of titles published annually: 1 Print
Bookshop(s): Les Belles Lettres, 95 Bd Raspai, 75006 Paris

Cercle de la Librairie
35 rue Gregoire-de-Tours, 75006 Paris
Tel: (01) 44 41 28 00 *Fax:* (01) 44 41 28 65
E-mail: commercial@electre.com
Web Site: www.electre.com
Telex: Lifran 270838 F
Key Personnel
President: Charles Henri Flammarion
Publication(s): La Bibliographie de la France (Bibliography of France); Catalogue general des ouvrages parus en langue francaise (General Catalog of Works Which Have Appeared in the French Language); Donnees statistiques sur l'edition du Livre en France (French Book Production Statistics); Les Livres Disponibles (French Books in Print); Repertoire des Livres au Format de Poche (List of Paperback or Pocket Edition Books); Le Repertoire International des Editeurs et Diffuseurs de Langue Francaise (International List of French Language Publishers & Distributors); Repertoire international des Librairies de Langue francaise (International List of French Language Bookshops)
Associate Companies: Booksellers' Circle Association of Book Trades & Industries

†◇**CISAC (Confederation Internationale des Societes d'Auteurs et de Compesiteurs)** (International Confederation of Societies of Authors & Composers)
20-26 Blvd du Parc, 92200 Neuilly/sur/Seine
Tel: (01) 55 62 08 50 *Fax:* (01) 55 62 08 60
E-mail: cisac@cisac.org
Web Site: www.cisac.org
Key Personnel
Secretary General: Eric Baptiste
President: Jean Louis Tournier
Founded: 1926

CITL, see College International des Traducteurs Litteraires (CITL)

College International des Traducteurs Litteraires (CITL) (International College of Literary Translators)
Espace Van Gogh, 13200 Arles
Tel: (04) 90 52 05 50 *Fax:* (04) 90 93 43 21
E-mail: citl@provnet.fr
Key Personnel
Dir: Claude Bleton
Publication(s): Actes des Assises de la Traduction Litteraire a Arles (1 volume annually)
Parent Company: Assises de la Traduction Litteraire A Arles

Confederation Internationale des Societes d'Auteurs et de Compesiteurs, see CISAC (Confederation Internationale des Societes d'Auteurs et de Compesiteurs)

COPACEL, see Groupements Francais des Fabricants de Papiers d'Impression-Ecriture (COPACEL)

†**Council of Europe Publishing**
Palais de l'Europe, 67075 Strasbourg Cedex
Tel: (03) 88 41 25 81 *Fax:* (03) 88 41 39 10
E-mail: publishing@coe.int
Web Site: book.coe.int
Telex: 870943F
Key Personnel
Head of Division: Mrs E Lejard-Boutsavath
Marketing & Promotion: Mrs Sophie Lobey
 Tel: (0388) 41 22 63 *E-mail:* sophie.lobey@coe.int
Rights & Permissions Manager: Charalambos Papadopoulos *Tel:* (0388) 412952
 E-mail: charalambos.papadopoulos@coe.int
Editorial Manager: Francine Raveney *Tel:* (0388) 415114 *E-mail:* francine.raveney@coe.int
Founded: 1949
Official publisher of the Council of Europe & reflects many different aspects of the Council's work, addressing the main challenges facing European society & the world today. Our catalogue of over 1200 title in French & English includes topics ranging from international law, human rights, ethical & moral issues, society, environment, health, education & culture.
Subjects: Human Rights, Law, Criminology, Public Health, Sociology, Nature, Consumer Protection, Education, Sports, Culture, Social Security, Youth, Local Authorities
ISBN Prefix(es): 92-871

CPE (Conseil Permanent des Ecrivains)
53 rue de Verneuil, 75007 Paris
Tel: (01) 49 54 68 80 *Fax:* (01) 42 84 20 87
Key Personnel
President: Maurice Cury *Tel:* (01) 40 35 87 06

◇**Dilicom**
20, rue des Grands-Augustins, 75006 Paris
Tel: (01) 43 25 43 35 *Fax:* (01) 43 29 76 88
E-mail: contact@dilicom.net
Web Site: www.dilicom.net
Key Personnel
Dir General: Bernard de Freminville
Specialize in teleordering & teleinformation between booksellers & publishers
Electra Transmittal.

Conseil Permanent des Ecrivains, see CPE (Conseil Permanent des Ecrivains)

Association des Ecrivains de Langue Francaise (ADELF) (French Language Writers' Association)
14, rue Broussais, 75014 Paris
Tel: (01) 43 21 95 99 *Fax:* (01) 43 20 12 22
Key Personnel
President: Edmond Jouve
Secretary General: Simone Freyfus
Founded: 1926

French Language Writers' Association.
Publication(s): *Lettres et cultures de langue francaise* (biannually)

Editions du Conseil de l'Europe, see Council of Europe Publishing

Federation de l'Imprimerie et de la Communaute Graphique-FICG (Federation of French Printers & Trade Writers)
115, blvd Saint-Germain, 75006 Paris
Tel: (01) 46 34 21 15 *Fax:* (01) 46 33 73 34
E-mail: ficg@ficg.fr
Key Personnel
President: Francois Gutle
Chief Executive: Pascal Bovero

Federation francaise des syndicats de librairies, see FFSL (Federation francaise des syndicats de libraires)

FFSL (Federation francaise des syndicats de libraires)
43 rue de Chateaudun, 75009 Paris
Tel: (01) 42 82 00 03 *Fax:* (01) 42 82 10 51
Key Personnel
President: Jean-Luc Dewas

FNPS (Federation nationale depresse d'information specialisee)
37 rue de Rome, 75008 Paris
Tel: (01) 44 90 43 60 *Fax:* (01) 44 90 43 72
E-mail: contact@fnps.fr
Web Site: www.fnps.fr
Key Personnel
President: Jean-Marc Detailleur
Dir: Jean-Michel Huan
French National Federation of Special Interest Press.

◇**France Edition**
115, bd Saint-Germain, 75006 Paris
Tel: (01) 44 41 13 13 *Fax:* (01) 46 34 63 83
E-mail: info@franceedition.org
Web Site: www.franceedition.org
Telex: Lifran 270838 F
Key Personnel
President: Liana Levi
Man Dir, French Publishers Agency: Kathryn Nanovic-Morlet *Tel:* 212-254-4540
E-mail: kathryn@blf.org
Specializing in promoting French books around the world, the organization of trade fairs, exhibitions, symposia, conferences & training sessions, production of catalogues devoted to specific themes, publication of a newsletter & marketing studies.
Publication(s): *La Lettre de France Edition* (marketing studies)
Branch Office(s)
30, rue Dinh Ngang, Hanoi, Viet Nam
Tel: (04) 826 4862 *Fax:* (04) 825 3411
E-mail: lanfevn@hn.vnn.vn
U.S. Office(s): French Publishers Agency/France Edition Inc, 853 Broadway, Suite 1509, New York, NY 10003-4703, United States *Tel:* 212-254-4540 *Fax:* 212-254-4540 *Web Site:* www.frenchpubagency.com

GFFDIE, see Groupements Francais des Fabricants de Papiers d'Impression-Ecriture (COPACEL)

Groupements Francais des Fabricants de Papiers d'Impression-Ecriture (COPACEL)
154, bd Haussmann, 75008 Paris
Tel: (01) 53 89 24 00 *Fax:* (01) 53 89 24 01
E-mail: info@copacel.fr
Web Site: www.copacel.fr
Telex: 651544

Key Personnel
President: M Claude Prince
French Manufacturer of Pocket Editions Group.

IIEP, see International Institute for Educational Planning (IIEP)

Intergovernmental Copyright Committee, see United Nations Educational, Scientific & Cultural Organization (UNESCO)

†◇**International Association of Literary Critics**
Affiliate of UNESCO
Hotel de Massa, 38, rue du Faubourg, St Jacques, 75014 Paris
Tel: (01) 40513300 *Fax:* (01) 43549299
E-mail: aicl.org@tiscalinet.it
Web Site: www.aicl.org
Telex: 206963
Key Personnel
President: Yves Gandon
Vice President: Fernando Martinho; Ryszard Matuszewski
Founded: 1970
Publication(s): *Revue* (biannually)

†‡**International Association of Universities**
One Rue Miollis, 75732 Paris Cedex 15
Tel: (01) 45 68 48 00 *Fax:* (01) 47 34 76 05
E-mail: iau@unesco.org
Web Site: www.unesco.org/iau
Key Personnel
Secretary General: Eva Egron-Polak
  E-mail: eegron.iau@unesco.org
Dir, Research: Guy R Neave *E-mail:* neave.iau@unesco.org
Founded: 1950
International non-governmental organization.
Publication(s): *Higher Education Policy* (quarterly, journal); *International Handbook of Universities* (biannually); *Monographs: Issues in Higher Education* (biannually); *World List of Universities*

†‡**International Chamber of Commerce**
38 Cours Albert 1er, 75008 Paris
Tel: (01) 49 53 28 28 *Fax:* (01) 49 53 28 59
E-mail: icclib@ibnet.com; icc@iccwbo.org
Web Site: www.iccwbo.org
Telex: 650770 ICCHQ *Cable:* INCOMERC-PARIS
Key Personnel
Secretary General: Maria Livanos
ISBN Prefix(es): 92-842

†◇**International Council on Archives** (Conseil International des Archives)
60 rue des Francs-Bourgeois, 75003 Paris
Tel: (01) 40 27 63 49; (01) 40 27 63 06; (01) 40 27 61 34 *Fax:* (01) 42 72 20 65
E-mail: ica@ica.org
Web Site: www.ica.org
Key Personnel
Secretary General: Mrs Joan Van Albada *Tel:* (01) 40276349 *E-mail:* vanalbada@ica.org
Publication(s): *Archivum*; *Janus*; *N'Existe Plus*

†‡**International Institute for Educational Planning (IIEP)**
7-9, rue Eugene-Delacroix, 75116 Paris
Tel: (01) 45 03 77 00 *Fax:* (01) 40 72 83 66
E-mail: information@iiep.unesco.org
Web Site: www.unesco.org/iiep
Telex: 620074 *Cable:* EDUPLAN PARIS
Key Personnel
Assistant Programme Specialist: Estelle Zadra
  E-mail: e.zadra@iiep.unesco.org
Chief, Communication & Publications: Ian Denison
Founded: 1963

Established by UNESCO, IIEP is an international center for advanced training & research in educational planning. The Institute's aim is to contribute to the development of education by expanding both knowledge & the supply of competent professionals in the field of educational planning. In this endeavor the Institute cooperates with interested training & research institutions throughout the world. IIEP is financed by UNESCO & by voluntary contributions from individual member states. The program & budget of the Institute are approved by its own Governing Board. A catalogue of publications is available on request.
Subjects: Educational Planning (Administration & Management, Methologies, Manpower & Employment, School Locations, Non-formal, Adult & Rural Education & Literacy)
ISBN Prefix(es): 92-803

†**ISSN International Centre**
20 rue Bachaumont, 75002 Paris
Tel: (01) 44 88 22 20 *Fax:* (01) 44 88 60 96; (01) 40 26 32 43
E-mail: issnic@issn.org
Web Site: www.issn.org
Key Personnel
Dir: Francoise Pelle *E-mail:* pelle@issn.org
International Bibliographic database regarding serial publications.
Publication(s): *ISSN Register* (quarterly on CD-ROM (ISSN compact) or frequently on the web (ISSN online)); *List of Serial Title Word Abbreviations-Cumulated Edition* (1998)

Ministere des Affaires Etrangeres Division de L'Ecrit et des Mediatheques
244, bd Saint-Germain, 75007 Paris
Tel: (01) 43 17 53 53 *Fax:* (01) 43 17 88 83
Web Site: www.france.diplomatie.gouv.fr
Key Personnel
Dir: Yves Mabin
Ministry of Foreign Affairs.
Parent Company: Association pour la diffusion de la pensee francaise (ADPF), 6 rue Ferrus, 75683 Paris Cedex 14

OECD, see Organization for Economic Cooperation & Development (OECD)

†**Office International des Epizooties** (World Organisation for Animal Health)
12 Rue de Prony, 75017 Paris
Tel: (01) 44 15 18 88 *Fax:* (01) 42 67 09 87
E-mail: oie@oie.int
Web Site: www.oie.int
Telex: EPIZOTI 642285F
Key Personnel
Editorial Dir: Dr Bernard Vallat
Sales & Marketing Agent: Ms Tamara Benicasa
Founded: 1924
Subjects: Veterinary science & world animal health
Publication(s): *Disease Information* (weekly, periodical); *World Animal Health in 2001* (periodical, 2002)
ISBN Prefix(es): 92-9044
Total Titles: 44 Print
Distributed by SMPF Inc

†**Organization for Economic Cooperation & Development (OECD)**
2, rue Andre-Pascal, 75775 Paris Cedex 16
Tel: (01) 45 24 82 00 *Fax:* (01) 45 24 85 00
E-mail: news.contact@oecd.org
Web Site: www.oecd.org
Telex: 640048 *Cable:* DEVELOPECONOMIE
Key Personnel
Secretary General: Donald Johnston
Founded: 1960
Subjects: Economics, Statistics, Environment, Energy, Education, Transportation, Agriculture, Development, Finance, Urban Affairs, Labor,

Science & Technology, Tourism, Consumer policy, Social problems
ISBN Prefix(es): 92-64; 92-821
Showroom(s): 33 rue Octave Feuillet, 75016 Paris
Bookshop(s): 33 rue Octave Feuillet, 75016 Paris

SACEM (Societe des Auteurs Copositeurs et Editeurs de Musique)
225 av Charles de Gaulle, 92528 Neuilly-sur-Seine Cedex
Tel: (01) 47 15 47 15 *Fax:* (01) 47 15 47 86
E-mail: communication@sacem.fr
Web Site: www.sacem.fr
Telex: 630 312 musica
Key Personnel
President: Jacques Demarny

SELF Syndicate of French Language Authors
18 rue Theodore Deck, 75015 Paris
Tel: (01) 40600501 *Fax:* (01) 46707395
Key Personnel
President: Benjamin Lambert; Victoria Therame; Maguelonne Toussaint-Samat
Secretary General: Gerard Gaillaguet
Publication(s): Ecrivains

SLAM, see Syndicat National de la Librairie Ancienne et Moderne (SLAM)

SLUT, see Syndicat des Libraires Universitaires et Techniques

Societe des auteurs dans les arts graphiques, plastiques et photographiques, see ADAGP (Societe des Auteurs dans les Arts Grarphiques et Plastiques)

Societe des Auteurs Compositeurs et Editeurs de Musique, see SACEM (Societe des Auteurs Copositeurs et Editeurs de Musique)

Standard Book Numbering Agency, see Agence Francophone pour la Numerotation Internationale du Livre (AFNIL)

Standard Book Numbering Agency, see Unesco Books & Copyright Division, USBN agency

Syndicat des ecrivains de langue francaise, see SELF Syndicate of French Language Authors

Syndicat des Libraires Universitaires et Techniques
40, rue Gregoire de Tours, 75006 Paris
Tel: (01) 43 29 88 79 *Fax:* (467) 525905
Key Personnel
President: Dominique Torreilles
Secretary: Janine de Puniet

Syndicat National de la Librairie Ancienne et Moderne (SLAM) (National Association of Antiquarian & Modern Booksellers)
4, rue Git-le-Coeur, 75006 Paris
Tel: (01) 43 29 46 38 *Fax:* (01) 43 25 41 63
E-mail: slam-livre@wanadoo.fr
Web Site: www.slam-livre.fr
Key Personnel
President: Alain Marchiset
Publication(s): Guide du Livre Ancien et des libraires membres du Syndicat national de la Librairie Ancienne et Moderne

◇**Syndicat National de l'Edition** (National Union of Publishers)
115 Blvd Saint-Germain, 75006 Paris
Tel: (01) 4441 4050 *Fax:* (01) 4441 4077
Web Site: www.snedition.fr

Key Personnel
President: Serge Eyrolles
Deputy General: Jean Sarzana
Publication(s): Aberviations des principales references en matiere juridique (1993); *Actes du colloque sur l'edition scientifique francaise*; *L'edition de livres en France* (annually, statistics); *Fiches techniques-pays (etudes du marche du livre a l'etranger)* (RFA, Espagne, Royaume-Uni); *Plaquette de representation de l'edition francaise*
ISBN Prefix(es): 2-909677

ULF (Union des Libraires de France), see Union des Libraires de France (ULF)

UNESCO, see United Nations Educational, Scientific & Cultural Organization (UNESCO)

Unesco Books & Copyright Division, USBN agency
35 rue Gregoire de Tour, 75279 Paris Cedex 06
Tel: (01) 44 41 29 19 *Fax:* (01) 44 41 29 03
E-mail: afnil@electre.com
Web Site: www.afnil.org; www.afnil.com
Telex: 204461; 270602
Key Personnel
Contact: Michele Fournier

Union des Libraires de France (ULF)
40 rue Gregoire-de-Tours, 75006 Paris
Tel: (01) 43 29 88 79 *Fax:* (01) 43 29 88 79
Key Personnel
President: Eric Hardin
General Delegate: Marie-Dominique Doumenc
Union of French Booksellers.
Publication(s): La Voix des Libraires; Le Bullentin de l'ULF

†◇**United Nations Educational, Scientific & Cultural Organization (UNESCO)**
7 Place de Fontenoy, 75352 Paris 07-SP
Tel: (01) 45 68 10 00 *Fax:* (01) 45 67 16 90
E-mail: clearing-house@unesco.org
Web Site: www.unesco.org
Telex: 204461; 270602 *Cable:* UNESCO PARIS
Key Personnel
Dir-General: Koichiro Matsuura
Dir, UNESCO Publishing: Milagros Del Corral
Rights: Alastair McLurg; Michiko Tanaka
Promotion: Cristina Laje; Jeanette Coulibaly
Founded: 1946
To date, UNESCO books have been translated into more than seventy languages. UNESCO acts as Standard Book Numbering Agency, administering ISBNs for UN publications. It also maintains responsibility, within its Copyright Division, for the Intergovernmental Copyright Committee. UNESCO publishes seven periodicals, including the illustrated monthly reviews, The Unesco Courier & World Heritage Review.
Subjects: Education, Science, Technology, Social Science, Culture, Communications, Human Rights, Art
ISBN Prefix(es): 92-3
Number of titles published annually: 152 Print
Total Titles: 6,000 Print

Gambia

Standard Book Numbering Agency
Gambia National Library, RG Pye Lane, Banjul
Tel: 226491 *Fax:* 223776
E-mail: national.library@ganet.gm
Key Personnel
Chief Librarian: Abdou Wally Mbye
Founded: 1946

National/public library service.
Branch Office(s)
Brikama Branch Library *Tel:* 484111 (Western division)

Germany

AG BDB, see Arbeitsgemeinschaft der Blindenschrift-Druckereien und Bibliotheken (AG BDB)

Arbeitsgemeinschaft der Blindenschrift-Druckereien und Bibliotheken (AG BDB) (Association of Braille Publishing Houses & Libraries)
c/o Deutsche Blindenstudienanstalt (BLISTA), Am Schlag 8, 35037 Marburg
Tel: (06421) 60 60 *Fax:* (06421) 60 62 29
E-mail: info@blista.de
Web Site: www.blista.de
Key Personnel
President: Rainer F V Witte

Arbeitsgemeinschaft von Jugendbuchverlagen e v (The Alliance of Publishers of Children's Books)
c/o Thienemann Verlag, Blumenstr 36, 70182 Stuttgart
Tel: (0711) 2843 440 *Fax:* (0711) 2483 622
E-mail: info@avj-online.de
Web Site: www.avj-online.de
Key Personnel
Chairman: Mathias Berg
Manager: Susanne Ziemer
Publication(s): Kinder und Jugendbuchverlage von A bis Z

Arbeitskreis fur Jugendliteratur eV
Metzstr 14c, 81667 Munich
Tel: (089) 45 80 80 6 *Fax:* (089) 45 80 80 88
E-mail: info@jugendliteratur.org
Web Site: www.jugendliteratur.org
Key Personnel
Man Dir: Franz Meyer
Youth Literature Committee (Section of IBBY).
Publication(s): Auswahlliste zum Deutschen Jugendliteraturpreis (annually); *Buch fur Jugend* (annually); *Das Bilderbuch; Das blane Buch; Das Kinderbuch; Julet* (quarterly)

◇**Borsenverein des Deutschen Buchhandels eV**
Grosser Hirschgraben 17-21, 60313 Frankfurt am Main
Tel: (069) 1306-0 *Fax:* (069) 1306-201
Key Personnel
General Manager: Dr Harald Heker
Head Information Department: Eugen Emmerling
Tel: (069) 1306291 *Fax:* (069) 1306294
E-mail: emmerling@boev.de
Publication(s): Adressbuch fuer den deutschsprachigen Buchhandel (German-Speaking Book Trade Directory); *Archiv fuer Geschichte des Buchwesens* (Book History Archives); *Boersenblatt fuer den Deutschen Buchhandel* (German Book Trade Journal); *Buch und Buchhandel in Zahlen* (Books & the Book Trade in Figures); *BuchJournal* (a general magazine for booksellers' customers); *Deutsche Bibliographie* (German Bibliography); *Neuerscheinungen-Sofortdienst (CIP)* (New Titles Express Service CIP); *VLB Verzeichnis lieferbarer Buecher* (German Books in Print)
Branch Office(s)
Berliner Bureau, Schiffbauerdamm 5, 10117

GERMANY

Berlin *Tel:* (030) 2800783-0 *Fax:* (030) 2800783-50
Leipziger Buero, Gerichtsweg 28, 04103 Leipzig *Tel:* (0341) 9954-110 *Fax:* (0341) 9954-113

Boersenverein des Deutschen Buchhandels, Landesverband Baden-Wuerttemberg eV (Association of Publishers & Booksellers in Baden-Wuerttemberg e V)
Paulinenstr 53, 70178 Stuttgart
Tel: (0711) 619410 *Fax:* (0711) 6194144
E-mail: post@buchhandelsverband.de
Web Site: www.buchhandelsverband.de
Key Personnel
Man Dir: Johannes Scherer
Association of Publishers & Booksellers in Baden-Wuerttemberg.

Borromausverein eV
Wittelsbacherring 9, 53115 Bonn
Tel: (0228) 7258-0 *Fax:* (0228) 7258-189
E-mail: info@borro.de
Web Site: www.borro.de
Key Personnel
President: Norbert Trippen
Publisher: Rolf Pitsch

Bundesverband Deutscher Kunstverleger eV (Association of German Art Editors)
Darmstaedter Landstr 3, 60594 Frankfurt Main
Mailing Address: Postfach 700 210, 60552 Frankfurt Main
Tel: (069) 629120 *Fax:* (069) 629120
Web Site: www.bdkv.de
Key Personnel
Chairman: Klaus Gerrit Friese; Ruth Leuchter
Contact: Birgit Maria Sturm *E-mail:* sturm@bdkv.de
Founded: 1989
The Federal Association of German Art Publishers is the ideal Sponsor of Kunstkoeln-International Art Fair for Art Brut, Editions & Art after 1980.
Membership(s): Arbeitskreis Deutscher Kusthandelsverbande.

†◇Conseil International des Associations de Bibliotheques de Theologie
Postfach 250104, 50517 Cologne
Tel: (0221) 3382109 *Fax:* (0221) 3382103
Key Personnel
President: Dr Andre J Geuns
Secretary: Dr I Dumke

Deutscher Komponisten-Interessenverband eV (German Composers Association)
kadettenweg 80 b, 12205 Berlin
Tel: (030) 84 31 05 80 *Fax:* (030) 84 31 05 82
E-mail: info@komponistenverband.org
Web Site: www.dkiv.allmusic.de
Key Personnel
President: Karl Heinz Wahren
Vice President: Prof Harald Banter
Manager: Manuel Neuendorf
Publication(s): Handbuch "Komponisten der Gegnwart im Deutschen Komponisten-Interessenverband" (1995)

†◇Gutenberg-Gesellschaft eV (Gutenberg Society)
Liebfrauenplatz 5, 55116 Mainz
Tel: (06131) 22 64 20 *Fax:* (06131) 23 35 30
E-mail: gutenberg-gesellschaft@freenet.de
Web Site: www.gutenberg-gesellschaft.uni-mainz.de
Key Personnel
President: Jens Beutel
Vice President: Hannetraud Schultheiss
Secretary General: Karl Delorme
Founded: 1901

International Association for Past & Present History of the Art of Printing.
Subjects: Past & Present History of the Art of Printing & of the Book
Publication(s): *Gutenberg-Jahrbuch*; *Kleine Drucke*; *Sonder-Veroeffentlichungen*
ISBN Prefix(es): 3-7755

Hessischer Verleger- und Buchhandler-Verband eV
Hessischer Verleger-und Buchhandler-Verband eV, Villa Clementine, Frankfurterstr 1, 65189 Wiesbaden
Tel: (0611) 166 600 *Fax:* (0611) 166 6059
E-mail: briefe@hessenbuchhandel.de
Web Site: www.hessenbuchhandel.de
Key Personnel
Chairman: Michael Lemling
Manager: Peter Brunner
Hessen Publishers' & Booksellers' Federation.

I A S A, see International Association of Sound & Audiovisual Archives

†International Association of Sound & Audiovisual Archives
c/o Suedwestrundfunk, Documentation & Archives Dept, 76522 Baden-Baden
Mailing Address: Postfach 820, 76522 Baden-Baden
Tel: (07221) 9293487 *Fax:* (07221) 9294199
Web Site: www.llgc.org.uk/iasa/
Key Personnel
Secretary General: Albrecht Haefner
 E-mail: albrecht.haefner@swr.de
Founded: 1969
A non-governmental UNESCO-affiliated organization established to function as a medium for international co-operation between archives which preserve recorded sound & audiovisual documents.
Publication(s): *IASA Information Bulletin* (quarterly); *IASA Journal* (biannual)
ISBN Prefix(es): 0-946475

International Council of Theological Library Associations, see Conseil International des Associations de Bibliotheques de Theologie

†◇International ISBN Agency, International ISMN Agency
Staatsbibliothek zu Berlin - Preussischer Kulturbesitz, Potsdamerstr 33, 10785 Berlin
Tel: (030) 266 2498 *Fax:* (030) 2662378
E-mail: isbn@sbb.spk-berlin.de; ismn@sbb.spk.berlin.de
Web Site: isbn-international.org; ismn-international.org
Key Personnel
Dir: Dr Hartmut Walravens
Contact: Carolin Unger *E-mail:* isbn3@sbb.spk-berlin.de
Founded: 1972
This is the international ISBN office. For national offices & further details please see the ISBN System section of this book.
Publication(s): *International ISBN Users' Manual*; *International ISMN Users' Manual*; *ISBN Newsletter*; *ISMN Newsletter*; *Music Publishers' International ISMN Directory*; *Publishers' International ISBN Directory*; *The ISBN & its Uses* (video-film & sound-slide-show)

†International ISMN Agency
Potsdamer Str 33, 10785 Berlin
Tel: (030) 266 2496; (030) 266 2498; (030) 266 2338 *Fax:* (030) 266-2378
E-mail: ismn@sbb.spk-berlin.de
Web Site: ismn-international.org
Key Personnel
Dir: Dr Hartmut Walravens

BOOK TRADE

Founded: 1994
Agency for the standard numbering of sheet music.
Publication(s): *ISMN Newsletter*; *ISMN Users' Manual*; *Publishers' International ISMN Directory*

†◇Internationale Jugendbibliothek (International Youth Library)
Schloss Blutenburg, 81247 Munich
Tel: (089) 891211-0 *Fax:* (089) 8117553
E-mail: bib@ijb.de
Web Site: www.ijb.de
Key Personnel
Chairwoman Foundations Board of Governors: Christa Spangenberg
Dir: Dr Barbara Scharioth
Publicity: Carola Gade *Tel:* (089) 891211-30
 E-mail: presse@ijb.de
Founded: 1949
Publication(s): *IJB Report* (biannually); *The White Ravens* (annual selection of international children's & youth literature)

Internationale Vereinigung fuer Geschichte und Gegenwart der Druckkunst eV, see Gutenberg-Gesellschaft eV

ISBN, see International ISBN Agency, International ISMN Agency

ISMN, see International ISMN Agency

Landesverband der Verleger und Buchhaendler Rheinland-Pfalz eV
Frankfurter Str 1, 65189 Wiesbaden
Tel: (06131) 234035 *Fax:* (06131) 230364
Rhineland-Palatinate Provincial Federation of Publishers & Booksellers.

LIBER, see Ligue des Bibliotheques Europeennes de Recherche (LIBER)

†◇Ligue des Bibliotheques Europeennes de Recherche (LIBER) (League of European Research Libraries)
Universitat Bremen, FB 10, GW 1, B 1200, 28334 Bremen
Mailing Address: Postfach 330440, 28334 Bremen
Tel: (0421) 2183361
Web Site: www.kb.dk/guests/intl/liber
Key Personnel
President: Erland Kolding Nielsen *Tel:* (045) 33 47 4301 *Fax:* (045) 33 32 98 46 *E-mail:* ekn@kb.dk
Vice President: Hans Geleijnse *Tel:* (031) 13 466 2240 *E-mail:* hans.geleijnse@uvt.nl
Publication(s): *European Research Libraries Co-operation* (The Liber Quarterly)

Norddeutscher Verleger- und Buchhaendler-Verband eV
Schwanenwik 38, 22087 Hamburg
Tel: (040) 22 54 79 *Fax:* (040) 2 29 85 14
North German Publishers' and Booksellers' Federation.

◇O Gracklauer Verlag und Bibliographische Agentur GmbH (O Gracklauer Publishers & Bibliographic Agency)
Wallotstr 7A, 14193 Berlin
Tel: (030) 825 81 39 *Fax:* (030) 826 20 39
E-mail: info@gracklauer.de
Web Site: www.gracklauer.de
Key Personnel
Owner & Man Dir: Rose M Meerwein
Suppliers of bibliographic information, title & copyright research.

ORGANIZATIONS

†◇PEN Club-German Speaking Writers Abroad
Wurmbachstr 3, 60487 Frankfurt
E-mail: intpen@dircon.co.uk
Web Site: www.oneworld.org/internatpen/centers.htm
Key Personnel
President: Fritz Beer
Secretary: Uwe Westphal
Founded: 1934
Writers association.

Presse-Grosso, see Presse-Grosso-Bundesverband Deutscher Buch-, Zeitungs-und Zeitschriften-Grossisten eV

Presse-Grosso-Bundesverband Deutscher Buch-, Zeitungs-und Zeitschriften-Grossisten eV
Haendelstr 25-29, 50674 Cologne
Tel: (0221) 9213370 *Fax:* (0221) 92133744
E-mail: bvpg@bvpg.de
Web Site: www.pressegrosso.de
Key Personnel
Chairman: Weiner Schiessl
Manager: Gerd Kapp
Founded: 1950
Federation of German Wholesalers of Books, Newspapers and Periodicals (also known as Presse-Grosso).

International Standard Book Numbering Agency, see International Standard Buchnummer GmbH

International Standard Buchnummer GmbH
Grosser Hirschbraben 17-21, 60311 Frankfurt am Main
Mailing Address: Postfach 100442, 60004 Frankfurt am Main
Tel: (069) 1306-387 *Fax:* (069) 1306-258
E-mail: lehr@bhv.de
Web Site: www.german-isbn.org
Key Personnel
Dir: Manfred Gravelius
The Booksellers' Association, Documentation & Data Processing Department (Standard Book Numbering Agency).

Stiftung Lesen
Fischtorplatz 23, 55116 Mainz
Tel: (06131) 2 88 90-0 *Fax:* (06131) 23 03 33
E-mail: mail@stiftunglesen.de
Web Site: www.stiftunglesen.de
Key Personnel
Manager: Prof Hilmar Hoffmann

UIE, see UNESCO Institute for Education (UIE)

†◇UNESCO Institute for Education (UIE)
Feldbrunnenstr 58, 20148 Hamburg
Tel: (040) 4480410 *Fax:* (040) 4107723
E-mail: uie@unesco.org
Web Site: www.unesco.org/education/uie
Key Personnel
Dir: Dr Adama Ouane *E-mail:* a.ouane@unesco.org
Founded: 1951
The UIE was created in 1951 with the financial support of UNESCO & a number of member states. It is funded by Germany, UNESCO & other donors, & housed in premises provided by the City of Hamburg. It is a research, training & dissemination center which has enabled more than 2000 scholars to participate in international cooperative research projects & has developed a particular interest in lifelong education. Major areas of the current research program include the development of nonconventional approaches to primary education for out-of-school children, post-literacy & functional literacy for adults & young people, monitoring & evaluation of nonformal education programs, literacy exchange network, the legislative environment for adult education, the empowerment of women through education. Publications include over 120 titles in English, French, Spanish & Arabic & the bimonthly International Review of Education, for which there are concessionary subscription rates for developing countries. In the field of lifelong education & related aspects, it has published over 60 books under the series of UIE Monographs, Case Studies, Advances in Lifelong Education, UIE-Studies on Post-literacy in Industrialized Countries, other theoretical studies on Post-literacy & Continuing Education, & UIE-Studies on Functional Illiteracy in Industrialized Countries & Handbooks & Reference books, based on both theoretical & operational research.
Subjects: Literacy, Non Formal Basic Education, Continuing Education, Functional Illiteracy in Industrialized Countries, Nonformal Education, Adult Education & lifelong learning
ISBN Prefix(es): 92-820
Parent Company: UNESCO, Paris, France

Verband der Schulbuchverlage eV (Association of Text Book Publishers)
Zeppelinallee 33, 60325 Frankfurt am Main
Tel: (069) 70 30 75 *Fax:* (069) 70 79 01 69
E-mail: verband@vds-bildungsmedien.de
Web Site: www.vds-bildungsmedien.de
Key Personnel
Chairman: Gerd-Dietrich Schmidt
Man Dir: Andreas Baer *E-mail:* baer@vds-bildungsmedien.de

Verband der Verlage- und Buchhaendlungen Berlin-Brandenburg eV
Luetzowstr 33, 10785 Berlin
Tel: (030) 26 39 18 0 *Fax:* (030) 26 39 18 18
E-mail: verband@berliner-buchhandel.de
Web Site: www.berliner-buchhandel.de
Key Personnel
President: Dietrich Simon
Manager: Detlef Bluhm
Publishers' & Booksellers' Association Berlin-Brandenburg.

Verband der Verlage und Buchhandlungen in Nordrhein-Westfalen eV (Association of Publishers & Booksellers at North Rhine Westphalia)
Marienstr 41, 40210 Duesseldorf
Tel: (0211) 8 64 45-22 *Fax:* (0211) 32 44 97
E-mail: info@buchnrw.de
Web Site: www.buchnrw.de
Key Personnel
Secretary: Herbert Becker

◇Verband Deutscher Antiquare eV (German Antiquarian Booksellers' Association)
Geschaftsstelle, Herr Norbert Munsch, Seeblick 1, 56459 Elbingen
Tel: (06435) 909147 *Fax:* (06435) 909148
E-mail: buch@antiquare.de
Web Site: www.antiquare.de
Key Personnel
President: Herrn Jochen Granier
Vice President: Fr Inge Utzt
Founded: 1952
Publication(s): *Katalog zur Stuttgarter Antiquariatsmesse* (annually); *Mitgliederverzeichnis* (biannually); *zur Koelner Antiquariatsmesse empfohlen von der Internationalen Liga der Antiquariatsbuchhaendler ILAB*; *Katalog zu den Antiquariatstagen in Koeln* (annually)

Verband Deutscher Auskunfts und Verzichnismedien
Heerdter Sandberg 30, 40549 Duesseldorf
Tel: (0211) 577995-0 *Fax:* (0211) 577995-44
E-mail: info@vdav.org
Web Site: www.vdav.de
Key Personnel
Secretary: Petra Felkowski
Association of German Directory Publishers.

Verband katholischer Verleger und Buchhaendler eV
Adenauerallee 176, 53113 Bonn
Tel: (0228) 2421560 *Fax:* (0228) 2421561
E-mail: vkb2000@aol.com
Key Personnel
Manager: Peter J Kerp
Federation of Catholic Publishers & Booksellers.

Verlegervereinigung Rechtsinformatik eV
c/o Carl Heymanns Verlag, Luxemburger Str 449, 50939 Cologne
Tel: (0221) 94373-0 *Fax:* (0221) 94373-901
E-mail: marketing@heymanns.com
Web Site: www.heymanns.com
Key Personnel
Chairman: Bertram Gallus
Association of Publishers of Legal Documentation.

Verwertungsgesellschaft Wort (Collecting Society Word)
Goethestr 49, 80336 Munich
Tel: (089) 5 14 12-0 *Fax:* (089) 5141258
E-mail: vgw@vgwort.de
Web Site: www.vgwort.de
Key Personnel
Chairman: Lutz Franke
General Manager: Prof Ferdinand Melichar, PhD *E-mail:* f.melichar@vgwort.de
Founded: 1958
Copyright society representing authors & publishers of literary & scientific works.
Branch Office(s)
Verwertungsgesellschaft Wort Berliner Buero, Koethener Str 44, 10963 Berlin
Tel: (030) 261 27 51 *Fax:* (030) 23 00 36 29
E-mail: vgbuero@t-online.de

Ghana

†Association of African Universities (Association des Universites Africaines)
African Universities House, 11 Aviation Rd, Airport Residential Area, Accra
Mailing Address: PO Box 5744, Accra-North
Tel: (021) 774495; (021) 761588 *Fax:* (021) 774821
E-mail: info@aau.org
Web Site: www.aau.org
Telex: 2284 Adua *Cable:* AFUNIV ACCRA
Key Personnel
President: Prof George Benneh
Secretary-General: Prof Akilagpa Sawyerr *E-mail:* secgen@aau.org
Founded: 1967
Subjects: Higher Education in Africa

Standard Book Numbering Agency
c/o Ghana Library Board, George Padmore Research Library on African Affairs, PO Box 2970, Accra
Tel: (021) 223526; (021) 228402 *Fax:* (021) 247768
E-mail: GeorgePadmore@Africanmail.com; Padmoreslib@yahoo.co.uk
Key Personnel
Contact: Sarah Dorothy Kanda; Omari Mensah Tenkovang
Parent Company: Ghana Library Board

GHANA   BOOK TRADE

†◇**Union of Writers of the African Peoples**
  (Union des Ecrivains Negro Africains)
c/o Ghana Association of Writers, PO Box 4414, Accra
Tel: (021) 774944 *Fax:* (021) 774250
Key Personnel
President: Atukwei Okai
General Secretary: J E Allotey-Pappoe
Objectives include the operation of a writers' publishing co-operative & the encouragement of the use of Swahili as the common language of all black African peoples.
Publication(s): *African World Alternatives*

†◇**University Bookshop**
University of Ghana, PO Box 25, Legon
Tel: (021) 500398 *Fax:* (021) 500398
E-mail: unibks@ug.gn.apc.org
Key Personnel
Manager: Emmanuel K H Tonyigah
Founded: 1948

Greece

Hellenic Federation of Publishers & Booksellers
73 Themistocleous St, 10683 Athens
Tel: (01) 33 00 924; (01) 33 00 926 *Fax:* (01) 33 01 617
E-mail: poev@otenet.gr
Key Personnel
President: Georgios Dardanos
Dir: Ms E Filippopoulos
Member of: International Association of Publishers; Federation of European Publishing; Federation of European Booksellers.
Publication(s): *Catalogue of the Greek Children's Books*; *General Catalogue of Greek Publishers*

Standard Book Numbering Agency
National Library of Greece, National Centre of ISBN, 32 Panepistimiou Ave, 106 79 Athens
Tel: (01) 33 82 601; (01) 33 82 581 *Fax:* (01) 36 08 495
E-mail: ebe@nlg.gr
Web Site: www.nlg.gr
Telex: 216270 ypth gr
Key Personnel
ISBN Administrator: Mrs Stauroula Verveniotou
  E-mail: verveniotou@nlg.gr

Syllogos Ekdoton Bibliopolon Athinon
  (Publishers & Booksellers' Association of Athens)
73 Themistokleous St, 10683 Athens
Tel: (01) 3830029; (01) 3303268 *Fax:* (01) 3823222
E-mail: seva@otenet.ge
Key Personnel
President: Eleni Kanaki
Membership(s): Hellenic Federation of Publishers & Booksellers.
Subjects: Issues concerning the book industry

Guatemala

Comite Gremial de Editores de Guatemala
10a Calle 7-55 Z, Zona 1, Guatemala City
Tel: (02) 82 68 15 *Fax:* (02) 2329053; (02) 2518381
Key Personnel
President: Santa Irene Piedra

Guinea

SAEC, see La Societe Africaine d'Edition et de Communication (SAEC)

La Societe Africaine d'Edition et de Communication (SAEC)
BP 6826, Conakry
Tel: 45 34 44 *Fax:* 45 34 44
E-mail: dtniane@eti-bull.net
Key Personnel
PDG de la SAEC: Mr Djibril Tamsir Niane
Editorial Secretary: Mr Daouda Tamsir Niane

Guyana

CARICOM, see Regional ISBN Agency (CARICOM)

Regional ISBN Agency (CARICOM)
Caribbean Community Secretariat, Avenue of the Republic, Georgetown
Mailing Address: PO Box 10827, Georgetown
Tel: (02) 226 9280 *Fax:* (02) 226 7816
E-mail: carisec1@caricom.org; carisec2@caricom.org; carisec3@caricom.og
Web Site: www.caricom.org *Cable:* CARIBSEC GUYANA
Key Personnel
ISBN Administrator: Maureen Newton
Publication(s): *Aging in the Commonwealth Caribbean*; *The Caribbean Community in the 1980s: report by a group of Caribbean experts*; *Caribbean development to the Year 2000: challenges, prospects and policies*; *CARICOM Model Legislation on Citzenship; Domestic Violence; Equality for Women in Employment; Equal Pay; Inheritance; Maintenance & Maintenance Order; Sexual Harassment & Sexual Offences*; *CARICOM Perspective*; *CARICOM Secretary-General's report* (annually); *CARICOM'S trade: a quick reference to some summary data: 1980-1996*; *CCS Current Awareness Service: New Additions: Articles* (occasional); *Charter of Civil Society for the Caribbean Community*; *Common External Tariff of the Caribbean Common Market: based on the Harmonised Commodity Description & Coding System (HS) 2nd ed*; *Curriculum Guidelines for Family Life Education in the Caribbean: Education for Living*; *Directory of Caribbean Publishers, 3rd ed*; *Employment Problem in CARICOM Countries: the Role of Education & Training in its Existence & its Solution*; *External Public Debt & Balance of Payment of CARICOM Member States 1980-1996*; *National Accounts Digest 1980-1994*; *Regional Census Office, Volume of Basic Tables for Sixteen CARICOM Countries*; *Regional Cultural Policy of the Caribbean Community*; *Removing the Barriers: facts on the CARICOM Single Market & Economy*; *REPORT on a Comprehensive Review of the Programmes, Institutions and Organisations of the Caribbean Community*; *Socio-economic Conditions of Children & Youth in CARICOM Countries: a Situational Analysis*; *Towards Equity in Development: a Report on the Status of Women in Sixteen Commonwealth Caribbean Countries*; *Treaty Establishing the Caribbean Community, Chaguaramas, 4th July 1973*

Standard Book Numbering Agency, see Regional ISBN Agency (CARICOM)

Hong Kong

Books Registration Office
Leisure & Cultural Services Dept, Room 805, 8/F, Lai Chi Kok Government Offices, 19 Lai Wan Rd, Lai Chi Kok, Kowloon
Tel: 218 09 145; 218 09 146 *Fax:* 218 09 841
E-mail: bro@lcsd.gov.hk
Key Personnel
ISBN Administrator & Librarian: Miss Chow Kam-sheung

Government Information Services
3rd-8th floors, Murray Bldg, Garden Road, Central
Tel: 2842 8777 *Fax:* 2845 9078
Web Site: www.info.gov.hk/isd
Key Personnel
Dir of Information Services: Miss Yvonne Choi
  Tel: 2842 8728 *E-mail:* ypchoi@isd.gov.uk

Standard Book Numbering Agency, see Books Registration Office

Hungary

Magyar Iroszoevetseg
Bajza utca 18, 1062 Budapest
Mailing Address: Pf 546, 1397 Budapest
Tel: (01) 322-8840; (01) 322-0631 *Fax:* (01) 321-3419
Key Personnel
President: Marton Kalasz
Hungarian Writers' Association.
Publication(s): *Kortars*; *Magyar Naplo* (journal)

◇**Magyar Koenyvkiadok es Koenyvterjesztoek Egyesuelese**
Kertesz u 41, 1073 Budapest
Tel: (01) 343 25 40 *Fax:* (01) 343 25 41
E-mail: mkke@mkke.hu
Web Site: www.mkke.hu
Key Personnel
President: Istvan Bart
Secretary General: Peter Zentai
Editor-in-Chief: Tarjan Tamas
Publication(s): *Koenyvvilag*
ISBN Prefix(es): 963-7002; 963-7409

Orszagos Szechenyi Konyvtar (National Szechenyi Library)
Budavari Palota F epuelet, 1827 Budapest
Tel: (01) 224-3700 *Fax:* (01) 202-0804
E-mail: isbn@oszk.hu
Web Site: www.oszk.hu
Key Personnel
Head of Division: Susanne Berke *E-mail:* berk@oszk.hu
ISBN Prefix(es): 963-201

Standard Book Numbering Agency, see Orszagos Szechenyi Konyvtar

Iceland

Felag Islenskra Bokautgefenda (Icelandic Publishers' Association)
Baronsstig 5, 101 Reykjavik

Tel: 511 8020 Fax: 511 5020
E-mail: baekur@mmedia.is
Key Personnel
Chairman: Sigurdur Svavarsson
General Manager: Vilborg Hardardottir
Founded: 1889
Publication(s): Bokatidindi (annually)

Standard Book Numbering Agency of Iceland
National & University Library of Iceland, Arngrimsgata 3, 107 Reykjavik
Tel: 525 5600 Fax: 525 5615
E-mail: lbs@bok.hi.is; isbn@bok.hi.is
Web Site: www.bok.hi.is
Telex: 2111 iskult
Key Personnel
Departmental Chief: Ms Nanna Bjarnadottir
  E-mail: nannab@bok.hi.is

India

AABC, see Afro-Asian Book Council (AABC)

†◇**Afro-Asian Book Council (AABC)**
4835/24 Ansari Rd, Daryaganj, New Delhi 110002
Tel: (011) 3261487 Fax: (011) 3267437
E-mail: sdas@ubspd.com
Key Personnel
Secretary General: Sukumar Das
Dir: Abul Hasan E-mail: kiran@ubspd.com
Founded: 1990
Nonprofit book promotion organization for South-South dialogue for the development of indigenous authorship & national book industries in Asia & Africa; International Book Development
Member of African Publishers Network (APNET), Asia-Pacific Cooperative Programme for Reading Promotion & Book Development (APPREB) & World Intellectual Property Organisation (WIPO).
Publication(s): AABC Newsletter (quarterly, newsletter)
Number of titles published annually: 3 Print
Total Titles: 8 Print

Assam Publishers' Association
College Hostel Rd, Panbazar, Guwahati 781 001
Tel: (0361) 23995
Founded: 1977

Delhi State Booksellers' & Publishers' Association
3027/7H Ranjit Nagar, Shiv Chowk, New Delhi 110008
Tel: (011) 231867; (011) 2515726 Fax: (011) 2936758
Key Personnel
President: Devendra Sharma
Honorary Secretary: Bhupinder Chowdhri

Federation of Indian Publishers
18/1C, Institutional Area, Aruna Asaf Ali Marg, New Delhi 110067
Tel: (011) 26964847; (011) 26852263 Fax: (011) 26864054
E-mail: fip1@satyam.net.in
Web Site: www.fiponweb.com
Key Personnel
President: Shri Anand Bhushan
Vice President (E): Amitabha Sen
Vice President (S): Prof H R Dase Gowda
Vice President (N): Shri Narender Kumar
Vice President (W): Shri Anil Gala
Publication(s): Indian Book Industry Journal

Gujarat Book Trade Federation
Navajivan Trust, PO Navajivan, Ahmedabad 380014
Tel: (079) 447 634; (079) 447 635
Key Personnel
Honorary Secretary: R N Shah
Representative body of the book trade in Gujarat.

ICRISAT, see International Crops Research Institute for the Semi-Arid Tropics (ICRISAT)

†‡**International Crops Research Institute for the Semi-Arid Tropics (ICRISAT)**
Patancheru 502 No 324, Andhra Pradesh
Tel: (040) 3296161 Fax: (040) 3241239; (040) 3296182
E-mail: icrisat@cgnet.com
Web Site: www.icrisat.org
Key Personnel
Dir General: William D Dar E-mail: w.dar@cgiar.org
Manager: C Geetha E-mail: c.geetha@cgiar.org
Subjects: Agriculture
ISBN Prefix(es): 92-9066

Meerut Publishers' Association
Shivaji Rd, Meerut, 250 002 Uttar Pradesh
Tel: (0121) 51 0688; (0121) 51 6080 Fax: (0121) 52 1545
E-mail: vrastogi@vsnl.com
Telex: 0549-209
Key Personnel
Partner: Mr Vipin Rastogi
Specializing in the field of bio-sciences, agriculture, environment & genetics for undergraduate & post graduate courses of studies in colleges & universities.
Parent Company: M/S Rastogi Publications
Associate Companies: M/S Pioneer Printers, Shiuasi Rd, Meerut

National Agency for ISBN
Ministry of Human Resource Development, Government of India, New Delhi 110001
Mailing Address: A2, W4 Curzon Rd Barracks, New Delhi 110001
Tel: (011) 2338-4687 Fax: (011) 2338 7934
E-mail: isbn@sb.nic.in
Telex: 031-61336
Key Personnel
Contact: Dr Suresh Chand
Publication(s): National Catalogue of ISBN Titles

Standard Book Numbering Agency, see National Agency for ISBN

Indonesia

IKAPI, see Ikatan Penerbit Indonesia (IKAPI)

Ikatan Penerbit Indonesia (IKAPI)
Jl Kalipasir 32, Jakarta 10330
Tel: (021) 3141907; (021) 3146050 Fax: (021) 3146050
E-mail: sekretariat@ikapi.or.id
Web Site: www.ikapi.or.id
Key Personnel
President: Arselan Harahap
Secretary General: Robinson Rusdi
Association of Indonesian Book Publishers.

Indonesian ISBN Agency
Jl Salemba Raya 28A, Jakarta Pusat 10430
Tel: (021) 3154864; (021) 3154870 Fax: (021) 3103554
E-mail: info@pnri.go.id
Web Site: www.pnri.go.id
Telex: 07345875
Key Personnel
Head, Sub Directorate of Bibliography: Sauliah Saleh E-mail: sauliah@pnri.go.id

Standard Book Numbering Agency, see Indonesian ISBN Agency

Islamic Republic of Iran

Standard Book Numbering Agency
1178 Enqulab Ave, Tehran 13156
Tel: (021) 6414991 Fax: (021) 6415360
E-mail: dariushmatlabi@yahoo.com; isbn@ketab.org.ir; dmatlabi@yahoo.com
Web Site: www.ketab.ir
Telex: 224581-IBFS-IR
Key Personnel
Contact: Mr Vahraz Nowruzpur Deilami

Ireland

CLE: The Irish Book Publishers' Association
43/44 Temple Bar, Dublin 2
Tel: (01) 670-7393 Fax: (01) 670-7642
E-mail: info@publishingireland.com
Web Site: www.publishingireland.com
Key Personnel
Contact: Orla Martin

Cumann Leabharfhoilsitheoiri Eireann, see CLE: The Irish Book Publishers' Association

Irish Educational Publishers' Association
c/o Gill & Macmillan Ltd, 10 Hume Ave, Park West, Dublin 12
Tel: (01) 500 9509; (01) 500 9555 (cust serv) Fax: (01) 500 9598; (01) 500 9596 (cust serv)
Key Personnel
Secretary: Hubert Mahony E-mail: hmahony@gillmacmillan.ie

Israel

Book & Printing Center - Israel Export Institute
29 Hamered St, 61500 Tel Aviv
Mailing Address: PO Box 50084, 61500 Tel Aviv
Tel: (03) 514 2830 Fax: (03) 514 2902; (03) 514 2815
E-mail: export-institute@export.gov.il; pama@export.gov.il
Web Site: www.export.gov.il; duns100.dundb.co.il/1483
Telex: 35613 Cable: MEMEX
Key Personnel
Chairman of the Board: Shraga Brosh
Dir General: Yechiel Assia
Founded: 1958
Division of the Israel Export Institute. Organizes & promotes activities relating to the export of Israeli books, publishing & printing services.
Publication(s): Israel Book Trade Directory (biennially)

ISRAEL

Book Publishers' Association of Israel
29 Carlebach St, Tel Aviv 67132
Mailing Address: PO Box 20123, Tel Aviv 61201
Tel: (03) 5614121 *Fax:* (03) 5611996
E-mail: info@tbpai.co.il
Web Site: www.tbpai.co.il
Key Personnel
Man Dir: Amnon Ben-Shmuel
Chairman: Shai Hausman
Key Representative: Lorna Soifer
The Association administers two subsidiary co-operative associations & two joint publishing companies - Ma'alot & Yachdav.

Hebrew Writers Association of Israel
PO Box 7098, Tel Aviv 61070
Tel: (03) 6953256 *Fax:* (03) 6919681
Key Personnel
President: Nathan Yonathan
Chairman: Dr Zahava Ben-Dov
Publication(s): *Moznayim* (monthly)

The Institute for the Translation of Hebrew Literature
23 Baruch Hirsch St, Bnei Brak
Mailing Address: PO Box 1005 1, 52001 Ramat Gan
Tel: (03) 579 6830 *Fax:* (03) 579 6832
E-mail: hamachon@inter.net.il
Web Site: www.ithl.org.il
Key Personnel
Man Dir: Nilli Cohen
Office Manager: Debbie Dagan
Activities of the Institute include promotion of modern Hebrew literature in translation & co-publishing projects, literary agency services, subsidies to authors & publishers for translations of Hebrew literary works & their publication abroad
Also acts as literary agent.
Publication(s): *Bibliography of Modern Hebrew Literature in Translation* (annually); *Modern Hebrew Literature* (semiannually)

Israel ISBN Group Agency
Israeli Center for Libraries, 5 Havazelet St, Jerusalem 91002
Mailing Address: PO Box 801, Bnei Brak 51108
Tel: (03) 6180151 *Fax:* (03) 5798048
E-mail: isbn@ici.org.il; icl@icl.org.il
Web Site: www.icl.org.il
Key Personnel
Dir, Consulting & Publication: Ariella Z Barrett
  Tel: (03) 6180151 (ext 106)
Contact: Haviva Shmueli *Tel:* (03) 6180151 (ext 115)
Parent Company: Israeli Center for Libraries
Branch Office(s)
28 Baruch Hirsh St, Bnei Brak 51131 *Tel:* (03) 6180151 (ext 106) *E-mail:* ariella@icl.org.il
Web Site: www.icl.org.il

Standard Book Numbering Agency, see Israel ISBN Group Agency

Italy

◇**Agenzia ISBN per l'Area di Lingua Italiana** (ISBN Agency for the Area of Italian Language)
Vie Bergonzoli 1/5, 20127 Milan
Tel: (02) 28315996 *Fax:* (02) 28315906
E-mail: bibliografica@bibliografica.it
Web Site: www.aie.it/ISBN/intro.asp
Key Personnel
ISBN Administrator: Dr Michele Costa
  E-mail: michele.costa@bibliografica.it
Run by Editrice Bibliografica.
Parent Company: Associazione Italiana Editori

ALAI, see Associazione Librai Antiquari d'Italia

Associazione Italiana Editori
Via delle Erbe 2, 20121 Milan
Tel: (02) 86463091 *Fax:* (02) 89010863
E-mail: aie@aie.it
Web Site: www.aie.it
Key Personnel
Dir: Ivan Cecchini *E-mail:* ivan.cecchini@aie.it
Italian Publishers' Association.
Publication(s): *Catalogo dei Libri Italiani in Commercio*; *Giornale Della Libreria*
Branch Office(s)
Via Crescenzio 19, 00193 Rome
  Tel: (06) 68806298 *Fax:* (06) 6872426
  E-mail: aieroma@aie.it

Associazione Librai Antiquari d'Italia
(Antiquarian Booksellers' Association of Italy)
Via del Parione, 11, 50123 Florence
Tel: (055) 282635 *Fax:* (055) 214831
E-mail: alai@alai.it
Web Site: www.alai.it
Key Personnel
President: Francesco Chellini *E-mail:* president@alai.it
Vice President: Umberto Pregliasco
  E-mail: preglias@fileita.it

†‡**Food & Agriculture Organization of the United Nations (FAO)**
Viale delle Terme di Caracalla, 00100 Rome
Tel: (06) 57054350 *Fax:* (06) 57053360
E-mail: telex-room@fao.org
Web Site: www.fao.org
Telex: 610181 FAO I *Cable:* FOODAGRI ROME
Key Personnel
Dir General: Dr Jacques Diouf
Dir Information: Christina Engfeldt
Chief, Sales & Marketing Group: R Sutton
Founded: 1945
FAO Publications reflect the Organization's principal aims: to increase world agriculture production; raise levels of nutrition; & improve the conditions of rural populations. Titles include books, monographs, periodicals, technical documents, annuals, yearbooks & reports of FAO conferences & meetings. Major publications are produced in the five official UN languages (Arabic, Chinese, English, French & Spanish) & all publications & documents are available on microfiche. Unsolicited manuscripts are automatically rejected. Articles of a technical nature of no more than 2500 words on international aspects of the animal industry, food & nutrition are occasionally accepted. No payment is made.
Subjects: Agriculture, Plant Production & Protection, Animal Production & Health, Forestry, Fisheries, Land & Water Development, Economic & Social Development, Food & Nutrition, Computerized Information Series, Educational & Training Materials
ISBN Prefix(es): 92-5; 92-851; 92-852; 92-853; 92-854; 92-855

Institute Propaganda Libraria, see IPL - Istituto Propaganda Libraria

†**International Centre Study Preservation & Restoration of Cultural Property (ICCROM)**
Via di San Michele 13, 00153 Rome
Tel: (06) 585531 *Fax:* (06) 58553349
E-mail: iccrom@iccrom.org
Web Site: www.iccrom.org
Key Personnel
Dir General: Nicholas Stanley-Price
Founded: 1959
Subjects: Heritage Preservation & Intergovernmental Organization
ISBN Prefix(es): 92-9077

◇**IPL - Istituto Propaganda Libraria** (Institute of Bookshop Advertising)
Via Mercalli 23, 20122 Milan
Tel: (02) 58301960 *Fax:* (02) 58301960
Key Personnel
Editorial Dir: Nicola Cerbino
Subjects include literature, literary criticism, fiction, history, essays, religion & philosophy.

Standard Book Numbering Agency, see Agenzia ISBN per l'Area di Lingua Italiana

Jamaica

Booksellers' Association of Jamaica
c/o Noveltry Trading Co Ltd, 53 Hanover St, Kingston
Mailing Address: PO Box 80, Kingston
Tel: (876) 922-5883 *Fax:* (876) 922-4743
Key Personnel
President: Keith Shervington

COMLA, see The Commonwealth Library Association (COMLA)

†◇**The Commonwealth Library Association (COMLA)**
PO Box 144, Mona, Kingston 7
Tel: (876) 927-2123 *Fax:* (876) 927-1926
E-mail: nkpodo@uwimona.edu.jm
Key Personnel
President: Anthony Evans
Vice President: Elizabeth Watson
Executive Secretary: Norma Y Amenu-Kpodo
Founded: 1972
Publication(s): *COMLA Newsletter* (3 issues/yr, newsletter)

◇**University of the West Indies Publishers' Association**
PO Box 42, Mona, Kingston
Tel: (876) 977-2659 *Fax:* (876) 977-2660
Key Personnel
Publication Officer: Annie Paul
University of the West Indies, Mona Campus.
Publication(s): *Caribbean Geography*

Japan

ACCU, see Asia/Pacific Cultural Centre for UNESCO (ACCU)

Antiquarian Booksellers' Association of Japan
29 San-ei-cho, Shinjuku-ku, Tokyo 160-0008
Tel: (03) 3357-1411 *Fax:* (03) 3351-5855
E-mail: kikuo@sc4.so-net.ne.jp
Web Site: www.abaj.gr.jp
Key Personnel
President: Tsukasa Maeda
Founded: 1964

†‡**Asia/Pacific Cultural Centre for UNESCO (ACCU)**
Japan Publishers Bldg, 6 Fukuromachi, Shinjuku-ku, Tokyo 162-8484
Tel: (03) 3269-4435 *Fax:* (03) 3269-4510
E-mail: general@accu.or.jp

Web Site: www.accu.or.jp *Cable:* ASCULCENTRE TOKYO
Key Personnel
Dir General: Muneharu Kusaba
Founded: 1971
Asian/Pacific Copublication Programme (ACP) is a joint program of UNESCO member states in Asia & the Pacific to produce good children's books. Regional training course on book production organized annually & Noma Concours for Picture Book Illustrations biennially.
Publication(s): Asian/Pacific Book Development (ABD); Asian/Pacific Culture (APC)
ISBN Prefix(es): 4-946438

†The Asian Productivity Organization
1-2-10 Hirakawacho, Chiyoda-ku, Tokyo 102-0093
Tel: (03) 5226 3920 *Fax:* (03) 5226 3950
E-mail: apo@apo-tokyo.org
Web Site: www.apo-tokyo.org
Key Personnel
Secretary General: Takashi Tajima
Dir, Administration & Finance Department: Nagare Gamage Kularatne
Dir, Information & Public Relations: Kenneth Mok *Tel:* (03) 5226 3927 *E-mail:* ipr@apo-tokyo.com
Founded: 1961
Subjects: Productivity Improvement in APO Member Countries
ISBN Prefix(es): 92-833
Bookshop(s): Quality Resources, One Water St, White Plains, NY 10601, United States
Tel: 212-979-8600 *Fax:* 914-791-9467

JAIP, see Japan Association of International Publications

Japan Association of International Publications
Chiyoda Kaikan, 21-4 Nihonbashi 1-chome, Chuo-ku, Tokyo 103-0027
Tel: (03) 3271 6901 *Fax:* (03) 3271 6920
E-mail: jaip@poppy.ocn.ne.jp
Web Site: www.jaip.gr.jp
Key Personnel
Chairman Board: Seishiro Murata
Secretary General: Hiroshi Takahashi
Founded: 1941
Subjects: Association of those who import & sell foreign publications, represent foreign publishers & support import of such publications
Publication(s): JAIP Directory
ISBN Prefix(es): 4-931516

Japan Book Publishers Association
6 Fukuro-machi, Shinjuku-ku, Tokyo 162-0828
Tel: (03) 3268-1303 *Fax:* (03) 3268-1196
E-mail: rd@jbpa.or.jp
Web Site: www.jbpa.or.jp *Cable:* SHOSEKIKYO TOKYO
Key Personnel
President: Kunizo Asakura
Executive Dir: Tadashi Yamashita
Founded: 1957
Publication(s): Bulletin of Japan Book Publishers Association; The Catalogue of Books in the Near Future; Introduction to Publishing in Japan 2002-2003; Japanese Books in Print CD-ROM Edition

Japan Electronic Publishing Association
Surugadai-Sunrise Bldg 2-11-1, Kanda Surugadal, Chiyoda-ku, Tokyo 101-0062
Tel: (03) 3219-2958 *Fax:* (03) 3219-2940
Web Site: www.jepa.or.jp
Key Personnel
Chairman of Board: Mr Hideki Hasegawa

Japan ISBN Agency
c/o Japan Library Publishers Bldg, 6 Fukuro-machi, Shinjuku-ku, Toyko 162-0828
Tel: (03) 326 72 301 *Fax:* (03) 326 72 304
E-mail: info@isbn-center.jp
Web Site: www.isbn-center.jp
Key Personnel
Secretary General: Naotoshi Matsudaira

Nihon Shoten Shogyo Kumiai Rengokai
2 Kanda-Surugadai 1 chome, Chiyoda-ku, Tokyo 101
Tel: (03) 32940388
Japan Federation of Commercial Co-operative of Bookstores.
Publication(s): Kodomohon Long-seller-list (Children's Books: A List of Best Sellers); *Zenkoku Shoten Meibo* (Address Book of Japan Booksellers); *Zenkoku Shoten Shinbun* (Newspaper for booksellers)

◇Publishers' Association for Cultural Exchange, PACE, Japan
1-2-1, Sarugaku-cho, Chiyoda-ku, Tokyo 101-0064
Tel: (03) 32915685 *Fax:* (03) 32333645
E-mail: office@pace.or.jp
Web Site: www.pace.or.jp
Key Personnel
President: Tatsuro Matsumae
Man Dir: Yasuko Korenaga
Founded: 1953
European Representation: Euro-Japanische Gesellschaft e.V. (Ohnichi Kyokai), Rossmarkt 15, 6000 Frankfurt am Main 1, Germany. Tel: (069) 285644.
Publication(s): Directory of Japanese Publishers (biennially); *Practical Guide to Publishing in Japan* (annually)

Standard Book Numbering Agency, see Japan ISBN Agency

Kazakstan

Book Chamber of Kazakhstan ISBN Agency
Ulica Puskina 2, Almaty 480016
Tel: (03272) 306 421 *Fax:* (03272) 304 265
E-mail: rntb@kaznet.kz
Web Site: www.isbn-international.org
Key Personnel
Contact: Ms K M Mukhataeva

Standard Book Numbering Agency, see Book Chamber of Kazakhstan ISBN Agency

Kenya

†◇Eastern & Southern Africa Regional Branch of the International Council on Archives (ESARBICA)
c/o Kenya National Archives & Documentation Service Archives Bldg, Moi Ave, Nairobi
Mailing Address: PO Box 49210, Nairobi 00100
Tel: (02) 228959 *Fax:* (02) 240059
E-mail: knarchives@form-net.com
Web Site: www.kenyarchives.go.ke *Cable:* ARCHIVES NAIROBI

ESARBICA, see Eastern & Southern Africa Regional Branch of the International Council on Archives (ESARBICA)

†International Livestock Research Institute
Old Naivasha Rd, Nairobi 00100
Mailing Address: PO Box 30709, Nairobi
Tel: (020) 630 743 *Fax:* (020) 631 499
E-mail: ilri-kenya@cgiar.org
Web Site: www.cgiar.org/ilri
Key Personnel
Dir General: Carlos Sere
Sales, Production, Information, Rights & Permissions: Michael Smalley
Founded: 1974
Subjects: Livestock Research & Development in Africa
ISBN Prefix(es): 92-9053
Branch Office(s)
PO Box 5689, Addis Ababa, Ethiopia *Tel:* (01) 463 215 *Fax:* (01) 461 252 *E-mail:* ilri-ethiopia@cgiar.org

Kenya Literature Bureau
PO Box 30022, Nairobi
Tel: (02) 608806; (02) 605595 *Fax:* (02) 605600
E-mail: klb@onlinekenya.co.ke
Key Personnel
Man Dir: M A Karauri
Chief Editor: A S Githenji
Founded: 1980
ISBN Prefix(es): 9966-44

Kenya Publishers Association
Occidental Plaza, 4th floor, Westlands, Nairobi
Mailing Address: PO Box 42767, Nairobi 00100
Tel: (020) 375 2344 *Fax:* (020) 375 4076
E-mail: kenyapublishers@wananchi.com
Web Site: www.kenyabooks.org
Key Personnel
Executive Secretary: Lynnette Kariuki
Founded: 1971
Membership(s): National Book Development Council of Kenya.

Standard Book Numbering Agency
Kenya National Library Services, Ngong Rd, Nairobi
Mailing Address: PO Box 30573, Nairobi
Tel: (02) 718012; (02) 718013; (02) 725550
Fax: (02) 721749
E-mail: knls@nbnet.co.ke
Web Site: www.knls.or.ke
Telex: 23278 afrec ke
Key Personnel
Dir: S K Nganga
Publication(s): Kenya National Bibliography

UNEP, see United Nations Environment Programme (UNEP)

†‡United Nations Environment Programme (UNEP)
PO Box 30552, Nairobi
Tel: (02) 621234 *Fax:* (02) 624489; (02) 624490
E-mail: eisinfo@unep.org
Web Site: www.unep.org
Telex: 22068 *Cable:* UNITERRA NAIROBI
Key Personnel
Editor: Naomi Poulton *E-mail:* naomi.poulton@unep.org
Founded: 1972
Subjects: Environmental Literature
ISBN Prefix(es): 92-807
Number of titles published annually: 100 Print
U.S. Office(s): United Nations Environment Programme, Regional Office for North America, 1707 "H" St NW, Suite 300, Washington, DC 20006, United States *Tel:* 202-785-0465
E-mail: brennan.vandyke@rona.unep.org

Republic of Korea

ISBN Agency - Korea
The National Library of Korea, 60-1 Banpo-dong, Seocho-gu, Seoul 137-702
Tel: (02) 590 06 27; (02) 590 06 28 *Fax:* (02) 590 06 22; (02) 590 06 21
E-mail: ISSNKC@mail.nl.go.kr
Web Site: www.nl.go.kr
Key Personnel
Contact: Mrs Nam-Sook Kim
Founded: 1990

Korean Publishers Association
105-2 Sagan-Dong, Chongno-Gu, Seoul 110-190
Tel: (02) 735-2701; (02) 735-2704 *Fax:* (02) 738-5414
E-mail: kpa@kpa21.or.kr
Web Site: www.kpa21.or.kr
Key Personnel
President: Choon Ho Na
Secretary General: Jong Jin Jung
Founded: 1947
ISBN Prefix(es): 89-85231

Korean Publishing Research Institute
3 F Daehan Chulpan Munhwa Hoegwan, 105-2 Sagan-dong, Jongro-gu, Seoul 110-190
Tel: (02) 7399040 *Fax:* (02) 7376187
E-mail: p715@chollian.net
Key Personnel
Chief Dir: Yoon Chung-Kwang
Researcher: Park Hyun-Na

Standard Book Numbering Agency, see ISBN Agency - Korea

Kuwait

†‡Arab Centre for Medical Literature
PO Box 5225, Safat 13053
Tel: 5338610; 5338611 *Fax:* 5338618; 5338619
Key Personnel
Secretary General: Dr Abdel Rahman Al-Awadi
Subjects: Arabizing Medical Literatures
Publication(s): *Atlas of Eye Diseases in Arab Countries* (undergoing publication); *Lecture Notes on Gynaecology*; *Teeth & Health*

Latvia

†Latvian Publishers Association (Latvieas Gramatizdevefu Asociacifa)
K Barona iela 36-4, 1011 Riga
Tel: (0371) 7282392 *Fax:* (0371) 7280549
E-mail: lga@gramatizdeveji.lv
Web Site: www.gramatizdeveji.lv
Key Personnel
Executive Dir: Dace Pugaca
President: Anita Rozkalne
Founded: 1993
Protection of rights & interests of publishers.
Membership(s): International Publishers Association.

Standard Book Numbering Agency
Unit of Latvijas bibliografijas Instituts
Latvijas Bibliografijas Instituts, Anglikanu iela 5 (Bibliotekas iela), Riga LV-1816
Tel: (02) 7212668 *Fax:* (02) 7224587
E-mail: anitag@lbi.lnb.lv
Web Site: www.lnb.lv/eng/centrala.htm
Key Personnel
Dir, Latvian ISBN Agency: Ms Laimdota Pruse
E-mail: laimdotap@lbi.lnb.lv
Founded: 1993
ISBN Numbering.
Parent Company: National Library of Latvia, K Barona 14, Riga LV-1235
Ultimate Parent Company: Ministry of Culture of the Republic of Latvia

Lesotho

◇Standard Book Numbering Agency
National University of Lesotho Library, Thomas Mofolo Library, Roma
Mailing Address: National University of Lesotho, PO Roma 180, Roma
Tel: (022) 340601; (022) 340468 *Fax:* 340000
E-mail: isbn@lib.nul.ls
Web Site: www.nul.ls
Telex: 4303 lo
Key Personnel
Contact: Ms Mamothepane Kotele *E-mail:* mt.kotele@nul.ls
Founded: 1964
Education, humanities, law, science & technology, social sciences, agriculture & health sciences.

Lithuania

Lithuanian ISBN Agency
Centre of Bibliography & Book Science, Gedimino pr 51, 2600 Vilnius
Tel: (05) 2497023 *Fax:* (05) 2496129
E-mail: isbnltu@lnb.lt
Web Site: www.lnb.lt
Key Personnel
Head of Agency: Dalia Smoriginiene
ISBN Prefix(es): 9986-530

Lithuanian Publishers' Association
K Sirbydo 6, 2600 Vilnius
Tel: (05) 2617740 *Fax:* (05) 2617740
E-mail: lla@centras.lt
Web Site: www.lla.lt
Key Personnel
President: Aleksandras Krasnovas
Dir: Ms V Misiuniene
Represents the interests of Lithuanian publishers.

Luxembourg

Federation Luxembourgeoise des Editeurs de Livres, ASBL
7 Rue Alcide de Gasperi, 2014 Luxemburg
Mailing Address: BP 482, 2014 Luxemburg
Tel: 439444 *Fax:* 439450
E-mail: promoculture@ibm.net
Key Personnel
General Secretary: Jean-Paul Schortgen
Economic Advisor: Romain Jeblick
Luxemburgish Publishers' Association.
Parent Company: Confederation Luxembourgeoise du Commerce

ISBN Agency - Luxembourg
Bibliotheque Nationale, 37 Blvd F D Roosevelt, L-2450 Luxembourg
Tel: 22 97 55-1 *Fax:* 47 56 72
E-mail: bib.nat@bi.etat.lu
Web Site: www.bnl.lu
Key Personnel
Dir: F F Monique Kieffer
Parent Company: Bibliotheque nationale

†Office des Publications Officielles des Communautes Europeennes (Office for Official Publications of the European Communities)
2, rue Mercier, 2985 Luxembourg
Tel: 2929-1 *Fax:* 292944619
E-mail: opoce-info-info@cec.eu.int
Web Site: www.eur-op.eu.int
Key Personnel
Dir: Lucien Emringer
Chief of Sales: Serge Brack
Chief of Marketing: N Reinert
Founded: 1969
Subjects: Economy, Law, Finance, Enterprises & Business, Energy, Foreign Relations, Agriculture, Fishing, Forestry, Tax, Employment, Labor, Environment, Scientific Research & Techniques, Information, Education, Culture, Statistics
U.S. Office(s): Unipub, 4611-F Assembly Dr, Lanham, MD 20706-4391, United States
Fax: 301-459-0056

Standard Book Numbering Agency, see ISBN Agency - Luxembourg

The Former Yugoslav Republic of Macedonia

Standard Book Numbering Agency
Narodna i Univerzitetska Biblioteka, Bul Goce Delcev, br 6, 91000 Skopje
Tel: (02) 3115 177; (02) 3133 418 *Fax:* (02) 3226 846
E-mail: kliment@nubsk.edu.mk
Web Site: www.nubsk.edu.mk
Key Personnel
Dir: Vera Kaljlieva

Madagascar

Fiantsorohana NY Boky Malagasy, Office du Livre Malgache
Lot 111, H29 Andrefran' Ambohijanahary, Tananrive 101
Mailing Address: BP 617, Tananrive 101
Tel: (02) 24449
Key Personnel
Secretary General: Juliette Ratsimandrava
E-mail: ratsimandrav@initel.refer.org

Malawi

ISBN Agency (International Standard Book Number National Agency)
National Archives of Malawi, PO Box 62, Zomba
Tel: (01) 525 240; (01) 524 148; (01) 524 184
Fax: (01) 525 362; (01) 524 148
E-mail: archives@sdnp.org.mw
Web Site: chambo.sdnp.org.mw
Key Personnel
Acting Dir: Mr O W Ambali
Administer the issuing of ISBNs to publishers in Malawi.
Membership(s): ICA (International Council on Archives).
Publication(s): *National Bibliography Archives of Malawi, Zomba* (annually)
Parent Company: Ministry of Sports & Culture, Pvt Bag 384, Lilongwe 3

Standard Book Numbering Agency, see ISBN Agency (International Standard Book Number National Agency)

Malaysia

Malaysian Book Importers & Distributors Association
45 Jalan Tun Mudh 2, Taman Tun Dr Ismail, 60000 Kuala Lumpur
Tel: (03) 7193485 *Fax:* (03) 7181664
Key Personnel
President: Mr K Arul
Secretary: Mr Leong Fook Kwong

Malaysian Book Publishers' Association
No 39, Jln Nilam 1/2, Subang Square, Subang High-Tech Industrial Park Batutiga, 40000 Shah Alam, Selangor
Tel: (03) 56379044 *Fax:* (03) 56379043
E-mail: inquiry@cerdik.com.my
Web Site: www.mabopa.com.my
Key Personnel
President: Ng Tieh Chuan
Vice President: Peter Paul
Honorary Secretary: Zainora Muhamad
Honorary Treasurer: Sumangala Pilai
Founded: 1969
Publish textbooks, revision course books, workbooks, encyclopedias, readers, magazines & multimedia products.
Publication(s): *Malaysian Publishers Directory*

SARBICA, see Southeast Asian Regional Branch of the International Council on Archives (SARBICA)

†◇Southeast Asian Regional Branch of the International Council on Archives (SARBICA)
c/o National Archives of Malaysia, Jalan Duta, 50568 Kuala Lumpur
Tel: (03) 651 0688 *Fax:* (03) 651 5679
E-mail: sarbica.sec@arkib.gov.my
Web Site: arkib.gov.my/sarbica/index.html
Key Personnel
Chairman, Malaysia: Lily Tan
Publication(s): *Southeast Asian Archives*; *Southeast Asian Microfilms Newsletter*

Standard Book Numbering Agency
c/o National Library of Malaysia, 232, Jalan Tun Razak, 50572 Kuala Lumpur
Tel: (03) 26871700 *Fax:* (03) 26927082
E-mail: pnmweb@www1.pnm.my
Web Site: www.pnm.my
Telex: MA 30092 *Cable:* NATLIB KUALALUMPUR

Maldive Islands

Standard Book Numbering Agency
Ministry of Education, Ghaazee Bldg, Ameeru Ahmed Magu, Male 20-05
Tel: 323261 *Fax:* 321201
E-mail: educator@dhivehinet.net.mv
Web Site: www.moe.gov.mv

Malta

Maltese Publishers Association, see Periodical & Book Publishers Association

◇Periodical & Book Publishers Association
The Terrace, Ta'Xbiex MSD 11
Fax: (507) 295 9217
E-mail: bookpub@cwebdesign.com
Web Site: www.cwebdesign.com/pbpa
Key Personnel
Founder & Chairman: Joseph John Meli
Founded: 1989
Member association of "Kopjamalt" - the Copyright Licensing Agency for the Maltese Islands.

Standard Book Numbering Agency
Publishers Enterprises Group (PEG) Inc, PEG Bldg, UB 7 Industrial Estate, San Gwann SGN09
Tel: (021) 440083; (021) 448539; (021) 490540
Fax: (021) 488908
E-mail: contact@peg.com.mt
Web Site: www.peg.com.mt
Key Personnel
Man Dir: Emanuel Debattista
Publishers & printers.

Mauritius

National ISBN Agency
Editions de l'Ocean Indien Ltee, Stanley, Rose Hill
Tel: (0230) 4646761; (0230) 4643959; (0230) 4643452 *Fax:* (0230) 4643445
E-mail: eoibooks@intnet.mu
Telex: mesynd 4739
Key Personnel
Contact: Mr C Colimalay
Publishers & Distributors of books/private company.
ISBN Prefix(es): 99903-0
Parent Company: Editions de L'Ocean Indien Ltee (Publishers & Distributors)
Associate Companies: Mauritius Printing Specialists (Pte) Ltd, Stanley, Rose-Hill
Branch Office(s)
Curepipe
Flacq
Goodlands
Port Louis
Rose Hill

Standard Book Numbering Agency, see National ISBN Agency

Mexico

Camara Nacional de la Industria Editorial Mexicana
Holanda No 13, col San Diego Churubusco, Del Coyoacan, 04120 Mexico
Tel: (05) 6 88 24 34; (05) 6 88 22 21; (05) 6 88 2011 *Toll Free Tel:* (800) 714-5352 *Fax:* (055) 5604-4347; (05) 6 04 31 47
E-mail: cepromex@caniem.com
Web Site: www.caniem.com
Telex: 1772969
Key Personnel
Dir: R Servin
President: A H Gayosso; J C Cramerez
Mexican Publishers' Association.
Publication(s): *Books of Mexico; How to obtain Mexican books and periodicals*

Centro Nacional de Informacion, Agencia Nacional ISBN
Calle Dinamarca 84, 2° Piso Colonia Juarez Delegacion Cuauhtemoc, 06600 Mexico, DF
Tel: (0555) 230 7632 *Fax:* (0555) 230 7634
Web Site: www.sep.gob.mx
Telex: 1773860 psep me
Key Personnel
ISBN Administrator: Alejandra Martinez Gamboa; Ketty Garcia Agut
National Center of Information, National Agency ISBN.

†◇Consejo Interamericano de Archiveros (CITA)
c/o Archivo General de la Nacion, Eduardo Molina y Albaniles s/n Col Penitenciaria Ampliacion, Delegacion Venustiano Carranza, 15350 Mexico, DF
Tel: (05) 51 33 99 00 (ext 19327); (05) 57 95 70 80 (ext 19424) *Fax:* (05) 57 89 52 96
Web Site: www.agn.gob.mx
Key Personnel
Dir General: Patricia Galeana
Publication(s): *Boletin del AGN y Colecciones Graficas; Documentos de Archivonomia; Estudios Historicos; Guias y Catalogos; Informacion de Archivos Estatales y Municipales*

Standard Book Numbering Agency, see Centro Nacional de Informacion, Agencia Nacional ISBN

Republic of Moldova

Camera Nationala a Cartii din Republica Moldova, see Chambre Nationale du Livre Agence ISBN

Chambre Nationale du Livre Agence ISBN
Subsidiary of Ministry of Culture
bd Stefan cel Mare 180, 2004 Chisinau
Tel: (02) 24 65 42 *Fax:* (02) 24 65 11
E-mail: cncm@moldova.cc
Web Site: www.iatp.md/cnc
Key Personnel
Dir: Valentina Chitoroaga *E-mail:* chitoroaga_v@moldova.cc
Founded: 1957
ISBN Prefix(es): 9975-9532

Standard Book Numbering Agency, see Chambre Nationale du Livre Agence ISBN

Morocco

African Training and Research Centre in Administration for Development, Documentation Centre, see Centre Africain de Formation et de Recherche Administratives pour le Developpement, Centre de Documentation

Agence Marocaine de l'ISBN
Bibliotheque Generale et Archives, Service du depot legal, Av Ibn Battouta, Rabat
Mailing Address: BP 1003, Rabat
Tel: (07) 771 890; (07) 772 152 *Fax:* (07) 776 062
E-mail: biblio1@onpt.net.ma
Key Personnel
ISBN Dir: Ahmed Toufiq
Contact: Meryem Moussaid
ISBN Agency of Morocco.
Publication(s): *Bibliographie Nationale Retrospective du Marco* (1986-1995)
Parent Company: Biliotheque Generale et Archives

†◇**Centre Africain de Formation et de Recherche Administratives pour le Developpement, Centre de Documentation**
PO Box 310, Tangier 90001
Tel: (061) 30 72 69 *Fax:* (039) 32 57 85
E-mail: cafrad@cafrad.org
Web Site: www.cafrad.org
Telex: 33664 *Cable:* CAFRAD TANGIER
Key Personnel
President: Mansouri Messaoud
Publication(s): *Directory of Administrative Information Services in Africa*

Standard Book Numbering Agency, see Agence Marocaine de l'ISBN

Namibia

ISBN Agency - Namibia
National Library of Namibia, Pvt Bag 13349, 9000 Windhoek
Tel: (061) 293 53 05 *Fax:* (061) 293 53 08
Web Site: www.isbn-international.org
Key Personnel
Contact: Werner Hillebrecht
 E-mail: whillebrecht@mec.gov.na
Publication(s): *Namibia National Bibliography* (1996-)

Standard Book Numbering Agency, see ISBN Agency - Namibia

Nepal

◇**National Federation of Standard Editor's Association in Nepal (NAFSEEN)**
Kamabakshee Tole, Gha 3-333, Kathmandu 44601-3000
Mailing Address: PO Box 3000-NFSEA Katmandu-3-30-15B, Kathmandu 44601-3000
Tel: (01) 212289; (01) 223036; (01) 224005
 Fax: (01) 223036
Telex: 3000 1-SB-ASS-NP *Cable:* NAFSEAN
Key Personnel
Secretary General: Ganesh Lall Chhipa
Editorial Dir: Ganesh Dass Chhipa

Branch Office(s)
09/63-09 Dathwee Chhen Twa Gallee, Chowk Bhitra 2nd Floor Puranco Bazaar, Arniiko-Barhabise VDC-9, Arniko Rajmarg-87 KM, Bagmati Anchal, Barhabise Mail PO Code 45303, Kathmandu Mail Centre

National Federation of Standard Periodicals Publishers Association of Nepal
Kamabakohee Tole, GHA 3-333, Kathmandu 44601-3000
Mailing Address: PO Box 3000-NFFSPP Kathmandu-3-30-15B, Kathmandu 44601-3000
Tel: (01) 212289; (01) 223036; (01) 224005
 Fax: (01) 223036
Telex: 3000 1-SB-ASS-NP *Cable:* NAPSPEPAN
Key Personnel
Secretary General: Ganesh Lall Singh
Dir: Ganesh Dass
Branch Office(s)
Arniko-Barhabise VDC-9, Arniko Rajmarg-87 KMArniko Rajmarg-87 KM, Bagmati Anchal Barhamise Mail

◇**National Federation of Standard Translator's Association in Nepal**
Kamabakshee Tole, Gha 3-333, Kathmandu 44601-3000
Mailing Address: PO Box 3000-NFSTA Kathmandu-3-30-15B, Kathmandu 44601-3000
Tel: (01) 212289; (01) 223036; (01) 224005
 Fax: (01) 223036 ISB-ASS
Telex: 3000 1-SB-ASS-NP *Cable:* NAFSTAN
Key Personnel
Secretary General: Ganesh Lall Chhipa
Dir: Ganesh Dass Chhipa
Branch Office(s)
09/63-16 Dathwee Chhen Twa Gallee, Chowk Bhitra 4th Floor Puranco Bazaar, Arniiko-Barhabise VDC-9, Arniko Rajmarg-87 KM, Bagmati Anchal, Barhabise Mail PO Code 45303, Kathmandu Mail Centre

◇**National Standards Wholesaler's Distributor's & Subscriber's Association of Nepal (NASWDISAN)**
Kamabakshee Tole, Gha 3-333, Kathmandu 44601-3000
Mailing Address: PO Box 3000-NSWDS Kathmandu-3-30-15B, Kathmandu 44601-3000
Tel: (01) 212289; (01) 223036; (01) 224005
 Fax: (01) 223036
Telex: 3000 1-SB-ASS-NP
Key Personnel
Secretary General: Ganesh Lall Chhipa
Dir: Ganesh Dass Chhipa
Branch Office(s)
09/63-08 Dathwee Chhen Twa Gallee, Chowk Bhitra 5th floor Puranco Bazaar, Arniiko-Barhabise VDC-9, Arniko Rajmarg-87 KM, Bagmati anchal, Barhabise Mail PO Code 45303, Kathmandu Mail Centre

Netherlands

Centraal Boekhuis BV
Erasmusweg 10, 4104 AK Culemborg
Mailing Address: Postbus 125, 4100 AC Culemborg
Tel: (0345) 47 59 11 *Fax:* (0345) 47 56 90
E-mail: info@centraal.boekhuis.nl
Web Site: www.centraalboekhuis.nl
Key Personnel
Man Dir: C J Hagenbeek
Dir, Sales & Marketing: S Berkina
Contact: Jaco Gulmans *Tel:* (0345) 47 56 50
 E-mail: j.gulmans@centraal.boekhuis.nl

Collectieve Propaganda van het Nederlandse Boek (CPNB) (Foundation for the Collective Promotion of the Dutch Book)
Keizersgracht 391, 1016 EJ Amsterdam
Mailing Address: Postbus 10576, 1001 EN Amsterdam
Tel: (020) 626 49 71 *Fax:* (020) 623 16 96
E-mail: info@cpnb.nl
Web Site: www.cpnb.nl
Key Personnel
Man Dir: Henk Kraima
Publication(s): *Children's Bookweek; Kinderboekenmolen, Voorleesgids* (annually); *Premium Bookweek*

†‡**Cour Internationale de Justice**
Palais de la Paix/Peace Palace, 2517 KJ The Hague
Tel: (070) 302 23 23 *Fax:* (070) 364 99 28
E-mail: mail@icj-cij.org; information@icj-cij.org
Web Site: www.icj-cij.org
Telex: 32323 *Cable:* INTERCOURT THE HAGUE
Key Personnel
Registrar & Contact: M Philippe Couvreur

CPNB, see Collectieve Propaganda van het Nederlandse Boek (CPNB)

ESOMAR, see European Society for Opinion & Marketing Research

†‡**Universala Esperanto-Asocio** (World Esperanto Association)
176 Nieuwe Binnenweg, 3015 BJ Rotterdam
Tel: (010) 4361044 *Fax:* (010) 4361751
E-mail: info@uea.org
Web Site: www.uea.org *Cable:* ESPERANTO ROTTERDAM
Key Personnel
President: Dr Renato Corsetti
Vice President: Prof Lee Chong-Yeong; Prof Humphrey Tonkin
Secretary General: Ivo Osibov
Editor: Stano Marchek
Founded: 1908
Subjects: Language problems & Esperanto as a possible solution
ISBN Prefix(es): 92-9017

†◇**European Association for Health Information & Libraries**
EAHIL Secretariat, c/o NVB Bureau, Nieuwegracht 15, 3512 LC Utrecht
Tel: (030) 2619663 *Fax:* (030) 2311830
E-mail: EAHIL-secr@nic.surfnet.nl
Web Site: www.eahil.org
Key Personnel
President: Arne Jakobsson
Secretary: Suzanne Bakker

European Association of Information Services, see EUSIDIC (European Association of Information Services)

†**European Society for Opinion & Marketing Research**
Vondelstr 172, 1054 GV Amsterdam
Tel: (020) 664 21 41 *Fax:* (020) 664 29 22
E-mail: email@esomar.nl
Web Site: www.esomar.org
Key Personnel
President: Fredrik Nauckhoff
Dir General: Ted Vonk *E-mail:* t.vonk@esomar.org
Founded: 1948
Subjects: Marketing & opinion research

†◇**EUSIDIC (European Association of Information Services)**
CAOS, WG Plein 475, 1054 SH Amsterdam

Tel: (020) 589 32 32 *Fax:* (020) 589 32 30
E-mail: eusidic@caos.nl
Web Site: www.eusidic.org
Key Personnel
Chair: Johan van Halm *Tel:* (033) 47 00671 *Fax:* (033) 47 01123 *E-mail:* johanvanhalm@cs.com
Vice Chair: Frank Spellerberg *Tel:* (0170) 3821 779 *Fax:* (06198) 57 66 95 *E-mail:* spellerberg.frank@web.de
Treasurer: Irja Laamanen *Tel:* (09) 5418 138 *Fax:* (09) 5418 167 *E-mail:* irja.laamanen@occuphealth.fi

IEA, see International Association for the Evaluation of Educational Achievement (IEA)

IFLA, see International Federation of Library Associations & Institutions (IFLA)

International Association for the Evaluation of Educational Achievement (IEA)
Herengracht 487, 1017 BT Amsterdam
Tel: (020) 6253625 *Fax:* (020) 4207136
E-mail: department@iea.nl
Web Site: www.iea.nl
Key Personnel
Chairman: Dr Alejandro Tiana *E-mail:* atiana@edu.und.es
Executive Dir: Dr Hans Wagemaker
  E-mail: hanswagemaker@compuserve.com
Manager Membership Relations: Dr Barbara Malak-Minkiewicz *E-mail:* b.malak@iea.nl
Founded: 1954
Research on educational outcomes.
Subjects: Education & various school subjects
Publication(s): *International Reports of IEA Studies*

†◇International Association of Scientific, Technical & Medical Publishers (STM)
Prins Willem Alexanderhof 5, 2595 BE The Hague
Mailing Address: POB 90407, 2509 LK The Hague
Tel: (070) 314 09 30 *Fax:* (070) 314 09 40
E-mail: info@stm-assoc.org
Web Site: www.stm-assoc.org
Key Personnel
Chairman: Eric Swanson
Secretary: Lex Lefebvre
International Trade Organization for STM, professional & scholarly publishers. Focus on copyright & legal issues, technology development & industry standards & library & users relations.

International Court of Justice, see Cour Internationale de Justice

†◇International Federation of Library Associations & Institutions (IFLA)
Postbus 95312, 2509 CH The Hague
Tel: (070) 3140884 *Fax:* (070) 3834827
E-mail: ifla@ifla.org
Web Site: www.ifla.org
Key Personnel
President: Christine Deschamps
Secretary General: R Ramachandran
Founded: 1927
Federation internationale des associations de bibliothecaires et des bibliotheques.
Publication(s): *IFLA Annual Report*; *IFLA Directory* (biennially); *IFLA Journal*; *IFLA Professional Reports*; *IFLA Publications* (series of monographs, published by K G Saur Verlag KG, Germany); *International Cataloguing & Bibliographic Control* (quarterly)

Bureau ISBN
Centraal Boekhuis, Erasmusweg 10, 4104 AK Culemborg
Mailing Address: Postbus 360, 4100 AJ Culemborg
Tel: (0345) 475855 *Fax:* (0345) 475895
E-mail: isbn@centraal.boekhuis.nl
Web Site: www.isbn.nl
Key Personnel
ISBN Administrator: Ben Klomp
Contact: Mr M G van den Heuvel
  E-mail: heuvm@centraal.boekhuis.nl
Publication(s): *ISBN Manual* (2002); *ISBN Publishers List* (on diskette & computer printout)
Parent Company: Centraal Boekhuis BV

KVB Koninklijke Vereeniging van het Boekenvak (Royal Dutch Book Trade Organization)
Fredriksplein 1, 1017 XK Amsterdam
Mailing Address: Postbus 15007, 1001 MA Amsterdam
Tel: (020) 624 02 12 *Fax:* (020) 620 88 71
E-mail: info@kvb.nl
Web Site: www.kvb.nl
Key Personnel
Executive Dir: Mrs C Verberne
Founded: 1815
Association for the Promotion of the Interests of Booksellers & Publishers.
Publication(s): *Adresboek* (Address book for the Dutch Book Trade); *Boekblad* (News Magazine for the Book Trade, weekly & monthly & website www.boekblad.nl)

Nederlands Uitgeversverbond (Dutch Publishers Association)
Atlas Kantorenpark, gebouw Azie, Hoogoorddreef 5, 1101 BA Amsterdam
Mailing Address: Postbus 12040, 1100 AA Amsterdam
Tel: (020) 43 09 150 *Fax:* (020) 43 09 179
E-mail: info@nuv.nl
Web Site: www.nuv.nl; www.uitgeversverbond.nl
Key Personnel
President: Prof Henk J L Vonhoff
Man Dir: J Bommer
Public Relations Secretary: Jaap Roorda
  E-mail: j.roorda@uitgeversverbond.nl
Founded: 1880
Royal Dutch Publishers' Association.

Nederlandsche Vereeniging van Antiquaren (Dutch Antiquarian Booksellers' Association)
Postbus 364, 3500 AJ Utrecht
Tel: (030) 231 92 86 *Fax:* (030) 234 33 62
E-mail: bestbook@wxs.nl
Web Site: www.nvva.nl
Key Personnel
President: Ton Kok *E-mail:* kok@xs4all.nl
Secretary: Drs PAGWE Pruimers
Founded: 1935

Nederlandsche Vereeniging voor Druk- en Boekkunst
van Banningstraas 2c, 2381 AV Zoeterwoude
Tel: (071) 5809634
Key Personnel
Secretary: Kees Thomassen
Netherlands Society for the Art of Printing and Book Production.
Publication(s): *Mededelingen* (irregularly)

Nederlandse Boekverkopersbond (Dutch Booksellers Association)
Prins Hendriklaan 72, 3721 AT Bilthoven
Tel: (030) 228 79 56 *Fax:* (030) 228 45 66
E-mail: nbb@boekbond.nl
Web Site: www.boekbond.nl
Key Personnel
President: W Karssen
Executive Secretary: Mr A C Doeser

Speurwerk Stitching betreffende het Boek
Frederiksplein 1, 1017 XK Amsterdam
Tel: (020) 625 49 27 *Fax:* (020) 620 88 71
E-mail: info@speurwerk.kvb.nl
Web Site: www.speurwerk.nl
Key Personnel
Dir: A A Herpers
Foundation for Bookmarket Research in the Netherlands.
Publication(s): *Boekenvakboek 1980, 1986-88* (Publishing Industry Statistics); *Gids voor de Informatiesector 1990, 1991, 1992, 1993, 1994*; *Speurwerk Boeken Omnibus* (quarterly, The Dutch Book Market); *Structural Analysis of the Book Market in Netherlands*
Branch Office(s)
Documentation Department Speurwerk/FE, Herengracht 330, 1016 CE Amsterdam, 1016 CE Amsterdam *Tel:* (020) 6247676 *Fax:* (020) 6238869

Standard Book Numbering Agency, see Bureau ISBN

STM, see International Association of Scientific, Technical & Medical Publishers (STM)

†Technical Centre for Agricultural & Rural Co-operation
Agro Business Park 2, Wageningen
Mailing Address: Postbus 380, 6700 AJ Wageningen
Tel: (0317) 467100 *Fax:* (0317) 460067
E-mail: cta@cta.nl
Web Site: www.cta.nl
Telex: (044) 30169 cta nl
Key Personnel
Head: A C Jackson *Tel:* (0317) 467127
  E-mail: jackson@cta.nl
Founded: 1984
Subjects: Tropical Agriculture, Rural Development & Information & Communication Management
ISBN Prefix(es): 92-9081
Branch Office(s)
Rue Montoyer, 39, 1000 Bruxelles, Belgium
  Tel: (02) 5137436 *Fax:* (02) 580868

Netherlands Antilles

†Bureau Intellectual Property
Berg Carmelweg 10-A, Curacao
Tel: (09) 465 7800 *Fax:* (09) 465 7815
E-mail: info@bureau-intellectual-property.org
Key Personnel
Dir: Mr Juny J Sluis
Founded: 1893
Registration of trademarks.
Publication(s): *Merkenblad* (Trademark journal)
Number of titles published annually: 161 Print
Total Titles: 296 Print

New Zealand

Booksellers New Zealand
Level 1, Survey House, 21-29 Broderick Rd, Wellington
Mailing Address: PO Box 13 248, Wellington
Tel: (04) 478 5511 *Fax:* (04) 478 5519
E-mail: enquiries@booksellers.co.nz
Web Site: www.booksellers.co.nz

NEW ZEALAND

Key Personnel
Chairperson: Tony Moores
Chief Executive: Alice Heather

Booksellers New Zealand
Level 1, E Wing Survey House, 21-29 Broderick Rd, Johnsonville 9
Mailing Address: PO Box 13-248, Johnsonville 1
Tel: (04) 4478-5511 *Fax:* (04) 4478-5519
Publication(s): *NZ Publishing News* (members only)
Associate Companies: Copyright Licensing Ltd

Christian Booksellers' Association (NZ Chapter)
71 Rata St, Matamata 2711
Tel: (07) 888 6010
E-mail: info@cbaonline.org
Web Site: www.cbaonline.org
Key Personnel
Secretary & Treasurer: Roger McRae
Currently have 54 retail members & 27 wholesale members.
Publication(s): *Newsletters* (bimonthly)

IAML, see International Association of Music Libraries, Archives & Documentation Centres (IAML)

†◇International Association of Music Libraries, Archives & Documentation Centres (IAML)
National Library of New Zealand, PO Box 1467, Wellington
Tel: (04) 474 3039 *Fax:* 613-520-2750
Web Site: www.iaml.info
Key Personnel
Secretary General: Roger Flury *E-mail:* roger.flury@natlib.govt.nz
Founded: 1951
Association internationale des bibliotheques, archives et centres de documentation musicaux (AIBM)
Internationale Vereinigung der Musikbibliotheken, Musikarchive und Musikdokumentations Zentren (IVMB).
Publication(s): *Fontes artis musicae*

◇New Zealand Council for Educational Research
10th floor, West Block, Education House, 178-182 Willis St, Wellington
Mailing Address: PO Box 3237, Wellington
Tel: (04) 384 7939 *Fax:* (04) 384 7933
Web Site: www.nzcer.org.nz
Key Personnel
Dir: Robyn Baker *E-mail:* robyn.baker@nzcer.org.nz
Publications Officer: Peter Ridder
Founded: 1934
Publication(s): *New Zealand Journal of Educational Studies* (set)
ISBN Prefix(es): 0-908567; 0-908916; 1-877140

New Zealand Press Council
79 Boulcott St, Wellington
Mailing Address: Box 10879, The Terrace, Wellington
Tel: (04) 4735220 *Fax:* (04) 4711785
E-mail: presscouncil@asa.co.nz
Web Site: www.presscouncil.org.nz
Key Personnel
Chairman: Sir John Jeffries
Secretary: Mary Major
Founded: 1972

†◇South Pacific Association for Commonwealth Literature & Language Studies (SPACLALS)
University of Waikato, Private Bag 3105, Hamilton
Tel: (07) 838-4466 *Fax:* (07) 838 4722
Founded: 1975
Publication(s): *Journal & Spaccals* (biannually); *Span*

SPACLALS, see South Pacific Association for Commonwealth Literature & Language Studies (SPACLALS)

Standard Book Numbering Agency
National Library of New Zealand, Molesworth & Aitken Sts, Wellington 6001
Mailing Address: PO Box 1467, Wellington 6001
Tel: (04) 474 3074 *Fax:* (04) 474 3161
E-mail: isbn@natlib.govt.nz
Web Site: www.natlib.govt.nz
Key Personnel
ISBN Librararian: Joy Grove

Nigeria

Children's Literature Association of Nigeria
c/o Institute of African Studies, University of Ibadan, Ibadan, Oyo State
Tel: (022) 400550; (022) 400614 *Fax:* (022) 711254
Key Personnel
President: Mabel Segun

Children's Literature Documentation & Research Centre, Ibadan
UIPO Box 20744, Ibadan, Oyo State
Fax: (022) 711254
Key Personnel
Dir: Mabel Segun

Christian Booksellers Association of Nigeria
c/o Potters House Bookshop, PO Box 13328, Jos, Plateau State
Tel: (073) 452387
E-mail: cban@bwave.net
Web Site: www.cbaonline.org
Key Personnel
President: Thomas A Sule
Administrative Secretary: Justice Okonkwo
Parent Company: Christian Booksellers Association USA, United States

CLIDORC, see Children's Literature Documentation & Research Centre, Ibadan

Nigerian Book Development Council
6, Obanta Rd, Apapa, Lagos
Tel: (01) 862269; (01) 862272
Key Personnel
Secretary: Alhaja M M Musa

Nigerian ISBN Agency
National Library of Nigeria, Ijora Lilipond Office, Otto Rd, Ijora Olopa, Lagos
Mailing Address: PMB 12626, Lagos
Tel: (01) 5850657; (01) 5850649
Web Site: www.nlbn.org
Telex: 21746 *Cable:* Biblios
Key Personnel
Agency Head: S E A Sonaike
Publication(s): *Nigerian ISBN Manual & Directory*

Nigerian Publishers Association
Book House: Quarter 673, Jericho GRA, Old Bodija, Ibadan
Mailing Address: GPO Box 2541, Ibadan
Tel: (02) 2414427 *Fax:* (02) 2413396

BOOK TRADE

E-mail: nigpa@skannet.com; nigpa@steineng.net; nigpa@freemail.nig.com
Telex: 31113
Key Personnel
President: V Nwankwo
Chief: Mrs F O Orikan
Publication(s): *The Publisher* (biannually)

SCAUL, see Standing Conference of African University Libraries (SCAUL)

Standard Book Numbering Agency, see Nigerian ISBN Agency

†◇Standing Conference of African University Libraries (SCAUL)
c/o E Bejide Bankole, Editor African Journal of Academic Librarianship, University of Lagos, Akoka, Yaba, Lagos
Mailing Address: PO Box 46, Akoka, Yaba, Lagos
Tel: (01) 524968 *Fax:* (01) 822644

University Booksellers Association of Nigeria
c/o Benin University Bookshop, PMB 1154, Ugbowo Campus, Benin City
Tel: (052) 200250 (Ugbowo); (052) 200480 (Ekehuan) *Fax:* (052) 241156
Telex: 41365

Norway

Bok Og Papiransattes Forening
Ovre Vollgate 15, N-0158 Oslo
Tel: 22205197 *Fax:* 22400033
Norwegian Book Trade Employees' Association.
Publication(s): *Norsk Bokhandlermatrikkel*; *Norsk Boknokkel*

Den Norske Bokhandlerforening (Norwegian Booksellers Association)
Ovre Vollgt 15, 0158 Oslo
Tel: 22 00 75 80 *Fax:* 22 33 38 30
E-mail: dfn@forleggerforeningen.no
Web Site: www.forleggerforeningen.no
Key Personnel
Dir: Kristin C Slordahl *E-mail:* kristin.slordahl@forleggerforeningen.no
Publication(s): *Bok og Samfunn*

ISBN-Kontoret Norge
National Library of Norway Oslo Division, Postbox 2674, N-0203 Oslo
Tel: 23 27 62 17 *Fax:* 23 27 60 10
E-mail: isbn-kontoret@nb.no
Web Site: www.nb.no/html/isbn_eng.html
Telex: 76078 ub n
Key Personnel
Administrator & Senior Librarian: Ms Ingebjoerg Rype
ISBN Agency.
Publication(s): *ISBN-Internasjonalt standard boknummer*
Parent Company: National Library of Norway

Norsk Musikkforleggerforening
c/o Musikk-Husets Forlag AS, PO Box 822, Sentrum, N-0104 Oslo
Tel: (022) 42 50 90 *Fax:* (022) 42 55 41
Web Site: www.mic.no/mic.nsf
Norwegian Music Publishers' Association.

Den Norske Forfatterforening
Radhusgata 7, Oslo
Mailing Address: Boks 327 Sentrum, N-0103 Oslo

Tel: 23357620; 22 42 40 77; 22 41 11 97 *Fax:* 22 42 11 07
E-mail: post@forfatterforeningen.no; forfatterforeningen@online.no
Web Site: skrift.no/dnf
Key Personnel
Secretary General: Lars Haavik
Office Manager: Tordis Fjeldstad
Founded: 1893
Norwegian Authors' Union.

Den Norske Forleggerforening
Ovre Vollgt 15, 0158 Oslo
Tel: 22 00 75 80 *Fax:* 22 33 38 30
E-mail: dnf@forleggerforeningen.no
Web Site: www.forleggerforeningen.no
Key Personnel
Dir: Kristin Cecilie Shordahl *E-mail:* kristin.shordahl@forleggerforeningen.no
Secretary: Astri Skarde *E-mail:* astri.skarde@forleggerforeningen.no
Memberships: IPA; FEP.

Standard Book Numbering Agency, see ISBN-Kontoret Norge

Pakistan

Standard Book Numbering Agency
National Library of Pakistan, Constitution Ave, Islamabad 44000
Mailing Address: PO Box 1982, Islamabad 44000
Tel: (051) 921 4523; (051) 920 2544; (051) 920 2549 *Fax:* (051) 922 1375
E-mail: nlpiba@paknet2.ptc.pk
Web Site: www.nlp.gov.pk
Key Personnel
Dir General: Mr M A Zaheer

Urdu Science Board
299 Upper Mail, Lahore
Tel: (042) 5758674; (042) 878168 *Fax:* (042) 5758674
Branch Office(s)
Gari Khata, Manzoor Chambers, Hyderabad
Khyber Bazar, Peshawar Branch, Peshawar

Papua New Guinea

Standard Book Numbering Agency
National Library Service of Papua New Guinea, 131, National Capital District, Waigani
Mailing Address: PO Box 734, Waigani
Tel: 3256200 *Fax:* 3251331
E-mail: paraide@datec.com.pg
Web Site: www.dg.com.pg/ola
Telex: NE 22234
Key Personnel
Contact: Mr Chris Kelly Meti
Publication(s): *ISBN Users Manual* (Second Edition, 1991)

Peru

Camara Peruana del Libro (Peruvian Publishers' Association)
Av Abancay 4ta cuadra, Lima
Tel: (01) 428 7690; (01) 428 7696 *Fax:* (01) 427 7331
E-mail: dn@binape.gob.pe
Web Site: www.binape.gob.pe
Key Personnel
President: Julio Cesar Flores Rodriguez
Executive Dir: Dra Loyda Moran Bustamente
Administrator: Guerra Raul Guerra

Standard Book Numbering Agency, see Camara Peruana del Libro

Philippines

†◇**Congress of South-East Asian Librarians IV (CONSAL IV)**
National Historic Institute of the Philippines, T M Kalaw St, 100 Ermita, Manila
Mailing Address: PO Box 2926, 100 Ermita, Manila
Tel: (02) 590646 *Fax:* (02) 572644
Key Personnel
Chairman: Dr Serafin D Quiason

Philippine Educational Publishers' Association
84 P Florentino St, Sta Mesa Heights, Quezon City
Tel: (02) 7124106 *Fax:* (02) 7313448; (02) 7437687
Web Site: nbdb.gov.ph/pubindust.htm
Key Personnel
President: Dominador D Buhain
 E-mail: dbuhain@cnl.net
Founded: 1950
Memberships: International Trade Association; IPA.

Standard Book Numbering Agency, The National Library of the Philippines
Division of Bibliographic Services Division
TM Kalaw St, 1000 Ermita, Manila
Mailing Address: PO Box 2926, Manila
Tel: (02) 5253196; (02) 5251748 *Fax:* (02) 5242324
E-mail: director@nlp.gov.ph
Web Site: www.nlp.gov.ph
Telex: 40726 nalib pm
Key Personnel
ISBN Administrator: Leonila DA Tominez
 E-mail: leat@nlp.gov.ph
Founded: 1900
National library.
Publication(s): *Directory of Printers & Publishers*; *Philippine National Bibliography* (annually, Bibliography of works written by Filipino authors about the Philippines, cumulated quarterly)
Parent Company: The National Library of the Philippines
Ultimate Parent Company: National Commission for Culture & the Arts

Poland

AGPOL (Przedsiebiorstwo Reklamy i Wydawnictw Handlu Zagranicznego)
ul St Kierbedzia 4, skr poczt 7, 00957 Warsaw
Tel: (022) 416061 *Fax:* (022) 405607
Telex: 813364 *Cable:* Agpol Warszawa
Key Personnel
Dir: Mieczyslaw Kroker
Founded: 1956
Offers publicity services abroad for Polish foreign trade & in Poland for foreign companies.

Istytut Bibliograficzny Biblioteka Narodowa, Krajowe Biuro ISBN
al Niepodleglosci 213, 02-086 Warsaw
Tel: (022) 608-2999 *Fax:* (022) 825-5251
E-mail: biblnar@bn.org.pl
Web Site: www.bn.org.pl
Telex: 816761 bn pl
Key Personnel
Dir: Michal Jagiello *Tel:* (022) 608 2233
 E-mail: bndyrekt@bn.org.pl

Krajowe Biuro Miedzynarodowego Numeru Ksiazki ISBN
Biblioteka Narodowa, al Niepodleglosci 213, 02-086 Warsaw
Tel: (022) 608-2410; (022) 608-2433 *Fax:* (022) 608-2433
E-mail: bnisbn@bn.org.pl
Web Site: www.bn.org.pl
Key Personnel
Librarian: Jadwiga Sadowska

National ISBN Agency, see Krajowe Biuro Miedzynarodowego Numeru Ksiazki ISBN

Polish Chamber of Books
Krakowskie Przdmiescie 7, PL-00 068 Warsaw
Tel: (022) 826 12 01 *Fax:* (022) 826 78 55
E-mail: pik@arspolona.com.pl
Web Site: www.pik.org.pl
Key Personnel
President: Mr Andrzej Nowakowski
Vice President: Grzegorz Majerowicz; Krzysztof Raniowski
Executive Dir: Regina Malgorzata Greda
Founded: 1990
Chamber of Commerce.

Polskie Towarzystwo Wydawcow Ksiazek
Mazowiecka 2/4, 00048 Warsaw
Tel: (022) 826 72 71 (ext 345); (022) 826 07 35 *Fax:* (022) 826 07 35 *Cable:* PETEWUKA
Key Personnel
President: Janusz Fogler
Deputy President: Aniela Topulos
General Secretary: Donat Chruscicki
Dir: Maria Kuisz
Polish Society of Book Editors.

Przedsiebiorstwo Reklamy i Wydawnictw Handlu Zagranicznego, see AGPOL (Przedsiebiorstwo Reklamy i Wydawnictw Handlu Zagranicznego)

Standard Book Numbering Agency, see Istytut Bibliograficzny Biblioteka Narodowa, Krajowe Biuro ISBN

Stowarzyszenie Ksiegarzy Polskich (Association of Polish Booksellers)
ul Mokotowska 4/6, 00641 Warsaw
Tel: (022) 252-871; (022) 256-061
Web Site: www.bookweb.org/orgs/1322.html
Key Personnel
President: Tadeusz Hussak
Social organization for State book trade employees.
Publication(s): *Ksiegarz*
ISBN Prefix(es): 83-85020

Zwiazek Literatow Polskich (Union of Polish Letters)
Krakowskie Przedmiescie 87/89, 00-079 Warsaw
Tel: (022) 8260589; (022) 8260866; (022) 8262504
Key Personnel
President: Piotr Kuncewicz
Founded: 1920

POLAND

Union of Polish Writers.
Membership(s): EWC (European Writers' Congress).

Portugal

Associacao Portuguesa de Editores e Livreiros
(Portuguese Publishers & Booksellers Association)
Av dos Estados Unidas da America, n° 97, 6° Esq°, 1700-167 Lisbon
Tel: (021) 843 51 80 *Fax:* (021) 848 93 77
E-mail: geral@apel.pt
Web Site: www.apel.pt
Telex: 62735 Apel P *Cable:* APEL
Key Personnel
President: Graca Didier
Secretary: Joao Miguel Guedes; Vasco Teixeira
Publication(s): *Livros Disponiveis*; *Livros de Portugal, Boletim Bibliografico* (Portuguese Books in Print, monthly)

Standard Book Numbering Agency
Associacao Portuguesa de Editores e Livreiros,
Av dos Estados Unidos da America, n° 97, 6° Esq°, 1700-167 Lisbon
Tel: (021) 843 51 80 *Fax:* (021) 848 93 77
E-mail: isbn@apel.pt
Web Site: www.apel.pt
Key Personnel
ISBN Administrator: Ms Conceicao Tome
Publication(s): *Livros Disponiveis* (Books in Print); *Portuguese Books* (CD Rom)

Puerto Rico

†◇ACURIL
PO Box 23317, UPR Station, San Juan 00931-3317
Tel: (787) 790-8054; (787) 764-0000 (ext 3319)
Fax: (787) 764-2311
E-mail: acuril@rrpac.upr.clu.edu; acuril@coqui.net
Web Site: acuril.rrp.upr.edu
Key Personnel
President: Lucero Arboleda De Roa
Executive Secretary: Oneida R Ortiz
Treasurer: Neida Pagan-Jimenez
Association of Caribbean University, Research & Institutional Libraries.
Publication(s): *ACURIL Newsletter*; *Proceedings of Annual Conference*

Association of Caribbean University, Research & Institutional Libraries, see ACURIL

Ateneo Puertorriqueno
PO Box 9021180, San Juan 00902-1180
Tel: (787) 722-4839; (787) 721-3877 *Fax:* (787) 725-3873
E-mail: info@ateneopr.com
Web Site: www.ateneopr.com
Key Personnel
President: Eduardo Morales, Esq
Vice President: Eladio Rivera Quinones
Executive Dir: Prof Roberto Ramos Perea
Founded: 1876
Puerto Rican Society of Writers. A depository of treasures in works of art, literature, historical documents & memorabilia. Offers literary contests, annual art competitions & short academic courses.

Qatar

Standard Book Numbering Agency
Qatar National Library, PO Box 205, Doha
Tel: 42 9955 *Fax:* 42 9976
E-mail: qanali@qatar.net.qa
Telex: 4743 qanali
Key Personnel
Contact: Mr Sami Abdel Jawad

Romania

†‡Centre Europeen pour l'Enseignement Superieur
39, Stirbei Voda St, 70732 Bucharest
Tel: (01) 3130839; (01) 3130698; (01) 3159956
Fax: (01) 3123567
E-mail: cepes@cepes.ro
Web Site: www.cepes.ro
Key Personnel
Dir: Jan Sadlak
Founded: 1972
Subjects: Higher Education
ISBN Prefix(es): 0-379
Number of titles published annually: 6 Print
Total Titles: 42 Print

Centrul National de Numerotare Standardizata Biblioteca Nationala (National Centre for Standard Numbering ISBN-ISSN-CIP)
Unit of Biblioteca Nationala A Romaniei
Str Ion Ghica 4, sect 3, 79708 Bucharest
Tel: (021) 3112635 *Fax:* (021) 3124990
E-mail: isbn@bibnat.ro; issn@bibnat.ro
Web Site: www.bibnat.ro
Key Personnel
Coordinator & Librarian: Aurelia Persinaru
CIP, Librarian: Laura Margarit
ISBN Librarian: Mihaela Laura Stanciu
Member of ISBN International Agency & ISSN International Centre. Activities for a national ISBN & ISSN agency (record all the Romanian publishers, assign ISBN & ISSN codes, etc). In charge with the management of Romanian Cataloguing in Publication Programme & editor of CIP National Bibliography.
Publication(s): *Bibliografia Cartilor in Curs de Aparitie* (monthly, journal)
ISBN Prefix(es): 973

Societa Ziaristilor din Romania
Piata Presei Libere 1, 71341 Bucharest
Mailing Address: Oficial Postal 33, 71341 Bucharest
Tel: (01) 222 83 51; (01) 222 38 71; (01) 315 24 82 *Fax:* (01) 222 42 66
E-mail: szrpress@moon.rol
Key Personnel
President: Cornelius Popa
First Vice President: Radu Sorescu
Journalists Society of Romania.

Standard Book Numbering Agency, see Centrul National de Numerotare Standardizata Biblioteca Nationala

Uniunea Scriitorilor din Romania (Romanian Writer's Union)
Piata Sf Gheorghe, nr3, 1900 Timisoara
Tel: (0256) 294895 *Fax:* (0256) 294895
Web Site: www.infotim.ro/usrt/usrt.htm
Telex: 11796
Key Personnel
President: Laurentiu Ulici
Secretary: Cornel Ungureanu
Publication(s): *Convorbiri Literare* (Literary Conversations); *Igaz Szo*; *Knijevni Jivot*; *Luceafarul*; *Neue Literatur*; *Orizont* (Horizon); *Romania Literara* (Literary Romania); *Secolul XX* (Twentieth Century); *Steaua* (The Star); *Utunk*; *Vatra*; *Viata Romaneasca* (Romanian Life)

Russian Federation

†◇Association of Research Libraries & Libraries for Science & Technology in the CIS
c/o Russian National Public Library for Science & Technology, 12 Kuznetski most, Moscow 103919
Tel: (095) 925 9288; (095) 924 9458 *Fax:* (095) 921 9862; (095) 925 9750
E-mail: gpntb@gpntb.ru
Web Site: www.gpntb.ru
Key Personnel
President: Andrei Zemskov

†◇International Association of Orientalist Librarians
Oriental Center, Russian State Library, 6/8 Mokhovaya St, Moscow 103009
Tel: (095) 2028852 *Fax:* (095) 2029187
E-mail: oricen@mail.ru
Web Site: www.orient.ru/eng/org/oricen/index.htm
Key Personnel
Librarian: Mrs Benedicte Vaerman
E-mail: benedicte.vaerman@bib.kuleuven.ac.be
Publication(s): *International Association of Orientalist Librarians Bulletin* (biannually)

International Community of Writers' Unions
Ul Povarskaja 52, 121825 Moscow
Tel: (095) 2916307 *Fax:* (095) 2919760
Key Personnel
First Secretary: T Pulator

◇The Press & Publishing Engineering Society
c/o Union of Scientific and Engineering Associations, Kursovoi per 17, 119034 Moscow
Tel: (095) 290-62-86; (095) 291-42-42 *Fax:* (095) 291-85-06
E-mail: sitsev@mail.sitek.ru
Web Site: usea.mailru.com
Key Personnel
Chairman: A Yu Ishlinskii
Scientific & production activities in book publishing.
Parent Company: Union of Scientific & Engineering Societies
Associate Companies: Ministry of Printing & Information of the Russian Federation

Publishers Association
B Nikitskaya St 44, 121069 Moscow
Tel: (095) 2021174 *Fax:* (095) 2023989
Key Personnel
Dir: Mr V Shibaev
Contact: Mr I Laptev

Publishing Council of the Academy of Sciences of the Russian Academy of Sciences
Leninsky prospekt 14, 117901 Moscow
Tel: (095) 952905 *Fax:* (095) 2379107

◇Rossiiskaya Knizhnaya Palata (Russian Book Chamber)
ul Ostozhenka, d ya, 119034 Moscow
Tel: (095) 2911278; (095) 291-96-30 *Fax:* (095) 291-96-30; (095) 202-67-25

E-mail: bookchyu@postman.ru
Web Site: www.bookchamber.ru/international
The Russian Book Chamber
All books & publications are registered & described.
Publication(s): *Knizhnava Letopis'* (Book Chronicle, weekly bulletin & 5 indexes, journal, 2002, informs about all types of books & booklets published in Russia)

Russian Book Chamber
Kremlevskaja nab 1/9, 119019 Moscow
Tel: (095) 2034653; (095) 2035608 *Fax:* (095) 2982576; (095) 2982590
E-mail: chamber@aha.ru
Web Site: www.bookchamber.ru
Key Personnel
Dir-General: Boris Lenski
Chamber also administers Russian National ISBN Agency.

Standard Book Numbering Agency
Russian ISBN Agency, Russian Book Chamber, Kremlevskaja Nab 1/9, 119019 Moscow
Tel: (095) 2034653; (095) 2035608 *Fax:* (095) 2982576; (095) 2982590
E-mail: chamber@aha.ru
Key Personnel
ISBN Administrator: N Smourova
Dir General: Boris Lenski

Saudi Arabia

Standard Book Numbering Agency
King Fahd National Library, Registration & Book Numbering Department, Riyadh 11472
Mailing Address: PO Box 7572, Riyadh 11472
Tel: (01) 464 51 97; (01) 462 48 88 (ext 224); (01) 462 48 88 (ext 601); (01) 462 48 88 (ext 238) *Fax:* (01) 464 53 41; (01) 462 27 07
E-mail: saudi-isbn@kfnl.gov.sa *Cable:* 407599 KFNLR S.J.
Key Personnel
General Dir: Mr Ali S Al-Sowaine

Senegal

†◇**Commission des Bibliotheques de l'AIDBA**
BP 375, Dakar
Tel: 240954
Key Personnel
Secretary: Emmanuel K W Dadzie
Association internationale pour le Developpement de la Documentation des Bibliotheques et des Archives en Afrique
International Association for the Development of Libraries and Archives in Africa.

†◇**Standing Conference of African Library Schools (SCALS)**
Universite Cheikh Anta Diop de Darkar, BP 5005, Dakar
Tel: (08) 250530 *Fax:* (08) 255219
Telex: 51-262

Serbia and Montenegro

Association of Yugoslav Publishers & Booksellers
Kneza Milosa 25, 11000 Belgrade
Mailing Address: POB 570, 11000 Belgrade
Tel: (011) 642-248; (011) 642-533 *Fax:* (011) 646-339
E-mail: ognjenl@eunet.yu
Web Site: www.beobookfair.co.yu
Key Personnel
General Dir: Mr Ognjen Lakicevic
 E-mail: ognjenl@eunet.yu
Publisher: Mrs Mirjana Popovic
Founded: 1954
Voluntary non-governmental organization. Represents members at home, abroad & by international organizations (IPA, Geneva). Organizer of the International Book Fair in Belgrade, Publishing activities
Membership(s): International Publishers Association, Geneva.
Publication(s): *Catalog of Yugoslav Books in Print*; *Catalogue of Book Fairs in Belgrade*; *Directory of Exhibitors at the International Book Fair in Belgrade*; *Directory of Members of the Association of Yugoslav Publishers & Booksellers* (annually)
ISBN Prefix(es): 86-7115

Jugoslovenski Bibliografsko-informacijski institut, Yubin, Agencija za ISBN (Yugoslav Institute for Bibliography & Information)
Terazije 26, 11000 Belgrade
Tel: (011) 687 836; (011) 688 840 *Fax:* (011) 687 760; (011) 688 840
E-mail: yubin@jbi.bg.ac.yu
Web Site: www.jbi.bg.ac.yu/
Key Personnel
Dir: Dr Radomir Glavicki
Head of International Exchange Dept: Tanja Ostojic *E-mail:* tanya@jbi.bg.ac.yu
Founded: 1950
Specializes in the production of National bibliography.
Publication(s): *Bibliography of Yugoslavia* (Bibliografija Jugoslavije)
Number of titles published annually: 8 Print
Total Titles: 8 Print

Standard Book Numbering Agency, see Jugoslovenski Bibliografsko-informacijski institut, Yubin, Agencija za ISBN

Singapore

SBPA, see Singapore Book Publishers' Association

Singapore Book Publishers' Association
c/o Cannon International, Block 86, Marine Parade Central No 03-213, Singapore 440086
Tel: (065) 3447801; (065) 4407409 *Fax:* (065) 4470897
E-mail: twcsbpa@singnet.com.sg
Key Personnel
President: K P Siram
Dir: Mr Tan Wu Cheng
Founded: 1966
Memberships: International Publishers Association (Geneva); Asia Pacific Publishers Association (Seoul).

Standard Book Numbering Agency
National Library Board, No 3 Changi South St 2, Tower B, Level 3, Singapore 486548
Tel: 6546 7271 *Fax:* 6546 7262
E-mail: legaldep@nlb.gov.sg
Web Site: www.nlb.gov.sg
Telex: Rs 26620 *Cable:* NATLIB SINGAPORE
Key Personnel
ISBN Administrators: Mrs Lim Siew Kim; Ms N Dana Lashmi
Publication(s): *Books About Singapore* (biannually); *Singapore National Bibliography* (quarterly/annually); *Singapore: National Library*; *Singapore Periodicals Index* (annually)

Slovakia

ISBN National Agency
Slovak National Library, Nam J C Hronskeho 1, 036 01 Martin
Tel: (043) 430 1802 *Fax:* (043) 430 1802
E-mail: snk@snk.sk
Web Site: www.snk.sk
Key Personnel
Contact: Jarmila Majerova *E-mail:* majerova@snk.sk
Founded: 1989
Parent Company: Slovak National Library

◇**Spolok slovenskych spisovatel'ov**
Laurinska 2, 815 08 Bratislava
Tel: (07) 533 53 71
Key Personnel
Honor Chairman: Ladislav Tazky
Chairman: Jaroslav Reznik
President: Mr Vincent Sikula
Founded: 1949
Association of Slovak Writers.
Publication(s): *Literarny Tyzdhennik* (Literary Weekly)
Associate Companies: Asociacia organizacii1 Slovenska, Ste Fanikova 14, 81508 Bratislava

Slovenia

Gospodarska Zbornica Slovenije, see Zdruzenie Zaloznikov in Knjigotrzcev Slovenije Gospodarska Zbornica Slovenije

Standard Book Numbering Agency
National & University Library, Turjaska 1, p p 259, 1000 Ljubljana
Tel: (01) 5861 333 *Fax:* (01) 5861 311
E-mail: isbn@nuk.uni-lj.si
Web Site: www.nuk.uni-lj.si

◇**Zdruzenie Zaloznikov in Knjigotrzcev Slovenije Gospodarska Zbornica Slovenije**
(Association of Publishers & Booksellers of Slovenia)
Dimiceva 13, Ljubljana 1504
Tel: (01) 5898 474 *Fax:* (01) 5898 100
E-mail: info@gzs.si
Web Site: www.gzs.si
Key Personnel
President, Association: Milan Matos
Membership(s): International Publishers Association.
Publication(s): *Knjiga*

South Africa

CDNL, see Conference of Directors of National Libraries (CDNL)

†◇Conference of Directors of National Libraries (CDNL)
The State Library of South Africa, Andries & Vermeulen Sts, 0001 Pretoria
Mailing Address: PO Box 397, Pretoria 0001
Tel: (012) 21 8931 *Fax:* (012) 32 5594
E-mail: postmaster@statelib.pwv.gov.za
Key Personnel
Chairperson: P J Lor
Vice Chairperson: M A Kadir; W van Drimmelen
Founded: 1980

The Director State Library
Vermeulen St 239, Pretoria
Tel: (012) 321 8931 *Fax:* (012) 321 8931
E-mail: postmaster@statelib.pwv.gov.za
Web Site: www.nlsa.ac.za

International Standard Book Numbering Agency
Vermeulen St 239, Pretoria
Mailing Address: PO Box 397, 0001 Pretoria
Tel: (012) 321 8931 *Fax:* (012) 325 5984
E-mail: therese@statelib.pwv.gov.za
Web Site: www.nlsa.ac.za
Branch Office(s)
5 Queen Victoria St, PO Box 496, 8000 Cape Town *Tel:* (021) 424 6320 *Fax:* (021) 423 3359

PASA, see Publishers' Association of South Africa (PASA)

Publishers' Association of South Africa (PASA)
7 Warick House, 150 Main Rd, Fish Hoek
Mailing Address: PO Box 22640, Fish Hoek, Cape Town 7974
Tel: (021) 782 7677 *Fax:* (021) 782 7679
E-mail: pasa@publishsa.co.za
Web Site: www.publishsa.co.za
Key Personnel
Manager: Louise Gain *E-mail:* louise@publishsa.co.za
Administrator: Desiree Murdoch
  E-mail: desiree@publishsa.co.za
Founded: 1992
Publication(s): *PASA Directory* (annually, list of members)

South African Booksellers' Association
PO Box 870, Bellville 7530
Tel: (021) 918 8616 *Fax:* (021) 951 4903
E-mail: fnel@naspers.com
Web Site: sabooksellers.com
Key Personnel
Chairman & President: Guru Redhi
Secretary: Peter Adams
Founded: 1998

Standard Book Numbering Agency, see The Director State Library

Spain

Agencia Espanola del ISBN
Santiago Rusinol, 8, 28040 Madrid
Tel: (091) 536 88 00 *Fax:* (091) 553 99 90
Web Site: www.mcu.es/bases/spa/isbn/ISBN.html
Telex: 47891 fcli e

Key Personnel
Head of Service: Maria Yribarren *E-mail:* maria.yribarren@cll.mcu.es
Ministerio de Educacion y Cultura.

Asociacion de Escritores y Artistas Espanoles
  (Spanish Writers' & Artists' Association)
Leganitos 10, 28013 Madrid
Tel: (091) 5599067 *Fax:* (091) 5599067
Key Personnel
Secretary: Jose Lopez Martinez
ISBN Prefix(es): 84-404; 84-398; 84-87857

Associacio d'Editors en Llengua Catalana
  (Association of Publishers in Catalan)
Valencia 279, 1r, 08009 Barcelona
Tel: (093) 155091 *Fax:* (093) 155273
E-mail: info@gremieditorscat.es
Web Site: www.gremieditorscat.es

Federacion de Gremios de Editores de Espana (FGEE) (Spanish Publishers Association)
Cea Bermudez, 44-2° Dehe, Madrid 20003
Tel: (091) 5345195 *Fax:* (091) 5352625
E-mail: fgee@fge.es
Web Site: www.federacioneditores.org
Telex: 48457 Fgee E
Key Personnel
President: D Emiliano Martinez
Executive Dir: Antonio Ma Avila
Founded: 1978
Professional Association of Publishers.
Subjects: To represent & defend the general interests of the Spanish publishing industry

Standard Book Numbering Agency, see Agencia Espanola del ISBN

UMA, see World Blind Union (WBU) - Union Mondiale des Aveugles (UMA)

WBU, see World Blind Union (WBU) - Union Mondiale des Aveugles (UMA)

†◇World Blind Union (WBU) - Union Mondiale des Aveugles (UMA)
c/o CPB Organization Nacional de Ciegos Espanoles, La Coruna 18, 28020 Madrid
Tel: (091) 5713685; (091) 5711236 *Fax:* (091) 5715777
E-mail: umc@once.es
Web Site: www.once.es/wbu
Key Personnel
Secretary General: Pedro Zurita
Founded: 1984
Publication(s): *The World Blind* (2 times/yr, Les Aveugles dans le Monde & Los Ciegos en el Mundo)

Sri Lanka

†◇The International Irrigation Management Institute
127, Sunil Mawatha, Pelawatte, Battaramulla
Mailing Address: PO Box 2075, Colombo
Tel: (011) 2787404; (011) 2784080 *Fax:* (011) 2786854
E-mail: iwmi@cgiar.org
Web Site: www.cgiar.org
Telex: 22318; 22907 IIMIHQCE
Key Personnel
Dir General: Prof Frank Rijsberman
Head of Information: Dr James K Lenahan
Founded: 1956

An autonomous nonprofit International Organization. Member of the Consultative Group on International Agricultural Research (CGIAR).
ISBN Prefix(es): 92-9090

Sri Lanka Association of Publishers
112 S Mahinda Mawatha, Colombo 10
Tel: (01) 695773 *Fax:* (01) 696653
Key Personnel
Dir: Dayawansa Jayakody
  E-mail: dayawansajay@hotmail.com
General Secretary: Gamini Wijesuriya
Publication(s): *Hela Bima* (newspaper); *Publishing Scene* (newsletter)

†◇Standard Book Numbering Agency (ISBN Agency-Sri Lanka)
14 Independence Ave, Colombo 7
Mailing Address: PO Box 1764, Colombo
Tel: (01) 698847; (01) 685198 *Fax:* (01) 685201
E-mail: natlib@slt.lk *Cable:* NATLIB
Key Personnel
Dir: Matarage Sarath Upali Amarasiri
Founded: 1990
Subjects: Social Sciences, Humanities, Science & Technology, Computer Science, Library & Information Science, Literature, Regional Interests, Mass Communication (mainly material on Sri Lanka)
Publication(s): *International Standard Book numbering in Sri Lanka* (2nd edition, brochure); *Sri Lanka (ISBN) Publishers Directory* (1991 & 1999 editions)
ISBN Prefix(es): 955-9011

Sudan

Sudanese Publishers' Association
c/o Institute of African & Asian Studies, Khartoum University, PO Box 321, Khartoum 11115
Tel: (0249) 11-7780031 *Fax:* (0249) 11-770358
Key Personnel
Dir: Abel Rahim Makkawi *E-mail:* makkawi@sudanmail.net

Suriname

Standard Book Numbering Agency
Publishers' Association Suriname, Domineestr 32 boven, Paramaribo
Mailing Address: PO Box 1841, Paramaribo
Tel: 472545 *Fax:* 410563
E-mail: postmaster@interfundgroup.com
Telex: 123 inco-sn
Key Personnel
ISBN Administrator: Mr E Hogenboom
ISBN Prefix(es): 99914

Swaziland

The Librarian, University College of Swaziland
Private Bag 4, Kwaluseni
Tel: 5184011 *Fax:* 5185276
E-mail: kwaluseni@uniswa.sz
Web Site: www.uniswa.sz
Telex: 2087
Key Personnel
Librarian: M R Mavuso *E-mail:* mmavuso@uniswac1.uniswa.sz

Sweden

Foreningen Svenska Laromedelsproducenter (The Swedish Association of Educational Publishers
Drottninggatan 97, 2nd floor, 113 60 Stockholm
Tel: (08) 736 19 40 *Fax:* (08) 736 19 44
E-mail: fsl@fsl.se
Web Site: www.fsl.se
Key Personnel
Dir: Jerker Fransson *Tel:* (08) 736 19 46
 E-mail: jerker.fransson@forlagskansli.se
Founded: 1974
Trade association for educational publishers.
ISBN Prefix(es): 91-85386
Associate Companies: The Swedish Publishers Association

Svenska Forlaggareforeningen (Swedish Publishers' Association)
Drottninggatan 97, 113 60 Stockholm
Tel: (08) 736 19 40 *Fax:* (08) 736 19 44
E-mail: info@forlaggareforeningen.se
Web Site: www.forlaggareforeningen.se
Key Personnel
Dir: Kristina Ahlinder
Founded: 1843
Publication(s): *Svensk Bokhandel* (jointly with the Swedish Booksellers' Association)

The Swedish Association of Educational Publishers (Foreningen Svenska Laromedelsproducenter), see Foreningen Svenska Laromedelsproducenter (The Swedish Association of Educational Publishers

Switzerland

AIESI, see Association Internationale des Ecoles des Sciences de l'Information

ASELF, see Association Suisse des Editeurs de Langue Francaise

†◇**Association Internationale des Ecoles des Sciences de l'Information** (International Association of Information Science Schools)
Unit of Agence Universitaire de la Francophonie
Haute Ecole de Gestion, Information et documentation, 7, route de Drize, 1227 Carouge
Tel: (022) 705 99 77 *Fax:* (022) 705 99 98
Web Site: www.aiesi.refer.org
Key Personnel
President: Jacqueline Deschamps *Tel:* (022) 705 99 69 *E-mail:* jacqueline.deschamps@heg.ge.ch
Founded: 1977

Association Suisse des Editeurs de Langue Francaise (Swiss Publishers' Association (French Language))
2, ave Agassiz, 1001 Lausanne
Tel: (021) 319 71 11 *Fax:* (021) 319 79 10
Telex: 455730
Key Personnel
Secretary General: Philippe Schibli
 E-mail: pschibli@centrezational.cl
ISBN Prefix(es): 2-88303

Association Suisse des Libraires de Langue Francaise (Association of Swiss French-Language Bookshops)
2 ave Agassiz, 1001 Lausanne
Tel: (021) 319 71 11 *Fax:* (021) 319 79 10
E-mail: aself@centrezational.cl
Telex: 455730
Key Personnel
Secretary: Philippe Schibli *E-mail:* pschibli@centrezational.cl
ISBN Prefix(es): 2-88303

Association Suisse Romande des Diffuseurs et Distributeurs de Livres (Association of Book Distributors of French-Speaking Switzerland)
2 ave Agassiz, 1001 Lausanne
Tel: (021) 319 71 11 *Fax:* (021) 319 79 10
E-mail: aself@centrezational.ch
Telex: 455730
Key Personnel
President: Antonio Jaccheo
Contact: Philippe Schibli *E-mail:* pschibli@centrezational.cl

Buchverleger-Verband der Deutschsprachigen Schweiz (VVDS) (Swiss Publishers Association)
Alderstr 40, 8034 Zurich
Tel: (01) 421 28 00 *Fax:* (01) 421 28 18
E-mail: sbvv@swissbooks.ch
Web Site: www.swissbooks.ch
Key Personnel
ISBN Administrator: Stefanie Nuebling *Tel:* (01) 421 28 01 *E-mail:* isbn@swissbooks.ch
This is the agency for German-language ISBNs.
Parent Company: Swiss Booksellers & Publishers Association

†**Conference of European Churches**
150 route de Ferney, 1211 Geneva 2
Mailing Address: PO Box 2100, 1211 Geneva 2
Tel: (022) 791 61 11 *Fax:* (022) 791 62 27
E-mail: cec@cec-kek.org
Web Site: www.cec-kek.org
Telex: 415 730 0IK CH *Cable:* OIKOUMENE, GENEVA
Key Personnel
General Secretary: Rev Keith Winston Clements
Associate General Secretary: Rev Ruediger Noll
Communications Secretary: Mr Robin Gurney
 Tel: (022) 791 6485 *E-mail:* reg@cec-kek.org
Founded: 1959
Subjects: Ecumenical Theology, International Relationships
Publication(s): *God Unites; In Christ a New Creation* (1992, English, French & German); *Springs Within the Valleys* (1997, English, French & German); *Working Together With Him* (1997, English, French & German)
ISBN Prefix(es): 2-88070
Branch Office(s)
Strasbourg, France
Brussels, Belgium

†◇**Distripress**
Beethovenstr 20, 8002 Zurich
Tel: (0411) 202 41 21 *Fax:* (0411) 202 10 25
E-mail: info@distripress.ch
Web Site: www.distripress.ch
Key Personnel
Man Dir: Dr Peter Emod *E-mail:* peter.emod@distripress.ch
Founded: 1955
Association pour la Promotion de la Diffusion Internationale de la Presse
Vereinigung zur Foerderung des internationalen Pressevertriebes
Membership(s): World Association of Newspapers; European Newspaper Publishers' Association.
Publication(s): *Distripress Gazette* (3 times/yr); *Who's Who in Distripress* (annually)

IBBY, see International Board on Books for Young People (IBBY)

ILO, see International Labour Organization (ILO)

†**Inter-Parliamentary Union**
5, chemin du Pommier, 1218 Le Grand Saconnex/Geneva
Mailing Address: PO Box 330, 1218 Le Grand Saconnex/Geneva
Tel: (022) 919 41 50 *Fax:* (022) 919 41 60
E-mail: postbox@mail.ipu.org
Web Site: www.ipu.org
Key Personnel
Secretary General: Anders B Johnsson
Information Officer: Luisa Ballin *Tel:* (022) 919 41 16 *E-mail:* lb@mail.ipu.org
Founded: 1889
World organization of national parliaments.
Publication(s): *Codes of Conduct for Elections* (1998, CS Goodwin-Gill); *The Conference of Presiding Officers of National Parliaments* (2001); *Declaration on Criteria for Free & Fair Elections* (1994); *Democracy: Its Principles & Achievement* (1998); *Free & Fair Elections: International Law & Practice* (1994, GS Goodwin-Gill); *Handbook for Parliamentarians: Eliminating the Worst Forms of Child Labour* (2002); *Handbook for Parliamentarians: Refugee Protection, A Guide to International Refugee Law* (2001); *Handbook for Parliamentarians: Respect for International Humanitarian Law* (1999); *The Parliamentary Mandate* (2000); *Presiding Officers of National Parliamentary Assemblies* (1997, G Bergougnous); *Universal Declaration on Democracy* (1997)
ISBN Prefix(es): 92-9142

†◇**International Board on Books for Young People (IBBY)**
Nonnenweg 12, 4003 Basel
Tel: (061) 272 29 17 *Fax:* (061) 272 27 57
E-mail: ibby@ibby.org
Web Site: www.ibby.org
Key Personnel
Executive Dir: Kimete Basha
Administrative Dir: Elizabeth Page
Founded: 1953
Publication(s): *Bookbird: A Journal of International Children's Literature* (quarterly); *Congress Proceedings* (biennially); *IBBY Honour List* (biennially)

†‡**International Commission of Jurists**
81a Ave de Chatelaine, 1219 Geneva
Mailing Address: PO Box 216, 1219 Geneva
Tel: (022) 979 38 00 *Fax:* (022) 979 38 01
E-mail: info@icj.org
Web Site: www.icj.org
Telex: 418 531 ICJ CH *Cable:* INTERJURISTS, GENEVA
Key Personnel
Secretary-General: Ernst Lueber
Founded: 1952
Subjects: Human Rights, International Law
Publication(s): *ICJ Newsletter; The Review*
ISBN Prefix(es): 92-9037

†‡**International Institute for Labour Studies**
4, route des Morillons, 1211 Geneva 22
Tel: (022) 799 6111 *Fax:* (022) 798 8685
E-mail: ilo@ilo.org
Web Site: www.ilo.org
Telex: 415647 ilo ch
Key Personnel
Dir: Padmanabha Gopinath
Founded: 1960
Publication(s): *The Bibliography Series; Discussion Papers; Organized Labour in the 21st Century; The Research Series*

†◇**International Labour Organization (ILO)**
4, route des Morillons, 1211 Geneva 22
Tel: (022) 799 6111 *Fax:* (022) 798 8685
E-mail: ilo@ilo.org
Web Site: www.ilo.org
Telex: 415 647 ilo ch *Cable:* INTERLAB GENEVA
Key Personnel
Dir: Ms L Stoddart *Tel:* (022) 799 6092
 E-mail: stoddart@ilo.org
Dir-General: Michel Hansenne
Chief, Publications Bureau: David Freedman
Chief, Marketing Operations: Luisito Cabrera
Rights Services: Susan Peters
Business Manager: Neal Thornton
Production Editor: May Ballerio
Editor: Francois Crozon; John Myers; Lillian Nell; Carlos Sebilla
Sales: Denis Brodier; Gloria Manghinang; Nicole Vallee
Founded: 1919
From the creation of the ILO in 1919, publishing has formed an important part of its activities. The ILO publishes books, reports & periodicals of international interest on major social, labor & economic problems & trends falling within their competence. This substantial publishing program has over 1300 titles in English, 827 in French & 650 in Spanish (editions in print) which cover studies, monographs, handbooks, training materials & periodicals.
Subjects: Reports for the *International Labor Conference,* Regional Conferences & Sectoral Meetings, Equality of Rights, International Labor Standards, Conditions of Work & Welfare Facilities, Cooperatives, Developing Countries & Technical Cooperation, Economics, Industrial Relations, Intermediate Technology, Employment Development, Structural Adjustment, Rural Development & Employment Planning, Human Rights & Apartheid, Labor Law & Labor Administration, International Migration & Population Questions, Multinationals, Productivity & Management Development & Training, Occupational Safety & Health, Social Security, Trade Unions, Vocational Guidance & Training, Wages & Hours of Work, Vocational Rehabilitation, Workers' Education, Women's Questions, Labor Information, Statistics, Bibliographies & Periodicals, Audiovisual Material, Microfiches & CD-ROM
ISBN Prefix(es): 92-2
Branch Office(s)
Guillermo Prieto No 94, Colonia San Rafael, Ave Cordoba 950, 06470 Mexico DF, Mexico
Piso 13 y 14, 1054 Buenos Aires, Argentina
Hohenzollernstr 21, 53173 Bonn, Germany
East Court, 3rd floor, India Habitat Centre, Lodi Rd, New Delhi 110 003, India
8th floor, UNU Headquarters Bldg, 53-70 Jingumae 5-chome, Shibuya-ku, Toyko 150, Japan
Millbank Tower, 21-24 Millbank, London SWlP 4QP, United Kingdom
U.S. Office(s): ILO Publications Center, 49 Sheridan Ave, Albany, NY 12210, United States

†**International Organization for Standardization (ISO)**
CP 56, One rue de Varembe, 1211 Geneva 20
Tel: (022) 749 01 11 *Fax:* (022) 733 34 30
E-mail: central@iso.org
Web Site: www.iso.org
Key Personnel
Secretary General: Alan Bryden
Founded: 1947
Worldwide Federation of national standards bodies with some 140 members (one per country).
Subjects: Development of International Standards in all fields except electrical & electronic engineering
ISBN Prefix(es): 92-67
U.S. Office(s): American National Standards Institute (ANSI), 1819 "L" St, NW, Washington, DC 20036, United States *Tel:* 212-642-4900 *Fax:* 212-398-0023 *E-mail:* info@ansi.org *Web Site:* www.ansi.org (Postal Address: 25 W 23 St, 4th floor, New York, NY 10036)

†◇**International Publishers Association**
Av de Miremont 3, 1206 Geneva
Tel: (022) 346 3018 *Fax:* (022) 347 5717
E-mail: secretariat@ipa-uie.org
Web Site: www.ipa-uie.org
Key Personnel
President: Pere Vicens Rahola
Vice President: Dr Ana Maria Cabanellas de las Cuevas; Asoke K Ghosh
Treasurer: Hans-Peter Thur
Secretary General: Jens Bammel
Founded: 1896

†‡**International Road Federation**
chemin de Blandonnet 2, 1214 Vernier (Geneva)
Tel: (022) 306 0260 *Fax:* (022) 306 0270
E-mail: info@irfnet.org
Web Site: www.irfnet.org
Key Personnel
Dir General & Chief Executive Officer: Wim Westerhuis
President: Alain Dupont
Publications: C de Jong Bozkurt
Founded: 1948
Subjects: Road Transport; Road Infrastructure
ISBN Prefix(es): 92-9106
U.S. Office(s): The Watergate Office Bldg, 2600 Virginia Ave NW, Suite 208, Washington, DC 20037, United States *Tel:* 202-338-4641 *Fax:* 202-338-8104

†‡**International Telecommunication Union (ITU)**
Place des Nations, 1211 Geneva 20
Tel: (022) 730 5111 *Fax:* (022) 733 7256
E-mail: itumail@itu.int
Web Site: www.itu.int/home/contact/index.html
Telex: 421000 Uit
Key Personnel
Executive Manager: Claus Ilg *E-mail:* claus.ilg@itu.int
The ITU was founded in 1865 as the International Telegraphic Union. It became the International Telecommunication Union in 1934 & a specialized agency of the UN in 1947. Structure: 4 permanent organizations - General Secretariat, International Telegraph & Telephone Consultative Committee (CCITT), International Radio Consultative Committee (CCIR) & the International Frequency Registration Board (IFRB). It regulates, plans, coordinates & standardizes international telecommunications.
ISBN Prefix(es): 92-61; 92-71; 92-72; 92-73; 92-74

†‡**International Union Against Cancer**
Affiliate of Council for International Organizations of Medical Sciences
3 Rue du Conseil General, 1205 Geneva
Tel: (022) 809 18 11 *Fax:* (022) 809 18 10
E-mail: info@uicc.org
Web Site: www.uicc.org
Key Personnel
Communications Manager: Steve Donnet
 Tel: (022) 809 18 75 *E-mail:* donnet@uicc.org
Founded: 1933
Objectives are to advance scientific & medical knowledge in research, diagnosis, treatment & prevention of cancer & promote all other aspects of the campaign against cancer throughout the world.
Publication(s): *Association of UICC Fellows Membership Directory* (2000); *International Directory of Cancer Institutes & Organizations* (online only)

ISO, see International Organization for Standardization (ISO)

IUCN, see World Conservation Union (IUCN)

◇**Schweizerischer Buchhaendler- und Verleger-Verband SBVV** (Swiss Booksellers' & Publishers' Association (German Language))
Alderstr 40, 8034 Zurich
Tel: (01) 421 28 00 *Fax:* (01) 421 28 18
E-mail: sbvv@swissbooks.ch
Web Site: www.swissbooks.ch
Key Personnel
Executive Dir: Dr Martin Jann
Secretary: Eva Heberlein
Further Education: Susanne Weibel
Accountant: Ernst Kaeppeli
ISBN Agentur: Stefanie Nuebling
 E-mail: stefanie.nuebling@swissbooks.ch
Publication(s): *Adressbuch des Schweizer Buchhandels; Das Schweizer Buch; Der Schweizer Buchhandel* (bimonthly, Official organ of this association, also its French equivalent SLESR & its Italian equivalents SESI & ALSI); *Schweizer Buecherverzeichnis; Verzeichnis der Auslieferungsstellen*

SLESR, see Societe des Libraires et Editeurs de la Suisse Romande (SLESR)

Societe des Libraires et Editeurs de la Suisse Romande (SLESR) (Booksellers' & Publishers' Association of French-Speaking Switzerland)
2 Ave Agassiz, 1001 Lausanne
Tel: (021) 319 71 11 *Fax:* (021) 319 79 10
E-mail: aself@centrezational.cl
Web Site: www.culturactif.ch/editions/asef1.htm
Key Personnel
Dir: Philippe Schibli
Publication(s): *La Librairie suisse* (official organ of this association, also its German equivalent SBVV & its Italian equivalents SESI & ALSI)
ISBN Prefix(es): 2-88303

Standard Book Numbering Agency, see Buchverleger-Verband der Deutschsprachigen Schweiz (VVDS)

UNCTAD, see United Nations Conference on Trade and Development (UNCTAD)

UNECE, see United Nations Economic Commission for Europe (UNECE)

Union Interparlementaire, see Inter-Parliamentary Union

†‡**United Nations Conference on Trade and Development (UNCTAD)**
Palais des Nations, 8-14, Av de la Paix, 1211 Geneva 10
Tel: (022) 917 1234; (022) 917 5809 *Fax:* (022) 907 0043
E-mail: info@unctad.org
Web Site: www.unctad.org
Telex: 412962 *Cable:* UNATIONS GENEVA
Key Personnel
Secretary-General: Edna Dos Santos-Duisenberg
Chief Reference Service: A Von Wartensleben
 E-mail: wartensleben@unctad.org
Founded: 1964
Subjects: Trade & Development

†‡**United Nations Economic Commission for Europe (UNECE)**
Palais des Nations, 1211 Geneva 10
Tel: (022) 917 12 34 *Fax:* (022) 917 05 05
E-mail: info.ece@unece.org
Web Site: www.unece.org
Telex: 41 29 62

Key Personnel
Executive Secretary: Brigita Schmoegnerova
Information Officer: Jean Michel Jakobowicz
Founded: 1947
Provides technical assistance to countries in transition & regional framework for the elaboration of conventions, norms & standards.
Subjects: Economic Analysis, Environmental, Transport, Energy, Timber, Statistics, Trade
ISBN Prefix(es): 92-1
U.S. Office(s): Regional Commissions New York Office, New York, NY 10017, United States, Director: Ms S Al-Bassam *Tel:* 212-963-8090 *Fax:* 212-963-1500 *E-mail:* rcnyo@un.org

†‡United Nations Research Institute for Social Development (UNRISD)
Palais des Nations, 1211 Geneva 10
Tel: (022) 917 3020 *Fax:* (022) 917 0650
E-mail: info@unrisd.org
Web Site: www.unrisd.org
Telex: 412962 UNOCH *Cable:* UNATIONS GENEVA
Key Personnel
Dir: Thandika Mkandawire
Deputy Dir: Peter Utting
Information Officer: Nicolas Bovay *Tel:* (022) 917 1143 *E-mail:* bovay@unrisd.org
Founded: 1963
Engages in multidisciplinary research on the social dimensions of contemporary problems affecting development.
Subjects: Technology & society; social policy & development; civil society & social movements; democracy & human rights; identities, conflict & cohesion
Publication(s): *The Accommodation of Cultural Diversity* (Case studies & public policy); *Agricultural Expansion & Tropical Deforestation: Poverty, International Trade & Land Use*; *Cambodia Reborn? The Transition to Democracy & Development*; *Derechos@Glob.net: Globalizacion y derechos humanos en America latina*; *Discours et realites des politiques participatives de gestion de l'environnement: Le cas du Senegal*; *Discours et Realites des Politiques Participatives de Geston de L'Environment*; *Ethnic Diversity & Public Policy: A Comparative Inquiry*; *Forest Policy & Politics in the Philippines: The Dynamics of Participatory Conservation*; *Gendered Poverty & Well-Being*; *Ghana's Adjustment Experience*; *La mano visible: Asumir la responsabilidad por el desarrollo social*; *Land Reform & Peasant Livelihoods: The Social Dynamics of Rural Poverty & Agrarian Reforms in Developing Countries*; *Le conflit libanais: Communautes religieuses, classes sociales et identite nationale*; *Lima megaciudad: Democracia, desarrollo y descentralizacion en sectores populares*; *Mains visibles: Assumer la responsabilite du developpement social*; *Missionaries & Mandarins: Feminist Engagement with Development Institutions*; *The Native Tourists: Mass Tourism within Developing Countries*; *Post-Conflict Eritrea: Prospects for Reconstruction & Development*; *Rebuilding Social & Economic Progress in Africa: Essays in the Memory of Philip Ndegwa*; *Renewing Social & Economic Transformation in East Central Europe*; *Rights@Glob.Net: Globalization & Human Rights in Latin America*; *Social Development & Public Policy*; *UNRISD News* (biannually, newsletter); *Visible Hands: Taking Responsibility for Social Development*; *Whose Land? Civil Society Perspective on Land Reform & Rural Poverty Reduction, Regional Experiences from Africa, Asia & Latin America*
ISBN Prefix(es): 92-9085
Total Titles: 95 Print

†‡Universal Postal Union (UPU)
CP 13, 3000 Berne 15
Tel: (031) 350 31 11 *Fax:* (031) 350 31 10
E-mail: info@upu.int
Web Site: www.upu.int *Cable:* UPU BERNE
Key Personnel
Dir-General: Thomas E Leavey
Head External Communications: James H Gunderson *Tel:* (031) 350 32 01 *E-mail:* james.gunderson@upu.int
Founded: 1874
Subjects: Postal matters
Publication(s): *Union Postale* (quarterly)
ISBN Prefix(es): 92-62

UNRISD, see United Nations Research Institute for Social Development (UNRISD)

UPU, see Universal Postal Union (UPU)

Vereinigung der Buchantiquare und Kupferstichhaendler in der Schweiz
(Association of Swiss Antiquarian Book & Print Dealers)
Kirchgasse 22, 8001 Zurich
Mailing Address: PO Box 675, 8001 Zurich
Tel: (01) 261 57 50 *Fax:* (01) 793 19 33
E-mail: eos@eos.ch
Web Site: www.vebuku.ch
Key Personnel
President: Marcus Benz
Founded: 1939
Membership(s): International League of Antiquarian Booksellers (ILAB).

Vereinigung des katholischen Buchandels der Schweiz
Perolles 42, CH-1705 Fribourg
Tel: (026) 4 26 43 11 *Fax:* (026) 4 26 43 00
Association of Swiss Catholic Booksellers & Publishers.

VVDS, see Buchverleger-Verband der Deutschsprachigen Schweiz (VVDS)

WARC, see World Alliance of Reformed Churches

Weltverband der Lehrmittelfirmen, see Worlddidac

WHO, see World Health Organization (WHO)

WIPO, see World Intellectual Property Organization (WIPO)

WMO, see World Meteorological Organization

†World Alliance of Reformed Churches
150 Route de Ferney, 1211 Geneva 2
Mailing Address: PO Box 2100, 1211 Geneva 2
Tel: (022) 791 6240 *Fax:* (022) 791 6505
E-mail: warc@warc.ch
Web Site: www.warc.ch *Cable:* WARC GENEVA
Key Personnel
Secretary General: Rev Setri Nyomi
Administrative Assistant & Communications Office: Sally J Redondo *Tel:* (022) 791 6235 *E-mail:* sjr@warc.ch
Founded: 1875
Subjects: Biblical Studies, Regional Interests, Protestant Religion, Theology, Women's Studies, Ecological Issues, Economic & Social Justice
Publication(s): *Reformed World* (quarterly, journal, Annual subscription); *Update* (quarterly, newsletter, Annual subscription)
ISBN Prefix(es): 92-9075

World Association of Publishers, Manufacturers & Distributors of Educational Materials, see Worlddidac

†World Conservation Union (IUCN)
Rue Mauverney 28, 1196 Gland
Tel: (022) 999 0000 *Fax:* (022) 999 0002
E-mail: mail@iucn.org
Web Site: www.iucn.org *Cable:* IUCNATURE GLAND
Key Personnel
President: Yolanda Kakabadse Navarro *E-mail:* president@iucn.org
Dir-General: Achim Steiner *Tel:* (022) 999 0297 *Fax:* (022) 999 0029 *E-mail:* achim.steiner@iucn.org
Founded: 1948
Subjects: Analytical reports on Eastern Europe; Biodiversity; Ecosystems; Forests; Mountains; Wetlands, Coastal & Marine Areas; Environmental Education; Environmental Law & Policy; Social Policy; Sustainable use initiatives & threatened species
ISBN Prefix(es): 2-8317; 2-88032

†‡World Health Organization (WHO)
(Organisation mondiale de la Sante)
Ave Appia, 20, 1211 Geneva 27
Tel: (022) 791 2111 *Fax:* (022) 791 3111
E-mail: publications@who.int
Web Site: www.who.int *Cable:* UNISANTE-GENEVE
Key Personnel
Dir General: Dr G H Brundtland
Chief, Marketing: A C Wieboldt *Tel:* (022) 791 2476 *E-mail:* wieboldta@who.int
Founded: 1948
The WHO is a specialized agency of the United Nations with primary responsibility for international health matters & public health. Through this organization the health professions of member states exchange their knowledge & experience with the aim of making possible the attainment by all citizens of the world of a level of health that will permit them to lead a socially & economically productive lives.
Subjects: Public Health, Reference, Medicine, Environmental Health
ISBN Prefix(es): 92-4
Number of titles published annually: 100 Print
Total Titles: 10,000 Print
Parent Company: Publicacoes Europa-America
U.S. Office(s): WHO Publications Center, 49 Sheridan Ave, Albany, NY 12210, United States *Tel:* 518-436-9686 *Fax:* 518-436-7433 *E-mail:* qcorp@compuserve.com

†◊World Intellectual Property Organization (WIPO)
34, chemin des Colombettes, 1211 Geneva 20
Mailing Address: PO Box 18, 1211 Geneva 20
Tel: (022) 338 95 20 *Fax:* (022) 740 14 29
E-mail: info@wipo.int
Web Site: www.wipo.org
Key Personnel
Dir General: Dr Kamil Idris
Founded: 1967
World Intellectual Property Organization (WIPO) Responsible for the promotion of the protection of intellectual property (industrial property & copyright & neighboring rights) throughout the world. Administers, among other international conventions, the Paris Convention for the Protection of Industrial Property & the Berne Convention for the Protection of Literary & Artistic Works.
Publication(s): *Industrial Property & Copyright* (La Propriete industrielle et le Droit d'auteur, monthly in English & French, bimonthly in Spanish); *Intellectual Property in Asia & the Pacific* (quarterly in English); *International Designs Bulletin* (monthly, bilingual French &

English); *PCT Gazette* (weekly in English & French); *PCT Newsletter* (monthly in English); *WIPO Gazette of International Marks-Gazette OMPI des Marques internationales* (monthly in English & French)

†◇World Meteorological Organization
CP 2300, 1211 Geneva 2
Tel: (022) 730 8111 *Fax:* (022) 730 8181
E-mail: pubsales@gateway.wmo.ch
Web Site: www.wmo.ch
Telex: 44 41 99 OMM CH *Cable:* METEOMOND GENEVE
Key Personnel
President: John Zillman
Secretary General: G O P Obasi
The publications of WMO include basic documents, operational publications, official records, WMO guides, technical notes, annual reports & the WMO Bulletin.
ISBN Prefix(es): 92-63
U.S. Office(s): AMS, 45 Beacon St, Boston, MA 02108, United States *Tel:* 617-227-2425 *Fax:* 617-742-8718 *E-mail:* wmopubs@9metsoc.org

World Trade Organization, see WTO (World Trade Organization)

†◇Worlddidac
Bollwerk 21, 3001 Bern
Tel: (031) 311 76 82 *Fax:* (031) 312 17 44
E-mail: info@worlddidac.org
Web Site: www.worlddidac.org
Key Personnel
Dir: Beat Jost

†‡WTO (World Trade Organization)
Centre William Rappard, 154 rue de Lausanne, 1211 Geneva 21
Tel: (022) 739 51 11 *Fax:* (022) 731 42 06
E-mail: info@wto.org
Web Site: www.wto.org
Telex: 412324 OMC; WTOCH *Cable:* OMC/WTO GENEVE
Key Personnel
Dir General: Dr Supachai Panitchpakdi
Dir Information: Keith Rockwell
Founded: 1948
Accord general sur les Tarifs douaniers et le Commerce; Examination & negotiations of various aspects of international trade policies & practices.
Publication(s): *Basic Instruments & Selected Documents (BISD) Series* (annually); *GATT Activities* (annually); *The International Markets for Meat* (annually); *International Trade Report* (annually); *International Trade Statistics* (annually); *Trade Policy Review series* (about 14 countries reviewed annually); *The World Market for Dairy Products* (annually)
ISBN Prefix(es): 92-870

Taiwan, Province of China

Standard Book Numbering Agency
National Central Library, 20 Chungshan S Rd, Taipei 100-01
Tel: (02) 2361 9132 ext 701 *Fax:* (02) 2311 5330
E-mail: isbn@msg.ncl.edu.tw
Web Site: www.ncl.edu.tw/isbn

Key Personnel
Dir: Dr Chuang Fang-Jung
Publication(s): *ISBN Publishers' Directory* (annually); *National Central Library Newsletter* (quarterly, newsletter)

United Republic of Tanzania

National Bibliographic Agency
Tanzania Library Service, 51 Uporoto St, Ursino Estates, Dar Es Salaam
Mailing Address: PO Box 31226, Dar Es Salaam
Tel: (051) 150048; (051) 110573 *Fax:* (022) 2151100
E-mail: tlsb@africaonline.co.tz; library@esrf.or.tz
Key Personnel
Dir: E A Mwinyimvua
ISBN Administrator: Mr M S Mkenga

Standard Book Numbering Agency, see Tanzania Library Service

Tanzania Library Service
PO Box 9283, Dar es Salaam
Tel: (022) 215 09 23; (022) 215 00 48 *Fax:* (022) 215 11 00
E-mail: tlsb@africaonline.co.tz
Key Personnel
Head, Bibliographic & Documentation Service
Dir: Irene Minja
ISBN Prefix(es): 9976-65

Thailand

National Library
Samsen Rd, Bangkok 10300
Tel: (02) 2810263; (02) 2815999; (02) 2815450 *Fax:* (02) 2810263; (02) 2815999; (02) 2815450
E-mail: suwaksin@emisc.moe.go.th
Web Site: www.ifla.org/VI/2/p2/natlibs.htm#T
Telex: 84189 depfiar th
Key Personnel
Dir: Suwakhon Siriwongworawat
Also acts as Standard Book Numbering Agency.

Publishers' & Booksellers' Association of Thailand
947/158-159 Moo 12, Bang Na-Trad Rd, Bang Na, Bangkok 10260
Tel: (02) 954-9560-4 *Fax:* (02) 954-9565-6
E-mail: info@pubat.or.th
Web Site: www.pubat.or.th

C/O Seames, see Southeast Asian Ministers of Education Organization Regional Language Centre (SEAMEO RELC)

†◇Southeast Asian Ministers of Education Organization Regional Language Centre (SEAMEO RELC)
Mom Luang Pin Malakul Centenery Bldg, 920 Sukhumvit Rd, Bangkok 10110
Tel: (02) 3910144; (02) 3910554; (02) 3916413 *Fax:* (02) 3812587
E-mail: secretariat@seameo.org
Web Site: www.seameo.org

Key Personnel
Dir: Dr Arief S Sadiman
Publications Officer: Wilfredo O Pascual, Jr
Founded: 1965
Subjects: Language Teaching & Research, Linguistics, English in multilingual, multicultural situations

Standard Book Numbering Agency
The National Library of Thailand, Samsen Rd, Bangkok 10300
Tel: (02) 2810263; (02) 6285196 *Fax:* (02) 2810263
E-mail: suwksir@emisc.moe.go.th; suwaksir@yahoo.com
Web Site: www.isbn.org
Telex: 84189 Natlib Th
Key Personnel
Dir: Suwakhon Siriwongorawat *Tel:* (062) 2817543

†‡United Nations Library, Bangkok
United Nations Bldg, Rajadamnern Ave, Bangkok 10200
Tel: (02) 2881360; (02) 2881341 *Fax:* (02) 2883036
E-mail: libref@un.org; library-escap@un.org
Web Site: www.unescap.org/unis/lib.htm; www.unescap.org/unis/library/net08.asp
Telex: 82392; 82315 Escap *Cable:* ESCAP BANGKOK
Key Personnel
Chief Librarian: Evelyn Domingo-Barker *Tel:* (02) 2881799 *E-mail:* domingo-barker@un.org
Founded: 1950
Subjects: Economic & Social Development in Asia & the Pacific Region
Publication(s): *Asia & Pacific Bibliography* (biannually); *ESCAP Publications* (biannually)

Tunisia

Agence Tunisienne de l'ISBN
Bibliotheque Nationale, 20 Souk El Attarine, 1008 Tunis
Mailing Address: BP 42, 1008 Tunis
Tel: (071) 57 2706 *Fax:* (071) 57 2887
E-mail: bibliotheque.nationale@email.ati.tn
Web Site: www.bibliotheque.nat.tn
Key Personnel
Contact: Mdme Ben Sedrine Nabiha
Founded: 1988

†◇Arab Regional Branch of the International Council on Archives
122 Blvd 9 avril 1938, 1030 Tunis
Tel: (071) 575 834 *Fax:* (071) 569 175
E-mail: archives.nationales@email.ati.tn; enquiry@dm.gov.ae
Web Site: www.archives-dgan.gov.dz/
Key Personnel
President: Abdulla A Kareem
Secretary: Rabbi Bannouri *E-mail:* rab_ban@yahoo.fr

Standard Book Numbering Agency, see Agence Tunisienne de l'ISBN

Turkey

Standard Book Numbering Agency
Kultur Bakanligi, Kutuphaneler Genel Mudurlugu, Necatibey Cad No:55, 06440 Ankara

Tel: (0312) 231 78 26; (0312) 231 78 29
 Fax: (0312) 231 35 64
E-mail: kultur@kutuphanelergm.gov.tr
Web Site: www.kutuphanelergm.gov.tr
Key Personnel
General Dir: Ms Gokcin Yalcin

Tuerk Editoerler Dernegi
No 12-3 Cagaloglu, Istanbul
Tel: (0212) 5125602 *Fax:* (0212) 5117794
Turkish Publishers' Association.

Uganda

Standard Book Numbering Agency, see Uganda Publishers & Booksellers Association

Uganda Publishers & Booksellers Association
PO Box 7732, Kampala
Tel: (041) 259 163 *Fax:* (041) 251 160
E-mail: mbd@infocom.co.ug
Telex: 61272
Key Personnel
Contact: Martin Okia
ISBN Prefix(es): 9970-04

Ukraine

Book Chamber of Ukraine, National ISBN Agency
Knyzkova Palata Ukrainy, 27 Yuri Gagarin Ave, Kiev 02660
Tel: (044) 573 52 36; (044) 573 01 84 *Fax:* (044) 573 52 36
E-mail: office@ukrbook.net
Web Site: www.ukrbook.net
Key Personnel
Head of ISBN Agency: Iryna Pogorelovska
Publication(s): *Economics, Economic Science*; *Germans in Ukraine*; *Market Economy*; *New Editions of Ukraine*; *Politics, Political Sciences*; *Publishing Business*; *Tartars in Ukraine*; *Turks in Ukraine*; *Ukraine's Ethnic Communities*

Standard Book Numbering Agency, see Book Chamber of Ukraine, National ISBN Agency

United Kingdom

†African Books Collective Ltd
The Jam Factory, 27 Park End St, Oxford OX1 1HU
Tel: (01865) 726686 *Fax:* (01865) 793298
E-mail: abc@africanbookscollective.com
Web Site: www.africanbookscollective.com
Key Personnel
Head: Mary Jay *E-mail:* mary.jay@africanbookscollective.com
Marketing: Ejemhen Esangbedo
Customer Services: Krisia Cook *E-mail:* krisia.cook@africanbookscollective.com; Naomi Robertson
Founded: 1989
Donor-funded organization owned by member publishers. Has exclusive distribution rights of member publishers titles outside Africa.

Subjects: Scholarly & Academic, Literary (including Criticism), Children's Books
ISBN Prefix(es): 91-7106; 0-949229; 0-908311; 9966-831; 1-870784; 978-2601; 978-2266; 0-947479; 0-947009; 978-2264; 978-2299; 978-2321; 978-2494; 9964-970; 978-2711; 1-870716; 0-949225; 99916-31; 0-908307; 0-949932; 0-906968; 99911-31; 9964-978; 978-2492; 978-2323; 978-2276

ALPSP, see Association of Learned & Professional Society Publishers

Antiquarian Booksellers' Association
Sackville House, 40 Piccadilly, London W1J 0DR
Tel: (020) 7439 3118 *Fax:* (020) 7439 3119
E-mail: info@aba.org.uk
Web Site: www.aba.org.uk
Key Personnel
President: Jonathan Potter
Administrator: Philippa Gibson; Deborah Stratford

Association of Authors' Agents
AP Watt Ltd, 20 John St, London WC1N 2DR
Tel: (020) 7405 6774 *Fax:* (020) 7836 9541
E-mail: aaa@apwatt.uk
Web Site: www.agentsassoc.co.uk
Key Personnel
President: Derek Jones
Treasurer: Barbara Levy
Secretary: Sarah Lutyens
Trade association representing the interests of UK based literary agents.

Association of Learned & Professional Society Publishers
South House, The Street, Clapham, Worthing, West Sussex BN13 3UU
Tel: (01903) 871 686 *Fax:* (01903) 871 457
E-mail: chief-exec@alpsp.org
Web Site: www.alpsp.org/default.htm
Key Personnel
Secretary-General: Sally Morris *E-mail:* sec-gen@alpsp.org
Business Manager: Jill Tolson
Editor: Robert Welham
Trade association for not-for-profit publishers international.
Publication(s): *ALPSP Alert* (monthly); *Learned Publishing* (quarterly); *Serial Publications* (2nd Edition, 2003)

Association of Little Presses
86 Lylton Rd, Oxford OX4 3N2
Tel: (01865) 718266
E-mail: alp@melloworld.com
Web Site: www.melloworld.com/alp
Key Personnel
Chairman: Lawrence Upton
Coordinator & Membership Secretary: Chris Jones
Treasurer: Peter Finch
Editor: Paul Green; Stan Trevor
Founded: 1971
Organizes book fairs.
Publication(s): *Catalogue of Little Press Books in Print* (biennially); *Getting Your Poetry Published*; *Poetry & Little Press Information (PALPI)* (biannually); *Publishing Yourself-Not Too Difficult After All*; *Small Presses and Little Publications of the UK and Ireland - an Address list*
Branch Office(s)
Consortium of London Presses, 89a Petherton Rd, London N5 2QT

Authors' Licensing & Collecting Society
Marlborough Court, 14-18 Holborn, London EC1N 2LE
Tel: (020) 7395 0600 *Fax:* (020) 7395 0660

E-mail: alcs@alcs.co.uk
Web Site: www.alcs.co.uk
Key Personnel
Chief Executive: Jane Carr
Head of Communications: Sandy Teli
Founded: 1977

Book Development Council International (BDCI)
29B Montague St, London WC1B 5BH
Tel: (020) 7691 9191 *Fax:* (020) 7691 9199
E-mail: mail@publishers.org.uk
Web Site: www.publishers.org.uk
Key Personnel
Chairman: Chris Paterson
Dir: Ian Taylor *Tel:* (020) 7691 1373
 E-mail: itaylor@publishers.org.uk
Executive Assistant: Kate Bostock *Tel:* (020) 7691 1375 *E-mail:* kbostock@publishers.org.uk
International Division of the Publishers Association.
Parent Company: International Division of the Publishers Association UK

†◇Book Industry Communication
39-41 North Rd, London N7 9DP
Tel: (020) 7607 0021 *Fax:* (020) 7607 0415
Web Site: www.bic.org.uk
Key Personnel
Chairman: Roger Woodham
Managing Agent: Brian Green *E-mail:* brian@bic.org.uk

Book Marketing Ltd
7 John St, London WC1N 2ES
Tel: (020) 7440 8931 *Fax:* (020) 7242 7485
E-mail: bml@bookmarketing.co.uk
Web Site: www.bookmarketing.co.uk
Key Personnel
Man Dir: Jo Henry
Chairman: Tim Rix
Deputy Chairman: Clare Harrison
Founded: 1989
Market research agency specializing in the book industry.
ISBN Prefix(es): 1-873517

Book Tokens Ltd
Minster House, 272-274 Vauxhall Bridge Rd, London SW1V 1BA
Tel: (020) 7802 0802 *Fax:* (020) 7802 0803
Web Site: www.booktokens.co.uk
Key Personnel
Man Dir: Stuart Mathews *E-mail:* stuart.mathews@booktokens.co.uk
Marketing & Sales Dir: Matthew Graham-Clare *E-mail:* matthew.graham-clare@booktokens.co.uk
Serves more than 3000 bookshops.
Parent Company: Booksellers Association of Great Britain & Ireland
Associate Companies: Booksellers Clearing House

The Book Trade Benevolent Society
Dillon Lodge, The Retreat, Abbots Rd, Kings Langley, Herts WD4 8LT
Tel: (01923) 263128 *Fax:* (01923) 270732
E-mail: btbs@booktradecharity.demon.co.uk
Web Site: www.booktradecharity.demon.co.uk
Key Personnel
President: Sally Whitaker
Chief Executive: David Hicks *Tel:* (01923) 299731
Founded: 1837
Charity-Occupational Benevolent Fund.

Books for Keeps
6 Brightfield Rd, Lee, London SE12 8QF
Tel: (020) 8852 4953 *Fax:* (020) 8318 7580
E-mail: booksforkeeps@btinternet.com

UNITED KINGDOM

BOOK TRADE

Web Site: www.booktrusted.com/handbook/journals/bookskeeps.html
Key Personnel
Man Dir: Richard Hill
Founded: 1976
Children's Book Review Magazine.
Publication(s): *A Multicultural Guide to Children's Books: 0-16*; *Books for Keeps* (bi-monthly); *Children's Books About Bullying*; *Poetry 0-13*
Parent Company: School Bookshop Association

◊Booktrust
45 East Hill, London SW18 2QZ
Tel: (020) 8516 2977 *Fax:* (020) 8516 2978
Web Site: www.booktrust.org.uk
Key Personnel
Prizes Administrator: Tarryn McKay *Tel:* (020) 8516 2972 *E-mail:* tarryn@booktrust.org.uk
Prizes Manager: Kate Mervyn-Jones *Tel:* (020) 8516 2973 *E-mail:* kate@booktrust.org.uk
Supported by the Arts Council of England with activities which include literary prizes such as The Man Booker Prize, The Orange Prize for Fiction & the Nestle Smarties Book Prize. Booktrust also runs the Book Information Service.
Publication(s): *The Authors & Bank Directory*; *Children's Books of the Year*; *Grants & Awards Annotated*; *Guide to Literary Prizes*
Divisions: Children's Literature Team at Booktrust (Reading-based projects & publications related to children under 16)

BPIF, see British Printing Industries Federation (BPIF)

British Association of Communicators in Business Ltd (CIB)
Suite A, 1st floor, Auriga Bldg, Davy Ave, Knowlhill, Milton Keynes MK5 8ND
Tel: (0870) 121 7606 *Fax:* (0870) 121 7601
E-mail: enquiries@cib.uk.com
Web Site: www.cib.uk.com
Key Personnel
Chairman: Alison Crossley
President: Alan Peaford
Secretary General: Kathie Jones
Founded: 1949
Publication(s): *CiB News* (monthly); *Communicators in Business Magazine* (quarterly)

British Copyright Council
29-33 Berners St, London W1T 3AB
Tel: (020) 788 122 *Fax:* (020) 788 847
E-mail: copyright@bcc2.demon.co.uk
Web Site: www.editor.net/bcc
Key Personnel
Vice President: Geoffrey Adams; Maureen Duffy

British Guild of Travel Writers
BGTW Secretariat, 51b Askew Crescent, London W12 9DN
Tel: (020) 8749 1128 *Fax:* (020) 8749 1128
E-mail: bgtw@garlandintl.co.uk
Web Site: www.bgtw.org
Key Personnel
Chairman: Mary Johns
Secretary: Melissa Shales
Founded: 1960
Publication(s): *Year Book* (annually)

British Printing Industries Federation (BPIF)
Farringdon Point, 29-35 Farringdon Rd, London EC1M 3JF
Tel: (020) 7915 8300 *Fax:* (020) 7405 7784
E-mail: info@bpif.org.uk
Web Site: www.bpif.org.uk
Key Personnel
Chief Executive: Michael Johnson
Dir General: Tom Machin

Deputy Dir: David Padbury
Marketing Executive: Ruth Yarnit
Publication(s): *Introduction to Printing Technology*; *Print Buyers Directory*; *Printing Industries* (monthly); *UK Periodical Printers*

Bryntirion Press
Bryntirion, Bridgend CF31 4DX
Tel: (01656) 655886 *Fax:* (01656) 656095
E-mail: office@emw.org.uk
Key Personnel
Press Manager: Huw Kinsey *Tel:* (01656) 665916 *E-mail:* huw@emw.org.uk
Secretary: Manon Lloyd Owen *Tel:* (01656) 665911 *E-mail:* manon@mudiad-efengylaidd.org
Publication(s): *Christian Handbook*; *From Shore to Shore*; *Heaven*; *Heirs of Salvation*; *A Light in the Land*; *On the Wings of the Dove*
ISBN Prefix(es): 0-900898; 1-85049

BSI British Standards Institution
389 Chiswick High Rd, London W4 4AL
Tel: (020) 8996 9000 *Fax:* (020) 8996 7001
E-mail: info@bsi-global.com; cservices@bsi-global.com
Web Site: www.bsi-global.com
Telex: 266933
Key Personnel
Chairman: David John
Man Dir: Stevan Breeze
Secretary: Stanley Williams
Founded: 1901
National Standards Body.
Publication(s): *Business Standards Magazine*; *13,000 British Standards*
U.S. Office(s): BSI Inc, 12110 Sunset Hills Rd, Suite 140, Reston, VA 20190-2131, United States

BTBS The Book Trade Charity, see The Book Trade Benevolent Society

†CAB International
Nosworthy Way, Wallingford, Oxon OX10 8DE
Tel: (01491) 832111 *Fax:* (01491) 833508
E-mail: corporate@cabi.org
Web Site: www.cabi.org
Telex: 847964 Comagg *Cable:* COMAG
Key Personnel
Dir General: Dr Denis Blight
Assistant Dir: Dr Ruth Ibbotson
Distribution Manager: Roger Farnell
Journals Production Manager: Pippa Smart
Contact: Angie Barker *E-mail:* a-barker@cabi.org
Publisher: Tim Hardwick *E-mail:* t.hardwick@cabi.org
Founded: 1929
Subjects: Agriculture, Agricultural Economics, Animal Health, Animal Science, Forestry, Rural Sociology, Nutrition, Environmental Science, Human, Horticulture Health
ISBN Prefix(es): 0-85198; 0-85199

†◊The Lewis Carroll Society
The Secretary, 69 Cromwell Rd, Hertford, Herts SG13 7DP
E-mail: aztec@compuserve.com
Web Site: lewiscarrollsociety.org.uk
Key Personnel
Honorary Secretary: Alan White
Chairman: Mark Richards
Treasurer: Roger Allen
Founded: 1969
The Ellis Hillman Memorial Award was established to honour significant & original contributions to the appreciation & enjoyment of Lewis Carroll & his works.

Chartered Institute of Journalists (CIJ)
2 Dock Offices, Surrey Quays Rd, London SE16 2XU
Tel: (020) 7252 1187 *Fax:* (020) 7232 2302
E-mail: memberservices@ioj.co.uk
Web Site: www.ioj.co.uk
Key Personnel
President: M Moriarty
General Secretary: C J Underwood
Founded: 1884
Professional body/independent trade union.
Subjects: Journalism & Broadcasting
Publication(s): *The Journal*

Children's Book Circle
80 Strand, London WC2R 0RL
Tel: (020) 7416 3130 *Fax:* (020) 7739 2318
Web Site: www.booktrusted.com/handbook/journals/bookskeeps.html
Key Personnel
Co-Chairperson: Susan Barry *E-mail:* susan.barry@wattspub.co.uk; Kirsten Grant

Children's Writers & Illustrators Group
Society of Authors, 84 Drayton Gardens, London SW10 9SB
Tel: (020) 7373 6642 *Fax:* (020) 7373 5768
Web Site: www.booktrusted.com/booklists/listindex.html
Key Personnel
Secretary: Jo Hodder *Tel:* (020) 7373 6647 *E-mail:* johodder@societyofauthors.org
Parent Company: The Society of Authors

Christian Booksellers Association
Grampian House, 144 Deansgate, Manchester M3 3ED
Mailing Address: PO Box 30, Manchester M60 3BX
Tel: (0161) 434 7000 *Fax:* (0161) 445 2911
E-mail: info@cba-ukeurope.org
Web Site: www.cba-ukeurop.org
Key Personnel
Executive Vice Chairman: John F Macdonald
General Secretary: Barry Holmes
Founded: 1984
International trade association. Not for profit, offering a trade service to the Christian sector & some at the general sector of publishing, distribution, retailing. In UK & over 70 countries.
Publication(s): *Christian Bookstore Journal* (monthly, trade publications)

CICI, see Confederation of Information Communication Industries

CIJ, see Chartered Institute of Journalists (CIJ)

Circle of Wine Writers
393 Ham Green, Holt, Trowbridge, Wilts BA14 6PX
Tel: (01225) 783007 *Fax:* (01225) 783152
E-mail: administrator@winewriters.org
Web Site: www.winewriters.org
Key Personnel
President: Hugh Johnson
Chairman: Andrew Henderson *E-mail:* andyh@mailbox.co.uk; Steven Spurrier
Honorary Secretary: Christopher Fielden *E-mail:* secretary@winewriters.org

†CODE - Europe
The Jam Factory, 27 Park End St, Oxford OX1 1HU
Tel: (01865) 202438 *Fax:* (01865) 2024390
E-mail: code_europe@compuserve.com
Web Site: www.oneworld.org/code_europe/code_news10.html
Key Personnel
Editor: Kevin Smith
Publication(s): *Tailor-Made Textbooks*

ORGANIZATIONS

UNITED KINGDOM

Comhairle nan Leabhraichean - The Gaelic Books Council
22 Mansfield St, Glasgow G11 5QP
Tel: (0141) 337 6211 *Fax:* (0141) 341 0515
E-mail: fios@gaelicbooks.net
Web Site: www.gaelicbooks.net
Key Personnel
Chairman: Donalda MacKinnon
Dir: Ian MacDonald
Retails all Gaelic & Gaelic related titles in print.
Publication(s): *Catalog of Gaelic Books in print*; *Gaelic Poetry Posters*

Confederation of Information Communication Industries
39-41 North Rd, London N7 9DP
Tel: (020) 7607 0021 *Fax:* (020) 7607 0415
Key Personnel
Manager: Brian Green *E-mail:* brian@bic.org.uk
Chairman: Peter Lalster
Dir: Clive Bradley
Operates CICInet, containing reference databases.

◇**Copyright Licensing Agency**
90 Tottenham Court Rd, London W1T 4LP
Tel: (020) 7631 5555 *Fax:* (020) 7631 5500
E-mail: cla@cla.co.uk
Web Site: www.cla.co.uk
Key Personnel
Office Manager: K Gardner
Collective administration of rights. Membership(s): International Federation of Reproduction Rights Organizations (IFRRO).
Publication(s): *CLArion* (biannually)
Associate Companies: Authors' Licensing & Collecting Society; Publishers Licensing Society

◇**Council of Academic & Professional Publishers**
Division of The Publishers Association
29 B Montague St, London WC1B 5BH
Tel: (020) 4691 9191 *Fax:* (020) 7691 9199
E-mail: mail@publishers.org.uk
Web Site: www.publishers.org.uk
Key Personnel
Chairman: Philip Shaw
Vice Chairman: Richard Stileman
Dir: Graham Taylor
Founded: 1977
Academic/Professional Publishing Division of The Publishers Association.
Associate Companies: Serial Publishers Executive

Crime Writers' Association
PO Box 63, Wakefield WF2 0YW
E-mail: info@theCWA.co.uk
Web Site: www.thecwa.co.uk
Key Personnel
Chairman: Hilary Bonner
Secretary: Judith Cutler *Tel:* (07227) 709 782
  E-mail: judith.cutler@virgin.net
Founded: 1953

Cyngor Llyfrau Cymru, see Welsh Books Council

Cyngor Llyfrau Cymru Canolfan Dosbarthu, see Welsh Books Council

DACS, see Design & Artists Copyright Society (DACS)

Design & Artists Copyright Society (DACS)
Parchment House, 13 Northburgh St, London EC1V 0JP
Tel: (020) 7336 8811 *Fax:* (020) 7336 8822
E-mail: info@dacs.co.uk
Web Site: www.dacs.co.uk

Telex: 885130 FABRIX G
Key Personnel
Chief Executive: Rachel Duffield

Directory & Database Publishers Association
PO Box 23034, London W6 0RJ
Tel: (020) 8846 9707 *Fax:* (020) 0870 168 0552
Web Site: www.directory-publisher.co.uk
Key Personnel
Chairman: John Condron
Secretary: Rosemary Pettit
  E-mail: RosemaryPettit@onetel.net.uk
Founded: 1970
Trade association for directory & database publishers
Membership(s): Advertising Association, Periodical Publishers Association, European Association of Directory Publishers, Advertising Standards Board of Finance, Confederation of Information Communication Industries, Digital Content Forum, Publishing National Training Organization.
Publication(s): *DPA News* (quarterly, newsletter); *Membership Book* (annually)
ISBN Prefix(es): 0-906247; 0-900247

Educational Publishers Council
29B Montague St, London WC1B 6BH
Tel: (020) 7691 9191 *Fax:* (020) 7691 9199
E-mail: mail@publishers.org.uk
Web Site: www.publishers.org.uk *Cable:* PUBLASOC, LONDON WC1
Key Personnel
Chairman: Philip Walters
Dir: Graham Taylor
School Books Division of The Publishers Association.
Parent Company: The Publishers Association

Educational Writers' Group
84 Drayton Gardens, London SW10 9SB
Tel: (020) 7373 6642 *Fax:* (020) 7373 5768
E-mail: info@societyofauthors.org
Web Site: www.societyofauthors.org
Key Personnel
General Secretary: Mark Le Fanu
Parent Company: The Society of Authors

Effective Publishing
58 Saint Wulszan Way, Southam, Leamington Spa, Warks CV33 0TQ
Tel: (01926) 812110
Key Personnel
Dir: Mr Chris Pratt
ISBN Prefix(es): 0-9518558; 1-900319
Associate Companies: Effective Services

†**European Information Association**
Central Library, Saint Peter's Sq, Manchester M2 5PD
Tel: (0161) 228 3691 *Fax:* (0161) 236 6547
E-mail: eia@libraries.manchester.gov.uk
Web Site: www.eia.org.uk/
Key Personnel
Manager: Catherine Webb *E-mail:* cwebb@librairies.manchester.gov.uk
Founded: 1991
Subjects: European Union Information
Publication(s): *Basic Sources of EU Information*; *EIA European Information Guides*; *EIA Quick Guides* (self-help reference cards series)
ISBN Prefix(es): 0-948272

Federation of Children's Book Groups
2 Bridge Wood View, Horsforth Leeds, West Yorks LS18 5PE
Tel: (0113) 2588910 *Fax:* (0113) 2588920
E-mail: info@fcbg.org.uk
Web Site: www.fcbg.org.uk
Key Personnel
Secretary: Alison Dick

†◇**The Folklore Society**
Warburg Institute, Woburn Sq, London WC1H 0AB
Tel: (020) 7862 8564; (020) 7862 8562
E-mail: folklore.society@talk21.com
Web Site: www.folklore-society.com
Key Personnel
President: Dr Marion Bowman
Vice President: Prof W F H Nicolaisen; Dr Jacqueline Simpson
Secretary: Juliette Wood
Treasurer: Robert McDowall
Information Officer, Librarian: Caroline Oates
  E-mail: c.oates@folklore-society.com
Administrator: Susan Vass *E-mail:* s.vass@folklore-society.com
Founded: 1878
Publication(s): *Aspect of British Calendar Customs*; *Folklore (Journal of the Folklore Society)* (FLS News); *Ribbons, Bells & Squeaking Fiddlers*

The Gaelic Books Council, see Comhairle nan Leabhraichean - The Gaelic Books Council

IATUL, see International Association of Technological University Libraries (IATUL)

IBD, see International Book Development (IBD)

IMO, see International Maritime Organization (IMO)

Independent Publishers Guild
PO Box 93, Royston SG8 5GH
Tel: (01763) 247014 *Fax:* (01763) 246293
E-mail: info@ipg.uk.com
Web Site: www.ipg.uk.com/
Key Personnel
Secretary: Y S Messenger

Institute of Printing
The Mews, Hill House, Clanricarde Rd, Tunbridge Wells, Kent TN1 1NU
Tel: (01892) 538118 *Fax:* (01892) 518028
E-mail: admin@instituteofprinting.org
Web Site: www.instituteofprinting.org/
Key Personnel
Chairman: Tony White
Secretary General & Administrator: David Freeland
Marketing: Sally Winser
Founded: 1980
Publication(s): *Professional Printer*

Institute of Scientific & Technical Communicators (ISTC)
PO Box 522, Peterborough PE2 5WX
Tel: (01733) 390141 *Fax:* (01733) 390126
E-mail: istc@istc.org.uk
Web Site: www.istc.org.uk
Key Personnel
President: Iain Wright
Editor: Colin Battson
Executive Secretary: Carol Battson
Founded: 1972
Subjects: Technical & Communication
Publication(s): *Communicator Journal* (quarterly)

†**International African Institute**
SOAS, Thornhaugh St, Russell Sq, London WC1H 0XG
Tel: (020) 7898 4420; (020) 7898 4435
  Fax: (020) 7898 4419
E-mail: iai@soas.ac.uk; ed2@soas.ac.uk
Web Site: www.iaionthe.net
Key Personnel
Chairman: Prof V Y Mudimbe
Chairman, Publications Committee: Dr Elizabeth Dunstan *Tel:* (020) 7898 4435
Honorary Dir: Prof Paul Spencer
Honorary Editor, Africa: Prof Richard Fardon

UNITED KINGDOM / BOOK TRADE

Founded: 1926
1200 institutions & individuals are subscribing & the Council includes representatives from Africa & elsewhere.
Subjects: Academic books on Africa, including History, Ethnography, Environmental Studies, Bibliography
Publication(s): *Africa* (quarterly, journal); *The Africa Bibliography* (annually); *African Issues* (biannually, paperback); *Classics in African Anthropology Series*; *International African Library Series* (biannually, paperback); *International African Seminars*; *Monographs from the IAI*
ISBN Prefix(es): 0-85302

†◇**International Association of Agricultural Information Specialists** (Association Internationale des Specialistes de l'Information Agricoles)
14 Queen St, Wallingford, Dorchester-on-Thames OX10 7HR
Tel: (01865) 340054
Web Site: www.iaald.org
Telex: 847965 (COMAGG G)
Key Personnel
Secretary-Treasurer: Margot Bellamy
  E-mail: margot.bellamy@fritillary.demon.co.uk
Founded: 1955
Publication(s): *Quarterly IAALD Bulletin* (2/yr (one combined issue), newsletter, 2000); *World Directory of Agricultural Information Resource Centres* (1/5 yrs, 2000, Available in hard copy & on CD Rom)

†**International Association of Technological University Libraries (IATUL)**
c/o Heriot-Watt University Library, EH14 4AS Edinburgh
Mailing Address: Radcliffe Science Library, Oxford University, Parks Rd, Oxford OX1 3QP
Tel: (0131) 449 5111 *Fax:* (0131) 451 3164
E-mail: iatul@qut.edu.au
Web Site: www.iatul.org
Key Personnel
President: Michael L Breaks *E-mail:* m.l.breaks@hw.ac.uk
Secretary: Judith Palmer *E-mail:* judith.palmer@bodley.ox.ac.uk
Founded: 1955
Publication(s): *IATUL Conference Proceedings*; *IATUL News* (quarterly)

International Book Development (IBD)
CfBT, 60 Queens Rd, Reading RG1 4BS
Tel: (0118) 902 1000 *Fax:* (0118) 902 1434
E-mail: enquiries@cfbt.com
Web Site: www.cfbt.com
Key Personnel
Man Dir: Tony Read
Dir: Amanda Buchan; Carmelle Denning; David Foster; Euan Henderson
Founded: 1990 (Now owned by the Centre for British Teachers (CfBT))
Provides consultancy, advisory, research, management & training services to international agencies, governments & trade organisations.

†‡**International Maritime Organization (IMO)**
4 Albert Embankment, London SE1 7SR
Tel: (020) 7735 7611 *Fax:* (020) 7587 3210
E-mail: publications-sales@imo.org
Web Site: www.imo.org
Telex: 04423588 *Cable:* INTERMAR
Key Personnel
Information Officer: Roger Kohn *E-mail:* rkohn@imo.org
Head of Publications: Harald Grell
Founded: 1959
Subjects: Texts of International Maritime Treaties concluded under its auspices, Maritime Technical Publications, Oil Pollution Prevention, Maritime Safety
ISBN Prefix(es): 92-801

†‡**The International Molinological Society**
125 Parkside Dr, Watford, Herts WD17 3BA
Mailing Address: Groothertoginnelaan 174B, 2517 EV The Hague, Netherlands
Tel: (070) 3460885
Web Site: tims.geo.tudelft.nl
Key Personnel
President: Michael Harverson
  E-mail: HarversonTims@aol.com
Publications Officer: Leo van der Drift
  E-mail: leo.diederik@consunet.nl
Founded: 1973
Subjects: Mills (Windmills, Watermills, Animal-Powered Mills) Technique, History, Sociology

†◇**International PEN**
9-10 Charterhouse Bldgs, Goswell Rd, London EC1M 7AT
Tel: (020) 7253 4308 *Fax:* (020) 7253 5711
E-mail: info@internatpen.org
Web Site: www.internatpen.org
Key Personnel
International President: Homero Aridjis
General-Secretary: Terry Carlbom
Contact: Sara Whyatt
Founded: 1921
A World Association of Writers.
Publication(s): *PEN International* (in English & French, issued with the assistance of UNESCO)

IOJ, see Chartered Institute of Journalists (CIJ)

ISSN UK Centre
British Library, Boston Spa, Wetherby, West Yorks LS23 7BQ
Tel: (0870) 444 1500 *Fax:* (01937) 546562
E-mail: issn-uk@bl.uk
Web Site: www.bl.uk/services/bibliographic/issn.html
Telex: 557381
Key Personnel
Director: David Baron
Allocates International Standard Serial Numbers (ISSN) to serials published in UK.

ISTC, see Institute of Scientific & Technical Communicators (ISTC)

LAB, see Latin America Bureau

†◇**Latin America Bureau**
One Amwell St, London EC1R 1UL
Tel: (020) 7278 2829 *Fax:* (020) 7833 0715
E-mail: info@lab.org.uk
Web Site: www.lab.org.uk
Key Personnel
Researcher & Editor: Marcela Lopez
Founded: 1977
Subjects: Political, Social & Economic Issues in contemporary Latin America & the Caribbean, Environmental & Women's studies

†◇**Maritime Information Association**
c/o Marine Society, 202 Lambeth Rd, London SE1 7JW
Tel: (020) 7261 9535 *Fax:* (020) 7401 2537
E-mail: enq@marine-society.org
Web Site: www.marine-society.org.uk/
Key Personnel
Dir: Jeremy Howard
Founded: 1972
Publication(s): *Marine Information* (guide to libraries & sources of information in the UK)

◇**Music Publishers Association**
20 York Bldg, 3rd floor, London WC2N 6JU
Tel: (020) 7839 7779 *Fax:* (020) 7839 7776
E-mail: info@mpaonline.org.uk
Web Site: www.mpaonline.org.uk
Key Personnel
Chairman: Andrew Potter
Deputy Chair: Jane Dyball
Chief Executive: Sarah Faulder
Trade organization for music publishers.
Publication(s): *Catalogue of Printed Music on CD-ROM*; *List of Members*; *Printed Music Distributors*

National Acquisitions Group
12 Holm Oak Dr, Madeley, Nr Crewe CW3 9HR
Tel: (01782) 750462 *Fax:* (01782) 750462
E-mail: nag@btconnect.com
Web Site: www.nag.org.uk
Key Personnel
Chair: Jo Grocott
Administration: Marie Hackett; Diane Roberts
Publication(s): *Directory of Acquisitions Librarians in the UK & Republic of Ireland* (biannually); *NAG News* (quarterly); *Taking Stock* (biannually)

National Federation of Retail Newsagents
Yeoman House, Sekforde St, London EC1R 0HF
Tel: (0207) 253 4225 *Fax:* (0207) 250 0927
Web Site: www.nfrn.org.uk
Key Personnel
Dir: David Daniels

National Union of Journalists (Book Branch)
Headland House, 308 Gray's Inn Rd, London WC1X 8DP
Tel: (020) 7278 7916 *Fax:* (020) 7873 8143
E-mail: book_branch@hotmail.com
Web Site: www.nujbook.org
Key Personnel
Branch Secretary: Nick Bardsley
Membership Secretary: Cath Rasbash
Founded: 1973
Trade Union.
Publication(s): *Comrade Moss* (1990, biography)

†◇**PEN Club-Writers in Exile London Branch**
10 Melfort Dr, Leighton Buzzard, Beds LU7 7XN
Tel: (020) 8340 5279
Key Personnel
President: Velta Snikere
Secretary: Robert Fearnley
Total Titles: 8 Print

Picture Research Association
One Willow Court, off Willow St, London EC2A 4QB
Tel: (01883) 730123 *Fax:* (01883) 730144
E-mail: chair@picture-research.org.uk
Web Site: www.picture-research.org.uk
Key Personnel
Chair: Charlotte Lippmann
Treasurer: Christine Hinze *E-mail:* christine@hinze.fsbusiness.co.uk
Publication(s): *Montage* (quarterly, magazine)

PLA, see Private Libraries Association (PLA)

†◇**Private Libraries Association (PLA)**
49 Hamilton Park W, London N5 1AE
Web Site: www.the-old-school.demon.co.uk/pla.htm
Key Personnel
Executive Secretary: James Brown
American Membership Secretary: William A Klutts *Tel:* 901-635-2544
Canadian Membership Secretary: Alan J Horne
Editor, Private Press Books: Paul W Nash
Founded: 1956

An international society of book collectors.
Publication(s): *The Private Library* (journal); *Private Press Books* (checklist of privately printed books)

Public Lending Right
Richard House, Sorbonne Close, Stockton-on-Tees, Cleveland TS17 6DA
Tel: (01642) 604699 *Fax:* (01642) 615641
E-mail: registrar@plr.uk.com
Web Site: www.plr.uk.com
Key Personnel
Registrar: Dr James Parker *E-mail:* jim.parker@plr.uk.com
Reports & Press Releases.
Publication(s): *Report on the Public Lending Right Scheme, 2000-01* (annually, 2002); *Whose Loan Is It Anyway? Essays in Celebration of PLR's 20th Anniversary* (1998)

The Publishers Association
29b Montague St, London WC1B 5BH
Tel: (020) 7691 9191 *Fax:* (020) 7691 9199
E-mail: mail@publishers.org.uk
Web Site: www.publishers.org.uk
Key Personnel
President: Anthony Forbes-Watson
Chief Executive: Ronnie Williams
 E-mail: rwilliams@publishers.org.uk
Dir: Graham Taylor *E-mail:* gtaylor@publishers.org.uk; Ian Taylor *E-mail:* itaylor@publishers.org.uk
Trade association for UK publishers of books, journals & electronic publications.
Publication(s): *Annual Book Trade Year Book*

Publishers Licensing Society Ltd
37-41 Gower St, London WC1E 6HH
Tel: (020) 7299 7730 *Fax:* (020) 7299 7780
E-mail: info@pls.org.uk
Web Site: www.pls.org.uk
Key Personnel
Chairman: Neil McRae
Consultant: Richard Balkwill
Chief Executive: Jens Bammel
Founded: 1981
PLS has non-exclusive licences from 1600 publishers to include their works in photocopying & digitisation licences negotiated by the Copyright Licensing Agency. PLS ensures publishers receive their share of fees collected by CLA.
Publication(s): *PLS Plus* (newsletter)
Associate Companies: Copyright Licensing Agency

SCOLMA, see Standing Conference on Library Materials on Africa

Scottish Book Marketing Group
Scottish Book Centre, 137 Dundee St, Edinburgh EH11 1BG
Tel: (0131) 228 6866 *Fax:* (0131) 228 3220
Publication(s): *Directory of Publishing in Scotland* (annually); *New Scottish Books* (bimonthly, leaflet); *Scottish Bestseller List* (fortnightly listing of bestselling books on Scotland); *Scottish Books Direct* (Home-Shopping facility for readers at home & abroad)
Associate Companies: Scottish Publishers Association *E-mail:* enquiries@scottishbooks.org *Web Site:* www.scottishbooks.org

Scottish Book Trust
Sandeman House, Trunks Close, 55 High St, Edinburgh EH1 1SR
Tel: (0131) 524 0160 *Fax:* (0131) 228 4293
E-mail: info@scottishbooktrust.com
Web Site: www.scottishbooktrust.com
Publication(s): *Off The Shelf: A Guide To Books & Writers for Children From Scotland*; *Shelf Life: Information, Author Information, Reviews on Books for Children in Scotland*
Parent Company: Book Trust

Scottish Newspaper Publishers' Association
48 Palmerston Pl, Edinburgh EH12 5DE
Tel: (0131) 220 4353 *Fax:* (0131) 220 4344
E-mail: info@snpa.org.uk
Web Site: www.snpa.org.uk
Key Personnel
Dir: Mr J B Raeburn *E-mail:* jraeburn@spef.org.uk
Trade association representing publishers of local newspapers throughout Scotland.

◊**Scottish Publishers Association**
Scottish Book Centre, 137 Dundee St, Edinburgh EH11 1BG
Tel: (0131) 2286866 *Fax:* (0131) 2283220
E-mail: info@scottishbooks.org
Web Site: www.scottishbooks.org
Key Personnel
Dir: Lorraine Fannin
Chairman: Timothy Wright
Founded: 1973
Trade association with 80 members.
Publication(s): *Directory of Publishing in Scotland* (annually); *New Scottish Books* (6 times/yr)
Associate Companies: Scottish Book Marketing Group

SIBMAS, see Societe Internationale des Bibliotheques et des Musees des Arts du Spectacle (SIBMAS)

†◊**Societe Internationale des Bibliotheques et des Musees des Arts du Spectacle (SIBMAS)**
(International Association of Libraries & Museums of the Performing Arts)
Theatre Museum, 1E Tavistock St, London WC2E 7PR
Tel: (020) 7943 4720 *Fax:* (020) 7943 4777
Web Site: www.theatrelibrary.org/sibmas/sibmas.html
Key Personnel
President: Dr Claudia Balk
Secretary General: Maria Teresa Iovinelli
Founded: 1954
International Society of Libraries & Museums for the Performing Arts.
Subjects: Performing Arts Collections, Worldwide
Publication(s): *Proceedings Bi-Annual Congresses*; *SIBMAS International Directory of Performing Arts Collections/Emmett Publishing Ltd* (Haslemere 1996)

Society of Authors
84 Drayton Gardens, London SW10 9SB
Tel: (020) 7373 6642 *Fax:* (020) 7373 5768
E-mail: info@societyofauthors.org
Web Site: www.societyofauthors.org/prizes.htm
Key Personnel
General Secretary: Mark Le Fanu
Manager: Kate Pool *E-mail:* kpool@societyofauthors.org
Publication(s): *The Author* (quarterly)

Society of Indexers
Blades Enterprise Centre, John St, Sheffield S2 4SU
Tel: (0114) 292 2350 *Fax:* (0114) 292 2351
E-mail: admin@indexers.org.uk
Web Site: www.socind.demon.co.uk
Key Personnel
President: Doreen Blake
Secretary: Liza Weinkoe
Administrator: P W Burrow
Founded: 1957
Publication(s): *The Indexer*; *Training in Indexing*
Associate Companies: American Society of Indexers; Australian Society of Indexers; Indexing & Abstracting Society of Canada; Association of Southern African Indexers & Bibliographers

†◊**Standing Conference on Library Materials on Africa**
Commonwealth Secretariat, Marlborough House, Pall Mall, London SW14 5HX
Tel: (020) 7747 6164 *Fax:* (020) 7747 6168
E-mail: scolma@hotmail.com
Web Site: www.soas.ac.uk/scolma/
Key Personnel
Chair: Sheila Allcock *E-mail:* sheila.allcock@qeh.ox.ac.uk
Secretary: David Blake
Publication(s): *African Research & Documentation*

UK International Standard Book Numbering Agency Ltd
Woolmead House W Bear Lane, Farnham GU9 7LG
Tel: (01252) 742525 *Fax:* (01252) 742526
E-mail: isbn@whitaker.co.uk
Web Site: www.whitaker.co.uk/isbn.htm
Key Personnel
Manager: Stella Griffiths
Publication(s): *International Standard Book Numbering*
Parent Company: J Whitaker & Sons Ltd

Union of Welsh Publishers & Booksellers
c/o Gomer Press, Llandysul, Ceredigion SA44 4BQ
Tel: (01559) 362371 *Fax:* (01559) 363758

†**VSO Books**
Voluntary Service Overseas, 317 Putney Bridge Rd, London SW15 2PN
Tel: (020) 8780 7200 *Fax:* (020) 8780 7300
E-mail: enquiry@vso.org.uk
Web Site: www.vso.org.uk
Key Personnel
Editor: Silke Bernau *Tel:* (020) 8780 7342
Founded: 1990
Subjects: Education, Development (Health, Agriculture, Technical, Community Development)
ISBN Prefix(es): 0-9509050; 1-903697
Number of titles published annually: 3 Print
Total Titles: 22 Print

Welsh Books Council (Cyngor Llyfrau Cymru)
Castell Brychan, Aberystwyth, Ceredigion SY23 2JB
Tel: (01970) 624151 *Fax:* (01970) 625385
E-mail: castellbrychan@wbc.org.uk
Web Site: www.cllc.org.uk
Key Personnel
Dir: Gwerfyl Pierce Jones
Head of Marketing: D Philip Davies *E-mail:* phil.davies@wbc.org.uk
Founded: 1963
Branch Office(s)
Distribution Center, Glanyrafon Enterprise Park, Aberystwyth, Ceredigion SY23 3AQ
 E-mail: distribution.centre@cllc.org.uk

Women in Publishing
Membership Officer, PO Box 402, West Byfleet KT14 7ZF
E-mail: wipub@hotmail.com; info@wipub.org.uk
Web Site: www.cyberiacafe.net/wip
Key Personnel
Membership Secretary: Natalie McCormack
 Tel: (020) 8923 2386 *E-mail:* nmccormack@waterlow.com
Founded: 1979
Promote the status of women within publishing & related fields.

UNITED KINGDOM — BOOK TRADE

†◇Writers & Scholars International
Lancaster House, 33 Islington High St, London N1 9LH
Tel: (020) 7278 2313 *Fax:* (020) 7278 1878
E-mail: natasha@indexoncensorship.org
Web Site: www.indexonline.org/
Key Personnel
Editor: Ursula Owen
Marketing Dir: Henderson Mullin
Founded: 1972
Information about censorship in the world today, covering subjects such as free speech, human rights, literature, freedom of information.
Subjects: Censorship, Current Affairs, Literature, Politics
Publication(s): *Index on Censorship* (quarterly, magazine)
Number of titles published annually: 4 Print

Writers' Guild of Great Britain
15 Britannia St, London WC1X 9JN
Tel: (020) 7833 0777 *Fax:* (020) 7833 4777
E-mail: admin@writersguild.org.uk
Web Site: www.writersguild.org.uk
Key Personnel
President: John Wilsher
Chairman: Bill Morrison
General Secretary: Bernie Corbett
 E-mail: corbett@writersguild.org.uk

United States

†American-Scandinavian Foundation
58 Park Ave, New York, NY 10016
Tel: 212-879-9779 *Fax:* 212-879-2301
E-mail: info@amscan.org; asf@amscan.org
Web Site: www.amscan.org
Key Personnel
Executive Vice President: Lynn Carter
 E-mail: carter@amscan.org
Publication(s): *Scan* (quarterly, newsletter); *Scandinavian Review* (triannually, cultural/literary/political magazine)

†Bernan Associates, Div of Kraus Organization, Ltd
4611-F Assembly Dr, Lanham, MD 20706-4391
Tel: 301-459-7666 *Toll Free Tel:* 800-274-4888 (USA); 800-233-0504 (Canada) *Fax:* 301-459-0056
E-mail: query@berman.com
Web Site: www.eurunion.org/publicat/sales.htm
Telex: 7108260418
Key Personnel
Sales & Publicity: Christopher Zahn
There are OAS offices/bookstores in 31 countries outside the USA.
Subjects: Development of American Nations (Regional, Social, Historical), Bibliography, Cultural Affairs, Economics, Education, Human Rights, Law, Sciences, Statistics
Publication(s): *Inter-American Review of Bibliography*
ISBN Prefix(es): 0-8270; 0-8171

IALL, see International Association of Law Libraries (IALL)

IASP, see International Association of Scholarly Publishers (IASP)

ILAB, see International League of Antiquarian Booksellers (ILAB)

†◇International Association of Law Libraries (IALL) (Association Internationale des Bibliotheques de Droit)
PO Box 5709, Washington, DC 20016-1309
Tel: 804-924-3384 *Fax:* 804-982-2232
E-mail: lbw@virginia.edu
Web Site: www.iall.org
Key Personnel
President: Holger Knudsen *Tel:* 856-225-6457
 E-mail: knudsen@mpipriv-hh.mpg.de
Treasurer: Gloria F Chao
Secretary: Ann Morrison *Tel:* 902-494-2640
 E-mail: morriso6@is.dal.ca
Founded: 1959
Publication(s): *The IALL Messenger* (irregularly); *International Journal of Legal Information* (tri-annually, Membership)

†◇International Association of Scholarly Publishers (IASP)
c/o Michigan State University Press, 1405 S Harrison Rd, East Lansing, MI 48823-5202
Tel: 517-355-9543 *Fax:* 517-432-2611
E-mail: bohm@pilot.msu.edu
Key Personnel
Dir: Mr F C Bohm
Founded: 1972

†◇International Comparative Literature Association (Association Internationale de Litterature Comparee)
Catholic University, Washington, DC 20064
Tel: 416-487-6727 *Fax:* 416-487-6786
E-mail: icla@byu.edu
Web Site: www.byu.edu/~icla
Key Personnel
President: Kawamoto Koji *E-mail:* kojik@aurora.dti.ne.jp
Vice President: Virgil Nemoianu
 E-mail: nemoianu@cua.edu
Founded: 1954

†◇International Institute of Iberoamerican Literature
University of Pittsburgh, 728 Cathedral of Learning, Pittsburgh, PA 15260-0001
Tel: 412-624-5246; 412-624-6100 *Fax:* 412-624-0829
E-mail: iili+@pitt.edu
Web Site: www.pitt.edu
Key Personnel
Dir: Jinx P Walton *E-mail:* jpw@pitt.edu
Administrator: Erika Braga
Contact: Mabel Morana *E-mail:* mabel@pitt.edu
Founded: 1938
Publication(s): *Memorias*; *Revista Iberoamericana* (quarterly, 1938, literary criticism journal)

†◇International League of Antiquarian Booksellers (ILAB)
400 Summit Ave, St Paul, MN 55102
Tel: 800-441-0076; 612-290-0700 *Fax:* 612-290-0646
E-mail: info@ilab-lila.com
Web Site: www.ilab.org
Key Personnel
Secretary General: Steven Temple *Tel:* 416-703-9908 *E-mail:* books@steventemplebooks.com
Founded: 1947
Publication(s): *Dictionary of the Antiquarian Book Trade* (in Danish, Dutch, English, French, German, Italian, Japanese, Spanish, Swedish); *International Directory of Antiquarian Booksellers*

†International Monetary Fund
700 19 St NW, Washington, DC
Tel: 202-623-7000; 202-623-7430 *Fax:* 202-623-4661; 202-623-7201
E-mail: publicaffairs@imf.org
Web Site: www.imf.org

Key Personnel
Acting Man Dir: Anne O Krueger
Chief, Publication Services: Lori Michele Newsom
Editor, Rights & Permissions: Ian S McDonald
Founded: 1946
Subjects: Economics, International monetary & trade issues, Domestic fiscal & monetary topics, Activities & operations of the International Monetary Fund, Balance of payments & external adjustment problems, International finance, International statistics
Publication(s): *Annual Report on Exchange Arrangements & Exchange Restrictions*; *Direction of Trade Statistics*; *Finance & Development* (published jointly with World Bank); *World Economic Outlook*
ISBN Prefix(es): 0-939934; 1-55775

†◇International Reading Association
800 Barksdale Rd, Newark, DE 19714
Mailing Address: PO Box 8139, Newark, DE 19714-8139
Tel: 302-731-1600 *Fax:* 302-731-1057
Web Site: www.reading.org
Telex: 5106002813
Key Personnel
President: Lesley Mandel Morrow
Executive Dir: Alan Farstrup
Public Information Associate: Janet Butler
 Tel: 302-731-1600 (ext 293) *E-mail:* jbutler@reading.org
Founded: 1956
Publication(s): *Journal of Adolescent & Adult Literacy*; *Lectura y vida*; *Newspaper Reading Today*; *Reading Research Quarterly*; *The Reading Teacher*

†◇Middle East Librarians Association
University of Washington Libraries, Monographic Services, Campus Box 352900, Seattle, WA 98195-2900
Tel: (206) 543-8407 *Fax:* (206) 685-8049
Web Site: www.depts.washington.edu/wsx9/melahp.html
Key Personnel
Editor, Near East Division: Jonathan Rodgers
 Tel: (734) 764-7555 *Fax:* (734) 763-6743
 E-mail: jrodgers@umich.edu
Secretary-Treasurer: Janet Heineck
 Tel: (206) 543-1642 *Fax:* (206) 685-8782
 E-mail: janeth@u.washington.edu
Publication(s): *MELA Notes* (Journal of Middle Eastern Librarianship)

SALALM, see Seminar on the Acquisition of Latin American Library Materials (SALALM)

†◇Seminar on the Acquisition of Latin American Library Materials (SALALM)
Secretariat, General Library, University of New Mexico, Albuquerque, NM 87131-1466
Tel: 505-277-5102 *Fax:* 505-277-0646
Key Personnel
Executive Secretary: Sharon A Moynahan
Publication(s): *Bibliography & Reference Series*

†◇United Nations Publications
Two UN Plaza, Room DC2-853, New York, NY 10017
Tel: 212-963-8302 *Toll Free Tel:* 800-253-9646 (orders US only) *Fax:* 212-963-3489
E-mail: publications@un.org
Web Site: www.un.org/Pubs/sales.htm
Telex: 62450 *Cable:* UNATIONS NYK
Key Personnel
Chief of Section: Susanna H Johnston
Marketing & Product Development: Christopher Woodthorpe
Rights & Permissions, US: Claudia Kaiser
 Tel: 212-963-5455 *Fax:* 212-963-4116
 E-mail: kaiser@un.org

Rights & Permissions, Geneva: Patricia Piguet
External Publications Officer: Renata Morteo
Tel: 212-963-5455 *Fax:* 212-963-3489
Founded: 1945
Since 1946, United Nations has published more than 10,000 reports, studies, annual surveys, yearbooks & monthly & quarterly periodicals in addition to the United Nations Official Records.
Reflecting the varied work of the Organization, the subjects include international trade, world & regional economic questions, international law, social questions, atomic energy, public administration & literature concerning the role & activities of the United Nations.
Subjects: Reference, Economics, International Trade, International Law, Political Science, Social Science, Environment, Educational
ISBN Prefix(es): 92-1
Branch Office(s)
Publications des Nations Unies, Section des Ventes et Commercialisation, Bureau E-4, 1211 Geneva 10, Switzerland *Tel:* (022) 917 2600; (022) 917 2614 *Fax:* (022) 917 0027 *E-mail:* unpubli@unog.ch
Bookshop(s): United Nations Bookshop, United Nations Concourse Level, First Ave & 46 St - Visitors Entrance, New York, NY 10017

Uruguay

Camara Uruguaya del Libro (Uruguayan Publishers' Association)
Juan D Jackson 1118, 11 200 Montevideo
Tel: (082) 41 57 32 *Fax:* (082) 41 18 60
E-mail: camurlib@adinet.com.uy
Key Personnel
President: Ernesto Sanjines

Standard Book Numbering Agency
Biblioteca Nacional, Casilla de Correo 452, 11200 Montevideo
Tel: (02) 402 08 12; (02) 408 50 30 *Fax:* (02) 409 69 02; (02) 401 67 16
E-mail: bibna@adinet.com.uy
Telex: 26991 biname uy
Key Personnel
Dir General: Luis Alberto Musso

Venezuela

Camara Venezolana del Libro (Venezuelan Publishers' Association)
Ave Andres Bello, Edificio Centro Andres Bello, Torre Oeste 11, piso 11, ofic 112-0, Caracas 1050
Tel: (0212) 7931347; (0212) 7931368 *Fax:* (0212) 7931368
E-mail: cavelibro@cantv.net
Key Personnel
Dir: M P Vargas

Standard Book Numbering Agency
Parque Central, Torre Este, Piso 3, Caracas 1011
Tel: (0212) 576 5650; (0212) 576 5370; (0212) 576 7120; (0212) 577 5106 *Fax:* (0212) 576 8720
E-mail: isbn_cenal@platino.gov.ve
Web Site: www.bnv.bib.ve; www.cenal.gov.ve
Telex: 24621 iabn vc
Key Personnel
Contact: Angela Negrin

Zambia

Booksellers' & Publishers' Association of Zambia (BPAZ)
Haile Selassie Ave, Lusaka
Mailing Address: PO Box 31838, Lusaka
Tel: (01) 255166 *Fax:* (01) 255166
E-mail: bpaz@zamnet.zm; longman@zamnet.zm
Web Site: www.africanpublishers.org
Key Personnel
Executive Dir: Basil Mbewe
Contact: Christine Kasonde

BPAZ, see Booksellers' & Publishers' Association of Zambia (BPAZ)

Standard Book Numbering Agency
c/o University of Zambia Library, PO Box 32379, Lusaka
Tel: (01) 292 837 (ext 1342); (01) 253 952; (01) 250 845 *Fax:* (01) 295 038
E-mail: library@unza.zm
Web Site: www.unza.zm/
Telex: ZA 40370 *Cable:* UNZA
Key Personnel
ISBN Administrator: Dr H Mwacalimba
Parent Company: Booksellers & Publishers Association of Zambia

Zimbabwe

†African Publishers' Network (APNET)
7e etage, Immeuble Roume, Abidjan, 01 Cote d'Ivoire
Mailing Address: BP 3429, Abidjan 01, Cote d'Ivoire
Tel: (04) 20211801; (04) 20211802 *Fax:* (04) 20211803
E-mail: apnetes@yahoo.com
Web Site: www.freewebs.com/africanpublishers
Key Personnel
Chairman: Mamadou Aliou Sow
Executive Secretary: Akin Fasemore
Membership & Trade Promotion Officer: Tainie Mundondo *E-mail:* apnettrade@yahoo.com
Treasurer: Janet Njoroge
Training Coordinator: Alice Mouko *E-mail:* apnettraining@yahoo.fr
Founded: 1992
Publication(s): *African Publishing Review* (6 times/yr); *Indaba Papers*; *Thematic Catalogues*; *Trade Directory 2000* (Repertoire Commercial/O Directorio Comercial, biannually, book, 2000)
Branch Office(s)
CP 1248, Luanda, Angola, Contact: Antonio de Brito *Tel:* (02) 331371 *Fax:* (02) 895162; (02) 332714 *E-mail:* infosec@ebonet.net
BP 1501, Yaounde, Cameroon, Contact: Freddy Ngandu *Tel:* 223554; 2223554 *Fax:* 2221761 *E-mail:* ngan_fred@yahoo.fr
PO Box 33 Panorama, Cairo, Egypt (Arab Republic of Egypt), Contact: Ashraf Hamouda *Tel:* (02) 4023399 *Fax:* (02) 4037567 *E-mail:* ahamouda@link.net
BP 542, Conakry, Guinea, Contact: Mamadou Aliou Sow *Tel:* 463507; 402849 *Fax:* 412012; 463507 *E-mail:* ganndal@mirinet.net.gn
PO Box 18033, Nairobi, Kenya, Contact: Janet Njoroge *Tel:* (02) 533665 *Fax:* (02) 540037 *E-mail:* longhorn@iconnect.co.ke
Private Bag 39, Blantyre, Malawi, Contact: Egidio Mpanga *Tel:* 670880; 670855 *Fax:* 671114 *E-mail:* dzuka@malawi.net
Ighodaro Rd, No 1, Jericho Layout, PMB 5205, Ibadan, Nigeria, Contact: Ayo Ojeniyi *Tel:* (02) 2412268; (02) 2410943 *Fax:* (02) 2411089; (02) 2413237 *E-mail:* info@heinemannbooks.com

APNET, see African Publishers' Network (APNET)

Standard Book Numbering Agency
National Archives of Zimbabwe, Causeway, Private Bag 7729, Harare
Tel: (04) 792 741 *Fax:* (04) 792 398
E-mail: nat.archives@gta.gov.zw
Publication(s): *Zimbabwe National Bibliography*

ZBPA, see Zimbabwe Book Publishers Association (ZBPA)

Zimbabwe Book Publishers Association (ZBPA)
Fidelity Life Tower, 4th floor, Corner Raleigh/Luck Sts, Harare
Mailing Address: PO Box 3041, Harare
Tel: (04) 754256 *Fax:* (04) 754256
E-mail: engelbert@collegepress.co.zw
Publication(s): *Directory of Zimbabwe Publishers 1995*; *Making Books*; *Zimbabwe: Books In Print 1995*

Major Book Dealers

This section contains active book dealers in one or more of the following categories: distribution, exporting, importing, major book chains, major independent booksellers, remainder dealers, and wholesalers.

Argentina

Librerias ABC SA
Ave Cordoba 685, 1054 Buenos Aires
Mailing Address: Casilla Correo Central 4452, C1000WBS Buenos Aires
Tel: (011) 4314-8106 *Fax:* (011) 4314-8106
E-mail: libabcc@datamarkets.com.ar
Web Site: www.libreriasabc.com.ar *Cable:* MOLAGENT
Key Personnel
President: Horst Stephan
Founded: 1969

Cosmos Libros SRL
Av Callao 737, 1023 Buenos Aires
Tel: (011) 48127364; (011) 48155347
E-mail: contactenos@cosmoslibros.com.ar
Web Site: www.cosmoslibros.com.ar
Key Personnel
Dir: Hugo Emilio Palacios
 E-mail: palacioshugo@arnet.com.ar
Founded: 1984
Subjects: Specialize in education
Type of Business: Distributor, Exporter, Importer, Major Independent Bookseller

Cuspide Libros SA
Suipacha 764 Piso Bajo Oficina 2, 1008 Buenos Aires
Tel: (011) 43228868 *Fax:* (011) 43223456
E-mail: distribuidora@cuspide.com
Web Site: www.cuspide.com
Telex: 25477 Dicus
Key Personnel
President: Joaquin M Gil Paricio
Founded: 1960
Branch Office(s)
Suipacha 1045, 1008 Buenos Aires *Tel:* (011) 3130486
Portugal 18 Santiago, Chile *Tel:* (02) 2224978 *Fax:* (02) 2250435

Libreria Huemul SA
Ave Santa Fe 2237, 1123 Buenos Aires
Tel: (011) 4822-1666; (011) 4825-2290
 Fax: (011) 822-1666
E-mail: libreriahuemul@arnet.com.ar
Key Personnel
President & Manager: Antonio Rego
Also Publisher.

Libreria Kier
Don Felipe 9, 1059 Buenos Aires
Tel: (091) 5227335
E-mail: info@libreriakier.com
Web Site: www.libreriakier.com
Founded: 1907
Type of Business: Distributor, Exporter, Importer, Major Independent Bookseller
Owned by: Editorial Kier SACIFI

H F Martinez de Murguia SAC y E
Av Cordoba 2270, 1120 Buenos Aires
Tel: (011) 4952-1088; (011) 4952-6173 (sales)
 Fax: (011) 4952-1088
E-mail: info@murguia.com.ar

Web Site: www.murguia.com.ar
Key Personnel
President: Agustin T Aparicio

Nueva Vision
Tucaman 3748, 1189 Buenos Aires
Tel: (011) 8631461; (011) 8635980
Key Personnel
Manager: Hector Yanover

Libreria General de Tomas Pardo SRL
Maipu 618, 1006 Buenos Aires
Tel: (011) 4322-0496 *Fax:* (011) 4393-6759

Riverside Agency SAC
Mexico 3080 PB, C1223ABL Buenos Aires
Tel: (011) 4957-2336 *Fax:* (011) 4956-1985
E-mail: riverside@laisla.net
Key Personnel
President: Juan Carlos Zaragoza
Vice President: Carlos Miguel Zaragoza
Dir: Gabriela Zaragoza
Founded: 1958
Type of Business: Distributor, Importer, Wholesaler

Libreria Rodriguez SA, Dto Suscripciones
Sarmiento 835, 1041 Buenos Aires
Tel: (011) 4326-3725; (011) 4326-3826
 Fax: (011) 4326-1959
E-mail: librerod@ssdnet.com.ar
Telex: 22087 Elerre
Key Personnel
General Manager: Bautista L Tello
Founded: 1903
Also Publisher (see Ediciones L R SA).

Libreria Santa Fe
Ave Santa Fe 2582, 1123 Buenos Aires
Tel: (011) 4824-5005; (011) 4829-2545 (virtual store) *Fax:* (011) 824-7932
E-mail: info@lsf.com.ar
Web Site: www.lsf.com.ar; www.libreriasantafe.com
Key Personnel
Contact: Juan Pablo Aisenberg; Ruben Aisenberg
Founded: 1957
Type of Business: Importer
Branch Office(s)
Ave Santa Fe 2376, Buenos Aires *Tel:* (011) 4827-0100
Alto Palermo Shopping Local 78, Ave Santa Fe 3253, Buenos Aires *Tel:* (011) 5777-8078
Ave Callao 335, Buenos Aires *Tel:* (011) 4371-8391
Ave Cordoba 2064, Buenos Aires *Tel:* (011) 4372-7609

Australia

Academic & General Bookshop
259 Swanston St, Melbourne, Victoria 3000
Tel: (03) 96633231 *Fax:* (03) 96637234
E-mail: info@academicbooks.com.au
Key Personnel
Owner: Anthony Kyriacou

Founded: 1974
Branch Office(s)
Caledonia Lane, Melbourne, Victoria *Tel:* (03) 6637229 *Fax:* (03) 6637234
Bookshop(s): 196 Elgin St, Carlton 3053

Angus & Robertson Bookshops
379 Collins St, Level 14, Melbourne, Victoria 3000
Mailing Address: GPO Box 82A, Melbourne, Victoria 3001
Tel: (03) 86231111 *Fax:* (03) 86231150
E-mail: info@angusrobertson.com.au
Web Site: www.angusrobertson.com.au
Key Personnel
General Manager: David Conners
Founded: 1882
170 stores in Australia & online bookstore.
Owned by: Brasch Pty Ltd

Australian Book Collector, imprint of Burnet's Books

Banyan Tree Book Distributors
13 College Rd, Kent Town, SA 5067
Tel: (08) 8363-4244 *Fax:* (08) 8363-4255
E-mail: enquiries@banyantreebooks.com.au; orders@banyantreebooks.com.au
Web Site: banyantreebooks.predelegation.com
Key Personnel
Dir: Susan Vanderheiden
Founded: 1989
Large, independent national Australian distributor of spiritual books.
Type of Business: Distributor

James Bennett Pty Ltd
3 Narabang Way, Belrose, NSW 2085
Mailing Address: Locked Bag 537, Frenchs Forest, NSW 2086
Tel: (02) 9986 7000 *Fax:* (02) 9986 7031
E-mail: customerservice@bennett.com.au
Web Site: www.bennett.com.au
Key Personnel
Man Dir: Chris von Hinckeldey *Tel:* (02) 9986 7036 *E-mail:* cvh@bennett.com.au
National Sales & Marketing Manager: Nada Novakov *Tel:* (02) 9986 7064 *E-mail:* nada@bennett.com.au
Operations & Logistics Controller: Frank Peard *Tel:* (02) 9986 7054 *E-mail:* fpeard@bennett.com.au
Founded: 1958
Library supplier.
Type of Business: Distributor, Exporter, Importer, Wholesaler
Owned by: B H Blackwell Ltd

Bibliotech
Division of ANUTECH
Corner Daley & Barry Drive, Acton, ACT 2601
Mailing Address: GPO Box 4, Canberra ACT 2601
Tel: (02) 62492479 *Fax:* (02) 62575088
E-mail: books@bibliotech.com.au
Key Personnel
Manager: Cathy Teager *Tel:* (02) 6249 4005
 E-mail: cathy.teager@anutech.com.au
Book Distribution Service.

AUSTRALIA

Type of Business: Distributor
Bookshop(s): Anutech Court, CNR Barry Dr & Daley Rd, Canberra ACT 2601 *Web Site:* www.anutech.com.au

Biramo Book Distributors
5 King St, Warners Bay, NSW 2282
Mailing Address: PO Box 95, Warners Bay, NSW 2282
Tel: (02) 49542626 *Fax:* (02) 49565398
E-mail: biramobooks@tpg.com.au
Key Personnel
Dir: Mr A F Rich
Founded: 1985
Type of Business: Distributor, Exporter, Importer, Wholesaler
Branch Office(s)
PO Box 14 640, Panmure, Auckland, New Zealand *Tel:* (09) 570 9089 *Fax:* (09) 570 4604

Birchalls
PO Box 170, Launceston, Tas 7250
Tel: (03) 63313011 *Toll Free Tel:* 800 806867 *Fax:* (03) 63317165
E-mail: enquiry@birchalls.com.au
Web Site: www.birchalls.com.au
Key Personnel
Man Dir: Graeme R Tilley *E-mail:* gtilley@birchalls.com.au
Founded: 1844
Australia's oldest online bookseller.
Type of Business: Importer, Major Book Chain Headquarters, Major Independent Bookseller, Wholesaler
Branch Office(s)
Students Bookshop, Burnie Tafe College, Mooreville Rd, Burnie *Tel:* (03) 64333602 *Fax:* (03) 64333716
Students Bookshop, Devonport Tafe College, 20 Valley Rd, Devonport *Tel:* (03) 64215518 *Fax:* (03) 64242581
Students Bookshop, Don College, Watkinson St, Devonport *Tel:* (03) 64244072 *Fax:* (03) 64244072
Birchalls Education Centre, 147 Bathurst St, Hobart, Tasmania 7250 *Tel:* (03) 62342122 *Fax:* (03) 62348719
Hobart Tafe Student Bookshop, 75 Campbell St, Hobart, Tasmania *Tel:* (03) 62337405 *Fax:* (03) 62311067
Bookshop(s): Students Bookshop, Alanvale Tafe College, Alanvale, Tasmania *Tel:* (03) 63364284 *Fax:* (03) 63364284

Books Australasia, see Gaston Renard Pty Ltd

Bookwise International
174 Cormack Rd, Wingfield SA 5013
Mailing Address: PO Box 2164, Regency Park SA 5942
Tel: (08) 8268 8222 *Fax:* (08) 8268 8704
E-mail: customer.service@bookwise.com.au
Web Site: www.bookwise.com.au
Key Personnel
Man Dir: Patricia Genat *E-mail:* patricia.genat@bookwise.com.au
Marketing Dir: Andrew Easton
Founded: 1957
Type of Business: Wholesaler
Branch Office(s)
62 Wellington Parade, East Melbourne, Victoria 3002
4124 Hood St, Sherwood 4075
428 George St, Sydney 2000

Burgewood Books
4 Diane Court, Warrandyte, Victoria 3113
Tel: (03) 98442512 (Australia); (03) 9844 2512 (International) *Fax:* (03) 98440664 (Australia); (03) 9844 0664 (International)

Key Personnel
President & Partner: Doreen Burge *E-mail:* dburge@iprimus.com.au
Vice President: Nell Charlwood
Author: Don Charlwood
Founded: 1996
Publishing.

Burnet's Books
100 Bridge St, Uralla, NSW 2358
Tel: (02) 6778 4682 *Fax:* (02) 6778 4516
E-mail: burnet@ozbook.com
Web Site: www.ozbook.com
Key Personnel
Man Dir & Editor: Ross Burnet *E-mail:* burnet@ozbook.com
Founded: 1986
Antiquarian & secondhand bookdealer.
Type of Business: Distributor, Exporter, Importer, Major Independent Bookseller, Wholesaler
Imprints: Australian Book Collector; Idriess Enterprises
Branch Office(s)
Gatherum Books, 62 Bridge St, Uralla, NSW 2358 *Tel:* (02) 6778 4376 *E-mail:* gatherum@dodo.com.au

Collins Booksellers Pty Ltd
86 Bourke St, 2nd floor, Melbourne, Victoria 3000
Tel: (03) 96629472 *Fax:* (03) 96622527
E-mail: enquiries@collinsbooks.com.au
Web Site: www.collinsbooks.com.au
Key Personnel
Chairman & Chief Executive, OBE: Michael G Zifcak
Secretary: T J McCarthy
Founded: 1929
Type of Business: Major Book Chain Headquarters
Branch Office(s)
Canberra
New South Wales
Victoria, Queensland
Western Australia (Western Australia)

Continental Bookshop
1292 Malvern Rd, Malvern, Victoria 3144
Tel: (03) 98247711 *Fax:* (03) 98247855
Key Personnel
Owner: Harry Raynor
Owner & Mgr: Christopher Raynor *E-mail:* audio@vicnet.com.au
Founded: 1962
Foreign language books & language learning media.
Type of Business: Distributor, Exporter, Importer, Major Independent Bookseller

DA Information Services Pty Ltd
648 Whitehorse Rd, Mitcham, Victoria 3132
Mailing Address: PO Box 163, Mitcham, Victoria 3132
Tel: (03) 9210-7777 *Fax:* (03) 9210-7788
E-mail: service@dadirect.com.au
Web Site: www.dadirect.com.au
Key Personnel
Chief Executive: Kim Hunt
Founded: 1951
Subscription agents, Library suppliers, Electronic Information Suppliers.
Type of Business: Distributor, Importer

Daltons Books
54 Marcus Clarke St, Canberra City, ACT 2601
Mailing Address: GPO Box 549, Canberra City ACT 2601
Tel: (02) 62491844 *Fax:* (02) 62475753
E-mail: daltons@daltons.com.au
Web Site: www.daltons.com.au

MAJOR

Key Personnel
Dir: Meredith Wright *E-mail:* meredith@daltons.com.au
Founded: 1968
Computer & Business, Book Specialists, Rare & Limited Edition Books.
Type of Business: Distributor, Exporter, Importer, Major Independent Bookseller
Owned by: T J Dalton Pty Ltd, PO Box 189, Claremont, WA 6010
Branch Office(s)
Dalton Books Pty Ltd

Dominie
8 Cross St, Brookvale, NSW 2100
Mailing Address: PO Box 33, Brookvale, NSW 2100
Tel: (02) 9050201 *Fax:* (02) 9055209

Dymocks Pty Ltd
428 George St, 6th floor, Sydney, NSW
Mailing Address: GPO Box 1521, Sydney, NSW 2001
Tel: (02) 9224 0411 *Toll Free Tel:* 800 805 711 *Fax:* (02) 9224 9401
E-mail: feedback@dymocks.com.au; service@dymocks.com.au
Web Site: www.dymocks.com.au
Key Personnel
Chairman: J P C Forsyth
Man Dir: K B Terry

Foreign Language Bookshop
259 Collins St, Melbourne, Victoria 3000
Tel: (03) 96542883 *Fax:* (03) 96507664
E-mail: flb@ozonline.com.au
Web Site: www.languages.com.au
Key Personnel
Man Dir: Annette Monester
Founded: 1938
Bookstore with stock in 90 languages-books, audio learning kits software.
Type of Business: Exporter, Importer, Major Independent Bookseller

Gaanetgetal Books
21 National St, Leichhardt, NSW 2040
Tel: (02) 4234-0865 *Fax:* (02) 4234-0875
E-mail: enquiries@books-on-rugs.com
Key Personnel
President: Geoffrey Long
Vice President: Ann Long
Manager: Naomi Jacobs
Type of Business: Distributor, Importer, Major Independent Bookseller, Wholesaler
Branch Office(s)
Bolvanna, Lot 2, Foxground Rd, Foxground, NSW 2536
Bookshop(s): 22 National St, Leichhardt, NSW 2040

Gaston Renard Pty Ltd
PO Box 1030, Ivanhoe, Melbourne, Victoria 3079
Tel: (03) 9459 5040 *Fax:* (03) 9459 6787
E-mail: books@gastonrenard.com.au
Web Site: www.gastonrenard.com.au
Key Personnel
Owner: Julien Renard
Founded: 1945
Specialize in antiquarian bookseller & publisher
Membership(s): ANZAAB.
Type of Business: Distributor, Exporter, Importer, Major Independent Bookseller

Grahames Bookshop
Division of Horwitz Grahame Pty Ltd
506 Miller St, Cammeray, NSW 2062
Tel: (02) 9296144 *Fax:* (02) 9571814
Ten company & franchise stores nationwide.

BOOK DEALERS   AUSTRIA

Branch Office(s)
MLC Bldg, 105 Miller S, North Sydney, NSW 2060
Bankstown Shopping Square, Bankstown, NSW 2200
Imperial Centre, Gosford, NSW 2250
City Tatts, 200 Pitt St, Sydney, NSW 2000
Mid-City Centre, 197 Pitt St, Sydney, NSW 2000

Identic Books
Formerly Mason's Book Centre
PO Box 323, Pymble NSW 2073
Tel: (02) 8901 3466 *Fax:* (02) 8901 3404
E-mail: enquiries@identic.com.au
Web Site: www.identic.com.au
Key Personnel
Man Dir: W A T Mason
Dir & Secretary: D W Mason
Founded: 1967
Type of Business: Distributor, Exporter, Importer, Major Independent Bookseller

Idriess Enterprises, *imprint of* Burnet's Books

Kirby Book Co Pty Ltd
Suite 704, 7 Hele St, Chatswood NSW 2067
Mailing Address: Private Bag No 19, PO Alexandria, Sydney, NSW 2067
Tel: (02) 9698 2377 *Toll Free Tel:* 800 225271 *Fax:* (02) 9698 8748
Key Personnel
Chairman: John D C Reid
Co Man Dir: John A D Reid; Peter N D Reid
  E-mail: preid@kirby.com.au
Founded: 1951
Australia's leading specialist wholesale distributor of oversea publications.
Type of Business: Wholesaler

Koorong Books Pty Ltd
28 West Parade, West Ryde, NSW 2114
Tel: (02) 9857 4477 *Fax:* (02) 9857 4499
E-mail: west_ryde@koorong.com.au; koorong@koorong.com.au
Web Site: www.koorong.com.au
Key Personnel
Managing Dir: Paul Bootes *E-mail:* pb@koorong.com.au
Buying & Marketing Manager: Gavin Shume
  E-mail: ga@koorong.com.au
Store Manager: Rob Morris *E-mail:* ro@koorong.com.au
Founded: 1975
Type of Business: Importer, Major Book Chain Headquarters
Branch Office(s)
198 Waymouth St, Adelaide, SA 5000, Store Manager: Christine DeBruyn *Tel:* (08) 8239 6777 *Fax:* (08) 8239 6788 *E-mail:* adelaide@koorong.com.au
120 Rusden St, Armidale, NSW 2350, Store Manager: Pete Hansen *Tel:* (02) 6772 2622 *Fax:* (02) 6772 7608 *E-mail:* armidale@koorong.com.au
4-8 Vicki St, Blackburn South, Victoria 3130, Store Manager: Matthew Hart *Tel:* (03) 9262 7444 *Fax:* (03) 9262 7499 *E-mail:* blackburn@koorong.com.au
Unit 1, 26 Maryborough St, Fyshwick, ACT 2609, Store Manager: Rod Brewe *Tel:* (02) 6280 3477 *Fax:* (02) 6280 3488 *E-mail:* fyshwick@koorong.com.au
31 Criterion St, Hobart, Tas 7000, Store Manager: Peter Atkinson *Tel:* (03) 6231 0992 *Fax:* (03) 6231 0993 *E-mail:* hobart@koorong.com.au
663 Newcastle St, Leederville, WA 6007, Store Manager: Mary Wright *Tel:* (08) 9427 9777 *Fax:* (08) 9427 9788 *E-mail:* leederville@koorong.com.au
Unit 3b, Henry Lawson Centre, 61-79 Henry St, Penrith, NSW 2750, Store Manager: Brad Johnson *Tel:* (02) 4724 4477 *Fax:* (02) 4724 4488 *E-mail:* penrith@koorong.com.au
141 Gordon St, Port Macquarie, NSW 2444, Store Manager: Rod Lampard-Mills *Tel:* (02) 6584 4977 *Fax:* (02) 6583 6235 *E-mail:* port-macquarie@koorong.com.au
837 Ruthven St, Toowoomba, Qld 4350, Store Manager: Cheryl Hansen *Tel:* (07) 4636 2177 *Fax:* (07) 4636 2188 *E-mail:* toowoomba@koorong.com.au
7 Broadway St, Wooloongabba, Qld 4102, Store Manager: Jenny Graf *Tel:* (07) 3896 8777 *Fax:* (07) 3896 8788 *E-mail:* wooloongabba@koorong.com.au

Landmark Education Supplies Pty Ltd
Princes Hwy, Drouin, Victoria 3818
Tel: (056) 251701
Key Personnel
Owner: Russell Porch

Language Book Centre
Division of Abbey's Bookshops Pty Ltd
131 York St, Sydney, NSW 2000
Tel: (02) 92671397 *Toll Free Tel:* 800 802 432 (outside Sydney & within Australia) *Fax:* (02) 92648993
E-mail: language@abbeys.com.au
Web Site: www.languagebooks.com.au
Key Personnel
Manager: Jacqueline Rychner *E-mail:* jacquir@abbeys.com.au
Man Dir: Jack Winning *Tel:* (02) 9264 3260
  E-mail: jackw@abbeys.com.au
Founded: 1976
Type of Business: Major Independent Bookseller

Magpie Books
PO Box 2038, Brighton 3186
Tel: (03) 95929931 *Fax:* (03) 95922045
E-mail: admin01@magpiebooks.com.au
Web Site: www.magpiebooks.com.au
Key Personnel
Proprietor: Brian Howes *E-mail:* brhowes@dove.net.au
Founded: 1986
Publishers of directories & price guides for the antiquarian book trade.
Type of Business: Distributor
Bookshop(s): Barossa Vintage Books, 111 Murray St, Angaston 5353 *Tel:* (08) 8564 3633 *E-mail:* brhowes@ozemail.com.au

Mason's Book Centre, see Identic Books

Robert Muir Old & Rare Books
69 Broadway, Nedlands 6009
Tel: (08) 9386 5842 *Fax:* (08) 9386 8211
E-mail: books@muirbooks.com
Web Site: www.muirbooks.com
Key Personnel
Owner: Helen Muir; Robert Muir
Founded: 1973
Member of ILAB, ABA, ANZAAB.
Type of Business: Exporter, Importer, Major Independent Bookseller

The Open Book
110 Gawler Pl, Adelaide, SA 5000
Mailing Address: GPO Box 1368, Adelaide, SA 5001
Tel: (08) 8124 0049 *Fax:* (08) 8223 4552
E-mail: openbook@openbook.com.au; service@openbook.com.au
Web Site: www.openbook.com.au
Key Personnel
National Retail Manager: Kevin Reichelt *Tel:* (08) 82239140 *E-mail:* kreichelt@openbook.com.au
Trade Sales Manager: Mike Grieger
  E-mail: mgrieger@openbook.com.au
Founded: 1913
Christian, religious bookstore - theological books & resources - specialty. Branch offices in Aubury, Brisbane, Hamilton, Melbourne, Sydney, Tanunda, & Toowoomba.
Type of Business: Distributor, Exporter, Importer, Major Book Chain Headquarters, Major Independent Bookseller, Wholesaler
Owned by: Openbook Publishers, 205 Halifax St, Adelaide, SA 5000

Soundbooks
1292 Malvern Rd, Malvern, Victoria 3144
Tel: (03) 98247711 *Fax:* (03) 98247855
E-mail: audio@vicnet.com.au
Web Site: www.soundbooks.com.au
Key Personnel
Dir: Christopher Raynor *E-mail:* audio@vicnet.com.au
Founded: 1982
Specialize in audiobooks.
Type of Business: Distributor, Exporter, Importer, Major Independent Bookseller

Michael Treloar Antiquarian Booksellers
196 North Terrace, Adelaide SA 5000
Mailing Address: GPO Box 2289, Adelaide SA 5001
Tel: (08) 82231111 *Fax:* (08) 82236599
E-mail: treloars@treloars.com
Web Site: www.treloars.com
Key Personnel
Owner: Michael Treloar
Founded: 1976
Type of Business: Major Independent Bookseller

La Trobe University Bookshop
La Trobe University, Plenty Rd, The Agora, Bundoora, Victoria 3083
Tel: (03) 94791234 *Fax:* (03) 94702011
E-mail: enquiries@bookshop.latrobe.edu.au
Web Site: www.bookshop.latrobe.edu.au
Key Personnel
General Manager: I Patterson
Branch Office(s)
La Trobe University Bendigo Campus, Edwards Rd, Student Union floor, Bendigo 3550 *Tel:* (03) 5444 7516 *Fax:* (03) 5444 7825 *E-mail:* bendigo@bookshop.latrobe.edu.au
Wodonga TAFE Campus, 15 McKoy St, Wodonga 3690 *Tel:* (02) 6058 3899 *Fax:* (02) 6056 2380 *E-mail:* wodonga@bookshop.latrobe.edu.au

University Co-operative Bookshop Ltd
235 Jones St, Level 10, Ultimo NSW 2007
Tel: (02) 93259600 *Fax:* (02) 92123372
E-mail: webhelp@coop-bookshop.com.au
Web Site: www.coop-bookshop.com.au
Key Personnel
Chief Executive Officer: Duncan Maclellan
Founded: 1958
Over 40 co-op stores located across Australia.
Type of Business: Major Book Chain Headquarters, Major Independent Bookseller

Austria

Aichinger, Bernhard & Co GmbH
Weihburggasse 16, 1010 Vienna
Tel: (01) 5128853 *Fax:* (01) 5128853-13
Key Personnel
Manager: Mag Veronika Aichinger

Buchhandlung Bayer
Formerly Buchhandlung Wolfgang Neugebauer
Kreuzgasse 6, 6800 Feldkirch
Tel: (05522) 74770 *Fax:* (05522) 74770
E-mail: bayer.buch@utanet.at
Key Personnel
Contact: Irmgard Neugebauer

AUSTRIA

Founded: 1973
Also library supplier.
Type of Business: Distributor, Exporter, Importer, Major Independent Bookseller
Parent Company: W Neugebauer Verlag GesmbH

Blackwell & Hadwiger GesmbH British Bookshop
Weihburggasse 24-26, 1010 Vienna
Tel: (01) 5121945; (01) 5132933 *Fax:* (01) 5121026
E-mail: britbook@netway.at
Key Personnel
Contact: Margaret Hofmaier
Founded: 1974
Type of Business: Importer, Major Independent Bookseller

British Bookshop, see Blackwell & Hadwiger GesmbH British Bookshop

Bucher-Stierle GesmbH
Kaigasse 1 - Mozartplazt, A-5010 Salzburg
Mailing Address: Postfach 245, A-5010 Salzberg
Tel: (0662) 840114 *Fax:* (0662) 8401149
E-mail: buecher-stierle@members.debis.at
Key Personnel
Owner: Vivienne Stierle
Founded: 1988
Type of Business: Exporter, Importer, Major Independent Bookseller

Der Buchfreund Universitats-Buchhandlung u Antiquariat Walter R Schaden
Sonnenfelsgasse 4, 1010 Vienna
Tel: (01) 512 48 56; (01) 513 82 89 *Fax:* (01) 512 60 28
E-mail: buch.schaden@vienna.at
Web Site: www.buch-schaden.at
Key Personnel
Owner: Rainer Schaden
Founded: 1955
Member of JLAB.
Type of Business: Importer, Major Independent Bookseller
Owned by: Rainer Schaden
Bookshop(s): Lugeck 7, 1010 Vienna

Dietz GmbH
Bahnstr 1, A-2351 Wiener Neudorf
Tel: (02236) 22596 *Fax:* (02236) 47127
Key Personnel
Manager: Horst Jansa; Walter Dietz
Founded: 1978
Type of Business: Importer, Wholesaler
Branch Office(s)
Airport Vienna, Vienna
Graz
Salzburg
Bookshop(s): American Discount, Rechte Wienzeile 5, 1040 Vienna

Fachbuchhandlung fur Wirtschaft und Recht Dr Karl Stropek GmbH
Waehringerstr 122, Postfach 84, A-1181 Vienna
Tel: (01) 4795495 *Fax:* (01) 4796230
Key Personnel
Proprietor: Eleonore Stropek
Founded: 1863
Library supplier.
Type of Business: Major Independent Bookseller

Gerold & Co
Graben 13, A-1010 Vienna
Mailing Address: Postfach 597, 1011 Vienna
Tel: (01) 5335014-0
E-mail: buch@gerold.at
Web Site: www.gerold.at
Telex: 847136157 Gerol *Cable:* Geroldbuch Vienna

Key Personnel
Man Dir: Hans Neusser
Subscription agent & library jobber for European books & periodicals; also publisher.

Hans Furstelberger
Kaufmaennisches Vereinhaus, Landstr 49, 4013 Linz
Tel: (0732) 773177 *Fax:* (0732) 784485
Type of Business: Major Independent Bookseller

A Hartleben Inhaber Dr Walter Rob
Schwarzenbergstr 6, Postfach 309, A-1010 Vienna
Tel: (01) 512-62-41 *Fax:* (01) 513-94-98
Key Personnel
Owner: Dr Walter Rob; Dr Marion Unger-Rob
Founded: 1803
Type of Business: Distributor, Importer, Major Independent Bookseller
Branch Office(s)
Huetteldorfer Str 114, 1140 Vienna

Verlag Johannes Heyn
Kramergasse 2-4, 9020 Klagenfurt
Tel: (0463) 54249 *Fax:* (0463) 542491
E-mail: buch@heyn.at; technik@heyn.at
Web Site: www.heyn.at
Key Personnel
Owner: Gert Zechner; Volkmar Zechner
Type of Business: Major Independent Bookseller

Buchhandlung Karl Hofbauer KG
Hauptplatz 31, 8430 Leibnitz
Tel: (03452) 82793; (03452) 82177 *Fax:* (03452) 71218
E-mail: hofbauer.buch@magnet.at
Key Personnel
Manager: Jutta Hofbauer
Founded: 1963
Type of Business: Importer, Major Independent Bookseller
Branch Office(s)
A-8430 Leibnitz, Grazerg 73 *Tel:* (03452) 83166

Friedrich Hofmeister-Figaro Verlag Grossortiment und Musikalienhandlung GesmbH
Seikrgasse 12, 1015 Vienna
Tel: (01) 50576510 *Fax:* (01) 5059185
Key Personnel
Contact: Ferdinand Walcher
Type of Business: Importer, Wholesaler

Innverlag + Gatt
Hunoldstr 12, 6020 Innsbruck
Tel: (0512) 34 53 31 *Fax:* (0512) 34 12 90
E-mail: info@innverlag.at
Web Site: www.innverlag.at
Key Personnel
Production: Klaus Hagleitner
Founded: 1947
Type of Business: Distributor, Importer, Major Independent Bookseller, Wholesaler

Alexander Kerbiser KG
Wiener Str 17, Hammerpark 10, 8680 Muerzzuschlag
Tel: (03852) 2204 *Fax:* (03852) 5349
Key Personnel
Contact: E M Mueck
Founded: 1936
Type of Business: Major Independent Bookseller

Walter Klugel
Gumpendorferstr 33, A-1060 Vienna
Tel: (0222) 573 03 42
Founded: 1921
Type of Business: Major Independent Bookseller

Antiquariat Walter Krieg Verlag
Karntner Str 4/III, A-1010 Vienna
Tel: (01) 5121093 *Fax:* (01) 5123266
Also library supplier.
Type of Business: Exporter

Leopold Stocker Verlag
Hofgasse 5, 8011 Graz
Mailing Address: Postfach 189, 8011 Graz
Tel: (0316) 82 16 36 *Fax:* (0316) 83 56 12
E-mail: buecherquelle@stocker-verlag.com
Web Site: www.buecherquelle.at
Key Personnel
Publisher: Wolfgang Dvorak-Stocker
Founded: 1917
Type of Business: Major Independent Bookseller
Bookshop(s): Buecherquelle Buchhandlungs GmbH, Graz

MANZ'sche Verlags- und Universitaetsbuchhandlung GMBH
Kohlmarkt 16, Postfach 163, 1010 Vienna
Tel: (01) 531 61-161 *Fax:* (01) 531 61-181
E-mail: bestellen@manz.co.at
Web Site: www.manz.at
Telex: 75310631
Also publisher & library supplier.
Type of Business: Exporter

Mohr-ZA Verlagsauslieferungen Ges mbH
Singerstr 12, 1010 Vienna
Mailing Address: Postfach 771, 1010 Vienna
Tel: (01) 5121676; (01) 5125711; (01) 5126994 *Fax:* (01) 111859
Key Personnel
Proprietor: Dr Gottfried Berger
Type of Business: Wholesaler

Buchhandlung Wolfgang Neugebauer, see Buchhandlung Bayer

Osterreichische Bibelgesellschaft (Austrian Bible Society)
Breite Gasse 8, 1070 Vienna
Tel: (01) 5238240 *Fax:* (01) 5238240-20
E-mail: bibelhaus@bibelgesellschaft.at
Web Site: www.oesterrbibelges.at
Key Personnel
Contact: Dr Jutta Henner
Founded: 1970
Type of Business: Major Independent Bookseller

Max Pock, Universitaetsbuchhandlung
Hauptplatz 1, 8010 Graz
Tel: (0316) 825254-0 *Fax:* (0316) 825258; (0316) 825254-8
Telex: 031873
Key Personnel
Manager: Dr Maximilian Pock
Also library supplier.
Type of Business: Exporter

Georg Prachner KG
Kaerntner Str 30, 1015 Vienna
Tel: (01) 5128549-0 *Fax:* (01) 5120158
Key Personnel
Man Dir: O G Prachner
Also Publisher.
Type of Business: Exporter, Importer, Major Independent Bookseller, Wholesaler

Styria Medien AG
Schonaugasse 64, 8010 Graz
Tel: (0316) 8063-1012 *Fax:* (0316) 8063-3034
E-mail: medien.ag@styria.com
Web Site: www.styria.com
Key Personnel
Contact: Wolfgang Habenschuss
Owned by: Styria Druck und Verlagshaus
Branch Office(s)
Hauptpl 15, 8720 Judenburg, Australia

Kaerntnerstr 2, 8720 Knittelfeld
Wollzeille 2, 1010 Vienna

J G Sydy's Buchhandlung Ludwig Schubert GmbH Nachfolge KG
Wienerstr 19, 3100 St Poelten
Tel: (02742) 35 31 89 *Fax:* (02742) 35 31 89; (02742) 35 31 85
E-mail: schubert.sydys@aon.at; info@buchandlung-schubert.at
Web Site: www.buchhandlung-schubert.at
Key Personnel
Contact: Susanne Sandler
Founded: 1837
Membership(s): Hauptverband des Oesterreichischen Buchhandels.
Type of Business: Exporter, Importer, Major Independent Bookseller

Tyrolia Verlagsanstalt GmbH
Exlgasse 20, 6020 Innsbruck
Tel: (0512) 2233-0 *Fax:* (0512) 2233-501
E-mail: tyrolia@tyrolia.at
Web Site: www.tyrolia.at
Telex: 053620
Key Personnel
Manager: Thaler Franz
Owned by: Verlagsanstalt Tyrolia
Branch Office(s)
Ehrwald
Fulpmes
Imst
Kufstein
Landeck
Lienz
Mayrhofen
Reutte
Schwaz
St Johann
Telfs
Vienna
Wattens
Woergl

Urban und Schwarzenberg GmbH
Frankgasse 4, 1096 Vienna
Tel: (01) 4052731 *Fax:* (01) 405272441
Key Personnel
Manager: Gunter Royer
Also Publisher.
Owned by: Williams & Wilkins Ltd

Buchhandlung Veritas
Hafenstr 1-3, 4010 Linz
Mailing Address: Postfach 50, 4010 Linz
Tel: (0732) 776451-280 *Fax:* (0732) 776451-239
E-mail: veritas@veritas.at
Web Site: www.veritas.at
Key Personnel
Manager: Klaus Radler
Owned by: Veritas GesmbH & Co KG

Wagner'sche Universitaetsbuchhandlung
Museumstr 4, 6020 Innsbruck
Tel: (0512) 59505-0 *Fax:* (0512) 59505-38
E-mail: buch@wagnersche.at
Web Site: www.wagnersche.at
Telex: 75311457
Key Personnel
Dir: Martin Flatscher
Also library supplier.
Type of Business: Exporter

Rupertusbuchhandlung Augustin Weis und Soehne KG
Dreifaltigkeitsgasse 12, A-5024 Salzburg
Tel: (0662) 878733-0 *Fax:* (0662) 871661
E-mail: info@rupertusbuch.at
Key Personnel
Manager: Bernhard Weis *E-mail:* b.weis@rupertusbuch.at

Also library supplier.
Type of Business: Exporter

Kunstverlag Wolfrum
Augustinerstr 10, 1010 Vienna
Tel: (01) 5125398-0 *Fax:* (01) 5125398-57
E-mail: your-welcome@wolfrum.at
Web Site: www.wolfrum.at
Telex: 75311081 Wolb *Cable:* WITWOLF VIENNA
Key Personnel
Man Dir: Monika Engel
Manager: Peter Engel; Erich Pospisil
Founded: 1919
Also Publisher of posters, note-cards, calendars & library supplier of art books.
Type of Business: Distributor, Exporter, Importer, Major Independent Bookseller
Owned by: Monika Engel & Hubert Wolfrum

Bangladesh

Adeyle Brothers & Co
60 Patuatuly, Dhaka 1100
Tel: (02) 233508
Owned by: Genclik Kitabevi

Bangladesh Books International Ltd
73-74 Patuatuli, Dhaka 1100
Tel: (02) 232252 (ext 31); (02) 232229; (02) 256071 (ext 19)
Key Personnel
Manager: Abdul Hafiz
Also publisher.

Dhaka Book Mart
38-2 Banglabazar, Dhaka 1100
Tel: (02) 259173

Kathakali (Bud of Spoken World)
18 Momin Rd, Chittagong 4000
Tel: (031) 619476; (031) 619006; (031) 612625
Key Personnel
Dir, Author & Editor: Mahbubul Haque
E-mail: mhaque@abnetbd.com
Founded: 1982
Managing Authority of Chittagong University Book Center, Publisher of Chittagong Guide.
Membership(s): Bangladesh Book Sellers' & Publishers' Association.
Type of Business: Distributor, Importer, Major Independent Bookseller, Wholesaler
Owned by: Mashuda Yasmin

Mullick Bros
160-161 Dhaka New Market, Dhaka 1205
Tel: (02) 8619125; (02) 507434 *Fax:* (02) 8610562
E-mail: mullick@bd.com
Also Publisher.

Puthigar Ltd
74 Farashganj, Dhaka 1100
Tel: (02) 231374; (02) 235333; (02) 259867

Barbados

The Book Source
9100407 Barbados Community College Campus, Howells Cross Rd, St Michael
Mailing Address: PO Box 964E, Belleville, Saint Michael

Tel: 4310379 *Fax:* 4261855
E-mail: bksource@caribsurf.com
Web Site: www.booksourceonline.com
Key Personnel
Dir: Beverly Smith-Hinkson *E-mail:* beverly.bksource@caribsurf.com
Founded: 1989
Book ordering service; college bookshop; online bookstore.
Type of Business: Major Independent Bookseller
Owned by: Datalore Inc

Christian Literature Crusade
Constitution Rd, Bridgetown
Mailing Address: PO Box 1239, Bridgetown
Tel: 429-5630 *Fax:* 426-9254
Key Personnel
Manager: Pauline Sealy
Founded: 1941
Type of Business: Distributor, Importer, Major Book Chain Headquarters

Cloister Bookstore Ltd
Hincks & Cowell Sts, Bridgetown
Tel: (246) 426-2662 *Fax:* (246) 429-7269
E-mail: cloisterbookstore@caribsurf.com
Key Personnel
Man Dir: A Musgrave
Founded: 1957
Type of Business: Distributor, Importer, Major Independent Bookseller, Wholesaler

Belgium

Uitgeverij Acco
Tiensestr 134, 3000 Leuven
Tel: (016) 29 11 00 *Fax:* (016) 20 73 89
E-mail: papierhandel@acco.be
Web Site: www.acco.be
Key Personnel
Dir: Herman Peeters *Tel:* (016) 62 80 10
E-mail: herman.peeters@acco.be
Founded: 1960
Type of Business: Distributor, Exporter, Major Independent Bookseller, Wholesaler

Agence et Menageries de la Prense
One Rue de Petite Ile, 1070 Brussels
Tel: (02) 52 51 641 *Fax:* (02) 52 34 863
Key Personnel
Contact: Jean-Pierre Verbeeck; Mr Sheridan
Founded: 1850
Type of Business: Distributor, Exporter, Importer, Major Book Chain Headquarters, Wholesaler

Agora bvba
Ninovesteenweg 24, 9320 Aalst-Erembodegem
Tel: (053) 78-87-00 *Fax:* (053) 78-26-91
E-mail: info@agorabooks.com
Web Site: www.agorabooks.com
Key Personnel
Dir: Jacques Van Mello
Founded: 1985
Type of Business: Distributor, Importer, Major Independent Bookseller

Altiora Averbode Uitgeverij nv
PB 54, 3271 Averbode
Tel: (013) 780 182 *Fax:* (013) 780 179
E-mail: averbode.publ@verbode.be
Web Site: www.averbode.be
Key Personnel
Contact: Karolien Van Geldre

Aquila BVBA, see Boekhandel Johannes

BELGIUM

NV Artis-Historia
Postbus 150, 2800 Mechelen 1
Tel: (078) 150 150 *Fax:* (078) 150 050
E-mail: info@artis-historia.be
Web Site: www.artis-historia.be
100 Bookshops throughout Belgium; Also Publisher.

Audivox
Rubenslei 23, 2018 Antwerp
Tel: (03) 470 1784
E-mail: info@audivox.net
Key Personnel
Dir: Robert Gonnissen
Founded: 1953
Specialize in the import & distribution of English & American books.

Boekhandel Johannes
Formerly Aquila BVBA
Alfons Smetsplein 10, 3000 Leuven
Tel: (016) 229501 *Fax:* (016) 208419
E-mail: info@johannes.be
Web Site: www.johannes.be
Key Personnel
Manager: Jos Maes *E-mail:* j.maes@johannes.be
Founded: 1977
Type of Business: Distributor, Importer, Major Independent Bookseller
Owned by: Aquila bvba, de Beriotstr 2, 3000 Leuven
Branch Office(s)
Boekhandel de Kleine Johannes, Tiensestr 47, 3000 Leuven *Tel:* (016) 206046 *Fax:* (016) 208419

Bredero
Rozenberg 15, 2400 Mol
Tel: (014) 31-84-61 *Fax:* (014) 70-02-05
Web Site: www.bredero.be
Key Personnel
Contact: E De Ridder
Type of Business: Major Independent Bookseller

De Plukvogel nv
Mechelsesteenweg 9, 1800 Vilvoorde
Tel: (02) 253-06-58 *Fax:* (02) 253-06-58
Key Personnel
Contact: P Steyaert

Exhibitions International NV/SA
Kolonel Begaultlaan 17, 3012 Leuven (Wilsele)
Tel: (016) 296900 *Fax:* (016) 296129
E-mail: orders@exhibitionsinternational.be
Web Site: www.exhibitionsinternational.be
Key Personnel
Dir: Marleen Geukens *E-mail:* marleen.geukens@exhibitionsinternational.be
Founded: 1988
Acts as distributor for art books, catalogues & illustrated books on gardens, travel, architecture, design, etc.
Type of Business: Distributor

Uitgeverij Het-Volk
Forelstr 22, 9000 Ghent
Tel: (09) 2656424; (09) 2656420 *Fax:* (09) 2258406
Key Personnel
Publishing Dept Manager: F Nauwelaerts
General Manager: E Korntheuer
Publishers of newspapers, magazines, books & comics.
Owned by: Drukkerij Het Volk NV
Bookshop(s): Brusselsestr 11, B-9200 Dendermonde; Kortedagsteeg 16, B-9000 Gent; Rijselstr 20, B-8900 Ieper; Markstr 24, B-8870 Izegem; Voorstr 35, B-8500 Kortrijk; Noordstr 6, B-8800 Roeselare; Maastrichtstr 65, B-3700 Tongeren; Korte Gasthuisstr 13, B-2300 Turnhout

J Story-Scientia BVBA
Van Duyseplein 8, 9000 Ghent
Tel: (09) 2255757 *Fax:* (09) 2331409
E-mail: bookshop@story.be
Web Site: www.story.be
Key Personnel
Manager: J Story
Founded: 1962
Scientific booksellers & subscription agents & publishers.
Type of Business: Distributor, Exporter, Importer, Major Independent Bookseller

Librairie des Presses Universitaires de Bruxelles
42 ave Paul Heger, 1000 Brussels
Tel: (02) 641 1440 *Fax:* (02) 6477962
Web Site: www.ulb.ac.be
Key Personnel
Contact: Paulette Biondi *E-mail:* pbiondi@ulb.ac.be
Scientific books.
Owned by: Presses universitaires de Bruxelles ASBL

Licap CVBA
Guimardstraat 1, 1040 Brussels
Tel: (02) 5099672 *Fax:* (02) 5099704; (02) 5099780
E-mail: info@licap.be
Key Personnel
Contact: Herman Deben
Founded: 1973
Type of Business: Major Independent Bookseller

Maison des Langues Vivantes-Intertaal SA
Steenstraat, 9, Rue des Pierres, 1000 Brussels
Tel: (02) 5117117 *Fax:* (02) 5145820
E-mail: mlv.i@skynet.be
Web Site: maison-des-langues.com
Key Personnel
Man Dir: Pierre De Laet
Founded: 1960
Specialize in modern languages.
Type of Business: Importer, Major Independent Bookseller

Oneindige Verhaal, t bvba (The Neverending Story)
Nieuwstraat 17, 9100 Sint-Niklaas
Tel: (03) 7765225 *Fax:* (03) 7765225
E-mail: oneindigeverhaal@boekenbank.be
Key Personnel
Dir: Herwig Staes
Assistant Manager: Tim Staes *Tel:* (03) 7651730 *E-mail:* timstaes@planetinternet.be
Founded: 1996
Bookstore.

Pijl Boekbedrijf nv
Bleekhofstraat 87, 2140 Antwerp
Tel: (03) 236-98-30; (03) 270-02-70 *Fax:* (03) 235-90-02
E-mail: booksell@innet.be
Key Personnel
Contact: Johan Van Hemeldonck
Type of Business: Major Book Chain Headquarters, Wholesaler

Simon Stevin NV
Zennestraat 37, 1000 Brussels
Tel: (02) 5121085; (02) 5138295 *Fax:* (02) 5117015
Key Personnel
Dirs: L Van Hoorick; J De Hertogh
Founded: 1930

Libris Toison d'Or SA
Espace Louise, 40-42 ave de la Toison d'Or, 1050 Brussels
Tel: (02) 5116400 *Fax:* (02) 5140961

Key Personnel
Manager: Jacqueline Evrard
Founded: 1961
Type of Business: Major Book Chain Headquarters, Wholesaler
Owned by: Librairies du Savoir

VTB-Travel Bookshop
Division of Tui Germany
Osystraat 35, 2060 Antwerp
Tel: (03) 224 10 52 *Fax:* (03) 224 10 56
E-mail: info.cultuur@vtb.be
Web Site: www.vtb.be
Key Personnel
Manager: Bert van Uytsel *Tel:* (03) 220-33-68 *E-mail:* bert.vanuytsel@vtb.be
Founded: 1929
Travel Bookshop; Travel Guides-Maps-Travel Necessities.
Membership(s): IMTA; VBVB.
Type of Business: Major Book Chain Headquarters, Major Independent Bookseller, Wholesaler

Wouters Import NV
Naamsestraat 48, 3000 Leuven
Tel: (016) 233481 *Fax:* (016) 229841
E-mail: info@bookshop.wouters.be
Web Site: www.wouters.be
Key Personnel
Dir: L Verwimp *E-mail:* ludov@bookshop.wouters.be
Founded: 1989
Type of Business: Distributor, Exporter, Importer, Wholesaler
Owned by: Wouters BVBA

Benin

Libraira-Papeterie ABM
BP 889, Cotonou
Tel: 330690 (voice & fax)
Key Personnel
Vice President: Michel Goussanou
Type of Business: Distributor, Exporter, Importer, Wholesaler
Owned by: Maison d'Edition ABM
Branch Office(s)
Porto Novo
Bookshop(s): BP 889, C138 Guinkomey, Cotonou

Bolivia

Libreria los Amigos del Libro
Casilla de Correo 450, Cochabamba 15
Tel: (04) 4504150; (04) 4504151 *Fax:* (04) 4115128
E-mail: gutten@amigol.bo.net *Cable:* AMIGOL
Key Personnel
Owner: Ingrid Guttentag
Manager: Petra Guttentag; Sonia Laguna
Founded: 1945
Type of Business: Distributor, Exporter, Importer, Major Book Chain Headquarters, Wholesaler
Branch Office(s)
Airport Jorge Wilstermann, Cochabamba
Shopping Center S O F E R, Cochabamba
Av Ayacucho S-0156, Cochabamba
Bookstore San Miguel, La Paz
Bookstore en Avd 16 de Julio Edificio Alameda, La Paz
Bookstore Calle, Ingavi No 14, Santa Cruz
Calle Mercado 1315, Aerport El Alto, La Paz

Gisbert y Cia SA
Calle Comercio 1270, Plaza Murillo La Paz, La Paz
Mailing Address: Casilla Postal 195, La Paz
Tel: (02) 220 26 26 *Fax:* (02) 220 29 11
E-mail: libgis@ceibo.entelnet.bo
Key Personnel
President: Javier Gisbert
Founded: 1907
Also Publisher.
Type of Business: Distributor, Importer, Major Independent Bookseller, Wholesaler

Libreria Juventud
Plaza Murillo 519, Casilla de Correo 1489, La Paz
Tel: (02) 2406248 *Fax:* (02) 2406248
Key Personnel
Manager: Gustavo Urquizo Mendoza
Founded: 1948
Type of Business: Importer, Wholesaler
Owned by: Libreria y Editorial Juventud

Libreria la Paz
Calle Colon 618, Casilla, 539 La Paz
Tel: (02) 353323; (02) 357109 *Fax:* (02) 391513
Key Personnel
Manager: Carlos Burgos Munoz
Founded: 1900
Type of Business: Distributor, Importer, Major Independent Bookseller, Wholesaler

Bosnia and Herzegovina

Veselin Maslesa
Ul Obala V Stepe Br 4, 71000 Sarajevo
Mailing Address: Pro Boks 237, 71000 Sarajevo
Tel: (071) 214633
Telex: 41154
Also publisher.
Type of Business: Exporter, Importer
Branch Office(s)
Maksima Gorkog 2, Pavla Goranina 2, Sarajevo
Terazije 38, Belgrade, Serbia and Montenegro (over 30 group bookshops)

Sarajevo Publishing, see Veselin Maslesa

Svjetlost
Muhamede Kantardzica 3, 71000 Sarajevo
Tel: (071) 443 419; (071) 664 535; (071) 664 066; (071) 214 578; (071) 207 352 *Fax:* (071) 443 435
Also Publisher.
Type of Business: Exporter, Importer

Botswana

Botswana Book Centre
c/o Pula Press, The Main Mall Plot 1178, Gaborone
Mailing Address: PO Box 91, Gaborone
Tel: 3952931 *Fax:* 3974315
E-mail: pulapress@botsnet.bw
Web Site: www.bbc.co.bw
Telex: 2327 Books *Cable:* Books
Key Personnel
Manager: Sedilame Dhliwayo
Founded: 1826
Membership(s): BOPIA.
Also acts as publisher.
Owned by: Botswana Book Centre Trust
Bookshop(s): Botswana Book Centre-Westgate *Tel:* 3500290; Francistown Shop; Lobatse Book Shop; Maun Shop
Warehouse: Broadhurst Industrial, Gaborone *Tel:* 3912130 *Fax:* 3912029
E-mail: bookcenter@botsnet.bw

Brazil

Livraria Brasiliense Editora SA
Av Marques do Sao Vicente 1771, 01139-003 Sao Paulo-SP
Tel: (011) 8250122 *Fax:* (011) 673024
Telex: 33271 *Cable:* DBL
Key Personnel
Contact: Claiton Celso Guerrato; Caio Graco Prado
Founded: 1943
Owned by: Editora Brasiliense SA

COLIVRO - Comercio e Distribuicao de Livros Ltda
Rua Miquel Couto, 35 SL 201/7, 20070030 Rio de Janeiro
Tel: (021) 2243177 *Fax:* (021) 2424517
Key Personnel
Manager: Fernando Jorge da Silva
Type of Business: Distributor, Wholesaler

Columbus Cultural Editora Comercial Importacao e Exporta
Rua Alves Guimaraes, 1297 Jardim America, 05410-002 Sao Paulo-SP
Tel: (011) 8648777 *Fax:* (011) 8646531
Key Personnel
Editor: Luiz Carlos Cardoso
Editor Assistant: Renata Farhat Borges
Founded: 1987
Type of Business: Exporter, Importer, Major Independent Bookseller
Owned by: Grupo Cardapio de Alimentacao

Cortez Editora e Livraria Ltda
Rua Bartira, 317 Perdizes, 05009-000 Sao Paulo-SP
Tel: (011) 3864 0111 *Fax:* (011) 3864 4290
E-mail: livraria@cortezeditora.com.br
Web Site: www.cortezeditora.com.br; www.livrariacortez.com.br
Key Personnel
Proprietor: Jose Xavier Cortez; Potira Beserra X Cortez
Editor: Danilo A Morales
Founded: 1980
Member of Brazilian Book Association.

Disal S/A Distribuidores Associados de Livros
Av Marques de Sao Vicente 182, Sao Paulo SP 01139-000
Tel: (011) 3226-3111 *Fax:* (011) 0800-7707106
E-mail: disal@disal.com.br
Web Site: www.disal.com.br
Key Personnel
President: Francisco S Canato
Founded: 1968
Type of Business: Distributor, Importer, Wholesaler
Bookshop(s): Rua Marcondes Salgado, 1.209, Centro, 14010-150 Ribeirao Preto/SP *Tel:* (016) 610-6536 *Fax:* (016) 3931-3031; Rua Maria Antonia, 380, 01222-010 Sao Paulo/SP *Tel:* (011) 3256-7293; (011) 3256-0264 *Fax:* (011) 3256-4127; Rua Deputado Lacerda Franco, 365, 05418-000 Sao Paulo/SP *Tel:* (011) 3816-6096 *Fax:* (011) 3813-5761; Rua Brasilia Castanho de Oliveira, 141, 07115-010 Sao Paulo *Tel:* (011) 6440-0555 *Fax:* (011) 6409-1753; Rua Emilio Malet, 1.196, 03320-001 Sao Paulo *Tel:* (011) 6193-0233 *Fax:* (011) 6192-4062

Livraria Duas Cidades Ltda
Rua Bento Freitas, 158, 01220-000 Sao Paulo
Tel: (011) 3331-5134 *Fax:* (011) 3331-4702
Also Publisher.

Editora Letraviva Importacao Distribuidora Livros Ltd
Av Reboucas 1986, 05402-300 Sao Paulo-SP
Tel: (011) 3088 7992; (011) 3088 7832 *Fax:* (011) 3088 7780
E-mail: letraviva@letraviva.com.br
Web Site: www.letraviva.com.br
Key Personnel
Contact: Bernardo J I Gurbanov
Founded: 1979
Type of Business: Distributor, Importer

Ernesto Reichmann Distribuidores de Livros LTDA
Rua Coronel Marques, 335, Tatuape, 03440-000 Sao Paulo
Tel: (011) 61982122 *Fax:* (011) 61982122
E-mail: rrr@erdl.com
Key Personnel
Dir: Reichmann Renato
Manager: Antonio Francisco; Hannelore Reichmann
Founded: 1936
Specialize in Medical & Allied Literature.
Subjects: Health & Fitness; Medical; Psychology & Psychiatry
Type of Business: Distributor, Exporter, Importer, Wholesaler
Branch Office(s)
Livraria Cientifica Ernesto Reichmann LTDA, R Pedro de Toledo, 597, V Mariana, 04039-031 Sao Paulo-SP
Bookshop(s): Livraria Cientifica Ernesto Reichmann LTDA, Rua Dom Jose de Barros, 158, Centro, 01038-000 Sao Paulo-SP

Global Editora e Distribuidora Ltda
Rua Pirapitingui 111, CEP 01508-020 Liberdade, Sao Paulo
Tel: (011) 3277-7999
Key Personnel
Man Dir, Sales: Luis Alves, Jr
Founded: 1973
Type of Business: Distributor, Exporter, Importer

Livro Ibero-Americano Ltda
Rua Hermenegildo de Barros 40, Rio de Janeiro CEP 20241-040
Tel: (021) 2221 2026 *Fax:* (021) 2252 8814
E-mail: ibero_ceramica@hotmail.com
Web Site: www.ceramicanorio.com/miscelanea/livroiberoamericano/livroiberoamericano.htm
Cable: NEBRIJA
Key Personnel
Man Dir: Sir Joao Francisco J Gomes
Founded: 1946
Also Publisher.
Type of Business: Distributor, Importer, Wholesaler
Branch Office(s)
Rua Conselheiro Crispiniano 29 - 1 pav, Sao Paulo-SP

ISAEC, see Editora Sinodal

LITEC (Livraria Editora Tecnica) Ltda
Rua Vitoria, 374, Santa Ifigenia, 01210-001 Sao Paulo
Tel: (011) 223-7872 *Fax:* (011) 222-6728
E-mail: litec@litec.com.br
Web Site: www.litec.com.br

BRAZIL

Key Personnel
Manager: Vainer Cavalheri; Antonio Clara Dos Santos
Founded: 1971
Type of Business: Importer
Owned by: Livraria Editora Tecnica Ltda
Branch Office(s)
Rua Marechal Floriano, 151 Centro, 20080-005 Rio de Janeiro-RJ *Tel:* (021) 2223-9425
Fax: (021) 2253-8005

Livraria Alema Buecherstube Brooklin Ltda
Rua Bernardino de Campos, 215, Brooklin, Sao Paulo-SP CEP 04620-001
Tel: (011) 5543 3829 *Fax:* (011) 5041 4315
E-mail: buchlbb@uol.com.br
Web Site: www.buchlbb.com/
Key Personnel
Contact: Ursula Hellner; Erica Richter

Livraria Cientifica Ernesto Reichmann Ltda
Rua Dom Jose de Barros 158 andar-Centro, 01.038-000 Sao Paulo SP
Mailing Address: PO Box 3935, 01038 Sao Paulo
Tel: (011) 3255-1342; (011) 3214-3167
Fax: (011) 3255-7501
E-mail: rrr@erdl.com
Web Site: www.ernestoreichmann.com.br
Key Personnel
Manager: Antonio Francisco; Hannelore Reichmann; Renato Reichmann
Founded: 1936
Specialize in Medical & Allied Literature.
Type of Business: Distributor, Exporter, Importer, Major Book Chain Headquarters, Wholesaler
Branch Office(s)
Rua Pedro de Toledo, 597-Vila Mariana, 04.039-031 Sao Paulo SP *Tel:* (011) 5575-8283
Fax: (011) 5575-9037

Livraria Cultura Editora Ltda
Av Paulista, 2073 Conjunto Nacional, 01311-940 Sao Paulo-SP
Tel: (011) 3170-4033 *Fax:* (011) 3285-4457
E-mail: livros@livrariacultura.com.br
Telex: 1138632 *Cable:* BOOKS-S.PAULO
Key Personnel
Dir: Pedro Herz
Founded: 1969
Type of Business: Importer

Livraria Editora Tecnica Ltd, see LITEC (Livraria Editora Tecnica) Ltda

Livraria Kosmos Editora Ltda
Rua do Rosario 155 Centro, 20041-005 Rio de Janeiro
Tel: (021) 2224-8616 *Fax:* (021) 2221-4582
Cable: EIKOS
Founded: 1935
Type of Business: Distributor, Exporter, Importer, Major Book Chain Headquarters

Livraria Nobel S/A
Rua Pedroso Alvarenga, 1046 9 andar, Sao Paulo CEP 04531-004
Tel: (011) 3706 1469 *Fax:* (011) 3218-2833
E-mail: ary@editoranobel.com.br
Web Site: www.livrarianobel.com.br
Key Personnel
Dir, Publicity: Ary Kuflik Benclowicz
Founded: 1943
Number of titles published annually: 80 Print
Total Titles: 230 Print
Type of Business: Distributor

Papirus Editora
R Dr Gabriel Penteado, 253, Campinas SP CEP 13001 970
Mailing Address: Caixa postal 736, CEP 13001 970 Campinas SP

Tel: (0192) 3272 4500; (0192) 3272 4534
Fax: (0192) 3272 7578
E-mail: editora@papirus.com.br
Web Site: www.papirus.com.br/
Key Personnel
Contact: Eliane Camargo
Founded: 1976
Branch Office(s)
Rua Jose Antonio Coelho, 386 Sao Paulo SP
Bookshop(s): Rua Sacramento 202, Campinas SP; Rua Sacramento 114, Campinas SP; Rua Barao de Jaguara 1331, Campinas SP

PTI, see PTI - Publicacoes Tecnicas Internacionais Ltda

PTI - Publicacoes Tecnicas Internacionais Ltda
Rua Peixoto Gomide, 209, 01409-901 Sao Paolo SP
Tel: (011) 3159 2535 *Fax:* (011) 3159 2450
E-mail: info@pti.com.br
Web Site: www.pti.com.br
Key Personnel
Contact: Pierre Grossmann
Founded: 1972
Type of Business: Distributor, Exporter, Importer
Branch Office(s)
Rua Herculano De Freitas 390, Sao Paulo, SP

Sagra-D C Luzzatto Livreiros, Editores e Distribuidores Ltda
Rua Joao Alfredo, 448 Cidade Baixa, 90050-230 Porto Alegre-RS
Tel: (051) 3227 5222 *Fax:* (051) 3227 4438
E-mail: atendimento@sagra-luzzatto.com.br
Web Site: www.sagra-luzzatto.com.br
Key Personnel
Dir: Antonio Wenzel Luzzatto; Fernanda Dora Luzzatto
Founded: 1967
Type of Business: Distributor, Exporter, Importer

Saraiva SA, Livreiros Editores
Rua Maestro Gabriel Migliori 380, 02712-140 Bairro Limao
Tel: (011) 3933-3300 *Fax:* (011) 3662-2062
E-mail: atendimento@livrariasaraiva.com.br
Web Site: www.livrariasaraiva.com.br; www.saraiva.com.br
Telex: 1126789
Key Personnel
Man Dir: Wander Soares
Founded: 1914
Subjects: Auxiliary textbooks; administration; economics; legal; primary & secondary school books
Type of Business: Distributor

Editora Sinodal
Rua Amadeo Rossi, 93001-970 Sao Leopoldo-RS
Mailing Address: 467 Caixa Postal 11, 93001-970 Sao Leopoldo-RS
Tel: (051) 590 2366 *Fax:* (051) 590 2664
E-mail: editora@editorasinodal.com.br
Web Site: www.editorasinodal.com.br
Key Personnel
General Dir: Eloy Teckemeier *E-mail:* diretor@editorasinodal.com.br
Founded: 1948
Type of Business: Exporter, Wholesaler

Sulina Livraria Editora
Av Borges de Medeiros 1030-1036, 90000 Porto Alegre RS
Tel: (0512) 254765; (0512) 250287 *Fax:* (0512) 280734
Key Personnel
President: Vilson Nailor Noer
Founded: 1946
Type of Business: Distributor, Exporter, Importer, Major Book Chain Headquarters

Owned by: Organizacao Sulina de Representacoes SA (see Livraria Sulina Editora)
Branch Office(s)
Rua Julio de Castilbos 1657, Caxias do Sul (nine other bookshops in Porto Alegre)
AV: Nacoes Unidas, 2001 Lj 1062

Livraria Triangulo Ltda
Rua Barao de Itapetininga, 274 Centro, 01042-000 Sao Paulo-SP
Tel: (011) 3231-0922; (011) 3231-0362; (011) 3231-0552 *Fax:* (011) 3231-0162
E-mail: livraria.triangulo@terra.com.br
Web Site: www.livrariatriangulo.com.br
Key Personnel
Contact: Carlos Roberto Gomes
Founded: 1985
Type of Business: Importer

Brunei Darussalam

The Brunel Press
PO Box 69, Kuala Belait
Tel: (03) 2344
Key Personnel
Manager: Ian MacGregor
Stockists & dealers for books handled by the Strait Times Press, Singapore.

Bulgaria

Hemus Co Inc
14 Benkovski Str, 1000 Sofia
Tel: (02) 981 1769 *Fax:* (02) 981 3341
E-mail: hemusb@pbitex.com
Telex: 22267 Hemkik
Key Personnel
Executive Dir: Anastasia Boneva
Founded: 1967
Art products, souvenirs, photo materials, records, compact discs, numismatic items, musical instruments. State owned.
Type of Business: Distributor, Exporter, Importer, Major Independent Bookseller
Bookshop(s): Hemus Books, 1b Raiko Daskalov Sq, Sofia 1000

Burundi

Imparudi (Imprimerie et Papeterie du Burundi)
BP 3010, Bujumbura
Tel: (02) 3125; (02) 7381 *Fax:* (02) 2572
Key Personnel
Contact: Mutambuka Theoneste
Type of Business: Distributor, Exporter, Importer, Wholesaler

Cameroon

Librairie Bilingue/The Bilingual Bookshop
BP 727, Yaounde
Tel: 224899 *Fax:* 232903
Telex: 8438 kn

Type of Business: Distributor, Importer, Major Independent Bookseller, Wholesaler
Owned by: Buma Kor & Co Ltd (SARL)
Branch Office(s)
Bomenda
Limbe

Presbyterian Book Depot & Printing Press Ltd (PRESBOOK)
BP 13, Limbe
Tel: 332114 *Fax:* 332694
Telex: 5952 *Cable:* PRESBOOK
Key Personnel
General Manager: W Abange
Founded: 1968
Also publishers & printers.
Type of Business: Distributor, Importer
Owned by: Presbyterian Church in Cameroon
Branch Office(s)
Presbook Mankon, BP 39, Bamenda
Presbook Buea, BP 19, Buea
Presbook Douala, BP 18, Douala
Presbook Kumba, BP 87, Kumba
Presbook Kumbo, BP 4, Kumbo
Presbook Mamfe, BP 114, Mamfe
Presbook Tiko, BP 28, Tiko
Presbook Yaounde, BP 1467, Yao Unde

Chile

Libreria Eduardo Albers Ltda
Vitacura 5648, Santiago 6640785
Mailing Address: Casilla 17, Santiago 30
Tel: (02) 218 5371 *Fax:* (02) 218 1458
Web Site: www.albers.cl
Key Personnel
Manager: Eduardo Albers *E-mail:* ealbers@albers.cl
Founded: 1943
Type of Business: Distributor, Exporter, Importer, Major Independent Bookseller, Wholesaler

Libreria Andres Bello
Editorial Juridica de Chile, Avda Ricardo Lyon, 946, Casilla 4256
Tel: (02) 2049900 *Fax:* (02) 2253600
Key Personnel
Manager: Francisco Hoyl Sotomayor

Berenguer Editorial
Correo 9, Casilla 16598-9, Santiago

Editorial Francesa Espanola SA
Huelen 10 piso 3 of A, Santiago
Tel: (02) 235-0911; (02) 235-9734 *Fax:* (02) 236-0900
Key Personnel
General Manager: Maria Isabel Castillo
Dir, Administration & Finance: Manuel Prietu
Type of Business: Distributor, Exporter, Importer, Wholesaler
Branch Office(s)
Av Valparaiso 152, Vina del Mar

Libreria Esoterica
Huerfanos 786, Local 19, Santiago
Tel: (02) 6338430 *Fax:* (02) 6397933
E-mail: wzzdarmd@entelchile.net
Telex: 240201
Key Personnel
Owner: Walter Zuniga Zavala
Founded: 1985
Type of Business: Distributor, Exporter, Importer, Major Independent Bookseller, Wholesaler

Feria Chilena del Libro Ltda
Huerfanos 623, Casilla 10225, Santiago
Tel: (02) 632 7334; (02) 639 6758 *Fax:* (02) 633 9374
E-mail: ventas@feriachilenadellibro.cl
Web Site: www.feriachilenadellibro.cl
Key Personnel
Chief Executive Officer: Juan Aldea Perez *Tel:* (0562) 6323465 *E-mail:* juanaldeap@feriachilenadellibro.cl
Head: Manuel Vilches
Sales Manager: Carlos Diaz
Founded: 1952
Type of Business: Distributor, Importer, Major Book Chain Headquarters, Wholesaler
Branch Office(s)
Isidora Goyenechea 3162, Las Condes, Santiago, Head: Eric Maxwell *Tel:* (02) 335 3693; (02) 335 3647 *Fax:* (02) 335 3694 *E-mail:* isidora@feriachilenadellibro.cl
Santa Magdalena 50, Providencia, Santiago, Head: Mirta Aldea *Tel:* (02) 232 1422; (02) 232 1426 *Fax:* (02) 232 1422 *E-mail:* magdalena@feriachilenadellibro.cl
Nueva York 3, Santiago, Head: Matilde Garay *Tel:* (02) 687 4270; (02) 697 2751 *Fax:* (02) 697 2751 *E-mail:* nuevayork@feriachilenadellibro.cl
Providencia 2124, Santiago, Head: Juan Carlos Fau *Tel:* (02) 335 3697; (02) 231 7197 *Fax:* (02) 231 7197 *E-mail:* drugstore@feriachilenadellibro.cl
Agustinas 859, Santiago, Sales Manager: Jorge Godoy *Tel:* (02) 664 3371; (02) 639 5354 *Fax:* (02) 639 5354 *E-mail:* agustinas@feriachilenadellibro.cl
Estado 22, Santiago, Sales Manager: Eduardo Jara *Tel:* (02) 639 6396; (02) 639 6536 *Fax:* (02) 639 6536 *E-mail:* estado@feriachilenadellibro.cl
Galeria Pleno Centro, Av Valparaiso 595, Vina del Mar, Sales Manager: Luis Cisternas *Tel:* (032) 694583; (032) 683093 *Fax:* (032) 683093 *E-mail:* vina@feriachilenadellibro.cl
Mall Marina Arauco Local 108, Vina del Mar, Sales Manager: Rafael Gonzalez *Tel:* (032) 382266; (032) 382267 *Fax:* (032) 382267 *E-mail:* marina@feriachilenadellibro.cl

Fondo de Cultura Economica SA
Paseo Bulnes 152, Casilla 10249
Tel: (02) 695 4843
E-mail: fcechile@ctcinternet.cl
Founded: 1953
Type of Business: Distributor, Exporter, Importer

Libreria Internacional Estudio
Anibal Pinto 345, Concepcion
Tel: (041) 225 533 *Fax:* (041) 244 542
Key Personnel
Contact: Jorge Jimenez Arriola
Founded: 1962
Type of Business: Major Independent Bookseller

Libreria Universitaria
Maria Luisa Santander 0447, Cassilla de Correo, Providencia, Santiago 10220
Tel: (02) 2234555; (02) 2236980 *Fax:* (02) 2099455; (02) 499455
Telex: 10220
Owned by: Editorial Universitaria SA

Lila Libreria de Mujeres
Providencia 1652, Local 3, Santiago
Tel: (02) 2361725 *Fax:* (02) 2361725
Key Personnel
Manager: Jimena Pizarro
Type of Business: Major Independent Bookseller

Libreria San Pablo
Avda L B O'Higgins 1626, Casilla 3746, Correo Central, Santiago
Tel: (02) 698 9145 *Fax:* (02) 671 6884
E-mail: alameda@san-pablo.cl
Web Site: www.san-pablo.cl
Key Personnel
Manager: Antonio Taconi
Type of Business: Distributor, Exporter, Importer, Wholesaler
Owned by: Ediciones San Pablo
Branch Office(s)
Benavente 383, Puerto Montt *Tel:* (065) 310154 *E-mail:* pmontt@san-pablo.cl
Av Vicuna Mackenna 779, Temuco *Tel:* (045) 210371 *E-mail:* temuco@san-pablo.cl
Avda Providencia 2343, Casilla 3746, Santiago *Tel:* (02) 232 4350 *E-mail:* providencia@san-pablo.cl
Gamero 498 Esquina Campos, Rancagua *Tel:* (072) 221063 *Fax:* (072) 221828 *E-mail:* rancagua@san-pablo.cl
Lautaro 517, Los Angeles *Tel:* (043) 315626

China

China International Book Trading Corporation
35 Chegongzhuang Xilu, Beijing 100044
Mailing Address: PO Box 399, Beijing 100044
Tel: (010) 68412026 *Fax:* (010) 68475199
E-mail: sinda@mail.cnokay.com
Web Site: chinabooks.cnokay.com *Cable:* CIBTC BEIJING
Key Personnel
President: Zhi Bin Liu
Contact: Ming Liang Yang
Founded: 1949
Type of Business: Distributor, Exporter, Importer, Major Independent Bookseller, Wholesaler
Branch Office(s)
China Book Trading GmbH, Postfach 200114, 63307 Rodermark, Germany *Tel:* (06074) 95564 *Fax:* (06074) 95271 *E-mail:* chinabook@aol.com
Cyress Book Co Ltd, London, United Kingdom
Peace Book Co Ltd, Wingon House, 71 Desvouex Rd, Rm 901-3 & 916, Central, Hong Kong, Hong Kong *Tel:* 25222130
CIBTC Tokyo Renrakujimucho, 1-29-12 Aobadai Meguro-ky, Tokyo, Japan *Tel:* (03) 57216536 *Fax:* (03) 57216537
Cypress Book (US) Company Inc, 3450 Third St, Unit 4B, San Francisco, CA 94124, United States

China National Publications Import & Export Corp
16 Gongti East Rd, Chaoyang District, Beijing 100020
Tel: (010) 65082324; (010) 65086873; (010) 65086874 *Fax:* (010) 65086860
E-mail: info-center@cnpeak.com
Web Site: www.cnpiec.com.cn
Telex: 22313 CPC CN *Cable:* PUBLIMEX
Key Personnel
President: Chen Weijiang
Type of Business: Distributor, Exporter, Importer, Wholesaler
Subsidiaries: Beijing Book Co Inc
Branch Office(s)
20 W Guangyuan Rd, Guangzhou, Guangdong Province 510300 *Tel:* (020) 86522185 *Fax:* (020) 86505965 *E-mail:* gzcnpiec@public.guangzhou.gd.cn
555 Wu Ding Rd, Shanghai 200040 *Tel:* (021) 62551599 *Fax:* (021) 62552697
No 17, South St, Xi'an 710001 *Tel:* (029) 7279743 *Fax:* (029) 7279755 *E-mail:* cnpiecx@public.xa.sn.cn
Rm 8, No 10 Bldg, Baoshiyilu Rest House, Provincial Organs Management Bureau, Hangzhou, Zhejiang 100020 *Tel:* (0571)

5114218 *Fax:* (0571) 5211780 *E-mail:* sales@cnpzjb.com *Web Site:* www.cnpzjb.com
Siemensstr 4, Postfach 1131, 63329 Egelsbach, Germany
3F9, Shibaura 2-chome, Minato-ku, Tokyo 108, Japan *Tel:* (030) 5476-0981 *Fax:* (030) 5476-4394 *E-mail:* jp-office@21cn.com
Unit 4, 55-57 Park Royal Rd, London NW10 7LR, United Kingdom *Tel:* (020) 8961 9283 *Fax:* (020) 8961 9282
Beijing Jiang Dong Crystal-Color Arts & Crafts Corp, 20A, 1st China Commercial Bldg, No 6, Xiaozhuang, Chaoyang District, Beijing 100026 *Tel:* (010) 65301191; (010) 65301555; (010) 63721298 *Fax:* (010) 65301555; (010) 63721298
Beijing Xing Tu Property Management Co Ltd
China Scientific & Cultural Audio-Video Publishing House, Chaoyang-mennei St 137, Beijing 100020 *Tel:* (010) 64038374 *Fax:* (010) 64017393 *E-mail:* cscavph@263.net
China Wan Da Trading Co, ZAO PTK Venera Rm 106-9a, St M Kalitnikovskaya, Moscow 109029, Russian Federation *Tel:* (095) 2700760 *Fax:* (095) 2700760 *E-mail:* kiepmos@aha.ru
CNPIEC (HK) Development Co Ltd
CNPIEC Information Technology Co Ltd
Culture & Art Co Ltd, No 15 Mingze St, Zhongshan District, Dalian 116001 *Tel:* (0411) 2807891; (0411) 2645663 *Fax:* (0411) 2650090 *E-mail:* cdtl@mail.dlptt.ln.cn
National Certification & Authentication Co Ltd, West Rm 6, Huhongzhuyuan Hotel, Xiaoshiqiao, Old Galou St, West District, Beijing 100009 *Tel:* (010) 64010515 *Fax:* (010) 64032229-218 *E-mail:* chinaca@publica.bj.cninfo.net
SCM Investment Co Ltd, Shenzhen Special Zone Newspaper Bldg, Floor 25, Section F, Shennan Ave, Shenzhen 518009 *Tel:* (0755) 3516683 *Fax:* (0755) 3516716
Shanghai Book Co Pte Ltd, Blk 231, Bain St, 04-41, 01-57, 2-73, Bras Basah Complex, Singapore 180231, Singapore *Tel:* 3360144 *Fax:* 3360490 *E-mail:* gntjoa@cnpiec.com.cn
Shenzen Branch *Tel:* (010) 65063069 *Fax:* (010) 65063069 *E-mail:* export@cnpiec.com.cn
16 Gongti East Rd, Chaoyang District, Beijing 100020 *Tel:* (010) 65002959 *Fax:* (010) 65001291 *E-mail:* wanxun2000@sina.com
World Publishing Corp, 137 Chaonei Dajie, Beijing 100010 *Tel:* (010) 64038365; (010) 64038373 *Fax:* (010) 64016320 *E-mail:* wpc@china.kw.com.cm

CIBTC, see China International Book Trading Corporation

CNPIEC, see China National Publications Import & Export Corp

Hubei Publications Import & Export Corporation
11, Zhongnan Rd, Wuchang, Wuhan 430071-027
Tel: (027) 87825561 *Fax:* (027) 87815557
E-mail: hbwwsdjkb@163.com
Key Personnel
Manager, Import & Export Dept: Shao-Zhang He
Founded: 1994
Books printing materials, audio-video products & other related goods both in wholesale & retail.
Type of Business: Distributor, Exporter, Importer, Major Independent Bookseller, Wholesaler
Owned by: State-owned, Manager of Import & Export Dept: Shao-zhang He

Jiang Xi Copyright Agency
Xin Wei Rd, Suite 17, Nanchang City, Jiang Xi Province 330002
Tel: (0791) 8528405 *Fax:* (0791) 8508901
E-mail: jxcopyright@hotmail.com
Web Site: www.jxbqzx.com

Key Personnel
Dir: Nie Wen Xing *Tel:* (0791) 8508901
Manager: Maggie Wan; Jiang Zhi Fei
Founded: 2001
Import foreign copyrights to all Jiang Xi Provincial publishers & export provincial copyrights to foreign publishers. Organize Jiang Xi Province News & Publishing Delegates to visit foreign counterparts, attend book exhibitions & have training.
Type of Business: Exporter, Importer
Parent Company: Jiang Xi Province Copyright Bureau

Xiamen International Book Exchange Center
No 809, East Section, South Hubin Rd, Xiamen, 361004 Fujian
Tel: (0592) 5061401 *Fax:* (0592) 5061400
E-mail: xibc@xpublic.fz.fj.cn
Key Personnel
President: Shu Yan Zhang
Type of Business: Distributor, Exporter, Importer, Major Independent Bookseller, Wholesaler

Colombia

Libreria Aguirre
Obispo Aguirre, 8, 27002 Lugo
Tel: (04) 2220336 *Cable:* Laguirre
Key Personnel
Manager: Aura Lopez Posada
Type of Business: Importer, Major Independent Bookseller

Circulo de Lectores SA
Calle 57 No 6-35, Apdo 52111, SantaFe de Bogota Cundinamarca
Tel: (01) 2173211; (01) 2177720 *Fax:* (01) 2178157
Telex: 41255
Key Personnel
General Manager: Eduardo Polo
Dir Marketing: Rafael Vargas
Founded: 1969
Also Book Club. Branch offices in Barranquilla, Bogota, Cali, Cartagena, Manizales, Medellin, Pereira, & Tunja.
Type of Business: Distributor, Exporter, Importer, Major Book Chain Headquarters, Wholesaler
Owned by: Diario el Tiempo

Distribuidoras Unidas SA
Transversal 93 N° 52-03, Bogota
Tel: 413 8079 *Fax:* 413 8502
E-mail: ibernal@disunidas.com.co
Web Site: www.disunidas.com.co
Key Personnel
Contact: Sr Hernando Trivino

Eurolibros
Calle 40 No 20-27, Bogota
Tel: (01) 2886400 *Fax:* (01) 2450291; (01) 3401811; (01) 3401830; (01) 2886400
Key Personnel
General Dir: Carlos Roberto Jimenez
 E-mail: carlosji@latino.net.co
Founded: 1983
Type of Business: Distributor, Wholesaler

Grupo Editorial Iberoamerica de Colombia SA
Carrer 2a1 No 54-78, Bogota
Mailing Address: Apdo Aereo 513, Bogota
Tel: (01) 3106553 *Fax:* (01) 3106553
E-mail: geicol@colomsat.net.co
Key Personnel
Dir General: Hernandez Rico Victor Manuel

Founded: 1991
Type of Business: Distributor, Exporter, Importer, Wholesaler

Grupo Noriega Editores de Colombia Ltda
Calle 40 No 22-44, Bogota
Tel: (01) 3689036 *Fax:* (01) 3377788
E-mail: gnoriega@unete.com.co
Key Personnel
Legal Representative: Gustavo Rodriguez Garcia
Founded: 1993
Type of Business: Distributor, Importer, Wholesaler
Owned by: Editorial Limusa SA DE CV

Editorial y Libreria Herder Ltda
Carrera 11, No 73-61, SantaFe de Bogota, DC
Tel: (01) 3344853 *Fax:* (01) 2832272
Key Personnel
Legal Representative: Alvaro Gomez Robayo
Type of Business: Distributor, Exporter, Importer
Owned by: Hermann Herder e Instituto Literario

Libreria Nacional Ltda
Unicentro-Local 1-146, Bogota
Tel: (01) 825829; (01) 833849; (01) 2139842; (01) 2139882 *Fax:* (01) 822404; (01) 2138404
Cable: LINALCO AA CALI
Key Personnel
Manager: Hernando Ordonez
Administrator General: Aura Bustamante
Gerente Bogota: Felipe Ossa
Administrador Libreria Barranquilla: Edgar Ramirez
Branch Office(s)
Carrera 53 No 75-129, Barranquilla
Unicentro Local No 1-146, Apdo Aereo 100778, Bogota *Fax:* (01) 2130484

Libreria y Distribuidora Lerner Ltda
Av Jimenez No 4-35, Bogota DC
Mailing Address: Apdo 8304, Bogata DC
Tel: (01) 243 0567; (01) 334 7826 *Fax:* (01) 281 4319
Telex: 43195
Key Personnel
Manager: Luis A Burgos H
Founded: 1957
Type of Business: Importer, Major Independent Bookseller
Branch Office(s)
Calle 92 No 15-23, Cundinamarca, Bogota
 Tel: (01) 2360580 *Fax:* (01) 6364362
 E-mail: lerner-norte@librerialerner.com.co

Panamericana Libreria y Papeleria SA
 (Panamericana Bookshop & Stationery Shop)
Calle 12, No 34-20, Apdo Aereo 6210, Cundinamarca
Tel: (01) 3649000 (ext 213) *Fax:* (01) 3600885
Web Site: www.panamericana.com.co
Key Personnel
Contact: Carlos Federico Ruiz *Tel:* (01) 3649000 (ext 257); Fernando Rojas Acosta
 E-mail: frojas@panamericana.com.co
Founded: 1997
Type of Business: Exporter, Importer, Major Independent Bookseller
Bookshop(s): Panamericana Libreria y Paleria Contamos Con

Ediciones Paulinas (Libreria San Pablo)
Carrera 46 No 22A-90, SantaFe de Bogota Cundinamarca
Tel: (01) 2444516 *Fax:* (01) 2684288
Key Personnel
Manager: Esther Guzman
Branch offices in Barranquilla, Bogota, Cali, Cucuta, Manizales, & Medellin.
Type of Business: Distributor, Exporter, Importer, Major Book Chain Headquarters, Wholesaler

Branch Office(s)
Barranquilla
Medellin
Bogota
Cali
Cucuta
Manizales
Bookshop(s): Carrera 13 No 72-41, Bogota; Carrera 32 No 161A-04, Bogota

Libreria Temis SA
Calle 13, No 6-45, Apdo Aereo, 5941 y 12008, 1 Bogota
Tel: (01) 341 3225 *Fax:* (01) 269 0793
Founded: 1951
Type of Business: Distributor, Exporter, Importer, Wholesaler
Owned by: Editorial Temis SA, Transv 39B 17-98, SantaFe de Bogota; Nomos Impresores, SA
Branch Office(s)
Calle 52 No 42-68, Medellin
Calle 12 No 5-33, Avda Pepe Sierra No 24-25

Libreria Tercer Mundo
Transv 2a A, No 67-27, Bogota
Tel: (01) 255 1539; (01) 255 0737 *Fax:* (01) 212 5976
E-mail: tmundoed@polcola.com.co
Key Personnel
General Manager: Santiago Pombo Vejarano
Library Dir: Juan Manuel Borda de Francisco
Founded: 1962
Owned by: Tercer Mundo Editores SA
Bookshop(s): Cra 7, No 16-91, Bogota; Cra 13, No 44-70, Bogota

Libreria Uniandes
Carrera 1 No 18A82, Bogota
Tel: (01) 2824066 (ext 2197); (01) 2824066 (ext 2198) *Fax:* (01) 2841890 *Cable:* UNIANDES
Key Personnel
General Manager: Arcesio Rodriguez P
Marketing & Sales Manager: Cesar Augusto Pena
International Trade: Luz Marina Cortes
Spanish & Latin American trade books; importers & subscription agents of academic & scientific publications.
Type of Business: Importer

Congo

Office national des Librairies Populaires (ONLP)
PB 1489, Brazzaville
Tel: 833 485 *Fax:* 831 879
Telex: 5379 *Cable:* Lipolaire Brazzaville
Key Personnel
Dir General: Ignace Taliane-Tchibamba

ONLP, see Office national des Librairies Populaires (ONLP)

The Democratic Republic of the Congo

Librairie des Presses Universitaires
Blvd du 30 Juin 4113, Kinshasa
Mailing Address: BP 1682, Kinshasa
Tel: (012) 30652
Owned by: Presses universitaires du Zaiire et l'Office du Livre (PUZ)

Librairie les Volcans
22 Ave President Mobutu, Goma
Mailing Address: BP 105, Goma
Tel: 366
Key Personnel
President: Kakule Tatsopa wa Mughalitsa
Type of Business: Distributor, Major Independent Bookseller
Owned by: Librairie Les Volcans, Publisher
Bookshop(s): Cereva

Okapi Centre de Diffusion
BP 11398, Kinshasa
Tel: (012) 31457

Librairie Saint-Paul
c/o Editions Paulines, Ave du Commerce 76, BP 335, Kinshasa
Mailing Address: BP 8505, Kinshasa
Tel: 77726
Founded: 1958
Type of Business: Distributor, Exporter, Importer, Major Independent Bookseller, Wholesaler
Owned by: Filles de Saint Paul - Congr. Internat. au service de la promotion et de l'evangelisation par les medias
Branch Office(s)
BP 505, Kisangani
BP 2447, Lubumbashi

Costa Rica

Libreria Universal Carlos Federspiel
Apdo 1532, Edificio Central, San Jose

Libreria Imprenta y Litografia Lehmann SA
Apdo 10011, San Jose
Tel: 2231212
Also Publisher.

Libreria Trejos SA

Cote d'Ivoire

CEDA, see Centre d'Edition et de Diffusion Africaines

Centre d'Edition et de Diffusion Africaines
BP 541, Abidjan 04
Tel: 22 22 42; 22 20 55 *Fax:* 21 72 62
Web Site: www.mbendi.co.za/orgs/cg01.htm

Key Personnel
Dir: Mr Venance Kacou
Also Publisher.
Type of Business: Distributor, Exporter, Importer, Wholesaler

Croatia

Tehnicka Knjiga
Jurisiceva 10, 10000 Zagreb
Tel: (041) 4810818 *Fax:* (041) 481 0821
Key Personnel
General Manager: Zvonimir Vistricka
Owned by: Tehnicka Knjiga, Zagreb

Cuba

Ediciones Cubanas
Obispo No 527 (altos) esq a Bernaza, Habana Vieja, Habana
Tel: (07) 63 1981; (07) 33 8942; (07) 63 1989 *Fax:* (07) 338 943
E-mail: edicuba@artsoft.cult.cu
Telex: 0512337 *Cable:* LIBROCUBA
Key Personnel
Dir: Nancy Matos Lacosta
Books, periodicals & printing material.
Type of Business: Distributor, Exporter, Importer, Major Book Chain Headquarters, Wholesaler
Owned by: Empresa de Comercio Exterior de Publicaciones
Bookshop(s): Libreria Internacional, Obispo No 528 e/ Vernaza y Villegas, Habana; Libreria La Bella Habana, Palacio del Segundo Cabo, O'Reilly No 4 Esq a Tacon, Habana Vieja

Cyprus

K P Kyriakou (Books - Stationery) Ltd
Panagides Bldg, 3 Crivas Digenis Ave, 3601 Limassol
Mailing Address: PO Box 159, 3601 Limassol
Tel: (025) 747555 *Fax:* (025) 747047
E-mail: cybooks@logos.cy.net
Key Personnel
Man Dir: Kyriakos P Kyriakou
  E-mail: kyriakospk@webnmedia.com
Founded: 1947
Type of Business: Distributor, Exporter, Importer, Major Independent Bookseller, Wholesaler

MAM (The House of Cyprus & Cyprological Publications)
19 Konstantinou Palaiologou Ave, 1015 Nicosia
Mailing Address: PO Box 21722, Nicosia 1512
Tel: (022) 753536
E-mail: mam@mam.com.cy
Web Site: www.mam.com.cy
Key Personnel
Manager: Fryni Michaelidou
Secretary: Mikis Michaelides
Founded: 1965
Specialize in all kinds of publications on Cyprus & in all publications by Cypriots. Authorized distributors of Cyprus Government publications & other Cypriot publishers.
Also publisher.

Type of Business: Distributor, Exporter, Importer, Wholesaler
Bookshop(s): MAM Cyprus Publications, Stoa tou Vivliou, 5 Pesmazoglou, 10564 Athens, Greece, Contact: Ms Koula Kyziakou

K Rustem & Bro
21-26 Kyrenia St, Nicosia
Mailing Address: PO Box 239, Nicosia
Tel: (022) 71041; (022) 71418; (022) 52085
Cable: RUSTEM BR 4
Bookshop(s): Tofarides Bookshop, PO Box 278, Larnaca *Tel:* (041) 54144

Czech Republic

Knihkupectvi - Antikvariat Galerie
Masarykova 15, 415 01 Teplice
Tel: (0417) 537 370 *Fax:* (0417) 537 370
E-mail: kniha.ln@antikteplice.cz; kniha.ln@worldonline.cz
Web Site: www.antikteplice.cz/
Key Personnel
Manager: Milos Novotny
Owned by: Martina Uldrychova
Branch Office(s)
Teplice, Kapelnii 4

Denmark

Arnold Busck International Boghandel A/S
Kobmagergade 49, 1150 Copenhagen K
Tel: 33733500 *Fax:* 33733535
E-mail: arnold@busck.dk
Web Site: www.busck.dk
Key Personnel
Manager & Bookseller: Troels Bek *Tel:* 33733525
Founded: 1896
Export Division is at above address.
Type of Business: Exporter, Major Book Chain Headquarters, Major Independent Bookseller
Owned by: Ole Arnold Busck

Gads Forlag
Kloster Str 9, 1157 Copenhagen K
Tel: (03) 7766 6000 *Fax:* (033) 7766 6001
E-mail: kundeservice@gads-forlag.dk.ell
Web Site: www.gads-forlag.dk
Key Personnel
Dir: Peter Hartmann
Manager: Erling Sievert *E-mail:* ES@gad.dk
Owned by: G E C Gads Foundation (see also G E C Gads Forlag)

Magasin du Nord A/S
Kongens Nytorv 13, 1095 Copenhagen K
Tel: (03) 33 11 44 33 *Fax:* (03) 33 15 18 40
E-mail: kundeservice@magasinkort.dk
Web Site: www.magasin.dk *Cable:* MAGDUNORD TELEX 15975
Key Personnel
Buyer: Alfred Jensen *Tel:* 033 182121 *Fax:* 033 182215

Nyt Nordisk Forlag Arnold Busck A/S, Publishers, see Arnold Busck International Boghandel A/S

Polyteknisk Boghandel og Forlag
Anker Engelunds Vej 1, Bygn 101 A, 2800 Lyngby
Tel: 77 42 44 44 *Fax:* 77 42 43 54

E-mail: polybog@pb.dtu.dk
Web Site: www.pf.dtu.dk/
Key Personnel
Dir: Lotte Lonver *E-mail:* lotte@poly.dtu.dk
Founded: 1960
Type of Business: Distributor, Importer, Major Independent Bookseller, Wholesaler

C A Reitzel Boghandel & Forlag A/S
Norregade 20, 1165 Copenhagen K
Tel: 33 12 24 00 *Fax:* 33 14 02 70
Web Site: www.careitzel.dk
Key Personnel
Man Dir: Svend Olufsen
Supplies universities, scientific libraries & institutions worldwide
Also Publisher.
Type of Business: Exporter, Importer

Scanvik Books Import ApS
Esplanaden 8 B, 1263 Copenhagen K
Tel: 3312 7766 *Fax:* 3391 2882
E-mail: mail@scanvik.dk
Web Site: www.scanvik.dk
Key Personnel
Dir: John Roberts; Uwe Schultheiss
Founded: 1980
Also agent.
Type of Business: Distributor, Exporter, Importer, Wholesaler

SKT's Boghandel
Lautrupvang 15, 2750 Ballerup
Tel: 44686662 *Fax:* 44686660
E-mail: skt@sktbooks.dk
Web Site: www.sktbooks.dk
Key Personnel
Contact: Mark Bentley
Founded: 1968
Type of Business: Major Independent Bookseller

Studenterboghandelen ved Odense Universitet
Campusvej 55, 5230 Odense M
Tel: 6550 1700 *Fax:* 6550 1701
E-mail: studenter@boghandel.sdu.dk
Web Site: www.boghandel.sdu.dk/
Key Personnel
Man Dir: Niels Lindberg
Founded: 1981
Type of Business: Importer, Major Independent Bookseller

Svensk-Norsk Bogimport A/S (Swedish Norwegian Bookimport)
Esplanaden 8 B, 1263 Copenhagen K
Tel: 33142666 *Fax:* 33143588
E-mail: snb@bog.dk
Web Site: www.snbog.dk
Key Personnel
President: Poul Brehmer
Founded: 1968
Type of Business: Distributor, Exporter, Importer, Major Independent Bookseller, Wholesaler

Tysk Bogimport ApS
Storeholm 51, 2670 Greve
Tel: 7020 4990 *Fax:* 7020 4991
E-mail: kontakt@tyskforlaget.dk
Web Site: www.tyskforlaget.dk
Key Personnel
Contact: Eberhard Riedel
Founded: 1958
Type of Business: Distributor, Importer, Major Independent Bookseller, Wholesaler

Universitetsbogladen
Blegdamsvej 3, 2200 Copenhagen N
Mailing Address: Postboks 716, 2200 Kopenhagen N
Tel: 3524 0444; 3532 6570 *Fax:* 3532 6571
E-mail: panum@unibog.dk

Web Site: www.universitetsbogladen.dk
Key Personnel
Manager: Henrik Larsen
Founded: 1968
Type of Business: Exporter, Importer, Major Independent Bookseller
Branch Office(s)
Universitetsparken 13, 2100 Copenhagen O
Tel: 3537 1133; 3532 0035 *Fax:* 3539 5459

Dominican Republic

Editorial Padilla
Prol Ave 27 de Febrero, Santo Domingo
Mailing Address: Apdo Postal 468, Santo Domingo
Tel: 379-1550 *Fax:* 379-2631
E-mail: edpadilla@codetel.net.do
Key Personnel
Contact: Carretera Manoguayabo, Esq
Also Publisher.
Branch Office(s)
El Conde 109, Santo Domingo *Tel:* (809) 6880303

Ecuador

CD Remain Cia Ltda
Ave Repulbica 740 y Eloy Alfaro, Profesional Piso 7, Ofc 702 Casilla, 17-17-1548 Quito
Tel: (02) 224973; (02) 239328 *Fax:* (02) 505760
Type of Business: Distributor

Libreria Cientifica SA
Casilla 2905, Quito
Tel: (02) 12556
Key Personnel
Manager: Alicia de Pino
Branch Office(s)
Luque 223, Guayaquil *Tel:* (04) 324650

Libreria Cima
Carlos Ibarra 200 y 10 de Agosto, Casilla 17-15-87C, Quito
Tel: (02) 571218; (02) 571318 *Cable:* CIMALE
Key Personnel
Manager: Luis A Carrera
Assistant Manager: Edgar R Freire
Type of Business: Exporter

De Cervantes Ediciones SA
Orellana 1811 y 10 de Agosto, primer piso, Quito
Tel: (02) 522 956 *Fax:* (02) 523 452; (02) 223 062
Key Personnel
Contact: Ismael Cervantes Quintero
Type of Business: Distributor, Exporter, Importer

Ecuazeta De Publicaciones Cia Ltda
Mariano Andrade 250 y Villalengua, Quito
Tel: (02) 443074 *Fax:* (02) 443074
Key Personnel
President: Jorge Zavaleta Salvador
Manager: Rocio Vacas de Alvarez
Founded: 1989
Type of Business: Distributor, Importer, Wholesaler

Edimecien Cia Ltda
Aguirre 178 y Av 10 de Agosto, Quito

Tel: (02) 250 2427; (02) 250 2428; (02) 250 2431
Fax: (02) 250 2429
Key Personnel
Contact: Sr Alfredo Montoya Gral
Type of Business: Distributor, Importer, Wholesaler

Promociones Culturales Gitral SA
Ave Machala 1024 y Velez Casilla, 09-01-7278 Guayaquil
Mailing Address: PO Box 09-01-7278, Guayaquil
Tel: (02) 510510; (02) 532060; (02) 32644
Fax: (02) 510510; (02) 326733
Key Personnel
President: Ramon Cedeno Galarza
Type of Business: Distributor, Importer

Libreria Universitaria
Garcia Moreno 739, Apdo 2982, Quito
Tel: (02) 212521
Key Personnel
Dir: Ing Carlos E Wong Flores
Founded: 1951
Type of Business: Distributor, Exporter, Importer, Wholesaler

Ediciones Monserrat
Ave 10 de Agosto 1831 y San Gregorio, Quito
Tel: (02) 222 667; (02) 505 685; (02) 222 567
Fax: (02) 541 294
E-mail: edimon@uio.satnet.net
Key Personnel
Contact: Claudio C Gustavo
Type of Business: Distributor
Owned by: Monica Claudio Cando

Egypt (Arab Republic of Egypt)

Al Arab Bookshop
Add 29, El Fagalah St, Cairo
Tel: (02) 5915315 *Cable:* ARABUKSHOP CAIRO
Key Personnel
Manager: Prof Saladin Boustany, PhD
Founded: 1900
Agent of the Library of Congress PL 480.
Type of Business: Distributor, Exporter
Owned by: Al Arab Publishing House

FHB Exporter
Ramsis Center, PO Box 159-11794, Cairo
Tel: (02) 2358329 *Fax:* (02) 2358329
E-mail: fhb@link.net
Key Personnel
Manager: Fouad H Baskharoun
Founded: 1970
Books, magazines & periodicals published in Egypt & the Arab World.
Type of Business: Distributor, Exporter, Wholesaler

Lehnert & Landrock, Bookshop and Art Publishers
44, Sherif St, Cairo
Tel: (02) 3927606; (02) 3935324 *Fax:* (02) 3934421
Key Personnel
Owner & Manager: Dr E Lambelet
Manager: Mahmud Abdel Aziz
Founded: 1924
Bookshop & art publisher.

Type of Business: Importer, Major Independent Bookseller, Wholesaler
Owned by: Edouard Lambelet & Co

Livres de France
36 rue Kasr el-Nil, Cairo
Tel: (02) 3935512

Misr Bookshop
3 Kamel Sidkey St, Al-Fagalah, Cairo
Tel: (02) 908920
Key Personnel
Manager: Amir Saiid El-Sahhar

El Salvador

Clasicos Roxsil Editorial SA de CV
Cuarta Avenida Sur 2-3, La Libertad, Santa Tecla
Tel: 228 1832; 229 3621 *Fax:* 228 1212
Fax on Demand: 228 1212
Key Personnel
Manager: Rosa Serrano de Lopez
Chief Editorial Dept: Roxana Beatriz Lopez
E-mail: roxanabe@navegante.com.sv
Founded: 1969
Type of Business: Distributor, Exporter, Importer, Wholesaler

Libreria UCA
Universidad Centroamericana Jose Simeon Canas, Autopista Sur, Jardines de Guadalupe, Apdo 01-575, 168 San Salvador
Tel: 240011 (ext 193); 234491 *Fax:* 2731010

Libreria Universitaria de l'Universidad de El Salvador
Ciudad Universitaria, Apdo 1703, San Salvador
Tel: 259427; 256604 *Fax:* 259427
Telex: 20794

Ethiopia

ECA Bookshop Co-op Society
PO Box 3001, Addis Ababa
Tel: (01) 517200 *Fax:* (01) 510365; (212) 963-4957 (New York)
E-mail: ecainfo@uneca.org
Web Site: www.uneca.org *Cable:* ECA ADDIS ABABA

Finland

Akateeminen Kirjakauppa
Keskuskatu 1, Pohjoisesplanadi 39, PL 128, 00101 Helsinki
Tel: (09) 121 4252 *Fax:* (09) 121 4322
E-mail: tilaukset@akateeminen.com
Web Site: www.akateeminen.com *Cable:* AKATEEMINEN
Key Personnel
Chief Executive: Stig-Bjorn Nyberg
Assistant: Anu Hantala
Founded: 1893
Subscriptions, CD-ROM.
Type of Business: Major Book Chain Headquarters, Major Independent Bookseller
Owned by: OY Stockmann AB

Branch Office(s)
Itakeskus, Itakatu 1 C, 00930 Helsinki *Tel:* (09) 121 4761
Tampere, Hameenkatu 6, 33100 Tampere *Tel:* (03) 248 0300 *Fax:* (03) 222 8602
Tapiola, Lansituulentie 10, 02100 Espoo *Tel:* (09) 121 451 *Fax:* (09) 121 4520
Turku, Eerikinkatu 15, 20100 Turku *Tel:* (02) 265 6811 *Fax:* (02) 265 6820

Oy Satusiivet - Sagovingar AB (Lasten Parhaat Kirjat)
Simonkatu 12B-27, SF-00100 Helsinki
Tel: (09) 6933267 *Fax:* (09) 6944186
Key Personnel
President: Ritva Lemonen
Editoial Manager: Leena Jaervenpaeae
Children's Bookclub.
Owned by: Kustannus Oy Tammi

Suomalainen Kirjakauppa Oy
Verkkokauppa, Koivuvaarankuja 2, 01640 Vantaa
Tel: (09) 852 751 *Fax:* (09) 852 7980
E-mail: etunimi.sukunimi@suomalainenkk.fi
Web Site: www.suomalainen.com
Telex: 121841
Key Personnel
Man Dir: Hannu Syrjaenen
Marketing Manager: Lisbeth Kuitunen; Alto Lahdenpere
Contact: Toimitusjohtaja Raimo Kurri
E-mail: raimo.kurri@suomalainenkk.fi
Branch offices in Espoo (3), Forssa, Hameenlinna, Hamina, Heinola, Helsinki (11), Iisalmi, Imatra, Javenpaa, Joensuu, Jyvaskyla, Kajaani, Kerava, Kotka (3), Kouvola, Kuopio, Lahti, Lappeenranta, Mikkeli (2), Pori, Raahe, Rovaniemi, Salo, Savonlinni, Seinaajoki, Tampere, Turku, Vaasa, Vantaa, Varkaus.
Type of Business: Major Book Chain Headquarters
Owned by: Rautakirja Oy

Tampereen Kirjakauppa Oy
Haemeenkatu 27, PL 21, 33200 Tampere
Tel: (03) 2128380 *Fax:* (03) 2122136
E-mail: trekirja@vip.fi
Web Site: www.tampereenkirjakauppa.fi
Key Personnel
Manager: Martti Helminen
Founded: 1910
Type of Business: Exporter, Importer, Major Independent Bookseller

Turun Kansallinen Kirjakauppa Oy
Linnankatu 16, 20101 Turku
Mailing Address: PL 135, 20101 Turku
Tel: (02) 2831000 *Fax:* (02) 2831010
E-mail: info@kansallinenkirjakauppa.fi
Web Site: www.kansallinenkirjakauppa.fi
Key Personnel
Manager: Paula Palmroth *E-mail:* paula.palmroth@kansallinenkirjakauppa.fi
Branch Office(s)
Hameenkatu 7, Turku *Tel:* (02) 2831 050 *Fax:* (02) 2831 051
Lansikeskus Viilarinkatu 1, Turku *Tel:* (02) 2831 060

France

Critiques Livres Distribution SAS
24 rue Malmaison, BP 93, 93172 Bagnolet Cedex
Tel: (01) 43603910 *Fax:* (01) 48973706
E-mail: critiques.livres@wanadoo.fr
Key Personnel
President: Rosalind Fay-Boehlinger
Founded: 1976

FRANCE

Books in the visual arts in English, French, German & Italian.
Type of Business: Distributor, Exporter, Importer, Wholesaler

Distique
5, rue du Mal Leclerc, 28600 Luisant
Tel: (02) 3730 5700 *Fax:* (02) 3730 5712
Type of Business: Distributor

Flammarion
26, rue Racine, 75278 Paris Cedex 06
Tel: (01) 40 51 31 00; (01) 40 51 30 41 *Fax:* (01) 43 29 21 48
Web Site: www.flammarion.com/
Telex: Flamlyo 300460 F
Key Personnel
Manager: Jean-Noel Flammarion
Also Publisher. Branches in Bordeaux, Dijon, Grenoble, Lyon, Marseilles, Montreal (Canada), & Paris.

A Van Ginneken
BP 532, 21014 Dijon Cedex
Tel: (0380) 789595 *Fax:* (0380) 740700
E-mail: hexalivre@axnet.fr
Telex: 341429
Key Personnel
Man Dir: Andries Van Ginneken
Type of Business: Distributor, Exporter, Importer, Wholesaler

Hachette Livre SA - H E D
43, Quai de Grenelle, 75905 Paris Cedex 15
Tel: (01) 43923000 *Fax:* (01) 43923030
Web Site: www.hachette.com
Key Personnel
Director: Isabelle Magnac

Editions Lavoisier
Formerly Editions Tec & Doc - Lavoisier
14 rue de Provigny, 94236 Cachan Cedex
Tel: (01) 47 40 67 00 *Fax:* (01) 47 40 67 03
E-mail: edition@tec-et-doc.com
Web Site: www.tec-et-doc.com/fr
Telex: 632020 F TDL
Key Personnel
Dir: Jacques Besnault
Founded: 1947
Type of Business: Distributor, Exporter, Importer, Major Independent Bookseller

Librairie FNAC
95, bd Jean-Jaures, 92110 Clichy Cedex
Tel: (01) 42 70 56 90
E-mail: service-clientele@fnac.com
Web Site: www.fnac.com
Key Personnel
Manager: Bertrand Picard
Assistant Dir: Garrigou Martine *E-mail:* marie-martine.garrigou@fnac.tm.fr

Librairie Generale des PUF
49 blvd Saint-Michel, 75005 Paris
Tel: (01) 44418120 *Fax:* (01) 43546481
E-mail: puf-lib@puf.worldnet.net
Owned by: Presses Universitaires de France, 12 rue Jean de Beauvais, 75006 Paris

Librairie la Hune
170, Blvd Saint-Germain, F 75006 Paris
Tel: (01) 45483585
Key Personnel
Man Dir: Georges Dupre
Owned by: Flammarion

Librairie Mollat
11-15 rue Vital Carles, 33080 Bordeaux Cedex
Tel: (0556) 564040 *Fax:* (0556) 564088
E-mail: mollat@mollat.com
Web Site: www.mollat.com
Telex: 541542 F
Branch Office(s)
83-91 rue Porte-Dijeaux, 33080 Bordeaux Cedex

Office International de Documentation et Librairie (OFFILIB)
48, rue Gay Lussac, 75240 Paris Cedex 05
Tel: (01) 55 42 73 00 *Fax:* (01) 43 29 91 67
E-mail: info@offilib.com
Web Site: www.offilib.com
Key Personnel
Dir: Stephanie Boudon
Type of Business: Importer, Major Independent Bookseller

OFFILIB, see Office International de Documentation et Librairie (OFFILIB)

Librairie Sauramps Medical
11 Bd Henri IV, 34000 Montpellier
Tel: (04) 67636880 *Fax:* (04) 67525905
E-mail: librairie-sauramps-medical@wanadoo.fr
Web Site: www.livres.medicaux.com
Telex: (04) 480728
Key Personnel
Manager: Dominique Torreilles
Founded: 1977
Publisher & bookseller.
Subjects: Specialize in medicine
Type of Business: Importer, Major Independent Bookseller

Editions Tec & Doc - Lavoisier, see Editions Lavoisier

Librairie de l'Universite
2 place Dr Leon Martin, 38000 Grenoble Cedex
Tel: (0476) 46 61 63 *Fax:* (0476) 46 14 59
Founded: 1964
Type of Business: Major Independent Bookseller
Owned by: Flammarion

Gambia

The Gambia Methodist Bookshop Ltd
16 Nelson Mandela St, Banjul
Mailing Address: PO Box 203, Banjul
Tel: 28179
Key Personnel
Manager: James Heffernan

Germany

Artibus et Literis
Friedrichstr 22-26, 40001 Duesseldorf
Tel: (0211) 388-10 *Fax:* (0211) 3881280
E-mail: webmaster@artibus.de
Web Site: www.artibus.de
Key Personnel
Managing Partner: Horst Janssen; Klaus Janssen
Books & journals.
Type of Business: Exporter, Importer

Buchhandlung G D Baedeker
Kettwiger Str 35, 45127 Essen
Tel: (0201) 20680 *Fax:* (0201) 2068-100
E-mail: service.gdb.essen@baedeker.de
Web Site: www.baedeker.de

Bertelsmann Distribution GmbH
And der Autobahn, 33310 Guetersloh
Mailing Address: PO Box 7777, 33310 Guetersloh
Tel: (05241) 805 718 *Fax:* (05241) 46970
Web Site: www.bertelsmann-distribution.de
Telex: 933827
Key Personnel
Man Dir: Dr Hans-Joachim Herzog; Hartmut Ostrowski
Also publishers' delivery service.
Type of Business: Wholesaler
Owned by: Bertelsmann AG

Blazek und Bergmann
c/o Hunzinger Information AG, Holzhausenstr 21, 60322 Frankfurt
Mailing Address: Postfach 50 05 54, 60394 Frankfurt
Tel: (069) 152003-0 *Fax:* (069) 152003-44
E-mail: info@blazek-und-bergmann.de
Web Site: www.blazek-und-bergmann.de
Owned by: Hunziger Information AG

Bouvier GmbH & Co KG
Am Hof 28, 53113 Bonn
Tel: (0228) 72901-0; (01803) 258940 (orders) *Fax:* (0228) 72901-178
E-mail: bouvier@books.de
Web Site: www.books.de
Key Personnel
Manager: Thomas Grundmann
Man Dir: Richard Feldmann
Type of Business: Major Independent Bookseller
Branch Office(s)
Bouvier Buechermarkt, Am Hof 20, 53113 Bonn *Tel:* (0228) 72901-156 *Fax:* (0228) 72901-178
Bouvier Duisdorf, Rochusstr 175, 53123 Bonn *Tel:* (0228) 72901-510 *Fax:* (0228) 72901-511
Bouvier Hamm, Richard-Matthaei-Platz 1, 59065 Hamm *Tel:* (02381) 92021-0 *Fax:* (02381) 92021-530
Bouvier Juridicum, Nassestr 1, 53113 Bonn *Tel:* (0228) 2420772 *Fax:* (0228) 72901-178
Bouvier Koblenz, Loehrstr 30, 56068 Koblenz *Tel:* (0261) 30337-0 *Fax:* (0261) 30337-577
Bouvier Science-Center, Endenicher Allee 19, 53115 Bonn *Tel:* (0228) 72901-158 *Fax:* (0228) 72901-178
Bouvier Siegburg, Markt 16-19, 53721 Siegburg *Tel:* (02241) 9667-0 *Fax:* (02241) 9667-524
Buchhaus Gonski, Neumarkt Passage, Neumarkt 18a, 50667 Cologne *Tel:* (0221) 20909-0 *Fax:* (0221) 20909-359

Fachverlag Hans Carl GmbH
Andernacher Str 33a, 90411 Nuernberg
Tel: (0911) 95285-0 *Fax:* (0911) 95285-48
E-mail: info@hanscarl.com
Web Site: www.hanscarl.com *Cable:* CARLVERLAG
Key Personnel
Contact: Wolfgang Illguth; Traudel Schmitt
Founded: 1861
Type of Business: Distributor, Major Independent Bookseller

Dokumente Verlag Import-Exportbuchhandlung, see Dokumente Verlag Versandbuchhandlung Librairie

Dokumente Verlag Versandbuchhandlung Librairie
Postfach 1340, 77603 Offenburg
Tel: (0781) 923699-0 *Fax:* (0781) 923699-70
E-mail: info@dokumente-verlag.de
Web Site: www.dokumente-verlag.de
Key Personnel
President: Michael Schlageter *Tel:* (0781) 92369918 *E-mail:* ms@dokumente-verlag.de
Contact: Heribert Jager
Founded: 1945
Library.
Owned by: Michael Schlageter & Heribert Jager

BOOK DEALERS — GERMANY

Erich-Weinert Universitatsbuchhandlung
Ulrichplatz 4-6, 39104 Magdeburg
Tel: (0391) 568590 *Fax:* (0391) 5685923
E-mail: e.angerer@weinert.de
Web Site: www.weinert.de
Founded: 1960
Type of Business: Major Independent Bookseller
Owned by: Ernst Angerer

Werner Flach Internationale Fachbuchhandlung
Humboldtstr 57, 60318 Frankfurt am Main
Tel: (069) 9591750 *Fax:* (069) 95917522
E-mail: fachbuch@flachbuch.com
Web Site: www.flachbuch.com
Key Personnel
President: Werner Flach
Founded: 1957
Type of Business: Major Independent Bookseller

R Friedlaender & Sohn GmbH Buchhaunlung & Antiquariat
Dessauer St 28-29, 10963 Berlin
Tel: (030) 2622328
Key Personnel
International Rights: Hans-Werner Kyrieleis

Graff Buchhandlung
Sack 15, 38100 Braunschweig
Tel: (0531) 480 89-0 *Fax:* (0531) 480 89-89
E-mail: infos@graff.de
Web Site: www.graff.de
Key Personnel
Contact: Joachim Wrensch; Thomas Wrensch
Founded: 1867
Type of Business: Major Independent Bookseller

Otto Harrassowitz KG Wissenschaftliche Buchhandlung & Zeitschriftenagentur
Kreuzberger Ring 7 b-d, 65205 Wiesbaden
Tel: (0611) 5300 *Fax:* (0611) 530560
E-mail: service@harrassowitz.de
Web Site: www.harrassowitz.de
Key Personnel
Dir & Managing Partner: Dr Knut Dorn
 Tel: (0611) 530800 *E-mail:* kdorn@harrassowitz.de
EDP: Friedemann Weigel
Administrative Dir: Detlef Dorn
Accounting & Finances: Ruth Becker-Scheicher
Founded: 1872
Service of Books & Scholarly Journals to Academic & Research Libraries.
Subjects: Library Service Agency; Subscription Agency
Type of Business: Exporter, Importer, Major Independent Bookseller
Owned by: Ruth Becker-Scheicher, Dr Knut Dorn, Friedemann Weigel

Anton Hiersemann, Verlag
Haldenstr 30, 70376 Stuttgart
Tel: (0711) 5499710; (0711) 5499711 *Fax:* (0711) 54997121
E-mail: hiersemann.hauswedell.verlage@t-online.de
Web Site: www.hiersemann.de
Key Personnel
Contact: Karl G Hiersemann
Founded: 1884
Owned by: Dr Ernst Hauswedell und Co

Heinrich Hugendubel
Verlagshaus Holzstr 28, 80469 Munich
Tel: (089) 235586-0 *Fax:* (089) 235586-111
 Cable: HUGENDUBEL MUNICH

Iberoamericana Editorial Vervuert
Wielandstr 40, 60318 Frankfurt
Tel: (069) 5974617 *Fax:* (069) 5978743
E-mail: info@iberoamericanalibros.com
Web Site: www.ibero-americana.net
Founded: 1975
Specialize in books & journals, Latin American & Spanish books.
Type of Business: Distributor, Exporter, Importer, Major Independent Bookseller
Parent Company: Iberoamericana de Libros y Ediciones, Amor de Dios 1, 28014 Madrid, Spain

Von Kloeden KG
Wielandstr 24, 10707 Berlin-Charlottenburg
Tel: (030) 887 125 18 *Fax:* (030) 887 125 19
E-mail: vkloeden@t-online.de
Web Site: www.vonkloeden.de
Key Personnel
Man Dir, Rights & Permissions: Friedrich Von Kloeden
Editorial: Uta Grabe Von Kloeden
Founded: 1967
Bookshop(s): Berlin

Koch, Neff und Oetinger & Co
Schockenriedstr 37, 70565 Stuttgart
Tel: (0711) 78600 *Fax:* (0711) 78602800
Web Site: www.buchkatalog.de
Telex: 07255684 knov d stgt
Subjects: Bibliography
Type of Business: Distributor, Wholesaler

Kreuz Verlag GmbH & Co KG
Liebknechtstr 33, 70565 Stuttgart
Tel: (0711) 788030 *Fax:* (0711) 7880310
E-mail: service@kreuzverlag.de
Web Site: www.kreuzverlag.de
Key Personnel
Manager: Olaf Carstens; Bernd Friedrich; Sabine Schubert
Sales: Heike Donner
Editor: Thomas Schmitz
Founded: 1945
Owned by: Verlagsgruppe Dornier, Dircksenstr 48, 10178 Berlin

Kubon & Sagner Buchexport-Import GmbH
Hessstr 39/41, 80798 Munich
Tel: (089) 54 218-0 *Fax:* (089) 54 218-218
E-mail: postmaster@kubon-sagner.de
Web Site: www.kubon-sagner.de
Key Personnel
Manager: Otto Sagner; Sabine Sagner-Weigl
Founded: 1947
Specialize in publications from East & Southeast Europe.
Subjects: Albanian, Hungarian, Romanian & Slavic studies
Type of Business: Distributor, Exporter, Importer, Major Independent Bookseller, Wholesaler
Subsidiaries: Verlag Otto Sagner

Lange & Springer Antiquariat
Hegelplatz 1, 10117 Berlin
Tel: (030) 31504196; (030) 3422011 *Fax:* (030) 3410440; (030) 31504197
E-mail: buchladen@lange-springer-antiquariat.de
Web Site: www.lange-springer-antiquariat.de
Founded: 1980
Type of Business: Major Independent Bookseller

Leipziger Kommissions- und Grossbuchhandelsgesellschaft mbH, see LKG (Leipziger Kommissions- und Grossbuchhandelsgesellschaft mbH)

Georg Lingenbrink GmbH & Co, Libri
Friesenweg 1, 22763 Hamburg
Tel: 0180-53 69 800 *Fax:* (040) 853 98 300
E-mail: service@libri.de
Web Site: www.libri.de
Key Personnel
Manager: Alfred Becht; Holger Bellmann; Dr Markus Conrad; Dr Gerhard Dust; Marga Winkler
Founded: 1928
Type of Business: Exporter, Importer, Wholesaler
Branch Office(s)
August-Schanz-Str 33, 60433 Frankfurt *Tel:* (069) 954 22 0 *Fax:* (069) 954 22 300
Europeaallee, 36244 Bad Hersfeld *Tel:* (06621) 890 *Fax:* (06621) 89 13 12

LKG (Leipziger Kommissions- und Grossbuchhandelsgesellschaft mbH)
Poetzschauer Weg, 04579 Espenhain
Tel: (034206) 65135 *Fax:* (034206) 65110
E-mail: lkg@lkg-service.de
Key Personnel
Dir: Juergen Petry
Founded: 1946
Type of Business: Distributor, Exporter

J A Mayersche Buchhandlung GmbH & Co KG Abt Verlag
Matthiashofstr 28-30, 52064 Aachen
Tel: (0241) 4777 499 *Fax:* (0241) 4777 467
E-mail: info@mayersche.de
Web Site: www.mayersche.de
Key Personnel
Man Dir, Publicity: Helmut Falter
Founded: 1817
Branch offices in Bochum, Cologne, Dortmund, Duisburg, Essen, Gelsenkirchen & Monchengladbach.
Type of Business: Distributor, Exporter, Importer, Major Independent Bookseller

Minerva KG Internationale Fachliteratur fur Medizin und Naturwissenschaften Neue Medien
Bunsenstr 6, 64293 Darmstadt
Tel: (06151) 9880 *Fax:* (06151) 98839
E-mail: minerva@minerva.de
Web Site: www.minerva.de
Key Personnel
Contact: Christoph Gude; Stefan Gude
Founded: 1949
Type of Business: Distributor, Major Independent Bookseller
Owned by: Helmut Gude

Heinrich Petersen Hans Buchimport GmbH
Meessen 10, 22113 Oststeinbek
Mailing Address: Postfach 1119, 22109 Oststeinbek
Tel: (040) 71003-0 *Fax:* (040) 71003-141
E-mail: vertrieb@petersen-buchimport.com
Web Site: www.petersen-buchimport.com
Key Personnel
Contact: Johann Christian Peterson

Pociao's Books
Prinz Albrechtstr 65, 53113 Bonn
Mailing Address: Postfach 190136, 53037 Bonn
Tel: (0228) 229583 *Fax:* (0228) 219507
E-mail: pociao@t-online.de
Web Site: www.sanssoleil.de
Founded: 1975
Type of Business: Distributor, Exporter, Importer, Major Independent Bookseller
Owned by: Expanded Media Editions Sans Soleil

Sachse & Heinzelmann Kunst- und Buchhandlung GmbH
Koenigstr 20, 30175 Hannover
Tel: (0511) 360240 *Fax:* (0511) 324167
E-mail: info@sachse-heinzelmann.de
Web Site: www.sachse-heinzelmann.de
Type of Business: Major Independent Bookseller

Sandila Import-Export Handels-GmbH
Sagestr 37, 79737 Herrischried
Tel: (07764) 93970 *Fax:* (07764) 939739

GERMANY

E-mail: info@sandila.de
Web Site: www.sandila.de
Founded: 1984
Type of Business: Distributor, Exporter, Importer, Wholesaler

Kurt Scholl
Steinhofweg 20, 69123 Heidelberg
Tel: (06221) 707661
Founded: 1964
Type of Business: Major Independent Bookseller

SPS Verlaggsservice GmbH
Karl-Mand-Str 2, 56070 Koblenz
Tel: (0261) 80706-0 *Fax:* (0261) 80706-54
Key Personnel
Owner: Hansjochen Keilholz
Founded: 1979
Type of Business: Distributor

Stern-Verlag Janssen & Co
Friedrichstr 24-26, 40001 Duesseldorf
Tel: (0211) 3881-0 *Fax:* (0211) 3881-200
E-mail: buchhaus-sternverlag@t-online.de
Web Site: www.buchsv.de
Key Personnel
Managing Partner: Horst Janssen; Klaus Janssen
Founded: 1900
New & antiquarian/second-hand books; journals.
Type of Business: Distributor, Exporter, Importer
Bookshop(s): Friedrichstr 22-26, 40217 Duesseldorf; Universitatsbuchhandlung, Universitatsstr 1, 40225 Duesseldorf *Tel:* (0211) 346161 *Fax:* (0211) 340360 *E-mail:* unibuch@buchhaus-sternverlag.de

G Umbreit GmbH & Co KG
Mundelsheimer Str 3, 74321 Bietigheim-Bissingen
Tel: (07142) 596-0 *Fax:* (07142) 596-200
E-mail: info@umbreit-kg.de
Web Site: www.umbreit-kg.de
Key Personnel
Man Dir & Associate: Thomas Bez
Assistant Mgr, Buying Department: Martina Schlaud-Weisensee
Contact: Torben Merklinghaus *Tel:* (07142) 596 115
Founded: 1912
Type of Business: Distributor, Wholesaler

Vervuert Verlag, see Iberoamericana Editorial Vervuert

Berthold Winter
Wilzenweg 17, 13595 Berlin
Tel: (030) 362 35 30 *Fax:* (030) 362 96 93
Founded: 1920
Type of Business: Distributor, Exporter, Importer, Wholesaler

Verlags -und Sortiments-Buchhandlung Konrad Wittwer GmbH & Co KG
Postfach 105343, 70046 Stuttgart
Tel: (0711) 25 07 0 *Fax:* (0711) 25 07 145
E-mail: info@wittwer.de
Web Site: www.wittwer.de
Key Personnel
Man Dir: Christian Wittwer; Dr Konrad M Wittwer; Konrad P Wittwer; Michael Wittwer
Founded: 1867
Type of Business: Major Independent Bookseller
Branch Office(s)
Koenigstr 30, 70173 Stuttgart *E-mail:* buchhans@wittwer.de *Web Site:* www.wittwer.de

Ghana

Ghana Publishing Corporation, Distribution and Sales Division
c/o Publishing Div, Private Post Bag, Tema
Tel: (022) 812921
Branches throughout Ghana.

Presbyterian Book Depot Ltd
Box 4276, Accra
Tel: (021) 662707 *Fax:* (021) 665594
E-mail: pcg@africaonline.com.gh
Telex: 2525 *Cable:* BOOKS ACCRA
Key Personnel
Ag Man Dir: E Anim-Ansah
Founded: 1870
The organization comprises bookselling, stationery supply, printing (Presbyterian Press) & publishing activities (see Waterville Publishing House) Newspapers-Christian Messenger & The Presbyterian.
Type of Business: Distributor, Importer, Major Book Chain Headquarters, Major Independent Bookseller, Wholesaler
Owned by: Presbyterian Church of Ghana, PO Box 1800, Accra
Branch Office(s)
PO Box 70, Akim Oda, Contact: Mr Boakye Yiadom *Tel:* (0882) 2181
PO Box 219, Koforidua, Contact: Ms Makafui Acolatse *Tel:* (081) 22434
PO Box 1999, Kumasi, Contact: Mr G K Aboa *Tel:* (051) 28145
PO Box 16, Nkawkaw, Contact: S O Lartey *Tel:* (0842) 22010
PO Box 7, Odumase, Contact: Mr F T Lowor
PO Box 27, Tamale, Contact: K Mate *Tel:* (071) 22382
PO Box 10, Berekum, Contact: Mr Francis Yeboan *Tel:* (0642) 22029
PO Box GP 195, Accra, Contact: Twum Barima J *Tel:* (021) 663124

Queensway Bookshop & Stores Ltd
Bank Lane, Accra
Mailing Address: PO Box 4276, Accra
Tel: (021) 62707 *Cable:* Success Accra
Key Personnel
Manager: Kwaku Mensah
Suppliers of educational, library & HMSO publications.
Branch Office(s)
Bank St, PO Box 20, Kumasi *Tel:* (051) 4047

University Bookshop
Kwame Nkrumah University of Science & Technology, University Post Office, Kumasi
Tel: (051) 60223 *Fax:* (051) 60137
E-mail: library@knust.edu.gh
Web Site: www.knust.edu.gh *Cable:* KUMASITECH KUMASI
Key Personnel
Manager: Robert Reddick Mensah
Type of Business: Major Independent Bookseller

University Bookshop
University Sq, University of Ghana, PO Box LG 1, Legon
Tel: (021) 500398 *Fax:* (021) 500774
E-mail: bookshop@ug.edu.gh
Web Site: www.ghanaweb.com/GhanaHomePage/education/legon.html
Key Personnel
Manager: Emmanuel Tonyigah
Founded: 1950
Type of Business: Major Independent Bookseller
Owned by: University of Ghana, PO Box LG 25, Legon

Gibraltar

Gibraltar Bookshop
300 Main St, Gibraltar
Mailing Address: PO Box 816, Gibraltar
Tel: 71894 *Fax:* 75554
Key Personnel
Manager: A Benady
Founded: 1973
Type of Business: Distributor, Major Independent Bookseller

Greece

Agyra (Atkypa)
85 Kifissou Ave, 122 41 Athens
Tel: (01) 3459321; (01) 3478044; (01) 3428595 *Fax:* (01) 3474732
E-mail: info@agyra.gr
Web Site: www.agyra.gr
Bookshop(s): Pesmazoglou 5, Athens 105 64 *Tel:* (01) 3213507

Aithra Scientific Bookstore
One Messologiou St, 106 81 Athens
Tel: (01) 3301269 *Fax:* (01) 3302622
Key Personnel
President: Prof Vangelis Spourdagos
Founded: 1984
Specialize in books of Mathematics, Physics, Chemistry, Astronomy, Geology & Meteorology.
Type of Business: Exporter, Importer, Major Independent Bookseller, Wholesaler

Akti-Oxy Publications
79 Emmanouil Mpenaki, 106 81 Athens
Tel: (0210) 8658502; (0210) 8676125 *Fax:* (0210) 8644679
E-mail: info@oxy.gr
Web Site: www.oxy.gr
Key Personnel
President: Nikos Hatzopoulos
Vice President: Paris Coutsikos
Editor: Arhondi Korka; Tassos Nickogiannis
Secretary: Tina Anapnioti
Founded: 1995
Experimental, cultural & underground publication.
Bookshop(s): Oxy, Asklipiou 22, 10680 Athens

Alexiadou Vefa
Zefxidos 3, 546 22 Thessaloniki
Tel: (01) 224642 *Fax:* (01) 2828431
E-mail: vefaeditions@ath.forthnet.gr
Web Site: www.addgr.com/comp/vefa/index.htm
Key Personnel
President, Author & Editor: Vefa Alexiadou
Vice President: Koszas Alexiades
Marketing Dir: Alexia Alexiadou
Founded: 1979
Type of Business: Exporter, Wholesaler
Branch Office(s)
Nevrokopiou 16, Thessaloniki

Alpha-Delta
6, Sarantaporou St, 111 44 Athens
Tel: (01) 2280027 *Fax:* (01) 2280027
Key Personnel
President: Dr Ath I Delikostopoulos
Founded: 1966
Type of Business: Wholesaler
Owned by: Alamoheilas Ltd

Anastasiadis Publications
306 Patission St, 111 41 Athens
Tel: (01) 2284013 *Fax:* (01) 2236442

BOOK DEALERS — GREECE

Key Personnel
Contact: Pantelis Anastasiadis
Type of Business: Distributor, Wholesaler

Angeletos Sokzates
68-70 Ipirou St, 163 42 Ilioupoli, Athens
Tel: (01) 9928100 *Fax:* (01) 9940530

Aquarious
One Notara, 106 83 Athens
Tel: (01) 3842354; (01) 3617360 *Fax:* (01) 3303890

Athina
43, Emm Benaki St, 106 81 Athens
Tel: (01) 3821308 *Fax:* (01) 3807220
Key Personnel
Contact: Mary G Mavrogianni
Type of Business: Exporter
Owned by: George Mavrogianni, 27, Emm Benaki St, 106 81 Athens

Bacharakis
13 v Konstantinou, 546 23 Thessaloniki
Mailing Address: Imeras 4, 55236 Panorama, Thessaloniki
Tel: (031) 263776 *Fax:* (031) 263776
Founded: 1967
Also Publisher.
Type of Business: Distributor, Wholesaler

Typothito G Dardanos
37 Didotou, 10680 Athens
Tel: (0210) 3642003 *Fax:* (0210) 3642030
E-mail: info@dardanosnet.gr
Web Site: www.dardanosnet.gr
Founded: 1993
Also acts as Publisher.
Type of Business: Distributor, Exporter, Importer, Major Book Chain Headquarters, Major Independent Bookseller

Diavlos
10 Valtetsiou St, 106 80 Athens
Tel: (0210) 3631169; (0210) 3625315 *Fax:* (0210) 3617473
E-mail: info@diavlos-books.gr
Web Site: www.diavlos-books.gr
Key Personnel
President & Man Dir: Mr E Deligiannakis
Founded: 1988
Publication of scientific, computer, popular science, academic, short guides, humor books.
Type of Business: Distributor, Exporter, Major Independent Bookseller
Bookshop(s): 5 Pesmazoglov St, Athens 10564

Dion
39 Filikis Etaireias, 546 21 Thessaloniki
Tel: (02310) 265042 *Fax:* (02310) 265083
E-mail: info@psarasbooks.gr
Web Site: www.psarasbooks.gr
Key Personnel
Public Relations: Maria Psara
Founded: 1978
Bookshop & publications.
Type of Business: Distributor, Major Independent Bookseller, Wholesaler
Owned by: Psaras Evangelos
Parent Company: Bookshop Psaras, Albania
Warehouse: Tzabela 25, Thessaloniki

Efstathiadis Group SA
88 Drakontos St, 104 42 Athens
Tel: (0210) 515 4650 *Fax:* (0210) 515 4657
E-mail: info@efgroup.gr
Web Site: www.efgroup.gr
Telex: 216176
Key Personnel
President: Panos Efstathiadis
Vice President & Sales Dir: Thanos Efstathiadis
Founded: 1930
Type of Business: Distributor, Exporter, Importer, Wholesaler
Branch Office(s)
14 Valtetsious St, 106 80 Athens
4 C Cristali St, Antigonidon Sq, 546 30 Thessaloniki
Bookshop(s): 84 Academias St, 106 78 Athens; 14 Ethnikis Aminis St, 546 21 Thessaloniki

Eleftheri Skepsis
112 Ippokratous St, 114 72 Athens
Tel: (0210) 3614736; (0210) 3630697
E-mail: info@eleftheriskepsis.gr
Web Site: www.eleftheriskepsis.gr

G C Eleftheroudakis Co Ltd
International Bookstore, Constitution Sq, Nikis 4, GA 105 63 Athens
Tel: (01) 3222255; (01) 3229388 *Fax:* (01) 3231401; (01) 3229388
Key Personnel
Man Dir: Virginia Eleftheroudakis-Gregou
Also Publisher.

Enalios
4 El Venizelou, 143 43 Athens
Tel: (01) 2531614 *Fax:* (01) 2184854
Founded: 1996
Type of Business: Wholesaler
Owned by: Eleni Kekropoulou

Erevnites
3-5 Gravias St, 105 52 Athens
Tel: (0210) 5234 415; (0210) 5234 232 *Fax:* (0210) 5241 863
E-mail: erevnite@otenet.gr
Web Site: www.erevnites.gr
Founded: 1991

Esoptron
14 Armodiou St, Athens 10552
Tel: (01) 6442169 *Fax:* (01) 9028895
Key Personnel
Publisher: Stamos Stinis; Pavlos Voudouris
Type of Business: Wholesaler
Bookshop(s): 49 Panepistimiou Str, 106 78 Athens (Stoa Orfeos)

Eurodiastasi
49 Kallifrona, 106 77 Athens
Tel: (01) 3844695 *Fax:* (01) 3844888
E-mail: eurodiastasi@internet.gr; eurodiastasi@galaxynet.gr
Web Site: www.eurodiastasi.gr
Key Personnel
Sales Manager: Yanni Mitsios
Type of Business: Exporter, Wholesaler
Owned by: Loukia Mitsa & Takis Michalopoulos

Filistor Publishing
31 Themistokleous St, 106 77 Athens
Tel: (01) 3818457
Founded: 1995
Owned by: Charalabos Grammenos

Grivas Publications
3 Irodotou St, 193 00 Aspropyrgos, Attiki
Mailing Address: PO Box 72, 193 00 Aspropyrgos, Attiki
Tel: (0210) 5573470 *Fax:* (0210) 5573076
E-mail: info@grivas.gr
Web Site: www.grivas.gr
Key Personnel
Man Dir: N Grivas *E-mail:* grivas@otenet.gr
Founded: 1985
Publisher of ELT Book.
Owned by: Nick & Costas Grivas

Harry Joe Patsis' European Publications' Center Ltd
62 Panepistimiou Str, 106 77 Athens
Tel: (0210) 3841040; (0210) 3841050 *Fax:* (0210) 6232194; (0210) 3841050
Key Personnel
Foreign Affairs Dir: Harry Joe Patsis
Contact: Helen Patsis; Theoharis Patsis
Founded: 1996
Type of Business: Distributor, Exporter, Importer, Major Book Chain Headquarters, Major Independent Bookseller, Wholesaler
Showroom(s): 62 Panepistiniou Str, Athens 106 77 (Same location for bookshop)

Iamvlichos
5-7 Marni St, 104 33 Athens
Tel: (01) 5227678 *Fax:* (01) 5226581
Key Personnel
General Manager: P Michalitsis
Sales Manager: K Pachidis
Founded: 1981
Owned by: P Michalitsis, K Pachidis, K Kalogeropoulos & D Doulgaridis
Bookshop(s): Sirius, Marni S, 10433 Athens

Ikaros
4 Voulis St, 105 62 Athens
Tel: (01) 3225152
Founded: 1943
Owned by: K Karydi & Ch Karydi

J M Pantelides Booksellers Ltd
11 Amerikis St, 106 72 Athens
Tel: (01) 363 9560 *Fax:* (01) 363 6453
Telex: 224609 Paza gr
Key Personnel
Man Dir: Mrs Maro Pantelides
Founded: 1948
Type of Business: Importer, Major Book Chain Headquarters, Major Independent Bookseller, Wholesaler

Kanakis Publications & Bookshop
24 Z Pigis St, 10561 Athens
Tel: (01) 3302385 *Fax:* (01) 3811902

Kapon Editions
23-27 Makriyianni St, 117 42 Athens
Tel: (01) 92-35-098 *Fax:* (01) 92-14-089
Web Site: www.homemarket.gr
Key Personnel
Contact: Rachel Kapon *E-mail:* kapon_ed@otenet.gr
Founded: 1970
Also publisher.
Type of Business: Wholesaler

Kritiki
1-3 Tsamadou St, 106 83 Athens
Tel: (0210) 3803730 *Fax:* (01) 3803740
E-mail: biblia@kritiki.gr
Web Site: www.kritiki.gr

Kyriakidis Brothers sa
Melenikou 5, 546 35 Thessaloniki
Tel: (031) 208 540 *Fax:* (031) 245 541
E-mail: info@kyriakidis.gr
Web Site: www.kyriakidis.gr
Type of Business: Major Independent Bookseller, Wholesaler
Owned by: Dimitrios Kyriakidis; Tasos Kyriakidis

Librairie Kaufmann SA
28, Stadiou St, 105 64 Athens
Tel: (0210) 3236817 *Fax:* (0210) 3230320
E-mail: ccaldi@otenet.gr
Telex: 218187
Branch Office(s)
Academias 76, 106 78 Athens *Tel:* (01) 3627844
Siha 54 106 72 *Tel:* (01) 3643433

GREECE

Malliaris - Pedia
10 Aristotelous St, 546 24 Thessaloniki
Tel: (02310) 262 485 *Fax:* (02310) 264 856
E-mail: info@malliaris.gr
Web Site: www.malliaris.gr
Key Personnel
President: Antonis Malliaris
Founded: 1985
Branch Office(s)
11 Mavromihalis St, Athens *Tel:* (01) 3605874
Aristotelous Corner & Ermou 53, Thessaloniki
 Tel: (02310) 252 888 *Fax:* (02310) 252 890
Bookshop(s): 11th Saint Minas St, 54624 Thessaloniki; 57 So Fouli St, Kalamaria, Thessaloniki *Tel:* (02310) 424 277 *Fax:* (02310) 424 294; 22 Kolokotronis St, Stavroupoli *Tel:* (02310) 640 755 *Fax:* (02310) 640 757

Mavrogianni Publications
27 Emm Benaki & Solonos St, 106 81 Athens
Tel: (01) 3304628 *Fax:* (01) 3304628

Melissa Publishing House
58 Skoufa St, 106 80 Athens
Tel: (010) 3611692 *Fax:* (010) 3600865
E-mail: webmaster@melissabooks.com
Web Site: www.melissabooks.com
Founded: 1954

Olkos Editions
56 Sina Str, 106 72 Athens
Tel: (0210) 36 21 379 *Fax:* (0210) 36 25 576
Web Site: www.olkos.gr
Key Personnel
Contact: Irene Louvzou
Founded: 1973
Type of Business: Distributor, Major Independent Bookseller, Wholesaler
Showroom(s): 5 Pezmantzoglou St, 105 64 Athens
Bookshop(s): 5 Pezmantzoglou St, 105 64 Athens

Pournaras Panagiotis
12 Kastritsiou Str, 546 23 Thessaloniki
Tel: (031) 0270941 *Fax:* (031) 0228922
E-mail: pournarasbooks@the.forthnet.gr
Founded: 1962
International library suppliers & publisher.
Type of Business: Distributor, Exporter, Importer, Major Independent Bookseller

Press Photo Publications
One Tpounakn, 104 45 Athens
Tel: (0210) 8541400 *Fax:* (0210) 8541485
E-mail: photomag@photo.gr
Web Site: www.photo.gr
Founded: 1989
Type of Business: Major Independent Bookseller

Road Editions
39 Ippokratous Str, 106 80 Athens
Tel: (0210) 3613242 *Fax:* (0210) 3614681
E-mail: roadsales@road.gr
Web Site: www.road.gr
Key Personnel
President & General Manager: Stephanos Psimenos
Editor: Ioannis Tegopoulos
Founded: 1994
Publish & retailer of maps & travel guides.
Type of Business: Exporter

Salto Publishers
33, Angelaki St, 546 21 Thessaloniki
Tel: (031) 262854 *Fax:* (031) 285879
E-mail: saltos@spocrk.net.gr
Key Personnel
Contact: Marina Mouratidou

Vlassi
116 Solwnos & 2-4 Lontoy, 10681 Athens
Tel: (0210) 3812900; (01) 3833013 *Fax:* (0210) 3827557
Web Site: www.vlassi.gr
Key Personnel
President: Nikos Vlassis
Author: G R Enopoulos; K Palamas; S Melas; Oswalt Kolle
Founded: 1964

Votsis Nikos
16 Emm Benaki St, 106 78 Athens
Fax: (01) 3820646
E-mail: mvotsis@otenet.gr
Founded: 1958
Type of Business: Importer, Wholesaler

IE Zachariadou OHG (Bucherstube)
Prox Koromila 20, GR 54622 Thessaloniki
Tel: (0310) 276334 *Fax:* (0310) 229936
E-mail: info@lillisbookstore.gr
Web Site: www.lillisbookstore.gr
Key Personnel
Owner: Evangelia (Lilli) Zachariadou
 E-mail: lilli@lillisbookstore.gr
Founded: 1972
German Book & Information Center, Greek General bookstore, Italian bookstore.
Type of Business: Exporter, Importer, Major Independent Bookseller

Guatemala

Piedra Santa Editorial
7a Ave 4-45, Zona 1
Tel: (02) 232-9053 *Fax:* (02) 232-9053
E-mail: piedrasanta@guate.net
Key Personnel
Dir: Irene Piedra Santa
 E-mail: irene_piedra_santa@hotmail.com
Founded: 1947
Also Publisher.
Type of Business: Distributor, Exporter, Importer, Major Book Chain Headquarters
Showroom(s): 11 Calle 6-50, Zona 1, Guatemala City

Libreria Tuncho Granados G
Apdo 13, Guatemala City
Tel: (02) 24736; (02) 27269; (02) 21181
Branch Office(s)
La Plaza del Sol, Calle Montufar y 2 Ave, Zona 9 Guatemala City CA

Libreria Universal
13 Calle 4-16, Zona 1, Guatemala City
Tel: (02) 28 484
Key Personnel
Manager: Olga A de Manrique
Owned by: Distribuidora General Universal

Guyana

Austin's Book Services
190 Church St, South Cummingsburg, Georgetown
Tel: (02) 27 7395; (02) 26 7350 *Fax:* (02) 27 7396
E-mail: austins@guyana.net.gy
Key Personnel
Man Dir: Lloyd F Austin
Founded: 1993

Type of Business: Distributor, Importer, Major Independent Bookseller
Bookshop(s): Austin's Book Services, 190 Church, Cummingsburg, Georgetown (wholesale & retail)

Christian Book Service
242 Albert St & South Rd, Border, Georgetown
Tel: (02) 52521 *Fax:* (02) 54039
Key Personnel
Manager: Wesley Rowe
Type of Business: Major Independent Bookseller
Owned by: Full Gospel Fellowship

National Bookseller
78 Church St, Georgetown
Tel: (02) 71244 *Fax:* (02) 57309

Honduras

Libreria Universitaria Jose T Reyes
Universidad Nacional Autonoma de Honduras, Blvd Suyapa, Edificio Administrativo, Planta Baja, Tegucigalpa DC
Tel: 232-2110 *Fax:* 235-3361
Web Site: www.unah.hn
Telex: 1289

University Library, see Libreria Universitaria Jose T Reyes

Hong Kong

Enterprise International
1604 Eastern Commercial Centre, 16th floor, 393-407 Hennessy Rd, Wan Chai
Tel: 25734161 *Fax:* 28383469 *Cable:* EINPRISE HONG KONG
Key Personnel
Proprietor: C P Ho
Founded: 1978

Hong Kong Book Centre Ltd
On Lok Yuen Bldg, Basement, 25 Des Voeux Rd, Central Hong Kong
Tel: 2522-7064 *Fax:* 2868-5079
E-mail: orders@hkbookcentre.com.hk
Web Site: www.swindonbooks.com
Key Personnel
Dir: Annabella Lee
Founded: 1962

Swindon Book Co Ltd
13-15 Lock Rd, Kowloon
Tel: 2366 8001 *Fax:* 2739 4978
E-mail: swindon@netvigator.com
Web Site: www.swindonbooks.com
Telex: 50441 swin hx *Cable:* SWINDON
Key Personnel
Dir: Annabella Li
Manager: Daisy K Y Li
Book & stationery retail & distribution; filofax agency; OECD publications.
Branch Office(s)
University Book Store

> BOOK DEALERS — INDIA

Hungary

Talentum Konyves es Kereskedo Kft
Bartok B ut 106/110, Budapest 1113
Tel: (01) 2057077; (01) 2057138
Type of Business: Distributor, Importer, Wholesaler

Iceland

Bokabud Mals og menningar
Laugavegi 18, 101 Reykjavik
Mailing Address: Posthof 392, 121 Reykjavik
Tel: 519 2777 *Fax:* 562 3523
E-mail: mm@centrum.is
Key Personnel
Manager: Arni Einarsson
Founded: 1937
Type of Business: Distributor, Exporter, Importer, Wholesaler
Owned by: Mal og menning
Branch Office(s)
Sidumula 7-9, 108 Reykjavik

Boksala Studenta (The University Bookstore)
V/Hringbraut, 101 Reykjavik
Tel: (05) 700 777 *Fax:* (05) 700 778
E-mail: boksala@boksala.is
Web Site: www.boksala.is
Key Personnel
Man Dir: Sigurdur Palsson
Buyer: Eysteinn Bjornsson
Founded: 1968
All subjects with a concentration on Academic & Professional Literature, Textbooks.
Type of Business: Distributor, Importer, Major Independent Bookseller
Owned by: Felagsstofnun Studenta

Vaka-Helgafell
Sueurlandsbraut 12, 108 Reykjavik
Tel: 522 2000 *Fax:* 522 2022
E-mail: vaka@edda.is
Web Site: vaka.is
Key Personnel
Chairman of the Board: Olafur Ragnarsson
Man Dir: Bernhard Petersen
Dir - Publishing & Rights: Petur Mar Olafsson
Marketing Manager: Kjartan Orn Olafsson
Editor-in-Chief: Bjarni Thorsteinsson
Production Manager: Unnur Agustsdottir
Founded: 1981
Type of Business: Distributor, Importer, Wholesaler

India

Affiliated East West Press Pvt Ltd
G-1/16 Ansari Rd, Darya Ganj, New Delhi 110 002
Tel: (011) 23279113; (011) 23264180 *Fax:* (011) 23260538
E-mail: affiliat@vsnl.com
Key Personnel
Man Dir: Sunny Malik
Founded: 1962
Expertise in society publications & distribution; publishers of undergraduate & graduate STM Books.
Type of Business: Distributor, Importer, Wholesaler

Allied Publishers Pvt Ltd
13-14 Asaf Ali Rd, New Delhi 110002
Tel: (011) 3239001; (011) 3233002; (011) 3233004; (011) 323006667 *Fax:* (011) 3235967
E-mail: aplnd@del2.vsnl.net.in
Web Site: www.alliedpublishers.com
Key Personnel
Man Dir: S M Sachdev
Dir: Ravi Sachdev; Sunil Sachdev
Founded: 1934
Also printers.
Type of Business: Distributor, Exporter, Importer, Wholesaler
Owned by: Allied Chambers (India) Ltd
Branch Office(s)
Prarthana Flats, Navrangpura, Ahmedabad 380009
  Tel: (079) 646 5916; (079) 663 0079
Bangalore
751 Anna Salai, Chennai 600002 *Tel:* (044) 8523938; (044) 8523984 *Fax:* (044) 8520649
3-5-1129 Kachiguida Cross Rd, Hyderabad 500027 *Tel:* (040) 4619079; (040) 4619081 *Fax:* (040) 4619079; (040) 4619081
17 Chittaranjan Ave, Kolkata 700072 *Tel:* (033) 2257023; (033) 2252514 *Fax:* (033) 261158
  E-mail: alliedcal@vsnl.com
Patiala House, 16-A Ashok Marg, Lucknow 226001 *Tel:* (0522) 214253; (0522) 280358 *Fax:* (0522) 214253
Ballard Estate, 15, JN Heredia Marg, Mumbai 400038 *Tel:* (022) 2617926; (022) 2617927 *Fax:* (022) 2617928 *E-mail:* alliedpl@vsnl.com
18 Hill Rd, Ramnagar, Nagpur 440010
  Tel: (0712) 521122; (0712) 542625 *Fax:* (0712) 542625

Atma Ram & Sons
Kashmere Gate, Delhi 110006
Tel: (011) 2523082 *Cable:* BOOKS
Key Personnel
Man Dir, Publicity, Rights & Permissions: Sushil Kumar Puri
Also publisher.
Type of Business: Importer

Biblia Impex Pvt Ltd
2/18 Ansari Rd, New Delhi 110002
Tel: (011) 327-8034; (011) 326-2515 *Fax:* (011) 328-2047
E-mail: info@bibliaimpex.com
Web Site: www.bibliaimpex.com *Cable:* ELYSIUM
Key Personnel
Man Dir: P K Goel
Founded: 1980
International bookseller & subscription agent.
Type of Business: Distributor, Exporter, Major Independent Bookseller

Books & Periodicals Agency
B-1 Inder Puri, New Delhi 110012
Tel: (011) 205624 *Fax:* 801-881-6189 (US Fax)
E-mail: bpage@del2.vsnl.net.in
Web Site: www.bpagency.com *Cable:* BACKVOLUME
Key Personnel
Proprietor: Girish Gupta
Founded: 1973
Exporter of books on South Asia & Southeast Asia. Over 100,000 titles in 356 subjects at www.bpagency.com.
Type of Business: Distributor, Exporter, Major Independent Bookseller

Books India
J-19/835 Mandir Marg, New Delhi 110 001
Tel: (011) 327 7463 *Fax:* (011) 241 2912
Key Personnel
Dir: Mr Baxi Himanshu
Founded: 1969
Type of Business: Exporter, Major Independent Bookseller

Nem Chand & Bros
Civil Lines, Roorkee 247667
Tel: (01332) 272258; (01332) 272752; (01322) 264343 *Fax:* (01332) 273258
E-mail: ncb_rke@rediffmail.com *Cable:* ENGINJOUR
Founded: 1951
Type of Business: Distributor, Exporter, Importer, Major Independent Bookseller, Wholesaler

Current Technical Literature Co (Pvt) Ltd
Malhotra House, Opp GPO, Mumbai, Maharashtra 400 001
Mailing Address: PO Box 1374, Mumbai, Maharashtra 400 001
Tel: (022) 2611045 *Fax:* (022) 2679786
  Cable: Cutelico
Key Personnel
Man Dir: R K Murti
Scientific, technical & medical books.
Branch Office(s)
Narayanguda, Opp Blood Bank, PO Box No 1030, Hyderabad 500 029 *Tel:* (040) 591516
152 Thambu Chetti St, PO Box No 128, Chennai 600 001 *Tel:* (044) 5342897
22 Chittaranjan Ave, Kolkata 700 072 *Tel:* (033) 273138
4676 Ansari Rd, 21 Daryaganj, PO Box No 7008, New Delhi 110 002 *Tel:* (011) 3278737

DK Agencies (P) Ltd
A/15-17 DK Ave, Mohan Garden, Najafgarh Rd, New Delhi 110 059
Tel: (011) 2535-7104; (011) 2535-7105
  Fax: (011) 2535-7103
E-mail: custserv@dkagencies.com
Web Site: www.dkagencies.com
Key Personnel
Dir: Jaswant Rai Mittal; Ramesh K Mittal
  E-mail: rkmittal@dkagencies.com
Senior Executive: Surya P Mittal *E-mail:* surya@dkagencies.com
Founded: 1968
Indian books & periodicals. Also multi-media (audio, video, CDs & microfilms from India). Also publisher & subscription agent.
Type of Business: Distributor, Exporter, Major Independent Bookseller, Wholesaler
Branch Office(s)
4788-90/23 Ansari Rd, Daryagarj, New Delhi 110 002 *Tel:* (011) 2326-6890
Bookshop(s): 4788-90/23 Ansari Rd, Darya Ganj, New Delhi 110002 *Tel:* (011) 2326-6890

E D Galgotia & Sons
17-B Connaught Pl, New Delhi 110 001
Tel: (011) 3322876 *Fax:* (011) 3755150
E-mail: galgotia@ndf.vsnl.net.in
Telex: 71161 Star In
Key Personnel
Dir: Suneel Galgotia; Neeraj Galgotia
Manager: P Paul
Subjects: Technical, scientific, medical & management
Type of Business: Importer, Major Independent Bookseller, Wholesaler

English Book Store
17-L Connaught Circus, New Delhi 110001
Tel: (011) 332 9126 *Fax:* (011) 332 1731
Key Personnel
Proprietor: Bhupinder Chowdhri
Importer - military science, aviation, nursing, foreign languages, travel, religion.

General Book Depot
1691 Nai Sarak, Delhi 110007
Tel: (011) 3263695; (011) 3250635 *Fax:* (011) 2394 0861

German Book Centre
8 II Main Rd CIT (East), Chennai 600 035
Tel: (044) 2434-6244; (044) 2434-6266
  Fax: (044) 2434-6529
E-mail: germanbk@vsnl.com
Web Site: germanbookcentre.com
Key Personnel
Contact: R Seshadri
Type of Business: Distributor, Importer, Wholesaler

Giri Trading Agency Pvt Ltd
58/2 TSV Koil St, Mylapore, Chennai 600004
Tel: (044) 4943551; (044) 4953817; (044) 4953823 *Fax:* (044) 4953823
E-mail: giritrading@vsnl.com
Web Site: www.giritrading.com
Key Personnel
Dir: T S V Hari *Tel:* (044) 46116110
  E-mail: tsvhari@eth.net; T S Srinivasan
General Manager: V Subramanian
Founded: 1951
Producers of audio cassettes specializing in all (A-Z) items pertaining to Hindu Religion; also acts as Publisher of English & all South Indian Language Books. Supply all items pertaining to Hindu worship.
Membership(s): Booksellers & Publishers of South India.
Type of Business: Distributor, Exporter, Major Independent Bookseller, Wholesaler
Owned by: Gitaa Cassettes, T S Ranganathan; Giri Publications; Kamakoti-Tamil Monthly Magazine
Parent Company: Giri Trading Agency
Ultimate Parent Company: Giri Trading Agency Pvt. Ltd
Branch Office(s)
Modi Nivas, Bhandarkar Rd, Matunga, Mumbai 400019 *Tel:* (022) 4141344; 4122316 *Fax:* (022) 4143140 *E-mail:* giri@bom8.vsnl.net.in
Bookshop(s): 10 Kapaleeshwarar Sannadth St, Mylapore, Chennai 600004 *Tel:* 4953820, 4953816

GOYL Saab, Publishers and Distributors, see General Book Depot

Health-Harmony, *imprint of* B Jain Publishers Overseas

Higginbothams Ltd
814 Anna Salai, Chennai 600 002
Tel: (044) 852 1841 *Fax:* (044) 852 8101 *Cable:* BOOKLOVER
Key Personnel
Dir: K A Arjun
Type of Business: Importer

Hindi Book Centre
4/5-B Asaf Ali Rd, New Delhi 110 002
Tel: (011) 328 6757; (011) 325 8993; (011) 326 1696 *Fax:* (011) 327 3335; (011) 648 1565
E-mail: info@hindibook.com
Web Site: www.hindibook.com *Cable:* STARPUBLIS
Key Personnel
Man Dir: Mr Amarnath
Executive Dir Sales: Mr Anil Varma
General books in Hindi.
Owned by: Star Publications (Pvt) Ltd, 55 Warren St, London W1T 5NW

Hindustan Book Agency
P19, Green Park Extension, New Delhi 110 016
Tel: (011) 6163294; (011) 6163296 *Fax:* (011) 6193297
E-mail: hindbook@nda.vsnl.net.in
Web Site: www.hindbook.com

Key Personnel
Partner: D K Jain; J K Jain
Founded: 1947
American Mathematical Society, Birkhauser Verlag, Cambridge University Press, IOP, Kluwer Academic Publisher, Oxford University Press, Princeton University Press, Springer Verlag, Elsevier Science.
Type of Business: Distributor

International Book House Pvt Ltd
Indian Mercantile Mansions (Extn), Madame Cama Rd, Mumbai, Maharashtra State 400 001
Tel: (022) 22021634; (022) 22021795 *Fax:* (022) 22851109
E-mail: ibh@vsnl.com
Web Site: www.intbh.com *Cable:* Interbook
Key Personnel
Dir: Sanjeev Gupta
Manager: T R B Vathsal
Founded: 1941
Trade books, book distributors, retailers, direct mail, direct to home, magazine subscriptions.
Type of Business: Distributor, Importer
Branch Office(s)
97 Residency Rd, Bangalore 560 025 *Tel:* (080) 22210193
Shop 5 Palace Court, One Kyd St, Kolkata 700 016 *Tel:* (033) 22294493
Bookshop(s): 13, S N Banejeer Rd, 2nd floor, Kolkata 700 013 *Tel:* (033) 216 26 78

Jaico Publishing House
127 Mahatma Gandhi Rd, Mumbai 400 023
Tel: (022) 267 6702; (022) 267 6802; (022) 267 4501 *Fax:* (022) 265 6412
E-mail: jaicowbd@vsnl.com
Web Site: www.jaicobooks.com
Telex: 118-6398 JAI IN *Cable:* JAICOBOOKS
Key Personnel
Man Dir: Ashwin Shah
Editor: R H Sharma
Type of Business: Importer
Owned by: Jaico Publishing House
Branch Office(s)
Jaico Book Agency, No 57, Dr Giri Rd, T Nagar, Chennai 600 017, Manager: Mr A R Sivaraman *Tel:* (044) 2826 2874; (044) 2822 2653; (044) 2822 4582 *E-mail:* jaicoche@md3.vsnl.net.in
Jaico Book Distributors, 194, Patpar Ganj Indl Area, Delhi *Tel:* (011) 2214 4204; (011) 2214 4205 *Fax:* (011) 2214 4206 *E-mail:* jaicobook@vsnl.net
Jaico Book Distributors, G-2, 16 Ansari Rd, Darya Ganj, New Delhi 110 002, Manager: Mr Sanjay Verma *Tel:* (011) 2326 0651; (011) 2326 0618; (011) 2326 4748 *Fax:* (011) 2327 8469 *E-mail:* sethidel@del6.vsnl.net.in
Jaico Book Enterprises, 302, Acharya Prafulla Chandra Roy Rd, Kolkata 700 009, Manager: Mr M K Bal *Tel:* (033) 2360 0542; (033) 2360 0543 *E-mail:* jaicocal@cal2.vsnl.net.in
Jaico Book House, 14/1 1st Main Rd, 6th Cross, Gandhi Nagar, Bangalore 560 009, Manager: Mr Hemant Sharma *Tel:* (080) 226 7016; (080) 225 7083 *Fax:* (080) 228 5492 *E-mail:* jaicobgr@blr.vsnl.net.in
Jaico Book House, 3-4-494/1/2 Barkatpura, Hyderabad 500 027, Manager: Mr K S Anand *Tel:* (040) 2755 1992 *E-mail:* hyd1_jaicohyd@sancharnet.in
Jaicos' Wholesale Book Distributors, ELGI House, 2 Mill Officers' Colony, Ahmedabad 380 009, Contact: Mr Sujesh Kumar *Tel:* (079) 657 9865; (079) 657 5262 *E-mail:* jaicoahm@vsnl.com

B Jain Publishers Overseas
1921/10, Chuna Mandi, Paharganj, New Delhi 110050
Tel: 23583100; 23581300 *Fax:* (011) 23580471
E-mail: bjain@vsnl.com

Web Site: www.bjainbooks.com
Key Personnel
Owner: Dr P N Jain *Tel:* (011) 22542967
Chief Executive Officer: Sh Kuldeep Jain
Founded: 1967
Books, handcraft items & globules.
Subjects: Medical, health & new age
Imprints: Health-Harmony
Branch Office(s)
7, FIE Patparganj, Delhi 110092
Showroom(s): 1921/10, Chuna Mandi, Paharganj, New Delhi 110055

Krishnamurthy K
23 Thanikachalam Rd, Chennai 600017
Tel: (044) 2434 4519 *Fax:* (044) 2434 2009
E-mail: ksm@md2.vsnl.net.in; service@kkbooks.com
Web Site: www.kkbooks.com
Founded: 1944
Type of Business: Importer
Branch Office(s)
Shop No 31, Lal Bahadur Stadiom, Hyderabad 500001 *Tel:* (040) 231447

The Modern Book Depot
15A, J L Nehru Rd, Kolkata 700013
Tel: (033) 2493102; (033) 2490933 *Fax:* (033) 2497455
E-mail: modcal@vsnl.com
Key Personnel
Owner: Dewan Chand; Prem Prakash
Founded: 1949
Type of Business: Importer, Major Independent Bookseller, Wholesaler
Owned by: Om Prakash
Branch Office(s)
Station Sq, Unit III, Bhubaneswar, Orissa 751001 *E-mail:* modbooks@cal2.vsnl.net.in

Motilal Banarsidass
41-UA Bungalow Rd, Jawahar Nagar, Delhi 110 007
Tel: (011) 23851985; (011) 23858335; (011) 23854826; (011) 23852747 *Fax:* (011) 23850689; (011) 25797221
E-mail: mlbd@vsnl.com
Web Site: www.mlbd.com *Cable:* GLORYINDIA
Key Personnel
Managing Partner: R P Jain
Founded: 1903
Indological books including Indian literature, religion, philosophy, history, culture, etc; also a publisher.
Type of Business: Distributor, Exporter, Importer, Wholesaler
Branch Office(s)
236, Ninth Main III Block, Jayanagar, Bangalore 560 0111 *Tel:* (080) 6542591
  E-mail: mlbdbgl@vsnl.com
120 Royapettah High Rd, Mylapore, Chennai 600004 *Tel:* (044) 4982315 *Fax:* (044) 4940066 FDA 48 *E-mail:* mlbdbook@sancharnet.in
PO Box 75, Chowk, Varanasi 221 001 *Tel:* (0542) 352331 *Fax:* (0542) 321806 *E-mail:* varanasi@mlbd.com
8 Camac St, Kolkata 700 017 *Tel:* (033) 2434874; (033) 2427457 *Fax:* (033) 2425291 *E-mail:* bpb_kol@vsnl.net
8 Mahalakshmi Chambers, 22 Warden Rd, Mumbai 400026 *Tel:* (022) 4923526; (022) 4982583 *Fax:* (022) 4963850 *E-mail:* mlbdmumbai@vsnl.net
Ashok Raipath, opposite Patna College, Patna, Bihar 800 004 *Tel:* (0612) 671442 *Fax:* (0612) 657641 *E-mail:* patna@mlbd.com
Sanas Plaza, Shop 11-12, 1302 Baji Rao Rd, Pune 411 002 *Tel:* (0212) 4486190 *Fax:* (0212) 660557 *E-mail:* mlbdpune@vsnl.net

Munshiram Manoharlal Publishers Pvt Ltd
54 Rani Jhansi Rd, New Delhi 110055

BOOK DEALERS

Mailing Address: PO Box 5715, New Delhi 110055
Tel: (011) 7771668 *Fax:* (011) 3612745
E-mail: mml@mantraonline.com *Cable:*
 LITERATURE NEW DELHI
Key Personnel
Man Dir: Devendra Jain
Sales Dir: Ashok Jain; Pankaj D Jain
Founded: 1952
Booksellers & publishers.
Type of Business: Major Independent Bookseller
Bookshop(s): 4416 Nai Sarak, Delhi 110006

Narosa Book Distributors Pvt Ltd
22, Daryaganj, Delhi Medical Association Rd, Delhi 110002
Tel: (011) 23243224; (011) 23243415; (011) 23243416 *Fax:* (011) 23243225; (011) 23258934
E-mail: narosa@ndc.vsnl.net.in/narosadl@nda.vsnl.net.in
Web Site: www.narosa.com *Cable:* NAROSA NEW DELHI
Key Personnel
Man Dir: N K Mehra
Marketing Manager: S Mehra
Senior Executive: P.K. Chopra
Branch Office(s)
35-36 Greams Rd, Thousand Lights, Chennai 600 006 *Tel:* (044) 28295362 *Fax:* (044) 28290377 *E-mail:* narosamds@vsnl.net
2F-2G Shivam Chambers, 53 Syed Amir Ali Ave, Kolkata 700 019 *Tel:* (033) 22814809 *Fax:* (033) 22814778
306 Shiv Centre, DBC Sector 17, PO KU Bazar, New Bombay 400 705 *Tel:* (022) 27890977 *Fax:* (022) 27891930

Navakarnataka Publications (P) Ltd
Embassy Centre, 11 Crescent Rd, Kumara Park East, PB 5159, Bangalore, Karnataka 560001
Tel: (080) 22203580; (080) 22203581; (080) 22203582 *Fax:* (080) 22203582
E-mail: nkp@bgl.vsnl.net.in
Web Site: www.navakarnatakabooks.com *Cable:* BOOKCENTRE
Key Personnel
Man Dir: R S Rajaram
Founded: 1960
Subscriptions, publications & distribution.
Type of Business: Distributor, Exporter, Importer, Major Independent Bookseller, Wholesaler
Branch Office(s)
5th Main, Gandhinagar, Bangalore, Karnataka 560009 *Tel:* (080) 22251382
Moquaddam Trade Centre, Station Rd, Gulbarga, Karnataka 585102 *Tel:* (08472) 224302
K S R Road, Mangalore, Karnataka 575001 *Tel:* (0824) 2441016
Ramaswamy Circle, Mysore, Karnataka 570024 *Tel:* (0821) 2424094

Oxford & IBH Publishing Co Pvt Ltd
66 Janpath, New Delhi 110001
Tel: (011) 3320518; (011) 3324578; (011) 3357791; (011) 3315310 *Fax:* (011) 3710090
E-mail: oxfordpubl@axcess.net.in *Cable:* INDAMER
Key Personnel
Man Dir: Gulab Primlani
Founded: 1921
Distributing agents for FAO, ICAO, OECD, IDRC.
Type of Business: Exporter, Importer, Major Independent Bookseller, Wholesaler
Owned by: Oxford & IBH Publishing Co Pvt Ltd
Branch Office(s)
17 Park St, Kolkata 700016

Popular Book Depot
217 Raja Rammohan Roy Marg, Mumbai 400 007
Tel: (022) 382 9401; (022) 382 6762
Key Personnel
Partner: Manmohan S Bhatkal *E-mail:* bhatkal@vsnl.com
Founded: 1924
Distribution of books, journals & educational aids.
Type of Business: Exporter, Importer
Branch Office(s)
Subscription Division, Saraswati Mandir, Jaganath Shankarshet Rd, Mumbai *Tel:* (022) 3879402
Bookshop(s): Nehru Planetarium, Worli, Mumbai 400018 *E-mail:* bhatkal@vsnl.com

Prints India
Prints House, 11 Darya Ganj, New Delhi 110 002
Tel: (011) 3268645 *Fax:* (011) 3275542
Telex: 31-61087 *Cable:* INDOLOGY
Key Personnel
Contact: V K Gupta
Founded: 1966
Also subscription agent & publisher.
Type of Business: Distributor, Exporter, Major Book Chain Headquarters, Major Independent Bookseller, Wholesaler
Owned by: MD Publications Pvt Ltd Co, MD House, 11 Darya Ganj, New Delhi 110002

Rupa & Co
15 Bankim Chatterjee St, College Sq, Kolkata 700 073
Mailing Address: PO Box 7071, Daryaganj, New Delhi 110 002
Tel: (011) 3278588; (011) 3272161 *Fax:* (033) 3277294
E-mail: rupa@ndb.vsnl.net.in
Telex: 3166641 *Cable:* RUPANCO
Key Personnel
Man Dir: D Mehra
All subjects; also publisher.
Type of Business: Distributor, Exporter, Importer, Wholesaler
Branch Office(s)
94 South Malaka, Allahabad
G1 & 2 Ghaswalla Tower, P G Solanki Path, Off Lamington Rd, Near Minerva Cinema, Mumbai 400 007

Scientific Book Agency
56-D Mirza Ghalib St, Kolkata 700016
Mailing Address: PO Box 239, Kolkata 700001
Tel: (033) 292915; (033) 4642206; (033) 4638273
E-mail: psjs@cal3.usnl.net.in
Key Personnel
Editor: J Sinha; Mrs Prakriti Sinha
Founded: 1954
Also acts as publishers.
Type of Business: Distributor, Exporter, Importer, Major Independent Bookseller, Wholesaler
Bookshop(s): 79/2 Mahatma Gandhi Rd, Kolkata 700009

R R Sheth & Co
PO Box 4060, Ashram Rd, Riverside, Ahmedabad 380009
Tel: (079) 5356573
E-mail: chintan@rrsheth.com
Web Site: www.rrsheth.com
Key Personnel
Proprietor: Bhagatbhai Bhuralal Sheth *Tel:* (022) 6183182
Export Manager: P V Katira
Founded: 1926
Gujarati & Hindi books, also publisher.
Type of Business: Wholesaler
Branch Office(s)
Opp Phuvara, Gandhi Marg, Ahmedabad 380001 *Tel:* (079) 5356573

Star Publications (P) Ltd
4/5 B Asaf Ali Rd, New Delhi 110002
Tel: (011) 328 6757; (011) 23258993; (011) 326 1696; (011) 326 8651 *Fax:* (011) 23273335; (011) 648 1565
E-mail: starpub@satyam.net.in
Web Site: www.starpublic.com *Cable:* STARPUBLIS
Key Personnel
Man Dir: Mr Amarnath Varma
All types of Indian Books, in all Indian languages & English
Also acts as publisher.
Type of Business: Distributor, Exporter

Super Book House
Sind Chambers, Shahid Bhagat Singh Rd, Colaba, Mumbai, Maharashtra 400 005
Tel: (022) 2830560 *Fax:* (022) 2834452
Telex: 011-83850
Key Personnel
Contact: Shoaib S Ranalui; M S Lehri
Branch Office(s)
5-8-548/A, 1st floor, Arastu Trust Bldg, Abid Rd, Hyderabad 500 001 *Tel:* (040) 203123
27/25 Shakti Nagar, New Delhi 110 007 *Tel:* (040) 203123 *Fax:* (040) 203724
Bookshop(s): Ideas, 1st floor, Doli Chambers, Next to Strand Cinema, Mumbai 400005

TBI Publishers' Distributors
M-33, Connaught Place, New Delhi 110 001
Tel: (011) 3325247 *Fax:* (011) 3325247
Key Personnel
Contact: Ravi Sabharwal
Founded: 1985
Type of Business: Distributor, Importer, Wholesaler
Branch Office(s)
46 Housing Society, South Extension I, New Delhi 110 001 *Tel:* (011) 4632903

N M Tripathi Pvt Ltd Publishers & Booksellers
164 Shamaldas Gandhi Marg, Mumbai 400002
Tel: (022) 22013651; (022) 22050048
Key Personnel
Man Dir: Kartik R Tripathi
Founded: 1888
Only Gujrati literature & publications. Gujrati is a local Indian language.

UBS Publishers' Distributors Pvt Ltd
5 Ansari Rd, New Delhi 110002
Mailing Address: PO Box 7015, New Delhi 110002
Tel: (011) 3273601; (011) 3266646 *Fax:* (011) 3276593; (011) 3274261
E-mail: ubspd@ubspd.com
Web Site: www.gobookshopping.com; www.ubspd.com *Cable:* ALLBOOKS
Key Personnel
Chairman: Mr C M Chawla
Man Dir: Mr Sukumas Das *Tel:* (011) 3276585 *E-mail:* sdas@ubspd.com
General Manager, Export Marketing: Amrit Sharma *Tel:* (011) 3271485 *E-mail:* alsharma@ubspd.com
Dir: M K Kalsi *Tel:* (011) 3245477 *E-mail:* mkkalsi@ubspd.com
Founded: 1963
Type of Business: Distributor, Exporter, Importer, Wholesaler
Branch Office(s)
10 First Main Rd, PO Box 9713, Gandhi Nagar, Bangalore 560 009 *Tel:* (080) 2253903, 2263901, 2263902 *Fax:* (080) 2263904 *E-mail:* ubspdbng@bgl.vsnl.net.in
No 60, Nelson Manickam Rd, Aminji Karai, Chennai 600029 *Tel:* (044) 3746222, 3746351 *Fax:* (044) 3746287 *E-mail:* vijayan@che.ubspd.com
80 Noronha Rd, Cantonment, Kanpur *Tel:* (0512) 315122

8/1-B, Chowringhee Lane, Kolkata 700 016
Tel: (033) 2521821, 2522910, 2529473
Fax: (033) 2523027 *E-mail:* ubspdcal@cal.vsnl.net.in

Universal Book Shop
c/o Chugh Publications, PB No 101, 2 Starchey Rd, Civil Lines, Allahabad 21101
Tel: (0532) 603012
Key Personnel
Partner: Ramesh Chugh
Owned by: Chugh Publications

Universal Book Traders
80 Gokhale Market, Opp Tishazari Courts, Delhi 110 054
Tel: (011) 2396 1288; (011) 2391 1966; (011) 2399 0487 *Fax:* (011) 2392 4152; (011) 2745 9023
E-mail: unilaw@vsnl.com
Web Site: www.unilawbooks.com
Key Personnel
Partner: Manish Arora; M G Arora; Pradeep Arora; Sanjeev Arora
Founded: 1956
Type of Business: Distributor, Exporter, Importer, Major Independent Bookseller, Wholesaler
Branch Office(s)
C-27, Connaught Pl, (between Odeon & Plaza) Middle Circle, New Delhi 110 001 *Tel:* (011) 2341 6277; (011) 2341 8671 *Fax:* (011) 2341 8014

Visalaandhra Publishing House
4-1-435, Vignana Bhavan, Bank St, Hyderabad 500 001
Tel: (040) 24744580 *Fax:* (040) 4735905
Founded: 1953
Publishing & marketing of general books in Telugu language.
Type of Business: Distributor, Importer, Wholesaler
Branch Office(s)
Sultan Bazar, Hyderabad 500 095 *Tel:* (040) 24751462
Visalaandhra Book House, College Rd, Anantapur 515001 *Tel:* (08554) 220614
Visalaandhra Book House, Arundelpet, Guntur 522 002 *Tel:* (0863) 2233297
Visalaandhra Book House, Main Rd, Hanmakonda 506 001 *Tel:* (08712) 2577156
Visalaandhra Book House, Bank St, Hyderabad 500001 *Tel:* (040) 24602946
Visalaandhra Book House, Kakinada 533 001 *Tel:* (0884) 2378992
Visalaandhra Book House, Gandhi Rd, Tirupati 517 501 *Tel:* (08574) 2222475
Visalaandhra Book House, Karl Marx Rd, Vijayawada 520002 *Tel:* (0866) 2572949
Visalaandhra Book House, Main Rd, Visakhapatnam 530002 *Tel:* (0891) 2502534

Indonesia

C V Toko Buku Tropen
Jl Pasar Baru 113, Jakarta 10710
Mailing Address: Tromol Pos 3604, Jakarta 10036
Tel: (021) 381 1669; (021) 381 3543; (021) 380 5938 *Fax:* (021) 380 0566
E-mail: tropen@cbn.net.id
Telex: 44122 Tropen IA *Cable:* TROPEN
Key Personnel
General Manager: Mr Yohan Slamet
Man Dir: Jani Dipokusumo
Founded: 1939
Type of Business: Distributor, Exporter, Importer, Major Independent Bookseller, Wholesaler

Effendi Harahap Bookstore
Jl Abimanyu Raya 17-19, Semarang
Tel: (024) 3544694

Gramedia Bookshop
109 Jln Palmerah, Selatan 22, Lantai IV, Jakarta 10270
Tel: (021) 5300545 *Fax:* (021) 5486085
Key Personnel
General Manager: Indra Gunawan
Owned by: PT Gramedia
Branch Office(s)
Jl Merdeka 43, Bandung
Jl Melawai IV/13, Jakarta
Jl Pintu Air 72, Jakarta
Jl Jendral Sudirman 56, Jogjakarta
Jl Basuki Rachmat 95, Surabaya

PT BPK Gunung Mulia (Gunung Mulia Christian Publishing House Limited Company)
Jln Kwitang 22-23, Jakarta Pusat 10420
Tel: (021) 3901208 *Fax on Demand:* (021) 3901633
E-mail: trade@bpkgm.com
Web Site: www.bpkgm.com
Key Personnel
President & Dir: Ichsan Gunawan
 E-mail: ichsan@bpkgm.com
Finance & Administration Dir: Viveka Nanda Leimena
Founded: 1951
Also publisher & printer.
Membership(s): CBA.
Type of Business: Distributor, Importer, Major Book Chain Headquarters, Major Independent Bookseller
Owned by: PT BPK Gunung Mulia
Branch Office(s)
Benedict A Salindeho, Jl Cendrawasih 267 B-C-D, Makassar 90134 *Tel:* (0411) 853586 *Fax:* (0411) 855717 *E-mail:* bpkgbupg@indosat.net.id
Carolus Wirto, Jl Genteng Besar No 28, Surabaya 60275 *Tel:* (031) 5342534 *Fax:* (031) 5342534 *E-mail:* bpkgmsby@sbycentrin.net.id
Rejeki Barus, Jl Nibung II/78, Komp Medan Plaza, Medan *Tel:* (0614) 524157 *E-mail:* bpkgmmdn@indosat.net.id
Showroom(s): Jl Kwitang 22-23, Jakarta Pusat 10420

PT Indira
Jln Borobudur 20, Jakarta
Tel: (021) 3148868; (021) 3904290 *Fax:* (021) 3929373
E-mail: indirawb@mweb.co.id
Importers of General/Trade books & Educational/Scientific/Technical books & textbooks. Library suppliers to foreign libraries of Indonesian printed books; also publisher.
Type of Business: Distributor
Branch Office(s)
Jogjakarta
Bookshop(s): JLn Borobudur 20, Jakarta

Java Books
PT Wira Mandala Pustaka, Kepala Cading Kiram Blok A-14 No 17, Jakarta 14240
Tel: (021) 4515351 (Hunting) *Fax:* (021) 4534987
E-mail: mndl@indo.net.id
Key Personnel
Contact: Eric Oey; Johannes Minarwan; Judo Suwidji
Founded: 1985
Type of Business: Distributor, Importer
Branch Office(s)
Bali
Bandung
Jakarta
Lombok
Medan
Surabaya
Ujung Pandang
Yogyakarta

Pembimbing Masa PT
Pusat Perdagangan Senen, Blok 1, Lantai IV No 2, Jakarta Pusat
Mailing Address: PO Box 3281, Jakarta Pusat
Tel: (021) 367645
Bookshop, subscription agency.
Type of Business: Importer
Owned by: Pembimbing Masa PT
Branch Office(s)
Jl Raya Pajajaran 7, Bogor

PT Pradnya Paramita
Jln Bunga No 8 A Matraman, Jakarta 13140
Tel: (021) 8583369 *Fax:* (021) 8583369
 Cable: PRADNYA JKT
Key Personnel
General Manager: Soehardjo
Administration Manager: W Moedjiono
Marketing Manager: M N Supomo
Production Manager: R E S Bujung
Also Publisher.
Branch Office(s)
Jl Kyai Maja 2A, Kebayoran Baru, Jakarta 12120, India

Islamic Republic of Iran

Nayiri Bookshop
1022 Enghelab Ave, Tehran 11339
Mailing Address: PO Box 11365-4631, Tehran 11339
Tel: (021) 677578; (021) 7536802; (021) 7537029 *Fax:* (021) 677578
Key Personnel
President: Sebouh Amirkhanian
Vice President: Mrs Seda Hartounian
Founded: 1931
Printing & Publishing of Magazines, Newspapers, in many languages, Greeting Cards, Gregorian-Armenian Art Calendars.
Type of Business: Distributor, Exporter, Importer, Major Independent Bookseller, Wholesaler

Ireland

AIS
7 Merrion Sq, Dublin 2
Tel: (01) 6616522 *Fax:* (01) 6612378
Type of Business: Distributor

Book Stop
Dun Laoghaire Shopping Centre, Dun Laoghaire, Dublin
Tel: (01) 2809917 *Fax:* (01) 2844863
E-mail: bookstop@indigo.ie
Key Personnel
Manager: John Davey
Branch Office(s)
Blackrock Shopping Centre, Blackrock, Co Dublin *Tel:* (01) 2832193 *Fax:* (01) 2782796 *E-mail:* bookstopbr@indigo.ie
Craysfort Park, Blackrock Teachers Center

The Columba Book Service
55A Spruce Ave, Stillorgan Industrial Park, Blackrock, Dublin
Tel: (01) 2942556 *Fax:* (01) 2942564
E-mail: info@columba.ie
Web Site: www.columba.ie
Key Personnel
Sales Dir: Cecilia West *E-mail:* west@columba.ie
Founded: 1986
Type of Business: Distributor

Eason & Son Ltd
80 Middle Abbey St, Dublin 1
Tel: (01) 873 3811 *Fax:* (01) 873 3545
E-mail: info@eason.ie
Web Site: www.eason.ie
Telex: 32566
Key Personnel
Chairman: Michael Ryder
Man Dir: Gordon Bolton
Founded: 1856
29 outlets in both the Republic of Ireland & Northern Ireland.
Type of Business: Distributor, Importer, Major Book Chain Headquarters, Major Independent Bookseller, Wholesaler

Gill & Macmillan Distribution
10 Hume Ave, Park West, Dublin 12
Tel: (01) 500 9500 *Fax:* (01) 500 9599
E-mail: sales@gillmacmillan.ie
Web Site: www.gillmacmillan.ie
Key Personnel
Distribution Dir: Dermot O'Brien
 E-mail: dobrien@gillmacmillan.ie
Type of Business: Distributor

Greene's Bookshop Ltd
16 Clare St, Dublin 2
Tel: (01) 6762554 *Fax:* (01) 6789091
E-mail: info@greenesbookshop.com
Web Site: www.greenesbookshop.com
Key Personnel
Managing Dir: David H Pembrey *Tel:* (01) 6760476 *E-mail:* dave@greenesbookshop.com
Dir & Financial Controller: Diarmuid Byrne
 E-mail: diarmuuid@greenesbookshop.com
Secondhand & Antiquarian Books: Fred Collins
 E-mail: fred@greenesbookshop.com
Library & Special Order Dept: Catherine Boyd
 E-mail: catherine@greenesbookshop.com
Founded: 1843
New & Secondhand Booksellers.
Type of Business: Major Independent Bookseller

Hodges Figgis & Co
56-58 Dawson St, Dublin 2
Tel: (01) 6774754 *Fax:* (01) 6792810; (01) 6793402
E-mail: books@hfiggis.ir
Key Personnel
Manager: Walter Pohli
Deputy Manager: Joseph Collins
Bookstall, National Institute of Higher Education, Dublin 9.
Owned by: EMI Group
Bookshop(s): Dublin City University, Dublin 9

The Library Shop
Trinity College, College St, Dublin 2
Tel: (01) 608 1171 *Fax:* (01) 6081016
Web Site: www.tcd.ie/library/shop/
Telex: 93782
Key Personnel
Manager: J G Duffy *Tel:* (01) 608 1650
 E-mail: jduffy@tcd.ie
contact: Paul Corrigan *E-mail:* paul.corrigan@tcd.ie
Type of Business: Major Independent Bookseller

O'Mahony & Co Ltd
120 O'Connell St, Limerick
Tel: (061) 418155 *Fax:* (061) 414558
E-mail: info@omahonys.ie
Web Site: www.omahonys.ie
Key Personnel
Chairman: David O'Mahony
Man Dir: Frank O'Mahony *E-mail:* frank.omahony@omahonys.ie
Founded: 1902
School & library suppliers.
Type of Business: Major Independent Bookseller
Branch Office(s)
Market Square, Parnell St, Ennis, Co Clare
 Tel: (065) 6828355 *Fax:* (065) 6820074
 E-mail: ennis.branch@omahonys.ie
University of Limerick Bookshop, National Technological Park, Limerick *Tel:* (061) 202048 *Fax:* (061) 335147 *E-mail:* university.branch@omahonys.ie
Castle St, Tralee, Co Kerry *Tel:* (066) 7122266 *Fax:* (066) 7129442 *E-mail:* tralee.branch@omahonys.ie

Veritas Co Ltd
Veritas House, 7-8 Lower Abbey St, Dublin 1
Tel: (01) 878 8177 *Fax:* (01) 874 4913
E-mail: sales@veritas.ie
Web Site: www.veritas.ie
Key Personnel
Dir: Maura Hyland
Sales & Operations Manager: Maureen Sanders
Owned by: The Catholic Communications Institute of Ireland
Branch Office(s)
Carey's Lane, Cork *Tel:* (021) 425 1255
 Fax: (021) 427 9165
Butcher St, Derry BT48 6HL *Tel:* (028) 71 266 888 *Fax:* (028) 71 365 120
83 O'Connell St, Ennis, Co Clare *Tel:* (065) 682 8696 *Fax:* (065) 682 0176
13 Lower Main St, Letterkenny, Co Donegal
 Tel: (074) 91 24814 *Fax:* (074) 91 22716
Adelaide St, Sligo *Tel:* (071) 91 61800 *Fax:* (071) 91 60121

Israel

Academon Publishing House
PO Box 24130, Jerusalem
Tel: (02) 5882163 *Fax:* (02) 5815558
Web Site: www.academon.co.il
Key Personnel
Import Manager: Richard Sherman
 E-mail: richard@academon.co.il
Founded: 1952
Academic & General Bookstore chain serving Hebrew University.
Type of Business: Importer, Major Book Chain Headquarters

Librairie Francaise Alcheh
55 Nahalat Benjamin St, 65163 Tel Aviv
Mailing Address: PO Box 1550, Tel Aviv
Tel: (03) 5604173 *Fax:* (03) 6 994526
E-mail: alcheh@zahav.net.il
Key Personnel
Man Dir: Yohanan Djerassi
Founded: 1939
French & English Books.
Type of Business: Major Book Chain Headquarters
Branch Office(s)
30, Jaffa Rd, Jerusalem
55 Nachlat Banyamin St, 68020 Tel Aviv-Jaffa
 Tel: (03) 5609817 *Fax:* (03) 5606218

Books International
1204/1 Grofit St (Commercial Center), Eilat
Mailing Address: PO Box 1950, Eilat 88000
Tel: (08) 633 0205 *Fax:* (08) 633 0204
E-mail: info@booksinternational.com
Web Site: www.booksinternational.com
Key Personnel
Man Dir: Shulamit Koretz
Exporter of Israeli books.
Type of Business: Distributor, Exporter

Eric Cohen Books Ltd
27 Hata'asia St, Ra'anana 43650
Mailing Address: PO Box 2325, Ra'anana 43650
Tel: (09) 747 8000 *Fax:* (09) 747 8001
E-mail: info@ecb.co.il
Web Site: www.ecb.co.il
Key Personnel
Man Dir: Eric Cohen

Dyonon/Papyrus Publishing House of the Tel-Aviv
Tel Aviv University, Entin Plaza, Gate 7, Tel Aviv 61392
Mailing Address: University Student's Union, PO Box 39287, Tel Aviv 61392
Tel: (03) 6410351; (03) 6410352; (03) 6427545 (head office); (03) 6422667 (import office)
 Fax: (03) 6423149
Telex: 342171 Versy Il attn Dyonon
Key Personnel
General Manager: Eitan Zinger
Import Manager: Rachel Hamo
Founded: 1972
Also publisher.
Type of Business: Distributor, Exporter, Importer, Major Book Chain Headquarters, Major Independent Bookseller, Wholesaler
Branch Office(s)
Bar-Ilan University Campus

F Fischer Book Service
PO Box 7346, Haifa 31071
Tel: (04) 255830 *Fax:* (04) 244970
Key Personnel
Manager: F Fischer
Founded: 1941
Type of Business: Importer, Major Independent Bookseller

Yozmot Heiliger Ltd
PO Box 56055, Tel Aviv 61560
Tel: (03) 5284851 *Fax:* (03) 5285397
E-mail: books@yozmot.com
Web Site: www.yozmot.com
Key Personnel
Dir: Avi Chamo; Jacob Merynger
Founded: 1989
Subscription center. Specialize in scientific & medical books.
Type of Business: Distributor, Exporter, Importer, Major Book Chain Headquarters, Major Independent Bookseller, Wholesaler

Israbook
Gefen Publishing House, PO Box 36004, Jerusalem 91360
Tel: (02) 5380247 *Fax:* (02) 5388423
E-mail: isragefen@netmedia.net.il
Web Site: www.israelbooks.com
Key Personnel
Publisher: Dror Greenfield; Ilan Greenfield
Founded: 1981
Type of Business: Distributor, Importer, Major Book Chain Headquarters, Major Independent Bookseller, Wholesaler
Owned by: Greenfield

Jerusalem Books Ltd
PO Box 26190, Jerusalem 91261
Tel: (02) 643-3580 *Fax:* (02) 643 3580

ISRAEL

E-mail: jerbooks@netmedia.co.il
Web Site: www.jerusalembooks.co.il
Key Personnel
Contact: Jeffrey Spitzer
Type of Business: Distributor, Exporter

Lonnie Kahn Ltd
20 Eliyahu Eitan St, Rishon Lezion 75703
Tel: (03) 9518418 Fax: (03) 9518415; (03) 9518416
E-mail: lonikahn@netvision.net.il
Key Personnel
General Manager: Mr Itamar Karlinski
Founded: 1943
Type of Business: Distributor, Importer, Major Independent Bookseller, Wholesaler

Landsberger
9 Ben-Yehuda St, Tel Aviv
Tel: (03) 5176330 Fax: (03) 5222646
Key Personnel
Man Dir: Esther Parnes

Ludwig Mayer Jerusalem Ltd
4 Shlomzion Hamalka St, 91010 Jerusalem
Mailing Address: PO Box 1174, 91010 Jerusalem
Tel: (02) 625-2628 Fax: (02) 623-2640
E-mail: mayerbks@netvision.net.il
Key Personnel
Contact: Marcel Marcus
Founded: 1908
Academic bookstore.
Type of Business: Exporter, Importer

Michlol Ltd
Technion, Haifa 32000
Tel: (04) 8322970 Fax: (04) 8223854
E-mail: ws2@isdn.net.il
Key Personnel
General Dir: Samuel Weissbach
Import Manager: Daniel Ran Tel: (04) 8322970

Mossad Harav Kook, see Rav Kook Institute

Palphot Ltd
PO Box 2, Herzlia 46100
Tel: (09) 9525252 Fax: (09) 9525277
E-mail: palphot@palphot.com
Web Site: www.palphot.com
Founded: 1934
Type of Business: Distributor, Exporter, Importer, Wholesaler

Rav Kook Institute
Maimon St, Jerusalem 910066
Mailing Address: PO Box 642, Jerusalem 910066
Tel: (02) 6526231 Fax: (02) 6526968
E-mail: mosad-haravkook@neto.bezeqint.net
Key Personnel
Chairman: Yehuda Raphael
Executive Dir: Yosef Movshovitz
Founded: 1935
Type of Business: Exporter, Wholesaler

J Robinson & Co
31 Nachlat Benyamin St, Tel Aviv 65162
Mailing Address: PO Box 4308, Tel Aviv 61042
Tel: (03) 5605461; (03) 5601626 Fax: (03) 5660439
E-mail: rob_book@netvision.net.il
Web Site: www.robinson.co.il
Key Personnel
Man Dir: Yehuda Robinson
Founded: 1889
Also antiquarian bookseller.
Total Titles: 100,000 Print
Type of Business: Exporter

Bookshop(s): Safra Tava Baita, 140 Ibn Gvirol St, Tel Aviv Tel: (03) 6021391; Sfat Em, 54 Ibn Gvirol St, Tel Aviv Tel: (03) 6961074; Vayikra, 90 Frishman St, Tel Aviv Tel: (03) 5238501

Rubin Mass Ltd
PO Box 990, Jerusalem 91009
Tel: (02) 627-7863 Fax: (02) 627-7864
E-mail: rmass@barak.net.il
Web Site: www.rubin-mass.com
Key Personnel
Man Dir: Mr Oren Mass E-mail: rmass@barak.net.il
Contact: Ilana Zin
Founded: 1927
Exporter of all Israeli books & periodicals.
Type of Business: Distributor, Exporter, Major Independent Bookseller, Wholesaler

Steimatzky Group Ltd
11 Hakishon St, 51114 Bnei Brak
Mailing Address: PO Box 1444, 51114 Bnei Brak
Tel: (03) 5775777 Fax: (03) 5794567
E-mail: info@steimatzky.co.il
Web Site: www.steimatzky.com
Key Personnel
Chairman: Eri M Steimatzky
Founded: 1925
Publishers' Representative & Publisher.
Type of Business: Distributor, Exporter, Importer, Major Book Chain Headquarters, Wholesaler

Yavneh Publishing House Ltd
4 Mazeh St, 65213 Tel Aviv
Tel: (03) 6297856 Fax: (03) 6293638
Founded: 1932
Type of Business: Distributor, Exporter, Importer, Major Book Chain Headquarters, Major Independent Bookseller, Wholesaler
Owned by: Aushalom Orenstein, Nira Prieskel

Italy

Libreria All'Accademia di Randi Lorenzo & Elena snc
Via S Lucia 1, 35139 Padova
Tel: (049) 8760306 Fax: (049) 8751825
E-mail: libreria@libreriadraghi.it Cable: DRAGHI PADOVA
Key Personnel
Manager: Lorenzo Randi; Elena Randi
Type of Business: Exporter, Importer, Major Book Chain Headquarters, Major Independent Bookseller
Bookshop(s): Libreria Draghi-Randi, Via Cavour 17-19, 1, 35122 Padova (established 1850; general bookshop, foreign dept, art books, law, finance); Libreria Universitaria, Via 8 Febbraio 10, 35122 Padova Tel: (049) 8757244 (law, literature, university textbooks); Libreria DRAGHI-GALLERIA, Galleria S Lucia 6, 35122 Padova (children books, guide books, dictionary, VHS films, gadgets, law, finance)

Athesia Buchhandlung
Via Portici, 41, 39100 Bozen
Tel: (0471) 927280 Fax: (0471) 927229
E-mail: buch@athesia.it
Web Site: www.athesiabuch.it
Telex: 400161
Key Personnel
Head of Library: Peter Matzneller
Founded: 1907
Type of Business: Distributor, Importer, Major Book Chain Headquarters, Major Independent Bookseller, Wholesaler
Owned by: Athesiabuch GmbH

MAJOR

Branch Office(s)
Bressanone
Brunico
Merano
Silandro
Vipiteno

Casalini Libri
Via Benedetto da Maiano, Suite 3, 50014 Florence
Tel: (055) 5018 1 Fax: (055) 5018 201
E-mail: info@casalini.it
Web Site: www.casalini.it
Key Personnel
Man Dir: Barbara Casalini E-mail: barbara@casalini.it; Michele Casalini E-mail: michele@casalini.it
Dir of Sales & Customer Services: Joachim Bartz E-mail: jbartz@casalini.it
Also publisher.
Type of Business: Exporter

Libreria Dante di A M Longo
Via P Costa, 39, I-48100 Ravenna
Tel: (0544) 33500 Fax: (0544) 217554
E-mail: longo-ra@linknet.it
Key Personnel
Manager: Alfio Longo Tel: (0544) 217026 E-mail: longo-ra@linknet.it
Founded: 1950
Type of Business: Exporter, Importer, Major Independent Bookseller
Owned by: Angelo Longo Editore

DEA, see DEA Diffusione Edizioni Anglo-Americane

DEA Diffusione Edizioni Anglo-Americane
Sede Legale e Amministrativa, Via Lima, 28, 00198 Rome
Tel: (06) 852121 Fax: (06) 8543228
E-mail: deanet@deanet.it; info@deanet.it
Web Site: www.deanet.it
Key Personnel
Contact: Enrico Ligi
Subjects: agriculture, architecture, archaeology, arts, astronomy, biology, botany, business, chemistry, computer science, earth sciences, economics, engineering, environment, fiction, finance, geography, history, languages, law, library science, literature, management, mathematics, medicine, philosophy, physics, political science, psychology, reference, religion, social science, sports & travel, veterinary, zoology

Libreria Feltrinelli
Via Andegari 6, 20121 Milan
Tel: (02) 86463485 Fax: (02) 72001064
Web Site: www.feltrinelli.it
Branch Office(s)
Piazza Porta Ravegnana 1, Bologna
Via Cavour 12-20, 50129 Florence Tel: (055) 292196
Via Carlo Alberto 2, Turin

Libreria S F Flaccovio
di via Ruggiero Settimo, 37, a Palermo
Tel: (091) 589442 Fax: (091) 331992
E-mail: info@flaccovio.com
Web Site: www.flaccovio.com
Key Personnel
Administrator: Sergio Flaccovio
Manager: Francesco Flaccovio
Founded: 1938
Owned by: S F Flaccovio Editore
Branch Office(s)
Libreria Dante, Quattro Canti di Citta, a Palermo Tel: (091) 585927 Fax: (091) 323103
P zza Vittorio Emanuele Orlando, 15/19, a Palermo Tel: (091) 334323 Fax: (091) 6112750

di via Ernesto Basile, 136, a Palermo *Tel:* (091) 420363 *Fax:* (091) 420363
di via Maqueda, 172, a Palermo *Tel:* (091) 585927 *Fax:* (091) 323103

FMR Ricci
Via Montecuccoli 32, 20147 Milan
Tel: (02) 48301246 *Fax:* (02) 48301473
E-mail: ricci@fmrmagazine.it
Key Personnel
President: Franco Maria Ricci *E-mail:* ricci@fmrmagazine.it
Contact: Raffaella Russo
Bookshop(s): 12 rud des Beaux-Arts, Paris 75001, France *Tel:* 01 4633963; Via Farini 27, Bologna 40124 *Tel:* (05) 1231811; Via delle Belle Donne 41/R, Florence 50123 *Tel:* (05) 5283312; Via Durini 19, Milano 20122 *Tel:* (02) 798444; Via Affo 1, Parma 43100 *Tel:* (05) 1287023; Via Borgognona 4/D, Rome 00187 *Tel:* (06) 6793466; Via Carlo Alberto 12, Turin 10123 *Tel:* (01) 15629171

Gregoriana Libreria Editrice
Via Roma, 82, 35122 Padova
Tel: (049) 657493 *Fax:* (049) 662089
Founded: 1922
Type of Business: Major Independent Bookseller
Owned by: Euganea Editoriale Comunicazioni SRL, Via Roma, 82, 35122 Padova
Branch Office(s)
Via Vescovado 33, I-35100 Padua
Piazza Duomo 5, 1-35100 Padua

Herder Editrice e Libreria
Piazza Montecitorio 120, 00186 Rome
Tel: (06) 679 53 04; (06) 679 46 28 *Fax:* (06) 678 47 51
E-mail: distr@herder.it; distr@herder.it
Web Site: www.herder.it
Key Personnel
Manager: Bettina Bolli
Administration: Paul Hermann Koellner
Founded: 1925
Book commerce, publishing house & distributor.
Type of Business: Distributor, Exporter, Importer, Major Independent Bookseller

Ilisso Edizioni di Vanna Fois & CSNC
Via Guerrazzi 6, 08100 Nuoro
Tel: (0784) 33033 *Fax:* (0784) 35413
E-mail: ilisso@ilisso.it
Web Site: www.ilisso.it
Key Personnel
Contact: Tiziana Serra
Founded: 1985
Art Books.
Owned by: Sebastiano Congiu & Vanna Fois

Libreria Editrice Minerva
Vicolodeli Archi 1, 1-06081 Assisi
Tel: (075) 812381 *Fax:* (075) 816564

Opus Libri SRL
Via della Torretta 16, 50137 Florence
Tel: (055) 660833 *Fax:* (055) 670604
E-mail: opuslib@dada.it
Key Personnel
Contact: Piero Riccetti
Founded: 1980
Type of Business: Distributor, Exporter, Importer, Major Independent Bookseller, Wholesaler

Libreria Commissionaria Internazionale di Raffaele Pancaldi
Via San Petronio Vecchio n 3, 40125 Bologna
Tel: (051) 229466 *Fax:* (051) 229466
Key Personnel
Manager: Raffaele Pancaldi
Founded: 1975
Type of Business: Importer, Major Independent Bookseller, Wholesaler

Libreria Internazionale Patron
Via Zamboni, 24, Bologna
Tel: (051) 223208 *Fax:* (051) 223208
Owned by: Patron Editore SRL

Libreria Rizzoli della Rizzoli Editore SpA
Via Mecenate, 91, 20138 Milan
Tel: (02) 50951 *Fax:* (02) 5065361
Key Personnel
Manager: Aldo Allegri
Owned by: R C S Rizzoli Libri SpA
Branch Office(s)
Libreria Internazionale Rizzoli SRL, Galleria Colonna, Largo Chigi 15, Rome *Tel:* (06) 6796641

Rosenberg e Sellier SpA
Via Andrea Doria 14, 10123 Turin
Tel: (011) 812 76 56 *Fax:* (011) 812 77 44
Key Personnel
Proprietor: Ugo Gianni Rosenberg; Elvi Rosenberg
International bookseller & subscription agent.
Type of Business: Exporter, Importer

Rux Guru srl
Via A Manna, 25/27, 06132 Perugia
Tel: (075) 5270257; (075) 5270258 *Fax:* (075) 5288244
E-mail: ruxinfo@rux-distribuzione.com
Web Site: www.rux-distribuzione.com
Key Personnel
President: Gastone Chellini
Administrator: Sara Maria Chellini
Founded: 1989
Distributor of books & didactical material for learning Italian as a foreign language. Media formats include audio, books, CD-ROM, online & video.
Subjects: linguistics
Type of Business: Distributor, Wholesaler

Libreria Internazionale Sperling e Kupfer
Via Durazzo, 4, 20134 Milan
Tel: (02) 21721-1 *Fax:* (02) 21721-277
Web Site: www.sperling.it
Key Personnel
Manager: Francesco Bogliari

Ulrico Hoepli - Libreria Internazionale
Via Hoepli 5, 20121 Milan
Tel: (02) 864871 *Fax:* (02) 8052886; (02) 864322 (library)
E-mail: libreria@hoepli.it
Web Site: www.hoepli.it *Cable:* HOEPLI MILAN
Key Personnel
Manager: Dr Ulrico Carlo Hoepli; Roberto Taneggi; Susanna Schwarz
Contact: Daniela Grazi
Founded: 1870
Owned by: Casa Editrice Libraria Ulrico Hoepli SpA

Jamaica

Bolivar Bookshop
1D Grove Rd, Kingston 10
Mailing Address: PO Box 413, Kingston 10
Tel: (876) 926-8799 *Fax:* (876) 968-1874
E-mail: bolivar-jamaica@colis.com
Key Personnel
Owner & Manager: Hugh Dunphy
Founded: 1965
Bookshop, Art Gallery & Antique Shop.
Parent Company: Jacaranda Holdings Ltd

Kingston Bookshop Ltd
74 King St, Kingston
Tel: 876-938-0005
E-mail: info@kingstonbookshop.com
Web Site: www.kingstonbookshop.com *Cable:* FUTURITY JAMAICA
Key Personnel
Manager: S A R Fuller
Branch Office(s)
The Pavillon Shopping Center, Halfway Tree Kingston *Tel:* 876-960-5376; 876-968-4591 *Fax:* 876-968-2325
Bookshop(s): Postal Corporation Commercial Centre, Liguanea, Kingston 6 *Tel:* 876-978-7261 *Fax:* 876-946-0914; The Springs, 17 Constant Spring Rd, Kingston 10 *Tel:* 876-920-1529; 876-960-7104 *Fax:* 876-968-6277

Sangster's Book Stores Ltd
101 Water Lane, Kingston
Tel: (876) 922-3648; (876) 922-3640
Toll Free *Tel:* 888-269-2665 *Fax:* (876) 922-3813
E-mail: info@sangstersbooks.com
Web Site: www.sangstersbooks.com
Key Personnel
Man Dir: S Kumaraswamy
Publishing & Publisher Representation.
Owned by: Gleaner Co Ltd, 7 North St, PO Box 40, Kingston
Branch Office(s)
33 King St, Kingston *Tel:* (876) 967-1930; 967-1931 *Fax:* (876) 967-9776
Mall Plaza, 20 Constant Spring, Kingston 10 *Tel:* (876) 926-2271 *Fax:* (876) 968-7155
Soverign Centre, 106 Hope Rd, Kingston 6 *Tel:* (876) 978-7825
97 Harbour St, Kingston *Tel:* (876) 922-3810 *Fax:* (876) 922-3813
2 St James St, Montego Bay, St James *Tel:* (876) 952-0319 *Fax:* (876) 940-0182
Lot 8 Portmore Plaza, St Catherine *Tel:* (876) 704-5450; 704-5371 *Fax:* (876) 704-5459
Bookshop(s): Springs Plaza, Shop 6, 17 Constant Spring Rd, Kingston 10 *Tel:* (876) 926-1800 *Fax:* (876) 968-5516; 28 Barbados Ave, Kingston 5 *Tel:* (876) 950-2489 *Fax:* (876) 960-2490; Mall, Sovereign, King St, Montego Bay; Spanish Town, Shop 28, 17 Burke Rd, St Catherine *Tel:* (876) 984-5003

Japan

Academia Scientific Book Inc
Shichi Bldg, 2-10-15 Kasuga, Bunkyo-Ku, Tokyo
Tel: (03) 3819805 *Fax:* (03) 38128509
Key Personnel
Owner: Satoshi Nakai
Branch Office(s)
Ohhomachi Hanahata 3-9-21, Tsukuba-City

Asahiya Shoten Ltd (Booksellers)
Asahi Bldg, 3-17-19 Toyosaki, Kita-ku, Osaka 531-0072
Tel: (06) 3131191; (06) 3727251; (06) 3727253 *Fax:* (06) 3755650
Key Personnel
President: Takeshi Hayashima

Bookman's & Co Ltd
Yodogawa Bldg, 3-1-18 toyosaki, Kita-ku, Osaka 531-0072
Tel: (06) 6371-4164 *Fax:* (06) 6371-4174

E-mail: info@bookmans.co.jp; bookman@osk3.3web.ne.jp
Web Site: www.bookmans.co.jp
Key Personnel
President: Mr Mitsunobu Nakamura
Founded: 1967
Art & architecture & graphical, industrial design photography. Textile, fashion, & interior design & human science.
Subjects: Human Science: Art & Architecture, Graphic design Industrial Design, Social Science
Type of Business: Importer, Wholesaler
Owned by: Mr M Nakamura

Christian Literature Society of Japan, see Kyobunkan Inc (Christian Literature Society of Japan)

France Tosho
1-12-9, Nishi-Shinjuku, Shinjuku-ku, Tokyo 160-0023
Mailing Address: PO Box 103, Shinjuuku, Tokyo
Tel: (03) 3346-0396 *Fax:* (03) 3346-9154
E-mail: frtosho@blue.ocn.ne.jp
Key Personnel
Chief of the Purchase Section: Fumisate Konodo
Founded: 1967
Type of Business: Importer, Major Independent Bookseller, Wholesaler

Ikubundo Publishers Co
Hongo 5-30-21, Bunkyo-ku, Tokyo 113-0033
Tel: (03) 3814-5571 *Fax:* (03) 3814-5576
E-mail: webmaster@ikubundo.com
Web Site: www.ikubundo.com

Japan Publications Trading Co Ltd (Import & Export)
1-2-1 Sarugaku-cho, Chiyoda-ku, Tokyo 101-0064
Tel: (03) 3292-3751 *Fax:* (03) 3292-0410
E-mail: jpt@jptco.co.jp
Web Site: www.jptco.co.jp
Key Personnel
President: Shin-ichiro Yonekura
Export Dir: Masatoshi Sato
Import Dir: Akira Sugiyama
Founded: 1942
Importer & exporter of general & academic books & periodicals, language learning textbooks & materials, audio/visual discs & other general merchandise. Also deals in rental & management of real estate.
Type of Business: Distributor, Exporter, Importer, Wholesaler
Sales Office(s): Maeda Bldg, 5-40-11 Maidashi, Higashi-ku, Fukuoka 812-0054 *Tel:* (092) 651-3785 *Fax:* (092) 651-1191 *E-mail:* kyushu@jptco.co.jp
701 Arai Bldg No 10, 3-5-2 Nishi-Nakajima, Yodogawa-ku, Osaka 532-0011 *Tel:* (06) 6886-7177 *Fax:* (06) 6886-7131 *E-mail:* osaka@jptco.co.jp

Kaigai Publications Ltd (Kaigai Shuppan Boeki Kabushiki Kaisha)
2-21 Kanda-Tsukasa-cho, Chiyoda-ku, Tokyo 101-0048
Tel: (03) 32924271 *Fax:* (03) 32924278
E-mail: admin@kaigai-pub.co.jp *Cable:* OVERSISPUB TOKYO
Founded: 1949
Type of Business: Importer, Major Independent Bookseller
Branch Office(s)
Sendai
Tsukuba

Kaigai Shuppan Boeki Kabushiki Kaisha, see Kaigai Publications Ltd (Kaigai Shuppan Boeki Kabushiki Kaisha)

Kanda Bookshop
Tanikawa Bldg, 3-2, Kanda Surugadai, Chiyoda-ku, Tokyo 101
Tel: (03) 3291-7071 *Fax:* (03) 3293-8005
E-mail: kanda@bookshop.co.jp
Web Site: www.bookshop.co.jp
Owned by: Charles E Tuttle Co Inc
Branch Office(s)
American Club Shop, 1-2 Azabu-dai 2-chome, Minato-ku, Tokyo 106 *Tel:* (03) 5848938
Okinawa Plaza Book Shop, 242 Yamazato, Okinawa-shi, Okinawa 904 *Tel:* (0988) 333520

Kinokuniya Co Ltd
3-17-7 Shinjuku, Shinjuku-ku, Tokyo 163-8636
Tel: (03) 3354-0141 *Fax:* (03) 3439-3955
E-mail: info@kinokuniya.co.jp
Web Site: www.kinokuniya.co.jp
Key Personnel
President: Osamu Matsubara
Founded: 1927
Also Publisher.
Type of Business: Distributor, Exporter, Importer, Major Book Chain Headquarters, Wholesaler

KPT InfoTrader Inc
501 Naniwasuji Bldg, 1-20-13, Utsubohonmachi, Nishi-Ku, Osaka 550-0004
Mailing Address: CPO Box 936, Osaka 530-8694
Tel: (06) 6479 7160 *Fax:* (06) 6479 7163
E-mail: osaka@infotrader.jp
Key Personnel
Chief Executive Officer: Yoshitaka Kitao
Chief Operating Officer: Yukichi Ohtsuka
Founded: 1956
Importing books & periodicals from all over the world, for world-famous enterprises, universities, government organizations, on firm-order basis.
Type of Business: Importer
Branch Office(s)
Tokyo *Tel:* (03) 5842 3150 *Fax:* (03) 5842 3153 *E-mail:* tokyo@infotrader.jp
Tsukuba *Tel:* (0298) 51 8145 *Fax:* (0298) 52 9873 *E-mail:* tsukuba@infotrader.jp

Kyobunkan Inc (Christian Literature Society of Japan)
4-5-1, Chuo-ku, Ginza, Tokyo 104-0061
Tel: (03) 3561-8449 *Fax:* (03) 5250-5109
E-mail: fbooks@kyobunkwan.co.jp
Web Site: www.kyobunkwan.co.jp
Key Personnel
Vice President: Hideo Usui
Founded: 1885
Branch offices in Fukuoka, Hiroshima, Kanazawa, Kobe, Kyoto, London (UK), Nagoya, New York (USA), Okayama, Osaka, Sapporo, Sendai, Singapore, Tsukuba, & Yokohama.
Type of Business: Distributor, Importer, Major Independent Bookseller, Wholesaler

Maruzen Co Ltd
PO Box 5050, Tokyo International 100-3191
Tel: (03) 3275 8595 *Fax:* (03) 3274 3239
E-mail: media@maruzen.co.jp
Web Site: www.maruzen.co.jp *Cable:* MARUYA TOKYO
Key Personnel
President: Nobuo Suzuki
Executive Dir: Atsushi Suzuki
Senior General Manager: Yusaku Takahashi
General Manager, Information Resources Navigation Division: Tetsuro Konno
 E-mail: t_konno@maruzen.co.jp
Dir, Information Resources Navigatioin Division: Nobuji Ebisui
Founded: 1869
Sales of foreign & Japanese books & journals; scientific information retrieval services; publishing.
Type of Business: Exporter, Importer
Branch Office(s)
Kanazawa
Kobe
Kyoto

Nankodo Co Ltd
42-6, Hongo 3-Chrome, Bunkyo-ku, Tokyo 113-8410
Tel: (03) 3811-9957 *Fax:* (03) 3811-5031
E-mail: yoshohp@nankodo.co.jp
Web Site: www.nankodo.co.jp
Key Personnel
President: Nobuhiko Hongo
Executive Dir, Foreign Division: Masao Takahashi
Founded: 1879
Also medical publishers.
Type of Business: Distributor, Importer, Wholesaler

Nauka Ltd
2-30-19 Minami-Ikebukuro, Toshima-ku, Tokyo 171-8551
Tel: (03) 3981-5261 *Fax:* (03) 3981-5361
E-mail: tokyo@nauka.co.jp
Web Site: www.nauka.co.jp
Telex: 524432 *Cable:* NAUKAINCO TOKYO
Key Personnel
President: Shuichi Sugawara
Founded: 1952
Type of Business: Distributor, Exporter, Importer, Major Book Chain Headquarters, Wholesaler
Bookshop(s): 1-34 Kanda-Jinbocho, Chiyoda-ku, Tokyo 101-0051 *Tel:* (03) 5259-2711 *Fax:* (03) 5259-2714 *E-mail:* shop@nauka.co.jp

Nihon-Shoseki Ltd
12-6 Esakacho 2-chome, Suita City, Osaka 564-0063
Tel: (06) 6386-8601 *Fax:* (06) 6386-8620
E-mail: nihonsho@mtci.ne.jp
Web Site: www.nihon-shoseki.co.jp
Key Personnel
President: Shin Tamaki
Purchasing Manager: I Tamaki
Founded: 1959
Scientific backfiles, rare & modern books, microforms & electromedias.
Membership(s): Japan Association of International Publications.
Type of Business: Distributor, Exporter, Wholesaler
Branch Office(s)
Toyko

Nippon Shuppan Hanbai Inc
3000 11-6 Iidabashi, Chiyoda-ku, Tokyo
Tel: (03) 3233-1111 *Fax:* (03) 3292-8571
E-mail: press@nippan.co.jp
Web Site: www.nippan.co.jp
Key Personnel
Contact: Ishikawa Masakatsu
Founded: 1949
Type of Business: Distributor, Exporter, Importer

Osaka Oviss Inc
Central PO Box 292, Osaka 530-8692
Tel: (06) 352 7090 *Fax:* (06) 352 8898
E-mail: ovissbk@osk.3web.ne.jp
Type of Business: Importer, Major Independent Bookseller

Sanseido Bookstore Ltd
11-8, Kouhoku 7-chome, Adachi-ku, Tokyo 123-0872
Tel: (03) 3896 6332 *Fax:* (03) 5839 0292
E-mail: fbook_stock@mail.books-sanseido.co.jp
Web Site: www.books-sanseido.co.jp
Key Personnel
President: Tadao Kamei
Dir, Sales Dept: Ryosuke Suzuki

Manager: Osamu Suzuki
Founded: 1881
Membership(s): Japan Association of International Publications.
Type of Business: Importer, Major Book Chain Headquarters, Major Independent Bookseller
Bookshop(s): 1-1 Kanda Jimbocho, Chiyoda-ku, Tokyo 101

Sanyo Shuppan Boeki Co Inc
Taiko Bldg 3F 11-16, 3 Nishishinjuku, Shinjuku-ku, Tokyo 160-0023
Tel: (03) 5351 3021 *Fax:* (03) 5351 3028
E-mail: ssb01@mx1.alpha-web.ne.jp
Key Personnel
President: Takeshi Katsukawa
Senior Man Dir: Koichi Ohnishi
Founded: 1956
Also publisher.
Type of Business: Distributor, Importer, Major Independent Bookseller, Wholesaler
Branch Office(s)
Niihama
Osaka

Shinko Tsusho Co Ltd
1-7-1 Wakaba, Shinjuku-ku, Tokyo 160
Tel: (03) 33531751 *Fax:* (03) 33532205
E-mail: shinko@tokyo.e-mail.ne.jp
Key Personnel
President: Ms Keiko Nagato
Founded: 1960
Type of Business: Distributor, Importer, Wholesaler

Shiseido Booksellers Ltd
55 Koyama-Minamikazusa, Kita-ku, Kyoto 603-8149
Tel: (075) 431 2345 *Fax:* (075) 432 6588
E-mail: shiseido@jd5.so-net.ne.jp
Web Site: www.shiseido-book.co.jp
Key Personnel
President: Tatsuro Sugaura
Import Dir: Hiromitsu Hori
Founded: 1947
Booksellers for scholars on the field of humanities
Membership(s): Japan Association of International Publications.
Type of Business: Importer, Major Independent Bookseller

Tohan Corporation
6-24 Higashigoken-cho, Shinjuku-ku, Tokyo 162-0813
Tel: (03) 3269-6111 *Fax:* (03) 3235-1337
Key Personnel
President: Hirotaka Kotaki
Manager, Overseas Business Dept: Kainan Tanaka
Overseas Business Development: Takako Yuasa
Tel: (03) 3266-9593 *Fax:* (03) 3266-8943
Overseas Sales Div: *Tel:* (03) 3266-9573 *Fax:* (03) 3266-8943
Also acts as literary agent.
Type of Business: Distributor, Exporter, Wholesaler

Tokyo Publications Service Ltd
Daiichi-Takiguchi Bldg, 20-7, Ginza 1-chome, Chuo-ku, Tokyo 104-0061
Tel: (03) 3561-9741 *Fax:* (03) 3561-9743
E-mail: tps@cf.mbn.or.jp
Web Site: plaza8.mbn.or.jp/~tokyoyosho
Key Personnel
President: Kunio Kihara
Founded: 1968
Type of Business: Distributor, Exporter, Importer, Major Independent Bookseller, Wholesaler

Charles E Tuttle Publishing Co Inc
RK Bldg, 2nd floor, 2-12-10 Shimo-Meguro, Meguro-Ku, Tokyo 153
Tel: (03) 5437-0171 *Fax:* (03) 5437-0755
E-mail: info@tuttlepublishing.com
Web Site: www.tuttlepublishing.com
Key Personnel
President, Singapore: Eric Oey
Man Dir: Kazuo Maekawa
Founded: 1948
English-language books in Japan.
Type of Business: Distributor, Exporter, Importer, Major Independent Bookseller, Wholesaler
Branch Office(s)
Jakarta, Indonesia
Osaka
Berkeley Books Pte Ltd, No 06-01/03 Olivine Bldg, 130 Joo Seng Rd, Singapore 368357, Singapore *Tel:* (06) 280-3320 *Fax:* (06) 280-6290
153 Milk St, Boston, MA 02109, United States *Fax:* 617-951-4045
Rutland, VT, United States
Sales Office(s): Airport Industrial Park, 364 Innovation Dr, North Clarendon, VT 05759-9436, United States
Bookshop(s): Kanda Shop, 1-3 Kanda-Jimbocho, Chiyoda-ku, Tokyo 100

United Publishers Services Ltd
Member of Times Publishing Group, Republic of Singapore
1-32-5 Higashi-shinagawa, Shinagawa-ku, Tokyo 140-0002
Tel: (03) 5479-7251 *Fax:* (03) 5479-7307
E-mail: general@ups.co.jp
Key Personnel
President: Mark Gresham
Vice President: Junichi Takayori
The largest stock holding agent of overseas publishers in the Japanese foreign book market.
Type of Business: Distributor, Importer, Wholesaler
Owned by: Times Publishing Ltd, Singapore

Yohan (Western Publications Distribution Agency)
3-14-9 Okubo, Shinjuku-ku, Tokyo 169-0072
Tel: (03) 3208-0181 *Fax:* (03) 3208-5308
Web Site: www.yohan.co.jp
Telex: 2324818 Yohan J *Cable:* BOOKYOHAN TOKYO
Key Personnel
Chairman: Masahiro Watanabe
President: Masanori Watanabe
Founded: 1953
Books & magazines, stocklist for publishers.
Type of Business: Distributor, Exporter, Importer, Wholesaler
Branch Office(s)
Nagoya
Osaka
Sapporo

Yushodo Co Ltd
29, San-ei-Cho, Shinjuku-ku, Tokyo 160-0008
Tel: (03) 3357-1411 *Fax:* (03) 3351-5855
E-mail: ysdhp@yushodo.co.jp; antiq@yushodo.co.jp; intl@yushodo.co.jp
Web Site: www.yushodo.co.jp
Telex: 02324136
Key Personnel
President: Mitsuo Nitta
Founded: 1932
Branch offices in Kansai, Ohtsuka, & Toyko. Importer & Exporter of Western Antiquarian & Rare Books.
Type of Business: Distributor, Exporter, Importer, Wholesaler

Jordan

Jordan Book Centre Co Ltd
University St, Amman 11941
Mailing Address: PO Box 301 (Al-Jubeiha), Amman 11941
Tel: (06) 5151882; (06) 5155882 *Fax:* (06) 5152016
E-mail: jbc@go.com.jo
Telex: 21153 *Cable:* JORDAN BOOK CENTRE/AMMAN
Key Personnel
Chief Executive: I Sharbain
Founded: 1958
Also Publisher.
Subjects: education, historical fiction, history, religion, theology, science, biology, chemistry, technology, engineering
Type of Business: Distributor, Wholesaler

Jordan Distribution Agency Co Ltd
PO Box 375, Amman 11118
Tel: (06) 4630191; (06) 4630192 *Fax:* (06) 4635152
E-mail: jda@go.com.jo
Telex: 22083 Distag Jo *Cable:* JODISTAG AMMAN
Key Personnel
Chairman: Raja Elissa
General Manager: Wadie Sayegh
Founded: 1951
Type of Business: Distributor, Exporter, Importer, Major Book Chain Headquarters, Major Independent Bookseller, Wholesaler
Owned by: Raja Elissa
Bookshop(s): Hotel Jordan Intercontinental, Amman

Sharbain's Bookshop
Jebel Amman, 1st Circle, Rainbow St, Amman
Mailing Address: PO Box 2427, Amman
Tel: (06) 638709 *Fax:* (06) 699119
Telex: 21153 sharbn jo-Bgrh-Inh *Cable:* SHARBAIN, AMMAN
Key Personnel
Owner: J I Sharbain
Founded: 1963
Type of Business: Distributor, Exporter, Importer, Major Independent Bookseller, Wholesaler

University of Jordan Bookshop
University of Jordan, Amman 11943
Mailing Address: PO Box 13307, Amman
Tel: (06) 843555 (ext 3339) *Fax:* (06) 836446
E-mail: admin@ju.edu.jo
Telex: 21153 *Cable:* UNIVERSITY OF JORDAN BOOKSHOP/AMMAN
Key Personnel
President: J J Sharbain
Founded: 1978
Owned by: JBC Co Ltd
Bookshop(s): PO Box 19903, Amman

Kenya

Book Sales (K) Ltd
PO Box 20377, Nairobi
Tel: (02) 221031; (02) 226543
Key Personnel
Chief Executive: Adrian Louis
Founded: 1976
Also Publishes.

Bookpoint Ltd
Loans House, Moi Ave, GPO 00100 Nairobi

Mailing Address: PO Box 46449, GPO 00100 Nairobi
Tel: (02) 211156; (02) 220221; (02) 226680 *Fax:* (02) 211029
E-mail: books@africaonline.co.ke
Key Personnel
Chairman: Mohinderlal Shah
Chief Executive: Sudhir Shah
Dir: Dipak Shah
Retail-Booksellers & Stationers.
Type of Business: Exporter, Importer, Major Independent Bookseller, Wholesaler

City Bookshop Ltd
Nkrumah Rd, Mombasa, City Centre
Mailing Address: PO Box 90512, Mombasa, City Centre
Tel: (011) 313 149; (011) 225548 *Fax:* (011) 314815 *Cable:* CITYBOOK
Key Personnel
Man Dir: Moez T Dungerwalla
Founded: 1953
Subjects: fiction, non fiction, magazines, greeting cards
Type of Business: Distributor, Importer, Major Independent Bookseller, Wholesaler

Keswick Books & Gifts Ltd
PO Box 10242, Nairobi
Tel: (02) 226-047; (02) 331-692 *Fax:* (02) 728-557
E-mail: keswick@swiftkenya.com
Key Personnel
Chief Executive: Margareta Hakanson
Founded: 1959
Type of Business: Distributor, Importer, Major Independent Bookseller
Branch Office(s)
Gospel Centre, Box 90310, Mombasa

Prestige Booksellers & Stationers
Mama Ngina St Prudential Bldg, Nairobi
Mailing Address: PO Box 45425, Nairobi
Tel: (02) 223515 *Fax:* (02) 2246796
E-mail: prest@iconnect.co.ke
Key Personnel
Chief Executive: R M Upadhyay
Contact: Dipak Upadhyay
Founded: 1972
Type of Business: Exporter, Importer, Major Independent Bookseller

Text Book Centre Ltd
Kijabe St, Nairobi
Mailing Address: PO Box 47540, Nairobi
Tel: (02) 330340 *Fax:* (02) 225779
E-mail: admin@tbc.co.ke
Web Site: www.textbook.centre.com *Cable:* TEXTBOOKS
Key Personnel
General Manager: C D Shah
Founded: 1964
Also Publisher.
Type of Business: Distributor, Exporter, Importer, Major Independent Bookseller, Wholesaler
Branch Office(s)
Sarit Centre Westlands

University of Nairobi Bookshop
PO Box 30197, Nairobi
Tel: (02) 334244 *Fax:* (02) 336885
E-mail: webmaster@uonbi.ac.ke
Web Site: www.uonbi.ac.ke
Telex: 22095 VARSITY KE
Key Personnel
Contact: Mrs M N Muriuki
Founded: 1974
Bookseller.
Owned by: University of Nairobi

Democratic People's Republic of Korea

Korea Publications Export & Import Corporation
Yonggwang Str, Central District, Yokjon-dong, Pyongyang
Tel: (02) 3818536 *Fax:* (02) 3814404
Telex: 36062 CH KP *Cable:* CHULPHANMUL, PYONGYANG
Key Personnel
Dir: Ri Yong
Head of Export Dept: Sin Hak Chol
Head of Import Dept: Jong Yong
Exporter: Mrs Kim Hye Son
Type of Business: Distributor, Exporter, Importer, Major Book Chain Headquarters, Major Independent Bookseller, Wholesaler
Bookshop(s): Changgwang Bookshop, Chollima St, Central District, Dongsong-dong

Republic of Korea

Daejon Trading Co Ltd
783-20 Pangbae-bondong, Socho-ku, Seoul
Tel: (02) 536-9555 *Fax:* (02) 536-0025
Key Personnel
Contact: Yoo Jung-Sun
Founded: 1981
Type of Business: Distributor, Importer

International Publications Service Inc (IPS)
Gongpyong Bldg, 11th floor, 5-1 Gongpyong-dong, Jongro-gu, Seoul 110-160
Mailing Address: KPO Box 496, Seoul 110-604
Tel: (02) 2115-8800 *Fax:* (02) 2273-8048
Web Site: www.ipsbook.com
Key Personnel
President: Yong-Kook Kim
General Manager: Dong-Hyun Lee
Founded: 1983
Distributions & subscription promotions for foreign publications.
Exclusive distributor for Newsweek, Reader's Digest, National Geographic & 63 other foreign periodicals.
Type of Business: Distributor, Importer, Wholesaler
Branch Office(s)
Kwangju
Kyungin
Pusan
Taejon
Taeku

IPS Inc, see International Publications Service Inc (IPS)

Kyobo Book Centre Co Ltd
1, 1-Ka Chongno, Chongno-ku, Seoul 110-714
Tel: (02) 397-3481; (02) 397-3482; (02) 397-3483; (02) 397-3484; (02) 397-3485 *Fax:* (02) 735-0030
E-mail: kyobofbd@kyobobook.co.kr
Key Personnel
President: Kun-Lyu
Dir: Byung Ha-Yu; Seong Ryoung-Kim
Supervisor: Sang Sik-Ahn
Vice President: Mun Jae-Shin
Manager Information Business Team: Mr T K Kim
Type of Business: Distributor, Exporter, Importer, Major Book Chain Headquarters, Wholesaler
Owned by: Kyobo Life Insurance Co Ltd

Panmun Book Co Ltd
40, Chongro 1-ka, Chongro-ku, Seoul
Mailing Address: CPO Box 1016, 136-074 Sungbuk-ku, Seoul
Tel: (02) 953-2451-5 *Fax:* (02) 953-2456-7
E-mail: panmunex@unitel.co.kr
Telex: K27546 *Cable:* PANMUSE
Branch Office(s)
16 Kwangbok-dong, 1-ka Pusan

Science Publications Centre
201 Taegyeong Bldg 364-28, Habjeong-dong, Mapo-gu, Seoul 121-220
Tel: (02) 3254015; (02) 7336719; (02) 3254017 *Fax:* (02) 3335799

Sophia Book Service
Golden Tower 1319, 191, 2-ka Chung Jung Rd, Sodaemun Ku, Seoul 120-722
Tel: (02) 362-2036 *Fax:* (02) 362-2036
Key Personnel
Owner: Eui-Soon Chang
General Manager: Hwan Kyu Paik
Founded: 1957
Type of Business: Distributor, Exporter, Importer, Wholesaler

Universal Publications Agency Press
UPA Bldg, No 2, Suite 1001, 20 Hyoje-dong, Seoul 110-850
Tel: (02) 3672 0044 *Fax:* (02) 3672 1222
E-mail: upa@upa.co.kr
Web Site: www.upa.co.kr
Telex: K28504 Unipub *Cable:* CHANGHOSHIN SEOUL
Key Personnel
Chairman: Chang-Ho Shin
Also Publisher.
Type of Business: Distributor

Kuwait

The Kuwait Book Shop Company Ltd
Sour-Al-Ghanem Bldg, Al-Sour St, Ahmadi-Souk Al-Ahmadi
Mailing Address: PO Box 2942, 13030 Safat
Tel: 2424687; 2424266 *Fax:* 2420558
E-mail: kbs@ncc.moc.kn
Telex: 30860 *Cable:* FARATOURS
Key Personnel
Owner: Bashir N Khatib

Lebanon

Librairies Antoine SAL/Librairie Antoine, A. Naufal & Freres
BP 11-656, Beirut
Tel: (01) 48 10 72; (01) 48 35 13 *Fax:* (01) 49 26 25

Librairie du Liban Publishers (Sal)
Sayegh Bldg Zouk Mosbeth, Kesrouwan
Mailing Address: PO Box 11-9232, Beirut
Tel: (09) 217 735; (09) 217 944; (09) 217 745; (09) 217 946 *Fax:* (09) 217 734

E-mail: info@ldlp.com
Web Site: www.ldlp.com
Telex: 45297 Libsay
Key Personnel
Man Dir: Pierre Sayegh *E-mail:* psayegh@ldlp.com
Founded: 1944
Bookseller
Also acts as Publisher.
Type of Business: Distributor, Exporter, Importer, Major Independent Bookseller, Wholesaler
Branch Office(s)
Rubeiz Bldg, Hamra St, Beirut *Tel:* (01) 344 070
Bookshop(s): 42 Bliss St, Beirut *Tel:* (01) 344 968

Lesotho

Mazenod Book Centre
PO Box 39, Mazenod 160
Tel: 35 0224 *Fax:* 35 0010 *Cable:* Mazbooks
Key Personnel
Manager: Rev Fr M Gareau

Morija Sesuto Book Depot
Church St, PO Box 4, Morija 190
Tel: 76204 *Fax:* 360009
Publishers, Books & Stationery Retailers.
Parent Company: Lesotho Evangelical Church (KEL), PO Box 260, Masery

Liberia

University Bookstore
University of Liberia, Monrovia
Mailing Address: PO Box 9020
Tel: 224671

Lithuania

Giliukas Ltd
S Lozoraicio 13, 3009 Kaunas
Tel: (07) 709560 *Fax:* (07) 709560
E-mail: giliukas@isi.kvn.lt
Key Personnel
Dir: Vyturys Jarutis
Founded: 1991
Type of Business: Distributor, Exporter, Importer, Wholesaler

Humanitas Ltd
Donelaicio 52, 3000 Kaunas
Tel: (07) 220333 *Fax:* (07) 423653
E-mail: beata@humanitas.lt
Key Personnel
Dir: Saulius Stogevicius
Founded: 1994
Type of Business: Distributor, Importer, Major Book Chain Headquarters, Wholesaler
Bookshop(s): Tunstantis ir Viena Naktis Bookshop, Vilnius g 11, 3000 Kaunas; Vilnius Art Bookshop, Vokieciy 2, Vilnius

Luxembourg

Librairie Bourbon
11, rue Bourbon, 1249 Luxembourg
Tel: 40 30 30-21 *Fax:* 40 30 30-45
E-mail: librairies@isp.lu
Web Site: www.librairie.lu
Key Personnel
Manager: Charles Jourdain
Founded: 1982
Owned by: Imprimerie Saint-Paul SA, 2988

Ernster Sarl
27 rue du Fosse, 1536 Luxembourg
Tel: 225077-1 *Fax:* 225073
E-mail: librairie@ernster.com
Web Site: www.ernster.com
Key Personnel
Manager: Fernand Ernster *Tel:* 262740 *E-mail:* f.ernster@ernster.com
Founded: 1889
Stationary: supplies for schools, bookshop.
Bookshop(s): Ernster Belle Etoile, 8050 Bertrange

Librairie Promoculture
14 rue Duchscher, 1424 Luxembourg
Mailing Address: BP 1142, L-1011 Luxembourg
Tel: 480691 *Fax:* 400950
E-mail: promocul@pt.lu
Key Personnel
Dir: Albert P Daming *E-mail:* daming@pt.lu
Founded: 1972
Subscription agency & technical bookshop. Also book publisher.
Subjects: Law
Type of Business: Major Independent Bookseller
Owned by: Albert Daming, 4, Avalaon St, Luxembourg L-1159

The Former Yugoslav Republic of Macedonia

Kultura
JNA 68a, Postanski fah 298, 91000 Skopje
Tel: (091) 111332 *Fax:* (091) 228608
Key Personnel
Dir: Dimitar Basevski
Commercial Dir: Arso Kokaleski
Editor: Branko Cvetkovski
Founded: 1945
Also Publisher & stationery goods supplier.
Type of Business: Distributor, Exporter, Importer, Major Independent Bookseller, Wholesaler

Makedonska kniga
11-ti Oktomvri, 1000 Skopje
Tel: (02) 224-055 *Fax:* (091) 1212 77
Telex: 51637
Key Personnel
Man Dir: Branislav Mihajlovic
Thirty-one bookshops in Skopje & in all major towns in Macedonia.
Type of Business: Exporter, Importer, Wholesaler
Owned by: Makedonska kniga (Knigoizdatelstvo)

Madagascar

La Librairie de Madagascar
38 Ave de l'Independance, Tananrive 101
Mailing Address: BP 402, Tananrive 101
Tel: (020) 222454 *Fax:* (020) 2264395; (020) 224395
Key Personnel
Manager: Yves Balanche
Founded: 1936

Librairie Mixte Sarl
Analakely, Tananrive 101
Tel: (020) 22 251-30
Key Personnel
Manager: Jean Razakasoa

Librairie Universitaire
BP 566, 101 Tananrive
Tel: (020) 24114

Societe Malgache d'Edition
Route des Hydrocarbures, Ankorondrano, BP 659, Antananarivo/Tananrive 101
Tel: (020) 2222635 *Fax:* (020) 2222254
E-mail: tribune@bow.dts.mg
Web Site: www.madagascar-tribune.com
Telex: 22340 RAMEX MG TANANARIVE
Key Personnel
Dir of Publication: Rahaga Ramaholimihaso
Founded: 1943
Also Publisher.
Type of Business: Exporter

Trano Printy Fiahyohana Loterana Malagasy
9 ave Grandidier, Tananrive 101
Mailing Address: BP 533, Tananrive
Tel: (020) 223340; (020) 24569
Also Publisher.

Malawi

Central Bookshop Ltd
PO Box 264, Blantyre
Tel: 621 447 *Fax:* 633 863
Key Personnel
Man Dir: A Hamid Sacranie *E-mail:* hamidcbs@malawi.net
Founded: 1960
School supplies, books, stationary & cards, Africana.
Type of Business: Distributor, Importer, Major Independent Bookseller
Branch Office(s)
City Centre, Lilongwe *Tel:* 784 343
Bookshop(s): Livingston Ave, Blantyre

CLAIM Bookshop
PO Box 503, Blantyre
Tel: 620839
Key Personnel
Manager: J T Matenje
Sales Manager: E C Mtumbati
Owned by: Christian Literature Association in Malawi

Malaysia

S Abdul Majeed & Co
No 7, Jalan 3/82B, Bangsar Utama, Off Jalan Bangsar, 59000 Kuala Lumpur

MALAYSIA

Tel: (03) 2832230 Fax: (03) 2822567
E-mail: peer@pc.jaring.my
Key Personnel
Man Dir: A M S Alaudeen
Type of Business: Distributor, Wholesaler
Branch Office(s)
35 Jalan Sekarat, Penang

Antara Publications (M) Sdn Bhd
10th floor, Wisma Muisan, 300 Jalan Raja Laut, 50350 Kuala Lumpur
Tel: (03) 2913188 Fax: (03) 2913299
Key Personnel
Man Dir: Kevin Sugumaran
Type of Business: Distributor, Importer, Wholesaler
Owned by: Antara Publications (M) S/B, Singapore
Bookshop(s): BBC English Shop, Lot 2.52, 2nd floor, Mall Complex, 100 Jalan Putra, Kuala Lumpur

Badan Bookstore Sdn Bhd
28 Tingkat Bawah, Kompleks Tun Abdul Razak, 80000 Johur Bahru, Johor
Tel: (07) 2234796; (07) 2377562; (07) 2330241; (07) 330241 Fax: (07) 2238188
Key Personnel
Dir: Encik Saadon
Branch Office(s)
63, Jalan Perang, Taman Pelangi, Johor Bahru

Flo Enterprise Sdn Bhd
24 Lorong PJS 1/2A Taman Perangsang Batu 7, Jalan Kelang Lama, 46000 Petaling Jaya
Tel: (03) 77833118 Fax: (03) 77831066
Key Personnel
Man Dir: Johnny Leong
Type of Business: Distributor, Importer

IBS Buku Sdn Bhd
B3-06, P J Industrial Park, Jalan Kemajuan, 46200 Petaling Jaya, Selangor, Darul Ehsan
Tel: (03) 79579282; (03) 79579470 Fax: (03) 79576026
E-mail: info@ibsbuku.com; ibsbuku@po.janing.my; hibs@tm.net.my
Key Personnel
Man Dir: Mohamed Mustafa
Founded: 1971
Type of Business: Distributor, Exporter, Importer, Wholesaler
U.S. Office(s): 6102 Gardenia Court, Alexandria, VA 22310, United States Tel: 703-313-8334 Fax: 703-295-4352 E-mail: agil@ibsbuku.com

International Book Service, see IBS Buku Sdn Bhd

Mahir Marketing Services Sdn Bhd
7 Jl 3/82B, Bangsar Utama, Off Jalan Bangsar, 59000 Kuala Lumpur
Tel: (088) 2827372 Fax: (088) 718067
Telex: MA 30226 MAHIR
Key Personnel
President: Tham Ban Hing
Owned by: Mahir Holdings Sdn Bhd
Branch Office(s)
Stadrum Shah Alam, Arasi, Quadran B Seksyen 13, Shah Alam Selangor Tel: (03) 5501755 (03) 5501442 Fax: (03) 5501826

Marican Sdn Bhd
321 Jalan Tuanku Abdul Rahman, 50100 Kuala Lumpur
Tel: (03) 2981133
Telex: MA 31697 Manews Cable: Maricanews
Key Personnel
General Manager: C C Lo
Also Publisher.
Type of Business: Wholesaler

Branch Office(s)
171 Middle Rd, Singapore 0718, Singapore
4th floor, Ruby Warehouse Complex, 8 Kaki Bukit Rd 2, Singapore 1441, Singapore

Mawaddah Enterprise Sdn Bhd
75 Jalan Kapitan Tam Yeong, 70000 Seremban, Negeri Sembilan Darul Khusus
Tel: (06) 7611062 Fax: (06) 7633062
E-mail: azhari@mawadah.pc.my
Key Personnel
Man Dir: Haji Azhari Hamzah
Founded: 1977
Type of Business: Distributor, Exporter, Importer, Wholesaler

MPH Distributors Sdn Bhd
Unit JA1, Ground floor, Mid Valley Megamall, Mid Valley City, 58000 Kuala Lumpur
Tel: (03) 2938 3800; (03) 2938 3818 Fax: (03) 2938 3811; (03) 2938 3817
E-mail: contact@mph.com.my; customerservice@mph.com.my
Web Site: www.mphonline.com; www.mph.com
Telex: Jcm MA 37402
Key Personnel
General Manager: Francis Heng Siang Goh
Group Financial Controller: Wong Paw
Manager: Tai Kwai Meng
Founded: 1963
Type of Business: Distributor, Importer, Major Book Chain Headquarters, Wholesaler
Owned by: MPH Group Malaysia Sdn Bhd
Bookshop(s): F39, 1st floor, Kinta Shopping Centre, No 2, Jalan Teh Lean Swee, Off Jalan Sultan Azlan Shah Utara, 34100 Ipoh Tel: (05) 545 1452 Fax: (05) 545 1386; F38, 1st floor, Bukit Raja Shopping Centre, Persiaran Bukit Raja 2, Bandar Baru Klang, 41150 Klang Tel: (03) 3342 8580 Fax: (03) 3343 1345; F02 & F03, 1st floor, Klang Parade, No 2112, KM2, Jalan Meru, 41050 Klang Tel: (03) 3343 7872 Fax: (03) 3343 7879; F1 & F2, 1st floor, Taman Maluri Shopping Centre, Jalan Jejaka, Taman Maluri, Cheras, 55100 Kuala Lumpur Tel: (03) 9285 1317 Fax: (03) 9285 1069; Jalan Telawi 2, No 2, Bangsar Baru, 59100 Kuala Lumpur Tel: (03) 2282 7300 Fax: (03) 2282 7293; F11-12, 1st floor, Alpha Angle Shopping Centre, Jalan R1, Section 1, Bandar Baru Wangsa Maju, 53300 Kuala Lumpur Tel: (03) 4142 1246 Fax: (03) 4142 1245; Lots 5 & 6, Level 1, Great Eastern Mall, No 303, Jalan Ampang, 50450 Kuala Lumpur Tel: (03) 4253 4835 Fax: (03) 4253 4204; GF002, Ground floor, Bukit Bintang Plaza, Jalan Bkt Bintang, 55100 Kuala Lumpur Tel: (03) 2142 8231 Fax: (03) 2142 8206; Unit 24, Departure Hall, Level 1, KL City Air Terminal, KL Sentral Station, 50470 Kuala Lumpur Tel: (03) 2273 0560 Fax: (03) 2273 0569; 673B, Ground floor, Mahkota Parade, No 1, Jalan Merdeka, 75000 Melaka Tel: (06) 283 3050 Fax: (06) 283 3003; Lot 170-3-76/79/81/82, 3rd floor, Gurney Plaza, Gurney Dr, 10250 Penang Tel: (04) 227 4202 Fax: (04) 227 4303; Lot 18-1-A, 1st floor, Gurney Tower, 18 Persiara Gurney, 10250 Penang Tel: (04) 370 2115 Fax: (04) 370 2116; LL2.05, Lower Level 2, Sunway Pyramid, 3 Jalan PJS 11/15, Bandar Sunway, 46150 Petaling Jaya Tel: (03) 7492 5805 Fax: (03) 7492 5806; G33 & 34, Ground floor, 1 Utama Shopping Centre, No 1, Lebuh Bandar Utama, Bandar Utama Damansara, 47800 Petaling Jaya Tel: (03) 7726 4352; (03) 7728 4406 Fax: (03 7726 4554; No 5, Ground floor, Jalan 14120, 46100 Petaling Jaya Tel: (03) 7957 3735 Fax: (03) 7957 2187; G26(1), G26B-C & G26D(1), Ground floor, Subang Parade, No 5, Jalan SS16/1, Subang Jaya, 47500 Petaling Jaya; Unit 1F & 2F, Anjung, Blok E16, Parcel E, Presint 1, Persiaren Sultan Salahudin Abd Aziz Shah, 6200 Putrajaya; Lot A22-A24, Giant Hypermarket Stadium Shah Alam, Lot 2 Jalan Persiaran Sukan, Seksyen 13, 40100 Shah Alam Tel: (03) 5511 8978 Fax: (03) 5511 8976; LGSOA, LG56 & LG57, Lower Ground floor, The Summit, Subang USJ, Persiaran Kewajipan, USJ1, 47600 UEP Subang Jaya Tel: (03) 8024 2261 Fax: (03) 8024 1442

Parry's Book Center Sdn Bhd
60 Jalan Negara, 53100 Kuala Lumpur
Mailing Address: PO Box 10960, 50730 Kuala Lumpur
Tel: (03) 4079179; (03) 4087235; (03) 4079176; (03) 4087528 Fax: (03) 4079180
E-mail: haja@pop3.jaring.my
Telex: Parry's MA Cable: PABOKCENT
Founded: 1993
University & library suppliers.

Pearson Education Malaysia Sdn Bhd
Lot 2, Jalan 215, Off Jalan Templer, 46050 Petaling Jaya, Selangor Darul Ehsan
Tel: (03) 77820466
E-mail: inquiry@personed.com.my
Web Site: www.pearson.com
Key Personnel
International Business: Wendy Spiegel Tel: 212-782-3482 E-mail: wendy.spiegel@pearsoned.com
Type of Business: Distributor, Exporter

University of Malaya Co-operative Bookshop Ltd
Jalan Pantai Baru, 59700 Kuala Lumpur
Mailing Address: PO Box 1127, 59700 Kuala Lumpur
Tel: (03) 756 5000; (03) 756 5425 Fax: (03) 755 4424
Telex: Unimal MA 39845
Key Personnel
Chairman: Royal Prof Ungku A Aziz
Type of Business: Distributor, Exporter, Importer, Major Independent Bookseller, Wholesaler

Mali

Librairie Deves et Chaumet
BP 64, Bamako
Tel: 222784

Malta

Audio Visual Centre Ltd
Mayflower Mansions, Bisazza St, Sliema SLM 01
Mailing Address: PO Box 58, Sliema SLM 01
Tel: 21330886 Fax: 21346945
E-mail: info@avc.com.mt
Key Personnel
Owner: Simon Bonello
Founded: 1972

The Ideal Bookshop
Main Gate St, Victoria, Gozo
Mailing Address: PO Box 20, Victoria, Gozo
Tel: 553944
Key Personnel
Manager: A Vassallo
Owned by: A Vassallo and Sons Ltd
Branch Office(s)
Bxara T-Tajba, Charity St, Victoria, Gozo Tel: (356) 553944 (Christian Bookshop)

Merlin Library Ltd
Mountbatten Str, Blata 1-Badja
Tel: 21 234438; 21 221202 *Fax:* 21 221135
E-mail: mail@merlinlibrary.com
Web Site: www.merlinlibrary.com
Key Personnel
Dir: Arthur J Gruppetta
Founded: 1964
Also Remainder Dealers.
Type of Business: Distributor, Importer, Major Independent Bookseller, Wholesaler

Giov Muscat & Co Ltd
213 St Ursula St, Valletta
Mailing Address: PO Box 348, Valletta
Tel: 247 380 *Fax:* 240 496
Key Personnel
Man Dir: J A Muscat
Founded: 1874
Type of Business: Importer, Major Independent Bookseller
Bookshop(s): 48 Merchants St, Valletta

Mauritius

Editions de l'Ocean Indien
Stanley, Rose Hill
Tel: 4646761 *Fax:* 4643445
E-mail: eoibooks@intnet.mu
Telex: MESYND 4739 IW *Cable:* EOI MAURITIUS
Key Personnel
Chairman: Mr Surendra Bissoondoyal
General Manager: Damie Ramtohul; Mr Samrat C Servansingh
Senior Marketing Manager: Amritlall Kundun
Founded: 1977
Also acts as publisher.
Branch offices in Curepipe, Flacq, Goodlands, Port Louis, & Rose Hill.
Type of Business: Distributor, Exporter, Importer, Major Book Chain Headquarters, Major Independent Bookseller, Wholesaler
Owned by: EPB, Singapore; Government of Mauritius (60%); Longman, United Kingdom; Macmillan, United Kingdom; Nathan, France
Bookshop(s): NPF Shopping Centre, J Koenig S Port Louis; Arcades Rond Point, Rose Hill; Arcades Salaffa, Curepipe; Arcades Virginie, Flacq; Jugadambi Sharma SSS, Goodlands

Mexico

Libreria Acuario SA de CV
Tehuantepec 34, Col Roma Sur, 06760 Mexico, DF
Tel: (05) 5742966; (05) 5741137 *Fax:* (05) 2642882
Founded: 1974
Type of Business: Distributor, Exporter, Importer
Bookshop(s): Ave Baja California 37-B, Col Roma Sur, 06760 Mexico, DF

American Book Store SA de CV
Madero No 25, Mexico 06000
Tel: (05) 512-6350; (05) 512-0306 *Fax:* (05) 518-6931
Founded: 1928
Type of Business: Importer, Major Independent Bookseller
Branch Office(s)
Av Eugenio Garza Sada No 2404, Col Roma, Monterrey, NL *Tel:* (08) 3588028
Circuito Medicos No 2, Ciudad Satelite, 53100 Edo de Mexico *Tel:* (05) 3930682 *Fax:* (05) 5624692
Insurgentes Sur 1636, Col Credito Constructo, 03940 Mexico, DF *Tel:* (05) 6614611 *Fax:* (05) 6615109
Quintana Roo 861, Las Fuentes, Celaya, Gto *Tel:* (0461) 47301 *Fax:* (0461) 47049

Libreria Bellas Artes
Av Juarez No 20, 06050 Cuauhtemoc 06050
Tel: (05) 510-2276 *Fax:* (05) 518-3755
Key Personnel
Manager: Miguel Noriega
Founded: 1946
Owned by: Editorial Limusa SA de CV

Central de Publicaciones SA
Ave Juarez No 4-B, 06050 Mexico, DF
Tel: (05) 5104231
Owned by: Galeria de Arte Misrachi SA, Genova No 20-A, Col Jaurez 06600

Librerias de Cristal, sa de cv (Cristal Bookstores)
Tehuantepec No 170, 06760 Mexico
Tel: (05) 5644100 *Fax:* (05) 2640983; (05) 5644100 ext 287 (fax on demand)
E-mail: biblio10@prodigy.net.mx *Cable:* EDIAPSA
Key Personnel
Dir: Benito Zychlinski
Information Bibliography Manager: Gabriel Rodriquez *Tel:* (05) 5644100 ext 210
Founded: 1939
Bookstores.
Owned by: Editorial Limusa SA de CV
Branch Office(s)
Tehuantepec 170, Col Roma Sur, 06760 Mexico City 49 MX *Tel:* (05) 6008390

Librerias Gonvill SA de CV
8 de Julio, No 825, Guadalajara, JAL
Tel: (033) 83-72-309 *Fax:* (033) 3837-2309
E-mail: librosbooks@gonvill.com.mx
Web Site: www.gonvill.com.mx
Key Personnel
General Dir: Jorge E Gonzalez Villalobos
Administrative Dir: Tirzo F Gonzaez Letechipia
Founded: 1967
Type of Business: Distributor, Exporter, Importer, Major Book Chain Headquarters, Wholesaler

Grupo Cultural Especializado, SA
Av Popocaltepetl 510, Col Xoco, Del Benito Juarez, 03330 Mexico, DF
Tel: (05) 6889831 *Fax:* (05) 6889965
Key Personnel
Dir: Mr Adrian Garcia Valades
General Manager: Ing Meliton Cross
Type of Business: Distributor, Importer, Wholesaler

Libreria Hamburgo SA
Insurgentes Sur 58, Mexico
Tel: (05) 5126796; (05) 5218265
Branch Office(s)
Insurgentes Sur 317, Mexico 11, DF *Tel:* (05) 5744015
Ribera de San Cosme 133, Mexico 4, DF *Tel:* (05) 5464736

Libreria Interacademica SA de CV
Ave Sonora 206, Col Hipodromo, Mexico, DF 06100
Tel: (05) 265-1165 *Fax:* (05) 265-1164
Telex: 1773596 Aldime *Cable:* LIBINTER
Key Personnel
Administrative Manager: Lourdes Reyes

Librolandia del Centro SA de CV
Matamoros 83 Retorno Gaston Madrid No 4, 83000-18 Hermosillo, Sonora 83000-18
Tel: (062) 135646; (062) 170236 *Fax:* (062) 170236
Key Personnel
Dir: Miguel A Castellanos Araujo
Type of Business: Major Independent Bookseller

MACH, see Mexican Academic Clearing House (MACH)

Mexican Academic Clearing House (MACH)
Apdo 13-319, Deleg Benito Juarez, 03500 Mexico, DF
Tel: (05) 674 0779; (05) 674 0567 *Fax:* (05) 673 6209
E-mail: hpadilla@spin.com.mx
Key Personnel
Dir General: Lic Hugo Padilla Chacon
Technical Consultant: Ario Garza Mercado
Founded: 1969
Type of Business: Exporter

Libreria Patria
Renacimiento Room 180, Col San Juan Tlihuaca, Mexico, DF 02400
Tel: (05) 5613446
Key Personnel
Dir General: Rene Solis
Also Publisher.

Libreria de Porrua Hermanos y Cia, SA
Justo Sierra No 36, Col Centro, 06020 Mexico, DF
Tel: (05) 7024574 *Fax:* (05) 7026529
E-mail: porrua@porrua.com
Web Site: www.porrua.com *Cable:* PORRUAS, MEXICO
Key Personnel
President & Dir General: Jose Antonio Perez Porrua
Founded: 1900
Branch Office(s)
Av Juarez No 16
Bookshop(s): Av Rep, Argentina 15

SCRIPTA - Distribucion y Servicios Editoriales, SA de CV
Copilco 178, Edis 22 Local D, Col Copilco Universidad, 04340 Mexico, DF
Tel: (05) 5481716 *Fax:* (05)5500564
Key Personnel
President & Dir: Bertha R Alavez Magana
Worldwide to academic libraries of scholarly books published in Latin America.
Type of Business: Distributor, Importer
U.S. Office(s): Scripta, 4011 Creek Rd, Youngstown, NY 14174, United States, Book Trade Counsellor: Lyman W Newlin *Tel:* 716-754-8145 *Fax:* 716-754-8145

Servicio a La Iglesia Catolica AC Edicion y Distribucion de Libros Religiosos
Viaducto Tlaplan No 20, Col Ejidos de Huipulco, Mexico
Mailing Address: PO Box 22-897, Tlalpan 14370
Tel: (05) 6710269 *Fax:* (05) 5441675
Key Personnel
President: Mrs Amalia R Pino

Servicios Especializados y Representacionesen Comercio Exterior SA de CV
Norte 198 No 691 Esq, Con Av Tahel, 15510 Mexico
Tel: (05) 7609129; (05) 7605149
Key Personnel
Dir: Filiberto Vargas
Manager: Julia Gutierrez

Mongolia

State Book Trading Office
Leniny gudamch 41, Ulan-Bator
Tel: (01) 22312 *Cable:* Mongolbook

Morocco

Librairie des Colonnes
54, rue Pasteur, Tanger
Tel: (09) 93 69 55 *Fax:* (099) 936955
Key Personnel
Dir: Mrs Rachel Muyal
Founded: 1947
Type of Business: Importer, Major Independent Bookseller
Owned by: Nouvelle Societe Kalila wa Dimna

Librairie des Ecoles
12 Ave Hassan II, Casablanca
Tel: (02) 22 25 22; (02) 26 67 41 *Fax:* (02) 20 10 03
Founded: 1947
Type of Business: Distributor, Exporter, Importer, Wholesaler

Librairie Internationale
70 rue T'ssoule, Rabat Maroc
Mailing Address: BP 302, Rabat Maroc
Tel: (07) 75 01 83 *Fax:* (07) 75 86 61
E-mail: Libinter@iam.net.ma
Key Personnel
President & Owner: Mohamed Kerouach
Vice President: Brigitte Kerouach
Founded: 1960
Specialize in scientific books, CD-ROMs & multimedia.
Type of Business: Distributor, Exporter, Importer, Major Book Chain Headquarters, Major Independent Bookseller
Owned by: Kerouach Mohamed
Branch Office(s)
V Continents, 3 rue T'ssoule, Rabat (Souissi)

Librairie Livre-Service
11, rue Tata (ex Poincare), Casablanca
Tel: (02) 262072 *Fax:* (02) 473089
Key Personnel
Executive & General Manager: Faouzi Slaoui
Type of Business: Exporter, Importer, Major Book Chain Headquarters

SMER Diffusion
3 rue Ghazza, Rabat
Tel: (07) 723725; (07) 725960 *Fax:* (07) 701643
Telex: 3274
Key Personnel
Dir: Youssef Slaoui
Branch Office(s)
13 Ave Alaouyine, Rabat
Bookshop(s): Librarie Livre-Service, 11 rue Tata, Casablanca *Tel:* (02) 25975; Librarie de L'Agdal, angle Ave de France, Agdal, Rabat

Societe Cherifienne de Distribution et de Presse Sochepress
Angle Rues Rahal Ben Ahmed et St-Saens, Casablanca 21700
Mailing Address: BP 13683, 20300 Casablanca
Tel: (02) 22400223 *Fax:* (02) 22404032
E-mail: infolivre@sochepress.co.ma
Telex: 26660 28019 *Cable:* SOCHEPRESS CASABLANCA
Key Personnel
President, Dir General: Abdallah Lahrizi
Dir: Zhor Alaoui Belghiti; Mohamed Gounajjar; Meriem Kabbaj; Hassan Lahrizi; Maati Taimouri
Type of Business: Distributor, Exporter, Importer, Wholesaler

Myanmar

Hanthawaddy Bookshop
157 Bo Aung Gyaw St, Rangoon
Owned by: Hanthawaddy Book House

Knowledge Book House
130, Bogyoke Aung San St, Pazundaung Tsp
Tel: (01) 290927
Owned by: Knowledge Printing & Publishing House

Sabe U
200 50 St, Rangoon

Sarpay Beikman Bookshop
529-531 Merchand St, Rangoon
Tel: (01) 83611; (01) 16611
Key Personnel
Manager: U Tin Gyi
Founded: 1956
Owned by: Sarpay Beikman Board

Sarpay Lawka
173, 33rd St, KTDA, Yangon
Tel: (01) 274391; (01) 285166

Thwe Thauk
185 48 St, Rangoon

Namibia

Central News Agency (CNA)
Kaiserstra Be Nord Private Bag 13176, Windhoek 9000
Tel: (061) 25625 *Fax:* (061) 227210

ELCIN Book Depot
PB 2013, Ondangwa 9000
Tel: (065) 240211 *Fax:* (065) 240536
Key Personnel
Contact: Anna K Kapenda
Type of Business: Major Book Chain Headquarters
Owned by: ELCIN

Swakopmunder Buchhandlung
PO Box 500, Kaiser Wilhelm St, Swakopmund
Tel: 402613 *Fax:* 404183
Key Personnel
Owner: H U Delius
Founded: 1900
Type of Business: Major Independent Bookseller

Windhoeker Buchhandlung
Independence Ave 69, Windhoek
Mailing Address: PO Box 1327, Windhoek
Tel: (061) 225216 *Fax:* (061) 225011
Type of Business: Distributor, Importer, Major Independent Bookseller
Owned by: Bertermann

Nepal

National Standards Publisher's & Bookseller's Association Nepal (NASPUBAN)
Kamabakshee Tole, Gha 3-333, Chowk Bitra, Kathmandu 44601
Mailing Address: PO Box 3000, 15B Kathmandu 44601
Tel: (01) 212289; (01) 223036; (01) 224005 *Fax:* (01) 223036
Telex: 3000 1-SB-ASS-NP *Cable:* ANTERPRAGATISHEELSAPHOOPASA KATMANDU NEPAL
Key Personnel
Secretary General: Ganesh Lall Chhipa
Executive Man Dir: Chandra Lall Ranjitkar
Dir: Ganesh Daas Chhipa
Editorial: Aneeta Shobha Tuladhar
Sales: Padma L Tuladhar; Suneeta D Tuladhar; Parbatee S Ranjitkar
Production: Shanta S Ranjitkar
Publicity: Chandrawatee C Ranjitkar
Rights & Permissions: Renooka S Tuladhar
Founded: 1963
Centre for Central General Selling. Order Supplies, Subscriptions & Publications.
Branch Office(s)
09-63-07, Dathwee Chhen Twa Gallee
Chowk Bhitra Purano Bazar, Arniko-Barhabise-9, Arniko Rajmarg-87K M Bagmati Anchal, Barhabise, 45303 Katmandu Mail Centre
Bookshop(s): People's Friendship Books & Periodicals Shop, Dathwee Chhen Twa Gallee, Purano Bazar, Arniko Barhabise 9, Barhabise 45303; Nepal Books & Periodicals House, Maisthan Tole, Birganj; People's Books & Periodicals Centre, Datraya Square, Bhaktapur; Banepa Books Depot, Banepa Nayan Bazar, Kavrepalanchok Dist; Jagriti Books Centre, Itahary Sunsary, Koshee Zone; People's Books Centre, Chenpur, Sakhuwa Sabha, Koshee Zone; Janapriya Pustak Bhandar, Patan Dhoka, Lalitpur

Ratna Book Distributors (Pvt) Ltd
PO Box 1080, Bagbazaar, Kathmandu
Tel: (01) 223026
E-mail: rpb@wlink.com.np
Key Personnel
Manager: Govinda P Shrestha
Contact: Roshan P Shrestha
Founded: 1945
Type of Business: Distributor, Importer, Wholesaler
Branch Office(s)
Saraswati Book Centre, Near UNDP Bldg, Pulchowk, Lalitpur, Kathmandu
Ratna Pustak Bhandar, Bhotahity PO Box 98, Kathmandu *Fax:* (01) 248421 *E-mail:* rpb@wlink.com.np

Netherlands

Athenaeum Boekhandel
Spui 14-16, 1012 XA Amsterdam
Tel: (020) 6226248 *Fax:* (020) 6384901
E-mail: info@athenaeum.nl
Web Site: www.athenaeum.nl
Key Personnel
Man Dir: M Asscher *Tel:* (020) 6226210
Founded: 1966
Type of Business: Importer, Major Independent Bookseller
Branch Office(s)
Athenaeum Boekhandel Haarlem, Gedempte Oude Gracht 70, 2011 GT Haarlem

BOOK DEALERS — NETHERLANDS

Tel: (023) 5318755 *Fax:* (023) 5322603
E-mail: haarlem@athenaeum.nl
Athenaeum Boekhandel Hogeschoolboekhandel, Kohnstammhuis DO.31, Wibautstraat 2-4, 1091 GM Amsterdam *Tel:* (020) 5995553 *Fax:* (020) 4686186 *E-mail:* wibaut@athenaeum.nl

John Benjamins Publishing Co
Klaprozenweg 105, 1033 NN Amsterdam
Mailing Address: Postbus 36224, 1020 ME Amsterdam
Tel: (020) 6304747 *Fax:* (020) 6739773 (publishing); (020) 6792956 (antiquariat)
E-mail: customer.services@benjamins.nl
Web Site: www.benjamins.com
Key Personnel
Dir: John Benjamins
Also Publisher & Antiquarian.
Branch Office(s)
Benjamins North America Inc, PO Box 27519, Philadelphia, PA 19118-0519, United States, Manager: Paul Peranteau *Tel:* 215-836-1200 *Fax:* 215-836-1204 *E-mail:* paul@benjamins.com

Broese BV
Stadhuisbrug 5, 3511 KP Utrecht
Tel: (030) 2335200 *Fax:* (030) 2314071
E-mail: info@broese.net
Web Site: www.broese.net
Telex: 40411 Boek
Key Personnel
Man Dir: Hylco Wijnants
Type of Business: Distributor, Exporter, Importer
Owned by: Boekhandels Groep Nederland
Bookshop(s): Minrebroederstr 13, 3512 GS Utrecht *Tel:* (030) 2336500 *Fax:* (030) 2316000; Heidelberglaan 2, 3584 CS Utrecht *Tel:* (030) 2155400 *Fax:* (030) 2540303

Bruna BV
Croeselaan 15, 3521 BJ Utrecht
Mailing Address: Postbus 30130, 3503 AC Utrecht
Tel: (0900) 1200 100
E-mail: klantenservice@bruna.com
Web Site: www.bruna.nl
Telex: 47518
Key Personnel
President: J V Hanegem
Owned by: Buehrmann-Tetterode NV
Bookshop(s): A P Standaard Boekhandel (Delft, Zaandam); Boekhandel Bergmans (Maastricht); Boekhandel H Coebergh Haarlem; Boekhandel Hugo Jonkers (Eindhoven); Moderne Boekhandel (Amsterdam); Boekhandel Mosmans ('s Hertogenbosch); Boekhandel Revers en van Brummen (Dordrecht); Boekhandel F Schoth (Boxmeer); Ten Have en Hoofdstadboekhandel (Amsterdam); Boekhandel Van Broek (Zeist); Boekhandel Van Leeuwen (Roosendaal)

Dekker v d Vegt
Marikenstr 29, 6511 PX Nijmegen
Tel: (024) 322 10 10 *Fax:* (024) 324 21 11
E-mail: mariken@dekker.nl
Web Site: www.dekker.nl
Key Personnel
Manager: P H M Hooghof
Founded: 1856
Type of Business: Major Independent Bookseller
Owned by: Boekhandels Groep Nederland
Branch Office(s)
Koningstr 31, 6811 DG Arnhem *Tel:* (026) 445 23 45 *Fax:* (026) 351 10 18 *E-mail:* arnhem@dekker.nl
Thomas van Aquinostr 1a, 6525 GD Nijmegen *Tel:* (024) 355 11 27 *Fax:* (024) 356 07 20 *E-mail:* campus@dekker.nl

European Book Service
PO Box 130, 3454 ZJ De Meern
Tel: (030) 6660211 *Fax:* (030) 6662674
Key Personnel
Man Dir: S Valk
Export Manager: R Puyk

Boekhandel Gianotten BV
Emmapassage 17, 5038 XA Tilburg
Tel: (013) 465 11 11 *Fax:* (013) 535 59 62
E-mail: emma@gianotten.nl
Web Site: www.gianotten.nl
Key Personnel
Manager: A J H Gunsing
Owned by: Boekhandels Groep Nederland
Branch Office(s)
De Barones 29 & 63, 4811 XZ Breda
Tel: (076) 514 97 00 *Fax:* (076) 514 15 19
E-mail: breda@gianotten.nl
Warandelaan 2, 5037 AB Tilburg *Tel:* (013) 465 11 11 *Fax:* (013) 463 54 04 *E-mail:* acad@gianotten.nl

Ginsberg Univ Boekhandel
Breestr 127-129, 2311 CM Leiden
Tel: (071) 5160562 *Fax:* (071) 5127505
E-mail: bree127@kooyker.nl
Key Personnel
Manager: R Egan
Type of Business: Major Independent Bookseller

ICOB/Atrium
Ondernemingsweg 60, 2404 HN Alphen aan den Rijn
Mailing Address: Postbus 392, 2400 AJ Alphen aan den Rijn
Tel: (0172) 43 72 31 *Fax:* (0172) 43 93 79
E-mail: icobal@xs4all.nl
Key Personnel
Man Dir: Hans Meijer
Publisher: Dennis Friedhoff
Founded: 1965
Also publisher.
Type of Business: Remainder Dealer

Nilsson & Lamm BV, Algemene Import Boekhandel
Pampuslaan 212, 1382 JS Weesp
Mailing Address: Postbus 195, 1380 AD Weesp
Tel: (0294) 49 49 49 *Fax:* (0294) 49 44 55
E-mail: info@nilsson-lamm.nl
Web Site: www.nilsson-lamm.nl
Key Personnel
Man Dir: M Brouwer
Sales & Distribution Dir: W J van Loon
Founded: 1880
Also acts as Publisher.
Type of Business: Distributor, Wholesaler

Pegasus Publishers & Booksellers
Singel 367, 1012 WL Amsterdam
Mailing Address: PO Box 11470, 1001 GL Amsterdam
Tel: (020) 6231138 *Fax:* (020) 6203478
E-mail: pegasus@pegasusboek.nl
Web Site: www.pegasusboek.nl
Key Personnel
Dir: Joop F Yisberg
Founded: 1945
Type of Business: Exporter, Importer, Major Independent Bookseller

Van Piere Boeken
Heuvel Galerie 190 & 232, 5611 DK Eindhoven
Tel: (040) 244 40 45 *Fax:* (040) 246 39 49
E-mail: info@vanpiere.nl
Web Site: www.vanpiere.nl
Key Personnel
Manager: Chris de Plot
Founded: 1848
Type of Business: Major Independent Bookseller
Owned by: Boekhandels Groep Nederland
Branch Office(s)
Rachelsmolen 1, 5612 MA Eindhoven *Tel:* (0877) 876277 *Fax:* (0877) 876266 *E-mail:* fontys1@vanpiere.nl
Ds Th Fliednerstr 2, 5631 DN Eindhoven
Tel: (0877) 876211 *Fax:* (0877) 876200
E-mail: fontys2@vanpiere.nl
Den Dolech 2, 5612 AZ Eindhoven
Tel: (040) 244 24 39 *Fax:* (040) 245 41 84
E-mail: tuboek@vanpiere.nl

Scheltema
Koningsplein 20, 1017 BB Amsterdam
Tel: (020) 5231411 *Fax:* (020) 6227684
E-mail: scheltema@scheltema.nl; informatie@scheltema.nl
Web Site: www.scheltema.nl
Key Personnel
General Manager: H Wijnants
Sales Manager: A Luinstra; C Noordhoek; Mrs T Scholtens
Founded: 1853
Type of Business: Major Independent Bookseller
Owned by: Boekhandels Groep Nederland
Branch Office(s)
Meibergdreef 9, 1105 AZ Amsterdam *Tel:* (020) 566 27 77 *Fax:* (020) 696 87 90 *E-mail:* amc@scheltema.nl
Roeterstr 41, 1030 BH Amsterdam *Tel:* (020) 420 53 67 *Fax:* (020) 420 64 27 *E-mail:* sarphati@scheltema.nl
Tafelbergweg 51, 1105 BD Amsterdam
Tel: (020) 652 12 94 *Fax:* (020) 652 12 93
E-mail: tafelbergweg@scheltema.nl
Weesperzijde 188, 1097 DZ Amsterdam
Tel: (020) 468 60 68 *Fax:* (020) 468 60 69
E-mail: leeuwenburg@scheltema.nl

Schuyt & Co Uitgevers en Importeurs BV
Nieuwe Gracht 56, 3512 LT Utrecht
Mailing Address: Postbus 404, 3500 AK Utrecht
Tel: (030) 7508273 *Fax:* (030) 7508327
E-mail: info@schuytco.nl
Web Site: www.schuyt-co.nl
Key Personnel
Man Dir: Patrick van Buuren *E-mail:* p.buuren@schuytco.nl
Owned by: Schuyt & Co Beheer BV

Valeton b v
Nes 35, Amsterdam
Tel: (020) 6201454 *Fax:* (020) 6279209
Key Personnel
President: Alexander Valeton
Vice President: Heleen Van Ketwich-Verschuur
Founded: 1990
Type of Business: Distributor, Exporter, Importer, Major Book Chain Headquarters, Wholesaler
Owned by: Alexander Valeton
Bookshop(s): Dam 8, 1012 CG Amsterdam; Westzeeoyk 20, Rotterdam

H de Vries Boeken
Gedempte Oude Gracht 27, 2011 GK Haarlem
Mailing Address: Postbus 274, 2000 AG Haarlem
Tel: (023) 5319458 *Fax:* (023) 5311680
E-mail: boeken@vries-boeken.com
Web Site: www.vries-boeken.com
Key Personnel
Man Dir: R H C de Vries; K de Vries Kuijper
Manager, General Bookshop: G Braaksma
Manager, School Textbooks: A Kroenburg
Founded: 1905
Type of Business: Major Independent Bookseller

Netherlands Antilles

De WitAruba Boekhandel
L G Smith Blvd 110, Oranjestad, Aruba
Mailing Address: PO Box 386, Oranjestad, Aruba
Tel: (0297) 823500 *Fax:* (0297) 821575
Cable: DEWITSTORES
Key Personnel
Man Dir: R de Zwart
Stationery, souvenirs, gifts, clothing.
Type of Business: Distributor, Importer, Major Independent Bookseller
Owned by: De Wit Stores NV

New Zealand

Arts Centre Bookshop
28 Worcester Blvd, Christchurch
Tel: (03) 365 5277 *Fax:* (03) 365 3293
E-mail: info@booksnz.com
Web Site: www.booksnz.com
Type of Business: Major Independent Bookseller

Bennetts Bookshop Ltd
Massey University Tritea Campus, Commercial Complex, Palmerston North
Tel: (06) 354 6020 *Fax:* (06) 354 6716
Toll Free Fax: 0800 118 333
E-mail: books@bennetts.co.nz; massey@bennetts.co.nz
Web Site: www.bennetts.co.nz *Cable:* Bennibooks
Key Personnel
Group General Manager: Trevor Day
Owned by: Blue Star Consumer Retailing Ltd
Branch Office(s)
Massey University Albany Campus, Albany, Auckland *Tel:* (09) 443 9707 *Fax:* (09) 443 9708 *E-mail:* aku@bennetts.co.nz
Auckland University of Technology, Commerce House, 360 Queen St, Auckland City *Tel:* (09) 307 9802 *Fax:* (09) 307 9927 *E-mail:* qau@bennetts.co.nz
Auckland University of Technology, Student Plaza Gate 2, Wellesley St, Auckland City *Tel:* (09) 307 9801 *Fax:* (09) 307 9986 *E-mail:* wau@bennetts.co.nz
Christchurch Polytechnic Institute of Technology, Madras St, Christchurch *Tel:* (03) 365 1394 *Fax:* (03) 365 7314 *E-mail:* chp@bennetts.co.nz
University of Waikato, Gate 5, Hillcrest Rd, Hamilton *Tel:* (07) 856 6813 *Fax:* (07) 856 2255 *E-mail:* wku@bennetts.co.nz
Walkato Institute of Technology, Gate 5, Tristram St, Hamilton *Tel:* (07) 839 0003 *Fax:* (07) 834 1291 *E-mail:* wkp@bennetts.co.nz
Manukau Institute of Technology, Gate 11, NP Block, Otara Rd, Manukau City *Tel:* (09) 274 8627 *Fax:* (09) 274 8830 *E-mail:* mkp@bennetts.co.nz
Auckland University of Technology Akoranga Campus, Gate 1, Akoranga Drive, Northcote *Tel:* (09) 307 9803 *Fax:* (09) 307 9967 *E-mail:* aau@bennetts.co.nz
Corner Lambton Quay & Bowen St, Wellington *Tel:* (04) 499 3433 *Fax:* (04) 499 3375 *E-mail:* gbs@bennetts.co.nz
Massey University Wellington, Gate E, Tasman St, Wellington *Tel:* (04) 384 1407 *Fax:* (04) 384 1408 *E-mail:* wgp@bennetts.co.nz

Blackmore's Booksellers BLA
284 Trafalgar St, Nelson
Tel: (03) 5489992 *Fax:* (03) 5466779
Key Personnel
Partner: Tim Blackmore; Jennifer Blackmore
Type of Business: Major Independent Bookseller

Hedley's Bookshop Ltd
150 Queen St, Masterton
Tel: (06) 3782875 *Fax:* (06) 3782570
E-mail: sales@hedleysbooks.co.nz
Web Site: www.hedleysbooks.co.nz
Key Personnel
Manager: David Hedley *Tel:* (061) 3 9499 2645
E-mail: david@hedleysbooks.com.au
Founded: 1907
Also publisher.
Type of Business: Distributor, Major Independent Bookseller
Branch Office(s)
Hedley Australia, PO Box 1058, Melbourne, Victoria 3079, Australia *Tel:* (02) 4992645 *Fax:* (03) 4994060
Bookshop(s): Hedley's Bookshop (BAM), Mezzanine level, Central Library Bldg, 65 Victoria St, Wellington *Tel:* (04) 4731730 *Fax:* (04) 4711635

Janeff Books (JM & MJ Books Ltd)
16 Te Mata Rd, Havelock North 4230
Tel: (070) 777783
Key Personnel
Owner: Max Dempsey; Margaret Dempsey
Type of Business: Major Independent Bookseller

JM & MJ Books Ltd, see Janeff Books (JM & MJ Books Ltd)

Kydds Paper Plus
77 Hakiaha St, Taumarunui
Tel: (07) 8957430 *Fax:* (07) 8957977
E-mail: kyddpp@xtra.co.nz
Web Site: www.middle-of-everywhere.co.nz/kyddspp.htm
Key Personnel
Owner: Mrs J J Kydd
Type of Business: Major Independent Bookseller

Lincoln University Bookshop
Lincoln University, Ellesmere Junction Rd/Springs Rd, Lincoln, Canterbury
Mailing Address: PO Box 94, Canterbury 8150
Tel: (03) 3252811 *Fax:* (03) 3252944
E-mail: info@lincoln.ac.nz
Web Site: www.lincoln.ac.nz
Key Personnel
Supervisor: Bronwyn Mclean *E-mail:* mcleanb@lincoln.ac.nz
Type of Business: Major Independent Bookseller

Living Word Distribution
52 Collingwood St, Hamilton 2001
Tel: (07) 839 5607 *Fax:* (07) 834 3916
E-mail: livingword.ltd@xtra.co.nz
Key Personnel
Executive Dir: G T Hooper
Founded: 1977
Subjects: Books, gifts, music & video, retailer
Type of Business: Distributor, Exporter, Importer, Major Independent Bookseller, Wholesaler
Parent Company: Living Word Distributors Ltd

McLeods Booksellers
1269 Tutanekai St, Rotorua
Mailing Address: PO Box 623, Rotorua
Tel: (07) 3485388 *Fax:* (07) 3490288
E-mail: mcleods@clear.net.nz
Web Site: www.mcleodsbooks.co.nz
Key Personnel
Manager: D C Thorp
Founded: 1944
Traditional, stock-holding combining selection & service with latest bibliographic technology. Specialise in: Maori books & floral art books.
Type of Business: Major Independent Bookseller

Omega Distributors Ltd
10 Andrew Baxter Dr, Mangere, 1701 Auckland
Mailing Address: PO Box 107025, Airport Oaks Mangere, 1730 Auckland
Tel: (09) 2570081 *Fax:* (09) 2570082
E-mail: books@omegavision.co.nz
Web Site: www.omegavision.co.nz/omega.html
Key Personnel
Executive Dir: Graham Walker
General Manager: M J Frith
Founded: 1958
Christian book/Bible/gift distributors.
Memberships: Booksellers Association of New Zealand; Christian Booksellers Association of New Zealand.
Type of Business: Distributor, Importer
Owned by: Vision Resources Ltd

One Way Book Centre
33 Formby Rd, Devonport 7310
Tel: (03) 64245731 *Fax:* (03) 64245731
E-mail: devcommchurch@hotmail.com
Web Site: www.devonport.tco.asn.au/commchurch/oneway.htm
Type of Business: Distributor, Importer, Major Independent Bookseller, Wholesaler

Pathfinder Bookshop
New Gallery Bldg, 38 Lorne St, Auckland Central
Tel: (09) 3790147 *Toll Free Tel:* 0800 55 44 55 *Fax:* (09) 3098167
E-mail: Tim@pathfinder.co.nz; Jennifer@pathfinder.co.nz
Web Site: www.pathfinder.co.nz
Founded: 1981
Type of Business: Major Independent Bookseller

Peaceful Living Publications
Unit 7B 42 Courtney Rd, Tauranga, BOP
Mailing Address: PO Box 300, Tauranga, BOP
Tel: (071) 5718105 *Fax:* (071) 5718513
E-mail: books@peaceful-living.co.nz
Key Personnel
Manager: Wayne Morgan
Office Manager: Maria Rawson
Metaphysics, mysticism, health, tarot cards, audio cassettes & CDs, self awareness & New Age literature.
Type of Business: Distributor

School Supplies (NZ) Ltd
13 Sir William Ave, East Tamaki, Auckland
Mailing Address: PO Box 58004, Greenmount
Tel: (03) 273 9883 *Toll Free Tel:* 800 577 700 *Fax:* (09) 273 9884 *Toll Free Fax:* 800 367 724
E-mail: orders@schoolsupplies.co.nz
Web Site: www.schoolsupplies.co.nz
Telex: NZ 63426
Key Personnel
General Manager: Graham Wadams
Curriculum Resource Manager: Michaela Davis
Type of Business: Distributor, Importer, Wholesaler
Owned by: New Zealand Office Products Ltd
Branch Office(s)
108 Bamford St, PO Box 19645, Woolston, Christchurch *Tel:* (03) 384-6499 *Fax:* 800-249-850
196-208 Middleton Rd, Churton Park, PO Box 50-384, Johnsonville, Wellington *Tel:* (04) 232 8680 *Fax:* (04) 232 9469

South Pacific Books Imports Ltd
PO Box 303 243, North Harbour, Auckland 1330
Tel: (09) 649 448 1591 *Fax:* (09) 649 448 1592

E-mail: sales@soupacbooks.co.nz
Web Site: www.soupacbooks.co.nz
Key Personnel
Man Dir: Alan McEldowney
Founded: 1984
Book wholesaler.
Warehouse: 6 King St, Grey Lynn, Auckland

South Sea Books
37 Holliss Ave, Cashmere, Christchurch
Tel: (03) 3317630
E-mail: southsea@ihug.co.nz
Web Site: www.abebooks.com/home/southsea
Key Personnel
Owner: Glenn Haszarde
Founded: 1984
Type of Business: Exporter, Importer, Major Independent Bookseller, Wholesaler

Techbooks
378 Broadway, Newmarket, Auckland
Mailing Address: Private Bag 99939, Newmarket, Auckland
Tel: (09) 524-0132 Fax: (09) 523-3769
E-mail: techbooks@techbooks.co.nz
Web Site: www.techbooks.co.nz
Key Personnel
Man Dir: Colin Greenwood
Founded: 1983
Type of Business: Major Independent Bookseller
Branch Office(s)
82 Waring Taylor St, Welington
Bookshop(s): 378-380 Broadway, Newmarket

Unity Books Ltd
57 Willis St, Wellington
Tel: (04) 499 4245 Fax: (04) 499 4246
E-mail: unity.books@clear.net.nz
Key Personnel
Dir: A H Preston
Manager: Tilly Lloyd
Type of Business: Major Independent Bookseller
Bookshop(s): Unity Books, 19 High St, Auckland
Tel: (09) 3070731 Fax: (09) 3734883

University Book Shop (Auckland) Ltd
Kate Edgar Bldg, 2 Alfred St, Auckland Central 1001
Mailing Address: PO Box 90944, Auckland Mail Centre, Auckland 1001
Tel: (09) 306 2700 Fax: (09) 306 2701
E-mail: campus@ubsbooks.co.nz
Web Site: www.ubsbooks.co.nz Cable: UNIBOOKS
Key Personnel
Manager: Ken McIntyre
Founded: 1966
Type of Business: Importer, Major Independent Bookseller
Owned by: Whitcoulls Ltd/Auckland University Students Association
Bookshop(s): Tamaki Campus, The Hub, Merton Rd, Auckland Tel: (09) 3737599 (ext 85295); Waiariki Campus, Mokoia Dr, Auckland Tel: (07) 3468806 Fax: (07) 3468806 E-mail: ubsbooks@ubsbooks.com

University Book Shop (Canterbury) Ltd
University of Canterbury, Private Bag 4800, Christchurch
Tel: (03) 3667001 Fax: (03) 3642999
E-mail: info@canterbury.ac.nz
Web Site: www.canterbury.ac.nz
Key Personnel
Manager: David Ault E-mail: david@ubscan.co.nz
Founded: 1971
Type of Business: Exporter, Importer, Major Independent Bookseller

University Book Shop (Otago) Ltd
378 Great King St, Dunedin
Mailing Address: PO Box 6060, Dunedin
Tel: (03) 4776976 Fax: (03) 4776571
E-mail: ubs@unibooks.co.nz
Web Site: www.unibooks.co.nz
Key Personnel
Manager: Bill Noble Tel: (03) 474 5401 (ext 888) E-mail: billn@unibooks.co.nz
Founded: 1945
Type of Business: Major Independent Bookseller

Whitcoulls Ltd
Level 5, Synergy House, 131 Queen St, Auckland
Mailing Address: Private Bag 92098, Auckland
Tel: (09) 356 5410 Fax: (09) 356 5423
E-mail: feedback@whitcoulls.co.nz
Web Site: www.whitcoulls.co.nz
Telex: NZ 60402
Key Personnel
Chief Executive: David Brown
General Manager: David Worley
Contact: Simone Howett
59 Stores nationwide.
Owned by: W H Smith

Nicaragua

Libreria Tecnologica Universitaria
Universidad Centroamericana, Pista de la Resistencia, Managua
Mailing Address: Apdo 69, Managua
Tel: (02) 773026 Fax: (02) 670106

Libreria Universitaria
Universidad Nacional Autonoma de Nicaragua, Recinto Universitario-Ruben, Dario, Managua
Tel: (0311) 2612; (0311) 2613

Nigeria

Ahmadu Bello University Bookshop Ltd
PMB 1094, Samaru, Zaria, Kaduna State
Tel: (069) 550054
Key Personnel
General Manager: K A Momoh

Benin University Bookshop
Ugbowo-Lagos Rd, Ugobowo, Benin City, Edo State
Tel: (052) 600443 Fax: (052) 602370
E-mail: registra@uniben.edu
Web Site: www.uniben.edu
Telex: 41365
Key Personnel
Manager: S O Ehiede

Challenge Bookshops
c/o ECWA Productions Ltd, 10, Kano Rd, Jos
Mailing Address: PMB 2010, Jos
Tel: (073) 53897; (073) 52230
Key Personnel
General Manager: E C Nwobilo
Type of Business: Wholesaler
Owned by: ECWA Productions Ltd

CSS Bookshops
Division of CSS Limited
19 Broad St, Lagos
Mailing Address: PO Box 174, Lagos
Tel: (01) 2633081; (01) 2637009; (01) 2637023; (01) 2633010 Fax: (01) 2637089
E-mail: cssbookshops@skannet.com.ng
Key Personnel
Chief Executive: Kola Olaitan
Secretary: Dotun Adegboyega
Founded: 1869
Also Publisher.
Type of Business: Distributor, Importer, Major Book Chain Headquarters, Wholesaler
Owned by: The Church of Nigeria

Fola Abbey Educational Book Services, Fola Abbey Bookshops Ltd
One Odulami Lane, off Kakawa St, Lagos, Lagos State
Tel: (01) 2636679 Fax: (01) 825268
Key Personnel
Chief Executive: Hakeem A Sanni
Suppliers of all Nigerian publications to Universities, Libraries & individuals.
Type of Business: Exporter

Mabrochi International Co Ltd
143 Moshood Abiola Way, Ebute Metta (West), Lagos, Lagos State
Mailing Address: PO Box 1509, Surulere PO, Lagos, Lagos State
E-mail: mabrochiadol@yahoo.com
Key Personnel
Sales Executive: Adol C Ofoegbu
Founded: 1976
Specialize in mail order services worldwide. Academic jobber for overseas universities & libraries. Subscription agent for Nigerian publications.
Type of Business: Distributor, Exporter, Importer, Major Independent Bookseller, Wholesaler
Branch Office(s)
7 Oyabiyi St, Yaba, Lagos, Lagos State (Tertiary textbooks)

Nigerian Book Suppliers Ltd
28, Akinremi St, Ikeja
Mailing Address: PO Box 4440, Ikeja
Tel: (01) 22407
Telex: 20202 Tds Box 052 Ikeja
Key Personnel
Man Dir: B Fatayi-Williams
Bookseller & library supplier specializing in professional books (especially legal, management, banking & accountancy), Africana, mass market paperback fiction & library titles for tertiary level libraries.

Odusote Bookstores Ltd
68 Obafemi Awolowo Way, Oke-Ado, Ibadan
Mailing Address: PO Box 244, Ibadan
Tel: (02) 2316451 Fax: (02) 2318781
E-mail: odubooks@infoweb.abs.net
Telex: 31215 (Odbook NG) Cable: ODBOOK, IBADAN
Key Personnel
Man Dir: Ola Odusote
Manager: Olufemi Odusote
Founded: 1964
Type of Business: Distributor, Wholesaler
Branch Office(s)
177 Herbert Macaulay St, Yaba, Lagos State
Tel: (01) 861248

University Bookshop Ltd
Obafemi Awolowo University, Ile-Ife, Osun State
Tel: (036) 230290 Cable: BOOKSHOP IFEVARSITY
Key Personnel
Man Dir: Oyeniyi Osundina
Founded: 1964
Type of Business: Major Independent Bookseller
Owned by: Obafemi Awolowo University
Branch Office(s)
Ado-Ekiti
Osogbo

NIGERIA

University Bookshop (Nigeria) Ltd
University of Ibadan, Ibadan, Oyo State
Tel: (02) 400550 (ext 1208); (02) 400550 (ext 1047); (02) 400614 (ext 1244); (02) 400614 (ext 1042)
Key Personnel
General Manager: Akin Aqbebi
Branch Office(s)
University College Hospital

University of Lagos Bookshop
PMB 1013, University of Lagos, Idiaraba, Lagos
Tel: (01) 820279 *Fax:* (01) 822644
Telex: 26983 Unilag.NG *Cable:* UNIVERSITY OF LAGOS
Key Personnel
Manager: Mrs Oluronke Orimalade
Founded: 1966
Type of Business: Importer
Branch Office(s)
College of Medicine, University of Lagos, Idi-Araba, Surulere, Lagos

University of Nigeria Bookshop Ltd
Nsukka, Enugu State
Tel: (042) 332077; (042) 771911
Key Personnel
Manager: B U Ezugwu
Founded: 1963
Books, stationery & related goods.
Membership(s): United Educational Institute Ltd.
Type of Business: Distributor, Major Independent Bookseller

John West Publications Co Ltd
Acme Rd, Lagos
Mailing Address: PO Box 2416, Lagos
Tel: (01) 932011
Telex: John West Ikeja
Key Personnel
Man Dir: Alhaji Lateef Kayode Jakande

Norway

A/L Biblioteksentralen (The Norwegian Library Bureau)
Malerhaugveien 20, 0661 Oslo
Mailing Address: Postboks 6142, Etterstad, 0602 Oslo
Tel: (022) 08 34 00 *Fax:* (022) 08 39 01
E-mail: bs@bibsent.no
Web Site: www.bibsent.no
Key Personnel
Administrative Dir: Borge Hofset *E-mail:* bho@bibsent.no
Head of Book/Media Dept: Toril Anderson
Founded: 1952
Bibliographic products & service; Materials, furnishings & interior architects for libraries.

Forlagsentralen ANS
Karihaugveien 22, 1086 Oslo
Mailing Address: Postboks 1, Furuset, 1001 Oslo
Tel: (022) 32 96 00 *Fax:* (022) 32 96 01
E-mail: firmapost@forlagsentralen.no
Web Site: www.forlagsentralen.no
Key Personnel
President: Eivind T Skogseide
Founded: 1964
Type of Business: Distributor

ARK Bokhandel
Formerly F Beyer Bok og Papirhandel A/S
Posboks 6693, St Olavs Plass, 0129 Oslo
Tel: 22 99 07 50 *Fax:* 22 99 07 51
E-mail: resepsjon@ark.no
Web Site: www.arkbokhandel.no *Cable:* BOKBEYER BERGEN
Key Personnel
Dir: Arne Henrik Frogh
Bookshop(s): Ark Aker Brygge, Fjordalleen 10, 0250 Oslo *Tel:* 22 83 81 33 *Fax:* 22 83 82 42 *E-mail:* aker.brygge@ark.no; Ark Amanda, Longhammerveien 27, 5536 Haugesund *Tel:* 52 71 98 11 *Fax:* 52 71 21 19 *E-mail:* amanda@ark.no; Ark Asker, Stroket 5, 1383 Asker *Tel:* 66 79 95 70 *Fax:* 66 90 05 80; 66 79 95 80 *E-mail:* asker@ark.no; Ark Bekkestua, Gamle Ringeriksv 37, 1357 Bekkestua *Tel:* 67 12 02 05 *Fax:* 67 12 30 42 *E-mail:* bekkestua@ark.no; Ark Berge, Prostebakken 3, 4006 Stavanger *Tel:* 51 89 52 50 *Fax:* 51 89 52 52 *E-mail:* berge@ark.no; Ark Berge avd BI, Hesbygt 5, 4014 Stavanger *Tel:* 51 55 02 21 *E-mail:* ark.bi@ark.no; Ark Beyer Asane, Asane Senter, 5116 Ulset *Tel:* 55 18 26 40 *Fax:* 55 19 49 25 *E-mail:* ark.beyer.aasane@ark.no; Ark Beyer Nesttun Senter, Nesttun Senter, Ostre Nesttunv 16, 5221 Nesttun *Tel:* 55 13 28 95 *Fax:* 55 13 28 96 *E-mail:* nesttun.senter@ark.no; Ark Beyer Strandgaten, Strandgt 4, 5013 Bergen *Tel:* 55 30 77 00 *Fax:* 55 30 77 10 *E-mail:* beyer@ark.no; Ark Beyer Vestkanten, Vestkanten, 5171 Loddefjord *Tel:* 55 26 90 92 *Fax:* 55 26 56 84 *E-mail:* vestkanten@ark.no; Ark Brundalen, Brundalen Videregaende skole, 7458 Jakobsli *Tel:* 73 91 37 80 *Fax:* 73 91 37 80 *E-mail:* brundalen@ark.no; Ark Bruns Brunhjornet, Kongensgt 10/14, 7484 Trondheim *Tel:* 73 87 93 00 *Fax:* 73 87 93 05 *E-mail:* bruns@ark.no; Ark Bruns City Syd, City Syd, Ostre Rosten, 7075 Tiller *Tel:* 72 88 88 84 *Fax:* 72 88 13 50 *E-mail:* citysyd@ark.no; Ark Bruns Melhus, Melhus torget, 7224 Melhus *Tel:* 72 87 09 90 *Fax:* 72 87 28 68 *E-mail:* melhus@ark.no; Ark Bruns Moholt, Moholt storsenter, Brosetvn 177, 7048 Trondheim *Tel:* 73 93 15 70 *Fax:* 73 93 15 65 *E-mail:* moholt@ark.no; Ark Bruns Torget, Trondheim Torg, Tinghusplassen 1, 7013 Trondheim *Tel:* 73 87 93 27 *Fax:* 73 50 50 53 *E-mail:* torget@ark.no; Ark City Nord, City Nord Stormyra, 8013 Bodo *Tel:* 75 50 80 40 *Fax:* 75 50 80 41 *E-mail:* citynord@ark.no; Ark Dahl, Storgt 29, 6413 Molde *Tel:* 71 20 55 00 *Fax:* 71 20 55 01; 71 20 55 02 *E-mail:* dahl@ark.no; Ark Down Town, Storgt 70, 3921 Porsgrunn *Tel:* 35 55 76 70 *Fax:* 35 55 76 70 *E-mail:* down.town@ark.no; Ark Dyring, Storgt 154, 3915 Porsgrunn *Tel:* 35 56 98 50 *Fax:* 35 56 98 60 *E-mail:* dyring@ark.no; Ark Egertorget, Ovre Slottsgt 23/25, 0157 Oslo *Tel:* 22 47 32 00 *Fax:* 22 47 32 49 *E-mail:* egertorget@ark.no; Ark Farris, Yttersovn 2, 3274 Larvik *Tel:* 33 11 66 00 *Fax:* 33 11 66 05 *E-mail:* farris@ark.no; Ark Futura, Industrivn 17, 6517 Kristiansund *Tel:* 71 58 44 80 *Fax:* 71 58 44 81 *E-mail:* futura@ark.no; Ark Glasshuset, Storgt 5, 8006 Bodo *Tel:* 75 54 97 00 *Fax:* 75 54 97 01 *E-mail:* glasshuset@ark.no; Ark Glemmen vgs, Glemmen videregaende skole, Taraveien 13, 1601 Fredrikstad *Tel:* 69 31 52 94; Ark Grunerlokka, Thorvald Meyersgt 46, 0552 Oslo *Tel:* 22 71 85 90 *Fax:* 22 71 85 91 *E-mail:* grunerlokka@ark.no; Ark Herkules, Ulefossvn 32B, 3730 Skien *Tel:* 35 53 41 80 *Fax:* 35 53 20 22 *E-mail:* herkules@ark.no; Ark Holmen, Holmensenteret, Vogellund 6, 1394 Nesbru *Tel:* 66 84 77 24 *Fax:* 66 84 96 80 *E-mail:* holmen@ark.no; Ark Homansbyen, Hegdehaugsveien 32, 0352 Oslo *Tel:* 22 46 53 35 *Fax:* 22 46 53 15 *E-mail:* homansbyen@ark.no; Ark Jessheim, Furusethgt 5, 2050 Jessheim *Tel:* 63 99 69 30 *Fax:* 63 99 69 35 *E-mail:* jessheim@ark.no; Ark Just, Torget 1, 3256 Larvik *Tel:* 33 18 44 20 *Fax:* 33 13 02 24 *E-mail:* just@ark.no; Ark Kilden, Gartnervn 16, 4016 Stavanger *Tel:* 51 90 61 80 *Fax:* 51 90 61 81 *E-mail:* kilden@ark.no; Ark Klofta, Trondheimsveien 86, 2040 Klofta *Tel:* 63 98 12 01 *Fax:* 63 98 24 84 *E-mail:* klofta@ark.no; Ark Kohns, Torvet 6, 2000 Lillestrom *Tel:* 63 81 60 05 *Fax:* 63 81 60 81 *E-mail:* kohns@ark.no; Ark Kvadrat, Gamle Stokkav 1, 4313 Sandnes *Tel:* 51 96 04 90 *Fax:* 51 96 04 91 *E-mail:* kvadrat@ark.no; Ark Majorstuen, Valkyriegt 1, 0366 Oslo *Tel:* 22 93 16 80 *Fax:* 22 93 16 99; 22 93 16 90 *E-mail:* majorstuen@ark.no; Ark Manglerud, Manglerud senter, Plogveien 6, 0679 Oslo *Tel:* 22 26 43 35 *E-mail:* manglerud@ark.no; Ark Metro, Solheimsvn 85, 1473 Lorenskog *Tel:* 67 97 14 14 *Fax:* 67 97 48 78 *E-mail:* metro@ark.no; Ark Nordstrand, Ekebergvn 228B, 1112 Oslo *Tel:* 22 28 80 10 *Fax:* 22 28 80 25 *E-mail:* nordstrand@ark.no; Ark Odds, Storgt 7, 8039 Bodo *Tel:* 75 54 99 00 *Fax:* 75 54 99 01 *E-mail:* odds@ark.no; Ark Osteras, Osterassenteret, Otto Rugesv 80, 1361 Osteras *Tel:* 67 14 48 06 *Fax:* 67 14 97 10 *E-mail:* ark.osteraas@ark.no; Ark Qvist, Drammensveien 16, 0255 Oslo *Tel:* 22 54 26 00 *Fax:* 22 54 26 11 *E-mail:* qvist@ark.no; Ark Roseby, Lingedalsvn 6/10, 6415 Molde *Tel:* 71 25 92 40 *Fax:* 71 25 92 41 *E-mail:* roseby@ark.no; Ark Sandvika, Radmann Halmrastv 7, 1337 Sanvika *Tel:* 67 54 05 80 *Fax:* 67 54 58 92 *E-mail:* sandvika@ark.no; Ark Sartor, Sartor Senter, 5353 Straume *Tel:* 56 38 19 55 *Fax:* 56 33 26 99 *E-mail:* sartor@ark.no; Ark Selbu, 7580 Selbu *Tel:* 73 81 75 20 *Fax:* 73 81 75 20 *E-mail:* selbu@ark.no; Ark Sjolyst, Karenlyst Alle 16, 0278 Oslo *Tel:* 22 56 09 85 *Fax:* 22 56 09 86 *E-mail:* sjolyst@ark.no; Ark Solli Plass, Drammensvn 20, 0255 Oslo *Tel:* 22 44 17 50 *Fax:* 22 56 07 04 *E-mail:* solli.plass@ark.no; Ark Steinkjer, Globus Storsenter, Sjofartsgt 2, 7729 Steinkjer *Tel:* 74 13 51 50 *Fax:* 74 13 51 51 *E-mail:* steinkjer@ark.no; Ark Stjordal, Torgkvartalet, Stokmovn 2, 7500 Stjordal *Tel:* 74 84 03 30 *Fax:* 74 84 03 31 *E-mail:* stjordal@ark.no; Ark Stord, Osen 3, 5411 Stord *Tel:* 53 41 14 11 *Fax:* 53 41 39 50 *E-mail:* stord@ark.no; Ark Storgata, Storgata 33, 0184 Oslo *Tel:* 22 11 34 05 *Fax:* 22 11 04 46 *E-mail:* storgata@ark.no; Ark Stovner, Stovner Senter 3, 0985 Oslo *Tel:* 22 10 09 50 *Fax:* 22 10 20 29 *E-mail:* stovner@ark.no; Ark Strommen, Stoperiveien 5, 2010 Strommen *Tel:* 63 81 66 60 *Fax:* 63 81 93 50 *E-mail:* strommen@ark.no; Ark Student Haugesund, Bjornsonsgt 45, 5528 Haugesund *Tel:* 52 70 26 91 *Fax:* 52 70 26 92 *E-mail:* student.haugesund@ark.no; Ark Student Rommetveit, Hogskolen, 5414 Stord *Tel:* 53 49 14 17 *Fax:* 53 49 15 17 *E-mail:* student.rommetveit@ark.no; Ark Sund, Haraldsgt 157, 5527 Haugesund *Tel:* 52 70 41 50 *Fax:* 52 71 59 66 *E-mail:* sund@ark.no; Ark Sverdrup, Nedre Enggt 5, 6509 Kristiansund *Tel:* 71 57 09 60 *Fax:* 71 57 09 70 *E-mail:* sverdrup@ark.no; Ark Torvbyen, Torvbyen kjopesenter, Brochsgt 7/11, 1607 Fredrikstad *Tel:* 69 30 14 70 *Fax:* 69 30 14 79 *E-mail:* torvbyen@ark.no; Ark Tveita, Tvetenvn 150, 0617 Oslo *Tel:* 22 75 66 50 *Fax:* 22 75 66 51 *E-mail:* tveita@ark.no; Ark Ulleval, Sognsvn 75, Pb 3863, 0855 Oslo *Tel:* 23 00 99 50 *Fax:* 22 56 59 83 *E-mail:* ullevaal@arkbokhandel.no; Ark Vestnes, 6390 Vestnes *Tel:* 71 18 01 15 *Fax:* 71 18 90 04 *E-mail:* vestnes@ark.no; Ark Vinterbro, Vinterbrosenteret, Sjoskogvn 7, 1407 Vinterbro *Tel:* 64 96 31 11 *Fax:* 64 96 31 12 *E-mail:* vinterbro@ark.no

F Beyer Bok og Papirhandel A/S, see ARK Bokhandel

BOOK DEALERS — PAKISTAN

Gardum A/S
Soregata 22-24, 4002 Stavanger
Mailing Address: Postboks 242 Sentrum, 4002 Stavinger
Tel: 51894440 *Fax:* 51894404
E-mail: firmapost@gardum.no
Key Personnel
Manager: Rein Fridtjot Gardum Gardum
Fantasy & Science Fiction, both in English & Norwegian.

Libris Emo AS
Boks 40, 2013 Skjetten
Tel: 63849200 *Fax:* 63849345
Key Personnel
President: Torgeir Daal
Chain Dir: Morten Aas
Founded: 1972
Type of Business: Major Book Chain Headquarters
Owned by: Aker RGI

Lyngs Bokhandel A/S
Postboks 327, 7001 Trondheim
Tel: 73512544 *Fax:* 73512544
Key Personnel
Manager: Ragnvald C Knudsen
Founded: 1927
Type of Business: Major Independent Bookseller

Olaf Norlis Bokhandel A/S
Universitetsgt 20-24, 0162 Oslo
Mailing Address: Postboks 1990 Vika, 0125 Oslo
Tel: (022) 004300 *Fax:* (022) 422651
E-mail: info@norli.no
Web Site: www.norli.no
Key Personnel
Manager: Tom Vister
Marketing Manager: Hans Petter Yssen
Founded: 1890
Specialize in medicine, education, business, computers, travel, Scandinavian literature, books in minority & immigrant languages & library supplier.
Type of Business: Distributor, Exporter, Importer, Major Independent Bookseller, Wholesaler
Owned by: H Aschehoug & Co W Nygaard A/S

Norsk Bokdistribusjon
Vakaasveien 7, Hvalstad (Asker)
Mailing Address: Postboks 203, 1379 Nesbru
Tel: 66 84 90 40 *Fax:* 66 84 55 90
E-mail: vv@vettviten.no
Web Site: www.vettviten.no
Key Personnel
Publisher: Jan Lien
Sales & Marketing Manager: Jo Lien
Founded: 1987
Specialize in computer science, technology & medicine.
Type of Business: Distributor, Importer, Wholesaler
Owned by: Vett & Viten as

Sentraldistribusjon ANS
Ostre Akerv 61, 0582 Oslo
Tel: (022) 98 57 10 *Fax:* (022) 98 57 20
E-mail: sdinfo@sd.no
Web Site: www.sd.no
Key Personnel
President: Roland Hellberg
Vice President: Jan Erik Stokke
Type of Business: Distributor
Owned by: Cappelens Publishing

SiT Tapir Fagbokhandel
Formerly Tapir Trykkeri
Nardoveien 12, 7005 Trondheim
Tel: 73598420 *Fax:* 73598495
E-mail: forlag@tapir.no
Web Site: www.campus.tapir.no
Key Personnel
Manager: Hans G Auganaes
Founded: 1921
Type of Business: Distributor, Exporter, Importer, Major Independent Bookseller, Wholesaler
Branch Office(s)
Alfred Getz vei 3, Gloshaugen, Manager: Svanhild H Karlsen *Tel:* 73593231 *E-mail:* svanhild.h.karlsen@tapir.no
Gunnerus Gate 1, Kalvskinnet, Manager: Randi Wist *Tel:* 73559780 *E-mail:* randi.wist@tapir.no
Leangen Alle 2, 2nd floor, Leangen, Manager: Inger J Nordvik *Tel:* 7359370 *E-mail:* inger.j.nordvik@tapir.no
Jonsvannsveien 82, Moholt, Manager: Anne B Michalsen *Tel:* 73559086 *E-mail:* anne.b.michalsen@tapir.no
Rotvoll Alle, Rotvoll, Manager: Charlotte Oiesvold *Tel:* 73559826 *E-mail:* charlotte.oiesvold@tapir.no
Queen Maud's College of Early Childhood Education (DMMH), Thoning Owesens Gate 18, 7044 Trondheim, Manager: Karin Keiseraas *Tel:* 73805276 *E-mail:* karin.keiseraas@tapir.no
Universitetet Dragvoll, Trondheim, Manager: Ian Page *Tel:* 73598451 *E-mail:* ian.page@tapir.no

Tanum Karl Johan A/S
Karl Johans gate 37-41, 0162 Oslo
Mailing Address: Postboks 1743, Vika, 0121 Oslo
Tel: (022) 41 11 00 *Fax:* (022) 33 32 75
E-mail: karl.johan@tanum.no; nettservice@tanum.no
Web Site: www.tanum.no
Telex: 72427 Tanum N *Cable:* TANUMBOK
Key Personnel
Dir: Petter A Knudsen
Manager: Bjorg Andreassen
Type of Business: Exporter, Importer, Wholesaler

Tapir Trykkeri, see SiT Tapir Fagbokhandel

Unipa A/S
Bredalsmarken 15-17, 5006 Bergen
Mailing Address: Postboks 2607 Mohlenpris, N-5836 Bergen
Tel: (05) 31 84 05 *Fax:* (05) 32 42 70
E-mail: unipa@online.no
Key Personnel
Man Dir: Terje Bergesen *E-mail:* terje.bergesen@unipa.com
Type of Business: Major Book Chain Headquarters

Wennergren-Cappelen A/S
Ovre Vollgate 15, Sentrum, 0105 Oslo
Mailing Address: Postboks 738 Sentrum, 0105 Oslo
Tel: (022) 35 72 50 *Fax:* (022) 33 71 04
E-mail: wenca@wenca.no
Web Site: www.wenca.no
Key Personnel
President: Glenn Andersen
Founded: 1829
Also Publishers, Stamp Dealers & Antiquariat.
Type of Business: Distributor, Importer, Wholesaler
Parent Company: Cap AS
Ultimate Parent Company: J W Cappelen, Universitetsgaten 20, 0162 Oslo (Also owner)

Pakistan

Comprehensive Book Service
56-New Urdu Bazar, Mohan Rd, Karachi 74200
Tel: (021) 214682 *Fax:* (021) 2632131
E-mail: shahzad@cbs.khi.sdnpk.undp.org
Telex: 23035 Pcokr *Cable:* GOODBOOKS
Key Personnel
Proprietor: Shahzad Najmee
Publishers, booksellers and library suppliers.
Type of Business: Distributor, Exporter, Importer, Major Independent Bookseller, Wholesaler

Ferozsons (Pvt) Ltd
60 Shahrah-e-Quaid-e-Azam, Lahore
Tel: (042) 6301196; (042) 6301197; (042) 6301198; (042) 111-62-62-62 *Fax:* (042) 6369204
E-mail: ferozsons@showroom.edunet.sdnpk.undp.org
Web Site: www.ferozsons.com.pk *Cable:* FEROZSONS
Key Personnel
Dir: Mr Zaheer Salam
Man Dir & Publicity: A Salam
Dir, Business Development: Muqeet Salam
Manager, Karachi: Ms Gul Afshan
Manager, Rawalpindi: Aftab A Tariq
Founded: 1894
Also Publisher & Printer.
Type of Business: Distributor, Exporter, Importer, Major Independent Bookseller, Wholesaler
Branch Office(s)
1st floor, Mehran Heights, Main Clifton Rd, Karachi, Sindh *Fax:* (042) 5835170
277 Peshawar Rd, Rawalpindi, Punjab *Fax:* (051) 5564273

Liberty Books (Pvt) Ltd
3 Rafiq Plaza, M R Kayani Rd, Saddar, Karachi
Mailing Address: PO Box 7427, Saddar, Karachi
Tel: (021) 111-311-113; (021) 5671240; (021) 5671244 *Fax:* (021) 5684319
E-mail: info@libertybooks.com
Web Site: www.libertybooks.com
Key Personnel
Man Dir: A Hussein
Sales Dir: Saleem Hussein
Founded: 1948
Type of Business: Distributor, Importer, Wholesaler
Branch Office(s)
Alternate Book Shop, Near Pizza Hut Boat Basin, Clifton, Karachi *Tel:* (021) 5373443
Book Land, Jinnah Rd, Quetta *Tel:* (081) 824295
Books & More, Shop No 125, Park Towers, LG 16 Lower Ground floor, Clifton, Karachi *Tel:* (021) 5832525 (ext 125)
International Book Service, Al-Mustafa Plaza Chandni Chowk, Room 11, Ground floor, Rawalpindi *Tel:* (051) 4420924
Liberty Books, Shop No G-1, Plot No GP-5, Block 5, Clifton, Karachi *Tel:* (021) 5374153
Liberty Books Dolmen Mall, Shop No G 101, Dolmen Mall, Tariq Rd, PECHS, Karachi *Tel:* (021) 4387085
Liberty Books Park Towers, Shop No A-11, Park Towers, Ground floor, Clifton, Karachi *Tel:* (021) 5832525 (ext 111)
London Book Co, 3, Kohsar Market, F 6/3, Islamabad *Tel:* (051) 2823852
Marriott Book Shop, Lobby Karachi Marriott Hotel, Abdullah Haroon Rd, Karachi *Tel:* (021) 5216532
Pearl Continental Book Shop, Lobby Pearl Continental Hotel Rd, Karachi *Tel:* (021) 5219829
Sheraton Book Shop, Lobby Karachi Sheraton Hotel, Club Rd, Karachi *Tel:* (021) 5688374
Variety Books, Liberty Market, Lahore *Tel:* (042) 5758355
Agha's Super Market, Uzma Court DC3 Block 8, Kehkashan 5, Clifton, Karachi 75600 *Tel:* (021) 5833119; (021) 5833120; (021) 5833121
The Forum, Suite No 123-124, G-20, Block 9, Clifton, Karachi *Tel:* (021) 5831275; (021) 5831276; (021) 5832687; (021) 5832688

NGM Communication
Gulberg Colony, Lahore 54660

PAKISTAN

Mailing Address: PO Box 3033, Lahore, Punjab 54660
Tel: (042) 5713849
E-mail: ngm@shoa.net; anjeeam@yahoo.com
Web Site: www.geocities.com/angeeam
Key Personnel
Editor: Andy Nizami
Founded: 1980
Member of The Pakistan Publishers & Booksellers Association (Karachi Zone). Commercial & Government Booksellers. Dealers in Back issues. International subscription Agents for Pakistani Journals, Periodicals, Serials & Newspapers. Library Suppliers. Publishers' Representatives. Bankers; Habib Bank Limited.
Type of Business: Distributor, Exporter, Major Book Chain Headquarters, Major Independent Bookseller, Wholesaler
Owned by: Fatima Nizami

Pak American Commercial (Pvt) Ltd
53/2 Kashmir Rd, Rawalpindi
Tel: (051) 563709 *Fax:* (051) 565190 *Cable:* PAKACINC KARACHI
Key Personnel
Dir: Ahsan Jaffri
Retail bookseller & subscription agent; also publisher.
Type of Business: Importer, Major Independent Bookseller, Wholesaler
Branch Office(s)
1st floor, Pak Chambers, 5 Temple Rd, Lahore

Pak Book Corporation
Aziz Chambers, 21 Queen's Rd, 54000 Lahore
Tel: (042) 111 636 636 *Fax:* (042) 6362328
E-mail: pbc@brain.net.pk
Key Personnel
Man Dir: M A Khan Akter
Dir: M Iqbal Cheema
Founded: 1975
Deal with scientific books, journals & films & CD-ROM databases.
Type of Business: Distributor, Exporter, Importer, Wholesaler
Branch Office(s)
G-6/1/1, Khayaban-E-Suharwardy, Islamabad
Star Centre, Main Tariq Rd, PECHS, Karachi

Paramount Books (Pvt) Ltd
PECH Society, 152/0 Block 1, Karachi 75400
Tel: (021) 455 0661 *Fax:* (021) 455 3772
E-mail: parabks@cyber.net.pk
Telex: 25856 PBL PAK *Cable:* PARABOOKS KARACHI
Key Personnel
Dir: Iqbal S Mohammad
Manager: Saleem A Latif
Founded: 1947
Type of Business: Distributor, Wholesaler
Branch Office(s)
Lahore
Rawalpindi

Royal Book Co
232 Saddar Co-operative Market, Abdullah Haroon Rd, Karachi 74400
Mailing Address: PO Box 7737, Karachi 74400
Tel: (021) 5684244 *Fax:* (021) 5683706
E-mail: royalbook@hotmail.com
Leading Publisher.
Type of Business: Distributor, Exporter, Importer, Major Independent Bookseller, Wholesaler
Branch Office(s)
402 Rehman Centre, Zaibunnisa St, Karachi 74400 *Tel:* (021) 5670628
Showroom(s): BE 5 Rex Centre, Zaibunnisa St, Karachi 74400

West-Pakistan Publishing Co (Pvt) Ltd
17 Urdu Bazar, Lahore
Mailing Address: GPO Box No 374, Lahore
Tel: (042) 52427 *Cable:* WESPUBLISH LAHORE
Key Personnel
Chief Executive: Syed Ahsan Shah
Founded: 1932
Also publisher.
Type of Business: Exporter, Importer, Wholesaler

Panama

Libreria Cultural Panamena SA
Via Espana 16, Apdo 2018, Panama
Tel: 2235628; 2236267 *Fax:* 2237280 *Cable:* CULPASA
Key Personnel
Manager: Amador j Fraguela
Founded: 1955
Type of Business: Distributor, Exporter, Importer, Major Book Chain Headquarters, Wholesaler
Owned by: Libreria Cultural Panamena SA, Distribudoira Cultural y Manfer SA

Libreria Menendez
Galerias Obarrio, Via Brasil, Panama
Tel: 2258996
Branch Office(s)
Libreria Menendez Paitilla
Libreria Santa Ana, Plaza Santa Ana
Ave Justo Arosemena y Calle 36

Papua New Guinea

University Book Shop Inc
University Papua New Guinea, Waigani Dr, Waigani
Mailing Address: PO Box 114, University, Waigani
Tel: 326 7375 *Fax:* 326 0961
Telex: NE 22366
Key Personnel
Manager: E Guy

Paraguay

Libreria Comuneros
Cerro Cora 289, Casella Correo 930, Asuncion
Tel: (021) 446-176; (021) 444-667 *Fax:* (021) 444-667
Web Site: www.uiowa.edu
Key Personnel
Proprietor: Oscar R Rolon
Type of Business: Distributor, Exporter, Importer, Major Independent Bookseller, Wholesaler

Libreria Internacional SA
Estrella 723, Asuncion
Tel: (021) 491 423; (021) 491 424 *Fax:* (021) 449 730
Key Personnel
Manager: Victor Buzo
Founded: 1953
Type of Business: Distributor, Importer, Wholesaler
Bookshop(s): Casa Central, Estrella 723, Asuncion

Agencia de Librerias Nizza SA
Eligio Ayala 1073, Casilla de Correo 2596, Asuncion
Tel: (021) 47160
Owned by: Ediciones Nizza

Peru

Librerias ABC SA
Sta Catalina 217, Apdo 53, Arequipa
Tel: (054) 422900; (054) 422902 *Fax:* (054) 422901 *Cable:* MOLAGENT LIMA
Key Personnel
Man Dir: Herbert H Moll
Branch Office(s)
Edificio El Pacifico, Miraflores
Centro Comercial Todos, San Isidro

Adriatica
Jiron Junin 565, Trujillo
Tel: (044) 291569 *Fax:* (044) 294242
E-mail: libreria@adriaticaperu.com
Web Site: www.adriaticaperu.com
Key Personnel
Manager: Adriana Doig Mannucci
Founded: 1994
Type of Business: Distributor, Importer, Major Independent Bookseller
Branch Office(s)
Av Larco 857, 2 do Piso, Trujillo

Distribuidora Importadora Durand SA
Jr San Pedro 311-313, Lima 34
Tel: (014) 4452113 *Fax:* (014) 4463190
Key Personnel
General Dir: Arturo Durand Gamero
Type of Business: Distributor, Importer, Wholesaler

Ediciones Euroamericanas SA
Av Emancipacion 234, Lima 1
Tel: (014) 4274686 *Fax:* (014) 4280545
Key Personnel
Manager: Juan Moncayo Larrea
Founded: 1985
Type of Business: Distributor, Importer, Wholesaler

Ediciones Zeta SCR Ltda
Pachacutec 1414, Jesus Maria, Lima
Mailing Address: PO Box 4050, Lima
Tel: (014) 472-5942; (014) 472-7778 *Fax:* (014) 472-9890; (014) 472-0781 *Cable:* EDIZETA LIMA
Key Personnel
Manager: Jorge Zavaleta
Founded: 1978
Type of Business: Distributor, Importer, Wholesaler
Bookshop(s): Zeta Bookstore SRL, Cmdte Espinar 219, Miraflores, Lima

Liberia Editorial Minerva-Miraflores
Av Larco No 299, Miraflores, Lima 18
Tel: (014) 4475499 *Fax:* (014) 4458583
E-mail: minerva@chavin-rcp-net-pe
Key Personnel
General Dir: Sandro Mariategui Chiappe
Type of Business: Distributor, Importer, Major Book Chain Headquarters, Major Independent Bookseller, Wholesaler
Branch Office(s)
Miraflores, Surquillo San Borja
Bookshop(s): Av La Paz Nro 210, Miraflores; Av Primavera 2593, San Borja

Libreria l'Universidad, Nicolas Ojeda Fierro e Hijos SRL Ltda
Ave Nicolas de Pierola 639, Lima
Tel: (014) 282461; (014) 282036
Branch Office(s)
Ave Nicolas de Pierola 681, Lima *Tel:* 282036

Sociedad Biblica Peruana Asociacion Cultural
Av Petit Thouars 991, Lima
Tel: (014) 4330232 *Fax:* (014) 4336389
E-mail: sbpac01@telemail.telematic.edu.pe
Key Personnel
General Secretary: Ing P A Quiroz
Founded: 1947
Type of Business: Distributor, Exporter, Importer
Owned by: SBP

Libreria Studium SA
Pl Francia 1164, Lima 1
Mailing Address: PO Box 2139, Lima 1
Tel: (01) 275960; (01) 326278; (01) 325528
Fax: (01) 4325354
Key Personnel
Purchasing & Exporting Manager: Sergio Costa B
Also Publisher.
Branch Office(s)
Calle Moral 107A-107B, Arequipa
Calle Arequipa 110, Ayacucho
Saenz Pena 625, Callao
Elias Aguirre 251, Chiclayo
Meson de la Estrella 144, Cuzco
Calle Real 377, Huancayo
Tacna 145, Ica
Prospero 268-270, Iquitos
Colmena 626, Lima
Jiron de la Union 560, Lima
Ave Larco 720, Miraflores
Tacna 216, Piura
Francisco Pizarro 533, Trujillo

Libreria y Distribuidora de la Universidad Nacional Mayor de San Marcos
Av Venezuela cdra 34, Ciudad Universitaria-costado de la piscina, Lima 1
Tel: (01) 464-0560 *Fax:* (014) 464-0560
E-mail: libreria@unmsm.edu.pe
Web Site: www.unmsm.edu.pe
Key Personnel
Administrator: Edilberto Chuchon Huamani
Type of Business: Distributor, Importer

Philippines

Bookmark Inc
264-A Pablo Ocampo Sr Ave, Makati City
Tel: (02) 8958061; (02) 8958062; (02) 8958063; (02) 8958064; (02) 8958065 *Fax:* (02) 8970824
E-mail: bookmark@info.com.ph
Web Site: www.bookmark.com.ph
Key Personnel
General Manager: Jose Maria Lorenzo Tan
Founded: 1945
Also Bookselling, Publishing & Retailing.
Type of Business: Exporter
Bookshop(s): Puso ng Baguio Bldg, Session Rd, Baguio City *Tel:* (074) 442-4912; T Pinpin St, Binondo, Manila *Tel:* (02) 241-5071; 35-H Amon Court Gate 1, Salinas Drive, Lahug, Cebu City *Tel:* (032) 233-6679 *Fax:* (032) 231-0428; 260 Osmena Blvd, Cebu City *Fax:* (032) 253-1395; The Filipino Bookstore, City Triangle, C M Recto Ave, Davao City *Tel:* (082) 224-4000; (082) 224-4180; The Filipino Bookstore, G-72, Glorietta 1, Ayala Center, Makati City *Tel:* (02) 867-2260; (02) 867-2261; 254 Sen Gil Puyat Ave, Makati City *Tel:* (02) 843-1126; Bistro Remedios M Adriatico St, 2nd floor, Remedios Circle, Malate, Manila *Tel:* (02) 522-5663; The Filipino Bookstore, Unit 123-B, Level 1, Shangri La Plaza, EDSA cor Shaw Blvd, Mandaluyong *Tel:* (02) 638-4469; (02) 638-4470; Brgy Tambaling, El Salvador, Misamis Oriental *Tel:* (08822) 755-652; (08822) 755-496; Benmar Bldg 1, Door E, Concepcion Grande, Naga City *Tel:* (054) 472-3665; Lim Bldg Sevilla Norte, Door 6P, National Rd, San Fernando City *Tel:* (072) 242-0640; Brgy Uno, Gen Malvar Ave, Sto Tomas, Batangas *Tel:* (043) 778-3723; (043) 778-3725; University Parkway, Fort Bonifacio Global City, Taguig, Metro Manila

Felta Book Sales Inc
Windsor Tower, Rm 204, Legaspi St, Legaspi Village, Makati City
Tel: (02) 912-1397; (02) 438-1756 *Fax:* (02) 912-7633
Key Personnel
President: Felicito Abiva
Founded: 1969
US & UK Publisher's Representative (Educational, Children's Books, Mass Paperback); Licensee of Educational Materials (Elem - High School); Journal Subscription Agent (Medical & Professional).
Type of Business: Distributor, Wholesaler
Branch Office(s)
110 Nathan St, White Plains, Quezon City

Goodwill Bookstore
Goodwill Bldg, 4th floor, 393 Gil Puyat Ave, Makati City
Tel: (02) 895-8684 *Fax:* (02) 895-7854
E-mail: gbs@goodwillbookstore.net
Web Site: www.goodwillbookstore.com
Telex: 27302 Gtc Ph *Cable:* Gotrade Manila
Key Personnel
President & General Manager: Manuel Cancio
Founded: 1938
Branch Office(s)
Pavillion Mall, Barangay San Antonio, BiOan, Laguna, Branch Manager: Ethel Mallabo *Tel:* (049) 520-8240 *Fax:* (049) 411-7147
SM Southmall, Zapote-Alabang Rd, Brgy Talon, Las PiOas City, Branch Manager: Peria Mondejar *Tel:* (02) 800-4044 *Fax:* (02) 800-4045
49 P del Rosario St, Cebu City, Wholesale Dir: Rose Rubio *Tel:* (032) 254-5547 *Fax:* (032) 255-0826
WVSU, Luna St, La Paz, Iloilo City, Branch Manager: Ronnie Bansale *Tel:* (033) 320-8570 *Fax:* (033) 320-8540
Glorietta 3, Ayala Center, Makati City, Retail Sales Dir: Joan L Cruz *Tel:* (02) 813-4956; (02) 813-4957 *Fax:* (02) 810-5926; (02) 810-9033
SM Megamall, Bldg A, EDSA corner J Vargas Ave, Mandaluyong City, Branch Manager: Bella Obispo *Tel:* (02) 633-6372 *Fax:* (02) 633-6371
513 Rizal Ave, Manila, Branch Manager: Peggy Calilong *Tel:* (02) 733-4089 *Fax:* (02) 733-4090
380 Quezon Ave, Quezon, Wholesale Dir: Archie Abad *Tel:* (02) 732-7433; (02) 732-7436; (02) 732-7437 *Fax:* (02) 741-4289
SM Annex, SM City, North EDSA, Quezon City, Branch Manager: Lorrie Palencia *Tel:* (02) 926-4047 *Fax:* (02) 927-0366
2164 Legarda St, Quiapo, Manila, Branch Manager: Minda Munion *Tel:* (02) 734-7477; (02) 735-8385 *Fax:* (02) 733-1428

G Miranda & Sons
12 UP Shopping Center, Laurel St, UP Diliman, Quezon City
Tel: (02) 7121620 *Fax:* (02) 7120502 *Cable:* MIRANDASONS
Key Personnel
Manager: Eloisa D Miranda
Branch Office(s)
Miranda Davao, C M Recto Ave, Davao City
Miranda Espana, 1404 Espana St, Manila
Miranda Recto, 1887 C M Recto Ave, Manila
Miranda Morayta, 844 N Reyes St, Morayta, Manila
Miranda Cubao, Aurora Blvd, Cubao, Quezon City

National Book Store Inc
Quad Alpha Centrum, 125 Pioneer St, Mandaluyong City 1550
Tel: (02) 6318061 *Fax:* (02) 6318079
E-mail: info@nationalbookstore.com.ph
Web Site: www.nationalbookstore.com.ph
Telex: 27890 NBS-PH; 41144 NBS-PM
Cable: Nabost Manila
Key Personnel
General Manager: Mrs Socorro C Ramos
Also Publisher.

Philippine Education Co Inc
140 Amorsolo St, Metro Manila
Tel: (02) 487215; (02) 487317
Telex: 7222321 *Cable:* Pecoi Manila
Key Personnel
General Manager: Antero L Soriano
Also Publisher.
Branch Office(s)
Araneta Center, Cubao
Makati Commercial Center, West Drive Arcade, Makati
Broadway Centrum, Dona Juana Rodriguez & Aurora Blvd, Quezon City

Popular Book Store
305 Tomas Morato St, Quezon City
Tel: (02) 372-2162 *Fax:* (02) 372-2050
E-mail: popular@pworld.net.ph *Cable:* POBOST
Key Personnel
Pres & Gen Mgr: Katherine Ann Po
Type of Business: Distributor, Importer, Major Independent Bookseller, Wholesaler
Owned by: Popular Trading Corporation

Rex Book Store Inc
86 P Florentino St, 1008 Quezon City
Tel: (02) 712-41-06; (02) 711-57-02
Key Personnel
President: Dominador D Buhain
Vice President & General Manager: Mario D Buhain
Editorial Manager: Mrs Flor Cabangis
Marketing Dir: Don Timothy I Buhain
Branch Office(s)
Rex Miscellaneous & Book Store, Greenhills, San Juan
Rex Book Store Cebu
Rex Book Store Davao
Rex Book Store Makati
Rex Book Store Mandaluyong
Bookshop(s): Rex Book Store, Recto, 1977 C M Recto Ave, Manila

Reyes Publishing Inc
Mariwasa Bldg, 717 Aurora Blvd, 1112 Quezon City
Tel: (02) 721-7492 *Fax:* (02) 721-8782
E-mail: reyespub@skyinet.net
Telex: 63740 Vri pn *Cable:* VERAREYES MANILA
Key Personnel
President: Luis Reyes
Manager: Paolo Reyes
Founded: 1986

Poland

ABE Marketing
ul Grzybowska 37A, 00-855 Warsaw
SAN: 128-0031
Tel: (022) 6540675 *Fax:* (022) 6520767
E-mail: info@abe.com.pl
Web Site: www.abe.com.pl/
Key Personnel
President: Marek Nowakowski *E-mail:* marek.nowakowski@abe.com.pl
Subscription Manager: Irena Ksiezopolska *E-mail:* irena.ksiezopolska@abe.com.pl
Founded: 1991
Polish sole agent for K G Saur Verlag Munich; subscription services.
Type of Business: Importer, Major Independent Bookseller
Branch Office(s)
ul Legionow Pilsudskiego 17, 30-509 Krakow *Tel:* (012) 296 3336 *Fax:* (012) 296 3337 *E-mail:* krakow@abe.pl
ul Wincentego Pola 16, 44-100 Gliwice *Tel:* (032) 3393151 *Fax:* (032) 3393151 *E-mail:* gliwice@abe.pl
Al Niepodleglosci 767, 81-868 Sopot *Tel:* (058) 5500936 *E-mail:* trojmiasto@abe.pl
Bookshop(s): Academic Bookstore Gliwice, ul Wincentego Pola 16, 44-100 Gliwice *Tel:* (032) 339 3150 *Fax:* (032) 339 3150 *E-mail:* gliwice@abe.pl; Academic Bookstore Warsaw

Centrala Handlu Zagranicznego ARS Polona SA (Foreign Trade Enterprise ARS Polona Joint Stock Company)
25, Obroncow St, 03-933 Warsaw
Tel: (022) 509 86 20 *Fax:* (022) 509 86 20
E-mail: arspolona@arspolona.com.pl
Web Site: www.arspolona.com.pl *Cable:* ARS POLONA WARSZAWA
Key Personnel
President: Magdalena Slusarska
Vice President: Grzegorz Guzowski
Founded: 1953
Export & import of books & periodicals as well as publish books. Export & import of musical instruments & philately. Organizer of Warsaw International & National Book Fairs.
Type of Business: Distributor, Exporter, Importer, Wholesaler

Dom Ksiazki, Panstwowe Przedesiebiorstwo
ul Jasna Nr 26, 00-054 Warsaw
Tel: (022) 826 8559 *Fax:* (022) 826 7117
E-mail: info@domksiazki.pl
Web Site: www.domksiazki.pl
Key Personnel
Dir General: Janusz Wojcikowski
Vice Manager: Stanislaw Zahorodny
Founded: 1950
Type of Business: Major Book Chain Headquarters, Wholesaler

Polish Chamber of Books (Polska Izba Ksiazki)
ul Oleandrow 8, 00-629 Warsaw
Tel: (022) 8759497 *Fax:* (022) 8759496
E-mail: biuro@pik.org.pl
Web Site: www.pik.org.pl
Key Personnel
President: Dorota Malinowska-Grupinska
Vice President: Piotr Marciszuk; Danuta Skora
Founded: 1990

Portugal

Centro Antiquar do Alecrim A Trindade
Rua do Alecrim, 79-81, 1200 Lisbon
Tel: (021) 3424660 *Fax:* (021) 3470180
E-mail: np75ae@mail.telepac.pt
Key Personnel
Contact: Antonio Trindade
Type of Business: Major Independent Bookseller

Sociedades Livreiras Bertrand
Rua Anchieta 15, 1249 060 Lisbon
Tel: (021) 0305592 *Fax:* (021) 0305596
E-mail: info@bertrand.pt
Web Site: www.bertrand.pt
Telex: 42748
Key Personnel
Man Dir: Antero Braga
Assistant Dir: Carlos Vilar
Founded: 1727
Owned by: Bertrand Editora Lda
Branch Office(s)
Algarveshopping, Lanka Parque Tavagueria, Guia, 8200 Albufeira
Loja 0.079, Estrada Nacional 9, 2645 543 Alcabideche *Tel:* (021) 460 70 92
Almada Forum, Loja 1.20, Estrada do Caminho Municipal 1011, Vale de Morelos, 2800 Almada
CC Continente da Amadora Loja nº 14-A, EN 249/1, 2724 510 Amadora *Tel:* (021) 425 47 42
Av dr Lourenco Peixinho 87 C, 3800 165 Aveiro *Tel:* (0234) 428 280
Braga Parque, Qt Dos Congregados loja 210, 4710 427 Braga *Tel:* (0253) 257 105
Rua D Diogo de Sousa, 133, 4700 422 Braga *Tel:* (0253) 218 115
Av Valbom, 19, 2750 508 Cascais
Coimbra Shopping, Loja 0.117, Av Dr Mendes Silva, 3030 193 Coimbra *Tel:* (0239) 401 933
Largo da Portagem 9, 3000 337 Coimbra *Tel:* (0239) 823 014
Forum Algarve, Loja 025, Estrada Nacional 125, Km 103, 8000 Faro *Tel:* (028) 986 51 87
Rua Dr Francisco Gomes 27, 8000 306 Faro *Tel:* (0289) 828 147
Madeira Shopping, Loja 0016, Caminho de Sta Quiteria, Sto Antº, 9000 283 Funchal *Tel:* (0291) 765 031
Guimaraes Shopping, Quinta das Lameiras, Creixomil, 4810 058 Guimaraes *Tel:* (0253) 511 909
CC Continente Leiria, loja 19/20, estrada nacional, nº1, Alto do Vieiro, 2400 441 Leiria *Tel:* 244824562 *Fax:* 244833857 *E-mail:* leiria.livraria@bertrand.pt
Amoreiras Shopping, Loja 2.108, Av Duarte Pacheco, 1070 103 Lisbon *Tel:* (021) 383 80 34
Centro Colombo, loja 0.135, Av Lusiada, 1500 392 Lisbon *Tel:* (021) 716 71 52
Centro Vasco da Gama, Loja 0.11, Av D Joao II, Lote 1.05.02, 1990 000 Lisbon *Tel:* (021) 895 13 21
Chiado, Rua Garrett 73-75, 1200 203 Lisbon *Tel:* (021) 346 86 46
Centro Cultural del Belem, Praca do Imperio, 1449 003 Lisbon *Tel:* (021) 364 56 37
Av de Roma 13B, 1000 261 Lisbon *Tel:* (021) 796 92 71
Olivais Shopping, Loja nº 23, Rua Cidade de Bolama, 1800 079 Lisbon *Tel:* (021) 855 11 61
Picoas Plaza, Loja C 0.9 Rua Tomas Ribeiro, 1050 000 Lisbon
Maia Shopping, Loja nº 139, Lugar de Ardegaes, 4445 000 Maia *Tel:* (022) 975 97 78
Norteshopping, Loja 0.120, Rua Sara Afonso, 105 a 117, 4250 446 Matosinhos *Tel:* (022) 955 97 78
Forum Montijo, loja 0.31, Zona industrial do Pau, Queimado, Rua da Azinheira, 2870 100 Montijo *Tel:* 212301603 *Fax:* 212301876 *E-mail:* montijo.livraria@bertrand.pt
Shopping Odivelas Parque, loja 1.007, Estrada da Paia, 2679 461 Odivelas *Tel:* 219316566 *Fax:* 219316582 *E-mail:* odivelas.livraria@bertrand.pt
Parque Atlantico, Loja 043, Rua da Juventude, 9500 211 Ponta Delgada, Ilha de Sao Miguel *E-mail:* acores.livraria@bertrand.pt
CC Portimao, Quinta da Malata, lote 1, loja 105/108, 8500 510 Portimao *Tel:* (0282) 418 929 *Fax:* (0282) 483 661 *E-mail:* portimao.livraria@bertrand.pt
Rua 31 Janeiro 65, 4000 543 Porto *Tel:* (022) 200 43 39
Shopping Brasilia, Piso 4, loja 55, P Mouzinho de Albuquerque 113, 4100 359 Porto *Tel:* (022) 609 90 18
Shopping Center Cidade do Porto, loja 223, Rua Goncalo Sampaio, 350, 4150 368 Porto *Tel:* (022) 600 94 27
Viacatarina Shopping, Piso 1, Loja 1, Rua de Santa Catarina, 312/350, 4000 443 Porto *Tel:* (022) 338 97 04
CC Parque Nascente, Loja 534b, Estrada Exterior da Circunvalacao, 4435 Rio Tinto *Tel:* 224801575 *Fax:* 224801579 *E-mail:* gondomar.livraria@bertrand.pt
W Shopping, Rua Pedro Santarem, nº 9 Loja 147D, 2000-220 Santarem *Tel:* 243322828 *Fax:* 243325322 *E-mail:* santarem.livraria@bertrand.pt
Estacao Viana Shopping, loja 1.128, Av Huberto Delgado, 4900 Viana do Castelo *Tel:* 258829726 *Fax:* 258829374 *E-mail:* vianaestacao@bertrand.pt
Rua Sacadura Cabral, 32, 4900 517 Viana do Castelo *Tel:* (0258) 822 838
Gaia Shopping, Av Descobrimentos, 549, 4404 503 Vila Nova de Gaia *Tel:* (022) 372 01 79

A Tavares de Carvalho
Av da Republica, 46-3, 1050-195 Lisbon
Tel: (021) 797 0377 *Fax:* (021) 795 8880
Key Personnel
Owner: A Tavares de Carvalho
Founded: 1959
Medium stock of old rare books in all fields, but mainly in Portuguese & Spanish 16th Century books.

CDL (Central Distribuidora Livreira) Sarl
Bairro Bela Vista Arm 2 P-30, 2735 Cacem Agualua-Cacem
Tel: (01) 4264422; (01) 769744; (01) 779825
Key Personnel
Dir: Mario Lino

Central Distribuidora Livreira, see CDL (Central Distribuidora Livreira) Sarl

Destarte, Lda
Rua Sto Antonio da Gloria, 90, 1250-218 Lisbon
Tel: (01) 347 9164 *Fax:* (01) 347 5811
E-mail: destarte@esoterica.pt
Key Personnel
Man Dir: Jorge Linhares *Tel:* (021) 3479164
Founded: 1980
Type of Business: Distributor, Importer
Imprints: Edicoes Destarte
Branch Office(s)
Livraria Linhares

Dinapress
Largo Dr Antonio de Sousa Macedo, 2, 1200 Lisbon
Tel: (021) 3955270 *Fax:* (021) 3950390
E-mail: dinalivro@ip.pt
Key Personnel
Marketing: Joel Antero D'Aguiar S Amaro
Founded: 1989

BOOK DEALERS — PORTUGAL

Type of Business: Exporter, Wholesaler
Owned by: Sr Silverio Pedroso Amaro
Bookshop(s): Centro Cultural Brasi Leiro

Distri Cultural Lda
Rua Vasco da Gamma, 4-4A, 2685 Sacavem
Tel: (021) 942 53 94 *Fax:* (021) 941 98 93
E-mail: cultural@electroliber.pt
Telex: 16588 Eliber
Key Personnel
Man Dir: Karl-Heinz Petzler
Sales Dir: Carlos Alberto
Marketing & Promotion: Martin E Wragg
Founded: 1980
Main Agencies: Oxford University Press, Hachette, Lanenscheidt, Max Hueber, Kuemmerly & Frey, Berlitz, Pan MacMillan, Harper Collins, RandomHouse, Bantom Doubleday Dell.
Type of Business: Distributor

Distri Lojas-Sociedade Livreira Lda
c/o Distri Cultural, Rue Vasco de Gama 4-4A, 2685 Sacavem
Tel: (021) 940 65 00 *Fax:* (021) 942 59 90
Telex: 62483
Key Personnel
Man Dir: Luis Santos
Sales Manager: Luis Alves
Commercial Contact: Jorge Mourao
Founded: 1977
Bookshops in Cascais, Coimbra, Estoril, & Sintra Porto (1); Braga, & Algarve (6); Lisbon (11).
Owned by: Grupo Distri

Distribuidora Editora Vral, Lda
Pcta Cesario Verde, 5, 2745 Queluz
Mailing Address: Apdo 119, 2745 Queluz Codex
Tel: (01) 4393978 *Fax:* (01) 4373558
Key Personnel
Contact: Victor Martins
Type of Business: Distributor, Exporter, Importer, Major Independent Bookseller

Domingos Castro
Travessa dos Frois, 3-2, 2000 Santarem
Tel: (043) 332920 *Fax:* (043) 27406
Founded: 1984
Type of Business: Distributor, Wholesaler
Branch Office(s)
Rua da Costa, 14-1 Fre, Lisbon
Rua Nartiags Lizgadade, 190-3, 4000 Porto

ECL
Rua D Manuel II, 33-5°, 4050-345 Porto
Tel: (022) 600 40 01; (022) 609 01 71 *Fax:* (022) 609 96 15
E-mail: ecl@mail.telepac.pt
Founded: 1990
Type of Business: Distributor

EDC -Empresa De Divulgacao Cultural, SA
c/o Editorial Verbo, Av August Antonio de Aguiar, 148, 1069-019 Lisbon
Tel: (021) 380 1100 *Fax:* (021) 386 5397
Web Site: www.editorialverbo.pt
Telex: 15177
Owned by: Editorial Verbo SA

Edicoei Tecnicas & Culturais, Lda, see Domingos Castro

Edicoes Destarte, *imprint of* Destarte, Lda

Electroliber Lda
Rua Vasco da Gama 4, Apdo 164, 2685 Sacavem Codex, Lisbon
Tel: (021) 940 6750 *Fax:* (021) 942 52 14
E-mail: electrliber@mail.telepac.pt
Telex: 16588 *Cable:* TELEGRAMAS ELECTROLIBER
Key Personnel
Contact: Pedro R de Vasconcelos; Antonio J Faria
Type of Business: Distributor
Branch Office(s)
Porto-Albufeira-Funchal

Empresa de Comercio Livreiro, see ECL

Esquina-Livraria e Papelaria Lda
Rua Afonso Lopes Vieira, 126 (AO FOCO), 4100-020 Porto
Tel: (022) 6065234 *Fax:* (022) 6053878
E-mail: livrariaesquina@mail.telepac.pt
Web Site: www.esquina-livraria.com
Key Personnel
Manager: Luis Barroso *Tel:* (022) 6065314
Also deals in secondhand books.
Type of Business: Wholesaler

Livraria Ferin Ltda
R Nova do Almada 70-74, 1249-098 Lisbon
Tel: (021) 3424422; (021) 3469033 *Fax:* (021) 3471101
E-mail: livraria.ferin@mail.telepac.pt
Key Personnel
President & General Manager: Margarida Dias Pinheiro
Founded: 1840
Type of Business: Exporter, Importer, Wholesaler

Julio de Figueiredo, Lda
Campo Grande 380, Lote 3C, Escritorio A, 1700-097 Lisbon
Tel: (021) 754 16 00 *Fax:* (021) 754 16 09
E-mail: info@jlf.pt
Web Site: www.jlf.pt
Key Personnel
Contact: Julio Figueiredo
Type of Business: Distributor, Importer

Figueirinhas, Lda
Rua do Almada 47, 4000 Porto
Tel: (022) 53 325 300 *Fax:* (022) 53 325 907
E-mail: correio@liv_figueirinhas.pt
Key Personnel
Contact: Francisco Pimenta
Type of Business: Distributor

Livraria Guimaraes
Rua da Misericordia, 68-70, 1200 Lisbon
Tel: (021) 3462436 *Fax:* (021) 3462620
Key Personnel
Man Dir: Isabel Leao
Founded: 1899
Also publishes under Guimaraes Editores Lda.

Hipocrates - Livros Tecnicos, Lda
Av Defensores Chaves 16A, 1000 117 Lisbon
Tel: (021) 3571247 *Fax:* (021) 3580902
E-mail: info@hipocrates.pt
Web Site: www.hipocrates.pt
Key Personnel
Contact: Norberto Boletas
Founded: 1976
Subjects: Medical
Type of Business: Importer

International Book Centre
c/o Distri Cultural, Rua Vasco de Gama, 4-4A, 2685 Sacavem
Tel: (021) 942 53 94 *Fax:* (021) 941 98 93
Key Personnel
Man Dir: Karl-Heinz Petzler
Assistant Dir: Beatriz Mestrinho
Owned by: Distri Cultural (Grupo Distri)

Jayantilal Jamnadas, Lda
Estrada de Benfica, 488A, 2700 Benfica, Lisbon
Tel: (01) 4960951
Founded: 1987
Type of Business: Major Independent Bookseller

Livraria Barata, Antonio D M Barata
Ave de Roma 11 - A-D, 1000 Lisbon
Tel: (021) 848 16 31 *Fax:* (021) 80 33 44
Key Personnel
Contact: Graca Didier

Livraria Buchholz, Lda
Rua Duque de Palmela, 4, 1250 098 Lisbon
Tel: (021) 3170580 *Fax:* (021) 3522634
E-mail: buchholz@mail.telepac.pt
Web Site: www.buchholz.pt
Key Personnel
Man Dir: Karin Sousa Ferreira *Tel:* (021) 3170589
Founded: 1943
General & academic titles in Portuguese, English/American, French, German & Spanish language.
Type of Business: Exporter, Importer

Livraria Caravana
Rua Jose da Costa Guerreiro, 8100 Loule
Tel: (089) 462879 *Fax:* (089) 462871
Founded: 1996
Also Tobacco & Stationer's Shop.
Type of Business: Major Independent Bookseller

Livraria Latina
Rua de Sta Catarina, 24000 Porto
Tel: (022) 2001294 *Fax:* (022) 2086053
Key Personnel
Contact: Henrique Perdigao
Founded: 1941
Also book publisher.
Type of Business: Importer, Major Independent Bookseller, Wholesaler

Livraria Ler, Lda
Rua Almeida Sousa, 24-E, 1350 Lisbon
Tel: (021) 60 69 96
Key Personnel
Dir: Luis Alves Dias
Founded: 1970
Type of Business: Distributor

Livraria Manuel Ferreira (Manuel Ferreira Bookshop)
Rua Dr Alves Veiga, 89, 4000 073 Porto
Tel: (021) 5363237 *Fax:* (022) 5364406
E-mail: livrariaferreira@hotmail.com
Key Personnel
Contact: Herculano Ferreira
Founded: 1959
Antiquarian Bookseller, Portuguese Culture.
Membership(s): ILAB-LILA; APLA; AILA.

Livraria Teorema 1-Cogitum Livrarias Lda
Shopping Center Massama, Loja 41, 2745 Queluz
Tel: (021) 4394912 *Fax:* (021) 4394909
E-mail: cogitum@ip.pt
Key Personnel
Contact: Joao Nuno Cruz
Founded: 1991
Owned by: Cogitum Uvrarias Lda

Lojas Europa-America
Apdo 8, Mem Martins Codex
Tel: (01) 9211461 *Fax:* (01) 9217940
Owned by: Publicacoes Europa-America Lda
Branch Office(s)
Ave 25 de Abril 48, Almada
Centro Comercial Pao de Acucar, Lojas 6,7 - Estrade a Nacional 6, Cascais
Ave 28 de Maio 61, Castelo Branco
Arcadas do Parque, Estoril
Pr Ferreira de Almeida 21-22, Faro
Rua Jose Relvas 15 B-C, Parede

PORTUGAL

Ave Antonio Enes 14-B, Queluz
Ave Elias Garcia 104-B, Queluz

Editorial Noticias
Rua Cruz Carriera, No 4-B, 1150 Lisbon
Tel: (01) 352 2066

Editorial O Livro Lda
Rua Major Neutel de Abreu, nº 16 A/B/C, 1500 Lisbon
Tel: (021) 778 35 77 *Fax:* (021) 778 35 36
E-mail: prof@editorialolivro.pt
Web Site: www.editorialolivro.pt
Key Personnel
Man Dir: Carlos de Moura
Also publisher.
Branch Office(s)
Rua da Boa Hora, 36 & 68, 4050 Porto *Tel:* (022) 2005739 *Fax:* (022) 2005736

Patio-Livraria Inglesa
Rua da Carreira, 43, 9000 Funchal, Madeira
Tel: (0291) 224490 *Fax:* (0291) 232077
E-mail: patiolivros@hotmail.com
Founded: 1981
Specialize in exporting books worldwide & in the supply of Portuguese/Brazilian publications. Carry in stock all available books on Madeira.
Type of Business: Distributor, Exporter, Importer, Major Book Chain Headquarters

Livraria Portugal (Dias e Andrade Lda)
Rua do Carmo 70-74, 1117 Lisbon Codex
Tel: (01) 3474982 *Fax:* (01) 3470264
E-mail: liv.portugal@mail.telepac.pt
Key Personnel
Manager: Henrique Arronches; Jose Simocs; Jose Reis; Manuel Dias
Founded: 1941
Type of Business: Distributor, Exporter, Importer

Livraria Sa da Costa
R Garrett, 100, 1200 Lisbon
Tel: (021) 346 07 21
Key Personnel
Manager: Manuel F da Costa
Owned by: Sa da Costa Editora

Sodilivros
Rua de Campolide, 183-B, 1070-029 Lisbon
Tel: (021) 3878902; (021) 3878903 *Fax:* (021) 3876281
E-mail: sodilivros@mail.telepac.pt
Key Personnel
Contact: Jorge De Azevedo
Founded: 1985
Type of Business: Distributor

Livraria Sousa e Almeida Lda
Rau da Fabrica 42, 4050-245 Porto
Tel: (022) 2050073 *Fax:* (022) 2050073
E-mail: sousaealmeida@net.sapo.pt; geral@sousaealmeida.com
Web Site: www.sousaealmeida.com

Puerto Rico

Bookstore, Institute of Puerto Rican Culture
Apdo 4184, San Juan 00902-4184
Tel: (809) 723-2115
Key Personnel
Owner & Manager, Institute de Cultura Puertoriquena: Rene Grullon Nunez
Stock includes subjects on music, Puerto Rico, history, humanities, short stories, poetry & literature. Also carry maps & sheet music.

Qatar

Arabian Bookshop
PO Box 7884, Doha
Tel: 442648 *Fax:* 449653
Telex: 5078 Majed DH

Reunion

Cazal SA
42 Rue Alexis de Villeneuve, Saint-Denis
Tel: 213264 *Fax:* 410977
Telex: 916453
Key Personnel
President: Philippe Baloukjy
Imprints, Printing, Advertising.

Librairie Universsitaire de la Reunion
29, Av de la Victoire, Saint Denis 97489
Tel: 210758
Key Personnel
Manager: Apavou

Romania

Artexim - Foreign Trade Co
Piata Scienteii, No 1, Bucharest
Mailing Address: PO Box 33-16, 70005 Bucharest
Tel: (01) 157672
Telex: 011191
Carries out all the commercial operations connected with book import & export.

Libraria Universitatii
Str Universitatii 1, R-3400 Cluj-Napoca
Tel: (064) 198 107
Libraria Universitatii belongs to the state & is under the rule of the Bookshops' Center, Dostoievski St No 71.

Russian Federation

Mezhdunarodnaya Kniga
39 Bolshaya Yakimanka St, Moscow 117049
Tel: (095) 238-46-00 *Fax:* (095) 230-21-17
E-mail: info@mkniga.msk.su
Web Site: www.mkniga.msk.su
Telex: 411160 MKN RU
Key Personnel
Dir: Yuri V Kurenkov
Export organization for books, periodicals, printing equipment, audio & video recordings, & other cultural goods. Other services include co-editions, copyright, & arranging of fairs & exhibitions abroad & in Russia.

Rwanda

Librairie Universitaire
BP 117, Butare
Tel: 530330 *Fax:* 530210
E-mail: biblio@nur.ac.rw
Web Site: www.lib.nur.ac.rw
Owned by: Universite Nationale du Rwanda, faculte du Droit

Saudi Arabia

Dar Al-Ulum Publishers, Booksellers & Distributors
PO Box 1050, Riyadh 11431
Tel: (01) 4777121 *Fax:* (01) 4793446
Telex: 203094 *Cable:* OHALI RIYADH
Key Personnel
Proprietor: Abdulla N Al-Ohali; Mohammad S Al-Kadi
Manager, Foreign Books: Gaafar I At-Tai
Also Publishers.
Type of Business: Distributor
Bookshop(s): Sitteen St, Sitteen St

International Bookshops
PO Box 22348, Riyadh 11495
Tel: (03) 4641851 *Fax:* (03) 4641851
Key Personnel
Owner: Said H AlSalah
General Manager: Basim S AlSalah
Also publisher.
Type of Business: Distributor, Importer, Major Independent Bookseller
Branch Office(s)
Dana Shopping Center, Damman
4 Seasons Center, Rakah
King Fahd St & 28 St

Tihama Bookstores
PO Box 8963, Jeddah 21482
Tel: (02) 6444444 *Fax:* (02) 6519277
E-mail: info@tihama.com
Web Site: www.tihama.com/book/book.htm
Key Personnel
Manager: Bassam Dayani *Tel:* (02) 651 7164 *Fax:* (02) 651 6917 *E-mail:* dayani@tihama.com
Owned by: Tihama Advertising Co

Senegal

Librairie Clairafrique
2, rue El Hadj Mbaye Gueye, BP 2005, Dakar
Tel: (08) 222169 *Fax:* (08) 218409
E-mail: clairafrique@le-senegal.com
Web Site: www.le-senegal.com/clairafrique
Telex: 21403 Clairaf
Key Personnel
Manager: Pauline Kemayi
Founded: 1951
Type of Business: Distributor, Major Independent Bookseller
Owned by: Archdiocese de Dahar

Serbia and Montenegro

Forum
Vojvode Misica 1, 22100 Novi Sad

Tel: (021) 57 216 *Fax:* (021) 57 216
Also Publisher.
Type of Business: Exporter, Importer

Nolit Publishing House
Terazije 27/II, 11000 Belgrade
Tel: (011) 345 017; (011) 355 510 *Fax:* (011) 627 285
Telex: 11-603 *Cable:* NOLIT BGD
Key Personnel
General Manager: Radivoje Nesic
Editor-in-Chief: Milos Stambolic
30 bookshops throughout Serbia and Montenegro.
Type of Business: Distributor, Exporter, Importer, Major Book Chain Headquarters, Major Independent Bookseller, Wholesaler

Prosveta
Cika Ljubina 1, 11000 Belgrade
Tel: (011) 629 843; (011) 631 566 *Fax:* (011) 182 581
E-mail: prosveta@eunet.yu
Web Site: www.prosveta.co.yu
Also publisher. Over 50 bookshops throughout Serbia and Montenegro.
Type of Business: Exporter, Importer

Vuk Karadzic
Kraljevica Marka 9, Postanski fah 762, 11000 Belgrade
Tel: (011) 628066; (011) 628043 *Fax:* (011) 623150
Key Personnel
Man Dir: Ancic Vojin
Also publisher.
Type of Business: Exporter, Importer

Sierra Leone

Njala University College Bookshop
PMB, Freetown
Tel: (022) 228788
E-mail: nuc@sierratel.sl; nuclib@sierratel.sl
Web Site: www.nuc-online.com *Cable:* Njalunbooks
Key Personnel
Manager: J D Kappia

Singapore

Info Access & Distribution
31, Kaki Bukit Rd 3, No 06-07, Techlink, Singapore 471818
Tel: 6741 8422 *Fax:* 6741 8821
E-mail: info.sg@igroup.net.com
Web Site: www.igroup.net
Key Personnel
Contact: Mr Lee Pit Teong
Founded: 1990
Type of Business: Remainder Dealer
Owned by: iGroup
Branch Office(s)
Polly Commercial Bldg, 21-23A Prat Ave, Room 1007-08, Hong Kong, Hong Kong *Tel:* 2572 7228 *Fax:* 2575 8822 *E-mail:* info.hk@igroupnet.com *Web Site:* hk.igroupnet.com
55A Phan Chu Trinh St, Hoan Kiem District, Hanoi, Viet Nam *Tel:* 9435472 *Fax:* 9435475 *E-mail:* info.vn@igroupnet.com

Marketasia Distributors (S) Pte Ltd
Pan-I Complex, 601 Sims Dr, No 04-05, Singapore 387382
Tel: 67448483; 67448486 *Fax:* 67448497; 67443690
E-mail: marketasia@pacific.net.sg
Web Site: www.marketasia.com.sg
Key Personnel
Dir: Johnson Lee *E-mail:* jl@marketasia.com.sg
Founded: 1987
Specialize in the publishing & distributing of books & magazines.
Type of Business: Distributor, Exporter, Importer
Owned by: Johnson Lee & Quek Chin Hu

Masagung Books Pte Ltd
41 Sixth Ave, Off Bukit Timah Rd, Singapore 276483
Tel: 4683276
Telex: rs 34500 A; B Gasing
Also Publisher.

MPH Bookstores (S) Pte Ltd
12 Tagore Dr, No 03-00, Singapore 787621
Tel: 6453 8200
E-mail: mphbooks@singnet.com.sg
Telex: RS 35853 Mphmag *Cable:* EMPRESS SINGAPORE
Key Personnel
Marketing Manager: Lawrence Geoffrey
Bookshop(s): 71-77 Stamford Rd, Singapore 178895; Cold Storage Jelita, 293 Holland Rd, Jalan Jelita 278628 *Tel:* 4689405; Isetan Dhoby Ghavt, B1-01-20-11, Orchard Rd, Singapore 238824 *Tel:* 3381888

Pacific Book Centre (S) Pte Ltd
Blk 73, Ayer Rajah Crescent, 03-01/09 Ayer Rajah Industrial Estate, Singapore 139952
Tel: 6464 0111 *Fax:* 6464 0110
E-mail: enquiries@snpcorp.com
Web Site: www.snp.com.sg
Telex: 36496
Key Personnel
Man Dir: Low Tai Ee
Manager: Lawrence Tan
Owned by: Pan Pacific Publications Pte Ltd, 16 Fan Yoong Rd, Singapore 629793
Branch Office(s)
Queenstown Branch, Apt Blk 6C, 01-48 Margaret Drive, Singapore 142006 *Tel:* 4745701
Alexandra Branch, Apt Blk 136, 01-155 Alexandra Rd, Singapore 150136 *Tel:* 4740577
Havelock Branch, Apt Blk 22, 01-675 Havelock Rd, Singapore 160022 *Tel:* 2724326
Pasir Panjang Branch, 02-02 PSA Bldg, 460 Alexandra Rd, Singapore 119963 *Tel:* 2781090
Bras Basah Branch, Bain St, 02-69 Block 231, Bras Basah Complex, Singapore 180231 *Tel:* 3381024
Jurong East Branch, Block 130 01-221, Jurong East St 13, Singapore 600130 *Tel:* 5666153
Bukit Batok Branch, Blk 283, Bukit Batok East Ave 3 01-275, Singapore 650283 *Tel:* 5674649

Publishers Marketing Services Pte Ltd
10-C Jalan Ampas, No 07-01, Ho Seng Lee Flatted Warehouse, Singapore 329513
Tel: 62565166 *Fax:* 62530008
E-mail: info@pms.com.sg
Web Site: www.pms.com.sg
Key Personnel
Man Dir: Brian Lim
Office Manager: Nicklaus Tan
Deputy Man Dir: Raymond Lim
Founded: 1980
Type of Business: Distributor, Exporter, Importer, Wholesaler
Owned by: Brian Lim

Select Books Pte Ltd
19 Tanglin Rd No 03-15, Tanglin Shopping Centre, Singapore 247909
Tel: 6732 1515 *Fax:* 6736 0855
E-mail: info@selectbooks.com.sg
Web Site: www.selectbooks.com.sg
Key Personnel
Executive Dir: Nancy Chng Way Song
Man Dir: Lena U Wen Lim
Administrative Manager: Mrs Ng San May
Founded: 1976
Distributor & Retailer of books about SE Asia.
Type of Business: Distributor, Exporter, Importer, Major Independent Bookseller

STM Publishers Services Pte Ltd
Affiliate of i Group Books Asia Pacific
352 Larong Chuan, No 01-05 Laurel Park, Singapore 556783
Tel: 62864998 *Fax:* 62882116
Key Personnel
Dir: Tony Poh *E-mail:* tonypoh@pacific.net.sg
Founded: 1993
Subjects: STM, Social Science, Arts, Education, Agriculture & Humanities-Publishers representing agent for SE & NE Asia Laws.
Type of Business: Distributor
Branch Office(s)
Chin Shan Information Service Ltd, 10F-1 No 166 Jiang Yi Rd, Chong Ho 235, Taipei Hsien, Taiwan, Province of China *E-mail:* csis@csis.com.tw

STP Distributors Pte Ltd
Times Centre, One New Industrial Rd, Singapore 536196
Tel: 6213 9288 *Fax:* 6281 3991
E-mail: stpds@tpl.com.sg
Web Site: www.tpl.com.sg
Telex: rs 28068 STP *Cable:* STPSALES SINGAPORE
Key Personnel
Senior Vice President: Michael Kok Pun Liew
Owned by: Times Publishing Group

Times The Bookshop
Times Centre, One New Industrial Rd, Singapore 536196
Tel: 6213 9288 *Fax:* 6382 2571
E-mail: ttb@tpl.com.sg
Web Site: www.timesone.com.sg
Telex: RS 25713 *Cable:* Times Singapore
Owned by: Times Publishing Ltd
Branch Office(s)
Centerpoint, 176 Orchard Rd, No 04-08/16, Singapore, Manager: Christopher Tong *Tel:* 67349022 *Fax:* 67349313
Plaza Singapura, 68 Orchard Rd, No 06-11/14, Singapore, Manager: Wan Salmiyah *Tel:* 68370552 *Fax:* 68370556
Suntec City Mall, 3 Temasek Blvd, No 02-054/056/058/060, Singapore, Manager: Kevin Han *Tel:* 63369391 *Fax:* 63369394
Tampines Mall, 4 Tampines Central 5, No 03-26/27, Singapore, Manager: Simon Pang *Tel:* 67833106 *Fax:* 67833917

The World Book Co (Pte) Ltd
Bras Basah Complex, Block 231, Bain St No 04-57, Singapore 180231
Tel: 3382323 *Fax:* 3371186
Telex: rs 36020 Wbksin
Key Personnel
General Manager: H P Foo

Slovakia

Slovart Co Ltd
Majernikova 4, 841 05 Bratislava 4
Tel: (02) 5479 1528 *Fax:* (02) 6541 1375
E-mail: slovart-expo@zutom.sk
Web Site: www.slovart-expo.sk

Telex: 93394 Slov
Type of Business: Exporter, Importer

Slovenia

Cankarjeva Zalozba
Kopitarjeva 2, SI-1512 Ljubljana
Tel: (01) 3603 720 *Fax:* (01) 3603 787
E-mail: info@cankarjeva-z.si
Web Site: www.cankarjeva-z.si
Also publisher & antiquarian bookseller.
Type of Business: Exporter, Importer
Branch Office(s)
Miklosiceva 16, Ljubljana
Slovenska 37, Ljubljana
Trg osvoboditve 7, Ljubljana
Trzaska 59, Ljubljana
Zaloska 35, Ljubljana
One junija 27, Trbovlje
Usnjarska stolpic S 15, Vrhnika

Co Libri
Presernova 5, 1000 Ljubljana
Tel: (01) 1255111 *Fax:* (01) 224454
Key Personnel
Man Dir: Mrs Majda Sikosek
Editor: Mr Vasja Krasevec
Founded: 1946
Also publisher.
Type of Business: Distributor, Exporter, Importer, Wholesaler

Sraka International
Valanticevo 17, 8000 Novo Mesto
Tel: (07) 3342 274 *Fax:* (07) 3342 094
Key Personnel
Dir & Editor: Drago Vovk
Founded: 1990
Type of Business: Distributor, Exporter, Importer
Owned by: Drago & Bozica Vovk

Tehniska Zalozba Slovenije
Lepi pot 6, PP 541, SI-1000 Ljubljana
Tel: (01) 4790211 *Fax:* (01) 4790230
E-mail: info@tzs.si
Web Site: www.tzs.si
Type of Business: Distributor, Major Independent Bookseller, Wholesaler

South Africa

Aloe Educational
PO Box 4349, Johannesburg 2000
Tel: (011) 8393719 *Fax:* (011) 8393720
Key Personnel
Chief Executive: Lionel N Schroder
Founded: 1968
Library suppliers & booksellers.
Owned by: Aloe Book Agency (Pty) Ltd

Book Promotions (Pte) Ltd
PO Box 5, Plumstead 7801
Tel: (021) 7060949 *Fax:* (021) 7060940
E-mail: enquiries@bookpro.co.za
Web Site: www.bookpro.co.za
Key Personnel
Man Dir: Roy G Mansell *Tel:* (021) 7060949 (ext 231) *E-mail:* roy@bookpro.co.za
Distributor, Importer.
Type of Business: Distributor, Importer

Central News Agency Ltd
PO Box 10799, Johannesburg 2000
Tel: (011) 4933200 *Fax:* (011) 4931438
Branch Office(s)
PO Box 9, Cape Town 8000 *Tel:* (021) 541261
PO Box 938, Durban 4000 *Tel:* (031) 451875
(also 250 branches throughout the country)

CNA, see Central News Agency Ltd

Faradawn cc
PO Box 1903, Saxonwold 2132
Tel: (011) 885-1847 *Fax:* (011) 885-1829
E-mail: faradawn@icon.co.za
Web Site: www.faradawn.co.za
Key Personnel
Contact: Lorraine Shalekoff; Lesley Thomas
Founded: 1983
Publishers Representatives, Book & Map Distributors.
Type of Business: Distributor, Importer, Wholesaler

Fogarty's Bookshop
Shop 20, Walmer Park Shopping Centre, Main St, Walmer-Port Elizabeth 6070
Mailing Address: PO Box 1881, Port Elizabeth 6000
Tel: (041) 3681425; (041) 3681454 *Fax:* (041) 3681279
E-mail: fogartys@global.co.za
Key Personnel
Manager: Teresa Fogarty
Type of Business: Major Independent Bookseller

Juta & Co Ltd
Juta House, 55 Wierda Rd E, Corner Albertyn, Wierda Valley, Sandton 2196
Mailing Address: PO Box 14373, Lansdowne 7779
Tel: (011) 217-7200 *Fax:* (011) 883-7623
E-mail: books@juta.co.za
Web Site: www.tmza.co.za/juta
Key Personnel
Man Dir: Andrew Cruick Shank
Marketing Manager: Chris Napier
Type of Business: Major Independent Bookseller
Owned by: Juta Holdings (Pty) Ltd
Bookshop(s): RAU Campus, Shop 21, Entrance 6, 1st floor, Student Center, Akademie Rd, Auckland Park, Johannesburg *Tel:* (011) 482-3566; (011) 489-3463 *Fax:* (011) 482-3565 *E-mail:* raubooks@juta.co.za; Provideamus Bldg, Shop 6A, 169 Zastron St, Bloemfontein 9301 *Tel:* (051) 448-6565 *Fax:* (051) 448-9068 *E-mail:* bloembooks@juta.co.za; Shop 10, Corner K90 & N Rand Rd, Boksburg 1460 *Tel:* (011) 823-1539; (011) 823-1530 *Fax:* (011) 823-1506 *E-mail:* bokbooks@juta.co.za; 47 Bree St, PO Box 30, Cape Town 8000 *Tel:* (021) 418-3260 *Fax:* (021) 418-1282 *E-mail:* ctbooks@juta.co.za; 216 Stanger St, PO Box 50197, Durban 4001 *Tel:* (031) 37-3970 *Fax:* (031) 37-1819 *E-mail:* dbnbooks@juta.co.za; Hatfield Plaza, 1122 Burnett St, 1st floor, Private Bag 12, Hatfield 0083 *Tel:* (012) 362-5800 *Fax:* (012) 362-5744 *E-mail:* ptabooks@juta.co.za; Balfour Shopping Centre, Shop 207, 2 Balfour Close, Highlands N Ext 9, Johannesburg 2192 *Tel:* (011) 786-8873; (011) 786-5377 *Fax:* (011) 786-8874 *E-mail:* balbooks@juta.co.za; Mezzanine floor, 111 Commissioner St, PO Box 1010, Johannesburg 2000 *Tel:* (011) 333-5521 *Fax:* (011) 333-4810 *E-mail:* jhbbooks@juta.co.za; Promenade Shopping Centre, Shop 52, Corner Louis Trichardt & Henshall Sts, Nelspruit 1201 *Tel:* (013) 752-2231; (013) 752-6918 *Fax:* (013) 752-7817 *E-mail:* nelbooks@juta.co.za; Shoprite Park, Shop 19/20, 262 Voortrekker Rd, Parow 7500 *Tel:* (021) 418-3260 *Fax:* (021) 930-7962 *E-mail:* pabooks@juta.co.za; Middestad Centre, Shop 39, Corner Rissik & Marshall St, Pietersburg *Tel:* (015) 297-0240 *Fax:* (015) 297-3247 *E-mail:* pietbooks@juta.co.za; Pretoria Church Sq, 225 Church St, Pretoria *Tel:* (012) 3242422 *Fax:* (012) 3242293 *E-mail:* csqbooks@juta.co.za; Renaissance Pl, 444 Jan Smuts Ave, Randburg 2194 *Tel:* (011) 886-8595 *E-mail:* rbgbooks@juta.co.za; Riverside Mall, Upper Ground floor, Shop 36, Main Rd, Rondebosch *Tel:* (021) 686-2094; (021) 686-2095 *Fax:* (021) 686-2096 *E-mail:* rondebooks@juta.co.za; Coetzenberg Gallery, Eikestad Mall, Shop 13A, 43 Andringe St, Stellenbosch *Tel:* (021) 8833378 *Fax:* (021) 8833318 *E-mail:* stelbooks@juta.co.za; Seagate Centre, Shop 2, 7 Torquay St, Summerstrand, Port Elizabeth *Tel:* (041) 583-1732 *Fax:* (041) 583-1854 *E-mail:* pebooks@juta.co.za

Logans University Bookshop (Pty) Ltd
39 Gale St, Durban 4001
Tel: (031) 3076530 *Fax:* (031) 3073230
Owned by: The Literary Group (Pty) Ltd
Branch Office(s)
100 Mansfield Rd, Durban *Tel:* 218223 (Technikon)
660 Umbilo Rd, Durban (Medical Books)
Nedbank Plaza, Durban Rd, PMB 301 Pietermaritzburg *Tel:* (0331) 941588

Maskew Miller Longman
Corner Logan Way & Forest Dr, Pinelands 7405
Mailing Address: PO Box 396, Cape Town 8000
Tel: (021) 531 7750 *Fax:* (021) 5314049
E-mail: firstname@mml.co.za
Web Site: www.mml.co.za
Telex: 526053 SA *Cable:* MASKEWMILLER
Key Personnel
Chief Executive: Fatima Dada
Publishing Dir: J Pienaar
Founded: 1893
Also publisher.
Type of Business: Importer, Wholesaler
Branch Office(s)
PO Box 3068, Central Park, Block H, 16th St, Midrand 1685 *Tel:* 27-011-315-3647 *Fax:* 27-011-315-2757
PO Box 1701, 46 Alexandra Rd, King William's Town 5600 *Tel:* 27-043-643-3963 *Fax:* 27-043-643-3963
Norlaine, Suite 110, 7-15 Old Main Rd, Pinetown 3610 *Tel:* 27-031-701-8813 *Fax:* 27-031-702-9627
PO Box 3876, Nelspruit 1200 *Tel:* 083-633-2917 *Fax:* 013-753-3073
600 Moolman Bldg, 29 Market St, Pietersburg 0699 *Tel:* 27-015-295-9194 *Fax:* 27-015-295-6012
Sanlam Plaza, 1st floor, Corner Maitland & East Burger Sts, Bloemfontein 9301 *Tel:* 27-051-448-0424 *Fax:* 27-051-430-4130
Private Bag X2200, Merlite Bldg, Off 18, Corner Shippard & Warren Sts, Mafikeng 2745 *Tel:* 27-018-381-1118 *Fax:* 27-018-381-6029

Media House Publications Pty Ltd
PO Box 782395, Sandton 2146
Tel: (011) 8826237 *Fax:* (011) 8829652
Key Personnel
Contact: Kate Everingham
Founded: 1983
Type of Business: Distributor, Exporter, Importer, Wholesaler
Owned by: Book Services International SA Pty Ltd

Nasou Via Afrika
40 Heerengracht, Cape Town 8001
Mailing Address: PO Box 5197, Cape Town 8000
Tel: (021) 406-3314 *Fax:* (021) 406-2922; (021) 406-3086
E-mail: mdewitt@nasou.com (customer service)
Web Site: www.nasou-viaafrika.com

BOOK DEALERS

Key Personnel
Manager Administration & Retail: Mr G Naude
Type of Business: Distributor, Importer, Major Book Chain Headquarters
Owned by: Via Afrika
Branch Office(s)
PO Box 1058, Bloemfontein 9300 *Tel:* (051) 448-2345 *Fax:* (051) 448-4544 *E-mail:* bfn@afribooks.com
PO Box 5485, Cape Town 8000 *Tel:* (021) 406-3992 *Fax:* (021) 406-3371 *E-mail:* bvl@afribooks.com
PO Box 279, East London 5200 *Tel:* (043) 735-3888 *Fax:* (043) 735-4200 *E-mail:* el@afribooks.com
PO Box 82, George 6530 *Tel:* (044) 873-2812 *Fax:* (044) 873-2811 *E-mail:* grg@afribooks.com
Private Bag X5022, Kimberley 8300 *Tel:* (082) 254-5382 *Fax:* (082) 832-9475
PO Box 556, Pinetown 3600 *Tel:* (031) 705-2417 *Fax:* (031) 701-8300 *E-mail:* ptn@afribooks.com
PO Box 95, Port Elizabeth 6000 *Tel:* (041) 363-1163 *Fax:* (041) 363-1183 *E-mail:* pe@afribooks.com
PO Box 3626, Randburg 2125 *Tel:* (011) 792-2213 *Fax:* (011) 792-2239 *E-mail:* rbg@afribooks.com

Shuter & Shooter (Pty) Ltd
21C Cascades Crescent, Pietermaritzburg 3202
Mailing Address: PO Box 13016, Pietermaritzburg 3202
Tel: (033) 347 6100 *Fax:* (033) 347 6120
Web Site: www.shuter.co.za
Key Personnel
Man Dir: Dave Ryder
Also Publisher.
Branch Office(s)
Teachers Centre, 11 Molteno Rd, Claremont 7700, Agent: Sharifa Mowzer *Tel:* (021) 671 3455
PO Box 618, Ferndale 2194, Regional Manager: Themba Msimanga *Tel:* (011) 792 8363

The Struik Publishing Group
80 McKenzie St, Gardens 8001
Mailing Address: PO Box 1144, Cape Town 8000
Tel: (021) 462 4360 *Fax:* (021) 462 4379
Web Site: www.struik.co.za *Cable:* DEKENA
Key Personnel
Executive: Gerrit Struik

Technical Books Ltd
Anreith Corner, 10th floor, Hans Strijdom Ave, Cape Town 8001
Mailing Address: PO Box 2866, Cape Town 8000
Tel: (021) 216540 *Fax:* (021) 4216593
E-mail: techbkct@mweb.co.za
Key Personnel
Chief Executive: Anthony Shapiro *E-mail:* tony@techbooks.co.za
Founded: 1929
STM book specialist.
Type of Business: Distributor, Importer, Major Independent Bookseller, Wholesaler

Van Schaik Bookstore University Bookshop
On-the-Dot Bldg, Sacks Circle, Bellville South
Mailing Address: PO Box 2355, Bellville 7535
Tel: (021) 918 85 00 *Fax:* (021) 951 14 70
E-mail: vsblv@vanschaik.com; vsblv@vanschaiknet.com
Web Site: www.vsonline.co.za; www.vanschaik.com *Cable:* BOOKSCHAIK
Key Personnel
General Manager: Dirk Uys *E-mail:* dirkuys@vanschaik.com
Founded: 1917
Owned by: Nasionale Boekhandel Ltd
Branch Office(s)
34 Fawley St, PO Box 563, Aucklandpark 2006, Contact: Corina van der Spoel *Tel:* (011) 482-3609 *Fax:* (011) 482-3127 *E-mail:* boekehuis@vanschaik.com
Student Centre of RAU, Auckland Park, Johannesburg 2092, Contact: Tom Hicks *Tel:* (011) 726-1698 *Fax:* (011) 482-1407 *E-mail:* vsrau@vanschaik.com
9 Park Rd, Willows, Bloemfontein 9301, Contact: Elsa Bester *Tel:* (051) 447-6685 *Fax:* (051) 447-7837 *E-mail:* vsbloem@vanschaik.com
University of Free State, Student Center, Shop 19, Bloemfontein 9300, Contact: Rene Schoeman *Tel:* (051) 444-3048 *Fax:* (051) 444-3057 *E-mail:* vsbrand@vanschaik.com
Medical University of SA-Pretoria, PO Box 31361, Braamfontein 2017, Contact: Anos Nkambule *Tel:* (012) 521-4327 *E-mail:* ankambule@vanschaik.com
Wits University (East Campus), Matrix Bldg, Braamfontein 2001, Contact: Thomas Khadaba *Tel:* (011) 339-2775 *Fax:* (011) 339-7180 *E-mail:* vsmatrix@vanschaik.com
Braamfontein Centre, Jorissen Str, Braamfontein, Johannesburg 2000, Contact: Alan Somers *Tel:* (011) 339-1711 *Toll Free Tel:* ' *Fax:* (011) 339-7267 *E-mail:* vsbraam@vanschaik.com
Brandwag Shopping Centre, Brandhof, Bloemfontein 9300, Contact: Dave Kok *Tel:* (051) 444-5533 *Fax:* (051) 444-5534 *E-mail:* dkok@vanschaik.com
Cape Technikon, Keizer Gracht Rd, Cape Town 8001, Contact: Stanton Hermanus *Tel:* (021) 465-1697 *Fax:* (021) 465-5121 *E-mail:* kaaptech@vanschaik.com
Naspers Bldg, Ground floor, PO Box 5496, Cape Town 8001, Contact: Susan Parsons *Tel:* (021) 406-2118 *Fax:* (021) 406-2957 *E-mail:* bsentrum@boeksentrum.com
Port Elizabeth Technikon, Hurteria Bldg, York St, George, Contact: Doreen Coetzee *Tel:* (044) 874-2801
Nedbank Forum, Burnett St, Hatfield, Pretoria 0083, Contact: Billy Palk *Tel:* (012) 362-5701 *Fax:* (012) 362-5673 *E-mail:* vshat@vanschaik.com
Wits Medical School, 7 York Rd, Parktown, Johannesburg, Contact: Susannah Mbatha *Tel:* (011) 717-2012 *E-mail:* smbatha@vanschaik.com
Wits University (West Campus), DJ du Plessis Bldg, Johannesburg 2000, Contact: Zoe Marks *Tel:* (011) 339-2828 *Fax:* (011) 403-8087 *E-mail:* zmarks@vanschaik.com
Vaal University of Technology East Rand Campus, Room P014, Process House, c/o Plane & Isando Rd, Kemptonpark 1619, Contact: Elaine Dippenaar *Tel:* (011) 392-4652 *E-mail:* edippenaar@vanschaik.com
Vaal University of Technology, Senpark Bldg, Room 105, c/o Corrie de Kock & Margareth Prinsloo St, Klerksdorp 2520, Contact: Ina Greyvenstein *Tel:* (018) 462-8967 *E-mail:* igreyven@vanschaik.com
Tshwane University of Technology, General Dan Pienaar Rd, Nelspruit, Contact: Lizzy Phiri *Tel:* (013) 745-3552
Sanlam Centre, Voortrekker Rd, Parow 7500, Contact: Erika Burger *Tel:* (021) 930-2480 *Fax:* (021) 939-3767 *E-mail:* vsparow@vanschaik.com
Sanlam Student Village, University Way, Summerstrand, Port Elizabeth 6001, Contact: Seun Gerber *Tel:* (041) 583-3171 *Fax:* (041) 583-2418 *E-mail:* vspe@vanschaik.com
University of Port Elizabeth (Vista Branch), Uitenhage Rd, Missionvale, Port Elizabeth 6001, Contact: Doreen Coetzee *Tel:* (041) 408-3111 *Fax:* (041) 583-2418 *E-mail:* vspe@vanschaik.com
Cachetpark Centre, Tom St, Potchefstroom, Contact: Anne-Marie Viljoen *Tel:* (018) 294-8875 *Fax:* (018) 294-4445 *E-mail:* vspotch@vanschaik.com
Shop 2, Filkem House, c/o Church & Queen Sts, PO Box 724, Pretoria 0001, Contact: Rassie Erasmus *Tel:* (012) 321-2442 *Fax:* (012) 325-7832 *E-mail:* vskerk@vanschaik.com
Tshwane University of Technology, FCM Total Garage, 422 Rebecca St, Pretoria West 0183, Contact: Jaap Kampman *Tel:* (012) 327-1945 *E-mail:* ptatech@vanschaik.com
18 Main Rd, PO Box 279, Rondebosch 7700, Contact: Anand Pillay *Tel:* (021) 689-4112 *Fax:* (021) 686-3404 *E-mail:* vsrbosch@vanschaik.com
Port Elizabeth Technikon, Saasveld, Contact: Doreen Coetzee *Tel:* (044) 801-5111
Officer Commanding, Air Force Base, Langebaan Rd, Saldanha 7395, Contact: Piet Snyman *Tel:* (022) 706-2219
Vaal University of Technology, Vista Campus, Sebokeng, Contact: Gladys Morei *Tel:* (082) 753 4261
University of Stellenbosch, Langenhoven Centre, Stellenbosch 7600, Contact: Ermien Louw *Tel:* (021) 887-2830 *Fax:* (021) 886-6184 *E-mail:* vssbosch@vanschaik.com
Queensmead Mall Shopping Centre, Shop 4, Teigmouth Rd, Umbilo, Contact: Barbara Hoskins *Tel:* (031) 205-5821 *Fax:* (031) 205-5823 *E-mail:* bhoskins@vanschaik.com
North West University, Hendrik v Eck Blvd, PO Box 2850, Vanderbijlpark 1900, Contact: Judy Kuilder *Tel:* (016) 985-1144 *Fax:* (016) 985-1126 *E-mail:* vaalpukke@naspers.com
Vaal University of Technology, Andries Potgieter Blvd, PO Box 5865, Vanderbijlpark 1900, Contact: Magda McClintock *Tel:* (016) 985-2340 *Fax:* (016) 985-1210 *E-mail:* vsvaal@vanschaik.com
19 Swartbos Rd, Witbank 1043, Contact: Celeste Greeff *Tel:* (013) 690-2796 *E-mail:* cgreeff@vanschaik.com

Spain

Agencia General de Libreria Internacional SL (AGLI)
Islas Marshall 1, 28035 Madrid
Tel: (091) 373 66 40 *Fax:* (091) 373 27 40
E-mail: agli@senda.ari.es
Key Personnel
Contact: President
Bookshop(s): Libreria Jose Ma Padrino Barquillo, 21, 28004 Madrid *Tel:* (091) 5325361 *Fax:* (091) 5328569

AGLI - Agencia General de Libreria Internacional SL, see Agencia General de Libreria Internacional SL (AGLI)

Alibri Libreria, SL
Balmes 26, 08007 Barcelona
Tel: (093) 317 05 78 *Fax:* (093) 412 27 02
E-mail: books-world@books-world.com
Cable: HERDER
Key Personnel
General Manager: Gerardo Nahm
Founded: 1925
Academic bookshop.
Type of Business: Exporter, Importer, Major Independent Bookseller
Owned by: Andreas Valtl

Libreria Ancora y Delfin
Av Diagonal 564, 08021 Barcelona
Tel: (093) 2000746 *Fax:* (093) 2000757
E-mail: ancoraydelfin@ancoraydelfin.com

SPAIN

Key Personnel
Contact: Eulalia Teixidor de Ventos
Founded: 1956
Bookshop.
Owned by: Ancora y Delfin SL

Libreria Bosch
Ronda Universidad 11, 08007 Barcelona
Tel: (093) 394 3600 *Fax:* (093) 412 2764
E-mail: info@libreriabosch.es
Web Site: www.libreriabosch.es *Cable:* BOSLIBRI
Key Personnel
Manager: Javier Bosch
Founded: 1889
General Bookstore.
Type of Business: Distributor, Exporter, Importer, Major Independent Bookseller
Owned by: Libreria Bosch, SL

CELESA, see Centro de Exportacion de Libros Espanoles SA (CELESA)

Centro de Exportacion de Libros Espanoles SA (CELESA) (Spanish Books Export Center)
Calle Laurel Nº 21, 28005 Madrid
Tel: (091) 517 01 70 *Fax:* (091) 517 34 81
E-mail: celesa@celesa.com
Web Site: www.celesa.es
Key Personnel
Dir: D Jose Maria Redondo Suarez
Founded: 1986
Specialize in the export of any book published in Spain.
Type of Business: Exporter
Owned by: 100 Editoriales Espanolas y Ministerio Cultura

Libreria DELSA
Serrano 80, 28006 Madrid
Tel: (091) 575 15 41 *Fax:* (091) 575 84 14
Key Personnel
Contact: Silvela Sonsoles
21 Branches throughout Spain DELSA de Publicaciones SA is also at the above address.

Diaz de Santos SA - Libreria Cientifico-Tecnica
Dona Juana I de Castilla, 22, 28027 Madrid
Tel: (091) 743 48 90 *Fax:* (091) 743 40 23
E-mail: librerias@diazdesantos.es
Web Site: www.diazdesantos.es
Telex: 45141 Dsan E
Key Personnel
Dir General: Joaquin Diaz Gomez
  E-mail: joaquin.diaz@diazdesantos.es
Owned by: Diaz de Santos SA
Branch Office(s)
Diaz de Santos SA - Libreria Cientifico-Tecnica, Calle Balmes 417-419, 08022 Barcelona
  Tel: (093) 212 86 47 *Fax:* (093) 211 49 91
  E-mail: barcelona@diazdesantos.es
UPC-Universitaria, Jordi Gironda Salgado, s/n, Campus Nord, 08034 Barcelona *Tel:* (093) 204 13 24 *Fax:* (093) 204 13 69 *E-mail:* upc@diazdesantos.es
Diaz de Santos SA - Agropecuaria, Calle Lagasca 95, 28006 Madrid *Tel:* (091) 576 73 82 *Fax:* (091) 576 73 16 *E-mail:* madrid@diazdesantos.es
c/ Rosalie de Castro, 36, 15706 Santiago de Compostela, Galicia *Tel:* (0981) 59 03 00 *Fax:* (0981) 59 03 70 *E-mail:* galicia@diazdesantos.es
Pl Ruiz de Alda, 11, 41004 Sevilla, Andalucia *Tel:* (095) 454 26 61 *Fax:* (095) 453 33 78 *E-mail:* andalucia@diazdesantos.es

EDHASA (Editora y Distribuidora Hispano-Americana SA)
Av Diagonal, 519-521, 2º piso, 08029 Barcelona
Tel: (093) 4949720 *Fax:* (093) 4194584
E-mail: info@edhasa.es
Web Site: www.edhasa.es
Key Personnel
Editorial Dir: Daniel Fernandez *E-mail:* d.fdez@edhasa.es
Publisher's Assistant: Virginia Elizondo *E-mail:* v.elizondo@edhasa.es
Founded: 1946
Subjects: Fine Editions, Illustrated Books, General Trade Books-Hardcover, Juvenile & Young Adult Books, Translations, Economics, Fiction, History, How-To, Literature, Literary, Literary Criticism, Essays, Management, Maritime, Philosophy, Romance, Science Fiction, Fantasy, Travel
Type of Business: Distributor, Exporter

Editora y Distribuidora Hispano Americana SA (EDHASA), see EDHASA (Editora y Distribuidora Hispano-Americana SA)

Enrique Libreria
Libreros 8, 28004 Madrid
Tel: (091) 522 80 88
Key Personnel
Contact: Enrique Bataller Ferrandiz
Founded: 1971
Type of Business: Exporter, Importer, Major Independent Bookseller

Casa del Libro Espasa-Calpe SA
Complejo Atica, Edificio 4, Via de las Dos Castillas, No 33, 28224 Pozuelo de Alarcon, Madrid
Tel: (091) 481 13 71
E-mail: casadellibro@casadellibro.com
Web Site: www.casadellibro.com
Telex: 48850 ESPACE *Cable:* ESPACALPE
Owned by: Editorial Espasa-Calpe SA
Branch Office(s)
Passeig de Gracia, 62, 08007 Barcelona
  Tel: (093) 272 34 80 *Fax:* (093) 487 14 26
  E-mail: pgracia@casadellibro.com
Alameda de Urquijo, 9, 48009 Bilbao
  Tel: (094) 415 32 00 *Fax:* (094) 415 32 22
  E-mail: alameda@casadellibro.com
Colon de Larreategui, 41, 48009 Bilbao
  Tel: (094) 424 07 04 *Fax:* (094) 424 38 12
  E-mail: colon@casadellibro.com
Plaza de Italia, 3, 33206 Gijon *Tel:* (098) 517 65 70 *E-mail:* gijon@casadellibro.com
Alcala, 96, 28009 Madrid *Tel:* (091) 432 26 10 *Fax:* (091) 578 19 90 *E-mail:* alcala@casadellibro.com
Gran via, 29, 28013 Madrid *Tel:* (091) 524 19 00 *Fax:* (091) 522 77 58 *E-mail:* granvia@casadellibro.com
Maestro Victoria, 3, 20813 Madrid *Tel:* (091) 521 48 98 *Fax:* (091) 521 91 81 *E-mail:* mvictoria@casadellibro.com
Salud, 17, 28013 Madrid *Tel:* (091) 524 19 39 *Fax:* (091) 522 77 88
Velazquez, 8, 41001 Sevilla *Tel:* (095) 450 29 50 *Fax:* (095) 422 24 96 *E-mail:* sevilla@casadellibro.com
Passeig Russafa, 11, 46002 Valencia *Tel:* (096) 353 00 20 *Fax:* (096) 352 84 12 *E-mail:* valencia@casadellibro.com
Velazquez Moreno, 27, 36202 Vigo *Tel:* (098) 644 16 79 *Fax:* (098) 644 18 53 *E-mail:* vigo@casadellibro.com
Arka, 11, 01005 Vitoria-Gasteiz *Tel:* (094) 515 81 75 *Fax:* (094) 513 36 78 *E-mail:* vitoria@casadellibro.com

Libreria Hispano Americana
Gran Via de Les Corts Catalanes 594, 08007 Barcelona
Tel: (093) 3175337; (093) 3180079 *Fax:* (093) 3189339
Key Personnel
Manager: Josep M Boixareu Vilaplana
Commercial Manager: Jose Romero Gonzalez
Founded: 1941
Specialize in Scientific & Technical Books.
Type of Business: Importer, Major Independent Bookseller

Hogar del Libro, SA
Ramelleres, 17, 08001 Barcelona
Tel: (093) 3182700 *Fax:* (093) 3010399
Key Personnel
Dir: Sebastia Fabregues
Branch Office(s)
Pg Placa Major 12, 08202 Sabadell
Pg Placa Major 34, 08202 Sabadell *Tel:* (03) 7255959
Hogar del Libro-Baricentro, Carretera Barcelona a Sabadell, Local No 135 *Tel:* (03) 7186310
Bookshop(s): Elisabets 6, 08001 Barcelona

Marcial Pons Librero
San Sotero, 6, 28037 Madrid
Tel: (091) 304 33 03 *Fax:* (091) 327 23 67
E-mail: librerias@marcialpons.es
Web Site: www.marcialpons.es
Founded: 1948
Type of Business: Distributor, Exporter, Importer, Major Independent Bookseller, Wholesaler
Bookshop(s): Law, Barbara de Braganza, 8, 28004 Madrid; Economics, Plaza de las Salesas, 10, 28004 Madrid; Humanities, Plaza Conde del Valle de Suchill, 8, 28015 Madrid

H F Martinez de Murguia SA
Valverde, 29, 28004 Madrid
Tel: (091) 522 66 34; (091) 532 39 71 *Fax:* (091) 531 37 86
Key Personnel
Manager: Francisco Gugel
Supplier of books published in Spain.
Type of Business: Distributor, Exporter, Importer, Wholesaler

Mundi-Prensa Libros, SA
Castello, 37, 28001 Madrid
Tel: (091) 436 37 00 *Fax:* (091) 575 39 98
E-mail: libreria@mundiprensa.es
Web Site: www.mundiprensa.com
Key Personnel
General Manager: Jose Maria Hernandez
  E-mail: hernandez@mundiprensa.es
Founded: 1948
Publisher, bookseller & subscription agency.
Type of Business: Distributor, Exporter, Importer, Major Book Chain Headquarters, Major Independent Bookseller, Wholesaler
Branch Office(s)
Consell de Cent, 391, 08009 Barcelona
  Tel: (0934) 88 34 92 *Fax:* (0934) 87 76 59
Rio Panuco, 141, 06500 Mexico City, Mexico
  Tel: (052) 5533 5658 *Fax:* (052) 5514 6799
Bookshop(s): Libreria Mundi-Prensa

Libreria Passim SA
Floridablanca 54-58, Ent 4a B, 08015 Barcelona
Tel: (093) 325 03 05 *Fax:* (093) 325 03 05
E-mail: passim@intercom.es
Key Personnel
Manager: Alex Pujol
Publishes catalogs of new & out-of-print books about Spain & Latin America published in Spain. Specialize in sales to universities & libraries.
Type of Business: Exporter, Major Independent Bookseller

Libreria Pons SL
Felix Latassa, 33, 50006 Zaragoza
Mailing Address: PO Box 10348, 50006 Zaragoza
Tel: (0976) 550 105; (0976) 350 037; (0976) 554 920 *Fax:* (0976) 356 072
E-mail: promedit@libreriapons-zaragoza.com; pedidos@liberiapons-zaragoza.com; admon@liberiapons-zaragoza.com

Web Site: www.libreriapons-zaragoza.com
Key Personnel
Dir: Juan F Pons
Founded: 1951
Library supplier.
Type of Business: Distributor, Importer, Major Independent Bookseller

PPC Editorial y Distribuidora, SA
Impresores, 15, Urbanizacion Prado del Espino, 28660 Boadilla del Monte (Madrid)
Tel: (091) 359 23 00 *Fax:* (091) 350 54 43
Telex: 45051 *Cable:* PEPECE
Key Personnel
President: Antonio Montero Moreno
Vice President: Juan Luis Acebal Lujan
Dir: Angel Alos Cortes
Type of Business: Distributor, Exporter, Major Book Chain Headquarters
Owned by: PPC
Branch Office(s)
Libreria Pastoral, Velazquez 2, 04002 Almeria
Libreria P P C, Canuda 9, 08002 Barcelona
Libreria Piedelatorre, 29015 Malaga
Libreria Selecta, San Felipe Neri 10, 07002 Palma de Mallorca
Libreria Concilio, Teniente Coronel Segui 1, 41001 Sevilla
Libreria Promocion, c/o Conde de Cardenas 5, 14002 Cordoba

Promocion Popular Cristiana, see PPC Editorial y Distribuidora, SA

Libreria Rubinos - 1860 SA
Alcala 98, 28009 Madrid
Tel: (091) 435 22 39 *Fax:* (091) 435 32 72
Key Personnel
Administrator: Antonio Rubinos Casanueva
Type of Business: Distributor, Exporter, Importer, Major Book Chain Headquarters, Major Independent Bookseller, Wholesaler

Sri Lanka

Bright Book Centre (Pvt) Ltd
S-27, 1st floor, Colombo Central Super Market Complex, Colombo 11
Tel: (0112) 434770 *Fax:* (0112) 333279; (0112) 43470
Key Personnel
President: Pon Sakthivel
Founded: 1990
Specialize in book publishing & distributing.
Type of Business: Distributor, Exporter, Importer, Major Independent Bookseller, Wholesaler
Branch Office(s)
77/24 Jampeetta Lane, Colombo 13

KVG de Silva & Sons
415 Galle Rd, Colombo 4
Tel: (01) 84146 *Fax:* (01) 588875
Telex: 22658 GLAXY CE
Key Personnel
President: K V J De Silva
Founded: 1898
Dealers in Rare Books & Maps of Sri Lanka & Sri Lankan Islands & old views of Sri Lanka.
Type of Business: Distributor, Importer, Major Independent Bookseller
Branch Office(s)
Serendib Gallery, 100 Galle Rd, Colombo 4
Bookshop(s): K V G's Bookstore, Liberty Plaza, Colombo 3

Lake House Bookshop
100, Sir Chittampalam A Gardiner Mawatha, Colombo 2
Tel: (01) 430581; (01) 432105; (01) 430582
Fax: (01) 432104
E-mail: bookshop@sri.lanka.net
Telex: 21266 Lakexpo Ce *Cable:* BOOKSALES
Key Personnel
Dir & General Manager: Victor Walatara
Founded: 1941
Also publisher.
Type of Business: Distributor, Exporter, Importer, Major Independent Bookseller, Wholesaler
Owned by: Lake House Investments Ltd, 40, WAD Ramanayake Mawatha, Colombo 2
Branch Office(s)
Liberty Plaza, Dehiwela, Hyde Park Corner

Sadeepa Bookshop
1060, Maradana Rd, Colombo 8
Tel: (011) 686114; (011) 694289; (011) 678043
Fax: (011) 683813; (011) 678044
E-mail: sadeepabk@itmin.com
Web Site: www.sadeepabooks.com
Key Personnel
Man Dir: Sarath Chandra Wanniatchi
Founded: 1987
Also printer & publisher.
Type of Business: Distributor, Importer, Major Book Chain Headquarters, Major Independent Bookseller, Wholesaler
Branch Office(s)
Sadeepa Print Shop, 1121, Maradana Rd, Colombo 8 *Tel:* (011) 683813
MBA Shopping Complex, Colombo 8 *Tel:* (011) 684241

Sarasavi Book Shop Pvt Ltd
Subsidiary of Sarasavi Group of Companies
30, Stanley Thilakarathna Mawatha, Nugegoda 10250
Tel: (01) 2852519; (01) 2820983; (01) 4304546
Fax: (01) 2509503; (01) 2821454
E-mail: sarasavi@slt.lk
Web Site: www.sarasavi.lk
Key Personnel
Chairman & Man Dir: Mr H D Premasiri
Founded: 1948
Membership(s): Sri Lanka Book Publishers' Association, Book Sellers Association of Ceylon, British Book Sellers Association, Sri Lanka Book Sellers Association.
Type of Business: Importer, Major Independent Bookseller
Imprints: Sarasavi Publishers
Branch Office(s)
Colombo Fort-44/9 YMBA Bldg, Colombo 1 *Tel:* (01) 2326831
Colombo 8-1/50 YMBA Bldg, Borella *Tel:* (01) 2698886
Bakeland Bldg, 87 Minuwangoda Rd, Gampaha *Tel:* (033) 2222376; (033) 4670236
86 D S Senanayake Veediya, Kandy *Tel:* (0812) 234036
74 Kumaratunga Mawatha, Matara *Tel:* (041) 2228406
74 High Level Rd, Maharagama *Tel:* (01) 2850340
Warehouse: 3/1 St John's Church Rd, Nugegoda

Sarasavi Publishers, *imprint of* Sarasavi Book Shop Pvt Ltd

Sudan

The Khartoum Bookshop, see The New Bookshop

The New Bookshop
Zubeir Pasha St, Khartoum
Mailing Address: PO Box 968, Khartoum
Tel: (011) 774425 *Cable:* Newstand Khartoum
Key Personnel
Owner: P N Flanginis
Founded: 1957
Subjects: Member of the Sudan Chamber of Commerce-Khartoum
Type of Business: Distributor, Importer, Wholesaler

The Nile Bookshop
New Extension, St 41, Khartoum
Mailing Address: PO Box 8036, Khartoum
Tel: (011) 463749 *Fax:* (011) 770821
E-mail: mohdelhag@yahoo.com; nilebookshop@yahoo.com *Cable:* NILE
Type of Business: Distributor, Importer, Major Independent Bookseller

The Sudan Bookshop Ltd
PO Box 156, Khartoum
Tel: (011) 74123; (011) 76781
Telex: 22480 sisco km *Cable:* Bookshop Khartoum
Key Personnel
Man Dir: Joseph A Tadros

University of Khartoum Bookshop
PO Box 321, Khartoum
Tel: (011) 80558
Key Personnel
Manager: Dr Khalid El-Mubarak
Owned by: Khartoum University Press

Sweden

Akerbloms Universitetsbokhandel
Affiliate of Bokia
Oestra Radhusgatan 6, Umea
Mailing Address: Box 83, S-90103 Umea
Tel: (090) 711250 *Fax:* (090) 711260
E-mail: swedish.books@akerbloms.se
Key Personnel
Manager: Mats Gyllengahm *E-mail:* mats.gyllengahm@bokia.se
Founded: 1843
Type of Business: Importer, Major Independent Bookseller

Akademibokhandeln/Almqvist & Wiksell
PO Box 7634, 103 94 Stockholm
Tel: (08) 613 61 00 *Fax:* (08) 24 25 43
Web Site: www.akademibokhandeln.se
Founded: 1953
Group Members: Akademibokhandeln/Eckersteins, Lundequistska.
Type of Business: Exporter, Importer, Major Book Chain Headquarters

Almqvist och Wiksell Bokhandel AB
Box 7634, 103 94 Stockholm
Tel: (08) 613 61 00 *Fax:* (08) 24 25 43
Web Site: www.akademibokhandeln.se
Telex: 12430
Key Personnel
Manager: Wojtek Boguslaw
Member of Esselte Bokhandel Group.

AB Gleerups Universitetsbokhandeln
Box 172, 221 00 Lund
Tel: (046) 46 19 60 00 *Fax:* (046) 46 15 94 03
Key Personnel
Manager: Peter Dahl
President: Kjell Dyster-Aas

SWEDEN

Contact: Lena Stenlund
Type of Business: Distributor, Importer, Major Independent Bookseller, Wholesaler

Soederbokhandeln Hansson och Bruce AB
Gotgatan 37, Stockholm
Tel: (08) 405432; (08) 6405433 *Fax:* (08) 6441315
Key Personnel
Manager: Stig Sunnerholm
Founded: 1874

Samdistribution AB
Norra Malmvaegen 82, Haeggvik, 191 24 Sollentuna
Mailing Address: Box 449, 191 24 Sollentuna
Tel: (08) 696 80 00 *Fax:* (08) 696 83 73
E-mail: samdistribution@bok.bonnier.se
Web Site: www.bok.bonnier.se
Key Personnel
President: Maria Curman
Man Dir: Eric Johansson
Founded: 1975
Warehousing of books (Book Trade, Book Services & Book Club Members).
Type of Business: Distributor
Owned by: Bonnierfoerlagen AB

Wettergrens Bokhandel AB
Avenyn 21, 411 36 Gothenburg
Tel: (031) 706 25 00 *Fax:* (031) 778 14 80
E-mail: info@wettergrens.se
Key Personnel
Contact: Carl Wettergren
Founded: 1882
Type of Business: Major Independent Bookseller

Switzerland

H R Balmer AG Buchhandlung Verlag Verlagauslieferung
Neugasse 12, Landsgemeindeplatz, 6301 Zug
Tel: (041) 726 97 97 *Fax:* (041) 726 97 98
E-mail: info@buecher-balmer.ch
Web Site: www.buecher-balmer.ch
Key Personnel
Contact: Christoph Balmer
Founded: 1864
Type of Business: Distributor, Importer, Major Independent Bookseller, Wholesaler
Bookshop(s): Buches Balmer, Einkaufs-Allee Metalli, 6304 Zug *Tel:* (041) 726 97 87 *Fax:* (041) 726 97 88

Brunnen Bibel Panorama
Formerly Pilgermission Buch & Brunnen-Verlag Basel
Wallstr 6, 4002 Basel
Tel: (061) 295 60 03 *Fax:* (061) 295 60 68
E-mail: info@bibelpanorama.ch
Web Site: www.bibelpanorama.ch
Key Personnel
Contact: Andreas Walter

Brunner Buecher AG, see Buchhandlung zum Elsasser AG

Buchhandlung zum Elsasser AG
Limmatquai 18, 8001 Zurich
Tel: (01) 261 08 47; (01) 251 16 12 *Fax:* (01) 261 08 97
Telex: 57268
Key Personnel
Manager: Mr Hansruedi Brunner

Fehr'sche Buchhandlung AG
Schmiedgasse 1, 9000 St Gallen
Tel: (071) 222 11 52; (071) 222 53 81
Key Personnel
Manager: B Brun

Huber & Lang
Schanzenstr 1, 3000 Bern 9
Tel: (031) 300 4646 *Fax:* (031) 300 4656
E-mail: contactbern@huberlang.com
Web Site: www.huberlang.com
Founded: 1927
Also publisher.
Type of Business: Distributor, Exporter, Importer, Major Independent Bookseller
Owned by: Hans Huber AG, Laenggass-str 76, 3000 Bern 9
Branch Office(s)
Stadelhoferstr 28, Postfach, 8021 Zurich 1
Tel: (043) 268 3222 *Fax:* (043) 268 3220
E-mail: contact.zurich@huberlang.com
(Medicine, Psychology, Science)

Buchhaus Meili AG
Fronwagplatz 13, 8201 Schaffhausen
Tel: (052) 625 41 44 *Fax:* (052) 625 47 46
E-mail: info@buchhausmeli.ch
Web Site: www.buchhausmeili.ch
Telex: 76777 Meibuch
Owned by: Peter Meili & Co

No Name Photo Gallery, see PEP Buchhandlung & No Name Photo Gallery

Orell Fuessli Buchhandlungs AG
Dietzingerstr 3, 8036 Zurich
Tel: (0848) 849 848 *Fax:* (01) 455 56 20
E-mail: orders@books.ch; info@ofv.ch
Web Site: www.ofv.ch; www.books.ch
Telex: (01) 813021 orla ch
Key Personnel
Manager: Dr Manfred Hiefner *E-mail:* mhiefner@ofv.ch
Also Publisher.

PEP Buchhandlung & No Name Photo Gallery
Unterer Heuberg 2, CH-4051 Basel
Tel: (061) 261 51 61 *Fax:* (061) 261 51 61
E-mail: pepnoname@balcab.ch
Web Site: www.pepnoname.ch
Key Personnel
Vice President: Victor Zwimpfer
Founded: 1980
Bookstore specializing in photo, film, art, tattoo, Indian literature & photo gallery.
Type of Business: Distributor, Exporter, Importer, Major Book Chain Headquarters, Major Independent Bookseller
Owned by: Tobias Toggweiler

Pilgermission Buch & Brunnen-Verlag Basel, see Brunnen Bibel Panorama

Quellen-Verlag
Gallusstr 20, 9001 St Gallen
Tel: (071) 227 47 77 *Fax:* (071) 227 47 58

Schweizer Buchzentrum (Swiss Book Centre)
Postfach 522, CH-4600 Olten
Tel: (062) 476161 *Fax:* (062) 465676
Type of Business: Distributor

Buchhandlung Staeheli AG
Bederstr 77, 8021 Zurich 2
Tel: (01) 2099111 *Fax:* (01) 2099112
E-mail: info@staehelibooks.ch
Web Site: www.staehelibooks.ch *Cable:* STAEHELIBOOKS

Key Personnel
Chief Executive Officer: Claus Gretener
E-mail: claus.gretener@staehelibooks.ch
Founded: 1934
Booksellers & Subscription Agents
Online Bookshop.
Type of Business: Importer, Major Independent Bookseller
Bookshop(s): 4/5 Am Weinplatz, 8021 Zurich 1

Staeheli's Bookshops Ltd, see Buchhandlung Staeheli AG

Centre Suisse du Livre, see Schweizer Buchzentrum

Centro Svizzero del Libro, see Schweizer Buchzentrum

Swiss Book Centre, see Schweizer Buchzentrum

Wepf & Co AG
Eisengasse 5, 4001 Basel
Tel: (061) 269 85 15 (Germany) *Fax:* (061) 261 35 97 (Germany)
E-mail: wepf@dial.eunet.ch
Web Site: www.wepf.ch *Cable:* WEPFCO BASEL
Key Personnel
Dir: H U Herrmann
Also Publisher & Antiquarian Bookshop.
Branch Office(s)
Freiburgerstr 83, 79576 Weil am Rhein, Germany *Tel:* (07621) 75028 *Fax:* (07621) 75992
E-mail: info@buchhandlung-wepf.de
5, quai des Bateliers, 67000 Strasbourg, France
Tel: (0388) 371327 *Fax:* (0388) 240096

Syrian Arab Republic

Avicenne Librairie Internationale
PO Box 2456, Damas
Tel: (011) 221 29 11; (011) 224 44 77 *Fax:* (011) 221 98 33
E-mail: avicenne@net.sy
Telex: Ortexo 419120 SY
Key Personnel
General Manager: Jean-Pierre Dummar
Founded: 1963
Entertainment Articles.
Type of Business: Distributor, Importer, Major Book Chain Headquarters
Owned by: Meridien Bookshop, Kuwatly St, Jean Pierre Dummar
Branch Office(s)
Sheraton Bookshop, Amawiia Sq, Damascus
Tel: (011) 2229300
Amir Poloee Bookshop, Aleppo *Tel:* (021) 2246510
Safir Bookshop, Homs *Tel:* (031) 412400

Taiwan, Province of China

The Children's Book Store Company Ltd
10, Lane 144 Section 5, Min Sheng East Rd, Taipei 105 ROC

Tel: (02) 2762-8222 *Fax:* (02) 2760-4322
Web Site: www.tong-nian.com.tw
Key Personnel
Chief Exec: Chang Yao-Hwa
Founded: 1955
Type of Business: Wholesaler

Mei Ya Publications Inc (Sueling Inc)
10F 82 Fuhsing S Rd, Sec 2, Taipei 106
Tel: (02) 7037481 *Fax:* (02) 7033847
Telex: 11240 Sueling
Key Personnel
Manager: Julia Lee
Specialize in college & university textbook reprints (all copyrighted).

United Republic of Tanzania

The Dar Es Salaam Bookshop
PO Box 9030, Dar Es Salaam
Tel: (051) 23416
Key Personnel
Manager: C Salu

Readit Books
PO Box 21100, Dar es Salaam
Tel: (022) 2184077 *Fax:* (022) 2181077
E-mail: readit@raha.com
Founded: 1993

University of Dar Es Salaam Bookshop
Unit of Dar es Salaam University Press Ltd
PO Box 35182, Dar Es Salaam
Tel: (022) 2410093; (022) 2410500 (ext 2568) *Fax:* (022) 2410137
Key Personnel
Ag Marketing Manager: Mr A Kanuya *Tel:* (022) 2410300
Type of Business: Importer, Major Independent Bookseller
Owned by: University of Dar Es Salaam

Thailand

Asia Books Co Ltd
No 5 Sukhumvit Rd, SOI 61 Wattana, Bangkok 10110
Tel: (02) 715-9000 *Fax:* (02) 391-2277
E-mail: information@asiabooks.com
Web Site: www.asiabooks.com
Key Personnel
Owner: Vinai Suttharoj
Assistant Man Dir: Rachanee Anakepeerasak *Tel:* (02) 715-9166 *E-mail:* rachanee@asiabooks.com
Founded: 1969
Publisher, Distributor & chain of English language bookshops in Thailand.
Type of Business: Distributor, Importer, Major Book Chain Headquarters, Wholesaler
Showroom(s): 3rd floor, Central City Plaza, Room 309, Bangna-Trat Rd, KM 3 Bangkok *Tel:* (02) 3610743; (02) 3610744 *Fax:* (02) 3610745; 3rd floor, Emporium Shopping Complex, Sukhumvit Rd, Bangkok *Tel:* (02) 6648565-7 *Fax:* (02) 6648548; 1st floor, Landmark Hotel, Sukhumvit Rd, Bangkok *Tel:* (02) 2525839; (02) 2525456 *Fax:* (02) 2515993; 3rd floor, Landmark Hotel, Sukhumvit Rd, Bangkok *Tel:* (02) 2525655; (02) 2529901 *Fax:* (02) 2515993; 2nd floor, Peninsula Plaza, Rajdamri Rd, Bangkok *Tel:* (02) 2539786; (02) 2539788 *Fax:* (02) 2540737; 2nd floor, Seacon Sq, Srinakarin Rd, Bangkok *Tel:* (02) 7218867-8 *Fax:* (02) 7218869; 4th floor, Siam Discovery Center, Rama1 Rd, Bangkok *Tel:* (02) 6580418-20 *Fax:* (02) 6580421; 221 Sukhumvit Rd (Between Sois 15-17), Bangkok *Tel:* (02) 2527277; (02) 6510428 *Fax:* (02) 2516042; 3rd floor, Thaniya Plaza Bldg, Silom Rd, Bangkok *Tel:* (02) 2312106; (02) 2312107 *Fax:* (02) 2312108; 2nd floor, Time Square Bldg, Sukhumvit Rd (between Sois 12-14), Bangkok *Tel:* (02) 2500162; (02) 2500163 *Fax:* (02) 2500164; 3rd floor, World Trade Centre (Skydome Zone C), Rajdamri Rd, Bangkok *Tel:* (02) 2556209; (02) 2556210 *Fax:* (02) 2556211

Central Book Distribution Co, Ltd
306 Silom Rd, Bangkok 10500
Tel: (02) 235-5400 *Fax:* (02) 237-8321
Telex: 82768 Cetrac Th *Cable:* CETRAC BANGKOK
Key Personnel
Owner: Tieng Chirathivat
Man Dir: Ratana Norabhanlobh *E-mail:* ratanan@cmg.co.th
Founded: 1948
Type of Business: Distributor, Exporter, Importer, Wholesaler

Christian Bookstore
14 Pramuan Rd, Bangkok 10500
Tel: (02) 234-7991
Key Personnel
Manager: Urai Kithpraditkul
Type of Business: Distributor, Importer, Major Book Chain Headquarters, Wholesaler

Nibondh Co Ltd
PO Box 402, Bangkok GPO
Tel: (02) 221-2611; (02) 221-1553 *Fax:* (02) 224-6889
E-mail: kongsiri@mozart.inet.co
Web Site: www.uiowa.edu/~lawlib/vendors/nibondh.htm
Key Personnel
Manager: Sumetra Kongsiri
English books at the company's main address; English, Thai books & magazines at Nibhondh (sikak), 40-42 New Rd, Bangkok.

Odeon Book Store Lp
Opp Odeon Theatre, Wang Burapha, Bangkok 10500
Tel: (02) 2210742; (02) 2216567 *Fax:* (02) 2253300; (02) 2548806
Key Personnel
Manager: Prasarn Santiwathana
Branch Office(s)
218/10-2 soil Siam Sq, Rama I Rd, Bangkok 10500

Suksit Siam Co Ltd
113, 115 Fung Nakorn Rd, Opp, Wat Rajbopith, Bangkok 10200
Tel: (02) 225-9531-2 *Fax:* (02) 222 5188
Key Personnel
Manager, Publicity: Mrs Nilchawee Sivaraksa
Also library suppliers.
Type of Business: Importer

Suriwong Book Centre, Ltd
54 Sridonchai Rd, Chiang Mai 50100
Mailing Address: PO Box 44, Chiang Mai 50000
Tel: (053) 281052 *Fax:* (053) 271902
E-mail: suriwong@loxinfo.co.th
Key Personnel
Man Dir: Joy Jittidecharaks
Book Retailer in Thai & English, medical journals agent.
Bookshop(s): 54 Sridonchai Rd, Chiang Mai 50100 *E-mail:* suriwong@loxinfo.co.th

Suriyaban Bookstore
c/o Suriyaban Publishers, 14 Pramuan Rd, Bangkok 10500
Tel: (02) 2347991; (02) 2347992
Key Personnel
Manager: Surapon Byboribankul
Owned by: Suriyaban Publishers

White Lotus Co Ltd
GPO Box 1141, Bangkok 10501
Tel: (02) 332-4915; (02) 741-6288; (02) 741-6289 *Fax:* (02) 311-4575; (02) 741-6287; (02) 741-6607
Web Site: thailine.com/lotus
Key Personnel
Chief Executive: D Ande *E-mail:* ande@loxinfo.ch.th
Founded: 1972
Also acts as Publisher.
Type of Business: Distributor, Exporter, Importer, Wholesaler

Togo

Librairie/Editions Nouvelles Editions Africaines du TOGO
239 Bd du 13 Janvier, Lome
Mailing Address: BP 4862, Lome
Tel: 21 67 61 *Fax:* 22 10 03
Key Personnel
Contact: Fatai Joseph Aguiar
Sales Administrator: Takougnadi
Owned by: Les Nouvelles Editions Africaines du TOGO (NEA-TOGO)
Bookshop(s): 239 Blvd du 13 Janvier, Lome; Tokoin Doumassesse VB, Lome

Librairie Walter
25 rue du Grand Marche, BP 397, Lome

Trinidad & Tobago

Campus Corner Ltd
72 Pembroke St, Port of Spain
Tel: (868) 623-1678 *Fax:* (868) 623-1678
Key Personnel
Manager: Hilton S Young
Founded: 1973
Type of Business: Distributor, Importer, Major Independent Bookseller, Wholesaler

Charran's Bookshop (1978) Ltd
53 Eastern Main Rd, Tunapuna
Tel: (868) 663-1884
Key Personnel
Manager: Betty Charran
Owned by: Charran Educational Publishers
Bookshop(s): Muir Marshall Ltd, 64a Independence Sq, Port of Spain

Tunisia

Librairie Art et Culture
24 Ave Taieb M'hiri, 7000 Bizerte
Tel: (02) 31072 *Fax:* (02) 431372
Key Personnel
Contact: Mr Limam Nouredine
Type of Business: Distributor

Editions Bouslama
15 Av de France, 1000 Tunis
Tel: (01) 245612
Also publisher.
Branch Office(s)
53 rue Nahas Pacha, Tunis
7 rue Amilcar, Tunis

Societe Nationale d'Edition et de Diffusion
5, ave de Carthage, 1000 Tunis
Tel: (01) 255000; (01) 261799
Also publisher.

Turkey

ABC Kitabevi Sanayi Tic AS
Tunel Meydani 1, 1 80030 Beyoglu, Istanbul
Tel: (0212) 2762404 *Fax:* (0212) 2851860
Telex: 46963 Abca Tr
Key Personnel
Manager: Hamit Calcskan
Owned by: Genclik Kitabevi

Arkadas Ltd
Mithatpasa cad 28/C, 06441 Yenisehir, Ankara
Tel: (0312) 4344624; (0312) 3548300 *Fax:* (0312) 4356057 *Fax on Demand:* (0312) 3548309
E-mail: arkadas@arkadas.com.tr
Web Site: www.arkadas.com.tr
Key Personnel
Chairman & Owner: Cumhur Ozdemir
  E-mail: cumhuro@arkadas.com.tr
Editor: Meltem Ozdemir *E-mail:* meltemo@arkadas.com.tr
Retail Trade of Book Stationery, Music Cassettes, Compact Discs, Import Diskettes, Poster & Print, Publishing.
Type of Business: Distributor, Importer, Major Independent Bookseller, Wholesaler

Fen Kitabevi
Milli Muedafaa Cad 14/7, Ankara
Tel: (0312) 425311 *Fax:* (0312) 4185109; (0312) 4171733
Founded: 1975
Type of Business: Importer, Major Independent Bookseller, Wholesaler
Owned by: Guellueoglu/Mehmet S

Redhouse Bookstore
SEV Matbaacilik ve Yayincilik AS, Rizapasa Yokusu No 50 Mercan, 34450 Istanbul
Tel: (0212) 520 7778; (0212) 520 2960; (0212) 520 0090 *Fax:* (0212) 522 1909
E-mail: info@redhouse.com.tr
Web Site: www.redhouse.com.tr
Telex: 23554 Peet Tr *Cable:* PEET ISTANBUL TR
Key Personnel
Manager: Charles H Brown
Owned by: Redhouse Press

Uganda

Uganda Bookshop
PO Box 7145
Tel: (041) 243756 *Fax:* (041) 245597 *Cable:* BOOKSHOP
Key Personnel
General Manager: Stephen Rostron
Founded: 1927
Type of Business: Distributor, Importer, Major Book Chain Headquarters, Major Independent Bookseller, Wholesaler
Owned by: Church of Uganda, PO Box 6246, Kampala

United Kingdom

Abbeydale, *imprint of* Bookmart Ltd

Africa Book Centre
38 King St, Covent Garden, London WC2E 8JT
Tel: (020) 7240 6649 *Toll Free Tel:* 0845 458 1581 (UK only) *Fax:* (020) 7497 0309
Toll Free Fax: 0845 458 1579 (UK only)
E-mail: orders@africabookcentre.com; info@africabookcentre.com
Web Site: www.africabookcentre.com
Key Personnel
Man Dir: Anthony W Zurbrugg *Tel:* (020) 7836 3020 *E-mail:* tz@africabookcentre.com
Founded: 1989
Member of Booksellers' Association (UK)
Also Publishers' Agent.
Type of Business: Distributor, Exporter, Importer, Major Independent Bookseller, Wholesaler
Warehouse: Central Books Ltd, 99 Wallis Rd, London E9 5LN *Tel:* (020) 8986 4854
E-mail: orders@centralbooks.com (Also distribution)

African Books Collective Ltd
The Jam Factory, 27 Park End St, Oxford OX1 1HU
Tel: (01865) 726686 *Fax:* (01865) 793298; (01993) 709265
E-mail: abc@africanbookscollective.com
Web Site: www.africanbookscollective.com
Key Personnel
Head: Mary Jay *E-mail:* mary.jay@africanbookscollective.com
Marketing: Ejemhen Esangbedo
Customer Services: Krisia Cook *E-mail:* krisia.cook@africanbookscollective.com; Naomi Robertson
Founded: 1989
Marketing & distribution of books published in Africa by 51 publishers from 12 countries. Scholarly, literature & children's, English language titles & Swahiti children's books.
Type of Business: Distributor
Owned by: African Publishers Collective
Warehouse: Unit 9, Green Farm, Fritwell, Bicester, Oxon OX27 7QU *Tel:* (07719) 792669

Afterhurst Ltd
c/o the Book Ordering Dept, Taylor & Francis Ltd, Rankine Rd, Basingstoke, Hants RG24 8PR
Tel: (01256) 813000 *Fax:* (01256) 479438
E-mail: book.orders@tandf.co.uk
Key Personnel
Sales Manager: Linda Jarrett
Type of Business: Distributor
Owned by: Taylor & Francis Ltd, 1 Gunpowder Sq, London EC4A 3DE

Airlift Book Co
8 The Arena, Mollison Ave, Enfield, Middx EN3 7NL
Tel: (020) 8804 0400 *Fax:* (020) 8804 0044
E-mail: customercare@airlift.co.uk
Web Site: www.airlift.co.uk
Key Personnel
Man Dir: J Bailey
Founded: 1979
Type of Business: Distributor

Albany Book Co Ltd
30 Clydeholm Rd, Clydeside Industrial Estate, Glasgow G14 0BJ
Tel: (0141) 9542271
Telex: 777253
Key Personnel
Man Dir: Andrew T Haigh
Dir: Jonathan Ridge; Mike Jones; Joseph Halpin
Bookshop(s): Book Services (Scotland) Ltd, 32 Finlas St, Glasgow G22 5DU (School Textbook Supply); College Bookshop, Jordanhill College, Southbrae Dr, Glasgow GI3 1PP (Educational Book Supply)

Aldington Books Ltd
Unit 3b, Frith Business Centre, Frith Rd, Aldington, Ashford, Kent TN25 7HJ
Tel: (01233) 720123 *Fax:* (01233) 721272
E-mail: sales@aldingtonbooks.co.uk
Web Site: www.aldingtonbooks.co.uk
Key Personnel
Dir: Jan Barker; Ashley Lennox-Kay
Type of Business: Distributor, Importer
Associate Companies: Bay Foreign Language Books *Web Site:* baylanguagebooks.co.uk

The Anglo American Book Company Ltd
Crown Buildings, Bancyfelin, Carmarthenshire SA33 5ND
Tel: (01267) 211880 *Fax:* (01267) 211882
E-mail: books@anglo-american.co.uk
Web Site: www.anglo-american.co.uk
Key Personnel
Man Dir: Dr Martin Roberts
Marketing Dir: David Bowman
Founded: 1992
Mail order book seller & distributor.
Type of Business: Distributor, Exporter, Importer

Apex Books Concern
Darus Salaam, 89 Norfolk Rd, Littlehampton, West Sussex BN17 5HE
Tel: (01903) 734432 *Fax:* (01903) 734432
E-mail: enquiries@apexbooks.co.uk
Web Site: www.apexbooks.co.uk
Key Personnel
Man Dir: S Dean *Tel:* (01903) 734682
Dir: A Dean; Ms M Hughes
Founded: 1950
Specialist in religious & cultural studies. Books, journals, videos, slides, microforms in all subjects.
Type of Business: Distributor, Exporter, Importer

Art Books International Ltd
Unit 14 Groves Business Centre, Shipton Rd Miltonunder-Wychwood, Chipping Norton Oxon OX7 6JP
Tel: (01993) 830000 *Fax:* (01993) 830007
E-mail: sales@art.bks.com
Web Site: www.art-bks.com
Key Personnel
Man Dir: Stanley Kekwick *E-mail:* stanley@art-bks.com
Sales Manager: Fiona Smith
Head of Accounts: Stephen Coke

BOOK DEALERS   UNITED KINGDOM

Founded: 1991
Type of Business: Distributor

Art Data
12 Bell Industrial Estate, 50 Cunnington St, London W4 5HB
Tel: (020) 87471061 *Fax:* (020) 87422319
E-mail: ibf@artdata.co.uk
Web Site: www.artdata.co.uk
Key Personnel
Contact: Tim Borton *E-mail:* tim@artdata.co.uk; Liana Sperow *E-mail:* liana@artdata.co.uk
Type of Business: Distributor, Wholesaler

Ashgrove Publishing
Imprint of Hollydata Publishers Ltd
27 John St, London WC1N 2BX
Tel: (01373) 834900 *Fax:* (01373) 834900
Web Site: www.ashgrovepublishing.com
Founded: 1980

Aspect Marketing Services
Orbital Park, Ashford, Kent TN24 0GA
Tel: (01233) 500 800 *Fax:* (01233) 500 700
E-mail: mail@aspectmarketing.co.uk
Web Site: www.aspectmarketing.co.uk
Founded: 1995
Provides a broad range of Direct Mail, response handling, fulfilment & data services as well as specialist services for publishers to promote new book titles & distribute catalogues to libraries & booksellers.

Austicks Headrow Bookshop
91 The Headrow, Leeds LS1 6LJ
Tel: (0113) 243-9607 *Fax:* (0113) 245-8837
Key Personnel
Manager: John Prime

B McCall Barbour
28 George IV Bridge, Edinburgh EH1 1ES
Tel: (0131) 2254816 *Fax:* (0131) 2254816
Key Personnel
Partner: Dr T C Danson-Smith
Founded: 1900
Christian Publishers.
Type of Business: Distributor, Exporter, Importer, Major Independent Bookseller, Wholesaler

Bargain Book Sales
2b Moore Park Rd, London SW6 2JT
Tel: (020) 7385 7007 *Fax:* (020) 7385 7007; (020) 7385 9727
Key Personnel
Owner & Dir: Graham Snell
Founded: 1975
Specialize in high-quality remainders, especially illustrated books on the Fine & Applied Arts, Graphics, Architecture, Photography, the Cinema & Music.
Type of Business: Remainder Dealer

Bay Foreign Language Books
Unit 3B Frith Business Centre, Frith Rd Aldington, Ashford Kent TN25 7HJ
Tel: (01233) 720020 *Fax:* (01233) 721272
E-mail: sales@baylanguagebooks.co.uk
Web Site: www.baylanguagebooks.co.uk
Key Personnel
Partner & Dir: Jan Barker
Dir: A R P Lennox-Kay
Founded: 1990
Publishers, University Library supply; over 480 languages in 2000-2001 catalogue.
Membership(s): Bookseller's Association.
Type of Business: Distributor, Exporter, Importer, Major Independent Bookseller, Wholesaler

George Bayntun Booksellers
Manvers St, Bath BA1 1JW
Tel: (01225) 466000 *Fax:* (01225) 482122
E-mail: ebc@georgebayntun.com
Web Site: www.georgebayntun.com
Key Personnel
Proprietor & Owner: Edward Bayntun Coward
Founded: 1894
Rare Books, First Editions & Fine Bindings.

BEBC Distribution
Albion Close, Newtown Business Park, Parkstone Poole, Dorset BH12 3LL
Mailing Address: PO Box 1496, Parkstone Poole Dorset BH12 3LL
Tel: (01202) 712934 *Fax:* (01202) 712913
E-mail: webenquiry@bebc.co.uk
Web Site: www.bebc.co.uk
Key Personnel
Distribution Manager: Charles Kipping *E-mail:* charlesk@bebc.co.uk
Founded: 1974
Provides order fulfillment service to publishers & book clubs.
Owned by: Bournemouth English Book Centre
Bookshop(s): BEBC Bookshop, 125 Charminster Rd, Bournemouth Dorset BH8 8UH, Manager: Alice Rowlands *Tel:* (01202) 523103 *Fax:* (01202) 523103 *E-mail:* charminster@bebc.co.uk; BEBC Bookshop at International House, One Yarmouth Pl, London W1V 7DW, Manager: Michael Keenan *Tel:* (0207) 493 5226 *Fax:* (0207) 493 5226 *E-mail:* piccadilly@bebc.co.uk

Bertrams
One Broadland Business Park, Norwich, Norfolk NR7 0WG
Tel: (0870) 4296666 *Fax:* (0870) 4296667
E-mail: books@bertrams.com
Web Site: www.bertrams.com
Key Personnel
Chairman: Kip Bertram
Chief Executive Officer: Terry Reilly
Dir: Nigel Bertram
Buying Manager: Adrian Stimpson
Sales Dir: Marcus Whewell
Marketing: Tanya DuRose
Founded: 1967
Type of Business: Exporter, Wholesaler

Bibliophile Books
5 Thomas Rd, London E14 7BN
Tel: (020) 7515 9222 *Fax:* (020) 7538 4115
E-mail: customercare@bibliophilebooks.com
Web Site: www.bibliophilebooks.com
Key Personnel
Chief Executive: Anne Quigley
Founded: 1978
Type of Business: Remainder Dealer

Birmingham Museums & Art Gallery
Chamberlain Sq, Birmingham B3 3DH
Tel: (0121) 303 2834; (0121) 303 1966; (0121) 464 9885 (shop) *Fax:* (0121) 303 1394
E-mail: info@bmag.co.uk
Web Site: www.bmag.org.uk; www.bmagshop.co.uk
Key Personnel
Senior Assistant Dir: Mr G Allen
Administrator: J Swancutt *Tel:* (0121) 303 3964 *E-mail:* jackie_swancutt@birmingham.gov.uk
Founded: 1885
Museum & art gallery.

Blackwell Retail
48-51 Broad St, Oxford, Oxon OX1 3AJ
Tel: (01865) 792792 *Fax:* (01865) 794143
E-mail: sales@blackwell.co.uk
Web Site: www.blackwell.co.uk
Telex: 83118 *Cable:* BOOKS OXFORD
Key Personnel
Man Dir: Dominic Myers
Founded: 1879
Booksellers.
Type of Business: Exporter, Major Book Chain Headquarters
Bookshop(s): Blackwell's Bookshop, Faculty of Management Bldg, The Robert Gordon University, Garthdee Campus, Garthdee Rd, Aberdeen AB10 7QE *Tel:* (01224) 263987 *Fax:* (01224) 263986 *Web Site:* www.blackwell.co.uk; Blackwell's Medical Bookshop, University Medical School, Polwarth Bldg, Foresterhill, Aberdeen AB25 2ZD *Tel:* (01224) 683431 *Fax:* (01224) 690794 *E-mail:* aberdeen.med@blackwell.co.uk; Blackwell's Reading College, Reading College School of Arts & Design, Kings Rd, Reading, Berkshire RG1 4HU, Manager: Chris Lawson; Alden & Blackwell, Eton College, Windsor, Berkshire SL4 6DF *Tel:* (01753) 863849 *Fax:* (01753) 832453 *E-mail:* eton@blackwell.co.uk *Web Site:* www.blackwell.co.uk; Blackwell's Business & Law Bookshop, 3 Windsor Arcade, Birmingham B2 5LG *Tel:* (0121) 2334969 *Fax:* (0121) 2363652 *E-mail:* birmingham@blackwell.co.uk *Web Site:* www.blackwell.co.uk; Blackwell's University Bookshop, University of Brighton, Mezzanine Floor, Cockroft Bldg, Moulsecoomb, Brighton BN2 4GJ *Tel:* (01273) 571974 *Fax:* (01273) 620556 *E-mail:* brighton@blackwell.co.uk *Web Site:* www.blackwell.co.uk; Blackwell's, 89 Park St, Bristol BS1 5PW *Tel:* (0117) 9276602 *Fax:* (0117) 9251854; Blackwell's University Bookshop, The University of the West of England, Coldharbour Lane, Bristol BS16 1QY *Tel:* (0117) 9652573 *Fax:* (0117) 9750437 *E-mail:* uweb@blackwell.co.uk *Web Site:* www.blackwell.co.uk; Blackwell's Map Centre, Unite 3, The Enterprise Centre, 61 Ditton Walk, Cambridge CB5 8QD, Manager: Sarah Copsey *Tel:* (01223) 568417 *Fax:* (01223) 568416 *E-mail:* ordsvy@blackwell.co.uk; Heffers: Academic + General Books, 20 Trinity St, Cambridge CB2 1TY, Manager: Mary McIntosh *Tel:* (01223) 568568 *Fax:* (01223) 568591 *E-mail:* heffers@heffers.co.uk; Heffers: Art + Graphics, 15-21 King St, Cambridge CB1 1LH, Manager: Michele Thomas *Tel:* (01223) 568495 *Fax:* (01223) 568411 *E-mail:* art@heffers.co.uk; Heffers: Grafton Centre Bookshop, 28B The Grafton Centre, Cambridge CB1 1PS, Manager: Erika McKay *Tel:* (01223) 568573 *Fax:* (01223) 568572 *E-mail:* grafton@heffers.co.uk; Heffers: Plus (Cambridge Paperback), 31 St Andrew's St, CB2 3AX Cambridge, Manager: Terrie Rodgers *Tel:* (01223) 568598 *Fax:* (01223) 568593 *E-mail:* plus@heffers.co.uk; Heffers: Sound, 19 Trinity St, Cambridge CB2 1TB, Manager: Tony McGeorge *Tel:* (01223) 568562 *Fax:* (01223) 568591 *E-mail:* sound@heffers.co.uk; Blackwell's University Bookshop, University of Wales, College of Cardiff, University Union, Senghennydd Rd, Cardiff CF2 4AZ *Tel:* (01222) 340673 *Fax:* (01222) 382533 *E-mail:* cardiff@blackwell.co.uk *Web Site:* www.blackwell.co.uk; Blackwell's Medical Bookshop, Sir Herbert Duthie Library, University of Wales College of Medicine, Heath Park, Cardiff CF4 4XN *Tel:* (01222) 762878 *E-mail:* cardiff.med@blackwell.co.uk *Web Site:* www.blackwell.co.uk; Blackwell's Medical Bookshop, Ninewells Hospital, Dundee DD1 9SY *Tel:* (01382) 566551 *Fax:* (01382) 669812; Blackwell's Bookshop Edinburgh Academy, Edinburgh Academy, 42 Henderson Row, Edinburgh EH3 5BL, Manager: Robina Brown *Tel:* (0131) 557 9610 *Fax:* (0131) 557 9610 *E-mail:* academy.edinburgh@blackwell.co.uk; Blackwell's Bookshop Fettes College, Fettes College, Comely Bank, Edinburgh EH4 1QX, Manager: Liz Marchant *Tel:* (0131) 332 5657 *Fax:* (0131) 332 5657 *E-mail:* fettes.edinburgh@blackwell.co.uk; Blackwell's Bookshop Heriot Watt University,

1347

Heriot Watt University, Hugh Nisbet Bldg, Riccarton Campus, Edinburgh EH14 4AS, Manager: Alistair Millar *Tel:* (0131) 451 5287 *Fax:* (0131) 451 5287 *E-mail:* heriotwatt@blackwell.co.uk; Blackwell's Bookshop King's Buildings, King's Buildings, University of Edinburgh, West Mains Rd, Edinburgh EH9 3JR, Acting Manager: Tom Tivan *Tel:* (0131) 667 0432 *Fax:* (0131) 667 0432 *E-mail:* kings.edinburgh@blackwell.co.uk; Blackwell's Bookshop Merchiston Castle, Merchiston Castle School, 294 Colinton Rd, Edinburgh EH13 0PU, Manager: Loata Millard *Tel:* (0131) 441 4752 *Fax:* (0131) 441 4752 *E-mail:* merchiston.edinburgh@blackwell.co.uk; Blackwell's Bookshop QMUC, Queen Margaret University College, 36 Clerwood Terrace, Edinburgh EH12 8TS, Manager: Liz Marchant *Tel:* (0131) 334 3818 *Fax:* (0131) 334 3818; Blackwell's Bookshop South Bridge, 53-62 South Bridge, Edinburgh EH1 1YS, Manager: Anne Watson *Tel:* (0131) 622 8222 *Fax:* (0131) 557 8149 *E-mail:* edinburgh@blackwell.co.uk; Blackwell's Edinburgh Royal Infirmary, Unite GF 319, 51 Little France Crescent, Little France, Edinburgh EH16 4SA, Manager: Bob Carroll *Tel:* (0131) 666 1764 *E-mail:* edinburgh.med@blackwell.co.uk; Blackwell's Napier University Craighouse, c/o Anne Watson, Blackwell's Bookshop South Bridge, 53-62 South Bridge, Edinburgh EH1 1YS; Blackwell's Napier University Merchiston, c/o Anne Watson, Blackwell's Bookshop South Bridge, 53-62 South Bridge, Edinburgh EH1 1YS; Blackwell's Napier University Sighthill, c/o Anne Watson, Blackwell's Bookshop South Bridge, 53-62 South Bridge, Edinburgh EH1 1YS; Blackwell's University Bookshop, University of Exeter, St Luke's College, Stocker Rd, Exeter EX4 4QA *Tel:* (01392) 59456 *Fax:* (01392) 411207 *E-mail:* exeter@blackwell.co.uk *Web Site:* www.blackwell.co.uk; Blackwell's University Bookshop, School of Education, St Luke's College, University of Exeter, Exeter EX1 2LU *Tel:* (01392) 264956; Blackwell's, Students' Union, St Mary's Pl, St Andrews, Fife KY16 9UZ, Manager: Barbara Dumbleton *Tel:* (01334) 476367 *Fax:* (01334) 476367 *E-mail:* st.andrews@blackwell.co.uk; Blackwell's, 21 Blenheim Terrace, Woodhouse Lane, Leeds LS2 9HJ, Manager: Andrew Lilley *Tel:* (0113) 243 2446 *Fax:* (0113) 243 0661 *E-mail:* leeds@blackwell.co.uk; Blackwell's University Bookshop, University of Liverpool, Alsop Bldg, Brownlow Hill, Liverpool L3 5TX *Tel:* (0151) 7098146 *Fax:* (0151) 7096653 *E-mail:* liverpool@blackwell.co.uk; Blackwell's, 100 Charing Cross Rd, London WC2H 0JG *Tel:* (0207) 2925100 *Fax:* (0207) 2409665 *E-mail:* london@blackwell.co.uk *Web Site:* www.blackwell.co.uk; Blackwell's London Business School, 18-22 Park Rd, London NW1 4SH, Manager: Tina Scott *Tel:* (020) 7723 6953 *Fax:* (020) 7723 7017 *E-mail:* lbs@blackwell.co.uk; Blackwell's Medical Bookshop, 2nd floor, Hunter Wing, Cranmer Terrace, Tooting, London SW15 0RE *Tel:* (020) 8725 0813; Blackwell's University Bookshop, University of North London, 158 Holloway Rd, London N7 8DD *Tel:* (0207) 7004786 *Fax:* (0207) 7007687 *E-mail:* unl@blackwell.co.uk *Web Site:* www.blackwell.co.uk; Blackwell's University Bookshop, University of North London, Ladbroke House, 62-66 Highbury Grove, London N5 2AD *Tel:* (0207) 3144215; Blackwell's University Bookshop, 119-122 London Rd, London SE1 6LF *Tel:* (0207) 9285378 *Fax:* (0207) 2619536 *E-mail:* sbu@blackwell.co.uk *Web Site:* www.blackwell.co.uk; Blackwell's Business & Law Bookshop, 243-244 High Holborn, London WC1V 7DZ *Tel:* (0207) 8319501 *Fax:* (0207) 4059412 *E-mail:* holborn@blackwell.co.uk; Blackwell's Academic Bookshop, Union Bldg, Loughborough University, Ashby Rd, Loughborough LE11 3TT *Tel:* (01509) 219788 *Fax:* (01509) 219754 *E-mail:* loughborough@blackwell.co.uk; Blackwell's University Bookshop, Faculty of Agriculture & Food Sciences, Sutton Bonington, Loughborough LE12 5RD *Tel:* (0115) 9516017; Blackwell's University Bookshop, The Precinct Centre, Oxford Rd, Manchester M13 9RN *Tel:* (0161) 2743331 *Fax:* (0161) 2743228 *E-mail:* manchester@blackwell.co.uk; Blackwell's, University Library, UMIST, Sackville St, Manchester M60 1QD *Tel:* (0161) 2004936 *E-mail:* umist@blackwell.co.uk; Blackwell's Academic Bookshop, The Elizabeth Gaskell Site, Manchester Metropolitan University, Hathersage Rd, Manchester M13 0JA; Blackwell's, 141 Percy St, Newcastle Upon Tyne NE1 7RS *Tel:* (0191) 232 6421 *Fax:* (0191) 260 2536 *E-mail:* newcastle@blackwell.co.uk; Blackwell's University Bookshop, University of Nottingham, Portland Bldg, University Park, Nottingham NG7 2RD *Tel:* (0115) 9580272 *Fax:* (0115) 9587063 *E-mail:* nottingham@blackwell.co.uk *Web Site:* www.blackwell.co.uk; Blackwell's Medical Bookshop, Queen's Medical Centre, Clifton Blvd, Nottingham NG7 2UH *Tel:* (0115) 9780938 *Fax:* (0115) 9709980 *E-mail:* nottingham.med@blackwell.co.uk; Blackwell's University Bookshop, Nottingham Trent University, Chaucer Bldg, Goldsmith St, Nottingham NG1 5LT *Tel:* (0115) 9417307 *Fax:* (0115) 9417311 *E-mail:* trent@blackwell.co.uk; Blackwell's University Bookshop, Nottingham Trent University, Clifton Campus, Clifton Lane, Clifton, Nottingham NG11 8NS *Tel:* (0115) 9844474 *Fax:* (0115) 9211410 *E-mail:* clifton@blackwell.co.uk; Blackwell's University Bookshop, 99 High St, Old Aberdeen AB25 3EN *Tel:* (01224) 486102 *Fax:* (01224) 276162 *E-mail:* aberdeen.ub@blackwell.co.uk *Web Site:* blackwell.co.uk; Blackwell's, 48-51 Broad St, Oxford OX1BQ *Tel:* (01865) 792792 *Fax:* (01865) 794143 *E-mail:* oxford@blackwell.co.uk *Web Site:* www.blackwell.co.uk; Blackwell's University Bookshop, Oxford Brookes University, Gipsy Lane, Headington, Oxford OX3 0BP *Tel:* (01865) 483063; (01865) 792792; Blackwell's Medical Bookshop, John Radcliffe Hospital, Headington, Oxford OX3 9DU *Tel:* (01865) 741663 *Fax:* (01865) 741663 *E-mail:* oxford.med@blackwell.co.uk; Blackwell's Art Bookshop, 27 Broad St, Oxford OX1 2AS *Tel:* (01865) 792792 *Fax:* (01865) 794143 *E-mail:* art@blackwell.co.uk *Web Site:* www.blackwell.co.uk; Blackwell's Rare Books, 48-51 Broad St, Oxford OX1 3SW *Tel:* (01865) 333555 *Fax:* (01865) 248833; Blackwell's Music Bookshop, 23-25 Broad St, Oxford OX1 3AX *Tel:* (01865) 333580 *Fax:* (01865) 728020 *E-mail:* music.ox@blackwell.co.uk; Blackwell's University Bookshop, University of Glamorgan, Llantwit, Treforest, Pontypridd, Mid-Glamorgan CF37 1DL *Tel:* (01443) 401502 *Fax:* (01443) 400791 *E-mail:* glamorgan@blackwell.co.uk; Blackwell's Academic Bookshop, University of Portsmouth, Students Centre, Unit 1, Cambridge Rd, Portsmouth PO1 2EF *Tel:* (023) 92832813 *Fax:* (023) 92851032 *E-mail:* portsmouth@blackwell.co.uk; Blackwell's University Bookshop, University Library Bldg, University of Central Lancashire, 52 St Peter's Square, Preston PR1 2HZ *Tel:* (01772) 254462; (01772) 893990 *Fax:* (01772) 202313 *E-mail:* preston@blackwell.co.uk; The Friar Street Bookshop, 142-143 Friar St, Reading RG1 1EX *Tel:* (0118) 9573082; Blackwell's University Bookshop, University of York, The Market Sq, Vanbrugh Way, Heslington, York YO10 5NM *Tel:* (01904) 432715 *Fax:* (01904) 413420 *E-mail:* york@blackwell.co.uk; Blackwell's University Bookshop, University of Salford, Horlock Court, University Rd, Salford M5 4WT *Tel:* (0161) 7374565 *Fax:* (0161) 7430566 *E-mail:* salford@blackwell.co.uk; Blackwell's University Bookshop, University of Sheffield, Mappin St, Sheffield S1 4DT *Tel:* (0114) 2787211 *Fax:* (0114) 2787629 *E-mail:* sheffield@blackwell.co.uk; Blackwell's University Bookshop, Sheffield Hallam University, City Campus, Pond St, Sheffield S1 1WB *Tel:* (0114) 2752152 *Fax:* (0114) 2798950 *E-mail:* hallam@blackwell.co.uk; Blackwell's, Broomhill, 220 Fulwood Rd, Sheffield S10 3BB *Tel:* (0114) 2660820 *E-mail:* broomhill@blackwell.co.uk; Blackwell's Academic Bookshop, Southampton Institute, Sir James Matthews Bldg, 157-187 Above Bar St, Southampton SO14 7JT *Tel:* (01703) 631806 *Fax:* (01703) 631787 *E-mail:* southampton@blackwell.co.uk

Roy Bloom Ltd
Fanshaw House, 3-9 Fanshaw St, London N1 6HX
Tel: (0207) 7295373 *Fax:* (0207) 7292375
E-mail: info@roybloom.com
Web Site: www.remainder-books.com
Key Personnel
Chairman: Roy Bloom *E-mail:* roybloom@roybloom.com
Man Dir: Adam Bloom
Sales Dir: Paul White *E-mail:* paul.white@roybloom.com
Founded: 1969
Specialize in publishers' overstocks & remainders.
Type of Business: Remainder Dealer

Book Representation & Distribution Ltd
Hadleigh Hall, London Rd, Hadleigh, Essex SS7 2DE
Tel: (01702) 552912 *Fax:* (01702) 556095
E-mail: mail@bookreps.com; info@bookreps.com
Web Site: www.bookreps.com
Key Personnel
Man Dir: Dan Levey
Secretary: Doreen Mann
Accountant: Richard Foster
Sales Manager: Celia Stocks
Marketing Manager: Don Brown
Founded: 1988
Type of Business: Distributor, Exporter, Importer

Bookmark Remainders
Rivendell Illand, Launceston, Cornwall PL15 7LS
Tel: (01566) 782728 *Fax:* (01566) 782059
E-mail: info@book-bargains.co.uk
Web Site: book-bargains.co.uk
Key Personnel
Man Dir: Andrew Rattray *E-mail:* andrew@book-bargains.co.uk
Founded: 1954
Remainder specialists.
Type of Business: Remainder Dealer

Bookmart Ltd
Blaby Rd, Wigston, Leicester LE18 4SE
Tel: (0116) 2759060 *Fax:* (0116) 2759090
E-mail: books@bookmart.co.uk
Key Personnel
Man Dir: Philip E Parkin
Finance Dir: Andrew Painter
Co-Edition Sales Manager: Linda Williams
Founded: 1989
Publisher & distributor, promotional books.
Imprints: Abbeydale; Silverdale
Branch Office(s)
Regent St, London

Bookpoint Ltd
39 Milton Park, Abingdon, Oxon OX14 4TD
Tel: (01235) 400400 *Fax:* (01235) 832068;
(01235) orders 821511

BOOK DEALERS UNITED KINGDOM

E-mail: firstname.lastname@bookpoint.co.uk
Web Site: www.oxfordshire.co.uk
Telex: 837091 bookpt g
Key Personnel
Man Dir: Tony Bryars
Founded: 1973
Type of Business: Distributor
Owned by: Hodder Headline PLC

Books for Europe Ltd
3 Sutton Court, Grange Rd, London W5 3PG
Tel: (020) 8840 6672
Key Personnel
Man Dir: Juliusz Komarnicki *Tel:* (091) 9671539
 Fax: (091) 9667865
Type of Business: Exporter

Books from India (UK) Ltd
45 Museum St, London WC1A 1LR
Tel: (071) 4053784 *Fax:* (071) 8314517
Key Personnel
Contact: Shreeram Vidyarthi
Founded: 1978
Also publisher.
Type of Business: Distributor, Exporter, Importer, Major Independent Bookseller, Wholesaler
Branch Office(s)
Asia Publishing House Ltd, Borden Villa, Borden Lane, Sittingbourne, Kent ME10 1BY
 Tel: (01795) 473149 *Fax:* (01795) 473149

Bookworld Wholesale Ltd
Unit 10, Hodfar Rd, Sandy Lane Industrial Estate, Stourport-on-Severn, Worcs DY13 9QB
Tel: (01299) 823330 *Fax:* (01299) 829970
Key Personnel
Dir: Lian Clark; Justin Gainham
Founded: 1988
Specialize in transport, military & modelling books.
Type of Business: Distributor, Exporter, Importer, Wholesaler

Booth-Clibborn Editions, see Internos Books

Botes Librair
Parkhurst Mews, Parkhurst Rd, Bexhill, East Sussex TN40 1DW
Mailing Address: PO Box 22, Bexhill, East Sussex TN40 1DW
Tel: (01424) 210871 *Fax:* (01424) 734506;
 (01424) 731262
E-mail: 100450.3641@compuserve.com
Key Personnel
President: David L Gould
Founded: 1964
Library suppliers, educational supplies & specialists in medical & scientific publications.
Type of Business: Exporter, Wholesaler
Branch Office(s)
Botes Unifoyle Ltd, International School Book Distributors
Bookshop(s): Books Unlimited, PO Box 22, Bexhill, East Sussex TN40 1DW

BPL Remainders
Princess House, 50 Eastcastle St, Suite 275, London W1N 7AP
Tel: (020) 7636 5070; (020) 7631 5070
 Fax: (020) 7580 3001
Telex: 22303
Key Personnel
General Manager: K Fox
Export Sales Administrator: Francesca Ferguson
Founded: 1982
Type of Business: Remainder Dealer

Bradt Travel Guides Ltd
19 High St, Chalfont St Peter, Saint Peter Bucks SL9 9QE
Tel: (01753) 893444 *Fax:* (01753) 892333
E-mail: info@bradtguides.com; enquiries@bradt-travelguides.com
Web Site: www.bradtguides.com
Key Personnel
President: Hilary Bradt
Office Manager: Debbie Hunter
Founded: 1972
US Distributor: Globe Pequot Press.
Type of Business: Exporter

The Bridge Book Co Ltd
10 Blenheim Court, Brewery Rd, London N7 9NT
Tel: (0207) 697-3000 *Fax:* (0207) 700-4552
E-mail: bridgepem@aol.com
Key Personnel
Man Dir: Mike Pemberton
Founded: 1962
Type of Business: Distributor, Exporter, Importer, Remainder Dealer
Parent Company: Chrysalis Books Ltd

Bridge Bookshop Ltd
Shore Rd, Pt Erin IM9 6HL
Tel: (01624) 833378 *Fax:* (01624) 835381
Key Personnel
Manager: Joan Hook
Dir: Rosemary Pickard
Founded: 1953
Type of Business: Exporter, Major Independent Bookseller
Owned by: Rosemary & Alan Pickard

Browne's Bookstore
56 Mill Rd, Cambridge CB1 2AS
Tel: (01223) 350968 *Fax:* (01223) 353456
E-mail: brownes_books@msn.com
Key Personnel
Contact: Mrs G H Browne
Founded: 1976
Specialize in mail order, library supplies.
Type of Business: Exporter, Major Independent Bookseller

Bushwood Books
6 Marksbury Ave, Kew Gardens, Surrey TW9 4JF
Tel: (0208) 3928585 *Fax:* (0208) 3929876
E-mail: bushwd@aol.com
Key Personnel
Contact: Richard Hansen; Victoria Hansen
Founded: 1984
Type of Business: Distributor
Owned by: Ultraco Ltd

Cedar Media
7-9 Church Hill, Loughton, Essex IG10 1QP
Tel: (020) 8508 8856 *Fax:* (020) 8508 8856
E-mail: cedarmedia@btinternet.com
Key Personnel
Dir: Marie L Barnett; Roger Barnett
Founded: 1987
Marketing, distribution of reference publication concerning EU & Europe as a whole.
Type of Business: Distributor, Exporter, Importer

Central Books
99 Wallis Rd, London E9 5LN
Tel: (0845) 458 9910 *Fax:* (0845) 458 9912
E-mail: orders@centralbooks.com
Web Site: www.centralbooks.co.uk; www.centralbooks.com
Key Personnel
Man Dir: William Norris
Sales Manager: Mark Chilver
Accounts: Dave Cope
Founded: 1939
Type of Business: Distributor, Exporter, Importer, Major Independent Bookseller

Clarke Associates Ltd
2-3 Denmark St, 3rd floor, Bristol BS1 5DQ
Tel: (0117) 926 8864 *Fax:* (0117) 922 6437
E-mail: enq@clarkeassoc.com
Web Site: www.clarkeassoc.demon.co.uk
Key Personnel
Chairman, Man Dir: Malcolm Clarke
Dir: Susan C Phillips
Founded: 1982
Publishing Consultants.
Type of Business: Distributor, Exporter, Importer
Owned by: Clarke Associates Ltd

Clipper Distribution Services
Windmill Grove, Portchester, Hants PO16 9HT
Tel: (0705) 200080 *Fax:* (0705) 200090
Key Personnel
Man Dir: John P C Delieu
Founded: 1988
Type of Business: Distributor

Colt Associates
The Old School, Brewhouse Hill, Wheathampstead, St Albans, Herts AL4 8AN
Tel: (0158) 2834292 *Fax:* (0158) 825778
Key Personnel
President: Roger Lloyd-Taylor
Founded: 1977
Other branch offices located in China, Hong Kong & Manila.
Branch Office(s)
Toyko, Japan

Combined Book Services
Units 1/K, Paddock Wood Distribution Center, Paddock Wood, Tonbridge, Kent TN12 6UU
Tel: (01892) 839819 *Fax:* (01892) 837272
E-mail: info@combook.co.uk
Web Site: www.combook.co.uk
Key Personnel
Man Dir: Charles Turner
Mail order book distribution.
Type of Business: Distributor, Exporter, Importer, Wholesaler

Commonwealth Education Foundation
PO Box 367, Edgware, Middlesex HA8 7AK
Tel: (0208) 9312359 *Fax:* (0208) 9592137
E-mail: cefoundation@aol.com
Key Personnel
Secretary: Nina Novy
Founded: 1989
Suppliers of any book to any country, single volume to complete libraries, free of charge.

Computer Bookshops Ltd
205 Formans Rd, Sparkhill, Birmingham B11 3AX
Tel: (0121) 778 3333 *Fax:* (0121) 606 0476
E-mail: info@computerbookshops.com
Web Site: www.computerbookshops.com
Key Personnel
Chairman: Ian Maclean
Man Dir: Donna Jones
Head of Marketing: Paul Savill *E-mail:* pauls@compbook.co.uk
Founded: 1978
Type of Business: Distributor, Wholesaler

Coningsby International Bookshop Services
22 School Lane, Coningsby, Lincoln LN4 4WX
Tel: (01526) 342231 *Fax:* (01526) 344367
E-mail: service@coningsby.com
Web Site: www.coningsby.com
Key Personnel
Owner: Clive Sharples; Ruth Sharples
Founded: 1976
Type of Business: Exporter, Major Independent Bookseller

Cordee Ltd
3a De Montfort St, Leicester LE1 7HD
Tel: (0116) 2543579 *Fax:* (0116) 2471176

E-mail: info@cordee.co.uk
Web Site: www.cordee.co.uk
Founded: 1973
Specialize in recreation & travel.
Type of Business: Distributor, Wholesaler

The Crafts Council
44a Pentonville Rd, Islington, London N1 9BY
Tel: (020) 7278 7700 *Fax:* (020) 7837 6891
Web Site: www.craftscouncil.org.uk
Key Personnel
Manager: Jo Swait *Tel:* (020) 7806 2557
 E-mail: j-swait@craftscouncil.org.uk
Contact: Lisa Daniel
Founded: 1971
Government-financed body promoting Britain's artist craftsman, craft books & catalogs.
Bookshop(s): The Gallery Shop

Crofthouse Books Ltd
39 Alexandra Rd, Addlestone, Surrey KT15 2PQ
Tel: (01932) 845559 *Fax:* (01932) 849528; (01932) 830006
E-mail: croft@crofthouse.co.uk
Web Site: www.crofthouse.co.uk
Key Personnel
Dir: David H Smith *E-mail:* david.smith@crofthouse.co.uk
Book supply service for commercial, industrial & academic libraries.
Type of Business: Distributor, Exporter, Importer, Major Independent Bookseller

Cyngor Llyfrau Cymru, see Welsh Books Council

Cyngor Llyfrau Cymru Canolfan Dosbarthu, see Welsh Books Council

Cypher Library Books
Elmfield Rd, Morley, Leeds LS27 0NN
Tel: (0113) 2012900 *Fax:* (0113) 2012929
E-mail: enquiries@cyphergroup.com
Web Site: www.cyphergroup.com
Key Personnel
Man Dir: Michael Robinson
Head of Sales & Marketing: Jackie Aspinall
Founded: 1947

Dawson UK Ltd, Books Division
Foxhills House, Brindley Close, Rushden, Northants NN10 6DB
Tel: (01933) 417500 *Fax:* (01933) 417501
E-mail: bkcustserv@dawsonbooks.co.uk
Web Site: www.dawsonbooks.co.uk
Key Personnel
Chief Executive: David Blundell
European Book Division Manager: Diane Kerr
European Publisher Relations Manager: Eric Le Strat
Marketing Manager: Steven Welch
Sales Manager: George Hammond
 E-mail: george.hammond@dawsonbooks.co.uk
Founded: 1809
Subscription Agent.
Type of Business: Distributor, Exporter, Importer
Owned by: Dawson Holdings Plc
Associate Companies: Dawson UK Subscription & Technology Divisions, Cannon House, Folkestone, Kent CT19 5EE

Delta Books Worldwide
39 Alexandra Rd, Addlestone, Surrey KT15 2PQ
Tel: (01932) 854 776 *Fax:* (01932) 849 528
E-mail: info@deltabooks.co.uk
Web Site: www.deltabooks.co.uk
Key Personnel
Contact: Eileen Fryer *E-mail:* eileen.fryer@deltabooks.co.uk
Type of Business: Distributor, Exporter, Wholesaler

Dillons, The Bookstore
128 New St, Birmingham B2 4DB
Tel: (0121) 6314333 *Fax:* (0121) 6432441
E-mail: bhamnew@dillons.eunet.co.uk
Branch offices in Aberdeen, Birmingham, Bromley, Cambridge, Canterbury, Charing Cross, Chichester, Coventry, Crawrey, Croydon, Derby, Ealing, Egham, Harrogate, Leicester, Liverpool, London, Manchester, Nottingham, Oxford, & Wolverhampton.
Owned by: THORN EMI Home Electronics (UK) Ltd
Branch Office(s)
Charing Cross
Chichester
Coventry

Dillons City Business Book Store
72 Park Rd, London WC2N 5EJ
Tel: (020) 7628 7479 *Fax:* (020) 7628 7871
E-mail: loncbus@dillons.eunet.co.uk
Key Personnel
Manager: Amanda Panedli

The Economists' Bookshop
Clare Market, Portugal St, London WC2A 2AB
Tel: (0171) 405 5531 *Fax:* (0171) 482 4873
E-mail: economists@waterstones.co.uk
Key Personnel
General Manager: Sue Tarratt
Owned by: The EMI Group -Dillons Group, Royal House, Prince's Gate House Rd, Solihull, W Ruplands BG1 3QQ
Branch Office(s)
The Barbican Business Book Centre, 9 Moorfields, London *Tel:* (020) 7628 7479
Bookshop(s): City Poly Bookshop, Moorgate, London EC2; City University Bookshop, Northampton Sq, London EC1V 0HB; Queen Mary & Westfield College Bookshop, Mile End Rd, London E1 4NS; Brunel University Bookshop, Cleveland Rd, Uxbridge, Middlesex

Electronica Books & Media Ltd
Sunbury International Business Center, Brookland Close, Sunbury-on-Thames, Middlesex TW16 7DX
Tel: (01932) 765119 *Fax:* (01932) 765429
Key Personnel
Dir: Michael Geelan
Founded: 1988
Type of Business: Distributor, Exporter, Importer, Wholesaler

Elstead Maps
Badgery Hookley Lane, Elstead, Godalming, Surrey GU8 6JE
Mailing Address: PO Box 52, Elstead, Godalming, Surrey GU8 6JJ
Tel: (01252) 703472 *Fax:* (01252) 703971
E-mail: enquiry@elstead.co.uk
Web Site: www.elstead.co.uk
Key Personnel
Proprietor: Stephen Colebrooke *E-mail:* stephen@elstead.co.uk
Founded: 1981
Mail order retailers.

European Schoolbooks Ltd
The Runnings, Cheltenham GL51 9PQ
Tel: (01242) 245252 *Fax:* (01242) 224137
E-mail: direct@esb.co.uk
Web Site: www.eurobooks.co.uk
Key Personnel
Man Dir: Frank A Preiss *E-mail:* fap@esb.co.uk
Founded: 1964
Specialists in major European languages other than English.
Type of Business: Distributor, Importer, Wholesaler

Bookshop(s): The European Bookshop, 5 Warwick St, London W1B 5LU *Tel:* (020) 7734 5259 *Fax:* (020) 7287 1720 *E-mail:* mrg@esb.co.uk; The Italian Bookshop, 7 Cecil Court, London WC2N 4EZ *Tel:* (020) 7240 1634 *Fax:* (020) 7240 1635 *E-mail:* italian@esb.co.uk; Young Europeans Bookstore, 5 Cecil Court, London WC2N 4EZ *Tel:* (020) 7836 6667 *Fax:* (020) 7240-1635 *E-mail:* yeb@esb.co.uk

Eurospan Distribution Center Ltd
3 Henrietta St, Covent Garden, London WC2E 8LU
Tel: (0161) 7642296 *Fax:* (0161) 7648213
E-mail: info@eurospan.co.uk
Web Site: www.eurospan.co.uk
Key Personnel
Man Dir: Peter Kershaw Taylor
Founded: 1969
Type of Business: Distributor

Extenza-Turpin
Formerly Turpin Distribution Services Ltd
Stratton Business Park, Pegasus Drive, Biggleswade, Beds SG18 8GB
Tel: (01767) 604 806 *Fax:* (01767) 601 640
Web Site: www.extenza-turpin.com
Key Personnel
Man Dir: Lorna M Summers
Operations Manager: Tim Richards
Information Technology Manager: Bill Pease
Accounting: Ruth Campbell
Sales: Kathy Law *E-mail:* lawk@extenza-turpin.com
Founded: 1968
Provide worldwide distribution of books & fulfillment of journals for academic & learned publishers from US & UK locations. Customized service includes invoicing in the publisher's name & using the publisher's own trading terms. Management reports are available 24/7 via internet. Mulilingual customer care & customer stationery. Multiple currencies.
Type of Business: Distributor
Parent Company: Royal Swets & Zeitlinger BV
Branch Office(s)
Turpin Distribution Services Ltd, 56 Industrial Park Dr, Pembroke, MA 12359, United States *Tel:* 781-829-8973 *Fax:* 781-829-9052
E-mail: turpin@turpinna.com

Clive Farahar & Sophie Dupre Booksellers
Horsebrook House, XV The Green, Calne, Wilts SN11 8DQ
Tel: (01249) 821121 *Fax:* (01249) 821202
E-mail: sophie@farahardupre.co.uk
Web Site: www.farahardupre.co.uk
Key Personnel
Contact: Sophie Dupre
Founded: 1981
Antiquarian books on voyages & travels. Autograph letters, signed photos, signed books, photography in all fields especially royalty & literature.
Type of Business: Major Independent Bookseller

T C Farries & Co Ltd
Irongray Rd, Lochside, Dumfries DG2 0LH
Tel: (01387) 720755 *Fax:* (01387) 721105
Key Personnel
Chairman: D W N Landale
Sales Dir: Mrs L Bennett
Man Dir: P D R Landale
Finance Dir: J McGrillis
Founded: 1982
Type of Business: Distributor, Exporter, Major Independent Bookseller, Wholesaler

David Flatman Ltd, see Lomond Books

FOYLES
113-119 Charing Cross Rd, London WC2H 0EB

BOOK DEALERS — UNITED KINGDOM

Tel: (020) 7437 5660 *Fax:* (020) 7434 1580
E-mail: sales@foyles.co.uk
Web Site: www.foyles.co.uk
Key Personnel
Manager: John Cruickshanks

Walter H Gardner & Co
16 Chalton Dr, London N2 0QW
Tel: (20) 8458 3202 *Fax:* (20) 8458 8499
E-mail: walterhgardnerco@aol.com
Key Personnel
Man Partner: Walter H Gardner
Sales & Marketing: Mrs D Gardner
Type of Business: Remainder Dealer

Gardners Books
One Whittle Dr, Eastbourne, East Sussex BN23 6QH
Tel: (01323) 521666; (01323) 521555
 Fax: (01323) 521666
E-mail: marketing@gardners.com
Web Site: www.gardners.com
Key Personnel
Dir, Export Sales: Warwick Bailey
 E-mail: wbailey@gardners.com
Contact: Mike Burge
International Book Wholesalers.
Type of Business: Exporter, Wholesaler

Gazelle Book Services Ltd
White Cross Mills High Town, Lancaster LA1 4XS
Tel: (01524) 68765 *Fax:* (01524) 63232
E-mail: sales@gazellebooks.co.uk
Web Site: www.gazellebook.co.uk
Key Personnel
Man Dir: Trevor Witcher *E-mail:* trevor.gazelle@talk21.com
Dir: Brian Haywood; Mark Trotter
Founded: 1988
Type of Business: Distributor

George Gregory Bookseller
Manvers St, Bath BA1 1JW
Tel: (01225) 466000 *Fax:* (01225) 482122
Key Personnel
President: Mrs C A W Bayntun-Coward
Founded: 1846
Old Books, Maps & Prints.

William George's Sons Ltd
89 Park St, Bristol BS1 5PW
Tel: (0117) 9276602
Key Personnel
Manager: Duncan Dewfall

Godfrey Cave Associates Ltd
27 Wrights Lane, London W8 5TZ
Tel: (020) 7416 3000 *Fax:* (020) 7416 3289
Key Personnel
Man Dir: Kevin Binston
Sales Dir: Deborah Wright
Sales Manager: Patrick Duffin
Publishing, Liason Manager: Roz Scott
Founded: 1972
Type of Business: Remainder Dealer

Godfrey Cave Holdings Ltd
27 Wrights Lane, London W8 5TZ
Tel: (020) 7416 3000 *Fax:* (020) 7416 3099
Comprised of Godfrey Cave Associates, Bloomsbury Editions, Omega Books, Benson Books.
Type of Business: Remainder Dealer

Gracewing/Fowler Wright Books
Gracewing House, 2 Southern Ave, Leominster, Herefordshire HR6 0QF
Tel: (01568) 616835 *Fax:* (01568) 613289
Web Site: www.gracewing.co.uk

Key Personnel
Man Dir: Tom Longford
Founded: 1958
Type of Business: Distributor, Exporter, Importer, Major Independent Bookseller, Wholesaler

Grange Books PLC
The Grange, Units 1-6, Kingsnorth Industrial Estate, Hoo, Nr Rochester, Kent ME3 9ND
Tel: (01634) 256 000 *Fax:* (01634) 255 500
E-mail: grangebooks@aol.com
Web Site: www.grangebooks.co.uk
Key Personnel
Man Dir: Michael Ash
Administrative Dir: Heather Staples
 E-mail: heather.staples@grangebooks.co.uk
Founded: 1972
Specialize in Illustrated Adult Nonfiction, Children's, Promotional, Reprint & Remainder Books; Publisher of promotional books co-editions.
Type of Business: Remainder Dealer

Grantham Book Services Ltd
Isaac Newton Way, Alma Park Industrial Estate, Grantham, Lincs NG31 9SD
Tel: (01476) 541000; (01476) 541 080 (orders)
 Fax: (01476) 541061
E-mail: orders@gbs.tbs-ltd.co.uk
Key Personnel
Chairman: David Pemberton
Man Dir: Graham Miller
Founded: 1975
Contract Distribution (Publishing).
Type of Business: Distributor
Owned by: Random House Group

Haigh & Hochland Ltd
Harniman House, 391-401 Oxford Rd, Manchester M13 9QA
Tel: (061) 2734156 *Fax:* (061) 2734340
Key Personnel
Man Dir: Michael Beattie
Founded: 1951
Type of Business: Distributor, Exporter, Importer, Major Independent Bookseller

Hatchards Ltd
187 Piccadilly, London W1J 9LE
Tel: (020) 7439 9921 *Fax:* (020) 7494 1313
E-mail: books@hatchards.co.uk
Web Site: www.hatchards.co.uk
Key Personnel
General Manager: Roger Katz
Marketing Assistant: Mark Hammett
Founded: 1797
Booksellers.
Owned by: EMI
Ultimate Parent Company: HMV Media Group

Health Sciences Associates International
15 Roehampton Lane, London SW15 5LS
Tel: (020) 8876 2340 *Fax:* (020) 8392 9845
Key Personnel
Contact: Neville Mendelson
Founded: 1982
Specialize in marketing, promote & sell by direct mail & displays medical veterinary & nursing journals, books & electronic publications direct to doctors & allied professions throughout Europe. Also offers US professional medical societies & publishers an office address in Europe, London, for receipt of orders & inquiries.
Type of Business: Distributor

Heffers:
20 Trinity St, Cambridge CB2 1TY
Tel: (01223) 568568 *Fax:* (01223) 568591
E-mail: heffers@heffers.co.uk
Web Site: www.heffers.co.uk
Telex: 81298

Key Personnel
Manager: Mary McIntosh
Founded: 1876
Type of Business: Exporter, Major Independent Bookseller
Owned by: Blackwell's Bookshops
Branch Office(s)
Heffers: Grafton Centre Bookshop, 28B The Grafton Centre, Cambridge CB1 1PS, Manager: Erika McKay *Tel:* (01223) 568573 *Fax:* (01223) 568572 *E-mail:* grafton@heffers.co.uk
Heffers: Plus, 31 St Andrews St, Cambridge CB2 3AX *Tel:* (01223) 568598 *Fax:* (01223) 568593 *E-mail:* plus@heffers.co.uk (paperbacks, audio books, video & DVDs)
Heffers: Sound, 19 Trinity St, Cambridge, Manager: Tony McGeorge *Tel:* (01223) 568562 *Fax:* (01223) 568591 *E-mail:* sound@heffers.co.uk (recorded music on cassette & compact disc, spoken word cassettes, DVDs)

Hellenic Bookservice
91 Fortess Rd, Kentish Town, London NW5 1AG
Tel: (020) 72679499 *Fax:* (020) 72679498
E-mail: info@hellenicbookservice.com
Web Site: www.hellenicbookservice.com
Key Personnel
Partner: Monica Williams
Founded: 1966
Independent Bookseller.

Thomas Heneage Art Books
42 Duke St, St James's, London SW1Y 6DJ
Tel: (020) 7930 9223 *Fax:* (020) 7839 9223
E-mail: artbooks@heneage.com
Web Site: www.heneage.com
Key Personnel
Man Dir: Thomas Heneage
Founded: 1977
Sells art books, catalogue raisonnes, monographs & exhibition catalogues.
Type of Business: Major Independent Bookseller
Owned by: Thomas Heneage

The Holt Jackson Book Co Ltd
Preston Rd, Lytham, Lancs FY8 5AX
Tel: (01253) 737464 *Fax:* (01253) 733361
E-mail: info@holtjackson.co.uk
Web Site: www.holtjackson.co.uk
Key Personnel
Chairman: Kevin Holden *E-mail:* kholden@holtjackson.co.uk
Deputy Chairman: Jonathan Pewtress
Acquisitions Manager: Tom Lee
Sales & Customer Care Dir: Anne Ollier
Finance Dir: Carole Park
Founded: 1932
Suppliers of shelf-ready books to public, business, academic & school libraries throughout the UK & overseas.
Type of Business: Exporter, Major Independent Bookseller, Wholesaler

Brian Inns Booksales & Services
9 Ashley Crescent, Warwick CV34 6QH
Tel: (01926) 498428 *Fax:* (01926) 498428
Key Personnel
Man Dir: Brian Inns
Founded: 1989
Sales consultant & sales agency.

Internos Books
12 Percy St, London W1P 9FB
Tel: (020) 7637 4255 *Fax:* (020) 7637 4251
Key Personnel
President: E Booth-Clibborn
Editor: M Sutcliffe
Sales Dir: J Booth-Clibborn
Founded: 1987
Type of Business: Distributor, Exporter, Importer, Wholesaler
Owned by: Booth-Clibborn Editions

UNITED KINGDOM   MAJOR

Richard Joseph Publishers Ltd
PO Box 15, Torrington, Devon EX38 8ZJ
Tel: (01805) 625750 *Fax:* (01805) 625376
E-mail: sheppardsdir@aol.com
Web Site: www.sheppardsworld.com
Key Personnel
Man Dir: Richard Joseph *E-mail:* rjoe01@aol.com
Founded: 1990
Also acts as print consultant.
Joint owner of Sheppard's Book Search with Nielson Book Data Ltd.

Kuperard
Division of Bravo Ltd
311 Ballards Lane, London N12 8LY
Tel: (020) 8446 2440 *Fax:* (020) 8446 2441
E-mail: kuperard@bravo.clara.net
Web Site: www.kuperard.co.uk
Key Personnel
Man Dir: Joshua Kuperard *E-mail:* joshua@bravo.clara.net
Sales & Marketing Manager: Martin Kaye
Founded: 1986
Publisher.
Type of Business: Distributor, Exporter, Importer

Lavis Marketing
73 Lime Walk, Headington, Oxford OX3 7AD
Tel: (01865) 767575 *Fax:* (01865) 750079
E-mail: orders@lavismarketing.co.uk
Key Personnel
Contact: James H Lavis *E-mail:* jim@lavismarketing.co.uk
Founded: 1982
Type of Business: Distributor

The Lexicon Bookshop
63 Strand St, Douglas, Isle of Man IM1 2RL
Tel: (01624) 673004 *Fax:* (01624) 661959
E-mail: manxbooks@lexiconbookshop.co.im
Web Site: www.lexiconbookshop.co.im
Key Personnel
Proprietor: D W Ashworth
Founded: 1936
Type of Business: Major Independent Bookseller

Lister Art Books of Southport
PO Box 31, Southport, Lancs PR9 8BF
Tel: (01704) 232033 *Fax:* (01704) 505926
E-mail: sales@laboox.demon.co.uk
Key Personnel
Contact: Graham Lister
Books on Antiques & Collecting; USA Co represented.
Type of Business: Distributor, Importer

Littlehampton Book Services Ltd
Faraday Close, Worthing, West Sussex BN13 3RB
Tel: (01903) 828500 *Fax:* (01903) 828802
E-mail: enquiries@lbsltd.co.uk
Web Site: www.lbsltd.co.uk
Key Personnel
Man Dir: Martin Evans
Publishing Services Dir: Bridget Radnedge
Finance Dir: Basil May
Type of Business: Distributor
Owned by: Orion Publishing Group, 5 Upper St Martin's Lane, London WC2H 9EA

Chris Lloyd Sales & Marketing Services
Stanley House, 1st floor, 3 Fleets Lane, Poole, Dorset BH15 3AJ
Tel: (01202) 649930 *Fax:* (01202) 649950
E-mail: chrlloyd@globalnet.co.uk
Founded: 1986
Type of Business: Distributor, Importer

Lomond, *imprint of* Lomond Books

Lomond Books
36 West Shore Rd, Granton, Edinburgh EH5 1QD
Tel: (0131) 551 2261 *Fax:* (0131) 559 2042
E-mail: info@flatman.co.uk; sales@lomond-books.co.uk
Web Site: www.lomond-books.co.uk; www.scottishbookstore.com
Key Personnel
Man Dir: David Flatman
Sales & Marketing Dir: Trevor Maher
Sales Manager: Duncan Baxter
Also retailer & publisher.
Type of Business: Remainder Dealer, Wholesaler
Imprints: Lomond

Mallory International Ltd
Aylesbeare Common Business Park, Exmouth Rd, Aylesbeare, Devon EX5 2DG
Tel: (01395) 239199 *Fax:* (01395) 239168
E-mail: sales@malloryint.co.uk
Web Site: www.malloryint.co.uk
Key Personnel
Executive Dir: Norman Guthrie
Dir: Mrs Clare Guthrie *E-mail:* clare@malloryint.co.uk; Julian Hardinge; Mrs Ulrike Hardinge
Founded: 1984
International booksellers.
Type of Business: Distributor, Exporter, Importer, Major Independent Bookseller

Marston Book Services Ltd
PO Box 269, Abingdon, Oxon OX14 4YN
Tel: (01235) 465500 *Fax:* (01235) 465555
E-mail: trade.enquiry@marston.co.uk
Web Site: www.marston.co.uk
Telex: 837515
Key Personnel
Chairman: John Holloran
Man Dir: Ross Clayton
Type of Business: Distributor

Menoshire Ltd
Unit 13, 21 Wadsworth Rd, Perivale, Middx UB6 7LQ
Tel: (020) 85667344 *Fax:* (020) 89912439
E-mail: sales@menoshire.com
Web Site: www.menoshire.com
Key Personnel
Man Dir: J M Treacy
Founded: 1975
Type of Business: Exporter, Importer, Wholesaler

Meresborough Books Ltd
17-25 Station Rd, Rainham, Kent ME8 7RS
Tel: (01634) 371591 *Fax:* (01634) 262114
E-mail: shop@rainhambookshop.co.uk
Web Site: www.rainhambookshop.co.uk
Key Personnel
Manager: Hamish Mackay-Miller
Founded: 1977
Independent bookshop & school books supplier.
Type of Business: Major Independent Bookseller, Wholesaler

Millbank Books Ltd
The Court Yard, The Old Monastery, Windhill, Bishop's Stortford, Herts CM23 2PE
Tel: (01279) 655233 *Fax:* (01279) 655244
E-mail: caw@millbank.demon.co.uk
Key Personnel
Dir: Diana Walsh; Christine Walsh
Founded: 1987
Distributors of General Nonfiction in the UK, Europe & Middle East; Import Specialist Titles from USA, Singapore, Malaysia, Australia & South Africa; Also act as UK agents for overseas publishers to sell the rights of their titles to UK publishers.
Type of Business: Distributor, Exporter, Importer

Motilal (UK) Books of India
PO Box 324, Borehamwood, Herts WD6 1NB
Tel: (020) 8905-1244 *Fax:* (020) 8905-1108
E-mail: info@mlbduk.com
Web Site: www.mlbduk.com
Key Personnel
Owner & Distribution Dir: Ray McLennan
Founded: 1982
Import, Export & Distribution Agency for books published in India.
Type of Business: Distributor, Exporter, Importer
Parent Company: Money Savers (London) Ltd

Music Book Distributors Ltd
44 Station Way, Buckhurst Hill, Essex IG9 6LN
Tel: (0181) 559 1522 *Fax:* (0181) 559 1522
Key Personnel
Dir: Neil Taylor
Founded: 1988
Type of Business: Wholesaler

NBN Plymbridge
Formerly Plymbridge Distributors Ltd
Plymbridge House, Estover Rd, Plymouth PL6 7PY
Tel: (01752) 202300 *Fax:* (01752) 202330
E-mail: enquiries@plymbridge.com; orders@plymbridge.com
Web Site: www.plymbridge.com
Key Personnel
Man Dir: Irv Myers
Type of Business: Distributor
Owned by: Rowman & Littlefield Group, Inc

Northern Map Distributors
101 Broadfield Rd, Sheffield S8 0XH
Tel: (0114) 2582660 *Toll Free Tel:* 800 834920
Key Personnel
Partner: David N Smith
Founded: 1975
Map & Guide Wholesaler.
Subjects: LAM-FORD Maps
Type of Business: Wholesaler

Orbis Books (London) Ltd
206 Blythe Rd, London W14 0HH
Tel: (020) 7602 5541 *Fax:* (020) 8742 7686
E-mail: bookshop@orbis-books.co.uk
Key Personnel
Dir: Jerzy Kulczycki
Specialize in books in English on Central & Eastern Europe. Stockholders of books in Polish, Czech, Slovak & Bulgarian.
Type of Business: Exporter, Importer, Major Independent Bookseller

Parfitts Book Services
50 Imber Rd, Warminster, Wilts BA12 0BN
Tel: (01985) 216371 *Fax:* (01985) 212982
E-mail: parfitts@cix.compulink.co.uk
Key Personnel
Dir: J E Parfitt
Type of Business: Distributor, Exporter, Importer, Major Independent Bookseller, Wholesaler

Plymbridge Distributors Ltd, see NBN Plymbridge

H Pordes Ltd
58-60 Charing Cross Rd, London WC2H 0BB
Tel: (020) 8445 1273 *Fax:* (020) 8445 5510
Key Personnel
Dir: Henry Pordes; N Pordes
Manager: Gino Della Ragione
Founded: 1975
Wholesale only-buying & selling of remainders. Also publisher.
Type of Business: Remainder Dealer

BOOK DEALERS — UNITED KINGDOM

Promotional Reprint Co Ltd
Kiln House, 210 New Kings Rd, London SW6 4NZ
Tel: (020) 7736 5666 *Fax:* (020) 7736 5777
Type of Business: Remainder Dealer

Rainham Bookshop, see Meresborough Books Ltd

Ramboro Books Plc
10 Blenheim Court, Brewery Rd, London N7 9NT
Tel: (020) 7700 7444 *Fax:* (020) 7700 4552
E-mail: enquiries@ramboro.co.uk
Web Site: www.ramborobooks.com
Key Personnel
International Sales Dir: Tim Finch
    E-mail: tfinch@chrysalisbooks.co.uk
Type of Business: Remainder Dealer

Randall & Swift Ltd
Pioneer Market 4, Winston Way, Ilford, Essex IG1 2RD
Tel: (020) 8553 3030 *Fax:* (020) 8559 1522
Key Personnel
Dir: Neil Taylor
Founded: 1979
Supplier of printed music & music books to libraries.

The Richmond Publishing Co Ltd
PO Box 963, Slough SL2 3RS
Tel: (01753) 643104 *Fax:* (01753) 646553
E-mail: rpc@richmond.co.uk
Key Personnel
Man Dir: Mrs S J Davie
Founded: 1970
Type of Business: Distributor, Exporter, Importer, Major Independent Bookseller, Wholesaler

RICS Books
Surveyor Court, Westwood Business Park, Coventry CV4 8JE
Tel: (0870) 333 1600 *Fax:* (020) 7334 3851
E-mail: weborders@rics.org.uk
Web Site: www.ricsbooks.com
Key Personnel
Dir of Operations: Angela Hartland *Tel:* (020) 7222 7000 (ext 744) *Fax:* (020) 7334 3840
    E-mail: ahartland@rics.org
Managing Editor: Toni Gill *Tel:* (020) 7222 7000 (ext 686) *Fax:* (020) 7334 3840 *E-mail:* tgill@rics.org
Founded: 1981
Distributor for 11 US publishers.
Type of Business: Distributor, Major Independent Bookseller
Owned by: Royal Institution of Chartered Surveyors (RICS)
Bookshop(s): 7 St Andrews Pl, Cardiff CF10 3BE *Tel:* (029) 2022 4414 *Fax:* (029) 2022 4416; RICS Coventry Bookstall *Tel:* (020) 7222 7000 (ext 198); 12 Great George St, Parliament Sq, London SW1P 3AD *Tel:* (020) 7334 3776 *Fax:* (020) 7222 9430 *E-mail:* bookshop@rics.org

Louise Ross & Co, Ltd
Mulberry House, 8 Mount Rd, Lansdown, Bath, Avon BA1 5PW
Tel: (0225) 44 87 86 *Fax:* (0225) 44 87 89
E-mail: louise.ross@btinternet.com
Key Personnel
Man Dir: Louise Ross *E-mail:* louise.ross@btinternet.com
Founded: 1977
Antiquarian & literary books, first editions only; also acts as publisher.
Type of Business: Major Independent Bookseller
Owned by: Ross Press

Roundhouse Group
Millstone, Limers Lane, Northam, North Devon EX39 2RG
Tel: (01237) 474474 *Fax:* (01237) 474774
E-mail: roundhouse.group@ukgateway.net
Web Site: www.roundhouse.net
Key Personnel
President & Chief Executive: Alan T Goodworth
Founded: 1991
Distributor of small/medium publisher lists from USA, Canada & Australia.
Type of Business: Distributor, Exporter, Importer, Wholesaler
Parent Company: Roundhouse Publishing Ltd
Warehouse: Orca Book Services, Stanley House, 3 Fleets Lane, Poole, Dorset BH15 3AJ
    Tel: (01202) 665 432 *Fax:* (01202) 666 219
    E-mail: orders@orca-book-services.co.uk

Royal Institution of Chartered Surveyors, see RICS Books

Sandpiper Books Ltd
24 Langroyd Rd, London SW17 7PL
Tel: (020) 8767 7421 *Fax:* (020) 8682 0280
E-mail: enquiries@sandpiper.co.uk
Key Personnel
Sales Manager: Chris Harley *E-mail:* charley@sandpiper.co.uk
Contact: Juliet Morgan
Founded: 1984
Specializing in scholarly & literary remainders, good quality arts, reprints of academic monographs with Oxford University Press.
Type of Business: Remainder Dealer
Showroom(s): 4/5 Academy Buildings, Lower Ground floor, Fanshaw St, London N1 6LQ
    Tel: (020) 7613 4446 *Fax:* (020) 7613 4513

Saqi Books
26 Westbourne Grove, London W2 5RH
Tel: (020) 7229 8543; (020) 7221 9347
Fax: (020) 7229 7492
E-mail: saqibooks@dial.pipex.com
Web Site: www.saqibooks.com
Key Personnel
Contact: Mai Ghoussoub
Editorial Manager: Sarah Al-Hamad
    E-mail: sarah@saqibooks.com
Founded: 1979
Type of Business: Exporter, Importer, Major Independent Bookseller
Owned by: A & S Gaspard; M Ghoussoub; K & H Makija

Derek Searle Associates
The Coach House, Cippenham Lodge, Cippenham Lane, Slough, Berks SL1 5AN
Tel: (01753) 539295 *Fax:* (01753) 551863
E-mail: dsapublish@aol.com
Key Personnel
Contact: Mrs Maureen Corrington
Founded: 1991
Act as Independent Sales & Marketing Agents on behalf of client Publishers.

Send the Light Ltd
Kingstown Broadway, Carlisle, Cumbria CA3 OHA
Tel: (01228) 512 512 *Fax:* (01228) 514 949
E-mail: info@stl.org
Web Site: www.stl.org
Key Personnel
Chief Executive: Keith Danby
Man Dir, Publishing: Mark Finnie
Founded: 1965
Publish & distribute books to advance the Christian faith.
Type of Business: Distributor, Wholesaler
Subsidiaries: Paternoster Publishing

Sherratt & Hughes
c/o WHSmith Retail Ltd, Freepost (sce 4410), Swindon, Wilts SN3 3XS
Tel: (01793) 695195
Key Personnel
Manager: J D Siverns
Incorporating Bowes & Bowes Books.
Owned by: WHSmith & Son Ltd

Shogun International Ltd
87 Gayford Rd, London W12 9BY
Tel: (020) 8749 2022 *Fax:* (020) 8740 1086
Key Personnel
Manager: P Tai
Founded: 1974
Manufactured supply of martial arts equipment, clothing & books (on martial arts only).
Type of Business: Distributor, Exporter, Importer, Wholesaler

Silverdale, *imprint of* Bookmart Ltd

John Smith & Son Booksellers
Ash House, Headlands Business Park, Ringwood, Hants BH24 3PB
Tel: (01425) 471160 *Fax:* (01425) 471718
Web Site: www.johnsmith.co.uk
Telex: 778881 Jssglw G *Cable:* BOOKS: GLASGOW
Key Personnel
Chairman: Peter Gray *E-mail:* pgray@johnsmith.co.uk
Deputy Chairman: Willie Anderson
    E-mail: wtca@johnsmith.co.uk
Man Dir: Terry Field *E-mail:* tfield@johnsmith.co.uk
Business Development Manager: Chris Sugden
    E-mail: crs@johnsmith.co.uk
Founded: 1751

Springfield Books Ltd
Norman Rd, Denby Dale, Huddersfield, West Yorks HD8 8TH
Tel: (01484) 864955 *Fax:* (01484) 865443
Key Personnel
Sales Manager, Publicity: Paula Brennan
Founded: 1984
Type of Business: Distributor

The Stationery Office, see TSO (The Stationery Office)

STL, see Send the Light Ltd

THE, see Total Home Entertainment

James Thin, Bookseller
53-62 South Bridge, Edinburgh EH1 1YS
Tel: (0131) 622 8222 *Fax:* (0131) 557 8149
E-mail: enquiries@jthin.co.uk
Key Personnel
Non-Exec Chmn: D Ainslie Thin
Man Dir: Jackie Thin
Dirs: Malcolm Gibson; Ken Lemond; Andrew Thin; James Thin; Graham White
Assistant to Man Dir: Dayle Coltman *Tel:* (0131) 622 8281 *E-mail:* dayle.coltman@jthin.co.uk
Founded: 1848
Specialize in the publication of Scottish interest & outdoor books under the Mercat Press imprint.
Type of Business: Major Independent Bookseller
Bookshop(s): James Thin Ltd, Unit 21-23, Sovereign S/Ctr, Weston-Super-Mare, Avon BS23 1HL; James Thin Ltd, 15 Sandgate, Ayr KA7 1BG; The Lanes, 77 Lowther St, Carlisle CA3 8EF; James Thin Ltd, 18/26 Church Crescent, Dumfries DG1 1DQ; James Thin Ltd, 7/8 High St, Dundee DD1 1SS; James Thin Ltd, 53/59 South Bridge, Edinburgh EH1 1YS; James Thin Ltd, 59 George St, Edinburgh

EH2 2JQ; James Thin Ltd, 29-31 Buccleuch St, Edinburgh EH8 9LT *Tel:* (0131) 667 6253 *Fax:* (0131) 667 6253 *E-mail:* buccleuchst@jthin.co.uk; James Thin Ltd, Hugh Nisbet Bldg, Heriot-Watt University, Riccarton Campus, Edinburgh EH14 2AS; James Thin Ltd, Kings Bldg Bookshop, University of Edinburgh, W Mains Rd, Edinburgh EH9 3JR *Tel:* (0131) 667 0432 *Fax:* (0131) 667 0432 *E-mail:* kingsbuilding@jthin.co.uk; Gyle, 35 Gyle Ave, South Gyle Broadway, Edinburgh EH12 9JT; James Thin Ltd, 22/24 Thackery Mall, Fareham Shopping Centre, Fareham, Hants PO16 OPQ; James Thin Ltd, Unit SU45, The Lakeside Centre, West Thurrock, Grays, Essex RM16 1ZF; James Thin Ltd, Mid Level, Unit 55-56, The Exchange, Ilford, Essex IGI IAA; James Thin Ltd, 29 Union St, Inverness IVI 1QA; James Thin Ltd, 87 Grampian Rd, Aviemore, Inverness-shire PH22 1RH; James Thin Ltd, Unit LSU 2, Centre Court Shopping Centre, Wimbledon, London SW19 8YE; James Thin Ltd, Unit 26, Treaty Centre, Hounslow, Middlesex TW3 IES; James Thin Ltd, 2A Mercer Walk, The Pavilions, Uxbridge, Middlesex 1LU 1LY; James Thin Ltd, 20/21 Castle Mall, Norwich, Norfolk NR1 3XJ; James Thin Ltd, Unit SU44, The Peacocks Centre, Woking, Surrey GU21 1GD; James Thin Ltd, University Bookshop, Student's Union, St Mary Pl, St Andrews, Fife KY16 9UY, Manager: Barbara Dumbleton *Tel:* (01334) 476367 *Fax:* (01334) 478367 *E-mail:* standrews@jthin.co.uk; James Thin, 176 High St, Perth PH1 5UN; James Thin, 5 New St, Huddersfield, Yorkshire HD1 2AX

Thomson Publishing Services
Cheriton House, North Way, Andover, Hants SP10 5BE
Tel: (01264) 332424 *Fax:* (01264) 364418
Key Personnel
General Manager: Barry Hinchmore
Customer Service Dir: Carrie Willicome
Chief Accountant: Jo Jewell
Founded: 1988
Type of Business: Distributor
Owned by: The Thomson Corp

Thornton's of Oxford Ltd
126-B Milton Park, Abingdon-upon-Thames OX14 4SA
Tel: (01235) 821994
E-mail: thorntons@booknews.demon.co.uk
Web Site: www.thorntonsbooks.co.uk
Key Personnel
Man Dir: Willem A Meeuws
Founded: 1835
Also Publisher.
Type of Business: Distributor, Exporter, Importer, Major Independent Bookseller

Tiger Books International PLC
26A York St, Twickenham, Middlesex TW1 3LJ
Tel: (0181) 8925577 *Fax:* (0181) 8916550
Key Personnel
Man Dir: Grahame Parish
Founded: 1985
Type of Business: Remainder Dealer

Titles Old and Rare Books of Oxford
15 Turl St, Oxford OX1 3DQ
Tel: (01865) 727928 *Fax:* (01865) 727928
Key Personnel
Contact: G Stone; R Stone
Founded: 1972
Specialize in History of Science, Travel, Agriculture, Literature, General Antiquarian & Secondhand Books.
Type of Business: Major Independent Bookseller

Total Home Entertainment
Rosevale Business Park, Newcastle-under-Lyme, Staffs ST5 7QT
Tel: (01782) 566566 *Fax:* (01782) 565400
E-mail: thenews@the.co.uk
Key Personnel
Man Dir: Alasdair Ogilvie
Sales & Marketing Dir, Books: Phil Scarlet
Wholesaler for Home Entertainment software including books, videos, music, multimedia products, electronic games & accessories. Multilingual export service & advice centre based in London.
Type of Business: Distributor, Exporter, Wholesaler
Owned by: John Menzies (UK) Ltd
Branch Office(s)
The International Export Office, Unit 4, Elsinore House, 77 Fulham Palace Rd, London W6 8JA

Troika
United House, North Rd, London N7 9DP
Tel: (020) 7619 0800 *Fax:* (020) 7619 0801
E-mail: troika@sellbooks.demon.co.uk
Key Personnel
Man Dir: Aidan Lunn
Founded: 1983
Independent Representatives.

John Trotter Books
80 East End Rd, Finchley, London N3 2SY
Tel: (020) 8349 9484 *Fax:* (020) 8346 7430
E-mail: John.Trotter@bibliophile.net
Web Site: www.bibliophile.net/John-Trotter-Books.html
Founded: 1973
Also acts as publisher & remainder dealer.
Type of Business: Major Independent Bookseller

TSO (The Stationery Office)
51 Nine Elms Lane, London SW8 5DR
Tel: (020) 7873 8787; (0870) 600 5522 (orders) *Fax:* (0870) 600 5533 (orders)
E-mail: customer.services@tso.co.uk
Web Site: www.theso.co.uk
Key Personnel
Chairman: Rupert Pennant-Rea
Chief Executive Officer: Tim Hailstone
Man Dir: Keith Burbage; Jeremy Hook; Dr Shane O'Neill
Chief Financial Officer: Richard Dell
Human Resources Dir: David Orr
Export Manager: Brian Tierney *Tel:* (020) 7873 8211 *Fax:* (020) 7873 8203 *E-mail:* brian.tierney@theso.co.uk
Sales Manager: Rebecca Barley
Publicity Manager: Michelle Brown
Bibliographics Manager: Peter Gutteridge
Editorial: Philip Brooks *Tel:* (01603) 605532 *E-mail:* phil.brooks@theso.co.uk
Contact: Jamie Precious
Founded: 1996
Publishes for UK government departments & a wide variety of public bodies on subjects covering academic & general interests. Also UK distributor for international organizations including UN, UNESCO, FAO, WHO, OECD, EU & IMF.
Type of Business: Distributor, Exporter
Branch Office(s)
TSO Ireland, 16 Arthur St, Belfast BT1 4GD, Ireland *Tel:* (02890) 238451
TSO - Norwich, St Crispins, Duke St, Norwich NR3 1PD *Tel:* (01603) 622211
TSO Scotland, 71-73 Lothian Rd, Edinburgh EH3 9AZ *Tel:* (0870) 6065566
TSO Wales, G50, Phase Two, Government Bldgs, Ty-Glas, Llanishen, Cardiff CF14 5ST *Tel:* (02920) 765892
Bookshop(s): TSO Scotland Bookshop, 71 Lothian Rd, Edinburgh EH3 9AZ, Manager: Ron Wilson *Tel:* (0870) 606 5566 *Fax:* (0870) 606 5588 *E-mail:* edinburgh.bookshop@tso.co.uk; 16 Arthur St, Belfast BT1 4GD, Ireland, Manager: Sharon Barnes *Tel:* (02890) 238451 *Fax:* (02890) 235401 *E-mail:* belfast.bookshop@tso.co.uk; 68-69 Bull St, Birmingham B4 6AD, Manager: James Furnival *Tel:* (0121) 236 9696 *Fax:* (0121) 236 9699 *E-mail:* birmingham.bookshop@tso.co.uk; 18-19 High St, Cardiff CF10 1PT, Manager: Joanne Fowler *Tel:* (02920) 39 5548 *Fax:* (02920) 38 4347 *E-mail:* cardiff.bookstore@tso.co.uk; 123 Kingsway, London WC2B 6PQ, Manager: Anya Somerville *Tel:* (020) 7242 6393; (020) 7242 6410 *Fax:* (020) 7242 6394 *E-mail:* london.bookshop@tso.co.uk; 9-21 Princess St, Albert Sq, Manchester M60 8AS, Manager: Ian Penney *Tel:* (0161) 834 7201 *Fax:* (0161) 833 0634 *E-mail:* manchester.bookshop@tso.co.uk

Turnaround Publisher Services Ltd
Unit 3, Olympia Trading Estate, Coburg Rd, Wood Green, London N22 6TZ
Tel: (020) 8829 3000 *Fax:* (020) 8881 5088
E-mail: enquires@turnaround-uk.com
Web Site: www.turnaround-uk.com
Key Personnel
Man Dir: Bill Godber *E-mail:* bill@turnaround-uk.com
Marketing Dir: Claire Thompson *E-mail:* claire@turnaround-uk.com
Founded: 1984
Book distributor of a wide range of US, UK & Irish based publishers to the UK & continental Europe.
Membership(s): Publishers' Association (UK); Bookseller's Association (UK).
Type of Business: Distributor, Exporter, Importer, Wholesaler

Turpin Distribution Services Ltd, see Extenza-Turpin

UBS Publishers' Distributors Ltd
475 N Circular Rd, London NW2 7QG
Tel: (020) 8450 8667 *Fax:* (020) 8452 6612
Key Personnel
Dir: M K Kalsi *E-mail:* mkkalsi@ubspd.com
Founded: 1937
Represent over 400 Indian publishers, stocks 2 million books in India & has constant liaisons with over 2000 commercial publishers, research institutions & government depts & disseminate information about their new publications through their weekly bulletins as well as their subject-wise catalogs.
Type of Business: Distributor, Exporter, Importer, Wholesaler

United Book Suppliers
689 Antrim Rd, Newtownabbey, Co Antrim BT36 8RN
Tel: (01232) 832362 *Fax:* (01232) 848780
Key Personnel
Man Dir: John Lindsay
Founded: 1981
Type of Business: Distributor, Exporter, Wholesaler

University of London
Central Printing Service, Room P1, Senate House, Malet St, London WC1E 7HU
Tel: (020) 7862 8000 *Fax:* (020) 7636 5874
E-mail: enquiries@lon.ac.uk
Web Site: www.lon.ac.uk
Key Personnel
Acting Manager: Allan Kendall
Publications Officer: S M Masters
Type of Business: Major Independent Bookseller

Robert Vaughan Antiquarian Booksellers
20 Chapel St, Stratford-Upon-Avon, Warwicks CV37 6EP
Tel: (01789) 205312
Key Personnel
Contact: Colleen M Vaughan
Founded: 1953
Subjects: Fine & First Editions of English Literature, Theatre & Allied Arts
Type of Business: Major Independent Bookseller

Vine House Distribution Ltd
Affiliate of Vine House Book Promotion
Waldenbury, North Common, Chailey, East Sussex BN8 4DR
Tel: (01825) 723 398 *Fax:* (01825) 724 188
E-mail: sales@vinehouseuk.co.uk
Web Site: www.vinehouseuk.co.uk
Key Personnel
Man Dir: Richard Squibb
Founded: 1988
International book distributors, including representation & public relations.
Type of Business: Distributor, Exporter, Importer
Warehouse: Mullany Business Park, Deanland Rd, Golden Cross, Nr Hailsham, East Sussex BN27 3RP *Tel:* (01825) 873 133

Peter Ward Book Exports
Unit 3, Taylors Yard, 67 Alderbrook Rd, London SW12 8AD
Tel: (020) 8772 3300 *Fax:* (020) 8772 3309
E-mail: pwbookex@dircon.co.uk
Key Personnel
Partner & President: Peter Ward
Vice President: Richard Ward
Founded: 1974
Publishers' representatives.
Type of Business: Exporter, Major Independent Bookseller, Wholesaler

Waterstone & Co Ltd
Capital Court, Capital Interchange Way, Brentford, Middlesex TW8 0EX
Tel: (020) 8742 3800
Numerous branches throughout the UK.

Welsh Books Council (Cyngor Llyfrau Cymru)
Castell Brychan, Aberystwyth, Ceredigion SY23 2JB
Tel: (01970) 624151 *Fax:* (01970) 625385
E-mail: castellbrychan@wbc.org.uk
Web Site: www.cllc.org.uk
Key Personnel
Manager: Dafydd Charles Jones *E-mail:* dafydd.jones@wbc.org.uk
Founded: 1963
Type of Business: Distributor, Wholesaler

Whitaker Information Services
Woolmead House, Bear Lane, Farnham, Surrey GU9 7LG
Tel: (01252) 742525 *Fax:* (01252) 742526
E-mail: custserv@whitaker.co.uk
Web Site: www.whitaker.co.uk
Key Personnel
Man Dir: Paul Pounsford
Order Routing & EDI Communication Network.
Owned by: J Whitaker & Sons Ltd

WHSmith PLC
Nations House PLC, 103 Wigmore St, London W1U 1WH
Tel: (020) 7409 3222 *Fax:* (020) 7514 9633
E-mail: customer.relations@whsmith.co.uk
Web Site: www.whsmith.co.uk
Key Personnel
Chairman: Jeremy Hardie
Corporate Affairs Dir: Tim Blythe
Founded: 1792

There are 553 High Street Stores & 100 airport & station bookstores throughout the UK & 100 specialist bookshops, operating under the name of Waterstones.
Type of Business: Distributor, Major Independent Bookseller

Wisdom Books
25 Stanley Rd, Ilford, Essex IG1 1RW
Tel: (020) 8553 5020 *Fax:* (020) 8553 5122
E-mail: sales@wisdom-books.com
Web Site: www.wisdom-books.com
Key Personnel
Man Dir: Dennis Heslop
Sales Manager: Mike Gilmore
Title Research: Leigh Wyman
Office Manager: Philip Bradley
Orders: Jonathon Steyn
Founded: 1989
Specialize in all traditions of Buddhism.
Type of Business: Distributor, Importer, Wholesaler

Witherby & Co Ltd
Book Dept, 2nd floor, 32-36 Aylesbury St, London EC1R 0ET
Tel: (020) 7251 5341 *Fax:* (020) 7251 1296
E-mail: books@witherbys.co.uk
Web Site: www.witherbys.com
Key Personnel
Man Dir & Publisher: Alan Witherby
 E-mail: alanw@witherbys.co.uk
Founded: 1740
Specialize in insurance & shipping publications.
Subjects: Risk management
Type of Business: Exporter, Major Independent Bookseller
Bookshop(s): 20 Aldermanbury, London EC2V 7HY *Tel:* (020) 7417 4431 *Fax:* (020) 7417 4431

Woodfield & Stanley Ltd
Broad Lane, Moldgreen, Huddersfield HD5 9BX
Tel: (01484) 421467; (01484) 532401
 Fax: (01484) 510237
Web Site: www.woodfield-stanley.co.uk
Key Personnel
Man Dir: P G Chadwick
Founded: 1946
Type of Business: Distributor, Major Independent Bookseller, Wholesaler

World Leisure Marketing
Unit 11, New Market Court, Derby DE24 8NW
Tel: (01332) 573737 *Fax:* (01332) 573399
E-mail: office@wlmsales.co.uk
Key Personnel
Man Dir: John Whitby
Sales Dir: John Grundy
Founded: 1991
Type of Business: Distributor, Exporter, Importer

Roy Yates Books
Smallfields Cottage, Cox Green, Rudgwick, Horsham, West Sussex RH12 3DE
Tel: (01403) 822299 *Fax:* (01403) 823012
Key Personnel
Proprietor: Roy Yates
Founded: 1987
Type of Business: Distributor, Exporter, Importer, Major Independent Bookseller, Wholesaler

Uruguay

Albe Libros Tecnicos SRL
Cerrito 564/566, Casilla de Correos 1601, 11000 Montevideo
Tel: (02) 95 75 28 *Fax:* (02) 95 75 28
Key Personnel
Bookstore & Editorial: Daniel Aljanati
Distributor: Jaime Daniel Aljanati
Founded: 1950
Type of Business: Distributor, Exporter, Importer, Major Independent Bookseller, Wholesaler
Owned by: Nuestra Tierra (publishing) & Distribuidora Albe SRL (distribution), Cerrito 566, Montevideo 1100

America Latina
18 de Julio 2089, Montevideo
Tel: (02) 415127 *Fax:* (02) 495568
Key Personnel
Manager: Ismael Munoz
Founded: 1962
Type of Business: Distributor, Importer, Major Independent Bookseller, Wholesaler

Barreiro y Ramos SA
25 de Mayo, 604 Montevideo
Tel: (02) 95 01 50 *Fax:* (02) 96 23 58
Key Personnel
Pres: Dr Gaston Barreiro Zorrilla
Also Publisher.
Branch Office(s)
Ave General Artigas 714, Las Piedras
Arocena 1599, Montevideo
Ave 18 de Julio 1852, Montevideo
Ave 18 de Julio 941, Montevideo
Ave 8 de Octubre 3728, Montevideo
Ave Agraciada 3945, Montevideo
Ave Rivera 2684, Montevideo
Calle 21 de Setiembre 2753, Montevideo
Minas 1491, Montevideo

Feria del Libro
Ave 18 de Julio 1308, Montevideo
Tel: (02) 900 42 48 *Fax:* (02) 900 20 70
Key Personnel
Manager: Domingo A Maestro
Type of Business: Distributor, Importer, Major Book Chain Headquarters, Wholesaler

Libreria Amalio M Fernandez SRL
25 de Mayo 477, planta baja ofic 2, 11000 Montevideo
Tel: (02) 95 26 84 *Fax:* (02) 95 17 82
Founded: 1951
Type of Business: Distributor, Exporter, Importer, Major Independent Bookseller, Wholesaler

El Galeon
Juan Carlos Gomez 1327, 11000 Montevideo
Tel: (02) 9156139; (02) 9157909 *Fax:* (02) 9157909
E-mail: elgaleon@netgate.com.uy *Cable:* GALLEONBOOK MONTEVIDEO
Key Personnel
Proprietor: Roberto Cataldo
Founded: 1973
Antiquarian bookseller specializing in history, literature, art, politics; also chart engraving.
Type of Business: Distributor, Exporter, Importer, Major Independent Bookseller, Wholesaler

Libreria Linardi y Risso
Juan Carlos Gomez 1435, 11000 Montevideo
Tel: (02) 915 7129; (02) 915 7328 *Fax:* (02) 915 7431
E-mail: lyrbooks@linardiyrisso.com
Web Site: www.linardiyrisso.com
Key Personnel
Manager: Andres Linardi; Alvaro J Risso
Founded: 1944
Antiquarian bookseller; Uruguayan Current Books.
Type of Business: Distributor, Exporter, Major Independent Bookseller

Palacio del Libro
25 de Mayo 577, Casilla 371, Montevideo
Tel: (02) 959019 *Fax:* (02) 957543
Key Personnel
Man Dir: Daniel Mussini
Vice President: Liliana Mussini
Editorial Graphic Bindery workshop.
Type of Business: Distributor, Exporter, Importer, Major Independent Bookseller, Wholesaler

Venezuela

Libreria del Este
52 Avda Francisco de Miranda, Edificio Galipan, Caracas 106
Mailing Address: Apdo 60337, Caracas 106
Tel: (02) 951 2307; (02) 951 1297
Key Personnel
Manager: Tomas Pericas
Exclusive distributors of World Bank, United Nations, UNESCO, OIT publications.
Type of Business: Distributor

Fundacion Kuai-Mare
c/o Instituto Autonomo Biblioteca Nacional y de Servicios de Bibliotecas, Calla Soledad, Edif Rogi I, Piso 3, Zona Industrial la Trinidad, Apdo 80593, Caracas 1080
Tel: (02) 938535 ext 213; (02) 9418011 (ext 227) *Fax:* (02) 9415219
Telex: 24621
This is the distribution side of the Instituto Autonomo Biblioteca Nacional y de Servicios de Bibliotecas, specializing in publications by Venezuelan official, cultural & university organizations. There are five other branches.

Libreria Medica Paris
Grand Ave, Edif Medica Paris, Caracas 106
Tel: (02) 781-6044 *Fax:* (02) 7931753
Telex: 21420 DISME VC
Key Personnel
Manager: Pierre Paneyko
Founded: 1975

OBE, see Organizacion de Bienestar Estudiantil (OBE)

Organizacion de Bienestar Estudiantil (OBE)
Universidad Central de Venezuela Ciudad Universitaria, Los Chaguaranos, Caracas 1050
Tel: (02) 6054050 (ext 4200); (02) 6054050 (ext 4201); (02) 6054050 (ext 4202) *Fax:* (02) 6930638
Web Site: www.ucv.ve/ftproot/obe/obe.htm
Key Personnel
Dir: Prof Arelis L Figueroa

Libreria Tecnica Vega
Plaza Las Tres Gracias, Edificio Odeon, Los Chagauramos, Caracas 1010-A
Mailing Address: Apdo 51662, Caracas, Los Chaguaramos 1010-A
Tel: (02) 6221397 *Fax:* (02) 6622092 *Cable:* EDIVEGA
Key Personnel
Manager: Lucia Ribas
Owned by: Fernando Vega, Ediciones Vega SRL

Zambia

Q & B Books
19 Njoka Rd, Olympia Park, Lusaka
Mailing Address: PO Box 46 unza, Lusaka
Tel: (01) 290032; (096) 747187 *Fax:* (01) 290032
E-mail: qbbooks@yahoo.com
Key Personnel
Dir, Operations: Queen Lutwi Unene
  E-mail: lutwiunene@yahoo.com
Dir: Bertha Mulowa
Sales Executive: Ashery Mambwe
Membership(s): Booksellers Association of Zambia (BAZA).
Type of Business: Distributor, Exporter, Importer, Major Independent Bookseller

University Bookshop
University of Zambia, Lusaka
Mailing Address: PO Box 32379, Lusaka
Tel: (01) 294690; (01) 290319 *Fax:* (01) 253952; (01) 294690
Telex: ZA 44370
Key Personnel
Bookshop Manager: Hudson Unene
  E-mail: hunene@admin.unza.zm
Accountant: Kenneth Phiri
Bookshop Supervisor: Raphael Makuya
Founded: 1967
Membership(s): Booksellers & Publishers Association of Zambia (BPAZ); Pan African Booksellers Association (PABA).
Type of Business: Distributor, Exporter, Importer, Major Independent Bookseller
Owned by: The University of Zambia
Branch Office(s)
Pakati Arcade-Lusaka Hotel Outlet, Box 32379, Lusaka

Zambia Catholic Bookshop (Mission Press)
Franciscan Centre, Chifubu Rd, Ndola
Mailing Address: PO Box 71581, Ndola
Tel: (02) 680456; (02) 680466 *Fax:* (02) 680484
E-mail: mpress@zamnet.zm
Type of Business: Distributor, Exporter, Importer, Wholesaler

Zimbabwe

Book Centre, Textbook Sales (Pvt) Ltd
Affiliate of Tutorial Press
4 Conald Rd, Harare
Mailing Address: PO Box 37799, Harare
Tel: (04) 790691 *Fax:* (04) 751690 *Cable:* TEXTBOOK
Key Personnel
Man Dir: A Wallace
Publisher: Mr G McCullough
Founded: 1956
Branch offices in Bulawayo, Gweru, Masvingo, Mutare, & Rusape.
Type of Business: Distributor, Importer, Major Book Chain Headquarters, Wholesaler
Bookshop(s): 16 George Silundika Ave, Harare

Kingstons Ltd
Kingstons House, 34 Union Ave, Harare
Mailing Address: PO Box 2374, Harare
Tel: (04) 750547; (04) 750548; (04) 750549; (04) 750550 *Fax:* (04) 775533
Key Personnel
Man Dir: Elliot Mugamu
Also retailer with 19 branches in Zimbabwe & one in Bobwana.
Type of Business: Wholesaler

Mambo Bookshop
Senga Rd, Gweru
Mailing Address: PO Box 779, Gweru
Tel: (054) 4016; (054) 4017 *Fax:* (054) 51991
E-mail: mambo@icon.co.zw
Key Personnel
General Manager: Fr Ron Gentile
Type of Business: Distributor, Exporter, Importer, Major Independent Bookseller, Wholesaler
Owned by: Mambo Press
Bookshop(s): Speke Ave/First St, Harare *Tel:* (0154) 705899; Gweru Bookshop, PO Box 779, Gweru *Tel:* (0154) 705899; Mambo Masvingo Bookshop, PO Box 1010, Masvingo *Tel:* (0139) 64566; Bulawago, PO Box 799, Gweru (19) 61162

Book Trade Reference Books & Journals

Featuring publications for and about the book trade and book publishing industries, titles listed may be relative to one specific country or may be of international relevance. Titles are arranged alphabetically by the country where the publisher is located or the country to which the title relates.

ƒ indicates those publications of international scope.

The type of publication appears in parentheses after the title:

(B) - Book   (J) - Journal   (P) - Periodical

For library-related publications see **Library Reference Books & Journals**.

Albania

Bibliografia kombetare e Librit Shqip
(Albanian National Bibliography of Books) (J)
Published by National Library
Sheshi Skenderbej, Tirana
Tel: (042) 23 843 *Fax:* (042) 23 843
Key Personnel
Dir: Mrs Nermin Basha *E-mail:* BashaN@natlib.tirana.al
Quarterly.

Drita (P)
Published by Union of Writers & Artists of Albania
Baboci 37 z, Tirana
Key Personnel
Editor: Zija Cela
First published 1960.
Daily.
232 USD (Europe); 297 USD (elsewhere)

Kultura Popullore (P)
Published by Academie des Sciences de la RPSA, Institut de Culture Populaire
Sheshi "Fan S NOLI", 7 Tirane
Tel: (04) 227476 *Fax:* (04) 22 74 76
E-mail: esulstar@akad.edu.al
Web Site: www.academyofsciences.net
Key Personnel
Contact: Dr Afrim Karagjozi *Tel:* (04) 230305
E-mail: akaragjozi@akad.edu.al
A scientific review which comprises Albanian ethnographic studies.
First published 1980.
Annually.

Les Lettres Albanaises (P)
Published by Union of Writers & Artists of Albania
Baboci 37 z, Tirana
Tel: (042) 27989
Key Personnel
Editor: Diana Culi
Published in French.
Quarterly.
12 USD

Libri (The Book) (J)
Published by National Library
Sheshi Skenderbej, Tirana
Tel: (042) 23 843 *Fax:* (042) 23 843
E-mail: BashaN@natlib.tirana.al
Key Personnel
Dir: Mrs Nermin Basha *E-mail:* BashaN@natlib.tirana.al

Nentori (P)
Published by Union of Writers & Artists of Albania
Baboci 37 z, Tirana
Tel: (042) 27989
Key Personnel
Editor: Kico Blushi
Text in Albanian.
First published 1954.
Monthly.
20 USD
ISSN: 0548-1600

Algeria

Bibliographie de l'Algerie (J)
Published by Bibliotheque Nationale
One Ave Frantz Fanon, 16000 Algiers
Tel: (021) 630632
Published in Arabic & French (Selon lalangue du document).
First published 1964.
Biannually.
40 DZD or 20 USD
ISSN: 0523-2392

Argentina

Boletin (Bulletin) (P)
Published by Sociedad Argentina de Escritores (SADE)
Uruguay 1371, 1016 Buenos Aires
Tel: 4813 0773 *Fax:* 4813 0773
E-mail: sadecentral@hotmail.com
Web Site: www.paralelo42.com/sade/
Key Personnel
President: Orlando Guzman
Vice President: Leonardo Tasca
Secretary General: Antonio Las Heras
Treasurer: Abelardo Garcia
Bimonthly.

Boletin de la Academia Argentina de Letras
(Bulletin of the Argentine Academy of Letters) (P)
Published by Academia Argentina de Letras (Argentine Academy of Letters)
Sanchez de Bustamante 2663, 1425 Buenos Aires
Tel: (011) 4802-3814; (011) 4802-7509; (011) 4802-5161 *Fax:* (011) 4-8028340
E-mail: aaldespa@fibertel.com.ar; aaladmin@fibertel.com.ar; aalbibl@fibertel.com.ar; despacho@aal.universia.com.ar
Web Site: aal.universia.com.ar/aal
Key Personnel
Librarian: Alejandro E Parada
Quarterly.
ISSN: 0001-3757

Criterio (P)
Published by Kriterion SA
Junin 627, Capital Federal, 1026 Buenos Aires
Tel: (011) 43747975
Text in Spanish.
First published 1928.
21 times/yr.
100 USD
ISSN: 0011-1473

Davar (P)
Published by Fundacion Sociedad Hebraica Argentina
Sarmiento 2233, 1044 Buenos Aires
Tel: 4952 5886; 4952 5887 *Fax:* 4953 4117
E-mail: hebraica@hebraica.org.ar
Web Site: www.hebraica.org.ar

Australia

APA Directory of Members (B)
Published by Australian Publishers Association Ltd
60/89 Jones St, Ultimo, NSW 2007
Tel: (02) 9281 9788 *Fax:* (02) 9281 1073
E-mail: apa@publishers.asn.au
Web Site: www.publishers.asn.au
Key Personnel
Chief Executive: Susan Bridge
Annually.
128 pp, 27.50 AUD

AUMLA (P)
Published by Australasian Universities Language & Literature Association
c/o Bruce Parr, EMSAH School, University of Queensland, Brisbane, Qld 4072
Tel: (07) 3365 2552 *Fax:* (07) 3365 2799
Key Personnel
Managing Editor: Bruce Parr *E-mail:* b.parr@mailbox.uq.edu.au
Editor: Lloyd Davis *E-mail:* lloyd.davis@mailbox.ug.edu.au
Journal of literary criticism, language & cultural studies; published in English with occasional articles in French, German or Spanish.
First published 1951.
Biannually.
170 pp
ISSN: 0001-2793

AUSTRALIA

The Australian Author (P)
Published by The Australian Society of Authors Ltd
PO Box 1566, Strawberry Hills, NSW 2012
Tel: (02) 93180877 *Fax:* (02) 93180530
E-mail: office@asauthors.org
Web Site: www.asauthors.org
Key Personnel
Editor: Helen Stanwix
Quarterly.

Australian Book Review (J)
Published by Australian Book Review Inc
193A Lennox St, Suite 6, Richmond, Victoria 3121
Mailing Address: PO Box 2320, Richmond, South Victoria 3121
Tel: (03) 9429 6700 *Fax:* (03) 9429 2288
E-mail: abr@vicnet.net.au
Web Site: home.vicnet.net.au/~abr
Key Personnel
Editor: Peter Rose
Deputy Editor: Aviva Tuffield
Publishes reviews & articles on Australian books & writing.
First published 1962.
10 times/yr.
67 AUD (domestic individuals); 87 AUD (Asia & Pacific individuals); 115 AUD (individuals elsewhere); 76 AUD (domestic insitutions); 95 AUD (Asia & Pacific institutions); 125 AUD (institutions elsewhere)
ISSN: 0155-2864

Australian Books in Print (B)
Published by Thorpe-Bowker
85 Turner St, Bldg C3, Port Melbourne, Victoria 3207
Tel: (03) 8645 0300; (03) 8645 0389 (customer service) *Fax:* (03) 8645 0333
E-mail: yoursay@thorpe.com.au; customer.service@thorpe.com.au
Web Site: www.thorpe.com.au
Key Personnel
Publisher: Andrew Wilkins *Tel:* (03) 8645 0392
  E-mail: andrew.wilkins@thorpe.com.au
Information on over 100,000 Australian titles in print as well as publisher & distributor information. Other useful book trade related information included. Also available on microfiche & CD-ROM.
First published 1956.
Annually.
2,500 pp
ISBN(s): 1-86452-041-8 (2 vol set)
ISSN: 0067-172X

Australian Bookseller & Publisher (P)
Published by Thorpe-Bowker
85 Turner St, Bldg C3, Port Melbourne, Victoria 3207
Tel: (03) 8645 0300; (03) 8645 0389 (customer service) *Fax:* (03) 8645 0333
E-mail: bookseller.publisher@thorpe.com.au; yoursay@thorpe.com.au; customer.service@thorpe.com.au
Web Site: www.thorpe.com.au
Key Personnel
Publisher: Andrew Wilkins *Tel:* (03) 8645 0392
  E-mail: andrew.wilkins@thorpe.com.au
First published 1921.
11 times/yr.
ISSN: 0004-8763

Australian Literary Studies (P)
Published by University of Queensland Press
The University of Queensland, Saint Lucia, Qld 4072
Mailing Address: PO Box 6042, Saint Lucia, Qld 4067
Tel: (07) 3365 2452 *Fax:* (07) 3365 7579
Web Site: www.uq.edu.au
Key Personnel
Publisher: Rosemary Chay *E-mail:* rosiec@uqp.uq.edu.au
Editor: Dr Leigh Dale
Academic/scholarly publication.
Biannually.
Vol 20, Nos 3 & 4, 2002, 43.80 AUD (domestic individuals & school libraries); 50 AUD (foreign individuals); 82.10 AUD (domestic tertiary institutions & libraries); 90 AUD (foreign institutions)
ISSN: 0004-9697

Australian Society of Indexers Newsletter (J)
Published by Australian Society of Indexers
GPO Box 2069, Canberra, ACT 2601
Tel: (02) 4268-5335
E-mail: secretary@aussi.org
Web Site: www.aussi.org/anl
Key Personnel
Editor: Frances Paterson *E-mail:* newsletter@bigpond.com
Also available in electronic format (ISSN 1326-2718).
Monthly; excluding Jan & Dec.
ISSN: 0314-3767

ʃ**Bibliographical Society of Australia & New Zealand Bulletin** (J)
Published by Bibliographical Society of Australia & New Zealand (BSANZ)
Baillieu Library, University of Melbourne, Melbourne, Victoria 3000
Tel: (03) 8344-5366 *Fax:* (03) 9347-8627
Web Site: www.csu.edu.au/community/BSANZ
Key Personnel
Editor: Ian Morrison *E-mail:* i.morrison@lib.unimelb.edu.au
First published 1970.
Quarterly.
Free to members
ISSN: 0084-7852

Biblionews & Australian Notes & Queries (J)
Published by Book Collectors' Society of Australia
16 Edwin St (South), Croydon, NSW 2132
Tel: (02) 9798 8984 *Fax:* (02) 9798 8984
E-mail: jeff@bcspl.com.au
Key Personnel
Ed: Brian Taylor
Secretary: Jeff Bidgood *E-mail:* bidgood@bigpond.net.au
Quarterly, to members.

Guide to New Australian Books (P)
Published by Thorpe-Bowker
85 Turner St, Bldg C3, Port Melbourne, Victoria 3207
Tel: (03) 8645 0300; (03) 8645 0389 (customer service) *Fax:* (03) 8645 0333
E-mail: yoursay@thorpe.com.au; customer.service@thorpe.com.au
Web Site: www.thorpe.com.au
Key Personnel
Editor: Andrew Wilkins *E-mail:* andrew.wilkins@thorpe.com.au
Listings & descriptions for newly published Australian books, along with information about forthcoming titles. Additional information includes author & editor.
First published 1990.
6 times/yr.
ISSN: 1035-5391

Introduction to Book Publishing (B)
Published by Australian Publishers Association Ltd
60/89 Jones St, Ultimo, NSW 2007
Tel: (02) 9281 9788 *Fax:* (02) 9281 1073
E-mail: apa@publishers.asn.au

BOOK TRADE REFERENCE

Web Site: www.publishers.asn.au
Key Personnel
Chief Executive: Susan Bridge
55 pp, 16.50 AUD

Island (P)
Published by Island Magazine Inc
PO Box 210, Sandy Bay, Tas 7006
Tel: (03) 6226 2325 *Fax:* (03) 6226 2172
E-mail: island@tassie.net.au
Web Site: www.islandmag.com
Key Personnel
Editor: David Owen
Literary Magazine.
Quarterly.

New Ceylon Writing (P)
Published by Macquarie University
Balaclava Rd, North Ryde, NSW
Mailing Address: Macquarie University, NSW 2109
Tel: (02) 9850 7111
E-mail: mqinfo@mq.edu.au
Web Site: www.mq.edu.au
Key Personnel
Editor: Yasmine Gooneratne
Creative & critical writing.

Overland (P)
Published by The O L Society Ltd
PO Box 14146, Melbourne, Victoria 8001
Tel: (03) 96884163 *Fax:* (03) 96877614
E-mail: overland@vu.edu.au
Web Site: www.overlandexpress.org
Key Personnel
Editor: Nathan Hollier; Katherine Wilson
First published 1954.
Quarterly.
42 AUD (individuals); 45 AUD (institutions); 32 AUD (students); 60 USD (foreign)
ISSN: 0030-7416

Periodicals in Print & Online: Australia, New Zealand & Asia Pacific (B)
Published by Bookman Health
Bookman Health, Level 9, Trak Centre, 443-449 Toorak Rd, Toorak, Victoria 3142
Toll Free *Tel:* 800 060 555 *Fax:* (03) 9826 1744
E-mail: bookman@bookman.com.au; sales@bookman.com.au
Web Site: www.bookman.com.au
First published 1981.
ISSN: 1322-3895

Quadrant (P)
Published by Quadrant Magazine Co Inc
46 George St, Fitzroy, Victoria 3065
Tel: (03) 94176855 *Fax:* (03) 94162980
E-mail: quadrantmonthly@ozemail.com.au
Key Personnel
Editor: P P McGuinness
Independent review of controversy, ideas, literature, poetry & the arts.
10 times/yr.
50 AUD (domestic); 60 USD (foreign)

Reading Time (P)
Published by Children's Book Council of Australia
PO Box 62, Ashmont, NSW 2650
Tel: (02) 6925 4907 *Fax:* (02) 6925 4907
E-mail: readingtime@cbc.org.au
Web Site: www.cbc.org.au/readtime.htm
Key Personnel
Editor & Publisher: Dr John Cohen
  E-mail: jcohen@ozemail.com.au
Yearly index to reviews & articles.
Quarterly.
44 pp
ISSN: 0155-218X

Southerly (P)
Published by English Association, Sydney Branch
c/o Halstead Press, 300/3 Smail St, Broadway,
   NSW 2007
Tel: (02) 9211 3033
E-mail: halstead@halstedpress.com.au
Web Site: www.arts.usyd.edu.au/departs/english/
   southerly
Key Personnel
Editor: David G Brooks *Tel:* (02) 9351 2569
   E-mail: david.brooks@english.usyd.edu.au;
   Noel Rowe *Tel:* (02) 9351 2270 *E-mail:* noel.
   rowe@english.usyd.edu.au
Short stories, poetry & literary criticism about
   Australian writers.
First published 1923.
Quarterly.

Sydney Studies in English (B)
Published by University of Sydney, Department
   of English
Dept of English, A20, University of Sydney,
   NSW 2006
Tel: (02) 9351 2349 *Fax:* (02) 9351 2434
E-mail: english.enquiries@arts.usyd.edu.au
Web Site: www.arts.usyd.edu.au/departs/english
Key Personnel
Editor: Prof Margaret Harris *Tel:* (02) 9351 2163
   E-mail: margaret.harris@arts.usyd.edu.au
Devoted to criticism & scholarship in English literature & drama.
First published 1975.
Annually.
16.50 AUD
ISSN: 0156-5419

Victorian Government Publications (VGP) (J)
Published by State Library of Victoria
328 Swanston St, Melbourne, Victoria 3000
Tel: (03) 8664 7000
Web Site: www.statelibrary.vic.gov.au
Telex: AA38104
Key Personnel
Government Publications Librarian: Dianne Beaumont *E-mail:* dianneb@slv.vic.gov.au
Monthly.

Weekly Book Newsletter (P)
Published by Thorpe-Bowker
85 Turner St, Bldg C3, Port Melbourne, Victoria
   3207
Tel: (03) 8645 0300; (03) 8645 0389 (customer
   service) *Fax:* (03) 8645 0395
E-mail: blue.newsletter@thorpe.com.au;
   yoursay@thorpe.com.au; customer.service@
   thorpe.com.au
Web Site: www.thorpe.com.au
Key Personnel
Publisher: Andrew Wilkins *Tel:* (03) 8645 0392
   E-mail: andrew.wilkins@thorpe.com.au
First published 1972.
Weekly (49 issues/yr).
ISSN: 0812-7042
Parent Company: R R Bowker
Ultimate Parent Company: Cambridge Information Group

Westerly (P)
Published by The Center for Studies in Australian
   Literature
English Communication & Cultural Studies, University of Western Australia, Crawley, WA
   6009
Tel: (08) 9380 2101 *Fax:* (08) 9380 1030
E-mail: westerly@cyllene.uwa.edu.au
Web Site: westerly.uwa.edu.au
Key Personnel
Editor: Delys Bird; Dennis Haskell
Annually.
ISSN: 0043-324X

**Writers and Photographers Marketing Guide:
Directory of Australian and New Zealand
Literary and Photo Markets** (B)
Published by Australian Writers' Professional
   Service
Stott House, 140 Flinders St, Melbourne, Victoria
   3000
Tel: (03) 6546211; (054) 468275 *Fax:* (03)
   6509648

Austria

Adressbuch des oesterreichischen Buchhandels
   (Directory of Austrian Book Trade) (B)
Published by Hauptverband des Oesterreichischen
   Buchhandels (Austrian Publishers' & Booksellers' Association)
Gruenangergasse 4, 1010 Vienna
Tel: (01) 512 15 35 *Fax:* (01) 512 84 82
E-mail: hvb@buecher.at
Web Site: www.buecher.at

Anzeiger des oesterreichischen Buchhandels
   (Austrian Book Trade Gazette) (J)
Published by Hauptverband des Oesterreichischen
   Buchhandels (Austrian Publishers' & Booksellers' Association)
Gruenangergasse 4, 1010 Vienna
Tel: (01) 512 15 35 *Fax:* (01) 512 84 82
E-mail: hvb@buecher.at
Web Site: www.buecher.at
Bimonthly.

**Anzeiger des Verbandes der Antiquare
Oesterreichs** (Austrian Antiquarian
   Booksellers' Association Gazette) (J)
Published by Verband der Antiquare Oesterreichs
   (Antiquarian Booksellers Association of Austria)
Grunangergasse 4, 1010 Vienna
Tel: (01) 512 15 35 *Fax:* (01) 512 84 82
E-mail: hvb@buecher.at
Web Site: www.buecher.at

Autorensolidaritaet (Solidarity of Authors) (P)
Published by Interessengemeinschaft oesterreichischer Autorinnen und Autoren
Literaturhaus, Seidengasse 13, 1070 Vienna
Tel: (01) 526204413 *Fax:* (01) 526204455
E-mail: ig@literaturhaus.at
Quarterly.

Die Rampe (P)
Published by Amt der Ooe Landesregierung, Institut fuer Kulturfoerderung
Spittelwiese 4, 4010 Linz
Tel: (0732) 772015491 *Fax:* (0732) 772011786
E-mail: k.post@ooe.gv.at
Web Site: www.ooe.gv.at
First published 1975.
Biannually.
5.20 EUR

**Die Literatur der oesterreichischen Kunst-,
Kultur- und Autorenverlage** (Austrian
   Publishing in Arts, Culture & Literature) (B)
Published by Interessengemeinschaft oesterreichischer Autorinnen und Autoren
Literaturhaus, Seidengasse 13, 1070 Vienna
Tel: (01) 526204413 *Fax:* (01) 526204455
E-mail: ig@literaturhaus.at
Web Site: www.literaturhaus.at/lh/ig

Literatur und Kritik (Literature & Criticism) (P)
Published by Otto Mueller Verlag
Ernest-Thun-Str 11, 5020 Salzburg
Tel: (0662) 881974-0 *Fax:* (0662) 872387
E-mail: otto.muellerverlag@salzburg.co.at
Web Site: www.onb.ac.at/biblos/omvs/litkrit1.htm
Key Personnel
Editor: Karl-Markus Gauss
Reviews German language literature & literary
   criticism.
First published 1966.
5 times/yr.
28 EUR; 6.80 EUR/issue
ISSN: 0024-466X

Manuskripte: Zeitschrift fuer Literatur
   (Manuscripts) (P)
Published by Alfred Kolleritsch Manuskripte
Sackstr 17, 8010 Graz
Tel: (0316) 82 56 08 *Fax:* (0316) 82 56 05
E-mail: lz@manuskripte.at
Web Site: www.manuskripte.at
Key Personnel
Editor: Alfred Kolleritsch; Guenter Waldorf
Journal for literature, art & criticism.
Quarterly.
27 EUR (domestic); 32 EUR (foreign)
ISSN: 0025-2638

Modern Austrian Literature (P)
Published by International Arthur Schnitzler Research Association
c/o Donald G Daviau, Dept of Comparative Literature, University of California, Riverside, CA
   92521
Tel: (909) 787-4314 *Fax:* (909) 787-2160
E-mail: austrian@citrus.ucr.edu
Key Personnel
Editor: Donald G Daviau
Text & summaries in English & German. Focuses
   on 19th & 20th century Austrian literature &
   culture.
Quarterly.
25 USD (individuals); 30 USD (foreign individuals); 35 USD (institutions); 40 USD (foreign
   institutions)

**Sprachkunst, Beitraege zur
Literaturwissenschaft** (Art of Language,
   Contributions to the Study of Literature) (P)
Published by Verlag der Oesterreichischen
   Akademie der Wissenschaften (Austrian
   Academy of Sciences Press)
PO Box 471, Postgasse 7, 1011 Vienna
Tel: (01) 512 9050; (01) 51581-3401; (01) 51581-
   3402; (01) 51581-3405; (01) 51581-3406
   Fax: (01) 51581-3400
E-mail: verlag@oeaw.ac.at
Web Site: www.verlag.oeaw.ac.at
Publication of articles particularly on poetical
   works, on literary history & poetics, reviews
   in addition. The language is German, English,
   French & Russian.
Biannually.
ISSN: 0038-8483

Stueckeboerse Katalog (J)
Published by Gerhard Ruiss
im Literaturhaus, Seidengasse 13, 1070 Vienna
Tel: (01) 52620440 *Fax:* (01) 526204430
E-mail: ig@literaturhaus.at
Web Site: www.literaturhaus.at/lh/ig
Catalogue of unpublished & published Austrian
   dramatic works.

Bangladesh

Bangladesh National Bibliography (J)
Published by National Library of Bangladesh, Directorate of Archives & Libraries
32 Justice Sayed Mahbub Murshed Sarani, Sher-
   e-Bangla Nagar (Agargaon), Dhaka 1207

Bangladesh

Tel: (02) 326572; (02) 318704
Key Personnel
Dir: Mr Hahashinur Rahman Khan
Text in Bengali & English.
First published 1972.
Annually.

Barbados

National Bibliography of Barbados (B)
Published by Naional Library Service
Culloden Farm, Culloden Rd, St Michael
Tel: 4295716 *Fax:* 4361501
E-mail: smith_a@caribsurf.com
Telex: WB 2222
Key Personnel
Contact: Mrs June Ward
Text in English.
First published 1975.
Biannually.
10 USD
ISSN: 0256-7709

Belarus

Letopis Pechati Belarusi (Byelorussian National Bibliography) (J)
Published by Nationalnaya Knizhnaya Palata Belarus (National Book Chamber of Belarus)
ul v Karuzhai, 31a, 220002 Minsk
Tel: (0172) 289-33-96 *Fax:* (0172) 289-33-96
E-mail: palata@palata.beipak.mihsk.BY
ISSN: 0130-9218

Neman (P)
Published by Ministry of Culture
Pro Skaryny 39, 220005 Minsk
Tel: (0172) 2331032
Literary, artistic, socio-political magazine. Text in Russian.
First published 1952.
Monthly.
120 USD (foreign)

Belgium

Adresgids Voor Het Boekenvak (B)
Published by Boek.be
Hof ter Schrieklaan 17, 2600 Berchem, Antwerp
Tel: (03) 230 89 23 *Fax:* (03) 281 22 40
E-mail: info@boek.be
Web Site: www.boek.be
A list of Dutch booksellers & publishers.
First published 1929.
Annually.

Annuaire (B)
Published by Commission Belge de Bibliographie et de Bibliologie (Belgian Commission of Bibliography & Bibliology)
4 blvd de l'Empereur, B-1000 Brussels
Tel: (02) 80510464 *Fax:* (02) 5195610; (02) 5131503
Annually.

Belgische Bibliografie (J)
Published by Koninklijke Bibliotheek Alber I
Keizerslaan 4, 1000 Brussels
Tel: (02) 519 57 15; (02) 519 53 11; (02) 519 53 05; (02) 519 53 08 *Fax:* (02) 519 55 33
E-mail: contacts@kbr.be
Web Site: www.kbr.be
Key Personnel
Contact: Willy Vanderpijpen *E-mail:* vdpijpen@kbr.be
Monthly.

Dietsche Warande en Belfort (P)
Published by Uitgeverij Peeters Leuven (Belgie) (Peeters Publishers & Booksellers)
Bondgenotenlaan 153, 3000 Leuven
Tel: (016) 235170 *Fax:* (016) 228500
E-mail: peeters@peeters-leuven.be
Web Site: www.peeters-leuven.be
Journal for literature, art & spiritual life.

Gulden Passer (P)
Published by Vereeniging der Antwerpsche Bibliophielene (Association of Antwerp Bibliophiles)
Museum Plantin-Moretus, Vrijdagmarkt 22, 2000 Antwerp
Tel: (03) 2330294; (03) 2322455 *Fax:* (03) 2262516
Key Personnel
Editor: Francine de Nave; Marcus de Schepper
Text in Dutch, English, French & German.
First published 1878.
Annually.
ISSN: 0777-5067

Le Livre et l'Estampe (The Book & The Print) (P)
Published by Societe Royale des Bibliophiles et Iconophiles de Belgique
blvd de l'Empereur 4, 1000 Brussels
Key Personnel
Editor: A Grisay
Text in French.
First published 1954.
Biannually.
50 EUR (European Union); 55 EUR (elsewhere)
ISSN: 0024-533X

Neerlandia (P)
Published by Algemeen-Nederlands Verbond
Gallaitstraat 86, 1030 Brussels
Tel: (02) 241 31 64 *Fax:* (02) 241 31 64
E-mail: anv.vlaanderen@edpnet.be
Web Site: www.algemeennederlandsverbond.org
5 times/yr.

Revue generale (General Review) (P)
Published by De Boeck et Larcier SA
Fond Jean-Paques 4, B-1348 Louvain-la-Neuve
Tel: (010) 48 25 00 *Fax:* (010) 48 25 19; (010) 48 25 70
E-mail: acces+cde@deboeck.be
Web Site: www.deboeck.be
Key Personnel
Contact: Agnes Duquenne *Tel:* (010) 48 26 10 *E-mail:* agnes.duquenne@deboeck.be
Publication includes general information on Belgian politics, economics, literature, etc.
First published 1865.
6 times/yr.
ISSN: 0777-2287

Streven (P)
Prinsstraat 15, 2000 Antwerp
Tel: (03) 212 10 20 *Fax:* (03) 212 10 22
E-mail: streven@skynet.be
Web Site: www.come.to/streven
Magazine on culture & society.
First published 1933.
Monthly (except Aug).
96 pp
ISSN: 0039-2324

Bolivia

Bio Bibliografia Boliviana (Bolivian Bibliography) (J)
Published by Los Amigos del Libro
Casilla de Correo 450, Cochabamba 15
Tel: (04) 2504150 *Fax:* (04) 115128
Key Personnel
Owner: Werner T Guttentag *E-mail:* gutten@amigol.bo.net
Text in Spanish.
First published 1962.
Annually.
170 USD

Bolivian Booknews (B)
Published by Los Amigos del Libro Ediciones
Calle Heroinas, No E-0311, esquina Espana, Cochabamba
Mailing Address: Apdo Aereo 450, Cochabamba
Tel: (04) 254114; (04) 251140 *Fax:* (04) 0411-5128
Key Personnel
President & Man Dir: Werner Guttentag *E-mail:* gutten@amigol.bo.net
Monthly.

Bosnia and Herzegovina

Izraz (P)
Published by SOUR Svjetlost
Petra Preradovica 3, 71000 Sarajevo
Mailing Address: PO Box 129, 71000 Sarajevo
Key Personnel
Editor: Dzevad Karahasan
Journal of literary & artistic criticism.
First published 1957.
Monthly.
15 USD
ISSN: 0021-3381

Botswana

National Bibliography of Botswana (P)
Published by Botswana National Library Service
Private Bag 0036, Gaborone
Tel: 352-397 *Fax:* 301-149
E-mail: natlib@global.bw; automate@global.bw
Web Site: www.gov.bw
Key Personnel
Dir: Mrs Constance B Modise *E-mail:* cbmodise@gov.bw
Editor: Gertrude Kayaga Mulindwa
First published 1969.
Triannually.
6 USD
ISSN: 0027-8777

Brazil

Bibliografia Brasileira (Brazilian Bibliography) (J)
Published by Biblioteca Nacional
Av Rio Branco, 219, 22040-008 Rio de Janeiro-RJ
Tel: (021) 2220-9367 *Fax:* (021) 2220-4173

E-mail: inter@bn.br
Web Site: www.bn.br
Quarterly.

Jornal do SNEL/Producao Editorial Brasileria
(SNEL Newspaper/Brazilian Editorial Production) (B)
Published by Sindicato Nacional dos Editores de Livros (SNEL)
Av Rio Branco, 37, Sala 1.504, 20090-003 Rio de Janeiro-RJ
Tel: (021) 2238-6481 *Fax:* (021) 2253-8502
E-mail: snel@snel.org.br
Web Site: www.snel.org.br
Telex: (021) 37063

Veritas (P)
Published by Editora da PUCRS
c/o Antoninho M Naime, Partenon, Porto Alegre-RS 90651-970
Mailing Address: CP 12001, Porto Alegre-RS 90651-970
Tel: (051) 3391511 *Fax:* (051) 3391564
Telex: (051) 3349
Education, Human Sciences, Philosophy. Text in Portuguese.
First published 1955.
Quarterly.
ISSN: 0042-3955

Bulgaria

Balgarski disertacii (Bulgarian Dissertations) (P)
Published by Cyril & Methodius National Library
88 Vasil Levski Blvd, 1504 Sofia
Tel: (02) 9882811 *Fax:* (02) 435499
E-mail: nbkm@nationallibrary.bg
Web Site: www.nationallibrary.bg
Key Personnel
Contact: Eli Popova *E-mail:* popova@online.bg
Editor-in-Chief: Alexandra Dipchikova *Tel:* (02) 9882811 ext 206 *E-mail:* alex@daisy.nl.acad.bg
First published 1973.
Annually.
ISSN: 0323-9411

Balgarski knigopis, Seria 1 (B)
Published by Cyril & Methodius National Library
88 Vasil Levski Blvd, 1504 Sofia
Tel: (02) 9882811 *Fax:* (02) 435499
E-mail: nbkm@nationallibrary.bg
Web Site: www.nationallibrary.bg
Key Personnel
Contact: Efrosina Angelova *E-mail:* angelova@nl.oltel.net
First published 1969.
Annually.
ISSN: 0323-9713

Balgarski periodichen Pechat, Seria 4
(Bulgarian Periodicals, Series 4) (P)
Published by Cyril & Methodius National Library (Narodna Biblioteka Kirili i Metodi)
88 Vassil Levski Blvd, 1504 Sofia
Tel: (02) 9882811 *Fax:* (02) 435499
E-mail: nbkm@nationallibrary.bg
Web Site: www.nationallibrary.bg
Key Personnel
Contact: Ilona Kalojanova *Tel:* (02) 9882811 (ext 273); (02) 9882811 (ext 281)
(Bulgarian Periodicals), part of *Bulgarska Nacionalna Bibliografija*.
First published 1967.
Annually.
ISSN: 0032-9764

Bibliographia na Balgarskata Bibliographia
(Bibliography of Bulgarian Bibliographies) (B)
Published by Cyril & Methodius National Library
88 Vasil Levski Blvd, 1504 Sofia
Tel: (02) 9882811 *Fax:* (02) 435499
E-mail: nbkm@nationallibrary.bg
Web Site: www.nationallibrary.bg
Key Personnel
Contact: Tzvetanka Pancheva
First published 1965.
Annually.
ISSN: 0204-7373

Bulgarski knigopis, Seria 1 (The National Bibliography) (P)
Published by Cyril & Methodius National Library
88 Vasil Levski Blvd, 1504 Sofia
Tel: (02) 9882811 *Fax:* (02) 435499
E-mail: nbkm@nationallibrary.bg
Web Site: www.nationallibrary.bg
Key Personnel
Contact: Eli Popova *E-mail:* popova@online.bg
Editor-in-Chief: Alexandra Dipchikova *Tel:* (02) 9882811 ext 206 *E-mail:* alex@daisy.nl.acad.bg
First published 1897.
Monthly.
ISSN: 0323-9616

Diskographia (B)
Published by Cyril & Methodius National Library
88 Vasil Levski Blvd, 1504 Sofia
Tel: (02) 9882811 *Fax:* (02) 435499
E-mail: nbkm@nationallibrary.bg
Web Site: www.nationallibrary.bg
Key Personnel
Contact: Eli Popova *E-mail:* popova@online.bg
Editor-in-Chief: Alexandra Dipchikova *Tel:* (02) 9882811 ext 206 *E-mail:* alex@daisy.nl.acad.bg
Annually.
ISSN: 1310-9154

Letopis na Statiite ot Balgarskite Spisania i Sbornici (Articles from Bulgarian Journals & Collections) (P)
Published by Cyril & Methodius National Library
88 Vasil Levski Blvd, 1504 Sofia
Tel: (02) 9882811 *Fax:* (02) 435499
E-mail: nbkm@nationallibrary.bg
Web Site: www.nationallibrary.bg
Key Personnel
Contact: Liulia Kostova
First published 1952.
Monthly.
ISSN: 0324-0398

Letopis na statiite ot balgarskite vestnici
(Articles from Bulgarian Newspapers) (P)
Published by Cyril & Methodius National Library
88 Vasil Levski Blvd, 1504 Sofia
Tel: (02) 9882811 *Fax:* (02) 435499
E-mail: nbkm@nationallibrary.bg
Web Site: www.nationallibrary.bg
Key Personnel
Contact: Maria Gavrilova
First published 1952.
Monthly.
ISSN: 0324-0347

Literaturen Forum (P)
Published by Literaturen Forum OOD
136 Rakovski Str, Sofia 1000
Tel: (02) 870293 *Fax:* (02) 988 10 69
E-mail: forum@isoc.bg
Web Site: www.bol.bg/forum
Key Personnel
Editor-in-Chief: Marin Georgiev
First published 1991.
Weekly (except July & Aug).

Literaturna Misal (Literary Thought) (P)
Published by Bulgarian Academy of Sciences, Institute of Literature
52 Shipchenski prohod blvd, bl 17, 7th & 8th floors, 1113 Sofia
Tel: (02) 70 18 30 *Fax:* (02) 70 18 30
E-mail: director@ilit.bas.bg
Web Site: www.cl.bas.bg
Key Personnel
Dir, Associate Prof: Raya Kuncheva *Tel:* 9792990
Text in Bulgarian. Contents page in English & French.
First published 1957.
Monthly.

Chile

Bibliografia chilena (Chilean Bibliographies) (J)
Published by Biblioteca Nacional de Chile
Ave B O'Higgins 651, Clasificador 1400, Santiago
Tel: (02) 338 957 *Fax:* (02) 381 957
E-mail: biblioteca.nacional@bndchile.cl
Web Site: www.dibam.cl/biblioteca_nacional
Key Personnel
Contact: Pedro Pablo Zegers
First published 1976.
Annually.

Efimeros (Ephemerals) (P)
Published by Biblioteca del Congreso Nacional
Compania 1175 & Huerfanos 1117-2° piso, Santiago
Tel: (02) 2701700 *Fax:* (02) 2701766
E-mail: direcbcn@congreso.cl
Web Site: www.bcn.cl

Mapocho (P)
Published by Biblioteca Nacional de Chile
Av Bernardo O'Higgins 651, Santiago
Tel: (02) 6380461 *Fax:* (02) 6380461
E-mail: biblioteca.nacional@bndechile.cl
Web Site: www.dibam.cl
Key Personnel
Dir: Alfonso Calderon Squadritto
Distributor Editorial University.
First published 1998.
Irregularly.
ISSN: 0716-2510

Revista Chilena de Literatura (Chilean Review of Literature) (P)
Published by Universidad de Chile Facultad de Filosofia y Humanidades, Departmento de Literatura
Ignacio Carrera Pinto 1025, Santiago
Fax: (02) 2716823
E-mail: deptolit@uchile.cl
Web Site: www.uchile.cl/facultades/filosofia/revista_literaria/
Key Personnel
Dir: Hugo Montes
Biannually.
ISSN: 0048-7651

China

China Today (P)
Published by China Welfare Institute
24 Baiwanzhuang Rd, Beijing 100037
Tel: (010) 68996217 *Fax:* (010) 68997796
E-mail: chinatoday@263.net; wandi@china.org.cn
Web Site: www.china.org.cn

CHINA

Published in English, French, Arabic, German, English braille & Chinese.
Monthly.

Chinese Literature (P)
Published by Chinese Literature Press
24 Baiwanzhuang Rd, Beijing 100037
Tel: (010) 8326678 *Fax:* (010) 8326678
Key Personnel
Editor: Jialong Tang
English & French editions.
First published 1951.
Quarterly.
ISSN: 0009-4617

ƒCommunications in Theoretical Physics (J)
Published by International Academic Publishers (IAP)
137 Chaonei Dajie, Beijing 100010
Tel: (010) 4038366 *Fax:* (010) 64014877
E-mail: wgxs@public3.bta.net.cn
Key Personnel
Editor: T H Ho
Presents important new developments in the area of theoretical physics. Papers published in this journal are devoted mainly to the fields of atomic & molecular physics, condensed matter & theory of statistical physics, nuclear theory, fluid theory & plasmas, elementary particle physics & quantum field theory, quantum mechanics & quantum optics, theoretical astrophysics, cosmology & relativity. Text in English.
First published 1981.
8 times/yr.
128 pp, 768 EUR or 769 USD (institutions for print or online edition); 921.60 EUR or 922.80 USD (institutions for both print & online editions)
ISSN: 0253-6102

Directory of Publishers in China (B)
Published by Foreign Languages Press (FLP)
24 Baiwanzhuanglu Rd, Beijing 100037
Tel: (010) 8320579 *Fax:* (010) 8317390
E-mail: flpcn@public3.bta.net.cn

Journal of Partial Differential Equations (J)
Published by International Academic Publishers (IAP)
137 Chaonei Dajie, Beijing 100010
Tel: (010) 4038366 *Fax:* (010) 64014877
E-mail: wgxs@public3.bta.net.cn
Key Personnel
Editor-in-Chief: Ding Weiyue
Associate Editor-in-Chief: Li Daqian; Chen Guowang; Jiang Song
Academic journal principally concerned with research in both theory & applications of partial differential equations.
First published 1988.
Quarterly.
96 pp, 160 USD (annual subscription)
ISSN: 1000-940X

Journal of Systems Science & Systems Engineering (J)
Published by International Academic Publishers (IAP)
137 Chaonei Dajie, Beijing 100010
Tel: (010) 4038366 *Fax:* (010) 64014877
E-mail: wgxs@public3.bta.net.cn
Key Personnel
Editor-in-Chief: Liu Bao
Associate Editor-in-Chief: Chai Benliang; Gu Jifa; Wang Zhongtuo
Carries papers on both theory & methodologies of Systems Science & Systems Engineering & also their applications to planning & management of R&D, production, economy, education, demography & military activities involving interdisciplinary theories, methodologies & techniques ranging from natural science to social science. Text in English.
First published 1992.
Quarterly.
96 pp, $140 USD (annual subscription)
ISSN: 1004-3756

Zhongguo jia shu mu (Chinese National Bibliography) (B)
Published by Beijing Library Press
7 Wenjin St, Xicheng District, Beijing 100034
Tel: (010) 66126146; (010) 66174391 *Fax:* (010) 66174391
E-mail: btsfxb@publicf.gov.cn
Web Site: www.nlcpress.com
Telex: 222211 NLC CN *Cable:* 0848

Colombia

Anuario Bibliografico Colombiano (Colombian Bibliographical Annual) (J)
Published by Instituto Caro y Cuervo
Carrera 11 No 64-37 Apdo Aereo 51502, Santafe de Bogota, Cundinamarca
Tel: (01) 255-82-89; (01) 558289 *Fax:* (01) 2170243
Annually.

ƒBoletin Informativo CERLALC (J)
Published by Centro Regional para el Fomento del Libro en America Latina y el Caribe (Regional Center for the Promotion of Books in Latin America & the Caribbean)
Calle 70 No 9-52, Bogota DC
Tel: (01) 540 2071
E-mail: libro@cerlalc.org
Web Site: www.cerlalc.org
Key Personnel
Editor: Margarita Mendieta

Directorio Latinoamericano de Editoriales, Distribuidoras y Librerias (B)
Published by Centro Regional para el Fomento del Libro en America Latina y el Caribe (Regional Center for the Promotion of Books in Latin America & the Caribbean)
Calle 70 No 9-52, Bogota DC
Tel: (01) 540 2071
E-mail: libro@cerlalc.org
Web Site: www.cerlalc.org
Key Personnel
Dir: Carmen Barvo
Dos nuevos publicaciones en Dd-Rom, anexo folletos. Para titulos no en inges, favor de proveer traduccion en Asimismo, el libro Manual de edicio.

Tinta Fresca (ISBN Bibliographical Bulletin/Editorial Mail) (J)
Published by Camara Colombiana del Libro
Carrera 17A No 37-27, Bogota
Tel: (01) 288 6188 *Fax:* (01) 287 3320
E-mail: camlibro@camlibro.com.co
Web Site: www.camlibro.com.co
Quarterly.

The Democratic Republic of the Congo

Bibliographie Nationale (B)
Published by Bibliotheque Nacionale
BP 3090, Kinshasa-Gombe
Telex: 21216 CAU ZR
Zaire Bibliography. Text in French.
First published 1971.
Irregularly.

Costa Rica

Anuario bibliografico costarricense (Annual Costa Rican Bibliography) (J)
Published by Asociacion Costarricense de Bibliotecarios (Costa Rican Association of Librarians)
Apdo 3308, San Jose
Text in Spanish.
First published 1956.
Free
ISSN: 0066-5010

Catalogo Nacional ISBN (National ISBN Catalog) (J)
Published by Direccion General de Bibliotecas y Biblioteca Nacional
Ap 10008, 1000 San Jose
Tel: 2331706; 2212436; 2212479 *Fax:* 2235510
Key Personnel
Contact: Marco A Chacon Monge

Indice de Revistas Nacionales (Catalog of National Periodicals) (J)
Published by Direccion General de Bibliotecas y Biblioteca Nacional
Apdo 10008-1000, San Jose
Tel: 2212436; 2212479 *Fax:* 2235510

Cote d'Ivoire

Bibliographie de la Cote-d'Ivoire (Ivory Coast Bibliography) (J)
Published by Bibliotheque Nationale
BP V180, Abidjan
Tel: 32 38 72
Text in French.
First published 1969.
Annually in two volumes.
ISSN: 0084-7860

Revue de Litterature de l'esthetique negre-africaines & edition de livres Scolaires, de litterature Jenerale et d'encyclopedie (P)
Published by Les Nouvelles Editions Ivoiriennes
One blvd de Marseille, 01 Abidjan
Mailing Address: BP 3525, 01 Abidjan
Tel: 32-12-51; 32-16-22; 32-60-09
Telex: Cote d Ivoire 22564

Croatia

Forum (J)
Published by Hrvatska Akademija Zhanosti i Umjetnosti, Razred Za Suvremenu knjizevnost
Zrinski trg 11, 10000 Zagreb
Tel: (01) 48 95 111 *Fax:* (01) 481 99 79
E-mail: kabpred@hazu.hr
Web Site: www.hazu.hr
Key Personnel
Editor: Slavko Mihalic
Journal of the Section for Contemporary Literature of the Croatian Academy of Sciences & Arts. Text in Croatian.

Cuba

Taller Literario (Literary Workshop) (P)
Published by Universidad de Oriente, Escuela de Letras
Avda Patricio Lumumba s-n, CP 90500 Santiago de Cuba Oriente
Tel: (0226) 31973
Key Personnel
Dir: Dr Bayardo Dupotey Rivas
Librarian: Caridad Velaquez Alazar
Text in Spanish.
First published 1971.
Quarterly.

Union (P)
Published by Ediciones Union, Union de Escritores y Artistas de Cuba
Calle 17 No 351 e/H, Plaza de la Revolucion, Havana
Tel: (07) 324551; (07) 324571 *Fax:* (07) 333158
E-mail: informatica@uneac.co.cu
Web Site: www.uneac.com
Key Personnel
Dir: Jorge Lois Arcos

Czech Republic

Casopis Narodniho muzea Rada historicka (Journal of the National Museum Series: History) (P)
Published by Narodni Muzeum
Vaclavske namesti 68, 115 79 Prague 1
Tel: (02) 24497111; (02) 24497212; (02) 24497352; (02) 2449376 *Fax:* (02) 22246047; (02) 24226488
Web Site: www.nm.cz
Key Personnel
Dir: Lukas Viktora *E-mail:* lukas.viktora@nm.cz
Secretary: Dr Libuse Ziebikerova, PhD
Summaries in English, French, German & Russian.
Quarterly.

Casopis Narodniho muzea Rada prirodovedna (Journal of the National Museum Series: Natural Science) (P)
Published by Narodni Muzeum
Vaclavske namesti 68, 115 79 Prague 1
Tel: (02) 24497111; (02) 24497212; (02) 24497352; (02) 2449376 *Fax:* (02) 22246047; (02) 24226488
Web Site: www.nm.cz
Key Personnel
General Dir: Michal Lukes *Tel:* (02) 4497310
E-mail: michal.lukes@nm.cz
Secretary: Radaria Valisova *Tel:* (02) 24497310
E-mail: sekretariat@nm.cz
Summaries in English, French, German & Russian.
Quarterly.

Czech Books For You (J)
Published by Artia Pegas Press Co Ltd
Palac Metro, Narodnitrida 25, 111 21 Prague
Mailing Address: PO Box 825, 110 00 Prague
Tel: (02) 266568; (02) 262081 *Fax:* (02) 266568
Telex: 161065 ARTA C *Cable:* ARTIASPOL PRAHA
Bulletin with annotations & prices of approximately 200 of the most interesting books published in the Czech Republic during the previous quarter. Text in Czech.
First published 1974.
Quarterly.
Free

Muzejni a vlastivedna prace (Museum & Local History) (P)
Published by Narodni Muzeum
Vaclavske namesti 68, 115 79 Prague 1
Tel: (02) 24497111; (02) 24497212; (02) 24497352; (02) 2449376 *Fax:* (02) 22246047; (02) 24226488
Web Site: www.nm.cz
Key Personnel
Dir: Lukas Viktora *E-mail:* lukas.viktora@nm.cz
Secretary: Dr Libuse Ziebikerova, PhD
Summaries in English, French, German & Russian.
Quarterly.

Numismaticke listy (Numismatics Journal) (P)
Published by Narodni Muzeum
Vaclavske namesti 68, 115 79 Prague 1
Tel: (02) 24497111; (02) 24497212; (02) 24497352; (02) 2449376 *Fax:* (02) 22246047; (02) 24226488
Web Site: www.nm.cz
Key Personnel
Dir: Lukas Viktora *E-mail:* lukas.viktora@nm.cz
Secretary: Dr Libuse Ziebikerova, PhD
Summaries in English, French, German & Russian.
6 times/yr.

Sbornik Narodniho muzea Rada A: Historie (Collection of the National Museum Series A: History) (P)
Published by Narodni Muzeum
Vaclavske namesti 68, 115 79 Prague 1
Tel: (02) 24497111; (02) 24497212; (02) 24497352; (02) 2449376 *Fax:* (02) 22246047; (02) 24226488
Web Site: www.nm.cz
Key Personnel
Dir: Lukas Viktora *E-mail:* lukas.viktora@nm.cz
Secretary: Dr Libuse Ziebikerova, PhD
Summaries in English, French, German & Russian.
Quarterly.

Sbornik Narodniho muzea Rada B: Prirodni vedy (Collection of the National Museum Series B: Natural Science) (P)
Published by Narodni Muzeum
Vaclavske namesti 68, 115 79 Prague 1
Tel: (02) 24497111; (02) 24497212; (02) 24497352; (02) 2449376 *Fax:* (02) 22246047; (02) 24226488
Web Site: www.nm.cz
Key Personnel
Dir: Lukas Viktora *E-mail:* lukas.viktora@nm.cz
Secretary: Dr Libuse Ziebikerova, PhD
In English or German, also in Czechoslovakian with English & German summaries.
Quarterly.

Sbornik Narodniho muzea Rada C: Literarni historie (Magazine of the National Museum of Prague, Series C: Literary History) (P)
Published by Narodni Muzeum
Vaclavske namesti 68, 115 79 Prague 1
Tel: (02) 24497111; (02) 24497212; (02) 24497352; (02) 2449376 *Fax:* (02) 22246047; (02) 24226488
Web Site: www.nm.cz
Key Personnel
Dir: Lukas Viktora *E-mail:* lukas.viktora@nm.cz
Secretary: Dr Libuse Ziebikerova, PhD
Summaries in English, French, German & Russian.
Quarterly.

Svetova Literatura (P)
Published by Spolecnost pro Svetovou Literaturu
Masarykovo nabr 26, 110 00 Prague 1
Tel: (02) 422912999 *Fax:* (02) 422912999
E-mail: furek@ius.prf.cuni.cz
Web Site: www.ff.cuni.cz/~furek/www4.htm
Review of Foreign Literature.
First published 1956.
Irregular.
240 CZK; 50 USD
ISSN: 0039-7075

Denmark

Bogormen (J)
Published by Danske Boghandler Medhjaelperforening (The Bookworm, Journal for Book Trade Employees)
Siljangade 6-8, 2300 Copenhagen S
Tel: 31542255 *Fax:* 31572422
For booksellers' assistants as well as other members of the book trade.
First published 1903.
Quarterly.
100 DKK
ISSN: 0006-5706

Born og Boger (Children & Books) (P)
Published by Danmarks Skolebiblioteksforening
Vesterbrogade 20, 5 sal, 1620 Copenhagen V
Tel: 33253222 *Fax:* 33253223
E-mail: dbf@dbf.dk
Web Site: www.ksbf.dk
Key Personnel
Editor: Niels Jacobsen
English Summary. Periodical concerning books & other cultural values for children & young adults.

Danish Literary Magazine (P)
Published by The Danish Arts Agency-The Literature Center
Kongens Nytorv 3, 1050 Copenhagen K
Tel: (033) 74 45 00 *Fax:* (033) 74 45 45
E-mail: literature@danish-arts.dk
Web Site: www.danlit.dk
Key Personnel
Dir: Marianne Krukow
Consultant: Annette Bach *E-mail:* annette.bach@danlit.dk
Excerpts from new Danish books, in addition to news about Danish books being published in other countries.
Biannually.

Dansk Bogfortegnelse (Danish National Bibliography, Books) (J)
Published by Danish Bibliographic Centre
Tempovej 7-11, 2750 Ballerup
Tel: 4486 7777 *Fax:* 44867891
E-mail: dbc@dbc.dk

Denmark

Web Site: www.dbc.dk
Key Personnel
Contact: Kirsten Waneck *E-mail:* kw@dbc.dk

Hvedekorn (P)
Published by Borgens Forlag A/S
Valbygardsvej 33, 2500 Valby
Tel: 36153615 *Fax:* 36153616
E-mail: kunst@hvedekorn.dk
Web Site: www.hvedekorn.dk
Magazine for poetry & graphics.

Nordisk Exlibris Tidsskrift (Scandinavian Bookplate Periodical) (P)
Published by Dansk Exlibris Selskab
PO Box 1519, 2700 Copenhagen
Tel: 46769166 *Fax:* 46769167
E-mail: 113071.3716@compuserve.com
Key Personnel
Editor: Klaus Roedel
Text in Danish, English & German.
First published 1946.
Quarterly.
250 DKK
ISSN: 0029-1323

Orbis Litterarum (P)
Published by Blackwell
One Rosenorns Alle, DK-1502 Copenhagen V
Mailing Address: PO Box 227, DK-1502 Copenhagen V
Tel: 7733 3333 *Fax:* 7733 3377
E-mail: info@mks.blackwellpublishing.com
Web Site: www.blackwellmunksgaard.com
Key Personnel
Editor: Prof Morton Nojgard
International Review of literary studies; text mainly in English, occasionally in French & German.

Produktionshaandbogen (Production Handbook) (B)
Published by Forlaget de Grafiske Haandboeger
Finsensvej 80, 2000 Frederiksberg
Tel: 38883222 *Fax:* 38883038
Key Personnel
Contact: Ilse Rosenback
Directory of prepress, printing & print-finishing companies in Denmark. Text in Danish.
Annually.
ISSN: 0105-7758

Egypt (Arab Republic of Egypt)

Lotus: Afro-Asian Writings (P)
Published by Permanent Bureau of Afro-Asian Writers
104 Sharia Kasr El-Aini, Cairo
Key Personnel
Editor: Youssef El Sebal
Important quarterly review published for the Permanent Bureau of Afro-Asian Writers. Text in Arabic.
First published 1968.
Quarterly.

Ethiopia

Ethiopian Publications: Books, Pamphlets, Annuals & Periodical Articles (P)
Published by Addis Ababa University, Institute of Ethiopian Studies
PO Box 1176, Addis Ababa
Tel: (01) 119469 *Fax:* (01) 552688
E-mail: ics@padis.gn.apc.org
Ethiopian National Bibliography.
Annually.

List of Ethiopian Authors (B)
Published by Addis Ababa University Press, Institute of Ethiopian Studies
PO Box 1176, Addis Ababa
Tel: (01) 119469 *Fax:* (01) 552688
E-mail: IES@padis.gn.apc.org
ISSN: 0071-1772

Fiji

Publications Bulletin (J)
Published by Fiji Government Printing Department
Government Buildings, PO Box 2353, Suva
Tel: 3211 201 *Fax:* 3306 034
E-mail: info@fiji.gov.fj
Web Site: www.fiji.gov.fj
Key Personnel
President: Ratu Josefa
Biannually.

ⓕSouth Pacific Bibliography (J)
Published by University of the South Pacific Library
Suva
Tel: 313 900 *Fax:* 3300 830
E-mail: library@usp.ac.fj
Web Site: www.usp.ac.fj/~library
Biennially.

ⓕSouth Pacific Periodicals Index (B)
Published by University of the South Pacific Library
Suva
Tel: 313 900 *Fax:* 3300 830
E-mail: library@usp.ac.fj
Web Site: www.usp.ac.fjl~library

Finland

Bokvaennen (The Bibliophile) (J)
Published by Boknoje, Barnens
Box 1253, 251-12 Helsinki
Tel: (042) 136415 *Fax:* (042) 147132
Key Personnel
Editor: Lars Forsberg

Books from Finland (J)
Published by Helsinki University Library
University of Helsinki, Unioninkatu 36, FIN-00014 Helsinki
Mailing Address: University of Helsinki, PO Box 15, FIN-00014 Helsinki
Tel: (09) 1357942 *Fax:* (09) 1357942
E-mail: bff@helsinki.fi
Web Site: www.lib.helsinki.fi/bff
Key Personnel
Editor-in-Chief: Kristina Carlson
Editor: Soila Lehtonen

Editor (London): Hildi Hawkins
A literary journal published in English of books from & about Finland.
First published 1967.
Quarterly.
80 pp, Annual subscription 27 euros, 20 euros in Finland & Scandinavia
ISSN: 0006-7490

The Finnish National Bibliography (P)
Published by Helsinki University Library
Slavonic Library, PB 15, Helsingin Yliopisto, 00014 Unioninkatu 36
Tel: (09) 191 23196 *Fax:* (09) 191 22719
E-mail: hyk-palvelu@helsinki.fi
Web Site: www.lib.helsinki.fi
Also on microfiche; monthly with annual cumulation.

Horisont (P)
Published by Svenska Oesterbottens Litteraturfoerening
Radhusgatan 50 c 53, 65100 Vasa
Tel: (061) 3128426 *Fax:* (061) 3242210
E-mail: horisont50@hotmail.com
Literary magazine.
First published 1954.
Quarterly.
30 euros/4 issues
ISSN: 0439-5530

Kirjakauppalehti (Book Trade Journal) (J)
Published by Kirjamedia Oy
Eerikinkatu 15-17 D 43, 00100 Helsinki
Tel: (09) 6859 9112; (09) 6859 9111 *Fax:* (09) 6859 9119
E-mail: toimisto@kirjakauppaliitto.fi
Web Site: www.kirjakauppalehti.net/; www.kirjakauppaliitto.fi
Key Personnel
Editor-in-Chief: Annika Asvik *Tel:* (09) 6859 9114 *E-mail:* annika.asvik@kirjakauppalehti.net

Parnasso (P)
Published by Yhtyneet Kuvalehdet Oy
Maistraatinportti 1, 00015 Helsinki
Tel: (09) 15 661; (09) 156 665 *Fax:* (09) 145 650; (09) 156 6511
Web Site: www.kuvalehdet.fi
Key Personnel
President: Pauli Leimio
Vice President: Ilkka Seppaelae
Content Dir: Harri Saukkomaa
Development Dir: Jouni Lojander
Branch Office(s)
Esterinportti 1, 00015 Helsinki

Skrifter utgivna av Svenska Litteratursaellskapet i Finland (P)
Published by Svenska Litteratursaellskapet i Finland (Society of Swedish Literature in Finland)
Riddareg 5, FIN 00170 Helsinki 17
Tel: (09) 618777 *Fax:* (09) 6187 7277
Key Personnel
Editor: Nina Edgren-Henrichson *E-mail:* nina.edgren-henrichson@sls.fi
Scholarly publications in history, literature, ethnology, Scandinavian languages, social & political sciences.
ISSN: 0039-6842

Virittaejae (P)
Published by Society for the Study of Finnish
Castrenianum, PO Box 3, 00014 University of Helsinki
Tel: (09) 191 24342 *Fax:* (09) 191 3329
Web Site: www.helsinki.fi/jarj/kks/virittaja
Key Personnel
Editor: Marja-Liisa Helasvuo *E-mail:* mlhelas@utu.fi; Susanna Shore *E-mail:* susanna.shore@helsinki.fi

Summaries in English, French & German
The Kinder.
First published 1897.
Quarterly (4 numbers per vol).
54 euros (47 euros if paid through a Finnish bank)
ISSN: 0042-6806

France

Annales de la Recherche Urbaine (P)
Published by Plan Urbanisme Contruction Architecture (PUCA)
Arche de la Defense-Paroi Nord, 92055 Paris la Defense Cedex
Tel: (01) 40 81 63 71 *Fax:* (01) 40 81 63 78
Web Site: www.equipement.gouv.fr
Key Personnel
Editor: Pierre Lassave *Tel:* (01) 40 81 63 70
 E-mail: pierre.lassave@equipement.gouv.fr; Anne Querrien *Tel:* (01) 40 81 24 46
 E-mail: anne.querrien@equipement.gouv.fr
First published 1979.
ISSN: 0180-930X
Parent Company: Ministere de l'Equipement, des Transports, du Logement, du Tourisme et de la Mer
Distributed by Lavoisier Abonnements

ƒ**Bibliotheques et Musees des Arts du Spectacle dans le Monde** (Performing Arts Libraries & Museums of the World) (B)
Published by Societe Internationale des Bibliotheques-Musees des Arts du Spectacle
Centre National de la Recherche Scientifique (CNRS), 3-5 rue Michel-Ange, 75794 Paris
Tel: (01) 44964000 *Fax:* (01) 44965000

ƒ**Bulletin du Bibliophile** (J)
Published by Electre-Editions du Cercle de la Librarie
35 rue Gregoire-de-Tours, 75006 Paris
Tel: (01) 44 41 28 00 *Fax:* (01) 43 29 68 95
Key Personnel
Secretary/Administration: Annie Charon
 E-mail: abcharon@club-internet.fr
Published in English, French & German.
First published 1834.
Biannually (June & Dec).
ISSN: 0399-9742

Choisir (P)
Published by Centre National de Documentation Pedagogique (CNDP)
29 rue d'Ulm, 75230 Paris Cedex 05
Tel: (01) 46349000 *Fax:* (01) 46345544
Key Personnel
Editor: J Lanfranchi

ƒ**Copyright Bulletin** (J)
Published by UNESCO
Division of Art & Cultural Enterprise
Unit of Creativity & Copyright
7, Place de Fontenoy, 75352 Paris 07-SP
Tel: (01) 45 68 10 00; (01) 45 68 11 78 *Fax:* (01) 45 67 16 90; (01) 45 68 55 40
 E-mail: publishing.promotion@unesco.org; natcom.ncp@unesco.org; m.e.guerassimos@unesco.org
Web Site: www.unesco.org/publications; www.unesco.org/culture/copyright
Articles & recent news on international conventions & developments in the field of copyright.
Published in English, French, Spanish, Chinese & Russian.
Quarterly.
80 pp

ƒ**Copyright Laws & Treaties of the World** (B)
Published by UNESCO Publishing
7 Place de Fontenoy, 75352 Paris 07-SP
Tel: (01) 45 68 10 00; (01) 45 68 11 78 *Fax:* (01) 45 67 16 90; (01) 45 68 55 40
 E-mail: publishing.promotion@unesco.org; natcom.ncp@unesco.org
Web Site: www.unesco.org/publications
Telex: 204461
Key Personnel
Dir General: Koichiro Matsuura
Dir, UNESCO Publishing: Chandran Nair
Editorial Dir: Michiko Tanaka
Rights & Permissions: Georgina Almeida
Promotion & Sales: Cristina Laje
Annually.

Critique (P)
Published by Les Editions de Minuit SA
7 rue Bernard-Palissy, 75006 Paris
Tel: (01) 44 39 39 20 *Fax:* (01) 45 44 82 36
 E-mail: contact@leseditionsdeminuit.fr
Web Site: www.leseditionsdeminuit.fr
Key Personnel
Contact: Isabelle Chave
General review of publications in France & abroad.

ƒ**Directory of Documentation, Libraries & Archives Services in Africa** (B)
Published by UNESCO Publishing
Office of Public Information, 7 Place de Fontenoy, 75352 Paris 07-SP
Tel: (01) 45 68 10 00; (01) 45 68 11 78 *Fax:* (01) 45 67 16 90; (01) 45 68 55 40
 E-mail: publishing.promotion@unesco.org
Web Site: www.unesco.org/publications
Telex: 204461

Documentation, technique scientifique et commerciale (J)
Published by Librairie Lavoisier
11 rue Lavoisier, 75384 Paris Cedex 08
Tel: (01) 47 40 67 00 *Fax:* (01) 47 40 67 88
 E-mail: edition@tec-et-doc.com
Web Site: www.lavoisier.fr
Documentation - Technical, Scientific & Commercial. Text & summaries in English, French & German.

Donnees statistiques sur l'edition du Livre en France (French Book Production Statistics) (B)
Published by Syndicat National de l'Edition (National Union of Publishers)
115 Blvd Saint Germain, 75006 Paris
Tel: (01) 44 41 40 50 *Fax:* (01) 44 41 40 77
Web Site: www.snedition.fr
Key Personnel
President: Serge Eyrolles

ƒ**Index Translationum, International Bibliography of Translations** (B)
Published by UNESCO
7, Place de Fontenoy, 75352 Paris 07-SP
Tel: (01) 45684310; (01) 45684311 *Fax:* (01) 45685591
 E-mail: index@unesco.org
Web Site: www.unesco.org/culture/xtrans
Cumulative bibliography available on CD-ROM & Internet only.
Annually.
8, $45 (US)
ISBN(s): 92-3-003809-1
ISSN: 1020-1386

ƒ**International Association of Literary Critics Review** (J)
Published by International Association of Literary Critics
Hotel de Massa, 38 rue du Faubourg, St Jacques, 75014 Paris
Tel: (01) 40513300 *Fax:* (01) 43549299
Web Site: www.aicl.org
Key Personnel
Founder & President: Yves Gandon

ƒ**Lettre Internationale (Revue)** (International Letter Review) (J)
41, rue Bobillot, 75013 Paris
Mailing Address: 27, rue St Ambroise, 75011 Paris
Tel: (01) 42470200; (01) 42470734 *Fax:* (01) 42338324
Published in 9 languages.

L'Information litteraire (P)
Published by Societe d'Edition Les Belles Lettres
95 Blvd Raspail, 75006 Paris
Tel: (01) 44398420 *Fax:* (01) 45449288
 E-mail: courrier@lesbelleslettres.com
Web Site: www.lesbelleslettres.com
Key Personnel
Founder: Paul Mazon
Dir: Michel Desgranges

Litterature (P)
Published by Editions Larousse
21 rue du Montparnasse, 75283 Paris Cedex 06
Tel: (01) 44 39 44 00 *Fax:* (01) 44 39 43 43
 E-mail: tleridon@larousee.fr
Web Site: www.larousse.fr
Key Personnel
Editor: Francois Tremollieres
Text in French.
First published 1971.
Quarterly.
55 EUR (domestic individuals); 65 EUR (foreign individuals); 70 EUR (domestic institutions); 80 EUR (foreign institutions)
ISSN: 0047-4800

Livres au Format de Poche (Paperback Books) (B)
Published by Electre
35, rue Gregoire-de-Tours, 75279 Paris Cedex 06
Tel: (01) 44 41 28 00 *Fax:* (01) 44 41 28 65
 E-mail: commercial@electre.com
Annually.
$43.61 F
ISBN(s): 2-7654-0590-5

Livres de France (Books of France) (J)
Published by Electre
35 rue Gregoire-de-Tours, 75006 Paris
Tel: (01) 44 41 28 00 *Fax:* (01) 44 41 28 55
Web Site: www.imaginet.fr/electre
Key Personnel
Chief Editor: Marianne Grangie
Guide to published books & trade information.
Monthly.

Livres Disponibles (B)
Published by Editions du Cercle de la Librairie
35, rue Gregoire-de-Tours, 75279 Paris Cedex 06
Tel: (01) 44 41 28 00 *Fax:* (01) 44 41 28 65
French Books in Print. Also available on microfiche, from database (Electre), & CD-ROM.
Annually.

Livres Hebdo (Weekly Books) (J)
Published by Electre
35 rue Gregoire-de-Tours, 75006 Paris
Tel: (01) 44 41 28 00 *Fax:* (01) 44 41 28 55
 E-mail: livreshebdo@electre.com
Web Site: www.imaginet.fr/electre
Key Personnel
Dir: Jean-Marie Doublet
Editor: Pierre Louis Rozynes
Book market trade journal.
Weekly.

FRANCE

Magazine litteraire (Literary Magazine) (P)
Published by Magazine-Expansion
4, rue du Texel, 75014 Paris
Tel: (01) 40 47 44 90 *Fax:* (01) 40 47 44 98
E-mail: magazine@magazine-litteraire.com
Web Site: www.magazine-litteraire.com
Monthly.
108 pp
ISSN: 0024-9807

La Nouvelle Revue francaise (P)
Published by Editions Gallimard
5 rue Sebastien-Bottin, 75328 Paris Cedex 07
Tel: (01) 49544200
Web Site: www.gallimard.fr
Key Personnel
Editor: Michel Braudeau
First published 1909.
Quarterly.
352 pp
ISSN: 0029-4802

Quinzaine litteraire (Literary Fortnightly) (P)
Published by Selis la Quinzaine Litteraire
135 rue Saint-Martin, 75194 Paris Cedex 04
Tel: (01) 48 87 75 87 *Fax:* (01) 48 87 13 01
Web Site: www.quinzaine-litteraire.presse.fr
Reviews & summaries of recently published books.
Bimonthly.
30 pp

Repertoire international des Editeurs et Diffuseurs de Langue francaise (International List of French Language Publishers & Distributors) (B)
Published by Editions du Cercle de la Librairie
35, rue Gregoire-de-Tours, 75279 Paris Cedex 06
Tel: (01) 44 41 28 00 *Fax:* (01) 44 41 28 65
Telex: lifran 270838
Annually.

Revue de Litterature comparee (Review of Comparative Literature) (P)
Published by Didier Erudition
6 rue de la Sorbonne, F-75005 Paris
Tel: (01) 43 54 47 57 *Fax:* (01) 40 51 73 85
E-mail: diderkkk@easynet.fr
Key Personnel
Editor: Pierre Brunel
Text in English & French.
ISSN: 0035-1466

Revue des Etudes Italiennes (Review of Italian Studies) (P)
Published by Societe des Etudes Italiennes (Paris)
Centre Malesherbes, 108, Blvd Malesherbes, 75850 Paris Cedex 17
Tel: (01) 43 18 41 69 *Fax:* (01) 43 18 41 71
E-mail: centr-rechesche.italian@parisa.sofbonne.fr
Key Personnel
Dir: Francois Livi *E-mail:* francois.livi@paris4.sorbonne.fr
Text in French.
First published 1936.
Biannually.
160 pp, 40 EUR
ISSN: 0035-2047

La Revue des Livres pour Enfants (Children's Books Review Magazine) (P)
Published by La Joie par les Livres
8 rue St-Bon, 75004 Paris
Tel: (01) 48 87 61 95 *Fax:* (01) 48 87 08 52
E-mail: cnle@lajoieparleslivres.com
Web Site: www.cockpit.fr/lajoie
Key Personnel
Contact: Jacques Vidal-Naquet

Gambia

National Bibliography of the Gambia (B)
Published by Gambia National Library
Reg Pye Lane, Banjul
Tel: 22 64 91; 22 83 12 *Fax:* 22 37 76
E-mail: national.library@qanet.gm
Web Site: www.dpb.dpu.dk/survey/gambia_desc.html
Key Personnel
Dir: Abdou W Mbye

Georgia

Sakmatsvilo Literaturis Moambe (Bulletin of Children's Literature) (J)
Published by Nakaduli
Ketskhoveli 5, 380007 Tbilisi

Germany

ƒAdressbuch fuer den deutschsprachigen Buchhandel (B)
Published by Buchhaendler-Vereinigung Verlag GmbH
Grosser Hirschgraben 17/21, 60311 Frankfurt am Main
Mailing Address: Postfach 10 04 42, 60004 Frankfurt am Main
Tel: (069) 1306 0 *Fax:* (069) 1306 201
E-mail: info@buchhandel.de
Web Site: www.buchhandel.de
Telex: 413573 buchvd
Directory of the German-language Book Trade.

The African Book Publishing Record (ABPR) (P)
Published by K G Saur Verlag GmbH, A Gale/Thomson Learning Company
Unit of Thomson Learning
Ortlerstr 8, 81373 Munich
Mailing Address: Postfach 70 16 20, 81316 Munich
Tel: (089) 76902-0 *Fax:* (089) 76902-150
E-mail: info@saur.de
Web Site: www.saur.de
Telex: 5212067
Bibliographical tool which offers systematic & comprehensive coverage of new & forthcoming African publications in a single source, providing full bibliographic & acquisitions data. Also includes an extensive book review section & features news, reports & articles about African book trade activities & developments.
Quarterly.
Parent Company: Gale
Ultimate Parent Company: The Thomson Corporation

African Books in Print/Livres Africains Desponibles (5th ed) (B)
Published by K G Saur Verlag GmbH, A Gale/Thomson Learning Company
Unit of Thomson Learning
Ortlerstr 8, 81373 Munich
Mailing Address: Postfach 70 16 20, 81316 Munich
Tel: (089) 76902-0 *Fax:* (089) 76902-150
E-mail: info@saur.de
Web Site: www.saur.de
Telex: 5212067
Major reference work containing full bibliographic details on 24,000 books, published in 45 African countries by more than 700 publishers & research institutions with publishing programs.
5th edition
ISBN(s): 3-598-07684-3
Parent Company: Gale
Ultimate Parent Company: The Thomson Corporation

African Studies Abstracts (J)
Published by K G Saur Verlag GmbH, A Gale/Thomson Learning Company
Unit of Thomson Learning
Ortlerstr 8, 81373 Munich
Mailing Address: Postfach 70 16 20, 81316 Munich
Tel: (089) 76902-0 *Fax:* (089) 76902-150
E-mail: info@saur.de
Web Site: www.saur.de
Abstracting journal providing coverage of all the leading journals in the field of African Studies, Third World countries & development issues. Each issue contains approximately 450 abstracts Published on behalf of the African Studies Centre, Leiden, Netherlands.
Parent Company: Gale
Ultimate Parent Company: The Thomson Corporation

Akzente (P)
Published by Carl Hanser Verlag
Kolbergerstr 22, 81679 Munich
Tel: (089) 998300 *Fax:* (089) 984809
E-mail: info@hanser.de
Web Site: www.hanser.de/verlag

Archiv fuer Geschichte des Buchwesens (Archive for History Books) (J)
Published by Buchhaendler-Vereinigung Verlag GmbH
Grosser Hirschgraben 17/21, 60311 Frankfurt am Main
Mailing Address: Postfach 10 04 42, 60004 Frankfurt am Main
Tel: (069) 1306 0 *Fax:* (069) 1306 201
E-mail: agb@buchhaendler-vereinigung.de; info@buchhandel.de
Web Site: www.buchhandel.de
Telex: 413573 buchvd
First published 1958.
Biannually.
ISBN(s): 3-7657-2187-5
ISSN: 0066-6327

Besprechungen Annotationen (P)
Published by Einkaufszentrale fur offentliche Bibliotheken BmbH
Bismarckstr 3, 72764 Reutlingen
Tel: (07121) 144-0 *Fax:* (07121) 144-280
E-mail: info@ekz.de
Web Site: www.ekz.de

Boersenblatt fuer den Deutschen Buchhandel/Frankfurt am Main und Leipzig (Official Journal of the German Book Trade) (J)
Published by Borsenverein des Deutschen Buchhandels eV
Grosser Hirschgraben 17-21, 60313 Frankfurt am Main
Tel: (069) 1306 363 *Fax:* (069) 2899 86
E-mail: boersenblatt@buchhandles-veseinigung.de
Web Site: www.boersenblatt.net
Telex: 413573 buchvd
First published 1834.
ISSN: 0940-0044

Buch Aktuell (Topical Book) (P)
Published by Harenberg Kommunikation Verlags- und Medien GmbH & Co KG

Koenigswall 21, 44137 Dortmund
Tel: (0231) 9056-0 *Fax:* (0231) 9056-110
E-mail: post@harenberg.de
Web Site: www.harenberg.de

Buch und Buchhandel in Zahlen (Books & the Book Trade in Figures) (B)
Published by Borsenverein des Deutschen Buchhandels eV
Grosser Hirschgraben 17-21, 60313 Frankfurt am Main
Tel: (069) 13 06-0 *Fax:* (069) 13 06-201
E-mail: info@boev.de
Web Site: www.buchhandel.de
Telex: 413573 buchvd
Key Personnel
Contact: Eva Martin
ISBN(s): 3-7657-2357-6

Buchhaendler heute (The Bookseller Today) (J)
Published by Vereinigten Verlagsanstalten GmbH
VVA Kommunikation, Hoeherweg 278, 40231 Duesseldorf
Tel: (0211) 7357-0 *Fax:* (0211) 7357-123
E-mail: info@vva.de
Web Site: www.vva.de
Book Trade.
Monthly.

BuchJournal (J)
Published by Borsenverein des Deutschen Buchhandels eV
Grosser Hirschgraben 17/21, 60311 Frankfurt am Main
Tel: (069) 1306-0 *Fax:* (069) 1306201
E-mail: info@buchhaendler-vereinigung.de
Web Site: www.buchhandel.de
Key Personnel
Management: Dr Michael Schoen; Peter Schuck
General magazine for booksellers' customers.
Quarterly.

BuchMarkt (Book Market) (J)
Published by Verlag K Werner GmbH
Sperberweg 4a, 40668 Meerbusch
Tel: (02150) 9191-0 *Fax:* (02150) 919191
E-mail: redaktion@buchmarkt.de
Web Site: www.buchmarkt.de
Key Personnel
Publisher, Man Dir & Editor-in-Chief: Christian von Zittwitz *Tel:* (02150) 9191-19
E-mail: cvz@buchmarkt.de
Journal for the book trade in German-speaking areas.

Buchreport (Book Report) (J)
Published by Harenberg Kommunikation Verlags- und Medien-GmbH & Co KG
Koenigswall 21, 44137 Dortmund
Tel: (0231) 9056-0 *Fax:* (0231) 9056-110
E-mail: harenberg@harenberg.de
Web Site: www.harenberg.de
Key Personnel
Publisher: Bodo Harenberg *Tel:* (0231) 9056-104 *Fax:* (0231) 9056-112
Magazine for booksellers in German-speaking areas.
First published 1970.
Weekly.
ISSN: 1615-0732

Buecherkarren (Book Cart) (J)
Published by Verlag Volk & Welt GmbH
Oranienstr 164/165, 10969 Berlin
Tel: (030) 61689530 *Fax:* (030) 61689540 *Cable:* VOLKWELT BERLIN
List of company publications to the general reader.
Quarterly.
Free

Buecherkommentare (Book Commentaries) (P)
Published by Rombach GmbH Druck und Verlagshaus & Co
Unterwerkstr 5, 79115 Freiburg
Tel: (0761) 4500-0 *Fax:* (0761) 4500-2125
E-mail: info@buchverlag.rombach.de
Web Site: www.rombach.de/buchverlag
Telex: uber 772728
Key Personnel
Management: Andreas Hodeige
Sales: Melanie Panzer *Tel:* (0761) 4500-2135
E-mail: panzer@buchverlag.rombach.de

Bulletin Jugend und Literatur (Youth & Literature Bulletin) (P)
Published by Neuland-Verlagsgesellschaft mbH
PO Box 1422, 21496 Geesthacht
Tel: (04152) 81342 *Fax:* (04152) 81343
E-mail: vertrieb@neuland.com
Web Site: www.neuland.com
Key Personnel
Editor: Frank Lindermann
First published 1969.
Monthly.
36 pp
ISSN: 0045-351X

Deutsche Nationalbibliographie (German National Bibliography) (J)
Published by Deutsche Bibliothek Frankfurt am Main
Grosser Hirschgraben 17/21, 60311 Frankfurt am Main
Mailing Address: Postfach 10 04 42, 60004 Frankfurt am Main
Tel: (069) 1306-0 *Fax:* (069) 1306-201
E-mail: info@buchhaendler-vereinigung.de
Web Site: www.buchhaendler-vereinigung.de
Key Personnel
Contact: Marlies Ney

ƒ**Dictionnaire pratique de l'Edition en 20 Langues** (Woerterbuch des Verlagswesens in 20 Sprachen) (Publishers Practical Dictionary in Twenty Languages) (B)
Published by K G Saur Verlag GmbH, A Gale/Thomson Learning Company
Unit of Thomson Learning
Ortlerstr 8, 81373 Munich
Mailing Address: Postfach 70 16 20, 81316 Munich
Tel: (089) 76902-0 *Fax:* (089) 76902-150
E-mail: info@saur.de
Web Site: www.saur.de
Telex: 5212067
Parent Company: Gale
Ultimate Parent Company: The Thomson Corporation

Directory of Special Collections in Western Europe (B)
Published by K G Saur Verlag GmbH, A Gale/Thomson Learning Company
Unit of Thomson Learning
Ortlerstr 8, 81373 Munich
Mailing Address: Postfach 70 16 20, 81316 Munich
Tel: (089) 76902-0 *Fax:* (089) 76902-150
E-mail: info@saur.de
Web Site: www.saur.de
Parent Company: Gale
Ultimate Parent Company: The Thomson Corporation

Flugpost - Informationsdienst Luftfahrt (Airmail-Aviation Information Service) (P)
Published by Flugpost Verlag Peter Pletschacher
Kolpingring 16, 82041 Oberhaching
Tel: (089) 613890-0 *Fax:* (089) 613890-10
E-mail: aviatic@t-online.de
Web Site: www.aviatic.de
Key Personnel
Man Dir: Peter Pletschacher
Newsletter.
First published 1989.
Weekly.
ISSN: 0938-3883

ƒ**Frankfurter Book Fair** (Frankfurt Book Fair) (B)
Published by Ausstellungs-und Messe-GmbH des Borsenvereins des Deutschen Buchhandels
Reineckstr 3, 63013 Frankfurt am Main
Mailing Address: Postfach 100116, 60001 Frankfurt am Main
Tel: (069) 2102-0 *Fax:* (069) 2102-227; (069) 2102-277
E-mail: info@book-fair.com
Web Site: www.frankfurter-buchmesse.de
Key Personnel
President & Chief Executive Officer: Volker Neumann
Vice President: Joachim Kehl
Chief Financial Officer: Gabriele Teucher

ƒ**Gesamtverzeichnis des deutschsprachigen Schrifttums** (Bibliography of German Language Publications) (B)
Published by K G Saur Verlag GmbH, A Gale/Thomson Learning Company
Unit of Thomson Learning
Ortlerstr 8, 81373 Munich
Mailing Address: Postfach 70 16 20, 81316 Munich
Tel: (089) 76902-0 *Fax:* (089) 76902-150
E-mail: info@saur.de
Web Site: www.saur.de
Telex: 5212067
Covers 1700-1965.
Parent Company: Gale
Ultimate Parent Company: The Thomson Corporation

ƒ**Gesamtverzeichnis des deutschsprachigen Schrifttums ausserhalb des Buchhandels** (Bibliography of German Language Publications Outside the Booktrade) (B)
Published by K G Saur Verlag GmbH, A Gale/Thomson Learning Company
Unit of Thomson Learning
Ortlerstr 8, 81373 Munich
Mailing Address: Postfach 70 16 20, 81316 Munich
Tel: (089) 76902-0 *Fax:* (089) 76902-150
E-mail: info@saur.de
Web Site: www.saur.de
Telex: 5212067
Covers 1966-1980.
Parent Company: Gale
Ultimate Parent Company: The Thomson Corporation

ƒ**Gesamtverzeichnis Deutschsprachiger Hochschulschriften 1966-1980** (Bibliography of German Language Academic Publications 1966-1980) (B)
Published by K G Saur Verlag GmbH, A Gale/Thomson Learning Company
Unit of Thomson Learning
Ortlerstr 8, 81373 Munich
Mailing Address: Postfach 70 16 20, 81316 Munich
Tel: (089) 76902-0 *Fax:* (089) 76902-150
E-mail: info@saur.de
Web Site: www.saur.de
Telex: 5212067
Parent Company: Gale
Ultimate Parent Company: The Thomson Corporation

ƒ**Guide to Microforms in Print** (B)
Published by K G Saur Verlag GmbH, A Gale/Thomson Learning Company

Unit of Thomson Learning
Ortlerstr 8, 81373 Munich
Mailing Address: Postfach 70 16 20, 81316 Munich
Tel: (089) 76902-0 *Fax:* (089) 76902-150
E-mail: info@saur.de
Web Site: www.saur.de
Telex: 5212067
Parent Company: Gale
Ultimate Parent Company: The Thomson Corporation

Guide to Microforms in Print: Author/Title (P)
Published by K G Saur Verlag GmbH, A Gale/Thomson Learning Company
Unit of Thomson Learning
Ortlerstr 8, 81373 Munich
Mailing Address: Postfach 70 16 20, 81316 Munich
Tel: (089) 76902-0 *Fax:* (089) 76902-150
E-mail: info@saur.de
Web Site: www.saur.de
Telex: 5212067
Cumulative alphabetical list of books, journals & other materials available from US & foreign publishers in microform.
Annual.
1999: 2,100 pp, $430
ISBN(s): 3-598-11392-7
Parent Company: Gale
Ultimate Parent Company: The Thomson Corporation

Hebbeljahrbuch (Hebbel Year Book) (P)
Published by Westholsteinische Verlagsanstalt und Verlagsdruckerei Boyens & Co
Wulf-Isebrand-Platz, 25767 Heide
Tel: (0481) 6886-0 *Fax:* (0481) 6886-469
E-mail: buchverlag@boyens-medien.de
Web Site: www.sh-nordsee.de
ISSN: 0073-1560

Die Horen (P)
Published by Wirtschaftsverlag NW, Verlag Fuer neue Wissenschaft GmbH
Buergermeister-Smidtstr 74-76, 27568 Bremerhaven
Mailing Address: Postfach 101110, 27511 Bremerhaven
Tel: (0471) 945440 *Fax:* (0471) 9454477
E-mail: vertrieb@nw-verlag.de
Web Site: www.nw-verlag.de
First published 1955.
Quarterly.
31 euros & postage (1 year subscription)
ISSN: 0018-4942

Imprimatur (J)
Published by Gesellschaft der Bibliophilen
Harrasowitz Verlag, 65174 Wiesbaden
Tel: (0611) 530570
E-mail: verlag@harrassowitz.de
Web Site: www.harrassowitz.de
Among other things history of books, printers, bookmindedness.
ISSN: 0073-5620

International African Bibliography (J)
Published by K G Saur Verlag GmbH, A Gale/Thomson Learning Company
Unit of Thomson Learning
Ortlerstr 8, 81373 Munich
Mailing Address: Postfach 70 16 20, 81316 Munich
Tel: (089) 76902-0 *Fax:* (089) 76902-150
E-mail: info@saur.de
Web Site: www.saur.de
Telex: 5212067
Indexes the latest books, articles & papers published internationally on Africa.
Quarterly.

Parent Company: Gale
Ultimate Parent Company: The Thomson Corporation

ʃ**International Book Trade Directory** (B)
Published by K G Saur Verlag GmbH, A Gale/Thomson Learning Company
Unit of Thomson Learning
Ortlerstr 8, 81373 Munich
Mailing Address: Postfach 70 16 20, 81316 Munich
Tel: (089) 76902-0 *Fax:* (089) 76902-150
E-mail: info@saur.de
Web Site: www.saur.de
Telex: 5212067
Listing details of booksellers in 134 countries outside the USA & Canada.
Parent Company: Gale
Ultimate Parent Company: The Thomson Corporation

ʃ**International Cataloguing & Bibliographic Control (ICBC)** (J)
Published by IFLA UBCIM Programme
c/o Die Deutsche Bibliothek, Adickesallee 1, 60322 Frankfurt am Main
Tel: (069) 1525 1140; (069) 1525 1141
Fax: (069) 1525 1142
E-mail: iflaubcim@dbf.ddb.de
Web Site: www.ifla.org/vi/3/admin/icbc.htm
Key Personnel
Program Dir: Marie-France Plassard
E-mail: plassard@dbf.ddb.de
International forum for the exchange of views & research results by members of the library & information management profession.
Quarterly.

ʃ**Jahrbuch der Auktionspreise fuer Buecher, Handschriften und Autographen** (German Book Prices Current) (B)
Published by Dr Ernst Hauswedell & Co
Haldenstr 30, 70376 Stuttgart
Mailing Address: Postfach 140155, 70071 Stuttgart
Tel: (0711) 54 99 71-11 *Fax:* (0711) 54 99 71-21
E-mail: info@hiersemann.de
Web Site: www.hauswedell.de
Key Personnel
Contact: Reinhold Busch
Publication contains Book auction prices in Germany, Austria, Switzerland & the Netherlands.

LiteraturNachrichten (Literary News) (P)
Published by Society for the Promotion of African, Asian & Latin American Literature
Reineckstr 3, 60313 Frankfurt am Main
Mailing Address: Postfach 10 01 16, 60001 Frankfurt am Main
Tel: (069) 2102247 *Fax:* (069) 2102227
E-mail: litprom@book-fair.com
Web Site: www.litprom.de
The only quarterly in Germany to report about literary developments in the Southern hemisphere.
First published 1983.
quarterly.
36 pp, Euro 15.00 aq
ISSN: 0935-7807

ʃ**Microform & Imaging Review** (J)
Published by K G Saur Verlag GmbH, A Gale/Thomson Learning Company
Unit of Thomson Learning
Ortlerstr 8, 81373 Munich
Mailing Address: Postfach 70 16 20, 81316 Munich
Tel: (089) 76902-0 *Fax:* (089) 76902-150
E-mail: info@saur.de
Web Site: www.saur.de
Telex: 5212067

Parent Company: Gale
Ultimate Parent Company: The Thomson Corporation

Neue deutsche Literatur (New German Literature) (P)
Published by Aufbau-Verlag GmbH
Neue Promenade 6, 10178 Berlin
Tel: (030) 28394238 *Fax:* (030) 28394100
E-mail: ndl@aufbau-verlag.de
Web Site: www.aufbau-verlag.de
Key Personnel
Editor: Juergen Engler
Periodical for German literature & reviews.
First published 1953.
Bimonthly.
192 pp, L10 (15.37 USD)
ISSN: 0028-3150

Neue Rundschau (New Review) (P)
Published by Martin Bauer
Hedderrichstr 114, 60596 Frankfurt am Main
Tel: (069) 6062-222 *Fax:* (069) 6062-214
E-mail: bauersfv@aol.com
Web Site: www.fischerverlage.de
First published 1890.
Quarterly.
ISBN(s): 3-10-809045-3
ISSN: 0028-3347
Parent Company: S Fischer Verlag, Berlin

ʃ**Publishers' International ISBN Directory** (B)
Published by K G Saur Verlag GmbH, A Gale/Thomson Learning Company
Unit of Thomson Learning
Ortlerstr 8, 81373 Munich
Mailing Address: Postfach 70 16 20, 81316 Munich
Tel: (089) 76902-0 *Fax:* (089) 76902-150
E-mail: info@saur.de
Web Site: www.saur.de
Telex: 5212067
Parent Company: Gale
Ultimate Parent Company: The Thomson Corporation

Quickborn (P)
Published by Quickborn, Vereinigung fuer Niederdeutsche Sprache und Literatur eV
Alexanderstr 16, 20099 Hamburg
Tel: (040) 24 08 09 *Fax:* (040) 3603 0767 15
E-mail: info@quickborn-ev.de
Key Personnel
Editor: Dirk Roemmer
Magazine for low-German language & literature, theatre & radio. Text in German.
First published 1907.
Quarterly.
ISSN: 0170-7558

Schriften und Zeugnisse zur Buchgeschichte (B)
Published by Harrassowitz Verlag
Taunusstr 14, 65183 Wiesbaden
Tel: (0611) 5300 *Fax:* (0611) 530570
E-mail: verlag@harrassowitz.de
Web Site: www.harrassowitz.de
History of books, the booktrade, publishers & printers. Text in German.
First published 1992.
Irregular.
ISSN: 0942-4709

Sinn und Form (Contents & Form) (P)
Published by Akademie der Kunste, Aufbau-Verlag Berlin-Brandenburg
Tucholskystr 2, 10117 Berlin
Tel: (030) 28884880 *Fax:* (030) 28884884
E-mail: sinnform@adk.de
Web Site: www.sinn-und-form.de
Key Personnel
Chief Editor: Sebastian Kleinschmidt

Contributions to literature. Articles on literature & humanities.
First published 1949.
Bimonthly.
144 pp, 9 euros
ISSN: 0037-5756

ƒ**Subject Guide to Microforms in Print** (B)
Published by K G Saur Verlag GmbH, A Gale/ Thomson Learning Company
Unit of Thomson Learning
Ortlerstr 8, 81373 Munich
Mailing Address: Postfach 70 16 20, 81316 Munich
Tel: (089) 76902-0 *Fax:* (089) 76902-150
E-mail: info@saur.de
Web Site: www.saur.de
Telex: 5212067
Parent Company: Gale
Ultimate Parent Company: The Thomson Corporation

Der Uebersetzer (The Translator) (J)
Published by Verband Deutschsprachiger Uebersetzer Literarischer und Wissenschaftlicher Werke eV (VDU)
Fuerstrstr 17, 72072 Tuebingen
Tel: (089) 2710994 *Fax:* (089) 2718272
Key Personnel
Editor: Klaus Birkenhauer; Eva Bornemann
Text in German.
First published 1964.
Monthly.

Verlage 2002/2003, Deutschland, Oesterreich, Schweiz und auslaendischer Verlage mit deutschen Auslieferungen (Publishers 2002/2003 Germany, Austria, Switzerland & Foreign Publishers with German Distributions) (B)
Published by Verlag der Schillerbuchhandlung Hans Banger OHG
Guldenbachstr 1, 50935 Cologne
Tel: (0221) 46014-0 *Fax:* (0221) 46014-25
E-mail: banger@banger.de
Web Site: www.banger.de
Key Personnel
Editor: Ruth Jepsen
Available on CD-ROM.
Annually.
1,008 pp
ISBN(s): 3-87856-096-6
ISSN: 1439-0736

Verlagsventretungen 2002/2003, Deutschland, Oesterreich, Schweiz (B)
Published by Verlag der Schillerbuchhandlung Hans Banger OHG
Guldenbachstr 1, 50935 Cologne
Tel: (0221) 46014-0 *Fax:* (0221) 46014-25
E-mail: banger@banger.de
Web Site: www.banger.de
Key Personnel
Editor: Ruth Jepsen
Annually.
448 pp
ISBN(s): 3-87856-098-2
ISSN: 0944-3754

Verzeichnis Lieferbarer Buecher (German Books in Print) (B)
Published by K G Saur Verlag GmbH, A Gale/ Thomson Learning Company
Unit of Thomson Learning
Ortlerstr 8, 81373 Munich
Mailing Address: Postfach 70 16 20, 81316 Munich
Tel: (089) 76902-0 *Fax:* (089) 76902-150
E-mail: info@saur.de
Web Site: www.saur.de
Telex: 5212067

Editor, Buchhaendler-Verinigung, Frankfurt.
Parent Company: Gale
Ultimate Parent Company: The Thomson Corporation

ƒ**Who's Who at the Frankfurt Book Fair** (B)
Published by K G Saur Verlag GmbH, A Gale/ Thomson Learning Company
Unit of Thomson Learning
Ortlerstr 8, 81373 Munich
Mailing Address: Postfach 70 16 20, 81316 Munich
Tel: (089) 76902-0 *Fax:* (089) 76902-150
E-mail: info@saur.de
Web Site: www.saur.de
Telex: 5212067
An international publishers' guide. A listing of publishers at the Frankfurt Book Fair, their addresses & the representatives chosen to attend the fair & their functions.
Parent Company: Gale
Ultimate Parent Company: The Thomson Corporation

Wolfenbuetteler Notizen zur Buchgeschichte (Wolfenbuetteler Notes on the History of Books) (J)
Published by Harrassowitz Verlag
Taunusstr 14, 65183 Wiesbaden
Tel: (0611) 530-0 *Fax:* (0611) 530570; (0611) 530-560 (orders)
E-mail: verlag@harrassowitz.de; service@harrassowitz.de
Web Site: www.harrassowitz.de
Biannually.
ISSN: 0341-2253

Zeitschriften 2002 Deutserland-Oesterreich-Schweiz (German Language Periodical) (B)
Published by Verlag der Schillerbuchhandlung Hans Banger OHG
Guldenbachstr 1, 50935 Cologne
Tel: (0221) 46014-0 *Fax:* (0221) 46014-25
E-mail: banger@banger.de
Web Site: www.banger.de
Key Personnel
Editor: Ruth Jepsen
Available on CD-ROM.
Annually.
1,427 pp
ISBN(s): 3-87856-094-X
ISSN: 1439-0728

Ghana

Asemka (J)
Published by University of Cape Coast
University Post Office, Cape Coast
Tel: (042) 32483; (042) 32480 (ext 220) *Fax:* (042) 32485
E-mail: ucclib@ucc.gn.apc.org
Telex: 2552
Key Personnel
Editor: Y S Boafo
Publishes studies in literature (mostly African) & languages.
First published 1974.
Annually.
10 USD (individuals); 20 USD (institutions)
ISSN: 0855-000X

Ghana National Bibliography (J)
Published by George Padmore Research Library on African Affairs
PO Box 2970, Accra
Tel: (021) 223526
First published 1965.

Biannually with annual cummulation.
60 USD
ISSN: 0855-0993

Greece

Nea Hestia (P)
Published by G C Eleftheroudakis SA
Nikis 4, 10563 Athens
Tel: (01) 3222255 *Fax:* (01) 3239821
Key Personnel
Editor: P Charis
Text in Greek.
First published 1927.
Bimonthly.
324 USD
ISSN: 0028-1735

Guatemala

Alero (Eaves) (P)
Published by Universidad de San Carlos de Guatemala
Ciudad Universitaria, Zona 12, Edificio de Rectoria Of 307, 01012 Guatemala
Tel: (02) 760790 *Fax:* (02) 767221
Text in Spanish.
First published 1973.
Bimonthly.
3.50 GTQ
ISSN: 0252-8711

Guyana

Guyanese National Bibliography (B)
Published by National Library
76-77 Main & Church St, Georgetown
Mailing Address: PO Box 10240, Georgetown
Tel: (02) 227-4053; (02) 226-2690; (02) 226-2699; (02) 227-4052 *Fax:* (02) 227-4053
E-mail: natlib@sdnp.org.gy
Key Personnel
Editor: Karen Sills
Text in English.
First published 1973.
Quarterly.
100 GYD or 30 USD

Hong Kong

PEN News (P)
Published by Hong Kong PEN Centre (Chinese-Speaking)
Mongkok Post Office, Kowloon
Mailing Address: PO Box 78521, Mongkok Post Office, Kowloon
Text in Chinese.

Hungary

⨏**Helikon Irodalomtudomanyi Szemle** (Helikon Review of General & Comparative Literature) (J)
Published by Magyar Tudomanyos Akademia Irodalomtudomanyi Intezete (Institute of Literary Studies of the Hungarian Academy of Sciences)
Menesi ut 11-13, 1118 Budapest
Tel: (01) 1665938
Summaries published in French, Russian & German.

The Hungarian Quarterly (P)
Published by The Hungarian Quarterly Society
Naphegy Tier 8, Budapest 1016
Tel: (01) 3756722 *Fax:* (01) 3188297
E-mail: hungq@hungary.com
Web Site: www.hungarianquarterly.com
Telex: 224371; 225859
Key Personnel
Editor: Miklos Vajda
Text in English.
ISBN(s): 963-7262; 963-7560

Literatura (P)
Published by Akademiai Kiado
Prielle Kornelia u 19/D, 1117 Budapest
Mailing Address: PO Box 245, 1516 Budapest
Tel: (01) 4648282 *Fax:* (01) 464 8251
E-mail: info@akkrt.hu
Web Site: www.akkrt.hu
Telex: 226228 aknyoh
Warehouse: Szentendrei str 89-93, H-1033 Budapest *Tel:* (01) 437-2443
Orders to: Fax: (01) 464 8221 *E-mail:* journals@akkrt.hu

Iceland

Arsskyrsla (B)
Published by Borgarbokasafn
Thingholtsstr 27, 101 Reykjavik
Tel: 5257155 *Fax:* 114643
ISBN(s): 9979-9326

Skirnir: Journal of the Icelandic Literary Society (J)
Published by Hid Islenzka Bokmenntafelag (Icelandic Literary Society)
Sidumula 21, 128 Reykjavik
Mailing Address: PO Box 8935, 128 Reykjavik
Tel: 5889060 *Fax:* 5889095
E-mail: hib@islandia.is
Web Site: www.hib.is
Key Personnel
Editor: Sveinn Yngvi Egilsson; Svavar H Svavarsson
Icelandic cultural studies.
First published 1827.
Biannually.
41 USD
ISSN: 0256-8446

India

⨏**African Books Newsletter** (J)
Published by Intertrade Publications Pvt Ltd
55 Gariahat Rd, Kolkata 700019
Mailing Address: PO Box 10210, Kolkata 700019
Tel: (033) 475-4872; (033) 475-5069
Check list of recent books published in English, arranged according to subject.

⨏**Akavita** (Blank Verse) (P)
Published by Samkaleen Prakashan
2762, Rajguru Marg, Paharganj, New Delhi 110055
Tel: (011) 3523520; (011) 3518197
Text in Hindi.
First published 1976.
Quarterly.
Annual subscription - Inland: Rs 80; Overseas: $24 US (seamail); $32 (airmail)
ISSN: 0970-096X

⨏**Art & Poetry Today** (P)
Published by Samkaleen Prakashan
2762, Rajguru Marg, Paharganj, New Delhi 110055
Tel: (011) 3523520; (011) 3518197
Text in English.
First published 1976.
Quarterly.
Annual subscription - Inland: Rs 80; Overseas: $24 US (seamail); $32 (airmail)
ISSN: 0970-1001

⨏**Asian Books Newsletter** (J)
Published by Intertrade Publications Pvt Ltd
55 Gariahat Rd, Kolkata 700019
Mailing Address: PO Box 10210, Kolkata 700019
Tel: (033) 475-4872; (033) 475-5069
Checklist of recent books published in English, arranged according to subject.

Creative Forum (P)
Published by Bahri Publications
997A/9 Gobindpuri, Kalkaji, New Delhi 110019
Mailing Address: PO Box 4453, Kalkaji, New Delhi 110019
Tel: (011) 6445710; (011) 6448606 *Fax:* (011) 6445710
E-mail: bahrius@vsnl.com
Web Site: bahripublications.org
Key Personnel
Publisher & Editor: Ujjal Singh Bahri
A journal of current literary practices.
First published 1989.
Quarterly.
400 INR or 90 USD (institutions); 300 INR or 60 USD (individuals)

D K Fortnight (J)
Published by D K Publishers' Distributors (P) Ltd
4834/24, Ansari Rd, Darya Ganj, New Delhi 110 002
Tel: (011) 23278368; (011) 23278584; (011) 23279215; (011) 23261465 *Fax:* (011) 23264368
E-mail: info@dkpd.com; order@dkpd.com (orders)
Web Site: www.dkpdindia.com
Telex: 31-66778
Key Personnel
Editor: Praveen Mittal
Lists the new books released during each fortnight in the market by various publishers to reach the information to the target audience as early as possible; also contains an editorial on book industry.

⨏**D K Yearbook** (B)
Published by D K Publishers' Distributors (P) Ltd
4834/24, Ansari Rd, Darya Ganj, New Delhi 110 002
Tel: (011) 23278368; (011) 23278584; (011) 23279215; (011) 23261465 *Fax:* (011) 23264368
E-mail: info@dkpd.com; order@dkpd.com (orders)
Web Site: www.dkpdindia.com
Telex: 31-66778
Key Personnel
Chief Editor: Parmil Mittal
Published in English; covers social sciences, humanities & sciences.
Annually.

Directory of Indian Publishers & Distributors (B)
Published by Indian Bibliographic Centre
GPO Box 1130, Varanasi 221 001
Tel: (0542) 221337 *Fax:* (0542) 221337
E-mail: rishipub@satyam.net.in
Reference book for librarians, publishers, distributors & booksellers.

Indian Author (P)
Published by Authors Guild of India
F-12 Jangpura Ext, New Delhi 110014
Tel: (011) 4315063; (011) 6847950 *Fax:* (011) 3321189
Newsletter.
First published 1976.
Quarterly.
30 INR

Indian Book Industry (J)
Published by Federation of Indian Publishers
18/6 Institutional Area, near JNU, New Delhi 110 067
Tel: (011) 6964847; (011) 6852263 *Fax:* (011) 6864054
The journal is a publication devoted to production, promotion, & distribution of books. There are six issues in a year & every issue has a focus on a particular subject. For example, the issue of April 1995 was a special issue on the National Convention of Indian Language Publishers held from 7-9 April 1995.
Bimonthly.

Indian Books & Foreign Books (B)
Published by Researchco Reprints
25-B/2, New Rohtak Rd, New Delhi 110005
Tel: (011) 5781565 *Fax:* (011) 7276256
Telex: 31-79055 *Cable:* SEARCHBOOK
Annual bibliography of books in English.

Indian Books in Print (J)
Published by Indian Bibliographies Bureau
219 Kadambari, 19 IX Rohini, Delhi 110085
Tel: (011) 7564112; (011) 7553211 *Fax:* (011) 7256502
E-mail: ibb_indian_bibliographies@hotmail.com
Key Personnel
Assistant Manager: Ms Bimla Rawat
Bibliography of Indian books published in English.
First published 1969.
Annually.
21st: 3,400 pp, 250 USD
ISSN: 0971-1589

Indian Horizons (J)
Published by Indian Council for Cultural Relations
Indraprastha Estate, New Delhi 110002
Tel: (011) 3379309 *Fax:* (011) 3778639
E-mail: iccr@vsnl.com
A journal in English on Indian Culture & the arts & of cultural relations past & present between India & the world. Contents include articles, fiction & review.
40 USD
ISBN(s): 0019-7203

Indian Journal of Applied Linguistics (P)
Published by Bahri Publications
997A/9 Gobindpuri, Kalkaji, New Delhi 110019
Mailing Address: PO Box 4453, Kalkaji, New Delhi 110019

Tel: (011) 6445710; (011) 6448606 *Fax:* (011) 6445710
E-mail: bahrius@vsnl.com
Web Site: bahripublications.org
Key Personnel
Editor: Mr Ujjal Singh Bahri
New theoretical & methodologist ideas & research from several disciplines engaged in Applied Linguistics.
Biannually.
160 pp, 400 INR or 90 USD (institutions); 300 INR or 60 USD (individuals)
ISSN: 0379-0037

Indian Literary Review (P)
Published by Indian Literary Review Editions
T-58 D C M School Marg, New Rohtak Rd, New Delhi 110005
Key Personnel
Editor: Devindra Kohli; Suresh Kohli
First published 1978.
Triannually.
60 INR (individuals); 75 INR (institutions)

Indian Literature (P)
Published by National Academy of Letters: Sahitya Akademi
Rabindra Bhavan, 35, Ferozeshah Rd, New Delhi 110001
Tel: (011) 3386626; (011) 3386627; (011) 3386628; (011) 3386629; (011) 3387386; (011) 3386088 *Fax:* (011) 3382428
E-mail: secy@sahitya-akademi.org
Web Site: www.sahitya-akademi.org
Telex: 31; 65445 SAND IN
Text in English.
Bimonthly.

Indian National Bibliography (J)
Published by Central Reference Library
Dept of Culture, Belvedere, Kolkata 700027
Tel: (033) 4791721; (033) 4481529; (033) 4791722 *Fax:* (033) 4791722
E-mail: crlinb@cal3.vsnl.net.in
Web Site: www.crlindia.org
Key Personnel
Contact: K K Kochukoshy
Index Indiana: journal for Indian language periodicals, published quarterly in Roman s cript.
Monthly with annual cumulation.

The Indian PEN (P)
Published by All-India PEN Centre
Theosophy Hall, 40 New Marine Lines, Mumbai 400 020
Tel: (022) 2032175
Key Personnel
Editor: Mr Nissim Ezekiel
Text in English.
First published 1934.
Quarterly.
42 INR or 9 USD
ISSN: 0019-6053

Indian Publishers' Directory (B)
Published by Mukherjee & Co Pvt Ltd
P-27B, CIT Rd, Scheme 52, Kolkata WB 700014
Tel: (033) 341606

International Journal of Communication (P)
Published by Bahri Publications
997A/9 Gobindpuri, Kalkaji, New Delhi 110019
Mailing Address: PO Box 4453, Kalkaji, New Delhi 110019
Tel: (011) 6445710; (011) 6448606 *Fax:* (011) 6445710
E-mail: bahrius@vsnl.com
Web Site: bahripublications.org
Key Personnel
Publisher & Editor: Ujjal Singh Bahri
First published 1990.
Biannually.
240 pp, 400 INR or 90 USD (institutions); 300 INR or 60 USD (individuals)

International Journal of Translation (P)
Published by Bahri Publications
997A/9 Gobindpuri, Kalkaji, New Delhi 110019
Mailing Address: PO Box 4453, Kalkaji, New Delhi 110019
Tel: (011) 6445710; (011) 6448606 *Fax:* (011) 6445710
E-mail: bahrius@vsnl.com
Web Site: bahripublications.org
Key Personnel
Publisher & Editor: Ujjal Singh Bahri
A review of translation studies.
Biannually.
160 pp, 400 INR or 90 USD (institutions); 300 INR or 60 USD (individuals)
ISSN: 0970-9819

Katha-Sahitya (J)
Published by Mitra & Ghosh Publishers Pvt Ltd
10 Shyama Charan Dey St, Kolkata 700073
Tel: (033) 316420
Key Personnel
Contact: Roy Sabitendranath *Tel:* (033) 415 5889; 415 4597
Monthly literary journal. Regular features: editorial, book review, magazine review, news about authors. Special issues: Puja issue, published on the eve of Durga Puja & book fair issue published on the eve of Kolkata Book Fair.
First published 1949.
Monthly.
128 pp, IRS $6.00 per copy. Annual subscriptions IRS $145.00 for India
ISSN: 0971-7137

Lalit Kala (P)
Published by Lalit Kala Akademi
c/o National Academy of Art, Rabindra Bhavan, New Delhi 110001
Tel: (011) 23387241
Web Site: www.lalitkala.org.in
Ancient arts.

Language Forum (P)
Published by Bahri Publications
997A/9 Gobindpuri, Kalkaji, New Delhi 110019
Mailing Address: PO Box 4453, Kalkaji, New Delhi 110019
Tel: (011) 6445710; (011) 6448606 *Fax:* (011) 6445710
E-mail: bahrius@vsnl.com
Web Site: bahripublications.org
Key Personnel
Editor: Mr Ujjal Singh Bahri
Journal of language & literature. Publishes papers on curriculum planning, linguistic analyses of Indian languages & dialects, comparative literature & linguistics & literature in general.
First published 1975.
Biannually.
200 pp, 400 INR or 90 USD (institutions); 300 INR or 60 USD (individuals)
ISSN: 0253-9071

ƒ**Latin American Books Newsletter** (J)
Published by Intertrade Publications Pvt Ltd
55 Gariahat Rd, Kolkata 700019
Mailing Address: PO Box 10210, Kolkata 700019
Tel: (033) 475-4872; (033) 475-5069
Key Personnel
Editor: John A Gillard

Literary Criterion (P)
c/o English Dept, Bangalore University, Jnana Bharathi, Bangalore, Karnataka 560056
Tel: (080) 3215299
Key Personnel
Editor: Prof C D Narasimhaiah; C N Srinath
Text in English.
First published 1952.
Quarterly.
250 INR or 40 USD
ISSN: 0024-452X

Literary Half-Yearly (P)
Published by Literary Press
c/o The Institute of Commonwealth & American Studies & English Language, Literary Press, Anjali 96, 7th Main, Jayalakshmipuram, Mysore, Karnataka 570012
Tel: 513030
Key Personnel
Editor: H H Anniah Gowda
Text in English.
First published 1960.
Biannually.
80 INR; 20 USD
ISSN: 0024-4554

ƒ**Marg** (P)
Published by Marg Publications
Army & Navy Bldg, 3rd floor, 148 Mahatma Gandhi Rd, Fort Mumbai 400001
Tel: (022) 842520; (022) 821151; (022) 045947; (022) 045948; 56657828 *Fax:* (022) 047102
E-mail: margpub@tata.com; margpub@vsnl.com
Web Site: www.marg-art.org
Key Personnel
Business Development Manager: Baptist Sequeira
Administration & Circulation Manager: Asha Shiralikar
Publication on Indian art, culture & related civilizations.
First published 1946.
Quarterly.
140 pp
ISSN: 0972-1444

Miscellany (P)
Published by Writers Workshop
162-92 Lake Gardens, Kolkata 700045
Tel: (033) 4734325; (033) 4732683
Key Personnel
Editor: P Lal
First published 1960.
Bimonthly.
18 USD
ISSN: 0026-5896

MIWA: Major Indian Works Annual (J)
Published by D K Agencies (P) Ltd
Mohan Garden, A/15-17, DK Ave, Najafgarh Rd, New Delhi 110059
Tel: (011) 2535-7104; (011) 2535-7105 *Fax:* (011) 2535-7103; (011) 2564 8053 (orders)
E-mail: information@dkagencies.com
Web Site: www.dkagencies.com
A bibliography of significant English language works from India.
Annually.
ISSN: 0971-4669

ƒ**Pacific Islands Books News Letters** (J)
Published by Intertrade Publications Pvt Ltd
55 Gariahat Rd, Kolkata 700019
Mailing Address: PO Box 10210, Kolkata 700019
Tel: (033) 475-4872; (033) 475-5069

Pustak Parichaya (J)
Published by Indian Publishing House
93 A Lenin Sarani, Kolkata 700013
Tel: (033) 3275267
Text in Hindi.

Recent Indian Books (J)
Published by Federation of Indian Publishers & Booksellers Associations

Federation H S C, 18/1-C Institutional Area,
    Aruna Asif Ali Marg, New Delhi 110067
Key Personnel
Editor: J C Mehta
First published 1975.
Quarterly.

ƒ**Samkaleen Kala Aur Kavita** (Contemporary
    Art & Poetry) (P)
Published by Samkaleen Prakashan
2762, Rajguru Marg, Paharganj, New Delhi
    110055
Tel: (011) 3523520; (011) 3518197
Key Personnel
Editor: Krishan Khullar
Text in Hindi.
First published 1976.
Quarterly.
32 pp
ISBN(s): 81-7083
ISSN: 0970-0986

Samkalin Bharatiya Sahitya (Contemporary
    Indian Literature) (P)
Published by National Academy of Letters:
    Sahitya Akademi
Rabindra Bhavan, 35, Ferozeshah Rd, New Delhi
    110001
Tel: (011) 3386626; (011) 3386627; (011)
    3386628; (011) 3386629; (011) 3386088; (011)
    3387386 *Fax:* (011) 3382428
E-mail: secy@sahitya-akademi.org
Web Site: www.sahitya-akademi.org
Telex: SAHITYAKAR
Creative & critical writings in Hindi & translation
    into Hindi from all the Indian languages.
First published 1980.
Bimonthly.
200 pp, 10 USD or 6 GBP; 50 USD or 30 GBP
    (airmail)
ISSN: 0970-8367
Branch Office(s)
YA-4 Sahvikas, 68 Patparganj, I P Extension,
    Delhi 10092

Samskrit Pratibha (P)
Published by National Academy of Letters:
    Sahitya Akademi
Rabindra Bhavan, 35, Ferozeshah Rd, New Delhi
    110001
Tel: (011) 3386088; (011) 3386626; (011)
    3386627; (011) 3386628; (011) 3386629; (011)
    3387386 *Fax:* (011) 3382428
E-mail: secy@sahitya-akademi.org
Web Site: www.sahitya-akademi.org
Telex: 31; 65445 SAND IN *Cable:*
    SAHITYAKAR
Key Personnel
Chief Editor: Prof S B Raghunathacharya
Journal of creative & critical writing in Sanskrit.
    Also publishes scholarly articles on Sanskrit
    literature of medieval & ancient periods.
First published 1964.
Biennially.

ƒ**Yuva Kavi** (Young Poets) (P)
Published by Samkaleen Prakashan
2762, Rajguru Marg, Paharganj, New Delhi
    110055
Tel: (011) 3523520 *Fax:* (011) 3518197
Text in Hindi.
First published 1976.
Quarterly.
32 pp
ISBN(s): 81-7083
ISSN: 0970-0978

Islamic Republic of Iran

**Bibliography of Customs & Manners in
    Isphahan** (B)
Published by The National Library of Iran
Anahita Alley, Africa St, PO Box 11365/9597,
    19176 Tehran
Mailing Address: Shahid Bahonar St, 19548
    Tehran
Tel: (021) 8881966 *Fax:* (021) 8786859
E-mail: nli@nli.ir
Key Personnel
Senior Research Librarian: Mrs Poori Soltani
    E-mail: poorisoltani@yahoo.com
Author: Ms Nahid Habibi Azad
First, $20

A Bibliography of Mathematics (B)
Published by The National Library of Iran
Anahita Alley, Africa St, PO Box 11365/9597,
    19176 Tehran
Mailing Address: Shahid Bahonar St, 19548
    Tehran
Tel: (021) 8881966 *Fax:* (021) 8786859
E-mail: nli@nli.ir
Web Site: www.nli.ir
Key Personnel
Senior Research Librarian: Mrs Poori Soltani
    E-mail: poorisoltani@yahoo.com
Compiler: M Rahbari
$30

**Bibliography of the Medical Manuscripts in
    Iran** (B)
Published by The National Library of Iran
Anahita Alley, Africa St, PO Box 11365/9597,
    19176 Tehran
Mailing Address: Shahid Bahonar St, 19548
    Tehran
Tel: (021) 8881966 *Fax:* (021) 8786859
E-mail: nli@nli.ir
Web Site: www.nli.ir
Key Personnel
Senior Research Librarian: Mrs Poori Soltani
    E-mail: poorisoltani@yahoo.com
First published 1992.
1st: 325 pp, 36001 IRR

**Catalogue de Precieux Ouvrages Scientifiques
    Francais de la Bibliotheque National de la
    Republique Islamique d'Iran** (Catalog of
    Valuable French Works in the National Library
    of Iran) (B)
Published by The National Library of Iran
Anahita Alley, Africa St, PO Box 11365/9597,
    19176 Tehran
Mailing Address: Shahid Bahonar St, 19548
    Tehran
Tel: (021) 8881966 *Fax:* (021) 8786859
E-mail: nli@nli.ir
Web Site: www.nli.ir
Key Personnel
Senior Research Librarian: Mrs Poori Soltani
    E-mail: poorisoltani@yahoo.com
Compiler: Ms Shohreh Taravatil
First published 1993.
$25

**Catalogue of Newspapers in the National
    Library of Iran** (Directory of Iranian
    Newspapers) (B)
Published by The National Library of Iran
Anahita Alley, Africa St, PO Box 11365/9597,
    19176 Tehran
Mailing Address: Shahid Bahonar St, 19548
    Tehran
Tel: (021) 8881966 *Fax:* (021) 8786859
E-mail: nli@nli.ir
Web Site: www.nli.ir
First published 1977.
1st: 3,341 pp

**Class PQ: French Literature, Individual
    Authors 18, 19, 20th Centuries: Based on the
    Library of Congress Classification** (B)
Published by The National Library of Iran
Anahita Alley, Africa St, PO Box 11365/9597,
    19176 Tehran
Mailing Address: Shahid Bahonar St, 19548
    Tehran
Tel: (021) 8881966 *Fax:* (021) 2288680
E-mail: nli@nli.ir
Web Site: www.nli.ir
Key Personnel
Senior Research Librarian: Mrs Poori Soltani
    E-mail: poorisoltani@yahoo.com
First published 1994.
1st: 185 pp, $25

**Directory of Documentation Centres, Special
    Libraries & University Libraries of Iran,
    2nd Edition** (B)
Published by The National Library of Iran
Anahita Alley, Africa St, PO Box 11365/9597,
    19176 Tehran
Mailing Address: Sh Bahonar Str, 19548 Tehran
Tel: (021) 8881966 *Fax:* (021) 8786859
E-mail: nli@nli.ir

**A Directory of Iranian Periodicals &
    Newspapers** (B)
Published by The National Library of Iran
Anahita Alley, Africa St, PO Box 11365/9597,
    19176 Tehran
Mailing Address: Shahid Bahonar St, 19548
    Tehran
Tel: (021) 8881966 *Fax:* (021) 8786859
E-mail: nli@nli.ir
Web Site: www.nli.ir
Key Personnel
Senior Research Librarian: Mrs Poori Soltani
    E-mail: poorisoltani@yahoo.com
First published 1994.
Annually.
50 USD
ISBN(s): 964-446-040-5
ISSN: 1028-7035

The Iranian National Bibliography (P)
Published by The National Library of Iran
Anahita Alley, Africa St, PO Box 11365/9597,
    19176 Tehran
Mailing Address: Shahid Bahonar St, 19548
    Tehran
Tel: (021) 8881966 *Fax:* (021) 2288680
E-mail: nli@nli.ir
Web Site: www.nli.ir
Key Personnel
Senior Research Librarian: Mrs Poori Soltani
    E-mail: poorisoltani@yahoo.com
First published 1963.
Biannually.
ISSN: 0075-0522

Pahlavi Text: Transcript, Translation (B)
Published by The National Library of Iran
Anahita Alley, Africa St, PO Box 11365/9597,
    19176 Tehran
Mailing Address: Sh Bahonar Str, 19548 Tehran
Tel: (021) 8881966 *Fax:* (021) 2288680
E-mail: nli@nli.ir
Key Personnel
Senior Research Librarian: Mrs Poori Soltani
    E-mail: poorisoltani@yahoo.com

First published 1992.
1st edition: 563 pp

Political Life of Imam Khomeini (B)
Published by The National Library of Iran
Anahita Alley, Africa St, PO Box 11365/9597, 19176 Tehran
Mailing Address: Shahid Bahonar St, 19548 Tehran
Tel: (021) 8881966 *Fax:* (021) 8786859
E-mail: nli@nli.ir

Rules & Standards for Publishing Books (B)
Published by The National Library of Iran
Anahita Alley, Africa St, PO Box 11365/9597, 19176 Tehran
Mailing Address: Shahid Bahonar St, 19548 Tehran
Tel: (021) 8881966 *Fax:* (021) 8786859
E-mail: nli@nli.ir
Key Personnel
Senior Research Librarian: Mrs Poori Soltani
E-mail: poorisoltani@yahoo.com
2nd (1988): 42 pp, $10

Ruznameye Dowlat-e Alliyah Iran (B)
Published by The National Library of Iran
Anahita Alley, Africa St, PO Box 11365/9597, 19176 Tehran
Mailing Address: Shahid Bahonar St, 19548 Tehran
Tel: (021) 8881966 *Fax:* (021) 2288680
E-mail: nli@nli.ir
Web Site: www.nli.ir
This is a reprint of an old newspaper.
1st, $50

Iraq

Iraqi National Bibliography (J)
Published by National Library
Bab-el-Muaddum, Baghdad
Tel: (01) 4164190
Triannually.

Ireland

Books Ireland (J)
Published by Jeremy Addis
11 Newgrove Ave, Dublin 4
Tel: (01) 2692185 *Fax:* (01) 2604927
E-mail: booksi@eircom.net
The trade journal & review medium of the Irish publishing industry.
First published 1976.
9 times/yr.
3 EUR
ISSN: 0376-6039

Comhar (Cooperation) (P)
5 Rae Mhuirfean, Baile Atha Cliath 2
Tel: (01) 678 5443 *Fax:* (01) 678 5443
E-mail: eolas@comhar-iris.ie
Web Site: www.comhar-iris.ie
Text in Irish, covering current affairs, the arts & literature.
Monthly.

Journal of the Irish Colleges of Physicians & Surgeons (J)
Published by Irish Colleges of Physicians & Surgeons
The Mercer Library, Mercer St Lower, Dublin 2
Tel: (01) 402 2196 *Fax:* (01) 402 2457
E-mail: jicps@rcsi.ie
Web Site: www.rcsi.ie
Quarterly.

Israel

Ariel: The Israel Review of Arts & Letters (P)
Published by The Israel Foreign Ministry
9 Yitzhak Rabin Blvd, Kiryat Ben-Gurion, 91035 Jerusalem
Tel: (02) 530 3111 *Fax:* (02) 530 3367
E-mail: ask@israel-info.gov.il
Web Site: www.mfa.gov.il
Key Personnel
Editor: Asher Weill
Published in six separate language editions - English, French, German, Spanish, Russian & Arabic - with occasional issues in other languages (i.e., Chinese & Japanese).
First published 1962.
Quarterly.
96 pp
ISSN: 0004-1343

Israel Book Trade Directory (B)
Published by Weill Publishers
PO Box 7705, Jerusalem 91076
Tel: (02) 6432147 *Fax:* (02) 6437502
E-mail: debasher@netvision.net.il
Biennially.

Jerusalem Report (P)
PO Box 1805, Jerusalem 91017
Tel: (02) 531-5440 *Fax:* (02) 537-9489; (02) 531-5425 (advertising)
E-mail: jrep@jreport.co.il (editorial); jsubs@jrport.co.il (subscriptions)
Web Site: www.jrep.com
Key Personnel
Editor: Hirsh Goodman

Kiryat Sefer (P)
Published by Jewish National & University Library
Edmond J Safra Campus, 91341 Jerusalem
Mailing Address: PO Box 34165, 91341 Jerusalem
Tel: (02) 6585019 *Fax:* (02) 6511771
E-mail: jnl@savion.huji.ac.il
Web Site: jnul.huji.ac.il/rambi
Telex: 25307
Database which catalogs documents acquired by the Library, including bibliographic descriptions for books, dissertations, periodicals & non-printed publications.
National bibliography of the State of Israel & the Jewish people.
First published 1925.

Modern Hebrew Literature (P)
Published by The Institute for the Translation of Hebrew Literature
23 Baruch Hirsch St, Bnei Brak
Mailing Address: PO Box 1005 1, 52001 Ramat Gan
Tel: (03) 579 6830 *Fax:* (03) 579 6832
E-mail: hamachon@inter.net.il
Web Site: www.ithl.org.il
Telex: 341118 BXTV IL ext 1272 *Cable:* TARGUM TELAVIV
Key Personnel
Man Dir: Mrs Nilli Cohen
English-language journal of contemporary Hebrew literature.
Biennially.

Italy

Andersen-Il Mondo dell'Infanzia (Andersen-The Newspaper of Books for Boys) (J)
Published by Feguagiskia' Studios
via Crosa di Vergagni 3, R16124 Genova
Tel: (010) 2510829; (010) 2757544 *Fax:* (010) 2510838
E-mail: info@andersen.it
Web Site: www.andersen.it
Text in Italian. Contains articles on CYL, teaching, theatre & film as well as literary competitions. Includes reviews & news.

Belfagor (P)
Published by Casa Editrice Leo S Olschki
Viuzzo del Pozzetto, 50126 Florence
Tel: (055) 6530684 *Fax:* (055) 6530214
E-mail: celso@olschki.it
Web Site: www.olschki.it
Key Personnel
Publisher: Leo S Olschki
Review of literature & information.
First published 1946.
6x/yr.
128 pp
ISSN: 0005-8351

La Bibliofilia (P)
Published by Casa Editrice Leo S Olschki
Viuzzo del Pozzetto, 50126 Florence
Tel: (055) 6530684 *Fax:* (055) 6530214
E-mail: celso@olschki.it
Web Site: www.olschki.it
Key Personnel
Publisher: Leo S Olschki
Text in English, French, German & Italian. Bibliophily, History of Printing.
First published 1899.
Triannually.
110 pp
ISSN: 0006-0941

Bibliografia Nazionale Italiana (Italian National Bibliography) (J)
Published by Central Institute of the Union Catalog of Italian Libraries & Bibliographical Information
Piazza dei Cavalleggeri, 1, 50122 Florence
Tel: (055) 24919 1 *Fax:* (055) 2342 482
E-mail: info@itcaspur.caspur.it
Web Site: www.bncf.firenze.sbn.it

Catalogo dei Libri in Commercio (Catalog of Books in Print) (B)
Published by Editrice Bibliografica SpA
Via Bergonzoli, 1/5, 20127 Milan
Tel: (02) 28315996 *Fax:* (02) 28315906
E-mail: bibliografica@bibliografica.it
Web Site: www.alice.it/eb
Sponsored by Associazone Italiana Editori, listing 325,000 Italian titles.
ISBN(s): 88-7075-552-5

Catalogo del Periodici Italiani (Catalogue of Italian Periodicals) (B)
Published by Editrice Bibliografica SpA
Via Bergonzoli, 1/5, 20127 Milan
Tel: (02) 28315996 *Fax:* (02) 28315906
E-mail: bibliografica@bibliografica.it
Web Site: www.alice.it/eb
ISBN(s): 88-7075-558-4

Cenobio (P)
Published by Ignazio Bonoli, Flavio Catenazzi, Franco Lanza, Carlo Monti, Marcello Ostinelli
via Streccia 4, 6943 Vezia

ITALY

Mailing Address: PO Box 174, 6903 Lugano 3, Switzerland
Tel: (091) 966 85 08 *Fax:* (091) 966 51 56
Web Site: www.culturactif.ch/revues/cenobio.htm
Cable: CH-6943 VEZIA
Key Personnel
Editor: Ignazio Bonoli; Flavio Catenazzi; Marcello Ostinelli; Manuel Rossello
Text in French & Italian.

Giornale della Libreria (Book Trade Journal) (J)
Published by Editrice Bibliografica SpA
Via Bergonzoli, 1/5, 20127 Milan
Tel: (02) 28315996 *Fax:* (02) 28315906
E-mail: bibliografica@bibliografica.it
Web Site: www.alice.it/eb
Monthly.
102.30 EUR

Giornale Storico della Letteratura Italiana (Historical Journal of Italian Literature) (P)
Published by Loescher Editore SRL
Via Vittorio Amedeo II, 18, 10121 Turin
Tel: (011) 5654111 *Fax:* (011) 56 25822
E-mail: mail@loescher.it
Web Site: www.loescher.it

Gli Editori Italiani (The Italian Publishers) (B)
Published by Editrice Bibliografica SpA
Via Bergonzoli, 1/5, 20127 Milan
Tel: (02) 28315996 *Fax:* (02) 28315906
E-mail: bibliografica@bibliografica.it
Web Site: www.alice.it/eb
3,200 Italian publisher listings.

Lettere Italiane (P)
Published by Casa Editrice Leo S Olschki
Viuzzo del Pozzetto, 50126 Florence
Tel: (055) 6530684 *Fax:* (055) 6530214
E-mail: celso@olschki.it
Web Site: www.olschki.it
History of Italian Literature.
First published 1949.
Quarterly.
170 pp
ISSN: 0024-1334

Letture: Mensile di Informazione Culturale, Letteratura e Spettacolo (P)
Published by Periodici San Paolo srl
Via Giotto 36, 20145 Milan
Tel: (02) 48071 *Fax:* (02) 48072568
E-mail: letture@stpauls.it
Web Site: www.stpauls.it/letture
Key Personnel
Dir: Antonio Rizzolo *Tel:* (02) 48072518
   Fax: (02) 48072515
First published 1946.
ISSN: 0024-144X

Libri e Riviste d'Italia (Italian Books & Periodicals) (J)
Published by Instituto Poligrafico Dello Stato SpA
Piazza Verdi 10, 00198 Rome
Tel: (06) 85081 *Fax:* (06) 85082517
E-mail: gestionegu@ipzs.it
Web Site: www.ipzs.it
Available in Italian editions & international editions in English, French, German & Spanish.
Biannually.

Nuova Corrente (New Current) (J)
Published by Tilgher-Genova sas
Via Assarotti 31/15, 16122 Genova
Tel: (010) 8391140 *Fax:* (010) 870653
E-mail: tilgher@tilgher.it
Web Site: www.tilgher.it
Key Personnel
Editor: Tiziana Arvigo; Pierfrancesco Fiorato; Santino Mele; Luigi Surdich; Enrico Tacchella; Stefano Verdino; Luisa Villa
Literary/philosophical topics. Text in Italian, but occasional issues in French & English.
First published 1954.
Biennially.

Paideia (P)
Published by Carlo Cordie-Giuseppe Scarpat
Via Manzoni 20, 25020 Flero
Tel: (030) 3582434 *Fax:* (030) 3582691
E-mail: paideiaeditrice@tin.it
Key Personnel
Dir: Giuseppe Scarpat
Literary review with bibliographical information; text in English, French, German & Italian.
First published 1946.

La Rassegna della Letteratura Italiana (Italian Literature Review) (P)
Published by Casa Editrice le Lettere
Costa San Giorgio 28, 50125 Florence
Tel: (055) 2342710; (055) 2476319 *Fax:* (055) 2346010
E-mail: staff@lelettere.it
Web Site: www.lelettere.it
Key Personnel
Dir: E Ghidetti
First published 1883.
ISSN: 0033-9423

Rivista di Letteratura Moderne e Comparate (Review of Modern & Comparative Literature) (P)
Published by Pacini Editore Srl
Via Gherardesca, 56121 Ospedaletto, Pisa
Tel: (050) 313011 *Fax:* (050) 3130300
E-mail: pacini.editore@pacinieditore.it
Web Site: www.pacinieditore.it
Text in English, French & Italian.
First published 1946.
4 times/yr.
21 euros (one issue); 57 euros (Italy-4 issues); 77 euros (abroad-4 issues)

Uomini e Libri (Men and Books) (P)
Published by Edizioni Effe Emme
Viale E Caldara 8, 20122 Milan

Jamaica

Book Production in Jamaica: A Select List of Jamaican Publications (B)
Published by Jamaica Library Service
2 Tom Redcam Dr, Cross Roads, Kingston 5
Mailing Address: PO Box 58, Kingston 5
Tel: (876) 926-3310 *Fax:* (876) 926-2188
E-mail: jamlibs@cwjamaica.com
Web Site: www.jamlib.org.jm

∮**Caribbean Quarterly** (J)
Published by Cultural Studies Initiative, Vice Chancellery
University of the West Indies, Mona, Kingston 7
Tel: (876) 977 1689 *Fax:* (876) 977 6105
Key Personnel
Managing Editor: Dr Veronica Salter
   E-mail: vsalter@uwimona.edu.jm
Editor: Rex Nettleford
First published 1949.
Quarterly.
120 pp
ISSN: 0008-6495

Jamaican National Bibliography (J)
Published by National Library of Jamaica
12 East St, Kingston
Tel: (876) 967-1526; (876) 967-2516; (876) 967-2496 *Fax:* (876) 922-5567
E-mail: nlj@infochan.com
Web Site: www.nlj.org.jm *Cable:* NALIBJAM
Key Personnel
Editor: Byron Palmer *Tel:* (876) 967-2494
Lists all material published in Jamaica, works by Jamaicans published outside of the country, as well as works about Jamaica.

Japan

Asian/Pacific Book Development (ABD) (J)
Published by Asia/Pacific Cultural Centre for UNESCO (ACCU)
Japan Publishers Bldg, 6 Fukuromachi, Shinjuku-ku, Tokyo 162-8484
Tel: (03) 3269-4435 *Fax:* (03) 3269-4510
E-mail: general@accu.or.jp
Web Site: www.accu.or.jp *Cable:* ASCULCENTRE
Key Personnel
Editor-in-Chief: Shigeo Miyamoto
Provides information, news items relating to books, publishing & promotional activities in Asia & the Pacific contributed by 25 national correspondents.
First published 1969.
Quarterly.

Biblia (J)
Published by Tenri University Press
Tenri Central Library, Tenri-SHI Nara 632-8577
Tel: (0743) 631515 *Fax:* (0743) 637728
E-mail: info@tcl.gr.jp
Web Site: www.tcl.gr.jp
Text in Japanese.
ISSN: 0006-0860

Bulletin of Japan Book Publishers Association (J)
Published by Japan Book Publishers Association
6 Fukuro-machi, Shinjuku-ku 162-0828
Tel: (03) 3268-1303 *Fax:* (03) 3268-1196
E-mail: rd@jbpa.or.jp
Web Site: www.jbpa.or.jp
Monthly.

The Catalog of Books in the Near Future (Korekara deru Hon) (P)
Published by Japan Book Publishers Association
6 Fukuro-machi, Shinjuku-ku, Tokyo 162-0828
Tel: (03) 3268-1303 *Fax:* (03) 3268-1196
E-mail: rd@jbpa.or.jp
Web Site: www.jbpa.or.jp
Bimonthly.

A Comprehensive Bibliography of Japanese Periodicals (P)
Published by The Shuppan News Co Ltd
3-2-4 Misaki-cho 3 chome, Chiyoda-ku, Tokyo 101
Tel: (03) 32622076

A Comprehensive Catalog of Collected Works, Publishers in Japan (J)
Published by The Shuppan News Co Ltd
3-2-4 Misaki-cho 3 chome, Chiyoda-ku, Tokyo 101
Tel: (03) 32622076

Directory of Japanese Publishing Industry (J)
Published by Publishers' Association for Cultural Exchange, PACE, Japan
1-2-1, Sarugaku-cho, Chiyoda-ku, Tokyo 101-0064
Tel: (03) 3291-5685 *Fax:* (03) 3233-3645

Web Site: www.pace.or.jp
Statistics of the Japanese publishing world.
Free

Doitsu Bungaku (P)
Published by Nippon Dokubungakkai
c/o Ikubundo, Hongo 5-30-21, Bunkyo-ku, Tokyo 113-0033
Key Personnel
President: Prof Takao Tsunekawa
German Literature.
First published 1947.
ISSN: 0419-5825

Doshisha Literature (J)
Published by Doshisha University, English Literary Society
Karasuma-Higashi-iru, Imadegawa-dori, Kamigyo-ku, Kyoto 602-8580
Tel: (075) 251 3260 *Fax:* (075) 251 3057
E-mail: ji-kksai@mail.doshisha.ac.jpkkitao@mail.doshisha.ac.jp
Web Site: www.doshisha.ac.jp/english
Journal of English literature & philology; text in English.

An Introduction to Publishing in Japan (B)
Published by Japan Book Publishers Association
6 Fukuro-machi, Shinjuku-ku, Tokyo 162-0828
Tel: (03) 3268-1303 *Fax:* (03) 3268-1196
Web Site: www.jbpa.or.jp *Cable:* SHOSEKIKYO TOKOYO 1

Japan Directory of Professional Associations (B)
Published by Intercontinental Marketing Corp
Centre Bldg, 2nd floor, 1-14-13 Taitoku, Tokyo 110-0013
Mailing Address: IPO Box 5056, Tokyo 100-3191
Tel: (03) 3876-3073 *Fax:* (03) 3876-3627
E-mail: imcbook@attglobal.net; kunikoi@attglobal.net
Web Site: jpgsonline.com; imcbook.net
Key Personnel
Editor: Warren E Ball
Lists important associations, societies & institutions, many of which are significant publishers or otherwise valuable information sources.
Annually.
ISBN(s): 4-900178-16-0

Japan English Publications in Print (B)
Published by Intercontinental Marketing Corp
Centre Bldg, 2nd floor, 1-14-13 Taitoku, Tokyo 110-0013
Mailing Address: IPO Box 5056, Tokyo 100-3191
Tel: (03) 3876-3073 *Fax:* (03) 3876-3627
E-mail: imcbook@attglobal.net; kunikoi@attglobal.net
Web Site: jpgsonline.com; imcbook.net
Key Personnel
Editor: Warren E Ball
English journals, books, directories & other publications, published in Japan.
Annually.
ISBN(s): 4-900178-15-2

Japanese Books in Print (B)
Published by Japan Book Publishers Association
6 Fukuro-machi, Shinjuku-ku, Tokyo 162-0828
Tel: (03) 3268-1303 *Fax:* (03) 3268-1196
E-mail: rd@jbpa.or.jp
Web Site: www.jbpa.or.jp

Japanese Literature Today (P)
Published by Japanese PEN Centre
Akasaka Residential Hotel-265, 9-1-7 Akasaka, Minato-ku, Tokyo 107-0052
Tel: (03) 3402-1171 *Fax:* (03) 3402-5951
E-mail: penclub@asahi-net.email.ne.jp; japan-pen@asahi-net.email.ne.jp
Web Site: www.jinjapan.org; www.mmjp.or.jp/japan-penclub
Annually.

Japanese Publications News and Reviews (J)
Published by Shuppan News Co Ltd
3-2-4 Masaki-cho 3 Chome, Chiyoda-ku, Tokyo 101
Tel: (03) 32622076

JPG Letter (J)
Published by Intercontinental Marketing Corp
Centre Bldg, 2nd floor, 1-14-13 Taitoku, Tokyo 110-0013
Mailing Address: IPO Box 5056, Tokyo 100-3191
Tel: (03) 3876-3073 *Fax:* (03) 3876-3627
E-mail: imcbook@attglobal.net; kunikoi@attglobal.net
Web Site: jpgsonline.com; imcbook.net
Key Personnel
Editor: Warren E Ball
Newsletter containing information on new English publications (periodicals & books) that are published in Japan & other southeast & east Asian countries.
Monthly.

Practical Guide to Publishing in Japan (B)
Published by Publishers' Association for Cultural Exchange, PACE, Japan
1-2-1, Sarugaku-cho, Chiyoda-ku, Tokyo 101-0064
Tel: (03) 3291-5685 *Fax:* (03) 3233-3645
Web Site: www.pace.or.jp

Shinkan News (J)
Published by Tohan Corporation
6-24 Higashigoken-cho, Shinjuku-ku, Tokyo 162-8710
Tel: (03) 3269-6111 *Fax:* (03) 3235-1337

Shuppan Nenkan (J)
Published by Shuppan News Co Ltd
3-2-4 Masaki-cho 3 Chome, Chiyoda-ku, Tokyo 101
Tel: (03) 32622076
Information on publishing for the previous year.
Annually.

Shuppan Nyusu (J)
Published by Shuppan News Co Ltd
3-2-4 Masaki-cho 3 Chome, Chiyoda-ku, Tokyo 101
Tel: (03) 32622076
Publishers' News.
Three times a month.

Studies in English Literature (P)
Published by Nihon Eibungakkai (English Literary Society of Japan)
501 Kenkyusha Bldg, 9 Surugadai 2-chome, Kanda, Chiyoda-ku, Tokyo 101-0062
Tel: (03) 32937528 *Fax:* (03) 32937539
Published annually in Japanese & English.

Umi (P)
Published by Chuokoron-Shinsha Inc
2-8-7 Kyobashi, Chuo-ku, Tokyo 104
Tel: (03) 3563-3666 *Fax:* (03) 3561-5920

Jordan

Palestinian Bibliography: A List of Books Published by the Arabs in Palestine 1948-1980 (B)
Published by Jordan Library Association
PO Box 6289, Amman
Tel: (06) 462 9412 *Fax:* (06) 462 9412

Palestinian-Jordanian Bibliography (B)
Published by Jordan Library Association
PO Box 6289, Amman
Tel: (06) 462 9412 *Fax:* (06) 462 9412

Kazakstan

Prostor (The Expose) (P)
Published by Kazakh Writers' Union
Dr Albai Khana, 105, 480091 Almaty
Tel: (3272) 696319 *Fax:* (3272) 691058
Web Site: prostor.samal.kz
Literary, artistic, socio-political magazine.
Monthly.

Kenya

African Journal of Health Sciences (J)
Published by African Forum for Health Sciences
PO Box 54840, Nairobi
Tel: (02) 722541 *Fax:* (02) 720030
E-mail: afhes@nairobi.mimcom.net; kemri-hq@nairobi.mimcom.net
Web Site: www.kemri.org
Key Personnel
Editor-in-Chief: Dr Davy Koech
First published 1994.
ISSN: 1022-9272

African Urban Quarterly (J)
Published by African Urban Quarterly Ltd, Centre for Urban Research
Private Bag 51366, Nairobi
Tel: (02) 216574 *Fax:* (02) 444110
International & interdisciplinary journal that covers all aspects of urbanization & regional planning from the most theoretical to the most imperical. AUQ serves as a central clearing house for research with analytical, descriptive, evaluative, & prescriptive problems concerned with comparative urbanization & regional planning in Africa with the rest of the world. Topics covered include agriculture, demography, transportation, medicine, politics, geography, history, sociology, economics, mathematics, urbanization, anthropology, archeology, education, law & environmental studies as they affect the quality of human life in both rural as well as in urban areas.
Quarterly.
130 USD
ISSN: 0747-6108

Kenya National Bibliography (B)
Published by Kenya National Library Service
PO Box 30573, Nairobi
Tel: (02) 725550; (02) 725551; (02) 718177; (02) 718012; (02) 718013 *Fax:* (02) 721749
E-mail: knls@nbnet.co.ke
Web Site: www.knls.or.ke
Key Personnel
Dir: S K Ng'anga

Republic of Korea

Books from Korea (B)
Published by Korean Publishers Association
105-2 Sagan-Dong, Chongno-Gu, Seoul 110-190
Tel: (02) 735-2701 *Fax:* (02) 738-5414
E-mail: kpa@kpa21.or.kr; kpasibf@soback.kornet.nm.kr
Web Site: www.kpa21.or.kr
Key Personnel
Secretary General: Jong Jin Jung
Text in English.
First published 1971.
Annually.

Catalog of Government Publications (B)
Published by National Assembly Library
Yoido-dong 1, Youngdeungpo-gu, Seoul 150-703
Tel: (02) 788-4143 (English assistance); (02) 788-3961 *Fax:* (02) 7884193
E-mail: question@nanet.go.kr
Web Site: www.nanet.go.kr
Telex: 25849
Includes University Publications.

Korean National Bibliography (J)
Published by The National Library of Korea
San 60-1, Banpo-dong, Seocho-gu, Seoul 137-702
Tel: (02) 590-0517 *Fax:* (02) 590-0530
E-mail: nlkpc@sun.nl.or.kr
Web Site: www.nl.go.kr
Annually.

Korean Publication Yearbook (B)
Published by Korean Publishers Association
105-2 Sagan-Dong, Chongno-Gu, Seoul 110-190
Tel: (02) 735-2701 *Fax:* (02) 738-5414
E-mail: kpa@kpa21.or.kr; kpasibf@soback.kornet.nm.kr
Web Site: www.kpa21.or.kr
Key Personnel
Secretary General: Jong Jin Jung
Text in Korean.
Annually.

Korean Publishers Directory (B)
Published by Korean Publishers Association
105-2 Sagan-Dong, Chongno-Gu, Seoul 110-190
Tel: (02) 735-2701 *Fax:* (02) 738-5414
E-mail: kpa@kpa21.or.kr
Web Site: www.kpa21.or.kr
Key Personnel
Secretary General: Jong Jin Jung
Published annually; text in English.

KPA Journal (J)
Published by Korean Publishers Association
105-2 Sagan-Dong, Chongno-Gu, Seoul 110-190
Tel: (02) 735-2701 *Fax:* (02) 738-5414
E-mail: kpa@kpa21.or.kr
Web Site: www.kpa21.or.kr
Key Personnel
Secretary General: Jong Jin Jung
Published monthly, in Korean.

Latvia

Daugava (P)
Published by Daugava Ltd
Balasta dambis 3, Riga LV-1081
Tel: 7280290
E-mail: ravdin@mailbox.riga.lv
Literary magazine.

Bimonthly.
ISSN: 0207-4001

Luxembourg

Bibliographie Luxembourgeoise (Luxembourg Bibliography) (J)
Published by Bibliotheque Nationale du Grand-Duche de Luxembourg
37 blvd F D Roosevelt, 2450 Luxembourg
Tel: 22 97 55-1 *Fax:* 47 56 72
E-mail: bib.nat@bi.etat.lu
Web Site: www.bibnatlux.etat.lu

Kritikon Litterarum (P)
Published by Thesen Verlag Vowinckel
3 pl de la Gare, 6674 Mertert
Tel: 748715 *Fax:* 26740429
First published 1972.
Biannually.
173 euros/vol
ISSN: 0340-9767

The Former Yugoslav Republic of Macedonia

Macedonian Review (P)
Published by Macedonian Scientific Institute
5 Pirotska Str, Sofia 1301
Tel: (02) 878 708
E-mail: mni@olb.net
Web Site: www.macedoniainfo.com
Cultural Life.
Quarterly.

Razgledi (P)
Ul Ivo Ribar-Lola 66, 91000 Skopje
Mailing Address: PO Box 345, 91000 Skopje
Review of literature, art & culture; text in Macedonian.
First published 1958.
Monthly.

Stremez (P)
Published by Interesna Zaednica na Kulturata Pri Lep
Joska Jordanoski 2, 97500 Prilep
Tel: 27308; 21703 *Fax:* 21703
Journal for literature & culture; text in Macedonian.
First published 1957.
10 times/yr.
ISSN: 0039-2294

Madagascar

Bibliographie annuelle de Madagascar (Madagascar Annual Bibliography) (B)
Published by Bibliotheque Universitarie, Campus Universitaire
Universite de Madagascar, Bibliotheque Universitaire, BP 908, Tananrive
Tel: (02) 23228
E-mail: buunivtanamg@minitel.refer.org
Annual.
ISSN: 0067-6926

Bibliographie Nationale de Madagascar (Madagascar National Bibliography) (B)
Published by Bibliotheque Nationale (Sous la Direction de Ralaisaholimanana Louis)
Bibliotheque Nationale, BP 257, Anosy, Tananrive
Tel: (02) 258 72 *Fax:* (02) 29448

Malaysia

Bibliografi Negara Malaysia (Malaysian National Bibliography) (J)
Published by Perpustakaan Negara Malaysia, Technical Services Div
232, Jalan Tun Razak, 50572 Kuala Lumpur
Tel: (03) 26943488; (03) 26943234; (03) 26871700 *Fax:* (03) 26942490
E-mail: pnmweb@www1.pnm.my
Web Site: www.pnm.my
Telex: 30092
Key Personnel
Editor: Nafisah Ahmad
40 MYR or 50 USD
ISSN: 0126-5210

Malay Literature (P)
Published by Dewan Bahasa dan Pustaka
Peti Surat 10803, 50926 Kuala Lumpur
Tel: (03) 21481011; (03) 21447269 *Fax:* (03) 2482726
Web Site: www.dbp.gov.my
Key Personnel
Head, Comparative Literature Dept: Mrs Zalila Shariff *E-mail:* zalila@dbp.gov.my
National Language & Literary Agency of Malaysia.
First published 1967.
June & Dec.
RM 10.00
ISSN: 0128-1186

ƒ**Southeast Asian Archives** (J)
Published by Southeast Asian Regional Branch of the International Council on Archives (SARBICA)
c/o National Archives of Malaysia, Jalan Duta, 50568 Kuala Lumpur
Tel: (03) 62010688 *Fax:* (03) 62015679
E-mail: query@arkib.gov.my
Web Site: www.arkib.gov.my

Malta

Malta National Bibliography (B)
Published by Malta National Library
36 Old Treasury St, Valletta CMR 02
Tel: 22 43 38 *Fax:* 23 59 92
Key Personnel
Contact: M Mallia
Annually.

Mauritius

Memorandum of Books Printed in Mauritius & Registered in the Archives (J)
Published by Mauritius Archives
Development Bank of Mauritius Complex, Petite Riviere
Tel: 233-7341; 233-4469 *Fax:* 233-4299
Key Personnel
Deputy Chief Archivist: Mr Gheeandut Suneechur
Acting Chief Archives Officer: Pierre Roland Chung Sam Wan
First published 1894.
Quarterly.

Mexico

Bibliografia Mexicana (Mexican Bibliography) (B)
Published by Biblioteca Nacional de Mexico
Centro Cultural Universitario, CU, Delegacion Coyoacan, 04510 Mexico, DF
Tel: (055) 5622-6818 *Fax:* (055) 5665-0951
E-mail: libros@biblional.bibliog.unam.mx
Web Site: biblional.bibliog.unam.mx
Key Personnel
Contact: Roxana L Mejia Murillo

Boletin Bibliografico Mexicano (Mexican Bibliographical Bulletin) (J)
Published by Libreria de Porrua Hermanos y Cia, SA
Av Republica De Argentina No 15, Col Centro, 06020 Mexico, DF
Tel: (05) 7024574 *Fax:* (05) 7026529; (05) 702-43-15
Web Site: www.porrua.com *Cable:* PORRAUS MEXICO
Key Personnel
Ed: Jose Antonio Perez Porrua
Monthly.

Boletin del Instituto de Investigaciones Bibliograficas (Bulletin of the Institute of Bibliographic Research) (J)
Published by Instituto de Investigaciones Bibliograficas (Institute of Bibliographic Research)
Hemeroteca Nacional de Mexico, Centro Cultural Universitario, 04510 Mexico, DF
Tel: (055) 5622-6818 *Fax:* (055) 5622-6869; (055) 5665-0951
E-mail: hemerote@biblional.bibliog.unam.mx
Web Site: biblional.bibliog.unam.mx
Book review & historic articles on Mexico & Latin America.

Como Comprar Libros y Publicaciones Periodicas de Mexico (How to Obtain Mexican Books & Periodicals) (B)
Published by Camara Nacional de la Industria Editorial Mexicana
Holanda numero 13, col San Diego Churubusco, Del Coyoacan, 04120 Mexico, DF
Tel: (055) 5688-2434; (055) 5688-2221; (055) 5688-2011 *Toll Free Tel:* (800) 714-5352
Fax: (055) 5604-4347; (055) 5604-3147
E-mail: cepromex@caniem.com
Web Site: www.caniem.com
Information on the Mexican publishing industry, including a list of principal exporters of Mexican books.
ISBN(s): 968-6276-01-7

Cuadernos Americanos (American Notebooks) (P)
Published by Universidad Nacional Autonoma de Mexico (National University of Mexico)
Torre I de Humanidades, 2°, piso Ciudad Universitaria, 04510 Mexico, DF
Tel: (055) 616-2515 *Fax:* (055) 616-2515
E-mail: cuadamer@servidor.unam.mx
Web Site: www.libros.unam.mx
Our America, Monograph; Our America, Permanent collection; 500 Years After, Commemorative collection of the 500 years of the arrival of Columbus to America; Annual Latin America, permanent collection.
Bimonthly.
200 MXP or 133 USD per year
ISSN: 0011-2356

Libros de Mexico (Books of Mexico) (J)
Published by Camara Nacional de la Industria Editorial Mexicana
Holanda numero 13, col San Diego Churubusco, Del Coyoacan, 04120 Mexico, DF
Tel: (055) 5688-2434; (055) 5688-2221; (055) 5688-2011 *Fax:* (055) 5604-4347; (055) 5604-3147
E-mail: ciecprom@inetcorp.net.mx
Web Site: www.caniem.com
Review of book trade.
Quarterly.

Morocco

Bibliographie Nationale Marocaine (Moroccan National Bibliography) (B)
Published by Bibliotheque Generale et Archives du Maroc
5, Ave Ibn Batouta, Rabat
Mailing Address: CP 1003, Rabat
Tel: (07) 77 18 90; (07) 77 21 52; (07) 77 60 62
Fax: (07) 77 60 62
E-mail: biblio1@onpt.net.ma
Biannually.

Nepal

Nepalese National Bibliography (B)
Published by Tribhuvan University Central Library
Kirtipur, Kathmandu
Tel: (01) 331317 *Fax:* (01) 331964
E-mail: tucl@healthnet.org.np
Web Site: www.tucl.org.np
Key Personnel
Chief: Mr Krishna Mani Bhandari
First published 1981.
Annually.
3rd: 120 pp, 20 USD
ISBN(s): 99933-51-00-8

Netherlands

Amsterdamer Publikationen zur Sprache und Literatur (P)
Published by Rodopi
Tijnmuiden 7, 1046 AK Amsterdam
Tel: (020) 611 48 21 *Fax:* (020) 447 29 79
E-mail: info@rodopi.nl
Web Site: www.rodopi.nl
Germanic Languages & Literatures.
ISSN: 0169-0221

ƒ**Babel (International Journal of Translation)** (J)
Published by Federation Internationale des Traducteurs (FIT)
John Benjamins Publishing Co, Klaprozenweg 105, 1033 NN Amsterdam
Mailing Address: PO Box 36224, 1020 ME Amsterdam
Tel: (020) 6304747 *Fax:* (020) 6739773
Web Site: www.benjamins.nl
Key Personnel
Journal Subscriptions: Mr Timo Taal
E-mail: subscription@benjamins.nl
Scholarly journal concerned with current issues & events in the field of translation.
Quarterly.
ISSN: 0521-9744

ƒ**Bibliotheca Orientalis** (J)
Published by Nederlands Instituut voor Het Nabije Oosten (Netherlands Institute for the Near East)
PB 9515, 2300 RA Leiden
Tel: (071) 527 20 36 *Fax:* (071) 527 20 38
E-mail: ninopublications@let.leidenuniv.nl
Web Site: www.leidenuniv.nl/nino/ninopubs/publ.html
Key Personnel
Editor: R E Kon; A van der Kooij; D J W Meijer; H J A de Meulenaere; J J Roodenberg; J de Roos; M Stol
International bibliographical & reviewing journal for Near Eastern & Mediterranean studies, published in English, French & German.
Bimonthly.
ISSN: 0006-1913

Boekblad (J)
Published by Koninklijke Vereeniging ter bevordering van de belangen des Boekhandels/Boekblad bv
Frederiksplein 1, 1017 XK Amsterdam
Mailing Address: Postbus 15007, 1001 MA Amsterdam
Tel: (020) 625 31 31 *Fax:* (020) 622 09 08
E-mail: redactie@boekblad.kvb.nl
Web Site: www.boekblad.nl
News-sheet for the book trade.
Daily, weekly, monthly.

Brinkman's Cumulatieve Catalogus (Brinkman's Cumulative Book Catalog) (J)
Published by Uitgeverij Bohn Stafleu Van Loghum BV
PO Box 4, 2400 MA Alphen aan den Rijn
Tel: (0172) 466811 *Fax:* (0172) 466770
Web Site: www.kb.nl/kb
Netherlands national bibliography.

Castrum Peregrini (P)
Published by Castrum Peregrini Presse
PO Box 645, 1000 AP Amsterdam
Tel: (020) 623 52 87 *Fax:* (020) 624 70 96
E-mail: mail@castrumperegrini.nl
Web Site: www.castrumperegrini.nl
Journal for literature & art. Text in German.

Deutsche Buecher (The German Books) (J)
Published by Rodopi
Tijnmuiden 7, 1046 AK Amsterdam
Tel: (020) 611 48 21 *Fax:* (020) 447 29 79
E-mail: info@rodopi.nl
Web Site: www.rodopi.nl
Key Personnel
Publisher & Editor: Ferdinand van Ingen; Hartmut Laufhuette; Hendrik Meijering
Editor: Andrea Kunne; Achim Nuber

Text in German.
ISSN: 0167-2185

Forum der Letteren (P)
Published by Smits BV
Westeinde 135, 2512 The Hague
Tel: (070) 3895390 *Fax:* (070) 3802135
First published 1960.
Quarterly.
ISSN: 0015-8496

Gids voor de Informatiesector (B)
Published by NBLC
Platinaweg 10, 2544 EZ The Hague
Mailing Address: Postbus 43300, 2504 AH The Hague
Tel: (070) 30 90 100 *Fax:* (070) 30 90 200
E-mail: infolijn@nblc.nl
Web Site: www.nblc.nl
(Boekenvakboek, 1991) Publishing Industry Statistics.

Het Nederlandse Boek (The Dutch Book) (J)
De Lairessestr 108, 1071 PK Amsterdam
Tel: (020) 6233187
New Pocket-Books & Paperbacks included.
First published 1852.
Bimonthly.
24 pp, 10 EUR
ISSN: 0166-0586

Hollands Maandblad (Holland Monthly) (P)
Published by Stichting Hollands Maandblad
Herengracht 481, 1017 BT Amsterdam
Tel: (020) 5249800 *Fax:* (020) 6276851
E-mail: hollandsmaandblad@contact-bv.nl
Web Site: www.hollandsmaandblad.nl

ƒ**IFLA Directory** (J)
Published by International Federation of Library Associations & Institutions
c/o Koninklijke Bibliotheek, Prins Willem-Alexanderhof 5, The Hague
Mailing Address: PO Box 95312, 2509 The Hague
Tel: (070) 3140884 *Fax:* (070) 3834827
E-mail: ifla@ifla.org
Web Site: www.ifla.org
Biennially.
ISSN: 0074-6002

ƒ**International Information & Library Review** (J)
Published by Academic Press Ltd
PO Box 211, Amsterdam 1000
Tel: (020) 485 3757 *Fax:* (020) 485 3432
E-mail: nlinfo-f@elsevier.com
Web Site: www.elsevier.com/locate/issn/1057-2317
Quarterly.
ISSN: 1057-2317
Ultimate Parent Company: Elsevier Science

LIBER Quarterly: The Journal of European Research Libraries (J)
Published by Igitur, Utrecht Publishing & Archiving Services
University Library, Vrije Universiteit Amsterdam, De Boelelaan 1103, 1081 HV Amsterdam
Tel: (020) 444 5220 *Fax:* (020) 444 5259
E-mail: info@igitur.uu.nl
Web Site: liber.library.uu.nl; www.igitur.nl
Key Personnel
Managing Editor: Trix Bakker *E-mail:* t.bakker@ubvu.vu.nl
Promotes cooperation among European research libraries. Mainly in English.
First published 1991.
Quarterly.
215 EUR per year; 59 EUR single copy
ISSN: 1435-5205

De negentiende EEUW (The Nineteenth Century) (P)
Published by Maatschappij der Nederlandse Letterkunde, Werkgroep Negentiende Eeuw
Groothertoginnelaan 260, 2517 EZ The Hague
Tel: (70) 3106455
Web Site: www.leidenuniv.nl/host/mnl/wkgrp19/
Key Personnel
Contact: Dr A van Kalmthout *E-mail:* a.b.g.m.van.kalmthout@let.rug.nl
First published 1977.
240 pp
ISSN: 1381-8546

Quaerendo (P)
Published by Brill Academic Publishers
Plantijnstr 2, 2321 JC Leiden
Mailing Address: PO Box 9000, 2300 PA Leiden
Tel: (071) 53 53 500 *Fax:* (071) 53 17 532
E-mail: cs@brill.nl
Web Site: www.brill.nl
Key Personnel
Editor: A R A Croiset van Uchelen
Journal from the Low Countries devoted to manuscripts & printed books; text mainly in English, occasionally in French & German. Also available online.
First published 1971.
Quarterly.
ISSN: 0014-9527

De Revisor (P)
Published by Em Querido's Uitgeverij BV
Singel 262, 1016 AC Amsterdam
Tel: (020) 55 11 262 *Fax:* (020) 63 91 968
Web Site: www.revisor.nl
Key Personnel
President: Ary T Langbroek *E-mail:* b.langbroek@querido.nl
Editor-in-Chief: Jacques Dohmen *E-mail:* j.dohmen@querido.nl
Publisher: Baerbel Dorweiler *E-mail:* b.dorweiler@querido.nl
Foreign Rights: Lucienne van der Leije *E-mail:* l.van.der.leije@querido.nl
First published 1971.

Speurwerk Boeken Omnibus (SBO) (The Dutch Book Market) (J)
Published by Stichting Speurwerk betreffende het Boek
Frederiksplein 1, 1017 XK Amsterdam
Tel: (020) 625 49 27 *Fax:* (020) 620 88 71
E-mail: info@speurwerk.kvb.nl
Web Site: www.speurwerk.nl
Quarterly.

New Zealand

New Zealand Books in Print (B)
Published by Thorpe-Bowker
85 Turner St, Bldg C3, Port Melbourne, Victoria, Australia 3207
Tel: (03) 8645 0300; (03) 8645 0389 (customer service) *Fax:* (03) 8645 0333
E-mail: yoursay@thorpe.com.au; customer.service@thorpe.com.au
Web Site: www.thorpe.com.au
Key Personnel
Editor: Andrew Wilkins *E-mail:* andrew.wilkins@thorpe.com.au
Bibliographic data on over 14,000 books in print from New Zealand & the Pacific Island states. Includes information on publishers, distributors, trade associations, as well as information about booksellers, literary awards & other book trade related information.
First published 1964.
Annually.
29: 850 pp, L55
ISBN(s): 1-86452-036-1
ISSN: 0157-7662

Te Rarangi Pukapuka Matua o Aotearoa (New Zealand National Bibliography) (J)
Published by National Library of New Zealand (Te Puna Matauranga o Aotearoa)
PO Box 1467, Wellington
Tel: (04) 474 3000 *Fax:* (04) 474 3035
E-mail: information@natlib.govt.nz
Web Site: www.natlib.govt.nz
First published 1961.
Monthly online version; cumulative on CD-ROM.
830 NZD or 405.29 USD for 1 CD-ROM annually; 1200 NZD or 585.96 USD for 2 CD-ROMs annually; monthly website version free & free on CD-ROM for International clients
ISSN: 0028-8497

Nigeria

ƒ**African Journal of Academic Librarianship** (P)
Published by Standing Conference of African University Libraries (SCAUL)
PO Box 46, Akoka, Yaba, Lagos
Tel: (01) 524968
First published 1983.
Biannually.
ISSN: 0189-6709

Benin Review (J)
Published by Ethiope Publishing Corporation
34 Murtala Mohammed St, Benin City
Mailing Address: PMB 1332, Benin City, Bendel State
Tel: (052) 253036
Telex: 41110
Key Personnel
Editor: Abiola Irele
Covers traditional & modern arts in Africa as well as cultural life in the Black World.
First published 1974.
Biannually.
ISSN: 0331-0213

ƒ**Heritage** (J)
Published by Heritage Books
2-8 Calcutta Crescent, Gate 1, 101251 Apapa, Lagos
Mailing Address: PO Box 610, 101251 Apapa, Lagos
Tel: (01) 5871333
Key Personnel
Editor: Naiwu Osahon
African arts & letters.
First published 1970.
Quarterly.
ISSN: 0794-3415

The Muse (P)
Published by English Association at Nsukka
University of Nigeria, Dept of English, Nsukka
Tel: 771911
Telex: 51496
Key Personnel
Editor: Onyedika L Okwuonu
Irregularly.

National Bibliography of Nigeria (J)
Published by National Library of Nigeria-Research & Development Dept
4, Wesley St, PMB 12626, Lagos

Mailing Address: Sanusi Dantata House, Plot 274 Central Business Area, PMB 1, Garki District, Abuja
Tel: (01) 2600220 *Fax:* (01) 63 1563
Web Site: www.nlbn.org
Cumulations before 1971 published by the Ibadan University Press.
First published 1950.
Annually, also available as a weekly service.

Northern Nigerian Publications (J)
Published by Ahmadu Bello University Press Ltd
PMB 1094, Zaria, Kaduna State
Tel: (069) 50054
E-mail: abupl@abu.edu.ng
Telex: 75241
Annually.

Publishing in Nigeria (B)
Published by Ethiope Publishing Corporation
34 Murtala Mohammed St, Benin City, Edo State
Mailing Address: PMB 1332, Benin City, Bendel State
Tel: (052) 253036
Telex: 41110

Serials in Print in Nigeria (B)
Published by National Library of Nigeria- Research & Development Dept
4, Wesley St, PMB 12626, Lagos
Mailing Address: Sanusi Dantata House, Plot 274 Central Business Area, PMB 1, Garki District, Abuja
Tel: (01) 2600220 *Fax:* (01) 63 1563
Web Site: www.nlbn.org

Norway

Bok Og Samfunn (J)
Published by Norwegian Booksellers Association
Ovre Vollgate 15, 0158 Oslo
Tel: (22) 40 45 40 *Fax:* (22) 41 12 89
E-mail: post@bokogsamfunn.no
Web Site: www.bokogsamfunn.no
Trade journal for the Norwegian book trade.

Edda (P)
Published by Scandinavian University Press
Universitetsforlaget AS, Sehesteds gate 3, 0105 Oslo
Mailing Address: Postboks 508 sentrum, 0105 Oslo
Tel: (024) 14 75 00 *Fax:* (024) 14 75 01
E-mail: post@universitetsforlaget.no
Web Site: www.universitetsforlaget.no
Literary research.
Scandinavian.
745 NOK
ISSN: 0013-0818

The Norseman (P)
Published by Nordmanns-Forbundet (The Norse Federation)
Raadhusgate 23B, 0158 Oslo
Tel: (023) 35 71 70 *Fax:* (023) 35 71 75
E-mail: norseman@norseman.no
Web Site: www.norseman.no
Key Personnel
Editor-in-Chief: Kjetil A Flatin
Editor: Gunnar Gran
5 times/yr.
64 pp
ISSN: 0029-1846

Norsk Bokhandlermatrikkel (Norwegian Booksellers Membership List) (B)
Published by Bok Og Papiransattes Forening
Ovre Vollgate 15, N-0158 Oslo
Tel: 22205197 *Fax:* 22420033

Samtiden (J)
Published by H Aschehoug & Co (W Nygaard)
Sehstedsgt 3, Oslo
Mailing Address: PB 363, Sentrum, 0102 Oslo
Tel: (022) 40 04 06 *Fax:* (022) 20 63 95
E-mail: knut.olav.ames@samtiden.no
Web Site: www.samtiden.no
Key Personnel
Assistant Editor: Erik V Jacobsen *E-mail:* erik.jacobsen@aschehoug.no
Journal for politics, literature & other social questions.

*§***Scandinavian Public Library Quarterly (SPLQ)** (J)
Published by Statens Bibliotektilsyn
Kronprinsens gate 9, 0033 Oslo
Mailing Address: PO Box 8145 Dep, 0033 Oslo
Tel: (021) 02 17 00 *Fax:* (021) 02 17 01
E-mail: splq@bs.dk
Web Site: www.splq.info
Key Personnel
Editor: Jens Thorhauge
First published 1968.

Syn og Segn (Vision & Tradition) (P)
Published by Det Norske Samlaget
Postboks 4672 Sofienberg, 0506 Oslo
Tel: (022) 70 78 00 *Fax:* (022) 68 75 02
E-mail: syn.og.segn@samlaget.no
Web Site: www.samlaget.no
Major Norwegian review on political & cultural affairs.
Quarterly.

Vinduet (The Window) (P)
Published by Gyldenal Norsk Forlag
Postboks 6860, St Olavs plass, 0164 Oslo
Tel: (022) 03 42 44; (022) 034100 *Fax:* (022) 034105
E-mail: vinduet@vinduet.no; gnf@gyldendal.no
Web Site: www.vinduet.no
Telex: 72 880 gyldn n
First published 1947.
Triannually.
ISSN: 0042-6288

Pakistan

Ham Qalam (P)
Published by Pakistan Writers' Guild
11 Abbok Rd Anarkali/ One Mentgomrey Rd, Lahore
Tel: 6367124
Monthly.

Pakistan Book Trade Directory (B)
Published by Library Promotion Bureau
Karachi University Campus, Dastagir Society, Federal B Area, Karachi 75270
Mailing Address: PO Box 8421, Karachi 75270
Tel: (021) 479001 *Fax:* (021) 473226
Key Personnel
Chief Editor: Mr Adil Usmani

Pakistan National Bibliography (Qaumi Kitabiaat-E-Pakistan) (J)
Published by Department of Libraries, National Library of Pakistan
Constitution Ave, Islamabad

Tel: (051) 92026436; (051) 9206440 *Fax:* (051) 9221375
E-mail: nlpiba@isb.paknet.com.pk
Web Site: www.nlp.gov.pk
Key Personnel
Editor: Muhammad Abas Khan Sherwani
First published 1962.
Annually.
1996: 300 pp, 60 USD

Papua New Guinea

Bikmaus (P)
Published by National Research Institute of Papua New Guinea
PO Box 5854, Boroko, NCD
Tel: 326 0061; 326 0079; 326 0083 *Fax:* 326 0213
E-mail: nri@global.net.pg
Web Site: www.nri.org.pg
First published 1980.
Quarterly.
ISSN: 0255-7231

Office of Libraries and Archives, Papua, New Guinea (J)
Published by National Library Service of Papua New Guinea
PO Box 734, Waigani NCD
Tel: 3256200 *Fax:* 3251331
Telex: NE 22234
Key Personnel
Dir General: Daniel Paraide *Tel:* 3258013
E-mail: paraide@daltron.com.ps
Annually.

Peru

Bibliografia Peruana (Peruvian National Bibliography) (J)
Published by Biblioteca Nacional del Peru
Av Abancay 4ta cuadra, Lima
Tel: (01) 428-7690; (01) 428-7696 *Fax:* (01) 427-7331
E-mail: dn@binape.gob.pe
Web Site: www.binape.gob.pe
Key Personnel
Dir: Sinesio Lopez Jimenez
First published 1943.
Annually.
2000, 50 PEN

Textual: Revista del Instituto Nacional de Cultura (P)
Published by Instituto Nacional de Cultura
Av Javier Prado Este 2465, Lima 41
Tel: (01) 476-9933 *Fax:* (01) 476-9888
Web Site: inc.perucultural.org.pe
Key Personnel
Dir: Dr Fernando Silva Santisteban

Philippines

Diliman Review (P)
Published by University of the Philippines, Sciences, Arts, & Letters, & Social Sciences & Philosophy

PHILIPPINES

College of Science, Velasquez St, Diliman, 1101 Quezon City
Tel: (02) 924-7392 *Fax:* (02) 929-1266
Web Site: www.upd.edu.ph
Key Personnel
Editor: Eddie E Eswetura

Philippine Studies (P)
Published by Ateneo de Manila University Press
Ground floor, Bellarmine Hall, Katipunan Ave, Loyola Heights, 1109 Quezon City
Tel: (02) 4265984; (02) 4266001 (ext 4613); (02) 4266001 (ext 4614 or 4615, editorial); (02) 4266001 (ext 4612 or 4616, business & marketing) *Fax:* (02) 4265909
E-mail: unipress@admu.edu.ph
Web Site: www.ateneopress.com
Publishes articles, notes & reviews in the humanities, literature, history, social sciences, philosophy & Philippine arts.
First published 1953.
Quarterly.
140 pp, 600 PHP or 40 USD per year; 50 PHP per back issue
ISSN: 0031-7837

Poland

Ksiegarz (The Bookseller) (J)
Published by Stowarzyszenie Ksiegarzy Polskich (Association of Polish Booksellers)
ul Batorego 24, 43-100 Tychy
Tel: (022) 252-874
E-mail: sklep@ksiegarz.com
Web Site: www.ksiegarz.com.pl

Pamietnik Teatralny (The Atrical Diary) (P)
Published by Polish Academy of Sciences, Institute of Art
ul Dluga 26/28, 00-950 Warsaw
Tel: (022) 831 80 56 *Fax:* (022) 831 31 49
E-mail: ispan@ispan.pl
Web Site: www.ispan.uw.edu.pl
History of Polish Theatre.
First published 1952.
Quarterly.

Polish Publishers and Booksellers (B)
Published by Panstwowy Instytut Wydawniczy (PIW) (National Publishing Institute)
ul Foksal 17, 00-372 Warsaw
Tel: (022) 826-02-01; (022) 826-02-05 *Fax:* (022) 826-15-36
Web Site: www.piw.pl
Telex: 814306
Text in English.

Ruch Wydawniczy w Liczbach (Polish Publishing in Figures) (B)
Published by Biblioteka Narodowa
al Niepodleglosci 213, 02 086 Warsaw 22
Tel: (022) 6082639 *Fax:* (022) 6082408
E-mail: statystyka@bn.org.pl
Web Site: www.bn.org.pl
Key Personnel
Editor: Krystyna Bankowska-Bober
First published 1955.
Annually.
102 pp
ISSN: 0511-1196

Soon to Appear (J)
Published by AGPOL (Przedsiebiorstwo Reklamy i Wydawnictw Handlu Zagranicznego)
ul Kerbedzia 4, 00-957 Warsaw
Tel: (022) 416061 *Fax:* (022) 405607
Telex: 813364

French, German & Russian editions.
ISSN: 0239-0345

Portugal

Livros de Portugal (Portuguese Books) (J)
Published by Associacao Portuguesa de Editores e Livreiros
Av Dos Estados Unidos da America, 97-6° Esq, 1700-167 Lisbon
Tel: (021) 843 51 80 *Fax:* (021) 848 93 77
E-mail: adm@apel.pt
Web Site: www.apel.pt
Telex: 62735
First published 1940.
Monthly.
50 USD
ISSN: 0870-5259

Livros Disponiveis (B)
Published by Associacao Portuguesa de Editores e Livreiros
Av Estados Unidos da America, 97 6 Esq, 1700-004 Lisbon
Tel: (021) 843 51 80 *Fax:* (021) 848 93 77
E-mail: adm@apel.pt
Web Site: www.apel.pt
Portuguese Books in Print (CD-ROM).
Annually.
36.41 EUR
ISSN: 0870-6093

O Mundo do Edicao Luso-Brasileira (B)
Published by Publicacoes Europa-America Lda
Apdo 8, Mem Martins Cedex
Tel: (01) 9211461 *Fax:* (01) 9217940
Telex: 42255 peap
The World of Publishing, Portugal & Brazil.

Puerto Rico

Atenea (P)
Published by University of Puerto Rico at Mayaguez, College of Arts & Sciences
Dept of English, Chardon 323, Mayaguez 00680
Mailing Address: Dept of English, Box 9265, Mayaguez 00681
Tel: (787) 832-4040 (ext 3076) *Fax:* (787) 265-3847
E-mail: atenea@uprm.edu
Web Site: mayaweb.upr.clu.edu/artssciences/atenea/atenea.htm
Key Personnel
Editor: Nandita Batra
Text in Spanish & English.
Biannually.
ISSN: 0885-6079

§**Guide to Review of Books From And About Hispanic America** (B)
Published by AMM Editions
c/o Pontifical Catholic University of Puerto Rico, Ponce 00732
Mailing Address: Box 151, Sta 6, Ponce 00732
Tel: (787) 841-2000 *Fax:* (787) 840-4295
Bibliography.
First published 1965.
Annually.

Romania

Bibliografia Romaniei (J)
Published by National Library
Str Ion Ghica 4, Sec 3, 79708 Bucharest
Tel: (01) 3157063; (01) 3142434 (ext 232) *Fax:* (01) 312 33 81
E-mail: go@bibnat.ro
Web Site: www.bibnat.ro
Romanian National Bibliography.
First published 1952.
Bimonthly.
156 pp
ISSN: 1221-9126

Convorbiri Literare (Literary Conversations) (P)
Published by Uniunea Scriitorilor din Romania
Calea Victoriei 115, Bucharest
Tel: (01) 650 72 45 *Fax:* (01) 312 96 34
E-mail: romlit@romlit.ro
Web Site: www.romlit.ro
Telex: 11796
Key Personnel
Editor-in-Chief: Cassian Maria Spiridon
First published 1867.
Monthly.
ISSN: 0010-8243

Euresis - Cahiers Roumains d'Etudes Litteraires (P)
Published by Editura Univers SA
Piata Presei Libere 1, Casa Presei Libere, corp central, et 4, sec 1, 79739 Bucharest
Tel: (01) 224 32 86 *Fax:* (01) 222 56 52
E-mail: univers@rnc.ro
Text in French & English, occasionally in German, Russian, Spanish & Italian.
Biannually.
ISSN: 1223-1193

Manuscriptum (P)
Published by Muzeul Literaturii Romane
B-dul Dacia, nr 12, sector 1, Cod 71116 Bucharest
Tel: (004) 021-2125845 *Fax:* (004) 021-2125846
E-mail: edit@mlr.ro
Web Site: www.mlr.ro
Manuscripts, Literary documents in Romanian, or bilingual, if necessary; Summaries in French, English, German & Russian.
First published 1970.
Triannually.

Revista de Istorie si Teorie Literara (Review of Literary History & Theory) (P)
Published by Academia Romana
Str 13 Septembrie nr 13, sector 5, 76117 Bucharest
Tel: (01) 411 90 08 *Fax:* (01) 410 39 83
E-mail: edacad@ear.ro
Web Site: www.ear.ro
Summaries in French & Russian.
Annually.

Romania Literara (Literary Romania) (P)
Published by Uniunea Scriitorilor din Romania
Calea Victoriei 115, Bucharest
Tel: (01) 650 72 45 *Fax:* (01) 312 96 34
E-mail: romlit@romlit.ro
Web Site: www.romlit.ro
Telex: 11796
Key Personnel
Dir: Nicolae Manolescu
First published 1954.
Weekly.
ISSN: 1220-6318

Romanian Review (P)
Published by Foreign Languages Press Romania

PO Box 33-28, Bucharest 71341
Tel: (01) 2228481 *Fax:* (01) 3110526
E-mail: rps@dialkappa.ro
Web Site: www.wsp.ro/rps
Text in English, French & German (monthly), Russian (quarterly).
First published 1946.
Monthly.
ISSN: 0035-8088

Secolul XX (Twentieth Century) (P)
Published by Uniunea Scriitorilor din Romania
Calea Victoriei 115, Bucharest
Tel: (01) 650 72 45 *Fax:* (01) 312 96 34
E-mail: romlit@romlit.ro
Web Site: www.romlit.ro
Telex: 11796
Key Personnel
Editor: Don Haulica
First published 1961.
Monthly.
ISSN: 0037-0517

Steaua (P)
Published by Uniunea Scriitorilor din Romania
Calea Victoriei 115, Bucharest
Tel: (01) 650 72 45 *Fax:* (01) 312 96 34
E-mail: romlit@romlit.ro
Web Site: www.romlit.ro
Telex: 11796
Key Personnel
Editor-in-Chief: Aurel Rau
First published 1953.
Monthly.
ISSN: 0039-0852

Russian Federation

Avrora (Aurora) (J)
Published by Russian Federation Union of Writers
Ul Millionnaya 4, St Petersburg 191186
Tel: (0812) 3121323
E-mail: sekretar@avrora.ru
Web Site: www.avrora.ru
Key Personnel
Editor: E Shevelyov
Contact: Mrs Marina Zurzumija
Literary, artistic & socio-political journal.
First published 1969.
Monthly.
ISSN: 0320-6858

Bibliografiia (Bibliography) (J)
Published by Rossiiskaya Knizhnaya Palata (Russian Book Chamber)
Ostogenka, 4, Moscow
Tel: (095) 2911278 *Fax:* (095) 2919630
E-mail: bookch@postman.ru
Web Site: www.bookchamber.ru/international
Contains articles on history, theory, methods & organization of bibliography, tells about the interesting experience of bibliographical work in libraries, & helps in work with catalogues, bibliographical aids & documents.
First published 1929.
Bimonthly.
ISSN: 0869-6020

Druzhba Narodov (People's Friendship) (P)
Published by Aspext Press Ltd
Povarskaya ul, 52, 121827 Moscow
Tel: (095) 291-62-27; (095) 291-62-49 *Fax:* (095) 291-63-54
Literary, artistic, socio-political magazine.
First published 1938.
Monthly.
ISSN: 0012-6756

Knizhnaya Letopis' (Book Chronicle) (J)
Published by Rossiiskaya Knizhnaya Palata (Russian Book Chamber)
Ostogenka, 4, Moscow
Tel: (095) 2911278 *Fax:* (095) 2919630
E-mail: bookch@postman.ru
Web Site: www.bookchamber.ru/international
Book Annals; published by Book Chamber International.
First published 1907.
Weekly.
160 pp, 520 USD
ISSN: 0869-5962

Knizhnaya Moskva: Putevoditel'-Spravochnik (Books in Moscow A Guide and Handbook) (B)
Published by Reklama
ul Cajkouskogo 7, 121099 Moscow
Tel: (095) 2052101

Knizhnoe Obozrenie (J)
Published by Ministerstvo Pechati i Informatsii Rossii
Sushchevskiival, 64, 129272 Moscow
Tel: (095) 2816266 *Fax:* (095) 2816266
Web Site: www.rusf.ru/ko
Telex: 411167 GBLSU
Book Reviews.
First published 1966.
Weekly.
132 USD a year
ISSN: 0023-2378

Letopis' Periodicheskikh i Prodolzhaiushchikhsya Izdanii (Chronicle of Periodical & Continual Editions) (J)
Published by Rossiiskaya Knizhnaya Palata (Russian Book Chamber)
Ostozhenka, 4, Moscow 119034
Tel: (095) 2911278; (095) 2919630 *Fax:* (095) 2919630
E-mail: bookch@postman.ru
Web Site: www.bookchamber.ru/international
Contains information about magazines & newspapers which have changed their name or which have ceased publication in Russia, in addition to other changes in periodicals.
First published 1933.
Annually.
ISSN: 0201-6265

Literaturnaya Rossiya (Literary Russia) (P)
Published by Izdatel'sko-Poligraficheskoe Ob'edinenie Pisatelei Rossii
Tsvetnoi Blvd, 30, Moscow 103662
Tel: (095) 200-4005; (095) 200-2309 (advertising); (095) 200-2467 (advertising) *Fax:* (095) 200-2755
E-mail: litrossia@litrossia.ru; info@periodicals.ru
Web Site: www.litrossia.ru; www.mkniga.ru
Key Personnel
Editor-in-Chief: Vladmir Yeryomenko
  E-mail: eremenko@litrossia.ru
First published 1958.
Weekly.
126 USD per year
ISSN: 1560-6856

Molodaya Gvardiya (The Young Guards) (P)
Published by Redaktsiya Molodaya Gvardiya
Novodmitrovskaya ul 5-a, Moscow 125015
Tel: (095) 2858829 *Fax:* (095) 285-56-90
Literary, artistic, socio-political magazine.
First published 1922.
Monthly.
ISSN: 0131-2251

Moskva (Moscow) (P)
Published by Soyuz Pisatelei Rossii, Moskovskoe Otdelenie
Arbat 20, Moscow 121918
Tel: (095) 9219626 *Fax:* (095) 291-07-32
E-mail: moskva@jurmos.msk.ru
Key Personnel
Editor: L I Borodin
Literary, artistic, socio-political illustrated magazine.
First published 1957.
Monthly.
ISSN: 0131-2332

Nash Sovremennik (Our Contemporary) (P)
Tsvetnoi bul, 32, Moscow 103750
Tel: (095) 200-24-24 *Fax:* (095) 200-23-05
E-mail: info@periodicals.ru
Web Site: www.friends-partners.org/partners/rpiac/nashsovr; www.mkniga.ru
Literary, artistic, socio-political magazine.
First published 1963.
Monthly.
126 USD per year
ISSN: 0027-8238

Neva (P)
Published by NEVA Magazin Ltd
Nevskii prospekt, 3, St Petersburg 191186
Tel: (0812) 312-70-35 *Fax:* (0812) 312-65-37
E-mail: redaktion@nevajournal.spb.ru; nevajournal@online.ru
Web Site: www.nevajournal.spb.ru
Literary, artistic, socio-political illustrated magazine, black & white photos.
First published 1955.
Monthly.
106 USD annually
ISSN: 0130-741X

Novyi Mir (P)
Published by Sergei/Yakovlev
Maly Putinkovsky per, 1/2, Moscow 103806
Tel: (095) 209-57-02 *Fax:* (095) 200-08-29
E-mail: nmir@aha.ru
Literary, artistic & socio-political illustrated journal.
First published 1925.
Monthly.
ISSN: 0130-7673

Russkaya Literatura (Russian Literature) (P)
Published by Academy of Sciences, Institute of Russian Literature, Pushkin's House
Makarova nab 4, Saint-Petersburg 199034
Tel: (0812) 218-16-01
Key Personnel
Dir: Prof Nikolaj N Skatov *Tel:* (0812) 218-19-01
Historical & literary journal.
Quarterly.
99 USD annually
ISSN: 0131-6095

Slovo (P)
Published by Slovo (Moscow)
Sushchevskii val 64, Moscow 129272
Tel: (095) 2815098 *Fax:* (095) 2384634
Telex: 411 169 GBLSU
Now Word.

Staroe Literaturnoe Obozrenie (P)
Published by Literaturnoe Obozrenie
ul Dobroljubova, 9/11, Moscow 127254
Tel: (095) 219-9263 *Fax:* (095) 218-0398
E-mail: info@periodicals.ru
Web Site: www.rema.ru/komment/litoboz/litoboz.htm; www.mkniga.ru
Key Personnel
Editor-in-Chief: Viktor Kulle
Journal of critics & bibliography.
First published 1973.

RUSSIAN FEDERATION

Bimonthly.
99.95 USD annually
ISSN: 1680-6077

Voprosy Literatury (Questions of Literature) (P)
Published by Fond Literaturnaya Mysl
B Gnezdnikovskii per, 10, Moscow 103009
Tel: (095) 229-49-77 *Fax:* (095) 229-64-71
E-mail: voplit@dionis.iasnet.ru
Telex: 411950POEMA SU *Cable:* 103009
Key Personnel
Editor-in-Chief: L Lazarev
First published 1957.
Bimonthly.
ISSN: 0042-8795

Znamya (The Banner) (P)
Nikolskaya ul, 8/1, Moscow 103863
Tel: (095) 924-13-46 *Fax:* (095) 921-32-72
E-mail: znamlit@dialup.ptt.ru
Literary, artistic, socio-political magazine. Contains short stories, archives, memoirs, fiction, documentaries & criticism.
First published 1931.
Monthly.
149.95 USD annually
ISSN: 0130-1616

Zvezda (The Star) (P)
Mokhovaya ul, 20, D28, St Petersburg 191028
Tel: (095) 272-89-48 *Fax:* (0812) 273-52-56
E-mail: arjev@zveza.spb.su; gordin@zvezda.spb.su
Literary, artistic, socio-political magazine.
Monthly.
123 USD annually
ISSN: 0321-1878

Senegal

Bibliographie du Senegal (Bibliographies of Senegal) (J)
Published by Archives Nationales du Senegal
Bldg Administratif, Ave Leopold Sedar Senghor, Dakar
Tel: (0221) 8217021 *Fax:* (0221) 8217021
E-mail: bdas@telecomplus.sn
Web Site: www.archivesdusenegal.gouv.sn
First published 1962.
ISBN(s): 0378-9942

ƒ**Bibliographie nationale courante de l' Annee...des pays d' Afrique d' expression francaise** (National Bibliography for the Year...of Francophone African Countries) (B)
Published by Ecole de Bibliothecaires, Archivistes, et Documentalistes de Dakar
EBAD/UCAD, BP 3252, Dakar
Tel: 825 76 60; 864 21 22 *Fax:* 824 05 42
E-mail: ebad@ebad.ucad.sn
Web Site: www.ebad.ucad.sn
Key Personnel
Dir: Mbaye Thiam
Bibliography covering books & other materials published in Francophone Africa.
First published 1967.
Annually.

Serbia and Montenegro

Bibliografija Jugoslavije (Bibliography of Yugoslavia) (J)
Published by Jugoslovenski Bibliografsko Informacijski Institut (Yugoslav Institute for Bibliography & Information)
Terazije 26, 11000 Belgrade
Tel: (011) 687 836; (011) 687 760 *Fax:* (011) 687 760; (011) 688 840
E-mail: suzana@jbi.bg.ac.yu
Web Site: www.yu-yubin.org
Key Personnel
Dir: Dr Radomir Glavicki
National Bibliography of Yugoslavia/Production.
First published 1949.
Bimonthly.
100 pp
ISSN: 0523-2201

Catalogue of Books Published by Yugoslav Publishers (B)
Published by Association of Yugoslav Publishers & Booksellers
Kneza Milosa 25, 11000 Belgrade
Tel: (011) 642248; (011) 642-533 *Fax:* (011) 646-339
E-mail: ognjenl@eunet.yu
Web Site: www.beobookfair.co.yu
Key Personnel
General Dir: Mr Ognjen Lakicevic
E-mail: ognjenl@eunet.yu

Knjizevne Novine (Literary News) (P)
Published by Serbian Unity Congress
Dositejeva 12, 11000 Belgrade
Tel: (011) 3282 893; (011) 3282 960 *Fax:* (011) 624 129
E-mail: office@bgd.serbianunity.net
Web Site: www.serbianunity.net
Key Personnel
Editor: Dragan M Jeremic

Lumina (P)
Published by Libertatea
str Z Zrenjanina nr 7, 26000 Panciova
Tel: 13 353 401; 13 346 447 *Fax:* 21 51 897
E-mail: lumina@libertatea.co.yu
Web Site: www.libertatea.co.yu
Key Personnel
Editor: Ion Balan
Literary & cultural review.
First published 1947.

Savremenik (P)
Published by Knjizevne Novine
pf 23, Gospodar Jovanova 5, 11000 Belgrade
Tel: (011) 637-518; (011) 638-159; (011) 639-631 *Fax:* (011) 637-518; (011) 638-168
Text in Serbo-Croatian.
Monthly.
ISSN: 0036-519X

Sierra Leone

Sierra Leone Publications (J)
Published by Sierra Leone Library Board
PO Box 326, Freetown
Tel: (022) 226 993; (022) 223 848 *Fax:* (022) 224 439
National bibliography.

First published 1962.
Annually.

Singapore

Books about Singapore (B)
Published by National Reference Library
91 Stamford Rd, Singapore 178896
Tel: 6332-3255 *Fax:* 6332-3248
E-mail: ref@nlb.gov.sg
Web Site: www.lib.gov.sg
Biennially.
ISSN: 0068-0176
Parent Company: National Library Board

NBDCS News (J)
Published by National Book Development Council of Singapore
Geylang East Community Library, National Library Board 50 Geylang East Ave 1, Singapore 38977
Tel: 6848 8290 *Fax:* 6742 9466
E-mail: nbdcs@nbdcs.org.sg
Web Site: www.NBDCS.org.sg
First published 1981.
Quarterly.
ISSN: 0129-9239

Singapore Book World (J)
Published by National Book Development Council of Singapore
Geylang East Community Library, National Library Board 50 Geylang East Ave 1, Singapore 38977
Tel: 6848 8290 *Fax:* 6742 9466
E-mail: nbdcs@nbdcs.org.sg
Web Site: www.nbdcs.org.sg
Reviews of Singapore published books & articles on the book trade & reading trends.
First published 1970.
Annually.
ISSN: 0080-9659

Singapore National Bibliography (SNB) (J)
Published by National Library Board Singapore, Library Support Services
No 3, Changi South St 2, Tower B, Level 3, Singapore 486548
Tel: 6546-7275 *Fax:* 6546-7262
E-mail: gifts_exchanges@nlb.gov.sg
Web Site: www.nlb.gov.sg
Telex: RS 26620 NATLIB
Annual accumulation.
Biannually.
ISSN: 0129-315X

Singapore Periodicals Index (B)
Published by National Reference Library
91 Stamford Rd, Singapore 178896
Tel: 6332-3255 *Fax:* 6332-3248
E-mail: ref@nlb.gov.sg
Web Site: www.lib.gov.sg
Telex: RS 26620 NATLIB
Key Personnel
Contact: Jeff Graf *E-mail:* libref@indiana.edu
Annually.

Slovakia

Kniha (The Book) (P)
Published by Slovenska Narodna Kniznica, Martin (Slovak National Library, Martin)
Nam J C Hronskeho 1, 036 01 Martin

Tel: (043) 422 07 20; (043) 430 18 02 *Fax:* (043) 422 07 20; (043) 430 18 02
E-mail: snk@snk.sk
Web Site: www.snk.sk

Literatura (Slovak Literature) (P)
Published by Veda Publishing House of the Slovak Academy of Sciences
Bradacova 7, 852 86 Bratislava
Tel: (02) 6383 2259 *Fax:* (02) 6383 2259
E-mail: markova@centrum.sk
Web Site: www.veda-sav.sk
Contents page & summaries in German & Russian.

Slovak Books in Print (J)
Published by Slovart Co Ltd
Pekna cesta 6/b, 830 04 Bratislava 34
Mailing Address: PO Box 14, 830 04 Bratislava 34
Tel: (02) 44 87 12 10 *Fax:* (02) 44 87 12 46
E-mail: pobox@slovart.sk
Web Site: www.slovart.sk; www.slovart.com
Telex: 93394 slov c

Slovenske pohlady na literaturu a umenie
(Slovak View on Literature & Art) (P)
Published by Asociacia Slovenskych Spisovatelov
Laurinska 2, 813 08 Bratislava
Tel: (07) 334316; (07) 334374; (07) 332334; (07) 5332671 *Fax:* (07) 335411
First published 1864.
Monthly.
ISSN: 0037-7007

Slovenia

Slovenska Bibliografija (J)
Published by Narodna in Univerzitetna Knjiznica, Ljubljana (National & University Library)
Narodna in Univerzitetna Knjiznica, Turjaska 1, 1001 Ljubljana
Tel: (01) 2001 110 *Fax:* (01) 4257 293
E-mail: info@nuk.uni-lj.si
Web Site: www.nuk.uni-lj.si/vstop.cgi
Slovene Bibliography.
Quarterly.
ISSN: 0353-1716

South Africa

Acta Classica (P)
Published by Classical Association of South Africa
c/o The Managing Editor, Acta Classica, Dept of Greek & Latin Studies, Rand Africkaans University, PO Box 524, 2006 Aucland Park
Tel: (012) 420-2368 *Fax:* (011) 489-2797
E-mail: wjh@lw.rau.ac.za
Web Site: www.sun.ac.za/as/casa
Key Personnel
Managing Editor: W J Henderson
Treasurer: J Christoff Zietsman
Annually.
Subscription - 100 ZAR per annum
ISSN: 0065-1141

Akroterion (P)
Published by University of Stellenbosch Dept of Ancient Studies
Private Bag X1, Matieland 7602
Tel: (021) 808-3203 *Fax:* (021) 808-3480
E-mail: jct@maties.sun.ac.za

Web Site: www.sun.ac.za/AS/journals/akro
Publishes articles in English or Afrikaans aimed at the non-specialist, covering all aspects of ancient Greek & Roman civilization, but focussing especially on the influence & reception of the Classics.
First published 1956.
Annually.
ISSN: 0303-1896

Catalog of Books (English) Published in Southern Africa, Still in Print (1970) (B)
Published by Struik Publishers (Pty) Ltd
80 McKenzie St, Gardens, Cape Town 8001
Mailing Address: PO Box 1144, Cape Town 8000
Tel: (021) 462-4360 *Fax:* (021) 216744; (021) 462-4379
Web Site: www.struik.co.za

English in Africa (P)
Published by Institute for the Study of English in Africa, Rhodes University
St Peter's Bldg (off Somerset St), Grahamstown 6140
Mailing Address: PO Box 94, Grahamstown 6140
Tel: (046) 6038565 *Fax:* (046) 6038566
E-mail: j.king@ru.ac.za
Web Site: www.ru.ac.za
Key Personnel
Managing Editor: Prof Laurence Wright
Editor: Craig Mackenzie
Editorial Assistant: Marion Baxter
Primary source material: critical articles & book reviews on all aspects of African literature written in English.
First published 1974.
Biannually in May & Oct.
Individuals 60 ZAR, Institutions 70 ZAR (Africa); Individuals & Institutions 16 GBP or 22 USD (Overseas)
ISSN: 0376-8902

Journal of Literary Studies (P)
Published by University of South Africa, Department of Literary Theory
PO Box 392, Pretoria 0003
Tel: (012) 429 6401; (012) 429 6700; (012) 429 6058 *Fax:* (012) 429 3221
E-mail: unisa-press@unisa.ac.za
Web Site: www.unisa.ac.za
Key Personnel
Editor: Ina Grabe *E-mail:* graberc@alpha.unisa.ac.za
Journal to provide a forum for the discussion of literary theory, methodology, research & related matters, features articles, commentary, book reviews & general announcements.
First published 1985.
Vol 17, 100 ZAR
ISSN: 0256-4718

New Coin Poetry (P)
Published by Institute for the Study of English in Africa, Rhodes University
St Peter's Bldg (off Somerset St), Grahamstown 6140
Mailing Address: PO Box 94, Grahamstown 6140
Tel: (046) 6038565 *Fax:* (046) 6038566
E-mail: j.king@ru.ac.za
Web Site: www.ru.ac.za
Key Personnel
Managing Editor: Prof Laurence Wright
Editor: Joan Metelerkamp
Editorial Assistant: Marion Baxter
Collection of South African poetry, reviews & interviews.
Biannually in June & Dec.
90 pp, 50 ZAR (Africa); 8.50 GBP or 15 USD (Overseas)
ISSN: 0028-4459

New Contrast (J)
Published by South African Literary Journal Ltd
PO Box 3841, Cape Town 8000
E-mail: newcontrast@mailbox.co.za
Publishes South African poetry, short fiction, essays, criticisms, book reviews, graphic art & general cultural commentary. Does not discriminate on the basis of race, gender, political persuasion or religious creed.
First published 1960.
Quarterly.
ISSN: 1017-5415

scrutiny2: issues in English studies in Southern Africa (P)
Published by University of South Africa Press
Dept of English, PO Box 392, Pretoria 0003
Tel: (012) 429 6702 *Fax:* (012) 429 3221
E-mail: unisa-press@unisa.ac.za
Web Site: www.unisa.ac.za/dept/press/onjourn.html
Telex: 3777 *Cable:* UNISA
Key Personnel
Editor: Prof Leon de Kock *Tel:* (012) 429 6294
E-mail: dkockl@unisa.ac.za
Literary articles & reviews.
First published 1996.
Biannually in May & Sept.
80 pp, 30 USD
ISSN: 0041-5359

∮**Shakespeare in Southern Africa** (P)
Published by Shakespeare Society of Southern Africa
c/o ISEA, Rhodes University, Grahamstown 6140
Mailing Address: PO Box 94, Grahamstown 6140
Tel: (0461) 6038565 *Fax:* (0461) 6038566
E-mail: b.cummings@ru.ac.za
Web Site: www.ru.ac.za/affiliates/isea/shake
Key Personnel
Editor: Prof Brian Pearce *E-mail:* brianp@dit.ac.za
Contact: Prof Laurence Wright *E-mail:* l.wright@ru.ac.za
Articles, commentary & reviews on all aspects of Shakesperean studies & performance, with a particular emphasis on the response to Shakespeare in Southern Africa.
First published 1987.
Annually.
100 pp, $120 per annum
ISSN: 1011-582X

South African Journal of African Languages (P)
Published by African Language Association of Southern Africa
Dept of African Languages, UNISA, PO Box 392, Pretoria 0003
Tel: (012) 429 8070 *Fax:* (012) 429 3355
E-mail: mww@unisa.ac.za
Web Site: www.alasa.org.za
Quarterly.

Staffrider (P)
Published by Cosaw Publishing (Pty) Ltd
PO Box 421007, Fordsburg 2033
Tel: 833 2530 *Fax:* 833 2532
First published 1978.
Quarterly.
ISSN: 0258-7211

Spain

Bibliografia Espanola Monografias (Spanish Bibliography) (J)
Published by Biblioteca Nacional de Espana

SPAIN

Paseo De Recoletos 20, Madrid 28071
Tel: (01) 5807706 *Fax:* (01) 5807712
E-mail: info.publicaciones@bne.es
Web Site: www.bne.es
Monthly.
ISSN: 0214-2694

Bibliografia Espanola: Suplemento de Publicaciones Periodicas (Periodical Publications Supplement to Spanish Bibliography) (J)
Published by Biblioteca Nacional de Espana
Paseo de Recoletos 20, Madrid 28071
Tel: (091) 5807706 *Fax:* (091) 5807712
E-mail: info.publicaciones@bne.es
Web Site: www.bne.es

Catalan Review (P)
Published by North American Catalan Society, Publicacions de L'Abadia de Montseriat
Ausias March 92-98 interior, 08013 Barcelona
Tel: (093) 2450303; (093) 2314001 *Fax:* (093) 247-3594
E-mail: pamsa@pamsa.com
Web Site: cr.middlebury.edu/catalan/CReview.htm; www.pamsa.com
Current & past issues of Catalan Review can be purchased from: Merce Vidal Tibbits, Dept of Modern Languages & Literatures, Howard University, Washington, DC 20059.

Delibros (J)
Published by Delibros SA
RDM, SL, Eloy Gonzalo, 27-3°, 28010 Madrid
Tel: (091) 591 4258 (subscriptions) *Fax:* (091) 594 3053
E-mail: info@delibros.com
Web Site: www.delibros.com
Key Personnel
Publisher: Jaime Brull
Dir: Teresa M Peces *E-mail:* direccion@delibros.com
Publicity Dir: Monica Lizana
 E-mail: publicidad@delibros.com
Editor: Virginia de Pablo *E-mail:* redaccion@delibros.com
Design: Jose Maria Cerezo
 E-mail: maquetacion@delibros.com
Illustration: Blanca Ortega
Subscriptions Coordinator: Nuria Garcia
 E-mail: suscripciones@delibros.com
Monthly.
ISSN: 0214-2694

Libros Espanoles en Venta: Repertorio Anual (Spanish Books in Print) (B)
Published by Agencia Espanola del ISBN
Santiago Rusinol, 8, 28040 Madrid
Tel: (091) 536 88 00 *Fax:* (091) 553 99 90
Web Site: www.mcu.es/bases/spa/isbn/ISBN.html
Annual three volume compilation of over 266,000 in-print titles from over 10,000 publishers. Also included are 23,000 recent out-of-print titles.
518.52 USD for print edition, 1,112 USD for CD-ROM

Litoral (P)
Published by Visor Libros
Isacc Peral, 18, 28015 Madrid
Tel: (091) 549 34 09 *Fax:* (091) 544 86 95
E-mail: visor-libros@visor-libros.com
Web Site: www.visor-libros.com
Poetry review.
Monthly.

Nuestro Tiempo (Our Time) (P)
Published by Servicio de Publicaciones de la Universidad de Navarra, SA
Carretera del Sadar, s/n, Campus Universitario, 31080 Pamplona-Navarra
Tel: (048) 425 600 *Fax:* (048) 425 718

E-mail: nuestrot@unav.es; cbulnes@unav.es
Web Site: www.unav.es/nt
50 EUR (subscription)
ISSN: 0029-5795

Razon y Fe (Reason & Faith) (P)
Published by Centro Loyola de Estudios y Communicacion Social
Pablo Aranda, 3, 28006 Madrid
Tel: (091) 5624930 *Fax:* (091) 5634073
E-mail: celomad@jesuitas.es
Web Site: www.jesuitas.es/razonyfe.htm
Spanish-American review.

Revista de Occidente (Review of the West) (P)
Published by Instituto Universitario Ortega y Gasset
C/Fortuny, 53, 28010 Madrid
Tel: (091) 700 4100 *Fax:* (091) 700 3530
E-mail: fogrocci@accessnet.es
Web Site: www.ortegaygasset.edu
Key Personnel
Dir: Soledad Ortega
First published 1923.

Serra d'Or (P)
Published by Publicacions de l'Abadia de Montserrat
Ausias March 92-98, interior, 08013 Barcelona
Tel: (093) 245 03 03; (093) 231 40 01 *Fax:* (093) 247 35 94
E-mail: pamsa@pamsa.com
Web Site: www.pamsa.com/rev/serrador.asp
Key Personnel
Dir: Josep Massot i Muntaner
Editor: Maur M Boix
First published 1955.
80 pp
ISSN: 0037-2501

Sri Lanka

Sri Lanka ISBN Publishers Directory (B)
Published by National Library & Documentation Centre
No 14, Independence Ave, Colombo 07
Tel: (01) 698847; (01) 685197 *Fax:* (01) 685201
E-mail: natlib@slt.lk
Web Site: www.natlib.lk
Key Personnel
Dir General: Mr M S U Amarasiri *E-mail:* dg@mail.natlib.lk
Deputy Dir: Mr G G Upasena *E-mail:* ddadmin@mail.natlib.lk
Assistant Librarian: Ms D Daniel
 E-mail: libdev@mail.natlib.lk
This directory includes 1080 Sri Lankan Publishers. It is divided into two parts: namely, Alphabetical Section & Numerical Section. In each section, the publishers are categorized into three groups: Commercial, Governmental & Non-Governmental Institutions & Author/Private Publishers. The ISBN Publishers Directory is computerized & the database is updated monthly.

Sri Lanka National Bibliography (J)
Published by National Library & Documentation Centre
No 14, Independence Ave, Colombo 07
Mailing Address: PO Box 1764, Colombo 07
Tel: (01) 698847 *Fax:* (01) 685201
E-mail: natlib@slt.lk
Web Site: www.natlib.lk
Key Personnel
Dir General: Mr M S U Amarasiri *E-mail:* dg@mail.natlib.lk

Deputy Dir: Mr G G Upasena *E-mail:* ddadmin@mail.natlib.lk
Text in English, Sinhala & Tamil. Contains information of the latest publications in Sri Lanka.
First published 1962.
Monthly.
420 LKR or 50 USD

Vidyodaya Journal of Social Sciences (J)
Published by University of Sri Jayewardenepura
Gangodawila, Nugegoda
Tel: (01) 802695; (01) 802696; (01) 803191; (01) 803192 *Fax:* (01) 852604
E-mail: unisjay@sjp.ac.lk
Web Site: www.sjp.ac.lk *Cable:* UNISJAY
Key Personnel
Editor-in-Chief: Winston E Ratnayake
Librarian/Coordinating Editor: Mr P Vidanapathirana
First published 1968.
Biannually.
ISSN: 1391-1937

Swaziland

Swaziland National Bibliography (J)
Published by University of Swaziland Library
Private Bag 4, Kwaluseni
Tel: 518-5108; 518-4011; 518-5356 *Fax:* 518-5276
E-mail: kwaluseni@uniswa.sz
Web Site: www.uniswa.sz
Telex: 222087WD
Irregularly.

Sweden

Bonniers Litteraera Magasin (Bonniers Literary Magazine) (P)
Published by Albert Bonniers Forlag AB
Box 3159, 103 63 Stockholm
Tel: (08) 696 86 20 *Fax:* (08) 696 83 61
E-mail: info@abforlag.bonnier.se
Web Site: www.bok.bonnier.se/new/albertbonniersforlag.htm

Svensk Bokfoerteckning (Swedish National Bibliography) (J)
Published by Kungliga Biblioteket, Tidnings AB Svensk Bokhandel
PO Box 5039, 102 41 Stockholm
Tel: (08) 463 40 00 *Fax:* (08) 463 40 04
E-mail: kungl.biblioteket@kb.se
Web Site: www.kb.se
ISSN: 0039-6443

Svensk Bokhandel (Swedish Book Trade) (J)
Published by Tidnings AB Svensk Bokhandel
Birkagatan 16 C, 113 86 Stockholm
Mailing Address: PO Box 6888, 113 86 Stockholm
Tel: (08) 545 417 70 *Fax:* (08) 545 417 75
Web Site: www.svb.se
Published jointly with Swedish Booksellers' Association.

Svenska Bokfoerlaeggarefoereningen (B)
Published by Swedish Publishers' Association
Drottninggatan 97 2tr, 113 60 Stockholm
Tel: (08) 736 19 40 *Fax:* (08) 736 19 44
E-mail: svf@forlagskansli.se
Web Site: www.forlagskansli.se
Key Personnel
Dir: Kristina Ahlinder *E-mail:* kristina.ahlinder@forlagskansli.se

Swedish Publishers' Association list of members & agents, together with book trade associates & organizations.
First published 1843.

Tex, Svensk Tidskrift foer Bibliografi (Text, Swedish Journal of Bibliography) (J)
Published by Dahlia Books, International Publishers & Booksellers
Box 1025, 751 40 Uppsala
Tel: (018) 101098 *Fax:* (018) 100525
E-mail: dahlia@telia.com
Bibliographical journal, in English & Swedish.
First published 1974.
Irregularly.
ISSN: 0345-0112

Switzerland

Bookbird: A Journal of International Children's Literature (J)
Published by International Board on Books for Young People (IBBY)
Nonnenweg 12, 4003 Basel
Tel: (061) 272 29 17 *Fax:* (061) 272 27 57
E-mail: ibby@ibby.org
Web Site: www.ibby.org
Key Personnel
President: Peter Schneck
Executive Dir: Kimete Basha
Editor: Evelyn B Freeman; Barbara A Lehman; Lilia Ratcheva-Stratieva; Patricia L Scharer
Covers many facets of international children's literature & includes news from IBBY & the IBBY National Sections.
Quarterly.
Back Issues $11.50
ISSN: 0006-7377

Drehpunkt (Pivot) (P)
Published by Lenos Verlag
Spalentorweg 12, 4051 Basel
Tel: (061) 261 34 14 *Fax:* (061) 261 35 18
E-mail: lenos@lenos.ch
Web Site: www.lenos.ch

Etudes de Lettres (Literary Studies) (P)
Published by Universite de Lausanne
Faculte des Lettres, BFSH2 bureau 2050, Universite' de Lausanne Dorigny, 1015 Lausanne
Tel: (021) 692-2978; (021) 692-2905 *Fax:* (021) 692-3045
E-mail: lidia.peytrignet@dlett.unil.ch
Web Site: www.unil.ch
Key Personnel
Editor: Johannes Bronkhorst
First published 1960.
Quarterly.
170 pp, 18 CHF (single vol), 26 CHF (double vol)
ISSN: 0014-2026

ƒ**International Publishers Association Proceedings of Congress** (B)
Published by International Publishers Association
Av de Miremont 3, 1206 Geneva
Tel: (022) 346 3018 *Fax:* (022) 347 5717
E-mail: secretariat@ipa-uie.org
Web Site: www.ipa-uie.org
Telex: 3421883 *Cable:* INPUBLASS
Key Personnel
Secretary-General: J Alexis Koutchoumow

Jugendliteratur (J)
Published by Schweizerischer Bund fuer Jugendliteratur (Swiss Federation for Youth Literature)
Gewerbestr 8, 6330 Cham
Tel: (041) 741 31 40 *Fax:* (041) 740 01 59
E-mail: sbj@bluewin.ch
Key Personnel
Chief Editor: Jutta Radel
Quarterly.
ISSN: 0256-6532

Librarium (J)
Published by Schweizerische Bibliophilen - Gesellschaft
Hoffnungsstr 3, 8038 Zurich
Text in German, French, Italian & English.
Triannually.
ISSN: 0024-2152

orte (P)
Published by orte-Verlag
Wirtschaft Kreuz, 9427 Wolfhaden
Tel: (071) 888 15 56
E-mail: info@orteverlag.ch
Web Site: www.orteverlag.ch

ƒ**La Propriete industrielle et le droit d'auteur** (Industrial Property & Copyright) (P)
Published by World Intellectual Property Organization (WIPO)
34, chemin des Colombettes, 1211 Geneva 20
Mailing Address: PO Box 18, 1211 Geneva 20
Tel: (022) 338 91 11 *Fax:* (022) 733 54 28
E-mail: info@wipo.int
Web Site: www.wipo.org
Telex: 412912 ompi ch
Key Personnel
Head Information Section: Laurent Manderieux
Monthly, English & French; Bimonthly, Spanish.

Pruefen & Handeln (P)
Published by Pruefen & Handeln/Examiner et Agir
8215 Hallau
Tel: (052) 6813144 *Fax:* (052) 6814014
E-mail: memopress@klettgau.ch
Web Site: www.klettgau.ch/pruefen&handeln
Cable: MEMOPRESS; Prufen & Handeln; Aktion Volk & Parlament
Journalism & literature; text in German. Short information on politics, economics & religion with commentary. Summary in French.
Parent Company: Aktion Volk und Parlament

Schweizer Buch (The Swiss Book) (J)
Published by Schweizerischer Buchhaendler- und Verleger-Verband SBVV (Swiss Booksellers' & Publishers' Association (German Language))
Hallwylstr 15, 3003 Bern
Tel: (031) 322 89 11 *Fax:* (031) 322 84 63
E-mail: slb-bns@slb.admin.ch
Web Site: www.snl.ch
Bibliographical bulletin. Cosponsored by Schweizerische Landesbibliothek.
First published 1943.
Bimonthly.
ISSN: 0036-732X

Schweizer Buchhandel (The Swiss Book Trade) (J)
Published by Schweizerischer Buchhaendler- und Verleger-Verband SBVV (Swiss Booksellers' & Publishers' Association (German Language))
Alderstr 40, 8034 Zurich
Tel: (01) 421 28 00 *Fax:* (01) 421 28 18
E-mail: sbvv@swissbooks.ch
Web Site: www.swissbooks.ch

Schweizer Buchhandels-Adressbuch (B)
Published by Schweizerischer Buchhaendler- und Verleger-Verband SBVV (Swiss Booksellers' & Publishers' Association (German Language))
Alderstr 40, 8034 Zurich
Tel: (01) 421 28 00 *Fax:* (01) 421 28 18
E-mail: sbvv@swissbooks.ch
Web Site: www.swissbooks.ch
Directory of the Swiss book trade, containing lists of publishers, booksellers, distributors, trade organizations & cross-reference indexes.
First published 1966.
Annually.
ISSN: 0080-7230

Schweizer Monatshefte (Swiss Monthly Magazine) (P)
Published by Gesellschaft Schweizer Monatshefte
Vogelsangstr 52, 8006 Zurich
Tel: (01) 361 26 06 *Fax:* (01) 363 70 05
E-mail: schweizermonatshefte@swissonline.ch
Web Site: www.schweizermonatshefte.ch
Monthly.
110 CHF

Taiwan, Province of China

Chinese National Bibliography (J)
Published by National Central Library
20 Chung-shan South Rd, Taipei
Tel: (02) 2361 9132 *Fax:* (02) 382 1489
E-mail: reader@msg.ncl.edu.tw
Web Site: www.ncl.edu.tw
Text in Chinese.

The Chinese PEN (P)
Published by International PEN, Taipei Chinese Center
4th floor, 4 Lane 68, When Chou St, Taipei
Tel: (02) 7219101 *Fax:* (02) 7219101
E-mail: taipen@tpts5.seed.net.tw
Key Personnel
Editor: Nancy C Ing
Text in English.
First published 1972.
Quarterly.

Counter Attack (P)
Published by National Institute for Compilation & Translation
247 Chou Shan Rd, Taipei
Tel: (02) 33225558 *Fax:* (02) 33225559
Web Site: www.nict.gov.tw
Key Personnel
Dir: Chi-chun Tseng
First published 1932.

Shu mo chi kan (J)
Published by Student Book Co Ltd
198, Sec 1, Ho-ping East Rd, Taipei 10610
Tel: (02) 3634156 *Fax:* (02) 3636334
E-mail: studentbook@web66.com.tw
Web Site: studentbook.web66.com.tw
Bibliography, text in Chinese.
First published 1966.
Quarterly.
ISSN: 0006-1581

Tamkang Review (P)
Published by Tamkang University, Graduate Institute of Western Languages & Literature
Tamkang University, Ching Sheng Bldg, Room 1101, 25137 Taipei
Tel: (02) 6215656 (ext 2329) *Fax:* (02) 6209912
E-mail: jwu@mail.tku.edu.tw
Web Site: www2.tku.edu.tw/~tfwx/trreview.htm

Journal mainly devoted to comparative studies between Chinese & foreign literatures; text in English.
Quarterly.

United Republic of Tanzania

Tanzania National Bibliography (J)
Published by Tanzania Library Service
Bibi Titi Mohamed St, Dar es Salaam
Mailing Address: PO Box 9283, Dar es Salaam
Tel: (022) 215 00 48; (022) 2150049 *Fax:* (022) 215 11 00
E-mail: tlsb@africaonline.co.tz
First published 1974.
Annually.
ISSN: 0856-003X

Umma (P)
Published by University of Dar Es Salaam
PO Box 35182, Dar es Salaam
Tel: (051) 410137 *Fax:* (051) 410137
E-mail: director@udsm.ac.tz
Web Site: www.udsm.ac.tz
Literary magazine published under the auspices of the Department of Literature, University of Dar Es Salaam.
Biannually.

Turkey

Turkiye Bibliyografyasi (Turkish National Bibliography) (J)
Published by National Library of Turkey
Bahcelievler, 06490 Ankara
Tel: (0312) 2126200 *Fax:* (0312) 2230451
E-mail: katalog@mkutup.gov.tr
Web Site: www.mkutup.gov.tr
Key Personnel
Librarian: Nurhan Naneci
First published 1928.
Monthly.
Annual subscription 48 USD foreign countries
ISSN: 0041-4328

Varlik (Existence) (P)
Published by Varlik Yayinlari AS
Cagaloglu, Yokusu 40/2, Istanbul
Tel: (0212) 518-0048 (Direct); (0212) 516-2004; (0212) 516-2013 *Fax:* (0212) 516-2005
E-mail: varlik@isbank.net.tr; varlik@varlik.com.tr
Web Site: www.varlik.com.tr
Key Personnel
Editor-in-Chief: Osman Deniztekin
Editor: Filiz Nayir Deniztekin; Enver Ercan
First published 1933.
Monthly.
2,500,000 TRL or 2 USD
ISSN: 1300-1728

United Kingdom

ƒ**AAB's British Bibliography of Rare & Out-of-Print Titles** (P)
Published by Magna Graecia's Publishers (UK)
PO Box 342, Oxford OX2 7YF
Tel: (01865) 553 653 *Fax:* (01865) 553 653
E-mail: orders@magnagraciaspublishers.co.uk
Web Site: www.magnagraeciaspublishers.co.uk
Key Personnel
Editor: Luigi Gigliotti
General Editor: Louis de Sybaris
First published 1975.
Weekly.
ISBN(s): 0-86340-002-7
ISSN: 1362-8534

ƒ**AAB's British Register of Wanted Publications** (B)
Published by Magna Graecia's Publishers (UK)
PO Box 342, Oxford OX2 7YF
Tel: (01865) 553 653 *Fax:* (01865) 553 653
E-mail: orders@magnagraciaspublishers.co.uk
Web Site: www.magnagraeciaspublishers.co.uk
Key Personnel
Editor: Luigi Gigliotti
General Editor: L de Sybaris
First published 1976.
Weekly.
ISBN(s): 0-86340-020-5
ISSN: 0966-2413

ƒ**AAB's Guide to Private English Language Schools in the United Kingdom for Overseas Students** (B)
Published by Magna Graecia's Publishers (UK)
PO Box 342, Oxford OX2 7YF
Tel: (01865) 553 653 *Fax:* (01865) 553 653
E-mail: orders@magnagraciaspublishers.co.uk
Web Site: www.magnagraeciaspublishers.co.uk
Key Personnel
Editor: Luigi Gigliotti
General Editor: Louis de Sybaris
First published 1975.
Annually.
ISBN(s): 0-95077-280-1
ISSN: 1363-1993

ƒ**Abstracts in New Technologies & Engineering** (J)
Published by CSA (Cambridge Scientific Abstracts)
3rd floor, Farringdon House, Wood St, East Grinstead, West Sussex RH19 1UZ
Tel: (01342) 326972 *Fax:* (01342) 310485
E-mail: service@csa.com
Web Site: www.csa.com
An index, with abstracts, to scientific & technical periodicals, published in the UK & US.
Bimonthly (journal); Quarterly (CD-ROM); Monthly (web).
$1145 euros, $1750 US, $1170 euros (rest of world)
ISSN: 1367-9899
Parent Company: Cambridge Information Group

ƒ**Advertiser's Annual 2003-2004** (B)
Published by Hollis Publishing Ltd
Harlequin House, 7 High St, Teddington, Middlesex TW11 8EL
Tel: (020) 8977 7711 *Fax:* (020) 8977 1133
E-mail: orders@hollis-pr.co.uk
Web Site: www.hollis-pr.com
Annually.
275 GBP (includes p&p)

ƒ**African Publishers Networking Directory** (B)
Published by African Books Collective Ltd
The Jam Factory, 27 Park End St, Oxford OX1 1HU
Tel: (01865) 726686 *Fax:* (01865) 793298
E-mail: abc@africanbookscollective.com
Web Site: www.africanbookscollective.com
Key Personnel
Head: Mary Jay *E-mail:* mary.jay@africanbookscollective.com
Resource directory of major African publishers.

The African Publishing Companion: A Resource Guide (B)
Published by Hans Zell Publishing Consultants
Glais Bheinn, Locharron, Ross-shire IV54 8YB
Tel: (01520) 722951 *Fax:* (01520) 722953
E-mail: hanszell@hanszell.co.uk
Web Site: www.hanszell.co.uk; www.africanpublishingcompanion.com
Key Personnel
Publisher & Editor: Hans M Zell *E-mail:* hzell@dial.pipex.com
Concise yet detailed information about many aspects of African publishing & book trade. Over 1,600 entries, extensively cross referenced. Purchase of book includes 24 month access to the online version.
First published 2002.
Biannually.
258 pp, 80 GBP or 130 USD
ISBN(s): 0-9541029-0-8

ƒ**African Research & Documentation** (J)
Published by Standing Conference on Library Materials on Africa (SCOLMA)
Commonwealth Secretariat, Marlborough House, Pall Mall, London SW1Y 5HX
Tel: (020) 7747 6164 *Fax:* (020) 7747 6168
E-mail: scolma@hotmail.com
Web Site: www.lse.ac.uk/library/scolma
Key Personnel
Editor: John McIlwaine *E-mail:* j.mcilwaine@ucl.ac.uk
First published 1973.
Triannually.
20 GBP or 48 USD

Agenda (P)
Published by The Agenda & Editions Charitable Trust
5 Cranbourne Court, Albert Bridge Rd, London SW11 4PL
Tel: (020) 228 0700 *Fax:* (020) 228 0700
First published 1959.
Quarterly.
Individuals: 26 GBP (UK), 28 GBP (Europe), 30 GBP (elsewhere); Libraries & Institutions: 30 GBP (UK), 32 GBP (Europe), 34 GBP (elsewhere)
ISSN: 0002-0796

ƒ**Alexandria: Journal of National & International Library & Information Issues** (J)
Published by Ashgate Publishing Ltd
Gower House, Croft Rd, Aldershot, Hants GU11 3HR
Tel: (01252) 331551 *Fax:* (01252) 344405
E-mail: journals@ashgatepub.co.uk
Web Site: www.ashgate.com
Key Personnel
Editor: Ian McGowan
ISSN: 0955-7490

Ambit (P)
Published by Dr Martin Bax
17 Priory Gardens, London N6 5QY
Tel: (020) 8340 3566
Web Site: www.ambitmagazine.co.uk

Key Personnel
Editor: Martin Bax
Poetry, prose, short fiction, illustration & reviews.
First published 1959.
Quarterly.
96 pp, 24 GBP (UK); 26 GBP or 52 USD (USA)
ISSN: 0002-6972

The Author (P)
Published by Society of Authors
84 Drayton Gardens, London SW10 9SB
Tel: (020) 7373 6642 *Fax:* (020) 7373 5768
E-mail: info@societyofauthors.org
Web Site: www.societyofauthors.org/prizes.htm
Key Personnel
Manager: Kate Pool *E-mail:* kpool@societyofauthors.org
First published 1890.
Quarterly.
30 GBP (UK); 35 GBP (overseas)
ISSN: 0005-0628

Best Book Guide (B)
Published by BookTrust
Book House, 45 East Hill, Wandsworth, London SW18 2QZ
Tel: (020) 8516 2977 *Fax:* (020) 8516 2978
Web Site: www.booktrust.org.uk; www.booktrusted.co.uk
Key Personnel
Contact: Ann Newton
Young Book Trust selection of paperbacks for children 12 & under.
Annually.

Book & Magazine Collector (J)
Published by Diamond Publishing Group Ltd
45 St Mary's Rd, Ealing, London W5 5RQ
Tel: (0208) 579 1082 *Fax:* (0208) 566 2024
E-mail: janice.mayne@dpgsubs.co.uk
Monthly.
3.50 GBP (UK); 3.95 GBP (Europe)
ISSN: 0952-8601

The Book Collector (P)
Published by The Collector Ltd
PO Box 12426, London W11 3GW
Tel: (020) 8200 5004 *Fax:* (020) 7792 3492
E-mail: info@thebookcollector.co.uk
Web Site: www.thebookcollector.co.uk
Key Personnel
Editor: Nicolas J Barker *E-mail:* nicolasb@nixnet.clara-co.uk
Antiquarian books & bibliography.
First published 1952.
Quarterly.
152 pp

BookBank (J)
Published by Nielsen BookData
Editorial Dept, 89-95 Queensway, Stevenage SG1 EA
Tel: (0870) 777 8710 *Fax:* (0870) 777 8711
E-mail: customerservices@nielsenbooknet.co.uk
Web Site: www.whitaker.co.uk
Key Personnel
Man Dir: Francis Bennett
CD-ROM containing bibliographic information on over 1,000,000 UK published titles, plus details of over 35,000 publishers' names & addresses.
Monthly or bimonthly.
Parent Company: Nielsen BookData
Ultimate Parent Company: VNU Business Media Inc

BookBank Global (J)
Published by Nielsen BookData
Editorial Dept, 89-95 Queensway, Stevenage SG1 EA
Tel: (01438) 744100 *Fax:* (01438) 745578
E-mail: customerservices@nielsenbooknet.co.uk
Web Site: www.whitaker.co.uk
CD-ROM containing bibliographic information on over 2,000,000 English language titles from the UK, Europe, USA, Australia, New Zealand & Southern Africa.
Monthly on 2 CD-ROMs.
Parent Company: Nielsen BookData
Ultimate Parent Company: VNU Business Media Inc

BookBank Global Compact (J)
Published by Nielsen BookData
Editorial Dept, 89-95 Queensway, Stevenage SG1 EA
Tel: (01438) 744100 *Fax:* (01438) 745578
E-mail: customerservices@nielsenbooknet.co.uk
Web Site: www.whitaker.co.uk
CD-ROM containing bibliographic information on over 2,000,000 English language titles from the UK, Europe, USA, Australia, New Zealand & Southern Africa.
Monthly on 1 CD-ROM.
Parent Company: Nielsen BookData
Ultimate Parent Company: VNU Business Media Inc

BookBank OP (J)
Published by Nielsen BookData
Editorial Dept, 89-95 Queensway, Stevenage SG1 EA
Tel: (0870) 777 8710 *Fax:* (0870) 777 8711
E-mail: customerservices@nielsenbooknet.co.uk
Web Site: www.whitaker.co.uk
Key Personnel
Man Dir: Francis Bennett
CD-ROM containing details of over 1.4 million out of print titles.
Quarterly.
Parent Company: Nielsen BookData
Ultimate Parent Company: VNU Business Media Inc

Books & Publishing in Argentina (B)
Published by Euromonitor PLC
60-61 Britton St, London EC1M 5UX
Tel: (020) 7251 8024 *Fax:* (020) 7608 3149
E-mail: info@euromonitor.com
Web Site: www.euromonitor.com
Analysis of retail, institutional, mail order & internet distribution channels; forecast sales data & trends to watch; title output by subject statistics; investigation into import & export sales.
1,500 USD

Books & Publishing in Australia (B)
Published by Euromonitor PLC
60-61 Britton St, London EC1M 5UX
Tel: (020) 7251 8024 *Fax:* (020) 7608 3149
E-mail: info@euromonitor.com
Web Site: www.euromonitor.com
Analysis of retail, institutional, mail order & internet distribution channels; forecast sales data & trends to watch; title output by subject statistics; investigation into import & export sales.
1,500 USD

Books & Publishing in Austria (B)
Published by Euromonitor PLC
60-61 Britton St, London EC1M 5UX
Tel: (020) 7251 8024 *Fax:* (020) 7608 3149
E-mail: info@euromonitor.com
Web Site: www.euromonitor.com
Analysis of retail, institutional, mail order & internet distribution channels; forecast sales data & trends to watch; title output by subject statistics; investigation into import & export sales.
1,500 USD

Books & Publishing in Belgium (B)
Published by Euromonitor PLC
60-61 Britton St, London EC1M 5UX
Tel: (020) 7251 8024 *Fax:* (020) 7608 3149
E-mail: info@euromonitor.com
Web Site: www.euromonitor.com
Analysis of retail, institutional, mail order & internet distribution channels; forecast sales data & trends to watch; title output by subject statistics; investigation into import & export sales.
1,500 USD

Books & Publishing in Brazil (B)
Published by Euromonitor PLC
60-61 Britton St, London EC1M 5UX
Tel: (020) 7251 8024 *Fax:* (020) 7608 3149
E-mail: info@euromonitor.com
Web Site: www.euromonitor.com
Analysis of retail, institutional, mail order & internet distribution channels; forecast sales data & trends to watch; title output by subject statistics; investigation into import & export sales.
1,500 USD

Books & Publishing in Canada (B)
Published by Euromonitor PLC
60-61 Britton St, London EC1M 5UX
Tel: (020) 7251 8024 *Fax:* (020) 7608 3149
E-mail: info@euromonitor.com
Web Site: www.euromonitor.com
Analysis of retail, institutional, mail order & internet distribution channels; forecast sales data & trends to watch; title output by subject statistics; investigation into import & export sales.
1,500 USD

Books & Publishing in China (B)
Published by Euromonitor PLC
60-61 Britton St, London EC1M 5UX
Tel: (020) 7251 8024 *Fax:* (020) 7608 3149
E-mail: info@euromonitor.com
Web Site: www.euromonitor.com
Analysis of retail, institutional, mail order & internet distribution channels; forecast sales data & trends to watch; title output by subject statistics; investigation into import & export sales.
1,500 USD

Books & Publishing in France (B)
Published by Euromonitor PLC
60-61 Britton St, London EC1M 5UX
Tel: (020) 7251 8024 *Fax:* (020) 7608 3149
E-mail: info@euromonitor.com
Web Site: www.euromonitor.com
Analysis of retail, institutional, mail order & internet distribution channels; forecast sales data & trends to watch; title output by subject statistics; investigation into import & export sales.
1,500 USD

Books & Publishing in Germany (B)
Published by Euromonitor PLC
60-61 Britton St, London EC1M 5UX
Tel: (020) 7251 8024 *Fax:* (020) 7608 3149
E-mail: info@euromonitor.com
Web Site: www.euromonitor.com
Analysis of retail, institutional, mail order & internet distribution channels; forecast sales data & trends to watch; title output by subject statistics; investigation into import & export sales.
1,500 USD

Books & Publishing in Italy (B)
Published by Euromonitor PLC
60-61 Britton St, London EC1M 5UX
Tel: (020) 7251 8024 *Fax:* (020) 7608 3149
E-mail: info@euromonitor.com
Web Site: www.euromonitor.com
Analysis of retail, institutional, mail order & internet distribution channels; forecast sales data & trends to watch; title output by subject statistics; investigation into import & export sales.
1,500 USD

UNITED KINGDOM

Books & Publishing in Japan (B)
Published by Euromonitor PLC
60-61 Britton St, London EC1M 5UX
Tel: (020) 7251 8024 *Fax:* (020) 7608 3149
E-mail: info@euromonitor.com
Web Site: www.euromonitor.com
Analysis of retail, institutional, mail order & internet distribution channels; forecast sales data & trends to watch; title output by subject statistics; investigation into import & export sales.
1,500 USD

Books & Publishing in Mexico (B)
Published by Euromonitor PLC
60-61 Britton St, London EC1M 5UX
Tel: (020) 7251 8024 *Fax:* (020) 7608 3149
E-mail: info@euromonitor.com
Web Site: www.euromonitor.com
Analysis of retail, institutional, mail order & internet distribution channels; forecast sales data & trends to watch; title output by subject statistics; investigation into import & export sales.
1,500 USD

Books & Publishing in Netherlands (B)
Published by Euromonitor PLC
60-61 Britton St, London EC1M 5UX
Tel: (020) 7251 8024 *Fax:* (020) 7608 3149
E-mail: info@euromonitor.com
Web Site: www.euromonitor.com
Analysis of retail, institutional, mail order & internet distribution channels; forecast sales data & trends to watch; title output by subject statistics; investigation into import & export sales.
1,500 USD

Books & Publishing in Russia (B)
Published by Euromonitor PLC
60-61 Britton St, London EC1M 5UX
Tel: (020) 7251 8024 *Fax:* (020) 7608 3149
E-mail: info@euromonitor.com
Web Site: www.euromonitor.com
Analysis of retail, institutional, mail order & internet distribution channels; forecast sales data & trends to watch; title output by subject statistics; investigation into import & export sales.
1,500 USD

Books & Publishing in Spain (B)
Published by Euromonitor PLC
60-61 Britton St, London EC1M 5UX
Tel: (020) 7251 8024 *Fax:* (020) 7608 3149
E-mail: info@euromonitor.com
Web Site: www.euromonitor.com
Analysis of retail, institutional, mail order & internet distribution channels; forecast sales data & trends to watch; title output by subject statistics; investigation into import & export sales.
1,500 USD

Books & Publishing in Switzerland (B)
Published by Euromonitor PLC
60-61 Britton St, London EC1M 5UX
Tel: (020) 7251 8024 *Fax:* (020) 7608 3149
E-mail: info@euromonitor.com
Web Site: www.euromonitor.com
Analysis of retail, institutional, mail order & internet distribution channels; forecast sales data & trends to watch; title output by subject statistics; investigation into import & export sales.
1,500 USD

Books & Publishing in Taiwan (B)
Published by Euromonitor PLC
60-61 Britton St, London EC1M 5UX
Tel: (020) 7251 8024 *Fax:* (020) 7608 3149
E-mail: info@euromonitor.com
Web Site: www.euromonitor.com
Analysis of retail, institutional, mail order & internet distribution channels; forecast sales data & trends to watch; title output by subject statistics; investigation into import & export sales.
1,500 USD

Books & Publishing in United Kingdom (B)
Published by Euromonitor PLC
60-61 Britton St, London EC1M 5UX
Tel: (020) 7251 8024 *Fax:* (020) 7608 3149
E-mail: info@euromonitor.com
Web Site: www.euromonitor.com
Analysis of retail, institutional, mail order & internet distribution channels; forecast sales data & trends to watch; title output by subject statistics; investigation into import & export sales.
1,500 USD

Books & Publishing in United States (B)
Published by Euromonitor PLC
60-61 Britton St, London EC1M 5UX
Tel: (020) 7251 8024 *Fax:* (020) 7608 3149
E-mail: info@euromonitor.com
Web Site: www.euromonitor.com
Analysis of retail, institutional, mail order & internet distribution channels; forecast sales data & trends to watch; title output by subject statistics; investigation into import & export sales.
1,500 USD

Books for Keeps (J)
Published by School Bookshop Association
6 Brightfield Rd, Lee, London SE12 8QF
Tel: (020) 8852 4953 *Fax:* (020) 8318 7580
E-mail: booksforkeeps@btinternet.com
Web Site: www.suffolkcc.gov.uk
Key Personnel
Man Dir: Richard Hill
Reviews of Children's Books.
6 times/yr.
18.60 GBP (UK); 22.50 GBP (overseas)
ISSN: 0143-909X

Books in Scotland (J)
Published by Ramsay Head Press
15 Gloucester Pl, Edinburgh EH3 6EE
Tel: (0131) 225 5646 *Fax:* (0131) 225 5646
E-mail: ramsayhead@btinternet.com
Key Personnel
Editorial Dir & International Rights: Conrad K Wilson
First published 1968.
Quarterly.
ISSN: 0143-1285

Books In The Media (J)
Published by VNU Entertainment Media UK Ltd
Endeavour House, 5th floor, 189 Shaftesbury Ave, London WC2H 8TJ
Tel: (020) 7420 6178 *Fax:* (020) 7836 2909
E-mail: bimsubs@galleon.co.uk
Web Site: www.thebookseller.com
Key Personnel
Editor: Tom Holman *E-mail:* t.holman@bookseller.co.uk
Listings of all National Daily & Sunday Press Reviews, TV & Radio Program Tie-ins, Serializations, Best Seller Lists & some Trade News & Comment, Inc Sales Index.
First published 1979.
Weekly.
128 GBP

The Bookseller (P)
Published by VNU Entertainment Media UK Ltd
5th floor, Endeavour House, 189 Shaftesbury Ave, London WC2H 8TJ
Tel: (020) 7420 6006 *Fax:* (020) 7836 6781; (020) 7420 6102 (advertising); (020) 7420 6103 (editorial)
E-mail: information@bookseller.co.uk
Web Site: www.thebookseller.com
Book trade newspaper.
First published 1858.
Weekly.
170 GBP (UK); 311 EUR (Europe); 406 USD (USA, Canada & elsewhere); 722 AUD (Australia & New Zealand)
ISSN: 0006-7539
Parent Company: VNU Business Media Inc
Ultimate Parent Company: VNU NV

Bookselling (J)
Published by Booksellers Association of the United Kingdom & Ireland Ltd
Minster House, 272 Vauxhall Bridge Rd, London SW1V 1BA
Tel: (020) 7802 0802 *Fax:* (020) 7802 0803
E-mail: mail@booksellers.org.uk
Web Site: www.booksellers.org.uk
Quarterly.
ISSN: 0969-4862

BPIF List of Members (B)
Published by British Printing Industries Federation (BPIF)
Farringdon Point, 29-35 Farringdon Rd, London EC1M 3JF
Tel: (0870) 240 4085
E-mail: info@bpif.org.uk
Web Site: www.bpif.org.uk
Directory of information on the BPIF & the Printing Industry.

British Humanities Index (BHI) (J)
Published by CSA (Cambridge Scientific Abstracts)
3rd floor, Farringdon House, Wood St, East Grinstead, West Sussex RH19 1UZ
Tel: (01342) 326972 *Fax:* (01342) 310485
E-mail: service@csa.com
Web Site: www.csa.com
Indexes humanities-related articles published by British newspapers & journals.
Quarterly (journal & CD-ROM), Monthly (web).
Print subscription: $750 euros, $1160 US, $775 euros (rest of world); CD-ROM $1250 euros; Web $1425 euros
ISSN: 0007-0815
Parent Company: Cambridge Information Group

British National Bibliography (J)
Published by The British Library
Boston Spa, Wetherby, W Yorks LS23 7BQ
Tel: (01937) 546070 *Fax:* (01937) 546586
E-mail: nbs-info@bl.uk
Web Site: www.bl.uk
British National Bibliography is available in-print, on-line & on CD-ROM.
First published 1950.
Weekly with 2 interim cumulations for Jan-April & May-Aug; annual volume.
ISSN: 0007-1544

Carousel - The Guide to Children's Books (B)
Published by David & Jenny Blanch
The Saturn Centre, 54-76 Bissell St, Birmingham B5 7HX
Tel: (0121) 622 7458 *Fax:* (0121) 622 7526
E-mail: carousel.guide@virgin.net
Web Site: www.carouselguide.co.uk
Triannually.
9.75 GBP (UK); 15 GBP (Europe & Ireland); 16 GBP (elsewhere)

Cencrastus (P)
Abbey Mount Techbase, Unit 1, Easter Rd, Edinburgh EH8 8EJ
Tel: (0131) 661 5687 *Fax:* (0131) 661 5687
E-mail: cencrastus@hotmail.com
Web Site: www.applegate.co.uk/company
Key Personnel
Editor: Raymond Ross
Scottish & International literature, arts & affairs.
First published 1979.

Triannually.
2.95 GBP

Chapman (P)
Published by Chapman Magazine
4 Broughton Pl, Edinburgh EH1 3RX
Tel: (0131) 5572207 *Fax:* (0131) 5569565
E-mail: admin@chapman-pub.co.uk
Web Site: www.chapman-pub.co.uk
Key Personnel
Editor: Joy Hendry
Assistant Editor: Gerry Stewart
Literary/magazine publisher.
First published 1970.
Triannually.
94th: 144 pp, One yr, 4 issues (personal): 16 GBP, 35 USD (USA), 21 GBP (overseas); Institutions: 20 GBP (UK), 43 USD (USA), 25 GBP (overseas)
ISSN: 0308-2695

ʃ**The Clio Montessori Series** (B)
Published by ABC-CLIO
c/o BR&D Ltd, Hadleigh Hall, London Rd, Hadleigh SS7 2DE
Tel: (01702) 552912 *Fax:* (01702) 556095
E-mail: mail@bookreps.com
Web Site: www.abc-clio.com
Collection of paperbacks, aimed at both teacher & parents, which covers Montessori's teachings & beliefs.

Critical Quarterly (P)
Published by Blackwell Publishing Ltd
108 Cowley Rd, Oxford OX4 1JF
Tel: (01865) 791100 *Fax:* (01865) 791347
E-mail: customerservices@oxon.blackwellpublishing.com
Web Site: www.blackwellpublishers.co.uk
Telex: 837022 OXBOOK G
Key Personnel
Editor: Colin MacCabe
Publishing Editor: Joanna Jellinek
ISSN: 0011-1562 (print); 1467-8705 (online).
Quarterly.
187 USD (Americas); 110 GBP (Europe); 123 GBP (elsewhere)

Current British Directories (B)
Published by CBD Research Ltd
Chancery House, 15 Wickham Rd, Beckenham, Kent BR3 5JS
Tel: (0871) 222 3440 *Fax:* (020) 8650 0768
E-mail: cbd@cbdresearch.com
Web Site: www.cbdresearch.com
Guide to directories published in the UK & Ireland.
First published 1952.
Irregularly.
14
ISBN(s): 0-900-246-936

ʃ**Dictionary of International Biography** (B)
Published by Melrose Press Ltd
St Thomas Pl, Ely, Cambs CB7 4GG
Tel: (01353) 646600 *Fax:* (01353) 646601
E-mail: info@melrosepress.co.uk
Web Site: www.melrosepress.co.uk
General reference publication listing leading individuals from all fields of interest.
29th, 199.50 USD, 135 GBP or 219 EUR
ISBN(s): 0-948875-19-4

Directory of BA Members (B)
Published by Booksellers Association of the United Kingdom & Ireland Ltd
Minster House, 272 Vauxhall Bridge Rd, London SW1V 1BA
Tel: (020) 7802 0802 *Fax:* (020) 7802 0803
E-mail: mail@booksellers.org.uk
Web Site: www.booksellers.org.uk

2002, 32 GBP plus 5 GBP overseas delivery
ISBN(s): 0-907972-83-7

Directory of Publishing in Scotland (B)
Published by Scottish Publishers Association
Scottish Book Centre, 137 Dundee St, Edinburgh EH11 1BG
Tel: (0131) 2286866 *Fax:* (0131) 2283220
E-mail: info@scottishbooks.org
Web Site: www.scottishbooks.org
Key Personnel
Administrator: Carol Lothian *E-mail:* carol.lothian@scottishbooks.org
Handbook for the Scottish book world, listing Scottish publishers, details of related organizations, the addresses of major Scottish bookshops, & information on support services.
Annually.

Directory of Publishing: United Kingdom, Commonwealth & Overseas (B)
Published by The Continuum International Publishing Group Ltd
The Tower Bldg, 11 York Rd, London SE1 7NX
Tel: (0207) 922 0880 *Fax:* (0207) 922 0881
Web Site: www.continuumbooks.com
Key Personnel
Editorial Dir: Philip Law

Directory of UK & Irish Book Publishers including distributors, sales agents & wholesalers (B)
Published by Booksellers Association of the United Kingdom & Ireland Ltd
Minster House, 272 Vauxhall Bridge Rd, London SW1V 1BA
Tel: (020) 7802 0802 *Fax:* (020) 7802 0803
E-mail: mail@booksellers.org.uk
Web Site: www.booksellers.org.uk
Full details on over 3000 UK & Irish publishers & their UK distributors, including imprints.
First published 1954.
Annually.
2002: 900 pp, 62.50 GBP
ISBN(s): 0-907972-78-0

ʃ**The Europa World Yearbook** (B)
Published by Europa Publications
Member of Taylor & Francis Group
11 New Fetter Lane, London EC4P 4EE
Tel: (020) 7842 2110 *Fax:* (020) 7842 2249
E-mail: info.europa@tandf.co.uk
Web Site: www.europapublications.co.uk
Over 4000 pages of up-to-date statistics & directory information surveying over 250 countries & territories & outlines over 1650 international organizations.
First published 1926.
Annually.
44th, 2 vols, 570 GBP
ISBN(s): 185743-175-8
ISSN: 0071-2302

ʃ**European Book World** (B)
Published by Anderson Rand Ltd
10 Willow Walk, Cambridge CB1 1LA
Tel: (01223) 566640 *Fax:* (01223) 566643
E-mail: info@andrand.com
Web Site: www.andrand.com
Detailed information on Publishers, Libraries & Booksellers throughout West & Eastern Europe, including former USSR. Details on over 150,000 organizations. Printed & CD-ROM.

The Good Book Guide (P)
24 Seward St, London EC1V 3GB
Tel: (0171) 490 9900 *Fax:* (0171) 490 9908
E-mail: enquiries@gbgdirect.com
Web Site: www.thegoodbookguide.com
Book review magazine, subscription only.
Monthly.

Granta (P)
Published by Granta Publications Ltd
2-3 Hanover Yard, Noel Rd, London N1 8BE
Tel: (0207) 704 9776 *Fax:* (0207) 704 0474
Web Site: www.granta.com
Key Personnel
Editor: Ian Jack
First published 1979.
Quarterly.
256 pp

ʃ**The Indexer** (J)
Published by Society of Indexers
Blades Enterprise Centre, John St, Sheffield S2 4SU
Tel: (0114) 292 2350 *Fax:* (0114) 292 2351
E-mail: admin@indexers.org.uk
Web Site: www.socind.demon.co.uk/indexer/indexer.htm
Journal of Australian, American, Canadian & Southern African & British Societies of Indexers.
First published 1958.
Biannually.
72 pp, 40 GBP
ISSN: 0019-4131

ʃ**Information Europe** (J)
Published by Beishon Publications Ltd
15 Micawber St, London N1 7TB
Tel: (0171) 336 6650 *Fax:* (0171) 336 6640
E-mail: beishon@mcmail.com
Web Site: www.biznet.maximizer.com/beishon
51 GBP

ʃ**Information Research Watch International (IRWI)** (J)
Published by CSA (Cambridge Scientific Abstracts)
3rd floor, Farringdon House, Wood St, East Grinstead, West Sussex RH19 1UZ
Tel: (01342) 310469 *Fax:* (01342) 310485
E-mail: service@csa.com, tjones@csa.com (sales); support@csa.com (technical support); eurosupport@csa.com (support in Europe)
Web Site: www.csa.com
Key Personnel
Editor: Mrs Pirkko Elliott *E-mail:* pirkko@dial.piper.com
Newsletter providing brief reports of research in library & information science, electronic publishing & use of the internet, & related fields such as publishing, museums, archives, records management, & information industry. Also includes an editorial & two articles per issue on aspects of research in library & information science.
First published 1980.
Bimonthly.
24 pp, Annual subscription includes access to a web database. Europe 350 GBP, 1535 USD, other nations 360 GBP
ISSN: 1470-1391
Parent Company: Cambridge Information Group

ʃ**International Printing Sourcebook** (B)
Published by Pira International
Randalls Rd, Leatherhead, Surrey KT22 7RU
Tel: (01372) 802080 *Fax:* (01372) 802079
E-mail: publications@pira.co.uk
Web Site: www.piranet.com
Covers pulp & paper, packaging, publishing & printing.
3rd, 150 GBP

IRWI, see Information Research Watch International (IRWI)

ʃ**The Journal of Commonwealth Literature** (J)
Published by SAGE Publications Ltd
1 Oliver's Yard, 55 City Rd, London EC1Y 1SP

Tel: (020) 7374 8500; (020) 7374 0645 (customer service) *Fax:* (020) 7374 8600
E-mail: info@sagepub.co.uk; orders@sagepub.co.uk
Web Site: www.sagepub.co.uk
Key Personnel
Man Dir: Stephen Barr
Editorial Dir: Ziyad Marar
Editor: John Thieme; Geraldine Stoneham
Critical & bibliographical forum in the field of Commonwealth writing. Published triannually, the first two issues contain critical comment on all aspects of Commonwealth & related literatures. The third issue contains a comprehensive bibliography of publications in the field.
4x/yr.
63 GPB/yr (individual), 220 GBP/yr (institutional)
ISSN: 0021-9894

Learned Publishing (J)
Published by Association of Learned & Professional Society Publishers
South House, The Street, Clapham, Worthing, West Sussex BN13 3UU
Tel: (01903) 871 686 *Fax:* (01903) 871 457
E-mail: sec-gen@alpsp.org
Web Site: www.alpsp.org/journal.htm
Key Personnel
Editor: Robert Welham
US Editor: Alma Wills
First published 1977.
Quarterly.
80 pp, 57 GBP, 92 USD or 92 EUR (individuals); 115 GBP, 185 USD or 185 EUR (institutions)
ISSN: 0953-1513

ʃ**Library & Information Update** (J)
Published by Chartered Institute of Library & Information Professionals (CILIP)
7 Ridgmount St, London WC1E 7AE
Tel: (020) 7255 0500 *Fax:* (020) 7255 0501
E-mail: update@cilip.org.uk
Web Site: www.cilip.org.uk/update
Key Personnel
Editor: Elspeth Hyams *E-mail:* elspeth.hyams@cilip.org.uk
News Editor: Matthew Mezey *E-mail:* matthew.mezey@cilip.org.uk
Associate Editor: Christina Brockhurst *E-mail:* christina.brockhurst@cilip.org.uk
Managing Editor, Production: Rachel Middleton *E-mail:* rachel.middleton@cilip.org.uk
Mediawatching: Laura Swaffield *E-mail:* laura.swaffield@cilip.org.uk
Art/Design Editor: Marianne Nyman *E-mail:* marianne.nyman@cilip.org.uk
Book Reviews Editor: Diana Dixon *E-mail:* diana.dixon@cilip.org.uk
Head of Advertising: Andrew Nelson-Cole *Tel:* (020) 7255 0550 *Fax:* (020) 7255 0551 *E-mail:* advertising@cilip.org.uk
Industry news, comment & debate within the library & information profession.
First published 2002.
Monthly.
Non-member subscription: 85 GBP (UK), 98 GBP (outside UK), 180 USD (North America)

Literary Review (J)
Published by The Literary Review & Quarto Ltd
44 Lexington St, London W1R 3LW
Tel: (020) 7437 9392 *Fax:* (020) 7734 1844
E-mail: litrev@dircon.co.uk; lindar@warnes.co.uk
Reviews of the best newly published fiction & nonfiction.
First published 1979.
Monthly.
64 pp, 30 GBP (UK), 36 GBP (Europe), 39 GBP (North America), 50 GBP (rest of world)
ISSN: 0144-4360

ʃ**LOGOS** (J)
Published by Whurr Publishers Ltd
19b Compton Terrace, London N1 2UN
Tel: (020) 7359 5979 *Fax:* (020) 7226 5290
E-mail: info@whurr.co.uk
Web Site: www.whurr.co.uk
Quarterly.
Vol 15, 45 GBP (individuals); 120 GBP (institutions)
ISSN: 0957-9650

London Review of Books (P)
Published by LRB Ltd
28 Little Russell St, London WC1A 2HN
Tel: (020) 7209 1141 *Fax:* (020) 7209 1151
E-mail: edit@lrb.co.uk
Web Site: www.lrb.co.uk
Key Personnel
Editor: Mary-Kay Wilmers
Bimonthly.
63.72 GBP (UK); 72.90 GBP (Europe); 42 USD (USA); 50 USD (Canada); 76.50 GBP (elsewhere)
ISSN: 0260-9592

New Books in German (J)
Published by British Centre for Literary Translation
c/o Goethe Institute, 50 Princes Gate, Exhibition Rd, London SW7 2PH
Tel: (020) 7596 4023 *Fax:* (020) 7594 0245
E-mail: nbg@london.goethe.org
Web Site: www.new-books-in-german.com
Key Personnel
Editor: Sally-Ann Spencer
Reviews German language literature (Swiss, Austrian & German) in English to promote sales into the British & USA markets.
Biannually.

ʃ**New Review of Academic Librarianship** (J)
Published by Taylor Graham Publishing
48 Regent St, Cambridge CB2 1FD
Web Site: www.taylorgraham.com
Key Personnel
Editor: Colin Harris
First published 1995.
Biannually.
Vol 10, 2004, 195 USD or 112 GBP (institutional); 41 USD or 25 GBP (individual)
ISSN: 1361-4533
Branch Office(s)
PMB 187, 12021 Wilshire Blvd, Los Angeles, CA 90025, United States

ʃ**New Review of Children's Literature & Librarianship** (J)
Published by Taylor Graham Publishing
48 Regent St, Cambridge CB2 1FD
Web Site: www.taylorgraham.com
Key Personnel
Editor: Dr Sally Maynard
First published 1995.
Biannually.
Vol 10, 2004, 195 USD or 112 GBP (institutional); 41 USD or 25 GBP (individual)
ISSN: 1361-4541
Branch Office(s)
PMB 187, 12021 Wilshire Blvd, Los Angeles, CA 90025, United States

ʃ**New Review of Hypermedia & Multimedia** (J)
Published by Taylor Graham Publishing
48 Regent St, Cambridge CB2 1FD
Web Site: www.taylorgraham.com
Key Personnel
Editor: Douglas Tudhope
First published 1995.
Biannually.
Vol 10, 2004, 224 USD or 136 GBP (institutional); 132 USD or 80 GBP (individual)
ISSN: 1361-4568
Branch Office(s)
PMB 187, 12021 Wilshire Blvd, Los Angeles, CA 90025, United States

ʃ**New Review of Information & Library Research** (J)
Published by Taylor Graham Publishing
48 Regent St, Cambridge CB2 1FD
Web Site: www.taylorgraham.com
Key Personnel
Editor: Peter Brophy
First published 1995.
Biannually.
Vol 10, 2004, 195 USD or 112 GBP (institutional); 41 USD or 25 GBP (individual)
ISSN: 1361-455X

ʃ**New Review of Information Networking** (J)
Published by Taylor Graham Publishing
48 Regent St, Cambridge CB2 1FD
Web Site: www.taylorgraham.com
Key Personnel
Editor: Michael Breaks
First published 1995.
Biannually.
Vol 10, 2004, 195 USD or 112 GBP (institutional); 41 USD or 25 GBP (individual)
ISSN: 1361-4576
Branch Office(s)
PMB 187, 12021 Wilshire Blvd, Los Angeles, CA 90025, United States

Orbis (P)
17 Greenhow Ave, West Kirby, Wirral CH48 5EL
Tel: (0191) 4897055 *Fax:* (0191) 4897055; (0191) 4301297
Web Site: www.orbisbooks.com
Key Personnel
Editor: Carole Baldock *E-mail:* carolebaldock@hotmail.com
Independent British literary quarterly with international connections; publishes mainly poetry, but uses some prose & letters; also features news, educational & review columns.
Quarterly.
15 GBP; 28 USD (overseas)

Outlets for Specialist New Books in the UK: A Subject Classified, Descriptive Directory (B)
Published by Peter Marcan Publications
PO Box 3158, London SE1 4RA
Tel: (020) 7357 0368
Entries on some 800 businesses of many kinds (including museum/art gallery shops, periodicals & associations, as well as related directories).

Outposts Poetry Quarterly (P)
Published by Hippopotamus Press
22, Whitewell Rd, Frome, Frome, Somerset BA11 4EL
Tel: (01373) 466653 *Fax:* (01373) 466653
Key Personnel
Editor: Roland John
New poetry, translations, essays & reviews.
Quarterly.
ISSN: 0950-7264

ʃ**PEN International Magazine** (J)
Published by International PEN
9-10 Charterhouse Bldgs, Goswell Rd, London EC1M 7AT
Tel: (020) 7253 4308 *Fax:* (020) 7253 5711
E-mail: info@internatpen.org
Web Site: www.internatpen.org
Published in English & French & issued with the assistance of UNESCO.
First published 1981.
Semiannual.
100 pp, 8 GBP or 13 USD
ISSN: 1010-4534

Phillip's International Paper Directory (B)
Published by CMP Data & Information Services
Division of CMP Information Ltd
Riverbank House, Angel Lane, Tonbridge, Kent TN9 1SE
Tel: (01732) 377591 *Fax:* (01732) 367301
E-mail: orders@cmpinformation.com
Web Site: www.cmpdata.co.uk
Key Personnel
Commerical Dir: Duncan Clark
Available in print & on CD-ROM.
First published 1904.
Annually.
2003: 752 pp, 149 GBP
ISBN(s): 0-86382-488-9
ISSN: 0954-8521

Planet - The Welsh Internationalist (P)
Published by Berw Cyf
PO Box 44, Aberystwyth, Ceredigion SY23 3ZZ
Tel: (01970) 611255 *Fax:* (01970) 611197
E-mail: planet.enquiries@planetmagazine.org.uk
Web Site: www.planetmagazine.org.uk
Key Personnel
Editor: John Barnie
Associate Editor: Helle Michelsen; Dafydd Prys
First published 1970.
6 times/yr.
128 pp
ISSN: 0048-4288

PN Review (P)
Published by Carcanet Press Ltd
4th floor, Alliance House, Cross St, Manchester M2 7AP
Tel: (0161) 834 8730 *Fax:* (0161) 832 0084
E-mail: info@carcanet.u-net.com
Web Site: www.carcanet.co.uk; www.pnreview.co.uk
Key Personnel
Editorial & Man Dir: Michael Schmidt
Features poetry & literary criticism.
First published 1972.
Bimonthly.
29.50 GBP

Poetry Now (P)
Published by Forward Press Ltd
Remus House, Coltsfoot Drive, Woodston, Peterborough PE2 7BU
Tel: (01733) 898101 *Fax:* (01733) 313524
E-mail: pnmag@forwardpress.co.uk
Web Site: www.forwardpress.co.uk
First published 1991.
Bimonthly.
15 GBP (UK); 25 USD (USA); 21 GBP (overseas)
Parent Company: Forward Press Ltd

Poetry Review (P)
Published by The Poetry Society Inc
22 Betterton St, London WC2H 9BX
Tel: (020) 7420 9880 *Fax:* (020) 7240 4818
E-mail: info@poetrysociety.org.uk
Web Site: www.poetrysociety.org.uk/review/review.htm
Key Personnel
Editor: David Herd; Robert Potts
Poetry & reviews.
Quarterly.

PR Planner (J)
Published by Waymaker Ltd
Chess House, 34 Germain St, Chesham, Bucks HP5 1SJ
Tel: (0870) 736 0010 *Fax:* (0870) 736 0011
E-mail: info@waymaker.co.uk
Web Site: www.waymaker.co.uk/prplanner
Key Personnel
Man Dir: Neil Palfreeman
CD-based media directory.
Quarterly.
1255 GBP (UK & Europe); 730 GBP (UK only/ Europe only); 940 GBP (any 5 countries)

Printing Trades Directory (B)
Published by CMP Data & Information Services
Riverbank House, Angel Lane, Tonbridge, Kent TN9 1SE
Tel: (01732) 377591 *Fax:* (01732) 367301
E-mail: orders@cmpinformation.com
Web Site: www.cmpdata.co.uk
Key Personnel
Commercial Dir: Duncan Clark *Tel:* (01732) 377423 *Fax:* (01732) 368324
Editor: Philip Dury *Tel:* (01732) 377542 *Fax:* (01732) 377483
Marketing Manager: Alison Prangnell *Tel:* (01732) 377627 *Fax:* (01732) 368324
E-mail: aprangnell@cmpinformation.com
Comprehensive directory on the UK print industry. Used by manufacturers, printers & print buyers.
First published 1960.
2003, 115 GBP
ISBN(s): 0-86382-502-8
ISSN: 0079-5372

Printing World (J)
Published by United Business Media International plc
Sovereign House, Sovereign Way, Tonbridge, Kent TN9 1RW
Tel: (01732) 377329 *Fax:* (01732) 377552
Web Site: www.dotprint.com
Key Personnel
Editor: Gareth Ward *E-mail:* gward@cmpinformation.com
The oldest weekly magazine serving the printing industry in the UK.
Weekly.
94.50 GBP (UK); 142 GBP (rest of world)

ƒPrivate Press Books (B)
Published by Private Libraries Association (PLA)
49 Hamilton Park W, London N5 1AE
Web Site: www.the-old-school.demon.co.uk/pla.htm
Key Personnel
Executive Secretary: James Brown
Editor, Private Press Books: Paul W Nash
Publications Secretary: David Chambers *E-mail:* dchambers@aol.com
Bibliography of the work of private presses throughout the world.
Annually.
25 GBP or 40 USD
ISSN: 0079-5402

ƒThe Rialto (P)
PO Box 309, Aylsham, Norwich, Norfolk NR11 6LN
Web Site: www.therialto.co.uk
Key Personnel
Editor: Michael Mackmin
Poetry magazine.
First published 1984.
Triannually.
56 pp, 12 GBP (UK); 14 GBP (Europe); 18 GBP (USA & Canada); 19 GBP (Australia & Japan)
ISSN: 0268-5981

ƒThe School Librarian (P)
Published by School Library Association
Lotmead Business Village, Unit 2, Lotmead Farm, Wanborough, Swindon SN4 0UY
Tel: (01793) 791787 *Fax:* (01793) 791786
E-mail: publications@sla.org.uk
Web Site: www.sla.org.uk
Key Personnel
Editor: Ray Lonsdale
Articles relating to school libraries & publishing for children. Reviews of books, websites & CD-ROMs.
First published 1937.
Quarterly.
56 pp, GBP 45
ISSN: 0036-6595

ƒSerials In The British Library (J)
Published by The British Library
Boston Spa, Wetherby, W Yorks LS23 7BQ
Tel: (01937) 546070 *Fax:* (01937) 546586
E-mail: nbs-info@bl.uk
Web Site: www.bl.uk
List all new serial titles acquired by the British Library reference departments & all UK serials received through legal deport. Coverage is worldwide & all subject areas.
Three printed issues, annual cumulation.
245 GBP (domestic); 305 GBP (foreign)
ISSN: 0260-0005

Sheppard's Book Dealers in Australia & New Zealand (B)
Published by Richard Joseph Publishers Ltd
PO Box 15, Torrington, Devon EX38 8ZJ
Tel: (01805) 625750 *Fax:* (01805) 625376
E-mail: sheppardsdir@aol.com
Web Site: www.sheppardsdirectories.co.uk
Key Personnel
Editor: Richard Joseph *E-mail:* rjoe01@aol.com
Advertising: Claire Brumham
Directory of antiquarian & secondhand book dealers in Australia & New Zealand. E-mail & web sites included.
4th: 252 pp, 27 GBP or 54 USD
ISBN(s): 1-872699-76-6

ƒSheppard's Book Dealers in Europe (B)
Published by Richard Joseph Publishers Ltd
PO Box 15, Torrington, Devon EX38 8ZJ
Tel: (01805) 625750 *Fax:* (01805) 625376
E-mail: sheppardsdir@aol.com
Web Site: www.sheppardsdirectories.co.uk
Key Personnel
Editor: Richard Joseph *E-mail:* rjoe01@aol.com
Advertising: Claire Brumham
Antiquarian & second hand book dealers on the continent of Europe.
First published 1967.
11th: 318 pp, 27 GBP or 54 USD
ISBN(s): 1-872699-65-0

Sheppard's Book Dealers in India & the Orient (B)
Published by Richard Joseph Publishers Ltd
PO Box 15, Torrington, Devon EX38 8ZJ
Tel: (01805) 625750 *Fax:* (01805) 625376
E-mail: sheppardsdir@aol.com
Web Site: www.sheppardsdirectories.co.uk
Key Personnel
Editor: Richard Joseph *E-mail:* rjoe01@aol.com
Advertising: Claire Brumham
A directory of antiquarian and secondhand book dealers in India & oriental countries.
Occasionally.
2nd, 24 GBP or 48 USD
ISBN(s): 1-872699-08-1

Sheppard's Book Dealers in Japan (B)
Published by Richard Joseph Publishers Ltd
PO Box 15, Torrington, Devon EX38 8ZJ
Tel: (01805) 625750 *Fax:* (01805) 625376
E-mail: sheppardsdir@aol.com
Web Site: www.sheppardsdirectories.co.uk
Key Personnel
Editor: Richard Joseph *E-mail:* rjoe01@aol.com
Advertising: Claire Brumham
Directory of antiquarian & secondhand book dealers in Japan.
2nd: 200 pp, 27 GBP or 48 USD
ISBN(s): 1-872699-66-9

UNITED KINGDOM

Sheppard's Book Dealers in Latin America & Southern Africa (B)
Published by Richard Joseph Publishers Ltd
PO Box 15, Torrington, Devon EX38 8ZJ
Tel: (01805) 625750 *Fax:* (01805) 625376
E-mail: sheppardsdir@aol.com
Web Site: www.sheppardsdirectories.co.uk
Key Personnel
Editor: Richard Joseph *E-mail:* rjoe01@aol.com
Advertising: Claire Brumham
Directory of antiquarian & secondhand book dealers in South America, South Africa & other countries.
88 pp, 21 GBP or 42 USD
ISBN(s): 1-872699-67-7

Sheppard's Book Dealers in North America (B)
Published by Richard Joseph Publishers Ltd
PO Box 15, Torrington, Devon EX38 8ZJ
Tel: (01805) 625750 *Fax:* (01805) 625376
E-mail: sheppardsdir@aol.com
Web Site: www.sheppardsdirectories.co.uk
Key Personnel
Editor: Richard Joseph *E-mail:* rjoe01@aol.com
Advertising: Claire Brumham
Directory of antiquarian & secondhand book dealers in the USA & Canada. E-mail & web sites included.
15th: 560 pp, 30 GBP or 60 USD
ISBN(s): 1-872699-72-3

Sheppard's Book Dealers in the British Isles (B)
Published by Richard Joseph Publishers Ltd
PO Box 15, Torrington, Devon EX38 8ZJ
Tel: (01805) 625750 *Fax:* (01805) 625376
E-mail: sheppardsdir@aol.com
Web Site: www.sheppardsdirectories.co.uk
Key Personnel
Editor: Richard Joseph *E-mail:* rjoe01@aol.com
Advertising: Claire Brumham
Antiquarian & secondhand book dealers in the British Isles, The Channel Islands, The Isle of Man & the Republic of Ireland.
Annually.
27th: 440 pp, 30 GBP or 60 USD
ISBN(s): 1-872699-78-2

ƒ**Sheppard's Dealers in Collectables (UK)** (B)
Published by Richard Joseph Publishers Ltd
PO Box 15, Torrington, Devon EX38 8ZJ
Tel: (01805) 625750 *Fax:* (01805) 625376
E-mail: sheppardsdir@aol.com
Web Site: www.sheppardsdirectories.co.uk
Key Personnel
Editor: Richard Joseph *E-mail:* rjoe01@aol.com
Advertising: Claire Brumham
Dealers of new & old collectables.
2nd, 18 GBP or 36 USD
ISBN(s): 1-872699-55-3

ƒ**Sheppard's International Directory of Ephemera Dealers** (B)
Published by Richard Joseph Publishers Ltd
PO Box 15, Torrington, Devon EX38 8ZJ
Tel: (01805) 625750 *Fax:* (01805) 625376
E-mail: sheppardsdir@aol.com
Web Site: www.sheppardsdirectories.co.uk
Key Personnel
Editor: Richard Joseph *E-mail:* rjoe01@aol.com
Advertising: Claire Brumham
Dealers of Ephemera.
First published 1994.
Every 6 years.
300 pp, 27 GBP or 56 USD

ƒ**Sheppard's International Directory of Print & Map Sellers** (B)
Published by Richard Joseph Publishers Ltd
PO Box 15, Torrington, Devon EX38 8ZJ
Tel: (01805) 625750 *Fax:* (01805) 625376
E-mail: sheppardsdir@aol.com
Web Site: www.sheppardsdirectories.co.uk
Key Personnel
Editor: Richard Joseph *E-mail:* rjoe01@aol.com
Advertising: Claire Brumham
Antiquarian & second hand print & map sellers.
4th, 27 GBP or 54 USD

Signal (P)
Published by Thimble Press
Lockwood, Station Rd, Woodchester, Stroud, Glos GL5 5EQ
Tel: (01453) 755566 *Fax:* (01453) 878599
E-mail: mail@thimblepress.biz
Web Site: www.thimblepress.biz
Approaches to children's books.
Triannually.
L17.50 (UK), L22 (elsewhere)

ƒ**Slavonica** (J)
Published by Maney Publishing
Hudson Rd, Leeds LS9 7DL
Tel: (0113) 249 7481 *Fax:* (0113) 248 6983
E-mail: maney@maney.co.uk
Web Site: www.maney.co.uk
Key Personnel
Editor: Jekaterina Young *E-mail:* katya.young@man.ac.uk
Academic publication on the languages, literature, history & culture of Russia & Central & Eastern Europe.
First published 1983.
Biannually.
120 pp, 28 GBP (individuals); 68 GBP (institutions)
ISSN: 1361-7427

Stand Magazine (P)
School of English, Leeds University, Leeds LS2 9JT
Tel: (0113) 233 4794 *Fax:* (0113) 233 2791
E-mail: stand@leeds.ac.uk
Web Site: www.people.vcu.edu/~dlatane/stand.html
Key Personnel
Managing Editor: Jon Glover
Literary magazine.
First published 1952.
Quarterly.
25 GBP (individuals); 35 GBP (institutions)

Swedish Book Review (P)
Published by Swedish-English Literary Translators Association
85 Ediva Rd, Meopham, Kent DA13 0ND
Tel: (01603) 593356 (subscriptions) *Fax:* (01603) 250599 (subscriptions)
E-mail: editor@swedishbookreview.com
Web Site: www.swedishbookreview.com
Key Personnel
Editor: Sarah Death
Translators review, in English, of works written in Swedish, originating from Sweden or Swedish writers in Finland.
First published 1983.
Biannually.
15 GBP, 25 USD or 200 SEK
ISSN: 0265-8119

The Times Literary Supplement (P)
Published by The Times Supplements Ltd
Admiral House, 66-68 East Smithfield, London E1W 9BX
Tel: (020) 7782 3000 *Fax:* (020) 7782 3100
Web Site: www.the-tls.co.uk
First published 1902.
Weekly.

UK Book Printers (B)
Published by Book Production Section BPIF
British Printing Industries Federation, Farringdon Point, 29-35 Farringdon Rd, London EC1M 3JF
Tel: (020) 7915 8300 *Fax:* (020) 7405 7784
E-mail: info@bpif.org.uk
Web Site: www.britishprint.com
Key Personnel
Editor: Leigh Martins
Biannually.

ƒ**UKBookWorld 2003 CD-ROM** (B)
Published by Clique Ltd
7 Pulleyn Dr, York Y024 1DY
Tel: (01904) 631752 *Fax:* (01904) 651325
E-mail: cole@clique.co.uk
Web Site: www.clique.co.uk
Price guide/reference 1.2 million+ books (second-hand/rare/out of print) on CD.
Annually in April.
36 GBP or 65 USD

Vigil (P)
Published by Vigil Publications
Station Rd, Gillingham SP8 4QA
Key Personnel
Editor: John Howard-Greaves
Poetry & Prose with the accent on developments in form & structure applied to contemporary themes.
Biannually.
6 GBP; 8 GBP (overseas)
ISSN: 0954-0881

Walford's Guide to Reference Material (B)
Published by Facet Publishing
7 Ridgmount St, London WC1E 7AE
Tel: (020) 7255 0590 *Fax:* (020) 7255 0591
E-mail: info@facetpublishing.co.uk
Web Site: www.facetpublishing.co.uk
Key Personnel
Production Manager: Kathryn Beecroft *Tel:* (020) 7255 0595 *E-mail:* k.beecroft@facetpublishing.co.uk
First published 1959.
Annually.
8th, 3 vols

Whitaker's Almanac (B)
Published by A & C Black Publishers Ltd
37 Soho Sq, London W1D 3QZ
Tel: (020) 7758 0200
E-mail: wayb@acblack.com
Web Site: www.acblack.com
Key Personnel
Editor: Lauren Hill
General reference book including information on British government.
First published 1868.
Annually.
135th: 1,300 pp, 40 GBP
ISBN(s): 0-7136-6497-5

ƒ**Whitaker's Books In Print: The Reference Catalogue of Current Literature** (B)
Published by Nielsen BookData
Editorial Dept, 89-95 Queensway, Stevenage SG1 EA
Tel: (0870) 777 8710 *Fax:* (0870) 777 8711
E-mail: customerservices@nielsenbooknet.co.uk
Web Site: www.whitaker.co.uk
Complete listing (5 volumes) of European English Language books in print. Contains details of over 1,110,000 titles from 41,273 publishers.
Annually.
14,523 pp, 580 GBP
ISBN(s): 0-85021-329-0
Parent Company: Nielsen BookData
Ultimate Parent Company: VNU Business Media Inc

Whitaker's Red Book - The Directory of Publishers (B)
Published by Nielsen BookData
Editorial Dept, 89-95 Queensway, Stevenage SG1 EA
Tel: (0870) 777 8710 *Fax:* (0870) 777 8711
E-mail: customerservices@nielsenbooknet.co.uk
Web Site: www.whitaker.co.uk
Complete listing of publishers & book trade organizations in the UK. Lists over 4,000 publishers, including addresses, e-mail, websites & contact details.
150 pp, 16.50 GBP
ISBN(s): 0-85021-328-2
Parent Company: Nielsen BookData
Ultimate Parent Company: VNU Business Media Inc

ƒ**Who's Who in Asia & the Pacific Nations** (B)
Published by Melrose Press Ltd
St Thomas Pl, Ely, Cambs CB7 4GG
Tel: (01353) 646600 *Fax:* (01353) 646601
E-mail: info@melrosepress.co.uk
Web Site: www.melrosepress.co.uk
Career profiles of leading achievers from this increasingly influential region.
First published 1989.
5th, 135 GBP, 219 EUR or 199.50 USD
ISBN(s): 1-903986-01-X

ƒ**Willing's Press Guide** (J)
Published by Waymaker Ltd
Chess House, 34 Germain St, Chesham, Bucks HP5 1SJ
Tel: (0870) 736 0010 *Fax:* (0870) 736 0011
E-mail: info@waymaker.co.uk
Web Site: www.willingspressguide.com
Media directory containing over 65,000 entries covering publications, organizations & media outlets.
Annually.
325 GBP (3 vols), 299 GBP (2 vols), 199 GBP (1 vol)

The World Market for Books & Publishing (B)
Published by Euromonitor PLC
60-61 Britton St, London EC1M 5UX
Tel: (020) 7251 8024 *Fax:* (020) 7608 3149
E-mail: info@euromonitor.com
Web Site: www.euromonitor.com
Global Reports incorporating: analysis of retail, institutional, mail order & internet distribution channels; forecast sales data & trends to watch; title output by subject statistics; investigation into import & export sales.
7,900 USD

ƒ**The World of Learning** (B)
Published by Europa Publications
Member of Taylor & Francis Group
11 New Fetter Lane, London EC4P 4EE
Tel: (020) 7842 2110 *Fax:* (020) 7842 2249
E-mail: info.europa@tandf.co.uk
Web Site: www.europapublications.co.uk
Directory lists over 30,000 academic institutions world-wide together with more than 150,000 staff & officials.
Annually.
53rd, 365 GBP
ISBN(s): 1-85743-135-9
ISSN: 0084-2117

ƒ**Writers' & Artists' Yearbook** (B)
Published by A & C Black Publishers Ltd
37 Soho Sq, London W1D 3QZ
Tel: (020) 7758 0200
E-mail: wayb@acblack.com
Web Site: www.acblack.com
Key Personnel
Editorial: Christine Robinson
Expert advice on writing techniques, research & markets.
Annually in Sept.
96th, 12.99 GBP
ISBN(s): 0-7136-6281-6
Parent Company: Bloomsbury Publishing PLC

Writers' Circles Handbook (B)
Published by Jill Dick
Oldacre, Horderns Park Rd, Chapel-en-le Frith, High Peak SK23 9SY
Tel: (01298) 812305
E-mail: oldacre@btinternet.com
Web Site: www.cix.co.uk/~oldacre
Key Personnel
Editor: Jill Dick *E-mail:* jillie@cix.co.uk
L5 post free

Writers News (P)
Published by Warners Group Publications plc
Wellington St, Leeds, West Yorks LS1 1RF
Mailing Address: PO Box 168, Leeds, West Yorks LS1 1RF
Tel: (0113) 238 8333 *Fax:* (0113) 238 8330
E-mail: letters@writersnews.co.uk
Web Site: www.writersnews.co.uk
Key Personnel
Editor: Derek Hudson *E-mail:* derek.hudson@writersnews.co.uk
Information on Markets, Competitions, Short Story Competitions, How-To Articles, for both the established & aspiring writer.
27.95 GBP

Writing Magazine (J)
Published by Warners Group Publications plc
Wellington St, Leeds, West Yorks LS1 1RF
Mailing Address: PO Box 168, Leeds, West Yorks LS1 1RF
Tel: (0113) 238 8333 *Fax:* (0113) 238 8330
E-mail: letters@writersnews.co.uk
Web Site: www.writersnews.co.uk
Key Personnel
Editor: Derek Hudson *E-mail:* derek.hudson@writersnews.co.uk
Commercial Manager: Janet Davison
Senior Sales Executive: Karen Chambers
Subscriptions: Christine Sheppard
Offers interviews with famous authors, writer profiles, how-to articles on poety, fiction, short stories, photojournalism, technology, nonfiction writing & more competitions.
Bimonthly.
14.95 GBP (6 issues)

United States

ƒ**Book Review Index** (B)
Published by The Gale Group
27500 Drake Rd, Farmington Hills, MI 48331-3535
Tel: 248-699-4253 *Fax:* (248) 699-8061
E-mail: galeord@gale.com
Web Site: www.gale.com
Telex: (313) 961-6637
Includes listings from outside the USA & Canada.

ƒ**Bookman's Price Index** (B)
Published by The Gale Group
27500 Drake Rd, Farmington Hills, MI 48331-3535
Tel: 248-699-4253 *Toll Free Tel:* 800- 877-4253 *Fax:* (248) 699-8061
E-mail: galeord@gale.com
Web Site: www.gale.com

ƒ**Contemporary Authors** (B)
Published by The Gale Group
27500 Drake Rd, Farmington Hills, MI 48331-3535
Tel: 248-699-4253 *Toll Free Tel:* 800- 877-4253 *Fax:* (248) 699-8061
E-mail: galeord@gale.com
Web Site: www.gale.com
Includes listings also from outside the US & Canada. There are three separate publications under this title: Regular Series, New Revisions & Autobiographies.

ƒ**Directory of Special Libraries and Information Centers** (B)
Published by The Gale Group
27500 Drake Rd, Farmington Hills, MI 48331-3535
Tel: 248-699-4253 *Toll Free Tel:* 800- 877-4253 *Fax:* 248-699-8061
E-mail: galeord@gale.com
Web Site: www.gale.com
US, Canada & International.

The Historical Novels Review (J)
Published by Historical Novel Society
824 Heritage Dr, Addison, IL 60101
Mailing Address: Booth Library, Eastern Illinois University, 600 Lincoln Ave, Charleston, IL 61920
Tel: 217-581-7538 *Fax:* 217-581-7534
E-mail: cfsln@eiu.edu (editorial); timarete@earthlink.net (subscription)
Web Site: www.historicalnovelsociety.org
Key Personnel
Coordinating Editor (UK): Sara Bowker
Coord Ed (USA): Sarah Johnson
Reviews of currently published historical fiction from the USA & Great Britain.
First published 1997.
Quarterly.
54 pp, 38 USD (airmail); 30 USD (surface), available with membership only
ISSN: 1471-7492

ƒ**International Literary Market Place** (B)
Published by Information Today, Inc
630 Central Ave, New Providence, NJ 07974
Tel: 908-286-1090 *Toll Free Tel:* 800-409-4929; 800-300-9868 (cust serv) *Fax:* 908-219-0192
E-mail: custserv@infotoday.com
Web Site: www.literarymarketplace.com
Directory of companies & individuals in the book publishing trade, covering 180 countries outside the US & Canada. Entries included for more than 10,000 publishers & 4300 book organizations, including agents, booksellers & library associations. The US & Canada are covered by Literary Market Place. Web version, which includes Literary Market Place, also available.
Annually.
38th: 1,790 pp, $239.00 USD/print, $399 USD/web
ISBN(s): 1-57387-205-9
ISSN: 0074-6827

Literary Market Place (B)
Published by Information Today, Inc
630 Central Ave, New Providence, NJ 07974
Tel: 908-286-1090 *Toll Free Tel:* 800-409-4929; 800-300-9868 (cust serv) *Fax:* 908-219-0192
E-mail: custserv@infotoday.com
Web Site: www.literarymarketplace.com
Directory of over 40,000 companies & individuals US & Canadian publishing. A two volume set, each containing two alphabetical names & numbers indexes, one for key companies listed & one for individuals. The rest of the world is covered by International Literary Market Place. Web version, which includes International Literary Market Place, also available.
Annually.

UNITED STATES

64th: 2,072 pp, $299.00 USD/print, $399 USD/web
ISBN(s): 1-57387-178-8 (2 volume set)
ISSN: 0000-1155

ƒReview - Latin American Literature & Arts (J)
Published by Americas Society
680 Park Ave, 4th floor, New York, NY 10021-5009
Tel: 212-249-8950 *Fax:* 212-517-6247
E-mail: inforequest@as-coa.org
Web Site: www.americas-society.org
Key Personnel
Managing Editor: Daniel Shapiro *Tel:* 212-249-8950 (ext 366) *Fax:* 212-249-5868
  E-mail: dshapiro@as-coa.org
Contemporary Latin American literature in English translation.
Biannually, mid-May & mid-Nov.
22 USD (domestic individuals); 32 USD (domestic institutes); 34 USD (foreign)

ƒScandinavian Review (J)
Published by American-Scandinavian Foundation
58 Park Ave, New York, NY 10016
Tel: 212-879-9779 *Fax:* 212-879-2301; 212-249-3444
E-mail: info@amscan.org
Web Site: www.amscan.org
Key Personnel
Editor: Adrienne Gyongy *E-mail:* agyongy@amscan.org
Cultural/literary/political magazine.
First published 1913.
Triannually.
15 USD (domestic individuals); 22 USD (foreign)

Solander
Published by Historical Novel Society
824 Heritage Dr, Addison, IL 60101
Mailing Address: 7 Ticehurst Close, Worth, Crawley, West Sussex RH10 7GN, United Kingdom
Tel: 217-581-7538 *Fax:* 217-581-7534
E-mail: histnovel@aol.com
Web Site: www.historicalnovelsociety.org
Key Personnel
Editor: Sarah Cuthbertson
  E-mail: sarah76cuthbert@aol.com
Publisher: Richard Lee
US Membership Secretary: Tracey Callison
  E-mail: hns@folkandfairy.org
Literary magazine for historical fiction, with articles, interviews & short fiction.
First published 1997.
Biannually.

38 pp, 38 USD airmail; 30 USD surface, available with membership only
ISSN: 1471-7484

Ulrich's International Periodicals Directory, see Ulrich's Periodicals Directory

ƒUlrich's Periodicals Directory (B)
Published by R R Bowker LLC
Subsidiary of Cambridge Information Group Inc
630 Central Ave, New Providence, NJ 07974
Tel: 908-286-1090 *Toll Free Tel:* 800-521-8110; 888-Bowker2; 888-269-5372 *Fax:* 908-219-0812
E-mail: ulrichs@bowker.com
Web Site: www.bowker.com; www.ulrichsweb.com
Key Personnel
Dir, Cust Serv, Fulfillment & Print Sales: Serge Sarkis
Four-volume set, arranged by subject classification, includes periodicals, newsletters, newspapers, annuals & irregular serials published worldwide. Also available on the Internet, CD-ROM, online & magnetic tape.
First published 1932.
Annual.
42nd, 2004: 11,600 pp, $749.00
ISBN(s): 0-8352-4591-8 (4 vol set)
ISSN: 0000-2100

ƒUnited Nations Publications (B)
2 United Nations Plaza, Sales Section, Rm DC2-853, New York, NY 10017
Tel: 212-963-8302 *Toll Free Tel:* 800-253-9646 *Fax:* 212-963-3489
E-mail: publications@un.org
Web Site: www.un.org/Pubs/index.html

Uruguay

Anuario Bibliografico Uruguayo (Uruguayan Bibliographical Annual 1968-) (B)
Published by Biblioteca Nacional del Uruguay
Ave 15 de Julio 1790, Casilla de Correo 452, 11200 Montevideo
Mailing Address: CP 11200, Montevido
Tel: (02) 48 50 30 *Fax:* (02) 49 69 02
First published 1946.
Annually.
400 pp
ISSN: 0304-8861

Venezuela

Bibliografia Venezolana (Venezuelan Bibliography) (B)
Published by Instituto Autonomo Biblioteca Nacional y de Servicios de Bibliotecas
Apdo 80593, Caracas 1080
Tel: (02) 943-1361 *Fax:* (02) 941-5219
Telex: 24621 VC
Biannually.
650 VEB or 30 USD
ISSN: 0798-0086

Zambia

National Bibliography of Zambia (B)
Published by National Archives of Zambia
Government Rd, Ridgeway, 10101 Lusaka
Mailing Address: PO Box 50010, 10101 Lusaka
Tel: (01) 254081 *Fax:* (01) 254080
E-mail: naz@zamnet.zm

Zimbabwe

ƒAfrican Publishing Review (J)
Published by African Publishers' Network (APNET)
18 Van Praagh Ave, Milton Park, Harare
Mailing Address: PO Box 3773, Harare
Tel: (04) 708413; (04) 20211801; (04) 708405 *Fax:* (04) 20211803
E-mail: apnetes@yahoo.com; apnet@harare.iafrica.com
Web Site: www.africanpublishers.org
Newsletter.
Bimonthly.

Zimbabwe National Bibliography (B)
Published by National Archives of Zimbabwe
PB 7729, Causeway, Harare
Tel: (04) 792741 *Fax:* (04) 792398
E-mail: archives@zim.gov.zw
Web Site: www.zim.gov.zw
Key Personnel
Dir: M I Murambiwa
Annually.
15 USD

Literary Associations & Prizes

Literary Associations & Societies

Listed in this section are literary associations and societies. Listings appear alphabetically under the country in which they are located. Other book trade associations and organizations can be found in the sections **Book Trade Organizations** and **Library Associations**.

Argentina

Academia Argentina de Letras (Argentine Academy of Letters)
Sanchez de Bustamante 2663, 1425 Buenos Aires
Tel: (011) 4802-3814; (011) 4802-5161; (011) 4802-7509 *Fax:* (011) 4802-8340
E-mail: aaldespa@fibertel.com.ar; aaladmin@fibertel.com.ar; aalbibl@fibertel.com.ar
Web Site: www.aal.universia.com.ar/aal
Key Personnel
President: Pedro Luis Barcia
General Secretary: Rodolfo Modern
Treasurer: Federico Peltzer
Founded: 1931
Specialize in philosophy, literature & linguistics.
Publication(s): *Boletin de la Academia Argentina de Letras* (Bulletin of the Argentine Academy of Letters, quarterly); *Serie de acuerdos acerca del Idioma*; *Serie de Clasicos Angentinos*; *Serie Estudios academicos y otras publicaciones*; *Serie Estudios Linguisticos y Filologicos*; *Serie Homenajes*

Argentinian PEN Centre
Member of International PEN
Coronel Diaz 2089, 17C, 1425 Buenos Aires
Web Site: www.oneworld.org
Key Personnel
President: Miguel A Olivera
Secretary: Alicia Bermolen; Luis Ricardo Furlan
Publication(s): *Boletin*

Australia

ASAL, see Association for the Study of Australian Literature Ltd (ASAL)

Association for the Study of Australian Literature Ltd (ASAL)
University of Queensland, Michie Bldg, St Lucia, Brisbane, Qld 4072
Tel: (07) 3665 1369 *Fax:* (07) 3665 2799
Web Site: www.asc.uq.edu.au
Key Personnel
President: Chris Lee *Tel:* (07) 4631 1045 *Fax:* (07) 4631 1063 *E-mail:* leec@usq.edu.au
Vice President: Lyn McCredden *Tel:* (03) 9244 3960 *Fax:* (03) 9481 6717 *E-mail:* lynmcr@deakin.edu.au
Treasurer: Simon Ryan *E-mail:* s.ryan@mcauley.acu.edu.au
Secretary: Paul Genoni *Tel:* (08) 9266 7256 *E-mail:* p.genoni@curtin.edu.au
Dir: Dr David Carter *E-mail:* david.carter@mailbox.uq.edu.au
Deputy Dir: Dr Martin Crotty *E-mail:* m.crotty@uq.edu.au
Executive Manager: Kerry Kilner *E-mail:* k.kilner@uq.edu.au
Founded: 1899
Publication(s): *Notes & Furphies*

Australasian Association for Lexicography (Australex)
Bond University, Gold Coast, Qld 4229
Tel: (07) 5595 2502 *Fax:* (07) 5595 2545
Web Site: www.anu.edu.au
Key Personnel
President: Bruce Moore
Vice President: Pam Peters
Treasurer: Julia Robinson
Secretary: Dr Pauline Bryant *Tel:* (02) 6125 5134 *Fax:* (02) 6279 8214 *E-mail:* pauline.bryant@anu.edu.au
Founded: 1990
Publication(s): *Australex* (newsletter)

Australex, see Australasian Association for Lexicography (Australex)

Australian Library Publishers' Society
Barr Smith Library, University of Adelaide, N Terrace, Adelaide, SA 5005
Tel: (08) 8303 5372 *Fax:* (08) 8303 4369
E-mail: library@adelaide.edu.au
Web Site: www.library.adelaide.edu.au/ual/publ/alps/
Key Personnel
Convener & University Librarian: Ray Choate *Tel:* (08) 8303 4064 *E-mail:* ray.choate@adelaide.edu.au
Represents 25 library publishers & markets approximately 300 publications.
Publication(s): *Catalogue of Members' Publications* (5th edition)

Australian Literature Society, see Association for the Study of Australian Literature Ltd (ASAL)

The Australian Society of Authors Ltd
PO Box 1566, Strawberry Hills, NSW 2012
Tel: (02) 93180877 *Fax:* (02) 93180530
E-mail: asa@asauthors.org
Web Site: www.asauthors.org
Key Personnel
Chair: Susan Hayes
Deputy Chair: Georgia Blain
Executive Dir: Jose Borghino *E-mail:* jose@asauthors.org
Treasurer: Libby Gleeson
Founded: 1963
Publication(s): *Australian Author* (triannually, magazine); *Australian Book Contracts*

Australian Writers' Guild Ltd
8/50 Reservoir St, Surrey Hills, NSW 2010
Tel: (02) 92811554 *Fax:* (02) 92814321
E-mail: admin@awg.com.au
Web Site: www.awg.com.au
Key Personnel
Executive Dir: Megan Elliott *E-mail:* melliott@awg.com.au
Publication(s): *A Matter of Cultural Sovereignty*; *The Writers' Directory: Writers for Screen, Stage, Radio & Television in Australia*

Bibliographical Society of Australia & New Zealand (BSANZ)
PO Box 1463, Waga Waga, NSW 2650
Tel: (03) 96699032 *Fax:* (03) 96699032
Web Site: www.csu.edu.au/community/BSANZ
Key Personnel
President: Prof Dirk H R Spennemann *E-mail:* dspennemann@csu.edu.au
Vice President: Prof Ross Harvey *E-mail:* rharvey@csu.edu.au
Secretary & Treasurer: Rachel Salmond *E-mail:* rsalmond@pobox.com
Founded: 1969
Publication(s): *Broadsheet* (triannually); *Bulletin* (quarterly)

BSANZ, see Bibliographical Society of Australia & New Zealand (BSANZ)

The Children's Book Council of Australia
PO Box 3203, Norwood, SA 5067
Tel: (08) 8332 2845 *Fax:* (08) 8333 0394
E-mail: office@cbc.org.au
Web Site: www.cbc.org.au
Key Personnel
President: Judy Moss *E-mail:* president@cbc.org.au
Secretary: Chris Donnelly *E-mail:* secretary@cbc.org.au
Treasurer: Kay Allport *E-mail:* treasurer@cbc.org.au
Awards Coordinator: Maureen Mann *E-mail:* awards@cbc.org.au
Branches in New South Wales, Queensland, South Australia, Tasmania, Victoria, Western Australia, Australian Capital Territory, Northern Territory.
Publication(s): *Reading Time* (quarterly)

Fellowship of Australian Writers
PO Box 3036, Ripponlea, Victoria 3138
Tel: (03) 9528 7088 *Fax:* (03) 9528 7088
E-mail: faw@ozemail.com.au

AUSTRALIA

Web Site: www.writers.asn.au
Key Personnel
President & Treasurer: Philip Rainford
Vice President: Michael Dugan
Vice President & Executive Officer: Marcus Niski
Awards Coordinator: Adrian Peniston-Bird
Twenty-one regional branches in suburbs of Sydney & country towns; 1,000 members.
Publication(s): *The Australian Writer* (bimonthly)

Fellowship of Australian Writers (Vic) Inc
PO Box 3036, Ripponlea, Victoria 3183
Tel: (03) 9528 7088 *Fax:* (03) 9528 7088
Web Site: www.writers.asn.au
Key Personnel
President: Philip Rainford *E-mail:* rainfordp@aol.com
Founded: 1928
All awards open the second week of September & close the third week of November each year.
Publication(s): *The Australian Writer* (bimonthly)

Melbourne PEN Centre
Member of International PEN
PO Box 2273, Caulfield Junction, Victoria 3161
Tel: (03) 95097257 *Fax:* (03) 95097257
Web Site: www.pen.org.au
Key Personnel
President: Judith Buckrich *E-mail:* buckrich@netspace.net.au
Secretary: Danik Bancilhon

NSW Writers' Centre
Rozelle Hospital, Balmain Rd, Rozelle, NSW 2039
Mailing Address: PO Box 1056, Rozelle, NSW 2039
Tel: (02) 95559757 *Fax:* (02) 98181327
E-mail: nswwc@ozemail.com.au
Web Site: www.nswwriterscentre.org.au
Key Personnel
Chairman: Angelo Loukakis
Deputy Chair: Pat Woolley
Treasurer: David LePage
Secretary: Alan Russell
Executive Dir: Irina Dunn
Founded: 1991
Resource & information centre for emerging & professional writers.
Publication(s): *Newswrite* (monthly)

Poetry Society of Australia
Grosvenor St, Sydney, NSW 2000
Mailing Address: PO Box N110, Sydney, NSW 2000
Tel: (02) 423861
Key Personnel
Joint Secretary: Robert Adamson; Debra Adamson
Publication(s): *New Poetry* (quarterly; also poems, articles, reviews, notes & comments, interviews)

Sydney PEN Centre
Member of International PEN
University of Technology, Sydney, PO Box 123, Broadway, NSW 2007
Tel: (02) 9514 2738 *Fax:* (02) 9514 2778
E-mail: sydney@pen.org.au
Web Site: www.pen.org.au
Key Personnel
President: Nicholas Jose
Vice President: Mary Cunnane; Rosie Scott
Honorary Secretary: Wilda Moxham
Honorary Treasurer: Chip Rolley
Founded: 1931
Publication(s): *Newsletter* (quarterly)

Austria

Austrian PEN Centre (Oesterreichischer PEN-Club)
Member of International PEN
Concordia Haus, Bankgasse 8, 1010 Vienna
Tel: (01) 5334459 *Fax:* (01) 5328749
E-mail: oepen.club@netway.at
Web Site: www.penclub.at
Key Personnel
President: Dr Wolfgang Georg Fischer
Secretary: Dr Peter Marginter
Publication(s): *Pen-Nachrichten* (biannually)

Institut fur Oesterreichkunde (Institute for the Knowledge of Austria)
Hanuschgasse 3/3, A-1010 Vienna
Tel: (01) 512-79-32 *Fax:* (01) 512-79-32
E-mail: loek.wirtschaftsgeschichte@univie.ac.at
Key Personnel
President: Prof Ernst Bruckmueller, PhD *Tel:* (01) 4277 41312 *E-mail:* ernst.bruckmueller@univie.ac.at
Secretary General: Bernhard Zimmermann
Founded: 1957
Publication(s): *Oesterreich Archiv* (yearly, book); *Oesterreich in Geschichte und Literatur (mit Geographie)* (bimonthly, journal); *Schriften des Institutes fuer Oesterreichkunde* (yearly, book); *Schriftenreihe Literatur des Institutes fuer Oesterreichkunde*

Oesterreichische Gesellschaft fuer Literatur (Austrian Literary Society)
Herrengasse 5, 1010 Vienna
Tel: (01) 5338159 *Fax:* (01) 5334067
E-mail: office@ogl.at
Web Site: www.ogl.at
Key Personnel
President: Marianne Gruber
Vice President: Helmuth A Niederle
Founded: 1961

Bahrain

Bahrain Writers & Literators Association
PO Box 1010, Manama
Key Personnel
President: Ali al-Shargawi
Secretary: Fareed Ramadan
Founded: 1969

Bangladesh

Society of Arts, Literature & Welfare
Society Park, K C Dey Rd, Chittagong
Web Site: www.bjfao.gov.cn
Key Personnel
General Secretary: Nesar Ahmed Chowdhury

Belgium

Academie Royale de Langue et de Litterature Francaises (Royal Academy of French Language & Literature)
Palais des Academies, One rue Ducale, 1000 Brussels
Tel: (02) 550-2277 *Fax:* (02) 550-2275
Key Personnel
Dir: Raymond Trousson
Vice Dir: Georges-Henri Dumont
Secretary: Andre Goosse
Publication(s): *Bulletin, Annuaire, Memoires*

Academie Royale des Sciences, des Lettres et des Beaux-Arts de Belgique (Belgian Royal Academy of Sciences, Letters & Fine Arts)
Palais des Academies, rue Ducale, One, 1000 Brussels
Tel: (02) 5502211; (02) 5502212; (02) 5502213 *Fax:* (02) 5502205
Web Site: www.cfwb.be/arb
Key Personnel
Secretary: Leo Houziaux *Tel:* (02) 5502203 *E-mail:* leo.houziaux@ulq.ac.be
Founded: 1772
Publication(s): *Biannual Bulletins, Memoirs, Year Book*

AEBLF, see Association des Ecrivains Belges de Langue Francaise (AEBLF)

Antwerp Bibliophile Society
Museum Plantin-Moretus, Vrijdagmarkt 22, 2000 Antwerp
Tel: (03) 2330294 *Fax:* (03) 2262516
E-mail: francine.demav@amtwerpa.be
Key Personnel
President: Prof L Voet, PhD
Secretary: Prof G Persoons, PhD; Prof L De Pavw-De Veen, PhD
Founded: 1877
Vereeniging der Antwerpsche Bibliophielen.
Publication(s): *De Gulden Passer* (annually)

Association des Ecrivains Belges de Langue Francaise (AEBLF) (Association of the Belgian Writers of French Language)
chaussee de Wavre, 150, 1050 Brussels
Tel: (02) 512 29 68 *Fax:* (02) 512 29 68
E-mail: aeb@euronet.be
Key Personnel
President: France Bastia *E-mail:* france.bastia@euronet.be
Vice President: Prof Emile Kesteman; Marie Nicolai
Secretary General: Jean Lacroix
Treasurer: Jean Pirlet
Publication(s): *Nos Lettres* (10 times/yr)

Belgian PEN Centre (French-Speaking)
Member of International PEN
10 Ave des Cerfs, 1950 Kraainem (Bx)
Tel: (02) 7314847 *Fax:* (02) 7314847
Web Site: www.oneworld.org/internatpen/centres.htm
Key Personnel
President: Huguette de Broqueville
E-mail: huguette.db@skynet.be
Founded: 1922
A voice of literature worldwide, bringing together poets, novelists, essayists, historians, critics, translators, editors, journalists & screenwriters. Members are united in a common concern for the craft & art of writing & a commitment to freedom of expression through the written word.

Belgian PEN Centre (French-Speaking)
Member of International PEN
10 Ave des Cerfs, 1950 Kraainem
Tel: (052) 351118 *Fax:* (052) 351119
Key Personnel
President: Huguette de Broqueville
E-mail: huguettedb@skynet.be
Secretary: M Fernand Auwera
Dutch-speaking.

Commission Belge de Bibliographie et de Bibliologie (Belgian Commission of Bibliography & Bibliology)
4 blvd de l'Empereur, 1000 Brussels
Tel: (02) 5195311 *Fax:* (02) 5195533
Web Site: www.kbr.be; opac.kbr.be/ekbr1.htm (web catalogue)
Key Personnel
Contact: Dr Raphael De Smedt
Founded: 1837
Publication(s): *Annuaire* (annually); *Coll: Bibliographia Belgica*

KANTL, see Koninklijke Academie voor Nederlandse Taal- en Letterkunde

Koninklijke Academie voor Nederlandse Taal-en Letterkunde (Royal Academy of Dutch Language & Literature)
Koningstr 18, 9000 Gent
Tel: (09) 265 93 40 *Fax:* (09) 265 93 49
E-mail: info@kantl.be
Web Site: www.kantl.be
Key Personnel
Permanent Secretary: Prof Dr Georges de Schutter *Tel:* (09) 265 93 42 *E-mail:* secretariaat@kantl.be
Librarian: Marijke de Wit *Tel:* (09) 265 93 43 *E-mail:* mdewit@kantl.be
Founded: 1886
Publication(s): *Jaarboek van de Koninklijke Academie voor Nederlandse Taal-en Letterkunde* (annually); *Verslagen en Mededelingen van de Koninklijke Academie voor Nederlandse Taal-en Letterkunde* (triannually)

Koninklijke Academie voor Wetenschappen Letteren en Schone Kunsten Van Belgie (Royal Belgian Academy of Sciences, Letters & Fine Arts)
Paleis der Academien, Hertogsstr 1, 1000 Brussels
Tel: (02) 550 23 23 *Fax:* (02) 550 23 25
E-mail: info@kvab.be
Web Site: www.kvab.be
Key Personnel
Publications Officer: Gilbert Reynderg *Tel:* (02) 550 23 32 *E-mail:* gilbert.reynderg@kvab.be
Permanent Secretary: Niceas Schamp
Dutch-speaking Royal Belgian Academy of Sciences, Letters & Fine Arts.
Publication(s): *Collectanea Biblica et Religiosa Antiqua*; *Collectanea Hellenistica*; *Collectanea Maritima*; *Corpus Catalogorum Belgii*; *Fontes Historiae Artis Neerlandicae*; *Iuris Scripta Historica*; *Iusti Lipsi Epistolae (The Correspondence of J Lipsius)*; *(Memoirs) & Fine Arts*; *National Biography*; *Proceedings Department of Letters*; *Studia Europea*; *Studies in Belgian Economic History*; *Year Book*

SABAM, see Societe Belge des Auteurs, Compositeurs et Editeurs (SABAM)

SLLW, see Societe de Langue et de Litterature Wallonnes ASBL

Societe Belge des Auteurs, Compositeurs et Editeurs (SABAM) (Belgian Society of Authors, Composers & Publishers)
Rue d'Arlon 75-77, 1040 Brussels
Tel: (02) 230 2640 *Fax:* (02) 231 1800
E-mail: 101641.2761@compuserve.com
Web Site: www.sabam.be
Key Personnel
President: Jacques Leduc
Man Dir: Thierry Dachelet *E-mail:* thierry.dachelet@sabam.be
General Manager: Peter Van Rompaey
Contact: Jean Darlier; Joseph Dethier
Publication(s): *Bulletin* (quarterly)

Societe de Langue et de Litterature Wallonnes ASBL (Society for Walloon Language & Literature)
Universite de Liege, 7 place du XX Aout, 4000 Liege
Tel: (086) 344432
E-mail: sllw.be@skynet.be
Web Site: users.skynet.be/sllw
Key Personnel
President: Guy Belleflamme *E-mail:* guy.belleflamme@skynet.be
Vice President & Editor: Marie-Guy Boutier *E-mail:* marie-guy.boutier@skynet.be
Secretary: Victor George
Publication(s): *Chronique de la Societe de Langue et de Litterature wallonnes* (Irregularly); *Dialectes de Wallonie* (Irregularly)

Bolivia

Bolivian PEN Centre (PEN Club de Bolivia (Centro Internacional de Escritores))
Member of International PEN
Casilla Postal 5920, Cochabamba
Key Personnel
President: Gaby Vallejo Canedo *E-mail:* gabyvall@supernet.com.bo

Brazil

Academia Amazonense de Letras
Rua Ramos Ferreira 1009 Terreo, CEP 69010-120 Manaus, AM
Tel: (092) 234-0584
Key Personnel
President: Djalma Batista
Secretary: Genesino Braga
Librarian: Mario Ypiranga Monteiro
Amazonas Academy of Letters.
Publication(s): *Revista*

Academia Brasileira de Letras
Ave Presidente Wilson 204-4° Andar, 20030-021 Rio de Janeiro-RJ
Tel: (021) 220-5391 *Fax:* (021) 220-6695
E-mail: academia@academia.org.br
Web Site: www.academia.org.br
Key Personnel
Secretary General: Abgar Renault
Librarian: Barbosa Lima Sobrinho
Publication(s): *Revista*

Academia Catarinense de Letras (Santa Catarina Academy of Letters)
c/o Prof Enrique Da Silva Sources, Integrated Center of Culture, Av Irineu Bornhausen 5600, 88010-970 Florianopolis SC
Tel: 2342166
Web Site: www.acle.com.br
Key Personnel
President: Doris Becke Machado Freitas
Founded: 1968
Publication(s): *Revista* (annually)

Academia Cearense de Letras (Ceara Academy of Letters)
Palacio da Luz, Rua do Rosario 1, 60005-590 Cortaleza, CE
Tel: (085) 2315669
E-mail: acletras@accvia.com.br
Web Site: www.secrel.com.br
Key Personnel
President: Artur Eduardo Benevides
Vice President: Ribeiro Branches
General Secretary: Cesar Loyal Barros
Founded: 1894
Publication(s): *Colecao Antonio Sales*; *Colecao Dolor Barreira*; *Revista da Academia Cearense de Letras*

Academia de Letras da Bahia (Bahia Academy of Letters)
Palacete Goes Calmon, Av Joana Angelica 198, 40050-000 Nazare, Salvador BA
Tel: (071) 321-4308 *Fax:* (071) 321-4308
E-mail: alb@stn.com.br
Key Personnel
President: Claudio Veiga
Vice President: Wilson Lins
Secretary: Edivaldo M Boaventura
Publication(s): *Revista* (annually)

Academia de Letras de Piaui
64000-490 Teresina, PI
Key Personnel
President: Jose de Arimathea Tito Filho
Piaui Academy of Letters.
Publication(s): *Revista*

Academia Mineira de Letras (Minas Gerais Academy of Letters)
Rua da Bahia 1466, Lourdes, 30160-011 Belo Horizonte-MG
Tel: (031) 3222-5764
E-mail: amletras@task.com.br
Web Site: www.academiamineiradeletras.org.br
Key Personnel
President: Murilo Badaro
Vice President: Miguel Augusto Goncalves; Raul Machado Horta

Academia Paraibana de Letras (Parabia Academy of Letters)
Rua Duque de Caxias 25, CP 334, 58000 Joao Pessoa, PB
E-mail: fsatiro@openline.com.br
Web Site: www.pbnet.com.br/openline/fsatiro/academia.html
Key Personnel
President: Wellington Hermes de Aguiar
Vice President: Claudio Santa Cruz Costa
Secretary: Humberto Cavalcante de Melo
Treasurer: Sergio de Castro Pinto
Founded: 1941
Publication(s): *Revista*

Academia Paulista de Letras (Sao Paulo Academy of Letters)
Largo do Arouche 312/324, 01219-010 Sao Paulo-SP
Tel: (011) 3331-7222 *Fax:* (011) 3331-7401
E-mail: acadsp@terra.com.br
Web Site: www.academiapaulistadeletras.org.br
Key Personnel
President: Erwin Theodor Rosenthal
Founded: 1909
Publication(s): *Biblioteca Academia Paulista de Letras*; *Revista da Academia Paulista de Letras*

Academia Pernambucana de Letras (Pernambuco Academy of Letters)
Ave Rui Barbosa 1596, Gracias, Barrio da Jaqueira, 52050-000 Recife-PE
Tel: (081) 3268-2211
Key Personnel
President: Luiz de Magalhaes Melo
Secretary: Dr Lucilo Varejao Filho
Founded: 1901
Publication(s): *Revista*

Brazilian PEN Centre (PEN Clube do Brasil (Associacao Universal de Escritores))
Member of International PEN

Praia do Flamengo 172-11° andar, Rio de Janeiro 2000
Key Personnel
President: Prof Marcos Almir Madeira
Secretary: Maria Cecilia Ribas Carneiro
Publication(s): *Boletim*

Bulgaria

Bulgarian Academy of Sciences, Institute of Literature
1, 15 Noemvri Str, 1040 Sofia
Tel: (02) 989-84-46 *Fax:* (02) 981-66-29; (02) 986-25-23; (02) 988-04-48
Web Site: www.bas.bg
Telex: (067) 224-24 BG
Key Personnel
Scientific Secretary General: Prof Naumya Yakimoff *Tel:* (02) 987-70-87 *E-mail:* yakimoff@eagle.cu.bas.bg
Founded: 1869
Publication(s): *Literatourna Missul* (Literary Thought)

Bulgarian Writers' Union
5 Anguel Kanchev, 1000 Sofia
Tel: (02) 898346 *Fax:* (02) 835411
Key Personnel
President: N Haitov
Publication(s): *Literaturen Front* (weekly); *Obzor* (Survey, quarterly, text in English, Spanish & French); *Plamak* (The Flame, monthly); *Savremennik* (quarterly); *Septemvri* (monthly); *Slaveiche* (monthly, for children)

China

China PEN Centre
Member of International PEN
Chinese Writers Activity Centre, 25 Dongtuchenglu, Beijing 10013
Fax: 8610 64221704
Key Personnel
President: Mr Ba Jin
Secretary: Jin Jianfan

Hong Kong PEN Centre (English-Speaking)
Member of International PEN
1/F, West, Lok Yen Bldg, 23D Peak Rd, Cheung Chau, Hong Kong
Tel: 25774168 *Fax:* 25774168
E-mail: hkpen_eng@yahoo.com
Key Personnel
President: Fred S Armentrout
Vice President: Peter Stambler
Secretary: Ruth Barzel
Publication(s): *Vietnamese Writers in Hong Kong's Camps, A Caselist*

Colombia

Colombian PEN Centre (PEN Internacional de Colombia)
Member of International PEN
PO Box 101830, Zona 10, Bogota
Tel: (01) 2846761; (01) 2561540 *Fax:* (01) 2184136
E-mail: pencolombia@hotmail.com
Key Personnel
President: Cecilia Balcazar de Bucher, PhD
Secretary: Gloria Guardia

Instituto Caro y Cuervo
Carrera 11, No 64-37, Apdo Aereo 51502, Bogota
Tel: (01) 3456004 *Fax:* (01) 2170243
E-mail: secretariagenera@caroycuervo.gov.co
Web Site: www.caroycuervo.gov.co
Key Personnel
Dir: Ignacio Chaves Cuevas
Secretary General: Carlos Julio Luque Cagua
Founded: 1942
Linguistics, Philology & Literature.

Instituto Colombiano de Cultura Hispanica
Calle 12, No 2-41, Apdo 5454, Bogota
Tel: (01) 3413857 *Fax:* (01) 2811051
Key Personnel
Dir: William Jaramillo Meja
General Secretary: Clemencia Vallejo de Meja
Publication(s): *Flora de la Real Expedicion Botanica del Nuevo*

Congo

Congolese PEN Centre
Member of International PEN
BP 2181, Brazzaville
Tel: 813601 *Fax:* 813601
Key Personnel
President: Emmanuel B Dongala

Czech Republic

Czech PEN Centre
Member of International PEN
28 rijna 9, 11000 Prague 1
Tel: (02) 24235546; (02) 24234343 *Fax:* (02) 24221926
E-mail: centrum@pen.cz
Web Site: www.pen.cz
Key Personnel
President: Jiri Stransky *E-mail:* jiri@pen.cz
Secretary: Libuse Ludvikova *E-mail:* libuse@pen.cz
Founded: 1925

Matice moravska
Arne Novaka 1, 60200 Brno
Tel: (05) 4949 1511 *Fax:* (05) 4949 1520
E-mail: bronek@phil.muni.cz
Web Site: www.phil.muni.cz
Key Personnel
President: Prof Jan Janak, Jr
Secretary: Dr Jiri Malir
Publication(s): *Casopis Matice moravske* (biannually)

Denmark

Dansk Forfatterforening (The Danish Writers Association)
Tordenskjolds Gard, Strandgade 6, Stuen, 1401 Copenhagen K
Tel: 32 95 51 00 *Fax:* 32 54 01 15
E-mail: danskforfatterforening@danskforfatterforening.dk
Web Site: www.danskforfatterforening.dk
Key Personnel
President: Mr Knud Vilby *E-mail:* knud@vilby.dk
Founded: 1894
Professional organization for authors, translators & illustrators of books for children & young people.
Publication(s): *Forfatteren* (8 times/yr)

Det Danske Sprog - og Litteraturselskab (Society for Danish Language & Literature)
Christians Brygge 1, 1219 Copenhagen K
Tel: 33130660 *Fax:* 33140608
E-mail: sekretariat@dsl.dk
Web Site: www.dsl.dk
Key Personnel
Dir: Jorn Lund *E-mail:* jl@dsl.dk
Secretary: Maria Krogh Langner *E-mail:* mkl@dsl.dk
Founded: 1911

Det Kongelige Danske Videnskabernes Selskab (The Royal Danish Academy of Sciences & Letters)
H C Andersens Blvd 35, 1553 Copenhagen V
Tel: 33435300 *Fax:* 33435301
E-mail: email@royalacademy.dk
Web Site: www.royalacademy.dk
Key Personnel
President: Prof Birger Munk Olsen
Secretary: Prof Ole Hansen *E-mail:* oleh@nbi.dk
Editor: Prof Flemming Lundgreen-Nielsen *E-mail:* flemnil@hum.ku.dk
Founded: 1742
Publication(s): *Biologiske Skrifter; Historisk-filosofiske Meddelelser; Historisk-filosofiske Skrifter; Matematisk-fysiske Meddelelser; Oversigt* (annually with an English summary, report); *Saerpublikationer*

Nyt Dansk Literaturselskab (New Danish Society for Literature)
Hotelvej 9, 2640 Hedehusene
Tel: 4659 5520 *Fax:* 4659 5520
E-mail: ndl@ndl.dk
Web Site: www.ndl.dk
Key Personnel
President: Morten Bagger *E-mail:* mba@fkb.dk
Manager: Anne Warming
Aims, Publication/Republication of books in short supply in libraries. Special activity, Magnaprint (large print books for partially sighted).

Ecuador

Academia Ecuatoriana de la Lengua
Roca E 960 y Tamayo, Quito
Tel: (02) 2901518 *Fax:* (02) 2543234
Key Personnel
President: Galo Rene Perez
Secretary: Piedad Larrea Borja
Publication(s): *Memorias de la Academia de la hengua*

Casa de la Cultura Ecuatoriana Benjamin Carrion
Av 6 de Diciembre 794, Apdo 67, Quito
Tel: (02) 2902262 *Fax:* (02) 2566070
E-mail: info@cce.org.ec
Web Site: cce.org.ec
Key Personnel
President: Raul Perez Torres
Secretary General: Dr Marco Antonio Rodriguez
Founded: 1944

Egypt (Arab Republic of Egypt)

Atelier, L
8 Victor Bassili St, 6 Pharaana St, Azarita, Alexandria
Tel: (03) 4820526 *Fax:* (03) 4837662
Key Personnel
Honorary President: Prof Naima El-Shishiny
Honorary Secretary: D Farouk Wahba
Society of Artists & Writers.

Finland

Finlands svenska forfattareforening (Society of Swedish Authors in Finland)
Uhro Kekkonens gata 8 B 14, 00100 Helsingfors
Tel: (09) 446266 *Fax:* (09) 446871
Key Personnel
President: Thomas Wulff
Vice President: Monika Fagerholm; Nalle Valtiala
Secretary: Merete Jensen
Founded: 1919
Membership(s): The Three Seas Writer's & Translator's Council; European Writer's Congress; Baltic Writer's Council; Nordic Writer's Council.

Finnish PEN Centre
Member of International PEN
Kauppakartanonkatu 25 G 86, 00930 Helsinki
Mailing Address: PO Box 84, 00131 Helsinki
Tel: (09) 3431186 *Fax:* (09) 3431186
Key Personnel
President: Elisabeth Nordgren *E-mail:* elisabeth.nordgren@pp.inet.fi
Secretary: Sanna Jaatinen

Kirjallisuudentutkijain Seura (Finnish Literary Research Society)
Dept of Finnish Literature, University of Helsinki, PL 3, Fabianink 33, 00014 Helsinki
Tel: (09) 19122658 *Fax:* (09) 19123008
Web Site: www.helsinki.fi/jarj/skts
Telex: 124690
Key Personnel
President: Prof Kaimikkoven *Tel:* (09) 40 8289924
Secretary: Mirjam Ilvas
Founded: 1929
Publication(s): *Kirjallisuudentutkijain Seuran Vuosikirja* (The Yearbook of the Literary Research Society)

Suomalainen Tiedeakatemia (Finnish Academy of Science & Letters)
Mariankatu 5, 00170 Helsinki
Tel: (09) 636800 *Fax:* (09) 660117
E-mail: acadsci@acadsci.fi
Web Site: www.acadsci.fi
Key Personnel
President: Mauno Koivisto
Secretary General: Matti Saarnisto *Tel:* (09) 636806 *E-mail:* matti.saarnisto@acadsci.fi
Founded: 1908
Publication(s): *Annales Academiae Scientiarium Gennicae, Geologica*; *Annales Academiae Scientiarium, Humaniora*; *Annales Academiae Scientiarum Fennicae, Mathematica*; *Folklore Fellows' Communications, FFC*; *Vuosikirja* (Yearbook)

Suomalaisen Kirjallisuuden Seura (Finnish Literature Society)
Hallituskatu 1, 00170 Helsinki
Tel: (09) 131231 *Fax:* (09) 13123220
E-mail: sks-fls@finlit.fi
Web Site: www.finlit.fi
Key Personnel
Secretary-General: Urpo Vento
Publisher: Matti Suurpaeae
Librarian: Henni Ilomaeki
Dir, Finnish Literature Information Centre: Marja-Leena Rautalin
Dir, Folklore Archive: Pekka Laaksonen
Dir, Literature Archive: Kaarina Sala
Specialize in folklore, ethnology, literary research, Finnish language, cultural history.
Publication(s): *Studia Fennica*; *Suomi*; *Tietolipas*; *Toimituksia* (irregular)

Svenska Litteratursaellskapet i Finland (Society of Swedish Literature in Finland)
Riddaregatan 5, 00170 Helsinki
Tel: (09) 618777 *Fax:* (09) 6187 7277
E-mail: sls@mail.sls.fi
Web Site: www.sls.fi
Key Personnel
Editor: Nina Edgren-Henrichson *E-mail:* nina.edgren-henrichson@sls.fi
Founded: 1885
Swedish Literary Society in Finland.
Publication(s): *Skrifter utgivna av Svenska Litteratursaellskapet i Finland* (Writings)

Svenska Oesterbottens Litteratufoerening (Swedish Oesterbottens Literary Association)
Stagnasvagen 85, 66640 Maxmo
Tel: (06) 3450286
Key Personnel
Contact: Gun Anderssen
Publication(s): *Horisont*

France

Academie Goncourte, Societe de gens de Lettres
c/o Drouant, Place Gaillon, 75002 Paris
Key Personnel
Presidents: Herve Bazin; Francis Nourissier
Responsible for annual prizes-poetry scholarships, best romance novels, biographies.

CALCRE, Association d'Information et de Defense des Auteurs
BP 17, 94404 Vitry Cedex
E-mail: secr@calcre.com
Web Site: www.calcre.com
Key Personnel
President: Roger Gaillard
Secretary: Claude Aubert
Treasurer: Andre Muriel
Founded: 1979
Publication(s): *Arlit - Annuaire des Revues Litteraires & Cie* (triannually); *Audace - Annuaire a l'Usage des Auteurs Cherchant un Editeur* (triannually); *Ecrire & Editer* (bimonthly, magazine); *Savelivre - Guide des Salons et des Fetes du Livre* (quarterly)

Centre National du Livre
Hotel de Avejan, 53 rue de Verneuil, 75343 Paris Cedex 07
Tel: (01) 49546868 *Fax:* (01) 45491021
Web Site: www.centrenationaldulivre.fr
Key Personnel
President: Eric Gross *Tel:* (01) 49 54 68 20
Secretary General: Michel Marian *Tel:* (01) 49 54 68 59 *E-mail:* michel.marian@culture.gouv.fr
National Literary Centre.

French PEN Centre (PEN Club Francais)
Member of International PEN
6 rue Francois-Miron, 75004 Paris
Tel: (01) 42773787 *Fax:* (01) 42786487
Key Personnel
Secretary: Sylvestre Clancier

Maison des Ecrivains (Writers' House)
Hotel d'Avejan, 53 rue de Verneuil, 75007 Paris
Tel: (01) 49546880 *Fax:* (01) 42842087
E-mail: courrier@maison-des-ecrivains.asso.fr
Web Site: www.maison-des-ecrivains.asso.fr
Key Personnel
President: Claude Esteban
Dir: Eric Gross

SACD, see Societe des Auteurs et Compositeurs Dramatiques (SACD)

SNAC, see Syndicat National des Auteurs et Compositeurs

Societe des Auteurs et Compositeurs Dramatiques (SACD)
11 bis rue Ballu, 75442 Paris Cedex 09
Tel: (01) 40 23 44 44 *Fax:* (01) 45 26 74 28
E-mail: infosacd@sacd.fr
Web Site: www.sacd.fr
Key Personnel
Dir General: Pascal Rogard
Dir, Communications: Dominique Racle
Publication(s): *SACD*
Subsidiaries:

Societe des Gens de Lettres de France
Hotel de Massa, 38, rue du Faubourg Saint-Jacques, 75014 Paris
Tel: (01) 53 10 12 00 *Fax:* (01) 53 10 12 12
E-mail: depot.sgdlf@wanadoo.fr
Web Site: www.sgdl.org
Telex: 206 963 F
Key Personnel
President: Alain Absire
First Vice President: Marie-France Briselance
Secretary General: Jean Claude Bologne
Treasurer: Francois Taillandier
Founded: 1838
Publication(s): *Journal des Lettres et de l'Audiovisuel*; *Revue des Lettres et de l'Audiovisuel*

la Societe des Poetes Francais
Hotel de Massa, 38, rue du Faubourg Saint-Jacques, 75014 Paris
Tel: (01) 60 29 46 06
E-mail: poetesfrancais@aol.com
Key Personnel
President: Vital Heurtebize
Secretary General: Linda Bastide
Founded: 1902
Publication(s): *Bulletin* (triannually)

Societe d'Etudes Dantesques
Centre Universitaire Mediterraneen, 65 Promenade des Anglais, 06000 Nice
Tel: 497134610; 497134611 *Fax:* 497134640
E-mail: cum@ville-nice.fr
Web Site: www.cum-nice.org
Key Personnel
Secretary General: Simon Lorenzi

Societe d'Histoire Litteraire de la France
112 rue Monge, F-75005 Paris
Mailing Address: BP 173, F-75005 Paris
Tel: (01) 45872330 *Fax:* (01) 45872330
E-mail: srhlf@aol.com
Key Personnel
President: R Pomeau

Founded: 1893
French Literary History Association.
Publication(s): *Revue d'Histoire litteraire de la France* (alternate months)

Syndicat National des Auteurs et Compositeurs
80 rue Taitbout, 75442 Paris Cedex 09
Tel: (01) 48 74 96 30 *Fax:* (01) 42 81 40 21
E-mail: snac.fr@wanadoo.fr
Web Site: www.snac.fr
Key Personnel
President: Maurice Cury
Publication(s): *Bulletin des Auteurs*

Germany

Adalbert Stifter Verein eV (Adalbert Stifter Association)
Hochstr 8, 81669 Munich
Tel: (089) 4489807 *Fax:* (089) 4891148
E-mail: asv.@asv-muen.de
Web Site: www.asv-muen.de
Key Personnel
Chairman: Prof Otto Herbert Hajek
Manager: Dr Peter Becher
Founded: 1947
Information brochure in German, Czech & English; literature, art, cultural history of Bohemia & Moravia.
Publication(s): *Stifter-Jahrbuch/Neue Folge* (since 1987)

Bundesverband junger Autoren und Autorinnen eV
Kannenbaeckerstr 9, 53340 Meckenheim
Mailing Address: Postfach 200303, 53133 Bonn
Tel: (02225) 7889 *Fax:* (02225) 7889
E-mail: bvjaa@t-online.de
Web Site: www.bvja-online.de
Key Personnel
Chairman: Heike Prassel *E-mail:* heike.prassel@bvja-online.de
Secretary: Michael Graf *E-mail:* michael.graf@bvja-online.de
Manager: Thomas Stichtenoth *E-mail:* thomas.stichtenoth@bvja-online.de
Founded: 1987
Publication(s): *Konzepte*; *LiteraturMagazin*

Deutsche Akademie fuer Sprache und Dichtung (German Academy of Language & Poetry)
Alexandraweg 23, 64287 Darmstadt
Tel: (06151) 40920 *Fax:* (06151) 409299
E-mail: sekretariat@deutscheakademie.de
Web Site: www.deutscheakademie.de
Key Personnel
President: Prof Dr Christian Meier
Secretary-General: Dr Bernd Busch
Founded: 1949
Publication(s): *Dichtung & Sprache* (irregularly); *Jahrbuch der Deutschen Akademie fuer Sprache & Dichtung* (annually); *Preisschriften* (annually); *Veroeffentlichungen der Deutschen Akademie fuer Sprache & Dichtung* (irregularly)

Deutscher Literaturfonds eV
Alexandraweg 23, 64287 Darmstadt
Tel: (06151) 40930 *Fax:* (06151) 409333
E-mail: deutscher.literaturfonds@t-online.de
Web Site: www.deutscher-literaturfonds.de
Key Personnel
Secretary General: Bernd Busch *E-mail:* dette@deutscher-literaturfonds.de

Gesellschaft fur Interkulturelle Germanistik eV (GIG)
c/o Institut fur Literaturwissenschaft der Universitat, Universitat Friderciana-Karlsruhe, Kaiserstr 12, 76128 Karlsruhe
Tel: (0721) 6080 *Fax:* (0721) 6084290
Key Personnel
President, University Bayreuth: Prof A Wierlacher, PhD
Vice President, University Karlsruhe: Prof B Thum, PhD

Gesellschaft zur Foerderung der Literatur aus Afrika Asien und Lateinamerika eV (Society for the Promotion of African, Asian & Latin American Literature)
Reineckstr 3, 60313 Frankfurt am Main
Mailing Address: Postfach 100116, 60001 Frankfurt am Main
Tel: (069) 2102 247; (069) 2102 250 *Fax:* (069) 2102 227; (069) 2102 277
E-mail: litprom@book-fair.com
Web Site: www.litprom.de
Key Personnel
President: Peter Weidhaas
Dir: Peter Ripken
The Society seeks to promote German translations of creative writing from Africa, Asia & Latin America. It works as a non-profit agency & as a consultant for German language publishers & Third World publishers who have translation rights to offer. It is organizing reading tours & special promotion campaigns & is also in charge of a special programme for translations grants into German.
Publication(s): *Literaturnachrichten* (quarterly in German)

Goethe-Gesellschaft in Weimar eV
Burgplatz 4, 99423 Weimar
Mailing Address: Postfach 2251, 99403 Weimar
Tel: (03643) 20 20 50 *Fax:* (03643) 20 20 61
E-mail: goetheges@aol.com
Web Site: www.goethe-gesellschaft.de
Key Personnel
President (Weimar): Dr Jochen Golz
Vice President (Dusseldorf): Dr Volkmar Hansen
Contact: Dr Petra Oberhauser
Founded: 1885
Publication(s): *Goethe-Jahrbuch (yearbook)* (annually)

Gutenberg-Gesellschaft eV (Gutenberg Society)
Liebfrauenplatz 5, 55116 Mainz
Tel: (06131) 22 64 20 *Fax:* (06131) 23 35 30
E-mail: gutenberg-gesellschaft@freenet.de
Web Site: www.gutenberg-gesellschaft.uni-mainz.de
Key Personnel
President: Jens Beutel
Vice President & Treasurer: Hannetraud Schultheiss
Publishing Manager: Dr Stephan Fuessel *E-mail:* fuessel@mail.uni-mainz.de
Secretary General: Karl Delorme
Founded: 1901
Publication(s): *Gutenberg-Jahrbuch (Gutenberg Yearbook)*: *Kleine Drucke der Gutenberg-Gesellschaft* (annually)

Internationale Vereinigung fuer Geschichte und Gegenwart der Druckkunst eV, see Gutenberg-Gesellschaft eV

Literarischer Verein in Stuttgart eV
Haldenstr 30, 70376 Stuttgart
Mailing Address: Postfach 140155, 70071 Stuttgart
Tel: (0711) 5499710 *Fax:* (0711) 54997121
Key Personnel
President: Gerd Hiersemann *E-mail:* hiersemann.hauswedell.verlage@t-online.de

The Society's goal (founded in 1839) is to publish the texts of valuable unpublished manuscripts & old printed texts in a new form - especially with regard to old German literature.
Publication(s): *Bibliothek des Literarischen Vereins in Stuttgart* (Vol 1 1842 - Vol 318 1996)

Literarisches Colloquium Berlin
Am Sandwerder 5, 14109 Berlin
Tel: (030) 8169960 *Fax:* (030) 81699619
E-mail: mail@lcb.de
Web Site: www.lcb.de
Key Personnel
Contact: Thomas Geiger *Tel:* (030) 81699613 *E-mail:* geiger@lcb.de
Founded: 1963
Publication(s): *Sprache im technischen Zeitalter* (quarterly)

Maximilian-Gesellschaft eV (Book Collectors Society)
Haldenstr 30, 70376 Stuttgart
Mailing Address: Postfach 140155, 70071 Stuttgart
Tel: (0711) 5499710 *Fax:* (0711) 54997121
E-mail: hiersemann.hauswedell.verlage@t-online.de
Web Site: www.maximilian-gesellschaft.de
Key Personnel
Chairman: Prof Horst Gronemeyer, PhD
Producer: Reinhold Busch

German PEN Centre (Deutsches PEN-Zentrum)
Member of International PEN
Kasinostr 3, 64293 Darmstadt
Tel: (06151) 23120 *Fax:* (06151) 293414
E-mail: pen-germany@t-online.de
Key Personnel
President: Johano Strasser
Secretary: Wilfried F Schoeller

Greece

Kentron Ekdoseos Ellinon Syngrafeon
Akadimia Athinon, Odos Anagnostopoulou 14, 10673 Athens
Tel: (01) 3612541 *Fax:* (01) 3602691
Centre for the Publication of Ancient Greek Authors.

Haiti

Le Bibliophile (The Book Lover)
Caphaitien
Key Personnel
President: Silvio Faschi
Secretary: Louis Toussaint
Publication(s): *La Citadelle* (weekly); *Stella* (monthly)

Hong Kong

Chinese Language Society of Hong Kong
18/F Kam Chung Bldg, 19-21 Hennessy Rd, Hong Kong
Tel: (02) 5284853
Key Personnel
Secretary: Leung Nga Mei

Hong Kong PEN Centre (Chinese-Speaking)
Member of International PEN
c/o Patrick Woo Chun Hoi, Chairman, Flat A, 22/F, Blk 4, Cityone Shatin, Shatin NT
Key Personnel
President: Pui Yau Ming
Secretary: Susie Chiang
Publication(s): *PEN News* (weekly in Chinese)

Hungary

Hungarian PEN Centre
Member of International PEN
VII Kertesz u 36, Budapest 1073
Tel: (01) 3184143 *Fax:* (01) 1171722
Key Personnel
President: Gabor Gorgey
Secretary: Eva Toth
Publication(s): *The Hungarian PEN, Le PEN hongrois* (annually, bulletin)

Magyar Irodalomtoerteneti Tarsasag (Society of Hungarian Literary History)
Piarista Koez 1, 1052 Budapest
Tel: (01) 377819 *Fax:* (01) 3377819
Key Personnel
President: Sandor Ivan Kovacs
General Secretary: Praznovszky Mihaly
Founded: 1912
Publication(s): *Irodalomtoertenet*

Magyar Tudomanyos Akademia Irodalomtudomanyi Intezete (Institute of Literary Studies of the Hungarian Academy of Sciences)
Menesi ut 11-13, 1118 Budapest
Tel: (01) 4665938 *Fax:* (01) 3853876
Web Site: www.mta.hu/kutatohelyek/intezetek/iti.htm
Key Personnel
Dir: Prof Laszlo Szorenyi *Tel:* (01) 3858970
Publication(s): *Helikon* (bimonthly); *Irodalomtoerteneti Fuezetek*; *Irodalomtoerteneti Koenyvtar*; *Irodalomtoerteneti Koezlemenyek* (quarterly); *Literatura* (quarterly); *Neohelicon* (quarterly)
Ultimate Parent Company: Hungarian Academy of Science (HAS)

Iceland

Hid Islenzka Bokmenntafelag (Icelandic Literary Society)
Sidumula 21, 128 Reykjavik
Tel: 5889060 *Fax:* 5889095
E-mail: hib@islandia.is
Web Site: www.hib.is
Key Personnel
President: Sigurdur Lindal
Secretary: Reynir Axelsson
Founded: 1816
Publication(s): *Skirnir* (biannually in 2 parts)

Icelandic PEN Centre
Member of International PEN
PO Box 33, Reykjavik
Key Personnel
President: Thor Vilhjalmsson
Secretary: Einar Karason

Rithofundasamband Islands (The Icelandic Writers' Union)
Dyngjuvegi 8, 104 Reykjavik
Tel: 5683190 *Fax:* 5683192
E-mail: rsi@rsi.is
Web Site: www.rsi.is
Key Personnel
Chairman: Adalsteinn Asberg Sigurdsson
Man Dir: Ragnheidur Tryggvadottir
Founded: 1974
Publication(s): *Frettabref* (newsletter)

India

All-India PEN Centre
Member of International PEN
Theosophy Hall, 40 New Marine Lines, Mumbai 400020
Tel: (022) 2032175
E-mail: ambika.sirkar@gems.vsnl.net.in
Cable: CARE ARYAHATA BOMBAY
Key Personnel
President: Annada Sankar
Acting Secretary & Treasurer: Ranjit Hoskote
Honorary Secretary-Treasurer: Prof Nissim Ezekiel
Member, Executive Committee: Rameshchandra Sirkar
Publication(s): *Asian Liturature: Poetry, Short Stories & Essays*; *Assamese Literature*; *Bengali Literature*; *Drama in Modern India & Writer's Responsibility in a Rapidly Changing World*; *India Writers Meet*; *Indian Literature of Today*; *The Indian PEN* (quarterly); *Indian Writers at Chidambaram*; *Indian Writers in Conference*; *Indian Writers in Council*; *Indo-Anglian Literature*; *The Novel in Modern India*; *Telugu Literature*; *Writers in Free India*; *Writing in India*

National Academy of Letters, India, see Sahitya Akademi

Sahitya Akademi (National Academy of Letters)
Rabindra Bhavan, 35 Ferozeshah Rd, New Delhi 110001
Tel: (011) 3386626; (011) 3386627; (011) 3386628; (011) 3386629; (011) 3387386; (011) 3386088 *Fax:* (011) 3382428
Web Site: www.sahitya-akademi.org *Cable:* SAHITYAKAR
Key Personnel
President: Ramakanta Rath
Vice President: Gopichand Narang
Secretary: Prof K Satchidanandan *E-mail:* secy@sahitya-akademi.org
Founded: 1954
Regional offices in Bangalore, Chennai, Kolkata & Mumbai.
Publication(s): *Indian Literature* (bimonthly); *Samkaleen Bharateeya Sahitya* (bimonthly); *Samskrita Pratibha* (biannually)

Indonesia

Indonesian PEN Centre
Member of International PEN
Jalan Camara 6, Jakarta, Pusat
Tel: (093) 3905837 *Fax:* (093) 325890
Key Personnel
Secretary: Dr Toeti Heraty Noerhadi

Ireland

Irish Academy of Letters
4 Ailesbury Grove, Dundum, Dublin 14
Key Personnel
Secretary: Sean J White

Irish PEN Centre
Member of International PEN
26 Rosslyn, Killarney Rd, Bray, Co Wicklow
Key Personnel
President: Mr O Z Whitehead
Secretary: Arthur Flynn

Israel

ACUM Ltd (Society of Authors, Composers & Music Publishers in Israel)
ACUM House, 9 Tuval St, 52117 Ramat-Gan
Tel: (03) 6113400 *Fax:* (03) 6122629
E-mail: info@acum.org.il
Web Site: www.acum.org.il
Key Personnel
Chairman: Hana Goldberg
Chief Executive Officer: Yorik Ben-David
Deputy Chief Executive Officer: Reuven Ratson
Head of Finances: Dafna Ramchurn
Manager, Licensing Performing Rights: Daliah Hadar
Manager, Radio/TV Licensing & Distribution: Brigitte Rayn
Manager, Reprint & Multimedia: Hany Moshe
Marketing & Business Development: Assaf Nahum
Founded: 1936
Administration of authors & composers' rights
Membership(s): BIEM & CISAC.

ELEAS, see English Language Editors' Association (ELEAS)

English Language Editors' Association (ELEAS)
PO Box 6925, Jerusalem
Tel: (02) 586-5772 *Fax:* (02) 586-6411
Web Site: www.geocities.com/athens/stage/4942/8Eleas.html
Key Personnel
Contact: David Grossman *E-mail:* davidg@macam.ac.il

Israeli PEN Centre
Member of International PEN
6 Kaplan St, Tel Aviv 61070
Mailing Address: PO Box 7203, Tel Aviv 61070
Tel: (03) 6964937 *Fax:* (03) 6964937
Key Personnel
President: Mr Sandu David
Secretary: Ms Shulamit Kuriansky

Mekize Nirdamim Society
PO Box 4344, Jerusalem
Tel: (02) 636072
Key Personnel
President: Prof S Abramson
Secretary: Prof I Tashma
Founded: 1864
International society publishes Hebrew works of the older classical Jewish literature.

Palestinian PEN Centre
Member of International PEN
Al Khaldi St No 4, Wadi Joz, Jerusalem
Tel: (02) 6262970 *Fax:* (02) 6264620

ISRAEL

E-mail: palpenc@palnet.com
Key Personnel
President: Hanan Awwad *Tel:* (02) 5813698 *Fax:* (02) 5894620

Italy

Accademia Nazionale di Scienze Lettere e Arti Modena (National Academy of Sciences, Literatures & Arts)
Palazzo Coccapani, Corso Vittorio Emanuele II, 59, 41100 Modena
Tel: (059) 225566 *Fax:* (059) 225566
E-mail: info@accademiasla-mo.it
Web Site: www.accademiasla-mo.it
Key Personnel
President: Prof Ferdinando Taddei
Publication(s): *Atti e Memorie* (annually)

Accademia Nazionale Virgiliana di Scienze, Lettere e Arti
Via dell'Accademia 47, Mantova 46100
Tel: (0376) 320314 *Fax:* (0376) 222774
Web Site: www.accademiavirgiliana.it/index.htm
Key Personnel
President: Prof Claudio Gallico
Founded: 1863
Publication(s): *Atti di Convegni tenuti presso l'Accademia Virgiliana; Atti e Memorie NS* (annually)

Accademia Petrarca di Lettere, Arti e Scienze (Petrarch Academy of Letters, Arts & Science)
Via dell'Orto n 28, 52100 Arezzo
Tel: (0575) 24700 *Fax:* (0575) 298846
Web Site: www.accademiapetrarca.it
Key Personnel
President: Prof Giulio Firpo
Secretary: Prof Antonio Batinti
Founded: 1787
Publication(s): *Atti e Memorie della Accademia, Studi Petrarcheschi*

Istituto Lombardo Accademia di Scienze e Lettere
Via Borgonuovo, 25, 20121 Milan
Tel: (02) 864087 *Toll Free Tel:* (02) 86461388
E-mail: istituto.lombardo@unimi.it
Web Site: www.istitutolombardo.it
Key Personnel
President: Prof Emilio Gatti
Vice President: Prof Alberto Quadrio Curzio

Italian PEN Centre
Member of International PEN
Via Daverio 7, 20122 Milan
E-mail: fmormando@planet.it
Key Personnel
President: Mario Luzi
Secretary General: Federica Mormando

Societa Dantesca Italiana (Italian Dante Society)
Palagio dell'Arte della Lana, Via Arte della Lana 1, 50123 Florence FI
Mailing Address: PO Box 739, 50123 Florence FI
Tel: (055) 287134 *Fax:* (055) 211316
E-mail: sdi@leonet.it; sdi.biblio@leonet.it (library)
Web Site: www.danteonline.it
Key Personnel
President: Prof Francesco Mazzoni, PhD
Founded: 1888
Publication(s): *Edizione Nazionale delle Opere di Dante Alighieri; Quaderni degli Studi Danteschi; Quaderni del Centro Studi e Documentazione Dantesca e Medievale; Studi Danteschi* (annually)

Japan

Japanese PEN Centre
Member of International PEN
Rm 265, Akasaka Residential Hotel, 9-1-7 Akasaka, Minato-Ku, Tokyo 107-0052
Tel: (03) 34021171; (03) 34021172 *Fax:* (03) 34025951
E-mail: japan-pen@asahi-net.email.ne.jp
Key Personnel
Secretary: Nobuhiro Akio
Publication(s): *Japanese Literature Today* (annually since 1976)

Nihon Eibungakkai (English Literary Society of Japan)
501 Kenkyusha Bldg, 9, Surugadai 2-chome, Kanda, Chiyoda-ku, Tokyo 101-0062
Tel: (03) 32937528 *Fax:* (03) 32937539
Key Personnel
President: Kazuhisa Takahashi
Founded: 1917
Publication(s): *Studies in English Literature* (tri-annually)

Nippon Dokubungakkai (Japanese Society of German Literature)
c/o Ikubundo, Hongo 5-30-21, Bunkyo-ku, Tokyo 113-0033
Tel: (03) 3813 5861 *Fax:* (03) 3813 5861
E-mail: e-mail@jgg.jp
Key Personnel
Contact: Prof Takao Tsunekawa
Publication(s): *Doitsu Bungaku* (biannually)

Nippon Hikaku Bungakukai (Comparative Literature Society of Japan)
Aoyama Gakuin University, Shibuya-ku, Tokyo
Key Personnel
President: K Nakajam
Secretary General: Saburo Ota

Nippon Rosiya Bungakkai (Russian Literary Society in Japan)
c/o Baba-ken, Tokyo Institute of Technology, 2-12-1 O-okayama, Meguro-ku, Tokyo 152-8552
Key Personnel
President: Togo Masanobu
Secretary General: T Egawa

Republic of Korea

Korean PEN Centre
Member of International PEN
Rm 1105, Oseong B/D, 13-5 Youido-dong, Yongdungpo-ku, Seoul 150010
Tel: (02) 782 1337; (02) 782 1338 *Fax:* (02) 786 1090
E-mail: penkon2001@yahoo.co.kr
Key Personnel
Secretary: Prof Chung-ho Chung
Publication(s): *Korean Literature Today* (quarterly)

Liechtenstein

Liechtenstein PEN Centre
Member of International PEN
Postfach 416, FL-9490 Vaduz
Tel: (0423) 2327271 *Fax:* (0423) 2328071
E-mail: info@pen-club.li *Cable:* PEN CLUB
Key Personnel
Secretary: Werner Fuld
Publication(s): *Zifferblatt* (annually)

The Former Yugoslav Republic of Macedonia

Dru-stvo na Pisatelite na Makedonija (Macedonian Writers Association)
Maksim Gorki 18, Skopje 1000
Tel: (02) 228039
E-mail: contact@dpism.org.mk
Web Site: www.dpism.org.mk
Key Personnel
President: Vele Smilevski *E-mail:* vsmil@dpism.org.mk
Secretary: Paskal Gilovski; Svetlana Hristova-Jocic
Founded: 1947

Macedonian PEN Centre
Member of International PEN
Str Maksim Gorki 18, 1000 Skopje
Tel: (02) 130054 *Fax:* (02) 130054
E-mail: macedpen@unet.com.mk
Web Site: www.pen.org.mk
Key Personnel
President: Dimitar Basevski
Secretary: Zoran Ancevski; Ivan Dzeparovski

Sojuz na drustvata za makedonski jazik i literatura
Filolski fakultet, 91000 Skopje
Key Personnel
President: Elena Bendevska
Secretary: Ljupco Mitrevski
Union of Associations for Macedonian Language & Literature.
Publication(s): *Literaturen zbor* (Literary Word)

Malaysia

Dewan Bahasa dan Pustaka
Peti Surat 10803, 50926 Kuala Lumpur
Tel: (03) 21481011; (03) 2484211; (03) 2481820 *Fax:* (03) 2482726; (03) 2142005; (03) 21414109; (03) 2148420
Web Site: www.dbp.gov.my
Telex: MA 32683
Key Personnel
Dir General: Haji Jumaat Moho Noor
National Language & Literary Agency.
Publication(s): *Dewan Bahasa; Dewan Budaya; Dewan Masyarakat; Dewan Pelajar; Dewan Sastera* (monthly); *Dewan Siswa* (monthly); *Tenggara* (biannually)

Mexico

Mexican PEN Centre
Member of International PEN
Heriberto Frias 1452-407, Col Del Valle, Mexico 03100 DF
Tel: (05) 574-4882 *Fax:* (05) 264-0813
E-mail: maleona@hotmail.com
Key Personnel
President: Maria Elena Ruiz Cruz
Publication(s): *Directorio de Escritores* (annually)

Nepal

Nepal PEN Centre
Member of International PEN
PO Box 8975 EPC 533, Kathmandu
Fax: (01) 522346
E-mail: archana@icimod.org.np; grana@saligram.mos.com.np; shaligrm@mos.com.np
Key Personnel
President: Dr D C Gautam
Vice President: Nagendra Raj Sharma
Secretary General: Greta Rana
Secretary: Archana Singh Karki
Publication(s): *Jane Eyre (in Nepali)* (With help from the Bronte Society, Translator-S Rai)

Netherlands

Maatschappij der Nederlandse Letterkunde
(Society of Netherlands Literature)
Universiteitsbibliotheek, Witte Singel 27, 2311 BG Leiden
Mailing Address: Postbus 9501, 2300 RA Leiden
Tel: (071) 527 2801; (071) 527 2814 *Fax:* (071) 527 2836
E-mail: mnl@library.leidenuniv.nl
Web Site: www.leidenuniv.nl/host/mnl
Key Personnel
Secretary: Dr Leo L van Maris
Founded: 1766
Publication(s): *Indische Letteren* (quarterly); *Jaarboek der Maatschappij* (annually); *De negentiende eeuw* (quarterly); *Tijdschrift voor Nederlandse Taal- en Letterkunde* (quarterly)

Netherlands PEN Centre
Member of International PEN
Graafseweg 3, 6512 BM Nijmegen
Tel: (043) 433498 *Fax:* (043) 433498
Key Personnel
President: Hans Van de Waarsenburg
Secretary: Daan Cartens

New Zealand

New Zealand Book Council
Old Wool House, 5th floor, 139-141 Featherson St, Wellington
Tel: (04) 499 1569 *Fax:* (04) 499 1424
E-mail: admin@bookcouncil.org.nz
Web Site: www.bookcouncil.org.nz
Key Personnel
President: Sir Kenneth Keith
Vice President: Chris Price
Executive Dir: Karen Ross *E-mail:* director@bookcouncil.org.nz
Publication(s): *Book Buyers in New Zealand*; *Books You Couldn't Buy*; *Landmarks of New Zealand Writing to 1945*; *Writers in Schools*

New Zealand Council for Educational Research
10th floor, West Block, Education House, 178-182 Willis St, Wellington
Mailing Address: PO Box 3237, Wellington
Tel: (04) 384 7939 *Fax:* (04) 384 7933
Web Site: www.nzcer.org.nz
Key Personnel
Dir: Robyn Baker *E-mail:* robyn.baker@nzcer.org.nz
Founded: 1934

New Zealand Society of Authors (NZSA)
PO Box 67013, Mount Eden, Auckland 3
Tel: (09) 356 8332 *Fax:* (09) 356 8332
E-mail: nzsa@clear.net.nz
Web Site: www.authors.org.nz
Key Personnel
President: William Taylor
Vice President: Maxine Alterio; Stephen Stratford
Executive Dir: Liz Allen
Membership Secretary: Jan Hughes
Publication(s): *New Zealand Author* (bimonthly)

New Zealand Writers Guild
1/243 Ponsonby Rd, Ponsonby, Auckland 1034
Mailing Address: PO Box 47 886, Ponsonby, Auckland 1034
Tel: (09) 360 1408 *Fax:* (09) 360 1409
E-mail: info@nzwritersguild.org.nz
Web Site: www.nzwritersguild.org.nz
Key Personnel
President: Denis Edwards
Vice President: Kathryn Burnett
Secretary: Dominic Sheehan

NZSA, see New Zealand Society of Authors (NZSA)

PEN NZ Inc, see New Zealand Society of Authors (NZSA)

Norway

Information Office for Norwegian Literature Abroad, see NORLA (Information Office for Norwegian Literature Abroad)

NORLA (Information Office for Norwegian Literature Abroad)
Victoria terr 11, 0203 Solli, Oslo
Mailing Address: PO Box 2663, 0203 Solli, Oslo
Tel: 23 27 63 50 *Fax:* 23 27 63 51
E-mail: firmapost@norla.no
Web Site: www.norla.no
Key Personnel
Man Dir: Kristin Brudevoll
Literary Advisor: Andrine Pollen
Secretary: Ingrid Overwien
Founded: 1978
State supported foundation offering grants to translations of Norwegian literature.
Publication(s): *Selected Norwegian Fiction*

Norske Akademi for Sprog og Litteratur
(Norwegian Academy for Language & Literature)
Inkognitogaten 24, 0256 Oslo
Tel: 22 56 29 50 *Fax:* 22 55 37 43
E-mail: ordet@riksmalsforbundet.no
Web Site: www.riksmalsforbundet.no
Key Personnel
President: Helge Nordahl
Secretary: Prof Sissel Lange-Nielsen

Det Norske Videnskaps-Akademi (The Norwegian Academy of Science & Letters)
Drammensveien 78, 0271 Oslo
Tel: 22121090 *Fax:* 22121099
E-mail: dnva@online.no
Web Site: www.dnva.no
Key Personnel
President: Prof Lars Walloe
Vice President: Prof Jan Fridthjof Bernt
Secretary General: Prof Reidun Sirevag
Publication(s): *Arbok*; *Avhandlinger*; *Skrifter*

Norwegian PEN Centre
Member of International PEN
Urtegaten 50, 0187 Oslo
Tel: 22194551 *Fax:* 22194551
E-mail: PEN@norskpen.no
Key Personnel
President: Kjell Olaf Jensen

Pakistan

Anjuman Taraqqi-e-Urdu Pakistan
Baba-e-Urdu Rd, D-159 Block 7, Gulshan-e Iqbal, Karachi 75300
Tel: (021) 461406; (021) 4973296; (021) 7724023
Key Personnel
President: N H Jafarey
Secretary: Jamiluddin A'Ali
Founded: 1903
For the promotion of the Urdu language & literature.
Publication(s): *Qaumi Zaban* (monthly); *Urdu* (quarterly)

Pakistan Writers' Guild
One Mentgomrey Rd, Lahore
Tel: 6367124
Key Personnel
Research Officer: Inamul Haq Javeid
Secretary General: Mohamed Tufail
Founded: 1959
Publication(s): *Ham Qalam* (monthly)

Sindhi Adabi Board
Station Rd, Sindhi University Campus, Hyderabad
Mailing Address: PO Box 12, Jamshoro, Hyderabad
Tel: (0221) 771276; (0221) 771465; (0221) 771600
Key Personnel
Chairman: Muhammad Ibrahim Joyo
Secretary: Ghulam Rabbani Agro
To promote the language, literature & culture of the Sind region.

Panama

Panamanian PEN Centre
Member of International PEN
PO Box 1824, Panama 1
Tel: 263-8822 *Fax:* 263-9918
Key Personnel
President: Jose Franco
Secretary: Dr Juan David Morgan

Philippines

Philippine PEN Centre
Member of International PEN
531 Padre Faura, 1099 Ermita, Manila
Mailing Address: PO Box 3959, 1099 Manila
Tel: (02) 5230870 *Fax:* (02) 5255038 *Cable:* SOLDAD MANILA
Key Personnel
President: Alejandro Roces
National Secretary: Francisco Sionil Jose

Poland

Instytut Badan Literackich PAN (Institute of Literary Research of the Polish Academy of Sciences)
ul Nowy Swiat 72, 00-330 Warsaw
Tel: (022) 8269945; (022) 6572895 *Fax:* (022) 8269945
E-mail: ibadlit@ibl.waw.pl
Web Site: www.ibl.waw.pl
Key Personnel
Dir: Prof Alina Witkowska; Prof Elzbieta Sarnawska-Temeriusz
Publication(s): *Kwartalnik Historii Prasy Polskiej* (Quarterly of the History of the Polish Press); *Literary Studies in Poland* (biannually); *Pamietnik Literacki* (Literary Journal, quarterly)

Polish PEN Centre (Polski PEN Club)
Member of International PEN
Krakowskie Przedmiescie 87/89, 00-079 Warsaw
Tel: (022) 8265784; (022) 8282823 *Fax:* (022) 8265784
E-mail: penclub@ikp.atm.com.pl
Web Site: www.penclub.atomnet.pl
Key Personnel
President: Wladyslaw Bartoszewski
Vice President: Adam Pomorski; Kazimierz Traciewicz
Secretary: Krzysztof Dorosz
Treasurer: Iwona Smolka
Founded: 1925

Towarzystwo Literackie im Adama Mickiewicza (Mickiewicz Literary Society)
ul Nowy Swiat 72, Palac Staszica, 00-330 Warsaw
Tel: (022) 265231 (ext 279)
Key Personnel
President: Prof Zdzislaw Libera, PhD
Publication(s): *Rocznik* (Yearbook)

Portugal

Instituto Portugues da Sociedade Cientifica de Goerres (Portuguese Institute of the Goerres Research Society)
c/o Universidade Catolica Portuguesa, Palm de Cima, 1600 Lisbon
Tel: (021) 7265554 *Fax:* (021) 7260546
E-mail: mrato@reitoria.ucp.pt
Key Personnel
Contact: Maria Eugenia Rato
Research in Portuguese.
Publication(s): *Portugiesische Forschungen der Goerres Gesellschaft*

Portuguese PEN Centre
Member of International PEN
York House, Rua das Janelas Verdes, 32, 1200 Lisbon
Tel: (021) 7573452 *Fax:* (021) 7573452
E-mail: penclube@mail.telepac.pt
Key Personnel
President: Casimiro de Brito
Secretary: Annabel Rita
Founded: 1978
Writers' Association.

Sociedade Portuguesa de Autores
Av Duque de Loule 31, 1069-153 Lisbon, Codex
Tel: (021) 3594400 *Fax:* (021) 3530257
E-mail: geral@spautores.pt
Web Site: www.spautores.pt *Cable:* AUTORES
Key Personnel
President: Dr Luiz Francisco Rebello
Vice President: Dr Alvaro Salazar
Publication(s): *Autores*

Puerto Rico

Puerto Rican PEN Centre (PEN Club of Puerto Rico)
Member of International PEN
721 Calle Hernandez, apt 11N, San Juan 00907
Tel: (787) 724-0869 *Fax:* (787) 724-2060
E-mail: saturno@prtc.net
Key Personnel
President: Juan Duchesne-Winter
Secretary: Maria E Ramos

Romania

Romanian PEN Centre
Member of International PEN
Bdul Ferdinand 29 ap 3, 70313 Bucharest
Tel: (01) 3111112 *Fax:* (01) 3125854
E-mail: univers@rnc.ro
Key Personnel
President: Ana Blandiana
Secretary: Denisa Comanescu

Societatea de Stiinte Filologice din Romania (SSF) (Romanian Philological Sciences Society)
Mendeleev Str, nr 21-25, sector 1, 70761 Bucharest 1
Tel: (021) 3123148
Key Personnel
President: Paul Cornea
Secretary General: Mircea Franculescu
Contact: Florentina Samihaian
Publication(s): *Buletinul SSF*; *Limba si literatura* (quarterly, journal); *Limba si Literatura Romania*

SSF, see Societatea de Stiinte Filologice din Romania (SSF)

Russian Federation

Russian PEN Centre
Member of International PEN
Neglinnaya St 18/1 Bldg 2, 103031 Moscow
Tel: (095) 2094589; (095) 2093171 *Fax:* (095) 2000293
E-mail: penrussian@dol.ru; penrus@aha.ru
Web Site: www.penrussia.org
Key Personnel
Dir General: Alexandr Tkachenko
Editor: Mikhail Kaminsky
Contact: Y Tutchaninova
Founded: 1921

Senegal

Senegal PEN Centre
Member of International PEN
Rue 1 Prolongee Pointe, Dakar
Tel: 8256700; 8258009 *Fax:* 8643375
E-mail: memgoree@sonatel.senet.net
Key Personnel
President: Ousmane Sembene
Secretary: Alioune Badara Beye

Serbia and Montenegro

Serbian PEN Centre
Member of International PEN
Milutina Bojica 4, 11000 Belgrade
Tel: (011) 626081 *Fax:* (011) 635979
E-mail: pencent@bitsyu.net
Key Personnel
President: Jovan Hristic
Secretary: Dr Kosta Cavoski
Publication(s): *Pismo* (quarterly, published jointly with "Jovan Popovic" Library, Zemun)

Slovenia

Slovene PEN Centre
Member of International PEN
Tomsiceva 12, 61000 Ljubljana
Tel: (01) 4254847
E-mail: slopen@guest.arnes.si
Key Personnel
President: Veno Taufer
Secretary: Iztok Ososnik
Publication(s): *Litterae Slovenicae*

Spain

Ateneo Cientifico, Literario y Artistico (Scientific, Literary & Artistic Athenaeum)
Calle del Prado 21, 28014 Madrid
Tel: (09142) 974 42
Key Personnel
President: Jose Prat Garcia
General Secretary: David M Rivas Infante
Founded: 1837

Ateneo Cientifico, Literario y Artistico (Scientific, Literary & Artistic Athenaeum)
Sa Rovellada de Dalt, 25, 07701 Mahon, Minorca, Balearic Islands
Tel: (071) 360553 *Fax:* (071) 352194
E-mail: ateneo@intercom.es
Web Site: www.usuarios.intercom.es/ateneo
Key Personnel
President: Francesc Tutzo Bennasar

Secretary: Miguel Angel Limon Pons
Founded: 1905
Publication(s): *Revista de Menorca* (quarterly)

Galician PEN Centre
Member of International PEN
Rep El Salvador, 14-1° izda, 15701 Santiago de Compostela
Tel: (081) 587750
E-mail: pengalicia@mundo-r.com
Key Personnel
President: Luis G Tosar
Secretary: Helena Villa Maneiro

Real Academia de Bones Lletres de Barcelona (Barcelona Royal Academy of Literature)
Carrer Bisbe Cassador 3, 08002 Barcelona
Tel: (093) 3150010 *Fax:* (093) 3102349
Key Personnel
President: Eduard Ripoll
Secretary: Frederic Udina
Librarian: Francisco Marsa
Publication(s): *Boletin, Memorias*

Real Academia Sevillana de Buenas Letras (Seville Royal Academy of Literature)
Casa de los Pinelo, Abades, 14, 41004 Seville
Tel: (09542) 21198
E-mail: insacan@insacan.org
Web Site: www.insacan.org
Key Personnel
Dir: Dr Rogelio Reyes Cano
Vice Dir: Dr Jose Luis Comellas Garcia-Llera
Secretary: Dr Jacabo Cortines; Enriqueta Vila Vilar
Founded: 1752
Publication(s): *Boletin de Buenas Letras* (quarterly)

Sociedad de Ciencias, Letras y Artes El Museo Canario
Dr Verneau, 2 Vegueta, 35001 Las Palmas, Canary Islands
Tel: (0928) 336800 *Fax:* (0928) 336801
E-mail: info@elmuseocanario.com
Web Site: www.elmuseocanario.com
Key Personnel
Chairman: Victor Montelongo Parada
Man Dir: Diego Lopez Diaz
Scientific, Literary & Art Society.
Publication(s): *El Museo Canario* (quarterly)

Sweden

Kungl Vitterhets Historie och Antikvitets Akademien (The Royal Academy of Letters, History & Antiquities)
Villagatan 3, 114 86 Stockholm
Mailing Address: PO Box 5622, 114 86 Stockholm
Tel: (08) 440 42 80 *Fax:* (08) 440 42 90
E-mail: kansli@vitterhetsakad.se
Web Site: www.vitterhetsakad.se
Key Personnel
President: Prof Anders Jeffner
Secretary-General: Prof Ulf Sporrong *Tel:* (08) 440 42 81 *E-mail:* sekreteraren@vitterhetsakad.se
Founded: 1753
Publication(s): *Arkiv (Archives)* (irregularly); *Arsbok (Yearbook)* (annually); *Fornvaennen (Journal of Swedish Antiquarian Research)* (quarterly); *Handlingar (Proceedings)* (irregularly); *Monografier (Monographs)* (irregularly)

Samfundet De Nio (The Academy of the Nine)
Villagatan 14, 114 32 Stockholm
Tel: (08) 411 15 42 *Fax:* (08) 21 19 15
Web Site: www.samfundetdenio.com
Key Personnel
President: Inge Jonsson
Secretary: Anders R Oehman
Founded: 1913

Swedish PEN Centre (Svenska Penklubben)
Member of International PEN
c/o Bokforlaget Natur och Kultur, Box 27 323, 102 54 Stockholm
Tel: (08) 453 86 80
E-mail: info@pensweden.org
Web Site: www.pensweden.org
Key Personnel
President: Ljiljana Dufgran *E-mail:* dufgran@telia.com

Switzerland

Ecrivains Suisses du Groupe d'Olten, see Schweizer Autorinnen und Autoren Gruppe Olten

Gesellschaft fur deutsche Sprache und Literatur in Zurich
Deutsches Seminar der Universitaet Zuerich, Schonberggasse, CH-8001 Zurich
Tel: (01) 6342571 *Fax:* (01) 6344905
E-mail: uguenthe@ds.unizh.ch
Key Personnel
President: Dr Ulla Gunther
Society for German Language & Literature in Zurich.

Schweizer Autorinnen und Autoren Gruppe Olten
Nordstr 9, 8035 Zurich
Tel: (01) 350 04 60 *Fax:* (01) 350 04 61
E-mail: sekretariat@a-d-s.ch
Web Site: www.a-d-s.ch
Key Personnel
Dir: Peter A Schmid *E-mail:* paschmid@a-d-s.ch
Secretary: Verena Roethlisberger *E-mail:* vroethlisberger@a-d-s.ch

Swiss German PEN Centre (Deutschweizer PEN Zentrum)
Member of International PEN
Zypressenstr 76, 8004 Zurich
Tel: (031) 3724085 *Fax:* (031) 3723032
E-mail: infopen@datacomm.ch
Key Personnel
President: Brechbuehl Beat
Secretary: Sebastian Hefti
Publication(s): *PEN-Brief*

Swiss Italian & Reto-Romansh PEN Centre
Member of International PEN
CP 107, 6903 Lugano
Tel: (091) 8039325 *Fax:* (091) 8039300
E-mail: p.e.n.lugano@ticino.com
Key Personnel
President: Franca Tiberto
Secretary: Attilia F Venturini
Publication(s): *Viceversa PEN International Centro Della Svizzera Italiana e Retoromancia, 1997*

Schweizerische Bibliophilen-Gesellschaft (Swiss Society of Bibliophiles)
Had Laubstr 42, 8044 Zuerich
Key Personnel
President: Dr Conrad Ulrich *Tel:* (01) 252 6349
Publication(s): *Librarium* (published triannually since 1958)

Schweizerischer Bund fuer Jugendliteratur (Swiss Federation for Youth Literature)
Gewerbestr 8, 6330 Cham
Tel: (041) 741 31 40 *Fax:* (041) 740 01 59
E-mail: sbj@bluewin.ch
Publication(s): *Autoren und Referenten der Deutschschweiz*; *Das Buch-Dein Freund* (yearbook for lower & middle grades); *Das Buch fuer Dich* (list of recommended books; yearly); *Information Buch Oberstufe* (yearbook for upper grades); *Jugendliteratur* (quarterly journal)

Schweizerischer Schriftstellerinnen und Schriftsteller-Verband (Swiss Writers' Union)
Nordstr 9, 8035 Zurich
Tel: (01) 3500460 *Fax:* (01) 3500461
E-mail: letter@ch-s.ch
Web Site: www.ch-s.ch
Key Personnel
Secretary: Peter A Schmid
Founded: 1912
Publication(s): *Neuer Judische Literatur in der Switzerland*; *Zweifache Eigenheit*

Suisse Romand PEN Centre (PEN Club de Suisse romande)
Member of International PEN
14 rue Crespin, 1206 Geneva
Key Personnel
President: Alexis Koutchoumow *E-mail:* jakoutchoumow@bluewin.ch
PEN Club for French-speaking Switzerland.
Publication(s): *PEN Club romand Newsletter* (biannually)

Taiwan, Province of China

China National Association of Literature and the Arts
No 4, Lane 22, Nuigpo St West, Taipei

Taipei Chinese PEN Centre
Member of International PEN
4 Lane 68, 4th floor, When Chou St, Taipei
Tel: (02) 23693609 *Fax:* (02) 23699948
E-mail: taipen@tpts5.seed.net.tw *Cable:* TAIPENCLUB
Key Personnel
President: Yu Chen
Secretary: Sarah Jen-Hui Hsiang
Publication(s): *The Chinese PEN* (quarterly)

Thailand

Thai PEN Centre
Member of International PEN
2/49 Ranong 1 Rd, Khet Dusit, Bangkok 10300
Mailing Address: PO Box 81, Dusit Post Office, Bangkok 10300
Tel: (02) 6685147; (02) 2792621
Key Personnel
President: Srisurang Poolthupya
Secretary: Dr Wareeya Bhavabhutananda Na Mahasarakham *E-mail:* wareeya@hotmail.com
Founded: 1958
Nonprofit literary society.
Publication(s): *Thailand PEN Journal* (journal)

The Siam Society
131 Soi Asoke, Sukhumvit 21 Rd, Bangkok 10110
Tel: (02) 66164707 *Fax:* (02) 2583491
E-mail: info@siam-society.org
Web Site: www.siam-society.org
Key Personnel
President: Bangkok Chowkwanyun
Publications Coordinator: Kanitha Kasina-ubol
Founded: 1904
Publication(s): *Journal of the Siam Society* (annually); *Natural History Bulletin of the Siam Society* (annually)

Tunisia

IBLA, see Institut des Belles Lettres Arabes (IBLA)

Institut des Belles Lettres Arabes (IBLA)
(Arabic Institute of Literature)
12 rue Jamaa El-Haoua, 1008 Tunis
Tel: (01) 560133 *Fax:* (01) 572683
E-mail: ibla@gnet.tn
Key Personnel
Dir: Jean Fontaine
Founded: 1960
Publication(s): *Revue IBLA*

Union des Ecrivains Tunisiens (Tunisian Writers' Union)
Avenue de Paris, Tunis 1000
Tel: (01) 257591 *Fax:* (01) 257807
E-mail: koutteb@planet.tn
Web Site: www.alkhadra.com/ittihad-koutteb
Key Personnel
President: Midani Ben Salah
Vice President: Mohammed El Kadhi
Secretary General: Souf Abid

Turkey

Turkish PEN Centre
Member of International PEN
General Yazgan Sokak 10/10, Tunel, 80050 Istanbul
Tel: (0212) 2526314 *Fax:* (0212) 2526315
Key Personnel
President: Nebile Direkcigil *E-mail:* n.direkcigil@iku.edu.tr
Secretary: Suat Karantay

United Kingdom

Yr Academi Gymreig (The Welsh Academy)
Mount Stuart House, 3rd floor, Mount Stuart Sq, Cardiff CF10 5FQ
Tel: (029) 20472266 *Fax:* (029) 20492930
E-mail: post@academi.org
Web Site: www.academi.org
Key Personnel
Chief Executive Officer: Peter Finch
Founded: 1959
The Welsh National Literature Promotion Agency & Society of Writers.
Publication(s): *Auto*; *Taliesin*

The Alliance of Literary Societies
22 Belmont Grove, Havant, Hants PO9 3PU
Tel: (023) 92 475855 *Fax:* (0870) 056 0330
Web Site: www.sndc.demon.co.uk/als.htm
Key Personnel
President: Aeronwy Thomas
Honorary Secretary: Rosemary Culley
 E-mail: rosemary@sndc.demon.co.uk
Founded: 1973
Publication(s): *Open Book* (annually)

Arts Council of Wales
9 Museum Pl, Cardiff CF10 3NX
Tel: (02920) 376500 *Fax:* (02920) 221447
Web Site: www.ccc-acw.org.uk
Key Personnel
Chief Executive: Peter Tyndall *E-mail:* peter.tyndall@artswales.org.uk

Aslib, The Association for Information Management
Temple Chambers, 3-7 Temple Ave, London EC4Y 0HP
Tel: (020) 7583 8900 *Fax:* (020) 7583 8401
E-mail: pubs@aslib.com
Web Site: www.aslib.co.uk; www.managinginformation.com
Key Personnel
Chief Executive: Roger Bowes
Head of Publications: Sarah Blair
Publication(s): *Directory of Information Sources in the UK* (biennially); *Managing Information* (10 times/yr)

The Association for Information Management, see Aslib, The Association for Information Management

Association for Scottish Literary Studies
c/o Dept of Scottish History, University of Glasgow, 9 University Gardens, Glasgow G12 8QH
Tel: (0141) 330 5309 *Fax:* (0141) 330 5309
Web Site: www.asls.org.uk
Key Personnel
General Manager: Duncan Jones *E-mail:* djones@scothist.arts.gla.ac.uk
Secretary: Jim Alison
Honorary Treasurer: Tom Ralph
Membership Secretary: Isobel McCallum
Founded: 1970
Also Publisher.
Publication(s): *New Writing Scotland* (annually); *Scottish Language* (annually); *Scottish Literary Journal* (biannually); *Scottish Studies Review* (biannually)

Association of Art Historians
70 Cowcross St, Clerkenwell, London EC1M 6EJ
Tel: (020) 7490 3211 *Fax:* (020) 7490 3277
E-mail: admin@aah.org.uk
Web Site: www.aah.org.uk
Key Personnel
Chair: Shearer West *E-mail:* chair@aah.org.uk
Vice Chair: Gen Doy *E-mail:* vice-chair@aah.org.uk
Honorary Secretary: Christiana Payne
 E-mail: honsec@aah.org.uk
Honorary Treasurer: Peter Baitup
 E-mail: hontreas@aah.org.uk
Administrator: Claire Davies
Founded: 1974
Professional arts organization which promotes the study of art history.
Publication(s): *The Art Book* (quarterly); *Art History* (5 times/yr); *Bulletin* (triannually)

Association of British Science Writers
Wellcome Wolfson Bldg, 165 Queen's Gate, London SW7 5HE
Tel: (0870) 770 3361
E-mail: absw@absw.org.uk

Web Site: www.absw.org.uk
Key Personnel
Chairman: Pallab Ghosh
Vice Chairman: Peter Wrobel
Secretary: Fabian Acker
Treasurer: Peter Briggs
Publication(s): *Science Reporter* (monthly)

Authors' Club
40 Dover St, London W1X 3RB
Tel: (020) 7408 5092
Key Personnel
Secretary: Lucy Jane Tetlow

Francis Bacon Society Inc
Canonbury Tower, Islington, London N1 2NQ
Tel: (020) 7359 6888 *Fax:* (020) 7704 1896
Web Site: www.sirbacon.org/links/bmembership.htm
Key Personnel
Honorary Vice President: Mary Brameld
Chairman: T D Bokenham, Esq
Designated Chairman: P A Welsford
Librarian: Prof John Spiers
Founded: 1886
Old Established Society; Custodians of the Francis Bacon Tradition.
Publication(s): *Baconiana* (periodically)

E F Benson, see The Tilling Society

E F Benson Society
The Old Coach House, High St, Rye, East Sussex TN31 7JF
Tel: (01797) 223114
E-mail: info@efbensonsociety.org
Web Site: www.efbensonsociety.org
Key Personnel
President: Gwen Watkins
Chair: Keith Cavers
Secretary: Allan Downend
Treasurer: Chris Roby
Founded: 1984
Publication(s): *Bensoniana Onwards Now 3*; *The Benson's*; *The Dodo* (annually, journal)

BookPower
305-307 Chiswick High Rd, London W4 4HH
Tel: (020) 8742 8232 *Fax:* (020) 8747 8715
E-mail: bookpower@ibd.uk.net
Web Site: www.bookpower.org
Key Personnel
Head Administration: Eileen Gillow
Founded: 1996
Charity. Administered by International Book Development Ltd.

Books Across the Sea
The English-Speaking Union, Dartmouth House, 37 Charles St, London W1X 8AB
Tel: (020) 7529 1550 *Fax:* (020) 7495 6108
E-mail: esu@mailbox.ulcc.ac.uk
Web Site: www.libfl.ru/eng/esu
Key Personnel
President: HRH, Prince Philip, The Duke of Edinburgh, KG, KT
Dir General: Valerie Mitchell
Chairman: The Lord Watson
Librarian: Andrea K Wathern
Founded: 1941
Publication(s): *Ambassador Booklist*

British Fantasy Society (BFS)
201 Reddish Rd, South Reddish, Stockport SK5 7HR
Tel: (0161) 6004125
E-mail: info@britishfantasysociety.org.uk
Web Site: www.britishfantasysociety.org.uk
Key Personnel
Chair: Nicki Robson
President: Ramsey Campbell

Secretary & Treasurer: Robert Parkinson
Publication(s): *Chills*; *Dark Horizons Newsletter*; *Mystique*

The British Science Fiction Association Ltd (BSFA Ltd)
97 Sharp St, Newland Ave, Hull HU5 2AE
E-mail: bsfa@enterprise.net
Web Site: www.bsfa.co.uk
Key Personnel
Membership Secretary: Estelle Roberts
Administrator: Vikki Lee France
Founded: 1948
Publication(s): *Focus* (biannually, magazine); *Matrix* (bimonthly, newsletter); *Vector* (bimonthly, journal)

The Bronte Society
The Bronte Parsonage Museum, Church St, Haworth, Keighley, West Yorks BD22 8DR
Tel: (01535) 642323 *Fax:* (01535) 647131
E-mail: info@bronte.info
Web Site: www.bronte.info
Key Personnel
Membership Development Officer: Rebecca Bishop *Tel:* (01535) 640195 *E-mail:* rebecca.bishop@bronte.org.uk
Founded: 1893
Publication(s): *Bronte Studies* (triannually); *Gazette* (biannually)

BSFA Ltd, see The British Science Fiction Association Ltd (BSFA Ltd)

Byron Society (International)
Byron House, 6 Gertrude St, London SW10 0JN
Tel: (01636) 816855 *Fax:* (01636) 816844
Web Site: www.byronsociety.com
Key Personnel
President: The Lord Byron
Chairman: Lord Gilmour
Honorary Dir: Elma Dangerfield
Publication(s): *The Byron Journal* (annually)

Randolph Caldecott Society
17 Home Rule Rd, Locks Heath, Southampton SO3 6LH
Tel: (01606) 891303
E-mail: charles.caldecott@lineone.net
Web Site: www.randolphcaldecott.org.uk
Key Personnel
Secretary: Kenn N Oultram
Treasurer: Charles Caldecott
Founded: 1983
Publication(s): *Caldecott Sketch*

Cambridge Bibliographical Society
University Library, West Rd, Cambridge CB3 9DR
Tel: (01223) 333000 *Fax:* (01223) 333160
E-mail: cbs@ula.cam.ac.uk
Key Personnel
Honorary Secretary: N A Smith
E-mail: nas1000@cam.ac.uk
Founded: 1949
Publication(s): *Monographs* (irregularly); *Transactions* (annually)

The Centre for Creative Communities
118 Commercial St, London E1 6NF
Tel: (020) 7247 5385 *Fax:* (020) 7247 5256
E-mail: info@creativecommunities.org.uk
Web Site: www.creativecommunities.org.uk
Key Personnel
Dir: Jennifer Williams
Research Dir: Cristina Losito
Research Officer: Joanna Cottingham
Information & Communications Manager: Antonio Molina-Vazquez

Children's Books History Society
25 Field Way, Hoddesdon, Herts EN11 0QN
Tel: (01992) 464885 *Fax:* (01992) 464885
E-mail: cbhs@abcgarrelt.demon.co.uk
Key Personnel
Chairman: Morna Daniels
Secretary: Mrs Pat Garrett
Treasurer: Sarah Jardine-Willoughby
Founded: 1969
In 1990, a biennial Harvey Darton Award was established for a book published in English, which extends our knowledge of some aspect of British children's literature of the past.
Publication(s): *CBHS Newsletter* (triannually, newsletter)

The John Clare Society
The Stables, 1a West St, Helpston, Peterborough PE6 7DU
Web Site: freespace.virgin.net/linda.curry/jclare.htm
Key Personnel
President: Ronald Blythe
Vice President: Prof Eric Robinson; Edward Storey; Prof Kelsey Thornton
Chairman: Paul Chirico *Tel:* (01223) 339494 *E-mail:* pac17@cam.ac.uk
Vice Chairman: Emma Trehane
Honorary Secretary: Sue Holgate *Tel:* (01223) 518989 *Fax:* (01223) 509870
Honorary Treasurer & Membership Secretary: Linda Curry *Tel:* (0121) 475 1805 *E-mail:* l.j.curry@bham.ac.uk
Journal Editor & Archivist: Prof John Goodridge *Tel:* (0115) 9418418 *E-mail:* john.goodridge@ntu.ac.uk
Sales Officer: Peter Moyse *Tel:* (01733) 252678 *Fax:* (01733) 252678 *E-mail:* moyse.helpston@talk21.com
Founded: 1981
To promote a wider & deeper knowledge of the poet, John Clare (1793-1864).
Publication(s): *The John Clare Society Journal* (annually)

The Joseph Conrad Society (UK)
c/o POSK, 238-46 King St, London W6 0RF
Web Site: www.bathspa.ac.uk/conrad/
Key Personnel
Chairman: Dr Keith Carabine *E-mail:* k.carabine@ukc.ac.uk
President: Philip Conrad
Secretary: Dr Tim Middleton *E-mail:* t.middleton@bathspa.ac.uk
Founded: 1973
Literary society devoted to all aspects of the study of the works & life of Joseph Conrad (1857-1924).
Publication(s): *The Conradian* (biannually)

Critics' Circle
51 Vartry Rd, London N15 6PS
Tel: (0171) 403 1818 *Fax:* (020) 7357 9287
E-mail: info@criticscircle.org.uk
Web Site: www.criticscircle.org.uk
Key Personnel
President: Charles Osborne
Vice President: Mike Dixon
Secretary: Charles Hedges
Treasurer: Peter Cargin
Founded: 1907
Professional association of critics of drama, music, the cinema & dance.

Daresbury Lewis Carroll Society
Blue Grass, Little Leigh, Northwich, Cheshire CW8 4RJ
Tel: (01606) 891303
Web Site: lewiscarrollsociety.org.uk
Key Personnel
Secretary: Kenneth N Oultram

Founded: 1970
Publication(s): *Stuff & Nonsense*

The Dickens Fellowship
Dickens House Museum, 48 Doughty St, London WC1N 2LF
Tel: (020) 7405 2127 *Fax:* (020) 7831 5175
E-mail: dickens.fellowship@btinternet.com
Web Site: www.dickens.fellowship.btinternet.co.uk
Key Personnel
President: Dr Paul Schlicke
Honorary General Secretary: Thelma Grove *E-mail:* hongensec@aol.com; Dr Tony R Williams *E-mail:* arwilliams33@compuserve.com
Honorary Treasurer: George Wright
Editor: Prof Malcolm Andrews
Founded: 1902
Affiliated to the Alliance of Literary Societies, The Birmingham & Midland Institute, 9 Margaret St, Birmingham, B 3BS.
Publication(s): *The Dickens Magazine* (6 times/yr); *The Dickensian* (triannually); *Mr Dick's Kite* (triannually, newsletter)

Early English Text Society
Christ Church, Oxford OX1 1DP
Web Site: www.eets.org.uk
Key Personnel
Honorary Dir: Prof John Burrow
Executive Secretary: R F S Hamer *E-mail:* richard.hamer@chch.ox.ac.uk
Editorial Secretary: Dr H L Spencer
Membership Secretary: Jane Watkinson
Founded: 1864

Edinburgh Bibliographical Society
c/o National Library of Scotland, George IV Bridge, Edinburgh EH1 1EW
Tel: (0131) 226 4531 *Fax:* (0131) 466 2807
E-mail: exkb33@srv1.lib.ed.ac.uk
Web Site: www.edbibsoc.lib.ed.ac.uk
Telex: 727442
Key Personnel
President: Dr Murray C T Simpson
Vice President: Prof David Finkelstein; Brenda E Moon
Acting Honorary Secretary: Dr Warren McDougall *E-mail:* warrenmcdougall@aol.com
Honorary Treasurer: Peter B Freshwater
Founded: 1890
Publication(s): *Transactions* (biennially)

The Eighteen Nineties Society
PO Box 97, High Wycombe, Bucks HP14 4GH
Tel: (01869) 248340
Web Site: www.1890s.org
Key Personnel
Founder: Dr G Krishnamurti
President: Elizabeth The Countess of Longford
Chair: Martyn Goff
Secretary & Treasurer: Steven Halliwell *E-mail:* steve@ft-1890s-society.demon.co.uk
Founded: 1963
Publication(s): *The Journal of the Eighteen Nineties Societies* (annually); *Keynotes* (quarterly, newsletter)

The George Eliot Fellowship
71 Stepping Stones Rd, Coventry, Warwicks CV5 8JT
Tel: (024) 7659 2231
Web Site: www.sndc.demon.co.uk/alsdef.htm#e
Key Personnel
President: Jonathan G Ouvry
Vice President: A S Byatt; Tenniel Evans; Beryl Gray, PhD; Graham Handley, PhD; Prof Barbara Hardy; F B Pinion; Ann Reader; Harriet Williams; Michael Wolff; Margaret Wolfit; Gabriel Woolf
Secretary: Hr Kathleen Adams
Founded: 1930

Publication(s): *George Eliot Review* (annually); *Pitkin Guide to George Eliot (illustrated)*; *Those Of Us Who Loved Her: The Men In George Eliot's Life*

Thomas Ellis Memorial Fund
University Registry, University of Wales, Cathays Park, Cardiff CF10 3NS
Tel: (029) 2038 2656 *Fax:* (029) 2039 6040
E-mail: awards@wales.ac.uk
Web Site: www.wales.ac.uk/newpages/external/E5536.asp
Key Personnel
Secretary General: Dr Lynn Williams
Grants to assist research into the language, literature, history & antiquities of Wales & Monmouthshire, & the publication of the results of such research. Applications should be sent to the Secretary General at the University Registry.

The English Association
University of Leicester, University Rd, Leicester LE1 7RH
Tel: (0116) 252 3982 *Fax:* (0116) 252 2301
E-mail: engassoc@le.ac.uk
Web Site: www.le.ac.uk/engassoc
Key Personnel
Chair of the Executive Committee: Prof Elaine Treharne
Chief Executive & Company Secretary: Helen Lucas *Tel:* (0116) 252 2300 *E-mail:* hl11@le.ac.uk
President: Martin Blocksidge
Honorary Treasurer: Roger J Claxton
Membership Coordinator: Jeremy Wiltshire *E-mail:* jnw4@le.ac.uk
Founded: 1906
Publication(s): *EA Newsletter* (triannually); *English* (triannually); *English 4-11* (triannually); *Essays & Studies* (annually); *The Use of English* (triannually); *The Year's Work in Critical & Cultural Theory* (annually); *The Year's Work in English Studies* (annually)

The English-Speaking Union of the Commonwealth
Dartmouth House, 37 Charles St, London W1J 5ED
Tel: (020) 7529 1550 *Fax:* (020) 7495 6108
E-mail: esu@esu.org
Web Site: www.esu.org
Key Personnel
Chairman: The Lord Watson of Richmond
Dir General: Valerie Mitchell
Librarian: Gill Hale *E-mail:* gill_hale@esu.org
Membership Secretary: Margaret Garrett
Founded: 1918
Branches worldwide in 52 countries.
Publication(s): *Concord*

Hakluyt Society
c/o Map Library, The British Library, 96 Euston Rd, London NW1 2DB
Tel: (01428) 641850 *Fax:* (01428) 641933
E-mail: office@hakluyt.com
Web Site: www.hakluyt.com
Key Personnel
President: Prof R C Bridges
Administrator: Richard Bateman
Founded: 1846
Publications of scholarly editions of records of voyages, travels & other geographical material of the past.
Publication(s): *The Hakluyt Society* (3rd series)

The Thomas Hardy Society
PO Box 1438, Dorchester, Dorset DT1 1YH
Tel: (01305) 251501 *Fax:* (01305) 251501
E-mail: info@hardysociety.org
Web Site: www.hardysociety.org

Key Personnel
Dir: Rosemarie Morgan *E-mail:* rm82@pantheon.yale.edu
Founded: 1968
List of publications available.
Publication(s): *The Thomas Hardy Journal* (triannually)

Jane Austen Society
Jane Austen's House, Chawton, Alton, Hants GU34 1SD
Tel: (01420) 83262 *Fax:* (01420) 83262
E-mail: museum@janeausten.demon.co.uk
Web Site: www.janeaustensoci.freeuk.com/index.htm
Key Personnel
Chairman: Patrick Stokes
President: Richard Knight
Honorary Secretary: Maggie Lane
Membership Secretary: Rosemary Culley *Tel:* (01705) 475855 *Fax:* (01705) 788842 *E-mail:* rosemary@sndc.demon.co.uk
Founded: 1940
Publication(s): *Jane Austen's House* (book)

The Richard Jefferies Society
Eidsvoll, Bedwells Heath, Boars Hill, Oxford OX1 5JE
Tel: (01865) 735678
Web Site: www.treitel.org/Richard/jefferies.html
Key Personnel
President: Prof Jeremy Hooker
Secretary: Phyllis Treitel
Founded: 1950
Publication(s): *The Richard Jefferies Society Journal*

Keats-Shelley Memorial Association (KSMA)
One Satchwell Walk, Leamington Spa, Warwicks CV32 4QE
Tel: (01892) 533452 *Fax:* (01892) 519142
Web Site: www.keats-shelley.co.uk
Key Personnel
Honorary Treasurer: Charles Cary-Elwes
Founded: 1903
Publication(s): *Keats-Shelley Review* (annually)

Kipling Society
6 Clifton Rd, London W9 1S5
Tel: (020) 7286 0194 *Fax:* (020) 7286 0194
Web Site: www.kipling.org.uk
Key Personnel
Honorary Secretary: Jane Keskar *E-mail:* jane@keskar.fsworld.co.uk
Founded: 1927
Publication(s): *The Kipling Journal* (quarterly)

Charles Lamb Society
Guildhall Library, Aldermanbury, London EC2P 2EJ
Tel: (020) 7332 1868; (020) 7332 1870
Web Site: users.ox.ac.uk/~scat1492/clsoc.htm
Key Personnel
Chairman: N R D Powell
Editor: Richard S Tomlinson *E-mail:* romanticism@ameritech.net
Membership Secretary: Robin Healey
Founded: 1935
Publication(s): *The Charles Lamb Bulletin* (quarterly)

Lancashire Authors' Association
Heatherslade, 5 Quakerfields, Westhoughton, Bolton, Lancs BL5 2BJ
Tel: (01254) 56788
E-mail: laa@lancs.communigate.co.uk
Web Site: www.communigate.co.uk/lancs/laa/index.phtml
Key Personnel
Chairman & Librarian: George W White
Deputy Chairman & Treasurer: T Halsall

President & General Secretary: Eric Holt
Joint Librarian: B Atkinson
Membership Secretary: B Holt
Founded: 1909
Publication(s): *Lancashire Miscellany* (1987/8/90 cassette tapes); *The Record* (quarterly)

Friends of Arthur Machen
78 Greenwich South St, Greenwich, London SE10 8UN
Tel: (01633) 422520 *Fax:* (0633) 421055
Web Site: www.machensoc.demon.co.uk
Key Personnel
Treasurer: Jeremy Cantwell
Publication(s): *Faunus* (biannually, journal); *Machenalia* (biannually, newsletter)

Medical Writers Group
Society of Authors, 84 Drayton Gardens, London SW10 9SB
Tel: (020) 7373 6642 *Fax:* (020) 7373 5768
E-mail: info@societyofauthors.org
Web Site: www.societyofauthors.org
Key Personnel
Chairman: Antony Beevor
Secretary: Mark Le Fanu *E-mail:* mlefanu@societyofauthors.org
Unit of The Society of Authors.
Divisions: The Society of Authors

William Morris Society
Kelmscott House, 26 Upper Mall, Hammersmith, London W6 9TA
Tel: (020) 8741 3735 *Fax:* (020) 8748 5207
Web Site: www.morrissociety.org
Key Personnel
President: Linda Parry
Editor: Dr Rosie Miles
Publication(s): *Journal* (quarterly, newsletter)

Oxford Bibliographical Society
c/o Bodleian Library, Oxford OX1 3BG
Tel: (01865) 277069 *Fax:* (01865) 277182
E-mail: membership@oxbibsoc.org.uk
Web Site: www.oxbibsoc.org.uk
Telex: 83656
Key Personnel
President: Prof Nigel Palmer
Secretary: Dr Julia Walworth *E-mail:* secretary@oxbibsoc.org.uk
Treasurer: David Thomas *E-mail:* treasurer@oxbibsoc.org.uk
Founded: 1922

English PEN Centre
Member of International PEN
Lancaster House, 33 Islington High St, London N1 9LH
Tel: (020) 7713 0023 *Fax:* (020) 7713 0005
E-mail: enquiries@englishpen.org
Web Site: www.englishpen.org
Key Personnel
President: Dr Alastair Niven
Executive Dir: Susanna Nicklin *E-mail:* susie@englishpen.org
Programme Dir, Writers in Prison Committee: Lucy Popescu
Membership Secretary: Simon Burt
Artistic Dir: Diana Reich
Publication(s): *PEN News* (biannually, newsletter)

The Poetry Society Inc
22 Betterton St, London WC2H 9BX
Tel: (020) 7420 9880 *Fax:* (020) 7240 4818
E-mail: info@poetrysociety.org.uk
Web Site: www.poetrysociety.org.uk
Key Personnel
Dir: Jules Mann
Membership Manager: Carl Dhiman
Publications Manager: Janet Phillips
Press & Marketing Manager: Lisa Roberts

Publication(s): *Jumpstart: Poetry in the Secondary School*; *Poems on the the Underground Posters*; *The Poetry Book for Primary Schools*; *Poetry News*; *Poetry Review*

The Beatrix Potter Society
9 Broadfields, Harpenden, Herts AL5 2HJ
Tel: (01625) 267880 *Fax:* (01625) 267879
E-mail: info@beatrixpottersociety.org.uk
Web Site: www.beatrixpottersociety.org.uk
Key Personnel
Chair: Judy Taylor
Founded: 1980
The Society promotes study & appreciation of Potter's life & works, holds regular talks & biennial Study Conference in Lake District.
Publication(s): *Books about Beatrix Potter's Life & Work* (quarterly, newsletter)

The Arthur Ransome Society Ltd (TARS)
Abbot Hall Museum, Kendal, Cumbria LA9 5AL
Tel: (01539) 722464
E-mail: tarsinfo@arthur-ransome.org
Web Site: www.arthur-ransome.org/ar
Key Personnel
President: Norman Willis
Company Secretary: Dr W H Janes
Publication(s): *Literary Transactions* (biannually); *Mixed Moss* (biannually); *The Outlaw* (biannually); *Ship's Log* (annually); *Signals* (annually)

RNA, see Romantic Novelists' Association (RNA)

Romantic Novelists' Association (RNA)
38 Stanhope Rd, Reading, Berks RG2 7HN
Tel: (01827) 714776 *Fax:* (01827) 714776
Web Site: www.rna-uk.org
Key Personnel
President: Diane Pearson
Chairman: Anthea Kenyon
Contact: Trisha Ashley *E-mail:* trisha-ashley@hotmail.com

Royal Literary Fund
3 Johnson's Court (off Fleet St), London EC4A 3EA
Tel: (020) 7353 7150 *Fax:* (020) 7353 1350
E-mail: rlitfund@btconnect.com
Web Site: www.rlf.org.uk
Key Personnel
President: Sir Stephen Tumim
General Secretary: Eileen Gunn
  E-mail: egunnrlf@globalnet.co.uk
Fellowship & Education Officer: Steve Cook
Publication(s): *Archives of the Royal Literary Fund 1790-1918*

The Royal Society for the Encouragement of Arts, Manufactures & Commerce (RSA)
8 John Adam St, London WC2N 6EZ
Tel: (020) 7930 5115 *Fax:* (020) 7839 5805
E-mail: general@rsa.org.uk
Web Site: www.rsa.org.uk
Key Personnel
Dir: Penny Egan *Tel:* (020) 7451 6883
  E-mail: director@rsa.org.uk
Encourages the development of a principled, prosperous society & the release of human potential through a program of projects & events with the support of influential fellows from every field & every background.
Publication(s): *RSA Journal*

Royal Society of Literature
Somerset House, Strand, London WC2R 1LA
Tel: (020) 7845 4676 *Fax:* (020) 7845 4679
E-mail: info@rslit.org
Web Site: www.rslit.org
Key Personnel
President: Michael Holroyd
Chairman of Council: Maggie Gee
Secretary: Maggie Fergusson
Founded: 1820
Registered charity. Administers & awards three literary prizes & confers the honor "Companion of Literature" on selected writers.
Publication(s): *News From the Royal Society of Literature*

RSA, see The Royal Society for the Encouragement of Arts, Manufactures & Commerce (RSA)

The Ruskin Society of London
Subsidiary of The Royal Society of Literature
Affiliate of British Italian Society
351 Woodstock Rd, Oxford OX2 7NX
Tel: (01865) 310987; (01865) 515962
  Fax: (01865) 240448
Key Personnel
Dir: A Hardy
Founded: 1980
Articles & news of Ruskinian interest & 19th century literary history.
Publication(s): *The Ruskin Gazette* (annually, journal)

The Dorothy L Sayers Society
Rose Cottage, Malthouse Lane, Hurstpierpoint, West Sussex BN6 9JY
Tel: (01273) 833444 *Fax:* (01273) 835988
E-mail: info@sayers.org.uk
Web Site: www.sayers.org.uk
Key Personnel
Chairman: Christopher Dean
Membership Secretary: Lenelle Davis
  Tel: (01252) 626619
Bulletin Secretary: Jasmine Simeone *Tel:* (01248) 714940 *Fax:* (01248) 714940
Publications: Janet Hunt
Founded: 1976
Publication(s): *Poetry of Dorothy L Sayers*; *Sidelights on Sayers* (annually)

Scottish PEN Centre
Member of International PEN
Greenleaf Editorial, 15A Lynedoch St, Glasgow G3 6EF
Tel: (01436) 672010
E-mail: info@scottishpen.org
Web Site: www.scottishpen.org
Key Personnel
President: Tessa Ransford
Vice President: Jenni Calder; Douglas Dunn
Secretary: Harry Watson
Treasurer: Mary Baxter

Shakespearean Authorship Trust
c/o Shakespeare's Globe Theater, 21 New Globe Walk, London SE1 9DT
Tel: (01473) 890264; (020) 7902 1403
  Fax: (01473) 890803
E-mail: info@shakespeareanauthorshiptrust.org.uk
Web Site: www.shakespeareanauthorshiptrust.org.uk
Key Personnel
Chairman: Mark Rylance

The Shaw Society
6 Stanstead Grove, Catford, London SE6 4UD
Tel: (020) 86973619 *Fax:* (020) 86973619
E-mail: bernardshawinfo@netscape.net
Web Site: www.sndc.demon.co.uk/shawsub.htm
Key Personnel
Secretary: Barbara Smoker
Treasurer: A J L Gayfer *E-mail:* anthnyellis@aol.com
Editor: T F Evans
Publication(s): *The Shavian* (every nine months)

Society for Editors & Proofreaders
Riverbank House, One Putney Bridge Approach, Fulham, London SW6 3JD
Tel: (020) 7736 3278 *Fax:* (020) 7736 3318
E-mail: administration@sfep.org.uk
Web Site: www.sfep.org.uk
Key Personnel
Chair: Naomi Laredo
Founded: 1988
Professional body providing training, information, support, electronic resources & newsletters.
Publication(s): *CopyRight* (magazine)

Society for the Study of Medieval Languages & Literature
c/o Dr D G Pattison, Magdalen College, Oxford OX1 4AU
Tel: (01865) 276087 *Fax:* (01865) 276087
Web Site: www.mod-langs.ox.ac.uk/ssmll
Key Personnel
President: Mr AVC Schmidt
Secretary: Dr Roger Dalrymple *E-mail:* roger.dalrymple@st-hughs.ox.ac.uk
Treasurer: Dr D G Pattison
Publication(s): *Medium Aevum* (biannually)

The Society of Women Writers & Journalists
Calvers Farm, Thelveton, Diss, Norfolk IP23 4NG
Tel: (01379) 740550 *Fax:* (01379) 741716
Web Site: www.swwj.co.uk
Key Personnel
Chairman: Jean Hawkes
Vice Chairman: Valerie Dunmore
President: Nina Bawden
Secretary: Zoe King *E-mail:* zoe@zoeking.com
Treasurer: Greg Hawkes
Membership Secretary: Wendy Hughes
  E-mail: wendy@stickler.org.uk
Publication(s): *The Woman Writer* (6 times/yr)

TARS, see The Arthur Ransome Society Ltd (TARS)

The Tilling Society
5 Friars Bank, Guestling, Hastings, East Sussex TN35 4EJ
Fax: (01424) 813237
E-mail: society@tilling.org.uk
Web Site: www.tilling.org.uk/society
Key Personnel
Joint-Secretary: Cynthia Reavell; Tony Reavell
Founded: 1982
Publication(s): *E F Benson as Mayor of Rye* (book); *Tilling Society Newsletter* (biannually, newsletter)

The Tolkien Society
65 Wentworth Crescent, Ash Vale, Surrey GU12 5LF
Tel: (01242) 529757
E-mail: membership@tolkiensociety.org
Web Site: www.tolkiensociety.org
Key Personnel
Chairman: Chris Cranshaw
Secretary: Sally Kennett
Membership Secretary: Trevor Reynolds
Publication(s): *Amon Hen* (bimonthly, bulletin); *Mallorn* (annually, journal)

Translators Association
c/o Society of Authors, 84 Drayton Gardens, London SW10 9SB
Tel: (020) 7373 6642 *Fax:* (020) 7373 5768
E-mail: info@societyofauthors.org
Web Site: www.societyofauthors.org
Key Personnel
Chairman: Antony Beever
Awards Secretary: Dorothy Sym *E-mail:* dsym@societyofauthors.org

UNITED KINGDOM

The Association is a specialist group representing published literary translators within the Society of Authors.
Publication(s): *In Other Words* (journal); *Quick Guide to Literary Translation*

Edgar Wallace Society
84 Ridgefield Rd, Oxford OX4 3DA
E-mail: info@edgarwallace.org
Web Site: www.edgarwallace.org
Key Personnel
President: Penelope Wyrd
Founded: 1969
Publication(s): *The Crimson Circle* (quarterly, magazine)

H G Wells Society
Dept of English Literature, Shearwood Mount, Shearwood Rd, Sheffield S10 2TD
Web Site: hgwellsusa.50megs.com
Key Personnel
Secretary: Steve McLean
Sales Officer: John Green
Founded: 1960
Publication(s): *H G Wells: A Comprehensive Bibliography*; *The Wellsian* (annually, journal)

The Welsh Academy, see Yr Academi Gymreig

West Country Writers' Association
High Wotton, Wotton Lane, Lympstone, Exmouth, Devon EX8 5AY
Tel: (01395) 222749
E-mail: wcwa@westcountrywriters.co.uk
Web Site: www.author.co.uk/wcwa
Key Personnel
Secretary: Judy Joss
Founded: 1951

Uruguay

Academia Nacional de Letras (National Academy of Literature)
Ituziango 1255, 11000 Montevideo 11000
Tel: (02) 9152374 *Fax:* (02) 9167460
E-mail: academia@montevideo.com.uy
Telex: 23133 Mec Ug
Key Personnel
President: Antonio Cravotto
Secretary: Carlos Jones
Founded: 1946
Publication(s): *Boletin de la Academia Nacional de Letras*; *Revista Nacional*

Venezuela

Venezuelan PEN Centre (Centro Venezolano del PEN Internacional)
Member of International PEN
10° Transversal con 7° Ave, Residencias Villas Ines, Piso 3, Altamira, Caracas 1010
Tel: (02) 5616691; (02) 5617589; (02) 5617287 *Fax:* (02) 5718064
Telex: 26217 Biaya *Cable:* BIAYACUCH
Key Personnel
President: Dr Jose Ramon Medina
Secretary: Oswaldo Trejo
Publication(s): *Con Textos; Coleccion Plural*

Zimbabwe

The Zimbabwe Writers Union
12 Shurugwi Rd, Gweru
Mailing Address: PO Box 6170, Gweru
Tel: (054) 23284
Key Personnel
President: D Mungoshi
Secretary General: Pathisa Nyathi

Literary Prizes

Prizes and awards are listed alphabetically under the country where the sponsor is located. In some instances, recipients are restricted to the country in which the prize or award is presented.

☆ indicates those prizes with no geographical restriction placed upon recipients.

Argentina

Concurso Literario Premio Emece
Emece Editores SA
Av Independencia 1668, 1100 Buenos Aires
Tel: (011) 4382-4043; (011) 4382-4045
    Fax: (011) 4383-3793
Web Site: www.emece.com.ar
Key Personnel
Editorial Department: Mirta Mallo
    E-mail: mmallo@eplaneta.com.ar
Established: 1954
For the best unpublished novel or book of short stories in the Spanish language.

National Prize for Literature
Argentina Ministry of Education, Science & Technology
Subsecretary of Culture, Pizzurno 935, 1020 Buenos Aires
Awarded triennially for best works of prose & poetry.

Premio Academia Nacional de la Historia
(National Academy of History Award)
Academia Nacional de la Historia (National Academy of History)
Balcarce 139, 1064 Buenos Aires
Tel: (01) 4343-4416; (01) 4331-4633; (01) 4331-5147 (ext 110) *Fax:* (01) 4331-5147 (ext 0)
E-mail: admite@an-historia.org.ar
Web Site: www.an-historia.org.ar

Australia

The Age Book of the Year Awards
The Age
250 Spencer St, Melbourne, Victoria 3000
Mailing Address: PO Box 257C, Melbourne, Victoria 8001
Tel: (03) 9600 4211 *Fax:* (03) 9670 7514
Web Site: www.theage.com.au
Two prizes awarded to the two Australian books of outstanding literary merit which best express Australia's identity or character: one prize for a work of imaginative writing, the other for a nonfiction work.
Award: One work to be named 'The Age' Book of the Year & 4,000 AUD; other, best work in its category, 3,000 AUD

Alexander Henderson Award
Australian Institute of Genealogical Studies Inc
1/41 Railway Rd, Blackburn, Melbourne, Victoria 3130
Mailing Address: PO Box 339, Blackburn, Melbourne, Victoria 3130
Tel: (03) 9877 3789 *Fax:* (03) 9877 9066
E-mail: info@aigs.org.au
Web Site: www.aigs.org.au/
Established: 1973
Best Australian family history book, written & entered for the award.
Closing Date: Nov 30 annually
Presented: Last Friday of May

The Alice Literary Award
Society of Women Writers (Australia)
73 Church Rd, Carrum, Victoria 3197
Tel: (03) 9772 2389
Web Site: home.vicnet.net.au/~swwvic
Key Personnel
President: Judy Keighran *Tel:* (03) 5975 6564
    E-mail: judyk@surf.net.au
Secretary: Judy Bartosy *E-mail:* fbartosy@surfnetcity.com.au
Established: 1978
Presented biennially for a distinguished & long-term contribution to literature by an Australian woman.

APA Book Design Awards
Australian Publishers Association Ltd
60/89 Jones St, Ultimo, NSW 2007
Tel: (02) 9281 9788 *Fax:* (02) 9281 1073
E-mail: apa@publishers.asn.au
Web Site: www.publishers.asn.au
Key Personnel
Contact: Angela Wong
Recognizes creativity, excellence & innovation in contemporary Australian book design. Books entered must have been designed in Australia & published for the first time during the preceding calendar year. Entries open in October & close in January.
Award: 20 award categories which feature prizes to the value of $1,000
Closing Date: April 16
Presented: Book Design Awards, held in conjunction with the Australian Book Fair at Darling Harbour in June

APA Campus Bookstore of the Year Award
Australian Publishers Association Ltd
60/89 Jones St, Ultimo, NSW 2007
Tel: (02) 9281 9788 *Fax:* (02) 9281 1073
E-mail: apa@publishers.asn.au
Web Site: www.publishers.asn.au
Key Personnel
President: Greg Browne
Chief Executive: Susan Bridge

APA Publisher of the Year Award
Australian Publishers Association Ltd
60/89 Jones St, Ultimo, NSW 2007
Tel: (02) 9281 9788 *Fax:* (02) 9281 1073
E-mail: apa@publishers.asn.au
Web Site: www.publishers.asn.au
Key Personnel
President: Greg Browne
Chief Executive: Susan Bridge
Peer-assessment award, acknowledging professional performance by organizations during the previous calendar year.
Presented: Australian Book Industry Awards Dinner at the Australian Book Fair in June, Annually in June

Arts Queensland Judith Wright Calanthe Award for Poetry
Brisbane Writers Festival Association Inc
PO Box 3567, South Brisbane, Qld 4101
Tel: (07) 3255 0254 *Fax:* (07) 3255 0362
E-mail: writers@qpac.com.au
Web Site: www.brisbanewritersfestival.com.au
Key Personnel
Festival Dir: Rosemary Cameron
Festival Manager: Rhiannon Phillips
Marketing: Gabe Cramb; Lisa Wickbold
Chairman: Sallyanne Atkinson
Deputy Chair: Helenka King
Secretary: Kristy Vernon
Treasurer: Karen Mitchell
Established: 1997
Award for poetry by an Australian author.
Other Sponsor(s): Arts Queensland
Award: 15,000 AUD & certificate
Closing Date: July
Presented: Oct

Australian Literature Society Gold Medal
Association for the Study of Australian Literature
School of English & European Languages, University of Tasmania, GPO Box 252-82, Hobart, Tas 7001
Tel: (03) 6226 2352 *Fax:* (03) 6226 7631
Web Site: www.asc.uq.edu.au/asal
Key Personnel
President: Lyn McCredden *E-mail:* lynmcr@deakin.edu.au
Vice President: Peter Kirkpatrick *Tel:* (02) 4736 0112 *E-mail:* p.kirkpatrick@uws.edu.au
Treasurer: Simon Ryan
Secretary: Paul Genoni *Tel:* (08) 9266 7526
    E-mail: p.genoni@curtin.edu.au
Award originated by Colonel, the Honourable R A Crouch in 1899 & continued by the Australian Literature Society until 1983 when the ALS incorporated with the Association for the Study of Australian Literature. It is awarded annually for the most outstanding Australian literary work, or for outstanding services to Australian literature.

Australian Vogel Literary Award
Allen & Unwin Pty Ltd
PO Box 8500, Saint Leonards, NSW 1590
Tel: (02) 8425 0100 *Fax:* (02) 99062218
Web Site: www.allenandunwin.com
Key Personnel
Contact: Emma Sorensen *E-mail:* emmas@allenandunwin.com
Established: 1980
Literary Award for an unpublished manuscript by Australian authors under 35 years of age.
Other Sponsor(s): The Australian Newspaper; Vogel Breads
Closing Date: May annually
Presented: Sept/Oct

The Marten Bequest Travelling Scholarships
Trust
35 Clarence St, Sydney, NSW 2000
Mailing Address: GPO Box 4270, Sydney 2001
Tel: (02) 8295 8100 *Fax:* (02) 8295 8659
Web Site: www.permanentgroup.com.au

AUSTRALIA   LITERARY

Key Personnel
Awards Administrator: Petrea Salter
Six scholarships awarded annually for study in the following area(s): singing, instrumental music, painting, ballet, sculpture, architecture, prose, poetry & acting. Entrants must be born in Australia & between the ages of 21-35 (except in the field of ballet: ages 17-35).
Award: Each scholarship 18,000 AUD
Closing Date: Oct/Nov of year previous

Bronze Swagman Award
Winton Tourist Promotion Association
PO Box 44, Winton, Qld 4735
Tel: (07) 4657 1466 *Fax:* (07) 4657 1886
E-mail: matilda@thehub.com.au
Web Site: www.patsopals.com
Key Personnel
Contact: M Nowland
Annual award for Bush Verse. Book verse available in December of each year.
Award: 2500 AUD Bronze statuette of The Swagman, sculpted by Daphne Mayo & a 250 AUD Winton Opal
Closing Date: Jan 31
Presented: Easter

R Carson Gold Short Story Competition
Fellowship of Australian Writers Queensland (FAWQ)
14 Cassowary Court, Caboolture, Qld 4510
Key Personnel
Receiving Officer: Nancy Cox-Millner
E-mail: nancycm@hotmail.com
Awarded annually for a short story by an Australian with Australian setting. Administered by the Union Fidelity Trust Company of Australia. Open only to persons born in Australia.
Award: 1st prize 1,000 AUD
Closing Date: April 23

Children's Book of the Year Awards
Children's Book Council of Australia
13 High St, Launceston, Tas 7250
Mailing Address: PO Box 325, Lenah Valley, Tas 7008
Tel: (03) 6223 1298
E-mail: office@cbc.org.au
Web Site: www.cbc.org.au
Key Personnel
Contact: Maureen Mann *Tel:* (03) 6334 2794
E-mail: maureen.mann@education.tas.gov.au
Awarded annually.
(1) Book of the Year, established 1946; (2) Junior Book of the Year, established 1982; (3) Picture Book of the Year, established 1952. $30,000 to be distributed amongst the winners & honor books (possibility of two) in each category.
(4) The Eve Pownall Information Book Award (nonfiction) established 1993. $10,000 to be distributed between winner & up to two honor books.
Closing Date: Dec 31

The Abbie Clancy Award
Society of Women Writers NSW Inc
GPO Box 1388, Sydney, NSW 2001
Web Site: www.womenwritersnsw.org/awards.html
Awarded annually to a needy & deserving English honours student studying at an Australian university.
Award: 1,000 AUD to 1,500 AUD

Tom Collins Poetry Prize
Western Australia Fellowship of Australian Writers
Tom Collins House, 88 Wood St, Swanbourne, WA 6010
Tel: (08) 9384 4771 *Fax:* (08) 9384 4854
E-mail: fawwa@iinet.net.au
Web Site: members.iinet.net.au/~fawwa

Key Personnel
President: Trisha Kotai-Ewers
Established: 1977
Administered by Western Australia FAW & sponsored by J Furphy & Sons, Shepparton, Victoria, since 1984, for a poem of up to 60 lines.
Award: 1st prize $1,000; 2nd prize $400; Highly Commended $150
Closing Date: Dec 31

C H Currey Memorial Fellowship
State Library of NSW Press
Macquarie St, Sydney, NSW 2000
Tel: (02) 9273 1414 *Fax:* (02) 9273 1255
E-mail: library@sl.nsw.gov.au
Web Site: www.sl.nsw.gov.au
Established: 1974
For the writing of Australian history from original sources, preferably making use of the State Library's resources.
Award: $20,000

Emeritus Awards
Australia Council Literature Board
372 Elizabeth St, Surry Hills, NSW 2010
Mailing Address: PO Box 788, Strawberry Hills, NSW 2012
Tel: (02) 9215 9000 *Fax:* (02) 9215 9111
E-mail: mail@ozco.gov.au
Web Site: www.ozco.gov.au
Key Personnel
Administrator: Maggie Joel *E-mail:* m.joel@ozco.gov.au
Open to Australian writers over the age of 65 who must be nominated by other people. They must have produced a critically acclaimed body of work over a long creative life. Nominators must give evidence that the maximum annual income of the nominated writer is less than $40,000.
Award: Up to $40,000
Closing Date: Nomination May 15
Presented: Nov

FAW Alan Marshall Short Story Award
Fellowship of Australian Writers (Vic) Inc
PO Box 3036, Ripponlea, Victoria 3183
Tel: (03) 9528 7088 *Fax:* (03) 9528 7088
Web Site: www.writers.asn.au
Key Personnel
Awards Coordinator: Adrian Peniston-Bird
Award to a young writer (10-14 years). One copy of each story is required. No word limit.
Other Sponsor(s): Penguin Books Australia
Award: 150 AUD & 50 AUD
Closing Date: Nov 30

FAW Anne Elder Poetry Award
Fellowship of Australian Writers (Vic) Inc
PO Box 3036, Ripponlea, Victoria 3183
Tel: (03) 9528 7088 *Fax:* (03) 9528 7088
Web Site: www.writers.asn.au
Key Personnel
Awards Coordinator: Adrian Peniston-Bird
Awarded to a first book of poetry. An award is possible where up to four poets contribute to a book, providing it is the first published book-length collection of poetry by the authors concerned. Book must be at least 20 pages. Self-published works are eligible. Publishers & authors can also submit entries. Two copies of each book required & will not be returned. Open to Australia residents only.
Award: 1000 AUD
Closing Date: Nov 30

FAW C J Dennis Poetry Award
Fellowship of Australian Writers (Vic) Inc
PO Box 3036, Ripponlea, Victoria 3183
Tel: (03) 9528 7088 *Fax:* (03) 9528 7088
Web Site: www.writers.asn.au

Key Personnel
Awards Coordinator: Adrian Peniston-Bird
Award to a young writer (10-14 years). Only one copy of poem required. Open to Australia residents only.
Award: 125 AUD & 75 AUD
Closing Date: Nov 30

FAW Christina Stead Award
Fellowship of Australian Writers (Vic) Inc
PO Box 3036, Ripponlea, Victoria 3183
Tel: (03) 9528 7088 *Fax:* (03) 9528 7088
Web Site: www.writers.asn.au
Key Personnel
Awards Coordinator: Adrian Peniston-Bird
For an autobiography, biography or memoir first published after Nov 18, 2001. Books published overseas are ineligible. Two copies of the book required & they will not be returned.
Other Sponsor(s): Merchant of Fairness Bookshop
Award: 500 AUD
Closing Date: Nov 30

FAW Colin Thiele Poetry Award
Fellowship of Australian Writers (Vic) Inc
PO Box 3036, Ripponlea, Victoria 3183
Tel: (03) 9528 7088 *Fax:* (03) 9528 7088
Web Site: www.writers.asn.au
Key Personnel
Awards Coordinator: Adrian Peniston-Bird
Award to a young writer (15-20 years). One copy of each poem is required. No word limit.
Other Sponsor(s): Michael Dugan
Award: 200 AUD & 100 AUD
Closing Date: Nov 30

FAW Jennifer Burbidge Short Story Award
Fellowship of Australian Writers (Vic) Inc
PO Box 3036, Ripponlea, Victoria 3183
Tel: (03) 9528 7088 *Fax:* (03) 9528 7088
Web Site: www.writers.asn.au
Key Personnel
Awards Coordinator: Adrian Peniston-Bird
Awarded in honour of Jenny Burbidge for a short story, up to 3,000 words, that deals with any aspect of the lives of those who suffer some form of physical or mental disability &/or its impact on their families in the Australian situation. One copy of each story is required. More than one entry may be submitted.
Other Sponsor(s): Mary Burbidge
Award: 250 AUD
Closing Date: Nov 30

FAW Jim Hamilton Award
Fellowship of Australian Writers (Vic) Inc
PO Box 3036, Ripponlea, Victoria 3183
Tel: (03) 9528 7088 *Fax:* (03) 9528 7088
Web Site: www.writers.asn.au
Key Personnel
Awards Coordinator: Adrian Peniston-Bird
Award honours the contribution Jim Hamilton OAM & his family have made to Australian writers & writing. 1st & 2nd prize will be awarded for a previously unpublished novel or a book-length collection (not less than 30,000 words) of short stories. The manuscript should be aimed at teenage or adult readers.
Other Sponsor(s): Eltham High School; Clare Mendes
Award: 1st prize 1,000 AUD; 2nd prize 500 AUD
Closing Date: Nov 30

FAW John Morrison Short Story Award
Fellowship of Australian Writers (Vic) Inc
PO Box 3036, Ripponlea, Victoria 3183
Tel: (03) 9528 7088 *Fax:* (03) 9528 7088
Web Site: www.writers.asn.au
Key Personnel
Awards Coordinator: Adrian Peniston-Bird
Award to a young writer (15-20 years). One copy of each story is required. Limit of 3,000 words per entry.

Other Sponsor(s): Paul Jennings
Award: 1st prize 200 AUD; 2nd prize 100 AUD
Closing Date: Nov 30

FAW John Shaw Neilson Poetry Award
Fellowship of Australian Writers (Vic) Inc
PO Box 3036, Ripponlea, Victoria 3183
Tel: (03) 9528 7088 *Fax:* (03) 9528 7088
Web Site: www.writers.asn.au
Key Personnel
Awards Coordinator: Adrian Peniston-Bird
For a poem of between 14 & 60 lines (inclusive). A suite of poems may be entered as one entry provided the individual parts of the suite are linked thematically & the total length is not more than 60 lines. Thematically separate poems must be submitted as separate entries. No limit to the number of entries.
Other Sponsor(s): Collected Works Bookshop
Award: 1st prize 500 AUD; others may be highly commended or commended
Closing Date: Nov 30

FAW Mary Grant Bruce Story Award for Children's Literature
Fellowship of Australian Writers (Vic) Inc
PO Box 3036, Ripponlea, Victoria 3183
Tel: (03) 9528 7088 *Fax:* (03) 9528 7088
Web Site: www.writers.asn.au
Key Personnel
Awards Coordinator: Adrian Peniston-Bird
Award to recognize & honor the contribution by Mary Grant Bruce to children's literature & to encourage the writing of quality children's short stories. The trust is administered by Wellington Shire Council. The story should be aimed at young readers aged 10-15 years. Entries may be no longer than 5000 words. Two copies of the story are required. More than one entry may be submitted. 600 AUD award to winner of open section. 2nd prize 300 AUD. Others may be commended. Writers living in the Gippsland area, as described by Municipal boundaries, are also eligible for separate 200 AUD award. Open to Australia residents only.
Closing Date: Nov 30

FAW Mavis Thorpe Clark Award
Fellowship of Australian Writers (Vic) Inc
PO Box 3036, Ripponlea, Victoria 3183
Tel: (03) 9528 7088 *Fax:* (03) 9528 7088
Web Site: www.writers.asn.au
Key Personnel
Awards Coordinator: Adrian Peniston-Bird
Awarded to postprimary students. Part 1 is for an individual submission & Part 2 is for a group entry. With the exception of school newspapers, all other kinds of creative writing are eligible. At least 10 items required, but volume is not of great importance. Individual submissions are restricted to one per student, but schools may submit more than one group entry. All entrants must be attending the same postprimary school in Australia & the work original & written in the current calendar year. Presentation, layout & design are not key criteria, but entries should be securely bound in some way. Only one copy of each entry required. Open to Australia residents only.
Award: Individual 350 AUD & framed certificate; Group 200 AUD & framed certificate
Closing Date: Nov 30

The Festival Awards for Literature
Arts South Australia
West's Coffee Palace, 110 Hindley Street, Adelaide, SA
Mailing Address: GPO Box 2308, Adelaide, SA 5001
Tel: (08) 8463 5444 *Fax:* (08) 8463 5420
E-mail: artssa@saugov.sa.gov.au
Web Site: www.arts.sa.gov.au
Key Personnel
Project Manager: Gail Kovatseff
The awards are offered biennially by the South Australian Government & announced during Writers' Week of the Adelaide Festival of Arts. The seven awards offered are: (1) The National Fiction Award for a published novel or a collection of short stories (15,000 AUD); (2) The John Bray Award for Poetry for a published collection of poetry (15,000 AUD); (3) The National Children's Literature Award for a published children's book, fiction or nonfiction (15,000 AUD); (4) The National Nonfiction Award for a published work of nonfiction (16,000 AUD); (5) The Jill Blewett Playwright's Award for a play script performed by a professional theatre company or a professional production unit (16,000 AUD); (6) Carclew Fellowship, a fellowship of up to 6 months at Carclew, open to writers resident in South Australia (15,000 AUD); (7) South Australian Premier's Literary Award for the most outstanding published work submitted to the Festival for Literature (extra 5000 AUD added to winner's 15,000 AUD category prize). Authors of published works must be citizens or residents of Australia.
Closing Date: Oct 31, 2005

The Miles Franklin Literary Award
Trust
35 Clarence St, Sydney, NSW 2000
Mailing Address: GPO Box 4270, Sydney 2001
Tel: (02) 8295 8100 *Fax:* (02) 8295 8659
Web Site: www.permanentgroup.com.au
Key Personnel
Awards Administrator: Petrea Salter
Established: 1954
Australia's most prestigious literary award. Annual award to the novel or play which is the best for its year & which represents Australia's life in any of its phases.
Award: 28,000 AUD
Closing Date: Dec 15
Presented: State Library of NSW, May/June

The Mary Gilmore Award
Association for the Study of Australian Literature
School of Literary & Communications Studies, Deakin University (Burwood Campus), Burwood, Victoria 3125
Tel: (03) 9244 3960 *Fax:* (03) 9481 6717
Web Site: www.asc.uq.edu.au/asal
Key Personnel
President: Lyn McCredden *E-mail:* lynmcr@deakin.edu.au
Established: 1985
Awarded annually for the best first book of poetry published in the preceding two calendar years.

Grants for Writers (New Work & Fellowships)
Australia Council Literature Board
372 Elizabeth St, Surry Hills, NSW 2010
Mailing Address: PO Box 788, Strawberry Hills, NSW 2012
Tel: (02) 9215 9000 *Fax:* (02) 9215 9111
E-mail: mail@ozco.gov.au
Web Site: www.ozco.gov.au
Key Personnel
Administrator: Maggie Joel *E-mail:* m.joel@ozco.gov.au
New Work & Fellowship categories offer grants ranging from $5,000 to $80,000 to Australian writers. Projects are accepted in the following areas: fiction, literary nonfiction, poetry, children's literature, writing for stage or radio. Minimum publication/performance requirements apply. One closing date per year.
Award: $40,000 per year for 2 years
Closing Date: May 15
Presented: Nov

Greater Dandenong Writing Awards
City of Greater Dandenong
397-405 Springvale Rd, Springvale, Victoria 3171
Mailing Address: PO Box 200, Dandenong, Victoria 3175
Tel: (03) 9239 5100 *Fax:* (03) 9329 5196
E-mail: cultural.development@cgd.vic.gov.au
Web Site: www.greaterdandenong.com
Key Personnel
Project Officer: Sarah Portanier *Tel:* (03) 9239-5141
Established: 1979
National competition with categories for short stories & poetry.
Award: Up to 4,500 AUD in cash prizes & publish winning writers in an anthology
Closing Date: April 30 annually

Grenfell Henry Lawson Festival of Arts Awards
Henry Lawson Festival of the Arts
Main St, Grenfell, NSW 2810
Mailing Address: PO Box 125, Grenfell, NSW 2810
Tel: (063) 431779 *Fax:* (063) 431548
E-mail: grenfelltourism@tpg.com.au
Web Site: www.henrylawsonfestival.asn.au
Telex: 437156
Key Personnel
President: Glenice Clarke *Tel:* (02) 6343 1326 *Fax:* (02) 6343 1421
Promotions Officer: Fiona Last *Tel:* (063) 431403 *Fax:* (063) 431421
Coordinator: Marion Knapp *E-mail:* knappdm@tpg.com.au
Awards are made for short story up to 5000 words, verse, art & the words & music of an Australian popular song; also a bush ballad.
Award: Cash & engraved bronze statuette created by Sydney sculptor Alan Ingham
Closing Date: March
Presented: Annually in June

Lyndall Hadow/Donald Stuart Short Story Award
Western Australia Fellowship of Australian Writers
Tom Collins House, 88 Wood St, Swanbourne, WA 6010
Tel: (08) 9384 4771 *Fax:* (08) 9384 4854
E-mail: fawwa@iinet.net.au
Web Site: members.iinet.net.au/~fawwa
Key Personnel
President: Trisha Kotai-Ewers
Executive Officer: Alethea Sheehan
Award for a short story not exceeding 3000 words. Alternates (even years) with Donald Stuart Short Story Award (odd years).
Award: 1st prize $400; 2nd prize $100; Highly Commended $50
Closing Date: June 15

The Grace Leven Prize for Poetry
Perpetual Trustee Co Ltd
39 Hunter St, Sydney, NSW 2000
Tel: (02) 9229 3951 *Toll Free Tel:* 800 501 227 *Fax:* (02) 9229 3957
E-mail: foundations@perpetual.com.au; info@perpetual.com.au; giftfund@perpetual.com.au
Web Site: www.perpetual.com.au
Instituted under the will of William Baylebridge, the Australian poet, who died in 1942. This prize is offered annually for the best volume of poetry published during the twelve months immediately preceding the year in which the award is made. Competitors must be either Australian born, & writing as Australians, or they must be naturalized in Australia & have lived in that country for at least ten years. The volume chosen may have been published in any country, but copies of it must be freely obtainable in Australia.
Award: $400

AUSTRALIA

The Walter McRae Russell Award
Association for the Study of Australian Literature
School of English, Art History, Film & Media Studies, John Woolley Bldg A20, University of Sydney, Sydney 2006
Tel: (02) 9351 8068 *Fax:* (02) 9351 2434
Web Site: www.asc.uq.edu.au/asal
Key Personnel
Chairman: Ian Henderson *E-mail:* ian.henderson@english.usyd.edu.au
President: Lyn McCredden *E-mail:* lynmcr@deakin.edu.au
Vice President: Peter Kirpatrick *Tel:* (02) 4736 0112 *E-mail:* p.kirpatrick@uws.edu.au
Treasurer: Simon Ryan
Secretary: Paul Genoni *Tel:* (08) 9266 7526 *E-mail:* p.genoni@curtin.edu.au
Established: 1983
Awarded annually for an outstanding work of literary scholarship by a young or unestablished author on an Australian subject published during the previous calendar year.
Award: $1,000

Malvern Newsheet Award
Fellowship of Australian Writers (Vic) Inc
PO Box 3036, Ripponlea, Victoria 3183
Tel: (03) 9528 7088 *Fax:* (03) 9528 7088
Web Site: www.writers.asn.au
Key Personnel
Awards Coordinator: Adrian Peniston-Bird
For a book of short stories &/or poems authored by a Writers' Group. All contributors must be members of the group. Maximum length of book is 30,000 words. Individual contributions to the anthology may not exceed 3,000 words. Each group may only submit one entry & one copy is required. Entries will not be returned.
Other Sponsor(s): Malvern Newsheet; Victorian Community Writers
Award: 1st prize 500 AUD; 2nd prize 200 AUD
Closing Date: Nov 30

Melbourne University Press Award
Fellowship of Australian Writers (Vic) Inc
PO Box 3036, Ripponlea, Victoria 3183
Tel: (03) 9528 7088 *Fax:* (03) 9528 7088
Web Site: www.writers.asn.au
Key Personnel
Awards Coordinator: Adrian Peniston-Bird
For a nonfiction work of sustained quality & distinction with an Australian theme first published after Nov 18, 2001. Books previously published overseas are ineligible. Two copies of the book are required & they will not be returned. Judges are independent of Melbourne University Press & books published by MUP are eligible.
Other Sponsor(s): Melbourne University Press
Award: 1,000 AUD
Closing Date: Nov 30

Metcalfe Medallion
Australian Library & Information Association (ALIA)
ALIA House, 9-11 Napier Close, Deakin, ACT 2600
Mailing Address: PO Box E441, Kingston, ACT 2604
Tel: (02) 6215 8222 *Fax:* (02) 6282 2249
E-mail: awards@alia.org.au
Web Site: www.alia.org.au
Recognizes high achievement by a personal financial member in their first five years of practice in libraries & information services. Peer nominations only.
Closing Date: Nominations - Aug 1

The Kathleen Mitchell Award
Trust
35 Clarence St, Sydney, NSW 2000
Mailing Address: GPO Box 4270, Sydney 2001
Tel: (02) 8295 8100 *Fax:* (02) 8295 8659
Web Site: www.permanentgroup.com.au
Key Personnel
Awards Administrator: Petrea Salter
Established: 1996
Biannual award for published authors under the age of 30 in the two calendar years preceding the award.
Award: 5,000 AUD

Angelo B Natoli Short Story Award
Fellowship of Australian Writers (Vic) Inc
PO Box 3036, Ripponlea, Victoria 3183
Tel: (03) 9528 7088 *Fax:* (03) 9528 7088
Web Site: www.writers.asn.au
Key Personnel
Awards Coordinator: Adrian Peniston-Bird
In honour of the late Angelo B Natoli, who for many years served as the Honorary Solicitor to Fellowship of Australian Writers (Vic) Inc. Awarded for a short story, open theme, to a maximum of 3,000 words. Other entries may be highly commended or commended. One copy of each story is required. More than one story may be submitted.
Award: 600 AUD
Closing Date: Nov 30

New South Wales Premier's Literary Awards
New South Wales Ministry for the Arts
St James Centre, Level 9, 111 Elizabeth St, Sydney, NSW 2000
Mailing Address: PO Box A226, Sydney South, NSW 1235
Tel: (02) 9228 5533 *Toll Free Tel:* 800 358 594 *Fax:* (02) 9228 4722
E-mail: ministry@arts.nsw.gov.au
Web Site: www.arts.nsw.gov.au
Established: 1979
Presented by the New South Wales Government to honor distinguished achievement by Australian writers. The Ethnic Affairs Commission Award of $10,000 is offered for a work which reflects an aspect of Australia's multicultural society. In addition, the committee judging the book awards may propose that a special award, (usually $5,000), with or without prize money, be made for a work not readily covered by the existing categories, or in recognition of a writer's achievements generally. Winners in all categories also receive commemorative medallions.
Award: Fiction $20,000; Non-fiction $20,000; Poetry $15,000; A Children's Book $15,000; Play, film, television or radio script $15,000; Literary Critism $15,000; Book of the year an additional $2,000; Ethnic Affairs Commission Award about Australia's multiculture $10,000

New South Wales Writer's Fellowship
New South Wales Ministry for the Arts
St James Centre, Level 9, 111 Elizabeth St, Sydney, NSW 2000
Mailing Address: PO Box A226, Sydney South, NSW 1235
Tel: (02) 9228 5533 *Fax:* (02) 9228 4722
E-mail: ministry@arts.nsw.gov.au
Web Site: www.arts.nsw.gov.au
Awarded by the New South Wales Government in conjunction with the New South Wales Premier's Literary Awards, to assist the writing of new literary work by a writer living in New South Wales. Applicants must demonstrate their project is likely to result in work of significant quality & be of lasting benefit to the applicant's experience & development as a writer or the advancement of Australian literature in general. Applicants are required to have been resident three years prior to & at the time of application.
Award: $20,000
Closing Date: June

Poetry Competition
Society of Women Writers NSW Inc
GPO Box 1388, Sydney, NSW 2001
Web Site: www.womenwritersnsw.org/awards.html
Annual competition which, in alternate years, is closed to members only or open to all Australian citizens. In years open to all, it is called the National Poetry Competition. Members only competitions in even-numbered years; National competitions in odd-numbered years.

Colin Roderick Award
Foundation for Australian Literary Studies
School of Humanities, James Cook University, Townsville, Qld 4811
Tel: (07) 4781 4451; (07) 4781 4426 *Fax:* (07) 4781 5655
Web Site: www.faess.jcu.edu.au/soh
Established: 1967
Award to the author of the best book in any field of writing dealing with any aspect of Australian life.
Award: 10,000 AUD & the H T Priestley Medal from the Townsville Foundation for Australian Literary Studies at the James Cook University
Closing Date: Feb 29
Presented: Townsville, Australia, Sept 13

Society of Women Writers Biennial Book Awards
Society of Women Writers NSW Inc
GPO Box 1388, Sydney, NSW 2001
Web Site: www.womenwritersnsw.org/awards.html
Established: 1925
Every second year, members are invited to submit books published over the previous two years. Separate awards are given for fiction, non-fiction, poetry & children's books. Two Children's Book Awards may be given - one for a book for younger readers & one for an adolescent/young adult book. Next award to be given in 2005.

Victorian Premier's Literary Awards
State Library of Victoria
328 Swanston St, Melbourne, Victoria 3000
Tel: (03) 8664 7000 *Fax:* (03) 9639 7006
E-mail: pla@slv.vic.gov.au
Web Site: www.statelibrary.vic.gov.au/pla
Established: 1985
Founded in 1985 on the occasion of the centenary of the births of Vance & Nettie Palmer. Open to Australian writers with works first published or performed between May 1, 2001 & April 30, 2002. The annual awards are (1) Vance Palmer Prize for a work of fiction ($30,000), (2) Nettie Palmer Prize for a work of non-fiction ($30,000), (3) Louis Esson Prize for Drama ($15,000), (4) C J Dennis Prize for Poetry ($15,000), (5) Kraft Foods Prize for Young Adult Fiction ($12,000), (6) Dinny O'Hearn/SBS Book Prize for Literary Translation ($15,000) & (7) Alfred Deakin Prize for an Essay Advancing Public Debate ($15,000). The applications are to be given to the Project Officer.
Closing Date: April 30
Presented: Mid-Oct

Patrick White Literary Award
Perpetual Trustee Co Ltd
39 Hunter St, Sydney, NSW 2000
Tel: (02) 9229 3951 *Toll Free Tel:* 800 501 227 *Fax:* (02) 9229 3957
E-mail: foundations@perpetual.com.au; info@perpetual.com.au; giftfund@perpetual.com.au
Web Site: www.perpetual.com.au
Key Personnel
Charitable Trusts Manager: Susan Ahmelman

Patrick White applied his Nobel Prize money to establish a trust to make an annual award to an Australian writer who has not been adequately recognized. Submissions are not required.

Young Australians Best Book Award
Young Australians Best Book Award Council
PO Box 238, Kew, Victoria 3101
Tel: (03) 98897749 *Fax:* (03) 9889 3665
E-mail: yabbabooks@yahoo.com
Web Site: www.vicnet.net.au/~yabba
Key Personnel
President: Graham Davey *E-mail:* daveyg@netspace.net.au
Treasurer: Richard Bennett
Established: 1986
Citation from Children.
Awarded annually.
Closing Date: Student nominations are sought in Term 1 (Feb-April)
Presented: Awards Ceremony, November

Austria

Austrian Award of Merit for Children's Literature
Bundeskanzleramt-Kunstsektion
Sektion II-Kunstangelegenheiten, Abteilung II/5, Schottengasse 1, 1014 Vienna
Tel: (01) 531 15-0 *Fax:* (01) 53 115-7620; (01) 531 15-7561
Web Site: www.art.austria.gv.at
Key Personnel
Contact: Dr Robert Stocker *E-mail:* robert.stocker@bka.gv.at
Established: 1980
Awarded biennially to an author, illustrator & translator in appreciation of his life's work.
Award: 11,000 EUR

Austrian Children's & Juvenile Book Awards
Bundeskanzleramt-Kunstsektion
Sektion II-Kunstangelegenheiten, Abteilung II/5, Schottengasse 1, 1014 Vienna
Tel: (01) 531 15-0 *Fax:* (01) 53 115-7620; (01) 531 15-7561
Web Site: www.art.austria.gv.at
Key Personnel
Contact: Dr Robert Stocker *E-mail:* robert.stocker@bka.gv.at
Established: 1955
Seven categories: four for books for children & young people, an "Austrian Children's & Young People's Nonfiction Book Prize," "Austrian Children's & Young People's Translation Prize" & an "Austrian Children's & Young People's Prize" for book illustration.
Award: 18,200 EUR to be shared by the prize winners. Prizewinning books are purchased by the Ministry of Education Arts in the amount of 10,200 EUR

Austrian National Award for Poetry for Children
Bundeskanzleramt-Kunstsektion
Sektion II-Kunstangelegenheiten, Abteilung II/5, Schottengasse 1, 1014 Vienna
Tel: (01) 531 15-0 *Fax:* (01) 53 115-7620; (01) 531 15-7561
Web Site: www.art.austria.gv.at
Key Personnel
Contact: Dr Robert Stocker *E-mail:* robert.stocker@bka.gv.at
Established: 1993
For the complete works of an author of poetry for children in German language.
Award: 7,300 EUR biennially

Austrian Promotional Award for Children's Literature
Bundeskanzleramt-Kunstsektion
Sektion II-Kunstangelegenheiten, Abteilung II/5, Schottengasse 1, 1014 Vienna
Tel: (01) 531 15-0 *Fax:* (01) 53 115-7620
Web Site: www.art.austria.gv.at
Key Personnel
Contact: Dr Robert Stocker *E-mail:* robert.stocker@bka.gv.at
Established: 1996
Biennial award to an author, illustrator or translator in appreciation of his outstanding contributions to children's literature.
Award: 7,300 EUR

☆**Austrian State Prize for European Literature**
Bundeskanzleramt-Kunstsektion
Sektion II-Kunstangelegenheiten, Abteilung II/5, Schottengasse 1, 1014 Vienna
Tel: (01) 531 15-0 *Fax:* (01) 53 115-7620; (01) 531 15-7561
Web Site: www.art.austria.gv.at
Key Personnel
Contact: Dr Robert Stocker *E-mail:* robert.stocker@bka.gv.at
Established: 1965
Presented by the Austrian Minister of Education to a European author (with the exception of an Austrian national) whose work has also been acclaimed outside his own country; this must be demonstrated by translation. No applications; The prize is awarded on the recommendation of an independent jury.
Award: 21,802 EUR & testimonial awarded annually

Ehrenpreis des oesterreichischen Buchhandels
The Austrian Booksellers & Publishers Association
Gruenangergasse 4, 1010 Vienna
Tel: (01) 512 15 35 *Fax:* (01) 512 84 82
E-mail: hvb@buecher.at
Web Site: www.buecher.at

☆**FIT Astrid Lindgren Translation Prize**
Federation internationale des Traducteurs (FIT) (International Federation of Translators)
Dr Heinrich Maierstr 9, 1180 Vienna
Mailing Address: PO Box 21, 1184 Vienna
Tel: (01) 4403607; (01) 4709819 *Fax:* (01) 4403756
Web Site: www.fit-ift.org
An international translation prize designed to promote the translation of children's literature, improve the quality thereof & draw attention to the role of translators in bringing the peoples of the world closer together in terms of culture. The prize may be awarded either for a single translation of outstanding quality or for the entire body of work of a translator of books written for children or young people. Candidates must be nominated by an FIT member & must be members in good standing of such an organization. The prize is awarded by a jury.
Award: Certificate of Merit & sum of money
Presented: FIT World Congresses

☆**FIT Best Periodical Award**
Federation internationale des Traducteurs (FIT) (International Federation of Translators)
Dr Heinrich Maierstr 9, 1180 Vienna
Mailing Address: PO Box 21, 1184 Vienna
Tel: (01) 4403607 *Fax:* (01) 4403756
Web Site: www.fit-ift.org
Key Personnel
President: Betty Cohen
Established: 1970
Awarded every three or four years, for both a literary & a nonliterary translation which make an outstanding contribution to the improvement of the quality of translation.
Other Sponsor(s): Carol-Bertil Nathhorst-Stiftelser

Foerderungspreis fuer Literatur (Recognition Prize for Literature)
Bundeskanzleramt-Kunstsektion
Sektion II-Kunstangelegenheiten, Abteilung II/5, Schottengasse 1, 1014 Vienna
Tel: (01) 53 115-0 *Fax:* (01) 53 115-7620
Web Site: www.art.austria.gv.at
Key Personnel
Contact: Dr Robert Stocker *E-mail:* robert.stocker@bka.gv.at
Awarded by jury. No applications.
Award: 7,267 EUR

Great Austrian State Prize
Bundeskanzleramt-Kunstsektion
Sektion II-Kunstangelegenheiten, Abteilung II/5, Schottengasse 1, 1014 Vienna
Tel: (01) 53 115-0 *Fax:* (01) 53 115-7620
Web Site: www.art.austria.gv.at
Key Personnel
Contact: Dr Robert Stocker *E-mail:* robert.stocker@bka.gv.at
Established: 1965
This prize alternates between literature, music & the fine arts. Awarded by Oesterreichischer Kunstsenat. No applications.
Award: 21,802 EUR for life's work

Grosse Literaturstipendien des Landes Tirol
Amt der Tiroler Landesregierung
Abteilung Kultur, Sillgasse 8, 6020 Innsbruck
Tel: (0512) 508-3756 *Fax:* (0512) 508 3755
Web Site: www.tirol.gv.at
Key Personnel
Contact: Dr Nikolaus Duregger *E-mail:* n.duregger@tirol.gv.at

Michael Haberlandt Medal
Verein fur Volkskunde
Laudongasse 15-19, 1080 Vienna
Tel: (01) 406 89 05 *Fax:* (01) 408 53 42
E-mail: office@volkskundemuseum.at
Web Site: www.volkskundemuseum.at

Oesterreichischer Staatspreis fuer literarische Ubersetzungen (Austrian State Prize for Literary Translators)
Bundeskanzleramt-Kunstsektion
Sektion II-Kunstangelegenheiten, Abteilung II/5, Schottengasse 1, 1014 Vienna
Tel: (01) 53 115-0 *Fax:* (01) 53 115-7620; (01) 531 15-7561
Web Site: www.art.austria.gv.at
Key Personnel
Contact: Dr Robert Stocker *E-mail:* robert.stocker@bka.gv.at
Award: 7,267 EUR

Rauriser Encouragement Award
Salzburger Landesregierung
Kulturabteilung, Postfach 527, 5010 Salzburg
Tel: (0662) 8042-2035; (0662) 8042-2100 *Fax:* (0662) 8042-3070
E-mail: kultur@salzburg.gv.at
Web Site: www.salzburg.gv.at/kultur
Key Personnel
Contact: Dr Herbert Mayrhofer *Tel:* (0662) 8042-2729 *E-mail:* herbert.mayrhofer@salzburg.gv.at
Annual literary award sponsored by the Salzburg provincial government & the village of Rauris. Awarded for a specific topic, as decided by jury.
Award: 3,634 EUR

Rauriser Literature Prize
Salzburger Landesregierung
Kulturabteilung, Postfach 527, 5010 Salzburg

AUSTRIA

Tel: (0662) 8042-2035; (0662) 8042-2100
Fax: (0662) 8042-3070
E-mail: kultur@salzburg.gv.at
Web Site: www.salzburg.gv.at/kultur
Key Personnel
Contact: Dr Herbert Mayrhofer *Tel:* (0662) 8042-2729 *E-mail:* herbert.mayrhofer@salzburg.gv.at
For an outstanding first publication in prose, as decided by jury.
Other Sponsor(s): Salzburg Provincial Government
Award: 7,270 EUR annually

State Scholarship for Literature
Bundeskanzleramt-Kunstsektion
Sektion II-Kunstangelegenheiten, Abteilung II/5, Schottengasse 1, 1014 Vienna
Tel: (01) 53 115-0 *Fax:* (01) 53 115-7620
Web Site: www.art.austria.gv.at
Key Personnel
Contact: Dr Robert Stocker *E-mail:* robert.stocker@bka.gv.at
Twenty annual awards by jury. Submissions accepted.
Award: Twenty annual awards of 1,090 EUR each month for one year

Otto Stoessl-Preis
Otto Stoessl-Stiftung
Semmelweisgasse 9, 8010 Graz
Tel: (0316) 8016-4611 *Fax:* (0316) 8016-4633
Web Site: www.literaturhaus.at
Key Personnel
Contact: Dr Christoph Binder *E-mail:* christoph.binder@stmk.gv.at
Established: 1981
Literature prize for unpublished German stories.
Award: 4,000 EUR
Closing Date: End of every 2nd year (2005, 2007...)
Presented: Vienna, End of every second year (2004, 2006...)

Georg Trakl Prize
Salzburger Landesregierung
Kulturabteilung, Postfach 527, 5010 Salzburg
Tel: (0662) 8042-2035; (0662) 8042-2100
Fax: (0662) 8042-3070
E-mail: kultur@salzburg.gv.at
Web Site: www.salzburg.gv.at/kultur
Key Personnel
Contact: Dr Herbert Mayrhofer *Tel:* (0662) 8042-2729 *E-mail:* herbert.mayrhofer@salzburg.gv.at
An irregular award to a writer of lyric poetry for his/her complete poetical works.
Award: 7,270 EUR

Upper Austria Culture Prize for Literature
Upper Austria State Government
Institut fuer Kulturfoerderung, Spittelwiese 4/2, 4020 Linz
Tel: (0732) 77 20-0 *Fax:* (0732) 77 20-17 86
Web Site: www.ooe.gv.at

City of Vienna Encouragement Prize
City of Vienna Magistrate
Kulturabteilung Magistratsabteilung 7, 8, Friedrich-Schmidt-Platz 5, Mezzanin 1-3 Stock, 1082 Vienna
Tel: (01) 4000-84766 *Fax:* (01) 4000-99-8007 (national); (01) 4000-7216 (international)
E-mail: post@m07.magwien.gv.at
Web Site: www.magwien.gv.at/ma07/index.htm
Established: 1951
Awarded annually to talented young writers (under 40 years of age) whose previous work is worthy of recognition & whose development shows promise. Candidates must be Austrian citizens who have either lived for three years in Vienna or who work in the city.
Award: 2,907 EUR

City of Vienna Prize
City of Vienna Magistrate
Kulturabteilung Magistratsabteilung 7, 8, Friedrich-Schmidt-Platz 5, Mezzanin 1-3 Stock, 1082 Vienna
Tel: (01) 4000-84766 *Fax:* (01) 4000-7216 (international); (01) 4000-99-8007 (national)
E-mail: post@m07.magwien.gv.at
Web Site: www.magwien.gv.at/ma07/index.htm
Established: 1947
Annual award to an author for total literary output.
Award: 7,267 EUR

City of Vienna Prize for Books for Children & Young People
City of Vienna Magistrate
Kulturabteilung Magistratsabteilung 7, 8, Friedrich-Schmidt-Platz 5, Mezzanin 1-3 Stock, 1082 Vienna
Tel: (01) 4000-84766 *Fax:* (01) 4000-7216 (international); (01) 4000-99-8007 (national)
E-mail: post@m07.magwien.gv.at
Web Site: www.magwien.gv.at/ma07/index.htm
Key Personnel
Contact: Ernestine Pecksteiner
Awarded annually by the City of Vienna for distinguished books for children & young people, including illustration.

Anton Wildgans Prize of Austrian Industry
Vereinigung der Oesterreichischen Industrie
Schwarzenbergplatz 4, 1031 Vienna
Tel: (01) 711 35 *Fax:* (01) 713 6899
E-mail: iv.office@iv-net.at
Web Site: www.iv-net.at
Key Personnel
Marketing & Communication: Ilse Steiner *E-mail:* i.steiner@iv-net.at
Awarded annually, at the beginning of the autumn, to an Austrian lyric poet, dramatist, novelist or essayist, young or middle aged. The author must be an Austrian citizen, writing in German, who lives either in Austria or abroad. Awarded by a committee. No applications.
Award: Maximum prize 7,500 EUR

Writers Scholarship for Literature
Bundeskanzleramt-Kunstsektion
Sektion II-Kunstangelegenheiten, Abteilung II/5, Schottengasse 1, 1014 Vienna
Tel: (01) 53 115-0 *Fax:* (01) 53 115-7620
Web Site: www.art.austria.gv.at
Key Personnel
Contact: Dr Robert Stocker *E-mail:* robert.stocker@bka.gv.at
Awarded by jury. Submissions accepted.
Award: 10 annual awards of 291 EUR each month for one year

Wuerdigungspreis (Lower Austria Prize of Honor)
AMT der Niederosterreichischen Landesregierung-Kulturabteilung
Landhausplatz 1, Haus Franz-Schubert-Platz 3 (NOE Landesbibliothek), 3109 St Poelten
Tel: (02742) 9005-12847 *Fax:* (02742) 9005-13860
E-mail: post.noevbb@noel.gv.at
Web Site: www.noe.gv.at

Bangladesh

Bangla Academy Literary Awards
Bangla Academy
Language & Literary Section, Old High Court Rd, Dhaka 1000
Tel: (02) 861 9577
Web Site: www.banglarepublic.com *Cable:* ACADEMY, DHAKA
Two awards annually for an overall outstanding contribution to Bangla literature.
Award: 100,000 BDT

Belgium

Goblet d'Alviella Prize (Prix Goblet d'Alviella)
Academie Royale de Belgique
Palais des Academies, One rue Ducale, 1000 Brussels
Tel: (02) 550 22 20; (02) 550 22 00 *Fax:* (02) 550 22 05
E-mail: arb@cfwb.be
Web Site: www.cfwb.be/arb
Key Personnel
Secretary: Leo Houziaux *Tel:* (02) 550 22 03 *E-mail:* leo.houziaux@ulg.ac.be
Established: 1926
For the best work of a strictly scientific & objective character relating to the history of religions, published by a Belgian author. Awarded every five years.
Award: 1,500 EUR
Closing Date: Dec 31, 2005

Lode Baekelmans Prize
Koninklijke Academie voor Nederlandse Taal- en Letterkunde (Royal Academy of Dutch Language & Literature)
Koningstr 18, 9000 Gent
Tel: (09) 265 93 40 *Fax:* (09) 265 93 49
E-mail: info@kantl.be
Web Site: www.kantl.be
Key Personnel
Librarian: Marijke De Wit *Tel:* (09) 265 93 43 *E-mail:* mdewit@kantl.be
Established: 1940
For the best literary work in Dutch - novel, poetry, play, radio play, essay, etc - dealing with the sea, sailors, navigation, the harbor, inland navigation or related topics. Recipients must be Belgian nationals. Awarded triennially.
Award: 1,860 EUR

Internationale Eugene Baie Prijs (International Eugene Baie Prize)
Province of Antwerp/Eugene Baie Foundation
Koningin Elisabethlei 22, 2018 Antwerp
Tel: (03) 2405011 *Fax:* (03) 2406470

Karel Barbier Prize
Koninklijke Academie voor Nederlandse Taal- en Letterkunde (Royal Academy of Dutch Language & Literature)
Koningstr 18, 9000 Gent
Tel: (09) 265 93 40 *Fax:* (09) 265 93 49
E-mail: info@kantl.be
Web Site: www.kantl.be
Key Personnel
Librarian: Marijke De Wit *Tel:* (09) 265 93 43 *E-mail:* mdewit@kantl.be
Established: 1927
For the best historical novel in Dutch, with a national-historical theme. Short stories & romanticized biographies also taken into consideration. Recipients must be Belgian nationals. Awarded biannually.
Award: 500 EUR

August Beernaert Prize
Koninklijke Academie voor Nederlandse Taal- en Letterkunde (Royal Academy of Dutch Language & Literature)
Koningstr 18, 9000 Gent

Tel: (09) 265 93 40 *Fax:* (09) 265 93 49
E-mail: info@kantl.be
Web Site: www.kantl.be
Key Personnel
Librarian: Marijke De Wit *Tel:* (09) 265 93 43
 E-mail: mdewit@kantl.be
Established: 1912
For the best literary work in Dutch, irrespective of the genre, published or unpublished. Recipients must be Belgian nationals. Awarded biennially.
Award: 1,240 EUR

Prix Auguste Beernaert (Auguste Beernaert Prize)
Academie Royale de Langue et de Litterature Francaises (Royal Academy of French Language & Literature)
Palais des Academies, One rue Ducale, 1000 Brussels
Tel: (02) 550 22 72 *Fax:* (02) 550 22 75
E-mail: alf@cfwb.be
Web Site: www.academielanguelitteraturefrancaises.be
Established: 1941
Awarded every four years for the most outstanding work of a Belgian author written in French language. Awarded by a jury.
Award: 1,000 EUR

☆**Anton Bergmann Prize** (Prix Anton Bergmann)
Academie Royale de Belgique
Palais des Academies, One rue Ducale, 1000 Brussels
Tel: (02) 550 22 00; (02) 550 22 20 *Fax:* (02) 550 22 05
E-mail: arb@cfwb.be
Web Site: www.cfwb.be/arb
Key Personnel
Secretary: Leo Houziaux *Tel:* (02) 550 22 03
 E-mail: leo.houziaux@ulg.ac.be
Established: 1875
For the author of a historical account or monograph, written in Dutch & relating to a Flemish town or community in Belgium. Awarded every five years for a work appearing in print or (provisionally) in manuscript form, during the period. Foreign authors may also compete, provided work is in Dutch & is published in Belgium or the Netherlands.
Award: 1,250 EUR
Closing Date: Dec 31, 2004

Prix Bouvier-Parvillez (Bouvier-Parvillez Prize)
Academie Royale de Langue et de Litterature Francaises (Royal Academy of French Language & Literature)
Palais des Academies, One rue Ducale, 1000 Brussels
Tel: (02) 550 22 72 *Fax:* (02) 550 22 75
E-mail: alf@cfwb.be
Web Site: www.academielanguelitteraturefrancaises.be
For the entire work of a Belgian author written in French. Awarded every four years.
Award: 850 EUR

Prix Alix Charlier-Anciaux (Alix Charlier-Anciaux Prize)
Academie Royale de Langue et de Litterature Francaises (Royal Academy of French Language & Literature)
Palais des Academies, One rue Ducale, 1000 Brussels
Tel: (02) 550 22 72 *Fax:* (02) 550 22 75
E-mail: alf@cfwb.be
Web Site: www.academielanguelitteraturefrancaises.be
Awarded every 5 years to a Belgian author for the whole of their work in the French language.
Award: 1,000 EUR

Constant de Horion Prize
Association des Ecrivains Belges de Langue Francaise (AEBLF) (Association of the Belgian Writers of French Language)
Camille Lemonnier-Maison des Ecrivains, 150 Chaussee de Wavre, 1050 Brussels
Tel: (02) 512 29 68 *Fax:* (02) 512 29 68
Web Site: www.ecrivainsbelges.be
Key Personnel
President: France Bastia *E-mail:* france.bastia@euronet.be
Secretary General: Jean Lacroix
Established: 1977
Founded by Baron Jean Constant (the writer Constant de Horion), for recognition of the best essay on literary history or literary criticism by an established Belgian writer, or a literary aspect of French expressionism. Belgian writers over 40 years of age are eligible. Awarded biennially.
Award: 1,239 EUR

Prix Henri Cornelus (Henri Cornelus Prize)
Academie Royale de Langue et de Litterature Francaises (Royal Academy of French Language & Literature)
Palais des Academies, One rue Ducale, 1000 Brussels
Tel: (02) 550 22 72 *Fax:* (02) 550 22 75
E-mail: alf@cfwb.be
Web Site: www.academielanguelitteraturefrancaises.be
Awarded triennially.
Award: 3,000 EUR

Arthur H Cornette Prize
Koninklijke Academie voor Nederlandse Taal- en Letterkunde (Royal Academy of Dutch Language & Literature)
Koningstr 18, 9000 Gent
Tel: (09) 265 93 40 *Fax:* (09) 265 93 49
E-mail: info@kantl.be
Web Site: www.kantl.be
Key Personnel
Librarian: Marijke De Wit *Tel:* (09) 265 93 43
 E-mail: mdewit@kantl.be
Established: 1950
For the best literary essay, written in Dutch, published or unpublished. Recipients must be Belgian nationals. Awarded every 5 years.
Award: 1,500 EUR
Closing Date: Feb 1, 2006

☆**Prix Albert Counson** (Albert Counson Prize)
Academie Royale de Langue et de Litterature Francaises (Royal Academy of French Language & Literature)
Palais des Academies, One rue Ducale, 1000 Brussels
Tel: (02) 550 22 72 *Fax:* (02) 550 22 75
E-mail: alf@cfwb.be
Web Site: www.academielanguelitteraturefrancaises.be
For a scholarly work on romance languages, in relation to or connected with Belgium. Monetary prize. Awarded every five years.
Award: 1,500 EUR

☆**Franz Cumont Prize** (Prix Franz Cumont)
Academie Royale de Belgique
Palais des Academies, One rue Ducale, 1000 Brussels
Tel: (02) 550 22 00; (02) 550 22 20 *Fax:* (02) 550 22 05
E-mail: arb@cfwb.be
Web Site: www.cfwb.be/arb
Key Personnel
Secretary: Leo Houziaux *Tel:* (02) 550 22 03
 E-mail: leo.houziaux@ulg.ac.be
Established: 1937
For a work by a Belgian or foreign author dealing with the history of religion or science in antiquity, ie in the Mediterranean area prior to the time of Mohammed. No application necessary. The prize cannot be divided, except where one or more authors have acted in collaboration. Awarded triennially.
Award: 2,500 EUR
Closing Date: Dec 31, 2005

Prix Henri Davignon (Henri Davignon Prize)
Academie Royale de Langue et de Litterature Francaises (Royal Academy of French Language & Literature)
Palais des Academies, One rue Ducale, 1000 Brussels
Tel: (02) 550 22 72 *Fax:* (02) 550 22 75
E-mail: alf@cfwb.be
Web Site: www.academielanguelitteraturefrancaises.be
Awarded every 5 years to a work of religious inspiration.
Award: 850 EUR

Nestor de Tiere Prize
Koninklijke Academie voor Nederlandse Taal- en Letterkunde (Royal Academy of Dutch Language & Literature)
Koningstraat 18, 9000 Ghent
Tel: (09) 265 93 40 *Fax:* (09) 265 93 49
E-mail: info@kantl.be
Web Site: www.kantl.be
Key Personnel
Librarian: Marijke De Wit *Tel:* (09) 265 93 43
 E-mail: mdewit@kantl.be
Established: 1930
For the best play written in Dutch. Recipients must be Belgian nationals. Awarded biennially.
Award: 500 EUR

Prix Felix Denayer (Felix Denayer Prize)
Academie Royale de Langue et de Litterature Francaises (Royal Academy of French Language & Literature)
Palais des Academies, One rue Ducale, 1000 Brussels
Tel: (02) 550 22 72 *Fax:* (02) 550 22 75
E-mail: alf@cfwb.be
Web Site: www.academielanguelitteraturefrancaises.be
For a single work or the entire literary work of a Belgian written in French. Awarded annually.
Award: 850 EUR

☆**Ernest Descailles Prize**
Academie Royale de Belgique
Palais des Academies, One rue Ducale, 1000 Brussels
Tel: (02) 550 22 00; (02) 550 22 20 *Fax:* (02) 550 22 05
E-mail: arb@cfwb.be
Web Site: www.cfwb.be/arb
Key Personnel
Secretary: Leo Houziaux *Tel:* (02) 550 22 03
 E-mail: leo.houziaux@ulg.ac.be
Established: 1907
Awarded every 5 years for a distinguished literary work written in French, preferably by a poet.
Award: 1,500 EUR
Closing Date: Dec 31, 2006

Jules Duculot Prize (Prix Jules Duculot)
Academie Royale de Belgique
Palais des Academies, One rue Ducale, 1000 Brussels
Tel: (02) 550 22 20; (02) 550 22 00 *Fax:* (02) 550 22 05
E-mail: arb@cfwb.be
Web Site: www.cfwb.be/arb
Key Personnel
Secretary: Leo Houziaux *Tel:* (02) 550 22 03
 E-mail: leo.houziaux@ulg.ac.be
Established: 1965

Awarded every 5 years for a work in print or manuscript form, written in French, dealing with the history of philosophy. Awarded only to Belgians, or to foreigners holding an academic grade granted by a Belgian university. Printed work must have been published in the 5 years prior to the end of the relevant period. The prize is awarded for what appears the most deserving work, irrespective of whether it has been submitted for entry or not.
Award: 3,000 EUR
Closing Date: Dec 31, 2005

Prix Robert Duterne (Robert Duterne Prize)
Academie Royale de Langue et de Litterature Francaises (Royal Academy of French Language & Literature)
Palais des Academies, One rue Ducale, 1000 Brussels
Tel: (02) 550 22 72 *Fax:* (02) 550 22 75
E-mail: alf@cfwb.be
Web Site: www.academielanguelitteraturefrancaises.be
Awarded every 4 years.
Award: 2,500 EUR

Charles Duvivier Prize (Prix Charles Duvivier)
Academie Royale de Belgique
Palais des Academies, One rue Ducale, 1000 Brussels
Tel: (02) 550 22 00; (02) 550 22 20 *Fax:* (02) 550 22 05
E-mail: arb@cfwb.be
Web Site: www.cfwb.be/arb
Key Personnel
Secretary: Leo Houziaux *Tel:* (02) 550 22 03
 E-mail: leo.houziaux@ulg.ac.be
Established: 1905
Awarded triennially for the Belgian author of the best work on the history of Belgian or foreign law, or on the history of Belgian political, judicial or administrative institutions.
Award: 1,250 EUR
Closing Date: Dec 31, 2005

Joris Eeckhout Prize
Koninklijke Academie voor Nederlandse Taal- en Letterkunde (Royal Academy of Dutch Language & Literature)
Koningstr 18, 9000 Gent
Tel: (09) 265 93 40 *Fax:* (09) 265 93 49
E-mail: info@kantl.be
Web Site: www.kantl.be
Key Personnel
Librarian: Marijke De Wit *Tel:* (09) 265 93 43
 E-mail: mdewit@kantl.be
Established: 1937
For the best literary essay about an author, written in Dutch, at least 100 pages, published or unpublished. Recipients must be Belgian nationals. Awarded biennially.
Award: 500 EUR

Leon Elaut Prize (Leon Elaut Prijs)
Koninklijke Academie voor Nederlandse Taal- en Letterkunde (Royal Academy of Dutch Language & Literature)
Koningstr 18, 9000 Gent
Tel: (09) 265 93 40 *Fax:* (09) 265 93 49
E-mail: info@kantl.be
Web Site: www.kantl.be
Key Personnel
Librarian: Marijke De Wit *Tel:* (09) 265 93 43
 E-mail: mdewit@kantl.be
Established: 1981
For the best monograph, written in Dutch, about cultural history of Flanders, 1815-1940 in connection with the Flemish movement. Awarded biennially.
Award: 2,480 EUR

Joseph Gantrelle Prize (Prix Joseph Gantrelle)
Academie Royale de Belgique
Palais des Academies, One rue Ducale, 1000 Brussels
Tel: (02) 550 22 00; (02) 550 22 20 *Fax:* (02) 550 22 05
E-mail: arb@cfwb.be
Web Site: www.cfwb.be/arb
Key Personnel
Secretary: Leo Houziaux *Tel:* (02) 550 22 03
 E-mail: leo.houziaux@ulg.ac.be
Established: 1890
Awarded biennially to Belgian authors for a work in classical philology.
Award: 1,500 EUR
Closing Date: Dec 31

Prix Georges Garnir (Georges Garnir Prize)
Academie Royale de Langue et de Litterature Francaises (Royal Academy of French Language & Literature)
Palais des Academies, One rue Ducale, 1000 Brussels
Tel: (02) 550 22 72 *Fax:* (02) 550 22 75
E-mail: alf@cfwb.be
Web Site: www.academielanguelitteraturefrancaises.be
Awarded triennially.
Award: 850 EUR

Prix Gaston et Mariette Heux (Gaston et Mariette Heux Prize)
Academie Royale de Langue et de Litterature Francaises (Royal Academy of French Language & Literature)
Palais des Academies, One rue Ducale, 1000 Brussels
Tel: (02) 550 22 72 *Fax:* (02) 550 22 75
E-mail: alf@cfwb.be
Web Site: www.academielanguelitteraturefrancaises.be
Awarded every 4 years.
Award: 1,800 EUR

Guido Gezelle Prize
Koninklijke Academie voor Nederlandse Taal- en Letterkunde (Royal Academy of Dutch Language & Literature)
Koningstr 18, 9000 Gent
Tel: (09) 265 93 40 *Fax:* (09) 265 93 49
E-mail: info@kantl.be
Web Site: www.kantl.be
Key Personnel
Librarian: Marijke De Wit *Tel:* (09) 265 93 43
 E-mail: mdewit@kantl.be
Established: 1941
Awarded every 5 years for the best volume of Dutch poetry, published or unpublished. Recipients must be Belgian nationals.
Award: 1,240 EUR

Maurice Gilliams Prize
Koninklijke Academie voor Nederlandse Taal- en Letterkunde (Royal Academy of Dutch Language & Literature)
Koningstr 18, 9000 Gent
Tel: (09) 265 93 40 *Fax:* (09) 265 93 49
E-mail: info@kantl.be
Web Site: www.kantl.be
Key Personnel
Librarian: Marijke De Wit *Tel:* (09) 265 93 43
 E-mail: mdewit@kantl.be
Established: 1985
Awarded every 4 years for the best volume of poetry, the best essay about poetry or for a complete poetical work, written in Dutch. Nationality of the recipient is not taken into account.
Award: 2,480 EUR

Grand Prix de Litterature Francaise Hors de France (Fondation Nessim Habif)
Academie Royale de Langue et de Litterature Francaises (Royal Academy of French Language & Literature)
Palais des Academies, One rue Ducale, 1000 Brussels
Tel: (02) 550 22 72 *Fax:* (02) 550 22 75
E-mail: alf@cfwb.be
Web Site: www.academielanguelitteraturefrancaises.be
Awarded biennially.
Award: 3,000 EUR

Prix Nicole Houssa (Nicole Houssa Prize)
Academie Royale de Langue et de Litterature Francaises (Royal Academy of French Language & Literature)
Palais des Academies, One rue Ducale, 1000 Brussels
Tel: (02) 550 22 72 *Fax:* (02) 550 22 75
E-mail: alf@cfwb.be
Web Site: www.academielanguelitteraturefrancaises.be
Awarded triennially.
Award: 850 EUR

Prize Joseph Houziaux (Prix Joseph Houziaux)
Academie Royale de Belgique
Palais des Academies, One rue Ducale, 1000 Brussels
Tel: (02) 550 22 11 *Fax:* (02) 550 22 05
E-mail: arb@cfwb.be
Web Site: www.cfwb.be/arb
Key Personnel
Secretary: Leo Houziaux *Tel:* (02) 550 22 03
 E-mail: leo.houziaux@ulg.ac.be
Established: 1994
Awarded triennially.
Award: 1,500 EUR

Tobie Jonckheere Prize (Prix Tobie Jonckheere)
Academie Royale de Belgique
Palais des Academies, One rue Ducale, 1000 Brussels
Tel: (02) 550 22 00; (02) 550 22 20 *Fax:* (02) 550 22 05
E-mail: arb@cfwb.be
Web Site: www.cfwb.be/arb
Key Personnel
Secretary: Leo Houziaux *Tel:* (02) 550 22 03
 E-mail: leo.houziaux@ulg.ac.be
Established: 1957
For a work, in published or manuscript form, devoted to the educational sciences. Awarded triennially.
Award: 1,500 EUR
Closing Date: Dec 31

Prix Jean Kobs (Jean Kobs Prize)
Academie Royale de Langue et de Litterature Francaises (Royal Academy of French Language & Literature)
Palais des Academies, One rue Ducale, 1000 Brussels
Tel: (02) 550 22 72 *Fax:* (02) 550 22 75
E-mail: alf@cfwb.be
Web Site: www.academielanguelitteraturefrancaises.be
Awarded triennially.
Award: 1,200 EUR

Hubert Krains Prize
Association des Ecrivains Belges de Langue Francaise (AEBLF) (Association of the Belgian Writers of French Language)
Camille Lemonnier-Maison des Ecrivains, 150 Chaussee de Wavre, 1050 Brussels
Tel: (02) 512 29 68 *Fax:* (02) 512 29 68
Web Site: www.ecrivainsbelges.be

Key Personnel
President: France Bastia *E-mail:* france.bastia@euronet.be
Secretary General: Jean Lacroix
Established: 1950
For the unpublished work of a writer below the age of 40. Founded by the Association of Belgian Writers in the French Language in memory of one of its presidents.
Award: 500 EUR awarded biennially (alternately prose & poetry)

Prize Henri Lavachery
Academie Royale de Belgique
Palais des Academies, One rue Ducale, 1000 Brussels
Tel: (02) 550 22 00; (02) 550 22 20 *Fax:* (02) 550 22 05
E-mail: arb@cfwb.be
Web Site: www.cfwb.be/arb
Key Personnel
Secretary: Leo Houziaux *Tel:* (02) 550 22 03
 E-mail: leo.houziaux@ulg.ac.be
Established: 1961
Awarded every 5 years to honor a work on ethnology. Prize confined to Belgians. Written work drafted in French only.
Award: 1,500 EUR
Closing Date: Dec 31, 2007

Rene Lyr Prize for Poetry
Association des Ecrivains Belges de Langue Francaise (AEBLF) (Association of the Belgian Writers of French Language)
Camille Lemonnier-Maison des Ecrivains, 150 Chaussee de Wavre, 1050 Brussels
Tel: (02) 512 29 68 *Fax:* (02) 512 29 68
Web Site: www.ecrivainsbelges.be
Key Personnel
President: France Bastia *E-mail:* france.bastia@euronet.be
Secretary General: Jean Lacroix
Established: 1959
Founded under Friends of Rene Lyr patronage & awarded triennially to a French-language poet for published or unpublished, non-prize-winning work. All poets of French expressionism are eligible.
Other Sponsor(s): The Family of Rene Lyr
Award: 875 EUR

Prix Lucien Malpertuis (Lucien Malpertuis Prize)
Academie Royale de Langue et de Litterature Francaises (Royal Academy of French Language & Literature)
Palais des Academies, One rue Ducale, 1000 Brussels
Tel: (02) 550 22 72 *Fax:* (02) 550 22 75
E-mail: alf@cfwb.be
Web Site: www.academielanguelitteraturefrancaises.be
For an outstanding contribution to Belgian literature in the field of drama, poetry, short story or essay written in French. Awarded biennially.
Award: 850 EUR

Joseph-Edmond Marchal Prize (Prix Joseph-Edmond Marchal)
Academie Royale de Belgique
Palais des Academies, One rue Ducale, 1000 Brussels
Tel: (02) 550 22 21 *Fax:* (02) 550 22 05
E-mail: arb@cfwb.be
Web Site: www.cfwb.be/arb
Key Personnel
Secretary: Leo Houziaux *Tel:* (02) 550 22 03
 E-mail: leo.houziaux@ulg.ac.be
Established: 1918
Awarded every 5 years for the Belgian author of the best work, in print or in manuscript form, on national antiques or archaeology.
Award: 1,500 EUR
Closing Date: Dec 31, 2007

Fondation Arthur Merghelynck (Arthur Merghelynck Foundation)
Academie Royale de Belgique
Palais des Academies, One rue Ducale, 1000 Brussels
Tel: (02) 550 22 11 *Fax:* (02) 550 22 05
E-mail: arb@cfwb.be
Web Site: www.cfwb.be/arb
Key Personnel
Secretary: Leo Houziaux *Tel:* (02) 550 22 03
 E-mail: leo.houziaux@ulg.ac.be
Established: 1999
Awarded annually.
Award: Subsidy allotted for research or to publication of works

Arthur Merghelynck Prize
Koninklijke Academie voor Nederlandse Taal- en Letterkunde (Royal Academy of Dutch Language & Literature)
Koningstr 18, 9000 Gent
Tel: (09) 265 93 40 *Fax:* (09) 265 93 49
E-mail: info@kantl.be
Web Site: www.kantl.be
Key Personnel
Librarian: Marijke De Wit *Tel:* (09) 265 93 43
 E-mail: mdewit@kantl.be
Established: 1946
Awarded triennially for the two best literary works, one prose the other poetry, including essays about prose or poetry, written in Dutch, published or unpublished. Recipients must be Belgian nationals.
Award: 2,480 EUR for each prize

Prix Auguste Michot (Auguste Michot Prize)
Academie Royale de Langue et de Litterature Francaises (Royal Academy of French Language & Literature)
Palais des Academies, One rue Ducale, 1000 Brussels
Tel: (02) 550 22 72 *Fax:* (02) 550 22 75
E-mail: alf@cfwb.be
Web Site: www.academielanguelitteraturefrancaises.be
Awarded biennially.
Award: 850 EUR

Grand prix de poesie Albert Mockel (Albert Mockel Grand Prize for Poetry)
Academie Royale de Langue et de Litterature Francaises (Royal Academy of French Language & Literature)
Palais des Academies, One rue Ducale, 1000 Brussels
Tel: (02) 550 22 72 *Fax:* (02) 550 22 75
E-mail: alf@cfwb.be
Web Site: www.academielanguelitteraturefrancaises.be
For the best Belgian poet writing in French. Awarded every five years.
Award: 2,500 EUR

Gilles Nelod Prize
Association des Ecrivains Belges de Langue Francaise (AEBLF) (Association of the Belgian Writers of French Language)
Camille Lemonnier-Maison des Ecrivains, 150 Chaussee de Wavre, 1050 Brussels
Tel: (02) 512 29 68 *Fax:* (02) 512 29 68
Web Site: www.ecrivainsbelges.be
Key Personnel
President: France Bastia *E-mail:* france.bastia@euronet.be
Secretary General: Jean Lacroix
Established: 1984
Founded by Gilles Nelod & administered by the Association of Belgian Writers in the French Language. Awarded biennially for a previously unpublished work of fiction.
Award: 250 EUR

Order of the Crown Prize
Belgium Ministry of Foreign Affairs
Service des Ordres, Rue Belliard 65, 1040 Brussels
Tel: (02) 5013511 *Fax:* (02) 5013669
Web Site: www.belgium-emb.org

Alex Pasquier Prize
Association des Ecrivains Belges de Langue Francaise (AEBLF) (Association of the Belgian Writers of French Language)
Camille Lemonnier-Maison des Ecrivains, 150 Chaussee de Wavre, 1050 Brussels
Tel: (02) 512 29 68 *Fax:* (02) 512 29 68
Web Site: www.ecrivainsbelges.be
Key Personnel
President: France Bastia *E-mail:* france.bastia@euronet.be
Secretary General: Jean Lacroix
Established: 1972
Established in memory of Association president Alex Pasquier, by his widow, for recognition of the best historical novel, published or unpublished, during the preceding five years by a Belgian writer in the French language.
Award: 625 EUR

Prix Sander Pierron (Sander Pierron Prize)
Academie Royale de Langue et de Litterature Francaises (Royal Academy of French Language & Literature)
Palais des Academies, One rue Ducale, 1000 Brussels
Tel: (02) 550 22 72 *Fax:* (02) 550 22 75
E-mail: alf@cfwb.be
Web Site: www.academielanguelitteraturefrancaises.be
Awarded biennially.
Award: 850 EUR

Prix Emile Polak (Emile Polak Prize)
Academie Royale de Langue et de Litterature Francaises (Royal Academy of French Language & Literature)
Palais des Academies, One rue Ducale, 1000 Brussels
Tel: (02) 550 22 72 *Fax:* (02) 550 22 75
E-mail: alf@cfwb.be
Web Site: www.academielanguelitteraturefrancaises.be
Biennial award to a poet of Belgian nationality.
Award: 850 EUR

Prix Andre Praga (Andre Praga Prize)
Academie Royale de Langue et de Litterature Francaises (Royal Academy of French Language & Literature)
Palais des Academies, One rue Ducale, 1000 Brussels
Tel: (02) 550 22 72 *Fax:* (02) 550 22 75
E-mail: alf@cfwb.be
Web Site: www.academielanguelitteraturefrancaises.be
Biennial award for a Belgian theatrical work.
Award: 850 EUR

Prix baron de Saint-Genois
Academie Royale de Belgique
Palais des Academies, One rue Ducale, 1000 Brussels
Tel: (02) 550 22 00; (02) 550 22 20 *Fax:* (02) 550 22 05
E-mail: arb@cfwb.be
Web Site: www.cfwb.be/arb
Key Personnel
Secretary: Leo Houziaux *Tel:* (02) 550 22 03
 E-mail: leo.houziaux@ulg.ac.be
Established: 1867

BELGIUM

For the author of the best historical or literary work written in Dutch. Awarded every five years.
Award: 1,250 EUR

Prix Georges Lockem (Georges Lockem Prize)
Academie Royale de Langue et de Litterature Francaises (Royal Academy of French Language & Literature)
Palais des Academies, One rue Ducale, 1000 Brussels
Tel: (02) 550 22 72 *Fax:* (02) 550 22 75
E-mail: alf@cfwb.be
Web Site: www.academielanguelitteraturefrancaises.be
Annual award to a French-speaking Belgian, age 25 or under for a manuscript or work published in the preceeding year.
Award: 850 EUR

Prize for Literature of the Parliament of the French Community of Belgium
Parliament of the French Community of Belgium (Prix litteraire de Parlement de la Communaute francais de Belgique)
Rue de la Loi 6, 1000 Brussels
Tel: (02) 213 35 11 *Fax:* (02) 213 35 13
Web Site: www.pcf.be
Key Personnel
Contact: N Ryelandt *E-mail:* ryelandtn@pcf.be
Awarded annually.
Award: 1,239 EUR
Closing Date: Feb 1

Victor Rossel Prize
Le Soir
rue Royale 112, 1000 Brussels
Tel: (02) 225 52 21 *Fax:* (02) 225 59 19
E-mail: nathalie.malice@rossel.be
Web Site: www.lesoir.be
Established: 1938
Annual award for the best novel or collection of short stories published during the year, written in French by a Belgian author.
Award: 4,958 EUR

Prix Leopold Rosy (Leopold Rosy Prize)
Academie Royale de Langue et de Litterature Francaises (Royal Academy of French Language & Literature)
Palais des Academies, One rue Ducale, 1000 Brussels
Tel: (02) 550 22 72 *Fax:* (02) 550 22 75
E-mail: alf@cfwb.be
Web Site: www.academielanguelitteraturefrancaises.be
Awarded triennially.
Award: 750 EUR

Prix Eugene Schmits (Eugene Schmits Prize)
Academie Royale de Langue et de Litterature Francaises (Royal Academy of French Language & Literature)
Palais des Academies, One rue Ducale, 1000 Brussels
Tel: (02) 550 22 72 *Fax:* (02) 550 22 75
E-mail: alf@cfwb.be
Web Site: www.academielanguelitteraturefrancaises.be
Awarded triennially.
Award: 850 EUR

Ary Sleeks Prize
Koninklijke Academie voor Nederlandse Taal- en Letterkunde (Royal Academy of Dutch Language & Literature)
Koningstr 18, 9000 Gent
Tel: (09) 265 93 40 *Fax:* (09) 265 93 49
E-mail: info@kantl.be
Web Site: www.kantl.be

Key Personnel
Librarian: Marijke De Wit *Tel:* (09) 265 93 43
E-mail: mdewit@kantl.be
Established: 1974
Triennial award which recognizes the best novel, volume of short stories or an essay, published or unpublished. Recipients must be Belgian nationals.
Award: 620 EUR

Prix de Stassart
Academie Royale de Belgique
Palais des Academies, One rue Ducale, 1000 Brussels
Tel: (02) 550 22 00; (02) 550 22 20 *Fax:* (02) 550 22 05
E-mail: arb@cfwb.be
Web Site: www.cfwb.be/arb
Key Personnel
Secretary: Leo Houziaux *Tel:* (02) 550 22 03
E-mail: leo.houziaux@ulg.ac.be
Established: 1851
Awarded every 5 years.
Award: 1,500 EUR
Closing Date: Dec 31

Suzanne Tassier Prize (Prix Suzanne Tassier)
Academie Royale de Belgique
Palais des Academies, One rue Ducale, 1000 Brussels
Tel: (02) 550 22 00; (02) 550 22 20 *Fax:* (02) 550 22 05
E-mail: arb@cfwb.be
Web Site: www.cfwb.be/arb
Key Personnel
Secretary: Leo Houziaux *Tel:* (02) 550 22 03
E-mail: leo.houziaux@ulg.ac.be
Established: 1956
Biennial award to a Belgian woman who, following study at a Belgian university, has obtained at least a Doctorate. The prize is awarded for a major scientific work, dealing with a subject from history, law, philology or the social sciences: failing a meritorious work from one of these branches, then for a subject from the natural sciences, medicine or mathematics. Preference will be given to a work of an historical nature, in its widest sense.
Award: 1,750 EUR
Closing Date: Dec 31, 2004

Auguste Teirlinck Prize (Prix Auguste Teirlinck)
Academie Royale de Belgique
Palais des Academies, One rue Ducale, 1000 Brussels
Tel: (02) 550 22 00; (02) 550 22 20 *Fax:* (02) 550 22 05
E-mail: arb@cfwb.be
Web Site: www.cfwb.be/arb
Key Personnel
Secretary: Leo Houziaux *Tel:* (02) 550 22 03
E-mail: leo.houziaux@ulg.ac.be
Established: 1907
For a contribution to Flemish literature. Awarded every five years.
Award: 1,250 EUR
Closing Date: Dec 31, 2005

Troubadour de la SABAM
Belgische Vereniging van Auteurs, Componisten en Uitgevers (Socete Belge des Auteurs, Compositeurs et Editeurs)
Rue d'Arlon 75-77, 1040 Brussels
Tel: (02) 286 82 11 *Fax:* (02) 230 05 89
E-mail: info@sabam.be
Web Site: www.sabam.be
Established: 1951
Biennial award which recognizes living poets of any nationality whose works have significantly influenced world poetry.
Award: 2,479 EUR

LITERARY

Prix Georges Vaxelaire (Georges Vaxelaire Prize)
Academie Royale de Langue et de Litterature Francaises (Royal Academy of French Language & Literature)
Palais des Academies, One rue Ducale, 1000 Brussels
Tel: (02) 550 22 72 *Fax:* (02) 550 22 75
E-mail: alf@cfwb.be
Web Site: www.academielanguelitteraturefrancaises.be
Biennial award for a theatrical work by a Belgian author represented in Belgium in the theatre or on radio/TV.
Award: 850 EUR

Prix Emmanuel Vossaert (Emmanuel Vossaert Prize)
Academie Royale de Langue et de Litterature Francaises (Royal Academy of French Language & Literature)
Palais des Academies, One rue Ducale, 1000 Brussels
Tel: (02) 550 22 72 *Fax:* (02) 550 22 75
E-mail: alf@cfwb.be
Web Site: www.academielanguelitteraturefrancaises.be
Awarded biennially.
Award: 850 EUR

Prix Frans de Wever (Frans de Wever Prize)
Academie Royale de Langue et de Litterature Francaises (Royal Academy of French Language & Literature)
Palais des Academies, One rue Ducale, 1000 Brussels
Tel: (02) 550 22 72 *Fax:* (02) 550 22 75
E-mail: alf@cfwb.be
Web Site: www.academielanguelitteraturefrancaises.be
Annual award to an author under the age of 40 for a collection of poems.
Award: 850 EUR

Prix Carton de Wiart (Carton de Wiart Prize)
Academie Royale de Langue et de Litterature Francaises (Royal Academy of French Language & Literature)
Palais des Academies, One rue Ducale, 1000 Brussels
Tel: (02) 550 22 72 *Fax:* (02) 550 22 75
E-mail: alf@cfwb.be
Web Site: www.academielanguelitteraturefrancaises.be
Awarded every 10 years.
Award: 750 EUR

Bolivia

Premios Nacionales de Cultura
Ministerio de Educacion
Palacio Chico, calle Ayacucho esq Potosi, La Paz
Tel: (02) 220 0910; (02) 220 0949 *Fax:* (02) 220 0948
E-mail: mnarql@caoba.entelnet.bo
Web Site: www.bolivia.com/empresas/cultura
Established: 1969
For recognition of achievements in literature, the arts or science. Awarded biannually.
Award: Monetary prizes & a medal

Concurso Nacional de Novela Erich Guttentag (Erich Guttentag National Novel Competition)
Editorial Los Amigos del Libro
Av Ayacucho S-0156, Casilla 450, Cochabamba
Casilla 450
Tel: (042) 4-504150; (042) 4-504151 *Fax:* (591) 411 5128

E-mail: gutten@amigol.bo.net
Key Personnel
President: Werner Guttentag

Franz Tamayo Prize
La Paz Municipal Mayor's Office
Oficial Mayor de Cultura, La Paz
For outstanding literary work.
Award: 15,000 & 5000 Bolivian pesos
Presented: annually

Brazil

Afonso Arinos Prize
Academia Brasileira de Letras
Av Pres Wilson 203, Castelo, 20030-021 Rio de Janeiro-RJ
Tel: (021) 3974 2500
E-mail: academia@academia.org.br
Web Site: www.academia.org.br
For the best work of fiction published or written during the two years preceding the year of award. Awarded annually.

Olavo Bilac Prize
Academia Brasileira de Letras
Av Pres Wilson 203, Castelo, 20030-021 Rio de Janeiro-RJ
Tel: (021) 3974 2500
E-mail: academia@academia.org.br
Web Site: www.academia.org.br
For the best book of poetry. Awarded annually.

Jabuti Prize (Premio Jabuti)
Camara Brasileira do Livro (Brazilian Book Association)
Depto de Marketing, Alameda Santos 1000, 10º andar, 01418-100 Sao Paulo-SP
Tel: (011) 3069-1300 *Fax:* (011) 3069-1300
E-mail: jabuti@cbl.org.br
Web Site: www.cbl.org.br
Established: 1959
Awarded annually for best literary composition published in previous year.

Monteiro Lobato Prize
Fundacao do Libro Infantil e Juvenil (FNLIJ)
Rua da Imprensa 16/12º andar-Centro, 20030-120 Rio de Janeiro-RJ
Tel: (021) 2262-9130 *Fax:* (021) 2240-6649
E-mail: informacao@fnlij.org.br
Web Site: www.fnlij.org.br
For children's literature. Awarded annually.

Julia Lopes de Ameida Prize
Academia Brasileira de Letras
Av Pres Wilson 203, Castelo, 20030-021 Rio de Janeiro-RJ
Tel: (021) 3974 2500
E-mail: academia@academia.org.br
Web Site: www.academia.org.br
For the best unpublished or published literary work written by a woman, preferably for a novel or collection of short stories. Awarded annually.

Machado de Assis Prize
Academia Brasileira de Letras
Av Pres Wilson 203, Castelo, 20030-021 Rio de Janeiro-RJ
Tel: (021) 3974 2500
E-mail: academia@academia.org.br
Web Site: www.academia.org.br
Established: 1943
Awarded annually to an outstanding Brazilian writer for the sum of his work. One of Brazil's highest literary honors.

Odorico Mendes Prize
Funarte Fudacao Nacional De Arte
Rua da Imprensa, 16, 5º andar Centro, 20030-120 Rio de Janeiro-RJ
Tel: (021) 2279-8003; (021) 2279-8004; (021) 2279-8005; (022) 2532-7144 *Fax:* (021) 2262-5547
Web Site: www.funarte.gov.br
For the best translation from foreign literature into the Portuguese language. Awarded annually.

National Book Institute Prizes
Instituto Nacional do Livro
SCRN, 704/705, B1 C, No 40, 2 andaer, 70730 Brasilia DF
Tel: (061) 2742315
For outstanding unpublished literary works of fiction, poetry, history & essays. In addition, one prize is awarded for the best unpublished work of children's literature & another for illustrations of books for children. Awarded annually.

Luisa Claudio de Sousa Prize
Brazilian PEN Centre (PEN Clube do Brasil (Associacao Universal de Escritores))
Praia do Flamengo 172 - 10 andar, 2000 Rio de Janeiro RJ
Tel: (021) 2850491
For the best book published in the previous year. Novels, plays, literary history & criticism works are considered.

Jose Verissimo Prize
Funarte Fudacao Nacional De Arte
Rua da Imprensa, 16, 5º andar Centro, 20030-120 Rio de Janeiro-RJ
Tel: (021) 2279-8005; (021) 2279-8004; (021) 2279-8003; (022) 2532-7144 *Fax:* (021) 2262-5547
Web Site: www.funarte.gov.br
For the best essay & a work of scholarship. Awarded annually.

Bulgaria

International Vaptsarov Prize
Union of Bulgarian Writers
Angel Kanchev 5, 1040 Sofia
Tel: (02) 874711 *Fax:* (02) 874757
Web Site: www.art.bg/lit.htm

Canada

☆**Lorne Pierce Medal**
Royal Society of Canada
283 Sparks St, Ottawa, ON K1R 7X9
Tel: 613-991-6990 *Fax:* 613-991-6996
E-mail: adminrsc@rsc.ca
Web Site: www.rsc.ca
Key Personnel
Publications & Awards Coordinator: Genevieve Gouin *Tel:* 613-991-5760 *E-mail:* ggouin@rsc.ca
Established: 1926
Awarded biennially for achievement & conspicuous merit in the field of imaginative or critical literature, in English or French.
Award: Medal

Chile

National Prize for Literature (Premio Nacional de Literatura)
Ministerio de Educacion de Chile
Alameda 1371, Santiago
Tel: (02) 3904000
Web Site: www.mineduc.cl
Established: 1942
Awarded annually to recognize an author's sum of work.
Award: Monetary prize

Colombia

☆**Felix Restrepo Prize**
Academia Colombiana
Carrera 3A, Numero 17-34, Piso 3, Apdo Aereo 44763, Bogota, DC
Tel: (01) 3414805 *Fax:* (01) 2838552
E-mail: accefyn@colciencias.gov.co
Web Site: www.accefyn.org.co
For distinguished contributions to philology.
Award: 100,000 Colombian pesos & publication of work, awarded annually

Costa Rica

Editorial Costa Rica Literary Prize
Editorial Costa Rica
Apdo 10,010, 1000 San Jose
Tel: 253-5354 *Fax:* 253-5091
E-mail: administrativos@editorialcostarica.com
Web Site: www.editorialcostarica.com
Key Personnel
Management: Habib Succar *E-mail:* editocr@racsa.co.cr
Established: 1973
Annual award is to encourage creative writing generally. The prize is rotated in order to be open to all genres - fiction, stories, theatre, essays, short stories, poetry, biography, history. The most recent winner was Eduardo Oconitrillo.
Award: 700,000 CRC

Aquileo J Echeverria Prize
Costa Rican Ministry of Culture, Youth & Sport
Avenidas 3 y 7, calles 11 y 15, frente al parque, Espana, San Jose 1000
Tel: 255 3188 *Fax:* 255 3252
E-mail: info@mcjdcr.go.cr
Web Site: www.mcjdcr.go.cr
For Costa Rican citizens who have excelled in the fields of literature (novel, short story, poetry, essay, scientific literature), history, theatre, music, fine arts. 40,000 CRC divided between the selected works. Total sum of awards cannot exceed 8,000,000 CRC. Awarded annually.
Award: 8,000,000 CRC

Joven Creacion Literary Prize
Editorial Costa Rica
Apdo 10,010, 1000 San Jose
Tel: 253-5354 *Fax:* 253-5091
E-mail: administrativos@editorialcostarica.com
Web Site: www.editorialcostarica.com
Key Personnel
Management: Habib Succar *E-mail:* editocr@racsa.co.cr
Established: 1976
Formed in collaboration with the Associacion de Autores, with the aim of stimulating

young writing in the fields of poetry & narrative/stories.
Award: 350,000 CRC

Carmen Lyra Literary Prize (Premio Carmen Lyra - Literatura Infantil)
Editorial Costa Rica
Apdo 10,010, 1000 San Jose
Tel: 253-5354 *Fax:* 253-5091
E-mail: administrativos@editorialcostarica.com
Web Site: www.editorialcostarica.com
Key Personnel
Management: Habib Succar
Established: 1974
Founded in honour of the writer Maria Isabel Carvajal (pseudonym Carmen Lyra), this annual award is to encourage the writing of literature intended for children & young people.
Award: 450,000 CRC
Closing Date: June 14

Premio Poesia y Narrativa
Editorial Universitaria Centroamericana (EDUCA)
Ciudad Universitatar Rodrigo Facio, Apdo 64, San Jose 2060
Tel: 2243727 *Fax:* 2539141
E-mail: educacr@sol.racsa.co.cr
Key Personnel
Dir: Sebastian Vaquerano

Cuba

☆**Casa de las Americas Literary Award**
Casa de las Americas
3ra y G, El Vedado, Havana 10400
Tel: (07) 56 2706; (07) 56 2709 *Fax:* (07) 33 4554
E-mail: casa@casa.cult.cu
Web Site: www.casa.cult.cu
Key Personnel
President: Roberto Fernandez Retamar
Annual prize awarded to an author for unpublished work in one or other of the following genres: novels, plays, 'testimonial' books, essays on artistic & literary themes - Brazilian & French Caribbean (or national language) works; short stories, poetry, essays on historical & social themes, books for children & young people & Anglo-Caribbean (or national language) works. The winning work will be published.
Award: $3,000 USD (or equivalent in national currency)

Czech Republic

Mlada Fronta Publishing House Prize
Mlada Fronta Publishing House
Radlicka 61, 15000 Prague 5
Tel: (02) 2527 6120 *Fax:* (02) 2527 6176
Key Personnel
Dir: Martina Hartova *E-mail:* hartova@mf.cz
Awarded annually for literary works of prose, poetry, journalism, popular science, also translations, published by them during the preceding year.

Jaroslav Seifert Prize
Charta 77 Foundation
Melantrichova 5, 110 00 Prague 1
Tel: (02) 24 21 44 52; (02) 24 23 02 16; (02) 24 22 50 92 *Fax:* (02) 24 21 36 47
Web Site: www.bariery.cz

Key Personnel
Program Dir: Indira Bornova *E-mail:* indira.bornova@bariery.cz
Established: 1986
For recognition of the best work in Czech & Slovak literature.
Other Sponsor(s): Zivnostenska Banka, Prague
Award: 250,000 CZK & a diploma made by one of the well known Czechoslovak artists
Closing Date: Spring every year
Presented: Zivnostenska Banka, Prague, Autumn

Denmark

Emil Aarestrup Prize (Emil Aarestrup Medaillen)
Dansk Forfatterforening (The Danish Writers Association)
Strandgade 6, 1401 Copenhagen K
Tel: 32 95 51 00; 32 95 59 89 *Fax:* 32 54 01 15
E-mail: danskforfatterforening@danskforfatterforening.dk
Web Site: www.danskforfatterforening.dk
For outstanding poetry. Awarded annually.

The H C Andersen Prize (H C Andersens Legat)
Dansk Forfatterforening (The Danish Writers Association)
Strandgade 6, 1401 Copenhagen K
Tel: 32 95 51 00; 32 95 59 89 *Fax:* 32 54 01 15
E-mail: danskforfatterforening@danskforfatterforening.dk
Web Site: www.danskforfatterforening.dk
For scientists & writers connected with H C Andersen, for outstanding contributions to Danish literature. Awarded annually.
Award: Prize varies

Martin Andersen Nexo Prize (Martin Andersen Nexo Legatet)
Dansk Forfatterforening (The Danish Writers Association)
Strandgade 6, 1401 Copenhagen K
Tel: 32 95 51 00; 32 95 59 89 *Fax:* 32 54 01 15
E-mail: danskforfatterforening@danskforfatterforening.dk
Web Site: www.danskforfatterforening.dk
Awarded annually.
Award: 10,000 DKK

Herman Bang Memorial Prize (Herman Bangs Mindelegat)
Dansk Forfatterforening (The Danish Writers Association)
Strandgade 6, 1401 Copenhagen K
Tel: 32 95 51 00; 32 95 59 89 *Fax:* 32 54 01 15
E-mail: danskforfatterforening@danskforfatterforening.dk
Web Site: www.danskforfatterforening.dk
For works of prose. Awarded annually.
Award: 5,000 DKK

Danish Academy Prize for Literature
Danish Academy (Danske Akademi)
Vognmagergade 7, 1120 Copenhagen K
Tel: 33131112 *Fax:* 33328045
E-mail: administrator@danskeakademi.dk
Web Site: www.danskeakademi.dk *Cable:* LAWOFF
Key Personnel
Administrator: Prof Allan Philip
Awarded biannually for an outstanding work of literature.
Award: 300,000 DKK

Danish Prize for Children's Literature
Danish Ministry of Cultural Affairs
The Media & Grants Secretariat, Nybrogade 10, 1203 Copenhagen K
Tel: 33923040 *Fax:* 33146428
E-mail: tips@kulturtilskud.dk
Web Site: www.kulturtilskud.min.dk
Key Personnel
Consultant: Eva Jensen *Tel:* 33923583
E-mail: ej@kulturtilskud.dk
Established: 1954
Annual award for the best Danish books for children & teenagers.
Award: 30,000 DKK

Danish Writers' Association Non-Fiction Prize
Dansk Forfatterforening (The Danish Writers Association)
Strandgade 6, 1401 Copenhagen K
Tel: 32 95 51 00; 32 95 59 89 *Fax:* 32 54 01 15
E-mail: danskforfatterforening@danskforfatterforening.dk
Web Site: www.danskforfatterforening.dk
Awarded annually.
Award: 30,000 DKK

Danmarks Skolebibliotekarforenings Bornebogspris
Danish School Librarian Association
Kaervej 113, 7190 Billund
Mailing Address: Postboks 44, 7190 Billund
Tel: 7533 1337
Web Site: www.skole-biblioteket.ffw.dk
Key Personnel
Contact: Karen Odegaard *E-mail:* karen.odegaard@skolekom.com

Dansk Oversaetterforbunds Aerespris
Dansk Forfatterforening (The Danish Writers Association)
Strandgade 6, 1401 Copenhagen K
Tel: 32 95 51 00; 32 95 59 89 *Fax:* 32 54 01 15
E-mail: danskforfatterforening@danskforfatterforening.dk
Web Site: www.danskforfatterforening.dk
For the outstanding translation into Danish of one or more significant works. Awarded annually.
Award: 30,000 DKK

Johannes Ewald Prize (Johannes Ewald Legatet)
Dansk Forfatterforening (The Danish Writers Association)
Strandgade 6, 1401 Copenhagen K
Tel: 32 95 51 00; 32 95 59 89 *Fax:* 32 54 01 15
E-mail: danskforfatterforening@danskforfatterforening.dk
Web Site: www.danskforfatterforening.dk
For prose, poetry & dramatic works. Awarded annually.
Award: 10,000 DKK

Soren Gyldendal Prize
Gyldendalske Boghandel - Nordisk Forlag A/S
Klareboderne 3, 1001 Copenhagen K
Tel: 33755555 *Fax:* 33755556
E-mail: gyldendal@gyldendal.dk
Web Site: www.gyldendal.dk
Telex: 15887 Gyldal Dk
Key Personnel
Man Dir: Stig Andersen
Secretary: Annie Auhagen *Tel:* 33755523
E-mail: annie_auhagen@gyldendal.dk
For Danish authors from any field whose work is of great literary value - Nominations only.
Award: 150,000 DKK

Holberg Medal (Holberg-Medaljen)
Dansk Forfatterforening (The Danish Writers Association)
Strandgade 6, 1401 Copenhagen K
Tel: 32 95 51 00; 32 95 59 89 *Fax:* 32 54 01 15

E-mail: danskforfatterforening@danskforfatterforening.dk
Web Site: www.danskforfatterforening.dk
For outstanding contributions to Danish literature. Awarded annually.
Award: 35,000 DKK & medal

☆Nordic Council Literature Prize
Nordic Council, Swedish Delegation
Store Strandstr 18, 1255 Copenhagen
Tel: 33 96 04 00 *Fax:* 33 11 18 70
Web Site: www.norden.org
Key Personnel
Secretary General: Eva Smekal *E-mail:* eva.smekal@riksdagen.se
Established: 1961
Awarded annually for a literary work in the fiction, genre, written in one of the languages of the Nordic countries. It can be a novel, a play, a collection - of poems, short stories or essays - or another work which meets high literary & artistic standards. The aim is to increase interest in Nordic literature & establish a Nordic book marker.
Award: 350,000 DKK
Presented: Nordic Council Conference or a session in Feb or March

Adam Gottlob Oehlenschlaeger Prize (Adam Oehlenschlaeger Legatet)
Dansk Forfatterforening (The Danish Writers Association)
Strandgade 6, 1401 Copenhagen K
Tel: 32 95 51 00; 32 95 59 89 *Fax:* 32 54 01 15
E-mail: danskforfatterforening@danskforfatterforening.dk
Web Site: www.danskforfatterforening.dk
For prose works & poetry. Awarded annually.
Award: 10,000 DKK

Edvard Pedersens Biblioteksfonds Forfatterpris
Danish Library Association
c/o Det nordjyske Landsbibliotek, Rendsburggade 2, 9100 Aalborg
Mailing Address: Postboks 839, 9100 Aalborg
Tel: 33250935 *Fax:* 33257900
E-mail: dkf@dlf.dk
Web Site: www.litteraturpriser.dk/pris/epfond.htm; www.edvardp.dk; www.dbf.dk
Key Personnel
Secretary: Jane Rasmussen *Tel:* 45858105
E-mail: jr-kultur@aalborg.dk

Henrik Pontoppidan Memorial Prize (Henrik Pontoppidans Mindefond)
Dansk Forfatterforening (The Danish Writers Association)
Strandgade 6, 1401 Copenhagen K
Tel: 32 95 51 00; 32 95 59 89 *Fax:* 32 54 01 15
E-mail: danskforfatterforening@danskforfatterforening.dk
Web Site: www.danskforfatterforening.dk
For outstanding contributions to Danish literature. Awarded annually.
Award: 10,000 DKK

Finland

Finlandia Junior Prize
Suomen Kirjasaatio (Finnish Book Foundation)
Lonnrotinkatu 11 A, 00120 Helsinki
Mailing Address: PO Box 177, 00121 Helsinki
Tel: (09) 228 77 250 *Fax:* (09) 612 1226
Web Site: www.skyry.net
Key Personnel
Man Dir: Veikko Sonninen *E-mail:* veikko.sonninen@skyry.net
Annual award for the outstanding Finnish children's book of the year.
Award: 26,000 EUR

Rudolf Koivu Prize
Grafia Ry
Uudenmaankatu 11B9, 00120 Helsinki
Tel: (09) 601 941; (09) 601 942 *Fax:* (09) 601 140
E-mail: grafia@grafia.fi
Web Site: www.grafia.fi
Key Personnel
Chairman: Mr Kari Kakko
Biennial award for the illustrator of the year's best Finnish picture-book for children.

Arvid Lydecken Prize
Suomen Nuorisokirjailijat ry
Palomaeentie 13 B, 02730 Espoo
Tel: (09) 852 2176
Web Site: www.nuorisokirjailijat.fi
Key Personnel
Chairman: Mrs Tuija Lehtinen *E-mail:* tuija.lehtinen@nuorisokirjailijat.fi
Annual award for the writer of the year's best Finnish book for children.

State Prizes for Literature
Ministry of Education, Finland
Meritullinkatu 10, Main Bldg, 00171 Helsinki
Mailing Address: PO Box 29, 00023 Helsinki
Tel: (09) 160 04; (09) 578 14 *Fax:* (09) 135 9335
E-mail: esa@rantanen.minedu.fi
Web Site: www.minedu.fi
Key Personnel
Minister of Education & Science: Tuula Haatainen *E-mail:* tuula.haatainen@minedu.fi
Annual prizes for the best literary works.
Award: 13,000 EUR

France

Prix de l'Academie des Sciences Arts et Belles Lettres de Dijon (Dijon Academy of Sciences, Art & Literature Prize)
Academie des Sciences Arts et Belles Lettres de Dijon
Bibliotheque Municipale de Dijon, 5 Rue de l'Ecole de Droit, 21000 Dijon
Tel: (080) 44 94 14 *Fax:* (080) 44 94 34
E-mail: bmdijon@ville-dijon.fr
Web Site: www.ville-dijon.fr

Prix de l'Academie Mallarme
Academie Mallarme
Espace Culturel, 16 rue Monsieur Le Prince, 75006 Paris
Tel: (01) 46227125
Key Personnel
Secretary General: Charles Dobzynski
Mallarme Academic Prize.

Prix ALPHA de la Nouvelle (ALPHA Prize for News)
ALPHA Association
9 Ave Pierre-Curie, 59190 Hazebrouck
Tel: 28410744

Prix Guillaume Apollinaire
22 rue Felibres, 91600 Savigny-Orge
Tel: (01) 6996 3524

Prix Antonin Artaud
Association des Ecrivains du Rouergue
BP 307, 12003 Rodez Cedex
Tel: (05) 65781307; (05) 65778849 (Secretary)

Francois-Joseph Audiffred Prize (Prix Francois-Joseph Audiffred)
Academie des Sciences Morales et Politiques, Institut de France
23 quai de Conti, 75006 Paris
Tel: (01) 44 41 43 26; (01) 44 41 44 41 *Fax:* (01) 44 41 43 27; (01) 44 41 43 41
E-mail: com@institut-de-france.fr
Web Site: www.asmp.fr; www.institut-de-france.fr
Key Personnel
Secretaire perpetuel: Jean Cluzel
  E-mail: secretaireperpetuel@asmp.fr
Annual award for a published work best qualified to inspire love of ethics & virtue & to discourage egoism & envy; or to stimulate knowledge & appreciation of France.

Prix Baudelaire
Societe des Gens de Lettres de France
Hotel de Massa, 38 rue du Faubourg Saint-Jacques, 75014 Paris
Tel: (01) 53 10 12 00 *Fax:* (01) 53 10 12 12
Web Site: www.sgdl.org
Key Personnel
President: Alain Absire
First Vice President: Marie-France Briselance
Secretary General: Jean Claude Bologne
Treasurer: Francois Taillandier
Awarded each spring to the best French translation of an English work to which the author is native of the United Kingdom or one of the Commonwealth Countries.
Award: 2,250 EUR
Presented: British Council, Paris

Prix Bordin
Academie des Beaux Arts, Institut de France
23 quai de Conti, 75006 Paris
Tel: (01) 44 41 44 41; (01) 44 41 43 26 *Fax:* (01) 44 41 43 41; (01) 44 41 43 27
E-mail: com@institut-de-france.fr
Web Site: www.academie-des-beaux-arts.fr; www.institut-de-france.fr
Key Personnel
Secretaire perpetuel: Arnaud d' Hauterives

Louis Castex Prize (Prix Louis Castex)
Academie Francaise, Institut de France
23 quai de Conti, 75006 Paris
Tel: (01) 44 41 44 41 *Fax:* (01) 44 41 43 41
E-mail: com@institut-de-france.fr
Web Site: www.institut-de-france.fr
For a literary work celebrating a major voyage of exploration or archaeological or ethnological discovery. Fictional romance excluded. Awarded annually.

Honore Chavee Prize
Academie des Inscriptions et Belles Lettres, Institut de France
23 quai de Conti, 75006 Paris
Tel: (01) 44 41 43 10; (01) 44 41 44 41 *Fax:* (01) 44 41 43 11; (01) 44 41 43 41
E-mail: com@institut-de-france.fr
Web Site: www.aibl.fr; www.institut-de-france.fr
Key Personnel
Secretaire perpetuel: M Jean Leclant *E-mail:* j.leclant.aibl@dial.oleane.com
Established: 1821
Biennial award to encourage work in linguistics & in particular, research on romance languages.

Prix Maurice-Edgar Coindreau
Societe des Gens de Lettres de France
Hotel de Massa, 38 rue du Faubourg Saint-Jacques, 75014 Paris
Tel: (01) 53 10 12 00 *Fax:* (01) 53 10 12 12
Web Site: www.sgdl.org
Key Personnel
President: Alain Absire
First Vice President: Marie-France Briselance
Secretary General: Jean Claude Bologne

FRANCE

Treasurer: Francois Taillandier
Rewards a literary translation for American work.
Award: 2,250 EUR

Concours de Nouvelles
Mairie de Palaiseau
Service culturel, BP 6, 91125 Palaiseau Cedex
Tel: (01) 60143960 *Fax:* (01) 60143960
E-mail: villepalaiseau@lemel.fr
Web Site: www.lemel.fr

Eve Delacroix Prize (Eve Delacroix Prize)
Academie Francaise, Institut de France
23 quai de Conti, 75006 Paris
Tel: (01) 44 41 43 00; (01) 44 41 44 41 *Fax:* (01) 43 29 47 45; (01) 44 41 43 41
E-mail: contact@academie-francaise.fr; com@institut-de-france.fr
Web Site: www.academie-francaise.fr; www.institut-de-france.fr
Key Personnel
Administration: Claude-Marie Durix
Annual award for a literary work, essay or novel combining literary quality, a sense of human dignity & the responsibilities of authorship.
Award: 762 EUR

Deux Magots Prize (Prix des Deux Magots)
Cafe des Deux Magots
6 Pl Saint Germain des Pres, 75006 Paris
Tel: (01) 45 48 55 25 *Fax:* (01) 45 49 31 29
E-mail: cafe.lesdeuxmagots@free.fr
Web Site: www.lesdeuxmagots.com
Key Personnel
Dir: M J Mathivat
Established: 1933
The prize originated in Paris.
Award: 7,700 EUR

Alfred Dutens Prize (Prix Alfred Dutens)
Academie des Inscriptions et Belles Lettres, Institut de France
23 quai de Conti, 75006 Paris
Tel: (01) 44 41 43 10; (01) 44 41 44 41 *Fax:* (01) 44 41 43 11; (01) 44 41 43 41
E-mail: com@institut-de-france.fr
Web Site: www.aibl.fr; www.institut-de-france.fr
Key Personnel
Secretaire perpetuel: M Jean Leclant *E-mail:* j.leclant.aibl@dial.oleane.com
Awarded every ten years for the most useful work on linguistics.

Prix Paul Feval de Litterature Populaire
Societe des Gens de Lettres de France
Hotel de Massa, 38 rue du Faubourg Saint-Jacques, 75014 Paris
Tel: (01) 53 10 12 00 *Fax:* (01) 53 10 12 12
Web Site: www.sgdl.org
Key Personnel
President: Alain Absire
First Vice President: Marie-France Briselance
Secretary General: Jean Claude Bologne
Treasurer: Francois Taillandier
For a translated German work.
Award: 3,000 EUR

Jean Finot Prize (Prix Jean Finot)
Academie des Sciences Morales et Politiques, Institut de France
23 quai de Conti, 75006 Paris
Tel: (01) 44 41 43 26; (01) 44 41 44 41 *Fax:* (01) 44 41 43 27; (01) 44 41 43 41
E-mail: com@institut-de-france.fr
Web Site: www.asmp.fr; www.institut-de-france.fr
Key Personnel
Secretaire perpetuel: Jean Cluzel
  E-mail: secretaireperpetuel@asmp.fr
Biennial award for a work of a humanitarian social trend.

Marshal Foch Prize (Prix du marechal Foch)
Academie Francaise, Institut de France
23 quai de Conti, 75006 Paris
Tel: (01) 44 41 43 00; (01) 44 41 44 41 *Fax:* (01) 43 29 47 45; (01) 44 41 43 41
E-mail: contact@academie-francaise.fr; com@institut-de-france.fr
Web Site: www.academie-francaise.fr; www.institut-de-france.fr
Key Personnel
Administration: Claude-Marie Durix
Biennial award for a book on the future of the nation's defence by a French officer, engineer, scholar or philosopher.

Gegner Prize (Prix Gegner)
Academie des Sciences Morales et Politiques, Institut de France
23 quai de Conti, 75006 Paris
Tel: (01) 44 41 43 26; (01) 44 41 44 41 *Fax:* (01) 44 41 43 27; (01) 44 41 43 41
E-mail: com@institut-de-france.fr
Web Site: www.asmp.fr; www.institut-de-france.fr
Key Personnel
Secretaire perpetuel: Jean Cluzel
  E-mail: secretaireperpetuel@asmp.fr
Awarded annually to a philosopher-writer whose works contribute to the progress of philosophic science.

Giles Prize (Prix Giles)
Academie des Inscriptions et Belles Lettres, Institut de France
23 quai de Conti, 75006 Paris
Tel: (01) 44 41 43 10; (01) 44 41 44 41 *Fax:* (01) 44 41 43 11; (01) 44 41 43 41
E-mail: com@institut-de-france.fr
Web Site: www.aibl.fr; www.institut-de-france.fr
Key Personnel
Secretaire perpetuel: M Jean Leclant *E-mail:* j.leclant.aibl@dial.oleane.com
Biennial award to a French National for a work on China, Japan or the Far East.

Goncourt Prize (Prix Goncourt)
Academie Goncourte, Societe de gens de Lettres
c/o Drouant, Place Gaillon, 75002 Paris
Tel: (01) 42651516 *Fax:* (01) 4703498
Web Site: www.academic-goncourt.fr
Founded by E de Goncourt, 1914, the annual prize honors a prose work by a younger writer with originality of spirit & form. The novel is the preferred medium. The Academy also awards each year, in various French towns, prizes for short story, biography, historical novel & poetry.
Award: 1,524 EUR to 7,622 EUR

☆Grand Prix de la Francophonie
Academie Francaise, Institut de France
23 quai de Conti, 75006 Paris
Tel: (01) 44 41 43 00; (01) 44 41 44 41 *Fax:* (01) 43 29 47 45; (01) 44 41 43 41
E-mail: contact@academie-francaise.fr; com@institut-de-france.fr
Web Site: www.academie-francaise.fr; www.institut-de-france.fr
Key Personnel
Administration: Claude-Marie Durix
Established: 1986
Annual award established by the Government of Canada in collaboration with the Academie Francaise. The Government of Canada donated 400,000 CAD as a founding sum with the expectation that other countries, organizations & groups would make further contributions. The prize is to reward the work of a French-speaking writer who has contributed in an outstanding manner to the upholding & exemplification of the French language. The prize can also be for literary or philosophical work which individually or collectively has assured the regeneration of the French language in the fields of science, technology or information.
Award: 45,735 EUR

Grand Prix de la Nouvelle
Societe des Gens de Lettres de France
Hotel de Massa, 38 rue du Faubourg Saint-Jacques, 75014 Paris
Tel: (01) 53 10 12 00 *Fax:* (01) 53 10 12 12
Web Site: www.sgdl.org
Key Personnel
President: Alain Absire
First Vice President: Marie-France Briselance
Secretary General: Jean Claude Bologne
Treasurer: Francois Taillandier
Award: 3,000 EUR

Grand Prix de la Societe des Poetes Francais
(Grand Prize of the French Poet's Society)
la Societe des Poetes Francais
Siege social, 16, rue Monsieur le Prince, 75006 Paris
Tel: (01) 60 29 46 06 *Fax:* (01) 40 46 99 82
E-mail: poetesfrancais@aol.com
Web Site: www.societedespoetesfrancais.asso.fr
Key Personnel
President: Vital Heurtebize
Secretary General: Linda Bastide
Established: 1936
Awarded annually for the whole body of a poet's work, as decided by the Committee of the Societe des Poetes (no applications allowed).

Grand Prix de Litterature de la Societe des Gens de Lettres pour l'ensemble de l'oeuvre
Societe des Gens de Lettres de France
Hotel de Massa, 38 rue du Faubourg Saint-Jacques, 75014 Paris
Tel: (01) 53 10 12 00 *Fax:* (01) 53 10 12 12
Web Site: www.sgdl.org
Key Personnel
President: Alain Absire
First Vice President: Marie-France Briselance
Secretary General: Jean Claude Bologne
Treasurer: Francois Taillandier
Award: 7,000 EUR

Grand Prix de Poesie de la Societe des Gens de Lettres
Societe des Gens de Lettres de France
Hotel de Massa, 38 rue du Faubourg Saint-Jacques, 75014 Paris
Tel: (01) 53 10 12 00 *Fax:* (01) 53 10 12 12
Web Site: www.sgdl.org
Key Personnel
President: Alain Absire
First Vice President: Marie-France Briselance
Secretary General: Jean Claude Bologne
Treasurer: Francois Taillandier
Award: 7,000 EUR

Grand Prix International de Poesie de la Ville de Grenoble
Societe des Poetes et Artistes de France
30 CRS-J-Jaures, 38000 Grenoble
Tel: (01) 76475483

Grand Prix Litteraire de l'Afrique Noire
(Black Africa Literary Prize)
Association des Ecrivains de Langue Francaise (ADELF) (French Language Writers' Association)
14 rue Broussais, 75014 Paris
Tel: (01) 43219599 *Fax:* (01) 43201222
Web Site: www.ecrivains-nc.org

Grand Prix SGDL de l'Essai
Societe des Gens de Lettres de France
Hotel de Massa, 38 rue du Faubourg Saint-Jacques, 75014 Paris
Tel: (01) 53 10 12 00 *Fax:* (01) 53 10 12 12

Web Site: www.sgdl.org
Key Personnel
President: Alain Absire
First Vice President: Marie-France Briselance
Secretary General: Jean Claude Bologne
Treasurer: Francois Taillandier
Established: 1984
For recognition of an outstanding essay.
Award: 3,000 EUR

Grand Prix SGDL de l'oeuvre Multimedia
Societe des Gens de Lettres de France
Hotel de Massa, 38 rue du Faubourg Saint-Jacques, 75014 Paris
Tel: (01) 53 10 12 00 *Fax:* (01) 53 10 12 12
Web Site: www.sgdl.org
Key Personnel
President: Alain Absire
First Vice President: Marie-France Briselance
Secretary General: Jean Claude Bologne
Treasurer: Francois Taillandier
Award: 3,000 EUR

Grand Prix SGDL du Livre des Arts
Societe des Gens de Lettres de France
Hotel de Massa, 38 rue du Faubourg Saint-Jacques, 75014 Paris
Tel: (01) 53 10 12 00 *Fax:* (01) 53 10 12 12
Web Site: www.sgdl.org
Key Personnel
President: Alain Absire
First Vice President: Marie-France Briselance
Secretary General: Jean Claude Bologne
Treasurer: Francois Taillandier
For recognition of outstanding works completed in the past year.
Award: 3,000 EUR

Grand Prix SGDL du Livre d'Histoire
Societe des Gens de Lettres de France
Hotel de Massa, 38 rue du Faubourg Saint-Jacques, 75014 Paris
Tel: (01) 53 10 12 00 *Fax:* (01) 53 10 12 12
Web Site: www.sgdl.org
Key Personnel
President: Alain Absire
First Vice President: Marie-France Briselance
Secretary General: Jean Claude Bologne
Treasurer: Francois Taillandier
To recognize the author of an historical work.
Award: 3,000 EUR

Grand Prix SGDL du Livre Jeunesse
Societe des Gens de Lettres de France
Hotel de Massa, 38 rue du Faubourg Saint-Jacques, 75014 Paris
Tel: (01) 53 10 12 00 *Fax:* (01) 53 10 12 12
Web Site: www.sgdl.org
Key Personnel
President: Alain Absire
First Vice President: Marie-France Briselance
Secretary General: Jean Claude Bologne
Treasurer: Francois Taillandier
Established: 1982
Annual award to recognize a book intended for young people by its qualities of invention, writing & presentation. Works written in French & published before March of the preceding year may be submitted by the author or editor.
Award: 3,000 EUR

Grand Prix SGDL du Roman
Societe des Gens de Lettres de France
Hotel de Massa, 38 rue du Faubourg Saint-Jacques, 75014 Paris
Tel: (01) 53 10 12 00 *Fax:* (01) 53 10 12 12
Web Site: www.sgdl.org
Key Personnel
President: Alain Absire
First Vice President: Marie-France Briselance
Secretary General: Jean Claude Bologne
Treasurer: Francois Taillandier
For recognition of an outstanding novel. Works published within the preceding year may be submitted.
Award: 3,000 EUR

Grand Prix SGDL du site Internet litteraire
Societe des Gens de Lettres de France
Hotel de Massa, 38 rue du Faubourg Saint-Jacques, 75014 Paris
Tel: (01) 53 10 12 00 *Fax:* (01) 53 10 12 12
E-mail: sgdlf@wanadoo.fr
Web Site: www.sgdl.org
Key Personnel
President: Alain Absire
First Vice President: Marie-France Briselance
Secretary General: Jean Claude Bologne
Treasurer: Francois Taillandier
Award: 3,000 EUR

Grand Prize for Literature (Grand Prix de Litterature)
Academie Francaise, Institut de France
23 quai de Conti, 75006 Paris
Tel: (01) 44 41 43 00; (01) 44 41 44 41 *Fax:* (01) 43 29 47 45; (01) 44 41 43 41
E-mail: contact@academie-francaise.fr; com@institut-de-france.fr
Web Site: www.academie-francaise.fr; www.institut-de-france.fr
Key Personnel
Administration: Claude-Marie Durix
Biennial award to a prose-writer for one or more works noteworthy in form & inspiration.

Grand Prize for Poetry (Grand prix de Poesie)
Academie Francaise, Institut de France
23 quai de Conti, 75006 Paris
Tel: (01) 44 41 43 00; (01) 44 41 44 41 *Fax:* (01) 43 29 47 45; (01) 44 41 43 41
E-mail: contact@academie-francaise.fr; com@institut-de-france.fr
Web Site: www.academie-francaise.fr; www.institut-de-france.fr
Key Personnel
Administration: Claude-Marie Durix
Awarded annually.
Award: 7,600 EUR

☆**Grand Prize for the Influence of the French Language** (prix du rayonnement de la langue et de la litterature francaises)
Academie Francaise, Institut de France
23 quai de Conti, 75006 Paris
Tel: (01) 44 41 43 00; (01) 44 41 44 41 *Fax:* (01) 43 29 47 45; (01) 44 41 43 41
E-mail: contact@academie-francaise.fr; com@institut-de-france.fr
Web Site: www.academie-francaise.fr; www.institut-de-france.fr
Key Personnel
Administration: Claude-Marie Durix
For work contributing to the influence of the French language. Monetary prize awarded annually.

Grands Prix d'Histoire Chateaubriand - la Vallee-aux-Loups
Maison de Chateaubriand
87 rue Chateaubriand, 92290 Chatenay-Malabry
Tel: (01) 47 02 58 61 *Fax:* (01) 47 02 05 57
E-mail: chateaubriand@cg92.fr
Web Site: 194.254.135.72/chateaubriand
Key Personnel
Dir: M Jean-Paul Clement

Cardinal Grente Prize (Prix du Cardinal Grente)
Academie Francaise, Institut de France
23 quai de Conti, 75006 Paris
Tel: (01) 44 41 43 00; (01) 44 41 44 41 *Fax:* (01) 43 29 47 45; (01) 44 41 43 41
E-mail: contact@academie-francaise.fr; com@institut-de-france.fr
Web Site: www.academie-francaise.fr; www.institut-de-france.fr
Key Personnel
Administration: Claude-Marie Durix
Awarded biennially for the entire works of a regular or secular member of the Roman Catholic clergy.

☆**Heredia Prize** (Prix Heredia)
Academie Francaise, Institut de France
23 quai de Conti, 75006 Paris
Tel: (01) 44 41 43 00; (01) 44 41 44 41 *Fax:* (01) 43 29 47 45; (01) 44 41 43 41
E-mail: contact@academie-francaise.fr; com@institut-de-france.fr
Web Site: www.academie-francaise.fr; www.institut-de-france.fr
Key Personnel
Administration: Claude-Marie Durix
Monetary award given in alternate years to (1) a Latin American writer for a piece of prose or poetry written in French, (2) the author of a collection of printed sonnets.

Grand Prix d'Histoire Nationale Maurice Payard (Maurice Payard National History Grand Prize)
Academie Nationale de Reims
7 rue des Ecoles, 51100 Reims
Mailing Address: 38 rue Gambetta, 51100 Reims
Tel: (0326) 910449 *Fax:* (0326) 910449
Key Personnel
Secretary General: Patrick Demouy *Tel:* (0326) 479819 *E-mail:* patrick.demouy@laposte.net
Administrative Secretary: Philippe Petit-Stervinou
Established: 1978
Champagne history.
Award: 1,500 EUR
Presented: July

Interallie Prize
Cercle Interallie
33 rue du Fauborg St Honore, 75008 Paris
Tel: (01) 42659600
Awarded since 1930 for a high quality novel, preferably written by a journalist. Awarded annually.

☆**Stanislas Julien Prize** (Prix Stanislas Julien)
Academie des Inscriptions et Belles Lettres, Institut de France
23 quai de Conti, 75006 Paris
Tel: (01) 44 41 43 10; (01) 44 41 44 41 *Fax:* (01) 44 41 43 11; (01) 44 41 43 41
E-mail: com@institut-de-france.fr
Web Site: www.aibl.fr; www.institut-de-france.fr
Key Personnel
Secretaire perpetuel: M Jean Leclant *E-mail:* j.leclant.aibl@dial.oleane.com
Monetary prize, awarded annually, for the best work related to China.

☆**Kalinga Prize for the Popularization of Science**
UNESCO Publishing
One rue Miollis, 75015 Paris
Tel: (01) 45 68 35 47 *Fax:* (01) 53 69 99 49
E-mail: dl.france@unesco.org
Web Site: www.unesco.org/science/ips/science_prizes/kalinga_science_prize.html; www.unesco.org/science/unesco_intern_sc_prizes.htm
Key Personnel
Contact: Yoslan Nur *E-mail:* y.nur@unesco.org
Established: 1952
Annual award established by the Kalinga Foundation Trust. The recipient must have distinguished him or herself in the course of a brilliant career as science writer, editor, lecturer, film producer, radio/TV program director or presenter. The National Commission for UN-

FRANCE

ESCO within each country forwards a single nomination to UNESCO on the basis of recommendations from national bodies, including science journals, national associations for the advancement of science.
Other Sponsor(s): Kalinga Foundation Trust (India)
Award: 2,000 GBP
Closing Date: June
Presented: India in even years; Paris (UNESCO Headquarters) in odd years, Nov

Prix Halperine Kaminsky
Societe des Gens de Lettres de France
Hotel de Massa, 38 rue du Faubourg Saint-Jacques, 75014 Paris
Tel: (01) 53 10 12 00 *Fax:* (01) 53 10 12 12
Web Site: www.sgdl.org
Key Personnel
President: Alain Absire
First Vice President: Marie-France Briselance
Secretary General: Jean Claude Bologne
Treasurer: Francois Taillandier
Composed of two prizes: Le Prix Halperine-Kaminsky Consecration & Le Prix Halperine-Kaminsky Decouverte.
Award: Le Prix Halperine-Kaminsky Consecration 7,000 EUR; Le Prix Halperine-Kaminsky Decouverte 1,500 EUR

Prix Roger Kowalski (Roger Kowalski Prize)
Ville de Lyon
Universite Lumiere Lyon 2, Faculte des arts, 18 quai Claude Bernard, 69007 Lyon
Annual prize awarded to a living poet for a French language manuscript.

Prix Valery Larbaud (Valery Larbaud Prize)
Association International des Amis de Valery Larbaud
Les Eygalades B, 116 rue Edmond-Carrieu, 30900 Nimes
Tel: (01) 04 6664 9402

Maison de Poesie (House of Poetry)
Emile Blemont Foundation
11 bis rue Ballu, 75009 Paris
Tel: (01) 40234599
Established: 1928

☆**Mandat des Poetes Prize**
Pierre Bearn
60 rue Monsieur-le-Prince, 75006 Paris
Tel: (01) 43262273
Founded in 1950 by Pierre Bearn, to aid a French-language poet of talent, young or old, in time of need. Awarded annually.

Medaille de la ville de Avignon (Medal of the Town of Avignon)
la Societe des Poetes Francais
Siege social, 16, rue Monsieur le Prince, 75006 Paris
Tel: (01) 60 29 46 06 *Fax:* (01) 40 46 99 82
E-mail: poetesfrancais@aol.com
Web Site: www.societedespoetesfrancais.asso.fr
Key Personnel
President: Vital Heurtebize
Secretary General: Linda Bastide

Medaille de la ville de Bayonne (Medal of the Town of Bayonne)
la Societe des Poetes Francais
Siege social, 16, rue Monsieur le Prince, 75006 Paris
Tel: (01) 60 29 46 06 *Fax:* (01) 40 46 99 82
E-mail: poetesfrancais@aol.com
Web Site: www.societedespoetesfrancais.asso.fr
Key Personnel
President: Vital Heurtebize
Secretary General: Linda Bastide

Medaille de la Ville de Chatcauneuf du Pape
la Societe des Poetes Francais
Siege social, 16, rue Monsieur le Prince, 75006 Paris
Tel: (01) 60 29 46 06 *Fax:* (01) 40 46 99 82
E-mail: poetesfrancais@aol.com
Web Site: www.societedespoetesfrancais.asso.fr
Key Personnel
President: Vital Heurtebize
Secretary General: Linda Bastide
Instituted by the town of Chatcauneuf-du-Pape & other cities in the same area. Awarded annually for a poetic work (unpublished, or published in previous five years) which, irrespective of subject, appears most deserving for its formal purity & lofty sentiments. Awarded preferably to a young poet.
Award: 152 EUR

Medaille de la ville de Chatel-Guyon (Medal of the Town of Chatel-Guyon)
la Societe des Poetes Francais
Siege social, 16, rue Monsieur le Prince, 75006 Paris
Tel: (01) 60 29 46 06 *Fax:* (01) 40 46 99 82
E-mail: poetesfrancais@aol.com
Web Site: www.societedespoetesfrancais.asso.fr
Key Personnel
President: Vital Heurtebize
Secretary General: Linda Bastide

Medaille de la ville de Combo les bains (Medal of the Town of Combo baths)
la Societe des Poetes Francais
Siege social, 16, rue Monsieur le Prince, 75006 Paris
Tel: (01) 60 29 46 06 *Fax:* (01) 40 46 99 82
E-mail: poetesfrancais@aol.com
Web Site: www.societedespoetesfrancais.asso.fr
Key Personnel
President: Vital Heurtebize
Secretary General: Linda Bastide

Medaille de la ville de Dijon (Medal of the Town of Dijon)
la Societe des Poetes Francais
Siege social, 16, rue Monsieur le Prince, 75006 Paris
Tel: (01) 60 29 46 06 *Fax:* (01) 40 46 99 82
E-mail: poetesfrancais@aol.com
Web Site: www.societedespoetesfrancais.asso.fr
Key Personnel
President: Vital Heurtebize
Secretary General: Linda Bastide

Medaille de la ville de Douai (Medal of the Town of Douai)
la Societe des Poetes Francais
Siege social, 16, rue Monsieur le Prince, 75006 Paris
Tel: (01) 60 29 46 06 *Fax:* (01) 40 46 99 82
E-mail: poetesfrancais@aol.com
Web Site: www.societedespoetesfrancais.asso.fr
Key Personnel
President: Vital Heurtebize
Secretary General: Linda Bastide

Medaille de la ville de Gap (Medal of the Town of Gap)
la Societe des Poetes Francais
Siege social, 16, rue Monsieur le Prince, 75006 Paris
Tel: (01) 60 29 46 06 *Fax:* (01) 40 46 99 82
E-mail: poetesfrancais@aol.com
Web Site: www.societedespoetesfrancais.asso.fr
Key Personnel
President: Vital Heurtebize
Secretary General: Linda Bastide

Medaille de la ville de Melun (Medal of the Town of Melun)
la Societe des Poetes Francais
Siege social, 16, rue Monsieur le Prince, 75006 Paris
Tel: (01) 60 29 46 06 *Fax:* (01) 40 46 99 82
E-mail: poetesfrancais@aol.com
Web Site: www.societedespoetesfrancais.asso.fr
Key Personnel
President: Vital Heurtebize
Secretary General: Linda Bastide

Medaille de la ville de Metz (Medal of the Town of Metz)
la Societe des Poetes Francais
Siege social, 16, rue Monsieur le Prince, 75006 Paris
Tel: (01) 60 29 46 06 *Fax:* (01) 40 46 99 82
E-mail: poetesfrancais@aol.com
Web Site: www.societedespoetesfrancais.asso.fr
Key Personnel
President: Vital Heurtebize
Secretary General: Linda Bastide

Medaille de la ville de Pau (Medal of the Town of Pau)
la Societe des Poetes Francais
Siege social, 16, rue Monsieur le Prince, 75006 Paris
Tel: (01) 60 29 46 06 *Fax:* (01) 40 46 99 82
E-mail: poetesfrancais@aol.com
Web Site: www.societedespoetesfrancais.asso.fr
Key Personnel
President: Vital Heurtebize
Secretary General: Linda Bastide

Medaille de la ville de Reims (Medal of the Town of Rheims)
la Societe des Poetes Francais
Siege social, 16, rue Monsieur le Prince, 75006 Paris
Tel: (01) 60 29 46 06 *Fax:* (01) 40 46 99 82
E-mail: poetesfrancais@aol.com
Web Site: www.societedespoetesfrancais.asso.fr
Key Personnel
President: Vital Heurtebize
Secretary General: Linda Bastide

Medaille de la ville de Toulon (Medal of the Town of Toulon)
la Societe des Poetes Francais
Siege social, 16, rue Monsieur le Prince, 75006 Paris
Tel: (01) 60 29 46 06 *Fax:* (01) 40 46 99 82
E-mail: poetesfrancais@aol.com
Web Site: www.societedespoetesfrancais.asso.fr
Key Personnel
President: Vital Heurtebize
Secretary General: Linda Bastide

Medaille de la ville de Vittel (Medal of the Town of Vittel)
la Societe des Poetes Francais
Siege social, 16, rue Monsieur le Prince, 75006 Paris
Tel: (01) 60 29 46 06 *Fax:* (01) 40 46 99 82
E-mail: poetesfrancais@aol.com
Web Site: www.societedespoetesfrancais.asso.fr
Key Personnel
President: Vital Heurtebize
Secretary General: Linda Bastide

Medaille du Senat (Medal of the Senate)
la Societe des Poetes Francais
Siege social, 16, rue Monsieur le Prince, 75006 Paris
Tel: (01) 60 29 46 06 *Fax:* (01) 40 46 99 82
E-mail: poetesfrancais@aol.com
Web Site: www.societedespoetesfrancais.asso.fr
Key Personnel
President: Vital Heurtebize
Secretary General: Linda Bastide

Prix Medicis de l'Essai
Prix Medicis
25 rue Dombasle, 75015 Paris
Tel: (01) 48287690 *Fax:* (01) 48287690
Key Personnel
Secretary General: Francine Mallet
 E-mail: dominique.larre@wanadoo.fr
Established: 1985
For the best essay in French, including translated writing, appearing during the preceding year. Monetary prize. Awarded annually.
Presented: Paris, France, Annually in early November

Prix Medicis Etranger
Prix Medicis
25 rue Dombasle, 75015 Paris
Tel: (01) 48287690 *Fax:* (01) 48287690
Key Personnel
Secretary General: Francine Mallet
 E-mail: dominique.larre@wanadoo.fr
Established: 1970
For the best foreign novel appearing in French during the preceding year. Awarded annually.
Presented: Paris, France, November

Medicis Prize
Prix Medicis
25 rue Dombasle, 75015 Paris
Tel: (01) 48287690 *Fax:* (01) 48287690
Key Personnel
Secretary General: Francine Mallet
 E-mail: dominique.larre@wanadoo.fr
Established: 1958
Awarded to an avant-garde novel, story or collection whose publication has not been accompanied by the celebrity or fame the author's talent deserves.
Presented: Paris, France, Annually in November

Prix du Meilleur Livre Etranger
24, rue de Oudinot, F-75007 Paris
Tel: (01) 45671898 *Fax:* (01) 45447924
Prize for the best foreign book.

Grand Prix Thyde Monnier de la SGDL
Societe des Gens de Lettres de France
Hotel de Massa, 38 rue de Faubourg Saint-Jacques, 75014 Paris
Tel: (01) 53 10 12 00 *Fax:* (01) 53 10 12 12
Web Site: www.sgdl.org
Key Personnel
President: Alain Absire
First Vice President: Marie-France Briselance
Secretary General: Jean Claude Bologne
Treasurer: Francois Taillandier
Established: 1975
Annual award in recognition of a cycle of novels or for a separate work (novel, essay or collection of poems) published during the preceding two years. Writers whose talents have not brought them material success are eligible.
Award: 2,000 EUR

Prix de Poesie Louis Montalte
Societe des Gens de Lettres de France
Hotel de Massa, 38 rue du Faubourg Saint-Jacques, 75014 Paris
Tel: (01) 53 10 12 00 *Fax:* (01) 53 10 12 12
E-mail: sgdlf@wanadoo.fr
Web Site: www.sgdl.org
Key Personnel
President: Alain Absire
First Vice President: Marie-France Briselance
Secretary General: Jean Claude Bologne
Treasurer: Francois Taillandier
For recognition of the complete works of a known poet.
Award: 3,000 EUR

Montyon Prize (Prix Montyon)
Academie Francaise, Institut de France
23 quai de Conti, 75006 Paris
Tel: (01) 44 41 43 00; (01) 44 41 44 41 *Fax:* (01) 43 29 47 45; (01) 44 41 43 41
E-mail: contact@academie-francaise.fr; com@institut-de-france.fr
Web Site: www.academie-francaise.fr; www.institut-de-france.fr
Key Personnel
Administration: Claude-Marie Durix
Annual award for any work published by a French author showing qualities of practical idealism.

Prix Gerard de Nerval
Societe des Gens de Lettres de France
Hotel de Massa, 38 rue du Faubourg Saint-Jacques, 75014 Paris
Tel: (01) 53 10 12 00 *Fax:* (01) 53 10 12 12
E-mail: sgdlf@wanadoo.fr
Web Site: www.sgdl.org
Key Personnel
President: Alain Absire
First Vice President: Marie-France Briselance
Secretary General: Jean Claude Bologne
Treasurer: Francois Taillandier
Established: 1989
For recognition of an outstanding translation of a German work.
Award: 2,500 EUR

Grand Prix Poncetton de la SGDL
Societe des Gens de Lettres de France
Hotel de Massa, 38 rue du Faubourg Saint-Jacques, 75014 Paris
Tel: (01) 53 10 12 00 *Fax:* (01) 53 10 12 12
E-mail: sgdlf@wanadoo.fr
Web Site: www.sgdl.org
Key Personnel
President: Alain Absire
First Vice President: Marie-France Briselance
Secretary General: Jean Claude Bologne
Treasurer: Francois Taillandier
Established: 1970
For recognition of the total works of a writer whose value has not been recognized & whose situation has been seriously affected.
Award: 3,000 EUR

Prix Jeune Poesie
la Societe des Poetes Francais
Siege social, 16, rue Monsieur le Prince, 75006 Paris
Tel: (01) 60 29 46 06 *Fax:* (01) 40 46 99 82
E-mail: poetesfrancais@aol.com
Web Site: www.societedespoetesfrancais.asso.fr
Key Personnel
President: Vital Heurtebize
Secretary General: Linda Bastide

Prix Universalis
Encylopaedia Universalis
18, rue de Tilsitt, 75017 Paris
Tel: (01) 45 72 72 72 *Fax:* (01) 45 72 03 43
Web Site: www.universalis.fr

Concours Promethee (Prix Promethee)
L'Atelier Imaginaire
BP n°2, 65290 Juillan
Tel: (0562) 320 370 *Fax:* (0562) 320 370
E-mail: contact@atelier-imaginaire.com
Web Site: www.atelier-imaginaire.com
Key Personnel
President: Guy Rouquet
Annual short story competition.

Prix de la reedition
Societe des Gens de Lettres de France
Hotel de Massa, 38 rue du Faubourg Saint Jacques, F-75014 Paris

Tel: (01) 53 10 12 00 *Fax:* (01) 53 10 12 12
Key Personnel
President: Alain Absire
First Vice President: Marie-France Briselance
Secretary General: Jean Claude Bologne
Treasurer: Francois Taillandier
Award: 1,500 EUR

☆**Lucien de Reinach Prize** (Prix Lucien de Reinach)
Academie des Sciences Morales et Politiques, Institut de France
23 quai de Conti, 75006 Paris
Tel: (01) 44 41 43 26 *Fax:* (01) 44 41 43 27
E-mail: com@institut-de-france.fr
Web Site: www.asmp.fr; www.institut-de-france.fr
Key Personnel
Secretaire perpetuel: Jean Cluzel
 E-mail: secretaireperpetuel@asmp.fr
Biennial award for the best original work written in French in the most recent two years on an overseas subject.

Prix Tristan Tzara de Traduction (Franco-Hongrois)
Societe des Gens de Lettres de France
Hotel de Massa, 38 rue du Faubourg Saint-Jacques, 75014 Paris
Tel: (01) 53 10 12 00 *Fax:* (01) 53 10 12 12
E-mail: sgdlf@wanadoo.fr
Web Site: www.sgdl.org
Key Personnel
President: Alain Absire
First Vice President: Marie-France Briselance
Secretary General: Jean Claude Bologne
Treasurer: Francois Taillandier
Established: 1986
For recognition of the Hungarian translation of a French work.
Award: 1,500 EUR

Prix de Poesie Charles Vildrac
Societe des Gens de Lettres de France
Hotel de Massa, 38 rue du Faubourg Saint-Jacques, 75014 Paris
Tel: (01) 53 10 12 00 *Fax:* (01) 53 10 12 12
E-mail: sgdlf@wanadoo.fr
Web Site: www.sgdl.org
Key Personnel
President: Alain Absire
First Vice President: Marie-France Briselance
Secretary General: Jean Claude Bologne
Treasurer: Francois Taillandier
Established: 1973
Annual award to recognize a writer of a collection of poems published during the year preceding the award. Writers under 40 years of age are eligible.
Award: 1,500 EUR

Volney Prize (Prix Volney)
Academie des Inscriptions et Belles Lettres, Institut de France
23 quai de Conti, 75006 Paris
Tel: (01) 44 41 43 10; (01) 44 41 44 41 *Fax:* (01) 44 41 43 11; (01) 44 41 43 41
E-mail: com@institut-de-france.fr
Web Site: www.aibl.fr; www.institut-de-france.fr
Key Personnel
Secretaire perpetuel: M Jean Leclant *E-mail:* j.leclant.aibl@dial.oleane.com
For a work in comparative philology.

Germany

Adelbert-von-Chamisso-Preis der Robert Bosch Stiftung
Bavarian Academy of Fine Arts

Max-Joseph-Platz 3, 80539 Munich
Tel: (089) 29 00 77-0 *Fax:* (089) 29 00 77-23
E-mail: info@badsk.de
Web Site: www.badsk.de
Key Personnel
Contact: Dr Oswald Georg Bauer
Annually.
Other Sponsor(s): Robert Bosch Stiftung

Andreas-Gryphius-Preis
Art Society
Hafenmarkt 2, 73728 Esslingen
Tel: (0711) 3969010 *Fax:* (0711) 39690123
E-mail: kuenstlergilde@t-online.de

Grosser Literaturpreis der Bayerischen Akademie der Schonen Kunste
Bavarian Academy of Fine Arts
Max-Joseph-Platz 3, 80539 Munich
Tel: (089) 29 00 77-0 *Fax:* (089) 29 00 77-23
E-mail: info@badsk.de
Web Site: www.badsk.de
Key Personnel
Contact: Dr Oswald Georg Bauer
Annually.

Berlin Art Prizes
Akademie der Kunste, Berlin
Hanseatenweg 10, 10557 Berlin
Tel: (030) 390 76-0 *Fax:* (030) 390 76-175
E-mail: info@adk.de
Web Site: www.adk.de
Established: 1948
Major literary award given for a body of work by the Akademie der Kuenste (Academy of Arts). The award, Fontane-Preis, is made once every six years (a similar award being made in other disciplines in the intervening five years). In addition, 'encouragement' prizes of 10,000 DM are given annually by the Akademie in each of the six disciplines - this includes one for literature & one for film/TV/radio work (which may be for writing).
Award: 15,339 EUR
Presented: March 18 annually

Horst Bienek Award for Poetry
Bavarian Academy of Fine Arts
Max-Joseph-Platz 3, 80539 Munich
Tel: (089) 29 00 77-0 *Fax:* (089) 29 00 77-23
E-mail: info@badsk.de
Web Site: www.badsk.de
Key Personnel
Contact: Dr Oswald Georg Bauer
Annually.
Other Sponsor(s): Robert Bosch Stiftung

☆Bremen Literatur Prize
Bremen City Council
c/o Stadtbibliothek Bremen, Friedrich-Ebert-Str 101/105, 28199 Bremen
Tel: (0421) 3614046; (0421) 3614757 *Fax:* (0421) 3616903
E-mail: barbara.lison@stadtbibliothek.bremen.de
Established by Senat der Frein Hansestadt Foundation to encourage German-speaking poets & writers. Awarded annually for a single work.
Award: 15,389 EUR

☆Bremen Literature Encouragement Prize
Bremen City Council
c/o Stadtbibliothek Bremeen, Friedrich-Ebert-Str 101/105, 28199 Bremen
Tel: (0421) 3614046; (0421) 3614757 *Fax:* (0421) 3616903
E-mail: barbara.lison@stadtbibliotkek.bremen.de
Established: 1977
Established by Rudolf-Alexander-Schroeder Foundation to encourage young German-speaking poets & writers. Awarded annually for a single work.
Award: 5,113 EUR

Georg-Buechner Preis
Deutsche Akademie fuer Sprache und Dichtung (German Academy of Language & Poetry)
Alexandraweg 23, 64287 Darmstadt
Tel: (06151) 40920 *Fax:* (06151) 409299
E-mail: sekretariat@deutscheakademie.de
Web Site: www.deutscheakademie.de
Key Personnel
Secretary-General: Dr Bernd Busch
Press Officer: Corinna Blattmann *Tel:* (06151) 409216
Established: 1951
Award: 40,000 EUR
Presented: Autumn annually

Buxtehuder Bulle
Stadt Buxtehude
Postfach 15 55, 21605 Buxtehude
Tel: (04161) 5 01-0 *Fax:* (04161) 5 01-3 18
E-mail: stadtverwaltung@stadt.buxtehude.de
Web Site: www.stadt.buxtehude.de
Established: 1971
Annual literary prize given to the best book (young readers aged 14-18) published in Germany during the preceding year. By internal nomination only.
Award: 5,000 EUR & plaque

Christoph-Martin-Wieland-Preis
Freundeskreis zur Internationalen Forderung Literarischer und Wissenschaftlicher Uebersetzungen
Implerstr 28, 81371 Munich
Tel: (0049) 89 763098
Key Personnel
President: Rosemarie Tietze
Established: 1979
Award: Awarded biennially

City of Munich Prizes
Landeshauptstadt Muenchen Kulturreferat
Burgstr 4, 80331 Munich
Tel: (089) 233 26991; (089) 233 21262
Web Site: www.muenchen.de
Established: 1977
Biennial awards for recognition of lifetime achievement in the arts by authors & artists of Munich. Prizes awarded for each of eight categories.
Literature: to honor an outstanding literary collection, established in 1991
Film: to honor special achievements in film, established in 1992
Journalism: to honor an outstanding journalistic work in print, radio, or television, established in 1992
Art: for special achievements in the field of fine arts, established in 1991
Architecture: for an outstanding exceptional project designed & constructed in Munich, established in 1977
Design: for an outstanding design achievement, established in 1992
Music: for deserving musicians & musical groups in all fields & all genres of music, established in 1992
Theatre, established in 1992.
Award: 7,500 EUR

Deutscher Jugendliteratur Preis
Arbeitskreis fur Jugendliteratur eV
Metzstr 14c, 81667 Munich
Tel: (089) 4580806 *Fax:* (089) 45808088
E-mail: info@jugendliteratur.org
Web Site: www.jugendliteratur.org
Key Personnel
Project Leader: Kristin Bernd
German Section of the International Board on Books for Young People.

Alfred-Doeblin Preis
Akademie der Kunste, Berlin
Hanseatenweg 10, 10557 Berlin
Tel: (030) 390 76-0 *Fax:* (030) 390 76-175
E-mail: info@adk.de
Web Site: www.adk.de
Established: 1983
This award will generally be made every one or two years for unpublished work of an epic nature.
Award: Up to 10,226 EUR

Annette von Droste Huelshoff Preis
Landschaftsverband Westfalen - Lippe Abteilung Kulturpflege
Warendorfer Str 24, 48133 Muenster
Tel: (0251) 591-5985 *Fax:* (0251) 591-268
E-mail: kultur@lwl.org
Web Site: www.lwl.org/kultur
Key Personnel
Contact: Prof Karl Teppe
Established: 1946
Biennial award for recognition of special achievement in poetry written in either high or low German. Every third time it can be awarded for creative musical achievement. Recipients must be natives or residents of the Westfalian - Lippe region of Germany. Established by Provinzialverband Westfalen in memory of the German & Westfalian poetess, Annette von Droste-Hulshoff (1797-1848). Formerly: Westfaelischer Literaturpreis.
Award: 12,782 EUR & certificate

Konrad Duden Prize
Stadt Mannheim, Amt fuer Rats und Oeffentlichkeitsarbeit
Rathaus E5, 68159 Mannheim
Tel: (0621) 293 9654 *Fax:* (0621) 293 9532
E-mail: masta@mannheim.de
Web Site: www.mannheim.de
Key Personnel
Contact: Kirsten Batzler *E-mail:* kirsten.batzler@mannheim.de
Awarded biennially to personalities who have particularly contributed to the German language. The award is noncompetitive.
Award: 12,500 EUR

Sigmund Freud Preis Fluer Wissenschaftliche Prosa
Deutsche Akademie fuer Sprache und Dichtung (German Academy of Language & Poetry)
Alexandraweg 23, 64287 Darmstadt
Tel: (06151) 40920 *Fax:* (06151) 409299
E-mail: sekretariat@deutscheakademie.de
Web Site: www.deutscheakademie.de
Key Personnel
Secretary-General: Dr Bernd Busch
Press Officer: Corinna Blattmann *Tel:* (06151) 409216
Established: 1964
Award: 12,500 EUR
Presented: Autumn annually

Friedenspreis des Deutschen Buchhandels
(Peace Prize of the German Book Trade)
Borsenverein des Deutschen Buchhandels eV
Grosser Hirschgraben 17/21, 60311 Frankfurt am Main
Tel: (069) 1306-0 *Fax:* (069) 1306-201
E-mail: info@boev.de
Web Site: www.boersenverein.de
Key Personnel
Acting Man Dir: Dr Harald Heker
Established: 1950

The prize is an amount made up exclusively of donations from publishers & booksellers. The Peace Prize is an impressive indication of the book trade's commitment to serve international understanding by its activities. According to tradition, the prize has been awarded annually.
Award: 15,000 EUR
Presented: The Frankfurt Book Fair, Autumn

Friedrich-Gerstaecker Preis-der Stadt Braunschweig
Stadt Braunschweig-Kulturinstitut
Steintorwall 3, 38100 Braunschweig
Tel: (0531) 470 4840 *Fax:* (0531) 470 4809
E-mail: kulturinstitut@braunschweig.de
Web Site: www.braunschweig.de
Award: 6,000 EUR awarded biennially

Friedrich Gundolf Preis fuer die Vermittlung Deutscher Kultur im Ausland (Friedrich Gundolf Prize for German Culture in Foreign Countries)
Deutsche Akademie fuer Sprache und Dichtung (German Academy of Language & Poetry)
Alexandraweg 23, 64287 Darmstadt
Tel: (06151) 40920 *Fax:* (06151) 409299
E-mail: sekretariat@deutscheakademie.de
Web Site: www.deutscheakademie.de
Key Personnel
Secretary-General: Dr Bernd Busch
Press Officer: Corinna Blattmann *Tel:* (06151) 409216
Established: 1964
Award: 12,500 EUR
Presented: Spring annually

Johann-Peter-Hebel-Preis
Ministerium fur Wisserschaft, Forschung und Kunst Baden-Wurttemberg
Koenigstr 46, 70173 Stuttgart
Tel: (0711) 279-0 *Fax:* (0711) 279-3081
E-mail: presse@mwk.bwl.de
Web Site: www.mwk-bw.de
Key Personnel
Publications: Dr Gunter Schanz

☆**Wilhelm Heinse Medal for Literature in Essay Form** (wilhelm-Heinse-Medaille)
Akademie der Wissenschaften und der Literatur, Klasse der Literatur
Geschwister-Scholl-Str 2, 55131 Mainz
Tel: (06131) 577-0 *Fax:* (06131) 577-206
Web Site: www.adwmainz.de
Established: 1978
Awarded biennially.

Ricarda-Huch-Preis
City of Darmstadt
Luisenplatz 5, 64283 Darmstadt 11
Tel: (06151) 131 *Fax:* (06151) 133777
E-mail: presseamt@darmstadt.de; info@darmstadt.de
Web Site: www.darmstadt.de
Established: 1978
Award: 10,250 EUR

☆**Inter Nationes Culture Prize**
Inter Nationes eV
Kennedyalle 91-103, 53175 Bonn
Tel: (0228) 8800 *Fax:* (0228) 880457
E-mail: info@inter-nationes.de
Web Site: www.inter-nationes.de
Established: 1968
Biennial award to recognize publishers, historians, writers, translators, etc., who have made a valuable contribution to international understanding in cultural fields. Awarded to foreign nationals only. Formerly:(1988) Inter Nationes - Preis fur Werke der Literatur und bildenden Kunst.
Award: 5,113 EUR & a personally dedicated booklet

International Youth Library, see White Ravens

Thomas Mann Prize
Hansestadt Lubeck-Bereich Kunst und Kultur
Breite Str 62, 23539 Luebeck
Tel: (0451) 12 21 300 *Fax:* (0451) 12 21 331
E-mail: kunst-und-kultur@luebeck.de; info@luebeck.de
Web Site: www.luebeck.de
Established: 1975
Founded in honor of Thomas Mann, to celebrate the 100th anniversary of his birth. The prize will be awarded to personalities who have, through their literary work, shown the humanitarian spirit set out in the work of Thomas Mann. No application fee. Awarded triennially.
Award: 7,669 EUR

Johann-Heinrich-Merck-Preis fuer literarische Kritik und Essay (J H Merck Prize for Literary Criticism & Essay)
Deutsche Akademie fuer Sprache und Dichtung (German Academy of Language & Poetry)
Alexandraweg 23, 64287 Darmstadt
Tel: (06151) 40920 *Fax:* (06151) 409299
E-mail: sekretariat@deutscheakademie.de
Web Site: www.deutscheakademie.de
Key Personnel
Secretary-General: Dr Bernd Busch
Press Officer: Corinna Blattmann *Tel:* (06151) 409216
Established: 1964
Award: 12,500 EUR
Presented: Autumn annually

Rolandpreis fur Kunst im offentlichen Raum
Senator for Bildung, Wissenschaft, Kunst und Sport
Rembertiring 8-12, 28195 Bremen
Tel: (0421) 361-4995; (0421) 361-2978 *Fax:* (0421) 361-15543
Established: 1989
Bremen City Council.

Literaturpreis der Stadt-Dortmund-Nelly-Sachs-Preis (The Literary Prize of Dortmund City-Nelly Sachs Prize)
Kulturbuero der Stadt Dortmund
Kleppingstr 21-23, 44135 Dortmund
Tel: (0231) 50-2 51 70 *Fax:* (0231) 50-2 24 97
E-mail: kulturbuero@dortmund.de
Web Site: www.dortmund.de/kulturbuero
Key Personnel
Contact: Hans-Georg Schuk *E-mail:* hg.schuk@t-online.de
Established: 1961
Instituted by the Dortmund City Council. Awarded biennially to personalities who have produced outstanding creative work in the art or cultural field.
Award: 15,000 EUR

Schiller Prize
Stadt Mannheim, Amt fuer Rats und Oeffentlichkeitsarbeit
Rathaus E5, 68159 Mannheim
Tel: (0621) 293 9654 *Fax:* (0621) 293-9532
E-mail: masta@mannheim.de
Web Site: www.mannheim.de
Key Personnel
Contact: Rainer Gluth *E-mail:* rainer.gluth@mannheim.de
Prize awarded to persons who have contributed. Awarded every four years significantly to cultural development by their total works or an individual work of outstanding quality, or whose previous work shows promise in the cultural field.
Award: 12,782 EUR

Literaturpreis der Landeshauptstadt Stuttgart (Stuttgart Literary Prize)
Landeshauptstadt Stuttgart
Interims-Rathaus, Heilbronner Str 7, 70174 Stuttgart
Tel: (0711) 216-0 *Fax:* (0711) 216-4773
E-mail: post@stuttgart.de
Web Site: www.stuttgart.de
Telex: 722854 Kult d

Thaddaeus-Troll-Preis
Foerderkreis Deutscher Schriftsteller in Baden-Wurttemberg eV
Rosenbergstr 96, 70176 Stuttgart
Fax: (0711) 6365364
E-mail: info@schriftsteller-in-bawue.de
Web Site: www.schriftsteller-in-bawue.de
Established: 1981
Applications not accepted for this award.
Award: Foerderpreis

Johann-Heinrich-Voss-Preis fuer Uebersetzung
Deutsche Akademie fuer Sprache und Dichtung (German Academy of Language & Poetry)
Alexandraweg 23, 64287 Darmstadt
Tel: (06151) 40920 *Fax:* (06151) 409299
E-mail: sekretariat@deutscheakademie.de
Web Site: www.deutscheakademie.de
Key Personnel
Secretary-General: Dr Bernd Busch
Press Officer: Corinna Blattmann *Tel:* (06151) 409216
Established: 1958
Award: 15,000 EUR
Presented: Spring annually

Walter Tiemann Award
Hochschule fuer Grafik und Buchkunst Leipzig (Academy of Visual Arts Leipzig)
Waechterstr 11, 04107 Leipzig
Tel: (0341) 21 35-0 *Fax:* (0341) 21 35-166
E-mail: hgb@hbg-leipzig.de
Web Site: www.hgb-leipzig.de
Key Personnel
Public Administration & Public Relations: Sibylle Schulz Shibru
To recognize independent publishers, small publishers & printing-presses. One to three different titles published within the preceding two years may be submitted. Established in honor of Walter Tiemann, a teacher & the rector from 1920 to 1945.
Award: A small sculpture & 1st prize 5,113 EUR; 2nd prize 1,534 EUR; 3rd prize 1,023 EUR

White Ravens
Internationale Jugendbibliothek (International Youth Library)
Schloss Blutenburg, 81247 Munich
Tel: (089) 8912110 *Fax:* (089) 8117553
E-mail: bib@ijb.de
Web Site: www.ijb.de
Established: 1983
Awarded annually to promote high quality children's books of international interest. About 250 children's books, by authors & illustrators from all over the world, are given recognition. Children's books submitted by publishers during the year prior to the award are considered. White Ravens books are listed in the annual international selected bibliography & exhibited during the Children's Book Fair in Bologna, Italy & thereafter upon request in libraries & other institutions. Titles in over 30 languages from 50 countries.
Closing Date: Dec
Presented: Bologna Children's Book Fair, Italy, April

Greece

Book Prizes of the Circle of the Greek Children's Book
Circle of the Greek Children's Book IBBY (Greek Section)
Bouboulinas 28, 10682 Athens
Tel: (0210) 8222296 *Fax:* (0210) 8222296
E-mail: kyklos@greekibby.gr
Web Site: www.greekibby.gr
Key Personnel
President: Loty Petrovits *Tel:* (0210) 8223008
E-mail: loty@eexi.gz
Established: 1970
Awarded annually for various types of children's literature.
Award: Prizes range from 1,000 EUR to 1,500 EUR

Parnassos Foundation Prize
Parnassos Literary Society
8 George Karytsis Sq, 105 61 Athens
Tel: (01) 32 13 363 *Fax:* (01) 32 49 398
Established: 1980
Annual award to provide recognition for the best play of the year.
Award: Monetary prize & honorary recognition

Haiti

Prix litteraire Henri Deschamps (Henri Deschamps Literary Prize)
Maison Henri Deschamps, Grand Rue
PO Box 164, Port-au-Prince
Tel: (509) 223-2215; (509) 223-2216 *Fax:* (509) 223-4975
E-mail: entdeschamps@gdfhaiti.com
Key Personnel
Secretary General: Paulette Poujol Oriol
Established: 1975
Annual award open to unpublished Haitian writers, on any subject.
Award: 1,000 USD & 1,000 free publishing copies

Hong Kong

Awards for Creative Writing in Chinese
Hong Kong Public Libraries
66 Causeway Rd, Causeway Bay, Hong Kong
Tel: 2921 0208 *Fax:* 2415 8211
E-mail: enquiries@lcsd.gov.hk
Web Site: www.hkpl.gov.hk
Key Personnel
Assistant Dir: Michael Mak *E-mail:* mklmak@lcsd.gov.hk
Senior Librarian (Extension Activities): Sun Tinny YM *Tel:* (02) 2921 2687
E-mail: tymsun@lcsd.gov.hk
Established: 1979
Biennial award to residents of Hong Kong aged 16 & over, under six categories (prose, poetry, fiction, literary criticism, children's storybook & children's picture book) to cultivate interest in creative writing in Chinese.
Award: 1st prize: 12,000 HKD for each category

Hong Kong Biennial Award for Chinese Literature
Hong Kong Public Libraries
66 Causeway Rd, Causeway Bay, Hong Kong
Tel: (02) 2921 0208 *Fax:* (02) 2415 8211
E-mail: enquiries@lcsd.gov.hk
Web Site: www.hkpl.gov.hk
Key Personnel
Senior Librarian (Extension Activities): Sun Tinny YM *Tel:* (02) 2921 2687
E-mail: tymsun@lcsd.gov.hk
Established: 1991
Award is by open nomination to give recognition to the outstanding achievements of established Hong Kong writers & to encourage them to write quality literary work. Awards presented biennially for fiction, prose, poetry, children's literature & literary criticism, published in Hong Kong in the previous two years & written in Chinese.
Award: 50,000 HKD

Hungary

Jozsef Attila Prize
Ministry of Culture & Education
Szalay-utca 10/14, 1055 Budapest
Tel: (01) 473-7000 *Fax:* (01) 473-7001
E-mail: info@om.hu
Web Site: www.om.hu
For highly significant work in prose or poetry. Given to writers, poets & critics. Since 1950 awarded to 8-10 people a year.

Robert Graves Prize
Hungarian Writers' Union
Magyar Iroszovetseg, Bajza utca 18, 1062 Budapest
Tel: (01) 322-8840; (01) 322-0631 *Fax:* (01) 321-3419
Key Personnel
President: Marton Kalasz

Kossuth Prize
Muvelodesi Miniszterium
Kossuth Lajos-Ter 1-3, 1055 Budapest, V
Tel: (01) 1120600 *Fax:* (01) 530124
Established: 1948
An irregular award to outstanding artists, including writers.

☆Hungarian PEN Club Medal
Hungarian PEN Centre
VII Kertesz u 36, 1073 Budapest
Tel: (01) 184143
For translation of Hungarian literary work into foreign languages. Awarded when merited.

State Prize
Office of the Prime Minister
Kossuth Lajos Ter 1-3, 1055 Budapest V
Tel: (01) 441-3000 *Fax:* (01) 441-3050
Web Site: www.meh.hu
Annual national prize for most exceptional & outstanding creative works. Of over a hundred recipients each year, one or more writers receive this award.

Szakszervezete Muveszeti Kulturalis Dij (Trade Union's Art & Cultural Prize)
National Confederation of Hungarian Trade Unions (Magyar Szakszervezetek Orszagos Szovetsege)
Magdolna u 5-7, 1086 Budapest
Tel: (01) 3232 656; (01) 309211189 *Fax:* (01) 3232 654
Web Site: www.mszosz.hu
Established: 1958
Awarded annually. Established by the Central Council of Hungarian Trade Unions, prizes are awarded to artists, scientists, educators, as well as for literary works. Nominees are people who excel in improving worker-artist contacts & in disseminating knowledge. Selection is by public opinion poll.

India

Bhai Santokh Singh Award
Haryana Punjabi Sahitya Akademi
Kothi No 897, Sector-2, Panchkula 134112
Tel: (0172) 565521; (0172) 563340
Key Personnel
Dir: A S Shergill
Awarded annually to an Indian national domiciled in Haryana State for contributions to the development of Panjabi literature. Presented for the life long contribution to the Panjabi writer once in a lifetime.
Award: 21,000 INR

I C Chacko Award
Kerala Sahitya Akademi
Town Hall Rd, Thrissur, Kerala 680020
Tel: (011) 331069
Web Site: www.keralasahityaakademi.org
Key Personnel
Secretary: P V Krishnan Nair
Awarded annually for the best book published in Malayalam during the preceding three years in the field of linguistics.
Award: 2,000 INR

Escorts Book Award
Delhi Management Association
India Habitat Centre, Core 6A, 1st floor, Lodhi Rd, New Delhi 110003
Tel: (011) 4649552; (011) 4649551 *Fax:* (011) 4649553
E-mail: dmadelhi@ndb.vsnl.net.in
Key Personnel
Program Manager: S Kumar
Established: 1965
Instituted by Escorts Ltd & administered by Delhi Management Association. For original books on management principles & practices by Indian writers. Awarded annually.
Award: 5,000 & 3,000 INR each

Indian Books Centre Oriental Studies Award
Sri Satguru Publications
40/5 Shakti Nagar, Delhi 110007
Tel: (011) 27434930; (011) 27126497 *Fax:* (011) 27227336
E-mail: ibcindia@vsnl.com
Web Site: www.indianbookscentre.com
For the best work in Oriental Studies, published in Sanskrit, English, Tibetan or Hindi.
Award: 1,100 INR, a shawl & a citation are awarded on a regular basis

Jnanpith Award
Bharatiya Jnanpith
18 Institutional Area, Lodi Rd, New Delhi 110 003
Tel: (011) 4626467; (011) 4654196; (011) 4656201; (011) 4698417 *Fax:* (011) 4654197
E-mail: jnanpith@satyam.net.in; jnanpith@satyam.com
Key Personnel
Dir: Aditya Sharma

Kerala Sahitya Akademi Awards
Kerala Sahitya Akademi
Town Hall Rd, Thrissur, Kerala 680020
Tel: (011) 331069
Web Site: www.keralasahityaakademi.org
Key Personnel
Secretary: P V Krishnan Nair

Annual awards for literary works in Malayalam published during the preceding three years, in the following categories: fiction; drama; poetry; short stories; novels; literary criticism; (biography; autobiography; travelogs & humor); scientific & scholarly works (including philosophy; education; sociology).
Award: varies

C B Kumar Award
Kerala Sahitya Akademi
Town Hall Rd, Thrissur, Kerala 680020
Tel: (011) 331069
Web Site: www.keralasahityaakademi.org
Key Personnel
Secretary: P V Krishnan Nair
Annual award for the best collection of essays in Malayalam.
Award: 1,500 INR

Kuttippuzha Award
Kerala Sahitya Akademi
Town Hall Rd, Thrissur, Kerala 680020
Tel: (011) 331069
Web Site: www.keralasahityaakademi.org
Key Personnel
Secretary: P V Krishnan Nair
Awarded annually for the best book of criticism published in Malayalam during the preceding three years.
Award: 2,000 INR

Law Books in Hindu Prize
Indian Law Institute
Bhagwan Das Rd, New Delhi 110 001
Tel: (011) 23387526 *Fax:* (011) 23782140
E-mail: ili@ilidelhi.org
Web Site: www.ilidelhi.org
Awarded annually for law books/manuscripts in Hindi. The first prize is 10,000 INR & prizes up to 100,000 INR may be awarded.

Mahrishi Vedvyasa Prize
Haryana Punjabi Sahitya Akademi
Kothi No 897, Sector-2, Panchkula 134112
Tel: (0172) 565521
Awarded annually to an Indian national domiciled in Haryana State for contribution towards the development of Sanskrit literature.
Award: 15,000 INR

Meera Award
Rajasthan Sahitya Akademi
Hiran Magri, Sector 4, Udaipur 313 002
Tel: (0294) 583717; (0294) 583629
Established: 1959
Awarded annually for the best literary work in Hindi.
Award: 11,000 INR

K R Namboodiri Award
Kerala Sahitya Akademi
Town Hall Rd, Thrissur, Kerala 680020
Tel: (011) 331069
Web Site: www.keralasahityaakademi.org
Key Personnel
Secretary: P V Krishnan Nair
Awarded annually for the best work on Vedic literature in Malayalam.
Award: 2,000 INR

Pandit Lakhmi Chand Prize
Haryana Punjabi Sahitya Akademi
Kothi No 897, Sector-2, Panchkula 134112
Tel: (0172) 565521
Awarded annually to an Indian national for outstanding work on literature, art, history & culture of Haryana.
Award: 15,000 INR

Sahitya Akademi Award
Sahitya Akademi (National Academy of Letters)
Rabindra Bhavan, 35 Ferozshah Rd, New Delhi 110 001
Tel: (011) 3386626; (011) 3386627; (011) 3386628; (011) 3386629; (011) 3387386; (011) 3386088 *Fax:* (011) 3382428
Web Site: www.sahitya-akademi.org
Key Personnel
Secretary: Prof K Satchidanandan *E-mail:* secy@sahitya-akademi.org
Established: 1955
For outstanding literary works written in each of the 22 languages of India recognized by the Indian National Academy of Letters (Sahitya Akademi). Awarded annually to Indian nationals only.
Award: 25,000 INR each
Closing Date: Dec annually
Presented: New Delhi, Feb annually

Sur Award
Haryana Punjabi Sahitya Akademi
Kothi No 897, Sector-2, Panchkula 134112
Tel: (0172) 565521
Awarded annually to an Indian national domiciled in Haryana State for outstanding contribution to development of Hindi, Sanskrit & Haryanvi.
Award: 50,000 INR

Sree Padmanabha Swami Prize
Kerala Sahitya Akademi
Town Hall Rd, Thrissur, Kerala 680020
Tel: (011) 331069
Web Site: www.keralasahityaakademi.org
Key Personnel
Secretary: P V Krishnan Nair
Awarded annually for the best drama literature published in Malayalam during the preceding three years.
Award: 2,500 INR

Tagore Literacy Award
Indian Adult Education Association
17-B, I P Estate, New Dehli 110 002
Tel: (011) 3319282; (011) 3722206; (011) 3721336 *Fax:* (011) 3366306
E-mail: iaea@vsnl.com
Key Personnel
President: B S Garg
Recognition of outstanding contribution to promotion of women's literacy & adult education in India.

Urdu Akademy Awards
Urdu Academy Delhi
Ghata Masjid Rd, Darya Ganj, New Delhi 110002
Tel: (011) 3276211; (011) 3262693; (011) 3251206
E-mail: urduacademy@yahoo.com
Awarded annually to Indian nationals for Urdu literature.

Islamic Republic of Iran

Children's Book Council Award (Jayezeh Showraye Ketabe Koodak)
Children's Book Council of Iran
PO Box 13145-133, Tehran 13158
Tel: (021) 6408074 *Fax:* (021) 6405878
E-mail: anmo@kanoon.net
Web Site: www.schoolnet.ir/~cbc

Key Personnel
General Secretary: Noushine Ansari
Established: 1963
For recognition of a contribution in the field of children's literature. Iranian writers, illustrators & translations are eligible. Established by A Yamini Sharif.
Award: A plaque or diploma is awarded annually
Presented: CBCI Annual Meeting, Jan annually

Ireland

Aosdana Membership
The Arts Council/An Chomhairle Ealaion
70 Merrion Sq, Dublin 2
Tel: (01) 618 0200 *Fax:* (01) 676 1302
E-mail: info@artscouncil.ie
Web Site: www.artscouncil.ie
Key Personnel
Arts Council Dir: Patricia Quinn *Tel:* (01) 618 0225 *E-mail:* patricia@artscouncil.ie
Special honorary affiliation of creative artists. To be eligible for membership, the artist must have been born in Ireland or been a resident of Ireland for five years, must not be less than 35 years of age & must have produced a body of works. Membership is by election.
Award: Annuities up to 11,072 EUR

The Clo Iar-Chonnacta Literary Award
Clo Iar-Chonnachta Teo
Indreabhan, Conamara, Co Galway
Tel: (091) 593 307 *Fax:* (091) 593 362
E-mail: cic@iol.ie
Web Site: www.cic.ie
Key Personnel
General Manager: Deirdre Thuathail
Presented annually for a newly written & unpublished work in the Irish language.
Award: 5,000 GBP
Closing Date: Dec

Denis Devlin Memorial Award for Poetry
The Arts Council/An Chomhairle Ealaion
70 Merrion Sq, Dublin 2
Tel: (01) 618 0200 *Fax:* (01) 676 1302
E-mail: info@artscouncil.ie
Web Site: www.artscouncil.ie
Key Personnel
Dir: Patricia Quinn *Tel:* (01) 618 0225 *E-mail:* patricia@artscouncil.ie
Given for the finest collection of poetry in the English language by an Irish citizen published in the previous three years.
Award: 1,500 GBP

Fish Short Story Prize
Fish Publishing
Durrus, Bantry, Co Cork
Tel: (027) 61246 *Fax:* (027) 61246
E-mail: story@fishpublishing.com
Web Site: www.fishpublishing.com
Key Personnel
Dir: Clem Cairns; Jula Walton
Established: 1994
Closing Date: Nov 30 annually

Fish Unpublished Novel Award
Fish Publishing
Durrus, Bantry, Co Cork
Tel: (027) 61246 *Fax:* (027) 61246
Web Site: www.fishpublishing.com
Key Personnel
Dir: Clem Cairns; Jula Walton
Closing Date: Sept

Fish VERY Short Story Prize
Fish Publishing
Durrus, Bantry, Co Cork

IRELAND

Tel: (027) 61246 *Fax:* (027) 61246
E-mail: VSSP@fishpublishing.com
Web Site: www.fishpublishing.com
Key Personnel
Dir: Clem Cairns; Jula Walton
Established: 2003
Closing Date: Feb 14 annually

Gregory Medal
Irish Academy of Letters, School of Irish Studies
4 Ailesbury Grove, Dundum, Dublin 14
For distinction in letters or outstanding literary work in Irish. Awarded periodically.

☆International Fiction Prize
Irish Times Ltd
10-16 D'Olier St, Dublin 2
Tel: (01) 6758000 *Fax:* (01) 6793910
Web Site: www.ireland.com
Awarded biannually for a work of fiction written in English & published in Ireland, the United Kingdom or the United States within a two year period from August 1 of the previous year to July 31 of the year of the prize. Four titles are shortlisted for this prize.

☆The Irish Literature Prize: Fiction
Irish Times Ltd
10-16 D'Olier St, Dublin 2
Tel: (01) 6758000 *Fax:* (01) 6773282
Web Site: www.ireland.com
Awarded biannually along with the Poetry Prize. Books can be in either English or Irish & published in Ireland, the United Kingdom or the United States within a two-year time period from August 1 & July 31 of the year of the prize. Three books are shortlisted for this prize.

☆The Irish Literature Prize: Nonfiction
Irish Times Ltd
10-16 D'Olier St, Dublin 2
Tel: (01) 6758000 *Fax:* (01) 6773282
Web Site: www.ireland.com
Awarded biannually along with the First Book Prize. Books can be in either English or Irish & published in Ireland, the United Kingdom or the United States within a two-year period from August 1 & July 31 of the year of the prize. Three books are shortlisted for this prize.

☆The Irish Literature Prize: Poetry
Irish Times Ltd
10-16 D'Olier St, Dublin 2
Tel: (01) 6758000 *Fax:* (01) 6773282
Web Site: www.ireland.com
Awarded biannually along with the Fiction Prize. Books can be in either English or Irish & published in Ireland, the United Kingdom or the United States within a two-year period from August 1 & July 31 of the year of the prize. Three books are shortlisted for this prize.

Macaulay Fellowship
The Arts Council/An Chomhairle Ealaion
70 Merrion Sq, Dublin 2
Tel: (01) 618 0200 *Fax:* (01) 676 1302
E-mail: info@artscouncil.ie
Web Site: www.artscouncil.ie
Key Personnel
Dir: Patricia Quinn *Tel:* (01) 618 0225
    E-mail: patricia@artscouncil.ie
Triennial award in literature to young Irish writers who are usually under 30 years of age.
Award: 3,500 GBP

Novel Prize
Irish Academy of Letters, School of Irish Studies
4 Ailesbury Grove, Dundum, Dublin 14
For the best novel written in Irish. Awarded annually.

☆The Prize for Poetry in Irish/An Duais don bhFiliíocht in Gaeilge
The Arts Council/An Chomhairle Ealaion
70 Merrion Sq, Dublin 2
Tel: (01) 618 0200 *Fax:* (01) 676 1302
E-mail: info@artscouncil.ie
Web Site: www.artscouncil.ie
Key Personnel
Dir: Patricia Quinn *Tel:* (01) 618 0225
    E-mail: patricia@artscouncil.ie
Established: 1962
Awarded to the author of the best book of poetry in the Irish language (Gaelic) published in the previous three years.
Award: 1,500 GBP

Rooney Prize for Irish Literature
Rooney Prize Committee
Strathin, Templecarrig, Delgany Co, Wicklow
Tel: (01) 2874769 *Fax:* (01) 2872595
E-mail: rooneyprize@ireland.com
Key Personnel
Chairman: Jim Sherwin *E-mail:* jsherwin@rol.ue
Annual award for Irish Literature. A noncompetitive prize to encourage young Irish creative talent. Enquiries to Jim Sherwin at above address.
Award: 5,000 IRL

Marten Toonder Award
The Arts Council/An Chomhairle Ealaion
70 Merrion Sq, Dublin 2
Tel: (01) 618 0200 *Fax:* (01) 676 1302
E-mail: info@artscouncil.ie
Web Site: www.artscouncil.ie
Key Personnel
Dir: Patricia Quinn *Tel:* (01) 618 0225
    E-mail: patricia@artscouncil.ie
Triennial literature award.
Award: 7,875 GBP - 10,000 GBP

Israel

ACUM Prize for Literature and Music
Society of Authors, Composers and Music Publishers in Israel
PO Box 14220, 61140 Tel Aviv
Tel: (03) 6850115 *Fax:* (03) 5620119
Established: 1957
To encourage creative work in the fields of literature & music. Israeli citizens are eligible.
Award: Monetary prizes annually

Award for Original Hebrew Novel
Mordechai Bernstein Literary Prizes Association
c/o The Book Publishers Association of Israel, 29 Carlebach St, 67132 Tel Aviv
Mailing Address: PO Box 20123, 61201 Tel Aviv
Tel: (03) 5614121 *Fax:* (03) 5611996
E-mail: info@tbpai.co.il
Established: 1981
To encourage authors under the age 50 who write Hebrew novels. Established to honor Mordechal Bernstein, an Israeli author.
Award: Monetary award, biennially

Award for Original Hebrew Poetry
Mordechai Bernstein Literary Prizes Association
c/o The Book Publishers Association of Israel, 29 Carlebach St, 67132 Tel Aviv
Mailing Address: PO Box 20123, 61201 Tel Aviv
Tel: (03) 5614121 *Fax:* (03) 5611996
E-mail: info@tbpai.co.il
Established: 1981
To encourage Hebrew poets under the age of 50. Established in honor of Mordechai Bernstein, an Israeli author.
Award: A monetary prize is awarded biennially

Bialik Prize for Literature
Tel-Aviv-Yafo Municipality
Dept of Municipal Prizes, Tel Aviv
The highest literary award of the Tel-Aviv-Yafo Municipality, awarded in two categories: belles-lettres & Jewish studies.
Award: 80,000 shekels awarded annually

Brenner Prize
Hebrew Writers' Association in Israel
PO Box 7111, Tel Aviv
Tel: (03) 253-256
In recognition of outstanding literary works.
Award: 12,000 shekels awarded annually

Israeli Prize in Humanities and Social Sciences
Israeli Ministry of Education and Culture
Rechov Shivtei Yisrael 34, 91911 Jerusalem
Tel: (02) 278211
For the most original, outstanding contribution to the humanities & social sciences. Prize awarded annually in each one of the following areas: (1) Judaica, Modern Hebrew Literature & Education; (2) the Humanities & the Social Sciences; (3) the Arts; (4) Science & Technology; (5) outstanding life-long service to the welfare of Israeli society.
Award: 110,000 shekels

☆The Jerusalem Prize For Freedom of the Individual in Society
Jerusalem International Book Fair
PO Box 775, Jerusalem 91007
Tel: (02) 629 7922; (02) 629 6412 *Fax:* (02) 624 3144
E-mail: jerfairs@jerusalem.muni.il
Web Site: www.jerusalembookfair.com
Key Personnel
Chairman & Man Dir: Zev Birger
Contact: Annette Aaronson
Established: 1963
Biennial award made to a world-renowned author whose works express the idea of the freedom of the individual in society.
Award: $5,000 cash
Presented: Jerusalem International Book Fair

Shazar Prize
Israel Ministry of Education & Culture
Rechov Shivtei Yisrael 34, 91911 Jerusalem
Tel: (02) 278-211
Awarded to immigrant writers, young authors & writers dealing with the Holocaust.
Award: 5,000 to 12,000 shekels to each author, awarded annually

Tchernichowsky Prize
Tel-Aviv-Yafo Municipality
Dept of Municipal Prizes, Tel Aviv
For outstanding translations into Hebrew. 60,000 shekels divided between two translators: one of belles-lettres & one of scientific material. Awarded biennially.
Award: 60,000 shekels divided

Italy

Andersen Prize
Sestri Levante Municipality
Piazza Matteotti 3, Sestri Levante, GE
Tel: (0187) 257213 *Fax:* (0187) 767378
E-mail: info@artificio23.it
Web Site: www.premioandersen.it

Key Personnel
Artistic Dir: Leonardo Pischedda
To recognize the year's best fairy tale for children. Professional or amateur writers are eligible.

Bagutta Prize
Bagutta Restaurant
via Bagutta 14, 20121 Milan
Tel: (02) 76000902; (02) 76002767 *Fax:* (02) 799613
Web Site: www.bagutta.it; www.acena.it/bagutta
Founded in 1926 for the best book of the year. Annual award given for several literary forms including the novel & poetry.

☆BolognaRagazzi Award
Bologna Children's Book Fair
Viale della Fiera 20, 40128 Bologna
Tel: (051) 282213; (051) 282111 *Fax:* (051) 6374040
Web Site: www.bookfair.bolognafiere.it
Key Personnel
Contact: Marisa del Todesco *E-mail:* marisa.deltodesco@bolognafiere.it
Established: 1966
Annual award aimed to focus attention on publishing houses of emerging countries (Arab world, Latin America, Asia & Africa) where children's literature offers new angles free of well-established traditions.

Isle of Elba - Rafaello Brignetti Literary Award
Premio Letterario Isola d'Elba - Raffaello Brignetti
c/o Consorzio Elba Promotion, Calata Italia 26, 57037 Portoferraio LI
Tel: (056) 5960157 *Fax:* (056) 5917632
E-mail: elbapro@elba2000.it
Annual award for recognition of outstanding works of prose, poetry, or literary essays. Works by European authors published in Italy or translated into Italian during the previous year are eligible. Formerly Premio Letterario Isola d'Elba. Renamed in 1984 in honor of Raffaello Brignetti.
Award: 5,165 EUR

Campiello Prize
Campiello Foundation
Via Torino, 151/c, 30172 Mestre-Venice
Tel: (041) 2517511 *Fax:* (041) 2517576
E-mail: campiello@industrialiveneto.org
Web Site: www.premiocampiello.org
Telex: 420380
Established: 1963
Promoted by the seven industrial association founder members of Fondazione Campiello. Annual award for a previously unpublished work of fiction.
Award: 8,263 EUR

☆Giosue Carduccie Prize
Bologna University
via Zamboni 33, I-40100 Bologna
Tel: (51) 228621
Established: 1950
For poetry, monographs & essays on poetry & poets. Awarded annually.
Award: 775 EUR

Castello-Sanguinetto Prize
Comune di Sanquinetto
Interno Castello 2, 37058 Sanguinetto VR
Tel: (0442) 81036 *Fax:* (0442) 365150
E-mail: info@comune.sanguinetto.vr.it
Web Site: www.comune.sanguinetto.vr.it
Established: 1951
Awarded annually to encourage the development of novels for young readers between 11 & 14 years of age. The novel must be published in Italy before July 15 of the current year. Established by Professor Giulletto Accordi.
Other Sponsor(s): Cassa di Risparmio di Verona - Vicenza e Belluno
Award: 1st prize 2,066 EUR

Certamen Capitolinum
Istituto Nazionale di Studi Romani
Piazza dei Cavalieri di Malta, 2, 00153 Rome
Tel: (06) 5743442; (06) 5743445 *Fax:* (06) 5743447
E-mail: studiromani@studiromani.it
Web Site: www.studiromani.it
Key Personnel
President: Prof Mario Mazza
Dir: Dr Fernanda Roscetti
Established: 1950
Awarded annually to provide recognition for the best works on the Latin language & literature. Teachers, scholars & students are eligible.
Award: 1st prize 600,000 ITL & a silver sculpture of a she-wolf; 2nd prize 300,000 ITL & a silver medallion; 3rd prize 100,000 ITL & a diploma (to students); Honorable Mentions

☆Antonio Feltrinelli Prize
Accademia Nazionale dei Lincei (National Italian Academy of Sciences)
Palazzo Corsini, Via della Lungara 10, 00165 Rome
Tel: (06) 68307831 *Fax:* (06) 6893616
E-mail: ufficio.premi@lincei.it
Web Site: www.lincei.it
Annual prizes for accomplishment in the various branches of sciences, humanities & literature. These prizes were instituted by an Italian businessman who died in 1942 & bequeathed his fortune to the academy for the purpose of "rewarding toil, study, intelligence . . . those men who with greater success distinguished themselves with high achievements in art & science, since they are the true benefactors of their own country as well as of all humanity". The literature award is granted every five years & the amount varies.

Grinzane Cavour Prize
Grinzane Cavour Prize Association (Premio Grinzane Cavour)
Via Montebello 21, 10124 Turin
Tel: (011) 8100111 *Fax:* (011) 8125456
E-mail: info@grinzane.it
Web Site: www.grinzane.it
Established: 1982
To encourage the diffusion of reading in the Italian school, especially of books of contemporary fiction. Literary critics, scholars, writers, journalists & people in the world of Italian culture judge the books. Established by Prof. Giuliano Soria. Awarded annually in five categories: contemporary Italian fiction; contemporary foreign fiction translated into Italian; an international prize for the complete works of a foreign writer; young beginning author, aged less than forty; essay writing.
Other Sponsor(s): Fondazione Cassa di Risparmio di Torino; Provincia di Torino; Regione Piemonte; SEAT
Award: International prize for the complete works of a foreign writer - 5,165 EUR; all others 3,615 EUR

☆Naples Prize
Fondazione Premio Napoli
Palazzo Reale, Piazza del Plebiscito, 80132 Naples
Tel: (081) 403187; (081) 422362 *Fax:* (081) 402023
E-mail: fnp@fondazionepremionapoli.it
Web Site: www.premionapoli.it
Key Personnel
Contact: Carmen Petillo
Established: 1954
Annual award for recognition of an outstanding work of literature in Italian. Italian & non-Italian authors are eligible.
Award: 10,000,000 ITL & plaque

Laura Orvieto Prize
Fondazione Premio Laura Orvieto
Archivo Contemporaneo del Gabinetto, GP Vieusseux, Via Maggio 42, I-50125 Florence
Tel: (055) 697877; (055) 697981; (055) 697946
Established: 1954
Monetary prize awarded biennially to provide recognition for the manuscript of a book of fiction for children from 8 to 11 years of age. Italian authors are eligible. Established by Adriana Guasconi Orvieto in memory of Laura Orvieto.

☆Premio Langhe Ceretto
Biblioteca Civica G Ferrero
Loc San Cassiano 34, 12051 Alba CN
Tel: (0173) 282582 *Fax:* (0173) 282383
E-mail: ceretto@ceretto.com
Web Site: www.ceretto.com
Key Personnel
Secretary: Dr Gianfranco Maggi
Established: 1991
Annual food & wine culture prize.

Strega Prize
Fondazione Marie e Goffredo Bellonci
via Marciana Marina, 58, 00138 Rome
Tel: (06) 88327652 *Fax:* (06) 8109668
E-mail: fond.bellonci@flashnet.it
Web Site: www.fondazionebellonci.com
Key Personnel
President: Antonio Maccanico
Dir: Anna Maria Rimoaldi
Established: 1947
Founded by Maria Bellonci & Guido Alberti for a work of fiction.

Viareggio Prizes
Premio Viareggio
Via Francesco Borgatti 25, 00191 Rome
Tel: (06) 3293736
Established: 1929
Since 1967, the annual award has been divided into three sections: fiction, nonfiction & poetry. Given to foreign writers & poets.
Award: 12,911 EUR

Japan

Female Writers Literary Award (Joryu Bungaku Award)
Chuokoron-Shinsha Inc
2-8-7 Kyobashi, Chou-ku, Tokyo 104-8320
Tel: (03) 3563-1261 *Fax:* (03) 3561-5920
E-mail: honyaku-irie@chuko.co.jp
Web Site: www.chuko.co.jp
Established: 1961
Annual award for the best work of fiction by a woman.
Award: 1,000,000 JPY & commemorative plaque

Gunzo for Fiction du Critique Prize
Kodansha Ltd
2-12-21 Otowa, Bunkyo-ku, Tokyo 112-8001
Tel: (03) 3946-6201 *Fax:* (03) 3944-9915
Web Site: www.kodansha.co.jp; www.kodanclub.com
Established: 1967

To provide recognition for an outstanding work of fiction by a new writer. Formerly known as the Gunzo Fiction Prize.
Award: 500,000 yen

Japan Translation Prize for Publisher
Japan Society of Translators
c/o Orion Press, 1-13 Kanda-Jimbocho, Chiyoda-ku, Tokyo 101
Tel: (03) 32943936 *Fax:* (03) 33061251
Awarded annually for outstanding translations.

Kodansha Cultural Prize in Publishing for Book Design
Kodansha Ltd
2-12-21 Otowa, Bunkyo-ku, Tokyo 112-8001
Tel: (03) 3946-6201 *Fax:* (03) 3944-9915
Web Site: www.kodansha.co.jp; www.kodanclub.com
Award: 1,000,000 yen

Kodansha Cultural Prize in Publishing for Illustrations
Kodansha Ltd
2-12-21 Otowa, Bunkyo-ku, Tokyo 112-8001
Tel: (03) 3946-6201 *Fax:* (03) 3944-9915
Web Site: www.kodansha.co.jp; www.kodanclub.com
Key Personnel
Contact: Tetsu Shirai
Established: 1970
Awarded annually to the best work of illustration.
Award: 1,000,000 yen

Kodansha Cultural Prize in Publishing for Photographs
Kodansha Ltd
2-12-21 Otowa, Bunkyo-ku, Tokyo 112-8001
Tel: (03) 3946-6201 *Fax:* (03) 3944-9915
Web Site: www.kodansha.co.jp; www.kodanclub.com
Award: 1,000,000 yen

Kodansha Cultural Prize in Publishing for Picture Books
Kodansha Ltd
2-12-21 Otowa, Bunkyo-ku, Tokyo 112-8001
Tel: (03) 3946-6201 *Fax:* (03) 3944-9915
Web Site: www.kodansha.co.jp; www.kodanclub.com
Key Personnel
Contact: Tetsu Shirai
Established: 1970
Awarded annually for the most outstanding picture book.
Award: 1,000,000 yen

Kodansha Essay Prize
Kodansha Ltd
2-12-21 Otowa, Bunkyo-ku, Tokyo 112-8001
Tel: (03) 3946-6201 *Fax:* (03) 3944-9915
Web Site: www.kodansha.co.jp; www.kodanclub.com
Key Personnel
Contact: Tetsu Shirai
Established: 1985
Annual award for the best essay.
Award: 1,000,000 yen

Kodansha Nonfiction Prize
Kodansha Ltd
2-12-21 Otowa, Bunkyo-ku, Tokyo 112-8001
Tel: (03) 3946-6201 *Fax:* (03) 3944-9915
Web Site: www.kodansha.co.jp; www.kodanclub.com
Key Personnel
Contact: Tetsu Shirai
Established: 1979
Annual award for the best nonfiction work.
Award: 1,000,000 yen

Kodansha Prize for Comics
Kodansha Ltd
2-12-21 Otowa, Bunkyo-ku, Tokyo 112-8001
Tel: (03) 3946-6201 *Fax:* (03) 3944-9915
Web Site: www.kodansha.co.jp; www.kodanclub.com
Award: 1,000,000 yen

Yukio Mishima Award
Shincho-Sha Co Ltd
71 Yaraicho, Shinjuku-ku, Tokyo 162-0805
Tel: (03) 3266-5411 *Fax:* (03) 3266-5534
E-mail: matsuie@shinchosha.co.jp
Web Site: www.shinchosha.co.jp
Established: 1987
Annual award for a literary work (novel, criticism, poetry, drama) written by a new or moderately well-known writer & published during the preceding year.
Award: 1,000,000 JPY & commemorative plaque

Noma Award for Publishing in Africa
Kodansha Ltd
2-12-21 Otowa, Bunkyo-ku, Tokyo 112-8001
Tel: (01993) 775235; (03) 3946-6201
   Fax: (01993) 709265; (03) 3944-9915
Web Site: www.nomaaward.org; www.kodanclub.com
Key Personnel
Secretary to the NOMA Award Managing Committee: Mary Jay *E-mail:* maryljay@aol.com
Established: 1979
Established by the late Shoichi Noma, former President of the Japanese publishing company Kodansha Ltd, for African writers & scholars whose work is published in Africa. The annual award is given for an outstanding work in any of the following categories: (1) scholarly or academic, (2) children's books, (3) literature & creative writing (including fiction, drama or poetry).
Award: 10,000 USD & commemorative plaque
Closing Date: Feb 28
Presented: Various places, mainly within Africa

Noma Award for the Translation of Japanese Literature
Kodansha Ltd
2-12-21 Otowa, Bunkyo-ku, Tokyo 112-8001
Tel: (03) 3946-6201 *Fax:* (03) 3944-9915
Web Site: www.kodansha.co.jp; www.kodanclub.com
Key Personnel
President: Sawako Noma
Established: 1990
For the best translation of a post-1926 Japanese novel or essay.
Award: 10,000 USD

Noma Concours for Children's Picture Book Illustrations
Kodansha Ltd
2-12-21 Otowa, Bunkyo-ku, Tokyo 112-8001
Tel: (03) 3946-6201 *Fax:* (03) 3944-9915
Web Site: www.kodansha.co.jp; www.kodanclub.com
Key Personnel
President: Sawako Noma
Established to promote high standards in children's book illustration.
Award: 2,000 USD

Noma Juvenile Literature Prize for New Writers
Kodansha Ltd
2-12-21 Otowa, Bunkyo-ku, Tokyo 112-8001
Tel: (03) 3946-6201 *Fax:* (03) 3944-9915
Web Site: www.kodansha.co.jp; www.kodansha.co.jp
Key Personnel
Contact: Tetsu Shirai
Established: 1963
Annual award for the best juvenile novel by a new writer.
Award: 1,000,000 yen

Noma Literacy Prize
Kodansha Ltd
2-12-21 Otowa, Bunkyo-ku, Tokyo 112-8001
Tel: (03) 3946-6201 *Fax:* (03) 3944-9915
Web Site: www.kodansha.co.jp; www.kodanclub.com
Key Personnel
President: Sawako Noma
Established to honor an individual or group working to improve literacy levels in the Third World.
Award: 10,000 USD

Noma Literature Prize for New Writers
Kodansha Ltd
2-12-21 Otowa, Bunkyo-ku, Tokyo 112-8001
Tel: (03) 3946-6201 *Fax:* (03) 3944-9915
Web Site: www.kodansha.co.jp; www.kodanclub.com
Key Personnel
Contact: Tetsu Shirai
Established: 1979
Annual award for the best novel by a new writer.
Award: 1,000,000 yen

Noma Prize for Juvenile Literature
Kodansha Ltd
2-12-21 Otowa, Bunkyo-ku, Tokyo 112-8001
Tel: (03) 3946-6201 *Fax:* (03) 3944-9915
Web Site: www.kodansha.co.jp; www.kodanclub.com
Key Personnel
Contact: Tetsu Shirai
Established: 1963
Annual award for the best juvenile novel.
Award: 2,000,000 yen

Noma Prize for Literature
Kodansha Ltd
2-12-21 Otowa, Bunkyo-ku, Tokyo 112-8001
Tel: (03) 3946-6201 *Fax:* (03) 3944-9915
Web Site: www.kodansha.co.jp; www.kodanclub.com
Key Personnel
Contact: Tetsu Shirai
Established: 1941
Annual award for the best Japanese novel of the year.
Award: 3,000,000 yen

Osaragi Jiro Prize
Asahi Shimbun Publishing Co
Osaragi Jiro Prize Office, 5-3-2 Tsukiji, Chou-ku, Tokyo 104-8011
Tel: (03) 3545-0131
Web Site: www.asahi.com
Established: 1974
Annual award for recognition of outstanding prose work. Established in memory of Jiro Osaragi, one of the most popular novelists in Japan.
Award: 2,000,000 yen & plaque

Oya Soichi Nonfiction Prize
The Society for the Promotion of Japanese Literature
c/o Bungei Shunju Bldg, 3-23 Kioi-cho, Chiyoda-ku, Tokyo 102-8008
Tel: (03) 3265-1211 *Fax:* (03) 3265-2624
Key Personnel
Contact: Kazukiyo Takahashi
Established: 1969
Annual award to encourage new nonfiction writers.
Award: 1,000,000 yen

Printing Culture Prize
Japan Federation of Printing Industries
1-16-8 Shintomi, Chuo-ku, Tokyo 104-0041
Tel: (03) 3552-4571
E-mail: info@jfpi.or.jp
Web Site: www.jfpi.or.jp
Established: 1987
To provide recognition in the field of printing for a work that is artistically, historically & academically valuable. Formerly, Insatsu Bunka Sho. Awarded every 4 years.
Award: Monetary award & plaque

Shincho Gakugei-Sho
Shincho-Sha Co Ltd
71 Yaraicho, Shinjuku-ku, Tokyo 162-0805
Tel: (03) 3266-5411 *Fax:* (03) 3266-5534
E-mail: matsuie@shinchosha.co.jp
Web Site: www.shinchosha.co.jp
Established: 1987
Annual award for a creative work of nonfiction contributing to Japanese art, literature or culture & published during the preceding year.
Award: 1,000,000 JPY & commemorative gift

Tanizaki Jun'ichiro Prize
Chuokoron-Shinsha Inc
2-8-7 Kyobashi, Chuo-ku, Tokyo 104-8320
Tel: (03) 3563-1261 *Fax:* (03) 3561-5920
E-mail: honyaku-irie@chuko.co.jp
Web Site: www.chuko.co.jp
Established: 1965
Annual award to recall the works by Tanizaki & to celebrate the publisher's birthday.
Award: 1,000,000 JPY & commemorative plaque

Shugoro Yamamoto Award
Shincho-Sha Co Ltd
71 Yaraicho, Shinjuku-ku, Tokyo 162-0805
Tel: (03) 3266-5411 *Fax:* (03) 3266-5534
E-mail: matsuie@shinchosha.co.jp
Web Site: www.shinchosha.co.jp
Established: 1987
Annual award for an outstanding novel written by a new or moderately well-known writer & published during the preceding year.
Award: 1,000,000 JPY & commemorative plaque

Yomiuri Literature Prize
Yomiuri Newspapers Publishing Co
c/o Office of International Affairs, 1-7-1 Otemachi, Chiyoda-ku, Tokyo 100-8055
Tel: (03) 3242-1111 *Fax:* (03) 3246-0888
Web Site: www.yomiuri.co.jp
Established: 1948
Annual award for the best work in six categories: novel, essay & travels, drama, literary study & translation, poetry & haiku, critique & biography.
Award: 1,000,000 yen, per category & commemorative inkstone

Yoshikawa Eiji Cultural Prize
Kodansha Ltd
2-12-21 Otowa, Bunkyo-ku, Tokyo 112-8001
Tel: (03) 3946-6201 *Fax:* (03) 3944-9915
Web Site: www.kodansha.co.jp; www.kodanclub.com
Award: 1,000,000 yen

Yoshikawa Eiji Literature Prize
Kodansha Ltd
2-12-21 Otowa, Bunkyo-ku, Tokyo 112-8001
Tel: (03) 3946-6201 *Fax:* (03) 3944-9915
Web Site: www.kodansha.co.jp; www.kodanclub.com
Key Personnel
Contact: Tetsu Shirai
Established: 1967
Annual award for a popular novel.
Award: 3,000,000 yen & commemorative plaque

Yoshikawa Eiji Literature Prize for New Writers
Kodansha Ltd
2-12-21 Otowa, Bunkyo-ku, Tokyo 112-8001
Tel: (03) 3946-6201 *Fax:* (03) 3944-9915
Web Site: www.kodansha.co.jp; www.kodanclub.com
Key Personnel
Contact: Tetsu Shirai
Established: 1980
Annual award to recognize the most promising work of fiction by a new writer published during the preceding year.
Award: 1,000,000 yen & commemorative plaque

Kenya

Jomo Kenyatta Prize for Literature
Kenya Publishers Association
Occidental Plaza, 4th floor, Muthithi Rd, East & Central Africa, Nairobi
Mailing Address: PO Box 42767, Nairobi 00100
Tel: (02) 3752344
E-mail: kenyapublishers@wananchi.com
Web Site: www.kenyabooks.org
Key Personnel
Executive Secretary: Lynnette Kariuki
Established: 1974
Awarded annually to provide recognition for an outstanding literary work written in the English or Swahili languages. Only Kenyan authors are eligible.
Other Sponsor(s): Text Book Centre
Award: Monetary
Closing Date: Mid-year, biannually
Presented: Nairobi International Book Fair, Late Sept, biannually

Republic of Korea

Korean Literature Translation Award
Korean Literature Translation Institute
Seojin Bldg, 5th floor, 149-1 Pyeong-dong, Jongno-gu, Seoul 110-102
Tel: (02) 732-1422 *Fax:* (02) 732-1443
E-mail: info@ltikorea.net
Web Site: www.ltikorea.net
Key Personnel
Contact: Park Eun Young
Established: 1993
Awarded biennially as part of the Korean government's efforts to introduce & promote Korean literary works overseas through translation.
Award: $60,000

Liechtenstein

Liechtenstein-Preis zur Foerderung Zeitgenoessischer Literatur (Liechtenstein Prize for the Advancement of Literature)
Liechtenstein PEN Centre
PO Box 416, 9490 Vaduz
Tel: (0423) 2327271 *Fax:* (0423) 2328071
E-mail: info@pen-club.li
Web Site: www.pen-club.li
Established: 1980

Luxembourg

Trophee International de la Reliure d'Art (Art of Bookbinding International Trophy)
ARA International
58, Domaine Mehlstrachen, 6942 Niederanven
Tel: 34 85 91 *Fax:* 34 85 91

Madagascar

Literature Prize
Malagasy Ministry of Culture, Communication & Leisure
Antsahovola, BP 305, 101 Tananrive
Tel: (02) 27092
For an outstanding novel. 130,000 Malagasy francs. Awarded every two years.

Malaysia

Anugerah Sastera Negara Prize
Dewan Bahasa dan Pustaka
Peti Surat 10803, 50926 Kuala Lumpur
Tel: (03) 21481011 *Fax:* (03) 2482726; (03) 2142005; (03) 21414109; (03) 2148420
Web Site: www.dbp.gov.my
Telex: 32683 DBP MA
Established: 1980
National Literary Award. The highest governmental award to an author writing in the national language, who has made a major contribution to the development of the country's literature.
Award: 30,000 MYR, publication facilities & other benefits

Dewan Bahasa Dan Pustaka Prize
Dewan Bahasa Dan Pustaka
Peti Surat 10803, 50926 Kuala Lumpur
Tel: (03) 21481011 *Fax:* (03) 21482726; (03) 2142005; (03) 21414109; (03) 2148420
Web Site: www.dbp.gov.my
Established: 1982
Malaysian Literary Prize. Awarded by the Malaysian Government biennially for creative writing in the national language, covering short story, novel, poetry & drama, & with the aim of encouraging new talent & enhancing the quality of the national literature.

Mexico

Concurso de Cuento de Ciencia Ficcion (Science Fiction Story Competition)
National Autonomous University of Mexico, Ciudad Universitaria
Delegacion - Coyoacan, 04510 Mexico, DF
Tel: (055) 5505215

Jorge Cuesta National Poetry Prize
Gobierno del Estado de Veracruz-Llave
Instituto Veracruzano de Cultura Francisco Canal s/n esq, 91700 Veracruz
Tel: (029) 316994; (029) 316967 *Fax:* (029) 316962

MEXICO

☆Rafael Heliodoro Valle Prize
National Library of Mexico
Insurgentes Sur 3000, Centro Cultural Universitario, 04510 Mexico, DF
Tel: (055) 6226801 *Fax:* (055) 650951
Established: 1976
Founded to reward an especially notable writer (in odd-numbered years; in even numbered years to an historian for research work & synthesis). The candidate must have been born in Latin America, over age 50 & the work written in Spanish or Portuguese.
Award: 20,000,000 MXN, plus diploma & gold medal

National Prize for Linguistics & Literature
Senate of the Republic
Insurgentes Sur No 2387, piso 3, Col San Angel, CP 01000 Mexico, DF
Tel: (05) 7236620; (05) 7236622
Annual award for the best literary works in the fields of the novel, poetry, essay, biography, drama & motion picture scriptwriting.
Award: 100,000 pesos

Premio Internacional de Novela Nuevo Leon
(Nuevo Leon International Novel Prize)
Ediciones Castillo SA de CV
Privada Francisco L Rocha No 7, Col San Jeronimo,, Monterrey CP 64630
Tel: (081) 8347-6215; (081) 8347-6275
Fax: (081) 8333-2804
E-mail: castillo@edicionescastillo.com.mx
Web Site: www.edicionescastillo.com

☆Alfonso Reyes Prize
Senate of the Republic
Consejo del Premio Nacional de Ciencias y Artes, Argentina 28, Oficina 124, 06029 Mexico, DF
Tel: (05) 7236620
Established: 1973
Awarded by the Federal Government of Mexico to an author of any nationality for his or her literary output on the study of the works of Alfonso Reyes or on Mexico.
Award: 20,000,000 pesos

Jose Ruben Romero (Premio de Novela Jose Ruben Romero)
Instituto Nacional de Bellas Artes
Morelos Norte No 485, Centro, Morelia Michoacan, CP 58000 Mexico
Tel: (05) 5207241 *Fax:* (05) 5202724
Established: 1978
Annual award to recognize unpublished novels of outstanding literary quality by authors in the Spanish language who are residents of Mexico. Works to be considered should be 120-300 pages in length. Established in memory of the Mexican author.
Other Sponsor(s): State of Michoacan
Award: 80,000,000 MXN & certificate
Closing Date: Aug 1

Juan Rulfo First Novel Prize (Premio Juan Rulfo Para Primera Novela)
Instituto Nacional de Bellas Artes
Av Juarez No 62, Centro, CP 90000 Tlaxcala
Tel: (05) 5207241 *Fax:* (05) 5202724
Established: 1980
Annual award to recognize the best first novel by an author in the Spanish language residing in Mexico. Works to be considered should be 120-300 pages in length. Established in memory of the Mexican author.
Other Sponsor(s): State of Guerrero
Award: 10,000,000 MXN & certificate
Closing Date: Aug 11

Premio Xavier Villaurrutia de Escritores para Escritores
Sociedad Alfonsina Internacional AC
Ave Transmisiones 42, 01790 Mexico, DF
Tel: (055) 6831217
Annual prizes for poetry, prose, novel, short story, drama or essays by new or young authors.
Award: 50,000 MXN

Monaco

☆Prix Litteraire Prince Pierre-de-Monaco
Foundation Prince Pierre de Monaco
Centre de Presse, 10, quai Antoine-ler, 98000 Monte Carlo
Tel: (093) 15 22 22 *Fax:* (093) 15 22 15
E-mail: lcalvas@gouv.mc
Key Personnel
Administrator: Beatrice Dunoyer *Tel:* (093) 158776
Secretary General: Rainier Rocchi
Established: 1951
Restricted to French-speaking writers. Annual award for the entire literary work of one author. No applications accepted.
Award: 100,000 FRF

Myanmar

National Literary Awards
Sarpay Beikman Public Library
529 Merchant St, Yangon
When the Burma Translation Society (now renamed Sarpay Beikman Board) was founded in 1947 it established the Best-Published-Novel-of-the-Year Prize with prize money of K1000. The awards were gradually increased & in 1962 Sarpay Beikman was offering nine awards.
When Sarpay Beikman was taken over by the Revolutionary Government in August 1963 the awards were transformed into National Literary Awards. More literary awards were gradually added & there are now 13 awards for the best published novel of the year, the best collection of short stories, the best belles letters, the best book of knowledge (arts), the best book of knowledge (science), the best book of poems, the best translation of a world classic, the best translation in the general knowledge field, the best published play, the best book for children, the best book for youth, the best book on Burmese culture & the best book on political affairs.
Each national literary award now draws prize money of K6000.

Netherlands

Henriette de Beaufort-prijs (Henriette de Beaufort Prize)
Maatschappij der Nederlandse Letterkunde (Society of Netherlands Literature)
Witte Singel 27, Universiteitsbibliotheek Leiden, 2300 RA Leiden
Mailing Address: PO Box 9501, 2300 RA Leiden
Tel: (071) 5272832 *Fax:* (071) 5272836
E-mail: mnl@library.leidenuniv.nl
Web Site: www.leidenuniv.nl/host/mnl
Key Personnel
Secretary: Dr Leo L van Maris
Established: 1985
Awarded triennially to recognize the author of a biographical work. Awarded alternately to a Dutch & a Flemish author.
Award: 2,500 EUR

F Bordewijk Prize
Jan Campert Foundation
PO Box 12654, 2500 DP The Hague
Tel: (070) 3533637 *Fax:* (070) 3533058
Key Personnel
Secretary: A P Spijkers
For the best Dutch novel.
Award: 10,000 Dutch florins awarded annually

Jan Campert Prize
Jan Campert Foundation
PO Box 12654, 2500 DP The Hague
Tel: (070) 3533637 *Fax:* (070) 3533058
Key Personnel
Secretary: A P Spijkers
For outstanding Dutch poetry.
Award: 10,000 Dutch florins awarded annually

Hendrik de Vries Award
City Council of Groningen
Trompsingel 27, 9724 DA Groningen
Tel: (050) 3676254 *Fax:* (050) 3676249
Established: 2001
To recognize achievement in or contribution to literature & the visual arts. The entry must, in some way, be related to Groningen or to the work of Hendrik de Vries. Established in honor of Hendrik de Vries (1896-1989), a poet & painter.
Award: 5,672 EUR awarded to young artists. The award has to be used to create some kind of art project

Frans Erensprijs
Stichting Frans Erensprijs
Europalaan 49, 6226 CN Maastricht
Tel: (043) 3635340
Established: 1986
Awarded every three years to recognize a Dutch author for memoirs, essays, or creative literary works in prose or poetry. Named for Frans Erens, a Dutch author (1857-1935).
Award: 5,165 EUR

Dr Wijnaendts Francken Prijs
Maatschappij der Nederlandse Letterkunde (Society of Netherlands Literature)
Universiteitsbibliotheek Leiden, Witte Singel 27, 2300 RA Leiden
Mailing Address: PO Box 9501, 2300 RA Leiden
Tel: (071) 5272832 *Fax:* (071) 5272836
E-mail: mnl@library.leidenuniv.nl
Web Site: www.leidenuniv.nl/host/mnl
Key Personnel
Secretary: Dr Leo L van Maris
Established: 1934
Awarded triennially for a work written in Dutch alternately in one of following categories: (1) essays & literary criticism, (2) cultural history.
Award: 2,500 EUR

Gold Pencil, Gouden Griffel
Collective Promotion of the Netherlands Book
Keizersgracht 391, 1016 EJ Amsterdam
Mailing Address: Postbus 10576, 1001 EN Amsterdam
Tel: (020) 6264971 *Fax:* (020) 6231696
E-mail: info@cpnb.nl
Web Site: www.cpnb.nl
Established: 1971
Award for the best Dutch children's books - A Golden Slate & 3,000 DFL. For Dutch or foreign, translated books - Silver Slate Pencils

(maximum 8). Also a Golden Brush & 3,000 DFL for the best Dutch illustrated children's book & two silver Brushes for Dutch or foreign, translated illustrated work. Awarded annually. Occasionally a Golden Key for children's/young persons' book with new developments (technically or in subject matter) is awarded.

☆Herman Gorterprijs (Poezie) (Herman Gorter Prize (Poetry))
Amsterdams Fonds voor de Kunst (Amsterdam Funds for the Arts)
Herengracht 609, 1017 CE Amsterdam
Tel: (020) 520 0520 *Fax:* (020) 623 8389
E-mail: afk@afk.nl
Web Site: www.afk.nl
Established: 1972
Subsidies, grants & prizes for the arts. Annual art awards of the city of Amsterdam; no application.

The G H's-Gravesande Prize
Jan Campert Foundation
PO Box 12654, 2500 DP The Hague
Tel: (070) 3533637 *Fax:* (070) 3533058
Key Personnel
Secretary: A P Spijkers
For special services to literature.
Award: 10,000 Dutch florins awarded triennially

J Greshoff Prize
Jan Campert Foundation
PO Box 12654, 2500 DP The Hague
Tel: (070) 3533637 *Fax:* (070) 3533058
Key Personnel
Secretary: A P Spijkers
For the best Dutch essay.
Award: 10,000 Dutch florins awarded biennially

Nienke van Hichtum Prize
Jan Campert Foundation
PO Box 12654, 2500 DP The Hague
Tel: (070) 3533637 *Fax:* (070) 3533058
Key Personnel
Secretary: A P Spijkers
For the best Dutch children's book.
Award: 10,000 Dutch florins awarded every two years

P C Hooft Prize for Literature
Boekblad
Frederiksplein 1, 1017 XK Amsterdam
Mailing Address: Postbus 15007, 1001 MA Amsterdam
Tel: (020) 625 31 31 *Fax:* (020) 622 09 08
E-mail: redactie@boekblad.kvb.nl
Web Site: www.boekblad.nl
For important & original literary works in Dutch. Awarded annually where possible: one year for poetry, the next year for prose, the next year for literary essay.

Lucy B & C W van der Hoogt Prize
Maatschappij der Nederlandse Letterkunde (Society of Netherlands Literature)
Universiteitsbibliotheek Leiden, Witte Singel 27, 2300 RA Leiden
Mailing Address: PO Box 9501, 2300 RA Leiden
Tel: (071) 5272832 *Fax:* (071) 5272836
E-mail: mnl@library.leidenuniv.nl
Web Site: www.leidenuniv.nl/host/mnl
Key Personnel
Secretary: Dr Leo L van Maris
Established: 1921
Awarded annually to a promising Dutch or Flemish writer.
Award: 6,000 EUR & a medal

Busken Huetprijs (Essay/biografie) (Busken Huet Prize (Essay/Biography))
Amsterdams Fonds voor de Kunst (Amsterdam Funds for the Arts)
Herengracht 609, 1017 CE Amsterdam
Tel: (020) 520 0520 *Fax:* (020) 623 8389
E-mail: afk@afk.nl
Web Site: www.afk.nl
Established: 1973
Subsidies, grants & prizes for the arts. Annual art awards of the city of Amsterdam; award cannot be applied for.

Constantijn Huygens Prize
Jan Campert Foundation
PO Box 12654, 2500 DP The Hague
Tel: (070) 3533637 *Fax:* (070) 3533058
Key Personnel
Secretary: A P Spijkers
To a distinguished Dutch author for all his works.
Award: 20,000 Dutch florins awarded annually

Charlotte Kohlerprijs
Stichting Charlotte Kohler
Postbus 19750, 1000 GT Amsterdam
Tel: (020) 5206130 *Fax:* (020) 6238499
E-mail: info@cultuurfonds.nl
Web Site: www.cultuurfonds.nl
Key Personnel
Contact: Mrs A de Boer
Award: 5,000 EUR

Multatuli Prize
Amsterdam City Government, Stichting Amsterdams Fonds voor de Kunst
Herengracht 609, 1017 CE Amsterdam
Tel: (020) 5200520 *Fax:* (020) 6238389
E-mail: afk@afk.nl
Web Site: www.afk.nl
Key Personnel
Contact: Desmond Spruyt
Established: 1972
Subsidies, grants & prizes for the arts.

Prijs der Nederlandse Letteren
Nederlandse Taalunie (Dutch Language Union)
Lange Voorhout 19, 2514 EB The Hague
Mailing Address: Postbus 10595, 2501 HN The Hague
Tel: (070) 346 95 48 *Fax:* (070) 365 98 18
E-mail: info@taalunie.org
Web Site: www.taalunie.org
Key Personnel
General Secretary: Koen Jaspaert
Established: 1956
Triennial award to the most outstanding prose writer, essay writer, drama writer or poet in the Netherlands or in Belgium writing in Dutch.
Award: 16,000 EUR

☆Martinus Nijhoff Prijs voor Vertalingen (Martinus Nijhoff Prize for Translators)
Prince Bernhard Cultural Foundation
Herengracht 476, 1017 CB Amsterdam
Mailing Address: Postbus 19750, 1000 GT Amsterdam
Tel: (020) 5206130 *Fax:* (020) 6238499
E-mail: info@cultuurfonds.nl
Web Site: www.cultuurfonds.nl
Established: 1953
Annual award for translation of literary work into & from Dutch.
Award: 50,000 EUR

Henriette Roland Holst Prijs
Maatschappij der Nederlandse Letterkunde (Society of Netherlands Literature)
Universiteitsbibliotheek Leiden, Witte Singel 27, 2300 RA Leiden
Mailing Address: PO Box 9501, 2300 RA Leiden
Tel: (071) 5272832 *Fax:* (071) 5272836
E-mail: mnl@library.leidenuniv.nl
Web Site: www.leidenuniv.nl/host/mnl
Key Personnel
Secretary: Dr Leo L van Maris
Established: 1957
Awarded triennially for a work written in Dutch & reflecting social concerns.
Award: 2,500 EUR

☆Jenny Smelik IBBY Prize
Dutch Section of the International Board on Books for Young People
PO Box 17162, 1001 JD Amsterdam
Tel: (071) 527 40 78 *Fax:* (071) 527 39 45
E-mail: ibbynederland@planet.nl
Web Site: www.ibby.org
Key Personnel
Dir: Toin Duijx
Established: 1983
To recognize alternately an author & an illustrator of children's books who contribute to a better understanding of minorities. Selection is by nomination & application. Established by Klasina Smelik in honor of the children's book author, Jenny Smelik-Kiggen. Formerly: Jenny Smilik-Kiggenprijs.
Award: 2,000 EUR biennial by the Dutch section of IBBY

Theo Thijssen Prize for Children's & Youth Literature
Postbus 90515, Prins Willem, Alexanderhof 5, 2595 LM The Hague
Tel: (070) 3339666 *Fax:* (070) 3477941
Key Personnel
Secretary: Aad Meinderts
For the best author's work for children & young people. Awarded triennially.
Award: 75,000 Dutch florins

New Zealand

Bank of New Zealand Essay Award
Bank of New Zealand
State Insurance Tower, One Willis St, Wellington
Mailing Address: PO Box 2392, Wellington
Tel: (04) 801 2400
Web Site: www.bnz.co.nz
Key Personnel
Sponsorship & Events Consultant: Lyndal McMeeking *E-mail:* lyndal_mcmeeking@bnz.co.nz
Biennial award open to essays on a topic of the writers choice. Entries must not have been published or broadcast. Entrants have to be either born in New Zealand or New Zealand citizens or residents for 3 years. Max length 2,500 words.
Award: 1st prize $1,000

Bank of New Zealand Katherine Mansfield Award
Bank of New Zealand
State Insurance Tower, One Willis St, Wellington
Mailing Address: PO Box 2392, Wellington
Tel: (04) 801 2400
Web Site: www.bnz.co.nz
Key Personnel
Sponsorship & Event Consultant: Lyndal McMeeking *E-mail:* lyndal_mcmeeking@bnz.co.nz
Biennial award for an unpublished short story. Sponsored by the Bank of New Zealand. Entrants to be either born in New Zealand or New Zealand citizens or residents for 3 years. Max length 3000 words.
Award: 1st prize $5,000; 2nd prize $1,500

NEW ZEALAND

Bank of New Zealand Novice Writer's Award
Bank of New Zealand
State Insurance Tower, One Willis St, Wellington
Mailing Address: PO Box 2392, Wellington
Tel: (04) 801 2400
Web Site: www.bnz.co.nz
Key Personnel
Sponsorship & Events Consultant: Lyndal McMeeking *E-mail:* lyndal_mcmeeking@bnz.co.nz
Biennial award open to writers whose works have not previously been published or broadcast for payment. Entrants must be either born in New Zealand, or New Zealand citizens or resident for 3 years. Max length 3000 words.
Award: 1st prize $1,500

Bank of New Zealand Young Writers' Award
Bank of New Zealand
State Insurance Tower, One Willis St, Wellington
Mailing Address: PO Box 2392, Wellington
Tel: (04) 801 2400
Web Site: www.bnz.co.nz
Key Personnel
Sponsorship & Event Consultant: Lyndal McMeeking *E-mail:* lyndal_mcmeeking@bnz.co.nz
Biennial award for an unpublished short story written by a secondary-school pupil (over 13 years). The entrant must be either born in New Zealand or a New Zealand citizen or resident for 3 years. Min length 750 words - max length 2000 words.
Award: 1st prize $1,000; Prize to school of winning student $500

Buckland Literary Award
Trustees Executors & Agency Company of New Zealand Ltd
24 Water St, Dunedin 9001
Tel: (03) 779 466 *Fax:* (03) 799 466
Founded in 1966 by the late Freda M Buckland for the work of the highest literary merit by a New Zealand writer. Awarded annually.

NZSA Hubert Church Best First Book of Fiction Award
Booksellers New Zealand
Level 1, Survey House, 21-29 Broderick Rd, Wellington
Mailing Address: PO Box 13 248, Wellington
Tel: (04) 478 5511 *Fax:* (04) 478 5519
E-mail: enquiries@booksellers.co.nz
Web Site: www.booksellers.co.nz
Key Personnel
Contact: Beth McGregor *E-mail:* beth.mcgregor@booksellers.co.nz
Established: 1944
Annual prize for the best first book of fiction, 48 pages or more (24 pages if a work of drama), written by a New Zealand citizen or a person resident in New Zealand for the previous five years.
Award: 1,000 NZD

Russell Clark Award
Library & Information Association of New Zealand Aotearoa (LIANZA)
Old Wool House, Level 6, 139-141 Featherston St, Wellington 6001
Mailing Address: PO Box 12-212, Wellington 6038
Tel: (04) 473 5834 *Fax:* (04) 499 1480
E-mail: office@lianza.org.nz
Web Site: www.lianza.org.nz
Key Personnel
Office Manager: Eve Young *E-mail:* eve@lianza.org.nz
Established: 1975
Annual award for the most distinguished illustrations for a children's book. Illustrator must be a citizen or resident of New Zealand.
Award: Bronze medal & 1,000 NZD

Esther Glen Award
Library & Information Association of New Zealand Aotearoa (LIANZA)
Old Wool House, Level 6, 139-141 Featherston St, Wellington 6001
Mailing Address: PO Box 12-212, Wellington 6038
Tel: (04) 473 5834 *Fax:* (04) 499 1480
E-mail: office@lianza.org.nz
Web Site: www.lianza.org.nz
Key Personnel
Office Manager: Eve Young *E-mail:* eve@lianza.org.nz
Established: 1944
Annual award for the best children's book of fiction by an author who is a citizen of, or resident in, New Zealand.
Award: $1,000 NZ & Bronze medal
Presented: Annual Conference

Elsie Locke Award
Library & Information Association of New Zealand Aotearoa (LIANZA)
Old Wool House, Level 6, 139-141 Featherston St, Wellington 6001
Mailing Address: PO Box 12-212, Wellington 6038
Tel: (04) 473 5834 *Fax:* (04) 499 1480
E-mail: office@lianza.org.nz
Web Site: www.lianza.org.nz
Key Personnel
Office Manager: Eve Young *E-mail:* eve@lianza.org.nz
Established: 1986
Awarded annually for the most distinguished contribution to nonfiction writing for young people. Author(s) must be a citizen or resident of New Zealand.
Award: 1,000 NZD & medal

NZSA Jessie Mackay Best First Book Award
Booksellers New Zealand
Level 1, Survey House, 21-29 Broderick Rd, Wellington
Mailing Address: PO Box 13 248, Wellington
Tel: (04) 478 5511 *Fax:* (04) 478 5519
E-mail: enquiries@booksellers.co.nz
Web Site: www.booksellers.co.nz
Key Personnel
Contact: Beth McGregor *E-mail:* beth.mcgregor@booksellers.co.nz
Established: 1940
Annual prize for the best first book of published poetry, of 24 pages or more, written by a New Zealand citizen or a person resident in New Zealand for the previous five years.
Award: 1,000 NZD

Montana New Zealand Book Awards
Booksellers New Zealand
Level 1, Survey House, 21-29 Broderick Rd, Wellington
Mailing Address: PO Box 13 248, Wellington
Tel: (04) 478 5511 *Fax:* (04) 478 5519
E-mail: enquiries@booksellers.co.nz
Web Site: www.booksellers.co.nz
Key Personnel
Contact: Beth McGregor *E-mail:* beth.mcgregor@booksellers.co.nz
Established: 1967
For the book of the year based on: (1) quality of writing & illustrations; (2) quality of editing, design & production; (3) impact on the community. Open only to books by New Zealand authors produced by New Zealand book publishers.
Other Sponsor(s): Creative New Zealand; Montana Wines
Award: $10,000
Presented: July

New Zealand Post Children's Book Awards
Booksellers New Zealand
Level One, Survey House, 21-29 Broderick Rd, Wellington
Mailing Address: PO Box 13 248, Wellington
Tel: (04) 478 5511 *Fax:* (04) 478 5519
E-mail: enquiries@booksellers.co.nz
Web Site: www.booksellers.co.nz
Key Personnel
Contact: Beth McGregor *E-mail:* beth.mcgregor@booksellers.co.nz
Sponsored by Aim Toothpaste Division of Lever Rexona Ltd & awarded annually. The awards aim to provide recognition & reward to New Zealand authors & illustrators of high-quality children's literature & are awarded in four categories:
5,000 NZD to the author of the best junior fiction book
2,500 NZD each to the author & illustrator of the best children's picture book (one award of 5,000 NZD where the author & illustrator are the same person)
5,000 NZD to the author of the best senior fiction book
5,000 NZD to the author of the best nonfiction book
1,000 NZD to a promising first children's book.
Other Sponsor(s): Creative New Zealand; New Zealand Post

PEN Best First Book Award
New Zealand Society of Authors (NZSA)
PO Box 67013, Mount Eden, Auckland 1030
Tel: (09) 356 8332 *Fax:* (09) 356 8332
E-mail: nzsa@clear.net.nz
Web Site: www.authors.org.nz
Key Personnel
Executive Dir: Liz Allen
Annual award for the best first book of published nonfiction of 48 pages or more, written by a New Zealand citizen or a person resident in New Zealand throughout the previous five years.
Award: $1,000 NZD
Closing Date: March 13

Nigeria

Concord Press Award for Academic Publishing
Concord Press Board of Trustees
Enuwa Sq, Ile-Ife
Mailing Address: PO Box 845, Ile-Ife
Tel: (036) 230190
Established 1984. Sponsored by M K O Abiola (founder & Chairman of the Concord Press of Nigeria Ltd). The principal aim of the Award is to encourage publication of works by Nigerian authors & scholars which are suitable as textbooks at University level. 25,000 naira awarded annually.

Delta Fiction Award
Delta Publications (Nigeria) Ltd
PO Box 1172, 172 Ogui Rd, Enugu
Tel: (042) 253215
For an unpublished novel on any subject, although theme should have an international flavor.
Award: 10,000 naira

Distinguished Authors Award
University Bookshop Ltd
c/o University Bookshop, Obafemi Awolowo University, Ile-Ife, Osun State
Tel: (036) 230290

Nigerian Book Development Council Book Prize
Nigerian Book Development Council
6 Obanta Rd, Apapa, Lagos
Tel: (01) 862269; (01) 862272
For the best book of social significance by a Nigerian author. 200 naira awarded annually.

Nigerian Book Development Council Literary Prize
Nigerian Book Development Council
6 Obanta Rd, Apapa, Lagos
Tel: (01) 862269; (01) 962272
For the best book written by a Nigerian & published in Nigeria (excluding children's books). 300 naira awarded annually.

Norway

Bastianprisen (Bastian Prize)
The Norwegian Association of Literary Translators
Postboks 579 Sentrum, 0150 Oslo
Tel: 22478090 *Fax:* 22420356
E-mail: post@translators.no
Web Site: skrift.no/no/english/index.asp
Key Personnel
Contact: Hilde Sveinsson *E-mail:* hilde@translators.no
Established: 1951
Awarded annually for an outstanding translation to Norwegian.
Closing Date: Jan 15 annually

N W Damm Children's Book Prize
N W Damm og Son A/S
Tordenskioldsgate 6B, 0055 Oslo
Tel: 22471000 *Fax:* 22471149; 22471142
E-mail: marked@damm.no
Established: 1952
Award: 60,000 Norwegian kroner biennially

Literature Awards for Children & Young People
Ministry of Cultural Affairs Norwegian Directorate for Public Libraries
Kronprinsens gate 9, 0251 Oslo
Mailing Address: PO Box 8145 DEP, 0033 Oslo
Tel: 23 11 75 00 *Fax:* 23 11 75 01
E-mail: post@abm-utvikling.no
Web Site: www.abm-utvikling.no
Key Personnel
Librarian: Elin Thomsen *Tel:* 21 02 17 25
  E-mail: elin.thomsen@bibtils.no
Established: 1949
Annual awards for the best books for children in the following categories: novel (ca 40,000 NOK), picture book (ca 40,000 NOK), illustrations, new-comer, translations (new Norwegian), translations (literary Norwegian), facts & comics.

Norske Akademis Pris Til Minne om Thorleif Dahl
Norwegian Academy for Language & Literature
Inkognitogaten 24, 0256 Oslo
Tel: (022) 56 29 50 *Fax:* (022) 55 37 43
E-mail: ordet@riksmalsforbundet.no
Web Site: www.riksmalsforbundet.no

Tarjei Vesaas Debutant Prize
Den Norske Forfatterforening
Radhusgata 7, Postboks 327, Sentrum, 0103 Oslo
Tel: 23357620
E-mail: post@forfatterforeningen.no
Web Site: skrift.no/dnf
Annual award to a writer under age 30 for the best first book of prose or poetry.
Award: 14,000 NOK

Pakistan

Adamjee Prize
Pakistan Writers' Guild
11 Abbok Rd, Anarkali, Lahore
Founded in 1960 for the best book of creative & progressive poetry, novel, short story, drama, travelogue or biography. 20,000 rupees. Awarded annually. Administered by the Pakistan Writers' Guild in Karachi.

Dawood Prize for Literature
Pakistan Writers' Guild
11 Abbok Rd, Anarkali, Lahore
Established: 1963
Founded for the best books on literary research, literary history, literary criticism; for research works on the Pakistan movement & for the best translation. Sponsored by the Dawood Foundation. Awarded annually.
Award: 25,000 rupees

Habib Bank Prize for Literature
Pakistan Writers' Guild
11 Abbok Rd, Anarkali, Lahore
Established: 1968
Founded for the best translation or adaptation of the year (into English or a Pakistani language) of a modern or classical work in any Pakistani language.
Award: 25,000 rupees awarded annually

National Bank of Pakistan Prize for Literature
Pakistan Writers' Guild
11 Abbok Rd, Anarkali, Lahore
Established: 1964
Founded for the best books on economics & scientific, technical & professional subjects.
Award: 25,000 rupees awarded annually

President's Award for Pride of Performance
Pakistan Ministry of Education
Block D Pakistan Secretariat, Islamabad
Tel: (051) 825001
For notable achievements in literature. Awarded annually.

Prizes for Manuscripts of Juveniles
Pakistan Writers' Guild
11 Abbok Rd, Anarkali, Lahore
Six prizes for creative writing in the field of children's literature in the Urdu language. Awarded annually.

Regional Literature Awards
Pakistan Writers' Guild
11 Abbok Rd, Anarkali, Lahore
For the best literary works, including the novel, short story, drama, poetry, biography, travel, literary criticism or research work, in each of the four regional languages of Punjabi, Pushto, Sindhi & Gujrati. Awarded annually.

United Bank Prize for Literature
Pakistan Writers' Guild
11 Abbok Rd, Anarkali, Lahore

Established: 1967
Founded for books in Urdu & Bengali in the following categories: for children up to 15 years of age; also poetry or prose, fiction or nonfiction, for young children.
Award: 20,000 rupees awarded annually

Panama

Literary Prize
Revista Nacional de Cultura, Instito Nacional de Cultura
Apdo 662, Panama 1
Tel: 2284362 *Fax:* 2288664
Key Personnel
Dir: A Ortega
Established: 1946
Annual award founded by Ricardo Miro to pay tribute to those who furthered the cause of learning, arts & sciences. Given in each of five sections: poetry, short story, fiction, theatre, essay.
Award: $2,000 Balboas for each section

Philippines

Cultural Centre of the Philippines Literary Awards/Literature Grants
Cultural Centre of the Philippines
CCP Complex, Roxas Blvd, 1300 Pasay City, Manila
Mailing Address: PO Box 310, 1004 Metro Manila
Tel: (02) 832-1125 *Fax:* (02) 832-3683
E-mail: ccp@culturalcenter.gov.ph
Web Site: www.culturalcenter.gov.ph
Telex: 40518 CULTURE PM *Cable:* CULTURE PM
Key Personnel
President: Nestor O Jardin
Division Chief, Literature Division: Herminio S Beltran, Jr *Tel:* (02) 832-1125 (ext 1706); (02) 832-1125 (ext 1707) *Fax:* (02) 832-3674
  E-mail: ccplit@hotmail.com
Awarded annually for the best volume of verse, essay, fiction & best play written in Filipino & other Philippine languages. Open to resident Filipino citizens. Winning works are published in the series of CCP literary quarterly journal, *Ani*.
Award: 10,000 PHP in each category. Prizes also for 2nd & 3rd places. CCP Literature Grants award 25,000 PHP for a novel & 15,000 each for poetry, short fiction, essay, play & children's literature

Don Carlos Palanca Memorial Awards for Literature Contest
Carlos Palanca Foundation Inc
Ground floor, CPJ Bldg, 105 Carlos Palanca Jr St, Legaspi Village, Makati, Metro Manila 1229
Tel: (02) 8183681 *Fax:* (02) 8174045
E-mail: cpawards@info.com.ph; palancaawards@yahoo.com
Web Site: www.viloria.com
Established: 1950
Open to all Philipino citizens except current officers of the Carlos Palanca Foundation.
Award: Cash, certificate & medals
Closing Date: Jan-April 30

Poland

Cracow City Literary Prize
Zwiazek Literatow Polskich (Union of Polish Letters)
Krakowskie Przedmiescie 87/89, 00-079 Warsaw
Tel: (022) 8265785 *Fax:* (022) 8260866
   Cable: ZLP KRAKOW KRUPNICZA 22 - PL
Key Personnel
Vice President, Writer & Journalist: Leszek Maruta *Tel:* (012) 423 43 55
For the entire work of an author whose life & writings were connected with Cracow. Awarded annually.

Nagroda Literacka SBP
Stowarzyszenie Bibliotekarzy Polskich (Polish Librarians Association)
Al Niepodleglosci 213, 02-086 Warsaw
Tel: (022) 825-97-05; (022) 825-50-24 (marketing) *Fax:* (022) 621-19-68; (022) 825-53-49 (marketing)
E-mail: biurozgsbp@wp.pl
Web Site: ebib.oss.wroc.pl/sbp
Established: 1983
Awarded annually for recognition of work that has had an impact on publishing activity. Outstanding works of fiction & nonfiction are considered. Opinions of the local branches of PLA are sought in the selection process.
Award: Plaque, diploma & registration

Jan Parandowski Prize
Polish PEN Centre (Polski PEN Club)
Krakowskie Przedmiescie 87/89, 00-079 Warsaw
Tel: (022) 8282823 *Fax:* (022) 8265784
E-mail: penclub@ikp.atm.com.pl
Web Site: www.penclub.atomnet.pl
Key Personnel
President: Wladyslaw Bartoszewski
Awarded annually to commemorate Jan Parandowski's personality & works. Every Polish author of literary merit is eligible.

PEN Club Prizes for Editors
Polish PEN Centre (Polski PEN Club)
Krakowskie Przedmiescie 87/89, 00-079 Warsaw
Tel: (022) 8282823 *Fax:* (022) 8265784
E-mail: penclub@ikp.atm.com.pl
Web Site: www.penclub.atomnet.pl
Key Personnel
President: Wladyslaw Bartoszewski
Awarded annually for the best editorial work. Every Polish editor of editorial merit is eligible.

PEN Club Prizes for Essay, Prose & Poetry
Polish PEN Centre (Polski PEN Club)
Krakowskie Przedmiescie 87/89, 00-079 Warsaw
Tel: (022) 8282823 *Fax:* (022) 8265784
E-mail: penclub@ikp.atm.com.pl
Web Site: www.penclub.atomnet.pl
Key Personnel
President: Wladyslaw Bartoszewski
Awarded annually for the best literary works in the year. Polish essayists, prose writers & poets are eligible.

PEN Club Prizes for Translators of Foreign Literature into Polish
Polish PEN Centre (Polski PEN Club)
Krakowskie Przedmiescie 87/89, 00-079 Warsaw
Tel: (022) 8282823 *Fax:* (022) 8265784
E-mail: penclub@ikp.atm.com.pl
Web Site: www.penclub.atomnet.pl
Key Personnel
President: Wladyslaw Bartoszewski
Annual awards to promote foreign literature in Poland. Open to all Polish translators of foreign literature into Polish.

PEN Club Prizes for Translators of Polish Literature into Foreign Languages
Polish PEN Centre (Polski PEN Club)
Krakowskie Przedmiescie 87/89, 00-079 Warsaw
Tel: (022) 8282823 *Fax:* (022) 8265784
E-mail: penclub@ikp.atm.com.pl
Web Site: www.penclub.atomnet.pl
Key Personnel
President: Wladyslaw Bartoszewski
Annual awards to promote Polish literature abroad. All foreign translators of Polish literature & poetry are eligible.

Polish Prime Minister Award for Literature for Children and Youth
Polish Prime Minister's Office
Al Ujazdowskie 1/3, 00-583 Warsaw
Tel: (022) 8413832; (022) 6946983 *Fax:* (022) 6252872; (022) 6947265
E-mail: cirinfo@kprm.gov.pl
Web Site: www.kprm.gov.pl
For the entire work of an author of books for children & young people. Awards biennially.

☆Polish Society of Authors (Zaiks) Prizes
Stowarzyszenie Autorow Zaiks (Nagrody i Wyrozniania Stowarzyszenia Autorow ZAIKS)
ul Hipoteczna 2, 00 092 Warsaw
Tel: (022) 8281705 *Fax:* (022) 8289204
E-mail: info@zaiks.org.pl
Web Site: www.zaiks.org.pl
Literary award for translators, est 1966, awarded annually; Award for the promotion of Polish creativity, est 1990, awarded annually; Varasviane Award: for works devoted to Warsaw, est 1988, awarded biannually; Award for creative achievements in choreography, est 2001, awarded biannually; Medal of ZAIKS.

Ksawery Pruszynski Prize
Polish PEN Centre (Polski PEN Club)
Krakowskie Przedmiescie 87/89, 00-079 Warsaw
Tel: (022) 8282823 *Fax:* (022) 8265784
E-mail: penclub@ikp.atm.com.pl
Web Site: www.penclub.atomnet.pl
Key Personnel
President: Wladyslaw Bartoszewski
Annual award to commemorate the personality & output of Ksawery Pruxzynski. Polish prose writers & essayists of editorial merit are eligible.

Jan Strzelecki Prize
Polish PEN Centre (Polski PEN Club)
Krakowskie Przedmiescie 87/89, 00-079 Warsaw
Tel: (022) 8282823 *Fax:* (022) 8265784
E-mail: penclub@ikp.atm.com.pl
Web Site: www.penclub.atomnet.pl
Key Personnel
President: Wladyslaw Bartoszewski
Awarded annually to commemorate Jan Strzelecki's personality & works. Polish authors, essayists & sociologists are eligible.

Commander Kazimierz Szczesny Prize
Polish PEN Centre (Polski PEN Club)
Krakowskie Przedmiescie 87/89, PL 00-079 Warsaw
Tel: (022) 8265784 *Fax:* (022) 8282823
E-mail: penclub@ikp.atm.com.pl
Web Site: www.penclub.atomnet.pl
Triennial award to commemorate Commander Kazimierz Szczesny. Polish marine writers & authors whose works are connected with the sea are eligible.

Portugal

Calouste Gulbenkian Translation Prize
Lisbon Academy of Sciences
Rua da Academie das Ciencias, nº 19, 1249-122 Lisbon
Tel: (021) 3219730 *Fax:* (021) 3420395
E-mail: geral@acad-ciencias.pt; biblioteca@acad-ciencias.pt
Web Site: www.acad-ciencias.pt
Annual award recognizes the best translator of a work of fiction, a play, or a work of poetry from a foreign language into Portuguese. Aesthetic & vernacular qualities of the translation are considered by the jury. Portuguese translators whose works are published during the year of the award are eligible.
Award: Two prizes of 100 EUR each, one for prose & one for poetry

Ricardo Malheiros Prize
Acedemia Das Ciencias De Lisboa
Rua da Academia das Ciencias, nº 19, 1249-122 Lisbon
Tel: (021) 3219730 *Fax:* (021) 3420395
E-mail: geral@acad-ciencias.pt; biblioteca@acad-ciencias.pt
Web Site: www.acad-ciencias.pt
Awarded annually to an author for a work of imaginative literature.
Award: 30 EUR

National Award for Poetry & the Novel
Associacao Portuguesa de Escritores (Portuguese Association of Writers)
Rua de S Domingos a Lapa 17, 1200 Lisbon
Tel: (021) 7932322 *Fax:* (021) 3972341
Annual award of two prizes, one for the best book of poetry & the other for the best novel or book of short stories.
Award: 249 EUR each

National Essay Award
Associacao Portuguesa de Escritores (Portuguese Association of Writers)
Rua de S Domingos a Lapa 17, 1200 Lisbon
Tel: (021) 7932322 *Fax:* (021) 3972341
Awarded biennially for the best essay written by a Portuguese author & printed in Portuguese.
Award: 300 EUR

Revelation Awards (Poetry & Prose)
Associacao Portuguesa de Escritores (Portuguese Association of Writers)
Rua de S Domingos a Lapa 17, 1200 Lisbon
Tel: (021) 7932322 *Fax:* (021) 3972341
Annual award with four prizes, two given for the best unpublished manuscript of poetry & two for prose.
Award: 30 EUR

Revelation Prize for Children's Literature
Associacao Portuguesa de Escritores (Portuguese Association of Writers)
Rua de S Domingos a Lapa 17, 1200 Lisbon
Tel: (021) 7932322 *Fax:* (021) 3972341
Annual award for the best book written for readers between four & sixteen.
Award: 601 EUR

Aquilino Ribeiro Literary Prize
Lisbon Academy of Sciences
Rua da Academia das Ciencias, nº 19, 1249-122 Lisbon
Tel: (021) 3219730 *Fax:* (021) 3420395
E-mail: geral@acad-ciencias.pt; biblioteca@acad-ciencias.pt
Web Site: www.acad-ciencias.pt

Romania

Romanian Writers' Union Prizes
Uniunea Scriitorilor din Romania (Romanian Writer's Union)
Calea Victoriei 115, 71102 Bucharest
Tel: (01) 6507249; (01) 6507198 *Fax:* (01) 3129634
For an outstanding contribution to Romanian literature in poetry, prose, drama, literary criticism, history of literature, literary reportage, literature for children & youth, translations from world literature & for a promising new literary work by a young writer. Awarded annually (separate prizes are awarded by Bucharest, Cluj, Jassy, Timisoara, Craiova, Sibiu, Brasov & Tiirgu-Mures Writers' Associations). Awarded annually. For further information contact the appropriate Associations of the Writers' Union of the Socialist Republic of Romania.

Singapore

National Book Development Council of Singapore Book Awards
National Book Development Council of Singapore
Geylang East Community Library, National Library Board 50 Geylang East Ave 1, Singapore 38977
Tel: 6848 8290 *Fax:* 6742 9466
Web Site: www.nbdcs.org.sg
Key Personnel
Dir: Prof Tommy Koh
Established: 1976
Awarded for outstanding works of creative & non creative writing by local authors in any of the four official languages (Malay, English, Chinese & Tamil). The awards are for fiction, poetry, drama, nonfiction, children's & young people's books. Up to 15 prizes awarded biennially.
Award: 500 SGD to 2,000 SGD

Slovakia

Mlade Ieta Prize
Young Years Publishing House
Peter Cacko, Nam SNP 12, CS-815 19 Bratislava
Tel: (07) 364475 *Fax:* (07) 364563
For existing works or for outstanding achievements in the field of juvenile literature. The executive body of the Frano Kral Prize is the Slovak Literary Fund, the Circle of Friends of Childrens Books in Slovakia & publishing house Mlade Ieta. The prize is awarded annually.

☆Pavol Orszagh-Hviezdoslav Prize
Association of Slovak Writers (Spolak Slovenskych Spisovatelov)
Stefanikova 14, 815 08 Bratislava
Tel: (07) 43615
Awarded annually by the Union of Slovak Writers to outstanding translators of Slovak literature abroad during the preceding year. 10,000 crowns, plus a fortnight in Slovakia.

Slovenia

International Literary Award Vilenica
Slovene Writers' Association
Tomsiceva 12, SI-1000 Ljubljana
Tel: (01) 4252340; (01) 2514144 *Fax:* (01) 4216430
E-mail: dsp@drustvo-dsp.si
Web Site: www.drustvo-dsp.si
Award for exceptional achievements in the field of poetry & prose.
Award: 1,500,000 SIT
Presented: International Literary gathering Vilenica

South Africa

Academy Prize for Translated Work
South African Academy for Science & Arts, Engelenburghuis
Ziervogelstr 574, Arcadia, Pretoria 0083
Mailing Address: Privaatsak X11, Arcadia 0007
Tel: (012) 3285082 *Fax:* (012) 3285091
E-mail: akademie@mweb.co.za
Web Site: www.akademie.co.za
Key Personnel
Contact: Dr D J C Geldenhuys
Established: 1948
For translations into Afrikaans of belletristic work from any other language. Awarded triennially.
Award: 2,500 ZAR

Alba Bouwer Prize
South African Academy for Science & Arts, Engelenburghuis
Ziervogelstr 574, Arcadia, Pretoria 0083
Mailing Address: Privaatsak X11, Arcadia 0007
Tel: (012) 3285082 *Fax:* (012) 3285091
E-mail: akademie@mweb.co.za
Web Site: www.akademie.co.za
Key Personnel
Contact: Dr D J C Geldenhuys
Established: 1989
For recognition of Afrikaans literature for children 7-12 years old. A monetary prize donated by the Akademie is awarded triennially.

CNA Literary Award
CNA (Central News Agency)
c/o Public Relations, Johannesburg 2000
Mailing Address: PO Box 10799, Johannesburg 2000
Tel: (011) 4917902 *Fax:* (011) 4930777
E-mail: angelaa@cna.co.za
Established in 1961 for the best original works, one in English & one in Afrikaans, published for the first time during the calendar year of the competition. R15,500 rand each for the winner & 3500 rand for the runners-up in both the English & Afrikaans categories, with an additional prize of 3000 rand for the best debut work published in each category. Awarded annually. Books must be in one of following categories: novel, short story, poetry, biography, drama, history, travel. Authors must be South African citizens or registered permanent residents of South Africa.

English Association (South African Branch) Literary Competition
English Association
B204 Devonshire Hill, Grotto Rd, Rondebosch, Cape Town 7700
Tel: (021) 6854242
For original unpublished manuscripts by residents of Southern Africa. Subject, literary form & amount of award vary from year to year. Three prizes are usually awarded annually according to the standard reached.

Percy FitzPatrick Prize
English Academy of Southern Africa
PO Box 124, Wits 2050
Tel: (011) 717-9339 *Fax:* (011) 717-9339
E-mail: engac@cosmos.wits.ac.za
Web Site: www.englishacademy.co.za
Key Personnel
Administrative Officer: Mrs C James
Awarded biennially. Recognizes achievement by Southern African writers publishing in South Africa in the field of children's books between the ages of 10-14 years.
Award: 2,000 ZAR

Katrine Harries Award
Library & Information Association of South Africa (LIASA)
PO Box 1598, Pretoria 0001
Tel: (012) 481 2870 *Fax:* (012) 481 2873
E-mail: liasa@liasa.org.za
Web Site: www.liasa.org.za
Key Personnel
Executive Dir: Gwenda Thomas
For outstanding illustrations in South African children's books, regardless of language. Awarded biennially.

Hertzog Prize
South African Academy for Science & Arts, Engelenburghuis
Ziervogelstr 574, Arcadia, Pretoria 0083
Mailing Address: Private Bag X11, Arcadia, Pretoria 0007
Tel: (012) 3285082 *Fax:* (012) 3285091
E-mail: akademie@mweb.co.za
Web Site: www.akademie.co.za
Established: 1914
A prestige prize for Afrikaans literature. Prizes are awarded in rotation for poetry, drama & prose. Awarded annually.
Award: 17,000 ZAR & 18 ct gold medal

Louis Hiemstra Prize for Nonfiction
South African Academy for Science & Arts, Engelenburghuis
Ziervogelstr 574, Arcadia, Pretoria 0083
Mailing Address: Private Bag X11, Arcadia, Pretoria 0007
Tel: (012) 3285082 *Fax:* (012) 3285091
E-mail: akademie@mweb.co.za
Web Site: www.akademie.co.za
Established: 2001
Awarded every three years for nonfiction work in Afrikaans.
Award: 20,000 ZAR

W A Hofmeyr Prize
Tafelberg Publishers Ltd
12 de Verdieping, 12th floor, Naspers, Heerengracht 40, Roggebaai 8012
Mailing Address: PO Box 879, Cape Town 8000
Tel: (021) 406 3033 *Fax:* (021) 406 3812
E-mail: tafelbrg@tafelberg.com
Web Site: www.nb.co.za/tafelberg
Established: 1954
Awarded annually for the best literary work published by Nasoek publishers, including Tafelberg, Human & Rousseau, Nasou Via Afrika, JL van Schaik, Jonathan Ball, Kwela, Queillerie, Pharos, Sunbird & Van Schaik Publishers.
Award: 5,000 ZAR & gold medallion (1 ounce pure gold)

Tienie Holloway Medal
South African Academy for Science & Arts, Engelenburghuis
Ziervogelstr 574, Arcadia, Pretoria 0083

SOUTH AFRICA

Mailing Address: Privaatsak X11, Arcadia 0007
Tel: (012) 3285082 *Fax:* (012) 3285091
E-mail: akademie@mweb.co.za
Web Site: www.akademie.co.za
Key Personnel
Contact: Dr D J C Geldenhuys
Established: 1969
Established by Dr J E Holloway & awarded triennially to a writer who has produced the best work in Afrikaans literature for infants.
Award: Gold medal

C P Hoogenhout Award
Library & Information Association of South Africa (LIASA)
PO Box 1598, Pretoria 0001
Tel: (012) 481 2870 *Fax:* (012) 481 2873
E-mail: liasa@liasa.org.za
Web Site: www.liasa.org.za
Key Personnel
Award Chair: G H Haffajee
To encourage the production of outstanding Afrikaans children's books appropriate for ages 7-12 years. Awarded biannually.
Award: Gold medal & certificate

C J Langenhoven Prize
South African Academy for Science & Arts, Engelenburghuis
Ziervogelstr 574, Arcadia, Pretoria 0083
Mailing Address: Privaatsak X11, Arcadia 0007
Tel: (012) 3285082 *Fax:* (012) 3285091
E-mail: akademie@mweb.co.za
Web Site: www.akademie.co.za
Key Personnel
Contact: Dr D J C Geldenhuys
For outstanding work in field of Afrikaans linguistics. Awarded triennially.

H Recht Malan Prize
Tafelberg Publishers Ltd
12 de Verdieping, 12th floor, Naspers, Heerengracht 40, Roggebaai 8012
Mailing Address: PO Box 879, Cape Town 8000
Tel: (021) 406 3033 *Fax:* (021) 406 3812
E-mail: tafelbrg@tafelberg.com
Web Site: www.nb.co.za/tafelberg
Awarded annually for the best nonfiction book published by Nasboek publishers, including Tafelberg, Human & Rousseau, Kwela, Queillerie, Pharos, JL van Schaik, Sunbird, Jonathan Ball, Van Schaik Publishers & Nasou Via Afrika.
Award: 5,000 ZAR & gold medallion (1 ounce pure gold)

Eugene Marais Prize
South African Academy for Science & Arts, Engelenburghuis
Ziervogelstr 574, Arcadia, Pretoria 0083
Mailing Address: Privaatsak X11, Arcadia 0007
Tel: (012) 3285082 *Fax:* (012) 3285091
E-mail: akademie@mweb.co.za
Web Site: www.akademie.co.za
Key Personnel
Contact: Dr D J C Geldenhuys
Established: 1961
For a first or early work of belletristic publication in Afrikaans. The prize can be awarded only once to any particular writer. Awarded annually.
Award: 11,000 ZAR

MER Prize
Tafelberg Publishers Ltd
12 de Verdieping, 12th floor, Naspers, Heerengracht 40, Roggebaai 8012
Mailing Address: PO Box 879, Cape Town 8000
Tel: (021) 406 3033 *Fax:* (021) 406 3812
E-mail: tafelbrg@tafelberg.com
Web Site: www.nb.co.za/tafelberg
Key Personnel
Contact: Riellela de Jage *E-mail:* rdejage@tafelberg.com
Awarded annually for the best children's book published by Nasboek publishers, including Tafelberg, Human & Rousseau, Kwela, Queillerie, Pharos, JL van Schaik, Sunbird, Jonathan Ball, Van Schaik Publishers & Nasou Via Afrikay.
Award: 5,000 ZAR & gold medallion (1 ounce pure gold)

Gustav Preller Prize
South African Academy for Science & Arts, Engelenburghuis
Ziervogelstr 574, Arcadia, Pretoria 0083
Mailing Address: Privaatsak X11, Arcadia 0007
Tel: (012) 3285082 *Fax:* (012) 3285091
E-mail: akademie@mweb.co.za
Web Site: www.akademie.co.za
Key Personnel
Contact: Dr D J C Geldenhuys
For literary science & literary criticism in Afrikaans. Awarded triennially.

Thomas Pringle Awards
English Academy of Southern Africa
PO Box 124, Wits 2050
Tel: (011) 717-9339 *Fax:* (011) 717-9339
E-mail: engac@cosmos.wits.ac.za
Web Site: www.englishacademy.co.za
Key Personnel
Administrative Officer: Mrs C James
Awarded every year in three of five categories, including play, book, film & television reviews in newspapers & periodicals; literary articles or substantial book reviews in academic & other journals & in newspapers; articles on language & the teaching of English in academic, teachers' & other journals & in newspapers; short stories & one-act plays in periodicals; & poetry in periodicals.
Other Sponsor(s): FNB Vita
Award: 2,000 ZAR in each category

Scheepers Prize
South African Academy for Science & Arts, Engelenburghuis
Ziervogelstr 574, Arcadia, Pretoria 0083
Mailing Address: Privaatsak X11, Arcadia 0007
Tel: (012) 3285082 *Fax:* (012) 3285091
E-mail: akademie@mweb.co.za
Web Site: www.akademie.co.za
Key Personnel
Contact: Dr D J C Geldenhuys
Established: 1956
Awarded triennially in recognition of excellence in children's literature to authors of Afrikaans.

Olive Schreiner Prize for English Literature
English Academy of Southern Africa
PO Box 124, Wits 2050
Tel: (011) 717-9339 *Fax:* (011) 717-9339
E-mail: engac@cosmos.wits.ac.za
Web Site: www.englishacademy.co.za
Key Personnel
Administrative Officer: Mrs C James
For original literary work in English by a promising South African writer & published in South Africa. Awarded annually in one of the following categories: prose, poetry, drama.
Other Sponsor(s): FNB Vita
Award: 5,000 ZAR

Spain

Miguel de Cervantes Prize
Direccion General del Libro y Bibliotecas, Ministerio de Cultura
Plaza del Rey 1, 28071 Madrid
Tel: (091) 7017000 *Fax:* (091) 7017003; (091) 7017004; (091) 7017005
Web Site: www.mcu.es
Annual award for the work of a writer who has made an outstanding contribution to Spanish Literature.
Award: 90,152 EUR

☆Premio Destino Infantil-Apel.les Mestres
(Destino Children's Book Prize)
Ediciones Destino
Provenza 260 5a Planta, 08008 Barcelona
Tel: (093) 496 70 01 *Fax:* (093) 496 70 02
E-mail: edicionesdestino@stl.logiccontrol.es
Web Site: www.edestino.es
Key Personnel
Editor: Joaquim Palau Fau
Established: 1980
Open to all illustrated literary works which have not been published in any form & are intended for children. Works can be in Spanish, Catalan, Basque, Galician, English, French or Italian. Exists to acknowledge creative effort in the world of illustrated books.
Award: 4,500 EUR
Closing Date: Sept
Presented: Oct annually

Espejo de Espana Prize
Editorial Planeta SA
Diagonal, 662-664, 08034 Barcelona
Tel: (093) 2283700 *Fax:* (093) 4151265
Web Site: www.planeta.es
Telex: 93458 EDTPE
Established: 1975
Awarded annually for an essay.
Award: 24,040 EUR

Fastenrath Prize
Real Academia Espanola
Felipe IV, 4, 28014 Madrid
Tel: (091) 4201478 *Fax:* (091) 4200079
Web Site: www.rae.es
Established: 1909
Annual award for works of excellence written in the Spanish language. Awarded in rotation for the following categories of writing: poetry; essays, criticism; novel or story; history, biography; drama.
Award: 12,000 EUR

Hucha de Oro Prize (Chest of Gold Prize)
Confederacion Espanola de Cajas de Ahorros (CECA)
19 Juan Hurtado de Mendoza, 28036 Madrid
Tel: (091) 3508306 *Fax:* (091) 3508040
Web Site: www.funcas.ceca.es
Telex: 27304
For an unpublished short story in Castilian. Annual awards are made in which the two main prize winners are selected from the previously chosen to the limit of 20 winners of the Hucha de Plata prizes (150 EUR & a chest of silver each).
Award: 1st prize: 6,000 EUR & chest of gold (hucha de oro); 2nd prize: 3,000 EUR & miniature chest of gold

Lazarillo Prize
Organizacion Espanola para Libro Infantily Juvenil
Santiago Rusinol 8, 28040 Madrid
Tel: (091) 5530821 *Fax:* (091) 5539990

E-mail: oepli@arrakis.es
Web Site: www.oepli.org
Established: 1982
Awarded for the author of narration, poetry or theater, of a children's or young adult book.
Award: 1st place 6,000 EUR; 2nd place 1,320 EUR

Ramon Llull Prize
Editorial Planeta SA
Diagonal, 662-664, 08034 Barcelona
Tel: (093) 2283700 *Fax:* (093) 4151265
Web Site: www.planeta.es
Telex: 93458 EDTPE
Key Personnel
Chairman: Jose Manuel Lara Hernandez
Established: 1968
Founded for the purpose of contributing to the increase & promotion of narrative in Catalan. Since 1995, it has accepted both fictional works (novels, narratives, etc) & nonfictional works (essays, memoirs, biographies, etc).
Award: 60,000 EUR
Presented: Jan annually

Premio Nadal (Nadal Prize)
Ediciones Destino
Provenza 260 5a Planta, 08008 Barcelona
Tel: (093) 496 70 01 *Fax:* (093) 496 70 02
E-mail: edicionesdestino@stl.logiccontrol.es
Web Site: www.edestino.es
Key Personnel
Editor: Joaquim Palau Fau
Secretary: Yolanda Bolsa *E-mail:* ybolsa@edestino.es
Established: 1944
The Nadal Prize is the oldest literary prize to be awarded to novels written in Spanish. Starting with the 2001 prize, novels presented for this award will also be competing for the Premio Destino-Guion script award, which will be awarded to the best novel according to its potential for adaptation to a film or audio-visual script.
Award: 18,030 EUR (winner); 4,988 EUR (runner-up)
Presented: Jan annually

National Prize for Illustration of Children's Literature
Direccion General del Libro y Bibliotecas, Ministerio de Cultura
Plaza del Rey 1, 28071 Madrid
Tel: (091) 7017000 *Fax:* (091) 7017003; (091) 7017004; (091) 7017005
Web Site: www.mcu.es
Annual award for the best illustrations in a book for children or young people. Awarded in alternate years in each category.
Award: 4,988 EUR

National Prize for Literature
Direccion General del Libro y Bibliotecas, Ministerio de Cultura
Plaza del Rey 1, 28071 Madrid
Tel: (091) 7017000 *Fax:* (091) 7017003; (091) 7017004; (091) 7017005
Web Site: www.mcu.es
Established: 1984
Three annual awards for the best books of poetry, fiction & essays published in the previous year in one of the official languages of Spain.
Award: 12,470 EUR each

National Prize of Spanish Letters
Direccion General del Libro y Bibliotecas, Ministerio de Cultura
Plaza del Rey 1, 28071 Madrid
Tel: (091) 7017000 *Fax:* (091) 7017003; (091) 7017004; (091) 7017005
Web Site: www.mcu.es
Established: 1986
Awarded in recognition of an author, writing in one of the official Spanish languages, for the whole of his work.
Award: 24,940 EUR

National Prizes for Children's Literature
Direccion General del Libro y Bibliotecas, Ministerio de Cultura
Plaza del Rey 1, 28071 Madrid
Tel: (091) 7017000 *Fax:* (091) 7017003; (091) 7017004; (091) 7017005
Web Site: www.mcu.es
Established: 1978
Two annual awards for the best literary works intended for children or young people, written in any of the official languages of Spain. Awarded in alternate years in each category.
Award: 7,482 EUR for original work; 4,988 EUR for a translation

☆**Leopoldo Panero Prize**
Instituto de Cooperacion Iberoamericana
Avda de los Reyes Catolicos 4, Ciudad Universitaria, 28040 Madrid
Tel: (091) 5838100 *Fax:* (091) 5838310
For poetry in Spanish, awarded annually.
Award: 7482 EUR

☆**Planeta Prize**
Editorial Planeta SA
Diagonal, 662-664, 08034 Barcelona
Tel: (093) 2283700 *Fax:* (093) 4151265
Web Site: www.planeta.es
Key Personnel
Chairman: Jose Manuel Lara Hernandez
Established: 1952
Spain: promotes Spanish authors. The award is presented annually in Oct
Argentina: given for previously unpublished works in Spanish, continuing in its objective of promoting the production of novels. Presented annually in Oct
Chile: awarded for the first time in 2000 for journalistic research. May be entered by journalists or writers with works referring to Chilean subject matter in any written journalistic genre: information, report, chronicle, biography, analysis or interview. Pieces may be the work of a single author or of several. Presented annually in Oct
Columbia: prize awarded in recognition of the life & works of, alternately, a journalist & historian. Presented annually in Dec.
Award: Cash

Premi Josep Pla (Josep Pla Prize)
Ediciones Destino
Provenza 260 5a Planta, 08008 Barcelona
Tel: (093) 496 70 01 *Fax:* (093) 496 70 02
E-mail: edicionesdestino@stl.logiccontrol.es
Web Site: www.edestino.es
Key Personnel
Editor: Joaquim Palau Fau
Secretary: Yolanda Bolsa *E-mail:* ybolsa@edestino.es
Established: 1969
Awarded for prose in Catalan without limits in terms of genre (novels, short stories, accounts, travel books, memoirs or biographies).
Award: 4,988 EUR
Presented: Jan annually

Prince of Austrias Prizes
Fundacion Principado de Asturias
General Yague 2, 33004 Oviedo
Tel: (08) 5258755 *Fax:* (08) 5242104
Web Site: www.sispain.org

Alvarez Quintero Prize
Real Academia Espanola
Felipe IV, 4, 28014 Madrid
Tel: (091) 4201478 *Fax:* (091) 4200079
Web Site: www.rae.es
Established: 1949
Biennial award for the best work in two categories alternately: novel or story collection & theatrical works.
Award: 600 EUR

Reading & Writing National Competition
Direccion General del Libro y Bibliotecas, Ministerio de Cultura
Plaza del Rey 1, 28071 Madrid
Tel: (091) 7017000 *Fax:* (091) 7017003; (091) 7017004; (091) 7017005
Web Site: www.mcu.es
Established: 1978
Annual competition for students at COU, BUP or equivalent levels of 'Formacion Profesional'. Prizes are given for literary works, in any of the official languages of Spain, related to an important figure in Spanish literature. Prize winners are selected from 150 qualifying works. A second group of awards is made for students at EGB level for illustrations related to an important figure in Spanish literature. Winners must use the prize money exclusively for the purchase of books.
Award: 1st prize 274 EUR; 2nd prize 249 EUR; 3rd prize 224 EUR for both literary & illustrations; 125 EUR for each additional prize

Rivadeneyra Prizes
Real Academia Espanola
Felipe IV, 4, 28014 Madrid
Tel: (091) 4201478 *Fax:* (091) 4200079
Web Site: www.rae.es
Established: 1940
Annual award for the best work on Spanish literature & linguistics.
Award: Two prizes: 1,800 EUR & 1,200 EUR

☆**La Sonrisa Vertical Prize**
La Sonrisa Vertical, Tusquets Editores
Cesare Cantu, 8, 08023 Barcelona
Tel: (093) 2530400 *Fax:* (093) 4176703; (093) 4188698
Web Site: www.tusquets-editores.es
Telex: 99061 TUSQ E
Established: 1978
Founded in homage to Lopez Barbadillo. Awarded annually for the best erotic novel written in Spanish or another language of the Spanish State. The prize is an advance on the work prior to publication, together with an artistic object.
Award: 6,000 EUR

Sri Lanka

Literary Prizes for Sinhala Literature
Ministry of Cultural Affairs
255, Bauddhaloka Mawatha, Colombo 7
Tel: (01) 545777
For the best books published in the previous year in the Sinhala language in the following categories: novels, short stories, poetry, translations, children's literature, scientific literature, drama; also three awards in miscellaneous literary areas & awards for original works in Pali, Sanskrit & Arabic. 5000 Sri Lanka rupees each, excepting children's literature for which the prize is 2000 rupees. Awarded annually.

D R Wijewardene Memorial Award
Lake House Bookshop
100 Ser Chittampalam, Gardines Mawatha, Colombo 2
Tel: (01) 432105 *Fax:* (01) 432104

SRI LANKA

E-mail: bookshop@sri.lanka.net
Telex: 21266 LAKEXPO CE BOOKSALES
Key Personnel
Chairman: Mr R S Wijewardena
General Manager: Mr Sarath de Silva
Established: 1984
Established by the Lake House Bookshop, Colombo, for the best unpublished manuscript of a novel or short story collection in Sinhala. Awarded annually.
Award: 50,000 LKR
Closing Date: Nov
Presented: Sri Lanka Foundation, Colombo 7, June

Sweden

Carl Akermarks Stipendium
Swedish Academy
PO Box 2118, 103 13 Stockholm
Tel: (08) 555 125 00 *Fax:* (08) 555 125 49
E-mail: sekretariat@svenskaakademien.se
Web Site: www.svenskaakademien.se
Reward for theatre. This award cannot be applied for. Awarded annually.
Award: Five prizes of 20,000 SEK

Aniara Priset
Svensk Biblioteksforening (Swedish Library Association)
Saltmaetargatan 3A, 103 62 Stockholm
Mailing Address: PO Box 3127, 103 62 Stockholm
Tel: (08) 545 132 30 *Fax:* (08) 545 132 31
E-mail: info@biblioteksforeningen.org
Web Site: www.biblioteksforeningen.org

Bellman Prize
Swedish Academy
PO Box 2118, 103 13 Stockholm
Tel: (08) 555 125 00 *Fax:* (08) 555 125 49
E-mail: sekretariat@svenskaakademien.se
Web Site: www.svenskaakademien.se
Annual award for poetry. This prize cannot be applied for.
Award: 200,000 SEK

Blekinge County Council Culture Prize
Blekinge County Council
Kansliet, 37181 Karlskrona
Tel: (0455) 734023 *Fax:* (0455) 80250
E-mail: landstinget.blekinge@ltblekinge.se
Web Site: www.ltblekinge.se
Established: 1964
Annual prize to recognize a person or organization for a valuable contribution to science, arts, poetry, literature, music, dance, theatre, journalism or free education.
Award: 50,000 SEK

Gerard Bonnier's Prize
Swedish Academy
PO Box 2118, 103 13 Stockholm
Tel: (08) 555 125 00 *Fax:* (08) 555 125 49
E-mail: sekretariat@svenskaakademien.se
Web Site: www.svenskaakademien.se
Annual prize to a writer active in the fields within the academy's mandate. This award cannot be applied for.
Award: 125,000 SEK

Dobloug Prize
Swedish Academy
PO Box 2118, 103 13 Stockholm
Tel: (08) 555 125 00 *Fax:* (08) 555 125 49
E-mail: sekretariat@svenskaakademien.se
Web Site: www.svenskaakademien.se
Annual prize for outstanding literary work by two Norwegian & two Swedish writers. This award cannot be applied for.
Award: Two prizes of 80,000 SEK in each category

Signe Ekblad-Eldh Prize
Swedish Academy
PO Box 2118, 103 13 Stockholm
Tel: (08) 555 125 00 *Fax:* (08) 555 125 49
E-mail: sekretariat@svenskaakademien.se
Web Site: www.svenskaakademien.se
To famous Swedish writers. This award cannot be applied for.
Award: 70,000 SEK annually

Gun & Olof Engqvist Prize
Swedish Academy
PO Box 2118, 103 13 Stockholm
Tel: (08) 555 125 00 *Fax:* (08) 555 125 49
E-mail: sekretariat@svenskaakademien.se
Web Site: www.svenskaakademien.se
For Swedish Literature & Cultural Journalism. This award cannot be applied for.
Award: 100,000 SEK awarded annually

Lydia & Herman Eriksson Prize
Swedish Academy
PO Box 2118, 103 13 Stockholm
Tel: (08) 555 125 00 *Fax:* (08) 555 125 49
E-mail: sekretariat@svenskaakademien.se
Web Site: www.svenskaakademien.se
Awarded to a Swedish writer for a work of prose or poetry. This prize cannot be applied for.
Award: 70,000 SEK every second year

Nils Holgersson Plaque
Svensk Biblioteksforening (Swedish Library Association)
Saltmaetargatan 3A, 103 62 Stockholm
Mailing Address: PO Box 3127, 103 62 Stockholm
Tel: (08) 54513230 *Fax:* (08) 54513231
E-mail: info@biblioteksforeningen.org
Web Site: www.biblioteksforeningen.org
Established: 1950

Kalleberger Prize
Swedish Academy
PO Box 2118, 103 13 Stockholm
Tel: (08) 555 125 00 *Fax:* (08) 555 125 49
E-mail: sekretariat@svenskaakademien.se
Web Site: www.svenskaakademien.se
An award in memory of Tekla Hansson to a Swedish writer for a work of prose or poetry. This prize cannot be applied for.
Award: 30,000 SEK annually

Kellgren Prize
Swedish Academy
PO Box 2118, 10313 Stockholm
Tel: (08) 555 125 00 *Fax:* (08) 555 125 49
E-mail: sekretariat@svenskaakademien.se
Web Site: www.svenskaakademien.se
Annual award for important achievements in any of the fields of the academy. This prize cannot be applied for.
Award: 125,000 SEK

Literary Award
Svenska Dagbladet
Master Samuelsgatan 56, 105 17 Stockholm
Tel: (08) 13 50 00 *Fax:* (08) 52 34 97
Web Site: www.svd.se
Established: 1944
To encourage Swedish theatre design & to recognize contributions during the preceding theatre season. Awarded annually.
Award: 25,000 SEK

☆**Nobel Prize for Literature**
Swedish Academy
PO Box 2118, 103 13 Stockholm
Tel: (08) 555 125 00 *Fax:* (08) 555 125 49
E-mail: sekretariat@svenskaakademien.se
Web Site: www.svenskaakademien.se
Of all the literary prizes, the Nobel Prize for Literature is the biggest in value & in honor bestowed. It is one of the five prizes founded by Alfred Nobel (1833-1896); the other four awards are for physics, chemistry, physiology or medicine, & peace. By the terms of Nobel's will, the prize for literature is to be given to the person "who shall have produced in the field of literature the most distinguished work of an idealistic tendency." No one may apply for the Nobel Prize, there is no competition. It is awarded to an author usually for their total literary output & not for any single work.
Award: A gold medal, a diploma & a sum of money
Presented: Dec 10, the anniversary of Nobel's death

Margit Pahlson Prize
Swedish Academy
PO Box 2118, 103 13 Stockholm
Tel: (08) 555 125 00 *Fax:* (08) 555 125 49
E-mail: sekretariat@svenskaakademien.se
Web Site: www.svenskaakademien.se
Annual award for achievements of particular significance for the Swedish language. This award cannot be applied for.
Award: 100,000 SEK

Swedish Academy Nordic Prize
Swedish Academy
PO Box 2118, 103 13 Stockholm
Tel: (08) 555 125 00 *Fax:* (08) 555 125 49
E-mail: sekretariat@svenskaakademien.se
Web Site: www.svenskaakademien.se
Annual award for important achievements in any of the fields of interest of the academy. Citizens of any of the Scandinavian countries are eligible. This award cannot be applied for.
Award: 250,000 SEK

Swedish Academy Prizes
Swedish Academy
PO Box 2118, 103 13 Stockholm
Tel: (08) 555 125 00 *Fax:* (08) 555 125 49
E-mail: sekretariat@svenskaakademien.se
Web Site: www.svenskaakademien.se
In addition to those fully listed individually, the Swedish Academy awards the following prizes: Ida Baeckman Prize (Literature/Journalism: biennial); Beskow Prize (Literary: biennial); Blom Prize (Swedish Language: annual); Karin Gierow Prizes (for (1) Cultural Information: annual; (2) Promotion of Knowledge: annual); Axel Hirsch Prize (Biographic/Historic: annual); Ilona Kohrtz Prize (Prose/Poetry: annual); Royal Prize (Cultural/Literary: annual); Birger Schoeldstroem Prize (Literary History/Biography: every 4 years); Schueck Prize (Literary History: annual); Swedish Language & Literature Teachers' Prize (annual); Swedish Linguistics Prize (annual); Swedish into Foreign Language Translation Prize (annual); Translation into Swedish Prize (annual); Zibet Prize (Literary/Historic referring to reign of Gustav III: biennial); miscellaneous prizes for work in literary or linguistic fields
These prizes cannot be applied for.

Swedish Authors' Fund Awards
Swedish Authors' Fund
Klara Norra Kyrkogata 29, Box 1106, 11181 Stockholm
Tel: (08) 4404550 *Fax:* (08) 4404565
E-mail: svff@svff.se
Web Site: www.svff.se

Key Personnel
Chairperson: Bengt Westerberg
To recognize authors, translators & illustrators who have made special contributions within their own fields. Main purpose of the fund is to administer the Swedish system of library loan compensation to authors, translators & book illustrators.
Award: 20,000 SEK

Lena Vendelfelt Prize
Swedish Academy
PO Box 2118, 103 13 Stockholm
Tel: (08) 555 125 00 *Fax:* (08) 555 125 49
E-mail: sekretariat@svenskaakademien.se
Web Site: www.svenskaakademein.se
For a literary work, mainly poetry. This prize cannot be applied for.
Award: 30,000 SEK annually

Switzerland

☆**Hans Christian Andersen Awards**
International Board on Books for Young People (IBBY)
Nonnenweg 12, Postfach, Basel 4003
Tel: (061) 272 29 17 *Fax:* (061) 272 27 57
E-mail: ibby@ibby.org
Web Site: www.ibby.org
Key Personnel
Administrative Dir: Elizabeth Page
Established: 1956
The International Board on Books for Young People (IBBY) gives these awards every two years to a living author & a living illustrator who, through their works, have made distinguished contributions to international children's & young adult literature. (Until 1966 a prize was awarded for a specific book & to an author only.) A jury of ten members, appointed by the Executive Committee of IBBY, makes the decision from nominations submitted from member countries all over the world.
Other Sponsor(s): Nissan Motor Corp
Award: Biennial, gold medal & diploma

Anne Frank Literary Award
Anne Frank-Fonds
Steinengraben 18, 4051 Basel
Tel: (061) 2741174 *Fax:* (061) 2741175
E-mail: info@annefrank.ch
Web Site: www.annefrank.ch
Key Personnel
President of the Board: Buddy Elias
Established: 1963

Grand Prix Ramuz
Foundation C F Ramuz
Case Postale 181, 1009 Pully
Tel: (021) 721 3643
Key Personnel
Contact: Rebetez Maurice
Established: 1955
To recognize a writer for his entire work. Swiss authors writing in the French language are eligible.
Award: 15,000 Swiss francs every five years

Grosser Schillerpreis
Schweizerische Schillerstiftung, Fondation Schiller Suisse
Mattenway 4, 8126-3270 Aarberg
Tel: 032 393 72 64
Key Personnel
Secretary: Agnes Aeschlimann
Prizes for Swiss citizens only.

☆**IBBY-Asahi Reading Promotion Award**
International Board on Books for Young People (IBBY)
Nonnenweg 12, 4003 Basel
Tel: (061) 272 29 17 *Fax:* (061) 272 27 57
E-mail: ibby@ibby.org
Web Site: www.ibby.org
Key Personnel
Administrative Dir: Elizabeth Page
Established: 1986
Presented annually to a group or institution that is making a significant contribution to book promotion programs for children & young adults.
Other Sponsor(s): Asahi Shimbun
Award: 1,000,000 JPY
Presented: Bologna Children's Book Fair

☆**IBBY Honour List**
International Board on Books for Young People (IBBY)
Nonnenweg 12, 4003 Basel
Tel: (061) 272 29 17 *Fax:* (061) 272 27 57
E-mail: ibby@ibby.org
Web Site: www.ibby.org
Key Personnel
Administrative Dir: Elizabeth Page
Biennial selection of outstanding, recently published books, honoring writers, illustrators & translators from IBBY member countries. Titles are selected by the National Sections. The Honor List Diplomas are presented to the recipients at the IBBY Congresses.

Inner Swiss Literature Award
Inner Swiss Cultural Foundation
Bildungs-und Kulturdepartement des Kantons Luzern, Kulturabteilung, Bahnhofstr 18, 6002 Lucerne
Tel: (041) 2285206 *Fax:* (041) 2100573
Key Personnel
Contact: Daniel Huber *E-mail:* daniel.huber@lu.ch
Established: 1951
Annual award for recognition of outstanding literary work. Authors living in the central part of Switzerland (Innerschweiz, cantons: Lucerne, Uri, Schwyz, Obwalden, Nidwalden, & Zug) or who originate from those areas are eligible.
Award: 20,000 CHF & certificate

International Award for the Promotion of Human Understanding
The International Organization for the Elimination of All Forms of Racial Discrimination (EAFORD)
5 Route des Morillons, burea No 475, 1211 Geneva 2
Mailing Address: Case Postale 2100, 1211 Geneva 2
Tel: (022) 7886233 *Fax:* (022) 7886233
E-mail: info@eaford.org
Web Site: www.eaford.org
Key Personnel
President: Mr Abdalla Sharafeddin
Secretary General: Dr Anis Al-Qasem
Established: 1978
Annual international award for outstanding published work in English, French, Arabic, Spanish or Portuguese dealing with questions of racism & racial discrimination.
Award: Monetary & certificate

☆**Gottfried Keller Prize**
Martin Bodmer-Stiftung fur einen Gottfried Keller-Preis
PO Box 1425, 8032 Zurich
Established: 1921
Founded by Martin Bodmer for Swiss & other writers who have honored the Swiss spirit. Awarded biennially.
Award: 25,000 CHF

Prix Liberte Litteraire
Foundation Armleder
Hotel Richemond, CH-1206 Geneva
Tel: (022) 7311400 *Fax:* (022) 7312414
Freedom Literary Prize.

Prix Litteraire de la Ville de La Chaux-de-Fonds et de la Revue (Literary Review Prize of La Chaux de Fronds)
Editions
19-21 Rue du Manege, 2301 La Chaux de Fonds
Tel: (032) 9682418 *Fax:* (032) 9682750

Preis der Schweizerische Schillerstiftung
Schweizerische Schillerstiftung, Fondation Schiller Suisse
Mattenway 4, 8126-3270 Aarberg
Tel: 032 393 72 64
Key Personnel
Secretary: Agnes Aeschlimann
Prize for Swiss citizens, or foreigners living in Switzerland for a minimum of five years.

City of Zurich Literary Prize
Praesidialdepartement der Stadt Zurich
Postfach, 8022 Zurich
Tel: (01) 2163125 *Fax:* (01) 2121404
E-mail: musik.literatur@prd.stzh.ch
Key Personnel
Contact: Roman Hess
Established: 1930
Founded by the city of Zurich to reward an author for his or her whole literary work. No applications or nominations accepted.
Award: 50,000 Swiss francs awarded at irregular intervals

Thailand

Bangkok Bank Foundation Prize
Bangkok Bank Foundation
333 Silom Rd, Bangkok 10500
Tel: (02) 645-5555; (02) 231-4333 *Fax:* (02) 236-5913
E-mail: info@bangkokbank.com
Web Site: www.bangkokbank.com
For prose or poetry in Thai concerning history, art, culture, religion, social affairs, philosophy or new creative ideas. Awarded annually.
Award: 50,000 THB

Turkey

Award for Literature & Scientific Publications
Turkish Language Institution (Turk Dil Kurumu)
Ataturk Bulvari, 217, Kavaklidere, 06680 Ankara
Tel: (0312) 4286100 *Fax:* (0312) 4285288
E-mail: bim@tdk.gov.tr
Web Site: www.tdk.gov.tr
Key Personnel
President: Dr Hasan Eren
To encourage & sponsor research & studies in Turkish language literature & linguistics.

United Kingdom

☆**Academi Cardiff International Poetry Competition**
Academi
Mount Stuart House, Mount Stuart Sq, Cardiff CF10 5FQ
Tel: (029) 20472266
E-mail: post@academi.org
Web Site: www.academi.org
Established: 1986
Awarded annually. Poems in the English language of no more than 50 lines on any subject. Open to all nationalities.
Other Sponsor(s): Cardiff Council
Award: 1st prize 5,000 GBP; 2nd prize 700 GBP; 3rd prize 300 GBP; five prizes of 200 GBP
Closing Date: Jan 30

J R Ackerley Prize for Autobiography
English PEN Centre
152-156 Kentish Town Rd, London NW1 9QB
Tel: (020) 7267 9444 *Fax:* (020) 7267 9304
E-mail: enquiries@pen.org.uk
Web Site: www.pen.org.uk
Key Personnel
President: Victoria Glendinning
Executive Dir: Susanna Nicklin *E-mail:* susie@englishpen.org
Established: 1982
Annual award for a literary autobiography written in English by an author of British nationality & published in the UK in the previous year.
Award: 1,000 GBP & a silver Dupont pen
Presented: PEN International Writers' Day

Airey Neave Research Award
The Airey Neave Trust
House of Commons, London SW1A 0AA
Tel: (020) 7495 0554 *Fax:* (020) 7491 1118
E-mail: info@aireyneavetrust.org.uk
Web Site: www.aireyneavetrust.org.uk
Award: 1-3 year research fellowship
Closing Date: May 1

Alexander Prize
The Royal Society
University College London, Gower St, London WC1E 6BT
Tel: (020) 7387 7532 *Fax:* (020) 7387 7532
E-mail: royalhistsoc@ucl.ac.uk; rhsinfo@rhs.ac.uk
Web Site: www.rhs.ac.uk
Key Personnel
Executive Secretary: Joy McCarthy
For an essay in English on a historical subject: must be a genuine work of original research. Candidates must either be under the age of 35 or be registered for a higher degree or have been registered for such a degree within the last three years. Must not exceed 8,000 words including foot-notes & can relate to any historical subject. Candidates are required to state the total number of words of their entry. It may be derived from a doctoral thesis (either in progress or completed) but it should be self-contained & suitable for reading as a lecture. No more than one essay submitted per year. To apply: send one typescript copy of the essay, without identification of the author, with a cover letter (stating name, address, date of birth, institution, details of degree registration where relevant & essay title).
Award: 250 GBP

☆**Arts Council Awards & Bursaries**
Arts Council of England
14 Great Peter St, London SW1P 3NQ
Tel: (0845) 300 6200 *Fax:* (020) 7973 6590
E-mail: enquiries@artscouncil.org.uk
Web Site: www.artscouncil.org.uk
Intended to provide experienced playwrights with an opportunity to research & develop work for theater independent of financial pressures & free from the need to write for a particular market. Full details of the help given to playwrights is available on request.
Award: Grants 500-5,000 GBP

The Arts Council of Wales Book of the Year Awards
Arts Council of Wales
Holst House, 9 Museum Pl, Cardiff CF10 3NX
Tel: (02920) 376500 *Fax:* (02920) 221447
Web Site: www.artswales.org
Key Personnel
Chief Executive: Peter Tyndall
Contact: Ms Lleucu Siencyn
Since 1968, The Arts Council of Wales has given awards to Welsh authors (by birth of residence) whose books are of exceptional literary merit. The books may be written in English or Welsh. The prizes are awarded to recognize achievement, to draw attention to writers of promise & to encourage the writing of creative literature in English & Welsh. Two prizes of 3,000 GBP are awarded annually to winners & 1,000 GBP to four other short-listed authors.
Other Sponsor(s): Hay-on-Wye Festival of Literature
Presented: Hay-on-Wye Festival of Literature

☆**Arvon Foundation International Poetry Competition**
Arvon Foundation Ltd
42A Buckingham Palace Rd, 2nd floor, London SW1W 0RE
Tel: (020) 7931 7611 *Fax:* (020) 7963 0961
E-mail: comps@arvonfoundation.org
Web Site: www.arvonfoundation.org
Key Personnel
Dir: Stephanie Anderson
Established: 1980
Entries for the competition must be previously unpublished poems of any length written in English. An anthology of winning poems, & those selected by the judges for special commendation, are published by the Arvon Foundation.

Authors' Club Best First Novel Award
Authors' Club
40 Dover St, London W1X 3RB
Tel: (020) 7408 5092
Key Personnel
Secretary: Lucy Jane Tetlow
Annual award for the most promising first novel published in English in the United Kingdom in the preceding year.
Award: 1,000 GBP
Closing Date: Nov

Authors' Club Sir Banister Fletcher Award
Authors' Club
40 Dover St, London W1X 3RB
Tel: (020) 7408 5092
Key Personnel
Secretary: Lucy Jane Tetlow
Annual award for the most deserving book on architecture or the arts.
Award: 1,000 GBP

Aventis Prizes for Science Books
The Royal Society
6-9 Carlton House Terrace, London SW1Y 5AG
Tel: (020) 7451 2513 *Fax:* (020) 7451 2693
E-mail: scottkeir@royalsoc.ac.uk
Web Site: www.aventissciencebookprizes.com
Key Personnel
Prize Administrator: Natasha Martineau *E-mail:* natashamartineau@yahoo.co.uk
Spirit Publicity: Reeta Bhatiani *E-mail:* reeta@spiritpublicity.com
Established: 1988
Prizes were established to celebrate the best in popular science writing & are awarded annually to books that make science more accessible to readers of all ages & backgrounds.
Other Sponsor(s): Aventis
Award: Up to 30,000 GBP awarded annually in two categories: General (10,000 GBP) for a book with a general readership; Junior (10,000 GBP) for a book for under-14's. Up to 5 short-listed authors in each category receive 1,000 GBP each

☆**BBC WILDLIFE Magazine Awards for Nature Writing**
BBC WILDLIFE Magazine
BBCi Nature, Broadcasting House, Whiteladies Rd, Bristol BS8 2LR
Tel: (0117) 9738402 *Fax:* (0117) 9467075
E-mail: wildlife.magazine@bbc.co.uk
Web Site: www.bbc.co.uk
Key Personnel
Editor: Rosamund Kidman Cox
Competition Organizer & Editorial Assistant: Nina Epton
Annual awards for essays of not more than 800 words based on personal observations or reflections on nature. Should the main award be won by a professional writer, a second award is made to the best essay by an amateur. There are also two awards for younger writers & a number of runner-up prizes.
Award: 1,000 GBP & 200 GBP
Closing Date: July 22

☆**Benson Medal**
Royal Society of Literature
Somerset House, Strand, London WC2R 1LA
Tel: (20) 7845 4676 *Fax:* (20) 7845 4679
E-mail: info@rslit.org
Web Site: www.rslit.org
Key Personnel
Chairman: Ronald Harwood
Assistant Secretary: Julia Abel Smith *Tel:* (020) 7845 4677 *E-mail:* julia@rslit.org
Established: 1961
Founded by Dr A C Benson. For a body of meritorious work in poetry, fiction, history, biography or belles lettres. A silver medal given periodically at the discretion of the Council of the Royal Society of Literature. Applications are not invited.

David Berry Prize
The Royal Society
University College London, Gower St, London WC1E 6BT
Tel: (020) 7387 7532 *Fax:* (020) 7387 7532
E-mail: royalhistsoc@ucl.ac.uk; rhsinfo@rhs.ac.uk
Web Site: www.rhs.ac.uk
Key Personnel
Executive Secretary: Joy McCarthy
For an essay in English on a subject, to be selected by the candidates, dealing with Scottish history. The essay submitted must be a genuine work of research based on original (manuscript or printed) materials. The essay should be between 6,000 & 10,000 words in length (excluding foot-notes & appendices). It must be submitted in typescript. The author's name should not appear on the typescript & should be submitted separately. No person to whom the prize has been awarded may enter for any subsequent competition for the prize.
Award: 250 GBP
Closing Date: Oct 31

PRIZES — UNITED KINGDOM

Besterman/McColvin Medal
Chartered Institute of Library & Information Professionals (CILIP)
7 Ridgmount St, London WC1E 7AE
Tel: (020) 7255 0650 *Fax:* (020) 7255 0501
E-mail: info@cilip.org.uk
Web Site: www.cilip.org.uk
Key Personnel
Marketing Manager: Louisa Myatt *E-mail:* louisa.myatt@cilip.org.uk
For outstanding works of reference published in the UK. One for print & one for electronic formats. The judges will assess the authority, scope & coverage, arrangement & currency of the information, quality of indexing, adequacy of references, physical presentation, originality & value for money.
Award: 500 GBP & certificate
Presented: Sept

James Tait Black Memorial Prizes
University of Edinburgh
David Hume Tower, George Sq, Edinburgh EH8 9JX
Tel: (0131) 650 3620 *Fax:* (0131) 650 6898
E-mail: english.literature@ed.ac.uk
Web Site: www.ed.ac.uk/~englitw3/jtbinf.htm
Key Personnel
Contact: Sheila Strathdee *E-mail:* s.strathdee@ed.ac.uk
Established: 1919
These literary prizes were founded by the late Mrs Janet Coats Black in memory of her husband, a partner in the publishing house of A&C Black Ltd, London. Mrs Black set aside 11,000 GBP to be used for two prizes of whatever income the fund would produce after paying expenses. The prizes, supplemented by the Scottish Arts Council, now amount annually to approximately 3,000 GBP each. Literary Prizes are awarded to the best biography & to the best work of fiction published during the calendar year Oct 1 to Sept 30.
Award: Approximately 3,000 GBP each
Closing Date: Sept 30

The K Blundell Trust
Society of Authors
84 Drayton Gardens, London SW10 9SB
Tel: (020) 7373 6642 *Fax:* (020) 7373 5768
E-mail: info@societyofauthors.org
Web Site: www.societyofauthors.org/prizes.htm
Provides grants to published British authors under 40 years of age & to published authors who need additional funding to write their next book.
Award: Generally 1,000-2,000 GBP (not to exceed 4,000 GBP)
Closing Date: April 30 & Oct 31

☆Boardman Tasker Prize for Mountain Literature
Boardman Tasker Charitable Trust
Pound House, Llangennith, Swansea SA3 1JQ
Tel: (01792) 386 215 *Fax:* (01792) 386 215
Web Site: www.boardmantasker.com
Key Personnel
Contact: Margaret Body *E-mail:* margaretbody@lineone.net
Established: 1983
Established to commemorate the lives of distinguished mountaineers Peter Boardman & Joe Tasker who died in 1982 on Mount Everest. Awarded annually to an author of a published work of nonfiction or fiction, written in the English language, initially or in translation, which makes an outstanding contribution to mountain literature; published between Nov 1 of previous year & Oct 31 of year of the prize.
Award: 2,000 GBP
Closing Date: Aug 1 of year in which the prize is offered
Presented: Alpine Club, London, UK, Nov

☆The Man Booker Prize
Booktrust
Book House, 45 East Hill, London SW18 2QZ
Tel: (020) 8516 2977 *Fax:* (020) 8516 2978
Web Site: www.booktrust.org.uk; www.themanbookerprize.com
Key Personnel
Prize Administrator: Tarryn McKay *Tel:* (020) 8516 2977 *E-mail:* tarryn@booktrust.org.uk
Established: 1969
Annual prize donated by the Man Group plc & administered by Booktrust, for any full-length novel, written in English by a citizen of The Commonwealth, or the Republic of Ireland. Any United Kingdom publisher who publishes works of fiction may enter up to two novels, with scheduled publication dates between October 1 & September 30. In addition, publishers may enter any current novel by an author who has previously been shortlisted or won the Booker Prize.
Other Sponsor(s): The Man Group plc
Award: 50,000 GBP

The Bridport Prize Poetry & Short Stories
Bridport Arts Centre
South St, Bridport, Dorset DT6 3NR
Tel: (01308) 459444 *Fax:* (01308) 459166
E-mail: info@bridport-arts.com
Web Site: www.bridportprize.org.uk
Established: 1973
Open writing competition for short stories (5,000 words maximum) & poetry (24 lines maximum).
Award: Prizes for both categories: 1st prize 3,000 GBP; 2nd prize 1,000 GBP; 3rd prize 500 GBP; 10 supplementary prizes
Closing Date: June 30th annually
Presented: Bridport Arts Centre, Last Saturday of Oct, annually

British Book Awards
Publishing News Ltd
39 Store St, London WC1E 7DB
Tel: (020) 7692 2900 *Fax:* (020) 7419 2111
Web Site: www.publishingnews.co.uk
Key Personnel
Organizer: Merric Davidson *Tel:* (01580) 212041 *E-mail:* nibbies@mdla.co.uk
Established: 1989
The UK Book Trade 'OSCARS'.
Other Sponsor(s): Activair; Baker Tilly; BCA; Blackwell's; The Bookseller; Borders (UK) Ltd; Butler & Tanner; Chrysalis Books; The Daily Mail; Expert Books; KPMG; Nielsen BookData; Nielsen BookScan; Oneword; Reader's Digest; Securicor Omega Express; W H Smith; The Spoken Word Publishing Association; Stora Enso; The Times; Virgin Books; VISTA International; Waterstone's
Closing Date: mid-Nov
Presented: Grosvenor House on Park Lane, February, annually

British Comparative Literature Association/British Centre for Literary Translation Prize
British Comparative Literature Association/British Centre for Literary Translation
UEA, Norwich NR4 7TJ
Tel: (01603) 592143 *Fax:* (01603) 250599
Web Site: www.bcla.org
Key Personnel
Contact: Dr Jean Boase-Beier *Tel:* (01603) 593360 *E-mail:* j.boase-beier@uea.ac.uk
Literary translation includes poetry, fiction or literary prose, from any period; maximum 25 typed pages.
Award: 1st prize 350 GBP; 2nd prize 200 GBP; 3rd prize 100 GBP; other entries may receive commendations
Closing Date: Jan 31 annually
Presented: BCLA Prize Giving, July

British Science Fiction Association Awards
The British Science Fiction Association Ltd (BSFA Ltd)
97 Sharp St, Newland Ave, Hull HU5 2AE
E-mail: bsfa@enterprise.net
Web Site: www.bsfa.co.uk
Key Personnel
Awards Administrator: Claire Brialey
Annual awards in four categories: best novel, best short fiction, best nonfiction & best artwork. Novel & nonfiction are for works first published in the UK in the previous year.
Closing Date: Jan 31
Presented: Eastercon

The Calouste Gulbenkian Foundation Prize
Society of Authors - Translators Association
84 Drayton Gardens, London SW10 9SB
Tel: (020) 7373 6642 *Fax:* (020) 7373 5768
E-mail: info@societyofauthors.org
Web Site: www.societyofauthors.org
The triennial prize is for translations of works from any period by a Portuguese national. The translation must have been first published in the UK.
Award: 1,000 GBP
Closing Date: Dec 20

The Carey Award
Society of Indexers
Blades Enterprise Centre, John St, Sheffield S2 4SU
Tel: (0114) 281 3060 *Fax:* (0114) 281 3061
E-mail: admin@socind.demon.co.uk
Web Site: www.socind.demon.co.uk
Key Personnel
Administrator: P W Burrow
The award is made by Council for services to indexing.

Carnegie Medal
Chartered Institute of Library & Information Professionals (CILIP)
7 Ridgmount St, London WC1E 7AE
Tel: (020) 7255 0650 *Fax:* (020) 7255 0501
E-mail: info@cilip.org.uk
Web Site: www.carnegiegreenaway.org.uk/carnegie/carn.html; www.cilip.org.uk
Key Personnel
Marketing Manager: Louisa Myatt *E-mail:* louisa.myatt@cilip.org.uk
Established: 1936
Established by The Library Association in memory of Scottish-born philanthropist, Andrew Carnegie (1835-1919). Awarded annually to the writer of an outstanding book for children.
Award: Golden medal & 500 GBP worth of books to donate to a library of their choice

Cartier Diamond Dagger Lifetime Achievement Award
Crime Writers' Association
PO Box 63, Wakefield WF2 0YW
E-mail: info@theCWA.co.uk
Web Site: www.thecwa.co.uk
Key Personnel
Chairman: Hilary Bonner
Secretary: Judith Cutler *Tel:* (07227) 709 782 *E-mail:* judith.cutler@virgin.net
Established: 1986
Annual award for outstanding contribution to crime fiction published in the English language, whether originally or in translation.
Other Sponsor(s): Cartier
Award: Silver book with diamond dagger

UNITED KINGDOM

LITERARY

Children's Award
Arts Council of England
14 Great Peter St, London SW1P 3NQ
Tel: (0845) 300 6200 *Fax:* (020) 7973 6590
E-mail: enquiries@artscouncil.org.uk
Web Site: www.artscouncil.org.uk
Celebrates the accomplishments & raises the profile of theatre for children & most especially, playwrights who work in this field.

☆Cholmondeley Awards for Poets
Society of Authors
84 Drayton Gardens, London SW10 9SB
Tel: (020) 7373 6642 *Fax:* (020) 7373 5768
E-mail: info@societyofauthors.org
Web Site: www.societyofauthors.org/prizes.htm
Established by the late Dowager Marchioness of Cholmondeley for the benefit & encouragement of poets of any age, sex or nationality. The noncompetitive award is for work generally, not for a specific book & submissions are not accepted. Awarded annually.
Award: Total of 8,000 GBP
Presented: 1966

Arthur C Clarke Award
Science Fiction Foundation, British Science Fiction Association, Science Museum
60 Bournemouth Rd, Folkestone, Kent CT 19 5AZ
Tel: (01303) 232939 *Fax:* (01303) 252939
E-mail: arthurclarkeaward@yahoo.co.uk
Web Site: www.clarkeaward.com
Key Personnel
Administrator: Paul Kincaid
Established: 1986
For the best science fiction novel published in the United Kingdom. The winner is chosen by a panel of six judges representing the Science Fiction Foundation, the British Science Fiction Association & the International Science Policy Foundation.
Award: Annual award of an engraved bookend & 2,005 GBP. (The amount of the award matches the year)
Presented: The Science Museum, London, Mid-May

David Cohen British Literature Prize
Arts Council of England
14 Great Peter St, London SW1P 3NQ
Tel: (0845) 300 6200 *Fax:* (020) 7973 6590
E-mail: enquiries@artscouncil.org.uk
Web Site: www.artscouncil.org.uk
Established: 1993
Administered by the Arts Council in association with Coutts & Co, this prize will be awarded biennially in recognition of the entire body of a writer's work.
Award: 40,000 GBP

Commonwealth Writers Prize
Commonwealth Foundation
Booktrust, Book House, 45 East Hill, London SW18 2QZ
Tel: (020) 8516 2972 *Fax:* (020) 8516 2978
E-mail: geninfo@commonwealth.int
Web Site: www.commonwealthwriters.com
Established: 1987
Annual award for a work of prose fiction, written by a citizen of the Commonwealth & published the previous year. The work must be in English & of reasonable length. Entries must be made by the publisher & are restricted to four entries per region.
Closing Date: Dec 31
Presented: May

☆Thomas Cook Travel Book Award
The Thomas Cook Group
Thomas Cook Business Park, Unit 19-21 Coningsby Rd, Peterborough PE3 8XX
Tel: (01733) 402009 *Fax:* (01733) 416688
Web Site: www.thetravelbookaward.com
Key Personnel
Prize Administrator: Joan Lee *Tel:* (01482) 610707 *E-mail:* ipmc@freenet.co.uk
Established: 1980
Awarded to the travel narrative which most inspires in the reader the desire to travel. Books must be published in English, or translated into English & published between Jan 1 - Dec 31 in the preceding year. Books may only be submitted by publishers & may only be entered once. Minimum 150 pages.
Other Sponsor(s): The Daily Telegraph
Award: 10,000 GBP plus a reproduction picture from the Thomas Cook company archives for the winner & shortlisted author
Closing Date: March 31

☆Duff Cooper Prize
Duff Cooper
54 St Maur Rd, London SW6 4DP
Tel: (020) 7736 3729 *Fax:* (020) 7731 7638
Key Personnel
Prize Administrator: Ms Artemis Cooper
Established: 1956
For a literary work of history, biography, poetry or politics supported by a recognized publisher in English or French. The prize is the interest from a trust fund. Awarded annually.
Award: 3,000 GBP & copy of Duff Cooper's autobiography, Old Men Forget
Closing Date: Nov 30
Presented: Feb

☆The Rose Mary Crawshay Prize
British Academy
The British Academy, 10 Carlton House Terrace, London SW1Y 5AH
Tel: (020) 7969 5200 *Fax:* (020) 7969 5300
E-mail: secretary@britac.ac.uk
Web Site: www.britac.ac.uk
Key Personnel
Administrator: Angela Pusey *Tel:* (020) 7969 5264 *Fax:* (020) 7969 5414 *E-mail:* a.pusey@britac.ac.uc
Established: 1888
Awarded by the Council of the British Academy to women writers of any nationality for an historical or critical work of value on any subject concerning English literature published within the preceding three years. Preference is given to works on Byron, Shelley or Keats. Two prizes awarded annually. Applications are not sought.
Award: 500 GBP

John Creasey Memorial Dagger
Crime Writers' Association
PO Box 63, Wakefield WF2 0YW
E-mail: info@theCWA.co.uk
Web Site: www.thecwa.co.uk
Key Personnel
Chairman: Hilary Bonner
Secretary: Judith Cutler *Tel:* (07227) 709 782 *E-mail:* judith.cutler@virgin.net
Established: 1973
Sponsored by Chivers Press. Annual award of magnifying glass with onyx handle & inscribed plate & check for best crime novel by author who has not previously published a full-length work of fiction. Submission by publishers only.
Other Sponsor(s): Chivers Press
Award: Ornamental dagger & 1,000 GBP

☆Isaac & Tamara Deutscher Memorial Prize
Lloyds Bank Ltd
School of Modern Languages, University of Southampton, Highfield, Southampton S017 1BJ
Web Site: www.deutscherprize.org.uk/home.htm
Established: 1968
For a work published or in typescript in any of the main European languages which contributes to the development of Marxist thought. Awarded annually.
Award: 250 GBP
Closing Date: May 1

Encore Award
Society of Authors
84 Drayton Gardens, London SW10 9SB
Tel: (020) 7373 6642 *Fax:* (020) 7373 5768
E-mail: info@societyofauthors.org
Web Site: www.societyofauthors.org/prizes.htm
Awarded to a second novel (or novels) judged to be the best first published in the UK during the year preceding the year in which the award is presented; publisher entry only.
Award: 10,000 GBP
Closing Date: Nov 30
Presented: Spring

☆Christopher Ewart-Biggs Memorial Prize
Hugo Arnold
The Secretary to the Judges Committee, Flat 3, 149 Hamilton Terrace, London NW8 9QS
Established: 1977
Awarded in memory of the British Ambassador to Ireland who was assassinated in Dublin in 1976. This award aims to create greater understanding between the peoples of Britain & Ireland, or co-operation between the partners of the European Community. Entries should be in English or French. Awarded biennially.
Award: 5,000 GBP
Closing Date: Dec 31

☆The Geoffrey Faber Memorial Prize
Faber & Faber Ltd
3 Queen Sq, London WC1N 3AU
Tel: (020) 7465 0045 *Fax:* (020) 7465 0043
Web Site: www.faber.co.uk
Key Personnel
Prize Administrator: Belinda Matthews *E-mail:* belinda.matthews@faber.co.uk
Established: 1963
Established as a memorial to the founder & first chairman of the firm. It is given in alternate years, for a volume of verse & for a volume of prose fiction. It is given to that volume of verse or prose fiction first published originally in the United Kingdom during the two years preceding the year in which the award is given which is, in the opinion of the judges, of the greatest literary merit. To be eligible for the prize the volume of verse or prose fiction in question must be by a writer who is: (a) not more than forty years old at the date of publication, (b) a citizen of the United Kingdom & Colonies, of any other Commonwealth state, of Ireland or of the Republic of South Africa. There are three judges, who are reviewers of poetry or fiction as the case may be, & they are nominated each year by the editors or literary editors of newspapers & magazines which regularly publish such reviews. Faber & Faber invite nominations from such editors & literary editors. No submissions for the prize are to be made.
Award: 1,000 GBP

Eleanor Farjeon Award
Scholastic UK Group
The Children's Book Circle, Orchard Books, 96 Leonard St, London EC2A 4RH
Tel: (020) 7739 2929 *Fax:* (020) 7739 2318
Web Site: www.booktrusted.com
Key Personnel
Promotions & Marketing: Susan Barry *E-mail:* susan.barry@wattspub.co.uk
Established: 1965

Established to commemorate the work of the late children's book author. The Children's Book Circle makes an annual award which may be given to a librarian, teacher, author, artist, publisher, reviewer, bookseller or television producer who, in the judgment of the Awards Committee, is considered to have done outstanding work for children's books.
Other Sponsor(s): Books for Children
Award: 500 GBP

The Fidler Award
Scottish Book Trust
Scottish Book Centre, 137 Dundee St, Edinburgh EH11 1BG
Tel: (0131) 229 3663 *Fax:* (0131) 228 4293
E-mail: info@scottishbooktrust.com
Web Site: www.scottishbooktrust.com
Established: 1983
Awarded to an unpublished novel written for 8-12 year olds. The author may have had previous books published, but this must be the first for this age range. Hodder Children's Books will publish the winning entry.
Other Sponsor(s): Hodder Children's Books
Award: Advance of 1,500 GBP, royalty package & rosewood/silver trophy, to be held for one year
Closing Date: Nov 30 annually

John Florio Prize
Society of Authors - Translators Association
84 Drayton Gardens, London SW10 9SB
Tel: (020) 7373 6642 *Fax:* (020) 7373 5768
E-mail: info@societyofauthors.org
Web Site: www.societyofauthors.org
Established: 1963
Established under the auspices of the Italian Institute & the British-Italian Society & named after John Florio. For the best translation into English of a 20th Century Italian work of literary merit & general interest, published by a British publisher during the preceding two years.
Award: 1,000 GBP
Closing Date: Dec 20

Fraenkel Prize in Contemporary History
Institute of Contemporary History & Wiener Library
4 Devonshire St, London W1W 5BH
Tel: (020) 7636 7247 *Fax:* (020) 7436 6428
E-mail: info@wienerlibrary.co.uk
Web Site: www.wienerlibrary.co.uk
Key Personnel
Administrative Co-ordinator: Rod Digges
Established: 1989
Inaugurated by Mr Ernst Fraenkel for an outstanding work in the field of contemporary history.
Award: Two awards: 6,000 USD (open to all entrants); 4,000 USD (entrants who have yet to publish a major work)
Closing Date: May 10

Gibb Memorial Trust
E J W Gibb Memorial Trust
2 Penarth Pl, Cambridge CB3 9LU
Tel: (01223) 566630 *Fax:* (01223) 511182
Web Site: www.gibbtrust.org
Key Personnel
Secretary to the Trustees: Robin Bligh
Established: 1902
Publishers of works about Persian, Turkish & Arabic history & religions.

The Gladstone History Book Prize
The Royal Society
University College London, Gower St, London WC1E 6BT
Tel: (020) 7387 7532 *Fax:* (020) 7387 7532

E-mail: royalhistsoc@ucl.ac.uk; rhsinfo@rhs.ac.uk
Web Site: www.rhs.ac.uk
Key Personnel
Executive Secretary: Joy McCarthy
Established: 1997
Based on any historical subject which is not primarily related to British history. Must be its author's first solely written history book & published in English during the calendar year by a scholar normally resident in the UK. Must be an original & scholarly work of historical research. Author or publisher should submit three copies (non-returnable) of an eligible book by the end of the year.
Award: 1,000 GBP
Closing Date: Dec 31 annually
Presented: Royal Historical Society Annual Reception, July

Glenfiddich Food & Drink Awards
William Grant & Sons
4 Bedford Sq, London WC1B 3RA
Tel: (020) 7255 1100 *Fax:* (020) 7436 4164
E-mail: lindsay.stewart@grayling.co.uk
Web Site: www.glenfiddich.com
Key Personnel
Chairman, Glenfiddich Food & Drink Awards: Heather Graham
Public Relations Officer: K Fiennes-Price
Established: 1970
Established to recognise excellence in writing, publishing & broadcasting on the subjects of food & drink.
Closing Date: January
Presented: January

Edgar Graham Book Prize
School of Oriental & African Studies
Geography Dept, Thornhaugh St, Russell Sq, London WC1H 0XG
Tel: (020) 7637 2388 *Fax:* (020) 7436 3844
Web Site: www.soas.ac.uk/
Key Personnel
Secretary: C Darfour *E-mail:* cd16@soas.ac.uk
Award is given biennially to a work of original scholarship published in English on agricultural &/or industrial development in Asia &/or Africa.
Award: 1,500 GBP

Kate Greenaway Medal
Chartered Institute of Library & Information Professionals (CILIP)
7 Ridgmount St, London WC1E 7AE
Tel: (020) 7255 0650 *Fax:* (020) 7255 0501
E-mail: info@cilip.org.uk
Web Site: www.carnegiegreenaway.org.uk/green/green.html; www.cilip.org.uk
Key Personnel
Marketing Manager: Louisa Myatt *E-mail:* louisa.myatt@cilip.org.uk
Established: 1955
Offered annually for the most distinguished work in the illustration of children's books first published in the United Kingdom during the preceding year.
Award: Golden medal & 500 GBP worth of books to donate to a library of their choice

Eric Gregory Trust Fund Awards
Society of Authors
84 Drayton Gardens, London SW10 9SB
Tel: (020) 7373 6642 *Fax:* (020) 7373 5768
E-mail: info@societyofauthors.org
Web Site: www.societyofauthors.org
A number of awards are made each year to encourage young British poets. Candidates for awards must be British subjects by birth, ordinarily resident in the United Kingdom & under the age of 30 on March 31 in the year of the award. Candidates must submit a published or unpublished volume of belles lettres, poetry or drama-poems.
Award: 25,000 GBP
Closing Date: Oct 31

☆**Guardian Children's Fiction Prize**
The Guardian
119 Farringdon Rd, London EC1R 3ER
Tel: (020) 7278 2332 *Fax:* (020) 7713 4368
Web Site: www.books.guardian.co.uk
Established: 1965
Awarded to an outstanding work of fiction (not picture books) for children written by a British or Commonwealth author, first published in the UK during the calendar year preceding the year in which the award is presented. The winner is chosen by a panel of authors & the review editor for The Guardian's children's books section. Awarded annually.
Award: 1,500 GBP

☆**The Guardian First Book Award**
The Guardian
119 Farringdon Rd, London EC1R 3ER
Tel: (020) 7278 2332 *Fax:* (020) 7713 4368
E-mail: sara@guardian.co.uk
Web Site: www.books.guardian.co.uk
Telex: 8811746
This award recognizes & rewards new writings by honouring an author's first book. Its aim is to reflect the breadth of coverage of all genres on The Guardian books pages & underpin the paper's commitment to new quality writing.
Award: 10,000 GBP plus an advertising package within The Guardian & Observer. Also, an endowment of 1,000 GBP worth of books will be made by The Guardian to a UK school of the author's choice

Hawthornden Prize
Hawthornden Literary Institute
Hawthornden Castle, Lasswade, Midlothian EH18 1EG
Tel: (0131) 4402180
Web Site: www.britishartsco.uk/literarycompetitions.htm
Established: 1919
Founded by Miss Alice Warrender, it is awarded annually to a British subject under age 41 for the best work of imaginative literature. It is especially designed to encourage young authors, & the word 'imaginative' is given a broad interpretation. Biographies are not excluded. Books do not have to be submitted for the prize; it is awarded without competition. A panel of judges chooses the winner.
Award: Annually

Francis Head Bequest
Society of Authors
84 Drayton Gardens, London SW10 9SB
Tel: (020) 7373 6642 *Fax:* (020) 7373 5768
E-mail: info@societyofauthors.org
Web Site: www.societyofauthors.org
Provides grants to professional authors over 35 years of age whose main source of income is from their writing & who, through accident, illness or other causes, are temporarily unable to write.

Heinemann Award for Literature
Royal Society of Literature
Somerset House, Strand, London WC2R 1LA
Tel: (020) 7845 4676 *Fax:* (020) 7845 4679
E-mail: info@rslit.org
Web Site: www.rslit.org
Key Personnel
Assistant Secretary: Julia Abel Smith *Tel:* (020) 7845 4677 *E-mail:* julia@rslit.org
Established: 1944
A foundation was established through a bequest in the will of the late William Heinemann, eminent British publisher. The Royal Society

of Literature administers the annual foundation award which is primarily to reward those classes of literature which are less remunerative, namely, poetry, criticism, biography, history, etc & to encourage the production of works of real merit. Submitted works must have been written originally in English & published during the calendar year previous to the year in which the prize is presented.
Award: 5,000 GBP
Closing Date: Dec 15 annually
Presented: June annually

Felicia Hemans Prize for Lyrical Poetry
University of Liverpool
PO Box 147, Liverpool L69 3BX
Tel: (0151) 794 2458 *Fax:* (0151) 794 3765
E-mail: wilder@liv.ac.uk
Web Site: www.liv.ac.uk
Telex: 627095
Annual prize is open to past & present members & students of the University of Liverpool only, is awarded to a lyrical poem, the subject of which may be chosen by the competitor. Only one poem, either published or unpublished, may be submitted. The prize shall not be awarded more than once to the same competition Poems, endorsed 'Hemans Prize'. Awarded annually.
Award: One year's income from the Felicia Hemans Memorial Fund
Closing Date: May 1

The Joan Hessayon New Writers' Award
Formerly New Writers Award
Romantic Novelists' Association (RNA)
16 St Briacway, Exmouth EX8 5RN
Tel: (01395) 279659
Web Site: www.rna-uk.org
Key Personnel
President: Diane Pearson
Established: 1960
For an unpublished romantic novel.
Award: Trophy & cash prize
Closing Date: Sept annually
Presented: Party in London, May annually

William Hill Sports Book of the Year
William Hill Organization
50 Station Rd, London N22 7TP
Tel: (020) 8918 3858 *Fax:* (020) 8889 0472
Key Personnel
Press Officer: Serena Momberg
Awarded annually to the best sports book published in the year preceding the year in which the prize is awarded. Publisher entry only.
Award: 15,000 GBP
Closing Date: Sept 12
Presented: Nov

Winifred Holtby Memorial Prize
Royal Society of Literature
Somerset House, Strand, London WC2R 1LA
Tel: (020) 7845 4676 *Fax:* (020) 7845 4679
E-mail: info@rslit.org
Web Site: www.rslit.org
Key Personnel
Assistant Secretary: Julia Abel Smith *Tel:* (020) 7845 4677 *E-mail:* julia@rslit.org
Established: 1966
Founded by Vera Brittain in memory of Winifred Holtby. An annual award for the best regional novel of its year; if no suitable work of fiction can be found the jury may consider works of nonfiction. Submissions by publishers, not by individual authors. Award Type is for regional fiction.
Closing Date: Dec 15 (entries are not accepted until mid-Oct)
Presented: St Bride Institute, London, June

The Independent Foreign Fiction Award
The Independent
Arts Council of England, 14 Great Peter St, London SW1P 3NQ
Tel: (020) 7973 5325 *Fax:* (020) 7962 0016
Web Site: www.artscouncil.org.uk
Annual prize for the best contemporary work of prose fiction translated into English from any other tongue, published between Jan 1 & Dec 31 each year. The prize is funded by the Arts Council & promoted by The Independent newspaper.
Award: 10,000 GBP to be divided equally between author & translator

International Short Story Competition/International Poetry Competition
Stand Magazine
Leeds University, School of English, Leeds LS2 9JT
Tel: (0113) 233 4794 *Fax:* (0113) 233 2791
E-mail: stand@leeds.ac.uk
Web Site: www.people.vcu.edu
Key Personnel
Administrator: Linda Goldsmith
Sample copies available for $13 US from David Latane, Dept of English, VCU, Richmond, VA 23284, USA.
Closing Date: March 31

☆Kraszna-Krausz Book Awards
Kraszna-Krausz Foundation
122 Fawnbrake Ave, London SE24 0BZ
Tel: (020) 7738 6701 *Fax:* (020) 7738 6701
E-mail: info@k-k.org.uk
Web Site: www.editor.net/k-k
Key Personnel
Contact: Andrea Livingstone
International awards made to encourage & recognize outstanding achievements in the publishing & writing of books on the art, history, practice & technology of photography & of the moving image. The Awards are made annually, with prizes for books on still photography alternating with those for books on the moving image (film, television, video). Publisher entry only.
Award: 5,000 GBP for each category winner; 1,000 GBP special commendations

Lakeland Book of the Year Awards
Cumbria Tourist Board
Ashleigh, Holly Rd, Windermere, Cumbria LA23 2AQ
Tel: (015394) 44444 *Fax:* (015394) 44041
Established: 1984
These annual awards were established by Hunter Davies & Cumbria Tourist Board. The Hunter Davies Award is for a book which best helps visitors or residents to enjoy a greater love or understanding of life in Cumbria - the Lake District. The Tullie House Prize is for a book which best helps develop a greater appreciation of the built &/or natural environment of Cumbria. The Barclays Bank Award is for the best small book on any aspect of Cumbria life, people or culture. The Border Television Prize is for a book which best illustrates the beauty & character of Cumbria.
Award: 100 GBP & a framed certificate

Lancashire County Library Children's Book of the Year Award
Lancashire County Library
County Library Manager, County Library Headquarters, County Hall, PO Box 61, Preston PR1 8RJ
Tel: (01772) 264018 *Fax:* (01772) 264880
E-mail: library@lcl.lancscc.gov.uk
Web Site: www.lancashire.gov.uk/libraries/
Key Personnel
Contact: David G Lightfoot *E-mail:* david.lightfoot@lcl.lancscc.gov.uk
Established: 1986
Annual award, sponsored by The University of Central Lancashire, given for a work of fiction or a collection of short stories by a single author. The book should be suitable for 11-14 year-olds.
Award: 500 GBP & an engraved decanter

Ralph Lewis Award
University of Sussex Library
Brighton BN1 9QL
Tel: (01273) 678163 *Fax:* (01273) 678441
E-mail: library@sussex.ac.uk
Web Site: www.sussex.ac.uk/library
Key Personnel
Contact: Pat Ringshaw *Tel:* (01273) 678158 *E-mail:* p.a.ringshaw@sussex.ac.uk
Established: 1985
Occasional award for promising manuscripts given to a UK-based publisher. No direct applications from writers.
Award: Grant

London Writers' Competition
Arts Office: Wandsworth Borough Council
Town Hall, Wandsworth High St, London SW18 2PU
Tel: (020) 8871 7380 *Fax:* (020) 8871 7630
E-mail: arts@wandsworth.gov.uk
Web Site: www.wandsworth.gov.uk/wbclondonwriters.htm
The competition is open to London writers only & has Poetry, Play, Short Story & Fiction for Children. All entries must be in English.
Award: 1st prize 600 GBP; 2nd prize 250 GBP; 3rd prize 100 GBP; two runners-up of 25 GBP
Closing Date: June 26

Macallan Gold Dagger for Fiction
Crime Writers' Association
PO Box 63, Wakefield WF2 0YW
E-mail: info@theCWA.co.uk
Web Site: www.thecwa.co.uk
Key Personnel
Chairman: Hilary Bonner
Secretary: Judith Cutler *Tel:* (07227) 709 782 *E-mail:* judith.cutler@virgin.net
Established: 1955
For the best crime-fiction novel of the year awarded annually by a panel of reviewers. Submission by publishers only.
Other Sponsor(s): The Macallan
Award: Ornamental dagger & 3,000 GBP

Macallan Gold Dagger for Non-Fiction
Crime Writers' Association
PO Box 63, Wakefield WF2 0YW
E-mail: info@theCWA.co.uk
Web Site: www.thecwa.co.uk
Key Personnel
Chairman: Hilary Bonner
Secretary: Judith Cutler *Tel:* (07227) 709 782 *E-mail:* judith.cutler@virgin.net
Established: 1978
Winner is selected by an independent panel. Submission by publishers only.
Other Sponsor(s): The Macallan
Award: 2,000 GBP & an ornamental dagger

Macallan Short Story Dagger
Crime Writers' Association
PO Box 63, Wakefield WF2 0YW
E-mail: info@theCWA.co.uk
Web Site: www.thecwa.co.uk
Key Personnel
Chairman: Hilary Bonner
Secretary: Judith Cutler *Tel:* (07227) 709 782 *E-mail:* judith.cutler@virgin.net

Established: 1955
Awarded for a short story published in a crime anthology. Submission by publishers only.
Other Sponsor(s): The Macallan
Award: 1,500 GBP & a gold pin of the CWA's crossed daggers emblem

Macallan Silver Dagger for Fiction
Crime Writers' Association
PO Box 63, Wakefield WF2 0YW
E-mail: info@theCWA.co.uk
Web Site: www.thecwa.co.uk
Key Personnel
Chairman: Hilary Bonner
Secretary: Judith Cutler *Tel:* (07227) 709 782
 E-mail: judith.cutler@virgin.net
Established: 1955
Other Sponsor(s): The Macallan
Award: Ornamental dagger & 2,000 GBP

☆Enid McLeod Literary Prize
Franco-British Society
Room 623 Linen Hall, 162-168 Regent St, London W1R 5TB
Tel: (020) 7734 0815 *Fax:* (020) 7734 0815
Web Site: www.booktrust.org.uk/prizes/mcleod.htm
Established: 1981
Awarded annually to a book that contributes the most to Franco-British understanding, written in English & published in the UK during the calendar year preceding the year in which the award is presented.
Closing Date: Dec 31

The Macmillan Prize for Children's Picture Book Illustration
Macmillan Children's Books
20 New Wharf Rd, London N1 9RR
Tel: (020) 7014 6124 *Fax:* (020) 7014 6142
Key Personnel
Contact: Imogen Blundell *E-mail:* i.blundell@macmillan.co.uk
Established: 1986
Annual award, established in order to stimulate new work from young illustrators in British art schools. Open to all art students in higher education establishments in the UK.
Award: 1000 GBP(winner), 500 GBP(runner-up) & 250 GBP(second runner-up)

Macmillan Silver Pen Award for Short Stories
English PEN Centre
Lancaster House, 33 Islington High St, London N1 9LH
Tel: (020) 7713 0023 *Fax:* (020) 7713 0005
E-mail: enquiries@englishpen.org
Web Site: www.englishpen.org
Key Personnel
President: Victoria Glendinning
Executive Dir: Susanna Nicklin *E-mail:* susie@englishpen.org
Presented annually for a collection of short stories written in English by an author of British nationality & published in the UK in the previous year.
Other Sponsor(s): Macmillan Publishers; S T Dupont; Stern Family (nonfiction award in memory of James Stern)
Award: 500 GBP & a silver Dupont pen
Presented: PEN International Writers' Day

Marsh Award for Children's Literature in Translation
Authors' Club
Digby Stuart College, University of Surrey Roehampton, Roehampton Lane, London SW15 5PU
Tel: (020) 8392 3008
E-mail: ncrcl@roehampton.ac.uk
Web Site: www.booktrusted.com

Key Personnel
Public Relations: Nicky Potter
Established: 1995
Awarded biennially to the best translation of a childrens book, by a British translator, from a foreign language into English, & published in the UK by a British publisher. Submissions are accepted from publishers for books produced for readers from 4-16 years of age. The award is made to the translator.
Other Sponsor(s): Marsh Christian Trust
Award: 750 GBP
Closing Date: June 30

Marsh Biography Award
The English Speaking Union
Dartmouth House, 37 Charles St, London W1X 8AB
Tel: (020) 7493 3328 *Fax:* (020) 7495 6108
E-mail: esu@esu.org
Web Site: www.booktrust.org.uk/prizes/marshbiog.htm
Key Personnel
Cultural Affairs Officer: Lucy Passmore
 E-mail: lucy_passmore@esu.org
Established: 1986
Awarded biennially to a signficant biography by a British author published in the UK in the two years prior to the year in which the prize is awarded. Publisher entry only.
Other Sponsor(s): B P Marsh & Co Ltd
Award: 3,500 GBP & silver trophy
Closing Date: April 1

☆MCA Book Prize
Management Consultancies Association (MCA)
49 Whitehall, London SW1A 2BX
Tel: (020) 7321 3990 *Fax:* (020) 7321 3991
E-mail: MCA@MCA.org.uk
Web Site: www.mca.org.uk
Key Personnel
Awards Administrator: Andrea Livingstone
 Tel: (020) 7738 6701 *Fax:* (020) 7738 6701
Deputy Dir: Sarah Taylor *Tel:* (020) 7321 3993
 E-mail: sarah.taylor@mca.org.uk
Established: 1993
Annual prize aimed to recognize & reward British writers of management books & to offer encouragement to writers whose books contribute stimulating, original & progressive ideas on management issues.
Award: 5,000 GBP

MIND Book of the Year
MIND Publications
15-19 Broadway, London E15 4BQ
Tel: (020) 8519 2122 *Fax:* (020) 8522 1725
E-mail: contact@mind.org.uk
Web Site: www.mind.org.uk
Key Personnel
Publicity: Anne McCarthy *Tel:* (020) 8522 1743
Established: 1981
Inaugurated by MIND & the National Book League in memory of Allen Lane. Awarded annually to the author of the book (fiction or nonfiction) which outstandingly furthers public awareness of mental health problems.
Award: 1,500 GBP

Scott Moncrieff Prize
Society of Authors - Translators Association
84 Drayton Gardens, London SW10 9SB
Tel: (020) 7373 6642 *Fax:* (020) 7373 5768
E-mail: info@societyofauthors.org
Web Site: www.societyofauthors.org
Established: 1964
Established under the auspices of the Translators Association of the Society of Authors to be awarded annually for the best translation published by a British publisher during the previous year. Only translations of French 20th Century works of literary merit & general interest will be considered. The work should be entered by the publisher & not the individual translator.
Closing Date: Dec 20

☆The Shiva Naipaul Memorial Prize
Spectator
56 Doughty St, London WC1N 2LL
Tel: (020) 7405 1706 *Fax:* (020) 7242 0603
E-mail: syndication@spectator.co.uk
Web Site: www.spectator.co.uk
Established: 1985
Awarded annually, this prize is given to an English-language writer of any nationality under 35 years of age best able to describe a visit to a foreign place or people. The award will not be for travel writing in the conventional sense, but for the most acute & profound observation of cultures &/or scenes (which could be within the writer's native country) evidently alien to the writer. Submissions should not previously have been published & should not be more than 4,000 words.
Award: 3,000 GBP & publication of winning entry in The Spectator
Closing Date: April 30

National Poetry Competition
The Poetry Society Inc
22 Betterton St, London WC2H 9BX
Tel: (020) 7420 9880 *Fax:* (020) 7240 4818
E-mail: competition@poetrysociety.org.uk; info@poetrysociety.org.uk
Web Site: www.poetrysociety.org.uk
Established: 1978
Awarded annually for a poem written in English. Send self-addressed envelope for entry form or visit website.
Award: 1st prize 5,000 GBP; 2nd prize 1,000 GBP; 3rd prize 500 GBP; 10 commendations 50 GBP
Closing Date: Oct 31

Natural World Book Prize
Booktrust
Book House, 45 East Hill, London SW18 2QZ
Tel: (020) 8516 2977 *Fax:* (020) 8516 2978
Web Site: www.booktrust.org.uk
Key Personnel
Prize Administrator: Tarryn McKay *Tel:* (020) 8516 2977 *E-mail:* tarryn@booktrust.org.uk
Established: 1987
Annual prize awarded to the author(s) of the book which most imaginatively promotes the conservation of the natural environment & all its animals & plants. The judges reserve the right to award a prize of 1,000 GBP for a runner-up. All entries must be published in the UK, by a UK publisher between June 1 & the following May 31. This award is open to any nationality. The author(s) must be alive at the time of submission.
Other Sponsor(s): BP, The Wildlife Trusts & Subbuteo Books
Award: 5,000 GBP

The Nestle Smarties Book Prize
Booktrust
Book House, 45 East Hill, London SW18 2QZ
Tel: (020) 8516 2977 *Fax:* (020) 8516 2978
Web Site: www.booktrust.org.uk
Key Personnel
Prize Administrator: Tarryn McKay *Tel:* (020) 8516 2977 *E-mail:* tarryn@booktrust.org.uk
Established: 1985
To encourage high standards & stimulate interest in children's books. The prize is only open to works of fiction or poetry for children, written in English by a citizen of the UK, or an author resident in the UK. The author of the book must be living at the time of publication. The adult panel must choose three from each category. The age categories are 5 & under, 6-8

& 9-11. The shortlisted books are then given to the Young Judges, who have to read the books & decide which book gets Gold, Silver & Bronze. The Young Judges are chosen from classes of school children, who have to complete tasks set for their age category. A new Young Judge category was added a couple of years ago, chosen from Kids' Club Networks. They read & judge the 6-8 books.
Other Sponsor(s): Nestle
Award: Gold prize 2,500 GBP; Silver prize 1,000 GBP; Bronze prize 500 GBP

New Writers Award, see The Joan Hessayon New Writers' Award

Observer National Children's Poetry Competition
The Observer
119 Farrington Rd, London EUR 3ER
Tel: (020) 7278 2332 *Fax:* (020) 7278 1449
First awarded in 1986 & sponsored then & in 1987 & 1988 by the Water Authorities Association. The competition is open to three age groups: 10 years & under, 11-14 years & 15-18 years. There is an additional prize for the best group of poems from any school.

Outposts Poetry Competition
Hippopotamus Press
22 Whitewell Rd, Frome, Somerset BA11 4EL
Tel: (0373) 466653 *Fax:* (0373) 466653
Web Site: www.jbwb.co.uk/poetpubs
Key Personnel
Competition Organizer: M Pargitter
Established: 1991
Awarded annually in the Autumn for new poetry adjudicated by a great poet.
Award: 1st prize 500 GBP; 2nd prize 200 GBP; 3rd prize 100 GBP

Parker Romantic Novel of the Year
Romantic Novelists' Association (RNA)
2 Broad Oak Lane, Wigginton, York Y032 2SB
Tel: (01904) 765035
Web Site: www.rna-uk.org/parkeraward.html
Key Personnel
President: Diane Pearson
Award Organizer: Joan Emery
Established: 1960
Established as the RNA Major Award. For the best romantic novel (modern or historical) published during the year. Open to non-members.
Other Sponsor(s): Parker Pen Co
Award: 10,000 GBP & a set of Parker Duofold pens worth over 400 GBP
Closing Date: Nov 30
Presented: Awards luncheon, London, April annually

The Michael Powell Book Award
British Film Institute
21 Stephen St, London W1T 1LN
Tel: (020) 7255 1444 *Fax:* (020) 7436 7950
Web Site: www.bfi.org.uk
Established: 1983
This annual award is given to a book published in Britain dealing with film or television by a UK author. The award takes the form of a specially commissioned plaque.

Premio Valle Inclan
Society of Authors - Translators Association
84 Drayton Gardens, London SW10 9SB
Tel: (020) 7373 6642 *Fax:* (020) 7373 5768
E-mail: info@societyofauthors.org
Web Site: www.societyofauthors.org
This annual prize is for published translations of full length Spanish works of literary merit & general interest (the original must have been written in Spanish but can be from any period & from anywhere in the world). The translation must have been first published in the UK.
Award: 1,000 GBP
Closing Date: Dec 20

☆**Quadrennial Prize for Bibliography**
International League of Antiquarian Booksellers
Wynches Barn, Herts SG10 6BA
Tel: (01424) 426146
Web Site: www.ilab-lila.com
Key Personnel
Prize Secretary: Raymond Kilgariff
To the author of the best work, published or unpublished, of learned bibliography, of research into the history of the book or typography, or a book of general interest on the subject. The competition is open, without restriction, but entries must be submitted in a language which is universally read. An already published work is eligible only if it has an imprint bearing a date within the four years preceding the closing date for submission. Entries in the form of a specialized catalogue of one or more books destined for sale are not eligible, nor periodicals or public library catalogues. Any further information relating to the prize for Bibliography awarded by ILAB can be obtained from the National Associations of Antiquarian Booksellers.
Award: 10,000 USD every four years
Presented: Summer 2006

Red House Children's Book Award
Red House
c/o The Federation of Children's Book Groups, 2 Bridge Wood View, Horsforth, Leeds LS18 5PE
Tel: (0113) 2588910 *Fax:* (0113) 2588920
E-mail: info@fcbg.org.uk
Web Site: www.fcbg.org.uk
Key Personnel
Coordinator: Marianne Adey
 E-mail: marianneadey@aol.com
Established: 1980
Coordinated by the Federation of Children's Book Groups, this award is given annually for the best work of fiction (published in the United Kingdom). Chosen by children for children.

☆**Trevor Reese Memorial Prize**
Institute of Commonwealth Studies
University of London, 28 Russell Sq, London WC1B 5DS
Tel: (020) 7862 8844 *Fax:* (020) 7862 8820
E-mail: ics@sas.ac.uk
Web Site: www.sas.ac.uk/commonwealthstudies/
Key Personnel
Events & Publicity Officer: Stephanie Kearins
 Tel: (020) 7862 8825 *E-mail:* skearins@sas.ac.uk
Established: 1976
The prize was established from a memorial fund to Dr Trevor Reese, Reader in Imperial Studies at the Institute of Commonwealth Studies, who died in 1976. The adjudicators are interested in wide-ranging publications, but the terms of the Prize specifically apply to scholarly works usually by a single author, in the field of Imperial & Commonwealth history. Awarded biennially.
Award: 1,000 GBP

☆**John Llewellyn Rhys Prize**
Booktrust
45 East Hill, London SW18 2QZ
Tel: (020) 8516 2977 *Fax:* (020) 8516 2978
Web Site: www.booktrust.org.uk/prizes/btprizes/mosjlr.htm
Key Personnel
Prize Administrator: Tarryn McKay *Tel:* (020) 8516 2977 *E-mail:* tarryn@booktrust.org.uk
Prize Manager: Susy Behr *Tel:* (020) 8516 2993 *E-mail:* susy@booktrust.org.uk
Established: 1942
Founded by Jane Oliver, the widow of John Llewellyn Rhys, a young writer killed in action in World War II. To be eligible, entries may be any work of literature written by a British or Commonwealth writer under the age of 35 at the time of publication. Books must be written in English & published in the UK during the year of the Prize. Previous winners of the prize may not enter. This prize is open to published works only, entries submitted by UK publisher only & is awarded annually.
Other Sponsor(s): The Mail on Sunday
Award: 5,000 GBP to the winner & 500 GBP to each of the other shortlisted authors

The Robinson Medal
Chartered Institute of Library & Information Professionals (CILIP)
7 Ridgmount St, London WC1E 7AE
Tel: (020) 7255 0650 *Fax:* (020) 7255 0501
E-mail: info@cilip.org.uk
Web Site: www.cilip.org.uk/practice/awards.html
Key Personnel
Marketing Manager: Louisa Myatt *E-mail:* louisa.myatt@cilip.org.uk
Awarded biennially to recognize innovation & excellence in library administration & administrative procedures. It is aimed specifically at attracting submissions from people working at paraprofessional levels in the library & information field.
Other Sponsor(s): Demco Group
Award: Trophy, certificate & 50 GBP book token
Presented: CILIP Awards Gala Ceremony, Landmark Hotel

Royal Historical Society/History Today Prize
The Royal Society
University College London, Gower St, London WC1E 6BT
Tel: (020) 7387 7532 *Fax:* (020) 7387 7532
E-mail: royalhistsoc@ucl.ac.uk
Web Site: www.rhs.ac.uk
Key Personnel
Executive Secretary: Joy McCarthy
For the best third year undergraduate dissertation in History in a higher education institution in the UK.
Award: 250 GBP

The Royal Society of Medicine Prizes for Medical Writing & Illustration
The Society of Authors, Medical Writers Group
84 Drayton Gardens, London SW10 9SB
Tel: (020) 7373 6642 *Fax:* (020) 7373 5768
E-mail: info@societyofauthors.org
Web Site: www.societyofauthors.org
Key Personnel
Contact: Dorothy Sym

Saltire History Book of the Year Award
The Saltire Society
9 Fountain Close, 22 High St, Edinburgh EH1 1TF
Tel: (0131) 556 1836 *Fax:* (0131) 557 1675
E-mail: saltire@saltiresociety.org.uk
Web Site: www.saltiresociety.org.uk
Key Personnel
Administrator: Kathleen Munro
Established: 1965
In memory of Dr Agnes Mure Mackenzie, this award is given biennially for a published work of Scottish Historical Research (including intellectual history & the history of science). Editions of texts are not eligible.
Award: A bound & inscribed copy of the winning publication

Sasakawa Prize
Society of Authors - Translators Association
84 Drayton Gardens, London SW10 9SB

Tel: (020) 7373 6642 *Fax:* (020) 7373 5768
E-mail: info@societyofauthors.org
Web Site: www.societyofauthors.org
This prize is for translations of full length Japanese works of literary merit & general interest, from any period. The translation must have been first published in the UK.
Award: 2,000 GBP

Schlegel-Tieck Prize
Society of Authors - Translators Association
84 Drayton Gardens, London SW10 9SB
Tel: (020) 7373 6642 *Fax:* (020) 7373 5768
E-mail: info@societyofauthors.org
Web Site: www.societyofauthors.org
Established under the auspices of the Translators Association, a subsidiary organization of the Society of Authors, to be awarded annually for the best translation published by a British publisher during the previous year. Only translations of German 20th Century works of literary merit & general interest will be considered. The work should be entered by the publisher & not the individual translator.
Closing Date: Dec 20

Scottish Arts Council Book Awards
The Scottish Arts Council
Literature Dept, 12 Manor Pl, Edinburgh EH3 7DD
Tel: (0131) 226 6051 *Fax:* (0131) 225 9833
E-mail: help.desk@scottisharts.org.uk
Web Site: www.sac.org.uk
Key Personnel
Literature Officer: Gavin Wallace *E-mail:* gavin.wallace@scottisharts.org.uk
Ten awards annually. Awarded in Spring & Autumn. Authors must be Scottish, resident in Scotland, or work must be of particular Scottish interest. Preference is given to literary fiction & poetry, but many other types of books are eligible for consideration. Reprints, technical or scientific books, & books that are highly specialized will not be considered. Works should be submitted by publishers on behalf of their authors. Publishers of children's books can submit titles to the SAC Children's Book Awards under separate guidelines.
Award: 1,000 GBP each
Closing Date: Spring Award: Jan 31 for books published between July & Dec; Autumn Award: July 31 for books published between Jan & June
Presented: April (Spring); Nov (Autumn)

Scottish Book of the Year Award & Scottish First Book of the Year
The Saltire Society
9 Fountain Close, 22 High St, Edinburgh EH1 1TF
Tel: (0131) 556 1836 *Fax:* (0131) 557 1675
E-mail: saltire@saltiresociety.org.uk
Web Site: www.saltiresociety.org.uk
Key Personnel
Administrator: Kathleen Munro
Established: 1982
Award established by The Saltire Society & now funded by The Scotsman. Awarded for a book of a literary nature written by an author of Scottish descent or living in Scotland, or a book which deals with the work or life of a Scot or with a Scottish problem, event or situation. The Scotsman contributes substantial monetary sums to be awarded annually.
Award: Scottish Book of the Year 5,000 GBP, Scottish First Book of the Year 1,500 GBP
Closing Date: Sept 7 for nominations

Scottish International Open Poetry Competition
Ayshire Writers & Artists Society
42 Tollerton Drive, Irvine, Ayrshire KA12 0ER
Tel: (01294) 276381
Web Site: www.irvineayrshire.org/openpoetry.htm
Established: 1972
Longest running poetry competition in UK. Free entry. Open to established & aspiring poets but two IRC's required.
Closing Date: Nov 30

Andre Simon Fund Book Awards
Andre Simon Memorial Fund
5 Sion Hill Pl, Bath BA1 5SJ
Tel: (01225) 336305 *Fax:* (01225) 421862
Key Personnel
Contact: Tessa Hayward *E-mail:* tessa@tantraweb.co.uk
Awards given annually for the best book on food or drinks.
Award: 2,000 GBP

Somerset Maugham Awards
Society of Authors
84 Drayton Gardens, London SW10 9SB
Tel: (020) 7373 6642 *Fax:* (020) 7373 5768
E-mail: info@societyofauthors.org
Web Site: www.societyofauthors.org
Established: 1946
Founded by Somerset Maugham to encourage young British writers to travel abroad. Given to a promising author of a published work of poetry, fiction, criticism, biography, history, philosophy, belles lettres or travel. Candidates must be British subjects by birth & ordinarily resident in the United Kingdom & under age 35. Awards must be used for foreign travel. Entry by publisher.
Award: Total of 12,000 GBP
Closing Date: Dec 20

☆**Stand Magazine International Short Story Competition**
Stand Magazine
Leeds University, School of English, Leeds LS2 9JT
Tel: (0113) 233 4794 *Fax:* (0113) 233 2791
E-mail: stand@leeds.ac.uk
Web Site: www.people.vcu.edu
Key Personnel
Administrator: Linda Goldsmith
Established: 1983
Hosted by the Cheltenham Festival of Literature to encourage & promote the work of new or unknown short-story writers. Awarded biennially. Please send UK stamped-addressed envelope or two international reply coupons.
Award: 1st prize 1,250 GBP; further prizes totaling 1,000 GBP: runners-up prizes of one-year magazine subscriptions to Stand Magazine

Sunday Times Small Publisher of the Year Award
The Sunday Times
Independent Publishers Guild, 4 Middle St, Great Gransden, Sandy, Beds SG19 3AD
Tel: (01767) 677753 *Fax:* (01767) 677069
Key Personnel
Administrator: Sheila Bounford *E-mail:* sheila@ipg.uk.com
Annual award for the best independent publisher in the UK which produces between 5 & 40 titles in a calendar year, with a maximum turnover of 1,500,000 GBP per year.
Award: 1,000 GBP
Closing Date: Jan 31
Presented: London Book Fair

☆**The Times Educational Supplement Information Book Award**
Times Educational Supplement
Admiral House, 66-68 East Smithfield, London E1W 1BX
Mailing Address: PO Box 495, London E1W 2XY
Tel: (020) 7782 3000 *Fax:* (020) 7782 3200
Web Site: www.tes.co.uk

☆**The Times Educational Supplement Schoolbook Award**
Times Educational Supplement
Admiral House, 66-68 East Smithfield, London E1W 1BX
Mailing Address: PO Box 495, London E1W 2XY
Tel: (020) 7782 3000 *Fax:* (020) 7782 3200
Web Site: www.tes.co.uk
The Award is administered jointly by the TES & the Educational Publishers Council. There are two categories, Primary, for children ages 5-11 & Secondary, for young people ages 11-16. Prizes are to be awarded to the authors of the most outstanding schoolbooks in the subject of National Curriculum Books (subject decided each year). The category changes annually. To be eligible, books must have originated in Great Britain, final entry date usually Dec 31. No proof copies can be considered. There is no limit to the number of entries but the publishers are asked to be selective in their entries & no books may be entered simultaneously for the Schoolbook Award & the TES Information Book Awards. One copy of each entry should be sent directly to TES & to each of the judges.

Tom-Gallon Trust Award
Society of Authors
84 Drayton Gardens, London SW10 9SB
Tel: (020) 7373 6642 *Fax:* (020) 7373 5768
E-mail: info@societyofauthors.org
Web Site: www.societyofauthors.org
Established: 1943
Awarded biennially to short story writers of limited means. Entrants must submit a list of already published fiction, one published or unpublished short story, & a brief statement of their financial position & willingness to devote substantial time to writing fiction as soon as they are financially able.
Award: 1,000 GBP
Closing Date: Sept 20

☆**The Betty Trask Prize & Awards**
Society of Authors
84 Drayton Gardens, London SW10 9SB
Tel: (020) 7373 6642 *Fax:* (020) 7373 5768
E-mail: info@societyofauthors.org
Web Site: www.societyofauthors.org
Established: 1983
Awards are for the benefit of authors under 35 years of age who are Commonwealth citizens & are given for a first novel (published or unpublished) of a romantic or traditional nature. All winners are required to use the money for a period or periods of foreign travel with a view to increasing their experience & knowledge for future literary benefit.
Award: Up to 25,000 GBP total value
Closing Date: Jan 31

Travelling Scholarships
Society of Authors
84 Drayton Gardens, London SW10 9SB
Tel: (020) 7373 6642 *Fax:* (020) 7373 5768
E-mail: info@societyofauthors.org
Web Site: www.societyofauthors.org/prizes.htm
Established: 1944
Annual awards to enable British writers to keep in touch with their colleagues abroad. Honorary Scholarships are awarded for a body of work & submissions are not accepted.
Award: 6,000 GBP

VER Poets Open Competition
VER Poets

UNITED KINGDOM   LITERARY

61-63 Chiswell Green Lane, St Albans, Herts AL2 3AL
Tel: (01727) 867005
Key Personnel
Chairman: Ray Badman
President: John Cotton
Vice President: John Mole
Editor & Organiser: May Badman
Established: 1966
Award: Total Prizes 1,000 GBP; 1st prizr 500 GBP; 2nd prize 300 GBP; two 3rd prizes 100 GBP each; plus publication in anthology
Closing Date: April 30
Presented: St Albans, June

Vondel Translation Prize
Society of Authors - Translators Association
84 Drayton Gardens, London SW10 9SB
Tel: (020) 7373 6642 *Fax:* (020) 7373 5768
E-mail: info@societyofauthors.org
Web Site: www.societyofauthors.org
The biennial prize is for translations of works into English of Dutch & Flemish works of literary merit & general interest. The translation must have been first published in the UK or the USA.
Award: Approximately 2,000 GBP
Closing Date: Dec 20

Walford Award
Chartered Institute of Library & Information Professionals (CILIP)
7 Ridgmount St, London WC1E 7AE
Tel: (020) 7255 0650 *Fax:* (020) 7255 0501
E-mail: info@cilip.org.uk
Web Site: www.cilip.org.uk
Key Personnel
Marketing Manager: Louisa Myatt *E-mail:* louisa.myatt@cilip.org.uk
Presented to an individual who has made a sustained & continual contribution to the science & art of bibliography in the UK. The nominee need not be a resident in the UK.
Award: 500 GBP & certificate

The David Watt Prize
Rio Tinto PLC
6 Saint James's Sq, London SW1Y 4LD
Tel: (020) 7930 2399 *Fax:* (020) 7930 3249
E-mail: davidwattprize@riotinto.com
Web Site: www.riotinto.com
Key Personnel
Contact: Celia Beale *E-mail:* celiabeale@globalnet.co.uk; Andrea Redfern
Established: 1988
Annual journalism prize for outstanding contributions towards the clarification of political issues & the promotion of their greater understanding.
Award: 7,500 GBP
Closing Date: March 31

Wheatley Medal
Chartered Institute of Library & Information Professionals (CILIP)
7 Ridgmount St, London WC1E 7AE
Tel: (020) 7255 0650 *Fax:* (020) 7255 0501
E-mail: info@cilip.org.uk
Web Site: www.cilip.org.uk
Key Personnel
Marketing Manager: Louisa Myatt *E-mail:* louisa.myatt@cilip.org.uk
Established: 1961
Presented in association with The Society of Indexers, for an outstanding printed index published in the UK between Jan 1 & April 27. Indexes will be judged on clarity, comprehensiveness, choice of terms & headings, use of cross reference, avoidance of strings of undifferentiated page references, layout, presentation, overall impact of the index & relevance to text.

Award: 500 GBP, certificate & gold medal
Presented: Awards ceremony, Sept

Whitbread Book Awards
Booksellers Association of the United Kingdom & Ireland Ltd
Minster House, 272 Vauxhall Bridge Rd, London SW1V 1BA
Tel: (020) 7802 0802 *Fax:* (020) 7802 0803
E-mail: mail@booksellers.org.uk
Web Site: www.whitbread-bookawards.co.uk
Key Personnel
Contact: Denise Bayat
Established: 1971
The awards celebrate & promote the best contemporary British writing. The awards are judged in two stages & open to five categories: Novel, Biography, Poetry & Children's Book of the Year. The Novel, First Novel, Biography & Poetry Awards are judged by a panel of three judges & the winner of each category receives an award of 5,000 GBP. Three adult judges & two young judges select a shortlist of four books for the Whitbread Children's Book of the Year. The final judges then select the Whitbread Children's Book of the Year, worth 5,000 GBP & then go on to choose the Whitbread Book of the Year from the winners of the Novel, First Novel, Biography & Poetry Awards & the winner of the Whitbread Children's Book of the Year. The winner receives a check for 25,000 GBP. Writers must have lived in Great Britain & Ireland for three or more years. Submissions must be received from publishers.
Award: Total of 50,000 GBP
Closing Date: Early July

Whitfield Prize
The Royal Society
University College London, Gower St, London WC1E 6BT
Tel: (020) 7387 7532 *Fax:* (020) 7387 7532
E-mail: royalhistsoc@ucl.ac.uk; rhsinfo@rhs.ac.uk
Web Site: www.rhs.ac.uk
Key Personnel
Executive Secretary: Joy McCarthy
Established: 1976
Annual prize for a new book on British history.
Award: 1,000 GBP
Closing Date: Dec 31
Presented: Royal Historical Society Annual Reception, July

John Whiting Award
Arts Council of England
14 Great Peter St, London SW1P 3NQ
Tel: (0845) 300 6200 *Fax:* (020) 7973 6590
E-mail: enquiries@artscouncil.org.uk
Web Site: www.artscouncil.org.uk
Award is intended to help future careers & enhance reputations of British playwrights & to draw to public attention the importance of writers in contemporary theatre.

Meyer Whitworth Award
Arts Council of England
14 Great Peter St, London SW1P 3NQ
Tel: (0845) 300 6200 *Fax:* (020) 7973 6590
E-mail: enquiries@artscouncil.org.uk
Web Site: www.artscouncil.org.uk
Intended to help further the careers of UK playwrights who are not yet established.

☆**WHSmith Literary Award**
WHSmith PLC
Nations House PLC, 103 Wigmore St, London W1U 1WH
Tel: (020) 7514 9623 *Fax:* (020) 7514 9635
Web Site: www.whsmith.co.uk

Established: 1959
The prize is awarded to a work of fiction or non-fiction that makes an outstanding contribution to English literature & written by an author from The UK, The Commonwealth or The Republic of Ireland. The winner is chosen by nomination; entries are not required.
Award: 10,000 GBP

WHSmith Young Writers' Competition
WHSmith PLC
Nations House PLC, 103 Wigmore St, London W1U 1WH
Tel: (020) 7514 9623 *Fax:* (020) 7514 9635
Web Site: www.whsmith.co.uk
Established: 1959
Established as the Children's Literary Competition & previously run by the 'Daily Mirror', the competition aims to encourage creativity in written English. Open to all children in the United Kingdom & of British nationality abroad, up to the age of 16 years. The award-winning work is published in book form.
Award: 93 awards totaling more than 7,000 GBP

Wolfson History Prize
The Wolfson Foundation
8 Queen Anne St, London W1M 9LD
Tel: (020) 7323 5730 *Fax:* (020) 7323 3241
Established: 1972
Two awards totaling up to 25,000 GBP are made annually to British authors of historical writing which is considered both scholarly & accessible to the general reader.
Award: 15,000 GBP & 10,000 GBP

Writers' Bursaries
Arts Council of England
14 Great Peter St, London SW1P 3NQ
Tel: (0845) 300 6200 *Fax:* (020) 7973 6590
E-mail: enquiries@artscouncil.org.uk
Web Site: www.artscouncil.org.uk
Fifteen awards: open to published writers resident in England who need funds to complete a work in progress.
Award: 7,000 GBP each

☆**Yorkshire Post Book of the Year Award**
Yorkshire Post Newspapers Ltd
Wellington St, Leeds LS1 1RF
Mailing Address: PO Box 168, Leeds LS1 1RF
Tel: (0113) 2432701 *Fax:* (0113) 2443430
Web Site: www.applegate.co.uk
Key Personnel
Organizer: Margaret Brown
Established: 1964
Awarded to the best book published each year in the United Kingdom called 'Book of the Year' Award. Translations, reissues & works of a strictly scientific or technical nature are excluded. In addition, there is a Best First Work Award for a new author. There are also special annual awards for books selected to advance the popular appreciation of art & music. Publisher entry only.
Award: 1,200 GBP

United States

☆**American-Scandinavian Foundation Translation Prize**
American-Scandinavian Foundation
58 Park Ave, New York, NY 10016
Tel: 212-879-9779 *Fax:* 212-879-2301; 212-249-3444
E-mail: asf@amscan.org
Web Site: www.amscan.org

Key Personnel
Editor: Adrienne Gyongy *E-mail:* agyongy@amscan.org
Established: 1980
Initiated by 'Scandinavian Review' (three per year) to bring best of contemporary Scandinavian literature to American readers. There is a prize either for poetry or fiction, in addition to publication. Awarded annually for the best translation of work by a Danish, Finnish, Icelandic, Norwegian or Swedish author born after 1800; for more details request rules.
Award: 2,000 USD
Closing Date: Postmark deadline of June 1

☆**The Bologna New Media Prize**
Children's Software Revue & The Bologna Children's Book Fair
44 Main St, Flemington, NJ 08822
Tel: 908-284-0404 *Fax:* 908-284-0405
Web Site: www.bolognanewmediaprize.com
Key Personnel
Editor: Warren Buckleitner *E-mail:* buckleit@aol.com
Established: 1997
Children's interactive media.
Closing Date: Dec 15 annually
Presented: Bologna, Italy, April annually

☆**Children's Book Award**
International Reading Association
800 Barksdale Rd, Newark, DE 19714
Mailing Address: PO Box 8139, Newark, DE 19714-8139
Tel: 302-731-1600 *Fax:* 302-731-1057
Web Site: www.reading.org
Key Personnel
Public Information Associate: Janet Butler
Tel: 302-731-1600 (ext 293) *E-mail:* jbutler@reading.org
Established: 1974
Awarded annually for a first or second book (any language) to authors who show unusual promise in the children's/young adult book field. There are three categories: Primary (ages preschool - 8), Intermediate (ages 9-13) & Young Adult (ages 14-17). Entries in languages other than English must include a one-page abstract in English & a translation into English of one chapter or similar selection.
Award: Four awards of 500 USD for 1st or 2nd published book
Presented: San Francisco

☆**Hugo Awards**
World Science Fiction Society
PO Box 426159, Kendall Square Station, Cambridge, MA 02142
Web Site: www.wsfa.org
Established: 1953
Established as Science Fiction Achievement Awards for the best science fiction writing in several categories. Chrome-plated rocket ship model awarded annually.

☆**IBC International Book Award**
International Book Committee (IBC)
800 Barksdale Rd, Newark, DE 19714
Mailing Address: PO Box 8139, Newark, DE 19714
Tel: 302-731-1600 *Fax:* 302-731-1057
Web Site: www.reading.org

Key Personnel
Chairman: Alan Farstrup
Vice Chairman: Leena Maissen
Established: 1972
Founded by book professionals as an outgrowth of the Support Committee for the Unesco International Book Year, the award is granted annually to outstanding persons or groups for their contribution to the promotion of books & reading internationally.

☆**The Irish American Cultural Institute Literary Awards**
The Irish American Cultural Institute
One Lackawanna Pl, Morristown, NJ
Tel: 973-605-1991 *Fax:* 973-605-8875
E-mail: irishway@aol.com
Web Site: www.iaci-usa.org
Established: 1966
For writers in the Irish or English language. Butler awards for each language in alternate years & O'Shaughnessy award for poetry. There is also funding to primary research on Irish-American themes. No application procedure.
Award: 10,000 USD for each language; 5,000 USD for poetry
Closing Date: Fall
Presented: Fall of the following year

☆**The Kiriyama Prize**
The Kiriyama Pacific Rim Institute
650 Delancey St, Suite 101, San Francisco, CA 94107-2082
Tel: 415-777-1628 *Fax:* 415-422-1646
E-mail: admin@pacificrimvoices.org; info@pacificrimvoices.org
Web Site: www.kiriyamaprize.org; www.pacificrimvoices.org
Key Personnel
Prize Administrator: Peter Coughlan
Prize Manager: Jeannine Cuevas
  E-mail: jeannine@kiriyamaprize.org
Established: 1996
Annual prize for the book judged to have contributed most to understanding among Pacific Rim countries. Books must be published in English, either originating in English or translated into English. Books must be published during the previous calendar year. Open to nonfiction or fiction of any genre.
Other Sponsor(s): Center for the Pacific Rim, University of San Francisco
Award: 30,000 USD (15,000 USD to winning authors, fiction & nonfiction)
Closing Date: July 3
Presented: Annually in spring

☆**Neustadt International Prize for Literature**
University of Oklahoma
University of Oklahoma, 110 Monnet Hall, Norman, OK 73019-4033
Tel: 405-325-4531 *Fax:* 405-325-7495
Web Site: www.ou.edu/worldlit
Key Personnel
Executive Dir: Robert Con Davis-Undiano
Established: 1969
'World Literature Today', an international literary quarterly, a biennial award for distinguished & continuing artistic achievement in the fields of poetry, drama or fiction. A new international jury of 12 is appointed for each successive award by the editor in consultation with the editorial board. Each juror presents one candidate for the prize. A majority (seven) of the jury must be present for the deliberations & the final voting. Representative selections of a candidate's work must be available to the jury in either French or English translation. Announcement of the winner is made in February or March, & the award is officially presented at The University of Oklahoma, Norman, Oklahoma, every other year. 'World Literature Today' dedicates one issue to the recipient. The University of Oklahoma Press will seriously consider the publication of a book by or on the winner. Prize not open to application.
Award: Certificate, replica of an eagle's feather in silver & 50,000 USD

Venezuela

☆**Romulo Gallegos Novel Prize**
National Council For Culture
Casa de Romulo Gallegos, Av Luis Roche con tercera transversal, Altamira, Caracas 1062
Tel: (02) 285 27 21; (02) 285 29 90; (02) 285 26 44 *Fax:* (02) 285 46 80; (02) 285 55 86
E-mail: celarg5@reacciun.ve
Web Site: www.celarg.org.ve
Established: 1964
Established by the National Institute of Culture & Fine Arts of the Republic of Venezuela. Originally instituted to mark the 80th anniversary of the birth of the illustrious author Romulo Gallegos, which was celebrated in August 1964, the first award was made in 1967, the 400th anniversary of the founding of Caracas - birthplace of the novelist. Competition is open to any writer from Latin America, Spain or the Philippines whose novel is written in Spanish & has been published originally in one of the countries of the above designated areas.
Award: 54,000 EUR

National Prize for Literature
Concejo Nacional de la Cultura (CONAC)
Centro Simon Bolivar, Torre Norte, Pisos 13-16, Caracas
Tel: (02) 484 21 72
Awarded annually to the best Venezuelan author. Also includes contestants in narrative prose & essays.
Award: 30,000 bolivares

Zimbabwe

The Literature Bureau Annual Literary Award
The Literature Bureau
Ministry of Education, Sport & Culture, Causeway, Harare
Mailing Address: PO Box CY121, Causeway, Harare
Tel: (04) 333812
Award for the best works in Shona & Ndebele. Most genres, including translations, qualify for entry.
Award: 500 Zimbabwe dollars

Book Trade Calendar

Calendar of Book Trade & Promotional Events—Alphabetical Index of Sponsors

Adelaide Festival Corp
Adelaide Bank Festival of Arts
March 2005, pg 1472

Advanstar Communications
AIIM 2005 Conference & Exposition
May 2005, pg 1475
ON DEMAND
May 2005, pg 1475

Advertising Research Foundation
Advertising Research Foundation Annual Convention & Trade Show
April 2005, pg 1473

ALA, see American Library Association (ALA)

American Association of Advertising Agencies (AAAA)
AAAA Management Conference
May 2005, pg 1475
AAAA Media Conference & Trade Show
March 2005, pg 1472
Creative Conference
November 2004, pg 1468

American Booksellers Association
ABA Convention & Trade Exhibit
June 2005, pg 1476

American Forest & Paper Association
Paper Week
April 2005, pg 1474
April 2006, pg 1482

American Institute of Graphic Arts (AIGA)
Business & Design Conference
Autumn 2006, pg 1483
National Design Conference
September 2005, pg 1479

American Library Association (ALA)
American Library Association Annual Conference
June 2005, pg 1476
June 2006, pg 1483
June 2007, pg 1485
June 2008, pg 1486
American Library Association Mid-Winter Meeting
January 2005, pg 1469
January 2006, pg 1481
January 2007, pg 1484
National Library Week
April 2005, pg 1474
April 2006, pg 1482
April 2007, pg 1485
April 2008, pg 1486
April 2009, pg 1487

American Medical Writers Association
American Medical Writers Association Annual Conference
October 2004, pg 1467

American Schools of Oriental Research
American Academy of Religion
November 2004, pg 1468
November 2005, pg 1480
November 2006, pg 1484
November 2007, pg 1486

American Society for Quality
ASQ World Conference on Quality & Improvement
May 2005, pg 1475
May 2006, pg 1482
The Quest for Excellence
April 2005, pg 1474

American Translators Association (ATA)
American Translators Association Annual Conference
October 2004, pg 1467
November 2005, pg 1481

Amsterdam RAI
Amsterdam International Printing Allied Industries Trade Fair (Grafivak)
May 2005, pg 1475

Antiquarian Booksellers' Association of America
California International Antiquarian Book Fair
February 2005, pg 1470

Arizona Humanities Council
Arizona Book Festival
April 2005, pg 1473

ARLIS/UK & Ireland Art Libraries Society
ARLIS/UK & Ireland Annual Conference
July 2005, pg 1478

Ars Polon SA - Warsaw International Book Fair Office
Warsaw International Book Fair
May 2005, pg 1476

Associated Collegiate Press (ACP)
National College Media Convention
November 2004, pg 1469
October 2005, pg 1480
November 2006, pg 1484
October 2007, pg 1486

Association of American Publishers Inc (AAP)
Association of American Publishers Annual Meeting
March 2005, pg 1472
Association of American Publishers Annual Meeting for Small & Independent Publishers
March 2005, pg 1472
Association of American Publishers Professional & Scholarly Publishing Divison Annual Meeting
February 2005, pg 1470
Association of American Publishers School Division Annual Meeting
February 2005, pg 1470

Association of American University Presses (AAUP)
Association of American University Presses Annual Meeting
June 2005, pg 1476

Association of Directory Publishers
Association of Directory Publishers Annual Meeting
April 2005, pg 1473

Association of Writers & Writing Programs (AWP)
Associated Writing Programs Annual Conference & Bookfair
March 2005, pg 1472

Association of Yugoslav Publishers & Booksellers
Belgrade International Book Fair
October 2004, pg 1467

Ausstellungs-und Messe-GmbH des Borsenvereins des Deutschen Buchhandels
Frankfurt Book Fair
October 2005, pg 1480
October 2006, pg 1484

BASH, see Booksellers Association of the United Kingdom & Ireland Ltd

BIBF Management Office, CNPIEC
Beijing International Book Fair
May 2005, pg 1475
September 2005, pg 1479

Bibliographical Society of Canada/La Societe bibliographique du Canada
Bibliographical Society of Canada/La Societe bibliographique du Canada Annual Meeting
July 2005, pg 1478

ALPHABETICAL INDEX OF SPONSORS / CALENDAR OF BOOK TRADE

Binding Industries Association International (BIA)
Binding Industries Association International Spring/Presidents Conference
March 2005, pg 1472

Bock.be
Antwerp Book Fair
October 2004, pg 1467

Boersenverein des Deutschen Buchhandels, Landesverband Baden-Wuerttemberg eV (Association of Publishers & Booksellers in Baden-Wuerttemberg e V)
Buch-IBO
March 2005, pg 1472
Karlsruher Buecherschau
November 2004, pg 1468
November 2005, pg 1481
November 2006, pg 1484
Stuttgarter Buchwochen (Stuttgart Bookweeks)
November 2004, pg 1469
November 2005, pg 1481
November 2006, pg 1484
November 2007, pg 1486

Bok & Bibliotek
Goteborg International Book Fair
September 2005, pg 1479
September 2006, pg 1483

BolognaFiere
Bologna Children's Book Fair
April 2005, pg 1473

Book Manufacturers' Institute Inc (BMI)
BMI Annual Conference
November 2004, pg 1468
BMI Management Conference
Spring 2005, pg 1471

Booksellers Association of the United Kingdom & Ireland Ltd
Booksellers Association of the United Kingdom & Ireland Annual Conference
April 2005, pg 1473

BookTech
BookTech Conference & Expo
March 2005, pg 1472

British & Irish Association of Law Librarians
British & Irish Association of Law Librarians Annual Conference
June 2005, pg 1477

The Bronte Society
The Bronte Society Annual General Meeting
June 2005, pg 1477

Bulgarian Book Publishers Association
Sofia International Book Fair
December 2004, pg 1469

Business & Industrial Trade Fairs Ltd
Graphic Arts
August 2005, pg 1478
Print & Pack Expo
August 2005, pg 1478

Canadian Library Association (CLA)
Canadian Library Association Annual Convention & Tradeshow
June 2005, pg 1477
June 2006, pg 1483

Canon Communications
Eastpack: The Power of Packaging
June 2005, pg 1477
SouthPack
April 2005, pg 1474
Westpack
January 2005, pg 1470

Catholic Press Association of the US & Canada
Catholic Press Association of the US and Canada Annual Convention
May 2005, pg 1475

CBA
CBA Advance
January 2005, pg 1470
January 2006, pg 1481
January 2007, pg 1484
CBA International Convention
July 2005, pg 1478
July 2006, pg 1483
July 2007, pg 1485
July 2008, pg 1486
July 2009, pg 1487

Chartered Institute of Library & Information Professionals (CILIP)
Umbrella 2005
June 2005, pg 1477

The Children's Book Council (CBC)
Children's Book Week
November 2004, pg 1468
November 2005, pg 1481
November 2006, pg 1484
Young People's Poetry Week
April 2005, pg 1475
April 2006, pg 1482
April 2007, pg 1485
April 2008, pg 1486
April 2009, pg 1487

Christian Booksellers Convention Ltd
Christian Booksellers Convention - UK
March 2005, pg 1472
March 2006, pg 1482

Church & Synagogue Library Association
Church & Synagogue Library Association Conference
July 2005, pg 1478
July 2006, pg 1483
July 2007, pg 1485

Ciana Ltd
Remainder & Promotional Book Fair
Spring 2005, pg 1471
Autumn 2005, pg 1479

CILIP, see Chartered Institute of Library & Information Professionals (CILIP)

Copywriter's Council of America (CCA)
Hall of Fame Awards & Annual Convention
November 2004, pg 1468

Deutsche Gesellschaft fur Informationswissenschaft und informationspraxis eV (German Society for Information Science & Information Practice)
DGI Annual Meeting & Online Conference
Spring 2005, pg 1471

The Direct Marketing Association Inc (The DMA)
DMA Annual Conference & Exhibition
October 2005, pg 1480

Distripress
Distripress Annual Congress
September 2005, pg 1479
October 2006, pg 1484

Docucorp International
Docugroup 2006
March 2006, pg 1482

Dog Writers' Association of America Inc (DWAA)
Dog Writers' Association of America Annual Meeting
February 2005, pg 1471

Edinburgh International Book Festival
Edinburgh International Book Festival
August 2005, pg 1478

The English Association
English Association Semiannual Teachers' Conference
March 2005, pg 1472
October 2005, pg 1480

European Association of Directory & Database Publishers (EADP)
European Association of Directory & Database Publishers Annual Congress
September 2005, pg 1479
Annual European Conference on Managing Directories
May 2005, pg 1475

Evangelical Christian Publishers Association
ECPA Management Seminar
April 2005, pg 1473
ECPA Publishing University
November 2004, pg 1468
November 2005, pg 1481
ECPA Trade Show
January 2005, pg 1470

Evangelical Press Association (EPA)
Evangelical Press Association Annual Conference
April 2005, pg 1473

Federacion de Gremios de Editores de Espana (FGEE) (Spanish Publishers Association)
LIBER Feria Internacional del Libro
October 2005, pg 1480
September 2006, pg 1484

Federation of Children's Book Groups
Federation of Children's Book Groups Annual Conference
April 2005, pg 1474

Feria Internacional del Libro Guadalajara
Feria Internacional del Libro
November 2004, pg 1468
November 2005, pg 1481

Football Writers Association of America
Football Writers Association of America Annual Meeting
January 2005, pg 1470

Fundacion El Libro
Buenos Aires International Children's Book Fair
Summer 2005, pg 1476

Garden Writers Association of America
Garden Writers Association of America Meeting & Symposium
September 2005, pg 1479

& PROMOTIONAL EVENTS

ALPHABETICAL INDEX OF SPONSORS

General Directorate of International Book Exhibitions & Fairs
Moscow International Book Fair
September 2005, pg 1479

General Egyptian Book Organization
Cairo International Book Fair
January 2005, pg 1470
Cairo International Children's Book Fair
November 2004, pg 1468

Ghana Trade Fair Co Ltd
Ghana International Book Fair
November 2004, pg 1468
November 2006, pg 1484

Graphic Arts Merchants Association of Australia Inc (GAMMA)
Pacprint
May 2005, pg 1475
PrintEx
May 2007, pg 1485

Graphic Arts Show Company
Graphic Arts/The Charlotte Show
March 2005, pg 1472
Gutenberg Festival
Spring 2005, pg 1471

Gravure Association of America Inc
GAA Expo 2005
May 2005, pg 1475

Gutenberg-Gesellschaft eV (Gutenberg Society)
Gutenberg Gesellschaft Annual General Meeting
June 2005, pg 1477

Hong Kong Trade Development Council
Hong Kong Book Fair
July 2005, pg 1478

IAML, see International Association of Music Libraries, Archives & Documentation Centres

IBBY, see International Board on Books for Young People (IBBY)

IDEAlliance
PRIMEX 2005 (Print Media Executive Summit)
February 2005, pg 1471
Spectrum 2005
September 2005, pg 1480

IDG World Expo
Macworld Conference & Expo
January 2005, pg 1470

IFLA, see International Federation of Library Associations & Institutions (IFLA)

Instituto Tecnologico y de Estudios Superiores de Monterrey
Monterrey International Book Fair
October 2004, pg 1467

Inter American Press Association (IAPA)
Inter American Press Association General Assembly
October 2004, pg 1467
Inter American Press Association Mid-Year Meeting
March 2005, pg 1472

International Association of Business Communicators (IABC)
International Association of Business Communicators Conference
June 2005, pg 1477

International Association of Music Libraries, Archives & Documentation Centres
International Association of Music Libraries, Archives & Documentation Centres Conference
July 2005, pg 1478

International Board on Books for Young People (IBBY)
International Board on Books for Young People Biennial Congress
September 2006, pg 1483
September 2008, pg 1486
International Children's Book Day
April 2005, pg 1474
April 2006, pg 1482

International Electronic Publishing Research Centre Ltd (IEPRC)
IEPRC Annual Conference
June 2005, pg 1477

International Federation of Library Associations & Institutions (IFLA)
World Library & Information Congress
August 2005, pg 1479
August 2006, pg 1483

International Newspaper Financial Executives
International Newspaper Financial Executives Annual Conference
June 2005, pg 1477

International Plate Printers', Die Stampers' & Engravers' Union of North America
International Plate Printers', Die Stampers' & Engravers' Union of North America Mini Meeting
June 2005, pg 1477
June 2006, pg 1483

International Publishers Association
IPA Congress
June 2008, pg 1486

International Reading Association
International Reading Association Annual Convention
May 2005, pg 1475

Internationale Vereinigung fuer Geschichte und Gegenwart der Druckkunst eV, see Gutenberg-Gesellschaft eV (Gutenberg Society)

Jerusalem International Book Fair
Jerusalem International Book Fair
February 2005, pg 1471

Jewish Book Council
Jewish Book Month
November 2004, pg 1468
November 2005, pg 1481

Don Johnson Inc
Technology, Reading & Learning Difficulties (TRLD)
January 2005, pg 1470
January 2006, pg 1481

Kids Cultural Books
African American Children's Book Festival
April 2005, pg 1473
April 2006, pg 1482
Multicultural Children's Book Festival
November 2004, pg 1469
November 2005, pg 1481

Latino Literacy Now
Latino Book & Family Festival
October 2004, pg 1467
November 2004, pg 1469
December 2004, pg 1469

Leipziger Messe GmbH, Projektteam Buchmesse
Leipzig Book Fair
March 2005, pg 1472
March 2006, pg 1482

Library Association of Alberta
Alberta Library Conference
April 2005, pg 1473

Luckwaldt Messen
Quod Libet/International Antiquarian Book Fair & Artists Books
October 2004, pg 1467

LUXEXPO
Antiques & Fine Arts Exhibition/Luxembourg Book Festival
February 2005, pg 1470

MediaLive International
Seybold Seminars
Summer 2005, pg 1476

Miami Book Fair International
Miami Book Fair International
November 2004, pg 1469

Modern Language Association of America (MLA)
Modern Language Association of America Annual Convention
December 2004, pg 1469

Montana Committee for the Humanities
Montana Festival of the Book
September 2005, pg 1479

NASW, see National Association of Science Writers (NASW)

National Association of College Stores (NACS)
CAMEX
February 2005, pg 1470

National Association of Printing Ink Manufacturers (NAPIM)
National Association of Printing Ink Manufacturers Annual Convention
April 2005, pg 1474

National Association of Science Writers (NASW)
National Association of Science Writers Annual Meeting
February 2005, pg 1471
February 2006, pg 1482
February 2007, pg 1484

National Federation of Press Women Inc (NFPW)
National Federation of Press Women National Conference
September 2005, pg 1480

National Newspaper Association
National Newspaper Association Annual Convention & Trade Show
October 2004, pg 1467
National Newspaper Association Annual Government Affairs Conference
March 2005, pg 1472

The National Press Foundation
National Press Foundation Annual Awards Dinner
February 2005, pg 1471

ALPHABETICAL INDEX OF SPONSORS

New Atlantic Independent Booksellers Association (NAIBA)
New Atlantic Independent Booksellers Association Annual Trade Show
October 2004, pg 1467
October 2005, pg 1480

New York Is Book Country
New York Is Book Country
Autumn 2005, pg 1479

Newsletter & Electronic Publishers Association
International Newsletter & Specialized - Information Conference
June 2005, pg 1477
NEPA's Annual Fall Conference
November 2004, pg 1469
Autumn 2005, pg 1479

Newspaper Association of America (NAA)
Newspaper Association of America Annual Convention
April 2005, pg 1474
April 2006, pg 1482
NEXPO®
March 2005, pg 1473
April 2006, pg 1482

North American Agricultural Journalists
North American Agricultural Journalists Spring Meeting
April 2005, pg 1474

NPES The Association for Suppliers of Printing, Publishing & Converting Technologies
NPES The Association for Suppliers of Printing, Publishing and Converting Technologies Annual Conference
October 2005, pg 1480

Outdoor Writers Association of America
Outdoor Writers Association of America Annual Conference
June 2005, pg 1477

Pacific Printing & Imaging Association
Print Buyers Conference
May 2005, pg 1476

Packaging Machinery Manufacturers Institute
PACK EXPO
November 2004, pg 1469

Penton Media
Internet World North
November 2004, pg 1468

Periodical Writers' Association of Canada
Periodical Writers' Association of Canada Annual General Meeting
May 2005, pg 1476

Photographic Society of America Inc (PSA)
PSA International Conference of Photography
August 2005, pg 1478
September 2006, pg 1484
September 2007, pg 1485

Post Newsweek Tech Media
FOSE
April 2005, pg 1474

Poznan International Fair Ltd
Infosystem Fairs
April 2005, pg 1474
Poligrafia
Spring 2005, pg 1471

Primedia Business Exhibitions
The National Center for Database Marketing (NCDM)
Winter 2004, pg 1469

PrintImage International
The Quick Print Show
February 2005, pg 1471

Printing Association of Florida Inc
Graphics of the Americas
February 2005, pg 1471

Printing Industries of America Inc
Print Sales & Marketing Executives Conference
June 2005, pg 1477

Publishers Association of the South (PAS)
Publishers Association of the South Fall Conference & Annual Meeting
September 2005, pg 1480
Publishers Winter Conclave
January 2005, pg 1470

Rain Taxi Review of Books
Twin Cities Book Festival
October 2004, pg 1468
Autumn 2005, pg 1479

Reed Exhibitions
BookExpo America (BEA)
June 2005, pg 1476

Reed Exhibitions Canada
BookExpo Canada
June 2005, pg 1477

Reed Exhibitions Japan Ltd
DP: Digital Publishing Fair
July 2005, pg 1478
TIBF: Tokyo International Book Fair
July 2005, pg 1478

Reed Exhibitions (UK)
London Book Fair
March 2005, pg 1472
Northprint
April 2005, pg 1474

Reed Expositions France
Salon du Livre de Jeunesse (Childrens Book Fair)
November 2006, pg 1484
Salon du Livre de Paris
March 2005, pg 1473

Reed Messe Salzburg GmbH
Dataprint
April 2005, pg 1473

Reed Midem
MILIA: World Interactive Content Forum
April 2005, pg 1474

Reed Tradex Co Ltd
AsiaPack AsiaPrint
June 2005, pg 1476

Research & Engineering Council of NAPL (National Association for Printing Leadership)
Binding, Finishing & Distribution Seminar
April 2005, pg 1473

Romance Writers of America
RWA Annual National Conference
July 2005, pg 1478
July 2006, pg 1483
July 2007, pg 1485
July 2008, pg 1486
July 2009, pg 1487

CALENDAR OF BOOK TRADE

SABEW, see Society of American Business Editors & Writers Inc

Salon du Livre de Montreal
Salon du Livre de Montreal
November 2004, pg 1469

The Dorothy L Sayers Society
The Dorothy L Sayers Society Annual Convention
August 2005, pg 1478
Summer 2007, pg 1485

School Library Association
School Library Association Annual Conference
Summer 2005, pg 1476

Science Fiction Research Association Inc
Science Fiction Research Association Annual Meeting
June 2005, pg 1477

Small Press Center
Small Press Book Fair
December 2004, pg 1469
December 2005, pg 1481

Small Publishers Association of North America (SPAN)
SPAN Conference
October 2004, pg 1467

Society for Imaging Science & Technology (IS&T)
Color Imaging Conference - Color Science Systems & Applications
November 2004, pg 1468
DPP 2005 - International Conference on Digital Production Printing
May 2005, pg 1475
IS&T Archiving Conference
April 2005, pg 1474
NIP 20: The 20th International Congress on Digital Printing Technologies
October 2004, pg 1467

Society for Scholarly Publishing
Society for Scholarly Publishing Annual Meeting
June 2005, pg 1477

Society of American Business Editors & Writers Inc
Society of American Business Editors & Writers Annual Convention and Exhibition
May 2005, pg 1476

Society of Children's Book Writers & Illustrators (SCBWI)
Winter Conference on Writing & Illustrating for Children
February 2005, pg 1471

The Society of Professional Journalists
Society of Professional Journalists National Convention
Autumn 2005, pg 1479

South African Booksellers Association
South African Booksellers Association Annual Conference
August 2005, pg 1478
August 2006, pg 1483

Southeast Booksellers Association (SEBA)
Southeast Booksellers Association Annual Meeting & Trade Show
September 2005, pg 1480
September 2006, pg 1484

Southern California Writers' Conference San Diego
Southern California Writers' Conference San Diego
February 2005, pg 1471

Southern Kentucky Book Fest
Southern Kentucky Book Fest
April 2005, pg 1474

Spanish Evangelical Publishers Association (SEPA)/Associacion de Editores Evangelicos and Editorial Unilit
EXPOLIT Exposicion de Literatura Cristiana Book Fair
May 2005, pg 1475
May 2006, pg 1483

Special Libraries Association (SLA)
Special Libraries Association Annual Conference
June 2005, pg 1477
June 2006, pg 1483
June 2007, pg 1485
July 2008, pg 1486
Special Libraries Association Leadership Summit
January 2005, pg 1470

SPIE - The International Society for Optical Engineering
IS&T/SPIE Electronic Imaging Science & Technology
January 2005, pg 1470

Technical Association of the Pulp & Paper Industry (TAPPI)
AICC/TAPPI SuperCorrExpo® 2004
November 2004, pg 1468
Papermakers Conference & Paper Expo - 2005 TAPPI
May 2005, pg 1476
TAPPI Fall Technical Conference & Trade Fair
October 2004, pg 1467

Texas Book Festival
Texas Book Festival
October 2005, pg 1480

Texas Graphic Arts Educational Foundation
Southwestern Graphics
May 2005, pg 1476

Texas Outdoor Writers Association
Texas Outdoor Writers Association Annual Conference
February 2005, pg 1471

Tuyap Fuar ve Kongre Merkezi
Istanbul Book Fair
October 2004, pg 1467
Izmir Book Fair
Spring 2005, pg 1471

UK Serials Group
UK Serials Group Annual Conference & Exhibition
April 2005, pg 1475
April 2006, pg 1482

Utah Humanities Council
Great Salt Lake Book Festival
September 2005, pg 1479

Virginia Foundation for the Humanities
Virginia Festival of the Book
March 2005, pg 1473
March 2006, pg 1482
March 2007, pg 1485
March 2008, pg 1486
March 2009, pg 1487

VNU Exhibitions Europe
Online Information & Content Management Europe
November 2004, pg 1469
November 2005, pg 1481

Vystaviste Flora Olomouc
Literary Festival
March 2005, pg 1472

Web Offset Association
Annual Web Offset Association Conference
May 2005, pg 1476
Spring 2006, pg 1482
April 2007, pg 1485

Weltverband der Lehrmittelfirmen, see Worlddidac

World Association of Publishers, Manufacturers & Distributors of Educational Materials, see Worlddidac

Worlddidac
China Didac/WORLDDIDAC
October 2005, pg 1480
WORLDDIDAC Brazil 2005
November 2005, pg 1481
WORLDDIDAC Mexico 2005
March 2005, pg 1473
WORLDDIDAC 2004 Basel
October 2004, pg 1468

Writer's Summer School
SWANICK: The Writer's Summer School
August 2005, pg 1478

Xplor International
Xplor Global Conference
October 2004, pg 1468
October 2005, pg 1480

Zimbabwe International Book Fair
Zimbabwe International Book Fair
August 2005, pg 1479

Calendar of Book Trade & Promotional Events—Alphabetical Index of Events

AAAA Management Conference
May 2005, pg 1475

AAAA Media Conference & Trade Show
March 2005, pg 1472

ABA Convention & Trade Exhibit
June 2005, pg 1476

Adelaide Bank Festival of Arts
Formerly Adelaide Writers' Week
March 2005, pg 1472

Adelaide Writers' Week, see Adelaide Bank Festival of Arts

Advertising Research Foundation Annual Convention & Trade Show
April 2005, pg 1473

African American Children's Book Festival
April 2005, pg 1473
April 2006, pg 1482

AICC/TAPPI SuperCorrExpo® 2004
November 2004, pg 1468

AIIM 2005 Conference & Exposition
May 2005, pg 1475

Alberta Library Conference
April 2005, pg 1473

American Academy of Religion
November 2004, pg 1468
November 2005, pg 1480
November 2006, pg 1484
November 2007, pg 1486

American Association of Advertising Agencies Management Conference, see AAAA Management Conference

American Association of Advertising Agencies Media Conference & Trade Show, see AAAA Media Conference & Trade Show

American Library Association Annual Conference
June 2005, pg 1476
June 2006, pg 1483
June 2007, pg 1485
June 2008, pg 1486

American Library Association Mid-Winter Meeting
January 2005, pg 1469
January 2006, pg 1481
January 2007, pg 1484

American Medical Writers Association Annual Conference
October 2004, pg 1467

American Translators Association Annual Conference
October 2004, pg 1467
November 2005, pg 1481

Amsterdam International Printing Allied Industries Trade Fair (Grafivak)
May 2005, pg 1475

Antiques & Fine Arts Exhibition/Luxembourg Book Festival
February 2005, pg 1470

Antwerp Book Fair
October 2004, pg 1467

Arizona Book Festival
April 2005, pg 1473

ARLIS/UK & Ireland Annual Conference
July 2005, pg 1478

AsiaPack AsiaPrint
June 2005, pg 1476

ASQ World Conference on Quality & Improvement
May 2005, pg 1475
May 2006, pg 1482

Associated Writing Programs Annual Conference & Bookfair
March 2005, pg 1472

Association of American Publishers Annual Meeting
March 2005, pg 1472

Association of American Publishers Annual Meeting for Small & Independent Publishers
March 2005, pg 1472

Association of American Publishers Professional & Scholarly Publishing Divison Annual Meeting
February 2005, pg 1470

Association of American Publishers School Division Annual Meeting
February 2005, pg 1470

Association of American University Presses Annual Meeting
June 2005, pg 1476

Association of Directory Publishers Annual Meeting
April 2005, pg 1473

Beijing International Book Fair
May 2005, pg 1475
September 2005, pg 1479

Belgrade International Book Fair
October 2004, pg 1467

Bibliographical Society of Canada/La Societe bibliographique du Canada Annual Meeting
July 2005, pg 1478

Binding, Finishing & Distribution Seminar
April 2005, pg 1473

Binding Industries Association International Spring/Presidents Conference
March 2005, pg 1472

BMI Annual Conference
November 2004, pg 1468

BMI Management Conference
Spring 2005, pg 1471

Bologna Children's Book Fair
April 2005, pg 1473

BookExpo America (BEA)
June 2005, pg 1476

BookExpo Canada
June 2005, pg 1477

Booksellers Association of the United Kingdom & Ireland Annual Conference
April 2005, pg 1473

BookTech Conference & Expo
March 2005, pg 1472

British & Irish Association of Law Librarians Annual Conference
June 2005, pg 1477

The Bronte Society Annual General Meeting
June 2005, pg 1477

Buch-IBO
March 2005, pg 1472

Buenos Aires International Children's Book Fair
Summer 2005, pg 1476

Business & Design Conference
Autumn 2006, pg 1483

Cairo International Book Fair
January 2005, pg 1470

Cairo International Children's Book Fair
November 2004, pg 1468

California International Antiquarian Book Fair
February 2005, pg 1470

CAMEX
February 2005, pg 1470

Canadian Library Association Annual Convention & Tradeshow
June 2005, pg 1477
June 2006, pg 1483

Catholic Press Association of the US and Canada Annual Convention
May 2005, pg 1475

ALPHABETICAL INDEX OF EVENTS

CBA Advance
Formerly CBA Expo
January 2005, pg 1470
January 2006, pg 1481
January 2007, pg 1484

CBA Expo, see CBA Advance

CBA International Convention
July 2005, pg 1478
July 2006, pg 1483
July 2007, pg 1485
July 2008, pg 1486
July 2009, pg 1487

Children's Book Week
November 2004, pg 1468
November 2005, pg 1481
November 2006, pg 1484

China Didac/WORLDDIDAC
October 2005, pg 1480

Christian Booksellers Convention - UK
March 2005, pg 1472
March 2006, pg 1482

Church & Synagogue Library Association Conference
July 2005, pg 1478
July 2006, pg 1483
July 2007, pg 1485

Color Imaging Conference - Color Science Systems & Applications
November 2004, pg 1468

Creative Conference
November 2004, pg 1468

Dataprint
April 2005, pg 1473

De Boekenbeurs, see Antwerp Book Fair

DGI Annual Meeting & Online Conference
Spring 2005, pg 1471

Distripress Annual Congress
September 2005, pg 1479
October 2006, pg 1484

DMA Annual Conference & Exhibition
October 2005, pg 1480

Docugroup 2006
March 2006, pg 1482

Dog Writers' Association of America Annual Meeting
February 2005, pg 1471

The Dorothy L Sayers Society Annual Convention
August 2005, pg 1478
Summer 2007, pg 1485

DP: Digital Publishing Fair
July 2005, pg 1478

DPP 2005 - International Conference on Digital Production Printing
May 2005, pg 1475

Eastpack: The Power of Packaging
June 2005, pg 1477

ECPA Management Seminar
April 2005, pg 1473

ECPA Publishing University
November 2004, pg 1468
November 2005, pg 1481

ECPA Trade Show
January 2005, pg 1470

Edinburgh International Book Festival
August 2005, pg 1478

English Association Semiannual Teachers' Conference
March 2005, pg 1472
October 2005, pg 1480

European Association of Directory & Database Publishers Annual Congress
September 2005, pg 1479

European Conference on Electronic Directories, see Annual European Conference on Managing Directories

Annual European Conference on Managing Directories
Formerly European Conference on Electronic Directories
May 2005, pg 1475

Evangelical Press Association Annual Conference
April 2005, pg 1473

EXPOLIT Exposicion de Literatura Cristiana Book Fair
May 2005, pg 1475
May 2006, pg 1483

Federation of Children's Book Groups Annual Conference
April 2005, pg 1474

Feria Internacional del Libro
November 2004, pg 1468
November 2005, pg 1481

Football Writers Association of America Annual Meeting
January 2005, pg 1470

FOSE
April 2005, pg 1474

Frankfurt Book Fair
October 2005, pg 1480
October 2006, pg 1484

GAA Expo 2005
Formerly Gravure Association of America Convention
May 2005, pg 1475

Garden Writers Association of America Meeting & Symposium
September 2005, pg 1479

Ghana International Book Fair
November 2004, pg 1468
November 2006, pg 1484

Goteborg International Book Fair
September 2005, pg 1479
September 2006, pg 1483

Grafivak, see Amsterdam International Printing Allied Industries Trade Fair (Grafivak)

Graphic Arts
August 2005, pg 1478

CALENDAR OF BOOK TRADE

Graphic Arts/The Charlotte Show
March 2005, pg 1472

Graphics of the Americas
February 2005, pg 1471

Gravure Association of America Convention, see GAA Expo 2005

Great Salt Lake Book Festival
September 2005, pg 1479

Guadalajara International Book Fair, see Feria Internacional del Libro

Gutenberg Festival
Spring 2005, pg 1471

Gutenberg Gesellschaft Annual General Meeting
June 2005, pg 1477

Hall of Fame Awards & Annual Convention
November 2004, pg 1468

Hong Kong Book Fair
July 2005, pg 1478

IEPRC Annual Conference
June 2005, pg 1477

Infosystem Fairs
April 2005, pg 1474

Inter American Press Association General Assembly
October 2004, pg 1467

Inter American Press Association Mid-Year Meeting
March 2005, pg 1472

International Association of Business Communicators Conference
June 2005, pg 1477

International Association of Music Libraries, Archives & Documentation Centres Conference
July 2005, pg 1478

International Board on Books for Young People Biennial Congress
September 2006, pg 1483
September 2008, pg 1486

International Children's Book Day
April 2005, pg 1474
April 2006, pg 1482

International Conference on Writing & Illustrating for Children, see Winter Conference on Writing & Illustrating for Children

International Newsletter & Specialized - Information Conference
June 2005, pg 1477

International Newspaper Financial Executives Annual Conference
June 2005, pg 1477

International Plate Printers', Die Stampers' & Engravers' Union of North America Mini Meeting
June 2005, pg 1477
June 2006, pg 1483

International Reading Association Annual Convention
May 2005, pg 1475

Internet World North
November 2004, pg 1468

IPA Congress
June 2008, pg 1486

IS&T Archiving Conference
April 2005, pg 1474

IS&T/SPIE Electronic Imaging Science & Technology
January 2005, pg 1470

Istanbul Book Fair
October 2004, pg 1467

Izmir Book Fair
Spring 2005, pg 1471

Jerusalem International Book Fair
February 2005, pg 1471

Jewish Book Month
November 2004, pg 1468
November 2005, pg 1481

Karlsruher Buecherschau
November 2004, pg 1468
November 2005, pg 1481
November 2006, pg 1484

Latino Book & Family Festival
October 2004, pg 1467
November 2004, pg 1469
December 2004, pg 1469

Leipzig Book Fair
March 2005, pg 1472
March 2006, pg 1482

LIBER Feria Internacional del Libro
October 2005, pg 1480
September 2006, pg 1484

Literary Festival
March 2005, pg 1472

London Book Fair
March 2005, pg 1472

Macworld Conference & Expo
January 2005, pg 1470

Miami Book Fair International
November 2004, pg 1469

MILIA: World Interactive Content Forum
April 2005, pg 1474

Modern Language Association of America Annual Convention
December 2004, pg 1469

Montana Festival of the Book
September 2005, pg 1479

Monterrey International Book Fair
October 2004, pg 1467

Montreal Book Show, see Salon du Livre de Montreal

Moscow International Book Fair
September 2005, pg 1479

Multicultural Children's Book Festival
November 2004, pg 1469
November 2005, pg 1481

National Association of Printing Ink Manufacturers Annual Convention
April 2005, pg 1474

National Association of Science Writers Annual Meeting
February 2005, pg 1471
February 2006, pg 1482
February 2007, pg 1484

The National Center for Database Marketing (NCDM)
Winter 2004, pg 1469

National College Media Convention
November 2004, pg 1469
October 2005, pg 1480
November 2006, pg 1484
October 2007, pg 1486

National Design Conference
September 2005, pg 1479

National Federation of Press Women National Conference
September 2005, pg 1480

National Library Week
April 2005, pg 1474
April 2006, pg 1482
April 2007, pg 1485
April 2008, pg 1486
April 2009, pg 1487

National Newspaper Association Annual Convention & Trade Show
October 2004, pg 1467

National Newspaper Association Annual Government Affairs Conference
March 2005, pg 1472

National Press Foundation Annual Awards Dinner
February 2005, pg 1471

NEPA's Annual Fall Conference
Formerly Newsletter Marketing Conference
November 2004, pg 1469
Autumn 2005, pg 1479

New Atlantic Independent Booksellers Association Annual Trade Show
October 2004, pg 1467
October 2005, pg 1480

New York Is Book Country
Autumn 2005, pg 1479

Newsletter Marketing Conference, see NEPA's Annual Fall Conference

Newspaper Association of America Annual Convention
April 2005, pg 1474
April 2006, pg 1482

NEXPO®
March 2005, pg 1473
April 2006, pg 1482

NIP 20: The 20th International Congress on Digital Printing Technologies
October 2004, pg 1467

North American Agricultural Journalists Spring Meeting
April 2005, pg 1474

Northprint
April 2005, pg 1474

NPES The Association for Suppliers of Printing, Publishing and Converting Technologies Annual Conference
October 2005, pg 1480

ON DEMAND
May 2005, pg 1475

Online Information, see Online Information & Content Management Europe

Online Information & Content Management Europe
Formerly Online Information
November 2004, pg 1469
November 2005, pg 1481

Outdoor Writers Association of America Annual Conference
June 2005, pg 1477

PACK EXPO
November 2004, pg 1469

Pacprint
May 2005, pg 1475

Paper Week
April 2005, pg 1474
April 2006, pg 1482

Papermakers Conference & Paper Expo - 2005 TAPPI
May 2005, pg 1476

Paris Book Fair, see Salon du Livre de Paris

Periodical Writers' Association of Canada Annual General Meeting
May 2005, pg 1476

Poligrafia
Spring 2005, pg 1471

PRIMEX 2005 (Print Media Executive Summit)
February 2005, pg 1471

Print & Pack Expo
August 2005, pg 1478

Print Buyers Conference
May 2005, pg 1476

Print Sales & Marketing Executives Conference
June 2005, pg 1477

PrintEx
May 2007, pg 1485

PSA International Conference of Photography
August 2005, pg 1478

ALPHABETICAL INDEX OF EVENTS

September 2006, pg 1484
September 2007, pg 1485

Publishers Association of the South Fall Conference & Annual Meeting
September 2005, pg 1480

Publishers Winter Conclave
January 2005, pg 1470

The Quest for Excellence
April 2005, pg 1474

The Quick Print Show
February 2005, pg 1471

Quod Libet/International Antiquarian Book Fair & Artists Books
October 2004, pg 1467

Remainder & Promotional Book Fair
Spring 2005, pg 1471
Autumn 2005, pg 1479

RWA Annual National Conference
July 2005, pg 1478
July 2006, pg 1483
July 2007, pg 1485
July 2008, pg 1486
July 2009, pg 1487

Salon du Livre de Jeunesse (Childrens Book Fair)
November 2006, pg 1484

Salon du Livre de Montreal
November 2004, pg 1469

Salon du Livre de Paris
March 2005, pg 1473

School Library Association Annual Conference
Summer 2005, pg 1476

Science Fiction Research Association Annual Meeting
June 2005, pg 1477

Seybold Seminars
Summer 2005, pg 1476

Small Press Book Fair
December 2004, pg 1469
December 2005, pg 1481

Society for Scholarly Publishing Annual Meeting
June 2005, pg 1477

Society of American Business Editors & Writers Annual Convention and Exhibition
May 2005, pg 1476

Society of Professional Journalists National Convention
Autumn 2005, pg 1479

Sofia International Book Fair
December 2004, pg 1469

South African Booksellers Association Annual Conference
August 2005, pg 1478
August 2006, pg 1483

Southeast Booksellers Association Annual Meeting & Trade Show
September 2005, pg 1480
September 2006, pg 1484

Southern California Writers' Conference San Diego
February 2005, pg 1471

Southern Kentucky Book Fest
April 2005, pg 1474

SouthPack
April 2005, pg 1474

Southwestern Graphics
May 2005, pg 1476

SPAN Conference
October 2004, pg 1467

Special Libraries Association Annual Conference
June 2005, pg 1477
June 2006, pg 1483
June 2007, pg 1485
July 2008, pg 1486

Special Libraries Association Leadership Summit
January 2005, pg 1470

Spectrum 2005
September 2005, pg 1480

Stuttgarter Buchwochen (Stuttgart Bookweeks)
November 2004, pg 1469
November 2005, pg 1481
November 2006, pg 1484
November 2007, pg 1486

SWANICK: The Writer's Summer School
August 2005, pg 1478

TAPPI Fall Technical Conference & Trade Fair
October 2004, pg 1467

Technology, Reading & Learning Difficulties (TRLD)
January 2005, pg 1470
January 2006, pg 1481

Texas Book Festival
October 2005, pg 1480

Texas Outdoor Writers Association Annual Conference
February 2005, pg 1471

TIBF: Tokyo International Book Fair
July 2005, pg 1478

Twin Cities Book Festival
October 2004, pg 1468
Autumn 2005, pg 1479

UK Serials Group Annual Conference & Exhibition
April 2005, pg 1475
April 2006, pg 1482

Umbrella 2005
June 2005, pg 1477

VABook!, see Virginia Festival of the Book

Virginia Festival of the Book
March 2005, pg 1473
March 2006, pg 1482
March 2007, pg 1485
March 2008, pg 1486
March 2009, pg 1487

Warsaw International Book Fair
May 2005, pg 1476

Annual Web Offset Association Conference
May 2005, pg 1476
Spring 2006, pg 1482
April 2007, pg 1485

Westpack
January 2005, pg 1470

Winter Conference on Writing & Illustrating for Children
Formerly International Conference on Writing & Illustrating for Children
February 2005, pg 1471

World Library & Information Congress
August 2005, pg 1479
August 2006, pg 1483

WORLDDIDAC Brazil 2005
November 2005, pg 1481

WORLDDIDAC Mexico 2005
March 2005, pg 1473

WORLDDIDAC 2004 Basel
October 2004, pg 1468

Xplor Global Conference
October 2004, pg 1468
October 2005, pg 1480

Young People's Poetry Week
April 2005, pg 1475
April 2006, pg 1482
April 2007, pg 1485
April 2008, pg 1486
April 2009, pg 1487

Zimbabwe International Book Fair
August 2005, pg 1479

Calendar of Book Trade & Promotional Events

Arranged chronologically by year and month, this section lists book trade events worldwide. Preceding this section are two indexes: the Sponsor Index is an alphabetical list of event sponsors followed by the names and dates of those events they sponsor; the Event Index is an alphabetical list of events along with the dates on which the events are held.

2004

OCTOBER

American Medical Writers Association Annual Conference
Sponsored by American Medical Writers Association
40 W Gude Dr, Suite 101, Rockville, MD 20850-1192, United States
Tel: 301-294-5303 *Fax:* 301-294-9006
E-mail: info@amwa.org
Web Site: www.amwa.org
Location: Adams Mark Hotel, St Louis, MO, USA
Oct 21-23, 2004

American Translators Association Annual Conference
Sponsored by American Translators Association (ATA)
225 Reinekers Lane, Suite 590, Alexandria, VA 22314, United States
Tel: 703-683-6100 *Fax:* 703-683-6122
E-mail: ata@atanet.org
Web Site: www.atanet.org
Key Personnel
Exec Dir: Walter Bacak *Tel:* 703-683-6100 ext 3006 *E-mail:* walter@atanet.org
Location: Sheraton Centre, Toronto, ON, Canada
Oct 13-16, 2004

Antwerp Book Fair
Sponsored by Bock.be
Hof ter Shrieklaan 17, 2600 Berchem/Antwerp, Belgium
Tel: (03) 2308923 *Fax:* (03) 2812240
E-mail: info@boek.be
Web Site: www.boek.be
Location: Bouwcentrum, Jan van Rijswijcklaan 191, Antwerp, Belgium
Oct 29-Nov 11, 2004

Belgrade International Book Fair
Sponsored by Association of Yugoslav Publishers & Booksellers
Kneza Milosa 25, 11000 Belgrade, Serbia and Montenegro
Tel: (011) 642248; (011) 642-533 *Fax:* (011) 646-339
Web Site: www.beobookfair.co.yu
Key Personnel
General Dir: Mr Ognjen Lakicevic
 E-mail: ognjenl@eunet.yu
Location: Belgrade, Serbia and Montenegro
Oct 2004

Inter American Press Association General Assembly
Sponsored by Inter American Press Association (IAPA)
Jules Dubois Bldg, 1801 SW Third Ave, Miami, FL 33129, United States
Tel: 305-634-2465 *Fax:* 305-635-2272
E-mail: info@sipiapa.org
Web Site: www.sipiapa.org
Key Personnel
Exec Dir: Julio E Munoz
Location: Antigua, Guatemala
Oct 22-25, 2004

Istanbul Book Fair
Sponsored by Tuyap Fuar ve Kongre Merkezi
E-S Karayolu Gurpinar Kavsagi, Beylikduzu/Buyukcekmece, 34900 Istanbul, Turkey
Tel: (0212) 886 68 43 *Fax:* (0212) 886 62 43
E-mail: artlink@tuyap.com.tr
Web Site: www.tuyap.com.tr
Location: Tuyap Fair Convention & Congress Center, Beylikduzu, Istanbul, Turkey
Oct 23-31, 2004

Latino Book & Family Festival
Sponsored by Latino Literacy Now
2777 Jefferson St, Suite 200, Carlsbad, CA 92008, United States
Tel: 760-434-4484
Web Site: www.latinobookfestival.com
Key Personnel
Mktg Dir: Jim Sullivan *Fax:* 760-434-7476
 E-mail: jim@lbff.us
Location: Houston, TX, USA
Oct 16-17, 2004

Monterrey International Book Fair
Sponsored by Instituto Tecnologico y de Estudios Superiores de Monterrey
Av Eugenio Garza Sada 2501, Col Tecnologico, 648497 Monterrey, Nuevo Leon, Mexico
Tel: (08) 328 43 28; (08) 328 42 82 *Fax:* (08) 359 96 23
E-mail: filmty@fil.mty.itesm.mx
Web Site: fil.mty.itesm.mx
Key Personnel
Opers Dir: Armando Ruiz
Location: Cintermex, Mexico
Oct 23-31, 2004

National Newspaper Association Annual Convention & Trade Show
Sponsored by National Newspaper Association
PO Box 7540, Columbia, MO 65205-7540, United States
Mailing Address: 127-129 Neff Annex, Columbia, MO 65211-1200, United States
Tel: 573-882-5800 *Toll Free Tel:* 800-829-4NNA
 Fax: 573-884-6490
E-mail: info@nna.org
Web Site: www.nna.org
Key Personnel
Exec Dir: Brian Steffens *E-mail:* briansteffens@nna.org
Location: Denver, CO, USA
Oct 13-16, 2004

New Atlantic Independent Booksellers Association Annual Trade Show
Sponsored by New Atlantic Independent Booksellers Association (NAIBA)
2667 Hyacinth St, Westbury, NY 11590, United States
Tel: 516-333-0681 *Fax:* 516-333-0689
E-mail: info@naiba.com; readingent@aol.com
Web Site: www.naiba.com
Key Personnel
Exec Dir: Eileen Dengler
Location: The Borgata, Atlantic City, NJ, USA
Oct 24-25, 2004

NIP 20: The 20th International Congress on Digital Printing Technologies
Sponsored by Society for Imaging Science & Technology (IS&T)
7003 Kilworth Lane, Springfield, VA 22151, United States
Tel: 703-642-9090 *Fax:* 703-642-9094
E-mail: info@imaging.org
Web Site: www.imaging.org
Location: Little America Hotel & Towers, Salt Lake City, UT, USA
Oct 31-Nov 5, 2004

Quod Libet/International Antiquarian Book Fair & Artists Books
Sponsored by Luckwaldt Messen
Bruechhorststr 34, 24641 Sieversbuetten, Germany
Tel: (04) 194 8101 *Fax:* (04) 194 636
E-mail: frauke@luckwaldt.de
Web Site: www.quod-libet.com
Key Personnel
Organizer: Frauke Luckwaldt
Location: Hamburger Boerse, Adolphsplatz 1, Hamburg, Germany
Oct 29-31, 2004

SPAN Conference
Sponsored by Small Publishers Association of North America (SPAN)
425 Cedar St, Buena Vista, CO 81211, United States
Mailing Address: PO Box 1306, Buena Vista, CO 81211-1306, United States
Tel: 719-395-4790 *Fax:* 719-395-8374
E-mail: span@spannet.org
Web Site: www.spannet.org
Key Personnel
Exec Dir: Scott Flora *E-mail:* scott@spannet.org
Busn Mgr: Debi Flora
A meaty, in-depth college for independent presses, authors & self-publishers. Emphasis is on "can-do" marketing/PR strategies.
Oct 22-24, 2004

TAPPI Fall Technical Conference & Trade Fair
Sponsored by Technical Association of the Pulp & Paper Industry (TAPPI)
15 Technology Pkwy S, Norcross, GA 30092, United States
Mailing Address: PO Box 105113, Atlanta, GA 30348-5113, United States
Tel: 770-446-1400 *Fax:* 770-446-6947
Web Site: www.tappi.org
Key Personnel
Publg Dir: Mary Beth Bennett
 E-mail: mbennett@tappi.org
Adv Asst: Vince Saputo *E-mail:* vsaputo@tappi.org
Corp Rel Dir: Clare Reagan *E-mail:* creagan@tappi.org
Admin: Wendy Cabral *E-mail:* wcabral@tappi.org
Location: Atlanta Marriott Marquis, Atlanta, GA, USA
Oct 17-21, 2004

Twin Cities Book Festival
Sponsored by Rain Taxi Review of Books
PO Box 3840, Minneapolis, MN 55403, United States
Tel: 612-825-1528 *Fax:* 612-825-1528
E-mail: bookfest@raintaxi.com
Web Site: www.raintaxi.com
Key Personnel
Dir: Eric Lorberer
Gala celebration of books, featuring large exhibition, author readings & signings, book art activities, panel discussions, used book sale & children's events.
Location: Minneapolis Community & Technical College, Minneapolis, MN, USA
Oct 16, 2004

WORLDDIDAC 2004 Basel
Sponsored by Worlddidac
Bollwerk 21, 3001 Bern, Switzerland
Mailing Address: PO Box 8866, 3001 Bern, Switzerland
Tel: (031) 311 76 82 *Fax:* (031) 312 17 44
E-mail: info@worlddidac.org
Web Site: www.worlddidac.org
International exhibition for educational materials, professional training & e-learning.
Location: Messe Basel, Basel, Switzerland
Oct 27-29, 2004

Xplor Global Conference
Sponsored by Xplor International
24238 Hawthorne Blvd, Torrance, CA 90505-6505, United States
Tel: 310-791-9521 *Toll Free Tel:* 800-669-7567 (ext 521) *Fax:* 310-375-4240
E-mail: info@xplor.org
Web Site: www.xplor.org
Key Personnel
Dir Opers: Ellen Dahlin
Location: Dallas Convention Center, Dallas, TX, USA
Oct 17-20, 2004

NOVEMBER

AICC/TAPPI SuperCorrExpo® 2004
Sponsored by Technical Association of the Pulp & Paper Industry (TAPPI)
15 Technology Pkwy S, Norcross, GA 30092, United States
Mailing Address: PO Box 105113, Atlanta, GA 30348-5113, United States
Tel: 770-446-1400 *Fax:* 770-446-6947
Web Site: www.tappi.org
Key Personnel
Publg Dir: Mary Beth Bennett
  E-mail: mbennett@tappi.org
Corp Rel Dir: Clare Reagan *E-mail:* creagan@tappi.org
Adv Asst: Vince Saputo *E-mail:* vsaputo@tappi.org
Location: Georgia World Congress Center, Atlanta, GA, USA
Nov 8-12, 2004

American Academy of Religion
Sponsored by American Schools of Oriental Research
825 Houston Mill Rd, Suite 201, Atlanta, GA 30329, United States
Tel: 404-727-3049 *Fax:* 404-727-7959
E-mail: aar@aarweb.org
Web Site: www.aarweb.org
Key Personnel
Prog Dir: Aislinn Jones
Location: San Antonio, TX, USA
Nov 20-23, 2004

BMI Annual Conference
Sponsored by Book Manufacturers' Institute Inc (BMI)
65 William St, Suite 300, Wellesley, MA 02481-3800, United States
Tel: 781-239-0103 *Fax:* 781-239-0106
E-mail: info@bmibook.com
Web Site: www.bmibook.org
Key Personnel
Exec VP: Stephen P Snyder
Location: Ventana Canyon Resort, Tucson, AZ, USA
Nov 7-10, 2004

Cairo International Children's Book Fair
Sponsored by General Egyptian Book Organization
Corniche el-Nil - Ramlet Boulac, Cairo 11221, Egypt (Arab Republic of Egypt)
Tel: (02) 5799635; (02) 5775228; (02) 5775109; (02) 5775367; (02) 5775436; (02) 5775545; (02) 5775000
E-mail: info@egyptianbook.org
Web Site: www.cibf.org; www.egyptianbook.org
Location: Cairo, Egypt
Nov 2004

Children's Book Week
Sponsored by The Children's Book Council (CBC)
12 W 37 St, 2nd fl, New York, NY 10118-7480, United States
Tel: 212-966-1990 *Toll Free Tel:* 800-999-2160 (orders only) *Fax:* 212-966-2073
Toll Free Fax: 888-807-9355 (orders only)
Web Site: www.cbcbooks.org
Key Personnel
Pres: Paula Quint
Location: Nationwide across the USA, Theme: "Book Time"
Nov 15-21, 2004

Color Imaging Conference - Color Science Systems & Applications
Sponsored by Society for Imaging Science & Technology (IS&T)
7003 Kilworth Lane, Springfield, VA 22151, United States
Tel: 703-642-9090 *Fax:* 703-642-9094
E-mail: info@imaging.org
Web Site: www.imaging.org
Key Personnel
Gen Co-chair: Ricardo Motta; Lindsay MacDonald
Location: Scottsdale, AZ, USA
Nov 2004

Creative Conference
Sponsored by American Association of Advertising Agencies (AAAA)
405 Lexington Ave, 18th fl, New York, NY 10174-1801, United States
Tel: 212-682-2500 *Fax:* 212-573-8968
E-mail: aaaaconferences@aaaa.org
Web Site: www.aaaa.org
Key Personnel
Pres & CEO: O Burtch Drake *E-mail:* obd@aaaa.org
VP & Dir, Pub Aff: Kipp Cheng
Nov 2004

ECPA Publishing University
Sponsored by Evangelical Christian Publishers Association
4816 S Ash Ave, Suite 101, Tempe, AZ 85282-7735, United States
Tel: 480-966-3998 *Fax:* 480-966-1944
E-mail: info@ecpa.org
Web Site: www.ecpa.org
Key Personnel
Pres: Mark Kuyper *E-mail:* mkuyper@ecpa.org

Excellence in Christian publishing through professional instruction, interactive learning & practical training.
Location: Indian Lakes Resort, Bloomingdale, IL, USA
Nov 7-9, 2004

Feria Internacional del Libro
Sponsored by Feria Internacional del Libro Guadalajara
Av Alemania 1370, Colonia Moderna, 44190 Guadalajara Jalisco, Mexico
Tel: (033) 3810 0291; (033) 3810 0331
  Fax: (033) 3810 0379
E-mail: fil@fil.com.mx; filny@aol.com
Web Site: www.fil.com.mx
Key Personnel
Pres: Raul Padilla Lopez
Dir: Nubia Edith Macias Navarro *E-mail:* dirfil@fil.com.mx
Gen Coord, Events & Prizes: Laura Niembro Diaz *E-mail:* eventsof@fil.com.mx
Location: Guadalajara, Mexico
Nov 27-Dec 5, 2004

Ghana International Book Fair
Sponsored by Ghana Trade Fair Co Ltd
PO Box NT601, Accra New Town, Accra, Ghana
Tel: (021) 227182; (012) 783421
E-mail: info@ghanainternationalbookfair.org
Web Site: www.ghanainternationalbookfair.org
Key Personnel
Mgr: Lawson Agana
Location: National Theatre, Accra, Ghana
Nov 9-14, 2004

Hall of Fame Awards & Annual Convention
Sponsored by Copywriter's Council of America (CCA)
Division of The Linick Group Inc
CCA Bldg, 7 Putter Lane, Middle Island, NY 11953-0102, United States
Mailing Address: PO Box 102, Middle Island, NY 11953-0102, United States
Tel: 631-924-8555 (ext 203) *Fax:* 631-924-3890
Key Personnel
VP: Roger Dextor
Dir, Spec Proj: Barbara Deal
Location: Orlando, FL, USA
Nov 2004

Internet World North
Sponsored by Penton Media
The Penton Media Bldg, 1300 E Ninth St, Cleveland, OH 44114, United States
Tel: 216-696-7000 *Fax:* 216-696-1752
E-mail: information@penton.com
Web Site: www.internetworld.co.uk
Location: G-Mex, Manchester, UK
Nov 3-4, 2004

Jewish Book Month
Sponsored by Jewish Book Council
15 E 26 St, New York, NY 10010-1579, United States
Tel: 212-532-4949 (ext 297) *Fax:* 212-481-4174
E-mail: jbc@jewishbooks.org
Web Site: www.jewishbookcouncil.org
Key Personnel
Exec Dir: Carolyn Starman Hessel
  E-mail: carolynhessel@jewishbooks.org
Nov 8-Dec 8, 2004

Karlsruher Buecherschau (Karlsruhe Book Exhibition)
Sponsored by Boersenverein des Deutschen Buchhandels, Landesverband Baden-Wuerttemberg eV (Association of Publishers & Booksellers in Baden-Wuerttemberg e V)
Paulinenstr 53, 70178 Stuttgart, Germany
Tel: (0711) 619410 *Fax:* (0711) 6194144

E-mail: post@buchhandelsverband.de
Web Site: www.buchhandelsverband.de
Key Personnel
Exhibition Mgr: Lisa Buchhorn *Tel:* (0711) 61941 26 *E-mail:* buchhorn@buchhandelsverband.de
Location: Landesgewerbeamt, Karl-Friedrich Str 17, Karlsruhe, Germany
Nov 12-Dec 5, 2004

Latino Book & Family Festival
Sponsored by Latino Literacy Now
2777 Jefferson St, Suite 200, Carlsbad, CA 92008, United States
Tel: 760-434-4484
Web Site: www.latinobookfestival.com
Key Personnel
Mktg Dir: Jim Sullivan *Fax:* 760-434-7476
  E-mail: jim@lbff.us
Location: Chicago, IL, USA
Nov 20-21, 2004

Miami Book Fair International
300 NE Second Ave, Suite 1515, Miami, FL 33132, United States
Tel: 305-237-3258 *Fax:* 305-237-3645
E-mail: bookfair@mdcc.edu
Web Site: www.miamibookfair.com
Key Personnel
Exec Dir: Magda Vergara
Location: Miami-Dade Community College, Wolfson Campus, Miami FL, USA
Nov 14-21, 2004

Multicultural Children's Book Festival
Sponsored by Kids Cultural Books
1081 Westover Rd, Stamford, CT 06902, United States
Tel: 203-359-6925 *Fax:* 203-359-3226
E-mail: info@kidsculturalbooks.org
Web Site: www.kidsculturalbooks.org/festivals.html
Location: Kennedy Center, Washington, DC, USA
Nov 6, 2004

National College Media Convention
Sponsored by Associated Collegiate Press (ACP)
Subsidiary of National Scholastic Press Assn
2221 University Ave SE, Suite 121, Minneapolis, MN 55414, United States
Tel: 612-625-8335 *Fax:* 612-626-0720
E-mail: info@studentpress.org
Web Site: studentpress.org
Key Personnel
Assoc Dir: Ann Akers
Also sponsored by College Media Advisors.
Location: Nashville Convention Center, Nashville, TN, USA
Nov 4-7, 2004

NEPA's Annual Fall Conference
Formerly Newsletter Marketing Conference
Sponsored by Newsletter & Electronic Publishers Association
1501 Wilson Blvd, Suite 509, Arlington, VA 22209, United States
Tel: 703-527-2333 *Toll Free Tel:* 800-356-9302
  Fax: 703-841-0629
E-mail: nepa@newsletters.org
Web Site: www.newsletters.org
Key Personnel
Exec Dir: Patti Wysocki
Location: InterContinental Hotel, New Orleans, LA, USA
Nov 3-5, 2004

Online Information & Content Management Europe
Formerly Online Information
Sponsored by VNU Exhibitions Europe
Subsidiary of VNU Business Media Europe
32-34 Broadwick St, London W1A 2HG, United Kingdom
Tel: (020) 7316 9539 *Fax:* (020) 7316 9598
E-mail: fiona.ashton@vnuexhibitions.co.uk
Web Site: www.online-information.co.uk; www.cme-expo.co.uk
Key Personnel
Event Dir: Vicky Bush *Tel:* (020) 7316 9585
  E-mail: victoria.bush@vnuexhibitions.co.uk
The show brings together hundreds of companies exhibiting the worlds best information resources, together with solutions for information management, knowledge exchange, content management, intranets & extranets & epublishing. It attracts thousands of international information managers, knowledge managers, librarians, academics, publishers, information users & IT professionals.
Location: Olympia Grand Hall, London, UK
Nov 30-Dec 2, 2004

PACK EXPO
Sponsored by Packaging Machinery Manufacturers Institute
4350 N Fairfax Dr, Suite 600, Arlington, VA 22203, United States
Tel: 703-243-8555 *Fax:* 703-243-3038
E-mail: expo@pmmi.org
Web Site: www.packexpo.com
Key Personnel
Exhibitor Servs Mgr: Kim Beaulieu
  E-mail: kim@pmmi.org
Location: McCormick Center, Chicago, IL, USA
Nov 4-7, 2004

Salon du Livre de Montreal (Montreal Book Show)
480 Boul St-Laurent, Suite 403, Montreal, PQ H2Y 3Y7, Canada
Tel: (514) 845-2365 *Fax:* (514) 845-7119
E-mail: slm.info@videotron.ca
Web Site: www.salondulivredemontreal.com
Key Personnel
Gen Mgr: Francine Bois
Location: La Place Bonaventure, Montreal, PQ, Canada
Nov 18-22, 2004

Stuttgarter Buchwochen (Stuttgart Bookweeks)
Sponsored by Boersenverein des Deutschen Buchhandels, Landesverband Baden-Wuerttemberg eV (Association of Publishers & Booksellers in Baden-Wuerttemberg e V)
Paulinenstr 53, 70178 Stuttgart, Germany
Tel: (0711) 619410 *Fax:* (0711) 6194144
E-mail: post@buchhandelsverband.de
Web Site: www.buchhandelsverband.de
Key Personnel
Contact: Maike Dreyer *Tel:* (0711) 619 41 28
  E-mail: dreyer@buchhandelsverband.de
Location: Haus der Wirtschaft, Stuttgart, Germany
Nov 18-Dec 12, 2004

WINTER

The National Center for Database Marketing (NCDM)
Sponsored by Primedia Business Exhibitions
11 River Bend Dr S, Stamford, CT 06907, United States
Mailing Address: PO Box 4254, Stamford, CT 06907-0254, United States
Tel: 203-358-9900 *Toll Free Tel:* 800-927-5007
  Fax: 203-358-5818
Web Site: www.primediabusiness.com
Winter 2004

DECEMBER

Latino Book & Family Festival
Sponsored by Latino Literacy Now
2777 Jefferson St, Suite 200, Carlsbad, CA 92008, United States
Tel: 760-434-4484
Web Site: www.latinobookfestival.com
Key Personnel
Mktg Dir: Jim Sullivan *Fax:* 760-434-7476
  E-mail: jim@lbff.us
Location: Inland Empire, CA, USA
Dec 11-12, 2004

Modern Language Association of America Annual Convention
Sponsored by Modern Language Association of America (MLA)
26 Broadway, 3rd fl, New York, NY 10004-1789, United States
Tel: 646-576-5000 *Fax:* 646-576-9930
E-mail: convention@mla.org
Web Site: www.mla.org
Key Personnel
Dir, Conventions: Maribeth T Kraus
Assoc Dir, Conventions: Karin Bagnall
Location: Philadelphia, PA, USA
Dec 27-30, 2004

Small Press Book Fair
Sponsored by Small Press Center
20 W 44 St, New York, NY 10036, United States
Tel: 212-764-7021 *Fax:* 212-354-5365
E-mail: info@smallpress.org
Web Site: www.smallpress.org
Key Personnel
Dir: Karin Taylor
Location: Small Press Center, New York, NY, USA
Dec 4-5, 2004

Sofia International Book Fair
Sponsored by Bulgarian Book Publishers Association
11 Slaveikov Sq, 1000 Sofia, Bulgaria
Mailing Address: PO Box 1046, 1000 Sofia, Bulgaria
Tel: (02) 986 79 93; (02) 986 79 70 *Fax:* (02) 986 79 93
E-mail: bba@otel.net; colibri@inet.bg
Web Site: www.bba-bg.org
Key Personnel
Dir: Raymond Wagenstein
Location: National Palace of Culture, Sofia, Bulgaria
Dec 2004

2005

JANUARY

American Library Association Mid-Winter Meeting
Sponsored by American Library Association (ALA)
50 E Huron St, Chicago, IL 60611, United States
Toll Free Tel: 800-545-2433 *Fax:* 312-944-6780
E-mail: ala@ala.org
Web Site: www.ala.org/events
Key Personnel
Public Info Dir: Mark Gould
Press Officer: Larra Clark
Location: Boston, MA, USA
Jan 14-19, 2005

Cairo International Book Fair
Sponsored by General Egyptian Book Organization
Corniche el-Nil - Ramlet Boulac, Cairo 11221, Egypt (Arab Republic of Egypt)
Tel: (02) 5799635; (02) 5775228; (02) 5775109; (02) 5775367; (02) 5775436; (02) 5775545; (02) 5775000 *Fax:* (02) 5765058; (02) 5799635
E-mail: info@egyptianbook.org
Web Site: www.cibf.org; www.egyptianbook.org
Cable: GEBO
Key Personnel
Chairman: Dr Mohamed Samir Sarhan
Location: Nasr City Fairground, Cairo, Egypt
Jan 26-Feb 8, 2005

CBA Advance
Formerly CBA Expo
Sponsored by CBA
9240 Explorer Dr, Colorado Springs, CO 80920-5001, United States
Mailing Address: PO Box 62000, Colorado Springs, CO 80962-2000, United States
Tel: 719-265-9895 *Toll Free Tel:* 800-252-1950 *Fax:* 719-272-3510
E-mail: info@cbaonline.org
Web Site: www.cbaonline.org
Key Personnel
Pres: William Anderson *E-mail:* banderson@cbaonline.org
VP & COO: Dorothy Gore
Convention & Expositions Mgr: Scott Graham
Location: Opryland Hotel, Nashville, TN, USA
Jan 31-Feb 4, 2005

ECPA Trade Show
Sponsored by Evangelical Christian Publishers Association
4816 S Ash Ave, Suite 101, Tempe, AZ 85282-7735, United States
Tel: 480-966-3998 *Fax:* 480-966-3417
E-mail: TradeShows@ecpa.org
Web Site: www.ecpa.org
Key Personnel
Pres: Mark Kuyper *E-mail:* mkuyper@ecpa.org
Location: Greensboro, NC, USA
Jan 5-7, 2005
Location: Hershey, PA, USA
Jan 9-11, 2005
Location: Arlington, TX, USA
Jan 12-14, 2005
Location: Chicago, IL, USA
Jan 17-19, 2005
Location: Riverside, CA, USA
Jan 20-22, 2005

Football Writers Association of America Annual Meeting
Sponsored by Football Writers Association of America
18652 Vista Del Sol, Dallas, TX 75287, United States
Tel: 972-713-6198 *Fax:* 972-713-6198
E-mail: tigerfwaa@aol.com
Web Site: www.fwaa.com; www.footballwriters.com
Key Personnel
Pres, New York Daily News: Dick Weiss
1st VP, Orlando Sentinel: Alan Schmadtke
2nd VP, CBS Sports Line: Dennis Dodd
Location: Miami, FL, USA
Jan 3-5, 2005

IS&T/SPIE Electronic Imaging Science & Technology
Sponsored by SPIE - The International Society for Optical Engineering
1000 20 St, Bellingham, WA 98225, United States
Mailing Address: PO Box 10, Bellingham, WA 98225-0010, United States
Tel: 360-676-3290 *Fax:* 360-647-1445
E-mail: exhibition@spie.org
Web Site: www.spie.org
Key Personnel
Gen Co-chair: Martin Freeman; Sethuraman Panchanathan
Exhibits Coord: Bonnie Peterson
Tech Coord: Jeanne Anderson
Location: San Jose, CA, USA
Jan 16-20, 2005

Macworld Conference & Expo
Sponsored by IDG World Expo
Unit of IDG
3 Speen St, Framingham, MA 01701, United States
Tel: 508-879-6700 *Toll Free Tel:* 800-645-EXPO *Fax:* 508-620-6668
Web Site: www.macworldexpo.com
Key Personnel
VP: Darrell Baker
Location: Moscone Convention Center, San Francisco, CA, USA
Jan 10-14, 2005

Publishers Winter Conclave
Sponsored by Publishers Association of the South (PAS)
4412 Fletcher St, Panama City, FL 32405-1017, United States
Tel: 850-914-0766 *Fax:* 850-769-4348
E-mail: executive@pubsouth.org
Web Site: www.pubsouth.org
Key Personnel
Pres: Beth Wright
Assn Exec: Pat Sabiston
Location: Marriott Riverside, Charleston, SC, USA
Jan 28-30, 2005

Special Libraries Association Leadership Summit
Sponsored by Special Libraries Association (SLA)
1700 18 St NW, Washington, DC 20009-2514, United States
Tel: 202-234-4700 *Fax:* 202-265-9317
E-mail: sla@sla.org
Web Site: www.sla.org
Key Personnel
Exec Dir: Janice LaChance *E-mail:* janice@sla.org
Location: Tampa, FL, USA
Jan 26-29, 2005

Technology, Reading & Learning Difficulties (TRLD)
Sponsored by Don Johnson Inc
26799 W Commerce, Volo, IL 60073, United States
Toll Free Tel: 888-594-1249 *Fax:* 847-740-7326
E-mail: info@trld.com
Web Site: www.trld.com
Key Personnel
Contact: Mary Krenz
TRLD is the only conference that integrates technology interventions with expert literacy strategies to ensure student success. The conference brings together educators, experienced literacy leaders & technology experts to share, discuss & work towards a solution to the nationwide concern of bringing literacy success to all students. Through quality speakers & relevant topics, TRLD gives educators ideas & strategies to immediately implement with students with high incidence disabilities.
Location: Grand Hyatt, Union Square, San Francisco, CA, USA
Jan 27-29, 2005

Westpack
Sponsored by Canon Communications
11444 W Olympic Blvd, Suite 900, Los Angeles, CA 90064, United States
Tel: 310-445-4200 *Fax:* 310-996-9499
Web Site: www.cancom.com; www.canontradeshows.com
Location: Anaheim Convention Center, Anaheim, CA, USA
Jan 10-12, 2005

FEBRUARY

Antiques & Fine Arts Exhibition/Luxembourg Book Festival
Sponsored by LUXEXPO
10 circuit de la Foire Internationale, 1347 Luxembourg-Kirchberg, Luxembourg
Tel: 43991 *Fax:* 4399315
E-mail: info@luxexpo.lu
Web Site: www.luxexpo.lu
Location: LUXEXPO Luxembourg Conference & Exhibition Center, Luxembourg, Luxembourg
Feb 17-20, 2005

Association of American Publishers Professional & Scholarly Publishing Divison Annual Meeting
Sponsored by Association of American Publishers Inc (AAP)
71 Fifth Ave, 2nd fl, New York, NY 10003-3004, United States
Tel: 212-255-0200 *Fax:* 212-255-7007
Web Site: www.publishers.org
Key Personnel
Pres & CEO: Patricia S Schroeder *Tel:* 202-347-3375 *Fax:* 202-347-3690
Location: Renaissance Mayflower Hotel, Washington, DC, USA
Feb 7-9, 2005

Association of American Publishers School Division Annual Meeting
Sponsored by Association of American Publishers Inc (AAP)
71 Fifth Ave, 2nd fl, New York, NY 10003-3004, United States
Tel: 212-255-0200 *Fax:* 212-255-7007
Web Site: www.publishers.org
Key Personnel
Pres & CEO: Patricia S Schroeder *Tel:* 202-347-3375 *Fax:* 202-347-3690
Location: Grand Hyatt Union Square, San Francisco, CA, USA
Feb 3-4, 2005

California International Antiquarian Book Fair
Sponsored by Antiquarian Booksellers' Association of America
20 W 44 St, 4th fl, New York, NY 10036, United States
Tel: 212-944-8291 *Fax:* 212-944-8293
E-mail: hq@abaa.org
Web Site: www.abaa.org
Key Personnel
Dir: Liane Wade
Location: 635 Eighth St, San Francisco, CA, USA
Feb 18-20, 2005

CAMEX
Sponsored by National Association of College Stores (NACS)
500 E Lorain St, Oberlin, OH 44074-1294, United States
Tel: 440-775-7777 *Toll Free Tel:* 800-622-7498 *Fax:* 440-775-4769
E-mail: info@nacs.org
Web Site: www.nacs.org; www.camex.org
Key Personnel
CEO: Brian Cartier

& PROMOTIONAL EVENTS

PR Dir: Laura Nakoneczny *Tel:* 440-775-7777, ext 2351 *E-mail:* lnakoneczny@nacs.org
Conference & tradeshow dedicated exclusively to the more than $10 billion collegiate retailing industry.
Location: New Orleans, LA, USA
Feb 27-March 3, 2005

Dog Writers' Association of America Annual Meeting
Sponsored by Dog Writers' Association of America Inc (DWAA)
173 Union Rd, Coatesville, PA 19320, United States
Tel: 610-384-2436 *Fax:* 610-384-2471
E-mail: rhydowen@aol.com
Web Site: www.dwaa.org
Key Personnel
Pres: Chris Walkowicz
Secy: Pat Santi
Location: Southgate Hotel, New York, NY, USA
Feb 13, 2005

Graphics of the Americas
Sponsored by Printing Association of Florida Inc
6095 NW 167 St, Suite D7, Hialeah, FL 33015, United States
Mailing Address: PO Box 170010, Hialeah, FL 33017-0010, United States
Tel: 305-558-4855 *Toll Free Tel:* 800-749-4855 *Fax:* 305-823-8965
E-mail: goa@pafgraf.org
Web Site: www.graphicsoftheamericas.com
Key Personnel
VP, Trade Shows: Chris Price *Tel:* 305-558-4855, ext 18 *E-mail:* cprice@pafgraf.org
Location: Miami Beach Convention Center, Miami Beach, FL, USA
Feb 4-6, 2005

Jerusalem International Book Fair
PO Box 775, Jerusalem 91007, Israel
Tel: (02) 6297922; (02) 6296412 *Fax:* (02) 6243144
E-mail: jerfairs@jerusalem.muni.il
Web Site: www.jerusalembookfair.com
Key Personnel
Chmn & Man Dir: Zev Birger
Location: Jerusalem International Convention Center, Jerusalem, Israel
Feb 13-18, 2005

National Association of Science Writers Annual Meeting
Sponsored by National Association of Science Writers (NASW)
PO Box 890, Hedgesville, WV 25427, United States
Tel: 304-754-5077 *Fax:* 304-754-5076
Web Site: www.nasw.org
Key Personnel
Exec Dir: Diane McGurgan *E-mail:* diane@nasw.org
Location: Washington, DC, USA
Feb 17-21, 2005

National Press Foundation Annual Awards Dinner
Sponsored by The National Press Foundation
1211 Connecticut Ave NW, Suite 310, Washington, DC 20036, United States
Tel: 202-663-7280 *Fax:* 202-530-2855
E-mail: npf@nationalpress.org
Web Site: www.nationalpress.org
Key Personnel
Dir of Opers: Donna Washington
Location: Washington Hilton, Washington, DC, USA
Feb 17, 2005

PRIMEX 2005 (Print Media Executive Summit)
Sponsored by IDEAlliance
100 Daingerfield Rd, Alexandria, VA 22314, United States
Tel: 703-837-1070 *Fax:* 703-837-1072
E-mail: info@idealliance.org
Web Site: www.idealliance.org
Key Personnel
Dir, Exec Programs: Georgia Volakis *Tel:* 703-837-1075 *E-mail:* gvolakis@idealliance.com
Location: Biltmore Hotel, Coral Gables, FL, USA
Feb 9-11, 2005

The Quick Print Show
Sponsored by PrintImage International
70 E Lake St, Suite 333, Chicago, IL 60601, United States
Tel: 312-726-8015 *Toll Free Tel:* 800-234-0040 *Fax:* 312-726-8113
E-mail: conferences@printimage.org
Web Site: www.printimage.org
Key Personnel
Pres & CEO: Steven D Johnson
Memb Progs Mgr: Jessica Grindell *E-mail:* jgrindell@printimage.org
Location: Orlando, FL, USA
Feb 18-24, 2005

Southern California Writers' Conference San Diego
Division of Random Cove, IE
1010 University Ave, Suite 54, San Diego, CA 92103, United States
Tel: 619-233-4651 *Fax:* 619-233-4651
E-mail: wewrite@writersconference.com
Web Site: www.writersconference.com
Key Personnel
Exec Dir: Michael Gregory *E-mail:* msg@writersconference.com
Location: San Diego, CA, USA
Feb 18-21, 2005

Texas Outdoor Writers Association Annual Conference
Sponsored by Texas Outdoor Writers Association
7503 Bayswater, Amarillo, TX 79119, United States
Tel: 806-345-3280 *Fax:* 806-372-3717
Web Site: www.towa.org
Key Personnel
Pres: Jonette Childs *E-mail:* saltex@pyramid3.net
Exec Dir & Treas: Lee Leschper *E-mail:* l.leschper@amarillonet.com
Location: Uvalde, TX, USA
Feb 2005

Winter Conference on Writing & Illustrating for Children
Formerly International Conference on Writing & Illustrating for Children
Sponsored by Society of Children's Book Writers & Illustrators (SCBWI)
8271 Beverly Blvd, Los Angeles, CA 90048, United States
Tel: 323-782-1010 *Fax:* 323-782-1892
E-mail: conference@scbwi.org
Web Site: www.scbwi.org
Key Personnel
Pres: Steve Mooser
Location: Hilton New York. Avenue of the Americas, New York, NY, USA
Feb 5-6, 2005

SPRING

BMI Management Conference
Sponsored by Book Manufacturers' Institute Inc (BMI)
65 William St, Suite 300, Wellesley, MA 02481-3800, United States
Tel: 781-239-0103 *Fax:* 781-239-0106
E-mail: info@bmibook.com
Web Site: www.bmibook.org
Key Personnel
Exec VP: Bruce W Smith
Spring 2005

DGI Annual Meeting & Online Conference
Sponsored by Deutsche Gesellschaft fur Informationswissenschaft und informationspraxis eV (German Society for Information Science & Information Practice)
Ostbahnhofstr 13, 60314 Frankfurt am Main, Germany
Tel: (069) 430313 *Fax:* (069) 4909096
E-mail: zentrale@dgi-info.de
Web Site: www.dgi-info.de
Location: Frankfurt Fairgrounds, Frankfurt, Germany
Spring 2005

Gutenberg Festival
Sponsored by Graphic Arts Show Company
1899 Preston White Dr, Reston, VA 20191-4367, United States
Tel: 703-264-7200 *Fax:* 703-620-9187
E-mail: info@gasc.org
Web Site: www.gasc.org
Key Personnel
Dir, Communs: David Poulos
Annual trade show for graphic design, digital prepress, printing, publishing & converting.
Location: Long Beach Convention Center, Long Beach, CA, USA
Spring 2005

Izmir Book Fair
Sponsored by Tuyap Fuar ve Kongre Merkezi
E-S Karayolu Gurpinar Kavsagi, Beylikduzu/Buyukcekmece, 34900 Istanbul, Turkey
Tel: (0212) 886 68 43 *Fax:* (0212) 886 62 43
E-mail: artlink@tuyap.com.tr
Web Site: www.tuyap.com.tr
Location: Izmir Culturepark Fair Venue, Izmir, Turkey
Spring 2005

Poligrafia
Sponsored by Poznan International Fair Ltd
ul Glogowska 14, 60-734 Poznan, Poland
Tel: (061) 869 2599; (061) 869 2295 *Fax:* (061) 866 5827
E-mail: poligrafia@mtp.pl
Web Site: poligrafiamtp.pl
Key Personnel
Proj Mgr: Krzysztof Slatala *Tel:* (061) 869 2196 *Fax:* (061) 869 2661 *E-mail:* krzysztof.slatala@mtp.pl
International fair of printing machines, materials & services.
Location: Poznan, Poland
Spring 2005

Remainder & Promotional Book Fair
Sponsored by Ciana Ltd
24 Langroyd Rd, London SW17 7PL, United Kingdom
Tel: (020) 8682 1969 *Fax:* (020) 8682 1997
E-mail: enquiries@ciana.co.uk
Web Site: www.ciana.co.uk
Location: Hilton Brighton Metropole Hotel, King's Rd, Brighton, UK
Spring 2005

MARCH

AAAA Media Conference & Trade Show
Sponsored by American Association of Advertising Agencies (AAAA)
405 Lexington Ave, 18th fl, New York, NY 10174-1801, United States
Tel: 212-682-2500 *Fax:* 212-573-8968
E-mail: aaaaconferences@aaaa.org
Web Site: www.aaaa.org
Key Personnel
Pres & CEO: O Burtch Drake *E-mail:* obd@aaaa.org
Sr VP, Conferences & Special Events: Karen Proctor *E-mail:* karen@aaaa.org
Conference Mgr: Michelle Montalto *E-mail:* michelle@aaaa.org
Conference Coord: Michelle James *E-mail:* mjames@aaaa.org
Location: Hilton Riverside, New Orleans, LA, USA
March 2-4, 2005

Adelaide Bank Festival of Arts
Formerly Adelaide Writers' Week
Sponsored by Adelaide Festival Corp
105 Hindley St, Adelaide, SA 5000, Australia
Mailing Address: PO Box 8221, Station Arcade, Adelaide, SA 5000, Australia
Tel: (08) 8216 4444 *Fax:* (08) 8216 4455
E-mail: afa@adelaidefestival.net.au
Web Site: www.adelaidefestival.com.au
Key Personnel
Artistic Dir: Brett Sheehy
Location: Pioneer Women's Memorial Gardens, King William St, Adelaide, Australia
March 3-19, 2005

Associated Writing Programs Annual Conference & Bookfair
Sponsored by Association of Writers & Writing Programs (AWP)
George Mason University, MS-1E3, Fairfax, VA 22030-4444, United States
Tel: 703-993-4301 *Fax:* 703-993-4302
E-mail: awp@gmu.edu
Web Site: www.awpwriter.org
Key Personnel
Exec Dir: D W Fenza
Dir of Conferences: Matt Scanlon
Association of writers & writing programs.
Location: Hyatt Regency, Vancouver, BC, Canada
March 30-April 2, 2005

Association of American Publishers Annual Meeting
Sponsored by Association of American Publishers Inc (AAP)
71 Fifth Ave, 2nd fl, New York, NY 10003-3004, United States
Tel: 212-255-0200 *Fax:* 212-255-7007
Web Site: www.publishers.org
Key Personnel
Pres & CEO: Patricia S Schroeder *Tel:* 202-347-3375 *Fax:* 202-347-3690
Location: New York, NY, USA
March 3, 2005

Association of American Publishers Annual Meeting for Small & Independent Publishers
Sponsored by Association of American Publishers Inc (AAP)
71 Fifth Ave, 2nd fl, New York, NY 10003-3004, United States
Tel: 212-255-0200 *Fax:* 212-255-7007
Web Site: www.publishers.org
Key Personnel
Pres & CEO: Patricia S Schroeder *Tel:* 202-347-3375 *Fax:* 202-347-3690
Location: New York, NY, USA
March 4, 2005

Binding Industries Association International Spring/Presidents Conference
Sponsored by Binding Industries Association International (BIA)
Affiliate of Special Industry Group of Printing Industries of America Inc
100 Daingerfield Rd, Alexandria, VA 22314, United States
Tel: 703-519-8137 *Fax:* 703-548-3227
E-mail: info@bindingindustries.org
Web Site: www.bindingindustries.org
Key Personnel
Exec Dir: Joanne Rock
Conference for top management held in conjunction with PIA/GATF Presidents Conference. Specially designed educational events & numerous networking activities for BIA members.
Location: The Ritz Carlton Golf Club, Naples, FL, USA
March 1-4, 2005

BookTech Conference & Expo
Sponsored by BookTech
401 N Broad St, 5th Fl, Philadelphia, PA 19108, United States
Toll Free *Tel:* 888-627-2630 *Fax:* 215-409-0100
E-mail: tradeshows@napco.com
Web Site: www.booktechexpo.com
BookTech incorporates the PrintMedia Conference & Expo & the In-Plant Graphics Conference plus a world-class expo on publishing & printing solutions providers.
Location: Hilton New York, 1335 Avenue of the Americas, New York, NY, USA
March 7-9, 2005

Buch-IBO
Sponsored by Boersenverein des Deutschen Buchhandels, Landesverband Baden-Wuerttemberg eV (Association of Publishers & Booksellers in Baden-Wuerttemberg e V)
Division of Internationale Bodensee-Messe, Friedrichshafen
Paulinenstr 53, 70178 Stuttgart, Germany
Tel: (0711) 619410 *Fax:* (0711) 6194144
E-mail: buchhorn@buchhandelsverband.de
Web Site: www.buchhandelsverband.de
Location: International Bodensee-Messe, Friedrichshafen, Germany
March 12-20, 2005

Christian Booksellers Convention - UK
Sponsored by Christian Booksellers Convention Ltd
Victoria House, Victoria Rd, Buckhurst Hill, Essex 1G9 5EX, United Kingdom
Tel: (020) 5592975; (020) 8559 1180 *Fax:* (020) 5029062
E-mail: 100067.1226@compuserve.com
Location: Doncaster Exhibition & Conference Center, Doncaster, UK
March 7-9, 2005

English Association Semiannual Teachers' Conference
Sponsored by The English Association
University of Leicester, University Rd, Leicester LE1 7RH, United Kingdom
Tel: (0116) 252 3982 *Fax:* (0116) 252 2301
E-mail: engassoc@le.ac.uk
Key Personnel
Chief Exec: Helen Lucas
Conference Org: Louise Callen
Membership Coord: Jeremy Wiltshire
Location: Oxford, UK
March 2005

Graphic Arts/The Charlotte Show
Sponsored by Graphic Arts Show Company
1899 Preston White Dr, Reston, VA 20191-4367, United States
Tel: 703-264-7200 *Fax:* 703-620-9187
E-mail: info@gasc.org
Web Site: www.gasc.org
Telex: NPES MCLN
Key Personnel
Pres: Regis J Delmontagne
Biennial event featuring equipment, products & services for graphic communications industry.
Location: Charlotte Convention Center, Charlotte, NC, USA
March 17-19, 2005

Inter American Press Association Mid-Year Meeting
Sponsored by Inter American Press Association (IAPA)
Jules Dubois Bldg, 1801 SW Third Ave, Miami, FL 33129, United States
Tel: 305-634-2465 *Fax:* 305-635-2272
E-mail: info@sipiapa.org
Web Site: www.sipiapa.org
Key Personnel
Exec Dir: Julio E Munoz
Meeting Coord: Angeles Mase *E-mail:* amase@sipiapa.org
March 2005

Leipzig Book Fair
Sponsored by Leipziger Messe GmbH, Projektteam Buchmesse
Messe-Allee 1, 04356 Leipzig, Germany
Mailing Address: Postfach 100 720, 04007 Leipzig, Germany
Tel: (0341) 6788240 *Fax:* (0341) 6788242
E-mail: info@leipziger-buchmesse.de
Web Site: www.leipziger-buchmesse.de
Key Personnel
Exhibition Dir: Oliver Zille *Tel:* (0341) 678 8241 *Fax:* (0341) 678 8242
Held annually in conjunction with The Leipzig Antiquarian Book Fair.
Location: Neues Messegelande, Leipzig, Germany
March 17-20, 2005

Literary Festival
Sponsored by Vystaviste Flora Olomouc
Wolkerova 17, 771 11 Olomouc, Czech Republic
Mailing Address: PO Box 46, 771 11 Olomouc, Czech Republic
Tel: (0585) 726 111 *Fax:* (0585) 413 370
E-mail: info@flora-ol.cz
Web Site: www.flora-ol.cz
March 2005

London Book Fair
Sponsored by Reed Exhibitions (UK)
Division of Reed Business
Oriel House, 26 The Quadrant, Richmond, Surrey TW9 1DL, United Kingdom
Tel: (020) 8910 7910 *Fax:* (020) 8940 2171
E-mail: lbfteam@reedexpo.co.uk
Web Site: www.lbf-virtual.com
Telex: 8951389 ITFLONG
Key Personnel
Key Acct Mgr: Catriana Stemp *E-mail:* catriana.stemp@reedexpo.co.uk
Sales Exec: Ruth Moses *E-mail:* ruth.moses@reedexpo.co.uk
Sponsored by The Booksellers Association of the United Kingdom & Ireland Limited. Spring publishing event attended by publishers, booksellers, literary agents, librarians, authors, production & content managers & international rights agents.
Location: Olympia Exhibition Centre, Hammersmith Rd, London, UK
March 13-15, 2005

National Newspaper Association Annual Government Affairs Conference
Sponsored by National Newspaper Association

PO Box 5737, Arlington, VA 22205-9998, United States
Tel: 703-534-1278 *Fax:* 703-534-5751
E-mail: info@nna.org
Web Site: www.nna.org
Location: Wyndham Washington, Washington, DC, USA
March 9-12, 2005

NEXPO®
Sponsored by Newspaper Association of America (NAA)
1921 Gallows Rd, Suite 600, Vienna, VA 22182, United States
Tel: 703-902-1600 *Fax:* 703-902-1843
E-mail: laths@naa.org
Web Site: www.nexpo.com
Key Personnel
Dir of Exhibition Sales: Brad Smith
Annual technical exposition & conference for newspapers.
Location: Dallas, TX, USA
March 19-22, 2005

Salon du Livre de Paris
Sponsored by Reed Expositions France
Subsidiary of Reed Exhibition Companies
11 rue du Colonel Pierre Avia, 75726 Paris Cedex 15, France
Tel: (01) 41 90 47 47 *Fax:* (01) 41 90 47 49
E-mail: salondulivre@reedexpo.fr; livre@reedexpo.fr
Web Site: www.salondulivreparis.com
Key Personnel
Fair Mgr: Taya de Reynies
  E-mail: taya_reynies@reedexpo.fr
Annual international publishing event for publishers, booksellers, teachers & librarians. Open to the trade & the public. Guest of honor: Russia.
Location: Paris Expo, Hall 1, Porte de Versailles, Paris, France
March 18-23, 2005

Virginia Festival of the Book
Sponsored by Virginia Foundation for the Humanities
145 Ednam Dr, Charlottesville, VA 22903, United States
Tel: 434-924-6890 *Fax:* 434-296-4714
E-mail: vabook@virginia.edu
Web Site: www.vabook.org
Key Personnel
Program Dir: Nancy Damon *Tel:* 434-924-7548
Program Assoc: Kevin McFadden
  E-mail: kjm7a@virginia.edu
Annual free public festival for children & adults featuring authors, illustrators, publishers, publicists, agents & other book professionals in panel discussions & readings for adults & children of all ages.
Location: Charlottesville, VA, USA
March 16-20, 2005

WORLDDIDAC Mexico 2005
Sponsored by Worlddidac
Bollwerk 21, 3001 Bern, Switzerland
Mailing Address: PO Box 8866, 3001 Bern, Switzerland
Tel: (031) 311 76 82 *Fax:* (031) 312 17 44
E-mail: info@worlddidac.org
Web Site: www.worlddidac.org
Key Personnel
Project Mgr: Esther Schindles *E-mail:* schindles@worlddidac.org
International exhibition for educational materials, professional training & e-learning.
Location: World Trade Center, Mexico City, Mexico
March 2005

APRIL

Advertising Research Foundation Annual Convention & Trade Show
Sponsored by Advertising Research Foundation
641 Lexington Ave, New York, NY 10022, United States
Tel: 212-751-5656 *Fax:* 212-319-5265
E-mail: info@thearf.org
Web Site: www.thearf.org
Key Personnel
Sr VP, Communs: Carol White *Tel:* 212-751-5656, ext 227 *E-mail:* carol@thearf.org
VP, Conference Brands: Ajay Durani *Tel:* 212-751-5656, ext 222 *E-mail:* ajay@thearf.org
Man Ed: Zena Pagan *Tel:* 212-751-5656, ext 216 *E-mail:* zena@thearf.org
Location: New York, NY, USA
April 2005

African American Children's Book Festival
Sponsored by Kids Cultural Books
1081 Westover Rd, Stamford, CT 06902, United States
Tel: 203-359-6925 *Fax:* 203-359-3226
E-mail: info@kidsculturalbooks.org
Web Site: www.kidsculturalbooks.org/festivals.html
Location: Cathedral of St John the Divine, New York, NY, USA
April 2005

Alberta Library Conference
Sponsored by Library Association of Alberta
80 Baker Crescent NW, Calgary, AB T2L 1R4, Canada
Tel: 403-284-5818 *Toll Free Tel:* 877-522-5550 *Fax:* 403-282-6646
E-mail: info@laa.ab.ca
Web Site: www.laa.ab.ca
Key Personnel
Pres: Pat Cavill
Exec Dir: Christine Sheppard *E-mail:* christine.sheppard@show.ca
Location: Jasper Park Lodge, Jasper, AB, Canada
April 2005

Arizona Book Festival
Sponsored by Arizona Humanities Council
1242 N Central, Phoenix, AZ 85004, United States
Tel: 602-257-0335
Web Site: www.azbookfestival.org/index.html
Location: Carnegie Center, Phoenix, AZ, USA
April 2, 2005

Association of Directory Publishers Annual Meeting
Sponsored by Association of Directory Publishers
116 Cass St, Traverse City, MI 49684-2505, United States
Mailing Address: PO Box 1929, Traverse City, MI 49685-1929, United States
Toll Free Tel: 800-267-9002 *Fax:* 231-486-2182
E-mail: hq@adp.org
Web Site: www.adp.org
Key Personnel
Pres & CEO: R Lawrence Angove *E-mail:* larry.angove@adp.org
Location: Ft Worth, TX, USA
April 2005

Binding, Finishing & Distribution Seminar
Sponsored by Research & Engineering Council of NAPL (National Association for Printing Leadership)
PO Box 1086, White Stone, VA 22578-1086, United States
Tel: 804-436-9922 *Toll Free Tel:* 8000-642-6275 (ext 1397) *Fax:* 804-436-9511
E-mail: recouncil@rivnet.net
Web Site: www.recouncil.org
Key Personnel
Man Dir: Ronald L Mihills
Seminar designed for bindery managers, manufacturing/operations executives & warehouse supervisors.
Location: Chicago, IL, USA
April 5-6, 2005

Bologna Children's Book Fair
Sponsored by BolognaFiere
Via della Fiera, 20, 40128 Bologna, Italy
Tel: (051) 282 111 *Fax:* (051) 637 40 04
E-mail: dir.gen@bolognafiere.it; bookfair@bolognafiere.it
Web Site: www.bookfair.bolognafiere.it
Location: Bologna Fiere Exhibition Centre, Bologna, Italy
April 13-16, 2005

Booksellers Association of the United Kingdom & Ireland Annual Conference
Sponsored by Booksellers Association of the United Kingdom & Ireland Ltd
Minster House, 272-274 Vauxhall Bridge Rd, London SW1V 1BA, United Kingdom
Tel: (020) 7802 0802 *Fax:* (020) 7802 0803
E-mail: mail@booksellers.org.uk
Web Site: www.booksellers.org.uk
Key Personnel
Contact: Anna O'Kane *E-mail:* anna.okane@booksellers.org.uk
Location: Glasgow, UK
April 10-12, 2005

Dataprint
Sponsored by Reed Messe Salzburg GmbH
Am Messezentrum 6, 5021 Salzburg, Austria
Mailing Address: Postfach 285, 5021 Salzburg, Austria
Tel: (0662) 44770 *Fax:* (0662) 4477161
E-mail: info@reedexpo.at; dataprint@reedexpo.at
Web Site: www.reedexpo.at; www.datapoint.at
Key Personnel
Dir: Johann Jungreithmair
Mgr: Max Poringer *E-mail:* max.poringer@reedexpo.at
Coord: Daniela Kogl-Egger *E-mail:* daniela.koegl@reedexpo.at
Trade fair for print media & digital production.
Location: Design Center, Linz, Austria
April 1, 2005

ECPA Management Seminar
Sponsored by Evangelical Christian Publishers Association
4816 S Ash Ave, Suite 101, Tempe, AZ 85282-7735, United States
Tel: 480-966-3998 *Fax:* 480-966-1944
E-mail: info@ecpa.org
Web Site: www.ecpa.org
Key Personnel
Pres: Mark Kuyper *E-mail:* mkuyper@ecpa.org
April 30-May 4, 2005

Evangelical Press Association Annual Conference
Sponsored by Evangelical Press Association (EPA)
PO Box 28129, Crystal, MN 55428-0129, United States
Tel: 763-535-4793 *Fax:* 763-535-4794
E-mail: director@epassoc.org
Web Site: www.epassoc.org
Key Personnel
Exec Dir: Doug Trouten
Location: Chicago, IL, USA
April 24-27, 2005

Federation of Children's Book Groups Annual Conference
Sponsored by Federation of Children's Book Groups
2 Bridge Wood View, Horsforth, Leeds, W Yorks LS18 5PE, United Kingdom
Tel: (0113) 2588910
E-mail: info@fcbg.org.uk
Web Site: www.fcbg.org.uk
Key Personnel
Contact: Jayne Truran
Theme "Windows on the World".
Location: The University of Hertfordshire, Hatfield, Herts, UK
April 1-3, 2005

FOSE
Sponsored by Post Newsweek Tech Media
10 G St NE, Suite 500, Washington, DC 20002-4228, United States
Tel: 202-772-2500 *Toll Free Tel:* 866-447-6864 *Fax:* 202-771-2511
E-mail: fose.exhibit@postnewsweektech.com
Web Site: www.fose.com; www.postnewsweektech.com
Key Personnel
VP, Trade Shows: Lorenz Hassenstein *Tel:* 202-772-5738 *E-mail:* lhassenstein@postnewsweektech.com
Dir: Gloria Lombardo *Tel:* 203-381-9245 *E-mail:* glombardo@postnewsweektech.com
Trade Show Opers Mgr: Lauri Nichols *Tel:* 202-772-5750 *E-mail:* lnichols@postnewsweektech.com
Location: Washington Convention Center, Washington, DC, USA
April 5-7, 2005

Infosystem Fairs
Sponsored by Poznan International Fair Ltd
ul Glogowska 14, 60-734 Poznan, Poland
Tel: (061) 869 2000; (061) 869 2599; (061) 869 2295 *Fax:* (061) 866 5827
E-mail: infosystem@mtp.pl
Web Site: www.mtp.pl; www.infosystem.pl
Telex: 413251
Key Personnel
Proj Mgr: Krzysztof Slatala *Tel:* (061) 869 2196 *Fax:* (061) 869 2661 *E-mail:* krzysztof.slatala@mtp.pl
International fair of telecommunications, information technology & electronics.
Location: Poznan International Fairground, Poznan, Poland
April 19-22, 2005

International Children's Book Day
Sponsored by International Board on Books for Young People (IBBY)
Nonnenweg 12, 4003 Basel, Switzerland
Mailing Address: Nonnenweg 12, Postfach, Basel 4003, Switzerland
Tel: (061) 272 29 17 *Fax:* (061) 272 27 57
E-mail: ibby@ibby.org
Web Site: www.ibby.org
On or around Hans Christian Andersen's birthday, April 2nd, International Children's Book day (ICBD) is celebrated to inspire a love of reading & to call attention to children's books. Each year a different national section has the opportunity to be the international sponsor. It decides upon a theme & invites a prominent author to write a message to the children of the world & a well-known illustrator to design a poster. These materials are used in different ways to promote books & reading around the world.
Location: India
April 2005

IS&T Archiving Conference
Sponsored by Society for Imaging Science & Technology (IS&T)
7003 Kilworth Lane, Springfield, VA 22151, United States
Tel: 703-642-9090 *Fax:* 703-642-9094
E-mail: info@imaging.org
Web Site: www.imaging.org
Location: Radisson Hotel Old Town, Alexandria, VA, USA
April 26-29, 2005

MILIA: World Interactive Content Forum
Sponsored by Reed Midem
Subsidiary of Reed Exhibition Companies
11 rue du Colonnel Pierre Avia, 75015 Paris, France
Mailing Address: BP 572, 75726 Paris Cedex 15, France
Tel: (01) 41 90 44 00 *Fax:* (01) 41 90 44 70
E-mail: info@milia.com; milia.conferences@reedmidem.com
Web Site: www.milia.com
Key Personnel
Exec Dir: Laurine Garaude *E-mail:* laurine.garaude@reedmidem.com
Location: Palais des Festivals, Cannes, France
April 11-15, 2005

National Association of Printing Ink Manufacturers Annual Convention
Sponsored by National Association of Printing Ink Manufacturers (NAPIM)
581 Main St, Woodbridge, NJ 07095, United States
Tel: 732-855-1525 *Fax:* 732-855-1838
E-mail: napim@napim.org
Web Site: www.napim.org
Key Personnel
Exec Dir: James E Coleman
Event Coord: Sue Coleman
Location: Hyatt Coconut Point, Bonita Springs, FL, USA
April 7-11, 2005

National Library Week
Sponsored by American Library Association (ALA)
50 E Huron St, Chicago, IL 60611, United States
Tel: 312-944-6780 *Toll Free Tel:* 800-545-2433 *Fax:* 312-944-8520
E-mail: pio@ala.org
Web Site: www.ala.org/events
Key Personnel
Public Info Dir: Mark Gould
Press Officer: Larra Clark *E-mail:* lclark@ala.org
Location: Nationwide throughout the USA
April 10-16, 2005

Newspaper Association of America Annual Convention
Sponsored by Newspaper Association of America (NAA)
1921 Gallows Rd, Suite 600, Vienna, VA 22182, United States
Tel: 703-902-1600 *Fax:* 703-902-1790
E-mail: laths@naa.org
Web Site: www.naa.org
Key Personnel
Pres & CEO: John Sturm
Location: Fairmont San Francisco, San Francisco, CA, USA
April 17-20, 2005

North American Agricultural Journalists Spring Meeting
Sponsored by North American Agricultural Journalists
Texas A & M University, 201 Reed Macdonald, 2112 TAMU, College Station, TX 77843-2112, United States
Mailing Address: 2604 Cumberland Ct, College Station, TX 77845, United States
Tel: 979-845-2872 *Fax:* 979-845-2414
Web Site: naaj.tamu.edu
Key Personnel
Exec Sec, Treas: Kathleen Phillips *E-mail:* ka-phillips@tamu.edu
April 2005

Northprint
Sponsored by Reed Exhibitions (UK)
Division of Reed Business
Oriel House, 26 The Quadrant, Richmond, Surrey TW9 1DL, United Kingdom
Tel: (020) 8910 7910 *Fax:* (020) 8940 2171
E-mail: northprint.helpline@reedexpo.co.uk
Web Site: www.northprintexpo.co.uk
Telex: 8951389 ITFLONG
Key Personnel
Exhibition Dir: Andrew Furness *Tel:* (020) 8910 7836 *Fax:* (020) 8334 0704 *E-mail:* andrew.furness@reedexpo.co.uk
Exhibition Administrator: Hannah Tranfield *Tel:* (020) 8910 7817 *Fax:* (020) 8910 7848 *E-mail:* hannah.tranfield@reedexpo.co.uk
Location: Harrogate Exhibition Centre, Harrogate, UK
April 19-21, 2005

Paper Week
Sponsored by American Forest & Paper Association
1111 19 St NW, Suite 800, Washington, DC 20036, United States
Tel: 202-463-2700 *Fax:* 202-463-4703
E-mail: info@afandpa.org
Web Site: www.afandpa.org; www.paperweek.org
Key Personnel
Pres & CEO: W Henson Moore
Location: Waldorf-Astoria Hotel & Towers, New York, NY, USA
April 10-13, 2005

The Quest for Excellence
Sponsored by American Society for Quality
600 N Plankinton Ave, Milwaukee, WI 53203, United States
Mailing Address: PO Box 3005, Milwaukee, WI 53201-3005, United States
Tel: 414-272-8575 *Toll Free Tel:* 800-248-1946 *Fax:* 414-272-1734
E-mail: cs@asq.org
Web Site: www.asq.org
Telex: 31-6567
Key Personnel
Exec Dir & Chief Strategic Officer: Paul Borawski
Location: Marriott Wardman Park Hotel, Washington, DC, USA
April 10-13, 2005

Southern Kentucky Book Fest
106 Cravens Library, One Big Red Way, Bowling Green, KY 42101, United States
Tel: 270-745-5016
Web Site: www.sokybookfest.org
Location: Sloan Convention Center, Bowling Green, KY, USA
April 15-16, 2005

SouthPack
Sponsored by Canon Communications
11444 W Olympic Blvd, Suite 900, Los Angeles, CA 90064, United States
Tel: 310-445-4200 *Fax:* 310-996-9499
E-mail: feedback@devicelink.com
Web Site: www.cancom.com; www.canontradeshows.com
Biennial.
Location: Georgia World Congress Center, Atlanta, GA, USA
April 13-14, 2005

& PROMOTIONAL EVENTS

UK Serials Group Annual Conference & Exhibition
Sponsored by UK Serials Group
PO Box 5594, Newbury RG20 0YP, United Kingdom
Tel: (01635) 254292 *Fax:* (01635) 253826
E-mail: uksg.admin@dial.pipex.com
Web Site: www.uksg.org
Key Personnel
Busn Mgr: Alison Whitehorn
Location: Heriot-Watt University, Edinburgh, UK
April 11-13, 2005

Young People's Poetry Week
Sponsored by The Children's Book Council (CBC)
12 W 37 St, 2nd fl, New York, NY 10118-7480, United States
Tel: 212-966-1990 *Toll Free Tel:* 800-999-2160 (orders only) *Fax:* 212-966-2073
Toll Free Fax: 888-807-9355 (orders only)
Web Site: www.cbcbooks.org/html/poetry_week.html
Key Personnel
Pres: Paula Quint
Location: Nationwide throughout the USA
April 11-17, 2005

MAY

AAAA Management Conference
Sponsored by American Association of Advertising Agencies (AAAA)
405 Lexington Ave, 18th fl, New York, NY 10174-1801, United States
Tel: 212-682-2500 *Fax:* 212-573-8968
E-mail: aaaaconferences@aaaa.org
Web Site: www.aaaa.org
Key Personnel
Pres & CEO: O Burtch Drake *E-mail:* obd@aaaa.org
Sr VP, Conferences & Special Events: Karen Proctor *E-mail:* karen@aaaa.org
Conference Mgr: Michelle Montalto *E-mail:* michelle@aaaa.org
Conference Coord: Michelle James *E-mail:* mjames@aaaa.org
Location: Fairmont Southampton, Southampton, Bermuda
May 4-6, 2005

AIIM 2005 Conference & Exposition
Sponsored by Advanstar Communications
70 Walnut St, Wellesley Hills, MA 02481, United States
Tel: 781-239-7510 *Fax:* 781-239-7511
E-mail: aiim@aiim.org
Web Site: www.aiim.org
Key Personnel
Gen Mgr: Brian Randall *E-mail:* brandall@advanstar.com
Location: Pennsylvania Convention Center, Philadelphia, PA, USA
May 17-19, 2005

Amsterdam International Printing Allied Industries Trade Fair (Grafivak)
Sponsored by Amsterdam RAI
PO Box 77777, Amsterdam 1070-MS, Netherlands
Tel: (020) 5491212 *Fax:* (020) 5491843
E-mail: grafivak@rai.nl
Web Site: www.grafivak.nl
Key Personnel
Prod Mgr: Xander de Bruine *Tel:* (020) 549 22 44 *E-mail:* x.d.bruine@rai.nl
Location: Amsterdam RAI Exhibition Center, Amsterdam, Netherlands
May 2005

ASQ World Conference on Quality & Improvement
Sponsored by American Society for Quality
600 N Plankinton Ave, Milwaukee, WI 53203, United States
Tel: 414-272-8575 *Toll Free Tel:* 800-248-1946 *Fax:* 414-272-1734
E-mail: cs@asq.org
Web Site: www.asq.org
Telex: 31-6567
Key Personnel
Exec Dir & Chief Strategic Officer: Paul Borawski
Events Mgmt Mgr: Shirley Krentz
Location: Washington State Convention & Trade Center, Seattle, WA, USA
May 16-18, 2005

Beijing International Book Fair
Sponsored by BIBF Management Office, CNPIEC
16 Gongti E Rd, Chaoyang District, Beijing 100020, China
Tel: (010) 6506 3080 *Fax:* (010) 6506 3101; (010) 6508 9188
E-mail: bibffo@bibf.net
Web Site: www.bibf.net
Key Personnel
Dir: Mr Zhu Zhigang
Location: Beijing Exhibition Center, Beijing, China
May 2005

Catholic Press Association of the US and Canada Annual Convention
Sponsored by Catholic Press Association of the US & Canada
3555 Veterans Memorial Hwy, Unit O, Ronkonkoma, NY 11779, United States
Tel: 631-471-4730 *Fax:* 631-471-4804
E-mail: cathjourn@aol.com
Web Site: www.catholicpress.org
Key Personnel
Pres: Helen Osman *Tel:* 512-476-4888 *E-mail:* helen_osman@austindiocese.org
Exec Dir: Owen McGovern *E-mail:* owen@catholicpress.org
May 2005

DPP 2005 - International Conference on Digital Production Printing
Sponsored by Society for Imaging Science & Technology (IS&T)
7003 Kilworth Lane, Springfield, VA 22151, United States
Tel: 703-642-9090 *Fax:* 703-642-9094
E-mail: info@imaging.org
Web Site: www.imaging.org
Key Personnel
Conference Mgr: Pamela Forness
Location: Amsterdam RAI Europa Complex, Amsterdam, The Netherlands
May 9-13, 2005

Annual European Conference on Managing Directories
Formerly European Conference on Electronic Directories
Sponsored by European Association of Directory & Database Publishers (EADP)
127 Ave Franklin Roosevelt, 1050 Brussels, Belgium
Tel: (02) 6463060 *Fax:* (02) 6463637
E-mail: mailbox@eadp.org
Web Site: www.eadp.org
Key Personnel
Congress & Conference Officer: Paola Caruso *E-mail:* paolacaruso@eadp.org
Location: Rome, Italy
May 2005

EXPOLIT Exposicion de Literatura Cristiana Book Fair
Sponsored by Spanish Evangelical Publishers Association (SEPA)/Associacion de Editores Evangelicos and Editorial Unilit
1360 NW 88 Ave, Miami, FL 33172, United States
Tel: 305-592-6136 (ext 105) *Toll Free Tel:* 800-767-7726 *Fax:* 305-592-0087
E-mail: info@expolit.com
Web Site: www.expolit.com
Key Personnel
Pres, EXPOLIT: David Ecklebarger
Program Dir: Marie Tanayo
Spanish Christian Literature Convention.
Location: Radisson Mart Plaza Hotel & Convention Centre, Miami, FL, USA
May 19-24, 2005

GAA Expo 2005
Formerly Gravure Association of America Convention
Sponsored by Gravure Association of America Inc
1200-A Scottsville Rd, Rochester, NY 14624, United States
Tel: 585-436-2150 *Fax:* 585-436-7689
E-mail: gaa@gaa.org
Web Site: www.gaa.org
Key Personnel
Meeting Planner: Pamela Schenk
Location: Adams Mark Hotel, Philadelphia, PA, USA
May 22-26, 2005

International Reading Association Annual Convention
Sponsored by International Reading Association
800 Barksdale Rd, Newark, DE 19714, United States
Mailing Address: PO Box 8139, Newark, DE 19714-8139, United States
Tel: 302-731-1600 *Fax:* 302-731-1057
E-mail: conferences@reading.org
Web Site: www.reading.org
Key Personnel
Pres: MaryEllen Vogt
Exec Dir: Alan E Farstrup
Location: San Antonio, TX, USA
May 1-5, 2005

ON DEMAND
Sponsored by Advanstar Communications
70 Walnut St, Wellesley Hills, MA 02481, United States
Tel: 781-239-7510 *Fax:* 781-239-7511
E-mail: ondemand@advanstar.com
Web Site: www.ondemandexpo.com
Key Personnel
Conference Dir: Tom Bliss
Gen Mgr: Brian Randall *E-mail:* brandall@advanstar.com
Digital printing & publishing.
Location: Pennsylvania Convention Center, Philadelphia, PA, USA
May 17-19, 2005

Pacprint
Sponsored by Graphic Arts Merchants Association of Australia Inc (GAMMA)
PO Box 1051, Crows Nest, NSW 2065, Australia
Tel: (02) 9417 7433 *Fax:* (02) 9417 7433
E-mail: enquiry@gamaa.net.au
Web Site: www.gamma.net.au; www.pacprint.com.au
Key Personnel
Chmn: Ron Patterson
Location: Melbourne Convention & Exhibition Centre, Melbourne, Australia
May 1, 2005

Papermakers Conference & Paper Expo - 2005 TAPPI
Sponsored by Technical Association of the Pulp & Paper Industry (TAPPI)
15 Technology Pkwy S, Norcross, GA 30092, United States
Tel: 770-446-1400 *Fax:* 770-446-6947
Web Site: www.tappi.org
Location: Hilton Milwaukee City Center, Milwaukee, WI, USA
May 22-26, 2005

Periodical Writers' Association of Canada Annual General Meeting
Sponsored by Periodical Writers' Association of Canada
54 Wolseley St, Suite 203, Toronto, ON M5T 1A5, Canada
Tel: 416-504-1645 *Fax:* 416-504-9079
E-mail: info@pwac.ca
Web Site: www.pwac.ca; www.writers.ca
Key Personnel
Exec Dir: Susan Stevenson
Location: Canada
May 2005

Print Buyers Conference
Sponsored by Pacific Printing & Imaging Association
1400 SW Fifth Ave, Suite 815, Portland, OR 97201, United States
Toll Free Tel: 877-762-7742 *Toll Free Fax:* 800-824-1911
E-mail: info@pacprinting.org
Web Site: www.ppi-assoc.org
Key Personnel
Exec Dir: Marcus Sassaman
Location: Portland, OR, USA
May 3, 2005
Location: Seattle, WA, USA
May 5, 2005

Society of American Business Editors & Writers Annual Convention and Exhibition
Sponsored by Society of American Business Editors & Writers Inc
University of Missouri, School of Journalism, 134 Neff Annex, Columbia, MO 65211-1200, United States
Tel: 573-882-7862 *Fax:* 573-884-1372
E-mail: sabew@missouri.edu
Web Site: www.sabew.org
Key Personnel
Exec Dir: Carrie M Paden *E-mail:* padenc@missouri.edu
Exec Asst: Vicky Edwards
Location: Red Lion Hotel, Seattle, WA, USA
May 1-3, 2005

Southwestern Graphics
Sponsored by Texas Graphic Arts Educational Foundation
13410 Preston Rd, No 1-100, Dallas, TX 75240-5299, United States
Tel: 940-763-8370 (Intl only) *Toll Free Tel:* 800-540-8280 *Fax:* 940-763-8395 (Intl Only)
Toll Free Fax: 800-540-5019
E-mail: info@swgraphics.com
Web Site: www.swgraphics.com
Key Personnel
Asst Show Mgr: Laura Bates
Location: Arlington Convention Center, Dallas, Ft Worth & Arlington, TX, USA
May 19-21, 2005

Warsaw International Book Fair
Sponsored by Ars Polon SA - Warsaw International Book Fair Office
Office for Domestic & International Book Fairs, 7 Krakowskie Przedmiescie St, 00-068 Warsaw, Poland
Tel: (022) 826-92-56 *Fax:* (022) 826-92-56
E-mail: mtk@arspolona.com.pl
Web Site: www.bookfair.pl
Key Personnel
Sec Gen: Ms Joanna Aleksandrowicz
Tel: (022) 826-97-12 *Fax:* (022) 826-97-12
E-mail: joannaa@arspolona.com.pl
Location: Palace of Culture & Science, Warsaw, Poland
May 19-22, 2005

Annual Web Offset Association Conference
Sponsored by Web Offset Association
Division of Printing Industries of America Inc
100 Daingerfield Rd, Alexandria, VA 22314, United States
Tel: 703-519-8100; 703-519-8142
Toll Free Tel: 800-742-2666 *Fax:* 703-519-7109
Web Site: www.gain.net
Key Personnel
Meetings Mgr: Bethany Forrest *E-mail:* bforrest@printing.org
Location: Opryland Grapevine, Grapevine, TX, USA
May 1-4, 2005

SUMMER

Buenos Aires International Children's Book Fair
Sponsored by Fundacion El Libro
Hipolito Yrigoyen 1628 - 5° piso, C1089AAF Buenos Aires, Argentina
Tel: (011) 4374 3288 *Fax:* (011) 4375 0268
E-mail: fundacion@el-libro.com.ar
Web Site: www.el-libro.com.ar
Key Personnel
Proj Mgr: Marta Diaz
Location: Centro de Exposiciones de la Ciudad de Buenos Aires, Avdas Figueroa Alcorta y Pueyrredón, Buenos Aires, Argentina
Summer 2005

School Library Association Annual Conference
Sponsored by School Library Association
Unit 2, Lotmead Business Village, Lotmead Farm, Wanborough, Swindon, Wilts SN4 0UY, United Kingdom
Tel: (01793) 791787 *Fax:* (01793) 791786
E-mail: info@sla.org.uk
Web Site: www.sla.org.uk
Key Personnel
Chief Executive: Kathy Lemaire *E-mail:* kathy@sla.org.uk
Summer 2005

Seybold Seminars
Sponsored by MediaLive International
795 Folsom St, 6th fl, San Francisco, CA 94107-1243, United States
Tel: 415-905-2300 *Fax:* 415-905-2329
Web Site: www.Seybold365.com
Key Personnel
VP & Gen Mgr: James Smith
Location: Moscone Convention Center, San Francisco, CA, USA
Summer 2005

JUNE

ABA Convention & Trade Exhibit
Sponsored by American Booksellers Association
828 S Broadway, Tarrytown, NY 10591, United States
Tel: 914-591-2665 *Toll Free Tel:* 800-637-0037
Fax: 914-591-2720
E-mail: info@bookweb.org
Web Site: www.bookweb.org
Key Personnel
Commns Mgr: Kristen Gilligan
Held in conjunction with BookExpo America.
Location: Jacob K Javits Convention Center, New York, NY, USA
June 2-5, 2005

American Library Association Annual Conference
Sponsored by American Library Association (ALA)
50 E Huron St, Chicago, IL 60611, United States
Tel: 312-280-3200 *Toll Free Tel:* 800-545-2433
Fax: 312-944-7841
E-mail: ala@ala.org
Web Site: www.ala.org
Key Personnel
Public Info Dir: Mark Gould
Press Officer: Larra Clark
Dir, Intl Rel: Michael Dowling
Location: Chicago, IL, USA
June 23-29, 2005

AsiaPack AsiaPrint
Sponsored by Reed Tradex Co Ltd
32nd fl, Sathorn Nakorn Tower, 100/68-69, North Sathorn Rd, Silom, Bangrak, Bangkok 10500, Thailand
Tel: (02) 636 7272 *Fax:* (02) 636 7282
E-mail: printpack@reedtradex.co.th
Web Site: www.asiapackasiaprint.com
Biennial international trade exhibition for printing, packaging & processing machinery, equipment materials, supplies & solutions. Co-organized by the Thai Printing Association.
Location: Bangkok International Trade & Exhibition Centre, Bangkok, Thailand
June 1, 2005

Association of American University Presses Annual Meeting
Sponsored by Association of American University Presses (AAUP)
71 W 23 St, Suite 901, New York, NY 10010, United States
Tel: 212-989-1010 *Fax:* 212-989-0176; 212-989-0275
E-mail: info@aaupnet.org
Web Site: www.aaupnet.org
Key Personnel
Exec Dir: Peter J Givler
Asst Dir: Timothy Muench
Admin Mgr: Linda McCall
Location: Philadelphia, PA, USA
June 16-19, 2005

BookExpo America (BEA)
Sponsored by Reed Exhibitions
Affiliate of Reed Exhibition Companies
383 Main Ave, Norwalk, CT 06851, United States
Tel: 203-840-5614 *Toll Free Tel:* 800-840-5614
Fax: 203-840-5580
E-mail: inquiry@bookexpo.america.com
Web Site: bookexpoamerica.com
Key Personnel
Sr VP: Tony Calanca
Industry VP & Show Mgr: Greg Topalian
E-mail: gtopalian@reedexpo.com
Mktg Dir: Tom Kobak *E-mail:* tkobak@reedexpo.com
Sales Dir: Steven Rosato *E-mail:* srosato@reedexpo.com
Produced & managed by Reed Exhibitions, BEA is sponsored by American Booksellers Association & Association of American Publishers.
Location: Jacob K Javits Convention Center, New York, NY, USA
June 2-5, 2005

& PROMOTIONAL EVENTS

BookExpo Canada
Sponsored by Reed Exhibitions Canada
3761 Victoria Park Ave, Unit 1, Toronto, ON M1W 3S2, Canada
Tel: 416-491-7565 (Toronto area); 514-845-1125 (Montreal area) *Toll Free Tel:* 888-322-7333 *Fax:* 416-491-7096 (Toronto area); 514-845-8089 (Montreal area) *Toll Free Fax:* 888-633-3376
Web Site: www.bookexpo.ca
Key Personnel
Show Mgr: Jennifer Sickinger *Tel:* 416-848-1692
    E-mail: jsickinger@reedexpo.com
Canada's largest book industry event. Sponsored by Canadian Booksellers Association.
Location: Metro Toronto Convention Centre, Toronto, ON, Canada
June 17-20, 2005

British & Irish Association of Law Librarians Annual Conference
Sponsored by British & Irish Association of Law Librarians
26 Myton Crescent, Warwick CV34 6QA, United Kingdom
Tel: (01926) 491717 *Fax:* (01926) 491717
Key Personnel
BIALL Administer: Susan Frost
    E-mail: susanfrost@compuserve.com
Location: Harrogate, UK
June 10-12, 2005

The Bronte Society Annual General Meeting
Sponsored by The Bronte Society
The Bronte Parsonage Museum, Church St, Haworth, Keighley, West Yorks BD22 8DR, United Kingdom
Tel: (01535) 642323 *Fax:* (01535) 647131
E-mail: bronte@bronte.org.uk
Web Site: www.bronte.info
Key Personnel
Museum Mgr: Alan Bentley
Location: Haworth, UK
June 4, 2005

Canadian Library Association Annual Convention & Tradeshow
Sponsored by Canadian Library Association (CLA)
328 Frank St, Ottawa, ON K2P 0X8, Canada
Tel: 613-232-9625 *Fax:* 613-563-9895
E-mail: info@cla.ca
Web Site: www.cla.ca
Key Personnel
Pres: Madeleine Lefebvre
Exec Dir: Don Butcher *E-mail:* dbutcher@cla.ca
Location: Calgary, AB, Canada
June 15-18, 2005

Eastpack: The Power of Packaging
Sponsored by Canon Communications
11444 W Olympic Blvd, Suite 900, Los Angeles, CA 90064, United States
Tel: 310-445-4200 *Fax:* 310-996-9499
Web Site: www.cancom.com; www.canontradeshows.com
Location: Jacob K Javits Convention Center, New York, NY, USA
June 13-15, 2005

Gutenberg Gesellschaft Annual General Meeting
Sponsored by Gutenberg-Gesellschaft eV (Gutenberg Society)
Liebfrauenplatz 5, 55116 Mainz, Germany
Tel: (06131) 22 64 20 *Fax:* (06131) 23 35 30
E-mail: gutenberg-gesellschaft@freenet.de
Web Site: www.gutenberg-gesellschaft.uni-mainz.de
Key Personnel
Sec Gen: Dr Cornelia Fischer
Location: Mainz, Germany
June 25, 2005

IEPRC Annual Conference
Sponsored by International Electronic Publishing Research Centre Ltd (IEPRC)
c/o David Haywood, LCP, Elephant & Castle, London SE1 6SB, United Kingdom
Tel: (020) 7514 6938 *Fax:* (020) 7514 6940
E-mail: admin@ieprc.org
Web Site: www.ieprc.org
Telex: 929810
Location: Jonkoping University, Stockholm, Sweden
June 10-11, 2005

International Association of Business Communicators Conference
Sponsored by International Association of Business Communicators (IABC)
One Hallidie Plaza, Suite 600, San Francisco, CA 94102, United States
Tel: 415-544-4700 *Toll Free Tel:* 800-776-4222 *Fax:* 415-544-4747
E-mail: conf@iabc.com
Web Site: www.iabc.com
Key Personnel
Pres: Julie Freeman
Location: Washington, DC, USA
June 2005

International Newsletter & Specialized - Information Conference
Sponsored by Newsletter & Electronic Publishers Association
1501 Wilson Blvd, Suite 509, Arlington, VA 22209, United States
Tel: 703-527-2333 *Toll Free Tel:* 800-356-9302 *Fax:* 703-841-0629
E-mail: nepa@newsletters.org
Web Site: www.newsletters.org
Key Personnel
Exec Dir: Patti Wysocki
Location: Mayflower Hotel, Washington, DC, USA
June 2005

International Newspaper Financial Executives Annual Conference
Sponsored by International Newspaper Financial Executives
21525 Ridgetop Circle, Suite 200, Sterling, VA 20166, United States
Tel: 703-421-4060 *Fax:* 703-421-4068
E-mail: infehq@infe.org
Web Site: www.infe.org
Key Personnel
VP & Exec Dir: Robert J Kasabian
    E-mail: bkasabian@infe.org
Location: Hilton in the Walt Disney World Resort, Orlando. FL, USA
June 25-29, 2005

International Plate Printers', Die Stampers' & Engravers' Union of North America Mini Meeting
Sponsored by International Plate Printers', Die Stampers' & Engravers' Union of North America
3957 Smoke Rd, Doylestown, PA 18901, United States
Tel: 215-340-2843
Key Personnel
Sec & Treas: James Kopernick
Location: Mont-Tremblant, Canada
June 2005

Outdoor Writers Association of America Annual Conference
Sponsored by Outdoor Writers Association of America
158 Lower Georges Valley Rd, Spring Mills, PA 16875, United States
Tel: 814-364-9557 *Fax:* 814-364-9558
E-mail: eking4owaa@cs.com
Web Site: www.owaa.org
Location: Madison, WI, USA
June 18-22, 2005

Print Sales & Marketing Executives Conference
Sponsored by Printing Industries of America Inc
100 Daingerfield Rd, Alexandria, VA 22314, United States
Tel: 703-519-8143 *Fax:* 703-548-3227
Web Site: www.gain.net
Location: Rancho Bernado Inn, San Diego, CA, USA
June 26-29, 2005

Science Fiction Research Association Annual Meeting
Sponsored by Science Fiction Research Association Inc
University of Guelph, Guelph, ON N1G 2W1, Canada
Tel: 519-824-4120 (ext 53251)
Web Site: www.sfra.org
Key Personnel
Pres: Peter Brigg *E-mail:* pbrigg@uoguelph.ca
Organizer: Elizabeth Hull *E-mail:* ehull@harpercollege.edu; Beverly Friend
    E-mail: friend@oakton.edu
Location: Imperial Palace Hotel & Casino, Las Vegas, NV, USA
June 23-26, 2005

Society for Scholarly Publishing Annual Meeting
Sponsored by Society for Scholarly Publishing
10200 W 44 Ave, Suite 304, Wheat Ridge, CO 80033-2840, United States
Tel: 303-422-3914 *Fax:* 303-422-8894
E-mail: ssp@resourcecenter.com; info@sspnet.org
Web Site: www.sspnet.org
Location: Westin Boston Copley, MA, USA
June 1-3, 2005

Special Libraries Association Annual Conference
Sponsored by Special Libraries Association (SLA)
1700 18 St NW, Washington, DC 20009-2514, United States
Tel: 202-234-4700 *Fax:* 202-234-2442
E-mail: sla@sla.org
Web Site: www.sla.org
Key Personnel
Exec Dir: Janice LaChance *E-mail:* janice@sla.org
Location: Toronto, ON, Canada
June 4-9, 2005

Umbrella 2005
Sponsored by Chartered Institute of Library & Information Professionals (CILIP)
7 Ridgmount St, London WC1E 7AE, United Kingdom
Tel: (020) 7255 0500 *Fax:* (020) 7255 0501
E-mail: umbrella@cilip.org.uk; conferences@cilip.org.uk
Web Site: www.umbrella2005.org.uk
Key Personnel
Contact: Joan Thompson *Tel:* (020) 7255 0544
Location: UMIST, Manchester, UK
June 30-July 2, 2005

JULY

ARLIS/UK & Ireland Annual Conference
Sponsored by ARLIS/UK & Ireland Art Libraries Society
The Courtauld Institute of Art, Somerset House, The Strand, WC2R ORN London, United Kingdom
Tel: (020) 7848 2703 *Fax:* (01527) 579298
Web Site: www.arlis.org.uk
Key Personnel
Administrator: Anna Mellows *E-mail:* arlis@courtauld.ac.uk
Chair: Margaret Young
Location: Aston, Birmingham, UK
July 7-10, 2005

Bibliographical Society of Canada/La Societe bibliographique du Canada Annual Meeting
Sponsored by Bibliographical Society of Canada/La Societe bibliographique du Canada
PO Box 575, Sta P, Toronto, ON M5S 2T1, Canada
E-mail: mcgaughe@yorku.ca
Web Site: www.library.utoronto.ca/bsc
Key Personnel
Pres: Carl Spadoni
Conference Coord: Mary F Williamson
 E-mail: mfw@yorku.ca; Joan Winearls
 E-mail: joan.winearls@utoronto.ca
Location: Halifax, NS, Canada
July 2005

CBA International Convention
Sponsored by CBA
9240 Explorer Dr, Colorado Springs, CO 80920-5001, United States
Mailing Address: PO Box 62000, Colorado Springs, CO 80962-2000, United States
Tel: 719-265-9895 *Toll Free Tel:* 800-252-1950
 Fax: 719-272-3510
E-mail: info@cbaonline.org
Web Site: www.cbaonline.org
Key Personnel
Pres: William Anderson *E-mail:* banderson@cbaonline.org
VP & COO: Dorothy Gore
Convention & Expositions Mgr: Scott Graham
For almost 50 years, the annual CBA International Convention has been our industry's single-most impacting week. During this week, people of the industry from all over the world meet face-to-face for buying & selling, education, inspiration, fellowship & future planning. Here individuals unite to further the mission of seeing Christian product impact lives for God's kingdom the world over. At this unique gathering, our industry's strength is most evident & our goals are most clearly in focus. It is, in short, the most important week in the ministry of your business & of the industry as a whole.
Location: Colorado Convention Center, Denver, CO, USA
July 9-14, 2005

Church & Synagogue Library Association Conference
Sponsored by Church & Synagogue Library Association
PO Box 19357, Portland, OR 97280-0357, United States
Tel: 503-244-6919 *Toll Free Tel:* 800-542-2752
 Fax: 503-977-3734
E-mail: csla@worldaccessnet.com
Web Site: www.worldaccessnet.com/~csla
Location: Embassy Suites Hotel, Portland, OR, USA
July 24-26, 2005

DP: Digital Publishing Fair
Sponsored by Reed Exhibitions Japan Ltd
18F Shinjuku Nomura Bldg, 1-26-2 Nishi-Shinjuku, Shinjuku-ku, Toyko 163-0570, Japan
Tel: (03) 3349 8507 *Fax:* (03) 3345 7929
E-mail: digi@reedexpo.co.jp
Web Site: www.reedexpo.co.jp/digi
Key Personnel
Deputy Show Dir: Keisuke Amano
Organized by Reed Exhibitions Japan Ltd, TIBF Executive Committee.
Location: Tokyo Big Sight, Tokyo, Japan
July 6-9, 2005

Hong Kong Book Fair
Sponsored by Hong Kong Trade Development Council
Unit 13, Expo Galleria, Hong Kong Convention & Exhibition Centre, One Expo Dr, Wanchai, Hong Kong
Tel: 2584-4333 *Fax:* 2824-0026; 2824-0249
E-mail: exhibitions@tdc.org.hk
Web Site: hkbookfair.tdc.org.hk
Key Personnel
Sales Adminstrator: Joyce P F Laing *Tel:* 2240-4018
Location: Hong Kong Convention & Exhibition Center, One Harbour Rd, Wanchai, Hong Kong
July 2005

International Association of Music Libraries, Archives & Documentation Centres Conference
Sponsored by International Association of Music Libraries, Archives & Documentation Centres
National Library of New Zealand, Music Room, PO Box 1467, Wellington 6001, New Zealand
Tel: (04) 474 3039 *Fax:* (04) 474 3035
Web Site: www.iaml.info
Key Personnel
Secretary General: Roger Flury *E-mail:* roger.flury@natlib.govt.nz
Location: Warsaw, Poland
July 10-15, 2005

RWA Annual National Conference
Sponsored by Romance Writers of America
16000 Stuebner Airline, Suite 140, Spring, TX 77379, United States
Tel: 832-717-5200 *Fax:* 832-717-5201
E-mail: info@rwanational.org
Web Site: www.rwanational.org
Key Personnel
Exec Dir: Allison Kelley *E-mail:* akelley@rwanational.org
Location: Reno Hilton Hotel, Reno, NV, USA
July 27-30, 2005

TIBF: Tokyo International Book Fair
Sponsored by Reed Exhibitions Japan Ltd
18F Shinjuku Nomura Bldg, 1-26-2 Nishi-Shinjuku, Shinjuku-ku, Toyko 163-0570, Japan
Tel: (03) 3349 8507 *Fax:* (03) 3345 7929
E-mail: tibf-eng@reedexpo.co.jp
Web Site: www.reedexpo.co.jp/tibf
Key Personnel
Deputy Show Dir: Keisuke Amano
Organized by Reed Exhibition Japan Ltd, TIBF executive committee.
Location: Tokyo Big Sight, Tokyo, Japan
July 6-9, 2005

AUGUST

The Dorothy L Sayers Society Annual Convention
Sponsored by The Dorothy L Sayers Society
Rose Cottage, Malthouse Lane, Hurstpierpoint, West Sussex BN6 9JY, United Kingdom
Tel: (01273) 833444 *Fax:* (01273) 835988
E-mail: info@sayers.org.uk
Web Site: www.sayers.org.uk
Key Personnel
Chairman: Christopher Dean
Location: Christ Church, Oxford, UK
Aug 12-15, 2005

Edinburgh International Book Festival
Scottish Book Centre, 137 Dundee St, Edinburgh EH11 1BG, United Kingdom
Tel: (0131) 228 5444 *Fax:* (0131) 228 4333
E-mail: admin@edbookfest.co.uk
Web Site: www.edbookfest.co.uk
Key Personnel
Dir: Catherine Lockerbie
PA to Dir: Lyn Trotter
The festival takes place in Charlotte Square Gardens (just off the West End of Princes St) over 17 days each August. An extensive program showcases the work of the world's authors & thinkers for people of all ages.
Location: Charlotte Square Gardens, Edinburgh, UK
Aug 13-29, 2005

Graphic Arts
Sponsored by Business & Industrial Trade Fairs Ltd
Unit 103-105, New East Ocean Centre, 9 Science Museum Rd, Tsimshatsui East, Kowloon, Hong Kong
Tel: 2865 2633 *Fax:* 2866 1770; 2866 2076
E-mail: enquiry@bitf.com.hk
Key Personnel
Senior Manager: Louis Leung
Location: Hong Kong Convention & Exhibition Centre, Hong Kong
Aug 2005

Print & Pack Expo
Sponsored by Business & Industrial Trade Fairs Ltd
Unit 103-105, New East Ocean Centre, 9 Science Museum Rd, Tsimshatsui East, Kowloon, Hong Kong
Tel: 2865 2633 *Fax:* 2866 1770; 2866 2076
E-mail: enquiry@bitf.com.hk
Web Site: www.printpackexpo.com
Key Personnel
Senior Manager: Louis Leung
Location: Hong Kong Convention & Exhibition Centre, Hong Kong
Aug 2005

PSA International Conference of Photography
Sponsored by Photographic Society of America Inc (PSA)
3000 United Founders Blvd, Suite 103, Oklahoma City, OK 73112-3940, United States
Tel: 405-843-1437 *Fax:* 405-843-1438
E-mail: psahg@theshop.net
Web Site: www.psa-photo.org
Key Personnel
VP, Conventions: Gerry Emmerich
Location: Sheraton City Centre Hotel, Salt Lake City, UT, USA
Aug 29-Sept 3, 2005

South African Booksellers Association Annual Conference
Sponsored by South African Booksellers Association
PO Box 870, Bellville 7535, South Africa
Tel: (021) 945 1572 *Fax:* (021) 945 2169
E-mail: saba@sabooksellers.com
Web Site: sabooksellers.com
Location: Cape Town, South Africa
Aug 16-17, 2005

SWANICK: The Writer's Summer School
Sponsored by Writer's Summer School

10 Stag Rd, Lake Dandown, Isle of Wight PO36 8PE, United Kingdom
Tel: (07050) 630949 *Fax:* (07050) 630949
E-mail: gxk@cs.nott.ac.uk
Web Site: www.wss.org.uk
Key Personnel
Sec: Jean Sutton *E-mail:* jean.sutton@lineone.net
A week-long summer school of informal talks & discussion groups, forums, panels, quizzes, competition & a lot of fun. Open to everyone, from absolute beginners to published authors. Held annually in August.
Location: The Hayes Conference Centre, Swanwick, Derbyshire, UK
Aug 2005

World Library & Information Congress
Sponsored by International Federation of Library Associations & Institutions (IFLA)
Postbus 95312, 2509 CH The Hague, Netherlands
Tel: (070) 3140884 *Fax:* (070) 3834827
E-mail: ifla@ifla.org
Web Site: www.ifla.org
Location: Oslo, Norway
Aug 2005

Zimbabwe International Book Fair
PO Box CY1179, Causeway, Harare, Zimbabwe
Tel: (04) 702104/8 *Fax:* (04) 702129
E-mail: information@zibf.org
Web Site: www.zibf.org
Location: Harare Sculpture Gardens, Harare, Zimbabwe
Aug 1-6, 2005

AUTUMN

NEPA's Annual Fall Conference
Formerly Newsletter Marketing Conference
Sponsored by Newsletter & Electronic Publishers Association
1501 Wilson Blvd, Suite 509, Arlington, VA 22209, United States
Tel: 703-527-2333 *Toll Free Tel:* 800-356-9302 *Fax:* 703-841-0629
E-mail: nepa@newsletters.org
Web Site: www.newsletters.org
Key Personnel
Exec Dir: Patti Wysocki
Autumn

New York Is Book Country
c/o C2 Media, 423 W 55 St, 6th fl, New York, NY 10019, United States
Tel: 646-557-6625 *Fax:* 646-557-6400
E-mail: nyibc@c2media.com
Web Site: www.nyisbookcountry.org
Key Personnel
Exec Dir: Ann Binkley
Annual five-day literary festival throughout the city, culminating in the Sunday, books-only street fair on Fifth Ave between 42nd & 57th Streets, New York, NY, USA.
Location: Fifth Ave, New York, NY, USA
Autumn

Remainder & Promotional Book Fair
Sponsored by Ciana Ltd
24 Langroyd Rd, London SW17 7PL, United Kingdom
Tel: (020) 8682 1969 *Fax:* (020) 8682 1997
E-mail: enquiries@ciana.co.uk
Web Site: www.ciana.co.uk
Location: Business Design Centre, Islington, London, UK
Autumn 2005

Society of Professional Journalists National Convention
Sponsored by The Society of Professional Journalists
Eugene S Pulliam National Journalism Center, 3909 N Meridian St, Indianapolis, IN 46208, United States
Tel: 317-927-8000 *Fax:* 317-920-4789
E-mail: spj@spj.org
Web Site: www.spj.org
Key Personnel
Exec Dir: Terrance G Harper
Deputy Dir: Julie Grimes
Programs Coord: Carrie Copeland
Location: Las Vegas, NV, USA
Autumn 2005

Twin Cities Book Festival
Sponsored by Rain Taxi Review of Books
PO Box 3840, Minneapolis, MN 55403, United States
Tel: 612-825-1528 *Fax:* 612-825-1528
E-mail: bookfest@raintaxi.com
Web Site: www.raintaxi.com
Key Personnel
Dir: Eric Lorberer
Gala celebration of books, featuring large exhibition, author readings & signings, book art activities, panel discussions, used book sale & children's events.
Location: Minneapolis, MN, USA
Autumn 2005

SEPTEMBER

Beijing International Book Fair
Sponsored by BIBF Management Office, CNPIEC
16 Gongti E Rd, Chaoyang District, Beijing 100020, China
Tel: (010) 6506 3080 *Fax:* (010) 6506 3101; (010) 6508 9188
E-mail: bibffo@bibf.net
Web Site: www.bibf.net
Key Personnel
Dir: Mr Zhu Zhigang
Location: China International Exhibition Center, Beijing, China
Sept 2005

Distripress Annual Congress
Sponsored by Distripress
Beethovenstr 20, CH-8002 Zurich, Switzerland
Tel: (01) 2024121 *Fax:* (01) 2021025
E-mail: info@distripress.ch
Web Site: www.distripress.ch
Key Personnel
Managing Dir: Dr Peter Emod *E-mail:* peter.emod@distripress.ch
Non-profit association promoting the free international circulation of the press.
Location: Nice, France
Sept 25-29, 2005

European Association of Directory & Database Publishers Annual Congress
Sponsored by European Association of Directory & Database Publishers (EADP)
127 Ave Franklin Roosevelt, 1050 Brussels, Belgium
Tel: (02) 6463060 *Fax:* (02) 6463637
E-mail: mailbox@eadp.org
Web Site: www.eadp.org
Key Personnel
Congress & Conference Officer: Paola Caruso *E-mail:* paolacaruso@eadp.org
Location: Stockholm, Sweden
Sept 14-17, 2005

Garden Writers Association of America Meeting & Symposium
Sponsored by Garden Writers Association of America
10210 Leatherleaf Ct, Manassas, VA 20111, United States
Tel: 703-257-1032 *Fax:* 703-257-0213
E-mail: info@gwaa.org
Web Site: www.gwaa.org
Key Personnel
Pres: Cathy Wilkerson Barash
Exec Dir: Robert LaGasse
Location: Vancouver, BC, Canada
Sept 2005

Goteborg International Book Fair
Sponsored by Bok & Bibliotek
412 94 Gothenburg, Sweden
Tel: (031) 7088400 *Fax:* (031) 209103
E-mail: info@goteborg-bookfair.com
Web Site: www.bok-bibliotek.se
Key Personnel
Man Dir: Anna Falck *E-mail:* af@goteborg-bookfair.com
Exhibition Mgr: Lisa Oden *E-mail:* lo@goteborg-bookfair.com
Sept 29-Oct 2, 2005

Great Salt Lake Book Festival
Sponsored by Utah Humanities Council
202 W300 N, Salt Lake City, UT 84103, United States
Tel: 801-359-9670 *Fax:* 801-531-7869
Web Site: www.utahhumanities.org/bookfestival/bookfestival2003_01.php
Key Personnel
Asst Dir & Dir of Progs: Jean Cheney *Tel:* 801-359-9670
Free literary event featuring nationally known authors.
Location: Salt Lake City Library, Salt Lake City, UT, USA
Sept 17-18, 2005

Montana Festival of the Book
Sponsored by Montana Committee for the Humanities
311 Brantly Hall, University of Montana, Missoula, MT 59812-8214, United States
Tel: 406-243-6022 *Toll Free Tel:* 800-624-6001 (MT only)
Web Site: www.bookfest-mt.org
Key Personnel
Coord: Kim Anderson
Two day celebration featuring over 70 authors & 50 events.
Location: Missoula, MT, USA
Sept 2005

Moscow International Book Fair
Sponsored by General Directorate of International Book Exhibitions & Fairs
16 Malaya Dmitrovka St, Moscow 127006, Russian Federation
Tel: (095) 2994034 *Fax:* (095) 9732132
E-mail: mibf@mibf.ru
Web Site: www.mibf.ru
Key Personnel
Gen Dir: Mr Nikolay Ph Ovsyannikov
Location: All Russian Exhibition Centre, Moscow, Russia
Sept 2005

National Design Conference
Sponsored by American Institute of Graphic Arts (AIGA)
164 Fifth Ave, New York, NY 10010, United States
Tel: 212-807-1990 (ext 223) *Fax:* 212-807-1799
E-mail: aiga@aiga.org; programs@aiga.org
Web Site: www.aiga.org
Key Personnel
Exec Dir: Richard Grefe

Biennial event.
Location: Boston, MA, USA
Sept 15-17, 2005

National Federation of Press Women National Conference
Sponsored by National Federation of Press Women Inc (NFPW)
PO Box 5556, Arlington, VA 22205-0056, United States
Tel: 703-534-2500 *Toll Free Tel:* 800-780-2715 *Fax:* 703-534-5751
E-mail: presswomen@aol.com
Web Site: www.nfpw.org
Key Personnel
Exec Dir: Carol Pierce
Location: Seattle, WA, USA
Sept 2005

Publishers Association of the South Fall Conference & Annual Meeting
Sponsored by Publishers Association of the South (PAS)
4412 Fletcher St, Panama City, FL 32405-1017, United States
Tel: 850-914-0766 *Fax:* 850-769-4348
E-mail: executive@pubsouth.org
Web Site: www.pubsouth.org
Key Personnel
Pres: Beth Wright
Assn Exec: Pat Sabiston
Location: Winston-Salem, NC, USA
Sept 15-16, 2005

Southeast Booksellers Association Annual Meeting & Trade Show
Sponsored by Southeast Booksellers Association (SEBA)
2611 Forest Dr, Suite 124, Columbia, SC 29204, United States
Tel: 803-779-0118 *Fax:* 803-779-0113
E-mail: info@sebaweb.org
Web Site: www.sebaweb.org
Key Personnel
Exec Dir: Wanda Jewell *E-mail:* sebajewell@aol.com
Location: Adam's Mark, Winston-Salem, NC, USA
Sept 15-19, 2005

Spectrum 2005
Sponsored by IDEAlliance
100 Daingerfield Rd, Alexandria, VA 22314, United States
Tel: 703-837-1070 *Fax:* 703-837-1072
E-mail: info@idealliance.org
Web Site: www.idealliance.org
Key Personnel
Dir, Exec Programs: Georgia Volakis *Tel:* 703-837-1075 *E-mail:* gvolakis@idealliance.com
Location: El Conquistador, Tucson, AZ
Sept 24-27, 2005

OCTOBER

China Didac/WORLDDIDAC
Sponsored by Worlddidac
Bollwerk 21, 3001 Bern, Switzerland
Mailing Address: PO Box 8866, 3001 Bern, Switzerland
Tel: (031) 311 76 82 *Fax:* (031) 312 17 44
E-mail: info@worlddidac.org
Web Site: www.worlddidac.org
Key Personnel
Proj Mgr: Madeleine Kihm *E-mail:* kihm@worlddidac.org
International exhibition for educational materials, professional training & e-learning.

Location: China
Oct 2005

DMA Annual Conference & Exhibition
Sponsored by The Direct Marketing Association Inc (The DMA)
1120 Avenue of the Americas, New York, NY 10036, United States
Tel: 212-768-7277 *Fax:* 212-302-6714
E-mail: conference@the-dma.org
Web Site: www.dmaannual.org
Key Personnel
VP, Conference Opers: Tana Stellato
Location: Georgia World Congress Center, Atlanta, GA, USA
Oct 16-19, 2005

English Association Semiannual Teachers' Conference
Sponsored by The English Association
University of Leicester, University Rd, Leicester LE1 7RH, United Kingdom
Tel: (0116) 252 3982 *Fax:* (0116) 252 2301
E-mail: engassoc@le.ac.uk
Key Personnel
Chief Exec: Helen Lucas
Conference Org: Louise Callen
Membership Coord: Jeremy Wiltshire
Location: London, UK
October 2005

Frankfurt Book Fair
Sponsored by Ausstellungs-und Messe-GmbH des Borsenvereins des Deutschen Buchhandels
Reineckstr 3, 63013 Frankfurt am Main, Germany
Mailing Address: Postfach 100116, 60001 Frankfurt am Main, Germany
Tel: (069) 21020 *Fax:* (069) 2102 227
E-mail: info@book-fair.com
Web Site: www.frankfurt-book-fair.com *Cable:* BUCHMESSE
Key Personnel
CEO & Dir: Volker Neumann
Location: Frankfurt Fairgrounds, Frankfurt, Germany
Oct 19-24, 2005

LIBER Feria Internacional del Libro
Sponsored by Federacion de Gremios de Editores de Espana (FGEE) (Spanish Publishers Association)
Cea Bermudez, 44-2° Dehe, Madrid 20003, Spain
Tel: (091) 5345195 *Fax:* (091) 5352625
E-mail: fgee@fge.es
Web Site: www.federacioneditores.org
Key Personnel
Executive Dir: Antonio Ma Avila
Location: Madrid, Spain
Oct 12-15, 2005

National College Media Convention
Sponsored by Associated Collegiate Press (ACP) Subsidiary of National Scholastic Press Assn
2221 University Ave SE, Suite 121, Minneapolis, MN 55414, United States
Tel: 612-625-8335 *Fax:* 612-626-0720
E-mail: info@studentpress.org
Web Site: studentpress.org
Key Personnel
Assoc Dir: Ann Akers
Also sponsored by College Media Advisors.
Location: Hyatt Regency, New Orleans, LA, USA
Oct 27-30, 2005

New Atlantic Independent Booksellers Association Annual Trade Show
Sponsored by New Atlantic Independent Booksellers Association (NAIBA)
2667 Hyacinth St, Westbury, NY 11590, United States
Tel: 516-333-0681 *Fax:* 516-333-0689

E-mail: info@naiba.com; readingent@aol.com
Web Site: www.naiba.com
Key Personnel
Exec Dir: Eileen Dengler
Location: Atlantic City, NJ, USA
Oct 23-24, 2005

NPES The Association for Suppliers of Printing, Publishing and Converting Technologies Annual Conference
Sponsored by NPES The Association for Suppliers of Printing, Publishing & Converting Technologies
1899 Preston White Dr, Reston, VA 20191-4367, United States
Tel: 703-264-7200 *Fax:* 703-620-0994
E-mail: npes@npes.org
Web Site: www.npes.org
Key Personnel
Pres: Regis J Delmontagne
Dir, Communs & Mktg: Carol J Hurlburt
E-mail: churlbur@npes.org
Trade Association representing companies which manufacture equipment, systems, software & supplies used in printing, publishing & converting.
Location: Key Biscayne, FL, USA
Oct 8-10, 2005

Texas Book Festival
610 Brazos St, Suite 200, Austin, TX 78701, United States
Tel: 512-477-4055 *Fax:* 512-322-0722
E-mail: bookfest@texasbookfestival.org
Web Site: www.texasbookfestival.org
Key Personnel
Dir: Mary Herman *Tel:* 512-320-5451
E-mail: maryherman@texasbookfestival.org
Prog Communs Mgr: Edward Nawotka *Tel:* 512-472-3808 *E-mail:* edward@texasbookfestival.org
Off Mgr: Andrea V Prestridge *E-mail:* andrea@texasbookfestival.org
The festival is a statewide program that promotes reading & literacy highlighted by a two-day festival featuring authors from Texas & across the country. Money raised from the festival is distributed as grants to public libraries throughout the state.
Location: State Capital Bldg, Austin, TX, USA
Oct 29-30, 2005

Xplor Global Conference
Sponsored by Xplor International
24238 Hawthorne Blvd, Torrance, CA 90505-6505, United States
Tel: 310-791-9521 *Toll Free Tel:* 800-669-7567 (ext 521) *Fax:* 310-375-4240
E-mail: info@xplor.org
Web Site: www.xplor.org
Key Personnel
Dir Opers: Ellen Dahlin
Location: Minneapolis Convention Center, Minneapolis, MN, USA
Oct 16-20, 2005

NOVEMBER

American Academy of Religion
Sponsored by American Schools of Oriental Research
825 Houston Mill Rd, Suite 201, Atlanta, GA 30329, United States
Tel: 404-727-3049 *Fax:* 404-727-7959
E-mail: aar@aarweb.org
Web Site: www.aarweb.org
Key Personnel
Prog Dir: Aislinn Jones

Location: Philadelphia, PA, USA
Nov 19-22, 2005

American Translators Association Annual Conference
Sponsored by American Translators Association (ATA)
225 Reinekers Lane, Suite 590, Alexandria, VA 22314, United States
Tel: 703-683-6100 *Fax:* 703-683-6122
E-mail: ata@atanet.org
Web Site: www.atanet.org
Key Personnel
Exec Dir: Walter Bacak *Tel:* 703-683-6100 ext 3006 *E-mail:* walter@atanet.org
Location: Seattle, WA, USA
Nov 9-12, 2005

Children's Book Week
Sponsored by The Children's Book Council (CBC)
12 W 37 St, 2nd fl, New York, NY 10118-7480, United States
Tel: 212-966-1990 *Toll Free Tel:* 800-999-2160 (orders only) *Fax:* 212-966-2073 *Toll Free Fax:* 888-807-9355 (orders only)
Web Site: www.cbcbooks.org
Key Personnel
Pres: Paula Quint
Location: Nationwide across the USA
Nov 14-20, 2005

ECPA Publishing University
Sponsored by Evangelical Christian Publishers Association
4816 S Ash Ave, Suite 101, Tempe, AZ 85282-7735, United States
Tel: 480-966-3998 *Fax:* 480-966-1944
E-mail: info@ecpa.org
Web Site: www.ecpa.org
Key Personnel
Pres: Mark Kuyper *E-mail:* mkuyper@ecpa.org
Excellence in Christian publishing through professional instruction, interactive learning & practical training.
Nov 6-8, 2005

Feria Internacional del Libro
Sponsored by Feria Internacional del Libro Guadalajara
Av Alemania 1370, Colonia Moderna, 44190 Guadalajara Jalisco, Mexico
Tel: (033) 3810 0291; (033) 3810 0331 *Fax:* (033) 3810 0379
E-mail: fil@fil.com.mx; filny@aol.com
Web Site: www.fil.com.mx
Key Personnel
Pres: Raul Padilla Lopez
Dir: Nubia Edith Macias Navarro *E-mail:* dirfil@fil.com.mx
Gen Coord, Events & Prizes: Laura Niembro Diaz *E-mail:* eventsof@fil.com.mx
Location: Guadalajara, Mexico
Nov 26-Dec 3, 2005

Jewish Book Month
Sponsored by Jewish Book Council
15 E 26 St, New York, NY 10010-1579, United States
Tel: 212-532-4949 (ext 297) *Fax:* 212-481-4174
E-mail: jbc@jewishbooks.org
Web Site: www.jewishbookcouncil.org
Key Personnel
Exec Dir: Carolyn Starman Hessel *E-mail:* carolynhessel@jewishbooks.org
Nov 26-Dec 26, 2005

Karlsruher Buecherschau (Karlsruhe Book Exhibition)
Sponsored by Boersenverein des Deutschen Buchhandels, Landesverband Baden-Wuerttemberg eV (Association of Publishers & Booksellers in Baden-Wuerttemberg e V)
Paulinenstr 53, 70178 Stuttgart, Germany
Tel: (0711) 619410 *Fax:* (0711) 6194144
E-mail: post@buchhandelsverband.de
Web Site: www.buchhandelsverband.de
Key Personnel
Exhibition Mgr: Lisa Buchhorn *Tel:* (0711) 61941 26 *E-mail:* buchhorn@buchhandelsverband.de
Location: Landesgewerbeamt, Karl-Friedrich Str 17, Karlsruhe, Germany
Nov 11-Dec 4, 2005

Multicultural Children's Book Festival
Sponsored by Kids Cultural Books
1081 Westover Rd, Stamford, CT 06902, United States
Tel: 203-359-6925 *Fax:* 203-359-3226
E-mail: info@kidsculturalbooks.org
Web Site: www.kidsculturalbooks.org/festivals.html
Location: Kennedy Center, Washington, DC, USA
Nov 2005

Online Information & Content Management Europe
Formerly Online Information
Sponsored by VNU Exhibitions Europe
Subsidiary of VNU Business Media Europe
32-34 Broadwick St, London W1A 2HG, United Kingdom
Tel: (020) 7316 9539 *Fax:* (020) 7316 9598
E-mail: fiona.ashton@vnuexhibitions.co.uk
Web Site: www.online-information.co.uk; www.cme-expo.co.uk
Key Personnel
Event Dir: Vicky Bush *Tel:* (020) 7316 9585 *E-mail:* victoria.bush@vnuexhibitions.co.uk
The show brings together hundreds of companies exhibiting the worlds best information resources, together with solutions for information management, knowledge exchange, content management, intranets & extranets & epublishing. It attracts thousands of international information managers, knowledge managers, librarians, academics, publishers, information users & IT professionals.
Location: Olympia Grand Hall, London, UK
Nov 28-Dec 1, 2005

Stuttgarter Buchwochen (Stuttgart Bookweeks)
Sponsored by Boersenverein des Deutschen Buchhandels, Landesverband Baden-Wuerttemberg eV (Association of Publishers & Booksellers in Baden-Wuerttemberg e V)
Paulinenstr 53, 70178 Stuttgart, Germany
Tel: (0711) 619410 *Fax:* (0711) 6194144
E-mail: post@buchhandelsverband.de
Web Site: www.buchhandelsverband.de
Key Personnel
Contact: Maike Dreyer *Tel:* (0711) 619 41 28 *E-mail:* dreyer@buchhandelsverband.de
Location: Haus der Wirtschaft, Stuttgart, Germany
Nov 10-Dec 4, 2005

WORLDDIDAC Brazil 2005
Sponsored by Worlddidac
Bollwerk 21, 3001 Bern, Switzerland
Mailing Address: PO Box 8866, 3001 Bern, Switzerland
Tel: (031) 311 76 82 *Fax:* (031) 312 17 44
E-mail: info@worlddidac.org
Web Site: www.worlddidac.org
International exhibition for educational materials, professional training & e-learning.
Location: Brazil
Nov 2005

DECEMBER

Small Press Book Fair
Sponsored by Small Press Center
20 W 44 St, New York, NY 10036, United States
Tel: 212-764-7021 *Fax:* 212-354-5365
E-mail: info@smallpress.org
Web Site: www.smallpress.org
Key Personnel
Dir: Karin Taylor
Location: Small Press Center, New York, NY, USA
Dec 4-5, 2005

2006

JANUARY

American Library Association Mid-Winter Meeting
Sponsored by American Library Association (ALA)
50 E Huron St, Chicago, IL 60611, United States
Toll Free Tel: 800-545-2433 *Fax:* 312-944-6780
E-mail: ala@ala.org
Web Site: www.ala.org/events
Key Personnel
Public Info Dir: Mark Gould
Press Officer: Larra Clark
Location: San Antonio, TX, USA
Jan 20-25, 2006

CBA Advance
Formerly CBA Expo
Sponsored by CBA
9240 Explorer Dr, Colorado Springs, CO 80920-5001, United States
Mailing Address: PO Box 62000, Colorado Springs, CO 80962-2000, United States
Tel: 719-265-9895 *Toll Free Tel:* 800-252-1950 *Fax:* 719-272-3510
E-mail: info@cbaonline.org
Web Site: www.cbaonline.org
Key Personnel
Pres: William Anderson *E-mail:* banderson@cbaonline.org
VP & COO: Dorothy Gore
Convention & Expositions Mgr: Scott Graham
Location: Opryland Hotel, Nashville, TN, USA
Jan 23-27, 2006

Technology, Reading & Learning Difficulties (TRLD)
Sponsored by Don Johnson Inc
26799 W Commerce, Volo, IL 60073, United States
Toll Free Tel: 888-594-1249 *Fax:* 847-740-7326
E-mail: info@trld.com
Web Site: www.trld.com
Key Personnel
Contact: Mary Krenz
TRLD is the only conference that integrates technology interventions with expert literacy strategies to ensure student success. The conference brings together educators, experienced literacy leaders & technology experts to share, discuss & work towards a solution to the nationwide concern of bringing literacy success to all students. Through quality speakers & relevant topics, TRLD gives educators ideas & strategies to immediately implement with students with high incidence disabilities.
Location: Hyatt Regency San Francisco, San Francisco, CA, USA
Jan 26-28, 2006

FEBRUARY

National Association of Science Writers Annual Meeting
Sponsored by National Association of Science Writers (NASW)
PO Box 890, Hedgesville, WV 25427, United States
Tel: 304-754-5077 *Fax:* 304-754-5076
Web Site: www.nasw.org
Key Personnel
Exec Dir: Diane McGurgan *E-mail:* diane@nasw.org
Location: St Louis, MO, USA
Feb 16-21, 2006

SPRING

Annual Web Offset Association Conference
Sponsored by Web Offset Association
Division of Printing Industries of America Inc
100 Daingerfield Rd, Alexandria, VA 22314, United States
Tel: 703-519-8100; 703-519-8142
  Toll Free Tel: 800-742-2666 *Fax:* 703-519-7109
Web Site: www.gain.net
Key Personnel
Meetings Mgr: Bethany Forrest *E-mail:* bforrest@printing.org
Spring 2006

MARCH

Christian Booksellers Convention - UK
Sponsored by Christian Booksellers Convention Ltd
Victoria House, Victoria Rd, Buckhurst Hill, Essex 1G9 5EX, United Kingdom
Tel: (020) 5592975; (020) 8559 1180 *Fax:* (020) 5029062
E-mail: 100067.1226@compuserve.com
Location: Doncaster Exhibition & Conference Center, Doncaster, UK
March 6-8, 2006

Docugroup 2006
Sponsored by Docucorp International
5910 N Central Expressway, Suite 800, Dallas, TX 75206-5140, United States
Tel: 214-891-6500 *Fax:* 214-987-8187
E-mail: info@docucorp.com
Web Site: www.docucorp.com
Key Personnel
Pres & CEO: Michael D Andereck
March 2006

Leipzig Book Fair
Sponsored by Leipziger Messe GmbH, Projektteam Buchmesse
Messe-Allee 1, 04356 Leipzig, Germany
Mailing Address: Postfach 100 720, 04007 Leipzig, Germany
Tel: (0341) 6788240 *Fax:* (0341) 6788242
E-mail: info@leipziger-buchmesse.de
Web Site: www.leipziger-buchmesse.de
Key Personnel
Exhibition Dir: Oliver Zille *Tel:* (0341) 678 8241 *Fax:* (0341) 678 8242
Held annually in conjunction with The Leipzig Antiquarian Book Fair.
Location: Neues Messegelande, Leipzig, Germany
March 16-19, 2006

Virginia Festival of the Book
Sponsored by Virginia Foundation for the Humanities
145 Ednam Dr, Charlottesville, VA 22903, United States
Tel: 434-924-6890 *Fax:* 434-296-4714
E-mail: vabook@virginia.edu
Web Site: www.vabook.org
Key Personnel
Program Dir: Nancy Damon *Tel:* 434-924-7548
Program Assoc: Kevin McFadden *E-mail:* kjm7a@virginia.edu
Annual free public festival for children & adults featuring authors, illustrators, publishers, publicists, agents & other book professionals in panel discussions & readings for adults & children of all ages.
Location: Charlottesville, VA, USA
March 22-26, 2006

APRIL

African American Children's Book Festival
Sponsored by Kids Cultural Books
1081 Westover Rd, Stamford, CT 06902, United States
Tel: 203-359-6925 *Fax:* 203-359-3226
E-mail: info@kidsculturalbooks.org
Web Site: www.kidsculturalbooks.org/festivals.html
Location: Cathedral of St John the Divine, New York, NY, USA
April 2006

International Children's Book Day
Sponsored by International Board on Books for Young People (IBBY)
Nonnenweg 12, 4003 Basel, Switzerland
Mailing Address: Nonnenweg 12, Postfach, Basel 4003, Switzerland
Tel: (061) 272 29 17 *Fax:* (061) 272 27 57
E-mail: ibby@ibby.org
Web Site: www.ibby.org
On or around Hans Christian Andersen's birthday, April 2nd, International Children's Book day (ICBD) is celebrated to inspire a love of reading & to call attention to children's books. Each year a different national section has the opportunity to be the international sponsor. It decides upon a theme & invites a prominent author to write a message to the children of the world & a well-known illustrator to design a poster. These materials are used in different ways to promote books & reading around the world.
Location: Slovakia
April 2006

National Library Week
Sponsored by American Library Association (ALA)
50 E Huron St, Chicago, IL 60611, United States
Tel: 312-944-6780 *Toll Free Tel:* 800-545-2433 *Fax:* 312-944-8520
E-mail: pio@ala.org
Web Site: www.ala.org/events
Key Personnel
Public Info Dir: Mark Gould
Press Officer: Larra Clark *E-mail:* lclark@ala.org
Location: Nationwide throughout the USA
April 2-8, 2006

Newspaper Association of America Annual Convention
Sponsored by Newspaper Association of America (NAA)
1921 Gallows Rd, Suite 600, Vienna, VA 22182, United States
Tel: 703-902-1600 *Fax:* 703-902-1790
E-mail: laths@naa.org
Web Site: www.naa.org
Key Personnel
Pres & CEO: John Sturm
Location: Fairmont Chicago, Chicago, IL, USA
April 2-5, 2006

NEXPO®
Sponsored by Newspaper Association of America (NAA)
1921 Gallows Rd, Suite 600, Vienna, VA 22182, United States
Tel: 703-902-1600 *Fax:* 703-902-1843
E-mail: laths@naa.org
Web Site: www.nexpo.com
Key Personnel
Dir of Exhibition Sales: Brad Smith
Annual technical exposition & conference for newspapers.
Location: Chicago, IL, USA
April 1-4, 2006

Paper Week
Sponsored by American Forest & Paper Association
1111 19 St NW, Suite 800, Washington, DC 20036, United States
Tel: 202-463-2700 *Fax:* 202-463-4703
E-mail: info@afandpa.org
Web Site: www.afandpa.org; www.paperweek.org
Key Personnel
Pres & CEO: W Henson Moore
Location: Waldorf-Astoria Hotel & Towers, New York, NY, USA
April 9-12, 2006

UK Serials Group Annual Conference & Exhibition
Sponsored by UK Serials Group
PO Box 5594, Newbury RG20 0YP, United Kingdom
Tel: (01635) 254292 *Fax:* (01635) 253826
E-mail: uksg.admin@dial.pipex.com
Web Site: www.uksg.org
Key Personnel
Busn Mgr: Alison Whitehorn
Location: University of Warwick, Coventry, UK
April 3-5, 2006

Young People's Poetry Week
Sponsored by The Children's Book Council (CBC)
12 W 37 St, 2nd fl, New York, NY 10118-7480, United States
Tel: 212-966-1990 *Toll Free Tel:* 800-999-2160 (orders only) *Fax:* 212-966-2073
  Toll Free Fax: 888-807-9355 (orders only)
Web Site: www.cbcbooks.org/html/poetry_week.html
Key Personnel
Pres: Paula Quint
Location: Nationwide throughout the USA
April 10-16, 2006

MAY

ASQ World Conference on Quality & Improvement
Sponsored by American Society for Quality
600 N Plankinton Ave, Milwaukee, WI 53203, United States
Tel: 414-272-8575 *Toll Free Tel:* 800-248-1946 *Fax:* 414-272-1734
E-mail: cs@asq.org
Web Site: www.asq.org
Telex: 31-6567

Key Personnel
Exec Dir & Chief Strategic Officer: Paul Borawski
Events Mgmt Mgr: Shirley Krentz
Location: Midwest Airlines Center, Milwaukee, WI, USA
May 1-3, 2006

EXPOLIT Exposicion de Literatura Cristiana Book Fair
Sponsored by Spanish Evangelical Publishers Association (SEPA)/Associacion de Editores Evangelicos and Editorial Unilit
1360 NW 88 Ave, Miami, FL 33172, United States
Tel: 305-592-6136 (ext 105) *Toll Free Tel:* 800-767-7726 *Fax:* 305-592-0087
E-mail: info@expolit.com
Web Site: www.expolit.com
Key Personnel
Pres, EXPOLIT: David Ecklebarger
Program Dir: Marie Tanayo
Spanish Christian Literature Convention.
Location: Radisson Mart Plaza Hotel & Convention Centre, Miami, FL, USA
May 18-23, 2006

JUNE

American Library Association Annual Conference
Sponsored by American Library Association (ALA)
50 E Huron St, Chicago, IL 60611, United States
Tel: 312-280-3200 *Toll Free Tel:* 800-545-2433 *Fax:* 312-944-7841
E-mail: ala@ala.org
Web Site: www.ala.org
Key Personnel
Public Info Dir: Mark Gould
Press Officer: Larra Clark
Dir, Intl Rel: Michael Dowling
Location: New Orleans, LA, USA
June 22-28, 2006

Canadian Library Association Annual Convention & Tradeshow
Sponsored by Canadian Library Association (CLA)
328 Frank St, Ottawa, ON K2P 0X8, Canada
Tel: 613-232-9625 *Fax:* 613-563-9895
E-mail: info@cla.ca
Web Site: www.cla.ca
Key Personnel
Pres: Madeleine Lefebvre
Exec Dir: Don Butcher *E-mail:* dbutcher@cla.ca
Location: Ottawa, ON, Canada
June 14-17, 2006

International Plate Printers', Die Stampers' & Engravers' Union of North America Mini Meeting
Sponsored by International Plate Printers', Die Stampers' & Engravers' Union of North America
3957 Smoke Rd, Doylestown, PA 18901, United States
Tel: 215-340-2843
Key Personnel
Sec & Treas: James Kopernick
Location: Washington, DC, USA
June 2006

Special Libraries Association Annual Conference
Sponsored by Special Libraries Association (SLA)
1700 18 St NW, Washington, DC 20009-2514, United States
Tel: 202-234-4700 *Fax:* 202-234-2442
E-mail: sla@sla.org
Web Site: www.sla.org
Key Personnel
Exec Dir: Janice LaChance *E-mail:* janice@sla.org
Location: Baltimore, MD, USA
June 10-15, 2006

JULY

CBA International Convention
Sponsored by CBA
9240 Explorer Dr, Colorado Springs, CO 80920-5001, United States
Mailing Address: PO Box 62000, Colorado Springs, CO 80962-2000, United States
Tel: 719-265-9895 *Toll Free Tel:* 800-252-1950 *Fax:* 719-272-3510
E-mail: info@cbaonline.org
Web Site: www.cbaonline.org
Key Personnel
Pres: William Anderson *E-mail:* banderson@cbaonline.org
VP & COO: Dorothy Gore
Convention & Expositions Mgr: Scott Graham
For almost 50 years, the annual CBA International Convention has been our industry's single-most impacting week. During this week, people of the industry from all over the world meet face-to-face for buying & selling, education, inspiration, fellowship & future planning. Here individuals unite to further the mission of seeing Christian product impact lives for God's kingdom the world over. At this unique gathering, our industry's strength is most evident & our goals are most clearly in focus. It is, in short, the most important week in the ministry of your business & of the industry as a whole.
Location: Colorado Convention Center, Denver, CO, USA
July 8-13, 2006

Church & Synagogue Library Association Conference
Sponsored by Church & Synagogue Library Association
PO Box 19357, Portland, OR 97280-0357, United States
Tel: 503-244-6919 *Toll Free Tel:* 800-542-2752 *Fax:* 503-977-3734
E-mail: csla@worldaccessnet.com
Web Site: www.worldaccessnet.com/~csla
Location: Greensboro, NC, USA
July 2006

RWA Annual National Conference
Sponsored by Romance Writers of America
16000 Stuebner Airline, Suite 140, Spring, TX 77379, United States
Tel: 832-717-5200 *Fax:* 832-717-5201
E-mail: info@rwanational.org
Web Site: www.rwanational.org
Key Personnel
Exec Dir: Allison Kelley *E-mail:* akelley@rwanational.org
Location: Atlanta Marriott Marquis, Atlanta, GA, USA
July 26-29, 2006

AUGUST

South African Booksellers Association Annual Conference
Sponsored by South African Booksellers Association
PO Box 870, Bellville 7535, South Africa
Tel: (021) 945 1572 *Fax:* (021) 945 2169
E-mail: saba@sabooksellers.com
Web Site: sabooksellers.com
Location: Durban, South Africa
Aug 15-16, 2006

World Library & Information Congress
Sponsored by International Federation of Library Associations & Institutions (IFLA)
Postbus 95312, 2509 CH The Hague, Netherlands
Tel: (070) 3140884 *Fax:* (070) 3834827
E-mail: ifla@ifla.org
Web Site: www.ifla.org
Location: Seoul, Korea
Aug 2006

AUTUMN

Business & Design Conference
Sponsored by American Institute of Graphic Arts (AIGA)
164 Fifth Ave, New York, NY 10010, United States
Tel: 212-807-1990 (ext 223) *Fax:* 212-807-1799
E-mail: aiga@aiga.org; programs@aiga.org
Web Site: www.aiga.org
Key Personnel
Exec Dir: Richard Grefe
Biennial event.
Autumn 2006

SEPTEMBER

Goteborg International Book Fair
Sponsored by Bok & Bibliotek
412 94 Gothenburg, Sweden
Tel: (031) 7088400 *Fax:* (031) 209103
E-mail: info@goteborg-bookfair.com
Web Site: www.bok-bibliotek.se
Key Personnel
Man Dir: Anna Falck *E-mail:* af@goteborg-bookfair.com
Exhibition Mgr: Lisa Oden *E-mail:* lo@goteborg-bookfair.com
Sept 21-24, 2006

International Board on Books for Young People Biennial Congress
Sponsored by International Board on Books for Young People (IBBY)
Nonnenweg 12, 4003 Basel, Switzerland
Mailing Address: Nonnenweg 12, Postfach, Basel 4003, Switzerland
Tel: (061) 272 29 17 *Fax:* (061) 272 27 57
E-mail: ibby@ibby.org
Web Site: www.ibby.org
IBBY's biennial congresses, hosted by different countries, are the most important meeting points for IBBY members & other people involved in children's books & reading development. They are wonderful opportunities to make contacts, exchange ideas & open horizons.
Location: Beijing, China
Sept 20-24, 2006

LIBER Feria Internacional del Libro
Sponsored by Federacion de Gremios de Editores de Espana (FGEE) (Spanish Publishers Association)
Cea Bermudez, 44-2° Dehe, Madrid 20003, Spain
Tel: (091) 5345195 *Fax:* (091) 5352625
E-mail: fgee@fge.es
Web Site: www.federacioneditores.org
Key Personnel
Executive Dir: Antonio Ma Avila
Location: Barcelona, Spain
Sept 27-30, 2006

PSA International Conference of Photography
Sponsored by Photographic Society of America Inc (PSA)
3000 United Founders Blvd, Suite 103, Oklahoma City, OK 73112-3940, United States
Tel: 405-843-1437 *Fax:* 405-843-1438
E-mail: psahg@theshop.net
Web Site: www.psa-photo.org
Key Personnel
VP, Conventions: Gerry Emmerich
Location: Hunt Valley Inn, Baltimore, MD, USA
Sept 4-9, 2006

Southeast Booksellers Association Annual Meeting & Trade Show
Sponsored by Southeast Booksellers Association (SEBA)
2611 Forest Dr, Suite 124, Columbia, SC 29204, United States
Tel: 803-779-0118 *Fax:* 803-779-0113
E-mail: info@sebaweb.org
Web Site: www.sebaweb.org
Key Personnel
Exec Dir: Wanda Jewell *E-mail:* sebajewell@aol.com
Location: Gaylord Palms Resort & Convention Center, Orlando, FL, USA
Sept 8-10, 2006

OCTOBER

Distripress Annual Congress
Sponsored by Distripress
Beethovenstr 20, CH-8002 Zurich, Switzerland
Tel: (01) 2024121 *Fax:* (01) 2021025
E-mail: info@distripress.ch
Web Site: www.distripress.ch
Key Personnel
Managing Dir: Dr Peter Emod *E-mail:* peter.emod@distripress.ch
Non-profit association promoting the free international circulation of the press.
Location: Barcelona, Spain
Oct 15-19, 2006

Frankfurt Book Fair
Sponsored by Ausstellungs-und Messe-GmbH des Borsenvereins des Deutschen Buchhandels
Reineckstr 3, 63013 Frankfurt am Main, Germany
Mailing Address: Postfach 100116, 60001 Frankfurt am Main, Germany
Tel: (069) 21020 *Fax:* (069) 2102 227
E-mail: info@book-fair.com
Web Site: www.frankfurt-book-fair.com *Cable:* BUCHMESSE
Key Personnel
CEO & Dir: Volker Neumann
Location: Frankfurt Fairgrounds, Frankfurt, Germany
Oct 4-9, 2006

NOVEMBER

American Academy of Religion
Sponsored by American Schools of Oriental Research
825 Houston Mill Rd, Suite 201, Atlanta, GA 30329, United States
Tel: 404-727-3049 *Fax:* 404-727-7959
E-mail: aar@aarweb.org
Web Site: www.aarweb.org
Key Personnel
Prog Dir: Aislinn Jones
Location: Washington, DC, USA
Nov 18-21, 2006

Children's Book Week
Sponsored by The Children's Book Council (CBC)
12 W 37 St, 2nd fl, New York, NY 10118-7480, United States
Tel: 212-966-1990 *Toll Free Tel:* 800-999-2160 (orders only) *Fax:* 212-966-2073 *Toll Free Fax:* 888-807-9355 (orders only)
Web Site: www.cbcbooks.org
Key Personnel
Pres: Paula Quint
Location: Nationwide across the USA
Nov 13-19, 2006

Ghana International Book Fair
Sponsored by Ghana Trade Fair Co Ltd
PO Box NT601, Accra New Town, Accra, Ghana
Tel: (021) 227182; (012) 783421
E-mail: info@ghanainternationalbookfair.org
Web Site: www.ghanainternationalbookfair.org
Key Personnel
Mgr: Lawson Agana
Location: Accra, Ghana
Nov 2006

Karlsruher Buecherschau (Karlsruhe Book Exhibition)
Sponsored by Boersenverein des Deutschen Buchhandels, Landesverband Baden-Wuerttemberg eV (Association of Publishers & Booksellers in Baden-Wuerttemberg e V)
Paulinenstr 53, 70178 Stuttgart, Germany
Tel: (0711) 619410 *Fax:* (0711) 6194144
E-mail: post@buchhandelsverband.de
Web Site: www.buchhandelsverband.de
Key Personnel
Exhibition Mgr: Lisa Buchhorn *Tel:* (0711) 61941 26 *E-mail:* buchhorn@buchhandelsverband.de
Location: Landesgewerbeamt, Karl-Friedrich Str 17, Karlsruhe, Germany
Nov 17-Dec 10, 2006

National College Media Convention
Sponsored by Associated Collegiate Press (ACP)
Subsidiary of National Scholastic Press Assn
2221 University Ave SE, Suite 121, Minneapolis, MN 55414, United States
Tel: 612-625-8335 *Fax:* 612-626-0720
E-mail: info@studentpress.org
Web Site: studentpress.org
Key Personnel
Assoc Dir: Ann Akers
Also sponsored by College Media Advisors.
Location: Adams Mark, St Louis, MO, USA
Nov 2-5, 2006

Salon du Livre de Jeunesse (Childrens Book Fair)
Sponsored by Reed Expositions France
Subsidiary of Reed Exhibition Companies
11 rue du Colonel Pierre Avia, 75726 Paris Cedex 15, France
Tel: (01) 41 90 47 47 *Fax:* (01) 41 90 47 00
E-mail: cplj@ldg.tm.fr; infos@reedexpo.fr
Web Site: www.reed-expo.fr; www.ldj.tm.fr
Key Personnel
Contact: Denis-Luc Panthin *E-mail:* panthin@ldj.tm.fr
France's leading publishing event dedicated to children's books.
Location: Rue de Paris, Montreuil, France
Nov 23-19, 2006

Stuttgarter Buchwochen (Stuttgart Bookweeks)
Sponsored by Boersenverein des Deutschen Buchhandels, Landesverband Baden-Wuerttemberg eV (Association of Publishers & Booksellers in Baden-Wuerttemberg e V)
Paulinenstr 53, 70178 Stuttgart, Germany
Tel: (0711) 619410 *Fax:* (0711) 6194144
E-mail: post@buchhandelsverband.de
Web Site: www.buchhandelsverband.de
Key Personnel
Contact: Maike Dreyer *Tel:* (0711) 619 41 28 *E-mail:* dreyer@buchhandelsverband.de
Location: Haus der Wirtschaft, Stuttgart, Germany
Nov 9-Dec 3, 2006

2007

JANUARY

American Library Association Mid-Winter Meeting
Sponsored by American Library Association (ALA)
50 E Huron St, Chicago, IL 60611, United States
Toll Free Tel: 800-545-2433 *Fax:* 312-944-6780
E-mail: ala@ala.org
Web Site: www.ala.org/events
Key Personnel
Public Info Dir: Mark Gould
Press Officer: Larra Clark
Location: Seattle, WA, USA
Jan 19-24, 2007

CBA Advance
Formerly CBA Expo
Sponsored by CBA
9240 Explorer Dr, Colorado Springs, CO 80920-5001, United States
Mailing Address: PO Box 62000, Colorado Springs, CO 80962-2000, United States
Tel: 719-265-9895 *Toll Free Tel:* 800-252-1950 *Fax:* 719-272-3510
E-mail: info@cbaonline.org
Web Site: www.cbaonline.org
Key Personnel
Pres: William Anderson *E-mail:* banderson@cbaonline.org
VP & COO: Dorothy Gore
Convention & Expositions Mgr: Scott Graham
Location: Indiana Convention Center, Indianapolis, IN, USA
Jan 29-Feb 3, 2007

FEBRUARY

National Association of Science Writers Annual Meeting
Sponsored by National Association of Science Writers (NASW)
PO Box 890, Hedgesville, WV 25427, United States
Tel: 304-754-5077 *Fax:* 304-754-5076
Web Site: www.nasw.org
Key Personnel
Exec Dir: Diane McGurgan *E-mail:* diane@nasw.org

& PROMOTIONAL EVENTS

Location: San Francisco, CA, USA
Feb 15-20, 2007

MARCH

Virginia Festival of the Book
Sponsored by Virginia Foundation for the Humanities
145 Ednam Dr, Charlottesville, VA 22903, United States
Tel: 434-924-6890 *Fax:* 434-296-4714
E-mail: vabook@virginia.edu
Web Site: www.vabook.org
Key Personnel
Program Dir: Nancy Damon *Tel:* 434-924-7548
Program Assoc: Kevin McFadden
 E-mail: kjm7a@virginia.edu
Annual free public festival for children & adults featuring authors, illustrators, publishers, publicists, agents & other book professionals in panel discussions & readings for adults & children of all ages.
Location: Charlottesville, VA, USA
March 21-25, 2007

APRIL

National Library Week
Sponsored by American Library Association (ALA)
50 E Huron St, Chicago, IL 60611, United States
Tel: 312-944-6780 *Toll Free Tel:* 800-545-2433
 Fax: 312-944-8520
E-mail: pio@ala.org
Web Site: www.ala.org/events
Key Personnel
Public Info Dir: Mark Gould
Press Officer: Larra Clark *E-mail:* lclark@ala.org
Location: Nationwide throughout the USA
April 15-21, 2007

Annual Web Offset Association Conference
Sponsored by Web Offset Association
Division of Printing Industries of America Inc
100 Daingerfield Rd, Alexandria, VA 22314, United States
Tel: 703-519-8100; 703-519-8142
 Toll Free Tel: 800-742-2666 *Fax:* 703-519-7109
Web Site: www.gain.net
Key Personnel
Meetings Mgr: Bethany Forrest *E-mail:* bforrest@printing.org
Location: Sheraton Centre Toronto, Toronto, Ontario, Canada
April 29-May 2, 2007

Young People's Poetry Week
Sponsored by The Children's Book Council (CBC)
12 W 37 St, 2nd fl, New York, NY 10118-7480, United States
Tel: 212-966-1990 *Toll Free Tel:* 800-999-2160 (orders only) *Fax:* 212-966-2073
 Toll Free Fax: 888-807-9355 (orders only)
Web Site: www.cbcbooks.org/html/poetry_week.html
Key Personnel
Pres: Paula Quint
Location: Nationwide throughout the USA
April 16-22, 2007

MAY

PrintEx
Sponsored by Graphic Arts Merchants Association of Australia Inc (GAMMA)
PO Box 1051, Crows Nest, NSW 2065, Australia
Tel: (02) 9417 7433 *Fax:* (02) 9417 7433
E-mail: enquiry@gamaa.net.au
Web Site: www.printex.net.au; www.gamma.net.au
PrintEx brings the latest printing & graphic communications technologies to the industry. Co-sponsored by The Printing Industries Association of Australia (PIAA).
Location: Sydney Convention & Exhibition Centre, Darling Harbour, Sydney, NSW, Australia
May 2007

SUMMER

The Dorothy L Sayers Society Annual Convention
Sponsored by The Dorothy L Sayers Society
Rose Cottage, Malthouse Lane, Hurstpierpoint, West Sussex BN6 9JY, United Kingdom
Tel: (01273) 833444 *Fax:* (01273) 835988
E-mail: info@sayers.org.uk
Web Site: www.sayers.org.uk
Key Personnel
Chairman: Christopher Dean
Location: Wheaton College, Wheaton, IL, USA
Summer 2007

JUNE

American Library Association Annual Conference
Sponsored by American Library Association (ALA)
50 E Huron St, Chicago, IL 60611, United States
Tel: 312-280-3200 *Toll Free Tel:* 800-545-2433
 Fax: 312-944-7841
E-mail: ala@ala.org
Web Site: www.ala.org
Key Personnel
Public Info Dir: Mark Gould
Press Officer: Larra Clark
Dir, Intl Rel: Michael Dowling
Location: Washington, DC, USA
June 21-27, 2007

Special Libraries Association Annual Conference
Sponsored by Special Libraries Association (SLA)
1700 18 St NW, Washington, DC 20009-2514, United States
Tel: 202-234-4700 *Fax:* 202-234-2442
E-mail: sla@sla.org
Web Site: www.sla.org
Key Personnel
Exec Dir: Janice LaChance *E-mail:* janice@sla.org
Location: Denver, CO, USA
June 2-7, 2007

JULY

CBA International Convention
Sponsored by CBA
9240 Explorer Dr, Colorado Springs, CO 80920-5001, United States
Mailing Address: PO Box 62000, Colorado Springs, CO 80962-2000, United States
Tel: 719-265-9895 *Toll Free Tel:* 800-252-1950
 Fax: 719-272-3510
E-mail: info@cbaonline.org
Web Site: www.cbaonline.org
Key Personnel
Pres: William Anderson *E-mail:* banderson@cbaonline.org
VP & COO: Dorothy Gore
Convention & Expositions Mgr: Scott Graham
For almost 50 years, the annual CBA International Convention has been our industry's single-most impacting week. During this week, people of the industry from all over the world meet face-to-face for buying & selling, education, inspiration, fellowship & future planning. Here individuals unite to further the mission of seeing Christian product impact lives for God's kingdom the world over. At this unique gathering, our industry's strength is most evident & our goals are most clearly in focus. It is, in short, the most important week in the ministry of your business & of the industry as a whole.
Location: Georgia World Congress, Atlanta, GA, USA
July 7-12, 2007

Church & Synagogue Library Association Conference
Sponsored by Church & Synagogue Library Association
PO Box 19357, Portland, OR 97280-0357, United States
Tel: 503-244-6919 *Toll Free Tel:* 800-542-2752
 Fax: 503-977-3734
E-mail: csla@worldaccessnet.com
Web Site: www.worldaccessnet.com/~csla
Location: Philadelphia, PA, USA
July 2007

RWA Annual National Conference
Sponsored by Romance Writers of America
16000 Stuebner Airline, Suite 140, Spring, TX 77379, United States
Tel: 832-717-5200 *Fax:* 832-717-5201
E-mail: info@rwanational.org
Web Site: www.rwanational.org
Key Personnel
Exec Dir: Allison Kelley *E-mail:* akelley@rwanational.org
Location: Hyatt Regency Dallas, Dallas, TX, USA
July 11-14, 2007

SEPTEMBER

PSA International Conference of Photography
Sponsored by Photographic Society of America Inc (PSA)
3000 United Founders Blvd, Suite 103, Oklahoma City, OK 73112-3940, United States
Tel: 405-843-1437 *Fax:* 405-843-1438
E-mail: psahg@theshop.net
Web Site: www.psa-photo.org
Key Personnel
VP, Conventions: Gerry Emmerich
Location: Starr Pass Marriott Resort & Spa, Tucson, AZ, USA
Sept 3-8, 2007

2007

OCTOBER

National College Media Convention
Sponsored by Associated Collegiate Press (ACP)
Subsidiary of National Scholastic Press Assn
2221 University Ave SE, Suite 121, Minneapolis, MN 55414, United States
Tel: 612-625-8335 *Fax:* 612-626-0720
E-mail: info@studentpress.org
Web Site: studentpress.org
Key Personnel
Assoc Dir: Ann Akers
Also sponsored by College Media Advisors.
Location: Washington Hilton, Washington, DC, USA
Oct 25-28, 2007

NOVEMBER

American Academy of Religion
Sponsored by American Schools of Oriental Research
825 Houston Mill Rd, Suite 201, Atlanta, GA 30329, United States
Tel: 404-727-3049 *Fax:* 404-727-7959
E-mail: aar@aarweb.org
Web Site: www.aarweb.org
Key Personnel
Prog Dir: Aislinn Jones
Location: San Diego, CA, USA
Nov 17-20, 2007

Stuttgarter Buchwochen (Stuttgart Bookweeks)
Sponsored by Boersenverein des Deutschen Buchhandels, Landesverband Baden-Wuerttemberg eV (Association of Publishers & Booksellers in Baden-Wuerttemberg e V)
Paulinenstr 53, 70178 Stuttgart, Germany
Tel: (0711) 619410 *Fax:* (0711) 6194144
E-mail: post@buchhandelsverband.de
Web Site: www.buchhandelsverband.de
Key Personnel
Contact: Maike Dreyer *Tel:* (0711) 619 41 28
  E-mail: dreyer@buchhandelsverband.de
Location: Haus der Wirtschaft, Stuttgart, Germany
Nov-Dec, 2007

2008

MARCH

Virginia Festival of the Book
Sponsored by Virginia Foundation for the Humanities
145 Ednam Dr, Charlottesville, VA 22903, United States
Tel: 434-924-6890 *Fax:* 434-296-4714
E-mail: vabook@virginia.edu
Web Site: www.vabook.org
Key Personnel
Program Dir: Nancy Damon *Tel:* 434-924-7548
Program Assoc: Kevin McFadden
  E-mail: kjm7a@virginia.edu
Annual free public festival for children & adults featuring authors, illustrators, publishers, publicists, agents & other book professionals in panel discussions & readings for adults & children of all ages.
Location: Charlottesville, VA, USA
March 26-30, 2008

APRIL

National Library Week
Sponsored by American Library Association (ALA)
50 E Huron St, Chicago, IL 60611, United States
Tel: 312-944-6780 *Toll Free Tel:* 800-545-2433
  Fax: 312-944-8520
E-mail: pio@ala.org
Web Site: www.ala.org/events
Key Personnel
Public Info Dir: Mark Gould
Press Officer: Larra Clark *E-mail:* lclark@ala.org
Location: Nationwide throughout the USA
April 13-19, 2008

Young People's Poetry Week
Sponsored by The Children's Book Council (CBC)
12 W 37 St, 2nd fl, New York, NY 10118-7480, United States
Tel: 212-966-1990 *Toll Free Tel:* 800-999-2160 (orders only) *Fax:* 212-966-2073
  Toll Free Fax: 888-807-9355 (orders only)
Web Site: www.cbcbooks.org/html/poetry_week.html
Key Personnel
Pres: Paula Quint
Location: Nationwide throughout the USA
April 14-20, 2008

JUNE

American Library Association Annual Conference
Sponsored by American Library Association (ALA)
50 E Huron St, Chicago, IL 60611, United States
Tel: 312-280-3200 *Toll Free Tel:* 800-545-2433
  Fax: 312-944-7841
E-mail: ala@ala.org
Web Site: www.ala.org
Key Personnel
Public Info Dir: Mark Gould
Press Officer: Larra Clark
Dir, Intl Rel: Michael Dowling
Location: Anaheim, CA, USA
June 26-July 2, 2008

IPA Congress
Sponsored by International Publishers Association
Av de Miremont 3, 1206 Geneva, Switzerland
Tel: (022) 3463018 *Fax:* (022) 3475717
E-mail: secretariat@ipa-uie.org
Web Site: www.ipa-uie.org
Key Personnel
Secretary General: Jens Bammel
Held every 4 years.
Location: Berlin, Germany
June 2008

JULY

CBA International Convention
Sponsored by CBA
9240 Explorer Dr, Colorado Springs, CO 80920-5001, United States
Mailing Address: PO Box 62000, Colorado Springs, CO 80962-2000, United States
Tel: 719-265-9895 *Toll Free Tel:* 800-252-1950
  Fax: 719-272-3510
E-mail: info@cbaonline.org
Web Site: www.cbaonline.org
Key Personnel
Pres: William Anderson *E-mail:* banderson@cbaonline.org
VP & COO: Dorothy Gore
Convention & Expositions Mgr: Scott Graham
For almost 50 years, the annual CBA International Convention has been our industry's single-most impacting week. During this week, people of the industry from all over the world meet face-to-face for buying & selling, education, inspiration, fellowship & future planning. Here individuals unite to further the mission of seeing Christian product impact lives for God's kingdom the world over. At this unique gathering, our industry's strength is most evident & our goals are most clearly in focus. It is, in short, the most important week in the ministry of your business & of the industry as a whole.
Location: Orange County Convention Center, Orlando, FL, USA
July 12-17, 2008

RWA Annual National Conference
Sponsored by Romance Writers of America
16000 Stuebner Airline, Suite 140, Spring, TX 77379, United States
Tel: 832-717-5200 *Fax:* 832-717-5201
E-mail: info@rwanational.org
Web Site: www.rwanational.org
Key Personnel
Exec Dir: Allison Kelley *E-mail:* akelley@rwanational.org
Location: San Francisco Marriott, San Francisco, CA, USA
July 30-Aug 2, 2008

Special Libraries Association Annual Conference
Sponsored by Special Libraries Association (SLA)
1700 18 St NW, Washington, DC 20009-2514, United States
Tel: 202-234-4700 *Fax:* 202-234-2442
E-mail: sla@sla.org
Web Site: www.sla.org
Key Personnel
Exec Dir: Janice LaChance *E-mail:* janice@sla.org
Location: Seattle, WA, USA
July 26-31, 2008

SEPTEMBER

International Board on Books for Young People Biennial Congress
Sponsored by International Board on Books for Young People (IBBY)
Nonnenweg 12, 4003 Basel, Switzerland
Mailing Address: Nonnenweg 12, Postfach, Basel 4003, Switzerland
Tel: (061) 272 29 17 *Fax:* (061) 272 27 57
E-mail: ibby@ibby.org
Web Site: www.ibby.org
IBBY's biennial congresses, hosted by different countries, are the most important meeting points for IBBY members & other people involved in children's books & reading development. They are wonderful opportunities to make contacts, exchange ideas & open horizons.
Location: Copenhagen, Denmark
Sept 7-11, 2008

2009

MARCH

Virginia Festival of the Book
Sponsored by Virginia Foundation for the Humanities
145 Ednam Dr, Charlottesville, VA 22903, United States
Tel: 434-924-6890 *Fax:* 434-296-4714
E-mail: vabook@virginia.edu
Web Site: www.vabook.org
Key Personnel
Program Dir: Nancy Damon *Tel:* 434-924-7548
Program Assoc: Kevin McFadden
 E-mail: kjm7a@virginia.edu
Annual free public festival for children & adults featuring authors, illustrators, publishers, publicists, agents & other book professionals in panel discussions & readings for adults & children of all ages.
Location: Charlottesville, VA, USA
March 18-22, 2009

APRIL

National Library Week
Sponsored by American Library Association (ALA)
50 E Huron St, Chicago, IL 60611, United States
Tel: 312-944-6780 *Toll Free Tel:* 800-545-2433
 Fax: 312-944-8520
E-mail: pio@ala.org
Web Site: www.ala.org/events
Key Personnel
Public Info Dir: Mark Gould
Press Officer: Larra Clark *E-mail:* lclark@ala.org
Location: Nationwide throughout the USA
April 12-18, 2009

Young People's Poetry Week
Sponsored by The Children's Book Council (CBC)
12 W 37 St, 2nd fl, New York, NY 10118-7480, United States
Tel: 212-966-1990 *Toll Free Tel:* 800-999-2160 (orders only) *Fax:* 212-966-2073
 Toll Free Fax: 888-807-9355 (orders only)
Web Site: www.cbcbooks.org/html/poetry_week.html
Key Personnel
Pres: Paula Quint
Location: Nationwide throughout the USA
April 13-19, 2009

JULY

CBA International Convention
Sponsored by CBA
9240 Explorer Dr, Colorado Springs, CO 80920-5001, United States
Mailing Address: PO Box 62000, Colorado Springs, CO 80962-2000, United States
Tel: 719-265-9895 *Toll Free Tel:* 800-252-1950
 Fax: 719-272-3510
E-mail: info@cbaonline.org
Web Site: www.cbaonline.org
Key Personnel
Pres: William Anderson *E-mail:* banderson@cbaonline.org
VP & COO: Dorothy Gore
Convention & Expositions Mgr: Scott Graham
For almost 50 years, the annual CBA International Convention has been our industry's single-most impacting week. During this week, people of the industry from all over the world meet face-to-face for buying & selling, education, inspiration, fellowship & future planning. Here individuals unite to further the mission of seeing Christian product impact lives for God's kingdom the world over. At this unique gathering, our industry's strength is most evident & our goals are most clearly in focus. It is, in short, the most important week in the ministry of your business & of the industry as a whole.
Location: Colorado Convention Center, Denver, CO, USA
July 11-16, 2009

RWA Annual National Conference
Sponsored by Romance Writers of America
16000 Stuebner Airline, Suite 140, Spring, TX 77379, United States
Tel: 832-717-5200 *Fax:* 832-717-5201
E-mail: info@rwanational.org
Web Site: www.rwanational.org
Key Personnel
Exec Dir: Allison Kelley *E-mail:* akelley@rwanational.org
Location: Marriott Wardman Park Hotel, Washington, DC, USA
July 15-18, 2009

Library Resources

Major Libraries

The majority of the libraries and archives listed are those associated with government or educational institutions. Many are also involved in publishing activities.

Afghanistan

Institute of Education Library, Kabul University
Jamal Mina, Kabul
Tel: 42594

Library of the Press & Information Department
Sanaii Wat, Kabul
Key Personnel
Dir: Mohammed Sarwar Rona

Ministry of Education Library
PO Box 717, Kabul
Key Personnel
Chief Officer: Mohamad Quasem Hilaman

Library of the National Bank
Ibn Sina Wat, Kabul
Key Personnel
Dir: A Aziz

Public Library
Charaii-i-Malik Asghar, Kabul
Key Personnel
Dir: Mohamad Omar Seddiqui

University Library
Kabul
Tel: 42594

Albania

Biblioteka Kombetare (National Library of the Republic of Albania)
Sheshi Skenderbej, Place Scanderbeg Tirana
Tel: 42 23 843 *Fax:* 42 23 843
E-mail: a_plasari@hotmail.com
Key Personnel
Dir: Dr Aurel Plasari
Founded: 1922
National Library.
Publication(s): *Bibliografia kombeetare e Republikees see Shipeerisee, Periodiku* (Albanian National Bibliography of Periodicals); *Bibliografia kombeetare e Republikees see Shqipeerise Libri* (Albanian National Bibliography of Books)

Shkoder Public Library
Shkoder

Algeria

Agence ISBN, see Bibliotheque Nationale

Bibliotheque Municipale de Constantine
Hotel de Ville, Constantine

Bibliotheque Nationale
One Ave Frantz Fanon, Algiers 1600
Tel: 630632
Key Personnel
Dir: Mahamed Aissamoussa
Founded: 1835
Total Titles: 350,000 Print
Publication(s): *Bibliographie de l'Algerie* (biannually, in Arabic & French)

Bibliotheque Universitaire Centrale (BUC)
Universite Mentouri, Route d'Ain El-Bey, 25000 Constantine
Mailing Address: BP 325, 25000 Constantine
Tel: (031) 61-42-05 *Fax:* (031) 61-21-90
E-mail: bucne@hotmail.com
Web Site: www.buc-constantine.edu.dz
Telex: 92436
Key Personnel
Chief Librarian: Noureddine Talhour
Founded: 1969
Publication(s): *Des Catalogues Thematiques*

Ecole nationale polytechnique, Bibliotheque
10, Ave Hassen Badi, El Harrach, 16200 Alger
Tel: (021) 52 14 94 *Fax:* (021) 52 29 73
E-mail: enp@ist.cerist.dz
Web Site: www.enp.edu.dz
Telex: 64147 Enp
Key Personnel
Librarian: K Amara

Institut National Agronomique, Bibliotheque
12 Avenue Hassen Badi, El-Harrach, Alger
Tel: (021) 52 47 81; (021) 52 47 84 *Fax:* (021) 52 59 04
Telex: 64143 DZ
Key Personnel
Chief Librarian: Rosa Issolah
Publication(s): *Annals de l'INA*

Institut Pasteur d'Algerie, Bibliotheque
One rue du Dr Laveran, El-Hamma, 16000 Alger
Tel: 21 67 25 02; 21 67 25 11; 21 67 23 44 *Fax:* 267 25 03
E-mail: ipa@ibnsima.ands.dz; ipabib@sante.dz
Web Site: www.ands.dz/ipa/pageaccueil.htm
Telex: 65-337; 65-627

Key Personnel
Dir: Prof F Boulahbal
Publication(s): *Archives de l'Institut Pasteur d'Algerie* (annually)

Archives Nationales d'Algerie
BP 61, Alger Gare
Tel: (02) 54-21-60 *Fax:* (02) 54-16-16
Web Site: www.archives-dgan.gov.dz
Telex: 62524
Key Personnel
Dir: Abdelkrim Badjada

Bibliotheque Centrale, Universite d'Alger
2 rue Didouche Mourad, Algiers
Tel: (021) 63-71-01 *Fax:* (021) 63-76-29
E-mail: bu@univ-alger.dz
Web Site: www.univ-alger.dz
Telex: 66529
Key Personnel
Librarian: Zoulikha Bekaddour

Universite d'Oran, Bibliotheque
BP 1524, El M'Naouer, 31000 Oran
Tel: (041) 41-69-39; (041) 41-66-44 *Fax:* (041) 41-60-21
E-mail: igmo@univ-oran.dz
Web Site: www.univ-oran.dz
Telex: 22993 UNIRX DZ

Angola

Direccao Provincial Servicos de Geologia e Minas de Angola Biblioteca
CP 1260, Luanda
Tel: (02) 323024 *Fax:* (02) 321655
Telex: 3324

Biblioteca Municipal de Luanda
CP 1227, Luanda
Tel: (02) 392297 *Fax:* (02) 33902
Key Personnel
Librarian: Antonio Jose Emidio De Brito

Biblioteca Nacional de Angola (Angola National Library)
Av Comandante Jika, Luanda
Mailing Address: CP 2915, Luanda
Tel: (02) 322 070 *Fax:* (02) 323 979
E-mail: biblioteca@netangola.com
Telex: 4129 Mincult
Key Personnel
Dir: Maria Jose Faria Ramos
Founded: 1968
Publication(s): *Novas* (News)

ANGOLA

Universidade Agostinho Neto Biblioteca
Av 4 de Fevereiro 7, Luanda
Mailing Address: CP 815, Luanda
Tel: (02) 330 517 *Fax:* (02) 330 520
Web Site: www.uan.ao
Telex: 3076
Key Personnel
Librarian: Jeronimo Octavio Xavier Belo

Argentina

Biblioteca Argentina Dr Juan Alvarez
Presidente Roca 731, 2000 Rosario
Tel: 4802538; 4802539 *Fax:* 4802561
E-mail: bibliarghem@rosario.gov.ar
Web Site: www.rosario.gov.ar
Key Personnel
Contact: Maria del Carmen D'Angelo

Biblioteca del Banco Central de la Republica Argentina (Library of the Central Bank of the Argentine Republic)
San Martin 216, 1004 Buenos Aires
Tel: (011) 4348 3500 (ext 2571); (011) 4348 3500 (ext 2801) *Fax:* (011) 4348 1200
E-mail: biblio@bcra.gov.ar
Web Site: www.bcra.gov.ar
Telex: 24031 BCFEXAR
Key Personnel
Chief Librarian: Marta S Gutierrez
  E-mail: mgutierrez@bcra.gov.ar
Publication(s): *Boletin Estadistico* (monthly); *Boletin Monetario y Financiero* (quarterly); *Central de Deudores* (monthly); *Informacion de Entidades Financieras* (monthly); *Informe Anual del Presidente al Congreso de la Nac* (annually); *Resumen de las Regulaciones del Sistema Financiero Argentino* (biannually)

Biblioteca Nacional
Aguero 2502, Buenos Aires 1425
Tel: (011) 4808-6000 *Fax:* (011) 4806-6157
E-mail: bibnal@red.bibnal.edu.ar
Web Site: www.bibnal.edu.ar
Key Personnel
Dir: Oscar Sbarra Mitre

Biblioteca Nacional de Maestros (National Teachers' Library)
Pizzurno 953, 1020 Buenos Aires
Tel: (011) 4129-1272 *Fax:* (011) 4129-1268
E-mail: bnmsecre@me.gov.ar
Web Site: www.bnm.me.gov.ar
Key Personnel
Dir: Dr R Levene
Publication(s): *Historia de la Biblioteca Nacional de Maestros*; *La Biblioteca* (monthly)

Biblioteca del Congreso de la Nacion (National Library of Congress)
Rivadavia 1850, Piso 3°, 1033 Buenos Aires
Tel: (011) 4372-1641 *Fax:* (011) 954-1067
E-mail: congreso@bcnbib.gov.ar
Web Site: www.bcnbib.gov.ar
Key Personnel
Dir of Technical Processes: Liliana Casteran Racedo

Sistema de Bibliotecas y de Informacion
Azcuenaga 280, C1029AAF Buenos Aires
Tel: (011) 4952-0078 *Fax:* (011) 4952-6557
E-mail: webmaster@sisbi.uba.ar
Web Site: www.sisbi.uba.ar
Telex: 18694-IBUBA-AR
Key Personnel
General Coordinator: Elsa Elena Elizalde

Biblioteca Central, Universidad del Salvador
Presidente Peron 1818, Lunes a Viernes de 10 a 17 hs, 1040 Buenos Aires
Tel: (011) 4371-0422 *Fax:* (011) 4371-0422
E-mail: uds-bibl@salvador.edu.ar
Web Site: www.salvador.edu.ar
Key Personnel
Dir: Laura Martino

Biblioteca Mayor de la Universidad Nacional de Cordoba (Principal Library of the National University of Cordoba)
Calle Obispo Trejo 242, ler Piso, 63 Cordoba X5000IYF
Tel: (351) 4331072 *Fax:* (351) 4331079
E-mail: biblio@bmayor.unc.edu.ar
Web Site: www.bmayor.unc.edu.ar
Key Personnel
Deputy Dir: Lic Rosa M Bestani
Founded: 1613
Collections from the 16th, 17th & 18th centuries.
Publication(s): *Informativo* (irregularly)

Biblioteca de la Universidad Nacional de La Plata
Plaza Rocha N° 137, 1900 La Plata
Tel: (021) 423-6600; (021) 423-6608; (021) 423-6607; (021) 423-6601 *Fax:* (021) 425-5004
E-mail: biblio@isis.unlp.edu.ar
Web Site: www.unlp.edu.ar
Telex: 31151 Bulap
Key Personnel
Dir: Prof Javier Fernandez

Universidad Nacional del Litoral
Blvd Pellegrini 2750, 3000 Santa Fe
Tel: (0342) 4571110 *Fax:* (0342) 4571110
E-mail: informes@unl.edu.ar
Web Site: www.unl.edu.ar
Key Personnel
Dir: Beatriz S Perez Risso de Costa

Aruba

Biblioteca Nacional Aruba (Aruba National Library)
George Madurostr 13, Oranjestad
Tel: 582-1580 *Fax:* 582-5493
E-mail: info@bibliotecanacional.aw
Web Site: www.bibliotecanacional.aw
Telex: bc 5060
Key Personnel
Dir: Astrid J T Britten
System Librarian: Lilian A Semeleer
Founded: 1949
National & Public Library
Membership(s): Acuril; IFLA.
Branch Office(s)
Filiaal San Nicolaas, Peter Stuyvesant Straat Z/N, San Nicolas *E-mail:* sn@setarnet.aw

Australia

Archives Office of New South Wales
2 Globe St, The Rocks, Sydney, NSW 2000
Mailing Address: PO Box 516, Kingswood, NSW 2747
Tel: (02) 9673-1788 *Fax:* (02) 9833-4518
E-mail: srecords@records.nsw.gov.au
Web Site: www.records.nsw.gov.au
Key Personnel
Dir: David Roberts
Branch Office(s)
76 Miller Red, Villawood

Australian National University Library
Cor Fellows & Garran Rd, Canberra, ACT 0200
Tel: (02) 6125 5111 *Fax:* (02) 6125 5931
E-mail: webmaster@anu.edu.au
Web Site: www.anu.edu.au
Key Personnel
University Librarian: C R Steele *Tel:* (02) 6125 8983 *E-mail:* colin.steele@anu.edu.au
Publication(s): *User response to URICA: a catalogue on line*

Barr Smith Press, University of Adelaide Library
Barr Smith Library, The University of Adelaide, Adelaide, SA 5005
Tel: (08) 8303 5372 *Fax:* (08) 8303 4369
E-mail: bslill@library.adelaide.edu.au
Web Site: www.library.adelaide.edu.au
Key Personnel
University Librarian: Ray Choate *Tel:* (08) 8303 4064 *E-mail:* ray.choate@adelaide.edu.au
Publication(s): *Joanna & Robert, the Barr Smith's Life in Letters, 1853-1919* (1996); *Poems & Recollections of the Past* (1996)

CSIRO (Commonwealth Scientific & Industrial Research Organization)
Bag 10, Clayton South, Victoria 3169
Tel: (03) 9545 2176 *Fax:* (03) 9545 2175
E-mail: enquiries@csiro.au
Web Site: www.csiro.au
Telex: 30236
Key Personnel
Chief Executive: Malcolm McIntosh
Chairman: Prof A Clarke
Library Network Services provides cost effective, specialized library services to CSIRO's Network of 45 libraries throughout Australia & delivery of a complete range of library services to staff of the Information Services Branch.

Monash University Library
Box 4, Monash University, Victoria 3800
Tel: (03) 9905 5054 *Fax:* (03) 9905 2610
E-mail: library@lib.monash.edu.au
Web Site: www.lib.monash.edu.au
Key Personnel
University Librarian: Cathrine Harboe-Ree

The State Library of New South Wales
Macquarie St, Sydney, NSW 2000
Tel: (02) 9273 1414 *Fax:* (02) 9273 1255
E-mail: library@sl.nsw.gov.au
Web Site: www.sl.nsw.gov.au
Key Personnel
State Librarian: Dagmar Schmidmaier
Founded: 1826
Publication(s): *Public Library News* (newsletter); *Public Library Statistics* (annually)

State Library of Queensland
South Bank Bldg, Level 2, South Brisbane, Qld 4101
Mailing Address: PO Box 3488, South Brisbane, Qld 4101
Tel: (07) 3840 7666 *Fax:* (07) 3846 2421
E-mail: srlenquiries@slq.qld.gov.au
Web Site: www.slq.qld.gov.au/
Key Personnel
State Librarian: Lea Giles-Peters
Includes the John Oxley Library of Queensland History.
Publication(s): *Annual Report of the Library Board of Queensland*; *The Development of State Libraries & Their Effect on the Public Library Movement in Australia* (1809-1964); *Directory of State & Public Library Service in Queensland* (annually); *North Queensland Towns & Districts Bibliography* (1975); *Pub-*

lic Libraries in Queensland: Statistical Bulletin (annually); Queensland Government Publications (quarterly)

State Library of South Australia
North Terrace, Adelaide, SA 5000
Mailing Address: GPO Box 419, Adelaide SA 5001
Tel: (08) 82077200 Toll Free Tel: 800-182-013 Fax: (08) 82077247
E-mail: info@slsa.sa.gov.au
Web Site: www.slsa.sa.gov.au
Key Personnel
Chairman: Peter Goldsworthy
Acting Dir: Margaret Allen
Founded: 1884
Publication(s): Collection Development Policy; Extra Extra (biannually); Strategic Plan (2001-04)

State Library of Tasmania
91 Murray St, Hobart, Tas 7000
Tel: (03) 6233 7511 Fax: (03) 6231 0927
E-mail: state.library@education.tas.gov.au
Web Site: www.statelibrary.education.tas.gov.au
Key Personnel
Dir: Siobhan Gaskell E-mail: siobhan.gaskell@education.tas.gov.au
Senior Librarian (Policy Planning): Bridget Hutton Tel: (03) 6233 6815 E-mail: bridget.hutton@education.tas.gov.au
Founded: 1850
State library & public library service.

State Library of Victoria
328 Swanston St, Melbourne, Victoria 3000
Tel: (03) 8664 7000 Fax: (03) 9639 3673
E-mail: info@slv.vic.gov.au
Web Site: www.statelibrary.vic.gov.au
Key Personnel
Chief Executive & State Librarian: Frances Awcock
Publication(s): La Trobe Library Journal (biannually); Victorian Government Publications (monthly)

State Library of Western Australia
Alexander Library Bldg, Perth Cultural Centre, Perth, WA 6000
Tel: (08) 9427 3111 Fax: (08) 9427 3256
E-mail: info@liswa.wa.gov.au
Web Site: www.liswa.wa.gov.au
Key Personnel
Chief Executive Officer & State Librarian: Claire Forte
Publication(s): The Genealogy Centre Resource List: Australasia (1999); Katatjin: A guide to the Indigenous Records in the Baltye Library (2003)

University of Melbourne Baillieu Library
Parkville Campus, Melbourne, Victoria 3010
Tel: (03) 8344 5378 Fax: (03) 9348 1142
Web Site: www.lib.unimelb.edu.au/
Telex: 30815
Library of arts, humanities & social sciences.

University of New South Wales Library
Sydney, NSW 2052
Tel: (02) 9385 1000
Web Site: www.info.library.unsw.edu.au
Key Personnel
University Librarian: Andrew Wells
Founded: 1948

University of Queensland Library
Level 1, Duhig North Bldg, Saint Lucia, Qld 4072
Tel: (07) 3365 6949 Fax: (07) 3365 1737
E-mail: universitylibrarian@library.uq.edu.au
Web Site: www.library.uq.edu.au
Key Personnel
University Librarian: Janine Schmidt Tel: (07) 3365 6342

University of South Australia Library
Holbrooks Rd, Underdale, SA 5032
Tel: (08) 8302 6661 Fax: (08) 8302 6250
Web Site: www.library.unisa.edu.au
Key Personnel
Librarian: Dr Alan Bundy E-mail: alan.bundy@unisa.edu.au
Publisher of library science texts & conference proceedings.

University of Sydney Library
Parramatta Rd, University of Sydney, NSW 2006
Tel: (02) 9351 2990 Fax: (02) 9351 2890
Web Site: www.library.usyd.edu.au
Key Personnel
University Librarian: John Shipp

University of Technology, Sydney Library
PO Box 123, Broadway, NSW 2007
Tel: 9514 2000
E-mail: info@uts.edu.au
Web Site: www.uts.edu.au
Key Personnel
Librarian: Stephen V O'Connor
Publication(s): Library Link (quarterly, newsletter)

University of Western Australia Library
35 Stirling Highway, Crawley, WA 6009
Tel: (08) 9380 1777 Fax: (08) 9380 1012
E-mail: uwalibrary@library.uwa.edu.au
Web Site: www.library.uwa.edu.au/
Telex: 92992 Uniwa Cable: Uniwest
Key Personnel
Librarian: John Arfield

Austria

Amtsbibliothek des Bundesministeriums fur Unterricht, und Kulturelle Angelegenheiten und des Bundesministeriums fur Wissenschaft und Verkehr
Minoritenplatz 5, 1014 Vienna
Tel: (01) 53 120-0 Fax: (01) 53 120-3099
E-mail: ministerium@bmbwk.gv.at
Web Site: www.bmbwk.gv.at/
Telex: 115532
Key Personnel
Manager: Dr Norbert Neumann
Publication(s): Euro-Dok: Bildung, Forschung, Kultur, Kunst, Unterricht, Wissenschaft; Forschungspolitische Dokumentation (Political Research Documentation); Veroeffentlichungen: Zuwachsverzeichnis

Bibliothek der Osterreichischen Akademie der Wissenschaften (Library of the Austrian Academy of Science)
Dr-Ignaz-Seipel-Platz 2, 1010 Vienna
Tel: (01) 51581-1262
E-mail: webmaster@oeaw.ac.at
Web Site: www.oeaw.ac.at
Telex: (01) 12628
Key Personnel
Contact: Dr Christine Harrauer E-mail: christine.harrauer@oeaw.ac.at
Publication(s): Kosmos und Mythos; Meliouchos

Bibliothek des Benediktinerklosters Melk in Niederoesterreich (Library of the Melk Benedictine Monastery in Lower Austria)
Abt Berthold Diemayrstr 1, 3390 Melk
Tel: (02752) 555-342 Fax: (02752) 555-52
E-mail: stiftsbibliothek.melk@nextra.at
Key Personnel
Librarian: P Gottfried Glassner
E-mail: gglassner@magnet.at
Publication(s): Die Anfaenge der Melker Bibliothek (1996)

Bibliothek des Osterreichischen Patentamtes
Osterreichisches Patentamt Dresdner Strar 87, PO Box 95, 1200 Vienna
Tel: (01) 53424 0 Fax: (01) 53424110
E-mail: info@patent.bmvit.gv.at
Web Site: www.patent.bmwa.gv.at
Telex: 136847 OEPA
Key Personnel
President: Dr Otmar Rafeiner
Librarian: Dr Ingrid Weidinger
Library of the Austrian Patent Office.
Publication(s): Oesterreichischer Musteronzeiger; Osterreichisches Gebroiuchsmusterblett; Oesterreichischer Markenanzeiger; Oesterreichisches Patentblatt; Patentschriften

Universitaetsbibliothek Graz (University Library Graz)
Universitaetsplatz 3a, 8010 Graz
Tel: (0316) 380 3102 Fax: (0316) 384 987
E-mail: ub.auskunft@uni-graz.at
Web Site: www.ub.uni-graz.at
Key Personnel
Librarian: Dr Werner Schlachee
Founded: 1573
Publication(s): Jahresbericht (annually, 1973); News (Informationsschrift der Universitaetsbibliothek Graz) (booklet, 1987)
Parent Company: Karl-Franzens Universitat Graz, Universitaetsplatz 3, 8010 Graz

IAEA Library, see Vienna International Centre Library

Universitaetsbibliothek Innsbruck
Innrain 50, 6010 Innsbruck
Tel: (0512) 507 2401 Fax: (0512) 507 2893
E-mail: ub-hb@uibk.ac.at
Web Site: ub.uibk.ac.at
Telex: 553708
Key Personnel
Dir: Dr Walter Neuhauser
Publication(s): Vom Codex zum Computer

Oberoesterreichische Landesbibliothek (Regional Library Upper Austria)
Schillerpl 2, Postfach 129, 4021 Linz 2
Tel: (0732) 664071-00 Fax: (0732) 664071-44
E-mail: landesbibliothek@ooe.gv.at
Web Site: www.landesbibliothek.at
Key Personnel
Dir: Dr Christian Enichlmayr Tel: (0732) 66407172 E-mail: christian.enichlmayr@ooe.gv.at
Founded: 1774
Reference Library.
Parent Company: Land Oberoesterreich

Oesterreichisches Staatsarchiv (Austrian State Archives)
Nottendorfer, Gasse 2, 1030 Vienna
Tel: (01) 79540 100 Fax: (01) 79540 199
E-mail: gdpost@oesta.gv.at
Web Site: www.oesta.gv.at
Key Personnel
General Dir: Dr Lorenz Mikoletzky
E-mail: lorenz.mikoletzky@oesta.gv.at
Personnel & Administrative Dir: Mag Luzia Owajko
Dir, Archives of the Republic: Hr Dr Manfred Fink
Dir, Finance Archives: Hr Dr Christian Sapper
Dir, War Archive: Hr Dr Christoph Tepperberg
Dir, Courthouse & State Archives: Hr Prof Dr Leopold Auer

AUSTRIA

Provisional Dir, General Adminstrative Archive: Dr Gerald Theimer
Founded: 1945
Publication(s): *Mitteilungen des Oesterreichischen Staatsarchivs* (Annually)

Osterreichische Nationalbibliothek (Austrian National Library)
Josefspl 1, 1015 Vienna
Mailing Address: PO Box 308, 1015 Vienna
Tel: (01) 534 10 *Fax:* (01) 534 10 280
E-mail: onb@onb.ac.at
Web Site: www.onb.ac.at
Telex: 112624 AOenb
Key Personnel
Dir General: Dr Johanna Rachinger
Publication(s): *Informationsfuehrer Bibliotheken und Dokumentations- stellen in Oesterreich* (Information Guide to Libraries and Documentation Centres in Austria)

Steiermaerkische Landesbibliothek
Kalchberggasse 2, 8010 Graz
Mailing Address: Postfach 861, 8010 Graz
Tel: (0316) 8770 *Fax:* (0316) 877-22
E-mail: post@stmk.gv.at
Web Site: www.verwaltung.steiermark.at
Key Personnel
Dir: Dr Joseph F Desput *E-mail:* joseph.desput@stmk.gv.at
Deputy Dir: Dr Christoph Binder *Tel:* (0316) 8016 4611 *E-mail:* christoph.binder@stmk.gv.at
Founded: 1811
Public scientific library.
Publication(s): *Geschichte und Gegenwart* (History & the Present, quarterly, 2000, scientific journal); *Veroeffentlichungen der Steiermaerkischen Landesbibliothek 24: Joerg-Martin Willnauer: Die Steiermark in Wort und Schild* (2000, scientific series concerning Styrian literature history & history of culture)

Universitaetsbibliothek der Technischen Universitaet Wien (Vienna University of Technology Library)
Resselgasse 4, 1040 Vienna
Tel: (01) 58801 44051 *Fax:* (01) 58801 44099
E-mail: info@mail.ub.tuwien.ac.at
Web Site: www.ub.tuwien.ac.at
Key Personnel
Librarian: Dr Peter Kubalek
Founded: 1815
Focuses on the Natural & Technical Sciences but also covers related subjects such as Environmental Technology.

Universitaetsbibliothek Salzburg
Hofstallgasse 2-4, 5020 Salzburg
Tel: (0662) 8044 77550 *Fax:* (0662) 8044 103
E-mail: info.hb@sbg.ac.at
Web Site: www.ubs.sbg.ac.at
Key Personnel
Librarian: Dr Christine Unterrainer *E-mail:* christine.unterrainer@sbg.ac.at

Vienna International Centre Library
Wagramer Str 5, 1400 Vienna
Mailing Address: PO Box 100, 1400 Vienna
Tel: (01) 2600-22620 *Fax:* (01) 2600-29584
E-mail: iaea.library.infodesk@iaea.org
Web Site: www.iaea.or.at
Telex: 112645 *Cable:* Inatom Vienna

Universitaetsbibliothek Wien (Vienna University Library)
D-Karl-Lueger-Ring 1, 1010 Vienna
Tel: (01) 427715001 *Fax:* (01) 42779150
E-mail: aer.ub@univie.ac.at; info.ub@univie.ac.at
Web Site: www.ub.unvie.ac.at

Key Personnel
Librarian: Maria Seissl *E-mail:* maria.seissl@univie.ac.at
Founded: 1365

Wiener Stadt- und Landesarchiv
Gasometer D, Guglgasse 14, Vienna 1082
Mailing Address: Rathaus, A-1082 Vienna
Tel: (01) 4000-84815 *Fax:* (01) 4000-7238
E-mail: post@m08.magwien.gv.at
Web Site: www.magwien.gv.at
Key Personnel
Dir: Dr Ferdinand Opll
Vienna Municipal Archives.
Publication(s): *Veroeffentlichungen des Wiener Stadt-und Landesarchivs*

Wiener Stadt- und Landesbibliothek
Rathaus, 1082 Vienna
Tel: (01) 4000-84920 *Fax:* (01) 4000-7219
E-mail: post@m09.magwien.gv.et
Web Site: www.stadtbibliothek.wien.at
Key Personnel
Man Dir: Gerhard Renner
Vienna Municipal & County Library.

Azerbaijan

Azerbaidzhanskaya respublikanskaya biblioteka im M F Akhundova (M F Achudova State Library of Azerbaijan Republic)
Ul Khagani 29, 370601 Baku
Tel: (012) 934 003
Key Personnel
Dir: Leyla Gafurova
Founded: 1923
Publication(s): *Azerbaijan in Foreign Press* (Bibliographic Indexes); *Scientific Transactions of M F Akhundov State Library*

Bahamas

The College of the Bahamas Library
Oakes Field Campus, PO Box N4912, Nassau
Tel: 302-4552 *Fax:* 326-7834
Web Site: www.cob.edu.bs/library
Key Personnel
Dir: Willamae Johnson *E-mail:* wjohnson@cob.edu.bs
Founded: 1975
Has branches in Freeport, Grand Bahama & New Providence.
Publication(s): *Bahamas Reference Collection: a Bibliography* (1980, with irregular supplements); *The Chickcharney Express* (irregular); *The Library Informer* (per semester, newsletter)

Sir Charles Hayward Library
The Mall, PO Box F-40040, Freeport
Tel: 352-7048
Key Personnel
Adult Librarian: Elaine B Talma

Nassau Public Library
Shirley St, Nassau, New Providence
Tel: 3224907; 85029
Founded: 1837

Bahrain

Bahrain Centre for Studies, Research Library & Information Dept
PO Box 496, Manama
Fax: (0973) 754678
E-mail: bcsr@batelco.com.bh
Web Site: www.batelco.com.bh/bcsr/
Telex: BCSR 9764 BN
Key Personnel
Library Dir: Najim Rashid

College of Medicine Library, Arabian Gulf University
PO Box 26671, Manama
Tel: 239 999 *Fax:* 272 555
E-mail: info@agu.edu.bh
Web Site: www.agu.edu.bh
Telex: 7319
Key Personnel
Librarian: Khushnud Hassan

Manama Central Library
PO Box 43, Manama
Tel: 231105 *Fax:* 274036
Key Personnel
Dir of Public Libraries: Monsoor Sarhan
Founded: 1946

University of Bahrain Library
PO Box 32038, Sukhair
Tel: 17438808 *Fax:* 17449838
E-mail: library@admin.uob.bh
Web Site: www.uob.edu.bh
Telex: 9258
Key Personnel
Dir: Hedi Talbi *E-mail:* talbi@admin.uob.bh
Deputy Dir: Tahani Hassan Al-Khalifa *E-mail:* tahanikh@admin.uob.bh
Founded: 1986
Membership(s): CILIP; SLA.
Publication(s): *Awan*; *Journal of Educational & Psychological Science*; *Journal of Human Sciences*; *Thaqafat*

Bangladesh

Bangladesh Central Public Library
Kazi Nazrul Islam Ave, Shahbagh, Dhaka 1000
Tel: (02) 50 08 19; (02) 50 08 39; (02) 50 28 16
Key Personnel
Librarian: Dr A F M Badiur-Rahman
Founded: 1958

Bangladesh Institute of Development Studies Library
E-17 Agargaon, Sher-e-Bangla Nagar, Dhaka 1207
Tel: (02) 9118999 *Fax:* (02) 8113023
E-mail: secy08bids@sdnbd.org
Web Site: www.bids-bd.org *Cable:* BIDECON DHAKA
Key Personnel
Chief Librarian: Nilufar Akhter *E-mail:* nilufar@sdnbd.org

National Library of Bangladesh, Directorate of Archives & Libraries
32 Justice Sayed Mahbub Murshed Sarini, Sher-e-Bangla Nagar (Agargaon), Dhaka 1207
Tel: (02) 232 6572
Key Personnel
Dir: Mr Hahashinur Rahman Khan

British Council Library
5 Fuller Rd, Dhaka 1000
Tel: (02) 861 8905-7; (02) 861 8867-8 *Fax:* (02) 861 3375; (02) 861 3255
E-mail: dhaka.enquiries@bd.britishcouncil.org
Web Site: www.britishcouncil.org/bangladesh/
Telex: 642470 Bric
Key Personnel
Dir: Dr June Rollinson
Deputy Dir: Charles Nuttall

Dhaka University Library
Ramna, Dhaka 1000
Tel: (02) 966-1900 *Fax:* (02) 865583
E-mail: duregstr@bangla.net
Web Site: www.univdhaka.edu
Key Personnel
Librarian: Dr Serajul Islam
Founded: 1921

University of Rajshahi Library
Rajshahi 6205
Tel: (0721) 750041; (0721) 750033 *Fax:* (0721) 750064
E-mail: rajcc@citechco.net
Web Site: www.ugc.org/rajsahai_uni.htm
Key Personnel
Administrator: Prof Abaydur Rahman Pramanik
Founded: 1955

Barbados

National Library Service
Coleridge St, Bridgetown 2
Tel: (0809) 436 6081; (0809) 426 1744; (0809) 426 3981 *Fax:* (0809) 436 1501
E-mail: natlib@caribsurf.com
Key Personnel
Dir: Dr J Y Blackman
Founded: 1847
Publication(s): *National Bibliography of Barbados*; *West Indian Collection*

University of the West Indies Library (Barbados)
Cave Hill Campus, St Michael
Tel: (0246) 425-1310 *Fax:* (0246) 425-1327
E-mail: webmaster@uwichill.edu.bb
Web Site: www.cavehill.uwi.edu
Telex: 2257 Univados *Cable:* UNIVADOS BARBADOS
Key Personnel
Librarian: Nel Bretney

Belarus

National Library of Belarus
Krasnoarmeyskaya St, 9, 220636 Minsk
Tel: (017) 227-54-63 *Fax:* (017) 229-24-94
E-mail: sol@nacbibl.minsk.by
Web Site: kolas.bas-net.by/bla/nb.htm
Key Personnel
Dir: Galina Nikolaevna Oleynik
Deputy Dir: Kiruchina Ludmila Gennadyevna *Tel:* (017) 227-53-16; Chernov Sergey Ivanovich *Tel:* (017) 227-56-84; Aksenova Tamara Vladimirovna *Tel:* (017) 227-87-43
Founded: 1922
Publication(s): *Chernobyl* (triannually, bibliographic index); *Cultural Life of Belarus* (monthly); *Current literature on the history of Belarus & its historical science* (triannually, bibliographic index); *Signal Information on Culture & Arts* (weekly); *Social Sciences* (monthly)

Belgium

AMVC-Letterenhuis (AMVC-Literary Centre)
Minderbroedersstraat 22, 2000 Antwerp
Tel: (03) 222 9320 *Fax:* (03) 222 9321
E-mail: amvc.letterenhuis@stad.antwerpen.be
Web Site: museum.antwerpen.be/amvc_letterenhuis
Key Personnel
Curator: Leen Van Dijck *Tel:* (03) 222 9329 *E-mail:* helena.vandijck@cs.antwerpen.be
Founded: 1933
Archives & Museum of Flemish Culture.

Archives generales du Royaume
Rue de Ruysbroeck 2, 1000 Brussels
Tel: (02) 513 76 80 *Fax:* (02) 513 76 81
E-mail: archives.generales@arch.be
National Archives.

Bibliotheque Central du Ministere de l'Education Nationale
Rue de Stassart, 43, 1050 Brussels
Tel: (02) 511 59 80 *Fax:* (02) 513 43 33
Key Personnel
Dir: J M Andrin

Bibliotheque du Musee Royal de Mariemont
100 chaussee de Mariemont, 7140 Morlanwelz-Mariemont
Tel: (064) 21 21 93 *Fax:* (064) 26 29 24
E-mail: info@musee-mariemont.be
Web Site: www.musee-mariemont.be
Key Personnel
Librarian: M B Delattre
Publication(s): *Bulletin d'Information* (quarterly); *Cahiers de Mariemont* (annually); *Catalogues d'Expositions, Monographies, Dossiers Pedagogiques*

Bibliotheque Fonds Quetelet
Rue de l'Industrie, 6, 1000 Brussels
Tel: (02) 506 60 54; (02) 506 61 51 *Fax:* (02) 502 84 25
E-mail: quetelet@mineco.fgov.be
Web Site: mineco.fgov.be
Key Personnel
Librarian: E Van Wesemael
Library of the Ministry of Economic Affairs.
Publication(s): *Accroissements de la Bibliotheque Fonds Quetelet* (monthly)

Bibliotheque Royale Albert Ier
4 Blvd de l'Empereur, 1000 Brussels
Tel: (02) 519 53 11 *Fax:* (02) 519 55 33
E-mail: contacts@kbr.be
Web Site: www.kbr.be
Telex: 21157
Key Personnel
Dir: Pierre Cockshaw
Koninklijke Bibliotheek Albert I.
Publication(s): *Bibliograhie de Belgique (Belgisch Bibliographie)* (monthly); *Bulletin de la BR (KB Bulletin)* (quarterly)

Bibliotheques de l'Universite Libre de Bruxelles
50 Ave Franklin D Roosevelt, 1050 Brussels
Tel: (02) 650 36 63 *Fax:* (02) 650 20 07
E-mail: mdesb@ulb.ac
Web Site: www.bib.ulb.ac.be/
Key Personnel
Librarian: Jean-Pierre Devroey

Centre d'Information et de Conservation de l'Universite de Liege
Place du 20-Aout, 7, 4000 Liege
Tel: (04) 366 52 18 *Fax:* (04) 366 57 98; (04) 366 44 22
E-mail: press@ulg.ac.be
Web Site: www.ulg.ac.be/hp.html
Key Personnel
Head Librarian: Nicole Haesenne
Chief Librarian: Dr J Denooz *E-mail:* joseph.denooz@ulg.ac.be
Publication(s): *Bibliotheca Universitatis Leodiensis*

Goethe-Institut
58 rue Belliard Str, 1040 Brussels
Tel: (02) 230 39 70 *Fax:* (02) 230 77 25
E-mail: eu@bruessel.goethe.org
Web Site: www.goethe.de/be/bru/deindex.htm
Key Personnel
Librarian: Margareta Hauschild
Founded: 1959

Institut Royal des Sciences Naturelles de Belgique, Bibliotheque (Royal Belgian Institute of Natural Sciences Library)
KBIN-Library/Documentation Service, Rue Vautier 29, 1000 Brussels
Tel: (02) 627 42 11 *Fax:* (02) 627 41 13
E-mail: bib@naturalsciences.be
Web Site: www.naturalsciences.be
Telex: INSNAT
Key Personnel
Librarian: Laurent Meese *Tel:* (02) 627 42 49 *E-mail:* laurent.meese@naturalsciences.be
Head Department Vertebrates: J Govaere
Founded: 1846
Publication(s): *Bulletin de L'Institut Royal des Sciences Naturelles de Belgique - Biology* (annually, 2003); *Bulletin de L Institut Royal des Sciences Naturelles de Belgique - Bulletin Van Het Koninkluk Belgisch Instituut Voor Natuurwetenschappen - Entomology* (annually, 2003); *Bulletin de L'Institut Royal des Sciences Naturelles de Belgique - Earth Sciences* (annually, 2004); *Documents de Travail de L'IR Sc N B*

Katholieke Universiteit Leuven
Centrale Bibliotheek, Mgr Ladeuzeplein 21, 3000 Leuven
Tel: (016) 32 46 60; (016) 32 46 01 *Fax:* (016) 32 46 16
E-mail: centrale.bibliotheek@bib.kuleuven.ac.be
Web Site: www.bib.kuleuven.ac.be
Key Personnel
Librarian: Raf Dekeyser *E-mail:* raf.dekeyser@bib.kuleuven.ac.be
University Library of Louvain.
Publication(s): *Ex officina* (Bulletin of the Friends of Louvain University Library)

Bibliotheque Universitaire Moretus Plantin (University Library Moretus Plantin)
Unit of The University of Namur
19 rue Grandgagnage, 5000 Namur
Tel: (081) 724646 *Fax:* (081) 724645
E-mail: infocentre@fundp.ac.be
Web Site: www.fundp.ac.be/bump
Key Personnel
Chief Librarian: Prof Rene Noel
Secretary: Yvette Deherve-Wilquet *E-mail:* yvettewilquet@fundp.ac.be
Academic library.

Bibliotheque du Parlement
Rue de la Loi 13, 1000 Brussels
Tel: (02) 5499271 *Fax:* (02) 5499498

BELGIUM

E-mail: bibliotheque@lachambre.be
Key Personnel
Librarian: Roland Van Nieuwenborgh

Museum Plantin-Moretus
Vrijdagmarkt 22, 2000 Antwerp
Tel: (03) 221 14 50; (03) 221 14 51 *Fax:* (03) 221 14 71
E-mail: museum.plantin.moretus@antwerpen.be
Web Site: museum.antwerpen.be
Key Personnel
Dir: Dr Francine de Nave
Publication(s): *About types, books & prints. Didactic brochure for the Plantin-Moretus Museum & City Prints Gallery* (1989, monograph); *The Illustration of Books Published by the Moretuses* (1996, monograph); *Plantin-Moretus Museum Antwerp (Musea Nostra)* (1995, monograph)

Stadsbibliotheek
Hendrik Conscienceplein 4, 2000 Antwerp
Tel: (03) 206 87 10 *Fax:* (03) 206 87 75
E-mail: stadsbibliotheek@stad.antwerpen.be
Web Site: stadsbibliotheek.antwerpen.be
Key Personnel
Dir: An Renard *Tel:* (03) 206 87 28 *E-mail:* an.renard@cs.antwerpen.be
Founded: 1481
Reference library of the city of Antwerp concentrating on humanities.

Bibliotheek Universitair Centrum
Middelheimlaan 1, 2020 Antwerp
Tel: (03) 265 37 94 *Fax:* (03) 265 36 52
E-mail: helpdesk@lib.ua.ac.be
Web Site: lib.ua.ac.be
Key Personnel
Contact: Dr B van Styvendaele

Universite Catholique de Louvain
Place de l'Universite 1, 1348 Louvain-la-Neuve
Tel: (010) 47 21 11
E-mail: sceb@sceb.ucl.ac.be
Web Site: www.ucl.ac.be
Key Personnel
Chief Librarian: Charles-Henri Nyns
  E-mail: nyns@sceb.ucl.ac.be

Universiteit Antwerpen Bibliotheek UFSIA
  (University of Antwerp UFSIA Library)
Prinsstr 9, 2000 Antwerp
Tel: (03) 2204996 *Fax:* (03) 2204437
E-mail: helpdesk@lib.ua.ac.be
Web Site: lib.ua.ac.be
Telex: 33599 Ufsia
Key Personnel
Chief Librarian: L Simons *Tel:* (03) 2224440
  E-mail: ludo.simons@ufsia.ac.be
Dir: Theo Boeckx *Tel:* (03) 2204448
  E-mail: theo.boeckx@ufsia.ac.be
Founded: 1852
Universiteit Antwerpen consists of Universitaire Faculteiten Sint-Ignatius (UFSIA), Universitaire Instelling Antwerpen (UIA), Rijksuniversitair Centrum Antwerpen (RUCA), each with its own library. The above entry details refer to UFSIA.

University Library of Louvain (Leuven), see Katholieke Universiteit Leuven

University Library of Louvain (Louvain-la-Neuve) Les Bibliotheques de l'Universite Catholique de Louvain, see Universite Catholique de Louvain

Vrije Universiteit Brussel Universiteitsbibliotheek
Campus Oefenplein, Pleinlaan 2, 1050 Brussels
Tel: (02) 629 21 11 *Fax:* (02) 629 22 82
E-mail: info@vub.ac.be
Web Site: www.vub.ac.be
Telex: 61051
Key Personnel
Rector: Prof Benjamin Van Camp, PhD

Belize

National Library Service of Belize
Princess Margaret Drive, Belize City
Mailing Address: PO Box 287, Belize City
Tel: (02) 34248; (02) 34249 *Fax:* (02) 34246
E-mail: nls@btl.net; leolibrary2003@yahoo.com
Web Site: www.nlsbze.bz
Key Personnel
Chief Librarian: Mrs Joy L Ysaguirre
Committed to the promotion of a more informed, aware & literate society & seeks to provide universal access to information through the maintenance of a National Library & Public Library service.
Memberships: Comla; ACURIL; ABINIA-AC; IFLA; INFOLAC.
Parent Company: Ministry of Education, Government of Belize

Benin

Bibliotheque Nationale du Benin
BP 401, Porto Novo
Tel: 22 25 85
E-mail: bn.benin@bj.refer.org
Web Site: www.bj.refer.org/benin_ct/tur/bnb/Pagetitre.htm
Key Personnel
Dir: H N Amoussou
Publication(s): *Les Numeras de la Bibliographie Nationale*

Bibliotheque Universitaire Centrale
Campus d'Abomey-Calavy, BP 04 789, Cotonou
Tel: 36 01 01 *Fax:* 36 01 01
Telex: 5010 *Cable:* Biblionationale
Key Personnel
Dir: Pascal Gandaho
Founded: 1970

Direction des Archives Nationales du Benin
BP 629, Porto Novo
Tel: 21 30 79 *Fax:* 21 30 79
Telex: 5347
Key Personnel
Dir: Elise R Paraiso *Tel:* 050266; 223497
Founded: 1913
Memberships: CIA; AIAF; WARBICA.
Publication(s): *Bulletin des Archives*; *Guide de l'usager*; *Memoire du Benin*; *Repertoire Serie E: Affaires politiques*; *Repertoire Serie N: Affaires Militaires*; *Repertoire Serie Q: Affaires Economiques*

Bermuda

Bermuda Archives
Government Administration Bldg, 30 Parliament St, Hamilton HM 13
Tel: 295-5151

Key Personnel
Archivist: Karla M Haywood
Publication(s): *A Guide to the Records of Bermuda* (1980)

Bermuda College Library
Stonington Ave, South Rd, Paget PG 04
Mailing Address: PO Box 297, Paget PG BX
Tel: (0441) 239-4033 *Fax:* (0441) 239-4034
E-mail: info@bercol.bm
Web Site: www.bercol.bm
Key Personnel
Dir: Daurene Aubrey
Librarian: Annette Lowe

Bermuda National Library
13 Queen St, Hamilton HM11
Tel: 295-2905 *Fax:* 292-8443
E-mail: bdanatlib@gov.bm
Web Site: www.bermudanationallibrary.bm
Telex: 3775 Modus
Key Personnel
Head Librarian: C Joanne Brangman
  E-mail: jbrangman@gov.bm
Technical Services Librarian: Patrice A Carvell
  E-mail: pcarvell@gov.bm
Adult Services Librarian: Julie Bean
  E-mail: jbean@gov.bm
Youth Services Librarian: Marla Smith
  E-mail: msmith@gov.bm
Publication(s): *Bermuda National Bibliography* (quarterly)
Branch Office(s)
Bermuda Youth Library, 74 Church St, Hamilton HM12 *Tel:* 295-0487 *Fax:* 296-0973
  E-mail: youthlib@gov.bm
Mobile Library

Bolivia

Biblioteca del Congreso Nacional
Mercado Esquina, Calle Ayacucho, No 308, La Paz
Tel: (02) 354108; (02) 392658 *Fax:* (02) 392402; (02) 341649
Web Site: www.congreso.gov.bo
Telex: 3204
Publication(s): *Fuentas del Congreso* (bulletin)

Biblioteca y Archivo Nacional de Bolivia
Calle Espana 43, Sucre
Mailing Address: Casilla 793, Sucre
Tel: (064) 21481 *Fax:* (064) 61208
E-mail: abnb@mara.scr.entelnet.bo
Key Personnel
Dir: Gunnar Mendoza
Founded: 1836

Biblioteca de la Direccion General de Cultura
Alcaldia Municipal, Casilla 1856, La Paz 1832
Library of Cultural Affairs Administration.

Universidad Boliviana Tomas Frias, Departmento de Bibliotecas
Av del Maestro, Casilla 36, Potosi
Tel: (062) 27300 *Fax:* (062) 27329; (062) 26663
Key Personnel
Dir: Julia B De Lopez
Publication(s): *Boletin del Departamento de Bibliotecas* (& occasional papers)

Biblioteca Central de la Universidad Mayor de San Andres
Ave Villazon 1995, Monoblock Central, La Paz
Tel: (02) 440047; (02) 352232 *Fax:* (02) 442505
E-mail: rector@umsanet.edu.bo

Web Site: www.umsanet.edu.bo; www.bc.umsanet.edu.bo
Key Personnel
Dir, Lic: Alberto Crespo Rodas

Biblioteca Central de la Universidad Mayor de San Francisco Xavier de Chuquisaca
Casilla 232, Sucre
Tel: (04) 6453308 *Fax:* (04) 6455308
Web Site: www.usfx.edu.bo
Key Personnel
Dir: Agar Penaranda

Biblioteca Central Universitaria 'Jose Antonio Arze'
Campus Universitaria Las Cuadras, Casilla 992, Cochabamba
Tel: (042) 232540
E-mail: biblioteca-c@umss.edu.bo
Web Site: www.umss.edu.bo
Telex: 6363
Key Personnel
Dir: Dr Luis Alberto Ponce
Founded: 1926
Publication(s): *Boletin Bibliografico*; *Notas Bibliotecologicas*

Bosnia and Herzegovina

Narodna i univerzitetska biblioteka Bosne i Hercegovine
Zmaja od Bosne 8B, 71000 Sarajevo
Tel: (071) 33 275 312 *Fax:* (071) 33 275 431
E-mail: nubbih@nub.ba
Web Site: www.nub.ba
Key Personnel
Dir: Dr Enes Kujundzjc
National & University Library of Bosnia & Herzegovina.

Botswana

Botswana National Archives & Records Services
PO Box 239, Gaborone
Tel: 391 820 *Fax:* 390 545
Web Site: www.gov.bw
Telex: 2994BD *Cable:* HOMES
Key Personnel
Dir: Ms K P Kgabi *E-mail:* kkgabi@gov.bw
Principal Archivist: A S B Akhaabi; C T Nengomasha
Librarian: A R Adekanmbi
Founded: 1967
Provides a national archives services to preserve for posterity historically important records & data for research, education & reference.
Publication(s): *Botswana National Archives & Records Services Library Accessions List* (annually)

Botswana National Library Service
Private Bag 0036, Gaborone
Tel: 352-397 *Fax:* 301-149
E-mail: natlib@global.bw; automate@global.bw
Web Site: www.gov.bw *Cable:* Bonalibs
Key Personnel
Dir: Ms C B Modise *E-mail:* cbmodise@gov.bw
Publication(s): *The National Bibliography of Botswana*

Geological Survey Department Library
Private Bag 14, Lobatse
Tel: 330327; 330428 *Fax:* 332013
E-mail: geosurv@global.bw
Web Site: www.gov.bw
Telex: 2293 Geo *Cable:* Rocks Lobatse
Key Personnel
Dir: T P Machacha *Tel:* 332495

University of Botswana Library
Private Bag 00390, Gaborone
Tel: 355-0000; 355-2304 *Fax:* 395-6591
Web Site: www.ub.bw
Telex: 2429
Key Personnel
Dir: H K Raseroka *E-mail:* raseroka@mopipi.ub.bw
Founded: 1971

Brazil

Arquivo Nacional
Rua Azeredo Coutinho, 77-3° Andar, Centro, 20230-170 Rio de Janeiro-RJ
Tel: (021) 3806-6171 *Fax:* (021) 2232-8430
E-mail: conarq@arquivonacional.gov.br
Web Site: www.arquivonacional.gov.br/
Telex: 2134103
Key Personnel
General Dir: Jaime Antones Da Silva
 E-mail: directorialgeral@arquivnacional.gov.br
Publication(s): *ACERVO-Revista do Arquivo Nacional*; *Serie de Publicacoes Historicas*; *Serie de Publicacoes Tecnicas*; *Serie Instrumentos de Trabalho*; *Serie Publicacoes Avulsas*

Biblioteca do Ministerio das Relacoes Exteriores
Esplanada dos Ministerios, Bloco H, 70170-900 Brasilia DF
Tel: (061) 2116359 *Fax:* (061) 2237362
Web Site: www.mre.gov.br *Cable:* 1319
Key Personnel
Dir, Librarian: Maria Salete Carvalho Reis
Publication(s): *Referencia de Periodicos* (monthly)

Biblioteca Municipal Mario de Andrade
Ave Sao Joao 473, Largo do Paissandu-Centro, 01035-000 Sao Paulo
Tel: (011) 3334-0001 *Fax:* (011) 3224-0009
E-mail: smc@prodam.pmsp.sp.gov.br
Web Site: www.prefeitura.sp.gov.br
Key Personnel
Dir: Lucia Neiza Pereira DaSilva
Contact: Marli Monteiro
Publication(s): *Boletim Bibliografico Biblioteca Mario de Andrade* (quarterly)

Biblioteca Publica do Estado do Rio de Janeiro
Ave Presidente Vargas 1261, 20071-004 Rio de Janeiro-RJ
Tel: (021) 2224-6184 *Fax:* (021) 2252-6810
E-mail: bibliotecapublica@bperj.rj.gov.br
Web Site: www.bperj.rj.gov.br
Key Personnel
Dir General: Ana Ligia Silva Medeiros

Centro de Documentacao e Informacao da Camara dos Deputados (House of Representatives' Centre of Documentation & Information)
Palacio do Congresso Nacional Edificio Principal, Praca dos Tres Ponderes, 70160-900 Brasilia-DF
Tel: (061) 216 0000 *Toll Free Tel:* 800 619 619
Web Site: www.camara.gov.br

Telex: 0611164
Key Personnel
Dir: Nelda Mendonca Raulino *E-mail:* nelda.raulino@camara.gov.br

Fundacao Biblioteca Nacional
Ave Rio Branco 219-39, 20040-008 Rio de Janeiro-RJ
Tel: (021) 22209367 *Fax:* (021) 22204173
Web Site: www.bn.br
Key Personnel
President: Eduardo Mattos Portella
 E-mail: portella@bn.br
Publication(s): *Anais da Biblioteca Nacional*; *Bibliografia Brasileira*; *Brazilian Book Magazine*; *revista "Poesia Sempre"*

SIBi/USP, see Sistema Integrado de Bibliotecas da Universidade de Sao Paulo (SIBi)

Sociedade Brasileira de Cultura Inglesa - Biblioteca
Rua Plinio Moscoso, 945, Rio de Janeiro-RJ
Tel: (071) 247-9788 *Fax:* (021) 245-3287
E-mail: culturainglesa@br.inter.net
Web Site: www.culturainglesa-ba.com.br
Key Personnel
Contact: Ma de Fatima B Goncalves
Publication(s): *Library News*

Universidade de Brasilia, Biblioteca Central
Campus Universitario Darcy Ribeiro Gleba "A" BCE, 70910-900 Brasilia DF
Tel: (061) 307-2417 *Fax:* (061) 274-2412
E-mail: informacoes@bce.unb.br
Web Site: www.bce.unb.br
Telex: 1083
Key Personnel
Dir: Pereira O'Dilon *Tel:* (061) 307 2400
 E-mail: direcao@bce.unb.br

Sistema Integrado de Bibliotecas da Universidade de Sao Paulo (SIBi) (University of Sao Paulo Integrated Library System)
Av Prof Luciano Gualberto, Trav J, 374/2 andar, Cidade Universitaria, 05508-900 Sao Paulo-SP
Tel: (011) 818-4194; (011) 818-4197 *Fax:* (011) 815-2142
E-mail: dtsibi@org.usp.br
Web Site: www.usp.br/sibi
Telex: 81465
Key Personnel
Dir: Teresinha Das Gracas Coletta
Publication(s): *SIBI Informa, Catalogos de Teses e Producao Docente, Intenacao* (available online)

Biblioteca Central da Universidade Federal do Parana
Rua XV de Novembro, 1299, 80060-000 Curitiba, Parana PR
Tel: (041) 360-5000 *Fax:* (041) 2627784
E-mail: webmaster@ufpr.br
Web Site: www.ufpr.br/
Telex: 5100
Key Personnel
Dir: Elayne Margareth Schloegel

Centro de Ciencias da Saude da Universidade Federal do Rio de Janeiro
Predio do CCS-Bloco L, Cidade Universitaria, 21949-900 Rio de Janeiro-RJ
Mailing Address: CP 68032, 21949-900 Rio de Janeiro-RJ
Tel: (021) 2562 6632; (021) 2562 6716; (021) 2562 6641 *Fax:* (021) 2270 0119
E-mail: ddbhome@sibi.ufrj.br
Web Site: www.sibi.ufrj.br *Cable:* C P 68032
Key Personnel
Librarian: Maria R A A Uriarte
Medical School Library of the University of Rio de Janeiro.

Universidade Federal do Rio Grande do Sul (UFRGS), Biblioteca Central
Av Paulo Gama, 110, Terreo de Reitoria Predio 12107, 90040-060 Porto Alegre, Rio Grande de Sul
Mailing Address: Cx Postal 2303, 90001-970 Porto Alegre-RS
Tel: (051) 3316-3065 *Fax:* (051) 3316-3984
E-mail: bcentral@bc.ufrgs.br
Web Site: www.biblioteca.ufrgs.br
Telex: 0511055
Key Personnel
Librarian: Ana Maria Galvao; Veleida Blank

Brunei Darussalam

Dewan Bahasa dan Pustaka
Ministry of Culture, Youth & Sports, Old Airport, Berakas, Negara Brunei Darussalam BB3510
Tel: (02) 235501 *Fax:* (02) 224763
E-mail: Chieflib@Brunei.bn
Web Site: www.kkbs.gov.bn; www.brunei.gov.bn/index.htm; dbp.gov.bn
Key Personnel
Librarian: Hj Abu Bakar Hj Zainal
National Language & Literature Bureau Library.
Publication(s): *Acquis List*; *Ind Exes*

Bulgaria

Bulgarian Academy of Sciences, Central Library
1, 15 Noemvri Str, 1040 Sofia
Tel: (02) 989-84-46 *Fax:* (02) 981-66-29; (02) 986-25-23; (02) 988-04-48
E-mail: webadmin@bas.bg
Web Site: www.bas.bg/
Telex: (067) 224-24 BG
Key Personnel
Associate Prof: Dincho Krastev *Tel:* (02) 987-89-66; (02) 989-84-46 (ext 250) *Fax:* (02) 986-25-00 *E-mail:* dincho@cl.bas.bg
Publication(s): *Bulgarian Academic Books* (catalog); *Problemi na specialnite biblioteki* (Problems of Special Libraries, irregularly); *Problems of Special Libraries; Collected Papers*

Central Agricultural Library
125, Tsarigadsko Shosse Blvd, Block 1, 1113 Sofia
Tel: (02) 70-55-17

Central State Archives
Division of General Department of Archives of the Republic of Bulgaria
Moskovska 5, 1000 Sofia
Tel: (02) 9400101; (02) 9400120; (02) 9400176 *Fax:* (02) 980 14 43
E-mail: gua@archives.government.bg
Web Site: www.archives.government.bg
Key Personnel
Dir: G Chernev
Founded: 1993
Collecting, registering, handling, preserving, using & making accessible to the public the archival holdings of the state agencies, public & private bodies.
Ultimate Parent Company: Council of Ministers

Central Technical Library
50, D-r GM Dimitrov Blvd, 1125 Sofia
Tel: (02) 702935; (02) 715247; (02) 718030 (Interlibrary loan) *Fax:* (02) 710157
E-mail: ctb@nacid.nat.bg; ctbloan@nacid.nat.bg (Interlibrary loan)
Web Site: www.nacid.nat.bg
Key Personnel
Dir: Valentina Slavcheva *E-mail:* vs@nacid.nat.bg
Founded: 1962
Parent Company: National Centre for Information & Documentation (NACID)

General Department of Archives of the Republic of Bulgaria
Moskovska 5, 1000 Sofia
Tel: (02) 940 0101; (02) 940 0102 *Fax:* (02) 980 14 43
E-mail: gua@archives.government.bg
Web Site: www.archives.government.bg
Key Personnel
Chairman: Atanas Atanassov *Tel:* (02) 940 0105
Deputy Chairman: Ventsislav Velchev
Secretary: Mr Panto Kolev
Founded: 1951
Administration, coordination, control & publishing of archival records.
Publication(s): *Archival Review* (quarterly); *Arhivite govoriat* (The Archives are Speaking); *Arhivni spravochnitsi* (Archival Finding Aids); *Journal of the State Archives* (biannually)

Medical University - Sofia, Central Medical Library
One, St G Sofiiski, 1431 Sofia
Tel: (02) 952 31 71 *Fax:* (02) 952 31 71
Web Site: www.medun.acad.bg/
Key Personnel
Dir: Dr Lydia Tacheva *E-mail:* lydia@medun.acad.bg
Deputy Dir: Dr Christo Mutafov *Tel:* (02) 522 342 *Fax:* (02) 52 2393 *E-mail:* mutafov@Sun.medun.acad.bg
Founded: 1918

National Library 'Ivan Vazov'
17 Avksentii Veleshki St, 4000 Plovdiv
Tel: (032) 62 29 15; (032) 62 50 46 *Fax:* (032) 62 47 25
E-mail: nbiv@plovdiv.techno-link.com
Web Site: fobos.primasoft.bg/libplovdiv
Key Personnel
Dir: Radka Videva Koleva *Tel:* (032) 62 68 46
Deputy Dir: Dimitar T Minev *Tel:* (032) 62 47 25 *E-mail:* dimin@abv.bg
Founded: 1879
Publication(s): *Plovdivski kraj* (annually)
Branch Office(s)
Children's Department, 15, Avksentii Veleshki St, 4000 Plovdiv *Tel:* (032) 622 045
Vustanicheski Residential District, 49, Dimitar Talev St, 4004 Plovdiv

Saints Cyril & Methodius National Library
88 Blvd Vasil Levski, 1037 Sofia
Tel: (02) 9882811 *Fax:* (02) 8435495
E-mail: nl@nationallibrary.bg
Web Site: www.nationallibrary.bg
Key Personnel
Librarian: Prof Boryana Hristova *Tel:* (02) 9881600 *E-mail:* hristova@nationallibrary.bg
Founded: 1878
Publication(s): *Biblioteka* (6 times/yr, journal, 1993, library sciences); *Bulgarska Nacionalna Bibliografija, Ser 1-8* (Bulgarian National Bibliography); *Bulgarski Knigopis* (monthly, bulletin, books, official, music, prints, maps); *Bulgarski periodicen Pecat* (annually, Bulgarian periodicals)

Sofia City & District State Archives
Moskovska 5, 1000 Sofia
Tel: (02) 940 01 06 *Fax:* (02) 980 14 43
Key Personnel
Dir: Kr Milcheva
Founded: 1952
Collecting, registering, handling, use & making available to the public the archives about Sofia & Sofia district.
Parent Company: General Department of Archives of the Republic of Bulgaria
Ultimate Parent Company: Council of Ministers

Sofia University Kliment Ohridski Biblioteka
Tzar Osvoboditel 15 Blvd, 1504 Sofia
Tel: (02) 467584; (02) 9443719 *Fax:* (02) 467170
E-mail: lsu@libsu.uni-sofia.bg
Web Site: www.libsu.uni-sofia.bg
Telex: 23296 Suko RBG
Key Personnel
Dir: Ivanka Yankova *E-mail:* yankova@libsu.uni-sofia.bg
Founded: 1888

Technical University of Sofia Library & Information Complex
8, Kliment Ohridski St, Sofia 1000
Tel: (02) 62 3073 *Fax:* (02) 68 5343
E-mail: office_tu@tu-sofia.bg
Web Site: www.tu-sofia.bg
Telex: 23574
Key Personnel
Dir: A Todorova
Founded: 1994

University of Sofia Library, see Sofia University Kliment Ohridski Biblioteka

Burkina Faso

Centre National des Archives
Presidence du Faso, BP 7030, Ouagadougou
Tel: 33-61-96; 32-47-12; 32-46-38 *Fax:* 31-49-26
Telex: 5221
Key Personnel
Dir: Assane Sawadogo *E-mail:* assaned49@yahoo.fr
Founded: 1970

Universite de Ouagadougou
BP 7021, Ouagadougou
Tel: 30 70 64; 30 70 65 *Fax:* 30 72 42
E-mail: info@univ-ouaga.bf
Web Site: www.univ-ouaga.bf
Telex: 5270 UV

Burundi

Bibliotheque Nationale du Burundi (National Library of Burundi)
BP 1095, Bujumbura
Tel: (02) 25051 *Fax:* (02) 26231
E-mail: biefbdi@cbinf.com

Bibliotheque Publique
BP 960, Bujumbura

Office National du Tourisme (ONT)
2, Avenue des Euphorbes, BP 902, Bujumbura
Tel: 222 023; 222 202; 229 390 *Fax:* 229 390
E-mail: ontbur@cbinf.com
Web Site: www.burundi.gov.bi/tourisme.htm
Telex: Cab Pub BDI 5081, 5082
Key Personnel
Dir: Hermenegilde Nimbona

Branch Office(s)
7, Boulevard de l'Uprona, Bujumbura
Aeroport International de Bujumbura

Bibliotheque de l'Universite du Burundi
BP 1320, Bujumbura
Tel: (022) 2857 *Cable:* UNIVARWA
Key Personnel
Chief Librarian: Tharlisse Nsabimana
Founded: 1964

Cameroon

Archives Bibliotheque nationales du Cameroon
BP 1053, Yaounde
Tel: 220078
Key Personnel
Dir: Emerant Mbon Mekompomb
Founded: 1952

Universite de Yaounde, Bibliotheque
BP 337, Yaounde
Tel: 222 1320 *Fax:* 222 1320
E-mail: rect.uyl@uycdc.uninet.cm
Web Site: www.uninet.cm/biblio.html
Telex: 8384
Key Personnel
Librarian: Peter Nkangafaok Chateh
Publication(s): Etudes et Recherches en Biblioth-economie

University of Dschang Central Library
PO Box 96, Dschang
Tel: 451092 *Fax:* 451202; 252751
Telex: 7013KN
Key Personnel
University Librarian: Joseph Elogo

Central African Republic

Bibliotheque Universitaire de Bangui
BP 1450, Bangui
Tel: 612 000 *Fax:* 61-78-90
Telex: 5283
Key Personnel
Dir: Thomas Poussoumandji

Chad

CDU, see Centre De Documentation Universitaire (CDU)

Centre De Documentation Universitaire (CDU)
(University Documentation Center)
Av Mobutu, N'Djamena
Mailing Address: BP 1117, N'Djamena
Tel: 5144 44; 5144 44 697 *Fax:* 514 033
E-mail: runiv.rectorat@sdnted.undp.org
Key Personnel
Chief Librarian: Mr Koulassim Doumtangar
Founded: 1972
Parent Company: Universite De N'Djamena

Centre de Recherche des Archives et de Documentation (CRAD)
731 Place Fontaine de l'Union, N'Djamena
Tel: 514 671 *Fax:* 516 079
Telex: 524 SKD UNESCO *Cable:* VNESCO NDJAMENA
Key Personnel
Chief of Center, Librarian: Ngaryaka Neldjita
Contact: Haroun Said
Publication(s): COMNAT

CRAD, see Centre de Recherche des Archives et de Documentation (CRAD)

Chile

Biblioteca del Congreso Nacional
Huerfanos 1117, 2° Piso, Santiago
Tel: (02) 2701700 *Fax:* (02) 2701766
Web Site: www.bcn.cl
Key Personnel
Dir: Soledad Ferreiro Serrano *E-mail:* sferreiro@bcn.cl
Library of Congress.
Publication(s): Boletin Informativo; Estudios; Serie Estudios; Temas de Actualidad (triannually)
Branch Office(s)
3° y 4° piso del Edificio del Congreso Nacional, Valparaiso *Tel:* (032) 263100

Biblioteca Nacional de Chile
Ave Libertador B O'Higgins 651, Santiago
Mailing Address: Clasificador 1400, Santiago
Tel: (02) 3605200; (02) 3605239; (02) 3605275 *Fax:* (02) 6380461; (02) 6381975; (02) 6321091; (02) 6381151
E-mail: bndir@bndechile.cl; subdir@bndechile.cl; ximena@bndechile.cl
Web Site: www.dibam.renib.cl
Key Personnel
Dir: Gonzalo Catalan Bertoni
National Library of the Office of Libraries, Archives & Museums.
Publication(s): Bibliografia chilena (formerly 'Anuario de la Prensa', 1982); *Referencias Criticas sobre Autores Chilenos* (annually, 1988)

Pontificia Universidad Catolica de Chile Sistema de Bibliotecas
Avda Vicuna Mackenna 4860, Santiago
Tel: (02) 6864616; (02) 6864762 *Fax:* (02) 6865852
Web Site: www.puc.cl
Key Personnel
Dir: Maria Luisa Arenas Franco

Biblioteca de la Universidad Catolica de Valparaiso
Ave Brasil 2950, Casilla 4059, Valparaiso
Tel: (032) 273261; (032) 273000 *Fax:* (032) 273183
Web Site: biblioteca.ucv.cl
Telex: 230389 Ucv
Key Personnel
Dir: Atilio Bustos Gonzalez *E-mail:* abustos@ucu.cl

Biblioteca Central de la Universidad de Chile
Av Diagonal Paraguay No 265 of 703, Santiago
Tel: (02) 6782583 *Fax:* (02) 6782574
E-mail: sisib@uchile.cl
Web Site: www.uchile.cl/bibliotecas
Key Personnel
Dir: Alamiro de Avila Martel
Founded: 1936

Universidad de Concepcion Direccion de Bibliotecas
Edificio Eula, Centro Eula, 2° Piso, Concepcion
Tel: (041) 20 41 15; (041) 20 43 93 *Fax:* (041) 24 60 76
E-mail: info@udec.cl
Web Site: www.bib.udec.cl
Key Personnel
Dir: Maria Nieves Alsonso Martinez

Universidad Technologica Metropolitana (UTEM), Sistema de Bibliotecas
Avda Jose Pedro Alessandri 1242-Nunoa, Santiago
Tel: (02) 272-40-32
Web Site: www.bibliotecautem.cl
Key Personnel
Dir: Ximena Sanchez *E-mail:* xsanchez@bibliotecautem.cl
Founded: 1989
Academic text in Humanities, Social Sciences, Pure & Applied Sciences.

China

Chongqing Library
11 First Section Changjiang Rd, Chongqing
Tel: (023) 6362-2596 *Fax:* (023) 6385-1474
Web Site: www.cqlib.org
Key Personnel
Dir: Shao Kangqing *E-mail:* skqcq@21cn.com
Founded: 1947

Dalian University of Technology Library
Linggong Rd 2, Ganjingzi District, Dalian City, Liaoning Province 116024
Tel: (0411) 84708620 *Fax:* (0411) 84708620; (0411) 84708626
E-mail: lib@dlut.edu.cn; libaqui4@dlut.edu.cn
Web Site: www.lib.dlut.edu.cn
Telex: 86231 DUTCN *Cable:* 7108
Key Personnel
Dir: Prof Liu Yuanfang
Founded: 1950
Publication(s): Chinese Journal of Computational Mechanics (bimonthly, periodical, 1984); *Journal of Dalian University of Technology* (bimonthly, periodical, 1950); *Journal of Mathematical Research & Exposition* (quarterly, periodical, 1981)

Fudan University Library
220 Han Dan Rd, Shanghai 200433
Tel: (021) 65642222; (021) 65643168 *Fax:* (021) 65649814
E-mail: libref@fudan.edu.cn
Web Site: www.library.fudan.edu.cn; www.fudan.edu.cn/english/index_en.html
Key Personnel
Professor: Xu Peng; Qin Zeng-Fu
Publication(s): Mathematical Analysis (Lectures on Higher Mathematics)

Liaoning Provincial Library
111 Wan Liu Tang Dong Ling, Shenyang, Liaoning Province
Tel: (024) 2482-2241
Web Site: www.lnlib.com
Founded: 1948

Library of Chinese Academy of Sciences
33 Beisihuan Xilu, Haidan Dist, Beijing 100080
Tel: (010) 82626684; (010) 82626611-6720 *Fax:* (010) 62566846
E-mail: office@mail.las.ac.cn; information@mail.las.ac.cn
Web Site: www.las.ac.cn
Telex: 83020
Key Personnel
Dir: Xu Yinchi
Membership(s): IFLA

Nanjing tushuguan (Nanjing Library)
66 Chengxian St, Nanjing, 210018 Jiangsu Province
Tel: (025) 83372163 *Fax:* (025) 83372163
E-mail: ntbgs@sina.com
Web Site: www.jslib.org.cn
Key Personnel
Executive Dir: Ma Ning *Tel:* (025) 83361845
Deputy Dir: Gong Aidong *Tel:* (025) 83617705; Yuan Dazhi *Tel:* (025) 84543649; Xu Jianye
Founded: 1907
Membership(s): IFLA; China Society for Library Science.
Publication(s): *Xin Shiji Tushuguan* (New Century Library, bimonthly, 2002, Co-sponser: Jiangsu Society for Library Science)

The National Library of China
33, Zhongguancun Nandajie, Haidian District, Beijing 100081
Tel: (010) 68415566 *Fax:* (010) 68419271
E-mail: webmaster@publicf.nlc.gov.cn
Web Site: www.nlc.gov.cn
Telex: 222211 NLC CN *Cable:* 0848
Key Personnel
Dir: Ren Jiyu
Founded: 1916
Zhongguo guojia tushuguan; formerly National Library of Beijing, Beijing Library, Peking Library, National Library of Peking, etc.
Publication(s): *Chinese Classification - A System Used in Chinese Libraries*; *Documentation* (series); *Journal of The National Library of China*; *The National Catalogue of Foreign Periodicals*

Peking University Library
Haidian District, Beijing 100871
Tel: (010) 62751051; (010) 62757223 *Fax:* (010) 62761008
E-mail: zxh@lib.pku.edu.cn
Web Site: www.lib.pku.edu.cn
Key Personnel
Dir: Prof Longji Dai *Tel:* (010) 62753503
E-mail: dailj@lib.pku.edu.cn
Founded: 1902

Qinghua daxue tushuguan (Qinghua University Library)
Tsinghua University Library, Beijing 100084
Tel: (010) 62782137 *Fax:* (010) 62781758
E-mail: tsg@mail.lib.tsinghua.edu.cn
Web Site: www.lib.tsinghua.edu.cn
Telex: 22617
Key Personnel
Dir: Xue Fangyu *Tel:* (010) 62771838
Founded: 1912

Library of the Renmin University of China
175 Haidian Rd, Beijing 100872
Tel: (010) 62511014 *Fax:* (010) 62515263; (010) 62515336
E-mail: rmdxxb@mail.ruc.edu.cn; leader@mail.ruc.edu.cn
Web Site: www.ruc.edu.cn
Key Personnel
Contact: Yang Dongliag *E-mail:* yangpj@sun.ihep.ac.cn
Founded: 1937

Shanghai Academy of Social Sciences Library
1610 Zhongshan W Rd, Shanghai
Tel: (021) 6486 2266 (ext 1305) *Fax:* (021) 6427 6018
E-mail: tsg@sass.stc.sh.cn
Web Site: www.sass.stc.sh.cn *Cable:* 7306
Key Personnel
Dir: Xie-Jun Chen
Librarian: Ms Zhang Jianfen

Shanghai tushuguan (Shanghai Library)
1555 Huai Hai Zhong Lu, Shanghai 200031
Tel: (021) 64455555 *Fax:* (021) 64455001
Web Site: www.libnet.sh.cn
Key Personnel
Dir: Shu Qing Zho
Hon Dir: Gu Ting-long

Xiamen University Library
422 Siming Rd S, Xiamen, Fujian 361005
Tel: (0592) 2085102 *Fax:* (0592) 2182360
E-mail: xiaodh@xmu.edu.cn
Web Site: www.xmu.edu.cn
Key Personnel
Chief Librarian: Dr Mingguang Chen
Founded: 1921
Specialize in book borrowing & reading, document, information services.

Yunnan Provincial Library
141 Cuihu Nan Rd, Kunming, Yunnan 650091
Tel: (0871) 532 2035; (0871) 532 3851
Web Site: www.ynu.edu.cn
Key Personnel
Dir: Wu Rui

ZheJiang Provincial Library
38 Shuguang Rd, Hangzhou, Zhejiang 310007
Tel: (0571) 799-9812 *Fax:* (0571) 7046263
Key Personnel
Chief Officer: Wang Xiaoliang
Chekiang Library, Hangchow.

Zhongguo guojia tushuguan, see The National Library of China

Zhongshan Library of Guangdong Province
213 Wenming Rd, Guangzhou, Guangdong Province 510110
Tel: (020) 83830676; (020) 83810164
E-mail: zxtxgwyh@163.net
Web Site: www.zslib.com.cn
Key Personnel
Dir: Huang Jungui
Also 81 Wende Rd, Guangdong (Canton) Tel: (020) 330349.

Colombia

Biblioteca Luis Angel Arango Banco de la Republica (Luis Angel Arango Library-Central Bank of Colombia)
Calle 11, No 4-14, Bogota
Mailing Address: CP 12362, Bogota
Tel: (01) 3431212 *Fax:* (01) 2863551
E-mail: wbiblio@banrep.gov.co
Web Site: www.banrep.gov.co *Cable:* REDESBANCO BIBLIOTECA
Key Personnel
Dir: Jorge Orlando Melo *E-mail:* jmelogo@banrep.gov.co
Publication(s): *Boletin Cultural y Bibliografico* (quarterly); *Estudios sobre Politica Economica* (biannually)

Archivo General de la Nacion de Colombia
Calle 24, 5-60, Bogota
Tel: (01) 2431336 *Fax:* (01) 3414030
E-mail: bnc@mincultura.gov.co
Web Site: www.bibliotecanacional.gov.co
Key Personnel
Dir: Lina Espitaleta *Tel:* (01) 3414029
E-mail: direccion.binal@mincultura.gov.co
National Archives.

BAC, see Biblioteca Agropecuaria de Colombia (BAC)

Biblioteca Agropecuaria de Colombia (BAC)
Centro de Investigacion Tibaitato, KM-14 via a Mosquera, Cundinamarca
Mailing Address: Apdo Aereo 240142, las Palmas, Bogata DC
Tel: (01) 4227373 (ext 1254) *Fax:* (01) 2813088
E-mail: bac@corpoica.org.co
Web Site: www.corpoica.org.co
Key Personnel
Dir: Francisco Salazar Alonso
Farming & Livestock Library of Colombia.
Parent Company: Corpoica-Corporacion Colombiana de Investigacion Agropecuaria

Biblioteca Nacional de Colombia
Calle 24 No 5-60, Bogota
Tel: (01) 2431336 *Fax:* (01) 3414030
E-mail: bnc@mincultura.gov.co
Web Site: www.bibliotecanacional.gov.co
Key Personnel
Dir: Lina Espitaleta *Tel:* (01) 3414029
E-mail: direccion.binal@mincultura.gov.co
Founded: 1777
Publication(s): *Revista Senderos*

British Council Library
Calle 87 No 12-79, Bogota
Tel: (01) 618 0118; (01) 618 7680 *Fax:* (01) 218 7754
E-mail: brit.council@bc-bogota.bcouncil.org; info@britishcouncil.org.co
Web Site: www.britishcouncil.org/colombia/
Telex: 45715 Bcoun
Key Personnel
Librarian: Maria Clemencia de Bohorquez
Dir: Joe Docherty

Centro de Estudios sobre Desarrollo Economico CEDE
Cra 1 E No 18A-1 0, Bogota
Tel: (01) 2849911; (01) 2824800 (ext 2461 & 2466) *Fax:* (01) 2841890
E-mail: cede@uniandes.edu.co
Web Site: wwwprof.uniandes.edu.co
Telex: 42343 Unand
Key Personnel
Coordinator: Miguel Angel Guerrero
E-mail: miguerre@uniandes.edu.co
Centre for Studies on Economic Development.

Pontificia Universidad Javeriana, Biblioteca General
Carrera 7 No 41-00, Bogota
Tel: (01) 320 8320 (ext 2135); (01) 320 8320 (ext 2150); (01) 320 8320 (ext 2151) *Fax:* (01) 320 8320 (ext 2131)
E-mail: biblioteca@javeriana.edu.co
Web Site: www.javeriana.edu.co
Key Personnel
Dir: Luz Maria Carbarcas Santoya

Universidad de los Andes, Biblioteca General, Ramon de Zubiria
10 Edificio Franco, Bloque G AA, Cra 1 Este No 18 A, 4976 Bogota
Tel: (01) 3394999; (01) 3394949 *Fax:* (01) 3324472
E-mail: sisbibli@uniandes.edu.co
Web Site: biblioteca.uniandes.edu.co
Telex: 42343
Key Personnel
Librarian: Angela Maria Mejia de Gutierrez
Tel: (01) 3394949 (ext 2147) *E-mail:* amejia@uniandes.edu.co

Universidad de Antioquia, Escuela Interamericana de Bibliotecologia, Biblioteca
Calle 67, No 53-108, Ciudad Universitaria Bloque 12, Of 324, 1226 Medellin
Tel: (04) 210 59 41 *Fax:* (04) 210 59 46
E-mail: bibeib@caribe.udea.edu.co
Web Site: caribe.udea.edu.co/~bibeib/principal.htm
Key Personnel
Dir: Carlos A Cadavid
Memberships: FID; ALA; AIBDA; IFLA; SALALM; Asociacion Latinoamericana de Archivos; The Library Association; ACURIL.
Publication(s): *Bibliografia Bibliotecologica*; *Bibliografica y de Obras de Referencia Colombianas* (Bibliography of Library Science, Bibliography and Colombian Works of Reference)

Universidad de los Andes, Centro de Estudios sobre Desarrollo Economico (CEDE), see Centro de Estudios sobre Desarrollo Economico CEDE

Universidad Externado de Colombia Biblioteca
Calle 12 N° 1-17 Este, Bogota
Tel: (01) 3420288; (01) 3419900 (ext 3350); (01) 3419900 (ext 3351)
E-mail: biblioteca@uexternado.edu.co
Web Site: www.uexternado.edu.co/biblioteca/
Key Personnel
Dir: Conrado Zuluaga Osorio *E-mail:* czuluaga@uexternado.edu.co

Universidad Nacional de Colombia, Biblioteca Central
Ciudad Universitaria, Cra 30, Calle 45, Bogota
Tel: (01) 2691743
E-mail: refer@biblioteca.campus.unal.edu.co
Web Site: www.unal.edu.co
Key Personnel
Dir: Jorge Aurelio Diaz

Congo

Bibliotheque Universitaire, Universite Marien Ngouabi
BP 69, Brazzaville
Tel: 814207; 812436 *Fax:* 814207
E-mail: unmgbuco@congonet.cg
Telex: 5331 KG
Key Personnel
Dir: F Wellot Samba
Librarian: Innocent Mabiala
Publication(s): *Annales*; *Dimi*; *Repertoire d'auteurs congolais*; *Revue d'histoire anthropologie* (Also other lists & catalogs)

Centre Culturel Francais, Bibliotheque
BP 2141, Brazzaville
Tel: 83 25 65 *Fax:* 83 06 18
Key Personnel
Contact: Andre Malraux

Bibliotheque Nationale Populaire
PB 1489, Brazzaville
Tel: 833485
Key Personnel
Dir: Pierre Mayola
Publication(s): *Repertorie bibliographique nationale*

The Democratic Republic of the Congo

Archives Nationales
42a Ave de la Justice, Kinshasa-Gombe
Mailing Address: BP 3428, Kinshasa-Gombe
Tel: (012) 31 083
Key Personnel
Librarian: Kiobe Lumenga-Neso
Founded: 1953
Publication(s): *Kinshasa. Genese et Sites Historiques* (Arnaza-Bief 1995)

Bibliotheque Centrale, Universite de Kinshasa
BP 190, Kinshasa 11
Tel: (012) 21361; (012) 21362 (ext 320)
E-mail: centreinfo@ic.cd
Web Site: unikin.sciences.free.fr
Publication(s): *Annales de la Bibliotheque Centrile de Kinshasa*

Bibliotheque Publique de Kinshasa
10 bd Tshatshi, BP 410, Kinshasa
Tel: (012) 3070
Key Personnel
Librarian: B Mongu

Institut Pedagogique National
BP 8815, Kinshasa-Binza
Tel: (012) 80573

Institut pour la Recherche Scientifique en Afrique Centrale (IRSAC)
Bibliotheque Centrale, Bukavu
Key Personnel
Chief Librarian: Mburunge Murhagane

IRSAC, see Institut pour la Recherche Scientifique en Afrique Centrale (IRSAC)

Universite de Kisangani Bibliotheque Centrale
Campus de Kisangani, BP 2012, Kisangani
Tel: 215-2
Key Personnel
Chief Librarian: Muzila Label Kakes

Bibliotheque Centrale de l'Universite de Lubumbashi
BP 1825, Lubumbashi, Katanga
Tel: (022) 22-5285
E-mail: unilu@unilu.net
Web Site: www.unilu.net
Key Personnel
Librarian: Mubadi Sule Mwanansuka

Costa Rica

Biblioteca Nacional
Calle 15-17, Av 3 y 3b, San Jose
Mailing Address: Apdo 10008-1000, San Jose
Tel: 233 1706; 221 2436; 221 2479 *Fax:* 223 5510
Telex: 3334 Dider
Key Personnel
Dir: Guadalupe Rodriguez
Contact: Marco A Chacon Monge
Publication(s): *Catalogo Nacional ISBN*; *Indice de Diarios y Semanarios de Costa Rica* (Catalog of Costa Rican Daily & Weekly Newspapers); *Indice de Revistas Nacionales* (Catalog of National Periodicals)

Biblioteca Mark Twain, Centro Cultural Costarricense-Norteamericano
Apdo 1489-1000, San Jose
Tel: 207-7574; 207-7577 Toll Free *Tel:* 800-207-7500 *Fax:* 224-1480
E-mail: info@cccncr.com
Web Site: www.cccncr.com
Key Personnel
Librarian: Guisella Ruiz

Universidad de Costa Rica Sistema de Bibliotecas, Documentacion e Informacion
Ciudad Universitaria Rodrigo Facio, Apdo 2060, San Jose
Tel: 253-6152; 207-5316; 207-4461 *Fax:* 204-2809
E-mail: marqueda@sibdi.bldt.ucr.ac.cr
Web Site: sibdi.bldt.ucr.ac.cr/sibdi.htm
Telex: UNICORI 2544
Key Personnel
Dir: Maria E Briceno Meza *Tel:* 207-5316 *E-mail:* mbriceno@sibdi.bldt.ucr.ac.cr; Maria Julia Vargas *Tel:* 207-4208 *E-mail:* mjvargas@sibdi.bldt.ucr.ac.cr
Publication(s): *Agronomia Costarricense* (biannually); *Annario del Cooperativismo en Costa Rica*; *Anuario de Estudios Centroamericanos* (annually); *Ciencia Y Tecnologia* (biannually); *Ciencias Economicas* (biannually); *Ciencias Matematicas* (biannually); *Educacion* (biannually); *Escena: Revista Teatral* (biannually); *Herencia* (biannually); *Ingenieria* (biannually); *Kanina: Revista de Artes Y Letras* (biannually); *Revista de Biologia Tropical* (biannually); *Revista de Filologia Y Linguistica* (biannually); *Revista de Filosofia* (biannually); *Revista de Historia* (biannually); *Revista Geologica de America Central* (biannually); *Revistas de Ciencias Sociales* (quarterly)

Cote d'Ivoire

Archives Nationales de Cote d'Ivoire
BP V126, Abidjan
Tel: 32 41 58 *Fax:* 21 50 13
Telex: 22296
Key Personnel
Dir: Missa Kouassi
Founded: 1957

Bibliotheque Centrale de la Cote d'Ivoire
BPV 6243, Abidjan-Treichville
Tel: 323872
Key Personnel
Librarian: P Zelli Any-Grah
Founded: 1963

Bibliotheque de l'Universite Nationale de Cote d'Ivoire
BP 859, 08 Abidjan
Tel: 439 000 *Fax:* 44 35 31
Telex: 3469
Key Personnel
Dir: Bakary Toure
Librarian: Francoise N'Goran
Founded: 1963
Publication(s): *Annales de l'Universite d'Abidjan*

Bibliotheque Municipale
BP 24, Plateau, Abidjan

COTE D'IVOIRE

Bibliotheque Nationale
BPV 180, Abidjan
Tel: 32 38 72
Key Personnel
Librarian: Ambroise Agnero
Publication(s): *Bibliographie de la Cote-d'Ivoire*

Centre Culturel Francais, Bibliotheque
01 BP 3995, 01 Abidjan
Tel: (020) 211699; (020) 225628 *Fax:* 227132
E-mail: ccf@netafric.ci
Telex: 22465 Miscop Ci
Key Personnel
Dir: Jean-Marc Fratani
Dir Adjoint: Jean-Michael Neher

INADES (Institut Africain pour le Developpment Economique et Social)
15 av Jean Jaures, Abidjan 08
Mailing Address: BP 2088, Abidjan 08
Tel: 22404720 *Fax:* 22448438
E-mail: inades@ci.refer.org; inades@africaonline.co.ci
Web Site: www.inades.ci.refer.org
Key Personnel
Dir: Michel Lambotte
Librarian: Nicole Vial
Publication(s): *COURRIER* (trimonthly); *Manuels de Bibliotheconomic* (quarterly)

Croatia

Nacionalna i Sveucilisna Knjiznica Biblioteka
(National & University Library)
Ulica Hrvatske bratske zajednice 4, 10000 Zagreb
Tel: (01) 61 64 111 *Fax:* (01) 61 64 186
E-mail: nsk@nsk.hr
Web Site: www.nsk.hr
Key Personnel
Contact: Prof Dubravka Fiala *E-mail:* dfiala@nsk.hr
Publication(s): *Bibliografija knjiga tiskanih u SR Hrvatskoj; Bibliografija rasprava, clanaka i knjizevnih radova u casopisima SR Hrvatske; Grada za hrvatsku retrospektivnu bibliografiju*

Cuba

Archivo Nacional de Cuba
Compostela 906, Esquina San Isidro Habana Vieja, Havana 10100
Tel: (07) 862 9436; (07) 636 489 *Fax:* (07) 33 8089
E-mail: arnac@ceniainf.cu
Key Personnel
Dir Dra: Berarda Salabarra Abraham

Biblioteca Central de la Universidad de Oriente
Ave Patricio Lumumba, Santiago 90 500
Tel: (022) 633013 *Fax:* (022) 633011
E-mail: marcosc@rect.uo.edu.cu
Web Site: www.uo.edu.cu
Key Personnel
Librarian: Maura Gonzalez

Biblioteca del Instituto Pre-Universitario de la Habana
Zulueta y San Jose, Havana
Key Personnel
Dir: Jose Manuel
Library of the Pre-University Institute of Education.

Biblioteca Historica Cubana y Americana
Municipio de la Habana, Oficina del Historiador de la Ciudad, Havana
Cuban & American Historical Library.

Biblioteca Nacional Jose Marti (Jose Marti National Library)
Apdo 6881, Havana
Tel: (07) 81 6224 *Fax:* (07) 33 5072
Telex: 511963 Bnjm
Key Personnel
Dir: Eliades Ignacio Acosta Matos
E-mail: eliadesa@jm.lib.cult.cu
Publication(s): *Bibliografia Cubana; Bibliografias Especializadas; Boletines Bibliograficas e Informacion Senal; Documentos Extranjeros Adquiridos; Ediciones Especializadas sobre la Cultura y el Arte; Indice General de Publicaciones Periodicas Cubanas; Revista de la Biblioteca Nacional Jose Marti*
Branch Office(s)
Ninguna

Biblioteca Jose Antonio Echeverria
Casa de las Americas, 3a y G, El Vedado, Havana 10400
Tel: (07) 3235 8789 *Fax:* (07) 334 554
E-mail: casa@tinored cu
Telex: 511019
Key Personnel
Dir: Ernest Sierra
Founded: 1959
Specialize in Latin-American Literature, History & Sociology.

IDICT, see Instituto de Informacion Cientifica y Tecnologica (IDICT)

Instituto de Informacion Cientifica y Tecnologica (IDICT)
Dept Comercial y de Marketing, Capitolio de la Habana, Prado Centre Dragones y San Jose, La Habana Vieja, Havana 10200
Mailing Address: Apdo 2213, La Habana Vieja, Havana 10200
Tel: (07) 862-6531; (07) 860-3411 *Fax:* (07) 862-6531
E-mail: andresdt@idict.cu; commercial@idict.cu
Web Site: www.idict.cu/
Telex: 511203 *Cable:* 62-6501 IDICT CU
Key Personnel
Gen Dir: Nicolas Garriga Mendez
E-mail: garriga@ceniai.inf.cu
Dir: Jesus Martinez; Luis A Mourelos; Eduardo Orozco; Gloria Ponjuan
Publication(s): *Cubaciencia; Directorio Biomundi*
Branch Office(s)
Biblioteca Nacional de Ciencia y Tecnica (BNCT)
Centro de Estudios y Desarollo Profesional en Ciencias de la Informacion (PROINFO)
Centro de Intercambio Automatizado (CENIAI)
Consultoria en Biotecnologia e Industria Medico-Farmaceutica (BIOMUNDI)

Instituto de Literatura y Lingueistica
Av Salvador Allende 710, Havana 3
Tel: (07) 75 485 *Fax:* (07) 338054; (07) 331325
E-mail: acc@ceniai.cu
Web Site: www3.cuba.cu/ciencia/acc/
Telex: 511290 acdcp cu
Key Personnel
Dir: Yolanda Ricardo Garcell
Vice Dir: Nuria Gregori Torada
Librarian: Pedro Luis Suarez Sola

Biblioteca Manuel Sanguily
Cuchillo de Zanja 19, Primer Piso entre Rayo y San Nichlas, Centro, Havana
Tel: (07) 63 3232
Key Personnel
Dir: Estrella Garcia

Biblioteca Central Ruben Martinez Villena, see Universidad de la Habana, Direccion de Informacion Cientifico Tecnica

UCLV, see Biblioteca General de la Universidad Central "Marta Abreu" de las Villas (UCLV)

Biblioteca General de la Universidad Central "Marta Abreu" de las Villas (UCLV)
(Central Library of Central Marta Abreu University of Las Villas)
Carretera de Camajuani, Km 5 5, Santa Clara, Villa Clara 54830
Tel: (0422) 81410; (0422) 81618; (0422) 8178
Fax: (0422) 81608; (0422) 22113
E-mail: luishs@dri.uclv.edu.cu
Key Personnel
Lib Inquiries: Jose Rivero Diaz
Founded: 1959
Subdivided into small branches for technical & social matters regarding careers studied in the University. Specific reference (eg cybernetics, economics, etc).

Universidad de la Habana, Direccion de Informacion Cientifico Tecnica
L y San Lazaro, Vedado, Havana
Tel: (07) 78-3231 *Fax:* (07) 33-5774
Telex: 0512210 Dict Uh
Key Personnel
Dir: Dr Maria Christina Santos *E-mail:* cristina@dict.uh.cu

Cyprus

The Library of the Archbishop Makarios III Foundation
Archbishopric, Archbishop Kyprianos Sq, 1505 Nicosia
Tel: (022) 430008 *Fax:* (022) 346753
Key Personnel
Dir: Dr Maria Stavrou

British Council Library
3 Museum St, 1097 Nicosia
Mailing Address: PO Box 25654, 1387 Nicosia
Tel: (022) 585000 *Fax:* (022) 677257
E-mail: enquiries@britishcouncil.org.cy
Web Site: www.britcoun.org/cyprus
Telex: 3911 Briconic
Key Personnel
Deputy Librarian: Joan Georghallides
Founded: 1940

Cyprus Library
Eleftherias Sq, 1011 Nicosia
Tel: (022) 303180; (022) 676118 *Fax:* (022) 304532
E-mail: cypruslibrary@cytanet.com.cy
Web Site: portico.bl.uk
Key Personnel
Librarian: Dr Antonis Maratheftis
E-mail: amaratheftis@hotmail.com
Founded: 1927
Membership(s): Conference of European National Librarians (CENL); IFLA.
Publication(s): *Cyprus Bibliography* (annually, 1999)
Parent Company: Ministry of Education & Culture

Library of the Cyprus Museum - Dept of Antiquities
Mouseiou 1, 1516 Lefkosia
Mailing Address: PO Box 22024, 1516 Lefkosia

Tel: (022) 865864; (022) 865888 *Fax:* (022) 303148
E-mail: roctarch@cytanet.com.cy
Key Personnel
Librarian: Maria Economidou
Founded: 1934

Municipal Library
PO Box 41, Famagusta
Key Personnel
Chief Librarian: Ch Christofides

Library of the Padagogic Institute Academia (College of Education)
c/o Ministry of Education, Tah Case 12720, 2252 Nicosia
Tel: (022) 402-300 *Fax:* (022) 480-505
E-mail: webmaster@cyearn.pi.ac.cy
Web Site: athena.pi.ac.cy/pedagogical/index.html
Key Personnel
Librarian: Soula Agdpiou; Maria Demetriou

Library of Phaneromeni, see The Library of the Archbishop Makarios III Foundation

Sultan's Library
Evcaf, Nicosia

Cyprus Turkish Public Library
Kizilay Ave, Nicosia
Tel: (022) 83257
Key Personnel
Chief Librarian: Fatma Oenen

Czech Republic

Knihovna Narodniho muzea (The National Museum Library)
Praha 1, Vaclavske namisti 68, 115 79 Prague
Tel: (02) 24497111 *Fax:* (02) 24497331
E-mail: nm@nm.cz
Web Site: www.nm.cz
Key Personnel
Dir: Helga Turkova, PhD *Tel:* (02) 24497343
 E-mail: helga.turkova@nm.cz
Publication(s): Sbornik Narodniho muzea, Rada C: literarni historie (Journal/Magazine of the National Museum Prague, series C: Literary History, annually, journal, 2003, summaries in English & German)

Mestska knihovna v Praze (The City Library in Prague)
Marianske Nam 1, 115 72 Prague 1
Tel: (02) 22113111 *Fax:* (02) 2328230
E-mail: informace@mlp.cz
Web Site: www.mlp.cz
Key Personnel
Dir: Tomas Rehak *E-mail:* reditel@mlp.cz

Moravska Zemska Knihovna (Moravian Library)
Kounicova 65a, 601 87 Brno
Tel: (05) 41646111 *Fax:* (05) 41646100
E-mail: mzk@mzk.cz
Web Site: www.mzk.cz
Key Personnel
Dir: Dr Jaromir Kubicek *Tel:* (05) 41646110
 E-mail: kubicek@mzk.cz
Founded: 1808

Narodni knihovna Ceske republiky (The National Library of the Czech Republic)
Klementinum 190, 110 01 Prague 1
Tel: (02) 21663111 *Fax:* (02) 21663267; (02) 21663277
E-mail: public.ur@nkp.cz
Web Site: www.nkp.cz
Key Personnel
Dir: Dr Vojtech Balik
Public Relations: Libuse Piherova, PhD
 E-mail: libuse.piherova@nkp.cz
Founded: 1777
Publication(s): Ceska narodni bibliografie Knihy (The Czech National Bibliography-Books, annually); Narodni bibliografie Ceske republiky, Hudebniny (The National Bibliography of the Czech Republic-Music, quarterly, Czech Music); Narodni Knihovna (National Library, quarterly)
Parent Company: The Ministry of Culture of the Czech Republic

Pamatnik narodniho pisemnictvi (Museum of Czech Literature)
Division of Ministry of Culture, Czech Rep
Strahovske nadvori 1/132, 118 38 Prague 1
Tel: (02) 20516695 *Fax:* (02) 20517277
E-mail: post@pamatniknarodnihopisemnictvi.cz
Web Site: www.pamatniknarodnihopisemnictvi.cz
Key Personnel
Dir: Dr Eva Wolfova *E-mail:* wolfova@pamatniknarodnihopisemnictvi.cz
Membership(s): ICOM.
Publication(s): Literarni Archiv-Almanac (annually)

Parlamentni Knihovna (Parliamentary Library)
Division of Office of the Chamber of Deputies
Snimovni 4, 118 26 Prague 1
Tel: (02) 57534 409 *Fax:* (02) 57534 408
E-mail: posta@psp.cz
Web Site: www.psp.cz
Key Personnel
Director: Dr Karel Sosna *E-mail:* sosna@psp.cz
Founded: 1857
Membership(s): IFLA; ECPRD.
Parent Company: Chamber of Deputies of the Czech Parliament

Statni technicka knihovna (State Technical Library)
Marianske namesti 5, 110 01 Prague 1
Mailing Address: PO Box 206, 110 01 Prague 1
Tel: (02) 21 663 111 *Fax:* (02) 22 221 340
E-mail: techlib@stk.cz
Web Site: www.stk.cz
Key Personnel
Dir: Martin Svoboda *Tel:* (02) 21 663 402
 E-mail: m.svoboda@stk.cz
Contact: Dr Jan Bayer *Tel:* (02) 21 663 480
 E-mail: j.bayer@stk.cz

Vedecka knihovna V olomouci (Research Library in Olomouc)
Bezrueova 2, Olomouc 9 779 11
Tel: (068) 585223441 *Fax:* (068) 585225774
E-mail: info@vkol.cz
Web Site: www.vkol.cz
Key Personnel
Contact: Dr Marie Nadvornikova, PhD *Tel:* (068) 5222328
Founded: 1573

Vysoka skola banska - Technicka Univerzita Ostrava (VSB - Technical University of Ostrava)
17 listopadu 15, 708 33 Ostrava-Poruba
Tel: (069) 596 991 111 *Fax:* (069) 596 998 507
Web Site: www.vsb.cz
Key Personnel
University Librarian: Daniela Tkacikova
 E-mail: daniela.tkacikova@vsb.cz

Denmark

Aalborg Universitetsbibliotek (Aalborg University Library)
Langagervej 2, 9220 Aalborg
Mailing Address: Postboks 8200, 9220 Aalborg
Tel: 96359400 *Fax:* 98156859
E-mail: aub@aub.aau.dk
Web Site: www.aub.aau.dk
Key Personnel
Chief Librarian: Niels-Henrik Gylstorff
Information Coordinator: Karen Dissing
 Tel: 96359343 *E-mail:* kd@aub.aau.dk

Arhus Kommunes Biblioteker (Arhus Public Library)
Mollegade 1, 8000 Aarhus C
Tel: 8940 9200 *Fax:* 8940 9393
Web Site: www.aakb.dk
Key Personnel
Chief Librarian: Rolf Hapel

Biblioteksstyrelsen (Danish National Library Authority)
Nyhavn 31 E, 1051 Copenhagen K
Tel: 33733373 *Fax:* 33733372
E-mail: bs@bs.dk
Web Site: www.bs.dk
Key Personnel
Dir: Jens Thorhauge
Contact: Vibeke Cranfield *E-mail:* vhc@bs.dk
Government agency under the Danish Ministry of Culture.
Publication(s): Nyt fra Nyhavn (Quarterly, Info on library related matters)

Danmarks BlindeBibliotek (The Danish National Library for the Blind)
Teglvaerksgade 37, 2100 Copenhagen O
Tel: 39 13 46 00 *Fax:* 39 13 46 01
E-mail: dbb@dbb.dk
Web Site: www.dbb.dk
Key Personnel
Dir: Elsebeth Tank *E-mail:* eta@dbb.dk
Head of Distribution & Projects: Lisbeth Trinskjer
 E-mail: lmt@dbb.dk

Danmarks Natur-og Laegevidenskabelige Bibliotek, Universitet de sbiblioteket (The Danish National Library of Science & Medicine)
Norre Alle 49, 2200 Copenhagen N
Tel: 35396523 *Fax:* 35391939
E-mail: dnlb@dnlb.dk
Web Site: www.dnlb.dk
Key Personnel
Advisory Librarian: Torsten Schlichtkrull
 Tel: 353-25070 *E-mail:* ts@dnlb.dk
Head Librarian: Mette Stockmarr *Tel:* 353-25001
 E-mail: ms@dnlb.dk
Founded: 1482
The Danish National Library of Science & Medicine, Copenhagen University Library.
Publication(s): Acta Historica Scientiarum Naturalium et Medicinalium; Skrifter Udgivet of Danmarks Natur-og Laegevedenskabelige Bibliotek, Kobenhavns Universitets Bibiotek

Danmarks Paedagogiske Bibliotek (National Library of Education)
Emdrupvej 101, 2400 Copenhagen NV
Mailing Address: PO Box 840, 2400 Copenhagen NV
Tel: 8888 9300 *Fax:* 8888 9391
E-mail: dpb@dpu.dk
Web Site: www.dpb.dpu.dk/
Key Personnel
Dir: Soren Carlsen *E-mail:* sca@dpu.dk
Deputy Dir: Jakob Andersen *E-mail:* jak@dpu.dk

DENMARK

Danmarks Statistik Biblioteket (National Statistical Library)
Sejrogade 11, 2100 Copenhagen O
Tel: 3917 3917 *Fax:* 3917 3999
E-mail: dst@dst.dk
Web Site: www.dst.dk/bibliotek
Key Personnel
Librarian: Per Knudsen *Tel:* 3917 3001
  E-mail: pkn@dst.dk

Danmarks Tekniske Videncenter (DTV)
Anker Engelunds Vej 1, 2800 Lyngby
Mailing Address: PO Box 777, 2800 Lyngby
Tel: 4525 7200 *Fax:* 4588 3040
E-mail: dtv@dtv.dk
Web Site: www.dtv.dk
Key Personnel
Dir: Annette Winkel Schwarz *E-mail:* aws@dtv.dk
Technical Knowledge Center & Library of Denmark.

DBB, see Danmarks BlindeBibliotek

Frederiksberg Kommunes Biblioteker
(Frederiksberg Public Library)
Solbjergvej 21-25, 2000 Frederiksberg
Tel: 38211800 *Fax:* 38211799
E-mail: bib@fkb.dk
Web Site: www.fkb.dk
Telex: 16548 fkbib
Key Personnel
Chief Librarian: Anne Moeller-Rasmussen
  E-mail: anra03@frederiksberg.dk
Founded: 1887

Gentofte Bibliotekerne (Gentofte Municipal Library)
Ahlmanns Alle 6, 2900 Hellerup
Tel: 39487500 *Fax:* 39487507
E-mail: bibliotek@gentofte.bibnet.dk
Web Site: www.gentofte.bibnet.dk
Key Personnel
Chief Librarian: Laone Gladbo
Branch Office(s)
Dyssegard Branch Library, Dyssegardsvej 22, 2900 Hellerup *Tel:* 39 65 58 90
  E-mail: dyssegaardbibliotek@gentofte.bibnet.dk
Gentofte Branch Library, Gentoftegade 45, 2820 Gentofte *Tel:* 39 65 03 23
  E-mail: gentoftebibliotek@gentofte.bibnet.dk
Jaegersborg Branch Library, Smakkegardsvej 112, 2820 Gentofte *Tel:* 39 65 05 10
  E-mail: jaegersborgbibliotek@gentofte.bibnet.dk
Ordrup Branch Library, Ordrupvej 121, 2920 Charlottenlund *Tel:* 39 64 14 40
  E-mail: ordrupbibliotek@gentofte.bibnet.dk
Vangede Branch Library, Vangede Bygade 45, 2820 Gentofte *Tel:* 39 65 38 47
  E-mail: vangedebibliotek@gentofte.bibnet.dk

Kobenhavns Kommunes Biblioteker
(Copenhagen Municipal Libraries)
Islands Brygge 37, 2300 Copenhagen S
Tel: 33664650 *Fax:* 33667061
E-mail: kkb@kkb.bib.dk
Web Site: www.kkb.bib.dk/
Telex: 16648
Key Personnel
City Librarian: Jan Ostergaard Bertelsen
  E-mail: kkb@bibliotek.kk.dk
Publication(s): *Arsberetning* (annual report)

Kobenhavns Stadsarkiv (City Archives of Copenhagen)
Radhus, 1599 Copenhagen
Tel: 33662370 *Fax:* 33667039
E-mail: stadsarkiv@kff.kk.dk
Web Site: www.ksa.kk.dk

Key Personnel
Head Archivist: Henrik Gautier
Copenhagen City Archives.
Publication(s): *Historiske Meddelelser om Kobenhavn* (Historical Yearbook)

Det Kongelige Bibliotek
Soren Kierkegaards Plads, 1016 Copenhagen K
Mailing Address: Postbox 2149, 1016 Copenhagen K
Tel: 33 47 47 47 *Fax:* 33 93 22 18
E-mail: kb@kb.dk
Web Site: www.kb.dk
Key Personnel
Dir-General: Erland Kolding Nielsen
Acquisitions: Jette Hagen *E-mail:* jh@kb.dk
Founded: 1648
Publication(s): *Catalogue of Oriental Manuscript; Xylographs, etc in Danish Collections* (irregular, 1966); *Fund og Forskning i Det Kongelige Biblioteks Samlinger* (annually, 1961, Discovery & Research in the Collections in the Royal Library)
Branch Office(s)
The Royal Library Amager, Njalsgade 80
  Tel: 3347 4747 *Fax:* 3393 2218
The Royal Library Fiolstraede, Fiolstraede 1
  Tel: 3347 4747 *Fax:* 3393 2218

Det nordjyske Landsbibliotek
Hovedbiblioteket, Rendsburggade 2, 9100 Aalborg
Mailing Address: PO Box 839, 9100 Aalborg
Tel: 99 31 44 00 *Fax:* 99 31 44 33
E-mail: njl@njl.dk
Web Site: www.njl.dk
Key Personnel
Librarian: Kirsten Boel
Central Library for the County of North Jutland.

Odense Centralbibliotek (Odense County Library)
Ostre Stationsvej 15, 5000 Odense C
Tel: 66514301 *Fax:* 66137337
E-mail: tele@fynbib.dk
Web Site: www.odensebib.dk
Key Personnel
Chief Librarian: Lene Byrialsen

Odense Universitetsbibliotek (University Library of Southern Denmark)
Campusvej 55, 5230 Odens M
Tel: 6550 2644 *Fax:* 6550 2601
E-mail: sdub@bib.sdu.dk
Web Site: www.bib.sdu.dk
Key Personnel
Dir & Librarian: Aase Lindahl *Tel:* 6550 2683
  E-mail: lindahl@bib.sdu.dk

Rigsarkivet (Danish National Archives)
Rigsdagsgarden 9, 1218 Copenhagen K
Tel: 33923310 *Fax:* 33153239
E-mail: mailbox@ra.sa.dk
Web Site: www.sa.dk
Key Personnel
National Archivist: Johan Peter Noack
Secretary: Helle Gjellerup *Tel:* 33922336
  E-mail: hg@ra.sa.dk
Danish National Archives.
Publication(s): *Siden Saxo*

Roskilde University Library
Universitetsvej 1, 4000 Roskilde
Mailing Address: PO Box 258, 4000 Roskilde
Tel: 46742007 *Fax:* 46742233
E-mail: rub@ruc.dk
Web Site: www.rub.ruc.dk
Key Personnel
Dir: Niels Senius Clausen *Tel:* 46742235
  E-mail: nsc@ruc.dk
Founded: 1971

Statsbiblioteket (State & University Library, Aarhus)
Universitetsparken, 8000 Aarhus
Tel: 89462022 *Fax:* 89462220
E-mail: sb@statsbiblioteket.dk
Web Site: www.statsbiblioteket.dk
Key Personnel
Chief Executive: Svend Larsen
State & University Library.
Publication(s): *Avismikrofilm i Statsbiblioteket; Journalism, Media & Communication; Ongoing Research in Denmark, Finland, Norway & Sweden; Nordicom; Bibliography of Nordic Mass Communication Literature* (ISSN 0105-1385)

Dominican Republic

Biblioteca Dominicana (Dominican Library)
Chapel of the Dominican Order, Santo Domingo
Key Personnel
Dir: Jose Rijo
Founded: 1914

Biblioteca Nacional (National Library)
Cesar Nicolas Penson 91, Santo Domingo
Tel: 688-4086
E-mail: biblioteca.nacional@dominicana.com
Key Personnel
Dir: Roberto DeSoto
Founded: 1971

Biblioteca de la Camara Oficial de Comercio, Agricultura e Industria del Distrito Nacional
Noel 52-Altos, Apdo 815, Santo Domingo
Tel: 682-2688; 682-7206 *Fax:* 685-2228
Library of the Chamber of Commerce, Agriculture and Industry.

Universidad Nacional Pedro Henriquez Urena
Campus 2, Edificio 3, Autopista Duarte km 6 1/2, Santo Domingo
Tel: (0809) 542-6888 (ext 2301-2315, 2320 & 2321) *Fax:* (0809) 566-2206; (0809) 540-3803
E-mail: biblioteca@unphu.edu.do
Web Site: www.unphu.edu.do/unphu/biblioteca
Key Personnel
Librarian: Carmen Iris Olivo
Founded: 1966
Publication(s): *Revista Aula 2da Epoca y Campus; Revista de Ciencias Juridicas y Politicas*

Biblioteca Municipal de Santo Domingo
Padre Billini 18, Santo Domingo
Key Personnel
Librarian: Luz Del Carmen Rijo

Biblioteca de la Secretaria de Estado de Relaciones Exteriores
752 Independencia Ave, Santo Domingo
Tel: 535-6280 *Fax:* 508-6863; 533-5772
E-mail: cmedina018@hotmail.com
Web Site: www.serex.gov.do
Key Personnel
Dir: Dr Prospero J Mella Chavier
Library of the Secretariat of Foreign Affairs.

Biblioteca de la Universidad Autonoma de Santo Domingo
Av Alma Mater, Ciudad Universitaria, Santo Domingo
Tel: 533-1104 *Fax:* 508-7374
E-mail: rectoria.uasd@codetel.net.do

Web Site: www.uasd.edu.do
Key Personnel
Dir: Martha Maria DeCastro Cotes

Ecuador

Archivo Nacional de Historia (National Historical Archives)
Av 10 de Agosto N11-539 y Santa Prisca Casilla 17-12-878, Quito
Tel: (02) 2280431 *Fax:* (02) 2280431
E-mail: ane@ane.gov.ec
Web Site: www.ane.gov.ec
Key Personnel
Dir: Grecia Vasco de Escudero
Founded: 1938

Biblioteca Ecuatoriana Aurelio Espinosa Polit'
Apdo 17-01-160, Quito
Tel: (02) 491156; (02) 491157 *Fax:* (02) 493928
E-mail: beaep@uio.satnet.net
Web Site: www.biblioespinosapolit.org
Key Personnel
Dir: Rev Julian G Bravo
Founded: 1928
Publication(s): *Diccionaris Bibliografico Ecuatoriano* (Vols I, II, III & IV)

Biblioteca Nacional del Ecuador (National Library of Ecuador)
Casa de la Cultura Ecuatoriana Benjamin Carrion, 12 de Octobre 555, Patria, Quito
Mailing Address: Casilla 67, Quito
Tel: (02) 2528840 *Fax:* (02) 2223391
E-mail: benjamincarrion@andinanet.net
Key Personnel
Dir: Laura de Crespo

Biblioteca de la Casa de la Cultura Ecuatoriana, see Biblioteca Nacional Eugenio Espejo de la Casa de la Cultura Ecuatoriana

Biblioteca Nacional Eugenio Espejo de la Casa de la Cultura Ecuatoriana
Avs 12 de Octubre 555 y Patria, Quito
Mailing Address: Apdo 67, Quito
Tel: (02) 2528-840 *Fax:* (02) 2223-391
E-mail: info@cce.org.ec
Web Site: cce.org.ec
Key Personnel
Dir Lic: Ruth Garaicoa Soria
Founded: 1792
Library of Ecuadorian Culture.

Museo y Biblioteca Municipal
Ave 10 de Agosto entre Chile y Calle Pedro Carbo Palacio, Municipal Apdo 6069, Guayaquil
Tel: (04) 515738
Key Personnel
Dir: Patricia De Quevedo

Biblioteca de la Universidad Central de Ecuador
Av America y Av Universitaria, Quito
Tel: (02) 2234 722 *Fax:* (02) 2236 367; (02) 2521 925
Web Site: www.ucentral.edu.ec

Biblioteca General, Universidad de Guayaquil
Chile 900 y Av Olmedo, Guayaquil
Tel: 2282440 *Fax:* 2391010
E-mail: zd@ug.edu.ec
Web Site: www.ug.edu.ec

Telex: 3179
Key Personnel
Dir: Leonor Villao de Santander

Egypt (Arab Republic of Egypt)

Alexandria Municipal Library
18 Sharia Menasce Moharrem Beey, Alexandria
Key Personnel
Chief Librarian: Sheikh Beshir Beshir El Shindi

Alexandria University Library
22 El-Geish Ave, El-Shatby, Alexandria
Tel: (03) 5971675 *Fax:* (03) 5960720
E-mail: postmaster@alex.eun.eg
Web Site: www.alex.edu.eg
Telex: 54467
Key Personnel
Chief Librarian: Khalid El Ramady

American University in Cairo Library
113 Sharia Kasr El Aini, Cairo 11511
Mailing Address: PO Box 2511, Cairo 11511
Tel: (02) 797-6904 *Fax:* (02) 792-3824
E-mail: aucpress@aucegypt.edu
Web Site: library.aucegypt.edu
Telex: 92224 AUCAI UN EGYPT
Key Personnel
Dean, Libraries & Learning Technologies: Shahira El Sawy *Tel:* (02) 797-6901
  E-mail: selsawy@aucegypt.edu
Head, ILL/Document Delivery & Electronic Resource Services: Hoda El Ridi *Tel:* (02) 797-6365 *E-mail:* elridhi@aucegypt.edu

Al- Azhar University Library
El-Nasr Rd, Cairo
Tel: (02) 904051; (02) 706097; (02) 261 1419
Web Site: www.alazhar.org
Key Personnel
Librarian: M E A Hady

Egyptian National Library (Dar-ul-Kutub)
Sharia Corniche El-Nil, Bulaq, Cairo
Tel: (02) 900 232
Key Personnel
General Dir: Ali Abdul Mohsen
Founded: 1870

Ein Shams University Library
Abbasiyah 11566, Cairo
Tel: (02) 4820230; (02) 6831474; (02) 6831231; (02) 6831492; (02) 6831417; (02) 6831090
  Fax: (02) 687824
E-mail: info@asunet.shams.eun.eg
Web Site: asunet.shams.eun.eg
Key Personnel
Librarian: Nasr El Din Abdel Rahman

Institute of Arab Research & Studies Arab League Educational, Cultural & Scientific Organization Library
One Tolombat St, Garden City, Cairo
Mailing Address: PO Box 229, Cairo
Tel: (02) 3551648 *Fax:* (02) 3562543
Telex: 92642 Alcso *Cable:* IREALEA CAIRO
Key Personnel
President: Prof M S Abulezz, PhD
Dir: Prof Ahmed Youssef
Founded: 1953

Library of the People's Assembly
Majilis al-Shab St, Cairo
Mailing Address: PO Box 1183, Cairo
Tel: (02) 3540279 *Fax:* (02) 3548977
Telex: 20054 EGYAS UN

Ministry of Education Library
12 El Falaki St, Cairo
Tel: (02) 516 9744 *Fax:* (02) 516 9560
E-mail: telecom@gega.net
Web Site: www.emoe.org
Key Personnel
Dir: Hassen Abdel Shafi

Ministry of Justice Library
Midan Lazoghli, Cairo
Tel: (02) 20806 *Fax:* (02) 795 8103
E-mail: mojeb@idsc1.gov.eg
Key Personnel
Librarian: Fekry Abou-El-Kheir

National Archives
Al-Qalcah, Cairo

National Information & Documentation Centre (NIDOC)
Al Tahrir St, Dokki, Cairo
Tel: (02) 3371696
Key Personnel
Dir: Dr Mostaga Esmat El-Sarha
Publication(s): *Directory of Scientific & Technical Libraries*

NIDOC, see National Information & Documentation Centre (NIDOC)

University of Ain Shams Library, see Ein Shams University Library

University of Cairo Library
Gameet el Qahira Street, Giza, Cairo
Tel: (02) 5729584 *Fax:* (02) 628884
Key Personnel
General Dir: Fatina Ibrahim

El Salvador

Biblioteca Nacional
Calle Delgado y 8A Ave Norte, San Salvador
Mailing Address: Apdo 2455, San Salvador
Tel: 221-6312; 221-4373; 271-5661; 272-2886
  Fax: 221-8847; 221-4419
E-mail: dibiaes@es.com.sv
Key Personnel
Dir: Manilo Argueta *E-mail:* manilo_a@yahoo.es
National Dir, Promotion & Diffusion: Silvia Martinez *E-mail:* silviamartinez@salnet.net

Biblioteca P Florentino Idoate, SJ, see Biblioteca de la Universidad Centroamericana Jose Simeon Canas

Biblioteca de la Universidad Centroamericana Jose Simeon Canas
Blvd Los Proceres, San Salvador
Mailing Address: Apdo 01-168, San Salvador
Tel: 210-6600 (ext 278) *Fax:* 210-6657
E-mail: ucabib.director@bib.uca.edu.sv
Web Site: www.uca.edu.sv
Key Personnel
Dir: Katherine Miller *E-mail:* kmiller@bib.uca.edu.sv
Publication(s): *Estudios Centro Americanas (ECA)*

Biblioteca Central de la Universidad de El Salvador
Sistema Bibliotecario, Apdo 2923, San Salvador
Tel: 503 2250278 *Fax:* 503 2250278
E-mail: sb@biblio.ues.edu.sv
Web Site: www.ues.edu.sv/biblio.html
Key Personnel
Dir: Carlos R Colindres *E-mail:* carlos@biblio.ues.edu.sv
Publication(s): *Boletin* (monthly); *Lista de Acquisiciones Recientes* (monthly)

Eritrea

University of Asmara Library
PO Box 1220, Asmara
Tel: (01) 161926; (01) 162553 *Fax:* (01) 162236
E-mail: assefawa@uoa.edu.er
Web Site: www.uoa.edu.er
Telex: 42091 *Cable:* ASMUNIV
Key Personnel
Dir & Librarian: Assefaw Abraha
 E-mail: assefawa@lib.usa.edu.er
Ultimate Parent Company: Ministry of Education

Estonia

Eesti Rahvusraamatukogu (National Library of Estonia)
Tonismaegi 2, 15189 Tallinn
Tel: 630 7611
E-mail: nlib@nlib.ee
Web Site: www.nlib.ee
Key Personnel
Dir General: Tiiu Valm *Tel:* 630 7600
 E-mail: tiiu.valm@nlib.ee
Dir of Library: Ene Loddes *Tel:* 372 631
 E-mail: ene.loddes@nlib.ee
The National Library of Estonia is also the Parliamentary Library of Estonia; it is the central library in the field of humanities & art.
Publication(s): *Eesti Rahvusbibliograafia: Artiklid* (The Estonian National Bibliography: Articles from Serials); *Eesti Rahvusraamatukogu: Raamatud* (The Estonian National Bibliography: Books)

Tartu University Library (Tartu Ulikooli Raamatukogu)
One W Struve Str, 50091 Tartu
Tel: (07) 375 702 *Fax:* (07) 375 701
E-mail: library@utlib.ee
Web Site: www.utlib.ee
Key Personnel
Library Dir: Toomas Liivamagi *Tel:* (07) 375 700
 E-mail: toomas.liivamagi@ut.ee
Founded: 1802
Membership(s): European Information Association (EIA) & its branch for Baltic & Nordic Countries; European Association for Health Information & Libraries Association (EAHIL); Association of Libraries of the Baltic Sea Region *Bibliotheca Baltica*; International Association of Music Libraries, Archives & Documentation Centres (IAML); International Association of Law Libraries (IALL); League of European Research Libraries (LIBER); Consortium of Legal Resource Centres & Legal Information Specialists of Central & Eastern Europe & Asia (CLCLIS CEEA).
Publication(s): *Eksliibrised Tartu Ulikooli Raamatukogus* (Bookplates in Tartu University Library, irregular, 1975, Four publications to introduce the collection); *Publicationes Bibliothecae Universitatis Litterarum Tartuensis* (irregular, 1973, Introduces Tartu University Library collections of manuscripts); *Raamat-aegrestaureerimine* (Book-Time-Restoration, irregular, 1969); *Raamatukogu toeid* (Publications of Tartu University Libary. I-XI, 1968, Papers on the library); *Tartu (Riiklik) Uelikool* (Tartu State University, The Bibliography of Works Published, irregular, Records all the works published by university faculty & students); *Tartu Uelikooli Raamatukogu vanagraafika kogu kataloogid* (Tartu University Library collections of graphic art since 15th centruy, irregular, 1974, Nine publications about English, German, Flemish, Dutch, Italian & French works of graphic art); *Tartu Ulikooli Raamatukogu aastaraamat* (Tartu University Library Yearbook, regular, 1996, Contains annual report, list of donations & research articles)

Ethiopia

Addis Adaba University Library
PO Box 1176, Addis Adaba
Tel: (01) 115673; (01) 550844 *Fax:* (01) 550655
Telex: 21205 *Cable:* AAUNIV
Key Personnel
Librarian: Adhana Mengsteab
Founded: 1950

African Union Library
Roosvelt St (Old Airport Area), PO Box 3243, W21 K19 Addis Ababa
Tel: (01) 51 77 00 *Fax:* (01) 51 78 44
Web Site: www.africa-union.org
Telex: 21046 *Cable:* OAU
Key Personnel
Chief Librarian: Mrs J C Ranaivoravelo

Agricultural Institute Library
PO Box 307, Jimma
Tel: (07) 11-00-19
Key Personnel
Librarian: Goitom Ghebru

Alemaya University of Agriculture Library
PO Box 138, Dire Dawa
Tel: (05) 11-14-00 *Fax:* (05) 11-40-08
Key Personnel
Assistant Librarian: Tesfaye Salilew
Founded: 1952
Publication(s): *The Alemayan*

British Council Library
Artistic Bldg, Adwa Ave, Addis Ababa
Mailing Address: PO Box 1043, Addis Ababa
Tel: (01) 55 00 22 *Fax:* (01) 55 25 44
E-mail: bc.addisababa@et.britishcouncil.org
Web Site: www.britishcouncil.org/ethiopia/index.htm
Telex: 21561
Key Personnel
Assistant Dir Knowledge & Learning Services: Hailemelekot Taye *E-mail:* hailemelekot.taye@bc-addis.bcouncil.org
Specialize in provision of library & information services.

Institute of Ethiopian Studies Library
PO Box 1176, Addis Ababa
Tel: (01) 55-05-44 *Fax:* 55-26-88
E-mail: ies.aau@telecom.net.et
Web Site: www.abyssiniagateway.net
Telex: 21205 *Cable:* AA N IV
Key Personnel
Librarian: Degife Gabre Tsadik
Founded: 1963

Publication(s): *Ethiopian Publications* (annually); *List of Current Periodical Publications* (biannually)
Parent Company: Addis Ababa University

National Archives & Library of Ethiopia
PO Box 717, Addis Ababa
Tel: (01) 516532 *Fax:* (01) 526411
E-mail: nale@telecom.net.et
Web Site: www.nale.gov.et
Key Personnel
Librarian: Almaz Mengistu
Founded: 1944

United Nations Economic Commission for Africa Library
PO Box 3001, Addis Ababa
Tel: (01) 51 72 00 *Fax:* (01) 51 22 33; (01) 51 03 65
E-mail: ecaweb@uneca.org
Web Site: www.uneca.org
Telex: 21029 *Cable:* ECA ADDIS ABABA
Key Personnel
Librarian: Fathi S Daif
Founded: 1958
Publication(s): *Africa Index: Selected articles on socio-economic development* (quarterly)

Faroe Islands

Foroya Landsbokasavn (National Library of the Faroe Islands)
J C Svabosgotu 16, FO-110 Torshavn
Mailing Address: PO Box 61, FO-110 Torshavn
Tel: 31 16 26 *Fax:* 31 88 95
E-mail: utlan@flb.fo
Web Site: www.flb.fo
Key Personnel
National Librarian: Martin Naes
 E-mail: marnes@mail.dk
Founded: 1828
Publication(s): *The Faroese* (book list)

Standard Book Numbering Agency, see Foroya Landsbokasavn

Fiji

Library Service of Fiji
PO Box 2526, Suva
Tel: 315 344 *Fax:* 314 994
Key Personnel
Chief Librarian: Humesh Prasad
Senior Librarian: Shafig Gafoor
Parent Company: Ministry of Education
Branch Office(s)
Northern Regional Library, Labasa
Western Regional Library, PO Box 150, Lautoka

National Archives of Fiji
25 Carnarvon St, Suva
Mailing Address: PO Box 2125, Suva
Tel: 304 144; 304 228 *Fax:* 307 066
Web Site: www.fiji.gov *Cable:* ARCHIVIST
Key Personnel
Archivist: Setareki Turnaceva
Founded: 1958

Suva City Library
Victoria Parade, Suva
Mailing Address: PO Box 176, Suva
Tel: 313 433 *Fax:* 302 158 *Cable:* TOWN CLERK SUVA

Key Personnel
Chief Librarian: Ms Lalita Sudhakar Lal
Founded: 1909
Publication(s): *Suva City Council* (annual report)

University of the South Pacific Library
Suva
Tel: 3313 900 *Fax:* 3300 830
E-mail: library@usp.ac.fj
Web Site: www.usp.ac.fj/library
Key Personnel
Dir: Dr Esther Williams *Tel:* 321 2282
 E-mail: williams_e@usp.ac.fj
Founded: 1969
Coordination Unit for Pacific Islands Marine Resources Information System (PIMRIS), Regional Center for Population Information Network (POPIN).
Publication(s): *PIC Newsletter* (quarterly); *PIMRIS Newsletter* (quarterly); *South Pacific Periodicals Index*; *South Pacific Research Register* (biennially)

Finland

Abo Akademis bibliotek (Abo Akademi University Library)
Domkyrkogt 2-4, 20500 Abo
Tel: (02) 2154180 *Fax:* (02) 2154795
E-mail: hblan@abo.fi
Web Site: www.abo.fi/library
Key Personnel
Librarian: Tore Ahlback
Contact: Anders Ekberg *E-mail:* anders.ekberg@abo.fi
Publication(s): *Skrifter utgivna av Abo Akademis bibliotek*

Eduskunnan Kirjasto (Library of Parliament, Finland)
Aurorankatu 6, 00102 Helsinki
Tel: (00) 4321 *Fax:* (00) 4323495
E-mail: kirjasto@eduskunta.fi
Web Site: www.eduskunta.fi/kirjasto/
Key Personnel
Library Dir: Tuula H Laaksovirta
Secretary: Satu Saarikivi *E-mail:* satu.saarikivi@eduskunta.fi
Publication(s): *Bibliographia iuridica Fennica*

Helsingin Kaupunginkirjasto - yleisten kirjastojen keskuskirjasto (Helsinki City Library - Central Library for Public Libraries)
Rautatielaisenkatu 8, 00520 Helsinki
Mailing Address: PO Box 4100, 00099 City of Helsinki
Tel: (09) 3108511 *Fax:* (09) 31085517
E-mail: city.library@hel.fi
Web Site: www.lib.hel.fi
Key Personnel
Library Dir: Ms Maija Berndtson
Executive Assistant: Reita Hamalainen *Tel:* (09) 31085520 *E-mail:* reita.hamalainen@hel.fi

Helsinki University Library
Unioninkatu 36, 00014 Helsingin, Yliopisto
Mailing Address: PL 15, 00014 Helsingin, Yliopisto
Tel: (09) 191 23196 *Fax:* (09) 191 22719
E-mail: hyk-palvelu@helsinki.fi
Web Site: www.lib.helsinki.fi
Telex: 121538 Hyk
Key Personnel
Dir: Kai Ekholm *Tel:* (09) 191 22721
Founded: 1640
Publication(s): *Books from Finland* (quarterly, mostly in English, but also in French & German); *The Finnish National Bibliography* (CD-ROM); *Publications of the University Library at Helsinki*
Branch Office(s)
Slavonic Library, PB 15, Helsingin Yliopisto, 00014 Unioninkatu 36 *Tel:* (09) 19123196
American Resource Center, Box 15, Helsingin Yliopisto, 00014 Unioninkatu 36 *Tel:* (09) 19124048 *Fax:* (09) 652940 *E-mail:* ARC@usembassy.fi

Joensuun Yliopisto (Joensuu University)
Yliopistokatu 2, PO Box 107, 80101 Joensuu
Tel: (013) 251 111 *Fax:* (013) 251 2050
E-mail: joyk@joyl.joensuun.ti
Web Site: www.joensuu.fi/
Telex: 46223
Key Personnel
Librarian: Helena Hamynen *Tel:* (013) 251 2660
 E-mail: helena.hamynen@joensuu.fi

Jyvaskylan Yliopiston Kirjasto (Jyvaskyla University Library)
Seminaarinkatu 15, 40014 Jyvaskylan Yliopisto
Mailing Address: PO Box 35 (B), 40014 Jyvaskyla
Tel: (014) 2601211 *Fax:* (014) 2603371
E-mail: jyk@Library.jyu.fi
Web Site: www.fyu.fi
Key Personnel
Dir: Pirjo Vatanen *Tel:* (014) 260-3373
 E-mail: pirjo.vatanen@library.jyu.fi
Librarian: Kaija Nygard *Tel:* (014) 260 3374
 E-mail: kaija.nygard@library.jyu.fi
Founded: 1863
Jyvaskyla University Library.
Parent Company: Jyvaskylan Yliopiston (Jyvaskyla University)

Kansallisarkisto Kirjasto (National Archives of Finland/Library)
Rauhankatu 17, 00170 Helsinki
Mailing Address: PO Box 258, 00171 Helsinki
Tel: (09) 228521 *Fax:* (09) 176302
E-mail: kansallisarkisto@narc.fi
Web Site: www.narc.fi
Key Personnel
Head of Library: Elisa Orrman *E-mail:* elisa.orrman@narc.fi
Library Assistant: Marjut Nuikka *E-mail:* marjut.nuikka@narc.fi
Founded: 1869
National Archives of Finland.

Library of Statistics, see Statistics Finland Library

Oulun Yliopiston Kirjasto (Oulu University Library)
PL 7500, 90014 Oulu
Tel: (08) 553 1011 *Fax:* (08) 556 9135
Web Site: www.kirjasto.oulu.fi/
Telex: 32256 Oyk
Key Personnel
Acting Chief Librarian: Paivi Kytomaki *Tel:* (08) 553 3500
Publication(s): *Acta Universitatis Ouluensis* (publications of Oulu University Library)

Sibelius-Akatemian Kirjasto (Sibelius Academy Library)
Toeoeloenkatu 28, 00260 Helsinki
Mailing Address: PL 86, 00251 Helsinki
Tel: (09) 4054 541 *Fax:* (09) 4054 542
E-mail: sibakirjasto@siba.fi
Web Site: www.siba.fi/Kirjastot
Key Personnel
Librarian: Irmeli Koskimies

Statistics Finland Library
Tyoepajakatu 13B, 00022 Helsinki
Mailing Address: PO Box 2B, 00022 Helsinki
Tel: (09) 1734 2220 *Fax:* (09) 1734 2279
E-mail: library@stat.fi
Web Site: www.stat.fi/tk/kk/index_en.html
Key Personnel
Chief Librarian: Hellevi Yrjoelae

Tampereen Yliopiston Kirjasto (Tampere University Library)
Yliopistonkatu 38, 33014 Tampere
Mailing Address: PL 617, 33101 Tampere
Tel: (03) 215 6434 *Fax:* (03) 215 7493
Web Site: www.uta.fi/~kimiii
Telex: 22263 Tayk
Key Personnel
Chief Librarian: Dr Mirja Iivonen *E-mail:* mirja.t.iivonen@uta.fi
Founded: 1925
Publication(s): *University Publications*

Teknillisen Korkeakoulun Kirjasto (Helsinki University of Technology Library)
Otaniementie 9, 02015 Hut
Mailing Address: PO Box 7000, 02015 Hut
Tel: (09) 451 4111 *Fax:* (09) 451 4132
E-mail: infolib@hut.fi
Web Site: lib.hut.fi
Key Personnel
Dir of Libraries: Ari Muhonen *E-mail:* ari.muhonen@hut.fi
Head of Information Services: Irma Pasanen
National Resource Library for Technology in Finland.
Publication(s): *Annual Bibliography of the Helsinki University of Technology* (online only); *Research at HUT* (annually, online only); *Tenttu* (online only)

TERKKO, see Terveystieteiden keskuskirjasto (TERKKO)

Terveystieteiden keskuskirjasto (TERKKO) (National Library of Health Sciences)
Haartmaninkatu 4, 00290 Helsinki
Mailing Address: PL 61, 00014 Helsinki
Tel: (09) 191 26643 *Fax:* (09) 241 0385
E-mail: terkko-info@helinski.fi
Web Site: www.terkko.helsinki.fi/
Key Personnel
Library Dir: Pirjo Rajakiili *Tel:* (09) 191 26646
 E-mail: pirjo.rajakiili@helsinki.fi
Publication(s): *FINMED/MEDIC* (bibliography & database)

Turun Yliopiston Kirjasto (Turku University Library)
Hallinto, 20014 Turku
Tel: (02) 333 51 *Fax:* (02) 333 5050
E-mail: kirjasto@utu.fi
Web Site: www.kirjasto.utu.fi
Telex: 62123 Tyk
Key Personnel
Librarian: Tuulikki Nurminen
Turku University Library.
Publication(s): *Annales Universitatis Turkuensis*

France

American Library in Paris
10, rue du General-Camou, 75007 Paris
Tel: (01) 53591260 *Fax:* (01) 45502583
E-mail: alparis@noos.fr
Web Site: www.americanlibraryinparis.org
Key Personnel
Dir: Shirley Lambert
Assistant Dir: Adele Witt
Reference Librarian: Kim LeMinh
Founded: 1920

Special Collections: Gregory Usher Cookbook Collection; Marlene Dietrich Collection
Specialize in social sciences, humanities, US history & civilization, literary criticism.

Bibliotheque Universitaire Antilles-Guyane (BUAG)
Campus de Schoelcher, BP 7210, 97275 Schoelcher Cedex
Tel: (0596) 727530 *Fax:* (0596) 727527
Web Site: www.univ-ag.fr
Key Personnel
Dir: Marie-Francoise Bernabe *E-mail:* marie-francoise.bernabe@martinique.univ-ag.fr
Librarian In-Charge, Martinique Section: Marie-France Grouvel *E-mail:* marie-france.grouvel@martinique.univ-ag.fr
Librarian In-Charge, Cayenne Section: Nicole Clement-Martin *Tel:* (0594) 252155 *Fax:* (0594) 309668 *E-mail:* nicole.clementmartin@guyane.univ-ag.fr
In-Charge, Guadeloupe Section: Catherine Vassilieff *Tel:* (0590) 489001 *Fax:* (0590) 489089 *E-mail:* catherine.vassilieff@univ-ag.fr

Archives Nationales
56 Rue des Francs Bourgeois, 75141 Paris Cedex 03
Tel: (01) 40 27 64 19 *Fax:* (01) 40 27 66 01
E-mail: chan.paris@culture.gouv.fr
Web Site: www.archivesnationales.culture.gouv.fr
Key Personnel
Dir: H Lerch
Branch Office(s)
09/63-02 Dathwee Chhen Twa Gallee, Chowk Bhitra 2nd floor Purano Bazaar, Arniko-Barhabise VDC-9, Arniko Rajmarg-87 K M, Bagmati Anchal, Barhabise Mail PO Code 45303,, Kathmandu, Nepal

Bibliotheque de l' Arsenal
Division of Bibliotheque Nationale de France
One Rue de Sully, 75004 Paris
Tel: (01) 53012525 *Fax:* (01) 53 01 25 07
E-mail: arsenal@bnf.fr
Web Site: www.ccfr.bnf.fr
Key Personnel
Dir & Chief Librarian: Bruno Blasselle *E-mail:* bruno.blasselle@bnf.fr

BDIC, see Bibliotheque de Documentation Internationale Contemporaine (BDIC)

Bibliotheque Centrale du Museum National d'Histoire Naturelle
38 rue Geoffry-Saint Hilaire, 75005 Paris
Tel: (01) 40 79 36 27 *Fax:* (01) 40 79 36 56
Web Site: www.mnhn.fr/mnhn/bcm
Key Personnel
Dir: Michele Mauries
Chief Librarian: Monique Duereux *E-mail:* ducreux@mnhn.fr

Bibliotheque d'Art et d'Archeologie Jacques Doucet
Division of Universites de Paris IV et Paris I
58, rue de Richelieu, Paris
Mailing Address: 2/4 rue Vivienne, 75083 Paris Cedex 02
Tel: (01) 47037628 *Fax:* (01) 47038925
E-mail: baa@bnf.fr
Web Site: www.paris4.sorbonne.fr (archives)
Key Personnel
Chief Librarian: Francoise Lemelle

Bibliotheque Historique de la Ville de Paris
(Historical Library of Paris)
24 rue Pavee, 75004 Paris
Tel: (01) 44 59 29 40 *Fax:* (01) 42 74 03 16
Key Personnel
Curator: Jean Derens

Bibliotheque Interuniversitaire de Montpellier
Bibliotheque Interuniversitaire, 60, rue des Etats Generaux, 34965 Montpellier Cedex 2
Tel: (04) 67 13 43 50 *Fax:* (04) 67 13 43 51
E-mail: biu.secretariat@univ-montpl.fr
Web Site: www.biu.montpellier.fr
Key Personnel
Chief Librarian: Pierre Gaillard

Bibliotheque Municipale de Besancon
One rue de la Bibliotheque, 25000 Besancon Cedex
Tel: (03) 81878140 *Fax:* (03) 81619877
E-mail: bib.etude@besancon.com
Web Site: www.besancon.com/biblio/francais/
Key Personnel
Librarian: Helene Richard *E-mail:* helene.richard@besancon.com
Dir: Marie-Claire Waille *E-mail:* marie-claire.waille@besancon.com

Bibliotheque Municipale de Grenoble
12 blvd Marechal Lyautey, 38021 Grenoble Cedex 1
Mailing Address: BP 1095, 38000 Grenoble Cedex 1
Tel: (04) 76862100 *Fax:* (04) 76862119
E-mail: bmei@upmf-grenoble.fr
Web Site: www.bm-grenoble.fr
Key Personnel
Librarians: Sylvie Crouzet; Catherine Pouyet
Publication(s): Bibliotheque municipale de Grenoble, Catalogue general auteurs des livres imprimes jusqu'a 1900 (1980, 12 vols available from K G Saur, Germany)

Bibliotheque Municipale de Lyon
30 blvd Vivier-Merle, 69431 Lyon Cedex 03
Tel: (07) 78621800 *Fax:* (07) 78621949
E-mail: bm@bm-lyon.fr
Web Site: www.bm-lyon.fr
Key Personnel
Librarian: Patrick Bazin *Tel:* (04) 7862 1924 *E-mail:* pbazin@bm-lyon.fr

Bibliotheque Municipale de Rennes (Rennes Public Library)
One rue de la Borderie, 35042 Rennes
Tel: (02) 99 63 09 09; (02) 99 87 98 98 *Fax:* (02) 99 36 05 96; (02) 99 87 98 99
E-mail: contact@bm-rennes.fr
Web Site: www.bm-rennes.fr
Key Personnel
Dir: Marie-Therese Pouillias *E-mail:* marie-therese.pouillias@bm-rennes.fr
Publication(s): Cinq cents ans d'imprimerie en Bretagne, 1484-1985 (catalog); *Jean Larcher* (catalog); *Le Femme 1900 dans les collections Henri Polles* (catalog); *Le Pelletier* (dictionary); *Le Romantisme breton: collection Henri Polles*; *L'itinerarie de Kenneth White* (catalog); *Paul Feval, 1816-1887*

Bibliotheque Nationale de France (National Library of France)
Quai Francois-Mauriac, 75706 Paris Cedex 13
Tel: (01) 53 79 59 59 *Fax:* (01) 47 03 77 34
Web Site: www.bnf.fr
Key Personnel
President: Jean Pierre Angremy
Dir General: Philippe Belaval

Bibliotheque Nationale et Universitaire de Strasbourg
5 rue du Marechal Joffre, BP 1029/F, 67070 Strasbourg Cedex
Tel: (03) 88 25 28 00 *Fax:* (03) 88 25 28 03
E-mail: bnus@bnus.u-strasbg.fr
Web Site: www-bnus.u-strasbg.fr

Key Personnel
Administrator: Bernard Falga *Tel:* (03) 88 25 28 10 *E-mail:* administrateur@bnus.u-strasbg.fr (main address & Management & Legal Section); 6 place de la Republique, BP 1029/F, 67070 Strasbourg cedex (Alsace Region Affairs Section); 3 bis rue du Marechal Joffre, BP 1029/F, 67070 Strasbourg Cedex Tel: (03) 88 25 28 46.
Publication(s): Bibliographie alsacienne; Catalogue critique des manuscrits persans; Papyrus grecs de la BNUS

Bibliotheque Universitaire Droit-Sciences Economiques
11, pl Carnot, 54042 Nancy Cedex
Mailing Address: BP 4232, Nancy Cedex
Tel: (03) 83 30 81 57 *Fax:* (03) 83 30 82 38
Web Site: www.univ-nancy2.fr/webbib/webbib/budroit.html
Key Personnel
Contact: Annie Kammerer *Tel:* (03) 83 30 82 30 *E-mail:* annie.kammerer@univ-nancy2.fr
Parent Company: Universites de Nancy

Bibliotheque Universite d'Avignon et des Pays du Vaucluse
74 Rue Louis Pasteur, 84029 Avignon Cedex 1
Tel: (04) 90 16 25 00 *Fax:* (04) 90 16 25 10
Web Site: www.univ-avignon.fr
Key Personnel
Dir: Francoise Febvre

Bibliotheque Municipale de Bordeaux
(Bordeaux Public Library)
85 Cours du Marechal Juin-F, 33000 Bordeaux
Tel: (05) 56103000 *Fax:* (05) 56103090
E-mail: bibli@mairie-bordeaux.fr
Web Site: www.bordeaux-city.com/bordeaux.htm
Key Personnel
Dir: Pierre Botineau
Founded: 1803

BUAG, see Bibliotheque Universitaire Antilles-Guyane (BUAG)

La Documentation Francaise
29 Quai Voltaire, 75007 Paris Cedex 07
Tel: (01) 40157110 *Fax:* (01) 40 15 72 30
E-mail: libparis@ladocumentationfrancaise.fr
Web Site: www.ladocumentationfrancaise.fr
Key Personnel
Man Dir: Sophie Moati
Commercial Dir: Alain-Marie Bassy
Editorial Dir: M Meusy
Chief Sales: Bernard Meunier

Bibliotheque de Documentation Internationale Contemporaine (BDIC)
Centre Universitaire, 6 allee de l'Universite, 92001 Nanterre Cedex
Tel: (01) 40 97 79 00 *Fax:* (01) 40 97 79 40
E-mail: courrier.bdic@u-paris10.fr
Web Site: www.bdic.fr/cermi/inter2.htm
Key Personnel
Dir: Genevieve Dreyfus-Armand *E-mail:* genevieve.dreyfus-amand@u-paris10.fr
This is a Paris University library.
Publication(s): Collection des Publications de la BDIC

Ecole Nationale Superieure des Sciences de l'information et des bibliotheques (ENSSIB)
17-21 Blvd du 11 Novembre 1918, 69623 Villeurbanne Cedex
Tel: (04) 72 44 43 43 *Fax:* (04) 72 44 43 44
E-mail: com@enssib.fr; dupuigre@enssib.fr
Web Site: www.enssib.fr
Key Personnel
Dir: Francois Dupuigrenet-Desroussilles
Dir, Publications: Pierre-Ives Duchemin

Publication(s): *Bulletin des bibliotheques de France*; *Monographies en sciences de l'information et des bibliotheques* (travaux d'etude et de recherche); *Presses de L'Enssib*

Bibliotheque de Geographie
191 rue St-Jacques, 75005 Paris
Tel: (01) 44 32 14 61; (01) 44 32 14 63 *Fax:* (01) 44 32 14 67
Web Site: margotte.univ-paris1.fr/ciolfi/sorbg1.htm
Key Personnel
Librarian: Joseph Maie
Parent Company: Universite de Paris

INIST, see Institut de l'Information Scientifique et Technique (INIST)

Bibliotheque de l'Institut de France
23 quai Conti, 75006 Paris
Tel: (01) 44 41 44 10 *Fax:* (01) 44 41 44 11
E-mail: bibliotheque@bif.univ-paris5.fr
Web Site: www.institut-de-france.fr/bibliotheques/institut.htm
Key Personnel
Dir & Librarian: Mireille Pastoureau
 E-mail: mireille.pastoureau@bif.univ-paris5.fr
Founded: 1795

Institut de l'Information Scientifique et Technique (INIST)
Affiliate of CNRS (French National Centre for Scientific Research)
2 Allee du Parc de Brabois, 54514 Vandoeuvre-les-Nancy Cedex
Tel: (03) 83 50 46 00 *Fax:* (03) 83 50 46 50
E-mail: webmaster@inist.fr
Web Site: www.inist.fr
Key Personnel
Dir: A Pain Chanudet
Founded: 1988
INIST-CNRS, a French scientific & technical information center, is a service unit of the French National Centre for Scientific Research (CNRS). It collects basic & applied research publications in cooperation with French & international organizations. Producer of multidisciplinary & multilingual bibliographical databases - PASCAL, FRANCIS & ARTICLE@INIST - listing documents published in most areas of science & technology, medicine, the humanities, social sciences & economics. Also acts as a scientific & technical document delivery service.
Publication(s): *Articlesciences* (1990, bibliographic database); *Francis* (1972, bibliographic database, monthly updates); *Pascal* (1973, bibliographic database, weekly updates)

Bibliotheque Interuniversitaire des Langues Orientales
Universite Sorbonne Nouvelle, 4, rue de Lille, 75007 Paris
Tel: (01) 44 77 87 20 *Fax:* (01) 44 77 87 30
E-mail: biulo@idf.ext.jussieu.fr
Web Site: www.univ-paris3.fr
Key Personnel
Dir: Nelly Guillaume *E-mail:* guillaum@idf.ext.jussieu.fr
Founded: 1868
Paris University Library.

Bibliotheque Mazarine
23 quai de Conti, 75006 Paris
Tel: (01) 44 41 44 06 *Fax:* (01) 44 41 44 07
Web Site: www.bibliotheque-mazarine.fr
Key Personnel
Chief Curator & Dir: Christian Peligry
 E-mail: christian.peligry@mazarine.univ-paris5.fr

Bibliotheque Interuniversitaire de Medecine
12 rue de l'Ecole de Medecine, 75270 Paris Cedex 06
Tel: (01) 40461951 *Fax:* (01) 44411020
Web Site: www.bium.univ-paris5.fr
Key Personnel
Dir & Chief Curator: P Casseyre
This is a Paris University library.
Publication(s): *Catalogue des Periodiques de la Bibliotheque (1976-1981)*; *Bibliotheque de l'ancienne Faculte de Medecine de Paris: Catalogue des Livres du XVIe siecle extrait du catalogue general du fonds ancien*

Bibliotheque Municipale de Nancy
43 rue Stanislas, CS 4230, 54042 Nancy Cedex
Tel: (03) 83373883 *Fax:* (03) 83379182
E-mail: bmnancy@mairie-nancy.fr
Web Site: www.nancy.fr
Key Personnel
Chief Librarian: Andre Markiewicz
Founded: 1750

Bibliotheque du Musee de l'Homme
Palais de Chaillot, 17 Pl du Trocadero, 75116 Paris
Tel: (01) 44 05 72 03 *Fax:* (01) 44 05 72 12
E-mail: bmhweb@mnhn.fr
Web Site: www.mnhn.fr
Key Personnel
Dir: Jacqueline Dubois
Contact: Prof A Langaney *E-mail:* langaney@mnhn.fr

Bibliotheque Interuniversitaire de Pharmacie
4 ave de l'Observatoire, 75270 Paris Cedex 6
Tel: (01) 53 73 95 22; (01) 53 73 95 23 *Fax:* (01) 53 73 99 05
E-mail: piketty@pharmacie.univ_paris5.fr
Web Site: www.biup.univ-paris5.fr
Key Personnel
Librarian: Francoise Malet
This is a Paris University library seat of CADIST for culture (Beauty culture: perfumes & cosmetics).

Bibliotheque Sainte-Genevieve
10 pl du Pantheon, 75005 Paris
Tel: (01) 44 41 97 97 *Fax:* (01) 44 41 97 96
E-mail: bsgmail@univ.paris1.fr
Web Site: www-bsg.univ-paris1.fr
Key Personnel
Librarian: Nathalie Jullian
This is a Paris University library & public library.

Service commun de la documentation de l'Universite de Lille III
Universite de Sciences et Technologies de Lille, BP 155, 59653 Villeneuve d'Ascq Cedex
Tel: (03) 20 43 44 10 *Fax:* (03) 20 33 71 04
Web Site: ustl.univ-lille1.fr
Key Personnel
Dir: Jean-Bernard Marino *Tel:* (03) 20 43 71 99
 E-mail: jean-bernard.marino@univ-lille1.fr

Bibliotheque de la Sorbonne
17 Rue de la Sorbonne, 75257 Paris Cedex 05
Tel: (01) 40 46 30 27 *Fax:* (01) 40 46 30 44
E-mail: adminst@biu.sorbonne.fr
Web Site: www.sorbonne.fr
Key Personnel
Chief Librarian: Catherine Gaillard
 E-mail: gaillard@biu.sorbonne.fr
Founded: 1762
This is a Paris Interuniversity library.
Branch Office(s)
Lettres et Sciences humaines

Universite de Toulouse-Mirail
5 allees Antonio Machado, 31058 Toulouse Cedex 09
Tel: (0561) 50 45 99 *Fax:* (0561) 50 35 20
E-mail: europe@univ-tlse2.fr
Web Site: www.univ-tlse2.fr/scd.html
Key Personnel
Dir & Chief Librarian: Jean-Claude Annezer
 Tel: (0561) 50 42 25 *E-mail:* jean-claude.annezer@univ-tlse2.fr
Librarian: Valerie Morell *Tel:* (0561) 50 44 63
 E-mail: valerie.morell@univ-tlse.fr
Publication(s): *Anglophonia*; *Caravelle*; *Champs du Signe*; *Criticon*; *Litteratures*; *Pallas*

French Guiana

Institut Francais de Recherche Scientifique pour le Developpement en Cooperation
(French Institute for Scientific Research for Cooperative Development)
Centre de Cayenne, BP 165, 97323 Cayenne Cedex
Tel: 299 292 *Fax:* 319 855
E-mail: dir.cayenne@cayenne.ird.fr
Web Site: www.cayenne.ird.fr
Key Personnel
Dir: M Georges-Henri Sala
Office of Scientific & Technical Research Overseas.
Publication(s): *La Nature et l'Homme* (irregularly)
Parent Company: Institut de Recherche pour le Developpement

Gabon

Bibliotheque de l'Universite Omar Bongo
Blvd Leon M'Ba, Libreville
Mailing Address: BP 13131, Libreville
Tel: 732956 *Fax:* 734530
E-mail: uob@internetgabon.cm
Web Site: www.uob.ga.refer.org
Telex: 5336
Key Personnel
Dir: Stary Mezeme Be'ndong
Founded: 1976
Publication(s): *Inventaire du fonds documentaire, par discipline* (annually); *Liste des nouvelles acquisitions* (quarterly); *Liste des periodiques en cours* (annually)

Centre Bibliotheque d'Information
BP 750, Libreville
Tel: 21115

Direction Generale des Archives Nationales, de la Bibliotheque Nationale et de la Documentation Gabonaise (DGABD) (Gabon National Archives, National Library)
BP 1188, Libreville
Tel: 732543; (0241) 730 239 *Fax:* 730239
Key Personnel
Archives Dir: Rene G Sonnet-Azize
Dir: Jean Paul Mifouna

Gambia

Gambia College Library
PO Box 144, Brikama
Tel: 484452; 484748; 484812 *Fax:* 483224
Key Personnel
Librarian: Rosanna A Jallon Ndaw-Jallow
President: N S Z Njie

The Gambia National Library
Reg Pye Lane, Banjul
Mailing Address: PMB 552, Banjul
Tel: 226491; 225876; 228312; 223776 *Fax:* 223 776
E-mail: national.library@qanet.gm
Key Personnel
Dir: Abdou W Mbye
Chief Librarian: Mary E Fye
Founded: 1946

Georgia

Gosudarstvennaya Respublikanskaya biblioteka Gruzinskoi SSR im K Marksai
Kecchoveli ul 5, Tblisi 700078
E-mail: navoi@physic.uzsci.net
Web Site: www.osi.uz/library
Key Personnel
Dir: Zukhriddin Nizomiddinovich *Tel:* (099871) 139 16 58 *Fax:* (099871) 133 09 08
Deputy Dir: Rasulov Khusan *Tel:* (099871) 139 40 36; Maminova Irina Zakirovna *Tel:* (098871) 139 40 20
Founded: 1998
State Republican Karl Marx Library of the Georgian SSR.

Germany

Badische Landesbibliothek
Erbprinzenstr 15, 76133 Karlsruhe
Mailing Address: Postfach 1429, 76033 Karlsruhe
Tel: (0721) 175-20 01; (0721) 175-22 22 *Fax:* (0721) 175-23 33
E-mail: informationszentrum@blb-karlsruhe.de
Web Site: www.blb-karlsruhe.de
Key Personnel
Dir: Dr Peter Michael Ehrle *Tel:* (0721) 175-22 00 *E-mail:* ehrle@blb-karlsruhe.de
Deputy Dir: Dr Ruediger Schmidt *Tel:* (0721) 175-22 10 *E-mail:* schmidt@blb-karlsruhe.de
Founded: 1500

Staatsbibliothek Bamberg
Neue Residenz, Domplatz 8, 96049 Bamberg
Tel: (0951) 95503-0 *Fax:* (0951) 95503-145
E-mail: info@staatsbibliothek-bamberg.de
Web Site: www.staatsbibliothek-bamberg.de
Key Personnel
Chief Librarian: Dr Bernhard Schemmel *E-mail:* bernhard.schemmel@staatsbibliothek-bamberg.de
Publication(s): *Auserlesene Schrift-Bilder; Bambergische Bildhauerzeichnungen des Rokoko und Klassizismus; Das Allgemeine Krankenhaus Fuerstbischof Franz Ludwig von Erthals in Bamberg von 1789; Der Bamberger Siddur; Die Ingenieur- und Zeichenakademie des Leopold Westen und ihre Entwicklung; Die Neuen Welten in alten Buechern; Duerer und die Literatur; Edler Schatz Holden Erinnerns; Fuers Schoene Geschlecht; Illuminierte Bologneser Handschriften 1260-1340; Johann Lukas Schoenlein; Karl Theodor von Buseck 1803-1860; Vergil 2000 Jahre*

Bayerische Staatsbibliothek (Bavarian State Library)
Ludwigstr 16, 80539 Munich, Bavaria
Tel: (089) 28638-0; (089) 28638-2322 *Fax:* (089) 28638-2200
E-mail: direktion@bsb-muenchen.de; info@bsb-muenchen.de
Web Site: www.bsb-muenchen.de
Key Personnel
General Director: Dr Hermann Leskien *Tel:* (089) 28638-2206 *E-mail:* leskien@bsb-muenchen.de
Founded: 1558
Publication(s): *Bayerische Staatsbibliothek (ein Selbstportrait); Jahresbericht* (annually)

Technische Universitat Bergakademie Freiberg
Akademiestr 6, 09599 Frieberg
Tel: (03731) 39 29 59 *Fax:* (03731) 39 43 60
E-mail: unibib@ub.tu-freiberg.de
Web Site: www.tu-freiberg.de
Key Personnel
Dir: Karin Mittenzwei *E-mail:* karin.mittenzwei@ub.tu-freiberg.de
Publication(s): *Veroeffentlichungen der Bibliothek "Georgius Agricola" der TU Bergakademie Freiberg*

Bibliothek des Instituts fuer Weltwirtschaft, see ZBW-Deutsche Zentralbibliothek fuer Wirtschaftswissenschaften/Bibliothek des Instituts fuer Weltwirtschaft

Bibliothek fur Zeitgeschichte/Library of Contemporary History
Konrad Adenauerstr 8, 70173 Stuttgart
Mailing Address: Postfach 10 54 41, 70047 Stuttgart
Tel: (0711) 212-4454; (0711) 212-4424 *Fax:* (0711) 212-4422
E-mail: bfz@wlb-stuttgart.de; information@wlb-stuttgart.de
Web Site: www.wlb-stuttgart.de/bfz
Key Personnel
Dir: Dr Hannsjoerg Kowark *E-mail:* kowark@wlb-stuttgart.de
Founded: 1915
This library is housed in same building as the Wuerttembergische Landesbibliothek, covering library (approx 310,000 books & approx 650 current periodicals), archives, documentation center for grey literature, research facilities, etc.
Publication(s): *Schriften der Bibliothek fuer Zeitgeschichte NF; Stuttgarter Vortraege zur Zeitgeschichte*
Parent Company: Wuerttembergische Landse Bibliothek
Ultimate Parent Company: Land Baden-Wuerttemberg

Bibliotheks und Informationssystem der Universitaet Oldenburg
Uhlhornsweg 49-55, Oldenburg 26129
Mailing Address: Postfach 2541, Oldenburg 26015
Tel: (0441) 798-2023 *Fax:* (0441) 798-4040
E-mail: zi@bis.uni-oldenburg.de
Web Site: www.bis.uni-oldenburg.de/
Telex: 25655 unoldd
Key Personnel
Dir: Hans-Joahim Waetjen *Tel:* (0441) 798-4010 *E-mail:* waetjen@bis.uni-oldenburg.de
Founded: 1974
Research library, scientific publishing house, media centre.
Parent Company: Carl von Ossietzky University Oldenburg

Universitaet Bonn
Universitaets -und Landesbibliothek, Adenaueralle 39-41, 53113 Bonn
Mailing Address: Postfach 2460, 53014 Bonn
Tel: (0228) 73-7352 *Fax:* (0228) 73-7546
E-mail: ulb@ulb.uni-bonn.de
Web Site: www.ulb.uni-bonn.de
Key Personnel
Dir: Dr Renate Vogt *E-mail:* renate.vogt@ulb.uni-bonn.de
Publication(s): *Universitaets -und Landesbibliothek Bonn*

Technische Universitaet Braunschweig
Pockelsstr 13, 38106 Braunschweig
Tel: (0531) 391-5018; (0531) 391-5011 *Fax:* (0531) 391-5836
E-mail: ub@tu-bs.de
Web Site: www.biblio.tu-bs.de
Key Personnel
Librarian: Prof Dietmar Brandes, PhD *E-mail:* d.brandes@tu-braunschweig.de
Publication(s): *Veroeffentlichungen der Universitaetsbibliothek Braunschweig*

Bucharchiv, see Deutsches Bucharchiv Muenchen, Institut fur Buchwissenschaften

Die Deutsche Bibliothek
Adickesallee 1, 60322 Frankfurt am Main
Tel: (069) 1525-0 *Fax:* (069) 1525-1010
E-mail: info@dbf.ddb.de
Web Site: www.ddb.de
Key Personnel
Dir General: Dr Elisabeth Niggemann
Contact: Kathrin Ansorge *Tel:* (069) 15251004 *E-mail:* ansorge@dbf.ddb.de
Founded: 1947
National Library & National Bibliographic Agency.
Publication(s): *Deutsche Nationalbibliografie* (brochure)
Branch Office(s)
Deutsches Musikarchiv Berlin, Gaertner St 25-32, 12207 Berlin, Acting Representative: Ingo Kolasa *Tel:* (030) 770020 *Fax:* (030) 77002299 *E-mail:* info@dma.ddb.de
Deutsche Buecherei Leipzig, Deutscher Platz 1, Leipzig, Deputy: Birgit Schneider *Tel:* (0341) 22710 *Fax:* (0341) 2271444 *E-mail:* info@dbl.ddb.de

Deutsche Buecherei Leipzig, see Die Deutsche Bibliothek

Deutscher Bundestag Bibliothek
Platz der Republik 1, 11011 Berlin
Tel: (030) 227 32624 *Fax:* (030) 227 36087
E-mail: bibliothek@bundestag.de
Web Site: www.bundestag.de
Key Personnel
Head of Library: Marga Coing

Deutsches Bucharchiv Muenchen, Institut fur Buchwissenschaften
Salvatorplatz 1, 80333 Munich
Mailing Address: Von-der-Tann-Str 5, 80539 Munich
Tel: (089) 29151-0; (089) 790 12 20 *Fax:* (089) 291951-95; (089) 790 14 19
E-mail: kontakt@bucharchiv.de
Web Site: www.bucharchiv.de
Key Personnel
Dir: Prof Ludwig Delp *Tel:* (089) 790 11 90
Founded: 1948
Institute for Book Research.
Publication(s): *Buchwissenschaftliche Beitraege aus dem Deutschen Bucharchiv Muenchen*

Deutsches Musikarchiv Berlin, see Die Deutsche Bibliothek

Die Deutsche Bibliothek/Deutsche Buecherei Leipzig
Deutscher Platz 1, 04103 Leipzig
Tel: (0341) 22710 *Fax:* (0341) 2271444
E-mail: info@dbl.ddb.de

Web Site: www.ddb.de
Key Personnel
Dir: Dr Elisabeth Niggemann
User Services & Archiving: Joerg Raeuber
National Library & National Bibliography Agency.
Publication(s): Deutsche Nationalbibliographie (German National Bibliography, weekly)

Universitaet Dortmund
Vogelpothsweg 76, 44227 Dortmund
Tel: (0231) 755-4001 *Fax:* (0231) 755-4007
Web Site: www.uni-dortmund.de
Key Personnel
Librarian: Marlene Nagelsmeier-Linke
 E-mail: marlene.nagelsmeier-linke@ub.uni-dortmund.de

Universitaetsbibliothek Eichstaett
Universitaetsallee 1, 85072 Eichstaett
Tel: (08421) 931330 *Fax:* (08421) 931791
E-mail: ub-direktion@ku-eichstaett.de
Web Site: www.ub.ku-eichstaett.de
Key Personnel
Dir: Hermann Holzbauer *Tel:* (08421) 931331
 E-mail: ub-direktion@ku-eichstaedtt.de
Founded: 1972

Ernst-Moritz-Arndt Universitat Greifswald, Universitatsbibliothek
Friedrich-Ludwig-Jahn-Str 14a, 17487 Greifswald
Tel: (03834) 86 1502 *Fax:* (03834) 86 1501
E-mail: ub@uni-greifswald.de
Web Site: web.ub.uni-greifswald.de
Key Personnel
Dir: Dr Hans-Armin Knoeppel *Tel:* (0384) 86 1500
Founded: 1604
Publication(s): Buchmalerei aus Handschriften und Drucken der Universitaetsbibliothek Greifswald; Die Vitae Pomeranorum

Fachhochschule Dortmund
 Hochschulbibliothek (University of Applied Sciences Dortmund Library)
Vogelpothsweg 76, 44227 Dortmund
Mailing Address: Postfach 105018, 44047 Dortmund
Tel: (0231) 7554047 *Fax:* (0231) 7554604
E-mail: bibliothek@fhb.fh-dortmund.de
Web Site: www.fh.dortmund.de
Key Personnel
Librarian: Dr Robert Klitzke *E-mail:* klitzke@fhb.fh-dortmund.de
Founded: 1972

Fachhochschule Stuttgart Hochschule der Medien (University of Applied Sciences School of Media)
Hochschule der Medien, Nobelstr 10, 70569 Stuttgart
Tel: (0711) 257060 *Fax:* (0711) 25706300
E-mail: office@hdm-stuttgart.de; friedling@hdm-stuttgart.de
Web Site: www.hdm-stuttgart.de
Key Personnel
Scientific Dir, Library: Prof Peter Vodosek
 E-mail: vodosek@hdm-stuggart.de
Library Manager: Friedling Erik *Tel:* (0711) 25706-123 *E-mail:* friedling@hdm-stuttgart.de
Founded: 1942
Information material on demand.
Publication(s): HDM aktuell (biannually)

Hamburgisches Welt-Wirtschafts-Archiv (HWWA) Bibliothek (Hamburg Institute of International Economics Library)
Neuer Jungfernstieg 21, 20347 Hamburg
Tel: (040) 42834-219 *Fax:* (040) 42834-550
E-mail: biblio@hwwa.de
Web Site: www.hwwa.de
Key Personnel
Head, Library: Hubert-Guenter Striefler
 E-mail: striefler@hwwa.de
Founded: 1908
Special library for economy.

Universitaetsbibliothek Hannover und Technische Informationsbibliothek (University Library of Hannover & Technical Information Library)
Universitatsbibliothek und TIB Welfengarten 1B, 30167 Hannover
Mailing Address: Postfach 6080, 30167 Hannover
Tel: (0511) 762 2268 *Fax:* (0511) 715936
E-mail: ubtib@tib.uni-hannover.de
Web Site: www.tib.uni-hannover.de
Key Personnel
Head Librarian: Uwe Rosemann *E-mail:* uwe.rosemann@tib.uni-hannover.de
Deputy Librarian: Petra Dueren *E-mail:* petra.deuren@tib.uni-hannover.de; Dr Irina Sens *E-mail:* irina.sens@tib.uni-hannover.de
Founded: 1831 (University Library of Hannover; Technical Information Library founded in 1959)
Document delivery.
Publication(s): TIBORDER-Document Delivery System (online catalog on STN International)

Herzog August Bibliothek
Lessingplatz 1, 38304 Wolfenbuettel
Mailing Address: Postfach 1364, 38299 Wolfenbuettel
Tel: (05331) 808-0 *Fax:* (05331) 808-302
E-mail: auskunft@hab.de
Web Site: www.hab.de
Key Personnel
Dir: Prof Helwig Schmidt-Olintzer
 E-mail: direktor@hab.de

Herzogin Anna Amalia Bibliothek
Platz der Demokratie 1, 99423 Weimar
Mailing Address: Postfach 2012, 99401 Weimar
Tel: (03643) 545-200 *Fax:* (03643) 545-220
E-mail: haab@swkk.de
Web Site: www.swkk.de
Key Personnel
Dir: Dr Michael Knoche *E-mail:* michael.knoche@swkk.de
Library is part of the Stiftung Weimarer Klassik und Kunstsammlungen.
Publication(s): Internationale Bibliographie zur Deutschen Klassik, 1750-1850
Parent Company: Stiftung Weimarer Klassik und Kunstsammlungen

Hessische Landes und Hochschulbibliothek, see Universitats und Landesbibliothe Darmstadt

Humboldt Universitaet zu Berlin
Universitaetsbibliothek, Dorotheenstr 27, 10117 Berlin 70099
Tel: (030) 2093 3212 *Fax:* (030) 2093 3207
E-mail: wwwadm.ub@ub.hu-berlin.de
Web Site: www.ub.hu-berlin.de
Key Personnel
Chief Librarian: Dr Milan Bulaty *Tel:* (030) 2093 3200 *E-mail:* milan.bulaty@ub.hu-berlin.de
Head of Library Administration: Gudrun von Garrel *Tel:* (030) 2093 3208 *E-mail:* gudrun.von.garrel@ub.hu-berlin.de

Ibero-Amerikanisches Institut Preussischer Kulturbesitz (Ibero American Institute)
Potsdamerstr 37, 10785 Berlin
Tel: (030) 266 2500 *Fax:* (030) 266 2503
E-mail: iai@iai.spk-berlin.de
Web Site: www.iai.spk-berlin.de
Telex: 183160 staab d
Key Personnel
Dir: Dr Gunther Maihold
Library Dir: Peter Altekrueger *Tel:* (030) 266 2533 *E-mail:* altekrueger@iai.spk-berlin.de
Founded: 1930
Research institute & special library for Latin America, Spain & Portugal
Membership(s): Lasa; Salalm; Redial; Adlaf; Liber.
Publication(s): Biblioteca Luso-Brasileira (book); *Bibliotheca Iberoamericana* (book); *Ibero-Analysen* (book); *Ibero-Bibliographien* (book); *Iberoamericana, Indiana* (journal)

Internationale Jugendbibliothek (International Youth Library)
Schloss Blutenburg, 81247 Munich
Tel: (089) 891211-0 *Fax:* (089) 8117553
E-mail: bib@ijb.de
Web Site: www.ijb.de
Key Personnel
Public Relations: Carola Gade *Tel:* (089) 89121130
Founded: 1949
International children & youth literature, posters, original illustrations, manuscripts & handwriting. 530,000 volumes in over 130 languages & 250 current magazines.
Publication(s): IJB Report (biannual report)

Universitat Konstanz
Universitaetsstr 10, 78464 Konstanz
Mailing Address: 78457 Konstanz
Tel: (07531) 88-0 *Fax:* (07531) 88-3688
E-mail: Posteingang@uni-konstanz.de
Web Site: www.uni-konstanz.de
Key Personnel
Librarian: Klaus Franken *E-mail:* klaus.franken@uni.konstanz.de

Leipziger Staedtische Bibliotheken, see Stadtbibliothek Leipzig

Library of Contemporary History, see Bibliothek fur Zeitgeschichte/Library of Contemporary History

Landesbibliothek Mecklenburg-Vorpommern
Am Dom 2, 19055 Schwerin
Tel: (0385) 558440 *Fax:* (0385) 5584424
E-mail: lb@lbmv.de
Web Site: www.lbmv.de
Key Personnel
Dir: Dr R Juergen Wegener *E-mail:* wegener@lbmv.de
Publication(s): CD-ROM Geschichtliche Bibliographie von Mecklenburg von den Anfangen bis 1945 (1998, bibiography); *Mecklenburg-Vorpommersche Bibliographie* (annually, bibliographical yearbook); *Periodica aus Mecklenburg-Vorpommern* (1996, bibliography of in Meckl-Vorp published newspapers, journals, yearbooks)
Branch Office(s)
Musikaliensammlung, Molkereistr 3, 19053 Schwerin, Herr Jedeck *Tel:* (0385) 5584431 *Fax:* (0385) 5584439 *E-mail:* jedeck@lbmv.de

Niedersaechsische Landesbibliothek (Lower Saxony State Library)
Waterloostr 8, 30169 Hannover
Tel: (0511) 1267-0 *Fax:* (0511) 1267-202
E-mail: nlb@mail.nlb-hannover.de
Web Site: www.nlb-hannover.de
Key Personnel
Deputy Dir: Peter Marmein *Tel:* (0511) 1267-341 *E-mail:* peter.marmein@mail.nlb-hannover.de
Dir: Dr Georg Ruppelt *Tel:* (0511) 1267-303 *Fax:* (0511) 1267-207
Founded: 1665

Niedersaechsische Staats- und Universitaetsbibliothek Goettingen
(Goettingen State & University Library)
Division of University of Goettingen
Platz der Goettinger Sieben 1, Papendiek 14, 37073 Goettingen
Mailing Address: 37070 Goettingen
Tel: (0551) 395212 (Secretariat); (0551) 393079 (chemistry); (0551) 392360 (physics); (0551) 395220 (medicine) *Fax:* (0551) 395222
E-mail: sub@sub.uni-goettingen.de
Web Site: www.sub.uni-goettingen.de
Key Personnel
Dir: Prof Elmar Mittler, PhD *Tel:* (0551) 395210
  E-mail: mittler@sub.uni-goettingen.de
Assistant Dir: Dr Klaus Ceynowa *Tel:* (0551) 395214 *E-mail:* ceynowa@sub.uni-goettingen.de
Founded: 1734

Universitatsbibliothek Regensburg
Universitaetsstr 31, 93053 Regensburg
Tel: (0941) 943-3901; (0941) 943-3902 *Fax:* (0941) 943-3285
Web Site: www.bibliothek.uni-regensburg.de
Key Personnel
Dir: Dr Friedrich Geisselmann
  E-mail: friedrichgeisselmann@bibliothek.uni-regensburg.de

Rheinisch-Westfaelische Technische Hochschule, see RWTH Aachen Hochschulbibliotek

Rheinische Landesbibliothek Koblenz (Rhenish Regional Library of the German 'Land' Rhineland Palatinate)
Bahnofplatz 14, 56068 Koblenz
Mailing Address: PO Box 201352, 56013 Koblenz
Tel: (0261) 91500 40 *Fax:* (0261) 91500 91
E-mail: info@rlb.de
Web Site: www.rlb.de
Key Personnel
Dir: Dr Ernst-Ludwig Berz *Tel:* (0261) 91500 14 *Fax:* (0261) 91500 90 *E-mail:* berz@rlb.de
General Research Library.

Universitaet Rostock Universitaetsbibliothek
Altbettelmoenschtr 4, 18051 Rostock
Tel: (0381) 4 98 22 83 *Fax:* (0381) 4 98 22 70
E-mail: ub-sekretariat@ub.uni-rostock.de00.de
Web Site: www.uni-rostock.de
Key Personnel
Dir: Dr Peter Hoffmann *E-mail:* peter.hoffmann@ub.uni-rostock.de

RWTH Aachen Hochschulbibliotek
Templergraben 61, 52062 Aachen
Mailing Address: Bibliothek, 52056 Aachen
Tel: (0241) 80-944 45 *Fax:* (0241) 80-92 273
E-mail: auskunft@bth.rwth-aachen.de
Web Site: www.rwth-aachen.de; www.bth.rwth-aachen.de
Telex: 0832704
Key Personnel
Dir: Ulrike Eich *Tel:* (0241) 80-94446
  E-mail: eich@bth.rwth-aachen.de
Founded: 1870

Saarlaendische Universitaets und Landesbibliothek (University & State Library of the Saarland)
Im Stadtisald, Geb 3, 66123 Saarbruecken
Mailing Address: Postfach 151141, 66041 Saarbruecken
Tel: (0681) 3022070 *Fax:* (0681) 3022796
E-mail: sulb@sulb.uni-saarland.de
Web Site: www.sulb.uni-saarland.de
Key Personnel
Dir: Prof Bernd Hagenau
Acquisitions: Gabriele Mohrbach *Tel:* (0681) 302 2087 *E-mail:* g.mohrbach@sulb.uni-saarland.de
Founded: 1950
Specialize in academic library.
Parent Company: Univsersitaet des Saarlandes
Branch Office(s)
Medizinische Bibliothek, 66421 Homburg, Contact: Reinhard Kraemer *Tel:* (0684) 162 6059 *Fax:* (0684) 162 6033 *E-mail:* m.kraemer@sulb.uni-saarland.de

Saechsische Landesbibliothek- Staats- und Universitaetsbibliothek Dresden
Zelleway 18, 01054 Dresden
Tel: (0351) 4677-123 *Fax:* (0351) 4677-111
E-mail: direktion@slub-dresden.de
Web Site: www.tu-dresden.de/slub
Key Personnel
Dir General: Prof Juergen Hering
Publication(s): Aurich, Frank; Die Anfange des Buchdrucks in Dresden; Bibliographie Geschichte der Technik; Saechsische Bibliographie; Schwarze Kopfe; SLUB-Kurier; Tradition und Herausforderung

Walther-Schuecking-Institut fuer Internationales Recht an der Universitaet Kiel
Christian-Albrechts-Universitaet zu Kiel, Westring 400, 24098 Kiel
Tel: (0431) 880 2367 *Fax:* (0431) 880 1619
E-mail: fb.internat-recht@ub.uni-kiel.de
Web Site: www.uni-kiel.de/internat-recht
Key Personnel
Dir: Dr Rainer Hofmann *Tel:* (0431) 880-1733 *E-mail:* hofmann-thies@internat-recht.uni-kiel.de; Dr Andreas Zimmermann *Tel:* (0431) 880-2152 *E-mail:* azimmermann@internat-recht.uni-kiel.de
Publication(s): German Yearbook Of International Law; Veroeffentlichungen des Walther-Schuecking-Instituts fuer Internationales Recht (series)

Staats- und Universitaetsbibliothek Hamburg Carl von Ossietzky (State & University Library)
Von-Melle Park 3, 20146 Hamburg
Tel: (040) 42838 2233 *Fax:* (040) 42838-3352
E-mail: auskunft@sub.uni-hamburg.de
Web Site: www.sub.uni-hamburg.de
Key Personnel
Dir: Prof Peter Rau, PhD
Founded: 1479
State & University Library. All areas of science; Special collections: Politics & Peace Research, Science of Administration, Spain & Portugal. Coastal & sea fishing, language & culture of North American Indians & Eskimos.

Staats- und Universitatsbibliothek Bremen
Bibliothekstr, 28359 Bremen
Tel: (0421) 2182601 *Fax:* (0421) 2182614
E-mail: suub@suub.uni-bremen.de
Web Site: www.suub.uni-bremen.de
Key Personnel
Library Dir: Annette Rath-Beckmann

Staatsbibliothek zu Berlin - Preussischer Kulturbesitz (Berlin State Library - Prussian Cultural Foundation)
Unter den Linden 8, 10117 Berlin
Mailing Address: Potsdamer Str 33, 10785 Berlin
Tel: (030) 266-0
Web Site: www.staatsbibliothek-berlin.de; www.sbb.spk-berlin.de
Key Personnel
General Dir: Dipl Ing Barbara Schneider-Kempf *E-mail:* barbara.schneider-kempf@sbb.spk-berlin.de
Founded: 1661
International Research Library.
Publication(s): Beitraege aus der Staatsbibliothek zu Berlin - PK (irregularly); International ISBN Publishers' Directory (annually); ISBN Newsletter (irregularly); ISBN Review (annually); ISMN Newsletter (irregularly); Jahresbericht (annually); Kartographische Bestandsverzeichnisse (irregularly); Kataloge der Handschriftenabteilung, Reihe 1: Handschriften & Reihe 2: Nachlaesse (irregularly); Kataloge der Musikabteilung (irregularly); Veroeffentlichungen der Osteuropa-Abteilung (irregularly)

Stadt Frankfurt a Main Stadt-und Universitaetsbibliothek
Bockenheimer Landstr 134-138, 60325 Frankfurt am Main
Tel: (069) 212-39-205 *Fax:* (069) 212-39-380
E-mail: auskunft@stub.uni-frankfurt.de
Web Site: www.stub.uni-frankfurt.de
Key Personnel
Dir: B Dugall *Tel:* (069) 21239-230
  E-mail: dugall@stub.uni-frankfurt.de

Stadt- und Universitaetsbibliothek
Bockenheimer Landstr 134-138, 60325 Frankfurt am Main
Tel: (069) 212-39-205; (069) 212-39-256; (069) 212-39-229; (069) 212-39-230; (069) 212-39-231 *Fax:* (069) 212-39-380; (069) 212-39-062
E-mail: direktion@uni-frankfurt.com; auskunft@stub.uni-frankfurt.de
Web Site: www.stub.uni-frankfurt.de
Key Personnel
Dir: Berndt Dugall *E-mail:* dugall@stub.uni-frankfurt.de

Stadtbibliothek Leipzig
Formerly Leipziger Staedtische Bibliotheken
Wilhelm-Leuschner-Platz 10/11, 04107 Leipzig
Mailing Address: Postfach 100927, 04009 Leipzig
Tel: (0341) 123 53 43 *Fax:* (0341) 123 53 05
E-mail: stadtbib@leipzig.de
Web Site: www.leipzig.de/stadtbib.htm
Key Personnel
Dir: Reinhard Stridde

Thueringer Universitaets- und Landesbibliothek
Bibliotheksplatz 2, 07743 Jena
Mailing Address: Postfach, 07740 Jena
Tel: (03641) 9-40000 *Fax:* (03641) 9-40002
E-mail: thulb_direktion@thulb.uni-jena.de; thulb_auskunft@thulb.uni-jena.de
Web Site: www.uni-jena.de/thulb
Key Personnel
Dir: Dr Sabine Wefers
Publication(s): Keine Aenderungen; Thueringen - Bibliographic (Online)

Universitat Ulm
89069 Ulm
Tel: (0731) 502-01 *Fax:* (0731) 5022038
E-mail: post@uni-ulm.de
Web Site: www.uni-ulm.de
Key Personnel
Dir: S Franke

Universitaets-Bibliothek Osnabrueck
(University of Osnabrueck Library)
49069 Osnabruck
Tel: (0541) 969-0 *Fax:* (0541) 969-4482
E-mail: aaa@uni-osnabrueck.de
Web Site: www.uni-osnabrueck.de
Key Personnel
Library Dir: Felicitas Hundhausen
  E-mail: felicitas.hundhausen@ub.uni-osnabrueck.de
Founded: 1974
Publication(s): Ausstellungs Kataloge

Universitaets- und Landesbibliothek Muenster
(University & Regional Library Muenster)
Krummer Timpen 3-5, 48143 Muenster
Tel: (0251) 83 224021 *Fax:* (0251) 83 28398
E-mail: sekretariat.ulb@uni-muenster.de
Web Site: www.uni-muenster.de/ULB
Key Personnel
Editor: Daniel Busse; Dr Stephanie Kloetgen; Dagmar Klose; Karin Vogel
Contact: Dr Beate Troeger *Tel:* (0251) 83 24022
Founded: 1588

Universitaets - und Landesbibliothek Sachsen-Anhalt
August-Bebel-Str 13, 06108 Halle (Saale)
Tel: (0345) 55 22000 *Fax:* (0345) 55 27140
E-mail: direktion@bibliothek.uni-halle.de; auskunft@bibliothek.uni-halle.de
Web Site: www.bibliothek.uni-halle.de
Key Personnel
Dir: Dr Heiner Schnelling *E-mail:* schnelling@bibliothek.uni-halle.de
Founded: 1696

Universitaets- und Stadtbibliothek Koeln
(Cologne University & City Library)
Universitaetsstr 33, 50931 Cologne
Tel: (0221) 470-2214; (0221) 470-2374; (0221) 470-3316 *Fax:* (0221) 470-5166
E-mail: auskunft@ub.uni-koeln.de; sekretariat@ub.uni-koeln.de
Web Site: www.ub.uni-koeln.de
Key Personnel
Dir & Professor: Dr Wolfgang Schmitz
 Tel: (0221) 470-2260 *E-mail:* schmitz@ub.uni-koeln.de
Founded: 1920

Universitaetsbibliothek Bamberg
Feldkirchenstr 21, 96052 Bamberg
Mailing Address: Postfach 2705, 96018 Bamberg
Tel: (0951) 863-1503; (0951) 863-1501
 Fax: (0951) 863-1565
E-mail: unibibliothek.bamberg@unibib.uni-bamberg.de
Web Site: www.uni.bamberg.de/unbib

Universitaetsbibliothek Bochum
Universitaetsstr 150, 44780 Bochum
Tel: (049234) 3222350; (049234) 3222351
 Fax: (049234) 3214736
E-mail: direktion-ub@rub.de
Web Site: www.ub.ruhr-uni-bochum.de
Key Personnel
Dir: Dr Erdmute Lapp *E-mail:* erda.lapp@ruhr-uni-bochum.de
Deputy Dir: George Sander

Universitaetsbibliothek Erlangen-Nuernberg
Schuhstr 1a, 91052 Erlangen
Tel: (09131) 85-22160 *Fax:* (09131) 85-29309
E-mail: direktion@bib.uni-erlangen.de
Web Site: www.ub.uni-erlangen.de
Key Personnel
Dir: Dr Hans-Otto Keunecke

Universitaetsbibliothek Freiburg
Werthmannplatz 2, 79098 Freiburg im Breisgau
Mailing Address: Postfach 1629, 79016 Freiburg im Breisgau
Tel: (0761) 2033918 *Fax:* (0761) 2033987
E-mail: info@ub.uni-freiburg.de
Web Site: www.ub.uni-freiburg.de
Key Personnel
Dir: Baerbel Schubel
Contact: Dr Wilfried Suehl-Strohmenger
 Tel: (0761) 203 3924 *E-mail:* suehl@ub.uni-freiburg.de
Publication(s): *Festschrift: Tradition-Organisation-Innovation; Reihe: Schriften der Universitaets Bibliothek Freiburg*

Universitaetsbibliothek Freie Universitaet Berlin
(Free University of Berlin)
Garystr 39, 14195 Berlin
Tel: (030) 838 54224; (030) 838 54273
 Fax: (030) 838 53738
E-mail: auskunft@ub.fu-berlin.de
Web Site: www.ub.fu-berlin.de
Key Personnel
Librarian: Ulrich Naumann *E-mail:* naumann@ub.fu-berlin.de
Founded: 1952
Parent Company: Freie Universitaet Berlin

Universitaetsbibliothek Heidelberg
Ploeck 107-109, 69117 Heidelberg
Mailing Address: Postfach 10 57 49, 69047 Heidelberg
Tel: (06221) 54 2380 *Fax:* (06221) 54 2623
E-mail: ub@ub.uni-hd.de
Web Site: www.ub.uni-heidelberg.de
Key Personnel
Dir: Dr Veit Probst *E-mail:* probst@ub.uni-heidelberg.de
Publication(s): *Bibliothek-Forschung und Praxis; Bibliothek und Wissenschaft; Heidelberger Bibliothehsschriften; Neuerwerbungslisten der Sondersammelgebiete Aegyptologie, Klassische Archaeologie, Mittlere und Neuere Kunstgeschichte; Zeitschriftenverzeichnis Aegyptologie, Klassische Archaeologie und Mittlere und Neuere Kunstgeschichte; Heidelberger Zeitschriftenverzeichnis*
Bookshop(s): Im Neuenheimer Feld 368, 69120 Heidelberg *Tel:* (06221) 544272 *Fax:* (06221) 544204 *Web Site:* ub.uni-hd.de

Universitaetsbibliothek Kaiserslautern
(University Library of Kaiserslautern)
Paul-Ehrlich-Str, 67663 Kaiserslautern
Mailing Address: Postfach 2040, 67608 Kaiserslautern
Tel: (0631) 205-2241 *Fax:* (0631) 205-2355
E-mail: unibib@ub.uni-kl.de
Web Site: www.uni-kl.de/bibliothek
Key Personnel
Dir: Ralf Werner Wildermuth
Founded: 1970
Parent Company: Technische Universitaet Kaiserslautern

Universitaetsbibliothek Leipzig
Beethovenstr 6, 04107 Leipzig
Tel: (0341) 97 30577 *Fax:* (0341) 97 30596
E-mail: auskunft@ub.uni-leipzig.de
Web Site: www.ub.uni-leipzig.de/ubl
Key Personnel
Dir: Dr Phil Ekkehard Henschke
Publication(s): *Geschriebenes aber bleibt*

Universitaetsbibliothek Mannheim
Schloss Ostfluegel und A3, 68131 Mannheim
Tel: (0621) 181-2941; (0621) 181-2948; (0621) 181-2989 *Fax:* (0621) 181-2939
E-mail: biblubma@bib.uni-mannheim.de
Web Site: www.bib.uni-mannheim.de
Key Personnel
Dir: Christian Benz *Tel:* (0621) 181-2941

Universitaetsbibliothek Tuebingen
(University Library)
Wilhelmstr 32, 72016 Tuebingen
Mailing Address: Postfach 2620, 72016 Tuebingen
Tel: (07071) 29-72846 *Fax:* (07071) 29-3123
E-mail: info-zentrum@ub.uni-tuebingen.de
Web Site: www.uni-tuebingen.de/ub
Key Personnel
Head Librarian: Dr Ulrich Schapka *Tel:* (07071) 29-72505 *E-mail:* ulrich.schapka@uni-tuebingen.de
Founded: 1477

Universitaetsbibliothek Wuppertal
Gauss-Str 20, 42119 Wuppertal
Mailing Address: Postfach 100127, 42001 Wuppertal
Tel: (0202) 439-2705 *Fax:* (0202) 439-2695
E-mail: information@bib.uni-wuppertal.de
Web Site: www.bib.uni-wuppertal.de
Key Personnel
Dir: Dr Dieter Staeglich *Tel:* (0202) 439-2691

Universitat Wuerzburg
Universitaetsbibliothek Am Hubland, 97074 Wuerzburg
Tel: (0931) 888-5906 *Fax:* (0931) 888-5970
E-mail: direktion@bibliothek.uni-wuerzburg.de; information@bibliothek.uni-wuerzburg.de
Web Site: www.bibliothek.uni-wuerzburg.de
Key Personnel
Librarian: Karl Suedekum *Tel:* (0931) 888-5942
 E-mail: suedekum@bibliothek.uni.wuerzburg.de
Publication(s): *Verzeichnis auf Anfrage*

Universitats und Landesbibliothe Darmstadt
(University & State Library Darmstadt)
Formerly Hessische Landes und Hochschulbibliothek
Division of Technische Universitat Darmstadt
Schloss, 64283 Darmstadt
Tel: (06151) 165850 *Fax:* (06151) 165897
E-mail: auskunft@ulb.tu-darmstadt.de
Web Site: www.ulb.tu-darmstadt.de
Key Personnel
Librarian: Dr Hans Georg Nolte-Fischer
Executive Secretary: Doris Michel *Tel:* (06151) 165801 *E-mail:* michel@ulb.tu-darmstadt.de
Founded: 1568
Branch Office(s)
Zweigbibliothek Lichtwiese, El Lissitzkystr 1, 64287 Darmstadt *Tel:* (06151) 165867 *E-mail:* zweigbib@ulb.tu-darmstadt.de
Patentinformationszentrum, Schoefferstr 8, 64295 Darmstadt *Tel:* (06151) 165427 *E-mail:* info@main-piz.de *Web Site:* www.main-piz.de

Universitatsbibliothek Augsburg
Universitatsstr 22, 86135 Augsburg
Mailing Address: Universitaetsbibliothek Augsburg, 86135 Augsburg
Tel: (0821) 598 5320; (0821) 598 5306; (0821) 598 5305 *Fax:* (0821) 598 5354
E-mail: dir@bibliothek.uni-augsburg.de
Web Site: www.bibliothek.uni-augsburg.de
Telex: 53830
Key Personnel
Contact: Eva Schoeppl *Tel:* (0821) 598 5304
 E-mail: eva.schoeppl@bibliothek.uni-augsburg.de
Founded: 1970

Wissenschaftliche Allgemeinbibliothek der Stadt Erfurt
Dompl 1, 99084 Erfurt
Tel: (0361) 562 48 76 *Fax:* (0361) 646 20 71
Key Personnel
Contact: Kerstin Weishaeupl

Wuerttembergische Landesbibliothek
Konrad-Adenauerstr 8, 70173 Stuttgart
Mailing Address: Postfach 105441, 70047 Stuttgart
Tel: (0711) 2124424 *Fax:* (0711) 2124422
E-mail: direktion@wlb-stuttgart.de; information@wlb-stuttgart.de
Web Site: www.wlb-stuttgart.de
Key Personnel
Dir: Dr H Kowark *E-mail:* kowark@wlb-stuttgart.de
Contact: Horst Hilger *Tel:* (0711) 2124390; (0711) 2124504 *E-mail:* hilger@wlb-stuttgart.de

Founded: 1765
Regional library for the state of Baden-Wurttemberg, currently comprised of 4.65 million media items.
Publication(s): *Ausstellungs- und Bestandskataloge*

ZBW-Deutsche Zentralbibliothek fuer Wirtschaftswissenschaften/Bibliothek des Instituts fuer Weltwirtschaft (German National Library of Economics/Library of the Kiel Institute for World Economics)
Duesternbrooker Weg 120, 24105 Kiel
Tel: (0431) 8814-383; (0431) 8814-555
Fax: (0431) 8814-520
E-mail: info@zbw.ifw-kiel.de
Web Site: www.zbw-kiel.de *Cable:* WELTWIRTSCHAFT KIEL
Key Personnel
Dir: Horst Thomsen *Tel:* (0431) 8814-444 *Fax:* (0431) 8814-530 *E-mail:* h.thomsen@zbw.ifw-kiel.de
Deputy Librarian: Ekkehart Seusing *Tel:* (0431) 8814-436 *E-mail:* e.seusing@zbw.ifw-kiel.de
Worldwide economics special library. Also provides document delivery services.
Publication(s): *ECONIS* (Database of references to literature in economics & adjacent subjects); *Thesaurus der ZBW*

Zentral- und Landesbibliothek Berlin (ZLB)
(Central & Regional Library of Berlin)
Bluecherplatz 1, 10961 Berlin
Tel: (030) 902260; (030) 90226-401 *Fax:* (030) 90226-163
E-mail: info@zlb.de
Web Site: www.zlb.de
Key Personnel
General Dir: Dr Claudia Lux *Tel:* (030) 90226-450 *E-mail:* lux@zlb.de
Founded: 1901
Full library & information services.

ZLB, see Zentral- und Landesbibliothek Berlin (ZLB)

Ghana

Balme Library, see University of Ghana Library

British Council Library
Bank Rd, Kumasi
Mailing Address: PO Box KS 1996, Kumasi
Tel: (051) 23462; (051) 37197 *Fax:* (051) 26725
E-mail: infokumasi@gh.britishcouncil.org
Web Site: www.britishcouncil.org/ghana
Telex: 2369 brico gh
Key Personnel
Education Information Officer: Benjamin Addo *E-mail:* benjaminaddo@bcgha.africainline.com.gh
Head Libraries & Information Services: Ruth Osci

Council for Scientific & Industrial Research-Institute for Scientific & Technological Information
PO Box M 32, Accra
Tel: (021) 777651-4; (021) 777655
E-mail: csir@ghana.com; cemensah@hotmail.com
Web Site: www.csir.org.gh
Telex: SCIENCES
Key Personnel
Acting Dir-General: Prof E Owusu Benoah
Publication(s): *CSIR Newsletter* (quarterly); *Directory of High Level Manpower* (every 5 years); *Directory of Research Projects (Science & Technology) in Ghana (1990)* (every 5 years); *Directory of Special & Research Libraries in Ghana*; *Ghana Journal of Agricultural Science* (biannually); *Ghana Journal of Science* (biannually); *Ghana Science Abstracts* (annually); *Union List of Scientific Serials in Ghanaian Libraries (1976)*

CSIR-INSTI, see Council for Scientific & Industrial Research-Institute for Scientific & Technological Information

Geological Survey Department Reference Library
Geological Survey Dept, PO Box M 80, Accra
Tel: (021) 228093; (021) 28079 *Fax:* (021) 228063; (021) 224676
E-mail: ghgeosur@ghana.com
Key Personnel
Librarian: E Hammond

Ghana Institute of Management & Public Administration, Library & Documentation Centre
Greenhill, Achimota, Accra
Mailing Address: PO Box 50, Achimota, Accra
Tel: (021) 401681; (021) 401682; (021) 401683 *Fax:* (021) 405805
E-mail: gimpa@excite.com
Telex: 2551 Gimpa Gh *Cable:* GIMPA ACHIMOTA
Key Personnel
Librarian: Theresa Gyedu

Ghana Library Board
Thorpe Rd, Accra
Mailing Address: PO Box 663, Accra
Tel: (021) 665 083 *Fax:* (021) 678 258 *Cable:* GHANLIB ACCRA
Key Personnel
Dir & Librarian: David Cornelius
The Research Library on African Affairs, a division of the Ghana Library Board performs some functions of a National Library for Ghana.
Publication(s): *Ghana National Bibliography, A Guide to Creative Writing by Africans in English* (Annual Report)

Institute of African Studies Library
University of Ghana, Legon, Accra
Mailing Address: PO Box LG 73, Legon, Accra
Tel: (021) 500512 *Fax:* (021) 502397
E-mail: asofo@ghana.com
Key Personnel
Director: Dr Irene Odotei
Assistant Librarian: Mrs Olive Adoah
Founded: 1961
Publication(s): *Research Review* (magazine)

Kwame Nkrumah University of Science & Technology Library
Private Post Bag, Kumasi
Tel: (051) 60199; (051) 60133 *Fax:* (051) 60358
E-mail: ustlib@libr.ug.edu.gh
Key Personnel
University Librarian: Mrs H R Asamoah-Hassan
Founded: 1951

George Padmore Research Library on African Affairs
PO Box 2970, Accra
Tel: (021) 228 402; (021) 223526 *Fax:* (021) 247 768
Key Personnel
Librarian: Omari Mensah Tenkorang
Founded: 1961
Publication(s): *Current Ghana Bibliography* (every two months, 1968); *Ghana National Bibliography* (annually)
Parent Company: Ghana Library Board

School of Administration Library
University of Ghana, PO Box 78, Legon, Accra
Fax: (021) 500024
E-mail: soa@libr.ug.edu.gh
Key Personnel
Librarian: Mr G Odartey-Cofie *Tel:* (021) 500591 *E-mail:* odarteycofiesoa@libr.ug.edu.gh
Founded: 1960
Publication(s): *Journal of Management Studies* (annually)

Statistical Service
PO Box 1098, Accra
Tel: (021) 682629 *Fax:* (021) 667069
E-mail: baahwadieh@yahoo.com
Telex: 2205 MIFAEP GH
Key Personnel
Government Statistician: Dr Oti Boateng Daasebre
Deputy Government Statisticians: Dr K A Twum-Baah; Mr K Addomah-Gyabaah
Information Officer: Mr J Y Amankrah
Collection, compilation, analysis, publication & dissemination of statistical information.

University of Cape Coast Library
PMB, University Post Office, Cape Coast
Tel: (042) 60133 *Fax:* (042) 32485
E-mail: Ucclib@ucc.gn.apc.org
Telex: 2552 UCC GH
Key Personnel
Librarian: Richard Arkaifie

University of Ghana Library
PO Box 25, Legon
Tel: (021) 502701 *Fax:* (021) 502701
E-mail: balme@ug.gn.apc.org
Web Site: www.ug.edu.gh *Cable:* UNIVERSITY LEGON
Key Personnel
Ag Librarian: Prof A A Alemna
Ag Dept Librarian: Mrs V Dodoo
Assistant Librarian: S K Asiedu
Founded: 1948

Gibraltar

Garrison Library
2 Library Gardens, Gibraltar 77418
Mailing Address: PO Box 374, Gibraltar
Tel: 77418 *Fax:* 79927
Key Personnel
Secretary: J M Searle
Gibraltor & Western Mediterranean Research by arrangement with secretary.

Gibraltar Library Service, see John Mackintosh Hall Library

John Mackintosh Hall Library
Knightsfield Holdings Ltd, 308 Main St, Gibraltar
Tel: 78000 *Fax:* 40843
Key Personnel
Dir: Geraldine Finlayson *E-mail:* gfjmh@gibnet.gi
Founded: 1964
Free lending library set up under will of late John Mackintosh, mainly adult fiction & nonfiction. Now incorporating the Gibraltar Library Service.

Greece

Athens Academy Library
28 Panepistimiou, 106 79 Athens
Tel: (01) 360-0209
Web Site: www.academyofathens.gr

British Council Library & Resource Centre
17 Kolonaki Sq, 106 73 Athens
Tel: (0210) 369 2333 *Fax:* (0210) 363 4769
E-mail: general.enquiries@britcoun.gr
Web Site: www.britishcouncil.gr/infoexch/greinfll.htm
Telex: 218799 Bric Gr
Key Personnel
Dir: Desmond Lauder *E-mail:* desmond.lauder@britishcouncil.gr
Branch Office(s)
9 Ethnikis Amnysis str, 540 13 Thessaloniki
Tel: (02310) 378 300 *Fax:* (02310) 282 498

Ethnikon Idryma Erevnon
48 Vassileou Voulgaroktonou Ave, 11635 Athens
Tel: (01) 7210554 *Fax:* (01) 7246212
Telex: 224064 EIE GR
Key Personnel
Man Dir: Prof B Maglaris
President: Prof Nikos Athanassiades
National Hellenic Research Foundation.

Eugenides Foundation Technical Library
387 Sygrou Ave, 17465 Athens
Tel: (01) 9411181 *Fax:* (01) 9417372
E-mail: lib@eugenfound.edu.gr
Web Site: www.eugenfound.edu.gr *Cable:* FONDATIONEVGE
Key Personnel
Librarian: Hara Brindesi

Gennadius Library
American School of Classical Studies at Athens, 61 Souidias St, Athens 106 76
Tel: (0210) 7210536 *Fax:* (0210) 7237767
E-mail: ascsa@ascsa.edu.gr
Web Site: www.ascsa.edu.gr/gennadius
Key Personnel
Dir: Dr Haris Kalligas *E-mail:* hkalligas@ascsa.edu.gr
Head Librarian: Sophie Papageorgiou
E-mail: spapageorg@ascsa.edu.gr
Publication(s): *The New Griffon, No 1, 1991* (in Greek)

National Library of Greece (Ethnike Bibliotheke tes Hellados)
Odos El Benizelu 32, 106 79 Athens
Tel: (0210) 3382566 *Fax:* (0210) 3382502
Web Site: www.nlg.gr
Key Personnel
Dir: Dr George Zachos *E-mail:* gzachos@nlg.gr
Founded: 1828

Library of the National Technological University of Athens
Zografou Campus 9 Heroon, Polytechniou Ave, 157 73 Zografos Athens
Tel: (0210) 772 1471 *Fax:* (0210) 772 1565
E-mail: pstath@softlab.ntua.gr
Web Site: www.lib.ntua.gr
Key Personnel
Dir: Prof E Galanis
Founded: 1836

Library of the Technical Chamber of Greece
23-25 Lekka Str, 10562 Athens
Tel: (0210) 3291701; (0210) 3245180 *Fax:* (0210) 3237525
E-mail: tee_lib@tee.gr
Web Site: www.tee.gr
Key Personnel
Head of Documentation & Information Unit: Katerina Toraki

Library of the University of Crete
Gallos Campus, GR 74100 Rethymnon
Tel: (02831) 077810 *Fax:* (02831) 077850
Web Site: www.libh.uoc.gr
Telex: 291145
Key Personnel
Dir: Eleni Diamantaki
Acquisitions Librarian: K Karadaki *Tel:* (0831) 77808 *E-mail:* karadaki@libr.uoc.gr

Library of the University of Thessaloniki
c/o Aristotle University of Thessaloniki, University Campus, 54006 Thessaloniki
Tel: (031) 995325; (031) 995327 *Fax:* (031) 995322
E-mail: syra@ipatia.ccf.auth.gr
Web Site: www.lib.auth.gr
Telex: 0412181 auth
Key Personnel
Dir: Syra Nikolakaki Fotini *E-mail:* syra@ipatia.ccf.auth.gr
Librarian: D Dimitriou
Founded: 1927
Contains resources for the region of Macedonia, from antiquity to the present, in Greek & other languages.
Total Titles: 150,000 Print

Guatemala

Archivo General de Centro America
4ta Av, 7-41, Zona 1, Guatemala City
Tel: 232-3037
Key Personnel
Dir: Arturo Valdes

Biblioteca Nacional de Guatemala (National Library of Guatemala)
5a Av 7-26, Zona 1, Guatemala City
Tel: (0502) 2322443 *Fax:* (0502) 2539071
E-mail: biblioguatemala@intelnett.com
Web Site: www.biblionet.edu.gt
Key Personnel
Dir: Victor Castillo Lopez
Founded: 1876

Biblioteca Central de la Universidad de San Carlos
Ciudad Universitaria, Zona 12, Guatemala City
Tel: (02) 460 611
E-mail: usacbibc@usac.edu.gt
Web Site: www.usac.edu.gt/dependencias/biblioteca
Key Personnel
Acting Dir: Lieda Ofelia Aguilar
Founded: 1974
Publication(s): *Boletin Bibliografico*; *Boletin Contenidos*

Guinea

Bibliotheque Nationale (National Library)
BP 561, Conakry
Tel: (01) 461 010
Key Personnel
Librarian: Lansana Sylla
Founded: 1958

Guyana

Guyana Medical Science Library
Georgetown Hospital Compound, Georgetown
Key Personnel
Librarian: Mrs Jennifer Wilson

National Library
76/77 Church & Main St, Georgetown
Tel: (02) 227-4053; (02) 227-4052; (02) 226-2690; (02) 227-2699 *Fax:* (02) 227-4053
E-mail: natlib@sdnp.org.gy
Web Site: www.natlib.gov.gy
Key Personnel
Chief Librarian: Karen Sills
Founded: 1909
Publication(s): *Guyanese National Bibliography*

Haiti

Bibliotheque du Petit Seminaire
Port-au-Prince

Bibliotheque Haitienne des Freres de l'I.C., Saint Louis de Gonzague
180 Rue du Centre, BP 1758, Port-au-Prince HT 6110
Tel: 2232148; 2237508 *Fax:* 2232029
Key Personnel
Dir: Br Ernest Even
Founded: 1920
Secteurs les plus importants du fonds documentaire; a) collections de journaux des XIXe et XXe siecles b) histoire de Saint-Domingue et de l'Haiti contemporaine c) litterature haitienne.

Bibliotheque Nationale d'Haiti (National Library of Haiti)
193 rue du Centre, Port-au-Prince
Tel: 220 236; 220 198 *Fax:* 238 773
Key Personnel
Dir: Francoise Beaulieu Thybulle
Founded: 1940

Holy See (Vatican City State)

Biblioteca Apostolica Vaticana (Vatican Apostolic Library)
Cortile del Belvedere, 00120 Vatican City
Tel: (06) 6987 9402 *Fax:* (06) 6988 4795
E-mail: bav@vatlib.it
Web Site: 212.77.1.230/it/v_home_bav/home_bav.shtml
Telex: 2024 Dirgental VA
Key Personnel
Dir: Raffaele Farina
Prefect: Prof Don Raffaele Farina
Founded: 1451

Honduras

Biblioteca Nacional de Honduras (National Library of Honduras)
Apdo 4563, Tegucigalpa
Tel: 228 02 41 *Fax:* 222 85 77
E-mail: binah@sdnhon.org.hn; binah@ns.hondunet.net
Web Site: www.binah.gob.hn
Key Personnel
Dir: Hector Roberto Luna

Sistema Bibliotecario
c/o Carretera a Suyapa, Ciudad Univeritaria, Tegucigalpa
Tel: 232-2204 *Fax:* 232-2204
E-mail: webmaster@biblio.unah.edu.hn
Web Site: www.biblio.unah.edu.hn
Telex: 1289 Unah Ho
Key Personnel
Dir: Orfylia S Pinel
Publication(s): *Boletin del Sistema Bibliotecario*

Hong Kong

British Council Library
3 Supreme Court Rd, Admirality, Hong Kong
Tel: 2913 5100 *Fax:* 2913 5102
E-mail: info@britishcouncil.org.hk
Web Site: www.britishcouncil.org.hk
Telex: 74141 bcoun hx
Key Personnel
Assistant Dir, Information: L J Nairn

Chinese University of Hong Kong Library System
Shatin, New Territories
Tel: 2609-7306 *Fax:* 2603-6952
E-mail: library@cuhk.edu.hk
Web Site: www.lib.cuhk.edu.hk
Telex: 50301 Cuhk Hx *Cable:* SINOVERSITY
Key Personnel
University Librarian: Dr Colin Storey *Tel:* 2609-7318 *E-mail:* storey@cuhk.edu.hk
Publication(s): *Catalogue of the Chinese Rare Books in the Libraries of The Chinese University of Hong Kong*; *History of Medicine: An Annotated Bibliography of Titles at The Chinese University of Hong Kong*; *Newspapers of Hong Kong, 1841-1979*; *Serials of Hong Kong, 1845*; *Union Catalogue of Asian Fine Arts Collection*
Branch Office(s)
Architecture Library *Tel:* 2609 6599 *Fax:* 2603 6584
Chung Chi College Library *Tel:* 2609 6969 *Fax:* 2603 5793
Li Ping Medical Library *Tel:* 2632 2459 *Fax:* 2637 7817
New Asia College Library *Tel:* 2609 7655 *Fax:* 2603 5796
United College Library *Tel:* 2609 7564 *Fax:* 2603 5729

The Hong Kong Polytechnic University Library
Hung Hom, Kowloon
Tel: 2766 6863
Web Site: www.polyu.edu.hk
Key Personnel
University Librarian: Barry Burton
E-mail: lbbarry@polyu.edu.hk
Publication(s): *Hongkongiana* (index to selected Hong Kong periodicals electronic database)

Hong Kong Public Libraries
11/F Hong Kong Central Library, 66 Causeway Rd, Hong Kong
Tel: 2921 0208 *Fax:* 2415 8211
E-mail: enquiries@lcsd.gov.hk
Web Site: www.hkpl.gov.hk
Key Personnel
Assistant Dir: Michael Mak *E-mail:* mklmak@lcsd.gov.hk
Provide free public library services through a network of 71 libraries.

Sun Yat-Sen Library
172-174 Boundary St, Kowloon
Tel: 23365291
Key Personnel
Librarian: Mrs Megie M L Tong

University of Hong Kong Libraries
University of Hong Kong, Main Library, Pokfulam
Tel: 2859 7000; 2859 2203 *Fax:* 2858 9420
E-mail: libadmin@hkucc.hku.hk
Web Site: lib.hku.hk
Key Personnel
Librarian: Dr Anthony W Ferguson
Deputy Librarian: Peter Sidorko; Lawrence Wai Hong Tam
Assistant Librarian (Administration): Esther Woo *Tel:* 2859 2206 *E-mail:* emwwoo@hkucc.hku.hk
Founded: 1912
Publication(s): *The University of Hong Kong Libraries Publications Series*

Hungary

BME KTK, see Budapesti Muszaki es Guzdasagtudomanyi Egyetem Orszagos Muszaki Informacios Kozpont es Konyvtar

Budapesti Kozgazdasagtudomanyi es Allamigazoatasi Luyutemi Egyetem Kozponti Konyvtar (Budapest University of Economic Science & Public Administration-Central Library)
Koezraktar U 18-20, Budapest 1093
Mailing Address: PF 489, Budapest 1828
Tel: (01) 2176827 *Fax:* (01) 2174910
E-mail: konyvtar@lib.bkae.hu
Web Site: www.lib.bke.hu
Key Personnel
Dir: Dr Hedvig Huszar *E-mail:* huszar@lib.bkae.hu
Central Library of Budapest University of Economic Sciences.

Budapesti Muszaki es Guzdasagtudomanyi Egyetem Orszagos Muszaki Informacios Kozpont es Konyvtar (Budapest University of Technology & Economics, National Technical Information Centre & Library)
Budafoki u 4-6, Budapest 1111
Mailing Address: PO Box 91, Budapest 1502
Tel: (01) 463-3534; (01) 463-1069 *Fax:* (01) 463-2440
E-mail: kolcs@omikk.bme.hu
Web Site: www.bme.hu; www.omikk.bme.hu
Key Personnel
Dir: Ilona Fonyo *E-mail:* ifonyo@omikk.bme.hu

Foszekesegyhazi Konyvtar (Cathedral Library)
Pazmany P U 2, H-2500 Esztergom
Tel: 33411891
E-mail: bibliotheca@ehf.hu *Cable:* BIBLIOTHECA ESZTERGOM
Key Personnel
Dir: Bela Czekli
Cathedral Library.

Fovarosi Szabo Ervin Konyvtar (Ervin Szabo Metropolitan Library)
Szabo Ervin ter 1, 1088 Budapest
Tel: (01) 1185815; (01) 411-5000 *Fax:* (01) 1185914
E-mail: info@fszek.hu
Web Site: www.fszek.hu
Key Personnel
Dir: Jenoe Kiss

Jozsef Attila Tudomanyegyetem Egyetemi Koenyvtar (University of Szeged University Library)
Dugonics Sq 13, 6720 Szeged
Mailing Address: Postfach 393, 6701 Szeged
Tel: (062) 544-036 *Fax:* (062) 544-035
E-mail: mader@bibl.u-szeged.hu
Web Site: www.bibl.u-szeged.hu
Key Personnel
Chief Librarian: Dr Bela Mader
Publication(s): *Acta Bibliothecaria* (irregularly); *Acta Universitatis Szegediensis de Attila Jozsef Nominatae*; *Dissertationes ex Bibliotheca Universitatis de Attila Jozsef nominatae*; *Koenyvtartoerteneti Fuezetek* (History of Libraries series, with German summaries)

Koezponti Statisztikai Hivatal Koenyvtar es Dokumentacios Szolgalat (Hungarian Central Statistical Office, Library & Documentation Service)
Keleti Karoly u 5, Budapest 1024
Tel: (01) 3456105 *Fax:* (01) 3456112
Web Site: www.ksh.hu; www.lib.ksh.hu
Key Personnel
Dir General: Dr Erzebet Nemes
Founded: 1867
Publication(s): *Magyarorszag toerteneti helysegnevtara 1773-1808* (Historical Gazetteer of Hungary, 2000); *Statisztikai modszerek-Temadokumentacio* (Statistical Methods-Surveys of Literature on Various Subjects, 2000); *Szakbibliografiak-Statisztikai adatforrasok bibliografia* (Special Bibliographies-Sources of Statistical Data Bibliography, 2002); *Toerteneti statisztikai fuezetek* (Papers on Historical Statistics, 2000); *Toerteneti statisztikai tanulmanyok* (Studies on Historical Statistics, 2000)

Kossuth Lajos Tudomanyegyetem Egyetemi Koenyvtar
Pf 39, 4010 Debrecen
Tel: (052) 316-835; (052) 316-666; (052) 512-900 *Fax:* (052) 410-443
E-mail: comp@lib.unideb.hu
Web Site: www.lib.unideb.hu
Telex: 72200
Key Personnel
Chief Librarian: Dr Olga Gomba
Dir General: Dr Iren Levay
Lajos Kossuth University Library.

Magyar Orszagos Leveltar (MOL) (National Archives of Hungary)
Becsi kapu ter 4, 1014 Budapest 1
Tel: (01) 225-2800 *Fax:* (01) 225-2805
E-mail: info@natarch.hu
Web Site: www.natarch.hu
Key Personnel
Dir: Prof Lajos Gecsenyi, PhD *Tel:* (01) 225-2803 *E-mail:* gecsenyi@natarch.hu
Founded: 1756
Publication(s): *Leveltari Kozlemenyek* (Archival Publications, biannually, 1923, academical & scholar); *Magyar Orszagos Leveltar Kiadvanyai* (Publications of National Archives of Hungary, biannually)

Magyar Tudomanyos Akademia Koenyvtara
(Library of the Hungarian Academy of Sciences)
Arany Janos u l, Budapest 1051
Mailing Address: PF 1002, 1245 Budapest
Tel: (01) 411 6100 *Fax:* (01) 311 6954
E-mail: mtak@vax.mtak.hu
Web Site: w3.mtak.hu
Key Personnel
Deputy Dir General: Dr Karolyne Domsa
 E-mail: domsa@vax.mtak.hu
Founded: 1826
Library of the Hungarian Academy of Sciences/Library of the HAS.
Publication(s): *Budapest Oriental Reprints Ser A & Ser B* (irregular, scientific monographs); *Oriental Studies* (irregular, scientific monographs); *Publicationes Bibliothecae Academiae Scientiarum Hungaricae* (irregular, scientific monographs)

MOL, see Magyar Orszagos Leveltar (MOL)

Orszagos Muoszaki, Informacios Koozpont es Koonyvtar (OMIKK) (National Technical Information Centre & Library)
Budafoki ut 4-6, 1111 Budapest
Mailing Address: Postafiok 91, 1502 Budapest
Tel: (01) 463-3534; (01) 463-1069 *Fax:* (01) 463-24-40
E-mail: kolcs@omikk.bme.hu
Web Site: www.omikk.bme.hu
Key Personnel
Dir General: Akos Robert Herman, PhD
 E-mail: har@omk.omikk.hu
Librarian: Peter Szanto
Translation Department, offers translation from Hungarian & other languages.
Publication(s): *Tudomanyos es Muoszaki Tajekoztatas* (scientific & technical information)

Orszagos Szechenyi Koenyvtar
Budavari Palota F epuelet, 1827 Budapest
Tel: (01) 224-3788 *Fax:* (01) 202-0804; (01) 375-9984
E-mail: kint@oszk.hu
Web Site: www.oszk.hu
Key Personnel
Dir General: Geza Poprady
National Center for Library Science & Methodology, Hungarian national ISBN & ISDS Center.
Publication(s): *A magyar irodalom es irodalomtudomany bibliografaja* (Bibliography of Hungarian Literature & Literary Studies); *Az Orszagos Szechenyi Koenyvtar evkoenyve* (National Szechenyi Library Year Book); *Hungariaka informacio* (Hungarica Information); *Kurrens Kuelfoeldi idoeszaki Kiadvanyok a Magyar Koenyvtarakban* (Current Foreign Periodical Publications in Hungarian Libraries); *Magyar Koenyveszet* (annually, Cumulation of Hungarian National bibliography); *Magyar nemzeti bibliografia Idoszaki kiadvanyok bibliografiaja* (Hungarian National Bibliography of Serials); *Magyar nemzeti bibliografia. Idoszaki kiadvanyok repertoriuma* (Hungarian National Bibliography. Repertory of Periodicals); *Magyar nemzeti bibliografia Koenyvek bibliografiaja* (Hungarian National Bibliography of Books); *Magyar nemzeti bibliografia. Zenemuvek bibliografiaja* (Hungarian National Bibliography of Music Scores & Records); *Mikrofilmek cimjegyzeke. Idoszaki kiadvanyok* (List of Microfilm Titles. Periodical Publications); *Mikrofilmek cimjegyzeke. Modern nyomtatvanyok* (List of Microfilm Titles. Modern Printed Matter); *Mikrofilmek cimjegyzeke. Szines grafikai plakatok* (List of Microfilm Titles. Colored Graphic Posters); *Mikrofilmek cimjegyzeke. Zenei gyujtemeny. Zenemukezira-tok* (List of Microfilm Titles. Music Collection. Music Manuscripts); *Uj periodikumok* (New Periodicals)

Sarospataki Reformatus- Kollegium Tudomanyos Gyuejtemenyei Nagykoenyvtar
Rakoczy ut 1, 3950 Sarospatak
Tel: 4111057
Key Personnel
Dir: Michael Szentimrel
The Library of Scientific Collections of the Reformed College of Saroapatak.

Iceland

Kennarahaskoli Islands (Iceland University of Education)
v/Stakkahlid, 105 Reykjavik
Tel: 5633800 *Fax:* 5633914
E-mail: vefur@khi.is
Web Site: www.khi.is
Key Personnel
Learning Center Dir: Kristin Indridadottir
 E-mail: kindr@khi.is

Landsbokasafn Islands-Haskolabokasafn
(National & University Library of Iceland)
Arngrimsgafa 3, 107 Reykjavik
Tel: 525 5600 *Fax:* 525 5615
E-mail: lbs@bok.hi.is
Web Site: www.bok.hi.is
Key Personnel
National Librarian: Sigrun Klara Hannesdottir
Deputy Librarian: Porsteinn Hallgrimsson
National Library & University Library of Iceland.
Publication(s): *Handritasafn Landsbokasafns* (catalog of manuscripts); *Islensk bokaskra* (Icelandic National Bibliography); *Islensk Hljodritaskra* (Bibliography of Icelandic Sound Recordings, supplement to Islensk bokaskra); *Ritmennf* (annually, journal)

Borgarbokasafn Reykjavikur (Reykjavik City Library)
Tryggvagata 15, 101 Reykjavik
Tel: 5631717 *Fax:* 5631705
E-mail: borgarbokasafn@borgarbokasafn.is
Web Site: www.borgarbokasafn.is
Key Personnel
City Librarian: Erla Kristin Jonasdottir
 E-mail: erla@borgarbokasafn.is
Founded: 1923
Publication(s): *Arsskyrsla*
Branch Office(s)
Foldasafn, Grafarvogskirkju Church, 112 Reykjavik *Tel:* 5675320 *Fax:* 5675356
Gerduberg, Gerduberg 3-5, 111 Reykjavik
 Tel: 5579122 *Fax:* 5579160
Kringlusafn, Borgarleikhus v/Listabraut, 104 Reykjavik *Tel:* 5806200 *Fax:* 5806219
Seljasafn, Holmascli 4-6, 109 Reykjavik
 Tel: 5873320
Solheimasafn, Solheimar 27, 104 Reykjavik
 Tel: 5536814 *Fax:* 5813780

India

American Information Resource Center
Division of Public Affairs Section, American Embassy
The American Center, 24 Kasturba Gandhi Marg, New Delhi 110001
Tel: (011) 2331-6841; (011) 2331-4251
 Fax: (011) 2332-9499
E-mail: libdel@pd.state.gov
Web Site: americanlibrary.in.library.net; newdelhi.usembassy.gov
Key Personnel
AIRC Dir: Veena Chawla
Public library.
Branch Office(s)
38-A Jawaharlal Nehra Rd, Kolkata 700071
 Tel: (033) 2245-1211; (033) 2245-1218
 Fax: (033) 2245 2445

The Asiatic Society of Mumbai
Town Hall, Mumbai 400 023
Tel: (022) 2660956 *Fax:* (022) 2665139
E-mail: asbl@bom2.vsnl.net.in
Web Site: education.vsnl.com/asbl/
Key Personnel
President: Mr B G Deshmukh
Vice President: Dr Devangana Desai; Mr Rajan M Jayakar; Dr Mani Kamerkar; Mr Eknath Kshirsagar
Honorary Secretary: Mrs Vimal Shah
Founded: 1804
Publication(s): *Journal of the Asiatic Society of Mumbai & Monographs*

British Council Libraries
17, Kasturba Gandhi Marg, New Delhi 110001
Tel: (011) 371 1401 *Fax:* (011) 371 0717
E-mail: delhi.library@in.britishcouncil.org
Web Site: www.bclindia.org/library
Key Personnel
Head, Library & Info Services: P Jayarajan
 E-mail: jayarajan@in.britishcouncil.org
Branch Office(s)
Bhaikaka Bhawan, Law Garden, Ellisbridge, 380 006 Ahmedabad, Gujarat *Tel:* (079) 6464693 *Fax:* (079) 6469493
Prestige Takt 23, Kasturba Rd Cross, Bangalore 560001 *Tel:* (080) 2240763 *Fax:* (080) 2240767
GTB Complex, Roshanpura Naka, Bhopal 462003 *Tel:* (0755) 553767 *Fax:* (0755) 765211
SCO 36-38, Sector 8C, Madhya Marg, Chandigarh 160008 *Tel:* (0172) 546540; (0172) 546541 *Fax:* (0172) 547540 *E-mail:* bl.chandigarh@in.britishcouncil.org
737 Anna Salai, Chennai 600002 *Tel:* (044) 8525002 *Fax:* (044) 8523234 *E-mail:* library.chennai@in.britishcouncil.org
5-9-22 Secretariat Rd, Sarovar Centre, Hyderabad 560001 *Tel:* (040) 23230774 *Fax:* (040) 23298273
L&T Chambers, 1st floor, 16 Camac St, Kolkata 700071 *Tel:* (033) 2825370 *E-mail:* kolkata.library@in.britishcouncil.org
Mittal Towers "A" Wing, 1st floor, Nariman Point, Mumbai 400021 *Tel:* (022) 2823530 *Fax:* (022) 2852024 *E-mail:* mumbai.library@in.britishcouncil.org
917/1 Ferugusson College Rd, Shivaji Nagar, Pune 411004 *Tel:* (020) 5654352 *Fax:* (020) 5654351
YMCA Bldg, Thiruvananthapuram 695001 *Tel:* (0471) 330716 *Fax:* (0471) 330717

Central Library
Vadodara, Gujaat, Baroda 390006
Tel: (0265) 540133
Key Personnel
State Librarian: Bakulesh Bhuta
Publication(s): *Granth Deep* (quarterly)

Central Secretariat Library
Dept of Culture, G Wing, Shastri Bhavan, New Delhi 110 001
Tel: (011) 338 9684 *Fax:* (011) 338 4846
E-mail: root%csl@delnet.ren.nic.in
Key Personnel
Dir: Kalpana Dasgupta

Delhi Public Library
S P Mukherjee Marg, New Delhi 110006
Tel: (011) 291 6881 *Fax:* (011) 294 3990

INDIA

Key Personnel
Dir: Dr Banwari Lal
Founded: 1951

Delhi University Library System
Delhi 110007
Tel: (011) 27667725 *Fax:* (011) 27667126
E-mail: crl@delnet.ven.nic.in
Web Site: www.du.ac.in
Key Personnel
University Librarian: M L Saini *Tel:* (011) 27667848 (ext 1127)

Gujarat Vidyapith Granthalaya
PO Navjivan, Ashram Rd, Ahmedabad, Gujarat 380014
Tel: (079) 7541148 *Fax:* (079) 7542547
E-mail: guivi@adinet.emet.in; gvpahd@ad1vsnl.net.in
Telex: 121-6254 GUVI IN
Key Personnel
Librarian: K K Bhausar
Combined university, state central & public library.
Publication(s): *Gujarati Samayik Lekh Suchi* (Gujarati Indexing of Articles from Selected Gujarati Journals); *Tapas Nibandh Suchi* (Gujarati Bibliography of Dissertations)

Indian Council of World Affairs Library
Sapru House, Barakhamba Rd, New Delhi 110001
Tel: (011) 3317246 *Fax:* (011) 3317248
Cable: INTERASIA
Key Personnel
Acting Librarian: Man Singh Deora
  E-mail: dgicwa@hotmail.com
Publication(s): *Documentation on Asia* (annually)

Indian Institute of Management
Vikram Sarabhai Library, Vastrapur, Ahmedabad 380 015
Tel: (079) 2630 7241 *Fax:* (079) 2630 6896
E-mail: director@iimahd.ernet.in
Web Site: www.iimahd.ernet.in
Key Personnel
Dir: Prof Bakul Dholakia
Founded: 1962

Indian Institute of Technology Madras Central Library
Central Library IITPO, Chennai 600 036
Tel: (044) 2578740 *Fax:* (044) 2350509
E-mail: libinfo@iitm.ac.in
Web Site: www.cenlib.iitm.ac.in
Telex: 418926 *Cable:* TECHNOLOGY
Key Personnel
Librarian: Dr Harish Chandra *E-mail:* hchandra@iitm.ac.in

Institute for Social & Economic Change Library
Nagarbhavi, Bangalore, Karnataka 560072
Tel: (080) 23215468; (080) 23215519; (080) 23215592; (080) 23215468 *Fax:* (080) 23217008
E-mail: admin@isec.ac.in
Web Site: www.isec.ac.in
Key Personnel
Librarian: TRB Sarma *Tel:* (080) 23215468 (ext 302) *E-mail:* trbsarma@isec.ac.in

Madras Literary Society Library
College Rd, Chennai 600 006
Tel: 827 9666
Key Personnel
Manager: P N Balasundaram

National Archives of India
Janpath, New Delhi 110001
Tel: (011) 23383436 *Fax:* (011) 23384127
E-mail: archives@ren02.nic.in
Web Site: nationalarchives.nic.in
Key Personnel
Librarian: R C Puri
Dir General: H D Singh

The National Library, Government of India
Belvedere, Kolkata 700027
Tel: (033) 2479 1381; (033) 2479 1384
  Fax: (033) 2479 1462
E-mail: nldirector@rediffmail.com; nldirector@nlindia.org
Web Site: www.nlindia.org
Telex: 021 8117 *Cable:* LIBRARIAN
Key Personnel
Dir: Dr Ramanuj Bhattacharjee *Tel:* (033) 479 2968
Principal Library & Information Officer: Dr R Ramachandran *Tel:* (033) 479 2467
Publication(s): *India's National Library*; *India's National Library: Systematization & Modernization*; *The National Library & Public Libraries in India*

Nehru Memorial Museum & Library (NMML)
Teen Murti House, New Delhi 110011
Tel: (011) 23017587 *Fax:* (011) 23015026
Key Personnel
Dir: Dr O P Kejariwal
Librarian: Mrs Kanwal Verma
Contact: Mrs Indu Jolly
Research Center on Modern Indian History, with emphasis on Indian Nationalism; 2, 09, 904 vols; large collections of newspapers, microfilms, private papers, institutional records, photographs & oral history recordings.

Pt Ravishankar Shukla University Library
Raipur, Madhya Pradesh 492010
Fax: (0771) 234283
E-mail: info@rsuniversity.com
Web Site: www.rsuniversity.com
Key Personnel
Librarian: Rameshwar Singh

Sahitya Akademi Library (National Academy of Letters Library)
Rabindra Bhavan, 35 Ferozeshah Rd, New Delhi 110001
Tel: (011) 3386626; (011) 3387386; (011) 3386088 *Fax:* (011) 3382428
E-mail: secy@sahitya-akademi.org
Web Site: www.sahitya-akademi.org *Cable:* SAHITYAKAR
Key Personnel
President: Ramakanta Rath
Librarian: K C Dutt
Publication(s): *Indian Literary Index* (biannually)

State Central Library
Afzalgunj, Hyderabad 500012
Tel: (040) 4600107; (040) 4615621
Key Personnel
Librarian: T V Vedamrutham

University of Mumbai Library
MG Rd, Fort, Mumbai 400032
Tel: (022) 2652819 *Fax:* (022) 2652832
Web Site: www.mu.ac.in
Key Personnel
Librarian: Dr S R Ganpule
Founded: 1879

Indonesia

Arsip Nasional Republik Indonesia
Jalan Ampera Raya, Cilandak Timar, Jakarta 12560
Tel: (021) 78 05 851 *Fax:* (021) 78 05 812
E-mail: anri@indo.net.id
Web Site: www.archivesindonesia.or.id
Key Personnel
Reference & Information Service: Dr Noerhadi Magetsari
National Archives.

British Council Library
S Widjojo Centre, 1st & 2nd floors, Jl Jenderal Sudirman 71, Jakarta 12190
Tel: (021) 252 4115 *Fax:* (021) 252 4129
E-mail: information@britishcouncil.or.id
Web Site: www.britishcouncil.or.id
Telex: 45246 BRICOUN JKT
Key Personnel
Librarian: Toosye Damayanti

CALTD, see Center for Agricultural Library & Technology Dissemination (CALTD)

Center for Agricultural Library & Technology Dissemination (CALTD) (Pusat Perpustakaan dan Penyebaran Teknalogi Pertanian)
Jl Ir Haji Juanda 20, Bogor 16122
Tel: (0251) 321746 (ext 66) *Fax:* (0251) 326561
E-mail: pustaka@bogor.net
Web Site: pustaka.bogor.net *Cable:* Pustaka
Key Personnel
Dir: Dr Tjeppy D Soedjana
Founded: 1842
Publication(s): *Indonesian Journal of Agricultural Science (IJAS)*
Parent Company: Agency for Agricultural Research & Development

Perpustakaan Dewan Perwakilan Rakjat - RI
Jalan Jenderal Gatot Subroto, Jakarta, Pusat 10270
Tel: (021) 5715220; (021) 5715224 *Fax:* (021) 5715884
Telex: 65396 RHM DPR-RI
Key Personnel
Chief Librarian: Mrs Roemningsih
Parliamentary Library of Indonesia.
Publication(s): *Aquisition List*

Pusat Dokumentasi dan Informasi Ilmiah
Jl Jend Gatot Subroto 10, Jakarta 12710
Tel: (021) 5733465; (021) 5733466; (021) 5250719 *Fax:* (021) 5733467
E-mail: info@pdii.lipi.go.id
Telex: 62875 IA *Cable:* PDII
Key Personnel
Contact: Mr B Sudarsono
Indonesian Centre for Scientific Documentation & Information.
Publication(s): *Baca* (bimonthly, Read); *Bibliografi Khusus* (Special Bibliographies, irregular); *Direktori Perpustakaan Khusus dan Sumber Informasi di Indonesia* (Directory of Special Libraries and Information Sources in Indonesia irregular); *Indeks Laporan Penelitian dan Survei* (Index of Research and Survey Report, annual, lists of acquisitions, books & microfiches); *Indeks Majalah Ilmiah Indonesia* (Index of Indonesian Learned Periodicals, semi-annual)

Library of Hasanuddin University
Gedung Perpustakaan UNHAS Lt 2-4, Kampus Tamalanrea, Jl Perintis Kemerdekaan, Ujung Pandang 90245

Tel: (0411) 512026; (0411) 512027 *Fax:* (0411) 512027
Web Site: www.unhas.ac.id/~perpus
Telex: 7179 UNHAS
Key Personnel
Head Librarian: Rosdiani Rachim

Hatta Foundation Library
Perpustakaan, Jl Solo 155, Yogyakarta 55281
Tel: (0274) 87747 *Fax:* (0274) 87747
Key Personnel
Librarian: R Soedjatmiko
Contact: Fauzie Ridjal
Hatta Foundation Library.
Branch Office(s)
Perpustakaan Yayasan Hatta, Jl Adisutjipto 155, Yogyakarta 55281

Perpustakaan Pusat Institut Teknologi Bandung (Central Library, Bandung Institute of Technology)
Jl Ganesha 10, Bandung 40132
Tel: (022) 250 0089 *Fax:* (022) 250 0089
E-mail: library@itb.ac.id
Web Site: www.lib.itb.ac.id
Telex: ITB BD 28324
Key Personnel
Chief Librarian: Dr Adjat Sakri
Librarian: Dr I Nyoman Susila
Publication(s): *Proceedings Institut Teknologi Bandung*

Perpustakaan Islam (Islamic Library)
Jl P Mangkubumi 38, Yogyakarta
Tel: (0274) 2078
Web Site: www.perpustakaan-islam.com
Key Personnel
Dir: Dr H Asyhuri Dahlan
Librarian: Moh Amien Mansoer

Perpustakaan Nasional
Jalan Salemba Raya 28A, Jakarta 10002
Mailing Address: PO Box 3624, Jakarta 10002
Tel: (021) 315-4863; (021) 315 4864; (021) 315 4870 *Fax:* (021) 310 3554
E-mail: pusnas@rad.net.id; info@pnri.go.id
Web Site: www.pnri.go.id
Key Personnel
Dir: Mr Dady Rachmananta
National Library of Indonesia.

National Library of Indonesia, see Perpustakaan Nasional

Library of Political and Social History
Medan Merdeka Selatan 11, Jakarta
Tel: (021) 360136
Key Personnel
Librarian: Dr Soekarman
Publication(s): *Index Pemilu* (Index of General Elections); *Press index; Index Artikel Tentang Negara* (Index of Official Publications)

Universitas Udayana Library
Jl PB Sudirman Denpasar, Bukit Jimbaran, Denpasar, Bali
Tel: (0361) 702772 *Fax:* (0361) 702-765
Web Site: www.unud.ac.id
Key Personnel
Librarian: Dr I Gusti Nyeman Tirtayasa
Publication(s): *Bibliografi*

Islamic Republic of Iran

Ferdowsi University of Mashhad Central Library & Information Centre
PO Box 331, 91735 Mashhad
Tel: (0511) 8789263; (0511) 8796798 *Fax:* (0511) 8796822
E-mail: centlib@ferdowsi.um.ac.ir
Web Site: c-library.um.ac.ir
Telex: 512271
Key Personnel
General Dir: Dr M T Eclalati
Founded: 1973

IRANDOC, see Iranian Information Documentation Centre

Iranian Information Documentation Centre
Affiliate of Ministry of Culture & Higher Education
1188, Enghelab Ave, Tehran
Mailing Address: PO Box 13185-1371, Tehran
Tel: (021) 6462548 *Fax:* (021) 6462254
E-mail: info@irandoc.ac.ir
Web Site: www.irandoc.ac.ir
Telex: 6415330 *Cable:* ASNDIRAN
Key Personnel
Dir: Prof Hussein Gharibi
International Relations Manager: Mr Mansoor Sheydaee
Contact: Ms Nastaron Sadeghi
Founded: 1968
Engaged in information sciences fields. Main activities include production & dissemination of Iranian scientific information (Persian); research on information science; Iranian dissertion abstracts (students graduated in Iran & abroad); research projects abstracts; Iranian scientific meetings & proceedings; Iranian government reports & other topics available for free online. Researchers can access the materials via the web page, periodicals & connecting to SABA intranet, a local network. They can also apply to search documents by letter or in person to the Search Unit of the library.
Publication(s): *The Abstract of Scientific & Technical Papers* (quarterly, 1993, bibliographic data & in some cases abstracts of the sci-tech articles published in Persian language journals); *Current Research in Iranian Universities and Research Centers* (quarterly, 1993, details with abstracts of the research project carried out in Iran); *Directory of Scientific Meeting Held In Iran* (quarterly, 1993, bibliographic data on the papers & lectures in the seminars held in Iran since 1989); *Dissertion Abstracts of Iranian Graduates Abroad* (quarterly, 1995, abstract of Masters & PhD dissertations of the Iranian graduates abroad since 1994); *Index to Latin periodicals available in Iranian special libraries* (electronic journal (www.irandoc.ac.ir)); *Iranian Dissertion Abstracts* (quarterly, 1973, bibliographic information & abstracts of the dissertation submitted by graduate students & PhD); *Iranian Government Report* (quarterly, 1998, reports gathered from ministries & governmental research organizations); *Iranian Scholars & Experts Database* (quarterly, 1996, name & details of selected Iranian experts holding Masters & PhD)

The Islamic Republic of Iran Parliament Library, No 1 (Ketabkhane-ye Majles-e Shora-ye Elsami, No 1) (Library, Museum & Documentation Center of the Islamic Consultative Assembly Number 1)
Baharestan Sq, Parliamentary Library, Tehran 11576-11119
Tel: (021) 3121805; (021) 3130911
E-mail: frelations@majlislib.com; irparlib@majlislib.com; info@majlislib.com
Web Site: www.majlislib.org
Key Personnel
Dir: Seyyed Mohammad Ali Ahmadi Abhari
Tel: (021) 3130920 *Fax:* (021) 3124339
E-mail: abhari@majlislib.com
Founded: 1923
Library & information services; manuscripts collection; indexing of the manuscripts; publishing; renovation, maintenance, disinfection & antiacidification of old books & manuscripts; making microfilms.
Ultimate Parent Company: Majles-e Shora-ye Eslami (The Islamic Consultative Assembly)

The Islamic Republic of Iran Parliament Library, No 2 (Ketab-Khane-ye Majles-e Shora-ye Eslami, no 2) (Library, Museum & Documentation Center of the Islamic Consultative Assembly, No 2)
Imam Khomeini Ave, Tehran 13174
Tel: (021) 6135335; (021) 3130919 *Fax:* (021) 3130919; (021) 3124339
E-mail: frelations@majlislib.com
Web Site: www.majlislib.com
Key Personnel
Dir: Seyyed Mohammad Ali Ahmadi Abhari
Tel: (021) 3130920 *E-mail:* Abhari@majlislib.com
Founded: 1950
Library & Information Services.
Ultimate Parent Company: Majles-e Shora-ye Eslami (The Islamic Consultative Assembly)

Mirzaye Shirazi Library
Eram Campus, Shiraz 71944
Tel: (0711) 6260011 *Fax:* (0711) 6287301
Web Site: www.shirazu.ac.ir
Telex: 65912; 332169
Key Personnel
President: Dr Zouhayr Hayati *E-mail:* zhayati@rose.shirazu.ac.ir; Dr M Ershad Langroodi
Acquisition Librarian: E Emami
Parent Company: Shiraz University

The National Library of the Islamic Republic of Iran
Anahita Alley, Africa Ave, 19176 Tehran
Tel: (021) 2288680 *Fax:* (021) 8088950
E-mail: natlibir@neda.net
Web Site: www.nli.ir
Key Personnel
Dir: Dr Mohammed Khatami
Publication(s): *A Bibliography of the Folklore of Isfahan; Catalog of Valuable French Works in the National Library of Iran; A Catalogue of the manuscripts in the National Library of Iran; A Directory of Iranian Periodicals & Newspapers; Glossary of Library Terms; The Iranian National Bibliography; List of Persian Subject Headings; The Name Authority List of Authors & Famous People; Persian Author Marks; Political Life of Imain Khomevni; Rules & Standards for Publishing Books; Technical Services* (8th ed)

Organizations of Libraries, Museums & Documentation Centre of Astan Quds
PO Box 91735-177, Mashhad
Tel: (098511) 2216009 *Fax:* (098511) 2220845
E-mail: webmaster@aqlibrary.org; info@aqlibrary.org
Web Site: www.aqlibrary.org
Key Personnel
Dir General: Dr A M Baradaran Rafiei

Publication(s): *Library & Information Science Quarterly* (quarterly)
Parent Company: Astan Quds Razavi

University of Isfahan Library
Hezar Jerib Ave, Isfahan
Tel: (0311) 684799; (0311) 792-2793 *Fax:* (0311) 275145
Telex: 312295 IREU IR
Key Personnel
Dir of Libraries: M Jamshidian, PhD

University of Tabriz Central Library
Central Library & Documentation Center, University of Tabriz, Tabriz
Tel: (0411) 3342199 *Fax:* (0411) 3355993
Web Site: www.tabrizu.ac.ir/centrallibrary/lib-general.htm
Telex: 412045 TBUN-IR
Key Personnel
Dir: A Adine Ghahramani; Dr G H Tasbihi

Central Library & Documentation Centre of University of Teheran
Enghelab Ave, 16 Azar St, Teheran
Tel: (021) 6462699; (021) 6419831; (021) 6405047 *Fax:* (021) 6409348
E-mail: publicrel@ut.ac.ir
Web Site: pages.ut.ac.ir/library/home.htm
Telex: 13944; 222966
Key Personnel
Head of Library: Dr Ali Akbar Enayati
Deputy: Dr Ziaee
Public Relations: Jabbar Khodadoost

Iraq

Al-Awqaf Central Library
Bab Al-Muadham, Baghdad
Mailing Address: PO Box 14146, Baghdad
Tel: (01) 4169362 *Fax:* (01) 4167790
Telex: 2785
Key Personnel
Librarian: Jassim M Al-Juboory
Dir: Afaf Abidul Latif
Founded: 1928
Library of Waqfs.
Branch Office(s)
Adhamiya, Mosul
Main Mosque, Anbar
Al-Qazzaza Library, Baghdad
Munier Al-Qadhi Library, Baghdad
Amarah
Diala
Kerkuk
Nasiriyah
Sulaymaniyah

The Diwan Library, Ministry of Education
PO Box 11317, Baghdad
Tel: (01) 8872949
Telex: 2259
Key Personnel
Librarian: Dr Kadhim G Al-Khazraji

Library of the Iraq Museum
Salhiya Quarter, Baghdad West
Tel: (01) 8879687
Key Personnel
Dir: Dr Muyad Said Damerji; Zounab Sadiq
Founded: 1934

Library of the Mosul Museum
Dawassa, Mosul
Key Personnel
Dir: Hazmin A Hameed

Mosul Public Library
1930 Abdul-Halim Al-Lawand, Mosul
Tel: (060) 810162 *Fax:* (060) 814765
Telex: 8011
Key Personnel
Gen Dir: Adran S Natheev

National Centre of Archives
National Library Bldg, 2nd floor, Bab-al-Muaddam, Baghdad
Mailing Address: POB 594, Baghdad
Tel: (01) 416 8440 *Cable:* CENTARCHIV
Key Personnel
Dir General: Salim Al-Alousi
Founded: 1972

National Library
Bab-el-Muaddum, Baghdad
Tel: (01) 416 4190
Key Personnel
Dir: Abdul Hameed Alwaehi
Founded: 1961
Publication(s): *al-Maktaba al-Arabia Journal*; *Iraqi National Bibliography* (triannually)

Scientific Documentation Centre
Central Science Library, Abu Nuas Rd, Baghdad
Mailing Address: PO Box 2441, Baghdad
Tel: (01) 7760023
Telex: 2187 Bathilmi IK
Key Personnel
Dir: Dr Faik Abdul S Razzaq

Central Library of the University of Baghdad
PO Box 47303, Baghdad
Tel: (01) 776 7819 *Fax:* (01) 776 3592
Telex: 2197
Key Personnel
Librarian: Dr Zeki Al-Werdi

Central Library of the University of Basrah
PO Box 49, Basrah
Tel: (01) 8868520 *Fax:* (01) 8868520
E-mail: basrahyni@uruklink.net
Telex: 207025
Key Personnel
Librarian: Dr Tarik Al-Manassir

Central Library of the University of Mosul
Mosul
Tel: (060) 810162 *Fax:* (060) 8011; (060) 8015
Telex: 8011
Key Personnel
Dir General: Dr Adnan S Natheev

Central Library of the University of Salahaddin
Arbil/Iraqi Kurdistan
Tel: 00873762566859 *Fax:* 00873762566861
Web Site: www.salun.org
Telex: 218510
Key Personnel
Dir: Dr Abdull S Abbas

Ireland

The Chester Beatty Library
Dublin Castle, Dublin 2
Tel: (01) 4070750 *Fax:* (01) 4070760
E-mail: info@cbl.ie
Web Site: www.cbl.ie
Key Personnel
Dir & Librarian: Dr Michael Ryan
Reference Librarian: Celine Ward *Tel:* (01) 4070757 *E-mail:* cward@cbl.ie

Among items on display at the Library is material showing the development of the written word from 2700 BC (the date of the Library's earliest clay tablet) down to modern times.

Boole Library, see University College Cork, Boole Library

Central Catholic Library
74 Merrion Sq, Dublin 2
Tel: (01) 676 1264
Key Personnel
Librarian: Teresa Whitington
E-mail: teresawhitington@eircom.net

Dublin City Public Libraries
Administrative Headquarters, 138-144 Pearse St, Dublin 2
Tel: (01) 674 4800 *Fax:* (01) 674 4879
E-mail: dublinpubliclibraries@dublincity.ie
Web Site: www.iol.ie/dublincitylibrary
Telex: 33287
Key Personnel
Dublin City Librarian & Dir: Deirdre Ellis-King
Headquarters of the International IMPAC Dublin Literary Awards.

James Hardiman Library, see National University of Ireland Galway (NUI, Galway)

Leabharlann Boole, see University College Cork, Boole Library

National Archives
Bishop St, Dublin 8
Tel: (01) 4072 300 *Fax:* (01) 4072 333
E-mail: mail@nationalarchives.ie
Web Site: www.nationalarchives.ie
Key Personnel
Dir: Dr David Craig

National Library of Ireland
Kildare St, Dublin 2
Tel: (01) 6030200 *Fax:* (01) 6766690
E-mail: info@nli.ie
Web Site: www.nli.ie
Key Personnel
Acting Dir: Aongus O hAonghusa
Editor: Dr Noel Kissane
Publishes material from its collection in the medium of folders, facsimile documents, illustrated booklets & books.
Publication(s): *Ex Camera, 1860-1960* (1990); *The Irish Face* (1987); *The Irish Famine: A Documentary History* (1995); *The Irish Publishing Record* (annually); *James Joyce* (1982); *The James Joyce/Paul Leon Papers* (1992); *Parnell - A Documentary History* (1991); *Treasures from the National Library of Ireland* (1994); *Writers, Racouteurs & Notable History* (1993); *W B Yeats & His Circle* (1989)

National University of Ireland Galway (NUI, Galway)
University Rd, Galway
Tel: (091) 524809 *Fax:* (091) 522394
Web Site: www.nuigalway.ie
Key Personnel
Chief Librarian: Marie Reddan *E-mail:* marie.reddan@nuigalway.ie
Founded: 1845

Oireachtas Library
Leinster House, Kildare St, Dublin 2
Tel: (01) 618 3412 *Fax:* (01) 661 5583
Web Site: www.irlgov.ie/oireachtas
Key Personnel
Librarian: Maura Corcoran *E-mail:* maura.corcoran@oireachtas.irlgov.ie
Selective works of parliamentary interest.

PRONI (Public Record Office of Northern Ireland)
66 Balmoral Ave, Belfast BT9 6NY
Tel: (02890) 255905 *Fax:* (02890) 255999
E-mail: proni@dcalni.gov.uk
Web Site: proni.nics.gov.uk
Key Personnel
Deputy Keeper & Chief Executive: Dr Gerry Slater *E-mail:* slaterg.proni@doeni.gov.uk

Public Record Office of Northern Ireland, see PRONI (Public Record Office of Northern Ireland)

Representative Church Body Library
Braemor Park, Churchtown, Dublin 14
Tel: (01) 4923979 *Fax:* (01) 4924770
E-mail: library@ireland.anglican.org
Web Site: www.ireland.anglican.org
Key Personnel
Librarian & Archivist: Raymond Refausse
Founded: 1932
Publication(s): *A Handlist of Church of Ireland Parish Registers in the Representative Church Body Library*; *A Handlist of Church of Ireland Vestry Minute Books in the Representative Church Body Library*; *A Library on the Move. Twenty Five Years of the Representative Church Body Library in Churchtown*; *Register of Holy Trinity Church, Cork, 1643-1668* (1998); *Register of the Cathedral Church of St Columb, Derry, 1703-1732*; *Register of the Cathedral Church of St Columb, Derry, 1732-1775*; *Register of the Church of St Thomas, Lisnagarvey, Co Antrim, 1637-1646*; *Register of the Parish of Leixlip, Co Kildare, 1665-1778*; *Register of the Parish of St Thomas, Dublin, 1750-1791*; *Registers of the Parish of St John the Evangelist, Dublin* (book)

Royal College of Surgeons in Ireland Library
123 St Stephens Green, Dublin 2
Tel: (01) 402 2100
E-mail: info@rcsi.ie
Web Site: www.rcsi.ie
Key Personnel
Librarian: Miss B M Doran
Deputy Librarian: Paul Murphy *Tel:* (01) 4022406 *E-mail:* pauljmurphy@rcsi.ie
Publication(s): *Journal of the Irish Colleges of Physicians & Surgeons*
Branch Office(s)
Beaumont Hospital Library, Beaumont Rd, Dublin 9 *Tel:* (01) 836 7396 *E-mail:* bhlibrary@rcsi.ie

Royal Dublin Society Library
Ballsbridge, Dublin 4
Tel: (01) 6680866; (01) 2407288 *Fax:* (01) 6604014
E-mail: info@rds.ie
Web Site: www.rds.ie *Cable:* SOCIETY, DUBLIN
Key Personnel
Librarian: Mary Kelleher *E-mail:* mary.kelleher@rds.ie
Founded: 1731
Private Society.

Trinity College Library Dublin
College St, Dublin 2
Tel: (01) 608 1665 *Fax:* (01) 608 3774
Web Site: www.tcd.ie/library
Telex: 93782
Key Personnel
Librarian & College Archivist: Robin Adams *Tel:* (01) 608 1661
Founded: 1592
Academic & legal deposit library.
Publication(s): *Long Room*
Parent Company: Trinity College Dublin

University College Cork, Boole Library
College Rd, Cork
Tel: (021) 4902919 *Fax:* (021) 4273428
E-mail: library@ucc.ie
Web Site: booleweb.ucc.ie
Telex: 7605 Unicei
Key Personnel
President: Dr Michael Mortell
Librarian: John Fitzgerald
Deputy Librarian: Edward Fahy

University College Dublin Library
Belfield, Dublin 4
Tel: (01) 716 7694 *Fax:* (01) 283 7667
E-mail: library@ucd.ie
Web Site: www.ucd.ie/library
Key Personnel
Librarian: S Phillips

Israel

Central Library of Agricultural Science
PO Box 12, 76100 Rehovot
Tel: (08) 9489906 *Fax:* (08) 9361348; (08) 9489399
E-mail: szekely@agri.huji.ac.il
Web Site: www.agri.huji.ac.il/library/menu.html
Telex: 381331
Key Personnel
Dir: N Barzely *E-mail:* barzely@agri.huji.ac.il

Aranne Library, see Ben-Gurion University of the Negev Aranne Library

Bar Ilan University Central Library
c/o Wurzweiler Central Library, PO Box 90000, 52900 Ramat-Gan
Tel: (03) 5318486 *Fax:* (03) 5349233
E-mail: barmae@mail.biu.ac.il
Web Site: www.biu.ac.il/lib
Key Personnel
University Librarian: Ya'akov Aronson *Tel:* (03) 5318357 *E-mail:* aronson@mail.biu.ac.il
Founded: 1955
Publication(s): *Hebrew Subject Headings for Use in Cataloging* (online); *Index to Literary Supplements of the Daily Hebrew Press* (internal online)

Ben-Gurion University of the Negev Aranne Library
PO Box 653, Beer-Sheva 84105
Tel: (08) 6461413 *Fax:* (08) 6472940
Web Site: www.bgu.ac.il/aranne/
Key Personnel
Dir: Avner Shmuelevitz *Tel:* (08) 6461432 *E-mail:* avner@bgumail.bgu.ac.il
Founded: 1965

Central Library for the Blind, Visually Impaired & Handicapped
4 Hahistadrut St, Netanya 42441
Tel: (09) 8617874 *Fax:* (09) 8626346
E-mail: office@clfb.co.il
Web Site: www.clfb.org.il
Key Personnel
Dir: Uri Cohen *Tel:* (03) 6315555 *Fax:* (03) 6315577
Branch Office(s)
Elinore & Athol Burns, 66 Moshe Dayan St, Yad-Eliyahu, Tel Aviv *Tel:* (03) 6315555 *Fax:* (03) 6315577

The Central Archives for the History of the Jewish People (CAHJP)
46 Jabotinsky St, Jerusalem
Mailing Address: PO Box 1149, Jerusalem 91010
Tel: (02) 5635716 *Fax:* (02) 5667686
E-mail: archives@vms.huji.ac.il
Web Site: www.sites.huji.ac.il/cahjp/index.htm
Key Personnel
Dir: Assouline Hadassah
Formerly Jewish Historical General Archives.

Dvir Bialik Municipal Central Public Library
14 Hibat-Zion St, Ramat Gan
Tel: (03) 786375
Key Personnel
Librarian: Hadassah Pelach

Hebrew University of Jerusalem
Edmond J Safra Campus, Givat Ram, Jerusalem 91904
Mailing Address: PO Box 34165, Jerusalem 91341
Tel: (02) 6585017 *Fax:* (02) 6511771
Web Site: www.huji.ac.il
Key Personnel
Dir: Prof Yoram Tsafrir *Tel:* (02) 6584651 *E-mail:* yoramt@savion.cc.huji.ac.il
Publication(s): *Index of Articles on Jewish Studies* (online); *Kiryat Sefer* (quarterly, bibliographical)

Israel State Archives
Quiryath Ben-Gurion, Bldg 3, Jerusalem 91919
Tel: (02) 568 06 80 *Fax:* (02) 679 33 75
Key Personnel
Dir: M Mossek
Publication(s): *Documents on the Foreign Policy of Israel* (series); *Israel Government Publications* (annually)

Jerusalem City (Public) Library
11 Bezalel St, Jerusalem 94591
Mailing Address: PO Box 1409, Jerusalem 94591
Tel: (02) 256 785 *Fax:* (02) 255 785
Key Personnel
Dir: A Vilner
Founded: 1964
Specialize in dramatic theatre, music & music performance.

Knesset Library
The Knesset, Kiryat Ben-Gurion, Hakiryah, Jerusalem 91950
Tel: (02) 6753246; (02) 6496043 *Fax:* (02) 662733
E-mail: sifria2@netvision.net.il
Web Site: www.knesset.gov.il
Key Personnel
Librarian: Sandra Fine
Founded: 1950

Pevsner Public Library
54 Pevsner St, Haifa 31053
Mailing Address: PO Box 5345, Haifa 31053
Tel: (04) 8667766; (04) 8667768 *Fax:* (04) 8666492
Key Personnel
Librarian: Dr S Back

Shaar Zion Library
Division of Culture
Beit Ariela, Shaul Hamelech Bd, Tel Aviv
Tel: 03 69101410
Key Personnel
Library Dir: Ora Nebenzahl
Ultimate Parent Company: Tel Aviv Municipality

Technion - Israel Institute of Technology Libraries
Elyachar Library, Technion City, Haifa 32000
Tel: (04) 8292507 *Fax:* (04) 8295662
E-mail: webteam@tx.technion.ac.il
Web Site: library.technion.ac.il

Telex: 46650
Key Personnel
Dir: Nurit Roitberg *E-mail:* roitberg@tx.technion.ac.il

Tel Aviv University Library
PO Box 39038, Tel Aviv 69978
Tel: (03) 640-8111 *Fax:* (03) 6407833
E-mail: tauinfo@post.tau.ac.il
Web Site: www.tau.ac.il
Telex: 342227 versy1L
Key Personnel
Dir: Dr Dan Simon

University of Haifa Library
PO Box 242, Jerusalem 91002
Tel: (04) 8240289 *Fax:* (04) 8257753
E-mail: info@mail.uhaifa.org
Web Site: lib.haifa.ac.il
Key Personnel
Dir: Prof Kipnis Baruch *E-mail:* baruch@univ.haifa.ac.il
Publication(s): *Index to Hebrew Periodicals* (online)

Weitz Center for Development Study
PO Box 2355, Rehovot 76122
Tel: (08) 9474111 *Fax:* (08) 9475884
E-mail: dsc@netvision.net.il
Key Personnel
Dir: Julia Margulis *Tel:* (08) 9474373
 E-mail: training@netvision.net.il

Weizmann Institute of Science Libraries
PO Box 26, 76100 Rehovot
Tel: (08) 9343583 (WIX Central Library); (08) 9343211 (Weizmann Institute) *Fax:* (08) 9344176
E-mail: hedva.milo@weizmann.ac.il
Web Site: www.weizmann.ac.il/WIS-library
Key Personnel
Chief Librarian: Ilana Pollack *Tel:* (08) 9343583
 E-mail: ilana.pollack@weizmann.ac.il

Italy

Biblioteca Ambrosiana
Piazza Pio XI 2, 20123 Milan
Tel: (02) 80 692 1 *Fax:* (02) 80 692 210
E-mail: info@ambrosiana.it
Web Site: www.ambrosiana.it
Key Personnel
Librarian: Gianfranco Ravasi *E-mail:* gfravasi@ambrosiana.it
Publication(s): *Fontes Ambrosiani*

Biblioteca Angelica
Piazza Sant' Agostino 8, 00186 Rome
Tel: (06) 6840801; (06) 68408069 *Fax:* (06) 68408053
E-mail: angelica.polosbn@inroma.roma.it
Web Site: biblioroma.sbn.it
Key Personnel
Dir: Marina Panetta *E-mail:* angelica.direzione@librari.beniculturali.it
Paola Munafo e Nicoletta Muratore: La Biblioteca Angelica, Roma, Instituto Poligrafico dello Stato (1989).

Biblioteca Comunale dell' Archiginnasio
Piazza Galvani 1, 40124 Bologna
Tel: (051) 276811 *Fax:* (051) 261160
E-mail: archiginnasio@comune.bologna.it
Web Site: www.archiginnasio.it
Key Personnel
Dir: Dr Pierangelo Bellettini
Founded: 1801
Publication(s): *L'Archiginnasio: Bollettino della Biblioteca Comunale di Bologna* (annually)

Archivio Centrale dello Stato
Piazzale degli Archivi, 27, 00144 Rome
Tel: (06) 545481 *Fax:* (06) 5413620
E-mail: acs@archivi.beniculturali.it
Web Site: www.archiviocentraledellostato.it; archivi.beniculturali.it/ACS
Key Personnel
Dir: Maurizio Fallace
Librarian: Eugenia Nieddu
National Archives.
Publication(s): *Bollettino Delle Nuove Accessioni*

Biblioteca dell'Archivio Storico Civico e Biblioteca Trivulziana
Castello Sforzesco, Cortile della Rocchetta I, 20121 Milan
Tel: (02) 86454638; (02) 89010293 *Fax:* (02) 875926
E-mail: marina_litrico@rcm.inet.it
Web Site: www.rcs.it/mimu/musei/biblioteca_trivulziana/info.htm
Key Personnel
Librarian: Dr Giovanni M Piazza
Library publications are sent free by request or in exchange for other publications.

Biblioteca Centrale della Regione Siciliana gia Biblioteca Nazionale di Palermo
Corso Vittorio Emanuele 429/431, 90134 Palermo
Tel: (091) 6967642 *Fax:* (091) 6967644
E-mail: bcrs@regione.sicilia.it
Web Site: www.regione.sicilia.it/beniculturali/bibliotecacentrale
Key Personnel
Dir DSSA: Carmela Perretta

Biblioteca Medicea Laurenziana
Affiliate of Ministero per i Beni e le Attivita Culturali
Piazza San Lorenzo n° 9, 50123 Florence
Tel: (055) 210760; (055) 211590; (055) 214443 *Fax:* (055) 2302992
E-mail: medicea@unifi.it
Web Site: www.bml.firenze.sbn.it
Key Personnel
Chief Librarian: Dr Franca Arduini
 E-mail: bmldirezione@unifi.it

Biblioteca Nazionale Braidense
Via Brera 28, 20121 Milan
Tel: (02) 86460907 *Fax:* (02) 72023910
E-mail: braidense@librari.beniculturali.it
Web Site: www.cilea.it/braidens/
Key Personnel
Dir: Dr Goffredo Dotti
Contact: Dr Arminda Batori

Biblioteca Nazionale Centrale Vittorio Emanuele II
Viale Castro Pretorio 105, 00185 Rome
Tel: (06) 49891 *Fax:* (06) 4457635
E-mail: bcrm@bnc.roma.sbn.it
Web Site: www.bncrm.librari.beniculturali.it
Key Personnel
Dir: Osvaldo Avallone
Publication(s): *Bollettino delle opere moderne straniere acquiste dalle Biblioteche Pubbliche statali Italiane; Quaderni della Biblioteca nazionale centrale di Roma; Studi guide, cataloghi*

Biblioteca Nazionale Vittorio Emanuele III
Piazza del Plebiscito 1, 80132 Naples
Tel: (081) 7819111 *Fax:* (081) 403820
E-mail: Emanuele@librari.beniculturali.it
Web Site: www.bnnonline.it
Key Personnel
Dir: Mauro Giancaspro
Librarian: Anna Giaccio *Tel:* (081) 7819215
Publication(s): *I Quaderni della Biblioteca Nazionale de Napoli*

Biblioteca Nazionale Centrale
Piazza dei Cavalleggeri 1, 50122 Florence
Tel: (055) 24919 1 *Fax:* (055) 2342 482
E-mail: info@bncf.firenze.sbn.it
Web Site: www.bncf.firenze.sbn.it
Key Personnel
Dir: Dr Antonia Ida Fontana

Biblioteca Nazionale Marciana
San Marco 7, 30124 Venice
Tel: (041) 5208788 *Fax:* (041) 5238803
E-mail: biblioteca@marciana.venezia.sbn.it
Web Site: www.marciana.venezia.sbn.it/
Key Personnel
Dir: Dr Marino Zorzi
Publication(s): *Miscellanea Marciana*

Biblioteca Nazionale Universitaria
Piazza Carlo Alberto 3, 10123 Turin
Tel: (011) 8101111 *Fax:* (011) 8121021
E-mail: bnto@librari.benicultural.it
Web Site: www.bnto.librari.beniculturali.it
Key Personnel
Dir: Aurelio Aghemo

Biblioteca Universitaria
Subsidiary of Biblioteca Estense
Biblioteca Estense Universitaria, Largo S Agostino 337, 41100 Modena
Tel: (059) 222248 *Fax:* (059) 230195
E-mail: biblio.estense@cedoc.mo.it
Web Site: www.cedoc.mo.it/estense
Key Personnel
Chief Librarian: Dr Ernesto Milano
 E-mail: estdir@cedoc.mo.it
Economics, medicine, engineering, mathematics.

Biblioteca Musicale S Cecilia
Via dei Greci 18, 00187 Rome
Tel: (06) 3609671 *Fax:* (06) 36001800
Web Site: www.santacecilia.it
Key Personnel
Librarian: Dr Domenico Carboni

Biblioteca Estense Universitaria
Largo S Agostino 337, 41100 Modena
Tel: (059) 222248 *Fax:* (059) 230195
E-mail: estense@kril.cedoc.unimo.it; biblio.estense@cedoc.mo.it
Web Site: www.cedoc.mo.it/estense
Key Personnel
Dir: Dr Ernesto Milano

European University Institute Library
Via dei Roccettini 9, 50016 San Domino
Tel: (055) 4685 340 *Fax:* (055) 4685 283
E-mail: euilib@iue.it
Web Site: www.iue.it
Telex: 571528 Iue *Cable:* UNIVEUR
Key Personnel
Interim Head: Andreas Frijdal
Deputy Dir: Tommaso Giordano

Biblioteca Comunale Malatestiana
Piazza Bufalini 1, 47023 Cesena (Forli)
Tel: (0547) 610 892 *Fax:* (0547) 421237
E-mail: malatestiana@sbn.provincia.ra.it
Web Site: www.malatestiana.it
Key Personnel
Dir: Daniela Savoia
Founded: 1452

Biblioteca Universitaria di Padua
Via S Biagio 7, 35121 Padua

Tel: (049) 8240211; (049) 8240241 *Fax:* (049) 8762711
E-mail: bupd@librari.beniculturali.it
Web Site: www.unipd.it/bibliotecauniversitaria
Key Personnel
Dir: Francesco Aliano
Librarian: Rosalba Suriano
Founded: 1629

Biblioteca Riccardiana
Palazzo Medici Riccardi, Via Ginori 10, 50123 Florence
Tel: (055) 212586; (055) 293385 *Fax:* (055) 211379
E-mail: riccardiana@riccardiana.firenze.sbn.it
Web Site: www.riccardiana.librari.beniculturali.it
Key Personnel
Dir: Dott Giovanna Lazzi

Biblioteca Nazionale Sagarriga Visconti Volpi
Piazza Umberto 1, 70122 Bari, Pugla
Tel: (080) 5212534; (080) 5211298 *Fax:* (080) 5211298
E-mail: visconti@librari.beniculturali.it
Key Personnel
Dir: Maria Teresa Tafuri di Melignano

Universita degli Studi di Firenze, Biblioteca di Lettre e Filosofia
Bologna Way 52, 50139 Florence
Tel: (055) 46 22 402 *Fax:* (055) 47 56 40
E-mail: bibfil@unifi.it
Web Site: www.unifi.it
Key Personnel
Dir: Floriana Tagliabue *E-mail:* floriana.tagliabuc@unifi.it

Universita di Roma 'La Sapienza'
Division of Uffieio Centrale Per I Beni Librari E Istituti Culturali
Piazzale Aldo Moro 5, 00185 Rome
Tel: (06) 4456820; (06) 4474021; (06) 4991 *Fax:* (06) 4474024
E-mail: alessandrina@librari.beniculturali.it
Web Site: www.alessandrina.librari.beniculturali.it; www.uniroma1.it
Key Personnel
Dir: Maria Concetta Petrollo *E-mail:* petrollo@uniroma1.it
Publication(s): *Catalogo Del Fondo Leopardiano*; *Inchiostri Per L'Infanzia*; *Voci Di Roma*
Parent Company: Ministero Per I Beni E Le Attivita Culturali

Jamaica

Jamaica Archives
Corner King & Manchester Sts, Spanish Town, St Catherine
Tel: (876) 984-2581; (876) 984-5001 *Fax:* (876) 984-8254
Key Personnel
Government Archivist: Elizabeth Williams

Jamaica Library Service
2 Tom Redcam Dr, Kingston 5
Mailing Address: PO Box 58, Kingston 5
Tel: (876) 926-3315 *Fax:* (876) 926-3354
E-mail: jamlibs@cwjamaica.com
Web Site: www.jamlib.org.jm
Key Personnel
Dir General: Patricia Roberts
Publication(s): *Book Production in Jamaica: A Select List of Jamaican Publications*; *Jamaica: A Select Bibliography 1900-1963*; *Jamaica Library Service 21 Years of Progress in Pictures 1948-1969*; *Jamaica Poetry: A Checklist, Slavery to the Present*; *Reflections on Black River*; *What's New in Librarianship*

National Library of Jamaica
12 East St, Kingston
Tel: (876) 967-1526; (876) 967-2516; (876) 967-2494; (876) 967-2496 *Fax:* (876) 922-5567
E-mail: nlj@infochan.com
Web Site: www.nlj.org.jm *Cable:* NALIBJAM
Key Personnel
Dir: John Aarons
Founded: 1979
The Library is the National Reference Library of Jamaica. Its main functions are to collect & preserve the national imprint, to serve as the bibliographic center for Jamaica & the focal point of the national information system.
Publication(s): *Gleaner* (of Jamaica); *Jamaican National Bibliography* (Occasional bibliography series); *The Gleaner* (Index monthly index to the)

Northern Caribbean University
Hiram S Walters Resource Center, Mandeville, Manchester
Tel: (876) 962-2204-7 *Fax:* (876) 962-0075
E-mail: info@ncu.edu.jm
Web Site: www.ncu.edu.jm
Key Personnel
Dir: Heather Rodriguez-James *Tel:* (876) 523-2101
Librarian: Hortense Riley; Ingrid Smith
Branch Office(s)
Andrews School of Nursing, Kingston

United Theological College of the West Indies
Golding Ave, Mona, Kingston 7
Mailing Address: PO Box 136, Kingston 7
Tel: (876) 927-2868; (876) 927-1724; (876) 977-0810 *Fax:* (876) 977-0812
E-mail: unitheol@cwjamaica.com
Web Site: www.utcwi.edu.jm
Key Personnel
President: Rev Howard Gregory *E-mail:* hkagregory@hotmail.com
Deputy President: Rev Lewin Williams *E-mail:* joylew@cwjamaica.com
Librarian: Miss Adenike Soyibo *E-mail:* asoyibo@hotmail.com
Founded: 1966
Theological Seminary.
Publication(s): *Caribbean Journal of Religious Studies* (biennially)

University of Technology, Jamaica
Calvin McKain Library, 237 Old Hope Rd, Kingston 6
Tel: (876) 927-1680-9 *Fax:* (876) 927-1614
E-mail: library@utech.edu.jm
Web Site: www.utechjamaica.edu.jm
Key Personnel
University Librarian: Hermine C Salmon
Founded: 1958

University of the West Indies Library (Jamaica)
Main Library, Mona Campus, Kingston 7
Tel: (876) 935-8294; (876) 935-8295; (876) 935-8296 *Fax:* (876) 927-1926
E-mail: manlibry@uwimona.edu.jm
Web Site: www.library.uwimona.edu.jm:1104
Telex: 2123 *Cable:* UNIVERS
Key Personnel
University/Campus Librarian: Stephney Ferguson *Tel:* (876) 970-2945 *E-mail:* sfergusn@uwimona.edu.jm
Founded: 1948
Educational Institution.
Publication(s): *Medical Caribbeana: An Index to Caribbean Health Sciences Literature* (Library Annual Report); *Research for Development, Vol 1* (1998, Bibliography of staff publications 1993-1998); *Research for Development: Strengthening Our Tourism Product* (Bibliography)
Branch Office(s)
Medical Library
Science Library

Japan

Gifu Diagaku Fuzoku Toshokan
Yanagido 1-1, Gifu 501-1193
Tel: (0582) 30-1111; (0582) 93-2191 *Fax:* (0582) 30-1107
E-mail: staff@acc.gifu-u.ac.jp
Web Site: www.gifu-u.ac.jp

Hokkaido University Library
Kita 8, Nishi 5, Kita-ku, Sapporo 060-0808
Tel: (011) 706-4998 *Fax:* (011) 747-2855
E-mail: bureau@hokudai.ac.jp
Web Site: www.lib.hokudai.ac.jp/index_e.html
Key Personnel
Dir: Yoshiro Inoue
Lib Prof: T Sanbong
Librarian: Hiroshi Yoshida
Founded: 1876
Publication(s): *Yuin* (Quarterly, The Hokkaido University Library Bulletin, in Japanese)

International Documentation Center, The University of Tokyo
7-3-1 General Library, 3rd floor, Hongo, Bunkyo-ku, Tokyo 113-0033
Tel: (03) 5841-2645 (ext 22645) *Fax:* (03) 5841-2658
E-mail: kokusai@lib.u-tokyo.ac.jp
Web Site: www.lib.u-tokyo.ac.jp/undepo
Key Personnel
Head Librarian: Akira Ohno
Librarian: Ms Kayu Sakata
Publication(s): *Watakushitachi no Kokuren* (1995, Japanese brochure about the United Nations)

Keio University School of Library & Information Science
2-15-45 Mita, Minato-ku, Tokyo 108
Tel: (03) 3453-4511 *Fax:* (03) 5427-1578
E-mail: slis-office@slis.keio.ac.jp
Web Site: www.slis.keio.ac.jp
Key Personnel
Librarian: Motoko Sekiguchi

Kokuritsu Kobunshokan (National Archives of Japan)
Kitanomaru Koen 3-2, Chiyoda-ku, Tokyo 102
Tel: (03) 3214-0621 *Fax:* (03) 3212-8806
Web Site: www.archives.go.jp/index_e.html
Key Personnel
Dir Gen: Kazumasa Iwahashi

Kyoto Sangyo University Library
Kamigamo-Motoyama, Kita-Ku, Kyoto 603-8555
Tel: (075) 7012151 *Fax:* (075) 7051447
E-mail: ksu-lib@star.kyoto-su.ac.jp
Web Site: www3.kyoto-su.ac.jp
Key Personnel
Dir: Satora Yabunaka
Founded: 1987

Kyushu University Library
6-10-1, Hakozaki, Higashi-ku, Fukuoka-shi 812-8581
Tel: (092) 6411101; (092) 6422111
E-mail: w3-admin@lib.kyushu-u.ac.jp
Web Site: www.lib.kyushu-u.ac.jp

JAPAN

Key Personnel
Librarian: S Arikana
Founded: 1903

National Diet Library
1-10-1 Nagata-cho, Chiyoda ku, Tokyo 100-8924
Tel: (03) 3581-2331 *Fax:* (03) 3508-2934
E-mail: kokusai@ndl.go.jp
Web Site: www.ndl.go.jp
Key Personnel
Librarian: Takao Kurosawa
Dir Planning & Cooperation Division: Hiroyuki Taya
Founded: 1948
As the only national library in Japan, provides services for the Diet, for the government & for the general public. As the only depository library in Japan, the library acquires all materials published in Japan, preserves them as national cultural heritage, compiles catalogs of these publications in a database or other format, & with these collections provides library services.
Publication(s): *Annual Report of the National Diet Library*; *Biburosu* (Biblos, quarterly, online (www.ndl.go.jp/jp/publication/biblos/index.html)); *Books on Japan* (quarterly, online (www.ndl.go.jp/en/publication/books_on_japan/boi_top_E.html)); *CDNLAO Newsletter*; *Current Awareness*; *Current Awareness-E*; *Kin gendai nihon seiji kankei jinbutsu bunken mokuroku* (Bibliography of Persons in Modern Japanese Politics, online (refsys.ndl.go.jp/hito.nsf/Internet?OpenFrameset)); *NDL Newsletter* (bi-monthly, online (www.ndl.go.jp/en/publication/ndl_newsletter/index.html)); *NDL Research Report*; *Nihon kagakugijutsu kankei chikuji kankobutsu soran* (Directory of Japanese Scientific Periodicals, online (refsys.ndl.go.jp/E001_EP01.nsf/PublicE?OpenFrameset)); *Nihon zenkoku shoshi* (Japanese National Bibliography, weekly, online (www.ndl.go.jp/jp/publication/inbwl/inb_top.html)); *Proceedings*; *Refarensu* (Reference, monthly)

Osaka Prefectural Nakanoshima Library
1-2-10 Nakanoshima, Kita-ku, Osaka 530
Tel: (06) 6203-0474 *Fax:* (06) 2034914
Web Site: www.library.pref.osaka.jp
Key Personnel
Head Librarian: Shigemitsu Nakayama
Founded: 1904

Osaka University Library
1-4 Machikaneyama, Toyonaka, Osaka 560-0043
Tel: (06) 6850-5066 *Fax:* (06) 6850-5069
Web Site: www.library.osaka-u.ac.jp
Key Personnel
Dir, Library Services: Takeshi Hayashi

Tenri Central Library
Tenri University, 1050 Soma-no-uchi, Tenri, Nara 632-8577
Tel: (0743) 63-9200 *Fax:* (0743) 63-7728
E-mail: info@tcl.gr.jp
Web Site: www.tcl.gr.jp
Key Personnel
Chief Librarian: Keiichiro Moroi

Tohoku University Library
UN Depository Library, Kawauchi, Aoba-ku, Sendai 980-8576
Tel: (022) 217 5935; (0221) 217 4844 *Fax:* (0222) 217 5949; (0222) 217846
E-mail: desk@library.tohoku.ac.jp
Web Site: www.library.tohoku.ac.jp

Tokyo Metropolitan Central Library
5-7-13 Minami-Azabu, Minato-ku, Tokyo 106-8575
Tel: (03) 3442-8451 *Fax:* (03) 3447-8924
Web Site: www.library.metro.tokyo.jp/
Key Personnel
Dir: Okabe Kazukuni
Founded: 1973

The Toyo Bunko
2-28-21 Honkomagome, Bunkyo-ku, Tokyo 113 0021
Tel: (03) 39420121 *Fax:* (03) 39420258
E-mail: webmaster@toyo-bunko.or.jp
Web Site: www.toyo-bunko.or.jp/toyobunko-e
Key Personnel
Dir: Yoshinobu Shiba
Founded: 1917
Also Centre for East Asian Cultural Studies for UNESCO, for which publications include various directories, bibliographies & monographs.
Publication(s): *Asian Research Trends: A Humanities & Social Science Review* (journal, annually); *Memoirs of the Research Department of the Toyo Bunko* (journal, annually)

University of Tokyo Library
7-3-1, Hongo, Bunkyo-ku, Tokyo 113-0033
Tel: (03) 5841 2612 *Fax:* (03) 3816 4208
E-mail: kikaku@lib.u-tokyo.ac.jp
Web Site: www.lib.u-tokyo.ac.jp
Key Personnel
Dir: K Rodumoto

Waseda University Library
1-6-1 Nishi-waseda, Shinjuku-ku, Tokyo 169-8050
Tel: (03) 32034141
E-mail: info@wul.waseda.ac.jp
Web Site: www.wul.waseda.ac.jp
Telex: 2323280
Key Personnel
Librarian: T Hamada
Publication(s): *Bulletin of Waseda University Library*

Jordan

Amman Public Library
PO Box 182181, Amman
Tel: (06) 637 111 *Fax:* (06) 649420
Telex: 21969 Amcity Jo
Key Personnel
City Librarian: Abdul-Fattah Al-Homran
Founded: 1960

British Council Library
Rainbow St, First Circle, Jebel Amman, Amman 11118
Mailing Address: PO Box 634, Amman 11118
Tel: (06) 4636147; (06) 4636148 *Fax:* (06) 4656413
E-mail: information@britishcouncil.org.jo
Web Site: www.britishcouncil.org.jo
Key Personnel
Information Officer: Sonia Kawas *E-mail:* sonia.kawas@britishcouncil.org.jo
Founded: 1950

The Department of the National Library
King Talal Circle (3rd Circle) Jabal Amman, Al-Hussein Bin Ali St, Amman
Tel: (06) 4610311 *Fax:* (06) 4616832
E-mail: nl@nic.net.jo
Web Site: www.nl.gov.jo
Key Personnel
Dir General: Ousama Mikadi

Jordan University of Science & Technology Library
PO Box 3030, Irbid 22110
Tel: (02) 295111 *Fax:* (02) 295123
Web Site: www.just.edu.jo
Telex: 21629
Key Personnel
Dir: Dr Salah Jarrar
Founded: 1986

Mu'tah University Library
PO Box 7, Mu'tah, 61710 Kerak
Tel: (06) 4617860 *Fax:* (03) 371651
E-mail: library@mutah.edu.jo
Telex: 63003 Mu'tah JO
Key Personnel
Dir: Amin Al-Najdawi *E-mail:* libdir@mutah.edu.jo
Founded: 1984

Public Library
PO Box 348, Irbid 1957
Key Personnel
Librarian: Anwar Ishaq Al-Nshiwat

Royal Scientific Society Library
Building Research Centre, PO Box 1438, Amman 11941
Tel: (06) 5344701 *Fax:* (06) 5344806
E-mail: kahhaleh@rss.gov.jo
Web Site: www.rss.gov.jo
Telex: 21276 RAMAH
Key Personnel
President: Dr Said Alloush *E-mail:* salloush@rss.gov.jo

University of Jordan Library
University of Jordan, Amman 11942
Tel: 5355000 (ext 3135) *Fax:* 5355570
E-mail: library@ju.edu.jo
Web Site: www.ju.edu.jo
Telex: 21629 Unvj jo
Key Personnel
Acting Dir: Dr Salah Jarrar
Founded: 1962
Publication(s): *Al-Maktaba* (monthly, newsletter); *Arab References till 1980* (in Arabic); *Jordanian Publications in 1982*; *The Library Guide* (in English & Arabic); *Periodical Holdings* (in English & Arabic)

Yarmouk University Library
Irbid
Tel: (02) 7271100 (ext 2878) *Fax:* (02) 7271273
E-mail: yarmouk@yu.edu.jo
Web Site: www.yu.edu.jo
Telex: 51566 Yarmuk Jo *Cable:* Yarmouk Jordan
Key Personnel
Dir: Dr Muhammad Saraireh *E-mail:* saraireh@yu.edu.jo
Founded: 1976
Specialize in education/library.

Kazakstan

Kazakhstan Academy of Sciences
National Academy of Sciences of the Republic of Kazakhstan, 28 Shevchenko St, Almaty 480021
Tel: (03272) 624871 *Fax:* (03272) 62500
E-mail: teta@nursat.kz
Web Site: www.president.kz
Key Personnel
Dir: K K Abugalieva

Kenya

Egerton University Library
PO Box 536, Njoro
Tel: (051) 62265; (051) 62491; (051) 62389; (051) 62278 *Fax:* (051) 62527
E-mail: eujdlib@africaonline.co.ke
Web Site: www.egerton.or.ke
Telex: 33075
Key Personnel
University Librarian: Sylvester C Otenya
Founded: 1939
Publication(s): *Egerton University Journal*

Kenya Agricultural Research Institute
PO Box 57811, Karihq, Nairobi
Tel: (02) 583301-20 *Fax:* (02) 583344
E-mail: resource.centre@kari.org
Web Site: www.hridir.org
Key Personnel
Head Librarian: Vivienne Ochieng
E-mail: vivienneo@kari.org

Kenya National Archives & Documentation Service
Kenya National Archives Bldg, Moi Ave, Nairobi 00100
Mailing Address: PO Box 49210, Nairobi 00100
Tel: (02) 228959 *Fax:* (02) 228020
E-mail: knarchives@kenyaweb.com
Web Site: www.kenyarchives.go.ke
Telex: 228020 *Cable:* ARCHIVES
Key Personnel
Dir: Musila Musembi
Librarian: Wekalao Namande
Founded: 1946
Publication(s): *Acquisitions guides*

Kenya National Library Service
Ngong Rd, Nairobi
Mailing Address: PO Box 30573, Nairobi 60100
Tel: (02) 725550; (02) 725551; (02) 718177; (02) 718012; (02) 718013 *Fax:* (02) 721749
E-mail: knls@nbnet.co.ke
Web Site: www.knls.or.ke *Cable:* KENLIB
Key Personnel
Dir: S K Ng'anga
Founded: 1969
Publication(s): *Kenya National Bibliography*; *Kenya Periodicals Directory*

Kenya Polytechnic Library
Haile Selassie Ave, Nairobi
Mailing Address: PO Box 52428, Nairobi
Tel: (02) 338231; (02) 338232 *Fax:* (02) 219689
Key Personnel
Librarian: P Okoth

Kenya School of Law
PO Box 30369, Nairobi
Tel: (02) 715895 *Fax:* (02) 714783
Key Personnel
Chief Librarian: Peter Okoth

Kenya Technical Teachers' College Library (KTTC)
Gigiri, PO Box 44600, Nairobi
Tel: (02) 520211-5 *Fax:* (02) 520037
Key Personnel
Librarian: G M King'ori
Publication(s): *Mwalimu Kenya Education Supplement* (monthly); *Secondary School Library Facilities in Central Province, Kenya*; *Serials Literature, Exploitation & Use in Libraries*; *The Problems of Providing Library Services to School Children in Developing Countries*

Kenyatta University Library
PO Box 43844, Nairobi
Tel: (02) 810901 *Fax:* (02) 811575
E-mail: info@ku.ac.ke
Telex: 25483
Key Personnel
Librarian: Alice R Bulogosi *E-mail:* arbulogosi@avu.org
Publication(s): *Directory of Research in the University*; *Education in Kenya: an Index* (1984); *Education in Kenya since Independence: a bibliography* (1963-1983)

McMillan Memorial Library
Banda St, Nairobi
Tel: (02) 21844
Key Personnel
Chief Librarian: A O Esilaba
Founded: 1931

Mines & Geological Department Library
Ministry of Environment & Natural Resources, Machakos Rd, Nairobi
Mailing Address: PO Box 30009, Nairobi
Tel: (02) 229261; (02) 541040 *Fax:* (02) 216951
Cable: Mineralogy
Key Personnel
Commissioner: C Y O Owayo

Ministry of Agriculture & Livestock Development Marketing Library
Kilimo House, Cathedral Rd, Nairobi
Mailing Address: PO Box 30028, Nairobi
Tel: (02) 718-870 *Fax:* (02) 725-774
Telex: 22766 minag ke
Under the charge of The Library Services Coordinator.
Publication(s): *Economic Review of Agriculture*

Mombasa Polytechnic Library
Tom Mboya Ave, Mombasa
Mailing Address: PO Box 90420, Mombasa
Tel: (011) 492222 *Fax:* (011) 495632
E-mail: msapoly@africaonline.com
Key Personnel
Librarian: R Kasina
Founded: 1972

National Public Health Laboratory Services (Medical Department)
Ministry of Health, Afya House, Cathedral Rd, Nairobi
Mailing Address: PO Box 30016, Nairobi
Tel: (02) 717077
E-mail: healthmin@nbnet.co.ke
Web Site: www.ministryofhealth.go.ke
Key Personnel
Dir: Dr Jack Nyamongo

University of Nairobi Libraries
PO Box 30197, Nairobi
Tel: (02) 334244 *Fax:* (02) 336885
E-mail: jkml@uonbi.ac.ke
Web Site: www.uonbi.ac.ke/jkml
Telex: 22095-Varsity KE *Cable:* VARSITY NAIROBI
Key Personnel
University Librarian: Salome W Mathangani *E-mail:* salma@uonbi.ac.ke
Specialize in supporting study, teaching & research needs of the University of Nairobi.
Branch Office(s)
Chiromo Library, College of Biological & Physical Sciences, Chiromo, Nairobi *Tel:* (02) 43181-90
Kabete Library, PO Box 30197, College of Agriculture & Veterinary Sciences, Kabete, Nairobi *Tel:* (02) 632211; (02) 631340
Kikuyu Library, College of Education & External Studies, PO Box 92, Kikuyu *Tel:* (02) 32021; (02) 32016; (02) 31117-8
Lower Kabete Library, Lower Kabete, Nairobi *Tel:* (02) 732160/5
Parklands Law Library, Parklands Campus, Parklands, Nairobi *Tel:* (02) 340859; (02) 340858; (02) 340477
ADD, State House Road, Nairobi *Tel:* (02) 724520/5 (Architecture Design & Development)
Medical, Ngong Rd, Nairobi *Tel:* (02) 726300

Upper Kabete Library
PO Box 30197, Nairobi
Tel: (02) 334244 *Fax:* (02) 336885
Web Site: www.uonbi.ac.ke/jkml
Key Personnel
University Librarian: S Mathangani *Tel:* (02) 334244 (ext 28501) *E-mail:* salma@uonbi.ac.ke

Democratic People's Republic of Korea

Grand People's Study House
PO Box 200, Pyongyang
Tel: (02) 84 4066
Key Personnel
Contact: Mr Choe Gwang Ryol
Founded: 1982

Republic of Korea

Dongguk University Central Library
26, 3-ga, Pil-dong, Chung-gu, Seoul 100-715
Tel: (02) 2260-3114 *Fax:* (02) 2277-1274
E-mail: dong0104@dongguk.edu
Web Site: lib.dgu.ac.kr; www.dongguk.edu

Ewha Womans University Central Library
11-1 Daehyun-dong, Seodaemun-gu, Seoul 120-750
Tel: (02) 3277-2114 *Fax:* (02) 3935903
E-mail: master@ewha.ac.kr
Web Site: lib.ewha.ac.kr
Key Personnel
Librarian: Bong Hee Kim

Korea Development Institute Library
207-41, Chongnyangri-Dong, Dongdaemun-gu, Seoul 130-012
Mailing Address: PO Box 113, Chongnyang, Seoul 130-012
Tel: (02) 958 4266 *Fax:* (02) 958 4261
E-mail: library@kdi.re.kr
Web Site: www.kdi.re.kr
Key Personnel
Chief Librarian: Hwajin Yoon
Founded: 1971
Economics Research Institution.

Korea University Library
1, 5-Ka Anam-dong, Sungbuk-ku, Seoul 136-701
Tel: 23 290 1499 *Fax:* 23 234 763
E-mail: unneu@korea.ac.kr
Web Site: library.korea.ac.kr

REPUBLIC OF KOREA

Kyungpook National University Central Library
1370 Sangyeok-dong, Buk-gu, Daegu 702-701
Tel: (053) 950-6510 *Fax:* (053) 950-6533
E-mail: mspark@kyungpook.ac.kr
Web Site: kudos.knu.ac.kr
Key Personnel
Dir: Chong-moon Seo *Tel:* (053) 955-5516
  E-mail: cmseo@kyungpook.ac.kr

National Assembly Library
Youido-dong 1, Yeongdeungpo-gu, Seoul 150-703
Tel: (02) 788-4143 (english service available)
  Fax: (02) 7884301; (02) 7884193
E-mail: question@nanet.go.kr
Web Site: www.nanet.go.kr
Telex: 25849
Key Personnel
Librarian: Ho-young Chung
Publication(s): *Acquisition List (in Korean)* (bimonthly & annually); *Index to Korean-Language Periodicals (in Korean)* (bimonthly & annually); *Index to Korean Laws and Statutes (in Korean)* (biennially); *Index to National Assembly Debates (in Korean)* (irregularly); *Index to Recent Periodical Articles of Major Interests (in Korean)* (monthly); *Issue Briefs (in Korean)* (irregularly); *Legislative Information Analysis (in Korean)* (quarterly); *List of Theses for Doctors' and Masters' Degrees Awarded in Korea (in Korean)* (annually); *National Assembly Library Review (in Korean)* (bimonthly)

The National Library of Korea
San 60-1 Banpo-Dong, Seocho-Gu, Seoul 137-702
Tel: (02) 590-0513; (02) 590-0514 *Fax:* (02) 590-0608
E-mail: yeolram@www.nl.go.kr
Web Site: www.nl.go.kr
Key Personnel
Librarian: Hyun_Taek Shin
Publication(s): *Bibliographie Index of Korea*; *Korean National Bibliography*
Branch Office(s)
635 Yeoksam-dong, Kangnam-gu, Seoul

Seoul National University Library
San 56-1, Shillim-dong, Kwanak-gu, Seoul 151-736
Tel: (02) 880-8070 *Fax:* (02) 878-2730
E-mail: kimya@plaza.snu.ac.kr
Web Site: library.snu.ac.kr/snu
Key Personnel
Dir General: Heo Seong-do *E-mail:* hsdhsd@snu.ac.kr
Secretary: Kim Hyun-mee *Tel:* (02) 880-5280
  E-mail: hyunmee@snu.ac.kr
Contact: Young-Aie Kim *E-mail:* kimya@plaza.snu.ac.kr

United Nations Depository Library
1, 5ka Anam-dong, Sungbuk-gu, Seoul 136-701
Tel: 23 290 1499 *Fax:* 29 234 763
E-mail: unneu@korea.ac.kr
Web Site: library.korea.ac.kr
Key Personnel
Chief Librarian: Kim Deoug Hoon

Yonsei University Library
134 Shinchon-dong, Seodaemun-gu, Seoul 120-749
Tel: (02) 2123-3486 *Fax:* (02) 393-7272
E-mail: ewebmaster@yonsei.ac.kr
Web Site: www.yonsei.ac.kr; library.yonsei.ac.kr
Key Personnel
Dir: Prof Young-mee Chung

Kuwait

Kuwait University Library
PO Box 5969, 13060 Safat
Tel: 4813182 *Fax:* 4816095
Web Site: www.kuniv.edu.kw
Telex: 22616
Key Personnel
Dir: Dr Husain A Al-Ansari
Publication(s): *The Library Bulletin*

National Library of Kuwait
Mubarakiya St, (Opposite) Al-Muzaini Exchange, Kuwait City
Mailing Address: PO Box 26182, 13122 Safat
Tel: 2415192 *Fax:* 2415195
E-mail: nccalknl@ncc.moc.kw *Cable:* Thaquf
Key Personnel
Dir General: Wafa'a H Al-Sane
Founded: 1994
National Depository, ISBN, UN Depository.
Parent Company: National Council for Culture, Arts & Letters

National Scientific & Technical Information Center (NSTIC)
Kuwait Institute for Scientific Research, 13109 Safat
Mailing Address: PO Box 24885, 13109 Safat
Tel: 4836100; 4818630 *Fax:* 4830643
E-mail: public_relations@safat.kisr.edu.kw
Web Site: www.kisr.edu.kw
Telex: Kisr Kt 22299 *Cable:* SCIENCE KUWAIT
Key Personnel
Dir: Mrs Ferial Al-Freih

NSTIC, see National Scientific & Technical Information Center (NSTIC)

Laos People's Democratic Republic

Bibliotheque Nationale (Bibliotheque nationale du Laos)
PO Box 122, Vientiane
Tel: (021) 212 452 *Fax:* (021) 212 408
Founded: 1957

Latvia

LNB, see National Library of Latvia

National Library of Latvia (Latvijas Nacionala Biblioteka)
Kr Barona 14 Str, Riga LV 1423
Tel: 7289 874 *Fax:* 7280 851
E-mail: lnb@lnb.lv
Web Site: www.lnb.lv
Key Personnel
Dir: Mr Andris Vilks *E-mail:* andrisv@lbi.lnb.lv
Founded: 1919
The National Library of Latvia is the keeper of all printed matter of the Republic of Latvia, the developer of national bibliographic resources & the center for development of a system of state libraries. NLL, coordinating with other libraries, forms a depository of national literature & performs the functions of an interlibrary loan center in Latvia.
Publication(s): *Latviesu zinatne un literatura*; *Latvijas preses hronika*

Lebanon

American University of Beirut Libraries
Bliss St, Riad El Solh, Beirut 1107 2020
Mailing Address: PO Box 11-0236, Riad El Solh, Beirut 1107 2020
Tel: (01) 340460 *Fax:* (01) 744703
E-mail: library@aub.edu.lb
Web Site: www.aub.edu.lb/
Telex: 20801 *Cable:* AMUNOB
Key Personnel
University Librarian: Helen Bikhazi
  E-mail: hb02@aub.edu.lb
Constituent Libraries: Jafet Memorial Library (Central Library), Farm Library; Science & Agriculture Library; Engineering & Architecture Library.

Library of Beirut Arab University
PO Box 11-5020, Beirut 1107 2089
Tel: (01) 300110 *Fax:* (01) 818402
E-mail: bau@inco.com.lb
Web Site: www.bau.edu.lb

Bibliotheque de l'Ecole Superieure des Lettres
rue de Damas, BP 1931, Beirut

Bibliotheque des Sciences Medicales
Campus des Sciences Medicales, Rue de Damas, BP 11-5076 Riyad El-Solh, Beirut
Tel: (01) 614001-2 *Fax:* (01) 614054
E-mail: csm.biblio@usj.edu.lb
Web Site: www.biblio-csm.usj.edu.lb
Key Personnel
Contact: May Harfouche Samaha
Parent Company: Universite Saint Joseph

Ecole Superieure d'Ingenieurs de Beyrouth (ESIB)
Universite de St Joseph (USJ), Campus des sciences et technologies, Mar Rou Kos-Mkalles, Beirut 1107 2050
Mailing Address: BP 11-514, Riad El Solh, Beirut 1107 2050
Tel: (04) 532662 (ext 427); (04) 532663 (ext 427) *Fax:* (04) 532645
E-mail: biblio-cst@usj.edu.lb
Web Site: www.fi.usj.lb
Key Personnel
Contact: Rose Saab
Parent Company: Universite Saint Joseph de Beyrouth

Library of the Faculty of Law
Universite St Joseph, Rue Huvelin, Mar Michael, Beirut 1104 2020
Mailing Address: BP 17-5208, Mar Michael, Beirut 1104 2020
Tel: (01) 200 625 *Fax:* (01) 215473
E-mail: css.biblio@usj.edu.lb
Web Site: www.biblio-css.usj.edu.lb
Publication(s): *Proche-Orient, Etudes Juridiques*

Bibliotheque de l'Institut Francais d'Archeologie du Proche Orient
Rue de Damas, Orient, Beirut
Tel: (01) 615 844; (01) 615 844 *Fax:* (01) 615 866
E-mail: ifapo@lb.refer.org

Key Personnel
Dir: Jean-Marie Dentzer
Publication(s): *Bibliotheque Archeologique et Historique* (147 titles); *Syria, Revue d'art oriental et d'archeologie* (annually, 2 vols)

Nami C Jafet Memorial Library, see American University of Beirut Libraries

Bibliotheque Nationale du Liban
BP 11-945, Beirut
Tel: (01) 862957 *Fax:* (01) 374079

Library of the Near East School of Theology
PO Box 13-5780, Chouran, Beirut
Tel: (01) 354194; (01) 349901 *Fax:* (01) 347129
E-mail: nest.lib@inco.com.lb
Telex: 44246 NEST LE
Key Personnel
Librarian: David A Kerry
Founded: 1932
Publication(s): *Theological Review*

Library of the Monastery of St-Saviour (Basilian Missionary Order of St-Saviour)
Saida

Bibliotheque Orientale (Oriental Library)
Quartier jesuite, Rue de l'Universite St Joseph, Beirut 1100 2150
Mailing Address: BP 16-6775 - Achrafieh, Beirut 1100 2150
Tel: (01) 202 421 *Fax:* (01) 339 287
E-mail: bo@usj.edu.lb
Web Site: www.usj.edu.lb
Key Personnel
Dir: May Seeman Seigneurie
Founded: 1875
University Research Library.
Publication(s): *Melanges de l'Universite Saint-Joseph (1906-)*
Parent Company: Compagnie de Jesus-Beyrouth (Beirut)
Ultimate Parent Company: Universite Saint-Joseph-Beyrouth

Lesotho

British Council Library
Hobson's Sq, Maseru 100
Mailing Address: PO Box 429, Maseru 100
Tel: 312609 *Fax:* 310363
E-mail: general.enquiries@bc-lesotho.bcouncil.org
Key Personnel
Library Supervisor: Zanedde Nsibirwa

Lesotho National Library Service
PO Box 985, Maseru 100
Tel: 322 592; 323 100 *Fax:* 323 100
Telex: 4228
Key Personnel
Librarian: Ms Dikeledi J Setlogelo
Founded: 1976

National University of Lesotho Library
PO Roma 180, Maseru
Tel: 340601 *Fax:* 340000
Web Site: www.nul.ls/library
Telex: 4303 10 *Cable:* UNITER
Key Personnel
Acting University Librarian: M M Moshoeshoe-Chadzingwa
Acting Department Librarian: Samuel M Mohai
E-mail: s.mohai@nul.ls

Liberia

Cuttington University College Library
Episcopal Church of Liberia, 1000 Monrovia 10
Mailing Address: PO Box 10-0277, 1000 Monrovia 10
Tel: 227-413 *Fax:* 226-059
Web Site: www.cuttington.org

Government Public Library
Ashmun St, Monrovia

University of Liberia Libraries
PO Box 9020, Monrovia
Tel: 226 418 *Fax:* 227 033; 226 418
Web Site: www.hometown.aol.com/dcronteh/myhomepage/index.html
Key Personnel
Dir: Dr C Wesley Armstrong

Libyan Arab Jamahiriya

Benghazi Public Library
Shar a Umar al-Mukhtar, Benghazi
Tel: (061) 96379

Al-Fateh University, The Central Library
PO Box 13482, Tripoli
Tel: (022) 605441 *Fax:* (022) 605460
Telex: 20629
Key Personnel
University Librarian: Dr Mohamed Abdul Jaleel

Government Library
14 Shar'a al-Jazair, Tripoli

National Archives
Castello, Tripoli
Tel: (021) 40 166
Founded: 1928

National Library of Libya
PO Box 9127, Benghazi
Tel: (061) 9097074 *Fax:* (061) 9097073
E-mail: nat_lib_libya@hotmail.com
Web Site: www.nll.8m.com
Telex: 40107

University of Garyounis Library
PO Box 1308, Benghazi
Tel: (061) 2220147 *Fax:* (061) 2229602
E-mail: info@garyounis.eu
Web Site: www.garyounis.edu
Telex: 40175 unigarly
Key Personnel
Librarian: Ahmed M Gallal
Founded: 1955

Liechtenstein

Liechtensteinische Landesbibliothek
Gerberweg 5, 9490 Vaduz
Mailing Address: Postfach 385, 9490 Vaduz
Tel: 236 63 62 *Fax:* 233 14 19
E-mail: info@landesbibliothek.li
Web Site: www.lbfl.li
Key Personnel
Librarian: Barbara Vogt
Founded: 1961
National Library.
Publication(s): *Liechtensteinische Bibliographie*

Lithuania

Martynas Mazvydas National Library of Lithuania (Lietuvos Nacionaline Martyno Mazvydo Biblioteka)
Gedimino pr 51, 01504 Vilnius
Tel: (02) 497023 *Fax:* (02) 496129
E-mail: biblio@lnb.lt
Web Site: www.lnb.lt
Key Personnel
Acting Dir: Vytautas Gudaitis
Deputy Dir: Algirdas Plioplys
Deputy Dir & Dir, Bibliography & Book Science Center: Dr Regina Varniene
Deputy Dir & Dir, Library Research Center: Vytautas Gudaitis
Founded: 1919
Library & information services.
Publication(s): *Bibliografijos Zinios* (Bibliographical News, monthly, 1947, Indices of current national bibliography); *Lietuvos Spaudos Statistika* (Lithuanian Press Statistics, annually, 1981, Publishing statistics); *Nacionalines Bibliografijos Duomenu Bankas (NBDB)* (National Bibliographic Data Bank (NBDB), online database (www.libis.lt:80821)); *Tarp Knygu* (In the World of Books, monthly, journal, 1949, Professional journal for librarians)

Vilnius University Library (Vilniaus Universiteto Biblioteka)
Universiteto 3, 2633 Vilnius
Tel: (085) 2687101 *Fax:* (085) 2687104
E-mail: mb@mb.vu.lt
Web Site: www.mb.vu.lt
Key Personnel
Dir & Librarian: B Butkeviciene *E-mail:* birute.butkeviciene@mb.vu.lt
Founded: 1570
Member of Lithuanian Academic Libraries Association.

Luxembourg

Bibliotheque de la Ville
26, rue Emile Mayrisch, L-4240 Esch/Alzette
Tel: 54 73 83-496 *Fax:* 55 20 37
Key Personnel
Librarian: Fernand Roeltgen

Bibliotheque nationale de Luxembourg (National Library of Luxembourg)
37, Bd F D Roosevelt, 2450 Luxembourg
Tel: 22 97 55-1 *Fax:* 47 56 72
E-mail: bib.nat@bi.etat.lu
Web Site: www.bnl.lu
Key Personnel
Dir: Dr Monique Kieffer
Publication(s): *Bibliographie d'histoire luxembourgeoise*; *Bibliographie luxembourgeoise*

Archives Nationales du Grand-Duche de luxembourg (National Archives)
Plateau du St-Esprit, 2010 Luxembourg
Mailing Address: BP 6, L-2010 Luxembourg
Tel: 4786660; 4786661 *Fax:* 474692
E-mail: archives.nationales@an.etat.lu
Web Site: www.etat.lu

Key Personnel
Dir: Dr Cornel Meder
Publication(s): *Publications des Anlux, Plusieurs Series* (catalogs, repertories, reprints)

Macau

Biblioteca Central de Macau
Av Conselheiro Ferreira de Almeida No 89A-B, Macao
Tel: 567576; 558049 *Fax:* 318756
Key Personnel
Chief Librarian: Ophelia Tang
Publication(s): *Boletim Bibliografico de Macau*

The Former Yugoslav Republic of Macedonia

Arhiv na Makedonija (Archives of Macedonia)
Grigor Prlichev, 3, 91000 Skopje
Tel: (091) 237-211; (091) 115-783; (091) 115-827
Fax: (091) 115-783
Web Site: www.arhiv.gov.mk
Key Personnel
Dir: Kiro Dojcinovski
Founded: 1951

Narodna i univerzitetska biblioteka Kliment Ohridski ('Kliment Ohridski' National & University Library)
bul "Goce Delcev" 6, 91000 Skopje
Tel: (02) 3115 177; (02) 3133 418 *Fax:* (02) 3226 846
E-mail: kliment@nubsk.edu.mk
Web Site: www.nubsk.edu.mk
Publication(s): *Bibliografija KPJ-SKM 1919-1979; Bilten na izdanija od oblasta na samoupravuvanjeto vo Jugoslavija; Katalog na staropecateni i retki knigi vo Narodnata i Univerzitetskata Biblioteka 'Kliment Ohridski' - Skopje; Makedonska Bibliografija*

Madagascar

Bibliotheque Universitaire d'Antananarivo
Campus Universitaire d'Ankatso, PO Box 908, 101 Tananrive
Tel: (020) 22 612 28 *Fax:* (020) 22 612 29
E-mail: bu@univ-antananarivo.mg
Web Site: www.bu.univ-antananarivo.mg
Key Personnel
Dir: Jean-Marie Andrianiaina
Founded: 1960
Publication(s): *Bibliographie annuelle de Madagascar*

Bibliotheque du Centre Culturel Albert Camus
14 ave de l'Independance, BP 488, Tananrive 101
Tel: 22 213 75; 22 236 47 *Fax:* 22 213 38
E-mail: medccac@dts.ng
Telex: 22507
Key Personnel
Contact: Singare Reinhard Veionique

Bibliotheque Nationale Malagasy
BP 257, Anosy, Tananrive
Tel: (02) 25872 *Fax:* (02) 22-9448
Key Personnel
Dir: Mr Louis-Dominique Ralaisaholimanana
Contact: Mr Roland Franck Ranaivoson

Bibliotheque Municipale
Av du 18 juin, BP 729, Tananrive
Tel: (04) 21176
Key Personnel
President: Julien Razafimandimbilaza
Librarian: Albert Denis Rakoto

Archives Nationales de Madagascar
23 rue Karija Tsaralalana, 101 Tananrive
Mailing Address: BP 3384, 101 Tananrive
Tel: (020) 22 235 34
E-mail: rijandriamihamina@malagasy.com
Key Personnel
Dir: Mdme Sahondra Andriamihamina

Malawi

British Council Library
PO Box 30222, Lilongwe 3
Tel: 773 244 *Fax:* 772 945
E-mail: info@britishcouncil.org.mw
Web Site: www.britishcouncil.org/malawi
Telex: 44476 Bricoun Ml

Bunda College of Agriculture Library
PO Box 219, Lilongwe
Tel: 277222 *Fax:* 277251
E-mail: bundalibrary@malawi.net
Web Site: www.unima.mw/bunda/library.htm
Telex: 43622 Bunda MI *Cable:* BUNDAGRIC
Key Personnel
University Librarian: S S Mwiyeriwa
College Librarian: Margaret E Ngwira
Parent Company: Bunda College of Agriculture, University of Malawi

Malawi National Library Service
PO Box 30314, Lilongwe, Lilongwe Central Region 3
Tel: 773 700 *Fax:* 771 616
E-mail: nls@malawi.net
Key Personnel
National Librarian: R S Mabomba

National Archives of Malawi
PO Box 62, Zomba
Tel: 525 240; 524 148 *Fax:* 524 148; 525 362
E-mail: archives@sdnp.org.mw
Web Site: chambo.sdnp.org.mw
Key Personnel
Acting Dir/Sr Librarian: O W Ambali
Publication(s): *Malawi National Bibliography*

University of Malawi Libraries
PO Box 278, Zomba
Tel: (01) 526 622; (01) 525 760
E-mail: university.office@unima.mw
Web Site: www.unima.mw
Telex: 44742
Key Personnel
Librarian: Steve S Mwiyeriwa
 E-mail: smwiyeriwa@unima.wn.apc.org; smwiyeriwa@chirunga.sdnp.org.mw
Founded: 1965
Publication(s): *An Annotated Bibliography of Education in Malawi; Directory of Malawi Libraries; Library Bulletin; Report on University Libraries*
Branch Office(s)
Bunda College of Agriculture Library, PO Box 219, Lilongwe, Geoffrey F Salanje *Tel:* (01) 277222 *Fax:* (01) 277251 *E-mail:* gsalanje@bunda.sdnr.org.mw
Chancellor College Library, PO Box 280, Zomba, Augustine Msiska *Tel:* (01) 524 222 *Fax:* (01) 524 046 *E-mail:* amsiska@chanco.unima.mw
College of Medicine Library, Private Bag 360, Chichiri, Blantyre 3, Ralph Masanjika *Tel:* (01) 677 245 *Fax:* (01) 674 700 *E-mail:* registrar@medcol.mw
Kamuzu College of Nursing Library, Private Bag 1, Lilongwe, Godwin Shaba
Polytechnic Library, PO Bag 303, Chichiri, Blantyre 3, Paul Kanthambi *Tel:* (01) 670411 *Fax:* (01) 674710

University of Malawi, Polytechnic Library
PB 303, Chichiri, Blantyre 3
Tel: 670411 *Fax:* 670578
Web Site: www.poly.ac.mw
Telex: 44613 Polytec
Key Personnel
Librarian: Paul Kanthambi

Malaysia

British Council Library
Ground floor, West Block Wisma Selangor Dredging, 142C Jalan Ampang, 50450 Kuala Lumpur
Tel: (03) 2723 7900 *Fax:* (03) 2713 6599
E-mail: information@britishcouncil.org.my
Web Site: www.britcoun.org/malaysia
Telex: MA 31052
Key Personnel
Librarian & Information Services Manager: Ms Gaik Sim Khoo
Branch Office(s)
3 World Quay, 10300 Penang
PO Box 10746, Sabah
PO Box 615, Sarawak

Ministry of Agriculture Library
Wisma Tani, 1st floor, Jalan Sultan Salahuddin, 50624 Kuala Lumpur
Tel: (03) 26954215 (ext 4216, 4217or 4298) *Fax:* (03) 26932220
E-mail: dahlia@agri.moa.my; lht@agri.moa.my; fuziah@agri.moa.my
Web Site: agrolink.moa.my/library
Telex: TANIAN MA 33045 *Cable:* TANI KUALA LUMPUR
Key Personnel
Librarian: Mrs Pathmavathy Satyahoorthy
Founded: 1905
Publication(s): *Bulletin of the Ministry of Agriculture* (irregular); *Malaysian Agricultural Journal* (biannual)

Ministry of Environment & Public Health, Library Division
Tingkat 2, Wisma Masja, Jalan Medan, 93360 Kuching Sarawak
Tel: (082) 319614; (082) 319613 *Fax:* (082) 311216
E-mail: info@moeswk.gov.my
Web Site: www.moeswk.gov.my
Key Personnel
Chief Librarian: Johnny Kueh

National Archives of Malaysia
Jalan Duta, 50568 Kuala Lumpur
Tel: (03) 62010688 *Fax:* (03) 62015679
E-mail: query@arkib.gov.my
Web Site: arkib.gov.my *Cable:* ARKIB KUALALUMPUR

Key Personnel
Dir-Gen: Mrs Zakiah Hanum Nor
Other publications include Acquisitions List, List of Record & Archives Groups available for researchs bibliographies & others.
Publication(s): *Annual Report of the National Archives* (Bulletins)

National Library of Malaysia (Gift & Exchange Unit)
232, Jalan Tun Razak, 50572 Kuala Lumpur
Tel: (03) 26871700 *Fax:* (03) 26927082
E-mail: pnmweb@www1.pnm.my
Web Site: www.pnm.my
Telex: MA NATLIB 30092
Key Personnel
Dir General: Zawiyah binti Baba
Publication(s): *Bibliography of books in Bahasa Malaysia*; *Directory of Librarians in Malaysia*; *Directory of Libraries in Malaysia*; *Index to Malaysian Conferences* (annually); *Malaysian National Bibliography* (quarterly, annually); *Malaysian Newspaper Index* (quarterly); *Malaysian Periodicals Index* (biannually)

National University of Malaysia Library
Universiti Kebangsaan Malaysia, 43600 UKM Bangi, Selangor Darul Ehsan
Tel: (03) 8921 3370; (03) 8921 5057 *Fax:* (03) 8925 4890
E-mail: puspa@pkrisc.cc.ukm.my
Web Site: www.ukm.my
Telex: MA 31496
Key Personnel
Chief Librarian: Muslim Norsham
 E-mail: norsham@pkrisc.cc.ukm.my
Holds Malay Library Collection (approx 30,000 titles).
Publication(s): *Katalog Koleksi Melayu, Penerbit Ukm 1990*

Perpustakaan Negeri Sabah, see Sabah State Library

Perpustakaan Sultanah Zanariah
Universiti Teknologi Malaysia, 81310 UTM Skudai, Johor
Tel: (07) 5533333 *Fax:* (07) 5572555
E-mail: psz@utm.my
Web Site: www.utm.my
Telex: MA 60205 *Cable:* UNITEK MA
Key Personnel
Chief Librarian: Rosna Binti Mohd Taib *Tel:* (07) 26154596 *E-mail:* rosna@psz.utm.my
Head Administration & Support Services: Kamariah BTE Nor Mohd Desa *Tel:* (07) 5502107 *E-mail:* kamariah@psz.tum.my
Assistant Registrar: Hazara Binti Sulaiman
 E-mail: hazara@mel.psz.utm.my
Publication(s): *Berita Unitek, Berita Satelit*; *Jurnal Teknologi*
Branch Office(s)
Kuala Lumpur Campus Branch, Universiti Teknologi Malaysia, Jalan Semarak, 54100 Kuala Lumpur *Tel:* (03) 26154100 *Fax:* (03) 26922186 *Web Site:* www.psz.utm.my/pszkl.html

Rubber Research Institute of Malaysia Library
260 Jalan Ampang, 50908 Kuala Lumpur
Mailing Address: PO Box 10150, 50908 Kuala Lumpur
Tel: (03) 4567033 *Fax:* (03) 4511301
Web Site: w3.itri.org.tw/k0000/apec/malaysia/malay-1.htm
Telex: Rrim MA 30369 *Cable:* SEARCHING
Key Personnel
Librarian: H S Kaw
Publication(s): *Journal Natural Rubber Research* (Planters' Bulletin)

Sabah State Library
Locked Bag 2023, 888999 Kota Kinabalu, Sabah
Tel: (088) 225865 *Fax:* (088) 270714
Web Site: www.ssl.sabah.gov.my
Key Personnel
Contact: Mrs Ku Joo Bee *E-mail:* joobee.ku@sabah.gov.my
Founded: 1953

SEACEN, see South East Asian Central Banks (SEACEN) Research & Training Centre

Selangor Public Library
c/o Perpustakaan Raja Tun Uda, Persiaran, Perdagangan, 40572 Shah Alam, Selangor
Tel: (03) 55197667 *Fax:* (03) 55196045
E-mail: ppas@sel.lib.edu.my; jothi@ppas.org.my
Web Site: www.ppas.org.my
Key Personnel
Dir: Mrs Shahaneem Mustafa

South East Asian Central Banks (SEACEN) Research & Training Centre
Lorong Universiti A, 59100 Kuala Lumpur
Tel: (03) 7958 5600 *Fax:* (03) 7957 4616
E-mail: info@seacen.org
Web Site: www.seacen.org
Key Personnel
Chief Librarian: Zainon Zubir *E-mail:* zzainon@seacen.po.my

Tun Razak Library
Jalan Kelab, 3000 Ipoh
Tel: (05) 508073
Publication(s): *Accession Lists* (in English, Malay, Chinese & Tamil); *Malaysiana Collection* (plus supplement)

Library Tun Seri Lanang
43600 UKM Bangi, Selangor DE
Tel: (03) 89250199 *Fax:* (03) 89256067
E-mail: kpustaka@pkrisc.cc.ukm.my
Web Site: www.ukm.my/library
Telex: 34196
Founded: 1970
Parent Company: Universiti Kebangsaan Malaysia

Universiti Putra Malaysia Library (UPM)
43400 UPM Serdang, Selangor Darul Ehsan
Tel: (03) 89468642 *Fax:* (03) 89483745
E-mail: lib@lib.upm.edu.my
Web Site: www.lib.upm.edu.my
Telex: Uniper MA 37454 *Cable:* UNIPERTAMA SUNGAI BESI
Key Personnel
Acting Chief Librarian: Badilah Saad *Tel:* (03) 894868601 *E-mail:* badilah@lib.upm.edu.my

University Library, Universiti Sains Malaysia
11800 Penang
Tel: (04) 6533888; (04) 6533700; (04) 6585518 *Fax:* (04) 6571526
E-mail: chieflib@notes.usm.my
Web Site: www.lib.usm.my *Cable:* UNISAINS
Key Personnel
Chief Librarian: Noor Ida Yang Rashdi *Tel:* (04) 6533888 (ext 3700)
Founded: 1969
Publication(s): *Bibliography series* (irregularly); *Midas Bulletin* (quarterly)

University of Malysia Library
Lembah Pantai, 50603 Kuala Lumpur
Tel: (03) 7956 7800 *Fax:* (03) 7957 3661
E-mail: query.perpustakaan@um.edu.my
Web Site: www.umlib.um.edu.my

Key Personnel
Librarian: Dr Zaiton Osman *E-mail:* zaiton@cc.um.edu.my
Publication(s): *Kekal Abadi* (quarterly newsletter); *Maklumat Semasa* (monthly)

University of Technology Malaysia Library, see Perpustakaan Sultanah Zanariah

UPM, see Universiti Putra Malaysia Library (UPM)

Mali

Bibliotheque du Centre Culturel Francais de Bamako
Blvd de l'independance, Bamako
Mailing Address: BP 1547, Bamako
Tel: 222 40 19 *Fax:* 222 58 28
E-mail: dir@ccfbko.org.ml
Web Site: www.ccfbko.org.ml
Telex: 2569
Key Personnel
Librarian: Veronique Reinhard-Singare

Bibliotheque Nationale
BP 159, Bamako
Tel: 22 49 63 *Fax:* 23 59 31
E-mail: info@culture.gov.ml
Web Site: w3.culture.gov.ml
Key Personnel
Dir: Bouna Boukary Diouara
Founded: 1962

Centre francais de Documentation, see Bibliotheque du Centre Culturel Francais de Bamako

Ecole normale superieure
BP 241, Bamako
Tel: 222189

Faculte de Medecine de Pharmuacie et d'Odonto-Stomatologie
Bibliotheque, BP 1805, Bamako
Tel: 22 52 77 *Fax:* 22 96 58
E-mail: codiawara@caramail.com
Key Personnel
Librarian: M Cheick Oumar Diawara

Malta

Gozo Public Library
Triq Vajringa, Victoria VCT 105
Tel: (021) 556200 *Fax:* (021) 560599
E-mail: gozo.libraries@gov.mt
Web Site: servicecharters.gov.mt
Key Personnel
Librarian: George V Borg *Tel:* (021) 561510
 E-mail: georgev.borg@magnet.mt
Founded: 1853

National Library of Malta (Bibljoteka Nazzjonali ta' Malta)
36, Old Treasury St, Valletta CMR 02
Tel: 21243297; 21236585; 21232691; 21245303 *Fax:* 21235992
E-mail: customercare.nlm@gov.mt
Web Site: www.libraries-archives.gov.mt
Key Personnel
Librarian: Joseph M Boffa *E-mail:* joseph.boffa@magnet.mt

MALTA

Contact: M Vella
Founded: 1555
Publication(s): *Malta National Bibliography*

University of Malta Library
Tal-Qroqq, MSD06 Msida
Tel: 3290 2316 *Fax:* 314 306
Web Site: www.lib.um.edu.mt
Telex: 407 Hieduc *Cable:* UNIVERSITY MALTA
Key Personnel
Dir, Library Services: Anthony Mangion *Tel:* 21 310 239 *E-mail:* dls@lib.um.edu.mt

Martinique

Archives Departementales de la Martinique
19 Ave Saint-John-Perse, Tartenson, 97263 Fort de France Cedex
Mailing Address: BP 649, Tartenson, 97263 Fort de France Cedex
Tel: 63 88 46 *Fax:* 70 04 50
E-mail: archives@cg972.fr
Key Personnel
Dir: Dominique Taffin
Founded: 1949
Publication(s): *Declaration des droits de l'homme et abolition de l'esclavage* (1998); *L'eglise martiniquaise et la piete populaire* (2001); *Enfances martiniquaises* (2001); *Guide des Archives de la Martinique* (1978); *L'immigration indienne a la Martinique* (2003); *Inventaire analytique du Conseil souverain de la Martinique - Tome 1* (1985); *Inventaire analytique du Conseil souverain de la Martinique - Tome 2* (1999); *Inventaire des sources de l'esclavage* (1998); *La Martinique de Pierre Verger* (2000); *1902 et apres* (2002)

Bibliotheque Schoelcher
One Rue de la Liberte, 97200 Fort-de-France
Mailing Address: BP 640, 97262 Fort-de-France Cedex
Tel: 702 667 *Fax:* 724 555
E-mail: biblio-schoelcher-dep@cg972.fr
Key Personnel
Librarian: Jacqueline Leger *E-mail:* legerbib@cg972.fr
Founded: 1883

Mauritania

Arab Library
Chinguetti
Key Personnel
Contact: M Abdallahi Ouid Fall

Bibliotheque Nationale
BP 20, Nouakchott
Tel: 24 35

Direction des Archives Nationales, Bibliotheque Publique et Centre du Documentation
ave de l'Independenance, Nouakchott
Mailing Address: BP 77, Nouakchott
Tel: 2523 1732
Telex: Prim 580 Mtn
Key Personnel
Dir: Moktar Ould Hemeina
Founded: 1955

Mauritius

British Council Library
Royal Rd, Rose Hill
Tel: 4549550; 4549551; 4549552 *Fax:* 4549553
E-mail: general.enquiries@mu.britishcouncil.org
Web Site: www.britishcouncil.org/mauritius
Key Personnel
Dir: Rosalind Burford *E-mail:* rosalind.burford@mu.britishcouncil.org

Carnegie Library
Queen Elizabeth II Ave, Curepipe
Tel: 6742 280; 6742 281 *Fax:* 676 5054
E-mail: contact@curepipe.org
Web Site: www.curepipe.org
Key Personnel
Senior Librarian: T K Ramnauth *Tel:* 674 2287
Founded: 1920
Large collection of material on historical background of Mauritius & original manuscripts, papers on colonization by French & British.
Parent Company: Municipal Council of Curepipe
Ultimate Parent Company: Ministry of Local Government & Environment

City Library
City Hall, Sir Jules Koenig St, Port Louis
Mailing Address: PO Box 422, Port Louis
Tel: 212 0831 (ext 163) *Fax:* 212 4258
E-mail: mpllib@intnet.mu
Web Site: mpl.intnet.mu *Cable:* CERNE/PORT LOUIS
Key Personnel
Librarian: Gaetan Benoit
Founded: 1851
Publication(s): *Bibliography: Mauritiana in City Library*; *Literary Publishing & Bibliographical Control in Mauritius*; *Newspapers Index: Mauritius*

Mauritius Archives
Development Bank of Mauritius Complex, Coromandel
Tel: 233-4469; 233 7341 *Fax:* 233 4299
Key Personnel
Deputy Chief Archivist: Mr Gheeandut Suneechur
Publication(s): *Annual Report of the Archives Department* (including a bibliographical supplement); *Quarterly Memorandum of Books Printed in Mauritius and Registered in the Archives*

Mauritius Institute Public Library
Chaussee St, Port Louis
Mailing Address: PO Box 54, Port Louis
Tel: 212 06 39 *Fax:* 212 57 17
Key Personnel
Head Librarian: Sewannah Ankiah
Founded: 1970

University Library
University of Mauritius, Reduit
Tel: 454 1041 (ext 1229) *Fax:* 454 0905
E-mail: int.libservice@uom.ac.mu
Web Site: www.uom.ac.mu
Telex: 4621
Publication(s): *Journal of the University of Mauritius* (irregular); *University of Mauritius Calendar*; *University of Mauritius Report* (annually)

Mexico

Biblioteca Nacional de Antropologia E Historia
Paseo de la Reforma y Calzada Gandhi s/n, Col Polanco, CP 11560, Mexico, DF
Tel: (055) 5536342; (055) 5536865
E-mail: ejuare@juarez.ciesas.edu.mx
Web Site: www.arts-history.mx
Key Personnel
Contact: Dr Cesar Moheno; Miguel Najera Perez
Founded: 1888
Parent Company: Instituto Nacional de Antropologia e Historia
Branch Office(s)
Subireccion de Documentacion

Archivo General de la Nacion
Eduardo Molina y Albaniles s/n, Col Penitenciaria Ampliacion Deleg Venustiano Carranza, 15350 Mexico, DF
Tel: 5133-9900 *Fax:* 5789-5296
E-mail: agn@segob.gob.mx
Web Site: www.agn.gob.mx
Key Personnel
Dir: Leonor Ortiz M Prieto
Publication(s): *Boletin*

Biblioteca Benjamin Franklin (USIS)
Londres 16, Col Juarez, Mexico, DF
Mailing Address: CP 06600, Mexico DF
Tel: 5080 2801 (ext 2802 & 2803) *Fax:* (055) 5910075
E-mail: garciae@state.gov
Web Site: www.usembassy-mexico.gov/biblioteca.htm
Publication(s): *Boletin de Seleccion de Adquisiciones Recientes* (quarterly)

Biblioteca Central
Campus Chapingo, Km 38 5 Carretera Mexico-Texcoco, CP 56230 Texcoco
Tel: (0595) 952-15-00 (exts 7111, 4741 & 5440) *Fax:* (0595) 952-15-01
Web Site: www.chapingo.mx
Key Personnel
Head of Library: Blanca Margarita Garcia Ocampo *E-mail:* blmgaro@chapingo.mx
Head of Consultation Office: Ramon Suarez Espinosa *E-mail:* rsuarez@chapingo.mx
Previously named Escuela Nacional de Agricultura Periodicals. Chapingo, Revista de Geografia Agricola, Textual.

Direccion General de Bibliotecas de la Universidad Nacional Autonoma de Mexico
Ciudad Universitaria, Circuito Interior, 04510 Mexico, DF
Tel: (055) 5622 1603 *Fax:* (055) 6160664
E-mail: webdgb@dgb.unam.mx
Web Site: www.dgbiblio.unam.mx
Key Personnel
Librarian: Silvia Gonzalez Marin
E-mail: marins@servidor.unam.mx
Publication(s): *Biblioteca Universitaria Revista de la Direccion General de Bibliotecas de la UNAM* (biannual, journal, 1986, specializes in library & information science); *Directorio de Bibliotecas UNAM* (directory for UNAM's library system, monthly, Directory fo the 139 libraries in UNAM's library system); *Librunam* (Database of books existing in UNAM's library system); *Seriunam* (Database of journals & serial publications existing in UNAM's library system); *Tesiunam* (Database of theses from UNAM & other Mexican universities)

Biblioteca de Mexico
Plaza de la Ciudadela No 4, Col Centro, 06040 Mexico, DF

Tel: (055) 7 09 11 01; (055) 7 09 10 85
  Fax: (055) 7 09 11 73
Web Site: www.cnca.gob.mx/bi.htm
Key Personnel
Librarian: Carmen E de Moreno
Founded: 1946

Biblioteca Nacional de Mexico
Centro Cultural Universitario, Delegacion Coyoacan 04510
Tel: (05) 6226818 *Fax:* (05) 6650951
E-mail: liceaj@biblional.bibliog.unam.mx
Web Site: biblional.bibliog.unam.mx
Key Personnel
Dir: Jose Guadalupe Moreno De Alba
Publication(s): *Bibliografia Mexicana*; *Boletin del Instituto de Investigaciones Bibliograficas* (annually)

Centro de Informacion Cientifica y Humanistica
Universidad Nacional Autonoma de Mexico, Ciudad Universitaria, Apdo 70-392, 04510 Mexico, DF
Tel: (055) 6223960 *Fax:* (055) 6162557
E-mail: admin@estadistica.unam.mx
Web Site: dgedi.estadistica.unam.mx
Telex: 01774523
Key Personnel
Dir: Mtro Juan Voutssas Marquez
Unidad de Bibliotecas de Investigacion Cientifica de la UNAM.

Biblioteca Francisco Xavier Clavigero, see Biblioteca de la Universidad Iberoamericana

Biblioteca del Congreso de la Union
Tacuba 29, Centro Historico de la Cuidad de Mexico, 06000 Mexico, DF
Tel: (05) 5 10 38 66; (05) 5 12 52 05 *Fax:* (05) 5 12 10 85
E-mail: emolina@servidor.unam.mx; emolina@cddhcu.gob.mx
Web Site: www.cddhcu.gob.mx/bibliot/

Hemeroteca Nacional de Mexico
Centro Cultural Universitario, CU, Del Coyoacan, 04510 Mexico, DF
Tel: (055) 622 6818 *Fax:* (055) 665 0951
Web Site: biblional.bibliog.unam.mx
Key Personnel
Dir: Jose Moreno de Alba
National Periodicals Library.

Biblioteca del Instituto Anglo-Mexicano de Cultura
Antonio Caso No 127, Colonia San Rafael, 06470 Mexico, DF
Tel: (05) 566-4500 *Fax:* (05) 566-6739
E-mail: biblioteca@theanglo.org.mx
Web Site: www.theanglo.org.mx/lib.html
Telex: 01772938 Brcome
Key Personnel
Head Librarian: Aurora P Vela
Anglo-Mexican Cultural Institute.

Instituto de Investigaciones Electricas
PO Box 475-1, 62001 Cuernavaca, Mor
Tel: (073) 18 38 11 *Fax:* (073) 182521
E-mail: garroyo@iie.org.mx
Web Site: www.iie.org.mx
Telex: 17-76352 IIEMME
Key Personnel
Executive Dir: Pablo Mulas

Biblioteca del Instituto Panamericano de Geografia e Historia (Library of the Pan American Institute of Geography & History)
Ex-Arzobispado 29, Col Observatorio, 11860 Mexico, DF
Tel: (055) 5277 5888; (055) 5277 5791; (055) 5515 1910 *Fax:* (055) 5271 6172
E-mail: info@ipgh.org.mx
Web Site: www.ipgh.org.mx
Key Personnel
Secretary General: Dr Chester J Zelaya-Goodman
  E-mail: secretariageneral@ipgh.org.mx
Publications Coordinator: Jaime Curenom
Publication(s): *Ver Informacion Adjunta*

Instituto Tecnologico y de Estdios Superiores de Monterrey Biblioteca
Ave Eugenio Garza Sada 2501 Sur, 64849 Monterrey, NL
Tel: (081) 8328-4096 *Fax:* (081) 8328-4067
Web Site: cib.mty.itesm.mx; biblioteca.itesm.mx
Key Personnel
Librarian: Miguel A Arreola
  E-mail: miguel_arreola@itesm.mx
Publication(s): *Transferencia* (Strategic Studies Center monthly)

ITESM Biblioteca, see Instituto Tecnologico y de Estdios Superiores de Monterrey Biblioteca

Biblioteca de la Universidad Iberoamericana
Prol Paseo de la Reforma 880, Lomas de Santa Fe, 01210 Mexico, DF
Tel: (055) 5950 4000 *Fax:* (055) 5950 4248
E-mail: buzon@uiacia.bib.uia.mx
Web Site: www.bib.uia.mx
Key Personnel
Dir: Mtro Fernando Alvarez Ortega

Biblioteca Daniel Cosio Villegas El Colegio de Mexico AC
Camino al Ajusco 20, Col Pedregal Sta Teresa, 10740 Mexico, DF
Mailing Address: Apdo 20-671, 01000 Mexico, DF
Tel: (055) 5449 3000; (055) 5449 2909; (055) 5449 2936; (055) 5449 2934 *Fax:* (055) 5645 0464; (055) 5645 4584
E-mail: biblio@colmex.mx
Web Site: biblio.colmex.mx
Telex: 1777585 COLME *Cable:* COLME
Key Personnel
Library Dir: Micaela Chavez Villa *E-mail:* mch@colmex.mx
Founded: 1940
Graduate institution for research & education in the social sciences & the humanities.
Publication(s): *Boletin de la BDCV*
Parent Company: El Colegio de Mexico

Monaco

Bibliotheque Louis Notari (Library Louis Notari)
8 rue Louis-Notari, 98000 Monaco
Tel: (093) 30-95-09 *Fax:* (093) 152941
Key Personnel
Dir: Herve Barral
Administrative Sectretary: Catherine Notari

Mongolia

State Archives
Ulan-Bator State Public Library of Mongolia, Chinggis Av 3, Ulan-Bator 11
Tel: (01) 323100
Key Personnel
Dir: M Bayaizul

Morocco

Bibliotheque Generale et Archives du Maroc
5, Ave Ibn Batouta, CP 1003, Rabat
Tel: (07) 77 18 90; (07) 77 21 52 *Fax:* (07) 77 60 62
E-mail: biblio1@onpt.net.ma
Key Personnel
Librarian: Ahmed Toufiq
Publication(s): *Bibliographie nationale marocaine*

British Council Library
36, Rue de Tanger, Rabat
Mailing Address: BP 427, Rabat
Tel: (037) 76 08 36 *Fax:* (037) 76 08 50
E-mail: bc@britishcouncil.org.ma
Web Site: www2.britishcouncil.org/morocco
Telex: 36293
Key Personnel
Dir: Steve McNulty
British Cultural Centre.
Branch Office(s)
87, Blvd Nador, Polo, Casablanca *Tel:* (022) 52 09 90 *Fax:* (022) 52 09 64 *E-mail:* casa.info@britishcouncil.org.ma

Centre National de Documentation
Ave Al Haj Ahmed Cherkaoui, 10004 Rabat
Mailing Address: BP 826, 10004 Rabat
Tel: (037) 77 30 13 *Fax:* (037) 77 31 34
E-mail: cndportal@cnd.mpep.gov.ma
Web Site: www.cndportal.net.ma
Key Personnel
Dir: Mr Adnan Benchekroun
Contact: Mr Ahmed Idouba *E-mail:* idouba@cnd.mpep.gov.ma
Publication(s): *voir liste jointe*

Bibliotheque de la Communaute Urbaine de Casablanca
142, Av des Forces Armees Royales, Casablanca
Tel: (02) 314 170
Key Personnel
Dir: Haj Mohamed Bouzid

Bibliotheque Generale et Archives
32 av Mohammed V, Tetouan
Mailing Address: BP 692, Tetouan
Tel: (0996) 3 258
Key Personnel
Librarian: M M Dellero

Institut Scientifique
Charia lbn Batouta, BP 703, 10106 Agdal-Rabat
Tel: (07) 77 45 48; (07) 77 45 49; (07) 77 45 50; (07) 77 45 55 *Fax:* (07) 77 45 70
Web Site: www.emi.ac.ma/univ-MdV/IS.html
Telex: MADILM 36361M
Key Personnel
Dir: Driss Najid
Founded: 1920
Publication(s): *Bulletin de l'Institut Scientifique*; *Documents de l'Institut Scientifique*; *Travaux de l'Institut Scientifique*

Bibliotheque de l'Universite Quaraouyine
Place des Seffarines, BP 790, Fes

Bibliotheque Ben Youssef
Ave 11 Janvier Hay Mohamadi Dauudiat, Marrakech
Tel: (04) 25465
Web Site: www.miniculture.gov.ma
Key Personnel
Dir: Seddik Bellarbi

Mozambique

Biblioteca Municipal
Pacos de Concelho, Maputo

Biblioteca Nacional de Mocambique
PO Box 141, Maputo
Tel: (01) 425 676
Key Personnel
Librarian: Joaquim Chigogoro Mussassa

Direccao Nacional de Geologia (Centro de Documentacao)
PO Box 217, Praca 25 de Junho, Maputo
Tel: (01) 427122 *Fax:* (01) 429216
E-mail: geologia@zebra.uem.mz
Telex: 6-584 GEOMI MO
Key Personnel
National Dir: Joao Marques
National Deputy Dir: Elias Daudi
Publication(s): *Boletim Geologico*

Arquivo Historico de Mocambique (Mozambique Historical Archives)
Division of Eduardo Mondlane University
Ave Filipe Magaia, 715, Maputo
Mailing Address: CP 2033, Maputo
Tel: (01) 321177; (01) 321178 *Fax:* (01) 323428
E-mail: jneves@zebra.uem.mz
Web Site: www.ahm.uem.mz
Key Personnel
Dir: Maria Ines Nogueira da Costa
Editor: J P Borges Coelho
Librarian: Antonio Sopa
Specialize in administrative & colonial archives 19th & 20th centuries. Bibliographic, cartographic, photographic & poster collectives.
Publication(s): *Arquivo* (Archive, every six weeks, bulletin, 1987); *Documentos* (annually, series); *Estudos* (Studies, 7 times/yr, series)

Bibliotecas da Universidade Eduardo Mondlane
Campus Universitario, Av Julius Nyerere, Maputo
Mailing Address: CP 1169, CP 257 Maputo
Tel: (01) 492875 *Fax:* (01) 493174
Web Site: www.uem.mz/reitoria/dsd/bibdsd.htm
Telex: 6-718 UEM MO
Key Personnel
Head of Services: Wanda do Amaral
E-mail: wanda@nambu.uem.mz
The University Eduardo Mondlane does not have a Central Library, but controls 15 departmental libraries; Direccao id responsible for all library & documentation services throughout the University.

Myanmar

Institute of Economics Library
Pyay Rd, Yangon
Tel: (01) 530376 *Fax:* (01) 664889
Web Site: www.aun.chula.ac.th/u_iey_mm.htm
Founded: 1964

Institute of Education Library
Pyay Rd, Yangon
Tel: (01) 31345

Magwe Degree College Library
University Campus, Magwe
Tel: (63) 21030
Key Personnel
Dir: Khin Myint Myint

Mandalay University Library
University Estate, Mandalay
Tel: (02) 21211
Key Personnel
Librarian: U Myint Thein
Founded: 1958

National Library
Six-Storeyed Bldg, Strand Rd, Yangon
Tel: (01) 283332; (01) 275997 *Fax:* (01) 212367
Web Site: www.myanmar.com/culture/text/P001.htm
Key Personnel
Dir: U Kyaw Oo
Founded: 1952

Universities' Central Library
Yangon University, PO 11041, Yangon
Tel: (01) 545 750 *Fax:* (01) 545 750
E-mail: ucl@mptmail.net.mm
Founded: 1929

Namibia

National Archives of Namibia
340 Mandume Ndemufayo Ave, Pioneers Park, Windhoek
Mailing Address: Private Bag 13301, Windhoek
Tel: (061) 2063874 *Fax:* (061) 2063876
E-mail: library@unam.na
Web Site: www.unam.na/ilrc/library/archives.html
Key Personnel
Head & Senior Archivist: Margaret Taylor
Tel: (061) 2063229 *Fax:* (061) 2063876
E-mail: mmtaylor@unam.na

National Library
PO Box 13349, Windhoek 9000
Tel: (061) 2934203; (061) 2934204 *Fax:* (061) 229808
E-mail: postmstr@natlib.mec.gov.na
Web Site: yaotto.natlib.mec.gov.na
Key Personnel
Chief, National Library: Mr J Loubser
Librarian: M K Hoffmann

Windhoek Public Library
4 Luederitz St, Private Bag 13183, Windhoek
Tel: (061) 224899 *Fax:* (061) 212169
E-mail: rviljoen@unam.na
Key Personnel
Librarian: Mrs L Hansmann

Nepal

British Council Library
PO Box 640, Kathmandu
Tel: (01) 4410 798 *Fax:* (01) 4410 545
Web Site: www.britishcouncil.org/nepal
Key Personnel
Information Services Manager: Raju Shakya
E-mail: raju.shakya@britishcouncil.org.np

Madan Puraskar Library
PO Box 42, Lalitpur 44702
Tel: (01) 5521014 *Fax:* (01) 5536390
E-mail: kmldxt@wlink.com.np
Key Personnel
Librarian: Kamalmani Dixit
E-mail: kamalmanidixit@hotmail.com
Founded: 1956

Nepal National Library
Harihar Bhawan, PO Box 182, Lalitpur
Tel: (01) 521132
Web Site: www.natlib.gov.np
Key Personnel
Chief Librarian: Dasharath Thapa
Founded: 1957

Tribhuvan University Central Library
Kirtipur, Katmandu
Tel: (01) 331317; (01) 330834 *Fax:* (01) 226964
E-mail: tucl@healthnet.org.np
Web Site: www.tucl.org.np
Key Personnel
Chief: Mr Krishna Mani Bhandari
Founded: 1959
Serves the university, government, ministries, foreign diplomatic missions, local & foreign researchers & the general public. Also is a depository for 11 international organizations including UN publications since 1965. The library has nearly 245,000 books at present. There are about 500 titles of learned periodicals, newspapers & valuable manuscripts. Nepal ISBN Agency is located here. Nepal National coordinating agency for the International Networking for the Availability of Scientific Publication. Depository Library of the voice records of the works of prominent Naplese authors in the Library of Congress website.
Publication(s): *Bibliography of non-alignment, 1982*; *Bibliography of Population & Family Planning, 1981*; *Nepalese National Bibliography* (annually, 1981, books published from Nepal, all subjects); *Nepal's Foreign Affaires* (bibliographical guide to resources in the Tucl, 1974); *Research on Nepal, a Bibliography of PhD Thesis* (2003, submitted by research scholars engaged in various fields of Nepal)

Netherlands

Bibliotheek van het Centraal Bureau voor de Statistiek (Statistics Netherlands Library)
Prinses Beatrixlaan 428, 2273 XZ Voorburg
Mailing Address: PO Box 4000, 2270 JM Voorburg
Tel: (070) 337 51 51 *Fax:* (070) 337 59 84
E-mail: bibliotheek@cbs.nl
Web Site: www.cbs.nl
Key Personnel
Librarian: Ms M F Wijngaarden *Tel:* (070) 337 51 49 *E-mail:* mwei@cbs.nl
Branch Office(s)
Kloosterweg 1, PO Box 4481, 6401 CZ Heerlen
Tel: (045) 5707187; (045) 5707188 *Fax:* (045) 5706280

Bibliotheek Wageningen UR (Wageningen University & Research Centre Library)
Jan Kopshuis, Bldg 356, Generaal Foulkesweg 19, 6703 BK Wageningen
Mailing Address: PO Box 9100, 6700 HA Wageningen
Tel: (0317) 484440 *Fax:* (0317) 484761
E-mail: helpdesk.library@wur.nl
Web Site: library.wur.nl
Key Personnel
Chief Librarian: Dr D van Zaane
Wageningen UR Library.

DBA, see Dienst Bibliotheek en Archief

Dienst Bibliotheek en Archief
Spui 68, 2511 BT The Hague
Tel: (070) 353 4401; (070) 353 4402 *Fax:* (070) 353 4504

Web Site: www.bibliotheekdenhaag.nl/dob/
Key Personnel
Librarian: W M Renes
Public Library.

Bibliotheek Technische Universiteit Eindhoven
(Eindhoven University of Technology Library)
De Hal Bldg, Het Kranenveld, 5612 AZ Eindhoven
Mailing Address: Postbus 90159, 5600 RM Eindhoven
Tel: (040) 2472381 *Fax:* (040) 2447015
E-mail: helpdesk.bib@tue.nl
Web Site: www.tue.nl/bib
Key Personnel
Head Librarian: C T J Klijs *Tel:* (040) 2472360

EVD eenheid Bibliotheek
Bezuidenhoutseweg 181, 2594 AH The Hague
Mailing Address: Postbus 20105, 2500 EC The Hague
Tel: (070) 778 8888 *Fax:* (070) 778 8889
E-mail: evd@info.evd.nl
Web Site: www.evd.nl
Telex: 31099 Ecza nl *Cable:* ECONINF
Key Personnel
Librarian: G P van der Sluys

Internationaal Instituut voor Sociale Geschiedenis (International Institute of Social History)
Cruquiusweg 31, 1019 AT Amsterdam
Tel: (020) 6685866; (020) 6928810 *Fax:* (020) 6654181; (020) 6630349; (020) 4680505
E-mail: info@iisg.nl; user.service@iisg.nl
Web Site: www.iisg.nl
Key Personnel
General Dir: Jaap Kloosterman *E-mail:* jkl@iisg.nl
Publication(s): Catalogs & Monograph Series; International Review of Social History

Koninklijke Bibliotheek
Prins Willem Alexanderhof 5, 2595 BE The Hague
Mailing Address: PO Box 90407, 2509 LK The Hague
Tel: (070) 3140911 *Fax:* (070) 3140450
E-mail: info@kb.nl
Web Site: www.kb.nl
Telex: 34402 KB NL
Royal (National) Library.
Publication(s): Bibliography of Translations (from the Dutch); *Dutch Bibliography - Brinkman's Cumulatieve Catalogues*

Museum Meermanno-Westreenianum
Prinsessegracht 30, 2514 AP The Hague
Tel: (070) 3462700 *Fax:* (070) 3630350
E-mail: info@meermanno.nl
Web Site: www.meermanno.nl/
Key Personnel
Dir: Dr Leo Voogt
Founded: 1848
National Book Museum.

Nederlands Instituut voor Wetenschappelijke Informatiediensten (Library of Royal Netherlands Academy of Arts & Sciences)
Joan Muyskenweg 25, 1096 CJ Amsterdam
Mailing Address: PO Box 95110, 1090 HD Amsterdam
Tel: (020) 4628600 *Fax:* (020) 6658013
E-mail: info@niwi.knaw.nl
Web Site: www.niwi.knaw.nl
Founded: 1997

NIWI, see Nederlands Instituut voor Wetenschappelijke Informatiediensten

Openbare Bibliotheek/Gemeentearchief, see Dienst Bibliotheek en Archief

Rijksmuseum Research Library
Frans van Mierisstr 92, 1071 RZ Amsterdam
Mailing Address: PO Box 74888, 1070 DN Amsterdam
Tel: (020) 6747047 *Fax:* (020) 6747001
E-mail: library@rijksmuseum.nl
Web Site: library.rijksmuseum.nl
Key Personnel
Contact: G J Koot *Tel:* (020) 6747250 *E-mail:* g.koot@rijksmuseum.nl
Founded: 1885
Art history.
Membership(s): IFLA (International Federation of Library Associations & Institutions).

Bibliotheek der Rijksuniversiteit Groningen
(University of Groningen Library)
Broerstr 4, 9712 CP Groningen
Mailing Address: Postbus 559, 9700 AN Groningen
Tel: (050) 363 50 20; (050) 363 3708 *Fax:* (050) 363 49 96; (050) 363 3720
E-mail: info@ub.rug.nl
Web Site: www.rug.nl/bibliotheek
Key Personnel
Librarian: A C Klugkist

Gemeentebibliotheek Rotterdam
Hoogstr 110, 3011 PV Rotterdam
Tel: (010) 281 61 00 *Fax:* (010) 2816181
Web Site: www.rotterdamnet.nl/bieb.htm
Telex: 25221 gbr nl
Key Personnel
Librarian: F H Meijer
Rotterdam Municipal Library.

Stichting Arnhemse Openbare en Gelderse Wetenschappelijke Bibliotheek
Koningstr 26, 6811 DG Arnhem
Tel: (026) 3543111 *Fax:* (026) 4458616
Web Site: www.biblioarnhem.nl
Key Personnel
Head: Dr Marc Wingens
Librarian: A J Hovy *E-mail:* j.hovy@biblioarnhem.nl
Founded: 1853
Public Library.

Bibliotheek van de Universiteit van Amsterdam (Amsterdam University Library)
Singel 425, 1012 WP Amsterdam
Tel: (020) 525 2301 *Fax:* (020) 525 2311
E-mail: secr-uba@uva.nl
Web Site: www.uba.uva.nl
Key Personnel
Librarian: Dr N Verhagen
Founded: 1578

Universiteitsbibliotheek Leiden (Leiden University Library)
WSD-Gebouw 1169, Witte Singel 27, 2311 BG Leiden
Mailing Address: Postbus 9501, 2300 RA Leiden
Tel: (071) 527 2832 *Fax:* (071) 527 2836
E-mail: secretariaat@library.leidenuniv.nl; helpdesk@library.leidenuniv.nl
Web Site: ub.leidenuniv.nl
Key Personnel
Librarian: P W J L Gerretsen

Universiteitsbibliotheek Nijmegen (University of Nijmegen Library)
Erasmuslaan 36, 6525 GG Nijmegen
Mailing Address: PO Box 9100, 6500 HA Nijmegen
Tel: (024) 3612400 *Fax:* (024) 3615944
E-mail: info@ubn.kun.nl

Web Site: www.kun.nl/ubn/
Key Personnel
Chief Librarian: Mrs H P A Smith

Universiteitsbibliotheek Utrecht (University Library Utrecht)
Wittevrouwenstr 7-11, 3512 CS Utrecht
Mailing Address: Postbus 16007, 3500 DA Utrecht
Tel: (030) 2536600; (030) 2536601; (030) 2537262 *Fax:* (030) 2538398
E-mail: info@library.nl; uitleen@library.uu.nl
Web Site: www.library.uu.nl
Telex: 47103
Key Personnel
Librarian: J S M Savenije *Tel:* (030) 2536502 *Fax:* (030) 2539292 *E-mail:* b.savenije@library.uu.nl
Publication(s): Handschriften en Oude Drukken van de Utrechtse Universiteits bibliothek (MSS & Old Books of University Library, Utrecht: Exhibition Catalogue 1984); *Illuminated & Decorated Medieval Manuscripts in the University Library Utrecht* (illustrated catalogue); *The Utrecht Psalter, Picturing the Psalms of David* (CD-ROM); *Vier eeuwen Universiteitsbibliotheek Utrecht (Four Centuries University Library, Utrecht: Part 1 1584-1878)* (summary in English)

Universiteit Wageningen, see Bibliotheek Wageningen UR

Netherlands Antilles

Openbare Bibliotheek
Abraham M Chumaceiro Blvd 17, Willemstad, Curacao
Tel: (09) 434 5200 *Fax:* (09) 465 6247
E-mail: publiclibrary@curinfo.an
Web Site: www.curacaopubliclibrary.an
Key Personnel
Librarian: Rose Marie de Paula
Founded: 1922
Branch Office(s)
Barber Branch, St Janschool, Barber 6, Curacao
Tel: (09) 8641606

Universiteits-Bibliotheek, Universiteit van de Nederlandse Antillen
Jan Noorduyweg 111, Curacao, NA
Mailing Address: PO Box 3059, Curacao, NA
Tel: (09) 8684422 *Fax:* (09) 8685465
E-mail: bibliotheek@una.an
Web Site: www.una.net
Telex: 110111
Key Personnel
Librarian: Dr Stanley R Criens *E-mail:* s.criens@una.an

New Caledonia

Bibliotheque Bernheim, Bibliotheque territoriale de la Nouvelle-Caledonie
BP G1, Noumea
Tel: 272 343 *Fax:* 276 588
E-mail: bibbern@canl.nc
Web Site: www.nla.gov.au/lap/libs/caledoniabb.html
Key Personnel
Librarian: Jean-Francois Carrez-Corral

Secretariat of the Pacific Community Library
BPD5, 98848 Noumea Cedex
Tel: 26 20 00 *Fax:* 26 38 18
E-mail: noumeaexternal@spc.int
Web Site: www.spc.int/library
Telex: 3139NM Sopacom *Cable:* SOUTH PACOM
Key Personnel
Librarian: Rachele Oriente
Founded: 1947
To support development in the Pacific via SPC programs.
Ultimate Parent Company: Pacific Community
Branch Office(s)
Suva, Fiji, Contact: Christina Tuitubou

New Zealand

Archives New Zealand (Te Whare Tohu Tohituhinga O Aotearoa)
10 Mulgrave St, Thorndon, Wellington
Mailing Address: PO Box 12-050, Wellington
Tel: (04) 4995595; (04) 4956226 (reference) *Fax:* (04) 4956210
E-mail: wellington@archives.govt.nz
Web Site: www.archives.govt.nz
Key Personnel
Chief Archivist: Dianne Macaskill
Specialize in the preservation of Government records.
Branch Office(s)
Auckland Regional Office, 525 Mt Wellington Highway, PO Box 91-220, Auckland, Regional Archivist: Mark Stoddart *Tel:* (09) 270-1100 *Fax:* (09) 276-4472 *E-mail:* auckland@archives.govt.nz
Christchurch Regional Office, 90 Peterborough St, Christchurch, Regional Archivist: Chris Adam *Tel:* (03) 377-0760 *Fax:* (03) 377-2662 *E-mail:* christchurch@archives.govt.nz
Dunedin Regional Offices, 556 George St, PO Box 6183, Dunedin North, Regional Archivist: Peter Miller *Tel:* (03) 477-0404 *Fax:* (03) 477-0422 *E-mail:* dunedin@archives.govt.nz

Auckland City Libraries
40-46 Lorne St, Auckland 1
Mailing Address: PO Box 4138, Auckland 1
Tel: (09) 377 0209 *Fax:* (09) 307 7741
E-mail: libraryreference@aucklandcity.govt.nz
Web Site: www.aucklandcitylibraries.com
Telex: 2750
Key Personnel
City Librarian: Barbara Birkbeck

Canterbury University Library
Private Bag 4800, Christchurch
Tel: (03) 364 2987 (ext 8723) *Fax:* (03) 3642055
E-mail: lending@libr.canterbury.ac.nz; helpdesk@libr.canterbury.ac.nz
Web Site: library.canterbury.ac.nz/
Telex: 4144 unicant
Key Personnel
University Librarian: Gail Pattie *Tel:* (03) 364 2987 (ext 8740) *E-mail:* gail.pattie@libr.canterbury.ac.nz

Christchurch City Libraries
PO Box 1466, Christchurch 1
Tel: (03) 941 7923 *Fax:* (03) 941 7848
E-mail: library@ccc.govt.nz
Web Site: library.christchurch.org.nz
Key Personnel
Library Manager: Sue Sutherland
Promotions & Publications Coordinator: Sasha Bowers *E-mail:* sasha.bowers@govt.nz
Marketing & Development Manager: Glenda Fulten *Tel:* (03) 3727840 *E-mail:* glenda.fulten@ccc.govt.nz
Publication(s): Bookmark (monthly); *Connect* (monthly)

Dunedin Public Libraries
Moray Pl, Dunedin
Mailing Address: PO Box 5542, Dunedin
Tel: (03) 4743690 *Fax:* (03) 4743660
E-mail: library@dcc.govt.nz
Key Personnel
Library Services Manager: Bernie Hawke *Tel:* (03) 4743657 *E-mail:* bhawke@dcc.govt.nz
Collection Development Librarian: Barbara Frame *Tel:* (03) 4743620 *E-mail:* bframe@dcc.govt.nz
Founded: 1908
Public Library.
Parent Company: Dunedin City Council

Napier Public Library
Station St, Napier
Mailing Address: PO Box 940, Napier
Tel: (06) 834 4180 *Fax:* (06) 834 4138
E-mail: library@napier.govt.nz
Web Site: www.napier.govt.nz/inlib.php
Key Personnel
Manager: Leslie Clague *Tel:* (06) 834 4142 *E-mail:* lesliec@napier.govt.nz
Branch Office(s)
Taradale Library, PO Box 7056, Taradale, Napier, Team Leader: Chrissy Arnold *Tel:* (06) 844 2363 *Fax:* (06) 844 7462 *E-mail:* carnold@napier.govt.nz

National Library of New Zealand (Te Puna Matauranga o Aotearoa)
Corner Molesworth & Aitken Sts, Wellington
Mailing Address: PO Box 1467, Wellington
Tel: (04) 474 3000 *Fax:* (04) 474 3035
E-mail: information@natlib.govt.nz; reference@natlib.govt.nz
Web Site: www.natlib.govt.nz
Telex: NZ (04) 4730-080
Key Personnel
Chief Executive: Penny Carnaby *E-mail:* carnabyp@natlib.govt.nz
National Librarian: Christopher Blake
Dir, Collection Services: Allison Elliott *E-mail:* elliotta@natlib.govt.nz
Founded: 1965

North Shore City Libraries
Private Bag 93-508, Takapuna, North Shore City
Tel: (09) 4868460 *Fax:* (09) 4868519
Web Site: www.shorelibraries.govt.nz
Key Personnel
City Librarian: Geoff Chamberlain *Tel:* (09) 4868461 *E-mail:* geoffc@shorelibraries.govt.nz
Founded: 1879
Branch Office(s)
Albany Village Library, Albany Village North Shore City
Birkenhead Library, PO Box 34-370, Birkenhead, North Shore City, Manager: Sharron Cleghorn *Tel:* (09) 486-8559 *E-mail:* sharronc@shorelibraries.govt.nz
Devonport Library, PO Box 32-003, Devonport, North Shore City, Manager: Sue Parr *Tel:* (09) 486-8527 *E-mail:* suep@shorelibraries.govt.nz
East Coast Bays Library, PO Box 35-017, Browns Bay, North Shore City, Manager: Ann Hill *Tel:* (09) 486-8577 *E-mail:* annh@shorelibraries.govt.nz
Glenfield Library, PO Box 40-099, Glenfield, North Shore City, Manager: Eileen O'loan *Tel:* (09) 486-8554 *E-mail:* eileeno@shorelibraries.govt.nz
Northcote Library, PO Box 36-001, Northcote, North Shore City, Manager: Kim Sipeli *Tel:* (09) 486-8490 *E-mail:* kims@shorelibraries.govt.nz

Palmerston North Public Library
4 The Square, Palmerston North
Mailing Address: PO Box 1948, Palmerston North
Tel: (06) 351 4100 *Fax:* (06) 351 4102
E-mail: pncl@pncc.govt.nz
Web Site: citylibrary.pncc.govt.nz
Key Personnel
City Librarian: Anthony Lewis *E-mail:* anthony.lewis@pncc.govt.nz
Administration Manager: Sarah Palmer
Advisory Services Manager: Lynette Collis *E-mail:* lynette.collis@pncc.govt.nz
Technical Services Manager: Mary Holmes *Fax:* mary.holmes@pncc.govt.nz
Childrens & Youth Librarian: Elizabeth Connelly
Founded: 1876

Parliamentary Library
Parliament Bldg, Wellington
Tel: (04) 471 9611 *Fax:* (04) 471 2551
E-mail: intdoc@parliament.govt.nz
Web Site: www.ps.parliament.govt.nz/library.htm
Key Personnel
Parliamentary Librarian: Moira Fraser

Alexander Turnbull Library
Division of National Library of New Zealand/Te Puna Matauranga o Aotearoa
National Library of New Zealand, National Library Bldg, Corner of Aitken & Molesworth Sts, Wellington
Mailing Address: PO Box 12349, Wellington North, Wellington
Tel: (04) 474 3000 *Fax:* (04) 474 3063
E-mail: atl@natlib.govt.nz
Web Site: www.natlib.govt.nz
Key Personnel
Chief Librarian: Margaret Calder *E-mail:* margaret.calder@natlib.govt.nz
Founded: 1918
Research library for NZ & the Pacific; John Milton's life & work; the history of the book.
Publication(s): Off the Record (annually, series); *Turnbull Library Record* (annually, series)

University of Auckland Library
5 Alfred St, Auckland
Mailing Address: PO Box 92019, Auckland
Tel: (09) 3737599 *Fax:* (09) 3737565
E-mail: library@auckland.ac.nz
Web Site: www.library.auckland.ac.nz
Key Personnel
University Librarian: Janet Copsey *Tel:* (09) 3737599 (ext 87352) *E-mail:* jl.copsey@auckland.ac.nz

University of Otago Library
65 Albany St, Dunedin
Mailing Address: PO Box 56, Dunedin
Tel: (03) 479 8916 *Fax:* (03) 479 8947
E-mail: library@otago.ac.nz; reference.central@library.otago.ac.nz
Web Site: www.library.otago.ac.nz
Key Personnel
University Librarian: Michael J Wooliscroft *Tel:* (03) 479 8916 (ext 8933) *E-mail:* michael.wooliscroft@library.otago.ac.nz
Founded: 1869

Wellington City Libraries
65 Victoria St, Wellington 1
Mailing Address: PO Box 1992, Wellington 1
Tel: (04) 801 4040 *Fax:* (04) 801 4047
E-mail: central@wcl.govt.nz
Web Site: www.wcl.govt.nz

Key Personnel
Manager, Libraries: Jane Hill *Tel:* (04) 801 4101
 E-mail: jane.hill@wcc.govt.nz
Branch Office(s)
Brooklyn Library, Corner of Harrison St & Cleveland St, Brooklyn, Wellington *Tel:* (04) 384 6814 *Fax:* (04) 384 2857 *E-mail:* brooklyn@wcl.govt.nz
Cummings Park Library, 1a Ottawa Rd, Ngaio, Wellington *Tel:* (04) 479 2344 *Fax:* (04) 479 4186 *E-mail:* cummingspark@wcl.govt.nz
Ruth Gotlieb (Kilbirnie) Library, 101 Kilbirnie Crescent, Kilbirnie *Tel:* (04) 387 1480 *Fax:* (04) 387 1490 *E-mail:* ruthgotlieb@wcl.govt.nz
Island Bay Library, 167 The Parade, Island Bay *Tel:* (04) 383 7216 *Fax:* (04) 383 7215 *E-mail:* islandbay@wcl.govt.nz
Johnsonville Library, 5 Broderick Rd, Wellington *Tel:* (04) 477 6151 *Fax:* (04) 477 6153 *E-mail:* johnsonville@wcl.govt.nz
Karori Library, 253 Karori Rd, Wellington *Tel:* (04) 476 7585 *Fax:* (04) 476 2265 *E-mail:* karori@wcl.govt.nz
Mervyn Kemp (Tawa) Library, Corner of Cambridge & Main Rd, Wellington *Tel:* (04) 232-1690 *Fax:* (04) 232-1699 *E-mail:* mervynkemp@wcl.govt.nz
Khandallah Library, 8 Ganges Rd, Wellington *Tel:* (04) 479 7535 *Fax:* (04) 479 2573 *E-mail:* khandallah@wcl.govt.nz
Miramar Library, 68 Miramar Ave, Wellington *Tel:* (04) 388 8005 *Fax:* (04) 388 4187 *E-mail:* miramar@wcl.govt.nz
Mobile Library *Tel:* (04) 801-4089
Newtown Library, 13 Constable St, Newtown, Wellington *Tel:* (04) 389 8220 *Fax:* (04) 389 8417 *E-mail:* newtown@wcl.govt.nz
Wadestown Library, Corner of Moorehouse St & Lennel Rd, Wellington *Tel:* (04) 473 5211 *Fax:* (04) 473 5389 *E-mail:* wadestown@wcl.govt.nz

Nicaragua

Archivo Nacional de Nicaragua
Del Cine Cabrera 2 1/2 C al lago, Managua
Tel: (02) 223 240 *Fax:* (02) 22722
E-mail: binanic@tmx.com.nic
Key Personnel
Dir: Alfredo Gonzalez Vilchez
Publication(s): Boletin

Biblioteca Nacional
C del Triunfo 302, Managua
Mailing Address: Apdo 101, Managua
Tel: (02) 897 517 *Fax:* (02) 894 387

INCAE, see Instituto Centroamericano de Administracion de Empresas (INCAE) Library

Instituto Centroamericano de Administracion de Empresas (INCAE) Library
Campus Francisco de Sola, Montefresco, Km 15 1/2 Carretera Sur, Managua
Mailing Address: Apdo 2485, Managua
Tel: (02) 65 8141; (02) 65 8149; (02) 65 8272 *Fax:* (02) 65 8617; (02) 65 8630
E-mail: biblioteca@mail.incae.edu.ni; incaeni@mail.incae.edu.ni
Web Site: www.incae.ac.cr/biblioteca
Telex: 2360
Key Personnel
Associate Dir: Antonio Acevedo E
Publication(s): Revista INCAE

Ruben Dario, see Biblioteca Nacional

Universidad Centroamericana
Pista de la Resistencia, Semaforos de ENEL 500mts al este, Managua
Mailing Address: Apdo 69, Managua
Tel: (02) 278-3923 *Fax:* (02) 267-0106
E-mail: comsj@ns.uca.edu.ni
Web Site: www.una.edu.ni
Telex: 2296
Key Personnel
Librarian: Conny Mendez R

Niger

Centre d'Enseignement Superieur de Niamey
Bibliotheque, BP 237, Niamey
Tel: 732713 *Fax:* 733862
Telex: uninim 5258 hi
University Education Centre.

Bibliotheqe l'Ecole nationale d'administration du Niger
Rue Martin Luther King Jr, Niamey
Mailing Address: BP 542, Niamey
Tel: 723183 *Fax:* 724383
Key Personnel
Librarian: Mme Yacouba Halimatou

Institut de Recherche en Sciences Humaines
BP 318, Niamey
Tel: 73-51-41
Telex: 5258
Key Personnel
Director: Zakari Maikorema
Publication(s): Etudes Nigeriennes

Bibliotheque de l'Universite de Niamey
BP 10 896, Niamey
Tel: 74-12-73 *Fax:* 73-38-62
Telex: 5258
Key Personnel
Contact: M Saidou Harouna

Nigeria

Ahmadu Bello University Library
Ahmadu Bello University, PMB 1044, Zaria
Tel: (069) 505-71; (069) 505-72; (069) 505-73; (069) 505-74 *Fax:* (069) 505-63
Telex: 75241 Zarabu Ng *Cable:* AGRICSEARCH, ZARIA
Founded: 1922
Publication(s): Agroclimatological Atlas of Northern States of Nigeria; NOMA (magazine, news); *Samaru Journal of Agricultural Research; Soil Survey Bulletin*

Anabra State Library Board
PMB 01026, Market Rd, Enugu
Tel: (042) 334 103 *Cable:* LIBRARIES ENUGU
Key Personnel
Librarian: C N Ekweozoh

Bendel State Library
PMB 1127, 17 James Watt Rd, Benin City, Bendel State
Tel: (052) 200 810 *Cable:* LIBRARY BENIN
Key Personnel
Dir: D O Oboro
Founded: 1971
Publication(s): Bendel Library Journal

Benin University Library
PMB 1154, Ugbowo-Lagos Rd, Ugbowo, Benin City, Edo State
Tel: (052) 600443 *Fax:* (052) 602370
E-mail: registra@uniben.edu; registra@uniben.edu.ng; library@uniben.edu
Web Site: www.uniben.edu
Telex: 41365 *Cable:* Uniben; Benin
Key Personnel
University Librarian: S A Tamah
Publication(s): List of Serials

IAR, see Institute for Agricultural Research (IAR)

Institute for Agricultural Research (IAR)
PMB 1044, Samaru-Zaria
Tel: (069) 550571; (069) 550572; (069) 550573; (069) 550574; (069) 550681 *Fax:* (069) 50563
E-mail: iar.abu@kaduna.rcl.ng.com
Key Personnel
Dir: Prof J P Voh
Publication(s): KWIC Index to the Abstracting & Indexing; Library Accession List (monthly); *List of Current Serials in the Library* (annually); *Subject Bibliographies on Nigeria Agriculture*

International Institute of Tropical Agriculture (IITA) Library
PMB 5320, Ibadan, Oyo State
Tel: (02) 241 2626 *Fax:* (02) 241 2221
E-mail: IITA@cgiar.org
Web Site: www.iita.org/info/libsrv.htm
Telex: 31417; 31159 Tropib Ng *Cable:* TROPFOUND IKEJA
Key Personnel
Head, Library & Documentation: Y Adedigba
 E-mail: y.adedigba@cgiar.org
Publication(s): IITA Annual Report; IITA Research

Library Board of Kaduna State
PMB 2061, Kaduna
Tel: (062) 242590
Key Personnel
Dir: J A Maigari
Publication(s): Biographies of Governors of Former Northern Nigeria & Kaduna State, 1960-1990; Meet Our Friends; Proceedings of the First Kaduna State Book Fair; Proceedings of the First Northern States Book Fair; Proceedings of the Second Kaduna State Book Fair

Kano State Library Board
PMB 3094, Kano
Tel: (064) 645614
Web Site: www.library.unt.edu/nigeria/Kano/Kano.htm
Key Personnel
Executive Director: Sanusi A Nassarawa
 E-mail: nassarawa2001@yahoo.com
Publication(s): Library Guide

Lagos City Council Libraries
48 Broad St, Lagos
Mailing Address: PMB 2025, Lagos
Tel: (01) 50246

National Archives of Nigeria Library
University of Ibadan, Chapel Rd, Ibadan
Tel: (022) 415000 *Cable:* DARCHNES
Key Personnel
Dir: Comfort Aina Ukwu

National Library of Nigeria-Research & Development Dept
Sanusi Dantata House, Plot 274 Central Business Area, PMB 1, Garki District, Abuja

Tel: (09) 2646773; (09) 2346774 *Fax:* (09) 2646772
E-mail: info@nlbn.org
Web Site: www.nlbn.org
Telex: 21746 Nat Lib Ng *Cable:* BIBLIOS
Key Personnel
National Librarian: Mrs O O Omolayde
Publication(s): *Afribiblios* (biannually); *Libraries in Nigeria, a Directory*; *National Bibliography of Nigeria*; *Nigerbiblios* (quarterly); *Nigerian Books in Print*; *Nominal List of Practicing Librarians in Nigeria*; *Serials in Print in Nigeria*

Nnamdi Azikiwe Library
University of Nigeria, Nsukka, Enugu State
Tel: (042) 771444 *Fax:* (042) 770644
E-mail: misunn@aol.com
Telex: Ulions 51496 *Cable:* NIGERSITY LIBRARY
Key Personnel
Acting Librarian: C C Uwechie
Collection includes 9000 items in microform; CD-ROM facilities available.
Publication(s): *Nsukka Library Notes*; *Readers' Guide* (Annual Report); *UNLAN* (University of Nigeria Library Accessions and News)

Obafemi Awolowo University Library
c/o Hezekiah Oluwasanmi Library, Ile-Ife, Osun State
Tel: (036) 230291 ext 2287; (036) 230290
Fax: (036) 230291 (ext 2287)
E-mail: ul@libraryoauife.edu.ng
Key Personnel
Librarian: Adedeji Adelabu

University of Ibadan, Kenneth Dike Library
Ibadan
Tel: (02) 810 3118 *Fax:* (02) 810 3118
E-mail: library@kdl.ui.edu.ng
Key Personnel
Librarian: Joseph Ezenwani Ikem
Founded: 1948
Publication(s): *Library Record* (monthly)

University of Jos Library
PMB 2084, Jos, Plateau State
Tel: (073) 610514; (073) 53724; (073) 44952 *Fax:* (073) 610514
Web Site: 128.255.135.155/libraries
Telex: 81136 Unijos NG *Cable:* LIBRARIAN UNIJOS
Key Personnel
University Librarian: Dr A Ochai
Publication(s): *Nigerian Periodicals Index* (1986)

University of Lagos Library
Akoka, Lagos
Tel: (01) 41 361 *Fax:* (01) 822644
Web Site: www.unilag.edu/library/index.asp
Telex: 26983
Key Personnel
Librarian: S A Orimoloye
Founded: 1962

University of Nigeria
Nnamdi Azikiwe Library, Enugu
Mailing Address: University of Nigeria, Nsukka
Tel: (042) 771444 *Fax:* (042) 770644; (042) 771500
E-mail: unnlibrary@yahoo.com
Web Site: www.unn-edu.net
Telex: 51496 ULIONS NG
Key Personnel
University Librarian: Emenike Ikeqbune
Founded: 1960

Norway

Bergen offentlige Bibliotek (Bergen Public Library)
Stromgaten 6, 5015 Bergen
Tel: 55 56 85 60; 55 56 85 50 *Fax:* 55 56 85 65
Web Site: www.bergen.folkebibl.no
Key Personnel
Dir: Trine Kolderup Flaten *E-mail:* trine@bergen.folkebib.no
Founded: 1872

Deichmanske Bibliotek
Henrik Ibsensgt 1, 0179 Oslo
Tel: (023) 43 29 00 *Fax:* (022) 11 33 89
E-mail: deichman@deich.folkebibl.no
Web Site: www.deich.folkebibl.no
Key Personnel
Chief Librarian: Liv Saeteren
City Library of Oslo.

Drammen Folkebibliotek
Gl Kirkeplass 7, Postboks 136-Bragernes, 3001 Drammen
Tel: (032) 80 63 03 *Fax:* (032) 80 64 53
E-mail: drm@drammen.folkebibl.no
Web Site: www.drammen.kommune.no/bibliotek
Key Personnel
Librarian: Karin Evant *E-mail:* karin@drammen.folkebibl.no
Public Library of Drammen; County Library of Buskerud.

Styret for det Industrielle Rettsvern Information Department
Kobehavngt 10, Postboks 8160 Dep, 0033 Oslo
Tel: (022) 38 73 00 *Fax:* (022) 38 73 01
Telex: 19152 nopat n
Key Personnel
Assistant Dir General: Per Olaf Ranger
Library of the Norwegian Patent Office.

Kristiansand Folkebibliotek
Radhusgt 11, 4611 Kristiansand
Mailing Address: Postboks 476, 4664 Kristiansand
Tel: (038) 12 49 10 *Fax:* (038) 12 49 49
E-mail: kristiansand.folkebibliotek@kristiansand.kommune.no
Web Site: www.kristiansand.kommune.no
Key Personnel
Chief Librarian: Oddhild Hildre
Municipal Library.

Nobelinstituttet (Nobel Institute)
Biblioteket, Drammensveien 19, 0255 Oslo
Tel: 22 12 93 20 *Fax:* 22 12 93 10
E-mail: library@nobel.no
Web Site: www.nobel.no
Key Personnel
Head Librarian: Anne C Kjelling *Tel:* 22 12 93 21 *E-mail:* ack@nobel.no
Founded: 1904
Library covers following fields: international relations, international law, peace, & international economics.

Norges Landbrukshogskoles Bibliotek (Agricultural University of Norway Library)
Postboks 5012, 1432 As
Tel: (064) 94 76 63 *Fax:* (064) 94 76 70
E-mail: biblutl@bibl.nlh.no
Web Site: www.nlh.no/biblioteket
Key Personnel
Librarian: Gerd Antonsen

Riksarkivet
Folke Bernadottes vei 21, Oslo
Mailing Address: Postboks 4013, Ulleval Stadion, 0806 Oslo
Tel: (022) 02 26 00 *Fax:* (022) 23 74 89
E-mail: riksarkivet@riksarkivaren.dep.no
Web Site: www.riksarkivet.no; www.arkivverket.no
National Archives of Norway.

Statistisk sentralbyras bibliotek og informasjonssenter (Statistics Norway-Library & Information Centre)
Kongens gate 6, 0033 Oslo
Mailing Address: Postboks 8131 Dep, 0033 Oslo 1
Tel: 21 09 46 42 *Fax:* 21 09 45 04
E-mail: biblioteket@ssb.no
Web Site: www.ssb.no/biblioteket
Key Personnel
Head of Division: Lars Rogstad *Tel:* 21 09 44 95 *E-mail:* rog@ssb.no
Founded: 1917

Universitetsbiblioteket i Bergen
Stein Rokkans hus, Nygardsgt 5, 5015 Bergen
Tel: 55 58 25 32 *Fax:* 55 58 97 03
E-mail: adm@ub.uib.no
Web Site: www.ub.uib.no
Telex: 42690 ubb n
Key Personnel
Dir: Kari Garnes *Tel:* 55 58 25 01 *E-mail:* kari.garnes@ub.uib.no
Founded: 1948

Universitetsbiblioteket i Oslo
Georg Sverdrups Hus, 4th floor, N-0317 Oslo
Mailing Address: PB 1085, Blindern, Oslo N-0317
Tel: (022) 85 50 50 *Fax:* (022) 85 90 50
E-mail: informasjon@uio.no
Web Site: www.ub.uio.no
Key Personnel
Dir: Jan Erik Roed *Tel:* (022) 84 40 01 *E-mail:* j.e.roed@ub.uio.no
Founded: 1811
Publication(s): *Bibliografi over Norges offentlige publikasjoner 1956-1990*; *Helse-NOTA 1992-*; *Kataloger pa mikrofilm kort*; *Maskinlesbare data*; *Mikrofilmer* (35mm Norske aviser, Norske tidsskrifter, Norske og utenlandske boker); *Nansen bilde data base pa CD-ROM*; *Nasjonalbibliografiske data NBDATA 1962-* (CD-ROM); *Nordisk samkatalog for periodika CDNOSP*; *Norsk bokfortegnelse*; *Norsk bokfortegnelse: Musikktrykk*; *Norsk lokalhistorisk litteratur 1946-1970*; *Norsk lokalhistorisk litteratur 1971-1990*; *Norsk musikkfortegnelse: lydfestinger*; *Norsk musikkfortegnelse: notetrykk*; *Norsk periodikafortegnelse 1993-* (annually); *Norsk samkatalog for boker CD-SAM 1981*; *Norsk samkatalog for boker CD-SAM 1983-*; *Norske tidsskriftartikler 1980-*; *Norske tidsskrifter 1971-1983*; *NOSP adresseliste* (annually); *UBO: Brosjyrer*; *UBO: Diverse publikasjonerk*; *UBO: Skrifter*; *UBO: Veiledninger*

Universitetsbiblioteket i Trondheim
7491 Trondheim
Tel: (073) 59 51 10 *Fax:* (073) 59 51 03
E-mail: ubit@ub.ntnu.no
Web Site: www.ub.ntnu.no
Key Personnel
Chief Librarian: Kari Christensen
Founded: 1768
University Library of Trondheim. Incorporating libraries of the College of Arts & Sciences & of the Museum (formerly Library of the Royal Norwegian Society of Sciences & Letters, DKNVS).

University of Oslo Library, see Universitetsbiblioteket i Oslo

Pakistan

British Council Library
House 1, St 61, F-6/3, PO Box 1135, Islamabad 44000
Tel: (051) 111 424 424 *Toll Free Tel:* 0800 22000
Fax: (051) 111 425 425
E-mail: info@britishcouncil.org.pk
Web Site: www.britishcouncil.org.pk
Telex: 54644
Key Personnel
Acting Dir: Andrew Picken
Deputy Dir: John Payne

Ewing Memorial Library
Forman Christian College, Ferezepur Rd, Lahore 54600
Key Personnel
Librarian: Jacob Lal Din
Founded: 1866

Dr Mahmud Husain Library
Karachi University, Karachi 32
Tel: (021) 474953 *Fax:* (021) 4969277
Web Site: www.un.org.pk/unic/hussainlibrary.htm
Key Personnel
Head Librarian: Prof Malahat Kaleem Sherwani
  E-mail: mksherwani@hotmail.com
Founded: 1952
Publication(s): *Guide to Bibliographical Sources* (Catalog of rare books)

Islamic Research Institute Library
PO Box 1035, Islamabad 44000
Tel: (051) 9261761-5; (051) 2252816
Web Site: www.iiu.edu.pk
Telex: 54068 IIU Pak *Cable:* ISLAMSERCH
Key Personnel
Rector: Mr Khalil-ur-Rehman Khan
Ultimate Parent Company: International Islamic University, Islamabad

National Archives of Pakistan
Administrative Block Area, N Block, Pakistan Secretariat, Islamabad 44000
Tel: (051) 920 2044 *Fax:* (051) 920 6349
Web Site: www.pakistan.gov.pk
Telex: ARCHIVES
Key Personnel
Dir General: Mr Antique Zafar Sheikh
Dir: Mr Mond Ramzan
Founded: 1951
Storage & presentation of historical & public records.
Membership(s): International Council on Archives (ICA).
Publication(s): *Pakistan Archives* (biannually, journal)
Branch Office(s)
Frere Market Rd, Karachi *Tel:* (021) 7765232

National Library of Pakistan
Constitution Ave, Islamabad 44000
Tel: (051) 9214523; (051) 92026436; (051) 9206440 *Fax:* (051) 9221375
E-mail: nlpiba@isb.paknet.com.pk
Web Site: www.nlp.gov.pk
Key Personnel
Dir General: Syed Irshad Ali Shah *Tel:* (051) 9202544 (ext 237)
Founded: 1993

Pakistan Institute of Development Economics (PIDE)
Quaid-i-Azam University Campus, PO Box 1091, Islamabad 44000
Tel: (051) 9206616 *Fax:* (051) 9210886
E-mail: pide@pide.org.pk
Web Site: www.pide.org.pk
Key Personnel
Acting Chief, Library & Documentation: Zafar Jared Naqvi *Tel:* (051) 9214041
  E-mail: naqviZJ@hotmail.com
Founded: 1957
Research.
Publication(s): *Pakistan Development Review* (quarterly)

Pakistan Institute of Nuclear Science & Technology Library, Science Information Division
Nilore, Islamabad
Tel: (051) 452350 *Fax:* (051) 429533
E-mail: ctc@shell.portal.com
Telex: 5725 Atcom Pk
Key Personnel
Head, Scientific Information Division: Dr Abdullah Sadiq
Principal Librarian: Mohammad Shafique

Pakistan Scientific & Technological Information Centre (PASTIC)
Quaid-I-Azam University Campus, PO Box 1217, Islamabad
Tel: (051) 920 1340; (051) 920 1341; (051) 920 7641 *Fax:* (051) 9207211
E-mail: pastic@isb.pol.com.pk
Web Site: www.psf.gov.pk/pastic
Key Personnel
Dir: Ms Nuzhat Yasmin
  E-mail: nuzhatyasmin_1@hotmail.com
Founded: 1974
Publication(s): *Directory of Scientific Periodicals of Pakistan*; *Pakistan Science Abstracts* (quarterly)
Parent Company: Pakistan Science Foundation (PSF)
Ultimate Parent Company: Ministry of Science & Technology

PASTIC, see Pakistan Scientific & Technological Information Centre (PASTIC)

Punjab Public Library
Library Rd, Lahore 54000
Tel: (042) 325487
E-mail: zilpk@yahoo.com
Key Personnel
Librarian: Hafiz Khuda Bakhsh
Founded: 1884

Punjab University Library
1-Quaid-e-Azam Campus, 54590 Lahore
Tel: (042) 923 1099 *Fax:* (042) 923 1101
E-mail: vc@pu.edu.pk
Web Site: www.pu.edu.pk/library.htm
Key Personnel
Chief Librarian: Abdul Waheed
Founded: 1882

Sind University Central Library
Allama ll Kazi Campus, Jamshoro, Sind
Tel: (0221) 771188
Key Personnel
Librarian: Mohammad IshaqueI Laghari

University of Baluchistan Library
Sariab Rd, Quetta
Tel: (081) 41770
Key Personnel
Librarian: Brohi Ghulam Murtaza
Founded: 1971

University of Engineering & Technology Central Library (UET)
Grand Trunk Rd, Lahore 54890
Tel: (042) 6829243 *Fax:* (042) 6822566
E-mail: central_library@yahoo.com
Web Site: www.uet.edu.pk *Cable:* UNIVENGTECH
Key Personnel
Librarian: Abdul Hameed
Assistant Librarian: Muhammad Saeed *Tel:* (042) 6822667
Founded: 1961
Publication(s): *Central Library Bulletin* (bi-monthly)

Panama

Biblioteca Nacional
Parque Recreativo y Cultural Omar, Via Porras, San Francisco, Ciudad de Panama
Mailing Address: Apdo 7906, Panama 9
Tel: 224-9466 *Fax:* 224-9988
E-mail: referencia@binal.ac.pa
Web Site: www.binal.ac.pa
Key Personnel
Dir: Algeria Pimentel S
Founded: 1942
Publication(s): *Bibliografias nacionales*

Biblioteca Bio-Medica del Laboratorio Conmemorativo Gorgas
Av Justo Arosemena 35-30, Apdo 6991, Panama 5
Tel: (02) 274111 *Fax:* (02) 254366
E-mail: igorgas@sin.fonet
Telex: 3433 *Cable:* GOMELA
Key Personnel
Dir: Dr Rolando E Saenz
Librarian: Nora E Osses; Gloria O de Cano
Branch Office(s)
PO Box 935, APO, Miami, FL, United States
Gorgas Memorial Laboratory
Bio-medical Research Library

Universidad de Panama, Biblioteca Interamericana Simon Bolivar
Estafeta Universitaria, Apdo 3277, Panama
Tel: 2636133
Key Personnel
Librarian: Nuria F de Gonzalez
Publication(s): *Boletin Bibliografico*

Papua New Guinea

Office of Libraries and Archives, Papua, New Guinea
PO Box 734, Waigani
Tel: 3256200 *Fax:* 3251331
E-mail: ola@datec.com.pg
Web Site: www.dg.com.pg/~ola *Cable:* PNG LIB BOROKO
Key Personnel
Dir General: Daniel Paraide
Founded: 1975
Publication(s): *Ola Nius (formerly National Library Nius)*; *Papua New Guinea National Bibliography*; *Selective Index to the Times of Papua New Guinea*

Papua New Guinea Institute of Public Administration Library (PNGIPA)
PO Box 1216, Boroko
Tel: 3260433; 3267345; 3267163 *Fax:* 3261654
E-mail: gaudichn@upng.ac.pg
Telex: 23011 *Cable:* PNGIPA
Key Personnel
Contact: Lewis Kusso-Alles

Publication(s): *Administration for Development* (college journal)
Branch Office(s)
Papua New Guinea Institute of Public Administration, Boroko

PNGIPA Library, see Papua New Guinea Institute of Public Administration Library (PNGIPA)

Michael Somare Library
PO Box 319, University Post Office, Waigani 134 NCD
Tel: 326 7280 *Fax:* 326 7187
E-mail: Library@upng.ac.pg
Web Site: www.theatrelibrary.org
Telex: ne 22366
Key Personnel
Contact: Florence J Griffin
Founded: 1966
Publication(s): *Guide to Manuscripts in the New Guinea Collection* (by Nancy Lutton 1980); *New Guinea Periodical Index* (quarterly)

Paraguay

Biblioteca y Archivo Nacionales (National Library & Archives)
Mariscal Estigarriba 95, Asuncion

Biblioteca de la Sociedad Cientifica del Paraguay
Avda Espana 505, Asuncion
Tel: (021) 24832
Library of the Paraguayan Scientific Society.

Peru

ALIDE, see Asociacion Latinoamericana de Instituciones Financieras Para El Desarrollo (ALIDE)

Archivo General de la Nacion del Peru
Jr Manuel Cuadros s/n Palacio de Justicia, Lima
Tel: (01) 427-5930; (01) 427-5939 *Fax:* (01) 428-2829
Web Site: agn.perucultural.org.pe
Key Personnel
Chief Librarian & Dir: Aida Mendoza Navarro

Asociacion Latinoamericana de Instituciones Financieras Para El Desarrollo (ALIDE) (Latin American Association of Development Financing Institutions)
Paseo de la Republica, Lima, San Isidro 3211
Mailing Address: Apartado Postal 3988, Lima 100
Tel: (01) 442 2400 *Fax:* (01) 442 8105
E-mail: sg@alide.org.pe
Web Site: www.alide.org.pe
Key Personnel
Secretary General: Rommel Acevedo
  E-mail: racevedo@alide.org.pe
Head, Institutional Relations Division: Eduardo Vasquez *E-mail:* dri@alide.org.pe
Founded: 1968
Represents institutions that finance development in Latin America & the Caribbean. Provides information & documentation related to development banking fields of interest, as well as having information on materials relative to specific economic sectors & technological aspects. Collects specialized documentation concerned with banking & financing development.
Membership(s): World Federation of Development Financing Institutions (WFDFI).
Publication(s): *Boletin Alide* (Alide Bulletin, 6 times/yr, dedicated to the provision of articles & analytical information, in depth studies & documents of a technical & legal nature related to banking & financing development); *Memoria Annual* (annually, report)

Biblioteca Central de la Universidad Nacional de San Agustin
Apdo 23, Arequipa
Tel: (054) 229 719
E-mail: sisbiblio@unmsm.edu.pe
Web Site: sisbib.unmsm.edu.pe/sbweb
Founded: 1828

Biblioteca Central de la Universidad Nacional Mayor de San Marcos
Simon Rodriquez 681, Apdo 454, Lima 1
Tel: (01) 4285210 *Fax:* (01) 4285210
E-mail: ogeibl@sanfer.edu.pe

Biblioteca Nacional
Av Abancay, 4ta cuadra, Lima
Tel: (01) 428-7690; (01) 428-7696 *Fax:* (01) 427-7331
E-mail: sg@binape.gob.pe
Web Site: www.binape.gob.pe
Key Personnel
Dir: Sinesio Lopez Jimenez
Publication(s): *Anuario Bibliografico Peruano* (Bibliographical Annual of Peru, annually); *Bibliografia Nacional* (annually, 2000, Peruvian monthly Bibliographical Information); *Boletin de la Biblioteca Nacional* (Bulletin of the National Library); *Gaceta Bibliotecaria* (Library Gazette, irregularly); *Revista Fenix* (Phoenix Magazine, magazine)

ESAN - Escuela de Administracion de Negocios para Graduados, Direccion de Investigacion
Alonso de Molina 1652, Monterrico, Surco, Lima
Mailing Address: Apdo 1846, Lima 100
Tel: (01) 317-7226 *Fax:* (01) 345-1328; (01) 345-1276
E-mail: cendoc@esan.edu.pe
Web Site: www.esan.edu.pe
Key Personnel
Dir: Santiago Roca, PhD

Fondo Editorial de le Pontificia Universidad Catolica del Peru
Plaza Francis 1164, Lima 1
Mailing Address: Apdo 1761, Lima 32
Tel: (01) 3307410; (01) 3307411 *Fax:* (01) 3307405
E-mail: feditor@pucp.edu.pe
Web Site: www.pucp.edu.pe
Key Personnel
Contact: Annie Ordonez *E-mail:* aordonez@pucp.edu.pe
Books & journals.
Publication(s): *Books* (13 academic journals)

Universidad del Pacifico Libreria
Av Salaverry 2020, Jesus Maria, Lima 100
Tel: (01) 471-2277; (01) 472-9635 *Fax:* (01) 470-6121
E-mail: Biblioteca@up.edu.pe
Web Site: www.up.edu.pe/biblioteca
Telex: 25650
Key Personnel
Dir: Maria C Bonilla de Gaviria
  E-mail: mbonilla@up.edu.pe
Publication(s): *Apuntes*; *Counterbalance Points* (monthly); *Intercampus*

Universidad Nacional San Antonio Abad del Cusco (UNSAAC)
Av De la Cultura s/n, Cusco
Mailing Address: Apdo 921, Cusco
Tel: (084) 222271; (084) 228661 *Fax:* (084) 238156
Web Site: www.unsaac.edu.pe

Philippines

Far Eastern University Library
Nicanor Reyes Sr, St Sampaloc, Manila
Tel: (02) 735-5649 *Fax:* (02) 732-0232
Web Site: www.feu.edu.ph/library.asp
Key Personnel
Chief Librarian: Zenaida M Galang
Founded: 1991
Publication(s): *Far Eastern University Journal*

Manila City Library
Alvarez St, Santa Cruz, Manila
Mailing Address: City Hall, Room 501, Manila
Web Site: www.cityofmanila.com.ph
Key Personnel
City Librarian: Paz C Gagolinan

National Library of the Philippines
TM Kalaw St, Ermita, 1000 Manila
Tel: (02) 525-3196 (Filipiniana); (02) 582271 (Reference); (02) 582660 (Public Documents); (02) 525-1748 *Fax:* (02) 524-2329
E-mail: amb@nlp.gov.ph
Web Site: www.nlp.gov.ph
Telex: (02) 505143 (Filipiniana); 582271 (Reference); 582660; 582511 (Public Documents)
Cable: NALIBPHILS
Key Personnel
Dir: Prudenciana C Cruz
Founded: 1901

Philippine Normal College Library & Library Science Departments
Taft Ave, Manila
Tel: (02) 5270372 *Fax:* (02) 5270372
Key Personnel
Contact: Calixta Aquirre

Rizal Library
Katipunan Rd, Loyola Heights, 1108 Quezon City, Metro Manila
Mailing Address: PO Box 154, 1099 Manila
Tel: (02) 426-6001; 5800-5816 (Local) *Fax:* (02) 426-5961
Web Site: rizal.lib.admu.edu.ph
Key Personnel
Dir: Mrs Lourdes T David *E-mail:* ltdavid@ateneo.edu
Founded: 1921
Educational institution.
Parent Company: Ateneo de Manila University

Science & Technology Information Institute Department of Science & Technology
DOST Complex, Bicutan, Taguig, Metro Manila
Mailing Address: PO Box 3596, Manila
Tel: (02) 837-2191 *Fax:* (02) 837-7520
Web Site: www.stii.dost.gov.ph
Key Personnel
Chief: Dr Irene D Amores
Publication(s): *Philippine Science & Technology Abstracts*; *R & D Philippines*; *SEA Abstracts*; *Series of Philippine Scientific Bibliographies*; *Union Catalogue of NISST*; *Union List of Serials of NSTA and its Agencies*

Silliman University Library
6200 Dumaguete City, Negros Oriental

Tel: (035) 4227208; (035) 4226002 *Fax:* (035) 4227208
E-mail: sulib@su.edu.ph
Web Site: su.edu.ph
Key Personnel
President: Agustin A Pulido *E-mail:* pres@su.edu.ph
University Librarian: Lorna T Yso *E-mail:* lty@su.edu.ph
Founded: 1901
Publication(s): *Convergence* (annually, journal, 1994, multidisciplinary journal of the arts & sciences); *Sands & Coral* (annually, journal, 1948, student literary journal); *Silliman Journal* (biannually, journal, 1954, humanities, sciences & social sciences); *Silliman University Library Bulletin* (bimonthly, newsletter, 1971, contains news about the library personnel, resources, services & facilities)

Ramona S Tirona Memorial Library
The Philippine Women's University, Taft Ave, 1004 Manila
Tel: (02) 5268421 (loc 176) *Fax:* (02) 5266935
Key Personnel
Librarian: Dionisia M Angeles
Publication(s): *Administrative Bulletin*; *Philippine Educational Forum*; *PWU Bulletin/FTB Bulletin*; *The Alumni Link and Philippine Women's University Forum*; *The Link*

University of Manila Central Library
546 MV delos Santos St, Sampaloc, Manila
Tel: (02) 7355256 *Fax:* (02) 7355089
E-mail: um@univman.edu.ph
Web Site: www.univman.edu.ph

University of San Carlos Library System
P del Rosario St, Cebu City 6000
Tel: (032) 254 0432 *Fax:* (032) 254 0432
E-mail: direklib@usc.edu.ph
Web Site: www.usc.edu.ph *Cable:* STEYL CEBU
Key Personnel
Dir, Libraries: Dr Marilou P Tadlip

University of Santo Tomas Library
Espana St, Sampaloc, Manila
Tel: (02) 731-3101 *Fax:* (02) 740-9709
E-mail: library@ust.edu.ph
Web Site: www.ust.edu.ph
Key Personnel
Chief Librarian: Angelita Timbangcaya
Prefect of Libraries: Fr Angel A Aparicio
 Tel: (02) 731-3034
Founded: 1611

University of the East Library
2219 C M Recto Ave, Manila
Tel: (02) 7358544 *Fax:* (02) 7356976
E-mail: webmaster@uec.edu.ph
Web Site: www.ue.edu.ph
Key Personnel
Dir: Sarah C De Jesus
Chief Librarian: Narcisa F Tioco

University of the Philippines Diliman University Library
Gonzalez Hall, Diliman, 1101 Quezon City
Tel: (02) 920-5301 *Fax:* (02) 926-1876
Web Site: www.mainlib.upd.edu.ph
Key Personnel
University Librarian: Salvacion M Arlante
 E-mail: salvacion.arlante@up.edu.ph
Founded: 1922
Publication(s): *Index to Philippine Periodicals (IPP)* (quarterly)

Poland

Naczelna Dyrekcja Archiwow Panstwowych
ul Dluga 6, 00-238 Warsaw
Mailing Address: PO Box 1005, 00-950 Warsaw
Tel: (022) 635-68-22 *Fax:* (022) 831-75-63
E-mail: coia-info@archiwa.gov.pl
Web Site: www.archiwa.gov.pl
Key Personnel
Contact: Doc dr hab Daria Nalecz
Main Directorate of the Polish State Archives.
Publication(s): *Archeion, Teki archiwalne*

Archiwum Glowne Akt Dawnych
ul Dluga 7, 00-263 Warsaw
Tel: (022) 831-54-91 *Fax:* (022) 831-16-08
Web Site: www.piasa.org/polisharchives/warsawhr.html
Key Personnel
Dir: Dr Hubert Wajs
Founded: 1808
Central Archives for Historical Documents.
Publication(s): *Miscellanea Historico-archivistica*

Biblioteka Jagiellonska (Jagiellonian Library)
al Mickiewicza 22, 30-059 Krakow
Tel: (012) 633-63-77; (012) 634-59-45 (ext 354, 355, 359, 360 & 361); (012) 633-09-03 *Fax:* (012) 633-09-03
Web Site: www.bj.uj.edu.pl
Key Personnel
Dir: Dr Krzysztof Zamorski *E-mail:* zamorski@if.uj.edu.pl
Deputy Dir: Ryszard Juchniewicz; Teresa Malik *Tel:* (012) 6339882 *E-mail:* malikter@if.uj.edu.pl; Zdislaw Pietrzyk, PhD
Founded: 1364
Publication(s): *Biuletyn Biblioteki Jagiellonskiej* (The Jagiellonian Library Bulletin, annually)
Parent Company: Uniwersytet Jagiellonski (Jagiellonian University)

Biblioteka Narodowa
al Niepodleglosci 213, 02-086 Warsaw
Tel: (022) 452-2999 *Fax:* (022) 825-5251
E-mail: biblnar@bn.org.pl
Web Site: www.bn.org.pl
Key Personnel
Dir: Prof Adam Manikowski
The National Library. See also Instytut Bibliograficzny, a division of the National Library.
Publication(s): *Biuletyn Informacyjny Biblioteki Narodowej* (The National Library Information Bulletin); *Rocznik Biblioteki Narodowej* (The National Library Yearbook)

Biblioteka Publiczna m st Warszawy - Biblioteka Glowna Wojewodztwa Mazowieckiego (The Warsaw Public Library-The Central Library of Masovia Province)
Ul Koszykowa 26/28, 00-553 Warsaw
Mailing Address: PO Box 365, 00-950 Warsaw
Tel: (022) 6217852 *Fax:* (022) 6211968
E-mail: Biblioteka@biblpubl.waw.pl
Web Site: www.biblpubl.waw.pl
Key Personnel
Manager: Michal Strak
Founded: 1907
Publication(s): *Prace Biblioteki Publicznej m st Warszawy* (The Works of Warsaw Public Library, irregularly); *Sesje varsavianistyczne* (Varsaviana Sessions, irregularly)

Biblioteka Uniwersytecka w Poznaniu (Poznan University Library)
Ul Ratajczaka 38-40, 61-816 Poznan
Tel: (061) 829-3800 *Fax:* (061) 829-3824
E-mail: library@amu.edu.pl
Web Site: lib.amu.edu.pl
Telex: 412714 Bup
Key Personnel
Dir: Dr Artur Jazdon *Tel:* (061) 852-2955
 E-mail: jazar@amu.edu.pl
Founded: 1919
Publication(s): *Biblioteka* (annually); *Zeszyty Naukowe Biblioteki Uniwersyteckiej w Pozniv* (irregularly)
Parent Company: Uniwersytek im Adama Mickiewicza w Poznaniu (UAM)

Biblioteka Gdanska PAN
Walowa 15, 80-858 Gdansk
Tel: (058) 312251-54 *Fax:* (058) 312970
E-mail: bgpan@task.gda.pl
Key Personnel
Librarian: Zbigniew Nowak
Publication(s): *Libri Gedanenses* (annually)

Politechnika Gdanska
ul Narutowicza 11/12, 80-952 Gdansk Wrzeszcz
Tel: (058) 3415791 *Fax:* (058) 3415821
E-mail: mainlibr@sunrise.pg.gda.pl; library@pg.gda.pl
Web Site: www.pg.gda.pl
Telex: 415821
Key Personnel
Manager: Miroslaw Komendecki
Publication(s): *Bibliografia publikacji pracownikow Politechniki Gdanskiej* (Bibliographic Publication of the Employees of the Technical University of Gdansk); *Raporty Wydzialow PG* (annually, Berichte der Fakultaten der TU Gdansk); *Wykaz nabytkow BG PG* (monthly, Directory of New Recruting of the Central Library of Gdansk); *Zhistorii Politechniki Gdanskiej* (The History of the Technical University of Gdansk, quarterly)

Glowna Biblioteka Lekarska
Chocimska 22, Warsaw
Tel: (022) 849-78-51 *Fax:* (022) 849-78-02
E-mail: gbl@gbl.waw.pl
Web Site: www.gbl.waw.pl
Telex: 814820
Key Personnel
Dir: Prof Janusz Kapuscik
Central Medical Library.
Publication(s): *Biuletyn GBL*; *Polska Bibliôgrafia Lekanska*

Biblioteka Glowna Politechniki Warszawskiej
Pl Politechniki 1, 00-661 Warsaw
Tel: (022) 6211370 *Fax:* (022) 6287184
E-mail: bgpw@bg.pw.edu.pl
Web Site: www.bg.pw.edu.pl
Library of the Technical University of Warsaw.

Instytut Bibliograficzny (Bibliographical Institute)
Division of National Library - Biblioteka Narodowa
Biblioteka Narodowa, al Niepodleglosci 213, 02-086 Warsaw
Tel: (022) 452-2999 *Fax:* (022) 825-5251
E-mail: biblnar@bn.org.pl
Web Site: www.bn.org.pl
Telex: 816761 Bn Pl
Key Personnel
Librarian: Jadwiga Sadowska, PhD
Publication(s): *Bibliografia Bibliografii Polskich* (Bibliography of Polish Bibliographies, Annually); *Bibliografia Wydawnictw Ciagych* (Bibliography of Serials, Quarterly); *Bibliografia Zawartosci Czasopism* (Index to Periodicals, Monthly); *Polonica Zagraniczne* (Foreign Polonica, Annually); *Polska Bibliografia Bibliologiczna* (Polish Bibliography of Library Science, Annually); *Przewodnik Bibliograficzny* (Bibliographical Guide, Weekly); *Ruch Wydawniczy w Liczbach* (Polish Publishing in Figures, Annually)

Politechnika Krakowska im Tadeusza Kosciuszki (Cracow University of Technology)
ul Warszawska 24, 31-155 Krakow
Tel: (012) 628-20-14 *Fax:* (012) 628-20-14
E-mail: listy@biblos.pk.edu.pl
Web Site: www.pk.edu.pl
Key Personnel
Librarian: Dorota Buzdygan *E-mail:* buzdygan@biblos.pk.edu.pl; Marek M Gorski *E-mail:* gorski@biblos.pk.edu.pl
Membership(s): International Association of Technological University Libraries (IATUL).

Politechnika Slaska (The Silesian Technical University)
Biblioteka Glowna, ul Kaszubska 23, Gliwice 44-100
Tel: (032) 237-12-69 *Fax:* (032) 237-15-51
E-mail: info@bibgl.polsl.gliwice.pl
Web Site: www.polsl.gliwice.pl/alma.mater/biblioteka.html
Key Personnel
Manager: Halina Baluka
Founded: 1945

Politechnika Wroclawska/Biblioteka Glowna i OINT (Wroclaw University of Technology/Main Library & Scientific Information Centre)
Wybrzeze Wyspianskiego 27, 50-370 Wroclaw
Tel: (071) 238-27-07; (071) 320-23-05; (071) 320-23-31 *Fax:* (071) 328-29-60
E-mail: bg@bg.pwr.wroc.pl
Web Site: www.bg.pwr.wroc.pl
Key Personnel
Dir: Henryk Szarski *E-mail:* szarski@bg.pwr.wroc.pl
Librarian: Lucja Talarczyk-Malcher
Publication(s): *Acta of Bioengineering and Biomechanics*; *Architectus*; *Badania Operacyjne i Decyzje*; *Environment Protection Engineering*; *Fizykochemiczne Problemy Mineralurgii*; *Inzynieria Chemiczna i Procesowa*; *Optica Applicata*; *Studia Geotechnica and Mechanica*; *Systems Science*

Polska Fundacja Spraw Miedzynarodowych (Polish Foundation of International Affairs)
Ul Warecka 1a, PL 00-950 Warsaw
Mailing Address: PO Box 1000, PL00-950 Warsaw
Tel: (022) 827 88 88; (022) 523 90 86 *Fax:* (022) 523 90 27
E-mail: warecka@qdnet.pl
Web Site: www.sprawymiedzynarodowe.pl
Key Personnel
Head of Publications: Aleksandra Zieleniec *Tel:* (022) 523 90 25 *E-mail:* aleksandra.zieleniec@msz.gov.pl
Publication(s): *The Polish Quarterly of International Affairs* (quarterly); *Yearbook of Polish Foreign Policy* (annually)

Biblioteka Slaska (Silesian Library)
Plac Rady Europy 1, 40-021 Katowice
Tel: (032) 208 38 75 *Fax:* (032) 208 37 20
E-mail: bsl@bs.katowice.pl
Web Site: www.bs.katowice.pl
Key Personnel
Dir: Prof Jan Malicki *Tel:* (032) 206 06 875
Research library. Main special collections covering: literature, history, law, religion, social science & economy, special Silesian collection.
Publication(s): *Bibliografia Slaska* (annually); *Ksiaznica Slaska* (irregularly, bulletin, information on the Silesian Library activites & articles on the history of Silesian books)

Uniwersytet Szczecinski
ul Mickiewicza 16, 70-384 Szczecin
Tel: (091) 444-23-61 *Fax:* (091) 444-23-62
E-mail: info@bg.univ.szczecin.pl
Web Site: www.univ.szczecin.pl/us/biblioteka.html
Cable: 422719
Key Personnel
Rector of University: Prof Tadeusz Wierzabicki
Dir: Jolanta Goc
Publication(s): *Przeglad Zachodniopomorski* (quarterly)

Biblioteka Uniwersytecka w Warszawie (Warsaw University Library)
Ul Dobra 56/60, 00-312 Warsaw
Tel: (022) 5525660; (022) 5525181 *Fax:* (022) 5525181
E-mail: buw@uw.edu.pl
Web Site: www.buw.uw.edu.pl
Key Personnel
Dir: Ewa Kobierska-Maciuszko *Tel:* (022) 5525663 *E-mail:* e.maciuszko@uw.edu.pl
Founded: 1817
Publication(s): *Prace Biblioteki Uniwersyteckiej w Warszawie - Acta Bibliothecae* (irregularly)

Biblioteka Uniwersytecka we Wroclawiu (Library of the University of Wroclaw)
Ul Karola Szajnochy 10, 50-076 Wroclaw
Tel: (071) 3463120 *Fax:* (071) 3463166
E-mail: infnauk@bu.uni.wroc.pl
Web Site: www.bu.uni.wroc.pl
Key Personnel
Director: Grazyna Piotrowicz
Founded: 1945
University Library Wroclaw.
Publication(s): *Bibliothecalia Wratlaviensia* (irregular, newspaper, 1995)

Uniwersytet Gdanski
Biblioteka Glowna UG, ul Armii Krajowej 110, 81824 Sopot
Tel: (058) 5509413 *Fax:* (058) 5515221
E-mail: bib@bg.univ.gda.pl; info@bg.univ.gda.pl
Web Site: www.bg.univ.gda.pl/library/
Key Personnel
Dir: Urszula Sawicka
Founded: 1970

Biblioteka Uniwersytecka w Torruniu (Nicholas Copernicus University Library)
Ul Gagarina 13, 87-100 Torun
Tel: (056) 61 14 408 *Fax:* (056) 652 04 19
E-mail: sekrretariat@bu.uni.torun.pl
Web Site: www.bu.uni.torun.pl/en
Key Personnel
Dir: Miroslaw Adam Suprуniuk, PhD
Founded: 1945
Library of the Mikolaj Kopernik University in Torun.
Parent Company: Uniwersytet Mikolaja Kopernika w Torruniu

Portugal

Biblioteca da Academia das Ciencias de Lisboa (Library of the Academy of Sciences of Lisbon)
Rua da Academia das Ciencias, 19, 1°, 1249-122 Lisboa
Tel: (021) 321 97 31; (021) 321 97 41 *Fax:* (021) 342 03 95
E-mail: biblioteca@acad-ciencias.pt
Web Site: www.acad-ciencias.pt

Biblioteca da Ajuda
Palacio Nacional da Ajuda, 1349-021 Lisbon
Tel: (021) 363 85 92 *Fax:* (021) 363 85 92
Key Personnel
Dir: Francisco Delfim Cunha Leao

Biblioteca Geral da Universidade de Coimbra
Largo da Porta Ferrea, 3000-447 Coimbra
Tel: (0239) 859800; (0239) 859815; (0239) 859831 *Fax:* (0239) 827135
E-mail: bguc@ci.uc.pt
Web Site: www.ci.uc.pt
Telex: (039) 52275
Key Personnel
Dir: Prof Anibal Pinto de Castro *E-mail:* acastro@ci.uc.pt
Publication(s): *Acta Universitatis Conimbrigensis*; *Biblioteca da Universidade de Coimbra*; *Biblioteca Geralda Universidade de Coimbra*; *Divulgacao Bibliografica*; *Revista da Universidade de Coimbra*; *Sumarios das Publicacoes Periodicas Portuguesas*

Biblioteca Nacional
Campo Grande 83, 1749-081 Lisbon
Tel: (021) 7982000 *Fax:* (021) 7982140
E-mail: bn@bn.pt
Web Site: www.bn.pt
Key Personnel
Deputy Dir: Fernanda Maria Campos *Tel:* (021) 7982022 *E-mail:* fcampos@bn.pt
Founded: 1796
National Library.
Publication(s): *Leituras: Revista da Biblioteca Nacional* (2x/yr)

Biblioteca Popular de Lisboa
R Academia Ciencias 19, 1200 Lisbon
Tel: (021) 346 98 83
Key Personnel
Contact: Belkiss Pousao Lopes

Biblioteca Publica de Evora (Public Library of Evora)
Largo Conde de Vila Flor, 7000 804 Evora
Tel: (0266) 769 330 *Fax:* (0266) 769 331
E-mail: bpevora@ptnetbiz.pt
Key Personnel
Dir: Jose Antonio Calixto *E-mail:* jac.bpe@ptnetbiz.pt
Public Library.
Publication(s): *Evora, BPADE, 1988*; *Isabel Cid-Incunabulos da Biblioteca Publica e Arquivo Distrital de Evora-Catalogo Abreviado*; *Isabel Cid-Incunabulos E Seus Possuidores, Estudo das marcas de posse dos incunabulos da Biblioteca Publica e Arquivo Distrital de Evora, Lisboa INIC, 1988*; *Isabel Cid-Lil Vicente e asua Epoca, Evora, 1992*
Parent Company: Instituto dos Arquivos Nacionais/Torre do Tombo

Biblioteca Publica Municipal do Porto
Jardim de Sao Lazaro, 4099 Porto
Tel: (02) 572147 *Fax:* (022) 5193488
Key Personnel
Dir: L Cabral
Municipal Library of Porto.

Fundacao para a Ciencia e a Tecnologia/Servico de Informacao e Documentacao(SID)
Av D Carlos I, 126, 1249-074 Lisbon
Tel: (01) 3924300 *Fax:* (01) 3907481
Web Site: www.fct.mct.pt
Telex: 12290 junic
Key Personnel
Dir: Dr Gabriela Lopes da Silva *E-mail:* g.l.silva@fct.mct.pt
Centre of Scientific & Technical Information, a branch of the Junta Nacional de Investigacao Cientifica e Technologia (National Council for Scientific & Technological Research).
Publication(s): *Guia de servicos di Documentacao e di Bibliotecas em Portugal*

Instituto dos Arquivos Nacionais/Torre do Tombo
Alameda da Universidade, 1600 Lisbon
Tel: (01) 7811500 *Fax:* (01) 7937230
E-mail: dc@iantt.pt
Telex: 65729 ANTTP
Key Personnel
Head of Division: Dr Maria de Lurdes Henriques

Biblioteca do Palacio Nacional de Mafra
Terreiro de D Joao V, 2640 Mafra
Tel: (0261) 817 550 *Fax:* (0261) 811947
Key Personnel
Dir: Maria Margarida Montenegro

Universidade do Minho (Minho University)
Largo do Paco, 4710 553 Braga
Tel: (0253) 604150 *Fax:* (0253) 604159
E-mail: sdum@sdum.uminho.pt
Web Site: www.sdum.uminho.pt
Telex: 132135
Key Personnel
Dir Documentation Services: Eloy Rodrigues
 E-mail: eloy@sdum.uminho.pt
Founded: 1973

Puerto Rico

Archivo General de Puerto Rico (Puerto Rican General Archive)
Apdo 9024184, San Juan 00902
Tel: (787) 724-0700 *Fax:* (787) 724-8393
Web Site: www.icp.gobierno.pr
Key Personnel
Dir: Ada T Rodriguez
National Archives of Puerto Rico.

Conrad F Asenjo Library, see University of Puerto Rico, Medical Sciences Campus Library

Biblioteca General de Puerto Rico (General Library of Puerto Rico)
Convento de los Dominicos No 98, San Juan 00902
Mailing Address: Apdo 9024184, San Juan 00902-4184
Tel: (787) 724-0700 *Fax:* (787) 724-8394
E-mail: www@icp.gobierno.pr
Web Site: www.icp.gobierno.pr/bge/index.htm
Key Personnel
Dir: Ada T Rodriguez
Founded: 1967
Library.

Caribbean & Latin American Studies Library
PO Box 21927, San Juan 00931-1927
Tel: (787) 764-0000 (ext 3319) *Fax:* (787) 763-5685
Key Personnel
Chief Librarian: Almaluces Figueroa
 E-mail: afiguer@upracd.upr.clu.edu
Research collection open to the general public.

Inter American University of Puerto Rico Library
Bo San Daniel Sector Las Canelas Carretera 2, Arecibo 00613
Tel: (787) 878-5475 (ext 320) *Fax:* (787) 880-1624
E-mail: sabreu@uiprl.inter.edu

University of Puerto Rico, General Library, Mayaguez Campus
PO Box 9022, Mayaguez 00681-9022
Tel: (787) 265-3810; (787) 832-4040 (ext 3810, 2151, 2155) *Fax:* (787) 265-5483
E-mail: library@rumlib.uprm.edu
Web Site: www.uprm.edu/library
Key Personnel
Library Dir: Prof Irma N Ramirez Aviles
 E-mail: irma@rumlib.uprm.edu

University of Puerto Rico, Library System, Rio Piedras Campus
PO Box 23302, San Juan 00931-3302
Tel: (787) 764-0000 (ext 3311); (787) 764-0000 (ext 5085); (787) 764-0000 (ext 5089) *Fax:* (787) 772-1479
Web Site: biblioteca.uprrp.edu
Key Personnel
Dir: Ramon A Budet Rodriguez *Tel:* (787) 764-0000 ext 5085 *E-mail:* rbudet@rrpac.upr.clu.edu
Associate Dir: Myra Torres Alamo
 E-mail: mytorres@rrpac.upr.clu.edu
Publication(s): *Al Dia*, *Entorno*; *Biblionotas*; *Boletines de Divulgacion*; *Lumbre*; *Perspectiva*; *Servicio de Alerta*

University of Puerto Rico, Medical Sciences Campus Library
PO Box 365067, San Juan 00936-5067
Tel: (787) 758-2525; (787) 751-8199 *Fax:* (787) 759-6713
E-mail: zgarcia@rcm.upr.edu
Web Site: rcm-library.rcm.upr.edu
Telex: 3859173
Key Personnel
Dir: Prof Victoria Delgado *E-mail:* vdelgado@rcm.upr.edu
Circulation & Reserve: Mrs Luz Evelyn Acevedo
 E-mail: eacevedo@rcm.upr.edu
Special Collections: Prof Carmen Santos Corrada
 E-mail: csantos@rcm.upr.edu
Technical Services: Prof Nilca Parrilla Diaz
 E-mail: nparrilla@rcm.upr.edu
Reference: Prof Margarita Gonzalez Perez
 E-mail: mmgonzalez@rcm.upr.edu
Serials: Prof Leticia Perez Guzman
 E-mail: lperez@rcm.upr.edu

Qatar

Qatar National Library
PO Box 205, Doha
Tel: 442 9955 *Fax:* 442 9976
E-mail: qanaly@qatar.net.qa
Telex: 4743 Qanali DH
Key Personnel
Dir: Mohammed Hamad Al-Nassr
Branch Office(s)
Al Khansa
Al- Shekh Ali
Al-Khore
Al-Rayyan
Al-Shamal
Al-Wakra

Qatar University Library
University St, Al-Dafana, Doha
Mailing Address: Libraries Administration, PO Box 2713, Doha
Tel: 4852405 *Fax:* 4835092
E-mail: postmaster@qu.edu.qa
Web Site: www.qu.edu.qa/english/library/libraries.htm
Telex: 4630 Unvsty DH
Key Personnel
Dir: Dr Ahmed M Al-Qattan *Tel:* 4852629
 E-mail: alqattan@qu.edu.qa

Reunion

Archives Departementales
rue Marcel Pagnol-Champ Fleuri, 97490 Sainte-Clotilde
Tel: 94 04 14 *Fax:* 94 04 21
E-mail: archives@cg974.fr
Key Personnel
Archivist: Nadine Rouayroux

Bibliotheque Departemental de Pret
One, place Joffre, 97400 Saint Denis
Tel: 21 03 24 *Fax:* 21 41 30
Key Personnel
Librarian: Marie-Colette Maujean

Mediatheque de Saint Pierre
BP 396, rue du College Arthur, 97458 St-Pierre Cedex
Tel: 96 71 91 *Fax:* 25 74 10
Web Site: www.mediatheque-saintpierre.fr
Key Personnel
Librarian: Linda Koo Seen Lin *E-mail:* ksl@mediatheque-saintpierre.fr

SCD, see Universite de la Reunion, Service Commun de la Documentation

Universite de la Reunion, Service Commun de la Documentation
15, ave Rene Cassin, 97715 Saint-Denis messag cedex 9
Mailing Address: BP 7152, 97715 Saint-Denis messag cedex 9
Tel: 93 83 83 *Fax:* 93 83 64
Web Site: www.univ-reunion.fr
Key Personnel
Dir: Lefe Bure
Conservateur General: Anne-Marie Blanc

Romania

Academia de Studii Economice, Biblioteca Centrala
Piata Romana nr 6, sector 1, Bucharest Cod 7000
Tel: (01) 211 26 50; (01) 211 26 55 *Fax:* (01) 312 95 49
Web Site: www.aseciti.ase.ro
Telex: Asero 11863

Arhivele Nationale ale Romaniei (National Archives of Romania)
Bulevardul Elisabeta, nr 49, sector 5, Bucharest
Tel: (01) 3152503 *Fax:* (01) 3125841
E-mail: webmaster@mai.gov.ro
Web Site: www.mai.gov.ro
Key Personnel
General Dir: Dr Costin Fenesan
Membership(s): International Association of Francopone Archives; International Council of Archives.
Publication(s): *Historical Abstract & America-History & Life* (article abstracts & index)

Biblioteca Centrala Universitara (Central University Library of Bucharest)
Str Boteanu, nr 1, sector 1, 010027 Bucharest
Tel: (021) 313 16 05; (021) 313 16 06 *Fax:* (021) 312 01 08
Web Site: www.bcub.ro
Key Personnel
Dir: Dr Mircea Regneala *E-mail:* regneala@bcub.ro
Deputy Dir: Robert Coravu; Voichita Dragomir
Publication(s): *Literatura romana*; *Ghid bibliografic Partea I: Surse. Partea a II-a: Scriitori. Vol.I: A-L. Vol.II: M-Z. 1979, 1982, 1983*

Biblioteca Nationala a Romaniei (National Library of Romania)
Str Ion Ghica 4, 030046 Bucharest
Tel: (01) 3157063 *Fax:* (01) 3123381
E-mail: go@bibnat.ro
Key Personnel
Dir: Mrs Rodica Maiorescu
Founded: 1955
National Library of Romania.

Biblioteca Centrala Universitara Mihail Eminescu (Central University Library)
Str Pacurari, nr 4, 6600 Iasi
Tel: (0232) 264245 *Fax:* (0232) 261796
E-mail: bcuis@bcu-iasi.ro
Web Site: www.bcu-iasi.ro
Key Personnel
Dir: Prof Al Calinescu *E-mail:* alcalinescu@bcu-iasi.ro
Parent Company: Ministry of Education & Research

INID, see Institutul National de Informare si Documentare (INID)

Institutul National de Informare si Documentare (INID) (National Institute for Information & Documentation)
Str I D Mendeleev nr 21-25, 010362 Bucharest
Tel: (01) 315 87 65 *Fax:* (01) 312 67 34
E-mail: inid@home.ro
Web Site: www.inid.ro
Key Personnel
General Dir: Ana-Eugenia Negulescu, MA
Publication(s): Asigurarea si Promovarea Calitatii (quarterly); *Informarea si Documentarea Moderna* (quarterly); *Management si Marketing Conpemporan* (quarterly)

Biblioteca Municipala Mihail Sadoveanu
Str Take Ionescu nr 4, 79711 Bucharest
Tel: (01) 2113625 *Fax:* (01) 2113625
Key Personnel
Assistant Dir: Rodica Cosmaciuc
Founded: 1935
Memberships: EBLIDA; IFLA; IMTAMEL.
Publication(s): *The Bibliography of Bucharest City* (1996); *Biblioteca Bucurestilor* (Bucharest's Library Review, monthly, 1998); *Foaia Cartierului* (Neighborhood's Review, monthly)

Universitatea Transilvania Din Brasov Biblioteca Centrala (Transylvania University of Brasov Central Library)
Bd Eroilor 29, 2200 Brasov
Tel: (068) 413 000 *Fax:* (068) 150 474
E-mail: libr@vega.unitbv.ro
Key Personnel
Dir: Aurel Negrutiu
Head, Library Service: Andrea Deaconescu *E-mail:* deacon@vega.unitbv.ro
Founded: 1948
Specialize in academic library, engineering, forestry, wood industry, humanities, sciences, medicine, music & economy.
Parent Company: Transilvania University of Brasov

Universitatea de Medicina si Farmacie Biblioteca Centrala (Central Library of the Univeristy of Medicine and Pharmacy)
Division of Government of Romania
Avram Iancu 31, 3400 Cluj-napoca
Tel: (064) 192629 *Fax:* (064) 190832
Web Site: www.bib.umfcluj.ro
Key Personnel
Dir: Iona Robu *E-mail:* irobu@umfcluj.ro
Founded: 1948

Central Library of the University of Medicine and Pharmacy.
Parent Company: University of Medicine & Pharmacy Ministry of Education

Biblioteca Universitatii Politehnica Bucuresti
Calea Grivitei, nr 132, corp I, etaj 2, camera 210, Bucharest
Tel: (021) 402 3982 *Fax:* (021) 312 70 44
Web Site: www.library.pub.ro
Telex: 10252 ipolb
Key Personnel
Dir: Dan-Radu Popescu *E-mail:* dr_popescu@library.pub.ro

Russian Federation

Fundamental Library of the Academy of Medical Sciences
Baltiiskaya Ul 8, 125874 Moscow
Tel: (095) 155-17-93
Key Personnel
Contact: G I Bakhereva

Biblioteka Akademii Nauk Rossii (Russian Academy of Sciences Library)
Birzevaja linija 1, 199034 St Petersburg
Tel: (0812) 3283592 *Fax:* (0812) 3287436
E-mail: ban@info.rasl.spb.ru
Web Site: www.ban.tu
Key Personnel
Contact: Dr Valerij Leonov
Founded: 1714

All-Russian Patent Technical Library
Berezhkovskaya naberezhnaya 24, 121857 Moscow
Tel: (095) 2406425 *Fax:* (095) 2404437
E-mail: vptb@aha.ru
Telex: 411774 bipat SU
Key Personnel
Library Dir: V I Amelkina
Deputy Dir: O I Kosolapov

Central State Archives
Vyborgskaya 3, 125212 Moscow
Tel: (095) 1597383
Key Personnel
Dir: A Prokopenko

Gosudarstvennaya publichnaya nauchno-tekhnicheskaya biblioteka SSSR
Kuznetskij most, 12, 103919 Moscow
Tel: (095) 9259288 *Fax:* (095) 9219862
E-mail: root@gpntb.msk.su
Telex: 411180
Key Personnel
Editor: A I Zemskov
Manager: N P Pavlova
State Public Scientific and Technical Library of the USSR.

Gosudarstvennaya publichnaya istoricheskaya biblioteka Rossii (State Public Historical Library of Russia)
Starosadskiy per 9, Moscow 101990
Tel: (095) 925-65-14; (095) 928-05-22 *Fax:* (095) 928-02-84
E-mail: info@shpl.ru
Web Site: www.shpl.ru
Key Personnel
Dir: Dr Mikhail Dmitriyevich Afanasiev

Institut Nauchnoy Informatsii po Obschestvennym Naukam, Rossijskoj Akademii Nauk RF
Nakhimovskii Prospeckt, d 51/21, 117997 Moscow
Tel: (095) 128-88-81; (095) 128-89-30 *Fax:* (095) 420-22-61
E-mail: info@inion.ru
Web Site: www.inion.ru
Institute of Scientific Information in the Social Sciences of the Russian Academie of Sciences, Russian Federation.

Nauchnaya biblioteka im M Gor'kogo Sankt-Petersburgskogo (Scientific Library of St Petersburg University)
Universitetskaya nab 7/9, Saint-Petersburg 199034
Tel: (0812) 328-27-41; (0812) 328-95-46 *Fax:* (0812) 328-27-41
E-mail: info@mail.lib.pu.ru
Web Site: www.lib.pu.ru
Key Personnel
Dir: Natalja A Sheshina
Vice Dir: Marina Karpova
M Gor'kii Scientific Library of the State University of St Petersburg.

Petrozavodskij Gosudarstvennyj Universitet
prospekt Lenina 33, Petrozavodsk 185640
Tel: (08142) 74-28-65 *Fax:* (08142) 71-10-00
E-mail: lib@mainpgu.karelia.ru
Web Site: www.karelia.ru
Key Personnel
Dir: Marina P Otlivanchik
Assistant Dir: Klaudia P Shirshina *Tel:* (08142) 71-10-44
Editor: Ludmila M Rots

Rossiiskaya Nacionalnaya biblioteka (National Library of Russia)
18, Sadovaya, St Petersburg 191069
Tel: (0812) 310-2856 *Fax:* (0812) 310-6148
E-mail: office@nlr.ru
Web Site: www.nlr.ru:8101
Key Personnel
Dir: Vladimir Zaitsev *Tel:* (0812) 118-85-00 *E-mail:* v.zaitsev@nlr.ru

Gosudarstvennaya publichnaya nauchno-tekhnicheskaya biblioteka Sibirskogo otdeleniya Rossiiskoi Akademii Nauk (State Public Scientific Technological Library of the Siberian Branch Academy of Sciences of Russia)
Voskhod 15, 200 Novosibirsk
Tel: (0382) 66-18-60 *Fax:* (0382) 66-33-65
E-mail: root@libr.nsk.su
Web Site: www.gpntb.ru
Telex: 133220 *Cable:* 1023 LIBRO
Key Personnel
Dir: Prof Boris Stepanovich Yelepov
Deputy Dir: Yelena Borisovna Soboleva
Secretary, International Ties: Vera Nicolaevna Cabanova
Founded: 1918

Russian State Historical Archives
Angliiskaya nab 4, 190000 St Petersburg
Tel: (0812) 311-09-26 *Fax:* (0812) 311-22-52
Key Personnel
Dir: V G Gerasimov

Sankt-Peterburgskogo Gosudarstvennogo Universiteta
7-9, Universitetskaya nab, St Petersburg 199034
Tel: (0812) 3262000 *Fax:* (0812) 2182741
E-mail: office@inform.pu.ru
Web Site: www.spbu.ru
Key Personnel
Vice Dir: M Karpova

Scientific Library of St Petersburg University, see Nauchnaya biblioteka im M Gor'kogo Sankt- Petersburgskogo

Scientific Library Voronezh State University
prospekt Revoljucii 24, 394000 Voronezh
Tel: (0732) 55-35-59 *Fax:* (0732) 208-258
E-mail: root@lib.vsu.ru
Web Site: www.lib.vsu.ru
Key Personnel
Librarian: Svetlana Yants
Founded: 1918

State Archives of the Russian Federation
Bolshaya Pirogovskaya ul 17, 119817 Moscow
Tel: (095) 245-81-41 *Fax:* (095) 245-12-87

Vserossijskaja gosudarstvennaja biblioteka inostrannoj literatury im M I Rudomino (M I Rudomino All-Russia State Library for Foreign Literature)
Nikolojamskaya ul, 1, Moscow 109189
Tel: (095) 9153621 *Fax:* (095) 9153637
E-mail: vgbil@libfl.ru
Web Site: www.libfl.ru
Key Personnel
Dir General: Ekaterina Genieva
Founded: 1922
General research & public library, an international cultural center
Member of International Federation of Library Associations & Institutions (IFLA), Russian Library Association.

Rwanda

Bibliotheque de l'Institut National de la Recherche Scientifique
BP 192, Butare
Tel: 30395 *Fax:* 30939
Telex: 22605

Service de l'Information et des Archives Nationales
Presidence de la Republique, BP 15, Kigali
Tel: 76 995 *Fax:* 82 162
Telex: 517 PRESIREP RW
Key Personnel
Dir: Charles Uyisenga

Bibliotheque de l'Universite Nationale du Rwanda
BP 117, Butare
Tel: 530330 *Fax:* 530210
E-mail: biblio@nur.ac.rw
Web Site: www.lib.nur.ac.rw
Telex: 22605
Key Personnel
Dir: Serugendo Emmanuel

Samoa

Nelson Memorial Public Library
PO Box 598, Apia
Tel: (0685) 21028 *Fax:* (0685) 21028
Web Site: www.samoa.com
Key Personnel
Chief Librarian: Ms Jacinta P Godinet
 E-mail: jpgodinet@lesamoa.net
Founded: 1960

Saudi Arabia

Imam Mohamed Bin Saud University Library
PO Box 5701, Riyadh 11432
Tel: (01) 258 0000 *Fax:* (01) 259 0271
Telex: 401166 Univer SJ
Key Personnel
Acting Dean of Library Affairs: Dr Mohamed Al Zeer

Institute of Public Administration Library
PO Box 205, Riyadh 11141
Tel: (01) 476 1600 *Fax:* (01) 479 2136
E-mail: library@ipa.edu.sa
Web Site: www.ipa.edu.sa
Telex: 404360 SJ *Cable:* IPADMIN
Key Personnel
Dir of Libraries: Mostafa M Sadhan
Publication(s): *Maktabat Al Idarah* (Library Administration, quarterly)

Islamic University Central Library
PO Box 170, Medina
Tel: (04) 847 4080 *Fax:* (04) 847 4560
Telex: 570022 Islami SJ
Key Personnel
University Rector: Dr Abdullah Saleh Alobeid
Dean & Library Affairs & Man Dir: Dr Mohammad Yakub Turkustani
Editor in Chief: Dr Ali Sultan Alhakamy
Founded: 1961

King Abdulasiz University Library
PO Box 3711, Jeddah 21481
Tel: (02) 695 2068 *Fax:* (02) 640 0169
E-mail: library@kaau.edu.sa
Web Site: www.kaau.edu.sa
Telex: 401141 Kauni SJ
Key Personnel
Administrator: Mohammed Ahmed Basager
 Tel: (02) 6952481 *Fax:* (02) 6400169
 E-mail: lia3003@kaau.edu.sa
A Central Library with 10 branches in various faculties.
Publication(s): *Annual Index of Umm Al-Qura* (Arabic); *Catalogue of MSS in the Central Library* (Arabic); *Dissertations on Saudi Arabia* (English)

King Abdulaziz Public Library
PO Box 86486, Riyadh 11622
Tel: (01) 4911300; (01) 4911304 *Fax:* (01) 4911949
E-mail: kapl@anet.net.sa
Telex: 406444 KAPL
Key Personnel
Dir General: Faisal A Al-Muammar

King Fahad National Library
King Faisal St, Riyadh
Web Site: www.kfnl.gov.sa

King Faisal University Library
PO Box 1758, Al-Hasa 31982
Tel: (03) 8574456 *Fax:* (03) 8576748
E-mail: library@kfu.edu.sa
Web Site: www.kfu.edu.sa
Telex: 870020 FAISAL SJ
Key Personnel
Dean of Library Affairs: Dr Mohammed Nassir Al-Dasari *Tel:* (03) 5801247 *E-mail:* mdosar@kfu.edu.sa
Vice Dean of Libraries: Dr Fares A Al-Faredi *E-mail:* vdean_library@damman.kfu.edu.sa
Librarian, College of Medicine: Mr Abdulhamid Abualsoud *Tel:* (03) 8577000 (ext 353)

King Saud University Library
PO Box 2454, Riyadh 11451
Tel: (01) 4676148 *Fax:* (01) 4676162
Web Site: www.ksu.edu.sa
Telex: 201019 Ksu SJ *Cable:* University
Key Personnel
Dean: Dr Sulaiman S Al-Ogla *E-mail:* sfalogla@.ksu.edu.sa
Founded: 1979
Publication(s): *Directory of Libraries in Saudi Arabia* (1979)

Umm al Qura University Library
PO Box 1629, Azizia, Makkah
Tel: (02) 5565621 *Fax:* (02) 5501000 (ext 5562)
E-mail: lib@uqu.edu.sa
Web Site: www.uqu.edu.sa
Telex: 540026 Jammka SJ
Key Personnel
Dean of Library Affairs: Dr Hammad M Ae-Thomaly

Senegal

L'Alliance francaise, Bibliotheque
2, rue Assane Ndoye, Dakar
Mailing Address: BP 1777, Dakar
Tel: 21 0822

Archives du Senegal
Immeuble administratif, ave Leopold Sedar Senghor, Dakar
Tel: 8235072 *Fax:* 8225126
E-mail: pmardi@primature.sn
Key Personnel
Dir: Saliou Mbaye
National Archives of Senegal.
Publication(s): *Bibliographie du Senegal* (annual report); *Dictionnaire de sigles et acronymes en usage au Senegal* (1990, monographic); *Guide de Archives de l'AOF* (monographic); *Histoire des institutions coloniales Francaise en Afrique de l'ouest (1816-1960)* (1991, monographic)

Ecole des Bibliothecaires, Archivistes et Documentalistes de l'Universite Cheikh Anta Diop de Dakar
BP 3252, Dakar
Tel: 825 76 60; 864 21 22 *Fax:* 824 05 42
E-mail: ebad@ebad.ucad.sn
Web Site: www.ebad.ucad.sn
Telex: 51-262 UNIVDAK SG
Key Personnel
Dir: Mbaye Thiam *E-mail:* mbaye.thiam@ebad.ucad.sn

IDEP, see Institut Africain de Developpement Economique et de Planification (IDEP), Bibliotheque

Institut Africain de Developpement Economique et de Planification (IDEP), Bibliotheque
BP 3186, Dakar
Tel: 823 10 20 *Fax:* 822 29 64
E-mail: idep@sonatel.senet.sn
Telex: 51579 Idep *Cable:* IDEP
Key Personnel
Dir: Dr Jeggan C Senghor

Institut Fondamental d'Afrique Noire, Bibliotheque
BP 206, Campus universitaire Dakar, Dakar
Tel: 825 00 90; 825 98 90; 825 71 24 *Fax:* 24 49 18
E-mail: bifan@telecomplus.sn
Web Site: www.refer.sn/ifan

Telex: 51262
Key Personnel
Librarian: Gora Dia

Universite Cheikh Anta Diop de Dakar, Bibliotheque Universitaire
BP 2006, Dakar
Tel: 825 02 79 *Fax:* 824 23 79
Web Site: www.bu.ucad.sn
Telex: 5126256 UNIVDAK
Key Personnel
Dir: Mr Henri Sene *Tel:* 824 69 81
 E-mail: hsene@bu.ucad.sn
Founded: 1957
University Library.
Publication(s): *Collective Catalogue of Memoires*; *Collective Catalogue of Periodicals*; *Collective National Catalogue of Periodical Publications*

Serbia and Montenegro

Centralna Narodna Biblioteka SR Crne Gore (Central National Library of Montenegro)
Bulevar Crnogorskih junaka 163, 81250 Cetinje
Tel: (086) 231 143 *Fax:* (086) 231 726
E-mail: cnb@cg.yu
Web Site: cnbct.cnb.cg.ac.yu
Key Personnel
Dir: Dr Cedomir Draskovic
Founded: 1946
Central National Library of Montenegro, national depository, general scientific library; special collection of Montenegrina, old & rare books.
Publication(s): *Bibliografski vjesnik* (Bibliographic Courier, 3x/yr)

Biblioteka Matice Srpske (Matica Srpska Library)
Ul Matice Srpska 1, 21000 Novi Sad
Tel: (021) 420 271; (021) 528 747 *Fax:* (021) 28 574; (021) 420 271
E-mail: bms@bms.ns.ac.yu
Web Site: www.bms.ns.ac.yu
Key Personnel
Dir: Miro Vuksanovic *Tel:* (021) 528 910
 E-mail: miro@bms.ns.ac.yu
Founded: 1826
Library & information work.
Membership(s): International Federation of Library Associations & Institutions (IFLA).
Publication(s): *Matica Srpska Library Guide*

Narodna Biblioteka Srbije (National Library of Serbia)
Skerliceva 1, Belgrade 11000
Tel: (011) 451-242; (011) 451-281; (011) 451-287 *Fax:* (011) 451-289; (011) 452-952
Web Site: www.nbs.bg.ac.yu
Telex: 12 208 NB SRB YU
Key Personnel
Dir: Milomar Petrovic; Mr Sreten Ugricic
 Tel: (011) 434-091 *E-mail:* sugricic@nbs.bg.ac.yu
Dir for International Relations: Vesna Injac
 Tel: (011) 453-843 *E-mail:* injac@nbs.bg.ac.yu
Head, Publishing & Editor: Djurdjic Ljiljana
Founded: 1832
Publishing Department of the National Library of Serbia.

Arhiv Srbije (Archives of Serbia)
Karnegijeva 2, 11000 Belgrade
Tel: (011) 33-70-781; (011) 33-70-782; (011) 33-70-879; (011) 33-70-880 *Fax:* (011) 33-70-246
E-mail: office@archives.org.yu

Web Site: www.archives.org.yu
Key Personnel
Dir: Vjera Mitrovic
Librarian: Tatjana Jovanovic
Founded: 1900
Publication(s): *Arhivski Pregled*

Biblioteka Srpske Akademije Nauka i Umetnosti (Library of the Serbian Academy of Sciences & Arts)
Knez Mihailova 35, 11000 Belgrade
Tel: (011) 33-42-400 *Fax:* (011) 639-120
E-mail: admin@bib.sanu.ac.yu
Web Site: www.bib.sanu.ac.yu
Key Personnel
Exchange Librarian (English-speaking Countries): Prof Spomenka Ninic *Tel:* (011) 33-42-400, ext 233 *E-mail:* ninic@bib.sanu.ac.yu
Dir, Library of SASA & Librarian: Prof Mr Niksa Stipcevic
Founded: 1842
Publication(s): *Izdanja Biblioteke Srske Akademije Nauka i Umetnosti*

Univerzitet u Beogradu biblioteka 'Svetozar Markovic'
Bulevar Kralja Aleksandra 71, 11000 Belgrade
Tel: (011) 3370-509 *Fax:* (011) 3370-354
Web Site: ns.unilib.bg.ac.yu
Key Personnel
Librarian: Ivan Gadjanski
University Library 'Svetozar Markovic'.

Sierra Leone

British Council Library
Tower Hill, Freetown
Mailing Address: PO Box 124, Freetown
Tel: (022) 222223; (022) 222227; (022) 2224683 *Fax:* (022) 224123
E-mail: bcouncil@sierratel.sl
Web Site: www.britishcouncil.org/sierraleone
Telex: 3453 Bricon SL
Key Personnel
Contact: Abator Thomas

Fourah Bay College Library
University of Sierra Leone, Mount Aureol, Freetown
Mailing Address: PO Box 87, Freetown
Tel: (022) 229471 *Cable:* FOURAH BAY
Key Personnel
Librarian: Deanna Thomas Lnm'jamtu-Sie
Founded: 1827

Milton Margai Teachers' College Library
Goderich hr, Freetown
Tel: (022) 024305

Njala University College Library (University of Sierra Leone)
PMB, Freetown
Tel: (022) 228788
E-mail: nuc@sierratel.sl; nuclib@sierratel.sl
Web Site: www.nuc-online.com
Key Personnel
Librarian: A N T Deen

Public Archives of Sierra Leone
University of Sierra Leone, Mount Aureol, Freetown
Mailing Address: PO Box 87, Mount Aureol, Freetown
Tel: (022) 229 471
Key Personnel
Hon Govt Archivist Prof: Akintola J G Wyse

Sierra Leone Library Board
PO Box 326, Freetown
Tel: (022) 226 993
Key Personnel
Chief Librarian: Mrs I O'Brien-Coker
Publication(s): *Sierra Leone Publications* (annually)

United States Information Service Library
c/o American Embassy, 8 Walpole, Freetown
Tel: 226481 *Fax:* 225471
Telex: 3509
Key Personnel
Librarian: Florence Nylander

University of Sierra Leone, see Njala University College Library (University of Sierra Leone)

Singapore

National Archives of Singapore
One Canning Rise, Singapore 179868
Tel: 6332 7909 *Fax:* 3393583
Web Site: www.nhb.gov.sg/NAS/nas.shtml
Founded: 1968

National University of Singapore Library
12 Kent Ridge Crescent, Singapore 119275
Tel: 6874-2028 *Fax:* 6777-3571
E-mail: clbsec@nus.edu.sg
Web Site: www.lib.nus.edu.sg
Telex: RS 33943 UNISPO
Key Personnel
Dir: Sylvia Yap *Tel:* 6874-2069 *Fax:* 6777-1272
 E-mail: clbyapsb@nus.edu.sg
Senior Librarian: Mrs Lin Lin Tey *Tel:* 6874-2018
 Fax: 6774-7180 *E-mail:* clbteyll@nus.edu.sg
Publication(s): *LINUS Newsletter of the NUS Library*; *NUS Library Guide*; *SMC Ondisc CD-ROM* (contains PERIND database: Index to Periodical Articles relating to Singapore, Malaysia, Brunei & ASEAN; Singapore/Malaysia Collection database; NUS Theses Collection database)
Branch Office(s)
Central Library
Chinese Library
Hon Sui Sen Memorial Library
C J Koh Law Library
Medical Library
Science Library

Slovakia

Centrum Vedecko-Technickych Informaci SR
Slovak Centre of Scientific & Technical Information, Namestie slobody 19, 81223 Bratislava
Tel: (02) 5292 3527 *Fax:* (02) 5292 3527; (02) 5296 4497
E-mail: cvti@tbb5.cvtisr.sk
Web Site: www.sltk.stuba.sk
Key Personnel
Dir: Dipl Ing Jan Kurak
Deputy Dir: Vlasta Cikatricisova
Slovak Centre of Scientific & Technical Information.
Publication(s): *Bulletin Centra VTI SR* (Signale informacie); *EURO-info*; *Infotrend*

Univerzitna Kniznica
Michalska 1, 814 17 Bratislava
Tel: (02) 59 804 100 *Fax:* (02) 54 434 246
E-mail: ukb@ulib.sk

Web Site: www.ulib.sk
Key Personnel
Librarian: Emil Vontorcik, PhD
Manager: Peter Tausche
Diplomat: Julius Balogh

Univerzita Pavla Jozefa Safarika
Srobarova 2, 041 80 Kosice
Tel: (055) 622 26 08 *Fax:* (055) 766 959
E-mail: sekretr@kosice.upjs.sk; rektor@kosice.upjs.sk
Web Site: www.upjs.sk
Key Personnel
Dir: Darina Kozuchova

Slovenska Narodna Kniznica, Martin (Slovak National Library, Martin)
Nam J C Hronskeho 1, 036 01 Martin
Tel: (043) 430 18 02 *Fax:* (043) 430 18 02
E-mail: snk@snk.sk
Web Site: www.snk.sk
Key Personnel
General Dir: Dusan Katuscak
Publication(s): *Hudobny archiv* (Music Archive); *Kniha* (The Book); *Kniznica* (monthly, Libraries & scientific information); *Literarny archiv* (Literary Archive); *Slovenska narodna bibliografia* (Print, CD-ROM, monthly, Slovak National Bibliography)

Ustredna kniznica Slovenskej akademie vied (Central Library of the Slovak Academy of Sciences)
Klemensova 19, 814 67 Bratislava
Tel: (02) 52926 321; (02) 52926 325 *Fax:* (02) 52921 733
E-mail: knizhorv@klemens.savba.sk
Web Site: www.uk.sav.sk/
Key Personnel
Dir: Dr Marcela Horvathova
Manager: Andrea Doktorova *E-mail:* andrea.doktorova@savba.sk
Publication(s): *Informacny Bulletin UK SAV* (Bulletin)
Parent Company: Slovak Academy of Sciences

Slovenia

Arhiv Republike Slovenije (Archives of the Republic of Slovenia)
Zvezdarska 1, pp 21, 1127 Ljubljana
Tel: (01) 24 14 218 *Fax:* (01) 24 14 269
E-mail: ars@gov.si
Web Site: www.sigov.si/ars
Key Personnel
Dir: Vladimir Zumer *E-mail:* vladimir.zumer@gov.si
Librarian: Alenka Hren *Tel:* (01) 24 12 218
E-mail: alenka.hren@gov.si
Founded: 1859
Publication(s): *Arhivi* (Archives); *Inventarji* (Inventories); *Katalogi* (Catalogs); *Viri* (Sources); *Vodniki* (Guides)

Narodna in Univerzitetna Knjiznica, Ljubljana (National & University Library)
Turjaska 1, 1000 Ljubljana
Tel: (01) 2001 110 *Fax:* (01) 4257 293
E-mail: info@nuk.uni-lj.si
Web Site: www.nuk.uni-lj.si/vstop.cgi
Telex: 32285 *Cable:* NUK LJUBLJANA
Key Personnel
Man Dir: Mr Lenart Setinc
Secretary: Mr Borut Abram

Publication(s): *Knjiznicarske novice*; *Signalne informacije*; *Slovenska bibliografija*
Branch Office(s)
Leskoskova 12, 1000 Ljubljana *Tel:* (01) 5861 300 *Fax:* (01) 5861 311

Univerza Ljubljana
Kongresni trg 12, 1000 Ljubljana
Tel: (01) 241 85 00 *Fax:* (01) 241 86 60
Web Site: www.uni-lj.si
Telex: 32285 NUK-LJB-YU *Cable:* NUK LJUBLJANA
Key Personnel
Librarian: Lenart Setinc

Somalia

Biblioteca dell'Universita Nazionale della Somalia
PO Box 15, Mogadishu
Tel: (01) 20535

National Library of Somalia
PO Box 1754, Mogadishu
Tel: (01) 227 58

South Africa

Bloemfontein Public Library
PO Box 1029, Bloemfontein 9300
Tel: (051) 405 8248
E-mail: pat@dux.bfncouncil.co.za
Key Personnel
City Librarian: P J van der Walt

Cape Provincial Library Service
c/o Hospital & Chiappini, Cape Town 8001
Mailing Address: PO Box 2108, Cape Town 8000
Tel: (021) 483 2271 *Fax:* (021) 419 7541
E-mail: capelib@pawc.wcape.gov.za
Web Site: www.westerncape.gov.za

Cape Town City Libraries
PO Box 3541, Cape Town 8000
Tel: (021) 462 44 00 *Fax:* (021) 461 5981
Key Personnel
Contact: Mrs M Raymond

The College of Education at Wits, Harold Holmes Library
27 St Andrews Rd, Parktown, Johannesburg 2193
Mailing Address: PB X1, Johannesburg 2050
Tel: (011) 717-3242; (011) 717-3240 *Fax:* (011) 717-3046
Web Site: www.wits.ac.za/library/campuslib/edulib.htm
Key Personnel
Librarian: Mark Sandham *Tel:* (011) 717-3239
E-mail: marks@library.wits.ac.za
Deputy Librarian: Alison Chisholm
E-mail: alisonc@library.wits.ac.za

Council for Scientific & Industrial Research, see CSIR Information Services

CSIR Information Services
Meiring Naude Rd, Brummeria, Pretoria
Mailing Address: PO Box 395, Pretoria 0001
Tel: (012) 841-2911 *Fax:* (012) 349-1153
Web Site: www.csir.co.za
Telex: 32043

Key Personnel
Dir: Roy Page-Shipp *Tel:* (012) 841-3070
Manager: Colleen Mogane *Tel:* (012) 841-2557
E-mail: cmogane@csir.co.za
Scientific, technological & business information, decision support value-added services, electronic real-time access to local & international databases.

Department of Science & Technology
Oranje Nassau Bldg, 188 Schoeman St, Pretoria
Mailing Address: Private Bag X894, Pretoria 0001
Tel: (012) 317 4300 *Fax:* (012) 323 8308
Web Site: www.dst.gov.za
Key Personnel
General Dir: Dr Robert Martin Adam
Publication(s): *Library News*

East London Municipal Library
Unisa Library Depot, PO Box 652, East London 5200
Tel: (043) 724991; (043) 724992 *Fax:* (043) 7431729
Web Site: www.unisa.ac.za/library
Key Personnel
Manager: Mrs M M Davidson

Education Library & Information Services, see EDULIS (Education Library & Information Services)

EDULIS (Education Library & Information Services)
15 Kruskal Ave, Bellville 7530
Mailing Address: Private Bag X9099, Cape Town 8000
Tel: (021) 957-9600 *Fax:* (021) 948-0748
E-mail: edulis@pgwc.gov.za
Web Site: wced.wcape.gov.za
Key Personnel
Head: Mrs Lyne Metcalfe *E-mail:* lmetcalf@pgwc.gov.za
Publication(s): *RESENSIONES: RECOMMENDED CURRICULUM RESOURCE MATERIAL FOR SECONDARY PRIMARY PREPRIMA* (annually)
Parent Company: Western Cape Education Department
Ultimate Parent Company: Western Cape Provincial Administration

Ethekwini Municipal Libraries
PO Box 917, Durban 4000
Tel: (031) 311 1111 *Fax:* (031) 311 2203
Key Personnel
Acting Dir Libraries: Ms Reigneth Nyongwana

Free State Provincial Library & Information Services
Private Bag X20606, Bloemfontein 9300
Tel: (051) 4054681 *Fax:* (051) 4033567
Web Site: www.sac.fs.gov.za *Cable:* ORANVRY
Key Personnel
Senior Manager: Ms J J Schimper
E-mail: jacomien@sac.fs.gov.za
Founded: 1948
Publication(s): *Free State Libraries* (quarterly, journal)

Harold Holmes Library, see The College of Education at Wits, Harold Holmes Library

Johannesburg Public Library
Library Gardens, Corner of Fraser & Market Streets, Johannesburg 2001
Mailing Address: PB X93, Marshalltown 2107
Tel: (011) 836 3787 *Fax:* (011) 836 6607
E-mail: library@mj.org.za

Key Personnel
Librarian: E J Bevan *E-mail:* jbevan@mj.org.za
Founded: 1890
Publication(s): *Local Government Library Bulletin* (irregular)

Kempton Park Public Library
CR Swart Dr/Pretoria Rd, Kempton Park 1620
Tel: (011) 9212173 *Fax:* (011) 9750921
Key Personnel
Chief Librarian: J H van der Walt

Kimberley Public Library
Chapel St, Kimberley 8300
Mailing Address: PO Box 627, Kimberley 8300
Tel: (053) 8306241 *Fax:* (053) 8331954
E-mail: fritz@kbymun.org.za
Key Personnel
City Librarian: Mr F H van Dyke
Founded: 1878
City Public Libraries including 6 branches & 18 depots.
Parent Company: Sol Plaatje Municipality
Branch Office(s)
Africana Library *E-mail:* afrilib@global.co.za
Judy Scott Library

Kwa-Zulu Natal Provincial Library Service
PB X9016, Pietermaritzburg 3200
Tel: (033) 3940241 *Fax:* (033) 3942237
E-mail: daviess@plho.kzntl.gov.za
Telex: 643030
Key Personnel
Deputy Dir: Dr Rookaya Bawa
Contact: Janet Hart *E-mail:* hartj@natalia.kzntl.gov.za
Publication(s): *KZN Librarian* (Journal of Kwa-Zulu Natal Provincial Library Service)

Library of Parliament
NCOP Wing, Ground floor, Parliament St, Cape Town
Mailing Address: PO Box 18, Cape Town 8000
Tel: (021) 403 2140; (021) 403 2141; (021) 403 2142 *Fax:* (021) 461 4331
E-mail: library@parliament.gov.za
Web Site: www.parliament.gov.za
Key Personnel
Chief Librarian: Albert Ntunja *Tel:* (021) 403 2126 *E-mail:* antunja@parliament.gov.za
Founded: 1854

Natal Archives Depot, see State Archives Service: Natal Archives Depot

Natal Society Library
Churchill Sq, Church St, Pietermaritzburg 3200
Mailing Address: PO Box 415, Pietermaritzburg 3200
Tel: (033) 345 2383 *Fax:* (033) 394 0095
E-mail: nsl@futurenet.co.za
Web Site: www.lawlibrary.co.za
Key Personnel
Dir: Mr J C Morrison
Founded: 1851
South African journals, legal books & pamphlets, South African trade & commercial directories.
Publication(s): *Aids Bibliography* (5 vols); *Natalia* (historical journal)

National Archives of South Africa, Orange Free State Archives Repository, Library/Free State Provincial Archives
29 Badenhorst St, Bloemfontein
Mailing Address: Private Bag X20504, Bloemfontein 9300
Tel: (051) 522 6762 *Fax:* (051) 522 6765
Fax on Demand: (051) 522 6765
E-mail: fsarch@sac.fs.gov.za

Web Site: www.national.archives.gov.za
Key Personnel
Contact: Mr P F Wheeler

National Archives Repository Library
24 Hamilton St, Arcadia, Pretoria 0001
Mailing Address: Private Bag X236, Pretoria 0001
Tel: (012) 323 5300 *Fax:* (012) 323 5287
E-mail: enquiries@dac.gov.za
Web Site: www.national.archives.gov.za
Key Personnel
National Archivist: Dr G A Dominy
Founded: 1909
Parent Company: National Archives & Record Services

National Library of South Africa
5 Queen Victoria St, Cape Town
Mailing Address: PO Box 496, Cape Town 8000
Tel: (021) 424 6320 *Fax:* (021) 423 3359
E-mail: macmahon@salib.ac.za
Web Site: www.nlsa.ac.za
Key Personnel
Dir: P E Westra
Founded: 1818

National Library of South Africa
239 Vermeulen St, Pretoria
Mailing Address: PO Box 397, 0001 Pretoria
Tel: (012) 321 8931 *Fax:* (012) 325 5984
E-mail: andrew.malotle@nlsa.ac.za
Web Site: www.nlsa.ac.za
Key Personnel
Dir: Dr Peter J Lor
Publication(s): *Directory of South African Publishers*; *Index to South African Periodicals (ISAP)*; *Micrographic Series Indexes*; *Periodicals in Southern African Libraries (PISAL)*; *Public & Community Libraries Inventory of South Africa*; *SANB (South African National Bibliography)*
Parent Company: National Department of Arts & Culture

Pretoria Public Library, see Tshwane Community Library & Information Service

Rhodes University Library
PO Box 184, Grahamstown 6140
Tel: (046) 603 8436 *Fax:* (046) 6223487
E-mail: library@ru.ac.za
Web Site: www.rhodes.ac.za/library/
Key Personnel
Chief Librarian: Margaret Kenyon *Tel:* (046) 6038079 *E-mail:* m.kenyon@ru.ac.za

Royal Society of South Africa Library
P D Hahn Bldg, UCT, 8000 Cape Town
Mailing Address: PO Box 594, 8000 Cape Town
Tel: (021) 650 2543 *Fax:* (021) 650 2710
E-mail: roysoc@science.uct.ac.za
Web Site: www.rssa.uct.ac.za
Telex: 5-214-39 SA
Key Personnel
President: L R Nassimbeni
Editor: J D Skinner
Honorary Librarian: D E Rawlings
Publication(s): *Transactions of the Royal Society of South Africa* (irregular)

South African Library for the Blind
PO Box 115, Grahamstown 6140
Tel: (046) 622 7226 *Fax:* (046) 622 4645
E-mail: blindlib@iafrica.com
Web Site: www.blindlib.org.za
Key Personnel
Dir: Johan Roos *E-mail:* director@blindlib.org.za
Founded: 1918

State Archives Service: Natal Archives Depot
Private Bag X9012, Pietermaritzburg 3200
Tel: (033) 342 4712 *Fax:* (033) 394 4352
Key Personnel
Chief Archivist: J N Hawley

Transvaal Museum Library
Paul Kruger St, Pretoria 0001
Mailing Address: PO Box 413, Pretoria 0001
Tel: (012) 322 7632 *Fax:* (012) 322 7939
Web Site: www.nfi.org.za
Telex: 30302 *Cable:* TRANSATOR
Key Personnel
Head Librarian: Tersia Perregil
Librarian: Jakkie Luus
Founded: 1937
Publication(s): *Overvaal Musea, Book parade*

Tshwane Community Library & Information Service
Formerly Pretoria Public Library
Sammy Marks Square, Pretoria 0002
Mailing Address: PO Box 2673, Pretoria 0001
Tel: (012) 3088837 *Fax:* (012) 3088873
Key Personnel
Library Manager: Johannes Magoro
Founded: 1964

University of Cape Town Libraries
Upper Campus, Library Rd, 7701 Rondebosch
Tel: (021) 650-3097 *Fax:* (021) 689-7568
E-mail: webco@uctlib.uct.ac.za
Web Site: www.lib.uct.ac.za/
Telex: 5720327
Key Personnel
Librarian: A S C Hooper
Publication(s): *Bibliographical series* (irregularly); *Jagger Journal* (annually); *Varia series* (irregularly)

University of Port Elizabeth Library
Private Bag X6058, Port Elizabeth 6000
Fax: (041) 504 2280
E-mail: library@upe.ac.za
Web Site: www.upe.ac.za/library *Cable:* UNIPE
Key Personnel
Scientific Editor: Mr S J Gerber
Publication(s): *UPE Publication Series*

University of Pretoria Academic Information Services
Hillcrest, Pretoria 0002
Tel: (012) 420 2241 *Fax:* (012) 362 5100
Web Site: www.ais.up.ac.za *Cable:* PUNIV
Key Personnel
Acting Dir: Prof J A Boon *E-mail:* jaboon@up.ac.za

University of South Africa Library
PO Box 392, Pretoria 0003
Tel: (012) 4293131 *Fax:* (012) 4292925
E-mail: willej@alpha.unisa.ac.za *Cable:* UNISA PRETORIA
Key Personnel
Executive Dir: Prof J Willemse
Publication(s): *Mousaion* (in collaboration with the University of South Africa's Dept of Information Science)

University of Stellenbosch Library
Private Bag X5036, Stellenbosch 7599
Tel: (021) 808 4385 *Fax:* (021) 808 4336
Web Site: www.sun.ac.za/library
Telex: 526661
Key Personnel
Senior Dir: Prof Hennie Viljoen *Tel:* (021) 808 4880 *E-mail:* jhvi@sun.ac.za
Deputy Dir: Mr Johan Engelbrecht *Tel:* (021) 808 4878 *E-mail:* jpe@sun.ac.za
Central library of the US Library Service.

University of the Western Cape Library
Modderdam Rd, Bellville 7535
Mailing Address: Private Bag X17, Bellville 7535
Tel: (021) 959 2947 *Fax:* (021) 959 2659
Web Site: www.uwc.ac.za/library
Telex: 576661
Key Personnel
University Librarian: Ms E R Tise *E-mail:* etise@uwc.ac.za
Deputy University Librarian: Mr J S Andrea; Ms K Kekana

University of the Witwaterstrand Library
One Jan Smuts Ave, Johannesburg 2001
Mailing Address: Private Bag 31550, Braamfontein
Tel: (011) 716-2400 *Fax:* (011) 403-1421
E-mail: 056heath@libris.wwl.wits.ac.za
Telex: 422460 *Cable:* UNIWITS
Key Personnel
Librarian: H M Edwards
Founded: 1934

Spain

Biblioteca de la Agencia Espanola de Cooperacion Internacional
Ave de Reyes Catolicos 4, 28040 Madrid
Tel: (091) 5838175 *Fax:* (091) 5838525
E-mail: biblioteca.hispanica@aeci.es
Web Site: www.aeci.es
Library of the Institute of Spanish-American Fellowship.

Archivo de la Corona de Aragon
Calle Almogaveres 77, 08018 Barcelona
Tel: (093) 4854 318; (093) 4854 285; (093) 3153 208 *Fax:* (093) 3001 252
E-mail: aca@cult.mec.es
Web Site: www.cultura.mecd.es/archivos/index.html
Key Personnel
Dir: Rafael Conde y Delgado de Molina
Royal Archives of Aragon.
Publication(s): Coleccion de Documentos Ineditos del Archivo de la Corona de Aragon (from 1847)

Archivo General de Indias
Avda de la Constitucion 3, 41071 Seville
Mailing Address: Edificio de la Cilla, Calle Santo Tomas 5, 41071 Seville
Tel: (05) 954 500 530; (05) 954 500 528 *Fax:* 954 219 485
E-mail: agi1@cult.mec.es
Web Site: www.cultura.mecd.es; www.mcu.es
Key Personnel
Contact: Rosario Parra Cala
Archives of the Indies.
Parent Company: Ministerio de Educacion, Cultura y Deporte

Archivo Historico Nacional
Calle Serrano 115, 28006 Madrid
Tel: (091) 7688 500 *Fax:* (091) 5631 199
Web Site: ahn.cult.mec.es
Founded: 1866
National Historical Archives; indexed genealogical records from the 15th to the 19th century.
Parent Company: Ministerio de Educacion, Cultura y Deporte

Archivo y Biblioteca Capitulares
Catedral de Toledo, Hombre de Palo, 2, 45001 Toledo
Tel: (0925) 21 24 23 *Fax:* (0925) 21 24 23
E-mail: archicapto@terra.es
Web Site: www.architoledo.org/catedral/archivos/textoarchivo.htm
Key Personnel
Dir: Dr Angel Fernandez Collado; Dr Ramon Gonzalvez
Archives & Library of the Cathedral Chapter.

Biblioteca Bergnes de las Casas - Bibioteca de Catalunya
Carrer de l'Hospital, 56, 08001 Barcelona
Tel: (093) 270 23 00 *Fax:* (093) 270 23 04
E-mail: bustia@bnc.es
Web Site: www.gencat.es/bc
Key Personnel
Librarian: Maria Artal
Library attached to Biblioteca de Catalunya.

The British Council Library
Pº General Martinez Campos 31, 28010 Madrid
Tel: (091) 337 3500 *Fax:* (091) 337 3573
E-mail: madrid@britishcouncil.es
Web Site: www.britishcouncil.es
Key Personnel
Contact: Antonia Dominguez

Biblioteca de Catalunya
Carrer of l'Hospital, 56, 08001 Barcelona
Tel: (093) 270 23 00 *Fax:* (093) 270 23 04
E-mail: bustia@bnc.es
Web Site: www.gencat.es/bc
Key Personnel
Dir: Mrs Vinyet Panyella
Chief of Difussion Area: Montserrat Fonoll *E-mail:* mfonoll@bnc.es
National Library of Catalonia.
Publication(s): Nota Bene (bimonthly, information bulletin of the biblioteca de Catalunya)

Biblioteca General de Humanidades Consejo Superior de Investigaciones Cientificas
(Spanish Council for Scientific Research)
Duque de Medinaceli, 6 planta baja, 28014 Madrid
Tel: (091) 360 18 10; (091) 360 18 12 *Fax:* (091) 369 09 40
E-mail: bghpre@bib.csic.es
Web Site: www.csic.es/cbic/BGH/bgh.htm
Key Personnel
Library Dir: Carmen M Perez-Montes Salmeron *E-mail:* carmela@bib.csic.es
Library of the Council for Scientific Research.
Parent Company: Ministerio de Educacion y Ciencia

Fundacion Esade
Marques de Mulhacen, 40-42, 08034 Barcelona
Tel: (093) 280 61 62 *Fax:* (093) 204 81 05
Web Site: www.esade.es/biblio
Telex: 98286
Key Personnel
Head Librarian: Francisca Buxo *E-mail:* buxo@esade.edu

Hemeroteca Municipal de Madrid
Calle Conde Duque 9-11, 28015 Madrid
Tel: (091) 588 57 74
Key Personnel
Director: Carlos Dorado Fernandez
Madrid Periodical Library.

Biblioteca y Casa - Museo de Menendez Pelayo
Rubio 6, 39003 Santander
Tel: (042) 23 45 34
E-mail: xjagenjo@sarenet.es
Web Site: www.turcantabria.com
Key Personnel
Librarian: Manuel Revuelta Sanudo
Publication(s): Boletin de la Biblioteca de Menendez Pelayo (annually); *Estudios de literatura y pensamiento hispanicos* (series); *La Biblioteca de Menendez Pelayo*

Biblioteca Nacional
Paseo de Recoletos 20, Madrid 28071
Tel: (091) 580 7800
Web Site: www.bne.es; www.mec.es
Key Personnel
Dir: Alicia Giron Garcia
Parent Company: Ministerio de Education, Cultura y Deporte

Patrimonio Nacional, Real Biblioteca
Palacio Real, Calle Bailen s/n, 28071 Madrid
Tel: (091) 454 87 00; (091) 454 87 32 *Fax:* (091) 454 87 21
E-mail: realbiblioteca@patrimonionacional.es
Web Site: www.patrimonionacional.es
Key Personnel
Dir: Maria Luisa Lopez-Vidriero *E-mail:* lvidriero@patrimonionacional.es
Library of the Royal Palace.

Servei de Biblioteques de la UAB
Universitat Autonoma de Barcelona, Edifici N, 08193 Bellaterra, Cerdanyola del Valles
Tel: (093) 581 1015 *Fax:* (093) 581 3219
E-mail: bib.utp@uab.es; s.biblioteques@uab.es
Web Site: www.bib.uab.es; www.uab.es
Telex: 52040 EDVCIE
Key Personnel
Dir: Joan Gomez Escofet *Tel:* (093) 581 10 71 *E-mail:* joan.gomez.escofet@uab.es
Deputy Librarian: Nuria Balague *E-mail:* nuria.balague@uab.es
Publication(s): Biblioteca Informacions

Servicio de Biblioteca
Hospital de Cruces, Apdo 69, 48080 Bilbao
Tel: (04) 6006125 *Fax:* (04) 6006049
E-mail: biblioteca.cruces@hcru.osakidetza.net
Web Site: www.osakidetza-svs.org
Service in information & scientific documentation in health sciences.
Publication(s): Catalogo Publicaciones y Series Periodicas Medicina

Universidad Autonoma - Biblioteca Universitaria
Carretera de Colmenar Viejo, Km 15, 28049 Madrid
Tel: (091) 3974399 *Fax:* (091) 3975058
E-mail: servicio.biblioteca@uam.es
Web Site: www.uam.es
Key Personnel
Contact: Maria Sintes *E-mail:* msintes@uam.es

Biblioteca de la Universidad Complutense
Cuidad Universitaria, 28040 Madrid
Tel: (091) 394 69 25; (091) 394 69 39 *Fax:* (091) 394 69 26
E-mail: bucweb@buc.ucm.es
Web Site: www.ucm.es/BUCM
Key Personnel
Dir: Jose Antonio Magan Wals *E-mail:* magan@buc.ucm.es
Head Librarian: Ana Delgado Perez

Universidad de Cantabria Biblioteca
Ave de Los Castros s/n, 39005 Santander
Tel: (0942) 201 180 *Fax:* (0942) 201 183
Web Site: www.buc.unican.es
Key Personnel
Dir: Javier Martinez *E-mail:* pvier.martinez@gastion.unican.es

Universidad Pontificia de Salamanca, Biblioteca
Compania 5, 37002 Salamanca
Tel: (0923) 277 118 *Fax:* (0923) 277 118
E-mail: bibliotecario.general@upsa.es
Web Site: www.upsa.es/biblioteca.html

Biblioteca de la Universitat de Barcelona
Baldiri Reixac 2, 08028 Barcelona
Tel: (093) 403 45 89 *Fax:* (093) 403 45 92
E-mail: sbib@org.ub.es
Web Site: www.bib.ub.es
Key Personnel
Dir: Dolors Lamarca *Tel:* (093) 403 57 15
 Fax: (093) 403 47 57 *E-mail:* dlamarca@ub.edu
Publication(s): Memoria; Red de Bibliothecas Universitarias

Sri Lanka

British Council Information Resource Centre
49 Alfred House Gardens, Colombo 3
Mailing Address: PO Box 753, Colombo 3
Tel: (01) 581171 *Fax:* (01) 587079
E-mail: enquiries@britishcouncil.lk
Web Site: www.britishcouncil.lk
Key Personnel
Dir: Tony O'Brien
Deputy Dir: Anna Searle
Library & Information Services Manager: Ranmali de Silva *E-mail:* library@britishcouncil.uk
Founded: 1949
Branch Office(s)
88/3 Kotugodella Veediya, Kandy, Branch Manager: Alison Markwick *Tel:* (081) 2222410; (081) 2234634 *Fax:* (081) 2234284 *E-mail:* bckandy@britishcouncil.lk

Colombo Public Library
No 15, Sir Marcus Fernando Mawatha, Colombo 07
Tel: (011) 2691968; (011) 2695156; (011) 2696530 *Fax:* (011) 2691968
Web Site: www.cmc.lk/library.asp
Key Personnel
Chief Librarian: Mr M D H Jayawardhana
Founded: 1925
Publication(s): Libraries & People: A Manual for Public Libraries in Sri Lanka; Road to Wisdom; Glimpses of Colombo
Parent Company: Colombo Municipal Council

Department of National Archives
Reid Ave, Colombo 7
Mailing Address: PO Box 1414, Colombo 7
Tel: (01) 694523; (01) 696917 *Fax:* (01) 694419
E-mail: narchive@slt.lk
Web Site: www.mca.gov.lk *Cable:* ARCHIVES
Key Personnel
Dir: Dr K D G Wimalaratne
Parent Company: Ministry of Cultural Affairs

Industrial Technology Institute Information Services Centre
363 Bauddhaloka Mawatha, Colombo 7
Tel: (01) 693807; (01) 693808; (01) 693809; (01) 698621; (01) 698622; (01) 698623
 Fax: (01) 686567
E-mail: info@iti.lk
Web Site: www.iti.lk *Cable:* CISIR
Key Personnel
Dir: Dr A M Mubarak *Tel:* (01) 691614
 E-mail: dir_ceo@iti.lk
Manager, Information Services: Dilmani Warnasuriya *E-mail:* dilmani@iti.lk
Founded: 1955

National Library & Documentation Centre
No 14, Independence Ave, Colombo 07
Tel: (01) 6852003; (01) 685199; (01) 698847
 Fax: (01) 685201
E-mail: natlib@sltnet.lk
Web Site: www.natlib.lk

Key Personnel
Chairman: Prof T Kariyawasam *E-mail:* ch@mail.natlib.lk
Dir General: Mr M S U Amarasiri *Tel:* (01) 687581 *E-mail:* dg@mail.natlib.lk
Founded: 1970
Publication(s): Directory of Social Science Libraries, Information Centres & Data Bases in Sri Lanka; International Standard Book Numbering in Sri Lanka (brochure); *Library News* (quarterly); *Sri Lanka Conference Index, 1976-1986, 1987-1990, 1991-1992* (Sri Lanka Newspaper article Index-1993); *Sri Lanka (ISBN) Publishers Directory, 1991 edition; Sri Lanka National Bibliography* (monthly)

National Museum Library of Sri Lanka (NMLSL)
Sir Marcus Fernando Mawatha, Colombo 07
Mailing Address: PO Box 854, Colombo 07
Tel: (01) 692092 *Fax:* (01) 695366
E-mail: cnmid@sltnet.lk
Web Site: www.mca.gov.lk
Key Personnel
Dir: Mrs N A Wikramasingha
See also Department of National Museums (Publisher).
Publication(s): Spolia Zeylanica: Bulletin of the National Museums of Sri Lanka; Sri Lanka Periodicals Index; Ceylon Periodicals Directory (Annual Supplements)
Parent Company: Ministry of Cultural Affairs

NMLSL, see National Museum Library of Sri Lanka (NMLSL)

University of Peradeniya Library
University Park, Peradeniya 20400
Mailing Address: PO Box 35, Peradeniya
Tel: (08) 388678 *Fax:* (08) 388678
E-mail: lib@mail.pdn.ac.lk
Web Site: www.pdn.ac.lk/library/main
Key Personnel
Librarian: N T S A Senadeera *E-mail:* lib@mail.pdn.ac.lk
Founded: 1921
Publication(s): Ceylon Journal of Science: Biological Sciences (irregularly, academic journal); *Ceylon Journal of Science: Physical Sciences* (irregularly, academic journal); *Modern Sri Lanka Studies* (irregularly, academic journal); *Sri Lanka Journals of the Humanities* (irregularly, academic journal)

Sudan

ACADI, see Arab Organization for Agricultural Development

Al-Neelain University
Affiliate of Ministry of Higher Education & Scientific Research
PO Box 12702, Khartoum
Tel: (011) 880055 *Fax:* (011) 776338
E-mail: neelain@an.mail.com
Telex: 23027 NILUN SD B
Founded: 1992
Academic teaching & lecturing.

AOAD, see Arab Organization for Agricultural Development

Arab Center for Agricultural Documentation, see Arab Organization for Agricultural Development

Arab Organization for Agricultural Development
St No 7, Al Alamarat, Khartoum
Mailing Address: PO Box 474, Khartoum
Tel: (011) 472176; (011) 472183 *Fax:* (011) 471402
E-mail: inquiry@aoad.org
Web Site: www.aoad.org
Telex: 22554 AOAD SD *Cable:* AOAD KHARTOUM
Key Personnel
Dir General: Dr Yahia Bakour

British Council Library
14 Abu Sinn St, Khartoum
Mailing Address: PO Box 1253, Khartoum
Tel: (0183) 780817; (0183) 777310 *Fax:* (0183) 774935
E-mail: info@sd.britishcouncil.org
Web Site: www.britishcouncil.org/sudan
Telex: 23114 Bckht Sd
Key Personnel
Dir: Paul Doubleday *E-mail:* paul.doubleday@sd.britishcouncil.org
Librarian: Ali Hassan Salih

Khartoum Polytechnic Library
PO Box 407, Khartoum
Tel: 78922
Key Personnel
Librarian: Mohammad Bakheit

National Records Office Library
PO Box 1914, Khartoum
Tel: (011) 784135; (011) 784255 *Fax:* (011) 778603
Key Personnel
Librarian: Abdel Aziz Gabir Mohamed
Founded: 1949

Omdurman Islamic University
PO Box 382, Omdurman 14415
Tel: 784348; 784365; 554272 *Fax:* 775253
Web Site: www.sudanembassy.org/contemporarylooks/umdurman.htm
Telex: 22527
Founded: 1921

University of Khartoum Library
PO Box 321, Khartoum
Web Site: www.sudan.net/uk
Key Personnel
Librarian: Dr Mohammed Nouri Al/Amin
Assistant Dir: Asma Ibrahim Al-Iman

Suriname

Bibliotheek Cultureel Centrum Suriname
Gravenstr 112-114, Paramaribo
Mailing Address: PO Box 1241, Paramaribo
Tel: 472369; 473309 *Fax:* 476516
E-mail: sccs@sr.net; stgccs1947@hotmail.com
Key Personnel
Dir: Johan Roozer
Founded: 1947
Library of the Cultural Centre Suriname.

Swaziland

Swaziland College of Technology Library
PO Box 69, Mbabane 14100
Tel: (040) 42681; (040) 43539 *Fax:* (040) 44521
E-mail: scotlibrary@africaonline.co.sz

Founded: 1946
Parent Company: Ministry of Education

Swaziland National Library Service
PO Box 1461, Mbabane
Tel: 42633 *Fax:* 43863
E-mail: snlssz@realnet.co.sz
Web Site: www.library.ohiou.edu/subjects/swaziland/snls.htm
Telex: 2270 Wd
Key Personnel
Dir: D Kunene *E-mail:* dijkunene@realnet.co.sz
Senior Librarian: Nomsa V Mkhwanazi *Tel:* 404 2633; 404 2757 *E-mail:* nomkhwa@realnet.co.sz
Librarian: N Fakudze *E-mail:* nqfakudze@realnet.co.sz

University of Swaziland Library
Private Bag 4, Kwaluseni
Tel: (051) 84011; (051) 85108 *Fax:* (051) 85276
E-mail: kwaluseni@uniswa.sz
Web Site: library.uniswa.sz
Telex: 2087 WD
Key Personnel
Librarian: Ms Makana R Mavuso
E-mail: mmavuso@uniswacc.uniswa.sz
Publication(s): *Serials in Swaziland University Libraries* (irregularly); *Swaziland National Bibliography* (irregularly)

Sweden

Goteborgs Stadsbibliotek
PO Box 5404, SE-40227 Gothenburg
Tel: (031) 61-65-00 *Fax:* (031) 61-66-93
Key Personnel
Contact: Anna Petren-Kihlstrom
City Library and County Library.

Goeteborgs Universitetsbibliotek
Centralbiblioteket, Renstroemsgatan 4, 405 30 Gothenburg
Mailing Address: Box 222, 40530 Gothenburg
Tel: (031) 7731000 *Fax:* (031) 16 37 97
E-mail: library@ub.gu.se
Web Site: www.ub.gu.se
Key Personnel
Librarian: Jon Erik Nordstrand *Tel:* (031) 773 1760
Publication(s): *Acta Bibliothecae Universitatis Gothoburgensis* (irregularly); *New Literature on Women. A Bibliography* (quarterly)

Kungl Tekniska Hoegskolan Biblioteket (Royal Institute of Technology Library)
Osquars backe 31, 100 44 Stockholm
Tel: (08) 790 7088 *Fax:* (08) 790 7122
E-mail: loandept@lib.kth.se
Web Site: www.lib.kth.se
Publication(s): *Stockholm Papers in History & Philosophy of Science & Technology*

Kungliga Biblioteket
Box 5039, 102 41 Stockholm
Tel: (08) 463 40 00 *Fax:* (08) 463 40 04
E-mail: kungl.biblioteket@kb.se
Web Site: www.kb.se
Key Personnel
National Librarian: Gunnar Sahlin
E-mail: gunnar.sahlin@kb.se
The Royal Library - National Library of Sweden.
Publication(s): *Acta Bibliothecae Regiae Stockholmiensis*; *Bibliography of Swedish Sheet Music* (On Line only); *Kungl Bibliotekets Utstaellningskatalog*; *Rapport*; *Suecana Extranea* (On Line only); *Svensk Bokfoerteckning* (On Line only); *Svensk Musikfoerteckning* (On Line only); *Svensk Periodicafoerteckning* (On Line only)

Lunds Universitets Bibliotek
Tornavaegen 9B, Lund
Mailing Address: PO Box 134, 221 00 Lund
Tel: (046) 222 00 00 *Fax:* (046) 222 36 82
E-mail: lub@lub.lu.se
Web Site: www.lub.lu.se
Key Personnel
Dir: Lars Bjornshauge *E-mail:* lars.bjornshauge@lub.lu.se
Senior Administrative Officer: Berit Nilsson *Tel:* (046) 222 92 04 *E-mail:* berit.nilsson@lub.lu.se
Publication(s): *Scripta Academica*

Malmoe Stadsbibliotek
Kung Oscars vaeg, 211 33 Malmoe
Tel: (040) 660 8500 *Fax:* (040) 660 8681
E-mail: info@mail.stadsbibliotek.org
Web Site: www2.malmo.stadsbibliotek.org
Key Personnel
Librarian: Ulla Brohed *Tel:* (040) 660 8680 *E-mail:* ulla.brohed@mail.stadsbibliotek.org; Gunilla Konradsson Mortin
City Library, Lending Centre for Southern & Western Sweden.

Riksarkivet
Fyrverkarbacken 13-17, 102 29 Stockholm
Mailing Address: PO Box 125 41, 102 29 Stockholm
Tel: (08) 737 63 50 *Fax:* (08) 737 64 74
E-mail: registry@riksarkivet.ra.se
Web Site: www.ra.se
National Record Office, National Archives of Sweden.

Statistics Sweden Library
Karlavaegen 100, 104 51 Stockholm
Mailing Address: Box 24 300, 104 51 Stockholm
Tel: (08) 506 940 00 *Fax:* (08) 661 5261
E-mail: scb@scb.se
Web Site: www.scb.se
Key Personnel
Chief Librarian: Rolf-Allan Norrmosse
Library of Statistics Sweden.
Publication(s): *Statistics from Individual Countries: National Statistics from Sweden and other Countries*; *Statistics from International Organizations and other (issuing) Bodies*

Stockholms Stadsbibliotek
Sveavaegen 73, 113 80 Stockholm
Tel: (08) 508 31 100 *Fax:* (08) 508 31 007
E-mail: info.ssb@kultur.stockholm.se
Web Site: www.ssb.stockholm.se
Telex: 19478
Key Personnel
City Librarian: Inga Lunden *E-mail:* inga.lunden@kultur.stockholm.se
City Library of Stockholm.

Stockholms Universitetsbibliotek
Universitetsvaegen 10, 106 91 Stockholm
Tel: (08) 16 28 00 *Fax:* (08) 15 77 76
Web Site: www.sub.su.se
Key Personnel
Head of Information & IT Department: Gunilla Lilie Bauer *Tel:* (08) 162747 *E-mail:* gunilla.lilie.bauer@sub.swe
Librarian: Gunnar Sahlin
This library incorporates the Library of the Royal Swedish Academy of Sciences (Kungliga Svenska Vetenskapsakadamiens Bibliotek) covering humanities, law, social sciences, mathematics & natural sciences, psychology & education.
Publication(s): *Stockholms universitetsbibliotek Rapport*

Svenska Barnboksinstitutet
Odengatan 61, 113 22 Stockholm
Tel: (08) 54 54 20 50 *Fax:* (08) 54 54 20 54
E-mail: info@sbi.kb.se; biblioteket@sbi.kb.se
Web Site: www.sbi.kb.se
Key Personnel
Dir: Sonja Svensson *E-mail:* sonja.svensson@sbi.kb.se
Head Librarian: Cecilia Ostlund *E-mail:* cecilia.ostlund@sbi.kb.se
Founded: 1965
Swedish Institute for Children's Books.
Publication(s): *Barnboken: Svenska Barnboksinstitutets Tidskrift* (ISSN 0347-772X) (biennually, 1978, English Summary)

Sveriges Lantbruksuniversitets Bibliotek
Undervisningsplan 10, 750 07 Uppsala
Mailing Address: Box 7071, 750 07 Uppsala
Tel: (018) 67 10 00 *Fax:* (018) 67 28 53
E-mail: infosok@bibul.slu.se
Web Site: www.bib.slu.se
Telex: 76062
Key Personnel
Dir: Sten F Vedi
Librarian: Bruno Johnsson *Tel:* (090) 786 65 58 *Fax:* (090) 786 59 25 *E-mail:* bruno.johnsson@bibum.slu.se
Libraries of the Swedish University of Agricultural Sciences.

Umea University Library
Samhaellsvetarhuset, 901 74 Umea
Tel: (090) 786 5693 *Fax:* (090) 786 6677
E-mail: laneexp@ub.unu.se; www.bibliotekschefen@ub.umu.se
Web Site: www.ub.umu.se
Key Personnel
Librarian: Lars-Ake Idahl *Tel:* (090) 786 9680 *E-mail:* lars-ake.idahl@ub.umu.se

Uppsala Universitetsbibliotek
Dag Hammarskjoelds vaeg 1, 751 20 Uppsala
Mailing Address: Box 510, 751 20 Uppsala
Tel: (018) 471 39 00
Web Site: www.ub.uu.se
Key Personnel
Librarian: Thomas Tottie
Publication(s): *Acta Bibliothecae R Universitatis Upsaliensis*; *Scripta Minora Bibliothecae R Universitatis Upsaliensis*; *Uppsala Universitetsbiblioteks Utstaellningskataloger*

Switzerland

Bibliotheca Bodmeriana (Fondation Martin Bodmer)
19-21, route du Guignard, 1223 Cologny
Mailing Address: CP 7, 1223 Cologny
Tel: (022) 707 44 33 *Fax:* (022) 707 44 30
E-mail: emacheret@fondationbodmer.ch
Web Site: www.unige.ch/biblio
Key Personnel
Dir: Dr Martin Bircher
Founded: 1972

Bibliotheque Cantonale et Universitaire de Lausanne
Pl de la Riponne 6, 1015 & 1003 Lausanne
Tel: (021) 3167880 *Fax:* (021) 3167870
Web Site: www.unil.ch/BCU
Key Personnel
Dir: Hubert Villard
Vice Dir: Silvia Kimmeier

SWITZERLAND

Bibliotheque Cantonale et Universitaire (Kantons- und Universitatsbibliothek)
Rue Joseph Piller 2, 1700 Fribourg
Tel: (026) 305 13 33 *Fax:* (026) 305 13 77
E-mail: bcu@fr.ch
Web Site: www.fr.ch/bcu/
Key Personnel
Dir: Martin Good *Tel:* (026) 305 13 05
 E-mail: goodm@fr.ch

Bibliotheque de la Ville, see Bibliotheque Publique et Universitaire de Neuchatel

Bibliotheque nationale suisse, see Schweizerische Landesbibliothek (Bibliotheque nationale suisse)

Bibliotheque Publique et Universitaire de Geneve (Geneva Public & University Library)
Promenade des Bastions, PO Box, 1211 Geneva 4
Tel: (022) 418 28 00 *Fax:* (022) 418 28 01
E-mail: info.bpu@ville-ge.ch
Web Site: www.ville-ge.ch/bpu/
Key Personnel
Dir: Alain L Jacquesson *Tel:* (022) 418 28 28
 E-mail: alain.jacquesson@bpu.ville-ge.ch
Founded: 1562
Publication(s): *Compte rendu* (annually)

Bibliotheque Publique et Universitaire de Neuchatel
rue Numa-Droz 3, 2000 Neuchatel
Tel: (032) 717-73-00; (032) 717 73 20 *Fax:* (032) 717-73-09
Web Site: bpun.unine.ch; rcbn.unine.ch
Key Personnel
Dir: Michel Schlup *E-mail:* michael.schlup@unine.ch
Publication(s): *Ville de Neuchatel: Bibliotheques et Musees* (annually)

Bureau International du Travail, see International Labour Office, Bureau of Library & Information Services

ETH- Bibliothek (Eidgenossische Technische Hochschule Bibliothek)
Raemistr 101, 8092 Zurich
Mailing Address: Post Box, 8092 Zurich
Tel: (01) 632 21 35 *Fax:* (01) 632 30 13
E-mail: info@library.ethz.ch
Web Site: www.ethbib.ethz.ch
Key Personnel
Dir: Dr Wolfram Neubauer *Tel:* (01) 632 25 49
 E-mail: neubauer@library.ethz.ch
Head, Collection Development: Dr Karin Assmann *Tel:* (01) 632 21 24 *E-mail:* assmann@library.ethz.ch
Library of the Swiss Federal Institute of Technology Zurich.
Parent Company: ETH Zurich (Swiss Federal Institute of Technology Zurich)

ILO, see International Labour Office, Bureau of Library & Information Services

International Labour Office, Bureau of Library & Information Services
4, route des Morillons, 1211 Geneva 22
Tel: (022) 799 8675 *Fax:* (022) 799 6516
E-mail: inform@ilo.org
Web Site: www.ilo.org/inform
Publication(s): *ILO Manual for Labour Information Centers (1992)* (available in English, French or Spanish); *ILO Thesaurus 1998: Labour, Employment & Training Terminology* (in English, French & Spanish); *Labordoc* (data base in English, French & Spanish)

Oeffentliche Bibliothek der Universitaet Basel (Public Library of Basel University)
Schoenbeinstr 18-20, 4056 Basel
Tel: (061) 267 3100 *Fax:* (061) 267 3103
E-mail: sekretariat-ub@unibas.ch
Web Site: www.ub.unibas.ch
Key Personnel
Dir: Hannes Hug *Tel:* (061) 267 3131
Founded: 1471
Publication(s): *Jahresbericht* (Occasional Papers & Indexes in the Series Publikationen der Universitaetsbibliothek)
Branch Office(s)
Medizinbibliothek, Hebelstr 20, 4031 Basel
WWZ-Bibliothek, Petersgraben 51, 4051 Basel

Schweizerische Landesbibliothek (Bibliotheque nationale suisse)
Division of Federal Office of Culture
Hallwylstr 15, 3003 Bern
Tel: (031) 322 89 11; (031) 3228979 (Lending Dept); (031) 3228935 (Information) *Fax:* (031) 322 84 63
E-mail: IZ-Helvetica@slb.admin.ch
Web Site: www.snl.ch
Key Personnel
Dir: Dr Jean-Frederic Jauslin
Swiss National Library.
Publication(s): *Das Schweizer Buch* (national bibliography); *The Swiss National Library*

Schweizerisches Bundesarchiv (Swiss Federal Archives)
Archivstr 24, 3003 Bern
Tel: (031) 322 89 89 *Fax:* (031) 322 78 23
E-mail: bundesarchiv@bar.admin.ch
Web Site: www.bundesarchiv.ch
Key Personnel
Contact: Hans von Ruette *E-mail:* hans.vonruette@bar.admin.ch
Founded: 1798

Schweizerisches Wirtschaftsarchiv (Archives Economiques Suisses)
Petersgraben 51, 4003 Basel
Tel: (061) 267 32 19 *Fax:* (061) 267 32 08
E-mail: info-wwzb@unibas.ch
Web Site: www.ub.unibas.ch/wwz
Key Personnel
Dir: Johanna Gisler *E-mail:* gisler@ubaclu.unibas.ch
Founded: 1910
Swiss Economic Archives.

Stadt- und Universitaetsbibliothek (Municipal & University Library of Berne)
Munstergasse 61, 3011 Berne
Mailing Address: Postfach, 3000 Berne
Tel: (031) 3203211 *Fax:* (031) 3203299
E-mail: info@stub.unibe.ch
Web Site: www.stub.unibe.ch
Key Personnel
Dir: Prof Robert Barth *Tel:* (031) 320 3201
 E-mail: robert.barth@stub.unibe.ch
Vice Dir: Anton Buchli *Tel:* (031) 320-3202
 E-mail: anton.buchli@stub.unibe.ch
Founded: 1528

Stiftsbibliothek (Abbey Library of St Gall)
Klosterhof 6d, 9004 St Gallen
Mailing Address: Postfach, 9004 St Gallen
Tel: (071) 227 34 16 *Fax:* (071) 227 34 18
E-mail: stibi@stibi.ch
Web Site: www.stibi.ch
Key Personnel
Librarian: Theres Flury *Tel:* (071) 227 34 17
 E-mail: theres.flury@kk-stibi.sg.ch; Prof Ernst Tremp
Historical library with a unique collection of early medieval manuscripts.

United Nations Library
Palais des Nations, 1211 Geneva 10
Tel: (022) 917 41 81 *Fax:* (022) 917 04 18
E-mail: library@unog.ch
Web Site: www.unog.ch/library
Telex: 412962

Universitat Zentralbibliothek Zuerich
Zaehringerplatz 6, 8025 Zurich
Tel: (01) 2683100 *Fax:* (01) 2683290
E-mail: zb@zb.unizh.ch
Web Site: www-zb.unizh.ch
Key Personnel
Dir: Dr Hermann Koestler *E-mail:* Hermann.Koestler@zb.unizh.ch
Vice-Dir: Christoph Meyer *E-mail:* christoph.meyer@zb.unizh.ch

Syrian Arab Republic

Al Maktabah Al Wataniah
Bab El-Faradj, Aleppo
Key Personnel
Librarian: Younis Roshdi
Founded: 1924
National Library.

Assad National Library
Malki St, Damascus
Mailing Address: PO Box 3639, Damascus
Tel: (011) 3320803 *Fax:* (011) 3320804
E-mail: contact@alassad-library.com
Web Site: www.alassad.library.com
Telex: 419134
Key Personnel
Librarian: Ghassan Lahham
Founded: 1984
Publication(s): *Analytical Index to Syrian Periodicals*; *List of Syrian Dissertations*; *Syrian National Bibliography*

Damascus University Library
Damascus University Library, Damascus, Baramkah
Tel: (011) 2215104; (011) 2215101 *Fax:* (011) 2236010
E-mail: info@damascus-online.com
Web Site: www.damascus-online/university.htm
Telex: 411971
Key Personnel
Contact: Nizar Oyoun El-Soud
Publication(s): *Bibliography of the Middle East*

Public Library of Latakia
Latakia, Syria
Key Personnel
Dir: Mohamad Ali Nitayfi

Al Zahiriah
Damascus
Tel: (011) 112813
National Library.

Taiwan, Province of China

Bureau of International Exchange of Publications
National Central Library, 20 Chungshan South Rd, Taipei
Tel: (02) 23169132 *Fax:* (02) 23110155
E-mail: shiny@msg.ncl.edu.tw
Web Site: www.ncl.edu.tw
Key Personnel
Bureau Chief: Teresa Wang Chang
   E-mail: teresa@msg.ncl.edu.tu
Publication(s): *Chinese Cultural Organizations Directory*; *National Central Library Newsletter*

Fu Ssu-Nien Library, Institute of History & Philology, Academia Sinica
Nankang, Taipei 11529
Tel: (02) 27829555 *Fax:* (02) 27868834
E-mail: fsndb@pluto.ihp.sinica.edu.tw
Web Site: www.saturn.ihp.sinica.edu.tw/~fsnlib
Key Personnel
Dir: Juei-hsiu Wu

National Central Library
20 Chung Shan S Rd, Taipei 100-01
Tel: (02) 2361 9132 *Fax:* (02) 382 1489
Web Site: www.ncl.edu.tw
Key Personnel
Dir: Dr Juang Fang-Rung
Founded: 1933
Publication(s): *Index to Chinese Periodical Literature*; *National Bibliography of the Republic of China*; *National Union List of Chinese Periodicals of the Republic of China*; *Union Catalog of Books in the Republic of China*; *Yearbook of Libraries in the Republic of China*

National Taiwan University Library
One Sec 4, Roosevelt Rd, Taipei 106
Tel: (02) 3366-2326
E-mail: tul@ntu.edu.tw
Web Site: www.lib.ntu.edu.tw
Key Personnel
Dir: Jieh Hsiang
Founded: 1915
Publication(s): *An Atlas Plants from the Tanaka Collection at National Taiwan Univeristy Library*; *Bibliography of the Works of Dr Tyozaburo Tanaka*; *Catalog of Chinese Stitched Binding Books in the National Taiwan University*; *Catalog of National Taiwan University Publications* (1946-1985); *Catalog of the Tanaka Collection at National Taiwan University Library*; *Ino Kanori & Taiwan Studies* (a special exhibition of Ino Collections); *List of Publications of the Faculty & Staff of the National Taiwan University Theses & Dissertations* (1959-1985); *National Taiwan University Catalog of Old Japanese Materials on Taiwan Studies*; *National Taiwan University Catalog of Rare Books Title Index*; *National Taiwan University Catalog of Rare Rooks*; *National Taiwan University College of Law Catalog of Old Japanese Materials on Taiwan Studies*; *National Taiwan University Library Newsletter* (monthly, newsletter); *National Taiwan University List of Serials in Chinese, Japanese & Korean Languages*; *National Taiwan University Union List of Collected Mainland Periodicals*; *Supplement & Index Report on the Present Status of Documents on Taiwanese History at the National Taiwan University*; *University Library Journal* (semiannually)

National War College Library
Yangmingshan, Taipei
Tel: (02) 3619132 *Fax:* (02) 3110155
Key Personnel
Contact: Lo Mou-pin

Sun Yat-sen Library
2F, 505 Jen-ai Rd, Sec 4, Taipei
Tel: (02) 2758 2045 *Fax:* (02) 2729 7030

Taiwan Branch Library, National Central Library
One Hsinshen S Rd, Section 1, Taipei 106
Mailing Address: PO Box 106, Taipei 106
Tel: (02) 771 8528
Key Personnel
Library Dir: Wei-jei Lin
Librarian: Hui-Hsien Jill Yu
Founded: 1915
List of Nonchinese serials of National Central Library Taiwan Branch.
Publication(s): *Catalog on China in Western Languages*; *N C L Taiwan Branch Bulletin*; *Southeast Asia Catalog*

Tajikistan

Gousudarstvennaja Biblioteka Respublika Tadzkistan im Firdousi
Rudaki 36, 734025 Dushanbe
Tel: (03772) 274 726
Key Personnel
Librarian: S Goibnazarov
Founded: 1933

United Republic of Tanzania

British Council Library
Samora Ave, Ohio St, Dar Es Salaam
Mailing Address: PO Box 9100, Dar Es Salaam
Tel: (022) 2116574; (022) 2118255; (022) 2138303; (022) 2116575; (022) 2116576 *Fax:* (022) 2112669; (022) 2116577
E-mail: info@britishcouncil.or.tz
Web Site: www.britishcouncil.org/tanzania
Telex: 41719 *Cable:* BRICO
Key Personnel
Librarian: Oreste Makafu

Eastern & Southern African Management Institute (ESAMI)
PO Box 3030, Arusha
Tel: (027) 250-8384; (027) 250-8388 *Fax:* (027) 250-8285
E-mail: esamihq@habari.co.tz
Web Site: www.esamihq.org
Telex: 42076
Key Personnel
Assistant Serials Librarian: Grace Lema
Publication(s): *African Management Development Forum* (biannual); *ESAMI Newsletter* (quarterly)
Branch Office(s)
Harare
Kampala
Lilongwe
Lusaka
Maputo
Mbabawe
Nairobi

Institute of Development Management Library (IDM), see Mzumbe University Library

Kivukoni College Library
PO Box 9193, Dar Es Salaam
Tel: (051) 820047
Telex: 41390
Key Personnel
Librarian: George M Gwahemba

Makumira Lutheran Theological College Library
Box 55, Usa River
Tel: (027) 255-3634; (027) 255-3635 *Fax:* (027) 255-3493
E-mail: library@makumira.ac.tz
Web Site: www.makumira.ac.tz
Telex: 42054
Key Personnel
Chief Librarian: Ndelilio Mbise *Tel:* 255 057 8599
Founded: 1947
Theology, East Africana.
Publication(s): *Africa Theological Journal & Larida la Uchungagi*

Mzumbe University Library
Formerly Institute of Development Management Library (IDM)
Mzumbe
Mailing Address: PO Box 1, Mzumbe
Tel: (023) 260-4380; (023) 260-4381; (023) 260-4383; (023) 260-4384 *Fax:* (023) 260-4382
E-mail: idm@raha.com
Telex: idm morogoro
Key Personnel
Dir: Matilda Kuzilwa *E-mail:* matildakuz@yahoo.co.uk
Founded: 1964
Academic Library.
Parent Company: Ministry of Science, Technology & Higher Education

Sokoine University of Agriculture Library
PO Box 3000, Morogoro
Tel: (056) 3510; (056) 3514
E-mail: usa@hnettan.gri.apc.org
Telex: 55308 Univmo Tz *Cable:* Uniagric Morogoro
Key Personnel
Librarian: Ms E V Chiduo
Publication(s): *Annual Record of Research*; *Bibliography of Higher Degree Theseses & Dissertations held by the Library of the Sokoine University of Agriculture*; *Library Accessions List* (quarterly); *The Green Revolution: A Bibliography*
Branch Office(s)
Mazimbu Library

Standard Book Numbering Agency, see Tanzania Library Service

Tanzania Library Service
PO Box 9283, Dar es Salaam
Tel: (022) 215 09 23; (022) 215 00 48 *Fax:* (022) 215 11 00
E-mail: tlsb@africaonline.co.tz
Telex: Tanlis
Key Personnel
Dir: E A Mwinyimvua
Publication(s): *Tanzania National Bibliography*; *Directory of Libraries in Tanzania* (1984)

University of Dar es Salaam Library
PO Box 35092, Dar Es Salaam
Tel: (051) 43241 *Fax:* (051) 43241

E-mail: libdirec@udsm.ac.tz; director@libis.udsm.ac.tz
Web Site: www.udsm.ac.tz/library
Telex: 41561
Key Personnel
Dir: Dr John M Newa
Publication(s): East Africana Accessions Bulletin; Tanzania Regional Bib Series; University of Dar Es Salaam Library Journal

Thailand

British Council Library
254 Chulalongkorn Soi 64, Siam Sq, Phyathai Rd, Pathumwan, Bangkok 10330
Tel: (02) 652 5480; (02) 652 5489 Fax: (02) 253 5312
E-mail: bc.bangkok@britcoun.or.th
Web Site: www.britishcouncil.or.th
Telex: 72058
Key Personnel
Dir: Bhaskar Chakravarti
British Education Information provider.

Centers of Academic Resources Chulalongkorn University
Phya Thai Rd, Bangkok 10330
Tel: (02) 218 2965; (02) 218 2964 Fax: (02) 215 3617
Web Site: www.car.chula.ac.th
Key Personnel
Dir: Dr Prachak Poomvises E-mail: prachak@chulkn.cav.chula.ac.th
Includes Central Library, Thailand Information Center & Audiovisual Center.
Publication(s): Academic Resources Journal; Union Catalog of Chulalongkorn University Libraries; Union List of Serials in Thailand (automated)

Main Library, Kasetsart University
Phahonyothin Rd, Chatuchak, Bangkok 10903
Mailing Address: PO Box 1084, Chatuchak, Bangkok 10903
Tel: (02) 9428615 Fax: (02) 5611369; (02) 9428614
E-mail: ospnk@ku.ac.th
Web Site: www.lib.ku.ac.th
Key Personnel
Librarian: Mrs Piboonsin Watanapongse

National Archives Division
Fine Arts Dept Samsen Rd, Bangkok 10300
Tel: (02) 281 1599; (02) 281 0263; (02) 281 5450
Fax: (02) 281 1599; (02) 281 0263; (02) 281 5450

The National Library of Thailand
Samsen Rd, Bangkok 10300
Tel: (02) 2810263; (02) 281 5999; (02) 281 5450
Fax: (02) 281 0263; (02) 281 5999; (02) 282 5450
E-mail: suwaksir@emisc.moe.go.th
Telex: 84189 DEPFIAR TH
Key Personnel
Dir: Mrs Kullasap Gesmankit

Siriraj Medical Library
Mahidol University, Siriraj Hospital, 2 Prannok Rd, Bangkoknoi, Bangkok 10700
Tel: (02) 411 3112; (02) 419 7635; (02) 419 7637
Fax: (02) 412 8418
E-mail: silib@diamond.mahidol.ac.th
Web Site: www.medlib.si.mahidol.ac.th
Key Personnel
Chief Librarian: Porntip Anaprayot
E-mail: lipan@mahidol.ac.th

Srinakharinwirot University, Central Library
Sukhumvit 23 Rd, Watthana, Bangkok 10110
Tel: (02) 2584002 (ext 160, 161, 162); (02) 2584003 (ext 160, 161, 162); (02) 6641000 (ext 5382) Fax: (02) 2604514; (02) 2584002
E-mail: library@swu.ac.th
Web Site: www.swu.ac.th/lib
Telex: 72270 Unisirin Th
Key Personnel
Dir: Mr Chaleo Pansida

Thai National Documentation Centre (TNDC)
Thailand Institute of Scientific & Technological Research, 196 Phaholyothin Rd, Chatuchak, Bangken, Bangkok 10900
Tel: (02) 579 1121; (02) 579 1130; (02) 579 5515; (02) 579 0160 Fax: (02) 561 4771
Telex: 21392 TISTR TH Cable: TISTR/BANGKOK
Key Personnel
Contact: Mrs Nongphanga Chitrakorn
Publication(s): Abstracts of TISTR Technical Reports; List of Scientific and Technical Literature Relating to Thailand; Scientific Serials in Thai Libraries; Thai Abstracts; TISTR Bibliographical Series

Thammasat University Libraries
2 Prachan Rd, Pranakorn, Bangkok 10200
Tel: (02) 623-5161; (02) 623-5167 Fax: (02) 623-5173
E-mail: tulib@alpha.tu.ac.th
Web Site: library2.tu.ac.th
Telex: 72432 TAMSAT TH
Key Personnel
Dir: Ms Nualchawee Suthamwong Tel: (02) 623-5171 E-mail: nsutham@alpha.tu.ac.th
Librarian: Mrs Chooman Thirakit Tel: (02) 613-3518
Founded: 1934
Academic libraries.
Publication(s): Dom Thad (biennial, journal)

TNDC, see Thai National Documentation Centre (TNDC)

Togo

Bibliotheque Nationale
Ave de la Victoire, PO Box 1002, Lome
Tel: 21 63 67; 21 04 10; 22 21 16 Fax: 22 19 67
Telex: 5322 Minedue
Key Personnel
Dir: Moussa Senghor
Founded: 1960
Publication(s): Bibliographie Nationale

Bibliotheque de l'Universite du Benin
BP 1515, Lome
Tel: 21 30 27 Fax: 21 85 95
E-mail: cafmicro@ub.tg
Web Site: www.ub.tg
Telex: 52 - 58

Trinidad & Tobago

Central Library of Trinidad & Tobago, see National Library & Information System Authority (NALIS)

National Archives
Unit of Ministry of Public Administration & Information
The Government Archivist, 105 St Vincent St, Port of Spain
Mailing Address: PO Box 763, Port of Spain
Tel: 625-2689 Fax: 625-2689
E-mail: natt@tstt.net.tt
Key Personnel
Government Archivist: Helena Leonce
Founded: 1960
Preserves the documentary heritage of Trinidad & Tobago.

National Library & Information System Authority (NALIS)
Hart & Abercromby Sts, Port of Spain
Tel: (0868) 623-6962; (0868) 624-4466 Fax: (0868) 625-6096 Fax on Demand: 624-3120
E-mail: nalis@nalis.gov.tt
Web Site: www.nalis.gov.tt Cable: Centralib Trinidad
Key Personnel
Executive Dir: Pamella Benson
Founded: 1998
National Library System.
Publication(s): Trinadad & Tabago National Bibliography (annually)

Trinidad Public Library, see National Library & Information System Authority (NALIS)

University of the West Indies Library (Trinidad & Tobago)
The Main Library, St Augustine
Tel: (0868) 662 2002 (ext 2132) Fax: (0868) 662-9238
E-mail: mainlib@library.uwi.tt
Web Site: www.mainlib.uwi.tt
Telex: 24520 Uwi-Wg Cable: STOMATA, PORT OF SPAIN
Key Personnel
Librarian: Dr Margaret D Rouse-Jones Tel: (0868) 662 2002, ext 2008
Publication(s): CARINDEX: Science & Technology; CARINDEX: Social Sciences & Humanities; Directory of Publishers, Printers & Booksellers in Trinidad & Tobago; OPreP Newsletter

Tunisia

Archives nationales
Le Premier Ministere, La Casbah, 1020 Tunis
Tel: (01) 560 556 Fax: (01) 569 175
Key Personnel
Dir: Moncef Fakhfakh
Founded: 1874

Bibliotheque Nationale
20 Souk el Attarine, Tunis
Mailing Address: BP 42, Tunis
Tel: (01) 245338 Fax: (01) 342700
Key Personnel
Librarian: Ibrahim M Chabbouh
Publication(s): Bibliographie Nationale: Publications en serie; Bibliographie nationale: Publications officielles et non officielles; Bibliographies Specialisees (Themes tunisiens notamment); Fahras al-Makhtuetat (catalogue des manuscrits); Informations bibliographiques; Repertoire des Unites de Documentation en Tunisie

British Council Library
c/o British Embassy, 5 pl de la Victoire, 1015 Tunis
Mailing Address: BP 229, 1015 Tunis
Tel: (01) 259 053; (01) 351 754 *Fax:* (01) 353 411
E-mail: info@tn.britishcouncil.org
Web Site: www.britishcouncil.org/tunisia

Centre de Recherches et d'Etudes Administratives
24, av docteur Calmette, Mutuelleville, 1002 Tunis
Tel: (01) 848 435; (01) 848 300 *Fax:* (01) 794 188
E-mail: webmaster@ena.nat.tn
Web Site: www.ena.nat.tn
Telex: Ena 13198
Key Personnel
Dir: Mohamed Hedi Touati
Founded: 1964
Publication(s): *Revue tunisienne d'Administration Publique* (biannually)

CREA, see Centre de Recherches et d'Etudes Administratives

Bibliotheque de la Faculte des Sciences de Tunis
University, El Manar-Tunis, 1060 Tunis
Tel: (01) 872600 *Fax:* (01) 885073

Institut de Presse & des Sciences de l'Information
7, impasse Mohamed Bachrouch, Montfluery, 1008 Tunis
Tel: (01) 33 52 16 *Fax:* (01) 34 85 96
Telex: 15254 IPSI.TN
Key Personnel
Director: Mustapha Hassen *E-mail:* mustapha.hassen@ipsi.rau.tn
Publication(s): *Revue Tunisienne de Communication*

Turkey

Ankara University Library
Tandogan, 06100 Ankara
Tel: (0312) 212 60 40 *Fax:* (0312) 212 60 49
Web Site: www.ankara.edu.tr
Key Personnel
Librarian: Dr Sekine Karakas
Founded: 1933

The Beyazit State Library
Imaret Sok 18, Istanbul-Beyazit
Tel: (0212) 522 2488 *Fax:* (0212) 526 1133
Key Personnel
Librarian: Yusuf Tavacl
Founded: 1882

Bilkent University Library
Bilkent, 06800 Ankara
Tel: (0312) 2664472 *Fax:* (0312) 2664391
Web Site: library.bilkent.edu.tr
Key Personnel
University Librarian: Dr Phyllis L Erdogan
  Tel: (0312) 290 1291; (0312) 290 1418
  E-mail: librdirector@bilkent.edu.tr
Founded: 1986
Membership(s): IFLA; LIBER; ALA; LA (UK); IATUL; MELA; IAML.
Branch Office(s)
Bilkent University East Campus Library, 06800 Ankara *Tel:* (312) 266-5117
  E-mail: eastlibrary@bilkent.edu.tr

Bogazici University Library
Bebek, 34342 Istanbul
Tel: (0212) 3581540 *Fax:* (0212) 2575016
Web Site: www.library.boun.edu.tr
Telex: 26411
Key Personnel
Dir: Guen Kut *E-mail:* kut@boun.edu.tr

The Grand National Assembly of Turkey Library & Documentation TBMM (TBMM Kutuephane Dokuemantasyon ve Tercueme Mueduerluegue)
Bakanliklar, Ankara 06543
Tel: (0312) 420 68 35 *Fax:* (0312) 420 75 48
E-mail: library@tbmm.gov.tr
Web Site: www.tbmm.gov.tr
Key Personnel
Dir: Ali Riza Cihan *E-mail:* acihan@tbmm.gov.tr
Memberships: APLAP; ECPRD; IFLA; LIBER.

Istanbul Universitesi Merkez Kuetuephanesi
Beyazit, 34452 Istanbul
Tel: (0212) 511 12 19 *Fax:* (0212) 511 12 19
E-mail: bilgi@library.istanbul.edu.tr
Web Site: www.istanbul.edu.tr/library
Key Personnel
Librarian: Guelguen Sayari
Istanbul University Central Library.

Library of the Mineral Research & Exploration General Directorate
MTA, 06520 Ankara
Tel: (0312) 287 34 30 *Fax:* (0312) 287 91 88
Web Site: www.mta.gov.tr
Telex: 42741 42060mta tr *Cable:* METEA/ANKARA
Key Personnel
Librarian: Gonul Kocer
Founded: 1935
Specialize in books on mining exploration, geological investigation, earth investigations.
Publication(s): *Bulletin of the Mineral Reserch & Exploration* (bulletin)
Parent Company: Bureau of Mines, USA
Ultimate Parent Company: BROM, France

Middle East Technical University Library
Inonu Bulvari, 06531 Ankara
Tel: (0312) 210 27 80; (0312) 210 27 82 *Fax:* (0312) 210 11 19
E-mail: lib-hot-line@metu.edu.tr
Web Site: www.metu.edu.tr
Telex: 42761
Key Personnel
Dir: Buelent Karasoezen *E-mail:* bulent@metu.edu.tr
Membership(s): IATUL (International Association of Technological University Libraries).

Milliii Kuetuephane
Baskanligi Bahcelievler Son Durak, 06490 Ankara
Tel: (0312) 212 62 00 *Fax:* (0312) 223 04 51
Web Site: www.mkutup.gov.tr
Key Personnel
Librarian: Sahika Unal
National Library.
Publication(s): *Turkiye Bibliyografyasi*

National Library of Izmir
Mill Kuetuephane Caddesi, no 39, Konak, Izmir
Tel: (0232) 4842002 *Fax:* (0232) 4821703
Key Personnel
Dir: Ali Riza Atay
Founded: 1912
Publication(s): *Izmir Milli Kuetuphanesi, Yazma Eserler Katalogu, Vol 1 ve 2* (manuscript catalogue of Izmir National Library Vol I & Vol II)

Sueleymaniye Kuetuephanesi
Aysekadin Hamami Sokak 35 Beyazit, Istanbul
Tel: (0212) 520 64 60 *Fax:* (0212) 520 64 62
Key Personnel
Librarian: Muammer Ulker
Library of the Sueleymaniye.
Publication(s): *Nail Bayraktar* (1984, catalog of the important Arabic manuscripts in Bagdatli Vehbi Efendi Library, Istanbul); *The Union Catalogue Islamic Medical Manuscripts in Turkish Library* (1984); *Turkiye Yazmalari Toplu Katalogiu (TUYATOK)* (The union catalogue of manuscripts in Turkey)

Technical University Library
Ayazaga Campus, 34469 Maslak/Istanbul
Tel: (0212) 285 35 96 *Fax:* (0212) 285 33 02
E-mail: library@papirus.library.itu.edu.tr
Web Site: www.library.itu.edu.tr
Key Personnel
Dir: Ayhan Kaygusuz *E-mail:* kaygusuz@itu.edu.tr
Contact: Nurten Atalik

Tuerdok (Turkish Scientific & Technical Documentation Centre)
Atatuerk Bulvari 221, Kavaklidere, 06100 Ankara
Tel: (0312) 468 5300 *Fax:* (0312) 427 7489
E-mail: www-adm@tubitak.gov.tr
Web Site: www.tubitak.gov.tr
Telex: 43186 Btak Tr *Cable:* TUBITAK, ANKARA

Turkmenistan

National Library of Turkmenistan
Pl K Marksa, 744000 Aschabad
Tel: (07) 3632 25 3254 *Fax:* (012) 257 481
Key Personnel
Dir: Nazar Atabaevich Kurbanov
Founded: 1895

Uganda

Central Reference Library
c/o Public Libraries Board Headquarters, 11-13 Buganda Rd, Kampala
Mailing Address: PO Box 4262, Kampala
Tel: (041) 233633 *Fax:* (041) 348625
E-mail: library@imul.com
Key Personnel
Dir: P Birungi
Founded: 1972

Albert Cook Medical Library
Makerere University Medical School, Kampala
Mailing Address: PO Box 7072, Kampala
Tel: (041) 534149 *Fax:* (041) 530024
E-mail: acook@uga.healthnet.org *Cable:* MAKUNIKA KAMPALA
Key Personnel
Deputy University Librarian: Maria Musoke
  E-mail: mmusoke@uga.healthnet.org
Publication(s): *East African Medical Bibliography* (bimonthly); *The Uganda Health Information Digest* (3 times/yr)

Makerere Institute of Social Research Library
PO Box 7062, Kampala
Tel: (041) 554582; (041) 53 28 30; (041) 53 28 37; (041) 53 28 38; (041) 53 28 39 *Fax:* (041) 53 28 21

UGANDA

E-mail: diremisr@infocom.co.ug
Web Site: www.makerere.ac.ug/research/misr.htm

Makerere University Library
PO Box 7062, Kampala
Tel: (041) 531041 *Fax:* (041) 540374
E-mail: librarian@mak.ac.ug
Web Site: www.makerere.ac.ug/mulib *Cable:* MAKUNIKA
Key Personnel
Librarian: James Mugasha
Founded: 1957

National Library of Uganda
Formerly Public Libraries Board
11-13 Buganda Rd, 11 Bombo Rd, Kampala
Mailing Address: PO Box 4262, Kampala
Tel: (041) 233633 *Fax:* (041) 348625
E-mail: library@imul.com *Cable:* LIBRARY, KAMPALA
Key Personnel
Dir: Ms G K Mulindwa
Founded: 1964 (as Public Libraries Board, established 2003 as National Library of Uganda)
Nationwide public library service & preservation of national heritage.
Parent Company: Ministry of Gender, Labour & Social Development

Public Libraries Board, see National Library of Uganda

Uganda Polytechnic Library at Uganda Technical College
PO Box 7181, Kampala
Tel: (041) 28 5211 *Cable:* TECHNICAL
Key Personnel
Chief Librarian: R Nganwa
Founded: 1954

Ukraine

Vernadsky Central Scientific Library of the National Academy of Sciences of Ukraine
Prospekt 40-richja Snavtnja 3, UA-252650 Kiev 34
Tel: (044) 285 81 64 *Fax:* (044) 264 33 98
E-mail: nlu@csl.freenet.kiev.ua
Key Personnel
Dir: Aleksei Semenovich Onischenko

United Arab Emirates

Centre for Documentation & Research
Abu Dhabi
Mailing Address: PO Box 5884, Abu Dhabi
Tel: (02) 444 5400 *Fax:* (02) 444 5811
Web Site: www.gebcad.com
Founded: 1988
Archival collections.
Publication(s): Documents of UAE (annually)
Ultimate Parent Company: Abu Dhabi Government

National Library
Zayed 1st St, Abu Dhabi
Mailing Address: PO Box 2380, Abu Dhabi
Tel: 6215300 *Fax:* 6336059
Web Site: www.cultural.org.ae/E/library.htm
Telex: 22414 Culcen Em

Key Personnel
Dir: Jumaa Alqubaisi
Total Titles: 800,000 Print

United Kingdom

Belfast Public Library
Royal Ave, Belfast BT1 1EA
Tel: (01232) 243 233 *Fax:* (01232) 332 819
Telex: 747359
Key Personnel
Chief Librarian: J N Montgomery
Founded: 1888

Birmingham Library Information Services
Main Library, Information Services, Edgbaston, Birmingham B15 2TT
Tel: (0121) 414 5817 *Fax:* (0121) 471 4691
E-mail: library@bham.ac.uk
Web Site: www.is.bham.ac.uk/mainlib
Telex: 337655
Key Personnel
Contact: Mrs Marjorie Westley *Tel:* (0121) 303 2868 *E-mail:* marje.westley@birmingham.gov.uk
Assistant Dir: V M Griffiths
Publication(s): Birmingham Between the Wars; Briefing (bimonthly); *Bygone Bartley Green; Directory of the Irish in Birmingham; In the Midst of Life; Lost Railways of Birmingham; National Socialist Literature in Birmingham Reference Library; News Review* (5 issues a week); *The Nine Days in Birmingham; Statistics & Market Research* (monthly); *Struggling Manor*

Bodleian Library
Broad St, Oxford OX1 3BG
Tel: (01865) 277000 *Fax:* (01865) 277182
E-mail: enquiries@bodley.ox.ac.uk
Web Site: www.bodley.ox.ac.uk
Telex: 83656
Key Personnel
Librarian: R P Carr

The British Library
St Pancras, 96 Euston Rd, London NW1 2DB
Tel: (0870) 444 1500
Web Site: www.bl.uk
Also publisher of books of interest to the general reader & collector, including facsimiles of items in the collection & works of general bibliography.
Publication(s): British National Bibliography (weekly); *Serials in the British Library* (quarterly); *The UKMARC Exchange Record Format* (1997); *UKMARC Manual: A Cataloguer's Guide to the Bibliographic Format* (1996)

British Library Document Supply Centre
Document Supply Centre, Boston Spa, Wetherby, West Yorks LS23 7BQ
Tel: (01937) 546060 *Fax:* (01937) 546333
E-mail: dsc-customer-services@bl.uk
Web Site: www.bl.uk/services/document/contact.html
Key Personnel
Publishing Officer: Dr Dorothy Dryden
Publications Officer: Andrea Seed
Also publisher.
Publication(s): Alphanumeric Reports Publications Index; Books at Boston Spa (on microfiche); *Boston Spa Books* (on CD-ROM); *Boston Spa Conferences* (on CD-ROM); *Boston Spa Serials* (on CD-ROM); *British Reports,*

MAJOR

Translations & Theses; Current Serials Received; Directory of Acronyms; Focus on British Biological & Medical Research; Focus on British Business & Management Science Research; Focus on British Engineering & Computer Sciences Research; East-West Links; Index of Conference Proceedings (monthly with annual cumulations); *Index of Conference Proceedings 1964-1988; Inside Conferences* (on CD-ROM); *Inside Information* (on CD-ROM); *Keyword Index to Serial Titles* (on microfiche); *POPSI-The Popular Song Index*

British Library, Newspaper Library
Colindale Ave, London NW9 5HE
Tel: (020) 7412 7353 *Fax:* (020) 7412 7379
E-mail: newspaper@bl.uk
Web Site: www.bl.uk
Telex: 21462
Key Personnel
Newspaper Librarian: Edmund King *Tel:* (020) 7412 7362 *E-mail:* ed.king@bl.uk
Editor of the Newsletter: Christopher Skelton-Foord
The national collection of British & overseas newspapers.

British Library of Political & Economic Science
London School of Economics, 10 Portugal St, London WC2A 2HD
Tel: (020) 7955 7229 *Fax:* (020) 7955 7454
E-mail: library@lse.ac.uk
Web Site: www.lse.ac.uk/library
Key Personnel
Librarian & Dir Information Services: Jean Sykes
Not a British Library division.
Publication(s): The International Bibliography of the Social Sciences

British Library Oriental & India Office Collections
96 Euston Rd, London NW1 2DB
Tel: (020) 7412 7873 *Fax:* (020) 7412 7641
E-mail: oioc-enquiries@bl.uk
Web Site: www.bl.uk
Key Personnel
Dir: G W Shaw
Publication(s): Calcutta: City of Palaces (1990); *Catalogue of the Nevill Collection of Sinhalese Mss* (4 vols, 1987-1990); *Catalogue of the Urdu, Panjabi, Pashto and Kashmiri Documents in the India Office Library and Records* (1990); *Descriptive Catalogue of the Batala Collection of Mughal Documents 1527-1757* (1990); *General Guide to the India Officer Records* (1988); *Oriental Gardens* (1991); *The Life of the Buddha* (1992)
Orders to: Turpin Distribution Services Ltd, Blackhorse Rd, Letchworth, Herts SG6 1HN
Tel: (01462) 672555 *Fax:* (01462) 480947

The British Library, Science Technology & Innovation Information Services
Science Technology & Innovation Information Services, 96 Euston Rd, London NW1 2DB
Tel: (020) 7412 7495; (020) 7412 7494; (020) 7412 7496
E-mail: scitech@bl.uk; social-policy@bl.uk; patents-information@bl.uk
Web Site: www.bl.uk
Key Personnel
Head of Library: Julia Stocken
List of seminars & publications available upon request. The national library for science, technology, business, patents & the social sciences, is the most comprehensive reference collection in Western Europe of such literature from the whole world. Inquiries are also handled by telephone, fax & e-mail. The library has inquiry & referral services (especially in business information, the environment, industrial prop-

LIBRARIES

UNITED KINGDOM

erty, health care & the social sciences); online database search, photocopy & linguistic aid services; runs courses & seminars & provides a wide range of publications from newsletters to definitive bibliographies.

Cambridge University Library
West Rd, Cambridge CB3 9DR
Tel: (01223) 333000 *Fax:* (01223) 333160
E-mail: library@lib.cam.ac.uk
Web Site: www.lib.cam.ac.uk
Key Personnel
Librarian: Mr P K Fox *Tel:* (01223) 333045
Deputy Librarian: Mr D J Hall *Tel:* (01223) 333047; Ms A E Murray *Tel:* (01223) 333083
Founded: 1400
List of publications available on request from the library offices or online.
Branch Office(s)
Medical Library, Addenbrooke's Hospital, Hills Rd, Cambridge CB2 2SP *Tel:* (01223) 336750 *Fax:* (01223) 331918 *E-mail:* library@medschl.cam.ac.uk
Betty & Gordon Moore Library, Wilberforce Rd, Cambridge CB3 OWD *Tel:* (01223) 765670 *Fax:* (01223) 765678 *E-mail:* moore-library@lib.cam.ac.uk
Scientific Periodicals Library, Arts School, Bene't St, Cambridge CB2 3PY *Tel:* (01223) 334742 *Fax:* (01223) 334748 *E-mail:* mlw1003@cam.ac.uk
Squire Law Library, 10 West Rd, Cambridge CB3 9DZ *Tel:* (01223) 330033 *Fax:* (01223) 330048 *E-mail:* dfus1003@cus.cam.ac.uk

Durham Chapter Library
The College, Durham DH1 3EH
Tel: (0191) 386 4266 *Fax:* (0191) 386 4267
E-mail: enquiries@durhamcathedral.co.uk
Web Site: www.durhamcathedral.co.uk/

Durham University Library
Stockton Rd, Durham DH1 3LY
Tel: (0191) 334 2968 *Fax:* (0191) 334 2971
E-mail: main.library@durham.ac.uk
Web Site: www.dur.ac.uk/library
Key Personnel
University Librarian: Dr John T D Hall *Tel:* (0191) 334 2960 *E-mail:* j.t.d.hall@durham.ac.uk

Edinburgh University Library
George Sq, Edinburgh EH8 9LJ
Tel: (0131) 650 3384; (0131) 650 3374 (reference & information services) *Fax:* (0131) 667 9780; (0131) 650 3380 (administration); (0131) 650 6863 (special collections)
E-mail: library@ed.ac.uk
Web Site: www.lib.ed.ac.uk
Key Personnel
Dir Library Services: Sheila E Cannell
E-mail: sheila.cannell@ed.ac.uk
Founded: 1580
Publication(s): *Catalogue of Printed Books* (1988 microfiche); *Catalogue of the Library of The Rev James Nairn* (Guides, Leaflets, Exhibition Catalogs); *Collection of Historical Essays* (1982); *Edinburgh University Library, 1580-1980*; *Manuscript Treasures of Edinburgh University Library* (1980)

Edinburgh City Library & Information Services
Central Library, George IV Bridge, Edinburgh EH1 1EG
Tel: (0131) 242 8020 *Fax:* (0131) 242 8009
E-mail: central.lending.library@edinburgh.gov.uk
Web Site: www.edinburgh.gov.uk/libraries
Key Personnel
Head, Lib & Info Servs: W Wallace
Founded: 1890

Public library service.
Parent Company: Culture & Leisure Dept
Ultimate Parent Company: City of Edinburgh Council

University of Exeter
University Library, Stocker Rd, Exeter EX4 4PT
Tel: (01392) 263867 *Fax:* (01392) 263871
E-mail: library@exeter.ac.uk
Web Site: www.ex.ac.uk/library/
Key Personnel
Librarian: Alasdair T Paterson

Glasgow City Libraries & Archives, the Mitchell Library
North St, Glasgow G3 7DN
Tel: (0141) 287 2913; (0141) 287 2905 *Fax:* (0141) 226 8452
E-mail: archives@cls.glasgow.gov.uk
Web Site: www.mitchelllibrary.org; www.glasgowlibraries.org
Key Personnel
Commercial Manager: Verina Litster
Publication(s): *West of Scotland Census Returns & Old Parochial Registers* (a directory of public library holdings in the West of Scotland)

University of Glasgow
University Library, Hillhead St, Glasgow G12 8QE
Tel: (0141) 330 6704 *Fax:* (0141) 330 4952
E-mail: library@lib.gla.ac.uk
Web Site: www.lib.gla.ac.uk
Key Personnel
Dir, Library Services: Chris Bailey
Founded: 1451
Specialize in university higher education.

Guildhall Library
Aldermanbury, London EC2P 2EJ
Tel: (020) 7332 1868; (020) 7332 1870; (020) 7332 1863; (020) 7332 1839 *Fax:* (020) 7600 3384
E-mail: printedbooks.guildhall@corpoflondon.gov.uk; manuscripts.guildhall@corpoflondon.gov.uk
Web Site: www.ull.ac.uk
Key Personnel
Librarian: Melvyn Barnes
Total Titles: 189,000 Print

Institute of Development Studies
University of Sussex, Brighton BN1 9RE
Tel: (01273) 606261 *Fax:* (01273) 621202; (01273) 691647
E-mail: blds@ids.ac.uk
Web Site: www.ids.ac.uk
Telex: 877997 IDSBTN G
Key Personnel
Head, Communications: Geoff Barnard
Founded: 1966

Leeds University Library
University of Leeds, Leeds LS2 9JT
Tel: (0113) 343 5663 *Fax:* (0113) 233 5561
E-mail: library@library.leeds.ac.uk
Web Site: www.leeds.ac.uk/library
Key Personnel
Dir, Library Services: J Wilkinson
Founded: 1874
Publication(s): *The Brotherton Collection*; *Catalogue of German Literature Printed in the 17th & 18th Centuries*; *A Catalogue of the Icelandic Collection*; *Catalogue of the Romany Collection*

University of Leicester
University Rd, Leicester LE1 9QD
Mailing Address: PO Box 248, Leicester LE1 9QD
Tel: (0116) 252 2043 *Fax:* (0116) 252 2066
E-mail: libdesk@le.ac.uk

Web Site: www.le.ac.uk/library
Key Personnel
Librarian: Christine Fyfe *Tel:* (0116) 252 2031

Liverpool Libraries & Information Services
Central Library, William Brown St, Liverpool L3 8EW
Tel: (0151) 233 5829 *Fax:* (0151) 233 5886
E-mail: refbt.central.library@liverpool.gov.uk
Key Personnel
Head of Library & Information Services: Joyce Little *Tel:* (0151) 233 6346 *E-mail:* joyce.little@liverpool.gov.uk
Publication(s): *Liverpool-Capital of the Slave Trade*; *Liverpool Women at War*; *The Battle of the Atlantic* (personal memories)

The Mitchell Library, see Glasgow City Libraries & Archives, the Mitchell Library

National Library for the Blind
Far Cromwell Rd, Bredbury, Stockport SK6 2SG
Tel: (0161) 355 2000 *Fax:* (0161) 355 2098
E-mail: enquiries@nlbuk.org
Web Site: www.nlb-online.org
Key Personnel
Chief Executive: Helen Brazier
Chairman: Dr Gillian Burrington
Dir, External Relations: Phil Robertshaw
Dir, ICT & Operations: Carol Pollitt
Dir, Library & Information Services: Pat Beech
Resources Dir: Susan Cohen
Founded: 1882
A leading national agency in the provision of library services for visually impaired people & Europe's largest lending library for people who cannot read print.
Publication(s): *Annual Review*; *Focus* (triannually, newsletter); *New Reading* (quarterly, catalog); *Read On* (quarterly, magazine)

National Library of Scotland
George IV Bridge, Edinburgh EH1 1EW
Tel: (0131) 226 4531 *Fax:* (0131) 622 4803
E-mail: enquiries@nls.uk
Web Site: www.nls.uk
Key Personnel
National Librarian: Martyn Wade
Publication(s): *Special & Named Printed Collections in the National Library of Scotland*, Ed G Hogg (1999)

National Library of Wales
Aberystwyth, Ceredigion, Cymru SY23 3BU
Tel: (01970) 632 800 *Fax:* (01970) 615 709
E-mail: holi@llgc.org.uk
Web Site: www.llgc.org.uk
Key Personnel
Librarian: Andrew M W Green
National Library.
Publication(s): *Llyfryddiaeth Cymru - A Bibliography of Wales* (no longer published on paper, available only as an online service on the web catalog); *The National Library of Wales Journal* (semiannually, academic, based on the library's holdings)

The Natural History Museum Library
Cromwell Rd, London SW7 5BD
Tel: (020) 7942 5011 *Fax:* (020) 7942 5559
E-mail: genlib@nhm.ac.uk
Web Site: www.nhm.ac.uk/library
Key Personnel
Head of Library & Information Services: Ray Lester
Founded: 1881

NLB, see National Library for the Blind

Oxford University, Taylor Institution Library
St Giles', Oxford OX1 3NA

Tel: (01865) 2-78154; (01865) 2-78158 (book enquiries) *Fax:* (01865) 2-78165
E-mail: enquiries@taylib.ox.ac.uk
Web Site: www.taylib.ox.ac.uk
Key Personnel
Acting Librarian: Ms A J Peters *Tel:* (01865) 2-78160 *E-mail:* amanda.peters@taylib.ox.ac.uk
Contact: Mrs E A C Baird *Tel:* (01865) 2-78162
 E-mail: liz.baird@taylib.ox.ac.uk
Founded: 1845
Graduate research library for modern languages.

Public Record Office
Kew, Richmond, Surrey TW9 4DU
Tel: (020) 8876 3444 *Fax:* (020) 8392 5286
E-mail: enquiry@nationalarchives.gov.uk
Web Site: www.pro.gov.uk
Key Personnel
Head of Enterprises: Anne Kilminster *Tel:* (0208) 3925206 *E-mail:* anne.kilminster@pro.gov.uk
Founded: 1838
National archive for the records of the British courts of law & central departments of state.

Reading University Library
The University of Reading, Whiteknights, PO Box 223, Reading RG6 6AE
Tel: (0118) 378 8770 *Fax:* (0118) 378 6636
E-mail: library@reading.ac.uk
Web Site: www.library.rdg.ac.uk
Key Personnel
Librarian: Julia Munro *Tel:* (0118) 378 8774
 E-mail: j.h.munro@rdg.ac.uk
Founded: 1892
University library.
Publication(s): *Beckett at Reading: catalogue of the Beckett manuscript collection at the University of Reading* (catalog, 1998); *Beckett's Dream Notebook* (1999); *Catalogue of the collection of children's books 1617-1939 in the Library of the University of Reading* (catalog, 1988); *The Cole Library of early medicine & zoology, Part 2, 1800 to present day & supplement* (catalog, 1975); *The Cole Library of early medicine & zoology, Part 1: 1472-1800* (catalog, 1969); *The Finzi book room at the University of Reading* (catalog, 1981); *Historical farm records: a summary guide to manuscripts and other material collected by the Institute of Agricultural History and Museum of English Rural Life* (1973); *The Ideal Core of the Onion: Reading Beckett Archives* (1992); *The Kingsley Read alphabet collection* (catalog, 1983); *Records management in British universities: a survey with some suggestions* (1978); *Robert Gibbings 1889-1958* (1989); *The Samuel Beckett collection* (catalog, 1978); *W M Childs: an account of his life and work* (1976)

John Rylands University Library of Manchester
Oxford Rd, Manchester M13 9PP
Tel: (0161) 275 3751 (Main Library Bldg); (0161) 834 5343 (Deansgate Bldg) *Fax:* (0161) 273 7488 (Main Library Bldg); (0161) 834 5574 (Deansgate Bldg)
E-mail: special.collections@man.ac.uk
Web Site: rylibweb.man.ac.uk
Key Personnel
Dir & University Librarian: Bill Simpson
 Tel: (0161) 275 3700 *E-mail:* bill.simpson@man.ac.uk
Assistant Dir & Deputy Librarian: Dr Diana Leitch *Tel:* (0161) 275 3737 *E-mail:* diana.leitch@man.ac.uk
General Administration: Peter Wadsworth
 Tel: (0161) 275 3760 *E-mail:* peter.wadsworth@man.ac.uk
Publication(s): *The Bulletin of the John Rylands University Library of Manchester*

School of Oriental & African Studies Library
University of London, Thornhaugh St, Russell Sq, London WC1H 0XG
Tel: (020) 7637 2388 *Fax:* (020) 7436 3844
E-mail: libenquiry@soas.ac.uk
Web Site: www.soas.ac.uk/library/home.html
Key Personnel
Head of Library Services: Anne Poulson
 Tel: (020) 7637 2388, ext 4150 *E-mail:* ap45@soas.ac.uk
Publication(s): *Library Catalogue* (1978-84 supplement on microfiche); *Library Guide*

Scottish Poetry Library
5 Crichton's Close, Canongate, Edinburgh EH8 8DT
Tel: (031) 557 2876 *Fax:* (031) 557 8393
E-mail: inquiries@spl.org.uk
Web Site: www.spl.org.uk
Key Personnel
Dir: Robyn Marsack *E-mail:* marsack@spl.org.uk
Librarian: Iain Young *E-mail:* librarian1@spl.org.uk
Assistant Dir: Ken Cockburn
 E-mail: kcockburn@spl.org.uk
Founded: 1984
Free lending & reference library specializing in Scottish & international poetry of mainly 20th century. Computer index to poetry now available online. Travelling van service provided. Stock includes books, audio & video tapes, periodicals, news cuttings. Workshops for children organized in term-time & holidays.
Publication(s): *Index to Scottish Poetry Magazines* (forthcoming, Vols 1-9 published)

Trinity College Library
Cambridge CB2 1TQ
Tel: (01223) 338488 *Fax:* (01223) 338532
E-mail: trin-lib@lists.cam.ac.uk
Web Site: library.trin.cam.ac.uk
Key Personnel
Librarian: D J McKitterick

ULL, see University of London Library

University of Aberdeen
Queen Mother Library, Meston Walk, Old Aberdeen AB24 3UE
Tel: (01224) 272580 *Fax:* (01224) 273956
E-mail: library@abdn.ac.uk
Web Site: www.abdn.ac.uk/diss/library
Key Personnel
Manager, Library Division: Ms Carole Munro
 Tel: (01224) 273321 *E-mail:* lib229@abdn.ac.uk
Contact: Christine A Miller *Tel:* (01224) 272572
 E-mail: c.a.miller@abdn.ac.uk
Founded: 1495
University library.
Publication(s): *George Washington Wilson Photographic Series* (irregular, Based on the Library's archive of Victorian glass plate negatives)
Branch Office(s)
Education Library (agriculture & forestry)
Medical Library
Taylor Library (law & European documentation centre)

University of London Library
Senate House, Malet St, London WC1E 7HU
Tel: (020) 7862 8500 *Fax:* (020) 7862 8480
E-mail: enquiries@ull.ac.uk
Web Site: www.ull.ac.uk
Key Personnel
Dir Library Services: Chris Hunt *Tel:* (020) 7862 8410 *E-mail:* cjhunt@ull.ac.uk
Founded: 1837

Academic research library.
Publication(s): *Catalogue of Goldsmiths' Library of Economic Literature, Vol I-V* (Guides; Brochures)

University of Southampton
University Library, University Rd, Highfield, Southampton SO17 1BJ
Tel: (01703) 22180 *Fax:* (01703) 23007
E-mail: libenqs@soton.ac.uk
Web Site: www.library.soton.ac.uk
Telex: 47661
Key Personnel
Librarian: Dr Mark Brown *Tel:* (0173) 22677
 E-mail: m.l.brown@soton.ac.uk

Wellcome Library for the History & Understanding of Medicine
Affiliate of Welcome Trust Centre for the History of Medicine at UCL
183 Euston Rd, London NW1 2BE
Tel: (020) 7611 8722 *Fax:* (020) 7611 8369
E-mail: library@wellcome.ac.uk
Web Site: library.wellcome.ac.uk
Key Personnel
Librarian: Frances Norton
Provides insight & information to anyone seeking to understand medicine & its role in society, past & present.
Parent Company: Wellcome Trust

Westminster Abbey Library
E Cloister, London SW1P 3PA
Tel: (020) 7654 4830 *Fax:* (020) 7654 4827
E-mail: library@westminster-abbey.org
Web Site: westminster-abbey.org
Key Personnel
Librarian: Dr Tony A Trowles

Uruguay

Biblioteca Nacional del Uruguay
Ave 15 de Julio 1790, Casilla de Correo 452, 11200 Montevideo
Tel: (02) 48 50 30 *Fax:* (02) 49 69 02
E-mail: bibna@adinet.com.uy
Web Site: www.mec.gub.uy/agn/sni/snipc.htm
Key Personnel
Dir: Prof Rafael Gomensoro
Founded: 1816
Publication(s): *Anuario Bibliografico Uruguayo 1968-*; *Directorio de Servicios de Informacion y Documentacion en el Uruquay, 1988-*; *Revista Archivo, 1987-*; *Revista Biblioteca Nacional 1966-*; *Uruquay: Indice de publicaciones periodicas en ciencia y tecnologia 1981-1983, 1986-*
Branch Office(s)
Oficina de Ventas, Instituto Nacional del Libro, San Jose, 1116 Montevideo *Tel:* (02) 986740

Centro Nacional de Documentacion Cientifica, Tecnica y Economics (CNDCTE)
18 de Julio 1790, Cassilla de Correo 452, Montevideo
Tel: (02) 484172 *Fax:* (02) 496902
Key Personnel
Dir: Elena Castro
Part of the National Library (Biblioteca National del Uruguay).
Publication(s): *Directorio de Servicios de Informacion y Documentacion en el Uruguay*; *Indice de publicaciones periodicas en ciencia y tecnologia 1981-1983*

Biblioteca Central y Publicaciones del Consejo de Educacion Secundaria
Eduardo Acevedo 1427, Planta Alta, 11200 Montevideo
Tel: (02) 408 42 73; (02) 408 30 51; (02) 408 12 52 *Fax:* (02) 408 12 52
Key Personnel
Dir: Juana Alekandronicius

Biblioteca Facultad de Humanidades y Ciencias de la Educacion
Magallanes 1577, Montevideo 11200
Tel: (02) 49 11 04; (02) 49 11 05; (02) 49 11 06 *Fax:* (02) 48 43 03
E-mail: biblio@fhudec.edu.uy
Web Site: www.rau.edu.uy/universidad/fhcet.htm
Key Personnel
Librarian: Margarita Llado

Biblioteca del Museo Historico Nacional
Rincon 437, CP 11000 Montevideo
Tel: (02) 95 10 51; (02) 915 33 16 *Fax:* (02) 915 68 63
Key Personnel
Contact: Luis Segarra

Biblioteca del Palacio Legislativo, see Biblioteca del Poder Legislativo

Biblioteca del Poder Legislativo (Library of the Legislative Power)
Av de las Leyes, s/n, 11800 Montevideo
Tel: (02) 208937 *Fax:* (02) 949162
Telex: 23203 CARE UY
Key Personnel
Librarian: Luis H Boions Pombo; Mazzeo Condenanza
Founded: 1928
Publication(s): *Anales Parlamentarios* (semestrial); *Bibliografia Uruguaya* (irregularly); *Boletin Bibliografico* (monthly); *Fichas Analiticas de Articulos de Publicaciones Periodicos* (monthly)

Biblioteca Municipal Dr Joaquin de Salterain
Solis 1456 y 25 de Mayo, Montevideo 11000
Tel: (02) 95 62 82
Web Site: www.mec.gub.uy/biblo.htm
Key Personnel
Contact: Graciela Fernandez Ribeiro

Uzbekistan

Alisher Navoi National Library of Uzbekistan
5 Mustakillik Sq, 700078 Tashkent
Tel: (099871) 139 16 58 *Fax:* (099871) 133 09 08
E-mail: navoi@physic.uzsci.net
Web Site: www.osi.uz/library
Key Personnel
Dir: A A Umarov
Founded: 1870

Venezuela

Archivo General de la Nacion (AG)
Esquinas de Santa Capilla y Carmelitas n° 15, Avenida Urdanata (Apdo 5935), Caracas 101
Mailing Address: PO Box 3910, Caracas 1010
Tel: (02) 862-99-07 *Fax:* (02) 81-93-28
Web Site: www.ucab.edu.ve/biblioteca
Key Personnel
Dir: Dr Mario Briceno Perozo

Biblioteca de la Universidad Catolica 'Andres Bello'
Montalban, La Vega Apdo 29068, Caracas 1020
Tel: (02) 4074190
Web Site: www.ucab.edu.ve/biblioteca
Key Personnel
Librarian: Emilio Piriz Perez *E-mail:* epiriz@ucab.edu.ve

Biblioteca del Congreso
Servicio Autonomo de Informacion Legislativa (SAIL), 3er piso, oficina 37, Caracas 1010
Tel: (02) 5645327 *Fax:* (02) 5636696
Telex: 21252 CCASSVC
Key Personnel
Contact: Bertha Pina Montes

Biblioteca Nacional
Final Av Panteon Foro Libertador, Edificio Sede, Caracas 1010
Tel: (02) 505 91 25 *Fax:* (02) 505 91 24
E-mail: vbetanc@reaccium.ve
Web Site: www.bnv.bib.ve
Telex: 24621 IASBN
Key Personnel
Dir: Virginia Betancourt

Instituto Autonomo, Biblioteca Nacional y de Servicios de Bibliotecas
Final Av Panteon Esq Fe a Remedios, Apdo 6525, Caracas 1010-DL
Tel: (02) 5059141 *Fax:* (02) 5059159
Telex: 24621 Iabn Vc
Key Personnel
Dir Lic: Virginia Betancourt
National Library, Public Library Services, Audio-visual Archive of Venezuela.
Publication(s): *Anuarios Bibliograficos* (to 1977); *Bibliografia Venezolana* (from 1978); *Catalogo de Publicaciones Oficiales*; *Informe Anual*

Biblioteca Marcel Roche del Instituto Venezolano de Investigaciones Cientificas (Marcel Roche Library of the Venezuelan Institute for Scientific Research)
Altos de Pipe, Km 11 Carretera Panamericana, Apdo 21827, Caracas 1020-A
Tel: (02) 5041512 *Fax:* (02) 504 14 23
E-mail: infoivic@ivic.ve
Web Site: biblioteca.ivic.ve
Telex: 21657 *Cable:* IVICSAS
Key Personnel
Librarian: Xiomara Jayaro *E-mail:* xjayaro@ivic.ve

Biblioteca Central de la Universidad Central de Venezuela
Biblioteca Central, Universidad Central de Venezuela, Caracas 1051
Tel: (02) 605-29-09; (02) 605-29-10 *Fax:* (02) 6622486
Web Site: www.ucv.ve
Telex: 28479
Key Personnel
Dir: Mercedes Sedano *E-mail:* msedano@reacciun.ve

Servicios Bibliotecarios Universidad de los Andes (Serbiula)
Edif Administrativo piso 5, Merida 5101
Tel: (0274) 2402731; (0274) 2402729 *Fax:* (0274) 2402507; (0274) 2402748
E-mail: adquisi@serbi.ula.ve
Web Site: www.serbi.ula.ve
Telex: 74206 BMULA-VC
Key Personnel
Coordinator: Jesus Rivero M
Head of Acquisitions: Crisalida Fuentes *Tel:* (0274) 2401227 *E-mail:* cfuentes@ula.ve
Founded: 1980
University library services.

Biblioteca Central de la Universidad de Zulia
Nucleo Humanistico, Maracaibo
Tel: (061) 596701 *Fax:* (061) 596700
Web Site: www.serbi.luz.ve/bibcentral
Key Personnel
Librarian: Elga Ortega
Publication(s): *Boletin* (biennially)

Viet Nam

General Sciences Library of Ho Chi Minh City
69 Ly Tu Trong, Ho Chi Minh City
Tel: (08) 822 5055 *Fax:* (08) 829 5632
Key Personnel
Dir: Nguyen Thi Bac
Founded: 1976

National Library of Vietnam
31 Trang Hi St, Hanoi
Tel: (04) 8248051 *Fax:* (04) 8253357
E-mail: info@nlv.gov.vn
Web Site: www.nlv.gov.vn
Key Personnel
Contact: Mr Pham The Khang
Founded: 1917
Publication(s): *Cong tac Thu' vien-Thu' muc* (Journal of Library and Bibliography); *Thu' muc quoc gia Viet nam* (National Bibliography)

Social Sciences Library
34 Ly Tu Trong, Ho Chi Minh City
Tel: (08) 20644 *Fax:* (08) 223735
Key Personnel
Dir: Tran Minh Duc

Yemen

British Council Library
Algiers St, Administrative Tower, 3rd floor, Sana'a Trade Centre, Sana'a
Mailing Address: PO Box 2157, Sana'a
Tel: (01) 448 356; (01) 448 357; (01) 448 358; (01) 448 359 *Fax:* (01) 448 360
E-mail: britishcouncil@ye.britishcouncil.org
Web Site: www.britishcouncil.org/yemen
Telex: 2748 Brcoun Ye

Library of the Great Mosque of Sana'a
Al Jamia al Kabir, Sana'a

Zambia

CBU Library, see The Copperbelt University Library

The Copperbelt University Library
Division of Ministry of Education
c/o Copperbelt University, Box 21692, Kitwe
Tel: (02) 222066; (02) 225155 *Fax:* (02) 222469; (02) 223972
E-mail: library@cbu.ac.zm
Web Site: www.cbu.edu.zm
Telex: ZA 53270
Key Personnel
Librarian: Charles B M Lungu
 E-mail: cbmlungu@cbu.ac.zm
Assistant Librarian: Nellie C Chiinza; Charles Maambo *E-mail:* maambo@cbu.ac.zm; Mwala

ZAMBIA

Sheba *E-mail:* shebamk@cbu.ac.zm; Hamaton Sitwala
Founded: 1987
Membership(s): Association of African Universities.
Ultimate Parent Company: Government of the Republic of Zambia

Hammarskjold Memorial Library
PO Box 21493, Kitwe
Tel: (02) 214572; (02) 219012; (02) 211488 *Fax:* (02) 211001
E-mail: daglib@zamnet.zm
Telex: 52050 Za *Cable:* MINCEN KITWE
Key Personnel
Librarian: Dunstan Chikonka
Founded: 1963
Information provision to the foundation's participant's & many other copperbelt residents interested in various research programs.
Publication(s): *Mindolo Weekly* (newsletter); *Mindolo World* (biannually, various reports of conferences & research programs)
Parent Company: Mindolo Ecumenical Foundation

Evelyn Hone College Library
PO Box 30029, Lusaka
Tel: (01) 225127 *Fax:* (01) 225127
Key Personnel
Librarian: Regina Shula

Kitwe Public Library
PO Box 20070, Kitwe
Tel: (02) 226162; (02) 221001; (02) 222927 *Fax:* (02) 224698

Lusaka City Library
PO Box 31304, Lusaka
Tel: (01) 227282
Telex: 40157 Za
Key Personnel
City Librarian: J C Nkole

National Archives of Zambia
PO Box 50010, 10101 Lusaka
Tel: (01) 254081 *Fax:* (01) 254080
E-mail: naz@zamnet.zm
Key Personnel
Acting Dir: Chrispin Hamooya
Publication(s): *List of Periodicals in the National Archives of Zambia*; *National Archives of Zambia Annual Reports*; *National Bibliography of Zambia*

National Institute of Public Administration Library
PO Box 31990, 10101 Lusaka
Tel: (01) 228802 *Fax:* (01) 27213
Telex: 40523
Key Personnel
Librarian: A G Kasonso

Natural Resources Development College Library
PO Box 310099, Lusaka
Tel: (01) 224610 *Fax:* (01) 224639 *Cable:* NATIVE LUSAKA
Key Personnel
Deputy Principal: Francis K Sinyangwe
Founded: 1964

Ndola Public Library
218 Independence Way, Ndola
Mailing Address: PO Box 70388, Ndola
Tel: 617173
Telex: 30270
Key Personnel
Librarian: K Mumba Chisaka

Northern Technical College Library
Chela Rd, Ndola
Mailing Address: PO Box KJ250093, Ndola
Tel: (02) 680141 *Fax:* (02) 680423
E-mail: nortec@zamtel.zm
Key Personnel
Librarian: P Nabombe

University of Zambia Press (UNZA Press)
PO Box 32379, Lusaka
Tel: (01) 290740; (01) 290409 *Fax:* (01) 253952
Telex: 44370 Za *Cable:* UNZA-Press
Key Personnel
Publisher: Samuel Kasankha
Membership(s): Book Sellers & Publishers Association of Zambia.
Publication(s): *Six Scholarly & Academic Journals* (biannual)
Parent Company: University of Zambia

Zambia Library Service
Division of Ministry of Education
PO Box 30802, Lusaka
Tel: (01) 254993 *Fax:* (01) 254993
E-mail: zamlibs@zamnet.zm *Cable:* ZAMLIBS
Key Personnel
Deputy Chief Librarian: E M Msadabwe
Publication(s): *Annual Report*; *Teacher/Librarians* (biannually, newsletter)

Zimbabwe

Bulawayo Public Library
100 Fort St, Bulawayo
Tel: (09) 60965 *Fax on Demand:* (09) 60965
E-mail: bpl@netconnect.co.zw
Web Site: www.angelfire.com/kg/bpl
Key Personnel
Librarian & Secretary: Robin W Doust
Founded: 1896
Public library & legal deposit (archive) collection.

Geological Survey of Zimbabwe
Box CY210, Causeway
Tel: (04) 726342; (04) 726343; (04) 252016; (04) 252017 *Fax:* (04) 739601
E-mail: zimgeosv@africaonline.co.zw
Web Site: www.geosurvey.co.zw
Telex: 22416 MINESZW *Cable:* MINES
Key Personnel
Dir: S M N Ncube

Harare City Library
PO Box 1087, Harare
Tel: (04) 751834; 751835
Key Personnel
Librarian: Mrs M Ross-Smith

Harare Polytechnic Library
Herbert Chitepo Ave, Harare
Mailing Address: PO Box CY-407, Causeway, Harare
Tel: (04) 752311
Key Personnel
Head: Mr P Chimanda
Founded: 1924
Ultimate Parent Company: Ministry of Higher Education

National Archives of Zimbabwe
Borrowdale Rd, Gunhill, Causeway, Harare
Mailing Address: Private Bag 7729, Causeway, Harare
Tel: (04) 792741; (04) 792742; (04) 792743 *Fax:* (04) 792398
Web Site: www.gta.gov.zw/NatArchives/home.htm
Key Personnel
Editor: O Wytete
Founded: 1935
Publication(s): *Guides to the National Archives collections* (series); *Zimbabwe National Bibliography*; *Directory of Libraries in Zimbabwe* (1986)

National Free Library of Zimbabwe
Dugald Niven Library, 12 Ave S Park, Bulawayo
Mailing Address: PO Box 1773, Bulawayo
Tel: (09) 69827; (09) 62359 *Fax:* (09) 77662
Telex: 33128
Key Personnel
Chief Librarian: D E Barron
Founded: 1944

NAZ, see National Archives of Zimbabwe

Library of Parliament
PO Box CY 298, Causeway, Harare
Tel: (04) 729722 ext 2131 *Fax:* (04) 795548
Telex: 24064
Key Personnel
Librarian: Mr Nelson Masawi
Founded: 1923

Turner Memorial Library
Queensway Civic Complex, Kingsway, POB 48, Mutare
Tel: (0120) 63412 *Fax:* (0120) 61002
Key Personnel
Head, Library Services: Mr Darlington Mandowo
Founded: 1936
Membership(s): Zimbabwe Library Association; United Nations Associated Libraries (UNAL).
Parent Company: City of Mutare (Municipality)
Branch Office(s)
Dangamvura Public Library & Sakubva Public Library, PO Box 448, Mutare

University of Zimbabwe Library
PO Box MP45, Mount Pleasant, Harare
Tel: (04) 303211 *Fax:* (04) 335383
E-mail: mainlib@uzlib.uz.zw
Web Site: uzweb.uz.ac.zw/library
Telex: 26580 Univ Z Zw *Cable:* UNIVERSITY
Key Personnel
Librarian: Dr B Mbambo *E-mail:* bmbambo@uzlib.uz.ac.zw

Library Associations

Listed below are library or library-related associations. Other book trade associations and organizations can be found in **Literary Associations & Societies** and **Book Trade Organizations**.

Albania

Council of Libraries
Ruga Abdi Toptani, no 3, Tirana
Tel: (042) 7984; (042) 7823
Key Personnel
President: M Domi

Algeria

Institut de Bibliotheconomie et des Sciences Documentaires (Institute of Library Economics & Documentation)
Universite d'Alger, 2 rue Didouche Mourad, Algiers
Tel: (021) 94 14 40 *Fax:* (021) 94 14 40
Key Personnel
Faculty: Annexe Bouzareah

Argentina

ABGRA (Asociacion de Bibliotecarios Graduados de la Republica Argentina) (Association of Graduate Librarians of Argentina)
Tucuman 1424, 8° piso, Dpto D, C1050AAB Buenos Aires
Tel: (011) 4371 5269; (011) 4373 0571
Fax: (011) 4371 5269
E-mail: info@abgra.org.ar
Web Site: abgra.sisbi.uba.ar
Key Personnel
President: Ana Maria Peruchena Zimmermann
Vice President: Alberto Ataulfo Lucero
Executive Secretary: Rosa Emma Monfasani
Founded: 1953
Publication(s): *Referencias*

Asociacion Argentina de Bibliotecas y Centros de Informacion Cientificos y Tecnicos
Ave Santa Fe 1145, 1059 Buenos Aires
Tel: (011) 3938406
Key Personnel
President: Abilio Bassets
Technical Secretary: Ernesto G Gietz
Argentian Association of Scientific & Technical Libraries & Information Centres.

Asociacion de Bibliotecarios Graduados de la Republica Argentina, see ABGRA (Asociacion de Bibliotecarios Graduados de la Republica Argentina)

Centro de Documentacion Bibliotecologica
Universidad Nacional del Sur, Avda Alem 1253, 8000 Bahia Blanca
Tel: (091) 28035 *Fax:* (091) 551447
Telex: 81712 ARDUIOR
Key Personnel
Dir: Atilio Peralta

Centre for Library Science Documentation.
Publication(s): *Bibliografia Bibliotecologica Argentina* (Argentine Library Science Bibliography); *Documentacion Bibliotecologica*; *Guia de las Bibliotecas Universitarias Argentinas* (Guide to Argentine University Libraries); *Junta de Bibliotecas Universitarias Nacionales Argentinas* (National Joint of Argentine University Libraries); *Quien es Quien en la Bibliotecologia Argentina* (Who's Who in Argentine Library Science)

Instituto de Bibliografia del Ministerio de Educacion de la Provincia de Buenos Aires
Calle 47 No 510 - 6 piso, 1900 La Plata
Tel: (021) 35915
Key Personnel
Dir: Maria del Carmen Crespi de Bustos
Publication(s): *Bibliografia Argentina de Historia*; *Boletin de Informacion Bibliografica*

Australia

ALIA, see Australian Library & Information Association

Australian Law Librarians' Group Inc
Law Courts Library, Level 15, Queens Sq, Sydney, NSW
Tel: (02) 9230 8675 *Fax:* (02) 9233 7952
Web Site: www.allg.asn.au
Key Personnel
National President: Vanessa O'Meara
 E-mail: vanessa_o'meara@agd.nsw.gov.au
National Vice President: Dorothy Shea
 E-mail: dorothy.shea@justice.tas.gov.au
National Secretary: Mary Greenfield
 E-mail: mary.greenfield@lexisnexis.com.au
National Treasurer: Niall O'Driscoll *E-mail:* niall.odriscoll@asic.gov.au
National Publishers' Liaison Coordinator: Sue Woodman *E-mail:* swoodman@liv.asn.au
Founded: 1969
Publication(s): *Australian Law Librarian* (quarterly)

Australian Library & Information Association
PO Box 6335, Kingston, ACT 2604
Tel: (02) 6215 8222 *Fax:* (02) 6282 2249
E-mail: enquiry@alia.org.au
Web Site: www.alia.org.au
Key Personnel
President: Christine Mackenzie
Executive Dir: Jennifer Nicholson
Founded: 1937
Publication(s): *Australian Academic & Research Libraries* (quarterly); *Australian Library Journal* (quarterly); *Australian Special Libraries News*; *Cataloguing Australia*; *Conference Proceedings* (biennially); *Directory of Special Libraries in Australia*; *inCite* (newsletter); *Library Services in Distance Education*; *Orana* (journal, school & children's librarianship & related issues); *Periodicals for School Libraries*

Australian Society of Archivists
Queensland State Archives, 435 Compton Rd, Runcorn, Qld 4113
Mailing Address: PO Box 1397, Sunnybank Hills, Qld 4109
Tel: (07) 3875 8755 *Fax:* (07) 3875 8764
E-mail: qsa@iie.qld.gov.au
Web Site: www.archives.qld.gov.au
Key Personnel
President: Kathryn Dan
Secretary: Fiona Burn
Man Editor: Shauna Hicks
Publication(s): *Archives and Manuscripts* (biannually); *ASA Bulletin* (6 times/yr); *Debates & Discourses: Selected Australian Writings in Archival Theory, 1951-1990*; *Directory of Archives in Australia*

CAVAL, see Cooperative Action by Victorian Academic Libraries (CAVAL)

Cooperative Action by Victorian Academic Libraries (CAVAL)
4 Park Dr, Bundoora, Victoria 3083
Tel: (03) 9459 2722 *Fax:* (03) 9459 2733
E-mail: caval@caval.edu.au
Web Site: www.caval.edu.au
Key Personnel
Chief Executive Officer: Steve O' Connor
 Tel: (03) 9450 5501 *E-mail:* steveo@caval.edu.au
Education & Business Development Manager: Sue Henczel *Tel:* (03) 9450 5505
 E-mail: sueh@caval.edu.au
Information Services Manager: Cathie Jilovsky
 Tel: (03) 9450 5504 *E-mail:* cathiej@caval.edu.au
Administrative Services Coordinator: David Noble
 Tel: (03) 9450 5528 *E-mail:* davidn@caval.edu.au
Publication(s): *CAVAL* (newsletter)

Council of Australian State Libraries
State Library of Victoria, 328 Swanston St, Melbourne, Victoria 3000
Tel: (03) 8664 7512 *Fax:* (03) 9639 4737
E-mail: casl@slv.vic.gov.au
Web Site: www.casl.org.au
Telex: 92231
Key Personnel
Chief Executive Officer & State Librarian: Frances Awcock *Tel:* (03) 9669 9888 *Fax:* (03) 9669 9958

National Library of Australia
Parkes Pl, Canberra, ACT 2600
Tel: (02) 6262 1111 *Fax:* (02) 6257 1703
E-mail: www@nla.gov.au
Web Site: www.nla.gov.au
Telex: 62100
Key Personnel
Dir General: Jan Fullerton
Assistant Dir General: Jasmine Cameron
Publications Dir: Dr Paul Hetherington *Tel:* (02) 6262 1474 *E-mail:* phetheri@nla.gov.au
Editorial & Production Coordinator: Heather Clark *Tel:* (02) 6262 1253 *E-mail:* hclark@nla.gov.au

Austria

Dokumentationsstelle fur neuere Osterreichische Literatur
Seidengasse 13, 1070 Vienna
Tel: (01) 526 20 44-0 *Fax:* (01) 526 20 44-30
E-mail: info@literaturhaus.at
Web Site: www.literaturhaus.at
Key Personnel
Dir: Dr Heinz Lunzer
Founded: 1965
Documentation Centre for Modern Austrian Literature.
Publication(s): *Zirkular* (quarterly)

Oesterreichische Gesellschaft fuer Dokumentation und Information (OGDI)
(Austrian Documentation Society)
c/o Wirtschaftuniversitaet Wien, Augasse 9, 1090 Vienna
Tel: (01) 31336 5107 *Fax:* (01) 31336 905107
E-mail: oegdi@termnet.at
Web Site: www.oegdi.at
Key Personnel
Pres: Gerhard Richter
Secretary: Hermann Huemer *E-mail:* hermann.huemer@wu-wien.ac.at
Founded: 1951
Membership(s): Austrian Society for Documentation & Information; FID.
Publication(s): *Oegdi Aktuell*

Oesterreichisches Institut fuer Bibliotheksforschung, Dokumentations- und Informationswesen
Resselgasse 4, 1040 Vienna
Key Personnel
Chairman: J Wawrosch
Austrian Institute for Library Research, Documentation and Information.

Vereinigung Oesterreichischer Bibliothekarinnen und Bibliothekare (VOEB) (Association of Austrian Librarians)
Voralberger Federal State Library, Fluherstr 4, 6900 Bregenz
E-mail: voeb@uibk.ac.at
Web Site: voeb.uibk.ac.at
Key Personnel
President: Dr Harald Weigel *E-mail:* harald.weigel@vorarlberg.at
Vice President: Dr Sigrid Reinitzer *Tel:* (0316) 380-3101; (0316) 380-3102; (0316) 380-3103 *Fax:* (0316) 38 49 87 *E-mail:* sigrid.reinitzer@kfunigraz.ac.at; Maria Seissl *E-mail:* maria.seissl@univie.ac.at
Secretary: Dr Werner Schlacher *E-mail:* werner.schlacher@kfunigraz.ac.at
Treasurer: Dr Gerhard Zechner *E-mail:* gerhard.zechner@voralberg.at
Founded: 1945
Publication(s): *Biblos* (quarterly, bulletin); *Mitteilungen* (quarterly, bulletin); *Verleger-Publisher: Gesellschaft der Freunde der Oesterreichischen National-bibliothek* (published in German)

VOEB, see Vereinigung Oesterreichischer Bibliothekarinnen und Bibliothekare (VOEB)

Bangladesh

National Library of Bangladesh, Directorate of Archives & Libraries
32 Justice Sayed Mahbub Murshed Sarani, Sher-e-Bangla Nagar (Agargaon), Dhaka 1207
Tel: (02) 326572 *Fax:* (02) 9118704
Key Personnel
Dir: Mr Hahashinur Rahman Khan
Founded: 1972
Collection, preservation & reproduction of books & other documents; reference & readers service. ISBN Agency of all publications. Hold seminars, exhibitions & workshops to create awareness of library services.
Membership(s): IFLA (International Federation of Library Associations & Institutions).
Publication(s): *Artical Index* (annually); *Bangladesh National Bibliography* (annually); *Public Library Directory* (annually)
Parent Company: Ministry of Cultural Affairs

The Library Association of Bangladesh
c/o Institute of Library & Information Science, Bangladesh Central Public Library Bldg, Shahbagh, Dhaka 1000
Tel: (02) 504269; (02) 8619408
E-mail: msik@icddrb.org
Key Personnel
President: M Shamsul Islam Khan
Vice President: Kazi Abdul Mazed; Dr Md Abdul Matir; Md Harun-ar-Rashid
General Secretary: Kh Fazlur Rahman
Treasurer: Md Abdul Latif
Founded: 1956
Work for the professional development in Bangladesh & offers training courses.
Publication(s): *The Eastern Librarian* (twice a year); *Upatta* (newsletter, quarterly, text in Bengali)

Barbados

Library Association of Barbados
PO Box 827E, Bridgetown
Key Personnel
President: Shirley Yearwood
Secretary: Hazelyn Devonish
Publication(s): *Bulletin* (irregular); *Update* (irregular, newsletter)

Belgium

APBD, see Association Professionnelle des Bibliothecaires et Documentalistes (APBD)

Archief- en Bibliotheekwezen in Belgie (Belgian Association of Archivists & Librarians)
Ruisbroekstr 2-10, 1000 Brussels
Tel: (02) 5195351 *Fax:* (02) 5195533
Telex: 21157
Key Personnel
General Secretary: Wim De Vos *E-mail:* wim.devos@kbr.be
Publication(s): *Archives et Bibliotheques de Belgique* (text in Dutch, English, French, German, Italian, Latin & Spanish)

Association Belgium de Documentation
(Belgian Association for Documentation)
Highwaye de Wavre 1683, Waversesteenweg, 1160 Brussels
Tel: (02) 675 58 62 *Fax:* (02) 672 74 46
E-mail: info@abd-bvd.be
Web Site: www.abd-bvd.be
Key Personnel
President: Philippians Laurent *Tel:* (010) 474262 *Fax:* (010) 474603 *E-mail:* laurent@spri.ucl.ac.be
Vice President: Paul Heyvaert *Tel:* (02) 519 54 86 *E-mail:* paul.heyvaert@kbr.be
Secretary: Vincent Maes *Tel:* (02) 246 45 31 *Fax:* (02) 246 39 58
Treasurer: Miguel Lambotte *Tel:* (02) 206 42 38 *E-mail:* miguel.lanbotte@tiscali.be
Founded: 1947
Membership(s): EBLIDA; ECIA.
Publication(s): *ABD-BVD Info* (newsletter); *Cahiers de la Documentation - Bladen voor Documentatie* (quarterly, text in Dutch, English & French)

Association des Archivistes et Bibliotheques, see Archief- en Bibliotheekwezen in Belgie

Association des Bibliothecaires Belges d'Expression Francaise
39 Emile Vandevandel Str, 1470 Genappe
Mailing Address: BP 20, 1470 Genappe
Tel: (067) 771477; (067) 790683 *Fax:* (067) 771477
E-mail: abbef.be@gate71.be; abbef@freeworld.be
Key Personnel
President: Michel Dagneau *E-mail:* dagneau.m@swing.be
Association of French-speaking Librarians from Belgium.
Publication(s): *Le Bibliothecaire: Revue d'Information culturelle et bibliographique*

Association Professionnelle des Bibliothecaires et Documentalistes (APBD)
Ave Reve d'or, 30, 7100 La Louviere
Tel: (071) 61 43 35 *Fax:* (071) 61 16 34
E-mail: biblio.hainaut@skynet.be
Web Site: www.apbd.be
Key Personnel
President: Jean-Claude Trefois *Tel:* (071) 21 55 18 *E-mail:* jean_claude.trefois@hainaut.be
Secretary: Laurence Hennaux *Tel:* (064) 45 87 76
Publication(s): *Bloc-notes*; *Un cadeau, un livre* (annual selection of children's books)

Scientific & Technical Information Service
Keizerslaan 4 Bld de l'Empereur, 1000 Brussels
Tel: (02) 519 56 40 *Fax:* (02) 519 56 45
E-mail: info@stis.fgov.be
Web Site: www.stis.fgov.be
Key Personnel
Dir: Dr Jean Moulin *Tel:* (02) 519 56 56 *E-mail:* jean.moulin@stis.fgov.be
Publication(s): *The Electronic Information Services Industry in Belgium 1997-1999*
Parent Company: Federal Office for Scientific, Technical & Cultural Affairs

SIST-DWTI, see Scientific & Technical Information Service

Vereniging van Religieus-Wetenschappelijke Bibliothecarissen (Association of Religious Academic Librarians)
Sint-Michielsstr 6, 3000 Leuven
Tel: (016) 323807 *Fax:* (016) 323862
Web Site: www.theo.kuleuven.ac.be/vrb
Key Personnel
President: Etienne D'hondt *E-mail:* etienne.dhondt@theo.kuleuven.ac.be
Secretary: Kris van de Casteele *Tel:* (03) 2873563 *Fax:* (03) 2873562 *E-mail:* kris.vandecasteele@ua.ac.be
Founded: 1965
Membership(s): Bibliotheques Europeennes de Theologie (BETH).
Publication(s): *VRB-Informatie* (quarterly)

Vlaamse Vereniging voor Bibliotheek-Archief-en Documentatiewezen (VVBAD)
(Flemish Association for Libraries, Archives & Documentation Centres)

Statiestr 179, 2600 Berchem Antwerp
Tel: (03) 2814457 *Fax:* (03) 2188077
E-mail: vvbad@vvbad.be
Web Site: www.vvbad.be
Key Personnel
President: Geert Puype
Executive Dir: Marc Storms *E-mail:* marc.storms@vvbad.be
Secretary: Marc Engels
Founded: 1921
Publication(s): *Archiefkunde* (monographs); *Bibliotheek- en Archiefgids* (Library & Archive Guide, 6 times/yr); *Bibliotheekkunde* (monographs); *INFO* (monthly, membership journal); *Vlaamse Archief-, Bibliotheek- en Documentatiegids* (biennially, address guide to archives, libraries & documentation centers in Dutch-speaking part of Belgium)

VRB, see Vereniging van Religieus-Wetenschappelijke Bibliothecarissen

Belize

Belize Library Association
c/o Bliss Institute, PO Box 287, Belize City
Tel: (02) 7267; (02) 34248; (02) 34249 *Fax:* (02) 34246
Key Personnel
President: H W Young
Secretary: Robert Hulse
Publication(s): *Belize Library Association Bulletin*

Bolivia

Asociacion Boliviana de Bibliotecarios (ABB) (Bolivia Association of Librarians)
c/o Efrain Virreira Sanchez, Casilla 992, Cochabamba
Tel: (064) 1481
Key Personnel
Dir: Gunnar Mendoza
Founded: 1836

Centro Nacional de Documentacion Cientifica y Tecnologica - Universidad Mayor De S an Andres
Av Mariscal Santa Cruz Nº 1175, esquina c, Ayacucho
Tel: (02) 359583 *Fax:* (02) 359586
E-mail: iiicndct@huayna.umsa.edu.bo
Telex: 3438 UMSA-BV
Key Personnel
Contact: Ruben Valle Vera
National Scientific & Technological Documentation Centre.
Publication(s): *Bibliography Series* (3-5 times/year); *Boletin Accesos* (quarterly); *Current Events* (annually)

Bosnia and Herzegovina

Drustvo Bibliotekara Bosne i Hercegovine (Librarians' Society of Bosnia & Herzegovina)
Zmaja od Bosne 8b, 71000 Sarajevo
Tel: (033) 275 312 *Fax:* (033) 218 431
E-mail: nubbih@nub.ba
Web Site: www.nub.ba
Key Personnel
President: Nevenka Hajdarovic *E-mail:* nevenka@nub.ba
Publisher: Emina Memija
Dir: Dr Enes Kujundzic
Founded: 1945
Publication(s): *Bibliotekarstvo* (annually)

Botswana

Botswana Library Association
PO Box 1310, Gaborone
Tel: (031) 3552295 *Fax:* (031) 357291
Web Site: www.bla.0catch.com
Telex: 2429BD
Key Personnel
Chairperson: Ms Bobana Badisang
Secretary: Peter Tshukudu
Founded: 1978
Publication(s): *Botswana Library Association Journal*

Brazil

Associacao dos Arquivistas Brasileiros (Association of Brazilian Archivists)
Av Presidente Vargas, 1733, Sala 903, 20210-030 Rio de Janeiro-RJ
Tel: (021) 2507-2239 *Fax:* (021) 3852-2541
E-mail: aab@aab.org.br
Web Site: www.aab.org.br
Key Personnel
President: Lia Temporal Malcher
Secretary: Laura Regina Xavier
Publication(s): *Associacao dos Arquivistas Brasileiros* (Association of Brazilian Archivists, bulletin); *Revista Arquivo & Administracao* (biannually)

Instituto Brasileiro de Informacao em Ciencia e Tecnologia
SAS Quadra 5 Lote 6 Bloco H, 70070-914 Brasilia DF
Tel: (061) 217-6360; (061) 217-6350 *Fax:* (061) 226-2677
E-mail: webmaster@ibict.br
Web Site: www.ibict.br
Telex: (061) 2481
Key Personnel
Dir: Nilson Lemos Lage *E-mail:* lage@ibict.br
Publication(s): *Bibliografia Brasileira de Ciencia da Informacao* (Brazilian Bibliography of Information Science, annually); *Bibliografic Brasileira de Politica Cientifica e Tecnologica* (Brazilian Bibliography of Political Science & Technology); *Boletim Qualidade & Produtividade* (Quality & Productivity Bulletin, quarterly); *Calendario de Eventos em C&T* (Calendar of Events in C&I, quarterly); *Ciencia da Informacao* (Information Science, biannually); *Informativo IBICT* (Informative IBICT, biannually)

Federacao Brasileira de Associacoes de Bibliotecarios - Comissao Brasileira de Documentacao Juridica (FEBAB/CBDJ) (Brazilian Federation of Library Associations - Brazilian Committee of Legal Documentation)
Rua Avanhandava, 40, cj 110, 01306-001 Sao Paulo-SP
Tel: (011) 3257-9979 *Fax:* (011) 3257-9979
E-mail: febab@febab.org.br
Web Site: www.febab.org.br
Key Personnel
President: Marcia Rosetto
Vice President: Carminda Nogueira de Castro Ferreira
Publication(s): *Noticias* (News)

IBICT, see Instituto Brasileiro de Informacao em Ciencia e Tecnologia

Brunei Darussalam

Persatuan Perpustakaan Kebangsaan Negara Brunei Darussalam (PPKNBD) (National Library Association of Brunei)
Perpustakaan Universiti Brunei Darussalam, Jalan Tungku Link Gadong BE 1410
Tel: (02) 223060 *Fax:* (02) 235472; (02) 241817
Key Personnel
President: Puan Nellie bte Dato Paduka Haji Sunny *Tel:* (02) 249001 *Fax:* (02) 249504
E-mail: chieflib@lib.ubd.edu.bn
Vice President: Pg Haji Mohd Shahminan bin Pg Haji Sulaiman *Tel:* (02) 380318 *Fax:* (02) 38200
Chief Librarian: Haji Abu Bakar Haji Zainal *Tel:* (02) 235501 *Fax:* (02) 224763
E-mail: chieflib@brunet.bn
Publication(s): *Wadah Pustaka* (newsletter, 1994)

PPKNBD, see Persatuan Perpustakaan Kebangsaan Negara Brunei Darussalam (PPKNBD)

Cameroon

Association des Bibliothecaires, Archivistes, Documentalistes et Museographes du Cameroon (ABADCAM) (Association of Librarians, Archivists, Documentalists & Museum Curators of Cameroon)
BP 4609, Nlongkak Centre Province
Tel: 222 6362 *Fax:* 222 4785; 222 6262
E-mail: abadcam@yahoo.fr
Telex: 8384
Key Personnel
President: Hilaire Omokolo
Librarian: P N Chateh
Works in collaboration with the Ministry of Culture in formulating policies for librarians, archivists, documentalists & museographers in Cameroon.
Publication(s): *Newsletter*

Chile

Colegio de Bibliotecarios de Chile AG
Paraguay 383, Torre 11 Oficina 122, 6510017 Santiago
Tel: (02) 222 56 52 *Fax:* (02) 635 50 23
E-mail: cdc@uplink.cl
Web Site: www.bibliotecarios.cl
Key Personnel
President: Marcia Marinovic Simunovic *Tel:* (02) 231 38 46 *E-mail:* mmarinovic@vtr.cl
Vice President: Claudia Cuevas Saavedra *Tel:* (02) 270 17 43 *Fax:* (02) 270 17 47
E-mail: ccuevas@bcn.cl

Secretary: Ana Maria Pino Yanez *Tel:* (02) 270 17 51 *Fax:* (02) 270 17 47 *E-mail:* apino@bcn.cl
Chilean Library Association.
Publication(s): *Indices de Publicaciones Periodicas en Bibliotecologia* (Catalogue of Periodical Publications on Librarianship); *Micronoticias*

Comision Nacional de Investigacion Cientifica y Technologica, see CONICYT

CONICYT (National Commission for Science & Technology)
Departamento de Informacion, Canada 308, Providencia, Santiago
Tel: (02) 3654400 *Fax:* (02) 6551396
E-mail: info@conicyt.cl
Web Site: www.conicyt.cl
Key Personnel
President: Sr Eric Goles Chacc
Head of Dept: Ana Maria Prat *Tel:* (02) 3654450
 E-mail: amprat@conicyt.cl
Founded: 1967
Publication(s): *Serie Directorios*; *Serie Informacion y Documentacion*

China

China Society for Library Science
33 Zhongguancun (S), Beijing 100081
Tel: (010) 6841 9270 *Fax:* (010) 6841 9271
E-mail: ztxhmsc@publicf.nlc.gov.cn
Web Site: www.nlc.gov.cn
Telex: 222211
Key Personnel
President: Liu Deyou
Secretary General: Gulian Li
Dir: Mr Ren Jiyu
Founded: 1979
Publication(s): *Journal of China Library Science*

Colombia

Asociacion Colombiana de Bibliotecologos y Documentalistas
Carrera 50, 27-70, modulo 1 nivel 4, bloque C-Colceincias, Bogota
Tel: (01) 3603077 (ext 326)
Web Site: www.biblio.ucaldas.edu.co
Key Personnel
President: Jaime Vasquez Restrepo
Vice President: Luis Alberto Becerra Hernandez
Colombian Library Association.
Publication(s): *Boletin*

Congo

Direction Generale des Services de Bibliotheques, Archives et Documentation
 (General Management of Library, Archives & Documentation Services)
Bibliotheque Nationale Populaire, BP 1489, Brazzaville
Tel: 833 485 *Fax:* 832 253

The Democratic Republic of the Congo

Association Zairoise des Archivistes, Bibliothecaires et Documentalistes
BP 805, Kinshasa X1
Tel: (012) 30123; (012) 30124
Key Personnel
Executive Secretary: E Kabeba-Bangasa
Zaire Association of Archivists, Librarians and Documentalists.
Publication(s): *Mukanda*

Costa Rica

Asociacion Costarricense de Bibliotecarios
 (Costa Rican Association of Librarians)
Apdo 3308, San Jose
Key Personnel
Secretary-General: Nelly Kopper
Publication(s): *Anuario bibliografico costarricense* (Boletin)

Cote d'Ivoire

ADBACI, see Association pour le Developpement de la Documentation, des Bibliotheques et Archives de la Cote d'Ivoire (ADBACI)

Association pour le Developpement de la Documentation, des Bibliotheques et Archives de la Cote d'Ivoire (ADBACI)
c/o Bibliotheque Nationale, BPV 180, Abidjan
Tel: 32 38 72
Key Personnel
Dir: Ambroise Agnero
Secretary General: Cangah Guy

Croatia

HKD, see Hrvatsko knjiznicarsko drustvo

Hrvatsko knjiznicarsko drustvo (Croatian Library Association)
c/o Nacionalna i sveucilisna knjiznica, Hrvatske bratske zajednice 4, 10 000 Zagreb
Tel: (01) 615 93 20; (01) 457 2344; (01) 457 2306 *Fax:* (01) 616 41 86
E-mail: hkd@nsk.hr
Web Site: pubwww.srce.hr/hkd
Key Personnel
President: Dubravka Stancin-Rosic *Tel:* (01) 616 40 37
Secretary: Dunja-Marija Gabriel
 E-mail: dgabriel@nsk.hr
Founded: 1940
Membership(s): IFLA (International Federation of Library Associations); EBLIDA (European Bureau of Library, Information & Documentation Associations).
Publication(s): *Vjesnik bibliotekara Hrvatske* (biannually, scientific magazine)

Cuba

Library Association of Cuba
c/o Direccion de Relaciones Internacionales, Ministerio de Culture, Calle 4 e/m 11y13, Vedado, Havana
Mailing Address: Apdo 6881, Havana
Tel: (07) 552244 *Fax:* (07) 662053
Telex: 0571963
Key Personnel
Dir: Marta Terry Gonzalez
Vice President: Elisa Masiques; Blanca Mercedes Mesa

Cyprus

Library Association of Cyprus
PO Box 1039, 1434 Nicosia
Tel: (022) 404849
Key Personnel
President: Costas D Stephanov
Secretary: Paris G Rossos
Publication(s): *Deltion Vivliothikarion* (Library Bulletin)

Czech Republic

Svaz knihovniku informacnich pracovniku Ceske republiky (SKIP) (Association of Library & Information Professionals of the Czech Republic)
National Library, Klementinum 190, 11001 Prague
Tel: (02) 21663111 *Fax:* (02) 21663261
Web Site: www.nkp.cz
Key Personnel
President: Vit Richter *E-mail:* vit.richter@nkp.cz
Honorary President: Dr Jarmila Burgetova
 Tel: (02) 3115030 *E-mail:* jarmila.burgetova@seznam.cz
Founded: 1968
Membership(s): IFLA.
Publication(s): *SKIP* (quarterly, bulletin)

Denmark

Arkivarforeningen
c/o Landsarkivet for Sjaelland, Jagtvej 10, 22 Copenhagen N
Tel: 31393520 *Fax:* 33153239
Key Personnel
President: Tyge Krogh
Secretary: Charlotte Steinmark
Archives Society.
Publication(s): *Kommunal opgavelosning 1842-1970* (Odense University Press, 1990)

Danmarks Biblioteksforening (Danish Library Association)
Vesterbrogade 20, 5 sal, 1620 Copenhagen V

Tel: 33 25 09 35 *Fax:* 33 25 79 00
Web Site: www.dbf.dk
Key Personnel
Dir: Winnie Vitzansky
Publication(s): *Biblioteksvejviser* (Library Guide); *Bogens Verden* (Library Journal); *Danmarks Biblioteker* (Members Magazine)

Danmarks Forskningsbiblioteksforening
c/o Statsbiblioteket, Universitetsparken, 8000 Arhus C
Tel: (045) 89 46 22 07 *Fax:* (045) 89 46 22 20
E-mail: df@statsbiblioteket.dk
Web Site: www.dfdf.dk
Key Personnel
President: Erland Kolding
Secretary: Hanne Dahl
Danish Research Library Association: Section 1 Research Libraries; Section 2 Staff members of Danish Research Libraries.
Publication(s): *DF-Revy*

Dansk Musikbiblioteks Forening (DMBF)
(Danish Music Library Association)
Nordjysk Musikkonservatorium, Ryesgade 52, 9000 Aalborg
Tel: 33 47 43 16 *Fax:* 33 47 47 10
E-mail: dmbf@kb.dk
Web Site: www.dmbf.nu
Key Personnel
President: Ole Bisbjerg *Tel:* 89 46 21 33 *E-mail:* ob@statsbiblioteket.dk
Vice President: Kirsten Husted *Tel:* 75 82 32 00, ext 135 *Fax:* 75 82 32 13 *E-mail:* kh@vejlebib.dk
Secretary General: Jane Mariegaard *Tel:* 96 31 31 61 *E-mail:* jane@hordkons.dk
Treasurer: Erling Dujardin *Tel:* 38 21 19 00 *Fax:* 38 21 19 99 *E-mail:* erdu01@frederiksberg.dk
Membership(s): Association of Danish Music Libraries (Danish section of AIBM/IAML).
Publication(s): *MusikBIB* (Journal for Music Libraries, quarterly, 2000, text in Danish)

Kommunernes Skolebiblioteksforening
(Association of Danish School Libraries)
Krimsvej 29 B 1, 2300 Copenhagen S
Tel: 33111391 *Fax:* 33111390
E-mail: komskolbib@ksbf.dk
Web Site: www.ksbf.dk
Key Personnel
Chief Executive: Paul Erik Sorensen
Editor: Niels Jacobsen
Publication(s): *Born og Boger* (Children & Books); *Skolebiblioteksarbogen* (School Libraries Annual)

Dominican Republic

Asociacion Dominicana de Bibliotecarios (ASODOBI) (Dominican Association of Librarians)
c/o Biblioteca Nacional, Cesar Nicolas Penson 91, Plaza de la Cultura, Santo Domingo
Tel: 6884086; 6884660 *Fax:* 685841
E-mail: biblioteca.nacional@dominicana.com; intec.biblioteca@codetel.net.do
Key Personnel
President: Prospero J Mella-Chavier
Secretary-General: Ms V Regus
Founded: 1971
Publication(s): *El Papiro*

ASODOBI, see Asociacion Dominicana de Bibliotecarios (ASODOBI)

Departamento de Documentacion y Bibliotecas
Galeria Nacional de Bellas Artes y Cultos, Santo Domingo
Key Personnel
Dir: Dr Jose de J Alvarez Valverde
Library and Documentation Service.

Grupo Bibliografico Nacional de la Republica Dominicana
Archivo General de la Nacion, Calle ME Diaz, Santo Domingo

Ecuador

Asociacion Ecuatoriana de Bibliotecarios (AEB) (Ecuadorian Library Association)
c/o Casa de la Cultura Ecuatoriana Benjamin Carrion, Av 12 de Octubre 555, Quito
Tel: 2528-840 *Fax:* 2223-391
E-mail: asoebfp@hotmail.com
Web Site: www.reicyt.org.ec/aeb
Key Personnel
President: Wilson Vega *Tel:* 446-233 (ext 132) *E-mail:* wilson_vega@ecuabox.com
Vice President: Eugenia Lopez *Tel:* 504-692 (ext 42)
Dir: Laura de Crespo
Secretary: Rosario Moreno E *Tel:* 502-456; 502-262
Treasurer: Cesar Calero *Tel:* 509-753; 509-754
Publication(s): *Unidad Bibliotecaria*

Egypt (Arab Republic of Egypt)

Egyptian Association for Library & Information Science
c/o Dept Archives, Librarianship & Information Science, Faculty of Arts, University of Cairo, Cairo
Tel: (02) 5676365 *Fax:* (02) 5729659
Key Personnel
President: Dr S Khalifa
Secretary: M Hosam El-Din
Publication(s): *Alam al-Maktabat* (Library World)

El Salvador

Asociacion de Bibliotecarios de El Salvador (El Salvador Library Association)
Apdo 2923, San Salvador
Tel: 216312 *Fax:* 225-02 78
Web Site: www.ues.edu.sv/abes/informacion.htm
Key Personnel
President: Olinda Estela Gomez Moran
Vice President: Salador Octavio Montes Figueroa
Publication(s): *Informa* (monthly, newsletter)

Asociacion General de Archivistas de El Salvador (Association of Archivists of El Salvador)
Archivo General de la Nacion, Direccion Nacional de Patrimonio Cultural, Palacio Nacional, Av Cuscatlan, San Salvador
Tel: 222 94 18 *Fax:* 281 58 60
E-mail: agnes@agn.gob.sv
Web Site: www.agn.gob.sv

Ethiopia

Ethiopian Library & Information Association
PO Box 30530, Addis Ababa
Tel: (01) 511344 *Fax:* (01) 552544
Key Personnel
President: Mulugeta Hunde
Secretary: Girma Makonnen
Founded: 1961
Publication(s): *Directory of Ethiopian Libraries*; *Ethiopian Library Association* (biannually, bulletin)

Finland

BMF, see Bibliothecarii Medicinae Fenniae (BMF)

Finnish Library Association, see Suomen Kirjastoseura

Bibliothecarii Medicinae Fenniae (BMF)
(Finnish Medical Librarians' Association)
PL 61, 00014 Helsingin Yliopisto
Tel: (09) 191 26645 *Fax:* (09) 191 26652
E-mail: etunimi.sukunimi@helsinki.fi
Web Site: www.terkko.helsinki.fi/bmf
Key Personnel
Chairman: Ulla Neuvonen
Founded: 1980
Membership(s): IFLA (International Federation of Library Associations & Institutions); EAHIL (European Association for Health Information & Libraries); NAMHI (Nordic Association for Medical & Health Information).

Suomen Kirjastoseura (Finnish Library Association)
Kansakoulukatu 10 A 19, 00100 Helsinki
Tel: (09) 694 1858 *Fax:* (09) 694 1859
E-mail: fla@fla.fi
Web Site: www.kaapeli.fi/~fla/presentation.html
Key Personnel
Secretary General: Tuula Haavisto
President: Mirja Ryynanen
Founded: 1910
Publication(s): *Kirjastolehti* (monthly, journal)

Suomen Tieteellinen Kirjastoseura ry (Finnish Research Library Association)
PO Box 217, 00171 Helsinki
Tel: (017) 34 22 25 *Fax:* (017) 34 22 79
E-mail: meri.kuula@arcada.fi
Web Site: pro.tsv.fi/stks
Key Personnel
Chairperson & President: Tuula Ruhanen *Tel:* (09) 191 280 51 *Fax:* (09) 191 280 86 *E-mail:* tuula.ruhanen@helsinki.fi

Secretary: Meri Kuula-Bruun *Tel:* (09) 52532 465 *Fax:* (09) 52532 444 *E-mail:* meri.kuula-bruun@arcada.fi
Publication(s): *Guide to Research Libraries & Information Services in Finland*; *Signum* (eight times/yr, text in Finnish)

Tietohuollon Neuvottelukunta
c/o Ministry of Education, Meritullinkatu 10, 00170 Helsinki
Mailing Address: PO Box 29, 00023 Helsinki
Tel: (09) 13 41 71 *Fax:* (09) 65 67 65
E-mail: jylha@csc.fi
Telex: 122109 Mined
Key Personnel
Chairman: Juhani Hakkarainen
Secretary General: Annu Jylhae-Pyykoenen
Finnish Council for Information Provision.

France

ABEF, see Association des Bibliotheques Chretiennes France (ABEF)

ADBS, see L'Association des Professionnels de l'Information et de la Documentation (ADBS)

ADEBD, see Association des Diplomes de l'Ecole de Bibliothecaires-Documentalistes

Association des Archivistes Francais (Association of French Archivists)
9 rue Montcalm, 75018 Paris
Tel: (01) 46 06 39 44 *Fax:* (01) 46 06 39 52
E-mail: secretariat@archivistes.org
Web Site: www.archivistes.org
Key Personnel
President: Elisabeth Verry
Vice President: Francois Gasnault; Anne-Catherine Marin; Henri Zuber
Secretary: Francoise Banat
Treasurer: Vincent Doom
Publication(s): *La Gazette des Archives*
Branch Office(s)
Centre de Formation, 9 rue Rodier, 75009 Paris

Association des Bibliothecaires Francais (Association of French Librarians)
31 rue de Chabrol, 75010 Paris
Tel: (01) 55 33 10 30 *Fax:* (01) 55 33 10 31
E-mail: abf@abf.asso.fr
Web Site: www.abf.asso.fr
Key Personnel
President: Gerard Briand
General Secretary: Jan-Francois Jacques
Founded: 1906
Publication(s): *Bulletin d'informations de l'ABF*

Association des Bibliotheques Chretiennes France (ABEF) (Association of Ecclesiastical Libraries in France)
6 rue du Regard, 75006 Paris
Tel: (01) 42 22 44 11 *Fax:* (01) 42 22 37 90
E-mail: agmd.bibliotheque@wanadoo.fr
Key Personnel
President: Paul de Crombrugghe
Vice President: Jerome Rousse-Lacordaire
Secretary: Colette Moron
Publication(s): *Bulletin de liaison de l'ABEF* (ISSN 0066-8958)

Association des Diplomes de l'Ecole de Bibliothecaires-Documentalistes (Association of Graduates of the School of Librarians and Documentalists)
c/o Bibliotheque du Saulchoir, 43 bis, rue de la Glaciere, 75013 Paris
Tel: (01) 45 87 05 33 *Fax:* (01) 43 31 07 56
E-mail: adbs@adbs.fr
Web Site: www.adbs.fr
Key Personnel
President: Marie-Cecile Comerre *Tel:* (01) 48 00 20 70
Secretary: M Potier
Publication(s): *Bulletin d'Information* (annually, text in French)

F A D B E N, see Federation des Enseignants Documentalistes de l'Education nationale

Federation des Enseignants Documentalistes de l'Education nationale (Federation of Associations of National Educational Record Clerks & Librarians)
25, rue Claude Tillier, 75012 Paris
Tel: (01) 43 72 45 60 *Fax:* (01) 43 72 45 60
E-mail: fadben@wanadoo.fr
Web Site: www.fadben.asso.fr
Key Personnel
President: Colette Charrier-Ligonat *Tel:* (05) 45 90 52 78 *E-mail:* c.charrier@wanadoo.fr
Vice President: Brigitte Bacconnier *Tel:* (04) 72 89 83 00 *E-mail:* brigitte.bacconnier@free.fr; Isabelle Fructus *Tel:* (04) 42 33 02 13 *Fax:* (04) 42 29 45 38 *E-mail:* fructus@club-internet.fr
Secretary: Isabelle Laudin *Tel:* (03) 29 45 32 00 *E-mail:* isabelle.laudin@ac-nancy-metz.fr
Publication(s): *La Lettre* (quarterly); *Mediadoc* (triannually)

L'Association des Professionnels de l'Information et de la Documentation (ADBS) (French Association of Information & Documentation Professionals)
25, rue Claude Tillier, 75012 Paris
Tel: (01) 43 72 25 25 *Fax:* (01) 43 72 30 41
E-mail: adbs@adbs.fr
Web Site: www.adbs.fr
Key Personnel
President: Florence Wilhelm
Publication(s): *Documentaliste - Sciences de l'Information et ouvrages Specialises*

Germany

A Sp B, see Arbeitsgemeinschaft der Spezialbibliotheken eV (ASpB)

Arbeitsgemeinschaft der Archive und Bibliotheken in der evangelischen Kirche (Joint Association of Archives & Libraries in the Evangelical Church)
Veilhofstr 28, 90489 Nuremberg
Mailing Address: Postfach 250429, 90129 Nuremburg
Tel: (0911) 58869-0 *Fax:* (0911) 58869-69
E-mail: LKANuernberg@t-online.de
Web Site: www.ekd.de/archive/deutsch/arbeitsg.htm
Key Personnel
President: Dr Helmut Baier
Publication(s): *Aus Evangelischen Archiven, Neue Folge der Allgemeinen Mitteilungen der AABevk*; *Veroeffenlichungen der AABevK* (Publications of the AABevK)

Arbeitsgemeinschaft der Regionalbibliotheken (Joint Association of Regional Libraries)
Konrad-Adenauer-Str 8, 70173 Stuttgart
Tel: (0711) 212-4423 *Fax:* (0711) 212-4422
Web Site: www.regionalbibliotheken.de
Key Personnel
Dir: Dr Hannsjoerg Kowark *E-mail:* kowark@wlb-stuttgart.de
Founded: 1983
German library federation.

Arbeitsgemeinschaft der Spezialbibliotheken eV (ASpB) (Association of Special Libraries, Germany)
c/o Forschungszentrum, Julich GmbH, Zentralbibliothek, 52425 Julich
Tel: (02461) 612907; (02461) 615368 *Fax:* (02461) 616103
Web Site: www.aspb.de
Key Personnel
Chairman: Dr Rafael Ball, PhD *E-mail:* r.ball@fz-juelich.de
Project Manager & Secretary Dir: Edith Salz *E-mail:* e.salz@fz-juelich.de
Founded: 1946
Membership(s): International Federation of Library Associations & Institutions (IFLA).
Publication(s): *Bericht ueber elie Tagungi elekrouischer* (biennially, newsletter, conference report)

Arbeitsgemeinschaft fur juristisches Bibliotheks- und Dokumentationswesen (Joint Association for Law Libraries & Legal Documentation)
Bibliot, Ismaninger Str 109, 81675 Munich
Tel: (089) 9231 358 *Fax:* (089) 9231 201
Web Site: www.ajbd.de
Key Personnel
Chairman: Dr Hans-Peter Ziegler *E-mail:* hans-peter.ziegler@bfh.bund.de
Vice Chairman: Dr Wolfgang Schwab *Tel:* (0316) 3801270 *Fax:* (0316) 3809160 *E-mail:* wolfgang.schwab@uni-graz.at
Secretary: Gerda Graf *Tel:* (0331) 9773571 *Fax:* (0331) 9773816 *E-mail:* ggraf@rz.uni-potsdam.de
Treasurer: Annette Schlag *Tel:* (030) 2025-9715 *Fax:* (030) 2025-9660 *E-mail:* kassenwartin@ajbd.de
Editor: Heinz-Guenther Black *Tel:* (0941) 943 2497 *Fax:* (0941) 943 3285 *E-mail:* herausgeber@ajbd.de; Cornelie Butz *Tel:* (0341) 2007 1600 *Fax:* (0341) 2007 1000 *E-mail:* butz@bverwg.bund.de
Publication(s): *Arbeitshefte* (irregularly); *Mitteilungen der Arbeitsgemeinschaft fuer juristisches Bibliotheks- und Dokumentationswesen* (triannually)

Arbeitsgemeinschaft fur medizinisches Bibliothekswesen
c/o Deutsche Zentralbibliothek fuer Medizin (DZM), Joseph-Stelzmann-Str 9, 50924 Cologne
Tel: (0621) 7592376 *Fax:* (0621) 7594419
Web Site: www.agmb.de
Key Personnel
Chairman: Ulrich Korwitz
Founded: 1970

Berufsverband Information Bibliothek (BIB)
Gartenstr 18, 72764 Reutlingen
Tel: (07121) 3491-0 *Fax:* (07121) 300433
E-mail: mail@bib-info.de
Web Site: www.bib-info.de
Key Personnel
President: Klaus-Peter Boettger *Tel:* (0208) 455-4141 *Fax:* (0208) 455-4125 *E-mail:* klaus.peter.boettger@sdadt-mh.de
Secretary: Katharina Boulanger
Association of Librarians.
Publication(s): *BuB-Forum for Bibliothek und Information*

BIB, see Berufsverband Information Bibliothek (BIB)

ASSOCIATIONS — GERMANY

Bibliothek & Information Deutschland (BID) - The Federal Union of German Library & Information Associations
Formerly Bundesvereinigung Deutscher Bibliotheksverbande (BDB)
Str des 17, Juni 114, 10623 Berlin
Tel: (030) 39 00 14 80; (030) 39 00 14 82
  Fax: (030) 39 00 14 84
E-mail: bdb@bdb-dachverband.de; gf@bdb-dachverband.de
Web Site: www.bdverband.de
Key Personnel
Speaker: Dr Georg Ruppelt *Tel:* (0511) 1267 303 *Fax:* (0511) 1267 207 *E-mail:* nlb@mail.nlb-hannover.de
Contact: Elke Daempfert *E-mail:* gs@bdb-dachverband.de
Formed by the joining of the German Association for Information Science & Practice (DGI) with the Federal Union of German Library Associations (BDB).
Publication(s): *Ausbildung im Europaeischen Rahmen-Abschlussbericht*; *BDB-Jahresbericht 1989/90*; *Bibklikotheken '93*; *Bibliotheken in der Informationsgesellschaft*; *Bibliotheksdienst* (monthly, journal, Official publication of BDB; Edited by Zentral- and Landesbibliothek Berlin); *Drehscheibe der Information*; *Menschen, Buecher und Computer*; *Umsetzung der EG-Richtlinien zum Vermiet-und Verleihrecht*
Branch Office(s)
Fadbodsdule Hamburg, Griudellof 30, 20146 Hamburg

BID, see Bibliothek & Information Deutschland (BID) - The Federal Union of German Library & Information Associations

Bundesvereinigung Deutscher Bibliotheksverbande (BDB), see Bibliothek & Information Deutschland (BID) - The Federal Union of German Library & Information Associations

DBV, see Deutscher Bibliotheksverband eV (DBV)

Deutsche Exlibris Gesellschaft ev (German Bookplate Society)
Joachim-Karnatz-Allee 19, 10557 Berlin
Tel: (030) 20 67 19 90 *Fax:* (030) 20 67 19 91
Web Site: www.exlibris-gesellschaft.de
Key Personnel
President: Dr Gernot Blum *E-mail:* info@exlibris-blum.de
Secretary: Birgit M A Goebel-Stiegler
  E-mail: birgit.goebel@t-online.de
Membership(s): FISAE (Federation International des Societes Amateurs d Exlibris).
Publication(s): *Jahrbuch Exlibriskunst und Graphik* (annually)

Deutsche Gesellschaft fur Informationswissenschaft und informationspraxis eV (German Society for Information Science & Information Practice)
Ostbahnhofstr 13, 60314 Frankfurt am Main
Tel: (069) 43 03 13 *Fax:* (069) 49 09 09 6
E-mail: zentrale@dgi-info.de
Web Site: www.dgd.de
Key Personnel
President: Dr Gabriele Beger *E-mail:* beger@dgi-info.de
Vice President: Dieter Mewes *E-mail:* mewes@dgi-info.de; Dr Ralph Schmidt *E-mail:* schmidt@dgi-info.de
Treasurer: Dr Klaus Steffen Dittrich
  E-mail: dittrich@dgi-info.de
Publication(s): *nfd-Information Wissenschaft und Praxis* (Documentation)

Deutscher Bibliotheksverband eV (DBV)
(Association of German Libraries)
Str des 17, Juni 114, 10623 Berlin
Tel: (030) 39 00 14 80; (030) 39 00 14 81
  Fax: (030) 39 00 14 84
E-mail: dbv@bibliotheksverband.de
Web Site: www.bibliotheksverband.de
Key Personnel
Chairman: Dr Georg Ruppelt
President: Brigitte soot Scherer
Contact: Elke Daempfert *E-mail:* daempfert@bdbibl.de
Publication(s): *D B V-Info* (annually)

Deutscher Verband Evangelischer Buechereien eV (German Association of Protestant Libraries)
Buergerstr 2a, 37073 Goettingen
Tel: (0551) 500759-0 *Fax:* (0551) 704415
E-mail: dveb@dveb.info
Web Site: www.dveb.info
Key Personnel
Chairman: Dr Eckart V Vietinghoff
Manager: Gabriele Kassenbrock
Publication(s): *Der Evangelische Buchberater* (quarterly); *Handwoerterbuch der evangelischen Buechereiarbeit 1980*

Deutsches Bibliotheksinstitut (German Library Institute)
Kurt-Schumacher-Damm 12-16, 13405 Berlin
Tel: (030) 410 34-0 *Fax:* (030) 410 34-100
E-mail: dbilink@dbi-berlin.de
Web Site: www.dbi-berlin.de
Key Personnel
Dir: Prof Gunter Beyersdorff
Also several reference books, monographs, bibliographical & statistical services.
Publication(s): *Bibliotheks Info* (monthly); *Bibliotheksdienst* (monthly, journal)
Branch Office(s)
Luisenstr 57, 10117 Berlin

GBDL, see Gesellschaft fur Bibliothekswesen und Dokumentation des Landbaues (GBDL)

Gesellschaft fur Bibliothekswesen und Dokumentation des Landbaues (GBDL)
(Society for Librarianship & Documentation in Agriculture)
Affiliate of Arbcitsgemeinschaft der Specialbibliotheken e v (ASpB)
c/o TU Muenchen, Informations- und Dokumentationszentrum Weihenstephan, 85350 Freising
Tel: (08161) 71 34 26 *Fax:* (08161) 71 44 09
Web Site: www.weihenstephan.de
Key Personnel
President: Prof W Laux, PhD
Secretary: Dr Birgid Schlindwein
  E-mail: schlind@weihenstephan.de
Publication(s): *Mitteilungen der Gesellschaft fuer Bibliothekswesen und Dokumentation des Landbaues*
Shipping Address: Voettingerstr 47, 85354 Freising

Informationszentrum fuer Informationswissenschaft und -praxis (IZ)
Fachhochschule Potsdam, Friedrich-Ebert-Str 4, 14467 Potsdam
Mailing Address: Postfach 600608, Pappelallee 8-9, 14469 Potsdam
Tel: (0331) 580-2210; (0331) 580-2230
  Fax: (0331) 580-2229
E-mail: iz@fh-potsdam.de
Web Site: www.fh-potsdam.de/~BIB/neu/iz
Documentation & Information Society.

IZ, see Informationszentrum fuer Informationswissenschaft und -praxis (IZ)

NABD, see Normenausschuss Bibliotheks- und Dokumentationswesen (NABD) im DIN Deutsches Institut fuer Normung eV

Normenausschuss Bibliotheks- und Dokumentationswesen (NABD) im DIN Deutsches Institut fuer Normung eV
Burggrafenstr 6, 10787 Berlin
Tel: (030) 2601-2305 *Fax:* (030) 2601-42860
Web Site: www.nabd.din.de *Cable:* DEUTSCHNORMEN BERLIN
Key Personnel
Contact: Dr Winfried Hennig *E-mail:* winfried.hennig@din.de

VdA - Verband deutscher Archivarinnen und Archivare e V (Association of German Archivists)
Marstallstr 2, 99423 Weimar 99423
Mailing Address: Postfach 2119, 99402 Weimar
Tel: (03643) 870-101 *Fax:* (03643) 870-164
E-mail: info@vda.archiv.net
Web Site: www.vda.archiv.net
Key Personnel
Chairman: Dr Volker Wahl *E-mail:* wahl@vda.archiv.net
Man Dir: Thilo Bauer *E-mail:* bauer@vda.archiv.net
Founded: 1946
Publication(s): *Archive in der Bundesrepublik Deutschland, Oesterreich & der Schweiz* (Register of Archives in Germany, Austria & Switzerland, at irregular intervals of several years)

Verein der Diplom-Bibliothekare an wissenschaftlichen Bibliotheken eV
c/o Stadtbuecherei Muelheim an der Ruhr, Friedrich-Ebert-Str 47, 45468 Muelheim an der Ruhr
Tel: (0221) 5747161 *Fax:* (0221) 5747110
Web Site: www.bibliothek.uni-regensburg.de/vddb
Key Personnel
Chairman: Klaus-Peter Boettger *Tel:* (0208) 455-4141 *Fax:* (0208) 455-4125 *E-mail:* klaus-peter.boettger@stadt-mh.de
Deputy Chairman: Kerstin Cevajka
  Tel: (07431) 579-179 *Fax:* (07431) 579-181
  E-mail: kcevajka@fh-albsig.de; Sabine Stummeyer *Tel:* (0511) 762-19870 *Fax:* (0511) 762-4075; (0511) 762-4076 *E-mail:* sabine.stummeyer@tib.uni-hannover.de
Association of Certified Librarians at Academic Libraries.
Publication(s): *Rundschreiben*

Verein Deutscher Bibliothekar eV (VDB)
(Association of German Librarians)
Unter den Linden 8, 10117 Berlin
Tel: (030) 266-1728 *Fax:* (030) 266-1717
E-mail: olaf.hanann@sbb.spk-berlin.de; info@vdb_online.de
Web Site: www.vdb-online.org
Key Personnel
Chairman: Annette Rath-Beckmann *Tel:* (0421) 218-2601; (0421) 218-2602 *E-mail:* rathb@uni-bremen.de
President: Dr Daniela Luelfing
1st Vice President: Dr Wilfried Suehl-Strohmenger
2nd Vice President: Dr Ulrich Hohoff
Secretary: Dr Thomas Elsmann
  E-mail: elsmann@uni-bremen.de
Founded: 1900
Publication(s): *Jahrbuch der deutschen Bibliotheken* (Yearbook of German Libraries, biennial); *Zeitschrift fuer Bibliothekswesen und Bibliographie* (Journal of Library Science & Bibliography)

Wuerttembergische Bibliotheksgesellschaft
Konrad-Adenauer-Str 8, 70173 Stuttgart

Mailing Address: Postfach 10 54 41, 70047 Stuttgart
Tel: (0711) 212-4454; (0711) 212-4424 *Fax:* (0711) 212-4422
E-mail: information@wlb-stuttgart.de
Web Site: www.wlb-stuttgart.de
Key Personnel
Secretary: Elisabeth Tosta
Society of Friends of the Wuerttemberg State Library.

Ghana

Ghana Library Association
PO Box 4105, Accra
Tel: (021) 764822 *Fax:* (021) 763523
Key Personnel
Secretary: A W K Insaidoo
President: E S Asiedo
Founded: 1962
Publication(s): *Ghana Library Journal* (irregularly)

Greece

Enosis Hellinon Bibliothekarion (Greek Library Association)
4 Skoulenion St, 10561 Athens
Tel: (01) 3226 625
Key Personnel
President: K Xatzopoulou
General Secretary: E Kalogeraky
Publication(s): *Greek Library Association Bulletin*

Guinea

Direction de la Recherche Scientifique et Techniques (National Research & Documentation Institute)
Bibliothelique Nationale, BP 561, Conakry
Tel: 46 10 10
Key Personnel
Dir: Lansana Sylla

Guyana

Guyana Library Association
c/o National Library, 76-77 Church & Main Sts, Georgetown
Tel: (0226) 2690; (0226) 2699; (0227) 4052 *Fax:* (0227) 4053
E-mail: natlib@sdnp.org.gy
Web Site: www.natlib.gov.gy
Key Personnel
President: Ivor Rodrigues
Secretary: Gwyneth George

Holy See (Vatican City State)

Biblioteca Apostolica Vaticana (Vatican Apostolic Library)
Cortile del Belvedere, 00120 Vatican City
Tel: (06) 6987 9402 *Fax:* (06) 6988 4795
E-mail: bav@librs6k.vatlib.it
Web Site: www.vatican.va
Telex: 2024 Dirgental VA
Key Personnel
Dir: Prof Don Raffaele Farina *Tel:* (06) 6987 9400 *Fax:* (06) 6988 5327 *E-mail:* prefetto@vatlib.it

Honduras

Asociacion de Bibliotecarios y Archivistas de Honduras (Association of Librarians & Archivists of Honduras)
11a Calle, Pritneray y Segunda Ave, No 105, Comayaguela DC, Tegucigalpa
Key Personnel
President: Francisca de Escoto Espinoza
Secretary General: Juan Angel R Ayes
Publication(s): *Catalogo de Prestamo*

Hong Kong

Hong Kong Library Association
GPO 10095, Hong Kong
E-mail: hklib@hklib.org.hk
Web Site: www.hklib.org.hk
Key Personnel
President: Tommy Yeung
Honorary Secretary: Venia Mak *Tel:* 26168562
Publication(s): *Journal of the Hong Kong Library Association* (irregularly)

Hungary

Magyar Koenyvtarosok Egyesuelete (Association of Hungarian Librarians)
Hold u 6, 1054 Budapest
Tel: (01) 311 8634 *Fax:* (01) 311 8634
E-mail: mke@oszk.hu
Web Site: www.mke.oszk.hu
Key Personnel
President: Bakos Klara *E-mail:* bakos@zmne.hu
General Secretary: Mrs Katalin Haraszti *Tel:* (01) 441 4854 *E-mail:* haraszti@ogyk.hu
Founded: 1935

Iceland

Upplysing - Felag bokasafns- og upplysingafraeoa (Information - the Icelandic Library & Information Science Association)
Lagmuli 7, 108 Reykjavik
Tel: 553-7290; 862-8627 *Fax:* 588-9239
E-mail: upplysing@bokis.is
Web Site: www.bokis.is
Key Personnel
President: H A Hardarson
Secretary: A Agnarsdottir
Publication(s): *Bokasafnid* (journal, yearbook of library & information science); *Fregnir* (3 times/yr, newsletter)

India

Documentation Research & Training Centre (DRTC)
Indian Statistical Institute, Eighth Mile Mysore Rd, RVCE Post, Bangalore 560 059
Tel: (080) 8483002 ((ext 490)); (080) 8483003 ((ext 490)); (080) 8483004 ((ext 490)); (080) 8483006 ((ext 490)) *Fax:* (080) 8484265
E-mail: drtc@isibang.ac.in
Web Site: www.isibang.ac.in/drtc/index.htm
Telex: 8458376 Isib In *Cable:* STATISTICA
Key Personnel
Head of Dept: I K Ravichandra Rao
Founded: 1962
Indian statistical institute.
Publication(s): *Annual Seminar, DRTC* (annually); *Refresher Seminar, DRTC* (annually)

DRTC, see Documentation Research & Training Centre (DRTC)

IASLIC, see Indian Association of Special Libraries & Information Centres (IASLIC)

Indian Association of Special Libraries & Information Centres (IASLIC)
P291, CIT Scheme 6M, Kankurgachi, Kolkata 700054
Tel: (033) 2352 9651; (033) 2354 9066
E-mail: iaslic@vsnl.net
Web Site: www.iaslic.org
Key Personnel
Publisher: J M Das
Publication(s): *Directory of Special & Research Libraries in India* (12 times/yr, newsletter); *Indian Library Science Abstracts* (quarterly)

Indian Association of Academic Librarians
c/o Jawaharlal Nehru University Library, New Mehrauli Rd, New Delhi 110067
Tel: (011) 6831717
Key Personnel
Secretary: M M Kashyap

Indian Library Association
A/40-1, Flat No 201, Ansal Bldg, Mukerjee Nagar, Delhi 110009
Tel: (011) 326 4748; (011) 765 1743
E-mail: ilanet1@nda.vsnl.net.in
Key Personnel
President: Ms Kalpana Dasgsupta

Indonesia

Ikatan Pustakawan Indonesia (Indonesian Library Association)
Jalan Merdeka Selatan No 11, 10110 Jakarta, Pusat
Tel: (021) 375718 *Fax:* (021) 3455611
Key Personnel
President: S Kartosdono
Publication(s): *Majalah Ikatan Pustakawan Indonesia*

Iraq

Arab Archivists Institute
c/o National Centre of Archives, National Library Bldg, 2nd floor, Bab-Al-Muaddum, Baghdad
Mailing Address: PO Box 594, Baghdad
Tel: (01) 416 8440
Key Personnel
Dir: Salim Al-Alousi
Founded: 1972

Ireland

Central Catholic Library Association Inc
74 Merrion Sq, Dublin 2
Tel: (01) 676 1264
Key Personnel
Librarian: Teresa Whitington
  E-mail: teresawhitington@eircom.net

An Chomhairle Leabharlanna (Library Council)
53/54 Upper Mount St, Dublin 2
Tel: (01) 6761963; (01) 6761167 *Fax:* (01) 6766721
E-mail: info@librarycouncil.ie
Web Site: www.librarycouncil.ie
Key Personnel
Dir: Mrs Norma McDermott
Research & Information Officer: Alun Bevan
  E-mail: abevan@librarycouncil.ie
Development agency for public libraries in Ireland.
Publication(s): *Annual Report*; *Irish Library News* (monthly)

Cumann Leabharlann na h-Eireann (Library Association of Ireland)
53 Upper Mount St, Dublin 2
Tel: (01) 61202193 *Fax:* (01) 61213090
Web Site: www.libraryassociation.ie
Key Personnel
President: Gobnait O'Riordan *E-mail:* president@libraryassociation.ie
Honorary Secretary: Denise Murphy
Founded: 1928
Membership(s): IFLA; EBLIDA.
Publication(s): *An Leabharlann* (published jointly with CILIP-Northern Ireland); *The Library Association of Ireland* (4 per year, published jointly with CILIP-Northern Ireland)

National Library of Ireland Society
Kildare St, Dublin 2
Tel: (01) 603 02 00 *Fax:* (01) 676 66 90
E-mail: info@nli.ie
Web Site: www.nli.ie
Key Personnel
Library Administration Officer: Kevin Browne
Executive Officer: Margaret Toomey

Israel

Israel Librarians & Information Specialists Association
The Isreal Center for Libraries, 9 Beit Hadfus St, Givaat Shaul, Jerusalem
Tel: (02) 6589515 *Fax:* (02) 6251628
E-mail: icl@icl.org.il
Web Site: www.icl.org.il
Key Personnel
President: Benjamin Schachter
Founded: 1965
Publication(s): *The Reader's Aid (Yad Lakore)-Israel Journal for Libraries and Archives*

Israel Society of Libraries & Information Centers (ASMI)
PO Box 28273, 91282 Jerusalem
Tel: (02) 6249421 *Fax:* (02) 6249421
E-mail: asmi@asmi.org.il
Web Site: www.asmi.org.il
Key Personnel
Chairperson: Shoshana Langerman *Tel:* (02) 5632756 *Fax:* (02) 5630640 *E-mail:* shala@barak-online.net
Founded: 1966
Membership(s): International Federation of Library Associations & Institutions (IFLA).
Publication(s): *Information & Librarianship* (irregularly, 2002, 2 issues per volume)

The Israeli Center for Libraries
28 Baruch Hirsh St, Benei-Berak 51131
Mailing Address: PO Box 3251, Bnei-Berak 51131
Tel: (03) 6180151 *Fax:* (03) 5798048
E-mail: icl@icl.org.il
Web Site: www.icl.org.il
Key Personnel
Chairman: Jacob Agmon
Dir: Orly Onn
Contact: Ariella Barrett
Founded: 1965
Publication(s): *Basifriot* (newspaper); *Yad-la-Kore* (The Reader's Aid Library Quarterly & Library Monographs)

Italy

Associazione Italiana Biblioteche (Italian Library Association)
c/o Biblioteca Nazionale Centrale, Viale Castro Pretorio 105, 00185 Rome
Mailing Address: CP 2461, 00100 Rome
Tel: (06) 4463532 *Fax:* (06) 4441139
E-mail: aib@aib.it
Web Site: www.aib.it
Key Personnel
President: Miriam Scarabo
Secretary: Marco Cupellaro
Editorial Office: Maria Teresa Natale
  E-mail: natale@aib.it
Publication(s): *AIB Notizie* (monthly); *Bollettino AIB* (quarterly); *Rapporti AIB* (irregularly)

Istituto Centrale per il Catalogo Unico delle Biblioteche Italiane e per le Informazioni Bibliografiche (Central Institute of the Union Catalog of Italian Libraries & Bibliographical Information)
Viale del Castro Pretorio, 105-00185 Rome
Tel: (06) 4989484 *Fax:* (06) 4959302
Web Site: www.iccu.sbn.it
Key Personnel
Dir: Dr Luciano Scala
Publication(s): *Bibliografia di Inventari e Cataloghi a Stampa dei Manoscritti*; *Bibliografia Nazionale Italiana*; *Catalogo Collettivo di Periodici - Archivio ISRDS/CNR*; *I Emilia Romagna - Il Friuli Venezia Giulia*; *Le Edizioni Italiane del XVI sec*, *Guida alla Catalogazione per Autori delle Stampe*, *Inventari Non a Stampa di Manoscritti*; *Periodici Italiani 1886-1981*; *Quaderno RICA*; *Regole Italiane di Catalogazione per Autori*; *Soggettario per i Cataloghi delle Biblioteche Italiane*

Jamaica

Jamaica Library Association
PO Box 125, Kingston 5
Tel: (876) 927-1614 *Fax:* (876) 927-1614
E-mail: liajapresident@yahoo.com
Web Site: www.liaja.org.jm
Key Personnel
President: Byron Palmer
Secretary: F Salmon
Honorary Secretary: Yulande Lindsay
Founded: 1949
Publication(s): *JLA Bulletin* (bulletin, 2002); *LIAJA Annual Report* (annually, report); *LIAJA News* (newsletter); *LIAJA Newslink* (2002)

Japan

Gakujutsu Bunken Fukyu-Kai (Association for Science Documents Information)
c/o Tokyo Institute of Technology, 2-12-1 Oh-Okayama, Meguro-Ku, Tokyo 152-8550
Tel: (03) 3726-3117 *Fax:* (03) 3726-3118
E-mail: gakujyutubunken@mvd.biglobe.ne.jp
Key Personnel
President: Shu Kanbara

Joho Kagaku Gijutsu Kyokai (Information Science & Technology Association (INFOSTA))
Sasaki Bldg, 2-5-7 Koishikawa, Bunkyo-ku, Tokyo 112-0002
Tel: (03) 3813-3791 *Fax:* (03) 3813-3793
E-mail: infosta@infosta.or.jp
Web Site: www.infosta.or.jp
Key Personnel
President: T Gondoh
General Manager: Yukio Ichikawa
Founded: 1950
Publication(s): *Journal of Information Science & Technology Association* (biannually, microfiche)

Joho Shori Gakkai (Information Processing Society of Japan)
Shibaura-Maekawa Bldg, 3-16-20, 7th floor, Shibaura, Minato-ku, Tokyo 108-0023
Tel: (03) 5484-3535 *Fax:* (03) 5484-3534
E-mail: intl@ipsj.or.jp
Web Site: www.ipsj.or.jp
Key Personnel
President: Dr Iwao Tada
Service Division Manager: Yoshio Tsuchikawa
Founded: 1960
Publication(s): *Joho-shori* (monthly, journal); *Transactions of IPSJ* (monthly)

Mita Toshokan Joho Gakkai (Mita Society for Library & Information Science)
c/o School of Library & Information Science, Keio University, 2-15-45 Mita, Minato-ku, Tokyo 108-8345
Tel: (03) 34533920
Key Personnel
President: Kimio Hosono
Secretary: Satoko Suzuki *E-mail:* mslis@slis.keio.ac.jp
Publication(s): *Library & Information Science* (biannually)

Nihon Igaku Toshokan Kyokai (Japan Medical Library Association)
Gakkai Center Bldg, 5F, 2-4-16 Yayoi, Bunkyo-ku, Tokyo 113-0032
Tel: (03) 38151942 *Fax:* (03) 38151608
E-mail: imlajimu@nisiq.net
Web Site: wwwsoc.nacsis.ac.jp/jmla

Key Personnel
Secretary: Junzo Tsuno
Publication(s): *Igakutoshokan*; *List of current periodicals acquired by the Japanese Medical, Dental & Pharmaceutical Libraries*; *Union Catalogue of Foreign Books in the Libraries of Japan Medical Schools*

Nihon Toshokan Joho Gakkai Shi (Japan Society of Library & Information Science)
c/o Aichi Shukutoku University, 9 Katahira Nagakute, Nagakute-cho, Aichi-gun, Aichi 480-1197
Tel: (0561) 62-4111 *Fax:* (0561) 63-9308
E-mail: muransky@asu.aasa.ac.jp
Web Site: www.soc.nii.ac.jp/jslis/
Key Personnel
President: Maso Nagasawa
Executive Secretary: Tomohide Muranushi
Contact: Shinichi Toda *Tel:* (03) 3945 7444
E-mail: toda@hakusrv.toyo.ac.jp
Founded: 1953
Publication(s): *Nihon Toshokan Joho Gakkaishi* (Journal of Japan Society of Library & Information Science, quarterly)

Nihon Toshokan Kyokai (Japan Library Association)
1-11-14 Shinkawa, Chuo-ku, Tokyo 104-0033
Tel: (03) 3523-0811 *Fax:* (03) 3523-0841
E-mail: info@jla.or.jp
Web Site: www.jla.or.jp
Key Personnel
Secretary-General: Reiko Sakagawa
Founded: 1892
Publication(s): *Basic Subject Headings (BSH)* (1983); *JLA Library & Information Science Text Series* (1999); *Librarianship in Japan* (1994); *Nihon No Sankotosho* (Guide to Japanese Reference Books, 1980); *Nihon no Toshokan* (Statistics on Libraries in Japan, annually); *Nippon Cataloging Rules (NCR)* (1987); *Nippon Decimal Classification (NDC)* (1996); *Sentei Tosho Somokuroku* (Standard Catalog of Selected Books, annually, catalog); *Toshokan Handobukku* (Librarian's Handbook, 1990); *Toshokan Nenkan* (Library Yearbook, annually); *Toshokan No Shigoto* (Library Work); *Toshokan Yogoshu* (Librarian's Glossary, 1988); *Toshokan'in No Tame No Eikaiwa Handobukku* (English Conversation Handbook for Librarians, 1991); *Toshokan'in Sensho* (Selective Books for Librarians)

Nippon Yakugaku Toshokan Kyogikai
c/o Library, Faculty of Pharmaceutical Sciences, University of Tokyo, 7-3-1 Hongo, Bunkyo-ku, Tokyo 113-0033
Tel: (03) 38122111
Web Site: wwwsoc.nii.ac.jp/jpla
Japan Pharmaceutical Library Association.
Publication(s): *Yakugaku Toshokan* (Pharmaceutical Library Bulletin)

Senmon Toshokan Kyogikai (SENTOKYO)
c/o Japan Library Association, Bldg F6, 1-11-14 Shinkawa, Chuo-ku, Tokyo 104-0033
Tel: (03) 3537-8335 *Fax:* (03) 3537-8336
E-mail: jsla@jsla.or.jp
Web Site: www.jsla.or.jp
Key Personnel
President: Kousaku Inaba
Executive Dir: Fumihisa Nakagawa
Japan Special Libraries Association.
Publication(s): *Hakusho: Nihon no Senmon Toshokan*; *Senmon Joho Kikan Soran* (triennially); *Senmon Toshokan* (6 times/yr, bulletin)

SENTOKYO, see Senmon Toshokan Kyogikai (SENTOKYO)

Jordan

Jordan Library Association
PO Box 6289, Amman
Tel: (06) 462 9412 *Fax:* (06) 462 9412
Key Personnel
President: Anwar Akroush
Secretary: Yousra Abu Ajamieh
Contact: Fadil Klayb
Publication(s): *Anglo-American Cataloguing Rules* (1983, 2nd ed, in Arabic); *Directory of Jordanian Periodicals* (1982); *Directory of Libraries & Librarians in Jordan* (1984); *Directory of Libraries in Jordan 1976*; *Introduction to Librarianship & Information Science* (1982, in Arabic); *Jordanian National Bibliography* (annually); *The Palestinian Bibliography: A List of Books Published by the Arabs in Palestine 1948-1980*; *Palestinian-Jordanian Bibliography 1900-1970 & 1971-1975*; *Rissalat al-Maktaba* (The Message of the Library, quarterly); *Technical Processing of Information* (in Arabic)

Kenya

Kenya Library Association
PO Box 46031, Nairobi
Tel: (02) 334244 *Fax:* (02) 336885
Key Personnel
Chairman: Jacinta Were *E-mail:* jwere@ken.healthnet.org
Secretary: Alice Bulogosi
Publication(s): *Kelias News* (bimonthly); *Maktaba Journal* (biannually)

Republic of Korea

Hanguk Seoji Hakhoe (Korean Bibliographical Society)
One Yoido-dong, Youngdeungpo-gu, Seoul 150-703
Tel: (02) 788-4143 *Fax:* (02) 788-3385
E-mail: w3@nanet.go.kr
Web Site: www.nanet.go.kr

Hanguk Tosogwan Hakhoe
c/o Dept of Library Science, Sung Kyun Kwan University, 53, 3-ga, Myungryun-dong, Chongro-ku, Seoul 110-745
Tel: (02) 7600114 *Fax:* (02) 7442453
Korean Library Science Society.
Publication(s): *Tosogwan Hak* (Journal of the Korean Library Science Society, Korean with English abstracts)

Korean Library Association (KLA)
1-KA, Hoehyun-Dong, Choong-ku, Seoul 100-177
Tel: (02) 5354868 *Fax:* (02) 5355616
E-mail: klanet@hitel.net
Web Site: www.korla.or.kr
Key Personnel
President: Ki Nam Shin
Executive Dir: Won Ho Jo
Publication(s): *KLA Bulletin* (bimonthly, text in Korean); *Korean Cataloguing Rules*; *Korean Decimal Classification*; *The Patterns of Book Cover Design in Korea (1392-1945)*; *Statistics on Libraries in Korea* (annually)

Korean Research & Development Library Association (KORDELA)
Room 0411 KIST Library, Cheongryang, Seoul
Mailing Address: POB 131, Cheongryang, Seoul
Tel: (02) 9673692 *Fax:* (02) 29634013
Telex: 27380 Kistrok K
Key Personnel
President: Ke Hong Park
Secretary: Keon Tak Oh

Kuwait

Kuwait University Library
PO Box 17140, 92452 Khaldiya
Web Site: www.kuniv.edu.kw
Key Personnel
Dir: Dr Husain A Al-Ansari
Publication(s): *The University Library*

Laos People's Democratic Republic

Association des Bibliothecaires Laotiens (Association of Laos Librarians)
c/o Direction de la Bibliotheque Nationale, Ministry of Information & Culture, PO Box 122, Vientiane
Tel: 212452 *Fax:* 212408
E-mail: pfd-mill@pan.laos.net.la

Latvia

Library Association of Latvia
Latvian National Library, Kr Barona 14, 2 Stavs, 205 telpa, 1423 Riga
Tel: (0371) 7287620 *Fax:* (0371) 7280851
E-mail: lnb@lbi.lnb.lv
Web Site: www.lnb.lv
Telex: TEMA SU
Key Personnel
President: Aldis Abele
Dir: Andris Vilks *E-mail:* andrisv@lbi.lnb.lv
Vice President: Silvia Linina
Editor: Antra Purina
Publication(s): *Nota Bene* (quarterly, journal)

Lebanon

The Lebanese Library Association
c/o American University of Beirut, University Library/Serials Dept, Beirut
Mailing Address: PO Box 11-0236, Beirut 1107 2020
Tel: (01) 350000; (01) 340460 *Fax:* (01) 351706
Web Site: www.aub.edu.lb
Telex: 20801
Key Personnel
President: Mr Fawz Abdalleh

Executive Secretary: Rudaynah Shoujah
Publication(s): *Al-Nashrah* (triannually, bulletin)

Lesotho

Lesotho Library Association
Private Bag A26, Maseru
Tel: 340 601 *Fax:* 340 601
E-mail: mmc@doc.isas.nul.ls
Web Site: www.sn.apc.org *Cable:* Lelia Maseru
Key Personnel
Chairman: S M Mohai
Secretary: N Taole
Publication(s): *Lesotho Library Association Newsletter* (annually)

Lithuania

Lithuanian Librarians Association
Sv Ignoto 6-108, 2600 Vilnius
Tel: (02) 750340 *Fax:* (02) 750340
E-mail: lbd@vpu.lt
Web Site: www.lbd.lt
Key Personnel
Vice President: Emilija Banionyte *E-mail:* emilija.banionyte@vpu.lt
Founded: 1935

The Former Yugoslav Republic of Macedonia

Bibliotekarsko Drustvo na Makedonija
(Macedonian Library Association)
Bul Goce Delcev 6, 91000 Skopje
Mailing Address: PO Box 566, 91000 Skopje
Tel: (091) 226846 *Fax:* (091) 232649
E-mail: mile@nubsk.edu.mk; bmile47@yahoo.com
Key Personnel
President: Mile Boseski
Secretary: Poliksena Matkovska
Union of Librarians' Associations of Macedonia Official titles: Savez drustava biblioteckih radnika Jugoslavije (Serbo-Croatian), Sojuz na drustvata na bibliotecnite rabotnici na Yugoslavija (Macedonian), Zveza durstev bibliotecnih delavcev Jugoslavije (Slovene). The headquarters of the League is situated in each of the six republics & two provinces of Serbia & Montenegro in turn & changes every two years.
Publication(s): *Bibliotekarska iskra*

Malawi

The Malawi Library Association
PO Box 429, Zomba
Tel: (050) 522222 *Fax:* (050) 523225
Key Personnel
Chairman: Joseph J Uta

Secretary: Vote D Somba
Publication(s): *Libraries in Malawi: Textbook for Library Assistants*; *MALA Bulletin*; *Manual for Small Libraries*

Malaysia

Persatuan Perpustakaan Malaysia
c/o Perpustakaan Negara Malaysia, 232 Jalan Tun Razak, 50572 Kuala Lumpur
Tel: (03) 26871700 *Fax:* (03) 26927082
E-mail: pnmweb@www1.pnm.my
Web Site: www.pnm.my
Key Personnel
President: Chew Wing Foong
Secretary: Leni Abdul Latif
Honorary Secretary: Ahmad Ridzuan Wan Chik
Library Association of Malaysia.
Publication(s): *Berita PPM* (bimonthly); *Majallah Perpustakaan Malaysia* (annually); *Sumber Pustaka* (newsletter)

Mali

AMBAD, see Association Malienne des Bibliothecaires, Archivistes et Documentalistes (AMBAD)

Association Malienne des Bibliothecaires, Archivistes et Documentalistes (AMBAD)
Rue Kasse Keita, Bamako
Tel: 22 49 63
Key Personnel
Dir: Mamadou Konoba Keiita

Malta

MaLIA, see Malta Library & Information Association (MaLIA)

Malta Library & Information Association (MaLIA)
c/o University of Malta Library, Tal-Qroqq, Msida MSD 06
Tel: 21322054
E-mail: mpar1@lib.um.edu.mt
Web Site: www.malia-malta.org
Key Personnel
Chairperson: Robert Mizzi *E-mail:* robmiz@mail.global.net.mt
Deputy Chairperson: Laurence Zerafa
Honorary Secretary: Ruth Muscat
Treasurer: Josephine Spiteri
Founded: 1969
Publication(s): *Directory of Libraries & Information Units in Malta* (1996); *Directory of Maltese Publishers, Printers, Book Designers & Book Dealers* (1981); *MaLIA Newletter* (quarterly)

Mauritania

Association Mauritanienne des Bibliothecaires, Archivistes et Documentalistes
c/o Bibliotheque Nationale BP 20, Nouakchott

Key Personnel
President: O Diouwara
Secretary: Sid'Ahmed Fall dit Dah

Mauritius

Mauritius Library Association
c/o The British Council, Royal Rd, Rose Hill
Mailing Address: POB 111, Rose Hill
Tel: 4549550; 4549551; 4549552 *Fax:* 4549553
E-mail: ielts@mu.britishcouncil.org
Web Site: www.britishcouncil.org/mauritius/
Key Personnel
President: K Appadoo
Secretary: S Rughoo
Publication(s): *Mauritius Library Association Newsletter* (quarterly)

Mexico

AMBAC, see Asociacion Mexicana de Bibliotecarios AC (AMBAC)

Asociacion Mexicana de Bibliotecarios AC (AMBAC)
Angel Urraza 817-A, Col Del Valle, 03100 Mexico, DF
Mailing Address: Apdo 80-065, Administracion de correos 80, 06001 Mexico, DF
Tel: (055) 55 75 33 96 *Fax:* (055) 55-75-11-35
E-mail: correo@ambac.org.mx
Web Site: www.ambac.org.mx
Key Personnel
President: Saul Armendariz Sanchez *E-mail:* asaul@xcaret.iqeofcu.unam.mx
Secretary: Graciela Tecuatt Quechol
Publication(s): *Memorias de Jornadas*; *Noticiero* (bulletin)

Escuela Nacional de Biblioteconomia y Archivonomia (National School of Librarianship & Archives)
Miguel Angel 94, Col Mixcoac, 13910 Mexico, DF
Tel: (055) 598-14-94
Key Personnel
Dir: Prof Eduardo Salas Estrada
Publication(s): *Bibliotecas y Archivos* (irregularly)

Instituto de Investigaciones Bibliograficas (Institute of Bibliographic Research)
Centro Cultural Universitario, Delagacion Coyoacan, 04510 Mexico, DF
Tel: (05) 6226818 *Fax:* (05) 6650951
Web Site: biblional.bibliog.unam.mx
Key Personnel
Dir: Vicente Quirarte
Coordinator: Aurora Cano Andaluz; Judith Licea De Arenas
Institute of Bibliographic Research.
Publication(s): *Bibliografia Mexicana*

Myanmar

Myanmar Library Association (MLA)
c/o National Library, Strand Rd, Yangon
Key Personnel
President: U Khin Maung Tin

Nepal

Nepal Library Association
GPO 2773, Kathmandu
Tel: (01) 331316 *Fax:* (01) 483720
Key Personnel
Contact: Rudra Prasad Dulal
Founded: 1980
Science & technology membership.
Publication(s): *Encyclopedia of Library & Information Science* (2nd ed, print & online)

Netherlands

Koninklijke Vereniging van Archivarissen in Nederland (Royal Association of Archivists in the Netherlands)
Cruquisweg 31, 1019 AT Amsterdam
Tel: (020) 462 77 27 *Fax:* (020) 462 77 28
E-mail: bureau@kvan.nl
Web Site: www.kvan.nl
Key Personnel
Office Dir: Mrs Marjoke de Roos
Publication(s): *Almanak van het Nederlands archiefwezen*; *Archievenblad*

FOBID, see Stichting Federatie van Organisaties van Bibliotheek-, Informatie-, Dokumentatiewezen (FOBID)

IFLA, see International Federation of Library Associations & Institutions (IFLA)

International Federation of Library Associations & Institutions (IFLA)
PO Box 95312, 2509 CH The Hague
Tel: (070) 3140884 *Fax:* (070) 3834827
E-mail: ifla@ifla.org
Web Site: www.ifla.org
Key Personnel
Secretary General: R Ramachandran
See also under International Organizations section.

NBBI, see Nederlands Bureau voor Bibliotheekwezen en Informatieverzorging (NBBI)

NBLC Vereniging van Openbare Bibliotheken (NBLC, Netherlands Public Library Association)
Grote Markstr 43, 1st floor, 2500 BC The Hague
Mailing Address: PO Box 16146, 2500 BC The Hague
Tel: (070) 30 90 100 *Fax:* (070) 30 90 200
E-mail: info@debibliotheken.nl
Web Site: www.debibliotheken.nl
Telex: nblc nl
Key Personnel
Executive Dir: J E van der Putten
Contact: Marian Koren *Tel:* (070) 3090115
  E-mail: koren@nblc.nl
Founded: 1972
Membership(s): National Association of Public Libraries; IFLA; EBLIDA.
Publication(s): *Bibliotheek Blad* (biweekly, journal)

Nederlands Bureau voor Bibliotheekwezen en Informatieverzorging (NBBI)
Burg Van Karnebeeclaan 19, 2585 The Hague
Mailing Address: PO Box 80544, 2585 The Hague
Tel: (070) 3607833 *Fax:* (070) 3615011
Web Site: www.stb.tno.nl

Key Personnel
Dir: Dr J DeVuyst
Contact: W Leys
Library & information science.

Nederlandse Vereniging voor beroepsbeoefenaren in de bibliotheeck-informatie-en kennissector (NVB) (The Netherland Association of Librarians, Documentalists & Information Specialists)
NVB-Nieuwegracht 15, 3512 LC Utrecht
Tel: (030) 2311263 *Fax:* (030) 2311830
E-mail: nvbinfo@wxs.nl
Web Site: www.nvb-online.nl
Key Personnel
President: Dr J S M Savenije *E-mail:* b.savenije@ubu.ruu.nl

Stichting Federatie van Organisaties van Bibliotheek-, Informatie-, Dokumentatiewezen (FOBID) (Federation of Organizations for Libraries, Information & Documentation)
Leidseveer 35, 3500 GG Utrecht
Mailing Address: Postbus 16146, 2500 The Hague
Tel: (070) 3090115 *Fax:* (030) 233 29 60; (070) 3090200
E-mail: vanwestrienen@surf.nl
Key Personnel
Chairman: Dr J H de Swart
Secretary: I Schultz *Tel:* (070) 3090121
Founded: 1974
National umbrella organization for cooperation between the national library organizations.
Publication(s): *Cataloguing Rules* (parts 1-8); *Library & Documentation Centres in the Netherlands*; *Library & Documentation Guide*

Netherlands Antilles

Antillion Library Association
c/o Openbare Bibliotheek Curacao, Abr M Chumaceiro Blvd, Willemstad, Curacao
Tel: (09) 4617055 *Fax:* (09) 4656247
Key Personnel
Secretary: Ms Marvis Amerikaan
Publication(s): *APLA Newsletter*

New Zealand

IAML, see International Association of Music Libraries, Archives & Documentation Centres

International Association of Music Libraries, New Zealand Branch, Inc
Christchurch City Libraries, Christchurch
Mailing Address: PO Box 1466, Christchurch
Tel: (03) 941 7923 *Fax:* (03) 941 7848
E-mail: library@ccc.govt.nz
Web Site: library.christchurch.org.nz
Key Personnel
President: Lisa Allcott *Tel:* (09) 524 3860
  E-mail: lisa.allcott@natlib.govt.nz
Secretary: Marilyn Hayr *Tel:* (09) 307 7751
  E-mail: hayrm@akcity.govt.nz
Treasurer: Freda Blanchard *Tel:* (09) 372 7645
  E-mail: f.blanchard@internet.co.nz
Publication(s): *Bibliography of Writings about New Zealand Music Published to end of 1983*; *Crescendo*; *Directory of New Zealand Musical Organizations*; *Orchestral Scores* (performing editions list); *Sing!* (choral scores Catalogue)

International Association of Music Libraries, Archives & Documentation Centres
National Library of New Zealand, PO Box 1467, Wellington
Tel: (04) 474 3039 *Fax:* (04) 474 3035
Web Site: www.iaml.info
Key Personnel
President: John H Roberts *E-mail:* jroberts@library.berkeley.edu
Secretary General: Roger Flury *E-mail:* roger.flury@natlib.govt.nz
Treasurer: Martie Severt *E-mail:* m.severt@mco.nl
Founded: 1951
Publication(s): *Fontes Artis Musicae* (quarterly, journal); *IAML-L Newsletter* (irregularly, electronic)

LIANZA, see Library & Information Association of New Zealand Aotearoa (LIANZA)

Library & Information Association of New Zealand Aotearoa (LIANZA)
Old Wool House, Level 6, 139-141 Featherston St, Wellington 6001
Mailing Address: PO Box 12-212, Wellington 6038
Tel: (04) 473 5834 *Fax:* (04) 499 1480
E-mail: office@lianza.org.nz
Web Site: www.lianza.org.nz
Key Personnel
President: Mirla Edmundson
Office Manager: Steve Williams *E-mail:* steve@lianza.org.nz
Founded: 1910
Professional association.
Publication(s): *DILSINZ* (Directory of Information & Library Services in New Zealand); *Library Life* (11 per year, magazine); *New Zealand Libraries* (biannually); *Public Libraries of New Zealand* (1995); *Public Library Statistics* (1999); *Valuing the Economic Costs & Benefits of Libraries* (1996); *Who's Who in New Zealand Libraries* (1990)

Nicaragua

Asociacion Nicaraguense de Bibliotecarios y Profesionales a Fines
Apdo 3257, Managua
Key Personnel
Executive Secretary: Susana Morales Hernandez
Nicaraguan Association of Librarians.

Nigeria

Anambra State School Libraries Association
c/o University of Nigeria, Enugu Campus Library, Enugu
Tel: (042) 252080; (042) 332091 *Cable:* Nigersity Enugu
Key Personnel
Honorary Secretary: Virginia W Dike
Publication(s): *Manual for School Libraries on Small Budgets*; *School Libraries Bulletin* (triannually)

Nigerian Library Association
c/o Kwara College of Technology, Ilorin
Tel: (01) 2360470 *Fax:* (01) 2631716
E-mail: nln@nlbn.org
Telex: 21746
Key Personnel
President: A O Banjo
Secretary: D D Bwayili
There are also regional associations in the various states under the umbrella of the Nigerian Library Association.
Publication(s): *Nigerian Libraries* (triannually); *NLA Newsletter*

Norway

Arkivarforeningen (The Association of Archivists)
Postboks 4015, Ulleval Station, 0806 Oslo
Tel: 22022657 *Fax:* 22237489
E-mail: synne.stavheim@riksarkivaren.dep.no
Publication(s): *Norsk arkivforum*

Norsk Biblioteforening (Norwegian Library Association)
Malerhaugveien 20, 0661 Oslo
Tel: 2324 3430 *Fax:* 2267 2368
E-mail: nbf@norskbiblioteforening.no
Web Site: www.norskbiblioteforening.no
Key Personnel
Dir: Berit Aaker
Publication(s): *Internkontakt*

Riksbibliotektjenesten
Kronprinsensgt 9, Vika, Oslo
Mailing Address: Postboks 8046 Dep, 0030 Oslo
Tel: 23 11 89 00 *Fax:* 23 11 89 01
E-mail: rbt@rbt.no
Key Personnel
Acting Dir General: Kirsten Engelstad
National Office for Research & Documentation, Academic & Professional Libraries.
Publication(s): *Handbook of Research & Special Libraries* (irregularly); *Skrifter fra Riksbibliotektjenesten* (irregularly); *Synopsis* (6 times/yr)

Pakistan

Government of Pakistan Department of Libraries
National Library of Pakistan, Constitution Ave, Islamabad 44000
Tel: (051) 9214523; (051) 92026436; (051) 9206440 *Fax:* (051) 9221375
E-mail: nlpiba@paknet2.ptc.pk
Web Site: www.nlp.gov.pk
Key Personnel
Dir General: Abdul Hafeez Akhtar
Editor: Amjad Majeed
Publication(s): *Accessions List Pakistan* (monthly); *Pakistan National Bibliography* (annually)

Karachi University Library Science Alumni Association
c/o University of Karachi, Dept of Library Science, Karachi 75270
Tel: (021) 479001 *Fax:* (021) 473226
Key Personnel
Secretary: S Zia Haider

Library Promotion Bureau
Karachi University Campus, Karachi 75270
Mailing Address: PO Box 8421, Karachi 75270
Tel: (021) 632-1959; (021) 6977737 *Fax:* (021) 632-1959
Key Personnel
President: Dr Ghaniul Akram Sabzwari
E-mail: gsabzwari@hotmail.com
Chief Editor: Dr Nasim Fatima
Founded: 1965
Publication(s): *Bibliographical Services Throughout Pakistan* (2nd Edition); *Documents Procurement Service*; *Libraries of Pakistan*; *Pakistan Book Trade Directory*; *Pakistan Library Bulletin* (quarterly); *Secondary School Library Resources & Services in Pakistan*; *University Librarianship in Pakistan*; *Who's Who in Library & Information Science*

Pakistan Library Association (PLA)
Constitution Ave, Islamabad 44000
Mailing Address: c/o Institute of Development Economics, PO Box 1091, Islamabad 44000
Tel: (051) 921-4523; (051) 920-2544; (051) 920-2549 *Fax:* (051) 922-1375
E-mail: nlpiba@isb.paknet.com.pk
Web Site: www.nlp.gov.pk
Key Personnel
President: Sain Malik
Secretary General: Atta Ullah
Vice President, Federal Branch: Zafar Javed Naqvi *E-mail:* pide@ish.paknet.com.pk
Founded: 1957
Professional body of Library & Information Managers of Pakistan.
Publication(s): *Code of Ethics for Librarians*; *PLA Newsletter* (bimonthly, text in English); *Public Libraries Facilities in Pakistan*; *Standards of College Libraries*; *Standards of Special Libraries*; *Standards of University Libraries*

PLA, see Pakistan Library Association (PLA)

Panama

Asociacion de Bibliotecarios Graduados del Istmo de Panama
c/o Director de la Biblioteca Bio-Medica de Laboratorio Conmemorativo Gorgas, Avda Justo Arosemena No 35-30, Apdo 6991, Panama 5
Tel: 2227411 *Fax:* 2254366
Key Personnel
President: Prof Manuel Victor De Las Casas
Secretary: Iris de Espinosa
Association of Graduate Librarians of the Isthmus of Panama (AGLIP).

Asociacion Panamena de Bibliotecarios
c/o Biblioteca Interamericana Simon Bolivar, Estafeta Universitaria, Panama City
Key Personnel
President: Bexie Rodriguez de Leon
Panama Library Association.
Publication(s): *Boletin*

Paraguay

Asociacion de Bibliotecarios Universitarios del Paraguay
c/o Prof Yoshiko M de Freundorfer, Head, Escuela de Bibliotecologia, Universidad Nacional de Asuncion, Asuncion Casilla 910, 2064 Asuncion
Tel: (021) 507080 *Fax:* (021) 213734
Key Personnel
President: Prof Gloria Ondina Ortiz C
Secretary: Celia Villamayor de Diaz
Paraguayan Association of University Librarians.

Peru

Asociacion de Archiveros del Peru (ADAP)
Archivo Central Salaverry 2020 Jesus Mario, Universidad del Pacifico, 11 Lima 11
Tel: (01) 4712277 *Fax:* (01) 2650958
E-mail: dri@u8p.edu.pe
Key Personnel
President: Jose Luis Abanto Arrelucea
1a Vocal: Yolanda Auqui Chayez
2a Vocal: Denise Ballivian Seminario
Peruvian Association of Archivists.

Asociacion Peruana de Bibliotecarios (APB)
Bellavista 561 Miraflores Apdo 995, Lima 18
Tel: (01) 474869
Key Personnel
President: Martha Fernandez de Lopez
Secretary: Luzmila Tello de Medina
Peruvian Association of Librarians.

Philippines

ASLP, see Association of Special Libraries of the Philippines (ASLP)

Association of Special Libraries of the Philippines (ASLP)
The National Library Bldg, Room 301, T M Kalaw St, 1100 Ermita, Manila
Tel: (02) 893-9590 *Fax:* (02) 893-9589
E-mail: vvt126_ph@yahoo.com
Key Personnel
President: Valentina Tolentino
Secretary: Socorro G Elevera
Publication(s): *ASLP Bulletin* (annually); *Directory of Special Library Resources and Research Facilities in the Philippines*

Bibliographical Society of the Philippines
National Library of the Philippines, T M Kalaw, Ermita, 1000 Manila
Tel: (02) 525-3196; (02) 525-1748 *Fax:* (02) 524-2324
E-mail: amb@nlp.gov.ph
Web Site: www.nlp.gov.ph
Key Personnel
Chief: Leonila D A Tominez *Fax:* (02) 524-1011

Philippine Librarians Association Inc
c/o National Library, T M Kalaw St, Room 301, 1000 Manila, Ermita
Tel: (02) 523-00-68
Web Site: www.dlsu.edu.ph/library/plai
Key Personnel
President: Fe Angelo Verzosa *E-mail:* libfamv@mail.dlsu.edu.ph
Vice President: Teresita C Moran
E-mail: tmoran@pusit.admu.edu.ph
Secretary: Shirley L Nava
Treasurer: Mona Lisa P Leguiab
Publication(s): *PLAI Bulletin* (annually); *PLAI Newsletter* (biannually)

Poland

Stowarzyszenie Bibliotekarzy Polskich (Polish Librarians Association)
al Niepodleglosci 213, 02-086 Warsaw
Tel: (022) 6082256 *Fax:* (022) 8259157
E-mail: biurozgsbp@wp.pl
Web Site: ebib.oss.wroc.pl/sbp/
Key Personnel
Chairman: Jan Wolosz *E-mail:* bnwolosz@bn.org.pl
Vice Chairman: Piotr Bierczynski
  E-mail: biercz@hiacynt.wimbp.lodz.pl; Jerzy Krawczyk *E-mail:* jurek@bg.agh.edu.pl; Stanislaw Krzywicki *E-mail:* ksiaznica@ksiaznica.szczecin.pl
Secretary General: Elzbieta Stefanczyk
  E-mail: bngroma@bn.org.pl
Treasurer: Andrzej Jopkiewicz *E-mail:* k.kruk@stat.gov.pl
Founded: 1946
Publication(s): *Bibliotekarz* (The Librarian); *Poradnik Bibliotekarza* (The Librarian's Adviser); *Przeglad Biblioteczny* (Library Review)

Portugal

Associacao Portuguesa de Bibliotecarios, Arquivistas e Documentalistas (The Portuguese Association of Librarians Archivists & Documentalists)
R Morais Soares, 43C-1 DTD, 1900-341 Lisbon Codex
Tel: (021) 816 19 80 *Fax:* (021) 815 45 08
E-mail: bad@apbad.pt; formacao@apbad.pt; contabilidade@apbad.pt
Web Site: www.apbad.pt
Key Personnel
President: Ernestina de Castro
Contact: Sandrine Jercaeret
Portuguese Association of Librarians, Archivists & Documentalists.
Publication(s): *Cadernos de Biblioteconomia, Arquivistica e Documentacao* (biannually)

Puerto Rico

Sociedad de Bibliotecarios de Puerto Rico (Society of Librarians of Puerto Rico)
PO Box 22898, San Juan 00931-2898
Tel: (787) 764-0000 (ext 5205) *Fax:* (787) 764-0000 (ext 5204)
E-mail: vtorres@upracd.upr.clu.edu
Web Site: www.geocities.com/sociedadsbpr
Key Personnel
President: Victor Federico Torres
Secretary: Doris E Rivera Marrero
Publication(s): *Boletin, Informa* (newsletter); *Cuadernos Bibliotecologicos, Cuadernos Bibliograficos*

Senegal

ASBAD, see Association Senegalaise des Bibliothecaires, Archivistes et Documentalistes (ASBAD)

Association Senegalaise des Bibliothecaires, Archivistes et Documentalistes (ASBAD)
c/o Ecole des Bibliothecaires, Archivistes et Documentalistes, Universite Cheikh Anta Diop de Dakar, BP 3252, Dakar
Tel: (0221) 864 27 73 *Fax:* (0221) 824 23 79
E-mail: ebad@ebad.ucad.sn
Web Site: www.ebad.ucad.sn
Key Personnel
President: Ndiaye Djibril
Publication(s): *Canal-ist*

Serbia and Montenegro

Jugoslovenski Bibliografsko Informacijski Institut (Yugoslav Institute for Bibliography & Information)
Terazije 26, 11000 Belgrade
Tel: (011) 687 836; (011) 687 760 *Fax:* (011) 687 760; (011) 688 840
E-mail: suzana@jbi.bg.ac.yu
Web Site: www.yu-yubin.org
Key Personnel
Dir: Dr Radomir Glavicki
Publication(s): *Belgrade*; *Bibliografija Jugoslavije* (Bibliography of Yugoslavia, includes books, pamphlets, music scores & articles of literary, scientific interest, philology, art & sport); *Universal Decimal Classification, International* (Serbocroatian version)

YUBIN, see Jugoslovenski Bibliografsko Informacijski Institut

Sierra Leone

Sierra Leone Association of Archivists, Librarians & Information Scientists (SLAALIS)
c/o COMAHS Library New England, Freetown
Tel: (022) 220758
Key Personnel
President: Deanna Thomas
Founded: 1987
Publication(s): *SLAALIS Bulletin* (quarterly)

SLAALIS, see Sierra Leone Association of Archivists, Librarians & Information Scientists (SLAALIS)

Singapore

Library Association of Singapore
Geylang East Community Library, 50 Geylang East Ave 1, 3rd floor, Singapore 389777
Tel: 6749 7990 *Fax:* 6749 7480
Web Site: www.las.org.sg
Publication(s): *Directory of Information Databases in Singapore*; *Directory of Libraries in Singapore*; *Singapore Libraries* (annually); *Singapore Libraries Bulletin* (quarterly)

Slovenia

ZBDS, see Zveza bibliotekarskih drustev Slovenije (ZBDS)

Zveza bibliotekarskih drustev Slovenije (ZBDS) (Union of Associations of Slovene Librarians)
Turjaska 1, 1000 Ljubljana
Tel: (01) 20 01 193 *Fax:* (01) 42 57 293
Web Site: www.zbds-zveza.si
Key Personnel
President: Srecko Macek *Tel:* (03) 426-17-18
  E-mail: srecko@ce.sik.si
Chief Editor: Stanislav Bahor *Tel:* (01) 58 61 345
  Fax: (01) 58 61 311
Founded: 1947
Publication(s): *Knjiznica* (Library, quarterly, 1957)

South Africa

LIASA, see Library & Information Association of South Africa (LIASA)

Library & Information Association of South Africa (LIASA)
PO Box 1598, Pretoria 0001
Tel: (012) 481 2870; (012) 481 2875; (012) 481 2876 *Fax:* (012) 481 2873
E-mail: liasa@liasa.org.za
Web Site: www.liasa.org.za
Key Personnel
Executive Dir: Gwenda Thomas
Publication(s): *LIASA-IN-Touch* (quarterly, magazine); *LIASA News* (quarterly, newsletter); *South African Journal of Library & Information Science* (biannually, journal)

Spain

Asociacion Espanola de Archiveros, Bibliotecarios, Museologos y Documentalistas (Spanish Association of Archivists, Librarians, Curators & Documentalists)
Recoletos 5, 28001 Madrid
Tel: (091) 5751727 *Fax:* (091) 5781615
E-mail: anabad@anabad.org
Web Site: www.anabad.org
Key Personnel
President: Julia M Rodriguez Barrero
Publication(s): *Boletin* (with bibliography section)

Sri Lanka

National Library & Documentation Services Board (NLDSB)
No 14, Independence Ave, Colombo 07
Mailing Address: PO Box 1764, Colombo 07
Tel: (01) 698847 *Fax:* (01) 685201
E-mail: nldsb@mail.natlib.lk
Web Site: www.natlib.lk
Key Personnel
Dir General: Mr M S U Amarasiri *Tel:* (01) 687581 *E-mail:* dg@mail.natlib.lk
Publication(s): *Directory of Social Science Libraries, Information Centres & Databases*

in Sri Lanka; International Standard Book Numbering in Sri Lanka (brochure); Library News (quarterly); Pustakala Dave Bhanda; Sri Lanka (ISBN) Publishers Directory; Sri Lanka National Bibliography (monthly); Sri Lanka Newspaper Article Index-1993 (conference index)

NLDSB, see National Library & Documentation Services Board (NLDSB)

Sri Lanka Library Association
Professional Center, 275/75 Bauddhaloka Mawatha, Colombo 7
Tel: (01) 2589103 Fax: (01) 2589103
E-mail: slla@operamail.com
Web Site: www.naresa.ac.lk/slla; www.nsf.ac.lk/slla
Key Personnel
President: Mr N U Yapa
Vice President: Ms D I D Andradi; Ms Sriyani Ileperuma
Secretary: Ms Deepali Talagala
Publication Officer: Mr M B M Fairooz
Assistant Secretary: Mr C Kuruppu
Education Officer: Ms Nanda P Wanasundera
Assistant Education Officer: Mr Ajith Leelarathne
Treasurer: Mr Anton D Nallathamby
Librarian: Mr J S K Weerawardane
Publication(s): SLLA News Letter (quarterly); Sri Lanka Library Review (biannually)

Swaziland

Swaziland Library Association
PO Box 2309, Mbabane H100
Tel: 404-2633 Fax: 404-3863
E-mail: sdnationalarchives@realnet.co.sz
Web Site: www.swala.sz
Key Personnel
Chairperson: Mrs Nomsa Mkhwanazi
Secretary: Sibongile Nxumalo
Founded: 1984

Sweden

Svensk Biblioteksforening (Swedish Library Association)
Saltmaetargatan 3A, 103 62 Stockholm
Mailing Address: PO Box 3127, 103 62 Stockholm
Tel: (08) 54513230 Fax: (08) 54513231
E-mail: info@biblioteksforeningen.org
Web Site: www.biblioteksforeningen.org
Key Personnel
Secretary General: Christina Stenberg Tel: (08) 54513233 E-mail: chs@sab.se
Editor & Chief: Marianne Steinsaphir E-mail: ms@bbl.sab.se
Publication(s): Biblioteksbladet (The Library Journal, 10 times/yr)

Svenska Arkivsamfundet (Swedish Society of Archivists)
c/o Landsarkivet i Lund, Anna-Christina Ulfsparre, Box 2016, 22002 Lund
Tel: (046) 197000 Fax: (046) 197070
E-mail: info@arkivsamfundet.org
Web Site: www.arkivsamfundet.org
Key Personnel
President: Berndt Fredriksson E-mail: berndt.fredriksson@foreign.ministry.se
Vice President: Carina Sjogren E-mail: carina.sjogren@srf.se
Secretary: Julia Aslund E-mail: julia.aslund@ssa.stockholm.se
Treasurer: Peter Nordstrom E-mail: peter.nordstrom@krigsarkivet.ra.se
Publication(s): Arkiv, Samhaelle, Forskning (Archives, Society, Research, biannually)

Tekniska Litteratursaellskapet (The Swedish Society for Technical Documentation)
Box 55580, 102 04 Stockholm
Tel: (08) 678 23 20 Fax: (08) 678 23 01
E-mail: kansliet@tls.se
Web Site: www.tls.se
Key Personnel
President: L Lindskog
Secretary: K Wahl
Publication(s): Tidskrift foer Dokumentation (quarterly)

Switzerland

Association des Bibliotheques et Bibliothecaires Suisses (Association of Swiss Librarians & Libraries)
Hallerstr 58, 3012 Bern
Tel: (031) 3824240 Fax: (031) 3824648
E-mail: bbs@bbs.ch
Web Site: www.bbs.ch
Key Personnel
General Secretary: Barbara Krauchi
Publication(s): Arbido (monthly, jointly with Swiss Association for Documentation & Swiss Association of Archivists)

Schweizerische Vereinigung fur Dokumentation
Schmidgasse 4, 6301 Zug
Tel: (041) 726 45 05 Fax: (041) 726 45 09
E-mail: svd-asd@hispeed.ch
Web Site: www.svd-asd.org
Key Personnel
President: Dr Urs Naegeli
Secretary: H Schweuk

Verband der Bibliotheken und der Bibliothekarinnen/Bibliothekare der Schweiz (BBS), see Association des Bibliotheques et Bibliothecaires Suisses

Verein Schweizerischer Archivarinnen und Archivare (Association of Swiss Archivists)
Schweizerisches Bundesarchiv, Aarchivsor 24, 3003 Bern
Tel: (031) 322 89 89; (031) 322 92 85
Web Site: www.staluzern.ch/vsa
Key Personnel
President: Andreas Kellerhals E-mail: andreas.kellerhals@bar.admin.ch
Founded: 1922
Membership(s): ICA.
Publication(s): Arbido

Taiwan, Province of China

LAC, see Library Association of China (LAC)

Library Association of China (LAC)
National Central Library, 20 Chung Shan S Rd, Taipei 100-01
Tel: (02) 23312675 Fax: (02) 2370-0899
E-mail: lac@msg.ncl.edu.tw
Web Site: www.ncl.edu.tw
Key Personnel
President: Huang Shih-wson
Secretary General: Teresa Wang Chang
Publication(s): Library Association of China Bulletin (semi-annually); Library Association of China Newsletter (quarterly)

United Republic of Tanzania

Tanzania Library Association
PO Box 33433, Dar Es Salaam
Tel: (022) 2775411
E-mail: tla_tanzania@yahoo.com
Web Site: www.angelfire.com/al4/tla/
Key Personnel
Chairman: Dr Alli Mcharazo E-mail: amcharazo@hotmail.com
Secretary: Matilda Kazilwa E-mail: kuz.idm@raha.com
Treasurer: Hermenegild Haule
Editor: Sam Kasulwa
Founded: 1975
Publication(s): Matukio (Events, biannually); Someni (Read, journal)

Thailand

Thai Library Association
1346 Akarnsongkrau Rd 5, Klongchan, Bangkapi, Bangkok 10240
Tel: (02) 734-8022; (02) 734-8023 Fax: (02) 734-8024
Web Site: tla.tiac.or.th
Key Personnel
President: Khunying Maenmas Chawalit
Executive Secretary: Mrs Vorrarat Srinamngern
Foreign Relations: Yupin Chancharoensin E-mail: yupin@car.chula.ac.th
Founded: 1954

Togo

Association Togolaise pour le Developpement de la Documentation des Bibliotheques, Archives et Musees
c/o Bibliotheque de l'Universite du Benin, BP 1515, Lome
Tel: 21 30 27 Fax: 21 85 95
E-mail: cafmicro@ub.tg
Web Site: www.ub.tg
Key Personnel
Secretary: E E Amah

ATODBAM, see Association Togolaise pour le Developpement de la Documentation des Bibliotheques, Archives et Musees

Trinidad & Tobago

Library Association of Trinidad & Tobago
PO Box 1275, Port of Spain
Tel: (0868) 687 0194
E-mail: secretary@latt.org.tt
Web Site: www.latt.org.tt/cms/
Key Personnel
President: Ernesta Greenidge
 E-mail: egreenidge@library.uwi.tt
Secretary: Sheryl Washington
 E-mail: swashington@ag.gov.tt
Founded: 1960
Publication(s): *Blatt* (annually, Bulletin of the Library Association of Trinidad & Tobago)

Tunisia

Association Tunisienne des Documentalistes, Bibliothecaires et Archivistes
Centre de Documentation Nationale, Rue 8004, Rue Sidi El Benna R P, 1000 Tunis
Tel: 651924
Key Personnel
President: Ahmed Ksibi
Tunisian Association of Record-Keepers, Librarians and Archivists.
Publication(s): *L'Enfant et la Lecture*; *RASSID*

Turkey

Tuerk Kueuephaneciler Dernegi (Turkish Librarians' Association)
Elguen Sok-8/8, 06442 Kizilay/Ankara
Tel: (0312) 230 13 25 *Fax:* (0312) 232 04 53
E-mail: tkd-o@tr.net
Web Site: www.kutuphaneci.org.tr
Key Personnel
President: A Berberoglu
Secretary: A Kaygusuz
Publication(s): *Tuerk Kuetuiphaneciligi* (quarterly)

Uganda

Uganda Library Association (ULA)
PO Box 5894, Kampala
Tel: (0141) 285001 (ext 4) *Fax:* (0141) 348625
E-mail: library@imul.com
Key Personnel
Chairman: Magara Elisam
 E-mail: magara_elisam@hotmail.com
Secretary: Charles Batambuze
Founded: 1972
Discussing the usage of libraries & their information resources in Uganda.
Publication(s): *Uganda Information Bulletin* (quarterly, newsletter); *Ugandan Libraries* (biannually)

ULA, see Uganda Library Association (ULA)

United Kingdom

ALCL, see Association of London Chief Librarians (ALCL)

ARLIS/UK & Ireland Art Libraries Society
18 College Rd, Bromsgrove, Worcs B60 2NE
Tel: (01527) 579298 *Fax:* (01527) 579298
Web Site: www.arlis.org.uk
Key Personnel
Chairperson: Margaret Young *Tel:* (0131) 667 5491 *E-mail:* margaret.young@edinburgh.gov.uk
Founded: 1969
Professional body for librarians & all concerned with the documentation of virtual art.
Publication(s): *ARLIS News-sheet* (6 times/yr); *Art Libraries Journal* (quarterly); *Annual Directory* (annually)

Aslib, The Association for Information Management
Temple Chambers, 3-7 Temple Ave, London EC4Y 0HP
Tel: (020) 7583 8900 *Fax:* (020) 7583 8401
E-mail: aslib@aslib.com
Web Site: www.aslib.co.uk
Key Personnel
Dir: R B Bowes
Head of Publications: Sarah Blair
Publication(s): *Aslib Book Guide* (monthly); *Aslib Proceedings* (monthly); *Current Awareness Abstracts* (monthly); *Forthcoming International Scientific & Technical References* (quarterly); *International Journal of Electronic Library Research* (quarterly); *IT Link* (monthly); *Journal of Documentation* (annually); *Managing Information* (monthly); *Program* (quarterly)

The Association for Information Management, see Aslib, The Association for Information Management

Association of British Theological & Philosophical Libraries
Dr Williams's Library, 14 Gordon Sq, London WC1H 0AR
Tel: (020) 7387 3727
Web Site: www.abtapl.org.uk
Key Personnel
Secretary: Colin Clarke *E-mail:* colin.clarke@dwlib.co.uk
Publication(s): *Bulletin of ABTAPL* (triannually)

Association of London Chief Librarians (ALCL)
Hall Place, Bourne Rd, Bexley DA5 1PQ

Bibliographical Society
Institute of English Studies, Senate House, Room 304, Malet St, London WC1E 7HU
Tel: (020) 7611 7244 *Fax:* (020) 7611 8703
E-mail: secretary@bibsoc.org.uk
Web Site: www.bibsoc.org.uk/bibsoc.htm
Key Personnel
Honorary Secretary: David Pearson *E-mail:* d.pearson@wellcome.ac.uk
Founded: 1892
Publication(s): *The Library* (quarterly, various books on bibliographical subjects)

Book Aid International
39-41 Coldharbour Lane, Camberwell, London SE5 9NR
Tel: (020) 7733 3577 *Fax:* (020) 7978 8006
E-mail: info@bookaid.org
Web Site: www.bookaid.org
Key Personnel
Chairman: Tim Rix
Dir: Sara Harrity
Deputy Dir: David Membrey *E-mail:* david.membrey@bookaid.org
Book aid charity sending about 750,000 new & used books a year to partners in developing world countries & supporting development of local publishing.

British & Irish Association of Law Librarians
26 Myton Crescent, Warwick CV34 6QA
Tel: (01926) 491717 *Fax:* (01926) 491717
E-mail: holborn@linclib.sonnet.co.uk
Web Site: www.biall.org.uk
Key Personnel
Chairman: Victoria Jannetta
Vice Chairman: Susan Doe
Administrator: Susan Frost
Treasurer: Alden Bowers
Founded: 1969
Publication(s): *The Law Librarian*

Chartered Institute of Library & Information Professionals (CILIP)
7 Ridgmount St, London WC1E 7AE
Tel: (020) 7255 0500; (020) 7255 0505 (textphone) *Fax:* (020) 7255 0501
E-mail: info@cilip.org.uk
Web Site: www.cilip.org.uk
Key Personnel
Chief Executive: Bob McKee
Member Services: Sue Brown
Founded: 2002
Professional body for librarians & information managers.
Publication(s): *Update* (monthly, magazine)
Imprints: Facet Publishing

CILIP, see Chartered Institute of Library & Information Professionals (CILIP)

Circle of State Librarians
Home Office Library, ISU Resources, Queen Anne's Gate, Room 1004, London SW1H 9AT
Tel: (020) 7273 4463 *Fax:* (020) 7273 3957
Web Site: www.circleofstatelibrarians.co.uk
Key Personnel
Chairperson: Ms Maewyn Cumming *Tel:* (020) 7276 3098 *E-mail:* maewyn.cumming@e-envoy.gsi.gov.uk
Vice Chairperson: Jan Parry *Tel:* (020) 7273 3883 *Fax:* (020) 7273 3957 *E-mail:* jan.parry@homeoffice.gsi.gov.uk
Secretary: Andrew Digby *Tel:* (020) 7438 8483 *Fax:* (020) 7438 9160 *E-mail:* andrew.digby@ir.gsi.gov.uk
Treasurer: Diane Murgatroyd *Tel:* (020) 7008 5943 *Fax:* (020) 7008 5935 *E-mail:* diane.murgatroyd@fco.gov.uk
Membership Secretary: Gillian Harrison
 E-mail: gillian.harrison2@homeoffice.gsi.gov.uk
Minutes Secretary: Lynda A Cooper
 E-mail: lynda.cooper@homeoffice.gsi.gov.uk
Editor State Librarian: Pat Bell *Tel:* (0161) 827 0243 *Fax:* (0161) 827 0491 *E-mail:* pat.bell@hmce.gsi.gov.uk
Business Manager: Peter Harvey *Tel:* (0870) 785 3621 *E-mail:* peter.harvey1@hmce.gsi.gov.uk
Publicity: Fiona Greig *Tel:* (020) 7944 6138 *Fax:* (020) 7944 6098 *E-mail:* fiona.greig@dtlr.gsi.gov.uk
Publication(s): *State Librarian* (triannually)

CSL, see Circle of State Librarians

Facet Publishing, *imprint of* Chartered Institute of Library & Information Professionals (CILIP)

Facet Publishing
Imprint of Chartered Institute of Library & Information Professionals (CILIP)
7 Ridgmount St, London WC1E 7AE
Tel: (020) 7255 0590 *Fax:* (020) 7255 0591
E-mail: info@facetpublishing.co.uk
Web Site: www.facetpublishing.co.uk
Key Personnel
Man Dir: Janet Liebster
Publisher: Helen Carley
Marketing Executive: Mark O'Loughlin *Tel:* (020) 7255 0597 *E-mail:* mark.o'loughlin@facetpublishing.co.uk
Professional body for librarians & information managers.
Publication(s): *A Directory of Libraries in the UK & Ireland*; *A Directory of Rare Books & Special Collections in the UK & Ireland*; *A Guide to World Language Dictionaries*; *The Successful LIS Professional Series*; *Walfords Guide to Reference Material* (3 vols)

Friends of the National Libraries
Dept of Manuscripts, The British Library, 96 Euston Rd, London NW1 2DB
Tel: (020) 7412 7559
Web Site: www.bl.uk/about/cooperation/friends2.html
Key Personnel
Chairman: Lord Egremont
Honorary Secretary: Michael Borrie
Founded: 1931

Impact
c/o The Library Association, 7 Ridgmount St, London WC1E 7AE
Mailing Address: Engineering Employer's Federation, Broadway House, Tothill St, London SW1H 9NQ
Tel: (020) 7222 7777; (020) 7636 7543 *Fax:* (020) 7222 2782; (020) 7436 7218
Key Personnel
President: Peter Loewenstein
Publication(s): *Adult Sequels*; *Children's Sequels*; *EU Information Sources*; *Counter Point Series*; *Cumulated Fiction Index*; *Fiction Index*; *Junior Fiction Index*; *Picture Book Index*

International Association of Music Libraries, Archives & Documentation Centres (UK & Ireland Branch)
Edinburgh City Libraries, 9 George IV Bridge, Edinburgh EH1 1EG
Tel: (0131) 242 8053 *Fax:* (0131) 242 8009
Web Site: www.iaml-uk-irl.org
Key Personnel
President: Susi Woodhouse *E-mail:* susi.woodhouse@btopenworld.com
President Elect: Kathy Adamson *E-mail:* k.adamson@ram.ac.uk
General Secretary: Peter Baxter *E-mail:* pbbaxter@hotmail.com
Treasurer: Peter Linnitt *E-mail:* peter.linnitt@bbc.co.uk
Membership Secretary: Almut Boehme *E-mail:* a.boehme@nls.uk
Press & Public Relations Officer: Chris Pressler *E-mail:* cpressler@ull.ac.uk
Publications Officer: Margaret Roll *E-mail:* mroll@buckscc.gov.uk
Editor: Geoff Thomason *E-mail:* geoff.thomason@rncm.ac.uk
Founded: 1953
Publication(s): *Brio* (biannually)

School Library Association
Unit 2, Lotmead Business Village, Lotmead Farm, Wanborough, Swindon, Wilts SN4 0UY
Tel: (01793) 791787 *Fax:* (01793) 791786
E-mail: info@sla.org.uk
Web Site: www.sla.org.uk
Key Personnel
President: Aidan Chambers
Chief Executive: Kathy Lemaire *E-mail:* kathy@sla.org.uk
Founded: 1937
Promote the development of effective school libraries through advocacy, publishing & training.
Publication(s): *The School Librarian* (quarterly)

SCONUL, see Society of College, National & University Libraries (SCONUL)

Scottish Library Association
1st floor, Bldg C, Brandon Gate, Leechlee Rd, Hamilton ML3 6AU
Tel: (01698) 458888 *Fax:* (01698) 283170
E-mail: slic@slainte.org.uk
Web Site: www.slainte.org.uk
Key Personnel
Dir: Elaine Fulton *E-mail:* e.fulton@slainte.org.uk
Publication(s): *Scottish Libraries* (bimonthly)

SHINE-Scottish Health Information Network
c/o Margaret Forrest, Health Promotion Library Scotland, Health Education Board for Scotland, The Priory, Canaan Lane, Edinburgh EH10 4SG
Tel: (0131) 536 5582 *Fax:* (0131) 536 5502
E-mail: mdg@ednet.co.uk
Web Site: www.shinelib.org.uk
Key Personnel
Chair: Margaret Forrest
Publication(s): *Directory of Health Information Resources in Scotland*
Branch Office(s)
Erskine Medical Library, Hugh Robson Bldg, George Sq, Edinburgh EH8 9XE *Tel:* (031) 650-3692

Society of Archivists
Prioryfield House, 20 Canon St, Taunton, Somerset TA1 1SW
Tel: (01823) 327030 *Fax:* (01823) 371719
E-mail: offman@archives.org.uk
Web Site: www.archives.org.uk
Key Personnel
Chairman: Elizabeth Rees *Tel:* (0191) 232 6789 *E-mail:* lizrees@gateshead.gov.uk
Vice Chairman: Peter Anderson *Tel:* (0131) 535 1406 *Fax:* (0131) 535 1430 *E-mail:* peter.anderson@nas.gov.uk
Executive Secretary: Patrick Cleary *Tel:* (0115) 962 6499 *Fax:* (0115) 962 6499 *E-mail:* pat.cleary@archives.org.uk
Publication(s): *Careers Opportunities* (monthly); *Journal of the Society of Archivists* (biannually, newsletter)

Society of College, National & University Libraries (SCONUL)
102 Euston St, London NW1 2HA
Tel: (020) 7387 0317 *Fax:* (020) 7383 3197
E-mail: info@sconul.ac.uk
Web Site: www.sconul.ac.uk
Key Personnel
Executive Secretary: A J C Bainton *E-mail:* toby.bainton@sconul.ac.uk
Founded: 1950

The Society of County Librarians
c/o Northamptonshire Libraries & Information Service, 27 Guildhall Rd, Northampton NN1 18A
Mailing Address: PO Box 259, Northampton NN1 18A
Tel: (0604) 20262
Key Personnel
Secretary: Keith Crawshaw; Derek Jones; Treyor Knight
Aim is to further the position of public libraries across England, Northern Ireland & Wales to influence decision makers.

Welsh Library Association
c/o Publications Office, Dept of Information & Library Studies, Llanbadarn Fawr, Aberystwyth Dyfed SY23 3AS
Tel: (01970) 622174 *Fax:* (01970) 622190
E-mail: hle@aber.ac.uk
Web Site: www.dil.aber.ac.uk/holi/wla/wla.htm
Key Personnel
President: Andrew Green *E-mail:* andrew.green@llgc.org.uk
Professional assocation.
Publication(s): *Y Ddolen* (journal); *The Festiniog Railway 1954-1994: A Bibliography*; *Mynegai-Y Cylchgrawn Efengylaidd 1948-1999*; *Newyddion* (newsletter); *Pwy yw Pwy yn Llyfrgelly-ddiaeth Cymru* (Who's Who In Welsh Librarianship); *Rhestr o Fynegeion: Gylchgronau a Phapurau Newydd Cymreig* (A List of Indexes to Welsch Periodicals & Newspapers, online); *Service Delivery Plans in Welsh Unitary Authorities for the Financial Year 1996/97 & their Relevance to Public Library Services* (1996); *The Teifi Library Project: An Investigation of the Library & Information Requirements of Mobile Library Users in South Ceredigion* (report); *Wales Unitary Public Library Authorities* (directory, 1996)

Uruguay

Agrupacion Bibliotecologica del Uruguay
(Group Librarian of Uruguay)
Cerro Largo 1666, Montevideo 11200
Tel: (02) 400 57 40
Key Personnel
President: Luis Alberto Musso
Founded: 1964
Uruguayan Library & Archive Science Association.
Publication(s): *Anales del Senado del Uruguay* (Annals of the Senate of Uruguay, 1971); *Aportes para la historia de la bibliotecologia en el Uruguay* (Library Proffesion story, 1969); *Archivos del Uruguay* (Uruguay archives, 1974); *Bibliografia bibliografica y bibliotecologica* (Bibliography, 1964); *Bibliografia de Historia del Uruguay* (Bibliography History, 1977); *Bibliografia uruguaya sobre Brasil* (Brasil Bibliography, 1973); *La Estrella del sur-Indice* (The Southern Star, 1968); *Colonizacion Canaria en la Banda Oriental del Uruguay* (Canary of Uruguay Colonization, 1997); *El Dia - Indice General Alfabetico* (The Day - Indice General Alfabetico); *Fernandez Saldana, relacion de su obra bibliografica* (Fernandez Saldana Bibliography, 1989); *El Rio de la Plata en el Archivo General de Indias* (The River Plate in Archive General of Indias, 1997); *De Libros y lectores* (Books and Readers, 2000); *Uruguay-Brasil y sus medallas* (Uruguay Brasil Medals, 1976)

Asociacion de Bibliotecologos del Uruguay
(Uruguayan Library Association)
Eduardo V Haedo 2255, 11200 Montevideo
Mailing Address: PO Box 1315, 11000 Montevideo
Tel: (02) 4099989 *Fax:* (02) 4099989
E-mail: ABU@adinet.com.uy
Key Personnel
President: Eduardo Correa

Venezuela

Colegio de Bibliotecologos y Archivologos de Venezuela, see Venezuelan Library & Archives Association

Venezuelan Library & Archives Association
Apdo 6283, Caracas
Tel: (02) 5721858
Key Personnel
President: Elsi Jimenez de Diaz
Founded: 1978
Professional Association.
Publication(s): *Panel de Noticias* (News Board, monthly; free to members only)

Viet Nam

Hoi Thu-Vien Vietnam (Vietnamese Library Association)
National Library of Vietnam, 31 Trang Thi, 10000 Hanoi
Tel: (04) 824 8051 *Fax:* (04) 825 3357
E-mail: info@nlv.gov.vn
Web Site: www.nlv.gov.vn
Publication(s): *Thu'-Vien Tap-san* (Library Bulletin)

Zambia

Zambia Library Association
PO Box 38636, Lusaka
Key Personnel
Chairman: Benson Njobvu
  E-mail: bensonnjobvu@hotmail.com
Publication(s): *Zambia Library Association Journal*; *Zambia Library Association Newsletter*

Zimbabwe

Library & Information Science Society
PO Box CY 407, Causeway, Harare
Tel: (04) 752311 *Fax:* (04) 720955
Key Personnel
Contact: Dakarai Mashava

Zimbabwe Library Association (ZLA)
PO Box 3133, Harare
Tel: (04) 692741
Key Personnel
Chairman: Driden Kunaka
Honorary Secretary: Albert Masheka
Publication(s): *The Zimbabwean Librarian*

ZLA, see Zimbabwe Library Association (ZLA)

Library Reference Books & Journals

The publications in this section are library related and are listed alphabetically under the country of the publisher.

The type of publication appears in parentheses after the title:

(B) - Book   (J) - Journal   (P) - Periodical

For information on reference books, journals and periodicals relating to the book publishing industry see **Book Trade Reference Books & Journals**.

Argentina

Guia de las Bibliotecas Universitarias Argentinas (Guide to Argentine University Libraries) (B)
Published by Centro de Documentacion Bibliotecologica, Universidad Nacional del Sur
Av Alem 1253, 8000 Bahia Blanca
Tel: (091) 4595111 *Fax:* (091) 4595110
E-mail: unsbc@criba.edu.ar
Web Site: bc.uns.edu.ar
Key Personnel
Chief Librarian: Marta Ibarlucca

Referencias (References) (J)
Published by AGBRA (Asociacion de Bibliotecarios Graduados de la Republica Argentina)
Tucuman 1424, 8° piso, D, 1050 Buenos Aires
Tel: (011) 4373 0571 *Fax:* (011) 4371 5269
E-mail: referencias@abgra.org.ar
Web Site: abgra.sisbi.uba.ar
Key Personnel
President: Ana Maria Peruchena Zimmermann
Vice President: Claudia Rodriguez
ISSN: 0328-1507

Australia

ABN Catalogue (J)
Published by Australian Bibliographic Network, National Library of Australia
Canberra, ACT 2600
Tel: (02) 6262 1111 *Fax:* (02) 6257 1703
E-mail: www@nla.gov.au
Web Site: www.nla.gov.au
Key Personnel
Dir General: Jan Fullerton *E-mail:* jfullert@nla.gov.au
Deputy Dir Gen: David Toll
Bimonthly.

Access (J)
Published by Australian School Library Association Inc
PO Box 5689, Mackay MC, Qld 4741
Tel: (07) 4953 1863 *Fax:* (07) 4953 1908
E-mail: asla@asla.org.au
Web Site: www.asla.org.au
Key Personnel
Executive Officer: Karen Bonanno
E-mail: kbonanno@bigpond.com
Editor: Margaret Butterworth *E-mail:* margaret@iinet.net.au
Quarterly.

Australian Academic & Research Libraries (J)
Published by Australian Library & Information Association
PO Box E441, Kingston, ACT 2604
Tel: (02) 6285 1877 *Fax:* (02) 6282 2249
E-mail: pre@comserver.canberra.edu.au
Web Site: www.alia.org.au
Key Personnel
Editor: Dr Peter Clayton
Quarterly.
106 AUD (Overseas air)
ISSN: 0004-8623

Australian Libraries: the Essential Directory (B)
Published by Auslib Press Pty Ltd
PO Box 622, Blackwood, SA 5051
Tel: (08) 8278 4363 *Fax:* (08) 8278 4000
E-mail: info@auslib.com.au
Web Site: www.auslib.com.au
Biennially.
6th: 300 pp, 70 AUD plus 8 AUD P&H
ISBN(s): 1-875145-51-6
ISSN: 1031-5187

Australian Library Journal (J)
Published by Australian Library & Information Association
9-11 Napier Close, Deakin, ACT 2600
Mailing Address: PO Box E441, Kingston, ACT 2604
Tel: (02) 6215 8222 *Fax:* (02) 6282 2249
E-mail: enquiry@alia.org.au
Web Site: www.alia.org.au/alj
Key Personnel
Editor: John Levett
Academic/scholarly publication.
First published 1951.
Quarterly.
106 AUD (Overseas air)

inCite (J)
Published by Australian Library & Information Association
9-11 Napier Close, Deakin, ACT 2600
Mailing Address: PO Box E441, Kingston, ACT 2604
Tel: (02) 6285 1877 *Fax:* (02) 6282 2249
E-mail: incite@alia.org.au
Web Site: www.alia.org.au
Key Personnel
Editor: Emma Davis
Managing Editor: Ivan Trundle
Newsletter.
First published 1980.
Monthly.
129 AUD (Overseas air)
ISSN: 0158-0876

Orana (J)
Published by Australian Library & Information Association
9-11 Napier Close, Deakin, ACT 2600
Tel: (02) 6285 1877 *Fax:* (02) 6282 2249
E-mail: enquiry@alia.org.au
Web Site: www.alia.org.au
Key Personnel
Editor: Margaret Steinberger
Production Editor: Shirley Campbell
E-mail: shirley.campbell@alianet.alia.org.au
Children's, youth services & school libraries journal.
Triannually.
ISSN: 0045-6705

Our Heritage: A Directory to Archives and Manuscript Repositories in Australia (B)
Published by Australian Society of Archivists
PO Box 77, Dickson, ACT 2602
Toll Free Tel: 800 622 251 *Fax:* (06) 2093931
E-mail: asa@asap.unimelb.edu.au
Web Site: www.archivists.org.au
Key Personnel
Dir General: G E Nichols
Provides archivists & other record keeping & information professionals with up to date material on professional issues & practice.
First published 1955.
Biannually.
ISSN: 0157-6895

La Trobe Journal (P)
Published by State Library of Victoria
328 Swanston St, Melbourne, Victoria 3000
Tel: (03) 8664 7000; (03) 9639 7006 (TTY)
Fax: (03) 9663 1480
E-mail: webinfo@slv.vic.gov.au
Web Site: www.slv.vic.gov.au
Key Personnel
Editor: Prof John Barnes *E-mail:* rjbarnes@latrobe.edu.au
First published 1968.
Biannually.
ISSN: 1441-3760

Austria

Biblos (J)
Published by Boehlau Verlag GmbH & Co KG
Sachsenplatz 4-6, 1201 Vienna
Mailing Address: Postfach 87, 1201 Vienna
Tel: (01) 330 24 27 *Fax:* (01) 330 24 32
E-mail: boehlau@boehlau.at
Web Site: www.boehlau.at
Austrian journal for book & library personnel, documentation, bibliography & bibliophily; published in English & German.
First published 1952.
Biannually.

Mitteilungen der Vereinigung Oesterreichischer Bibliothekarinnen und Bibliothekare (Bulletin of the Association of Austrian Librarians) (J)
Published by Vereinigung Oesterreichischer Bibliothekarinnen und Bibliothekare (VOEB) (Association of Austrian Librarians)
Innrain 50, 6010 Innsbruck
Tel: (0512) 507-2425 *Fax:* (0512) 507-2893

AUSTRIA

Key Personnel
Contact: Eva Ramminger *E-mail:* eva.ramminger@uibk.ac.at
Text in German.
First published 1948.
Quarterly.
ISSN: 1022-2588

Scrinium (J)
Published by Verband Oesterreichischer Archivare (Association of Austrian Archivists)
Postfach 164, 1014 Vienna
Tel: (01) 79540450 *Fax:* (01) 79540109
Key Personnel
Editor: Rainer Egger
Text in German.
First published 1969.
Biannually.
ISSN: 1012-0327

Bangladesh

Eastern Librarian (J)
Published by The Library Association of Bangladesh
c/o Institute of Library & Information Science, Bangladesh Central Public Library Bldg, Shahbagh, Dhaka 1000
Tel: (02) 504269
Key Personnel
Editor: M Shamsul Islam Khan *E-mail:* msik@icddrb.org
Research articles, case studies & short reports on library & information science & documentation. Text in English.
First published 1966.
Biannually.
30 USD
ISSN: 1021-3651

Barbados

Bulletin of the Library Association of Barbados (J)
Published by Library Association of Barbados
PO Box 827E, Bridgetown
Key Personnel
President: Shirley Yearwood
Text in English.
First published 1968.
Irregularly.
5 USD

Belgium

Archives et Bibliotheques de Belgique (Library Archives of Belgium) (J)
Published by Archives et Bibliotheques de Belgique a s b l
Blvd de l'Empereur 4, 1000 Brussels
Tel: (02) 5195393 *Fax:* (02) 5195533
Key Personnel
Chairman & Rights & Permissions: Frank Daelemans *E-mail:* frank.daelemans@klr.be
Text in Dutch, English, French, German, Italian, Latin & Spanish.
First published 1923.
Annually.
30 USD
ISSN: 0003-9748

Bibliotheek- & archiefgids (Library & Archive Guide) (J)
Published by Vlaamse Vereniging voor Bibliotheek- Archief-en Documentatiewezen (VVBAD) (Flemish Association for Libraries, Archives & Documentation Centres)
Statiestr 179, 2600 Antwerp
Tel: (03) 2814457 *Fax:* (03) 2188077
Web Site: www.vvbad.be
Key Personnel
Editor: Peter Van den Broeck
Editorial Secretary: Marijke Hoflack *E-mail:* marijke.hoflack@vvbad.be
First published 1922.
Bimonthly.
48 pp
ISSN: 0772-7003

Les Cahiers de la Documentation (J)
Published by Association Belgium de Documentation (Belgian Association for Documentation)
Chaussee de Wavre 1683, 1160 Brussels
Tel: (02) 675 58 62 *Fax:* (02) 672 74 46
E-mail: info@abd-bvd.be
Web Site: www.abd-bvd.be
Text in Dutch, English & French.
First published 1947.
Quarterly.
49.58 EUR per year
ISSN: 0007-9804

Bosnia and Herzegovina

Bibliotekarstvo (Librarianship) (J)
Published by Drustvo Bibliotekara Bosne i Hercegovine (Librarians' Society of Bosnia & Herzegovina)
Zmaja od Bosne 8b, 71000 Sarajevo
Tel: 33 275 312 *Fax:* 33 218 431
E-mail: nubbih@nub.ba
Web Site: www.nub.ba
Key Personnel
President: Nevenka Hajdarovic *E-mail:* nevenka@nub.ba
Dir: Dr Enes Kujundzic
First published 1956.
ISSN: 0006-1832

Brazil

Ciencia da Informacao (Information Science) (J)
Published by Instituto Brasileiro de Informacao em Ciencia e Tecnologia
SAS Qd 5, Lote 6, Bloco H - 5° andar, 70070-914 Brasilia-DF
Tel: (061) 217-6360; (061) 217-6350 *Fax:* (061) 226-2677
E-mail: webmaster@ibict.br
Web Site: www.ibict.br; www.ibict.br/cionline/inicio.htm
Key Personnel
Dir: Nilson Lemos Lage *E-mail:* lage@ibict.br
Triannually.

Bulgaria

Biblioteka (The Library) (J)
Published by St Cyril & St Methodius National Library
88 Levski Blvd, 1504 Sofia
Tel: (02) 9881600 *Fax:* (02) 435495
E-mail: nbkm@nl.otel.net
Key Personnel
Editor in Chief: Alexandra Dipchikova *E-mail:* dipchikova@nationallibrary.bg
First published 1954.
Bimonthly.
12 BGN (domestic); 48 USD (foreign)
ISSN: 0861-847X

China

Library & Information Service (J)
Published by Library of Chinese Academy of Sciences
33 Beisihuan xilu, Zhongguancum, Beijing 100080
Tel: (010) 62540371 *Fax:* (010) 62566846
E-mail: journal@mail.las.ac.cn; menggj@mail.las.ac.cn
Web Site: www.las.ac.cn
Key Personnel
Dir: Xu Yinchi
Monthly.
96 pp, $142

Colombia

ASCOLBI Revista (J)
Published by Asociacion Colombiana de Bibliotecologos y Documentalistas
Calle 12 No 34-20, Bogota
Tel: (01) 3603077 (ext 326) *Fax:* (01) 3600885
E-mail: lbecerra@panamerica.com.co
Web Site: biblio.ucaldas.edu.co/docs/ascolbi.htm
Quarterly.

Boletin Cultural y Bibliografico (Cultural & Bibliographical Bulletin) (J)
Published by Biblioteca Luis Angel Arango Banco de la Republica (Luis Angel Arango Library-Central Bank of Colombia)
Carrera 5 No 11-68, Bogota
Tel: (01) 3431202; (01) 2827840 *Fax:* (01) 2863551
E-mail: wbiblio@banrep.gov.co
Web Site: www.banrep.gov.co/blaa
Quarterly.

Croatia

Vjesnik bibliotekara Hrvatske (Croatian Librarians' Report) (J)
Published by Hrvatsko knjizincarsko drustvo (Croatian Library Association)
c/o Nacionalna i sveucilisna knjiznica, Hrvatske bratske zajednice 4, 10 000 Zagreb
Tel: (01) 615 93 20 *Fax:* (01) 616 41 86
E-mail: hkd@nsk.hr
Web Site: jagor.srce.hr/hkd; www.hkdrustvo.hr

Key Personnel
President: Dubravka Stancin-Rosic *Tel:* (01) 616 40 37
Editor-in-Chief: Tinka Katic *E-mail:* tkatic@nsk.hr
Text in Croatian, English, German; summaries in Croatian & English. Back issues available. Cumulative index every 5 years.
First published 1950.
Quarterly.
200 pp, 300 HRK or 50 USD
ISSN: 0507-1925

Cuba

Biblioteca Nacional Jose Marti Revista (Jose Marti National Library Review) (J)
Published by Biblioteca Nacional Jose Marti
Apdo 6881, Avda de Independencia y 20 de Mayo, Plaza de la Revolucion, Havana 10600
Tel: 79-6091
Web Site: www.lib.cult.cu
Telex: 511963
Key Personnel
Dir: Eliades Acosta Matos
Editor: Julio Le Riverend
Text in Spanish.
First published 1909.
Triannually.
15 USD
ISSN: 0006-1727

Denmark

Bibliotekspressen (The Library Press) (J)
Published by Bibliotekarforbundet
Lindevangs Alle 2, 2000 Frederiksberg
Tel: 38 88 22 33 *Fax:* 38 88 32 01
E-mail: bf@bf.dk
Web Site: www.bf.dk/bpr.htm
Key Personnel
Editor: Per Nyeng *E-mail:* pn@bf.dk; Hanne Folmer Schade *E-mail:* hfs@bf.dk
ISSN: 1395-0401

Biblioteksvejviser (Guide to Danish Libraries) (B)
Published by Danmarks Biblioteksforening (Danish Library Association)
Vesterbrogade 20, 5 sal, 1620 Copenhagen V
Tel: 33 25 09 35 *Fax:* 33 25 7900
E-mail: dbf@dbf.dk
Web Site: www.dbf.dk
Key Personnel
Dir: Winnie Vitzansky
Editor: Hanne Klemmed *E-mail:* hk@dbf.dk
Text in Danish; index in English.
First published 1970.
Annually.
385 DKK per year
ISSN: 0420-1108

Bogens Verden (Book Magazine) (J)
Published by Danmarks Biblioteksforening (Danish Library Association)
Vesterbrogade 20, 5 sal, 1620 Copenhagen V
Tel: 33 25 09 35 *Fax:* 33 25 7900
E-mail: dbf@dbf.dk
Web Site: www.dbf.dk
Key Personnel
Dir: Winnie Vitzansky
Editor: Bruno Svindborg
Magazine for Danish & foreign literature & culture.

First published 1918.
6 times/yr.
ISSN: 0006-5692

Danmarks Biblioteker (J)
Published by Danmarks Biblioteksforening (Danish Library Association)
Vesterbrogade 20, 5 sal, 1620 Copenhagen V
Tel: 33 25 09 35 *Fax:* 33 25 7900
E-mail: dbf@dbf.dk
Web Site: www.dbf.dk
Key Personnel
Dir: Winnie Vitzansky
Newsletter from the Danish Library Association.
First published 1987.
10 times/yr.
ISSN: 1397-1026

DF-Revy (J)
Published by Danmarks Forskningsbiblioteksforening
Handelshojskolens Bibliotek, Fuglesangs Alle 4, 8210 Aarhus V
Tel: 89 48 65 42 *Fax:* 86 15 96 27
E-mail: kin@asb.dk
Web Site: www.dfdf.dk/dfrevy.shtml
Key Personnel
President: Erland Kolding Nielsen
Editor: Kirsten Krogh Kruuse

Over Broen - Library Student's Journal (J)
Published by Danmarks Biblioteksskole/Royal School of Library & Information Science
Birketinget 6, 2300 Copenhagen S
Tel: 32 58 60 66 *Fax:* 32 84 02 01
E-mail: overbroen@hotmail.com
Web Site: www.db.dk
Key Personnel
Librarian: Ivar A L Hoel
ISSN: 0904-3853

Skolebiblioteksaarbog (School Libraries Annual) (B)
Published by Danmarks Skolebiblioteksforening
Vesterbrogade 20, 5 sal, 1620 Copenhagen V
Tel: 33 25 09 35 *Fax:* 33 25 79 00
E-mail: dbf@dbf.dk
Web Site: www.dbf.dk
First published 1969.
ISSN: 0900-9582

Ethiopia

Bulletin (J)
Published by Ethiopian Library & Information Association
PO Box 30530, Addis Ababa
Tel: (01) 511344
Key Personnel
President: Mulugeta Hunde
Biannually.

Bulletin (J)
Published by Ethiopian Manuscript Microfilm Library
PO Box 30274, Addis Ababa
Tel: (01) 110844
First published 1974.
Quarterly.

Fiji

Journal (P)
Published by Fiji Library Association (FLA)
Government Buildings, PO Box 2292, Suva
Tel: 304144 *Fax:* 304144
Telex: FJ2276 *Cable:* UNIVERSITY SUVA
First published 1979.
Biannually (June & Dec).
7 FJD per issue
ISSN: 1016-9989

Finland

Kirjastolehti (Bulletin) (J)
Published by Suomen Kirjastoseura (Finnish Library Association)
Vuorikatu 22 A18, 00100 Helsinki
Tel: (09) 6221 340 *Fax:* (09) 6221 466
E-mail: fla@fla.fi
Web Site: www.fla.fi/kirjastolehti
Key Personnel
President: Tarja Cronberg
First published 1908.
8 times/yr.
40 pp
ISSN: 0023-1843

Signum (J)
Published by Suomen Tieteellinen Kirjastoseura (Finnish Research Library Association)
Library of Parliament, Aurorankatu 6, 00102 Helsinki
Tel: (09) 432 3485 *Fax:* (09) 432 3495
Web Site: www.pro.tsv.fi/stks
Key Personnel
Editor: Paivikki Karhula *E-mail:* paivikki.karhula@eduskunta.fi
First published 1968.
8 times/yr.

France

Documentaliste - Sciences de l'Information (Documentalist - Information Sciences) (J)
Published by L'Association des Professionnels de l'Information et de la Documentation (ADBS) (French Association of Information & Documentation Professionals)
25 rue Claude Tillier, 75012 Paris
Tel: (01) 43 72 25 25 *Fax:* (01) 43 72 30 41
E-mail: adbs@adbs.fr
Web Site: www.adbs.fr
Key Personnel
President: Florence Wilhelm
Director of the Review: Jean-Claude Moal
Editor: Jean Michel Rauzier *E-mail:* jean-michel.rauzier@adbs.fr
General Manager: David Cayre
French review devoted to techniques, professions, services & policies in the information & library fields & to research in information sciences, with particular focus on European & French-speaking countries. Abstracts in English.
First published 1964.
5 times/yr.
80 pp
ISSN: 0395-3858

INTER BCD (J)
Published by Centre d'Etude de la Documentation et de l'Information Scolaires

FRANCE

16, rue des Belles-Croix, 91150 Etampes
Tel: (01) 64 94 39 51 *Fax:* (01) 64 94 49 35
E-mail: cedis@calvanet.calvacom.fr
Web Site: www.ac-versailles.fr/cedis
Key Personnel
Publisher: Michel Mouillet
Editor: Marie Noelle Michaut
Journal for specialist librarians.
Biannually.
ISSN: 1270-1467

INTER CDI (J)
Published by Centre d'Etude de la Documentation et de l'Information Scolaires
16, rue des Belles-Croix, 91150 Etampes
Tel: (01) 64 94 39 51 *Fax:* (01) 64 94 49 35
E-mail: cedis@calvanet.calvacom.fr
Web Site: www.ac-versailles.fr/cedis
Key Personnel
Publisher: Michel Mouillet
Journal for Specialist Librarians (second level).
First published 1972.
Bimonthly.
108 pp
ISSN: 0242-2999

Scribeco (J)
Published by Institut National de la Statistique et des Etudes Economiques (INSEE)
One rue Vincent Auriol, 80027 Amiens Cedex 01
Tel: (03) 22 92 73 22 *Fax:* (03) 22 97 92 95
E-mail: inseeactualites@insee.fr
Web Site: www.insee.fr
Bibliographic bulletin.
First published 1986.
6 times/yr.
ISSN: 0769-0509

Germany

Beitraege zum Buch-und Bibliothekswesen (B)
Published by Harrassowitz Verlag
Taunusstr 14, 65183 Wiesbaden
Tel: (0611) 530-0 *Fax:* (0611) 530570
E-mail: verlag@harrassowitz.de; service@harrassowitz.de
Web Site: www.harrassowitz.de
Key Personnel
Editor: Michael Knoche
Rights & Permissions: Michael Langfeld
  E-mail: mlangfeld@harrassowitz.de
This book series deals with, among other things, library science, bibliographies & the history of books, libraries & publishing houses.
First published 1965.
Irregularly.
ISSN: 0408-8107

Bibliothek und Wissenschaft (Libraries & Science) (J)
Published by Harrassowitz Verlag
Taunusstr 14, 65183 Wiesbaden
Tel: (0611) 530-0 *Fax:* (0611) 530570
E-mail: verlag@harrassowitz.de; service@harrassowitz.de
Web Site: www.harrassowitz.de
Key Personnel
Publicity Dir: Robert Gietz *Tel:* (0611) 530-551
  E-mail: rgietz@harrassowitz.de
History of books, libraries & science.
First published 1964.
Annually.
99 EUR or 168 CHF per vol
ISSN: 0067-8236

Buchprofile (J)
Published by Borromausverein eV
Wittelsbacherring 9, 53115 Bonn
Tel: (0228) 7258-0 *Fax:* (0228) 7258-189
E-mail: lektorat@borro.de
Web Site: www.buchprofile.de
Key Personnel
Dir: Rolf Pitsch
Editor: Herbert Stangl
Book profile for Catholic library work.

Buchwissenschaftliche Beitraege aus dem Deutschen Bucharchiv Muenchen (Articles of the German Archives in Munich) (B)
Published by Harrassowitz Verlag
Taunusstr 14, 65183 Wiesbaden
Tel: (0611) 530-0 *Fax:* (0611) 530570
E-mail: verlag@harrassowitz.de; service@harrassowitz.de
Web Site: www.harrassowitz.de
Key Personnel
Rights & Permissions: Robert Gietz
Editor: Ludwig Delp; Ursula Neumann
This book series deals, among other things, with the history of books, libraries, literature & publishing houses.
First published 1950.
Irregularly.
ISSN: 0724-7001

Erwerbung in Deutschen Bibliotheken (Acquisitions Departments of German Libraries) (J)
Published by Harrassowitz Verlag
Taunusstr 14, 65183 Wiesbaden
Tel: (0611) 530-0 *Fax:* (0611) 530570
E-mail: verlag@harrassowitz.de; service@harrassowitz.de
Web Site: www.harrassowitz.de
Key Personnel
Rights & Permissions: Robert Gietz
First published 1994.
Biennially.
20 EUR or 35.20 CHF per year
ISSN: 1434-792X

Geschichte des Buchhandels (History of the Book Trade) (B)
Published by Harrassowitz Verlag
Taunusstr 14, 65183 Wiesbaden
Tel: (0611) 530-0 *Fax:* (0611) 530570
E-mail: verlag@harrassowitz.de; service@harrassowitz.de
Web Site: www.harrassowitz.de
Key Personnel
Rights & Permissions: Robert Gietz
The series deals with the history of the international booktrade. Presently the following volumes are available Germany, Netherlands, Hungary, Norway, Russia & Soviet Union.
First published 1975.
Irregularly.
ISSN: 0941-7877

Gesellschaft fuer das Buch (Society for the Book) (J)
Published by Harrassowitz Verlag
Taunusstr 14, 65183 Wiesbaden
Tel: (0611) 530-0 *Fax:* (0611) 530570
E-mail: verlag@harrassowitz.de; service@harrassowitz.de
Web Site: www.harrassowitz.de
Key Personnel
Rights & Permissions: Robert Gietz
First published 1995.
Irregularly.
ISSN: 0948-5007

Handbuch der Bibliotheken (Directory of Libraries) (B)
Published by K G Saur Verlag GmbH, A Gale/Thomson Learning Company
Unit of Thomson Learning
Ortlerstr 8, 81373 Munich
Mailing Address: Postfach 70 16 20, 81316 Munich
Tel: (089) 76902-0 *Fax:* (089) 76902-150
E-mail: info@saur.de
Web Site: www.saur.de
Telex: 5212067
Bundesrepublik Deutschland, Oesterreich, Schweiz, Germany, Austria, Switzerland.
Parent Company: Gale
Ultimate Parent Company: The Thomson Corporation

IFLA Journal (J)
Published by K G Saur Verlag GmbH, A Gale/Thomson Learning Company
Unit of Thomson Learning
Ortlerstr 8, 81373 Munich
Mailing Address: Postfach 70 16 20, 81316 Munich
Tel: (089) 76902-0 *Fax:* (089) 76902-150
E-mail: info@saur.de
Web Site: www.saur.de
Telex: 5212067
Parent Company: Gale
Ultimate Parent Company: The Thomson Corporation

IFLA Publications (B)
Published by K G Saur Verlag GmbH, A Gale/Thomson Learning Company
Unit of Thomson Learning
Ortlerstr 8, 81373 Munich
Mailing Address: Postfach 70 16 20, 81316 Munich
Tel: (089) 76902-0 *Fax:* (089) 76902-150
E-mail: info@saur.de
Web Site: www.saur.de
Telex: 5212067
A series of publications related to the International Federation of Library Associations & Institutions.
Parent Company: Gale
Ultimate Parent Company: The Thomson Corporation

Jahrbuch der Deutschen Bibliotheken (Yearbook of German Libraries) (B)
Published by Harrassowitz Verlag
Taunusstr 14, 65183 Wiesbaden
Tel: (0611) 530-0 *Fax:* (0611) 530570
E-mail: verlag@harrassowitz.de; service@harrassowitz.de
Web Site: www.harrassowitz.de
Information about German Scientific Libraries.
First published 1902.
Biennially.
79 EUR
ISSN: 0075-2223

Leipziger Jahrbuch zur Buchgeschichte (J)
Published by Harrassowitz Verlag
Taunusstr 14, 65183 Wiesbaden
Tel: (0611) 530-0 *Fax:* (0611) 530570
E-mail: verlag@harrassowitz.de; service@harrassowitz.de
Web Site: www.harrassowitz.de
Key Personnel
Editor: Thomas Keiderling; Lothar Poethe; Volker Titel
History of books, of the booktrade, of publishers & of printers.
First published 1991.
Annually.
59 EUR
ISSN: 0940-1954

Librarianship and Information Work Worldwide (B)
Published by K G Saur Verlag GmbH, A Gale/Thomson Learning Company
Unit of Thomson Learning
Ortlerstr 8, 81373 Munich

Mailing Address: Postfach 70 16 20, 81316 Munich
Tel: (089) 76902-0 *Fax:* (089) 76902-150
E-mail: info@saur.de
Web Site: www.saur.de
Parent Company: Gale
Ultimate Parent Company: The Thomson Corporation

Marginalien Zeitschrift fuer Buchkunst und Bibliophilie (Marginal Notes - Journal for Book Art & Bibliophilic) (J)
Published by Harrassowitz Verlag
Taunusstr 14, 65183 Wiesbaden
Tel: (0611) 530-0 *Fax:* (0611) 530570
E-mail: verlag@harrassowitz.de; service@harrassowitz.de
Web Site: www.harrassowitz.de
First published 1948.
Quarterly.
69 EUR
ISSN: 0025-2948

Schulbibliothek aktuell (School Library Today) (J)
Published by Deutsches Bibliotheksinstitut (German Library Institute)
Kurt-Schumacher-Damm 12-16, 13405 Berlin
Tel: (030) 410 34-0 *Fax:* (030) 410 34-100
E-mail: publikationen@dbi-berlin.de
Web Site: www.dbi-berlin.de
Key Personnel
Dir: Prof Gunter Beyersdorff
First published 1975.
Quarterly.
ISSN: 0341-471X

Wolfenbuetteler Schriften zur Geschichte des Buchwesens (J)
Published by Harrassowitz Verlag
Taunusstr 14, 65183 Wiesbaden
Tel: (0611) 530-0 *Fax:* (0611) 530570
E-mail: verlag@harrassowitz.de; service@harrassowitz.de
Web Site: www.harrassowitz.de
Key Personnel
Rights & Permissions: Robert Gietz
This journal series deals with the history of books, libraries & publishing houses. Published in cooperation with Herzog August Bibliothek.
First published 1977.
Irregularly.
ISSN: 0724-9586

World Guide to Libraries (B)
Published by K G Saur Verlag GmbH, A Gale/Thomson Learning Company
Ortlerstr 8, 81373 Munich
Mailing Address: Postfach 70 16 20, 81316 Munich
Tel: (089) 76902-0 *Fax:* (089) 76902-150
E-mail: info@saur.de
Web Site: www.saur.de
Telex: 5212067
Furnishes details on 47,000 libraries in 167 countries. Covers national, general research, university, school, government, corporate, ecclesiastical, special & public libraries with over 30,000 volumes. Alphabetical index.
1,200 pp
ISBN(s): 3-598-20725-5
Parent Company: Gale
Ultimate Parent Company: The Thomson Corporation
U.S. Office(s): Thomson Learning

World Guide to Special Libraries (B)
Published by K G Saur Verlag GmbH, A Gale/Thomson Learning Company
Unit of Thomson Learning
Ortlerstr 8, 81373 Munich
Mailing Address: Postfach 70 16 20, 81316 Munich
Tel: (089) 76902-0 *Fax:* (089) 76902-150
E-mail: info@saur.de
Web Site: www.saur.de
Telex: 5212067
Parent Company: Gale
Ultimate Parent Company: The Thomson Corporation

Zeitschrift fuer Bibliothekswesen und Bibliographie (Journal of Library Science & Bibliography) (J)
Published by Vittorio Klostermann GmbH
Frauenlobstr 22, 60487 Frankfurt am Main
Mailing Address: Postfach 90 06 01, 60446 Frankfurt am Main
Tel: (069) 97 08 16-0 *Fax:* (069) 70 80 38
E-mail: verlag@klostermann.de
Web Site: www.klostermann.de
Key Personnel
Editor: Dr Elisabeth Niggemann
Publisher: Vittorio E Klostermann *Tel:* (069) 97 08 16-0 (ext 11) *E-mail:* vek@klostermann.de
Marketing: Martin Warny *Tel:* (069) 97 08 16-12 *E-mail:* m.warny@klostermann.de
6 times/yr.
ISSN: 0044-2380

Ghana

Directory of Research & Special Libraries in Ghana (B)
Published by Council for Scientific & Industrial Research
PO Box M32, Accra
Tel: (021) 777651-4 *Fax:* (021) 777655
Web Site: www.csir.org.gh
Key Personnel
Acting Dir General: Prof E Owusu Benoah

Guyana

Bulletin (J)
Published by Guyana Library Association
c/o National Library, 76-77 Church & Main Sts, Georgetown
Tel: (02) 227-4053; (02) 227-4052; (02) 226-2690; (0226) 2699 *Fax:* (02) 227-4053
E-mail: natlib@sdnp.org.gy
Web Site: www.natlib.gov.gy
Key Personnel
Editor: Wenda Stevenson
First published 1970.
Biannually.
ISSN: 1023-3385

Hungary

Hungarian Library & Information Science Abstracts (J)
Published by Orszagos Szechenyi Konyvtar (National Szechenyi Library)
Budavari Palota F Bldg, Room 801, 1827 Budapest
Tel: (01) 224-3793 *Fax:* (01) 224-3795
E-mail: racz@oszk.hu; fazokas@oszk.hu
Web Site: www.oszk.hu
Telex: 224226 bibln h
Key Personnel
Editor: Laszlo Nagypal *E-mail:* lnagypal@oszk.hu
Text in English.
First published 1972.
Biannually.
17 EUR
ISSN: 0046-8304

Koenyvtartoerteneti Fuezetek (History of Libraries series) (J)
Published by Jozsef Attila Tudomanyegyetem Egyetemi Koenyvtar
6720 Szeged, Dugonics Sq 13, 6720 Szeged
Mailing Address: PO Box 393, 6701 Szeged
Tel: (062) 544036 *Fax:* (062) 544035
E-mail: mader@bibl.u-szeged.hu
Web Site: www.bibl.u-szeged.hu

Konyvtari Figyelo Uj folyam (Library Review) (J)
Published by Orszagos Szechenyi Konyvtar (National Szechenyi Library)
Buda Royal Palace Wing F, 1827 Budapest
Tel: (01) 224-3793; (01) 224-3796 *Fax:* (01) 224-3795
E-mail: racz@oszk.hu; fazokas@oszk.hu
Web Site: www.oszk.hu
Telex: 224226 bibln h
Key Personnel
Editor-in-Chief: Dr Peter Dippold *E-mail:* dippold@oszk.hu
Text in Hungarian; summaries in English & German.
First published 1955.
Quarterly.
51 EUR
ISSN: 0023-3773

Magyar konyvtari szakirodalom bibliografiaja (Bibliography on Hungarian Library Literature) (J)
Published by Orszagos Szechenyi Konyvtar (National Szechenyi Library)
Budavari Palota F Bldg, Room 801, 1827 Budapest
Tel: (01) 224-3793 *Fax:* (01) 224-3795
E-mail: racz@oszk.hu; fazokas@oszk.hu
Web Site: www.oszk.hu
Telex: 224226 bibln h
Key Personnel
Editor: Ferencne Javori *E-mail:* javori@oszk.hu
Text in Hungarian.
First published 1969.
Quarterly.
20 EUR
ISSN: 0133-736X

Iceland

Bokasafnid
Published by Upplysing - Felag bokasafns- og upplysingafraeoa (Information - the Icelandic Library & Information Science Association)
Lagmuli 7, 108 Reykjavik
Mailing Address: Borgarbokasafn Reykjavikur, Tryggvagoetu 15, 101 Reykjavik
Tel: 553-7290; 862-8627 *Fax:* 588-9239
E-mail: upplysing@bokis.is
Web Site: www.bokasafnid.is
Key Personnel
President: H A Hardarson
Yearbook of library & information science.
Annually.
ISSN: 1670-0066

ICELAND

Fregnir (J)
Published by Upplysing - Felag bokasafns- og upplysingafraeoa (Information - the Icelandic Library & Information Science Association)
Lagmuli 7, 108 Reykjavik
Tel: 553-7290; 862-8627 *Fax:* 588-9239
E-mail: upplysing@bokis.is
Web Site: www.bokis.is
Key Personnel
President: H A Hardarson
Newsletter.
Triannually.
ISSN: 1605-4415

India

Annals of Library & Information Studies (J)
Published by National Institute of Science Communication & Information Resources (NISCAIR)
14 Satsang Vihar Marg, Off SJS Sansanwal Marg, New Delhi 110067
Tel: (011) 26560141; (011) 26560143; (011) 26560165 *Fax:* (011) 26862228
E-mail: sales@niscair.res.in
Web Site: www.niscair.res.in
Telex: 031-73099
Key Personnel
Dir: Mr V K Gupta
Text in English.
First published 1954.
Quarterly.
400 INR or 75 USD
ISSN: 0972-5423

Books of the Week Bulletin (J)
Published by D K Agencies (P) Ltd
Mohan Garden, A/15-17, DK Ave, Najafgarh Rd, New Delhi 110059
Tel: (011) 2535-7104; (011) 2535-7105 *Fax:* (011) 2535-7103
E-mail: information@dkagencies.com
Web Site: www.dkagencies.com
Source for bibliographical details of English language publications published from India.
Weekly.

Bulletin (J)
Published by Indian Library Association
A/40-41, Flat No 201, Ansal Bldg, Mukherjee Nagar, Delhi 110009
Tel: 27651743 *Fax:* 27651743
E-mail: info@ilaindia.org
Web Site: www.ilaindia.org
Key Personnel
President: Dr C R Karisiddappa
Editor: S Ansari
Text in English.
First published 1965.
Quarterly.
750 INR or 55 USD
ISSN: 0019-5782

D K Newsletter (J)
Published by D K Agencies (P) Ltd
Mohan Garden, A/15-17, DK Ave, Najafgarh Rd, New Delhi 110059
Tel: (011) 2535-7104; (011) 2535-7105 *Fax:* (011) 2535-7103
E-mail: information@dkagencies.com
Web Site: www.dkagencies.com
News & reviews of Indian publications in English.
First published 1975.
Quarterly.
ISSN: 0971-4448

IASLIC Bulletin (J)
Published by Indian Association of Special Libraries & Information Centres (IASLIC)
P291, CIT Scheme 6M, Kankurgachi, Kolkata 700054
Tel: (033) 2352 9651; (033) 2354 9066
E-mail: iaslic@vsnl.net
Web Site: www.iaslic.org
Key Personnel
President: Dr Prithvish Nag
Honorary Editor: Dr Arjun Dasgupta
Text in English.
First published 1956.
Quarterly.

Indian Library Science Abstracts (J)
Published by Indian Association of Special Libraries & Information Centres (IASLIC)
P291, CIT Scheme 6M, Kankurgachi, Kolkata 700054
Tel: (033) 2352 9651; (033) 2354 9066
E-mail: iaslic@vsnl.net
Web Site: www.iaslic.org
Key Personnel
President: Dr Prithvish Nag
Annually.
ISSN: 0019-5790

Journal of Library & Information Science (J)
Published by University of Delhi, Department of Library & Information Science
Delhi 110007
Tel: (011) 27666656 *Fax:* (011) 915250614
First published 1976.
Biannually.
80 INR or 14 USD
ISSN: 0970-714X

MIWA-Major Indian Works Annual (B)
Published by D K Agencies (P) Ltd
Mohan Garden, A/15-17, DK Ave, Najafgarh Rd, New Delhi 110059
Tel: (011) 2535-7104; (011) 2535-7105 *Fax:* (011) 2535-7103
E-mail: information@dkagencies.com
Web Site: www.dkagencies.com
Bibliographic guide to carefully chosen, genuinely significant works of higher academic/research/general value.
Annually.

The National Library & Public Libraries in India (B)
Published by The National Library
Belvedere, Kolkata 700027
Tel: (033) 24791381; (033) 24791384 *Fax:* (033) 24791462
E-mail: nldirector@rediffmail.com
Web Site: nlindia.org
Telex: 021-8117
Key Personnel
Dir: Dr Ramanuj Bhattacharjee

Special List (J)
Published by D K Agencies (P) Ltd
Mohan Garden, A/15-17, DK Ave, Najafgarh Rd, New Delhi 110059
Tel: (011) 2535-7104; (011) 2535-7105 *Fax:* (011) 2535-7103
E-mail: information@dkagencies.com
Web Site: www.dkagencies.com
Information by subject on books & back numbers of Indian periodicals.

Subscribers' Guide to Indian Periodicals/Serials (J)
Published by D K Agencies (P) Ltd
Mohan Garden, A/15-17, DK Ave, Najafgarh Rd, New Delhi 110059
Tel: (011) 2535-7104; (011) 2535-7105 *Fax:* (011) 2535-7103
E-mail: information@dkagencies.com
Web Site: www.dkagencies.com
Biennially.

Indonesia

Baca (Read) (J)
Published by Indonesian Institute of Sciences, Centre for Scientific Documentation & Information
PO Box 4298, 12042 Jakarta
Tel: (021) 573 34 65; (021) 573 34 66 *Fax:* (021) 573 34 67
E-mail: admin@pdii.lipi.go.id
Web Site: www.pdii.lipi.go.id
Key Personnel
Editor: Antari Wahyuning Mawarti
  E-mail: Antari_s@hotmail.com
First published 1974.
Quarterly.
ISSN: 0125-9008

Majalah Ikatan Pustakawan Indonesia (J)
Published by Indonesian Library Association
Jalan Salemba Raya 28A, Jakarta 10002
Mailing Address: PO Box 3624, Jakarta 10002
Key Personnel
President: Mr Dady P Rachmananta *Tel:* (021) 3101472 *E-mail:* pusnas@rad.net.id
Secretary-General: Mrs Zurniaty Nasrul *Tel:* (021) 5733465 *Fax:* (021) 5733467 *E-mail:* zurniaty@pdii.lipi.go.id
Indonesian Library Association Journal.
Irregularly.

Islamic Republic of Iran

A Catalog of the Manuscripts in the National Library of Iran (B)
Published by The National Library of Iran
Anahita Alley, Africa St, PO Box 11365/9597, 19176 Tehran
Mailing Address: Sh Bahonar Str, 19548 Tehran
Tel: (021) 8881966 *Fax:* (021) 8786859
E-mail: nli@nli.ir
Web Site: www.nli.ir
Key Personnel
Manuscript Dept: H Aximi

Class DSR: History of Iran (B)
Published by The National Library of Iran
Anahita Alley, Africa St, PO Box 11365/9597, 19176 Tehran
Mailing Address: Sh Bahonar Str, 19548 Tehran
Tel: (021) 8881966 *Fax:* (021) 8786859
E-mail: nli@nli.ir
Web Site: www.nli.ir
Key Personnel
Author & Research Librarian: Kamran Fani
An adaptation of Library of Congress Classification.
First published 1980.
3rd (2000): 198 pp, $50
ISBN(s): 964-446-056-1

Class PIR: Iranian Languages & Literature (B)
Published by The National Library of Iran

Anahita Alley, Africa St, PO Box 11365/9597, 19176 Tehran
Mailing Address: Sh Bahonar Str, 19548 Tehran
Tel: (021) 8881966 *Fax:* (021) 8786859
E-mail: nli@nli.ir
Web Site: www.nli.ir
Based on the Library of Congress Classification.
2nd

Dewey Decimal Classification: Geography of Iran (B)
Published by The National Library of Iran
Anahita Alley, Africa St, PO Box 11365/9597, 19176 Tehran
Mailing Address: Shahid Bahonar St, 19548 Tehran
Tel: (021) 8881966 *Fax:* (021) 8786859
E-mail: nli@nli.ir
Web Site: www.nli.ir
3rd

Dewey Decimal Classification: History of Iran (B)
Published by The National Library of Iran
Anahita Alley, Africa St, PO Box 11365/9597, 19176 Tehran
Mailing Address: Shahid Bahonar St, 19548 Tehran
Tel: (021) 8881966 *Fax:* (021) 8786859
E-mail: nli@nli.ir
Web Site: www.nli.ir
Key Personnel
Author & Research Librarian: Kamran Fani
Senior Research Librarian: Mrs Poori Soltani
    E-mail: poorisoltani@yahoo.com
First published 1982.
3rd (1999), $20
ISBN(s): 964-446-037-5

Dewey Decimal Classification: Iranian Languages (B)
Published by The National Library of Iran
Anahita Alley, Africa St, PO Box 11365/9597, 19176 Tehran
Mailing Address: Shahid Bahonar St, 19548 Tehran
Tel: (021) 8881966 *Fax:* (021) 8786859
E-mail: nli@nli.ir
Web Site: www.nli.ir
Key Personnel
Senior Research Librarian: Mrs Poori Soltani
    E-mail: poorisoltani@yahoo.com
First published 1988.
3rd (1998), $15
ISBN(s): 964-446-031-6

Dewey Decimal Classification: Iranian Literature (B)
Published by The National Library of Iran
Anahita Alley, Africa St, PO Box 11365/9597, 19176 Tehran
Mailing Address: Shahid Bahonar St, 19548 Tehran
Tel: (021) 8881966 *Fax:* (021) 8786859
E-mail: nli@nli.ir
Web Site: www.nli.ir
Key Personnel
Senior Research Librarian: Mrs Poori Soltani
    E-mail: poorisoltani@yahoo.com
Text in Persian.
First published 1972.
2nd (1998), $50
ISBN(s): 964-446-032-4

A Directory of Iranian Newspapers (B)
Published by The National Library of Iran
Anahita Alley, Africa St, PO Box 11365/9597, 19176 Tehran
Mailing Address: Shahid Bahonar St, 19548 Tehran
Tel: (021) 8881966 *Fax:* (021) 8786859

E-mail: nli@nli.ir
Web Site: www.nli.ir
Annually.

Farsi Author Numbers, to be used with the Library of Congress Classification Schedules (B)
Published by The National Library of Iran
Anahita Alley, Africa St, PO Box 11365/9597, 19176 Tehran
Mailing Address: Shahid Bahonar St, 19548 Tehran
Tel: (021) 8881966 *Fax:* (021) 8786859
E-mail: nli@nli.ir
Web Site: www.nli.ir
Key Personnel
Senior Research Librarian: Mrs Poori Soltani
    E-mail: poorisoltani@yahoo.com
First published 1997.
3rd: 34 pp

Faslname-ye Ketab (J)
Published by The National Library of Iran
Anahita Alley, Africa St, PO Box 11365/9597, 19176 Tehran
Mailing Address: Shahid Bahonar St, 19548 Tehran
Tel: (021) 8881966 *Fax:* (021) 8786859
E-mail: nli@nli.ir
Web Site: www.nli.ir
Key Personnel
Editor: Abbas Horri
Journal of The National Library of Iran.
First published 1990.
Quarterly.
ISSN: 1022-6451

List of Persian Subject Headings (B)
Published by The National Library of Iran
Anahita Alley, Africa St, PO Box 11365/9597, 19176 Tehran
Mailing Address: Shahid Bahonar St, 19548 Tehran
Tel: (021) 8881966 *Fax:* (021) 8786859
E-mail: nli@nli.ir
Web Site: www.nli.ir
Key Personnel
Senior Research Librarian: Mrs Poori Soltani
    E-mail: poorisoltani@yahoo.com
3 vols.
First published 1993.
3rd (2002), $50
ISBN(s): 964-446-070-7

Technical Services (B)
Published by The National Library of Iran
Anahita Alley, Africa St, PO Box 11365/9597, 19176 Tehran
Mailing Address: Shahid Bahonar St, 19548 Tehran
Tel: (021) 8881966 *Fax:* (021) 8786859
E-mail: nli@nli.ir
Web Site: www.nli.ir
8th, $501
ISBN(s): 964-446-029-4

Ireland

Directory of Libraries & Information Services in Ireland (B)
Published by Library Association of Ireland & CILIP (Northern Ireland)
53 Upper Mount St, Dublin 2
Tel: (061) 202193
E-mail: laisec@iol.ie
Web Site: www.libraryassociation.ie

Key Personnel
President: Gobnait O'Riordan *E-mail:* president@libraryassociation.ie
Available online only.
5th

Irish Library News (J)
Published by An Chomhairle Leabharlanna (Library Council)
53/54 Upper Mount St, Dublin 2
Tel: (01) 6761963; (01) 6761167 *Fax:* (01) 6766721
E-mail: info@librarycouncil.ie
Web Site: www.librarycouncil.ie
Key Personnel
Dir: Norma McDermott *E-mail:* nmcdermott@librarycouncil.ie
Newssheet issued free to libraries.
First published 1977.
Monthly.
ISSN: 0332-0049

An Leabharlann (Irish Library) (J)
Published by Library Association of Ireland & CILIP-Northern Ireland
53 Upper Mount St, Dublin 2
Tel: (061) 202193 *Fax:* (061) 213090
Web Site: www.libraryassociation.ie
Key Personnel
President: Gobnait O'Riordan *E-mail:* president@libraryassociation.ie
First published 1930.

Long Room (J)
Published by Friends of the Library
Trinity College, College St, Dublin 2
Tel: (01) 6772941 *Fax:* (01) 6719003
Web Site: www.tcd.ie
Telex: 93782
Key Personnel
Editor: Vincent Kinane *E-mail:* vkinane@lib1.tcd.ie
Ireland's Journal for the History of the Book.
Annually.

Israel

Bibliography of Modern Hebrew Literature in Translation (B)
Published by The Institute for the Translation of Hebrew Literature
23 Baruch Hirsch St, Bnei Brak
Mailing Address: PO Box 1005 1, 52001 Ramat Gan
Tel: (03) 579 6830 *Fax:* (03) 579 6832
E-mail: hamachon@inter.net.il; litscene@ithl.org.il
Web Site: www.ithl.org.il
Key Personnel
Man Dir: Mrs Nilli Cohen
First published 1979.
Annually.
ISSN: 0334-309X

Index to Hebrew Periodicals (P)
Published by University of Haifa Library
PO Box 242, Jerusalem 91002
Tel: (04) 8240289 *Fax:* (04) 8257753
Web Site: lib.haifa.ac.il
Key Personnel
Chairman: Jacob Agmon
Available online only. http://libnet.ac.il/libnet/ihp.
First published 1977.
Annually.
ISSN: 0334-2921

ISRAEL

Information & Librarianship (J)
Published by Israel Society of Libraries & Information Centers
PO Box 28273, Jerusalem 91281
Tel: (02) 6249421 *Fax:* (02) 6249421
E-mail: asmi@asmi.org.il
Web Site: www.asmi.org.il
Key Personnel
Chairperson: Shoshana Langerman
  E-mail: shola@barak-online.net
Biannually.

Yad La-Kore (Reader's Aid) (P)
Published by The Israeli Center for Libraries
5 Hachavatzelet St, 91002 Jerusalem
Mailing Address: PO Box 242, 91002 Jerusalem
Tel: (02) 6252949 *Fax:* (02) 3250620
E-mail: rochelle@actcom.co.il
Web Site: www.icl.org.il
Key Personnel
Dir: Dr Martin Weyl
Israel Journal for Libraries & Archives.
First published 1946.
Quarterly.
ISSN: 0334-200X

Italy

Accademie e Biblioteche d'Italia (Academies & Libraries of Italy) (J)
Published by Ministero per Beni Culturali e Ambientali
Palombi Editore, Via dei Gracchi 187, 00192 Rome
Tel: (06) 3214150 *Fax:* (06) 3214752
E-mail: flli.palombi@mail.stm.it
96 pp
ISSN: 0393-4451

Bollettino AIB (AIB Bulletin) (J)
Published by Italian Library Association (Associazione Italiana Biblioteche)
CP 24 61, 00100 Rome
Tel: (06) 4463532 *Fax:* (06) 4441139
E-mail: bollettino@aib.it
Web Site: www.aib.it/aib/boll/boll.htm
Key Personnel
Editor: Giovanni Solimine
Contact: Maria Teresa Natale
Quarterly.
ISSN: 1121-1490

Catalogo Collettivo di Periodici - Archivio ISRDS/CNR (Catalog of Collective Periodicals) (B)
Published by Istituto Centrale per il Catalogo Unico delle Biblioteche Italiane e per le Informazioni Bibliografiche (Central Institute of the Union Catalog of Italian Libraries & Bibliographical Information)
Viale del Castro Pretorio, 105-00185 Rome
Tel: (06) 4989484 *Fax:* (06) 4959302
Web Site: www.iccu.sbn.it
Key Personnel
Dir: Dr Luciano Scala
Contains listings of over 46,000 periodicals in 1500 libraries.

Periodici Italiani 1966-1981 (Italian Periodicals 1966-1981) (B)
Published by Istituto Centrale per il Catalogo Unico delle Biblioteche Italiane e per le Informazioni Bibliografiche (Central Institute of the Union Catalog of Italian Libraries & Bibliographical Information)
Viale del Castro Pretorio, 105-00185 Rome
Tel: (06) 4989484 *Fax:* (06) 4959302
Web Site: www.iccu.sbn.it
Key Personnel
Dir: Dr Luciano Scala

Regole Italiane di Catalogazione per Autori (Italian Rules of Cataloging by Author) (B)
Published by Istituto Centrale per il Catalogo Unico delle Biblioteche Italiane e per le Informazioni Bibliografiche (Central Institute of the Union Catalog of Italian Libraries & Bibliographical Information)
Viale del Castro Pretorio, 105-00185 Rome
Tel: (06) 4989484 *Fax:* (06) 4959302
Web Site: www.iccu.sbn.it
Key Personnel
Dir: Dr Luciano Scala

Soggettario per i Cataloghi delle Biblioteche Italiane (Subject Collections in Italian Libraries) (J)
Published by Istituto Centrale per il Catalogo Unico delle Biblioteche Italiane e per le Informazioni Bibliografiche (Central Institute of the Union Catalog of Italian Libraries & Bibliographical Information)
Viale del Castro Pretorio, 105-00185 Rome
Tel: (06) 4989484 *Fax:* (06) 4959302
Web Site: www.iccu.sbn.it
Key Personnel
Dir: Dr Luciano Scala

Jamaica

JLA Bulletin (J)
Published by Jamaica Library Association
PO Box 125, Kingston 5
Tel: (876) 927-1614 *Fax:* (876) 927-1614
E-mail: liajapresident@yahoo.com
Web Site: www.liaja.org.jm
Key Personnel
President: Byron Palmer
First published 1950.
Annually.
300 JMD

JLA News (B)
Published by Jamaica Library Association
PO Box 125, Kingston 5
Tel: (876) 927-1614 *Fax:* (876) 927-1614
E-mail: liajapresident@yahoo.com
Web Site: www.liaja.org.jm
Key Personnel
President: Byron Palmer
News of current events in the libraries of Jamaica.
Quarterly.

Japan

Biblos (J)
Published by National Diet Library
1-10-1 Nagata-cho, Chiyoda-ku, Tokyo 100-8924
Tel: (03) 3581-2331 *Fax:* (03) 3508-2934
E-mail: kokusai@ndl.go.jp
Web Site: www.ndl.go.jp/jp/publication/biblos
Key Personnel
Dir, Planning & Cooperation Dept: Yukiko Saito
Online magazine for branch, executive, judicial & other special libraries.
ISSN: 1344-8412

Bulletin of the Japan Special Libraries Association (J)
Published by Japan Special Libraries Association
c/o Japan Library Association Bldg F6, 1-11-14 Shinkawa, Chuo-ku, Tokyo 104-0033
Tel: (03) 35378335 *Fax:* (03) 35378336
E-mail: jsla@jsla.or.jp
Web Site: www.jsla.or.jp
Abstracts in English.
Bimonthly.

Directory of Special Information Institutions (B)
Published by Japan Special Libraries Association
c/o Japan Library Association Bldg F6, 1-11-14 Shinkawa, Chuo-ku, Tokyo 104-0033
Tel: (03) 35378335 *Fax:* (03) 35378336
E-mail: jsla@jsla.or.jp
Web Site: www.jsla.or.jp
Entry names also in English.
Triennially.

Gendai no Toshokan (Libraries Today) (J)
Published by Japan Library Association
1-11-14 Shinkawa, Chuo-ku, Tokyo 104-0033
Tel: (03) 3523 0811 *Fax:* (03) 3523 0841
E-mail: info@jla.or.jp
Web Site: www.jla.or.jp
First published 1963.
Quarterly.
ISSN: 0016-6332

Journal of Information Science & Technology Association (J)
Published by Information Science and Technology Association
Sasaki Bldg, 7 Koishiwawa-2, Bunkyo-ku, Tokyo 112
Tel: (03) 38133791 *Fax:* (03) 38133793
E-mail: infosta@infosta.or.jp
Web Site: www.infosta.or.jp
Features articles which review new technologies in the global information world.
Monthly.

Nihon no Sankotosho Shikiban (Guide to Japanese Reference Books) (J)
Published by Japan Library Association
1-11-14 Shinkawa, Chuo-ku, Tokyo 104-0033
Tel: (03) 3523 0811 *Fax:* (03) 3523 0841
E-mail: info@jla.or.jp
Web Site: www.jla.or.jp
First published 1962.
Irregularly.

Nihon no Toshokan (Statistics on Libraries in Japan) (B)
Published by Japan Library Association
1-11-14 Shinkawa, Chuo-ku, Tokyo 104-0033
Tel: (03) 3523 0811 *Fax:* (03) 3523 0841
E-mail: info@jla.or.jp
Web Site: www.jla.or.jp
Statistics & directory of public & university libraries.
First published 1952.
Annually.

Refarensu (Reference) (J)
Published by National Diet Library
1-10-1 Nagata-cho, Chiyoda-ku, Tokyo 100-8924
Tel: (03) 3581-2331 *Fax:* (03) 3508-2934
E-mail: kokusai@ndl.go.jp
Web Site: www.ndl.go.jp
Key Personnel
Dir, Planning & Cooperation Dept: Yukiko Saito
First published 1951.
Monthly.
ISSN: 0034-2912

Toshokan Zasshi (Library Journal) (J)
Published by Japan Library Association

1-11-14 Shinkawa, Chuo-ku, Tokyo 104-0033
Tel: (03) 3523 0811 *Fax:* (03) 3523 0841
E-mail: info@jla.or.jp
Web Site: www.jla.or.jp
First published 1907.
Monthly.

Jordan

Jordanian National Bibliography (B)
Published by Jordan National Library
King Talal Circle (3rd Circle) Jabal Amman, Al-Hussein Bin Ali St, Amman
Mailing Address: PO Box 6070, Amman
Tel: (06) 4610311 *Fax:* (06) 4616832
E-mail: nl@amra.nic.gov.jo
Web Site: www.nis.gov.jo/library
Annually.

Rissalat al-Maktaba (J)
Published by Jordan Library Association
PO Box 6289, Amman
Tel: (06) 4629412 *Fax:* (06) 4629412
Key Personnel
President: Anwar Akroush
The Message of the Library, text in Arabic, summaries in English.

Kenya

Accessions List of the Library of Congress Office, Nairobi, Kenya (P)
Published by US Library of Congress Office
Library of Congress Office, PO Box 30598, Nairobi
Tel: (02) 363 6300; (02) 363 6146 *Fax:* (02) 363 6321
E-mail: nairobi@libcon-kenya.org
Web Site: www.loc.gov/acq/ovop/nairobi/; www.icipe.org/locnairobi
Key Personnel
Field Director: Paul J Steere
Bimonthly.
ISSN: 1527-5396

Maktaba (J)
Published by Kenya Library Association
PO Box 46031, Nairobi
Tel: (02) 334244 *Fax:* (02) 336885
Key Personnel
Chairman: Jacinta Were *E-mail:* jwere@ken.healthnet.org
Official journal of the Kenya Library Association.
Biannually.
ISSN: 0070-7988

Republic of Korea

Bibliographic Index of Korea (B)
Published by The National Library of Korea
San 60-1, Banpo-dong, Seocho-gu, Seoul 137-702
Tel: (02) 5353702 (ext 522 or 524)
E-mail: nlkpc@sun.nl.or.kr
Web Site: www.nl.go.kr
Key Personnel
Dir: Gi-Young Jeong
Annually.

Journal of the Korean Society for Library & Information Science (J)
Published by Korean Society for Library & Information Science
Sungkyunkwan University, 53, 3-ga, Myungnyundong, Chongno-gu, Seoul 110-745
Tel: (02) 760-0330 *Fax:* (02) 760-0326
Key Personnel
President: Eun-Chul Lee *E-mail:* eclee@skku.ac.kr
Text in Korean with English abstracts.
First published 1970.
Quarterly.
300 pp
ISSN: 1225-598X

KLA Bulletin (J)
Published by Korean Library Association (KLA)
60-1, Panpo-dong, Seocho-ku, Seoul
Tel: (02) 5354868 *Fax:* (02) 5355616
E-mail: klanet@hitel.net
Key Personnel
President: Shin Ki Nam
Bimonthly.
ISSN: 0022-7358

Kukhoe Tosogwanbo (National Assembly Library Review) (J)
Published by National Assembly Library
One Yoido-dong, Yeongdeungpo-gu, Seoul 150-703
Tel: (02) 7884143 (english service); (02) 7883961 *Fax:* (02) 7884193
E-mail: w3@nanet.go.kr
Web Site: www.nanet.go.kr
Telex: 25849
Key Personnel
Librarian: Ho-young Chung
Bimonthly.
ISSN: 0027-8572

Statistics on Libraries in Korea (J)
Published by Korean Library Association (KLA)
60-1, Panpo-dong, Seocho-ku, Seoul
Tel: (02) 5354868 *Fax:* (02) 5355616
E-mail: klanet@hitel.net
Key Personnel
President: Shin Ki Nam
Annually.
ISSN: 1225-5521

Kuwait

The Library Bulletin (P)
Published by Kuwait University Library
PO Box 17140, 92452 Khaldiya
Key Personnel
Dir: Dr Husain A Al-Ansari

The University Library (P)
Published by Kuwait University Library
PO Box 17140, 92452 Khaldiya
Key Personnel
Dir: Dr Husain A Al-Ansari

Lebanon

Newsletter (J)
Published by The Lebanese Library Association
c/o American University of Beirut, University Library, Beirut
Tel: (01) 350000 *Fax:* (01) 351706
Telex: 2080
Key Personnel
President: Marouf Rafi

The Former Yugoslav Republic of Macedonia

Bibliotekarska iskra (Librarian Association of Macedonia) (J)
Published by Bibliotekarsko Drushtvo na Makedonija
Narodna i univerziteska biblioteka "Kliment Ohridski", Bul Goce Delcev-6, Skopje 91000
Tel: (091) 115-177 *Fax:* (091) 230-874

Malawi

Directory of Malawi Libraries (B)
Published by University of Malawi Libraries
Central Library, Box 280, Zomba
Tel: 522 222; 523 225 *Fax:* 523 225; 524 046
Web Site: www.sdnp.org.mw/webwshp/schinyamu

MALA Bulletin (J)
Published by Malawi Library Association
PO Box 429, Zomba
Tel: (050) 522222 *Fax:* (050) 523225
Key Personnel
President: Ralph Masanjika
First published 1978.
Biannually.
300 MWK or 20 USD per year

Malaysia

Directory of Libraries in Malaysia (B)
Published by National Library of Malaysia (Gift & Exchange Unit)
232 Jalan Tun Razak, 50572 Kuala Lumpur
Tel: (03) 26943488 (ext 274, 275); (03) 26943234 *Fax:* (03) 26927082
E-mail: pnmweb@www1.pnm.my
Web Site: www.pnm.my
Telex: 30092
Key Personnel
Dir-General: Mariam Abdul Kadir

Majallah Perpustakaan Malaysia (J)
Published by Persatuan Perpustakaan Malaysia
c/o Perpustakaan Negara Malaysia, 232 Jalan Tun Razak, 50572 Kuala Lumpur
Tel: (03) 2694 7390 *Fax:* (03) 2694 7390
E-mail: ppm55@po.jaring.my
Web Site: www.pnm.my/ppm/
Official journal, text in English & Malay.

Sumber Pustaka (J)
Published by Persatuan Perpustakaan Malaysia
c/o Perpustakaan Negara Malaysia, 232 Jalan Tun Razak, 50572 Kuala Lumpur
Tel: (03) 2694 7390 *Fax:* (03) 2694 7390
E-mail: ppm55@po.jaring.my

Web Site: www.pnm.my/ppm/
Malaysian Library Association official newsletter, text in English & Malay.

Malta

A Bibliography of Maltese Bibliographies (B)
Published by University of Malta Library
c/o University of Malta, Msida MSD 06
Tel: 32902316 *Fax:* 21314306
Web Site: www.lib.um.edu.mt
Key Personnel
Chancellor: Prof J Rizzo Naudi
Librarian: Dr Paul Xuereb *E-mail:* paul.m.xuereb@um.edu.mt
First published 1993.

Malia Newsletter (J)
Published by Malta Library & Information Association
c/o University of Malta Library, Tal-Qroqq, Msida MSD 06
E-mail: mpar1@lib.um.edu.mt
Web Site: www.malia-malta.org
Key Personnel
Chairman: Robert Mizzi
Honorary Secretary: Ruth Muscat
Quarterly.

Mauritius

Mauritius Library Association Newsletter (J)
Published by Mauritius Library Association
c/o British Council, Royal Rd, Rose Hill
Mailing Address: POB 111, Rose Hill
Tel: 4549550; 4549551; 4549552 *Fax:* 4549553
E-mail: general.equiries@mu.britishcouncil.org
Web Site: www.britishcouncil.org/mauritius/
Quarterly.

Memorandum of Books printed in Mauritius & Registered in the Archives Office (B)
Published by Mauritius Archives
Development Bank of Mauritius Complex, Petite Riviere
Tel: 233-4469 *Fax:* 233-4299
First published 1894.

Mexico

Boletin (Bulletin) (J)
Published by Instituto de Investigaciones Bibliograficas (Institute of Bibliographic Research)
Centro Cultural Universitario, CU, Delegacion Coyoacan, 04510 Mexico, DF
Tel: 5622 6818 *Fax:* (05) 6650951
Web Site: biblional.bibliog.unam.mx
Key Personnel
Dir: Vicente Quirarte

Centro de Bibliotecologia, Archivologia e Informacion Anuario (Annual of Library Science, Archives & Information Science) (B)
Published by Universidad Nacional Autonoma de Mexico (National University of Mexico)
Torre 1 de Humanidades PB 20 piso, Ciudad Universitaria, 04510 Mexico, DF
Tel: (05) 6221603 *Fax:* (05) 6160664

Web Site: www.unam.mx
Key Personnel
Dir: Adolfo Rodriquez Gallardo

Noticiero de la AMBAC (News of the Mexican Association of Librarians) (J)
Published by Asociacion Mexicana de Bibliotecarios AC (AMBAC)
Angel Urraza 817-A, Col Del Valle, 03100 Mexico, DF
Mailing Address: Apdo 80-065, Administracion de correos 80, 06001 Mexico, DF
Tel: (055) 55 75 33 96 *Fax:* (055) 55-75-11-35
E-mail: correo@ambac.org.mx
Web Site: www.ambac.org.mx
Key Personnel
President: Saul Armendariz Sanchez
  E-mail: asaul@xcaret.iqeofcu.unam.mx
Vice President: Felipe Becerril Torres

Netherlands

BibliotheckBlad (Library Journal) (J)
Published by Vereniging NBLC
Platinaweg 10, 2544 EZ The Hague
Mailing Address: PO Box 43300, 2504 AH The Hague 5
Tel: (070) 30 90 100 *Fax:* (070) 30 90 200
E-mail: bibliotheckblad@nblc.nl
Web Site: www.nblc.nl

Brinkman's Cumulative Catalog (B)
Published by Uitgeverij Bohn Stafleu Van Loghum BV
2400 MA Alphen aan den Rijn, PO Box 4, Holland
Tel: (0172) 466811 *Fax:* (0172) 466770
E-mail: klantenservice@bsl.nl
Web Site: www.kb.nl
Dutch National Bibliography.
Quarterly.

Informatie Professional (J)
Published by Nederlandse Vereniging voor beroepsbeoefenaren in de bibliotheeckinformatie-en kennissector (NVB) (The Netherland Association of Librarians, Documentalists & Information Specialists)
c/o NVB-Verenigingsbureau Plompetorengracht 11, Nieuwegracht 15, 3512 LC Utrecht
Tel: (030) 2311263 *Fax:* (030) 2311830
E-mail: nvbinfo@wxs.nl
Web Site: www.nvb-online.nl
Key Personnel
President: Dr J S M Savenije *E-mail:* b.savenije@ubu.ruu.nl
Professional journal for librarians, researchers & documentalists (joint publication).
Monthly.

Nederlands Archievenblad (Netherlands) (J)
Published by Vereniging van Archivaissen in Nederland
Cruquiusweg 31, 1019 AT Amsterdam
Tel: (020) 462 77 27 *Fax:* (020) 462 77 28
E-mail: bureau@kvan.nl
Web Site: www.kvan.nl
Key Personnel
Contact: Mathilda van Geem

New Zealand

Library Life (J)
Published by Library & Information Association of New Zealand Aotearoa (LIANZA)
Old Wool House, Level 6, 139-141 Featherston St, Wellington 6001
Mailing Address: PO Box 12-212, Wellington 6038
Tel: (04) 473 5834 *Fax:* (04) 499 1480
E-mail: office@lianza.org.nz
Web Site: www.lianza.org.nz
Key Personnel
President: Mirla Edmundson
  E-mail: edmundsonm@hermes.cpit.ac.nz
Office Manager: Eve Young *E-mail:* eve@lianza.org.nz
Editor: Jane Chapman
11 times a year (not January).
ISSN: 0110-4373

New Zealand Libraries (J)
Published by Library & Information Association of New Zealand Aotearoa (LIANZA)
Old Wool House, Level 6, 139-141 Featherston St, Wellington 6001
Mailing Address: PO Box 12-212, Wellington 6038
Tel: (04) 473 5834 *Fax:* (04) 499 1480
E-mail: office@lianza.org.nz
Web Site: www.lianza.org.nz
Key Personnel
Editor: Barbara Frame *E-mail:* frame@xtra.co.nz
Biannually.
ISSN: 0028-8381

Nigeria

Afribiblios (J)
Published by National Library of Nigeria-Research & Development Dept
Sanusi Dantata House, Plot 274 Central Business Area, PMB 1, Garki District, Abuja
Tel: (09) 2347714; (09) 2347900
E-mail: nln@nlbn.org
Web Site: www.nlbn.org
Key Personnel
Chairman: Francis Z Gana
Dir: Mr E N O Adimorah
Biannually.

Bendel Library Journal (J)
Published by Edo State Library
PMB 1127, Benin City
Tel: (052) 200810
Key Personnel
Dir: J O U oDiase

Libraries in Nigeria: A Directory (B)
Published by National Library of Nigeria-Research & Development Dept
Sanusi Dantata House, Plot 274 Central Business Area, PMB 1, Garki District, Abuja
Tel: (09) 2347714; (09) 2347900
E-mail: nln.rusd@nlbn.org
Web Site: www.nlbn.org
Telex: 21746
Key Personnel
Dir: Mr E N O Adimorah
National Librarian: Mrs O O Omolayole

Library Forum (J)
Published by Nigerian Library Association
c/o National Library Association, 4 Wesley St, PMB 12626, Lagos

Tel: (01) 2634704 *Fax:* (01) 616404
Telex: 21746
Key Personnel
Chairman: Francis Z Gana
Quarterly.

Library Record (J)
Published by University of Ibadan, Kenneth Dike Library
Ibadan
Tel: (02) 810 3118 *Fax:* (02) 810 3118
E-mail: library@kdl.ui.edu.ng
Web Site: www.ui.edu.ng/unitslibrary.htm
Key Personnel
Librarian: Joseph Ezenwani Ikem
Monthly.
ISSN: 0046-8436

Nigerian Libraries (J)
Published by Nigerian Library Association
c/o National Library of Nigeria, PMB 12626, 4 Wesley St, Lagos
Tel: (01) 2634704 *Fax:* (01) 616404
E-mail: library@unilag.edu
Telex: 21746
Key Personnel
Editor-in-Chief: Dr S Olajire Olanlokun
Official publication of the Nigerian Library Association.
Triannually.
ISSN: 0029-0122

Nigerian Periodicals Review (J)
Published by ABIC Books & Equipment Ltd
18 Kenyatta St, Nsukka Enugu
Mailing Address: PO Box 13740, Nsukka Enugu
Tel: (042) 331827 *Fax:* (042) 334811
First published 1986.
Quarterly.
ISSN: 0794-3865

Nominal List of Practicing Librarians in Nigeria (B)
Published by National Library of Nigeria-Research & Development Dept
Sanusi Dantata House, Plot 274 Central Business Area, PMB 1, Garki District, Abuja
Tel: (09) 2347714; (09) 2347900
E-mail: nln@nlbn.org
Web Site: www.nlbn.org
Telex: 21746
Key Personnel
Chairman: Francis Z Gana
Dir: Mr E N O Adimorah
Names & addresses of practicing librarians at 59 libraries in Nigeria.
Annually.

Nsukka Library Notes (J)
Published by Nnamdi Azikiwe Library
University of Nigeria, Nsukka, Enugu State
Tel: (042) 770 709 *Fax:* (042) 770 644
E-mail: misunn@aol.com
Telex: ULIONS NG 51496
Key Personnel
Librarian: C C Uwechie

Norway

Bok og Bibliotek (Books & Libraries) (J)
Published by Statens bibliotektilsyn
Postboks 8145 Dep, 0033 Oslo
Tel: 6 7 11 38 05 *Fax:* 6 7 11 38 01
E-mail: bob@abm-utvikling.no
Web Site: www.bibtils.no/bob

Key Personnel
Dir: Jon Birger Ostby
Contact: Chris Erichsen

Pakistan

Libraries of Pakistan (B)
Published by Library Promotion Bureau
Karachi University Campus, PO Box 8421, Karachi 75270
Tel: (021) 632-1959; (021) 6977737 *Fax:* (021) 632-1959
Key Personnel
Dir: Dr Manzoor Ahmed

Pakistan Library Bulletin (J)
Published by Library Promotion Bureau
Karachi University Campus, Dastagir Society, Federal B Area, Karachi 75270
Mailing Address: PO Box 8421, Karachi 75270
Tel: (021) 632-1959; (021) 6977737 *Fax:* (021) 632-1959
E-mail: samdani020@yahoo.com; dr_nf@yahoo.com
Key Personnel
Dir: Dr Manzoor Ahmed
Quarterly.

Plan for Development of Libraries in Pakistan (B)
Published by Library Promotion Bureau
Karachi University Campus, PO Box 8421, Karachi 75270
Tel: (021) 632-1959; (021) 6977737 *Fax:* (021) 632-1959
Key Personnel
President: Dr Ghaniul Akram Sabzwari
E-mail: gsabzwari@yahoo.com
Librarian: Dr Manzoor Ahmed

Papua New Guinea

Directory of Libraries in Papua New Guinea (B)
Published by National Library Service of Papua New Guinea
131 National Capital District, Waigani
Mailing Address: PO Box 734, Waigani
Tel: 325 6200 *Fax:* 325 1331
E-mail: ola@datec.com.pg
Telex: 23472
Key Personnel
Dir: Daniel Paraide

Guide to Manuscripts in the New Guinea Collection (B)
Published by University of Papua New Guinea Library
POB 320, Waigani NCD 134
Tel: 326 7280 *Fax:* 326 7187
E-mail: library@upng.ac.pg
Key Personnel
Librarian: Florence Griffin
By Nancy Lutton (1980).

Peru

Boletin Bibliografico (Bibliographical Bulletin) (J)
Published by Biblioteca Central de la Universidad Nacional Mayor de San Marcos
Pje Simon Rodriguez N°697, Lima
Mailing Address: Apdo 454, Lima 1
Tel: (014) 4285210 *Fax:* (014) 336337
Key Personnel
Dir: Dr Oswaldo Salaverry Garcia

Boletin de la Biblioteca Nacional del Peru (National Library of Peru Bulletin) (J)
Published by Biblioteca Nacional del Peru
Avda Abancay 4ta cuadra, Lima
Tel: (01) 428-7690; (01) 428-7696 *Fax:* (01) 427-7331
E-mail: dn@binape.gob.pe
Web Site: www.binape.gob.pe
Key Personnel
Dir: Sinesio Lopez Jimenez
First published 1943.
Irregularly.

FENIX Revista de la Biblioteca Nacional del Peru (FENIX National Library of Peru Review) (J)
Published by Biblioteca Nacional del Peru
Avda Abancay 4ta cuadra, Lima 1
Tel: (01) 428-7690; (01) 428-7696 *Fax:* (01) 427-7331
E-mail: dn@binape.gob.pe
Web Site: www.binape.gob.pe
Key Personnel
Dir: Sinesio Lopez Jimenez
First published 1944.
Irregularly.
42 (2001), $30
ISSN: 0015-0002

Philippines

ASLP Bulletin (J)
Published by Association of Special Libraries of the Philippines (ASLP)
National Library of the Philippines, TM Kalaw St, 1000 Ermita, Manila
Tel: (02) 525-3196; (02) 525-1748 *Fax:* (02) 524-2324
E-mail: director@nlp.gov.ph
Web Site: www.nlp.gov.ph
Key Personnel
President: Lilia F Echiverri
Dir: Adoracion B Mendoza
Quarterly.
30 PHP or 15 USD per year to members
ISSN: 0001-2548

Bulletin (J)
Published by Philippine Librarians Association Inc
The National Library Bldg, TM Kalaw St, Manila 1000
Tel: (02) 523-00-68 *Fax:* (02) 524-23-29
E-mail: amb@max.ph.net
Web Site: www.dlsu.edu.ph/library/plai
Key Personnel
President: Fe Angela Verzosa *Tel:* (02) 524-4611 *Fax:* (02) 524-8835 *E-mail:* libfamv@mail.dlsu.edu.ph

Index to Philippine Periodicals (IPP) (B)
Published by University of the Philippines Library, Indexing Section
Gonzalez Hall, Diliman, 1101 Quezon City

PHILIPPINES

Tel: (02) 920-5301 *Fax:* (02) 926-1876
E-mail: salvacion.arlante@up.edu.ph
Web Site: www.mainlib.upd.edu.ph
Key Personnel
University Librarian: Salvacion M Arlante
First published 1946.
Quarterly.

Journal of Philippine Librarianship (J)
Published by University of the Philippines, Institute of Library Science
Diliman, Quezon City 1101
Tel: (02) 920 5367 *Fax:* (02) 920 5367
Web Site: www.upd.edu.ph
Key Personnel
Business Manager: Nathalie N de la Torre
 E-mail: nathalie8_4@yahoo.com
Text in English.
Annually.
$15
ISSN: 0022-359X

Newsletter (J)
Published by University of the Philippines, Institute of Library Science
Diliman, Gonzalez Hall, 1101 Quezon City
Tel: (02) 920 5367 *Fax:* (02) 920 5367
Web Site: www.upd.edu.ph
Key Personnel
Business Manager: Nathalie N de la Torre
 E-mail: nathalie8_4@yahoo.com
Text in English.
ISSN: 0300-3612

Philippine National Bibliography (J)
Published by National Library of the Philippines
T M Kalaw St, 1000 Ermita, Manila
Tel: (02) 525-3196; (02) 525-1748 *Fax:* (02) 524-2324
E-mail: director@nlp.gov.ph; bibliography@nlp.gov.ph
Web Site: www.nlp.gov.ph
Key Personnel
Chief: Leonila D A Tominez
Quarterly with annual cumulation.
Parent Company: National Commission for Culture & the Arts

Poland

Bibliografia Wydawnictw CIAGLYCH
 (Bibliography of Polish Serials) (J)
Published by Biblioteka Narodowa
al Niepodleglosci 213, 02-086 Warsaw
Tel: (022) 608-2999 *Fax:* (022) 825-5251
E-mail: biblnar@bn.org.pl
Web Site: www.bn.org.pl
Telex: 813702 BNPL; 816761 *Cable:* AL NIEPODLEGLOSCI
Key Personnel
Dir: Michael Jagiello
Librarian: Ewa Krysiak *E-mail:* ekrysiak@biblnar.bn.org.pl
Available in CD-ROM or online only.
Annually.

Bibliotekarz (The Librarian) (J)
Published by Polish Librarians' Association
al Niepodleglosci 213, 02-086 Warsaw
Tel: (022) 827-52-96
E-mail: sbp@ceti.pl
Web Site: ebib.oss.wroc.pl/sbp/wydaw.htm
Key Personnel
President: Stanislaw Czajka
Dir: Janusz Nowicki *E-mail:* wyd.sbp-portal@wp.pl
Editor-in-Chief: Jan Wolosz

Text in Polish. Summaries in English & Russian.
Weekly.

Biblioteki Publiczne w Liczbach (Public Libraries in Figures) (B)
Published by Biblioteka Narodowa
al Niepodleglosci 213, 02-086 Warsaw
Tel: (022) 608-2999 *Fax:* (022) 825-5251
E-mail: biblnar@bn.org.pl
Web Site: www.bn.org.pl
Telex: 816761
Key Personnel
Dir: Prof Adam Manikowski
ISSN: 0137-2726

Informator Adresowy Podstawowych Placowek Informacji Naukowej i Technicznej (B)
Published by Centralne Laboratorium Przemyslu Ziemniacanego (Starch & Potato Products Research Laboratory)
ul Armii Poznari 49, 62-030 Lubon
Tel: (061) 8934605 *Fax:* (061) 8934608
E-mail: clpz@man.poznan.pl
Web Site: www.clpz.poznan.pl

Informator Biblioteczny (Library Guide) (B)
Published by Polish Librarians' Association
ul Konopczynskiego 5/7, 00-335 Warsaw
Tel: (022) 827-52-96
E-mail: sbp@ceti.pl
Web Site: ebib.oss.wroc.pl/sbp/wydaw.htm
Key Personnel
President: Stanislaw Czajka

Informator Nauki Polskiej (Polish Research Directory) (B)
Published by Osrodek Przetwarzania Informacji
Al Niepodleglosci 188 B, 00-950 Warsaw
Tel: (022) 825 12 40 *Fax:* (022) 825 33 19
E-mail: opi@opi.org.pl
Web Site: www.opi.org.pl
Key Personnel
Dir: Pawel Gierycz *Tel:* (022) 825 61 78
 E-mail: gierycz@opi.org.pl
Available in Polish & English language versions, four volumes.

Informator o Bibliotekach Wspolpracujacych w Ramach Specjalizacji Zbiorow (Information About Modern Libraries Working on Group Specializations) (B)
Published by Biblioteka Glowna Politechniki Warszawskiej
Plac Politechniki 1, 00-661 Warsaw
Tel: (022) 621-13-70 *Fax:* (022) 621-13-70
Web Site: www.bg.pw.edu.pl
Key Personnel
Dir: Elzbieta Dudzinska *E-mail:* dudz@bg.pw.edu.pl

Katalog Rozpraw Doktorskich i Habilitacyjnych (Science, Information, Business-Catalogue of Doctoral & Habilitational Dissertations) (P)
Published by Osrodek Przetwarzania Informacji
Al Niepodleglosci 188 B, 00-950 Warsaw
Mailing Address: PO Box 355, 00-950 Warsaw
Tel: (022) 825 12 40 *Fax:* (022) 825 33 19
E-mail: opi@opi.org.pl
Web Site: www.opi.org.pl
Key Personnel
Dir: Pawel Gierycz *Tel:* (022) 825 61 78
 E-mail: gierycz@opi.org.pl
Annually.

Komputerowe Bazy Danych o Nauce i Technice (Computerized Databases on Science & Technology) (B)
Published by Osrodek Przetwarzania Informacji
Al Niepodleglosci 188 B, 00-950 Warsaw
Mailing Address: PO Box 355, 00-950 Warsaw

Tel: (022) 825 12 40 *Fax:* (022) 825 33 19
E-mail: opi@opi.org.pl
Web Site: www.opi.org.pl
Key Personnel
Dir: Pawel Gierycz *Tel:* (022) 825 61 78
 E-mail: gierycz@opi.org.pl

Nauka, Informacja, Biznes (Science, Information, Business) (P)
Published by Osrodek Przetwarzania Informacji
Al Niepodleglosci 188 B, 00-950 Warsaw
Mailing Address: PO Box 355, 00-950 Warsaw
Tel: (022) 825 12 40 *Fax:* (022) 825 33 19
E-mail: opi@opi.org.pl
Web Site: www.opi.org.pl
Key Personnel
Dir: Pawel Gierycz *Tel:* (022) 825 61 78
 E-mail: gierycz@opi.org.pl
Seven mathematical series.
Quarterly.

Placowki Informacji Naukowej i Technicznej w Polsce (Scientific & Technical Information Centres in Poland) (B)
Published by Osrodek Przetwarzania Informacji
Al Niepodleglosci 188 B, 00-950 Warsaw
Mailing Address: PO Box 355, 00-950 Warsaw
Tel: (022) 825 12 40 *Fax:* (022) 825 33 19
E-mail: opi@opi.org.pl
Web Site: www.opi.org.pl
Key Personnel
Dir: Pawel Gierycz *Tel:* (022) 825 61 78
 E-mail: gierycz@opi.org.pl

Polska Bibliografia Bibliologiczna (Polish Bibliography of Library Science) (B)
Published by Biblioteka Narodowa
al Niepodleglosci 213, 02-086 Warsaw
Tel: (022) 608-2999 *Fax:* (022) 825-5251
E-mail: biblnar@bn.org.pl
Web Site: www.bn.org.pl
Telex: 816761
Key Personnel
Dir: Prof Adam Manikowski

Poradnik Bibliotekarza (The Librarian's Adviser) (J)
Published by Polish Librarians' Association
al Niepodleglosci 213, 02-086 Warsaw
Tel: (022) 827-52-96 *Fax:* (022) 223541
E-mail: sbp@ceti.pl
Web Site: ebib.oss.wroc.pl/sbp/wydaw.htm
Key Personnel
President: Stanislaw Czaja
Editor-in-Chief: Jadwiga Chruscinska *Tel:* (022) 822-43-49
Monthly.

Rocznik Biblioteki Narodowej (National Library Yearbook) (B)
Published by Biblioteka Narodowa
al Niepodleglosci 213, 02-086 Warsaw
Tel: (022) 608-2999 *Fax:* (022) 825-5251
E-mail: biblnar@bn.org.pl
Web Site: www.bn.org.pl
Telex: 816761
Covers scientific library science with text in Polish with English summaries.
Annually.
ISSN: 0083-7261

Portugal

Boletim de Bibliografia Portuguesa (J)
Published by Instituto da Biblioteca Nacional e do Livro
Campo Grande 83, 1751 Lisbon

Tel: (021) 7967639; (021) 7950134 *Fax:* (021) 7933607
E-mail: bn@bn.pt
Web Site: www.bn.pt
Key Personnel
Assistant Dir: Fernanda Maria Fields *Tel:* (021) 7982022 *E-mail:* fcampos@bn.pt
Portuguese Bibliographic Bulletin.

Cadernos de Biblioteconomia, Arquivistica e Documentacao (Library Management, Archives & Documentation) (J)
Published by Associacao Portuguesa de Bibliotecarios, Arquivistas e Documentalistas (The Portuguese Association of Librarians Archivists & Documentalists)
R Morais Soares, 43-C, 1° Dto, 1900-341 Lisbon
Tel: (021) 816 19 80 *Fax:* (021) 815 45 08
E-mail: bad@apbad.pt
Web Site: www.apbad.pt
Key Personnel
Dir: Antonio Pina Falcao
Triannually.

Guia de Servicios de Documentacao e de Bibliotecas em Portugal (List of Portuguese Libraries & Documentation Services) (B)
Published by Fundacao para a Ciencia e a Tecnologia/Servico de Informacao e Documentacao(SID)
Av D Carlos I, 126, 1249-074 Lisbon
Tel: (021) 3924440 *Fax:* (021) 3957284
E-mail: sid@fct.mces.pt
Web Site: www.fct.mct.pt
Key Personnel
President: Prof Fernando Ramoa Ribeiro
Dir: Dr Gabriela Lopes da Silva *E-mail:* g.l.silva@fct.mct.pt
Internet database only at www.fct.mct.pt, option: Bibliotecas com Revistas de C&T.

Sumarios das Publicacoes Periodicas Portuguesas (Current Contents of Portuguese Periodicals) (J)
Published by Biblioteca Geral da Universidade de Coimbra
Largo da Porta Ferrea, 3000-447 Coimbra
Tel: (0239) 859800; (0239) 859800/15 *Fax:* (0239) 827135
E-mail: bguc@ci.uc.pt
Web Site: www.uc.pt
Key Personnel
Dir: Prof Anibal Pinto de Castro
E-mail: acastro@ci.uc.pt

Romania

ABSI - Abstracte in bibliologie si stiinta informarii (ABSI - Abstracts in Library & Information Science) (J)
Published by National Library
Str Ion Ghica nr 4, 79708 Bucharest
Tel: (01) 314 24 34; (01) 314 24 33; (01) 315 70 63 *Fax:* (01) 312 33 81
E-mail: go@bibnat.ro
Web Site: www.bibnat.ro
Key Personnel
Dir General: Ion Dan Erceanu *Tel:* (021) 310 08 60
Chief Editor: Ioana Varlan
Contact: Dina Paladi *E-mail:* dina.paladi@bibnat.ro
First published 1960.
Monthly.
51 pp
ISSN: 1220-3092

Biblioteconomie Culegere de Traduceri Prelucrate (Librarianship: Collected Adapted Translations) (J)
Published by National Library
Str Ion Ghica nr 4, Sector 3, 79708 Bucharest
Tel: (01) 314 24 34; (01) 314 24 33; (01) 315 70 63 *Fax:* (01) 312 33 81
E-mail: go@bibnat.ro
Web Site: www.bibnat.ro
Key Personnel
Dir General: Ion Dan Erceanu *Tel:* (021) 310 08 60
Chief Editor: Anca Moraru
Librarianship: Collected adapted translations.
First published 1964.
Quarterly.
95 pp
ISSN: 1220-3076

Information & Documentation Problems (J)
Published by National Institute for Information & Documentation
21-25 Mendeleev St, Sector 1, Bucharest 70141
Tel: (01) 315 87 65 *Fax:* (01) 312 67 34
E-mail: inid@home.ro
Web Site: www.inid.ro
Key Personnel
Contact: Gheorghe Anghel
About 500 different publications in Romanian, periodicals (science, know-hows, machines, products, works, etc).

Russian Federation

Bibliotechnoe delo i Bibliografiya Bibliografieheskaya informatsiya (Library Science and Theory of Bibliography, Bibliographic Information) (B)
Published by Russian State Library
3/5 Vozdvizhenka St, Moscow 101000
Tel: (095) 222-83-40 (inquiries); (095) 202-73-71 (administration) *Fax:* (095) 202-35-65; (095) 290-60-62
E-mail: mbs@rsl.ru
Web Site: www.rsl.ru
Telex: 411167 GBL SU
Key Personnel
Dir: Victor Vasilyevich Fedorov, PhD

Biblioteka (The Librarian) (J)
Published by Ministry of Culture
Prospekt Marksa ll-1, 121019 Moscow
Tel: (095) 2026308
Telex: 411167 GBLSU

Biblioteka v epohu peremen, Informatsionnyj sbornik (J)
Published by Russian State Library
3/5 Vozdvizhenka St, Moscow 101000
Tel: (095) 222-83-40 (inquiries); (095) 202-73-71 (administration) *Fax:* (095) 202-35-65; (095) 290-60-62
E-mail: mbs@rsl.ru
Web Site: www.rsl.ru
Key Personnel
Dir: Vladimir Vasilyevich Fedorov, PhD
First published 1999.
Quarterly.
160 pp, $50

Bibliotekovedenie (Library Science) (J)
Published by Russian State Library
3/5 Vozdvizhenka St, Moscow 101000
Tel: (095) 222-83-40 (inquiries); (095) 202-73-71 (administration) *Fax:* (095) 202-35-65; (095) 290-60-62
E-mail: mbs@rsl.ru
Web Site: www.rsl.ru
Key Personnel
Dir: Victor Vasilyevich Fedorov, PhD

Bibliotekovedenie i Bibliografiya za Rubezhom-Librarianship & Bibliography Abroad (Librarianship & Bibliography Abroad) (B)
Published by Russian State Library
3/5 Vozdvizhenka St, Moscow 101000
Tel: (095) 222-83-40 (inquiries); (095) 202-73-71 (administration) *Fax:* (095) 202-35-65; (095) 290-60-62
E-mail: mbs@rsl.ru
Web Site: www.rsl.ru
Telex: 411167 GBL SU
Key Personnel
Dir: Victor Vasilyevich Fedorov, PhD

Esteticheskoe vospitanie Referativno-Bibliograficheskaya informatsiya (Aesthetic Education Bibliographic Information) (B)
Published by Russian State Library
3/5 Vozdvizhenka St, Moscow 101000
Tel: (095) 222-83-40 (inquiries); (095) 202-73-71 (administration) *Fax:* (095) 202-35-65; (095) 290-60-62
E-mail: mbs@rsl.ru
Web Site: www.rsl.ru
Telex: 411167 GBL SU
Key Personnel
Dir: Victor Vasilyevich Fedorov, PhD

Izobrazitelnoye Iskustvo, Bibliograficheskaya Informatsiya (Fine Art, Bibliographic Information) (B)
Published by Russian State Library
3/5 Vozdvizhenka St, Moscow 101000
Tel: (095) 222-83-40 (inquiries); (095) 202-73-71 (administration) *Fax:* (095) 202-35-65; (095) 290-60-62
E-mail: mbs@rsl.ru
Web Site: www.rsl.ru
Telex: 411167 GBL SU
Key Personnel
Dir: Victor Vasilyevich Fedorov, PhD
Theory & practice of fine art in Russia & abroad.

Kultura, Kulturologiya, Referativno-bibliograficheskaya informatsiya (Culture, Culturology, Bibliographic Information) (J)
Published by Russian State Library
3/5 Vozdvizhenka St, Moscow 101000
Tel: (095) 222-83-40 (inquiries); (095) 202-73-71 (administration) *Fax:* (095) 202-35-65; (095) 290-60-62
E-mail: mbs@rsl.ru
Web Site: www.rsl.ru
Key Personnel
Dir: Vladimir Vasilyevich Fedorov, PhD

Kultura v Sovremennom Mire, Informatsionni Sbornik (Culture in the Modern World, Serial Information) (B)
Published by Russian State Library
3/5 Vozdvizhenka St, Moscow 101000
Tel: (095) 222-83-40 (inquiries); (095) 202-73-71 (administration) *Fax:* (095) 202-35-65; (095) 290-60-62
E-mail: mbs@rsl.ru
Web Site: www.rsl.ru
Telex: 411167 GBL SU
Key Personnel
Dir: Victor Vasilyevich Fedorov, PhD
The world cultural process, cultural policy, views & analyses, innovation in culture & art.

RUSSIAN FEDERATION

Massovaya Biblioteca, Teoriya i Practica
(Public Library, Theory & Practice) (B)
Published by Russian State Library
3/5 Vozdvizhenka St, Moscow 101000
Tel: (095) 222-83-40 (inquiries); (095) 202-73-71 (administration) *Fax:* (095) 202-35-65; (095) 290-60-62
E-mail: mbs@rsl.ru
Web Site: www.rsl.ru
Key Personnel
Dir: Victor Vasilyevich Fedorov, PhD
Serial information publication.

Materialnaya Baza Sfery Kulturi, Informatsionni Sbornik (Material Base of the Cultural Sphere, Serial Information) (B)
Published by Russian State Library
3/5 Vozdvizhenka St, Moscow 101000
Tel: (095) 222-83-40 (inquiries); (095) 202-73-71 (administration) *Fax:* (095) 202-35-65; (095) 290-60-62
E-mail: mbs@rsl.ru
Web Site: www.rsl.ru
Telex: 411167 GBL SU
Key Personnel
Dir: Victor Vasilyevich Fedorov, PhD
Material & technical facilities, economy, management in culture.

Mir Bibliotek Segodnya (Library World Today) (J)
Published by Russian State Library
3/5 Vozdvizhenka St, Moscow 101000
Tel: (095) 222-83-40 (inquiries); (095) 202-73-71 (administration) *Fax:* (095) 202-35-65; (095) 290-60-62
E-mail: mbs@rsl.ru
Web Site: www.rsl.ru
Key Personnel
Dir: Victor Vasilyevich Fedorov, PhD
Original & abstract information on Russian & world libraries. Serial information publication.

Muzeynoe delo i ohrana pamyatnikov, Referativno-bibliograficheskaya informatsiya (Museums & Protection of Monuments, Bibliographic Information) (J)
Published by Russian State Library
3/5 Vozdvizhenka St, Moscow 101000
Tel: (095) 222-83-40 (inquiries); (095) 202-73-71 (administration) *Fax:* (095) 202-35-65; (095) 290-60-62
E-mail: mbs@rsl.ru
Web Site: www.rsl.ru
Key Personnel
Dir: Vladimir Vasilyevich Fedorov, PhD

Muzika, Bibliograficheskaya Informatsiya (Music, Bibliographic Information) (B)
Published by Russian State Library
3/5 Vozdvizhenka St, Moscow 101000
Tel: (095) 222-83-40 (inquiries); (095) 202-73-71 (administration) *Fax:* (095) 202-35-65; (095) 290-60-62
E-mail: mbs@rsl.ru
Web Site: www.rsl.ru
Telex: 411167 GBL SU
Key Personnel
Dir: Victor Vasilyevich Fedorov, PhD
Theory, history & genres of music.

Narodnoie Tvorchestvo: Sociokulturnaya Deyatelnost v Sfere Dosuga, Informatsionni Sbornik (Sociocultural Activity in the Sphere of Leisure, Serial Information) (B)
Published by Russian State Library
3/5 Vozdvizhenka St, Moscow 101000
Tel: (095) 222-83-40 (inquiries); (095) 202-73-71 (administration) *Fax:* (095) 202-35-65; (095) 290-60-62
E-mail: mbs@rsl.ru
Web Site: www.rsl.ru
Key Personnel
Dir: Victor Vasilyevich Fedorov, PhD
Folk art, amateur activity & national traditional art.

Nauchnye i tekhnicheskie biblioteki (Scientific & Technical Libraries) (J)
Published by GPNTB Rossii
Kuznetskii Most 12, Moscow 103031
Tel: (095) 2925570 *Fax:* (095) 9219862
E-mail: info@gpntb.ru
Web Site: www.gpntb.ru
Telex: 411167 GBLSU
Key Personnel
Dir & Editor-in-Chief: Dr A I Zemskov
Professional journal on library science & the practice of regional & metropolitan libraries of all types, sci-tech information centers, LIS colleges & universities.
First published 1961.
Monthly.
140 pp, 129.95 USD per year
ISSN: 0130-9765

Nauka o Kulture, Itogi i perspektivy, Informatsionnyj sbornik (Culture Science, Results & Perspectives, Serial Information) (J)
Published by Russian State Library
3/5 Vozdvizhenka St, Moscow 101000
Tel: (095) 222-83-40 (inquiries); (095) 202-73-71 (administration) *Fax:* (095) 202-35-65; (095) 290-60-62
E-mail: mbs@rsl.ru
Web Site: www.rsl.ru
Key Personnel
Dir: Vladimir Vasilyevich Fedorov, PhD

Panorama kulturnoi zhizni Rossiyskoi Federatsii, Informatsionnyj sbornik (Panorama of Cultural Life in Russian Federation, Serial Information) (J)
Published by Russian State Library
3/5 Vozdvizhenka St, Moscow 101000
Tel: (095) 222-83-40 (inquiries); (095) 202-73-71 (administration) *Fax:* (095) 202-35-65; (095) 290-60-62
E-mail: mbs@rsl.ru
Web Site: www.rsl.ru
Key Personnel
Dir: Victor Vasilyevich Fedorov, PhD

Panorama kulturnoi zhizni stran SNG i Baltii, Informatsionnyj sbornik (Panorama of Cultural Life in the States of the CIS & in the Baltic States, Serial Information) (J)
Published by Russian State Library
3/5 Vozdvizhenka St, Moscow 101000
Tel: (095) 222-83-40 (inquiries); (095) 202-73-71 (administration) *Fax:* (095) 202-35-65; (095) 290-60-62
E-mail: mbs@rsl.ru
Web Site: www.rsl.ru
Key Personnel
Dir: Victor Vasilyevich Fedorov, PhD

Panorama kulturnoi zhizni zarubezhnyh stran Informatsionnyj sbornik (Panorama of Cultural Life Abroad. Serial Information) (J)
Published by Russian State Library
3/5 Vozdvizhenka St, Moscow 101000
Tel: (095) 222-83-40 (inquiries); (095) 202-73-71 (administration) *Fax:* (095) 202-35-65; (095) 290-60-62
E-mail: mbs@rsl.ru
Web Site: www.rsl.ru
Key Personnel
Dir: Victor Vasilyevich Fedorov, PhD

Russkaya Kultura Vne Granits (Russian Culture Beyond Frontiers) (B)
Published by Russian State Library
3/5 Vozdvizhenka St, Moscow 101000
Tel: (095) 222-83-40 (inquiries); (095) 202-73-71 (administration) *Fax:* (095) 202-35-65; (095) 290-60-62
E-mail: mbs@rsl.ru
Web Site: www.rsl.ru
Key Personnel
Dir: Victor Vasilyevich Fedorov, PhD
Serial Information Culture, History & Policy.

Sociokulturnaya Deyatelnost v Sfere Dosuga, Referativno-Bibliograficheskaya Informatsiya (Sociocultural Activities in the Sphere of Leisure, Bibliographic Information) (B)
Published by Russian State Library
3/5 Vozdvizhenka St, Moscow 101000
Tel: (095) 222-83-40 (inquiries); (095) 202-73-71 (administration) *Fax:* (095) 202-35-65; (095) 290-60-62
E-mail: mbs@rsl.ru
Web Site: www.rsl.ru
Telex: 411167 GBL SU
Key Personnel
Dir: Victor Vasilyevich Fedorov, PhD
Problems of outdoor recreation.

Zrelischnie Iskustva Referativno-Bibliograficheskaya Informatsiya (Performing Arts, Bibliographic Information) (B)
Published by Russian State Library
3/5 Vozdvizhenka St, Moscow 101000
Tel: (095) 222-83-40 (inquiries); (095) 202-73-71 (administration) *Fax:* (095) 202-35-65; (095) 290-60-62
E-mail: mbs@rsl.ru
Web Site: www.rsl.ru
Telex: 411167 GBL SU
Key Personnel
Dir: Victor Vasilyevich Fedorov, PhD
Theatre, circus, dance & music hall art.

Saudi Arabia

Bulletin (J)
Published by King Fahad National Library
King Fahd Hwy, Riyadh
Mailing Address: PO Box 7572, Riyadh 11472
Tel: (01) 462 4888 *Fax:* (01) 464 5341
Key Personnel
Dir: Abdur Rahman Al Sarra

Directory of Libraries in Saudi Arabia (B)
Published by King Saud University Library
al-Jami'ah St, Riyadh 11495
Mailing Address: PO Box 22480, Riyadh 11495
Tel: (01) 4676148; (01) 4676 6149 *Fax:* (01) 467 6162
E-mail: sfalogia@ksu.edu.sa
Web Site: www.ksu.edu.sa
Key Personnel
Dean: Dr Sulaiman Al-Ogla
First published 1979.
215 pp

Senegal

Repertoire des Bibliotheques et Organismes de Documentation au Senegal (Catalogue of the Libraries and Documentation Centres of Senegal) (B)
Published by Ecole des Bibliothecaires, Archivistes et Documentalistes de l'Universite Cheikh Anta Diop de Dakar
Faculty of Arts & Social Sciences, BP 3252 Dakar
Tel: 825 76 60; 864 21 22 *Fax:* 824 05 42
E-mail: ebad@ebad.ucad.sn
Web Site: www.ebad.ucad.sn
Key Personnel
Dir: Mbaye Thiam *E-mail:* mbaye.thiam@ebad.ucad.sn
Archives & documentation centres throughout Senegal. Information on 124 libraries.

Serbia and Montenegro

Biblioteke u Jugoslaviji (Libraries in Yugoslavia) (B)
Published by Jugoslovenski Bibliografsko-informacijski institut, Yubin, Agencija za ISBN (Yugoslav Institute for Bibliography & Information)
Terazije 26, 1000 Belgrade
Tel: (011) 687 836 *Fax:* (011) 687 760
Web Site: www.jbi.bg.ac.yu

Biblioteke u SR Srbiji (Libraries in Serbia) (B)
Published by Narodna Biblioteka Srbije (National Library of Serbia)
Skerliceva 1, Belgrade 11000
Tel: (011) 451242
Key Personnel
Dir: Milomir Petrovic

Sierra Leone

SLAALIS Bulletin (J)
Published by Sierra Leone Association of Archivists, Librarians & Information Scientists (SLAALIS)
7 Percival St, Freetown
Tel: (022) 23848
Key Personnel
Chief Librarian: Irene O'Brien-Coker
First published 1987.
Quarterly.
1.50 SLL per year

Singapore

Directory of Libraries in Singapore (B)
Published by Library Association of Singapore
Geylang East Community Library, 50 Geylang East Ave 1, 3rd floor, Singapore 389777
Tel: 6749 7990 *Fax:* 6749 7480
Web Site: www.las.org.sg
Key Personnel
President: Mr Choy Fatt Cheong *Tel:* 780 5289
E-mail: choyfc@tp.edu.sg
Administrative Officer: Ms Azian Mohammad
E-mail: lassec@singnet.com.sg
80 SGD plus postage & admin

Singapore Journal of Library Information Management (B)
Formerly Singapore Libraries
Published by Library Association of Singapore
Geylang East Community Library, 50 Geylang East Ave 1, 3rd floor, Singapore 389777
Tel: 6749 7990 *Fax:* 6749 7480
Web Site: www.las.org.sg
Key Personnel
President: Mr Choy Fatt Cheong *Tel:* 780 5289
E-mail: choyfc@tp.edu.sg
Administrative Officer: Ms Azian Mohammad
E-mail: lassec@singnet.com.sg
Annually.
40 SGD (local & Malaysia); 60 SGD (other countries)

Singapore Libraries, see Singapore Journal of Library Information Management

Singapore Libraries Bulletin (P)
Published by Library Association of Singapore
Geylang East Community Library, 50 Geylang East Ave 1, 3rd floor, Singapore 389777
Tel: 6749 7990 *Fax:* 6749 7480
Web Site: www.las.org.sg
Key Personnel
Editor: Ms Zarinah Mohamed *E-mail:* zarinah@las.org.sg
Quarterly.

Singapore Periodicals Index (P)
Published by National Library Board Singapore, Library Supply Services
Tower B, 3rd Story, No 3, Changi South St 2, Singapore 486548
Tel: 6546 7275 *Fax:* 6546 7262
Web Site: www.nlb.gov.sg *Cable:* RS 26620 NATLIB
Serial (CD-ROM).
First published 1996.
Annually.
ISSN: 0218-902X

Slovenia

Knjiznica: Revija za Podrocje Bibliotekarstva in Informacijske Znanosti (Library: Journal for Library & Information Science) (J)
Published by Zveza bibliotekarskih drustev Slovenije (ZBDS) (Union of Associations of Slovene Librarians)
Turjaska 1, 1000 Ljubljana
Tel: (01) 2001 193 *Fax:* (01) 4257 293
Web Site: www.zbds-zveza.si
Key Personnel
Editor: Melita Ambrozic *E-mail:* melita.ambrozic@nuk.uni-lj.si
Text in Slovenian; summaries in English. Library & information sciences.
First published 1957.
Quarterly.
150 pp, $30 Vol
ISSN: 0023-2424

South Africa

Cape Librarian (P)
Published by Cape Provincial Library Service
c/o Hospital & Chiappini, Cape Town 8001
Mailing Address: PO Box 2108, Cape Town 8000
Tel: (021) 4102 446 *Fax:* (021) 419-7541
E-mail: capelib@pawc.wcape.gov.za
Web Site: www.westerncape.gov.za
Key Personnel
Dir: N F Van Der Merwe
Text in Afrikaans & English.
First published 1957.
Monthly (except July & Dec).
ISSN: 0008-5790

Free State Libraries (J)
Published by Department of Sport, Arts, Culture, Science & Technology Library, Information & Technology Services Directorate
Private Bag X20606, Bloemfontein 9300
Tel: (051) 4054681 *Fax:* (051) 4033567
E-mail: loader@majuba.ofs.gov.za; jacomien@majuba.ofs.gov.za
Web Site: www.mangung.ofs.gov.za/vpr
Telex: 267056t
Key Personnel
Editor: Adri Smuts
First published 1958.
Quarterly.
ISSN: 0016-0458

Index to South African Periodicals (ISAP) (J)
Published by National Library of South Africa
239 Vermeulen St, Pretoria
Mailing Address: PO Box 397, 0001 Pretoria
Tel: (012) 321 8931 *Fax:* (012) 325 5984
E-mail: askotze@statelib.pwv.gov.za
Web Site: www.nlsa.ac.za
Key Personnel
Dir: Dr Peter J Lor
First published 1940.

Kwaznaplis (J)
Published by Kwazulu Natal Provincial Library Services
PB X9016, Pietermaritzbur, Kwazulu-Natal 3200
Tel: (0331) 940241 *Fax:* (0331) 942237
E-mail: hartj@natalia.kzntl.gov.za
Key Personnel
Deputy Dir: Dr Rookaya Bawa
First published 1971.
6 times/yr.
Free to libraries in South Africa

LIASA News (J)
Published by Library & Information Association of South Africa (LIASA)
PO Box 1598, Pretoria 0001
Tel: (012) 481 2870; (012) 481 2875; (012) 481 2876 *Fax:* (012) 481 2873
E-mail: liasa@liasa.org.za
Web Site: www.liasa.org.za
Key Personnel
Executive Dir: Gwenda Thomas
Quarterly.

Local Government Library Bulletin (J)
Published by Johannesburg Public Library
Library Gardens, Corner Fraser & Market Sts, Johannesburg 2001
Mailing Address: PB X93, Marshalltown 2107
Tel: (011) 836 3787 *Fax:* (011) 836 6607
E-mail: library@mj.org.za
Key Personnel
Librarian: E J Bevan *E-mail:* jbevan@mj.org.za
Monthly.
Free

Mousaion (P)
Published by Unisa Press
Unisa Main Campus, Preller St, Nieu Muckleneuk, Pretoria 0003
Mailing Address: PO Box 392, Unisa 0001
Tel: (012) 429-3111 *Fax:* (012) 429-4111
E-mail: kempg@alpha.unisa.ac.za

SOUTH AFRICA

Web Site: www.unisa.ac.za
Telex: 350068 *Cable:* UNISA
Key Personnel
Editor: Prof J A Kruger
Biannually.
20 USD

Periodicals in Southern African Libraries (PISAL) (J)
Published by National Library of South Africa
239 Vermeulen St, Pretoria
Mailing Address: PO Box 397, 0001 Pretoria
Tel: (012) 321 8931 *Fax:* (012) 325 5984
Web Site: www.nlsa.ac.za
Key Personnel
Dir: Dr Peter J Lor

Quarterly Bulletin of the South African Library (J)
Published by National Library of South Africa
5 Queen Victoria St, Cape Town 8000
Mailing Address: PO Box 496, Cape Town 8000
Tel: (021) 424 6320 (ext 238) *Fax:* (021) 423 3359
E-mail: docdel@nlsa.ac.za
Web Site: www.nlsa.ac.za

South African Journal of Library & Information Science (J)
Published by Library & Information Association of South Africa (LIASA)
PO Box 1598, Pretoria 0001
Tel: (012) 481 2870; (012) 481 2875; (012) 481 2876 *Fax:* (012) 481 2873
E-mail: liasa@liasa.org.za
Web Site: www.liasa.org.za
Key Personnel
Executive Dir: Gwenda Thomas
Biannually.

South African Journal of Library & Information Science (J)
Published by Bureau for Scientific Publications
PO Box 11663, Pretoria, Hatfield 0028
Tel: (012) 3226404 *Fax:* (012) 3207803
E-mail: bspman@icon.co.za
Telex: 350068
First published 1933.
Quarterly.
ISSN: 0256-8861

South African National Bibliography (SANB) (J)
Published by National Library of South Africa
239 Vermeulen St, Pretoria
Mailing Address: PO Box 397, 0001 Pretoria
Tel: (012) 321 8931 *Fax:* (012) 325 5984
Web Site: www.nlsa.ac.za
Annual cumulation.
ISSN: 0085-5677

Spain

Biblioteca Hispana (Spanish Library) (B)
Published by Consejo Superior de Investigaciones Cientificas
Vitruvio, 8, 28006 Madrid
SAN: 001-1347
Tel: (091) 562 96 33 *Fax:* (091) 562 96 34
E-mail: publ@orgc.csic.es
Web Site: www.csic.es/publica
Key Personnel
Pres: Cesar Nombela Cano

Sri Lanka

Directory of Social Science Libraries, Information Centres and Data Bases in Sri Lanka 1990 (B)
Published by National Library & Documentation Centre
No 14, Independence Ave, Colombo 07
Tel: (01) 698847; (01) 685197 *Fax:* (01) 685201
E-mail: nldsb@mail.natlib.lk; nldsb@mail.natlib.lk
Web Site: www.natlib.lk
Key Personnel
Dir General: Mr M S U Amarasiri *E-mail:* dg@mail.natlib.lk
Other publications relevent to Social Sciences, Conference Index; Selected Bibliography on SAARC; Sri Lanka Pustakala Namawaliya; Sri Lanka Rajaye Prakashana Namawaliya; Directory of Libraries in Sri Lanka; Directory of Social Scientists in Sri Lanka Part I; Bibliography on Kataragama; Bibliography on Mahindagamanaya; Lama Grantha Namawaliaya; Pustakala Dave Bhanda; Sri Lanka Newspaper article index.

Library News (J)
Published by National Library & Documentation Centre
No 14, Independence Ave, Colombo 07
Tel: (01) 698847; (01) 685197 *Fax:* (01) 685201
E-mail: nldsb@mail.natlib.lk; nldsb@mail.natlib.lk
Web Site: www.natlib.lk
Key Personnel
Dir General: Mr M S U Amarasiri *E-mail:* dg@mail.natlib.lk
Quarterly.
ISSN: 1391-0000

Sri Lanka Library Review (J)
Published by Sri Lanka Library Association
275/75 Bauddhaloka Mawatha, Colombo 7
Tel: (01) 2589103 *Fax:* (01) 2589103
E-mail: sllibrary@mail.ewisl.net
Web Site: www.naresa.ac.lk/slla
Key Personnel
President: Mrs Daya Ratnayake
General Secretary: Ms Deepali Talagala

Sri Lanka Periodicals Directory (J)
Published by National Museum Library of Sri Lanka (NMLSL)
PO Box 854, Colombo 07
Tel: (01) 695 366 *Fax:* (01) 695 366
Annual supplements.

Sri Lanka Periodicals Index (P)
Published by National Museum Library of Sri Lanka (NMLSL)
PO Box 854, Colombo 07
Tel: (01) 695 366 *Fax:* (01) 695 366

Swaziland

Directory of Swaziland Libraries (B)
Published by University of Swaziland Library
Private Bag 4, Kwaluseni
Tel: 518-4011; 518-5108 *Fax:* 518-5276
E-mail: uniswapgs@uniswa.sz
Web Site: www.uniswa.sz
Key Personnel
Chancellor: HM King Mswati, III
Irregularly.

Serials in Swaziland University Libraries (B)
Published by University of Swaziland Library
Private Bag 4, Kwaluseni
Tel: 518-4011; 518-5108 *Fax:* 518-5276
E-mail: uniswapgs@uniswa.sz
Web Site: www.uniswa.sz
Telex: 2087
Irregularly.

Sweden

Biblioteksbladet (Library Journal) (J)
Published by Svensk Biblioteksforening (Swedish Library Association)
Saltmaetargatan 3 A, 111 60 Stockholm
Mailing Address: PO Box 3127, 103 62 Stockholm
Tel: (08) 545 132 30 *Fax:* (08) 545 132 31
E-mail: info@biblioteksforeningen.org
Web Site: www.biblioteksforeningen.org
Text in Scandinavian languages with summaries in English.

Svensk periodicafoerteckning (Current Swedish Periodicals) (B)
Published by Kungliga Biblioteket, Bibliografiska avdelningen
Box 5039, 102 41 Stockholm
Tel: (08) 463 40 00 *Fax:* (08) 463 40 04
E-mail: kungl.biblioteket@kb.se
Web Site: www.kb.se
Telex: 19640 KBS S
Key Personnel
Contact: Eva Crantz *Tel:* (08) 463-42 22
 E-mail: eva.crantz@kb.se
ISSN: 1104-1102

Tidskrift foer Dokumentation (Documentation Periodical) (J)
Published by Tekniska Litteratursaellskapet (The Swedish Society for Technical Documentation)
Grev Turegatan 14, Stockholm
Mailing Address: Box 55580, 102 04 Stockholm
Tel: (08) 678 23 20 *Fax:* (08) 678 23 01
E-mail: kansliet@tls.se
Web Site: www.tls.se
Text in Swedish, with summaries & occasional articles in English Nordic Journal of Documentation.
Quarterly.
ISSN: 0040-6872

Switzerland

Arbido (J)
Published by Association des Bibliotheques et Bibliothecaires Suisses (Association of Swiss Librarians & Libraries)
Hallerstr 58, 3008 Bern
Tel: (031) 382 42 40 *Fax:* (031) 382 46 48
E-mail: bbs@bbs.ch
Web Site: www.bbs.ch
Key Personnel
President: Dr Peter Wille

Syrian Arab Republic

Damascus University Library Review (J)
Published by Damascus University Press
Damascus University Library, Damascus, Baramkah
Tel: (011) 2215104; (011) 2215101 *Fax:* (011) 2236010
E-mail: info@damascus-online.com
Web Site: www.damascus-online/university.htm
Telex: 411971

Taiwan, Province of China

Chung-hua min-kuo t'u-shu-kuan nien-chien (B)
Published by National Central Library
20 Chung Shan S Rd, Taipei 100-01
Tel: (02) 2361 9132 (ext 250); (02) 2314 7322 *Fax:* (02) 382 1489
Web Site: www.ncl.edu.tw
Key Personnel
Dir: Dr Tseng Chi-Chun
Yearbook of Libraries in the Republic of China.

Chung-kuo t'u-shu-kuan hsueh-hui hui-pao (J)
Published by Library Association of China (LAC)
20 Chungshan S Rd, Taipei 10010
Tel: (02) 2331-2675; (02) 2361-9132 *Fax:* (02) 2370-0899
E-mail: lac@msg.ncl.edu.tw
Web Site: www.ncl.edu.tw
Key Personnel
President: James HC Hu
Secretary General: Teresa Wang Chang
Bulletin of the Library Association of China.

Journal of Library & Information Science (J)
Published by Department of Adult & Continuing Education, National Taiwan Normal University
162 Hoping East Rd, sec 1, Taipei 10610
Tel: (02) 321-8457; (02) 391-4248 *Fax:* (02) 341-8431
E-mail: mtc@mtc.ntnu.edu.tw
Web Site: www.mtc.ntnu.edu.tw
Key Personnel
President: Hsi-Muh Leu
CALA Editor: Wilfred W Fong *Tel:* (0414) 229-5421 *Fax:* (0414) 229-4848 *E-mail:* wfong@csd.uwm.edu
First published 1975.
Biannually.
ISSN: 0363-3640

Tseng-pu hsiu-ting Chung-hua min-kuo Chung-wen ch'i-k'an lien-ho mu-lu (B)
Published by National Central Library
20 Chung Shan S Rd, Taipei 100-01
Tel: (02) 2361 9132 (ext 250); (02) 2314 7322 *Fax:* (02) 382 1489
Web Site: www.ncl.edu.tw
Key Personnel
Dir: Tseng Chi-Chun
National Union List of Chinese Periodicals of the Republic of China.

United Republic of Tanzania

Directory of Libraries, Museums and Archives in Tanzania (B)
Published by Tanzania Library Service
Bibi Titi Mohamed St, Dar-es-Salaam
Mailing Address: PO Box 9283, Dar es Salaam
Tel: (022) 215 00 48; (022) 215 09 23
E-mail: tlsb@africaonline.co.tz
Key Personnel
Dir General: Ellezer A Mwinyimvua
First published 1979.

Matukio (J)
Published by Tanzania Library Association
PO Box 33433, Dar es Salaam
Tel: (022) 2775411
E-mail: tla_tanzania@yahoo.com
Web Site: www.angelfire.com/al4/tla/
Key Personnel
Chairman: Dr Alli Mcharazo
   E-mail: amcharazo@hotmail.com

Thailand

An Annotated Bibliography of Librarianship in Thailand (B)
Published by Department of Library Science, Chulalongkorn University, Faculty of Arts
c/o Chulalongkorn University, 254 Phyathai Rd Patumwan, Bangkok 10330
Tel: (02) 215-0871-3 *Fax:* (02) 215-4804
E-mail: info@chula.ac.th
Web Site: www.chula.ac.th
Telex: 20217
Key Personnel
Prof: Dr Boonrod Binson

Bulletin (J)
Published by Thai Library Association
1346 Akarnsongkrau Rd 5, Klongchan, Bangkapi Bangkok 10240
Tel: (0662) 734-8022-3 *Fax:* (02) 734-8024
Web Site: tla.tiac.or.th
Key Personnel
President: Khunying Maenmas Chawalit
Foreign Relations: Yupin Chancharoensin
   E-mail: yupin@car.chula.ac.th
Executive Secretary: Mrs Vorrarat Srinamngern
Quarterly.

List of Scientific Libraries in Thailand (B)
Published by Thai National Documentation Centre (TNDC)
196 Phahonyothin Rd, Chatuchak, Bangkok 10900
Tel: (02) 579 1121/30 (ext 1233) *Fax:* (02) 579 8594
Telex: 21392
Key Personnel
Dir: Mrs Nongphanga Chitrakorn

Trinidad & Tobago

Bulletin (J)
Published by Library Association of Trinidad & Tobago
PO Box 1275, Port of Spain
Tel: (868) 687-0194
E-mail: latt@mailcity.com
Web Site: www.latt.org.tt
Key Personnel
President: Ernesta Greenidge
   E-mail: egreenidge@library.uwi.tt
Secretary: Sheryl Washington
   E-mail: swashington@ag.gov.tt
First published 1964.
ISSN: 0521-9590

Tunisia

Rassid (J)
Published by Association Tunisienne des Documentalistes, Bibliothecaires et Archivistes
Centre de Documentation Nationale, Rue 8004, Rue Sidi El Benna R P, 1000 Tunis
Tel: (01) 245338
Key Personnel
Pres: Daly Abdelbaki
Chief Redactor: Mohamed Abdelsaoued
First published 1970.
Quarterly.
60 pp, $25/yr
ISSN: 0330-8782

United Kingdom

Archives (J)
Published by British Records Association
c/o Finsbury Library, 245 St John St, London EC1V 4NB
Tel: (020) 7833 0428 *Fax:* (020) 7833 0416
E-mail: britrecassoc@hotmail.com
Web Site: www.hmc.gov.uk/bra
ISBN(s): 0-900222

Art Libraries Journal (J)
Published by ARLIS/UK & Ireland Art Libraries Society
18 College Rd, Bromsgrove, Worcs B60 2NE
Tel: (01527) 579298 *Fax:* (01527) 579298
E-mail: info@arlis.org.uk
Web Site: www.arlis.org.uk
Key Personnel
Editor: Gillian Varley *E-mail:* g.varley@arlis2.demon.co.uk
First published 1976.
Quarterly.
52 GBP
ISSN: 0307-4722

Aslib Book Guide (J)
Published by Aslib, The Association for Information Management
Temple Chambers, 3-7 Temple Ave, London EC4Y 0HP
Tel: (020) 7583 8900 *Fax:* (020) 7583 8401
E-mail: pubs@aslib.com
Web Site: www.aslib.co.uk

Telex: 23667
Monthly.

Aslib Directory of Information Sources in the UK (B)
Published by Aslib, The Association for Information Management
Temple Chambers, 3-7 Temple Ave, London EC4Y 0HP
Tel: (020) 7583 8900 *Fax:* (020) 7583 8401
E-mail: pubs@aslib.com
Web Site: www.aslib.co.uk
Telex: 23667
Listing of over 9,000 organizations in the UK.
First published 1928.
1,577 pp
ISBN(s): 0-85142-472-4

Bibliography of Printed Works on London History to 1939 (B)
Published by Facet Publishing
7 Ridgmount St, London WC1 7AE
Tel: (020) 7255 0590 *Fax:* (020) 7255 0591
E-mail: info@facetpublishing.co.uk
Web Site: www.facetpublishing.co.uk
First bibliography on London History.
First published 1994.
895 pp, 89.95 GBP
ISBN(s): 1-85604-074-7

The Bibliotheck (P)
Published by Library Association, Scottish Group, University College & Research Section
c/o Scottish Centre for the Book, Napier University, Craighouse Rd, Edinburgh EH10 5LG
Tel: (0131) 455-6150 *Fax:* (0131) 455-6193
E-mail: scob@napier.ac.uk
Web Site: www.pmpc.napier.ac.uk/scob/bibliothek.html
Key Personnel
Editor: Dr William A Kelly; Prof Alistair McCleery
A Scottish journal of bibliography & allied topics.
15 GBP

Brio (J)
Published by International Association of Music Libraries Archives & Documentation Centres: UK & Ireland Branch
County Library HQ, Walton St, Aylesbury, Bucks HP20 1UU
Web Site: www.iaml-uk-irl.org
Key Personnel
Publications Officer: Margaret Roll
  E-mail: mroll@buckscc.gov.uk
Articles relevant to the music library profession, reviews of books & scores & news from music libraries.
First published 1964.
Biannually, May & Nov.
27 GBP or 56 USD; free with membership
ISSN: 0007-0173

Chartered Institute of Library & Information Professionals Yearbook, see CILIP Yearbook

CILIP Yearbook (B)
Published by Facet Publishing
7 Ridgmount St, London WC1E 7AE
Tel: (020) 7255 0590 *Fax:* (020) 7255 0591
E-mail: info@facetpublishing.co.uk
Web Site: www.facetpublishing.co.uk
Key Personnel
Production Manager: K A Beecroft
Listing of officers, members, Royal Charter & bylaws.
Annually.
464 pp, 39.95 GBP
ISBN(s): 1-85604-476-9

Directory of Acquisitions Librarians in the UK & Republic of Ireland (B)
Published by National Acquisitions Group
12 Holm Oak Dr, Madeley, Nr Crewe CW3 9HR
Tel: (01782) 750462 *Fax:* (01782) 750462
E-mail: nag@btconnect.com
Web Site: www.nag.org.uk
Key Personnel
Chair: Jo Grocott
Administration: Marie Hackett; Diane Roberts
Publications: Jonathan Earl
8th

Directory of Rare Book & Special Collections in the UK & Republic of Ireland (B)
Published by Facet Publishing
7 Ridgmount St, London WC1E 7AE
Tel: (020) 7255 0590 *Fax:* (020) 7255 0591
E-mail: info@facetpublishing.co.uk
Web Site: www.facetpublishing.co.uk
Key Personnel
Editor: Barry Bloomfield
Details of the rare & special collections of over 1200 libraries.

Impact: Journal of the Career Development Group (J)
Published by Chartered Institute of Library & Information Professionals (CILIP)
Music Library, University of Reading, 35 Upper Redlands Rd, Reading RG1 5JE
Tel: (0118) 931 8413
Web Site: www.careerdevelopmentgroup.org.uk
Bimonthly.
20 pp
ISSN: 1468-1625

Information Scotland (J)
Formerly Scottish Libraries
Published by Scottish Library Association
Bldg C, 1st floor, Brandon Gate, Leechlee Rd, Hamilton ML3 6AU
Tel: (01698) 458888 *Fax:* (01698) 458899
E-mail: slic@slainte.org.uk
Web Site: www.slainte.org.uk
Key Personnel
Dir: Elaine Fulton *E-mail:* e.fulton@slainte.org.uk
Assistant Dir: Rhona Arthur *E-mail:* r.arthur@slainte.org.ok

Interlending & Document Supply (J)
Published by Emerald
60/62 Toller Lane, Bradford, West Yorks BD8 9BY
Tel: (01274) 777700 *Fax:* (01274) 785201
E-mail: gcrawford@emeraldinsight.com
Web Site: www.emeraldinsight.com
Key Personnel
Man Dir: Dr Keith Howard
ISSN: 0264-1615

♩Journal of Documentation (J)
Published by Emerald
60/62 Toller Lane, Bradford, West Yorks BD8 9BY
Tel: (01274) 777700 *Fax:* (01274) 785201
E-mail: jdoc@emeraldinsight.com
Web Site: www.emeraldinsight.com
Key Personnel
Man Dir: Dr Keith Howard
Managing Editor: Diane Heath *E-mail:* dheath@emeraldinsight.com
First published 1944.
6 times/yr.
Vol 60, 2004: 720 pp
ISSN: 0022-0418

Journal of Information Science (J)
Published by SAGE Publications Ltd
1 Oliver's Yard, 55 City Rd, London EC1Y 1SP
Tel: (020) 7374 8500; (020) 7374 0645 (customer service) *Fax:* (020) 7374 8600
E-mail: info@sagepub.co.uk; orders@sagepub.co.uk
Web Site: www.sagepub.co.uk
Key Personnel
Man Dir: Stephen Barr
Editorial Dir: Ziyad Marar
Editor: Adrian Dale
Published in association with Chartered Institute of Library & Information Professionals.
Bimonthly.
241 GBP/yr (institutional)
ISSN: 0165-5515

Journal of the Society of Archivists (J)
Published by Carfax Publishing Co
4 Park Sq, Milton Park, Abingdon, Oxon OX14 4RN
Tel: (01235) 828600 *Fax:* (01235) 829000
Web Site: www.tandf.co.uk
Key Personnel
Editor: Cressida Annesley; Susan Corrigall; Andrew Flinn; Kate Manning
Journal for archivists, record managers & conservators worldwide.
Biannually.
ISSN: 0037-9816

Legal Information Management (P)
Published by British & Irish Association of Law Librarians/Sweet & Maxwell Ltd
c/o Aon Ltd, 21 Peterborough Rd, Harrow, Middx HA1 2AJ
Tel: (020) 8864 9966 *Fax:* (020) 8422 0760
Web Site: www.biall.org.uk
Telex: 335101 PINCO G
Key Personnel
Chair: Victoria Jannetta *E-mail:* victoria.jannetta@kpmq.co.uk
Quarterly.

The Libraries Directory (B)
Published by James Clarke & Co Ltd
PO Box 60, Cambridge CB1 2NT
Tel: (01223) 350865 *Fax:* (01223) 366951
E-mail: publishing@jamesclarke.co.uk
Web Site: www.jamesclarke.co.uk
Key Personnel
Man Dir: Adrian Brink
Editor: Iain Walker
Directory of Public Libraries, Special Libraries, Record Offices, Archives & Library Organizations in the UK & Ireland.
First published 1890.
Biennially.
2000-2002: 510 pp
ISBN(s): 0-227-67956-3 (Hardcover 99 GBP); 0-227-67957-1 (CD-ROM Reference Edition (Stand Alone) 99 GBP+VAT); 0-227-67958-X (CD-ROM Marketing Edition (Stand Alone) 175 GBP+VAT); 0-227-67959-8 (CD-ROM Reference Edition (Network) 150 GBP+VAT); 0-227-67960-1 (CD-ROM Marketing Edition (Network) 250 GBP+VAT)
ISSN: 0961-4575

Libraries in The United Kingdom & The Republic of Ireland (B)
Published by Facet Publishing
7 Ridgmount St, London WC1E 7AE
Tel: (020) 7255 0590 *Fax:* (020) 7255 0591
E-mail: info@facetpublishing.co.uk
Web Site: www.facetpublishing.co.uk
Listing of public library services & a select list of academic & other library addresses.
Annually.
29th: 464 pp, 39.95 GBP
ISBN(s): 1-85604-450-5

The Library (P)
Published by Bibliographical Society

Institute of English Studies, Senate House, Room 304, Malet St, London WC1E 7HU
Web Site: www.bibsoc.org.uk/library.htm
Key Personnel
Editor: Dr Oliver Pickering *Tel:* (01132) 336 377
  E-mail: o.s.pickering@leeds.ac.uk
Bibliography.
Quarterly.

Library and Information Science Abstracts (LISA) (J)
Published by CSA (Cambridge Scientific Abstracts)
3rd floor, Farringdon House, Wood St, East Grinstead, West Sussex RH19 1UZ
Tel: (01342) 336163 *Fax:* (01342) 310485
E-mail: service@csa.com; tjones@csa.com (sales); support@csa.com (technical support)
Web Site: www.csa.com
Key Personnel
Editor: Lilian Lincoln *E-mail:* llincoln@csa.com
Monthly publication. Indexes & abstracts 500 periodicals from over 65 countries in over 20 languages. Current awareness & search service for information about library & information science & related areas including the internet & information industry. Also available as a CD-ROM searchable database & as a web database.
First published 1969.
Monthly.
100 pp, Annual subscription for 11 issues plus cumulated annual index: Europe L650, $1010,
ISSN: 0024-2179
Parent Company: Cambridge Information Group

Library Review (J)
Published by Emerald
60/62 Toller Lane, Bradford, West Yorks BD8 9BY
Tel: (01274) 777700 *Fax:* (01274) 785201
E-mail: gcrawford@emeraldinsight.com
Web Site: www.emeraldinsight.com
Key Personnel
Man Dir: Dr Keith Howard
ISSN: 0024-2535

LISA, see Library and Information Science Abstracts (LISA)

Managing Information (J)
Published by Aslib, The Association for Information Management
Temple Chambers, 3-7 Temple Ave, London EC4Y 0HP
Tel: (020) 7583 8900 *Fax:* (020) 7583 8401
E-mail: pubs@aslib.com
Web Site: www.aslib.com
Biennially.

New Library World (J)
Published by Emerald
60/62 Toller Lane, Bradford, West Yorks BD8 9BY
Tel: (01274) 777700 *Fax:* (01274) 785201
E-mail: information@emeraldinsight.com (academic sales)
Web Site: www.emeraldinsight.com
Key Personnel
Managing Editor: Diane Heath *E-mail:* dheath@emeraldinsight.com
Editor: Linda Ashcroft *E-mail:* l.s.ashcroft@livjm.ac.uk

Assistant Editor: Stephanie McIvor *E-mail:* s.mcivor@ntlworld.com
Incorporates Information & Library Manager.
ISSN: 0307-4803

The Private Library (J)
Published by Private Libraries Association (PLA)
49 Hamilton Park W, London N5 1AE
Tel: (020) 7503 9827
Web Site: www.the-old-school.demon.co.uk/pla.htm
Key Personnel
Executive Secretary: James Brown
Editor, Private Press Books: Paul W Nash
Publications Secretary: David Chambers
  E-mail: dchambers@aol.com
Concerned with book collecting.
First published 1957.
Quarterly.
48 pp, 25 GBP or 40 USD
ISSN: 0032-8898

Reference Reviews (J)
Published by Emerald
60/62 Toller Lane, Bradford, West Yorks BD8 9BY
Tel: (01274) 777700 *Fax:* (01274) 785201
E-mail: information@emeraldinsight.com (academic sales)
Web Site: www.emeraldinsight.com
Key Personnel
Managing Editor: Diane Heath *E-mail:* dheath@emeraldinsight.com
Editor: Anthony Chalcraft *E-mail:* a.chalcraft@yorksj.ac.uk
Reviews of current reference materials, electronic version only.
ISSN: 0950-4125

Scottish Libraries, see Information Scotland

The SLG Directory to Children's and School Library Services in the British Isles (B)
Published by Library Association, School Libraries Group
7 Ridgmount St, London WC1E 7AE
Tel: (020) 7255 0500 *Fax:* (020) 7255 0501
E-mail: lapublishing@la-hq.org.uk
Web Site: www.la-hq.org.uk/directory/about/slg.html
Key Personnel
Chair: Glenys Willars *Tel:* (0116) 267 8008
  Fax: (0116) 267 8039 *E-mail:* gwillars@leicsgov.uk
Vice Chair: Gill Purbrick *Tel:* (0208) 859 2843
  E-mail: gill.urbrick@elthamhill.greenwich.sch.uk
2nd
ISBN(s): 0-85365; 0-948933

State Librarian (J)
Published by Circle of State Librarians
Mags Griffin HM Customs & Excise, 8th floor, Dorset House, 27-45 Stamford St, London SE1 9PY
Tel: (020) 8929-2825 *Fax:* (020) 8929-0762
E-mail: mags.griffin@hmce.gsi.gov.uk
Web Site: www.circleofstatelibrarians.co.uk
Key Personnel
Contact: Gareth Vaughan

Uruguay

Bibliografía y documentacion en el Uruguay (Bibliography and Documentation in Uruguay) (B)
Published by Agrupacion Bibliotecologica del Uruguay (Group Librarian of Uruguay)
Cerro Largo 1666, Montevideo 11200
Tel: (02) 400 57 40
Key Personnel
Pres: Luis Alberto Musso

Revista de la Biblioteca Nacional (National Library Review) (J)
Published by Biblioteca Nacional del Uruguay
Ave 15 de Julio 1790, Casilla de Correo 452, 11200 Montevideo
Tel: (02) 48 50 30 *Fax:* (02) 49 69 02
Bimonthly.
ISSN: 0797-9061

Zambia

Directory of Libraries in Zambia (B)
Published by Zambia Library Association
PO Box 38636, Lusaka
Key Personnel
Chairman: Benson Njobvu
  E-mail: bensonnjobvu@hotmail.com
Provides details on all the major libraries in the country.

Zambia Library Association Journal (J)
Published by Zambia Library Association
PO Box 38636, Lusaka
Key Personnel
Chairman: Benson Njobvu
  E-mail: bensonnjobvu@hotmail.com

Zimbabwe

Directory of Libraries (B)
Published by National Archives of Zimbabwe
Borrowdale Rd, Gunhill
Mailing Address: PB 7729, Causeway, Harare
Tel: (04) 792741 *Fax:* (04) 792398
E-mail: archives@gta.gov.zw
Web Site: www.gta.gov.zw
Key Personnel
Dir: M I Murambiwa

The Zimbabwe Librarian (P)
Published by Zimbabwe Library Association (ZLA)
PO Box 3133, Harare
Tel: (04) 788694 *Fax:* (04) 738693
Key Personnel
Editor: Sabelo Mapasure
Newsletter with text in English.
First published 1969.
Biannually.
30 ZWD; 30 USD to non-members

Notes

Notes

Notes

Notes

Notes

Notes

Notes

Notes

Industry Yellow Pages

Arranged alphabetically by company/organization name, the industry yellow pages include the page number(s) where the listing can be found as well as the organization's country, telephone, fax, e-mail address and web address. Companies/organizations listed in the following sections are excluded from the yellow pages: **Book Trade Reference Books and Journals**; **Literary Prizes**; **Calendar of Book Trade & Promotional Events** and **Library Reference Books & Journals**.

A A Publishing (United Kingdom) *Tel:* (01256) 491522 *Fax:* (01256) 322575 *E-mail:* aapublish@theaa.com *Web Site:* www.theaa.com; www.aanewsroom.com, pg 654

A & A (Italy) *Tel:* (02) 876 999 *Fax:* (02) 877 928, pg 374

A & A & A Edicoes e Promocoes Internacionais Ltda (Brazil) *Tel:* (024) 221-1467 *Fax:* (024) 221-3669, pg 76

A & A Farmar (Ireland) *Tel:* (01) 4963625 *Fax:* (01) 4970107 *E-mail:* afarmar@iol.ie *Web Site:* www.farmarbooks.com, pg 357

A & B Personal Management Ltd (United Kingdom) *Tel:* (020) 7734 6047; (020) 7734 6048 *Fax:* (020) 7734 6318 *E-mail:* admin@writewords.org.uk, pg 1138

A Francke Verlag (Tubingen und Basel) (Germany) *Tel:* (089) 718 747 *Fax:* (089) 7142039 *E-mail:* info@iudicium.de *Web Site:* www.geist.de, pg 190

A/L Biblioteksentralen (The Norwegian Library Bureau) (Norway) *Tel:* (022) 08 34 00 *Fax:* (022) 08 39 01 *E-mail:* bs@bibsent.no *Web Site:* www.bibsent.no, pg 1332

A-Mail Academic (United Kingdom) *Tel:* (020) 7871 9139 *Fax:* (020) 7871 9140 *E-mail:* a-mail@djlb.co.uk *Web Site:* www.a-mail.co.uk, pg 654

A-R Editions Inc (United States) *Tel:* 608-836-9000 *Toll Free Tel:* 800-736-0070 (US book orders only) *Fax:* 608-831-8200 *E-mail:* info@areditions.com *Web Site:* www.areditions.com, pg 1165, 1185, 1248

A R T Dialog (Czech Republic) *Tel:* (0420) 24148 2808 *Fax:* (0420) 24148 1442 *E-mail:* artdialog@mybox.cz *Web Site:* www.artdialog-literary.wz.cz, pg 1130

Aache Ediciones (Spain) *Tel:* (0949) 220 438 *Fax:* (0949) 220 438 *E-mail:* ediciones@aache.com *Web Site:* aache.iberlibro.net, pg 570

Aafzam Ltd (Zambia) *Tel:* (01) 223261, pg 781

Aalborg Universitetsbibliotek (Denmark) *Tel:* 96359400 *Fax:* 98156859 *E-mail:* aub@aub.aau.dk *Web Site:* www.aub.aau.dk, pg 1501

Aarachne Verlag (Austria) *Tel:* (01) 2855353 *Fax:* (01) 2855353 *E-mail:* spinne@aarachne.at *Web Site:* www.aarachne.at, pg 48

Aardvark Enterprises (Canada) *Tel:* 403-256-4639, pg 1153, 1175, 1215

Aare-Verlag (Switzerland) *Tel:* (062) 836 86 50 *Fax:* (062) 836 86 56 *E-mail:* bildung@sauerlaender.ch *Web Site:* www.sauerlaender.ch, pg 617

Aarhus Universitetsforlag (Denmark) *Tel:* 89425370 *Fax:* 89425380 *E-mail:* unipress@au.dk *Web Site:* www.unipress.dk, pg 128

Bokforlaget Atlantis AB (Sweden) *Tel:* (08) 7830440 *Fax:* (08) 6617285 *E-mail:* mail@atlantis-publishers.se, pg 609

The AB Book Club (BAB) (Iceland) *Tel:* 5643170 *Fax:* 5643190, pg 1253

AB Svenska Laromedel-Editum (Finland) *Tel:* (09) 8043188 *Fax:* (09) 8043257, pg 141

ABA Books (New Zealand) *Tel:* (07) 8549360 *Fax:* (07) 8549361 *Web Site:* www.ababooks.co.nz, pg 493

Editorial Abaco de Rodolfo Depalma SRL (Argentina) *Tel:* (011) 4371-1675 *Fax:* (011) 4371-5802 *E-mail:* info@abacoeditorial.com.ar *Web Site:* www.abacoeditorial.com.ar, pg 2

Mandira Jaya Abadi (Indonesia) *Tel:* (024) 3519547; (024) 3519548 *Fax:* (024) 3542189, pg 353

Publicacions de l'Abadia de Montserrat (Spain) *Tel:* (093) 2450303; (093) 2657923; (093) 2430302 *Fax:* (093) 2473594 *E-mail:* pamsa@pamsa.com *Web Site:* www.pamsa.com, pg 570

Abagar Pablioing (Bulgaria) *Tel:* (02) 702826 *Fax:* (02) 702926 *E-mail:* abagar@gti.bg, pg 92

Abagar, Veliko Tarnovo (Bulgaria) *Tel:* (062) 43936; (062) 47814 *Fax:* (062) 46993, pg 93

Abakus Musik Barbara Fietz (Germany) *Tel:* (06478) 2250 *Fax:* (06478) 1355 *E-mail:* hotline@abakus-musik.de *Web Site:* www.abakus-musik.de, pg 190

Abakus Verlag GmbH (Austria) *Tel:* (0662) 632076 *Fax:* (0662) 8044137, pg 48

Abbotsford Publishing (United Kingdom) *Tel:* (01543) 255749; (01543) 258903 *Web Site:* www.abbotsfordpublishing.com, pg 654

ABC Books (Australian Broadcasting Corporation) (Australia) *Tel:* (02) 8333 3959 *Fax:* (02) 8333 3999 *E-mail:* abcbooks@abc.net.au *Web Site:* abcshop.com.au, pg 10

ABC-CLIO (United Kingdom) *Tel:* (01865) 311350 *Fax:* (01865) 311358 *E-mail:* oxford@abc-clio.ltd.uk *Web Site:* www.abc-clio.com, pg 654

ABC der Deutschen Wirtschaft, Verlagsgesellschaft mbH (Germany) *Tel:* (06151) 389420 *Fax:* (06151) 33164; (06151) 389280 *E-mail:* info@abconline.de *Web Site:* www.abconline.de, pg 190

ABC Kitabevi AS (Turkey) *Tel:* (0212) 27 62 404, pg 648

ABC Kitabevi Sanayi Tic AS (Turkey) *Tel:* (0212) 2762404 *Fax:* (0212) 2851860, pg 1346

Librerias ABC SA (Argentina) *Tel:* (011) 4314-8106 *Fax:* (011) 4314-8106 *E-mail:* libabcc@datamarkets.com.ar *Web Site:* www.libreriasabc.com.ar, pg 1297

Librerias ABC SA (Peru) *Tel:* (054) 422900; (054) 422902 *Fax:* (054) 422901, pg 516, 1334

Ben Abdallah Editions (Tunisia) *Tel:* (01) 237 011 *Fax:* (01) 786 290, pg 647

S Abdul Majeed & Co (Malaysia) *Tel:* (03) 283-2230 *Fax:* (03) 282-5670 *E-mail:* peer@pc.jaring.my, pg 454

S Abdul Majeed & Co (Malaysia) *Tel:* (03) 2832230 *Fax:* (03) 2822567 *E-mail:* peer@pc.jaring.my, pg 1325

ABE Marketing (Poland) *Tel:* (022) 6540675 *Fax:* (022) 6520767 *E-mail:* info@abe.com.pl *Web Site:* www.abe.com.pl/, pg 1336

Gruppo Abele (Italy) *Tel:* (011) 3841066 *E-mail:* segreteria@gruppoabele.it *Web Site:* www.gruppoabele.it, pg 374

Abeledo-Perrot SAE e I (Argentina) *Tel:* (011) 4124-9750 *Fax:* (011) 4371-5156 *E-mail:* editorial@abeledo-perrot.com, pg 2

Edizioni Abete (Italy) *Tel:* (06) 225821 *Fax:* (06) 2282960, pg 374

ABG Professional Information (United Kingdom) *Tel:* 08707 772906 *Fax:* 08702 404388 *E-mail:* info@abgpublications.co.uk *Web Site:* www.abgpublications.co.uk, pg 655

ABGRA (Asociacion de Bibliotecarios Graduados de la Republica Argentina) (Argentina) *Tel:* (011) 4371 5269; (011) 4373 0571 *Fax:* (011) 4371 5269 *E-mail:* info@abgra.org.ar *Web Site:* abgra.sisbi.uba.ar, pg 1557

Abhinav Publications (India) *Tel:* (011) 26566387; (011) 26524658 *Fax:* (011) 26857009 *Web Site:* www.abhinavexports.com, pg 326

Abhishek Publications (India) *Tel:* (0172) 707562 *Fax:* (0172) 704668, pg 327

ABIC Books & Equipment Ltd (Nigeria) *Tel:* (042) 331827 *Fax:* (042) 334811, pg 503

Universite d'Abidjan (Cote d'Ivoire) *Tel:* 441285 *Fax:* 434254 *E-mail:* puci@africaonline.co.ci, pg 117

Abimo (Belgium) *Tel:* (052) 462407 *Fax:* (052) 461962 *E-mail:* info@abimo-uitgeverij.com *Web Site:* www.abimo-uitgeverij.com, pg 62

Abisega Publishers (Nigeria) Ltd (Nigeria) *Tel:* (022) 415802, pg 503

Editrice Abitare Segesta (Italy) *Tel:* (02) 210581 *Fax:* (02) 21058316 *Web Site:* www.abitare.it, pg 374

Abiva Publishing House Inc (Philippines) *Tel:* (02) 7120245 *Fax:* (02) 7320308 *E-mail:* info@abiva.com.ph *Web Site:* www.abiva.com.ph, pg 518

Libraira-Papeterie ABM (Benin) *Tel:* 330690 (voice & fax), pg 1302

Abo Akademis bibliotek (Finland) *Tel:* (02) 2154180 *Fax:* (02) 2154795 *E-mail:* hblan@abo.fi *Web Site:* www.abo.fi/library, pg 1505

Abo Akademis forlag - Abo Akademi University Press (Finland) *Tel:* (02) 215 3292 *Fax:* (02) 215 4490 *E-mail:* forlaget@abo.fi *Web Site:* www.abo.fi/stiftelsen/forlag, pg 141

Aboriginal Studies Press (Australia) *Tel:* (02) 6246 1226 *Fax:* (02) 6261 4285 *E-mail:* sales@aiatsis.gov.au *Web Site:* www.aiatsis.gov.au, pg 10

Editorial Abril SA (Argentina) *Tel:* (011) 3752450; (011) 3752451, pg 2

Abril SA (Brazil) *Tel:* (011) 877-1190 *Fax:* (011) 877-1640 *Web Site:* abril.com.br, pg 76

Absolute Press (United Kingdom) *Tel:* (01225) 316 013 *Fax:* (01225) 445 836 *E-mail:* info@absolutepress.co.uk *Web Site:* www.absolutepress.co.uk, pg 655

Absolutt Krim (Norway) *Tel:* 24051000 *Fax:* 24051099 *E-mail:* post@damm.no *Web Site:* www.dammbokklubb.no, pg 1254

Ediciones Abya-Yala (Ecuador) *Tel:* (02) 2506251; (02) 2506247 *Fax:* (02) 2506255 *E-mail:* editorial@abyayala.org *Web Site:* www.abyayala.org, pg 136

Yr Academi Gymreig (United Kingdom) *Tel:* (029) 20472266 *Fax:* (029) 20492930 *E-mail:* post@academi.org *Web Site:* www.academi.org, pg 1406

Academia (Czech Republic) *Tel:* (02) 24 941 976 *Fax:* (02) 24 212 582 *E-mail:* academia@academia.cz *Web Site:* www.academia.cz, pg 122

Academia (Lithuania) *Tel:* (02) 626851 *Fax:* (02) 226351, pg 448

Academia Amazonense de Letras (Brazil) *Tel:* (092) 234-0584, pg 1397

Academia Argentina de Letras (Argentina) *Tel:* (011) 4802-3814; (011) 4802-7509; (011) 4802-5161 *Fax:* (011) 4-8028340 *E-mail:* aaldespa@fibertel.com.ar; aaladmin@fibertel.com.ar; aalbibl@fibertel.com.ar, pg 2

Academia Argentina de Letras (Argentina) *Tel:* (011) 4802-3814; (011) 4802-5161; (011) 4802-7509 *Fax:* (011) 4802-8340 *E-mail:* aaldespa@fibertel.com.ar; aaladmin@fibertel.com.ar; aalbibl@fibertel.com.ar *Web Site:* www.aal.universia.com.ar/aal, pg 1395

Academia Brasileira de Letras (Brazil) *Tel:* (021) 220-5391 *Fax:* (021) 220-6695 *E-mail:* academia@academia.org.br *Web Site:* www.academia.org.br, pg 1397

Academia-Bruylant (Belgium) *Tel:* (010) 45 23 95 *Fax:* (010) 45 44 80 *E-mail:* academia.bruylant@skynet.be *Web Site:* www.academia-bruylant.be, pg 62

Academia Catarinense de Letras (Brazil) *Tel:* 2342166 *Web Site:* www.acle.com.br, pg 1397

Academia Cearense de Letras (Brazil) *Tel:* (085) 2315669 *E-mail:* acletras@accvia.com.br *Web Site:* www.secrel.com.br, pg 1397

Academia das Ciencias de Lisboa (Portugal) *Tel:* (021) 346-3866 *Fax:* (021) 342-0395, pg 528

Biblioteca da Academia das Ciencias de Lisboa (Portugal) *Tel:* (021) 321 97 31; (021) 321 97 41 *Fax:* (021) 342 03 95 *E-mail:* biblioteca@acad-ciencias.pt *Web Site:* www.acad-ciencias.pt, pg 1538

Academia de Centro America (Costa Rica) *Tel:* 283-1847 *Fax:* 283-1848 *E-mail:* info@academiaca.or.cr; rherrera@acedmiaca.or.cr, pg 114

Academia de la Llingua Asturiana (Spain) *Tel:* (0985) 211837 *Fax:* (0985) 226816 *E-mail:* alla@asturnet.es *Web Site:* www.asturnet.es/alla, pg 570

Academia de Letras da Bahia (Brazil) *Tel:* (071) 321-4308 *Fax:* (071) 321-4308 *E-mail:* alb@stn.com.br, pg 1397

Academia de Letras de Piaui (Brazil), pg 1397

Academia de Studii Economice, Biblioteca Centrala (Romania) *Tel:* (01) 211 26 50; (01) 211 26 55 *Fax:* (01) 312 95 49 *Web Site:* www.aseciti.ase.ro, pg 1539

Academia Ecuatoriana de la Lengua (Ecuador) *Tel:* (02) 2901518 *Fax:* (02) 2543234, pg 1398

Academia Mineira de Letras (Brazil) *Tel:* (031) 3222-5764 *E-mail:* amletras@task.com.br *Web Site:* www.academiamineiradeletras.org.br, pg 1397

Academia Nacional de la Historia (Venezuela) *Tel:* (02) 481-34-13; (02) 483-94-35; (02) 482-67-20; (02) 486720 *Fax:* (02) 481-75-47 *E-mail:* anhistoria@cantv.net, pg 778

Academia Nacional de Letras (Uruguay) *Tel:* (02) 9152374 *Fax:* (02) 9167460 *E-mail:* academia@montevideo.com.uy, pg 1410

Academia Nicaraguense de la Lengua (Nicaragua), pg 502

Academia Paraibana de Letras (Brazil) *E-mail:* fsatiro@openline.com.br *Web Site:* www.pbnet.com.br/openline/fsatiro/academia.html, pg 1397

Academia Paulista de Letras (Brazil) *Tel:* (011) 3331-7222 *Fax:* (011) 3331-7401 *E-mail:* acadsp@terra.com.br *Web Site:* www.academiapaulistadeletras.org.br, pg 1397

Academia Pernambucana de Letras (Brazil) *Tel:* (081) 3268-2211, pg 1397

Academia Press (Belgium) *Tel:* (09) 233.80.88 *Fax:* (09) 233.14.09 *E-mail:* info@academiapress.be *Web Site:* www.academiapress.be, pg 62

Academia Publications P Ltd (Malaysia) *Tel:* (03) 572455, pg 455

Academia Scientific Book Inc (Japan) *Tel:* (03) 3819805 *Fax:* (03) 38128509, pg 1321

Academic & General Bookshop (Australia) *Tel:* (03) 96633231 *Fax:* (03) 96637234 *E-mail:* info@academicbooks.com.au, pg 1297

Academic Book Corporation (India) *Tel:* (0522) 418421; (0522) 416584 *Fax:* (0522) 22061; (0522) 210376, pg 327

Academic Books (Pvt) Ltd (Zimbabwe) *Tel:* (04) 755034; (04) 754224 *Fax:* (04) 781913, pg 782

Academic Library of Tallinn Pedagogical University (Estonia) *Tel:* (02) 6659 401 *Fax:* (02) 6659 400 *E-mail:* ear@ear.ee *Web Site:* www.ear.ee, pg 139

The Academic Press (India) *Tel:* (0124) 6322779; (0124) 6322005 *Fax:* (0124) 6324782 *E-mail:* indoc@indiatimes.com, pg 327

Academic Publishers (Bangladesh) *Tel:* (02) 507355; (02) 507366 *Fax:* (02) 863060, pg 61

Academic Publishers (India) *Tel:* (033) 241-4857 *Fax:* (033) 241-3702 *E-mail:* acabooks@cal.vsnl.net.in, pg 327

Academie Goncourte, Societe de gens de Lettres (France), pg 1399

Academie Nationale de Reims (France) *Tel:* (0326) 910449 *Fax:* (0326) 910449 *E-mail:* academie.nationale.reims@wanadoo.fr, pg 145

Academie Royale de Langue et de Litterature Francaises (Belgium) *Tel:* (02) 550-2277 *Fax:* (02) 550-2275, pg 1396

Academie Royale des Sciences, des Lettres et des Beaux-Arts de Belgique (Belgium) *Tel:* (02) 5502211; (02) 5502212; (02) 5502213 *Fax:* (02) 5502205 *Web Site:* www.cfwb.be/arb, pg 1396

Academie Tunisienne des Sciences, des Lettres et des Arts Beit El Hekma (Tunisia) *Tel:* (71) 277 275; (71) 731 696; (71) 731 824 *Fax:* (71) 731 204, pg 647

Editura Academiei Romane (Romania) *Tel:* (0410) 411 90 08; (0410) 410 32 00 *Fax:* (0410) 410 39 83 *E-mail:* edacad@ear.ro *Web Site:* www.ear.ro, pg 538

Academon Publishing House (Israel) *Tel:* (02) 5882163 *Fax:* (02) 5815558, pg 364

Academon Publishing House (Israel) *Tel:* (02) 5882163 *Fax:* (02) 5815558 *Web Site:* www.academon.co.il, pg 1319

Academy of Education Planning & Management (AEPAM) (Pakistan) *Tel:* (051) 926-1096 *Fax:* (051) 926-1353; (051) 926-1359 *E-mail:* webinfo@aepam.gov.pk *Web Site:* www.aepam.gov.pk, pg 511

Academy of the Hebrew Language (Israel) *Tel:* (02) 6493555 *Fax:* (02) 5617065 *E-mail:* acad2u@vms.huji.ac.il *Web Site:* hebrew-academy.huji.ac.il, pg 364

Fundamental Library of the Academy of Medical Sciences (Russian Federation) *Tel:* (095) 155-17-93, pg 1540

Academy Science Publishers (Kenya) *Tel:* (020) 884401; (020) 884405 *Fax:* (020) 884406 *E-mail:* aas@africaonline.co.ke; asp@africaonline.co.ke *Web Site:* www.aasciences.org, pg 432

Academy of Sciences Publishing House (Democratic People's Republic of Korea) *Tel:* (02) 51956, pg 436

Acair Ltd (United Kingdom) *Tel:* (01851) 703 020 *Fax:* (07880) 725 320 *E-mail:* enquiries@acairbooks.com *Web Site:* www.acairbooks.com, pg 655

Acantilado (Spain) *Tel:* (093) 4144906 *Fax:* (093) 4147107 *E-mail:* correo@elacantilado.com *Web Site:* www.elacantilado.com, pg 570

Editorial Acanto SA (Spain) *Tel:* (093) 4189093 *Fax:* (093) 4189088 *E-mail:* acantocb@dtinf.net, pg 570

Accademia (Milano) (Italy) *Tel:* (02) 2552593, pg 374

Libreria All'Accademia di Randi Lorenzo & Elena snc (Italy) *Tel:* (049) 8760306 *Fax:* (049) 8751825 *E-mail:* libreria@libreriadraghi.it, pg 1320

Accademia Nazionale di Scienze Lettere e Arti Modena (Italy) *Tel:* (059) 225566 *Fax:* (059) 225566 *E-mail:* info@accademiasla-mo.it *Web Site:* www.accademiasla-mo.it, pg 1402

Accademia Nazionale Virgiliana di Scienze, Lettere e Arti (Italy) *Tel:* (0376) 320314 *Fax:* (0376) 222774 *Web Site:* www.accademiavirgiliana.it/index.htm, pg 1402

Accademia Petrarca di Lettere, Arti e Scienze (Italy) *Tel:* (0575) 24700 *Fax:* (0575) 298846 *Web Site:* www.accademiapetrarca.it, pg 1402

Accedo Verlagsgesellschaft mbH (Germany) *Tel:* (089) 935714 *Fax:* (089) 9294109 *E-mail:* accedoverlag@web.de *Web Site:* www.accedoverlag.de, pg 190

Access International Services (Morocco) *Tel:* (02) 316068 *Fax:* (02) 304685, pg 474

Access Press (Australia) *Tel:* (08) 9379 3188 *Fax:* (08) 9379 3199, pg 10

Uitgeverij Acco (Belgium) *Tel:* (016) 62 80 41 *Fax:* (016) 62 80 01 *E-mail:* uitgeverij@acco.be *Web Site:* www.acco.be, pg 62

Uitgeverij Acco (Belgium) *Tel:* (016) 29 11 00 *Fax:* (016) 20 73 89 *E-mail:* papierhandel@acco.be *Web Site:* www.acco.be, pg 1301

Acento Editorial (Spain) *Tel:* (091) 5088996; (091) 5085145; (091) 4228976 *Fax:* (091) 5089927; (091) 5084974 *E-mail:* informa@acento-editorial.com, pg 570

ACER Agencia Literaria (Spain) *Tel:* (091) 3692061 *Fax:* (091) 3692052, pg 1136

ACER Press (Australia) *Tel:* (03) 9277 5555; (03) 9835 7447 (customer service) *Toll Free Tel:* (800) 338 402 (customer service) *Fax:* (03) 9277 5500; (02) 9835 7499 (customer service) *E-mail:* sales@acer.edu.au *Web Site:* www.acer.edu.au, pg 10

Editorial Acervo SL (Spain) *Tel:* (093) 2122664 *Fax:* (093) 4174425 *E-mail:* acervo25@hotmail.com, pg 570

Ach Publishing House (Israel) *Tel:* (04) 8727227 *Fax:* (04) 8417839, pg 364

Achiasaf Publishing House Ltd (Israel) *Tel:* (09) 8851390 *Fax:* (09) 8851391 *E-mail:* info@achiasaf.co.il *Web Site:* www.achiasaf.co.il, pg 364

Achiever (Israel) *Tel:* (02) 6253627 *Fax:* (02) 6255740, pg 364

ACHPER Inc (Australian Council for Health, Physical Education & Recreation) (Australia) *Tel:* (08) 8340 3388 *Fax:* (08) 8340 3399 *E-mail:* achper@achper.org.au *Web Site:* www.achper.org.au, pg 10

Achterbahn AG Buch (Germany) *Tel:* (0431) 7028-200 *Fax:* (0431) 7028-228 *E-mail:* info@achterbahn.de *Web Site:* www.achterbahn.de, pg 190

ACI International Ltd (Australia) *Tel:* (03) 6058555, pg 1153

Joh van Acken GmbH & Co KG (Germany) *Tel:* (02151) 44 00-0 *Fax:* (02151) 44 00-11 *E-mail:* verlag@vanacken.de *Web Site:* www.spendengrusskarten.de/willkommen.html, pg 190

F A Ackermanns Kunstverlag GmbH (Germany) *Tel:* (089) 78580826 *Fax:* (089) 78580828 *E-mail:* info@ackermann-kalender.de *Web Site:* www.ackermann-kalender.de, pg 190

Editions ACLA (France) *Tel:* (01) 48 04 00 75 *Fax:* (01) 42 77 72 98, pg 145

Editorial Acme SA (Argentina) *Tel:* (011) 4328-1508; (011) 4328-1662 *Fax:* (011) 4328-9345 *E-mail:* acme@redynet.com.ar, pg 3

Aconcagua Ediciones y Publicaciones SA (Mexico) *Tel:* (05) 536-1660 *Fax:* (05) 5432280, pg 461

Acorn Books (South Africa) *Tel:* (011) 8805768 *Fax:* (011) 8805768 *E-mail:* acorbook@iafrica.com, pg 562

ACP Publishing Pty Ltd (Australia) *Tel:* (02) 9282 8000 *Fax:* (02) 9267 4361 *Web Site:* www.acp.com.au, pg 10

ACR Edition (France) *Tel:* (01) 47 88 14 92 *Fax:* (01) 43 33 38 81 *E-mail:* acredition@acr-edition.com *Web Site:* www.acr-edition.com, pg 145

Editorial Acribia SA (Spain) *Tel:* (0976) 232089 *Fax:* (0976) 219212 *E-mail:* acribia@infornet.es *Web Site:* www.editorialacribia.com, pg 571

Act 3 Publishing (United Kingdom) *Tel:* (020) 7402 5321, pg 655

Acta Universitatis Gothoburgensis (Sweden) *Tel:* (031) 7731000 *Fax:* (031) 163797 *E-mail:* library@ub.gu.se *Web Site:* www.ub.gu.se, pg 609

Actes-Graphiques (France) *Tel:* (04) 77 21 23 80; (06) 09 42 21 13 *Fax:* (04) 77 25 39 28 *Web Site:* www.actes-graphiques.com, pg 145

Editions Actes Sud (France) *Tel:* (04) 90 49 86 91 *Fax:* (04) 90 96 95 25 *E-mail:* contact@actes-sud.fr *Web Site:* www.actes-sud.fr, pg 145

Actinic Press Ltd (United Kingdom) *Tel:* (01684) 540154 *Fax:* (01684) 540154, pg 655

Action Artistique de la Ville de Paris (France) *Tel:* (01) 43 25 30 30 *Fax:* (01) 43 25 17 69 *E-mail:* aavp@club-internet.fr, pg 145

Action Editora Ltda (Brazil) *Tel:* (021) 3325-7229 *Fax:* (021) 3325-7229 *Web Site:* www.editora.com.br, pg 76

Action Magazine (Zimbabwe) *Tel:* (04) 747217 *Fax:* (04) 747409 *E-mail:* action@action.co.zw *Web Site:* www.action.co.zw, pg 782

Action Publications (Cyprus) *Tel:* (022) 818884 *Fax:* (022) 873634, pg 121

Action Publishers (Kenya) *Tel:* (020) 608-810 *Fax:* (020) 753-227 *E-mail:* actonpublishersinfo@acton.co.ke *Web Site:* www.acton.co.ke, pg 433

Actualquarto (Belgium) *Tel:* (071) 21 61 53 *Fax:* (071) 21 77 13, pg 63

Libreria Acuario SA de CV (Mexico) *Tel:* (05) 5742966; (05) 5741137 *Fax:* (05) 2642882, pg 1327

ACUM Ltd (Society of Authors, Composers & Music Publishers in Israel) (Israel) *Tel:* (03) 6113400 *Fax:* (03) 6122629 *E-mail:* info@acum.org.il *Web Site:* www.acum.org.il, pg 1401

Acumen Publishing Ltd (United Kingdom) *Tel:* (01494) 794398 *Fax:* (01494) 784850 *Web Site:* www.acumenpublishing.co.uk, pg 655

ACURIL (Puerto Rico) *Tel:* (787) 790-8054; (787) 764-0000 (ext 3319) *Fax:* (787) 764-2311 *E-mail:* acuril@rrpac.upr.clu.edu; acuril@coqui.net *Web Site:* acuril.rrp.upr.edu, pg 1282

Editions Ad Solem (Switzerland) *Tel:* (022) 321 19 30 *Fax:* (022) 321 19 31 *E-mail:* office@adsolem.ch *Web Site:* www.ad-solem.com, pg 617

ADA Edita Tokyo Co Ltd (Japan) *Tel:* (03) 3403-1581 *Fax:* (03) 3497-0649 *E-mail:* info@ga-ada.co.jp *Web Site:* www.ga-ada.co.jp, pg 415

Ada Korn Editora SA (Argentina) *Tel:* (011) 4374-6199 *Fax:* (011) 4374-9699 *E-mail:* adakorn@datamarkets.com.ar, pg 3

Ada Press Publishers (Turkey) *Tel:* (0212) 249 35 45, pg 648

Adaex Educational Publications Ltd (Ghana) *Tel:* (024) 367145 *E-mail:* epublication@yahoo.com, pg 302

ADAGP (Societe des Auteurs dans les Arts Grarphiques et Plastiques) (France) *Tel:* (01) 43590979 *Fax:* (01) 45634489 *E-mail:* adagp@adagp.fr *Web Site:* www.adagp.fr, pg 1266

Adalbert Stifter Verein eV (Germany) *Tel:* (089) 4489807 *Fax:* (089) 4891148 *E-mail:* asv.@asv-muen.de *Web Site:* www.asv-muen.de, pg 1400

Adamantine Press Ltd (United Kingdom), pg 655

Centro de Estudios Adams-Ediciones Valbuena SA (Spain) *Tel:* (093) 4465000; (0902) 333 543 *Fax:* (093) 4465004 *E-mail:* info@adams.es *Web Site:* www.adams.es, pg 571

Mario Adda Editore SNC (Italy) *Tel:* (080) 5539502 *Fax:* (080) 5539502 *E-mail:* info@addaeditore.it *Web Site:* www.addaeditore.it, pg 374

Addis Ababa University Press (Ethiopia) *Tel:* (01) 239746; (01) 239800 (ext 227) *Fax:* (01) 239729 *E-mail:* aau.pres@telecom.net.et, pg 140

Addis Adaba University Library (Ethiopia) *Tel:* (01) 115673; (01) 550844 *Fax:* (01) 550655, pg 1504

Addison-Wesley Pte Ltd (India) *Tel:* (011) 214 6067 *Fax:* (011) 214 6071 *E-mail:* info@pearsoned.co.in *Web Site:* www.pearsonedindia.com, pg 327

Adea Edizioni (Italy) *Tel:* (0372) 430402 *Fax:* (0372) 43363 *E-mail:* info@adea.it *Web Site:* www.adea.it/edizioni.html, pg 374

Adebara Publishers Ltd (Nigeria), pg 503

Adelphi Edizioni SpA (Italy) *Tel:* (02) 725731 *Fax:* (02) 89010337 *E-mail:* info@adelphi.it *Web Site:* www.adelphi.it, pg 374

ADEVA (Akademische Druck-u Verlagsanstalt) (Austria) *Tel:* (0316) 3644 *Fax:* (0316) 364424 *E-mail:* info@adeva.com *Web Site:* www.adeva.com, pg 1153, 1175, 1215

Adeyle Brothers & Co (Bangladesh) *Tel:* (02) 233508, pg 61, 1301

ADIRA (Switzerland) *Tel:* (022) 312 25 43 *Fax:* (022) 312 26 13 *E-mail:* adira@adira.net *Web Site:* www.adira.net, pg 617

Adivinar y Multiplicar, SA de CV (Mexico) *Tel:* (055) 5604-1005; (055) 1304-0802 (mobile) *Fax:* (055) 5604-1583 *E-mail:* multiplimx@msn.com, pg 461

Deborah Adlam (United Kingdom) *Tel:* (0131) 6676048, pg 1149

Adlard Coles Nautical (United Kingdom) *Tel:* (020) 7758 0200 *Fax:* (020) 7758 0222 *E-mail:* acn@acblack.com *Web Site:* www.adlardcoles.com, pg 655

ADMICAL (Association pour le Developpement du Mecenat Industriel et Commercial) (France) *Tel:* (01) 42552001 *Fax:* (01) 42557132 *E-mail:* contact@admical.org *Web Site:* www.admical.org, pg 1267

Adobe Systems GmbH (Germany) *Tel:* (089) 31 70 50 *Fax:* (089) 31 70 5705 *Web Site:* www.adobe.de, pg 1155

Adonia-Verlag (Switzerland) *Tel:* (01) 7207712 *Fax:* (01) 9800622 *Web Site:* www.libroplus.ch, pg 617

ADPF Publications (France) *Tel:* (01) 43 13 11 00 *Fax:* (01) 43 13 11 25 *Web Site:* www.france.diplomatie.fr; www.adpf.asso.fr, pg 145

ADR/BookPrint Inc (United States) *Tel:* 316-522-5599 *Toll Free Tel:* 800-767-6066 *Fax:* 316-522-5445 *E-mail:* info@adrbookprint.com *Web Site:* www.adrbookprint.com, pg 1165, 1186, 1228

Adrian (France) *Tel:* (01) 42 36 44 29 *Fax:* (01) 42 36 44 29, pg 145

Adriatica (Peru) *Tel:* (044) 291569 *Fax:* (044) 294242 *E-mail:* libreria@adriaticaperu.com *Web Site:* www.adriaticaperu.com, pg 1334

Adroit Birmingham Ltd (United Kingdom) *Tel:* (0121) 3596831 *Fax:* (0121) 3593974, pg 1182

Adsale Publishing Co Ltd (Hong Kong) *Tel:* 2811 8897 *Fax:* 2516 5024 *E-mail:* publicity@adsale.com.hk *Web Site:* www.adsale.com.hk, pg 315

Advaita Ashrama (India) *Tel:* (033) 22440898; (033) 22452383; (033) 22164000 *Fax:* (033) 22450050 *E-mail:* advaita@vsnl.com *Web Site:* www.advaitaonline.com, pg 327

The Advancement Centre (Australia) *Tel:* (02) 9896 2311 *Fax:* (02) 9368 323, pg 11

Advent Indonesia Publishing (Indonesia) *Tel:* (022) 630392; (022) 642006 *Fax:* (022) 630588, pg 353

Advent Kiado (Hungary) *Tel:* (01) 256-5205 *Fax:* (01) 2565205 *E-mail:* advent12@matavnet.hu, pg 320

The Advent Press (Ghana) *Tel:* (021) 777861; (021) 775327 *Fax:* (021) 774338; (021) 2119, pg 303

Adverbum SARL (France) *Tel:* (04) 92 81 28 81 *Fax:* (04) 92 81 37 11 *E-mail:* info@adverbum.fr *Web Site:* www.adverbum.fr, pg 146

Advisory Unit: Computers in Education (United Kingdom) *Tel:* (01707) 266714 *Fax:* (01707) 273684 *E-mail:* sales@advisory-unit.org.uk *Web Site:* www.advisory-unit.org.uk, pg 655

Adwinsa Publications (Ghana) Ltd (Ghana) *Tel:* (021) 221654; (021) 21577, pg 303

AE Expaideftikon Vivlion Kai Diskon (Greece) *Tel:* (010) 7239474 *Fax:* (010) 7239483, pg 305

AE Technical Translation Services (United Kingdom) *Tel:* (01286) 650667; (01286) 650555 *Fax:* (01286) 650500, pg 1149

Editorial AEDOS SA (Spain) *Tel:* (093) 488 34 92 *Fax:* (093) 487 76 59 *Web Site:* www.mundiprensa.es, pg 571

Aeneas Verlagsgesellschaft GmbH (Austria) *Tel:* (02236) 25422, pg 48

AENOR (Asociacion Espanola de Normalizacion y Certificacion) (Spain) *Tel:* (091) 4 32 60 00; (0902) 102 201 *Fax:* (091) 913 10 36 95 *E-mail:* info@aenor.es *Web Site:* www.aenor.es, pg 571

Aeolian Press (Australia) *Tel:* (08) 9761 2772 *Fax:* (08) 9761 4151, pg 11

Centre Aequatoria (Belgium) *Tel:* (016) 46 44 84 *E-mail:* info@abbol.com *Web Site:* www.aequatoria.be; www.abbol.com, pg 63

Aerogie-Verlag (Germany) *Tel:* (030) 6 76 32 00 *Fax:* (030) 6 76 32 00, pg 191

Aerospace Publications Pty Ltd (Australia) *Tel:* (02) 6280 0111 *Fax:* (02) 6280 0007 *E-mail:* mail@ausaviation.com.au *Web Site:* www.ausaviation.com.au, pg 11

AEskan (Iceland) *Tel:* 551-0248, pg 325

Aesthetica (Italy) *Tel:* (091) 308290 *Fax:* (091) 308290 *E-mail:* aesthetica@unipa.it, pg 374

Afa Yayincilik Sanayi Tic AS (Turkey) *Tel:* (0212) 276 27 67 *Fax:* (0212) 2444362, pg 648

Editorial Afers, SL (Spain) *Tel:* (0961) 26 86 54 *Fax:* (0961) 27 25 82 *E-mail:* afers@provicom.com *Web Site:* www.provicom.com/afers, pg 571

Affiliated East West Press Pvt Ltd (India) *Tel:* (011) 23315398; (011) 23279113; (011) 23264180 *Fax:* (011) 23260538 *E-mail:* aewp.newdel@axcess.net.in; affiliat@vsnl.com, pg 327

Affiliated East West Press Pvt Ltd (India) *Tel:* (011) 23279113; (011) 23264180 *Fax:* (011) 23260538 *E-mail:* affiliat@vsnl.com, pg 1315

Affonso & Reichmann Editores Associados (Brazil) *Tel:* (021) 507-1270 *Fax:* (021) 507-1270, pg 77

A4 Publications Ltd (United Kingdom) *Tel:* (01384) 440591 *Fax:* (01384) 440582, pg 656

Afram Publications (Ghana) Ltd (Ghana) *Tel:* (021) 412561; (021) 406060 *E-mail:* aframpub@punchgh.com, pg 303

Africa Book Centre (United Kingdom) *Tel:* (020) 7240 6649 *Toll Free Tel:* 0845 458 1581 (UK only) *Fax:* (020) 7497 0309 *Toll Free Fax:* 0845 458 1579 (UK only) *E-mail:* orders@africabookcentre.com; info@africabookcentre.com *Web Site:* www.africabookcentre.com, pg 1346

Africa Book Services (EA) Ltd (Kenya) *Tel:* (020) 223641 *Fax:* (020) 330272 *E-mail:* abs@mref.co.ke, pg 433

Africa Christian Press (Ghana) *Tel:* (021) 244147; (021) 244148 *Fax:* (021) 220271; (021) 668115 *E-mail:* acpbooks@ghana.com, pg 303

Africa Literatura Arte Cultura - ALAC (Portugal) *Tel:* (021) 4192274, pg 528

Books for Africa Publishing House (Zimbabwe) *Tel:* (04) 794329 *Fax:* (04) 61881, pg 782

Nouvelles Editions Africaines du Senegal (NEAS) (Senegal) *Tel:* 8211381; 8221580 *Fax:* 8223604, pg 551

African Association for Literacy & Adult Education (AALAE) (Kenya) *Tel:* (02) 222-391; (02) 331-512 *Fax:* (02) 340-849, pg 433

African Books Collective Ltd (United Kingdom) *Tel:* (01865) 726686 *Fax:* (01865) 793298 *E-mail:* abc@africanbookscollective.com *Web Site:* www.africanbookscollective.com, pg 1289

African Books Collective Ltd (United Kingdom) *Tel:* (01865) 726686 *Fax:* (01865) 793298; (01993) 709265 *E-mail:* abc@africanbookscollective.com *Web Site:* www.africanbookscollective.com, pg 1346

African Centre for Technology Studies (ACTS) (Kenya) *Tel:* (02) 524700; (02) 524000 *Fax:* (02) 524701; (02) 524001 *E-mail:* acts@cgiar.org *Web Site:* www.acts.or.ke, pg 433

African Council for Communication Education (Kenya) *Tel:* (020) 215270-33424 (ext 2068, 2328); (020) 227043 *Fax:* (020) 216135; (020) 750329; (020) 229168 *E-mail:* acceb@arcc.or.ke; acceb@form-net.com, pg 433

African Cultural Centre (Mauritius) *Tel:* 2124131 *Fax:* 2088620, pg 461

The African Literature Club (Germany) *Tel:* (06221) 411861 *Fax:* (06221) 411861, pg 191

African Publishers' Network (APNET) (Zimbabwe) *Tel:* (04) 20211801; (04) 20211802 *Fax:* (04) 20211803 *E-mail:* apnetes@yahoo.com *Web Site:* www.freewebs.com/africanpublishers, pg 1295

African Union Library (Ethiopia) *Tel:* (01) 51 77 00 *Fax:* (01) 51 78 44 *Web Site:* www.africa-union.org, pg 1504

African Universities Press (Nigeria) *Tel:* (022) 317218, pg 503

Africana-FEP Publishers Ltd (Nigeria) *Tel:* (046) 210669, pg 503

Afro-Asian Book Council (AABC) (India) *Tel:* (011) 3261487 *Fax:* (011) 3267437 *E-mail:* sdas@ubspd.com, pg 1273

Edicoes Afrontamento (Portugal) *Tel:* (02) 507 42 20 *Fax:* (02) 507 42 29 *E-mail:* afrontamento@mail.telepac.pt, pg 528

Afterhurst Ltd (United Kingdom) *Tel:* (01256) 813000 *Fax:* (01256) 479438 *E-mail:* book.orders@tandf.co.uk, pg 1346

Agalma Psicanalise Editora Ltda (Brazil) *Tel:* (071) 332-8776 *Fax:* (071) 245-7883 *E-mail:* pedidos@agalma.com.br *Web Site:* www.agalma.com.br, pg 77

Agam Kala Prakashan (India) *Tel:* (011) 713395 *Fax:* (011) 7401485, pg 327

AGAPE (Serbia and Montenegro) *Tel:* (021) 469-474 *Fax:* (021) 469-382 *E-mail:* agape@eunet.yu *Web Site:* www.agape.yu, pg 552

Agape Ferences Nyomda es Konyvkiado Kft (Hungary) *Tel:* (062) 444-002; (062) 323-002 *Fax:* (062) 442-592 *E-mail:* agape@tiszanet.hu, pg 320

Editorial AGATA SA de CV (Mexico) *Tel:* (033) 614-4902; (03) 614-4909 *Fax:* (033) 6138429, pg 462

Age Concern Books (United Kingdom) *Tel:* (020) 8765 7200 *Fax:* (020) 8765 7211 *E-mail:* infodep@ace.org.uk *Web Site:* www.ageconcern.org.uk, pg 656

Editions L'Age d'Homme - La Cite (Switzerland) *Tel:* (021) 312 00 95 *Fax:* (021) 320 84 40 *E-mail:* agedhomme@iprolink.ch, pg 617

Agence Bibliographique de l'Enseignement Superieur (France) *Tel:* (04) 67 54 84 10 *Fax:* (04) 67 54 84 14 *E-mail:* nom@abes.fr *Web Site:* www.abes.fr, pg 146

Agence de Distribution de Presse (Senegal) *Tel:* (08) 320278 *Fax:* (08) 324915 *E-mail:* adpresse@telecomplus.sn, pg 551

Agence de l'Est (France) *Tel:* (01) 46334816; (06) 6546 7928 *Fax:* (01) 46334816 *E-mail:* agencedelest1@wanadoo.fr, pg 1130

Agence et Menageries de la Prense (Belgium) *Tel:* (02) 52 51 641 *Fax:* (02) 52 34 863, pg 1301

Agence Francophone pour la Numerotation Internationale du Livre (AFNIL) (France) *Tel:* (01) 44 41 29 19 *Fax:* (01) 44 41 29 03 *E-mail:* afnil@electre.com *Web Site:* www.afnil.org; www.afnil.com, pg 1267

Agence Hoffman (Germany) *Tel:* (089) 3084807; (089) 3087469 *Fax:* (089) 3082108 *E-mail:* info@agencehoffman.de *Web Site:* www.agencehoffman.de, pg 1131

Agence Marocaine de l'ISBN (Morocco) *Tel:* (07) 771 890; (07) 772 152 *Fax:* (07) 776 062 *E-mail:* biblio1@onpt.net.ma, pg 1278

Agence Tunisienne de l'ISBN (Tunisia) *Tel:* (071) 57 2706 *Fax:* (071) 57 2887 *E-mail:* bibliotheque.nationale@email.ati.tn *Web Site:* www.bibliotheque.nat.tn, pg 1288

Agencia Brasileira do ISBN (Brazil) *Tel:* (021) 2220-9367 *Fax:* (021) 2220-4173 *E-mail:* isbn@bn.br *Web Site:* www.bn.br, pg 1263

Agencia Colombiana del ISBN, Camara Columbiana del Libro (Colombia) *Tel:* (01) 288-6188 *Fax:* (01) 287-3320 *E-mail:* agenciaisbn@camlibro.com.co *Web Site:* www.camlibro.com.co, pg 1264

Agencia Espanola de Cooperacion (Spain) *Tel:* (091) 5838100; (091) 5838254; (091) 5838101; (091) 5838102 *Fax:* (091) 5838310; (091) 5838311; (091) 5838313, pg 571

Biblioteca de la Agencia Espanola de Cooperacion Internacional (Spain) *Tel:* (091) 5838175 *Fax:* (091) 5838525 *E-mail:* biblioteca.hispanica@aeci.es *Web Site:* www.aeci.es, pg 1545

Agencia Espanola del ISBN (Spain) *Tel:* (091) 536 88 00 *Fax:* (091) 553 99 90 *Web Site:* www.mcu.es/bases/spa/isbn/ISBN.html, pg 1284

Agencia General de Libreria Internacional SL (AGLI) (Spain) *Tel:* (091) 373 66 40 *Fax:* (091) 373 27 40 *E-mail:* agli@senda.ari.es, pg 1341

Agencija Za Ikonomicesko Programirane i Razvitie (Bulgaria) *Tel:* (02) 9816597 *Fax:* (02) 466110 *E-mail:* aecd@sf.cit.bg, pg 93

The Agency (London) Ltd (United Kingdom) *Tel:* (020) 7727 1346 *Fax:* (020) 7727 9037 *E-mail:* info@theagency.co.uk *Web Site:* www.writersservices.com/wrhandbook/agency_london.htm, pg 1138

Agens-Werk, Geyer & Reisser, Druck und Verlagsgesellschaft mbH (Austria) *Tel:* (01) 5445641-46 *Fax:* (01) 5445641-46 *E-mail:* prepress@agens-werk.at, pg 48

Agentur des Rauhen Hauses Hamburg GmbH (Germany) *Tel:* (040) 53 53 88-0 *Fax:* (040) 53 53 88-43 *E-mail:* kundenservice@agentur-rauhes-haus.de *Web Site:* www.agentur-rauhes-haus.de, pg 191

Agenzia ISBN per l'Area di Lingua Italiana (Italy) *Tel:* (02) 28315996 *Fax:* (02) 28315906 *E-mail:* bibliografica@bibliografica.it *Web Site:* www.aie.it/ISBN/intro.asp, pg 1274

Agenzia Letteraria Internazionale (Italy) *Tel:* (02) 865445; (02) 861572 *Fax:* (02) 876222 *E-mail:* alidmb@tin.it, pg 1133

Agertofts Forlag A/S (Denmark) *Tel:* 4615 1248 *Fax:* 4615 2404, pg 128

AGIR S/A Editora (Brazil) *Tel:* (021) 221-6424 *Fax:* (021) 252-0410 *E-mail:* info@agireditora.com.br *Web Site:* www.visualnet.com.br/cmaya/cm-ft-01.htm, pg 77

AGIS Verlag GmbH (Germany) *Tel:* (07221) 95 75-0 *Fax:* (07221) 6 68 10 *E-mail:* info@agis-verlag.de *Web Site:* www.agis-verlag.de, pg 191

AGM doo (Croatia) *Tel:* (01) 4856309; (01) 4856307 *Fax:* (01) 4856316 *E-mail:* agm@agm.hr *Web Site:* www.agm.hr, pg 117

Edizioni della Fondazione Giovanni Agnelli (Italy) *Tel:* (011) 6500500 *Fax:* (011) 6502777 *E-mail:* staff@fga.it *Web Site:* www.fondazione-agnelli.it, pg 374

Agni Publishing House (Russian Federation) *Tel:* (08462) 70-32-87; (08462) 70-23-87 (ext 445 - Orders) *Fax:* (08462) 70-23-85 *E-mail:* cdk@transit.samara.ru; support@agniart.ru (distribution & ordering) *Web Site:* www.agni.samara.ru, pg 543

Uitgeversmaatschappij Agon B V (Netherlands) *Tel:* (020) 521 97 77 *Fax:* (020) 622 49 37 *E-mail:* info@boekboek.nl *Web Site:* www.boekboek.nl, pg 477

Agora bvba (Belgium) *Tel:* (053) 78-87-00 *Fax:* (053) 78-26-91 *E-mail:* info@agorabooks.com *Web Site:* www.agorabooks.com, pg 1301

Agora Editorial (Spain) *Tel:* (095) 2228699; (095) 2221847 *Fax:* (095) 2226411, pg 571

Editora Agora Ltda (Brazil) *Tel:* (011) 38723322 *Fax:* (011) 38727476 *E-mail:* agora@editoraagora.com.br *Web Site:* www.gruposummus.com.br/agora, pg 77

De Agostini Scolastica (Italy) *Tel:* (02) 380861 *Fax:* (02) 38086448 *Web Site:* www.scuola.com, pg 374

AGPOL (Przedsiebiorstwo Reklamy i Wydawnictw Handlu Zagranicznego) (Poland) *Tel:* (022) 416061 *Fax:* (022) 405607, pg 1281

Agrargazdsagi Kutato es Informatikai Intezet (Hungary) *Tel:* (01) 2171011 *Fax:* (01) 1177037, pg 320

Agricole Publishing Academy (India) *Tel:* (011) 692703, pg 327

Agricultural Institute Library (Ethiopia) *Tel:* (07) 11-00-19, pg 1504

Central Library of Agricultural Science (Israel) *Tel:* (08) 9489906 *Fax:* (08) 9361348; (08) 9489399 *E-mail:* szekely@agri.huji.ac.il *Web Site:* www.agri.huji.ac.il/library/menu.html, pg 1519

Agrivet Publishers (Namibia) *Tel:* (061) 228909 *Fax:* (061) 230619 *E-mail:* agrivet@iafrica.com.na, pg 476

Ediciones Agrotecnicas, SL (Spain) *Tel:* (091) 5473515 *Fax:* (091) 5474506 *E-mail:* agrotecnicas@agrotecnica.com *Web Site:* www.agrotecnica.com, pg 571

Agrupacion Bibliotecologica del Uruguay (Uruguay) *Tel:* (02) 400 57 40, pg 1573

AGT Editor SA (Mexico) *Tel:* (05) 273-9228 *Fax:* (05) 2771696, pg 462

Editorial Aguaclara (Spain) *Tel:* (096) 524 00 64 *Fax:* (096) 525 93 02 *E-mail:* edit.aguaclara@natural.es, pg 571

Agudat Sabah (Israel) *Tel:* (09) 8620544 *Fax:* (09) 8620546, pg 364

Aguilar Altea Taurus Alfaguara SA de CV (Mexico) *Tel:* (05) 688 89 66; (05) 688 82 77; (05) 688 75 66 *Fax:* (05) 6042304; (05) 6886538 *E-mail:* info@editorialaguilar.com *Web Site:* www.alfaguara.com.mx, pg 462

Aguilar Altea Taurus Alfaguara SA de Ediciones (Argentina) *Tel:* (011) 4912-7220 *Fax:* (011) 4912-7440 *E-mail:* info@alfaguara.com.ar *Web Site:* www.alfaguara.com.ar, pg 3

Aguilar SA de Ediciones (Spain) *Tel:* (091) 7449060 *Fax:* (091) 7449093 *E-mail:* limarquezes@santillana.es *Web Site:* www.gruposantillana.com, pg 571

Libreria Aguirre (Colombia) *Tel:* (04) 2220336, pg 1306

Agyra (Greece) *Tel:* (01) 3459321; (01) 3478044; (01) 3428595 *Fax:* (01) 3474732 *E-mail:* info@agyra.gr *Web Site:* www.agyra.gr, pg 1312

AHB Publications (Australia), pg 11

Ahmadu Bello University Bookshop Ltd (Nigeria) *Tel:* (069) 550054, pg 1331

Ahmadu Bello University Library (Nigeria) *Tel:* (069) 505-71; (069) 505-72; (069) 505-73; (069) 505-74 *Fax:* (069) 505-63, pg 1533

Ahmadu Bello University Press Ltd (Nigeria) *Tel:* (069) 550054 *E-mail:* abupl@abu.edu.ng, pg 503

Ahn Graphics (Republic of Korea) *Tel:* (02) 743 8065; (02) 743 8066; (02) 743 4154; (02) 743 3353 *Fax:* (02) 743 3352 *E-mail:* ask@ag.co.kr *Web Site:* www.ag.co.kr, pg 437

Al Ahram Establishment (Egypt (Arab Republic of Egypt)) *Tel:* (02) 748248 *Fax:* (02) 745888 *E-mail:* ahram@ahram.org.eg, pg 137

Al Ahram Establishment (Egypt (Arab Republic of Egypt)) *Tel:* (02) 5786200; (02) 5786300; (02) 5786400; (02) 5786500 *Fax:* (02) 5786126; (02) 5786833 *E-mail:* ahram@ahram.org.eg *Web Site:* www.extra.ahram.org.eg, pg 1147

Ahriman-Verlag GmbH (Germany) *Tel:* (0761) 502303 *Fax:* (0761) 502247 *E-mail:* ahriman@t-online.de *Web Site:* www.ahriman.com, pg 191

Ai Chih Book Co Ltd (Taiwan, Province of China) *Tel:* (07) 8121571 *Fax:* (07) 8121534, pg 638

Ai Interactive Ltd (United Kingdom) *Tel:* (01235) 529595 *Fax:* (01235) 520205 *E-mail:* medical@andromeda-interactive.co.uk *Web Site:* www.andromeda-interactive.co.uk, pg 656

AIB Associazione Italiana Bibliotheche (Italy) *Tel:* (06) 4463532 *Fax:* (06) 4441139 *E-mail:* aib@aib.it *Web Site:* www.aib.it, pg 374

AIBDA (Costa Rica) *Tel:* (0506) 2160222 *Fax:* (0506) 2294741; (0506) 2160233 *E-mail:* iicahq@iica.ac.cr *Web Site:* www.iica.int/servicios/aibda, pg 1264

Aichinger, Bernhard & Co GmbH (Austria) *Tel:* (01) 5128853 *Fax:* (01) 5128853-13, pg 1299

aid infodienst - Verbraucherdienst, Ernaehrung, Landwirtschaft eV (Germany) *Tel:* (0228) 8499-0 *Fax:* (0228) 8499-177 *E-mail:* aid@aid.de *Web Site:* www.aid.de, pg 191

Aide Editora e Comercio de Livros Ltda (Brazil) *Tel:* (021) 2589-9926 *Fax:* (021) 2589-9926 *E-mail:* aideeditora@radnet.com.br *Web Site:* www.radnet.com.br/aideeditora, pg 77

Aikamedia Oy (Finland) *Tel:* (014) 7514751 *Fax:* (014) 7514757 *E-mail:* asiakaspalvelu@aikamedia.fi *Web Site:* www.aikamedia.fi, pg 1252

Aiki News (Japan) *Tel:* (042) 748-1240 *Fax:* (042) 748-2421, pg 415

Aina-e-Adab (Pakistan) *Tel:* (042) 54069, pg 511

Aion Verlag (Romania) *Tel:* (059) 147595, pg 538

Air Gallery Edition, Helmut Kreuzer (Germany) *Tel:* (08122) 84487 *Fax:* (08122) 84487, pg 191

Air Larko Panorama ALP (Cyprus) *Tel:* (06) 236181 *Fax:* (06) 245046, pg 121

Airis Press (Russian Federation) *Tel:* (095) 9561684; (095) 7852925 *Fax:* (095) 9561684; (095) 7852925 *E-mail:* rolf@airis.ru *Web Site:* www.airis.ru, pg 543

Airlife Publishing Ltd (United Kingdom) *Tel:* (01743) 235651 *Fax:* (01743) 232944 *E-mail:* info@airlifebooks.com *Web Site:* www.airlifebooks.com, pg 656

Airlift Book Co (United Kingdom) *Tel:* (020) 8804 0400 *Fax:* (020) 8804 0044 *E-mail:* customercare@airlift.co.uk *Web Site:* www.airlift.co.uk, pg 1346

L'Airone Editrice (Italy) *Tel:* (06) 6570758 *Fax:* (06) 65740509 *E-mail:* gremese@gremese.com *Web Site:* www.gremese.com, pg 375

AIS (Ireland) *Tel:* (01) 6616522 *Fax:* (01) 6612378, pg 358, 1318

Aisthesis Verlag (Germany) *Tel:* (0521) 172604 *Fax:* (0521) 172812 *E-mail:* aisthesis@bitel.net *Web Site:* www.aisthesis.de, pg 191

Aithra Scientific Bookstore (Greece) *Tel:* (01) 3301269 *Fax:* (01) 3302622, pg 1312

AITI (Associazione Italiana Traduttori e Interpreti) (Italy) *Tel:* (081) 7645362 *Fax:* (081) 7645362 *E-mail:* segreteria@aiti.org *Web Site:* www.aiti.org, pg 1148

AITIM (Asociacion de Investigacion Tecnica de las industrias de la Madera y Corcho) (Spain) *Tel:* (091) 5425864 *Fax:* (091) 5590512 *E-mail:* informame@aitim.es *Web Site:* www.aitim.es, pg 571

Gillon Aitken Associates Ltd (United Kingdom) *Tel:* (020) 7373 8672 *Fax:* (020) 7373 6002 *E-mail:* reception@gillonaitken.co.uk, pg 1138

Editura Aius (Romania) *Tel:* (051) 196136 *Fax:* (051) 196135 *E-mail:* aius@euroweb.ro, pg 538

Ajanta Books International (India) *Tel:* (011) 3926182 *Fax:* (011) 7415016 *E-mail:* ajantabi@ndf.vsnl.net.in; ajantabi@id.erh.net, pg 1132

Ajanta Publications (India) (India) *Tel:* (011) 2917375; (011) 2926182 *Fax:* (011) 741 5016; (011) 713 2908; (011) 7213076, pg 327

Ajstan Publishers (Armenia) *Tel:* (01) 528520, pg 10

Biblioteca da Ajuda (Portugal) *Tel:* (021) 363 85 92 *Fax:* (021) 363 85 92, pg 1538

AK Press & Distribution (United Kingdom) *Tel:* (0131) 5555165 *Fax:* (0131) 5555215 *E-mail:* help@akuk.com *Web Site:* www.akuk.com, pg 656

Akademiai Kiado (Hungary) *Tel:* (01) 4648220; (01) 4648282; (01) 4648221; (01) 4648231, pg 320

Akademie Verlag GmbH (Germany) *Tel:* (030) 4 22 00 60 *Fax:* (030) 422 00 657 *E-mail:* info@akademie-verlag.de *Web Site:* www.akademie-verlag.de, pg 191

Akademiforlaget Corona AB (Sweden) *Tel:* (040) 286161 *Fax:* (040) 286162 *E-mail:* kundservice@cor.se *Web Site:* www.cor.se, pg 609

Akademiforlaget Goteborgslitteratur (Sweden) *Tel:* (031) 81 34 10 *Fax:* (031) 81 14 92 *E-mail:* sales@akg.se, pg 609

Biblioteka Akademii Nauk Rossii (Russian Federation) *Tel:* (0812) 3283592 *Fax:* (0812) 3287436 *E-mail:* ban@info.rasl.spb.ru *Web Site:* www.ban.tu, pg 1540

Akademische Druck-u Verlagsanstalt Dr Paul Struzl GmbH (Austria) *Tel:* (0316) 3644 *Fax:* (0316) 3644-24 *E-mail:* info@adeva.com *Web Site:* www.adeva.com, pg 48

Akademisk Forlag A/S (Denmark) *Tel:* 33 43 40 80 *Fax:* 33 43 40 99 *E-mail:* akademisk@akademisk.dk *Web Site:* www.akademisk.dk, pg 128

Libreria Akadia Editorial (Argentina) *Tel:* (011) 4961-8614; (011) 4964-2230 *Fax:* (011) 4961-8614 *E-mail:* akadia@arnet.com.ar, pg 3

Akadoma CV (Indonesia) *Tel:* (021) 3904323, pg 353

Akajase Enterprises (United Republic of Tanzania) *Tel:* (051) 26121, pg 643

Ediciones Akal SA (Spain) *Tel:* (091) 8061996 *Fax:* (091) 6564911; (091) 8044028 *E-mail:* pedidos.akal@akal.com (orders); edicion@akal.com; universidad@akal.com; educacion@akal.com; prensa@akal.com *Web Site:* www.akal.com, pg 571

Akateeminen Kirjakauppa (Finland) *Tel:* (09) 121 4252 *Fax:* (09) 121 4322 *E-mail:* tilaukset@akateeminen.com *Web Site:* www.akateeminen.com, pg 1309

Akateeminen Kustannusliike Oy (Finland) *Tel:* (09) 434 2320 *Web Site:* www.spes.fi, pg 141

Akcali Copyright Agency (Turkey) *Tel:* (0216) 3388771; (0216) 3485160 *Fax:* (0216) 3490778 *E-mail:* akcali@attglobal.net, pg 1138

Akdeniz Yayincilik (Turkey) *Tel:* (0212) 629-0026 *Fax:* (0212) 629-0027, pg 648

Akerbloms Universitetsbokhandel (Sweden) *Tel:* (090) 711250 *Fax:* (090) 711260 *E-mail:* swedish.books@akerbloms.se, pg 1343

akg-images gmbh (Germany) *Tel:* (030) 80485200 *Fax:* (030) 80485500 *E-mail:* info@akg.de; info@akg-images.com *Web Site:* www.akg-images.com, pg 191

Akita Shoten Publishing Co Ltd (Japan) *Tel:* (03) 3264-7248 *Fax:* (03) 3265-9076, pg 415

Akohi Editions (Cote d'Ivoire) *Tel:* 24 39 54 79 *Fax:* 24 39 75 58, pg 117

Editions Akpagnon (Togo) *Tel:* 220244 *Fax:* 220244, pg 646

Akritas (Greece) *Tel:* (0210) 9314968; (0210) 9334554 *Fax:* (0210) 9311436, pg 305

M Akselrad (Germany) *Tel:* (06221) 183030 *Fax:* (06221) 181223 *E-mail:* makselrad@gmx.net, pg 191

Akshat Publications (India) *Tel:* (011) 7247234; (011) 7114425; (011) 7240483 *Fax:* (011) 7254734; (011) 7218836, pg 327

Akson Charerntat (S/B Akson) (Thailand) *Tel:* (02) 2214587 *Fax:* (02) 2255356, pg 645

Akti-Oxy Publications (Greece) *Tel:* (0210) 8658502; (0210) 8676125 *Fax:* (0210) 8644679 *E-mail:* info@oxy.gr *Web Site:* www.oxy.gr, pg 1312

Al Ahram Book Club (Egypt (Arab Republic of Egypt)) *Tel:* (02) 5786069 *Fax:* (02) 5786833 *E-mail:* ahram@ahram.org.eg *Web Site:* www.extra.ahram.org.eg, pg 1252

Al-Fatah University, General Administration of Libraries, Printing & Publications (Libyan Arab Jamahiriya) *Tel:* (02133) 621988, pg 447

Editions Al-Fourkane (Morocco) *Tel:* (02) 983351 *Fax:* (02) 983351, pg 474

Editions Al Liamm (France) *Tel:* (0298) 02 10 84, pg 146

Al Maktabah Al Wataniah (Syrian Arab Republic), pg 1548

Al-Neelain University (Sudan) *Tel:* (011) 880055 *Fax:* (011) 776338 *E-mail:* neelain@an.mail.com, pg 1546

AL Publishers (India) *Tel:* (040) 7611600, pg 327

Al-Tanwir Al Ilmi (Scientific Enlightenment Publishing House) (Jordan) *Tel:* (026) 4899619 *Fax:* (026) 4899619, pg 432

Aladdin Books Ltd (United Kingdom) *Tel:* (020) 7323 3319 *Fax:* (020) 7323 4829 *E-mail:* kerry.mciver@aladdinbooks.co.uk *Web Site:* www.aladdinbooks.co.uk, pg 656

Alamire vzw, Music Publishers (Belgium) *Tel:* (011) 610 510 *Fax:* (011) 610 511 *E-mail:* info@alamire.com *Web Site:* www.alamire.com, pg 63

Alamo Hellas (Greece) *Tel:* (01) 2280027 *Fax:* (01) 2280027, pg 305

Editorial 'Alas' (Spain) *Tel:* (093) 4537506; (093) 3233445 *Fax:* (093) 4537506 *E-mail:* sala@editorial-alas.com *Web Site:* www.editorial-alas.com, pg 571

Alba (Italy) *Tel:* (0532) 249854 *Fax:* (0532) 249854 *E-mail:* alba_editrice@virgilio.it, pg 375

Alba Fachverlag GmbH & Co KG (Germany) *Tel:* (0211) 5 20 13-0 *Fax:* (0211) 5 20 13-28 *E-mail:* oepnv@alba.verlag.de *Web Site:* www.alba-verlag.de, pg 191

Albah Publishers (Nigeria), pg 503

J H Goehre Albanus Verlag (Switzerland) *Tel:* (052) 293503, pg 617

Albany Book Co Ltd (United Kingdom) *Tel:* (0141) 9542271, pg 1346

Albarello Verlag GmbH (Germany) *Tel:* (0202) 2058 8279 *Fax:* (0202) 2058 80534 *Web Site:* www.vier-v.de, pg 191

Albatros (Poland) *Tel:* (022) 842-9867 *Fax:* (022) 842-9867, pg 522

Albatros AS (Czech Republic) *Tel:* (02) 34633261 *Fax:* (02) 34633262 *E-mail:* albatros@bonton.cz *Web Site:* www.albatros.cz, pg 122

Editura Albatros (Romania) *Tel:* (01) 2228493 *Fax:* (01) 2228493, pg 538

Editorial Albatros SACI (Argentina) *Tel:* (011) 4807-2030 *Fax:* (011) 4807-2010 *E-mail:* info@edalbatros.com.ar *Web site:* www.edalbatros.com.ar, pg 3

Albe Libros Technicos (Uruguay) *Tel:* (02) 915 75 28; (02) 915 74 85 *Fax:* (02) 915 75 28 *Web Site:* www.bosch.es/puntos_internacional.asp, pg 776

Albe Libros Tecnicos SRL (Uruguay) *Tel:* (02) 95 75 28 *Fax:* (02) 95 75 28, pg 1355

Verlag Karl Alber GmbH (Germany) *Tel:* (0761) 27 17-436 *Fax:* (0761) 27 17-212 *E-mail:* info@verlag-alber.de *Web Site:* www.verlag-alber.de, pg 191

Alberdania SL (Spain) *Tel:* (0943) 63 28 14 *Fax:* (0943) 63 80 55 *E-mail:* alberdania@ctv.es, pg 571

Libreria Eduardo Albers Ltda (Chile) *Tel:* (02) 218 5371 *Fax:* (02) 218 1458 *Web Site:* www.albers.cl, pg 1305

Albert Bonniers Forlag (Sweden) *Tel:* (08) 696 86 20 *Fax:* (08) 696 8369; (08) 696 8347 *E-mail:* info@abforlag.bonnier.se *Web Site:* www.albertbonniersforlag.com, pg 609

Albert Nauck & Co (Germany) *Tel:* (0221) 94373-0 *Fax:* (0221) 94373-901, pg 191

Ermanno Albertelli Editore (Italy) *Tel:* (0521) 290387 *Fax:* (0521) 290387 *E-mail:* info@tuttostoria.it *Web Site:* www.tuttostoria.it, pg 375

Alberti Libraio Editore (Italy) *Tel:* (0323) 402534 *Fax:* (0323) 401074 *E-mail:* info@albertilibraio.it *Web Site:* www.albertilibraio.it, pg 375

Alberts XII (Latvia) *Tel:* (02) 7205286 *Fax:* (02) 7205284 *E-mail:* alberts@internet.lv, pg 444

E Albrecht Verlags-KG (Germany) *Tel:* (089) 85853-0 *Fax:* (089) 85853199 *E-mail:* av@albrecht.de, pg 192

Verlag und Antiquariat Frank Albrecht (Germany) *Tel:* (06203) 65713 *Fax:* (06203) 65311 *E-mail:* albrecht@antiquariat.com *Web Site:* www.antiquariat.com, pg 192

Albyn Press (United Kingdom) *Tel:* (020) 7351 4995 *Fax:* (020) 7351 4995, pg 656

Librairie Francaise Alcheh (Israel) *Tel:* (03) 5604173 *Fax:* (03) 6 994526 *E-mail:* alcheh@zahav.net.il, pg 1319

Alcor-Edimpex (Verlag) Ltd (Romania) *Tel:* (01) 665-34-40 *Fax:* (01) 665 34 40 *E-mail:* ed_alcor@yahoo.com *Web Site:* www.rotravel.com/alcor, pg 538

The Alden Group Ltd (United Kingdom) *Tel:* (01865) 253 200 *Fax:* (01865) 249 070 *E-mail:* alden.press@alden.co.uk *Web Site:* www.alden.co.uk, pg 1182

The Alden Group Ltd (United Kingdom) *Tel:* (01865) 253 200 *Fax:* (01865) 249 070 *E-mail:* information@alden.co.uk *Web Site:* www.alden.co.uk, pg 1224

Aldington Books Ltd (United Kingdom) *Tel:* (01233) 720123 *Fax:* (01233) 721272 *E-mail:* sales@aldingtonbooks.co.uk *Web Site:* www.aldingtonbooks.co.uk, pg 1346

Aldwych Press Ltd (United Kingdom) *Tel:* (020) 7240 0856 *Fax:* (020) 7379 0609 *E-mail:* info@eurospan.co.uk *Web Site:* www.eurospan.co.uk, pg 656

Centro Antiquar do Alecrim A Trindade (Portugal) *Tel:* (021) 3424660 *Fax:* (021) 3470180 *E-mail:* np75ae@mail.telepac.pt, pg 1336

Aleks Print Publishing House (Bulgaria) *Tel:* (052) 823147 *Fax:* (052) 823147 *E-mail:* dstankov@ultranet.bg, pg 93

Aleks Soft (Bulgaria) *Tel:* (02) 328855 *Fax:* (02) 328855 *E-mail:* info@alexsoft.net, pg 93

Alekto Verlag GmbH (Austria) *Tel:* (0463) 591180 *Fax:* (0463) 593217 *E-mail:* bali@bali.co.at, pg 48

Livraria Alema Ltda Brasileitura (Brazil) *Tel:* (047) 326-4558 *Fax:* (0473) 3263062, pg 77

Alemar's Best Sellers Club (Philippines) *Tel:* (02) 592617, pg 1255

Alemaya University of Agriculture Library (Ethiopia) *Tel:* (05) 11-14-00 *Fax:* (05) 11-40-08, pg 1504

El Aleph Editores (Spain) *Tel:* (093) 443 71 00 *Fax:* (093) 443 71 30 *E-mail:* correu@grup62.com *Web Site:* www.grup62.com, pg 572

Aletheia Publishing (Australia) *Tel:* (07) 3855 2056 *E-mail:* aletheia@powerup.com.au, pg 11

Alexander Verlag Berlin (Germany) *Tel:* (030) 3021826 *Fax:* (030) 3029408 *E-mail:* info@alexander-verlag.com *Web Site:* www.alexander-verlag.com, pg 192

Alexandria Municipal Library (Egypt (Arab Republic of Egypt)), pg 1503

Alexandria University Library (Egypt (Arab Republic of Egypt)) *Tel:* (03) 5971675 *Fax:* (03) 5960720 *E-mail:* postmaster@alex.eun.eg *Web Site:* www.alex.edu.eg, pg 1503

Alexiadou Vefa (Greece) *Tel:* (01) 224642 *Fax:* (01) 2828431 *E-mail:* vefaeditions@ath.forthnet.gr *Web Site:* www.addgr.com/comp/vefa/index.htm, pg 1312

Vefa Alexiadou Editions (Greece) *Tel:* (0210) 2848 086 *Fax:* (0210) 2849 689 *E-mail:* vefaeditions@ath.forthnet.gr *Web Site:* www.addgr.com/comp/vefa/index.htm, pg 305

ALFA dd za izdavacke, graficke i trgovacke poslove (Croatia) *Tel:* (01) 4666 066; (01) 4666 077 *Fax:* (01) 4666 258 *E-mail:* alfa-zg@zg.tel.hr, pg 117

Alfa-Narodna Knjiga (Serbia and Montenegro) *Tel:* (011) 3221-484; (011) 3227-426; (011) 3223-910 *Fax:* (011) 3227-946 *E-mail:* alfankkl@eunet.yu *Web Site:* www.narodnaknjiga.co.yu, pg 552

Editora Alfa Omega Ltda (Brazil) *Tel:* (011) 3062-6400; (011) 3062-6690 *Fax:* (011) 3083-0746 *E-mail:* alfaomega@alfaomega.com.br *Web Site:* www.alfaomega.com.br, pg 77

Publicacoes Alfa SA (Portugal) *Tel:* (021) 7587320, pg 528

Alfabeta Bokforlag AB (Sweden) *Tel:* (08) 714 36 30 *Fax:* (08) 643 24 31 *E-mail:* info@alfamedia.se *Web Site:* www.alfamedia.se, pg 609

Alfabeta Impresores Ltda (Chile) *Tel:* (02) 6397765 *Fax:* (02) 6391752, pg 98

Alfadil Ediciones (Venezuela) *Tel:* (02) 762-3036; (02) 761-3576; (02) 763-5676 *Fax:* (02) 762-0210 *E-mail:* contacto@alfagrupo.com *Web Site:* www.alfagrupo.com, pg 778

Alfagrama SRL ediciones (Argentina) *Tel:* (011) 4342-2452; (011) 4345-2299 *Fax:* (011) 4345-5411 *E-mail:* libros@alfagrama.com.ar *Web Site:* www.alfagrama.com.ar, pg 3

Alfaguara Ediciones SA - Grupo Santillana (Spain) *Tel:* (091) 744 90 60 *Fax:* (091) 744 92 24 *E-mail:* loboan@santillana.es *Web Site:* www.santillana.es, pg 572

Libreria Alfani Editrice SRL (Italy) *Tel:* (055) 2398800 *Fax:* (055) 218251 *E-mail:* info@librerialfani.it *Web Site:* www.librerialfani.it, pg 375

Alfaomega Grupo Editor SA de CV (Mexico) *Tel:* (05) 5755022 (ext 126); (05) 5755022 (ext 222) *Fax:* (052) 5752490 *E-mail:* universitaria@alfaomega.com.mx *Web Site:* www.alfaomega.com.mx, pg 462

Ediciones Alfar SA (Spain) *Tel:* (095) 4406100; (095) 4406366; (095) 4406614 *Fax:* (05) 4402580, pg 572

Edicions Alfons el Magnanim, Institucio Valenciana d'Estudis i Investigacio (Spain) *Tel:* (096) 3883756 *Fax:* (096) 3883751 *Web Site:* www.alfonselmagnanim.com, pg 572

Algarve (Lithuania) *Tel:* (02) 725910; (02) 721635 *Fax:* (02) 721462, pg 448

Editorial Algazara (Spain) *Tel:* (095) 2358284 *Fax:* (095) 2333175, pg 572

Les Editions Algeriennes En-Nahdha (Algeria) *Tel:* (021) 737627 *Fax:* (021) 737627 *E-mail:* info@ennahdha.com, pg 2

Sheikh Shaukat Ali & Sons (Pakistan) *Tel:* (021) 214585; (021) 212289 *Fax:* (021) 2637877, pg 511

Alianza Editorial de Argentina SA (Argentina) *Tel:* (011) 4342-4426; (011) 4342-9029 *Fax:* (011) 4342-4426; (011) 4342-9025 *E-mail:* gconosur@satlink.com, pg 3

Alianza Editorial Mexicana, SA de CV (Mexico) *Tel:* (05) 5618333; (05) 6704712 *Fax:* (05) 5619797, pg 462

Alianza Editorial SA (Spain) *Tel:* (091) 3938888 *Fax:* (091) 3207480 *E-mail:* alianza@anaya.es; mmorales@anaya.es *Web Site:* www.alianzaeditorial.es, pg 572

Alibaba Verlag GmbH (Germany) *Tel:* (069) 590097 *Fax:* (069) 559855 *E-mail:* alibaba@alibaba-verlag.de *Web Site:* www.alibaba-verlag.de, pg 192

Alibri Libreria, SL (Spain) *Tel:* (093) 317 05 78 *Fax:* (093) 412 27 02 *E-mail:* books-world@books-world.com, pg 1341

Edizioni Alice (Italy) *Tel:* (02) 83 61 347 *E-mail:* info@hod.it *Web Site:* www.hod.it, pg 375

Alice-Kan (Japan) *Tel:* (03) 5976-7013 *Fax:* (03) 3943-8396, pg 415

Alinari Fratelli SpA Istituto di Edizioni Artistiche (Italy) *Tel:* (055) 23951 *Fax:* (055) 2382857 *E-mail:* info@alinari.it *Web Site:* www.alinari.com, pg 375

Alinco SA - Aura Comunicacio (Spain) *Tel:* (093) 2172054 *Fax:* (093) 2373469, pg 572

Alinea (Italy) *Tel:* (055) 333428 *Fax:* (055) 331013 *E-mail:* ordini@alinea.it; info@alinea.it *Web Site:* www.alinea.it, pg 375

Alinea A/S (Denmark) *Tel:* 33 69 46 66 *Fax:* 33 69 46 60 *E-mail:* alinea@alinea.dk; skoleservice@alinea.dk *Web Site:* www.alinea.dk, pg 128

Alisher Navoi National Library of Uzbekistan (Uzbekistan) *Tel:* (099871) 139 16 58 *Fax:* (099871) 133 09 08 *E-mail:* navoi@physic.uzsci.net *Web Site:* www.osi.uz/library, pg 1555

ALITHIA Publishing Co (Cyprus) *Tel:* (022) 463040 *Fax:* (022) 463945, pg 121

Alkem Company Pte Ltd (Singapore) *Tel:* 62656666 *Fax:* 62617875 *E-mail:* microsoft@alkem.com.sq, pg 1161

Alkem Company Pte Ltd (Singapore) *Tel:* 6265 6666 *Fax:* 6261-7875 *E-mail:* enquiry@alkem.com.sg, pg 1181

Alkem Company Pte Ltd (Singapore) *Tel:* 6265 6666 *Fax:* 6261 7875 *E-mail:* enquiry@alkem.com.sg *Web Site:* www.alkem.com.sg, pg 1237

Alkim Kitapcilik-Yayimcilik (Turkey), pg 649

Alkor-Edition Kassel GmbH (Germany) *Tel:* (0561) 3105-282 *Fax:* (0561) 37755 *E-mail:* alkor-edition@baerenreiter.com *Web Site:* www.alkor-edition.com, pg 192

Editora All (Romania) *Tel:* (01) 402 26 00 *Fax:* (01) 402 26 10 *E-mail:* info@all.ro *Web Site:* www.all.ro, pg 538

YELLOW PAGES

All-India PEN Centre (India) *Tel:* (022) 2032175 *E-mail:* ambika.sirkar@gems.vsnl.net.in, pg 1401

All'Insegna del Giglio (Italy) *Tel:* (055) 451593 *Fax:* (055) 450030, pg 375

All-Russian Patent Technical Library (Russian Federation) *Tel:* (095) 2406425 *Fax:* (095) 2404437 *E-mail:* vptb@aha.ru, pg 1540

Ian Allan Publishing Ltd (United Kingdom) *Tel:* (01932) 266600 *Fax:* (01932) 266601 *E-mail:* info@ianallanpub.co.uk *Web Site:* www.ianallan.com, pg 656

Umberto Allemandi & Co Publishing (United Kingdom) *Tel:* (020) 7735 3331 *Fax:* (020) 7735 3332 *E-mail:* contact@theartnewspaper.com *Web Site:* www.theartnewspaper.com, pg 656

Umberto Allemandi & C SRL (Italy) *Tel:* (011) 8199111 *Fax:* (011) 8193090 *E-mail:* info@allemandi.com *Web Site:* www.allemandi.com, pg 375

Allen & Unwin Pty Ltd (Australia) *Tel:* (02) 8425 0100 *Fax:* (02) 9906 2218 *E-mail:* frontdesk@allenandunwin.com *Web Site:* www.allenandunwin.com, pg 11

Allert de Lange BV (Netherlands) *Tel:* (020) 6246744 *Fax:* (020) 6384975, pg 477

L'Alliance francaise, Bibliotheque (Senegal) *Tel:* 21 0822, pg 1541

The Alliance of Literary Societies (United Kingdom) *Tel:* (023) 92 475855 *Fax:* (0870) 056 0330 *Web Site:* www.sndc.demon.co.uk/als.htm, pg 1406

Alliance West African Publishers & Co (Nigeria) *Tel:* (085) 230798, pg 503

Allied Book Centre (India) *Tel:* (0135) 656526; (0135) 650949; (0135) 9837066875 *Fax:* (0135) 656554 *E-mail:* abc_book@rediffmail.com, pg 328

Allied Mouse Ltd (United Kingdom) *Tel:* (01349) 865400 *Fax:* (01349) 866066 *E-mail:* info@heartstone.co.uk *Web Site:* www.heartstone.co.uk, pg 656

Allied Publishers Pvt Ltd (India) *Tel:* (011) 3239001; (011) 3233002; (011) 5402792 *Fax:* (011) 3235967 *E-mail:* allied.delhi@vsnl.com; delhi.allied@excess.net.in *Web Site:* www.alliedpublishers.com, pg 328

Allied Publishers Pvt Ltd (India) *Tel:* (011) 3239001; (011) 3233002; (011) 3233004; (011) 323006667 *Fax:* (011) 3235967 *E-mail:* aplnd@del2.vsnl.net.in *Web Site:* www.alliedpublishers.com, pg 1315

Allison & Busby (United Kingdom) *Tel:* (020) 7738 7888 *Fax:* (020) 7733 4244 *E-mail:* all@allisonbusby.co.uk *Web Site:* www.allisonandbusby.com, pg 656

Allt om Hobby AB (Sweden) *Tel:* (08) 99 93 33 *Fax:* (08) 99 88 66 *E-mail:* order@hobby.se *Web Site:* www.hobby.se, pg 609

Allt om Hobbys Publishing Co (Sweden) *Tel:* (08) 99 93 33 *Fax:* (08) 99 88 66 *E-mail:* order@hobby.se *Web Site:* www.hobby.se, pg 1256

Alma (Denmark) *Tel:* 48 25 54 41 *Fax:* 48 25 20 41, pg 128

Alma Littera (Lithuania) *Tel:* (05) 272 82 46; (05) 272 56 85 *Fax:* (05) 272 80 26 *E-mail:* post@almali.lt *Web Site:* www.almali.lt, pg 448

Alma'Arif PT (Indonesia) *Tel:* (022) 4207177; (022) 4203708 *Fax:* (022) 439194, pg 353

Livraria Almedina (Portugal) *Tel:* 239 851 903 *E-mail:* editora@almedina.net *Web Site:* www.almedina.net, pg 528

Almenna Bokafelagid (Iceland) *Tel:* 564-3170 *Fax:* 564-3190, pg 325

Akademibokhandeln/Almqvist & Wiksell (Sweden) *Tel:* (08) 613 61 00 *Fax:* (08) 24 25 43 *Web Site:* www.akademibokhandeln.se, pg 1343

Almqvist och Wiksell Bokhandel AB (Sweden) *Tel:* (08) 613 61 00 *Fax:* (08) 24 25 43 *Web Site:* www.akademibokhandeln.se, pg 1343

Almqvist och Wiksell International (Sweden) *Tel:* (08) 613 61 00 *Fax:* (08) 24 25 43 *E-mail:* scand.mongr@awi.se *Web Site:* www.akademibokhandeln.se, pg 609

Aloe Educational (South Africa) *Tel:* (011) 8393719 *Fax:* (011) 8393720, pg 1340

Forlaget alokke AS (Denmark) *Tel:* 75671119 *Fax:* 75671074 *E-mail:* alokke@get2net.dk, pg 129

Alouette Verlag (Germany) *Tel:* (040) 712 23 53 *Fax:* (040) 713 41 88 *E-mail:* webmaster@alouette-verlag.de *Web Site:* www.alouette-verlag.de, pg 192

Ediciones Alpe (Mexico) *Tel:* (05) 5365749; (05) 2033157 *Fax:* (05) 2033157, pg 462

Alpha-Delta (Greece) *Tel:* (01) 2280027 *Fax:* (01) 2280027, pg 1312

Alpha Literatur Verlag/Alpha Presse (Germany) *Tel:* (069) 555325 *Fax:* (069) 955130-99, pg 192

Editions Alphee (Monaco) *Tel:* (093) 30-40-06 *Fax:* (099) 99-67-18, pg 473

Alpina Color Graphics Inc (United States) *Tel:* 212-683-2535 *Toll Free Tel:* 866-338-1214 *Fax:* 212-683-3965 *E-mail:* info@alpina.net *Web Site:* www.alpina.net, pg 1186

AlpnetCompuType Ltd (United Kingdom) *Tel:* (01895) 440791 *Fax:* (01895) 441500 *E-mail:* computype@computype.co.uk, pg 1183

ALS-Verlag GmbH (Germany) *Tel:* (06074) 82 16-0; (06074) 82 16-50 (orders) *Fax:* (06074) 2 73 22 *E-mail:* info@als-verlag.de *Web Site:* www.als-verlag.de, pg 192

Alsatia SA (France) *Tel:* (03) 89 45 21 53 *Fax:* (03) 89 45 18 98, pg 146

Alta Fulla Editorial (Spain) *Tel:* (093) 4590708; (093) 4591363 *Fax:* (093) 2075203 *E-mail:* altafulla@altafulla.com *Web Site:* www.altafulla.com, pg 572

Altberliner Verlag GmbH (Germany) *Tel:* (030) 284 992-0 *Fax:* (030) 284 992-20 *E-mail:* presse@altberliner.de *Web Site:* www.altberliner.de, pg 192

Altea, Taurus, Alfaguara SA (Spain) *Tel:* (091) 744 90 60 *Fax:* (091) 744 92 24 *E-mail:* clientes@santillana.es *Web Site:* www.alfaguara.santillana.es, pg 572

Ediciones Altera SL (Spain) *Tel:* (093) 4519537 *Fax:* (093) 4517441 *E-mail:* editorial@altera.net, pg 572

Altera Forlag A/S (Norway) *Tel:* 22569590 *Fax:* 22565088, pg 508

Alternative Editura (Romania) *Tel:* (01) 2234966; (01) 2229468 *Fax:* (01) 6756074; (01) 2234971, pg 538

Editions Alternatives (France) *Tel:* (01) 43 29 88 64 *Fax:* (01) 43 29 02 70 *E-mail:* info@editionsalternatives.com *Web Site:* www.editionsalternatives.com, pg 146

Editions ALTESS (France) *Tel:* (01) 47 70 78 79 *Fax:* (01) 47 70 78 77 *E-mail:* eliaur@club-internet.fr *Web Site:* www.ifrance.com/3eMillenaire/altess/index.htm, pg 146

Altin Kitaplar Yayinevi (Turkey) *Tel:* (0212) 5206246; (0212) 5201588; (0212) 5268010 *Fax:* (0212) 5120266 *E-mail:* info@altinkitaplar.com.tr *Web Site:* www.altinkitaplar.com.tr, pg 649

Altina (Belgium) *Tel:* (059) 80-16-51 *Fax:* (059) 51-27-17, pg 63

Altiora Averbode Uitgeverij nv (Belgium) *Tel:* (013) 780 182 *Fax:* (013) 780 179 *E-mail:* averbode.publ@verbode.be *Web Site:* www.averbode.be, pg 1301

Aluminium-Verlag Marketing & Kommunikation GmbH (Germany) *Fax:* (0211) 15 91-379 *E-mail:* info@alu-verlag.de *Web Site:* www.alu-verlag.de, pg 192

Alumni PT (Indonesia) *Tel:* (022) 2501251; (022) 2503039; (022) 2503038 *Fax:* (022) 2503044, pg 353

Alun Books (United Kingdom) *Tel:* (01639) 886186 *E-mail:* enquiries@alunbooks.co.uk *Web Site:* www.alunbooks.co.uk, pg 657

Biblioteca Argentina Dr Juan Alvarez (Argentina) *Tel:* 4802538; 4802539 *Fax:* 4802561 *E-mail:* bibliarghem@rosario.gov.ar *Web Site:* www.rosario.gov.ar, pg 1490

Livraria Francisco Alves Editora SA (Brazil) *Tel:* (021) 221-3198 *Fax:* (021) 242-3438, pg 77

Alyssa Editions (Tunisia) *Tel:* 740989 *Fax:* 733659, pg 647

Editions Alzieu (France) *Tel:* (04) 76 51 09 51 *Fax:* (04) 76 51 09 51 *E-mail:* admin@editions-alzieu.com *Web Site:* www.editions-alzieu.com, pg 146

Am Oved Publishers Ltd (Israel) *Tel:* (03) 6291526 *Fax:* (03) 6298911 *E-mail:* info@am-oved.co.il *Web Site:* www.am-oved.co.il, pg 365

AMA nakladatelstvi (Czech Republic) *Tel:* (0618) 265 84 *Fax:* (0618) 228 31 *E-mail:* rstudio@login.cz, pg 122

Armenio Amado Editora de Simoes, Beirao & Ca Lda (Portugal) *Tel:* (039) 92150 *Fax:* (039) 851901, pg 528

Amalthea-Verlag (Austria) *Tel:* (01) 712 35 60 *Fax:* (01) 713 89 95 *E-mail:* amalthea.verlag@amalthea.at *Web Site:* www.amalthea.at, pg 48

Pustaka Aman Press Sdn Bhd (Malaysia) *Tel:* (09) 7481849 *Fax:* (09) 784058, pg 455

Amanda (Denmark) *Tel:* 3379-0110 *Fax:* 33790011 *E-mail:* forlag@dansklf.dk, pg 129

Amar Prakashan (India) *Tel:* (011) 713182, pg 328

Editions de l'Amateur (France) *Tel:* (01) 45 77 08 05 *Fax:* (01) 45 79 97 15, pg 146

Amazonas Editores Ltda (Colombia) *Tel:* (091) 6180256; (091) 2182760 *Fax:* (091) 6180326, pg 110

Ambar Prakashan (India) *Tel:* (011) 2362 5528 *Fax:* (011) 2574 3569 *E-mail:* pitambar@bol.net.in, pg 328

Amber Books Ltd (United Kingdom) *Tel:* (020) 7520 7600 *Fax:* (020) 7520 7606; (020) 7520 7607 *E-mail:* enquiries@amberbooks.co.uk *Web Site:* www.amberbooks.co.uk, pg 657

Amber Lane Press Ltd (United Kingdom) *Tel:* (01608) 810024 *Fax:* (01608) 810024 *E-mail:* info@amberlanepress.co.uk *Web Site:* www.amberlanepress.co.uk, pg 657

Amberwood Publishing Ltd (United Kingdom) *Tel:* (01634) 290115 *Fax:* (01634) 290761 *E-mail:* books@amberwoodpublishing.com *Web Site:* www.amberwoodpublishing.com, pg 657

Ambit Serveis Editorials, SA (Spain) *Tel:* (093) 4881342 *Fax:* (093) 4874772, pg 572

Uitgeverij Ambo BV (Netherlands) *Tel:* (020) 5245411 *Fax:* (020) 4200422 *E-mail:* info@amboanthos.nl *Web Site:* www.amboanthos.nl, pg 477

Amboss-Verlag E Widmer (Switzerland) *Tel:* (071) 711236; (071) 714590 *Fax:* (071) 714590, pg 617

Editions Ambozontany (Madagascar) *Tel:* (07) 50027; (07) 51441, pg 453

Librairie Ambozontany (Madagascar) *Tel:* (07) 50027; (07) 51441, pg 453

Biblioteca Ambrosiana (Italy) *Tel:* (02) 80 692 1 *Fax:* (02) 80 692 210 *E-mail:* info@ambrosiana.it *Web Site:* www.ambrosiana.it, pg 1520

Amebo Book Club (Nigeria), pg 1254

America Latina (Uruguay) *Tel:* (02) 415127 *Fax:* (02) 495568, pg 1355

American Book Store SA de CV (Mexico) *Tel:* (05) 512-6350; (05) 512-0306 *Fax:* (05) 518-6931, pg 1327

The American Chamber of Commerce in Hong Kong (Hong Kong) *Tel:* 2526-0165 *Fax:* 2810-1289 *E-mail:* amcham@amcham.org.hk *Web Site:* www.amcham.org.hk, pg 1155

The American Chamber of Commerce in Japan
(Japan) Tel: (03) 3433-5381 Fax: (03) 3433-8454
E-mail: info@accj.or.jp Web Site: www.accj.or.jp,
pg 415

American Chamber of Commerce of Jamaica (Jamaica)
Tel: 876-929-7866 Fax: 876-929-8597 E-mail: info@
amchamjamaica.org Web Site: www.amchamjamaica.
org, pg 413

American Information Resource Center (India) Tel: (011)
2331-6841; (011) 2331-4251 Fax: (011) 2332-9499
E-mail: libdel@pd.state.gov Web Site: americanlibrary.
in.library.net; newdelhi.usembassy.gov, pg 1515

American Library in Paris (France) Tel: (01) 53591260
Fax: (01) 45502583 E-mail: alparis@noos.fr
Web Site: www.americanlibraryinparis.org, pg 1505

American Pizzi Offset Corp (United States) Tel: 212-986-1658 Fax: 212-286-1887 E-mail: info@
americanpizzi.com, pg 1165

American Pizzi Offset Corp (United States) Tel: 212-986-1658 Fax: 212-286-1887 E-mail: apocnyusa@aol.
com, pg 1186

American-Scandinavian Foundation (United States)
Tel: 212-879-9779 Fax: 212-879-2301 E-mail: info@
amscan.org; asf@amscan.org Web Site: www.amscan.
org, pg 1294

American Technical Publishers (United Kingdom)
Tel: (01462) 437933 Fax: (01462) 433678
E-mail: atp@ameritech.co.uk Web Site: www.
ameritech.co.uk, pg 657

American University in Cairo Library (Egypt
(Arab Republic of Egypt)) Tel: (02) 797-6904
Fax: (02) 792-3824 E-mail: aucpress@aucegypt.edu
Web Site: library.aucegypt.edu, pg 1503

American University in Cairo Press (Egypt (Arab
Republic of Egypt)) Tel: (02) 797 6926; (02) 797
6895 (orders) Fax: (02) 794 1440 E-mail: aucpress@
aucegypt.edu Web Site: aucpress.com, pg 137

American University of Beirut Libraries (Lebanon)
Tel: (01) 340460 Fax: (01) 744703 E-mail: library@
aub.edu.lb Web Site: www.aub.edu.lb/, pg 1524

Amerindian Research Unit (Guyana) Tel: (02) 4930
Fax: (02) 54885 Web Site: www.wisard.org, pg 314

Editions d'Amerique et d'Orient, Adrien Maisonneuve
(France) Tel: (01) 43 26 86 35 Fax: (01) 43 54 59
54 E-mail: maisonneuve@maisonneuve-adrien.com,
pg 146

Editions Amez (France) Tel: (03) 88 84 56 56 Fax: (03)
88 84 56 84, pg 146

Amichai Publishing House Ltd (Israel) Tel: (09) 8859099
Fax: (09) 8853464, pg 365

Libreria los Amigos del Libro (Bolivia) Tel: (04)
4504150; (04) 4504151 Fax: (04) 4115128
E-mail: gutten@amigol.bo.net, pg 1302

Los Amigos del Libro Ediciones (Bolivia) Tel: (04)
254114 Fax: (04) 251140 Web Site: www.
librosbolivia.com, pg 75

Amir Kabir Book Publishing & Distribution Co (Islamic
Republic of Iran) Tel: (021) 3933996; (021) 3933997;
(021) 3900751-2; (021) 3112118 Fax: (021) 3903747,
pg 357

L'Amitie par le Livre (France) Tel: (03) 81820894
Fax: (03) 81820894, pg 146, 1252

Amiza Associate Malaysia Sdn Bhd (Malaysia) Tel: (03)
7036100 Fax: (03) 7034268, pg 455

AMK Interaksi Sdn Bhd (Malaysia) Tel: (03) 215306
Fax: (03) 718067, pg 455

Amman Public Library (Jordan) Tel: (06) 637 111
Fax: (06) 649420, pg 1522

Ammann Verlag & Co (Switzerland) Tel: (01) 268 10
40 Fax: (01) 268 10 50 E-mail: info@ammann.ch
Web Site: www.ammann.ch, pg 617

Amnesty International Publications (United Kingdom)
Tel: (020) 7814 6200 Fax: (020) 7833 1510
E-mail: information@amnesty.org.uk Web Site: www.
amnesty.org.uk, pg 657

Amnesty International VZW (Belgium) Tel: (03) 271
16 16 Fax: (03) 235 78 12 E-mail: amnesty@aivl.be
Web Site: www.aivl.be, pg 63

Amnistia Internacional Editorial SL (Spain) Tel: (091)
315 2851 Fax: (091) 323 2158 E-mail: amnistia.
internacional@a-i.es, pg 572

Amorrortu Editores SA (Argentina) Tel: (011) 4816-5812; (011) 4816-5869 Fax: (011) 4816-3321
E-mail: info@amorrortueditores.com Web Site: www.
amorrortueditores.com, pg 3

Amosium Servis (Czech Republic) Tel: (069) 624 55 01,
pg 122

Editions Amphora SA (France) Tel: (01) 43 29 03 04;
(01) 43 26 10 87 Fax: (01) 43 29 49 49; (01) 40 46
85 76 Web Site: www.ed-amphora.fr, pg 146

Editions Amrita SA (France) Tel: (05) 53 50 79 54
Fax: (05) 53 50 80 20 E-mail: amrita.editions@
perigord.com, pg 146

Amtsbibliothek des Bundesministeriums fur
Unterricht, und Kulturelle Angelegenheiten und des
Bundesministeriums fur Wissenschaft und Verkehr
(Austria) Tel: (01) 53 120-0 Fax: (01) 53 120-3099
E-mail: ministerium@bmbwk.gv.at Web Site: www.
bmbwk.gv.at/, pg 1491

AMV Ediciones (Spain) Tel: (091) 5336926; (091)
5349368 Fax: (091) 5530286 Web Site: www.
amvediciones.com, pg 572

AMVC-Letterenhuis (Belgium) Tel: (03) 222 9320
Fax: (03) 222 9321 E-mail: amvc.letterenhuis@
stad.antwerpen.be Web Site: museum.antwerpen.
be/amvc_letterenhuis, pg 1493

An Gum (Ireland) Tel: (01) 8734700 Fax: (01) 8731104
E-mail: gum@educ.irlgov.ie, pg 358

Anabas-Verlag Guenter Kaempf GmbH & Co KG
(Germany) Tel: (069) 94 21 98 71 Fax: (069) 94 21
98 72 E-mail: info@anabas-verlag.com, pg 192

L'Anabase (France) Tel: (04) 67561338 Fax: (01)
34858073, pg 146

Anabra State Library Board (Nigeria) Tel: (042) 334
103, pg 1533

Editorial Anagrama (Spain) Tel: (093) 2037652
Fax: (093) 2037738 E-mail: anagrama@anagrama-ed.es Web Site: www.anagrama-ed.es, pg 572

Anako Editions (France) Tel: (01) 43 94 92 88 Fax: (01)
43 94 02 45 E-mail: anako.editions@anako.com
Web Site: www.anako.com, pg 146

Anam Publishing Co (Republic of Korea) Tel: (02)
22380491 Fax: (02) 22524334, pg 437

Anambra State School Libraries Association (Nigeria)
Tel: (042) 252080; (042) 332091, pg 1568

Anand Book Club (India), pg 1253

Ananda Publishers Pvt Ltd (India) Tel: (033) 2241 4352;
(033) 2241 3417 Fax: (033) 2253240; (033) 2253241
E-mail: ananda@cal3.vsnl.net.in Web Site: www.
anandapub.com, pg 328

Anansi Uitgewers (South Africa) Tel: (021) 968411
Fax: (021) 969698, pg 562

Anastasiadis Publications (Greece) Tel: (01) 2284013
Fax: (01) 2236442, pg 1312

Ediciones Anaya SA (Spain) Tel: (091) 393 86 00
Fax: (091) 320 91 29; (091) 742 66 31 E-mail: cga@
anaya.es Web Site: www.anaya.es, pg 572

Anaya Educacion (Spain) Tel: (091) 393 86 00
Fax: (091) 320 91 29; (091) 742 66 31 E-mail: cga@
anaya.es Web Site: www.anaya.es, pg 573

Anaya-Touring Club (Spain) Tel: (091) 393 86 00
Fax: (091) 742 66 31; (091) 320 91 29 E-mail: cga@
anaya.es Web Site: www.anaya.es, pg 573

Libraire Ancienne Noel Anselot (Belgium) Tel: (061)
656091 Fax: (061) 656091, pg 63

Editrice Ancora (Italy) Tel: (02) 3456081 Fax: (02)
34560866 E-mail: editrice@ancora-libri.it
Web Site: www.ancora-libri.it, pg 375

Libreria Ancora y Delfin (Spain) Tel: (093) 2000746
Fax: (093) 2000757 E-mail: ancoraydelfin@
ancoraydelfin.com, pg 1341

Editions l'Ancre de Marine (France) Tel: (02) 32 25
45 97 E-mail: service-clients@ancre-de-marine.com
Web Site: www.ancre-de-marine.com, pg 147

Andersen Press Ltd (United Kingdom) Tel: (020) 7840
8701 Fax: (020) 7233 6263 E-mail: andersenpress@
randomhouse.co.uk Web Site: www.andersenpress.co.
uk, pg 657

Robert Andersen & Associates Pty Ltd (Australia)
Tel: (03) 9489 3968 Fax: (03) 9482 2416
E-mail: 100357.354@compuserve.com, pg 11

Darley Anderson Literary TV & Film Agency
(United Kingdom) Tel: (020) 7385 6652 Fax: (020)
7386 5571; (020) 7386 9689 E-mail: enquiries@
darleyanderson.com Web Site: www.darleyanderson.
com, pg 1138

Michelle Anderson Publishing (Australia) Tel: (03) 9826
9028 Fax: (03) 9826 8552 E-mail: mapubl@bigpond.
net.au Web Site: www.michelleandersonpublishing.
com, pg 11

Anderson Rand Ltd (United Kingdom) Tel: (01223)
566640 Fax: (01223) 316144; (01223) 566643
E-mail: info@andrand.com Web Site: www.andrand.
com, pg 657

Andi Offset (Indonesia) Tel: (0274) 561881 Fax: (0274)
588282 E-mail: andi_pub@indo.net.id, pg 353

Andina Publishing House (Bulgaria) Tel: (052) 630902,
pg 93

Andorran Standard Book Numbering Agency (Andorra)
Tel: 826445 Fax: 829445 E-mail: bncultura.gov@
andorra.ad Web Site: bibnac.andorra.ad, pg 1259

Andreas und Andreas Verlagsbuchhandel (Austria)
Tel: (0662) 6575-0 Fax: (0662) 6575-5, pg 48

Andrena Publishers (Lithuania) Tel: (02) 703834; (02)
627015 E-mail: andrena@takas.lt, pg 448

Andreou Chr Publishers (Cyprus) Tel: (022) 666877
Fax: (022) 666878 E-mail: andzeou2@cytanet.com.cy,
pg 121

Andresen & Butenschon AS (Norway) Tel: (047)
23139240 Fax: (047) 22335805 E-mail: abforlag@
abforlag.no, pg 508

Chris Andrews Publications (United Kingdom)
Tel: (01865) 723404 Fax: (01865) 725294
E-mail: enquiries@cap-ox.com Web Site: www.cap-ox.com, pg 657

Andromeda Oxford Ltd (United Kingdom) Tel: (01235)
550 296 Fax: (01235) 550 330 E-mail: mail@
andromeda.co.uk Web Site: www.andromeda.co.uk,
pg 658

K C Ang Publishing Pte Ltd (Singapore) Tel: 4741680
Fax: 2542002, pg 554

Angel Publications (Australia) Tel: (02) 4821 1463,
pg 11

Angeletos Sokzates (Greece) Tel: (01) 9928100 Fax: (01)
9940530, pg 1313

Franco Angeli SRL (Italy) Tel: (02) 28 37 141 Fax: (02)
26 14 47 93 E-mail: redazioni@francoangeli.it
Web Site: www.francoangeli.it, pg 375

Biblioteca Angelica (Italy) Tel: (06) 6840801; (06)
68408069 Fax: (06) 68408053 E-mail: angelica.
polosbn@inroma.roma.it Web Site: biblioroma.sbn.it,
pg 1520

Angelika und Lothar Binding (Germany) Tel: (06221)
20955 Fax: (06221) 181846 E-mail: Angelika.
Binding@gmx.net Web Site: www.binding-singles.de,
pg 192

Angkasa CV (Indonesia) Tel: (022) 4208955; (022)
4204795 Fax: (022) 439183, pg 353

The Anglo American Book Company Ltd (United Kingdom) *Tel:* (01267) 211880 *Fax:* (01267) 211882 *E-mail:* books@anglo-american.co.uk *Web Site:* www.anglo-american.co.uk, pg 1346

Anglo-Didactica, SL Editorial (Spain) *Tel:* (091) 3780188 *Fax:* (091) 3780188 *E-mail:* anglodidac@aregen.net, pg 573

Anglo-German Foundation for the Study of Industrial Society (United Kingdom) *Tel:* (020) 7823 1123 *Fax:* (020) 7823 2324 *E-mail:* info@agf.org.uk *Web Site:* www.agf.org.uk, pg 658

Angus & Robertson Bookshops (Australia) *Tel:* (03) 86231111 *Fax:* (03) 86231150 *E-mail:* info@angusrobertson.com.au *Web Site:* www.angusrobertson.com.au, pg 1297

Anhui Children's Publishing House (China) *Tel:* (0551) 2849306 *Fax:* (0551) 2849306 *E-mail:* ahsebwsh@mail.hf.ah.cn *Web Site:* www.ahse.cn, pg 101

Anhui People's Publishing House (China) *Tel:* (0551) 257134; (0551) 2653673, pg 101

Anixis Publications (Greece) *Tel:* (01) 6205436 *Fax:* (01) 8079357, pg 305

Anjuman Taraqqi-e-Urdu Pakistan (Pakistan) *Tel:* (021) 461406; (021) 4973296; (021) 7724023, pg 1403

Ankara University Library (Turkey) *Tel:* (0312) 212 60 40 *Fax:* (0312) 212 60 49 *Web Site:* www.ankara.edu.tr, pg 1551

Ankh-Hermes BV (Netherlands) *Tel:* (0570) 678911 *Fax:* (0570) 624632 *E-mail:* info@ankh-hermes.nl *Web Site:* www.ankh-hermes.com, pg 477

Ankur Prakashani (Bangladesh) *Tel:* (02) 250132 *Fax:* (02) 9567730 *E-mail:* ankur@bangla.net, pg 61

Ankur Publishing Co (India) *Tel:* (022) 543 2817; (022) 536 9907 *Fax:* (022) 543 2817 *E-mail:* ankur@bom3.vsnl.net.in *Web Site:* www.satyamplastics.com/ankurpublishing/, pg 328

Anmol Publications Pvt Ltd (India) *Tel:* (011) 3255577; (011) 3261597; (011) 3278000 *Fax:* (011) 3280289 *E-mail:* anmol@nde.vsnl.net.in, pg 328

Editions d'Annabelle (France) *Tel:* (01) 47420161 *Fax:* (01) 47424214, pg 147

Anowuo Educational Publications (Ghana) *Tel:* (021) 669961, pg 303

Anrich Verlag GmbH (Germany) *Tel:* (06201) 6007-0 *Fax:* (06201) 17464, pg 192

Forlagsentralen ANS (Norway) *Tel:* (022) 32 96 00 *Fax:* (022) 32 96 01 *E-mail:* firmapost@forlagsentralen.no *Web Site:* www.forlagsentralen.no, pg 1332

Ansay Pty Ltd (Australia) *Tel:* (02) 5602044 *Fax:* (02) 5694585, pg 11

Antara Publications (M) Sdn Bhd (Malaysia) *Tel:* (03) 2913188 *Fax:* (03) 2913299, pg 1326

Pustaka Antara (Malaysia) *Tel:* (03) 292 5823 *Fax:* (03) 291 7997, pg 455

PT Pustaka Antara Publishing & Printing (Indonesia) *Tel:* (021) 3156994; (021) 3156995 *Fax:* (021) 322745 *E-mail:* nacelod@indo.net.id, pg 353

Antenna Edicoes Tecnicas Ltda (Brazil) *Tel:* (021) 2223-2442 *Fax:* (021) 2263-8840 *E-mail:* antenna@anep.com.br *Web Site:* www.anep.com.br, pg 77

Antex Verlag-Hans Joachin Schuhmacher (Germany) *Tel:* (033603) 40410 *Fax:* (033603) 40400, pg 192

Edition Anthese (France) *Tel:* (01) 46 56 06 67 *Fax:* (01) 49 85 09 92, pg 147

Uitgeverij Anthos (Netherlands) *Tel:* (020) 5245411 *Fax:* (020) 4200422 *E-mail:* info@amboanthos.nl *Web Site:* www.amboanthos.nl, pg 477

Editorial Anthropos del Hombre (Spain) *Tel:* (093) 6972296 *Fax:* (093) 6972296, pg 573

Editions Anthropos (France) *Tel:* (01) 45781292 *Fax:* (01) 45750567, pg 147

Edicoes Antigona (Portugal) *Tel:* (021) 749483 *Fax:* (021) 749483, pg 528

Bibliotheque Universitaire Antilles-Guyane (BUAG) (France) *Tel:* (0596) 727530 *Fax:* (0596) 727527 *Web Site:* www.univ-ag.fr, pg 1506

Antillion Library Association (Netherlands Antilles) *Tel:* (09) 4617055 *Fax:* (09) 4656247, pg 1568

Antiqua-Verlag GmbH (Germany) *Tel:* (07746) 2273 *Fax:* (07746) 2260, pg 193

Antiquarian Booksellers' Association (United Kingdom) *Tel:* (020) 7439 3118 *Fax:* (020) 7439 3119 *E-mail:* info@aba.org.uk *Web Site:* www.aba.org.uk, pg 1289

Antiquarian Booksellers' Association of Japan (Japan) *Tel:* (03) 3357-1411 *Fax:* (03) 3351-5855 *E-mail:* kikuo@sc4.so-net.ne.jp *Web Site:* www.abaj.gr.jp, pg 1274

Antiquariats-Union Vertriebs GmbH & Co KG (Germany) *Tel:* (04131) 983504 *Fax:* (04131) 9835595 *E-mail:* webmaster@restauflagen.de *Web Site:* www.restauflagen.de, pg 193

Antique Collectors' Club Ltd (United Kingdom) *Tel:* (01394) 389950 *Fax:* (01394) 389999 *E-mail:* peter.hawk@antique-acc.com; sales@antique-acc.com *Web Site:* www.antique-acc.com, pg 658

Antiques & Collectors Guides Ltd (United Kingdom) *Tel:* (0141) 8480880 *Fax:* (0141) 8892063, pg 658

Librairies Antoine SAL/Librairie Antoine, A. Naufal & Freres (Lebanon) *Tel:* (01) 48 10 72; (01) 48 35 13 *Fax:* (01) 49 26 25, pg 1324

Antonius-Verlag (Switzerland) *Tel:* (065) 223912, pg 617

Biblioteca Nacional de Antropologia E Historia (Mexico) *Tel:* (055) 5536342; (055) 5536865 *E-mail:* ejuare@juarez.ciesas.edu.mx *Web Site:* www.arts-history.mx, pg 1528

Editora Antroposofica Ltda (Brazil) *Tel:* (011) 5687-9714; (011) 5686-4550 *Fax:* (011) 2479714 *E-mail:* editora@antroposofica.com.br *Web Site:* www.sab.org.br/edit; www.antroposofica.com.br, pg 77

Editrice Antroposofica SRL (Italy) *Tel:* (02) 7491197 *Fax:* (02) 70103173, pg 375

Antroposofsko Izdatelstvo Dimo R Daskalov OOD (Bulgaria) *Tel:* (042) 54481, pg 93

Maison d'Edition Protestante ANTSO (Madagascar) *Tel:* (022) 20886 *Fax:* (022) 26372 *E-mail:* fjkm@dts.mg, pg 453

Antwerp Bibliophile Society (Belgium) *Tel:* (03) 2330294 *Fax:* (03) 2262516 *E-mail:* francine.demav@amtwerpa.be, pg 1396

Anvil Books Ltd (United Kingdom) *Tel:* (020) 8829-3000 *Fax:* (020) 8881-5088, pg 658

Anvil Press (Zimbabwe) *Tel:* (04) 73-9681; (04) 78-1770; (04) 78-1771; (04) 792551 *Fax:* (04) 75-1202, pg 782

Anvil Press Poetry Ltd (United Kingdom) *Tel:* (020) 8469 3033 *Fax:* (020) 8469 3363 *E-mail:* info@anvilpresspoetry.com *Web Site:* www.anvilpresspoetry.com, pg 658

Anvil Publishing Inc (Philippines) *Tel:* (02) 671888 *Fax:* (02) 6719235 *E-mail:* anvil@fc.emc.com.ph; pubdept@anvil.com.ph, pg 518

Any Photo Type (United States) *Tel:* 212-244-1130 *Fax:* 212-594-4697, pg 1186

Anzea Publishers Ltd (Australia) *Tel:* (02) 7631211 *Fax:* (02) 7643201, pg 11

Ao Livro Tecnico Industria e Comercio Ltda (Brazil) *Tel:* (021) 580-6230; (021) 580-1168 *Fax:* (021) 580-9955 *E-mail:* contatos@editoraaolivrotecnico.com.br *Web Site:* www.editoraaolivrotecnico.com.br, pg 77

Aoki Shoten Co Ltd (Japan) *Tel:* (03) 32192341 *Fax:* (03) 32192585, pg 415

AOL-Verlag Frohmut Menze (Germany) *Tel:* (07227) 95 88-0 *Fax:* (07227) 95 88-95 *E-mail:* info@aol-verlag.de; bestellung@aol-verlag.de *Web Site:* www.aol-verlag.de, pg 193

Aoraki Press Ltd (New Zealand) *Tel:* (04) 3858528 *Fax:* (03) 3858528 *E-mail:* aoraki@actrix.gen.nz, pg 493

AP Information Services Ltd (United Kingdom) *Tel:* (020) 8349 9988 *Fax:* (020) 8349 9797 *E-mail:* info@apinfo.co.uk *Web Site:* www.apinfo.co.uk, pg 658

APA (Academic Publishers Associated) (Netherlands) *Tel:* (020) 626 5544 *Fax:* (020) 528 5298 *E-mail:* info@apa-publishers.com *Web Site:* www.apa-publishers.com, pg 477

APA Production Pte Ltd (Singapore) *Tel:* 8651600; 8651601 *Fax:* 8616438 *E-mail:* apasin@singnet.com.sg, pg 554

APAC Publishers Services Pte Ltd (Singapore) *Tel:* 6844 7333 *Fax:* 6747 8916 *E-mail:* service@apacmedia.com.sg, pg 554

Apaginastantas - Cooperativa de Servicos Culturais (Portugal) *Tel:* (021) 668987, pg 528

Editions APESS ASBL (Luxembourg) *Tel:* 80 8358 *Fax:* 80 2813 *E-mail:* apess@ci.edu.lu *Web Site:* www.restena.lu/apess, pg 450

Apex Books Concern (United Kingdom) *Tel:* (01903) 734432 *Fax:* (01903) 734432 *E-mail:* enquiries@apexbooks.co.uk *Web Site:* www.apexbooks.co.uk, pg 1346

Apex Press & Publishing (Oman) *Tel:* 799388 *Fax:* 793316 *E-mail:* apexoman@gto.net.om *Web Site:* www.apexstuff.com, pg 511

Apex Publishing Ltd (United Kingdom) *Tel:* (0870) 242 0938 *Fax:* (0870) 046 6536 *E-mail:* enquiry@apexpublishing.co.uk *Web Site:* www.apexpublishing.co.uk, pg 658

Verlag Der Apfel (Austria) *Tel:* (01) 52 661 52 *Fax:* (01) 52 287 18, pg 48

APH Publishing Corp (India) *Tel:* (011) 5100581; (011) 5410924; (011) 3285807 *Fax:* (011) 3274050 *E-mail:* aph@mantrasonline.com, pg 328

Verlag APHAIA Svea Haske, Sonja Schumann GbR (Germany) *Tel:* (030) 813 39 98 *Fax:* (030) 813 39 98 *E-mail:* info@aphaia-verlag.de *Web Site:* www.aphaia-verlag.de, pg 193

Apimondia (Italy) *Tel:* (06) 6852286 *Fax:* (06) 6852287 *E-mail:* apimondia@mclink.it *Web Site:* www.apimondia.org, pg 375

Apocalipis Digital (Cuba) *Tel:* (07) 816625 *E-mail:* adigital@tinored.cu; adigital@colombus.cu, pg 120

Apogeo srl - Editrice di Informatica (Italy) *Tel:* (02) 289981 *Fax:* (02) 26116334 *E-mail:* apogeo@apogeonline.com *Web Site:* www.apogeonline.com, pg 375

Apollo-Verlag Paul Lincke GmbH (Germany) *Tel:* (06131) 246300 *Fax:* (06131) 246861 *E-mail:* apollo@schott-musik.de, pg 193

Apollo's Reklame en Uitgeversburo (Suriname), pg 608

Apostolado da Oracao Secretariado Nacional (Portugal) *Tel:* (053) 22485 *Fax:* (053) 201221, pg 528

Apostolato della Preghiera (Italy) *Tel:* (06) 697 607 1 *Fax:* (06) 67 81 063 *E-mail:* adp@adp.it *Web Site:* www.adp.it, pg 375

Biblioteca Apostolica Vaticana (Holy See (Vatican City State)) *Tel:* (06) 6987 9402 *Fax:* (06) 6988 4795 *E-mail:* bav@vatlib.it, pg 314

Biblioteca Apostolica Vaticana (Holy See (Vatican City State)) *Tel:* (06) 6987 9402 *Fax:* (06) 6988 4795 *E-mail:* bav@vatlib.it *Web Site:* 212.77.1.230/it/v_home_bav/home_bav.shtml, pg 1513

Biblioteca Apostolica Vaticana (Holy See (Vatican City State)) *Tel:* (06) 6987 9402 *Fax:* (06) 6988 4795 *E-mail:* bav@librs6k.vatlib.it *Web Site:* www.vatican.va, pg 1564

Apostoliki Diakonia tis Ekklisias tis Hellados (Greece) *Tel:* (010) 7239417; (010) 7248681-9 *Fax:* (010) 7238149 *E-mail:* apostoliki-diakonia@ath.forthnet.gr *Web Site:* www.apostoliki-diakonia.gr, pg 305

Forlaget Apostrof ApS (Denmark) *Tel:* 3920 8420 *Fax:* 3920 8453 *E-mail:* info1@apostrof.dk *Web Site:* www.apostrof.dk, pg 129

Apotekarsocietetens Forlag (Sweden) *Tel:* (08) 7235000 *Fax:* (08) 205511, pg 609

Apple Books (Zambia) *Tel:* (01) 211216 *Fax:* (01) 224855, pg 781

Apple Press (United Kingdom) *Tel:* (01273) 727268 *Fax:* (01273) 727269 *E-mail:* information@quarto.com *Web Site:* www.quarto.com, pg 658

Appleby's Bindery Ltd (Canada) *Tel:* 506-488-2086 Toll Free *Tel:* 800-561-2005 (Canada only) *Fax:* 506-488-2086 *E-mail:* applbind@nbnet.nb.ca, pg 1215, 1235, 1245

Appletree Press Ltd (United Kingdom) *Tel:* (028) 9024 3074 *Fax:* (028) 9024 6756 *E-mail:* reception@appletree.ie *Web Site:* www.appletree.ie, pg 658

Appropriate Technology Development Group (Inc) WA (Australia) *Tel:* (08) 9336 1262 *Fax:* (08) 9430 5729 *E-mail:* apace@argo.net.au *Web Site:* www.argo.net.au/apace, pg 11

Aquamarin Verlag (Germany) *Tel:* (08092) 9444 *Fax:* (08092) 1614 *E-mail:* aquamarin-verlag@t-online.de, pg 193

Aquanut Agencies Pte Ltd (Singapore) *Tel:* 7753614 *Fax:* 7753614 *E-mail:* aquanut@singnet.com.sg *Web Site:* www.aquanut.com.sg, pg 555

Editora Aquariana Ltda (Brazil) *Tel:* (011) 288 7139 *Fax:* (011) 283 0476 *E-mail:* aquariana@ground.com.br, pg 77

Aquarious (Greece) *Tel:* (01) 3842354; (01) 3617360 *Fax:* (01) 3303890, pg 1313

Aquarius Ekdotiki Etaireia (Greece) *Tel:* (01) 3842354 *Fax:* (01) 8826060, pg 306

Aquila Press (Australia) *Tel:* (02) 8268 3333 *Fax:* (02) 8268 3357 *E-mail:* sales@youthworks.asn.au *Web Site:* www.youthworks.net.au, pg 11

ARA International (Luxembourg) *Tel:* 34 85 91 *Fax:* 34 85 91 *E-mail:* amisrelart@pt.lu *Web Site:* www.ara-international.lu, pg 450

Arab Archivists Institute (Iraq) *Tel:* (01) 416 8440, pg 1565

Arab Library (Mauritania), pg 1528

Al Arab Bookshop (Egypt (Arab Republic of Egypt)) *Tel:* (02) 5915315, pg 1309

Arab Centre for Medical Literature (Kuwait) *Tel:* 5338610; 5338611 *Fax:* 5338618; 5338619, pg 1276

Arab Communicators (Bahrain) *Tel:* (0973) 254 258 *Fax:* (0973) 531 837, pg 60

Arab Institute for Research & Publishing (Lebanon) *Fax:* (01) 751438; (01) 752308 *E-mail:* mkayyali@jonet.com, pg 445

Arab Organization for Agricultural Development (Sudan) *Tel:* (011) 78760; (011) 78761; (011) 78762; (011) 78763 *Fax:* (011) 471402 *E-mail:* inquiry@aoad.org; info@aoad.org *Web Site:* www.aoad.org, pg 608

Arab Organization for Agricultural Development (Sudan) *Tel:* (011) 472176; (011) 472183 *Fax:* (011) 471402 *E-mail:* inquiry@aoad.org *Web Site:* www.aoad.org, pg 1546

Al Arab Publishing House (Egypt (Arab Republic of Egypt)) *Tel:* (02) 908027, pg 137

Arab Regional Branch of the International Council on Archives (Tunisia) *Tel:* (071) 575 834 *Fax:* (071) 569 175 *E-mail:* archives.nationales@email.ati.tn; enquiry@dm.gov.ae *Web Site:* www.archives-dgan.gov.dz/, pg 1288

Arab Scientific Publishers BP (Lebanon) *Tel:* (01) 785107; (01) 785108; (01) 786607 *Fax:* (01) 786230; (01) 860138 *E-mail:* asp@asp.com.lb *Web Site:* www.asp.com.lb, pg 445

Arabian Bookshop (Qatar) *Tel:* 442648 *Fax:* 449653, pg 1338

ARADCO VSI Ltd (United Kingdom) *Tel:* (020) 7692 7700 *Fax:* (020) 7692 7711 *Web Site:* www.aradco.com, pg 1149

ARADCO VSI Ltd (United Kingdom) *Tel:* (020) 7692 7700 *Fax:* (020) 7692 7711 *E-mail:* aradco@compuserve.com *Web Site:* www.aradco.com, pg 1183

Arambol, SL (Spain) *Tel:* (091) 3194057 *Fax:* (091) 3194057 *E-mail:* arambolsl@hotmail.com, pg 573

Biblioteca Luis Angel Arango Banco de la Republica (Colombia) *Tel:* (01) 3431212 *Fax:* (01) 2863551 *E-mail:* wbiblio@banrep.gov.co *Web Site:* www.banrep.gov.co, pg 1498

arani-Verlag GmbH (Germany) *Tel:* (030) 691-7073 *Fax:* (030) 691-4067, pg 193

Aranyhal Konyvkiado Goldfish Publishing (Hungary) *Tel:* (01) 239-6721 *Fax:* (01) 239-6730 *E-mail:* sprinter@com.kibernet.hu, pg 320

Editorial Aranzadi SA (Spain) *Tel:* (0902) 444 144 *Fax:* (0948) 297 200 *E-mail:* clientes@aranzadi.es *Web Site:* www.aranzadi.es, pg 573

Editorial Franciscana Aranzazu (Spain) *Tel:* (043) 780797; (043) 780951 *Fax:* (043) 783370, pg 573

Ararat -Tiped, Editura (Romania) *Tel:* (01) 3111425; (01) 6134050 *Fax:* (01) 3111420, pg 538

Aratron, IK (Bulgaria) *Tel:* (02) 9807455 *Fax:* (02) 958-19-31 *E-mail:* aratron@techno-link.com, pg 93

M J Bezerra de Araujo Editora Ltda (Brazil) *Tel:* (021) 5024435 *Fax:* (021) 5024435, pg 77

L'Arbalete (France) *Tel:* (04) 72933434 *Fax:* (04) 72933400, pg 147

Uitgeverij de Arbeiderspers (Netherlands) *Tel:* (020) 5247500 *E-mail:* info@arbeiderspers.nl *Web Site:* www.ap-archipel.nl, pg 477

Arbeiterpresse Verlags- und Vertriebsgesellschaft mbH (Germany) *Tel:* (0201) 6462106 *Fax:* (0201) 6462108 *E-mail:* vertrieb@arbeiterpresse.de *Web Site:* www.arbeiterpresse.de, pg 193

Arbeitsgemeinschaft der Archive und Bibliotheken in der evangelischen Kirche (Germany) *Tel:* (0911) 58869-0 *Fax:* (0911) 58869-69 *E-mail:* LKANuernberg@t-online.de *Web Site:* www.ekd.de/archive/deutsch/arbeitsg.htm, pg 1562

Arbeitsgemeinschaft der Blindenschrift-Druckereien und Bibliotheken (AG BDB) (Germany) *Tel:* (06421) 60 60 *Fax:* (06421) 60 62 29 *E-mail:* info@blista.de *Web Site:* www.blista.de, pg 1269

Arbeitsgemeinschaft der Regionalbibliotheken (Germany) *Tel:* (0711) 212-4423 *Fax:* (0711) 212-4422 *Web Site:* www.regionalbibliotheken.de, pg 1562

Arbeitsgemeinschaft der Spezialbibliotheken eV (ASpB) (Germany) *Tel:* (02461) 612907; (02461) 615368 *Fax:* (02461) 616103 *Web Site:* www.aspb.de, pg 1562

Arbeitsgemeinschaft fur juristisches Bibliotheks- und Dokumentationswesen (Germany) *Tel:* (089) 9231 358 *Fax:* (089) 9231 201 *Web Site:* www.ajbd.de, pg 1562

Arbeitsgemeinschaft fur medizinisches Bibliothekswesen (Germany) *Tel:* (0621) 7592376 *Fax:* (0621) 7594419 *Web Site:* www.agmb.de, pg 1562

Arbeitsgemeinschaft von Jugendbuchverlagen e v (Germany) *Tel:* (0711) 2843 440 *Fax:* (0711) 2483 622 *E-mail:* info@avj-online.de *Web Site:* www.avj-online.de, pg 1269

Arbeitsgruppe LOK Report eV (Germany) *Tel:* (030) 86 40 92 63 *Fax:* (030) 86 40 92 64 *E-mail:* redaktion@lok-report.de *Web Site:* www.lok-report.de, pg 193

Arbeitskreis fur Jugendliteratur eV (Germany) *Tel:* (089) 45 80 80 6 *Fax:* (089) 45 80 80 88 *E-mail:* info@jugendliteratur.org *Web Site:* www.jugendliteratur.org, pg 1269

Arbol Editorial SA de CV (Mexico) *Tel:* (05) 6887677; (05) 6057600, pg 462

Uitgeverij Arbor (Netherlands) *Tel:* (035) 5422141 *Fax:* (035) 15433, pg 477

Les Editions de l'Arbre (Tunisia) *Tel:* (01) 753 209 *Fax:* (01) 887 927, pg 647

Editorial Arca SRL (Uruguay) *Tel:* (02) 9166966 int 110 *Fax:* (02) 901887; (02) 930188 *E-mail:* saroya@st.com.uy, pg 776

Arcadia Books Ltd (United Kingdom) *Tel:* (0207) 436 9898 *E-mail:* info@arcadiabooks.co.uk *Web Site:* www.arcadiabooks.co.uk, pg 659

Arcadia Edizioni Srl (Italy) *Tel:* (059) 76 60 34 *Fax:* (059) 77 92 79 *E-mail:* edizioni@arcadiabooks.com *Web Site:* www.arcadiabooks.com, pg 375

Arcadia Verlag GmbH (Germany) *Tel:* (040) 4141000 *Fax:* (040) 41410041 *E-mail:* contact@sikorski.de *Web Site:* www.sikorski.de, pg 193

Editions Arcam (France) *Tel:* (01) 42729312 *E-mail:* phreatiq@multimania.com, pg 147

Arcanta Aries Gruppo Editoriale (Italy) *Tel:* (049) 8712477 *Fax:* (049) 8713851, pg 375

AB Arcanum (Sweden) *Tel:* (0302) 242 70 *Fax:* (0302) 242 73 *E-mail:* info@arcanum-utbildning.se *Web Site:* www.arcanum-utbildning.se, pg 609

ARCHA sro Vydavatel'stro (Slovakia) *Tel:* (07) 5315586; (07) 54415609 *Fax:* (07) 5441586 *E-mail:* archa@internet.sk, pg 559

The Library of the Archbishop Makarios III Foundation (Cyprus) *Tel:* (022) 430008 *Fax:* (022) 346753, pg 1500

L'Arche Editeur (France) *Tel:* (01) 46 33 46 45 *Fax:* (01) 46 33 56 40 *E-mail:* contact@arche-editeur.com *Web Site:* www.arche-editeur.com, pg 147

Arche Verlag AG, Raabe und Vitali (Switzerland) *Tel:* (01) 252 24 10 *Fax:* (01) 261 11 15 *E-mail:* info@arche-verlag.com *Web Site:* www.arche-verlag.com, pg 617

Archief- en Bibliotheekwezen in Belgie (Belgium) *Tel:* (02) 5195351 *Fax:* (02) 5195533, pg 1558

Biblioteca Comunale dell' Archiginnasio (Italy) *Tel:* (051) 276811 *Fax:* (051) 261160 *E-mail:* archiginnasio@comune.bologna.it *Web Site:* www.archiginnasio.it, pg 1520

Archimede Edizioni (Italy) *Tel:* (02) 748231 *Fax:* (02) 74823278, pg 376

Rosellina Archinto Editore (Italy) *Tel:* (02) 86460237 *Fax:* (02) 86451955 *E-mail:* info@archinto.it *Web Site:* www.archinto.it, pg 376

Editions de l'Archipel (France) *Tel:* (01) 55 80 77 40 *Fax:* (01) 55 80 77 41 *E-mail:* ecricom@wanadoo.fr, pg 147

Archipelago Press (Singapore) *Tel:* 2248044 *Fax:* 2247400 *E-mail:* edm@pacific.net.sg, pg 555

Architectura & Natura (Netherlands) *Tel:* (020) 6236186 *Fax:* (020) 6382303 *E-mail:* info@architectura.nl *Web Site:* www.architectura.nl, pg 478

Architectural Association Publications (United Kingdom) *Tel:* (020) 7887 4021; (020) 7887 4000 *Fax:* (020) 7414 0783 *E-mail:* publications@aaschool.ac.uk *Web Site:* www.aaschool.ac.uk/publications, pg 659

Koninklijke Vereniging van Archivarissen in Nederland (Netherlands) *Tel:* (020) 462 77 27 *Fax:* (020) 462 77 28 *E-mail:* bureau@kvan.nl *Web Site:* www.kvan.nl, pg 1568

YELLOW PAGES

Archives Nationales de Cote d'Ivoire (Cote d'Ivoire) *Tel:* 32 41 58 *Fax:* 21 50 13, pg 1499

Archives Bibliotheque nationales du Cameroon (Cameroon) *Tel:* 220078, pg 1497

Archives Departementales (Reunion) *Tel:* 94 04 14 *Fax:* 94 04 21 *E-mail:* archives@cg974.fr, pg 1539

Archives Departementales de la Martinique (Martinique) *Tel:* 63 88 46 *Fax:* 70 04 50 *E-mail:* archives@cg972.fr, pg 1528

Archives du Senegal (Senegal) *Tel:* 8235072 *Fax:* 8225126 *E-mail:* pmardi@primature.sn, pg 1541

Archives generales du Royaume (Belgium) *Tel:* (02) 513 76 80 *Fax:* (02) 513 76 81 *E-mail:* archives.generales@arch.be, pg 1493

Archives Nationales (The Democratic Republic of the Congo) *Tel:* (012) 31 083, pg 1499

Archives Nationales (France) *Tel:* (01) 40 27 64 19 *Fax:* (01) 40 27 66 01 *E-mail:* chan.paris@culture.gouv.fr *Web Site:* www.archivesnationales.culture.gouv.fr, pg 1506

Archives nationales (Tunisia) *Tel:* (01) 560 556 *Fax:* (01) 569 175, pg 1550

Archives New Zealand (New Zealand) *Tel:* (04) 4995595; (04) 4956226 (reference) *Fax:* (04) 4956210 *E-mail:* wellington@archives.govt.nz *Web Site:* www.archives.govt.nz, pg 1532

Archives Office of New South Wales (Australia) *Tel:* (02) 9673-1788 *Fax:* (02) 9833-4518 *E-mail:* srecords@records.nsw.gov.au *Web Site:* www.records.nsw.gov.au, pg 1490

Archivio Centrale dello Stato (Italy) *Tel:* (06) 545481 *Fax:* (06) 5413620 *E-mail:* acs@archivi.beniculturali.it *Web Site:* www.archiviocentraledellostato.it; archivi.beniculturali.it/ACS, pg 1520

Archivio Guido Izzi Edizioni (Italy) *Tel:* (06) 39735580 *Fax:* (06) 39734433, pg 376

Archivio Segreto Vaticano (Holy See (Vatican City State)) *Tel:* (06) 69883314 *Fax:* (06) 69885574, pg 314

Biblioteca dell'Archivio Storico Civico e Biblioteca Trivulziana (Italy) *Tel:* (02) 86454638; (02) 89010293 *Fax:* (02) 875926 *E-mail:* marina_litrico@rcm.inet.it *Web Site:* www.rcs.it/mimu/musei/biblioteca_trivulziana/info.htm, pg 1520

Archivio Storico Ticinese (Switzerland) *Tel:* (091) 820 0101 *Fax:* (091) 825 1874 *E-mail:* casagrande@casagrande-online.ch *Web Site:* www.casagrande-online.ch, pg 617

Archivo de la Corona de Aragon (Spain) *Tel:* (093) 4854 318; (093) 4854 285; (093) 3153 208 *Fax:* (093) 3001 252 *E-mail:* aca@cult.mec.es *Web Site:* www.cultura.mecd.es/archivos/index.html, pg 1545

Archivo General de la Nacion (Mexico) *Tel:* 5133-9900 *Fax:* 5789-5296 *E-mail:* agn@segob.gob.mx *Web Site:* www.agn.gob.mx, pg 1528

Archivo General de la Nacion (AG) (Venezuela) *Tel:* (02) 862-99-07 *Fax:* (02) 81-93-28 *Web Site:* www.ucab.edu.ve/biblioteca, pg 1555

Archivo General de Centro America (Guatemala) *Tel:* 232-3037, pg 1513

Archivo General de Indias (Spain) *Tel:* (05) 954 500 530; (05) 954 500 528 *Fax:* 954 219 485 *E-mail:* agi1@cult.mec.es *Web Site:* www.cultura.mecd.es; www.mcu.es *pg* 1545

Archivo General de la Nacion de Colombia (Colombia) *Tel:* (01) 2431336 *Fax:* (01) 3414030 *E-mail:* bnc@mincultura.gov.co *Web Site:* www.bibliotecanacional.gov.co, pg 1498

Archivo General de la Nacion del Peru (Peru) *Tel:* (01) 427-5930; (01) 427-5939 *Fax:* (01) 428-2829 *Web Site:* agn.perucultural.org.pe, pg 1536

Archivo General de Puerto Rico (Puerto Rico) *Tel:* (787) 724-0700 *Fax:* (787) 724-8393 *Web Site:* www.icp.gobierno.pr, pg 1539

Archivo Historico Nacional (Spain) *Tel:* (091) 7688 500 *Fax:* (091) 5631 199 *Web Site:* ahn.cult.mec.es, pg 1545

Archivo Nacional de Cuba (Cuba) *Tel:* (07) 862 9436; (07) 636 489 *Fax:* (07) 33 8089 *E-mail:* arnac@ceniainf.cu, pg 1500

Archivo Nacional de Historia (Ecuador) *Tel:* (02) 2280431 *Fax:* (02) 2280431 *E-mail:* ane@ane.gov.ec *Web Site:* www.ane.gov.ec, pg 1503

Archivo Nacional de Nicaragua (Nicaragua) *Tel:* (02) 223 240 *Fax:* (02) 22722 *E-mail:* binanic@tmx.com.nic, pg 1533

Archivo y Biblioteca Capitulares (Spain) *Tel:* (0925) 21 24 23 *Fax:* (0925) 21 24 23 *E-mail:* archicapto@terra.es *Web Site:* www.architoledo.org/catedral/archivos/textoarchivo.htm, pg 1545

L'Archivolto (Italy) *Tel:* (02) 29010444; (02) 29010424 *Fax:* (02) 29001942 *E-mail:* info@archivolto.com *Web Site:* www.archivolto.com, pg 376

Naczelna Dyrekcja Archiwow Panstwowych (Poland) *Tel:* (022) 635-68-22 *Fax:* (022) 831-75-63 *E-mail:* coia-info@archiwa.gov.pl *Web Site:* www.archiwa.gov.pl, pg 1537

Archiwum Glowne Akt Dawnych (Poland) *Tel:* (022) 831-54-91 *Fax:* (022) 831-16-08 *Web Site:* www.piasa.org/polisharchives/warsawhr.html, pg 1537

Arcipelago Edizioni di Chiani Marisa (Italy) *Tel:* (02) 36525177 *Fax:* (02) 36553002 *E-mail:* arcipelago@arcipelagoedizioni.fastwebnet.it *Web Site:* www.arcipelagoedizioni.com, pg 376

Arco Libros SL (Spain) *Tel:* (091) 4153687; (091) 4161371 *Fax:* (091) 4135907 *E-mail:* arcolibros@arcomuralla.com *Web Site:* www.arcomuralla.com, pg 573

Arcs Editions (Tunisia) *Tel:* (01) 351617, pg 647

Arcturus Publishing Ltd (United Kingdom) *Tel:* (020) 7407 9400 *Fax:* (020) 7407 9444 *E-mail:* info@arcturuspublishing.com *Web Site:* www.arcturuspublishing.com, pg 659

ARCult Media (Germany) *Tel:* (0228) 211059 *Fax:* (0228) 217493 *E-mail:* info@arcultmedia.de *Web Site:* www.arcultmedia.de; www.kulturforschung.de; www.ericarts.org, pg 193

Ardey-Verlag GmbH (Germany) *Tel:* (0251) 4132-0 *Fax:* (0251) 4132-20 *Web Site:* www.ardey-verlag.de, pg 193

Publications Aredit (France) *Tel:* (03) 20 26 79 81, pg 147

Uitgeverij Arena BV (Netherlands) *Tel:* (020) 55 40 500 *Fax:* (020) 42 16 868 *E-mail:* info@boekenarena.nl *Web Site:* www.meulenhoff.nl; www.boekenarena.nl, pg 478

Arena Verlag GmbH (Germany) *Tel:* (0931) 79 644-0 *Fax:* (0931) 79 644-13, pg 193

Edizioni ARES (Italy) *Tel:* (02) 29514202; (02) 29526156 *Fax:* (02) 29520163 *E-mail:* aresed@tin.it; info@ares.mi.it *Web Site:* www.ares.mi.it, pg 376

Arevik (Armenia) *Tel:* (02) 524561 *Fax:* (02) 520536 *E-mail:* arevikp@freenet.am; arevick@netsys.am *Web Site:* www.arevik.am, pg 10

Argalia Editore delle Arti Grafiche Editoriali SRL (Italy) *Tel:* (0722) 328756 *Fax:* (0722) 328756 *Web Site:* www.culturitalia.uibk.ac.at, pg 376

Editorial Argentina Plaza y Janes SA (Argentina) *Tel:* (011) 4862-6769; (011) 4862-6785 *Fax:* (011) 4864-4970, pg 3

Argentine Bible Society (Argentina) *Tel:* (011) 4312-5787; (011) 4312-8558 *Fax:* (011) 4312-3400 *E-mail:* socbibliaarg@biblica.org *Web Site:* www.biblesociety.org, pg 3

Argentinian PEN Centre (Argentina) *Web Site:* www.oneworld.org, pg 1395

WYDAWNICTWO ARKADY

ARGO-RISK Publisher (Russian Federation) *Tel:* (095) 4768538 *Fax:* (095) 2926511 *E-mail:* zayats@glas.apc.org, pg 543

Argo Spoken Word (United Kingdom) *Tel:* (020) 8910 5000 *Fax:* (020) 8910 3130, pg 659

Argon Verlag GmbH (Germany) *Tel:* (030) 25 37 38-0 *Fax:* (030) 25 37 38-99 *E-mail:* info.argon@fischerverlage.de *Web Site:* www.fischerverlage.de, pg 194

Argosy Press (Zimbabwe) *Tel:* (04) 704715; (04) 704766 *Fax:* (04) 752162, pg 782

Argument-Verlag (Germany) *Tel:* (040) 401800-0 *Fax:* (040) 401800-20 *E-mail:* verlag@argument.de *Web Site:* www.argument.de, pg 194

Arguval Editorial SA (Spain) *Tel:* (095) 2318784; (095) 2360213 *Fax:* (095) 2323715 *E-mail:* editorial@arguval.com *Web Site:* www.arguval.com, pg 573

Argyll Publishing (United Kingdom) *Tel:* (01369) 820229 *Fax:* (01369) 820372 *E-mail:* argyll.publishing@virgin.net *Web Site:* www.skoobe.biz, pg 659

Arhiv na Makedonija (The Former Yugoslav Republic of Macedonia) *Tel:* (091) 237-211; (091) 115-783; (091) 115-827 *Fax:* (091) 115-783 *Web Site:* www.arhiv.gov.mk, pg 1526

Arhiv Republike Slovenije (Slovenia) *Tel:* (01) 24 14 218 *Fax:* (01) 24 14 269 *E-mail:* ars@gov.si *Web Site:* www.sigov.si/ars, pg 1543

Arhivele Nationale ale Romaniei (Romania) *Tel:* (01) 3152503 *Fax:* (01) 3125841 *E-mail:* webmaster@mai.gov.ro *Web Site:* www.mai.gov.ro, pg 1539

Arhus Kommunes Biblioteker (Denmark) *Tel:* 8940 9200 *Fax:* 8940 9393 *Web Site:* www.aakb.dk, pg 1501

Editorial Ariel SA (Spain) *Tel:* (093) 496 70 30 *Fax:* (093) 496 70 32 *E-mail:* editorial@ariel.es *Web Site:* www.ariel.es, pg 573

Ariel Lydbokforlag (Norway) *Tel:* 64943510 *Fax:* 64943510, pg 508

Ariel Publishing House (Israel) *Tel:* (02) 6434540 *Fax:* (02) 6436164, pg 365

Aries-Verlag Paul Johannes Muller (Germany) *Tel:* (08661) 8209 *Fax:* (08661) 985980, pg 194

Arihant Publishers (India) *Tel:* (0141) 515192, pg 328

Ario Company Ltd (Republic of Korea) *Tel:* (02) 7122001; (02) 7122003 *Fax:* (02) 7023156, pg 437

Ariston Editions (Switzerland) *Tel:* (071) 6727218 *Fax:* (071) 6727219 *E-mail:* 106420.3235@compuserve.com, pg 617

Uitgevirj Aristos (Netherlands) *Tel:* (010) 243 73 70 *Fax:* (010) 243 76 00 *E-mail:* aristos@xs4all.nl *Web Site:* www.xs4all.nl/~feico/aristos, pg 478

Aritbus et Historiae, Rivista Internationale di arti visive ecinema, Institut IRSA - Verlagsanstatt (Poland) *Tel:* (012) 421 90 30; (012) 421 91 55 *Fax:* (012) 421 48 07 *E-mail:* irsa@irsa.com.pl *Web Site:* www.irsa.com.pl, pg 522

Ark Boeken (Netherlands) *Tel:* (020) 6114847 *Fax:* (020) 6114864 *E-mail:* arkboeken@wxs.nl, pg 478

ARK Bokhandel (Norway) *Tel:* 22 99 07 50 *Fax:* 22 99 07 51 *E-mail:* resepsjon@ark.no *Web Site:* www.arkbokhandel.no, pg 1332

Edizioni Arka SRL (Italy) *Tel:* (02) 4818230 *Fax:* (02) 4816752 *E-mail:* arka.edizioni@tin.it, pg 376

Arkadas Ltd (Turkey) *Tel:* (0312) 434 46 24 *Fax:* (0312) 435 60 57, pg 649

Arkadas Ltd (Turkey) *Tel:* (0312) 4344624; (0312) 3548300 *Fax:* (0312) 4356057 *E-mail:* arkadas@arkadas.com.tr *Web Site:* www.arkadas.com.tr, pg 1346

Wydawnictwo Arkady (Poland) *Tel:* (022) 8268980; (022) 8267079; (022) 8269316; (022) 635 83 44 *Fax:* (022) 827 41 94 *E-mail:* arkady@arkady.com.pl *Web Site:* arkady.com.pl, pg 522

1605

Arkana Verlag Tete Boettger Rainer Wunderlich GmbH (Germany) *Tel:* (0551) 41709 *Fax:* (0551) 43868, pg 194

Uitgeverij Jan van Arkel (Netherlands) *Tel:* (030) 2731840 *Fax:* (030) 2733614 *E-mail:* i-books@antenna.nl *Web Site:* www.antenna.bl/i-books, pg 478

Arkeoloji Ve Sanat Yayinlari (Turkey) *Tel:* (212) 293 0378 *Fax:* (212) 245 6877 *E-mail:* info@arkeolojisanat.com *Web Site:* www.arkeolojisanat.com, pg 649

Arkin Kitabevi (Turkey) *Tel:* (0212) 522 92 24 *Fax:* (0212) 512 19 01, pg 649

Arkitektens Forlag (Denmark) *Tel:* 32836970 *Fax:* 32836940 *E-mail:* eksp@arkfo.dk; red@arkfo.dk *Web Site:* www.arkfo.dk, pg 129

Arkitektur Forlag AB (Sweden) *Tel:* (08) 7027850 *Fax:* (08) 6115270 *E-mail:* redaktionen@arkitektur.se *Web Site:* www.arkitektur.se, pg 609

Arkivarforeningen (Denmark) *Tel:* 31393520 *Fax:* 33153239, pg 1560

Arkivarforeningen (Norway) *Tel:* 22022657 *Fax:* 22237489 *E-mail:* synne.stavheim@riksarkivaren.dep.no, pg 1569

Arktos (Italy) *Tel:* (011) 9773941 *Fax:* (011) 9715340, pg 376

Arlekin-Wydawnictwo Harlequin Enterprises sp zoo (Poland) *Tel:* (022) 8499557; (022) 8499498; (022) 8498630 *Fax:* (022) 8499557, pg 522

ARLIS/UK & Ireland Art Libraries Society (United Kingdom) *Tel:* (01527) 579298 *Fax:* (01527) 579298 *Web Site:* www.arlis.org.uk, pg 1572

Armada Publishing House (Russian Federation) *Tel:* (095) 4544301; (095) 45431526 *Fax:* (095) 4542481 *E-mail:* riv@armada.msk.ru, pg 543

Editions de l'Armancon (France) *Tel:* (03) 80 64 41 87 *Fax:* (03) 80 64 46 96 *Web Site:* www.editions-armancon.fr, pg 147

Editore Armando Armando SRL (Italy) *Tel:* (06) 5894525 *Fax:* (06) 5818564 *E-mail:* info@armandoeditore.com *Web Site:* www.armando.it, pg 376

Armenia Editions (France) *Tel:* (06) 08 22 71 50 *Fax:* (06) 08 27 85 94, pg 147

Gruppo Editoriale Armenia SpA (Italy) *Tel:* (02) 683911 *Fax:* (02) 6684884 *E-mail:* armenia@armenia.it *Web Site:* www.armenia.it, pg 376

Armitano Editores CA (Venezuela) *Tel:* (02) 2342565; (02) 2340870; (02) 2340865 *Fax:* (02) 2341647 *E-mail:* armiedit@telcel.net.ve *Web Site:* www.armitano.com, pg 779

Grupo Editorial Armonia (Mexico) *Tel:* 54 42 96 00 *E-mail:* corporativo@grupoarmonia.com.mx *Web Site:* www.grupoarmonia.com.mx, pg 462

Arms & Armour Press (United Kingdom) *Tel:* (020) 7420 5555 *Fax:* (020) 7420 7261, pg 659

Livraria Arnado Lda (Portugal) *Tel:* (0239) 27573 *Fax:* (0239) 22598, pg 528

Arnaud Editore SRL (Italy) *Tel:* (055) 216485 *Fax:* (055) 260466, pg 376

Arnette (France) *Tel:* (01) 45496500 *Fax:* (01) 45491288, pg 147

Arnkrone Forlaget A/S (Denmark) *Tel:* 32507000 *Fax:* 32522652, pg 129

Arnold (United Kingdom) *Tel:* (020) 7873 6000 *Fax:* (020) 7873 6325 *E-mail:* feedback.arnold@hodder.co.uk *Web Site:* www.arnoldpublishers.com, pg 659

Edward Arnold (Australia) Pty Ltd (Australia) *Tel:* (03) 9859 9011 *Fax:* (03) 9859 9141, pg 12

Arnoldsche Verlagsanstalt GmbH (Germany) *Tel:* (0711) 645618-0 *Fax:* (0711) 645618-79 *E-mail:* art@arnoldsche.com *Web Site:* www.arnoldsche.com, pg 194

Aromolaran Publishing Co Ltd (Nigeria) *Tel:* (02) 24392, pg 503

Arpeco Engineering (Canada) *Tel:* 905-564-5150 *Toll Free Tel:* 800-387-4806 *Fax:* 905-564-2943 *E-mail:* sales@arpeco.com *Web Site:* www.arpeco.com, pg 1215

Arpoador (Uruguay) *Tel:* (02) 707826 *Fax:* (02) 717278, pg 777

Arquivo Nacional (Brazil) *Tel:* (021) 232-6938 *Fax:* (021) 224-4525 *E-mail:* arqnacdg@rio.com.br, pg 78

Arquivo Nacional (Brazil) *Tel:* (021) 3806-6171 *Fax:* (021) 2232-8430 *E-mail:* conarq@arquivonacional.gov.br *Web Site:* www.arquivonacional.gov.br/, pg 1495

Arquivo Universidade de Coimbra (Portugal) *Tel:* (0239) 25422 *Fax:* (0239) 25841 *Web Site:* www.uc.pt, pg 528

Arrayan Editores (Chile) *Tel:* (02) 4314200 *Fax:* (02) 2741041 *E-mail:* web@arrayan.cl *Web Site:* www.arrayan.cl, pg 98

J W Arrowsmith Ltd (United Kingdom) *Tel:* (0117) 966 7545 *Fax:* (0117) 963 7829 *E-mail:* jw@arrowsmith.co.uk *Web Site:* www.arrowsmith.co.uk, pg 1162, 1183, 1224, 1247

Ars Edition GmbH (Germany) *Tel:* (089) 3810060 *Fax:* (089) 381006-58, pg 194

Ars Longa Publishing House (Romania) *Tel:* (0232) 215078 *Fax:* (0232) 215078 *E-mail:* arslonga@mail.dntis.ro, pg 538

Ars Poetica Editora Ltda (Brazil) *Tel:* (011) 2405598 *Fax:* (011) 5312648, pg 78

Ars Scribendi bv Uitgeverij (Netherlands) *Tel:* (0348) 443998 *Fax:* (0348) 444076 *E-mail:* info@arsscribendi.com *Web Site:* www.arsscribendi.com, pg 478

Ars Vivendi Verlag (Germany) *Tel:* (09103) 719 29 0 *Fax:* (09103) 719 59 19 *E-mail:* ars@arsvivendi.com *Web Site:* www.arsvivendi.com, pg 194

Bibliotheque de l' Arsenal (France) *Tel:* (01) 53012525 *Fax:* (01) 53 01 25 07 *E-mail:* arsenal@bnf.fr *Web Site:* www.ccfr.bnf.fr, pg 1506

Arsenale Editrice SRL (Italy) *Tel:* (04) 5545166 *Fax:* (04) 5545057, pg 376

D I Arsenidis Publications (Greece) *Tel:* (01) 36-29-538; (01) 36-33923 *Fax:* (01) 36-18-707 *Web Site:* www.arsenidis.gr, pg 306

Arsip Nasional Republik Indonesia (Indonesia) *Tel:* (021) 78 05 851 *Fax:* (021) 78 05 812 *E-mail:* anri@indo.net.id *Web Site:* www.archivesindonesia.or.id, pg 1516

Arsorigo Co Ltd (Taiwan, Province of China) *Tel:* (02) 2735-1274 *Fax:* (02) 2725-2387, pg 638

Editions Art & Metiers Du Livre (France) *Tel:* (01) 42 27 32 36 *Fax:* (01) 47 63 25 52 *E-mail:* infos@faton.fr *Web Site:* www.art-metiers-du-livre.com, pg 147

Art Book Co Ltd (Taiwan, Province of China) *Tel:* (02) 23620578 *Fax:* (02) 23623594 *E-mail:* artbook@ms43.hinet.net, pg 638

Art Books International Ltd (United Kingdom) *Tel:* (020) 7720 1503; (020) 7578 1222 *Fax:* (020) 7720 3158 *E-mail:* sales@art-bks.com *Web Site:* www.artbooksinternational.co.uk, pg 659

Art Books International Ltd (United Kingdom) *Tel:* (01993) 830000 *Fax:* (01993) 830007 *E-mail:* sales@art.bks.com *Web Site:* www.art-bks.com, pg 1346

Art Data (United Kingdom) *Tel:* (020) 87471061 *Fax:* (020) 87422319 *E-mail:* ibf@artdata.co.uk *Web Site:* www.artdata.co.uk, pg 1347

Art Directors Club Verlag GmbH (Germany) *Tel:* (030) 59 00 31 0 *Fax:* (030) 59 00 31 0 *E-mail:* adc@adc.de *Web Site:* www.adc.de, pg 194

Librairie Art et Culture (Tunisia) *Tel:* (02) 31072 *Fax:* (02) 431372, pg 1346

Art Gallery of South Australia Bookshop (Australia) *Tel:* (08) 8207 7029 *Fax:* (08) 8207 7069 *E-mail:* agsa.bookshop@saugov.sa.gov.au *Web Site:* www.artgallery.sa.gov.au, pg 12

Art Gallery of Western Australia (Australia) *Tel:* (08) 9492 6600 *Fax:* (08) 9492 6655 *E-mail:* admin@artgallery.wa.gov.au *Web Site:* www.artgallery.wa.gov.au, pg 12

Art House Group (Finland) *Tel:* (09) 9800 2500 *Fax:* (09) 693 3762, pg 141

Art on the Move (Australia) *Tel:* (08) 9227 7505 *Fax:* (08) 9227 5304 *E-mail:* artmoves@highwayl.com.au, pg 12

Art Sales Index Ltd (United Kingdom) *Tel:* (01784) 451145 *Fax:* (01784) 451144 *E-mail:* sales@art-sales-index.com *Web Site:* www.art-sales-index.com, pg 659

The Art Trade Press Ltd (United Kingdom) *Tel:* (023) 9248 4943, pg 659

Artava Ltd (Latvia) *Tel:* (02) 7222472 *Fax:* (02) 7830254 *E-mail:* arta@com.latnet.lv, pg 444

Artcolor (Germany) *Tel:* (02381) 980190 *Fax:* (02381) 9801999, pg 194

Artech House (United Kingdom) *Tel:* (020) 7596 8750 *Fax:* (020) 7630 0166 *E-mail:* artech-uk@artechhouse.com *Web Site:* www.artechhouse.com, pg 659

Artel (Belgium) *Tel:* (081) 21 37 00 *Fax:* (081) 21 23 72 *E-mail:* erasme@skynet.be, pg 63

Artema (Italy) *Tel:* (011) 3853656 *Fax:* (011) 3853244 *E-mail:* cse@estorinese.inet.it, pg 376

Artemis Verlag (Romania) *Tel:* (01) 2226661, pg 538

Artes de Mexico y del Mundo SA de CV (Mexico) *Tel:* (05) 208 3684; (05) 525 4036; (05) 525 5905 *Fax:* (05) 525 5925 *E-mail:* artesmex@internet.com.mx; artesdemexico@artesdemexico.com *Web Site:* www.artesdemexico.com, pg 462

Artes e Oficios Editora Ltda (Brazil) *Tel:* (051) 311 0832; (051) 311 5442 *Fax:* (051) 311 0832 *E-mail:* artesofi@pro.via-rs.com.br, pg 78

Edi.Artes srl (Italy) *Tel:* (02) 70209917 *Fax:* (02) 70209919, pg 376

Editora Artes Medicas Ltda (Brazil) *Tel:* (011) 221-9033 *Fax:* (011) 223-6635 *E-mail:* artesmedicas@artesmedicas.br *Web Site:* www.artesmedicas.br, pg 78

Artetech Publishing Co (United Kingdom) *Tel:* (01225) 862482 *Fax:* (01225) 865601, pg 660

Artexim - Foreign Trade Co (Romania) *Tel:* (01) 157672, pg 1338

Arthur James Ltd (United Kingdom) *Tel:* (01962) 736880 *Fax:* (01962) 736881 *E-mail:* office@johnhunt-publishing.com *Web Site:* www.johnhunt-publishing.com, pg 660

Artibus et Literis (Germany) *Tel:* (0211) 388-10 *Fax:* (0211) 3881280 *E-mail:* webmaster@artibus.de *Web Site:* www.artibus.de, pg 1310

Artioli Editore (Italy) *Tel:* (059) 827181 *Fax:* (059) 826819 *E-mail:* artiolip@pianeta.it, pg 377

NV Artis-Historia (Belgium) *Tel:* (02) 2409200 *Fax:* (02) 2480818 *E-mail:* info@artis-historia.be *Web Site:* www.artis-historia.be, pg 63

NV Artis-Historia (Belgium) *Tel:* (078) 150 150 *Fax:* (078) 150 050 *E-mail:* info@artis-historia.be *Web Site:* www.artis-historia.be, pg 1302

Artisjus (Hungary) *Tel:* (01) 488 2600 *Fax:* (01) 212 1544 *E-mail:* info@artisjus.com *Web Site:* www.artisjus.hu, pg 1132

The Artist Publishing Co (Taiwan, Province of China) *Tel:* (02) 23932780 *Fax:* (02) 23932012 *E-mail:* artvenue@tpts6.seed.net.tw, pg 638

ARTMED Editora (Brazil) *Tel:* (051) 33303444 *Fax:* (051) 3302378 *E-mail:* artmed@artmed.com.br *Web Site:* www.artmed.com.br, pg 78

Artmoves Inc (Australia) *Tel:* (03) 9882 8116 *Fax:* (03) 9882 8162 *E-mail:* artmoves@bigpond.com, pg 12

Artprice (France) *Tel:* (04) 72 421 706 *Fax:* (04) 78 220 606 *Web Site:* www.artprice.com, pg 147

ArTresor naklada (Croatia) *Tel:* (01) 487 2917 *Fax:* (01) 487 2916 *E-mail:* artresor@zg.tel.hr, pg 117

Arts Centre Bookshop (New Zealand) *Tel:* (03) 365 5277 *Fax:* (03) 365 3293 *E-mail:* info@booksnz.com *Web Site:* www.booksnz.com, pg 1330

Arts Council of England (United Kingdom) *Tel:* (020) 7333 0100 *Fax:* (020) 7973 6590 *E-mail:* enquiries@artscouncil.org.uk *Web Site:* www.artscouncil.org.uk, pg 660

Arts Council of Wales (United Kingdom) *Tel:* (02920) 376500 *Fax:* (02920) 221447 *Web Site:* www.ccc-acw.org.uk, pg 1406

Wydawnictwa Artystyczne i Filmowe (Poland) *Tel:* (022) 8455301; (022) 8455584; (022) 8455465; (022) 8453936 *Fax:* (022) 8455584; (022) 8455465; (022) 8453936, pg 522

Arun-Verlag (Germany) *Tel:* (036743) 233-0 *Fax:* (036743) 233-17 *E-mail:* info@arun-verlag.de *Web Site:* www.arun-verlag.de, pg 194

Arvore Coop de Actividades Artisticas, CRL (Portugal) *Tel:* (02) 383867 *Fax:* (02) 2002684, pg 528

Arya Medi Publishing House (India) *Tel:* (011) 5717012 *Fax:* (011) 5715850, pg 328

AS Narbuto Leidykla (AS Narbutas' Publishers) (Lithuania) *Tel:* (075) 420868 *Fax:* (075) 429335, pg 448

AS Publishing (United Kingdom) *Tel:* (020) 8458 3552 *Fax:* (020) 8458 0618 *E-mail:* asp@dircon.co.uk, pg 660

ASA Editions (France) *Tel:* (01) 47 70 42 90 *Fax:* (01) 47 70 42 98 *E-mail:* info@asaeditions.fr *Web Site:* www.asaeditions.fr, pg 147

Asahiya Shoten Ltd (Booksellers) (Japan) *Tel:* (06) 3131191; (06) 3727251; (06) 3727253 *Fax:* (06) 3755650, pg 1321

Asahiya Shuppan (Japan) *Tel:* (03) 3267-0865 *Fax:* (03) 3267-0875 *Web Site:* www.amgakuin.com, pg 415

Asakura Publishing Co Ltd (Japan) *Tel:* (03) 32600141 *Fax:* (03) 32600180, pg 415

Asam Establishment for Publishing & Distribution (Saudi Arabia) *Tel:* (01) 4453732 *Fax:* (01) 4412583, pg 550

Asamblea Legislativa, Biblioteca Monsenor Sanabria (Costa Rica) *Tel:* 223-2396 *Fax:* 243-2400 *E-mail:* jvolio@congreso.aleg.go.cr; vvargas@congreso.aleg.go.cr; epaniagu@congreso.aleg.go.cr, pg 115

Roland Asanger Verlag GmbH (Germany) *Tel:* (08744) 7262 *Fax:* (08744) 967755 *E-mail:* verlag@asanger.de *Web Site:* www.asanger.de, pg 194

The Asano Agency, Inc (Japan) *Tel:* (03) 39434171 *Fax:* (03) 39437637, pg 1134

Aschehoug Dansk Forlag A/S (Denmark) *Tel:* 33305522; 33305822 *Fax:* 33305823 *E-mail:* info@ash.egmont.com *Web Site:* www.aschehoug.dk, pg 129

Aschehoug Forlag (Norway) *Tel:* 22400400 *Fax:* 22206395 *E-mail:* epost@aschehoug.no *Web Site:* www.aschehoug.no, pg 508

H Aschehoug & Co (W Nygaard) A/S (Norway) *Tel:* 22400400 *Fax:* 22206395 *E-mail:* epost@aschehoug.no *Web Site:* www.aschehoug.no, pg 508

Aschendorffsche Verlagsbuchhandlung GmbH & Co KG (Germany) *Tel:* (0251) 690101 *Fax:* (0251) 690143 *E-mail:* buchverlag@aschendorff.de *Web Site:* www.aschendorff.de/buch, pg 194

Asclepios Edition Lothar Baus (Germany) *Tel:* (06841) 71863 *Web Site:* www.asclepiosedition.de, pg 194

Ascona Presse (Switzerland) *Tel:* (091) 791 13 34 *Fax:* (091) 791 13 34 *E-mail:* info@rmeuter.ch *Web Site:* www.rmeuter.ch, pg 617

Asempa Publishers (Ghana) *Tel:* (021) 221706 *E-mail:* asempa@ghana.com, pg 303

ASFORED (Association Nationale pour la Formation et le Perfectionnement Professionnels dans les Metiers de l'Edition) (France) *Tel:* (01) 45883981 *Fax:* (01) 45815492 *E-mail:* info@asfored.org *Web Site:* www.asfored.org, pg 1267

Asgard Publishing Services (United Kingdom) *Tel:* (0113) 262 8373 *Fax:* (0113) 262 8373 *Web Site:* www.asgardpublishing.co.uk, pg 1150

Asgard-Verlag Dr Werner Hippe GmbH (Germany) *Tel:* (02241) 3164-0 *Fax:* (02241) 316436 *E-mail:* service@asgard.de, pg 194

Ashanti Publishing (South Africa) *Tel:* (011) 8032506 *Fax:* (011) 8035094, pg 562

Ashgate Publishing Ltd (United Kingdom) *Tel:* (01252) 331551 *Fax:* (01252) 344405 *E-mail:* info@ashgatepub.co.uk *Web Site:* www.ashgate.com, pg 660

Ashgrove Publishing (United Kingdom) *Tel:* (020) 7831 5013 *Fax:* (020) 7831 5011 *Web Site:* www.ashgrovepublishing.com, pg 660

Ashgrove Publishing (United Kingdom) *Tel:* (01373) 834900 *Fax:* (01373) 834900 *Web Site:* www.ashgrovepublishing.com, pg 1347

Ashling Books (Australia) *Tel:* (02) 6259 1027, pg 12

Ashmolean Museum Publications (United Kingdom) *Tel:* (01865) 278010 *Fax:* (01865) 278018 *E-mail:* publications@ashmus.ox.ac.uk *Web Site:* www.ashmol.ox.ac.uk/ash/publications, pg 660

Sheikh Muhammad Ashraf Publishers (Pakistan) *Tel:* (042) 353171; (042) 353489 *Fax:* (042) 353489, pg 511

Ashton & Denton Publishing Co (CI) Ltd (United Kingdom) *Tel:* (01534) 735461; (01534) 727976 *Fax:* (01534) 875805, pg 660

Asia Books Co Ltd (Thailand) *Tel:* (02) 715-9000 *Fax:* (02) 391-2277 *E-mail:* information@asiabooks.com *Web Site:* www.asiabooks.com, pg 1345

Asia Pacific Business Press Inc (India) *Tel:* (011) 23845886; (011) 23845654; (011) 23843955; (011) 23844729 *Fax:* (011) 23841561 *E-mail:* niir@vsnl.com *Web Site:* www.niir.org, pg 328

Asia Pacific Communications Ltd (Hong Kong) *Tel:* 2861 0102 *Fax:* 2529 6816 *E-mail:* asiapac@attglobal.net, pg 315

Asia/Pacific Cultural Centre for UNESCO (ACCU) (Japan) *Tel:* (03) 3269-4435 *Fax:* (03) 3269-4510 *E-mail:* general@accu.or.jp *Web Site:* www.accu.or.jp, pg 1274

Asia Pacific Offset Inc (United States) *Tel:* 202-462-5436 *Toll Free Tel:* 800-756-4344 *Fax:* 202-986-4030 *Web Site:* www.asiapacificoffset.com, pg 1165, 1186, 1228

Asia 2000 Ltd (Hong Kong) *Tel:* 2530 1409 *Fax:* 2526 1107 *E-mail:* info@asia2000.com.hk; editor@asia2000.com.hk *Web Site:* www.asia2000.com.hk, pg 315

Asian Culture Co Ltd (Taiwan, Province of China) *Tel:* (02) 2507-2606 *Fax:* (02) 2507-4260 *E-mail:* asian@asianculture.com.tw *Web Site:* www.asianculture.com.tw, pg 638

Asian Educational Services (India) *Tel:* (011) 661493 *Fax:* (011) 6852805; (011) 6855499 *E-mail:* asianeds@nda.vsnl.net.in, pg 329

The Asian Productivity Organization (Japan) *Tel:* (03) 5226 3920 *Fax:* (03) 5226 3950 *E-mail:* apo@apo-tokyo.org *Web Site:* www.apo-tokyo.org, pg 1275

Asian Trading Corporation (India) *Tel:* (080) 5487444; (080) 5490444 *Fax:* (080) 5479444 *E-mail:* mail@atcbooks.net; sales@atcbooks.net *Web Site:* www.atcbooks.net, pg 329

Asiapac Books Pte Ltd (Singapore) *Tel:* 63928455 *Fax:* 63926455 *E-mail:* asiapacbooks@pacific.net.sg *Web Site:* www.asiapacbooks.com, pg 555

The Asiatic Society of Mumbai (India) *Tel:* (022) 2660956 *Fax:* (022) 2665139 *E-mail:* asbl@bom2.vsnl.net.in *Web Site:* education.vsnl.com/asbl/, pg 1515

ASK Ltd (Ukraine) *Tel:* (044) 241-94-96; (044) 456-72-51 *Fax:* (044) 455-58-89 *E-mail:* ask.sale@i.com.ua, pg 653

Aslib, The Association for Information Management (United Kingdom) *Tel:* (020) 7583 8900 *Fax:* (020) 7583 8401 *E-mail:* aslib@aslib.com; pubs@aslib.com *Web Site:* www.aslib.co.uk, pg 660

Aslib, The Association for Information Management (United Kingdom) *Tel:* (020) 7583 8900 *Fax:* (020) 7583 8401 *E-mail:* pubs@aslib.com *Web Site:* www.aslib.co.uk; www.managinginformation.com, pg 1406

Aslib, The Association for Information Management (United Kingdom) *Tel:* (020) 7583 8900 *Fax:* (020) 7583 8401 *E-mail:* aslib@aslib.com *Web Site:* www.aslib.co.uk, pg 1572

Asociacion de Bibliotecarios Graduados del Istmo de Panama (Panama) *Tel:* 2227411 *Fax:* 2254366, pg 1569

Asociacion de Bibliotecarios Universitarios del Paraguay (Paraguay) *Tel:* (021) 507080 *Fax:* (021) 213734, pg 1569

Asociacion Argentina de Bibliotecas y Centros de Informacion Cientificos y Tecnicos (Argentina) *Tel:* (011) 3938406, pg 1557

Asociacion Bautista Argentina de Publicaciones (Argentina) *Tel:* (011) 4863-8924 *Fax:* (011) 4863-6745, pg 3

Asociacion Boliviana de Bibliotecarios (ABB) (Bolivia) *Tel:* (064) 1481, pg 1559

Asociacion Colombiana de Bibliotecologos y Documentalistas (Colombia) *Tel:* (01) 3603077 (ext 326) *Web Site:* www.biblio.ucaldas.edu.co, pg 1560

Asociacion Costarricense de Bibliotecarios (Costa Rica), pg 1560

Asociacion de Archiveros del Peru (ADAP) (Peru) *Tel:* (01) 4712277 *Fax:* (01) 2650958 *E-mail:* dri@u8p.edu.pe, pg 1569

Asociacion de Bibliotecarios de El Salvador (El Salvador) *Tel:* 216312 *Fax:* 225-02 78 *Web Site:* www.ues.edu.sv/abes/informacion.htm, pg 1561

Asociacion de Bibliotecarios y Archivistas de Honduras (Honduras), pg 1564

Asociacion de Bibliotecologos del Uruguay (Uruguay) *Tel:* (02) 4099989 *Fax:* (02) 4099989 *E-mail:* ABU@adinet.com.uy, pg 1573

Asociacion de Escritores y Artistas Espanoles (Spain) *Tel:* (091) 5599067 *Fax:* (091) 5599067, pg 1284

Asociacion Dominicana de Bibliotecarios (ASODOBI) (Dominican Republic) *Tel:* 6884086; 6884660 *Fax:* 685841 *E-mail:* biblioteca.nacional@dominicana.com; intec.biblioteca@codetel.net.do, pg 1561

Asociacion Ecuatoriana de Bibliotecarios (AEB) (Ecuador) *Tel:* 2528-840 *Fax:* 2223-391 *E-mail:* asoebfp@hotmail.com *Web Site:* www.reicyt.org.ec/aeb, pg 1561

Asociacion Espanola de Archiveros, Bibliotecarios, Museologos y Documentalistas (Spain) *Tel:* (091) 5751727 *Fax:* (091) 5781615 *E-mail:* anabad@anabad.org *Web Site:* www.anabad.org, pg 1570

Asociacion General de Archivistas de El Salvador (El Salvador) *Tel:* 222 94 18 *Fax:* 281 58 60 *E-mail:* agnes@agn.gob.sv *Web Site:* www.agn.gob.sv, pg 1561

Asociacion Latinoamericana de Instituciones Financieras Para El Desarrollo (ALIDE) (Peru) *Tel:* (01) 442 2400 *Fax:* (01) 442 8105 *E-mail:* sg@alide.org.pe *Web Site:* www.alide.org.pe, pg 1536

Asociacion Instituto Linguistico de Verano (Colombia) *Tel:* (01) 2821047; (01) 3416185 *E-mail:* sil_colombia@sil.org *Web Site:* www.sil.org/americas/colombia, pg 110

Asociacion Mexicana de Bibliotecarios AC (AMBAC) (Mexico) *Tel:* (055) 55 75 33 96 *Fax:* (055) 55-75-11-35 *E-mail:* correo@ambac.org.mx *Web Site:* www.ambac.org.mx, pg 1567

Asociacion Nicaraguense de Bibliotecarios y Profesionales a Fines (Nicaragua), pg 1568

Asociacion Panamena de Bibliotecarios (Panama), pg 1569

Asociacion para el Progreso de la Direccion (APD) (Spain) *Tel:* (094) 423 22 50 *Fax:* (094) 423 62 49 *E-mail:* apd@bil.apd.es *Web Site:* www.apd.es, pg 573

Asociacion Peruana de Bibliotecarios (APB) (Peru) *Tel:* (01) 474869, pg 1569

Editores Asociados Mexicanos SA de CV (EDAMEX) (Mexico) *Tel:* (05) 5598588 *Fax:* (05) 5757035; (05) 5750555 *Web Site:* www.edamex.com, pg 462

Aspect Marketing Services (United Kingdom) *Tel:* (01233) 500 800 *Fax:* (01233) 500 700 *E-mail:* mail@aspectmarketing.co.uk *Web Site:* www.aspectmarketing.co.uk, pg 1347

Aspect Press (New Zealand) *Tel:* (06) 368-2887, pg 493

Aspect Press Ltd (Russian Federation) *Tel:* (095) 3094062 *Fax:* (095) 3091166 *E-mail:* info@aspectpress.ru *Web Site:* www.aspectpress.ru, pg 543

ASR Publications (Pakistan) *Tel:* (042) 877613; (042) 877496 *Fax:* (042) 5711575, pg 512

Assad National Library (Syrian Arab Republic) *Tel:* (011) 3320803 *Fax:* (011) 3320804 *E-mail:* contact@alassad-library.com *Web Site:* www.alassad.library.com, pg 1548

Assam Publishers' Association (India) *Tel:* (0361) 23995, pg 1273

Peter Asschenfeldts Bokklubb (Norway) *Tel:* 22429165 *Fax:* 22471098, pg 1254

Assemblies of God Mission (Papua New Guinea) *Tel:* 881256, pg 515

Assimil NV (Belgium) *Tel:* (02) 5114502 *Fax:* (02) 5129138 *E-mail:* contact@assimil.be *Web Site:* www.assimil.be, pg 63

Editions Assimil SA (France) *Tel:* (01) 45 76 87 37 *Fax:* (01) 45 94 06 55 *E-mail:* contact@assimil.com *Web Site:* www.assimil.com, pg 148

Assimil GmbH (Germany) *Tel:* (02426) 94000 *Fax:* (02426) 4862 *E-mail:* kontakt@assimil.com *Web Site:* www.assimil.com, pg 195

Assirio & Alvim (Portugal) *Tel:* (021) 555580 *Fax:* (021) 3152935, pg 528

Asso Verlag (Germany) *Tel:* (0208) 802356 *Fax:* (0208) 809882, pg 195

Associacao Arvore da Vida (Brazil) *Tel:* (011) 2185399 *Fax:* (011) 2181401 *E-mail:* editora@eavida.com.br, pg 78

Associacao Brasileira dar Editoras Universitarias (ABEU) (Brazil) *Tel:* (011) 32427171 *Fax:* (011) 32427172 *E-mail:* feu@editora.unesp.br, pg 1263

Associacao dos Arquivistas Brasileiros (Brazil) *Tel:* (021) 2507-2239 *Fax:* (021) 3852-2541 *E-mail:* aab@aab.org.br *Web Site:* www.aab.org.br, pg 1559

Associacao dos Escritores Mocambicanos (AEMO) (Mozambique) *Tel:* (01) 420727, pg 475

Associacao Palas Athena do Brasil (Brazil) *Tel:* (011) 3209-6288 *Fax:* (011) 3277-8137 *E-mail:* grafica@palasathena.org; editora@palasathena.org *Web Site:* www.palasathena.org, pg 78

Associacao Portuguesa de Bibliotecarios, Arquivistas e Documentalistas (Portugal) *Tel:* (021) 816 19 80 *Fax:* (021) 815 45 08 *E-mail:* bad@apbad.pt; formacao@apbad.pt; contabilidade@apbad.pt *Web Site:* www.apbad.pt, pg 1570

Associacao Portuguesa de Editores e Livreiros (Portugal) *Tel:* (021) 843 51 80 *Fax:* (021) 848 93 77 *E-mail:* geral@apel.pt *Web Site:* www.apel.pt, pg 1282

Associacio d'Editors en Llengua Catalana (Spain) *Tel:* (093) 155091 *Fax:* (093) 155273 *E-mail:* info@gremieditorscat.es *Web Site:* www.gremieditorscat.es, pg 1284

Associated Educational Distributors (M) Sdn Bhd (Malaysia) *Tel:* (06) 2844786 *Fax:* (06) 2844697, pg 455

Associated Publishing House (India) *Tel:* (011) 2429392, pg 329

Associated Translation & Typesetting (United Kingdom) *Tel:* (0121) 603 6344 *Fax:* (0121) 603 6399 *E-mail:* ATTEuro@aol.com (European translation); ATTAsia@aol.com (Eastern/Asian translation); ATTgraphic@jaure.demon.com (web design/graphics) *Web Site:* www.jaure.demon.co.uk, pg 1150

Associated Translation & Typesetting (United Kingdom) *Tel:* (0121) 603 6344 *Fax:* (0121) 603 6399 *E-mail:* ATTEuro@aol.com (European translation); ATTAsia@aol.com (Eastern/Asian translation) *Web Site:* www.jaure.demon.co.uk, pg 1183

L'Association (France) *Tel:* (01) 43558587 *Fax:* (01) 43558621 *E-mail:* lassocia@club-internet.fr, pg 148

Association Belgium de Documentation (Belgium) *Tel:* (02) 675 58 62 *Fax:* (02) 672 74 46 *E-mail:* info@abd-bvd.be *Web Site:* www.abd-bvd.be, pg 1558

Association de la Recherche Historique et Sociale (Morocco) *Tel:* 918239, pg 474

Association des Archivistes Francais (France) *Tel:* (01) 46 06 39 44 *Fax:* (01) 46 06 39 52 *E-mail:* secretariat@archivistes.org *Web Site:* www.archivistes.org, pg 1562

Association des Auteurs Autoedites (France) *Tel:* (01) 43 27 20 35 *Fax:* (01) 43 27 20 35 *Web Site:* www.auteurs-autoedites.com, pg 1267

Association des Bibliothecaires Laotiens (Laos People's Democratic Republic) *Tel:* 212452 *Fax:* 212408 *E-mail:* pfd-mill@pan.laos.net.la, pg 1566

Association des Bibliothecaires, Archivistes, Documentalistes et Museographes du Cameroon (ABADCAM) (Cameroon) *Tel:* 222 6362 *Fax:* 222 4785; 222 6262 *E-mail:* abadcam@yahoo.fr, pg 1559

Association des Bibliothecaires Belges d'Expression Francaise (Belgium) *Tel:* (067) 771477; (067) 790683 *Fax:* (067) 771477 *E-mail:* abbef.be@gate71.be; abbef@freeworld.be, pg 1558

Association des Bibliothecaires Francais (France) *Tel:* (01) 55 33 10 30 *Fax:* (01) 55 33 10 31 *E-mail:* abf@abf.asso.fr *Web Site:* www.abf.asso.fr, pg 1562

Association des Bibliotheques Chretiennes France (ABEF) (France) *Tel:* (01) 42 22 44 11 *Fax:* (01) 42 22 37 90 *E-mail:* agmd.bibliotheque@wanadoo.fr, pg 1562

Association des Bibliotheques et Bibliothecaires Suisses (Switzerland) *Tel:* (031) 3824240 *Fax:* (031) 3824648 *E-mail:* bbs@bbs.ch *Web Site:* www.bbs.ch, pg 1571

Association des Diplomes de l'Ecole de Bibliothecaires-Documentalistes (France) *Tel:* (01) 45 87 05 33 *Fax:* (01) 43 31 07 56 *E-mail:* adbs@adbs.fr *Web Site:* www.adbs.fr, pg 1562

Association des Ecrivains Belges de Langue Francaise (AEBLF) (Belgium) *Tel:* (02) 512 29 68 *Fax:* (02) 512 29 68 *E-mail:* aeb@euronet.be, pg 1396

Association des Ecrivains Reunionnais (ADER) (Reunion) *Tel:* (0262) 213317 *Fax:* (0262) 431601, pg 537

Association des Editeurs Belges (Belgium) *Tel:* (02) 241 65 80 *Fax:* (02) 216 71 31 *E-mail:* adeb@adeb.be *Web Site:* www.adeb.irisnet.be, pg 1262

Association for Scottish Literary Studies (United Kingdom) *Tel:* (0141) 330 5309 *Fax:* (0141) 330 5309 *Web Site:* www.asls.org.uk, pg 661, 1406

Association for the Study of Australian Literature Ltd (ASAL) (Australia) *Tel:* (07) 3665 1369 *Fax:* (07) 3665 2799 *Web Site:* www.asc.uq.edu.au, pg 1395

Association Francaise du Multimedia (France) *Tel:* (01) 48242991 *Fax:* (01) 45231337 *E-mail:* info@afee.org *Web Site:* www.afee.org, pg 1267

Association Internationale de Bibliophilie (France) *Tel:* (01) 44412800 *Fax:* (01) 43296895, pg 1267

Association Internationale des Ecoles des Sciences de l'Information (Switzerland) *Tel:* (022) 705 99 77 *Fax:* (022) 705 99 98 *Web Site:* www.aiesi.refer.org, pg 1285

Association Internationale des Etudes Francaises (AIEF) (France) *Fax:* (01) 40462588 *Web Site:* www.aief.eu.org, pg 1267

Association Malienne des Bibliothecaires, Archivistes et Documentalistes (AMBAD) (Mali) *Tel:* 22 49 63, pg 1567

Association Mauritanienne des Bibliothecaires, Archivistes et Documentalistes (Mauritania), pg 1567

Association of African Universities (Ghana) *Tel:* (021) 774495; (021) 761588 *Fax:* (021) 774821 *E-mail:* info@aau.org *Web Site:* www.aau.org, pg 1271

Association of Art Historians (United Kingdom) *Tel:* (020) 7490 3211 *Fax:* (020) 7490 3277 *E-mail:* admin@aah.org.uk *Web Site:* www.aah.org.uk, pg 1406

Association of Authors' Agents (United Kingdom) *Tel:* (020) 7405 6774 *Fax:* (020) 7836 9541 *E-mail:* aaa@apwatt.uk *Web Site:* www.agentsassoc.co.uk, pg 1289

Association of British Science Writers (United Kingdom) *Tel:* (0870) 770 3361 *E-mail:* absw@absw.org.uk *Web Site:* www.absw.org.uk, pg 1406

Association of British Theological & Philosophical Libraries (United Kingdom) *Tel:* (020) 7387 3727 *Web Site:* www.abtapl.org.uk, pg 1572

Association of Commonwealth Universities (ACU) (United Kingdom) *Tel:* (020) 7380 6700 *Fax:* (020) 7387 2655 *E-mail:* info@acu.ac.uk *Web Site:* www.acu.ac.uk, pg 661

Association of Development Agencies (Jamaica) *Tel:* 876-960-2319; 876-968-3605 *Fax:* 876-929-8773, pg 413

Association of Learned & Professional Society Publishers (United Kingdom) *Tel:* (01903) 871 686 *Fax:* (01903) 871 457 *E-mail:* chief-exec@alpsp.org *Web Site:* www.alpsp.org/default.htm, pg 1289

Association of Little Presses (United Kingdom) *Tel:* (01865) 718266 *E-mail:* alp@melloworld.com *Web Site:* www.melloworld.com/alp, pg 1289

Association of London Chief Librarians (ALCL) (United Kingdom), pg 1572

Association of Research Libraries & Libraries for Science & Technology in the CIS (Russian Federation) *Tel:* (095) 925 9288; (095) 924 9458 *Fax:* (095) 921 9862; (095) 925 9750 *E-mail:* gpntb@gpntb.ru *Web Site:* www.gpntb.ru, pg 1282

Association of Special Libraries of the Philippines (ASLP) (Philippines) *Tel:* (02) 893-9590 *Fax:* (02) 893-9589 *E-mail:* vvt126_ph@yahoo.com, pg 1569

Association of Yugoslav Publishers & Booksellers (Serbia and Montenegro) *Tel:* (011) 642-533; (011) 642 248 *Fax:* (011) 646-339 *E-mail:* ognjenl@eunet.yu *Web Site:* www.beobookfair.co.yu, pg 552

Association of Yugoslav Publishers & Booksellers (Serbia and Montenegro) *Tel:* (011) 642-248; (011) 642-533 *Fax:* (011) 646-339 *E-mail:* ognjenl@eunet.yu *Web Site:* www.beobookfair.co.yu, pg 1283

Association pour la Recherche et l'Information demographiques (APRD) (France) *Tel:* (01) 44321400 *Fax:* (01) 40462588, pg 148

Association pour le Developpement de la Documentation, des Bibliotheques et Archives de la Cote d'Ivoire (ADBACI) (Cote d'Ivoire) *Tel:* 32 38 72, pg 1560

Association Professionnelle des Bibliothecaires et Documentalistes (APBD) (Belgium) *Tel:* (071) 61 43 35 *Fax:* (071) 61 16 34 *E-mail:* biblio.hainaut@skynet.be *Web Site:* www.apbd.be, pg 1558

Association for Science Education (United Kingdom) *Tel:* (01707) 283000 *Fax:* (01707) 266532 *E-mail:* info@ase.org.uk *Web Site:* www.ase.org.uk, pg 661

Association Senegalaise des Bibliothecaires, Archivistes et Documentalistes (ASBAD) (Senegal) *Tel:* (0221) 864 27 73 *Fax:* (0221) 824 23 79 *E-mail:* ebad@ebad.ucad.sn *Web Site:* www.ebad.ucad.sn, pg 1570

Association Suisse des Editeurs de Langue Francaise (Switzerland) *Tel:* (021) 3197111 *Fax:* (021) 7963311 *E-mail:* pschibli@centrepatronal.ch, pg 618

Association Suisse des Editeurs de Langue Francaise (Switzerland) *Tel:* (021) 319 71 11 *Fax:* (021) 319 79 10, pg 1285

Association Suisse des Libraires de Langue Francaise (Switzerland) *Tel:* (021) 319 71 11 *Fax:* (021) 319 79 10 *E-mail:* aself@centrezational.cl, pg 1285

Association Suisse des Traducteurs Terminologues et Interpretes (ASTTI) (Switzerland) *Tel:* (031) 313 88 10 *Fax:* (031) 313 88 99 *E-mail:* astti@astti.ch *Web Site:* www.astti.ch, pg 1149

Association Suisse Romande des Diffuseurs et Distributeurs de Livres (Switzerland) *Tel:* (021) 319 71 11 *Fax:* (021) 319 79 10 *E-mail:* aself@centrezational.ch, pg 1285

Association Togolaise pour le Developpement de la Documentation des Bibliotheques, Archives et Musees (Togo) *Tel:* 21 30 27 *Fax:* 21 85 95 *E-mail:* cafmicro@ub.tg *Web Site:* www.ub.tg, pg 1571

Association Tunisienne des Documentalistes, Bibliothecaires et Archivistes (Tunisia) *Tel:* 651924, pg 1572

Association Zairoise des Archivistes, Bibliothecaires et Documentalistes (The Democratic Republic of the Congo) *Tel:* (012) 30123; (012) 30124, pg 1560

Associazione Carmelo Teresiano Italiano, OCD (Italy) *Tel:* (06) 7989081 *Fax:* (06) 79890840, pg 377

Associazione Internazionale di Archeologia Classica (Italy) *Tel:* (06) 6798798 *Fax:* (06) 69789119 *E-mail:* info@aiac.org; segreteria@aiac.org *Web Site:* www.aiac.org, pg 377

Associazione Italiana Biblioteche (Italy) *Tel:* (06) 4463532 *Fax:* (06) 4441139 *E-mail:* aib@aib.it *Web Site:* www.aib.it, pg 1565

Associazione Italiana Editori (Italy) *Tel:* (02) 86463091 *Fax:* (02) 89010863 *E-mail:* aie@aie.it *Web Site:* www.aie.it, pg 1274

Associazione Librai Antiquari d'Italia (Italy) *Tel:* (055) 282635 *Fax:* (055) 214831 *E-mail:* alai@alai.it *Web Site:* www.alai.it, pg 1274

Astor-Verlag, Willibald Schlager (Austria) *Tel:* (01) 9144281 *Fax:* (01) 9144281, pg 48

Editorial Astrea de Alfredo y Ricardo Depalma SRL (Argentina) *Tel:* (011) 4382-1880 *Toll Free Tel:* 800-345-278732 *Fax:* (011) 4382-4203 *E-mail:* info@astrea.com.ar *Web Site:* www.astrea.com.ar, pg 3

Editorial Astri SA (Spain) *Tel:* (093) 6801207 *Fax:* (093) 6803194 *E-mail:* astri@astri.es *Web Site:* www.astri.es, pg 573

Astrodata AG (Switzerland) *Tel:* (043) 343 33 33 *Fax:* (043) 343 33 43 *E-mail:* info@astrodata.ch *Web Site:* www.astrodata.ch, pg 618

Casa Editrice Astrolabio-Ubaldini Editore (Italy) *Tel:* (06) 855 21 31 *Fax:* (06) 855 27 56, pg 377

Astrolog Publishing House (Israel) *Tel:* (09) 7412044 *Fax:* (09) 7442044, pg 365

AT Verlag (Switzerland) *Tel:* (062) 836 6666 *Fax:* (062) 836 6667 *E-mail:* info.buchverlag@azag.ch *Web Site:* www.at-verlag.ch, pg 618

Editrice Atanor SRL (Italy) *Tel:* (06) 7024595 *Fax:* (06) 7014422, pg 377

Ataturk Kultur, Dil ve Tarih, Yusek Kurumu Baskanligi (Turkey) *Tel:* (0312) 428 61 00 *Fax:* (0312) 428 52 88 *E-mail:* bim@tdk.gov.tr *Web Site:* www.tdk.gov.tr, pg 649

Ataturk Universitesi (Turkey) *Tel:* (0442) 231 11 11 *Fax:* (0442) 236 10 14 *E-mail:* webadmin@atauni.edu.tr *Web Site:* www.atauni.edu.tr/, pg 649

Verlag Atelier im Bauernhaus Fischerhude Wolf-Dietmar Stock (Germany) *Tel:* (04293) 491; (04293) 493 *Fax:* (04293) 1238, pg 195

Atelier Books (United Kingdom) *Tel:* (0131) 5574050 *Fax:* (0131) 5578382 *E-mail:* mail@bournefineart.co.uk *Web Site:* www.bournefineart.co.uk/books.html, pg 661

Editions de l'Atelier (France) *Tel:* (01) 44089515 *Fax:* (01) 44089500, pg 148

Atelier, L (Egypt (Arab Republic of Egypt)) *Tel:* (03) 4820526 *Fax:* (03) 4837662, pg 1399

Atelier National de Reproduction des Theses (France) *Tel:* (03) 20 30 86 73 *Fax:* (03) 20 54 21 95 *E-mail:* anrt@univ-lille3.fr *Web Site:* www.anrtheses.com.fr, pg 148

Atelier Publishing Co Ltd (Japan) *Tel:* (03) 3357-2741 *Fax:* (03) 3357-2194, pg 415

Atelier Verlag Andernach (AVA) (Germany) *Tel:* (02632) 44432 *Fax:* (02632) 31383, pg 195

Editura si Atelierele Tipografice Metropol SRL (Romania) *Tel:* (01) 2104593; (01) 2108433 *Fax:* (01) 2106987, pg 1161

Ateliers et Presses de Taize (France) *Tel:* (03) 85 50 30 50 *Fax:* (03) 85 50 30 55 *E-mail:* editions@taize.fr *Web Site:* www.taize.fr, pg 148

Atena (Poland) *Tel:* (061) 228685 *Fax:* (061) 524082 *E-mail:* atena@poz1.commet.pl, pg 522

Atena Kustannus Oy (Finland) *Tel:* (014) 620192 *Fax:* (014) 620190 *E-mail:* atena@atenakustannus.fi *Web Site:* www.atenakustannus.fi, pg 141

Sociedad de Educacion Atenas SA (Spain) *Tel:* (091) 5480127 *Fax:* (091) 5591771, pg 573

Ateneo Cientifico, Literario y Artistico (Spain) *Tel:* (09142) 974 42, pg 1404

Ateneo Cientifico, Literario y Artistico (Spain) *Tel:* (071) 360553 *Fax:* (071) 352194 *E-mail:* ateneo@intercom.es *Web Site:* www.usuarios.intercom.es/ateneo, pg 1404

Editorial Atenco de Caracas (Venezuela) *Tel:* (02) 5734622; (02) 5734400; (02) 5734600 *Fax:* (02) 5754475 *E-mail:* webmaster@ateneo.org.ve, pg 779

Ateneo de Manila University Press (Philippines) *Tel:* (02) 4265984; (02) 4261238 *Fax:* (02) 4265909 *E-mail:* unipress@pusit.admu.edu.ph (business/operations) *Web Site:* www.admu.edu.ph, pg 518

Ateneo Puertorriqueno (Puerto Rico) *Tel:* (787) 722-4839; (787) 721-3877 *Fax:* (787) 725-3873 *E-mail:* info@ateneopr.com *Web Site:* www.ateneopr.com, pg 1282

Athena Press (Australia) *Tel:* (02) 9357 3720 *Fax:* (02) 9357 3720, pg 12

Athenaeum Boekhandel (Netherlands) *Tel:* (020) 6226248 *Fax:* (020) 6384901 *E-mail:* info@athenaeum.nl *Web Site:* www.athenaeum.nl, pg 1328

Athenaeum Verlag AG (Switzerland) *Tel:* (091) 571536, pg 618

Editora Atheneu Ltda (Brazil) *Tel:* (011) 220-9186 *Fax:* (011) 221-3389 *E-mail:* atheneau@nutecnet.com.br *Web Site:* www.atheneu.com.br, pg 78

Atheneum Forlag A/S (Norway) *Tel:* 23292072; 23291900 *Fax:* 23291901, pg 508

Athens Academy Library (Greece) *Tel:* (01) 360-0209 *Web Site:* www.academyofathens.gr, pg 1513

Athesia Buchhandlung (Italy) *Tel:* (0471) 927280 *Fax:* (0471) 927229 *E-mail:* buch@athesia.it *Web Site:* www.athesiabuch.it, pg 1320

Athesia Verlag Bozen (Italy) *Tel:* (0471) 92 72 03 *Fax:* (0471) 92 72 07 *E-mail:* buchverlag@athesia.it, pg 377

Athina (Greece) *Tel:* (01) 3821308 *Fax:* (01) 3807220, pg 1313

Athina, Mary Mavrogiannis (Greece) *Tel:* (010) 3821308 *Fax:* (010) 3838228, pg 306

Editions Athina-Mavrogianni (Greece) *Tel:* (01) 3304628; (01) 3821308 *Fax:* (01) 3838228, pg 306

The Athlone Press Ltd (United Kingdom) *Tel:* (020) 7922 0888 *Fax:* (020) 7922 0881 *E-mail:* athlonepress@btinternet.com *Web Site:* www.transcomm.ox.ac.uk/wwwroot/athlone_press.htm, pg 661

Editora Atica SA (Brazil) *Tel:* (011) 278 93 22 *Fax:* (011) 277 41 46, pg 78

Atica, SA Editores e Livreiros (Portugal) *Tel:* (021) 8153220 *Fax:* (021) 8153219, pg 529

Atlantic Transport Publishers (United Kingdom) *Tel:* (01326) 373656 *Fax:* (01326) 378309; (01326) 373656, pg 661

Atlantica Editrice SARL (Italy), pg 377

Editions Atlantica Seguier (France) *Tel:* (05) 59 52 84 00 *Fax:* (05) 59 52 84 01 *E-mail:* atlantica@atlantica.fr *Web Site:* www.atlantica.fr, pg 148

Editorial Atlantida SA (Argentina) *Tel:* (011) 4331-4591; (011) 4331-4599 *Fax:* (011) 3313341 *Web Site:* www.atlantida.com.ar, pg 3

Atlantis M Pechlivanides & Co SA (Greece) *Tel:* (010) 9220071; (010) 9220073 *Fax:* (01) 9025773, pg 306

Atlantis Musikbuch (Switzerland), pg 618

Atlantis sro (Czech Republic) *Tel:* (05) 422 132 21 *Fax:* (05) 422 132 21 *E-mail:* atlantis-brno@volny.cz *Web Site:* www.volny.cz/atlantis/, pg 122

Atlantis-Verlag AG (Switzerland) *Tel:* (01) 2622717 *Fax:* (01) 2512615, pg 618

Atlantisz Kiado (Hungary) *Tel:* (01) 4065645 *Fax:* (01) 4065645 *E-mail:* atlantis@budapest.hu, pg 320

Atlas (Greece) *Tel:* (01) 3627342 *Fax:* (01) 3300257 *E-mail:* c_poulos@hotmail.com, pg 306

Editions Atlas (France) *Tel:* (01) 40 74 38 38 *Fax:* (01) 45 61 19 85 *E-mail:* contact@editionsatlas.fr *Web Site:* www.editionsatlas.fr, pg 148

Editora Atlas SA (Brazil) *Tel:* (011) 3357-9144 *E-mail:* edatlas@editora-atlas.com.br *Web Site:* www.edatlas.com.br; www.atlasnet.com.br, pg 78

Atlas Press (United Kingdom) *Tel:* (020) 7490 8742 *Fax:* (021) 7490 8742 *E-mail:* enquiries@atlaspress.co.uk *Web Site:* www.atlaspress.co.uk, pg 661

Atma Ram & Sons (India) *Tel:* (011) 223092 *E-mail:* yogesh2@ndf.vsnl.net.in, pg 329

Atma Ram & Sons (India) *Tel:* (011) 2523082, pg 1315

ATP - Packager (France) *Tel:* (0473) 19 58 80 *Fax:* (0473) 195899 *E-mail:* atp.chamalieres@wanadoo.fr, pg 148

Ediciones Atril (Spain) *Tel:* (091) 6911000 *Fax:* (091) 6916380, pg 574

Atrium Group (Spain) *Tel:* (093) 2540099 *Fax:* (093) 2118139 *E-mail:* atrium@atriumgroup.org *Web Site:* www.atriumbooks.com, pg 574

Atrium Verlag AG (Switzerland) *Tel:* (01) 473035, pg 618

Attic Press Ltd (Ireland) *Tel:* (021) 4321 725 *Fax:* (021) 315 329 *E-mail:* corkunip@ucc.ie *Web Site:* www.corkuniversitypress.com, pg 358

Atuakkiorfik A/S Det Greenland Publishers (Denmark) *Tel:* 32 21 22 *Fax:* 32 25 00 *E-mail:* henri@atuakkiorfik.gl *Web Site:* www.atuakkiorfik.gl, pg 129

Scoop/Au Vent des Iles (French Polynesia) *Tel:* 50 95 95 *Fax:* 50 95 97 *E-mail:* contact@tahiti-books.com *Web Site:* www.tahiti-books.com, pg 189

Aubanel Editions (France) *Tel:* (04) 78 94 61 42; (04) 78 94 21 73, pg 148

Editions de l'Aube (France) *Tel:* (04) 90 07 46 60 *Fax:* (04) 90 07 53 02, pg 148

Editions Aubier-Montaigne SA (France) *Tel:* (01) 40 51 31 00 *Fax:* (01) 43 29 21 48, pg 148

Auckland City Libraries (New Zealand) *Tel:* (09) 377 0209 *Fax:* (09) 307 7741 *E-mail:* libraryreference@aucklandcity.govt.nz *Web Site:* www.aucklandcitylibraries.com, pg 1532

Auckland University Press (New Zealand) *Tel:* (09) 373 7528 *Fax:* (09) 373 7465 *E-mail:* aup@auckland.ac.nz *Web Site:* www.auckland.ac.nz/aup/, pg 493

Audio-Forum - The Language Source (United Kingdom) *Tel:* (020) 586 4499 *Fax:* (020) 722 1068 *E-mail:* microworld@ndirect.co.uk *Web Site:* www.microworld.ndirect.co.uk, pg 661

Audio Visual Centre Ltd (Malta) *Tel:* 21330886 *Fax:* 21346945 *E-mail:* info@avc.com.mt, pg 1326

Audivox (Belgium) *Tel:* (03) 470 1784 *E-mail:* info@audivox.net, pg 1302

AUE-Verlag GmbH (Germany) *Tel:* (06298) 1328 *Fax:* (06298) 4298 *E-mail:* aue-verlag@web.de *Web Site:* www.aue-verlag.com, pg 195

Ludwig Auer GmbH (Germany) *Tel:* (0906) 73-0 *Fax:* (0906) 73-130 (management); (0906) 73-184 (sales) *E-mail:* org@auer-medien.de *Web Site:* www.auer-medien.de, pg 1155

Auer Verlag GmbH (Germany) *Tel:* (0906) 73-240 *Fax:* (0906) 73177; (0906) 73178 *E-mail:* info@auer-verlag.de *Web Site:* www.auer-verlag.de, pg 195

Aufbau Taschenbuch Verlag GmbH (Germany) *Tel:* (030) 283 94-0 *Fax:* (030) 283 94 100 *E-mail:* info@aufbau-verlag.de *Web Site:* www.aufbau-verlag.de, pg 195

Aufbau-Verlag GmbH (Germany) *Tel:* (030) 28 394-0 *Fax:* (030) 28 394-100 *E-mail:* info@aufbau-verlag.de *Web Site:* www2.aufbauverlag.de, pg 195

Aufstieg-Verlag GmbH (Germany) *Tel:* (0871) 54112 *Fax:* (0871) 54112 *Web Site:* www.aufstieg-verlag.de, pg 195

August Guese Verlag GmbH (Germany) *Tel:* (06039) 48 01 10 *Fax:* (06039) 48 01 48 *E-mail:* info@guese.de *Web Site:* www.guese.de, pg 195

J J Augustin Verlag GmbH (Germany) *Tel:* (04124) 20 44-46 *Fax:* (04124) 47 09, pg 195

Augustin-Verlag (Switzerland) *Tel:* (052) 6492340 *Fax:* (052) 649 31 94 *E-mail:* augustin@augustin.ch, pg 618

Augustinus-Verlag Wurzburg Inh Augustinerprovinz (Germany) *Tel:* (0931) 3097-400 *Fax:* (0931) 3097-401 *E-mail:* verlag@augustiner.de *Web Site:* www.augustiner.de, pg 195

Augustus Verlag (Germany) *Tel:* (089) 9271-0 *Fax:* (089) 9271-168 *Web Site:* www.droemer-weltbild.de, pg 195

Editions d'Aujourd'hui (Les Introuvables) (France) *Tel:* (01) 43547910 *Fax:* (01) 43298620, pg 148

Aulis Publishers (United Kingdom) *Tel:* (01672) 539 041 *Fax:* (01373) 452 888 *E-mail:* info@aulis.com *Web Site:* www.aulis.com, pg 661

Aulis Verlag Deubner & Co KG (Germany) *Tel:* (0221) 9514540 *Fax:* (0221) 518443 *E-mail:* info@aulis.de *Web Site:* www.aulis.de, pg 195

AULOS sro (Czech Republic) *Tel:* (02) 536863 *Fax:* (02) 90004536 *E-mail:* aulos@volny.cz, pg 122

Aurelia Books PVBA (Belgium) *Tel:* (091) 82 55 82 *Fax:* (091) 82 72 47, pg 63

Aurora (Czech Republic) *Tel:* (02) 24 21 43 26; (02) 24 21 46 24 *Fax:* (02) 24 21 43 26 *E-mail:* eaurora@eaurora.cz *Web Site:* www.eaurora.cz, pg 122

Aurora (Indonesia) *Tel:* (021) 5810413, pg 353

Aurora Art Publishers (Russian Federation) *Tel:* (0812) 312-3753 *Fax:* (0812) 312-5460, pg 544

Aurora Semanario Israeli de Actualidad (Israel) *Tel:* (03) 5462785; (03) 5463297 *Fax:* (03) 5625082 *E-mail:* aurorail@netvision.net.il, pg 365

Aurum Press Ltd (United Kingdom) *Tel:* (020) 7637 3225 *Fax:* (020) 7580 2469 *Web Site:* www.aurumpress.co.uk, pg 661

Auslib Press Pty Ltd (Australia) *Tel:* (08) 8278 4363 *Fax:* (08) 8278 4000 *E-mail:* info@auslib.com.au *Web Site:* www.auslib.com.au, pg 12

Ausmed Publications Pty Ltd (Australia) *Tel:* (03) 9375 7311 *Fax:* (03) 9375 7299 *E-mail:* ausmed@ausmed.com.au *Web Site:* www.ausmed.com.au, pg 12

Aussaat Verlag (Germany) *Tel:* (02845) 392222 *Fax:* (02845) 33689 *E-mail:* info@neukirchener-verlag.de *Web Site:* www.aussaat-verlag.de, pg 195

Aussie Books (Australia) *Tel:* (07) 3345 4253 *Fax:* (07) 3344 1582 *E-mail:* sildale@yahoo.com *Web Site:* www.treasureenterprises.com, pg 12

Aussies Afire Publishing (Australia) *Tel:* (02) 6581 0654 *Fax:* (02) 6581 0745 *Web Site:* www.gracechurchpm.org.au, pg 12

Austed Publishing Co (Australia) *Tel:* (08) 9203 6044 *Fax:* (08) 9203 6055 *E-mail:* net@austed.com.au *Web Site:* www.austed.com.au, pg 12

Austicks Headrow Bookshop (United Kingdom) *Tel:* (0113) 243-9607 *Fax:* (0113) 245-8837, pg 1347

Austin's Book Services (Guyana) *Tel:* (02) 27 7395; (02) 26 7350 *Fax:* (02) 27 7396 *E-mail:* austins@guyana.net.gy, pg 1314

Australasian Association for Lexicography (Australex) (Australia) *Tel:* (07) 5595 2502 *Fax:* (07) 5595 2545 *Web Site:* www.anu.edu.au, pg 1395

Australasian Medical Publishing Company Ltd (AMPCO) (Australia) *Tel:* (02) 9562 6666 *Fax:* (02) 9562 6699 *E-mail:* medjaust@ampco.com.au *Web Site:* www.mja.com.au, pg 12

Australasian Textiles & Fashion Publishers (Australia) *Tel:* (03) 5261 3966 *Fax:* (03) 5261 6950 *Web Site:* www.atfmag.com, pg 12

Australia Council Literature Board (Australia) *Tel:* (02) 9215 9000 *Toll Free Tel:* 800 226 912 *Fax:* (02) 9215 9111 *E-mail:* mail@ozco.gov.au *Web Site:* www.ozco.gov.au, pg 1259

Australian Academic Press Pty Ltd (Australia) *Tel:* (07) 3257 1176 *Fax:* (07) 3252 5908 *E-mail:* info@australianacademicpress.com.au *Web Site:* www.australianacademicpress.com.au, pg 13

Australian Academy of Science (Australia) *Tel:* (02) 6247 5777 *Fax:* (02) 6257 4620 *E-mail:* eb@science.org.au; aas@science.org.au *Web Site:* www.science.org.au, pg 13

The Australian & New Zealand Association of Antiquarian Booksellers (Australia) *Tel:* (03) 9525 1649 *Fax:* (03) 9529 1298 *E-mail:* admin@anzaab.com; bookshop@hincebooks.com.au *Web Site:* www.anzaab.com, pg 1259

Australian Booksellers Association Inc (Australia) *Tel:* (03) 9859 7322 *Fax:* (03) 9859 7344 *E-mail:* mail@aba.org.au *Web Site:* www.aba.org.au, pg 1260

Australian Broadcasting Authority (Australia) *Tel:* (02) 9344 7700 *Toll Free Tel:* 800 22 6667 (Australia only) *Fax:* (02) 9334 7799 *E-mail:* info@aba.gov.au *Web Site:* www.aba.gov.au, pg 13

Australian Chart Book Pty Ltd (Australia) *Tel:* (02) 9489 4786 *Fax:* (02) 9487 2089 *Web Site:* www.austchartbook.com.au, pg 13

Australian Copyright Council (Australia) *Tel:* (02) 9318 1788 (copyright); (02) 9699 3247 (sales) *Fax:* (02) 9698 3536 *E-mail:* info@copyright.org.au *Web Site:* www.copyright.org.au, pg 1260

Australian Film Television & Radio School (Australia) *Tel:* (02) 9805 6611 *Fax:* (02) 9805 1275 *E-mail:* info_nsw@aftrs.edu.au *Web Site:* www.aftrs.edu.au, pg 13

Australian Institute of Criminology (Australia) *Tel:* (02) 6260 9200 *Fax:* (02) 6260 9201 *E-mail:* aicpress@aic.gov.au *Web Site:* www.aic.gov.au, pg 13

Australian Institute of Family Studies (AIFS) (Australia) *Tel:* (03) 9214 7888 *Fax:* (03) 9214 7839 *E-mail:* publications@aifs.org.au *Web Site:* www.aifs.org.au, pg 13

Australian Law Librarians' Group Inc (Australia) *Tel:* (02) 9230 8675 *Fax:* (02) 9233 7952 *Web Site:* www.allg.asn.au, pg 1557

Australian Library & Information Association (Australia) *Tel:* (02) 6215 8222 *Fax:* (02) 6282 2249 *E-mail:* enquiry@alia.org.au *Web Site:* www.alia.org.au, pg 1557

Australian Library Publishers' Society (Australia) *Tel:* (08) 8303 5372 *Fax:* (08) 8303 4369 *E-mail:* library@adelaide.edu.au *Web Site:* www.library.adelaide.edu.au/ual/publ/alps/, pg 1395

Australian Licensing Corp (Australia) *Tel:* (02) 9280 2220 *Fax:* (02) 9280 2223 *E-mail:* rodhare@alc-online.com *Web Site:* www.alc-online.com, pg 1129

Australian Marine Conservation Society Inc (AMCS) (Australia) *Tel:* (07) 3848 5235 *Toll Free Tel:* 800 066 299 *Fax:* (07) 3892 5814 *E-mail:* amcs@amcs.org.au *Web Site:* www.amcs.org.au, pg 13

Australian National University Library (Australia) *Tel:* (02) 6125 5111 *Fax:* (02) 6125 5931 *E-mail:* webmaster@anu.edu.au *Web Site:* www.anu.edu.au, pg 1490

Australian Press Council (Australia) *Tel:* (02) 9261 1930 *Toll Free Tel:* 800-02-5712 *Fax:* (02) 9267 6826 *E-mail:* info@presscouncil.org.au *Web Site:* www.presscouncil.org.au, pg 1260

Australian Publishers Association Ltd (Australia) *Tel:* (02) 9281 9788 *Fax:* (02) 9281 1073 *E-mail:* apa@publishers.asn.au *Web Site:* www.publishers.asn.au, pg 1260

Australian Rock Art Research Association (Australia) *Tel:* (03) 9523 0549 *Fax:* (03) 9523 0549 *E-mail:* auraweb@hotmail.com *Web Site:* mc2.vicnet.net.au/home/aura/web/index.html, pg 13

Australian Scholarly Publishing (Australia) *Tel:* (03) 98175208 *Fax:* (03) 8176431 *E-mail:* aspic@ozemail.com.au, pg 13

Australian Society of Archivists (Australia) *Tel:* (07) 3875 8755 *Fax:* (07) 3875 8764 *E-mail:* qsa@iie.qld.gov.au *Web Site:* www.archives.qld.gov.au, pg 1557

The Australian Society of Authors Ltd (Australia) *Tel:* (02) 93180877 *Fax:* (02) 93180530 *E-mail:* office@asauthors.org *Web Site:* www.asauthors.org/cgi-bin/asa/information.cgi, pg 1260

The Australian Society of Authors Ltd (Australia) *Tel:* (02) 93180877 *Fax:* (02) 93180530 *E-mail:* asa@asauthors.org *Web Site:* www.asauthors.org, pg 1395

Australian Society of Indexers (Australia) *Tel:* (02) 4268-5335 *Web Site:* www.aussi.org, pg 1260

Australian Writers' Guild Ltd (Australia) *Tel:* (02) 92811554 *Fax:* (02) 92814321 *E-mail:* admin@awg.com.au *Web Site:* www.awg.com.au, pg 1395

Austrian PEN Centre (Austria) *Tel:* (01) 5334459 *Fax:* (01) 5328749 *E-mail:* oepen.club@netway.at *Web Site:* www.penclub.at, pg 1396

Authors' Club (United Kingdom) *Tel:* (020) 7408 5092, pg 1406

Authors' Licensing & Collecting Society (United Kingdom) *Tel:* (020) 7395 0600 *Fax:* (020) 7395 0660 *E-mail:* alcs@alcs.co.uk *Web Site:* www.alcs.co.uk, pg 1289

Authorspress (India) *Tel:* (011) 22436299; (011) 22460145 *Fax:* (011) 22460145 *E-mail:* authorspress@yahoo.com, pg 329

Automobilia srl (Italy) *Tel:* (02) 4802 1671 *Fax:* (02) 4819 4968 *E-mail:* automobilia@tin.it, pg 377

Bundesverband junger Autoren und Autorinnen eV (Germany) *Tel:* (02225) 7889 *Fax:* (02225) 7889 *E-mail:* bvjaa@t-online.de *Web Site:* www.bvja-online.de, pg 1400

Autoren- und Verlags-Agentur GmbH (AVA) (Germany) *Tel:* (08152) 925883 *Fax:* (08152) 3076 *E-mail:* avagmbh@aol.com, pg 1131

Verlag der Autoren GmbH & Co KG (Germany) *Tel:* (069) 23 85 74-0 *Fax:* (069) 24 27 76 44 *E-mail:* buch@verlag-der-autoren.de *Web Site:* www.verlag-der-autoren.de, pg 196

Autorensolidaritat - Verlag der Interessengemeinschaft osterreichischer Autorinnen und Autoren (Austria) *Tel:* (01) 526 20 44-13 *Fax:* (01) 526 20 44-55 *E-mail:* ig@literaturhaus.at, pg 48

Biblioteca de Autores Cristianos (Spain) *Tel:* (091) 3090862; (091) 3090973 *Fax:* (091) 3091980 *E-mail:* bac@planalfa.es, pg 574

Autorinnen und Autoren der Schweiz AdS (Switzerland) *Tel:* (01) 350 04 60 *Fax:* (01) 350 04 61 *E-mail:* sekretariat@a-d-s.ch *Web Site:* www.a-d-s.ch, pg 1162

Autovision Verlag Guenther & Co (Germany) *Tel:* (040) 810327 *Fax:* (040) 87932995 *Web Site:* www.autovision-verlag.de, pg 196

Autrement Editions (France) *Tel:* (01) 44 73 80 00 *Fax:* (01) 44 73 00 12 *E-mail:* contact@autrement.com *Web Site:* www.autrement.com, pg 148

Autres Temps (France) *Tel:* (0491) 26 80 33 *Fax:* (0491) 41 11 01, pg 148

Autumn Publishing Ltd (United Kingdom) *Tel:* (01243) 531660 *Fax:* (01243) 774433 *E-mail:* autumn@autumnpublishing.co.uk *Web Site:* www.autumnpublishing.co.uk, pg 662

Editions Philippe Auzou (France) *Tel:* (01) 40338400 *Fax:* (01) 47972008, pg 148

AV Studio Reklamno-vydavatel 'ska agentura (Slovakia) *Tel:* (07) 726297 *Fax:* (07) 726297, pg 559

AVACO - Christian Mass Communications Center (Japan) *Tel:* (03) 3203-4121 *Fax:* (03) 3203-4186 *E-mail:* avaco@ppp.fastnet.ne.jp *Web Site:* www.fastnet.ne.jp, pg 415

Editions l'Avant-Scene de Prette Technique (France) *Tel:* (01) 46342820 *Fax:* (01) 43545014, pg 149

Editorial Avante SA de Cv (Mexico) *Tel:* (05) 5214548; (05) 5217563; (05) 5127634; (05) 5127563 *Fax:* (05) 5215245 *E-mail:* editorialavante@infosel.net.mx *Web Site:* www.editorialavante.com.mx, pg 462

AVCR Historicky ustav (Czech Republic) *Tel:* (02) 868 821 21; (02) 838 813 73 *Fax:* (02) 887 513 *E-mail:* panek@hiu.cas.cz, pg 122

Aventinum Nakladatelstvi spol sro (Czech Republic) *Tel:* (02) 4021907; (02) 4019069; (02) 40193056 *Fax:* (02) 4018534, pg 122

NV Uitgeverij Altiora Averbode (Belgium) *Tel:* (013) 780156 *Fax:* (013) 776837 *E-mail:* averbode.publ@verbode.be, pg 63

Avero Publications Ltd (United Kingdom) *Tel:* (0191) 2615790 *Fax:* (0191) 2611209 *E-mail:* nstc@newcastle.ac.uk, pg 662

Avgvstinvs (Spain) *Tel:* (091) 5342070 *Fax:* (091) 5544801 *E-mail:* revista@avgvstinvs.org *Web Site:* www.avgvstinvs.org, pg 574

Aviatic Verlag GmbH (Germany) *Tel:* (089) 613890-0 *Fax:* (089) 613890-10 *E-mail:* aviatic@aviatic.de *Web Site:* www.aviatic.de, pg 196

Aviation Industry Press (China) *Tel:* (010) 64918415 *Fax:* (010) 64922211, pg 101

Avicenne Librairie Internationale (Syrian Arab Republic) *Tel:* (011) 221 29 11; (011) 224 44 77 *Fax:* (011) 221 98 33 *E-mail:* avicenne@net.sy, pg 1344

Monte Avila Editores Latinoamericana CA (Venezuela) *Tel:* (02) 265-6020; (02) 265-9871 *E-mail:* maelca@telcel.net.ve, pg 779

Avinash Reference Publications (India) *Tel:* (0231) 21024 *Fax:* (0231) 27262, pg 329

AvivA Britta Jurgs GmbH (Germany) *Tel:* (030) 39 73 13 72 *Fax:* (030) 39 73 13 71 *E-mail:* aviva@txt.de *Web Site:* www.aviva-verlag.de, pg 196

Avoca Publications (Ireland) *Tel:* (01) 889218, pg 358

Avots (Latvia) *Tel:* (02) 7211394 *Fax:* (02) 7225824 *E-mail:* avots@apollo.lv *Web Site:* www.vardnicas.lv, pg 444

Award Publications Ltd (United Kingdom) *Tel:* (020) 7388 7800 *Fax:* (020) 7388 7887 *E-mail:* info@award.abel.co.uk, pg 662

Al-Awqaf Central Library (Iraq) *Tel:* (01) 4169362 *Fax:* (01) 4167790, pg 1518

AWT World Trade (United States) *Tel:* 773-777-7100 *Fax:* 773-777-0909 *E-mail:* sale@awt-gpi.com *Web Site:* www.awt-gpi.com, pg 1248

Axel Juncker Verlag Jacobi KG (Germany) *Tel:* (089) 360960 *Fax:* (089) 36096222, pg 196

Axicon Auto ID Ltd (United Kingdom) *Tel:* (01869) 351155 *Fax:* (01869) 351205 *E-mail:* sales@axicon.com *Web Site:* www.axicon.com, pg 1183

Axiom Publishers & Distributors (Australia) *Tel:* (08) 83627052 *Fax:* (08) 83629430 *E-mail:* axiompub@camtech.net.au, pg 14

Axiotelis G (Greece) *Tel:* (010) 3610091; (010) 3636264; (010) 3634264 *Fax:* (010) 3610887, pg 306

Bokforlaget Axplock (Sweden) *Tel:* (0152) 150 60 *Fax:* (0152) 151 40 *E-mail:* post@axplock.se *Web Site:* www.axplock.se, pg 609

Biblioteca Ayacucho (Venezuela) *Tel:* (02) 5644402; (02) 5643583 *Fax:* (02) 5634223, pg 779

Ayalga Ediciones SA (Spain) *Tel:* (085) 5500599; (085) 501299 *Fax:* (085) 5500869, pg 574

Al-Ayam Press Co Ltd (Sudan) *Web Site:* www.alayam.com, pg 608

Aydin Yayincilik (Turkey) *Tel:* (0312) 2873402; (0312) 2873403 *Fax:* (0312) 2873402, pg 649

Editorial Ayuso (Spain) *Tel:* (091) 2228080, pg 574

AZ Bertelsmann Direct GmbH (Germany) *Tel:* (05241) 805438 *Fax:* (05241) 8066962 *E-mail:* az@bertelsmann.de *Web Site:* www.az.bertelsmann.de, pg 196

AZ Editora SA (Argentina) *Tel:* (011) 4961-4036; (011) 4961-4037; (011) 4961-4038; (011) 4961-0088 *Fax:* (011) 4961-0089 *E-mail:* correo@az-editora.com *Web Site:* www.az-editora.com.ar, pg 3

Azerbaidzhanskaya respublikanskaya biblioteka im M F Akhundova (Azerbaijan) *Tel:* (012) 934 003, pg 1492

Azernesr (Azerbaijan) *Tel:* (012) 925015, pg 60

Al- Azhar University Library (Egypt (Arab Republic of Egypt)) *Tel:* (02) 904051; (02) 706097; (02) 261 1419 *Web Site:* www.alazhar.org, pg 1503

La Azotea Editorial Fotografica SRL (Argentina) *Tel:* (011) 4811-0931 *Fax:* (011) 4811-0931 *E-mail:* azotea@laazotea.com.ar *Web Site:* www.laazotea.com.ar, pg 4

Editorial Azteca SA (Mexico) *Tel:* (05) 5261157, pg 462

B & B (Republic of Korea) *Tel:* (02) 540-4425 *Fax:* (02) 517-8793 *E-mail:* bbpress-98@hanmail.net, pg 437

Ediciones B, SA (Spain) *Tel:* (093) 484 66 00 *Fax:* (093) 232 46 60 *Web Site:* www.edicionesb.es; www.edicionesb.com, pg 574

B I Publications Pvt Ltd (India) *Tel:* (011) 3274443; (011) 3259352; (011) 3255118 *Fax:* (011) 3261290 *E-mail:* bigroup@del3.vsnl.net.in, pg 329

B M Israel BV (Netherlands) *Tel:* (020) 624 70 40 *Fax:* (020) 507 20 32 *E-mail:* bmisrael@xs4all.nl *Web Site:* www.nvva.nl/israelbm, pg 478

b small publishing (United Kingdom) *Tel:* (020) 8974 6851 *Fax:* (020) 8974 6845 *E-mail:* info@bsmall.co.uk *Web Site:* homepage.ntlworld.com/codework/welcome.htm, pg 662

Ba-reunsa Publishing Co (Republic of Korea) *Tel:* (031) 792-0185, pg 437

BAAF Adoption & Fostering (United Kingdom) *Tel:* (020) 7593 2000 *Fax:* (020) 7593 2001 *E-mail:* mail@baaf.org.uk *Web Site:* www.baaf.org.uk, pg 662

Auteursbureau Greta Baars-Jelgersma (Netherlands) *Tel:* (024) 6963336 *Fax:* (024) 6963293 *E-mail:* 6963336@hetnet.nl *Web Site:* home.hetnet.nl/~jelgersma696, pg 1135

Bernard Babani (Publishing) Ltd (United Kingdom) *Tel:* (020) 7603 2581; (020) 7603 7296 *Fax:* (020) 7603 8203 *E-mail:* enquiries@babanibooks.com *Web Site:* www.babanibooks.com, pg 662

Babel Verlag Kevin Perryman (Germany) *Tel:* (08243) 961691 *Fax:* (08243) 961614 *E-mail:* info@babel-verlag.de *Web Site:* www.babel-verlag.de, pg 196

Baberu Inc (Japan) *Tel:* (03) 5530-2205 *Fax:* (03) 5530-2204 *E-mail:* buc@babel.co.jp *Web Site:* www.babel.co.jp, pg 415

Babtext Nakladatelska Spolecnost (Czech Republic) *Tel:* (02) 435 992 *Fax:* (02) 768992; (02) 61221868, pg 122

Joan Bacchus-Xavier (Trinidad & Tobago) *Tel:* 6225588 *Fax:* 6251330, pg 646

Bacharakis (Greece) *Tel:* (031) 263776 *Fax:* (031) 263776, pg 1313

J P Bachem Verlag GmbH (Germany) *Tel:* (0221) 1619-0 *Fax:* (0221) 1619-159 *E-mail:* info@bachem-verlag.de *Web Site:* www.bachem-verlag.de, pg 196

Dr Bachmaier Verlag GmbH (Germany) *Tel:* (089) 685120 *Fax:* (089) 685120 *E-mail:* contact@verlag-drbachmaier.de *Web Site:* www.verlag-drbachmaier.de, pg 196

Backhuys Publishers BV (Netherlands) *Tel:* (071) 5170208 *Fax:* (071) 5171856 *E-mail:* info@backhuys.com *Web Site:* www.backhuys.com, pg 478

Francis Bacon Society Inc (United Kingdom) *Tel:* (020) 7359 6888 *Fax:* (020) 7704 1896 *Web Site:* www.sirbacon.org/links/bmembership.htm, pg 1406

Editions de la Baconniere SA (Switzerland) *Tel:* (022) 8690029 *Fax:* (022) 8690015 *E-mail:* DEB@medecinehygiene.ch, pg 618

Badan Bookstore Sdn Bhd (Malaysia) *Tel:* (07) 2234796; (07) 2377562; (07) 2330241; (07) 330241 *Fax:* (07) 2238188, pg 1326

Badan Penerbit Kristen Gunung Mulia (Indonesia) *Tel:* (021) 3901208 *Fax:* (021) 3901633 *E-mail:* corp.off@bpkgm.com *Web Site:* www.bpkgm.com, pg 353

Badenia Verlag und Druckerei GmbH (Germany) *Tel:* (0721) 95 45-0 *Fax:* (0721) 95 45-125 *E-mail:* verlag@badeniaverlag.de *Web Site:* www.badeniaverlag.badeniaonline.de, pg 196

Badische Landesbibliothek (Germany) *Tel:* (0721) 175-20 01; (0721) 175-22 22 *Fax:* (0721) 175-23 33 *E-mail:* informationszentrum@blb-karlsruhe.de *Web Site:* www.blb-karlsruhe.de, pg 1508

Badischer Landwirtschafts-Verlag GmbH (Germany) *Tel:* (0761) 271330 *Fax:* (0761) 2713372 *E-mail:* redaktion@blv-freiburg.de, pg 196

Buchhandlung G D Baedeker (Germany) *Tel:* (0201) 20680 *Fax:* (0201) 2068-100 *E-mail:* service.gdb.essen@baedeker.de *Web Site:* www.baedeker.de, pg 1310

U Baer Verlag (Switzerland) *Tel:* (01) 3835500 *Fax:* (01) 3836883, pg 618

Barenreiter Verlag Basel AG (Switzerland) *Tel:* (061) 395898; (061) 395899 *Fax:* (061) 3079660 *E-mail:* info@baerenreiter.com *Web Site:* www.baerenreiter.com, pg 618

Buchhandlung Baeschlin (Switzerland) *Tel:* (055) 6401125 *Fax:* (055) 6406594 *Web Site:* www.baeschlin.ch, pg 618

K P Bagchi & Co (India) *Tel:* (033) 267474; (033) 269496 *Fax:* (033) 2482973, pg 329

Baha'i (Italy) *Tel:* (06) 9334334 *Fax:* (06) 9334335 *E-mail:* ceb@bahai.it *Web Site:* www.bahai.it, pg 377

Baha'i Publishing Trust (United Kingdom) *Tel:* (01572) 722780 *Fax:* (01572) 724280 *E-mail:* sales@bahaibooks.co.uk *Web Site:* www.bahai-publishing-trust.co.uk, pg 662

Baha'i Publishing Trust of India (India) *Tel:* (011) 26819391; (011) 26818990 *Fax:* (011) 26812703 *E-mail:* publisher@bahaindia.org; bptindia@del3.vsnl.net.in; nsaindia@bahaindia.org *Web Site:* www.bahaindia.org, pg 329

Baha'i Verlag GmbH (Germany) *Tel:* (06192) 22921 *Fax:* (06192) 22936 *E-mail:* info@bahai-verlag.de *Web Site:* www.bahaipublishers.org, pg 196

Maison d'Editions Baha'ies ASBL (Belgium) *Tel:* (02) 647 07 49 *Fax:* (02) 646 21 77 *E-mail:* meb@swing.be *Web Site:* www.adeb.irisnet.be, pg 63

Bahnsport Aktuell Verlag GmbH (Germany) *Tel:* (06184) 9233-30 *Fax:* (06184) 9233-50 *E-mail:* mce-aktuell@mce-online.de, pg 196

Bahrain Centre for Studies, Research Library & Information Dept (Bahrain) *Fax:* (0973) 754678 *E-mail:* bcsr@batelco.com.bh *Web Site:* www.batelco.com.bh/bcsr/, pg 1492

Bahrain Writers & Literators Association (Bahrain), pg 1396

Baifukan Co Ltd (Japan) *Tel:* (03) 3262-5270 *Fax:* (03) 3262-5276 *E-mail:* bfkeigyo@mx7.mesh.ne.jp *Web Site:* www.baifukan.co.jp/, pg 415

Baile del Sol, Colectivo Cultural (Spain) *Tel:* 676438253 *E-mail:* bailesol@yahoo.com, pg 574

Bill Bailey Publishers' Representatives (United Kingdom) *Tel:* (01626) 331079 *Fax:* (01626) 331080 *E-mail:* billbailey.pubrep@eclipse.co.uk, pg 662

Bailey Brothers & Swinfen Ltd (United Kingdom) *Tel:* (01797) 366905 *Fax:* (01797) 366638, pg 662

Editions J B Bailliere (France) *Tel:* (01) 55 33 69 00 *Fax:* (01) 55 33 68 07, pg 149

W & G Baird Ltd (United Kingdom) *Tel:* (028) 9446 3911 *Fax:* (028) 9446 6250 *E-mail:* wgbaird@wgbaird.com *Web Site:* www.wgbaird.org, pg 1183, 1224

Bakalar spol sro (Czech Republic) *Tel:* (019) 523197, pg 122

Baken-Verlag Walter Schnoor (Germany) *Tel:* (04822) 1671; (04192) 1784, pg 196

Bakermat NV (Belgium) *Tel:* (015) 42 05 08 *Fax:* (015) 42 05 73 *E-mail:* info@bakermat.com *Web Site:* www.bakermat.com, pg 63

Bakyoung Publishing Co (Republic of Korea) *Tel:* (02) 7336771 *Fax:* (02) 7364818 *E-mail:* psy@pakyoungsa.co.kr, pg 437

Bal-eon (Republic of Korea) *Tel:* (02) 293546; (02) 293547 *Fax:* (02) 293548, pg 437

Balai Pustaka (Indonesia) *Tel:* (021) 3447003; (021) 3447006 *Fax:* (021) 3446555 *E-mail:* mail@balaiperaga.com *Web Site:* www.balaiperaga.com, pg 353

Edition Balance Marion Guenther Bonsack (Germany) *Tel:* (03621) 750061 *Fax:* (03621) 151315156 *E-mail:* info@edition-balance.de *Web Site:* www.edition-balance.de, pg 196

Uitgeverij Balans (Netherlands) *Tel:* (020) 524 75 80 *Fax:* (020) 524 75 89 *E-mail:* balans@uitgeverijbalans.nl *Web Site:* www.uitgeverijbalans.nl, pg 478

Balassi Kiado Kft (Hungary) *Tel:* (01) 3518075; (01) 3518343 *E-mail:* balassi@mail.datanet.hu, pg 321

Carmen Balcells Agencia Literaria SA (Spain) *Tel:* (093) 2008565; (093) 2008933 *Fax:* (093) 2007041 *E-mail:* ag-balcells@mx2.redestb.es, pg 1136

Agencia Literaria Balcells Mello e Souza Riff S/C Ltda (Brazil) *Tel:* (021) 2287-6299 *Fax:* (021) 2287-6393 *E-mail:* bmsr@bmsr.com.br *Web Site:* www.bmsr.com.br, pg 1129

Izdatelstvo na Balgarskata Akademija na Naukite (Bulgaria) *Tel:* (02) 720922; (02) 9793449; (02) 9793441 *Fax:* (02) 704054, pg 93

A A Balkema Uitgevers BV (Netherlands) *Tel:* (0252) 435111 *Fax:* (0252) 435447 *E-mail:* orders@swets.nl *Web Site:* www.balkema.nl, pg 478

Jonathan Ball Publishers (South Africa) *Tel:* (011) 622-2900 *Fax:* (011) 622-7610, pg 562

Editions Balland (France) *Tel:* (01) 43 25 74 40 *Fax:* (01) 46 33 56 21 *E-mail:* info@balland.fr *Web Site:* www.balland.fr, pg 149

Ballinakella Press (Ireland) *Tel:* (061) 927030 *Fax:* (061) 927418 *E-mail:* info@ballinakella.com, pg 358

H R Balmer AG Verlag (Switzerland) *Tel:* (041) 726 9797 *Fax:* (041) 726 9798 *E-mail:* info@buecher-balmer.ch *Web Site:* www.buecher-balmer.ch, pg 618

H R Balmer AG Buchhandlung Verlag Verlagauslieferung (Switzerland) *Tel:* (041) 726 97 97 *Fax:* (041) 726 97 98 *E-mail:* info@buecher-balmer.ch *Web Site:* www.buecher-balmer.ch, pg 1344

Baltos Lankos (Lithuania) *Tel:* (05) 240 86 73; (05) 240 79 06 *Fax:* (05) 240 74 46 *E-mail:* leidykla@baltoslankos.lt *Web Site:* www.baltoslankos.lt, pg 449

Staatsbibliothek Bamberg (Germany) *Tel:* (0951) 95503-0 *Fax:* (0951) 95503-145 *E-mail:* info@staatsbibliothek-bamberg.de *Web Site:* www.staatsbibliothek-bamberg.de, pg 1508

Editorial Banca y Comercio SA de CV (México) *Tel:* (05) 2089692; (05) 2081785; (05) 2081705 *Fax:* (05) 2081803 *E-mail:* edbyc@prodigy.net *Web Site:* www.edbyc.com.mx, pg 462

Bancaria Editrice SpA (Italy) *Tel:* (06) 6767222; (06) 6767475 *Fax:* (06) 6767250 *Web Site:* www.bancariaeditrice.it, pg 377

Bandansan (Thailand) *Tel:* (02) 825511, pg 645

Bandicoot Books (Australia) *Tel:* (03) 6267 2530 *Fax:* (03) 6267 1223 *Web Site:* www.bandicootbooks.com, pg 14

Bang Printing Co Inc (United States) *Tel:* 218-829-2877 *Toll Free Tel:* 800-328-0450 *Fax:* 218-829-7145 *Web Site:* www.bangprinting.com, pg 1186, 1239

The Bangalore Printing & Publishing Co Ltd (India) *Tel:* (080) 6709638; (080) 6709027 *Fax:* (080) 6704053 *E-mail:* marketing@bangalorepress.com *Web Site:* www.bangalorepress.com, pg 329

C Bange GmbH & Co KG (Germany) *Tel:* (09274) 94130 *Fax:* (09274) 94132 *E-mail:* service@bange-verlag.de *Web Site:* www.bange-verlag.de, pg 196

Bangladesh Books International Ltd (Bangladesh) *Tel:* (02) 232252 (ext 31); (02) 232229; (02) 256071 (ext 19), pg 1301

Bangladesh Central Public Library (Bangladesh) *Tel:* (02) 50 08 19; (02) 50 08 39; (02) 50 28 16, pg 1492

Bangladesh Government Press, Ministry of Establishment, Government of the Peoples Republic of Bangladesh (Bangladesh) *Tel:* (02) 606 316 *Fax:* (02) 8113095 *E-mail:* adab@bdonline.com, pg 61

Bangladesh Institute of Development Studies Library (Bangladesh) *Tel:* (02) 9118999 *Fax:* (02) 8113023 *E-mail:* secy08bids@sdnbd.org *Web Site:* www.bids-bd.org, pg 1492

National Library of Bangladesh, Directorate of Archives & Libraries (Bangladesh) *Tel:* (02) 232 6572, pg 1492

National Library of Bangladesh, Directorate of Archives & Libraries (Bangladesh) *Tel:* (02) 326572 *Fax:* (02) 9118704, pg 1558

Bangladesh Publishers (Bangladesh) *Tel:* (02) 233135, pg 61

Bani Mandir, Book-Sellers, Publishers & Educational Suppliers (India) *Tel:* (0361) 520241; (0361) 513886 *E-mail:* utpal@gwl.vsnl.net.in *Web Site:* www.banimandir.cjb.net, pg 329

Bank-Verlag GmbH (Germany) *Tel:* (0221) 54 90-0 *Fax:* (0221) 54 90-120 *E-mail:* bank-verlag@bank-verlag.de *Web Site:* www.bank-verlag.de, pg 197

Bannakhan (Thailand) *Tel:* (02) 227796, pg 645

Bannakit Trading (Thailand) *Tel:* (02) 2825520; (02) 2827537; (02) 2814213 *Fax:* (02) 2820076, pg 645

The Banner of Truth Trust (United Kingdom) *Tel:* (0131) 337 7310 *Fax:* (0131) 346 7484 *E-mail:* info@banneroftruth.co.uk *Web Site:* www.banneroftruth.co.uk, pg 662

Banson (United Kingdom) *Tel:* (020) 7729 7315; (020) 7613 1388 *Fax:* (020) 7729 7870 *E-mail:* banson@ourplanet.com, pg 662

The Banton Press (United Kingdom) *Tel:* (01770) 820231 *Fax:* (01770) 820231 *E-mail:* bantonpress@btinternet.com *Web Site:* www.bantonpress.co.uk, pg 662

Banyan Tree Book Distributors (Australia) *Tel:* (08) 8363-4244 *Fax:* (08) 8363-4255 *E-mail:* enquiries@banyantreebooks.com.au; orders@banyantreebooks.com.au *Web Site:* banyantreebooks.predelegation.com, pg 1297

Dr Richard Bar di animali (Germany) *Tel:* (0911) 951 9490 *Fax:* (0911) 951 9489 *E-mail:* di.animali@web.de *Web Site:* www.zivilist.it, pg 197

Bar Ilan University Central Library (Israel) *Tel:* (03) 5318486 *Fax:* (03) 5349233 *E-mail:* barmae@mail.biu.ac.il *Web Site:* www.biu.ac.il/lib, pg 1519

Bar Ilan University Press (Israel) *Tel:* (03) 5318111 *Fax:* (03) 5353446 *E-mail:* press@mail.biu.ac.il *Web Site:* www.biu.ac.il/Press, pg 365

Editorial Barath SA (Spain) *Tel:* (091) 4496049, pg 574

Baraza la Kiswahili la Taifa (United Republic of Tanzania) *Tel:* (051) 23452; (051) 24139, pg 1149

The Barbados National Trust (Barbados) *Tel:* 246-426-2421 *Fax:* 246-429-9055 *E-mail:* natrust@sunbeach.net *Web Site:* trust.funbarbados.com, pg 1129

B McCall Barbour (United Kingdom) *Tel:* (0131) 2254816 *Fax:* (0131) 2254816, pg 1347

McCall Barbour (United Kingdom) *Tel:* (0131) 225-4816 *Fax:* (0131) 225-4816 *E-mail:* ashbethany43@hotmail.com, pg 663

Editorial Barcanova SA (Spain) *Tel:* (093) 2172054; (093) 2172550 *Fax:* (093) 2373469 *E-mail:* barcanova@barcanova.es *Web Site:* www.barcanova.es, pg 574

Editorial Barcino SA (Spain) *Tel:* (093) 2186888 *Fax:* (093) 2186888 *E-mail:* ebarcino@editorialbarcino.com *Web Site:* www.editorialbarcino.com, pg 574

Barcode Graphics Inc (Canada) *Tel:* 416-751-1474 *Toll Free Tel:* 800-263-3669 *Fax:* 416-751-1575 *E-mail:* info@barcodegraphics.com *Web Site:* www.barcodegraphics.com, pg 1175

Hjalmar R Bardarson (Iceland) *Tel:* 555-0729, pg 325

Bardi Editore srl (Italy) *Tel:* (06) 4817656 *Fax:* (06) 48912574 *E-mail:* bardied@tin.it *Web Site:* www.bardieditore.com, pg 377

Bardon-Chinese Media Agency (Taiwan, Province of China) *Tel:* (02) 33932585 *Fax:* (02) 23929577 *Web Site:* www.bardonchinese.com, pg 1137

Barefoot Books (United Kingdom) *Tel:* (01225) 322400 *Fax:* (01225) 322499 *E-mail:* info@barefootbooks.co.uk *Web Site:* www.barefootbooks.com, pg 663

Barenreiter-Verlag Karl-Votterle GmbH & Co KG (Germany) *Tel:* (0561) 3105-0 *Fax:* (0561) 3105-176 *E-mail:* info@baerenreiter.com *Web Site:* www.baerenreiter.com, pg 197

Bargain Book Sales (United Kingdom) *Tel:* (020) 7385 7007 *Fax:* (020) 7385 7007; (020) 7385 9727, pg 1347

Bargezzi-Verlag AG (Switzerland) *Tel:* (031) 221380; (031) 211434, pg 618

Barkfire Press (New Zealand) *Tel:* (09) 3031039 *Fax:* (09) 3031059 *E-mail:* info@barkfire.com *Web Site:* www.barkfire.com, pg 494

Barmarick Publications (United Kingdom) *Tel:* (01964) 630033 *Fax:* (01964) 631716 *Web Site:* www.barmarick.co.uk, pg 663

Barn Dance Publications Ltd (United Kingdom) *Tel:* (020) 8657 2813 *Fax:* (020) 8651 6080 *E-mail:* barndance@pubs.co.uk *Web Site:* www.barndancepublications.co.uk, pg 663

Barnas Hobbyklubb (Norway) *Tel:* 24051000 *Fax:* 24051099 *E-mail:* post@damm.no *Web Site:* www.dammbokklubb.no, pg 1254

Barnens Bokklubb (Sweden) *Tel:* (08) 506 304 00 *Fax:* (08) 506 304 01 *E-mail:* redaktionen@barnensbokklubb.se *Web Site:* www.barnensbokklubb.se, pg 1256

Baronet (Czech Republic) *Tel:* (02) 22310115 *Fax:* (02) 22310118 *E-mail:* baronet.odbyt@volny.cz *Web Site:* www.baronet-knihy.cz; www.baronet.cz, pg 122

Barr Smith Press, University of Adelaide Library (Australia) *Tel:* (08) 8303 5372 *Fax:* (08) 8303 4369 *E-mail:* bslill@library.adelaide.edu.au *Web Site:* www.library.adelaide.edu.au, pg 1490

Barreiro y Ramos SA (Uruguay) *Tel:* (02) 98 66 21 *Fax:* (02) 96 23 58, pg 777

Barreiro y Ramos SA (Uruguay) *Tel:* (02) 986621 *Fax:* (02) 962358, pg 1168, 1189, 1231

Barreiro y Ramos SA (Uruguay) *Tel:* (02) 96 23 58 *Fax:* (02) 96 23 58, pg 1241, 1250

Barreiro y Ramos SA (Uruguay) *Tel:* (02) 95 01 50 *Fax:* (02) 96 23 58, pg 1355

Barrister & Principal (Czech Republic) *Tel:* (05) 45211015 *Fax:* (05) 45210607 *E-mail:* barrister@barrister.cz *Web Site:* www.barrister.cz, pg 122

La Bartavelle (France) *Tel:* (02) 37821450 *Fax:* (02) 37821463, pg 149

Verlag Dr Albert Bartens KG (Germany) *Tel:* (030) 803 56 78 *Fax:* (030) 803 20 49 *E-mail:* info@bartens.com *Web Site:* www.bartens.com, pg 197

Otto Wilhelm Barth-Verlag KG (Germany) *Tel:* (089) 9271-0 *Fax:* (089) 9271-168, pg 197

Editions A Barthelemy (France) *Tel:* (04) 90 03 60 00 *Fax:* (04) 90036009 *E-mail:* infos@editions-barthelemy.com *Web Site:* www.editions-barthelemy.com, pg 149

Bartkowiaks Forum Book Art (Germany) *Tel:* (040) 2793674 *Fax:* (040) 2704397 *E-mail:* info@forumbookart.de *Web Site:* www.forumbookart.com, pg 197

Bartleby & Co (Belgium) *Tel:* (02) 538 10 51 *E-mail:* bartleby@skynet.be, pg 63

Bartschi Publishing (Switzerland) *Tel:* (01) 7373528, pg 618

BAS Printers Ltd (United Kingdom) *Tel:* (01722) 411711 *Fax:* (01722) 411727 *E-mail:* sales@basprint.co.uk *Web Site:* www.basprint.co.uk, pg 1163, 1183, 1224

Basam Books Oy (Finland) *Tel:* (09) 7579 3839 *Fax:* (09) 7579 3838 *E-mail:* bs@basambooks.com *Web Site:* www.basambooks.com, pg 141

Baseball Magazine-Sha Co Ltd (Japan) *Tel:* (03) 3238-0285 *Fax:* (03) 3238-0084 *Web Site:* www.bbm-japan.com, pg 415

Baseline Creative Ltd (United Kingdom) *Tel:* (0117) 962 0006 *Fax:* (0117) 962 5006 *E-mail:* contact@base.co.uk *Web Site:* www.base.co.uk, pg 1183

Basica Editora (Portugal) *Tel:* (021) 779273, pg 529

Basileia Verlag und Basler Missionsbuchhandlung (Switzerland) *Tel:* (061) 251766 *Fax:* (061) 2688321; (061) 232523, pg 618

Basilisken-Presse (Germany) *Tel:* 06421 15188, pg 197

Basilius Presse AG (Switzerland) *Tel:* (061) 228004; (061) 228005 *Fax:* (061) 232523, pg 618

BasisDruck Verlag GmbH (Germany) *Tel:* (030) 445 76 80 *Fax:* (030) 445 95 99 *E-mail:* basisdruck@onlinehome.de *Web Site:* www.basisdruck.de, pg 197

Bassermann Verlag (Germany) *Tel:* (089) 41 360 *E-mail:* vertrieb.verlagsgruppe@randomhouse.de *Web Site:* www.randomhouse.de/bassermann, pg 197

Bastei Luebbe Taschenbuecher (Germany) *Tel:* (02202) 121-293; (02202) 121-544 *Fax:* (02202) 121-927 *E-mail:* bastei.luebbe@luebbe.de *Web Site:* www.luebbe.de, pg 197

Bastei Verlag (Germany) *Tel:* (02202) 121-0 *Fax:* (02202) 121-936 *E-mail:* info@bastei.de *Web Site:* www.bastei.de, pg 197

Bastogi (Italy) *Tel:* (0881) 725070 *Fax:* (0881) 728119 *E-mail:* bastogi@tiscali.it *Web Site:* www.bastogi.it, pg 377

Ediciones Bat (Chile) *Tel:* (02) 2743171 *Fax:* (02) 2250261, pg 99

David Bateman Ltd (New Zealand) *Tel:* (09) 415 7664 *Fax:* (09) 415 8892 *E-mail:* bateman@bateman.co.nz *Web Site:* www.bateman.co.nz, pg 494

The Bath Press (United Kingdom) *Tel:* (01225) 428101 *Fax:* (01225) 312418 *E-mail:* bath@cpi-group.co.uk *Web Site:* www.cpi-group.net/bathbas.htm, pg 1163

The Bath Press (United Kingdom) *Tel:* (01225) 428101 *Fax:* (01225) 312418 *E-mail:* bath@cpi-group.co.uk *Web Site:* www.cpi-group.net, pg 1183, 1247

Batsford Ltd (United Kingdom) *Tel:* (020) 7221 2213; (020) 7314 1469 (sales) *Fax:* (020) 7221 6455; (020) 7314 1594 (sales) *E-mail:* enquiries@chrysalis.com *Web Site:* www.chrysalisbooks.co.uk/books/publisher/batsford, pg 663

Casa Editrice Luigi Battei (Italy) *Tel:* (0521) 233733 *Fax:* (0521) 231291, pg 377

Battre Ledarskap (Sweden) *Tel:* (040) 25 86 76 *Fax:* (040) 97 05 50 *E-mail:* export@liber.se *Web Site:* www.battreledarskap.net, pg 1256

Wydawnictwo Baturo (Poland) *Tel:* (033) 81 25 086; (033) 81 40 955; (033) 81 62 703 *Fax:* (033) 81 40 955 *E-mail:* baturo@baturo.com.pl *Web Site:* www.baturo.com.pl, pg 522

Societe Nouvelle Rene Baudouin (France) *Tel:* (01) 43290050 *Fax:* (01) 43257241, pg 149

Verlag Hermann Bauer Gmbh & Co KG (Germany) *Tel:* (0761) 7082-0 *Fax:* (0761) 701811 *E-mail:* info@hermann-bauer.de, pg 197

N E Bauman Moscow State Technical University Publishers (Russian Federation) *Tel:* (095) 263-67-98; (095) 263-60-45; (095) 265-37-97 *Fax:* (095) 265-42-98 *E-mail:* press@bmstu.ru *Web Site:* www.bmstu.ru, pg 544

Baumann GmbH & Co KG (Germany) *Tel:* (09221) 949413 *Fax:* (09221) 949352 *E-mail:* service@baumann-online.de *Web Site:* www.baumann-online.de, pg 197

Dr Wolfgang Baur Verlag Kunst & Alltag (Germany) *Tel:* (08171) 217514 *Fax:* (08171) 217515 *E-mail:* verlag@kunstalltag.de *Web Site:* www.kunstalltag.de, pg 198

Bautz Traugott (Germany) *Tel:* (05521) 57 00; (05521) 55 88 *Fax:* (05521) 16 73; (05521) 57 80 *E-mail:* bautz@bautz.de *Web Site:* www.bautz.de, pg 198

Bauverlag GmbH (Germany) *Tel:* (05241) 802119 *Fax:* (05241) 809582 *E-mail:* info@bauverlag.de *Web Site:* www.bauverlag.de, pg 198

Colin Baxter Photography Ltd (United Kingdom) *Tel:* (01479) 873999 *Fax:* (01479) 873888 *E-mail:* sales@colinbaxter.co.uk *Web Site:* www.colinbaxter.co.uk; www.worldlifelibrary.co.uk, pg 663

Bay Foreign Language Books (United Kingdom) *Tel:* (01233) 720020 *Fax:* (01233) 721272 *E-mail:* sales@baylanguagebooks.co.uk *Web Site:* www.baylanguagebooks.co.uk, pg 1347

Bay View Books Ltd (United Kingdom) *Tel:* (01237) 479225; (01237) 421285 *Fax:* (01237) 421286, pg 663

Bayard Presse (France) *Tel:* (01) 44 35 60 60 *Fax:* (01) 44 35 61 61 *Web Site:* www.bayardpresse.com, pg 149

Bayda Books (Australia) *Tel:* (0613) 9387-2799 *Fax:* (0613) 9387-2799 *Web Site:* www.bayda.com.au, pg 14

Buchhandlung Bayer (Austria) *Tel:* (05522) 74770 *Fax:* (05522) 74770 *E-mail:* bayer.buch@utanet.at, pg 1299

Bayerische Akademie der Wissenschaften (Germany) *Tel:* (089) 23031-0 *Fax:* (089) 23031-100 *E-mail:* webmaster@badw.de; presse@badw.de *Web Site:* www.badw.de, pg 198

Bayerische Staatsbibliothek (Germany) *Tel:* (089) 28638-0; (089) 28638-2322 *Fax:* (089) 28638-2200 *E-mail:* direktion@bsb-muenchen.de; info@bsb-muenchen.de *Web Site:* www.bsb-muenchen.de, pg 1508

Bayerische Verlagsanstalt GmbH (Germany) *Tel:* (0951) 967120 *Fax:* (0951) 96712235, pg 198

Bayerischer Schulbuch-Verlag GmbH (Germany) *Tel:* (089) 450510 *Fax:* (089) 45051-200, pg 198

Ebenezer Baylis & Son Ltd (United Kingdom) *Tel:* (01905) 357979 *Fax:* (01905) 354919 *E-mail:* theworks@ebaylis.demon.co.uk, pg 1224

Joycelyn Bayne (Australia) *Tel:* (08) 8356 1748, pg 14

George Bayntun Booksellers (United Kingdom) *Tel:* (01225) 466000 *Fax:* (01225) 482122 *E-mail:* ebc@georgebayntun.com *Web Site:* www.georgebayntun.com, pg 1347

BBC Audiobooks (United Kingdom) *Tel:* (01672) 562255 *Fax:* (01672) 564634 *E-mail:* bbc@covertocover.co.uk *Web Site:* bbcaudiobooks.com, pg 663

BBC English (United Kingdom) *Tel:* (020) 8576 2221 *Fax:* (020) 8576 3040 *Web Site:* www.bbcenglish.com, pg 663

BBC WORLDWIDE PUBLISHERS   INDUSTRY

BBC Worldwide Publishers (United Kingdom) *Tel:* (020) 8433 2000 *Fax:* (020) 8749 0538 *E-mail:* bbcsales@bbc.co.uk *Web Site:* www.bbcworldwide.com, pg 663

BCA - Book Club Associates (United Kingdom) *Tel:* (020) 7760 6500 *Fax:* (020) 7760 6501 *Web Site:* www.bca.co.uk, pg 663

BCM Media Inc (Republic of Korea) *Tel:* (02) 567-0644; (02) 533-0089 *Fax:* (02) 552-9169 *E-mail:* bcmpub@nuri.net *Web Site:* www.bcm.co.kr, pg 437

BCS Publishing Ltd (United Kingdom) *Tel:* (01869) 324423 *Fax:* (01869) 324385, pg 1163, 1183

be.bra verlag GmbH (Germany) *Tel:* (030) 440 23-810 *Fax:* (030) 440 23-819 *E-mail:* post@bebraverlag.de *Web Site:* www.bebraverlag.de, pg 198

Beacon Verlag Koerber OHG (Germany) *Tel:* (06322) 2056 *Fax:* (06322) 2056, pg 198

Beaconsfield Publishers Ltd (United Kingdom) *Tel:* (01494) 672118 *Fax:* (01494) 672118 *E-mail:* books@beaconsfield-publishers.co.uk *Web Site:* www.beaconsfield-publishers.co.uk, pg 664

Ruth Bean Publishers (United Kingdom) *Tel:* (01234) 720356 *Fax:* (01234) 720590 *E-mail:* ruthbean@onetel.net.uk, pg 664

Beas Ediciones SRL (Argentina) *Tel:* (011) 4923-4030; (011) 4924-5337 *Fax:* (011) 4924-0217, pg 4

Beascoa SA Ediciones (Spain) *Tel:* (093) 3196517; (093) 3934380 *Fax:* (093) 3107694; (093) 3934389 *E-mail:* info@beascoa.com, pg 574

Editions des Beatitudes, Pneumatheque (France) *Tel:* (02) 54 88 21 18 *Fax:* (02) 54 88 97 73 *E-mail:* edd.etrangers@wandadoo.com *Web Site:* www.editions-beatitudes.fr, pg 149

Beatriz Viterbo Editora (Argentina) *Tel:* (0341) 4487521 *Fax:* (0341) 4261919, pg 4

The Chester Beatty Library (Ireland) *Tel:* (01) 4070750 *Fax:* (01) 4070760 *E-mail:* info@cbl.ie *Web Site:* www.cbl.ie, pg 1518

Beauchesne Editeur (France) *Tel:* (01) 45 48 80 28 *Fax:* (01) 42 22 59 79, pg 149

Beazer Publishing Company Pty Ltd (Australia) *Tel:* (03) 5156 0556 *Fax:* (03) 5156 0556 *E-mail:* info@beazerpublishing.com *Web Site:* www.beazerpublishing.com, pg 14

Mitchell Beazley (United Kingdom) *Tel:* (020) 7531 8400; (020) 7531 8480 (UK sales); (020) 7531 8481 (special sales); (020) 7531 8479 (marketing); (020) 7531 8488 (publicity); (020) 7531 8482 (export sales); (020) 7531 8484 (foreign rights); (020) 7531 8476 (US sales) *Fax:* (020) 7531 8650 *E-mail:* enquiries@mitchell-beazley.co.uk *Web Site:* www.mitchell-beazley.com, pg 664

BEBC Distribution (United Kingdom) *Tel:* (01202) 712934 *Fax:* (01202) 712913 *E-mail:* webenquiry@bebc.co.uk *Web Site:* www.bebc.co.uk, pg 1347

Ludwig Bechauf Verlag (Germany) *Tel:* (0521) 130648 *Fax:* (0521) 139347, pg 198

Bechtermuenz Verlag (Germany) *Tel:* (089) 9271 312 *Fax:* (0821) 70 04-179, pg 198

Bechtle Graphische Betriebe und Verlagsgesellschaft GmbH und Co KG (Germany) *Tel:* (0711) 9310-0, pg 198

Beck & Gluckler Verlag GmbH & Co KG (Germany) *Tel:* (0761) 701530 *Fax:* (0761) 701580, pg 198

Verlag C H Beck oHG (Germany) *Tel:* (089) 38189-0 *Fax:* (089) 38189-402 *E-mail:* info.lsw@beck.de; bestellung@beck.de (orders) *Web Site:* www.beck.de, pg 198

Edition Monika Beck (Germany) *Tel:* (06848) 72152 *Fax:* (06848) 72159 *E-mail:* info@mathbeck.de *Web Site:* www.mathbeck.de/edmb, pg 198

Barbara Beckett Publishing Pty Ltd (Australia) *Tel:* (02) 93312871 *Fax:* (02) 93603106, pg 14

Bedout Editores SA (Colombia) *Tel:* (04) 5112900 *Fax:* (04) 2517946, pg 110

Bokklubben Bedre Ledelse (Norway) *Tel:* 24051000 *Fax:* 24051099 *E-mail:* post@damm.no *Web Site:* www.dammbokklubb.no, pg 1254

Beerenverlag (Germany) *Tel:* (069) 61009551 *Fax:* (069) 61009560, pg 198

Beginners Publishers (Ghana) *Tel:* (021) 503040 *Fax:* (051) 772642 Attn: Beginners Publishers, pg 303

Beijing Ancient Books Publishing House (China) *Tel:* (010) 2016699 313; (010) 2013122 *Fax:* (010) 2012339 *E-mail:* geo@bph.com.cn, pg 101

Beijing Arts & Crafts Publishing House (China) *Tel:* (010) 65230677; (010) 4031811, pg 101

Beijing Education Publishing House (China) *Tel:* (010) 2016699-268; (010) 62013122 *Fax:* (010) 2012339 *E-mail:* geo@bph.com.cn, pg 101

Beijing Fine Arts & Photography Publishing House (China) *Tel:* (010) 2016699; (010) 62016699-315 *Fax:* (010) 2012339 *E-mail:* geo@bph.com.cn, pg 101

Beijing Juvenile & Children's Books Publishing House (China) *Tel:* (010) 2016699-350; (010) 62013122 *Fax:* (010) 2012339 *E-mail:* geo@bph.com.cn, pg 101

Beijing Medical University Press (China) *Tel:* (010) 62092249 *Fax:* (010) 62029848 *E-mail:* bmupress@public.fhnet.cn.net *Web Site:* www.bjmu.edu.cn, pg 101

Beijing Publishing House (China) *Tel:* (010) 62003964 *Fax:* (010) 62012339; (010) 62016699 *E-mail:* geo@bph.com.cn; public@bphg.com.cn *Web Site:* www.bph.com.cn, pg 101

Beijing University Press (China) *Tel:* (010) 62752033 *Fax:* (010) 2564095 *E-mail:* psj@pup.pku.edu.cn, pg 101

Dr Ivanka Beil, Internationale Handelsvermittlung im Medien- und Verlagswesen (Germany) *Tel:* (06201) 14611 *Fax:* (06201) 16883, pg 1131

Library of Beirut Arab University (Lebanon) *Tel:* (01) 300110 *Fax:* (01) 818402 *E-mail:* bau@inco.com.lb *Web Site:* www.bau.edu.lb, pg 1524

Belarus (The Belorussia) (Belarus) *Tel:* (0172) 238742 *Fax:* (0172) 238731, pg 62

Verlag Beleke KG (Germany) *Tel:* (0201) 8130-0 *Fax:* (0201) 8130-108 *E-mail:* info@beleke.de *Web Site:* www.beleke.de, pg 198

Belfast Public Library (United Kingdom) *Tel:* (01232) 243 233 *Fax:* (01232) 332 819, pg 1552

Belforte Editore Libraio srl (Italy) *Tel:* (0586) 210919 *Fax:* (0586) 210349 *E-mail:* belforte@librinformatica.it *Web Site:* www.librinformatica.it, pg 377

Belgian PEN Centre (French-Speaking) (Belgium) *Tel:* (02) 7314847 *Fax:* (02) 7314847 *Web Site:* www.oneworld.org/internatpen/centres.htm, pg 1396

Belgian PEN Centre (French-Speaking) (Belgium) *Tel:* (052) 351118 *Fax:* (052) 351119, pg 1396

Editions Belin (France) *Tel:* (01) 55 42 84 00 *Fax:* (01) 43 25 18 29 *E-mail:* contact@edition-belin.fr *Web Site:* www.editions-belin.com, pg 149

Belitha Press Ltd (United Kingdom) *Tel:* (020) 7221 2213; (020) 7314 1469 (sales) *Fax:* (020) 7221 6455; (020) 7314 1594 (sales) *E-mail:* enquiries@chrysalis.com *Web Site:* www.chrysalis.co.uk/childrens/publisher/belitha, pg 664

Belize Library Association (Belize) *Tel:* (02) 7267; (02) 34248; (02) 34249 *Fax:* (02) 34246, pg 1559

Bell & Bain Ltd (United Kingdom) *Tel:* (0141) 649 5697 *Fax:* (0141) 632 8733 *E-mail:* info@bell-bain.demon.co.uk *Web Site:* www.bell-bain.co.uk, pg 1163, 1183

Bell & Bain Ltd (United Kingdom) *Tel:* (0141) 649 5697 *Fax:* (0141) 632 8733 *E-mail:* info@bell-bain.co.uk *Web Site:* www.bell-bain.co.uk, pg 1224

Bell & Bain Ltd (United Kingdom) *Tel:* (0141) 649 5697 *Fax:* (0141) 632 8733 *E-mail:* info@bell-bain.demon.co.uk *Web Site:* www.bell-bain.co.uk, pg 1238

Libreria Bellas Artes (Mexico) *Tel:* (05) 510-2276 *Fax:* (05) 518-3755, pg 1327

Ediciones Bellaterra SA (Spain) *Tel:* (093) 3390511; (093) 3499786 *Fax:* (093) 3520851 *E-mail:* bellaterra@retermail.es, pg 574

Bellcourt Books (Australia) *Tel:* (03) 5572 1310 *Fax:* (03) 5572 1310 *E-mail:* bellcourt@ansonic.com.au, pg 14

Editions Belle Riviere (Switzerland) *Tel:* (024) 498 40 49 *Fax:* (024) 498 40 46, pg 618

Societe d'Edition Les Belles Lettres (France) *Tel:* (01) 44398420 *Fax:* (01) 45449288 *E-mail:* courrier@lesbelleslettres.com *Web Site:* www.lesbelleslettres.com, pg 149

Bellew Publishing Co Ltd (United Kingdom) *Tel:* (020) 8673 5611 *Fax:* (020) 8675 2142 *E-mail:* bellewsubs@hotmail.com, pg 664

Biblioteca de la Universidad Catolica 'Andres Bello' (Venezuela) *Tel:* (02) 4074190 *Web Site:* www.ucab.edu.ve/biblioteca, pg 1555

Editorial Andres Bello/Editorial Juridica de Chile (Chile) *Tel:* (02) 2049900; (02) 4619500 *Fax:* (02) 2253600 *Web Site:* www.editorialjuridica.cl, pg 99

Clubs de Lectores Andres Bello (Chile) *Tel:* (02) 2049900; (02) 2049901 *Fax:* (02) 2253600, pg 1251

Libreria Andres Bello (Chile) *Tel:* (02) 2049900 *Fax:* (02) 2253600, pg 1305

Belaruskaya Encyklapedyya (Belarus) *Tel:* 2840600; 2841767 *Fax:* 2840983, pg 62

Belser Wissenschaftlicher Dienst (Germany) *Tel:* (07054) 2475 *Fax:* (07054) 2639 *E-mail:* 101553.3467@compuserve.com *Web Site:* www.belser.com, pg 199

Julius Beltz GmbH & Co KG (Germany) *Tel:* (06201) 60070 *E-mail:* info@beltz.de *Web Site:* www.beltz.de, pg 199

BeMa (Italy) *Tel:* (02) 252071 *Fax:* (02) 27000692 *E-mail:* segreteria@bema.it *Web Site:* www.bema.it, pg 377

Bemrose Booth (United Kingdom) *Tel:* (01332) 294242; (01332) 267245 *Fax:* (01332) 295848; (01332) 290367 *Web Site:* www.bemrose.co.uk, pg 1225

Bemust (Bosnia and Herzegovina) *Tel:* (033) 414-050; (061) 173780 *Fax:* (033) 414-050 *E-mail:* bemust@bih.net.ba, pg 76

Ben and Company Ltd (United Republic of Tanzania) *Tel:* (812) 781421 *Fax:* (511) 12440 *E-mail:* siggers@pearsoned.ema.com, pg 643

Ben-Gurion University of the Negev Aranne Library (Israel) *Tel:* (08) 6461413 *Fax:* (08) 6472940 *Web Site:* www.bgu.ac.il/aranne/, pg 1519

Ben-Zvi Institute (Israel) *Tel:* (02) 5398844; (02) 5398848; (02) 5639202; (02) 5639203; (02) 5639204 *Fax:* (02) 5612329 *E-mail:* mahonzvi@h2.hum.huji.ac.il *Web Site:* www.ybz.org.il, pg 365

Bendel State Library (Nigeria) *Tel:* (052) 200 810, pg 1533

James Bendon Ltd (Cyprus) *Fax:* (025) 632352 *E-mail:* books@jamesbendon.com *Web Site:* www.jamesbendon.com, pg 121

Imprimerie Bene (France) *Tel:* (04) 66294897 *Fax:* (04) 66382146, pg 1154, 1216

Benefit Publishing Co (Hong Kong), pg 315

Benghazi Public Library (Libyan Arab Jamahiriya) *Tel:* (061) 96379, pg 1525

Benin University Bookshop (Nigeria) *Tel:* (052) 600443 *Fax:* (052) 602370 *E-mail:* registra@uniben.edu *Web Site:* www.uniben.edu, pg 1331

YELLOW PAGES

Benin University Library (Nigeria) *Tel:* (052) 600443 *Fax:* (052) 602370 *E-mail:* registra@uniben.edu; registra@uniben.edu.ng; library@uniben.edu *Web Site:* www.uniben.edu, pg 1533

Eliane Benisti Literary Agency (France) *Tel:* (01) 42228533 *Fax:* (01) 45441817 *E-mail:* benisti@compuserve.com, pg 1130

Biblioteca Benjamin Franklin (USIS) (Mexico) *Tel:* 5080 2801 (ext 2802 & 2803) *Fax:* (055) 5910075 *E-mail:* garciae@state.gov *Web Site:* www.usembassy-mexico.gov/biblioteca.htm, pg 1528

John Benjamins BV (Netherlands) *Tel:* (020) 6304747 *Fax:* (020) 6739773 *E-mail:* customer.services@benjamins.nl *Web Site:* www.benjamins.com, pg 479

John Benjamins Publishing Co (Netherlands) *Tel:* (020) 6304747 *Fax:* (020) 6739773 (publishing); (020) 6792956 (antiquariat) *E-mail:* customer.services@benjamins.nl *Web Site:* www.benjamins.com, pg 1329

Petra Bornhauber Benleo Verlag (Germany) *Tel:* (02271) 4782-0 *Fax:* (02271) 4782-20 *Web Site:* www.benleo.de, pg 199

David Bennett Books (United Kingdom) *Tel:* (020) 7221 2213; (020) 7314 1469 (sales) *Fax:* (020) 7221 6455; (020) 7314 1594 (sales) *E-mail:* enquiries@chrysalis.com *Web Site:* www.chrysalisbooks.co.uk/childrens/publisher/davidbennett, pg 664

James Bennett Pty Ltd (Australia) *Tel:* (02) 9986 7000 *Fax:* (02) 9986 7031 *E-mail:* customerservice@bennett.com.au *Web Site:* www.bennett.com.au, pg 1297

Bennetts Bookshop Ltd (New Zealand) *Tel:* (06) 354 6020 *Fax:* (06) 354 6716 *Toll Free Fax:* 0800 118 333 *E-mail:* books@bennetts.co.nz; massey@bennetts.co.nz *Web Site:* www.bennetts.co.nz, pg 1330

E F Benson Society (United Kingdom) *Tel:* (01797) 223114 *E-mail:* info@efbensonsociety.org *Web Site:* www.efbensonsociety.org, pg 1406

Benteli Verlag (Switzerland) *Tel:* (031) 9608484 *Fax:* (031) 9617414 *E-mail:* info@benteliverlag.ch *Web Site:* www.benteliverlag.ch, pg 618

John Bentley Book Agencies (New Zealand) *Tel:* (09) 4736920 *Fax:* (09) 4736920 *E-mail:* sjsb@connected.net.nzed, pg 1135

Benziger Verlag AG (Switzerland) *Tel:* (01) 2527050 *Fax:* (01) 2624792, pg 619

Beobachter Buchverlag (Switzerland) *Tel:* (01) 8296111 *Fax:* (01) 8103791 *Web Site:* www.beobachter.ch, pg 619

Beogradski Izdavacko-Graficki Zavod (Serbia and Montenegro) *Tel:* (011) 650-235; (011) 651-666 *Fax:* (011) 651-841 *Web Site:* www.suc.org/biz/BIGZ/, pg 552

Berchtold Haller Verlag (Switzerland) *Tel:* (031) 334 03 03 *Fax:* (031) 334 03 06 *Web Site:* www.egw.ch, pg 619

Berenguer Editorial (Chile), pg 1305

Berg International Editeur (France) *Tel:* (01) 43267273 *Fax:* (01) 46339499, pg 149

Berg Publishers (United Kingdom) *Tel:* (01865) 245104 *Fax:* (01865) 791165 *E-mail:* enquiry@bergpublishers.com *Web Site:* www.bergpublishers.com, pg 664

Bergadis (Greece) *Tel:* (01) 3614263, pg 306

Technische Universitat Bergakademie Freiberg (Germany) *Tel:* (03731) 39 29 59 *Fax:* (03731) 39 43 60 *E-mail:* unibib@ub.tu-freiberg.de *Web Site:* www.tu-freiberg.de, pg 1508

Bergen offentlige Bibliotek (Norway) *Tel:* 55 56 85 60; 55 56 85 50 *Fax:* 55 56 85 65 *Web Site:* www.bergen.folkebibl.no, pg 1534

Berger-Levrault Editions SAS (France) *Tel:* (03) 83 38 83 83 *Fax:* (03) 83 38 86 10; (03) 83 38 37 12 *E-mail:* ble@berger-levrault.fr *Web Site:* www.berger-levrault.fr, pg 149

Berghahn Books Ltd (United Kingdom) *Tel:* (01865) 250011 *Fax:* (01865) 250056 *E-mail:* info@berghahnbooks.com *Web Site:* www.berghahnbooks.com, pg 665

Berghs (Sweden) *Tel:* (08) 31 65 59 *Fax:* (08) 32 77 45 *E-mail:* info@berghsforlag.se *Web Site:* www.berghsforlag.se, pg 610

Bergli Books AG (Switzerland) *Tel:* (061) 373 27 77 *Fax:* (061) 373 27 78 *E-mail:* info@bergli.ch *Web Site:* www.bergli.ch, pg 619

Bergmoser & Holler Verlag AG (Germany) *Tel:* (0241) 93888-10 *Fax:* (0241) 93888-134 *E-mail:* kontakt@buhv.de *Web Site:* www.buhv.de, pg 199

Biblioteca Bergnes de las Casas - Bibioteca de Catalunya (Spain) *Tel:* (093) 270 23 00 *Fax:* (093) 270 23 04 *E-mail:* bustia@bnc.es *Web Site:* www.gencat.es/bc, pg 1545

Bergstadtverlag Wilhelm Gottlieb Korn GmbH Wuerzburg (Germany) *Tel:* (0711) 4406-193 *Fax:* (0711) 4406-199, pg 199

Bergverlag Rother GmbH (Germany) *Tel:* (089) 608669-0 *Fax:* (089) 608669-69 *E-mail:* bergverlag@rother.de *Web Site:* www.rother.de, pg 199

Beri Publishing (Australia) *Tel:* (03) 9809 1434 *Fax:* (03) 9809 1434 *E-mail:* beripub@ozemail.com.au, pg 14

Berichthaus Verlag, Dr Conrad Ulrich (Switzerland) *Tel:* (01) 2526349 *Fax:* (01) 2526426, pg 619

Berita Publishing Sdn Bhd (Malaysia) *Tel:* (03) 7620 8111 *Fax:* (03) 7620 8026 *Web Site:* www.beritapublishing.com.my, pg 455

Berkeley Brasil Editora Ltda (Brazil) *Tel:* (011) 839-5525 *Fax:* (011) 261-1342 *E-mail:* berkeley@siciliano.com.br, pg 78

The Berlin Agency (Jung-Lindemann & Olechnowitz) (Germany) *Tel:* (030) 88702888 *Fax:* (030) 88702889 *E-mail:* junglindemann@berlinagency.de *Web Site:* www.berlinagency.de, pg 1131

Berliner Debatte Wissenschafts Verlag, GSFP-Gesellschaft fur Sozialwissen-schaftliche Forschung und Publizistik mbH & Co KG (Germany) *Tel:* (030) 44651355 *Fax:* (030) 44651358 *E-mail:* web@berlinerdebatte.de *Web Site:* www.berlinerdebatte.de, pg 199

Berliner Handpresse Wolfgang Joerg und Erich Schonig (Germany) *Tel:* (030) 6148728; (030) 6142605, pg 199

Berliner Wissenschafts-Verlag GmbH (BWV) (Germany) *Tel:* (030) 84 17 70-0 *Fax:* (030) 84 17 70-21 *E-mail:* bwv@bwv-verlag.de *Web Site:* www.bwv-verlag.de, pg 199

Berlitz (UK) Ltd (United Kingdom) *Tel:* (020) 7611 9640 *Fax:* (020) 7611 9656 *E-mail:* publishing@berlitz.co.uk *Web Site:* www.berlitz.co.uk; languagecenter.berlitz.com/holborn, pg 665

David Berman Developments Inc (Canada) *Tel:* 613-728-6777 *Fax:* 613-728-2867 *E-mail:* info@timewise.net *Web Site:* www.timewise.net, pg 1175

Bermuda Archives (Bermuda) *Tel:* 295-5151, pg 1494

Bermuda College Library (Bermuda) *Tel:* (0441) 239-4033 *Fax:* (0441) 239-4034 *E-mail:* info@bercol.bm *Web Site:* www.bercol.bm, pg 1494

Bermuda National Library (Bermuda) *Tel:* 295-2905 *Fax:* 292-8443 *E-mail:* bdanatlib@gov.bm *Web Site:* www.bermudanationallibrary.bm, pg 1494

The Bermudian Publishing Co (Bermuda) *Tel:* 295-0695 *Fax:* 295-8616 *E-mail:* info@thebermudian.com *Web Site:* www.thebermudian.com, pg 75

Luigi Bernabo Associates SRL (Italy) *Tel:* (02) 45473700 *Fax:* (02) 45473577 *E-mail:* bernabo.luigi@tin.it, pg 1133

Bernal Publishing (Australia) *Tel:* (0613) 9808-3775 *Fax:* (0613) 9888-7572 *E-mail:* sales@bernalpublishing.com *Web Site:* www.bernalpublishing.com, pg 14

SOCIEDADES LIVREIRAS BERTRAND

Bernan Associates, Div of Kraus Organization, Ltd (United States) *Tel:* 301-459-7666 *Toll Free Tel:* 800-274-4888 (USA); 800-233-0504 (Canada) *Fax:* 301-459-0056 *E-mail:* query@berman.com *Web Site:* www.eurunion.org/publicat/sales.htm, pg 1294

Bernard und Graefe Verlag (Germany) *Tel:* (0228) 64830 *Fax:* (0228) 6483109 *E-mail:* 101336.245@compuserve.com, pg 199

Berndtson & Berndtson GmbH Verlag-Publishing (Germany) *Tel:* (08141) 222 580 *Fax:* (08141) 902 41 *E-mail:* sales@berndtson.com *Web Site:* www.berndtson.com, pg 199

Bernecker Mediagruppe (Germany) *Tel:* (05661) 731-0 *Fax:* (05661) 731-111 *Web Site:* www.bernecker.de, pg 199

Verlag Alexander Bernhardt (Austria) *Tel:* (05242) 62131-0 *Fax:* (05242) 72801, pg 48

Bibliotheque Bernheim, Bibliotheque territoriale de la Nouvelle-Caledonie (New Caledonia) *Tel:* 272 343 *Fax:* 276 588 *E-mail:* bibbern@canl.nc *Web Site:* www.nla.gov.au/lap/libs/caledoniabb.html, pg 1531

Beroa-Verlag (Switzerland) *Tel:* (01) 4801313 *Fax:* (01) 4801312, pg 619

Bertello Edizioni (Italy) *Tel:* (0171) 699002 *Fax:* (0171) 697729, pg 377

Bertelsmann AG (Germany) *Tel:* (05241) 80-0 *Fax:* (05241) 80-9662 *E-mail:* info@bertelsmann.de *Web Site:* www.bertelsmann.de, pg 1155

C Bertelsmann Verlag GmbH (Germany) *Tel:* (089) 41360; (1805) 990505 (hotline for literature & nonfiction) *Fax:* (089) 4372-2812 *E-mail:* vertrieb.verlagsgruppe@randomhouse.de *Web Site:* www.randomhouse.de, pg 199

Bertelsmann Club (Germany) *Tel:* (05) 415 233 *Fax:* (05) 415 744 *E-mail:* service@derclub.de *Web Site:* www.bertelsmann-club.de, pg 1252

Bertelsmann de Mexico SA (Mexico) *Tel:* (05) 5501620; (05) 5489048, pg 1254

Bertelsmann Distribution GmbH (Germany) *Tel:* (05241) 805 718 *Fax:* (05241) 46970 *Web Site:* www.bertelsmann-distribution.de, pg 1310

Bertelsmann Lexikon Verlag GmbH (Germany) *Tel:* (05241) 800 *Fax:* (05241) 73075 *E-mail:* vertrieb.verlagsgruppe@bertelsmann.de *Web Site:* www.lexiconverlag.de/lexiconverlag.html, pg 200

Verlag Bertelsmann Stiftung (Germany) *Tel:* (05241) 8181197 *Fax:* (05241) 8181931 *E-mail:* sabine.klemm@bertelsmann.de *Web Site:* www.bertelsmann-stiftung.de/verlag, pg 200

W Bertelsmann Verlag GmbH & Co KG (Germany) *Tel:* (0521) 911-01-0 *Fax:* (0521) 911 01-79 *E-mail:* service@wbv.de *Web Site:* www.wbv.de; www.berufsbildung.de; www.berufe.net, pg 200

Robert Berthold Photography (Australia) *Tel:* (02) 9887 3986 *Fax:* (02) 9887 3986, pg 14

Editions Bertout (France) *Tel:* (02) 35 04 69 68 *Fax:* (02) 35 04 69 65 *Web Site:* www.editionsbertout.com, pg 149

Bertrams (United Kingdom) *Tel:* (0870) 4296666 *Fax:* (0870) 4296667 *E-mail:* books@bertrams.com *Web Site:* www.bertrams.com, pg 1347

Editora Bertrand Brasil Ltda (Brazil) *Tel:* (021) 2585 2000 *Fax:* (021) 2585 2085 *E-mail:* record@record.com.br *Web Site:* www.record.com.br, pg 78

Bertrand Editora Lda (Portugal) *Tel:* (021) 320084 *Fax:* (021) 3468286, pg 529

Editions Bertrand-Lacoste (France) *Tel:* (01) 53 40 53 53 *Fax:* (01) 42 33 82 47 *E-mail:* contact@bertrand-lacoste.fr *Web Site:* www.bertrand-lacoste.fr, pg 149

Sociedades Livreiras Bertrand (Portugal) *Tel:* (021) 0305592 *Fax:* (021) 0305596 *E-mail:* info@bertrand.pt *Web Site:* www.bertrand.pt, pg 1336

Verlag Beruf und Schule Belz KG (Germany) *Tel:* (04821) 40140 *Fax:* (04821) 4941 *E-mail:* info@vbus.de *Web Site:* www.verlag-beruf-schule.de, pg 200

Berufsverband Information Bibliothek (BIB) (Germany) *Tel:* (07121) 3491-0 *Fax:* (07121) 300433 *E-mail:* mail@bib-info.de *Web Site:* www.bib-info.de, pg 1562

Beta Editorial SA (Spain) *Tel:* (093) 2804640 *Fax:* (093) 2806320, pg 574

Beta Medical Publishers (Greece) *Tel:* (010) 6714340; (010) 6714371 *Fax:* (010) 6715015 *E-mail:* betamedarts@hol.gr *Web Site:* www.betamedarts.gr, pg 306

Editora Betania S/C (Brazil) *Tel:* (031) 3451-1122 *Fax:* (031) 3451-1638 *E-mail:* betanhdv@prover.com.br *Web Site:* www.editorabetania.com.br, pg 79

Bethania Verlag (Austria) *Tel:* (01) 6672216, pg 48

Better Music Type (United States) *Tel:* 615-833-0800, pg 1186

Bettex, Editions Medicales Roland (Switzerland) *Tel:* (022) 7029311 *Fax:* (022) 7029355, pg 619

Annette Betz Verlag im Verlag Carl Ueberreuter (Austria) *Tel:* (01) 40 444-172 *Fax:* (01) 40 444-5 *Web Site:* www.annettebetz.com; www.ueberreuter.at, pg 48

Betzel Verlag GmbH (Germany) *Tel:* (05021) 91 48 69 *Fax:* (05021) 91 48 68 *E-mail:* betzelverlag@proximedia.de, pg 200

Beust Verlag GmbH (Germany) *Tel:* (089) 230895-0 *Fax:* (089) 230895-131 *E-mail:* mail@beustverlag.de, pg 200

Beuth Verlag GmbH (Germany) *Tel:* (030) 26010 *Fax:* (030) 26011260 *E-mail:* info@beuth.de *Web Site:* www.beuth.de; www.mybeuth.de, pg 200

The Beyazit State Library (Turkey) *Tel:* (0212) 522 2488 *Fax:* (0212) 526 1133, pg 1551

Editions Beyeler (Switzerland) *Tel:* (061) 235412 *Fax:* (061) 229691, pg 619

Joachim Beyer Verlag (Germany) *Tel:* (09274) 95051 *Fax:* (09274) 95053 *E-mail:* info@beyerverlag.de *Web Site:* www.derschachladen.de, pg 200

Bezalel Academy of Arts & Design (Israel) *Tel:* (02) 589 3333 *Fax:* (02) 582 3094 *E-mail:* mail@bezalel.ac.il *Web Site:* www.bezalel.ac.il, pg 365

Bezerr-Editorae e Distribuidora de Abel Antonio Bezerra (Portugal) *Tel:* (0253) 22604 *Fax:* (0253) 617105, pg 529

De Bezige Bij B V Uitgeverij (Netherlands) *Tel:* (020) 3059810 *Fax:* (020) 3059824 *E-mail:* info@debezigebij.nl *Web Site:* www.debezigebij.nl, pg 479

BFI Publishing (United Kingdom) *Tel:* (020) 7957 4789 *Fax:* (020) 74367950; (020) 76362516 *E-mail:* publishing@bfi.org.uk *Web Site:* www.bfi.org.uk, pg 665

BBT Bhaktivedanta Book Trust (Sweden) *Tel:* (08) 530 257 72 *E-mail:* p.huy@t-online.de, pg 610

Bharat Law House Pvt Ltd (India) *Tel:* (011) 791 0001; (011) 791 0002; (011) 791 0003 *Fax:* (011) 791 0004 *E-mail:* blh@nda.vsnl.net.in, pg 330

Bharat Publishing House (India) *Tel:* (011) 25757081; (011) 23670067 *Fax:* (011) 23676058 *E-mail:* pitambar@bol.net.in, pg 330

Bharatiya Vidya Bhavan (India) *Tel:* (022) 3631261; (022) 8118261; (022) 8118262 *Fax:* (022) 3630058, pg 330

Bhawan Book Service, Publishers & Distributors (India) *Tel:* 2258836; 271559; 612-67-2506 *Fax:* 265315; 612-67-0010 *E-mail:* bbpdpat@glascl01.vsnl.net.in, pg 330

Mauritius Bhojpuri Institute (Mauritius) *Tel:* 2082956 *Fax:* 4643445, pg 461

Bhratara Karya Aksara (Indonesia) *Tel:* 021 81858, pg 354

Bi-bong Publishing Co (Republic of Korea) *Tel:* (02) 3142-6555 *Fax:* (02) 3142-6556 *E-mail:* beebook@hitel.net, pg 437

The Bialik Institute (Israel) *Tel:* (02) 6783554; (02) 6797942 *Fax:* (02) 6783706 *E-mail:* bialik@actcom.co.il *Web Site:* www.bialik-publishing.com, pg 365

Bianco (Italy) *Tel:* (06) 8554962 *Fax:* (06) 8844703, pg 377

Bianco Lunos Bogtrykkeri AS (Denmark) *Tel:* (03) 615 3300 *Fax:* (03) 615 3301 *Web Site:* www.aller.dk, pg 1176

Bianco Lunos Bogtrykkeri AS (Denmark) *Tel:* 33140781 *Fax:* 33913808, pg 1216

Bianco Lunos Bogtrykkeri AS (Denmark) *Tel:* 36 15 33 00 *Fax:* 36 15 33 01, pg 1235

Bibellesbund Verlag (Switzerland) *Tel:* (052) 245 14 45 *Fax:* (052) 245 14 46 *E-mail:* info@bibellesebund.ch *Web Site:* www.bibellesebund.ch, pg 619

Bible Reading Fellowship (United Kingdom) *Tel:* (01865) 319700 *Fax:* (01865) 319701 *E-mail:* enquiries@brf.org.uk *Web Site:* www.brf.org.uk, pg 665

Bible Society (United Kingdom) *Tel:* (01793) 418100 *Fax:* (01793) 418118 *E-mail:* info@bfbs.org.uk *Web Site:* www.biblesociety.org.uk, pg 665

Bible Society in Australia National Headquarters (Australia) *Tel:* (02) 9829 9001 *Fax:* (02) 9829 9020 *E-mail:* customer.service@bible.org.au; sdadm@boble.org.au *Web Site:* www.biblesociety.com.au, pg 14

Bible Society of Namibia (Namibia) *Tel:* (061) 235090 *Fax:* (061) 228663 *E-mail:* bsn@nambible.org.na *Web Site:* www.biblesociety.org, pg 476

Bible Society of South Africa (South Africa) *Tel:* (021) 421-2040 *Fax:* (021) 419-4846 *E-mail:* biblia@biblesociety.co.za *Web Site:* www.biblesociety.co.za, pg 562

Biblia Impex Pvt Ltd (India) *Tel:* (011) 23278034; (011) 23262515 *Fax:* (011) 2328-2047 *E-mail:* info@bibliaimpex.com *Web Site:* www.bibliaimpex.com, pg 330

Biblia Impex Pvt Ltd (India) *Tel:* (011) 327-8034; (011) 326-2515 *Fax:* (011) 328-2047 *E-mail:* info@bibliaimpex.com *Web Site:* www.bibliaimpex.com, pg 1315

Biblio Verlag (Germany) *Tel:* (05402) 641720 *Fax:* (05402) 641722 *E-mail:* info@militaria-biblio.de; biblio-verlag@t-online.de *Web Site:* www.militaria-biblio.de, pg 200

Bibliografica Internacional SA (Chile) *Tel:* (02) 6394057 *Fax:* (02) 6397693, pg 99

Editrice Bibliografica SpA (Italy) *Tel:* (02) 28315996 *Fax:* (02) 28315906 *E-mail:* bibliografica@bibliografica.it *Web Site:* www.bibliografica.it, pg 378

Bibliographical Society (United Kingdom) *Tel:* (020) 7611 7244 *Fax:* (020) 7611 8703 *E-mail:* secretary@bibsoc.org.uk *Web Site:* www.bibsoc.org.uk/bibsoc.htm, pg 1572

Bibliographical Society of Australia & New Zealand (BSANZ) (Australia) *Tel:* (02) 6931 8669 *Fax:* (02) 6931 8669 *E-mail:* rsalmond@pobox.com *Web Site:* www.csu.edu.au/community/BSANZ, pg 1260

Bibliographical Society of Australia & New Zealand (BSANZ) (Australia) *Tel:* (03) 96699032 *Fax:* (03) 96699032 *Web Site:* www.csu.edu.au/community/BSANZ, pg 1395

Bibliographical Society of the Philippines (Philippines) *Tel:* (02) 525-3196; (02) 525-1748 *Fax:* (02) 524-2324 *E-mail:* amb@nlp.gov.ph *Web Site:* www.nlp.gov.ph, pg 1569

Bibliographisches Institut & F A Brockhaus AG (Germany) *Tel:* (0621) 3901-01 *Fax:* (0621) 3901-3 91 *Web Site:* www.brockhaus.de, pg 200

Bibliographisches Institut & F A Brockhaus AG (Switzerland) *Tel:* (041) 7108375 *Fax:* (041) 7108325 *Web Site:* www.bifab.de, pg 619

Bibliographisches Institut GmbH (Germany) *Tel:* (0341) 97 86-30 *Fax:* (0341) 97 86-5 60, pg 201

Bibliography Institute of the National Library of Latvia (Latvia) *Tel:* (02) 7289874 *Fax:* (02) 7280851 *E-mail:* lnb@com.latnet.lv; lnb@lbi.lnb.lv *Web Site:* www.lnb.lv, pg 444

Bibliomed - Medizinische Verlagsgesellschaft mbH (Germany) *Tel:* (05661) 73440 *Fax:* (05661) 8360 *E-mail:* info@bibliomed.de *Web Site:* www.bibliomed.de, pg 201

Le Bibliophile (The Book Lover) (Haiti), pg 1400

Bibliophile Books (United Kingdom) *Tel:* (020) 7515 9222 *Fax:* (020) 7538 4115 *E-mail:* customercare@bibliophilebooks.com *Web Site:* www.bibliophilebooks.com, pg 1256, 1347

Verlag Bibliophile Drucke von Josef Stocker AG (Switzerland) *Tel:* (01) 7404444, pg 619

Bibliopolis - Edizioni di Filosofia e Scienze Srl (Italy) *Tel:* (081) 664606 *Fax:* (081) 7616273 *E-mail:* info@bibliopolis.it *Web Site:* www.bibliopolis.it, pg 378

Biblioteca Agropecuaria de Colombia (BAC) (Colombia) *Tel:* (01) 4227373 (ext 1254) *Fax:* (01) 2813088 *E-mail:* bac@corpoica.org.co *Web Site:* www.corpoica.org.co, pg 1498

Biblioteca Central (Mexico) *Tel:* (0595) 952-15-00 (exts 7111, 4741 & 5440) *Fax:* (0595) 952-15-01 *Web Site:* www.chapingo.mx, pg 1528

Biblioteca Central de la Universidad de Oriente (Cuba) *Tel:* (022) 633013 *Fax:* (022) 633011 *E-mail:* marcosc@rect.uo.edu.cu *Web Site:* www.uo.edu.cu, pg 1500

Biblioteca Central de la Universidad Nacional de San Agustin (Peru) *Tel:* (054) 229 719 *E-mail:* sisbiblio@unmsm.edu.pe *Web Site:* sisbib.unmsm.edu.pe/sbweb, pg 1536

Biblioteca Central de la Universidad Nacional Mayor de San Marcos (Peru) *Tel:* (01) 4285210 *Fax:* (01) 4285210 *E-mail:* ogeibl@sanfer.edu.pe, pg 1536

Biblioteca Central de Macau (Macau) *Tel:* 567576; 558049 *Fax:* 318756, pg 1526

Direccion General de Bibliotecas de la Universidad Nacional Autonoma de Mexico (Mexico) *Tel:* (055) 5622 1603 *Fax:* (055) 6160664 *E-mail:* webdgb@dgb.unam.mx *Web Site:* www.dgbiblio.unam.mx, pg 1528

Biblioteca Centrala Universitara (Romania) *Tel:* (021) 313 16 05; (021) 313 16 06 *Fax:* (021) 312 01 08 *Web Site:* www.bcub.ro, pg 1539

Biblioteca Centrale della Regione Siciliana gia Biblioteca Nazionale di Palermo (Italy) *Tel:* (091) 6967642 *Fax:* (091) 6967644 *E-mail:* bcrs@regione.sicilia.it *Web Site:* www.regione.sicilia.it/beniculturali/bibliotecacentrale, pg 1520

Biblioteca de Mexico (Mexico) *Tel:* (055) 7 09 11 01; (055) 7 09 10 85 *Fax:* (055) 7 09 11 73 *Web Site:* www.cnca.gob.mx/bi.htm, pg 1528

Biblioteca del Banco Central de la Republica Argentina (Argentina) *Tel:* (011) 4348 3500 (ext 2571); (011) 4348 3500 (ext 2801) *Fax:* (011) 4348 1200 *E-mail:* biblio@bcra.gov.ar *Web Site:* www.bcra.gov.ar, pg 1490

Biblioteca del Congreso (Venezuela) *Tel:* (02) 5645327 *Fax:* (02) 5636696, pg 1555

Biblioteca del Congreso Nacional (Bolivia) *Tel:* (02) 354108; (02) 392658 *Fax:* (02) 392402; (02) 341649 *Web Site:* www.congreso.gov.bo, pg 1494

Biblioteca del Congreso Nacional (Chile) *Tel:* (02) 2701700 *Fax:* (02) 2701766 *Web Site:* www.bcn.cl, pg 1497

Biblioteca del Instituto Pre-Universitario de la Habana (Cuba), pg 1500

YELLOW PAGES

Biblioteca dell'Universita Nazionale della Somalia (Somalia) *Tel:* (01) 20535, pg 1543

Biblioteca do Ministerio das Relacoes Exteriores (Brazil) *Tel:* (061) 2116359 *Fax:* (061) 2237362 *Web Site:* www.mre.gov.br, pg 1495

Biblioteca Dominicana (Dominican Republic), pg 1502

Biblioteca Ecuatoriana Aurelio Espinosa Polit' (Ecuador) *Tel:* (02) 492190 *Fax:* (02) 493928, pg 136

Biblioteca Ecuatoriana Aurelio Espinosa Polit' (Ecuador) *Tel:* (02) 491156; (02) 491157 *Fax:* (02) 493928 *E-mail:* beaep@uio.satnet.net *Web Site:* www.biblioespinosapolit.org, pg 1503

Biblioteca General de Puerto Rico (Puerto Rico) *Tel:* (787) 724-0700 *Fax:* (787) 724-8394 *E-mail:* www@icp.gobierno.pr *Web Site:* www.icp.gobierno.pr/bge/index.htm, pg 1539

Biblioteca Geral da Universidade de Coimbra (Portugal) *Tel:* (0239) 859800; (0239) 859900 *Fax:* (0239) 827135 *E-mail:* bguc@ci.uc.pt *Web Site:* www.uc.pt, pg 529

Biblioteca Geral da Universidade de Coimbra (Portugal) *Tel:* (0239) 859800; (0239) 859815; (0239) 859831 *Fax:* (0239) 827135 *E-mail:* bguc@ci.uc.pt *Web Site:* www.ci.uc.pt, pg 1538

Biblioteca Historica Cubana y Americana (Cuba), pg 1500

Biblioteca Medicea Laurenziana (Italy) *Tel:* (055) 210760; (055) 211590; (055) 214443 *Fax:* (055) 2302992 *E-mail:* medicea@unifi.it *Web Site:* www.bml.firenze.sbn.it, pg 1520

Biblioteca Municipal (Mozambique), pg 1530

Biblioteca Municipal Mario de Andrade (Brazil) *Tel:* (011) 3334-0001 *Fax:* (011) 3224-0009 *E-mail:* smc@prodam.pmsp.sp.gov.br *Web Site:* www.prefeitura.sp.gov.br, pg 1495

Biblioteca Nacional (Argentina) *Tel:* (011) 4808-6000 *Fax:* (011) 4806-6157 *E-mail:* bibnal@red.bibnal.edu.ar *Web Site:* www.bibnal.edu.ar, pg 1490

Biblioteca Nacional de Colombia (Colombia) *Tel:* (01) 2431336 *Fax:* (01) 3414030 *E-mail:* bnc@mincultura.gov.co *Web Site:* www.bibliotecanacional.gov.co, pg 1498

Biblioteca Nacional (Costa Rica) *Tel:* 233 1706; 221 2436; 221 2479 *Fax:* 223 5510, pg 1499

Biblioteca Nacional (Dominican Republic) *Tel:* 688-4086 *E-mail:* biblioteca.nacional@dominicana.com, pg 1502

Biblioteca Nacional (El Salvador) *Tel:* 221-6312; 221-4373; 271-5661; 272-2886 *Fax:* 221-8847; 221-4419 *E-mail:* dibiaes@es.com.sv, pg 1503

Biblioteca Nacional (Nicaragua) *Tel:* (02) 897 517 *Fax:* (02) 894 387, pg 1533

Biblioteca Nacional (Panama) *Tel:* 224-9466 *Fax:* 224-9988 *E-mail:* referencia@binal.ac.pa *Web Site:* www.binal.ac.pa, pg 1535

Biblioteca Nacional (Peru) *Tel:* (01) 4287690; (01) 4287696 *Fax:* (01) 4277331 *E-mail:* dn@binape.gob.pe *Web Site:* www.binape.gob.pe, pg 516

Biblioteca Nacional (Peru) *Tel:* (01) 428-7690; (01) 428-7696 *Fax:* (01) 427-7331 *E-mail:* sg@binape.gob.pe *Web Site:* www.binape.gob.pe, pg 1536

Biblioteca Nacional (Portugal) *Tel:* (021) 7982000 *Fax:* (021) 7982140 *E-mail:* bn@bn.pt *Web Site:* www.bn.pt, pg 1538

Biblioteca Nacional (Venezuela) *Tel:* (02) 505 91 25 *Fax:* (02) 505 91 24 *E-mail:* vbetanc@reaccium.ve *Web Site:* www.bnv.bib.ve, pg 1555

Biblioteca Nacional Aruba (Aruba) *Tel:* 582-1580 *Fax:* 582-5493 *E-mail:* info@bibliotecanacional.aw *Web Site:* www.bibliotecanacional.aw, pg 1490

Biblioteca Nacional de Angola (Angola) *Tel:* (02) 322 070 *Fax:* (02) 323 979, pg 2

Biblioteca Nacional de Chile (Chile) *Tel:* (02) 3605200; (02) 3605239; (02) 3605275 *Fax:* (02) 6380461; (02) 6381975; (02) 6321091; (02) 6381151 *E-mail:* bndir@bndechile.cl; subdir@bndechile.cl; ximena@bndechile.cl *Web Site:* www.dibam.renib.cl, pg 1497

Biblioteca Nacional de Guatemala (Guatemala) *Tel:* (0502) 2322443 *Fax:* (0502) 2539071 *E-mail:* biblioguatemala@intelnett.com *Web Site:* www.biblionet.edu.gt, pg 1513

Biblioteca Nacional de Honduras (Honduras) *Tel:* 228 02 41 *Fax:* 222 85 77 *E-mail:* binah@sdnhon.org.hn; binah@ns.hondunet.net *Web Site:* www.binah.gob.hn, pg 1514

Biblioteca Nacional de Maestros (Argentina) *Tel:* (011) 4129-1272 *Fax:* (011) 4129-1268 *E-mail:* bnmsecre@me.gov.ar *Web Site:* www.bnm.me.gov.ar, pg 1490

Biblioteca Nacional de Mexico (Mexico) *Tel:* (05) 6226818 *Fax:* (05) 6650951 *E-mail:* liceaj@biblional.bibliog.unam.mx *Web Site:* biblional.bibliog.unam.mx, pg 1529

Biblioteca Nacional de Mocambique (Mozambique) *Tel:* (01) 425 676, pg 1530

Biblioteca Nacional del Ecuador (Ecuador) *Tel:* (02) 2528840 *Fax:* (02) 2223391 *E-mail:* benjamincarrion@andinanet.net, pg 1503

Biblioteca Nacional del Uruguay (Uruguay) *Tel:* (02) 48 50 30 *Fax:* (02) 49 69 02 *E-mail:* bibna@adinet.com.uy *Web Site:* www.mec.gub.uy/agn/sni/snipc.htm, pg 1554

Biblioteca Nacional Jose Marti (Cuba) *Tel:* (07) 81 6224 *Fax:* (07) 33 5072, pg 1500

Biblioteca Nationala a Romaniei (Romania) *Tel:* (01) 3157063 *Fax:* (01) 3123381 *E-mail:* go@bibnat.ro, pg 1540

Biblioteca Nazionale Braidense (Italy) *Tel:* (02) 86460907 *Fax:* (02) 72023910 *E-mail:* braidense@librari.beniculturali.it *Web Site:* www.cilea.it/braidens/, pg 1520

Biblioteca Nazionale Centrale Vittorio Emanuele II (Italy) *Tel:* (06) 49891 *Fax:* (06) 4457635 *E-mail:* bncrm@bnc.roma.sbn.it *Web Site:* www.bncrm.librari.beniculturali.it, pg 1520

Biblioteca Nazionale Vittorio Emanuele III (Italy) *Tel:* (081) 7819111 *Fax:* (081) 403820 *E-mail:* Emanuele@librari.beniculturali.it *Web Site:* www.bnnonline.it, pg 1520

Biblioteca Nazionale Centrale (Italy) *Tel:* (055) 24919 1 *Fax:* (055) 2342 482 *E-mail:* info@bncf.firenze.sbn.it *Web Site:* www.bncf.firenze.sbn.it, pg 1520

Biblioteca Nazionale Marciana (Italy) *Tel:* (041) 5208788 *Fax:* (041) 5238803 *E-mail:* biblioteca@marciana.venezia.sbn.it *Web Site:* www.marciana.venezia.sbn.it/, pg 1520

Biblioteca Nazionale Universitaria (Italy) *Tel:* (011) 8101111 *Fax:* (011) 8121021 *E-mail:* bnto@librari.benicultural.it *Web Site:* www.bnto.librari.beniculturali.it, pg 1520

Editorial Biblioteca Nueva SL (Spain) *Tel:* (091) 3100436 *Fax:* (091) 3198235 *E-mail:* editorial@bibliotecanueva.com *Web Site:* www.bibliotecanueva.es, pg 574

Biblioteca Popular de Lisboa (Portugal) *Tel:* (021) 346 98 83, pg 1538

Biblioteca Publica de Evora (Portugal) *Tel:* (0266) 769 330 *Fax:* (0266) 769 331 *E-mail:* bpevora@ptnetbiz.pt, pg 1538

Biblioteca Publica do Estado do Rio de Janeiro (Brazil) *Tel:* (021) 2224-6184 *Fax:* (021) 2252-6810 *E-mail:* bibliotecapublica@bperj.rj.gov.br *Web Site:* www.bperj.rj.gov.br, pg 1495

Biblioteca Publica Municipal do Porto (Portugal) *Tel:* (022) 5193480 *Fax:* (022) 5193488 *E-mail:* bpmp@em-porto.pt, pg 529

Biblioteca Publica Municipal do Porto (Portugal) *Tel:* (02) 572147 *Fax:* (022) 5193488, pg 1538

BIBLIOTHEK FUR ZEITGESCHICHTE/LIBRARY OF CONTEMPORARY

Biblioteca Universitaria (Italy) *Tel:* (059) 222248 *Fax:* (059) 230195 *E-mail:* biblio.estense@cedoc.mo.it *Web Site:* www.cedoc.mo.it/estense, pg 1520

Biblioteca y Archivo Nacional de Bolivia (Bolivia) *Tel:* (064) 21481 *Fax:* (064) 61208 *E-mail:* abnb@mara.scr.entelnet.bo, pg 1494

Biblioteca y Archivo Nacionales (Paraguay), pg 1536

Bibliotech (Australia) *Tel:* (02) 62492479 *Fax:* (02) 62575088 *E-mail:* books@bibliotech.com.au, pg 1297

Biblioteka Jagiellonska (Poland) *Tel:* (012) 633-63-77; (012) 634-59-45 (ext 354, 355, 359, 360 & 361); (012) 633-09-03 *Fax:* (012) 633-09-03 *Web Site:* www.bj.uj.edu.pl, pg 1537

Biblioteka Kombetare (Albania) *Tel:* 42 23 843 *Fax:* 42 23 843 *E-mail:* a_plasari@hotmail.com, pg 1489

Biblioteka Narodowa (Poland) *Tel:* (022) 608-2999; (022) 452-2999 *Fax:* (022) 825-7751 *E-mail:* biblnar@bn.org.pl *Web Site:* www.bn.org.pl, pg 522

Biblioteka Narodowa (Poland) *Tel:* (022) 452-2999 *Fax:* (022) 825-5251 *E-mail:* biblnar@bn.org.pl *Web Site:* www.bn.org.pl, pg 1537

Biblioteka Publiczna m st Warszawy - Biblioteka Glowna Wojewodztwa Mazowieckiego (Poland) *Tel:* (022) 6217852 *Fax:* (022) 6211968 *E-mail:* Biblioteka@biblpubl.waw.pl *Web Site:* www.biblpubl.waw.pl, pg 1537

Biblioteka Uniwersytecka w Poznaniu (Poland) *Tel:* (061) 829-3800 *Fax:* (061) 829-3824 *E-mail:* library@amu.edu.pl *Web Site:* lib.amu.edu.pl, pg 1537

Bibliotekarsko Drustvo na Makedonija (The Former Yugoslav Republic of Macedonia) *Tel:* (091) 226846 *Fax:* (091) 232649 *E-mail:* mile@nubsk.edu.mk; bmile47@yahoo.com, pg 1567

Biblioteksstyrelsen (Denmark) *Tel:* 33733373 *Fax:* 33733372 *E-mail:* bs@bs.dk *Web Site:* www.bs.dk, pg 1501

Bibliotekstjaenst AB (Sweden) *Tel:* (046) 18 00 00 *Fax:* (046) 18 01 25 *E-mail:* btj@btj.se *Web Site:* www.btj.se, pg 610

Bibliotheca Bodmeriana (Switzerland) *Tel:* (022) 707 44 33 *Fax:* (022) 707 44 30 *E-mail:* emacheret@fondationbodmer.ch *Web Site:* www.unige.ch/biblio, pg 1547

Bibliotheek van het Centraal Bureau voor de Statistiek (Netherlands) *Tel:* (070) 337 51 51 *Fax:* (070) 337 59 84 *E-mail:* bibliotheek@cbs.nl *Web Site:* www.cbs.nl, pg 1530

Bibliotheek Wageningen UR (Netherlands) *Tel:* (0317) 484440 *Fax:* (0317) 484761 *E-mail:* helpdesk.library@wur.nl *Web Site:* library.wur.nl, pg 1530

Bibliothek & Information Deutschland (BID) - The Federal Union of German Library & Information Associations (Germany) *Tel:* (030) 39 00 14 80; (030) 39 00 14 82 *Fax:* (030) 39 00 14 84 *E-mail:* bdb@bdb-dachverband.de; gf@bdb-dachverband.de *Web Site:* www.bdverband.de, pg 1563

Bibliothek der Osterreichischen Akademie der Wissenschaften (Austria) *Tel:* (01) 51581-1262 *E-mail:* webmaster@oeaw.ac.at *Web Site:* www.oeaw.ac.at, pg 1491

Bibliothek des Benediktinerklosters Melk in Niederoesterreich (Austria) *Tel:* (02752) 555-342 *Fax:* (02752) 555-52 *E-mail:* stiftsbibliothek.melk@nextra.at, pg 1491

Bibliothek des Osterreichischen Patentamtes (Austria) *Tel:* (01) 53424 0 *Fax:* (01) 53424110 *E-mail:* info@patent.bmvit.gv.at *Web Site:* www.patent.bmwa.gv.at, pg 1491

Bibliothek fur Zeitgeschichte/Library of Contemporary History (Germany) *Tel:* (0711) 212-4454; (0711) 212-4424 *Fax:* (0711) 212-4422 *E-mail:* bfz@wlb-stuttgart.de; information@wlb-stuttgart.de *Web Site:* www.wlb-stuttgart.de/bfz, pg 1508

BIBLIOTHEKS UND INFORMATIONSSYSTEM DER UNIVERSITAET OLDENBURG INDUSTRY

Bibliotheks und Informationssystem der Universitaet Oldenburg (Germany) *Tel:* (0441) 798-2023 *Fax:* (0441) 798-4040 *E-mail:* zi@bis.uni-oldenburg.de *Web Site:* www.bis.uni-oldenburg.de/, pg 1508

Bibliotheque Cantonale et Universitaire de Lausanne (Switzerland) *Tel:* (021) 3167880 *Fax:* (021) 3167870 *Web Site:* www.unil.ch/BCU, pg 1547

Bibliotheque Cantonale et Universitaire (Kantons- und Universitatsbibliothek) (Switzerland) *Tel:* (026) 305 13 33 *Fax:* (026) 305 13 77 *E-mail:* bcu@fr.ch *Web Site:* www.fr.ch/bcu/, pg 1548

Bibliotheque Central du Ministere de l'Education Nationale (Belgium) *Tel:* (02) 511 59 80 *Fax:* (02) 513 43 33, pg 1493

Bibliotheque Centrale de la Cote d'Ivoire (Cote d'Ivoire) *Tel:* 323872, pg 1499

Bibliotheque Centrale du Museum National d'Histoire Naturelle (France) *Tel:* (01) 40 79 36 27 *Fax:* (01) 40 79 36 56 *Web Site:* www.mnhn.fr/mnhn/bcm, pg 1506

Bibliotheque Centrale, Universite de Kinshasa (The Democratic Republic of the Congo) *Tel:* (012) 21361; (012) 21362 (ext 320) *E-mail:* centreinfo@ic.cd *Web Site:* unikin.sciences.free.fr, pg 1499

Bibliotheque d'Art et d'Archeologie Jacques Doucet (France) *Tel:* (01) 47037628 *Fax:* (01) 47038925 *E-mail:* baa@bnf.fr *Web Site:* www.paris4.sorbonne.fr (archives), pg 1506

Bibliotheque de l'Institut National de la Recherche Scientifique (Rwanda) *Tel:* 30395 *Fax:* 30939, pg 1541

Bibliotheque de l'Universite Omar Bongo (Gabon) *Tel:* 732956 *Fax:* 734530 *E-mail:* uob@internetgabon.cm *Web Site:* www.uob.ga.refer.org, pg 1507

Bibliotheque de la Ville (Luxembourg) *Tel:* 54 73 83-496 *Fax:* 55 20 37, pg 1525

Bibliotheque de l'Ecole Superieure des Lettres (Lebanon), pg 1524

Bibliotheque de l'Universite Nationale de Cote d'Ivoire (Cote d'Ivoire) *Tel:* 439 000 *Fax:* 44 35 31, pg 1499

Bibliotheque Departemental de Pret (Reunion) *Tel:* 21 03 24 *Fax:* 21 41 30, pg 1539

La Bibliotheque des Arts (France) *Tel:* (01) 46331818 *Fax:* (01) 40469596, pg 150

La Bibliotheque des Arts (Switzerland) *Tel:* (021) 3123667 *Fax:* (021) 3123615 *Web Site:* www.archinform.net, pg 619

Bibliotheque des Sciences Medicales (Lebanon) *Tel:* (01) 614001-2 *Fax:* (01) 614054 *E-mail:* csm.biblio@usj.edu.lb *Web Site:* www.biblio-csm.usj.edu.lb, pg 1524

Bibliotheque du Centre Culturel Francais de Bamako (Mali) *Tel:* 222 40 19 *Fax:* 222 58 28 *E-mail:* dir@ccfbko.org.ml *Web Site:* www.ccfbko.org.ml, pg 1527

Bibliotheque du Musee Royal de Mariemont (Belgium) *Tel:* (064) 21 21 93 *Fax:* (064) 26 29 24 *E-mail:* info@musee-mariemont.be *Web Site:* www.musee-mariemont.be, pg 1493

Bibliotheque du Petit Seminaire (Haiti), pg 1513

Bibliotheque Fonds Quetelet (Belgium) *Tel:* (02) 506 60 54; (02) 506 61 51 *Fax:* (02) 502 84 25 *E-mail:* quetelet@mineco.fgov.be *Web Site:* mineco.fgov.be, pg 1493

Bibliotheque Generale et Archives du Maroc (Morocco) *Tel:* (07) 77 18 90; (07) 77 21 52 *Fax:* (07) 77 60 62 *E-mail:* biblio1@onpt.net.ma, pg 1529

Bibliotheque Haitienne des Freres de l'I.C., Saint Louis de Gonzague (Haiti) *Tel:* 2232148; 2237508 *Fax:* 2232029, pg 1513

Bibliotheque Historique de la Ville de Paris (France) *Tel:* (01) 44 59 29 40 *Fax:* (01) 42 74 03 16, pg 1506

Bibliotheque Interuniversitaire de Montpellier (France) *Tel:* (04) 67 13 43 50 *Fax:* (04) 67 13 43 51 *E-mail:* biu.secretariat@univ-montpl.fr *Web Site:* www.biu.montpellier.fr, pg 1506

Bibliotheque Municipale (Cote d'Ivoire), pg 1499

Bibliotheque Municipale de Besancon (France) *Tel:* (03) 81878140 *Fax:* (03) 81619877 *E-mail:* bib.etude@besancon.com *Web Site:* www.besancon.com/biblio/francais/, pg 1506

Bibliotheque Municipale de Constantine (Algeria), pg 1489

Bibliotheque Municipale de Grenoble (France) *Tel:* (04) 76862100 *Fax:* (04) 76862119 *E-mail:* bmei@upmf-grenoble.fr *Web Site:* www.bm-grenoble.fr, pg 1506

Bibliotheque Municipale de Lyon (France) *Tel:* (07) 78621800 *Fax:* (07) 78621949 *E-mail:* bm@bm-lyon.fr *Web Site:* www.bm-lyon.fr, pg 1506

Bibliotheque Municipale de Rennes (France) *Tel:* (02) 99 63 09 09; (02) 99 87 98 98 *Fax:* (02) 99 36 05 96; (02) 99 87 98 99 *E-mail:* contact@bm-rennes.fr *Web Site:* www.bm-rennes.fr, pg 1506

Bibliotheque Nationale (Algeria) *Tel:* (021) 671967; (021) 675781; (021) 671867 *Fax:* (021) 672999, pg 1259

Bibliotheque Nationale (Algeria) *Tel:* 630632, pg 1489

Bibliotheque Nationale (Cote d'Ivoire) *Tel:* 32 38 72, pg 1500

Bibliotheque Nationale (Guinea) *Tel:* (01) 461 010, pg 1513

Bibliotheque Nationale (Mali) *Tel:* 22 49 63 *Fax:* 23 59 31 *E-mail:* info@culture.gov.ml *Web Site:* w3.culture.gov.ml, pg 1527

Bibliotheque Nationale (Mauritania) *Tel:* 24 35, pg 1528

Bibliotheque Nationale (Togo) *Tel:* 21 63 67; 21 04 10; 22 21 16 *Fax:* 22 19 67, pg 1550

Bibliotheque Nationale (Tunisia) *Tel:* (01) 245338 *Fax:* (01) 342700, pg 1550

Bibliotheque Nationale de France (France) *Tel:* (01) 53 79 59 59; (01) 53 79 81 75; (01) 53 79 87 94 *Fax:* (01) 53 79 81 72 *E-mail:* commercial@bnf.fr *Web Site:* www.bnf.fr, pg 150

Bibliotheque Nationale de France (France) *Tel:* (01) 53 79 59 59 *Fax:* (01) 47 03 77 34 *Web Site:* www.bnf.fr, pg 1506

Bibliotheque nationale de Luxembourg (Luxembourg) *Tel:* 22 97 55-1 *Fax:* 47 56 72 *E-mail:* bib.nat@bi.etat.lu *Web Site:* www.bnl.lu, pg 1525

Bibliotheque Nationale d'Haiti (Haiti) *Tel:* 220 236; 220 198 *Fax:* 238 773, pg 1513

Bibliotheque Nationale du Benin (Benin) *Tel:* 22 25 85 *E-mail:* bn.benin@bj.refer.org *Web Site:* www.bj.refer.org/benin_ct/tur/bnb/Pagetitre.htm, pg 1494

Bibliotheque Nationale du Burundi (Burundi) *Tel:* (02) 25051 *Fax:* (02) 26231 *E-mail:* biefbdi@cbinf.com, pg 1496

Bibliotheque Nationale et Universitaire de Strasbourg (France) *Tel:* (03) 88 25 28 00 *Fax:* (03) 88 25 28 03 *E-mail:* bnus@bnus.u-strasbg.fr *Web Site:* www-bnus.u-strasbg.fr, pg 1506

Bibliotheque Publique (Burundi), pg 1496

Bibliotheque Publique de Kinshasa (The Democratic Republic of the Congo) *Tel:* (012) 3070, pg 1499

Bibliotheque Publique et Universitaire de Geneve (Switzerland) *Tel:* (022) 418 28 00 *Fax:* (022) 418 28 01 *E-mail:* info.bpu@ville-ge.ch *Web Site:* www.ville-ge.ch/bpu/, pg 1548

Bibliotheque Publique et Universitaire de Neuchatel (Switzerland) *Tel:* (032) 717-73-00; (032) 717 73 20 *Fax:* (032) 717-73-09 *Web Site:* bpun.unine.ch; rcbn.unine.ch, pg 1548

Bibliotheque Royale Albert Ier (Belgium) *Tel:* (02) 519 53 11 *Fax:* (02) 519 55 33 *E-mail:* contacts@kbr.be *Web Site:* www.kbr.be, pg 1493

Bibliotheque Universitaire Centrale (Benin) *Tel:* 36 01 01 *Fax:* 36 01 01, pg 1494

Bibliotheque Universitaire Centrale (BUC) (Algeria) *Tel:* (031) 61-42-05 *Fax:* (031) 61-21-90 *E-mail:* bucne@hotmail.com *Web Site:* www.buc-constantine.edu.dz, pg 1489

Bibliotheque Universitaire d'Antananarivo (Madagascar) *Tel:* (020) 22 612 28 *Fax:* (020) 22 612 29 *E-mail:* bu@univ-antananarivo.mg *Web Site:* www.bu.univ-antananarivo.mg, pg 1526

Bibliotheque Universitaire Droit-Sciences Economiques (France) *Tel:* (03) 83 30 81 57 *Fax:* (03) 83 30 82 38 *Web Site:* www.univ-nancy2.fr/webbib/webbib/budroit.html, pg 1506

Bibliotheque Universitaire, Universite Marien Ngouabi (Congo) *Tel:* 814207; 812436 *Fax:* 814207 *E-mail:* unmgbuco@congonet.cg, pg 1499

Bibliotheque Universite d'Avignon et des Pays du Vaucluse (France) *Tel:* (04) 90 16 25 00 *Fax:* (04) 90 16 25 10 *Web Site:* www.univ-avignon.fr, pg 1506

Bibliotheques de l'Universite Libre de Bruxelles (Belgium) *Tel:* (02) 650 36 63 *Fax:* (02) 650 20 07 *E-mail:* mdesb@ulb.ac *Web Site:* www.bib.ulb.ac.be/, pg 1493

Societe Biblique Francaise (France) *Tel:* (01) 39945051 *Fax:* (01) 39905351 *E-mail:* contacts@alliance-biblique-fr.org *Web Site:* www.la-bible.net, pg 150

Biblos srl (Italy) *Tel:* (049) 5975236 *Fax:* (049) 9409875, pg 378

Biddles Ltd (United Kingdom) *Tel:* (01553) 764 728 *Fax:* (01553) 764 633 *E-mail:* enquiries@biddles.co.uk *Web Site:* www.biddles.co.uk, pg 1163

Biddles Ltd (United Kingdom) *Tel:* (01553) 764 728 *Fax:* (01553) 764 633 *E-mail:* enquiries@biddles.co.uk *Web Site:* www.biddlesbooks.co.uk, pg 1225

Biddles Ltd (United Kingdom) *Tel:* (01553) 764 728 *Fax:* (01553) 764 633 *E-mail:* sales@biddles.co.uk; enquiries@biddles.co.uk *Web Site:* www.biddles.co.uk, pg 1238

Joseph Biddulph Publisher (United Kingdom) *Tel:* (01443) 662559, pg 665

Der Baum Wolfgang Biedermann Verlag (Austria) *Tel:* (01) 526 2720, pg 48

Bielefelder Verlagsanstalt GmbH & Co KG Richard Kaselowsky (Germany) *Tel:* (0521) 595 514 *Fax:* (0521) 595 518 *E-mail:* kontakt@bva-bielefeld.de *Web Site:* www.bva-bielefeld.de, pg 201

Bierman og Bierman I/S (Denmark) *Tel:* 75 32 02 88 *Fax:* 75 32 15 48 *E-mail:* mail@bierman.dk *Web Site:* www.bierman.dk, pg 129

Biermann Verlag GmbH (Germany) *Tel:* (02236) 376-0 *Fax:* (02236) 376-999 *E-mail:* info@biermann.net *Web Site:* www.biermann-online.de, pg 201

Big Apple Tuttle-Mori Agency Inc (Taiwan, Province of China) *Tel:* (02) 8990-1238 *Fax:* (02) 8990-1129 *E-mail:* bigapple1@worldnet.att.net *Web Site:* www.bigapple1.info, pg 1137

Big Balloon BV (Netherlands) *Tel:* (023) 5176620 *Fax:* (023) 5176630 *E-mail:* info@bigballoon.nl *Web Site:* www.bigballoon.nl, pg 479

Big Database Publishing Pvt Ltd (India), pg 330

Big Tree Publishing (Republic of Korea) *Tel:* (02) 7369653 *Fax:* (02) 7328694 *E-mail:* kennamu@unitel.co.kr, pg 437

The Big Word (United Kingdom) *Tel:* (0870) 7488000 *Fax:* (0870) 7488001 *E-mail:* production@thebigword.com *Web Site:* www.thebigword.com, pg 1150

Bihar Hindi Granth Akademi (India) *Tel:* (0612) 50390, pg 330

Erven J Bijleveld (Netherlands) *Tel:* (030) 2310800 *Fax:* (030) 2311774 *E-mail:* info@bijleveldbooks.nl *Web Site:* www.bijleveldbooks.nl, pg 479

YELLOW PAGES

Bijutsu Shuppan-Sha, Ltd (Japan) *Tel:* (03) 32342159 *Fax:* (03) 32349451 *Web Site:* www.bijutsu.co.jp, pg 415

Bilal Muslim Mission of Tanzania (United Republic of Tanzania) *Tel:* 21201111; 2112419; 2112420 *Fax:* 2116550 *E-mail:* bilal@raha.com, pg 643

Bilblioteka Nov den - Sajuz na Svobodnite Demokrati (Union of Free Democrats) (Bulgaria) *Tel:* (02) 773982; (02) 9814280 *Fax:* (02) 327972, pg 93

BILD Publications (United Kingdom) *Tel:* (01562) 723010 *Fax:* (01562) 723029 *E-mail:* enquiries@bild.org.uk *Web Site:* www.bild.org.uk, pg 665

Bild und Heimat Verlagsgesellschaft GmbH (Germany) *Tel:* (03765) 78 15-0 *Fax:* (03765) 1 22 45, pg 201

Bildarchiv Preussischer Kulturbesitz bpk (Germany) *Tel:* (030) 278 792 0 *Fax:* (030) 278 792 39 *E-mail:* bildarchiv@bpk.spk-berlin.de *Web Site:* www.bildarchiv-bpk.de, pg 201

Bilden Bilgisayar (Turkey) *Tel:* (0216) 449 52 50 *Fax:* (0216) 449 52 51 *E-mail:* bilden@bilden.com.tr *Web Site:* www.bilden.com.tr, pg 649

BW Bildung und Wissen Verlag und Software GmbH (Germany) *Tel:* (0911) 96 76-175 *Fax:* (0911) 96 76-189 *E-mail:* info@bwverlag.de *Web Site:* www.bwverlag.de, pg 201

Bilkent University Library (Turkey) *Tel:* (0312) 2664472 *Fax:* (0312) 2664391 *Web Site:* library.bilkent.edu.tr, pg 1551

Bina Aksara Parta (Indonesia) *Tel:* (361) 95240, pg 354

Bina Cipta PT (Indonesia) *Tel:* (022) 2504319 *Fax:* (022) 2504319, pg 354

Bina Ilmu (Indonesia) *Tel:* (031) 5323214; (031) 5340076 *Fax:* (031) 5315421, pg 354

Bina Rena Pariwara (Indonesia) *Tel:* (021) 7901938 *Fax:* (021) 7901939, pg 354

Bind-It Corp (United States) *Tel:* 631-234-2500 *Toll Free Tel:* 800-645-5110 *Web Site:* www.bindit.com, pg 1228

Bindernagelsche Buchhandlung (Germany) *Tel:* (06031) 7323-0 *Fax:* (06031) 734949, pg 201

Guy Binsfeld & Co Sarl (Luxembourg) *Tel:* 49 68 68-1 *Fax:* 40 76 09; 48 87 70 *E-mail:* editions@binsfeld.lu *Web Site:* www.editionsguybinsfeld.lu, pg 450

Bio Concepts Publishing (Australia) *Tel:* (07) 3868-0699 *Fax:* (07) 3868-0600 *E-mail:* info@bioconcepts.com.au *Web Site:* www.bioconcepts.com.au, pg 14

Biocommerce Data Ltd (United Kingdom) *Tel:* (020) 8332 4660 *Fax:* (020) 8332 4666 *E-mail:* biocom@pjbpubs.com; custserv@biocom.com (orders) *Web Site:* www.pjbpubs.com/bcd, pg 665

Editoriale Bios (Italy) *Tel:* (0984) 398300 *Fax:* (0984) 398300, pg 378

BIOS Scientific Publishers Ltd (United Kingdom) *Tel:* (01235) 828600 *Fax:* (01235) 829011 *E-mail:* sales@bios.co.uk *Web Site:* www.bios.co.uk, pg 665

Editorial Biosfera CA (Venezuela) *Tel:* (02) 751 9119; (02) 753 8892 *Fax:* (02) 751 9320, pg 779

Biramo Book Distributors (Australia) *Tel:* (02) 49542626 *Fax:* (02) 49565398 *E-mail:* biramobooks@tpg.com.au, pg 1298

Birchalls (Australia) *Tel:* (03) 63313011 *Toll Free Tel:* 800 806867 *Fax:* (03) 63317165 *E-mail:* enquiry@birchalls.com.au *Web Site:* www.birchalls.com.au, pg 1298

Birchgrove Books (Australia) *Tel:* (02) 9810 5040 *Fax:* (02) 9810 6053 *E-mail:* 100406.343@compuserve.com, pg 14

Birkhauser Verlag AG (Switzerland) *Tel:* (061) 2050707 *Fax:* (061) 2050799 *E-mail:* info@birkhauser.ch; sales@birkhauser.ch *Web Site:* www.birkhauser.ch, pg 619

Birkner & Co Zweigniederlassung Mecklenburg-Vorpommern (Germany) *Tel:* (040) 85308502 *Fax:* (040) 85308381, pg 201

Birlinn Ltd (United Kingdom) *Tel:* (0131) 668 4371 *Fax:* (0131) 668 4466 *E-mail:* info@birlinn.co.uk *Web Site:* www.birlinn.co.uk, pg 666

Birmingham Books (United Kingdom) *Tel:* (0121) 235 2868; (0121) 235 4511 *Fax:* (0121) 233 9702; (0121) 233 4458, pg 666

Birmingham Library Information Services (United Kingdom) *Tel:* (0121) 303 4511; (0121) 233 9702; (0121) 235 2868 *Fax:* (0121) 233 4458 *E-mail:* central.library@birmingham.gov.uk *Web Site:* www.birmingham.gov.uk; www.is.bham.ac.uk, pg 666

Birmingham Library Information Services (United Kingdom) *Tel:* (0121) 414 5817 *Fax:* (0121) 471 4691 *E-mail:* library@bham.ac.uk *Web Site:* www.is.bham.ac.uk/mainlib, pg 1552

Birmingham Museums & Art Gallery (United Kingdom) *Tel:* (0121) 303 2834; (0121) 303 1966; (0121) 464 9885 (shop) *Fax:* (0121) 303 1394 *E-mail:* info@bmagshop.co.uk *Web Site:* www.bmag.org.uk; www.bmagshop.co.uk, pg 1347

Adam Biro Editions (France) *Tel:* (01) 44 59 84 59 *Fax:* (01) 44 59 87 17, pg 150

Biro Penyediaan Teks Itm (Biroteks) (Malaysia) *Tel:* (03) 59271 ext 495 *Fax:* (03) 500226; (03) 55692733, pg 455

Biro Pusat Statistik (Indonesia) *Tel:* (021) 3507057 *Fax:* (021) 3857046 *E-mail:* bpsha@bps.go.id *Web Site:* www.bps.go.id, pg 354

Birsen Yayinevi (Turkey) *Tel:* (0212) 5278578; (0212) 5278522 *Fax:* (0212) 5270895 *Web Site:* www.geocities.com/birsen2us, pg 649

Biryongso Publishing Co (Republic of Korea) *Tel:* (02) 3443-4318; (02) 3443-4319 *Fax:* (02) 3442-4661 *Web Site:* www.bir.co.kr, pg 437

BIS Publishers (Netherlands) *Tel:* (020) 524 75 60 *Fax:* (020) 524 75 57 *E-mail:* bis@bispublishers.nl *Web Site:* www.bispublishers.nl, pg 479

Bishopsgate Press Ltd (United Kingdom) *Tel:* (01732) 833778 *Fax:* (01732) 833090, pg 666

Bitan Publishers Ltd (Israel) *Tel:* (03) 6040089; (054) 664575 *Fax:* (03) 5404792, pg 365

BKV-Brasilienkunde Verlag GmbH (Germany) *Tel:* (05452) 4598 *Fax:* (05452) 4357 *E-mail:* brasilien@T-Online.de *Web Site:* www.brasilienkunde.de; home.t-online.de/home/Brasilien, pg 201

BLA Publishing Ltd (United Kingdom) *Tel:* (01342) 318980 *Fax:* (01342) 410980, pg 666

A & C Black Publishers Ltd (United Kingdom) *Tel:* (020) 7758 0200 *Fax:* (020) 7758 0222 *E-mail:* enquiries@acblack.co.uk *Web Site:* www.acblack.co.uk, pg 666

Black Academy Press (Nigeria) *Tel:* (083) 230606; (083) 232606, pg 503

Black Ace Books (United Kingdom) *Tel:* (01307) 465096 *Fax:* (01307) 465494 *Web Site:* www.blackacebooks.com, pg 666

Black Bear Press Ltd (United Kingdom) *Tel:* (01223) 424571 *Fax:* (01223) 426877 *E-mail:* black_bear_pres@msn.com, pg 1183

Black Bear Press Ltd (United Kingdom) *Tel:* (01223) 424571 *Fax:* (01223) 426877 *E-mail:* black_bear_press@msn.com, pg 1225

Black Dog Books (Australia) *Tel:* (03) 9419 9406 *Fax:* (03) 9419 1214 *E-mail:* dog@bdb.com.au *Web Site:* www.bdb.com.au, pg 14

Black Mask Ltd (Ghana) *Tel:* (021) 500178 *Fax:* (021) 667701 *E-mail:* balme@ug.gn.apc.org, pg 303

BLAUKREUZ-VERLAG BERN

Black Spring Press Ltd (United Kingdom) *Tel:* (020) 7401 2044 *Fax:* (020) 7401 2055 *E-mail:* bsp@blackspring.demon.co.uk, pg 666

Blackbooks Co-operative for Aborigines Ltd (Australia) *Tel:* (0612) 9660 2396 *Fax:* (0612) 9660 1924 *E-mail:* tranby@tranby.com.au *Web Site:* www.tranby.com.au, pg 14

Blackie Children's Books (United Kingdom) *Tel:* (020) 7010 3000 *Fax:* (020) 7010 6060, pg 666

Blackmore Ltd (United Kingdom) *Tel:* (01747) 853034 *Fax:* (01747) 854500 *E-mail:* sales@blackmore.co.uk *Web Site:* www.blackmore.co.uk, pg 1183, 1225

Blackmore's Booksellers BLA (New Zealand) *Tel:* (03) 5489992 *Fax:* (03) 5466779, pg 1330

Blackstaff Press (United Kingdom) *Tel:* (028) 9066 8074 *Fax:* (028) 9066 8207 *E-mail:* info@blackstaffpress.com *Web Site:* www.blackstaffpress.com, pg 666

Blackstone Press Pty Ltd (Australia) *Tel:* (02) 9389 7677 *Fax:* (02) *E-mail:* c.l.e.@laams.com.au, pg 14

Blackwell & Hadwiger GesmbH British Bookshop (Austria) *Tel:* (01) 5121945; (01) 5132933 *Fax:* (01) 5121026 *E-mail:* britbook@netway.at, pg 1300

Blackwell Publishing Asia (Australia) *Tel:* (03) 8359 1011 *Fax:* (03) 8359 1120 *E-mail:* info@blackwellpublishingasia.com.au *Web Site:* www.blacksci.co.uk, pg 15

Blackwell Publishing Ltd (United Kingdom) *Tel:* (01865) 791100 *Fax:* (01865) 791347 *Web Site:* www.blackwellpublishers.co.uk, pg 666

Blackwell Retail (United Kingdom) *Tel:* (01865) 792792 *Fax:* (01865) 794143 *E-mail:* sales@blackwell.co.uk *Web Site:* www.blackwell.co.uk, pg 1347

Blackwell Science Ltd (United Kingdom) *Tel:* (01865) 206206 *Fax:* (01865) 721205 *E-mail:* shona.macdonald@blacksci.co.uk, pg 667

Blackwell Wissenschafts-Verlag GmbH (Germany) *Tel:* (030) 32 79 06-0 *Fax:* (030) 32 79 06-10 *E-mail:* verlag@blackwell.de *Web Site:* www.blackwis.de, pg 201

Bladkompaniet A/S (Norway) *Tel:* 24 14 68 00 *Fax:* 24 14 68 01 *E-mail:* bladkompaniet@bladkompaniet.no *Web Site:* www.bladkompaniet.no, pg 508

Edition Klaus Blahak Dr Fredric Kroll (Germany) *Tel:* (049) 761-244-73 *Fax:* (049) 761-244-73, pg 202

Horst Blaich Pty Ltd (Australia) *Tel:* (03) 9720 2658 *Fax:* (03) 9762 4225, pg 15

Joan Blair (Australia) *Tel:* (02) 4232 1642, pg 15

John Blake Publishing Ltd (United Kingdom) *Tel:* (020) 7381 0666 *Fax:* (020) 7381 6868 *E-mail:* words@blake.co.uk *Web Site:* www.blake.co.uk, pg 667

William Blake & Co (France) *Tel:* (05) 56 31 42 20 *Fax:* (05) 56 31 45 47 *E-mail:* editions.william.blake@wanadoo.fr *Web Site:* www.editions-william-blake-and-co.com, pg 150

Blaketon Hall Ltd (United Kingdom) *Tel:* (01392) 210 602 *Fax:* (01392) 421 165 *E-mail:* sales@blaketonhall.co.uk *Web Site:* www.blaketonhall.co.uk, pg 667

Editions Gerard Blanchart & Cie SA (Belgium) *Tel:* (02) 4783706 *Fax:* (02) 4786429, pg 63

Editions Blanco SA (Belgium) *Tel:* (02) 7720320 *Fax:* (02) 7706429, pg 64

Blandford Publishing Ltd (United Kingdom) *Tel:* (01202) 665432 *Fax:* (01202) 666219, pg 668

Blanvalet VerlagGmbH (Germany) *Tel:* (089) 41360; (089) 4372-0 (literature hotline) *Fax:* (089) 4372-2812 *E-mail:* vertrieb.verlagsgruppe@randomhouse.de *Web Site:* www.blanvalet-verlag.de, pg 202

Verlag Die Blaue Eule (Germany) *Tel:* (0201) 8 77 69 63 *Fax:* (0201) 8 77 69 64 *E-mail:* info@die-blaue-eule.de *Web Site:* www.die-blaue-eule.de, pg 202

Blaukreuz-Verlag Bern (Switzerland) *Tel:* (031) 300 58 66 *Fax:* (031) 300 58 69 *E-mail:* verlag@blaueskreuz.ch *Web Site:* www.blaueskreuz.ch, pg 619

Blaukreuz-Verlag Wuppertal (Germany) *Tel:* (0202) 6200370 *Fax:* (0202) 6200381 *E-mail:* bkv@blaukreuz.de *Web Site:* www.blaukreuz.de, pg 202

Blay Foldex (France) *Tel:* (01) 49 88 92 10 *Fax:* (01) 49 88 92 09, pg 150

Blaze International Productions Inc (United States) *Tel:* 212-967-7501 *Fax:* 212-967-7551, pg 1186, 1228, 1239, 1248

Blazek und Bergmann (Germany) *Tel:* (069) 152003-0 *Fax:* (069) 152003-44 *E-mail:* info@blazek-und-bergmann.de *Web Site:* www.blazek-und-bergmann.de, pg 1310

Bleicher Verlag GmbH (Germany) *Tel:* (07156) 43 08-0 *Fax:* (07156) 43 08-27 *E-mail:* info@bleicher-verlag.de *Web Site:* www.bleicher-verlag.de, pg 202

BLIC, russko-Baltijskij informaciionnyj centr, AO (Russian Federation) *Tel:* (0812) 3112252 *Fax:* (0812) 3112252; (0812) 1135896 *E-mail:* blitz@blitz.spb.ru, pg 544

Central Library for the Blind, Visually Impaired & Handicapped (Israel) *Tel:* (09) 8617874 *Fax:* (09) 8626346 *E-mail:* office@clfb.co.il *Web Site:* www.clfb.org.il, pg 1519

Blitzprint Inc (Canada) *Tel:* 403-253-5151 *Toll Free:* 866-479-3248 *Fax:* 403-253-5642 *E-mail:* blitzprint@blitzprint.com *Web Site:* www.blitzprint.com, pg 1215

Bloch Editores SA (Brazil) *Tel:* (021) 555-4167 *Fax:* (021) 555-4069 *E-mail:* blocheditores@ieg.com.br, pg 79

Blockfoil Ltd (United Kingdom) *Tel:* (01473) 721701 *Fax:* (01473) 270705 *E-mail:* info@blockfoil.com *Web Site:* www.blockfoil.com, pg 1225

Bloemfontein Public Library (South Africa) *Tel:* (051) 405 8248 *E-mail:* pat@dux.bfncouncil.co.za, pg 1543

H W Blok Uitgeverij BV (Netherlands) *Tel:* (020) 5159222 *Fax:* (020) 5159100, pg 479

Blondel La Rougery SARL (France) *Tel:* (01) 48 94 94 52 *Fax:* (01) 48 94 94 38, pg 150

Bloodaxe Books Ltd (United Kingdom) *Tel:* (01434) 240 500 *Fax:* (01434) 240 505 *E-mail:* editor@bloodaxebooks.demon.co.uk *Web Site:* www.bloodaxebooks.com, pg 668

Roy Bloom Ltd (United Kingdom) *Tel:* (0207) 7295473 *Fax:* (0207) 7292375 *E-mail:* info@roybloom.com *Web Site:* www.remainder-books.com, pg 1163, 1348

Bloomings Books (Australia) *Tel:* (03) 9427 1234 *Fax:* (03) 9427 9066 *E-mail:* sales@bloomings.com.au *Web Site:* www.bloomings.com.au, pg 15

Bloomsbury Publishing PLC (United Kingdom) *Tel:* (020) 7494 2111 *Fax:* (020) 7434 0151 *E-mail:* csm@bloomsbury.com *Web Site:* www.bloomsburymagazine.com, pg 668

Blorenge Books (United Kingdom) *Tel:* (01873) 856114, pg 668

Eberhard Blottner Verlag GmbH (Germany) *Tel:* (06128) 2 36 00 *Fax:* (06128) 21180 *E-mail:* blottner@blottner.de *Web Site:* www.blottner.de, pg 202

Blubber Head Press (Australia) *Tel:* (03) 6223 8644 *Fax:* (03) 6223 8644 *E-mail:* books@astrolabebooks.com.au *Web Site:* www.astrolabebooks.com.au, pg 15

Editora Edgard Blucher Ltda (Brazil) *Tel:* (011) 852-5366 *Fax:* (011) 852 2707 *E-mail:* eblucher@uol.com.br, pg 79

Blueprint (United Kingdom) *Tel:* (01372) 802080 *Fax:* (01372) 802079 *E-mail:* publications@pira.co.uk, pg 668

BLV Verlagsgesellschaft mbH (Germany) *Tel:* (089) 127050 *Fax:* (089) 12705354 *E-mail:* blv.verlag@blv.de *Web Site:* www.blv.de, pg 202

BMG Ricordi SpA (Italy) *Tel:* (02) 988131 *Fax:* (02) 88812212 *E-mail:* bmgricordi@bmg.com *Web Site:* www.bmgricordi.it, pg 378

BMJ Publishing Group (United Kingdom) *Tel:* (020) 7387 4499; (020) 7383 6245 *Fax:* (020) 7383 6661; (020) 7383 6662 *E-mail:* customerservices@bmjbooks.com *Web Site:* www.bmjpg.com, pg 668

BN International BV (Netherlands) *Tel:* (035) 524 84 00 *Fax:* (035) 525 60 04 *Web Site:* www.bninternational.com, pg 1237

Bo-jinjae Printing Co Ltd (Republic of Korea) *Tel:* (02) 6792351; (02) 6792355 *Fax:* (02) 6762821, pg 437

Bo Moon Dang (Republic of Korea) *Tel:* (02) 7047025 *Fax:* (02) 7042324, pg 437

Bo Ri Publishing Co Ltd (Republic of Korea) *Tel:* (02) 3233676 *Fax:* (02) 3240285, pg 437

Board of Studies (Australia) *Tel:* (02) 9367 8111 *Fax:* (02) 9367 8484 *E-mail:* customerliaison@boardofstudies.nsw.edu.au *Web Site:* www.boardofstudies.nsw.edu.au, pg 15

Boat Books Group (Australia) *Tel:* (02) 94391133 *Fax:* (02) 94398517 *E-mail:* boatbook@boatbooks-aus.com.au, pg 15

De Boccard Edition-Diffusion (France) *Tel:* (01) 43 26 00 37 *Fax:* (01) 43 54 85 83, pg 150

Verlag Erwin Bochinsky GmbH & Co KG (Germany) *Tel:* (069) 27 13 78 90 *Fax:* (069) 27 13 78 94 *Web Site:* www.bochinsky.de, pg 202

Bock und Herchen Verlag (Germany) *Tel:* (02224) 57 75 *Fax:* (02224) 7 83 10 *E-mail:* buh@bock-net.de *Web Site:* www.b-u-b.de, pg 202

Bodleian Library (United Kingdom) *Tel:* (01865) 277000 *Fax:* (01865) 277182 *E-mail:* enquiries@bodley.ox.ac.uk *Web Site:* www.bodley.ox.ac.uk, pg 1552

Les Editions de la Fondation Martin Bodmer (Switzerland) *Tel:* (022) 7362370 *Fax:* (022) 7001540, pg 619

De Boeck et Larcier SA (Belgium) *Tel:* (010) 48 2500 *Fax:* (010) 48 2519 *E-mail:* acces+cde@deboeck.be *Web Site:* www.larcier.be/larcier.html, pg 64

Boehlau-Verlag GmbH & Cie (Germany) *Tel:* (0221) 91 39 0-0 *Fax:* (0221) 91 39 0-32 *E-mail:* vertrieb@boehlau.de *Web Site:* www.boehlau.de, pg 202

Boehlau Verlag GmbH & Co KG (Austria) *Tel:* (01) 330 24 27 *Fax:* (01) 330 24 32 *E-mail:* boehlau@boehlau.at *Web Site:* www.boehlau.at, pg 48

Verlag Hermann Boehlaus Nachfolger Weimar GmbH & Co (Germany) *Tel:* (03643) 8508-90; (03643) 8508-91 *Fax:* (03643) 8508-92, pg 203

Boek Promotions BV (Netherlands) *Tel:* (035) 5310154, pg 479

Boek.be (Belgium) *Tel:* (03) 230 89 23 *Fax:* (03) 281 22 40 *E-mail:* info@boek.be *Web Site:* www.boek.be, pg 1262

Boekencentrum BV (Netherlands) *Tel:* (079) 3615481; (079) 3628282 (sales) *Fax:* (079) 3615489 *E-mail:* info@boekencentrum.nl *Web Site:* www.boekencentrum.nl, pg 479

De Boekerij BV (Netherlands) *Tel:* (020) 535 31 35 *Fax:* (020) 535 31 30 *E-mail:* info@boekerij.nl *Web Site:* www.boekerij.nl, pg 479

Boekhandel Johannes (Belgium) *Tel:* (016) 229501 *Fax:* (016) 208419 *E-mail:* info@johannes.be *Web Site:* www.johannes.be, pg 1302

BoekWerk (Netherlands) *Tel:* (050) 5265559 *Fax:* (050) 5268198, pg 479

Klaus Boer Verlag (Germany) *Tel:* (089) 13938099 *Fax:* (089) 13938098 *E-mail:* boerv@online.de *Web Site:* www.boerverlag.de, pg 203

Borsenverein des Deutschen Buchhandels eV (Germany) *Tel:* (069) 1306-0 *Fax:* (069) 1306-201, pg 1269

Boersenverein des Deutschen Buchhandels, Landesverband Baden-Wuerttemberg eV (Germany) *Tel:* (0711) 619410 *Fax:* (0711) 6194144 *E-mail:* post@buchhandelsverband.de *Web Site:* www.buchhandelsverband.de, pg 1270

Bogan's Forlag (Denmark) *Tel:* 48188055 *Fax:* 48188769, pg 129

Bogazici University Library (Turkey) *Tel:* (0212) 3581540 *Fax:* (0212) 2575016 *Web Site:* www.library.boun.edu.tr, pg 1551

Bogfabrikken Fakta ApS (Denmark) *Tel:* 3537 3533 *Fax:* 3537 3299, pg 129

Bohem Press Kinderbuchverlag (Switzerland) *Tel:* (01) 440 7000 *Fax:* (01) 440 7001 *E-mail:* art@bohem.ch *Web Site:* www.bohem.ch, pg 619

Bohmann Druck und Verlag GmbH & Co KG (Austria) *Tel:* (01) 74095 114 *Fax:* (01) 74095 111 *E-mail:* g.huber.zv@bohmann.at *Web Site:* www.bohmann.co.at, pg 49

Uitgeverij Bohn Stafleu Van Loghum BV (Netherlands) *Tel:* (030) 63 83 838 *Fax:* (030) 63 83 839 *Web Site:* www.bsl.nl, pg 479

Boighar (Bangladesh) *Tel:* (031) 252745, pg 61

Boinkie Publishers (Australia) *Tel:* (02) 588-7010 *Fax:* (02) 9311-3428, pg 15

Edition Boiselle (Germany) *Tel:* (06232) 629662 *Fax:* (06232) 629664 *E-mail:* info@edition-boiselle.de *Web Site:* www.edition-boiselle.de, pg 203

Bok Og Papiransattes Forening (Norway) *Tel:* 22205197 *Fax:* 22400033, pg 1280

Bokabud Mals og menningar (Iceland) *Tel:* 519 2777 *Fax:* 562 3523 *E-mail:* mm@centrum.is, pg 1315

Bokaforlag Birtingur (Iceland) *Tel:* 562-7700 *Fax:* 562-7710, pg 325

Bokautgafan Orn og Orlygur ehf (Iceland) *Tel:* 568-4866 *Fax:* 5671240, pg 325

Bokaverslun Sigfusar Eymundssonar (Iceland) *Tel:* 13135 *Fax:* 15078, pg 325

Bokklubb Bra Bockesr (Sweden) *Tel:* (042) 339000 *Fax:* (042) 330504, pg 1256

De norske Bokklubbene A/S (Norway) *Tel:* 02299 *Fax:* 02212 *Web Site:* www.bokklubbene.no, pg 1254

Boksamleren (Norway) *Tel:* 24051000 *Fax:* 24051099 *E-mail:* post@damm.no *Web Site:* www.dammbokklubb.no, pg 1254

Bolanz Verlag fur Alle (Germany) *Tel:* (07541) 33 6 99 *Fax:* (07541) 32467, pg 203

Bold ADS (Zimbabwe) *Tel:* (04) 62-1321; (04) 62-1326 *Fax:* (04) 62-1328 *E-mail:* shunidzarira@boldads.co.zw, pg 782

CB-Verlag Carl Boldt (Germany) *Tel:* (030) 833 70 87 *Fax:* (030) 833 91 25 *E-mail:* cb-verlag@t-online.de, pg 203

Boletin Oficial del Estado (Spain) *Tel:* (091) 902 365 303 *Fax:* (091) 5382349 *E-mail:* info@docu.boe.es *Web Site:* www.boe.es, pg 574

Bolinda Publishing Pty Ltd (Australia) *Tel:* (03) 9338 0666 *Fax:* (03) 9335 1903 *Web Site:* www.bolinda.com, pg 15

Bolivar Bookshop (Jamaica) *Tel:* (876) 926-8799 *Fax:* (876) 968-1874 *E-mail:* bolivar-jamaica@colis.com, pg 1321

Bolivian PEN Centre (Bolivia), pg 1397

Bollati Boringhieri Editore (Italy) *Tel:* (011) 55 91 711 *Fax:* (011) 54 30 24 *E-mail:* info@bollatiboringhieri.it *Web Site:* www.bollatiboringhieri.it, pg 378

Herbert Bolles (Australia) *Tel:* (02) 4567 7350 *Fax:* (02) 4567 7350 *E-mail:* bolles@pnc.com.au, pg 15

Bollmann-Bildkarten-Verlag GmbH & Co KG (Germany) *Tel:* (0531) 332069 *Fax:* (0531) 353064 *E-mail:* info@bollmann-bildkarten.de *Web Site:* www.bollmann-bildkarten.de, pg 203

Izdatelstvo Bolshaya Rossiyskaya Entsiklopedia (Russian Federation) *Tel:* (095) 9177582; (095) 9179009 *Fax:* (095) 9177139, pg 544

Bompiani-RCS Libri (Italy) *Tel:* (02) 50951 *Fax:* (02) 5065361 *Web Site:* www.rcslibri.it; www.bompiani.rcslibri.it, pg 378

Bonacci editore (Italy) *Tel:* (06) 68300004 *Fax:* (06) 68806382 *E-mail:* info@bonacci.it *Web Site:* www.bonacci.it, pg 378

Bonafides Verlags-Anstalt (Liechtenstein) *Tel:* (075) 82510, pg 447

Giuseppe Bonanno Editore (Italy) *Tel:* (095) 601984 *Fax:* (095) 604380 *Web Site:* www.bonannoedizioni.it, pg 378

Frances Bond Literary Services (South Africa) *Tel:* (031) 2662007 *Fax:* (031) 2662007 *E-mail:* fbond@mweb.com.za, pg 1136

Casa Editrice Bonechi (Italy) *Tel:* (055) 576841 *Fax:* (055) 5000766 *E-mail:* redazione@bonechi.it; informazioni@bonechi.it *Web Site:* www.bonechi.it, pg 378

Bonechi-Edizioni Il Turismo Srl (Italy) *Tel:* (055) 375739; (055) 3424527 *Fax:* (055) 374701 *E-mail:* info@bonechionline.com *Web Site:* www.bonechionline.com, pg 378

Bonifatius GmbH Druck-Buch-Verlag (Germany) *Tel:* (05251) 153 0 *Fax:* (05251) 153 104 *E-mail:* mail@bonifatius.de *Web Site:* www.bonifatius.de, pg 203

Universitaet Bonn (Germany) *Tel:* (0228) 73-7352 *Fax:* (0228) 73-7546 *E-mail:* ulb@ulb.uni-bonn.de *Web Site:* www.ulb.uni-bonn.de, pg 1508

Editions Andre Bonne (France) *Tel:* (01) 45150061 *Fax:* (01) 45218175, pg 150

Bonnier Audio (Sweden) *Tel:* (08) 6968700 *Fax:* (08) 6968757 *E-mail:* info@bonnieraudio.se *Web Site:* www.bonnieraudio.se, pg 610

Bonnier Carlsen Bokforlag AB (Sweden) *Tel:* (08) 59895500 *Fax:* (08) 59895545, pg 610

Bonnier Publications A/S (Denmark) *Tel:* 3917 2000 *Fax:* 3929 0199 *Web Site:* www.bonnierpublications.com, pg 129

Bonnier Utbildning AB (Sweden) *Tel:* (08) 696 85 90 *Fax:* (08) 696 86 55 *E-mail:* info@bonnierutbildning.se *Web Site:* www.bonnierutbildning.se, pg 610

Albert Bonniers Forlag AB (Sweden) *Tel:* (08) 696 86 20 *Fax:* (08) 696 83 61 *E-mail:* info@abforlag.bonnier.se *Web Site:* www.albertbonniersforlag.se, pg 610

Bonniers Bokklubb (Sweden) *Tel:* (08) 696 87 80 *Fax:* (08) 696 83 51; (08) 696 83 64 *E-mail:* medlemsservice@bbk.bonnier.se; best@bbk.bonnier.se; avbest@bbk.bonnier.se *Web Site:* www.bonniersbokklubb.se, pg 1256

Bonniers Specialmagasiner A/S Bogdivisionen (Denmark) *Tel:* 39295500 *Fax:* 39172300, pg 129

Bonsai-Centrum (Germany) *Tel:* (06221) 8491-0 *Fax:* (06221) 849130 *E-mail:* info@bonsai-centrum.de *Web Site:* www.bonsai-centrum.de, pg 203

Bonsignori Editore SRL (Italy) *Tel:* (06) 5881496 *Fax:* (06) 5882839 *E-mail:* redazione@bonsignori.it, pg 378

Bonum Editorial SACI (Argentina) *Tel:* (011) 4554-1414 *Fax:* (011) 4554-1414 *E-mail:* produccion@editorialbonum.com.ar *Web Site:* www.editorialbonum.com.ar, pg 4

Boobook Publications (Australia) *Tel:* (049) 97 0811 *Fax:* (049) 97 1089, pg 15

Book Agencies of Tasmania (Australia) *Tel:* (03) 6247 7405 *Fax:* (03) 6247 1116 *E-mail:* bookagencies@trump.net.au, pg 15

Book Aid International (United Kingdom) *Tel:* (020) 7733 3577 *Fax:* (020) 7978 8006 *E-mail:* info@bookaid.org *Web Site:* www.bookaid.org, pg 1572

Book & Printing Center - Israel Export Institute (Israel) *Tel:* (03) 514 2830 *Fax:* (03) 514 2902; (03) 514 2815 *E-mail:* export-institute@export.gov.il; pama@export.gov.il *Web Site:* www.export.gov.il; duns100.dundb.co.il/1483, pg 1273

Book Centre, Textbook Sales (Pvt) Ltd (Zimbabwe) *Tel:* (04) 790691 *Fax:* (04) 751690, pg 1356

Book Chamber of Kazakhstan ISBN Agency (Kazakstan) *Tel:* (03272) 306 421 *Fax:* (03272) 304 265 *E-mail:* rntb@kaznet.kz *Web Site:* www.isbn-international.org, pg 1275

Book Chamber of Ukraine, National ISBN Agency (Ukraine) *Tel:* (044) 573 52 36; (044) 573 01 84 *Fax:* (044) 573 52 36 *E-mail:* office@ukrbook.net *Web Site:* www.ukrbook.net, pg 1289

Book Circle (India) *Tel:* (011) 23266258; (011) 23288283; (011) 23257798 *Fax:* (011) 23263050 *E-mail:* info@meditechbooks.com *Web Site:* www.meditechbooks.com, pg 330

Book Club Associates (United Kingdom) *Tel:* (0870) 165 0292; (044) 1793 512100 *Fax:* (0870) 165 0222; (044) 1793 567711 *Web Site:* www.bca.co.uk, pg 1256

Book Collectors' Society of Australia (Australia) *Tel:* (02) 9807 5489 *Fax:* (02) 9807 5489, pg 15

The Book Company Publishing Pty Ltd (Australia) *Tel:* (02) 94863711 *Fax:* (02) 94863722 *E-mail:* sales@thebookcompany.com.au *Web Site:* www.thebookcompany.com.au, pg 15

Book Creation (United Kingdom) *Tel:* (020) 7583 0553 *Fax:* (020) 7583 9439, pg 1163

Book Creation (United Kingdom) *Tel:* (020) 7583 0553 *Fax:* (020) 7583 9439 *E-mail:* info@librios.com, pg 1183

Book Creation (United Kingdom) *Tel:* (020) 7583 0553 *Fax:* (020) 7583 9439, pg 1225

Book Creation (United Kingdom) *Tel:* (020) 7583 0553 *Fax:* (020) 7583 9439 *E-mail:* info@librios.com *Web Site:* www.librios.com, pg 1238

Book Development Council International (BDCI) (United Kingdom) *Tel:* (020) 7691 9191 *Fax:* (020) 7691 9199 *E-mail:* mail@publishers.org.uk *Web Site:* www.publishers.org.uk, pg 1289

Book Editore (Italy) *Tel:* (051) 71 47 20 *Fax:* (051) 71 12 16 *E-mail:* bookeditore@libero.it *Web Site:* web.tiscali.it/bookeditore, pg 378

Book Faith India (India) *Tel:* (011) 713-2459 *Fax:* (011) 724-9674 *E-mail:* pilgrim@del2.vsnl.net.in, pg 330

The Book Guild Ltd (United Kingdom) *Tel:* (01273) 472534 *Fax:* (01273) 476472 *E-mail:* info@bookguild.co.uk *Web Site:* www.bookguild.co.uk, pg 668

The Book House (Pakistan) *Tel:* (042) 61212; (042) 232415 *Fax:* (042) 6360955, pg 512

Book Industry Communication (United Kingdom) *Tel:* (020) 7607 0021 *Fax:* (020) 7607 0415 *Web Site:* www.bic.org.uk, pg 1289

Book Lovers Club (India) *Tel:* (011) 6910050; (011) 6916209 *Fax:* (011) 6331241 *E-mail:* ghai@nde.vsnl.net.in, pg 1253

Book Lovers' Club (Serbia and Montenegro) *Tel:* (011) 651666; (011) 650399, pg 1255

Book Marketing Ltd (Hong Kong) *Tel:* (02) 5620121 *Fax:* (02) 5650187, pg 315

Book Marketing Ltd (United Kingdom) *Tel:* (020) 7440 8931 *Fax:* (020) 7242 7485 *E-mail:* bml@bookmarketing.co.uk *Web Site:* www.bookmarketing.co.uk, pg 668, 1289

Book Packaging & Marketing (United Kingdom) *Tel:* (01327) 861300 *Fax:* (01327) 861300, pg 668

Book Production Consultants PLC (United Kingdom) *Tel:* (01223) 352790 *Fax:* (01223) 460718 *E-mail:* tl@bpccam.co.uk *Web Site:* www.bpccam.co.uk, pg 1138

Book Production Consultants PLC (United Kingdom) *Tel:* (01223) 352790 *Fax:* (01223) 460718 *Web Site:* www.bpccam.co.uk, pg 1163

Book Production Consultants PLC (United Kingdom) *Tel:* (01223) 352790 *Fax:* (01223) 460718 *E-mail:* bpc@bpccam.co.uk *Web Site:* www.bpccam.co.uk, pg 1183

Book Production Consultants PLC (United Kingdom) *Tel:* (01223) 352790; (01223) 323092 (ISDN) *Fax:* (01223) 460718 *E-mail:* tl@bpccam.co.uk *Web Site:* www.bpccam.co.uk, pg 1247

Book Promotions (Pte) Ltd (South Africa) *Tel:* (021) 7060949 *Fax:* (021) 7060940 *E-mail:* enquiries@bookpro.co.za *Web Site:* www.bookpro.co.za, pg 1340

The Book Publishers Association of Israel (Israel) *Tel:* (03) 5614121 *Fax:* (03) 5611996 *E-mail:* info@tbpai.co.il *Web Site:* www.tbpai.co.il, pg 365

Book Publishers' Association of Israel (Israel) *Tel:* (03) 5614121 *Fax:* (03) 5611996 *E-mail:* info@tbpai.co.il *Web Site:* www.tbpai.co.il, pg 1274

The Book Publishers' Association of Israel, International Promotion & Literary Rights Department (Israel) *Tel:* (03) 5614121 *Fax:* (03) 5611996 *E-mail:* hamol@tbpai.co.il *Web Site:* www.tbpai.co.il, pg 1133

Book Publishing Institute (Afghanistan), pg 1

Book Representation & Distribution Ltd (United Kingdom) *Tel:* (01702) 552912 *Fax:* (01702) 556095 *E-mail:* mail@bookreps.com; info@bookreps.com *Web Site:* www.bookreps.com, pg 1348

Book Representation & Publishing Co Ltd (Nigeria) *Tel:* (022) 710242, pg 503

Book Sales (K) Ltd (Kenya), pg 433

Book Sales (K) Ltd (Kenya) *Tel:* (02) 221031; (02) 226543, pg 1323

The Book Source (Barbados) *Tel:* 4310379 *Fax:* 4261855 *E-mail:* bksource@caribsurf.com *Web Site:* www.booksourceonline.com, pg 1301

Book Stop (Ireland) *Tel:* (01) 2809917 *Fax:* (01) 2844863 *E-mail:* bookstop@indigo.ie, pg 1318

Book Tokens Ltd (United Kingdom) *Tel:* (020) 7802 0802 *Fax:* (020) 7802 0803 *Web Site:* www.booktokens.co.uk, pg 1289

The Book Trade Benevolent Society (United Kingdom) *Tel:* (01923) 263128 *Fax:* (01923) 270732 *E-mail:* btbs@booktradecharity.demon.co.uk *Web Site:* www.booktradecharity.demon.co.uk, pg 1289

Bookbank SA (Spain) *Tel:* (091) 3733539 *Fax:* (091) 3165591 *E-mail:* bookbank@nexo.es, pg 1136

Bookbank SL Agencia Literaria (Spain) *Tel:* (091) 3733539 *Fax:* (091) 3165591 *E-mail:* bookbank@nexo.es, pg 574

Bookbuilders Ltd (Hong Kong) *Tel:* 27968123 *Fax:* 27968267; 27968690 *E-mail:* lph@netvigator.com, pg 1177, 1217

BookBuilders New York Inc (United States) *Tel:* 845-639-5316 *Fax:* 845-639-5318 *Web Site:* www.mcabooks.com, pg 1166, 1186

BookBuilders New York Inc (United States) *Tel:* 845-639-5316 *Fax:* 845-639-5318 *E-mail:* mcanewcity@aol.com *Web Site:* www.mcabooks.com, pg 1228

BookBuilders New York Inc (United States) *Tel:* 845-639-5316 *Fax:* 845-639-5318 *Web Site:* www.mcabooks.com, pg 1239, 1248

Bookionics (India) *Tel:* (040) 593654 *Fax:* (040) 595678 *E-mail:* bookionics@yahoo.com, pg 331

Booklink (United Kingdom) *Tel:* (01923) 828612 *Fax:* (01923) 828455 *E-mail:* info@booklink.co.uk *Web Site:* www.booklink.co.uk, pg 1138

Booklinks Corporation (India) *Tel:* (0842) 65021; (0842) 62282; (0842) 65550, pg 331

Bookmaker (France) *Tel:* (01) 43 54 84 34 *Fax:* (01) 43 54 71 02 *E-mail:* bookmake@club-internet.fr, pg 150

Bookman Books Ltd (Taiwan, Province of China) *Tel:* (02) 2368-7226; (02) 2365-8617 *Fax:* (02) 2363-6630; (02) 2365-3548 *Web Site:* www.bookman.tw, pg 639

Bookman Consultants Ltd (Kenya) *Tel:* (02) 336771 *Fax:* (02) 217267, pg 433

Bookman Health (Australia) *Tel:* (03) 9521 3250 *Toll Free Tel:* 800 060 555 *Fax:* (03) 9826 1744 *E-mail:* sales@bookman.com.au *Web Site:* www.bookman.com.au, pg 15

Bookman Literary Agency (Denmark) *Tel:* 45892520 *Fax:* 45892501 *Web Site:* www.bookman.dk, pg 1130

Bookman Printing & Publishing House Inc (Philippines) *Tel:* (02) 712-4813; (02) 712-4818; (02) 712-4843; (02) 740-8108; (02) 740-8107; (02) 712-3587 *Fax:* (02) 712-4843 *E-mail:* bookman@info.com.ph, pg 518

Bookman's & Co Ltd (Japan) *Tel:* (06) 6371-4164 *Fax:* (06) 6371-4174 *E-mail:* info@bookmans.co.jp; bookman@osk3.3web.ne.jp *Web Site:* www.bookmans.co.jp, pg 1321

Bookmark Inc (Philippines) *Tel:* (02) 8958061; (02) 8958062; (02) 8958063; (02) 8958064; (02) 8958065 *Fax:* (02) 8970824; (02) 8994248 *E-mail:* bookmark@info.com.ph; bookmktg@info.com.ph *Web Site:* www.bookmark.com.ph, pg 518

Bookmark Inc (Philippines) *Tel:* (02) 8958061; (02) 8958062; (02) 8958063; (02) 8958064; (02) 8958065 *Fax:* (02) 8970824 *E-mail:* bookmark@info.com.ph *Web Site:* www.bookmark.com.ph, pg 1335

Bookmark Remainders (United Kingdom) *Tel:* (01566) 782728 *Fax:* (01566) 782059 *E-mail:* info@book-bargains.co.uk *Web Site:* book-bargains.co.uk, pg 1348

Bookmarks Club (United Kingdom) *Tel:* (020) 7536 9696 *Fax:* (020) 7538 0018 *E-mail:* bookmarks@internationalsocialist.org *Web Site:* www.internationalsocialist.org, pg 1257

Bookmarks Publications (United Kingdom) *Tel:* (020) 7637 1848 *Fax:* (020) 7637 3416 *E-mail:* mailorder@bookmarks.uk.com *Web Site:* www.bookmarks.uk.com, pg 668

Bookmart Ltd (United Kingdom) *Tel:* (0116) 2759060 *Fax:* (0116) 2759090 *E-mail:* books@bookmart.co.uk, pg 1348

Bookpoint Ltd (Kenya) *Tel:* (02) 211156; (02) 220221; (02) 226680 *Fax:* (02) 211029 *E-mail:* books@africaonline.co.ke, pg 1323

Bookpoint Ltd (United Kingdom) *Tel:* (01235) 400400 *Fax:* (01235) 832068; (01235) orders 821511 *E-mail:* firstname.lastname@bookpoint.co.uk *Web Site:* www.oxfordshire.co.uk, pg 1348

BookPower (United Kingdom) *Tel:* (020) 8742 8232 *Fax:* (020) 8747 8715 *E-mail:* bookpower@ibd.uk.net *Web Site:* www.bookpower.org, pg 1406

Bookprint Consultants Ltd (New Zealand) *Tel:* (04) 381 3071 *Fax:* (04) 381 3067 *E-mail:* gstewart@iconz.co.nz, pg 1160, 1221, 1237, 1246

Books Across the Sea (United Kingdom) *Tel:* (020) 7529 1550 *Fax:* (020) 7495 6108 *E-mail:* esu@mailbox.ulcc.ac.uk *Web Site:* www.libfl.ru/eng/esu, pg 1406

Books & Books (India) *Tel:* (011) 551252, pg 331

Books & Periodicals Agency (India) *Tel:* (011) 205624 *Fax:* 801-881-6189 (US Fax) *E-mail:* bpage@del2.vsnl.net.in *Web Site:* www.bpagency.com, pg 1315

Books Exports (United Kingdom) *Tel:* (020) 8931 2359; (020) 8959 2137 *Fax:* (0181) 9592137 *E-mail:* roshanbp@aol.com, pg 1257

Books for Children (United Kingdom) *Tel:* (020) 8606 3090 *Fax:* (020) 8606 3099, pg 1257

Books for Europe Ltd (United Kingdom) *Tel:* (020) 8840 6672 *Fax:* (020) 8840 6672, pg 669

Books for Europe Ltd (United Kingdom) *Tel:* (020) 8840 6672, pg 1349

Books for Keeps (United Kingdom) *Tel:* (020) 8852 4953 *Fax:* (020) 8318 7580 *E-mail:* booksforkeeps@btinternet.com *Web Site:* www.booktrusted.com/handbook/journals/bookskeeps.html, pg 1289

Books for Pleasure Inc (Philippines) *Tel:* (02) 771807 *Fax:* (02) 7275240 *E-mail:* vromance@compass.com.ph, pg 518

Books from India (UK) Ltd (United Kingdom) *Tel:* (071) 4053784 *Fax:* (071) 8314517, pg 1349

Books in the Attic Publishers Ltd (Israel) *Tel:* (03) 248324 *Fax:* (03) 623630, pg 365

Books India (India) *Tel:* (011) 327 7463 *Fax:* (011) 241 2912, pg 1315

Books International (Israel) *Tel:* (08) 633 0205 *Fax:* (08) 633 0204 *E-mail:* info@booksinternational.com *Web Site:* www.booksinternational.com, pg 1319

Books International (United Kingdom) *Tel:* (01252) 376564 *Fax:* (01252) 370181 *E-mail:* booksinter@aol.com *Web Site:* www.books-international.co.uk/, pg 669

Books of Zimbabwe Publishing Co (Pvt) Ltd (United Kingdom) *Tel:* (01444) 455549 *E-mail:* info@booksofzimbabwe.com *Web Site:* www.booksofzimbabwe.com, pg 669

Books Registration Office (Hong Kong) *Tel:* 218 09 145; 218 09 146 *Fax:* 218 09 841 *E-mail:* bro@lcsd.gov.hk, pg 1272

Booksellers' & Publishers' Association of Zambia (BPAZ) (Zambia) *Tel:* (01) 255166 *Fax:* (01) 255166 *E-mail:* bpaz@zamnet.zm; longman@zamnet.zm *Web Site:* www.africanpublishers.org, pg 1295

Booksellers' Association of Jamaica (Jamaica) *Tel:* (876) 922-5883 *Fax:* (876) 922-4743, pg 1274

Booksellers New Zealand (New Zealand) *Tel:* (04) 478 5511 *Fax:* (04) 478 5519 *E-mail:* enquiries@booksellers.co.nz *Web Site:* www.booksellers.co.nz, pg 1279

Booksellers New Zealand (New Zealand) *Tel:* (04) 4478-5511 *Fax:* (04) 4478-5519, pg 1280

Bookservice (Italy) *Tel:* (0771) 744350 *Fax:* (0771) 744350, pg 378

Bookstore, Institute of Puerto Rican Culture (Puerto Rico) *Tel:* (809) 723-2115, pg 1338

Booktrust (United Kingdom) *Tel:* (020) 8516 2977 *Fax:* (020) 8516 2978 *Web Site:* www.booktrust.org.uk, pg 1290

Bookwise International (Australia) *Tel:* (08) 8268 8222 *Fax:* (08) 8268 8704 *E-mail:* customer.service@bookwise.com.au *Web Site:* www.bookwise.com.au, pg 1298

Bookworld Ltd (Zambia) *Tel:* (01) 225 282 *Fax:* (01) 225 195 *E-mail:* bookwld@zamtel.zm, pg 781

Bookworld Wholesale Ltd (United Kingdom) *Tel:* (01299) 823330 *Fax:* (01299) 829970, pg 1349

The Bookworm Club (United Kingdom) *Tel:* (01223) 568650 *Fax:* (01223) 568591 *E-mail:* clubs@heffers.co.uk, pg 1257

Boolarong Press (Australia) *Tel:* (07) 3848 8200 *Fax:* (07) 3848 8077, pg 15

Boom Uitgeverij (Netherlands) *Tel:* (020) 625 33 27 *Fax:* (020) 625 33 27 *E-mail:* info@uitgeverijboom.nl *Web Site:* www.uitgeverijboom.nl, pg 479

Boombana Publications (Australia) *Tel:* (07) 3289 8106 *Fax:* (07) 3289 8107 *Web Site:* www.boombanapublications.com, pg 16

Richard Boorberg Verlag GmbH & Co (Germany) *Tel:* (0711) 73 85-0 *Fax:* (0711) 73 85-100 *Web Site:* www.boorberg.de, pg 203

Boosey & Hawkes Music Publishers Ltd (United Kingdom) *Tel:* (020) 7580 2060 *Fax:* (020) 7291 7109 *E-mail:* information@boosey.com *Web Site:* www.boosey.com/publishing, pg 669

Boosey & Hawkes Music Publishers LTD, London (Germany) *Tel:* (030) 25001300 *Fax:* (030) 25001399 *E-mail:* musikverlag@boosey.com *Web Site:* www.boosey.com/publishing, pg 203

Boostan Publishing House (Israel) *Tel:* (03) 9221821 *Fax:* (03) 9221299, pg 365

BOOX (Sweden) *Tel:* (08) 411 37 00 *Fax:* (08) 411 53 30 *E-mail:* transbok@algonet.se, pg 610

Edizioni Bora SNC di E Brandani & C (Italy) *Tel:* (051) 356133 *Fax:* (051) 4159651 *E-mail:* daniele.brandani@mailbox.dsnet.it, pg 379

Borba (Serbia and Montenegro) *Tel:* (011) 3243-437 *Fax:* (011) 3244-913 *Web Site:* www.borba.co.yu, pg 552

Editions Bordas (France) *Tel:* (01) 44395445 *Fax:* (01) 44394350 *Web Site:* www.editions-bordas.com, pg 150

Pierre Bordas & Fils, Editions (France) *Tel:* (01) 43 25 04 51 *Fax:* (01) 43 25 47 84 *E-mail:* pierre.bordas.filsd@wanadoo.fr, pg 150

Bibliotheque Municipale de Bordeaux (France) *Tel:* (05) 56103000 *Fax:* (05) 56103090 *E-mail:* bibli@mairie-bordeaux.fr *Web Site:* www.bordeaux-city.com/bordeaux.htm, pg 1506

Presses Universitaires de Bordeaux (PUB) (France) *Tel:* (05) 57 12 44 22 *Fax:* (05) 57 12 45 34 *E-mail:* pub@montaigne.u-bordeaux.fr *Web Site:* www.pub.montaigne.u-bordeaux.fr, pg 150

Borgens Forlag A/S (Denmark) *Tel:* 36 15 36 15 *Fax:* 36 15 36 16 *E-mail:* post@borgen.dk *Web Site:* www.borgen.dk, pg 129

Borim Publishing Co (Republic of Korea) *Tel:* (02) 3141-2222 *Fax:* (02) 3141-8474 *E-mail:* namu@borimplc.co.kr *Web Site:* www.borimplc.co.kr, pg 437

Edizioni Borla SRL (Italy) *Tel:* (06) 39376728 *Fax:* (06) 39376620 *E-mail:* borla@edizioni-borla.it *Web Site:* www.edizioni-borla.it, pg 379

Born-Verlag (Germany) *Tel:* (0561) 4095107 *Fax:* (0561) 4095112 *E-mail:* info.born@ec-jugend.de *Web Site:* www.born-buch.de, pg 203

Bornegudstjeneste-Forlaget (Denmark) *Tel:* 75934455 *Fax:* 75924275 *E-mail:* lohse@imh.dk, pg 129

Editions Bornemann (France) *Tel:* (01) 42 82 74 44 *Fax:* (01) 48 74 14 88, pg 150

Borromausverein eV (Germany) *Tel:* (0228) 7258-0 *Fax:* (0228) 7258-189 *E-mail:* info@borro.de *Web Site:* www.borro.de, pg 1270

Editions Emile Borschette (Luxembourg) *Tel:* 87177 *Fax:* 879599, pg 450

Borsen Forlag (Denmark) *Tel:* 33 32 01 02 *Fax:* 33 12 24 45 *E-mail:* redaktionen@borsen.dk *Web Site:* www.borsen.dk, pg 129

Borthwick Institute Publications (United Kingdom) *Tel:* (01904) 321160 *Web Site:* www.york.ac.uk/borthwick, pg 669

Antoni Bosch Editor SA (Spain) *Tel:* (093) 206 07 30 *Fax:* (093) 206 07 31 *E-mail:* info@antonibosch.com *Web Site:* www.antonibosch.com, pg 574

Bosch Casa Editorial SA (Spain) *Tel:* (093) 4548437; (093) 4544629; (093) 4521050 *Fax:* (093) 3236736 *E-mail:* bosch@boschce.es *Web Site:* www.boschce.es, pg 575

Bosch en Keuning grafische bedrijven (Netherlands) *Tel:* (035) 5412050 *Fax:* (035) 2202446, pg 1160, 1181, 1221

J M Bosch Editor (Spain) *Tel:* (093) 3175308 *Fax:* (093) 4122764 *E-mail:* jmb@libreriabosch.es *Web Site:* www.libreriabosch.es/jmb, pg 575

Libreria Bosch (Spain) *Tel:* (093) 394 3600 *Fax:* (093) 412 2764 *E-mail:* info@libreriabosch.es *Web Site:* www.libreriabosch.es, pg 1342

Editorial M J Bosch, SL (Spain) *Tel:* (093) 4512335 *E-mail:* mjbosch@colon.net, pg 575

Gustav Bosse GmbH & Co KG (Germany) *Tel:* (0561) 31 05-0 *Fax:* (0561) 31 05-2 40 *E-mail:* info@bosse-verlag.de *Web Site:* www.bosse-verlag.de, pg 203

BOSZ scp (Poland) *Tel:* (013) 469 90 00 *Fax:* (013) 469 61 88 *E-mail:* biuro@ks.onet.pl *Web Site:* www.bosz.com.pl, pg 522

Botanisch-Zoologische Gesellschaft (Liechtenstein) *Tel:* (00423) 2324819 *Fax:* (00423) 2332819 *E-mail:* renat@pingnet.li, pg 447

Libreria y Ediciones Botas SA (Mexico) *Tel:* (05) 5702-4083; (05) 5702-5403 *Fax:* (02) 55101788 *E-mail:* botas@mail.nextgeninter.net.mx, pg 462

Bote & Bock Musikalienhandelsgesellschaft mbH (Germany) *Tel:* (030) 2500-1300 *Fax:* (030) 2500-1399 *E-mail:* musikverlag@boosey.com, pg 203

Ediciones Botella al Mar (Argentina) *Tel:* (011) 4803-8246 *E-mail:* edicionesbotellaalmar@hotmail.com, pg 4

Botes Librair (United Kingdom) *Tel:* (01424) 210871 *Fax:* (01424) 734506; (01424) 731262 *E-mail:* 100450.3641@compuserve.com, pg 1349

Botimpex Publications Import-Export Agency (Albania) *Tel:* (042) 34023 *Fax:* (042) 26886 *E-mail:* botimpex@albaniaonline.net; botimpex@icc-al.org; ebega@albmail.com *Web Site:* pages.albaniaonline.net/botimpex/, pg 1

Botswana Book Centre (Botswana) *Tel:* 3952931 *Fax:* 3974315 *E-mail:* pulapress@botsnet.bw *Web Site:* www.bbc.co.bw, pg 1303

Botswana Library Association (Botswana) *Tel:* (031) 3552295 *Fax:* (031) 357291 *Web Site:* www.bla.0catch.com, pg 1559

Botswana National Archives & Records Services (Botswana) *Tel:* 391 820 *Fax:* 390 545 *Web Site:* www.gov.bw, pg 1495

Botswana National Library Service (Botswana) *Tel:* 352-397 *Fax:* 301-149 *E-mail:* natlib@global.bw; automate@global.bw *Web Site:* www.gov.bw, pg 1495

The Botswana Society (Botswana) *Tel:* 3919673 *Fax:* 3919745 *E-mail:* botsoc@botsnet.bw *Web Site:* www.botswanasociety.com, pg 76

Bottin SA (France) *Tel:* (01) 49 81 56 56 *Fax:* (01) 49 81 56 76, pg 151

Boukoumanis' Editions (Greece) *Tel:* (01) 3618502; (01) 3637436 *Fax:* (01) 3630669 *E-mail:* info@boukoumanis.gr *Web Site:* www.boukoumanis.gr, pg 306

Boulevard Books UK/The Babel Guides (United Kingdom) *Tel:* (01865) 712931 *Fax:* (01865) 712931 *E-mail:* raybabel@dircon.co.uk *Web Site:* www.babelguides.com, pg 669

Bounty Books (United Kingdom) *Tel:* (020) 7531 8600 *Fax:* (020) 7531 8607 *Web Site:* www.bounty-publishing.co.uk, pg 669

Librairie Bourbon (Luxembourg) *Tel:* 40 30 30-21 *Fax:* 40 30 30-45 *E-mail:* librairies@isp.lu *Web Site:* www.librairie.lu, pg 1325

Bourdeaux-Capelle SA (Belgium) *Tel:* (082) 222283; (082) 222277 *Fax:* (082) 226378, pg 64

Christian Bourgois Editeur (France) *Tel:* (01) 45 44 09 13 *Fax:* (01) 45 44 87 86 *E-mail:* bourgois-editeur@wanadoo.fr *Web Site:* www.christianbourgois-editeur.fr, pg 151

Editions Bouslama (Tunisia) *Tel:* (01) 245612 *Fax:* (01) 381100, pg 647

Editions Bouslama (Tunisia) *Tel:* (01) 245612, pg 1346

Bouvier GmbH & Co KG (Germany) *Tel:* (0228) 72901-0; (01803) 258940 (orders) *Fax:* (0228) 72901-178 *E-mail:* bouvier@books.de *Web Site:* www.books.de, pg 1310

Bouvier Verlag (Germany) *Tel:* (0228) 72901124 *Fax:* (0228) 637909 *E-mail:* verlag@books.de *Web Site:* www.bouvier-online.de, pg 203

Bovolenta (Italy) *Tel:* (0532) 259386 *Fax:* (0532) 259387, pg 379

M J Bowen (Australia) *Tel:* (03) 9561 3425 *Fax:* (03) 9882 9405, pg 16

Bowerdean Publishing Co Ltd (United Kingdom) *Tel:* (020) 8788 0938 *Fax:* (020) 8788 0938 *Web Site:* www.bowerdean.co.uk/, pg 669

Boxtree Ltd (United Kingdom) *Tel:* (020) 7014 6000 *Fax:* (020) 7014 6001 *Web Site:* www.panmacmillan.com/imprints/boxtree.html, pg 669

Marion Boyars Publishers Ltd (United Kingdom) *Tel:* (020) 8788 9522 *Fax:* (020) 8789 8122 *Web Site:* www.marionboyars.co.uk, pg 669

David Boyce Publishing (Australia) *Tel:* (02) 6997484, pg 16

Boydell & Brewer Ltd (United Kingdom) *Tel:* (01394) 610 600 *Fax:* (01394) 610 316 *E-mail:* boydell@boydell.co.uk *Web Site:* www.boydell.co.uk, pg 669

BPB Publications (India) *Tel:* (011) 3281723; (011) 3254990; (011) 3254991 *Fax:* (011) 3266427 *E-mail:* admin@bpbonline.com *Web Site:* www.bpbonline.com, pg 331

BPL Remainders (United Kingdom) *Tel:* (020) 7636 5070; (020) 7631 5070 *Fax:* (020) 7580 3001, pg 1349

BPP Publishing Ltd (United Kingdom) *Tel:* (020) 8740 2222 *Fax:* (020) 8740 1111 *E-mail:* info@bpp.com *Web Site:* www.bpp.com, pg 670

BPS Books (British Psychological Society) (United Kingdom) *Tel:* (0116) 254 9568 *Fax:* (0116) 247 0787 *E-mail:* enquiry@bps.org.uk *Web Site:* www.bps.org.uk, pg 670

BR Publishing Corporation (India) *Tel:* (011) 7430113; (011) 7143353, pg 331

Bokforlaget Bra Bocker AB (Sweden) *Tel:* (040) 665 46 00 *Fax:* (040) 665 46 22 *E-mail:* kundservice@bbb.se *Web Site:* www.bbb.se, pg 610

Brabys Brochures (South Africa) *Tel:* (031) 717 4000 *Fax:* (031) 717 4001 *E-mail:* brabys@brabys.com *Web Site:* www.brabys.com, pg 563

Dr Barry Bracewell-Milnes (United Kingdom) *Tel:* (01737) 350736 *Fax:* (01737) 371415, pg 670

Bradt Travel Guides Ltd (United Kingdom) *Tel:* (01753) 893444 *Fax:* (01753) 892333 *E-mail:* enquiries@bradt-travelguides.com *Web Site:* www.bradtguides.com, pg 670

Bradt Travel Guides Ltd (United Kingdom) *Tel:* (01753) 893444 *Fax:* (01753) 892333 *E-mail:* info@bradtguides.com; enquiries@bradt-travelguides.com *Web Site:* www.bradtguides.com, pg 1349

Bragelonne (France) *Tel:* (01) 48 18 19 70; (01) 48 18 19 71 *Fax:* (01) 48 18 02 47 *E-mail:* info@bragelonne.fr *Web Site:* www.bragelonne.fr, pg 151

Louis Braille Audio (Australia) *Tel:* (03) 9864 9645 *Fax:* (03) 9864 9646 *E-mail:* lba.sales@visionaustralia.org.au *Web Site:* www.louisbrailleaudio.com, pg 16

Braintrust Marketing Services Ges mbH Verlag (Austria) *Tel:* (01) 40416-0 *Fax:* (01) 40416-33 *E-mail:* braintrust@magnet.at *Web Site:* www.braintrust.at, pg 49

J W Braithwaite & Son Ltd (United Kingdom) *Tel:* (01902) 452209 *Fax:* (01902) 352918, pg 1225

Verlag Brandenburger Tor GmbH (Germany) *Tel:* (030) 8557511 *Fax:* (030) 85605332 *E-mail:* info@verlag-brandenburger-tor.de, pg 203

Brandenburgisches Verlagshaus in der Dornier Medienholding GmbH (Germany) *Tel:* (030) 28447-112; (030) 28447-113 *Fax:* (030) 28447-123 *E-mail:* info@dornier-verlage.de *Web Site:* www.dornier-verlage.de, pg 204

Brandes & Apsel Verlag GmbH (Germany) *Tel:* (069) 957 301 86 *Fax:* (069) 957 301 87 *E-mail:* brandes-apsel@doodees.de *Web Site:* www.brandes-apsel-verlag.de, pg 204

Brandon Book Publishers Ltd (Ireland) *Tel:* (066) 9151463 *Fax:* (066) 9151234 *Web Site:* www.brandonbooks.com, pg 358

Christian Brandstaetter Verlagsgesellschaft mbH (Austria) *Tel:* (01) 512 15 43 *Fax:* (01) 512 15 43-231 *E-mail:* cbv@oebv.co.at *Web Site:* www.brandstaetter-verlag.at, pg 49

Oscar Brandstetter Verlag GmbH & Co KG (Germany) *Tel:* (0611) 9 91 20-0 *Fax:* (0611) 3 08 37 85 *E-mail:* brandstetter-verlag@t-online.de *Web Site:* www.brandstetter-verlag.de, pg 204

Editora Brasil-America (EBAL) SA (Brazil) *Tel:* (021) 5800303 *Fax:* (021) 5801637, pg 79

Editora do Brasil SA (Brazil) *Tel:* (011) 222 0211 *Fax:* (011) 222 5583, pg 79

Instituto Brasileiro de Informacao em Ciencia e Tecnologia (Brazil) *Tel:* (061) 217-6360; (061) 217-6350 *Fax:* (061) 226-2677 *E-mail:* webmaster@ibict.br *Web Site:* www.ibict.br, pg 79, 1559

Brasilia Editora (J Carvalho Branco) (Portugal) *Tel:* (02) 315854 *Fax:* (02) 2055854, pg 529

Editora Brasiliense SA (Brazil) *Tel:* (011) 6198-1488 *Fax:* (011) 6198-1488 *E-mail:* brasilienseedit@uol.com.br *Web Site:* www.editorabrasiliense.com.br, pg 79

Livraria Brasiliense Editora SA (Brazil) *Tel:* (011) 8250122 *Fax:* (011) 673024, pg 1303

Brasilivros Editora e Distribuidora Ltda (Brazil) *Tel:* (011) 3284-8155 *Fax:* (011) 2850305; (011) 2856406, pg 79

Brassey's UK Ltd (United Kingdom) *Tel:* (020) 7221 2213; (020) 7314 1469 (sales) *Fax:* (020) 7221 6455; (020) 7314 1594 (sales) *E-mail:* enquiries@chrysalis.com *Web Site:* www.chrysalis.co.uk/books/publisher/brasseys, pg 670

Technische Universitaet Braunschweig (Germany) *Tel:* (0531) 391-5018; (0531) 391-5011 *Fax:* (0531) 391-5836 *E-mail:* ub@tu-bs.de *Web Site:* www.biblio.tu-bs.de, pg 1508

Brazilian PEN Centre (Brazil), pg 1397

Breakthrough Ltd - Breakthrough Publishers (Hong Kong) *Tel:* 2632 0257 *Fax:* 2632 0288 *Web Site:* www.teachlikethis.com, pg 315

Editions Breal (France) *Tel:* (01) 48 12 22 22 *Fax:* (01) 48 12 22 39 *E-mail:* infos@editions-breal.fr *Web Site:* www.editions-breal.fr, pg 151

Nicholas Brealey Publishing (United Kingdom) *Tel:* (020) 7239 0360 *Fax:* (020) 7239 0370 *E-mail:* sales@nbrealey-books.com *Web Site:* www.nbrealey-books.com, pg 670

Bredero (Belgium) *Tel:* (014) 31-84-61 *Fax:* (014) 70-02-05 *Web Site:* www.bredero.be, pg 1302

Bredero (Netherlands Antilles) *Tel:* (09) 7376751, pg 493

Breedon Books Publishing Company Ltd (United Kingdom) *Tel:* (01332) 384235 *Fax:* (01332) 292755 *E-mail:* sales@breedonpublishing.co.uk *Web Site:* www.breedonbooks.co.uk, pg 670

Breese Books Ltd (United Kingdom) *Tel:* (020) 7727 9426 *Fax:* (020) 7229 3395 *E-mail:* mbreese999@aol.com *Web Site:* www.sherlockholmes.co.uk, pg 670

Breitkopf & Hartel (Germany) *Tel:* (0611) 450080 *Fax:* (0611) 4500859; (0611) 4500860; (0611) 4500861 *E-mail:* info@breitkopf.com *Web Site:* www.breitkopf.com; www.breitkopf.de, pg 204

Emgleo Breiz (France) *Tel:* (02) 98 44 89 42 *Fax:* (02) 98 02 68 17 *E-mail:* andrelemercier@hotmail.com; brud.nevez@wanadoo.fr *Web Site:* emgleo.breiz.online.fr, pg 151

Breklumer Buchhandlung und Verlag (Germany) *Tel:* (04671) 910020 *Fax:* (04671) 910030 *E-mail:* verlag@breklumer.de *Web Site:* www.breklumer.de, pg 204

Editions Jacques Bremond (France) *Tel:* (04) 66 57 45 61; (06) 78 51 48 15 *Fax:* (04) 66 37 27 40 *E-mail:* editions-jacques-bremond@wanadoo.fr, pg 151

Joh & Sohn Brendow Verlag GmbH (Germany) *Tel:* (02841) 809-0 *Fax:* (02841) 97761-30 *E-mail:* info@brendow-verlag.de *Web Site:* www.brendow.de, pg 204

Edizioni Brenner (Italy) *Tel:* (0984) 74537 *Fax:* (0984) 74537, pg 379

Verlag Das Brennglas (Germany) *Tel:* (09342) 915843 *Fax:* (09342) 915843 *E-mail:* info@das-brennglas.com *Web Site:* www.brennglas.com, pg 204

The Brenthurst Press (Pty) Ltd (South Africa) *Tel:* (011) 6466024 *Fax:* (011) 4861651 *E-mail:* orders@brenthurst.co.az *Web Site:* www.brenthurst.org.za, pg 563

Brepols Publishers NV (Belgium) *Tel:* (014) 448020 *Fax:* (014) 428919 *E-mail:* info@brepols.net *Web Site:* www.brepols.net, pg 64

Breslich & Foss Ltd (United Kingdom) *Tel:* (020) 7819 3990 *Fax:* (020) 7819 3998 *E-mail:* sales@breslichfoss.com, pg 671

Breslov Research Institute (Israel) *Tel:* (02) 5824641 *Fax:* (02) 5825542 *E-mail:* info@breslov.org *Web Site:* www.breslov.org/catalog.html, pg 365

Alain Brethes Editions (France) *Tel:* (02) 40 77 35 11; (02) 51 13 04 55, pg 151

Editore Giorgio Bretschneider (Italy) *Tel:* (06) 6879361 *Fax:* (06) 6864543 *E-mail:* info@bretschneider.it *Web Site:* www.bretschneider.it, pg 379

Brewin Books Ltd (United Kingdom) *Tel:* (01527) 854228 *Fax:* (01527) 852746 *E-mail:* enquiries@brewinbooks.com *Web Site:* www.brewinbooks.com, pg 671

Editions BRGM (France) *Tel:* (02) 38 64 30 28 *Fax:* (02) 38 64 36 82 *E-mail:* editions@brgm.fr *Web Site:* editions.brgm.fr, pg 151

Brick Row Publishing Co Ltd (New Zealand) *Tel:* (09) 4106993 *Fax:* (09) 4106993, pg 494

The Bridge Book Co Ltd (United Kingdom) *Tel:* (0207) 697-3000 *Fax:* (0207) 700-4552 *E-mail:* bridgepem@aol.com, pg 1349

Bridge Books (United Kingdom) *Tel:* (01978) 358661 *Fax:* (01978) 262377, pg 671

Bridge Bookshop Ltd (United Kingdom) *Tel:* (01624) 833378 *Fax:* (01624) 835381, pg 1349

Bridge To Peace Publications (Australia) *Tel:* (02) 9875 1912 *E-mail:* books@bridgetopeace.com.au; adesso@bridgetopeace.com.au *Web Site:* www.bridgetopeace.com.au, pg 16

Bridgeway Publications (Australia) *Tel:* (07) 3390 4323 *Fax:* (07) 3390 4323 *E-mail:* info@bridgeway.org.au *Web Site:* www.bridgeway.org.au, pg 16

Brigg Verlag Franz-Joset Buchler KG (Germany) *Tel:* (0821) 78094660 *Fax:* (0821) 78094661, pg 204

Bright Arts Hong Kong Ltd (Hong Kong) *Tel:* 25620119 *Fax:* 25657031 *E-mail:* william@brightartshk.com *Web Site:* www.brightartshk.com, pg 1177

Bright Book Centre (Pvt) Ltd (Sri Lanka) *Tel:* (0112) 434770 *Fax:* (0112) 333279; (0112) 43470, pg 1343

Bright Concepts Printing House (Philippines) *Tel:* (045) 9612865 *E-mail:* dawnphilatelics@yahoo.com, pg 518

Bright Future Printing Co Ltd (Hong Kong) *Tel:* 2515 1776 *Fax:* 2897 2799; 2558 1717, pg 1155, 1177

Brijbasi Printers Pvt Ltd (India) *Tel:* (011) 6914115; (011) 6841897 *Fax:* (011) 6837553, pg 331

Brill Academic Publishers (Netherlands) *Tel:* (071) 53 53 500 *Fax:* (071) 53 17 532 *E-mail:* cs@brill.nl *Web Site:* www.brill.nl, pg 479

E J Brill, Robert Brown & Associates (Australia) *Tel:* (063) 318577 *Fax:* (063) 321273, pg 16

Brilliant Publications (United Kingdom) *Tel:* (01525) 229720 *Fax:* (01525) 229725 *E-mail:* sales@brilliantpublications.co.uk *Web Site:* www.brilliantpublications.co.uk, pg 671

Brimax Books (United Kingdom) *Tel:* (01243) 792 489 *Fax:* (020) 7531 8607, pg 671

Brinque Book Editora de Livros Ltda (Brazil) *Tel:* (011) 8428142 *Fax:* (011) 8432235 *E-mail:* brinquebook@infantil.net, pg 79

The British Academy (United Kingdom) *Tel:* (020) 7969 5200 *Fax:* (020) 7969 5300 *E-mail:* secretary@britac.ac.uk *Web Site:* www.britac.ac.uk, pg 671

British & Irish Association of Law Librarians (United Kingdom) *Tel:* (01926) 491717 *Fax:* (01926) 491717 *E-mail:* holborn@linclib.sonnet.co.uk *Web Site:* www.biall.org.uk, pg 1572

British Association of Communicators in Business Ltd (CIB) (United Kingdom) *Tel:* (0870) 121 7606 *Fax:* (0870) 121 7601 *E-mail:* enquiries@cib.uk.com *Web Site:* www.cib.uk.com, pg 1290

British Copyright Council (United Kingdom) *Tel:* (020) 788 122 *Fax:* (020) 788 847 *E-mail:* copyright@bcc2.demon.co.uk *Web Site:* www.editor.net/bcc, pg 1290

British Council Library (Malaysia) *Tel:* (03) 2723 7900 *Fax:* (03) 2713 6599 *E-mail:* information@britishcouncil.org.my *Web Site:* www.britcoun.org/malaysia, pg 1526

British Council Library (Tunisia) *Tel:* (01) 259 053; (01) 351 754 *Fax:* (01) 353 411 *E-mail:* info@tn.britishcouncil.org *Web Site:* www.britishcouncil.org/tunisia, pg 1551

British Council Library (Yemen) *Tel:* (01) 448 356; (01) 448 357; (01) 448 358; (01) 448 359 *Fax:* (01) 448 360 *E-mail:* britishcouncil@ye.britishcouncil.org *Web Site:* www.britishcouncil.org/yemen, pg 1555

The British Council, Design, Publishing & Print Department (United Kingdom) *Tel:* (020) 7930 8466 *Fax:* (020) 7389 6347 *E-mail:* general.enquiries@britcoun.org *Web Site:* www.britishcouncil.org, pg 671

British Council Information Resource Centre (Sri Lanka) *Tel:* (01) 581171 *Fax:* (01) 587079 *E-mail:* enquiries@britishcouncil.lk *Web Site:* www.britishcouncil.lk, pg 1546

British Council Libraries (India) *Tel:* (011) 371 1401 *Fax:* (011) 371 0717 *E-mail:* delhi.library@in.britishcouncil.org *Web Site:* www.bclindia.org/library, pg 1515

British Council Library (Bangladesh) *Tel:* (02) 861 8905-7; (02) 861 8867-8 *Fax:* (02) 861 3375; (02) 861 3255 *E-mail:* dhaka.enquiries@bd.britishcouncil.org *Web Site:* www.britishcouncil.org/bangladesh/, pg 1493

British Council Library (Colombia) *Tel:* (01) 618 0118; (01) 618 7680 *Fax:* (01) 218 7754 *E-mail:* brit.council@bc-bogota.bcouncil.org; info@britishcouncil.org.co *Web Site:* www.britishcouncil.org/colombia/, pg 1498

British Council Library (Cyprus) *Tel:* (022) 585000 *Fax:* (022) 677257 *E-mail:* enquiries@britishcouncil.org.cy *Web Site:* www.britcoun.org/cyprus, pg 1500

British Council Library (Ethiopia) *Tel:* (01) 55 00 22 *Fax:* (01) 55 25 44 *E-mail:* bc.addisababa@et.britishcouncil.org *Web Site:* www.britishcouncil.org/ethiopia/index.htm, pg 1504

British Council Library (Ghana) *Tel:* (051) 23462; (051) 37197 *Fax:* (051) 26725 *E-mail:* infokumasi@gh.britishcouncil.org *Web Site:* www.britishcouncil.org/ghana, pg 1512

British Council Library (Hong Kong) *Tel:* 2913 5100 *Fax:* 2913 5102 *E-mail:* info@britishcouncil.org.hk *Web Site:* www.britishcouncil.org.hk, pg 1514

British Council Library (Indonesia) *Tel:* (021) 252 4115 *Fax:* (021) 252 4129 *E-mail:* information@britishcouncil.or.id *Web Site:* www.britishcouncil.or.id, pg 1516

British Council Library (Jordan) *Tel:* (06) 4636147; (06) 4636148 *Fax:* (06) 4656413 *E-mail:* information@britishcouncil.org.jo *Web Site:* www.britishcouncil.org.jo, pg 1522

British Council Library (Lesotho) *Tel:* 312609 *Fax:* 310363 *E-mail:* general.enquiries@bc-lesotho.bcouncil.org, pg 1525

British Council Library (Malawi) *Tel:* 773 244 *Fax:* 772 945 *E-mail:* info@britishcouncil.org.mw *Web Site:* www.britishcouncil.org/malawi, pg 1526

British Council Library (Mauritius) *Tel:* 4549550; 4549551; 4549552 *Fax:* 4549553 *E-mail:* general.enquiries@mu.britishcouncil.org *Web Site:* www.britishcouncil.org/mauritius, pg 1528

British Council Library (Morocco) *Tel:* (037) 76 08 36 *Fax:* (037) 76 08 50 *E-mail:* bc@britishcouncil.org.ma *Web Site:* www2.britishcouncil.org/morocco, pg 1529

British Council Library (Nepal) *Tel:* (01) 4410 798 *Fax:* (01) 4410 545 *Web Site:* www.britishcouncil.org/nepal, pg 1530

British Council Library (Pakistan) *Tel:* (051) 111 424 424 *Toll Free Tel:* 0800 22000 *Fax:* (051) 111 425 425 *E-mail:* info@britishcouncil.org.pk *Web Site:* www.britishcouncil.org.pk, pg 1535

British Council Library (Sierra Leone) *Tel:* (022) 222223; (022) 222227; (022) 2224683 *Fax:* (022) 224123 *E-mail:* bcouncil@sierratel.sl *Web Site:* www.britishcouncil.org/sierraleone, pg 1542

The British Council Library (Spain) *Tel:* (091) 337 3500 *Fax:* (091) 337 3573 *E-mail:* madrid@britishcouncil.es *Web Site:* www.britishcouncil.es, pg 1545

British Council Library (Sudan) *Tel:* (0183) 780817; (0183) 777310 *Fax:* (0183) 774935 *E-mail:* info@sd.britishcouncil.org *Web Site:* www.britishcouncil.org/sudan, pg 1546

British Council Library (United Republic of Tanzania) *Tel:* (022) 2116574; (022) 2118255; (022) 2138303; (022) 2116575; (022) 2116576 *Fax:* (022) 2116669; (022) 2116577 *E-mail:* info@britishcouncil.or.tz *Web Site:* www.britishcouncil.org/tanzania, pg 1549

British Council Library (Thailand) *Tel:* (02) 652 5480; (02) 652 5489 *Fax:* (02) 253 5312 *E-mail:* bc.bangkok@britcoun.or.th *Web Site:* www.britishcouncil.or.th, pg 1550

British Council Library & Resource Centre (Greece) *Tel:* (0210) 369 2333 *Fax:* (0210) 363 4769 *E-mail:* general.enquiries@britcoun.gr *Web Site:* www.britishcouncil.gr/infoexch/greinfll.htm, pg 1513

British Educational Communication & Technology Agency (BECTA) (United Kingdom) *Tel:* (024) 7641 6994 *Fax:* (024) 7641 1418 *E-mail:* becta@becta.org.uk *Web Site:* www.becta.org.uk, pg 671

British Fantasy Society (BFS) (United Kingdom) *Tel:* (0161) 6004125 *E-mail:* info@britishfantasysociety.org.uk *Web Site:* www.britishfantasysociety.org.uk, pg 1406

British Guild of Travel Writers (United Kingdom) *Tel:* (020) 8749 1128 *Fax:* (020) 8749 1128 *E-mail:* bgtw@garlandintl.co.uk *Web Site:* www.bgtw.org, pg 1290

British Horse Society (United Kingdom) *Tel:* (08701) 202 244 *Fax:* (01926) 707 800 *E-mail:* enquiry@bhs.org.uk *Web Site:* www.bhs.org.uk, pg 671

British Institute in Eastern Africa (Kenya) *Tel:* (02) 4343190; (02) 4343330 *Fax:* (02) 43365 *E-mail:* britinst@insightkenya.com *Web Site:* www.britac.ac.uk/institutes/eafrica, pg 433

The British Library (United Kingdom) *Tel:* (01937) 546585 *Fax:* (01937) 546586 *E-mail:* nbs-info@bl.uk *Web Site:* www.bl.uk, pg 671

The British Library (United Kingdom) *Tel:* (0870) 444 1500 *Web Site:* www.bl.uk, pg 1552

British Library Document Supply Centre (United Kingdom) *Tel:* (01937) 546060 *Fax:* (01937) 546333 *E-mail:* dsc-customer-services@bl.uk *Web Site:* www.bl.uk, pg 671

British Library Document Supply Centre (United Kingdom) *Tel:* (01937) 546060 *Fax:* (01937) 546333 *E-mail:* dsc-customer-services@bl.uk *Web Site:* www.bl.uk/services/document/contact.html, pg 1552

British Library, Newspaper Library (United Kingdom) *Tel:* (020) 7412 7353 *Fax:* (020) 7412 7379 *E-mail:* newspaper@bl.uk *Web Site:* www.bl.uk, pg 1552

British Library of Political & Economic Science (United Kingdom) *Tel:* (020) 7955 7229 *Fax:* (020) 7955 7454 *E-mail:* library@lse.ac.uk *Web Site:* www.lse.ac.uk/library, pg 1552

British Library Oriental & India Office Collections (United Kingdom) *Tel:* (020) 7412 7873 *Fax:* (020) 7412 7641 *E-mail:* oioc-enquiries@bl.uk *Web Site:* www.bl.uk, pg 1552

British Library Publications (United Kingdom) *Tel:* (020) 7412 7000 *Fax:* (020) 7412 7768 *E-mail:* enquiries@bl.uk *Web Site:* www.bl.uk, pg 672

The British Library, Science Technology & Innovation Information Services (United Kingdom) *Tel:* (020) 7412 7495; (020) 7412 7494; (020) 7412 7496 *E-mail:* scitech@bl.uk; social-policy@bl.uk; patents-information@bl.uk *Web Site:* www.bl.uk, pg 1552

British Museum Press (United Kingdom) *Tel:* (020) 7637 1292 *Fax:* (020) 7436 7315 *E-mail:* customerservices@bmcompany.co.uk; information@thebritishmuseum.ac.uk *Web Site:* www.britishmuseum.co.uk, pg 672

British Printing Industries Federation (BPIF) (United Kingdom) *Tel:* (020) 7915 8300 *Fax:* (020) 7405 7784 *E-mail:* info@bpif.org.uk *Web Site:* www.bpif.org.uk, pg 1290

The British Science Fiction Association Ltd (BSFA Ltd) (United Kingdom) *E-mail:* bsfa@enterprise.net *Web Site:* www.bsfa.co.uk, pg 1407

British Sisalkraft Ltd (United Kingdom) *Tel:* (01634) 292700 *Fax:* (01634) 291029 *E-mail:* sales@bsk-laminating.com *Web Site:* www.bsk-laminating.com, pg 1163

British Tourist Authority (United Kingdom) *Tel:* (020) 8846 9000 *Fax:* (020) 8846 0302 *Web Site:* www.visitbritain.com, pg 672

Verlag Ekkehard & Ulrich Brockhaus GmbH & Co KG (Germany) *Tel:* (0202) 44 74 74; (0172) 2 55 59 61 *Fax:* (0202) 42 82 82 *E-mail:* mail@verlag-brockhaus.de *Web Site:* www.verlag-brockhaus.de, pg 204

F A Brockhaus GmbH (Germany) *Tel:* (0621) 3901-01 *Fax:* (0621) 3901-391 *Web Site:* www.brockhaus.de, pg 204

Brockhaus/Kommission GmbH (Germany) *Tel:* (07154) 1327-0 *Fax:* (07154) 1327-13, pg 204

R Brockhaus Verlag (Germany) *Tel:* (02302) 930 93 800 *Fax:* (02302) 930 93 801 *E-mail:* info@brockhaus-verlag.de *Web Site:* www.brockhaus-verlag.de, pg 204

Brody (Czech Republic) *Tel:* (02) 22252077 *Fax:* (02) 22252077 *E-mail:* brody@draha.czcom.cz, pg 122

Vanden Broele NV (Belgium) *Tel:* (050) 456 177 *Fax:* (050) 456 199 *E-mail:* graphic.group@vandenbroele.be *Web Site:* www.vandenbroele.be, pg 64

Broese BV (Netherlands) *Tel:* (030) 2335200 *Fax:* (030) 2314071 *E-mail:* info@broese.net *Web Site:* www.broese.net, pg 1329

Brombergs Bokforlag AB (Sweden) *Tel:* (08) 562 62 080 *Fax:* (08) 562 62 085 *E-mail:* info@brombergs.se *Web Site:* www.brombergs.se, pg 610

Edicions Bromera SL (Spain) *Tel:* (096) 2402254 *Fax:* (096) 2403191 *E-mail:* illa@bromera.com; bromera@bromera.com *Web Site:* www.bromera.com, pg 575

The Bronte Society (United Kingdom) *Tel:* (01535) 642323 *Fax:* (01535) 647131 *E-mail:* info@bronte.info *Web Site:* www.bronte.info, pg 1407

Brookers Ltd (New Zealand) *Tel:* (04) 4998178 *Fax:* (04) 4998173 *E-mail:* service@brookers.co.nz *Web Site:* www.brookers.co.nz, pg 494

Brookfield Press (Australia) *Tel:* (07) 3374 1053 *Fax:* (07) 3374 2059, pg 16

Brookfield Press (New Zealand) *Tel:* (09) 5765438 *Fax:* (09) 5736222, pg 494

Brooklands Books Ltd (United Kingdom) *Tel:* (01932) 865051 *Fax:* (01932) 868803 *E-mail:* info@brooklands-books.com *Web Site:* www.brooklands-books.com, pg 672

Broteria Associacao Cultural e Cientifica (Portugal) *Tel:* (021) 3961660 *Fax:* (021) 3956629, pg 529

Curtis Brown (Australia) Pty Ltd (Australia) *Tel:* (02) 9331 5301 *Fax:* (02) 9360 3935 *E-mail:* info@curtisbrown.com.au, pg 1129

D Brown & Sons Ltd (United Kingdom) *Tel:* (01446) 771475 *Fax:* (01446) 771476, pg 1163, 1183, 1225

Ediciones Brown SA (Peru) *Tel:* (01) 4462753 *Fax:* (01) 4462753, pg 516

The Brown Reference Group PLC (United Kingdom) *Tel:* (020) 7920 7500 *Fax:* (020) 7920 7501 *E-mail:* info@brownreference.com *Web Site:* www.brownreference.com, pg 672

Brown, Son & Ferguson, Ltd (United Kingdom) *Tel:* (0141) 4291234 *Fax:* (0141) 4201694 *E-mail:* enquiry@skipper.co.uk *Web Site:* www.skipper.co.uk, pg 672

Brown Wells & Jacobs Ltd (United Kingdom) *Tel:* (020) 8771 5115 *Fax:* (020) 8771 9994 *E-mail:* postmaster@popking.demon.co.uk *Web Site:* www.bwj.org, pg 672

Browne's Bookstore (United Kingdom) *Tel:* (01223) 350968 *Fax:* (01223) 353456 *E-mail:* brownes_books@msn.com, pg 1349

F Bruckmann Munchen Verlag & Druck GmbH & Co Produkt KG (Germany) *Tel:* (089) 13 06 99 11 *Fax:* (089) 13 06 99 10 *E-mail:* info@bruckmann.de *Web Site:* www.bruckmann-verlag.de, pg 204

Brud Nevez (France) *Tel:* (02) 98 44 89 42 *Fax:* (02) 98 02 68 17, pg 151

Bruecke-Verlag Kurt Schmersow (Germany) *Tel:* (05121) 91 92 0 *Fax:* (05121) 91 92 20 *E-mail:* buchhaltung@bruecke-verlag.de *Web Site:* www.bruecke-verlag.de, pg 205

Bruehlsche Uni-Druckerei Verlag, der Giessener Anzeiger GmbH & Co KG (Germany) *Tel:* (0641) 95040 *Fax:* (0641) 9504100, pg 205

BRUEN-Verlag, Gorenflo (Germany) *Tel:* (06142) 61434 *Fax:* (06142) 61259 *E-mail:* 0614261434-1@t-online.de, pg 205

A W Bruna Uitgevers BV (Netherlands) *Tel:* (030) 2470411 *Fax:* (030) 2410018 *E-mail:* a.w.bruna@awbruna.nl *Web Site:* www.awbruna.nl, pg 480

Bruna BV (Netherlands) *Tel:* (0900) 1200 100 *E-mail:* klantenservice@bruna.com *Web Site:* www.bruna.nl, pg 1329

The Brunel Press (Brunei Darussalam) *Tel:* (03) 2344, pg 1304

Brunnen-Verlag Basel (Switzerland) *Tel:* (061) 234406 *Fax:* (061) 2956069 *E-mail:* brunnen-verlag@bluewin.ch, pg 620

Brunnen Bibel Panorama (Switzerland) *Tel:* (061) 295 60 03 *Fax:* (061) 295 60 68 *E-mail:* info@bibelpanorama.ch *Web Site:* www.bibelpanorama.ch, pg 1344

Brunnen-Verlag GmbH (Germany) *Tel:* (0641) 6059-0 *Fax:* (0641) 6059-100 *E-mail:* info@brunnen-verlag.de *Web Site:* www.brunnen-verlag.de, pg 205

Literaturagentur Andreas Brunner (Austria) *Tel:* (01) 5333191 *Fax:* (01) 5333191-15 *E-mail:* brunner@literaturagentur.at *Web Site:* www.literaturagentur.at, pg 1129

Editorial Bruno (Spain) *Tel:* (091) 724 48 00 *Fax:* (091) 361 31 33 *E-mail:* informacion@editorial-bruno.es *Web Site:* www.editorial-bruno.es, pg 575

Asociacion Editorial Bruno (Peru) *Tel:* (01) 4244134; (01) 4251248 *Fax:* (01) 4251248, pg 516

F Bruns Bokhandel og Forlag A/S (Norway) *Tel:* 73510022; 73509320 *Fax:* 73509320 *E-mail:* brunslb@online.no, pg 508

Etablissements Emile Bruylant SA (Belgium) *Tel:* (02) 512 98 45 *Fax:* (02) 511 72 02 *E-mail:* info@bruylant.be *Web Site:* www.bruylant.be, pg 64

Felicity Bryan (United Kingdom) *Tel:* (01865) 513816 *Fax:* (01865) 310055, pg 1138

Bryntirion Press (United Kingdom) *Tel:* (01656) 655886 *Fax:* (01656) 665919 *E-mail:* office@emw.org.uk *Web Site:* www.evangelicalmvt-wales.org/books/bryntirionpress/default.htm, pg 672

Bryntirion Press (United Kingdom) *Tel:* (01656) 655886 *Fax:* (01656) 656095 *E-mail:* office@emw.org.uk, pg 1290

Bryson Agency Australia Pty Ltd (Australia) *Tel:* (03) 9620 9100 *Fax:* (03) 9621 2788 *E-mail:* agency@bryson.com.au *Web Site:* www.bryson.com.au, pg 1129

BS Publications (India) *Tel:* (040) 23445600; (040) 23445601 *Fax:* (040) 23445611 *E-mail:* contactus@bspublications.net, pg 331

BSE Verlag Dr Bernhard Schuttengruber (Austria) *Tel:* (0316) 839600; (0316) 283170, pg 49

BSI British Standards Institution (United Kingdom) *Tel:* (020) 8996 9000 *Fax:* (020) 8996 7001 *E-mail:* info@bsi-global.com; cservices@bsi-global.com *Web Site:* www.bsi-global.com, pg 1290

BSMPS - M/s Bishen Singh Mahendra Pal Singh (India) *Tel:* (0135) 655748 *Fax:* (0135) 650107 *E-mail:* info@bishensinghbooks.com *Web Site:* www.bishensinghbooks.com, pg 331

Edizioni Bucalo SNC (Italy) *Tel:* (0773) 410036 *Fax:* (0773) 410036 *E-mail:* info@bucalo.it *Web Site:* www.bucalo.it, pg 379

C L Baader Buch & Offsetdruckere GmbH & Co KG (Germany) *Tel:* (07381) 791 *Fax:* (07381) 411412, pg 1155, 1176

C L Baader Buch & Offsetdruckere GmbH & Co KG (Germany) *Tel:* (07381) 791, pg 1216

C L Baader Buch & Offsetdruckere GmbH & Co KG (Germany) *Tel:* (07381) 791 *Fax:* (07381) 411412, pg 1235, 1245

Buch- und Kunstverlag Kleinheinrich (Germany) *Tel:* (0251) 4840193 *Fax:* (0251) 4840194, pg 205

Verlag Bucheli (Switzerland) *Tel:* (041) 741 77 55 *Fax:* (041) 741 71 15 *E-mail:* info@bucheli-verlag.ch *Web Site:* www.mueller-rueschlikon.ch/bucheli.htm, pg 620

Verlag C J Bucher GmbH (Germany) *Tel:* (089) 51480 *Fax:* (089) 5148-2229, pg 205

Bucher-Stierle GesmbH (Austria) *Tel:* (0662) 840114 *Fax:* (0662) 8401149 *E-mail:* buecher-stierle@members.debis.at, pg 1300

Buchervertriebsanstalt (Liechtenstein), pg 447

Editions Buchet-Chastel Pierre Zech Editeur (France) *Tel:* (01) 44 32 05 60 *Fax:* (01) 44 32 05 61 *E-mail:* buchet.chastel@wanadoo.fr *Web Site:* www.theatre-contemporain.net/editions/buchet/buchet.htm, pg 151

Der Buchfreund Universitats-Buchhandlung u Antiquariat Walter R Schaden (Austria) *Tel:* (01) 512 48 56; (01) 513 82 89 *Fax:* (01) 512 60 28 *E-mail:* buch.schaden@vienna.at *Web Site:* www.buch-schaden.at, pg 1300

Buchhandlung Holl & Knoll KG, Verlag Alte Uni (Germany) *Tel:* (07262) 4417 *Fax:* (07262) 7942 *E-mail:* alteuni@aol.com, pg 205

Buchheim-Verlag (Germany) *Tel:* (08157) 1221 *Fax:* (08157) 3143, pg 205

Buchkultur Verlags GmbH Zeitschrift fuer Literatur & Kunst (Austria) *Tel:* (01) 7863380 *Fax:* (01) 7863380-10 *E-mail:* office@buchkultur.net *Web Site:* www.buchkultur.net, pg 49

BuchMarkt Verlag K Werner GmbH (Germany) *Tel:* (02150) 9191-0 *Fax:* (02150) 919191 *E-mail:* redaktion@buchmarkt.de *Web Site:* www.buchmarkt.de, pg 205

C C Buchners Verlag GmbH & Co KG (Germany) *Tel:* (0951) 96 501-0 *Fax:* (0951) 61-774 *E-mail:* service@ccbuchner.de *Web Site:* www.ccbuchner.de, pg 205

Buchverlag Basler Zeitung (Switzerland) *Tel:* (061) 6391315 *Fax:* (061) 6391343 *E-mail:* order@baz.ch *Web Site:* www.baz.ch, pg 620

Buchverlag Junge Welt GmbH (Germany) *Tel:* (030) 231079 0 *Fax:* (030) 2826989 *E-mail:* bvjw.berlin@t-online.de *Web Site:* www.buchverlagjw.com, pg 205

Buchverlage Langen-Mueller/Herbig (Germany) *Tel:* (089) 2 90 88-0 *E-mail:* info@herbig.net *Web Site:* www.herbig.net, pg 205

Buchverleger-Verband der Deutschsprachigen Schweiz (VVDS) (Switzerland) *Tel:* (01) 421 28 00 *Fax:* (01) 421 28 18 *E-mail:* sbvv@swissbooks.ch *Web Site:* www.swissbooks.ch, pg 1285

The Buckman Agency (United Kingdom) *Tel:* (01608) 683677 *Fax:* (01608) 683449, pg 1139

Budapesti Kozgazdasagtudomanyi es Allamigazoatasi Luyutemi Egyetem Kozponti Konyvtar (Hungary) *Tel:* (01) 2176827 *Fax:* (01) 2174910 *E-mail:* konyvtar@lib.bkae.hu *Web Site:* www.lib.bke.hu, pg 1514

Budapesti Muszaki es Gazdasagtudomanyi Egyetem (Hungary) *Tel:* (01) 4632441; (01) 4632440, pg 321

Budapesti Muszaki es Guzdasagtudomanyi Egyetem Orszagos Muszaki Informacios Kozpont es Konyvtar (Hungary) *Tel:* (01) 463-3534; (01) 463-1069 *Fax:* (01) 463-2440 *E-mail:* kolcs@omikk.bme.hu *Web Site:* www.bme.hu; www.omikk.bme.hu, pg 1514

Buddhist Publication Society Inc (Sri Lanka) *Tel:* (08) 223679; (08) 237283 *Fax:* (08) 223679 *E-mail:* bps@ids.lk; bps@metta.lk *Web Site:* www.metta.lk, pg 605

Buechergilde Gutenberg (Germany) *Tel:* (069) 27 39 08-0 *Fax:* (069) 27 39 08-25; (069) 27 39 08-26 *E-mail:* service@buechergilde.de *Web Site:* www.buechergilde.de, pg 1252

Buchergilde Gutenberg AG (Switzerland), pg 1256

Buchergilde Gutenberg Verlagsgesellschaft mbH (Germany) *Tel:* (069) 27 39 08-0 *Fax:* (069) 27 39 08-26; (069) 27 39 08-25 *E-mail:* service@buechergilde.de *Web Site:* www.buechergilde.de, pg 205

Buechse der Pandora Verlags-GmbH (Germany) *Tel:* (06441) 911312 *Fax:* (06441) 911314, pg 205

Buffetti (Italy) *Tel:* (06) 231951 *Fax:* (06) 2389796 *Web Site:* www.buffetti.it, pg 379

Bugra Suisse Burchler Grafino AG (Switzerland) *Tel:* (031) 548111 *Fax:* (031) 544562, pg 620

Buijten en Schipperheijn BV Drukkerij en Uitgeversmaatschappij (Netherlands) *Tel:* (020) 5241010 *Fax:* (020) 5241011 *E-mail:* info@bijten.nl, pg 480

Building & Road Research Institute (BRRI) (Ghana) *Tel:* (051) 60064; (051) 60065 *Fax:* (051) 60080 *E-mail:* brri@ghana.com *Web Site:* www.csir.org.gh/brri.html, pg 303

Building Information Ltd (Finland) *Tel:* (09) 549 5570 *Fax:* (09) 5495 5320 *E-mail:* rakennustieto@rakennustieto.fi *Web Site:* www.rakennustieto.fi, pg 141

De l'edition Bukie Banane (Mauritius) *Tel:* 4542327 *E-mail:* limem@intnet.mu *Web Site:* pages.intnet.mu/develog/, pg 461

PT Bulan Bintang (Indonesia) *Tel:* (021) 3901651; (021) 3901652 *Fax:* (021) 3107027, pg 354

Bulawayo Public Library (Zimbabwe) *Tel:* (09) 60965 *E-mail:* bpl@netconnect.co.zw *Web Site:* www.angelfire.com/kg/bpl, pg 1556

Bulgarian Academy of Sciences, Central Library (Bulgaria) *Tel:* (02) 989-84-46 *Fax:* (02) 981-66-29; (02) 986-25-23; (02) 988-04-48 *E-mail:* webadmin@bas.bg *Web Site:* www.bas.bg/, pg 1496

Bulgarian Academy of Sciences, Institute of Literature (Bulgaria) *Tel:* (02) 989-84-46 *Fax:* (02) 981-66-29; (02) 986-25-23; (02) 988-04-48 *Web Site:* www.bas.bg, pg 1398

Bulgarian National ISSN Centre (Bulgaria) *Tel:* (02) 9461165; (02) 9882811 *Fax:* (02) 435495 *E-mail:* issn@nationallibary.bg *Web Site:* www.nationallibrary.bg, pg 1263

Bulgarian Writers' Union (Bulgaria) *Tel:* (02) 898346 *Fax:* (02) 835411, pg 1398

Bulgarski Houdozhnik Publishers (Bulgaria) *Tel:* (02) 467285; (02) 43351; (02) 43278 *Fax:* (02) 467285, pg 93

Bulgarski Pissatel (Bulgaria) *Tel:* (02) 875873; (02) 873454; (02) 874527 *Fax:* (02) 872495, pg 93

Bulvest 2000 Ltd (Bulgaria) *Tel:* (02) 9833286; (02) 9833169 *Fax:* (02) 9815464 *E-mail:* bulvest@internet-bg.net, pg 93

Bulzoni Editore SRL (Le Edizioni Universitarie d'Italia) (Italy) *Tel:* (06) 4455207 *Fax:* (06) 4450355 *E-mail:* bulzoni@bulzoni.it *Web Site:* www.bulzoni.it, pg 379

Bum-Woo Publishing Co (Republic of Korea) *Tel:* (02) 7172121; (02) 7172122 *Fax:* (02) 7170429 *E-mail:* yhd@bumwoos.co.kr, pg 437

Bumi Aksara PT (Indonesia) *Tel:* (021) 4717049; (021) 4700988 *Fax:* (021) 4700989, pg 354

Bun-ichi Sogo Shuppan (Japan) *Tel:* (03) 3235-7341 *Fax:* (03) 3269-1402 *E-mail:* bunichi@bun-ichi.co.jp *Web Site:* www.bun-ichi.co.jp/, pg 415

Bund demokratischer Wissenschaftlerinnen und Wissenschaftler eV (BdWi) (Germany) *Tel:* (06421) 2 13 95 *Fax:* (06421) 2 46 54 *E-mail:* verlag@bdwi.de *Web Site:* www.bdwi.de, pg 205

Bund Deutscher Schriftsteller (Germany) *Tel:* (06074) 47566 *Fax:* (06074) 47540 *Web Site:* www.bund-deutscher-schriftsteller.de, pg 206

Bund fuer deutsche Schrift und Sprache (Germany) *Tel:* (05381) 46355 *Fax:* (05381) 46355 *E-mail:* verwaltung@bfds.de *Web Site:* www.bfds.de, pg 206

Bund-Verlag GmbH (Germany) *Tel:* (069) 79 50 10 0 *Fax:* (069) 79 50 10 10 *E-mail:* kontakt@bund-verlag.de *Web Site:* www.bund-verlag.de, pg 206

Bunda College of Agriculture Library (Malawi) *Tel:* 277222 *Fax:* 277251 *E-mail:* bundalibrary@malawi.net *Web Site:* www.unima.mw/bunda/library.htm, pg 1526

Bundes-Verlag GmbH (Germany) *Tel:* (02302) 930 93-0 *E-mail:* info@bundesverlag.de *Web Site:* www.bundes-verlag.de, pg 206

Bundesanzeiger Verlagsgesellschaft (Germany) *Tel:* (0221) 9 76 68-0 *Fax:* (0221) 9 76 68-278 *E-mail:* vcotiicb@bundesanzeiger.de *Web Site:* www.bundesanzeiger.de, pg 206

Bundesverband der Dolmetscher und Ubersetzer eV (BDU) (Germany) *Tel:* (030) 88712830 *Fax:* (030) 88712840 *E-mail:* bgs@bdue.de *Web Site:* www.bdue.de, pg 1147

Bundesverband Deutscher Kunstverleger eV (Germany) *Tel:* (069) 629120 *Fax:* (069) 629120 *Web Site:* www.bdkv.de, pg 1270

Bunkasha Publishing Co Ltd (Japan) *Tel:* (03) 3222-5111 *Fax:* (03) 3222-3672 *E-mail:* fukai@bunkasha.co.jp *Web Site:* www.bunkasha.co.jp, pg 415

Bunkashobo-Hakubun-Sha (Japan) *Tel:* (03) 3947-2034 *Fax:* (03) 3947-4976, pg 415

Editions du Buot (France) *Tel:* (01) 53388110 *Fax:* (01) 53388119, pg 151

Burall Floraprint Ltd (United Kingdom) *Tel:* (0870) 728 72 22 *Fax:* (0870) 728 72 77 *E-mail:* floraprint@burall.com *Web Site:* www.bflora.com, pg 672

Burckhardthaus-Laetare Verlag GmbH (Germany) *Tel:* (069) 8400030 *Fax:* (069) 84000333, pg 206

Aenne Burda Verlag (Germany) *Tel:* (0781) 843322 *Fax:* (0781) 843386, pg 206

Bureau des Longitudes (France) *Tel:* (01) 43 26 59 02 *Fax:* (01) 43 26 80 90 *E-mail:* contact@bureau-des-longitudes.fr *Web Site:* www.bureau-des-longitudes.fr, pg 151

Bureau Intellectual Property (Netherlands Antilles) *Tel:* (09) 465 7800 *Fax:* (09) 465 7815 *E-mail:* info@bureau-intellectual-property.org, pg 1279

Bureau of Ghana Languages (Ghana) *Tel:* (021) 665461; (021) 65194, pg 303

Bureau of Ghana Languages (Ghana) *Tel:* (021) 665461, pg 1148

Bureau of International Exchange of Publications (Taiwan, Province of China) *Tel:* (02) 23169132 *Fax:* (02) 23110155 *E-mail:* shiny@msg.ncl.edu.tw *Web Site:* www.ncl.edu.tw, pg 1549

Bureau of Resource Sciences (Australia) *Tel:* (02) 6272 4282 *Fax:* (02) 6272 4747, pg 16

Bureau of Statistics (United Republic of Tanzania) *Tel:* (051) 111634; (051) 111635 *Fax:* (051) 112352 *E-mail:* kento@raha.com, pg 643

Ulrich Burgdorf/Homeopathic Publishing House (Germany) *Tel:* (0551) 796050 *Fax:* (0551) 796955 *E-mail:* Burgdorf-Verlag@t-online.de *Web Site:* www.burgdorf-verlag.de, pg 206

Fachverlag fur Burgerinformation, Eigenvelag (Austria) *Tel:* (0316) 686727 *Fax:* (0316) 6867274 *E-mail:* fachverlag@sime.com, pg 49

Burgewood Books (Australia) *Tel:* (03) 98442512 (Australia); (03) 9844 2512 (International) *Fax:* (03) 98440664 (Australia); (03) 9844 0664 (International), pg 1298

Edmund Burke Publisher (Ireland) *Tel:* (01) 2882159; (01) 6719777 *Fax:* (01) 2834080 *E-mail:* deburca@indigo.ie *Web Site:* www.deburcararebooks.com, pg 358

Burnet's Books (Australia) *Tel:* (02) 6778 4682 *Fax:* (02) 6778 4516 *E-mail:* burnet@ozbook.com *Web Site:* www.ozbook.com, pg 1298

Kartographischer Verlag Busche GmbH (Germany) *Tel:* (0231) 4 44 77-0 *Fax:* (0231) 4 44 77-77 *E-mail:* info@kvbusche.de *Web Site:* www.kvbusche.de, pg 206

Anita und Klaus Buscher B & B Verlag (Germany) *Tel:* (06321) 968485 *Fax:* (06321) 968486, pg 206

Arnold Busck International Boghandel A/S (Denmark) *Tel:* 33733500 *Fax:* 33733535 *E-mail:* arnold@busck.dk *Web Site:* www.busck.dk, pg 1308

Bush Press Communications Ltd (New Zealand) *Tel:* (09) 486 2667 *Fax:* (09) 486 2667 *E-mail:* bush.press@clear.net.nz, pg 494

Bushwood Books (United Kingdom) *Tel:* (0208) 3928585 *Fax:* (0208) 3929876 *E-mail:* bushwd@aol.com, pg 1349

Business & Industrial Publication Co Ltd (Hong Kong) *Tel:* 25273377 *Fax:* 28667732, pg 315

Business Bureau Christchurch Ltd (New Zealand) *Tel:* (03) 3585287, pg 494

YELLOW PAGES

Business Center for Academic Societies Japan (Japan) *Tel:* (03) 5814-5800 *Fax:* (03) 5814-5823 *E-mail:* nuehara@bcasj.or.jp; haraki@bcasj.or.jp *Web Site:* www.bcasj.or.jp, pg 416

Business Contact BV (Netherlands) *Tel:* (020) 5249800 *Fax:* (020) 6276851 *E-mail:* info@contact-bv.nl *Web Site:* www.boekenwereld.com, pg 480

Business Directory of Lanka Ltd (Sri Lanka) *Tel:* (01) 2695095; (074) 721560; (074) 721561 *Fax:* (074) 721560 *E-mail:* info@lanka.com *Web Site:* www.lanka.com, pg 606

Business Monitor International (United Kingdom) *Tel:* (020) 7248 0468 *Fax:* (020) 7248 0467 *E-mail:* subs@businessmonitor.com *Web Site:* www.businessmonitor.com, pg 672

Business Tutors (Barbados) *Tel:* (246) 428-5664 *Fax:* (246) 429-4854 *E-mail:* pchad@caribsurf.com, pg 62

Helmut Buske Verlag GmbH (Germany) *Tel:* (040) 2999580 *Fax:* (040) 29995820 *E-mail:* info@buske.de *Web Site:* www.buske.de, pg 206

Verlag Busse und Seewald GmbH (Germany) *Tel:* (05221) 77 5-0 *Fax:* (05221) 77 52 04 *E-mail:* info@busse-seewald.de *Web Site:* www.busse-seewald.de, pg 206

Butler & Tanner Inc (United States) *Tel:* 212-262-4753 *Fax:* 212-262-4779 *E-mail:* sales@nyc.butlerandtanner.com *Web Site:* www.butlerandtanner.com, pg 1228

Butler & Tanner Ltd (United Kingdom) *Tel:* (01373) 451500 *Fax:* (01373) 451333 *E-mail:* manufacturing@butlerandtanner.com *Web Site:* www.butlerandtanner.com, pg 1183, 1225, 1247

Butterworths Australia Ltd (Australia) *Tel:* (02) 9422 2189 *Toll Free Tel:* 800 772 772 *Fax:* (02) 9422 2406 *E-mail:* orders@butterworths.com; customer.relations@lexisnexis.com.au *Web Site:* www.butterworths.com.au, pg 16

Butterworths Hong Kong (Hong Kong) *Tel:* 2965-1400 *Fax:* 2976-0840 *E-mail:* customer.care@butterworths-hk.com *Web Site:* www.butterworths-hk.com, pg 316

Butterworths New Zealand Ltd (New Zealand) *Tel:* (04) 385 1479 *Fax:* (04) 385 1598 *E-mail:* Customer.Relations@butterworths.co.nz *Web Site:* www.butterworths.co.nz; www.lexisnexis.com/au/nz, pg 494

Butterworths Tolley (United Kingdom) *Tel:* (020) 8686 9141; (020) 8662 2000 (customer service) *Fax:* (020) 8686 3155; (020) 8662 2012 (customer service) *E-mail:* customer-services@butterworths.com, pg 673

Butzon & Bercker GmbH (Germany) *Tel:* (02832) 929-130 *Fax:* (02832) 929-139 *E-mail:* service@butzonbercker.de *Web Site:* www.butzonbercker.de, pg 206

BV Uitgevery NZV (Nederlandse Zondagsschool Vereniging) (Netherlands) *Tel:* (033) 460 60 11 *Fax:* (035) 460 60 20 *E-mail:* info@nzv.nl *Web Site:* www.nzv.nl, pg 480

Bwrdd Croeso Cymru (United Kingdom) *Tel:* (029) 2047 5214 *Fax:* (029) 2048 5031 *E-mail:* info@visitwales.com *Web Site:* www.visitwales.com, pg 673

Forlaget By och Bygd (Sweden) *Tel:* (08) 652 09 55, pg 610

Bycornute Books (United Kingdom) *Tel:* (01323) 649053, pg 1139

Byggforlaget (Sweden) *Tel:* (08) 665 36 50 *Fax:* (08) 667 39 49 *Web Site:* www.byggforlaget.se, pg 610

Byron Society (International) (United Kingdom) *Tel:* (01636) 816855 *Fax:* (01636) 816844 *Web Site:* www.byronsociety.com, pg 1407

BZZTOH Publishers (Netherlands) *Tel:* (070) 3632934 *Fax:* (070) 3631932 *E-mail:* info@bzztoh.nl *Web Site:* www.bzztoh.nl, pg 480

C & C Offset Printing Co Ltd (Hong Kong) *Tel:* 2666-4988 *Fax:* 2666-4938 *E-mail:* offsetprinting@candcprinting.com *Web Site:* www.ccoffset.com, pg 1155, 1177, 1217

C & C Offset Printing Co Ltd (United States) *Tel:* 503-233-1834 *Fax:* 503-233-7815 *E-mail:* portlandinfo@ccoffset.com *Web Site:* www.ccoffset.com, pg 1166, 1186, 1228

C&S Publications (New Zealand) *Tel:* (0812) 56807 *Fax:* (0812) 8966583, pg 494

C V Toko Buku Tropen (Indonesia) *Tel:* (021) 381 1669; (021) 381 3543; (021) 380 5938 *Fax:* (021) 380 0566 *E-mail:* tropen@cbn.net.id, pg 1318

Ca Luna Forlaget (Denmark) *Tel:* 86 82 86 88; 26 20 24 68 *Fax:* 86 82 86 64 *E-mail:* caluna@caluna.dk *Web Site:* www.caluna.dk, pg 130

Caann Verlag, Klaus Wagner (Germany) *Tel:* (08121) 9 32 71 *Fax:* (08121) 9 32 78 *E-mail:* info@caann-verlag.de *Web Site:* www.caann-verlag.de, pg 206

CAB International (United Kingdom) *Tel:* (01491) 832111 *Fax:* (01491) 833508 *E-mail:* corporate@cabi.org *Web Site:* www.cabi.org, pg 1290

Ediciones el Caballito SA (Mexico) *Tel:* (05) 5443284; (05) 5963400, pg 462

CABI Publishing (United Kingdom) *Tel:* (01491) 832111 *Fax:* (01491) 833508 *E-mail:* publishing@cabi.org *Web Site:* www.cabi-publishing.org, pg 673

Cabildo Insular de Gran Canaria Departamento de Ediciones (Spain) *Tel:* (0928) 219421 *Fax:* (0928) 381627 *E-mail:* webadmin@grancanaria.com *Web Site:* www.grancanaria.com, pg 575

Cabinet Conseil CCMLA (Morocco) *Tel:* (07) 770229; (07) 770264 *Fax:* (07) 770264, pg 474

Cacho Publishing House, Inc (Philippines) *Tel:* (02) 783011-13 *Fax:* (02) 6315244 *E-mail:* cacho@s.com.ph, pg 518

Cacho Publishing inc (Philippines) *Tel:* (02) 6318362; (02) 6318363; (02) 6318364; (02) 6318365 *Fax:* (02) 6315244 *E-mail:* cacho@mozcom.com, pg 1160

Cacho Publishing inc (Philippines) *Tel:* (02) 783011-13 *Fax:* (02) 6315244 *E-mail:* cacho@mozcom.com, pg 1222

Cacucci Editore (Italy) *Tel:* (080) 521 42 20 *Fax:* (080) 523 47 77 *E-mail:* info@cacucci.it *Web Site:* www.cacucci.it, pg 379

Cadans (Netherlands) *Tel:* (020) 6206263 *Fax:* (020) 4288540 *E-mail:* post@sjaloom.nl *Web Site:* www.sjaloom.com, pg 480

Cadence Publicacoes Internacionais Ltda (Brazil) *Tel:* (021) 2637885 *Fax:* (021) 2830812 *E-mail:* cadence@mtecnet.com.br, pg 79

Edizioni Cadmo SRL (Italy) *Tel:* (055) 50 18 1 *Fax:* (055) 50 18 201 *E-mail:* info@casalini.it *Web Site:* www.casalini.it, pg 379

Cadmos Verlag GmbH (Germany) *Tel:* (04131) 981 666 *Fax:* (04131) 981 668 *E-mail:* cadmos-verlag@tonline.de *Web Site:* www.cadmos.de, pg 206

Cadogan Guides (United Kingdom) *Tel:* (020) 8600 3550 *Fax:* (020) 8600 3599 *E-mail:* info@cadoganguides.com; editorial@cadoganguides.com; advertising@cadoganguides.com; publicity@cadoganguides.com; marketing@cadoganguides.com *Web Site:* www.cadoganguides.com, pg 673

Editions du Cadratin (France) *Tel:* (01) 42 81 52 23 *Fax:* (01) 42 82 17 01, pg 151

Caglayan Kitabevi (Turkey) *Tel:* (0212) 2454433 *Fax:* (0212) 1491794 *E-mail:* info@caglayan.com, pg 649

Editions des Cahiers Bourbonnais (France) *Tel:* (0470) 568 061 *Fax:* (0470) 568 080 *Web Site:* www.cahiers-bourbonnais.com, pg 151

Editions Cahiers d'Art (France) *Tel:* (01) 45487673 *Fax:* (01) 45449850 *E-mail:* cahiersart@aol.com, pg 151

Cahiers de la Renaissance Vaudoise (Switzerland) *Tel:* (021) 3121914 *Fax:* (021) 3126714 *E-mail:* courrier@ligue-vaudoise.ch *Web Site:* www.ligue-vaudoise.ch, pg 620

CAMARA BRASILEIRA DO LIVRO

Cahiers du Cinema (France) *Tel:* (01) 53 44 75 75 *Fax:* (01) 43 43 95 04, pg 151

Les Cahiers Fiscaux Europeens Sarl (France) *Tel:* (04) 93 53 89 39 *Fax:* (04) 93 53 66 28 *E-mail:* auteurs@fontaneau.com, pg 151

Cahiers Luxembourgeois (Luxembourg) *Tel:* 338885 *Fax:* 336513, pg 451

Cairns Art Society Inc (Australia) *Tel:* (07) 4039 1122 *E-mail:* cas@internetnorth.com.au, pg 16

Cairo University Press (Egypt (Arab Republic of Egypt)) *Tel:* (02) 846144, pg 137

Caja de Ahorros del Mediterraneo-Obras Sociales (Spain) *Tel:* (06) 5906363; (06) 5905785 *Fax:* (06) 5905828 *E-mail:* cam@cam.es *Web Site:* www.cam.es, pg 575

Calambur Editorial, SL (Spain) *Tel:* (091) 913553033 *Fax:* (091) 913553033 *E-mail:* calambur@calambureditorial.com *Web Site:* www.calambureditorial.com, pg 575

Calamo Editorial (Spain) *Tel:* (096) 5130581 *Fax:* (096) 5115345 *E-mail:* calamo@lobocom.es *Web Site:* www.lobocom.es/~calamo, pg 575

CALCRE, Association d'Information et de Defense des Auteurs (France) *E-mail:* secr@calcre.com *Web Site:* www.calcre.com, pg 1399

Randolph Caldecott Society (United Kingdom) *Tel:* (01626) 891303 *E-mail:* charles.caldecott@lineone.net *Web Site:* www.randolphcaldecott.org.uk, pg 1407

Calder Publications Ltd (United Kingdom) *Tel:* (020) 7633 0599 *E-mail:* info@calderpublications.com *Web Site:* www.calderpublications.com, pg 673

Calderini SRL (Italy) *Tel:* (051) 6226822 *Fax:* (051) 549329 *E-mail:* comm@calderini.agriline.it *Web Site:* www.calderini.it; www.gce.it, pg 1159

Caledonian International Book Manufacturing (United Kingdom) *Tel:* (0141) 7623000 *Fax:* (0141) 7620922 *E-mail:* 101622.235@compuserve.com, pg 1183, 1225

Calesa SA Editorial La (Spain) *Tel:* (0983) 548 102 *Fax:* (0983) 548 024 *E-mail:* editorial@la-calesa.com *Web Site:* www.la-calesa.com, pg 575

Callenbach BV (Netherlands) *Tel:* (038) 3392555 *Fax:* (038) 3311776 *E-mail:* algemeen@kok.nl, pg 480

Callis Editora Ltda (Brazil) *Tel:* (011) 3842-2066 *Fax:* (011) 3849-5882 *E-mail:* editorial@callis.com.br; callis@callis.com.br *Web Site:* www.callis.com.br, pg 79

Verlag Georg D W Callwey GmbH & Co (Germany) *Tel:* (089) 4360050 *Fax:* (089) 436005113 *Web Site:* www.callwey.de, pg 207

Editions Calmann-Levy SA (France) *Tel:* (01) 47 42 38 33 *Fax:* (01) 47 42 77 81, pg 152

Calosci (Italy) *Tel:* (0575) 678282 *Fax:* (0575) 678282 *E-mail:* info@calosci.com *Web Site:* www.calosci.com, pg 379

Calvary Press (Sri Lanka) *Tel:* (01) 553110, pg 606

Calwer Verlag GmbH (Germany) *Tel:* (0711) 167 22-0 *Fax:* (0711) 167 22 77 *E-mail:* info@calwer.com *Web Site:* www.calwer.com, pg 207

Edicions Camacuc (Spain) *Tel:* (096) 357 28 56 *Fax:* (096) 357 28 56, pg 575

Camara Argentina del Libro (Argentina) *Tel:* (011) 4381-8383 *Fax:* (011) 4381-9253 *E-mail:* cal@editores.com *Web Site:* www.editores.com, pg 1259

Camara Boliviana del Libro (Bolivia) *Tel:* (02) 44 4239; (02) 44 4077 *Fax:* (02) 44 1523 *E-mail:* cabolib@ceibo.entelnet.bo, pg 1263

Camara Brasileira do Livro (Brazil) *Tel:* (011) 3069-1300 *Fax:* (011) 3069-1300 *E-mail:* cbl@cbl.org.br *Web Site:* www.cbl.org.br, pg 1263

1627

Camara Chilena del Libro AG (Chile) *Tel:* (02) 6989519; (02) 6724088 *Fax:* (02) 6989226 *E-mail:* camlibro@terra.cl; prolibro@ctcreuna.cl *Web Site:* www.camlibro.cl, pg 1264

Camara Colombiana del Libro (Colombia) *Tel:* (01) 288 6188 *Fax:* (01) 287 3320 *E-mail:* camlibro@camlibro.com.co *Web Site:* www.camlibro.com.co, pg 1264

Camara Dos Deputados Coordenacao De Publicacoes (Brazil) *Tel:* (061) 216-0000 *Fax:* (061) 318-2190 *E-mail:* publicacoes.cedi@camara.gov.br *Web Site:* www.camara.gov.br, pg 79

Camara Ecuatoriana del Libro (Ecuador) *Tel:* (02) 553311; (02) 553314 *Fax:* (02) 222150 *E-mail:* celnp@hoy.net *Web Site:* www.celibro.org.ec, pg 1266

Camara Municipal de Castelo (Portugal) *Tel:* (058) 809300 *Fax:* (058) 809347, pg 529

Camara Nacional de la Industria Editorial Mexicana (Mexico) *Tel:* (05) 6 88 24 34; (05) 6 88 22 21; (05) 6 88 2011 *Toll Free Tel:* (800) 714-5352 *Fax:* (055) 5604-4347; (05) 6 04 31 47 *E-mail:* cepromex@caniem.com *Web Site:* www.caniem.com, pg 1277

Biblioteca de la Camara Oficial de Comercio, Agricultura e Industria del Distrito Nacional (Dominican Republic) *Tel:* 682-2688; 682-7206 *Fax:* 685-2228, pg 1502

Camara Peruana del Libro (Peru) *Tel:* (01) 428 7690; (01) 428 7696 *Fax:* (01) 427 7331 *E-mail:* dn@binape.gob.pe *Web Site:* www.binape.gob.pe, pg 1281

Camara Uruguaya del Libro (Uruguay) *Tel:* (082) 41 57 32 *Fax:* (082) 41 18 60 *E-mail:* camurlib@adinet.com.uy, pg 1295

Camara Venezolana del Libro (Venezuela) *Tel:* (0212) 7931347; (0212) 7931368 *Fax:* (0212) 7931368 *E-mail:* cavelibro@cantv.net, pg 1295

Cambridge Bibliographical Society (United Kingdom) *Tel:* (01223) 333000 *Fax:* (01223) 333160 *E-mail:* cbs@ula.cam.ac.uk, pg 1407

Cambridge University Press (Australia) *Tel:* (03) 8671 1400 *Fax:* (03) 9676 9966 *E-mail:* info@cambridge.edu.au; customerservice@cambridge.edu.au *Web Site:* www.cambridge.edu.au, pg 16

Cambridge University Library (United Kingdom) *Tel:* (01223) 333000 *Fax:* (01223) 333160 *E-mail:* library@lib.cam.ac.uk *Web Site:* www.lib.cam.ac.uk, pg 1553

Cambridge University Press (United Kingdom) *Tel:* (01223) 312393 *Fax:* (01223) 315052 *E-mail:* information@cup.cam.ac.uk; uksales@cambridge.org (sales); editorial@cambridge.org (editorial enquiries); rights@cambridge.org (rights & permission); web@cambridge.org (web services) *Web Site:* www.cambridge.org, pg 674

Cambridge University Press - Printing Division (United Kingdom) *Tel:* (01223) 358331 *Fax:* (01223) 325672 *E-mail:* info@cup.cam.ac.uk *Web Site:* printing.cambridge.org, pg 1183

Cambridge University Press - Printing Division (United Kingdom) *Tel:* (01223) 358331 *Fax:* (01223) 325672 *Web Site:* uk.cambridge.org, pg 1225

Cambridge University Press - Printing Division (United Kingdom) *Tel:* (01223) 312393 *Fax:* (01223) 315052 *Web Site:* uk.cambridge.org, pg 1247

Camden Press Ltd (United Kingdom) *Tel:* (020) 7226 2061 *Fax:* (020) 7226 2418, pg 674

Camera Austria (Austria) *Tel:* (0316) 81 55 50-0 *Fax:* (0316) 81 55 50-9 *E-mail:* office@camera-austria.at *Web Site:* www.camera-austria.at, pg 49

Camera dei Deputati Ufficio Pubblicazioni Informazione Parlamentare (Italy) *Tel:* (06) 67601 *Fax:* (06) 67603522; (06) 6783082 *Web Site:* www.camera.it, pg 379

Camerapix Publishers International Ltd (Kenya) *Tel:* (02) 4448923; (02) 4448924; (02) 4448925 *Fax:* (02) 4448818 *E-mail:* info@camerapix.com; camerapix@iconnect.co.ke *Web Site:* www.camerapix.com, pg 433

Camerapix Publishers International Ltd (United Kingdom) *Tel:* (020) 8449 5503 *Fax:* (020) 8449 8120 *E-mail:* camerapixuk@btinternet.com *Web Site:* www.camerapix.com, pg 674

Cameron & Hollis (United Kingdom) *Tel:* (01683) 220808 *Fax:* (01683) 220012 *E-mail:* editorial@cameronbooks.co.uk; sales@cameronbooks.co.uk (orders) *Web Site:* www.cameronbooks.co.uk, pg 674

Editorial Caminho SARL (Portugal) *Tel:* (021) 3152683 *Fax:* (021) 534346 *E-mail:* caminho@mail.telepac.pt, pg 529

Editora Caminho Suave Ltda (Brazil) *Tel:* (011) 2733377 *Fax:* (011) 2783537, pg 79

Campanotto (Italy) *Tel:* (0432) 699390; (0432) 690155 *Fax:* (0432) 644728 *E-mail:* edizioni@campanottoeditore.it *Web Site:* www.campanottoeditore.it, pg 379

Campbell Thomson & McLaughlin Ltd (United Kingdom) *Tel:* (020) 7242 0958 *Fax:* (020) 7242 2408, pg 1139

Les Editions Camphill (Switzerland) *Tel:* (021) 8062269 *Fax:* (021) 8061897, pg 620

Instituto Campineiro de Ensino Agricola Ltda (Brazil) *Tel:* (019) 3272-2280 *Fax:* (019) 3272-6004 *E-mail:* icea@icea.com.br *Web Site:* www.icea.com.br, pg 79

Campinia Media VZW (Belgium) *Tel:* (014) 59 09 59 *Fax:* (014) 59 03 44 *E-mail:* info@campiniamedia.be *Web Site:* www.campiniamedia.be, pg 64

Campus Corner Ltd (Trinidad & Tobago) *Tel:* (868) 623-1678 *Fax:* (868) 623-1678, pg 1345

Editora Campus Ltda (Brazil) *Tel:* (021) 3970-9300 *Fax:* (021) 2507-1991 *E-mail:* info@elsevier.com.br *Web Site:* www.campus.com.br, pg 79

Campus Evangelical Fellowship, Literature Department (Taiwan, Province of China) *Tel:* (02) 2368-2361 *Fax:* (02) 2367-2139 *E-mail:* info@cef.org.tw *Web Site:* www.cef.org.tw, pg 639

Campus Publishing Ltd (Ireland) *Tel:* (091) 524662; (091) 767408 *Fax:* (091) 527505, pg 358

Campus Verlag GmbH (Germany) *Tel:* (069) 976 516-0 *Fax:* (069) 976 516-78 *E-mail:* info@campus.de *Web Site:* www.campus.de, pg 207

Campusbooks Medien AG (Germany) *Tel:* (089) 18921730 *Fax:* (089) 18921731 *E-mail:* info@campusbooks.de *Web Site:* www.campusbooks.de/partner_main.html, pg 207

Bibliotheque du Centre Culturel Albert Camus (Madagascar) *Tel:* 22 213 75; 22 236 47 *Fax:* 22 213 38 *E-mail:* medccac@dts.ng, pg 1526

Editions Canal (France) *Tel:* (01) 42222730 *Fax:* (01) 42223025, pg 152

Canale G e C SpA (Italy) *Tel:* (011) 40 78 511 *Fax:* (011) 40 78 527 *E-mail:* info@canale.it *Web Site:* www.canale.it, pg 1159

Canale G e C SpA (Italy) *Tel:* (011) 40 78 511 *Fax:* (011) 40 78 527 *E-mail:* info@canale.it, pg 1180

Canale G e C SpA (Italy) *Tel:* (011) 40 78 511 *Fax:* (011) 40 78 527 *E-mail:* info@canale.it *Web Site:* www.canale.it, pg 1220

Candlelight Trust T/A Candlelight Farm (Australia) *Tel:* (08) 92944141 *Fax:* (08) 92944141, pg 17

Editorial Cangallo SACI (Argentina) *Tel:* (011) 4331-0204; (011) 4331-8848, pg 4

Canis Vydavatelstvi a Nakladatelstvi (Czech Republic) *Tel:* (02) 251096, pg 122

Cankarjeva Zalozba (Slovenia) *Tel:* (01) 4323 144 *Fax:* (01) 2318 782 *E-mail:* knjigarna.oxford@cankarjeva-z.si *Web Site:* www.cankarjeva-z.si, pg 561

Cankarjeva Zalozba (Slovenia) *Tel:* (01) 3603 720 *Fax:* (01) 3603 787 *E-mail:* info@cankarjeva-z.si *Web Site:* www.cankarjeva-z.si, pg 1340

Cannon International (Singapore) *Tel:* 6546 7271 *Fax:* 6546 7262 *E-mail:* legaldep@nlb.gov.sq *Web Site:* www.nlb.gov.sg, pg 555

Canoe Press (Jamaica) *Tel:* 876-935-8432; 876-935-8470; 876-977-2659 *Fax:* 876-977-2660 *E-mail:* uwipress_marketing@cwjamaica.com; cuserv@cwjamaica.com (customer service & orders) *Web Site:* www.uwipress.com, pg 413

Canongate Books Ltd (United Kingdom) *Tel:* (0131) 557 5111 *Fax:* (0131) 557 5211 *E-mail:* info@canongate.co.uk; customerservices@canongate.co.uk *Web Site:* www.canongate.net, pg 674

Editions Canope (France) *Tel:* (04) 73 93 82 90 *Fax:* (04) 73 39 33 00, pg 152

Canova SRL (Italy) *Tel:* (0422) 262397 *Fax:* (0422) 433673 *E-mail:* info@canovaedizioni.it *Web Site:* www.canovaedizioni.it, pg 379

Editorial Cantabrica SA (Spain) *Tel:* (04) 4245307 *Fax:* (04) 4231984, pg 575

Edizioni Cantagalli (Italy) *Tel:* (0577) 42102 *Fax:* (0577) 45363 *E-mail:* cantagalli@edizionicantagalli.com *Web Site:* www.edizionicantagalli.com, pg 379

Uitgeverij Cantecleer BV (Netherlands) *Tel:* (035) 5486600 *Fax:* (035) 5486615 *E-mail:* cancleer@worldonline.nl, pg 480

Canterbury University Library (New Zealand) *Tel:* (03) 364 2987 (ext 8723) *Fax:* (03) 3642055 *E-mail:* lending@libr.canterbury.ac.nz; helpdesk@libr.canterbury.ac.nz *Web Site:* library.canterbury.ac.nz/, pg 1532

Canterbury University Press (New Zealand) *Tel:* (03) 364-2914 *Fax:* (03) 364-2044 *E-mail:* mail@cup.canterbury.ac.nz *Web Site:* www.cup.canterbury.ac.nz, pg 494

Dr Cantz'sche Druckerei GmbH & Co (Germany) *Tel:* (0711) 4405-0; (0711) 4405-121 (Marketing & Sales) *Fax:* (0711) 4405-111 *E-mail:* bklein@jfink.de *Web Site:* www.jfink.de, pg 207

Capall Bann Publishing (United Kingdom) *Tel:* (01823) 401528 *Fax:* (01823) 401529 *E-mail:* enquiries@capallbann.co.uk *Web Site:* www.capallbann.co.uk, pg 674

Cape Catley Ltd (New Zealand) *Tel:* (09) 445-9668 *Fax:* (09) 445-9668 *E-mail:* cape.catley@xtra.co.nz *Web Site:* www.capecatleybooks.co.nz, pg 495

Cape Provincial Library Service (South Africa) *Tel:* (021) 5910095 *Fax:* (021) 4102261, pg 563

Cape Provincial Library Service (South Africa) *Tel:* (021) 483 2271 *Fax:* (021) 419 7541 *E-mail:* capelib@pawc.wcape.gov.za *Web Site:* www.westerncape.gov.za, pg 1543

Cape Town City Libraries (South Africa) *Tel:* (021) 462 44 00 *Fax:* (021) 461 5981, pg 1543

Editorial Capitan San Luis (Cuba) *Tel:* (07) 2034475 *Fax:* (07) 332070, pg 120

Capitol Publishing House Inc (Philippines) *Tel:* (02) 6712662 *Fax:* (02) 6712663 *E-mail:* capitolpublishing@e-yellowpages.ph, pg 518

Capone Editore SRL (Italy) *Tel:* (0832) 612618 *Fax:* (0832) 611877, pg 379

Cappelen akademisk forlag (Norway) *Tel:* 22985800 *Fax:* 22985841 *Web Site:* www.cappelen.no/main/info.asp, pg 508

J W Cappelens Forlag A/S (Norway) *Tel:* (022) 365000 *Fax:* (022) 365040 *E-mail:* web@cappelen.no *Web Site:* www.cappelen.no, pg 508

Cappelli Editore (Italy) *Tel:* (051) 239060 *Fax:* (051) 239286 *E-mail:* info@cappellieditore.com *Web Site:* www.cappellieditore.com, pg 380

Edizioni del Capricorno (Italy) *Tel:* (011) 386500 *Fax:* (011) 3853244 *E-mail:* cse@estorinese.inet.it, pg 380

YELLOW PAGES

Capstone Publishing Ltd (United Kingdom) *Tel:* (01865) 798623 *Fax:* (01865) 240941 *E-mail:* capstone_publishing@msn.com *Web Site:* www.capstone.co.uk, pg 674

Captain Jonas Publications (Australia) *Tel:* (07) 4956 5022 *Fax:* (07) 4956 2633 *E-mail:* aarfw@ozemail.com.au, pg 17

CAPU (Portugal) *Tel:* (021) 8429190 *Fax:* (021) 8409361 *E-mail:* capu@capu.pt *Web Site:* www.capu.pt, pg 529

Editions Capucines (Mauritius) *Tel:* 4641563 *Fax:* 4641563 *E-mail:* edcapsee@intnet.mu, pg 461

Editions Caracteres (France) *Tel:* (01) 43 37 96 98 *Fax:* (01) 43 37 26 10 *E-mail:* caracteres2000@aol.com *Web Site:* www.editions-caracteres.fr, pg 152

Editions Caraibes SA (Haiti) *Tel:* 23179, pg 314

Caramel, Uitgeverij (Belgium) *Tel:* (02) 2452427 *Fax:* (02) 2558493 *E-mail:* caramel@skynet.be, pg 64

Editora Caravela (Portugal) *Tel:* (01) 7155848 *Fax:* (021) 155848, pg 529

Carcanet Press Ltd (United Kingdom) *Tel:* (0161) 834 8730 *Fax:* (0161) 832 0084 *E-mail:* info@carcanet.u-net.com *Web Site:* www.carcanet.co.uk, pg 674

Cardiff Academic Press (United Kingdom) *Tel:* (029) 2056 03 *Fax:* (029) 2055 4909 *E-mail:* drakegroup@btinternet.com, pg 675

Careers & Educational Publishers Ltd (Ireland) *Tel:* (094) 71093, pg 358

Careers & Occupational Information Centre (COIC) (United Kingdom) *Tel:* (0114) 259 4564 *Fax:* (0114) 259 3439, pg 675

Carfax Publishing (United Kingdom) *Tel:* (020) 7583 9855 *Fax:* (020) 7842 2298 *E-mail:* sales@carfax.co.uk *Web Site:* www.carfax.co.uk, pg 675

Carib Publishing Ltd (Jamaica) *Tel:* 876-960-2602 *Fax:* 876-960-2602 *E-mail:* carib@toj.com, pg 413

Carib Research & Publications Inc (Barbados) *Tel:* 438-0580, pg 62

Caribbean & Latin American Studies Library (Puerto Rico) *Tel:* (787) 764-0000 (ext 3319) *Fax:* (787) 763-5685, pg 1539

Caribbean Authors Publishing (Jamaica) *Tel:* 876-926-6163 *Fax:* 876-929-1226, pg 413

Caribbean Community Secretariat (Guyana) *Tel:* (02) 26-9280; (02) 26-9281; (02) 26-9282; (02) 26-9283; (02) 26-9284; (02) 26-9285; (02) 26-9286; (02) 26-9287; (02) 26-9288; (02) 26-9289 *Fax:* (02) 26-7816; (02) 25-7341; (02) 25-8031 *E-mail:* carisec1@caricom.org; carisec2@caricom.org; carisec3@caricom.org *Web Site:* www.caricom.org, pg 314

Caribbean Epidemiology Centre (Trinidad & Tobago) *Tel:* (868) 622-4261; (868) 622-4262 *Fax:* (868) 622-2792 *E-mail:* postmaster@carec.paho.org *Web Site:* www.carec.org, pg 647

Caribbean Food & Nutrition Institute (Jamaica) *Tel:* 876-927-3829; 876-927-1927 *Fax:* 876-927-2657 *E-mail:* e-mail@cfni.paho.org, pg 413

Caribbean Telecommunications Union (Trinidad & Tobago) *Tel:* (868) 627-0281; (868) 627-0347 *Fax:* (868) 623-1523 *E-mail:* ctunion@c-t-u.org; secgen@c-t-u.org *Web Site:* www.c-t-u.org, pg 647

Carinthia Verlag (Austria) *Tel:* (0463) 50 12 20-220 *Fax:* (0463) 50 12 20-214 *Web Site:* www.verlag.carinthia.com, pg 49

Carit Andersens Forlag A/S (Denmark) *Tel:* 35436222 *Fax:* 35435151 *E-mail:* info@mercantila.dk *Web Site:* www.caritandersen.dk, pg 130

Caritas Printing Training Centre (Hong Kong) *Tel:* 2526 1148 *Fax:* 2537 1231 *E-mail:* info@caritas.org.hk *Web Site:* www.caritas.org.hk, pg 1156

Caritas Printing Training Centre (Hong Kong) *Tel:* 25261148 *Fax:* 25371231, pg 1177

Caritas Printing Training Centre (Hong Kong) *Tel:* 2526 1148 *Fax:* 2537 1231, pg 1217

Caritas Printing Training Centre (Hong Kong) *Tel:* 2524 2701 (ext 239) *Fax:* 2537 1231 *Web Site:* vtes.caritas.org.hk, pg 1236

Carl-Auer-Systeme Verlag (Germany) *Tel:* (06221) 64380 *Fax:* (06221) 643822 *E-mail:* info@carl-auer.de *Web Site:* www.carl-auer.de, pg 207

Fachverlag Hans Carl GmbH (Germany) *Tel:* (0911) 95285-0 *Fax:* (0911) 95285-48; (0911) 95285-71; (0911) 95285-61 *E-mail:* info@hanscarl.com *Web Site:* www.hanscarl.com, pg 207

Fachverlag Hans Carl GmbH (Germany) *Tel:* (0911) 95285-0 *Fax:* (0911) 95285-48 *E-mail:* info@hanscarl.com *Web Site:* www.hanscarl.com, pg 1310

Carl Link Verlag-Gesellschaft mbH Fachverlag fur Verwaltungsrecht (Germany) *Tel:* (089) 36007 0 *Fax:* (089) 36007 3310 *E-mail:* info@carllink.de *Web Site:* www.carllink.de, pg 207

Carlong Publishers (Caribbean) Ltd (Jamaica) *Tel:* (876) 923-7008 *Fax:* (876) 923-7003 *E-mail:* sales@carlpub.com, pg 413

Forlaget Carlsen A/S (Denmark) *Tel:* 4444 3233 *Fax:* 4444 3633 *E-mail:* carlsen@carlsen.dk *Web Site:* www.carlsen.dk, pg 130

Carlsen Verlag GmbH (Germany) *Tel:* (040) 39 804 0 *Fax:* (040) 39 804 390, pg 207

Carlsson Bokfoerlag AB (Sweden) *Tel:* (08) 411 23 49 *Fax:* (08) 796 84 57, pg 610

Carlton Publishing Group (United Kingdom) *Tel:* (020) 7612 0400 *Fax:* (020) 7612 0401 *E-mail:* enquires@carltonbooks.co.uk; sales@carltonbooks.co.uk; editorial@carltonbooks.co.uk *Web Site:* www.carltonint.co.uk, pg 675

Carmelitana VZW (Belgium) *Tel:* (09) 225.48.36 *Fax:* (09) 224.06.01 *E-mail:* boekhandel@carmelitana.be *Web Site:* www.carmelitana.be, pg 64

Edizioni Carmelitane (Italy) *Tel:* (06) 68100886 *Fax:* (06) 68100887 *E-mail:* edizioni@ocarm.org *Web Site:* www.carmelites.info/edizioni, pg 380

Carnegie Library (Mauritius) *Tel:* 6742 280; 6742 281 *Fax:* 676 5054 *E-mail:* contact@curepipe.org *Web Site:* www.curepipe.org, pg 1528

Carnell Literary Agency (United Kingdom) *Tel:* (01279) 723626 *Fax:* (01279) 600308, pg 1139

Jon Carpenter Publishing (United Kingdom) *Tel:* (01608) 811969 *Fax:* (01608) 811969, pg 675

Editions Didier Carpentier (France) *Tel:* (01) 48780072 *Fax:* (01) 42829199, pg 152

Alzira Chagas Carpigiani (Brazil) *Tel:* (011) 849-0189 *Fax:* (011) 227-3384 *E-mail:* kerredit@uol.com.br, pg 79

Carre d'Art Edition Archigraphie (Switzerland) *Tel:* (022) 311 57 50 *Fax:* (022) 312 21 21, pg 620

Carrick Media (United Kingdom) *Tel:* (01294) 311322 *Fax:* (01294) 311322 *E-mail:* enquiries@carrickmedia.demon.co.uk, pg 675

Edizioni Carroccio (Italy) *Tel:* (049) 700568 *Fax:* (049) 700568, pg 380

Carroggio SA de Ediciones (Spain) *Tel:* (093) 4949922 *Fax:* (093) 4949923 *E-mail:* carroggio@carroggio.com *Web Site:* www.carroggio.es, pg 575

Carroll & Brown Ltd (United Kingdom) *Tel:* (020) 7372 0900 *Fax:* (020) 7372 0460 *E-mail:* mail@carrollandbrown.co.uk *Web Site:* www.carrollandbrown.co.uk, pg 675

The Lewis Carroll Society (United Kingdom) *E-mail:* aztec@compuserve.com *Web Site:* lewiscarrollsociety.org.uk, pg 1290

Carta, The Israel Map & Publishing Co Ltd (Israel) *Tel:* (02) 678 3355 *Fax:* (02) 678 2373 *E-mail:* carta@carta.co.il *Web Site:* www.holyland-jerusalem.com, pg 365

EDIZIONI CASAGRANDE SA

Editura Cartea Moldovei (Republic of Moldova) *Tel:* (02) 246550 *Fax:* (02) 246411, pg 473

Editura Cartea Romaneasca (Romania) *Tel:* (01) 3123733; (01) 6148802 *Fax:* (01) 3110025, pg 538

Edizioni Cartedit SRL (Italy) *Tel:* (0373) 277410 *Fax:* (0373) 277405, pg 380

Carter's (Antiques & Collectibles) P/L (Australia) *Tel:* (02) 8850 4600 *Fax:* (02) 8850 4100 *E-mail:* info@carters.com.au *Web Site:* www.carters.com.au, pg 17

Carto BVBA (Belgium) *Tel:* (02) 2680345 *Fax:* (02) 2680345, pg 64

Cartoeristiek (Federatie van Belgische Autobus- en Autocarondernemers) (BAAV) (Belgium) *Tel:* (051) 226060 *Fax:* (051) 229273, pg 64

Edizioni Cartografiche Milanesi (Italy) *Tel:* (02) 9101649 *Fax:* (02) 9101118 *E-mail:* info@ortelio-ecm.it *Web Site:* www.ortelio-ecm.it, pg 380

Cartographia Ltd (Hungary) *Tel:* (01) 222-6727 *Fax:* (01) 222-6728 *E-mail:* mail@cartographia.hu *Web Site:* www.cartographia.hu, pg 321

Cartoon-Caricature-Contor (CCC) (Germany) *Tel:* (089) 3233669 *Fax:* (089) 3226859 *E-mail:* ccc@c5.net *Web Site:* www.c5.net, pg 1131

The Cartoon Cave (United Kingdom) *Tel:* (01780) 460689; (01780) 460757 *Fax:* (01780) 460689 *Web Site:* www.cartooncave.co.uk, pg 675

CartoTravel Verlag GmbH & Co KG (Germany) *Tel:* (06196) 6096-0 *Fax:* (06196) 27450 *E-mail:* info@cartotravel.de *Web Site:* www.cartotravel.de, pg 207

Carvajal SA (Peru) *Tel:* (01) 440 9685; (01) 440 9618 *Fax:* (01) 440 5871 *E-mail:* carvajal@correo.dnet.com.pe *Web Site:* www.carvajal.com.co, pg 516

Carvajal International Inc (United States) *Tel:* 305-448-6875 *Toll Free Tel:* 800-622-6657 *Fax:* 305-448-9942 *E-mail:* info@cargraphics.com *Web Site:* www.carvajal.com.co, pg 1228

A Tavares de Carvalho (Portugal) *Tel:* (021) 797 0377 *Fax:* (021) 795 8880, pg 1336

Casa de las Americas (Cuba) *Tel:* (07) 327271; (07) 323588 *Fax:* (07) 327272, pg 120

Casa de Velazquez (Spain) *Tel:* (091) 5433605 *Fax:* (091) 5446870 *E-mail:* bcv@bibli.cvz.es, pg 575

Casa Editora Abril (Cuba) *Tel:* (07) 8627871; (07) 8624359 *Fax:* (07) 335282 *E-mail:* eabril@jcc.org.cu *Web Site:* www.almamater.cu, pg 120

Casa Editoriala Independenta Europa (Romania) *Tel:* (051) 153487; (051) 425801 *Fax:* (051) 153487, pg 538

Casa Editrice Giuseppe Principato Spa (Italy) *Tel:* (02) 312025; (02) 3315309 *Fax:* (02) 33104295 *E-mail:* info@principato.it *Web Site:* www.principato.it, pg 380

Casa Editrice Libraria Ulrico Hoepli SpA (Italy) *Tel:* (02) 864871 *Fax:* (02) 864322 *E-mail:* hoepli@hoepli.it *Web Site:* www.hoepli.it, pg 380

Casa Editrice Lint Srl (Italy) *Tel:* (040) 360396 *Fax:* (040) 361354, pg 380

Casa Musicale Edizioni Carrara SRL (Italy) *Tel:* (035) 243618 *Fax:* (035) 270398 *E-mail:* info@edizionicarrara.it *Web Site:* www.edizionicarrara.it, pg 380

Casa Musicale G Zanibon SRL (Italy) *Tel:* (02) 88811 *Fax:* (02) 88814317, pg 380

Edizioni Casagrande SA (Switzerland) *Tel:* (091) 820 0101 *Fax:* (091) 825 1874 *E-mail:* casagrande@casagrande-online.ch *Web Site:* www.casagrande-online.ch, pg 620

Casalini Libri (Italy) *Tel:* (055) 5018 1 *Fax:* (055) 5018 201 *E-mail:* info@casalini.it *Web Site:* www.casalini.it, pg 380, 1320

Editorial Casals SA (Spain) *Tel:* (093) 2449550 *Fax:* (093) 2656895 *E-mail:* casals@editorialcasals.com *Web Site:* www.editorialcasals.com, pg 575

Editorial Casariego (Spain) *Tel:* (091) 4424339; (091) 4425178; (091) 4411330; (091) 4416829 *Fax:* (091) 4426224 *E-mail:* casariego@infonegocio.com *Web Site:* www.casariego.com, pg 576

Casarotto Ramsay & Associates Ltd (United Kingdom) *Tel:* (020) 7287 4450 *Fax:* (020) 7287 9128 *E-mail:* agents@casarotto.uk.com *Web Site:* www.casarotto.uk.com, pg 1139

Casket Publications (Australia) *Tel:* (02) 9805 8878; (02) 9481 9145 *Fax:* (02) 9875 5382, pg 17

Casopisni zavod Uradni list Republike Slovenije (Slovenia) *Tel:* (01) 1250 294 *Fax:* (01) 1251 418 *E-mail:* info@uradni-list.si *Web Site:* www.uradni-list.si, pg 561

Frank Cass Publishers (United Kingdom) *Tel:* (020) 8920 2100 *Fax:* (020) 8447 8548 *E-mail:* info@frankcass.com *Web Site:* www.frankcass.com, pg 675

Cassell & Co (United Kingdom) *Tel:* (020) 7420 5555 *Fax:* (020) 7240 7261; (020) 7240 8531, pg 675

Casset Ediciones SL (Spain) *Tel:* (091) 5043584 *Fax:* (091) 2508841, pg 576

Editorial Castalia (Spain) *Tel:* (091) 3195857 *Fax:* (091) 3102442 *E-mail:* castalia@infornet.es *Web Site:* www.castalia.es, pg 576

Casa Editrice Castalia (Italy) *Tel:* (011) 4374176 *Fax:* (011) 4374176, pg 380

Editions Casteilla (France) *Tel:* (01) 30 14 19 30 *Fax:* (01) 34 60 31 32 *E-mail:* info@casteilla.fr *Web Site:* www.casteilla.fr, pg 152

Il Castello srl (Italy) *Tel:* (02) 48401629 *Fax:* (02) 4453617 *E-mail:* il_castello@tin.it, pg 380

Editions Casterman (France) *Tel:* (01) 55 28 12 00 *Fax:* (01) 55 28 12 60 *Web Site:* www.casterman.com, pg 152

Editions Casterman SA (Belgium) *Tel:* (02) 209 83 00 *Fax:* (02) 209 83 01 *Web Site:* www.casterman.com, pg 65

Casterman NV (Netherlands) *Tel:* (0321) 313553 *Fax:* (0321) 318205, pg 480

Castle House Publications Ltd (United Kingdom) *Tel:* (01892) 539606 *Fax:* (01892) 517773; (01892) 517005 *E-mail:* enquiries@castlehouse.co.uk *Web Site:* www.castlehouse.co.uk, pg 676

Castle Publications SA (Switzerland) *Tel:* (022) 511036 *Fax:* (022) 7511111; (022) 7884240, pg 620

Castle Translations (United Kingdom) *Tel:* (01524) 841169 *Fax:* (01524) 381721 *E-mail:* info@castletranslations.co.uk *Web Site:* ukpetsearch.freeuk.com/castletrans, pg 1150

Castlemead Publications (United Kingdom) *Tel:* (01920) 465525 *Fax:* (01920) 465545 *E-mail:* sales@castlemeadpublications.fsnet.co.uk, pg 676

Le Castor Astral (France) *Tel:* (01) 48 40 14 95 *Fax:* (01) 48 45 97 52 *E-mail:* swproduction@magic.fr, pg 152

Editrice Il Castoro (Italy) *Tel:* (02) 29513529 *Fax:* (02) 29529896 *E-mail:* editrice.castoro@iol.it *Web Site:* www.castoro-on-line.it, pg 380

Edicios do Castro (Spain) *Tel:* (0981) 621494; (0981) 620937; (0981) 620200 *Fax:* (0981) 623804 *E-mail:* edicios.ocastro@sargadelos.com *Web Site:* www.sargadelos.com, pg 576

Castrum Peregrini Presse (Netherlands) *Tel:* (020) 235287 *Fax:* (020) 6247096 *E-mail:* mail@castrumperegrini.nl *Web Site:* castrumperegrini.nl, pg 480

Biblioteca de Catalunya (Spain) *Tel:* (093) 270 23 00 *Fax:* (093) 270 23 04 *E-mail:* bustia@bnc.es *Web Site:* www.gencat.es/bc, pg 576, 1545

Catchfire Press Inc (Australia) *Tel:* (02) 4951 8859 *E-mail:* catchfire@idl.com.au *Web Site:* www.cust.idl.com.au/catchfire, pg 17

Ediciones Catedra SA (Spain) *Tel:* (091) 3200119; (091) 3938800; (091) 3938787 *Fax:* (091) 7426631; (091) 7412118 *E-mail:* catedra@catedra.com *Web Site:* www.catedra.com, pg 576

Cathedral Books Ltd (Ireland) *Tel:* (01) 8787372 *Fax:* (01) 8787704 *E-mail:* cathedra@indigo.ie, pg 358

Kyle Cathie Ltd (United Kingdom) *Tel:* (020) 7692 7215 *Fax:* (020) 7692 7260 *E-mail:* general.enquiries@kyle-cathie.com *Web Site:* www.kylecathie.co.uk, pg 676

Catholic Institute for International Relations (United Kingdom) *Tel:* (020) 7354 0883 *Fax:* (020) 7359 0017 *E-mail:* ciir@ciir.org *Web Site:* www.ciir.org, pg 676

Catholic Institute of Sydney (Australia) *Tel:* (02) 9752 9500 *Fax:* (02) 9746 6022 *E-mail:* cisinfo@cis.catholic.edu.au *Web Site:* www.cis.catholic.edu.au, pg 17

Central Catholic Library Association Inc (Ireland) *Tel:* (01) 676 1264, pg 1565

The Catholic Truth Society (United Kingdom) *Tel:* (020) 7640 0042 *Fax:* (020) 7640 0046 *E-mail:* info@cts-online.org.uk *Web Site:* www.cts-online.org.uk, pg 676

Imprimerie Catholique (Madagascar) *Tel:* (02) 22304, pg 1160

Catia Monser Eggcup-Verlag (Germany) *Tel:* (0211) 215122 *Fax:* (0211) 215122 *E-mail:* cmonserev@aol.com *Web Site:* members.aol.com/CMonserEV, pg 207

Causeway Press Ltd (United Kingdom) *Tel:* (01695) 576048; (01695) 577360 *Fax:* (01695) 570714 *E-mail:* davidalcorn.causewaypress@btinternet.com, pg 676

Caux Books (Switzerland) *Tel:* (021) 9629469 *Fax:* (021) 9629465 *E-mail:* info@caux.ch *Web Site:* www.caux.ch, pg 620

Caux Edition SA (Switzerland) *Tel:* (021) 963 94 69 *Fax:* (021) 962 94 65 *E-mail:* info@caux.ch *Web Site:* www.caux.ch, pg 620

Paul Cave Publications Ltd (United Kingdom) *Tel:* (01703) 223591; (01703) 333457 *Fax:* (01703) 227190 *E-mail:* lanksmag@zone.co.uk, pg 676

Verlag Bo Cavefors (Switzerland) *Tel:* (01) 2017200, pg 620

Marshall Cavendish Books (Singapore) *Tel:* (065) 2848844 *Fax:* (065) 2854871 *E-mail:* te@corp.tpl.com.sg *Web Site:* www.timesone.com.sg/te, pg 555

Marshall Cavendish Partworks Ltd (United Kingdom) *Tel:* (020) 7565 6000 *Fax:* (020) 7734 6221 *E-mail:* info@marshallcavendish.co.uk *Web Site:* www.marshallcavendish.co.uk, pg 676

Cavendish Publishing Pty Ltd (Australia) *Tel:* (02) 9664 0909 *Fax:* (02) 9664 5420 *E-mail:* info@cavendishpublishing.com *Web Site:* www.cavendishpublishing.com.au, pg 17

Cavendish Publishing Ltd (United Kingdom) *Tel:* (020) 7278 8000 *Fax:* (020) 7278 8080 *E-mail:* info@cavendishpublishing.com *Web Site:* www.cavendishpublishing.com, pg 676

The Caxton Press (New Zealand) *Tel:* (03) 366 8516 *Fax:* (03) 365 7840 *E-mail:* print.design@caxton.co.nz *Web Site:* www.caxton.co.nz, pg 495

The Caxton Press (New Zealand) *Toll Free Tel:* 800 229 866 *Fax:* (03) 365 7840 *E-mail:* print.design@caxton.co.nz *Web Site:* www.caxton.co.nz, pg 1160

Editorial Caymi SACI (Argentina) *Tel:* (011) 4304-2474 *Fax:* (011) 4304-2474, pg 4

Cazal SA (Reunion) *Tel:* 213264 *Fax:* 410977, pg 1338

CB Print Finishers Ltd (United Kingdom) *Tel:* (0191) 2150101 *Fax:* (0191) 2701651 *E-mail:* sales@cbprint.co.uk *Web Site:* www.cbprint.co.uk, pg 1225

CBA Translations (United Kingdom) *Tel:* (01404) 822284 *Fax:* (01404) 823136 *E-mail:* info@cbatranslations.co.uk *Web Site:* www.cbatranslations.co.uk, pg 1150

CBD Research Ltd (United Kingdom) *Tel:* (020) 8650 7745 *Fax:* (020) 8650 0768 *E-mail:* cbd@cbdresearch.com *Web Site:* www.cbdresearch.com, pg 677

CCH Editions Ltd (United Kingdom) *Tel:* (020) 8547 3333 *Fax:* (020) 8547 1124 *E-mail:* customer.services@cch.co.uk *Web Site:* www.cch.co.uk, pg 677

CCH New Zealand Ltd (New Zealand) *Tel:* (09) 488 2760 *Toll Free Tel:* 800 500224 (New Zealand only) *Fax:* (09) 488 6911 *E-mail:* nzsales@cch.co.nz *Web Site:* www.cch.co.nz, pg 495

CD Remain Cia Ltda (Ecuador) *Tel:* (02) 224973; (02) 239328 *Fax:* (02) 505760, pg 1308

CDL (Central Distribuidora Livreira) Sarl (Portugal) *Tel:* (01) 4264422; (01) 769744; (01) 779825, pg 1336

CEAC, Grupo Editorial SA (Spain) *Tel:* (093) 3073004 *Fax:* (093) 2660067 *E-mail:* atencioncliente@ceacedit.com; info@ceacedit.com *Web Site:* www.ceacedit.com; www.editorialceac.com, pg 576

Editorial la Cebra (Mexico) *Tel:* (05) 2779529; (05) 2779797; (05) 2737717; (05) 2737888 *Fax:* (05) 2737866 *E-mail:* info@adcebra.com, pg 463

CEC-Cosmic Energy Connections (Switzerland) *Tel:* (0761) 7059 632 *Fax:* (0761) 7059 633, pg 620

Biblioteca Musicale S Cecilia (Italy) *Tel:* (06) 3609671 *Fax:* (06) 36001800 *Web Site:* www.santacecilia.it, pg 1520

CEDAM (Casa Editrice Dr A Milani) (Italy) *Tel:* (049) 8239111 *Fax:* (049) 8752900 *E-mail:* info@cedam.com *Web Site:* www.cedam.com, pg 380

Cedar Media (United Kingdom) *Tel:* (020) 8508 8856 *Fax:* (020) 8508 8856 *E-mail:* cedarmedia@btinternet.com, pg 1349

Cedel, Ediciones Jose O Avila Monteso ES (Spain) *Tel:* (093) 2156039 *Fax:* (093) 2156088 *E-mail:* cedel@wbsite.es, pg 576

CEEBA Publications Antenne d'Autriche (Austria) *Tel:* (02236) 803115 *Fax:* (02236) 8033 *E-mail:* svd@steyler.at *Web Site:* www.ceeba.at, pg 49

Editions du CEFAL (Belgium) *Tel:* (04) 254 25 20 *Fax:* (04) 254 24 40 *E-mail:* cefal.celes@skynet.be *Web Site:* www.cefal.com, pg 65

CEIC Alfons El Vell (Spain) *Tel:* (06) 2876551 *Fax:* (06) 2875286, pg 576

Cekit SA (Colombia) *Tel:* (06) 3253033; (06) 3348179; (06) 3348189 *Fax:* (06) 3348020 *E-mail:* comercial@cekit.com.co *Web Site:* www.cekit.com.co, pg 110

Celebrity Educational Publishers (Singapore) *Tel:* (06) 7857274 *Fax:* (06) 7489108, pg 555

Celeluck Co Ltd (Hong Kong) *Tel:* 2893 9197; 2893 9147 *Fax:* 2891 5591 *E-mail:* open@open.com.hk *Web Site:* www.open.com.hk, pg 316

Celeste Ediciones (Spain) *Tel:* (091) 3100599; (002) 118298 *Fax:* (091) 3100459 *E-mail:* info@celesteediciones.com, pg 576

CELID (Italy) *Tel:* (011) 447 47 74 *Fax:* (011) 447 47 59 *E-mail:* edizioni@celid.it *Web Site:* www.celid.it, pg 381

Celta Editora, Lda (Portugal) *Tel:* (021) 4417433 *Fax:* (021) 4467304 *E-mail:* mail@celtaeditora.pt; celtaeditora@mail.telepac.pt *Web Site:* www.celtaeditora.pt, pg 529

Celuc Libri (Italy) *Tel:* (02) 86 45 07 76 *Fax:* (02) 86 45 14 24, pg 381

CEM Publishers Ltd (Nigeria), pg 504

Cemagref Editions (France) *Tel:* (01) 4096 61 21 *Fax:* (01) 4096 60 36 *E-mail:* info@cemagref.fr *Web Site:* www.cemagref.fr, pg 152

Sociedad Fondo Editorial Cenamec (Venezuela) *Tel:* (02) 563-2591; (02) 563-3542; (02) 563-5597; (02) 563-8155; (02) 563-9997; (02) 563-8244 *E-mail:* cenamec@reacciun.ve *Web Site:* www.cenamec.org.ve/, pg 779

Editions Cenomane (France) *Tel:* (02) 43242157 *Fax:* (02) 43771916, pg 152

Department of Census & Statistics (Sri Lanka) *Tel:* (01) 675297 *Fax:* (01) 697594 *E-mail:* dcensus@lanka.ccom.lk *Web Site:* www.statistics.gov.lk, pg 606

Cent Pages (France) *Tel:* (04) 38 12 16 20 *Fax:* (04) 38 12 16 29 *E-mail:* editions@editions-centpages.fr *Web Site:* www.editions-centpages.fr, pg 152

Centaur Press (1954) (United Kingdom) *Tel:* (020) 7431 4391 *Fax:* (020) 7431 5129 *E-mail:* books@opengatepress.co.uk *Web Site:* www.opengatepress.co.uk, pg 677

Centaurus-Verlagsgesellschaft GmbH (Germany) *Tel:* (07643) 93 39-0 *Fax:* (07643) 93 39-11 *E-mail:* info@centaurus-verlag.de *Web Site:* www.centaurus-verlag.de, pg 207

Centenary of Technical Education in Bairnsdale Group (Australia) *Tel:* (03) 5152-4556, pg 17

Centenary Publishing House Ltd (Uganda) *Tel:* (041) 241599 *Fax:* (041) 250427, pg 652

Center for Advanced Welsh & Celtic Studies (United Kingdom) *Tel:* (01970) 626717 *Fax:* (01970) 627066 *E-mail:* cawcs@wales.ac.uk *Web Site:* www.aber.ac.uk/~awcwww/s/cyflwyniad.html, pg 677

Center for Agricultural Library & Technology Dissemination (CALTD) (Indonesia) *Tel:* (0251) 321746 (ext 66) *Fax:* (0251) 326561 *E-mail:* pustaka@bogor.net *Web Site:* pustaka.bogor.net, pg 1516

The Center for Romanian Studies (Romania) *Tel:* (032) 219000 *Fax:* (032) 219010, pg 539

Center Print Ltd (United Kingdom) *Tel:* (0115) 961 2277 *Fax:* (0115) 938 1424, pg 1163

Center Print Ltd (United Kingdom) *Tel:* (0115) 961 2277 *Fax:* (0115) 938 1424 *E-mail:* cprint@besharapress.co.uk *Web Site:* www.besharapress.com, pg 1183

Center Print Ltd (United Kingdom) *Tel:* (0115) 961 2277 *Fax:* (0115) 938 1424 *E-mail:* cprint@besharapress.co.uk, pg 1225

Centers of Academic Resources Chulalongkorn University (Thailand) *Tel:* (02) 218 2965; (02) 218 2964 *Fax:* (02) 215 3617 *Web Site:* www.car.chula.ac.th, pg 1550

Centraal Boekhuis BV (Netherlands) *Tel:* (0345) 47 59 11 *Fax:* (0345) 47 56 90 *E-mail:* info@centraal.boekhuis.nl *Web Site:* www.centraalboekhuis.nl, pg 1278

Central Library (India) *Tel:* (0265) 540133, pg 1515

Central de Publicaciones SA (Mexico) *Tel:* (05) 5104231, pg 1327

Central Africana Ltd (Malawi) *Tel:* 631509; 243595 *Fax:* 622236 *E-mail:* africana@sdwp.org.mw, pg 454

Central Agricultural Library (Bulgaria) *Tel:* (02) 70-55-17, pg 1496

The Central Archives for the History of the Jewish People (CAHJP) (Israel) *Tel:* (02) 5635716 *Fax:* (02) 5667686 *E-mail:* archives@vms.huji.ac.il *Web Site:* www.sites.huji.ac.il/cahjp/index.htm, pg 1519

Central Book Distribution Co, Ltd (Thailand) *Tel:* (02) 235-5400 *Fax:* (02) 237-8321, pg 1345

Central Books (United Kingdom) *Tel:* (0845) 458 9910 *Fax:* (0845) 458 9912 *E-mail:* orders@centralbooks.com *Web Site:* www.centralbooks.co.uk; www.centralbooks.com, pg 1349

Central Bookshop Ltd (Malawi) *Tel:* 621 447 *Fax:* 633 863, pg 1325

Central Catequistica Salesiana (CCS) (Spain) *Tel:* (091) 7252000 *Fax:* (091) 7262570 *E-mail:* apedidos@editorialccs.com; sei@editorialccs.com *Web Site:* www.editorialccs.com, pg 576

Central Catholic Library (Ireland) *Tel:* (01) 676 1264, pg 1518

Central European University Press (Hungary) *Tel:* (01) 327 3000 *Fax:* (01) 327 3183 *E-mail:* ceupress@ceupress.com *Web Site:* www.ceupress.com, pg 321

Central News Agency (CNA) (Namibia) *Tel:* (061) 25625 *Fax:* (061) 227210, pg 1328

Central News Agency Ltd (South Africa) *Tel:* (011) 4933200 *Fax:* (011) 4931438, pg 1340

Central Reference Library (Uganda) *Tel:* (041) 233633 *Fax:* (041) 348625 *E-mail:* library@imul.com, pg 1551

Central Secretariat Library (India) *Tel:* (011) 338 9684 *Fax:* (011) 338 4846 *E-mail:* root%csl@delnet.ren.nic.in, pg 1515

Central State Archives (Bulgaria) *Tel:* (02) 9400101; (02) 9400120; (02) 9400176 *Fax:* (02) 980 14 43 *E-mail:* gua@archives.government.bg *Web Site:* www.archives.government.bg, pg 1496

Central State Archives (Russian Federation) *Tel:* (095) 1597383, pg 1540

Central Tanganyika Press (United Republic of Tanzania) *Tel:* (061) 22140 *Fax:* (061) 324565, pg 643

Central Technical Library (Bulgaria) *Tel:* (02) 702935; (02) 715247; (02) 718030 (Interlibrary loan) *Fax:* (02) 710157 *E-mail:* ctb@nacid.nat.bg; ctbloan@nacid.nat.bg (Interlibrary loan) *Web Site:* www.nacid.nat.bg, pg 1496

Central Tibetan Secretariat (India) *Tel:* (01892) 22467 *Fax:* (01892) 23723 *E-mail:* ltwa@ndf.vsnl.net.in, pg 331

Centrala Handlu Zagranicznego ARS Polona SA (Poland) *Tel:* (022) 509 86 20 *Fax:* (022) 509 86 20 *E-mail:* arspolona@arspolona.com.pl *Web Site:* www.arspolona.com.pl, pg 1336

Biblioteca Centrala Universitara Mihail Eminescu (Romania) *Tel:* (0232) 264245 *Fax:* (0232) 261796 *E-mail:* bcuis@bcu-iasi.ro *Web Site:* www.bcu-iasi.ro, pg 1540

Istituto Centrale per il Catalogo Unico delle Biblioteche Italiane e per le Informazioni Bibliografiche (Italy) *Tel:* (06) 4989484 *Fax:* (06) 4959302 *Web Site:* www.iccu.sbn.it, pg 381, 1565

Centralna Narodna Biblioteka SR Crne Gore (Serbia and Montenegro) *Tel:* (086) 231 143 *Fax:* (086) 231 726 *E-mail:* cnb@cg.yu *Web Site:* cnbct.cnb.cg.ac.yu, pg 1542

Centre Africain d'Animation et d'Echanges Culturels Editions Khoudia (CAEC) (Senegal) *Tel:* 211023 *Fax:* 215109, pg 551

Centre Africain de Formation et de Recherche Administratives pour le Developpement, Centre de Documentation (Morocco) *Tel:* (061) 30 72 69 *Fax:* (039) 32 57 85 *E-mail:* cafrad@cafrad.org *Web Site:* www.cafrad.org, pg 1278

Centre Bibliotheque d'Information (Gabon) *Tel:* 21115, pg 1507

Centre Culturel De Differdange (Luxembourg) *Tel:* 587045 *Fax:* 580295, pg 451

Centre Culturel Francais, Bibliotheque (Congo) *Tel:* 83 25 65 *Fax:* 83 06 18, pg 1499

Centre Culturel Francais, Bibliotheque (Cote d'Ivoire) *Tel:* (020) 211699; (020) 225628 *Fax:* 227132 *E-mail:* ccf@netafric.ci, pg 1500

Centre De Documentation Universitaire (CDU) (Chad) *Tel:* 5144 44; 5144 44 697 *Fax:* 514 033 *E-mail:* runiv.rectorat@sdnted.undp.org, pg 1497

Centre de Librairie et d'Editions Techniques (CLET) (France) *Tel:* (01) 40926500 *Fax:* (01) 40926550, pg 152

Centre de Linguistique Appliquee (Senegal) *Tel:* 230126, pg 551

Centre de Publications Evangeliques (Cote d'Ivoire) *Tel:* 444805 *Fax:* 445817, pg 117

Centre de Recherche des Archives et de Documentation (CRAD) (Chad) *Tel:* 514 671 *Fax:* 516 079, pg 1497

Centre de Recherche, et Pedagogie Appliquee (The Democratic Republic of the Congo), pg 114

Centre de Recherches et d'Etudes Administratives (Tunisia) *Tel:* (01) 848 435; (01) 848 300 *Fax:* (01) 794 188 *E-mail:* webmaster@ena.nat.tn *Web Site:* www.ena.nat.tn, pg 1551

Centre de Vulgarisation Agricole (The Democratic Republic of the Congo) *Tel:* (012) 71165 *Fax:* (012) 21351, pg 114

Centre d'Edition et de Diffusion Africaines (Cote d'Ivoire) *Tel:* 21 24 65 10; 21 24 65 11 *Fax:* 21 25 05 67 *E-mail:* infos@ceda-ci.com *Web Site:* www.ceda-ci.com, pg 117

Centre d'Edition et de Diffusion Africaines (Cote d'Ivoire) *Tel:* 22 22 42; 22 20 55 *Fax:* 21 72 62 *Web Site:* www.mbendi.co.za/orgs/cg01.htm, pg 1307

Centre d'Edition et de Production pour l'Enseignement et la Recherche (CEPER) (Cameroon) *Tel:* (023) 221323, pg 98

Centre d'Enseignement Superieur de Niamey (Niger) *Tel:* 732713 *Fax:* 733862, pg 1533

Centre d'Etudes et Documentation Economique Juridique et Sociale (CEDEJ) (Egypt (Arab Republic of Egypt)) *Tel:* (02) 392 87 11; (02) 392 87 16; (02) 392 87 39; (02) 704641 *Fax:* (02) 392 87 91 *E-mail:* cedej@idsc.net.eg *Web Site:* www.cedej.org.eg, pg 137

Centre d'Information et de Conservation de l'Universite de Liege (Belgium) *Tel:* (04) 366 52 18 *Fax:* (04) 366 57 98; (04) 366 44 22 *E-mail:* press@ulg.ac.be *Web Site:* www.ulg.ac.be/hp.html, pg 1493

Centre Europeen pour l'Enseignement Superieur (Romania) *Tel:* (01) 3130839; (01) 3130698; (01) 3159956 *Fax:* (01) 3123567 *E-mail:* cepes@cepes.ro *Web Site:* www.cepes.ro, pg 1282

Centre for Alternative Technology (United Kingdom) *Tel:* (01654) 705980; (01654) 705959 (mail order); (01654) 705993 (CAT shop) *Fax:* (01654) 702782; (01654) 705999 (mail order); (01654) 703605 (education & courses) *E-mail:* pubs@cat.org.uk *Web Site:* www.cat.org.uk, pg 677

Centre for Basic Research (Uganda) *Tel:* (041) 231228; (041) 235533; (041) 342987 *Fax:* (041) 235413 *E-mail:* cbr@cbr-ug.org *Web Site:* www.cbr-ug.org, pg 652

Centre for Comparative Literature & Cultural Studies (Australia) *Tel:* (03) 9905 4000; (03) 9905 3059 *Fax:* (03) 9905 4007 *Web Site:* www.arts.monash.edu/au/cclcs, pg 17

Centre for Conflict Resolution (South Africa) *Tel:* (021) 6502503; (021) 6502750 *Fax:* (021) 6852142; (021) 6504053 *E-mail:* ccr@uctvax.uct.ac.za *Web Site:* www.uct.ac.za, pg 563

The Centre for Creative Communities (United Kingdom) *Tel:* (020) 7247 5385 *Fax:* (020) 7247 5256 *E-mail:* info@creativecommunities.org.uk *Web Site:* www.creativecommunities.org.uk, pg 1407

Centre for Documentation & Research (United Arab Emirates) *Tel:* (02) 444 5400 *Fax:* (02) 444 5811 *Web Site:* www.gebcad.com, pg 1552

Centre for Educational Technology (Israel) *Tel:* (03) 6460183 *Fax:* (03) 6460821, pg 366

Centre for European Policy Studies (Belgium) *Tel:* (02) 2293911 *Fax:* (02) 2194151; (02) 2293971 *E-mail:* info@ceps.be *Web Site:* www.ceps.be, pg 1262

Centre for Information on Language Teaching & Research (CILT) (United Kingdom) *Tel:* (020) 7379 5101; (020) 7379 5110 (resources library & information services) *Fax:* (020) 7379 5082 *E-mail:* publications@cilt.org.uk; library@cilt.org.uk (library information) *Web Site:* www.cilt.org.uk, pg 677

Centre for South Asian Studies (Pakistan) *Tel:* (042) 864014 *Fax:* (042) 5867206, pg 512

Centre International de Recherches 'Primitifs Flamands' ASBL (Belgium) *Tel:* (02) 7396866 *Fax:* (02) 7320105, pg 65

Centre National des Archives (Burkina Faso) *Tel:* 33-61-96; 32-47-12; 32-46-38 *Fax:* 31-49-26, pg 1496

Centre National de Documentation (Morocco) *Tel:* (037) 77 30 13 *Fax:* (037) 77 31 34 *E-mail:* cndportal@cnd.mpep.gov.ma *Web Site:* www.cndportal.net.ma, pg 1529

Centre National de Documentation Pedagogique (CNDP) (France) *Tel:* (01) 55 43 60 00 *Fax:* (01) 55 43 60 01 *Web Site:* www.cndp.fr/cndp_reseau, pg 152

Centre National de Production de Materiel Didactique (CNAPMAD) (Madagascar) *Tel:* (02) 289-54 *Fax:* (02) 200-53, pg 453

Centre National du Livre (France) *Tel:* (01) 49546868 *Fax:* (01) 45491021 *Web Site:* www.centrenationaldulivre.fr, pg 1399

Centre National Infor-Jeunes (CNIJ) (Belgium) *Tel:* (081) 22 08 72 *Fax:* (081) 22 82 64, pg 65

Centre of Legal Information (Lithuania) *Tel:* (02) 61 75 29; (02) 62 36 50 *Fax:* (02) 62 15 23 *E-mail:* webadm@utic.tm.lt, pg 449

Centre pour l'Innovation et la Recherche en Communication de l'Entreprise (CIRCE) (France) *Tel:* (01) 49 24 96 76, pg 152

Centre Protestant d'Editions et de Diffusion (CEDI) (The Democratic Republic of the Congo), pg 114

Centre Publications (Australia) *Tel:* (03) 8700149, pg 17

Centre Regional pour la Promotion du Livre en Afrique (CREPLA) (Cameroon) *Tel:* 224782; 2936, pg 1263

CentrePolygraph Traders & Publishers Co (Russian Federation) *Tel:* (095) 2817411 *Fax:* (095) 2844074, pg 544

Centro Agronomico Tropical de Investigacion y Ensenanza (CATIE) (Costa Rica) *Tel:* 556-6431 *Fax:* 556-1533 *E-mail:* comunicacion@catie.ac.cr *Web Site:* www.catie.ac.cr, pg 115

Centro Ambrosiano di Documentazione e Studi Religiosi (Italy) *Tel:* (02) 83.75.476 *Fax:* (02) 58.10.09.49 *E-mail:* cadr@cadr.it *Web Site:* www.cadr.it, pg 381

Centro Biblico (Italy) *Tel:* (081) 8048933 *Fax:* (081) 8048933, pg 381

Centro de Cultura Tradicional (Spain) *Tel:* (0923) 293255 *Fax:* (0923) 293256 *E-mail:* cct@dipsanet.es *Web Site:* www.dipsanet.es/cultura/culturatradicional/inicio.htm, pg 576

Centro de Documentacao e Informacao da Camara dos Deputados (Brazil) *Tel:* (061) 216 0000 *Toll Free Tel:* 800 619 619 *Web Site:* www.camara.gov.br, pg 1495

Centro de Documentacao e Informao para o Desenvolvimento (Cape Verde) *Tel:* 613969 *Fax:* 1527, pg 98

Centro de Documentacion Bibliotecologica (Argentina) *Tel:* (091) 28035 *Fax:* (091) 551447, pg 1557

Centro De Educacion Popular (Ecuador) *Tel:* (02) 525 521 *Fax:* (02) 542 818 *E-mail:* cedep@fmlaluna.com *Web Site:* www.jacomenet.com/laluna/cedep.html, pg 136

Centro de Estudios sobre Desarrollo Economico CEDE (Colombia) *Tel:* (01) 2849911; (01) 2824800 (ext 2461 & 2466) *Fax:* (01) 2841890 *E-mail:* cede@uniandes.edu.co *Web Site:* wwwprof.uniandes.edu.co, pg 1498

Centro de Estudios Avanzados en Ciencias Sociales (CEACS) del Instituto Juan March de Estudios e Investigaciones (Spain) *Tel:* (091) 4354240 *Fax:* (091) 5763420 *E-mail:* webmast@mail.march.es *Web Site:* www.march.es, pg 576

Centro de Estudios Mexicanos y Centroamericanos (Mexico) *Tel:* (05) 5 40 59 21; (05) 5 40 59 22 *Fax:* (05) 2 02 77 94 *E-mail:* cemca.lib@francia.org.mx *Web Site:* www.francia.org.mx/cemca, pg 463

Centro de Estudios Politicos Y Constitucionales (Spain) *Tel:* (091) 5401950 *Fax:* (091) 5419574 *E-mail:* cepc@cepc.es *Web Site:* www.cepc.es, pg 576

Centro de Estudos Juridicosdo Para (CEJUP) (Brazil) *Tel:* (091) 225-0355 *Fax:* (091) 241-3184, pg 79

Centro de Exportacion de Libros Espanoles SA (CELESA) (Spain) *Tel:* (091) 517 01 70 *Fax:* (091) 517 34 81 *E-mail:* celesa@celesa.com *Web Site:* www.celesa.es, pg 1342

Centro de Informacion Cientifica y Humanistica (Mexico) *Tel:* (055) 6223960 *Fax:* (055) 6162557 *E-mail:* admin@estadistica.unam.mx *Web Site:* dgedi.estadistica.unam.mx, pg 1529

Centro de la Mujer Peruana Flora Tristan (Peru) *Tel:* (01) 433-2765; (01) 433-1457; (01) 433-9060 *Fax:* (01) 433-9500 *E-mail:* postmast@flora.org.pe *Web Site:* www.flora.org.pe, pg 516

Centro de Planificacion y Estudios Sociales (CEPLAES) (Ecuador) *Tel:* (02) 548-547 *Fax:* (02) 566-207 *E-mail:* ceplaes@ceplaes.ec, pg 136

Centro de Traducciones y Terminologia Especializada (CTTE) (Cuba) *Tel:* (07) 862-6531; (07) 860-3411 *Fax:* (07) 862-6531 *E-mail:* comercial@idict.cu *Web Site:* www.cubaciencia.cu/, pg 1147

Centro Di (Italy) *Tel:* (055) 2342668 *Fax:* (055) 2342667, pg 381

Centro Documentazione Alpina (Italy) *Tel:* (011) 7720444 *Fax:* (011) 7732170 *Web Site:* www.cda.it, pg 381

Centro Editor de America Latina SA (Argentina) *Tel:* (011) 4371-2411, pg 4

Centro Editorial Mexicano Osiris SA (Mexico) *Tel:* (05) 5406902; (05) 2027185 *Fax:* (05) 2027185, pg 463

Centro Editoriale Valtortiano SRL (Italy) *Tel:* (0776) 807032 *Fax:* (0776) 809789 *E-mail:* cev@mariavaltorta.com *Web Site:* www.mariavaltorta.com, pg 381

Centro Estudos Geograficos (Portugal) *Tel:* (021) 778883 *Fax:* (021) 7938690 *E-mail:* ceg@mail.telepac.pt, pg 529

Centro Italiano Studi Alto Medioevo (Italy) *Tel:* (0743) 225630 *Fax:* (0743) 49902 *E-mail:* cisam@cisam.org *Web Site:* www.cisam.org, pg 381

Centro Latinoamericano de Demografia (CELADE) (Chile) *Tel:* (02) 4712000; (02) 2102000; (02) 2085051 *Fax:* (02) 2080252; (02) 2081946 *E-mail:* secepal@eclac.cl *Web Site:* www.eclac.org, pg 1264

Centro Nacional de Documentacion Cientifica, Tecnica y Economics (CNDCTE) (Uruguay) *Tel:* (02) 484172 *Fax:* (02) 496902, pg 1554

Centro Nacional de Documentacion Cientifica y Tecnologica - Universidad Mayor De S an Andres (Bolivia) *Tel:* (02) 359583 *Fax:* (02) 359586 *E-mail:* iiicndct@huayna.umsa.edu.bo, pg 1559

Centro Nacional de Informacion, Agencia Nacional ISBN (Mexico) *Tel:* (0555) 230 7632 *Fax:* (0555) 230 7634 *Web Site:* www.sep.gob.mx, pg 1277

Centro Programmazione Editoriale (CPE) (Italy) *Tel:* (059) 908065 *Fax:* (059) 908271, pg 381

Centro Psicologia Clinica (Portugal) *Tel:* (085) 4211986 *Fax:* (085) 4211986 *E-mail:* cdibera@tin.it *Web Site:* www.centro-psicologia.it, pg 529

Centro Regional para el Fomento del Libro en America Latina y el Caribe (Colombia) *Tel:* (01) 212 6056; (01) 249 5141; (01) 321 7501; (01) 540 2071; (01) 312 5690 *Fax:* (01) 255 4614 *E-mail:* cerlalc@impsat.net.co; info@cerlalc.org; libro@cerlalc.org *Web Site:* www.cerlalc.org, pg 110

Centro Regional para el Fomento del Libro en America Latina y el Caribe (Colombia) *Tel:* (01) 212-6056; (01) 249-5141 *Fax:* (01) 255-4614; (01) 321-7503 *E-mail:* libro@cerlalc.org *Web Site:* www.cerlalc.org, pg 1264

Centro Scientifico Torinese (Italy) *Tel:* (011) 3853656 *Fax:* (011) 3853244 *E-mail:* cse@estorinese.inet.it, pg 381

Edizioni Centro Studi Erickson (Italy) *Tel:* (0461) 950690 *Fax:* (0461) 950698 *E-mail:* info@erickson.it *Web Site:* www.erickson.it, pg 381

Centro Studi Terzo Mondo (Italy) *Tel:* (02) 29409041 *Fax:* (02) 29409041 *E-mail:* cstm@libero.it, pg 381

Centro UNESCO de San Sebastian (Spain) *Tel:* (0943) 427003 *Fax:* (0943) 427003 *E-mail:* unescoeskola@retemail.es *Web Site:* www.servicom.es/unesco, pg 577

Centrul National de Numerotare Standardizata Biblioteca Nationala (Romania) *Tel:* (021) 3112635 *Fax:* (021) 3124990 *E-mail:* isbn@bibnat.ro; issn@bibnat.ro *Web Site:* www.bibnat.ro, pg 1282

Forlaget Centrum (Denmark) *Tel:* 33 32 12 06 *Fax:* 33 32 12 07 *E-mail:* info@forlaget-centrum.dk *Web Site:* www.forlaget-centrum.dk, pg 130

Centrum Vedecko-Technickych Informaci SR (Slovakia) *Tel:* (02) 5292 3527 *Fax:* (02) 5292 3527; (02) 5296 4497 *E-mail:* cvti@tbb5.cvtisr.sk *Web Site:* www.sltk.stuba.sk, pg 1542

CEP Editions (France) *Tel:* (01) 42961550 *Fax:* (01) 48243489, pg 153

Cep Kitaplari AS (Turkey) *Tel:* (0212) 516 20 04 *Fax:* (0212) 516 20 05 *Web Site:* www.varlik.com.tr, pg 649

CEPA - Centro Editor de Psicologia Aplicada Ltda (Brazil) *Tel:* (021) 2220-6545 *Fax:* (021) 2262-2717 *E-mail:* psicocepa@psicocepa.com.br *Web Site:* www.psicocepa.com.br, pg 80

Cepadues Editions SA (France) *Tel:* (05) 61 40 57 36 *Fax:* (05) 61 41 79 89 *E-mail:* cepadues@cepadues.com *Web Site:* www.cepadues.com, pg 153

il Cerchio Iniziative Editoriali (Italy) *Tel:* (0541) 21158; (0541) 708190 *Fax:* (0541) 799173 *E-mail:* info@ilcerchio.it *Web Site:* www.ilcerchio.it, pg 381

Editions Cercle d'Art SA (France) *Tel:* (01) 48 87 92 12 *Fax:* (01) 48 87 47 79 *E-mail:* info@officieldesarts.com *Web Site:* www.officieldesarts.com/cercledart/, pg 153

Cercle de la Librairie (France) *Tel:* (01) 44 41 28 00 *Fax:* (01) 44 41 28 65 *E-mail:* commercial@electre.com *Web Site:* www.electre.com, pg 1267

CERDIC-Publications (France) *Tel:* (0388) 877107 *Fax:* (0388) 877125 *E-mail:* cerdic@wanadoo.fr, pg 153

Editura Ceres (Romania) *Tel:* (01) 2224836, pg 539

Editions du Cerf (France) *Tel:* (01) 44 18 12 12 *Fax:* (01) 45 56 04 27 *Web Site:* www.editionsducerf.fr, pg 153

Cesarini Hermanos (Argentina) *Tel:* (011) 4861-1152 *Fax:* (011) 4861-1152 *E-mail:* cesarinihnos@movi.com.ar, pg 4

Ceska Biblicka Spolecnost (Czech Republic) *Tel:* (02) 84 693 925 *Fax:* (02) 84 693 933 *E-mail:* cbs@dumbible.cz *Web Site:* www.dumbible.cz, pg 123

Ceska Expedice (Czech Republic) *Tel:* (02) 727 612 04, pg 123

Ceske Narodni Stredisko ISSN (Czech Republic) *Tel:* (02) 21 663 440 *Fax:* (02) 2222 1340 *E-mail:* issn@stk.cz *Web Site:* www.stk.cz/en/issn/index.htm, pg 1265

Cesoc Ltda (Chile) *Tel:* (02) 6391081; (02) 6336992 *Fax:* (02) 6325382 *E-mail:* cesoc@bellsouth.cl, pg 99

Cetal Ediciones (Chile) *Tel:* (032) 213360 *Fax:* (032) 214851, pg 99

Edicoes Cetop (Portugal) *Tel:* (021) 926 3222 *Fax:* (021) 921 7940, pg 529

The Ceylon Chamber of Commerce (Sri Lanka) *Tel:* (01) 2452183; (01) 2421745; (01) 2329143 *Fax:* (01) 2437477; (01) 2449352 *E-mail:* info@chamber.lk *Web Site:* www.chamber.lk, pg 606

CFM Publications (Jamaica) *Tel:* 876-927-1660; 876-927-1669 *Fax:* 876-927-0997 *E-mail:* helpdesk@uwimona.edu.jm *Web Site:* www.uwimona.edu.jm, pg 413

CFW Publications Ltd (Hong Kong) *Tel:* 2554 3004 *Fax:* 2543 8007, pg 316

CG Ediz Medico-Scientifiche (Italy) *Tel:* (011) 338507 *Fax:* (011) 3852750 *Web Site:* www.cgems.it, pg 381

Chadwyck-Healey France (CHF) (France) *Tel:* (01) 44 83 81 81 *Fax:* (01) 44 83 81 83, pg 153

Chadwyck-Healey Ltd (United Kingdom) *Tel:* (01223) 215512 *Fax:* (01223) 215514 *E-mail:* andrew.hall@proquest.co.uk *Web Site:* www.proquest.co.uk, pg 677

Chalantika (Bangladesh) *Tel:* (02) 257345 *Fax:* (02) 7115691, pg 61

Editions du Chalet (France) *Tel:* (01) 53263335 *Fax:* (01) 53263336, pg 153

Chalkface Press Pty Ltd (Australia) *Tel:* (08) 9385 1923 *Fax:* (08) 9385 1923 *E-mail:* info@chalkface.net.au; sales@wooldridges.com.au (orders) *Web Site:* www.chalkface.net.au, pg 17

Challenge Bookshops (Nigeria) *Tel:* (073) 53897; (073) 52230, pg 1331

Challenge Machinery Co (United States) *Tel:* 231-799-8484 *Fax:* 231-798-1275 *E-mail:* info@challengemachinery.com *Web Site:* www.challengemachinery.com, pg 1248

Chamaeleon Verlag AG (Switzerland) *Tel:* (01) 2525497 *Fax:* (01) 2725282, pg 620

Chambers Harrap Publishers Ltd (United Kingdom) *Tel:* (0131) 5565929 *Fax:* (0131) 5565313 *E-mail:* admin@chambers.co.uk; webmanager@chambers.co.uk *Web Site:* www.chambersharrap.co.uk, pg 677

Editions Jacqueline Chambon (France) *Tel:* (04) 23 23 27 *Fax:* (04) 26 55 02, pg 153

Editions de la Chambre de Commerce et d'Industrie SA (ECCI) (Belgium) *Tel:* (04) 344-50-88 *Fax:* (04) 343-05-53 *E-mail:* lvenanzi@ecci.be *Web Site:* www.ecci.be, pg 65

Chambre des Employes Prives (Luxembourg) *Tel:* 44 40 91-1 *Fax:* 44 40 91-250 *E-mail:* info@cepl.lu *Web Site:* www.cepl.lu, pg 451

Chambre Nationale du Livre Agence ISBN (Republic of Moldova) *Tel:* (02) 24 65 42 *Fax:* (02) 24 65 11 *E-mail:* cncm@moldova.cc *Web Site:* www.iatp.md/cnc, pg 1277

Editions Champ Vallon (France) *Tel:* (04) 50 56 15 51 *Fax:* (04) 50 56 15 64 *E-mail:* info@champ-vallon.com *Web Site:* www.champ-vallon.com, pg 153

Librairie des Champs-Elysees/Le Masque (France) *Tel:* (01) 44 41 74 50; (01) 44 41 74 00 *Fax:* (01) 43 26 91 04 *Web Site:* www.lemasque.com, pg 153

Chanakya Publications (India) *Tel:* (011) 711976, pg 331

Chancellor Publications (United Kingdom) *Tel:* (020) 7269 9150 *Fax:* (020) 7269 9151 *E-mail:* mail@chancellorpublication.com *Web Site:* www.chancellorpublication.com, pg 677

Chancerel International Publishers Ltd (Germany) *Tel:* (049711) 6672 5728 *Fax:* (049711) 6672 2004 *E-mail:* tvandree@klett-mail.de *Web Site:* www.chancerel.com, pg 208

Philippe Chancerel Editeur (France) *Tel:* (01) 39 65 69 18, pg 153

Nem Chand & Bros (India) *Tel:* (01332) 272258; (01332) 272752; (01322) 264343 *Fax:* (01332) 273258 *E-mail:* ncb_rke@rediffmail.com, pg 1315

S Chand & Co Ltd (India) *Tel:* (011) 3672080; (011) 3672081; (011) 3672082 *Fax:* (011) 3677446 *E-mail:* schand@vsnl.com, pg 331

Chang-josa Publishing Co (Republic of Korea) *Tel:* (02) 7380393, pg 438

Editions Chanlis (Belgium) *Tel:* (071) 326394, pg 65

Editions Chantecler (Belgium) *Tel:* (03) 8 70 44 00 *Fax:* (03) 8 77 21 15, pg 65

Chapman (United Kingdom) *Tel:* (0131) 5572207 *Fax:* (0131) 5569565 *E-mail:* admin@chapman-pub.co.uk *Web Site:* www.chapman-pub.co.uk, pg 677

Chapter Two (United Kingdom) *Tel:* (020) 8316 5389 *Fax:* (020) 8854 5963 *E-mail:* chapter2UK@aol.com *Web Site:* www.chaptertwo.org.uk, pg 678

Editions Chardon Bleu (France) *Tel:* (04) 72 39 02 13 *Fax:* (04) 72 39 04 03 *E-mail:* chardonbleued@aol.com *Web Site:* www.chardonbleu.com, pg 153

Editions du Chariot (France) *Tel:* (02) 37258989 *Fax:* (02) 37258900 *E-mail:* edchariot@aol.com *Web Site:* www.editions-du-chariot.com, pg 153

Deborah Charles Publications (United Kingdom) *Tel:* (0151) 724 2500 *Fax:* (0151) 729 0371 *E-mail:* dcp@legaltheory.demon.co.uk *Web Site:* www.legaltheory.demon.co.uk, pg 678

Editions Charles-Lavauzelle SA (France) *Tel:* (05) 55584500 *Fax:* (05) 55584543, pg 153

The Charlesworth Group (United Kingdom) *Tel:* (01484) 517077 *Fax:* (01484) 517068 *E-mail:* sales@charlesworth.com *Web Site:* www.charlesworth.com, pg 1184, 1225

Charotar Publishing House (India) *Tel:* (02692) 256237 *Fax:* (02692) 240089 *E-mail:* charotar@icenet.net; charotar@cphbooks.com *Web Site:* www.cphbooks.com, pg 332

Charran's Bookshop (1978) Ltd (Trinidad & Tobago) *Tel:* (868) 663-1884, pg 1345

Charran's Educational Publishers (Trinidad & Tobago) *Tel:* (868) 622-3832 *Fax:* (868) 623-5829, pg 647

La Charte Editions juridiques (Belgium) *Tel:* (02) 512 29 49 *Fax:* (02) 512 26 93 *E-mail:* info@lacharte.be *Web Site:* www.lacharte.be, pg 65

The Chartered Institute of Building (United Kingdom) *Tel:* (01344) 630700 *Fax:* (01344) 630777 *E-mail:* reception@ciob.org.uk *Web Site:* www.ciob.org.uk, pg 678

Chartered Institute of Journalists (CIJ) (United Kingdom) *Tel:* (020) 7252 1187 *Fax:* (020) 7232 2302 *E-mail:* memberservices@ioj.co.uk *Web Site:* www.ioj.co.uk, pg 1290

Chartered Institute of Library & Information Professionals (CILIP) (United Kingdom) *Tel:* (020) 7255 0500; (020) 7255 0505 (textphone) *Fax:* (020) 7255 0501 *E-mail:* info@cilip.org.uk *Web Site:* www.cilip.org.uk, pg 1572

Chartered Institute of Library & Information Professionals in Scotland (United Kingdom) *Tel:* (01698) 458888 *Fax:* (01698) 458899 *E-mail:* slic@slainte.org.uk *Web Site:* www.slainte.org.uk, pg 678

Chartered Institute of Personnel & Development (United Kingdom) *Tel:* (020) 8971 9000 *Fax:* (020) 8263 3333 *E-mail:* publish@cipd.co.uk *Web Site:* www.cipd.co.uk, pg 678

The Chartered Institute of Public Finance & Accountancy (United Kingdom) *Tel:* (020) 7543 5600 *Fax:* (020) 7543 5607 *E-mail:* publications@cipfa.org *Web Site:* www.cipfa.org.uk/shop, pg 678

Chase Publishing Services (United Kingdom) *Tel:* (01395) 514709 *Fax:* (01395) 514709 *E-mail:* r.addicott@btinternet.com, pg 1163

Chase Publishing Services (United Kingdom) *Tel:* (01395) 514709 *Fax:* (01395) 514709, pg 1184, 1247

Chasse Maree (France) *Tel:* (02) 98 92 66 33 *Fax:* (02) 98 92 04 34 *E-mail:* chasse-maree@glenat.com *Web Site:* www.chasse-maree.com, pg 153

Chatham Publishing (United Kingdom) *Tel:* (020) 8458 6314 *Fax:* (020) 8905 5245 *E-mail:* info@chathampublishing.com *Web Site:* www.chathampublishing.com, pg 678

Chemical Industry Press (China) *Tel:* (010) 64918054; (010) 4213641; (010) 4234411 *Fax:* (010) 64918054 *Web Site:* www.cip.com.cn, pg 101

Verlag fur chemische Industrie H Ziolkowsky GmbH (Germany) *Tel:* (0821) 325-830 *Fax:* (0821) 325-8323, pg 208

Editions du Chene (France) *Tel:* (01) 43 92 30 00 *Fax:* (01) 43 92 33 81, pg 154

Cheng Chung Book Co, Ltd (Taiwan, Province of China) *Tel:* (02) 2382-2815 *Fax:* (02) 2389-3571 *Web Site:* www.ccbc.com.tw, pg 639

Cheng Wen Publishing Company (Taiwan, Province of China) *Tel:* (02) 2362-8032 *Fax:* (02) 2366-0806 *E-mail:* ccicncwp@ms17.hinet.net, pg 639

Cheng Yun Publishing Company Ltd (Taiwan, Province of China) *Tel:* (02) 28117798 *Fax:* (02) 28123041 *E-mail:* toybook@ms34.hinet.net *Web Site:* www.toybook.com.tw, pg 639

Chengdu Maps Publishing House (China) *Tel:* (028) 485 2177; (028) 445 3030 *E-mail:* ccph@public.cd.sc.cn, pg 101

Cheong-mun-gag Publishing Co (Republic of Korea) *Tel:* (02) 9851451; (02) 9897423; (02) 9897421 *Fax:* (02) 9828679 *E-mail:* CMGbook@hitel.kol.co.kr, pg 438

Le Cherche Midi Editeur (France) *Tel:* (01) 42 22 71 20 *Fax:* (01) 45 44 08 38 *E-mail:* infos@cherche-midi.com *Web Site:* www.cherche-midi.com, pg 154

Cherokee Literary Agency (South Africa) *Tel:* (021) 671-4508 *Fax:* (021) 761-4329, pg 1136

Cherrytree Books (United Kingdom) *Tel:* (020) 7487 0920 *Fax:* (020) 7487 0921 *E-mail:* sales@evansbrothers.co.uk *Web Site:* www.evansbooks.co.uk, pg 678

Chetana Private Ltd Publishers & International Booksellers (India) *Tel:* (022) 228 81159; (022) 282 4983 *Fax:* (022) 262 4316 *E-mail:* orders@chetana.com; chetana1946@chetana.com *Web Site:* www.chetana.com, pg 332

Chiang Mai University Library (Thailand) *Tel:* (053) 944501 *Fax:* (053) 222766 *E-mail:* prasit@lib.cmunet.edu *Web Site:* www.lib.cmu.ac.th, pg 645

Chien Chen Bookstore Publishing Company Ltd (Taiwan, Province of China) *Tel:* (07) 3820363 *Fax:* (07) 3892816, pg 639

Chijin Shokan Co Ltd (Japan) *Tel:* (03) 3235-4422 *Fax:* (03) 3235-8984 *E-mail:* chijinshokan@nifty.com *Web Site:* www.chijinshokan.co.jp, pg 416

Chikuma Shobo Publishing Co Ltd (Japan) *Tel:* (03) 5687-2671 *Fax:* (03) 5687-1585 *Web Site:* www.chikumashobo.co.jp, pg 416

Chikyu-sha Co Ltd (Japan) *Tel:* (03) 3585-0087 *Fax:* (03) 3589-2902, pg 416

Wilfred Bwalya Chilangwa Publications (Zambia) *Tel:* (01) 282998 *E-mail:* hope@samnet.zm, pg 781

Child Honsha Co Ltd (Japan) *Tel:* (03) 3813-3781 *Fax:* (03) 3818-3778, pg 416

Childerset Publishers (Australia) *Tel:* (074) 425510 *Fax:* (074) 425512 *E-mail:* tessgsp@ozemail.com.au, pg 17

Children's Book Circle (United Kingdom) *Tel:* (020) 7416 3130 *Fax:* (020) 7739 2318 *Web Site:* www.booktrusted.com/handbook/journals/bookskeeps.html, pg 1290

The Children's Book Council of Australia (Australia) *Tel:* (08) 8332 2845 *Fax:* (08) 8333 0394 *E-mail:* office@cbc.org.au *Web Site:* www.cbc.org.au, pg 1395

The Children's Book Store Company Ltd (Taiwan, Province of China) *Tel:* (02) 2762-8222 *Fax:* (02) 2760-4322 *Web Site:* www.tong-nian.com.tw, pg 1344

Children's Book Trust (India) *Tel:* (011) 23316974; (011) 23316970 *Fax:* (011) 23721090 *E-mail:* cbtnd@vsnl.com *Web Site:* www.childrensbooktrust.com, pg 332

Children's Books History Society (United Kingdom) *Tel:* (01992) 464885 *Fax:* (01992) 464885 *E-mail:* cbhs@abcgarrelt.demon.co.uk, pg 1407

Children's Literature Association of Nigeria (Nigeria) *Tel:* (022) 400550; (022) 400614 *Fax:* (022) 711254, pg 1280

Children's Literature Documentation & Research Centre, Ibadan (Nigeria) *Fax:* (022) 711254, pg 1280

The Children's Press (Ireland) *Tel:* (01) 497-3628 *Fax:* (01) 496-8263 *E-mail:* cle@iol.ie *Web Site:* www.irelandseye.com, pg 358

Children's Writers & Illustrators Group (United Kingdom) *Tel:* (020) 7373 6642 *Fax:* (020) 7373 5768 *Web Site:* www.booktrusted.com/booklists/listindex.html, pg 1290

Child's Play (International) Ltd (United Kingdom) *Tel:* (01793) 616286 *Fax:* (01793) 512795 *E-mail:* allday@childs-play.com *Web Site:* www.childs-play.com, pg 679

Child's World Education Ltd (United Kingdom) *Tel:* (01753) 647060 *Fax:* (01753) 645522, pg 679

Chin Chin Publications Ltd (Taiwan, Province of China) *Tel:* (02) 25084331 *Fax:* (02) 25074902 *E-mail:* we122179@ms13.hinet.net *Web Site:* www.weichuan.org.tw, pg 639

China National Association of Literature and the Arts (Taiwan, Province of China), pg 1405

China Agriculture Press (China) *Tel:* (010) 5005665 *Fax:* (010) 5005894 *E-mail:* fcap@bj.col.com.cn, pg 102

China Books (Australia) *Tel:* (03) 9663 8822 *Fax:* (03) 9663 8821 *E-mail:* info@chinabooks.com.au *Web Site:* www.chinabooks.com.au, pg 17

China Braille Publishing House (China) *Tel:* (010) 6382 5214; (010) 6381 7417 *Fax:* (010) 6383 3585, pg 102

China Cartographic Publishing House (China) *Tel:* (010) 6356 4947 *Fax:* (010) 6352 9403 *E-mail:* fanyi@chinamap.com, pg 102

China Express Media Ltd (Hong Kong) *Tel:* 2575 7288 *Fax:* 2575 7088 *E-mail:* kcchan@ossima.com, pg 316

China Film Press (China) *Tel:* (010) 4216761; (010) 4219917 *Fax:* (010) 4219489, pg 102

China Foreign Economic Relations & Trade Publishing House (China) *Tel:* (010) 64248236; (010) 64219742; (010) 64245686 *Fax:* (010) 64219392 *E-mail:* cfertph@263.net *Web Site:* www.caitec.org.cn/cfertph/indexv3.htm, pg 102

China Forestry Publishing House (China) *Tel:* (010) 6013117; (010) 661884477 *Fax:* (010) 66180373 *E-mail:* cfph@public3.bta.net.cn, pg 102

China International Book Trading Corporation (China) *Tel:* (010) 68412026 *Fax:* (010) 68475199 *E-mail:* sinda@mail.cnokay.com *Web Site:* chinabooks.cnokay.com, pg 1305

China ISBN Agency (China) *Tel:* (010) 65127806; (010) 65212832 *Fax:* (010) 65127875, pg 1264

China Knowledge Press (Singapore) *Tel:* (065) 6310 8737 *Fax:* (065) 6310 8738 *E-mail:* info@chinaknowledge-press.com *Web Site:* www.chinaknowledge-press.com, pg 555

China Labour Publishing House (China) *Tel:* (010) 64911180; (010) 4910488, pg 102

China Law Magazine Ltd (Taiwan, Province of China) *Tel:* (02) 23814211 *Fax:* (02) 23814211 *E-mail:* chinals@hk.china.com, pg 639

China Light Industry Press (China) *Tel:* (010) 65271562 *Fax:* (010) 65121371, pg 102

China Machine Press (CMP) (China) *Tel:* (010) 88379973 *Fax:* (010) 68320405 (orders) *E-mail:* cjhui@mail.machineinfo.gov.cn *Web Site:* www.cmpbook.com; www.machineinfo.gov.cn, pg 102

China Materials Management Publishing House (China) *Tel:* (010) 68392913; (010) 68392825 *Fax:* (010) 8392911, pg 102

China National Publications Import & Export Corp (China) *Tel:* (010) 65082324; (010) 65086873; (010) 65086874 *Fax:* (010) 65086860 *E-mail:* info-center@cnpeak.com *Web Site:* www.cnpiec.com.cn, pg 1305

China Ocean Press (China) *Tel:* (010) 62112880-888 *Fax:* (010) 62112880-617 *E-mail:* zbs@oceanpress.com.cn *Web Site:* www.oceanpress.com.cn, pg 102

China Oil & Gas Periodical Office (China) *Tel:* (010) 64219111, pg 102

China PEN Centre (China) *Fax:* 8610 64221704, pg 1398

China Pictorial Publishing House (China) *Tel:* (010) 68412392; (010) 68414896; (010) 68412665 *Fax:* (010) 68413023 *E-mail:* wangjingtang@hotmail.com *Web Site:* www.china-pictorial.com, pg 102

China Social Sciences Publishing House (China) *Tel:* (010) 64031534 *Fax:* (010) 64074509, pg 103

China Society for Library Science (China) *Tel:* (010) 6841 9270 *Fax:* (010) 6841 9271 *E-mail:* ztxhmsc@publicf.nlc.gov.cn *Web Site:* www.nlc.gov.cn, pg 1560

China Textile Press (China) *Tel:* (010) 64168240 *Fax:* (010) 64168225 *Web Site:* www.c-textilep.com, pg 103

China Theatre Publishing House (China) *Tel:* (010) 62244207; (010) 62244208, pg 103

China Tibetology Publishing House (China) *Tel:* (010) 64917618; (010) 64932942 *Fax:* (010) 4917619, pg 103

China Times Publishing Co (Taiwan, Province of China) *Tel:* (02) 2304-7103 *Fax:* (02) 23027844 *Web Site:* www.chinatimes.com.tw, pg 639

China Translation & Publishing Corp (China) *Tel:* (010) 66168196; (010) 66168647 *Fax:* (010) 6022734 *E-mail:* ctpc@public.bta.net.cn, pg 103

China Youth Publishing House (China) *Tel:* (010) 64033812; (010) 64032266 *Fax:* (010) 4031803, pg 103

Chinese Christian Literature Council Ltd (Hong Kong) *Tel:* 2367 8031, pg 316

Chinese Christian Literature Council Taiwan Ltd (Taiwan, Province of China) *Tel:* (02) 7080230 *Fax:* (02) 7551895, pg 639

Chinese Language Society of Hong Kong (Hong Kong) *Tel:* (02) 5284853, pg 1400

Chinese Literature Press (China) *Tel:* (010) 68326678 *Fax:* (010) 68326678 *E-mail:* chinalit@public.east.cn.net, pg 103

Chinese Marketing & Communications (United Kingdom) *Tel:* (0161) 237 3821 *Fax:* (0161) 236 7558 *E-mail:* support@chinese-marketing.com *Web Site:* www.chinese-marketing.com, pg 1150

Chinese Pedagogics Publishing House (China) *Tel:* (010) 68326333 *Fax:* (010) 8317390, pg 103

Chinese University of Hong Kong Library System (Hong Kong) *Tel:* 2609-7306 *Fax:* 2603-6952 *E-mail:* library@cuhk.edu.hk *Web Site:* www.lib.cuhk.edu.hk, pg 1514

The Chinese University Press (Hong Kong) *Tel:* 2609 6508 *Fax:* 2603 6692; 2603 7355 *E-mail:* cup@cuhk.edu.hk *Web Site:* www.cuhk.edu.hk/cupress.w1.htm; www.chineseupress.com, pg 316

Chingchic Publishers (Australia) *E-mail:* chingchic@winshop.com.au *Web Site:* www.chingchic.com, pg 17

Editions Chiron (France) *Tel:* (01) 30141930 *Fax:* (01) 34603132 *E-mail:* chiron@wanadoo.fr, pg 154

Chiron Media (Australia) *Tel:* (074) 947311 *Fax:* (074) 947890 *E-mail:* chiron@acslink.net.au, pg 17

Chiron-Verlag Reinhardt Stiehle (Germany) *Tel:* (07071) 8884150 *Fax:* (07071) 8884151 *E-mail:* info@chironverlag.de *Web Site:* www.chironverlag.de, pg 208

Cedric Chivers Ltd (United Kingdom) *Tel:* (0117) 9371910 *Fax:* (0117) 9371920 *E-mail:* info@cedricchivers.co.uk *Web Site:* www.cedricchivers.co.uk, pg 1225

Chmielorz GmbH Verlag (Germany) *Tel:* (0611) 360980 *Fax:* (0611) 36098-17 *E-mail:* tme@chmielorz.de *Web Site:* www.chmielorz.de, pg 208

CHOICE Magazine (Australia) *Tel:* (02) 9577 3399 *Fax:* (02) 9577 3377 *E-mail:* ausconsumer@choice.com.au *Web Site:* www.choice.com.au, pg 17

Chokechai Theues Shop (Thailand) *Tel:* (02) 2225-7877, pg 645

An Chomhairle Leabharlanna (Ireland) *Tel:* (01) 6761963; (01) 6761167 *Fax:* (01) 6766721 *E-mail:* info@librarycouncil.ie *Web Site:* www.librarycouncil.ie, pg 1565

Chong Moh Offset Printing Ltd (Singapore) *Tel:* 8622701 *Fax:* 8624335 *E-mail:* chongmoh@singnet.com.sg, pg 1161, 1181, 1222

Chong No Books Publishing Co Ltd (Republic of Korea) *Tel:* (02) 7325381 *Fax:* (02) 7326202, pg 438

Chongqing Library (China) *Tel:* (023) 6362-2596 *Fax:* (023) 6385-1474 *Web Site:* www.cqlib.org, pg 1497

Chongqing University Press (China) *Tel:* (023) 65111125 *Fax:* (023) 65106879 *E-mail:* chenxy@cqup.com.cn *Web Site:* www.cqup.com.cn, pg 208

Chopsons Pte Ltd (Singapore) *Tel:* 64483634 *Fax:* 64481071 *E-mail:* chopsons@singnet.com.sg, pg 555

Chopsticks Publications Ltd (Hong Kong) *Tel:* 2336-8433 *Fax:* 2338-1462 *E-mail:* chopsticks1971@netvigator.com, pg 316

Chorion IP (United Kingdom) *Tel:* (020) 7434 1880 *Fax:* (020) 7434 1882 *E-mail:* info@enidblyton.co.uk *Web Site:* www.chorion.co.uk, pg 679

Chorus-Verlag (Germany) *Tel:* (089) 634 999 60 *Fax:* (089) 634 999 61 *Web Site:* www.chorus-verlag.de, pg 208

The Chosun Ilbo Co, Ltd (Republic of Korea) *Tel:* (02) 7245114 *Fax:* (02) 7246199, pg 438

Chotard et Associes Editeurs (France) *Tel:* (01) 41 29 96 05 *Fax:* (01) 41 29 98 15, pg 154

Chowkhamba Sanskrit Series Office (India) *Tel:* (0542) 2333458 *Fax:* (0542) 2333458 *E-mail:* cssoffice@satyam.net.in *Web Site:* www.chowkhambaseries.com, pg 332

Chr Belser AG fur Verlagsgeschaefte und Co KG (Germany) *Tel:* (0711) 2191-0 *Fax:* (0711) 2191-330, pg 208

Christchurch City Libraries (New Zealand) *Tel:* (03) 941 7923 *Fax:* (03) 941 7848 *E-mail:* library@ccc.govt.nz *Web Site:* library.christchurch.org.nz, pg 1532

Christian Audio-Visual Action (CAVA) (Zimbabwe) *Tel:* (04) 752233 *Fax:* (04) 727030 *E-mail:* cava@mango.zw, pg 783

The Christian Book Centre (Papua New Guinea) *Tel:* 852 2043 *Fax:* 852 3376, pg 515

Christian Book Service (Guyana) *Tel:* (02) 52521 *Fax:* (02) 54039, pg 1314

Christian Booksellers Association (United Kingdom) *Tel:* (0161) 434 7000 *Fax:* (0161) 445 2911 *E-mail:* info@cba-ukeurop.org *Web Site:* www.cba-ukeurop.org, pg 1290

Christian Booksellers' Association (NZ Chapter) (New Zealand) *Tel:* (07) 888 6010 *E-mail:* info@cbaonline.org *Web Site:* www.cbaonline.org, pg 1280

Christian Booksellers Association of Nigeria (Nigeria) *Tel:* (073) 452387 *E-mail:* cban@bwave.net *Web Site:* www.cbaonline.org, pg 1280

Christian Bookselling Association of Australia Inc (Australia) *Tel:* (02) 9524 3347 *Fax:* (02) 9540 3001 *E-mail:* info@cbaa.com.au *Web Site:* www.cbaa.com.au, pg 1260

Christian Bookstore (Thailand) *Tel:* (02) 234-7991, pg 1345

Christian Communications Ltd (Hong Kong) *Tel:* 2725-8558 *Fax:* 2386-1804 *Web Site:* www.ccfellow.org, pg 316

Christian Education (United Kingdom) *Tel:* (0121) 472 4242 *Fax:* (0121) 472 7575 *E-mail:* enquiries@christianeducation.org.uk *Web Site:* www.christianeducation.org.uk/cep/cep_about.htm, pg 679

Christian Focus Publications Ltd (United Kingdom) *Tel:* (01862) 871 011 *Fax:* (01862) 871 699 *E-mail:* info@christianfocus.com *Web Site:* www.christianfocus.com, pg 679

Christian Literature Association in Malawi (Malawi) *Tel:* 620839; 673091, pg 454

Christian Literature Crusade (Australia) *Tel:* (02) 9875 1330 *Fax:* (02) 9481 8304, pg 18

Christian Literature Crusade (Barbados) *Tel:* 429-5630 *Fax:* 426-9254, pg 1301

The Christian Literature Society (India) *Tel:* (044) 25354296; (044) 25354297 *Fax:* (044) 25354297, pg 332

The Christian Literature Society of Korea (Republic of Korea) *Tel:* (02) 553-0870 *Fax:* (02) 555-7721, pg 438

Christian Research Association (United Kingdom) *Tel:* (020) 8294 1989 *Fax:* (020) 8294 0014 *E-mail:* admin@christian-research.org.uk *Web Site:* www.christian-research.org.uk, pg 679

Christian Verlag GmbH (Germany) *Tel:* (089) 381803-17; (089) 381803-31 *Fax:* (089) 38180381 *E-mail:* info@christian-verlag.de *Web Site:* www.christian-verlag.de, pg 208

Christiana-Verlag (Switzerland) *Tel:* (052) 741 41 31 *Fax:* (052) 741 20 92 *E-mail:* info@christiana.ch *Web Site:* www.christiana.ch, pg 620

Hans Christians Druckerei und Verlag GmbH & Co KG (Germany) *Tel:* (040) 35 60 06-0 *Fax:* (040) 35 60 06-26 *E-mail:* verlag@christians.de *Web Site:* www.christians.de, pg 208

Christliche Verlagsgesellschaft mbH (Germany) *Tel:* (02771) 8302-0 *Fax:* (02771) 8302-30 *E-mail:* info@cv-dillenburg.de *Web Site:* www.cb-buchshop.de, pg 208

Christliches Verlagshaus GmbH (Germany) *Tel:* (0711) 830000 *Fax:* (0711) 830010, pg 208

Uitgeverij Christofoor (Netherlands) *Tel:* (030) 692 39 74 *Fax:* (030) 691 48 34 *E-mail:* info@christofoor.nl, pg 480

Christoph Merian Verlag (Switzerland) *Tel:* (061) 226 33 25 *Fax:* (061) 226 33 45 *E-mail:* verlag@merianstiftung.ch *Web Site:* www.christoph-merian-verlag.ch, pg 620

Christophorus-Verlag GmbH (Germany) *Tel:* (0761) 27170 *Fax:* (0761) 2717352, pg 208

Christusbruderschaft Selbitz ev, Abt Verlag (Germany) *Tel:* (09280) 68-34 *Fax:* (09280) 68-68 *E-mail:* info@verlag-christusbruderschaft.de *Web Site:* www.verlag-christusbruderschaft.de, pg 209

Chroma Graphics (Overseas) Pte Ltd (Singapore) *Tel:* 67423706 *Fax:* 67486712, pg 1181

Chronicles Publishers Ltd (Israel) *Tel:* (03) 5615052 *Fax:* (03) 5624104 *E-mail:* chronicl@inter.net.il, pg 1159

Chronique Sociale (France) *Tel:* (04) 78372212 *Fax:* (04) 78420318 *E-mail:* chroniquesociale@wanadoo.fr *Web Site:* www.chroniquesociale.com, pg 154

Chronos Verlag (Switzerland) *Tel:* (01) 265 4343 *Fax:* (01) 265 4344 *E-mail:* info@chronos-verlag.ch *Web Site:* www.chronos-verlag.ch, pg 621

The Chrysalis Press (United Kingdom) *Tel:* (01926) 855223 *E-mail:* chrysalis@margaretbuckley.com, pg 679

Chrysi Penna - Golden Pen Books (Greece) *Tel:* (01) 03805672 *Fax:* (01) 03825205 *E-mail:* xpenna@acci.gr; info@chrissipenna.com *Web Site:* www.chrissipenna.com, pg 306

Chrysopolitissa Publishers (Cyprus) *Tel:* (022) 353929 *Fax:* (022) 353929, pg 121

Chryssos Typos AE Ekodeis (Greece) *Tel:* (01) 3637945 *Fax:* (01) 3824417, pg 306

Chu Liu Book Company (Taiwan, Province of China) *Tel:* (02) 2371 1031 *Fax:* (02) 3815823 *E-mail:* chuliu@ms13.hinet.net, pg 639

Chugh Publications (India) *Tel:* (0532) 623561, pg 332

Chung Hwa Book Co (HK) Ltd (Hong Kong) *Tel:* 2715 0176 *Fax:* 2713 8202; 2713 4675 *E-mail:* info@chunghwabook.com.hk; pub-dept@chunghwabook.com.hk *Web Site:* www.chunghwabook.com.hk, pg 316

Chung Hwa Book Co Ltd (Taiwan, Province of China) *Tel:* (02) 8797 8669 *Fax:* (02) 8797 8909, pg 639

Chung Rim Publishing Co Ltd (Republic of Korea) *Tel:* (02) 544-4341 *Fax:* (02) 5468053, pg 438

Chuo-Tosho Co Ltd (Japan) *Tel:* (075) 441-2174 *Fax:* (075) 441-3300, pg 416

Chuokoron-Shinsha Inc (Japan) *Tel:* (03) 3563-1431 *Fax:* (03) 3561-5922 *E-mail:* honyaku-irie@chuko.co.jp *Web Site:* www.chuko.co.jp, pg 416

Church Archivists Press (Australia) *Tel:* (07) 3865 0466 *Fax:* (07) 3865 0458, pg 18

Church House Publishing (United Kingdom) *Tel:* (020) 7898 1300 *Fax:* (020) 7898 1305 *E-mail:* sales@c-of-e.org.uk *Web Site:* www.chpublishing.co.uk, pg 679

Church Mouse Press (New Zealand) *Tel:* (063) 357-2445 *Fax:* (063) 357-2445, pg 495

Church Society (United Kingdom) *Tel:* (01923) 235111 *Fax:* (01923) 800362 *E-mail:* enquiries@churchsociety.org *Web Site:* www.churchsociety.org, pg 679

Church Union (United Kingdom) *Tel:* (020) 7222 6952 *Fax:* (020) 7976 7180 *E-mail:* churchunion@care4free.net *Web Site:* www.churchunion.care4free.net, pg 680

Chvojkova nakladatelstvi (Czech Republic) *Tel:* (02) 225 169 65; (02) 717 430 23 *Fax:* (02) 225 169 65, pg 123

CIACO (Belgium) *Tel:* (018) 213700 *Fax:* (018) 212372, pg 65

CIAT - Centro Internacional de Agricultura Tropical (Colombia) *Tel:* (02) 445-0000 *Fax:* (02) 445-0073 *E-mail:* ciat@cgiar.org *Web Site:* www.ciat.cgiar.org, pg 110

CIC Edizioni Internazionali (Italy) *Tel:* (06) 8412673 *Fax:* (06) 8412688; (06) 8412687 *E-mail:* info@gruppocic.it *Web Site:* www.gruppocic.it, pg 381

Cicada Press (New Zealand) *Tel:* (09) 4180890 *Fax:* (09) 4181142, pg 495

CICC Book House, Leading Publishers & Booksellers (India) *Tel:* (0484) 353557; (0484) 355658, pg 332

Cicero-Chr Erichsens (Denmark) *Tel:* 3316-0308 *Fax:* 33160307 *E-mail:* info@cicero.dk *Web Site:* www.cicero.dk, pg 130

Cicero Editeurs (France) *Tel:* (01) 43544757 *Fax:* (01) 40517385, pg 154

Cicero Presse Verlag & Antiquariat (Germany) *Tel:* (04651) 890305 *Fax:* (04651) 890885 *E-mail:* ciceropresse@t-online.de *Web Site:* www.zvab.com, pg 209

Cicerone Press (United Kingdom) *Tel:* (01539) 562 069 *Fax:* (01539) 563 417 *E-mail:* info@cicerone.co.uk *Web Site:* www.cicerone.co.uk, pg 680

Editora Cidade Nova (Brazil) *Tel:* (011) 4158-2252 *Fax:* (011) 4158-2252 *E-mail:* editoria@cidadenova.org.br *Web Site:* www.cidadenova.org.br, pg 80

Cidade Nova Editora (Portugal) *Tel:* (01) 2478734 *Fax:* (01) 2476369 *Web Site:* perola.net-rubi.com.br, pg 529

CIDAP (Ecuador) *Tel:* (07) 829-451; (07) 828-878 *Fax:* (07) 831-450 *E-mail:* ciesa@pi.pro.ec, pg 136

Cideb Editrice SRL (Italy) *Tel:* (0185) 60241 *Fax:* (0185) 230100 *E-mail:* info@cideb.com *Web Site:* www.cideb.it, pg 382

CIE (International Commission on Illumination Central Bureau) (Austria) *Tel:* (01) 714 31 87 0 *Fax:* (01) 713 08 38 18 *E-mail:* ciecb@ping.at *Web Site:* www.cie.co.at/cie, pg 1261

Ciela Publishing House (Bulgaria) *Tel:* (02) 951 63 76; (02) 954 93 97; (02) 951 66 97 *Fax:* (02) 954 93 97 *E-mail:* ciela@bulnet.bg *Web Site:* www.ciela.net, pg 93

Publicacoes Ciencia e Vida Lda (Portugal) *Tel:* (021) 3427989 *Fax:* (021) 3460224, pg 529

Instituto de Ciencias de la Computacion (NCR) (Paraguay) *Tel:* (021) 490076 *Fax:* (021) 497849, pg 516

Editorial de Ciencias Sociales (Cuba) *Tel:* (07) 2036090; (07) 333441 *Fax:* (07) 2304801 *E-mail:* nuevomil@icl.cult.cu, pg 120

Libreria Cientifica SA (Ecuador) *Tel:* (02) 12556, pg 1308

Cientifica Interamericana SACI, Editorial (Argentina) *Tel:* (011) 4822-8883 *Fax:* (011) 4827-0486 *E-mail:* edit@interame.satlink.net, pg 4

Editora Cientifica Medica Latinoamerican SA de CV (Mexico) *Tel:* (05) 55206702 *Fax:* (05) 52020926, pg 463

Editorial Cientifico Tecnica (Cuba) *Tel:* (07) 2036090 *Fax:* (07) 333441 *E-mail:* nuevomil@icl.cult.cu, pg 120

Ediciones Cieplan (Chile) *Tel:* (02) 2323212; (02) 2324558; (02) 6333836 *Fax:* (02) 3340312 *E-mail:* cieplan@ctcreuna.cl, pg 99

Marianne Cieslik (Germany) *Tel:* (02461) 51222; (02461) 57661 *Fax:* (02461) 52772, pg 209

CIESPAL (Centro Internacional de Estudios Superiores de Comunicacion para America Latina) (Ecuador) *Tel:* (02) 2524177 *Fax:* (02) 2502487 *E-mail:* publicaciones@ciespal.net *Web Site:* www.ciespal.net, pg 136

Il Cigno Galileo Galilei-Edizioni di Arte e Scienza (Italy) *Tel:* (06) 6865493; (06) 6873842 *Fax:* (06) 6892109 *E-mail:* info@ilcigno.org, pg 382

Libreria Cima (Ecuador) *Tel:* (02) 571218; (02) 571318, pg 1308

Cimaise sarl (France) *Tel:* (01) 45437045 *Fax:* (01) 45437045, pg 154

Cinema (Czech Republic) *Tel:* (02) 627 83 95-6 *Fax:* (02) 627 72 39 *E-mail:* schur@comp.cz, pg 123

CIPG EDITORIAL & TRANSLATION RESEARCH CENTER INDUSTRY

CIPG Editorial & Translation Research Center (China) *Tel:* (010) 68326681 *E-mail:* ftrchina@public3.bta.net.cn *Web Site:* www.tac-online.org.cn, pg 1147

Cirad (France) *Tel:* (04) 67 61 58 00 *Fax:* (04) 67 61 55 47 *Web Site:* www.cirad.fr, pg 154

Ciranna e Ferrara (Italy) *Tel:* (0362) 230849 *Fax:* (0362) 326213, pg 382

Ciranna - Roma (Italy) *Tel:* (091) 224499 *Fax:* (091) 311064 *E-mail:* info@ciranna.it *Web Site:* www.ciranna.it, pg 382

Circe Ediciones, SA (Spain) *Tel:* (093) 2040990; (093) 2040659 *Fax:* (093) 2041183 *E-mail:* circe@oceano.com, pg 577

Circle of State Librarians (United Kingdom) *Tel:* (020) 7273 4463 *Fax:* (020) 7273 3957 *Web Site:* www.circleofstatelibrarians.co.uk, pg 1572

Circle of Wine Writers (United Kingdom) *Tel:* (01225) 783007 *Fax:* (01225) 783152 *E-mail:* administrator@winewriters.org *Web Site:* www.winewriters.org, pg 1290

Editions Circonflexe (France) *Tel:* (01) 46 34 77 77 *Fax:* (01) 43 25 34 67 *E-mail:* info@circonflexe.fr *Web Site:* www.circonflexe.fr, pg 154

Circulo de Lectores SA (Colombia) *Tel:* (01) 2173211; (01) 2177720 *Fax:* (01) 2178157, pg 1306

Circulo de Lectores SA (Colombia) *Tel:* 2173211; 2177720 *Fax:* 2178157, pg 1251

Circulo de Lectores SA (Spain) *Tel:* (0902) 22 33 55 *E-mail:* atencion-socios@circulo.es *Web Site:* www.circulo.es, pg 1255

Circulo de Leitores (Portugal) *Tel:* (021) 762 6100 *Fax:* (021) 760 7149 *E-mail:* correio@circuloleitores.pt *Web Site:* www.circuloleitores.pt, pg 1255

Circulo do Livro SA (Brazil) *Tel:* (011) 8513644 *Fax:* (011) 2827273, pg 1251

CIRIA (United Kingdom) *Tel:* (020) 7549 3300 *Fax:* (020) 7253 0523 *E-mail:* enquiries@ciria.org.uk *Web Site:* www.ciria.org.uk, pg 680

CIS Publishers (Australia) *Tel:* (03) 92467131 *Fax:* (03) 3470175 *E-mail:* samone.underwood@reeducation.com.au, pg 18

CISAC (Confederation Internationale des Societes d'Auteurs et de Compesiteurs) (France) *Tel:* (01) 55 62 08 50 *Fax:* (01) 55 62 08 60 *E-mail:* cisac@cisac.org *Web Site:* www.cisac.org, pg 1267

Cisalpino (Italy) *Tel:* (02) 2040 4031 *Fax:* (02) 2040 4044 *Web Site:* www.monduzzi.com/cisalpino, pg 382

CISAM (Italy) *Tel:* (0743) 225630 *Fax:* (0743) 49902 *E-mail:* cisam@cisam.org *Web Site:* www.cisam.org, pg 382

Cisneros (Spain) *Tel:* (091) 5619900 *Fax:* (091) 5613990, pg 577

Editions Citadelles & Mazenod (France) *Tel:* (01) 53043060 *Fax:* (01) 45220427 *E-mail:* info@citadelles-mazenod.com *Web Site:* www.citadelles-mazenod.com, pg 154

CITIC Publishing House (China) *Tel:* (010) 85323366 *Fax:* (010) 85322508 *E-mail:* g-office@citic.com.cn; mail@citicpub.com *Web Site:* www.citic.com.cn; www.publish.citic.com, pg 103

Citta Nuova Editrice (Italy) *Tel:* (06) 3216212 *Fax:* (06) 3207185 *E-mail:* segr.rivista@cittanuova.it *Web Site:* www.cittanuova.it, pg 382

Cittadella Editrice (Italy) *Tel:* (075) 813595 *Fax:* (075) 813719 *E-mail:* amministrazione@cittadellaeditrice.com *Web Site:* www.cittadellaeditrice.com, pg 382

City Bookshop Ltd (Kenya) *Tel:* (011) 313 149; (011) 225548 *Fax:* (011) 314815, pg 1324

City Library (Mauritius) *Tel:* 212 0831 (ext 163) *Fax:* 212 4258 *E-mail:* mpllib@intnet.mu *Web Site:* mpl.intnet.mu, pg 1528

Editorial Ciudad Nueva de la Sefoma (Argentina) *Tel:* (011) 4981-4885 *Fax:* (011) 4981-4885 *E-mail:* ciudadnueva@ciudadnueva.org.ar *Web Site:* www.ciudadnueva.org.ar, pg 4

Editorial Ciudad Nueva (Spain) *Tel:* (091) 725 95 30; (091) 356 96 12 *Fax:* (091) 713 04 52 *E-mail:* editorial@ciudadnueva.com *Web Site:* www.ciudadnueva.com, pg 577

Livraria Civilizacao (Americo Fraga Lamares & Ca Lda) (Portugal) *Tel:* (022) 20002286 *Fax:* (022) 312382, pg 529

Civitas SA Editorial (Spain) *Tel:* (091) 902 011 787 *Fax:* (091) 725 26 73 *E-mail:* clientes@civitas.es *Web Site:* www.civitas.es, pg 577

Claassen Verlag GmbH (Germany) *Tel:* (089) 5148-0 *Fax:* (089) 5148-2229 *E-mail:* info@ullstein-heyne-list.de *Web Site:* www.claassen-verlag.de, pg 209

CLAIM Bookshop (Malawi) *Tel:* 620839, pg 1325

Clairefontaine, Editions (Switzerland) *Tel:* (021) 323 08 79, pg 621

The John Clare Society (United Kingdom) *Web Site:* freespace.virgin.net/linda.curry/jclare.htm, pg 1407

Editorial Claret SA (Spain) *Tel:* (093) 3010887 *Fax:* (093) 3174830 *E-mail:* editorial@claret.es; admin@claret.es *Web Site:* www.claret.es, pg 577

Claretian Communications Inc (Philippines) *Tel:* (02) 9213984 *Fax:* (02) 9217429 *E-mail:* cci@claret.org; claret@info.com.ph *Web Site:* www.bible.claret.org, pg 518

Editorial Claretiana (Argentina) *Tel:* (011) 4305-9597; (011) 4305-9510 *Fax:* (011) 4305-6552 *E-mail:* editorial@editorialclaretiana.com.ar *Web Site:* www.editorialclaretiana.com.ar, pg 4

Editorial Claridad SA (Argentina) *Tel:* (011) 4371-5546 *Fax:* (011) 4375-1659 *E-mail:* editorial@heliasta.com.ar *Web Site:* www.heliasta.com.ar, pg 4

Clarke Associates Ltd (United Kingdom) *Tel:* (0117) 926 8864 *Fax:* (0117) 922 6437 *E-mail:* enq@clarkeassoc.com *Web Site:* www.clarkeassoc.demon.co.uk, pg 1349

James Clarke & Co Ltd (United Kingdom) *Tel:* (01223) 350865 *Fax:* (01223) 366951 *E-mail:* publishing@jamesclarke.co.uk *Web Site:* www.jamesclarke.co.uk, pg 680

Clasicos Roxsil Editorial SA de CV (El Salvador) *Tel:* 228-1832; 288-2646; 229-6742 *Fax:* 228-1212, pg 138

Clasicos Roxsil Editorial SA de CV (El Salvador) *Tel:* 228 1832; 229 3621 *Fax:* 228 1212, pg 1309

Class Publishing (United Kingdom) *Tel:* (020) 7371 2119 *Fax:* (020) 7371 2878 *E-mail:* post@class.co.uk *Web Site:* www.class.co.uk, pg 680

Werner Classen Verlag (Switzerland) *Tel:* (01) 2015606, pg 621

E W Classey Ltd (United Kingdom) *Tel:* (01367) 244700 *Fax:* (01367) 244800 *E-mail:* info@classeybooks.com *Web Site:* www.abebooks.com/home/bugbooks; www.classeybooks.com, pg 680

Classic (Pakistan) *Tel:* (042) 323963; (042) 312977 *Fax:* (042) 7238236, pg 512

Editora Classica (Portugal) *Tel:* (021) 372386 *Fax:* (021) 3474729, pg 530

Classical Publishing Co (India) *Tel:* (011) 563689, pg 332

Classikaletet (Israel) *Tel:* (03) 5616996 *Fax:* (03) 5615526 *E-mail:* kimbooks@netvision.net.it, pg 366

Claudiana Editrice (Italy) *Tel:* (011) 6689804 *Fax:* (011) 6504394 *E-mail:* info@claudiana.it *Web Site:* www.claudiana.it, pg 382

Claudius Verlag (Germany) *Tel:* (089) 12172-123 *Fax:* (089) 12172-138 *E-mail:* info@claudius.de *Web Site:* www.claudius.de, pg 209

Uitgeverij Clavis (Belgium) *Tel:* (011) 28 68 68 *Fax:* (011) 28 68 69 *E-mail:* info@clavis.be *Web Site:* www.clavis.be, pg 65

Clays Ltd (United Kingdom) *Tel:* (01986) 893211 *Fax:* (01986) 895293 *E-mail:* sales@clays.co.uk *Web Site:* www.clays.co.uk, pg 1163, 1225

Clays Ltd (United Kingdom) *Tel:* (01986) 893211 *Fax:* (01986) 89529 *E-mail:* sales@clays.co.uk *Web Site:* www.st-ives.co.uk; www.clays.co.uk, pg 1238

Clays Ltd (United Kingdom) *Tel:* (01986) 893211 *Fax:* (01986) 895293 *E-mail:* sales@clays.co.uk *Web Site:* www.clays.co.uk, pg 1247

CLD (France) *Tel:* (02) 47282068 *Fax:* (02) 47288548, pg 154

Editions CLE (Cameroon) *Tel:* (0237) 22-35-54 *Fax:* (0237) 23-27-09 *E-mail:* edition@iccnet.cm, pg 98

Cle International (France) *Tel:* (01) 45 87 44 00 *Fax:* (01) 45 87 44 10 *E-mail:* cle@vuef.fr *Web Site:* www.cle-inter.com, pg 154

CLE: The Irish Book Publishers' Association (Ireland) *Tel:* (01) 670-7393 *Fax:* (01) 670-7642 *E-mail:* info@publishingireland.com *Web Site:* www.publishingireland.com, pg 1273

R J Cleary Publishing (Australia) *Tel:* (02) 2643750, pg 18

Clerestory Press (New Zealand) *Tel:* (03) 3553588 *Fax:* (03) 3553588 *E-mail:* young.writers@xtra.co.nz, pg 495

CLEUP - Cooperative Libraria Editrice dell 'Universita di Padova (Italy) *Tel:* (049) 8753496 *Fax:* (049) 650261 *E-mail:* redazione@cleup.it, pg 382

The Cleveland Vibrator Co (United States) *Tel:* 216-241-7157 *Toll Free Tel:* 800-221-3298 *Fax:* 216-241-3480 *E-mail:* cvc@clevelandvibrator.com *Web Site:* www.clevelandvibrator.com, pg 1248

Clever Books (South Africa) *Tel:* (012) 3424715 *Fax:* (012) 432376, pg 563

Editorial Clie (Spain) *Tel:* (093) 7884262; (093) 7885722 *Fax:* (093) 7800514 *E-mail:* libros@clie.es *Web Site:* www.clie.es, pg 577

Editions Climats (France) *Tel:* (04) 99 58 30 91; (04) 67 45 37 90 *Fax:* (04) 99 58 30 92 *E-mail:* contact@editions-climats.com *Web Site:* www.editions-climats.com, pg 154

Climent, Eliseau Editor (Spain) *Tel:* (06) 3516492 *Fax:* (06) 3529872 *E-mail:* 3i4@arrakis.es, pg 577

Clipper Distribution Services (United Kingdom) *Tel:* (0705) 200080 *Fax:* (0705) 200090, pg 1349

De Clivo Press (Switzerland) *Tel:* (01) 8201124, pg 621

Clo Iar-Chonnachta Teo (Ireland) *Tel:* (091) 593 307 *Fax:* (091) 593 362 *E-mail:* cic@iol.ie *Web Site:* www.cic.ie, pg 358

Clodhanna Teoranta (Ireland), pg 358

Cloister Bookstore Ltd (Barbados) *Tel:* (246) 426-2662 *Fax:* (246) 429-7269 *E-mail:* cloisterbookstore@caribsurf.com, pg 1301

Jonathan Clowes Ltd (United Kingdom) *Tel:* (020) 7722 7674 *Fax:* (020) 7722 7677, pg 1139

William Clowes Ltd (United Kingdom) *Tel:* (01502) 712884 *Fax:* (01502) 717003 *E-mail:* william@clowes.co.uk *Web Site:* www.clowes.co.uk, pg 1163, 1184, 1225, 1238, 1247

Club de Lectores (Argentina) *Tel:* (011) 4342-6251; (011) 4342-3955, pg 4

Club de Lectores Extemporaneos (Mexico) *Tel:* (05) 5875424; (05) 5878785, pg 1254

Club du Livre SA (France) *Tel:* (01) 47638055 *Fax:* (01) 44404865, pg 1252

YELLOW PAGES COMHAIRLE NAN LEABHRAICHEAN - THE GAELIC BOOKS COUNCIL

CLUEB (Cooperativa Libraria Universitaria Editrice Bologna) (Italy) *Tel:* (051) 220736 *Fax:* (051) 237758 *E-mail:* clueb@clueb.com; info@clueb.com *Web Site:* www.clueb.com, pg 382

Editura Clusium (Romania) *Tel:* (064) 196940 *Fax:* (064) 196940 *E-mail:* clusium@codec.ro, pg 539

CLUT Editrice (Italy) *Tel:* (011) 5647980 *Fax:* (011) 542192 *E-mail:* informazioni@clut.it *Web Site:* www.clut.it, pg 383

CMA Edition (Germany) *Tel:* (0941) 23939; (0941) 34003; (08458) 8960 *Fax:* (08458) 8960; (0941) 34003, pg 209

CMC Publishing Co Ltd (Japan) *Tel:* (03) 3293-2065 *Fax:* (03) 3293-2069 *E-mail:* info@cmcbooks.co.jp *Web Site:* www.cmcbooks.co.jp, pg 416

CMP Information Ltd (United Kingdom) *Tel:* (01732) 377591 *Fax:* (01732) 377440 *Web Site:* www.cmpdata.co.uk, pg 680

CNRS Editions (France) *Tel:* (01) 53 10 27 00 *Fax:* (01) 53 10 27 27 *Web Site:* www.cnrseditions.fr, pg 155

Co-Fine Promotions (Hong Kong) *Tel:* 25180383 *Fax:* 25180361 *E-mail:* cofine@netvigator.com, pg 1245

Co Libri (Slovenia) *Tel:* (01) 1255111 *Fax:* (01) 224454, pg 1340

Coach House Printing (Canada) *Tel:* 416-979-2217 *Fax:* 416-977-1158 *E-mail:* mail@chbooks.com *Web Site:* www.chbooks.com, pg 1175, 1215

Coachwise Ltd (United Kingdom) *Tel:* (0113) 2311310 *Fax:* (0113) 2319606 *E-mail:* enquiries@coachwise.ltd.uk *Web Site:* www.coachwise.ltd.uk, pg 680

La Coccinella Editrice SRL (Italy) *Tel:* (0332) 224690 *Fax:* (0332) 222025, pg 383

Elspeth Cochrane Agency (United Kingdom) *Tel:* (020) 7622 0314 *Fax:* (020) 7622 5815 *E-mail:* info@elspethcochrane.co.uk, pg 1139

Cockatoo Press (Schweiz), Thailand-Publikationen (Switzerland) *Tel:* (01) 9841725 *Fax:* (01) 9843420 *E-mail:* cockatoo@thailine.com *Web Site:* www.thailine.com, pg 621

Cockbird Press (United Kingdom) *Tel:* (01435) 830430 *Fax:* (01435) 830027, pg 680

CODE - Europe (United Kingdom) *Tel:* (01865) 202438 *Fax:* (01865) 2024390 *E-mail:* code_europe@compuserve.com *Web Site:* www.oneworld.org/code_europe/code_news10.html, pg 1290

Codes Rousseau (France) *Tel:* (02) 51 23 11 00 *Fax:* (02) 51 21 31 02 *E-mail:* info@codes-rousseau.fr *Web Site:* www.codesrousseau.fr, pg 155

CODESRIA (Council for the Development of Social Science Research in Africa) (Senegal) *Tel:* 8259814; 8259822 *Fax:* 8241289; 8640143 *E-mail:* codesria@sonatel.senet.net *Web Site:* www.cordesria.org, pg 551

Codice Comercio Distriducaio e Casa Editorial Ltda (Brazil) *Tel:* (011) 5031-8033 *E-mail:* codice@codicenet.com.br, pg 80

Codra Enterprises Inc (United States) *Tel:* 714-891-5652 *Fax:* 714-891-5642 *E-mail:* codra@codra.com; sales@codra.com *Web Site:* www.codra.com, pg 1166

Rene Coeckelberghs Bokfoerlag AB (Sweden) *Tel:* (08) 7230880 *Fax:* (08) 7230311, pg 610

Rene Coeckelberghs Editions (Switzerland) *Tel:* (041) 515060 *Fax:* (041) 516645, pg 621

Coffee Industry Corporation (Papua New Guinea) *Tel:* 732 1266; 732 2466 *Fax:* 732 1431 *E-mail:* cicgka@daltron.com.pg *Web Site:* www.coffeecorp.org.pg, pg 515

Eric Cohen Books Ltd (Israel) *Tel:* (09) 747 8000 *Fax:* (09) 747 8001 *E-mail:* info@ecb.co.il *Web Site:* www.ecb.co.il, pg 1319

Coimbra Editora Lda (Portugal) *Tel:* (0239) 85 2650 *Fax:* (0239) 85 2651 *E-mail:* sede@mail.coimbraeditora.pt; revistas@mail.coimbraeditora.pt *Web Site:* www.coimbraeditora.pt, pg 530

Cole Publications (Australia) *Tel:* (03) 9830 4242 *Fax:* (03) 9830 4242, pg 18

Colegial Bolivariana CA (Venezuela) *Tel:* (02) 2391055; (02) 2391244; (02) 2391377; (02) 2391166; (02) 2391944; (02) 2391433; (02) 2391777; (02) 2391555 *Fax:* (02) 2396502; (02) 2379942 *Web Site:* co-bo.com, pg 779

Colegio de Bibliotecarios de Chile AG (Chile) *Tel:* (02) 222 56 52 *Fax:* (02) 635 50 23 *E-mail:* cdc@uplink.cl *Web Site:* www.bibliotecarios.cl, pg 1559

Ediciones Colegio De Espana (ECE) (Spain) *Tel:* (023) 21 47 88 *Fax:* (023) 21 87 91 *E-mail:* info@colesp.eurart.es *Web Site:* www.eurart.es/emp/colesp, pg 577

El Colegio de Mexico AC (Mexico) *Tel:* (05) 54953080 *Fax:* (05) 54493083 *E-mail:* fgomez@colmex.mx *Web Site:* www.colmex.mx, pg 463

Colegio de Postgraduados en Ciencias Agricolas (Mexico) *Tel:* (0595) 95 2 02 00; (055) 58 04 59 00 *E-mail:* seia@colpos.mx *Web Site:* www.colpos.mx, pg 463

Libreria del Colegio SA (Argentina) *Tel:* (011) 4300-5400; (011) 4362-1222 *Fax:* (011) 4362-7364 *E-mail:* edsudame@satlink.com, pg 4

Charles Coleman Verlag GmbH & Co KG (Germany) *Tel:* (0221) 5497-0 *Fax:* (0221) 5497-326 *E-mail:* coleman@rudolf.mueller.de *Web Site:* www.coleman-verlag.de; www.rudolf-mueller.de, pg 209

Edicoes Colibri (Portugal) *Tel:* (021) 7964038 *Fax:* (021) 7964038 *E-mail:* colibri@edi-colibri.pt *Web Site:* www.edi-colibri.pt, pg 530

Armand Colin, Editeur (France) *Tel:* (01) 44395447 *Fax:* (01) 44394343 *E-mail:* infos@armand-colin.com *Web Site:* www.armand-colin.com/pr/infosf.html, pg 155

Rosica Colin Ltd (United Kingdom) *Tel:* (020) 7370 1080 *Fax:* (020) 7244 6441, pg 680, 1139

COLIVRO - Comercio e Distribuicao de Livros Ltda (Brazil) *Tel:* (021) 2243177 *Fax:* (021) 2424517, pg 1303

Collectieve Propaganda van het Nederlandse Boek (CPNB) (Netherlands) *Tel:* (020) 626 49 71 *Fax:* (020) 623 16 96 *E-mail:* info@cpnb.nl *Web Site:* www.cpnb.nl, pg 1160, 1278

College International des Traducteurs Litteraires (CITL) (France) *Tel:* (04) 90 52 05 50 *Fax:* (04) 90 93 43 21 *E-mail:* citl@provnet.fr, pg 1267

The College of Education at Wits, Harold Holmes Library (South Africa) *Tel:* (011) 717-3242; (011) 717-3240 *Fax:* (011) 717-3046 *Web Site:* www.wits.ac.za/library/campuslib/edulib.htm, pg 1543

College of Medicine Library, Arabian Gulf University (Bahrain) *Tel:* 239 999 *Fax:* 272 555 *E-mail:* info@agu.edu.bh *Web Site:* www.agu.edu.bh, pg 1492

The College of the Bahamas Library (Bahamas) *Tel:* 302-4552 *Fax:* 326-7834 *Web Site:* www.cob.edu.bs/library, pg 1492

College Press Publishers (Pvt) Ltd (Zimbabwe) *Tel:* (04) 754145; (04) 773231; (04) 773236; (04) 757153; (04) 754255 *Fax:* (04) 754256 *E-mail:* nellym@collegepress.co.zw, pg 783

Peter Collin Publishing Ltd (United Kingdom) *Tel:* (020) 7494 2111 *Fax:* (020) 7434 0151 *E-mail:* order@petercollin.com *Web Site:* www.petercollin.com, pg 680

Collins Booksellers Pty Ltd (Australia) *Tel:* (03) 96629472 *Fax:* (03) 96622527 *E-mail:* enquiries@collinsbooks.com.au *Web Site:* www.collinsbooks.com.au, pg 1298

The Collins Press (Ireland) *Tel:* (021) 4347717 *Fax:* (021) 4347720 *E-mail:* enquiries@collinspress.ie *Web Site:* www.collinspress.com, pg 358

Colmegna SA (Argentina) *Tel:* (042) 523102; (042) 557345 *Fax:* (042) 4557345, pg 4

Colombian PEN Centre (Colombia) *Tel:* (01) 2846761; (01) 2561540 *Fax:* (01) 2184236 *E-mail:* pencolombia@hotmail.com, pg 1398

Colombo Book Association (Sri Lanka) *Tel:* (01) 686878; (01) 072270652 *Fax:* (01) 696578, pg 606

Colombo Public Library (Sri Lanka) *Tel:* (011) 2691968; (011) 2695156; (011) 2696530 *Fax:* (011) 2691968 *Web Site:* www.cmc.lk/library.asp, pg 1546

Librairie des Colonnes (Morocco) *Tel:* (09) 93 69 55 *Fax:* (099) 936955, pg 1328

Colonnese Editore (Italy) *Tel:* (081) 293900 *Fax:* (081) 455420 *E-mail:* info@colonnese.it *Web Site:* www.colonnese.it, pg 383

Colorcraft Ltd (Hong Kong) *Tel:* 25909033 *Fax:* 25909005; 25909271 *E-mail:* info.cc@colorcraft.com.hk *Web Site:* www.colorcraft.com.hk, pg 1245

Colorprint Offset (Hong Kong) *Tel:* 2896-7777 *Fax:* 2889-6606 *E-mail:* info@cpo.com.hk *Web Site:* www.cpo.com.hk, pg 1156, 1177, 1217

Colorprint Offset Inc (United States) *Tel:* 212-681-9400 *Fax:* 212-681-9362, pg 1166

Colorprint Offset Inc (United States) *Tel:* 212-681-9400 *Fax:* 212-681-9362 *Web Site:* www.cpo.hk, pg 1187

Colorprint Offset Inc (United States) *Tel:* 212-681-9400 *Fax:* 212-681-9362 *E-mail:* info@colorprintoffset.com, pg 1229

Colour Library Direct (United Kingdom) *Tel:* (01483) 426777 *Fax:* (01483) 426947 *E-mail:* prod@quad-pub.co.uk, pg 681

Colourpoint Books (United Kingdom) *Tel:* (028) 9182 0505 *Fax:* (028) 9182 1900 *E-mail:* info@colourpoint.co.uk; sales@colourpoint.co.uk *Web Site:* www.colourpoint.co.uk, pg 681

Colt Associates (United Kingdom) *Tel:* (0158) 2834292 *Fax:* (0158) 825778, pg 1349

The Columba Book Service (Ireland) *Tel:* (01) 2942556 *Fax:* (01) 2942564 *E-mail:* info@columba.ie *Web Site:* www.columba.ie, pg 359, 1319

The Columba Press (Ireland) *Tel:* (01) 2942556 *Fax:* (01) 2942564 *E-mail:* info@columba.ie *Web Site:* www.columba.ie, pg 359

Columbia Overseas Marketing Pte Ltd (Singapore) *Tel:* 7478607 *Fax:* 7458668, pg 1222

Columbus (Czech Republic) *Tel:* (02) 683 10 17; (02) 683 47 65; (02) 74771407 *Fax:* (02) 683 10 17; (02) 683 08 28 *E-mail:* columbus@alpha-net.cz, pg 123

Columbus Cultural Editora Comercial Importacao e Exporta (Brazil) *Tel:* (011) 8648777 *Fax:* (011) 8646531, pg 1303

Columbus Verlag Paul Oestergaard GmbH (Germany) *Tel:* (07576) 96 03-0 *Fax:* (07576) 96 03-29 *E-mail:* info@columbus-verlag.de *Web Site:* www.columbus-verlag.de, pg 209

Columna Edicions, Libres i Comunicacio, SA (Spain) *Tel:* (093) 4238761 *Fax:* (093) 4238761, pg 577

Combel Editorial SA (Spain) *Tel:* (093) 2449550 *Fax:* (093) 2656895 *E-mail:* casals@editorialcasals.com, pg 577

Combined Academic Publishers (United Kingdom) *Tel:* (01494) 581601 *Fax:* (01494) 581602 *Web Site:* www.combinedacademic.co.uk, pg 681

Combined Book Services (United Kingdom) *Tel:* (01892) 839819 *Fax:* (01892) 837272 *E-mail:* info@combook.co.uk *Web Site:* www.combook.co.uk, pg 1349

Editora Comercial de Publicaciones (Spain) *Tel:* (096) 3952045; (096) 3957293 *Fax:* (096) 3952297 *E-mail:* edicep@nexo.net, pg 577

Comhairle nan Leabhraichean - The Gaelic Books Council (United Kingdom) *Tel:* (0141) 337 6211 *Fax:* (0141) 341 0515 *E-mail:* fios@gaelicbooks.net *Web Site:* www.gaelicbooks.net, pg 1291

1637

Los Libros del Comienzo (Spain) *Tel:* (091) 5481079 *Fax:* (091) 5400378 *E-mail:* buzon@libroscomienzo.com *Web Site:* www.libroscomienzo.com, pg 577

Comision Nacional Forestal (Mexico) *Tel:* (05) 5349707; (05) 5247862, pg 463

Comissao Nacional de Energia Nuclear (CNEN) (Brazil) *Tel:* (021) 2295-9596 *Fax:* (021) 2295-8696 *E-mail:* macedo@cnen.gov.br *Web Site:* www.cnen.gov.br, pg 80

Comissao para a Igualdade e Direitos das Mulheres (Portugal) *Tel:* (021) 7983000 *Fax:* (021) 7983099 *E-mail:* cidm@mail.telepac.pt, pg 530

Editions du Comite des Travaux Historiques et Scientifiques (CTHS) (France) *Tel:* (01) 55 55 97 64 *Fax:* (01) 55 55 97 60 *E-mail:* cths.ventes@recherche.gouv.fr *Web Site:* www.cths.fr, pg 155

Comite Gremial de Editores de Guatemala (Guatemala) *Tel:* (02) 82 68 15 *Fax:* (02) 2329053; (02) 2518381, pg 1272

Comite National d'Evaluation (CNE) (France) *Tel:* (01) 55 55 60 97 *Fax:* (01) 55 55 63 94 *Web Site:* www.cne-evaluation.fr, pg 155

ComMedia & Arte Verlag Bernd Mayer (Germany) *Tel:* (07945) 950719 *Fax:* (07945) 950718, pg 209

Commercial Colorlab Ltd (Hong Kong) *Tel:* 2880 5128, pg 1217

Commercial Press (Hong Kong) Ltd (Hong Kong) *Tel:* 25651371 *Fax:* 25651113; 25654277 *E-mail:* info@commercialpress.com.hk *Web Site:* www.commercialpress.com.hk, pg 316

Commission Belge de Bibliographie et de Bibliologie (Belgium) *Tel:* (02) 5195311 *Fax:* (02) 5195533 *Web Site:* www.kbr.be; opac.kbr.be/ekbr1.htm (web catalogue), pg 1397

Commission des Bibliotheques de l'AIDBA (Senegal) *Tel:* 240954, pg 1283

Commission for Racial Equality (United Kingdom) *Tel:* (020) 7939 0000 *Fax:* (020) 7939 0001 *E-mail:* info@cre.gov.uk *Web Site:* www.cre.gov.uk, pg 681

Commonwealth Council for Educational Administration & Management (New Zealand) *Tel:* (09) 917 9568 *Fax:* (09) 917 9501 *Web Site:* www.cceam.org, pg 495

Commonwealth Education Foundation (United Kingdom) *Tel:* (0208) 9312359 *Fax:* (0208) 9592137 *E-mail:* cefoundation@aol.com, pg 1349

The Commonwealth Library Association (COMLA) (Jamaica) *Tel:* (876) 927-2123 *Fax:* (876) 927-1926 *E-mail:* nkpodo@uwimona.edu.jm, pg 1274

Commonwealth Publishing Company Ltd (Taiwan, Province of China) *Tel:* (02) 2517-3688 *Fax:* (02) 2517-3686 *Web Site:* www.bookzone.com.tw, pg 639

Commonwealth Secretariat (United Kingdom) *Tel:* (020) 7747 6500 *Fax:* (020) 7930 0827 *E-mail:* info@commonwealth.int *Web Site:* www.thecommonwealth.org, pg 681

Bibliotheque de la Communaute Urbaine de Casablanca (Morocco) *Tel:* (02) 314 170, pg 1529

Communication Art Design & Printing Ltd (Hong Kong) *Tel:* 2865 6787 *Fax:* 2866 3429 *E-mail:* cadesign@pacific.net.hk, pg 1256

Communication Foundation for Asia Media Group (CFAMG) (Philippines) *Tel:* (02) 607411; (02) 607412; (02) 607413; (02) 607414; (02) 607415; (02) 607416; (02) 7132981 *Fax:* (02) 612504; (02) 7132974 *E-mail:* cfa@mozcom.com, pg 518

Communication Par Livre (CPL) (France) *Tel:* (01) 42733047 *Fax:* (01) 42733047, pg 155

Editions Comp'Act (France) *Tel:* (04) 79 85 27 85 *Fax:* (04) 79 85 29 34 *E-mail:* contact@editionscompact.com *Web Site:* www.editionscompact.com, pg 155

Compact Verlag GmbH (Germany) *Tel:* (089) 7451610 *Fax:* (089) 756095 *E-mail:* info@compactverlag.de *Web Site:* www.compactverlag.de, pg 209

Compagnie d'Editions Libres, Sociales et Economiques (CELSE) (France) *Tel:* (01) 42674123 *Fax:* (01) 42274020 *E-mail:* celse@celsedit.com *Web Site:* www.celsedit.com, pg 155

Compagnie Francaise des Arts Graphiques SA (France) *Tel:* (05) 46243925, pg 155

Compagnie 12 (France) *Tel:* (01) 43 70 99 00 *Fax:* (01) 43 70 80 88, pg 155

Editora Companhia das Letras/Editora Schwarcz Ltda (Brazil) *Tel:* (011) 3707-3500 *Fax:* (011) 3707-3501 *E-mail:* editora@companhiadasletras.com.br *Web Site:* www.companhiadasletras.com.br, pg 80

Compania Editorial Continental SA de CV (Mexico) *Tel:* (05) 5442776; (05) 6890088 *Fax:* (05) 5618155, pg 463

Compania Literaria (Spain) *Tel:* (091) 4015312 *Fax:* (091) 4015312, pg 577

Companion Travel Guide Books (Australia) *Tel:* (02) 9608-1169 *Fax:* (02) 9608-1169 *E-mail:* 6LEI937764@aol.com, pg 18

Compass Equestrian Ltd (United Kingdom) *Tel:* (0156) 479 5136 *Fax:* (0156) 479 5136 *E-mail:* compbook@globalnet.co.uk *Web Site:* www.users.globalnet.co.uk/~compbook, pg 681

Compass Maps Ltd (United Kingdom) *Tel:* (01275) 474737 *Fax:* (01275) 474787 *E-mail:* info@papoutmaps.com *Web Site:* www.mapgroup.net, pg 681

Compass-Verlag GmbH (Austria) *Tel:* (01) 981 16-113; (01) 981 16-114 *Fax:* (01) 981 16-118; (01) 981 16-108 *E-mail:* hfu@compass.at; ssc@compass.at; office@compass.at *Web Site:* www.compass.at; www.cmd.at, pg 49

Compendium Publishing (United Kingdom) *Tel:* (020) 72874570 *Fax:* (020) 74940583 *E-mail:* compendium@compuserve.com, pg 681

Editions Complexe SPRL (Belgium) *Tel:* (02) 538 88 46 *Fax:* (02) 538 88 42, pg 65

Ediciones de la Universidad Complutense de Madrid (Spain) *Tel:* (091) 394 64 60; (091) 394 64 61 *Fax:* (091) 394 64 58 *E-mail:* ecsa@rect.ucm.es *Web Site:* www.ucm.es/info/ecsa, pg 577

Complutense, SA Editorial (Spain) *Tel:* (091) 3946460; (091) 3946461 *Fax:* (091) 3946458 *E-mail:* ecsa@eucemos.sim.ucm.es *Web Site:* www.ucm.es/info/ecsa, pg 577

Editions de Compostelle (France) *Tel:* (01) 64299404, pg 155

Comprehensive Book Service (Pakistan) *Tel:* (021) 214682 *Fax:* (021) 2632131 *E-mail:* shahzad@cbs.khi.sdnpk.undp.org, pg 1333

Computer Bookshops Ltd (United Kingdom) *Tel:* (0121) 778 3333 *Fax:* (0121) 606 0476 *E-mail:* info@computerbookshops.com *Web Site:* www.computerbookshops.com, pg 1349

Computer Step (United Kingdom) *Tel:* (01926) 817999 *Fax:* (01926) 817005 *E-mail:* publisher@ineasysteps.com *Web Site:* www.ineasysteps.com, pg 681

Libreria Comuneros (Paraguay) *Tel:* (021) 446-176; (021) 444-667 *Fax:* (021) 444-667 *Web Site:* www.uiowa.edu, pg 1334

Comunica Press SA (Spain) *Tel:* (091) 8591604 *Fax:* (091) 8595269 *E-mail:* info@comunica.es *Web Site:* www.comunica.es, pg 578

Comunidad Autonoma de Madrid, Servicio de Documentacion y Publicaciones (Spain) *Tel:* (091) 702 76 21 *Fax:* (091) 319 85 68, pg 578

Edizioni di Comunita SpA (Italy) *Tel:* (011) 5656363 *Fax:* (011) 5656351 *E-mail:* novarese@amemail.mondadori.it *Web Site:* www.comunita.einaudi.it, pg 383

Concept Publishing Ltd (New Zealand) *Tel:* (09) 489 1121 *Fax:* (09) 489 5335, pg 495

Concept Publishing Co (India) *Tel:* (011) 5648039 *Fax:* (011) 5648053 *E-mail:* publishing@conceptpub.com *Web Site:* www.conceptpub.com, pg 332

Concordia (Czech Republic) *Tel:* (02) 355241; (02) 7929747 *Fax:* (02) 7929747, pg 123

Concordia-Buchhandlung & Verlag (Germany) *Tel:* (0375) 21 28 50 *Fax:* (0375) 29 80 80; (0375) 21 28 50 *E-mail:* concordia@t-online.de *Web Site:* www.concordiabuch.de, pg 209

Concordia Editora Ltda (Brazil) *Tel:* (051) 3342 2699 *Fax:* (051) 3342 2699 *E-mail:* pedido@editoraconcordia.com.br; editora@editoraconcordia.com.br *Web Site:* www.editoraconcordia.com.br, pg 80

Concraid (Belgium) *Tel:* (065) 34-72-34 *Fax:* (065) 34-72-34, pg 65

Concrete Information Ltd (United Kingdom) *Tel:* (01276) 608770 *Fax:* (01276) 37369 *E-mail:* enquiries@concreteinfo.org *Web Site:* www.concreteinfo.org, pg 682

Coneco Litho Graphics (United States) *Tel:* 518-793-3823 *Fax:* 518-793-5823 *Web Site:* www.conecolithographics.com, pg 1166, 1187

Coneco Litho Graphics (United States) *Tel:* 518-793-3823 *Fax:* 518-793-5823 *E-mail:* support@conecolithographics.com *Web Site:* www.conecolithographics.com, pg 1229

Coneco Litho Graphics (United States) *Tel:* 518-793-3823 *Fax:* 518-793-5823 *Web Site:* www.conecolithographics.com, pg 1239

Confederacion de Cooperativas del Caribe y Centro America (CCCCA) (Costa Rica) *Tel:* 2404592 *Fax:* 2333122 *E-mail:* ccocca@sol.racsa.co.cr, pg 115

Confederation of Information Communication Industries (United Kingdom) *Tel:* (020) 7607 0021 *Fax:* (020) 7607 0415, pg 1291

Conference Interpreters Group (United Kingdom) *Tel:* (0208) 9950801 *Fax:* (0208) 7421066 *E-mail:* ciglondon@aol.com, pg 1150

Conference of Directors of National Libraries (CDNL) (South Africa) *Tel:* (012) 21 8931 *Fax:* (012) 32 5594 *E-mail:* postmaster@statelib.pwv.gov.za, pg 1284

Conference of European Churches (Switzerland) *Tel:* (022) 791 61 11 *Fax:* (022) 791 62 27 *E-mail:* cec@cec-kek.org *Web Site:* www.cec-kek.org, pg 1285

Editorial Confluencia Lda (Portugal) *Tel:* (021) 663853 *Fax:* (021) 326921 *E-mail:* livroshorizonte@mail.telepac.pt, pg 530

Congregacion Paulinas - Hijas de San Pablo (Chile) *Tel:* (02) 221 2832 *Fax:* (02) 221 2832 *E-mail:* paulinasedit@entelchile.net, pg 99

Biblioteca del Congreso de la Nacion (Argentina) *Tel:* (011) 4372-1641 *Fax:* (011) 954-1067 *E-mail:* congreso@bcnbib.gov.ar *Web Site:* www.bcnbib.gov.ar, pg 1490

Biblioteca del Congreso de la Union (Mexico) *Tel:* (05) 5 10 38 66; (05) 5 12 52 05 *Fax:* (05) 5 12 10 85 *E-mail:* emolina@servidor.unam.mx; emolina@cddhcu.gob.mx *Web Site:* www.cddhcu.gob.mx/bibliot/, pg 1529

Congress of South-East Asian Librarians IV (CONSAL IV) (Philippines) *Tel:* (02) 590646 *Fax:* (02) 572644, pg 1281

CONICYT (Chile) *Tel:* (02) 3654400 *Fax:* (02) 6551396 *E-mail:* info@conicyt.cl *Web Site:* www.conicyt.cl, pg 1560

Coningsby International Bookshop Services (United Kingdom) *Tel:* (01526) 342231 *Fax:* (01526) 344367 *E-mail:* service@coningsby.com *Web Site:* www.coningsby.com, pg 1349

Connaissance et Pratique du Droit Zairos (CDPZ) (The Democratic Republic of the Congo), pg 114

Connection Medien GmbH (Germany) *Tel:* (08639) 98 34-0 *Fax:* (08639) 1219 *E-mail:* seminare@connection.de *Web Site:* www.connection.de; www.seminar-connection.de, pg 209

Conquista, Empresa de Publicacoes Ltda (Brazil) *Tel:* (021) 228-6752 *Fax:* (021) 228-5709, pg 80

The Joseph Conrad Society (UK) (United Kingdom) *Web Site:* www.bathspa.ac.uk/conrad/, pg 1407

Conran Octopus (United Kingdom) *Tel:* (020) 7531 8400 *Fax:* (020) 7531 8627 *E-mail:* info@conran-octopus.co.uk *Web Site:* www.conran-octopus.co.uk, pg 682

Conseil International des Associations de Bibliotheques de Theologie (Germany) *Tel:* (0221) 3382109 *Fax:* (0221) 3382103, pg 1270

Biblioteca Central y Publicaciones del Consejo de Educacion Secundaria (Uruguay) *Tel:* (02) 408 42 73; (02) 408 30 51; (02) 408 12 52 *Fax:* (02) 408 12 52, pg 1555

Consejo Episcopal Latinoamericano (CELAM) (Colombia) *Tel:* (01) 6670050; (01) 6706416 *E-mail:* editora@celam.org; celam@celam.org; itepal@celam.org *Web Site:* www.celam.org, pg 110

Consejo Interamericano de Archiveros (CITA) (Mexico) *Tel:* (05) 51 33 99 00 (ext 19327); (05) 57 95 70 80 (ext 19424) *Fax:* (05) 57 89 52 96 *Web Site:* www.agn.gob.mx, pg 1277

Consejo Superior de Investigaciones Cientificas (Spain) *Tel:* (091) 561-2833; (091) 5629633 *Fax:* (091) 5629634 *E-mail:* publ@orgc.csic.es *Web Site:* www.csic.es/publica, pg 578

Biblioteca General de Humanidades Consejo Superior de Investigaciones Cientificas (Spain) *Tel:* (091) 360 18 10; (091) 360 18 12 *Fax:* (091) 369 09 40 *E-mail:* bghpre@bib.csic.es *Web Site:* www.csic.es/cbic/BGH/bgh.htm, pg 1545

Consello da Cultura Galega - CCG (Spain) *Tel:* (0981) 957202 *Fax:* (0981) 957205 *E-mail:* consello.cultura.galega@xunta.es *Web Site:* www.consellodacultura.org, pg 578

Conservart SA (Belgium) *Tel:* (02) 3322538 *Fax:* (02) 3322840 *E-mail:* conservart@skynet.be, pg 65

Conservation Resources International Inc (United States) *Tel:* 703-321-7730 *Toll Free Tel:* 800-634-6932 *Fax:* 703-321-0629 *E-mail:* criusa@conservationresources.com *Web Site:* www.conservationresources.com, pg 1240

Conservative Policy Forum (United Kingdom) *Tel:* (020) 7222 9000 *E-mail:* cpf@conservatives.com *Web Site:* www.conservatives.com, pg 682

Uitgeverij Conserve (Netherlands) *Tel:* (072) 5093693 *Fax:* (072) 5094370 *E-mail:* info@conserve.nl *Web Site:* www.conserve.nl, pg 481

Consiglio Nazionale delle Ricerche Rep Pubblicazioni e Informazioni Scientifiche (Italy) *Tel:* (06) 49932019 *Fax:* (06) 49933077 *E-mail:* pgiugni@dcire.cnr.it *Web Site:* www.urp.cnr.it, pg 383

Consolidated Printers Inc (United States) *Tel:* 510-843-8524; 510-843-8565 *Fax:* 510-486-0580 *E-mail:* cpi@consoprinters.com *Web Site:* www.consoprinters.com, pg 1166

Consolidated Printers Inc (United States) *Tel:* 510-843-8524 *Fax:* 510-486-0580 *E-mail:* cpi@consoprinters.com *Web Site:* www.consoprinters.com, pg 1229

Constable & Robinson Ltd (United Kingdom) *Tel:* (020) 8741 3663 *Fax:* (020) 8748 7562 *E-mail:* enquiries@constablerobinson.com *Web Site:* www.constablerobinson.com, pg 682

Constancia Editores, SA (Portugal) *Tel:* (021) 4246901; (021) 4246902 *E-mail:* info@constancia-editores.pt; prosa@santillana.pt *Web Site:* www.constancia-editores.pt; www.santillana.pt, pg 530

Editorial Constitucion y Leyes SA - COLEX (Spain) *Tel:* (091) 5813485 *Fax:* (091) 5813490 *E-mail:* colexeditor@interbook.net *Web Site:* www.colex.es, pg 578

Constitutional Publishing Co Pty Ltd (Australia) *Tel:* (08) 9421 6216 *Fax:* (08) 9221 1572, pg 18

Consultor Assessoria de Planejamento Ltda (Brazil) *Tel:* (021) 5893030 *Fax:* (021) 580-2163, pg 80

Ediciones Contables y Administrativas SA (Mexico) *Tel:* (05) 6040140; (05) 6041998; (05) 6040260 *Fax:* (05) 6056730, pg 463

Uitgeverij Contact NV (Belgium) *Tel:* (03) 4572024 *Fax:* (03) 4581327, pg 65

Contex Corporation (Japan) *Tel:* (03) 42-522-0051 *Fax:* (03) 42-526-2345; (03) 42-548-2400 *E-mail:* contex@jade.dt.ne.jp *Web Site:* contex.co.jp/, pg 416

Contexto Editora (Portugal) *Tel:* (021) 347 97 69 *Fax:* (021) 347 97 70 *E-mail:* context-editora@clix.pt, pg 530

Editora Contexto (Editora Pinsky Ltda) (Brazil) *Tel:* (011) 3832-5838 *Fax:* (011) 3832-1043 *E-mail:* contexto@editoracontexto.com.br *Web Site:* www.editoracontexto.com.br, pg 80

Continental Bookshop (Australia) *Tel:* (03) 98247711 *Fax:* (03) 98247855, pg 1298

Continental SRL Editrice (Italy) *Tel:* (035) 237088 *Fax:* (035) 237039, pg 383

The Continuum International Publishing Group Ltd (United Kingdom) *Tel:* (0207) 922 0880 *Fax:* (0207) 922 0881 *E-mail:* info@continuum-books.com *Web Site:* www.continuumbooks.com, pg 682

Jane Conway-Gordon (United Kingdom) *Tel:* (020) 7494 0148 *Fax:* (020) 7287 9264, pg 1139

Conway Maritime Press (United Kingdom) *Tel:* (020) 7221 2213; (020) 7314 1469 (sales) *Fax:* (020) 7221 6455; (020) 7314 1594 (sales) *E-mail:* enquiries@chrysalis.com *Web Site:* www.chrysalisbooks.co.uk/books/publisher/conway, pg 683

Albert Cook Medical Library (Uganda) *Tel:* (041) 534149 *Fax:* (041) 530024 *E-mail:* acook@uga.healthnet.org, pg 1551

Martin Cook Associates Ltd (United States) *Tel:* 845-639-5316 *Fax:* 845-639-5318 *E-mail:* mcanewcity@aol.com *Web Site:* www.mcabooks.com, pg 1166, 1187, 1229, 1240, 1248

Cookery Book (Australia) *Tel:* (02) 9439 3144 *Fax:* (02) 9439 3405 *E-mail:* answers@cookerybook.com.au *Web Site:* www.cookerybook.com.au, pg 18

Coolabah Publishing (Australia) *Tel:* (02) 6766 4420 *Fax:* (02) 6766 1058 *E-mail:* narnia@mpx.com.au, pg 18

Cooper Dale (United Kingdom) *Tel:* (020) 8748 6824 *Fax:* (020) 8748 5689, pg 1184

Leo Cooper (United Kingdom) *Tel:* (01226) 734555 *Fax:* (01226) 734438 *E-mail:* enquiries@pen-sword.demon.co.uk *Web Site:* www.pen-and-sword.co.uk, pg 683

Cooperative Action by Victorian Academic Libraries (CAVAL) (Australia) *Tel:* (03) 9459 2722 *Fax:* (03) 9459 2733 *E-mail:* caval@caval.edu.au *Web Site:* www.caval.edu.au, pg 1557

Cooperative Regionale de l'Enseignement Religieux (CRER) (France) *Tel:* (02) 41689140 *Fax:* (02) 41689141 *E-mail:* crer49@wanadoo.fr, pg 155

Edizioni Cooperative Scarl (Italy) *Tel:* (06) 844391 *Fax:* (06) 84439406, pg 383

Copenhagen Business School Press (Denmark) *Tel:* 38153960 *Fax:* 38153962 *E-mail:* cbspress@cbs.dk *Web Site:* www.cbspress.dk, pg 130

Editions Copernic (France) *Tel:* (01) 40 61 97 67 *Fax:* (01) 40 61 96 33, pg 155

Coppenrath Verlag (Germany) *Tel:* (0251) 41411-0 *Fax:* (0251) 4141120 *E-mail:* info@coppenrath.de *Web Site:* www.coppenrath.de, pg 209

Copper Beech Publishing Ltd (United Kingdom) *Tel:* (01342) 314734 *Fax:* (01342) 314794 *E-mail:* sales@copperbeechpublishing.co.uk *Web Site:* www.btinternet.com/~copperbeechpublishing, pg 683

The Copperbelt University Library (Zambia) *Tel:* (02) 222066; (02) 225155 *Fax:* (02) 222469; (02) 223972 *E-mail:* library@cbu.ac.zm *Web Site:* www.cbu.edu.zm, pg 1555

Copress Verlag (Germany) *Tel:* (089) 1257414 *Fax:* (089) 12162282 *E-mail:* verlag@stiebner.com *Web Site:* www.stiebner.com, pg 209

Editions Coprur (France) *Tel:* (03) 88 14 72 41 *Fax:* (03) 88 14 72 39 *E-mail:* coprur@editions-coprur.fr, pg 155

Copyright Agency Ltd (Australia) *Tel:* (02) 93947600 *Fax:* (02).93947601 *E-mail:* info@copyright.com.au *Web Site:* www.copyright.com.au, pg 1260

Copyright International Agency Corina GmbH (Germany) *Tel:* (030) 80902386 *Fax:* (030) 80902388 *E-mail:* info@corina.com *Web Site:* www.corina.com, pg 1131

Copyright Licensing Agency (United Kingdom) *Tel:* (020) 7631 5555 *Fax:* (020) 7631 5500 *E-mail:* cla@cla.co.uk *Web Site:* www.cla.co.uk, pg 1291

Copytrain (United Kingdom) *Tel:* (01844) 279345 *Fax:* (01844) 279345, pg 1139

Casa Editrice Corbaccio srl (Italy) *Tel:* (02) 80206338 *Fax:* (02) 804067 *E-mail:* info@corbaccio.it *Web Site:* www.corbaccio.it, pg 383

Cordee Ltd (United Kingdom) *Tel:* (0116) 2543579 *Fax:* (0116) 2471176 *E-mail:* info@cordee.co.uk *Web Site:* www.cordee.co.uk, pg 683, 1349

Bokforlaget Cordia AB (Sweden) *Tel:* (019) 333850 *Fax:* (019) 333859 *E-mail:* forlaget@cordia.se *Web Site:* www.cordia.se, pg 610

Editorial Cordillera Inc (Puerto Rico) *Tel:* 787-767-6188 *Fax:* 787-767-8646 *E-mail:* info@editorialcordillera.com *Web Site:* www.editorialcordillera.com, pg 537

Cordinata Ltd (Holy Land 2000) (Israel) *Tel:* (03) 5226885 *Fax:* (03) 5276661 *E-mail:* cordinata@isdn.net.il, pg 366

Coresi SRL (Romania) *Tel:* (01) 6386045; (01) 6386158; (01) 6386164; (00) 3127115; (00) 6154781 *Fax:* (01) 2230177, pg 539

Corian-Verlag Heinrich Wimmer (Germany) *Tel:* (08271) 5951 *Fax:* (08271) 6931 *E-mail:* 082716941-0001@t-online.de; 101374.1022@compuserve.com, pg 209

Corint Publishing Group (Romania) *Tel:* (0212) 11 97 66 *Fax:* (0212) 10 70 86 *E-mail:* corint@dnt.ro, pg 539

Cork University Press (Ireland) *Tel:* (021) 4902980 *Fax:* (021) 4315329 *E-mail:* corkunip@ucc.ie *Web Site:* www.corkuniversitypress.com, pg 359

Cornelsen und Oxford University Press GmbH & Co (Germany) *Tel:* (030) 827936-0 *Fax:* (030) 827936-36 *Web Site:* www.cornelsen.de, pg 210

Cornelsen Verlag GmbH & Co OHG (Germany) *Tel:* (030) 897 85-0 *Fax:* (030) 897 85-299 *E-mail:* c-mail@cornelsen.de *Web Site:* www.cornelsen.com, pg 210

Cornelsen Verlag Scriptor GmbH & Co KG (Germany) *Tel:* (030) 89 7858700 *Fax:* (030) 89 7858799 *E-mail:* c-mail@cornelsen.de *Web Site:* www.cornelsen.de, pg 210

Cornford Press (Australia) *Tel:* (03) 6331 9658 *Fax:* (03) 6331 9658 *E-mail:* info@cornfordpress.com *Web Site:* www.cornfordpress.com, pg 18

Cornucopia Press (Australia) *Tel:* (08) 9388 1965 *Fax:* (09) 3817341 *E-mail:* cornucop@aoi.com.au, pg 18

Corona Publishing Co Ltd (Japan) *Tel:* (03) 3941-3131 *Fax:* (03) 3941-3137 *E-mail:* info@coronasha.co.jp *Web Site:* www.coronasha.co.jp, pg 416

Corona Verlag (Germany) *Tel:* (040) 6424144 *Fax:* (040) 64221023, pg 210

Corporacion de Estudios y Publicaciones (Ecuador) *Tel:* (02) 221-711 *Fax:* (02) 226-256 *E-mail:* cep@accessinter.net, pg 136

Corporacion de Promocion Universitaria (Chile) *Tel:* (02) 2749022 *Fax:* (02) 2741828, pg 99

Ediciones Corregidor SAICI y E (Argentina) *Tel:* (011) 4374-5000; (011) 4374-4959 *Fax:* (011) 4374-5000 *E-mail:* corregidor@corregidor.com *Web Site:* www.corregidor.com, pg 4

Corsaire Editions (France) *Tel:* (02) 38 53 15 00 *Fax:* (02) 38 54 08 92 *E-mail:* corsaire.editions@wanadoo.fr *Web Site:* www.corsaire-editions.com, pg 156

Cortez Editora e Livraria Ltda (Brazil) *Tel:* (011) 3864 0111 *Fax:* (011) 3864 4290 *E-mail:* livraria@cortezeditora.com.br *Web Site:* www.cortezeditora.com.br; www.livrariacortez.com.br, pg 1303

Editions Jose Corti (France) *Tel:* (01) 43 26 63 00; (01) 43 26 80 48 *Fax:* (01) 40 46 89 24 *E-mail:* corti@noos.fr *Web Site:* www.jose-corti.fr, pg 156

Libreria Cortina Editrice SRL (Italy) *Tel:* (045) 594177 *Fax:* (045) 597551 *E-mail:* info@libreriacortina.it; cortinab@tin.it *Web Site:* www.libreriacortina.it, pg 383

Ediciones Corunda SA de CV (Mexico) *Tel:* (05) 6525511; (05) 6525581 *Fax:* (05) 6525211, pg 463

Corvina Books Ltd (Hungary) *Tel:* (01) 1184347 *Fax:* (01) 1184410 *E-mail:* corvina@axelero.hu, pg 321

Cosa-Verlag, Giusep Condrau SA (Switzerland) *Tel:* (081) 947 64 64; (081) 947 63 52 *Fax:* (081) 947 63 52 *E-mail:* condrau@cosa.ch *Web Site:* www.cosa.ch, pg 621

Cosmo Publications (India) *Tel:* (011) 3278779; (011) 3280455 *Fax:* (011) 3274597 *E-mail:* genesis.cosmo@axcess.net.in; genesis@ndb.vsnl.net.in, pg 332

Cosmopolita SRL (Argentina) *Tel:* (011) 4361-8925; (011) 4361-8049 *Fax:* (011) 4361-8049; (011) 4361-8925, pg 4

Cosmopolitan Publishers Ltd (Kenya) *Tel:* (020) 333448 *Fax:* (020) 333448, pg 433

Edicoes Cosmos (Portugal) *Tel:* (021) 3468201 *Fax:* (021) 799 99 79 *E-mail:* cosmos@liv-arcoiris.pt, pg 530

Cosmos Libros SRL (Argentina) *Tel:* (011) 48127364; (011) 48155347 *E-mail:* contactenos@cosmoslibros.com.ar *Web Site:* www.cosmoslibros.com.ar, pg 1297

Cosmos-Verlag AG (Switzerland) *Tel:* (31) 9506464 *Fax:* (31) 9506460 *E-mail:* info@cosmosverlag.ch, pg 621

Costa e Nolan SpA (Italy) *Tel:* (022) 9402156 *Fax:* (022) 047922, pg 383

Editorial Costa Rica (Costa Rica) *Tel:* 253-5354 *Fax:* 253-5091 *E-mail:* ventas@editorialcostarica.com; difusion@editorialcostarica.com *Web Site:* www.editorialcostarica.com, pg 115

Costaisa SA (Spain) *Tel:* (093) 536 100 *Fax:* (093) 057 917 *E-mail:* costaisa@costaisa.com *Web Site:* www.costaisa.com, pg 578

Cotidiano Mujer (Uruguay) *Tel:* (02) 9018782; (02) 9020393 *Fax:* (02) 4095651 *E-mail:* cotidian@chasque.apc.org.uy *Web Site:* chasque.chasque.apc.org/cotidian/, pg 777

Cottage Publications (United Kingdom) *Tel:* (01247) 888033; (0410) 057990 (mobile) *Fax:* (01247) 888063 *E-mail:* info@cottage-publications.com *Web Site:* www.cottage-publications.com, pg 683

J G Cotta'sche Buchhandlung Nachfolger GmbH (Germany) *Tel:* (0711) 6672-1256 *Fax:* (0711) 6672-2031 *E-mail:* info@klett-cotta.de *Web Site:* www.klett-cotta.de, pg 210

Council for British Archaeology (United Kingdom) *Tel:* (01904) 671417 *Fax:* (01904) 671384 *E-mail:* archaeology@compuserve.com; cbabooks@dial.pipex.com *Web Site:* www.britarch.ac.uk, pg 683

Council for Scientific & Industrial Research-Institute for Scientific & Technological Information (Ghana) *Tel:* (021) 777651-4; (021) 777655 *E-mail:* csir@ghana.com; cemensah@hotmail.com *Web Site:* www.csir.org.gh, pg 1512

Council of Academic & Professional Publishers (United Kingdom) *Tel:* (020) 4691 9191 *Fax:* (020) 7691 9199 *E-mail:* mail@publishers.org.uk *Web Site:* www.publishers.org.uk, pg 1291

Council of Australian State Libraries (Australia) *Tel:* (03) 8664 7512 *Fax:* (03) 9639 4737 *E-mail:* casl@slv.vic.gov.au *Web Site:* www.casl.org.au, pg 1557

Council of Europe Publishing (France) *Tel:* (0388) 41 25 81 *Fax:* (0388) 41 39 10 *E-mail:* publishing@coe.int *Web Site:* book.coe.int, pg 156

Council of Europe Publishing (France) *Tel:* (03) 88 41 25 81 *Fax:* (03) 88 41 39 10 *E-mail:* publishing@coe.int *Web Site:* book.coe.int, pg 1267

Council of Libraries (Albania) *Tel:* (042) 7984; (042) 7823, pg 1557

Counseil International de la Langue Francaise (France) *Tel:* (01) 48787395 *Fax:* (01) 48784928 *E-mail:* cilf@cilf.org *Web Site:* www.cilf.org, pg 156

Countryside Books (United Kingdom) *Tel:* (01635) 43816 *Fax:* (01635) 551004 *E-mail:* info@countrysidebooks.co.uk *Web Site:* www.countrysidebooks.co.uk, pg 683

Countyvise Ltd (United Kingdom) *Tel:* (0151) 6473333 *Fax:* (0151) 6478286 *E-mail:* info@countyvise.co.uk *Web Site:* www.countyvise.co.uk, pg 683

Cour Internationale de Justice (Netherlands) *Tel:* (070) 302 23 23 *Fax:* (070) 364 99 28 *E-mail:* mail@icj-cij.org; information@icj-cij.org *Web Site:* www.icj-cij.org, pg 1278

Editions Courrier du Livre (France) *Tel:* (01) 43 36 41 05 *Fax:* (01) 43 31 07 45 *E-mail:* info@tredaniel-courrier.com *Web Site:* www.tredaniel.com/, pg 156

Courseguides International Ltd (Hong Kong) *Tel:* 2737 3322 *Fax:* 2793 1188, pg 317

Uitgeverij Coutinho BV (Netherlands) *Tel:* (035) 6949991 *Fax:* (035) 6947165 *E-mail:* info@coutinho.nl *Web Site:* www.coutinho.nl, pg 481

Covenant Publishing Co Ltd (United Kingdom) *Tel:* (020) 8877 9010 *Fax:* (020) 8871 4770 *E-mail:* admin@britishisrael.co.uk *Web Site:* www.britishisrael.co.uk, pg 683

Covenanter Press (Australia) *Tel:* (02) 4257 9188 *Fax:* (02) 6351 4611 *Web Site:* www.covenanterpress.com.au, pg 18

Richard & Erika Coward Writing & Publishing Partnership (United Kingdom) *Tel:* (0208) 202 9592 *E-mail:* info@writers.net, pg 683

Cox & Wyman Ltd (United Kingdom) *Tel:* (0118) 953 0500 *Fax:* (0118) 950 7222 *E-mail:* enquiries@coxandwyman.co.uk; coxandwyman@cpi-group.net *Web Site:* www.cpi-group.net, pg 1163

Cox & Wyman Ltd (United Kingdom) *Tel:* (0118) 953 0500 *Fax:* (0118) 950 7222, pg 1184

Cox & Wyman Ltd (United Kingdom) *Tel:* (0118) 953 0500 *Fax:* (0118) 950 7222 *E-mail:* coxandwyman@cpi-group.net *Web Site:* www.cpi-group.net, pg 1225, 1238

CPE (Conseil Permanent des Ecrivains) (France) *Tel:* (01) 49 54 68 80 *Fax:* (01) 42 84 20 87, pg 1267

Cradley Print Ltd (United Kingdom) *Tel:* (01384) 414100; (01384) 414102 (sales) *Fax:* (01384) 414102 *E-mail:* sales@cradleygp.co.uk *Web Site:* www.cradleygp.co.uk, pg 1184

Cradley Print Ltd (United Kingdom) *Tel:* (01384) 414100 *Fax:* (01384) 414102 *E-mail:* sales@cradleygp.co.uk *Web Site:* www.cradleygp.co.uk, pg 1225

Cradley Print Ltd (United Kingdom) *Tel:* (01384) 414100 *Fax:* (01384) 414102 *Web Site:* www.cradleygp.co.uk, pg 1247

Craft Print Pte Ltd (Singapore) *Tel:* 861 4040 *Fax:* 861 0530 *E-mail:* craftprt@singet.com.sg, pg 1181

Craft Print Pte Ltd (Singapore) *Tel:* 861 4040 *Fax:* 861 0530 *E-mail:* info@craftprint.com *Web Site:* www.craftprint.com, pg 1222, 1246

The Crafts Council (United Kingdom) *Tel:* (020) 7278 7700 *Fax:* (020) 7837 6891 *Web Site:* www.craftscouncil.org.uk, pg 1350

Craig Potton Publishing (New Zealand) *Tel:* (03) 5489009 *Fax:* (03) 5489009 *E-mail:* info@cpp.co.nz *Web Site:* www.cpp.co.nz, pg 495

Craig Printing Co Ltd (New Zealand) *Tel:* (03) 211-0393 *Fax:* (03) 214-9930 *E-mail:* sales@craigsatlas.co.nz *Web Site:* www.craigprint.co.nz, pg 495

Otto Cramwinckel Uitgever (Netherlands) *Tel:* (020) 627 66 09 *Fax:* (020) 638 38 17 *E-mail:* info@cram.nl *Web Site:* www.cram.nl, pg 481

Wendy Crane Books (New Zealand) *Tel:* (04) 5664228, pg 495

Crathern Machinery Group Inc (United States) *Tel:* 603-746-4111 *Fax:* 603-746-4172 *E-mail:* info@crathern.com *Web Site:* www.crathern.com, pg 1248

Crawford House Publishing Pty Ltd (Australia) *Tel:* (08) 8370 0300; (08) 8370 3555 (orders) *Fax:* (08) 8370 0344; (08) 8370 3566 (orders) *Web Site:* www.crawfordhouse.com.au, pg 18

Creaciones Monar Editorial (Spain) *Tel:* (093) 2133928 *Fax:* (093) 2198460 *Web Site:* www.monar.com, pg 578

Creadif (Belgium) *Tel:* (02) 512 98 45 *Fax:* (02) 511 72 02, pg 65

Editure Ion Creanga (Romania) *Tel:* (01) 2231112, pg 539

Creation Books (United Kingdom) *Tel:* (020) 7430 9878 *Fax:* (020) 7242 5527 *E-mail:* info@creationbooks.com *Web Site:* www.creationbooks.com, pg 683

Creative Monochrome Ltd (United Kingdom) *Tel:* (020) 8686 3282 *Fax:* (020) 8681 0662 *E-mail:* sales@cremono.com; roger@cremono.demon.co.uk, pg 684

CREDES - Centre de Recherche d'Etude et de Documentation en Economie de la Sante (France) *Tel:* (01) 53 93 43 00 *Fax:* (01) 53 93 43 50 *Web Site:* www.credes.fr, pg 156

Cremers (Schoollandkaarten) PVBA (Belgium) *Tel:* (02) 2680345 *Fax:* (02) 2680345, pg 66

Edizioni Cremonese SRL (Italy) *Tel:* (055) 2476371 *Fax:* (055) 2476372 *E-mail:* cremonese@ed-cremonese.it *Web Site:* www.ed-cremonese.it, pg 383

Editeurs Crepin-Leblond (France) *Tel:* (03) 25 03 87 48 *Fax:* (03) 25 03 87 40 *E-mail:* crepin-leblond@graphycom.com *Web Site:* www.graphycom.com, pg 156

Editora Crescer Ltda (Brazil) *Tel:* (031) 221-9335 *Fax:* (031) 3227-0729 *E-mail:* crescer@crescer.com.br *Web Site:* www.crescer.com.br, pg 80

Cressrelles Publishing Company Ltd (United Kingdom) *Tel:* (01684) 540154 *Fax:* (01684) 540154, pg 684

Rupert Crew Ltd (United Kingdom) *Tel:* (020) 7242 8586 *Fax:* (020) 7831 7914 *E-mail:* rupertcrew@compuserve.com, pg 1139

Le Cri Editions (Belgium) *Tel:* (02) 6466533 *Fax:* (02) 6466607 *E-mail:* lecri@skynet.be, pg 66

Crime Writers' Association (United Kingdom) *E-mail:* info@theCWA.co.uk *Web Site:* www.thecwa.co.uk, pg 1291

Crisalide (Italy) *Tel:* (0771) 64463 *Fax:* (0771) 639121 *E-mail:* crisalide@crisalide.com *Web Site:* www.crisalide.com, pg 383

Crista International (Australia) *Tel:* (07) 5537 2956 *Fax:* (07) 5537 2956, pg 18

Librerias de Cristal, sa de cv (Mexico) *Tel:* (05) 5644100 *Fax:* (05) 2640983; (05) 5644100 ext 287 (fax on demand) *E-mail:* biblio10@prodigy.net.mx, pg 1327

Ediciones Cristiandad (Spain) *Tel:* (091) 781 99 70 *Fax:* (091) 781 99 77 *E-mail:* info@kgm.es *Web Site:* www.edicionescristiandad.com, pg 578

Cristy's Atelier (Hong Kong) *Tel:* 25418609 *Fax:* 28540995 *E-mail:* cristys@intercon.net, pg 1177

Editions Criterion (France) *Tel:* (01) 45443834 *Fax:* (01) 45499392, pg 156

Critica (Argentina) *Tel:* (011) 4382-4045; (011) 4382-4043 *Fax:* (011) 4383-3793 *E-mail:* info@grijalbo.com.ar, pg 5

Critics' Circle (United Kingdom) *Tel:* (0171) 403 1818 *Fax:* (0171) 7357 9287 *E-mail:* info@criticscircle.org.uk *Web Site:* www.criticscircle.org.uk, pg 1407

Critiques Livres Distribution SAS (France) *Tel:* (014) 360-3910 *Fax:* (014) 897-3706 *E-mail:* critiques.livres@wanadoo.fr, pg 1245

Critiques Livres Distribution SAS (France) *Tel:* (01) 43603910 *Fax:* (01) 48973706 *E-mail:* critiques.livres@wanadoo.fr, pg 1309

Croatian ISBN Agency (Croatia) *Tel:* (01) 6164087; (01) 6164288 *Fax:* (01) 6164371 *E-mail:* isbn@nsk.hr *Web Site:* www.nsk.hr, pg 1265

Studia Croatica (Argentina) *Tel:* (011) 4771-4954 *Fax:* (011) 4771-4954 *E-mail:* webmasters@studiacroatica.com, pg 5

Crofthouse Books Ltd (United Kingdom) *Tel:* (01932) 845559 *Fax:* (01932) 849528; (01932) 830006 *E-mail:* croft@crofthouse.co.uk *Web Site:* www.crofthouse.co.uk, pg 1350

Comite international de la Croix-Rouge (Switzerland) *Tel:* (022) 734 60 01 *Fax:* (022) 733 20 57; (022) 730 27 68 *Web Site:* www.icrc.org, pg 621

Paul H Crompton Ltd (United Kingdom) *Tel:* (020) 8780 1063 *Fax:* (020) 8780 1063 *E-mail:* cromptonph@aol.com, pg 684

Croner CCH Group Ltd (United Kingdom) *Tel:* (020) 85473333 *Fax:* (020) 85472637 *E-mail:* info@croner.co.uk *Web Site:* www.croner.co.uk, pg 684

Editura Cronos SRL (Romania) *Tel:* (044) 262245; (044) 7690952 *Fax:* (01) 2231025 *E-mail:* cronos@dial.kappa.ro, pg 539

Cross Continent Press Ltd (Nigeria) *Tel:* (01) 862437 *Fax:* (01) 685679, pg 504

Crossbridge Books (United Kingdom) *Tel:* (0121) 447 7897 *Fax:* (0121) 445 1063 *E-mail:* crossbridgebooks@btinternet.com *Web Site:* www.crossbridgebooks.com, pg 684

Crossroad Distributors Pty Ltd (Australia) *Tel:* (02) 8845 7744 *Fax:* (02) 8845 7755 *E-mail:* custserv@crossroad.com.au, pg 18

Crown House Publishing Ltd (United Kingdom) *Tel:* (01267) 211345 *Fax:* (01267) 211882 *E-mail:* books@crownhouse.co.uk *Web Site:* www.crownhouse.co.uk, pg 684

The Crowood Press Ltd (United Kingdom) *Tel:* (01672) 520320 *Fax:* (01672) 520280 *E-mail:* enquiries@crowood.com *Web Site:* www.crowood.com, pg 684

G L Crowther (United Kingdom) *Tel:* (01772) 257126, pg 684

Crucible Publishers (United Kingdom) *Tel:* (01373) 834900 *Fax:* (01373) 834900 *E-mail:* sales@cruciblepublishers.com *Web Site:* www.cruciblepublishers.com, pg 684

Ediciones Cruilla SA (Spain) *Tel:* (093) 2376344; (093) 2922172 *Fax:* (093) 2380116 *Web Site:* www.cruilla.com, pg 578

Publicaciones Cruz O SA (Mexico) *Tel:* (055) 56-80-61-22 *Fax:* (055) 56-80-61-22 *E-mail:* infolibros@libros.com.mx; atencionaclienteslibros@libros.com.mx *Web Site:* www.libros.com.mx, pg 463

Crystal Publishing (Australia) *Tel:* (03) 9525 4549 *E-mail:* minx@alphalink.com.au, pg 19

CS Graphics Pte Ltd (Singapore) *Tel:* 861-0100 *Fax:* 861-0190, pg 1161

CS Graphics Pte Ltd (Singapore) *Tel:* 6865 2010 *Fax:* 6861 0190 *Web Site:* ourworld.compuserve.com/homepages/csgraphics, pg 1181

CS Graphics Pte Ltd (Singapore) *Tel:* 6865 2010 *Fax:* 6861 0190 *Web Site:* www.csgraphics.us, pg 1222

CS Graphics Pte Ltd (Singapore) *Tel:* 6865 2010 *Fax:* 6861 0190 *E-mail:* rick@csgraphics.us *Web Site:* www.csgraphics.us, pg 1237

CS Graphics USA Inc (United States) *Tel:* 916-791-9066 *Fax:* 916-791-9112, pg 1166, 1187, 1229

CS Graphics USA Inc (United States) *Tel:* 916-791-9066 *Fax:* 916-791-9112 *E-mail:* csgraphics@mindspring.com, pg 1240

CSA (Cambridge Scientific Abstracts) (United Kingdom) *Tel:* (0441) 865 336250 *Fax:* (0441) 865 336258 *E-mail:* service@csa.com; tjones@csa.com (sales); marketing@bowker.uk.co *Web Site:* www.csa.com, pg 684

Verlag CSA Rosemarie Schneider (Germany) *Tel:* (06082) 970116 *Fax:* (06082) 970123 *E-mail:* csa-europa@csa-activ.de *Web Site:* www.csa-activ.de, pg 210

CSIR Information Services (South Africa) *Tel:* (012) 841-2911 *Fax:* (012) 349-1153 *Web Site:* www.csir.co.za, pg 1543

CSIRO (Commonwealth Scientific & Industrial Research Organization) (Australia) *Tel:* (03) 9545 2176 *Fax:* (03) 9545 2175 *E-mail:* enquiries@csiro.au *Web Site:* www.csiro.au, pg 1490

CSIRO Publishing (Commonwealth Scientific & Industrial Research Organisation) (Australia) *Tel:* (03) 9662 7500 *Fax:* (03) 9662 7555 *E-mail:* publishing@csiro.au *Web Site:* www.publish.csiro.au, pg 19

CSS Bookshops (Nigeria) *Tel:* (01) 2633081; (01) 2637009; (01) 2637023; (01) 2633010 *Fax:* (01) 2637089 *E-mail:* cssbookshops@skannet.com.ng, pg 504, 1331

CTBI Publications (United Kingdom) *Tel:* (020) 7523 2121 *Fax:* (020) 7928 0010 *E-mail:* info@ctbi.org.uk *Web Site:* www.ctbi.org.uk, pg 685

CTE-Centro de Tecnologia Educativa SA (Spain) *Tel:* (093) 217 75 01 *Fax:* (093) 217 62 53 *E-mail:* cte@mx2.redestb.es.com *Web Site:* www.centrocte.com, pg 578

CTIF (Center Technique Industriel de la Fonderie) (France) *Tel:* (01) 41 14 63 00 *Fax:* (01) 45 34 14 34 *E-mail:* contact@ctif.com *Web Site:* www.ctif.com, pg 156

CTL-Presse Clemens-Tobias Lange (Germany) *Tel:* (040) 39902223 *Fax:* (040) 39902224 *E-mail:* ctl@europe.com *Web Site:* www.ctl-presse.de, pg 210

CTNERHI - Centre Technique National d'Etudes et de Recherches sur les Handicaps et les Inadaptations (France) *Tel:* (01) 45 65 59 00 *Fax:* (01) 45 65 44 94 *E-mail:* ctnerhi@club-internet.fr *Web Site:* perso.club-internet.fr/ctnrhi, pg 156

CTP Book Printers (Pty) Ltd (South Africa) *Tel:* (011) 8890600 *Fax:* (011) 8890922 *E-mail:* ctpjhb@iafrica.com, pg 1182

CTP Book Printers (Pty) Ltd (South Africa) *Tel:* (021) 930 8820 *Fax:* (021) 939 1559 *E-mail:* ctp@ctpbooks.co.za, pg 1223

Editorial Cuarto Propio (Chile) *Tel:* (02) 204 7645 *Fax:* (02) 204 7622 *E-mail:* cuartopropio@cuartopropio.cl *Web Site:* www.cuartopropio.cl, pg 99

Editorial Cuatro Vientos (Chile) *Tel:* (02) 2258381; (02) 269 5343 *Fax:* (02) 3413107 *E-mail:* 4vientos@netline.cl *Web Site:* www.cuatrovientos.net, pg 99

Agencia Cubana del ISBN (Cuba) *Tel:* (07) 36034 *Fax:* (07) 333441 *E-mail:* cclfilh@ceniai.cu, pg 1265

Ediciones Cubanas (Cuba) *Tel:* (07) 63 1981; (07) 33 8942; (07) 63 1989 *Fax:* (07) 338 943 *E-mail:* edicuba@artsoft.cult.cu, pg 1307

Cuernavaca Editorial S A (Mexico) *Tel:* (05) 5113619; (05) 5142529; (05) 2867794 *Fax:* (05) 2117112, pg 463

Editions Cujas (France) *Tel:* (01) 44 24 24 36; (01) 44 24 24 37 *Fax:* (01) 44 24 24 38 *E-mail:* cujas@cujas.fr *Web Site:* www.cujas.fr, pg 156

Cultur Prospectiv, Edition (Switzerland) *Tel:* (01) 260 69 01 *Fax:* (01) 260 69 29 *E-mail:* cedition@culturprospectiv.ch *Web Site:* www.culturprospectiv.ch, pg 621

Cultura (Belgium) *Tel:* (032) 093691595 *Fax:* (032) 093695925 *E-mail:* info@cultura-net.com *Web Site:* www.cultura-net.com; www.cultura.be, pg 66

Edizioni Cultura della Pace (Italy) *Tel:* (055) 576149 *Fax:* (055) 5088003, pg 383

Casa de la Cultura Ecuatoriana Benjamin Carrion (Ecuador) *Tel:* (02) 2902262 *Fax:* (02) 2566070 *E-mail:* info@cce.org.ec *Web Site:* cce.org.ec, pg 1398

Editorial Cultura (Guatemala) *Tel:* (02) 692080 *Fax:* (02) 346135, pg 313

Editora Cultura Medica Ltda (Brazil) *Tel:* (021) 2567-3888 *Fax:* (021) 2569-5443 *E-mail:* atendimento@culturamedica.com.br *Web Site:* www.culturamedica.com.br, pg 80

Instituto de Cultura Puertoriquena (Puerto Rico) *Tel:* 787-724-0700 *Fax:* 787-724-8393 *E-mail:* www@icp.gobierno.pr *Web Site:* www.icp.gobierno.pr, pg 537

La Cultura Sociologica (Italy) *Tel:* (02) 29409041 *Fax:* (02) 29409041, pg 384

Ediciones Cultural Colombiana Ltda (Colombia) *Tel:* (01) 2116090 *Fax:* (01) 2176570, pg 110

Editorial Cultural Inc (Puerto Rico) *Tel:* 787-765-9767 *Fax:* 787-765-9767 *E-mail:* cultural@coqui.net *Web Site:* www.editorialcultural.com, pg 537

Cultural Relics Publishing House (China) *Tel:* (010) 64048057 *Fax:* (010) 64010698 *E-mail:* web@wenwu.com *Web Site:* www.wenwu.com, pg 103

Ediciones Culturales Internacionales SA de CV Edicion Compra y Venta de Libros, Casetes, Videos (Mexico) *Tel:* (05) 2508099 (ext 200) *Fax:* (05) 55311597, pg 463

Ediciones Culturales Ver Ltda (Colombia) *Tel:* (01) 2859362; (01) 2859204 *Fax:* (01) 2859362, pg 110

Culture et Bibliotheque pour Tous (France) *Tel:* (01) 45 33 07 07 *Fax:* (01) 45 33 45 76 *E-mail:* uncbpt.services@wanadoo.fr, pg 156

Bibliotheek Cultureel Centrum Suriname (Suriname) *Tel:* 472369; 473309 *Fax:* 476516 *E-mail:* sccs@sr.net; stgccs1947@hotmail.com, pg 1546

Cumann Leabharlann na h-Eireann (Ireland) *Tel:* (01) 61202193 *Fax:* (01) 61213090 *Web Site:* www.libraryassociation.ie, pg 1565

The Mary Cunnane Agency Pty Ltd (Australia) *Tel:* (02) 438599922 *Fax:* (02) 43651093 *E-mail:* info@cunnaneagency.com *Web Site:* www.cunnaneagency.com, pg 1129

Ediciones CUPSA, Centro de Comunicacion Cultural CUPSA, AC (Mexico) *Tel:* (05) 5925252; (05) 5662307; (05) 5462100, pg 463

Ediciones la Cupula SL (Spain) *Tel:* (093) 268 28 05 *Fax:* (093) 268 07 65 *E-mail:* lacupula@eix.intercom.es *Web Site:* www.lacupula.com, pg 578

Cura Verlag GmbH (Austria) *Tel:* (01) 7136480 *Fax:* (01) 7126258; (01) 7126219, pg 49

Edizioni Curci SRL (Italy) *Tel:* (02) 760361 *Fax:* (02) 76014504 *E-mail:* info@edizionicurci.it *Web Site:* www.edizionicurci.it, pg 384

Curiad (United Kingdom) *Tel:* (01286) 882166 *Fax:* (01286) 882692 *E-mail:* curiad@curiad.co.uk *Web Site:* www.curiad.co.uk, pg 685

Curial Edicions Catalanes SA (Spain) *Tel:* (093) 4588101 *Fax:* (093) 2077427 *E-mail:* curial@lix.intercom.es, pg 578

Currency Press Pty Ltd (Australia) *Tel:* (02) 9319 5877 *Fax:* (02) 9319 3649 *E-mail:* enquiries@currency.com.au *Web Site:* www.currency.com.au, pg 19

Current Books (India) *Tel:* (0487) 2444322 *E-mail:* info@dcbooks.com *Web Site:* www.dcbooks.com/currentbooks.htm, pg 332

Current Pacific Ltd (New Zealand) *Tel:* (09) 480-1388 *Fax:* (09) 480-1387 *E-mail:* info@cplnz.com *Web Site:* www.cplnz.com, pg 495

Current Science Group (United Kingdom) *Tel:* (020) 7323 0323 *Fax:* (020) 7580 1938 *E-mail:* info@current-science.com *Web Site:* www.current-science-group.com, pg 685

Current Technical Literature Co (Pvt) Ltd (India) *Tel:* (022) 2611045 *Fax:* (022) 2679786, pg 1315

James Currey Ltd (United Kingdom) *Tel:* (01865) 244 111 *Fax:* (01865) 246 454 *E-mail:* editorial@jamescurrey.co.uk *Web Site:* www.jamescurrey.co.uk, pg 685

Curriculum Corporation (Australia) *Tel:* (03) 9207 9600 *Fax:* (03) 9639 1616 *E-mail:* sales@curriculum.edu.au *Web Site:* www.curriculum.edu.au, pg 19

Eleanor Curtain Publishing (Australia) *Tel:* (03) 9822 0344 *Fax:* (03) 9824 8851, pg 19

Curtis Brown Group Ltd (United Kingdom) *Tel:* (020) 7393 4400 *Fax:* (020) 7393 4401 *E-mail:* cb@curtisbrown.co.uk, pg 1139

Cuspide Libros SA (Argentina) *Tel:* (011) 43228868 *Fax:* (011) 43223456 *E-mail:* distribuidora@cuspide.com *Web Site:* www.cuspide.com, pg 1297

Custom Services (United States) *Tel:* 845-365-0414 *Fax:* 845-365-0864, pg 1187

Cuttington University College Library (Liberia) *Tel:* 227-413 *Fax:* 226-059 *Web Site:* www.cuttington.org, pg 1525

CyberClub (United Kingdom) *Tel:* (020) 8731 6161 *Fax:* (020) 8905 5050 *Web Site:* www.astorlaw.com, pg 685

Cyhoeddiadau Barddas (United Kingdom) *Tel:* (01792) 792 829, pg 685

Cyhoeddiadau'r Gair (United Kingdom) *Tel:* (01248) 382947 *Fax:* (01248) 383954 *E-mail:* eds00e@bangor.ac.uk *Web Site:* www.ysgolsul.com, pg 685

Cymdeithas Lyfrau Ceredigion (United Kingdom) *Tel:* (01970) 617776 *Fax:* (01970) 624049; (01970) 625844 *E-mail:* clc.gyf@talk21.com, pg 685

Cynosure Publishing Inc (Taiwan, Province of China) *Tel:* 8862 2657 3275 *Fax:* (02) 2657 5300 *E-mail:* cynobook@tpts4.seed.net.tw, pg 639

Cypher Library Books (United Kingdom) *Tel:* (0113) 2012900 *Fax:* (0113) 2012929 *E-mail:* enquiries@cyphergroup.com *Web Site:* www.cyphergroup.com, pg 1350

Cyprus Library (Cyprus) *Tel:* (022) 303180; (022) 676118 *Fax:* (022) 304532 *E-mail:* cypruslibrary@cytanet.com.cy *Web Site:* portico.bl.uk, pg 1500

Library of the Cyprus Museum - Dept of Antiquities (Cyprus) *Tel:* (022) 865864; (022) 865888 *Fax:* (022) 303148 *E-mail:* roctarch@cytanet.com.cy, pg 1500

Cyprus Telecommunications Authority (CYTA) (Cyprus) *Tel:* (022) 701000 *Fax:* (022) 497155 *E-mail:* enquiries@cyta.com.cy *Web Site:* www.cyta.com.cy, pg 121

Czech PEN Centre (Czech Republic) *Tel:* (02) 24235546; (02) 24234343 *Fax:* (02) 24221926 *E-mail:* centrum@pen.cz *Web Site:* www.pen.cz, pg 1398

Czernin Verlag Ltd (Austria) *Tel:* (01) 403 35 63 *Fax:* (01) 403 35 63-15 *E-mail:* office@czernin-verlag.com *Web Site:* www.czernin-verlag.com, pg 49

Spoldzielnia Wydawnicza 'Czytelnik' (Poland) *Tel:* (022) 6281441 *Fax:* (022) 6283178 *E-mail:* sekretariat@czytelnik.pl *Web Site:* www.czytelnik.pl, pg 522

D&B Ltd (United Kingdom) *Tel:* (01494) 422000 *Fax:* (01494) 422260 *E-mail:* custserv@dnb.com *Web Site:* www.dnb.com, pg 685

D&B Marketing Pty Ltd (Australia) *Tel:* (03) 9828 3333 *Fax:* (03) 9828 3300 *E-mail:* csc.austral@dnb.com.au *Web Site:* www.dnb.com.au, pg 19

D & K Group (United States) *Tel:* 847-956-0160 *Toll Free Tel:* 800-632-2314 *Fax:* 847-956-8214 *E-mail:* info@dkgroup.net *Web Site:* www.dkgroup.com, pg 1229, 1240, 1248

D C Thomson & Co Ltd (United Kingdom) *Tel:* (01382) 223131 *Fax:* (01382) 462097 *E-mail:* shout@dcthomson.co.uk *Web Site:* www.dcthomson.co.uk, pg 685

DA Information Services Pty Ltd (Australia) *Tel:* (03) 9210-7777 *Fax:* (03) 9210-7788 *E-mail:* service@dadirect.com.au *Web Site:* www.dadirect.com.au, pg 1298

DA-Izdatelstvo Publishers (Bulgaria) *Tel:* (02) 988 1208 *Fax:* (02) 986 6290, pg 93

Ediciones Dabar, SA de CV (Mexico) *Tel:* (05) 6550396 *Fax:* (05) 6033674 *E-mail:* dabar@data.net.mx, pg 464

Dabill Publications (Australia) *Tel:* (02) 4228 8836 *Fax:* (02) 4226 9367 *Web Site:* www.dabill.com.au, pg 19

DachsVerlag GmbH (Austria) *Tel:* (01) 285 22 05-0 *Fax:* (01) 285 22 05-15 *E-mail:* office@dachs.at *Web Site:* www.dachs.at, pg 49

Editura Dacia (Romania) *Tel:* (0264) 452178 *Fax:* (0264) 452178 *E-mail:* office@edituradacia.ro *Web Site:* www.edituradacia.ro; www.cjnet.ro, pg 539

Daco Verlag Guenter Blase oHG (Germany) *Tel:* (0711) 96421-0 *Fax:* (0711) 96421-10 *E-mail:* info@daco-verlag.de *Web Site:* www.daco-verlag.de, pg 210

Les Editions Roger Dacosta (France) *Tel:* (01) 45441491, pg 156

Edizioni Armando Dado, Tipografia Stazione (Switzerland) *Tel:* (091) 751 48 02 *Fax:* (091) 752 10 26, pg 621

Dae Won Sa Co Ltd (Republic of Korea) *Tel:* (02) 7576717 *Fax:* (02) 7758043, pg 438

Daedalus Verlag (Germany) *Tel:* (0251) 231355 *Fax:* (0251) 232631 *E-mail:* info@daedalus-verlag.de *Web Site:* www.daedalus-verlag.com, pg 210

Daehan Printing & Publishing Co Ltd (Republic of Korea) *Tel:* (031) 730-3850 *Fax:* (031) 735-8104 *E-mail:* mschung@daehane.com; james@daehane.com; sabrachili@daehane.com *Web Site:* www.daehane.com, pg 438

Daehan Printing & Publishing Co Ltd (Republic of Korea) *Tel:* (031) 730-3850 *Fax:* (031) 735-8104 *E-mail:* mschung@daehane.com *Web Site:* www.daehane.com, pg 1159, 1180

Daehan Printing & Publishing Co Ltd (Republic of Korea) *Tel:* (031) 730-3850; (031) 730-3813 *Fax:* (031) 735-8104 *Web Site:* www.dhpop.com; www.daehane.com, pg 1221

Daehan Printing & Publishing Co Ltd (Republic of Korea) *Tel:* (031) 730-3850 *Fax:* (031) 735-8104 *Web Site:* www.daehane.com; www.dhpop.com, pg 1237

Daejon Trading Co Ltd (Republic of Korea) *Tel:* (02) 536-9555 *Fax:* (02) 536-0025, pg 1324

Daeyoung Munhwasa (Republic of Korea) *Tel:* (02) 716-3883 *Fax:* (02) 703-3839 *E-mail:* spotto29@hotmail.com, pg 438

Dafolo Forlag (Denmark) *Tel:* 9620 6666 *Fax:* 9842 9711 *E-mail:* dafolo@dafolo.dk *Web Site:* www.dafolo.dk; www.dafaloforlag.dk, pg 130

DAFSA (France) *Tel:* (01) 44 37 26 00 *Fax:* (01) 44 37 26 35 *E-mail:* dorra.medjani@dri-wefa.com *Web Site:* www.dafsa.fr, pg 156

Institut Dagang Muchtar (Indonesia) *Tel:* (031) 42973, pg 354

Klub-Dagbreek (South Africa) *Tel:* (011) 6736725 *Fax:* (011) 6736719, pg 1255

Dagmar Dreves Verlag (Germany) *Tel:* (04131) 248100 *Fax:* (04131) 248102, pg 210

Dagraja Press (Australia) *Tel:* (02) 6247 0782; (02) 6262 7533 *E-mail:* granorab@ozemail.com.au, pg 19

Dahlgaard Media BV (Denmark) *Tel:* 3537 3533 *Fax:* 3537 3299, pg 130

Dahlia Books, International Publishers & Booksellers (Sweden) *Tel:* (018) 101098 *Fax:* (018) 100525 *E-mail:* dahlia@telia.com, pg 611

Dai Hak Publishing Co (Republic of Korea) *Tel:* (02) 364-9788 *Fax:* (02) 393-9045, pg 438

Dai Nippon Printing Co (Hong Kong) Ltd (Hong Kong) *Tel:* 2408-0188 *Fax:* 2408-8479 *Web Site:* www.dnp.co.jp, pg 1156

Dai Nippon Printing Co (Hong Kong) Ltd (Hong Kong) *Tel:* 2408-0188 *Fax:* 2408-8479 *E-mail:* info@mail.dnp.co.jp *Web Site:* www.dnp.co.jp, pg 1177

Dai Nippon Printing Co (Hong Kong) Ltd (Hong Kong) *Tel:* 2408-0188 *Fax:* 2614-7585; 2407-6201 *Web Site:* www.dnp.co.jp, pg 1217, 1236

Dai Nippon Printing Co Ltd (Japan) *Tel:* (03) 3266 2111 *E-mail:* info@mail.dnp.co.jp *Web Site:* www.dnp.co.jp, pg 1221

Daiichi Media Pte Ltd (Singapore) *Tel:* 6849 8666 *Fax:* 6256 5922 *E-mail:* info@daiichimedia.com.sg; sales@daiichimedia.com.sg *Web Site:* www.daiichimedia.com, pg 555

Daiichi Shuppan Co Ltd (Japan) *Tel:* (03) 3291-4576 *Fax:* (03) 3291-4579 *Web Site:* www.daiichi-shuppan.co.jp, pg 416

Le Daily-Bul (Belgium) *Tel:* (064) 222973 *Fax:* (064) 222973, pg 66

Daily Times of Nigeria Ltd (Publication Division) (Nigeria) *Tel:* (01) 4977280 *Fax:* (01) 4977284 *Web Site:* www.dailytimesofnigeria.com, pg 504

Daimon Verlag AG (Switzerland) *Tel:* (055) 412 2266 *Fax:* (055) 412 2231 *E-mail:* daimon@compuserve.com *Web Site:* www.daimon.ch, pg 621

Dainippon Tosho Publishing Co, Ltd (Japan) *Tel:* (03) 3561-8672 *Fax:* (03) 3563-5596 *Web Site:* www.dainippon-tosho.co.jp, pg 416

Dalia Peled Publishers, Division of Modan (Israel) *Tel:* (08) 4221821 *Fax:* (08) 4221299, pg 366

Dalian Maritime University Press (China) *Tel:* (0411) 84729480; (0411) 84728394 *Fax:* (0411) 84727996 *E-mail:* dmup@dmupress.com; cbs@dmupress.com *Web Site:* www.dmupress.com, pg 104

Dalian University of Technology Library (China) *Tel:* (0411) 84708620 *Fax:* (0411) 84708620; (0411) 84708626 *E-mail:* lib@dlut.edu.cn; libaqui4@dlut.edu.cn *Web Site:* www.lib.dlut.edu.cn, pg 1497

Editions Dalloz Sirey (France) *Tel:* (01) 40 64 54 54 *Fax:* (01) 40 64 54 60 *E-mail:* ventes@dalloz.fr *Web Site:* www.dalloz.fr, pg 157

Rafael Dalmau, Editor (Spain) *Tel:* (093) 3173338 *Fax:* (093) 3173338, pg 578

Izdatel'stovo Dal'nevostonogo Gosudarstvennogo Universite (Russian Federation) *Tel:* 57779 (Director) *Fax:* 257200, pg 544

Terence Dalton Ltd (United Kingdom) *Tel:* (01787) 249290 *Fax:* (01787) 248267 *E-mail:* tdl@lavenhamgroup.cp.uk *Web Site:* www.terencedalton.co.uk, pg 685

Daltons Books (Australia) *Tel:* (02) 62491844 *Fax:* (02) 62475753 *E-mail:* daltons@daltons.com.au *Web Site:* www.daltons.com.au, pg 1298

Ediciones Daly S L (Spain) *Tel:* (095) 2582569 *Fax:* (095) 2583619 *E-mail:* daly@edicionesdaly.com *Web Site:* edicionesdaly.com, pg 578

Damanhur Edizioni (Italy) *Tel:* (0124) 512213 *Fax:* (0124) 512213 *E-mail:* dhbooks@damanhurbooks.com *Web Site:* www.damanhurbooks.com, pg 384

Damascus University Library (Syrian Arab Republic) *Tel:* (011) 2215104; (011) 2215101 *Fax:* (011) 2236010 *E-mail:* info@damascus-online.com *Web Site:* www.damascus-online/university.htm, pg 1548

Damascus University Press (Syrian Arab Republic) *Tel:* (011) 2215104; (011) 2215101 *Fax:* (011) 2236010 *E-mail:* info@damascus-online.com *Web Site:* www.damascus-online/university.htm, pg 638

Dami Editore SRL (Italy) *Tel:* (02) 76006533 *Fax:* (02) 784010 *E-mail:* damieditore@damieditore.it *Web Site:* www.damieditore.it, pg 384

N W Damm og Son A/S (Norway) *Tel:* 24 05 10 00 *Fax:* 24 05 10 99 *E-mail:* post@egmont.no *Web Site:* www.damm.no, pg 508

Dana Verlag (Germany) *Tel:* (05468) 1813 *Fax:* (05468) 239, pg 210

Dance Books Ltd (United Kingdom) *Tel:* (01420) 86138 *Fax:* (01420) 86142 *E-mail:* dl@dancebooks.co.uk *Web Site:* www.dancebooks.co.uk, pg 686

Dangaroo Press (Australia) *Tel:* (02) 49545938 *Fax:* (02) 49546531, pg 19

Editions Dangles SA-Edilarge SA (France) *Tel:* (02) 38864180 *Fax:* (02) 38837234 *E-mail:* dangles@wanadoo.fr *Web Site:* www.editions-dangles.com, pg 157

The C W Daniel Co Ltd (United Kingdom) *Tel:* (01799) 521909; (01799) 526216 *Fax:* (01799) 513462 *E-mail:* cwdaniel@dial.pipex.com *Web Site:* www.cwdaniel.com, pg 686

Ann-Christine Danielsson Agency (Sweden) *Tel:* (040) 482380 *Fax:* (040) 482190 *E-mail:* acd.agency@swipnet.se, pg 1137

The Danish Literature Centre (Denmark) *Tel:* 33744500 *Fax:* 33744565 *E-mail:* danlit@danlit.dk *Web Site:* www.literaturenet.dk, pg 130

DanKook University Press (Republic of Korea) *Tel:* (02) 793-5034 *Fax:* (02) 709-5814 *E-mail:* omslit@dankook.ac.kr; pencil58@yahoo.com *Web Site:* www.dankook.ac.kr, pg 438

Danmar Publishers (Kenya) *Tel:* (020) 504818, pg 433

Danmarks Biblioteksforening (Denmark) *Tel:* 33 25 09 35 *Fax:* 33 25 79 00 *Web Site:* www.dbf.dk, pg 1560

Danmarks BlindeBibliotek (Denmark) *Tel:* 39 13 46 00 *Fax:* 39 13 46 01 *E-mail:* dbb@dbb.dk *Web Site:* www.dbb.dk, pg 1501

Danmarks Forskningsbiblioteksforening (Denmark) *Tel:* (045) 89 46 22 07 *Fax:* (045) 89 46 22 20 *E-mail:* df@statsbiblioteket.dk *Web Site:* www.dfdf.dk, pg 1561

Danmarks Forvaltningshojskole Forlaget (Denmark) *Tel:* 38 14 52 00 *Fax:* 38 14 53 45 *E-mail:* dhf@dhfnet.dk; dspa@dspa.dk *Web Site:* www.dkdfh.dk, pg 130

Danmarks Natur-og Laegevidenskabelige Bibliotek, Universitet de sbiblioteket (Denmark) *Tel:* 35396523 *Fax:* 35391939 *E-mail:* dnlb@dnlb.dk *Web Site:* www.dnlb.dk, pg 1501

Danmarks Paedagogiske Bibliotek (Denmark) *Tel:* 8888 9300 *Fax:* 8888 9391 *E-mail:* dpb@dpu.dk *Web Site:* www.dpb.dpu.dk/, pg 1501

Danmarks Statistik Biblioteket (Denmark) *Tel:* 3917 3917 *Fax:* 3917 3999 *E-mail:* dst@dst.dk *Web Site:* www.dst.dk/bibliotek, pg 1502

Danmarks Tekniske Videncenter (DTV) (Denmark) *Tel:* 4525 7200 *Fax:* 4588 3040 *E-mail:* dtv@dtv.dk *Web Site:* www.dtv.dk, pg 1502

D'Anna (Italy) *Tel:* (055) 2335513 *Fax:* (055) 225932 *E-mail:* gdanna@tin.it; gdanna@mbox.vol.it, pg 384

Hristo G Danov State Publishing House (Bulgaria) *Tel:* (032) 632552; (032) 265421 *Fax:* (032) 260560, pg 93

Dansk Biblioteks Center (Denmark) *Tel:* 44 86 77 77 *Fax:* 44 86 78 91 *E-mail:* dbc@dbc.dk *Web Site:* www.dbc.dk, pg 130

Dansk Forfatterforening (Denmark) *Tel:* 32 95 51 00 *Fax:* 32 54 01 15 *E-mail:* danskforfatterforening@danskforfatterforening.dk *Web Site:* www.danskforfatterforening.dk, pg 1398

Dansk Historisk Handbogsforlag ApS (Denmark) *Tel:* 45 93 48 00 *Fax:* 45 93 47 47 *E-mail:* genos@worldonline.dk, pg 130

Dansk ISBN - Kontor (the Danish ISBN Agency) (Denmark) *Tel:* 44867725 *Fax:* 44867853 *E-mail:* isbn@dbc.dk *Web Site:* www.isbn-kontoret.dk, pg 1265

Dansk Musikbiblioteks Forening (DMBF) (Denmark) *Tel:* 33 47 43 16 *Fax:* 33 47 47 10 *E-mail:* dmbf@kb.dk *Web Site:* www.dmbf.nu, pg 1561

Dansk Psykologisk Forlag (Denmark) *Tel:* 3538 1665 *Fax:* 3538 1655 *E-mail:* salg@dpf.dk; dk-psych@dpf.dk *Web Site:* www.dpf.dk, pg 130

Dansk Teknologisk Institut, Forlaget (Denmark) *Tel:* 42 99 66 11 *Fax:* 42 99 54 36 *E-mail:* info@teknologisk.dk, pg 130

Den Danske Boghandlerforening (Denmark) *Tel:* 32542255 *Fax:* 32540041 *E-mail:* ddb@bogpost.dk *Web Site:* www.bogguide.dk, pg 1265

Den Danske Forlaeggerforening (Denmark) *Tel:* 33 15 66 88 *Fax:* 33 15 65 88 *E-mail:* publassn@webpartner.dk; jh@carlsen.dk, pg 1265

Det Danske Sprog - og Litteraturselskab (Denmark) *Tel:* 33130660 *Fax:* 33140608 *E-mail:* sekretariat@dsl.dk *Web Site:* www.dsl.dk, pg 1398

Libreria Dante di A M Longo (Italy) *Tel:* (0544) 33500 *Fax:* (0544) 217554 *E-mail:* longo-ra@linknet.it, pg 1320

Danubia Werbung und Verlagsservice (Austria) *Tel:* (01) 792666 *Fax:* (01) 792666443, pg 49

Danubiaprint (Slovakia) *Tel:* (07) 309167 *Fax:* (07) 362613, pg 559

Danuma Prakashakayo (Sri Lanka) *Tel:* (01) 686878 *Fax:* (01) 696578, pg 606

Daphne Diffusion SA (Belgium) *Tel:* (09) 221 45 91 *Fax:* (09) 220 16 12 *E-mail:* info@daphne.be, pg 66

Daphnis-Verlag (Switzerland) *Tel:* (01) 202 52 71 *Fax:* (01) 201 42 31, pg 621

Dar Al-Kitab Al-Loubnani (Lebanon) *Tel:* 861563; (01) 735732 *Fax:* (01) 351433 *E-mail:* info@daralkitab-online.com, pg 445

Dar Al-Kitab Al-Masri (Egypt (Arab Republic of Egypt)) *Tel:* (02) 742168; (02) 754301; (02) 744657 *Fax:* (02) 3924657 *E-mail:* info@daralkitab-online.com, pg 137

Dar Al-Maaref-Liban Sarl (Lebanon) *Tel:* (01) 931243, pg 446

Dar Al Maarifah (Syrian Arab Republic) *Tel:* (011) 44670278 *Fax:* (011) 2241615 *E-mail:* info@easyquran.com *Web Site:* www.dar-al-maarifah.com; www.easyquran.com, pg 638

Dar Al-Matbo at Al-Gadidah (Egypt (Arab Republic of Egypt)) *Tel:* (03) 4825508 *Fax:* (03) 4833819, pg 138

Dar Al-Mirrikh (Mars Publishing House) (Saudi Arabia) *Tel:* (01) 464 7531; (01) 465 7939; (01) 4658523 *Fax:* (01) 465 7939, pg 550

Dar al-Nahda al Arabia (Egypt (Arab Republic of Egypt)), pg 138

Dar Al-raed Al-Llubnani (Lebanon) *Tel:* (01) 450757; (01) 451581, pg 446

Dar Al-Rayah for Publishing & Distribution (Saudi Arabia) *Tel:* (01) 4931869 *Fax:* (01) 4911985, pg 550

Dar Al-Shareff for Publishing & Distribution (Saudi Arabia) *Tel:* (01) 4779491, pg 550

Dar Al-Thakafia Publishing (Egypt (Arab Republic of Egypt)) *Tel:* (02) 42718 *Fax:* (02) 4034694 *E-mail:* nassar@hotmail.com, pg 138

Dar Al-Ulum Publishers, Booksellers & Distributors (Saudi Arabia) *Tel:* (01) 4777121 *Fax:* (01) 4793446, pg 1338

Dar An-Nahar Sal (Lebanon) *Tel:* (01) 561 687 *Fax:* (01) 561 693, pg 446

Dar Arabia Lil Kitab (Tunisia) *Tel:* (01) 888255, pg 648

SARL DAR-Echihab (Algeria) *Tel:* (02) 626727; (02) 626734 *Fax:* (02) 574632, pg 2

Dar El Afaq (Tunisia) *Tel:* (01) 265904 *Fax:* (01) 569035, pg 648

Dar El Ilm Lilmalayin (Lebanon) *Tel:* (09611) 306666 *Fax:* (09611) 701657 *E-mail:* info@malayin.com *Web Site:* www.malayin.com, pg 446

Dar El Kitab (Morocco) *Tel:* (02) 304581; (02) 305419 *Fax:* (02) 304581, pg 474

Dar El Shorouk (Egypt (Arab Republic of Egypt)) *Tel:* (02) 4023399; (02) 4037567 *Fax:* (02) 3934814 *E-mail:* dar@shorouk.com *Web Site:* www.shorouk.com, pg 138

The Dar Es Salaam Bookshop (United Republic of Tanzania) *Tel:* (051) 23416, pg 1345

Dar Nachr Al Maarifa Pour L'Edition et La Distribution (Morocco) *Tel:* (07) 795702; (07) 796914 *Fax:* (07) 790343, pg 474

Typothito G Dardanos (Greece) *Tel:* (0210) 3642003 *Fax:* (0210) 3642030 *E-mail:* info@dardanosnet.gr *Web Site:* www.dardanosnet.gr, pg 1313

Daresbury Lewis Carroll Society (United Kingdom) *Tel:* (01606) 891303 *Web Site:* lewiscarrollsociety.org.uk, pg 1407

Darescheta Consulting und Handels GmbH (Germany) *Tel:* (0611) 9310992 *Fax:* (0611) 3082096, pg 210

Darf Publishers Ltd (United Kingdom) *Tel:* (020) 7431 7009 *Fax:* (020) 7431 7655 *E-mail:* darf@freeuk.com *Web Site:* home.freeuk.net/darf, pg 686

Dargaud (France) *Tel:* (01) 53 26 32 32 *Fax:* (01) 53 26 32 00 *E-mail:* contact@dargaud.fr *Web Site:* www.dargaud.fr, pg 157

Dargenis Publishers (Lithuania) *Tel:* (037) 205241 *Fax:* (037) 205241 *E-mail:* dargenis@kaunas.omnitel.net, pg 449

Ediciones de Juan Darien (Uruguay) *Tel:* (02) 2090223 *E-mail:* dayraq@chasque.apc.org, pg 777

Verlag Darmstaedter Blaetter Schwarz und Co (Germany) *Tel:* (06151) 48196, pg 210

D'Artagnan Publishing (Australia) *Tel:* (08) 2726718, pg 19

Darton, Longman & Todd Ltd (United Kingdom) *Tel:* (020) 8875 0155 *Fax:* (020) 8875 0133 *E-mail:* tradesales@darton-longman-todd.co.uk *Web Site:* www.darton-longman-todd.co.uk, pg 686

Darulfikir (Malaysia) *Tel:* (03) 2981636; (03) 26913892 *Fax:* (03) 26928757 *E-mail:* e-mel@darulfikir.com.my *Web Site:* www.darulfikir.com.my, pg 455

Darzhavno Izdatelstvo Zemizdat (Bulgaria) *Tel:* (02) 9867895 *Fax:* (02) 442319, pg 93

Das Arsenal, Verlag fuer Kultur und Politik GmbH (Germany) *Tel:* (030) 3441827; (030) 34651361 *Fax:* (030) 34651362, pg 210

D'Assis Books (Australia) *Tel:* (07) 5448 2145 *Fax:* (07) 5447 5200, pg 19

Dastane Ramchandra & Co (India) *Tel:* (020) 447 8193; (020) 448 5950; (020) 551 1964 *Fax:* (020) 4478193, pg 333

DAT Publications (Israel) *Tel:* (03) 5071239 *Fax:* (03) 5070458 *E-mail:* dat@y-dat.co.il *Web Site:* www.y-dat.co.il, pg 366

Data Becker GmbH & Co KG (Germany) *Tel:* (0211) 9331 800; (0211) 9334 900 (orders) *Fax:* (0211) 9331 444; (0211) 9334 999 (orders) *E-mail:* info@databecker.de *Web Site:* www.databecker.de, pg 210

Datacom Buchverlag GmbH (Germany) *Tel:* (02271) 6080 *Fax:* (02271) 608290, pg 211

DATAMAP - Europe (Bulgaria) *Tel:* (02) 510090 *Fax:* (02) 510090 *E-mail:* datamap@mail.techno-linek.com, pg 94

Datanews (Italy) *Tel:* (06) 70450318/9 *Fax:* (06) 70450320 *E-mail:* info@datanews.it *Web Site:* www.datanews.it, pg 384

Datapage Technologies International Inc (United States) *Tel:* 636-278-8888 *Toll Free Tel:* 800-876-3844 *Fax:* 636-278-2180 *Web Site:* www.datapage.com, pg 1187

Editions du Dauphin (France) *Tel:* (01) 43 27 79 00 *Fax:* (01) 43 27 76 31, pg 157

M d'Auria Editore SAS (Italy) *Tel:* (081) 5518963 *Fax:* (081) 5493827; (081) 5518963 *E-mail:* info@dauria.it *Web Site:* www.dauria.it, pg 384

Verlag Werner Dausien (Germany) *Tel:* (06181) 92810 *Fax:* (06181) 5070932, pg 211

Davaco Publishers (Netherlands) *Tel:* (0525) 661823 *Fax:* (0525) 662153 *E-mail:* main@davaco.com *Web Site:* www.davaco.com, pg 481

David & Charles Ltd (United Kingdom) *Tel:* (01626) 323200 *Fax:* (01626) 323319 *E-mail:* postermaster@davidandcharles.co.uk *Web Site:* www.davidandcharles.co.uk, pg 686

David Godwin Associates (United Kingdom) *Tel:* (020) 7240 9992 *Fax:* (020) 7395 6110 *E-mail:* assistant@davidgodwinassociates.co.uk, pg 1139

David's Marine Books (New Zealand) *Tel:* (09) 303 1459 *Toll Free Tel:* 508 242 787; 800 422 427 *Fax:* (09) 307 8170 *E-mail:* sales@transpacific.co.nz *Web Site:* www.transpacific.co.nz, pg 495

Davidsfonds Uitgeverij NV (Belgium) *Tel:* (016) 310600 *Fax:* (016) 310608 *E-mail:* informatie@davidsfonds.be *Web Site:* www.davidsfonds.be, pg 66

Christopher Davies Publishers Ltd (United Kingdom) *Tel:* (01792) 648825 *Fax:* (01792) 648825 *E-mail:* sales@cdaviesbookswales.com *Web Site:* www.cdaviesbookswales.com, pg 686

Dawson Books (United Kingdom) *Tel:* (01933) 417500 *Fax:* (01933) 417501 *E-mail:* contactus@dawson.co.uk; bksales@dawsonbooks.co.uk *Web Site:* www.dawson.co.uk, pg 686

Dawson UK Ltd, Books Division (United Kingdom) *Tel:* (01933) 417500 *Fax:* (01933) 417501 *E-mail:* bkcustserv@dawsonbooks.co.uk *Web Site:* www.dawsonbooks.co.uk, pg 1350

Daya Publishing House (India) *Tel:* (011) 23245578; (011) 23244987 *Fax:* (011) 23244987 *E-mail:* dayabooks@vsnl.com *Web Site:* www.dayabooks.com, pg 333

Dayi Information Co (Taiwan, Province of China) *Tel:* (02) 5796800 *Fax:* (02) 5796805, pg 639

Daystar Press (Publishers) (Nigeria) *Tel:* (022) 412670, pg 504

dbv-Druck Beratungs-und Verlags GmbH Verlag fur die Technische Universitaet Graz (Austria) *Tel:* (0316) 38 30 33 *Fax:* (0316) 38 30 43 *E-mail:* office@dbv.at *Web Site:* www.dbv.at, pg 49

DC Book Club (India) *Tel:* (0481) 2563114; (0481) 2563226; (0481) 2578214 *Fax:* (0481) 2564758 *E-mail:* ceo@dcbooks.com *Web Site:* www.dcbooks.com, pg 1253

DC Books (India) *Tel:* (0481) 2563114; (0481) 2301614 *Web Site:* www.dcbooks.com, pg 333

Editions De Boeck-Larcier SA (Belgium) *Tel:* (02) 548 07 11 *Fax:* (02) 513 90 09 *Web Site:* www.deboeck.be, pg 66

G De Bono Editore (Italy) *Tel:* (055) 576022 *Fax:* (055) 5001665, pg 384

De Cervantes Ediciones SA (Ecuador) *Tel:* (02) 522 956 *Fax:* (02) 523 452; (02) 223 062, pg 1308

Maria Esther De Fleischmann (Mexico) *Tel:* (05) 5852698; (05) 5852698 *Fax:* (05) 5854296 *E-mail:* fleischmann1@compuserve.com.mx, pg 464

De Graaf Publishers (Netherlands) *Tel:* (0172) 57 1461 *Fax:* (0172) 57 2231 *E-mail:* degraaf.books@wxs.nl *Web Site:* www.antiqbook.nl/degraafbooks, pg 481

De La Salle University (Philippines) *Tel:* (02) 741-9271; (046) 416-0338; (046) 416-3878 *Fax:* (02) 5264237 *E-mail:* mcovatg@dlsu.edu.ph *Web Site:* www.dasma.dlsu.edu.ph, pg 519

Michel De Maule Editions (France) *Tel:* (01) 42 97 93 56; (01) 42 97 93 48 *Fax:* (01) 42 97 94 90, pg 157

De Plukvogel nv (Belgium) *Tel:* (02) 253-06-58 *Fax:* (02) 253-06-58, pg 1302

De Vecchi Editions SA (France) *Tel:* (01) 69 34 12 01; (01) 44 76 88 88 *Fax:* (01) 64 48 24 97; (01) 44 76 88 89, pg 157

Giovanni De Vecchi Editore SpA (Italy) *Tel:* (02) 66984851 *Fax:* (02) 6701548, pg 384

De Walburg Pers (Netherlands) *Tel:* (0575) 510522 *Fax:* (0575) 542289 *E-mail:* info@walburgpers.nl *Web Site:* www.walburgpers.nl, pg 481

De Wit Stores NV (Netherlands Antilles) *Tel:* (0297) 823500 *Fax:* (0297) 821575 *E-mail:* dewitstores@sctarnet.aw, pg 493

De WitAruba Boekhandel (Netherlands Antilles) *Tel:* (0297) 823500 *Fax:* (0297) 821575, pg 1330

DEA Diffusione Edizioni Anglo-Americane (Italy) *Tel:* (06) 8551441 *Fax:* (06) 8543228 *E-mail:* info@deanet.it *Web Site:* www.deanet.com, pg 384

DEA Diffusione Edizioni Anglo-Americane (Italy) *Tel:* (06) 852121 *Fax:* (06) 8543228 *E-mail:* deanet@deanet.it; info@deanet.it *Web Site:* www.deanet.it, pg 1320

Deakin University Press (Australia) *Tel:* (03) 5227 8144 *Fax:* (03) 5227 2020 *E-mail:* lynnew@deakin.edu.au *Web Site:* www.deakin.edu.au, pg 19

Nouvelles Editions Debresse (France) *Tel:* (01) 45481047, pg 157

Debrett's Ltd (United Kingdom) *Tel:* (020) 7915 9633 *Fax:* (020) 7753 4212 *E-mail:* people@debretts.co.uk *Web Site:* www.debretts.co.uk, pg 687

Decanord (France) *Tel:* (03) 20 09 90 60 *Fax:* (03) 20 09 92 75, pg 157

Editions La Decouverte (France) *Tel:* (01) 44 08 84 01 *Fax:* (01) 44 08 84 17 *E-mail:* ladecouverte@ladecouverte-syros.com *Web Site:* www.editionsladecouverte.fr, pg 157

Edizioni Dedalo SRL (Italy) *Tel:* (080) 5311413; (080) 5311400; (080) 5311401 *Fax:* (080) 5311414 *E-mail:* info@edizionidedalo.it *Web Site:* www.edizionidedalo.it, pg 384

Dedalo Litostampa SRL (Italy) *Tel:* (080) 531 14 13; (080) 531 14 00; (080) 531 14 01 *Fax:* (080) 531 14 14 *E-mail:* info@edizionidedalo.it *Web Site:* www.edizionidedalo.it, pg 1159

Dedalo Litostampa SRL (Italy) *Tel:* (080) 531 14 13; (080) 531 1400 *Fax:* (080) 531 14 14 *E-mail:* info@edizionidedalo.it *Web Site:* www.edizionidedalo.it, pg 1180

Dedalo Litostampa SRL (Italy) *Tel:* (080) 531 14 13; (080) 531 14 00; (080) 531 14 01 *Fax:* (080) 531 14 14 *E-mail:* info@edizionidedalo.it *Web Site:* www.edizionidedalo.it, pg 1220

Dedalo Litostampa SRL (Italy) *Tel:* (080) 531 14 13; (080) 531 14 01; (080) 531 14 00 *Fax:* (080) 531 14 14 *E-mail:* info@edizionidedalo.it *Web Site:* www.edizionidedalo.it, pg 1237

Dedalus Ltd (United Kingdom) *Tel:* (01487) 832382 *Fax:* (01487) 832382 *E-mail:* info@dedalusbooks.com *Web Site:* www.dedalusbooks.com, pg 687

Dee-Jay Publications (Ireland) *Tel:* (0402) 39125 *Fax:* (0402) 39064, pg 359

DEF (De Blauwe Vogel) NV/SA (Belgium) *Tel:* (011) 685751-2 *Fax:* (011) 67-21-70, pg 66

Defiant Publications (United Kingdom) *Tel:* (0121) 745 8421 *E-mail:* info@defiantpublications.co.uk, pg 687

Degener & Co, Manfred Dreiss Verlag (Germany) *Tel:* (09161) 886039 *Fax:* (09161) 886057 *E-mail:* degener@degener-verlag.com *Web Site:* www.degener-verlag.com, pg 211

Edizioni Dehoniane Bologna (EDB) (Italy) *Tel:* (051) 4290011 *Fax:* (051) 4290099 *E-mail:* webmaster@dehoniane.it *Web Site:* www.dehoniane.it, pg 384

Edizioni Dehoniane (Italy) *Tel:* (06) 624996 *Fax:* (06) 6628326 *E-mail:* webmaster@dehoniane.it *Web Site:* www.dehoniane.it, pg 384

Editorial DEI (Departamento Ecumenico de Investigaciones) (Costa Rica) *Tel:* 253-0229; 253-9124 *Fax:* 2531541 *E-mail:* publicaciones@dei-cr.org *Web Site:* www.dei-cr.org, pg 115

DEI Tipographia del Genio Civile (Italy) *Tel:* (06) 44163792 *Fax:* (06) 4403307 *E-mail:* dei@build.it *Web Site:* www.build.it, pg 384

Deichmanske Bibliotek (Norway) *Tel:* (023) 43 29 00 *Fax:* (022) 11 33 89 *E-mail:* deichman@deich.folkebibl.no *Web Site:* www.deich.folkebibl.no, pg 1534

Verlag Horst Deike KG (Germany) *Tel:* (07531) 81550 *Fax:* (07531) 815581 *E-mail:* info@deike-verlag.de *Web Site:* www.deike-verlag.de, pg 211

Editorial Deimos, SL (Spain) *Tel:* (091) 479-23-42 *Fax:* (091) 5438214 *E-mail:* editorial@deimos-es.com *Web Site:* www.deimos-es.com, pg 578

Maison d'Editions Claude Dejaie (Belgium) *Tel:* (081) 460748, pg 66

Dekel Publishing House (Israel) *Tel:* (03) 5230063 *Fax:* (03) 5273011 *E-mail:* dekelpbl@netvision.net.il *Web Site:* www.dekelpublishing.com, pg 366

Marcel Dekker AG (Switzerland) *Tel:* (061) 260 63 00 *Fax:* (061) 260 63 33 *E-mail:* intlcustserv@dekker.com *Web Site:* www.dekker.com, pg 621

Dekker v d Vegt (Netherlands) *Tel:* (024) 322 10 10 *Fax:* (024) 324 21 11 *E-mail:* mariken@dekker.nl *Web Site:* www.dekker.nl, pg 1329

Instituto del Tercer Mundo (Uruguay) *Tel:* (02) 419 6192 *Fax:* (02) 411 9222 *E-mail:* item@chasque.apc.org; item@item.org.uy *Web Site:* www.chasque.apc.org/item/, pg 777

Del Verbo Emprender SA de CV (Mexico) *Tel:* (05) 294-1160; (05) 294-8633 *Fax:* (05) 294-8633, pg 464

Guy Delabergerie Editions Sarl (French Guiana) *Tel:* 311162 *Fax:* 311759, pg 189

Delabie Europrint SA (Belgium) *Tel:* (056) 84 10 00, pg 1215

Editions Delachaux et Niestle SA (Switzerland) *Tel:* (021) 8110711 *Fax:* (021) 8110712 *E-mail:* contact@delachaux-niestle.com, pg 621

Delancey Press Ltd (United Kingdom) *Tel:* (020) 7387 3544 *Fax:* (020) 8383 5314 *E-mail:* delanceypress@aol.com *Web Site:* www.delanceypress.com, pg 687

Editions Andre Delcourt & Cie (Switzerland) *Tel:* (021) 6479772 *Fax:* (021) 6478831, pg 621

Editions Delcourt (France) *Tel:* (01) 56 03 92 20 *Fax:* (01) 56 03 92 30 *Web Site:* www.editions-delcourt.fr, pg 157

Delectus Books (United Kingdom) *Tel:* (020) 8963 0979 *Fax:* (020) 8963 0502 *Web Site:* abebooks.com/home/delectus; www.delectusbooks.co.uk, pg 687

Delft University Press (Netherlands) *Tel:* (015) 2785706 *Fax:* (015) 2785678 *E-mail:* info@library.tudelft.nl *Web Site:* www.library.tudelft.nl, pg 481

Delhi Public Library (India) *Tel:* (011) 291 6881 *Fax:* (011) 294 3990, pg 1515

Delhi State Booksellers' & Publishers' Association (India) *Tel:* (011) 231867; (011) 2515726 *Fax:* (011) 2936758, pg 1273

Delhi University Library System (India) *Tel:* (011) 27667725 *Fax:* (011) 27667126 *E-mail:* crl@delnet.ven.nic.in *Web Site:* www.du.ac.in, pg 1516

La Delirante (France) *Tel:* (01) 43 54 47 97 *Fax:* (01) 43 54 06 97, pg 157

Delius, Klasing und Co (Germany) *Tel:* (0521) 55 90 *Fax:* (0521) 55 91 13 *E-mail:* info@delius-klasing.de *Web Site:* www.delius-klasing.de, pg 211

Delius Klasing Verlag (Germany) *Tel:* (0521) 55 90 *Fax:* (0521) 55 91 13 *E-mail:* info@delius-klasing.de *Web Site:* www.delius-klasing.de, pg 211

Casa Editrice Istituto della Santa (Italy) *Tel:* (0321) 22371, pg 385

Edizioni Della Torre di Salvatore Fozzi & C SAS (Italy) *Tel:* (070) 270507 *Fax:* (070) 270507, pg 385

Dellasta Publishing (Australia) *Tel:* (03) 9888 9188 *Fax:* (03) 9888 7806 *E-mail:* dellasta@publishaust.net.au *Web Site:* www.dellasta.com.au, pg 19

Edizioni dell'Orso (Italy) *Tel:* (0131) 252349 *Fax:* (0131) 257567 *E-mail:* direzione.commerciale@ediorso.it *Web Site:* www.ediorso.it, pg 385

Editions Delmas (France) *Tel:* (08) 20 80 00 17 *Fax:* (01) 40 64 89 90 *E-mail:* delmas@dalloz.fr *Web Site:* www.editions-delmas.com, pg 157

Delphin Verlag GmbH (Germany) *Tel:* (02236) 39990 *Fax:* (02236) 399997, pg 211

Delp'sche Verlagsbuchhandlung (Germany) *Tel:* (09841) 9030 *Fax:* (09841) 90315, pg 211

Libreria DELSA (Spain) *Tel:* (091) 575 15 41 *Fax:* (091) 575 84 14, pg 1342

Delta Books (Pty) Ltd (United Kingdom) *Tel:* (01865) 304059 *Fax:* (01865) 304035 *E-mail:* mail@premierbookmarketing.com, pg 687

Delta Books Worldwide (United Kingdom) *Tel:* (01932) 854 776 *Fax:* (01932) 849 528 *E-mail:* info@deltabooks.co.uk *Web Site:* www.deltabooks.co.uk, pg 1350

Editions Delta SA (Belgium) *Tel:* (02) 217 55 55 *Fax:* (02) 217 93 93 *E-mail:* editions.delta@skynet.be, pg 66

Delta Forlags AB (Sweden) *Tel:* (08) 25 47 81, pg 611

Delta Publications (Nigeria) Ltd (Nigeria) *Tel:* (042) 3606, pg 504

Delta Science Fiction Bok Klubb (Sweden) *Tel:* (08) 254781, pg 1256

Jean-P Delville Editions (France) *Tel:* (01) 42 22 72 90 *Fax:* (01) 42 22 65 62 *E-mail:* editions.delville@wanadoo.fr, pg 157

Demeter (Tunisia) *Tel:* 71 94 52 42; 71 94 52 46 *Fax:* 71 94 51 99, pg 648

Demetra SRL (Italy) *Tel:* (045) 6159711 *Fax:* (045) 6159700, pg 385

Editions du Demi-Cercle (France) *Tel:* (01) 42330685 *Fax:* (01) 42330862, pg 157

Demonvamp Publications (Australia) *Tel:* (03) 9802 3875, pg 20

Den Norske Bokhandlerforening (Norway) *Tel:* 22 00 75 80 *Fax:* 22 33 38 30 *E-mail:* dfn@forleggerforeningen.no *Web Site:* www.forleggerforeningen.no, pg 1280

Fundacion Omar Dengo (Costa Rica) *Tel:* 257 6263 *Fax:* 2221654 *E-mail:* info@fod.ac.cr *Web Site:* www.fod.ac.cr, pg 115

Denkmayr GmbH Druck & Verlag (Austria) *Tel:* (0732) 654511 *Fax:* (0732) 65451117 *E-mail:* denkmayr.linz@magnet.at, pg 50

Editions Denoel (France) *Tel:* (01) 44 39 73 73 *Fax:* (01) 44 39 73 90 *E-mail:* denoel@denoel.fr, pg 157

Denor Press (United Kingdom) *Tel:* (020) 8343 7368 *Fax:* (020) 8446 4504 *E-mail:* denor@dial.pipex.com *Web Site:* www.xhf37.dial.pipex.com, pg 687

Verlag Harald Denzel, Auto- und Freizeitfuehrer (Austria) *Tel:* (0512) 586880 *Fax:* (0512) 586880 *E-mail:* denzel-verlag@web.de *Web Site:* members.telering.at/denzel-verlag, pg 50

Depalma SRL (Argentina) *Tel:* (011) 5382-8806 *Fax:* (011) 5382-8888 *E-mail:* info@depalma.ssdnet.com.ar, pg 5

Departamento de Documentacion y Bibliotecas (Dominican Republic), pg 1561

Departamento Nacional do Livro (Brazil) *Tel:* (021) 2220-1707; (021) 2220-1683 *Fax:* (021) 2220-1702 *E-mail:* dnl@bn.br *Web Site:* www.bn.br, pg 1263

Departemento de Publicaciones de la Universidad de la Republica (Uruguay) *Tel:* (02) 408 2906; (02) 408 5714 *Fax:* (02) 408 0303 *E-mail:* infoed@edic.edu.uy *Web Site:* www.rau.edu.uy, pg 777

Book Club of the Dept of Cultural Affairs of Sri Lanka (Sri Lanka) *Tel:* (01) 872035 *Fax:* (01) 872035 *E-mail:* pltm1950@sltnet.lk; gsk@sltnet.lk *Web Site:* www.mca.gov.lk, pg 1256

Department of Culture & Information Government of Sharjah (United Arab Emirates) *Tel:* (06) 5671116; (06) 5673139 *Fax:* (06) 5662126; (06) 5660535 *E-mail:* shjbookfair@hotmail.com; cultural@emirates.net.ae *Web Site:* shjbookfair.gov.ae, pg 654

Department of Energy (NSW) (Australia) *Tel:* (02) 8281 7777 *Fax:* (02) 8281 7799 *E-mail:* information@deus.nsw.gov.au *Web Site:* www.doe.nsw.gov.au, pg 20

Department of National Archives (Sri Lanka) *Tel:* (01) 694523; (01) 696917 *Fax:* (01) 694419 *E-mail:* narchive@slt.lk *Web Site:* www.mca.gov.lk, pg 1546

Department of Primary Industries, Queensland (Australia) *Tel:* (07) 3239 3772 *Fax:* (07) 3239 6509 *E-mail:* books@dpi.qld.gov.au *Web Site:* www.dpi.qld.gov.au, pg 20

Department of Science & Technology (South Africa) *Tel:* (012) 317 4300 *Fax:* (012) 323 8308 *Web Site:* www.dst.gov.za, pg 1543

The Department of the National Library (Jordan) *Tel:* (06) 4610311 *Fax:* (06) 4616832 *E-mail:* nl@nic.net.jo *Web Site:* www.nl.gov.jo, pg 1522

Dervy Editions (France) *Tel:* (01) 42 79 25 21 *Fax:* (01) 42 78 25 39 *E-mail:* contact@dervy.fr, pg 158

Derzhavne Naukovo-Vyrobnyche Pidpryemstro Kartografia (Ukraine) *Tel:* (044) 5524033 *Fax:* (044) 2388314 *E-mail:* admin@ukrmap.com.ua *Web Site:* www.ukrmap.com.ua, pg 653

Editorial Desarrollo SA (Peru) *Tel:* (01) 428-5380 *Fax:* (01) 428-6628, pg 517

Desbooks Pty Ltd (Australia) *Tel:* (03) 9484 2465 *Fax:* (03) 9484 3877 *E-mail:* desb@alphalink.com.au, pg 20

Imprimerie Carlo Descamps SA (France) *Tel:* (03) 27400208 *Fax:* (03) 27405683, pg 1154

Deschamps Imprimerie (Haiti) *Tel:* 2461 905; 2501 474; 56-3853; 56-2253 *Fax:* 2491 225 *E-mail:* henrid@acn2.net, pg 314

Desclee de Brouwer SA (France) *Tel:* (01) 45 49 61 92 *Fax:* (01) 42 22 61 41 *E-mail:* direction@descleedebrouwer.com *Web Site:* www.descleedebrouwer.com, pg 158

Espanola Desclee De Brouwer SA (Spain) *Tel:* (094) 4233045; (094) 4246843 *Fax:* (094) 4237594 *E-mail:* info@desclee.com *Web Site:* www.desclee.com, pg 578

Desclee Editions (France) *Tel:* (01) 45443834 *Fax:* (01) 45499392, pg 158

Desert Research Foundation of Namibia (DRFN) (Namibia) *Tel:* (061) 229855 *Fax:* (061) 228286 *E-mail:* info@drfn.org.na *Web Site:* www.drfn.org.na, pg 476

Design & Artists Copyright Society (DACS) (United Kingdom) *Tel:* (020) 7336 8811 *Fax:* (020) 7336 8822 *E-mail:* info@dacs.co.uk *Web Site:* www.dacs.co.uk, pg 1291

Design Human Resources Training & Development (Hong Kong) *Tel:* 29877018 *Fax:* 29877018, pg 317

Designer Publisher Inc (Taiwan, Province of China) *Tel:* (02) 365 6268 *Fax:* (02) 365 6521, pg 639

Desktop Miracles Inc (United States) *Tel:* 802-253-7900 *Fax:* 802-253-1900 *Web Site:* www.desktopmiracles.com, pg 1187, 1240, 1249

Ediciones Desnivel, SL (Spain) *Tel:* (091) 3602242 *Fax:* (091) 3602264 *E-mail:* edicionesdesnivel@desnivel.com *Web Site:* www.desnivel.com, pg 578

Dessain - Departement de De Boeck & Larcier SA (Belgium) *Tel:* (02) 548 07 11 *Fax:* (02) 513 90 09 *E-mail:* adeb@adeb.be *Web Site:* www.adeb.irisnet.be, pg 66

Dessain et Tolra SA (France) *Tel:* (01) 44 39 44 00 *Fax:* (01) 44 39 43 43, pg 158

Destarte, Lda (Portugal) *Tel:* (01) 347 9164 *Fax:* (01) 347 5811 *E-mail:* destarte@esoterica.pt, pg 1336

Ediciones Destino SA (Spain) *Tel:* (093) 496 70 01 *Fax:* (093) 496 70 02 *E-mail:* edicionesdestino@stl.logiccontrol.es *Web Site:* www.edestino.es, pg 579

Editions Desvigne (France) *Tel:* (01) 30 14 19 30 *Fax:* (01) 34 60 31 32 *E-mail:* info@casteilla.fr *Web Site:* www.casteilla.fr, pg 158

Det Danske Bibelselskab (Denmark) *Tel:* 33 12 78 35 *Fax:* 33 93 21 50 *E-mail:* bibelselskabet@bibelselskabet.dk *Web Site:* www.bibelselskabet.dk, pg 130

Det Norske Samlaget (Norway) *Tel:* (022) 70 78 00 *Fax:* (022) 68 75 02 *E-mail:* det.norske@samlaget.no *Web Site:* www.samlaget.no, pg 508

Detska radost (The Former Yugoslav Republic of Macedonia) *Tel:* (091) 112394; (091) 213059 *Fax:* (091) 225830; (091) 213059 *E-mail:* detskaradost@yahoo.com *Web Site:* www.detskaradost.com, pg 452

Izdatelstvo Detskaya Literatura (Russian Federation) *Tel:* (095) 9280803 *Fax:* (095) 9213007, pg 544

Franz Deuticke Verlagsgesmbh (Austria) *Tel:* (01) 512 15 44 280 *Fax:* (01) 512 15 44 289 *E-mail:* info@deuticke.at *Web Site:* www.deuticke.at, pg 50

Andre Deutsch Ltd (United Kingdom) *Tel:* (020) 7612 0400 *Fax:* (020) 7612 0401 *Web Site:* www.carlton.com, pg 687

Verlag Harri Deutsch (Switzerland) *Tel:* (033) 2223975 *Fax:* (033) 2223950 *E-mail:* verlag@harri-deutsch.de *Web Site:* www.harri-deutsch.de, pg 622

Verlag Harri Deutsch (Germany) *Tel:* (069) 77015860 *Fax:* (069) 77015869 *E-mail:* verlag@harri-deutsch.de *Web Site:* www.harri-deutsch.de/verlag, pg 211

Deutsche Akademie fuer Sprache und Dichtung (Germany) *Tel:* (06151) 40920 *Fax:* (06151) 409299 *E-mail:* sekretariat@deutscheakademie.de *Web Site:* www.deutscheakademie.de, pg 1400

Deutsche Bibelgesellschaft (Germany) *Tel:* (0711) 7181-0 *Fax:* (0711) 7181-250 *E-mail:* infoabt@dbg.de *Web Site:* www.dbg.de, pg 211

Die Deutsche Bibliothek (Germany) *Tel:* (069) 1525-0 *Fax:* (069) 1525-1010 *E-mail:* info@dbf.ddb.de *Web Site:* www.ddb.de, pg 1508

Die Deutsche Bibliothek/Deutsche Buecherei Leipzig (Germany) *Tel:* (069) 1525-0 *Fax:* (069) 1525-1010 *E-mail:* info@dbf.ddb.de *Web Site:* www.ddb.de, pg 211

Deutsche Blinden-Bibliothek (Germany) *Tel:* (06421) 6060 *Fax:* (06421) 606259 *E-mail:* info@blista.de *Web Site:* www.blista.de, pg 211

Deutsche Buch-Gemeinschaft C A Koch's Verlag Nachfolger (Austria) *Tel:* (01) 8123730 *Fax:* (01) 811024, pg 1251

Deutsche Exlibris Gesellschaft ev (Germany) *Tel:* (030) 20 67 19 90 *Fax:* (030) 20 67 19 91 *Web Site:* www.exlibris-gesellschaft.de, pg 1563

Deutsche Gesellschaft fuer Eisenbahngeschichte eV (Germany) *Tel:* (02922) 84970 *Fax:* (02922) 84927 *E-mail:* info@dgeg.de *Web Site:* www.dgeg.de, pg 212

Deutsche Gesellschaft fuer Luft-und Raumfahrt Lilienthal Oberth eV (Germany) *Tel:* (0228) 30 80 5-0 *Fax:* (0228) 30 80 5-24 *E-mail:* geschaeftsstelle@dglr.de *Web Site:* www.dglr.de, pg 212

Deutsche Gesellschaft fur Informationswissenschaft und informationspraxis eV (Germany) *Tel:* (069) 43 03 13 *Fax:* (069) 49 09 09 6 *E-mail:* zentrale@dgi-info.de *Web Site:* www.dgd.de, pg 1563

Deutsche Landwirtschafts-Gesellschaft VerlagsgesGmbH (Germany) *Tel:* (069) 24 788-451 *Fax:* (069) 24 788-484 *E-mail:* dlg-verlag@dlg-frankfurt.de *Web Site:* www.dlg-verlag.de, pg 212

Verlag Deutsche Unitarier (Germany) *Tel:* (0751) 625 96 *Fax:* (0751) 672 01 *E-mail:* verlag@unitarier.de *Web Site:* www.unitarier.de, pg 212

Deutsche Verlags-Anstalt GmbH (DVA) (Germany) *Tel:* (089) 45554-0 *Fax:* (089) 45554-100; (089) 45554-111 *E-mail:* info@dva.de; buch@dva.de *Web Site:* www.dva.de, pg 212

Deutscher Adressbuch-Verlag fuer Wirtschaft und Verkehr GmbH (Germany) *Tel:* (040) 85308-410 *Fax:* (040) 85308-385 *E-mail:* info@businessdeutschland.de *Web Site:* www.businessdeutschland.de, pg 212

Deutscher Aerzte-Verlag GmbH (Germany) *Tel:* (02234) 7011-0 *Fax:* (02234) 7011-398; (02234) 7011-475 *E-mail:* zielinka@aerzteverlag.de *Web Site:* www.aerzteverlag.de, pg 212

Deutscher Apotheker Verlag Dr Roland Schmiedel GmbH & Co (Germany) *Tel:* (0711) 2582-0 *Fax:* (0711) 2582-290 *E-mail:* service@deutscher-apotheker-verlag.de *Web Site:* www.deutscher-apotheker-verlag.de, pg 212

Deutscher Betriebswirte-Verlag GmbH (Germany) *Tel:* (07224) 9397-151 *Fax:* (07224) 9397-905 *E-mail:* info@betriebswirte-verlag.de *Web Site:* www.betriebswirte-verlag.de, pg 212

Deutscher Bibliotheksverband eV (DBV) (Germany) *Tel:* (030) 39 00 14 80; (030) 39 00 14 81 *Fax:* (030) 39 00 14 84 *E-mail:* dbv@bibliotheksverband.de *Web Site:* www.bibliotheksverband.de, pg 1563

Deutscher Buchkreis (Germany) *Tel:* (07071) 96590 *Fax:* (07071) 965965, pg 1252

Deutscher Bundestag Bibliothek (Germany) *Tel:* (030) 227 32624 *Fax:* (030) 227 36087 *E-mail:* bibliothek@bundestag.de *Web Site:* www.bundestag.de, pg 1508

Deutscher Drucker Verlagsgesellschaft mbH & Co KG (Germany) *Tel:* (0711) 448170 *Fax:* (0711) 442099 *E-mail:* info@publish.de *Web Site:* www.publish.de, pg 212

Deutscher EC-Verband (Germany) *Tel:* (0561) 40950 *Fax:* (0561) 4095112 *E-mail:* info.dv@ec-jugend.de *Web Site:* www.ec-jugend.de, pg 212

Deutscher Fachverlag GmbH (Germany) *Tel:* (069) 7595-01 *Fax:* (069) 75952999 *E-mail:* info@dfv.de *Web Site:* www.dfv.de, pg 212

Deutscher Gemeindeverlag GmbH (Germany) *Tel:* (0711) 78630 *Fax:* (0711) 7863400, pg 212

Deutscher Instituts-Verlag GmbH (Germany) *Tel:* (0221) 49 81-0 *Fax:* (0221) 49 81 *E-mail:* div@iwkoeln.de *Web Site:* www.divkoeln.de, pg 213

Deutscher Klassiker Verlag (Germany) *Tel:* (069) 75601-0 *Fax:* (069) 75601-522 *Web Site:* www.suhrkamp.de, pg 213

Deutscher Komponisten-Interessenverband eV (Germany) *Tel:* (030) 84 31 05 80 *Fax:* (030) 84 31 05 82 *E-mail:* info@komponistenverband.org *Web Site:* www.dkiv.allmusic.de, pg 1270

Deutscher Kunstverlag GmbH (Germany) *Tel:* (089) 121516-0 *Fax:* (089) 121516-10; (089) 121516-16 *E-mail:* vertrieb@deutscher-kunstverlag.ccn.de, pg 213

Deutscher Literatur-Verlag (Germany) *Tel:* (040) 682895-0 *Fax:* (040) 68289550 *E-mail:* info@kelter.de *Web Site:* www.kelter.de, pg 213

Deutscher Literaturfonds eV (Germany) *Tel:* (06151) 40930 *Fax:* (06151) 409333 *E-mail:* deutscher.literaturfonds@t-online.de *Web Site:* www.deutscher-literaturfonds.de, pg 1400

Deutscher Psychologen Verlag GmbH (DPV) (Germany) *Tel:* (0228) 987310 *Fax:* (0228) 641023 *E-mail:* service@bdp-verband.org *Web Site:* www.bdp-verband.org, pg 213

Deutscher Sparkassenverlag GmbH (Germany) *Tel:* (0711) 782-0 *Fax:* (0711) 782-16 35 *E-mail:* webredaktion@dsv-gruppe.de *Web Site:* www.dsv-gruppe.de, pg 213

Deutscher Studien Verlag (Germany) *Tel:* (06201) 60070 *E-mail:* info@beltz.de *Web Site:* www.beltz.de, pg 213

Deutscher Taschenbuch Verlag GmbH & Co KG (dtv) (Germany) *Tel:* (089) 38167-0 *Fax:* (089) 346428 *E-mail:* verlag@dtv.de *Web Site:* www.dtv.de, pg 213

Deutscher Universitats-Verlag (Germany) *Tel:* (0611) 7878-0 *Fax:* (0611) 7878-400 *Web Site:* www.duv.de; www.gwv-fachverlage.de, pg 213

Deutscher Verband Evangelischer Buchereien eV (Germany) *Tel:* (0551) 500759-0 *Fax:* (0551) 704415 *E-mail:* dveb@dveb.info *Web Site:* www.dveb.info, pg 1563

Deutscher Verlag fur Grundstoffindustrie GmbH (Germany) *Tel:* (0711) 8931-0 *Fax:* (0711) 8931-298 *E-mail:* kunden.service@thieme.de *Web Site:* www.thieme.de, pg 213

Deutscher Verlag fur Kunstwissenschaft GmbH (Germany) *Tel:* (030) 25913864; (030) 25913865 *Fax:* (030) 25913537, pg 213

Deutscher Wanderverlag Dr Mair & Schnabel & Co (Germany) *Tel:* (0711) 455005 *Fax:* (0711) 4569952, pg 214

Deutscher Wirtschaftsdienst John von Freyend GmbH (Germany) *Tel:* (0221) 93763-0 *Fax:* (0221) 93763-99 *E-mail:* box@dwd-verlag.de *Web Site:* www.dwd-verlag.de, pg 214

Deutsches Bibliotheksinstitut (Germany) *Tel:* (030) 410 34-0 *Fax:* (030) 410 34-100 *E-mail:* dbilink@dbi-berlin.de *Web Site:* www.dbi-berlin.de, pg 1563

Deutsches Bucharchiv Muenchen, Institut fur Buchwissenschaften (Germany) *Tel:* (089) 291951-90; (089) 291951-91; (089) 291951-95 *E-mail:* kontakt@bucharchiv.de *Web Site:* www.bucharchiv.de, pg 214

Deutsches Bucharchiv Muenchen, Institut fur Buchwissenschaften (Germany) *Tel:* (089) 29151-0; (089) 790 12 20 *Fax:* (089) 291951-95; (089) 790 14 19 *E-mail:* kontakt@bucharchiv.de *Web Site:* www.bucharchiv.de, pg 1508

Deutsches Jugendinstitut (DJI) (Germany) *Tel:* (089) 62306-0 *Fax:* (089) 62306-265 *E-mail:* dji@dji.de *Web Site:* www.dji.de, pg 214

Les Editions des Deux Coqs d'Or (France) *Tel:* (01) 43923334 *Fax:* (01) 43923338, pg 158

Deva Wings Publications (Australia) *Tel:* (03) 5348 1414 *Fax:* (03) 5348 1414 *E-mail:* devawings@netconnect.com.au *Web Site:* www.spacountry.net.au/devawings, pg 20

Development News Ltd (Austria) *Tel:* (0222) 3880324 *Toll Free Tel:* (0222) 3880324, pg 50

Institut pour le Developpement Forestier (France) *Tel:* (01) 40622280 *Fax:* (01) 45559854 *E-mail:* paris@association-idf.com, pg 158

Les Devenirs Visuels (France) *Tel:* (01) 47 70 60 02 *Fax:* (01) 47 70 60 03, pg 158

Librairie Deves et Chaumet (Mali) *Tel:* 222784, pg 1326

Perpustakaan Dewan Perwakilan Rakjat - RI (Indonesia) *Tel:* (021) 5715220; (021) 5715224 *Fax:* (021) 5715884, pg 1516

Dewan Bahasa dan Pustaka (Brunei Darussalam) *Tel:* (02) 235501 *Fax:* (02) 224763 *E-mail:* Chieflib@Brunei.bn *Web Site:* www.kkbs.gov.bn; www.brunei.gov.bn/index.htm; dbp.gov.bn, pg 1496

Dewan Bahasa dan Pustaka (Malaysia) *Tel:* (03) 21481011; (03) 2481820; (03) 21483839 *Fax:* (03) 2482726; (03) 2142005; (03) 21414109; (03) 2148420; (03) 21444460 *Web Site:* www.dbp.gov.my, pg 455

Dewan Bahasa dan Pustaka (Malaysia) *Tel:* (03) 21481011; (03) 2484211; (03) 2481820 *Fax:* (03) 2482726; (03) 2142005; (03) 21414109; (03) 2148420 *Web Site:* www.dbp.gov.my, pg 1402

Dewan Pustaka Islam (Malaysia) *Tel:* (03) 755 7225 *Fax:* (03) 755 7871, pg 455

Dexia Bank (Belgium) *Tel:* (02) 222 54 89 *Fax:* (02) 222 57 52 *E-mail:* cultureline@dexia.be *Web Site:* www.dexia.be/culture, pg 66

Dhaka Book Mart (Bangladesh) *Tel:* (02) 259173, pg 1301

Dhaka University Library (Bangladesh) *Tel:* (02) 966-1900 *Fax:* (02) 865583 *E-mail:* duregstr@bangla.net *Web Site:* www.univdhaka.edu, pg 1493

Dharma Edition, Tibetisches Zentrum (Germany) *Tel:* (040) 6443585 *Fax:* (040) 6443515 *E-mail:* tz@tibet.de *Web Site:* www.tibet.de, pg 214

The Dharmasthiti Buddist Institute Ltd (Hong Kong) *Tel:* 2760 8878 *Fax:* 2760 1223, pg 317

Dhillon Publishers Ltd (Kenya) *Tel:* (020) 505393, pg 433

Di Baio Editore SpA (Italy) *Tel:* (02) 6692254 *Fax:* (02) 6709257, pg 385

Edition Dia (Germany) *Tel:* (030) 6235021; (030) 6235022 *Fax:* (030) 6235023 *E-mail:* info@editiondia.de *Web Site:* www.editiondia.de, pg 214

Diachronikes Ekdoseis (Greece) *Tel:* (01) 7213225 *Fax:* (01) 7246180, pg 306

Editorial Diagonal del grup 62 (Spain) *Tel:* (093) 4437100 *Fax:* (093) 4437129, pg 579

Diagonal-Verlag GbR Rink-Schweer (Germany) *Tel:* (06421) 681936 *Fax:* (06421) 681944 *E-mail:* info@diagonal-verlag.de *Web Site:* www.diagonal-verlag.de, pg 214

The Diagram Group (United Kingdom) *Tel:* (020) 7482 3633 *Fax:* (020) 7482 4932 *E-mail:* diagramuis@aol.com, pg 1184

YELLOW PAGES

Diagram Visual Information Ltd (United Kingdom) *Tel:* (020) 7482 3633 *Fax:* (020) 7482 4932 *E-mail:* diagramvis@aol.com, pg 687, 1139

Dialog-Verlag GmbH (Germany) *Tel:* (040) 7111424 *Fax:* (040) 7101267, pg 214

Diamond Comics (P) Ltd (India) *Tel:* 9810003062 (Mobile) *Fax:* (0120) 2401093; (0120) 2401094; (0120) 2401095; (0120) 2401073 *E-mail:* comicsdiamond@mantraonline.com *Web Site:* www.comicsdiamond.com, pg 333

Diamond Inc (Japan) *Tel:* (03) 5778-7232 *Fax:* (03) 5778-6612 *Web Site:* www.diamond.co.jp, pg 416

PT Dian Rakyat (Indonesia) *Tel:* (021) 460-4444, pg 354

Diana Argentina SA, Editorial (Argentina) *Tel:* (011) 4922-5035; (011) 4922-5036 *Fax:* (011) 4922-5035; (011) 4922-5036 *E-mail:* to_dianaarg@sinectis.com.ar, pg 5

Editorial Diana SA de CV (Mexico) *Tel:* (055) 5089-1220 *Fax:* (052) 5089-1230 *E-mail:* 4sales@diana.com.mx; editors@diana.com.mx *Web Site:* www.diana.com.mx, pg 464

Diario la Voz del Interior (Argentina) *Tel:* (011) 4382-2267 *Fax:* (011) 3822508 *E-mail:* info@nueva.com.ar, pg 5

Diavlos (Greece) *Tel:* (0210) 3631169 *Fax:* (0210) 3617473 *E-mail:* info@diavlos-books.gr *Web Site:* www.diavlos-books.gr, pg 306

Diavlos (Greece) *Tel:* (0210) 3631169; (0210) 3625315 *Fax:* (0210) 3617473 *E-mail:* info@diavlos-books.gr *Web Site:* www.diavlos-books.gr, pg 1313

Ediciones Diaz de Santos SA (Spain) *Tel:* (091) 7434890 *Fax:* (091) 7434023 *E-mail:* librerias@diazdesantos.es *Web Site:* www.diazdesantos.es, pg 579

Diaz de Santos SA - Libreria Cientifico-Tecnica (Spain) *Tel:* (091) 743 48 90 *Fax:* (091) 743 40 23 *E-mail:* librerias@diazdesantos.es *Web Site:* www.diazdesantos.es, pg 1342

Editorial Ruy Diaz SAEIC (Argentina) *Tel:* (011) 4567-4918; (011) 4567-2865 *Fax:* (011) 4567-4918 *E-mail:* editorial@ruydiaz.com.ar *Web Site:* www.ruydiaz.com.ar, pg 5

The Dickens Fellowship (United Kingdom) *Tel:* (020) 7405 2127 *Fax:* (020) 7831 5175 *E-mail:* dickens.fellowship@btinternet.com *Web Site:* www.dickens.fellowship.btinternet.co.uk, pg 1407

Dickson Price Publishers Ltd (United Kingdom) *Tel:* (01795) 597800 *Fax:* (01795) 597800, pg 687

Didaco Comunicacion y Didactica, SA (Spain) *Tel:* (093) 237 64 00 *Fax:* (093) 218 92 77 *E-mail:* didaco@cambrabcn.es *Web Site:* www.didaco.es, pg 579

Didactica Editora (Portugal) *Tel:* (021) 301 17 31 *Fax:* (021) 273 04 23 *E-mail:* didacticaeditora@mail.telepac.pt; info@didactica.pt *Web Site:* viriato.viatecla.pt/didactica, pg 530

Editura Didactica si Pedagogica (Romania) *Tel:* (01) 3150043 *Fax:* (01) 3122885 *E-mail:* edpdirector@mail.codecnet.ro, pg 539

Organizzazione Didattica Editoriale Ape (Italy) *Tel:* (055) 572584 *Fax:* (055) 578243, pg 385

Diderot sro (Czech Republic) *Tel:* (02) 55707711; (02) 55707703 *Fax:* (02) 55707700 *E-mail:* redakce@diderot.cz; obchod@bp.diderot.cz *Web Site:* www.diderot.cz, pg 123

Die Deutsche Bibliothek/Deutsche Bucherei Leipzig (Germany) *Tel:* (0341) 22710 *Fax:* (0341) 2271444 *E-mail:* info@dbl.ddb.de *Web Site:* www.ddb.de, pg 1508

Die Verlag H Schafer GmbH (Germany) *Tel:* (06172) 95830 *Fax:* (06172) 71288 *E-mail:* dieverlag@t-online.de, pg 214

Dienst Bibliotheek en Archief (Netherlands) *Tel:* (070) 353 4401; (070) 353 4402 *Fax:* (070) 353 4504 *Web Site:* www.bibliotheekdenhaag.nl/dob/, pg 1530

Diesterweg, Moritz Verlag (Germany) *Tel:* (069) 42081-0 *Fax:* (069) 42081-200 *Web Site:* www.diesterweg.de, pg 214

Sammlung Dieterich Verlagsgesellschaft mbH (Germany) *Tel:* (0341) 9954600 *Fax:* (0341) 9954620 *E-mail:* info@aufbau-verlag.de *Web Site:* www.aufbau-verlag.de, pg 214

Dieterichsche Verlagsbuchhandlung Mainz (Germany) *Tel:* (06131) 573276 *Fax:* (06131) 571061 *E-mail:* DVB~mainz@t-online.de, pg 214

Maximilian Dietrich Verlag (Germany) *Tel:* (08331) 2853 *Fax:* (08331) 490364, pg 214

Dietrich zu Klampen Verlag (Germany) *Tel:* (5041) 801133 *Fax:* (5041) 801336 *E-mail:* info@zuklampen.de *Web Site:* www.dan4u.de/zuklampen, pg 214

Dietz GmbH (Austria) *Tel:* (02236) 22596 *Fax:* (02236) 47127, pg 1300

Verlag J H W Dietz Nachf GmbH (Germany) *Tel:* (0228) 23 80 83 *Fax:* (0228) 23 41 04 *E-mail:* info@dietz-verlag.de *Web Site:* www.dietz-verlag.de, pg 214

Dietz Verlag Berlin GmbH (Germany) *Tel:* (030) 24 00 92 90 *Fax:* (030) 24 00 95 90 *E-mail:* info@dietzverlag.de *Web Site:* www.dietzverlag.de, pg 215

DIFEL - Difusao Editorial SA (Portugal) *Tel:* (021) 537677 *Fax:* (021) 545886 *E-mail:* difel.as@mail.telepac.pt, pg 530

Editions de la Difference (France) *Tel:* (01) 53 38 85 38 *Fax:* (01) 42 45 34 94 *E-mail:* editions-de-la-difference@wanadoo.fr *Web Site:* www.ladifference.fr, pg 158

Edition Diffusion de Livre au Maroc (Morocco) *Tel:* (02) 442375; (02) 442376; (02) 445986 *Fax:* (02) 313565 *E-mail:* info@eddif.net.ma, pg 474

Difros Publications (Greece) *Tel:* (01) 3610811, pg 306

Difusao Cultural (Portugal) *Tel:* (021) 7599364 *Fax:* (021) 7594418, pg 530

Wydawnictwo DiG (Poland) *Tel:* (022) 839 0838 *Fax:* (022) 828-00-96 *E-mail:* biuro@dig.com.pl *Web Site:* www.dig.com.pl, pg 522

Digital Publishing (Germany) *Tel:* (089) 747482-0 *Fax:* (089) 74792308 *E-mail:* info@digitalpublishing.de *Web Site:* www.digitalpublishing.de, pg 215

Digma Publications (South Africa) *Tel:* (011) 8834854 *Fax:* (011) 8836540, pg 563

Dilagro SA (Spain) *Tel:* (0973) 24 51 00; (0973) 23 34 80 *Fax:* (0973) 23 64 13 *Web Site:* www.dilagro.com, pg 579

Le Dilettante (France) *Tel:* (01) 43-37-98-98 *Fax:* (01) 43-37-06-10 *E-mail:* info@ledilettante.com *Web Site:* www.ledilettante.com, pg 158

DILIA (Czech Republic) *Tel:* (02) 83891587 *Fax:* (02) 826348; (02) 83893599; (02) 83890598; (02) 83890597 *E-mail:* chabr@dilia.cz *Web Site:* www.dilia.cz, pg 1130

Dilicom (France) *Tel:* (01) 43254335 *Fax:* (01) 43297688 *E-mail:* dilicom@edilectre.fr *Web Site:* www.dilicom.net, pg 158

Dilicom (France) *Tel:* (01) 43 25 43 35 *Fax:* (01) 43 29 76 88 *E-mail:* contact@dilicom.net *Web Site:* www.dilicom.net, pg 1267

Diligentia-Uitgeverij (Belgium) *Tel:* (052) 44 45 11 *Fax:* (052) 44 45 22 *E-mail:* diligentia.book@planetinternet.be, pg 66

Dillons, The Bookstore (United Kingdom) *Tel:* (0121) 6314333 *Fax:* (0121) 6432441 *E-mail:* bhamnew@dillons.eunet.co.uk, pg 1350

Dillons City Business Book Store (United Kingdom) *Tel:* (020) 7628 7479 *Fax:* (020) 7628 7871 *E-mail:* loncbus@dillons.eunet.co.uk, pg 1350

Editorial Dimensao Ltda (Brazil) *Tel:* (021) 233-2764 *Fax:* (021) 233-2570 *E-mail:* memoria@ig.com.br, pg 80

DIRECTION GENERALE DES ARCHIVES NATIONALES

Dimenze 2 Plus 2 Praha (Czech Republic) *Tel:* (02) 231 11 41 *Fax:* (02) 231 11 41 *Web Site:* www.dub.cz/dimenze.html, pg 123

Dinalivro (Portugal) *Tel:* (021) 670 348 *Fax:* (021) 60 84 89 *E-mail:* dinalivro@ip.pt, pg 530

Dinapress (Portugal) *Tel:* (021) 3955270 *Fax:* (021) 3950390 *E-mail:* dinalivro@ip.pt, pg 1336

Dinastindo (Indonesia) *Tel:* (021) 7250002; (021) 72799307 *Fax:* (021) 7262145 *E-mail:* dinastindo@yahoo.com, pg 354

Dinsic Publicacions Musicals (Spain) *Tel:* (093) 318 06 05 *Fax:* (093) 412 05 01 *E-mail:* dinsic@dinsic.com *Web Site:* www.dinsic.com/, pg 579

Diogenes Verlag AG (Switzerland) *Tel:* (01) 2548511 *Fax:* (01) 2528407 *E-mail:* info@diogenes.ch *Web Site:* www.diogenes.ch, pg 622

Dion (Greece) *Tel:* (02310) 265042 *Fax:* (02310) 265083 *E-mail:* info@psarasbooks.gr *Web Site:* www.psarasbooks.gr, pg 1313

Dioptra Publishing (Greece) *Tel:* (01) 33 02 828 *Fax:* (01) 3302882 *E-mail:* info@dioptra.gov *Web Site:* www.dioptra.gr, pg 306

Diotima Presse (Austria) *Tel:* (043) 2747-8528 *Fax:* (043) 2747-8528 *E-mail:* buecher4web@diotimapresse.com *Web Site:* www.diotimapresse.com, pg 50

Dipa-Verlag GmbH (Germany) *Tel:* (069) 95732044 *Fax:* (069) 576128, pg 215

Dipak Kumar Guha (India) *Tel:* (011) 2-553-1842 *Fax:* (011) 2-550-0998 *E-mail:* dkguha@eth.net; anybody@bol.net.in, pg 1132

Diponegoro CV (Indonesia) *Tel:* (022) 5201215 *Fax:* (022) 5201215, pg 354

Ediciones Diputacion de Salamanca (Spain) *Tel:* (0923) 29 31 00 *Fax:* (0923) 29 31 29 *E-mail:* informacion@dipsanet.es *Web Site:* www.dipsanet.es, pg 579

Diputacion Provincial de Cordoba (Spain) *Tel:* (0957) 211392; (0957) 211323 *Fax:* (0957) 211387, pg 579

Diputacion Provincial de Malaga (Spain) *Tel:* (0952) 069 207 *Fax:* (0952) 069 215 *E-mail:* cedma@cedma.com *Web Site:* cedma.com, pg 579

Diputacion Provincial de Sevilla, Servicio de Publicaciones (Spain) *Tel:* (095) 4550029 *Fax:* (095) 4550050 *E-mail:* caba174@dipusevilla.es *Web Site:* www.dipusevilla.es, pg 579

Direccao Geral Familia (Portugal) *Tel:* (021) 8470430 *Fax:* (021) 8491516, pg 530

Direccao Nacional de Geologia (Centro de Documentacao) (Mozambique) *Tel:* (01) 427122 *Fax:* (01) 429216 *E-mail:* geologia@zebra.uem.mz, pg 1530

Direccao Provincial Servicos de Geologia e Minas de Angola Biblioteca (Angola) *Tel:* (02) 323024 *Fax:* (02) 321655, pg 1489

Biblioteca de la Direccion General de Cultura (Bolivia), pg 1494

Direccion General de Publicaciones CNCA Coordinacion Juridica (Mexico) *Tel:* (05) 605-85-89 (ext 5127-149) *Fax:* (05) 605-87-31, pg 464

Direction de la Recherche Scientifique et Techniques (Guinea) *Tel:* 46 10 10, pg 1564

Direction des Archives Nationales, Bibliotheque Publique et Centre du Documentation (Mauritania) *Tel:* 2523 1732, pg 1528

Direction des Archives Nationales du Benin (Benin) *Tel:* 21 30 79 *Fax:* 21 30 79, pg 1494

Direction Generale des Archives Nationales, de la Bibliotheque Nationale et de la Documentation Gabonaise (DGABD) (Gabon) *Tel:* 732543; (0241) 730 239 *Fax:* 730239, pg 1507

Direction Generale des Services de Bibliotheques, Archives et Documentation (Congo) *Tel:* 833 485 *Fax:* 832 253, pg 1560

The Director State Library (South Africa) *Tel:* (012) 321 8931 *Fax:* (012) 321 8931 *E-mail:* postmaster@statelib.pwv.gov.za *Web Site:* www.nlsa.ac.za, pg 1284

Directory & Database Publishers Association (United Kingdom) *Tel:* (020) 8846 9707 *Fax:* (020) 0870 168 0552 *Web Site:* www.directory-publisher.co.uk, pg 1291

Direzione Generale Archivi (Italy) *Tel:* (06) 4742177 *Fax:* (06) 4742177 *E-mail:* studi@archivi.beniculturali.it *Web Site:* www.archivi.beniculturali.it, pg 385

Editions Dis Voir (France) *Tel:* (01) 48 87 07 09 *Fax:* (01) 48 87 07 14 *E-mail:* disvoir@aol.com *Web Site:* www.disvoir.com, pg 158

Disal S/A Distribuidores Associados de Livros (Brazil) *Tel:* (011) 3226-3111 *Fax:* (011) 0800-7707106 *E-mail:* disal@disal.com.br *Web Site:* www.disal.com.br, pg 1303

Discordia Verlagsgesellschaft mbH (Germany) *Tel:* (02291) 911024 *Fax:* (02291) 911925, pg 215

Discovery Walking Guides Ltd (United Kingdom) *Tel:* (01604) 244869 *Fax:* (01604) 752576 *Web Site:* www.walking.demon.co.uk, pg 687

Diseno Editorial SA (Spain) *Tel:* (091) 5533168, pg 579

Disha Prakashan (India) *Tel:* 7108832, pg 333

Edition Diskord (Germany) *Tel:* (07071) 40102 *Fax:* (07071) 44710 *E-mail:* ed.diskord@t-online.de *Web Site:* www.edition-diskord.de, pg 215

Editorial Dismar (Uruguay) *Tel:* (02) 407946, pg 777

Disney Hachette Edition (France) *Tel:* (01) 53898500 *Fax:* (01) 45632201, pg 158

Distique (France) *Tel:* (02) 3730 5700 *Fax:* (02) 3730 5712, pg 1310

Distri Cultural Lda (Portugal) *Tel:* (021) 942 53 94 *Fax:* (021) 941 98 93; (021) 942 52 14, pg 530

Distri Cultural Lda (Portugal) *Tel:* (021) 942 53 94 *Fax:* (021) 941 98 93 *E-mail:* cultural@electroliber.pt, pg 1337

Distri Lojas-Sociedade Livreira Lda (Portugal) *Tel:* (021) 940 65 00 *Fax:* (021) 942 59 90, pg 1337

Distribuidora Editora Vral, Lda (Portugal) *Tel:* (01) 4393978 *Fax:* (01) 4373558, pg 1337

Distribuidora Importadora Durand SA (Peru) *Tel:* (014) 4452113 *Fax:* (014) 4463190, pg 1334

Editora e Distribuidora Irradiacao Cultural Ltda (Brazil) *Tel:* (021) 5773522 *Fax:* (021) 5771249, pg 80

Distribuidoras Unidas SA (Colombia) *Tel:* 413 8079 *Fax:* 413 8502 *E-mail:* ibernal@disunidas.com.co *Web Site:* www.disunidas.com.co, pg 1306

Distripress (Switzerland) *Tel:* (0411) 202 41 21 *Fax:* (0411) 202 10 25 *E-mail:* info@distripress.ch *Web Site:* www.distripress.ch, pg 1285

Divadelni Ustav (Czech Republic) *Tel:* (02) 24809111 *Fax:* (02) 24811452 *E-mail:* divadelni.ustav@czech-theatre.cz *Web Site:* www.divadelni-ustav.cz, pg 123

Diversity Management (Australia) *Tel:* (02) 9130 4305 *Fax:* (02) 9365 1426, pg 1129

Divyanand Verlags GmbH (Germany) *Tel:* (07764) 93 97-0 *Fax:* (07764) 93 97-39 *E-mail:* info@sandila.de *Web Site:* www.sandila.de, pg 215

The Diwan Library, Ministry of Education (Iraq) *Tel:* (01) 8872949, pg 1518

Dix (United States) *Tel:* 315-478-4700 *Fax:* 315-703-0119 *Web Site:* www.dixtype.com, pg 1229

DIY Publishing (United Kingdom) *Tel:* (020) 7586 4499 *Fax:* (020) 7722 1068 *E-mail:* info@diypublishing.com *Web Site:* www.diypublishing.com, pg 688

Djambatan PT (Indonesia) *Tel:* (021) 7203199 *Fax:* (021) 7208562, pg 354

Djof Publishing Jurist-og Okonomforbundets Forlag (Denmark) *Tel:* 39 13 55 00 *Fax:* 39 13 55 55 *E-mail:* fl@djoef.dk *Web Site:* www.djoef-forlag.dk, pg 130

DK Agencies (P) Ltd (India) *Tel:* (011) 2535-7104; (011) 2535-7105 *Fax:* (011) 2535-7103 *E-mail:* custserv@dkagencies.com *Web Site:* www.dkagencies.com, pg 1315

DK Book House Co Ltd (Thailand) *Tel:* (02) 721-9190 *Fax:* (02) 247-1033, pg 645

DK Printworld (P) Ltd (India) *Tel:* (011) 25453975; (011) 25466019 *Fax:* (011) 25465926 *E-mail:* dkprintworld@vsnl.net, pg 333

DLV Deutscher Landwirtschaftsverlag GmbH (Germany) *Tel:* (0511) 678 06-0 *Fax:* (0511) 678 06-110 *E-mail:* dlv.hannover@dlv.de *Web Site:* www.dlv.de, pg 215

DMG Business Media Ltd (United Kingdom) *Tel:* (01737) 768611 *Fax:* (01737) 855477 *Web Site:* www.dmg.co.uk, pg 688

DMK-Verlag (Germany) *Tel:* (0911) 203946; (0911) 227698 *Fax:* (0911) 208897, pg 1131

Dnipro (Ukraine) *Tel:* (044) 224-31-82 *Fax:* (044) 224 41 57, pg 653

DNP America LLC (United States) *Tel:* 212-687-2746; 212-503-1060 *Fax:* 212-286-1505 *Web Site:* www.dnp.co.jp/, pg 1166, 1187

DNP America LLC (United States) *Tel:* 212-503-1074 *Fax:* 212-286-1505 *Web Site:* www.dnp.co.jp/, pg 1229

DNP America LLC (United States) *Tel:* 212-687-2746; 212-503-1060 *Fax:* 212-286-1505 *Web Site:* www.dnp.co.jp/, pg 1240

Doaba Publications (India) *Tel:* (011) 3274669; (011) 3259753, pg 333

Ludwig Doblinger (Bernhard Herzmansky) Musikverlag KG (Austria) *Tel:* (01) 515 03-0 *Fax:* (01) 515 03-51 *E-mail:* music@doblinger.at *Web Site:* www.doblinger.at, pg 50

Dobro Publishing (United Kingdom) *Tel:* (020) 8346 4010 *E-mail:* dobropublishing@aol.com *Web Site:* www.drsandradelroy.com, pg 688

Dobunshoin Publishers Co (Japan) *Tel:* (03) 3812-7777 *Fax:* (03) 3812-7792, pg 416

DOC 6, SA (Spain) *Tel:* (093) 215 43 13 *Fax:* (093) 488 36 21 *E-mail:* mail@doc6.es *Web Site:* www.doc6.es, pg 579

Ediciones Doce Calles SL (Spain) *Tel:* (091) 902 197 501 *Fax:* (091) 925 137 060 *E-mail:* docecalles@infonegocio.com *Web Site:* www.infonegocio.com/docecalles, pg 579

Docendo Finland Oy (Finland) *Tel:* (014) 339 7700 *Fax:* (014) 339 7755 *E-mail:* info@docendo.fi *Web Site:* www.docendo.fi, pg 141

Documenta CV (Belgium) *Tel:* (02) 5102313 *Fax:* (02) 5102497, pg 66

La Documentation Francaise (France) *Tel:* (01) 40 15 70 00 *Fax:* (01) 40 15 72 30 *E-mail:* contact@ladocumentationfrancaise.fr *Web Site:* www.ladocfrancaise.gouv.fr, pg 158

La Documentation Francaise (France) *Tel:* (01) 40157110 *Fax:* (01) 40 15 72 30 *E-mail:* libparis@ladocumentationfrancaise.fr *Web Site:* www.ladocumentationfrancaise.fr, pg 1506

Bibliotheque de Documentation Internationale Contemporaine (BDIC) (France) *Tel:* (01) 40 97 79 00 *Fax:* (01) 40 97 79 40 *E-mail:* courrier.bdic@u-paris10.fr *Web Site:* www.bdic.fr/cermi/inter2.htm, pg 1506

Documentation Research & Training Centre (DRTC) (India) *Tel:* (080) 8483002 ((ext 490)); (080) 8483003 ((ext 490)); (080) 8483004 ((ext 490)); (080) 8483006 ((ext 490)) *Fax:* (080) 8484265 *E-mail:* drtc@isibang.ac.in *Web Site:* www.isibang.ac.in/drtc/index.htm, pg 1564

Dodoni Publications (Greece) *Tel:* (01) 36 37 067 *Fax:* (01) 36 30 312, pg 306

Doecker Verlag GmbH & Co KG (Austria) *Tel:* (01) 7159200 *Fax:* (01) 715920076 *E-mail:* doecker@ping.at, pg 50

Dogakusha Inc (Japan) *Tel:* (03) 3816-7011 *Fax:* (03) 3816-7044 *E-mail:* eigyoubu@dogakusha.co.jp *Web Site:* www.dogakusha.co.jp, pg 416

Daniel Doglioli (Italy) *Tel:* (0382) 529317 *Fax:* (0382) 529317 *Web Site:* www.filastrocche.it/contempo/daniele/daniele.asp, pg 1133

Dohosha Publishing Co Ltd (Japan) *Tel:* (03) 5276 0831 *Fax:* (03) 5276 0840, pg 417

Christoph Dohr (Germany) *Tel:* (0221) 70 70 02 *Fax:* (0221) 70 43 95 *E-mail:* info@dohr.de *Web Site:* www.dohr.de, pg 215

Doin Editeurs (France) *Tel:* (01) 34 63 33 33 *Fax:* (01) 34 65 39 85, pg 159

Editura DOINA SRL (Romania) *Tel:* (01) 3228107 *Fax:* (01) 3227541, pg 539

Doko Video Ltd (Israel) *Tel:* (03) 5753555 *Fax:* (03) 5753189 *E-mail:* dokoa@ibm.net, pg 366

Pusat Dokumentasi dan Informasi Ilmiah (Indonesia) *Tel:* (021) 5733465; (021) 5733466; (021) 5250719 *Fax:* (021) 5733467 *E-mail:* info@pdii.lipi.go.id, pg 1516

Dokumentationsstelle fur neuere Osterreichische Literatur (Austria) *Tel:* (01) 526 20 44-0 *Fax:* (01) 526 20 44-30 *E-mail:* info@literaturhaus.at *Web Site:* www.literaturhaus.at, pg 1558

Dokumente Verlag Versandbuchhandlung Librairie (Germany) *Tel:* (0781) 923699-0 *Fax:* (0781) 923699-70 *E-mail:* info@dokumente-verlag.de *Web Site:* www.dokumente-verlag.de, pg 1310

Dokuz Eylul Universitesi (Turkey) *Tel:* (0232) 420 41 80 *Fax:* (0232) 420 18 27 *E-mail:* hukuk@deu.edu.tr *Web Site:* www.deu.edu.tr, pg 649

Dolling und Galitz Verlag GmbH (Germany) *Tel:* (040) 3893515 *Fax:* (040) 38904945 *E-mail:* doellingundgalitzverlag@compuserve.com *Web Site:* www.doellingundgalitz.com, pg 215

Wydawnictwo Dolnoslaskie (Poland) *Tel:* (071) 328 89 54; (071) 328 89 52; (071) 328 89 51 *Fax:* (071) 328 89 54 *E-mail:* sekretariat@wd.wroc.pl *Web Site:* ksiegarnia.bellona.pl, pg 522

Dolphin Books (China) *Tel:* (010) 68326332 *Fax:* (010) 8317390, pg 104

Dolphin Press Group Ltd (Bulgaria) *Tel:* (056) 45085 *Fax:* (056) 48481 *Web Site:* www.dolphin-press.com, pg 94

Dolphin Publications (India) *Tel:* (022) 6490184 *Fax:* (022) 6233674, pg 333

Dom, Izdatel'stvo sovetskogo deskkogo fonda im & I Lenina (Russian Federation) *Tel:* (095) 9236661 *Fax:* (095) 9285322, pg 544

Dom Ksiazki, Panstwowe Przedesiebiorstwo (Poland) *Tel:* (022) 826 8559 *Fax:* (022) 826 7117 *E-mail:* info@domksiazki.pl *Web Site:* www.domksiazki.pl, pg 1336

Dom Techniky Zvazu Slovenskych Vedeckotechnickych Spolocnosti Ltd (Slovakia) *Tel:* (02) 5022 4421 *Fax:* (02) 5542 4983 *E-mail:* zsvts@rainside.sk, pg 559

Dom Wydawniczy Bellona (Poland) *Tel:* (022) 6202044 *Fax:* (022) 6522695 *E-mail:* biuro@bellona.pl *Web Site:* ksiegarnia.bellona.pl, pg 522

Ekdoseis Domi AE (Greece) *Tel:* (01) 3637389; (01) 3672056 *Fax:* (01) 3601782, pg 306

Domingos Castro (Portugal) *Tel:* (043) 332920 *Fax:* (043) 27406, pg 1337

YELLOW PAGES

Dominican Publications (Ireland) *Tel:* (01) 872-1611; (01) 873-1355 *Fax:* (01) 873-1760 *E-mail:* sales@dominicanpublications.com *Web Site:* www.dominicanpublications.com, pg 359

Dominie (Australia) *Tel:* (02) 9050201 *Fax:* (02) 9055209, pg 1298

agenda Verlag Thomas Dominikowski (Germany) *Tel:* (0251) 79 96 10 *Fax:* (0251) 79 95 19 *E-mail:* info@agenda.de *Web Site:* www.agenda.de, pg 215

Domino Verlag, Guenther Brinek GmbH (Germany) *Tel:* (089) 179130 *E-mail:* info@domino-verlag.de *Web Site:* www.domino-verlag.de, pg 215

Domowina Verlag GmbH (Germany) *Tel:* (03591) 5770 *Fax:* (03591) 577243 *E-mail:* domowinaverlag@t-online.de *Web Site:* www.buchhandel.de/domowinaverlag, pg 215

Domus Academy (Italy) *Tel:* (02) 42414001 *Fax:* (02) 4222525 *E-mail:* info@domusacademy.it *Web Site:* www.domusacademy.com, pg 385

Editoriale Domus SpA (Italy) *Tel:* (02) 82472 1 *E-mail:* editorialedomus@edidomus.it *Web Site:* www.edidomus.it, pg 385

Editorial Don Bosco (Bolivia) *Tel:* (02) 357755; (02) 371149 *Fax:* (02) 362822, pg 75

Ediciones Don Bosco Argentina (Argentina) *Tel:* (011) 4981-7314; (011) 4981-1388 *Fax:* (011) 4958-1506 *E-mail:* e.d.b.sofrasa@interlink.com.ar, pg 5

Ediciones Don Bosco SA de C (Mexico) *Tel:* (05) 3963349, pg 464

Don Bosco Verlag (Germany) *Tel:* (089) 48008300 *Fax:* (089) 48008309 *Web Site:* www.donbosco.de, pg 215

Editorial Don Quijote (Spain) *Tel:* (05) 4235080, pg 579

Donald Duck's Bokklubb (Norway) *Tel:* 24051000 *Fax:* 24051099 *E-mail:* post@damm.no *Web Site:* www.dammbokklubb.no, pg 1255

John Donald Publishers Ltd (United Kingdom) *Tel:* (0131) 668 4371 *Fax:* (0131) 668 4466 *E-mail:* info@birlinn.co.uk *Web Site:* www.birlinn.co.uk, pg 688

Donat Verlag (Germany) *Tel:* (0421) 274886 *Fax:* (0421) 275106 *E-mail:* donatverlag@excite.de, pg 215

Buchgemeinschaft Donauland Kremayr & Scheriau (Austria) *Tel:* (01) 811 02 348 *Fax:* (01) 811 02 680 *E-mail:* donauland@donauland.at *Web Site:* www.donauland.at, pg 1251

Dong-A Publishing & Printing Co Ltd (Republic of Korea) *Tel:* (02) 3398-8800 *Fax:* (02) 3398-2660, pg 438

Dong Hwa Publishing Co (Republic of Korea) *Tel:* (02) 7135411; (02) 7135415 *Fax:* (02) 7017041, pg 438

Dongguk University Central Library (Republic of Korea) *Tel:* (02) 2260-3114 *Fax:* (02) 2277-1274 *E-mail:* dong0104@dongguk.edu *Web Site:* lib.dgu.ac.kr; www.dongguk.edu, pg 1523

Donhead Publishing Ltd (United Kingdom) *Tel:* (01747) 828422 *Fax:* (01747) 828522 *E-mail:* sales@donhead.com *Web Site:* www.donhead.com, pg 688

Ad Donker (Pty) Ltd (South Africa) *Tel:* (011) 622-2900 *Fax:* (011) 622-7610, pg 563

Uitgeversmaatschappij Ad Donker BV (Netherlands) *Tel:* (010) 4363009 *Fax:* (010) 4362963 *E-mail:* donker@bart.nl *Web Site:* www.uitgeverijdonker.nl, pg 481

R R Donnelley (United Kingdom) *Tel:* (01423) 796100; (01423) 866132 (ISDN) *Fax:* (01423) 796101 *E-mail:* gms.sales@rrd.com *Web Site:* www.rrdonnelley.co.uk, pg 1225

Editorial Donostiarra SA (Spain) *Tel:* (0943) 215 737; (0943) 213 011 *Fax:* (0943) 219 521 *E-mail:* info@donostiarra.com *Web Site:* www.donostiarra.com, pg 579

Doplnek (Czech Republic) *Tel:* (05) 452-424-55 *Fax:* (05) 452-424-55 *E-mail:* doplnek@doplnek.cz *Web Site:* www.doplnek.cz, pg 123

Dorikos Publishing House (Greece) *Tel:* (010) 6854726 *Fax:* (01) 3301866, pg 306

Dorleta SA (Spain) *Tel:* (094) 4218710 *Fax:* (094) 4322232 *E-mail:* dorletoi@sarenet.es, pg 579

Dorling Kindersley Ltd (United Kingdom) *Tel:* (020) 7010 3000 *Fax:* (020) 7010 6060 *E-mail:* customer.service@dk.com *Web Site:* www.dk.com, pg 688

Verlagsgruppe Dornier GmbH (Germany) *Tel:* (0711) 78803-0 *Fax:* (0711) 78803-10 *E-mail:* info@verlagsgruppe-dornier.de *Web Site:* www.verlagsgruppe-dornier.de, pg 216

Dorriston Publishers Ltd (United Kingdom) *Tel:* (020) 7272 2722 *Fax:* (020) 7272 7274, pg 1163

Universitaet Dortmund (Germany) *Tel:* (0231) 755-4001 *Fax:* (0231) 755-4007 *Web Site:* www.uni-dortmund.de, pg 1509

Dosmil Editora (Colombia) *Tel:* (01) 2694800, pg 110

Editorial Dossat SA (Spain) *Tel:* (091) 3694011 *Fax:* (091) 3691398, pg 580

Les Dossiers d'Aquitaine (France) *Tel:* (05) 56 91 84 98 *Fax:* (05) 56 91 64 92 *E-mail:* ddabx@wanadoo.fr *Web Site:* www.ddabordeaux.com, pg 159

Dost Kitabevi Yayinlari (Turkey) *Tel:* (0312) 4172901 *Fax:* (0312) 4199397, pg 649

Dost Yayinlari (Turkey) *Tel:* (0212) 245 31 41 *Fax:* (0212) 243 02 78, pg 650

Doubleday New Zealand Ltd, Book Club Division (New Zealand) *Tel:* (09) 4782846 *Fax:* (09) 4781609, pg 1254

Doubleday New Zealand Ltd (New Zealand) *Tel:* (09) 4782846; (09) 4792200 (member service hotline) *E-mail:* membercare@doubledayclubs.co.nz, pg 495

Doyle Graphics (Ireland) *Tel:* (0506) 21970 *Fax:* (0506) 51323, pg 1179

Ediciones Doyma SA (Spain) *Tel:* (093) 2000 711 *Fax:* (093) 2091 136 *Web Site:* www.doyma.es, pg 580

Dragon Press (Australia) *Tel:* (09) 9341 2004, pg 20

Drake Educational Associates Ltd (United Kingdom) *Tel:* (029) 2056 0333 *Fax:* (029) 2055 4909 *E-mail:* info@drakeav.com *Web Site:* www.drakegroup.co.uk, pg 688

Drake Educational Associates Ltd (United Kingdom) *Tel:* (029) 2056 0333 *Fax:* (029) 2055 4909 *E-mail:* info@drakeav.com *Web Site:* www.drakegroup.co.uk; www.drakeed.com, pg 1139

Dramatic Lines Publishers (United Kingdom) *Tel:* (020) 8296 9502 *Fax:* (020) 8296 9503 *E-mail:* mail@dramaticlines.co.uk *Web Site:* www.dramaticlines.co.uk, pg 688

Drammen Folkebibliotek (Norway) *Tel:* (032) 80 63 03 *Fax:* (032) 80 64 53 *E-mail:* drm@drammen.folkebibl.no *Web Site:* www.drammen.kommune.no/bibliotek, pg 1534

Dreamland Editeur (France) *Tel:* (01) 53 20 46 66 *Fax:* (01) 53 20 46 67 *E-mail:* dreamland@nous.fr, pg 159

Dreamland Publications (India) *Tel:* (011) 25106050; (011) 25435657 *Fax:* (011) 25428283 *E-mail:* dreamland@vsnl.com *Web Site:* www.dreamlandpublications.com, pg 333

Drei Brunnen Verlag GmbH & Co (Germany) *Tel:* (0711) 86020 *Fax:* (0711) 860229 *E-mail:* mail@drei-brunnen-verlag.de *Web Site:* www.drei-brunnen-verlag.de, pg 216

Drei-D-World und Foto-World Verlag und Vertrieb (Switzerland) *Tel:* (061) 424917, pg 622

Drei Eichen Verlag Manuel Kissener (Germany) *Tel:* (09732) 9142-0 *Fax:* (09732) 9142-20 *E-mail:* info@drei-eichen.de *Web Site:* www.drei-eichen.de, pg 216

DSI DATA SERVICE & INFORMATION

Drei Ulmen Verlag GmbH (Germany) *Tel:* (089) 3087911; (089) 3088343, pg 216

Dreisam Ratgeber in der Rutsker Verlag GmbH (Germany) *Tel:* (0221) 921635-0 *Fax:* (0221) 921635-24 *E-mail:* kontakt@hayit.com *Web Site:* www.hayit.com, pg 216

Cecilie Dressler Verlag GmbH & Co KG (Germany) *Tel:* (040) 607909-03 *Fax:* (040) 6072326 *E-mail:* dressler@vsg-hamburg.de *Web Site:* www.cecilie-dressler.de, pg 216

De Driehoek BV, Uitgeverij (Netherlands) *Tel:* (020) 624 64 26 *Fax:* (020) 638 71 55 *E-mail:* driehoek.uitgeverij@planet.nl, pg 481

Verlagsgruppe Droemer Knaur GmbH & Co KG (Germany) *Tel:* (089) 9271-0 *Fax:* (089) 9271-168 *E-mail:* info@droemer-knaur.de *Web Site:* www.droemer-knaur.de, pg 216

Editions Droguet et Ardant (France) *Tel:* (01) 45 44 38 34 *Fax:* (01) 45 49 93 92, pg 159

Literature Verlag Droschl (Austria) *Tel:* (0316) 32-64-04 *Fax:* (0316) 32-40-71 *E-mail:* droschl@droschl.com; literaturverlag@droschl.com *Web Site:* www.droschl.com, pg 50

Droste Verlag GmbH (Germany) *Tel:* (0211) 8605228 *Fax:* (0211) 3230098, pg 216

Librairie Droz SA (Switzerland) *Tel:* (022) 3466666 *Fax:* (022) 3472391 *E-mail:* droz@droz.org *Web Site:* www.droz.org, pg 622

Dru-stvo na Pisatelite na Makedonija (The Former Yugoslav Republic of Macedonia) *Tel:* (02) 228039 *E-mail:* contact@dpism.org.mk *Web Site:* www.dpism.org.mk, pg 1402

Druck & Verlagshaus Fromm GmbH & Co KG (Germany) *Tel:* (0541) 310-0 *Fax:* (0541) 310315 *E-mail:* druckhaus@fromm-os.de *Web Site:* www.fromm-os.de, pg 1155

Karl Elser Druck GmbH (Germany) *Tel:* (07041) 805-41 *Fax:* (07041) 805-50 *E-mail:* info@elserdruck.de *Web Site:* www.elserdruck.de, pg 216

Druckerei u Verlagsanstalt Bayerland GmbH (Germany) *Tel:* (08131) 7 20 66 *Fax:* (08131) 73 53 99 *E-mail:* zentrale@bayerland-amperbote.de *Web Site:* www.bayerland.de, pg 216

Druffel-Verlag (Germany) *Tel:* (08143) 992160 *Fax:* (08143) 992241; (08143) 992161, pg 216

Drukarnia I Ksiegarnia Swietego Wojciecha, Dziat Wydawniczy (Poland) *Tel:* (061) 8529186 *Fax:* (061) 8523746 *E-mail:* wydawnictwo.ksw@archpoznan.org.pl, pg 522

The Drummond Agency (Australia) *Tel:* (03) 5427 3644 *Fax:* (03) 5427 3655, pg 1129

Drustvo Bibliotekara Bosne i Hercegovine (Bosnia and Herzegovina) *Tel:* (033) 275 312 *Fax:* (033) 218 431 *E-mail:* nubbih@nub.ba *Web Site:* www.nub.ba, pg 1559

Druzhba Narodov (Russian Federation) *Tel:* (095) 9258671, pg 544

DRW-Verlag Weinbrenner-GmbH & Co (Germany) *Tel:* (0711) 75 91-0 *Fax:* (0711) 75 91-333 *E-mail:* info@weinbrenner.de *Web Site:* www.drw-verlag.de; www.weinbrenner.de, pg 216

Dryden Press (Australia) *Tel:* (02) 331-4571 *Fax:* (02) 398-9782, pg 20

Drzavna Uprava za Zastitu Prirode i Okolisa (State Directorate for the Protection of Nature & Environment) (Croatia) *Tel:* (01) 613 3444 *Fax:* (01) 611 2073 *E-mail:* duzo@ring.net *Web Site:* www.mzopu.hr, pg 118

DSI Data Service & Information (Germany) *Tel:* (049) 2843 3220 *Fax:* (049) 2843 3230 *E-mail:* dsi@dsidata.com *Web Site:* www.dsidata.com, pg 217

Du May (France) *Tel:* (01) 46992424 *Fax:* (01) 48255692, pg 159

Duang Kamon Co Ltd (Thailand) *Tel:* (02) 252-6261; (02) 253-1766, pg 645

Livraria Duas Cidades Ltda (Brazil) *Tel:* (011) 220 4702 *Fax:* (011) 220-5813, pg 80

Livraria Duas Cidades Ltda (Brazil) *Tel:* (011) 3331-5134 *Fax:* (011) 3331-4702, pg 1303

Dublin City Public Libraries (Ireland) *Tel:* (01) 674 4800 *Fax:* (01) 674 4879 *E-mail:* dublinpubliclibraries@dublincity.ie *Web Site:* www.iol.ie/dublincitylibrary, pg 1518

Dublin Institute for Advanced Studies (Ireland) *Tel:* (01) 6140100 *Fax:* (01) 6680561 *Web Site:* www.dias.ie, pg 359

Dubois Publishing (Australia) *Tel:* (02) 92111178 *Fax:* (02) 92111868, pg 20

Duboux Editions SA (Switzerland) *Tel:* (033) 2256060 *Fax:* (033) 2256066 *E-mail:* duboux-editions@duboux.ch *Web Site:* www.duboux.ch, pg 622

Gerald Duckworth & Co Ltd (United Kingdom) *Tel:* (020) 7490 7300 *Fax:* (020) 7490 0080 *E-mail:* info@duckworth-publishers.co.uk *Web Site:* www.ducknet.co.uk, pg 688

Verlag Duerr & Kessler GmbH (Germany) *Tel:* (0180) 304 14 20 *Fax:* (02241) 39 76 190 *E-mail:* info@wolfverlag.de *Web Site:* www.wolfverlag.de, pg 217

Dumara Distribuidora de Publicacoes Ltda (Brazil) *Tel:* (021) 5420248 *Fax:* (021) 2750294, pg 81

Dumjahn Verlag (Germany) *Tel:* (06131) 330810 *Fax:* (06131) 330811 *E-mail:* eisenbahn@dumjahn.de *Web Site:* www.dumjahn.de, pg 217

DuMont monte Verlag GmbH & Co KG (Germany) *Tel:* (0221) 224-1823 *Fax:* (0221) 224-1812 *E-mail:* info@dumontmonte.de *Web Site:* www.dumontmonte.de, pg 217

DuMont Reiseverlag GmbH & Co KG (Germany) *Tel:* (0221) 224-1839 *Fax:* (0221) 224-1855 *E-mail:* info@dumontreise.de *Web Site:* www.dumontreise.de, pg 217

Dorothy Duncan Braille & Transcription Library (Zimbabwe) *Tel:* (04) 251116; (04) 251117 *Fax:* (04) 251117 *E-mail:* chiedza@samara.co.zw, pg 783

Duncker und Humblot GmbH (Germany) *Tel:* (030) 79 00 06-0 *Fax:* (030) 79 00 06-31 *E-mail:* info@duncker-humblot.de *Web Site:* www.duncker-humblot.de, pg 217

Dunedin Academic Press (United Kingdom) *Tel:* (0131) 473 2397 *Fax:* (01250) 870920 *E-mail:* mail@dunedinacademicpress.co.uk *Web Site:* www.dunedinacademicpress.co.uk, pg 688

Dunedin Public Libraries (New Zealand) *Tel:* (03) 4743690 *Fax:* (03) 4743660 *E-mail:* library@dcc.govt.nz, pg 1532

Dunia Pustaka Jaya PT (Indonesia) *Tel:* (021) 3909322; (021) 3909284 *Fax:* (021) 3909320, pg 354

Dunmore Press Ltd (New Zealand) *Tel:* (06) 3579242 *Fax:* (06) 3579242 *E-mail:* books@dunmore.co.nz *Web Site:* www.dunmore.co.nz, pg 495

Dunod Editeur (France) *Tel:* (01) 40 46 49 02 *Fax:* (01) 40 46 49 90 *E-mail:* infos@dunod.com *Web Site:* www.dunod.com, pg 159

Kustannus Oy Duodecim (Finland) *Tel:* (09) 618451 *Fax:* (09) 61885400 *E-mail:* etunimi.sukunimi@duodecim.fi *Web Site:* www.duodecim.fi, pg 141

DUP (1996) Ltd (United Republic of Tanzania) *Tel:* (051) 410300 *Fax:* (051) 410137 *E-mail:* director@dup.udsm.ac.tz, pg 643

Editions Dupuis SA (Belgium) *Tel:* (071) 600 500 *Fax:* (071) 600 599 *E-mail:* info@dupuis.com *Web Site:* www.dupuis.com, pg 66

Editions J Dupuis (France) *Tel:* (01) 44 84 40 80 *Fax:* (01) 44 84 40 99 *Web Site:* www.dupuis-entertainment.com, pg 159

Durham Chapter Library (United Kingdom) *Tel:* (0191) 386 4266 *Fax:* (0191) 386 4267 *E-mail:* enquiries@durhamcathedral.co.uk *Web Site:* www.durhamcathedral.co.uk/, pg 1553

Durham University Library (United Kingdom) *Tel:* (0191) 334 2968 *Fax:* (0191) 334 2971 *E-mail:* main.library@durham.ac.uk *Web Site:* www.dur.ac.uk/library, pg 1553

Durieux d o o (Croatia) *Tel:* (01) 23 00 337; (01) 23 21 178 *Fax:* (01) 23 00 337 *E-mail:* durieux@durieux.hr *Web Site:* www.durieux.hr, pg 118

Durvan SA de Ediciones (Spain) *Tel:* (094) 4230777 *Fax:* (094) 4243832 *E-mail:* editorial@durvan.com *Web Site:* www.durvan.com, pg 580

Dustri-Verlag Dr Karl Feistle (Germany) *Tel:* (089) 61 38 61-0 *Fax:* (089) 613 54 12 *E-mail:* info@dustri.de *Web Site:* www.dustri.de, pg 217

Duta Wacana University Press (Indonesia) *Tel:* (0274) 563929 *Fax:* (0274) 513235 *E-mail:* humas@ukdw.ac.id *Web Site:* www.ukdw.ac.id, pg 354

Dutch Connection (United Kingdom) *Tel:* (01625) 610613 *Fax:* (01625) 610613 *E-mail:* dutchconnection@aol.com, pg 1150

Dutta Publishing Co Ltd (India) *Tel:* (0361) 543995, pg 333

Gottlieb Duttweiler Institute for Trends & Futures (Switzerland) *Tel:* (01) 7246111 *Fax:* (01) 7246262 *E-mail:* biblio@gdi.ch *Web Site:* www.gdi.ch, pg 622

Klaus D Dutz (Germany) *Tel:* (0251) 65514 *Fax:* (0251) 661692 *E-mail:* dutz.nodus@t-online.de, pg 217

DVG-Deutsche Verlagsgesellschaft mbH (Germany) *Tel:* (08031) 15643 *Fax:* (08031) 380662, pg 217

Dvir Bialik Municipal Central Public Library (Israel) *Tel:* (03) 786375, pg 1519

Dvir Publishing Ltd (Israel) *Tel:* (08) 9246565 *Fax:* (08) 9251770 *E-mail:* info@zmora.co.il, pg 366

Gwasg Dwyfor (United Kingdom) *Tel:* (01286) 881911 *Fax:* (01286) 880120 *E-mail:* argraff@gwasgdwyfor.demon.co.uk, pg 688

Dykinson SL (Spain) *Tel:* (091) 544 28 46; (091) 544 28 69 *Fax:* (091) 544 60 40 *E-mail:* info@dykinson.com *Web Site:* www.dykinson.es; www.dykinson.com, pg 580

Dymocks Pty Ltd (Australia) *Tel:* (02) 9224 0411 *Toll Free No:* 800 805 711 *Fax:* (02) 9224 9401 *E-mail:* feedback@dymocks.com.au; service@dymocks.com.au *Web Site:* www.dymocks.com.au, pg 1298

Dynamo House P/L (Australia) *Tel:* (03) 9427 0955; (03) 9428 3636 *Fax:* (03) 9429 8036 *E-mail:* info@dynamoh.com.au *Web Site:* www.dynamoh.com.au, pg 20

Dyonon/Papyrus Publishing House of the Tel-Aviv (Israel) *Tel:* (03) 6427545 (head office) *Fax:* (03) 6423149, pg 366

Dyonon/Papyrus Publishing House of the Tel-Aviv (Israel) *Tel:* (03) 6410351; (03) 6410352; (03) 6427545 (head office); (03) 6422667 (import office) *Fax:* (03) 6423149, pg 1319

Dzuka Publishing Co Ltd (Malawi) *Tel:* (01) 672548; (01) 670637 *Fax:* (01) 671114; (01) 670021 *E-mail:* dzuka@malawi.net, pg 454

E D Galgotia & Sons (India) *Tel:* (011) 3322876 *Fax:* (011) 3755150 *E-mail:* galgotia@ndf.vsnl.net.in, pg 1315

Edizioni E - Elle SRL (Italy) *Tel:* (040) 566821 *Fax:* (040) 566819, pg 385

Edizioni E/O (Italy) *Tel:* (06) 3722829 *Fax:* (06) 37351096 *E-mail:* info@edizionieo.it *Web Site:* www.edizioni-eo.it, pg 385

E P U Editora Pedagogica e Universitaria Ltd (Brazil) *Tel:* (011) 3168-6077 *Fax:* (011) 3078-5803 *E-mail:* epu@epu.com.br *Web Site:* www.epu.com.br, pg 81

EA Books (Australia) *Tel:* (02) 9438 1533 *Fax:* (02) 9438 5934 *E-mail:* eabooks@engaust.com.au *Web Site:* www.engaust.com.au, pg 20

EA EOOD (Bulgaria) *Tel:* (064) 22827 *Fax:* (064) 22528 *E-mail:* ea@famahold.com, pg 94

Toby Eady Associates Ltd (United Kingdom) *Tel:* (020) 7792 0092 *Fax:* (020) 7792 0879 *E-mail:* toby@tobyeady.demon.co.uk *Web Site:* www.tobyeadyassociates.co.uk, pg 1139

Eagle/Inter Publishing Service (IPS) Ltd (United Kingdom) *Tel:* (01483) 306309 *Fax:* (01483) 579196 *E-mail:* eagle_indeprint@compuserve.com, pg 689

Eagle Press (United Kingdom) *Tel:* (0115) 9552335 *Fax:* (0115) 9552336, pg 1225

Eaglemoss Publications Ltd (United Kingdom) *Tel:* (020) 7590 8300 *Fax:* (020) 7590 8301 *E-mail:* enquiries@woodgt.co.uk *Web Site:* www.eaglemoss.co.uk, pg 689

EAIS Literary Agents (France) *Tel:* (01) 47 88 08 40 *Fax:* (01) 47 88 08 40, pg 1130

Early English Text Society (United Kingdom) *Web Site:* www.eets.org.uk, pg 1407

Earthscan Publications Ltd (United Kingdom) *Tel:* (020) 7278 0433 *Fax:* (020) 7278 1142 *E-mail:* earthinfo@earthscan.co.uk *Web Site:* www.earthscan.co.uk, pg 689

Eason & Son Ltd (Ireland) *Tel:* (01) 873 3811 *Fax:* (01) 873 3545 *E-mail:* info@eason.ie *Web Site:* www.eason.ie, pg 359, 1319

East African Publishing House (United Republic of Tanzania) *Tel:* (02) 557417; (02) 557788, pg 643

East & West Publishing Co (Pakistan) *Tel:* (021) 212036 *Fax:* (021) 7784362, pg 512

East China Normal University Press (China) *Tel:* (021) 62232613 *Fax:* (021) 62864922 *E-mail:* lxb@ecnu.edu.cn *Web Site:* www.ecnu.edu.cn, pg 104

East China University of Science & Technology Press (China) *Tel:* (021) 64132885 *Fax:* (021) 64250735 *Web Site:* www.ecust.edu.cn, pg 104

East London Municipal Library (South Africa) *Tel:* (043) 724991; (043) 724992 *Fax:* (043) 7431729 *Web Site:* www.unisa.ac.za/library, pg 1543

East West Operation (EWO) Ltd (Slovenia) *Tel:* (01) 4256 272 *Fax:* (01) 2517 348 *E-mail:* ewo-arkadna@siol.net, pg 561

East-West Publications Fonds BV (Netherlands) *Tel:* (70) 364 45 90 *Fax:* (70) 361 48 64 *E-mail:* epublica@packardbell.org, pg 481

East-West Publications (UK) Ltd (United Kingdom) *Tel:* (01621) 782466 *Fax:* (01621) 782466, pg 689

East Word (United Kingdom) *Tel:* (020) 7582 9349 *Fax:* (020) 7793 0474 *E-mail:* info@eastword.uk.com, pg 1150

Eastern Africa Publications Ltd (United Republic of Tanzania) *Tel:* (057) 3176; (057) 26708, pg 643

Eastern & Southern Africa Regional Branch of the International Council on Archives (ESARBICA) (Kenya) *Tel:* (02) 228959 *Fax:* (02) 240059 *E-mail:* knarchives@form-net.com *Web Site:* www.kenyarchives.go.ke, pg 1275

Eastern & Southern African Management Institute (ESAMI) (United Republic of Tanzania) *Tel:* (027) 250-8384; (027) 250-8388 *Fax:* (027) 250-8285 *E-mail:* esamihq@habari.co.tz *Web Site:* www.esamihq.org, pg 1549

Eastern Book Centre (India) *Tel:* (011) 3314191, pg 333

Eastern Book Co (India) *Tel:* (0522) 2223171; (0522) 2226517 *Fax:* (0522) 2224328 *E-mail:* sales@ebc-india.com *Web Site:* www.ebc-india.com, pg 333

Eastern Law House Pvt Ltd (India) *Tel:* (033) 237 4989; (033) 237 2301 *Fax:* (033) 215 0491 *E-mail:* elh@cal.vsnl.net.in *Web Site:* easternlawhouse.com, pg 334

Eastview Productions Sdn Bhd (Malaysia) *Tel:* (03) 7762669; (03) 7762614; (03) 7556639 *Fax:* (03) 7550731, pg 455

Easy Computing NV (Belgium) *Tel:* (02) 346 52 52 *Fax:* (02) 346 01 20 *E-mail:* info@easycomputing.com *Web Site:* www.easycomputing.com, pg 67

Easy Finder Ltd (Hong Kong) *Tel:* 2990 7100 *Fax:* 2623 9315 *E-mail:* easybook@nextmedia.com.hk *Web Site:* www.nextmedia.hk, pg 317

Editions l'Eau Vive (Switzerland) *Tel:* (022) 7329847 *Fax:* (022) 7410482, pg 622

Edizioni EBE (Italy) *Tel:* (0766) 858878 *Fax:* (0766) 858877, pg 385

Ediciones Ebenezer (Spain) *Tel:* (093) 2133515 *Fax:* (093) 2131684 *E-mail:* 101745.1635@compuserve.com, pg 580

EBG Verlags GmbH (Germany) *Tel:* (07154) 1340, pg 1252

Eboris-Coda-Bompiani (Switzerland) *Tel:* (022) 7188820 *Fax:* (022) 7079199, pg 622

ECA Bookshop Co-op Society (Ethiopia) *Tel:* (01) 517200 *Fax:* (01) 510365; (212) 963-4957 (New York) *E-mail:* ecainfo@uneca.org *Web Site:* www.uneca.org, pg 1309

Ediciones Eca SA de CV (Mexico) *Tel:* (055) 5787325 *Fax:* (055) 6891826 *Web Site:* www.centroescolareca.edu.mx, pg 464

Biblioteca Jose Antonio Echeverria (Cuba) *Tel:* (07) 3235 8789 *Fax:* (07) 334 554 *E-mail:* casa@tinored.cu, pg 1500

Echo Publishing Company Ltd (Taiwan, Province of China) *Tel:* (02) 763-1452 *Fax:* (02) 27568712, pg 639

Echo Verlag (Germany) *Tel:* (0551) 796824 *Fax:* (0551) 74035 *E-mail:* clages.echoverlag@t-online.de *Web Site:* www.echoverlag.de, pg 217

Echter Wurzburg Frankische Gesellschaftsdruckerei und Verlag GmbH (Germany) *Tel:* (0931) 66068-0 *Fax:* (0931) 66068-23 *E-mail:* info@echterverlag.de *Web Site:* www.echter-verlag.de, pg 217

ECI voor Boeken en platen BV (Netherlands) *Tel:* (0347) 379214 *Fax:* (0347) 379380 *E-mail:* service@eci.nl *Web Site:* www.eci.nl, pg 481

ECI voor Boeken en platen BV (Netherlands) *Tel:* (0347) 379214 *Fax:* (0347) 379380, pg 1254

ECIG (Italy) *Tel:* (010) 2512399 *Fax:* (010) 2512398, pg 385

ECL (Portugal) *Tel:* (022) 600 40 01; (022) 609 01 71 *Fax:* (022) 609 96 15 *E-mail:* ecl@mail.telepac.pt, pg 1337

Editions de l'Eclat (France) *Tel:* (01) 45 77 04 04 *Fax:* (01) 45 75 92 51 *E-mail:* eclat@lyber-eclat.net *Web Site:* www.lyber-eclat.net, pg 159

Ediciones del Eclipse (Argentina) *Tel:* (011) 4771-3583 *Fax:* (011) 4771-3583 *E-mail:* info@deleclipse.com *Web Site:* www.deleclipse.com, pg 5

Eco Verlags AG (Switzerland) *Tel:* (01) 440400, pg 622

Ecobooks (Belgium) *Tel:* (052) 37 11 38 *Fax:* (052) 37 11 51 *E-mail:* ecobooks@ping.be, pg 67

Ecoe Ediciones Ltda (Colombia) *Tel:* (01) 2889821; (01) 2889871 *Fax:* (01) 3201377 *E-mail:* correo@ecoeediciones.com *Web Site:* www.ecoeediciones.com, pg 110

Editions de l'Ecole (France) *Tel:* (01) 42 22 94 10 *Fax:* (01) 45 48 04 99 *E-mail:* edl@ecoledesloisirs.com *Web Site:* www.ecoledesloisirs.fr, pg 159

Ecole de Traducteurs et d'Interpretes de Beyrouth-Universite Saint-Joseph (ETIB) (Lebanon) *Tel:* (01) 611 456 (ext 5512) *Fax:* (01) 611 360 *E-mail:* etib@usj.edu.lb *Web Site:* www.usj.edu.lb, pg 1149

Ecole des Bibliothecaires, Archivistes et Documentalistes de l'Universite Cheikh Anta Diop de Dakar (Senegal) *Tel:* 825 76 60; 864 21 22 *Fax:* 824 05 42 *E-mail:* ebad@ebad.ucad.sn *Web Site:* www.ebad.ucad.sn, pg 1541

Editions de l'Ecole des Hautes Etudes en Sciences Sociales (EHESS) (France) *Tel:* (01) 49 54 25 25 *Fax:* (01) 45 44 93 11 *E-mail:* editions@ehess.fr *Web Site:* www.ehess.fr, pg 159

Ecole francaise d'Athenes (Greece) *Tel:* (010) 36 79 900 *Fax:* (010) 36 32 101 *E-mail:* efa@efa.gr *Web Site:* www.efa.gr, pg 307

Ecole Francaise de Rome (Italy) *Tel:* (06) 68 60 11 *Fax:* (06) 687 48 34 *E-mail:* publ@ecole-francaise.it *Web Site:* www.ecole-francaise.it, pg 385

Editions et Publications de l'Ecole Lacanienne (EPEL) (France) *Tel:* (01) 45 49 29 36; (01) 45 44 24 00 *Fax:* (01) 45 44 22 85 *E-mail:* epel.paris@wanadoo.fr *Web Site:* www.ecole-lacanienne.net/popup-epel.html, pg 159

Bibliotheqe l'Ecole nationale d'administration du Niger (Niger) *Tel:* 723183 *Fax:* 724383, pg 1533

Ecole nationale polytechnique, Bibliotheque (Algeria) *Tel:* (021) 52 14 94 *Fax:* (021) 52 29 73 *E-mail:* enp@ist.cerist.dz *Web Site:* www.enp.edu.dz, pg 1489

Ecole Nationale Superieure des Beaux-Arts (France) *Tel:* (01) 47035000 *Fax:* (01) 47035080 *E-mail:* info@ensba.fr *Web Site:* www.ensba.fr, pg 159

Ecole Nationale Superieure des Sciences de l'information et des bibliotheques (ENSSIB) (France) *Tel:* (04) 72 44 43 43 *Fax:* (04) 72 44 43 44 *E-mail:* com@enssib.fr; dupuigre@enssib.fr *Web Site:* www.enssib.fr, pg 1506

Ecole normale superieure (Mali) *Tel:* 222189, pg 1527

Ecole Superieure d'Ingenieurs de Beyrouth (ESIB) (Lebanon) *Tel:* (04) 532662 (ext 427); (04) 532663 (ext 427) *Fax:* (04) 532645 *E-mail:* biblio-cst@usj.edu.lb *Web Site:* www.fi.usj.lb, pg 1524

Librairie des Ecoles (Morocco) *Tel:* (02) 22 25 22; (02) 26 67 41 *Fax:* (02) 20 10 03, pg 1328

Ecomed Verlagsgesellschaft AG & Co KG (Germany) *Tel:* (08191) 1250 *Fax:* (08191) 125492 *E-mail:* info@ecomed.de *Web Site:* www.ecomed.de, pg 218

Econ Taschenbuchverlag (Germany) *Tel:* (0211) 43596, pg 218

Econ Verlag GmbH (Germany) *Tel:* (089) 5148-0 *Fax:* (089) 5148-2229 *Web Site:* www.econ-verlag.de, pg 218

Economic & Business Research (Trinidad & Tobago) *Tel:* (868) 624-5064 *Fax:* (868) 623-4137 *E-mail:* maxifill@opus.co.tt *Web Site:* www.opus.co.tt./maxifill, pg 647

The Economic & Social Research Institute (Ireland) *Tel:* (01) 6671525 *Fax:* (01) 6686231 *E-mail:* admin@esri.ie *Web Site:* www.esri.ie, pg 359

The Economist Books (United Kingdom) *Tel:* (020) 7404 3001 *Fax:* (020) 7404 3003 *E-mail:* info@profilebooks.co.uk, pg 689

The Economist Intelligence Unit (United Kingdom) *Tel:* (020) 7830 1007 *Fax:* (020) 7830 1023 *E-mail:* london@eiu.com *Web Site:* www.eiu.com, pg 689

The Economists' Bookshop (United Kingdom) *Tel:* (0171) 405 5531 *Fax:* (0171) 482 4873 *E-mail:* economists@waterstones.co.uk, pg 1350

Economy and Press (Hong Kong) *Tel:* 28917556, pg 317

Association des Ecrivains de Langue Francaise (ADELF) (France) *Tel:* (01) 43 21 95 99 *Fax:* (01) 43 20 12 22, pg 1267

Ecuazeta De Publicaciones Cia Ltda (Ecuador) *Tel:* (02) 443074 *Fax:* (02) 443074, pg 1308

ECWA Productions Ltd (Nigeria) *Tel:* (073) 53897; (073) 52230, pg 504

Verlag ED Emmentaler Druck AG (Switzerland) *Tel:* (035) 21911 *Fax:* (035) 0524642, pg 622

Editorial EDAF SA (Spain) *Tel:* (091) 435 82 60 *Fax:* (091) 431 52 81 *E-mail:* edaf@edaf.net *Web Site:* www.edaf.es, pg 580

Edagricole - Edizioni Agricole (Italy) *Tel:* (051) 65751 *Fax:* (051) 6575800 *E-mail:* sede@gce.it *Web Site:* www.edagricole.it, pg 385

Edamex SA de CV (Mexico) *Tel:* (05) 55598588 *Toll Free Tel:* 800 024 8588 *Fax:* (05) 55750555; (05) 55757035 *E-mail:* info@edamex.com *Web Site:* www.edamex.com, pg 464

Edanim Publishers Ltd (Israel) *Tel:* (03) 688-8466 *Fax:* (03) 537-7820, pg 366

EDAS (Italy) *Tel:* (090) 675653 *Fax:* (090) 675653 *E-mail:* info@edas.it *Web Site:* www.edas.it, pg 385

EDC -Empresa De Divulgacao Cultural, SA (Portugal) *Tel:* (021) 380 1100 *Fax:* (021) 386 5397 *Web Site:* www.editorialverbo.pt, pg 1337

Eddison Sadd Editions Ltd (United Kingdom) *Tel:* (020) 7837 1968 *Fax:* (020) 7837 6844 *E-mail:* langel@eddisonsadd.co.uk, pg 689

Ede Vau Verlag GmbH (Germany) *Tel:* (02154) 490080 *Fax:* (02154) 490081 *E-mail:* evvgmbh@t-online.de, pg 218

Edebe (Spain) *Tel:* (093) 2037408 *Fax:* (093) 2054670 *E-mail:* editorial@edebe.com *Web Site:* www.edebe.com, pg 580

EDERSA (Editoriales de Derecho Reunidas SA) (Spain) *Tel:* (091) 5477961 *Fax:* (091) 5478001 *E-mail:* dijusa@dijusa.es, pg 580

Edeval (Universidad de Valparaiso) (Chile) *Tel:* (02) 250792 *Fax:* (02) 252125 *E-mail:* rrpp@uv.cl *Web Site:* www.uv.cl, pg 99

Edex, Centro de Recursos Comunitarios (Spain) *Tel:* (094) 442 57 84 *Fax:* (094) 441-7512 *E-mail:* edex@edex.es *Web Site:* www.edex.es, pg 580

EDHASA (Editora y Distribuidora Hispano-Americana SA) (Spain) *Tel:* (093) 4949720 *Fax:* (093) 4194584 *E-mail:* info@edhasa.es *Web Site:* www.edhasa.es, pg 580, 1342

Edi-Liber Irlan SA (Spain) *Tel:* (093) 4160641 *Fax:* (093) 4160774 *E-mail:* ediliber@mx3.redestb.es, pg 580

Ediart Editrice (Italy) *Tel:* (075) 8943594 *Fax:* (075) 8942411 *E-mail:* ediart@ediart.it *Web Site:* www.ediart.it, pg 386

Ediblanchart sprl (Belgium) *Tel:* (02) 4783706 *Fax:* (02) 4786429, pg 67

Edicart (Italy) *Tel:* (0331) 74291 *Fax:* (0331) 74292 *E-mail:* info@edicart.it *Web Site:* www.edicart.it, pg 386

Edicial SA (Argentina) *Tel:* (011) 4342-8481; (011) 4342-8482; (011) 4342-8483 *Fax:* (011) 4342-8481 *E-mail:* edicial@edicial.com.ar, pg 5

Ediciclo Editore SRL (Italy) *Tel:* (0421) 74475 *Fax:* (0421) 282070 *E-mail:* posta@ediciclo.it *Web Site:* www.ediciclo.it, pg 386

Ediciones Deusto SA (Spain) *Tel:* (094) 4356177 *Fax:* (094) 4356173 *E-mail:* edicio01@sarenet.es *Web Site:* www.ediciones-deusto.es, pg 580

Ediciones Ekare (Venezuela) *Tel:* (02) 263 00 80; (02) 263 61 70 *Fax:* (02) 263 00 91, pg 779

Ediciones El Almendro de Cordoba (Spain) *Tel:* (0957) 082 789; (0957) 274 692 *Fax:* (0957) 274 692 *E-mail:* ediciones@elalmendro.com *Web Site:* www.elalmendro.com, pg 580

Ediciones Euroamericanas SA (Peru) *Tel:* (014) 4274686 *Fax:* (014) 4280545, pg 1334

EDICIONES L'ISARD, S L

Ediciones l'Isard, S L (Spain) *Tel:* (093) 436 81 18 *Fax:* (093) 436 03 41 *E-mail:* isard@isard.net Web Site: www.isard.net, pg 580

Ediciones Zeta SCR Ltda (Peru) *Tel:* (014) 472-5942; (014) 472-7778 *Fax:* (014) 472-9890; (014) 472-0781, pg 1334

Institut d'Edicions de la Diputacio de Barcelona (Spain) *Tel:* (093) 4022 116 *Fax:* (093) 4022 290 *E-mail:* godovx@diba.es *Web Site:* www.diba.es, pg 581

Editorial Edicol SA (Mexico) *Tel:* (05) 55637203; (05) 55637900 *Fax:* (05) 5636966, pg 464

Edicomunicacion SA (Spain) *Tel:* (093) 3590866 *Fax:* (093) 3590004, pg 581

Edicon Editora e Consultorial Ltda (Brazil) *Tel:* (011) 3255-1002 *Fax:* (011) 3255-9822 *E-mail:* edicon@edicon.com.br *Web Site:* www.edicon.com.br, pg 81

EDIFIR SRL (Italy) *Tel:* (055) 289506 *Fax:* (055) 289478, pg 386

Edigol Ediciones SA (Spain) *Tel:* (093) 372 63 04 *Fax:* (093) 371 76 32 *E-mail:* info@edigol.com *Web Site:* www.edigol.com, pg 581

Edika-Med, SA (Spain) *Tel:* (093) 454 96 00 *Fax:* (093) 323 48 03 *E-mail:* info@edikamed.com *Web Site:* www.edikamed.com, pg 581

Edilesa-Ediciones Leonesas SA (Spain) *Tel:* (0987) 80 11 16 *Fax:* (0987) 84 00 28 *E-mail:* edilesa@edilesa.es *Web Site:* www.edilesa.es, pg 581

Edilux (Spain) *Tel:* (0958) 08 20 00; (0958) 184056 *Fax:* (0958) 184056; (0958) 082472 *E-mail:* ediluxsl@supercable.es, pg 581

EDIM SA (Mali) *Tel:* 225522 *Fax:* 238503, pg 460

Edimecien Cia Ltda (Ecuador) *Tel:* (02) 250 2427; (02) 250 2428; (02) 250 2431 *Fax:* (02) 250 2429, pg 1308

EDIMSA - Editores Medicos SA (Spain) *Tel:* (091) 376 81 40 *Fax:* (091) 373 99 07 *E-mail:* edimsa@edimsa.es *Web Site:* www.edimsa.es, pg 581

Edinburgh University Library (United Kingdom) *Tel:* (0131) 650 3384; (0131) 650 3374 (reference & information services) *Fax:* (0131) 667 9780; (0131) 650 3380 (administration); (0131) 650 6863 (special collections) *E-mail:* library@ed.ac.uk *Web Site:* www.lib.ed.ac.uk, pg 1553

Edinburgh Bibliographical Society (United Kingdom) *Tel:* (0131) 226 4531 *Fax:* (0131) 466 2807 *E-mail:* exkb33@srv1.lib.ed.ac.uk *Web Site:* www.edbibsoc.lib.ed.ac.uk, pg 1407

Edinburgh City Libraries (United Kingdom) *Tel:* (0131) 242 8000 *E-mail:* eclis@edinburgh.gov.uk *Web Site:* www.edinburgh.gov.uk/libraries, pg 689

Edinburgh City Library & Information Services (United Kingdom) *Tel:* (0131) 242 8020 *Fax:* (0131) 242 8009 *E-mail:* central.lending.library@edinburgh.gov.uk *Web Site:* www.edinburgh.gov.uk/libraries, pg 1553

Edinburgh University Press Ltd (United Kingdom) *Tel:* (0131) 650 4223 *E-mail:* marketing@eup.ed.ac.uk; journals@eup.ed.ac.uk (Orders) *Web Site:* www.eup.ed.ac.uk, pg 689

Ediciones Edinford SA (Spain) *Fax:* (095) 254689, pg 581

Edipro-Edicoes Profissionais Ltda (Brazil) *Tel:* (014) 232-3375 *Fax:* (014) 232-4684, pg 81

Edipuglia (Italy) *Tel:* (080) 5333056 *Fax:* (080) 5333057 *E-mail:* edipuglia@tin.it *Web Site:* www.edipuglia.it, pg 386

Edirisooriya & Company (Sri Lanka) *Tel:* (01) 522555; (01) 523216 *Fax:* (01) 446380; (01) 074618905, pg 606

Editrice Edisco (Italy) *Tel:* (011) 54 78 80 *Fax:* (011) 51 75 396 *E-mail:* info@edisco.it *Web Site:* www.edisco.it, pg 386

Editorial Ediseis SA (Spain) *Tel:* (091) 4165511; (091) 4165218 *Fax:* (091) 4165411, pg 581

Edisport Editoriale SpA (Italy) *Tel:* (02) 380851 *Fax:* (02) 38010393 *E-mail:* edisport@edisport.it *Web Site:* www.edisport.it, pg 386

Edistudio (Italy) *Tel:* (050) 48670; (050) 2208745 *Fax:* (050) 500585 *E-mail:* edistudio@edistudio.it, pg 386

Editions Edisud (France) *Tel:* (04) 42 21 61 44 *Fax:* (04) 42 21 56 20 *E-mail:* info@edisud.com *Web Site:* www.edisud.com, pg 159

Editions Edita (Switzerland) *Tel:* (021) 6251392 *Fax:* (021) 6254291, pg 622

Edita Publishing Oy (Finland) *Tel:* (020) 450 00 *Fax:* (020) 450 2396 *E-mail:* etunimi.sukunimi@edita.fi *Web Site:* www1.edita.fi, pg 142

Editalia (Edizioni d'Italia) (Italy) *Tel:* (06) 85081 *Toll Free Tel:* 800 01 4858 *Fax:* (06) 85085165 *Web Site:* www.editalia.it, pg 386

Editest, SPRL (Belgium) *Tel:* (02) 6476284 *Fax:* (02) 7325629, pg 67

Institute Editeur (France) *Tel:* (01) 40 87 17 17 *Fax:* (01) 40 87 17 18, pg 160

Les Editeurs Reunis (France) *Tel:* (01) 43 54 74 46; (01) 43 54 43 81 *Fax:* (01) 43 25 34 79, pg 160

Editorial Editex SA (Spain) *Tel:* (091) 7992040 *Fax:* (091) 7150444 *E-mail:* correo@editex.es *Web Site:* www.editex.es, pg 581

Edition (United Kingdom) *Tel:* (01683) 220808 *Fax:* (01683) 220012 *E-mail:* sales@cameronbooks.co.uk *Web Site:* www.cameronbooks.co.uk, pg 1163

Edition (United Kingdom) *Tel:* (01683) 220808 *Fax:* (01683) 220012 *E-mail:* editorial@cameronbooks.co.uk; sales@cameronbooks.co.uk *Web Site:* www.cameronbooks.co.uk, pg 1184

Edition Aragon-Verlagsgesellschaft mbH (Germany) *Tel:* (02841) 16561 *Fax:* (02841) 24336, pg 218

Edition Epoca (Switzerland) *Tel:* (01) 4511717 *Fax:* (01) 4511717 *E-mail:* info@epoca.ch *Web Site:* www.epoca.ch, pg 622

Edition1 (France) *Tel:* (01) 43923587 *Fax:* (01) 43923585, pg 160

Edition S der OSD (Austria) *Tel:* (01) 61077-315 *Fax:* (01) 61077-419 *E-mail:* office@verlagoesterreich.at, pg 50

Edition XII (United Kingdom) *Tel:* (020) 7229 6471; (020) 7833 0120 *Fax:* (020) 7229 5239; (020) 7923 5500; (020) 7923 5505 *E-mail:* info@editionxii.co.uk *Web Site:* www.editionxii.co.uk, pg 690

Les Editions de Minuit SA (France) *Tel:* (01) 44 39 39 20 *Fax:* (01) 45 44 82 36 *E-mail:* contact@leseditionsdeminuit.fr *Web Site:* www.leseditionsdeminuit.fr, pg 160

Editions d'Organisation (France) *Tel:* (01) 44 41 11 11 *Fax:* (01) 44 41 11 85 *E-mail:* service-lecteurs@editions-organisation.com *Web Site:* www.editions-organisation.com, pg 160

Les Editions du CFPJ (Centre de Formation et de Perfectionnement des Journalistes) - Sarl Presse et Formation (France) *Tel:* (01) 44 82 20 00 *Fax:* (01) 44 82 20 01 *Web Site:* www.cfpj.com, pg 160

Editions ELOR (France) *Tel:* (02) 99 91 22 80 *Fax:* (02) 99 91 34 45 *E-mail:* edit.elor@wanadoo.fr *Web Site:* www.elor.com, pg 160

Les Editions ESF (France) *Tel:* (02) 37 29 69 20 *Fax:* (02) 37 29 69 35 *E-mail:* info@esf-editeur.fr *Web Site:* www.esf-editeur.fr, pg 160

Editions Grund (France) *Tel:* (01) 53103600 *Fax:* (01) 43294986 *E-mail:* grund@grund.fr *Web Site:* www.grund.fr, pg 160

Editions Recherche sur les Civilisations (ERC) (France) *Tel:* (01) 43 13 11 00 *Fax:* (01) 43 13 11 25 *E-mail:* erc.edit@adpf.asso.fr *Web Site:* www.france.diplomatie.fr; www.adpf.asso.fr, pg 160

INDUSTRY

Editions rue d'Ulm (France) *Tel:* (01) 44 32 30 29 *Fax:* (01) 44 32 36 86 *E-mail:* ulm-editions@ens.fr *Web Site:* www.presses.ens.fr, pg 160

Editions Terrail/Finest SA (France) *Tel:* (01) 45 77 08 05 *Fax:* (01) 45 79 97 15, pg 160

Editions Unes (France) *Tel:* (04) 94673158 *Fax:* (04) 94673175, pg 160

Editogo (Togo) *Tel:* (08) 21-37-18 *Fax:* (08) 21-14-89, pg 646

Companhia Editora Forense (Brazil) *Tel:* (021) 2533-5537 *Fax:* (021) 2533-5537 *E-mail:* forense@forense.com.br *Web Site:* www.forense.com.br, pg 81

Editora Letraviva Importacao Distribuidora Livros Ltd (Brazil) *Tel:* (011) 3088 7992; (011) 3088 7832 *Fax:* (011) 3088 7780 *E-mail:* letraviva@letraviva.com.br *Web Site:* www.letraviva.com.br, pg 1303

Corporacion Editora Nacional (Ecuador) *Tel:* (02) 554358; (02) 554558; (02) 554658 *Fax:* (02) 566340 *E-mail:* cen@accessinter.net, pg 136

Editora Universidade De Brasilia (Brazil) *Tel:* (061) 226-6874 *Fax:* (061) 323-1017 *E-mail:* editora@unb.br *Web Site:* www.editora.unb.br, pg 1251

Editorama SA (Dominican Republic) *Tel:* 596-6669; 596-4274 *Fax:* 594-1421 *E-mail:* editorama@codetel.net.do *Web Site:* www.editorama.com, pg 135

Editori Laterza (Italy) *Tel:* (06) 3218393 *Fax:* (06) 3223853 *E-mail:* laterza@laterza.it *Web Site:* www.laterza.it, pg 386

Editorial Everest SA (Spain) *Tel:* (0987) 844200 *Fax:* (0987) 844202 *E-mail:* publicaciones@everest.es *Web Site:* www.everest.es, pg 581

Editorial Francesa Espanola SA (Chile) *Tel:* (02) 235-0911; (02) 235-9734 *Fax:* (02) 236-0900, pg 1305

Editoriale Bortolazzi-Stei srl (United States) *Tel:* 914-834-9594 *Fax:* 914-833-9106 *E-mail:* fulvioforcellini@ebs-bortolazzi.com, pg 1187

Editpress (Luxembourg) *Tel:* 547131 *Fax:* 547130 *E-mail:* tageblatt@tageblatt.lu, pg 451

Edizioni Associate/Editrice Internazionale Srl (Italy) *Tel:* (06) 44704513 *Fax:* (06) 44704513 *E-mail:* easso@tin.it, pg 386

Edizioni d'Arte Antica e Moderna EDAM (Italy) *Tel:* (055) 2298578 *Fax:* (055) 220837, pg 386

Edizioni del Centro Camuno di Studi Preistorici (Italy) *Tel:* (0364) 42091 *Fax:* (0364) 42572 *E-mail:* ccspreist@tin.it *Web Site:* www.rockart-ccsp.com, pg 386

Edizioni di Storia e Letteratura (Italy) *Tel:* (06) 39670307 *Fax:* (06) 39671250 *E-mail:* info@storiaeletteratura.it *Web Site:* www.storiaeletterature.it, pg 386

Edizioni Il Punto d'Incontro SAS (Italy) *Tel:* (0444) 239189 *Fax:* (0444) 239266 *E-mail:* ordini@edizionilpuntocontro.it *Web Site:* www.edizionilpuntodincontro.it, pg 386

Edizioni la Scala (Italy) *Tel:* (080) 4975838 *Fax:* (080) 4975839 *E-mail:* lascala@abbazialascala.com *Web Site:* www.abbazialascala.com, pg 387

Edizioni l'Arciere SRL (Italy) *Tel:* (0171) 905566 *Fax:* (0171) 905730, pg 387

Edizioni Qiqajon (Italy) *Tel:* (015) 679115 *Fax:* (015) 6794949 *E-mail:* acquisti@qiqajon.it *Web Site:* www.qiqajon.it, pg 387

Edizioni Studio Domenicano (ESD) (Italy) *Tel:* (051) 582034 *Fax:* (051) 331583 *E-mail:* esd@alinet.it *Web Site:* www.esd-domenicani.it, pg 387

EDP Sciences (France) *Tel:* (01) 69 18 75 75 *Fax:* (01) 69 28 84 91 *E-mail:* edps@edpsciences.org *Web Site:* www.edpsciences.org, pg 161

EDT Edizioni di Torino (Italy) *Tel:* (011) 5591816 *Fax:* (011) 2307034 *E-mail:* edt@edt.it *Web Site:* www.edt.it, pg 387

Educatieve Uitgeverij Edu'Actief BV (Netherlands)
Tel: (0522) 235235 *Fax:* (0522) 235222 *E-mail:* info@edu-actief.nl *Web Site:* www.edu-actief.nl, pg 481

Educatieve Partners Nederland bv (Netherlands)
Tel: (030) 6383001 *Fax:* (030) 6383004 *E-mail:* info@epn.nl *Web Site:* www.epn.nl, pg 481

Education Science Publishing House (China) *Tel:* (010) 62102454; (010) 62013803 *Fax:* (010) 62012454 *E-mail:* esph@public.net.china.com.cn, pg 104

Educational Advantage (Australia) *Tel:* (03) 5480 9466 *Fax:* (03) 5480 9462 *E-mail:* joe@mathsmate.net *Web Site:* www.mathsmate.net, pg 20

Educational Books Publishing House (Democratic People's Republic of Korea), pg 436

The Educational Company of Ireland (Ireland) *Tel:* (01) 4500611 *Fax:* (01) 4500993 *E-mail:* info@edco.ie *Web Site:* www.edco.ie, pg 359

Educational Distributors Ltd (New Zealand) *Tel:* (09) 818 4473 *Fax:* (09) 836 2399 *E-mail:* ed.nz@xtra.co.nz, pg 496

Educational Explorers (Publishers) Ltd (United Kingdom) *Tel:* (0118) 987 3101 *Fax:* (0118) 987 3103 *E-mail:* explorers@cuisenaire.co.uk *Web Site:* www.cuisenaire.co.uk, pg 690

Educational Press & Manufacturers Ltd (Ghana) *Tel:* (051) 5003; (051) 5845 *Fax:* (051) 227572 *Web Site:* www.diana.com.mx, pg 303

Educational Publishers Council (United Kingdom) *Tel:* (020) 7691 9191 *Fax:* (020) 7691 9199 *E-mail:* mail@publishers.org.uk *Web Site:* www.publishers.org.uk, pg 1291

Educational Publishers Ltd (Ghana) *Tel:* (021) 220395 *Fax:* (021) 227572, pg 303

The Educational Publishing House Ltd (Hong Kong) *Tel:* 24088801 *Fax:* 2810 4201, pg 317

Educational Research & Study Group (Nigeria), pg 504

Educational Supplies Pty Ltd (The Dominie Group) (Australia) *Tel:* (02) 99050201 *Fax:* (02) 99055209, pg 20

Educational Writers' Group (United Kingdom) *Tel:* (020) 7373 6642 *Fax:* (020) 7373 5768 *E-mail:* info@societyofauthors.org *Web Site:* www.societyofauthors.org, pg 1291

Educum Publishers Ltd (South Africa) *Tel:* (011) 3153647 *Fax:* (011) 3152757, pg 563

EDULIS (Education Library & Information Services) (South Africa) *Tel:* (021) 957-9600 *Fax:* (021) 948-0748 *E-mail:* edulis@pgwc.gov.za *Web Site:* wced.wcape.gov.za, pg 1543

EDUSC - Editora da Universidade do Sagrado Coracao (Brazil) *Tel:* (014) 3235-7111 *Fax:* (014) 3235-7219 *E-mail:* edusc@usc.br *Web Site:* www.edusc.com.br, pg 81

Eduskunnan Kirjasto (Finland) *Tel:* (00) 4321 *Fax:* (00) 4323495 *E-mail:* kirjasto@eduskunta.fi *Web Site:* www.eduskunta.fi/kirjasto/, pg 1505

Edwina Publishing (Australia) *Tel:* (03) 9836 3810 *Fax:* (03) 9830 1356 *Web Site:* www.edwinapublishing.com, pg 21

Eekhoorn BV Uitgeverij (Netherlands) *Tel:* (036) 610577 *Fax:* (036) 620982 *E-mail:* info@weton-wesgram.nl *Web Site:* www.eekhoorn.com, pg 482

Uitgeverij de Eenhoorn (Belgium) *Tel:* (056) 60 54 60 *Fax:* (056) 61 69 81 *E-mail:* info@eenhoorn.be *Web Site:* www.eenhoorn.be, pg 67

Eesti Entsuklopeediakirjastus (Estonia) *Tel:* 6999 620 *Fax:* 6999 621 *E-mail:* ene@ene.ee *Web Site:* www.ene.ee, pg 139

Eesti Piibliselts (Estonia) *Tel:* 631 1671 *Fax:* 631 1438 *E-mail:* eps@eps.ee *Web Site:* www.eps.ee, pg 139

Eesti Rahvusraamatukogu (Estonia) *Tel:* 630 7611 *Fax:* 631 1410 *E-mail:* nlib@nlib.ee *Web Site:* www.nlib.ee, pg 139

Eesti Rahvusraamatukogu (Estonia) *Tel:* 630 7611 *E-mail:* nlib@nlib.ee *Web Site:* www.nlib.ee, pg 1504

EFE Tres D-Pub Juridicas Ltda (Brazil) *Tel:* (084) 2233394 *Fax:* (084) 2232263 *E-mail:* f3dsat@truenetrn.com.br, pg 81

eFeF-Verlag/Edition Ebersbach (Switzerland) *Tel:* (056) 4260618 *Fax:* (056) 4270461 *E-mail:* info@efefverlag.ch *Web Site:* www.efefverlag.ch, pg 622

Effata Editrice (Italy) *Tel:* (0121) 353452 *Fax:* (0121) 353839 *E-mail:* info@effata.it *Web Site:* www.effata.it, pg 387

Effective Publishing (United Kingdom) *Tel:* (01926) 812110, pg 1291

Effendi Harahap Bookstore (Indonesia) *Tel:* (024) 3544694, pg 1318

EFR-Editrici Francescane (Italy) *Tel:* (049) 8225702 *Fax:* (049) 8225713 *E-mail:* info@bibliotecafrancescana.it *Web Site:* www.biblia.it, pg 387

Efstathiadis Group SA (Greece) *Tel:* (0210) 515 4650 *Fax:* (0210) 515 4657 *E-mail:* info@efgroup.gr *Web Site:* www.efgroup.gr, pg 1313

Ediciones Ega (Spain) *Tel:* (04) 4216787 *Fax:* (04) 4213010, pg 581

Egales (Editorial Gai y Lesbiana) (Spain) *Tel:* (093) 4127283 *Fax:* (093) 4127283 *E-mail:* egales@auna.com *Web Site:* www.editorialegales.com, pg 581

Egan Publishing Pty Ltd (Australia) *Tel:* (03) 5923451 *Fax:* (03) 95931026, pg 21

Egan-Reid Ltd (New Zealand) *Tel:* (09) 3784100 *Fax:* (09) 3784300 *E-mail:* publishing@eganreid.com *Web Site:* www.egan-reid.com, pg 1181

Egan-Reid Ltd (New Zealand) *Tel:* (09) 3784100 *Fax:* (09) 3784300 *E-mail:* publishing@eganreid.co.nz *Web Site:* www.egan-reid.com, pg 1246

Editions EGC (Monaco) *Tel:* (093) 97984006 *Fax:* (093) 92052422 *E-mail:* multip@webstore.mc, pg 473

EGEA (Edizioni Giuridiche Economiche Aziendali) (Italy) *Tel:* (02) 58365751 *Fax:* (02) 58365753 *E-mail:* egea.edizioni@egea.uni-bocconi.it, pg 387

Egerton University (Kenya) *Tel:* (051) 62265; (051) 622491; (051) 62271; (051) 62280 *Fax:* (051) 62527; (051) 62442; (051) 62389 *E-mail:* eujdlib@africaonline.co.ke, pg 433

Egerton University Library (Kenya) *Tel:* (051) 62265; (051) 62491; (051) 62389; (051) 62278 *Fax:* (051) 62527 *E-mail:* eujdlib@africaonline.co.ke *Web Site:* www.egerton.or.ke, pg 1523

Egmont EHAPA Verlag GmbH (Germany) *Tel:* (030) 24008-0 *Fax:* (030) 24008-599 *Web Site:* www.ehapa.de, pg 218

Egmont Franz Schneider Verlag GmbH (Germany) *Tel:* (089) 3 58 11-6 *Fax:* (089) 3 58 11-7 55 *E-mail:* postmaster@schneiderbuch.de *Web Site:* www.schneiderbuch.de, pg 218

Egmont International Holding A/S (Denmark) *Tel:* 33 30 55 50 *Fax:* 33 32 19 02 *E-mail:* egmont@egmont.com *Web Site:* www.egmont.com, pg 130

Egmont Lademann A/S (Denmark) *Tel:* 3615 6600 *Fax:* 3644 1162 *Web Site:* www.egmontbogklub.dk, pg 1255

Egmont Latvia SIA (Latvia) *Tel:* (07) 244066; (07) 467931; (07) 468671 *Fax:* (07) 860049 *E-mail:* egmont@egmont.lv *Web Site:* www.egmont.lv, pg 444

Egmont Lietuva (Lithuania) *Tel:* (02) 231265; (02) 231266; (02) 231267 *Fax:* (02) 231269 *E-mail:* egmont@egmont.com *Web Site:* www.egmont.com, pg 449

Egmont Neografia spol sro (Slovakia) *Tel:* (07) 02 4333 8064; (07) 02 4333 3933; (07) 295966 *Fax:* (07) 238755 *E-mail:* egmont@netlab.sk, pg 559

Egmont Pestalozzi-Verlag (Germany) *Tel:* (089) 35811-862 *Fax:* (089) 5811-869, pg 218

Egmont Serieforlaget A/S (Denmark) *Tel:* 70 20 50 35 *Fax:* 33 30 57 60; 36 18 58 90 *E-mail:* abonnement@tsf.egmont.com *Web Site:* www.serieforlaget.dk, pg 130

Egmont Serieforlaget (Sweden) *Tel:* (040) 6939400 *Fax:* (040) 6939498 *E-mail:* egmont@egmont.com *Web Site:* www.egmont.com, pg 611

Egmont vgs verlagsgesellschaft mbH (Germany) *Tel:* (0221) 20811-0 *Fax:* (0221) 20811-66 *E-mail:* info@vgs.de *Web Site:* www.vgs.de, pg 218

Egyptian Association for Library & Information Science (Egypt (Arab Republic of Egypt)) *Tel:* (02) 5676365 *Fax:* (02) 5729659, pg 1561

Egyptian National Library (Dar-ul-Kutub) (Egypt (Arab Republic of Egypt)) *Tel:* (02) 900 232, pg 1503

The Egyptian Society for the Dissemination of Universal Culture and Knowledge (ESDUCK) (Egypt (Arab Republic of Egypt)) *Tel:* (02) 35425079; (02) 3542 0295 *Fax:* (02) 3540295, pg 138

The Egyptian Society for the Dissemination of Universal Culture and Knowledge (ESDUCK) (Egypt (Arab Republic of Egypt)) *Tel:* (02) 3542 0295 *Fax:* (02) 3540295, pg 1130

The Egyptian Society for the Dissemination of Universal Culture and Knowledge (ESDUCK) (Egypt (Arab Republic of Egypt)) *Tel:* (02) 3542 0295; (02) 35425079, pg 1147

Ehrenwirth Verlag (Germany) *Tel:* (02202) 121-330 *Fax:* (02202) 121-920 *E-mail:* ehrenwirth@luebbe.de *Web Site:* www.luebbe.de, pg 218

Ehrenwirth Verlag GmbH (Germany) *Tel:* (02202) 121-0 *Fax:* (02202) 121 920 *Web Site:* www.ehrenwirth.de, pg 218

Eichborn AG (Germany) *Tel:* (069) 256003-0 *Fax:* (069) 256003-30 *E-mail:* rights@eichborn.de; vertrieb@eichborn.de *Web Site:* www.eichborn.de, pg 219

Eichosha Company Ltd (Japan) *Tel:* (03) 3263-1641 *Fax:* (03) 3263-6174 *E-mail:* info@eichosha.co.jp *Web Site:* www.eichosha.co.jp, pg 417

Universitaetsbibliothek Eichstaett (Germany) *Tel:* (08421) 931330 *Fax:* (08421) 931791 *E-mail:* ub-direktion@ku-eichstaett.de *Web Site:* www.ub.ku-eichstaett.de, pg 1509

J W Eides Forlag A/S (Norway) *Tel:* (05) 32 90 40 *Fax:* (05) 31 90 18 *Web Site:* www.eideforlag.no, pg 509

Drei Eidgenossen Verlag (Switzerland) *Tel:* (061) 475166 *Fax:* (061) 475166, pg 622

Eiffes Romain (Luxembourg) *Tel:* (023) 65 10 52 *E-mail:* rend@pt.lu, pg 451

The Eighteen Nineties Society (United Kingdom) *Tel:* (01869) 248340 *Web Site:* www.1890s.org, pg 1407

The Eihosha Ltd (Japan) *Tel:* (03) 5206-6020 *Fax:* (03) 5206-6022, pg 417

Eike-Boekklub (South Africa) *Tel:* (012) 401 0700 *Fax:* (012) 3255498 *E-mail:* lapa@atkv.org.za, pg 1255

Eiland-Verlag Sylt Frank Roseman (Germany) *Tel:* (04651) 936212 *Fax:* (04651) 936214 *E-mail:* info@eiland-verlag.de *Web Site:* www.eiland-verlag.de, pg 219

Ein Shams University Library (Egypt (Arab Republic of Egypt)) *Tel:* (02) 4820230; (02) 6831474; (02) 6831231; (02) 6831492; (02) 6831417; (02) 6831090 *Fax:* (02) 687824 *E-mail:* info@asunet.shams.eun.eg *Web Site:* asunet.shams.eun.eg, pg 1503

Giulio Einaudi Editore SpA (Italy) *Tel:* (011) 56561 *Fax:* (011) 542903, pg 387

Bibliotheek Technische Universiteit Eindhoven (Netherlands) *Tel:* (040) 2472381 *Fax:* (040) 2447015 *E-mail:* helpdesk.bib@tue.nl *Web Site:* www.tue.nl/bib, pg 1531

EinfallsReich Verlagsgesellschaft MbH (Germany) *Tel:* (05533) 2017, pg 219

Eironeia-Verlag (Germany) *Tel:* (0761) 581617 *Fax:* (0761) 3603474529, pg 219

Editions Eisele SA (Switzerland) *Tel:* (021) 6256324 *Fax:* (021) 6236359 *Web Site:* www.eisele.ch, pg 622

Christian Ejlers' Forlag aps (Denmark) *Tel:* 3312 2114 *Fax:* 3312 2884 *E-mail:* liber@ce-publishers.dk *Web Site:* www.ejlers.dk, pg 131

EK-Verlag GmbH (Germany) *Tel:* (0761) 70310-31 *Fax:* (0761) 70310-50, pg 219

Ekab Business Ltd (Ghana) *Tel:* (021) 225318, pg 303

Ekdoseis Kazantzaki (Kazantzakis Publications) (Greece) *Tel:* (01) 3642829 *Fax:* (01) 3642829, pg 307

Ekdoseis Thetili (Greece) *Tel:* (010) 3215229; (010) 7212226, pg 307

Ekdotike Athenon SA (Greece) *Tel:* (010) 360-8911 *Fax:* (010) 3606157, pg 307

Ekdotikos Oikos Adelfon Kyriakidi A E (Greece) *Tel:* (02310) 208540 *Fax:* (02310) 245541 *E-mail:* johnkyr@the.forthnet.gr, pg 307

Ekelunds Forlag AB (Sweden) *Tel:* (08) 821320 *Fax:* (08) 832956 *E-mail:* education@ekelunds.se, pg 611

Ekenas Tryckeri AB (Finland) *Tel:* (019) 222 800 *Fax:* (019) 222 815 *E-mail:* leif.rex@eta.fi, pg 142

Izdatelstvo Ekologija (Russian Federation) *Tel:* (095) 9287860, pg 544

Ekonomibok Forlag AB (Sweden) *Tel:* (042) 929 50 *Fax:* (042) 929 50, pg 611

Polskie Wydawnictwo Ekonomiczne PWE SA (Poland) *Tel:* (022) 827 80 01 *Fax:* (022) 827 55 67 *E-mail:* pwe@pwe.com.pl *Web Site:* www.pwe.com.pl, pg 522

Izdatelstvo 'Ekonomika' (Russian Federation) *Tel:* (095) 240-4877; (095) 240-4848 *Fax:* (095) 240-4817 *E-mail:* info@economizdat.ru *Web Site:* www.economizdat.ru, pg 544

El Ancora Editores (Colombia) *Tel:* (01) 283 9040; (01) 342 6224; (01) 283 9235 *Fax:* (01) 283 9235 *E-mail:* ancoraed@elancoraeditores.com *Web Site:* www.elancoraeditores.com, pg 111

EL Ciervo 96 (Spain) *Tel:* (093) 200 51 45; (093) 201 00 96 *Fax:* (093) 201 10 15 *E-mail:* redaccion@elciervo.es *Web Site:* www.elciervo.es, pg 581

El Colegio de Michoacan A C (Mexico) *Tel:* (0351) 515 71 00 *Fax:* (0351) 5157100 (ext 1742) *E-mail:* publica@colmich.cmich.udg.mx; publica@colmich.edu.mx *Web Site:* www.colmich.edu.mx, pg 464

El Hogar y la Moda SA (Spain) *Tel:* (093) 508 70 00 *Fax:* (093) 454 87 72 *E-mail:* hymsa@hymsa.com *Web Site:* www.hymsa.com, pg 581

Dar-El-Machreq Sarl (Lebanon) *Tel:* (01) 202423; (01) 202424 *Fax:* (01) 329348 *E-mail:* machreq@cyberia.net.lb *Web Site:* www.darelmachreq.com, pg 446

Editorial El Manual Moderno SA de CV (Mexico) *Tel:* (055) 2651100; (055) 2651124; (055) 2651121 *Fax:* (055) 2651175 *E-mail:* mmoderno@compuserve.com.ux *Web Site:* www.manualmoderno.com.mx, pg 464

El Viso, SA Ediciones (Spain) *Tel:* (091) 5196576; (091) 5196583 *Fax:* (091) 5196583 *E-mail:* lvisoh@anexo.es, pg 582

Eland Publishing Ltd (United Kingdom) *Tel:* (020) 7833 0762 *Fax:* (020) 7833 4434 *E-mail:* info@travelbooks.co.uk *Web Site:* www.travelbooks.co.uk, pg 690

Elanders Publishing AS (Norway) *Tel:* 22636400 *Fax:* 22636594, pg 509

ELC International (United Kingdom) *Tel:* (01865) 513186; (01865) 26520284 *Fax:* (01865) 513186; (01865) 26530180 *E-mail:* snyderpub@aol.com, pg 690

ELCE Editeurs et Libraires Catholiques d'Europe (Switzerland) *Tel:* (071) 279580 *Fax:* (071) 279580 *E-mail:* hawas@mhs.ch, pg 622

ELCIN Book Depot (Namibia) *Tel:* (065) 240211 *Fax:* (065) 240536, pg 1328

NV Drukkerij Eldorado (Suriname) *Tel:* (0597) 472362, pg 608

Electa (Italy) *Tel:* (02) 215631 *Fax:* (02) 26413121, pg 387

Electre (France) *Tel:* (01) 44 41 28 00 *Fax:* (01) 44 41 28 65 *E-mail:* biblio@electre.com *Web Site:* www.electre.com, pg 161

Electroliber Lda (Portugal) *Tel:* (021) 940 6750 *Fax:* (021) 942 52 14 *E-mail:* electrliber@mail.telepac.pt, pg 1337

Electronic Publishing Services Ltd (EPS) (United Kingdom) *Tel:* (020) 7837 3345 *Fax:* (020) 7837 8901 *E-mail:* eps@epsltd.com *Web Site:* www.epsltd.com, pg 690

Electronic Technology Publishing Co Ltd (Hong Kong) *Tel:* 2342 8298; 2342 8299; 2342 9845 *Fax:* 2341 4247 *E-mail:* info@electronictechnology.com *Web Site:* www.electronictechnology.com, pg 317

Electronica Books & Media Ltd (United Kingdom) *Tel:* (01932) 765119 *Fax:* (01932) 765429, pg 1350

Electronics Industry Publishing House (China) *Tel:* (010) 68253874; (010) 68233825 *Fax:* (010) 86106821-4062, pg 104

Edizioni dell'Elefante (Italy) *Tel:* (06) 68803710 *Fax:* (06) 6832526, pg 387

Eleftheri Skepsis (Greece) *Tel:* (0210) 3614736; (0210) 3630697 *E-mail:* info@eleftheriskepsis.gr *Web Site:* www.eleftheriskepsis.gr, pg 1313

G C Eleftheroudakis Co Ltd (Greece) *Tel:* (01) 3222255; (01) 3229388 *Fax:* (01) 3231401; (01) 3229388, pg 1313

Eleftheroudakis, GCSA International Bookstore (Greece) *Tel:* (01) 3229388 *Fax:* (01) 325 48 89 *E-mail:* elebooks@netor.gr, pg 307

Elegance Finance Printing Services Ltd (Hong Kong) *Tel:* 2283 2222 *Fax:* 2521 3616 *E-mail:* saledept@elegancefinptg.com, pg 1178

Elegance Finance Printing Services Ltd (Hong Kong) *Tel:* 2283 2222 *Fax:* 2283 2283; 2521 3616 *Web Site:* www.eleganceholdings.com, pg 1245

Elegance Printing & Book Binding (USA) (United States) *Tel:* 516-676-5941 *Fax:* 516-676-5973 *Web Site:* www.elegancebooks.com, pg 1166, 1187, 1229, 1240

Elektor-Verlag GmbH (Germany) *Tel:* (0241) 889090 *Fax:* (0241) 8890988 *E-mail:* redaktion@elektor.de *Web Site:* www.elektor.de, pg 219

Elektrowirtschaft Verlag (Switzerland) *Tel:* (01) 2994141 *Fax:* (01) 2994140 *E-mail:* redaktion@infel.ch *Web Site:* www.infel.ch, pg 623

Element Books Ltd (United Kingdom) *Tel:* (01747) 851448 *Fax:* (01747) 855721, pg 690

Element Uitgevers (Netherlands) *Tel:* (035) 6941750 *Fax:* (035) 6945824 *E-mail:* element@wxs.nl, pg 482

Elephas Books Pty Ltd (Australia) *Tel:* (08) 9370 1461 *Fax:* (08) 9341 8952, pg 21

Editora Elevacao (Brazil) *Tel:* (011) 3358-6868; (011) 3358-6875; (011) 3358-6869 *Fax:* (011) 3331-5803 *E-mail:* info@elevacao.com.br *Web Site:* www.elevacao.com.br, pg 81

Elf Exploration Production (France) *Tel:* (05) 59 83 65 80 *Fax:* (05) 59 83 58 11 *E-mail:* contact_ep@cgt-totalfina-elf.org *Web Site:* www.cgt-totalfina-elf.org, pg 161

Elfande Ltd (United Kingdom) *Tel:* (01372) 220330 *Fax:* (01372) 220340 *E-mail:* sales@contact-uk.com *Web Site:* www.contact-uk.com, pg 690

Ediciones Elfos SL (Spain) *Tel:* (093) 4069479 *Fax:* (093) 4069006 *E-mail:* eltos-ed@teleline.es *Web Site:* www.edicioneselfos.com, pg 582

Edward Elgar Publishing Ltd (United Kingdom) *Tel:* (01242) 226934 *Fax:* (01242) 262111 *E-mail:* info@e-elgar.co.uk *Web Site:* www.e-elgar.co.uk, pg 690

Elgin Consultants Ltd (Hong Kong) *Tel:* 2815 1680, pg 1156

Elias Modern Publishing House (Egypt (Arab Republic of Egypt)) *Tel:* (02) 5903756; (02) 5939544 *Fax:* (02) 5880091 *E-mail:* eliasmph@gega.net *Web Site:* www.eliaspublishing.com, pg 138

The George Eliot Fellowship (United Kingdom) *Tel:* (024) 7659 2231 *Web Site:* www.sndc.demon.co.uk/alsdef.htm#e, pg 1407

Elite Printing Co Ltd (Hong Kong) *Tel:* 2558 0119 *Fax:* 2897 2675 *E-mail:* sales@elite.com.hk *Web Site:* www.elite.com.hk, pg 1156

Elkar, Euskal Liburu eta Kantuen Argitaldaria, SL (Spain) *Tel:* (943) 310327 *Fax:* (943) 310345, pg 582

David Ell Press Pty Ltd (Australia) *Tel:* (02) 5551634 *Fax:* (02) 5557067, pg 21

Elle Di Ci - Libreria Dottrina Cristiana (Italy) *Tel:* (011) 9552111 *Fax:* (011) 9574048 *E-mail:* editoriale@elledici.org *Web Site:* www.elledici.org, pg 387

Ellebore Editions (France) *Tel:* (01) 40 01 09 49 *Fax:* (01) 40 01 09 94 *E-mail:* ellebore@wfi.fr; info@ellebore.fr *Web Site:* www.wfi.fr/ellebore, pg 161

Verlag Heinrich Ellermann GmbH & Co KG (Germany) *Tel:* (040) 607909-08 *Fax:* (040) 607909-59 *E-mail:* ellermann@vsg-hamburg.de *Web Site:* www.ellermann.de, pg 219

Ellerstroms (Sweden) *Tel:* (046) 323295 *Fax:* (046) 323295 *E-mail:* info@ellerstroms.se *Web Site:* www.ellerstroms.se, pg 611

Ellert & Richter Verlag GmbH (Germany) *Tel:* (040) 39 84 77-0 *Fax:* (040) 39 84 77-23 *E-mail:* info@ellert-richter.de *Web Site:* www.ellert-richter.de, pg 219

Elliniki Etaireia Metafraston Logotechnias (Greece) *Tel:* (01) 6717466 *Fax:* (01) 6717466, pg 1148

Elliniki Leschi Tou Vivliou (Greece) *Tel:* (01) 6463888 *Fax:* (01) 6463263 *E-mail:* elli@gezmanosnet.gz, pg 307

Elliot Right Way Books (United Kingdom) *Tel:* (01737) 832202 *Fax:* (01737) 830311 *E-mail:* info@right-way.co.uk *Web Site:* www.right-way.co.uk, pg 690

Ellipses - Edition Marketing SA (France) *Tel:* (01) 45 67 74 19 *Fax:* (01) 47 34 67 94 *E-mail:* info@editions-ellipses.com *Web Site:* www.editions-ellipses.fr, pg 161

Aidan Ellis Publishing (United Kingdom) *Tel:* (01548) 842755 *E-mail:* mail@aidanellispublishing.co.uk *Web Site:* www.demon.co.uk/aepub, pg 690

Thomas Ellis Memorial Fund (United Kingdom) *Tel:* (029) 2038 2656 *Fax:* (029) 2039 6040 *E-mail:* awards@wales.ac.uk *Web Site:* www.wales.ac.uk/newpages/external/E5536.asp, pg 1408

ELLUG (Editions Litteraires et Linguistiques de l'Universite de Grenoble III) (France) *Tel:* (04) 76 82 43 72; (04) 76 82 77 74 *Fax:* (04) 76 82 41 85 *E-mail:* ellug@u-grenoble3.fr *Web Site:* www-ellug.u-grenoble3.fr/ellug, pg 161

Elm Publications (United Kingdom) *Tel:* (01487) 773254; (01487) 773238 *E-mail:* elm@elm-training.co.uk *Web Site:* www.elm-training.co.uk, pg 691

Elmar BV (Netherlands) *Tel:* (015) 215 32 32 *Fax:* (015) 215 32 30 *E-mail:* elmar@elmar.nl *Web Site:* 212.83.197.79, pg 482

Edicoes ELO (Portugal) *Tel:* (061) 812 143; (061) 812 344 *Fax:* (061) 81 28 20 *E-mail:* eloag@elografica.pt *Web Site:* www.elografica.pt, pg 531

Elpis Verlag GmbH (Germany) *Tel:* (06221) 165789, pg 219

Buchhandlung zum Elsasser AG (Switzerland) *Tel:* (01) 261 08 47; (01) 251 16 12 *Fax:* (01) 261 08 97, pg 1344

Elsevier Advanced Technology (United Kingdom) *Tel:* (01865) 843848 *Fax:* (01865) 843010 *E-mail:* eatsales@elsevier.co.uk (sales) *Web Site:* www.nepcon.co.uk/ex0210g.htm, pg 691

Elsevier Australia (Australia) *Tel:* (029) 5178999 *Toll Free Tel:* 1-800 263 951 (within Australia); 0-800 170 165 (to Australia from New Zealand) *Fax:* (029) 5172249 *Toll Free Fax:* 0-800 170 160 (from Australia to New Zealand) *E-mail:* service@elsevier.com.au *Web Site:* www.elsevier.com.au, pg 21

Elsevier GmbH/Urban & Fischer Verlag (Germany) *Tel:* (089) 5383-0 *Fax:* (089) 5383-939 *E-mail:* info@elsevier-deutschland.de *Web Site:* www.elsevier.de, pg 219

Elsevier Ltd (United Kingdom) *Tel:* (01865) 843000 *Fax:* (01865) 843010 *E-mail:* initial.surname@elsevier.com *Web Site:* www.elsevier.com, pg 691

Elsevier SAS (Editions Scientifiques et Medicales Elsevier) (France) *Tel:* (01) 45589110 *Fax:* (01) 45589419 *Web Site:* www.elsevier.fr, pg 161

Elsevier Science (Japan) *Tel:* (03) 5561-5033 *Toll Free Tel:* (0120) 383-608 (within Japan) *Fax:* (03) 5561-5047 *E-mail:* info@elsevier.co.jp *Web Site:* www.elsevier.co.jp, pg 417

Elsevier Science BV (Netherlands) *Tel:* (020) 5862560 *Fax:* (020) 4852457 *E-mail:* nlinfo-f@elsevier.nl, pg 482

Elstead Maps (United Kingdom) *Tel:* (01252) 703472 *Fax:* (01252) 703971 *E-mail:* enquiry@elstead.co.uk *Web Site:* www.elstead.co.uk, pg 1350

Elton Publications (Australia) *Tel:* (08) 9 446 1328 *Fax:* (08) 9 445 8229 *E-mail:* elton@iinet.net.au *Web Site:* www.elton.iinet.net.au, pg 21

Elvetica Edizioni SA (Switzerland) *Tel:* (091) 6835056 *Fax:* (091) 6837605 *E-mail:* info@swissfinance.com *Web Site:* www.tinet.ch/swissfinance, pg 623

N G Elwert Verlag (Germany) *Tel:* (06421) 17090 *Fax:* (06421) 15487 *E-mail:* elwertmail@elwert.de *Web Site:* www.elwert.de, pg 219

Uitgeverij Elzenga (Netherlands) *Tel:* (020) 55 11 262, pg 482

Gholam Emami (Germany) *Tel:* (0911) 288356 *Fax:* (0911) 288356, pg 219

Emece Editores SA (Argentina) *Tel:* (011) 4382-4045; (011) 4382-4043 *Fax:* (011) 4383-3793 *E-mail:* info@eplaneta.com.ar; pasiusis@planeta.com.ar *Web Site:* www.emece.com.ar, pg 5

Emerald (United Kingdom) *Tel:* (01274) 777700 *Fax:* (01274) 785201 *E-mail:* info@emeraldinsight.com; information@emeraldinsight.com (academic sales); editorial@emeraldinsight.com (editorial) *Web Site:* www.emeraldinsight.com, pg 691

Emerald City Books (Australia) *Tel:* (02) 7641115 *Fax:* (02) 7641115 *E-mail:* emeraldcitybooks@hotmail.com, pg 21

Emerald Publications (Ireland) *Tel:* (021) 962853 *Fax:* (021) 310983 *E-mail:* alongk@iol.ie, pg 359

Editura Eminescu (Romania) *Tel:* (01) 2228540, pg 539

Emirates Printing Press (LLC) (United Arab Emirates) *Tel:* (04) 347 5550; (04) 347 5544 *Fax:* (04) 347 5959 *E-mail:* eppdubai@emirates.net.ae *Web Site:* www.eppdubai.com, pg 1224

Emmaus Bible School (United Republic of Tanzania) *Tel:* (061) 354500 *Fax:* (061) 350911 *E-mail:* CMML-Dodoma@maf.org, pg 643

Emons Verlag (Germany) *Tel:* (0221) 56977-0 *Fax:* (0221) 524937 *E-mail:* info@emons-verlag.de *Web Site:* www.emons-verlag.de, pg 219

Emperor Publishing (Australia) *Tel:* (02) 9261 4055 *Fax:* (02) 9264 9435 *E-mail:* pa@oxfordsquare.com.au, pg 21

Empire Printing Ltd (Hong Kong) *Tel:* 2665 5193 *Fax:* 2661 7722, pg 1156

Emporio de Promocoes Artistica Cultural e Editora Ltda (Brazil) *Tel:* (011) 8262992 *Fax:* (011) 661135, pg 81

Empresa Brasileira de Pesquisa Agropecuaria (Brazil) *Tel:* (061) 348-4113 *Fax:* (061) 347-1041 *E-mail:* webmaster@sct.embrapa.br *Web Site:* www.embrapa.br, pg 81

Empresa Moderna Lda (Mozambique) *Tel:* (01) 424594, pg 475

Empresas Editoriales SA (Mexico) *Tel:* (05) 5288979; (05) 5288417 *Fax:* (05) 5288417, pg 465

Editorial Empuries (Spain) *Tel:* (093) 4870062 *Fax:* (093) 4874147, pg 582

Enalios (Greece) *Tel:* (01) 2531614 *Fax:* (01) 2184854, pg 1313

Enciclopedia Catalana, SA (Spain) *Tel:* (093) 412 0030 *Fax:* (093) 301 4863 *Web Site:* www.enciclopedia-catalana.com, pg 582

Encres Vives (France) *Tel:* (05) 62740787 *E-mail:* encres@mygale.org, pg 161

Ediciones Encuentro SA (Spain) *Tel:* (091) 532 26 07 *Fax:* (091) 532 23 46 *E-mail:* encuentro@ediciones-encuentro.es *Web Site:* www.ediciones-encuentro.es, pg 582

Encyclopaedia Britannica (Australia) Inc (Australia) *Tel:* (02) 9923 5600 *Fax:* (02) 9929 3758 *Web Site:* www.britannica.com.au, pg 21

Encyclopaedia Britannica (UK) International Ltd (United Kingdom) *Tel:* (020) 7500 7800; (0845) 075 700 (orders CD or DVD inside UK); (0177) 901 3948 (orders CD or DVD outside UK); (0845) 075 8000 (order books inside UK); (0845) 901 3948 (order books outside UK) *Fax:* (020) 7500 7878 *E-mail:* enquiries@britannica.co.uk *Web Site:* www.britannica.co.uk, pg 691

Encyclopedia Britannica (Germany) *Tel:* (0251) 48 227-0 *Fax:* (0251) 48 227-27 *E-mail:* lexikadienst@aol.com *Web Site:* www.britannica.de, pg 219

Encyclopedia Judaica (Israel) *Tel:* (02) 6557822 *Fax:* (02) 6528962 *E-mail:* info@keter-books.co.il *Web Site:* www.keter-books.co.il, pg 366

Encyclopedia of China Publishing House (China) *Tel:* (010) 68315610 *Fax:* (010) 68316510 *E-mail:* ygh@bj.col.com.cn, pg 104

Encyclopedia Universalis France SA (France) *Tel:* (01) 45 72 72 72 *Fax:* (01) 45 72 03 43 *E-mail:* contact@universalis.fr *Web Site:* www.universalis.fr, pg 161

Les Encyclopedies du Patrimoine (France) *Tel:* (01) 42 60 66 63 *Fax:* (01) 42 60 66 73 *Web Site:* www.culture.gouv.fr, pg 161

Enda Tiers Monde (Senegal) *Tel:* (0221) 821-60-27; (0221) 822-42-29 *Fax:* (0221) 822-26-95 *E-mail:* enda@enda.sn *Web Site:* www.enda.sn, pg 551

Ediciones Endymion (Spain) *Tel:* (01) 5223668; (01) 5222210, pg 582

EnEffect, Center for Energy Efficiency (Bulgaria) *Tel:* (02) 963 17 14; (02) 963 07 23; (02) 963 21 69 *Fax:* (02) 963 25 74 *E-mail:* eneffect@mail.orbitel.bg *Web Site:* www.eneffect.bg, pg 94

Energeia sp zoo Wydawnictwo (Poland) *Tel:* (022) 847 00 53 *Fax:* (022) 847-00-53, pg 523

Energica Foerlags AB/Halsabocker (Sweden) *Tel:* (0250) 55 20 00 *Fax:* (0250) 43191 *Web Site:* www.energica.com, pg 611

Energoatomizdat (Russian Federation) *Tel:* (095) 9259993 *Fax:* (095) 2356585, pg 544

The Energy Information Centre (United Kingdom) *Tel:* (01638) 751 400 *Fax:* (01638) 751 801 *E-mail:* info@eic.co.uk *Web Site:* www.eic.co.uk, pg 691

Engel & Bengel Verlag (Germany) *Tel:* (06353) 8107 *Fax:* (06353) 507057 *E-mail:* verlag@engelundbengel.de *Web Site:* www.engelundbengel.de, pg 220

Engelhorn Verlag GmbH (Germany) *Tel:* (089) 45554-0 *Fax:* (089) 45554-111, pg 220

Englisch Verlag GmbH (Germany) *Tel:* (0611) 9 427 2-0 *Fax:* (0611) 9 42 72 30 *E-mail:* info@englisch-verlag.de *Web Site:* www.englisch-verlag.de, pg 220

The English Agency (Japan) Ltd (Japan) *Tel:* (03) 3406 5385 *Fax:* (03) 3406 5387 *E-mail:* info@eaj.co.jp, pg 1134

The English Association (United Kingdom) *Tel:* (0116) 252 3982 *Fax:* (0116) 252 2301 *E-mail:* engassoc@le.ac.uk *Web Site:* www.le.ac.uk/engassoc, pg 1408

English Book Store (India) *Tel:* (011) 332 9126 *Fax:* (011) 332 1731, pg 1315

English Language Editors' Association (ELEAS) (Israel) *Tel:* (02) 586-5772 *Fax:* (02) 586-6411 *Web Site:* www.geocities.com/athens/stage/4942/8Eleas.html, pg 1401

The English-Speaking Union of the Commonwealth (United Kingdom) *Tel:* (020) 7529 1550 *Fax:* (020) 7495 6108 *E-mail:* esu@esu.org *Web Site:* www.esu.org, pg 1408

English Teaching Professional (United Kingdom) *Tel:* (020) 7222 1155 *Fax:* (020) 7222 1551 *E-mail:* info@etprofessional.com *Web Site:* www.etprofessional.com, pg 691

Verlag Peter Engstler (Germany) *Tel:* (09774) 858490 *Fax:* (09774) 858491 *E-mail:* engstler-verlag@t-online.de *Web Site:* www.engstler-verlag.de, pg 220

Enkay Publishers Pvt Ltd (India) *Tel:* (011) 301-6994; (011) 301-2314 *Fax:* (011) 301-2314, pg 334

Enna (Italy) *Tel:* (0935) 500368 *Fax:* (0935) 500568, pg 388

Enne (Italy) *Tel:* (0874) 412357 *Fax:* (0874) 412357, pg 388

Ennsthaler GesmbH & Co KG (Austria) *Tel:* (07252) 52053-10 *Fax:* (07252) 52053-16 *E-mail:* buero@ennsthaler.at *Web Site:* www.ennsthaler.at, pg 50

Enosis Hellinon Bibliothekarion (Greece) *Tel:* (01) 3226 625, pg 1564

Enrique Libreria (Spain) *Tel:* (091) 522 80 88, pg 1342

Johan Enschede Amsterdam BV (Netherlands) *Tel:* (020) 585 86 00 *Fax:* (020) 585 86 01 *E-mail:* info@jea.nl *Web Site:* www.jea.nl, pg 482

Ensslin und Laiblin Verlag GmbH & Co KG (Germany) *Tel:* (07121) 98 98 0 *Fax:* (07121) 98 98 44 *E-mail:* ensslin-verlag@t-online.de *Web Site:* www.ensslin-verlag.de, pg 220

Editions Entente (France) *Tel:* (01) 55 42 84 00 *Fax:* (01) 40 49 01 02, pg 161

Enterprise International (Hong Kong) *Tel:* 25734161 *Fax:* 28383469, pg 1314

Enterprise Nationale du Livre (ENAL) (Algeria) *Tel:* (021) 737494; (021) 735841 *Fax:* (021) 735841, pg 2

Enterprise Publications (Australia) *Tel:* (08) 8261 9528 *Fax:* (08) 8261 9528, pg 21

Entretenlibro SA de CV (Mexico) *Tel:* (09183) 425570, pg 465

Envirobook (Australia) *Tel:* (02) 9518 6154 *Fax:* (02) 9518 6156 *E-mail:* trekaway@sia.net.au, pg 21

Environmental Research Unit (Ireland) *Tel:* (01) 660 25 11 *Fax:* (01) 668 00 09, pg 359

Enzyklopadie Verlag (Romania) *Tel:* (01) 2243667; (01) 2244014 *Fax:* (01) 2243667, pg 539

EOS Gabinete de Orientacion Psicologica (Spain) *Tel:* (091) 554 12 04 *Fax:* (091) 554 12 03 *E-mail:* eos@eos.es *Web Site:* www.eos.es, pg 582

EOS Verlag der Benefiktiner der Erzabtei St. Ottilien (Germany) *Tel:* (08193) 71261 *Fax:* (08193) 6844 *E-mail:* mail@eos-verlag.de *Web Site:* www.eos-verlag.de, pg 220

EP Graphics (United States) *Tel:* 260-589-2145 *Toll Free Tel:* 877-589-2145 *Fax:* 260-589-2810 *Web Site:* www.epgraphics.com, pg 1229

EPA (Editions Pratiques Automobiles) (France) *Tel:* (01) 43 92 30 00 *Fax:* (01) 43 92 33 81 *Web Site:* www.editionsduchene.fr, pg 161

Editions de l'Epargne (France) *Tel:* (01) 44 16 95 80 *Fax:* (01) 44 16 95 99, pg 161

EPB Publishers Pte Ltd (Singapore) *Tel:* 278 0881 *Fax:* 278 2456 *E-mail:* epb@sbg.com.sg, pg 555

EPER (United Kingdom) *Tel:* (0131) 650 6200 *Fax:* (0131) 667 5927 *E-mail:* ials.enquiries@ed.ac.uk *Web Site:* www.ials.ed.ac.uk, pg 691

Editions les Eperonniers (Belgium) *Tel:* (010) 813614 *Fax:* (010) 815386, pg 67

Epikerotita (Greece) *Tel:* (01) 3636083, pg 307

EPO Publishers, Printers, Booksellers (Belgium) *Tel:* (03) 2396874 *Fax:* (03) 2184604 *E-mail:* publishers@epo.be *Web Site:* www.epo.be, pg 67

EPP Books Services (Ghana) *Tel:* (021) 778853; (021) 778347 *Fax:* (021) 779099 *E-mail:* info@eppbooks.com *Web Site:* www.eppbooks.com, pg 304

Eppinger-Verlag OHG (Germany) *Tel:* (0791) 95061-0 *Fax:* (0791) 95061-41 *E-mail:* info@eppinger-verlag.de, pg 220

Epworth Press (United Kingdom) *Tel:* (01733) 325002 *Fax:* (01733) 384180 *E-mail:* comm.editor@mph.org.uk *Web Site:* www.mph.org.uk, pg 691

EQ Opciones en Educacion (Uruguay) *Tel:* (02) 4808720 *Fax:* (02) 4873965 *E-mail:* opciones@distrinet.com.uy, pg 777

Era Books (India) *Tel:* (011) 473993; (022) 5741764, pg 334

Era Publications (Australia) *Tel:* (08) 8352 4122 *Fax:* (08) 8234 0023 *E-mail:* admin@erapublications.com; service@erapublications.com *Web Site:* www.erapublications.com, pg 21

Ediciones Era SA de CV (Mexico) *Tel:* (055) 55 28 1221 *Fax:* (055) 56 06 2904 *E-mail:* erapedidos@laneta.apc.org *Web Site:* www.edicionesera.com.mx, pg 465

ERA Technology Ltd (United Kingdom) *Tel:* (01372) 367000 *Fax:* (01372) 367099 *E-mail:* info@era.co.uk *Web Site:* www.era.co.uk, pg 692

Editrice Eraclea (Italy) *Tel:* (02) 8693635 *Fax:* (02) 86453613 *E-mail:* cinquevie@libero.it, pg 388

Erasmus Grasser-Verlag GmbH (Germany) *Tel:* (08861) 241900 *Fax:* (08861) 241901, pg 220

ERB (Czech Republic) *Tel:* (02) 24009111 *Fax:* (02) 2320989, pg 1251

L'Ere Nouvelle (France) *Tel:* (04) 93 99 30 13 *E-mail:* lerenouvelle@wanadoo.fr *Web Site:* assoc.wanadoo.fr/lerenouvelle/pub, pg 161

Erein (Spain) *Tel:* (0943) 218300; (0943) 218211 *Fax:* (0943) 218311 *E-mail:* erein@erein.com *Web Site:* www.erein.com, pg 582

Eremiten-Presse und Verlag GmbH (Germany) *Tel:* (0211) 66 05 90 *Fax:* (0211) 698 94 70, pg 220

Eren Yayincilik ve Kitapcilik Ltd Sti (Turkey) *Tel:* (0212) 251-2858 *E-mail:* eren@turk.net, pg 650

Editions Eres (France) *Tel:* (05) 61 75 15 76 *Fax:* (05) 61 73 52 89 *E-mail:* eres@edition-eres.com *Web Site:* www.edition-eres.com, pg 162

Eres Editions-Horst Schubert Musikverlag (Germany) *Tel:* (04298) 1676 *Fax:* (04298) 5312 *E-mail:* info@eres-musik.de *Web Site:* www.eres-musik.de, pg 220

Eresco PT (Indonesia) *Tel:* (022) 5205985 *Fax:* (022) 5205984, pg 354

Eretz Hemdah Institute for Advanced Jewish Studies (Israel) *Tel:* (02) 537-1485 *Fax:* (02) 537-9626 *E-mail:* eretzhem@netvision.net.il *Web Site:* www.eretzhemdah.org, pg 366

Erevnites (Greece) *Tel:* (0210) 5234 415; (0210) 5234 232 *Fax:* (0210) 5241 863 *E-mail:* erevnite@otenet.gr *Web Site:* www.erevnites.gr, pg 1313

ERF-Verlag GmbH (Germany) *Tel:* (06441) 9570 *Fax:* (06441) 957120 *E-mail:* info@erf.de *Web Site:* www.erf.de, pg 220

ERGA SNC di Carla Ottino Merli & C (Edizioni Realizzazioni Grafiche - Artigiana) (Italy) *Tel:* (010) 8328441 *Fax:* (010) 8328799, pg 388

Ergebnisse Verlag GmbH (Germany) *Tel:* (040) 4801027 *Fax:* (040) 4801592, pg 220

Edition Ergo Sum (Austria) *Tel:* (02238) 77078 *Fax:* (02238) 77076 *E-mail:* apverlag@magnet.at, pg 50

Ergon Verlag Dr H J Dietrich (Germany) *Tel:* (0931) 280084 *Fax:* (0931) 282872 *E-mail:* service@ergon-verlag.de *Web Site:* www.ergon-verlag.de, pg 220

Erich-Weinert Universitatsbuchhandlung (Germany) *Tel:* (0391) 568590 *Fax:* (0391) 5685923 *E-mail:* e.angerer@weinert.de *Web Site:* www.weinert.de, pg 1311

Erika spol sro (Czech Republic) *Tel:* (02) 7950452 *Fax:* (02) 7929351, pg 123

Eriksson & Lindgren Bokforlag (Sweden) *Tel:* (08) 6523226; (08) 6523227 *Fax:* (08) 6523223 *E-mail:* info@eriksson-lindgren.se, pg 611

Erker-Verlag (Switzerland) *Tel:* (071) 227979 *Fax:* (071) 227919, pg 623

Erlanger Verlag Fuer Mission und Okumene (Germany) *Tel:* (09874) 9 17 00 *Fax:* (09874) 9 33 70 *E-mail:* verlagsleitung@erlanger-verlag.de *Web Site:* www.erlanger-verlag.de, pg 220

Penerbit Erlangga (Indonesia) *Tel:* (021) 8717006 *Fax:* (021) 8717011 *E-mail:* erlprom@rad.net.id *Web Site:* www.erlangga.com, pg 354

L'Erma di Bretschneider SRL (Italy) *Tel:* (06) 6874127 *Fax:* (06) 6874129 *E-mail:* edizioni@lerma.it *Web Site:* www.lerma.it, pg 388

Edi.Ermes srl (Italy) *Tel:* (02) 7021121 *Fax:* (02) 70211283 *E-mail:* eeinfo@eenet.it, pg 388

Ernest Press (United Kingdom) *Tel:* (0141) 637 5492 *Fax:* (0141) 637 5492 *E-mail:* sales@ernest-press.co.uk *Web Site:* www.ernest-press.co.uk, pg 692

Ernesto Reichmann Distribuidores de Livros LTDA (Brazil) *Tel:* (011) 61982122 *Fax:* (011) 61982122 *E-mail:* rrr@erdl.com, pg 1303

Ernst & Young (United Kingdom) *Tel:* (020) 7951 2000 *Fax:* (020) 7951 1345 *Web Site:* www.ey.com, pg 692

Ernst Kabel Verlag GmbH (Germany) *Tel:* (089) 381801-0 *Fax:* (089) 338704 *E-mail:* info@piper.de *Web Site:* www.piper.de, pg 221

Ernst-Moritz-Arndt Universitat Greifswald, Universitatsbibliothek (Germany) *Tel:* (03834) 86 1502 *Fax:* (03834) 86 1501 *E-mail:* ub@uni-greifswald.de *Web Site:* web.ub.uni-greifswald.de, pg 1509

Ernst, Wilhelm & Sohn, Verlag Architektur und technische Wissenschaft GmbH & Co (Germany) *Tel:* (030) 47031-200 *Fax:* (030) 47031-270 *E-mail:* info@ernst-und-sohn.de *Web Site:* www.wiley.vch.de/ernstsohn, pg 221

Ernster Sarl (Luxembourg) *Tel:* 225077-1 *Fax:* 225073 *E-mail:* librairie@ernster.com *Web Site:* www.ernster.com, pg 1325

Edition Hans Erpf Edition (Switzerland) *Tel:* (037) 711385 *Fax:* (037) 711968, pg 623

Editions Errance (France) *Tel:* (01) 43 26 85 82 *Fax:* (01) 43 29 34 88, pg 162

Errepar SA (Argentina) *Tel:* (011) 4370-2002 *Fax:* (011) 4307-9541 *E-mail:* clientes@errepar.com *Web Site:* www.errepar.com, pg 5

The Erskine Press (United Kingdom) *Tel:* (01953) 88 72 77 *Fax:* (01953) 88 83 61 *E-mail:* erskpres@aol.com *Web Site:* www.erskine-press.com, pg 692

Verlagsgesellschaft des Erziehungsvereins GmbH (Germany) *Tel:* (02845) 392-0 *Fax:* (02845) 392392 *E-mail:* info@neukirchener-verlag.de *Web Site:* www.neukirchener-verlag.de, pg 221

ESA Publications (NZ) Ltd (New Zealand) *Tel:* (09) 579 3126 *Fax:* (09) 579 4713 *E-mail:* info@esa.co.nz *Web Site:* www.esa.co.nz, pg 496

ESAN - Escuela de Administracion de Negocios para Graduados, Direccion de Investigacion (Peru) *Tel:* (01) 317-7226 *Fax:* (01) 345-1328; (01) 345-1276 *E-mail:* cendoc@esan.edu.pe *Web Site:* www.esan.edu.pe, pg 1536

Escala Ltda (Colombia) *Tel:* (01) 2878200 *Fax:* (01) 2325148, pg 111

Verlag am Eschbach GmbH (Germany) *Tel:* (07634) 1088 *Fax:* (07634) 3796 *E-mail:* vertrieb@verlag-am-eschbach.de *Web Site:* www.verlag-am-eschbach.de, pg 221

Esco BVBA (Belgium) *Tel:* (03) 2223800 *Fax:* (03) 2223838, pg 67

Escrituras Editora e Distribuidora de Livros Ltda (Brazil) *Tel:* (011) 5082-4190 *Fax:* (011) 5082-4190 *E-mail:* escrituras@escrituras.com.br *Web Site:* www.escrituras.com.br, pg 81

Escuela Nacional de Biblioteconomia y Archivonomia (Mexico) *Tel:* (055) 598-14-94, pg 1567

Asocicion Escuela Para Todos (Costa Rica) *Tel:* 2255438; 2255338; 2340530; 2341339 *Fax:* 2243014, pg 115

Escutcheon Press (Australia) *Tel:* (02) 4344 2304 *Fax:* (02) 4341 1248, pg 22

Ediciones Eseuve SA (Spain) *Tel:* (091) 539-01-03 *Fax:* (091) 528-87-59, pg 582

Editorial Esfinge SA de CV (Mexico) *Tel:* (05) 3591313; (05) 3591111; (05) 3591515 *Fax:* (05) 5761343 *E-mail:* editorial@esfinge.com.mx *Web Site:* www.esfinge.com.mx, pg 465

Eshkol Books Publishers & Printing Ltd (Israel) *Tel:* (02) 5370451; (02) 5370179 *Fax:* (02) 5372732, pg 367

Esic Editorial (Spain) *Tel:* (091) 4524100 *Fax:* (091) 3528534 *E-mail:* info.madrid@esic.es *Web Site:* www.esic.es, pg 582

Editorial Esin, SA (Spain) *Tel:* (093) 244 95 50 *Fax:* (093) 265 68 95 *E-mail:* combel@editorialcasals.com *Web Site:* www.editorialcasals.com, pg 582

Editions Eska (France) *Tel:* (01) 42 86 55 73 *Fax:* (01) 42 60 45 35 *E-mail:* eska@multimediart.fr *Web Site:* www.sybex.fr, pg 162

Esogetics GmbH (Germany) *Tel:* (07251) 8001-40 *Fax:* (07251) 8001-55 *E-mail:* info-de@esogetics.com *Web Site:* www.esogetics.com, pg 221

Esoptron (Greece) *Tel:* (01) 6442169 *Fax:* (01) 9028895, pg 1313

Libreria Esoterica (Chile) *Tel:* (02) 6338430 *Fax:* (02) 6397933 *E-mail:* wzzdarmd@entelchile.net, pg 1305

Verlag Esoterische Philosophie GmbH (Germany) *Tel:* (0511) 755331 *Fax:* (0511) 755334 *E-mail:* info@esoterische-philosophie.de *Web Site:* www.esoterische-philosophie.de, pg 221

Espace de Libertes (Belgium) *Tel:* (02) 6276860 *Fax:* (02) 6266861, pg 67

Editions Espaces 34 (France) *Tel:* (04) 67 84 11 23 *Fax:* (04) 67 84 00 74 *E-mail:* chesp34@club-internet.fr *Web Site:* www.editions-espaces34.fr, pg 162

Espasa-Calpe Argentina SA (Argentina) *Tel:* (011) 4382-4043; (011) 4382-4045 *Fax:* (011) 4383-3793 *E-mail:* info@eplaneta.com.ar, pg 5

Casa del Libro Espasa-Calpe SA (Spain) *Tel:* (091) 481 13 71 *E-mail:* casadellibro@casadellibro.com *Web Site:* www.casadellibro.com, pg 1342

Editorial Espasa-Calpe SA (Spain) *Tel:* (091) 3589689 *Fax:* (091) 3589364; (091) 3589505 *E-mail:* sagerencias@espasa.es *Web Site:* www.espasa.com, pg 582

Espasa-Calpe Mexicana SA (Mexico) *Tel:* (05) 5758585 *Fax:* (05) 5758980, pg 465

Editorial Espaxs SA (Spain) *Tel:* (093) 454 06 52 *Fax:* (093) 4510149, pg 582

Universala Esperanto-Asocio (Netherlands) *Tel:* (010) 4361044 *Fax:* (010) 4361751 *E-mail:* info@uea.org *Web Site:* www.uea.org, pg 1278

Esperanto Translating Service (United Kingdom) *Tel:* (020) 84282829 *Fax:* (020) 84282829 *E-mail:* espero@moose.co.uk, pg 1150

Espiritualidad (Spain) *Tel:* (091) 350-49-22 *Fax:* (091) 350-49-22 *E-mail:* ede@edespiritualidad.org *Web Site:* www.edespiritualidad.org, pg 583

Espresso Verlag GmbH (Germany) *Tel:* (030) 5333 4444 *Fax:* (030) 5333 4159 *E-mail:* info@espresso-verlag.de *Web Site:* www.espresso-verlag.de, pg 221

L'Esprit Du Temps (France) *Tel:* (0556) 02 84 19 *Fax:* (0556) 02 91 31 *E-mail:* espritemp@aol.com *Web Site:* www.psy-book.net, pg 162

Editions Esprit Ouvert (Switzerland) *Tel:* (021) 3208844 *Fax:* (021) 3235403, pg 623

Esquina-Livraria e Papelaria Lda (Portugal) *Tel:* (022) 6065234 *Fax:* (022) 6053878 *E-mail:* livrariaesquina@mail.telepac.pt *Web Site:* www.esquina-livraria.com, pg 1337

Ess Ess Publications (India) *Tel:* (011) 3260807 *Fax:* (011) 3274173 *E-mail:* sumitsethi@vsnl.com *Web Site:* www.essess.8m.com, pg 334

Essay und Zeitgeist Verlag (Luxembourg) *Fax:* 425227, pg 451

Essegi (Italy) *Tel:* (0544) 499203 *Fax:* (0544) 499076 *E-mail:* essegi_libri@libero.it, pg 388

Esselibri (Italy) *Tel:* (081) 5757255 *Fax:* (081) 5757944 *E-mail:* info@simone.it *Web Site:* www.simone.it, pg 388

Esslinger Verlag J F Schreiber GmbH (Germany) *Tel:* (0711) 310594-6 *Fax:* (0711) 310594-77; (0711) 310594-65 *E-mail:* esslinger@klett-mail.de, pg 221

Editions de L'Est (France) *Tel:* (03) 83598054 *Fax:* (03) 83598072, pg 162

estamp (United Kingdom) *Tel:* (020) 8994 2379 *Fax:* (020) 8994 2379 *E-mail:* st@estamp.demon.co.uk, pg 692

Editorial Estampa, Lda (Portugal) *Tel:* (021) 355 56 63 *Fax:* (021) 314 19 11 *E-mail:* estampa@mail.telepac.pt *Web Site:* www.browser.pt/estampa, pg 531

Estates Gazette (United Kingdom) *Tel:* (020) 8652 3500; (020) 7411 2540 (edit); (020) 7411 2626 (advertising); (01444) 445335 (subscriptions) *Fax:* (020) 7437 2432; (020) 7437 0294 (edit); (020) 7437 2432 (advertising); (01444) 445567 (subscriptions), pg 692

Libreria del Este (Venezuela) *Tel:* (02) 951 2307; (02) 951 1297, pg 1356

Biblioteca Estense Universitaria (Italy) *Tel:* (059) 222248 *Fax:* (059) 230195 *E-mail:* estense@kril.cedoc.unimo.it; biblio.estense@cedoc.mo.it *Web Site:* www.cedoc.mo.it/estense, pg 1520

Estonian Academy Publishers (Estonia) *Tel:* 645 4504 *Fax:* 646 6026 *E-mail:* niine@kirj.ee *Web Site:* www.kirj.ee, pg 139

Estonian ISBN Agency (Estonia) *Tel:* 630 7372 *Fax:* 631 1200 *E-mail:* eraamat@nlib.ee *Web Site:* www.nlib.ee, pg 139

Estonian Publishers Association (Estonia) *Tel:* (02) 6449866 *Fax:* (02) 6411443 *E-mail:* astat@eki.ee, pg 1266

Angel Estrada y Cia SA (Argentina) *Tel:* (011) 4344-5500 *Fax:* (011) 4331-6527 *E-mail:* editocom@estrada.com.ar *Web Site:* www.estrada.com.ar, pg 5

Estragon Press Ltd (Ireland) *Tel:* (027) 61186 *Fax:* (027) 61186 *E-mail:* estragon@iol.ie, pg 359

Estrella Publishing (Philippines), pg 519

Estudio de Bioinformacion, S L (Spain) *Tel:* (096) 351 46 27 *Fax:* (096) 394 37 27 *E-mail:* bioinformacion@bioinformacion.com *Web Site:* www.bioinformacion.com, pg 583

Instituto de Estudios Fiscales (Spain) *Tel:* (091) 5063740 (ext 51307) *Fax:* (091) 5273951 *E-mail:* ventas.campillo@sgt.meh.es *Web Site:* www.minhac.es/ief, pg 583

Centro de Estudios Monetarios Latinoamericanos (CEMLA) (Mexico) *Tel:* (05) 533-0300 *Fax:* (05) 525-4432 *E-mail:* cemlasub@mail.internet.com.mx *Web Site:* www.cemla.org, pg 465

Instituto de Estudios Peruanos (Peru) *Tel:* (01) 332-6194; (01) 332-2156; (01) 332-6173; (01) 431-3167 *Fax:* (01) 432-4981 *E-mail:* libreria@iep.org.pe *Web Site:* iep.perucultural.org.pe, pg 517

Instituto de Estudios Riojanos (Spain) *Tel:* (0941) 262064; (0941) 262065 *Fax:* (0941) 246667, pg 583

Institut d'Estudis Metropolitans de Barcelona (Spain) *Tel:* (093) 691 83 61; (093) 691 97 97; (093) 691 91 82 *Fax:* (093) 580 65 72 *E-mail:* iermb@uab.es *Web Site:* www.uab.es/iembl, pg 583

Centro De Estudos Africanos (Mozambique) *Tel:* (01) 490828; (01) 499876 *Fax:* (01) 491896 *E-mail:* ceadid@zebra.uem.mz *Web Site:* www.cea.uem.mz, pg 475

l'Eta dell'Acquario (Italy) *Tel:* (011) 6693910 *Fax:* (011) 6693929, pg 388

Etaireia Spoudon Neoellinikou Politismou Kai Genikis Paideias (Greece) *Tel:* (01) 06795 000 *Fax:* (01) 06795 090 *E-mail:* admin@moraitis.edu.gr *Web Site:* www.moraitis.edu.gr, pg 307

Etas Libri (Italy) *Tel:* (02) 50951 *Fax:* (02) 50952309 *E-mail:* etaslab@rcs.it *Web Site:* www.etaslab.it, pg 388

Publicaciones Etea (Spain) *Tel:* (0957) 222100 *Fax:* (0957) 222182 *E-mail:* comunica@etea.com *Web Site:* www.etea.com, pg 583

ETH- Bibliothek (Eidgenossische Technische Hochschule Bibliothek) (Switzerland) *Tel:* (01) 632 21 35 *Fax:* (01) 632 30 13 *E-mail:* info@library.ethz.ch *Web Site:* www.ethbib.ethz.ch, pg 1548

Ethekwini Municipal Libraries (South Africa) *Tel:* (031) 311 1111 *Fax:* (031) 311 2203, pg 1543

Ethics International Press Ltd (United Kingdom) *Tel:* (01223) 357458 *Fax:* (01223) 303598 *E-mail:* info@ethicspress.com *Web Site:* www.ethicspress.com, pg 692

Ethiope Publishing Corporation (Nigeria) *Tel:* (052) 253036, pg 504

Ethiopian Library & Information Association (Ethiopia) *Tel:* (01) 511344 *Fax:* (01) 552544, pg 1561

Ethiopian Nutrition Institute (ENI) (Ethiopia) *Tel:* (01) 151600 *Fax:* (01) 754744, pg 140

Ethnikon Idryma Erevnon (Greece) *Tel:* (01) 7210554 *Fax:* (01) 7246212, pg 1513

Institut d'Ethnologie du Museum National d'Histoire Naturelle (France) *Tel:* (01) 40 79 48 38 *Fax:* (01) 40 79 38 58 *E-mail:* diff.pub@mnhn.fr *Web Site:* www.mnhn.fr/publication, pg 162

Eton Press (Auckland) Ltd (New Zealand) *Tel:* (09) 4183635 *Fax:* (09) 4806488 *E-mail:* info@eton.co.nz *Web Site:* www.eton.co.nz, pg 496

ETR (Editrice Trasporti su Rotaie) (Italy) *Tel:* (03) 6541092 *Fax:* (03) 6541092 *E-mail:* etr@itreni.com *Web Site:* www.itreni.com, pg 388

Etu Ediciones SL (Spain) *Tel:* (093) 2741671 *Fax:* (093) 2741671 *E-mail:* etu@arrakis.es, pg 583

Institut d'Etudes Augustiniennes (France) *Tel:* (01) 43 54 80 25 *Fax:* (01) 43 54 39 55 *E-mail:* iea@wanadoo.fr, pg 162

Institut d'Etudes Slaves IES (France) *Tel:* (01) 43 26 50 89; (01) 43 26 79 18 *Fax:* (01) 43 26 16 23 *E-mail:* etudes.slaves@paris4.sorbonne.fr *Web Site:* www.etudes-slaves.paris4.sorbonne.fr, pg 162

EUDEBA (Editorial Universitaria de Buenos Aires) (Argentina) *Tel:* (011) 4383-8025 *Fax:* (011) 4383-2202 *E-mail:* eudeba@eudeba.com *Web Site:* www.eudeba.com.ar, pg 5

Eugenides Foundation Technical Library (Greece) *Tel:* (01) 9411181 *Fax:* (01) 9417372 *E-mail:* lib@eugenfound.edu.gr *Web Site:* www.eugenfound.edu.gr, pg 1513

Biblioteca Nacional Eugenio Espejo de la Casa de la Cultura Ecuatoriana (Ecuador) *Tel:* (02) 2528-840 *Fax:* (02) 2223-391 *E-mail:* info@cce.org.ec *Web Site:* cce.org.ec, pg 1503

Eugrimas (Lithuania) *Tel:* 52 733 955; 52 754 754 *Fax:* 52 733 955 *E-mail:* info@eugrimas.lt *Web Site:* www.eugrimas.lt, pg 449

Eulama Literary Agencies (Italy) *Tel:* (06) 5407309 *Fax:* (06) 5408772 *E-mail:* eulama@tiscalinet.it, pg 1133

Eular Verlag (Switzerland) *Tel:* (061) 251317 *Fax:* (061) 251286 *E-mail:* eular@reinhardt.ch, pg 623

Eulen Verlag (Germany) *Tel:* (089) 47 07 77 44 *Fax:* (089) 47 07 77 42 *E-mail:* info@eulenverlag.de *Web Site:* www.eulen-verlag.de, pg 221

Eulenhof-Verlag Wolfgang Ehrhardt Heinold (Germany) *Tel:* (040) 490005-14 *Fax:* (040) 490005-15 *E-mail:* w.e.heinold@eulenhof.de *Web Site:* www.eulenhof.de, pg 221

Eulyu Publishing Co Ltd (Republic of Korea) *Tel:* (02) 7338151; (02) 7338152; (02) 7338153 *Fax:* (02) 7329154, pg 438

Eumo Editorial (Spain) *Tel:* (093) 889 28 18; (093) 889 29 61 *Fax:* (093) 889 35 41 *E-mail:* eumoeditorial@eumoeditorial.com *Web Site:* www.eumoeditorial.com, pg 583

Ediciones Eunate (Spain) *Tel:* (0948) 272352 *Fax:* (0948) 172636 *E-mail:* eunate@cin.es *Web Site:* www.cin.es, pg 583

EUNSA (Ediciones Universidad de Navarra SA) (Spain) *Tel:* (0948) 256850 *Fax:* (0948) 256854 *E-mail:* eunsa@cin.es *Web Site:* www.eunsa.es, pg 583

Eurasia Academic Publishers (Bulgaria) *Tel:* (02) 241523 *E-mail:* eurasia@realsci.com *Web Site:* www.biblio.hit.bg, pg 94

Eurasia Press Pte Ltd (Singapore) *Tel:* 2805522 *Fax:* 2800593; 3825458 *E-mail:* eurasia@mbox3.singnet.com.sg, pg 1161, 1181

Eurasia Press Pte Ltd (Singapore) *Tel:* 90012349 *Fax:* 62931269, pg 1222

Eurasia Press Pte Ltd (Singapore) *Tel:* 2805522 *Fax:* 2800593 *E-mail:* eurasia@mbox3.singnet.com.sg, pg 1237

EURASIA PRESS PTE LTD

Eurasia Press Pte Ltd (Singapore) *Tel:* 2805522 *Fax:* 2800593, pg 1246

Eurasia Publishing House Private Ltd (India) *Tel:* (011) 7779891 *Fax:* (011) 7777446 *E-mail:* schandco@giasdl01.vsnl.net.in, pg 334

Eureka Press Ltd (Jamaica) *Tel:* 876-962-3947 *Fax:* 876-961-5383 *E-mail:* eurekapr@cwjamaica.com, pg 413

Euro Print Verlag (Romania) *Tel:* (01) 745-20-11 *Fax:* (01) 312-42-25, pg 539

Euro Translations (United Kingdom) *Tel:* (0208) 6686133 *Fax:* (0208) 6686133 *E-mail:* info@euro-translations.net *Web Site:* www.euro-translations.net, pg 1150

Ediciones Euroamericanas (Mexico) *Tel:* (05) 56 10 01 33 *Fax:* (05) 56 10 01 33 *E-mail:* thielemedina@prodigy.net.mx, pg 465

Eurobook Ltd (United Kingdom) *Tel:* (01865) 858333 *Fax:* (01865) 858263; (01865) 340087 *E-mail:* eurobook@compuserve.com, pg 692

Eurodiastasi (Greece) *Tel:* (01) 3844695 *Fax:* (01) 3844888 *E-mail:* eurodiastasi@internet.gr; eurodiastasi@galaxynet.gr *Web Site:* www.eurodiastasi.gr, pg 1313

EuroGeoGrafiche Mencattini (Italy) *Tel:* (0575) 900010 *Fax:* (0575) 911161 *E-mail:* eurogeo@egm.it *Web Site:* www.egm.it, pg 388

Eurohueco SA (Spain) *Tel:* (093) 7730700 *Fax:* (093) 7730708 *Web Site:* www.eurohueco.es, pg 1223

Eurolibros (Colombia) *Tel:* (01) 2886400 *Fax:* (01) 2450291; (01) 3401811; (01) 3401830; (01) 2886400, pg 1306

Eurolibros Ltda (Colombia) *Tel:* (01) 2886400; (01) 3401837 *Fax:* (01) 2886400, pg 111

Euromedia Group-Odeon (Czech Republic) *Fax:* (02) 241 623 28 *E-mail:* odeon@euromedia.cz, pg 123

Euromonitor PLC (United Kingdom) *Tel:* (020) 7251 8024 *Fax:* (020) 7608 3149 *E-mail:* info@euromonitor.com *Web Site:* www.euromonitor.com, pg 692

Europ Export Edition GmbH (Germany) *Tel:* (06151) 38920 *Fax:* (06151) 38 92 80 *E-mail:* info@abconline.de *Web Site:* www.abconline.de, pg 221

Publicacoes Europa-America Lda (Portugal) *Tel:* (01) 9211461; (01) 9211462 *Fax:* (01) 9217846, pg 531

Edizioni Europa (Italy) *Tel:* (06) 8419124, pg 388

Europa Konyvkiado (Hungary) *Tel:* (01) 331-2700 *Fax:* (01) 331-4162 *E-mail:* info@europakiado.hu *Web Site:* www.europakiado.hu, pg 321

Verlag Europa-Lehrmittel GmbH & Co KG (Germany) *Tel:* (02104) 6916-0 *Fax:* (02104) 6916-27 *E-mail:* info@europa-lehrmittle.de *Web Site:* www.europa-lehrmittel.de, pg 221

Europa Publications (United Kingdom) *Tel:* (020) 7842 2110; (020) 7842 2133 (marketing & sales) *Fax:* (020) 7842 2249 (marketing & sales) *E-mail:* info.europa@tandf.co.uk *Web Site:* www.europapublications.com, pg 692

Europa Union Verlag GmbH (Germany) *Tel:* (0228) 7 29 00 0 *E-mail:* Service@euverlag.de *Web Site:* www.europa-union-verlag.de, pg 222

Europa Verlag AG (Switzerland) *Tel:* (01) 471629, pg 623

Europa Verlag GmbH (Germany) *Tel:* (040) 355434-0 *Fax:* (040) 355434-66 *E-mail:* info@europaverlag.de *Web Site:* www.europaverlag.de, pg 222

Europaeische Verlagsanstalt GmbH & Rotbuch Verlag GmbH & Co KG (Germany) *Tel:* (040) 450194-0 *Fax:* (040) 450194-50 *E-mail:* info@rotbuch.de *Web Site:* www.rotbuch.de; www.europaeische-verlagsanstalt.de, pg 222

Verlag Europaeische Wehrkunde (Germany) *Tel:* (0228) 340884 *Fax:* (040) 79713304, pg 222

Europaring der Buch- und Schallplattenfreunde (Switzerland) *Tel:* (031) 584466, pg 1256

European Association for Health Information & Libraries (Netherlands) *Tel:* (030) 2619663 *Fax:* (030) 2311830 *E-mail:* EAHIL-secr@nic.surfnet.nl *Web Site:* www.eahil.org, pg 1278

European Association of Directory & Database Publishers (Belgium) *Tel:* (02) 6463060 *Fax:* (02) 6463637 *E-mail:* mailbox@eadp.org *Web Site:* www.eadp.be, pg 1262

European Book Service (Netherlands) *Tel:* (030) 6660211 *Fax:* (030) 6662674, pg 1329

European Booksellers Federation (EBF) (Belgium) *Tel:* (02) 223 49 40 *Fax:* (02) 223 49 38 *E-mail:* eurobooks@skynet.be *Web Site:* www.ebf-eu.org, pg 1262

European Foundation for the Improvement of Living & Working Conditions (Ireland) *Tel:* (01) 2043100 *Fax:* (01) 2826456 *E-mail:* postmaster@eurofound.eu.int *Web Site:* www.eurofound.ie, pg 360

European Healthcare Management Association (Ireland) *Tel:* (01) 283 9299 *Fax:* (01) 283 8653 *E-mail:* office@ehma.org *Web Site:* www.ehma.org, pg 360

European Information Association (United Kingdom) *Tel:* (0161) 228 3691 *Fax:* (0161) 236 6547 *E-mail:* eia@libraries.manchester.gov.uk *Web Site:* www.eia.org.uk/, pg 1291

European Schoolbooks Ltd (United Kingdom) *Tel:* (01242) 245252 *Fax:* (01242) 224137 *E-mail:* direct@esb.co.uk *Web Site:* www.eurobooks.co.uk, pg 692, 1350

European Society for Opinion & Marketing Research (Netherlands) *Tel:* (020) 664 21 41 *Fax:* (020) 664 29 22 *E-mail:* email@esomar.nl *Web Site:* www.esomar.org, pg 1278

European University Institute Library (Italy) *Tel:* (055) 4685 340 *Fax:* (055) 4685 283 *E-mail:* euilib@iue.it *Web Site:* www.iue.it, pg 1520

Europhone Language Institute (Pte) Ltd (Singapore) *Tel:* 3373617; 3363992 *Fax:* 3374506, pg 556

Europress Editores e Distribuidores de Publicacoes Lda (Portugal) *Tel:* (01) 9387180; (01) 9387190; (01) 9387317; (01) 9877560; (01) 9381450 *Fax:* (01) 9381452; (01) 9877560 *E-mail:* europress@mail.telepac.pt, pg 531

Eurospan Distribution Center Ltd (United Kingdom) *Tel:* (0161) 7642296 *Fax:* (0161) 7648213 *E-mail:* info@eurospan.co.uk *Web Site:* www.eurospan.co.uk, pg 1350

The Eurospan Group (United Kingdom) *Tel:* (020) 7240 0856 *Fax:* (020) 7379 0609 *E-mail:* info@eurospan.co.uk *Web Site:* www.eurospan.co.uk, pg 692

EUSIDIC (European Association of Information Services) (Netherlands) *Tel:* (020) 589 32 32 *Fax:* (020) 589 32 30 *E-mail:* eusidic@caos.nl *Web Site:* www.eusidic.org, pg 1278

Evagean Publishing (New Zealand) *Tel:* (07) 884-8783 *Fax:* (07) 884-8783 *E-mail:* alison.honeyfield@clear.net.nz *Web Site:* www.evagean.co.nz, pg 496

Evangel Publishing House (Kenya) *Tel:* (020) 860839; (020) 802033 *Fax:* (020) 802034 *E-mail:* evanglit@maf.or.ke; evanglit@panafricachristian.cominsightkenya.com, pg 433

Evangelical Press & Services Ltd (United Kingdom) *Tel:* (01325) 380232 *Fax:* (01325) 466153 *E-mail:* sales@evangelicalpress.org *Web Site:* www.evangelicalpress.org, pg 693

Evangelische Haupt-Bibelgesellschaft und von Cansteinsche Bibelanstalt (Germany) *Tel:* (030) 28878850-0 *Fax:* (030) 28878850-8 *E-mail:* kontakt@ehbg.de *Web Site:* www.ehbg.de, pg 222

Evangelische Verlagsanstalt GmbH (Germany) *Tel:* (0341) 71141-0 *Fax:* (0341) 7114150 *E-mail:* info@eva-leipzig.de *Web Site:* www.eva-leipzig.de, pg 222

INDUSTRY

Evangelischer Presseverband fuer Baden eV (Germany) *Tel:* (0721) 93 27 50 *Fax:* (0721) 9 32 75 20, pg 222

Evangelischer Presseverband fuer Bayern eV (Germany) *Tel:* (089) 121 72-0 *Fax:* (089) 121 72-138 *E-mail:* info@epv.de *Web Site:* www.epv.de, pg 222

Evangelischer Presseverband in Osterreich (Austria) *Tel:* (01) 712 54 61 *Fax:* (01) 712 54 75 *E-mail:* epv@evang.at, pg 50

Evans Brothers Ltd (United Kingdom) *Tel:* (020) 7487 0920 *Fax:* (020) 7487 0921 *E-mail:* sales@evansbrothers.co.uk *Web Site:* www.evansbooks.co.uk, pg 693

Evans Brothers (Nigeria Publishers) Ltd (Nigeria) *Tel:* (022) 417570; (022) 417601; (022) 407626, pg 504

Faith Evans Associates (United Kingdom) *Tel:* (020) 8340 9920 *Fax:* (020) 8340 9910, pg 1139

EVD eenheid Bibliotheek (Netherlands) *Tel:* (070) 778 8888 *Fax:* (070) 778 8889 *E-mail:* evd@info.evd.nl *Web Site:* www.evd.nl, pg 1531

Everbest Printing Co Ltd (Hong Kong) *Tel:* 2727 4433 *Fax:* 2772 7687 *E-mail:* sales@everbest.com.hk *Web Site:* www.everbest.com, pg 1156, 1178, 1218, 1236

Everest Editora (Portugal) *Tel:* (021) 9152483; (021) 9152510 *Fax:* (021) 9152525 *E-mail:* everesteditora@mail.telepac.pt *Web Site:* www.everest.pt, pg 531

Evrodiastasi (Greece) *Tel:* (01) 8611303, pg 307

EVT Energy Video Training & Verlag GmbH (Germany) *Tel:* (069) 431575 *Fax:* (069) 4950974, pg 222

Ewha Womans University Central Library (Republic of Korea) *Tel:* (02) 3277-2114 *Fax:* (02) 3935903 *E-mail:* master@ewha.ac.kr *Web Site:* lib.ewha.ac.kr, pg 1523

Ewha Womans University Press (Republic of Korea) *Tel:* (02) 3277-2114 *Fax:* (02) 393-5903 *Web Site:* www.ewha.ac.kr/, pg 438

Ewing Memorial Library (Pakistan), pg 1535

Ex Libris Forlag A/S (Norway) *Tel:* (022) 47 11 00 *Fax:* (022) 47 11 49 *E-mail:* nwd@egmont.no, pg 509

Ex Libris Press (United Kingdom) *Tel:* (01225) 863595 *Fax:* (01225) 863595 *E-mail:* roger.jonesW@ex-librisbooks.co.uk (orders) *Web Site:* www.ex-librisbooks.co.uk, pg 693

Exandas Publishers (Greece) *Tel:* (01) 3822064; (01) 3084885 *Fax:* (01) 3813065 *E-mail:* exandas@otenet.gr *Web Site:* www.exandasbooks.gr, pg 307

Excel United Company Ltd (Hong Kong) *Tel:* 2889 1078 *Fax:* 2889 1721 *E-mail:* info@excelunited.com *Web Site:* www.excelunited.com, pg 1218

Editura Excelsior Art (Romania) *Tel:* (0256) 201078 *Fax:* (0256) 201078 *E-mail:* edituraelcelsior@rdslink.ro, pg 539

Ediciones Exclusivas SA (Mexico) *Tel:* (05) 815878, pg 465

University of Exeter (United Kingdom) *Tel:* (01392) 263867 *Fax:* (01392) 263871 *E-mail:* library@exeter.ac.uk *Web Site:* www.ex.ac.uk/library/, pg 1553

Exhibitions International NV/SA (Belgium) *Tel:* (016) 296900 *Fax:* (016) 296129 *E-mail:* orders@exhibitionsinternational.be *Web Site:* www.exhibitionsinternational.be, pg 1302

Exil Verlag (Germany) *Tel:* (069) 751102 *Fax:* (069) 751547 *E-mail:* fs7a020@uni-hamburg.de, pg 222

Exisle Publishing Ltd (New Zealand) *Tel:* (09) 817 9192 *Fax:* (09) 817 2295 *E-mail:* admin@exisle.co.nz *Web Site:* www.exisle.co.nz, pg 496

Helen Exley Giftbooks (United Kingdom) *Tel:* (01923) 250505 *Fax:* (01923) 818733 *Toll Free Fax:* 800-440 *E-mail:* enquiry@exleypublications.co.uk, pg 693

Edition Exodus (Switzerland) *Tel:* (01) 2041774 *Fax:* (01) 2024933 *E-mail:* editionexodus@compuserve.com *Web Site:* www.kath.ch/exodus, pg 623

L'Expansion Scientifique Francaise (France) *Tel:* (01) 45 48 42 60 *Fax:* (01) 45 44 81 55 *E-mail:* expansionscientifiquefrancaise@wanadoo.fr *Web Site:* www.expansionscientifique.com, pg 162

Experimental Art Foundation (Australia) *Tel:* (08) 8211 7505 *Fax:* (08) 8211 7323 *E-mail:* eaf@eaf.asn.au *Web Site:* www.eaf.asn.au, pg 22

expert verlag GmbH, Fachverlag fuer Wirtschaft & Technik (Germany) *Tel:* (07159) 92 65-0 *Fax:* (07159) 92 65-20 *E-mail:* expert@expertverlag.de *Web Site:* www.expertverlag.de, pg 222

Expolibri GmbH (Germany) *Tel:* (0341) 2113 231 *Fax:* (0341) 2115 996, pg 222

Export Booksellers Group (United Kingdom) *Tel:* (020) 7834 5477 *Fax:* (020) 7834 8812 *E-mail:* mail@booksellers.org.uk *Web Site:* www.booksellers.org.uk, pg 1163

Exportradet Spraktjanst AB (Sweden) *Tel:* (08) 783 85 00 *Fax:* (08) 662 90 93 *E-mail:* infocenter@swedishtrade.se *Web Site:* www.swedishtrade.se, pg 1149

Express Media Corp (United States) *Tel:* 615-360-6400 *Toll Free Tel:* 888-EXPMEDIA (397-6342) *Fax:* 615-360-3140 *E-mail:* info@expressmedia.com *Web Site:* www.expressmedia.com, pg 1166, 1187

Express Media Corp (United States) *Tel:* 615-360-6400 *Fax:* 615-360-3140 *E-mail:* info@expressmedia.com *Web Site:* www.expressmedia.com, pg 1229

Express Media Corp (United States) *Tel:* 615-360-6400 *Toll Free Tel:* 888-EXPMEDIA (397-6342) *Fax:* 615-360-3140 *E-mail:* info@expressmedia.com *Web Site:* www.expressmedia.com, pg 1249

Express Newspapers (United Kingdom) *Tel:* (020) 7928 8000 *Fax:* (020) 7922 7966, pg 693

Editora Expressao e Cultura-Exped Ltda (Brazil) *Tel:* (021) 445-0333 *Fax:* (021) 445-0996, pg 81

Editorial Extemporaneos SA (Mexico) *Tel:* (05) 5875424 *Fax:* (05) 5878785, pg 465

Extent Verlag und Service Wolfgang M Flamm (Germany) *Tel:* (030) 3279805-0; (030) 3279805-11 *Fax:* (030) 3279805-35 *E-mail:* extent@t-online.de, pg 223

Extenza-Turpin (United Kingdom) *Tel:* (01767) 604 806 *Fax:* (01767) 601 640 *Web Site:* www.extenza-turpin.com, pg 1350

Universidad Externado de Colombia (Colombia) *Tel:* (01) 3428984; (01) 3420288 (ext 3151) *Fax:* (01) 3424948 *E-mail:* publicaciones@uexternado.edu.co *Web Site:* www.uexternado.edu.co, pg 111

Extraordinary People Press (Australia) *Tel:* (02) 9326 6609 *Fax:* (02) 9399 6587 *E-mail:* info@extraordinarypeoplepress.com *Web Site:* www.extraordinarypeoplepress.com, pg 22

Eye Books (United Kingdom) *Tel:* (020) 8743 3276 *Fax:* (020) 8743 3276 *E-mail:* info@eye-books.com *Web Site:* www.eye-books.com, pg 693

Editions Eyrolles (France) *Tel:* (01) 44 41 11 11 *Fax:* (01) 44 41 11 85 *E-mail:* service-lecteurs@editions-eyrolles.com *Web Site:* www.editions-eyrolles.com, pg 162

Ezel Erverdi (Dergah Yayinlari AS) Muessese Muduru (Turkey) *Tel:* (0212) 516 12 62; (0212) 516 00 47 *Fax:* (0212) 519 04 21 *Web Site:* www.dergahyayinlari.com, pg 650

Fabbri (GE) Ltd (United Kingdom) *Tel:* (020) 7836 0519; (020) 7468 5600 *Fax:* (020) 7836 0280 *E-mail:* mailbox@gefabbri.co.uk *Web Site:* www.gefabbri.co.uk, pg 693

Fabel-Verlag Gudrun Liebchen (Germany) *Tel:* (09701) 1463 *Fax:* (09701) 1463, pg 223

Faber & Faber Ltd (United Kingdom) *Tel:* (020) 7465 0045 *Fax:* (020) 7465 0034 *Web Site:* www.faber.co.uk, pg 694

Fabian Society (United Kingdom) *Tel:* (020) 7227 4900 *Fax:* (020) 7976 7153 *E-mail:* info@fabian-society.org.uk *Web Site:* www.fabian-society.org.uk, pg 694

Fabylon-Verlag (Germany) *Tel:* (0172) 8211847 *Fax:* (089) 8110882 *E-mail:* fabylon@t-online.de *Web Site:* www.fabylonzeitspur.de, pg 223

Facet NV (Belgium) *Tel:* (03) 227 40 28 *Fax:* (03) 227 37 92 *E-mail:* facet@village.uunet.be *Web Site:* www.mijnweb.nu/be021988, pg 67

Facet Publishing (United Kingdom) *Tel:* (020) 7255 0590 *Fax:* (020) 7255 0591 *E-mail:* info@facetpublishing.co.uk *Web Site:* www.facetpublishing.co.uk; www.cilip.org.uk, pg 694

Facet Publishing (United Kingdom) *Tel:* (020) 7255 0590 *Fax:* (020) 7255 0591 *E-mail:* info@facetpublishing.co.uk *Web Site:* www.facetpublishing.co.uk, pg 1573

Fachbuchhandlung fur Wirtschaft und Recht Dr Karl Stropek GmbH (Austria) *Tel:* (01) 4795495 *Fax:* (01) 4796230, pg 1300

Fachbuchverlag Leipzig GmbH (Germany) *Tel:* (0341) 4 90 34-0 *Fax:* (0341) 4 80 62 20 *E-mail:* voigt@hanser.de, pg 223

Fachbuchverlag Pfanneberg & Co (Germany) *Tel:* (02104) 6916-0 *Fax:* (02104) 6916-27 *E-mail:* gero.pfanneberg@giessen.netsurf.de *Web Site:* www.pfanneberg.de, pg 223

Fachhochschule Dortmund Hochschulbibliothek (Germany) *Tel:* (0231) 7554047 *Fax:* (0231) 7554604 *E-mail:* bibliothek@fhb.fh-dortmund.de *Web Site:* www.fh.dortmund.de, pg 1509

Fachhochschule Fur Druk, Studiengang Verlagswirtschaft und Verlagsherstellung (Germany) *Tel:* (0711) 685 2807 *Fax:* (0711) 685 6650 *E-mail:* info@hdm-stuttgart.de *Web Site:* www.hdm-stuttgart.de, pg 1176

Fachhochschule Fur Druk, Studiengang Verlagswirtschaft und Verlagsherstellung (Germany) *Tel:* (0711) 6852807 *Fax:* (0711) 6852834 *E-mail:* info@fhd-stuttgart.de *Web Site:* www.fhd-stuttgart.de, pg 1217

Fachhochschule Stuttgart Hochschule der Medien (Germany) *Tel:* (0711) 257060 *Fax:* (0711) 25706300 *E-mail:* office@hdm-stuttgart.de; friedling@hdm-stuttgart.de *Web Site:* www.hdm-stuttgart.de, pg 1509

Fachmedien Verlag Winfried Ruf (FMV) (Germany) *Tel:* (08233) 4924 *Fax:* (08233) 4789, pg 223

Fachverband der Buch und Medienwirtschaft (Austria) *Tel:* (01) 50105 DW 3331; (01) 50105 DW 3333 *Fax:* (01) 50105 DW 3043 *E-mail:* buchwirtschaft@wko.at *Web Site:* www.buchwirtschaft.at, pg 1261

Fachverlag fur das graphische Gewerbe GmbH (Germany) *Tel:* (089) 33036131 *Fax:* (089) 33036100, pg 223

Fachverlag Schiele & Schoen GmbH (Germany) *Tel:* (030) 253 75 20 *Fax:* (030) 251 72 48 *E-mail:* service@schiele-schoen.de *Web Site:* www.schiele-schoen.de, pg 223

Fackeltrager-Verlag GmbH (Germany) *Tel:* (0441) 980 66-0 *Fax:* (0441) 980 66-34 *E-mail:* info@lappan.de *Web Site:* www.lappan.de, pg 223

Factor-Alias (Bulgaria) *Tel:* (02) 747-891 *E-mail:* factoral@omega.bg, pg 94

The Factory Shop Guide (United Kingdom) *Tel:* (020) 7622 3722 *Fax:* (020) 7720 3536 *E-mail:* factshop@macline.co.uk, pg 694

Biblioteca Facultad de Humanidades y Ciencias de la Educacion (Uruguay) *Tel:* (02) 49 11 04; (02) 49 11 05; (02) 49 11 06 *Fax:* (02) 48 43 03 *E-mail:* biblio@fhudec.edu.uy *Web Site:* www.rau.edu.uy/universidad/fhcet.htm, pg 1555

Faculte de Medecine de Pharmacie et d'Odonto-Stomatologie (Mali) *Tel:* 22 52 77 *Fax:* 22 96 58 *E-mail:* codiawara@caramail.com, pg 1527

Bibliotheque de la Faculte des Sciences de Tunis (Tunisia) *Tel:* (01) 872600 *Fax:* (01) 885073, pg 1551

Faculte des Sciences Humaines et Sociales de Tunis (Tunisia) *Tel:* (01) 560 950; 71 56 08 58 *Fax:* 71 56 75 51, pg 648

Facultes catholiques de Kinshasa (The Democratic Republic of the Congo) *Tel:* (0243) 88 46 965 *Fax:* (0243) 88 46 965 *E-mail:* facakin@yahoo.fr, pg 114

Facultes Catoliques de Kinshasa (The Democratic Republic of the Congo) *Tel:* (088) 46 965 *Fax:* (088) 46 965 *E-mail:* facakin@ic.cd *Web Site:* www.cenco.cd/facultescath/, pg 114

Library of the Faculty of Law (Lebanon) *Tel:* (01) 200 625 *Fax:* (01) 215473 *E-mail:* css.biblio@usj.edu.lb *Web Site:* www.biblio-css.usj.edu.lb, pg 1524

FADL's Forlag A/S (Denmark) *Tel:* 35 35 62 87 *Fax:* 35 36 62 29 *E-mail:* forlag@fadl.dk *Web Site:* forlag.fadl.dk, pg 131

Forlaget Fag og Kultur (Norway) *Tel:* (022) 23 30 24 00 *Fax:* (022) 23 30 24 04 *E-mail:* firmapost@fagogkultur.no *Web Site:* www.fagogkultur.no, pg 509

Olaiya Fagbamigbe Ltd (Publishers) (Nigeria) *Tel:* (034) 2075, pg 504

Forlaget for Faglitteratur A/S (Denmark) *Tel:* 33137900 *Fax:* 33145156, pg 131

Fahrner & Fahrner (Germany) *Tel:* (069) 584777 *Fax:* (069) 584777 *E-mail:* mfahrner@t-online.de *Web Site:* www.themodernword.com/tlon/index.html, pg 223

Fairfield Marketing Group Inc (United States) *Tel:* 203-261-5585; 203-261-5568 *Fax:* 203-261-0884 *E-mail:* ffldmktgrp@aol.com *Web Site:* www.fairfieldmarketing.com, pg 1187, 1229

Fairfield Marketing Group Inc (United States) *Tel:* 203-261-5585; 203-261-5568 *Fax:* 203-261-0884 *E-mail:* ffijmktgrp@aol.com *Web Site:* www.fairfieldmarketing.com, pg 1249

Faksimile Verlag AG (Switzerland) *Tel:* (041) 4290820 *Fax:* (041) 4290840 *E-mail:* faksimile@faksimile.ch *Web Site:* www.faksimile.ch, pg 623

Christa Falk-Verlag (Germany) *Tel:* (08667) 14 13 *Fax:* (08667) 14 17 *E-mail:* email@chfalk-verlag.de *Web Site:* www.chfalk-verlag.de, pg 223

Falken-Verlag GmbH (Germany) *Tel:* (06127) 702-0 *Fax:* (06127) 702-133 *E-mail:* vertrieb.verlagsgruppe@bertelsmann.de *Web Site:* www.randomhouse.de/falken, pg 223

Editions Fallois (France) *Tel:* (01) 42669195 *Fax:* (01) 49240637, pg 162

C J Fallon (Ireland), pg 360

Fama (Bulgaria) *Tel:* (02) 881175; (02) 657006 *Fax:* (02) 657006, pg 94

Famedram Publishers Ltd (United Kingdom) *Tel:* (01651) 842429 *Fax:* (01651) 842180 *E-mail:* famedram@artwork.co.uk, pg 694

Family Health Publications (Australia) *Tel:* (08) 9389 8777 *Fax:* (08) 9389 8444 *Web Site:* www.familyhealth.info, pg 22

Family Reading Publications (Australia) *Tel:* (03) 5334 3244 *Fax:* (03) 5334 3299 *E-mail:* info@familyreading.com.au *Web Site:* www.familyreading.com.au, pg 22

Fan Noli Verlag Rexhep Hida (Albania) *Tel:* (042) 61673, pg 1

Editions Pierre Fanlac (France) *Tel:* (05) 53-53-41-90 *Fax:* (05) 53-08-05-85 *E-mail:* info@fanlac.com *Web Site:* www.fanlac.com, pg 162

Fanucci (Italy) *Tel:* (06) 639366384 *Fax:* (06) 6382998 *E-mail:* info@fanucci.it *Web Site:* www.fanucci.it, pg 388

Far East Book Co Ltd (Taiwan, Province of China) *Tel:* (02) 2311 8740 *Fax:* (02) 2311 4184 *E-mail:* service@mail.fareast.com.tw *Web Site:* www.fareast.com.tw, pg 639

Far Eastern University Library (Philippines) *Tel:* (02) 735-5649 *Fax:* (02) 732-0232 *Web Site:* www.feu.edu.ph/library.asp, pg 1536

Faradawn cc (South Africa) *Tel:* (011) 885-1847 *Fax:* (011) 885-1829 *E-mail:* faradawn@icon.co.za *Web Site:* www.faradawn.co.za, pg 1340

Clive Farahar & Sophie Dupre Booksellers (United Kingdom) *Tel:* (01249) 821121 *Fax:* (01249) 821202 *E-mail:* sophie@farahardupre.co.uk *Web Site:* www.farahardupre.co.uk, pg 1350

Editions Farel (France) *Tel:* (01) 64 68 46 44 *Fax:* (01) 64 68 39 90 *E-mail:* lire@editionsfarel.com *Web Site:* www.editionsfarel.com, pg 162

Farm-level Applied Methods for East & Southern Africa (FARMESA) (Zimbabwe) *Tel:* (04) 758051-4 *Fax:* (04) 758055 *E-mail:* fspzim@internet.co.zw; fspzim@harare.iafrica.com *Web Site:* www.farmesa.co.zw, pg 783

T C Farries & Co Ltd (United Kingdom) *Tel:* (01387) 720755 *Fax:* (01387) 721105, pg 1350

Farseeing Publishing Company Ltd (Taiwan, Province of China) *Tel:* (02) 23921167 *Fax:* (02) 3225455 *E-mail:* fars@msb.ninet.net *Web Site:* www.farseeing.com.tw, pg 639

Farsight Press (United Kingdom) *Tel:* (020) 8675 1693, pg 694

Fassbaender Verlag (Austria) *Tel:* (01) 8923546 *Fax:* (01) 8923546-22 *E-mail:* mail@fassbaender.com *Web Site:* www.fassbaender.com, pg 50

Editions Fata Morgana (France) *Tel:* (04) 67 54 40 40 *Fax:* (04) 67 04 14 91 *E-mail:* davidini@wanadoo.fr *Web Site:* perso.wanadoo.fr/fatamorgana, pg 162

Editorial Fata Morgana SA de CV (Mexico) *Tel:* (055) 52 80 08 29 *Fax:* (055) 52 80 81 37 *E-mail:* editorial@fatamorgana.com.mx *Web Site:* www.fatamorgana.com.mx, pg 465

Fatatrac (Italy) *Tel:* (055) 6810124 *Fax:* (055) 6810260 *E-mail:* info@fatatrac.com *Web Site:* www.fatatrac.com/, pg 388

Al-Fateh University, The Central Library (Libyan Arab Jamahiriya) *Tel:* (022) 605441 *Fax:* (022) 605460, pg 1525

Ekkehard Faude Verlag (Germany) *Tel:* (041 71) 6883555 *Fax:* (041 71) 6883565, pg 223

Faust Vrani (Croatia) *Tel:* (01) 231 3646; (01) 2332 302 *Fax:* (01) 231 3646; (01) 2332 302 *E-mail:* pontes@pontes.com, pg 118

Ediciones Librerias Fausto (Argentina) *Tel:* (011) 4372-4919 *Fax:* (011) 4372-3914 *E-mail:* fausto@fausto.com *Web Site:* www.fausto.com, pg 6

Favorit-Verlag Huntemann und Markus & Co GmbH (Germany) *Tel:* (07222) 2 22 54 *Fax:* (07222) 2 98 38 *E-mail:* info@favorit-verlag.de *Web Site:* www.favorit-verlag.de, pg 223

Librairie Artheme Fayard (France) *Tel:* (01) 45498200 *Fax:* (01) 42224017 *Web Site:* www.editions-fayard.fr, pg 163

Fazlee Sons (Pvt) Ltd (Pakistan) *Tel:* (021) 214585; (021) 212289 *Fax:* (021) 6640522 *E-mail:* fazlee@tarique.khi.sdnpk.undp.org, pg 512

FBT de R Editions (France) *Tel:* (01) 41 15 19 69; (06) 07 68 33 71 *Fax:* (01) 41 15 19 69, pg 163

FCA Editora de Informatica (Portugal) *Tel:* (021) 3151218 *Fax:* (021) 577827, pg 531

Editora FCO Ltda (Brazil) *Tel:* (031) 2131288 *Fax:* (031) 2243825, pg 81

Feakle Press (Australia) *Tel:* (02) 9557 3248, pg 22

Feather Books (United Kingdom) *Tel:* (01743) 872177 *Fax:* (01743) 872177 *E-mail:* john@waddysweb.freeuk.com *Web Site:* www.waddysweb.com, pg 694

FEDA SA (Switzerland) *Tel:* (091) 9235677 *Fax:* (091) 9220171, pg 623

Federacao Brasileira de Associacoes de Bibliotecarios - Comissao Brasileira de Documentacao Juridica (FEBAB/CBDJ) (Brazil) *Tel:* (011) 3257-9979 *Fax:* (011) 3257-9979 *E-mail:* febab@febab.org.br *Web Site:* www.febab.org.br, pg 1559

Federacion de Gremios de Editores de Espana (FGEE) (Spain) *Tel:* (091) 5345195 *Fax:* (091) 5352625 *E-mail:* fgee@fge.es *Web Site:* www.federacioneditores.org, pg 1284

Federal Publications (S) Pte Ltd (Singapore) *Tel:* 62139288 *Fax:* 62844733 *E-mail:* tpl@tpl.com.sg *Web Site:* www.tpl.com.sg, pg 556

Federal Publications Sdn Bhd (Malaysia) *Tel:* (03) 7351511 *Fax:* (03) 73 64620 *E-mail:* kesoon@pc.jaring.my, pg 455

Federation d'Activities Culturelles, Fac Editions (France) *Tel:* (01) 45 48 76 51 *Fax:* (01) 42 22 22 31, pg 163

Federation de l'Imprimerie et de la Communaute Graphique-FICG (France) *Tel:* (01) 46 34 21 15 *Fax:* (01) 46 33 73 34 *E-mail:* ficg@ficg.fr, pg 1268

Federation des Enseignants Documentalistes de l'Education nationale (France) *Tel:* (01) 43 72 45 60 *Fax:* (01) 43 72 45 60 *E-mail:* fadben@wanadoo.fr *Web Site:* www.fadben.asso.fr, pg 1562

Federation Francaise de la Randonnee Pedestre (France) *Tel:* (01) 44 89 93 90 *Fax:* (01) 40 35 85 48 *E-mail:* info@ffrp.asso.fr *Web Site:* asp.ffrp.asso.fr, pg 163

Federation Internationale des Traducteurs (FIT) (Austria) *Tel:* (01) 4403607; (01) 4709819 *Fax:* (01) 4403756; (01) 4708194 *E-mail:* info@fit.org *Web Site:* www.fit-ift.org/, pg 1261

Federation Luxembourgeoise des Editeurs de Livres, ASBL (Luxembourg) *Tel:* 439444 *Fax:* 439450 *E-mail:* promoculture@ibm.net, pg 1276

Federation of Children's Book Groups (United Kingdom) *Tel:* (0113) 2588910 *Fax:* (0113) 2588920 *E-mail:* info@fcbg.org.uk *Web Site:* www.fcbg.org.uk, pg 1291

Federation of European Publishers (FEP) (Belgium) *Tel:* (02) 7701110 *Fax:* (02) 7712071 *Web Site:* www.fep-fee.be, pg 1262

Federation of Indian Publishers (India) *Tel:* (011) 26964847; (011) 26852263 *Fax:* (011) 26864054 *E-mail:* fip1@satyam.net.in *Web Site:* www.fiponweb.com, pg 1273

The Federation Press (Australia) *Tel:* (02) 9552-2200 *Fax:* (02) 9552-1681 *E-mail:* info@federationpress.com.au *Web Site:* www.federationpress.com.au, pg 22

Federico Motta Editore SpA (Italy) *Tel:* (02) 300761; (02) 30076231 *Fax:* (02) 38010046; (02) 33403275 *E-mail:* info@mottaeditore.it *Web Site:* www.mottaeditore.it, pg 389

Libreria Universal Carlos Federspiel (Costa Rica), pg 1307

Feguagiskia' Studios (Italy) *Tel:* (010) 2757544 *Fax:* (010) 2510838, pg 389

Frank Fehmers Productions (Netherlands) *Tel:* (020) 6238766 *Fax:* (020) 6246262 *Web Site:* www.fbg.nl/34927, pg 482

Fehr'sche Buchhandlung AG (Switzerland) *Tel:* (071) 222 11 52; (071) 222 53 81, pg 1344

Editions Francois Feij (Switzerland) *Tel:* (021) 8254675, pg 623

Felag Islenskra Bokautgefenda (Iceland) *Tel:* 511 8020 *Fax:* 511 5020 *E-mail:* baekur@mmedia.is, pg 1272

Feldheim Publishers Ltd (Israel) *Tel:* (02) 6513947 *Fax:* (02) 6536061 *E-mail:* sales@feldheim.com *Web Site:* www.feldheim.com, pg 367

Fellowship of Australian Writers (Australia) *Tel:* (03) 9528 7088 *Fax:* (03) 9528 7088 *E-mail:* faw@ozemail.com.au *Web Site:* www.writers.asn.au, pg 1395

Fellowship of Australian Writers (Vic) Inc (Australia) *Tel:* (03) 9528 7088 *Fax:* (03) 9528 7088 *Web Site:* www.writers.asn.au, pg 1396

Felta Book Sales Inc (Philippines) *Tel:* (02) 912-1397; (02) 438-1756 *Fax:* (02) 912-7633, pg 1335

Giangiacomo Feltrinelli SpA (Italy) *Tel:* (02) 725721 *Fax:* (02) 72572500, pg 389

Libreria Feltrinelli (Italy) *Tel:* (02) 86463485 *Fax:* (02) 72001064 *Web Site:* www.feltrinelli.it, pg 1320

Feltron-Elektronik Zeissler & Co GmbH (Germany) *Tel:* (02241) 48670 *Fax:* (02241) 404241, pg 223

Editions Des Femmes (France) *Tel:* (01) 42 22 60 74 *Fax:* (01) 42 22 62 73 *E-mail:* info@desfemmes.fr *Web Site:* www.desfemmes.fr, pg 163

Fen Kitabevi (Turkey) *Tel:* (0312) 425311 *Fax:* (0312) 4185109; (0312) 4171733, pg 1346

Fenda Edicoes (Portugal) *Tel:* (021) 8823650 *Fax:* (021) 8823659 *E-mail:* info@fenda.pt, pg 531

Fenice 2000 (Italy) *Tel:* (02) 66984638; (02) 67075155 *Fax:* (02) 67074283, pg 389

Fenix-Kustannus Oy (Finland) *Tel:* (09) 420 8190 *Fax:* (09) 420 8045, pg 142

Editions Le Fennec (Morocco) *Tel:* (02) 220519; (02) 268008; (02) 264380 *Fax:* (02) 264941 *E-mail:* fennec@techno.net.ma, pg 474

FEP International Private Ltd (Singapore) *Tel:* 4743135 *Fax:* 4752389, pg 556

FEP International Sdn Bhd (Malaysia) *Tel:* (03) 7036150; (03) 7036152; (03) 7036154 *Fax:* (03) 7036989, pg 456

Ferd Dummler's Verlag (Germany) *Tel:* (02203) 3029-0 *Fax:* (02203) 3029-40, pg 223

Ferdinand Berger und Sohne (Austria) *Tel:* (02982) 4161-332 *Fax:* (02982) 4161-382 *E-mail:* druckerei.office@berger.at *Web Site:* www.berger.at, pg 50

Ferdinand Enke Verlag (Germany) *Tel:* (0711) 8931-0 *Fax:* (0711) 8931-706 *Web Site:* www.enke.de, pg 224

Ferdowsi University of Mashhad Central Library & Information Centre (Islamic Republic of Iran) *Tel:* (0511) 8789263; (0511) 8796798 *Fax:* (0511) 8796822 *E-mail:* centlib@ferdowsi.um.ac.ir *Web Site:* c-library.um.ac.ir, pg 1517

Feria Chilena del Libro Ltda (Chile) *Tel:* (02) 632 7334; (02) 639 6758 *Fax:* (02) 633 9374 *E-mail:* ventas@feriachilenadellibro.cl *Web Site:* www.feriachilenadellibro.cl, pg 1305

Feria del Libro (Uruguay) *Tel:* (02) 900 42 48 *Fax:* (02) 900 20 70, pg 1355

Livraria Ferin Ltda (Portugal) *Tel:* (021) 3424422; (021) 3469033 *Fax:* (021) 3471101 *E-mail:* livraria.ferin@mail.telepac.pt, pg 1337

Fern House (United Kingdom) *Tel:* (01353) 740222 *Fax:* (01353) 741987 *E-mail:* info@fernhouse.com *Web Site:* www.fernhouse.com, pg 1184

Editorial Libreria Amalio M Fernandez (Uruguay) *Tel:* (02) 9151782; (02) 295 26 84 *Fax:* (02) 295 17 82, pg 777

Libreria Amalio M Fernandez SRL (Uruguay) *Tel:* (02) 95 26 84 *Fax:* (02) 95 17 82, pg 1355

Fernandez Editores SA de CV (Mexico) *Tel:* (05) 6056557 *Fax:* (05) 6889173 *Web Site:* www.fernandezeditores.com.mx, pg 465

Fernfawn Publications (Australia) *Tel:* (07) 3202 6157 *Fax:* (07) 3202 6157, pg 22

Fernhurst Books (United Kingdom) *Tel:* (01903) 882277 *Fax:* (01903) 882715 *E-mail:* sales@fernhurstbooks.co.uk *Web Site:* www.fernhurstbooks.co.uk, pg 694

Fernwood Press (Pty) Ltd (South Africa) *Tel:* (021) 7948686 *Fax:* (021) 7948339 *E-mail:* ferpress@iafrica.com *Web Site:* www.fernwoodpress.co.za, pg 563

Ferozsons (Pvt) Ltd (Pakistan) *Tel:* (042) 6301196; (042) 6301197; (042) 6301198 *Fax:* (042) 6369204 *E-mail:* ferozsons@showroom.edunet.sdnpk.undp.org, pg 512

Ferozsons (Pvt) Ltd (Pakistan) *Tel:* (042) 6301196; (042) 6301197; (042) 6301198; (042) 111-62-62-62 *Fax:* (042) 6369204 *E-mail:* ferozsons@showroom.edunet.sdnpk.undp.org *Web Site:* www.ferozsons.com.pk, pg 1333

Chaves Ferreira Publicacoes SA (Portugal) *Tel:* (021) 3871373 *Fax:* (021) 7161396 *E-mail:* chavesferreira@mail.telepac.pt, pg 531

Franz Ferzak World & Space Publications (Germany) *Tel:* (09446) 1403, pg 224

Festina Lente Edizioni (Italy) *Tel:* (055) 292612 *Fax:* (055) 292612, pg 389

Festland Verlag GmbH (Germany) *Tel:* (0228) 36 20 21-23 *Fax:* (0228) 35 17 71 *E-mail:* verlag@festland-verlag.de *Web Site:* www.oeckl.de, pg 224

Festo Didactic GmbH & Co KG (Germany) *Tel:* (0711) 3467-0 *Toll Free Tel:* 800 5600967 (orders) *Fax:* (0711) 34754-88500 *Toll Free Fax:* 800 5600843 (orders) *E-mail:* did@festo.com *Web Site:* www.festo.com/didactic, pg 224

Editions du Feu Nouveau (France) *Tel:* (01) 44844797, pg 163

FF Press (Romania) *Tel:* (01) 6191544 *Fax:* (01) 3129694, pg 540

FFSL (Federation francaise des syndicats de libraires) (France) *Tel:* (01) 42 82 00 03 *Fax:* (01) 42 82 10 51, pg 1268

FGUP Izdatelstvo Mashinostroenie (Russian Federation) *Tel:* (095) 2683858 *Fax:* (095) 2694897 *E-mail:* mashpubl@mashin.ru *Web Site:* www.mashin.ru, pg 544

FHB Exporter (Egypt (Arab Republic of Egypt)) *Tel:* (02) 2358329 *Fax:* (02) 2358329 *E-mail:* fhb@link.net, pg 1309

FHG Publications Ltd (United Kingdom) *Tel:* (0141) 8870428 *Fax:* (0141) 8897204 *E-mail:* fhg@ipcmedia.com *Web Site:* www.holidayguides.com, pg 694

FIAF (International Federation of Film Archives) (Belgium) *Tel:* (02) 538 3065 *Fax:* (02) 534 4774 *E-mail:* info@fiafnet.org *Web Site:* www.fiafnet.org, pg 1262

Fiantsorohana NY Boky Malagasy, Office du Livre Malgache (Madagascar) *Tel:* (02) 24449, pg 1276

FiberMark Red Bridge International Ltd (United Kingdom) *Tel:* (01204) 556900 *Fax:* (01204) 384754 *E-mail:* sales@redbridge.co.uk *Web Site:* www.redbridge.co.uk, pg 1238

Fibre Leather Manufacturing Corp (United States) *Tel:* 508-997-4557 *Toll Free Tel:* 800-358-6012 *Fax:* 508-997-7268 *E-mail:* fibreleather@earthlink.net, pg 1240

Fibre Verlag (Germany) *Tel:* (0541) 431838 *Fax:* (0541) 432786 *E-mail:* info@fibre-verlag.de *Web Site:* www.fibre-verlag.de, pg 224

Fiction Factory International Ltd (Denmark) *Tel:* (043) 33 75 55 09 *Fax:* (043) 33 75 55 44, pg 1251

Sadie Fields Productions Ltd (United Kingdom) *Tel:* (020) 89969970 *Fax:* (020) 89969977 *E-mail:* edith@tangobooks.co.uk, pg 694

Wolfgang Fietkau Verlag (Germany) *Tel:* (033203) 71 105 *Fax:* (033203) 71 109 *E-mail:* fietkau@fietkau.de *Web Site:* www.fietkau.de, pg 224

Julio de Figueiredo, Lda (Portugal) *Tel:* (021) 754 16 00 *Fax:* (021) 754 16 09 *E-mail:* info@jlf.pt *Web Site:* www.jlf.pt, pg 1337

Figueirinhas, Lda (Portugal) *Tel:* (022) 53 325 300 *Fax:* (022) 53 325 907 *E-mail:* correio@liv_figueirinhas.pt, pg 1337

Livraria Editora Figueirinhas Lda (Portugal) *Tel:* (022) 324985 *Fax:* (022) 3325907 *E-mail:* correio@liv-figueirinhas.pt, pg 531

Filadelfia forlag (Iceland) *Tel:* 552-5155; 552-0735 *Fax:* 562-0735 *E-mail:* filadelfia-forlag@gospel.is, pg 325

Editions Filipacchi-Sonodip (France) *Tel:* (01) 41 34 90 69; (01) 41 34 90 55 *Fax:* (01) 41 34 90 70, pg 163

Filistor Publishing (Greece) *Tel:* (01) 3818457, pg 1313

Filmfaust Verlag - Internationale Filmzeitschrift (Germany) *Tel:* (069) 748305 *Fax:* (069) 564321 *E-mail:* info@filmfaust.de *Web Site:* www.filmfaust.de, pg 224

Ekdoseis Filon (Greece) *Tel:* (01) 3618705 *Fax:* (01) 3618705, pg 307

Filozofski Fakultet Sveucilista u Zagrebu (Croatia) *Tel:* (01) 6120111 *Fax:* (01) 6156879 *E-mail:* tajnik_fakultet@ffzg.hr *Web Site:* www.ffzg.hr, pg 118

Financial Training Co (United Kingdom) *Tel:* (020) 7481 6050 *Fax:* (020) 7265 0337 *Web Site:* www.financial-training.com, pg 694

Finansy i Statistika Publishing House (Russian Federation) *Tel:* (095) 925-47-08 *Fax:* (095) 925-09-57 *E-mail:* mail@finstat.ru *Web Site:* www.finstat.ru, pg 544

Finch Publishing (Australia) *Tel:* (02) 9418 6247 *Fax:* (02) 9418 8878 *E-mail:* info@finch.com.au *Web Site:* www.finch.com.au, pg 22

Findhorn Press Inc (United Kingdom) *Tel:* (01309) 690582 *Fax:* (01309) 690036 *E-mail:* info@findhornpress.com *Web Site:* www.findhornpress.com, pg 695

Fine Art Publishing Pty Ltd (Australia) *Tel:* (02) 99668400 *Fax:* (02) 99660355 *E-mail:* info@gbpub.com.au *Web Site:* www.gbpub.com.au, pg 22

Bokforlaget Fingraf AB (Sweden) *Tel:* (08) 550 300 23 *Fax:* (08) 550 695 70, pg 611

Emil Fink Verlag (Germany) *Tel:* (0711) 814646 *Fax:* (0711) 8106070 *E-mail:* info@fink-verlag.de *Web Site:* www.fink-verlag.de, pg 224

Verlagsgruppe J Fink GmbH & Co KG (Germany) *Tel:* (0711) 81 4646 *Fax:* (0711) 81 06070 *E-mail:* info@fink-verlag.de *Web Site:* www.fink-verlag.de, pg 224

Wilhelm Fink GmbH & Co Verlags-KG (Germany) *Tel:* (05251) 127-5; (05251) 127-842 *Fax:* (05251) 127-860 *E-mail:* kontakt@fink.de *Web Site:* www.fink.de, pg 224

Finken Verlag GmbH (Germany) *Tel:* (06171) 6388-0 *Fax:* (06171) 6388-44 *E-mail:* info@finken.de *Web Site:* www.finken.de, pg 224

The Arnold & Leona Finkler Institute of Holocaust Research (Israel) *Tel:* (03) 5340333 *Fax:* (03) 5351233 *E-mail:* michmad@mail.biu.ac.il *Web Site:* www.biu.ac.il, pg 367

Finlands svenska forfattareforening (Finland) *Tel:* (09) 446266 *Fax:* (09) 446871, pg 1399

Finnish ISBN Agency (Finland) *Tel:* (09) 19144327 *Fax:* (09) 19144341 *E-mail:* isbn-keskus@helsinki.fi *Web Site:* www.lib.helsinki.fi, pg 1266

Finnish PEN Centre (Finland) *Tel:* (09) 3431186 *Fax:* (09) 3431186, pg 1399

Firebird Books Ltd (United Kingdom) *Tel:* (01202) 715349 (sales); (01258) 454675 (editorial) *Fax:* (01202) 736191 *E-mail:* skboorh@bournemouth-net.co.uk, pg 695

Firma KLM Privatee Ltd, Publishers & International Booksellers (India) *Tel:* (033) 274391; (033) 4681209 *Fax:* (033) 276544, pg 334

First & Best in Education Ltd (United Kingdom) *Tel:* (01536) 399004 (editorial); (01536) 399005 (accounts) *Fax:* (01536) 399012 *E-mail:* anne@firstandbest.co.uk *Web Site:* www.firstandbest.co.uk, pg 695

First Edition Translations Ltd (United Kingdom) *Tel:* (01223) 356733 *Fax:* (01223) 321488 *E-mail:* info@firstedit.co.uk *Web Site:* www.firstedit.co.uk, pg 1150

Editions First (France) *Tel:* (01) 40 21 46 46 *Fax:* (01) 55 43 25 20 *E-mail:* firstinfo@efirst.com *Web Site:* www.efirst.com, pg 163

Librairie Fischbacher, International Art Book Distribution (import-export) (France) *Tel:* (01) 43 26 84 87 *Fax:* (01) 43 26 48 87, pg 163

F Fischer Book Service (Israel) *Tel:* (04) 255830 *Fax:* (04) 244970, pg 1319

Fischer & Co (Sweden) *Tel:* (08) 242160 *Fax:* (08) 247825 *E-mail:* bokforlaget@fischer-co.se *Web Site:* www.fischer-co.se, pg 611

Harald Fischer Verlag GmbH (Germany) *Tel:* (09131) 205620 *Fax:* (09131) 206028 *E-mail:* info@haraldfischerverlag.de *Web Site:* www.haraldfischerverlag.de, pg 224

Verkehrs-Verlag J Fischer GmbH & Co KG (Germany) *Tel:* (0211) 99193-0 *Fax:* (0211) 6801544; (0211) 9919327 *E-mail:* vvf@verkehrsverlag-fischer.de *Web Site:* www.verkehrsverlag-fischer.de, pg 224

Karin Fischer Verlag GmbH (Germany) *Tel:* (0241) 960 90 90 *Fax:* (0241) 960 90 99 *Web Site:* www.karin-fischer-verlag.de, pg 225

Fischer Media AG fur Verlag und Publishing (Switzerland) *Tel:* (031) 7205111 *Fax:* (031) 7205112 *E-mail:* info@fischerprint.ch *Web Site:* www.fischergroup.ch, pg 623

Verlag Reinhard Fischer (Germany) *Tel:* (089) 791 88 92 *Fax:* (089) 791 83 10 *E-mail:* verlagfischer@compuserve.de *Web Site:* www.verlag-reinhard-fischer.de, pg 225

Rita G Fischer Verlag (Germany) *Tel:* (069) 941942-0 *Fax:* (069) 941942-99; (069) 941942-98 *E-mail:* r.g.fischer.verlag@t-online.de *Web Site:* www.buchhandel.de/r.g.fischer/, pg 225

S Fischer Verlag GmbH (Germany) *Tel:* (069) 6062-0 *Fax:* (069) 6062-319 *Web Site:* www.fischerverlage.de, pg 225

Fischer Taschenbuch Verlag GmbH (Germany) *Tel:* (069) 60620 *Fax:* (069) 6062352 *Web Site:* www.s-fischer.de, pg 225

Anne Louise Fisher & Suzy Lucas (United Kingdom) *Tel:* (020) 7494 4609 *Fax:* (020) 7494 4611, pg 1139

Fishing News Books Ltd (United Kingdom) *Tel:* (01865) 206206 *Fax:* (01865) 721205 *E-mail:* fishing.newsbooks@oxon.blackwellpublishing.com *Web Site:* www.fishknowledge.com, pg 695

Fitzwilliam Publishing Co Ltd (Ireland) *Tel:* (01) 614575 *Fax:* (01) 614575, pg 360

The Five Mile Press Pty Ltd (Australia) *Tel:* (03) 8756 5500 *Fax:* (03) 8756 5588 *E-mail:* publishing@fivemile.com.au *Web Site:* www.fivemile.com.au, pg 22

Editions Fivedit (France) *Tel:* (04) 50 66 33 78 *Fax:* (04) 50 23 33 08 *E-mail:* fivedit.sa@wanadoo.fr, pg 163

Izdatelstvo Fizkultura i Sport (Russian Federation) *Tel:* (095) 2582690 *Fax:* (095) 2001217, pg 545

Fizmatlit Publishing Co (Russian Federation) *Tel:* (095) 3347151 *Fax:* (095) 3360666, pg 545

Fjolvi (Iceland) *Tel:* 5688433 *Fax:* 5588142 *E-mail:* fjolvi@fjolvi.is *Web Site:* www.fjolvi.is, pg 325

Flaccovio Dario (Italy) *Tel:* (091) 202533 *Fax:* (091) 227702 *E-mail:* press@darioflaccovio.com *Web Site:* www.darioflaccovio.com, pg 389

Flaccovio Editore (Italy) *Tel:* (091) 589442 *Fax:* (091) 331992 *E-mail:* info@flaccovio.com *Web Site:* www.flaccovio.com, pg 389

Libreria S F Flaccovio (Italy) *Tel:* (091) 589442 *Fax:* (091) 331992 *E-mail:* info@flaccovio.com *Web Site:* www.flaccovio.com, pg 1320

Werner Flach Internationale Fachbuchhandlung (Germany) *Tel:* (069) 9591750 *Fax:* (069) 95917522 *E-mail:* fachbuch@flachbuch.com *Web Site:* www.flachbuch.com, pg 1311

Ediciones FLACSO Costa Rica (Costa Rica) *Tel:* 2346890 *Fax:* 2256779, pg 115

Flactem (Australia) *Tel:* (03) 9889 6855 *Fax:* (03) 98888948, pg 22

Flambard Press (United Kingdom) *Tel:* (01434) 674360 *Fax:* (01434) 674178 *Web Site:* www.flambardpress.co.uk, pg 695

Les Editions du Flamboyant (Benin) *Tel:* 310220 *Fax:* 312079 *E-mail:* IPEC@leland.bj, pg 75

Flame Tree Publishing (United Kingdom) *Tel:* (020) 7386 4700 *Fax:* (020) 7386 4700 *E-mail:* info@flametreepublishing.com *Web Site:* www.flametreepublishing.com, pg 695

Flammarion SA (France) *Tel:* (01) 40513008; (01) 4053127 *Fax:* (01) 43250118; (01) 43292148, pg 163

Flammarion (France) *Tel:* (01) 40 51 31 00; (01) 40 51 31 41 *Fax:* (01) 43 29 21 48 *Web Site:* www.flammarion.com/, pg 1310

Flechsig Buchvertrieb (Germany) *Tel:* (0931) 385235 *Fax:* (0931) 385305 *E-mail:* info@verlagshaus.com *Web Site:* www.verlagshaus.com, pg 225

Erich Fleischer Verlag (Germany) *Tel:* (04202) 517-0 *Fax:* (04202) 517-41 *E-mail:* info@efv-online.de *Web Site:* www.efv-online.de, pg 225

Fleischhauer & Spohn GmbH & Co (Germany) *Tel:* (07142) 596161 *Fax:* (07142) 596280 *E-mail:* info@verlag-fleischhauer.de *Web Site:* www.verlag-fleischhauer.de, pg 225

Flensburger Hefte Verlag GmbH (Germany) *Tel:* (0461) 2 63 63; (0461) 2 14 72 *Fax:* (0461) 2 69 12 *E-mail:* flensburgerhefte@t-online.de *Web Site:* www.flensburgerhefte.de, pg 225

Flesch Financial Publications (Pty) Ltd (South Africa) *Tel:* (021) 4617472 *Fax:* (021) 4613758 *E-mail:* sflesch@aztec.co.za, pg 563

Editions Fleurus (France) *Tel:* (01) 45 44 38 34 *Fax:* (01) 45 49 93 92, pg 163

Flicks Books (United Kingdom) *Tel:* (01225) 767 728 *Fax:* (01225) 760 418 *E-mail:* flicks.books@pipex.com, pg 695

Flo Enterprise Sdn Bhd (Malaysia) *Tel:* (03) 77833118 *Fax:* (03) 77831066, pg 1326

La Flor del Itapebi (Uruguay) *Tel:* (02) 710 92 67 *Fax:* (02) 710 92 67 *E-mail:* itapebi@itapebi.com.uy *Web Site:* www.itapebi.com, pg 777

Ediciones de la Flor SRL (Argentina) *Tel:* (011) 4963-7950 *Fax:* (011) 4963-5616 *E-mail:* edic-flor@datamarkets.com.ar *Web Site:* www.edicionesdelaflor.com.ar, pg 6

Flora Publications International Pty Ltd (Australia) *Tel:* (07) 3229 6366 *Fax:* (07) 3378 7102 *E-mail:* info@flora.com.au, pg 22

Florilegium (Australia) *Tel:* (02) 95558589 *Fax:* (02) 98184409 *E-mail:* florileg@ozemail.com.au, pg 22

Floris Books (United Kingdom) *Tel:* (0131) 337 2372 *Fax:* (0131) 347 9919 *E-mail:* floris@floris.books.co.uk *Web Site:* www.florisbooks.co.uk, pg 695

Flugzeug Publikations GmbH (Germany) *Tel:* (07303) 964220 *Fax:* (07303) 964141 *E-mail:* flugzeug@charter.net *Web Site:* webpages.charter.net/flugzeug, pg 225

Empresa Literaria Fluminense, Lda (Portugal) *Tel:* (021) 601138 *Fax:* (021) 3963371, pg 531

Flyleaf Press (Ireland) *Tel:* (01) 2845906 *Fax:* (01) 2831693 *E-mail:* flyleaf@indigo.ie *Web Site:* www.flyleaf.ie, pg 360

FMR Ricci (Italy) *Tel:* (02) 48301246 *Fax:* (02) 48301473 *E-mail:* ricci@fmrmagazine.it, pg 1321

FN-Verlag der Deutschen Reiterlichen Vereinigung GmbH (Germany) *Tel:* (02581) 63 62-115 *Fax:* (02581) 63 31 46 *E-mail:* fnverlag@fn-dokr.de *Web Site:* www.fnverlag.de, pg 225

FNPS (Federation nationale depresse d'information specialisee) (France) *Tel:* (01) 44 90 43 60 *Fax:* (01) 44 90 43 72 *E-mail:* contact@fnps.fr *Web Site:* www.fnps.fr, pg 1268

Focus Publications International SA (Panama) *Tel:* 225 6638 *Fax:* 225 0466 *E-mail:* focusint@sinfo.net *Web Site:* focuspublicationsint.com, pg 515

Focus Publications Ltd (Kenya) *Tel:* (020) 600737 *E-mail:* focus@africaonline.co.ke, pg 433

Focus-Verlag Gesellschaft mbH (Germany) *Tel:* (0641) 76031; (0641) 68225 (orders) *Fax:* (0641) 76031; (0641) 68331 (orders) *E-mail:* info@focus-verlag.de *Web Site:* www.focus-verlag.de, pg 225

Foldmuvelesugyi Miniszterium Muszaki Intezet (Hungary) *Tel:* (028) 320-644 *Fax:* (028) 320-960 *E-mail:* dekani@eng.gau.hu, pg 321

Foereningen Auktoriserade Translatorer (Sweden) *E-mail:* info@eurofat.se *Web Site:* www.eurofat.se, pg 1149

Forlagshuset Norden AB (Sweden) *Tel:* (040) 93 42 50 *Fax:* (040) 93 01 56, pg 611

Foszekesegyhazi Konyvtar (Hungary) *Tel:* 33411891 *E-mail:* bibliotheca@ehf.hu, pg 1514

Maurice et Pierre Foetisch SA (Switzerland) *Tel:* (021) 3239444; (021) 3239445 *Fax:* (021) 3115011, pg 623

Fovarosi Szabo Ervin Konyvtar (Hungary) *Tel:* (01) 1185815; (01) 411-5000 *Fax:* (01) 1185914 *E-mail:* info@fszek.hu *Web Site:* www.fszek.hu, pg 1514

Fogarty's Bookshop (South Africa) *Tel:* (041) 3681425; (041) 3681454 *Fax:* (041) 3681279 *E-mail:* fogartys@global.co.za, pg 1340

Fogola Editore in Torino (Italy) *Tel:* (011) 535897 *Fax:* (011) 530305 *Web Site:* www.culturitalia.uibk.ac.at, pg 389

Foi-Commerce (Bulgaria) *Tel:* (02) 227116 *Fax:* (02) 227116 *E-mail:* foi@nlcv.net, pg 94

Foibe Filan-Kevitry NY Mpampianatra (FOFIPA) (Madagascar) *Tel:* (02) 27500 *Fax:* (02) 35788, pg 453

Fola Abbey Educational Book Services, Fola Abbey Bookshops Ltd (Nigeria) *Tel:* (01) 2636679 *Fax:* (01) 825268, pg 1331

Folens Ltd (United Kingdom) *Tel:* (0870) 609 1237 *Fax:* (0870) 609 1236 *E-mail:* folens@folens.com *Web Site:* www.folens.com, pg 695

Folens Publishers (Ireland) *Tel:* (01) 4137200 *Fax:* (01) 4137280 *E-mail:* info@folens.ie *Web Site:* www.folens.ie, pg 360

Editoriale Fernando Folini (Italy) *Tel:* (0131) 807001 *Fax:* (0131) 807001 *E-mail:* edifolini@edifolini.com *Web Site:* www.edifolini.com, pg 389

The Folio Society (United Kingdom) *Tel:* (020) 7400 4200 *Fax:* (020) 7400 4242 *E-mail:* enquiries@foliosoc.co.uk *Web Site:* www.foliosoc.co.uk, pg 1257

Folio Verlagsgesellschaft mbH (Austria) *Tel:* (01) 5813708-0 *Fax:* (01) 5813708-20 *E-mail:* office@folioverlag.com; folio@thing.at; folio@dialogon.at *Web Site:* www.folioverlag.com/books.php, pg 50

Folklore Comtois (France) *Tel:* (03) 81 55 29 77 *Fax:* (03) 81 55 23 97, pg 164

The Folklore Society (United Kingdom) *Tel:* (020) 7862 8564; (020) 7862 8562 *E-mail:* folklore.society@talk21.com *Web Site:* www.folklore-society.com, pg 1291

Folkuniversitetets foerlag (Sweden) *Tel:* (046) 148720 *Fax:* (046) 132904 *E-mail:* info@folkuniversitetsforlag.se *Web Site:* www.folkuniversitetsforlag.se, pg 611

Editions Foma SA (Switzerland) *Tel:* (021) 6351361 *Fax:* (021) 6351704, pg 623

Fondacija Zlatno Kljuce (Bulgaria) *Tel:* (02) 760-671; (02) 623517 *Fax:* (02) 623517 *E-mail:* ynfirst@mat.bg, pg 94

Institut Fondamental d'Afrique Noire, Cheikh Anta Diop (Senegal) *Tel:* 825 00 90; 825 98 90; 825 71 24 *Fax:* 24 49 18 *E-mail:* bifan@telecomplus.sn *Web Site:* www.refer.sn/ifan, pg 551

Fondation de l'Encyclopedie de Geneve (Switzerland) *Fax:* (022) 3273391; (022) 3273365, pg 623

Fondazzjoni Patrimonju Malti (Malta) *Tel:* 21231515 *Fax:* 21250118 *E-mail:* patrimonju@keyworld.net *Web Site:* www.patrimonju.org.mt, pg 460

Fondo de Cultura Economica SA (Chile) *Tel:* (02) 695 4843 *E-mail:* fcechile@ctcinternet.cl, pg 1305

Fondo de Cultura Economica (Mexico) *Tel:* (05) 2274672 *Fax:* (05) 2274640 *E-mail:* adiezc@fce.com.mx (editorial) *Web Site:* www.fondodeculturaeconomica.com, pg 465

Fondo de Cultura Economica de Espana, SL (Spain) *Tel:* (091) 7632800; (091) 7632766 *Fax:* (091) 7635133 *E-mail:* fcevent@interbook.es, pg 583

Fondo Editorial de la Plastica Mexicana (Mexico) *Tel:* (05) 5549-4291 *Fax:* (05) 5688-1168, pg 466

Fondo Editorial de la Pontificia Universidad Catolica del Peru (Peru) *Tel:* (01) 4602870 *Fax:* (01) 4626390 *Web Site:* www.pucp.edu.pe, pg 517

Fondo Educativo Interamericano SA (Colombia) *Tel:* (01) 3382577; (01) 3382877 *Fax:* (01) 2852891; (01) 2320191 *E-mail:* eeducativa@epm.net.co; educapyv@multi.net.co, pg 111

Fondo Educativo Interamericano (Panama) *Tel:* 2691511; 2230210, pg 515

Fong & Sons Printers Pte Ltd (Singapore) *Tel:* 2663688 *Fax:* 2664988, pg 1222

Fonna Forlag L/L (Norway) *Tel:* 22201303 *Fax:* 22201201, pg 509

Fono Forlag (Norway) *Tel:* 66846490 *Fax:* 66847507 *E-mail:* mail@fonoforlag.no *Web Site:* www.fonoforlag.no, pg 509

The Font Bureau Inc (United States) *Tel:* 617-423-8770 *Fax:* 617-423-8771 *E-mail:* info@fontbureau.com *Web Site:* www.fontbureau.com, pg 1187

Miguel Font Editor (Spain) *Tel:* (071) 477300 *Fax:* (071) 476805 *E-mail:* miquel@globalnet.es, pg 583

Uitgeverij De Fontein BV (Netherlands) *Tel:* (035) 5486311 *Fax:* (035) 5423855 *E-mail:* info@defonteinbaarn.nl *Web Site:* www.veenboschenkeuning.nl/pages/fontein.htm, pg 482

Livraria Martins Fontes Editora Ltda (Brazil) *Tel:* (011) 3241-3677 *Fax:* (0800) 11-605-6867 *E-mail:* info@martinsfontes.com.br *Web Site:* www.martinsfontes.com.br, pg 81

Food & Agriculture Organization of the United Nations (FAO) (Italy) *Tel:* (06) 57054350 *Fax:* (06) 57053360 *E-mail:* telex-room@fao.org *Web Site:* www.fao.org, pg 1274

Food Trade Press Ltd (United Kingdom) *Tel:* (01959) 563944 *Fax:* (01959) 561285 *E-mail:* ftpbooks@aol.com *Web Site:* foodtradepress.net, pg 696

Forbes Publications Ltd (United Kingdom) *Tel:* (020) 7495 7945 *Fax:* (020) 7495 7916 *E-mail:* editorial@rapportgroup.com, pg 696

Foreign Language Bookshop (Australia) *Tel:* (03) 96542883 *Fax:* (03) 96507664 *E-mail:* flb@ozonline.com.au *Web Site:* www.languages.com.au, pg 1298

The Foreign Language Press Group (Democratic People's Republic of Korea) *Tel:* (02) 841342 *Fax:* (02) 812100, pg 436

Foreign Language Teaching & Research Press (China) *Tel:* (010) 68420958; (010) 68420959 *Fax:* (010) 68420956, pg 104

Foreign Languages Press (China) *Tel:* (010) 68995852; (010) 68996188 *E-mail:* flpcn@public3.bta.net.cn *Web Site:* www.flp.com.cn, pg 104

Foreign Languages Publishing House (Democratic People's Republic of Korea) *Tel:* (02) 51-863, pg 436

Forening for Boghaandvaerk, Nordjysk afdeling (Denmark) *Tel:* 32 95 85 15 *Web Site:* www.boghaandvaerk.dk, pg 1265

Foreningen Svenska Laromedelsproducenter (The Swedish Association of Educational Publishers) (Sweden) *Tel:* (08) 736 19 40 *Fax:* (08) 736 19 44 *E-mail:* fsl@fsl.se *Web Site:* www.fsl.se, pg 1285

Foreningen Svenska Laromedelsproducenter (The Swedish Association of Educational Publishers) (Sweden) *Tel:* (08) 736 19 40 *Fax:* (08) 736 19 44 *E-mail:* fsl@fsl.se *Web Site:* www.fsl.se, pg 611

Editora Forense Universitaria Ltda (Brazil) *Tel:* (011) 580-0776 *Fax:* (011) 589-2084 *E-mail:* foruniv@unisys.com.br, pg 81

Forensic Science Society (United Kingdom) *Tel:* (01423) 506068 *Fax:* (01423) 566391 *E-mail:* tracey@forensic-science-society.org.uk *Web Site:* www.forensic-science-society.org.uk, pg 696

Forlagid (Iceland) *Tel:* 522 2000 *Fax:* 522 2022 *E-mail:* edda@edda.is, pg 325

Forma Edkotiki E P E (Greece) *Tel:* (01) 8327008 *Fax:* (01) 8325650, pg 307

FormAsia Books Ltd (Hong Kong) *Tel:* (02) 2525 8572 *Fax:* (02) 2522 4234 *E-mail:* formasia@hkstar.com *Web Site:* www.formasiabooks.com, pg 317

Formato Editorial ltda (Brazil) *Tel:* (011) 3613-3000 *Fax:* (011) 3611-3308 *E-mail:* falecom@formatoeditorial.com.br *Web Site:* www.formatoeditorial.com.br, pg 82

Arnaldo Forni Editore SRL (Italy) *Tel:* (051) 6814142; (051) 6814198 *Fax:* (051) 6814672 *E-mail:* info@fornieditore.com *Web Site:* www.fornieditore.com, pg 389

Foroya Landsbokasavn (Faroe Islands) *Tel:* (031) 311626 *Fax:* (031) 318895 *E-mail:* utlan@flb.fo *Web Site:* www.flb.fo, pg 1266

Foroya Landsbokasavn (Faroe Islands) *Tel:* 31 16 26 *Fax:* 31 88 95 *E-mail:* utlan@flb.fo *Web Site:* www.flb.fo, pg 1504

Forsamlingsforbundets Forlags AB (Finland) *Tel:* (09) 61261546 *Fax:* (09) 603963 *E-mail:* bokhandel@ff-forlag.fi, pg 142

Bengt Forsbergs Foerlag AB (Sweden) *Tel:* (040) 763 20 *Fax:* (040) 303939 *E-mail:* info@forsbergsforlag.se *Web Site:* www.forsbergsforlag.se, pg 611

Forth Naturalist & Historian (United Kingdom) *Tel:* (01786) 467755 *Fax:* (01786) 464994 *Web Site:* www.stir.ac.uk/departments/naturalsciences/forth_naturalist, pg 696

Fortuna Finanz-Verlag AG (Switzerland) *Tel:* (01) 9103102 *Fax:* (01) 9103353 *E-mail:* info@goldseiten.de *Web Site:* www.goldseiten.de, pg 623

Fortunajaya (Indonesia) *Tel:* (0272) 22030 *Fax:* (0272) 22543, pg 355

Forum (Serbia and Montenegro) *Tel:* (021) 57 286 *Fax:* (021) 57 691, pg 552

Forum (Serbia and Montenegro) *Tel:* (021) 57 216 *Fax:* (021) 57 216, pg 1338

Forum Artis, SA (Spain) *Tel:* (091) 4353180; (091) 4350548 *Fax:* (091) 4355124 *E-mail:* forum@adenet.es, pg 583

Bokforlaget Forum AB (Sweden) *Tel:* (08) 696 84 40; (08) 6968410 (Orders) *Fax:* (08) 696 83 67, pg 611

Forlaget Forum (Denmark) *Tel:* 33411830 *Fax:* 33411831 *E-mail:* kontakt@forlagetforum.dk *Web Site:* www.forlagetforum.dk, pg 131

Forum Publications (Malaysia) *Tel:* (03) 7554007 *Fax:* (03) 7561879 *E-mail:* g2jomo@umcsd.um.edu.my, pg 456

Forum Verlag GmbH & Co (Germany) *Tel:* (0711) 76727-0 *Fax:* (0711) 76727-28 *E-mail:* info@forumverlag.de *Web Site:* www.forumverlag.de, pg 225

Forum Verlag Leipzig Buch-Gesellschaft mbH (Germany) *Tel:* (0341) 9 80 50 08 *Fax:* (0341) 9 80 50 07 *E-mail:* info@forumverlagleipzig.de *Web Site:* www.forumverlagleipzig.de, pg 225

Editions Foucher (France) *Tel:* (01) 41 23 65 60 *Fax:* (01) 41 23 65 03 *E-mail:* contact@editions-foucher.fr *Web Site:* www.editions-foucher.fr, pg 164

Foulsham Publishers (United Kingdom) *Tel:* (01256) 329242 *Fax:* (01256) 812558; (01256) 812521 *E-mail:* mdl@macmillan.co.uk, pg 696

Foundation Books Ltd (Kenya) *Tel:* (020) 765485, pg 434

Foundation for the Production & Translation of Dutch Literature (Netherlands) *Tel:* (020) 6206261 *Fax:* (020) 6207179 *E-mail:* office@nlpvf.nl *Web Site:* www.nlpvf.nl, pg 1135

The Foundational Book Company for the John W Doorly Trust (United Kingdom) *Tel:* (020) 7584 1053, pg 696

Lora Fountain & Associates Literary Agency (France) *Tel:* (01) 43562196 *Fax:* (01) 43482272 *E-mail:* lora@fountlit.com, pg 1130

Fountain Publishers Ltd (Uganda) *Tel:* (041) 259163; (041) 251112; (031) 263041; (031) 263042 *Fax:* (041) 251160 *E-mail:* fountain@starcom.co.ug *Web Site:* www.fountainpublishers.co.ug, pg 652

Four Courts Press Ltd (Ireland) *Tel:* (01) 453-4668 *Fax:* (01) 453-4672 *E-mail:* info@four-courts-press.ie *Web Site:* www.four-courts-press.ie, pg 360

Four Seasons Publishing Ltd (United Kingdom) *Tel:* (020) 8942 4445 *Fax:* (020) 8942 4446 *E-mail:* info@fourseasons.net, pg 696

Fourah Bay College Library (Sierra Leone) *Tel:* (022) 229471, pg 1542

Naipes Heraclio Fournier SA (Spain) *Tel:* (0945) 465525 *Fax:* (0945) 465543 *E-mail:* fournier@nhfournier.es *Web Site:* www.nhfournier.es, pg 583

Fourth Dimension Publishing Co Ltd (Nigeria) *Tel:* (042) 459969 *Fax:* (042) 456904 *E-mail:* info@fdpbooks.com; fdpbook@aol.com *Web Site:* www.fdpbooks.com, pg 504

Fourth Estate (United Kingdom) *Tel:* (020) 8741 4414 *Fax:* (020) 8307 4466 *E-mail:* general@4thestate.co.uk *Web Site:* www.4thestate.co.uk, pg 696

W & G Foyle Ltd (United Kingdom) *Tel:* (020) 7437 5660 *Fax:* (020) 7434 1574 *E-mail:* administration@foyles.co.uk *Web Site:* www.foyles.co.uk, pg 696

FOYLES (United Kingdom) *Tel:* (020) 7437 5660 *Fax:* (020) 7434 1580 *E-mail:* sales@foyles.co.uk *Web Site:* www.foyles.co.uk, pg 1350

Editions Fragments (France) *Tel:* (01) 47 00 76 48 *Fax:* (01) 47 00 22 04 *E-mail:* art@fragmentseditions.com *Web Site:* www.fragmentseditions.com, pg 164

Fragua Editorial (Spain) *Tel:* (091) 544 22 97; (091) 549 18 06 *Fax:* (091) 549 18 06 *E-mail:* fragua@fragua.com *Web Site:* www.fragua.com, pg 583

Franc-Franc podjetje za promocijo kulture Murska Sobota d o o (Slovenia) *Tel:* (06) 922501 *Fax:* (06) 922501 *E-mail:* franc.franc@siol.net, pg 561

Institut Francais de Recherche pour l'Exploitation de la Mer (IFREMER) (France) *Tel:* (02) 98 22 40 13 *Fax:* (02) 98 22 45 86 *E-mail:* editions@ifremer.fr *Web Site:* www.ifremer.fr, pg 164

Institut Francais d'Etudes Arabes de Damas (Syrian Arab Republic) *Tel:* (011) 3330214; (011) 3331962 *Fax:* (011) 3327887 *E-mail:* ifead@net.sy *Web Site:* www.lb.refer.org/ifead, pg 638

Association Francaise de Normalisation (France) *Tel:* (01) 41 62 80 00 *Fax:* (01) 49 17 90 00 *Web Site:* www.afnor.fr, pg 164

Edition Francaise pour le Monde Arabe (EDIFRAMO) (Lebanon) *Tel:* (01) 862437; (01) 341650; (01) 441614, pg 446

France Edition (France) *Tel:* (01) 44 41 13 13 *Fax:* (01) 46 34 63 83 *E-mail:* info@franceedition.org *Web Site:* www.franceedition.org, pg 1268

France Edition Office de Promotion Internationale (France) *Tel:* (01) 44 41 13 13 *Fax:* (01) 46 34 63 83 *E-mail:* info@franceedition.com *Web Site:* bief.org, pg 164

Editions France-Empire (France) *Tel:* (01) 45 00 33 00 *Fax:* (01) 45 00 20 77 *E-mail:* france-empire@france-empire.fr *Web Site:* www.france-empire.fr, pg 164

France-Loisirs (France) *Tel:* (01) 45 68 60 00 *Fax:* (01) 42 73 14 38 *Web Site:* www.franceloisirs.com, pg 164

France Tosho (Japan) *Tel:* (03) 3346-0396 *Fax:* (03) 3346-9154 *E-mail:* frtosho@blue.ocn.ne.jp, pg 1322

Instituto Frances de Estudios Andinos, IFEA (Peru) *Tel:* (01) 447-6070 *Fax:* (01) 445-7650 *E-mail:* postmaster@ifea.org.pe *Web Site:* www.ifeanet.org, pg 517

Biblioteca Francescana (Italy) *Tel:* (02) 29002736 *Fax:* (02) 29002736 *E-mail:* info@bibliotecafrancescana.it *Web Site:* www.bibliotecafrancescana.it, pg 389

Francis Balsom Associates (United Kingdom) *Tel:* (01970) 636400 *Fax:* (01970) 636414 *E-mail:* info@fbagroup.co.uk *Web Site:* www.fbagroup.co.uk, pg 696

Les Editions Franciscaines SA (France) *Tel:* (01) 45407351 *Fax:* (01) 40447504 *E-mail:* editions-franciscaines@wanadoo.fr, pg 164

Editorial Franciscana (Portugal) *Tel:* (0253) 22490 *Fax:* (0253) 619735, pg 531

Verlag der Francke Buchhandlung GmbH (Germany) *Tel:* (06421) 17 25-0 *Fax:* (06421) 17 25-30 *E-mail:* info@francke-buch.de *Web Site:* www.francke-buch.de, pg 226

Franckh-Kosmos Verlags-GmbH & Co (Germany) *Tel:* (0711) 2191-0 *Fax:* (0711) 2191-422 *E-mail:* info@kosmos.de *Web Site:* www.kosmos.de, pg 226

Association Frank (France) *Tel:* (01) 43656405 *Fax:* (01) 48596668, pg 164

Frank Brothers & Co Publishers Ltd (India) *Tel:* (011) 263393; (011) 279936; (011) 278150; (011) 260796 *Fax:* (011) 3269032 *E-mail:* fbros@ndb.vsnl.net.in, pg 334

Frank Publishing Ltd (Ghana) *Tel:* (021) 240711, pg 304

Frankfurter Literaturverlag GmbH (Germany) *Tel:* (069) 40894-0 *Fax:* (069) 40894-194 *E-mail:* info@haensel-hohenhausen.de *Web Site:* www.cgl-verlag.de, pg 226

FVA-Frankfurter Verlagsanstalt GmbH (Germany) *Tel:* (069) 96220610 *Fax:* (069) 96220630 *E-mail:* info@frankfurter-verlagsanstalt.de *Web Site:* www.frankfurter-verlagsanstalt.de, pg 226

Franklin Book Programs Inc (Afghanistan), pg 1

Rodney Franklin Agency (Israel) *Tel:* (03) 5600724 *Fax:* (03) 5600479 *E-mail:* rodneyf@netvision.net.il, pg 367

Leanne Franson (Canada) *Tel:* 514-526-4236 *Fax:* 514-526-0972 *E-mail:* inksports@videotron.ca *Web Site:* www.theispot.com/artist/LFranson, pg 1175

Franz-Sales-Verlag (Germany) *Tel:* (08421) 9 34 89-31 *Fax:* (08421) 9 34 89-35 *E-mail:* info@franz-sales-verlag.de *Web Site:* www.franz-sales-verlag.de, pg 226

VERLAG FRANZ VAHLEN GMBH INDUSTRY

Verlag Franz Vahlen GmbH (Germany) *Tel:* (089) 38189-381 *Fax:* (089) 38189-402 *E-mail:* info@vahlen.de *Web Site:* www.vahlen.de, pg 226

Franzis-Verlag GmbH (Germany) *Tel:* (08121) 95 0 *Fax:* (08121) 95 16 96 *E-mail:* info@franzis.de *Web Site:* www.franzis.de, pg 226

Fraser Books (New Zealand) *Tel:* (06) 3771359 *Fax:* (06) 3771359, pg 496

The Fraser Press (United Kingdom) *Tel:* (0141) 3331992 *Fax:* (0141) 3331992, pg 697

Fraser Publications (Australia) *Tel:* (018) 039845 *Fax:* (057) 261775 *E-mail:* fraspub@albury.net.au, pg 22

Edizioni Frassinelli SRL (Italy) *Tel:* (02) 217211 *Fax:* (02) 21721277, pg 389

Fratelli Conte Editori SRL (Italy) *Tel:* (081) 7611858 *Fax:* (081) 7613667 *Web Site:* www.clio.it/sr/ce/conte/conte_ed.html, pg 389

Frati Editori di Quaracchi (Italy) *Tel:* (06) 94551259 *Fax:* (06) 94551267 *E-mail:* quaracchi@ofm.org *Web Site:* www.quaracchi.ofm.org, pg 389

Frauenoffensive Verlagsgesellschaft MbH (Germany) *Tel:* (089) 489500-48 *Fax:* (089) 489500-49, pg 226

Fraunhofer IRB Verlag Fraunhofer Informationszentrum Raum und Bau (Germany) *Tel:* (0711) 9 70-25 00 *Fax:* (0711) 9 70-25 07 *E-mail:* irb@irb.fhg.de *Web Site:* www.irbdirekt.de, pg 226

frechverlag GmbH (Germany) *Tel:* (0711) 83086-11 *Fax:* (0711) 83086-86 *E-mail:* kundenservice@frechverlag.de *Web Site:* www.frech.de, pg 226

Fredebeul und Koenen GmbH (Germany) *Tel:* (0201) 49821 *Fax:* (0201) 8492415, pg 226

Frederiksberg Kommunes Biblioteker (Denmark) *Tel:* 38211800 *Fax:* 38211799 *E-mail:* bib@fkb.dk *Web Site:* www.fkb.dk, pg 1502

Frederking & Thaler Verlag GmbH (Germany) *Tel:* (089) 4372-0 *Fax:* (089) 4372-2854, pg 226

Free Association Books Ltd (United Kingdom) *Tel:* (020) 7388 3182 *Fax:* (020) 7388 3187 *E-mail:* info@fabooks.com *Web Site:* www.fabooks.com, pg 697

Free State Provincial Library & Information Services (South Africa) *Tel:* (051) 4054681 *Fax:* (051) 4033567 *Web Site:* www.sac.fs.gov.za, pg 1543

Freedom Press (United Kingdom) *Tel:* (020) 7247 9249 *Fax:* (020) 7377 9526, pg 697

W H Freeman & Co Ltd (United Kingdom) *Tel:* (01256) 329242 *Fax:* (01256) 330688 *Web Site:* www.whfreeman.co.uk, pg 697

Erika G Freese Verlag (Germany) *Tel:* (030) 8333077 *Fax:* (030) 8333077 *E-mail:* eg.freese@t-online.de, pg 226

Verlag Freies Geistesleben (Germany) *Tel:* (0711) 28532 00 *Fax:* (0711) 28532 10 *E-mail:* info@geistesleben.com *Web Site:* www.geistesleben.com, pg 227

Freimund-Verlag der Gesellschaft fur Innere und Aeussere Mission im Sinne der Lutherischen Kirche eV (Germany) *Tel:* (09874) 6 89 39 80 *Fax:* (09874) 6 89 39 99 *E-mail:* info@freimund-verlag.de *Web Site:* www.freimund-buchhandlung.de/verlag, pg 227

Livraria Freitas Bastos Editora SA (Brazil) *Tel:* (021) 290-9949 *Fax:* (021) 290-9949 *E-mail:* fbastos@netfly.com.br; freitasbastos@freitasbastos.com.br, pg 82

Fremad A/S (Denmark) *Tel:* 33 41 18 10 *Fax:* 33 41 18 11 *Web Site:* www.fremad.dk, pg 131

Fremantle Arts Centre Press (Australia) *Tel:* (08) 9430 6331 *Fax:* (08) 9430 5242 *E-mail:* facp@iinet.net.au *Web Site:* facp.iinet.net.au, pg 23

Fremdenverkehrs Aktiengessellschaft (Austria) *Tel:* (0662) 88861011 *Fax:* (0662) 8886202, pg 51

French PEN Centre (France) *Tel:* (01) 42773787 *Fax:* (01) 42786487, pg 1399

Samuel French Ltd (United Kingdom) *Tel:* (020) 7387 9373 *Fax:* (020) 7387 2161 *E-mail:* theatre@samuelfrench-london.co.uk *Web Site:* www.samuelfrench-london.co.uk, pg 697

French's (United Kingdom) *Tel:* (020) 7483 4269 *Fax:* (020) 7722 0574, pg 1139

Frenckellin Kirjapaino Oy (Finland) *Tel:* (09) 887 3611 *Fax:* (09) 887 3670 *E-mail:* etunimi.sukunimi@frenckell.fi *Web Site:* www.frenckell.fi, pg 142

Freshet Press (Australia) *Tel:* (03) 53483085, pg 23

Sigmund Freud Copyrights (United Kingdom) *Tel:* (01206) 825433 *Fax:* (01206) 822990 *E-mail:* info@markpaterson.co.uk *Web Site:* www.markpaterson.co.uk/sigmund.htm, pg 697

Margarethe Freudenberger - selbstverlag fur jedermann (Germany) *Tel:* (09392) 8449, pg 227

Freund Publishing House Ltd (Israel) *Tel:* (03) 5662925 *Fax:* (03) 5605335, pg 367

Freund Publishing House Ltd (Israel) *Tel:* (03) 562-8540 *Fax:* (03) 562-8538 *E-mail:* h_freund@netvision.net.il *Web Site:* www.freundpublishing.com, pg 1148

Verlag Walter Frey (Germany) *Tel:* (030) 883 25 61 *Fax:* (030) 883 25 61 *E-mail:* tranvia@aol.com, pg 227

Freytag-Berndt und Artaria, Kartographische Anstalt (Austria) *Tel:* (01) 869 90 90-83 *Fax:* (01) 869 90 90-61 *E-mail:* office@freytagberndt.at, pg 51

FRICK Verlag-GmbH (Germany) *Tel:* (07231) 102842 *Fax:* (07231) 357744 *E-mail:* info@frickverlag.de *Web Site:* www.frickverlag.de, pg 227

R Friedlaender & Sohn GmbH Buchhaunlung & Antiquariat (Germany) *Tel:* (030) 2622328, pg 1311

Russel Friedman Books (South Africa) *Tel:* (011) 702-2300 *Fax:* (011) 702-1403 *E-mail:* rfbooks@iafrica.com *Web Site:* www.rfbooks.co.za, pg 564

S Friedman Publishing House Ltd (Israel) *Tel:* (03) 5176091 *Fax:* (03) 5179756, pg 367

Blake Friedmann Literary Agency Ltd (United Kingdom) *Tel:* (020) 7284 0408 *Fax:* (020) 7284 0442 *Web Site:* www.blakefriedmann.co.uk, pg 1140

Erhard Friedrich Verlag (Germany) *Tel:* (0511) 400040 *Fax:* (0511) 40004-119 *E-mail:* info@friedrich-verlag.de *Web Site:* www.friedrich-verlagsgruppe.de, pg 227

Friedrich Kiehl Verlag GmbH (Germany) *Tel:* (0621) 6 35 02-0 *Fax:* (0621) 6 35 02-22 *E-mail:* info@kiehl.de *Web Site:* www.kiehl.de, pg 227

Frieling & Partner GmbH (Germany) *Tel:* (030) 7 66 99 90 *Fax:* (030) 7 74 41 03 *Web Site:* www.frieling.de, pg 227

The Friendly Press (United Kingdom) *Tel:* (0117) 908-2281 *Fax:* (0117) 908-2282 *E-mail:* phgassoc@aol.com, pg 697

Friends of Antiquity (Czech Republic) *Tel:* (02) 24811549; (02) 24225143 *Fax:* (02) 24226026, pg 1251

Friends of the Earth (Charity) Ltd (Hong Kong) *Tel:* 2528 5588 *Fax:* 2529 2777 *E-mail:* foehk@hk.super.net, pg 317

Friends of the National Libraries (United Kingdom) *Tel:* (020) 7412 7559 *Web Site:* www.bl.uk/about/cooperation/friends2.html, pg 1573

Friesens Corp (Canada) *Tel:* 204-324-6401 *Fax:* 204-324-1333 *E-mail:* friesens@friesens.com, pg 1153

J Frimodt Forlag (Denmark) *Tel:* 75934455 *Fax:* 75924275 *E-mail:* lohse@imh.dk, pg 131

Paul und Peter Fritz AG Literary Agency (Switzerland) *Tel:* (01) 44 388 41 40 *Fax:* (01) 44 388 41 30 *E-mail:* info@fritzagency.com *Web Site:* www.fritzagency.com, pg 1137

C E Fritzes AB (Sweden) *Tel:* (08) 6909190 *Fax:* (08) 6909191 *E-mail:* order.fritzes@liber.se *Web Site:* www.fritzes.se, pg 611

Frjals fjolmiolun hf-Urvalsbaekur (Iceland) *Tel:* 550-500; 550-5999 *Fax:* 550-5022, pg 325

Frobenius AG (Switzerland) *Tel:* (061) 7715677 *Fax:* (061) 7116218, pg 623

Froebel - kan Co Ltd (Japan) *Tel:* (03) 5395-6600 *Fax:* (03) 5395-6627 *E-mail:* info-e@froebel-kan.co.jp *Web Site:* www.froebel-kan.co.jp, pg 417

Verlag A Fromm im Druck- u Verlagshaus Fromm GmbH & Co KG (Germany) *Tel:* (0541) 3100 *Fax:* (0541) 310315; (0541) 310440, pg 227

Friedrich Frommann Verlag (Germany) *Tel:* (0711) 955969-0 *Fax:* (0711) 955969-1 *E-mail:* info@frommann-holzboog.de *Web Site:* www.frommann-holzboog.de, pg 227

Georg Fromme und Co (Austria) *Tel:* (01) 5445641 *Fax:* (01) 544564166, pg 51

Frontier Publishing Ltd (United Kingdom) *Tel:* (01508) 558174 *E-mail:* frontier.pub@macunlimited.net *Web Site:* www.frontierpublishing.co.uk, pg 697

The FruitMarket Gallery (United Kingdom) *Tel:* (0131) 225 2383 *Fax:* (0131) 220 3130 *E-mail:* fruitmarket@fruitmarket.co.uk *Web Site:* www.fruitmarket.co.uk, pg 698

FT Caribbean (BVI) Ltd (Antigua & Barbuda) *Tel:* 462-3392; 462-3692 *Fax:* 462-3492 *E-mail:* ftcarib@candw.ag, pg 2

Editora FTD SA (Brazil) *Tel:* (011) 3284-8500 *Fax:* (011) 3283-5011 *E-mail:* ftd@dial&ta.com.br *Web Site:* www.ftd.com.br, pg 82

Fu Ssu-Nien Library, Institute of History & Philology, Academia Sinica (Taiwan, Province of China) *Tel:* (02) 27829555 *Fax:* (02) 27868834 *E-mail:* fsndb@pluto.ihp.sinica.edu.tw *Web Site:* www.saturn.ihp.sinica.edu.tw/~fsnlib, pg 1549

Edition Dr Heinrich Fuchs (Austria) *Tel:* (01) 4792381 *Fax:* (01) 4792381 *E-mail:* edition.h.fuchs@aon.at, pg 51

Fudan University Library (China) *Tel:* (021) 65642222; (021) 65643168 *Fax:* (021) 65649814 *E-mail:* libref@fudan.edu.cn *Web Site:* www.library.fudan.edu.cn; www.fudan.edu.cn/english/index_en.html, pg 1497

Fudan University Press (China) *Tel:* (021) 5484906-2842 *Fax:* (021) 65104812; (021) 65642840 *E-mail:* fupirc@fudan.edu.cn, pg 104

Fuh-Wen Book Co (Taiwan, Province of China) *Tel:* (06) 2744219; (06) 2351830 *Fax:* (06) 2347222, pg 639

Fuji Keizai Company Ltd (Japan) *Tel:* (03) 3644-5811 *Fax:* (03) 3661-0165 *Web Site:* www.fuji-keizai.co.jp, pg 417

Fujian Children's Publishing House (China) *Fax:* (0591) 7539070 *E-mail:* fcph@163.net, pg 104

Fujian Science & Technology Publishing House (China) *Tel:* (0591) 7538745; (0591) 7538623 *Fax:* (0591) 7538472, pg 104

Fukuinkan Ehon Library (Japan) *Tel:* (03) 39421226 *Fax:* (03) 39429691, pg 1253

Fukuinkan Shoten Publishers Inc (Japan) *Tel:* (03) 39420032 *Fax:* (03) 39421401 *Web Site:* www.fukuinkan.co.jp, pg 417

Fukumura Shuppan Inc (Japan) *Tel:* (03) 3813-3981 *Fax:* (03) 3818-2786 *Web Site:* www.fukumura.co.jp, pg 417

Fuldaer Verlagsanstalt GmbH (Germany) *Tel:* (0661) 295-0 *Fax:* (0661) 295-71 *E-mail:* info@fva.de *Web Site:* www.fva.de, pg 227

Full Circle Publications Co-Operative (Australia) *Tel:* (03) 9830 4253, pg 23

Full Circle Publishing (India) *Tel:* (011) 55654197 *Fax:* (011) 24645795 *E-mail:* gbp@del2.vsnl.com; fullcircle@vsnl.com *Web Site:* www.atfullcircle.com, pg 334

David Fulton Publishers Ltd (United Kingdom) *Tel:* (020) 8996 3610 *Fax:* (020) 8996 3622 *E-mail:* mail@fultonpublishers.co.uk *Web Site:* www.fultonpublishers.co.uk, pg 698

Michael Fulton Partners (United Kingdom) *Tel:* (01491) 680042 *Fax:* (01491) 680085 *Web Site:* www.foreignword.biz/cv/410.htm, pg 1150

Fumaido Publishing Company Ltd (Japan) *Tel:* (03) 3946-2345 *Fax:* (03) 3947-0110 *E-mail:* fumaido@tkd.att.ne.jp, pg 417

Fundacao Biblioteca Nacional (Brazil) *Tel:* (021) 22209367 *Fax:* (021) 22204173 *Web Site:* www.bn.br, pg 1495

Fundacao Cultural Avatar (Brazil) *Tel:* (021) 621-0217 *Fax:* (021) 2621-0217 *E-mail:* fcavatar@nitnet.com.br *Web Site:* www.nitnet.com.br/~fcavatar, pg 82

Fundacao de Assistencia ao Estudante (Brazil) *Tel:* (061) 223-9329 *Fax:* (061) 226-6270, pg 82

Fundacao Instituto Brasileiro de Geografia e Estatistica (IBGE - CDDI/DECOP) (Brazil) *Tel:* (021) 569-2043 *Fax:* (021) 234-6189 *Web Site:* www.ibge.gov.br, pg 82

Fundacao Joaquim Nabuco-Editora Massangana (Brazil) *Tel:* (081) 3441-5500 *Fax:* (081) 3441-5600 *E-mail:* editora@fundaj.gov.br *Web Site:* www.fundaj.gov.br, pg 82

Fundacao para a Ciencia e a Tecnologia/Servico de Informacao e Documentacao(SID) (Portugal) *Tel:* (01) 3924300 *Fax:* (01) 3907481 *Web Site:* www.fct.mct.pt, pg 1538

Fundacao Sao Paulo, EDUC (Brazil) *Tel:* (011) 3873-3359 *Fax:* (011) 38733359 *E-mail:* educsp@puc001.pucsp.ansp.br, pg 82

Fundacio La Caixa (Spain) *Tel:* (093) 404 6079 *Fax:* (093) 3395703 *E-mail:* info@lacaixa.es *Web Site:* portal1.lacaixa.es, pg 584

Fundacion Biblioteca Alemana Gorres (Spain) *Tel:* (091) 3668508; (091)3668509, pg 584

Fundacion Centro de Investigacion y Educacion Popular (CINEP) (Colombia) *Tel:* (02) 2456181 *Fax:* (01) 2879089 *E-mail:* info@cinep.org.co *Web Site:* www.cinep.org.co, pg 111

Fundacion Centro Gumilla (Venezuela) *Tel:* (02) 564 98 03; (02) 564 58 71; (02) 562 75 31 *Fax:* (02) 564 75 57 *E-mail:* comunicacion@gumilla.org.ve; centro@gumilla.org.ve *Web Site:* www.gumilla.org.ve, pg 779

Fundacion Coleccion Thyssen-Bornemisza (Spain) *Tel:* (091) 420 39 44 *Fax:* (091) 4202780 *E-mail:* umseo.thyssen-bornemisza@offcampus.es, pg 584

Fundacion de Cultura Universitaria (Uruguay) *Tel:* (02) 9152532; (02) 959038; (02) 9168360 *Fax:* (02) 9152549 *E-mail:* administrador@fcu.com.uy *Web Site:* www.fcu.com.uy, pg 777

Fundacion de Estudios Libertarios Anselmo Lorenzo (Spain) *Tel:* (091) 7970424 *Fax:* (091) 5052183 *E-mail:* fal@cnt.es *Web Site:* www.cnt.es/fal, pg 584

Fundacion de los Ferrocarriles Espanoles (Spain) *Tel:* (091) 1511 071 *Fax:* (091) 5284822; (091) 5391415 *E-mail:* fuccu20@ffe.es *Web Site:* www.ffe.es, pg 584

Fundacion Editorial de Belgrano (Argentina) *Tel:* (011) 4772-4014 *Fax:* (011) 4775-8788, pg 6

Fundacion El Libro (Argentina) *Tel:* (011) 43743288 *Fax:* (011) 43750268 *E-mail:* fundacion@el-libro.com.ar *Web Site:* www.el-libro.com.ar, pg 1259

Fundacion Esade (Spain) *Tel:* (093) 280 61 62 *Fax:* (093) 204 81 05 *Web Site:* www.esade.es/biblio, pg 1545

Fundacion Gratis Date (Spain) *Tel:* (0948) 123612 *Fax:* (0948) 123612 *E-mail:* fundacion@gratisdate.org *Web Site:* www.gratisdate.org, pg 584

Fundacion Juan March (Spain) *Tel:* (091) 435 42 40 *Fax:* (091) 576 34 20 *E-mail:* webmast@mail.march.es *Web Site:* www.march.es, pg 584

Fundacion Kuai-Mare (Venezuela) *Tel:* (02) 938535 ext 213; (02) 9418011 (ext 227) *Fax:* (02) 9415219, pg 1356

Fundacion Marcelino Botin (Spain) *Tel:* (0942) 226072 *Fax:* (0942) 226045 *E-mail:* fmabotin@fundacionmbotin.org *Web Site:* www.fundacionmbotin.org, pg 584

Fundacion para la Cultura y el Desarrollo (Guatemala) *Tel:* (02) 500216 *Fax:* (02) 325508, pg 313

Fundacion Rosacruz (Spain) *Tel:* (076) 589100 *Fax:* (076) 589161 *E-mail:* correo@fundacionrosacruz.org *Web Site:* www.fundacionrosacruz.org, pg 584

Fundacion Servicio para el Agricultor (Venezuela) *Tel:* (02) 2843089; (02) 2841134; (02) 2852016 *Fax:* (02) 2853946 *E-mail:* izamora@etheron.net, pg 779

Fundacion Universidad de la Sabana Ediciones INSE (Colombia) *Tel:* (01) 6760867 *E-mail:* susabana@col1.telcom.com.co, pg 111

Editorial Fundamentos (Spain) *Tel:* (091) 319 96 19 *Fax:* (091) 319 55 84 *E-mail:* fundamentos@editorialfundamentos.es *Web Site:* www.editorialfundamentos.es, pg 584

Funfax Ltd (United Kingdom) *Tel:* (020) 7836 5411 *Fax:* (020) 7836 7570 *E-mail:* clairrey@dk-uk.com, pg 698

Furco Ltd (United Kingdom) *Tel:* (04) 726795 *Fax:* (04) 726796 *E-mail:* info@africafilmtv.com *Web Site:* www.africafilmtv.com, pg 698

Furnival Press (United Kingdom) *Tel:* (020) 7274 2067 *Fax:* (020) 7274 6984 *E-mail:* furnprint@aol.com, pg 1226, 1238

Vernon Futerman Associates (United Kingdom) *Tel:* (020) 76292414 *Fax:* (020) 76297181, pg 1140

Editorial Futura (Portugal) *Tel:* (021) 7155848 *Fax:* (021) 155848, pg 531

Futuribles SARL (France) *Tel:* (01) 53 63 37 70 *Fax:* (01) 42 22 65 54 *E-mail:* revue@futuribles.com *Web Site:* www.futuribles.com, pg 164

Edizioni Futuro SRL (Italy) *Tel:* (045) 915622 *Fax:* (045) 8300261, pg 389

Fuzambo Publishing Co (Japan) *Tel:* (03) 3291-2171 *Fax:* (03) 3291-2179, pg 417

G+B Arts International (Switzerland) *Tel:* (061) 2610138 *Fax:* (061) 2610173, pg 623

G Braun (vormals G Braun'sche Hofbuchdruckerei und Verlag) (Germany) *Tel:* (0721) 1607320 *Fax:* (0721) 1607321 *E-mail:* info@gbraun-immo.de *Web Site:* www.gbraun.de, pg 1217

G Braun (vormals G Braun'sche Hofbuchdruckerei und Verlag) Gmbh (Germany) *Tel:* (0721) 1607320 *Fax:* (0721) 1607321 *E-mail:* kohler.buchverlag@gbraun.de *Web Site:* www.gbraun.de, pg 227

Gaanetgetal Books (Australia) *Tel:* (02) 4234-0865 *Fax:* (02) 4234-0875 *E-mail:* enquiries@books-on-rugs.com, pg 1298

Gaba Publications Amecea, Pastoral Institute (Kenya) *Tel:* (0321) 61218; (0321) 62153 *Fax:* (0321) 62570 *E-mail:* gabapubs@africaonline.co.ke *Web Site:* www.amecea.org, pg 434

Gabal-Verlag GmbH (Germany) *Tel:* (069) 84 000 66-0 *Fax:* (069) 84 000 66-66 *E-mail:* support@gabal-verlag.de *Web Site:* www.gabal-verlag.de, pg 227

Les Editions Gabalda et Cie (France) *Tel:* (01) 43 26 53 55 *Fax:* (01) 43 25 04 71 *E-mail:* editions@gabalda.com *Web Site:* www.gabalda.com, pg 164

Editions Jacques Gabay (France) *Tel:* (01) 43 54 64 64 *Fax:* (01) 43 54 87 00 *E-mail:* infos@gabay.com *Web Site:* www.gabay.com, pg 164

Verlagsbuchhandlung Megapress, Franz-J Gaber (Germany) *Tel:* (0610) 225951; (0610) 2327044 *Fax:* (0610) 231018, pg 228

Gaberbocchus Press (Netherlands) *Tel:* (020) 6245181 *Fax:* (020) 6230672 *E-mail:* info@deharmonie.nl *Web Site:* www.gaberbocchus.nl, pg 482

Betriebswirtschaftlicher Verlag Dr Th Gabler (Germany) *Tel:* (0611) 7878470 *Fax:* (0611) 787878400 *Web Site:* www.gwv-fachverlage.de, pg 228

Verlag Gachnang & Springer, Bern-Berlin (Switzerland) *Tel:* (031) 3518383 *Fax:* (031) 3518385 *E-mail:* verlag@gachnang-springer.com *Web Site:* www.gachnang-springer.com, pg 623

Editions Victor Gadoury (Monaco) *Tel:* (093) 251296 *Fax:* (093) 501339 *E-mail:* contact@gadoury.com *Web Site:* www.gadoury.com, pg 473

Gads Forlag (Denmark) *Tel:* 7766 6000 *Fax:* 7766 6001 *E-mail:* kuneservice@gads-forlag.dk *Web Site:* www.gads-forlag.dk, pg 131

Gads Forlag (Denmark) *Tel:* (03) 7766 6000 *Fax:* (033) 7766 6001 *E-mail:* kundeservice@gads-forlag.dk.ell *Web Site:* www.gads-forlag.dk, pg 1308

Ediciones de Arte Gaglianone (Argentina) *Tel:* (011) 4923-2579; (011) 4923-0150 *Fax:* (011) 4923-0150; (011) 4923-2579 *E-mail:* ediciones@gaglianone.ar, pg 6

Gaia Books Ltd (United Kingdom) *Tel:* (020) 7323 4010 *Fax:* (020) 7323 0435 *E-mail:* info@gaiabooks.com *Web Site:* www.gaiabooks.co.uk, pg 698

Editora Gaia Ltda (Brazil) *Tel:* (011) 2777999 *Fax:* (011) 2778141 *E-mail:* gaia@dialdata.com.br, pg 82

Gaia Media AG/Literary & Media Agency (Switzerland) *Tel:* (061) 2619119 *Fax:* (061) 2619117 *E-mail:* gaiamediaag@access.ch, pg 1137

Imprimerie Gaignault (France), pg 1216

Gairm Publications (United Kingdom) *Tel:* (0141) 221 1971 *Fax:* (0141) 221 1971, pg 698

Gakken Co Ltd (Japan) *Tel:* (03) 3726-8440 *Fax:* (03) 3726-8858, pg 417

Gakujutsu Bunken Fukyu-Kai (Japan) *Tel:* (03) 3726-3117 *Fax:* (03) 3726-3118 *E-mail:* gakujyutubunken@mvd.biglobe.ne.jp, pg 1565

GakuseiSha Publishing Co Ltd (Japan) *Tel:* (03) 3857-3031 *Fax:* (03) 3857-3037 *E-mail:* info@gakusei.co.jp *Web Site:* www.gakusei.co.jp, pg 417

Galago Publishing Pty Ltd (South Africa) *Tel:* (011) 9072029 *Fax:* (011) 8690890 *E-mail:* lemur@mweb.co.za *Web Site:* www.galago.co.za, pg 564

Galaktika Publishing House (Bulgaria) *Tel:* (052) 225077; (052) 241132; (052) 241156; (052) 604716; (052) 604715 *Fax:* (052) 234750, pg 94

Izdatelstvo Galart (Russian Federation) *Tel:* (095) 1512502; (095) 1514513 *Fax:* (095) 1513761, pg 545

Galaxia SA Editorial (Spain) *Tel:* (0986) 432100 *Fax:* (0986) 223205 *E-mail:* galaxia@editorialgalaxia.es *Web Site:* www.editorialgalaxia.es, pg 584

Galaxie, vydavatelství a nakladatelství (Czech Republic) *Tel:* (02) 2317801; (02) 2317875 *Fax:* (02) 2311351, pg 123

El Galeon (Uruguay) *Tel:* (02) 9156139; (02) 9157909 *Fax:* (02) 9157909 *E-mail:* elgaleon@netgate.com.uy, pg 1355

La Galera, SA Editorial (Spain) *Tel:* (093) 4120030 *Fax:* (093) 3173277; (093) 3014863 *E-mail:* lagalera@grec.com *Web Site:* www.enciclopedia-catalana.com, pg 584

Galerie Der Spiegel-Dr E Stunke Nachfolge GmbH (Germany) *Tel:* (0221) 25 55 52 *Fax:* (0221) 25 55 53 *E-mail:* der-spiegel@galerie.de *Web Site:* www.galerie.de/der-spiegel, pg 228

Galerie Editions Kutter (Luxembourg) *Tel:* 22 35 71 *Fax:* 47 18 84 *E-mail:* kuttered@pt.lu *Web Site:* www.kutter.lu, pg 451

Editorial Galerna SRL (Argentina) *Tel:* (011) 4867-1661 *Fax:* (011) 4862-5031 *E-mail:* gventas@hg.com.ar, pg 6

Galgotia Publications Pvt Ltd (India) *Tel:* (011) 589334 *Fax:* (011) 3281909; (011) 321909 *E-mail:* gppl.galgtia@axcess.net.in, pg 334

Editions Galilee (France) *Tel:* (01) 43 31 23 84 *Fax:* (01) 45 35 53 68 *E-mail:* editions.galilee@free.fr, pg 164

Galleon Publications (Philippines) *Tel:* (02) 592-519; (02) 523-1825 *Fax:* (02) 525-6129, pg 519

The Gallery Press (Ireland) *Tel:* (049) 8541779 *Fax:* (049) 8541779 *E-mail:* gallery@indigo.ie *Web Site:* www.gallerypress.com, pg 360

Galley Press Publishing (Australia) *Tel:* (02) 9698 9262 *Fax:* (02) 9360 1968 *E-mail:* isbin@ozemail.com.au, pg 23

Editions Gallimard (France) *Tel:* (01) 49 54 42 00 *Fax:* (01) 45 44 94 03 *Web Site:* www.gallimard.fr, pg 164

Adriano Gallina Editore sas (Italy) *Tel:* (081) 5496730 *Fax:* (081) 5448747, pg 389

Galrev Druck-und Verlagsgesellschaft Hesse & Partner OHG (Germany) *Tel:* (030) 44 65 01 83 *Fax:* (030) 44 65 01 84 *E-mail:* galrev@galrev.com *Web Site:* www.galrev.com, pg 228

Galzerano Editore (Italy) *Tel:* (0974) 62028 *Fax:* (0974) 62028, pg 390

Gamberetti Editrice SRL (Italy) *Tel:* (06) 3728394 *Fax:* (06) 3728394 *E-mail:* gamberetti@gamberetti.it *Web Site:* www.gamberetti.it, pg 390

The Gambia Methodist Bookshop Ltd (Gambia) *Tel:* 28179, pg 1310

Gambia College Library (Gambia) *Tel:* 484452; 484748; 484812 *Fax:* 483224, pg 1507

The Gambia National Library (Gambia) *Tel:* 226491; 225876; 228312; 223776 *Fax:* 223 776 *E-mail:* national.library@qanet.gm, pg 1508

Ediciones Gamma (Colombia) *Tel:* (01) 6227054; (01) 6227076 *Fax:* (01) 6227129 *E-mail:* diners@cable.net.co, pg 111

Editions Gamma (France) *Tel:* (03) 44806868 *Fax:* (03) 44806860, pg 165

Gamma Medya Agency (Turkey) *Tel:* (0212) 663 96 80 *Fax:* (0212) 663 96 81 *E-mail:* web@gammamedya.net *Web Site:* www.gammamedya.net, pg 1138

Gammaprim (France) *Tel:* (01) 49959492 *Fax:* (01) 40230134 *E-mail:* fgosselin@gammaprim.fr, pg 165

Gamsberg Macmillan Publishers (Pty) Ltd (Namibia) *Tel:* (061) 232165 *Fax:* (061) 233538 *E-mail:* gmp@iafrica.com.na *Web Site:* www.macmillan-africa.com, pg 476

Gandon Editions (Ireland) *Tel:* (021) 770830 *Fax:* (021) 770755, pg 360

Ganesh & Co (India) *Tel:* (044) 4344519 *Fax:* (044) 4342009 *E-mail:* ksm@md2.vsnl.net.in; service@kkbooks.com, pg 334

Gangan Publishing (Australia) *Tel:* (02) 9280 2120 *Fax:* (02) 9280 2130 *E-mail:* books@gangan.com *Web Site:* www.gangan.com, pg 23

Gangan Verlag (Austria) *Tel:* (0316) 670 4090 *Fax:* (0316) 670 4096 *Web Site:* www.gangan.com, pg 51

Gangemi Editore spa (Italy) *Tel:* (06) 6872774; (06) 68806189 (orders) *Fax:* (06) 68806189 *E-mail:* info@gangemieditore.it *Web Site:* www.gangemieditore.it, pg 390

A R Gantner Verlag KG (Liechtenstein) *Tel:* 377 1808 *Fax:* 377 1802 *E-mail:* bgc@adon.li *Web Site:* www.gantner-verlag.com, pg 447

Editions Ganymede (France) *Tel:* (01) 48945232 *Fax:* (02) 64 42 86 68 *E-mail:* rozeille.hatem@wanadoo.fr *Web Site:* www.hatem.com, pg 165

Garant Publishers Ltd (Belgium) *Tel:* (03) 231 29 00 *Fax:* (03) 233 26 59 *E-mail:* uitgeverij@garant.be *Web Site:* www.garant.be, pg 67

Garcia Hermanos Imprenta y Litografia (Costa Rica) *Tel:* 2202003; 2212223 *Fax:* 2310675 *E-mail:* info@novanet.co.cr *Web Site:* www.novanet.co.cr, pg 115

Vicent Garcia Editores, SA (Spain) *Tel:* (096) 361 9559; (096) 3691589; (096) 369 3246 *Fax:* (096) 393 00 57 *E-mail:* vgesa@combios.es *Web Site:* www.vgesa.com, pg 584

Editions du Garde-Temps (France) *Tel:* (01) 44788477 *Fax:* (01) 44788479 *E-mail:* studio-magnet@calva.net, pg 165

Garden Art Press Ltd (United Kingdom) *Tel:* (01394) 385501 *Fax:* (01394) 384434, pg 698

Gardenhouse Editions (United Kingdom) *Tel:* (020) 76221720 *Fax:* (020) 7720 9114, pg 1163

Imprimerie Librairie Gardet (France) *Tel:* (04) 50 53 67 47 *Fax:* (04) 50 53 67 47 *E-mail:* edimontagne@wanadoo.fr, pg 165

Walter H Gardner & Co (United Kingdom) *Tel:* (20) 8458 3202 *Fax:* (20) 8458 8499 *E-mail:* walterhgardnerco@aol.com, pg 698, 1351

Gardners Books (United Kingdom) *Tel:* (01323) 521666; (01323) 521555 *Fax:* (01323) 521666 *E-mail:* marketing@gardners.com *Web Site:* www.gardners.com, pg 1351

Gardum A/S (Norway) *Tel:* 51894440 *Fax:* 51894404 *E-mail:* firmapost@gardum.no, pg 1333

Editrice Garigliano SRL (Italy) *Tel:* (0776) 21869 *Fax:* (0776) 21869, pg 390

Garnet Publishing Ltd (United Kingdom) *Tel:* (0118) 959 7847 *Fax:* (0118) 959 7356 *E-mail:* enquiries@garnet-ithaca.demon.co.uk (general enquiries); orders@garnet-ithaca.demon.co.uk (ordering) *Web Site:* www.garnet-ithaca.co.uk, pg 698

Garolla (Italy) *Tel:* (02) 48005574 *Fax:* (02) 48003915, pg 390

Garotech (Philippines) *Tel:* (02) 993286, pg 519

Garr Publishing (Australia) *Tel:* (02) 4367 7762 *Fax:* (02) 4367 7223 *E-mail:* garrpublishing@mail2me.com.au *Web Site:* www.garrpublishing.com.au, pg 23

Garradunga Press (Australia) *Tel:* (0409) 320 619 (mobile) *Fax:* (07) 4032 5918 *E-mail:* bolton@iig.com.au, pg 23

John Garratt Publishing (Australia) *Tel:* (03) 9545 3111 *Toll Free No:* 300 650 878 *Fax:* (03) 9545 3222 *E-mail:* sales@johngarratt.com.au *Web Site:* www.johngarratt.com.au, pg 23

Garrison Library (Gibraltar) *Tel:* 77418 *Fax:* 79927, pg 1512

Gartaganis D (Greece) *Tel:* (02310) 209680, pg 307

Garuda-Verlag (Switzerland) *Tel:* (01) 7411287 *Fax:* (056) 6401012 *E-mail:* garuda@bluewin.ch, pg 624

Garzanti Libri (Italy) *Tel:* (02) 674171 *Fax:* (02) 67417323, pg 390

Verlag HP Gassner AG (Liechtenstein) *Tel:* (075) 2327253 *Fax:* (075) 2323720, pg 447

Gaston Renard Pty Ltd (Australia) *Tel:* (03) 9459 5040 *Fax:* (03) 9459 6787 *E-mail:* books@gastonrenard.com.au *Web Site:* www.gastonrenard.com.au, pg 1298

Gateway Books (United Kingdom) *Tel:* (01225) 835 127 *Fax:* (01225) 840 012 *E-mail:* sales@gatewaybooks.com, pg 698

Gatidhara (Bangladesh) *Tel:* (02) 7392077 (press); (02) 7113117 (res); (02) 7115630 (res); (02) 7117515 (showroom); (02) 7118273 (showroom) *Fax:* (02) 9134617; (02) 9566456 *E-mail:* akter@aitlbd.net; gatidara@bdonline.com, pg 61

Gatzanis Verlags GmbH (Germany) *Tel:* (0711) 9640570 *Fax:* (0711) 9640572 *E-mail:* info@gatzanis.de *Web Site:* www.gatzanis.de, pg 228

Gaulitana (Malta) *Tel:* 2155-4212 *Fax:* 2155-4598 *E-mail:* joseph.bezzina@um.edu.mt, pg 460

Ediciones Gaviota SA (Spain) *Tel:* (091) 358 01 08 *Fax:* (091) 729 38 58 *E-mail:* publicaciones@ediciones-gaviota.es *Web Site:* www.everest.es, pg 584

Gaya Favorit Press (Indonesia) *Tel:* (021) 513816 *Fax:* (021) 5209366; (021) 4609115 *E-mail:* ptgfp1@rad.net.id, pg 355

Gazelle Book Services Ltd (United Kingdom) *Tel:* (01524) 68765 *Fax:* (01524) 63232 *E-mail:* sales@gazellebooks.co.uk *Web Site:* www.gazellebook.co.uk, pg 1351

Edizioni GB (Italy) *Tel:* (049) 8647834 *Fax:* (049) 8647834, pg 390

Gbabeks Publishers Ltd (Nigeria) *Tel:* (062) 217976, pg 505

GCL Publishing (1997) Ltd (New Zealand) *Tel:* (09) 3092444 *Fax:* (09) 3092449 *E-mail:* info@gcl.co.nz *Web Site:* www.gcl.co.nz; www.auto.co.nz, pg 496

Biblioteka Gdanska PAN (Poland) *Tel:* (058) 312251-54 *Fax:* (058) 312970 *E-mail:* bgpan@task.gda.pl, pg 1537

Politechnika Gdanska (Poland) *Tel:* (058) 3415791 *Fax:* (058) 3415821 *E-mail:* mainlibr@sunrise.pg.gda.pl; library@pg.gda.pl *Web Site:* www.pg.gda.pl, pg 1537

Gdanskie Wydawnictwo Psychologiczne SC (Poland) *Tel:* (058) 551-61-04; (058) 550-16-04; (058) 551-11-01 *Fax:* (058) 551-61-04; (058) 550-16-04 *Web Site:* www.gwp.pl, pg 523

Gea-Libris Publishing House (Bulgaria) *Tel:* (02) 9863171; (02) 9864604 *Fax:* (02) 9866900 *E-mail:* emilgea@techno-link.com *Web Site:* www.gea-libris.search.bg, pg 94

Gebrueder Borntraeger Science Publishers (Germany) *Tel:* (0711) 3514560 *Fax:* (0711) 3515699 *E-mail:* mail@schweizerbart.de *Web Site:* www.schweizerbart.de, pg 228

GECTI (Gabinete de Especializacao e Cooperacao Tecnica Internacional L) (Portugal) *Tel:* (021) 7968877; (021) 7971940; (021) 7972154 *Fax:* (021) 7963465 *E-mail:* gecti@mail.telepac.pt *Web Site:* www.inedita.com/gecti, pg 531

Geddes & Grosset (United Kingdom) *Tel:* (01555) 665000 *Fax:* (01555) 665694 *E-mail:* info@gandg.sol.co.uk, pg 699

Gedins Forlag (Sweden) *Tel:* (08) 662 15 51 *Fax:* (08) 6637073 *E-mail:* gedins@perigab.se, pg 611

Editorial Gedisa SA (Spain) *Tel:* (093) 253 09 04 *Fax:* (093) 253 09 05 *E-mail:* gedisa@gedisa.com *Web Site:* www.gedisa.com, pg 584

Gee & Son (Denbigh) Ltd-Gwasg Gee-Gee's Press (United Kingdom) *Tel:* (01745) 812020 *Fax:* (01745) 812825, pg 1163

Uitgeverij Vrij Geestesleven (Netherlands) *Tel:* (030) 6924953 *Fax:* (030) 6932304, pg 482

Geeta Prakashan (India) *Tel:* (0821) 33589, pg 335

Geetha Publishers Sdn Bhd (Malaysia) *Tel:* (03) 4417073, pg 456

Gefen Publishing House Ltd (Israel) *Tel:* (02) 5380247 *Fax:* (02) 5388423 *E-mail:* info@gefenpublishing.com *Web Site:* www.israelbooks.com, pg 367

Konkursbuch Verlag Claudia Gehrke (Germany) *Tel:* (07071) 78779 *Fax:* (07071) 763780 *E-mail:* office@konkursbuch.com *Web Site:* www.konkursbuch.com, pg 228

SK-Gehrmans Musikforlag AB (Sweden) *Tel:* (08) 6100600 *Fax:* (08) 6100628 *E-mail:* order@sk-gehrmans.se *Web Site:* www.sk-gehrmans.se, pg 611

Geiser Productions (United Kingdom) *Tel:* (020) 8579 4653 *Fax:* (020) 8567 6593 *E-mail:* geiser@gxn.co.uk *Web Site:* www.geiserproductions.com; www.sidsjournal.com, pg 699

Uitgevery Gelbis NV (Belgium) *Tel:* (03) 2410202 *Fax:* (03) 2410200 *E-mail:* gelbis.boeken@lequana.com, pg 67

Caroline van Gelderen Literary Agency (Netherlands) *Tel:* (020) 6126475 *Fax:* (020) 6180843, pg 1135

Gembooks (United Kingdom) *Tel:* (01202) 399729 *Fax:* (01202) 399729 *E-mail:* readbooks@onmail.co.uk, pg 699

Verlag Junge Gemeinde E Schwinghammer GmbH & Co KG (Germany) *Tel:* (0711) 99078-0 *Fax:* (0711) 99078-25, pg 228

General Book Depot (India) *Tel:* (011) 2326 3695; (011) 2325 0635 *Fax:* (011) 2394 0861 *E-mail:* contact@goyalbookshop.com *Web Site:* www.goyalbookshop.com, pg 335

General Book Depot (India) *Tel:* (011) 3263695; (011) 3250635 *Fax:* (011) 2394 0861, pg 1315

General Department of Archives of the Republic of Bulgaria (Bulgaria) *Tel:* (02) 940 0101; (02) 940 0102 *Fax:* (02) 980 14 43 *E-mail:* gua@archives.government.bg *Web Site:* www.archives.government.bg, pg 1496

General Egyptian Book Organization (Egypt (Arab Republic of Egypt)) *Tel:* (02) 5799635; (02) 5775228; (02) 5775367; (02) 5775436; (02) 5775545; (02) 5775000; (02) 5775109 *Fax:* (02) 5765058; (02) 5799635 *E-mail:* info@egyptianbook.org *Web Site:* www.egyptianbook.org, pg 138

General Egyptian Book Organization (Egypt (Arab Republic of Egypt)) *Tel:* (02) 5775228; (02) 5775367; (02) 5775109; (02) 5799635; (02) 5775436; (02) 5775545; (02) 5775000 *Fax:* (02) 5765058; (02) 5799635 *E-mail:* info@egyptianbook.org *Web Site:* www.egyptianbook.org, pg 1266

General Printers & Publishers (India) *Tel:* (022) 2387 3113; (022) 2382 6854 *Fax:* (022) 2382 7197, pg 335

General Publications Ltd (United Republic of Tanzania) *Tel:* (0741) 6195 85; (0741) 6231 82, pg 643

General Sciences Library of Ho Chi Minh City (Viet Nam) *Tel:* (08) 822 5055 *Fax:* (08) 829 5632, pg 1555

Bibliotheque Generale et Archives (Morocco) *Tel:* (0996) 3 258, pg 1529

Librairie Generale Francaise SA (France) *Tel:* (01) 43 92 30 00 *Fax:* (01) 43 92 35 90, pg 165

Generalitat de Catalunya Diari Oficial de la Generalitat vern (Spain) *Tel:* (093) 302 64 62 *Fax:* (093) 318 62 21 *E-mail:* llibrbcn@gencat.net *Web Site:* www.gencat.net/diari, pg 584

Genesis Forlag (Norway) *Tel:* (022) 31 02 40 *Fax:* (022) 31 02 05 *E-mail:* genesis@genesis.no *Web Site:* www.genesis.no, pg 509

Genesis Publications Ltd (United Kingdom) *Tel:* (01483) 540970 *Fax:* (01483) 304709 *E-mail:* info@genesis-publications.com *Web Site:* www.genesis-publications.com, pg 699

Genius Verlag (Germany) *Tel:* (08386) 960401 *Fax:* (08386) 960402 *E-mail:* contact@genius-verlag.de *Web Site:* www.genius-verlag.de, pg 228

Genko-Sha (Japan) *Tel:* (03) 3263-3515 *Fax:* (03) 3239-5886 *E-mail:* gks@genkosha.co.jp *Web Site:* www.genkosha.co.jp, pg 417

Gennadius Library (Greece) *Tel:* (0210) 7210536 *Fax:* (0210) 7237767 *E-mail:* ascsa@ascsa.edu.gr *Web Site:* www.ascsa.edu.gr/gennadius, pg 1513

Uitgeverij en boekhandel Van Gennep BV (Netherlands) *Tel:* (20) 6247033 *Fax:* (20) 6247035 *E-mail:* vangennep@wxs.nl, pg 482

Editora Gente Livraria e Editora Ltda (Brazil) *Tel:* (011) 3675 2505 *Fax:* (011) 3675 0430 *E-mail:* gentedit@mandic.com.br, pg 82

Editorial Gente Nueva (Cuba) *Tel:* (07) 833-7676 *Fax:* (07) 33-8187 *E-mail:* gentenueva@icl.cult, pg 120

Alfons W Gentner Verlag GmbH & Co KG (Germany) *Tel:* (0711) 63672-0 *Fax:* (0711) 63672747 *E-mail:* gentner@gentnerverlag.de *Web Site:* www.gentnerverlag.de, pg 228

Gentofte Bibliotekerne (Denmark) *Tel:* 39487500 *Fax:* 39487507 *E-mail:* bibliotek@gentofte.bibnet.dk *Web Site:* www.gentofte.bibnet.dk, pg 1502

Geocart Uitg Cartogr AG Claus BVBA (Belgium) *Tel:* (03) 760 14 60 *Fax:* (03) 760 15 28 *E-mail:* site@geocart.be *Web Site:* www.geocart.be, pg 67

Geocarto International Centre (Hong Kong) *Tel:* 2546-4262 *Fax:* 2559-3419 *E-mail:* geocarto@geocarto.com *Web Site:* www.geocarto.com, pg 317

GeoCenter Touristik Medienservice GmbH (Germany) *Tel:* (0711) 781946 10 *Fax:* (0711) 7824375 *E-mail:* geocenterilh@t-online.de; vertrieb@geocenter.de *Web Site:* www.geokatalog.de, pg 228

Istituto Geografico de Agostini SpA (Italy) *Tel:* (0321) 4241 *Fax:* (0321) 471286 *E-mail:* info@deagostini.it *Web Site:* www.deagostini.it, pg 390

Instituto Geografico Militar (Chile) *Tel:* (02) 4606863 *Fax:* (02) 4608294 *E-mail:* clientes@igm.cl *Web Site:* www.igm.cl, pg 99

Geographers' A-Z Map Company Ltd (United Kingdom) *Tel:* (01732) 781000 *Fax:* (01732) 780677 *E-mail:* tradesales@a-zmaps.co.uk *Web Site:* www.azmaps.co.uk, pg 699

The Geographical Association (United Kingdom) *Tel:* (0114) 296 0088 *Fax:* (0114) 296 7176 *E-mail:* ga@geography.org.uk *Web Site:* www.geography.org.uk, pg 699

Bibliotheque de Geographie (France) *Tel:* (01) 44 32 14 61; (01) 44 32 14 63 *Fax:* (01) 44 32 14 67 *Web Site:* margotte.univ-paris1.fr/ciolfi/sorbg1.htm, pg 1507

Geological Publishing House (China) *Tel:* (010) 62351944 *Fax:* (010) 6024523, pg 105

Geological Society Publishing House (United Kingdom) *Tel:* (01225) 445046 *Fax:* (01225) 442836 *E-mail:* rebecca.toop@geolsoc.org.uk *Web Site:* www.geolsoc.org.uk, pg 699

Geological Survey Department (Zimbabwe) *Tel:* (04) 790701; (04) 726342; (04) 726343; (04) 252016; (04) 252017 *Fax:* (04) 739601 *E-mail:* zimeosv@africaonline.co.zw; zgs@samara.co.zw *Web Site:* www.geosurvey.co.zw, pg 783

Geological Survey Department Library (Botswana) *Tel:* 330327; 330428 *Fax:* 332013 *E-mail:* geosurv@global.bw *Web Site:* www.gov.bw, pg 1495

Geological Survey Department Reference Library (Ghana) *Tel:* (021) 228093; (021) 28079 *Fax:* (021) 228063; (021) 224676 *E-mail:* ghgeosur@ghana.com, pg 1512

Geological Survey of Zimbabwe (Zimbabwe) *Tel:* (04) 726342; (04) 726343; (04) 252016; (04) 252017 *Fax:* (04) 739601 *E-mail:* zimgeosv@africaonline.co.zw *Web Site:* www.geosurvey.co.zw, pg 1556

Wydawnictwa Geologiczne (Poland) *Tel:* (022) 495351 (ext 518), pg 523

GEOprojects Sarl (Lebanon) *Tel:* (01) 350721; (01) 344236 *Fax:* (01) 353000, pg 446

Georeto-Geogidsen (Belgium) *Tel:* (011) 37 52 54 *Fax:* (011) 37 52 54 *E-mail:* georeto@pandora.be *Web Site:* www.geogidsen.be, pg 67

Georg Editeur SA (Switzerland) *Tel:* (022) 8690029 *Fax:* (022) 8690015 *E-mail:* livres@medecinehygiene.ch *Web Site:* www.medecinehygiene.ch, pg 624

George Gregory Bookseller (United Kingdom) *Tel:* (01225) 466000 *Fax:* (01225) 482122, pg 1351

George Mann Publications (United Kingdom) *Tel:* (01622) 759591 *Fax:* (01622) 209193 *Web Site:* www.gmp.co.uk, pg 699

William George's Sons Ltd (United Kingdom) *Tel:* (0117) 9276602, pg 1351

Georgi GmbH (Germany), pg 228

Editions Gerard de Villiers (France) *Tel:* (01) 43 92 30 00 *Fax:* (01) 43 92 35 80 *Web Site:* www.editionsgerarddevilliers.com, pg 165

Gerhard Wolf Janus-Press GmbH (Germany) *Tel:* (030) 47535220 *Fax:* (030) 47533790, pg 228

German Book Centre (India) *Tel:* (044) 2434-6244; (044) 2434-6266 *Fax:* (044) 2434-6529 *E-mail:* germanbk@vsnl.com *Web Site:* germanbookcentre.com, pg 1316

Germanisches Nationalmuseum (Germany) *Tel:* (0911) 13310 *Fax:* (0911) 1331 200 *E-mail:* info@gnm.de *Web Site:* www.gnm.de, pg 228

Germinal Press (Australia), pg 23

Gerold & Co (Austria) *Tel:* (01) 532 0102 *Fax:* (01) 532 01 02-15; (01) 532 01 02-22 *E-mail:* office@gerold.at *Web Site:* www.gerold.at, pg 51

Gerold & Co (Austria) *Tel:* (01) 5335014-0 *E-mail:* buch@gerold.at *Web Site:* www.gerold.at, pg 1300

Gerstenberg Verlag (Germany) *Tel:* (05121) 1060 *Fax:* (05121) 106498 *E-mail:* verlag@gerstenberg-verlag.de *Web Site:* www.gerstenberg-verlag.de, pg 228

Klaus Gerth Musikverlag (Germany) *Tel:* (06443) 68-0 *Fax:* (06443) 68-34 *E-mail:* info@gerth.de *Web Site:* www.gerth.de, pg 229

Gerth Medien GmbH (Germany) *Tel:* (06443) 68-0 *Fax:* (06443) 68-34 *Web Site:* www.gerth.de, pg 229

Verlag fuer Geschichte der Naturwissenschaften und der Technik (Germany) *Tel:* (05441) 92 71 29 *Fax:* (05441) 92 71 27 *E-mail:* info@gnt-verlag.de *Web Site:* www.gnt-verlag.de, pg 229

Verlag fuer Geschichte und Politik (Austria) *Tel:* (01) 712 62 58 0 *Fax:* (01) 712 62 58 19 *E-mail:* office@oldenbourg.at, pg 51

Gesellschaft fur Bibliothekswesen und Dokumentation des Landbaues (GBDL) (Germany) *Tel:* (08161) 71 34 26 *Fax:* (08161) 71 44 09 *Web Site:* www.weihenstephan.de, pg 1563

Gesellschaft fur deutsche Sprache und Literatur in Zurich (Switzerland) *Tel:* (01) 6342571 *Fax:* (01) 6344905 *E-mail:* uguenthe@ds.unizh.ch, pg 1405

Gesellschaft fuer Organisationswissenschaft e V (Germany) *Tel:* (09206) 480 *Fax:* (09206) 628, pg 229

Gesellschaft fur Interkulturelle Germanistik eV (GIG) (Germany) *Tel:* (0721) 6080 *Fax:* (0721) 6084290, pg 1400

Verlag Lynkeus/H Hakel Gesellschaft (Austria) *Tel:* (01) 7342294, pg 51

Gesellschaft zur Foerderung der Literatur aus Afrika Asien und Lateinamerika eV (Germany) *Tel:* (069) 2102 247; (069) 2102 250 *Fax:* (069) 2102 227; (069) 2102 277 *E-mail:* litprom@book-fair.com *Web Site:* www.litprom.de, pg 1400

Ediciones Gestio 2000 SA (Spain) *Tel:* (093) 4106767 *Fax:* (093) 4109645 *E-mail:* info@gestion2000.com *Web Site:* www.gestion2000.com, pg 585

Gesundheits-Dialog Verlag GmbH (Germany) *Tel:* (089) 6 13 40 24 *Fax:* (089) 6 13 37 87 *E-mail:* dialog.top@t-online.de *Web Site:* www.gesundheits-dialog.de, pg 229

Uitgeverij De Geus BV (Netherlands) *Tel:* (076) 522 81 51 *Fax:* (076) 522 25 99 *E-mail:* email@degeus.nl *Web Site:* www.degeus.nl, pg 482

Paul Geuthner Librairie Orientaliste (France) *Tel:* (01) 43 29 75 64 *Fax:* (01) 46 34 71 30 *E-mail:* geuthner@geuthner.com *Web Site:* www.geuthner.com, pg 165

Ghana Publishing Corporation, Distribution and Sales Division (Ghana) *Tel:* (022) 812921, pg 1312

Ghana Academy of Arts & Sciences (Ghana) *Tel:* (021) 777651 *E-mail:* gaas@ghastinet.gn.apc.org, pg 304

Ghana Institute of Linguistics Literacy & Bible Translation (GILLBT) (Ghana) *Tel:* (021) 777525, pg 304

Ghana Institute of Management & Public Administration, Library & Documentation Centre (Ghana) *Tel:* (021) 401681; (021) 401682; (021) 401683 *Fax:* (021) 405805 *E-mail:* gimpa@excite.com, pg 1512

Ghana Library Association (Ghana) *Tel:* (021) 764822 *Fax:* (021) 763523, pg 1564

Ghana Library Board (Ghana) *Tel:* (021) 665 083 *Fax:* (021) 678 258, pg 1512

Ghana Publishing Corporation (Ghana) *Tel:* (021) 664338 *Fax:* (021) 664330 *E-mail:* asspcom@africaonline.com.gh *Web Site:* www.africaonline.com.gh/assembly, pg 304

Ghana Universities Press (GUP) (Ghana) *Tel:* (021) 22532, pg 304

Bruno Ghigi Editore (Italy) *Tel:* (0541) 791727 *Fax:* (0541) 791727, pg 390

Ghisetti e Corvi Editori (Italy) *Tel:* (02) 76006232 *Fax:* (02) 76009468 *E-mail:* sedes.spa@gpa.it *Web Site:* www.ghisetticorvi.it, pg 390

Giampiero Casagrande Editore (Switzerland) *Tel:* (091) 9235677 *Fax:* (091) 9220171, pg 624

Giancarlo Politi Editore (Italy) *Tel:* (02) 6887341 *Fax:* (02) 66801290 *E-mail:* politi@interbusiness.it *Web Site:* politi.undo.net, pg 390

Boekhandel Gianotten BV (Netherlands) *Tel:* (013) 465 11 11 *Fax:* (013) 535 59 62 *E-mail:* emma@gianotten.nl *Web Site:* www.gianotten.nl, pg 1329

Giao Duc Publishing House (Viet Nam) *Tel:* (04) 268151 *Fax:* (04) 262010, pg 780

G Giappichelli Editore SRL (Italy) *Tel:* (011) 8153111 *Fax:* (011) 8125100 *E-mail:* spedizioni@giappichelli.com *Web Site:* www.giappichelli.it, pg 390

E J W Gibb Memorial Trust (United Kingdom) *Tel:* (01985) 213409 *Fax:* (01985) 212910 *Web Site:* www.arisandphillips.com, pg 700

Stanley Gibbons Publications (United Kingdom) *Tel:* (01425) 472363 *Fax:* (01425) 470247 *E-mail:* sales@stangib.demon.co.uk *Web Site:* www.stanleygibbons.com, pg 700

Gibraltar Bookshop (Gibraltar) *Tel:* 71894 *Fax:* 75554, pg 1312

Gidlunds Bokforlag (Sweden) *Tel:* (0225) 77 11 55 *Fax:* (0255) 77 11 65 *E-mail:* utgivning@gidlunds.se *Web Site:* www.gidlunds.se, pg 612

Gidrometeoizdat (Russian Federation) *Tel:* (0812) 3520815 *Fax:* (0812) 3522688, pg 545

Gieck-Verlag GmbH (Germany) *Tel:* (089) 8415906 *Fax:* (089) 8403310, pg 229

Verlag Ernst und Werner Gieseking GmbH (Germany) *Tel:* (0521) 1 46 74 *Fax:* (0521) 14 37 15 *E-mail:* gieseking-verlag@t-online.de *Web Site:* www.gieseking-verlag.de, pg 229

H Gietl Verlag & Publikationsservice GmbH (Germany) *Tel:* (09402) 93 37-0 *Fax:* (09402) 93 37-24 *Web Site:* www.gietl-verlag.de, pg 229

Michael Gifkins & Associates (New Zealand) *Tel:* (09) 5235032 *Fax:* (09) 5235033 *E-mail:* michael.gifkins@xtra.co.nz, pg 1135

Gifu Diagaku Fuzoku Toshokan (Japan) *Tel:* (0582) 30-1111; (0582) 93-2191 *Fax:* (0582) 30-1107 *E-mail:* staff@acc.gifu-u.ac.jp *Web Site:* www.gifu-u.ac.jp, pg 1521

Gihan Book Shop (Sri Lanka), pg 606

Instituto de Cultura Juan Gil-Albert (Spain) *Tel:* (096) 5121 216; (096) 5121 300 *Fax:* (096) 5121 216 *E-mail:* galbert@dip-alicante.es *Web Site:* www.dip-alicante.es/galbert/, pg 585

Gildefachverlag GmbH & Co KG (Germany) *Tel:* (05181) 8004-0 *Fax:* (05181) 8004-90, pg 229

Editorial Gustavo Gili SA (Spain) *Tel:* (093) 3228161 *Fax:* (093) 3229205 *E-mail:* info@ggili.com *Web Site:* www.ggili.com, pg 585

Ediciones Gili SA de CV (Mexico) *Tel:* (05) 373-1744; (05) 5606011 *Fax:* (05) 3601453, pg 466

Giliukas Ltd (Lithuania) *Tel:* (07) 709560 *Fax:* (07) 709560 *E-mail:* giliukas@isi.kvn.lt, pg 1325

Gill & Macmillan Distribution (Ireland) *Tel:* (01) 500 9500 *Fax:* (01) 500 9599 *E-mail:* sales@gillmacmillan.ie *Web Site:* www.gillmacmillan.ie, pg 1319

Gill & Macmillan Ltd (Ireland) *Tel:* (01) 500 9500 *Fax:* (01) 500 9599 *E-mail:* sales@gillmacmillan.ie *Web Site:* www.gillmacmillan.ie, pg 360

Gilles und Francke Verlag (Germany) *Tel:* (0203) 362787 *Fax:* (0203) 355520 *E-mail:* verlag@gilles-francke.de *Web Site:* www.gilles-francke.de, pg 229

Gim-Yeong Co (Republic of Korea) *Tel:* (02) 7454823; (02) 7454825 *Fax:* (02) 7454826, pg 438

Gina Schlenz Literatur-Agentur Koln (Germany) *Tel:* (02206) 81125 *Fax:* (02206) 81125 *E-mail:* litschlenz@aol.com, pg 1131

Ginn & Co Ltd (United Kingdom) *Tel:* (01865) 888000 *Fax:* (01865) 314222 *E-mail:* enquiries@ginn.co.uk *Web Site:* www.ginn.co.uk, pg 700

A Van Ginneken (France) *Tel:* (0380) 789595 *Fax:* (0380) 740700 *E-mail:* hexalivre@axnet.fr, pg 1310

Ginninderra Press (Australia) *Tel:* (02) 6258 9060 *Fax:* (02) 6258 9069 *Web Site:* www.ginninderrapress.com.au, pg 23

Ginsberg Univ Boekhandel (Netherlands) *Tel:* (071) 5160562 *Fax:* (071) 5127505 *E-mail:* bree127@kooyker.nl, pg 1329

Giourdas Moschos (Greece) *Tel:* (01) 3624947 *E-mail:* mgiurdas@acci.gr *Web Site:* www.mgiurdas.gr, pg 307

Giovanis Publications, Pangosmios Ekdotikos Organismos (Greece) *Tel:* (01) 3825798; (01) 3301511 *Fax:* (01) 3824417 *E-mail:* giovani1@otenet.gr *Web Site:* www.geocities.com/giovanis_pub/en_main1.htm, pg 307

Edizioni del Girasole srl (Italy) *Tel:* (0544) 212830 *Fax:* (0544) 38432 *E-mail:* info@europart.it, pg 390

Girassol Edicoes, LDA (Portugal) *Tel:* (021) 41 43942 *Fax:* (021) 41 43518 *E-mail:* girassol@mail.telepac.pt, pg 532

Girault Gilbert bvba (Belgium) *Tel:* (02) 2171430; (02) 2175880 *Fax:* (02) 2173375, pg 67

Giri Trading Agency Pvt Ltd (India) *Tel:* (044) 4943551; (044) 4953817; (044) 4953823 *Fax:* (044) 4953823 *E-mail:* giritrading@vsnl.com *Web Site:* www.giritrading.com, pg 1316

Girol Books Inc (Canada) *Tel:* 613-233-9044 *Fax:* 613-233-9044 *E-mail:* info@girol.com *Web Site:* www.girol.com, pg 1175

Gisbert y Cia SA (Bolivia) *Tel:* (02) 20 26 26 *Fax:* (02) 20 29 11 *E-mail:* libgis@ceibo.entelnet.bo *Web Site:* www.sonnegocios.com, pg 75

Gisbert y Cia SA (Bolivia) *Tel:* (02) 220 26 26 *Fax:* (02) 220 29 11 *E-mail:* libgis@ceibo.entelnet.bo, pg 1303

Editions Jean Paul Gisserot (France) *Tel:* (01) 43 31 80 04 *Fax:* (01) 43 31 88 15 *E-mail:* editions-gisserot.com *Web Site:* www.editions-gisserot.com, pg 165

Gitanjali Publishing House (India) *Tel:* (011) 621991; (011) 6237555, pg 335

Promociones Culturales Gitral SA (Ecuador) *Tel:* (02) 510510; (02) 532060; (02) 32644 *Fax:* (02) 510510; (02) 326733, pg 1309

A Giuffre Editore SpA (Italy) *Tel:* (02) 380891 *Fax:* (02) 38009582 *E-mail:* giuffre@giuffre.it *Web Site:* www.giuffre.it, pg 390

Giunti Gruppo Editoriale (Italy) *Tel:* (055) 5062376 *Fax:* (055) 5062397 *E-mail:* informazioni@giunti.it *Web Site:* www.giunti.it, pg 390

Editrice la Giuntina (Italy) *Tel:* (055) 268684 *Fax:* (055) 219718 *E-mail:* giuntina@fol.it *Web Site:* www.giuntina.it, pg 391

Edizioni Giuridico Scientifiche (SRL) (Italy) *Tel:* (02) 55192219 *Fax:* (02) 76009444, pg 391

Gius Laterza e Figli SpA (Italy) *Tel:* (080) 5281211 *Fax:* (080) 5243461 *E-mail:* laterza@laterza.it *Web Site:* www.laterza.it, pg 391

Giuseppe Laterza Editore (Italy) *Tel:* (080) 5237936 *Fax:* (080) 5237360, pg 391

Gjurgja Journalistic & Publishing Firm (The Former Yugoslav Republic of Macedonia) *Tel:* (091) 228076, pg 452

Glad Sounds Sdn Bhd (Malaysia) *Tel:* (03) 7562901; (03) 7556442 *Fax:* (03) 7560528 *E-mail:* gladsnd@po.jaring.my, pg 456

Glas New Russian Writing (Russian Federation) *Tel:* (095) 441 9157 *Fax:* (095) 441 9157 *Web Site:* www.bham.ac.uk/glas; www.glas.msk.su, pg 545

Glasgow City Libraries & Archives, the Mitchell Library (United Kingdom) *Tel:* (0141) 287 2913; (0141) 287 2905 *Fax:* (0141) 226 8452 *E-mail:* archives@cls.glasgow.gov.uk *Web Site:* www.mitchelllibrary.org; www.glasgowlibraries.org, pg 1553

Glasgow City Libraries Publications (United Kingdom) *Tel:* (0141) 287 2846 *Fax:* (0141) 287 2815 *Web Site:* www.glasgowlibraries.org, pg 700

University of Glasgow (United Kingdom) *Tel:* (0141) 330 6704 *Fax:* (0141) 330 4952 *E-mail:* library@lib.gla.ac.uk *Web Site:* www.lib.gla.ac.uk, pg 1553

Eric Glass Ltd (United Kingdom) *Tel:* (020) 7229 9500 *Fax:* (020) 7229 6220, pg 1140

GLB Parkland Verlags-und Vertriebs GmbH (Germany) *Tel:* (0221) 96493-0 *Fax:* (0221) 964933, pg 229

Gleaner Co Ltd (Jamaica) *Tel:* 876-922-2340 *Fax:* 876-922-2319; 876-922-6297; 876-922-6223, pg 413

AB Gleerups Universitetsbokhandeln (Sweden) *Tel:* (046) 46 19 60 00 *Fax:* (046) 46 15 94 03, pg 1343

Verlag Gleitschirm (Switzerland) *Tel:* (081) 235241 *Fax:* (081) 221452, pg 624

Glenat Benelux SA (Belgium) *Tel:* (02) 7612640 *Fax:* (02) 7612645 *E-mail:* glenat@glenat.be *Web Site:* www.glenat.com, pg 67

Editions Glenat (France) *Tel:* (04) 76 88 75 75 *Fax:* (04) 76 88 75 70 *Web Site:* www.glenat.com, pg 165

Gloatz, Hille GmbH & Co KG fur Mehrfarben und Zellglasdruck (Germany) *Tel:* (030) 721 99 12; (030) 723 254 93 *Fax:* (030) 721 95 65 *E-mail:* gloatz.hille.gmbh@gmx.de; info@gloatz-hille.de *Web Site:* www.gloatz-hille.de, pg 229

Global Editora e Distribuidora Ltda (Brazil) *Tel:* (011) 2777999 *Fax:* (011) 2778141 *E-mail:* global@dialdata.com.br, pg 82

Global Editora e Distribuidora Ltda (Brazil) *Tel:* (011) 3277-7999, pg 1303

Global Educational Services Pte Ltd (Singapore) *Tel:* 7585086 *Fax:* 7586172 *E-mail:* global@signet.com.sg, pg 556

Global Kontakts Balgarija (Bulgaria) *Tel:* (02) 540636 *Fax:* (02) 528790, pg 94

Global Oriental Ltd (United Kingdom) *Tel:* (01303) 226799 *Fax:* (01303) 243087 *E-mail:* info@globaloriental.co.uk *Web Site:* www.globaloriental.co.uk, pg 700

Globi Verlag AG (Switzerland) *Tel:* (01) 4552130 *Fax:* (01) 4552188 *E-mail:* info@globi.ch *Web Site:* www.globi.ch, pg 624

Editora Globo SA (Brazil) *Tel:* (011) 3767-7886 *Fax:* (011) 3767-7870 *E-mail:* wcarelli@edglobo.com.br *Web Site:* www.editoraglobo.com.br, pg 82

Globus Buchvertrieb (Austria) *Tel:* (01) 513 96 92 0 *Fax:* (01) 513 96 92 9, pg 51

Casa de editura Globus (Romania) *Tel:* (01) 2231510; (01) 2231530 *Fax:* (01) 6664265, pg 540

Globus-Nakladni zavod (Croatia) *Tel:* (01) 462 8400 *Fax:* (01) 462 8400, pg 118

Glossa (Italy) *Tel:* (02) 877609 *Fax:* (02) 72003162 *E-mail:* informazioni@glossaeditrice.it *Web Site:* www.glossaeditrice.it, pg 391

Glowna Biblioteka Lekarska (Poland) *Tel:* (022) 849-78-51 *Fax:* (022) 849-78-02 *E-mail:* gbl@gbl.waw.pl *Web Site:* www.gbl.waw.pl, pg 1537

Biblioteka Glowna Politechniki Warszawskiej (Poland) *Tel:* (022) 6211370 *Fax:* (022) 6287184 *E-mail:* bgpw@bg.pw.edu.pl *Web Site:* www.bg.pw.edu.pl, pg 1537

Glowworm Books Ltd (United Kingdom) *Tel:* (01506) 857570 *Fax:* (01506) 858100 *E-mail:* admin@GlowwormBooks.co.uk; sales@amaising.co.uk (packaging); sales@glowwormbooks.co.uk (publishing & schools division) *Web Site:* www.GlowwormBooks.co.uk, pg 700

GLS Language Services (United Kingdom) *Tel:* (0141) 357 6611 *Fax:* (0141) 357 6605 *E-mail:* info@glslanguages.demon.co.uk *Web Site:* www.glslanguageservices.co.uk, pg 1150

Verlag Glueckauf GmbH (Germany) *Tel:* (02054) 924120 *Fax:* (02054) 924129 *E-mail:* info@vge.de; vertrieb@vge.de *Web Site:* www.vge.de, pg 229

Glydendal Akademisk (Norway) *Tel:* (022) 034300 *Fax:* (022) 034305 *E-mail:* akademisk@gyldendal.no *Web Site:* www.gyldendal.no/akademisk, pg 509

GMC Publications Ltd (United Kingdom) *Tel:* (01273) 477374; (01273) 488005 *Fax:* (01273) 478606 *E-mail:* pubs@thegmcgroup.com; theguild@thegmcgroup.com *Web Site:* www.thegmcgroup.com/pubsweb/, pg 700

Gmelin Verlag GmbH (Germany) *Tel:* (08152) 6671 *Fax:* (08152) 5120 *E-mail:* gerd.gmelin@gmelin-verlag.de *Web Site:* www.gmelin-verlag.de, pg 230

GMP Publishers Ltd (United Kingdom) *Tel:* (020) 8986 4854 *Fax:* (020) 8533 5821 *E-mail:* davidoraubrey@gmpub.demon.co.uk *Web Site:* www.gmppubs.co.uk, pg 700

Forlaget GMT (Denmark) *Tel:* 86386095, pg 131

Bruno Gmuender Verlag GmbH (Germany) *Tel:* (030) 615003-0 *Fax:* (030) 6159007 *E-mail:* info@brunogmuender.com *Web Site:* www.brunogmuender.com, pg 230

Gnostic Editions (Australia) *Tel:* (03) 9853 1401 *Fax:* (03) 9853 1481 *E-mail:* mail@gnoticeditions.com, pg 23

Gnostic Press Ltd (New Zealand) *Tel:* (09) 4838619 *Fax:* (09) 4190319 *E-mail:* gnostic.press@ihug.co.nz *Web Site:* homepages.ihug.co.nz/~gnosticpress, pg 496

Godfrey Cave Associates (United Kingdom) *Tel:* (020) 7416 3000 *Fax:* (020) 7416 3289, pg 1257

Godfrey Cave Associates Ltd (United Kingdom) *Tel:* (020) 7416 3000 *Fax:* (020) 7416 3289, pg 1351

Godfrey Cave Holdings Ltd (United Kingdom) *Tel:* (020) 7416 3000 *Fax:* (020) 7416 3099, pg 1351

Celia Godkin (Canada) *Tel:* 613-275-7204 *Fax:* 613-275-7204 *E-mail:* celia.godkin@utoronto.ca, pg 1175

Godord (Iceland) *Tel:* 551-6998, pg 325

Godsfield Press Ltd (United Kingdom) *Tel:* (01962) 735633; (01626) 323200 (general enquiries) *Fax:* (01962) 735320; (01626) 323319 (general enquiries) *E-mail:* mail@davidandcharles.co.uk *Web Site:* www.davidandcharles.co.uk, pg 701

Godwit Publishing Ltd (New Zealand) *Tel:* (09) 4805410 *Fax:* (09) 4805930, pg 496

BV Uitgeversbedryf Het Goede Boek (Netherlands) *Tel:* (35) 525 35 08 *Fax:* (35) 525 40 13, pg 482

Goel Prakashen (India) *Tel:* (0121) 642946; (0121) 644766 *Fax:* (0121) 645855, pg 335

Alois Goschl & Co (Austria) *Tel:* (01) 321180 *Fax:* (01) 651899, pg 51

Goteborgs Stadsbibliotek (Sweden) *Tel:* (031) 61-65-00 *Fax:* (031) 61-66-93, pg 1547

Goeteborgs Universitetsbibliotek (Sweden) *Tel:* (031) 7731000 *Fax:* (031) 16 37 97 *E-mail:* library@ub.gu.se *Web Site:* www.ub.gu.se, pg 1547

Cornelia Goethe Literaturverlag (Germany) *Tel:* (069) 40894-0 *Fax:* (069) 40894-169 *E-mail:* literatur@fouque-verlag.de *Web Site:* www.cornelia-goethe.de; www.fouque-verlag.de, pg 230

Goethe-Gesellschaft in Weimar eV (Germany) *Tel:* (03643) 20 20 50 *Fax:* (03643) 20 20 61 *E-mail:* goetheges@aol.com *Web Site:* www.goethe-gesellschaft.de, pg 1400

Goethe-Institut (Belgium) *Tel:* (02) 230 39 70 *Fax:* (02) 230 77 25 *E-mail:* eu@bruessel.goethe.org *Web Site:* www.goethe.de/be/bru/deindex.htm, pg 1493

Goethe-Verlag, Godhard von Heydebrand (Switzerland) *Tel:* (031) 833248, pg 624

Golden Cockerel Press Ltd (United Kingdom) *Tel:* (020) 7405 7979 *Fax:* (020) 7404 3598, pg 701

Golden Cup Printing Co Ltd (Hong Kong) *Tel:* 23434254 *Fax:* 23415426 *E-mail:* info@goldencup.com.hk *Web Site:* www.goldencup.com.hk, pg 1156

Golden Cup Printing Co Ltd (Hong Kong) *Tel:* 23434254; 23434255 *Fax:* 23415426 *E-mail:* sales@goldencup.com.hk *Web Site:* www.goldencup.com.hk, pg 1178, 1218

Golden Cup Printing Co Ltd (Hong Kong) *Tel:* 23434254 *Fax:* 23415426 *E-mail:* sales@goldencup.com.hk *Web Site:* www.goldencup.com.hk, pg 1236

Golden Cup Printing Co Ltd (Hong Kong) *Tel:* 23434254 *Fax:* 223415426 *E-mail:* info@goldencup.com.hk; sales@goldencup.com.hk *Web Site:* www.goldencup.com.hk, pg 1246

Golden Publications (Mauritius) *Tel:* 2416640, pg 461

Goldland Business Co Ltd (Nigeria) *Tel:* (01) 8023179087; (01) 821203 *E-mail:* goldland@consultant.com, pg 505

Wilhelm Goldmann Verlag GmbH (Germany) *Tel:* (089) 4136-0; (01805) 990505 (hot line) *Fax:* (089) 43722812 *E-mail:* vertrieb.verlagsgruppe@bertelsmann.de, pg 230

Victor Goldschmidt Verlagsbuchhandlung (Switzerland) *Tel:* (061) 236565 *Fax:* (061) 2616123, pg 624

Goldschneck Verlag (Germany) *Tel:* (07151) 66 01 19 *Fax:* (07151) 66 07 78 *Web Site:* www.goldschneck.de, pg 230

Goldshield Communications Ltd (United Kingdom) *Tel:* (0114) 2431000 *Fax:* (0114) 2433000, pg 1184, 1226

The Goldsmith Press Ltd (Ireland) *Tel:* (045) 433613 *Fax:* (045) 434648 *E-mail:* de@iol.ie, pg 360

Goll Bruno Verlag fur Aussergewoehnliche Perspektiven (VAP) (Germany) *Tel:* (05742) 93 04 44 *Fax:* (05742) 93 04 55 *Web Site:* www.vap-buch.de, pg 230

Gollancz/Witherby (United Kingdom) *Tel:* (020) 7240 3444 *Fax:* (020) 7240 4822 *E-mail:* info@orionbooks.co.uk *Web Site:* www.orionbooks.co.uk, pg 701

Gomer Press (J D Lewis & Sons Ltd) (United Kingdom) *Tel:* (01559) 362371 *Fax:* (01559) 363758 *E-mail:* gwasg@gomer.co.uk *Web Site:* www.gomer.co.uk, pg 701

Gomez Gomez Hermanos Editores S de RL Edicion de Libros y Revistas (Mexico) *Tel:* (05) 55225903; (05) 6123906 *Fax:* (05) 633786, pg 466

Gondolat Kiado (Hungary) *Tel:* (01) 38-3358 *Fax:* (01) 138-4540, pg 321

Gondrom Verlag GmbH & Co KG (Germany) *Tel:* (09208) 51-0 *Fax:* (09208) 51-21 *E-mail:* service@gondrom.de *Web Site:* www.gondrom.de, pg 230

Editions Gondwana (Martinique) *Tel:* 580676; 580014 *Fax:* 580014, pg 460

Gondwanaland Press (New Zealand) *Tel:* (04) 4758092 *Fax:* (04) 4756194, pg 496

Pierre Gonin Editions d'Art (Switzerland) *Tel:* (021) 7285948 *Fax:* (021) 7285948 *Web Site:* www.lemeilleur.ch/editionsgonin, pg 624

Gono Prakashani, Gono Shasthya Kendra (Bangladesh) *Tel:* (02) 500406; (02) 839366 *Fax:* (02) 863567; (02) 833182 *E-mail:* gk.mail@drik.bgd.toolnet.org, pg 61

Librerias Gonvill SA de CV (Mexico) *Tel:* (033) 83-72-309 *Fax:* (033) 3837-2309 *E-mail:* librosbooks@gonvill.com.mx *Web Site:* www.gonvill.com.mx, pg 1327

Good Earth Publishing Co Ltd (Hong Kong) *Tel:* 2338 6103 *Fax:* 2338 3610, pg 317

Goodbooks Publishing Co (Ghana) *Tel:* (021) 665629 *Fax:* (021) 302993 *E-mail:* allgoodbooks@hotmail.com, pg 304

Goodwill Bookstore (Philippines) *Tel:* (02) 895-8684 *Fax:* (02) 895-7854 *E-mail:* gbs@goodwillbookstore.net *Web Site:* www.goodwillbookstore.com, pg 1335

Van Goor BV (Netherlands) *Tel:* (020) 5353135 *Fax:* (020) 5353130 *E-mail:* boekerij@boekery.nl *Web Site:* www.van-goor.nl, pg 483

Uitgeverij CJ Goossens BV (Netherlands) *Tel:* (015) 2123623 *Fax:* (015) 2124295, pg 483

A H Gordon (United Kingdom) *Tel:* (01280) 848 650, pg 701

The Robert Gordon University (United Kingdom) *Tel:* (01224) 262000 *Fax:* (01224) 263553 *E-mail:* sim@rgu.ac.uk *Web Site:* www.rgu.ac.uk, pg 701

Gorenjski Tisk Printing House (Slovenia) *Tel:* (04) 2016300 *Fax:* (04) 2016301 *E-mail:* info@go-tisk.si *Web Site:* www.go-tisk.si, pg 1162, 1182, 1223

Gorenjski Tisk Printing House (Slovenia) *Tel:* (064) 263 0 *Fax:* (064) 241 323 *E-mail:* info@go-tisk.si *Web Site:* www.go-tisk.si, pg 1238, 1246

Biblioteca Bio-Medica del Laboratorio Conmemorativo Gorgas (Panama) *Tel:* (02) 274111 *Fax:* (02) 254366 *E-mail:* igorgas@sin.fonet, pg 1535

Gosudarstvennaya publichnaya nauchno-tekhnicheskaya biblioteka SSSR (Russian Federation) *Tel:* (095) 9259288 *Fax:* (095) 9219862 *E-mail:* root@gpntb.msk.su, pg 1540

Gosudarstvennaya publichnaya istoricheskaya biblioteka Rossii (Russian Federation) *Tel:* (095) 925-65-14; (095) 928-05-22 *Fax:* (095) 928-02-84 *E-mail:* info@shpl.ru *Web Site:* www.shpl.ru, pg 1540

Gosudarstvennaya Respublikanskaya biblioteka Gruzinskoi SSR im K Marksai (Georgia) *E-mail:* navoi@physic.uzsci.net *Web Site:* www.osi.uz/library, pg 1508

Gosudarstvenny Komitet Armjamskoj SSR po delam izdatel'stv, poligrafii, kniznoj targovli (Armenia) *Tel:* (02) 528660 *E-mail:* grapalat@arminco.com, pg 1259

Foerlagshuset Gothia (Sweden) *Tel:* (08) 4622660 *Fax:* (08) 4620322 *E-mail:* info.gothia@verbum.se *Web Site:* www.gothia.nu, pg 612

Gotthelf-Verlag (Switzerland) *Tel:* (01) 2428155 *Fax:* (01) 2646486 *E-mail:* rms@reinhardt.ch, pg 624

Gottmer Uitgevers Groep (Netherlands) *Tel:* (023) 541 11 90 *Fax:* (023) 527 44 04 *E-mail:* info@gottmer.nl *Web Site:* www.gottmer.nl, pg 483

Gould Genealogy (Australia) *Tel:* (08) 8396 1110 *Fax:* (08) 8396 1163 *E-mail:* inquiries@gould.com.au *Web Site:* www.gould.com.au, pg 23

Gousudarstvennaja Biblioteka Respublika Tadzkistan im Firdousi (Tajikistan) *Tel:* (03772) 274 726, pg 1549

Government Public Library (Liberia), pg 1525

Government Library (Libyan Arab Jamahiriya), pg 1525

Government Information Services (Hong Kong) *Tel:* 2842 8777 *Fax:* 2845 9078 *Web Site:* www.info.gov.hk/isd, pg 1272

Government of Pakistan Department of Libraries (Pakistan) *Tel:* (051) 9214523; (051) 92026436; (051) 9206440 *Fax:* (051) 9221375 *E-mail:* nlpiba@paknet2.ptc.pk *Web Site:* www.nlp.gov.pk, pg 1569

Government Press (Afghanistan) *Tel:* 26851, pg 1

Government Press (Kenya) *Tel:* 334075, pg 434

Government Printer (Ethiopia), pg 140

Government Printer (Gambia) *Tel:* 227399, pg 190

The Government Printer (Israel) *Tel:* (02) 5685111; (02) 5685200 *Fax:* (02) 5685226, pg 1159

Government Printer (Lesotho) *Tel:* 313023, pg 447

Government Printer (South Africa) *Tel:* (012) 323-9731; (012) 457-531; (021) 457-531 *Fax:* (012) 461-4404, pg 564

Government Printer (United Republic of Tanzania), pg 643

Government Printer (Zambia) *Tel:* (01) 215401; (01) 215805; (01) 215685; (01) 216972, pg 781

Government Printer (Imprimerie National du Rwanda) (Rwanda) *Tel:* 75350 *Fax:* 75820, pg 550

Government Printer (Imprimerie National Du Tchad) (Chad), pg 98

Government Printer (Imprimerie Nationale) (Madagascar) *Tel:* (02) 23675, pg 453

Government Printer (Imprimerie Nationale) (Malawi) *Tel:* (050) 523155 *Fax:* (050) 52230133, pg 454

Government Printer (Imprimerie Nationale) (Mauritius) *Tel:* 2345294; 2345295, pg 461

Government Printer (Imprimerie Officielle) (Morocco) *Tel:* (077) 65024, pg 475

Government Printer (Imprimerie Officielle de la Republique Tunisienne - IORT) (Tunisia) *Tel:* (01) 299914, pg 648

Government Printer (INABU) (Burundi) *Tel:* (02) 22214; (02) 24046, pg 97

Government Printer (Societe De L'Imprimerie Nationale Du Niger) (Niger) *Tel:* 734798, pg 503

Government Publications Ireland (Ireland) *Tel:* (01) 6476000 *Fax:* (01) 6610747 *E-mail:* info@opw.ie *Web Site:* www.opw.ie, pg 360

Govi-Verlag Pharmazeutischer Verlag GmbH (Germany) *Tel:* (06196) 9 28-2 0; (06196) 9 28-2 29 *Fax:* (06196) 9 28-2 33 *E-mail:* service@govi.de *Web Site:* www.govi.de, pg 230

Govinda-Verlag (Switzerland) *Tel:* (052) 6726677 *Fax:* (052) 6726678 *E-mail:* info@govinda.ch *Web Site:* www.govinda.ch, pg 624

Govostis Publishing SA (Greece) *Tel:* (010) 3816661, pg 307

Gower Publishing Ltd (United Kingdom) *Tel:* (01252) 331551 *Fax:* (01252) 344405 *E-mail:* info@gowerpub.com *Web Site:* www.gowerpub.com, pg 701

Gozo Press (Malta) *Tel:* 551534; 564395 *Fax:* 560857 *E-mail:* gozopress@orbit.net.mt, pg 460

Gozo Public Library (Malta) *Tel:* (021) 556200 *Fax:* (021) 560599 *E-mail:* gozo.libraries@gov.mt *Web Site:* servicecharters.gov.mt, pg 1527

Edicoes Graal Ltda (Brazil) *Tel:* (011) 7961-0006 *Fax:* (011) 7961-0006, pg 83

Ordem do Graal na Terra (Brazil) *Tel:* (011) 4781-0006 *Fax:* (011) 4781-0006 (ext 217) *E-mail:* graal@graal.org.br *Web Site:* www.graal.org.br, pg 83

Grabert-Verlag (Germany) *Tel:* (07071) 40700 *Fax:* (07071) 407026, pg 230

Gracewing/Fowler Wright Books (United Kingdom) *Tel:* (01568) 616835 *Fax:* (01568) 613289 *Web Site:* www.gracewing.co.uk, pg 1351

Gracewing Publishing (United Kingdom) *Tel:* (01568) 616835 *E-mail:* gracewingx@aol.com *Web Site:* www.gracewing.co.uk, pg 701

Grada Publishing (Czech Republic) *Tel:* (02) 20386401; (02) 20386402 *Fax:* (02) 20386400 *E-mail:* info@gradapublishing.cz; obchod@gradapublishing.cz *Web Site:* www.gradapublishing.cz; www.grada.cz, pg 123

Gradevinska Knjiga (Serbia and Montenegro) *Tel:* (011) 323 35 65; (011) 324 76 62 *Fax:* (011) 323 32 34, pg 552

Izdavacka preduzece Gradina (Serbia and Montenegro) *Tel:* (018) 25 864; (018) 25 456 *Fax:* (018) 25 456 *E-mail:* gradinar@bankerinter.net, pg 552

Gradiva-Publicacnoes Lda (Portugal) *Tel:* (021) 397 40 67; (021) 397 40 68; (021) 397 13 57 *Fax:* (021) 395 34 71 *E-mail:* geral@ip.pt *Web Site:* www.gradiva.pt, pg 532

Graduate Institute of International Studies (Switzerland) *Tel:* (022) 9085700 *Fax:* (022) 9085710 *E-mail:* info@hei.unige.ch *Web Site:* www.hei.unige.ch, pg 624

Graefe und Unzer Verlag GmbH (Germany) *Tel:* (089) 4 19 81-0 *Fax:* (089) 4 19 81-113 *E-mail:* leserservice@graefe-und-unzer.de *Web Site:* www.graefe-und-unzer.de, pg 230

Graf Editions (Germany) *Tel:* (089) 27 159 57 *Fax:* (089) 27 159 97 *Web Site:* www.graf-editions.de, pg 231

Graff Buchhandlung (Germany) *Tel:* (0531) 480 89-0 *Fax:* (0531) 480 89-89 *E-mail:* infos@graff.de *Web Site:* www.graff.de, pg 1311

Graffiti Publications (Australia) *Tel:* (03) 5472 3805 *E-mail:* graffiti@netcon.net.au *Web Site:* www.graffitipub.com.au, pg 23

Editora e Grafica Carisio Ltda, Minas Editora (Brazil) *Tel:* (034) 2413557 *Fax:* (034) 2413310, pg 83

Grafica e Arte srl (Italy) *Tel:* (035) 255014 *Fax:* (035) 250164 *E-mail:* info@graficaearte.it *Web Site:* www.graficaearte.it, pg 391

Grafica Editora Primor Ltda (Brazil) *Tel:* (021) 4744966, pg 83

Marchesi Grafiche Editoriali SpA (Italy) *Tel:* (06) 331359 *Fax:* (06) 3336505, pg 391

Graficki zavod Hrvatske (Croatia) *Tel:* (01) 2404 444; (01) 240 7166 *Fax:* (01) 240 4444, pg 118

Grafit Verlag GmbH (Germany) *Tel:* (0231) 7214650 *Fax:* (0231) 7214677 *E-mail:* info@grafit.de *Web Site:* www.grafit.de, pg 231

Grafo (Italy) *Tel:* (030) 393221 *Fax:* (030) 3701411, pg 391

Grafos SA Arte Sobre Papel (Spain) *Tel:* (093) 261 87 50 *Fax:* (093) 263 10 04 *E-mail:* info@grafos-barcelona.com *Web Site:* www.grafos-barcelona.com, pg 1223, 1238

Graham Brash Pte Ltd (Singapore) *Tel:* 6262 4843 *Fax:* 6262 1519 *E-mail:* graham_brash@giro.com.sg *Web Site:* www.grahambrash.com.sg, pg 556

Graham-Cameron Publishing & Illustration (United Kingdom) *Tel:* (01263) 821 333 *Fax:* (01263) 821 334 *E-mail:* enquiry@graham-cameron-illustration.com *Web Site:* www.graham-cameron-illustration.com, pg 701

The Graham Publishing Company (Pvt) Ltd (Zimbabwe) *Tel:* (04) 706207 *Fax:* (04) 752439, pg 783

W F Graham (Northampton) Ltd (United Kingdom) *Tel:* (01604) 645537 *Fax:* (01604) 648414, pg 701

Grahames Bookshop (Australia) *Tel:* (02) 9296144 *Fax:* (02) 9571814, pg 1298

Grainger Museum (Australia) *Tel:* (03) 8344 5270 *Fax:* (03) 9349 1707 *E-mail:* grainger@unimelb.edu.au *Web Site:* www.lib.unimelb.edu.au/collections/grainger, pg 24

Verlag der Stiftung Gralsbotschaft GmbH (Germany) *Tel:* (0711) 294355 *Fax:* (07156) 18663 *E-mail:* info@gral.de *Web Site:* www.gral.de, pg 231

Gram Editora (Argentina) *Tel:* (011) 4304-4833; (011) 4305-8397 *Fax:* (011) 4304-5692 *E-mail:* grameditora@infovia.com.ar *Web Site:* www.grameditora.com.ar, pg 6

Gramedia (Indonesia) *Tel:* (021) 5483008; (021) 5490666 *Fax:* (021) 5300545 *Web Site:* www.gramedia.co.id, pg 355

Gramedia Bookshop (Indonesia) *Tel:* (021) 5300545 *Fax:* (021) 5486085, pg 1318

Gran Enciclopedia-Asturiana Silverio Canada (Spain) *Tel:* (0985) 170921; (0985) 349684 *Fax:* (0985) 349542 *E-mail:* gea.edi@teleline.es; gea_edi@yahoo.es *Web Site:* www.enciclopediaasturiana.com, pg 585

Editions Jacques Grancher (France) *Tel:* (01) 42 22 64 80 *Fax:* (01) 45 48 25 03 *E-mail:* info@grancher.com *Web Site:* www.grancher.com, pg 165

The Grand National Assembly of Turkey Library & Documentation TBMM (Turkey) *Tel:* (0312) 420 68 35 *Fax:* (0312) 420 75 48 *E-mail:* library@tbmm.gov.tr *Web Site:* www.tbmm.gov.tr, pg 1551

Grand People's Study House (Democratic People's Republic of Korea) *Tel:* (02) 84 40 66 *Fax:* (08502) 381-4427; (08502) 381-2100, pg 1523

Grand People's Study House (Democratic People's Republic of Korea) *Tel:* (02) 84 4066, pg 1523

Editions du Grand-Pont (Switzerland) *Tel:* (021) 3123222 *Fax:* (021) 3113222, pg 624

Grande Loge de Luxembourg (Luxembourg) *Tel:* 463-566 *Fax:* 463566, pg 451

Grandi & Associati SRL (Italy) *Tel:* (02) 4695541; (02) 4818962 *Fax:* (02) 48195108 *E-mail:* agenzia@grandieassociati.it, pg 1133

Editions Grandir (France) *Tel:* (04) 66 84 01 19 *Fax:* (04) 66 26 14 50, pg 166

Grandreams Ltd (United Kingdom) *Tel:* (01225) 429383 *Fax:* (01225) 428161 *E-mail:* wrrake@robert-frederick.co.uk, pg 702

Grange Books PLC (United Kingdom) *Tel:* (01634) 256 000 *Fax:* (01634) 255 500 *E-mail:* grangebooks@aol.com *Web Site:* www.grangebooks.co.uk, pg 702, 1351

Granit Editions (France) *Tel:* (01) 40 71 98 75 *Fax:* (01) 46 51 30 06, pg 166

Granit sro (Czech Republic) *Tel:* (02) 27 018 361 *Fax:* (02) 27 018 361 *E-mail:* info@granit-publishing.cz *Web Site:* www.granit-publishing.cz, pg 123

Granrott Press (Australia) *Tel:* (08) 8383 6081 *Fax:* (08) 8383 6067, pg 24

Grant & Cutler Ltd (United Kingdom) *Tel:* (020) 7734 2012 *Fax:* (020) 7734 9272 *E-mail:* contactus@grantandcutler.com *Web Site:* www.grantandcutler.com, pg 702

Granta Books (United Kingdom) *Tel:* (020) 7704 9776 *Fax:* (020) 7704 0474 *E-mail:* info@granta.com *Web Site:* www.granta.com, pg 702

Grantham Book Services Ltd (United Kingdom) *Tel:* (01476) 541000; (01476) 541 080 (orders) *Fax:* (01476) 541061 *E-mail:* orders@gbs.tbs-ltd.co.uk, pg 1351

Grantham House Publishing (New Zealand) *Tel:* (04) 3813071 *Fax:* (04) 3813067 *E-mail:* gstewart@iconz.co.nz, pg 496

Grao Editorial (Spain) *Tel:* (093) 4080464; (093) 4050455 *Fax:* (093) 3524737 *E-mail:* grao@grao.com; editorial@grao.com *Web Site:* www.grao.com, pg 585

Grao Editorial (Spain) *Tel:* (093) 4080464; (093) 4050455 *Fax:* (093) 3524737 *E-mail:* grao@grao.com *Web Site:* www.grao.com, pg 585

Graphic Art (28) Co Ltd (Thailand) *Tel:* (02) 2330302, pg 645

Graphic Educational Publications (New Zealand) *Tel:* (09) 6300488 *Fax:* (09) 6234196, pg 496

Graphic Reproductions Ltd (Ireland) *Tel:* (01) 6230101 *Fax:* (01) 6166598; (01) 6166599, pg 1179

Graphic Services Corp (United States) *Tel:* 203-270-7578 *Fax:* 203-270-1578 *Web Site:* www.independentcartongroup.com, pg 1240

Edition Graphischer Zirkel (Austria) *Tel:* (01) 0277346615, pg 51

GRASPO CZ AS - Druckerei und Buchbinderei (Czech Republic) *Tel:* (0577) 606111 *Fax:* (0577) 104052 *E-mail:* graspo@graspo.com; mp@graspo.com *Web Site:* www.graspo.com, pg 1216

Grass Roots Publishing (Australia) *Tel:* (03) 5794 7256 *Fax:* (03) 5794 7285, pg 24

Grass-Verlag (Germany) *Tel:* (02173) 51305 *Fax:* (02224) 770515, pg 231

Sarl Editions Jean Grassin (France) *Tel:* (02) 97 52 93 63 *Fax:* (02) 97 52 83 90 *E-mail:* j.grassin@wanadoo.fr *Web Site:* www.editions-grassin.com, pg 166

Graton Editeur NV (Belgium) *Tel:* (02) 6756 666 *Fax:* (02) 6756 363 *E-mail:* graton.sa@skynet.be, pg 68

Graz Stadtmuseum (Austria) *Tel:* (0316) 822580 *Fax:* (0316) 822580-6 *Web Site:* homepage.sime.com, pg 51

Universitaetsbibliothek Graz (Austria) *Tel:* (0316) 380 3102 *Fax:* (0316) 384 987 *E-mail:* ub.auskunft@uni-graz.at *Web Site:* www.ub.uni-graz.at, pg 1491

Great China Book Company (Taiwan, Province of China) *Tel:* (02) 82263099 *Fax:* (02) 82265906, pg 640

Library of the Great Mosque of Sana'a (Yemen), pg 1555

Great Wall Graphics Ltd (Hong Kong) *Tel:* 2524 0014 *Fax:* 2845 3588, pg 1156

Great Western Press Pty Ltd (Australia) *Tel:* (02) 4124 394 *Fax:* (02) 9144 5566, pg 24

Greater Glider Productions Australia Pty Ltd (Australia) *Tel:* (07) 5494 3000 *Fax:* (07) 5494 3284, pg 24

Editorial Gredos SA (Spain) *Tel:* (091) 7444920 *Fax:* (091) 5192033 *E-mail:* comercial@editorialgredos.com *Web Site:* www.editorialgredos.com, pg 585

The Greek Bookshop (United Kingdom) *Tel:* (020) 8446 1986 *Fax:* (020) 8446 1985 *E-mail:* info@thegreekbookshop.com *Web Site:* www.thegreekbookshop.com, pg 702

Greek Institute (United Kingdom) *Tel:* (020) 8360 7968 *Fax:* (020) 8360 7968, pg 1150

Green Books Ltd (United Kingdom) *Tel:* (01803) 863260 *Fax:* (01803) 863843 *E-mail:* greenbooks@gn.apc.org *Web Site:* www.greenbooks.co.uk, pg 702

Christine Green Authors' Agent (United Kingdom) *Tel:* (020) 7041 8844 *Fax:* (020) 7686 8860 *E-mail:* info@christinegreen.co.uk *Web Site:* www.christinegreen.co.uk, pg 1140

The Green Pagoda Press Ltd (Hong Kong) *Tel:* 2561 1924 *Fax:* 2811 0946 *E-mail:* gpinfo@gpp.com.hk *Web Site:* www.greenpagoda.com, pg 1178

The Green Pagoda Press Ltd (Hong Kong) *Tel:* 2561 1924 *Fax:* 2811 0946 *E-mail:* gpinfo@gpp.com.hk *Web Site:* www.gpp.com.hk, pg 1218

The Green Pagoda Press Ltd (Hong Kong) *Tel:* 2561 1924 *Fax:* 2811 0946 *E-mail:* gpinfo@gpp.com.hk *Web Site:* www.greenpagoda.com, pg 1236

Green Street Bindery (United Kingdom) *Tel:* (01865) 243297 *Fax:* (01865) 791329, pg 1226

W Green The Scottish Law Publisher (United Kingdom) *Tel:* (0131) 225 4879 (orders); (0131) 225 4879 (marketing); (0207) 449 1104 (trade customers); (264) 342 828 (international book orders & information); (264) 342 766 (international subscription orders & information) *Fax:* (0131) 225 2104 (orders); (0131) 225 2104 (marketing); (0207) 449 1144 (trade customers); (264) 342 761 (international book orders & information); (264) 342 761 (international subscription orders & information) *E-mail:* enquiries@thomson.com; trade.sales@sweetandmaxwell.co.uk (trade customers) *Web Site:* www.wgreen.co.uk, pg 702

Greene & Heaton Ltd (United Kingdom) *Tel:* (020) 8749 0315 *Fax:* (020) 8749 0318 *Web Site:* www.greeneheaton.co.uk, pg 1140

Greene's Bookshop Ltd (Ireland) *Tel:* (01) 6762554 *Fax:* (01) 6789091 *E-mail:* info@greenesbookshop.com *Web Site:* www.greenesbookshop.com, pg 1319

Greenhill Books/Lionel Leventhal Ltd (United Kingdom) *Tel:* (020) 8458 6314 *Fax:* (020) 8905 5245 *E-mail:* info@greenhillbooks.com; sales@greenhillbooks.com *Web Site:* www.greenhillbooks.com, pg 703

Greger-Delacroix (Hungary) *Tel:* (01) 608936 *E-mail:* gregerdelacroix@compuserve.com; greger@elender.hu, pg 321

Gregg Publishing Co (United Kingdom) *Tel:* (01444) 445070 *Fax:* (01444) 445050 *E-mail:* Rdowling@gowerpub.com, pg 703

Libreria Editrice Gregoriana (Italy) *Tel:* (049) 657493 *Fax:* (049) 659777, pg 391

Gregoriana Libreria Editrice (Italy) *Tel:* (049) 657493 *Fax:* (049) 662089, pg 1321

Gregory & Company Authors' Agents (United Kingdom) *Tel:* (020) 7610 4676 *Fax:* (020) 7610 4686 *E-mail:* info@gregoryandcompany.co.uk *Web Site:* www.gregoryandcompany.co.uk, pg 1140

Ernesto Gremese Editore srl (Italy) *Tel:* (06) 65740507 *Fax:* (06) 65740509 *E-mail:* gremese@gremese.com *Web Site:* www.gremese.com, pg 391

Gremese International srl (Italy) *Tel:* (06) 65740507 *Fax:* (06) 65740509 *E-mail:* gremese@gremese.com *Web Site:* www.gremese.com, pg 391

Gresham Books Ltd (United Kingdom) *Tel:* (01865) 513582 *Fax:* (01865) 512718 *E-mail:* info@gresham-books.co.uk *Web Site:* www.gresham-books.co.uk, pg 703

Greuthof Verlag und Vertrieb GmbH (Germany) *Tel:* (07681) 6025 *Fax:* (07681) 6027, pg 231

Grevas Forlag (Denmark) *Tel:* 86997065 *Fax:* 86997265, pg 131

Greven Verlag Koeln GmbH (Germany) *Tel:* (0221) 20 33-161 *Fax:* (0221) 20 33-162 *E-mail:* greven.verlag@greven.de *Web Site:* www.greven-verlag.de, pg 231

Piero Gribaudi Editore (Italy) *Tel:* (02) 89302244 *Fax:* (02) 89302376 *E-mail:* info@gribaudi.it *Web Site:* www.gribaudi.it, pg 391

John Grieg Forlag AS (Norway) *Tel:* 55213181 *Fax:* 55218180, pg 509

Griese Ingolf Wipe Griese (Germany) *Tel:* (0231) 417412 *Fax:* (0231) 418461; (0231) 417418, pg 231

Editions du Griffon (Neuchatel) (Switzerland) *Tel:* (032) 7252204, pg 624

Grijalbo SA (Venezuela) *Tel:* (02) 238 15 42; (02) 238 17 32 *Fax:* (02) 239 03 08 *E-mail:* griven@etheron.net, pg 779

Grijalbo Mondadon SA Junior (Spain) *Tel:* (093) 4767100 *Fax:* (093) 4767121, pg 585

Grijalbo Mondadori SA (Chile) *Tel:* (02) 782-8200 *Fax:* (02) 782-8210 *E-mail:* editorial@randomhouse-mondadori.cl *Web Site:* www.grijalbo.com, pg 99

Grijalbo Mondadori SA (Spain) *Tel:* (093) 4767100 *Fax:* (093) 4767121 *E-mail:* marketing@grijalbo.com *Web Site:* www.grijalbo.com, pg 585

Editorial Grijalbo SA de CV (Mexico) *Tel:* (05) 3584355 *Fax:* (05) 3584312 *Web Site:* www.grijalbo.com.mx, pg 466

Grimm Press Ltd (Taiwan, Province of China) *Tel:* (02) 23517251 *Fax:* (02) 23517244 *E-mail:* ishbel@cite.com.tw, pg 640

Grivas Publications (Greece) *Tel:* (0210) 5573470 *Fax:* (0210) 5573076 *E-mail:* info@grivas.gr *Web Site:* www.grivas.gr, pg 1313

Groeninghe NV (Belgium) *Tel:* (056) 22 40 77 *Fax:* (056) 22 82 86 *Web Site:* www.groeninghe.com, pg 68

David Grossman Literary Agency Ltd (United Kingdom) *Tel:* (020) 7221 2770 *Fax:* (020) 7221 1445, pg 1140

Grote'sche Verlagsbuchhandlung GmbH & Co KG (Germany) *Tel:* (02234) 1060 *Fax:* (02234) 106284, pg 231

Groto Publikasi (Suriname) *Tel:* (0597) 493569, pg 608

Editions Francois Grounauer (Switzerland) *Tel:* (022) 447948, pg 624

Editora Ground Ltda (Brazil) *Tel:* (011) 5031-1500 *Fax:* (011) 5031-3462 *E-mail:* editora@ground.com.br; vendas@ground.com.br; marketing@ground.com.br *Web Site:* www.ground.com.br, pg 83

Groupe de Recherche et d'Echanges Technologiques (GRET) (France) *Tel:* (01) 40 05 61 61 *Fax:* (01) 40 05 61 10 *E-mail:* gret@gret.org; librairie@gret.org *Web Site:* www.gret.org, pg 166

Groupe des Editions du Rocher (France) *Tel:* (01) 40 46 54 00 *Fax:* (01) 40 46 91 36, pg 166

Groupe Express-Expansion (France) *Tel:* (01) 53 91 10 63 *Fax:* (01) 53 91 10 06 *Web Site:* www.groupe-expansion.com, pg 166

Groupe Hatier International (France) *Tel:* (01) 44 39 28 00 *Fax:* (01) 45 44 84 54 *E-mail:* hatier@intl.com, pg 166

Groupe Revue Fiduciaire (France) *Tel:* (01) 47 70 42 42 *Fax:* (01) 48 24 12 93 *E-mail:* courrier@grouperf.com *Web Site:* www.grouperf.com, pg 166

Groupement d'Information Promotion Presse Edition (GIPPE) (France) *Tel:* (01) 45 32 12 75 *E-mail:* gippe@free.fr *Web Site:* gippe.free.fr, pg 166

Groupements Francais des Fabricants de Papiers d'Impression-Ecriture (COPACEL) (France) *Tel:* (01) 53 89 24 00 *Fax:* (01) 53 89 24 01 *E-mail:* info@copacel.fr *Web Site:* www.copacel.fr, pg 1268

Grub Street (United Kingdom) *Tel:* (020) 7924 3966; (020) 7738 1008 *Fax:* (020) 7738 1009 *E-mail:* post@grubstreet.co.uk *Web Site:* www.grubstreet.co.uk, pg 703

Verlag Grundlagen und Praxis GmbH & Co (Germany) *Tel:* (0491) 6 18 86 *Fax:* (0491) 36 34 *E-mail:* grundlagen-praxis@t-online.de *Web Site:* www.grundlagen-praxis.de, pg 231

Gruner + Jahr AG & Co (Germany) *Tel:* (040) 37030 *Fax:* (040) 37036000 *E-mail:* oeffentlichkeiharbeit@guj.de *Web Site:* www.guj.de, pg 231

Grupo Bibliografico Nacional de la Republica Dominicana (Dominican Republic), pg 1561

Editorial Grupo Cero (Spain) *Tel:* (091) 758 19 40; (091) 5423349 *Fax:* (091) 758 19 41 *E-mail:* pedidos@editorialgrupocero.com *Web Site:* www.editorialgrupocero.com, pg 585

Grupo Comunicar (Spain) *Tel:* (0959) 248380 *Fax:* (0959) 248380 *E-mail:* info@grupocomunicar.com *Web Site:* www.grupo-comunicar.com, pg 585

Grupo Cultural Especializado, SA (Mexico) *Tel:* (05) 6889831 *Fax:* (05) 6889965, pg 1327

Grupo Editorial CEAC SA (Spain) *Tel:* (093) 2472424 *Fax:* (093) 2315115 *E-mail:* atencioncliente@ceacedit.com *Web Site:* www.ceacedit.com; www.editorialceac.com, pg 586

Grupo Editorial Iberoamerica, SA de CV (Mexico) *Tel:* (05) 5111267; (05) 5116760, pg 466

Grupo Editorial Iberoamerica de Colombia SA (Colombia) *Tel:* (01) 3106553 *Fax:* (01) 3106553 *E-mail:* geicol@colomsat.net.co, pg 1306

Grupo Editorial RIN-78 (Guatemala) *Tel:* (02) 692080 *Fax:* (02) 601834, pg 313

Grupo Editorial Z Zeta SA de CV (Mexico) *Tel:* (05) 6705627; (05) 5817929 *Fax:* (05) 5758280, pg 466

Grupo Noriega Editores de Colombia Ltda (Colombia) *Tel:* (01) 3689036 *Fax:* (01) 3377788 *E-mail:* gnoriega@unete.com.co, pg 1306

Grupo Santillana de Ediciones SA (Spain) *Tel:* (091) 7449060 *Fax:* (091) 3224475 *E-mail:* grupo@santillana.es *Web Site:* www.gruposantillana.com, pg 586

Schweizer Autorinnen und Autoren Gruppe Olten (Switzerland) *Tel:* (01) 350 04 60 *Fax:* (01) 350 04 61 *E-mail:* sekretariat@a-d-s.ch *Web Site:* www.a-d-s.ch, pg 1405

Gruppe 21 GmbH (Germany) *Tel:* (02054) 10489-0 *Fax:* (02054) 10489-29 *E-mail:* redaktion@info21.de *Web Site:* www.gruppe21.de, pg 232

Verlag Gruppenpaedagogischer Literatur (Germany) *Tel:* (06081) 5 67 40 *Fax:* (06081) 5 74 38 *E-mail:* info@vglw.de *Web Site:* www.vglw.de, pg 231

Gruppo Editoriale Faenza Editrice SpA (Italy) *Tel:* (0546) 670411 *Fax:* (0546) 660440 *E-mail:* info@faenza.com *Web Site:* www.faenza.com, pg 391

Walter de Gruyter GmbH & Co KG (Germany) *Tel:* (030) 260 05-0 *Fax:* (030) 260 05-251 *E-mail:* wdg-info@degruyter.de *Web Site:* www.degruyter.de, pg 231

Editura Gryphon (Romania) *Tel:* (0268) 313 642; (0268) 312 888 *Fax:* (0268) 312 888 *E-mail:* gryphon@gryphon.ro *Web Site:* www.gryphon.ro, pg 540

GSB (Ghana Standards Board) (Ghana) *Tel:* (021) 662942; (021) 665461, pg 304

GSMBA, Edition Bruno Gasser (Switzerland) *Tel:* (061) 6811103 *Fax:* (061) 6811103 *E-mail:* gasser@dial-switch.ck, pg 624

Guadalquivir SL Ediciones (Spain) *Tel:* (095) 422 19 76; (095) 422 19 17 *Fax:* (095) 421 33 20 *E-mail:* guadalquivir.ed@svq.servicom.es, pg 586

Editorial Guadalupe (Argentina) *Tel:* (011) 4826-8587 *Fax:* (011) 4826-8587 *E-mail:* ventas@editorialguadalupe.com.ar *Web Site:* www.editorialguadalupe.com.ar, pg 6

Editora Guadalupe Ltda (Colombia) *Tel:* (01) 2690788; (01) 2690211 *Fax:* (01) 2685308, pg 111

Editora Guanabara Koogan SA (Brazil) *Tel:* (021) 3970-9450 *Fax:* (021) 2252-2732 *E-mail:* gbk@editoraguanabara.com.br *Web Site:* www.editoraguanabara.com.br, pg 83

Ugo Guanda Editore (Italy) *Tel:* (02) 80206322 *Fax:* (02) 72000306 *E-mail:* info@guanda.it *Web Site:* www.guanda.it, pg 392

Guangdong Science & Technology Press (China) *Tel:* (020) 87768688; (020) 87618770 (Directorial Office); (020) 87769412 (Foreign Cooperation Editorial Office) *Fax:* (020) 87764169 *E-mail:* gdkjwb@ns.guangzhou.gb.com.cn *Web Site:* www.xwcbj.gd.gov.cn, pg 105

Guarro Casas SA (Spain) *Tel:* (093) 7767676 *Fax:* (093) 7767677 *E-mail:* guarro@guarro.com *Web Site:* www.guarro.com, pg 1238

Editorial Guaymuras (Honduras) *Tel:* 237 54 33 *Fax:* 238 45 78 *E-mail:* editorial@sigmanet.hn, pg 315

Librairie Guenegaud (France) *Tel:* (01) 43260791 *Fax:* (01) 40468872 *E-mail:* libraire.guenegaud@wanadoo.fr, pg 166

Gunter Olzog Verlag GmbH (Germany) *Tel:* (089) 71 04 66 60 *Fax:* (089) 71 04 66 61 *E-mail:* olzog.verlag@t-online.de *Web Site:* www.olzog.de, pg 231

Guenther Butkus (Germany) *Tel:* (0521) 69689 *Fax:* (0521) 174470 *E-mail:* pendragon.verlag@t-online.de *Web Site:* www.pendragon.de, pg 231

Edizioni Guerini e Associati SpA (Italy) *Tel:* (02) 582980 *Fax:* (02) 58298030 *E-mail:* info@guerini.it *Web Site:* www.guerini.it, pg 392

The Guernsey Press Co Ltd (United Kingdom) *Tel:* (01481) 240240; (01481) 243657 (ISDN) *Fax:* (01481) 240275 *E-mail:* books@guernsey-press.com *Web Site:* www.guernsey-press.com, pg 1163

The Guernsey Press Co Ltd (United Kingdom) *Tel:* (01481) 240240; (01481) 243657 (ISDN) *Fax:* (01481) 240290; (01481) 240275 *E-mail:* books@guernsey-press.com *Web Site:* www.guernsey-press.com, pg 1184

The Guernsey Press Co Ltd (United Kingdom) *Tel:* (01481) 240256; (01481) 243657 (ISDN) *Fax:* (01481) 240282 *E-mail:* books@guernsey-press.com *Web Site:* www.guernsey-press.com, pg 1226

The Guernsey Press Co Ltd (United Kingdom) *Tel:* (01481) 240240; (01481) 243657 (ISDN) *Fax:* (01481) 240275 *E-mail:* books@guernsey-press.com *Web Site:* www.guernsey-press.com, pg 1238

Guerra Edizioni GURU srl (Italy) *Tel:* (075) 5289090 *Fax:* (075) 5288244 *E-mail:* geinfo@guerra-edizioni.com *Web Site:* www.guerra-edizioni.com, pg 392

Guetersloher Verlagshaus (Germany) *Tel:* (05241) 74050 *Fax:* (05241) 740548 *E-mail:* info@gtvh.de *Web Site:* www.guetersloher-vh.de, pg 232

Verlag Klaus Guhl (Germany) *Tel:* (030) 3213062 *Fax:* (030) 30823868, pg 232

Guildhall Library (United Kingdom) *Tel:* (020) 7332 1868; (020) 7332 1870; (020) 7332 1863; (020) 7332 1839 *Fax:* (020) 7600 3384 *E-mail:* printedbooks.guildhall@corpoflondon.gov.uk; manuscripts.guildhall@corpoflondon.gov.uk *Web Site:* www.ull.ac.uk, pg 1553

Editions d'Art Albert Guillot (France) *Tel:* (04) 78521026, pg 166

Livraria Guimaraes (Portugal) *Tel:* (021) 3462436 *Fax:* (021) 3462620, pg 1337

Guimaraes Editores, Lda (Portugal) *Tel:* (021) 324 3120 *Fax:* (021) 324 3129 *E-mail:* guimaraes.ed@mail.telepac.pt *Web Site:* www.guimaraes-ed.pt, pg 532

Guinness World Records Ltd (United Kingdom) *Tel:* (020) 7891 4567 *Fax:* (020) 7891 4501, pg 703

Guizhou Education Publishing House (China) *Tel:* (0851) 627904; (0851) 524211, pg 105

Gujarat Book Trade Federation (India) *Tel:* (079) 447 634; (079) 447 635, pg 1273

Gujarat Vidyapith Granthalaya (India) *Tel:* (079) 7541148 *Fax:* (079) 7542547 *E-mail:* guivi@adinet.emet.in; gvpahd@ad1vsnl.net.in, pg 1516

Editorial Gulaab (Spain) *Tel:* (091) 6170867 *Fax:* (071) 61 86 55 *E-mail:* alfaomega@sew.es, pg 586

Gulur Raudur Grenn og Blar Childrens Bookclub (Iceland) *Tel:* 5102525 *Fax:* 5102525 *E-mail:* klubbar@mm.is, pg 1253

Gummerus Printing (Finland) *Tel:* (014) 683 500 *Fax:* (014) 676 770 *E-mail:* etunimi.sukunimi@gummerus.fi *Web Site:* www.gummerus.fi, pg 1176, 1216

Gummerus Publishers (Finland) *Tel:* (09) 584 301 *Fax:* (09) 5843 0200 *E-mail:* publisher@gummerus.fi *Web Site:* www.gummerus.fi, pg 142

M D Gunasena & Co Ltd (Sri Lanka) *Tel:* (01) 323981; (01) 323982; (01) 323983; (01) 323984 *Fax:* (01) 323336 *E-mail:* mdgunasena@mail.ewisl.net *Web Site:* mdgunasena.com, pg 606

Gundhild Lenz-Mulligan (United Kingdom) *Tel:* (020) 8543 7846 *Fax:* (020) 8543 8909 *E-mail:* glenz-mulligan@dial.pipex.com, pg 1140

Gunnar Lie & Associates Ltd (United Kingdom) *Tel:* (020) 8487 9020 *Fax:* (020) 8878 2832 *E-mail:* gunnarlie@compuserve.com, pg 1140

PT BPK Gunung Mulia (Indonesia) *Tel:* (021) 3901208 *Fax:* (021) 3901633 *E-mail:* corp.off@bpkgm.com *Web Site:* www.bpkgm.com, pg 355

PT BPK Gunung Mulia (Indonesia) *Tel:* (021) 3901208 *E-mail:* trade@bpkgm.com *Web Site:* www.bpkgm.com, pg 1318

Guru Publishers Ltd (Kenya) *Tel:* (020) 764146, pg 434

Verlag des Gustav-Adolf-Werks (Germany) *Tel:* (0341) 490 62 0 *Fax:* (0341) 4770505 *E-mail:* gaw-verlag@t-online.de, pg 232

Th Gut Verlag (Switzerland) *Tel:* (01) 9285211 *Fax:* (01) 9285200 *Web Site:* www.gutverlag.ch/, pg 624

Gutenberg-Gesellschaft eV (Germany) *Tel:* (06131) 22 64 20 *Fax:* (06131) 23 35 30 *E-mail:* gutenberg-gesellschaft@freenet.de *Web Site:* www.gutenberg-gesellschaft.uni-mainz.de, pg 232, 1270, 1400

Gutenberg Publications (Greece) *Tel:* (01) 3642003; (01) 3641979; (01) 3641996 *Fax:* (01) 3642030; (01) 3611384 *E-mail:* gut_ub@otenet.gr, pg 307

Gutersloher Verlaghaus GmbH /Chr Kaiser/Kiefel/Quell (Germany) *Tel:* (05241) 74050 *Fax:* (05241) 740548 *E-mail:* info@gtvh.de *Web Site:* www.gtvh.de, pg 232

Guthmann & Peterson Liber Libri, Edition (Austria) *Tel:* (01) 877 04 26 *Fax:* (01) 876 40 04 *E-mail:* verlag@guthmann-peterson.de *Web Site:* www.guthmann-peterson.de, pg 51

Guyana Community Based Rehabilitation Progeamme (Guyana) *Tel:* (022) 64004 *Fax:* (022) 62615, pg 314

Guyana Library Association (Guyana) *Tel:* (0226) 2690; (0226) 2699; (0227) 4052 *Fax:* (0227) 4053 *E-mail:* natlib@sdnp.org.gy *Web Site:* www.natlib.gov.gy, pg 1564

Guyana Medical Science Library (Guyana), pg 1513

GVA Publishers Ltd (Switzerland) *Tel:* (022) 3112424 *Fax:* (022) 3112556, pg 624

Gvanim Publishing House (Israel) *Tel:* (03) 5281044; (03) 5283648 *Fax:* (03) 5283648 *E-mail:* traklinm@zahav.net.il, pg 367

Gwasg Carreg Gwalch (United Kingdom) *Tel:* (01492) 642 031 *Fax:* (01492) 641 502 *E-mail:* llyfrau@carreg-gwalch.co.uk *Web Site:* www.carreg-gwalch.co.uk, pg 703

Gwasg Gwenffrwd (United Kingdom) *Tel:* (01490) 420 560; (0845) 330 6754, pg 703

Gwasg y Dref Wen (United Kingdom) *Tel:* (01222) 617860 *Fax:* (01222) 610507 *E-mail:* gwil-drefwen@btinternet.com, pg 703

Gyan Publishing House (India) *Tel:* (011) 23261060; (011) 23282060 *Fax:* (011) 23285914 *E-mail:* gyanbook@del2.vsnl.net.in *Web Site:* www.gyanbooks.com, pg 335

Gyeom-jisa (Republic of Korea) *Tel:* (02) 3351985 *Fax:* (02) 3351986, pg 438

Gyldendal Norsk Forlag A/S (Norway) *Tel:* 22034100 *Fax:* 22034105 *E-mail:* gnf@gyldendal.no *Web Site:* www.gyldendal.no, pg 509

Gyldendals Babybogklubben (Denmark) *Tel:* 70 11 00 33 *Fax:* 70 11 01 33 *E-mail:* boernebogklub@gyldendal.dk *Web Site:* www.gyldendal.dk, pg 1251

Gyldendals Bogklubben (Denmark) *Tel:* 70 11 00 33 *Fax:* 70 11 01 33 *E-mail:* gyldendals-bogklub@gyldendal.dk *Web Site:* www.gyldendal.dk, pg 1251

Gyldendals Borne Bogklubben (Denmark) *Tel:* 70 11 00 33 *Fax:* 70 11 01 33 *E-mail:* boernebogklub@gyldendal.dk *Web Site:* www.gyldendal.dk, pg 1252

Gyldendals Junior Bogklubben (Denmark) *Tel:* 70 11 00 33 *Fax:* 70 11 01 33 *E-mail:* boernebogklub@gyldendal.dk *Web Site:* www.gyldendal.dk, pg 1252

Gyldendalske Boghandel - Nordisk Forlag A/S (Denmark) *Tel:* 33755555 *Fax:* 33755556 *E-mail:* gyldendal@gyldendal.dk *Web Site:* www.gyldendal.dk, pg 131

Gylym, Izd-Vo (Kazakstan) *Tel:* (03272) 618005; (03272) 618845 *Fax:* (03272) 618845; (03272) 618005, pg 432

Gyosei Corporation (Japan) *Tel:* (03) 5349-6666 *Fax:* (03) 5349-6655 *E-mail:* eigyo1@gyosei.co.jp *Web Site:* www.gyosei.co.jp, pg 417

H & Y Printing Ltd (Hong Kong) *Tel:* 2870 2379 *Fax:* 2555 0028 *E-mail:* hyphk@netvigator.com, pg 1156

H B Verlags und Vertriebs-Gesellschaft mbH (Germany) *Tel:* (040) 4151-04 *Fax:* (040) 41513231, pg 232

H K Scanner Arts International Ltd (Hong Kong) *Tel:* 29760302 *Fax:* 29760292, pg 1178

H L Schlapp Buch- und Antiquariatshandlung GmbH und Co KG Abt Verlag (Germany) *Tel:* (06151) 17 90-0 *Fax:* (06151) 17 90 40 *E-mail:* darmstadt@schlapp.de *Web Site:* www.schlapp.de, pg 232

Verlag H M Hauschild GmbH (Germany) *Tel:* (0421) 1785-0 *Fax:* (0421) 1785-285 *E-mail:* info@hauschild-werbedruck.de *Web Site:* www.hauschild.werbedruck.de, pg 232

Haag und Herchen Verlag GmbH (Germany) *Tel:* (069) 550911-13 *Fax:* (069) 552601; (069) 554922 *E-mail:* verlag@haagundherchen.de *Web Site:* www.haagundherchen.de, pg 232

C W Haarfeld GmbH & Co (Germany) *Tel:* (0201) 720950 *Fax:* (0201) 7209533, pg 232

Wolfgang G Haas - Musikverlag Koeln ek (Germany) *Tel:* (02203) 98 88 3-0 *Fax:* (02203) 98 88 3-50 *E-mail:* info@haas-koeln.de *Web Site:* www.haas-koeln.de, pg 232

P Haase & Sons Forlag A/S (Denmark) *Tel:* 33 18 10 80 *Fax:* 33 11 59 59 *E-mail:* haase@haase.dk *Web Site:* www.haase.dk, pg 131

Dr Rudolf Habelt GmbH (Germany) *Tel:* (0228) 9 23 83-0 *Fax:* (0228) 9 23 83-6 *E-mail:* info@habelt.de *Web Site:* www.habelt.de, pg 232

Habermann Institute for Literary Research (Israel) *Tel:* (08) 9244569; (08) 9241160 *Fax:* (08) 9249466 *E-mail:* zmalachi@post.tau.ac.il, pg 367

Hachette Education (France) *Tel:* (01) 43923000; (01) 43923797 *Fax:* (01) 43923575 *Web Site:* www.hachette-education.com, pg 166

Hachette francais langue etrangere - FLE (France) *Tel:* (01) 43 92 30 00 *Fax:* (01) 43 92 39 20 *E-mail:* fle@hachette-livre.fr *Web Site:* www.fle.hachette-livre.fr, pg 166

Hachette Jeunesse Image (France) *Tel:* (01) 43923000 *Fax:* (01) 43923030 *Web Site:* www.hachettejeunesse.com, pg 166

Hachette Jeunesse Roman (France) *Tel:* (01) 43923000 *Fax:* (01) 43923222, pg 166

Hachette Livre (France) *Tel:* (01) 43923000 *Fax:* (01) 43923030, pg 167

Hachette Livre International (France) *Tel:* (01) 55 00 11 00 *Fax:* (01) 55 00 11 60, pg 167

Hachette Livre SA - H E D (France) *Tel:* (01) 43923000 *Fax:* (01) 43923030 *Web Site:* www.hachette.com, pg 1310

Hachette Pratiques (France) *Tel:* (01) 43923238 *Fax:* (01) 43923030, pg 167

Hachmeister Verlag (Germany) *Tel:* (0251) 51210 *Fax:* (0251) 57217 *E-mail:* hachmeister.galerie@t-online.de *Web Site:* www.hachmeister-galerie.de, pg 232

Hadar Publishing House Ltd (Israel) *Tel:* (03) 6812244 *Fax:* (03) 6826138 *E-mail:* info@zmora.co.il, pg 367

Peter Haddock Ltd (United Kingdom) *Tel:* (01262) 678121 *Fax:* (01262) 400043 *E-mail:* enquiries@peterhaddock.com *Web Site:* www.phpublishing.co.uk, pg 703

Walter Haedecke Verlag (Germany) *Tel:* (07033) 529830 *Fax:* (07033) 529831 *E-mail:* haedecke_vlg@t-online.de, pg 232

Haedong (Republic of Korea) *Tel:* (02) 953707 *Fax:* (02) 953707, pg 438

Dr Curt Haefner-Verlag GmbH (Germany) *Tel:* (06221) 6446-0 *Fax:* (06221) 6446-40 *E-mail:* info@haefner-verlag.de *Web Site:* www.haefner-verlag.de, pg 233

Haenssler Verlag GmbH (Germany) *Tel:* (09274) 95051 *Fax:* (09274) 95053 *E-mail:* info@haenssler.de *Web Site:* www.haenssler.de, pg 233

Haere Po Editions (French Polynesia) *Tel:* 582636 *Fax:* 582333 *E-mail:* haerepotahiti@mail.pf, pg 189

Heinz-Jurgen Hausser (Germany) *Tel:* (06151) 22824 *Fax:* (06151) 26854, pg 233

Haffmans Verlag AG (Switzerland) *Tel:* (01) 386 4000 *Fax:* (01) 386 4001 *E-mail:* verlag@haffmans.ch, pg 624

Hagaberg AB (Sweden) *Tel:* (08) 690 90 00 *Fax:* (08) 7021940, pg 612

Lehrmittelverlag Wilhelm Hagemann GmbH (Germany) *Tel:* (0211) 17 92 70-0 *Fax:* (0211) 17 92 70-70 *E-mail:* aktuell@hagemann.de *Web Site:* www.hagemann.de, pg 233

Hagen & Stam Uitgeverij Ten (Netherlands) *Tel:* (070) 3045700 *Fax:* (070) 3045800, pg 483

Hagenbach & Bender GMBH (Switzerland) *Tel:* (31) 3816666 *Fax:* (31) 3816677 *E-mail:* rights@hagenbach-bender.com *Web Site:* www.hagenbach-bender.com, pg 624

Hahner Verlagsgesellschaft mbH (Germany) *Tel:* (02408) 55 05 *Fax:* (02408) 58081 *E-mail:* office@hvg.de, pg 233

Mary Hahn's Kochbuchverlag (Germany) *Tel:* (089) 2 90 88-0 *E-mail:* l.eggs@herbig.net *Web Site:* www.herbig.net, pg 233

Hahnsche Buchhandlung (Germany) *Tel:* (0511) 80 71 80 40 *Fax:* (0511) 36 36 98 *E-mail:* verlag@hahnsche-buchhandlung.de *Web Site:* www.hahnsche-buchhandlung.de, pg 233

Chu Hai Publishing (Taiwan) Co Ltd (Taiwan, Province of China) *Tel:* (02) 7080290 *Fax:* (02) 7084804, pg 640

Haifa University Press (Israel) *Tel:* (04) 8240111 *Fax:* (04) 8342245 *Web Site:* www.haifa.ac.il, pg 367

Haigh & Hochland Ltd (United Kingdom) *Tel:* (061) 2734156 *Fax:* (061) 2734340, pg 1351

Hainaim Publishing Co Ltd (Republic of Korea) *Tel:* (02) 326-1600 *Fax:* (02) 326-1625 *Web Site:* www.hainaim.com, pg 439

Hak Won Publishing Co (Republic of Korea) *Tel:* (02) 741-4621; (02) 741-4623 *Fax:* (02) 765-1877 *E-mail:* ccnstar@hanmail.net, pg 439

Hakgojae Publishing Inc (Republic of Korea) *Tel:* (02) 7361713 *Fax:* (02) 7398592 *E-mail:* hkjass@hitel.kol.co.kr, pg 439

Hakibbutz Hameuchad Publishing House Ltd (Israel) *Tel:* (03) 5785810 *Fax:* (03) 5785811, pg 367

Hakluyt Society (United Kingdom) *Tel:* (01428) 641850 *Fax:* (01428) 641933 *E-mail:* office@hakluyt.com *Web Site:* www.hakluyt.com, pg 703, 1408

Hakmunsa Publishing Co (Republic of Korea) *Tel:* (02) 738-5118 *Fax:* (02) 733-8998 *E-mail:* hakmun@hakmun.co.kr *Web Site:* www.hakmun.co.kr, pg 439

Hakubunkan-Shinsha Publishers Ltd (Japan) *Tel:* (03) 3811-4721; (03) 3811-6693 *Fax:* (03) 3818-1431 *Web Site:* www.hakubunkan.co.jp, pg 417

Hakusui-Sha Co Ltd (Japan) *Tel:* (03) 3291-7811 *Fax:* (03) 3291-8448 *E-mail:* hpmaster@hakusuisha.co.jp *Web Site:* www.hakusuisha.co.jp, pg 417

Hakutei-Sha (Japan) *Tel:* (03) 3986-3271 *Fax:* (03) 3986-3272 *E-mail:* LDX00227@nifty.ne.jp, pg 418

Hakuyo-Sha (Japan) *Tel:* (03) 5281-9772 *Fax:* (03) 5281-9886 *E-mail:* hakuyo@mars.dti.ne.jp *Web Site:* www.hakuyo-sha.co.jp, pg 418

Hakuyu-Sha (Japan) *Tel:* (03) 3268-8271 *Fax:* (03) 3268-8273 *Web Site:* www.hakubunkan.co.jp, pg 418

Peter Halban Publishers Ltd (United Kingdom) *Tel:* (020) 7437 9300 *Fax:* (020) 7431 9512 *E-mail:* books@halbanpublishers.com *Web Site:* www.halbanpublishers.com, pg 703

Halbooks Publishing (Australia) *Tel:* (02) 9326 4250 *Fax:* (02) 9326 4250 *E-mail:* sean@iotaproductions.com.au, pg 24

Halcyon Publishing Ltd (New Zealand) *Tel:* (09) 4895337 *Fax:* (09) 4442399 *E-mail:* info@halcyonpublishing.co.nz, pg 496

Haldane Mason Ltd (United Kingdom) *Tel:* (020) 8459 2131 *Fax:* (020) 8728 1216 *E-mail:* haldane.mason@dial.pipex.com, pg 704

Hale & Iremonger Pty Ltd (Australia) *Tel:* (02) 9560 0470 *Fax:* (02) 9550 0097 *E-mail:* info@haleiremonger.com *Web Site:* www.haleiremonger.com, pg 24

Robert Hale Ltd (United Kingdom) *Tel:* (020) 7251 2661 *Fax:* (020) 7490 4958 *E-mail:* enquire@halebooks.com *Web Site:* www.halebooks.com, pg 704

Robert Hale Ltd (United Kingdom) *Tel:* (020) 7251 2661 *Fax:* (020) 7490 4958 *E-mail:* english@halebooks.com *Web Site:* www.halebooks.com, pg 1164

Herbert von Halem Verlag (Germany) *Tel:* (0221) 92 58 29 0 *Fax:* (0221) 92 58 29 29 *E-mail:* info@halem-verlag.de *Web Site:* www.halem-verlag.de; www.inpunkto.de, pg 233

Halldale Publishing & Media Ltd (United Kingdom) *Tel:* (01252) 532000 *Fax:* (01252) 512714 *Web Site:* www.halldale.com, pg 704

Hallgren och Fallgren Studieforlag AB (Sweden) *Tel:* (018) 50 71 00 *Fax:* (018) 12 72 70 *E-mail:* info@hallgren-fallgren.se *Web Site:* www.hallgren-fallgren.se, pg 612

Hallwag Kuemmerly & Frey AG (Germany) *Tel:* (031) 850 31 31 *Fax:* (031) 850 31 00 *E-mail:* info@swisstravelcenter.ch *Web Site:* www.swisstravelcenter.ch; www.hallwag.com, pg 1176

Hallwag Kuemmerly & Frey AG (Switzerland) *Tel:* (031) 423131 *Fax:* (031) 414133, pg 625

Hallwag Kuemmerly & Frey AG (Switzerland) *Tel:* (031) 335 55 55 *Fax:* (031) 414133, pg 1162

Hallwag Kuemmerly & Frey AG (Switzerland) *Tel:* (031) 850 31 31 *Fax:* (031) 850 31 00 *E-mail:* info@swisstravelcenter.com *Web Site:* www.swisstravelcenter.ch, pg 1224

F H Halpern (Australia) *Tel:* (03) 9596 1436 *Fax:* (03) 9596 1436, pg 24

Hambledon & London Ltd (United Kingdom) *Tel:* (020) 7586 0817 *Fax:* (020) 7586 9970 *E-mail:* office@hambledon.co.uk Web Site: www.hambledon.co.uk, pg 704

Hamburger Lesehefte Verlag Iselt & Co Nfl mbH (Germany) *Tel:* (04841) 8352-0 *Fax:* (04841) 8352-10 *E-mail:* verlagsgruppe.husum@t-online.de Web Site: www.verlagsgruppe.de, pg 233

The Hamburgh Register (Guyana) *Tel:* (02) 258486 *Fax:* (02) 258511 *E-mail:* wrma@sdup.org.gy, pg 314

Hamburgisches Welt-Wirtschafts-Archiv (HWWA) Bibliothek (Germany) *Tel:* (040) 42834-219 *Fax:* (040) 42834-550 *E-mail:* biblio@hwwa.de Web Site: www.hwwa.de, pg 1509

Libreria Hamburgo SA (Mexico) *Tel:* (05) 5126796; (05) 5218265, pg 1327

Hamdard Foundation Pakistan (Pakistan) *Tel:* (021) 6616001; (021) 6616002; (021) 6616003; (021) 6616004; (021) 6620945 *Fax:* (021) 6611755 *E-mail:* hamdard@khi.paknet.com.pk Web Site: www.hamdard.com.pk, pg 512

Liselotte Hamecher (Germany) *Tel:* (0561) 16611 *Fax:* (0561) 775262, pg 233

Kerri Hamer (Australia) *Tel:* (02) 9349 5170 *Fax:* (02) 9349 5170, pg 24

Hamilton Printing Co (United States) *Tel:* 518-732-4491 *Toll Free Tel:* 800-242-4222 *Fax:* 518-732-7714, pg 1167, 1229, 1249

Hamish Hamilton Ltd (United Kingdom) *Tel:* (020) 7010 3000 *Fax:* (020) 7010 6060 *E-mail:* customer.service@penguin.co.uk Web Site: www.penguin.co.uk, pg 704

Hamlyn (United Kingdom) *Tel:* (020) 7531 8400 *Fax:* (020) 7531 8650 Web Site: www.hamlyn.co.uk, pg 704

Geoffrey Hamlyn-Harris (Australia) *Tel:* (07) 4681 1450 *Fax:* (07) 4681 1450, pg 24

Hammarskjold Memorial Library (Zambia) *Tel:* (02) 214572; (02) 219012; (02) 211488 *Fax:* (02) 211001 *E-mail:* daglib@zamnet.zm, pg 1556

Alfred Hammer (Germany) *Tel:* (06078) 71622 *Fax:* (06078) 71655, pg 233

Peter Hammer Verlag GmbH (Germany) *Tel:* (0202) 505066; (0202) 505067 *Fax:* (0202) 509252 *E-mail:* info@peter-hammer-verlag.de Web Site: www.peter-hammer-verlag.de, pg 233

Maison d'Edition Mohamed Ali Hammi (Tunisia) *Tel:* 04224534 *Fax:* 74407441 *E-mail:* caeu@gnet.tn, pg 648

Hammond Bindery Ltd (United Kingdom) *Tel:* (01924) 369598 *Fax:* (01924) 298075; (01924) 364108 *E-mail:* sales@hammond-bindery.co.uk Web Site: www.hammpack.co.uk, pg 1226

Hammond Bindery Ltd (United Kingdom) *Tel:* (01924) 369598 *Fax:* (01924) 364108; (01924) 298075 Web Site: www.hammpack.co.uk, pg 1238

Hammond Bindery Ltd (United Kingdom) *Tel:* (01924) 369598 *Fax:* (01924) 298075 *E-mail:* sales@hammond-bindery.co.uk Web Site: www.hammpack.co.uk, pg 1247

Hammond Packaging Ltd (United Kingdom) *Tel:* (01924) 369598 *Fax:* (01924) 298075; (01924) 364108 *E-mail:* hammpack@dial.pipex.com Web Site: www.hammpack.co.uk; www.charlesworth.com, pg 1164

Hammond Packaging Ltd (United Kingdom) *Tel:* (01924) 369598 *Fax:* (01924) 298075 *E-mail:* hammpack@dial.pipex.com Web Site: www.hammpack.co.uk, pg 1184

Hammond Packaging Ltd (United Kingdom) *Tel:* (01924) 369598 *Fax:* (01924) 298075; (01924) 364108 *E-mail:* sales@hammond-bindery.co.uk Web Site: www.hammpack.co.uk, pg 1226

Hammonia-Verlag GmbH Fachverlag der Wohnungswirtschaft (Germany) *Tel:* (040) 520103-0 *Fax:* (040) 520103-30 *E-mail:* info@hammonia.de Web Site: www.hvh.de, pg 233

Otzar Hamore (Israel) *Tel:* (03) 6922983 *Fax:* (03) 6922903, pg 367

Hampden Press (Australia) *Tel:* (02) 9351 9070 *Fax:* 9351 9323 *E-mail:* j.higgs@cchs.usyd.edu.au, pg 24

Editions Viviane Hamy (France) *Tel:* (01) 53171600 *Fax:* (01) 53171609 *E-mail:* information@viviane-hamy.fr Web Site: www.viviane-hamy.fr/0000.html, pg 167

Hanjin Publishing Co (Republic of Korea) *Tel:* (02) 7137453 *Fax:* (02) 7135510, pg 439

Hand-Presse (Austria) *Tel:* (0512) 87975, pg 51

H&H Publishing (Australia) *Tel:* (03) 98774428 *Fax:* (03) 98774222, pg 24

The Handsel Press (United Kingdom) *Tel:* (01202) 665432 *Fax:* (01202) 666219 *E-mail:* handsel@dial.pipex.com Web Site: www.handselpress.co.uk, pg 704

Verlag Handwerk und Technik GmbH (Germany) *Tel:* (040) 5 38 08-0 *Fax:* (040) 5 38 08-101 Web Site: www.handwerk-technik-shop.de, pg 233

Hangil Art Vision (Republic of Korea) *Tel:* (02) 5154811; (02) 5154813 *Fax:* (02) 5154816, pg 439

Hanguk Seoji Hakhoe (Republic of Korea) *Tel:* (02) 788-4143 *Fax:* (02) 788-3385 *E-mail:* w3@nanet.go.kr Web Site: www.nanet.go.kr, pg 1566

Hanguk Tosogwan Hakhoe (Republic of Korea) *Tel:* (02) 7600114 *Fax:* (02) 7442453, pg 1566

Hanitzotz A-Sharara Publishing House (Israel) *Tel:* (03) 6839145 *Fax:* (03) 6839148 *E-mail:* oda@netvision.net.il Web Site: www.odaction.org; www.hanitzotz.com/challenge, pg 367

Hannibal-Verlag (Germany) *Tel:* (089) 24 245 415 *Fax:* (089) 24 245 294 *E-mail:* info@hannibal-verlag.de Web Site: www.hannibal-verlag.de, pg 234

The Hannon Press (Ireland) *Tel:* (0405) 46089 *Fax:* (0405) 46089, pg 361

Universitaetsbibliothek Hannover und Technische Informationsbibliothek (Germany) *Tel:* (0511) 762 2268 *Fax:* (0511) 715936 *E-mail:* ubtib@tib.uni-hannover.de Web Site: www.tib.uni-hannover.de, pg 1509

Hans Furstelberger (Austria) *Tel:* (0732) 773177 *Fax:* (0732) 784485, pg 1300

Hans Prakashan (India) *Tel:* (0532) 623077 *E-mail:* ar@nde.vsnl.net.in, pg 335

Hansa Verlag Ingwert Paulsen Jr (Germany) *Tel:* (04841) 8352-0 *Fax:* (04841) 8352-10 *E-mail:* verlagsgruppe.husum@t-online.de Web Site: www.verlagsgruppe.de, pg 234

Edition Wilhelm Hansen AS (Denmark) *Tel:* 33 11 78 88 *Fax:* 33 14 81 78 *E-mail:* ewh@ewh.dk Web Site: www.ewh.dk; www.wilhelm-hansen.dk, pg 131

Hanseproduktion AB (Sweden) *Tel:* (0498) 24 93 18 *Fax:* (0498) 24 93 18, pg 612

Carl Hanser Verlag (Germany) *Tel:* (089) 9 98 30 0 *Fax:* (089) 98 48 09 *E-mail:* info@hanser.de Web Site: www.hanser.de/verlag, pg 234

Soederbokhandeln Hansson och Bruce AB (Sweden) *Tel:* (08) 405432; (08) 6405433 *Fax:* (08) 6441315, pg 1344

Hanthawaddy Bookshop (Myanmar), pg 1328

Hanthawaddy Book House (Myanmar), pg 475

Hanul Publishing Co (Republic of Korea) *Tel:* (02) 3260095; (02) 3366183 *Fax:* (02) 3337543 *E-mail:* newhanul@nuri.net, pg 439

Happy Cat Books Ltd (United Kingdom) *Tel:* (01255) 870902 *Fax:* (01255) 870902 *E-mail:* mcwest@happycat.co.uk, pg 704

Happy Mental Buch- und Musik Verlag (Germany) *Tel:* (08158) 993303 *Fax:* (08158) 993305, pg 234

Har-El Printers & Publishers (Israel) *Tel:* (03) 681 6834 *Fax:* (03) 681 3563 Web Site: www.harelart.com, pg 1159

Har-El Printers & Publishers (Israel) *Tel:* (03) 681 6834 *Fax:* (03) 681 3563 *E-mail:* mharel@harelart.co.il Web Site: www.harelart.com, pg 1180, 1220

Harare City Library (Zimbabwe) *Tel:* (04) 751834; 751835, pg 1556

Harare Polytechnic Library (Zimbabwe) *Tel:* (04) 752311, pg 1556

Editora Harbra Ltda (Brazil) *Tel:* (011) 5084-2403; (011) 5084-2482; (011) 5571-1122; (011) 5549-2244; (011) 5571-0276 *Fax:* (011) 5575-6876; (011) 5571-9777 *E-mail:* editorial@harbra.com.br Web Site: www.harbra.com.br, pg 83

Harden's Ltd (United Kingdom) *Tel:* (020) 7839 4763 *Fax:* (020) 7839 7561 *E-mail:* mail@hardens.com Web Site: www.hardens.com, pg 704

Hardt und Worner Marketing fur das Buch (Germany) *Tel:* (06172) 7005 *Fax:* (01672) 71547 *E-mail:* hardt.woerner@t-online.de, pg 234

Norman Hardy Printing Group (United Kingdom) *Tel:* (020) 7378 1579 *Fax:* (020) 7378 6422 *E-mail:* info@thehardygroup.co.uk Web Site: www.thehardygroup.co.uk, pg 1226

Patrick Hardy Books (United Kingdom) *Tel:* (01223) 350865 *Fax:* (01223) 366951 *E-mail:* sales@lutterworth.com; publishing@lutterworth.com Web Site: www.lutterworth.com, pg 705

The Thomas Hardy Society (United Kingdom) *Tel:* (01305) 251501 *Fax:* (01305) 251501 *E-mail:* info@hardysociety.org Web Site: www.hardysociety.org, pg 1408

Harenberg Kommunikation Verlags- und Medien-GmbH & Co KG (Germany) *Tel:* (0231) 9056-0 *Fax:* (0231) 9056-110 *E-mail:* post@harenberg.de Web Site: www.harenberg.de, pg 234

Hargreen Publishing Co (Australia) *Tel:* (03) 9329 9714 *Fax:* (03) 9329 5295 *E-mail:* em@execmedia.com.au, pg 24

Siegfried Haring Literatten-Verlag Ulm (Germany) *Tel:* (0731) 9806040 *Fax:* (0731) 9806042 *E-mail:* ratart.edition@t-online.de, pg 234

Harlenic Hellas Publishing SA (Greece) *Tel:* (01) 3609438 *Fax:* (01) 3614846 *E-mail:* harlenic@otenet.gr Web Site: www.harlenic.gr, pg 308

Harlequin Books (Australia) *Tel:* (02) 9415 9230 *Fax:* (02) 9417 5232 *E-mail:* bhobbs@romance.net.au Web Site: www.eharlequin.com.au, pg 24

Harlequin Iberica SA (Spain) *Tel:* (091) 4358623 *Fax:* (091) 4310484 *E-mail:* atencionalcliente@harlequiniberica.com Web Site: www.harlequiniberica.com, pg 586

Harlequin SA (France) *Tel:* (01) 42166363 *Fax:* (01) 45828694, pg 167

Harley Books (United Kingdom) *Tel:* (01206) 271216 *Fax:* (01206) 271182 *E-mail:* harley@keme.co.uk Web Site: www.harleybooks.com, pg 705

L'Harmattan (France) *Tel:* (01) 40 46 79 11; (01) 40 46 79 20 *Fax:* (01) 43 25 82 03 *E-mail:* harmat@worldnet.fr Web Site: www.editions-harmattan.fr, pg 167

Harmi-Press Publications, Haroula D Papadimitriou G P (Greece) *Tel:* (01) 3456734 *Fax:* (01) 3474732, pg 308

De Harmonie Uitgeverij (Netherlands) *Tel:* (020) 6245181 *Fax:* (020) 6230672 *E-mail:* info@deharmonie.nl Web Site: www.deharmonie.nl, pg 483

Harmonie Verlag (Germany) *Tel:* (0761) 709667 *Fax:* (0761) 709662 *E-mail:* harmonieverlag@aol.com, pg 234

HarperCollins Publishers (New Zealand) Ltd (New Zealand) *Tel:* (09) 4439400 *Fax:* (09) 4439403 *E-mail:* editors@harpercollins.co.nz *Web Site:* www.harpercollins.co.nz, pg 497

HarperCollins Publishers (Australia) Pty Ltd (Australia) *Tel:* (02) 9952 5000 *Fax:* (02) 9952 5555 *Web Site:* www.harpercollins.com.au, pg 24

HarperCollins Publishers India Pty Ltd (India) *Tel:* (011) 3278586; (011) 3268185 *Fax:* (011) 3277294 *E-mail:* harper@ndf.vsnl.net.in, pg 335

HarperCollins Publishers Zimbabwe Pvt Ltd (Zimbabwe) *Tel:* (04) 755408; (04) 710017; (04) 755409; (04) 710018 *Fax:* (04) 72-1413; (04) 710019 *E-mail:* harpcoll@icon.co.zw, pg 783

HarperCollins UK (United Kingdom) *Tel:* (020) 8741 7070 *Toll Free Tel:* (0870) 900 2050 (customer service) *Fax:* (020) 8307 4813 *Toll Free Fax:* (0141) 306 3767 (customer service) *E-mail:* contact@harpercollins.co.uk *Web Site:* www.harpercollins.co.uk, pg 705

HarperCollinsReligious (Australia) *Tel:* (011) 6222900 *Fax:* (011) 6223553 *E-mail:* fiona.mclennan@harpercollins.com.au *Web Site:* www.harpercollinsreligious.com.au, pg 25

Otto Harrassowitz KG Wissenschaftliche Buchhandlung & Zeitschriftenagentur (Germany) *Tel:* (0611) 5300 *Fax:* (0611) 530560 *E-mail:* service@harrassowitz.de *Web Site:* www.harrassowitz.de, pg 1311

Harrassowitz Verlag (Germany) *Tel:* (0611) 530-0 *Fax:* (0611) 530-560 (orders) *E-mail:* service@harrassowitz.de *Web Site:* www.harrassowitz.de, pg 234

Harris (Indonesia) *Tel:* (061) 22272, pg 355

Harris-Elon Agency (Israel) *Tel:* (02) 563-3237 *Fax:* (02) 561-8711 *E-mail:* litagent@netvision.net.il, pg 1133

Harry Joe Patsis' European Publications' Center Ltd (Greece) *Tel:* (0210) 3841040; (0210) 3841050 *Fax:* (0210) 6232194; (0210) 3841050, pg 1313

Hart Publishing (United Kingdom) *Tel:* (01865) 245533 *Fax:* (01865) 794882 *E-mail:* mail@hartpub.co.uk *Web Site:* www.hartpub.co.uk; www.hartpublishingusa.com, pg 705

Harth Musik Verlag-Pro musica Verlag GmbH (Germany) *Tel:* (02204) 2003-0 *Fax:* (02204) 2003-33, pg 234

A Hartleben Inhaber Dr Walter Rob (Austria) *Tel:* (01) 512-62-41 *Fax:* (01) 513-94-98, pg 1300

Litteraturverlag Karlheinz Hartmann (Germany) *Tel:* (06007) 7622; (069) 96206013 (Frankfurt) *Fax:* (06007) 614606, pg 234

Hartys Creek Press (Australia) *Tel:* (02) 6587 1100, pg 25

Harvard University Press (United Kingdom) *Tel:* (020) 7306 0603 *Fax:* (020) 7306 0604 *E-mail:* info@hup-mitpress.co.uk *Web Site:* www.hup.harvard.edu, pg 705

Denise Harvey (Greece) *Tel:* (02270) 31154 *Fax:* (02270) 31154, pg 308

Harvey Map Services Ltd (United Kingdom) *Tel:* (01786) 841202 *Fax:* (01786) 841098 *E-mail:* winni@harveymaps.co.uk *Web Site:* www.harveymaps.co.uk, pg 705

Roland Harvey Studios (Australia) *Tel:* (03) 9836 6655 *Fax:* (03) 9836 6652 *E-mail:* sales@rolandharvey.com.au, pg 25

Harveys Ltd (United Kingdom) *Tel:* (0131) 440 0074 *Fax:* (0131) 440 3478 *E-mail:* sales@harveys.ltd.uk *Web Site:* www.harveys.ltd.uk, pg 1226

Harveys Ltd (United Kingdom) *Tel:* (0131) 440 0074; (0131) 440 0014 *Fax:* (0131) 440 3478 *E-mail:* sales@harveys.ltd.uk *Web Site:* www.harveys.ltd.uk, pg 1238

The Harvill Press (United Kingdom) *Tel:* (020) 7840 8893 *Fax:* (020) 7840 6117 *E-mail:* enquiries@randomhouse.co.uk/harvill/; www.harvill.com, pg 705

Library of Hasanuddin University (Indonesia) *Tel:* (0411) 512026; (0411) 512027 *Fax:* (0411) 512027 *Web Site:* www.unhas.ac.id/~perpus, pg 1516

Haschemi Edition Cologne Kunstverlag fuer Fotografie (Germany) *Tel:* (0221) 561007; (0221) 561008 *Fax:* (0221) 529282 *E-mail:* info@haschemi.de *Web Site:* www.haschemi.de, pg 234

von Hase & Koehler Verlag KG (Germany) *Tel:* (06131) 232334 *Fax:* (06131) 227952, pg 234

Hasefer (Romania) *Tel:* (021) 312 22 84 *Fax:* (021) 312 22 84 *E-mail:* hasefer@fx.ro, pg 540

Haseo Publishing Co (Republic of Korea) *Tel:* (02) 2378161; (02) 2378165 *Fax:* (02) 2376575 *E-mail:* haseo@haseo.co.kr *Web Site:* www.haseo.co.kr, pg 439

Drukkerij Scherpenheuvel Haseth (Netherlands Antilles) *Tel:* (09) 7671134, pg 493

Haskolautgafan - University of Iceland Press (Iceland) *Tel:* 5254003 *Fax:* 525-5255 *Web Site:* www.haskolautgafan.hi.is, pg 325

Hat Box Press (Australia) *Tel:* (03) 9749 2510, pg 25

Hatagu Sip Alapitvany (Hungary) *Tel:* (01) 1403728, pg 321

Hatchards Ltd (United Kingdom) *Tel:* (020) 7439 9921 *Fax:* (020) 7494 1313 *E-mail:* books@hatchards.co.uk *Web Site:* www.hatchards.co.uk, pg 1351

Beth Hatefutsoth (Israel) *Tel:* (03) 640 8000 *Fax:* (03) 640 5727 *E-mail:* bhwebmas@post.tau.ac.il *Web Site:* www.bh.org.il, pg 367

Editions Hatier SA (France) *Tel:* (01) 49 54 49 54 *Fax:* (01) 40 49 00 45 *E-mail:* enseignants@editions-hatier.fr *Web Site:* www.editions-hatier.fr, pg 167

Hatje Cantz Verlag (Germany) *Tel:* (0711) 44 05-0 *Fax:* (0711) 44 05-220 *E-mail:* contact@hatjecantz.de *Web Site:* www.hatjecantz.de, pg 234

Hatta Foundation Library (Indonesia) *Tel:* (0274) 87747 *Fax:* (0274) 87747, pg 1517

Hatter Lap- es Konyvkiado Kft (Hungary) *Tel:* (01) 3208230; (01) 3297293 *Fax:* (01) 3208230; (01) 3297293 *E-mail:* hatterkiado@matavnet.hu, pg 321

Haude und Spenersche Verlagsbuchhandlung (Germany) *Tel:* (030) 6917073 *Fax:* (030) 6914067, pg 235

Haufe Mediengruppe (Germany) *Tel:* (0761) 3683-0 *Fax:* (0761) 3683-195 *E-mail:* online-werburg@haufe.de *Web Site:* www.haufe.de, pg 235

Rudolf Haufe Verlag GmbH & Co KG (Germany) *Tel:* (0761) 3683-0 *Fax:* (0761) 3683-195 *E-mail:* online@haufe.de *Web Site:* www.haufe.de, pg 235

Karl F Haug Verlag GmbH & Co (Germany) *Tel:* (00711) 8931-0 *Fax:* (0711) 8931-706 *Web Site:* www.haug-verlag.de/, pg 235

HAUM - Daan Retiøf Publishers (Pty) Ltd (South Africa) *Tel:* (012) 3228474 *Fax:* (012) 3222424, pg 564

HAUM - De Jager Publishers (South Africa) *Tel:* (012) 3284620 *Fax:* (012) 3284706; (012) 3283809, pg 564

HAUM (Hollandsch Afrikaansche Uitgevers Maatschappij) (South Africa) *Tel:* (012) 32284620 *Fax:* (012) 3284706; (012) 3283809, pg 564

Paul Haupt Bern (Switzerland) *Tel:* (031) 3012425 *Fax:* (031) 3014669 *E-mail:* info@haupt.ch *Web Site:* www.haupt.ch, pg 625

Hauptverband des Oesterreichischen Buchhandels (Austria) *Tel:* (01) 512 15 35 *Fax:* (01) 512 84 82 *E-mail:* hvb@buecher.at *Web Site:* www.buecher.at, pg 1261

Dr Ernst Hauswedell & Co (Germany) *Tel:* (0711) 54 99 71-0; (0711) 54 99 71-11 *Fax:* (0711) 54 99 71-21, pg 235

Pierre Hautot Editions (France) *Tel:* (01) 42 61 10 15 *Fax:* (01) 49 27 00 06, pg 167

Uitgeverij Ten Have (Netherlands) *Tel:* (038) 3392556 *Fax:* (038) 3392518, pg 483

Hawk Books (United Kingdom) *Tel:* (01326) 376633 *Fax:* (01326) 376669, pg 706

Hawker Brownlow (Australia) *Tel:* (03) 9555 1344 *Toll Free Tel:* 800-334-603 *Fax:* (03) 9553 4538 *Toll Free Fax:* 800-150-445 *E-mail:* orders@hbe.com.au *Web Site:* www.hbe.com.au, pg 25

Hawker Publications Ltd (United Kingdom) *Tel:* (020) 7720 2108 *Fax:* (020) 7498 3023 *E-mail:* hawker@hawkerpubs.demon.co.uk *Web Site:* www.careinfo.org, pg 706

Hawthorn Press (United Kingdom) *Tel:* (01453) 757040 *Fax:* (01453) 751138 *E-mail:* info@hawthornpress.com *Web Site:* www.hawthornpress.com, pg 706

Hayakawa Publishing Inc (Japan) *Tel:* (03) 3252-3111 *Fax:* (03) 3254-1550, pg 418

Hayes Publishing Co (Australia) *Tel:* (07) 3379 4137 *Fax:* (07) 3379 4137, pg 25

Imprimerie Hayez SPRL (Belgium) *Tel:* (02) 413 02 00 *Fax:* (02) 411 23 78 *E-mail:* com@hayez.be *Web Site:* www.hayez.be, pg 68

Hayit Reisefuhrer in der Rutsker Verlag GmbH (Germany) *Tel:* (0221) 921635-0 *Fax:* (0221) 921635-24 *E-mail:* kontakt@hayit.com *Web Site:* www.hayit.com, pg 235

Haymon-Verlag GesmbH (Austria) *Tel:* (0512) 576300 *Fax:* (0512) 576300-14 *E-mail:* office@haymonverlag.at *Web Site:* www.haymonverlag.at, pg 51

Haynes Publishing (United Kingdom) *Tel:* (01963) 442030; (01963) 442080 (trade) *Fax:* (01963) 440001 (trade) *E-mail:* sales@haynes.co.uk *Web Site:* www.haynes.co.uk, pg 706

Hayward Gallery Publishing (United Kingdom) *Tel:* (020) 7921 0826 *Fax:* (020) 7401 2664 *E-mail:* dpower@hayward.org.uk *Web Site:* www.hayward.org.uk, pg 706

Sir Charles Hayward Library (Bahamas) *Tel:* 352-7048, pg 1492

Editions Hazan (France) *Tel:* (01) 49 61 92 08; (01) 49 61 90 90 *Fax:* (01) 45 97 83 47; (01) 45 97 83 45, pg 167

Hazard Press Ltd (New Zealand) *Tel:* (03) 3770370 *Fax:* (03) 3770390 *E-mail:* info@hazard.co.nz *Web Site:* www.hazardpress.com, pg 497

Hazleton Publishing Ltd (United Kingdom) *Tel:* (020) 7332 2000 *Fax:* (020) 7332 2003 *E-mail:* info@hazletonpublishing.com *Web Site:* www.hazletonpublishing.com, pg 706

HB Media Holdings Pte Ltd (Singapore) *Tel:* 62591919 *Fax:* 67443895, pg 1161

HB Publications (United Kingdom) *Tel:* (020) 8769 1585 *Fax:* (020) 8769 2320 *E-mail:* sales@hbpublications.com *Web Site:* www.hbpublications.com, pg 706

Headley Brothers Ltd (United Kingdom) *Tel:* (01233) 623131 *Fax:* (01233) 612345 *E-mail:* printing@headley.co.uk *Web Site:* www.headley.co.uk, pg 1184, 1226, 1247

Headline Book Publishing Ltd (United Kingdom) *Tel:* (020) 7873 6000 *Fax:* (020) 7873 6124 *E-mail:* headline.books@headline.co.uk *Web Site:* www.madaboutbooks.com, pg 706

Health Development Agency (United Kingdom) *Tel:* (020) 7430 0850 *Fax:* (020) 7061 3390 *E-mail:* communications@hda-online.org.uk *Web Site:* www.hda-online.org.uk, pg 706

Health Sciences Associates International (United Kingdom) *Tel:* (020) 8876 2340 *Fax:* (020) 8392 9845, pg 1351

Heartland Publishing Ltd (United Kingdom) *Tel:* (01622) 843040 *Fax:* (01622) 843040 *E-mail:* publish@heartland.co.uk *Web Site:* www.heartland.co.uk, pg 707

A M Heath & Co Ltd (United Kingdom) *Tel:* (020) 7836 4271 *Fax:* (020) 7497 2561 *E-mail:* amheath@demon.co.uk, pg 1140

Heavenly Lotus Publishing Co, Ltd (Taiwan, Province of China) *Tel:* (02) 2873-6629 *Fax:* (02) 8736709, pg 640

Agentur Literatur Gudrun Hebel (Germany) *Tel:* (030) 34 70 77 67 *Fax:* (030) 34 70 77 68 *E-mail:* info@agentur-literatur.de; gudrun.hebel@agentur-literatur.de *Web Site:* www.agentur-literatur.de, pg 1131

Hebrew University of Jerusalem (Israel) *Tel:* (02) 6585017 *Fax:* (02) 6511771 *Web Site:* www.huji.ac.il, pg 1519

Hebrew Writers Association of Israel (Israel) *Tel:* (03) 6953256 *Fax:* (03) 6919681, pg 1274

Heckners Verlag (Germany) *Tel:* (05331) 8008-0 *Fax:* (05331) 8008-58, pg 235

Hedley's Bookshop Ltd (New Zealand) *Tel:* (06) 3782875 *Fax:* (06) 3782570 *E-mail:* sales@hedleysbooks.co.nz *Web Site:* www.hedleysbooks.co.nz, pg 1330

Heel Verlag GmbH (Germany) *Tel:* (02223) 9230-0 *Fax:* (02223) 9230-13; (02223) 9230-26 *E-mail:* service@heel-verlag.de *Web Site:* www.heel-verlag.de, pg 235

Heffers: (United Kingdom) *Tel:* (01223) 568568 *Fax:* (01223) 568591 *E-mail:* heffers@heffers.co.uk *Web Site:* www.heffers.co.uk, pg 1351

Bokforlaget Hegas AB (Sweden) *Tel:* (042) 330 340 *Fax:* (042) 330 141 *E-mail:* kom.litt@helsingborg.se, pg 612

June Heggenhougen (Norway) *Tel:* 32832125 *Fax:* 32832125, pg 1135

Heibonsha Ltd, Publishers (Japan) *Tel:* (03) 3818-0873; (03) 3818-0874 (sales) *Fax:* (03) 3818-0857 *E-mail:* shop@heibonsha.co.jp *Web Site:* www.heibonsha.co.jp, pg 418

Heideland-Orbis NV (Belgium) *Tel:* (03) 3600211 *Fax:* (03) 3600212, pg 68

Joh Heider Verlag GmbH (Germany) *Tel:* (02202) 95 40-35 *Fax:* (02202) 2 15 31 *E-mail:* anzeigen@marburger-bund.de *Web Site:* www.heider-verlag.de/mb/mediadaten/, pg 235

Heigl Verlag, Horst Edition (Germany) *Tel:* (07554) 283 *Fax:* (07552) 938756 *E-mail:* info@heigl-verlag.de *Web Site:* www.heigl-verlag.de, pg 235

Yozmot Heiliger Ltd (Israel) *Tel:* (03) 5284851 *Fax:* (03) 5285397 *E-mail:* books@yozmot.com *Web Site:* www.yozmot.com, pg 1319

Heilongjiang Science & Technology Press (China) *Tel:* (0451) 3635613 *Fax:* (0451) 3642127, pg 105

Institut fuer Heilpaedagogik (Switzerland) *Tel:* (041) 3170033 *Fax:* (041) 3170034 *E-mail:* info@ihpl.ch *Web Site:* www.ihpl.ch, pg 625

Heima er Bezt Book Club (Iceland) *Tel:* 5531599; 5882400 *Fax:* 5888994, pg 1253

Max Heindel Verlag Rosenkreuzer Philosophie (Switzerland) *Tel:* (081) 834 20 03 *Fax:* (081) 834 20 04 *E-mail:* max_heindel_verlag@bluewin.ch *Web Site:* www.heindel-verlag.ch, pg 625

Heinemann Botswana (Botswana) *Tel:* 372305 *Fax:* 371832, pg 76

Heinemann Educational Publishers Southern Africa (South Africa) *Tel:* (011) 322 8600 *Fax:* (011) 322 8716 *E-mail:* customerliaison@heinemann.co.za *Web Site:* www.heinemann.co.za, pg 564

Heinemann Educational Publishing (United Kingdom) *Tel:* (01865) 888130 (General Inquiries) *Fax:* (01865) 314290 (General inquiries) *E-mail:* orders@heinemann.co.uk *Web Site:* www.heinemann.co.uk, pg 707

Heinemann Kenya Ltd (EAEP) (Kenya) *Tel:* (020) 222057; (020) 222144; (020) 228949 *Fax:* (020) 448753; (020) 226286, pg 434

Heinemann Library (Australia) *Tel:* (03) 92467131, pg 25

Heinemann Publishers (Pty) Ltd (South Africa) *Tel:* (011) 784 8619 *Fax:* (011) 784 8360 *E-mail:* bevw@heinemann.co.za, pg 564

William Heinemann Ltd (United Kingdom) *Tel:* (020) 7840 8548 *Fax:* (020) 7828 6127, pg 707

Verlag Otto Heinevetter Lehrmittel GmbH (Germany) *Tel:* (040) 25 90 19 *Fax:* (040) 251 2128 *E-mail:* info@heinevetter-verlag.de *Web Site:* www.heinevetter-verlag.de, pg 235

Arnold Heinman Publishers (India) Pvt Ltd (India) *Tel:* (011) 6383422; (011) 60780; (011) 664256 *Fax:* (011) 6877571, pg 335

Heinrich Hugendubel AG (Switzerland) *Tel:* (071) 67711-90 *Fax:* (071) 67711-91, pg 625

Heinrichshofen's Verlag GmbH & Co KG (Germany) *Tel:* (04421) 9267-0 *Fax:* (04421) 9267-99 *E-mail:* info@heinrichshofen.de *Web Site:* www.heinrichshofen.de, pg 236

Heinz-Theo Gremme Verlag (Germany) *Tel:* (02592) 984200 *E-mail:* theo.gremme@epost.de *Web Site:* www.gremme-verlag.de, pg 236

Heinze GmbH (Germany) *Tel:* (01805) 339833 *Fax:* (01805) 119877 *E-mail:* info@heinze.de; kundenservice@heinze.de *Web Site:* www.heinze.de/; www.heinzebauoffice.de, pg 236

Hekla Forlag (Denmark) *Tel:* 36 15 36 15 *Fax:* 36 15 36 16 *E-mail:* post@borgen.dk *Web Site:* www.borgen.dk, pg 131

Helbing und Lichtenhahn Verlag AG (Switzerland) *Tel:* (061) 2289070 *Fax:* (061) 2289071 *E-mail:* info@helbing.ch *Web Site:* www.helbing.ch, pg 625

Helbling Verlags-Gesellschaft mbH (Austria) *Tel:* (0512) 262333-0 *Fax:* (0512) 262333-111 *E-mail:* office@helbling.co.at *Web Site:* www.helbling.com, pg 51

HelfRecht Verlag und Druck (Germany) *Tel:* (09232) 6010 *Fax:* (09232) 601280 *E-mail:* info@helfrecht.de *Web Site:* www.helfrecht.de, pg 236

Editorial Heliasta SRL (Argentina) *Tel:* (011) 4371-5546 *Fax:* (011) 4375-1659 *E-mail:* editorial@heliasta.com.ar *Web Site:* www.heliasta.com.ar, pg 6

Helicon Publishing Ltd (United Kingdom) *Tel:* (08709) 200200 *Fax:* (01235) 826999 *E-mail:* helicon@rm.com *Web Site:* www.helicon.co.uk, pg 707

Helikon Kiado (Hungary) *Tel:* (01) 428-9450; (01) 428-9429 *Fax:* (01) 428-9481 *E-mail:* helikon@helikon.hu *Web Site:* www.helikon.hu, pg 321

Helion & Co (United Kingdom) *Tel:* (0121) 705 3393 *Fax:* (0121) 711 4075 *E-mail:* info@helion.co.uk *Web Site:* www.helion.co.uk, pg 707

Heliopol (Bulgaria) *Tel:* (02) 746850; (02) 718513 *E-mail:* heliopol@heliopol.bg, pg 94

Heliopolis-Verlag (Germany) *Tel:* (07473) 5427 *Fax:* (07473) 5427, pg 236

Uitgeverij Helios NV (Belgium) *Tel:* (03) 6645320, pg 68

Hellenic Bookservice (United Kingdom) *Tel:* (020) 72679499 *Fax:* (020) 72679498 *E-mail:* info@hellenicbookservice.com *Web Site:* www.hellenicbookservice.com, pg 1351

Hellenic Federation of Publishers & Booksellers (Greece) *Tel:* (01) 33 00 924; (01) 33 00 926 *Fax:* (01) 33 01 617 *E-mail:* poev@otenet.gr, pg 1272

Hellerau-Verlag Dresden GmbH (Germany) *Tel:* (0351) 803 5293 *Fax:* (0351) 826 0130 *E-mail:* info@hellerau-verlag.de *Web Site:* www.hellerau-verlag.de/, pg 236

Christopher Helm (Publishers) Ltd (United Kingdom) *Tel:* (020) 7758 0200 *Fax:* (020) 7758 0222 *E-mail:* customerservice@acblack.com; ornithology@acblack.com, pg 707

Helm Information Ltd (United Kingdom) *Tel:* (01580) 880 561 *Fax:* (01580) 880 541 *Web Site:* www.helm-information.co.uk, pg 707

Helsingin Kaupunginkirjasto - yleisten kirjastojen keskuskirjasto (Finland) *Tel:* (09) 3108511 *Fax:* (09) 31085517 *E-mail:* city.library@hel.fi *Web Site:* www.lib.hel.fi, pg 1505

Helsinki University Library (Finland) *Tel:* (09) 191 23196 *Fax:* (09) 191 22719 *E-mail:* hyk-palvelu@helsinki.fi *Web Site:* www.lib.helsinki.fi, pg 1505

Verlag Helvetica Chimica Acta (Switzerland) *Tel:* (01) 3602434 *Fax:* (01) 3602435 *E-mail:* info@wiley-vch.de *Web Site:* www.wiley-vch.de, pg 625

Helyode Editions (SA-ADN) (Belgium) *Tel:* (02) 3444934 *Fax:* (02) 3475534, pg 68

Hema Maps Pty Ltd (Australia) *Tel:* (07) 3340 0000 *Fax:* (07) 3340 0099 *E-mail:* manager@hemamaps.com.au *Web Site:* www.hemamaps.com, pg 25

Hemco Publications (Mauritius) *Tel:* 4643141, pg 461

Van Hemeldonck NV (Belgium) *Tel:* (014) 611034 *Fax:* (014) 620288 *E-mail:* booksell@innet.be, pg 68

Hemeroteca Municipal de Madrid (Spain) *Tel:* (091) 588 57 74, pg 1545

Hemeroteca Nacional de Mexico (Mexico) *Tel:* (055) 622 6818 *Fax:* (055) 665 0951 *Web Site:* biblional.bibliog.unam.mx, pg 1529

Hemisferio Sur Edicion Agropecuaria (Uruguay) *Tel:* (02) 916 45 15; (02) 916 45 20 *Fax:* (02) 916 45 20 *E-mail:* librperi@adinet.com.uy, pg 777

Editorial Hemisferio Sur SA (Argentina) *Tel:* (011) 49529825 *Fax:* (011) 49528454 *E-mail:* informe@hemisferiosur.com.ar *Web Site:* www.hemisferiosur.com.ar, pg 6

Editions Hemma (Belgium) *Tel:* (086) 43 01 01 *Fax:* (086) 43 36 40 *Web Site:* www.hemma.be, pg 68

Hemma Holland BV (Netherlands) *Tel:* (020) 675 53 26 *Fax:* (020) 679 62 54, pg 483

Hemming Information Services (United Kingdom) *Tel:* (020) 7973 6694 *Fax:* (020) 7233 5052 *E-mail:* customer@hqluk.com *Web Site:* www.h-info.co.uk, pg 707

Hemus Co Inc (Bulgaria) *Tel:* (02) 981 1769 *Fax:* (02) 981 3341 *E-mail:* hemusb@pbitex.com, pg 1304

Hemus Editora Ltda (Brazil) *Tel:* (011) 279-9911 *Fax:* (011) 279-9721, pg 83

Henan Science & Technology Publishing House (China) *Tel:* (0371) 5727616; (0371) 5721756-643 *Fax:* (0371) 5727616 *E-mail:* hnkj565@public2.zz.ha.cn, pg 105

Hendon Publishing Co Ltd (United Kingdom) *Tel:* (01282) 613129; (01282) 697725 *Fax:* (01282) 870215, pg 708

Thomas Heneage Art Books (United Kingdom) *Tel:* (020) 7930 9223 *Fax:* (020) 7839 9223 *E-mail:* artbooks@heneage.com *Web Site:* www.heneage.com, pg 1351

G Henle Verlag (Germany) *Tel:* (089) 759820 *Fax:* (089) 7598240 *E-mail:* info@henle.de *Web Site:* www.henle.de, pg 236

Ian Henry Publications Ltd (United Kingdom) *Tel:* (01708) 736213 *Fax:* (01621) 850862, pg 708

Edition Hentrich Druck & Verlag Gebr Hentrich und Tank GmbH & Co KG (Germany) *Tel:* (030) 84410001 *Fax:* (030) 84410002, pg 236

Heraldry Today (United Kingdom) *Tel:* (01672) 520617 *Fax:* (01672) 520183 *E-mail:* heraldry@heraldrytoday.co.uk *Web Site:* www.heraldrytoday.co.uk, pg 708

Herattaja-yhdistys Ry (Finland) *Tel:* (06) 438 8911 *Fax:* (06) 438 7430 *E-mail:* jormakka@nic.fi, pg 142

YELLOW PAGES

Editions Herault (France) *Tel:* (02) 41554590 *Fax:* (02) 41586228, pg 167

Herbert Press Ltd (United Kingdom) *Tel:* (020) 7758 0200 *Fax:* (020) 7758 0222 *E-mail:* customerservices@acblack.com *Web Site:* www.acblack.com, pg 708

F A Herbig Verlagsbuchhandlung GmbH (Germany) *Tel:* (089) 2 90 88-0 *E-mail:* l.eggs@herbig.net *Web Site:* www.herbig.net, pg 236

Herbita Editrice di Leonardo Palermo (Italy) *Tel:* (091) 6167732 *Fax:* (091) 6167716, pg 392

Hans-Alfred Herchen & Co Verlag KG (Germany) *Tel:* (069) 550911-13 *Fax:* (069) 552601; (069) 554922, pg 236

Hercules de Ediciones, SA (Spain) *Tel:* (0981) 220585; (0981) 226443 *Fax:* (0981) 220717 *E-mail:* empg05052@empresas-galicia.com, pg 586

Editorial y Libreria Herder Ltda (Colombia) *Tel:* (01) 3344853 *Fax:* (01) 2832272, pg 1306

Herder AG Basel (Switzerland) *Tel:* (061) 8210900 *Fax:* (061) 8279067 *E-mail:* verkauf@herder.ch, pg 625

Herder-Buchgemeinde (Germany) *Tel:* (0761) 27170 *Fax:* (0761) 2717520, pg 1252

Editorial Herder SA (Spain) *Tel:* (093) 476 26 26 *Fax:* (093) 207 34 48 *E-mail:* editorialherder@herder-sa.com *Web Site:* www.herder-sa.com, pg 586

Herder Editrice e Libreria (Italy) *Tel:* (06) 679 53 04; (06) 679 46 28 *Fax:* (06) 678 47 51 *E-mail:* distr@herder.it *Web Site:* www.herder.it, pg 392

Herder Editrice e Libreria (Italy) *Tel:* (06) 679 53 04; (06) 679 46 28 *Fax:* (06) 678 47 51 *E-mail:* distr@herder.it; distr@herder.it *Web Site:* www.herder.it, pg 1321

Verlag Herder GmbH & Co KG (Germany) *Tel:* (0761) 2717440 *Fax:* (0761) 2717360 *E-mail:* kundenservice@herder.de *Web Site:* www.herder.de/, pg 236

Heritage Books (Nigeria) *Tel:* (01) 5871333; (01) 5871333 *E-mail:* obw@infoweb.abs.net, pg 505

Heritage House Group Ltd (United Kingdom) *Tel:* (01332) 347087 *Fax:* (01332) 290688 *E-mail:* sales@hhgroup.co.uk *Web Site:* www.hhgroup.co.uk, pg 708

Heritage Press (United Kingdom) *Tel:* (01273) 731296 *Fax:* (01273) 731296, pg 708

Heritage Press Ltd (New Zealand) *Tel:* (09) 4137503; (09) 4139343 *Fax:* (09) 4137503; (09) 4139343 *E-mail:* heritagepressltd@xtra.co.nz *Web Site:* www.heritagepress.co.nz, pg 497

Heritage Publishers (India) *Tel:* (011) 23266258 *Fax:* (011) 23263050 *E-mail:* heritage@nda.vsnl.net.in; info@meditechbooks.com, pg 335

Heritage Publishing Co (Cote d'Ivoire) *Tel:* 433056 *Fax:* 433056, pg 117

Heritage Publishing House (Philippines) *Tel:* (02) 7248114 *Fax:* (02) 6471393 *E-mail:* heritage@iconn.com.ph *Web Site:* www.iconn.com.ph/heritage, pg 519

Hermagoras/Mohorjeva (Austria) *Tel:* (0463) 56515 21 *Fax:* (0463) 514189 *E-mail:* office@mohorjeva.at *Web Site:* www.mohorjeva.at, pg 51

Hermann editeurs des Sciences et des Arts SA (France) *Tel:* (01) 45 57 45 40 *Fax:* (01) 40 60 12 93 *E-mail:* hermann.sa@wanadoo.fr, pg 167

Editorial Hermes SA (Mexico) *Tel:* (05) 6741425; (05) 6741894; (05) 6744385 (ext 71) *Fax:* (05) 6743949, pg 466

Hermes Edizioni SRL (Italy) *Tel:* (06) 3235433 *Fax:* (06) 3236277 *E-mail:* info@ediz-mediterranee.com *Web Site:* www.ediz-mediterranee.com, pg 392

Hermes Publishing House (Bulgaria) *Tel:* (032) 630630 *Fax:* (032) 634095 *E-mail:* hermes@plovdiv.technolink.com *Web Site:* www.hermesbooks.com, pg 94

Editions Hermes Science Publications (France) *Tel:* (01) 53 10 15 20 *Fax:* (01) 53 10 15 21 *E-mail:* hermes@iway.fr *Web Site:* www.hermes-science.com; www.editions-hermes.fr, pg 167

Hermess Ltd (Latvia) *Tel:* (02) 7112743 *Fax:* (02) 7313130 *E-mail:* hermess@binet.lv, pg 444

Hermetische Truhe Buchhandlung fuer Esoterische Literatur Barbara Dethlefsen (Germany) *Tel:* (089) 2710650 *Fax:* (089) 2724627, pg 236

Nick Hern Books Ltd (United Kingdom) *Tel:* (020) 8749 4953 *Fax:* (020) 8735 0250 *E-mail:* info@nickhernbooks.demon.co.uk *Web Site:* www.nickhernbooks.co.uk, pg 708

Editions de l'Herne (France) *Tel:* (01) 42 61 25 06 *Fax:* (01) 42 60 10 00 *E-mail:* lherne@freesurf.fr, pg 167

Hernovs Forlag (Denmark) *Tel:* 32963314 *Fax:* 32960446 *E-mail:* admin@hernov.dk *Web Site:* www.hernov.dk, pg 132

Herodotus Press (Ireland) *Tel:* (01) 4540120 *Fax:* (01) 4541134, pg 361

Herold Business Data AG (Austria) *Tel:* (02236) 401-0 *Fax:* (02236) 401-8 *E-mail:* kundendienst@herold.at *Web Site:* www.herold.co.at, pg 52

Herold Druck-und Verlagsgesellschaft mbH (Austria) *Tel:* (01) 795 94 *Fax:* (01) 795 94-115, pg 52

Herold Verlag Dr Wetzel (Germany) *Tel:* (089) 7915774 *E-mail:* wetzel@herold-verlag.de *Web Site:* www.herold-verlag.de, pg 236

Heron Press Publishing House (Bulgaria) *Tel:* (02) 443368 *Fax:* (02) 443368 *E-mail:* heron_press@attglobal.net, pg 94

Editorial Herrero SA (Mexico) *Tel:* (05) 5664900 *Fax:* (05) 5664900, pg 466

Herscher (France) *Tel:* (08) 25 82 01 11 *Fax:* (01) 43 25 18 29 *E-mail:* contact@editions-belin.fr *Web Site:* www.editions-belin.fr, pg 168

Axel Hertenstein, Hertenstein-Presse (Germany) *Tel:* (07231) 2 70 84 *Fax:* (07231) 2 70 84, pg 237

Editions Hervas (France) *Tel:* (01) 43 79 10 95 *Fax:* (01) 43 79 77 10, pg 168

Herzog August Bibliothek (Germany) *Tel:* (05331) 808-0 *Fax:* (05331) 808-302 *E-mail:* auskunft@hab.de *Web Site:* www.hab.de, pg 1509

Herzogin Anna Amalia Bibliothek (Germany) *Tel:* (03643) 545-200 *Fax:* (03643) 545-220 *E-mail:* haab@swkk.de *Web Site:* www.swkk.de, pg 1509

HES & De Graaf Publishers BV (Netherlands) *Tel:* (030) 6011955 *Fax:* (030) 6011813 *E-mail:* info@hesdegraaf.com *Web Site:* www.hesdegraaf.com, pg 483

Hessischer Verleger- und Buchhandler-Verband eV (Germany) *Tel:* (0611) 166 600 *Fax:* (0611) 166 6059 *E-mail:* briefe@hessenbuchhandel.de *Web Site:* www.hessenbuchhandel.de, pg 1270

Hessisches Ministerium fuer Umwelt, Landwirtschaft und Forsten (Germany) *Tel:* (0611) 8150 *Fax:* (0611) 8151941 *E-mail:* poststelle@hmulu.hessen.de *Web Site:* www.mulf.hessen.de, pg 237

Hestia-I D Hestia-Kollaros & Co Corporation (Greece) *Tel:* (01) 3635970; (01) 36-15-077; (01) 360574 *Fax:* (01) 3606758; (01) 3606759 *Web Site:* www.ianos.gr, pg 308

Hestra-Verlag Hernichel & Dr Strauss GmbH & Co KG (Germany) *Tel:* (06151) 39070 *Fax:* (06151) 390777, pg 237

Uitgeverij Het-Volk (Belgium) *Tel:* (09) 2656424; (09) 2656420 *Fax:* (09) 2258406, pg 1302

Heuff Amsterdam Uitgever (Netherlands) *Tel:* (020) 620 46 25 *Fax:* (020) 620 46 25, pg 483

Uitgeverij Heureka (Netherlands) *Tel:* (0294) 480 000 *Fax:* (0294) 415 183 *E-mail:* heureka@belboek.com *Web Site:* www.belboek.com/heureka; www.belboek.com/index.html, pg 483

Hexaglot Holding GmbH (Germany) *Tel:* (040) 514560 *Fax:* (040) 51456991 *E-mail:* info@hexaglot.de *Web Site:* www.hexaglot.de/, pg 237

Heyden & Son (United Kingdom) *Tel:* (020) 8203 5171 *Fax:* (020) 8203 1027 *E-mail:* sales@heyden.com, pg 1184

Friedrich W Heye Verlag GmbH (Germany) *Tel:* (089) 6653201 *Fax:* (089) 66532210 *E-mail:* verlag@heye.de *Web Site:* www.heye-verlag.de, pg 237

Carl Heymanns Verlag KG (Germany) *Tel:* (0221) 94373-0 *Fax:* (0221) 94373-901 *E-mail:* marketing@heymanns.com *Web Site:* www.heymanns.com, pg 237

Verlag Johannes Heyn (Austria) *Tel:* (0463) 54249 *Fax:* (0463) 542491 *E-mail:* buch@heyn.at; technik@heyn.at *Web Site:* www.heyn.at, pg 1300

Johannes Heyn GmbH & Co KG (Austria) *Tel:* (0463) 54 2 49 *Fax:* (0463) 54 2 49-41 *E-mail:* buch@heyn.at *Web Site:* www.heyn.at, pg 52

Wilhelm Heyne Verlag (Germany) *Tel:* (089) 41 36 0 *Fax:* (089) 51 48 2229 *E-mail:* heyne-suedwest@randomhouse.de *Web Site:* www.heyne.de, pg 237

Monica Heyum Agency (Sweden) *Tel:* (08) 7451934 *Fax:* (08) 7771470, pg 1137

Hid Islenzka Bokmenntafelag (Iceland) *Tel:* 5889060 *Fax:* 5889095, pg 325

Hid Islenzka Bokmenntafelag (Iceland) *Tel:* 5889060 *Fax:* 5889095 *E-mail:* hib@islandia.is *Web Site:* www.hib.is, pg 1401

Max Hieber KG (Germany) *Tel:* (089) 29008023 *Fax:* (089) 229782 *E-mail:* info@eminent-orgeln.de *Web Site:* www.eminent-orgeln.de/kontakte.htm, pg 237

Anton Hiersemann, Verlag (Germany) *Tel:* (0711) 5499710; (0711) 5499711 *Fax:* (0711) 54997121 *E-mail:* info@hiersemann.de *Web Site:* www.hiersemann.de, pg 237

Anton Hiersemann, Verlag (Germany) *Tel:* (0711) 5499710; (0711) 5499711 *Fax:* (0711) 54997121 *E-mail:* hiersemann.hauswedell.verlage@t-online.de *Web Site:* www.hiersemann.de, pg 1311

Higginbothams Ltd (India) *Tel:* (044) 852 1841 *Fax:* (044) 852 8101, pg 1316

High Resolution Inc (United States) *Tel:* 207-236-3777 *Fax:* 207-236-2500 *Web Site:* www.highres.com, pg 1187

David Higham Associates Ltd (United Kingdom) *Tel:* (020) 7434 5900 *Fax:* (020) 7437 1072 *E-mail:* dha@davidhigham.co.uk *Web Site:* www.davidhigham.co.uk, pg 1140

Higher Education Press (China) *Tel:* (010) 58581862 *Fax:* (010) 82085552 *Web Site:* www.hep.edu.cn; www.hep.com.cn, pg 105

Highland Books Ltd (United Kingdom) *Tel:* (01483) 424560 *Fax:* (01483) 424388 *E-mail:* info@highlandbks.com *Web Site:* www.highlandbks.com, pg 708

Hihorse Publishing Pty Ltd (Australia) *Tel:* (03) 9397 3084 *Fax:* (03) 9397 3084 *E-mail:* hihorse@c031.aone.net.au, pg 25

Hikarinokuni Ltd (Japan) *Tel:* (06) 6768-1151 *Fax:* (06) 6768-6795 *E-mail:* hikari@skyblue.ocn.ne.jp *Web Site:* www.hikarinokuni.co.jp, pg 418

Al Hilal Publications (Bahrain) *Tel:* 231122, pg 60

Dar Al Hilal Publishing Institution (Egypt (Arab Republic of Egypt)) *Tel:* (02) 362 5450 *Fax:* (02) 362 5469, pg 138

AIG I Hilbinger Verlag GmbH (Germany) *Tel:* (0611) 4190088 *Fax:* (0611) 4190088, pg 237

Edition E Hilger (Austria) *Tel:* (01) 512 53 15-0 *Fax:* (01) 513 91 26 *E-mail:* hilger@hilger.at, pg 52

Hilit Publishing Co Ltd (Taiwan, Province of China) *Tel:* (02) 2362-6602 *Fax:* (02) 2365-2552 *E-mail:* hilit.publish@msa.hinet.net *Web Site:* www.hilit.com.tw, pg 640

Hill & Knowlton Asia Ltd (Hong Kong) *Tel:* 2894 6321 *Fax:* 2576 3551 *Web Site:* www.hillandknowlton.com, pg 1156

Hillelforlaget (Sweden) *Tel:* (08) 587 858 04 *Fax:* (08) 587 858 58, pg 612

Hillview Publications Pte Ltd (Singapore) *Tel:* 334 8996 *Fax:* 334 8997, pg 556

Hilmarton Manor Press (United Kingdom) *Tel:* (01249) 760208 *Fax:* (01249) 760379 *E-mail:* mailorder@hilmartonpress.co.uk *Web Site:* www.hilmartonpress.co.uk, pg 708

Hilt & Hansteen A/S (Norway) *Tel:* (022) 38 40 10 *Fax:* (022) 37 40 15 *Web Site:* hilt-hansteen.no, pg 509

Himalaya Publishing House (India) *Tel:* (011) 3270392; (011) 652225 *Fax:* (022) 3956286, pg 335

Himalayan Books (India) *Tel:* (011) 352126; (011) 351731 *Fax:* (011) 332-1731 *E-mail:* ebs@vsnl.com, pg 336

Himmelsturmer Verlag (Germany) *Tel:* (040) 48061717 *Fax:* (040) 48061799 *E-mail:* himmelstuermer@gmx.de, pg 237

Himpunan Masyarakat Pencinta Buku (Indonesia) *Tel:* (022) 470821; (022) 470287, pg 1253

Hind Pocket Books Private Ltd (India) *Tel:* (011) 202046; (011) 202332; (011) 202467 *Fax:* (011) 2282332, pg 336

Verlag Hinder und Deelmann (Germany) *Tel:* (06462) 1301 *Fax:* (06462) 3307 *Web Site:* www.hinderunddeelmann.de/, pg 237

Hindi Book Centre (India) *Tel:* (011) 328 6757; (011) 325 8993; (011) 326 1696 *Fax:* (011) 327 3335; (011) 648 1565 *E-mail:* info@hindibook.com *Web Site:* www.hindibook.com, pg 1316

Hindi Pracharak Sansthan (India) *Tel:* (0542) 54470; (0542) 52425; (0542) 52670; (0542) 355168; (0542) 56850; (0542) 361452, pg 336

Hindustan Book Agency (India) *Tel:* (011) 6163294; (011) 6163296 *Fax:* (011) 6193297 *E-mail:* hindbook@nda.vsnl.net.in *Web Site:* www.hindbook.com, pg 1316

Hindy's Enterprise (United States) *Tel:* 845-735-4666 *Fax:* 617-344-5905, pg 1167

Hindy's Enterprise (United States) *Tel:* 845-735-4666 *Fax:* 617-344-5905; 530-324-8964, pg 1187

Hindy's Enterprise (United States) *Tel:* 845-735-4666 *Fax:* 617-344-5905, pg 1229, 1240

Hindy's Enterprise Co Ltd (Hong Kong) *Tel:* 25166318 *Fax:* 25165161, pg 1178, 1218

Hing Yip Printing Co Ltd (Hong Kong) *Tel:* 25532432; 25532828 *Fax:* 28147887, pg 1218

Hinoki Publishing Co Ltd (Japan) *Tel:* (03) 32912488 *Fax:* (03) 32953554 *E-mail:* info@hinoki-shoten.co.jp *Web Site:* www.hinoki-shoten.co.jp, pg 418

Hinstorff Verlag GmbH (Germany) *Tel:* (0381) 49 69-0 *Fax:* (0381) 49 69-103 *E-mail:* sekretariat@hinstorff.de *Web Site:* www.hinstorff.de, pg 237

Hiotellis P (Greece) *Tel:* (01) 3638066; (01) 3611159 *Fax:* (01) 2113112 *E-mail:* panos-x@otenet.gr, pg 308

Ediciones Hiperion SL (Spain) *Tel:* (091) 577 60 15; (091) 577 60 16 *Fax:* (091) 435 86 90 *E-mail:* hiperion.com *Web Site:* www.hiperion.com, pg 586

Hipocrates - Livros Tecnicos, Lda (Portugal) *Tel:* (021) 3571247 *Fax:* (021) 3580902 *E-mail:* info@hipocrates.pt *Web Site:* www.hipocrates.pt, pg 1337

The Hippogriff Press CC (South Africa) *Tel:* (011) 6464229 *Fax:* (011) 6464229, pg 564

Hippokrates-Verlag GmbH (Germany) *Tel:* (0711) 8931-0 *Fax:* (0711) 8931-706 *Web Site:* www.hippokrates.de, pg 238

Hippopotamus Press (United Kingdom) *Tel:* (01373) 466653 *Fax:* (01373) 466653, pg 709

Hiralal Printing Works Ltd (India) *Tel:* (022) 7672726; (022) 7683012 *Fax:* (022) 7631191, pg 1159, 1179

Hiralal Printing Works Ltd (India) *Tel:* (022) 7672726; (022) 7683012, pg 1220

Hirmer Verlag GmbH (Germany) *Tel:* (089) 1215160 *Fax:* (089) 12151610; (089) 12151616 (distribution) *E-mail:* vertrieb@hirmerverlag.de *Web Site:* www.hirmerverlag.de; www.weltkunstverlag.de, pg 238

Hirokawa Publishing Co (Japan) *Tel:* (03) 38153651 *Fax:* (03) 38153650, pg 418

Harro V Hirschheydt (Germany) *Tel:* (05130) 36758 *Fax:* (05130) 36799 *E-mail:* kontakt@hirschheydt-online.de, pg 238

F Hirthammer Verlag GmbH (Germany) *Tel:* (089) 3233360 *Fax:* (089) 3241728 *E-mail:* info@hirthammerverlag.de *Web Site:* www.hirthammerverlag.de, pg 238

S Hirzel Verlag GmbH und Co (Germany) *Tel:* (0711) 25820 *Fax:* (0711) 2582290 *E-mail:* service@hirzel.de *Web Site:* www.hirzel.de, pg 238

Libreria Hispano Americana (Spain) *Tel:* (093) 3175337; (093) 3180079 *Fax:* (093) 3189339, pg 1342

Editorial Hispano Europea SA (Spain) *Tel:* (093) 2013709; (093) 2018500 *Fax:* (093) 4142635 *E-mail:* hispaneuropea@mx3.redestb.es, pg 586

Editorial Hispanoamerica (Colombia) *Tel:* (01) 2216694 *Fax:* (01) 2213020, pg 111

Histec Publications (Australia) *Tel:* (03) 9592 3787 *Fax:* (03) 9592 2823 *Web Site:* www.histec.com, pg 25

Editions d'Histoire Sociale (EDHIS) (France) *Tel:* (01) 42614778, pg 168

Historical Association of Zambia (Zambia), pg 781

Arquivo Historico de Mocambique (Mozambique) *Tel:* (01) 321177; (01) 321178 *Fax:* (01) 323428 *E-mail:* jneves@zebra.uem.mz *Web Site:* www.ahm.uem.mz, pg 1530

Institutum Historicum Societatis Iesu (Italy) *Tel:* (06) 689 77673 *Fax:* (06) 686 1342; (06) 689 77663 *E-mail:* ihsiroma@tin.it *Web Site:* space.tin.it/scuola/mmorales/ihsi.html, pg 392

Instytut Historii Nauki PAN (Poland) *Tel:* (022) 826 87 54; (022) 65 72 746 *Fax:* (022) 826 61 37 *E-mail:* ihn@ihnpan.waw.pl *Web Site:* www.ihnpan.waw.pl, pg 523

Historische Uitgeverij (Netherlands) *Tel:* (050) 3181700; (050) 3135258 *Fax:* (050) 3146383 *E-mail:* info@histuitg.nl *Web Site:* www.histuitg.nl, pg 483

Historischer Verein fur das Furstentum Liechtenstein (Liechtenstein) *Tel:* 392 17 47 *Fax:* 392 17 05 *E-mail:* info@hvfl.li *Web Site:* www.hvfl.li, pg 448

History House Publishing (Ireland) *Tel:* (065) 24066 *Fax:* (065) 20388, pg 361

Hjemmenes Forlag (Norway) *Tel:* 22143151 *Fax:* 22920738, pg 509

Forlaget Hjulet (Denmark) *Tel:* 31310900 *Fax:* 31310900 *E-mail:* aloa@gte2net.dk, pg 132

Galerie Hlavniho Mesta Prahy (Czech Republic) *Tel:* (02) 3332 1200 *Fax:* (02) 3332 3664 *E-mail:* ghmp@volny.cz *Web Site:* www.citygalleryprague.cz, pg 123

HLT Publications (United Kingdom) *Tel:* (020) 8317 6161 *Fax:* (020) 8317 6001 *E-mail:* obp@hltpublications.co.uk *Web Site:* www.holborncollege.ac.uk/OldbaileyPress.cfm, pg 709

HMR Publishing Co (Pakistan) *Tel:* (042) 7588972; (042) 7588967 *Fax:* (042) 7581212, pg 512

Ho-Chi Book Publishing Co (Taiwan, Province of China) *Tel:* (02) 2974-0168 *Fax:* (02) 2792-4702 *E-mail:* hochi@ms12.hinet.net; hochi@email.gcn.net.tw, pg 640

Ho Printing Singapore Pte Ltd (Singapore) *Tel:* 5429322 *Fax:* 5428322, pg 1161, 1181, 1222, 1237

Ho Printing Singapore Pte Ltd (Singapore) *Tel:* 65429322 *Fax:* 65428322, pg 1246

Hobbs The Printers Ltd (United Kingdom) *Tel:* (023) 8066 4800 *Fax:* (023) 8066 4801 *E-mail:* info@hobbs.uk.com *Web Site:* www.hobbstheprinters.co.uk; www.hobbs.uk.com, pg 1184

Hobbs The Printers Ltd (United Kingdom) *Tel:* (023) 8066 4800 *Fax:* (023) 8066 4801 *E-mail:* info@hobbs.uk.com *Web Site:* www.hobbs.uk.com, pg 1226

Hobbs The Printers Ltd (United Kingdom) *Tel:* (023) 8066 4800 *Fax:* (023) 8066 4801 *E-mail:* info@hobbs.uk.com *Web Site:* www.hobbs.uk.com; www.hobbstheprinters.co.uk, pg 1239, 1247

Hobbyglede (Norway) *Tel:* 24051000 *Fax:* 24051099 *E-mail:* post@damm.no *Web Site:* www.dammbokklubb.no, pg 1255

Hobsons (United Kingdom) *Tel:* (020) 7336 6633 *Fax:* (020) 7608 1034 *E-mail:* enquiries@hobsons.co.uk *Web Site:* www.hobsons.com, pg 709

Hod-Ami, Computer Books Ltd (Israel) *Tel:* (09) 9541207 *Fax:* (09) 9571582 *E-mail:* info@hod-ami.co.il *Web Site:* www.hod-ami.co.il, pg 368

Hodder & Stoughton General (United Kingdom) *Tel:* (020) 7873 6000 *Fax:* (020) 7873 6024, pg 709

Hodder & Stoughton Religious (United Kingdom) *Tel:* (020) 7873 6000 *Fax:* (020) 7873 6059 *E-mail:* firstname.surname@hodder.co.uk *Web Site:* www.headline.co.uk, pg 709

Hodder Children's Books (United Kingdom) *Tel:* (020) 7873 6000 *Fax:* (020) 7873 6225 *Web Site:* www.hodderheadline.co.uk, pg 709

Hodder Education (United Kingdom) *Tel:* (020) 7873 6272 *Fax:* (020) 7873 6299 *E-mail:* joanne.craik@hodder.co.uk *Web Site:* www.hodderheadline.co.uk, pg 709

Hodder Headline Australia (Australia) *Tel:* (02) 82480800; (02) 43901300 (customer service) *Fax:* (02) 82480810 *E-mail:* Auspub@hha.com.au (Australian publishing); hsales@alliancedist.com.au; adscs@alliancedist.com.au (customer service) *Web Site:* www.hha.com.au, pg 26

Hodder Headline Ltd (United Kingdom) *Tel:* (020) 7873 6000 *Fax:* (020) 7873 6024 *Web Site:* www.hodderheadline.co.uk, pg 709

Hodder Moa Beckett Publishers Ltd (New Zealand) *Tel:* (09) 4781000 *Fax:* (09) 4781010 *E-mail:* admin@hoddermoa.co.nz, pg 497

Hodges Figgis & Co (Ireland) *Tel:* (01) 6774754 *Fax:* (01) 6792810; (01) 6793402 *E-mail:* books@hfiggis.ir, pg 1319

Editions Hoebeke (France) *Tel:* (01) 42 22 83 81 *Fax:* (01) 45 44 04 96, pg 168

Lars Hoekerbergs Bokfoerlag (Sweden) *Tel:* (08) 244360 *Fax:* (08) 6503984 *E-mail:* hokerbook@ebox.tninet.se, pg 612

Verlag Hoelder-Pichler-Tempsky (Austria) *Tel:* (01) 401 36-139 *Fax:* (01) 401 36-128 *E-mail:* hpt@hpt.co.at, pg 52

Verlag Wolfgang Hoelker (Germany) *Tel:* (0251) 414110 *Fax:* (0251) 4141140 *E-mail:* info@coppenrath.de *Web Site:* www.coppenrath.de, pg 238

Verlag Peter Hoell (Germany) *Tel:* (06167) 912220 *Fax:* (06167) 912221 *E-mail:* hoell.verlag@t-online.de, pg 238

Hofbauer, Christoph und Trojanow Ilia, Akademischer Verlag Muenchen (Germany) *Tel:* (089) 51616151 *Fax:* (089) 51616199 *E-mail:* avm@druckmedien.de, pg 238

Buchhandlung Karl Hofbauer KG (Austria) *Tel:* (03452) 82793; (03452) 82177 *Fax:* (03452) 71218 *E-mail:* hofbauer.buch@magnet.at, pg 1300

Agence Hoffman (France) *Tel:* (01) 43265694 *Fax:* (01) 43263407 *E-mail:* info@agence-hoffman.com, pg 1130

Edition Hoffmann & Co (Germany) *Tel:* (06031) 2443 *Fax:* (06031) 62965, pg 238

Dieter Hoffmann Verlag (Germany) *Tel:* (06136) 95100 *Fax:* (06136) 951037, pg 238

H Hoffmann GmbH (Germany) *Tel:* (033203) 305810 *Fax:* (033203) 305820 *E-mail:* hhvberlin@t-online.de, pg 238

Hoffmann und Campe Verlag GmbH (Germany) *Tel:* (040) 441880 *Fax:* (040) 44188202 *E-mail:* email@hoca.de *Web Site:* www.hoca.de, pg 238

Verlag Karl Hofmann GmbH & Co (Germany) *Tel:* (07181) 4020 *Fax:* (07181) 402111 *E-mail:* info@hofmann-verlag.de *Web Site:* www.hofmann-verlag.de, pg 238

Friedrich Hofmeister-Figaro Verlag Grossortiment und Musikalienhandlung GesmbH (Austria) *Tel:* (01) 50576510 *Fax:* (01) 5059185, pg 1300

Friedrich Hofmeister Musikverlag (Germany) *Tel:* (0341) 9 60 07 50 *Fax:* (0341) 9 60 30 55 *E-mail:* info@hofmeister-musikverlag.com *Web Site:* www.friedrich-hofmeister.de; www.hofmeister-musikverlag.com, pg 238

Dr Verena Hofstaetter (Austria) *Tel:* (01) 370 33 02 *Fax:* (01) 370 59 34 *E-mail:* verlag@vh-communications.at, pg 52

Hogar del Libro, SA (Spain) *Tel:* (093) 3182700 *Fax:* (093) 3010399, pg 1342

Hogrefe Verlag GmbH & Co Kg (Germany) *Tel:* (0551) 496090 *Fax:* (0551) 4960988 *E-mail:* verlag@hogrefe.de *Web Site:* www.hogrefe.de/, pg 238

Hohenrain-Verlag GmbH (Germany) *Tel:* (07071) 40700 *Fax:* (07071) 407026, pg 239

Matth Hohner AG Verlag (Germany) *Tel:* (07425) 200 *Fax:* (07425) 249 *E-mail:* info@hohner.de *Web Site:* www.hohner.de, pg 239

Hoi Kwong Printing Co Ltd (Hong Kong) *Tel:* 2562-1641 *Fax:* 2564-2142 *E-mail:* sales@hoikwong.com *Web Site:* www.hoikwong.com, pg 1157

Hoi Kwong Printing Co Ltd (Hong Kong) *Tel:* 2562-1641; 2562-1096 *Fax:* 2564-2142 *E-mail:* sales@hoikwong.com *Web Site:* www.hoikwong.com, pg 1218

Hoi Thu-Vien Vietnam (Viet Nam) *Tel:* (04) 824 8051 *Fax:* (04) 825 3357 *E-mail:* info@nlv.gov.vn *Web Site:* www.nlv.gov.vn, pg 1574

Hoikusha Publishing Co Ltd (Japan) *Tel:* (06) 6788-4470 *Fax:* (06) 6788-4970 *Web Site:* www.hoikusha.co.jp, pg 418

Hoja Casa Editorial SA de CV (Mexico) *Tel:* (055) 688-4828; (055) 688-6458; (055) 605-7677; (055) 604-0843 *Fax:* (055) 605-7677 *E-mail:* editorialpax@editorialpax.com *Web Site:* www.editorialpax.com, pg 466

Ediciones Mil Hojas Ltda (Chile) *Tel:* (02) 2743172 *Fax:* (02) 2250261, pg 99

Hokkaido University Library (Japan) *Tel:* (011) 706-4998 *Fax:* (011) 747-2855 *E-mail:* bureau@hokudai.ac.jp *Web Site:* www.lib.hokudai.ac.jp/index_e.html, pg 1521

Hokkaido University Press (Japan) *Tel:* (011) 747-2308 *Fax:* (011) 736-8605, pg 278

Hokuryukan Co Ltd (Japan) *Tel:* (03) 5449-4591 *Fax:* (03) 5449-4950 *E-mail:* hk-ns@mk1.mqcnet.or.jp, pg 418

The Hokuseido Press (Japan) *Tel:* (03) 38270511 *Fax:* (03) 38270567 *E-mail:* info@hokuseido.com, pg 418

Holbrook Design (United Kingdom) *Tel:* (01865) 459000 *Fax:* (01865) 459006 *E-mail:* info@holbrook-design.co.uk *Web Site:* www.holbrook-design.co.uk, pg 1184

Holguin, Ediciones (Cuba) *Tel:* (024) 424974 *E-mail:* promotoraliteraria@baibrama.cult.cu, pg 120

Holkenfeldt 3 (Denmark) *Tel:* 931221 *Fax:* 938241, pg 132

Holland & Josenhans GmbH & Co (Germany) *Tel:* (0711) 6143920 *Fax:* (0711) 6143922 *E-mail:* verlag@huj.03.net *Web Site:* www.holland-josenhans.de/, pg 239

Holland Enterprises Ltd (United Kingdom) *Tel:* (020) 8551 7711 *Fax:* (020) 8551 1266 *E-mail:* sales@holland-enterprises.co.uk *Web Site:* www.holland-enterprises.co.uk, pg 709

Uitgeverij Holland (Netherlands) *Tel:* (023) 5323061 *Fax:* (023) 5342908 *E-mail:* info@uitgeverijholland.nl *Web Site:* www.uitgeverijholland.nl, pg 483

Holland University Press BV (APA) (Netherlands) *Tel:* (020) 626 5544 *Fax:* (020) 528 5298 *E-mail:* info@apa-publishers.com *Web Site:* www.apa-publishers.com, pg 483

Uitgeverij Hollandia BV (Netherlands) *Tel:* (023) 5257150 *Fax:* (023) 52574404 *E-mail:* gottmer@x54all.nl *Web Site:* www.hiswa.nl, pg 483

Hollinek Bruder & Co mbH Gesellschaftsdruckerei & Verlagsbuchhandring (Austria) *Tel:* (02231) 67365 *Fax:* (02231) 67365 *E-mail:* hollinek@via.at, pg 52

Hollis Publishing Ltd (United Kingdom) *Tel:* (020) 8977 7711 *Fax:* (020) 8977 1133 *E-mail:* hollis@hollis-pr.co.uk; orders@hollis-pr.co.uk *Web Site:* www.hollis-pr.co.uk, pg 709

Hollym Corporation; Publishers (Republic of Korea) *Tel:* (02) 735-7551-4 *Fax:* (02) 730-5149; (02) 730-8192 *E-mail:* hollym@chollian.net; info@hollym.co.kr *Web Site:* www.hollym.co.kr, pg 439

Holnap Kiado Vallalat (Hungary) *Tel:* (01) 666928 *Fax:* (01) 656624, pg 321

Holograms (M) Sdn Bhd (Malaysia) *Tel:* (03) 2824002 *Fax:* (03) 2822751, pg 456

Holos Verlag (Germany) *Tel:* (0228) 263020; (0228) 262332 *Fax:* (0228) 212435, pg 239

Holp Book Co Ltd (Japan) *Tel:* (03) 5285-5011 *Fax:* (03) 3225-1663 *E-mail:* holp@holp.co.jp *Web Site:* www.holp.co.jp, pg 418

The Holt Jackson Book Co Ltd (United Kingdom) *Tel:* (01253) 737464 *Fax:* (01253) 733361 *E-mail:* info@holtjackson.co.uk *Web Site:* www.holtjackson.co.uk, pg 1351

Vanessa Holt Ltd (United Kingdom) *Tel:* (01702) 473787 *Fax:* (01702) 471890 *E-mail:* vanessa@holtlimited.freeserve.co.uk, pg 1140

Verlagsgruppe Georg von Holtzbrinck GmbH (Germany) *Tel:* (0711) 2150-0 *Fax:* (0711) 2150-269 *E-mail:* info@holtzbrinck.com *Web Site:* www.holtzbrinck.com, pg 239

Holyoake Books (United Kingdom) *Tel:* (01509) 852333 *Fax:* (01509) 856500 *E-mail:* info@co-opu.demon.co.uk, pg 710

Hans Holzmann Verlag GmbH und Co KG (Germany) *Tel:* (08247) 35401 *Fax:* (08247) 354170 *E-mail:* info@holzmannverlag.de *Web Site:* www.holzmannverlag.de/, pg 239

Home Health Education Service (United Kingdom) *Tel:* (01476) 591700; (01476) 539900 (orders) *Fax:* (01476) 577144 *E-mail:* stanborg@aol.com, pg 710

Uitgeverij Homeovisie BV (Netherlands) *Tel:* (072) 566 1133 *Fax:* (072) 566 1295 *E-mail:* info@vsm.nl *Web Site:* www2.vsminfo.nl, pg 483

Homestead Books (Australia) *Tel:* (03) 9873 7202 *Fax:* (03) 9873-0542 *E-mail:* service@theruralstore.com.au *Web Site:* www.theruralstore.com.au, pg 26

Libros-Ediciones Homines (Puerto Rico) *Tel:* (787) 250-1912 (ext 2347), pg 537

Evelyn Hone College Library (Zambia) *Tel:* (01) 225127 *Fax:* (01) 225127, pg 1556

Honeyglen Publishing Ltd (United Kingdom) *Tel:* (020) 7602 2876 *Fax:* (020) 7602 2876, pg 710

Hong Kong Book Centre Ltd (Hong Kong) *Tel:* 2522-7064 *Fax:* 2868-5079 *E-mail:* orders@hkbookcentre.com.hk *Web Site:* www.swindonbooks.com, pg 1314

Hong Kong China Tourism Press (Hong Kong) *Tel:* 2561 8001 *Fax:* 2561 8196 *E-mail:* edit-e@hkctp.com.hk *Web Site:* www.hkctp.com.hk, pg 317

Hong Kong Christian Service (Hong Kong) *Tel:* 2731-6316 *Fax:* 2731-6333 *E-mail:* info@hkcs.org *Web Site:* www.hkcs.org, pg 1157

Hong Kong Christian Service (Hong Kong) *Tel:* 2731-6316; 2731-6360 *Fax:* 2731-6333; 2731-6363 *E-mail:* info@hkcs.org *Web Site:* www.hkcs.org, pg 1246

Hong Kong Library Association (Hong Kong) *E-mail:* hklib@hklib.org.hk *Web Site:* www.hklib.org.hk, pg 1564

Hong Kong PEN Centre (English-Speaking) (China) *Tel:* 25774168 *Fax:* 25774168 *E-mail:* hkpen_eng@yahoo.com, pg 1398

The Hong Kong Polytechnic University Library (Hong Kong) *Tel:* 2766 6863 *Web Site:* www.polyu.edu.hk, pg 1514

Hong Kong Public Libraries (Hong Kong) *Tel:* 2921 0208 *Fax:* 2415 8211 *E-mail:* enquiries@lcsd.gov.hk *Web Site:* www.hkpl.gov.hk, pg 1514

Hong Kong Publishing Co Ltd (Hong Kong) *Tel:* 25259053, pg 317

Hong Kong University Press (Hong Kong) *Tel:* 2550 2703 *Fax:* 2875 0734 *E-mail:* upweb@hkucc.hku.hk *Web Site:* www.hkupress.org, pg 317

Hongik Media Plus Ltd (Republic of Korea) *Tel:* (02) 786-1016 *Fax:* (02) 786-1709 *E-mail:* hongikcb@soback.kornet.nm.kr, pg 439

Honno Welsh Women's Press (United Kingdom) *Tel:* (01970) 623 150 *Fax:* (01970) 623 150 *E-mail:* post@honno.co.uk *Web Site:* www.honno.co.uk, pg 710

Editions Honore Champion (France) *Tel:* (01) 46340729 *Fax:* (01) 46346406 *E-mail:* champion@honorechampion.com *Web Site:* www.honorechampion.com, pg 168

Hook & Hatton Ltd (United Kingdom) *Tel:* (01604) 847278 *Fax:* (01604) 821486 *E-mail:* hook_hatton@compuserve.com, pg 1150

Hoover's Business Press (United Kingdom) *Tel:* (01865) 513186 *Fax:* (01865) 513186 *Web Site:* www.hoovers-europe.com, pg 710

Hopeful Monster Editore (Italy) *Tel:* (011) 4367197; (011) 4358519 *Fax:* (011) 4369025 *E-mail:* info@hopefulmonster.net *Web Site:* www.hopefulmonster.net, pg 392

Hoppenstedt GmbH & Co KG (Germany) *Tel:* (06151) 380-0 *Fax:* (06151) 380-360 *E-mail:* info@hoppenstedt.de *Web Site:* www.hoppenstedt.de, pg 239

Hora (Italy) *Tel:* (02) 26412203 *Fax:* (02) 26412203, pg 392

Horacek Ladislav-Paseka (Czech Republic) *Tel:* (02) 222 710 751-3; (02) 222 718 886 *Fax:* (02) 22718886 *E-mail:* paseka@paseka.cz *Web Site:* www.paseka.cz, pg 123

Horan Wall & Walker (Australia) *Tel:* (02) 8268 8268 *Fax:* (02) 8268 8267 *E-mail:* info@hww.com.au *Web Site:* www.hww.com.au, pg 26

Pierre Horay Editeur (France) Tel: (01) 43 54 53 90 Fax: (01) 43 54 63 50 E-mail: editions@horay-editeur.fr Web Site: www.horay-editeur.fr, pg 168

Kate Hordern (United Kingdom) Tel: (0117) 923 9368 Fax: (0117) 973 1941 E-mail: katehorden@blueyonder.co.uk, pg 1140

Horitsu Bunka-Sha (Japan) Tel: (075) 791-7131 Fax: (075) 721-8400 E-mail: eigy@hou-bun.co.jp Web Site: web.kyoto-inet.or.jp/org/houritu, pg 418

Horizon Scientific Press (United Kingdom) Tel: (01953) 601106 Fax: (01953) 603068 E-mail: mail@horizonpress.com Web Site: www.horizonpress.com, pg 710

Editorial Horizonte (Peru) Tel: (01) 427-9364 Fax: (01) 427-4341, pg 517

Horlemann Verlag (Germany) Tel: (02224) 5589 Fax: (02224) 5429 E-mail: horlemann@aol.com Web Site: www.horlemann-verlag.de/, pg 239

Editorial Horsori SL (Spain) Tel: (093) 3461997 Fax: (093) 3118498 E-mail: horsori@retemail.net Web Site: www.horsori.es, pg 586

Horus Editora Ltda (Brazil) Tel: (011) 288-7681 Fax: (011) 288-7681 E-mail: horus@horuseditora.com.br Web Site: www.horuseditora.com.br, pg 83

Hospitality Books (Australia) Tel: (02) 9809 5793 Fax: (02) 9809 4884 Web Site: www.hospitalitybooks.com.au, pg 26

Hospitality Training Foundation (United Kingdom) Tel: (020) 8579 2400 Fax: (020) 8840 6217 E-mail: info@htf.org.uk Web Site: www.htf.org.uk, pg 710

Host & Son Publishers Ltd (Denmark) Tel: 33382888 Fax: 33382898 E-mail: host@euroconnect.dk, pg 132

Hotei Publishing (Netherlands) Tel: (020) 568 8330 Fax: (020) 568 8286 Web Site: www.kit.nl/hotei, pg 484

House of Lochar (United Kingdom) Tel: (01951) 200232 Fax: (01951) 200232 E-mail: lochar@colonsay.org.uk Web Site: www.houseoflochar.com, pg 710

Uitgeverij Houtekiet (Belgium) Tel: (03) 2381296 Fax: (03) 2388041 E-mail: info@houtekiet.com Web Site: www.boekenwereld.be, pg 68

Forlaget Hovedland (Denmark) Tel: 86276500 Fax: 86276537 E-mail: mail@hovedland.dk Web Site: www.hovedland.dk, pg 132

How To Books Ltd (United Kingdom) Tel: (01865) 793806 Fax: (01865) 248780 E-mail: info@howtobooks.co.uk Web Site: www.howtobooks.co.uk, pg 710

Tanja Howarth Literary Agency (United Kingdom) Tel: (020) 7240 5553 Fax: (020) 7379 0969 E-mail: tanja.howarth@btinternet.com, pg 1140

Josef Hribal (Czech Republic) Tel: (02) 542731, pg 124

Hriker (Bulgaria) Tel: (02) 319-217, pg 94

Publishing House Hristo Botev (Bulgaria) Tel: (02) 9870810, pg 94

Izdavacka Delatnost Hrvatske Akademije Znanosti I Umjetnosti (Croatia) Tel: (01) 49 22 373; (01) 48 72 902 Fax: (01) 48 19 979 E-mail: stross@mahazu.hazu.hr, pg 118

Hrvatsko filozofsko drustvo (Croatia) Tel: (01) 612 0156 Fax: (01) 617 0682 E-mail: filozofska-istrazivanja@zg.tel.hr, pg 118

Hrvatsko knjizicarsko drustvo (Croatia) Tel: (01) 615 93 20; (01) 457 2344; (01) 457 2306 Fax: (01) 616 41 86 E-mail: hkd@nsk.hr Web Site: pubwww.srce.hr/hkd, pg 1560

Hsiao Yuan Publication Co, Ltd (Taiwan, Province of China) Tel: (02) 23676789 Fax: (02) 23628424 E-mail: vfafol30@ms5.hinet.net, pg 640

Hsin Yi Publications (Taiwan, Province of China) Tel: (02) 23965303 Fax: (02) 23910799 Web Site: www.hsin-yi.org.tw, pg 640

Hua Yang Printing Holding Co Ltd (Hong Kong) Tel: 24167591 Fax: 24110235, pg 1218

Hubei Publications Import & Export Corporation (China) Tel: (027) 87825561 Fax: (027) 87815557 E-mail: hbwwsdjkb@163.com, pg 1306

Verlag Huber & Co AG (Switzerland) Tel: (052) 723 5617 Fax: (052) 723 5619 E-mail: buchverlag@huber.ch Web Site: www.huber.ch, pg 625

Huber & Lang (Switzerland) Tel: (031) 300 4646 Fax: (031) 300 4656 E-mail: contactbern@huberlang.com Web Site: www.huberlang.com, pg 1344

Hans Huber (Germany) Tel: (031) 3004500 Fax: (031) 3004590 E-mail: verlag@hanshuber.com Web Site: www.hanshuber.com, pg 239

Volker Huber Edition & Galerie (Germany) Tel: (069) 814523 Fax: (069) 880155 E-mail: edition-huber@t-online.de Web Site: www.volkerhuber.de, pg 239

Hubsch (Luxembourg) E-mail: 101755.3213@compuserve.com, pg 451

Hudanuda Publishing Co Ltd (Nigeria) Tel: (069) 5141, pg 505

Angus Hudson Ltd (United Kingdom) Tel: (020) 8959 3668 Fax: (020) 8959 3678 E-mail: sales@angushudson.com Web Site: www.angushudson.com, pg 710

Hudson Publishing (Australia) Tel: (03) 9853 7753 Fax: (03) 9853 7290 E-mail: hudson@c031.aone.net.au, pg 26

Max Hueber Verlag GmbH & Co KG (Germany) Tel: (089) 9602-0 Fax: (089) 9602-358 E-mail: kundenservice@hueber.de Web Site: www.hueber.de, pg 239

Felicitas Huebner Verlag (Germany) Tel: (05695) 1028 Fax: (05695) 1027, pg 239

Verlag Uta Huelsey (Germany) Tel: (0281) 27227 Fax: (0281) 24682 E-mail: uta.hulsey@t-online.de, pg 240

Libreria Huemul SA (Argentina) Tel: (011) 4822-1666; (011) 4825-2290 Fax: (011) 822-1666, pg 6

Libreria Huemul SA (Argentina) Tel: (011) 4822-1666; (011) 4825-2290 Fax: (011) 822-1666 E-mail: libreriahuemul@arnet.com.ar, pg 1297

Hug & Co (Switzerland) Tel: (01) 269 41 41 Fax: (01) 269 41 06 E-mail: info@hug-musikverlage.ch Web Site: www.hug-musikverlage.ch, pg 625

Heinrich Hugendubel (Germany) Tel: (089) 235586-0 Fax: (089) 235586-111, pg 1311

Heinrich Hugendubel Verlag GmbH (Germany) Tel: (089) 235586-0 Fax: (089) 235586-111 Web Site: www.hugendubel.de, pg 240

Hugo's Language Books Ltd (United Kingdom) Tel: (020) 7010 3000 Fax: (020) 7010 6060 E-mail: customerservice@dk.com Web Site: uk.dk.com, pg 710

Editions Charles Huguenin Pro Arte (Switzerland) Tel: (038) 61 27 27 Fax: (038) 61 37 19, pg 625

Huia Publishers (New Zealand) Tel: (04) 473-9262 Fax: (04) 473-9265 E-mail: customer.services@huia.co.nz Web Site: www.huia.co.nz, pg 497

Huis Van Het Boek (Belgium) Tel: (03) 230 89 23 Fax: (03) 281 22 40 E-mail: info@boek.be Web Site: www.boek.be, pg 68

Human & Rousseau (Pty) Ltd (South Africa) Tel: (021) 424 1320; (021) 424 1323 Fax: (021) 424 2510; (021) 426 5744 E-mail: rhauman@nbh.naspers.co.za Web Site: www.humanrousseau.com, pg 564

Human Sciences Research Council (South Africa) Tel: (012) 302 2999 Fax: (012) 326 5362 Web Site: www.hsrc.ac.za, pg 565

Edition Humanistische Psychologie (EHP) (Germany) Tel: (02202) 981236 Fax: (02202) 981237 E-mail: info@ehp-koeln.com Web Site: www.ehp-koeln.com; www.ehp.biz, pg 240

Humanistischer Verband Deutschlands, Landesverband Berlin eV (Germany) Tel: (030) 6139040 Fax: (030) 61390450 E-mail: hvd@humanismus.de Web Site: www.humanismus.de, pg 240

Humanitas Ltd (Lithuania) Tel: (07) 220333 Fax: (07) 423653 E-mail: beata@humanitas.lt, pg 1325

Humanitas Publishing House (Romania) Tel: (01) 223-1501; (01) 222-8546 Fax: (01) 224-3632 E-mail: editors@agora.humanitas.ro Web Site: www.humanitas.ro, pg 540

Humboldt-Taschenbuch Verlag Jacobi KG (Germany) Tel: (089) 360960 Fax: (089) 36096-222 (general); (089) 36096-258 (orders) E-mail: redaktion@humboldt.de, pg 240

Humboldt Universitaet zu Berlin (Germany) Tel: (030) 2093 3212 Fax: (030) 2093 3207 E-mail: wwwadm.ub@ub.hu-berlin.de Web Site: www.ub.hu-berlin.de, pg 1509

Edition Hundertmark (Germany) Tel: (0221) 237944 Fax: (0221) 249146 E-mail: info@hundertmark-gallery.com Web Site: www.hundertmark-gallery.com, pg 240

Hundskolan i Solleftea AB (Sweden) Tel: (0620) 832 00 Fax: (0620) 832 29 E-mail: gundvald@hundskolan.se Web Site: www.humanitydog.se, pg 612

Hung Hing Off-set Printing Co Ltd (Hong Kong) Tel: 2664 8682 Fax: 2664 2070 E-mail: info@hhop.com.hk Web Site: www.hhop.com.hk, pg 1157, 1178, 1218

Hungarian PEN Centre (Hungary) Tel: (01) 3184143 Fax: (01) 1171722, pg 1401

John Hunt Publishing Ltd (United Kingdom) Tel: (01962) 736880; (01962) 736888 (orders) Fax: (01962) 736881 E-mail: office@johnhunt-publishing.com Web Site: www.johnhunt-publishing.com, pg 710

Hunter & Foulis Ltd (United Kingdom) Tel: (01620) 826379 Fax: (01620) 829485 E-mail: mail@hunterfoulis.co.uk Web Site: www.hunterfoulis.co.uk, pg 1226

Hunter & Foulis Ltd (United Kingdom) Tel: (01620) 826 379 Fax: (01620) 829 485 E-mail: mail@hunterfoulis.co.uk Web Site: www.hunterfoulis.co.uk, pg 1239

Hunter Books (Australia), pg 26

Hunter House Publications (Australia) Tel: (02) 4930 5992 Fax: (02) 4930 5993 E-mail: wf&mc@hunterlink.net.au, pg 26

Huntsmen Offset Printing Pte Ltd (Singapore) Tel: 2650600 Fax: 2658575, pg 1222

Ediciones Huracan Inc (Puerto Rico) Tel: (787) 763-7407 Fax: (787) 763-7407, pg 537

Huron Valley Graphics Inc (United States) Tel: 734-477-0448 Toll Free Tel: 800-362-9655 Fax: 734-477-0393 E-mail: custserv@hvg.com Web Site: www.hvg.com, pg 1187

C Hurst & Co (Publishers) Ltd (United Kingdom) Tel: (020) 7240 2666 Fax: (020) 7240 2667 E-mail: hurst@atlas.co.uk Web Site: www.hurstpub.co.uk, pg 711

Dr Mahmud Husain Library (Pakistan) Tel: (021) 474953 Fax: (021) 4969277 Web Site: www.un.org.pk/unic/hussainlibrary.htm, pg 1535

Huss-Medien GmbH (Germany) Tel: (030) 421510 Fax: (030) 42151332 E-mail: huss.medien@hussberlin.de Web Site: huss-medien.de, pg 240

Huss-Verlag GmbH (Germany) Tel: (089) 323910 Fax: (089) 32391416 E-mail: management@huss-verlag.de Web Site: www.huss-verlag.de/, pg 240

Husum Druck- und Verlagsgesellschaft mbH Co KG (Germany) Tel: (04841) 83520 Fax: (04841) 835210 E-mail: verlagsgruppe.husum@t-online.de Web Site: www.verlagsgruppe.de/, pg 240

YELLOW PAGES

Alan Hutchison Ltd (United Kingdom) *Tel:* (020) 7221 0129, pg 711

Huthig GmbH & Co KG (Germany) *Tel:* (06221) 4890 *Fax:* (06221) 489219 *E-mail:* info@huethig.de *Web Site:* www.huethig.de, pg 240

Hutton Press Ltd (United Kingdom) *Tel:* (01964) 550573 *Fax:* (01964) 550573, pg 711

Hutton-Williams Agency (United Kingdom) *Tel:* (020) 8879 0237 *Fax:* (020) 8879 3831, pg 1140

Hw Moon Publishing Co (Republic of Korea) *Tel:* (02) 724897, pg 439

Hyangmunsa Publishing Co (Republic of Korea) *Tel:* (02) 5385671; (02) 5385672 *Fax:* (02) 5385673, pg 439

Hyden House Ltd (United Kingdom) *Tel:* (01730) 823311 *Fax:* (01730) 823322 *E-mail:* info@permaculture.co.uk *Web Site:* www.permaculture.co.uk, pg 711

Hyein Publishing House (Republic of Korea) *Tel:* (02) 3836928 *Fax:* (02) 3836929 *E-mail:* vvh103@chollian *Web Site:* www.hyeinbooks.co.kr, pg 439

Hyland House Publishing Pty Ltd (Australia) *Tel:* (03) 9376 4461 *Fax:* (03) 9376 4461 *E-mail:* hyland3@netspace.net.au, pg 26

Hymns Ancient & Modern Ltd (United Kingdom) *Tel:* (01603) 612914 *Fax:* (01603) 624483 *E-mail:* admin@scm-canterburypress.co.uk *Web Site:* www.scm-canterburypress.co.uk, pg 711

Hyoronsha Publishing Co Ltd (Japan) *Tel:* (03) 3260-9401 *Fax:* (03) 3260-9408, pg 418

Editura Hyperion (Republic of Moldova) *Tel:* (02) 244259, pg 473

Hyperion - Verlag (Germany) *Tel:* (089) 32954165 *Fax:* (089) 32954175 *E-mail:* mail@hyperion-verlag.de *Web Site:* www.hyperion-verlag.de, pg 240

HYS Culture Co Ltd (Taiwan, Province of China) *Tel:* (07) 6914310 *Fax:* (02) 6914311 *E-mail:* hysccl@msl.hinet.net *Web Site:* www.hysbook.com.tw, pg 640

Hyun Am Publishing Co (Republic of Korea) *Tel:* (02) 877-2565 *Fax:* (02) 877-2566, pg 439

I Prooptiki, Ekdoseis (Greece) *Tel:* (01) 8226254 *Fax:* (01) 8226254 *E-mail:* info@prooptikibooks.gr *Web Site:* wwws.prooptikibooks.gr, pg 308

IAEA - International Atomic Energy Agency (Austria) *Tel:* (01) 2600-0; (01) 2600-22530 *Fax:* (01) 2600-7 *E-mail:* official.mail@iaea.org *Web Site:* www.iaea.org/worldatom/Books, pg 52

Iaith Cyf (United Kingdom) *Tel:* (01239) 711668 *Fax:* (01239) 711698 *E-mail:* ymhol@cwmni-iaith.com *Web Site:* www.cwmni-iaith.com, pg 711

Iamvlichos (Greece) *Tel:* (01) 5227678 *Fax:* (01) 5226581, pg 1313

Ianos (Greece) *Tel:* (02301) 284833 *Fax:* (02310) 284832 *E-mail:* internet@ianos.gr *Web Site:* www.ianos.gr, pg 308

IBA International Media & Book Agency (Germany) *Tel:* (030) 4437 9155 *Fax:* (030) 4437 9199 *E-mail:* office@iba-berlin.de *Web Site:* www.iba-berlin.de, pg 1131

Ibadan University Press (Nigeria) *Tel:* (022) 400550; (022) 400614 (ext 1244, 1042, 1032, 1093), pg 505

Ibaizabal Edelvives SA (Spain) *Tel:* (094) 6308036 *Fax:* (094) 6308028 *E-mail:* ibaizabal@ibaizabal.biz, pg 586

Ibcon SA (Mexico) *Tel:* (055) 5255 4577 *Fax:* (455) 5255 4577 *E-mail:* ibcon@ibcon.com.mx; ibcon@infosel.net.mx *Web Site:* www.ibcon.com.mx, pg 466

IBD Publisher & Distributors (India) *Tel:* (011) 3251094 *Fax:* (011) 3259102 *E-mail:* piyush_gahlot@rediffmail.com, pg 336

Ibera VerlagsgesmbH (Austria) *Tel:* (01) 513 19 72 *Fax:* (01) 513 19 72-28 *E-mail:* presse@ibera.at *Web Site:* www.ibera.at, pg 52

Editorial Iberia, SA (Spain) *Tel:* (093) 2010599; (093) 2013807 *Fax:* (093) 2097362 *E-mail:* omega@ediciones-omega.es *Web Site:* www.ediciones-omega.es, pg 586

Iberico Europea de Ediciones SA (Spain) *Tel:* (091) 4357243, pg 586

Livro Ibero-Americano Ltda (Brazil) *Tel:* (021) 2221 2026 *Fax:* (021) 2252 8814 *Web Site:* www.livroiberoamericano.com.br, pg 83

Livro Ibero-Americano Ltda (Brazil) *Tel:* (021) 2221 2026 *Fax:* (021) 2252 8814 *E-mail:* ibero_ceramica@hotmail.com *Web Site:* www.ceramicanorio.com/miscelanea/livroiberoamericano/livroiberoamericano.htm, pg 1303

Ibero-Amerikanisches Institut Preussischer Kulturbesitz (Germany) *Tel:* (030) 266 2500 *Fax:* (030) 266 2503 *E-mail:* iai@iai.spk-berlin.de *Web Site:* www.iai.spk-berlin.de, pg 1509

Iberoamericana Editorial Vervuert (Germany) *Tel:* (069) 5974617 *Fax:* (069) 5978743 *E-mail:* info@iberoamericanalibros.com *Web Site:* www.ibero-americana.net, pg 1311

IBIS (Denmark) *Tel:* 35358788 *Fax:* 35350696 *E-mail:* ibis@ibis.dk *Web Site:* www.ibis.dk, pg 132

Ibis (Italy) *Tel:* (031) 3371367; (031) 306836 *Fax:* (031) 306829 *E-mail:* info@ibisedizioni.it *Web Site:* www.ibisedizioni.it, pg 392

IBRASA (Instituicao Brasileira de Difusao Cultural Ltda) (Brazil) *Tel:* (011) 3107 41 00 *Fax:* (011) 3107 35 13 *E-mail:* editora.ibrasa@uol.com.br *Web Site:* www.ibrasa.com.br, pg 83

IBS Buku Sdn Bhd (Malaysia) *Tel:* (03) 7751763; (03) 775-1566; (03) 7760514 *Fax:* (03) 79576026; (03) 776-8551 *E-mail:* ibsbuku@po.jaring.my, pg 456

IBS Buku Sdn Bhd (Malaysia) *Tel:* (03) 79579282; (03) 79579470 *Fax:* (03) 79576026 *E-mail:* info@ibsbuku.com; ibsbuku@po.janing.my; hibs@tm.net.my, pg 1326

ICA bokforlag (Sweden) *Tel:* (021) 194278 *Fax:* (021) 194283 *E-mail:* bok@forlaget.ica.se *Web Site:* www.forlaget.ica.se/bok, pg 612

Icaria Editorial SA (Spain) *Tel:* (093) 3011723 *Fax:* (093) 3178242 *E-mail:* www.icariaeditorial.com, pg 587

ICBS/IBIS ApS (Denmark) *Tel:* 33114255 *Fax:* 33911167 *E-mail:* icbs@get2net.dk *Web Site:* www.icbs-ibis.dk, pg 1130

ICC United Kingdom (United Kingdom) *Tel:* (020) 7823 2811 *Fax:* (020) 7235 5447 *E-mail:* katharinehedger@iccorg.co.uk *Web Site:* www.iccwbo.org; www.iccuk.net, pg 711

Publicaciones ICCE (Spain) *Tel:* (091) 725 72 00 *Fax:* (091) 361 10 52 *E-mail:* info@ciberaula.net *Web Site:* www.ciberaula.net, pg 587

Iceland Review (Iceland) *Tel:* 512-7575 *Fax:* 561-8646 *E-mail:* icelandreview@icelandreview.com *Web Site:* www.icelandreview.com, pg 325

Icelandic PEN Centre (Iceland), pg 1401

ICG/Holliston (United States) *Tel:* 423-357-6141 *Toll Free Tel:* 800-251-0451 *Fax:* 423-357-8840 *Toll Free Fax:* 800-325-0351 *E-mail:* custserv@icgholliston.com *Web Site:* www.icgholliston.com, pg 1240

ICG Publications BV (Netherlands) *Tel:* (070) 4480203 *Fax:* (070) 4480177, pg 484

Ichiryu-Sha (Japan) *Tel:* (03) 3822-0585 *Fax:* (03) 3821-3964, pg 418

Ichtiar Baru I Van Hoeve (Indonesia) *Tel:* (021) 7511856, pg 1179

Ichtiar Baru I Van Hoeve (Indonesia) *Tel:* (021) 7511856; (021) 7511901 *Fax:* (021) 7511855, pg 1220

ISTITUTO IDROGRAFICO DELLA MARINA

Ichtiar Baru I Van Hoeve (Indonesia) *Tel:* (021) 7511856, pg 1237

Ici et Ailleurs-Vents d'Ailleurs (France) *Tel:* (04) 42533087 *Fax:* (04) 42533097 *E-mail:* info@kaona.com *Web Site:* www.kaona.com, pg 168

ICOB/Atrium (Netherlands) *Tel:* (0172) 43 72 31 *Fax:* (0172) 43 93 79 *E-mail:* icobal@xs4all.nl, pg 1329

Icon Press (United Kingdom) *Tel:* (01323) 507270 *Fax:* (01323) 507270 *E-mail:* iconpress@philipbrown.screaming.net *Web Site:* www.iconpress.co.uk, pg 711

Icone Editora Ltda (Brazil) *Tel:* (011) 826-7074; (021) 826-9510 *Fax:* (011) 826-9510, pg 83

ICPC Ltd (Ireland) *Tel:* (01) 8474711 *Fax:* (01) 8474546 *Web Site:* www.icpc.ie, pg 1180

ICSA Publishing Ltd (United Kingdom) *Tel:* (020) 7612 7020 *Fax:* (020) 7323 1132 *E-mail:* icsa.pub@icsa.co.uk *Web Site:* www.icsapublishing.co.uk, pg 711

ICSI Corp (United States) *Tel:* 330-645-0004; 330-786-0002 *Toll Free Tel:* 800-860-0709; 800-965-0004 *Fax:* 330-786-0056 *Web Site:* www.icsidata.com, pg 1188

Edition ID-Archiv/ID-Verlag (Germany) *Tel:* (030) 6947703 *Fax:* (030) 6947808 *E-mail:* id-verlag@mail.nadir.org *Web Site:* www.txt.de/id-verlag/, pg 240

Idara-e-Tehqiqat-e-Islami (Pakistan) *Tel:* (051) 850751-5; (051) 850755, pg 512

Idara Ishaat-E-Diniyat Ltd (India) *Tel:* (011) 26926832; (011) 26926833 (office); (011) 461676; (011) 4631786 (showroom) *Fax:* (011) 26932787; (011) 4632786 *E-mail:* sales@idara.com; idara@yahoo.com *Web Site:* www.idara.com, pg 336

Idara Siqafat-e-Islamia (Pakistan) *Tel:* (042) 53908, pg 512

Idea Books (Italy) *Tel:* (0584) 425410 *Fax:* (0178) 609 8685 *E-mail:* ideab@tiscali.it, pg 392

Idea Books, SA (Spain) *Tel:* (093) 4533002 *Fax:* (093) 4541895 *E-mail:* ideabooks@ideabooks.es *Web Site:* www.ideabooks.es, pg 587

Idea Verlag GmbH (Germany) *Tel:* (08141) 80939 *Fax:* (08141) 80939 *E-mail:* info@idea-verlag.de *Web Site:* www.idea-verlag.de, pg 240

The Ideal Bookshop (Malta) *Tel:* 553944, pg 1326

Editorial Idearium de la Universidad de Mendoza (EDIUM) (Argentina) *Tel:* (0261) 420-2017; (0261) 420-0740 *Fax:* (0261) 420-1100 *E-mail:* umimen@um.edu.ar *Web Site:* www.um.edu.ar/um/, pg 6

Idegenforgalmi Propaganda es Kiado Vallalat (Hungary) *Tel:* (01) 633652; (01) 633653 *Fax:* (01) 1837320, pg 321

Idegraf SA, Editions (Switzerland) *Tel:* (022) 792 03 96 *Fax:* (022) 793 63 30 *E-mail:* 101512.3363@compuserve.com, pg 625

Casa Editrice Libraria Idelson di G Gnocchi (Italy) *Tel:* (081) 5453443 *Fax:* (081) 5464991 *E-mail:* info@idelson-gnocchi.com *Web Site:* www.idelson-gnocchi.com, pg 392

Idelson-Gnocchi Edizioni Scientifiche (Italy) *Tel:* (081) 5453443 *Fax:* (081) 5464991 *E-mail:* ordini@idelson-gnocchi.com *Web Site:* www.idelson-gnocchi.com, pg 393

Identic Books (Australia) *Tel:* (02) 8901 3466 *Fax:* (02) 8901 3404 *E-mail:* enquiries@identic.com.au *Web Site:* www.identic.com.au, pg 1299

Editions Ides et Calendes SA (Switzerland) *Tel:* (032) 725 38 61 *Fax:* (032) 725 58 80 *E-mail:* info@idesetcalendes.com; artides@artides.com; ides@livre.net *Web Site:* www.artides.com; www.livre.net/ides, pg 625

Idmon Publications (Greece) *Tel:* (01) 5015550 *Fax:* (01) 5015550 *E-mail:* idmon@in.gr, pg 308

Istituto Idrografico della Marina (Italy) *Tel:* (010) 24431 *Fax:* (010) 261400 *E-mail:* iim.sre@marina.difesa.it *Web Site:* www.marina.difesa.it, pg 393

Idryma Meleton Chersonisou tou Aimou (Greece) *Tel:* (0310) 832143 *Fax:* (0310) 831429 *E-mail:* imxa@imxa.gr, pg 308

Idunn (Iceland) *Tel:* 5155500 *Fax:* 5155579 *E-mail:* idunn@idunn.is *Web Site:* www.idunn.is, pg 325

IDW-Verlag GmbH (Germany) *Tel:* (0211) 45610 *Fax:* (0211) 4541206 *E-mail:* post@idw-verlag.de *Web Site:* www.idw-verlag.de, pg 241

Ie-No-Hikari Association (Japan) *Tel:* (03) 3266-9029 *Fax:* (03) 3266-9053 *E-mail:* hikari@mxd.meshnet.or.jp *Web Site:* www.ienohikari.or.jp, pg 419

Ifjusagi Lap-eskonyvkiado Vallalat (Hungary) *Tel:* (01) 1116660 *Fax:* (01) 1530959, pg 321

IG Autorinnen Autoren (Austria) *Tel:* (01) 526 20 44-13 *Fax:* (01) 526 20 44-55 *E-mail:* ig@literaturhaus.at *Web Site:* www.literaturhaus.at/lh/ig, pg 52

Igaku-Shoin Ltd (Japan) *Tel:* (03) 38175600 *Fax:* (03) 38157791 *E-mail:* info@igaku-shoin.co.jp *Web Site:* www.igaku-shoin.co.jp, pg 419

Igel Verlag Literatur Michael Matthias Schardt (Germany) *Tel:* (0441) 6640262 *Fax:* (0441) 6640263, pg 241

Editorial Pablo Iglesias (Spain) *Tel:* (091) 104 313 *Fax:* (091) 194 585 *E-mail:* administracion@fpi.es *Web Site:* www.fpabloiglesias.es, pg 587

Iglu Editora Ltda (Brazil) *Tel:* (011) 3873-0227 *Fax:* (011) 3873-0227, pg 84

IHT Gruppo Editoriale SRL (Italy) *Tel:* (02) 794181 *Fax:* (02) 784021 *E-mail:* info@iht.it *Web Site:* www.iht.it, pg 393

Ikaros (Greece) *Tel:* (01) 3225152, pg 1313

Ikaros Ekdotiki (Greece) *Tel:* (01) 3225152 *Fax:* (01) 3235262, pg 308

Ikarus - Buchverlag (Germany) *Tel:* (06682) 919383 *Fax:* (06682) 919385 *E-mail:* ikarus-verlag@t-online.de *Web Site:* www.ikarus-verlag.de, pg 241

Ikatan Penerbit Indonesia (IKAPI) (Indonesia) *Tel:* (021) 3141907; (021) 3146050 *Fax:* (021) 3146050 *E-mail:* sekretariat@ikapi.or.id *Web Site:* www.ikapi.or.id, pg 1273

Ikatan Pustakawan Indonesia (Indonesia) *Tel:* (021) 375718 *Fax:* (021) 3455611, pg 1564

IKI Nokta Research Press & Publications Industry & Trade Ltd (Turkey) *Tel:* (0216) 349 01 41 *Fax:* (0216) 337 67 56 *E-mail:* ikinokta@superonline.com; ikinokta@turkinfo.com; ikinokta@gisoturkey.com; ikinokta @ turkgis.com; ikinokta@infoturk.com *Web Site:* www.ikinokta.com, pg 650

IKO Verlag fur Interkulturelle Kommunikation (Germany) *Tel:* (069) 784808 *Fax:* (069) 7896575 *E-mail:* info@iko-verlag.de *Web Site:* www.iko-verlag.de, pg 241

Ikon Document Management Services (United Kingdom) *Tel:* (0118) 9770510 *Fax:* (0118) 9770513, pg 1164

Ikon Document Management Services (United Kingdom) *Tel:* (0118) 9770510 *Fax:* (0118) 9770513 *E-mail:* pamh@ikonds.co.uk *Web Site:* www.ikon.com, pg 1184

Ikon Document Management Services (United Kingdom) *Tel:* (0118) 9770510 *Fax:* (0118) 9770513 *Web Site:* www.ikon.com, pg 1226

Ikon Document Management Services (United Kingdom) *Tel:* (020) 7336 6509 *Fax:* (020) 7336 7840 *Web Site:* www.uk.ikon.com, pg 1248

Ikon Document Services (United States) *Tel:* 978-562-9131 *Fax:* 978-562-4304, pg 1188

Ikon Document Services (United States) *Tel:* 978-562-9131 *Fax:* 978-562-4304 *Web Site:* www.ikon.com, pg 1229

Ikon Publishing Ltd (Hungary) *Tel:* (01) 1761404 *Fax:* (01) 1158089, pg 322

Ikubundo Publishers Co (Japan) *Tel:* (03) 3814-5571 *Fax:* (03) 3814-5576 *E-mail:* webmaster@ikubundo.com *Web Site:* www.ikubundo.com, pg 1322

ILA (International Literary Agency) USA (Italy) *Tel:* (0184) 484048; (0347) 9334966 *Fax:* (0184) 487292 *E-mail:* books@librigg.com, pg 1133

Ila - Palma, Tea Nova (Italy) *Tel:* (091) 332051 *Fax:* (091) 6259260, pg 393

Iletisim Yayinlari (Turkey) *Tel:* (0212) 516 22 60 *Fax:* (0212) 516 12 58 *E-mail:* iletisim@iletisim.tr *Web Site:* www.iletisim.com.tr, pg 650

Ilisso Edizioni di Vanna Fois & CSNC (Italy) *Tel:* (0784) 33033 *Fax:* (0784) 35413 *E-mail:* ilisso@ilisso.it *Web Site:* www.ilisso.it, pg 1321

Iljisa Publishing House (Republic of Korea) *Tel:* (02) 7329320 *Fax:* (02) 7222807, pg 439

Iljo-gag Publishers (Republic of Korea) *Tel:* (02) 7335430; (02) 7335431 *Fax:* (02) 7385857 *E-mail:* ilchokak@hitel.kol.co.kr; ilchokak@chollian.dacom.co.kr, pg 439

Illert Publications (Australia) *Tel:* (02) 4283 3009 *Fax:* (02) 4283 3009 *E-mail:* illert@keira.hotkey.net.au, pg 26

Ilmamaa (Estonia) *Tel:* (07) 427 290 *Fax:* (07) 427 320 *E-mail:* ilmamaa@ilmamaa.ee *Web Site:* www.ilmamaa.ee, pg 139

Iluminuras - Projetos e Producoes Editoriais Ltda (Brazil) *Tel:* (011) 3068-9433 *Fax:* (011) 3082-5317, pg 84

Image & Print Group Ltd (United Kingdom) *Tel:* (0141) 353 1900 *Fax:* (0141) 353 8611 *E-mail:* info@imageandprint.co.uk *Web Site:* www.imageandprint.co.uk, pg 1184

Image & Print Group Ltd (United Kingdom) *Tel:* (0141) 353 1900; (0141) 353 8620 (ISDN) *Fax:* (0141) 353 8611 *E-mail:* info@imageandprint.co.uk *Web Site:* www.imageandprint.co.uk, pg 1226, 1239

Image/Magie (France) *Tel:* (01) 66 80 34 02 *Fax:* (01) 66 80 34 56, pg 168

Image Printing Company Ltd (Hong Kong) *Tel:* 2873 2633 *Fax:* 2558 3044 *E-mail:* imageprt@pop3.hknet.com, pg 1157, 1178, 1218, 1236

Imagen y Deporte, SL (Spain) *Tel:* (0976) 75 40 00 *Fax:* (0976) 75 40 00 *Web Site:* www.imagenydeporte.com, pg 587

The Images Publishing Group Pty Ltd (Australia) *Tel:* (03) 9561 5544 *Fax:* (03) 9561 4860 *E-mail:* books@images.com.au *Web Site:* www.imagespublishinggroup.com, pg 26

Imago (United States) *Tel:* 212-921-4411 *Fax:* 212-921-8226 *E-mail:* sales@imagousa.com *Web Site:* www.imagousa.com, pg 1167, 1229, 1240

Editions Imago (France) *Tel:* (01) 46 33 15 33 *Fax:* (01) 60 23 87 51 *E-mail:* info@editions-imago.fr *Web Site:* www.editions-imago.fr, pg 168

Imago Editora Importacao e Exportacao Ltda (Brazil) *Tel:* (021) 2502-9092 *Fax:* (021) 2502-5435 *E-mail:* imago@imagoeditora.com.br *Web Site:* www.imagoeditora.com.br, pg 84

Imago Productions (Far East) Pte Ltd (Singapore) *Tel:* 67484433 *Fax:* 67486082 *Web Site:* www.imago.co.uk, pg 1246

Imago Publishing Ltd (United Kingdom) *Tel:* (01844) 337000 *Fax:* (01844) 339935 *E-mail:* sales@imago.co.uk *Web Site:* www.imago.co.uk, pg 711

Imago Services (HK) Ltd (Hong Kong) *Tel:* 2811 3316 *Fax:* 2597 5256 *E-mail:* enquiries@imago.com.hk *Web Site:* www.imago.co.uk, pg 1157

Imam Mohamed Bin Saud University Library (Saudi Arabia) *Tel:* (01) 258 0000 *Fax:* (01) 259 0271, pg 1541

IMEC (France) *Tel:* (01) 53 34 23 23 *Fax:* (01) 43-79-46-87 *E-mail:* bibliotheque@imec-archives.com *Web Site:* www.imec-archives.com, pg 168

Imge Kitabevi (Turkey) *Tel:* (0312) 419 46 10; (0312) 419 46 11 *Fax:* (0312) 425 29 87 *E-mail:* imge@www.imge.com.tr *Web Site:* www.imgekitabevi.com, pg 650

Immediate Publishing (United Kingdom) *Tel:* (01273) 207259; (01273) 207411 *Fax:* (01273) 205612, pg 712

Impact (United Kingdom) *Tel:* (020) 7222 7777; (020) 7636 7543 *Fax:* (020) 7222 2782; (020) 7436 7218, pg 1573

Impala (Portugal) *Tel:* (021) 4364401 *Fax:* (021) 4366572, pg 532

Impart Books (United Kingdom) *Tel:* (01686) 623484 *E-mail:* impart@books.mid-wales.net *Web Site:* www.books.mid-wales.net, pg 712

Imparudi (Imprimerie et Papeterie du Burundi) (Burundi) *Tel:* (02) 3125; (02) 7381 *Fax:* (02) 2572, pg 1304

Imperial College Press (United Kingdom) *Tel:* (020) 7836 3954 *Fax:* (020) 7836 2002 *E-mail:* edit@icpress.co.uk *Web Site:* www.icpress.co.uk, pg 712

IMPF bvba (Belgium) *Tel:* (09) 225 44 29 *Fax:* 058 315 77 *E-mail:* maarten@fotobeurs.com *Web Site:* www.fotobeurs.com, pg 1175

IMPF bvba (Belgium) *Tel:* (09) 225 44 29, pg 1215

IMPF bvba (Belgium) *Tel:* (09) 225 44 29; (09) 265 99 00 *Fax:* (09) 233 13 38 *E-mail:* impf@xs4all.be, pg 1245

Impredisur, SL (Spain) *Tel:* (0958) 202955; (0958) 290577, pg 587

Imprensa Nacional-Casa da Moeda (Portugal) *Tel:* (021) 781 07 00 *Fax:* (021) 781 07 54 *Web Site:* www.incm.pt, pg 532

Imprenta de la Universidad Nacional (Colombia) *Tel:* (01) 2686965; (01) 2699111 *Fax:* (01) 2441035, pg 111

Imprenta y Litografia Trejos SA (Costa Rica) *Tel:* 2242411 *Fax:* 2241528, pg 115

Imprima Korea Agency (Republic of Korea) *Tel:* (02) 325-9155 *Fax:* (02) 334-9160 *E-mail:* imprima@chollian.net *Web Site:* www.imprima.co.kr, pg 1134

Imprimerie Bietlot Freres SA (Belgium) *Tel:* (071) 283611 *Fax:* (071) 283620 *E-mail:* info@bietlot.be *Web Site:* www.bietlot.be, pg 1235

Imprimerie Commerciale et Administrative de Mauritanie (Mauritania), pg 461

Imprimerie de Kabgayi (Rwanda) *Tel:* 62252; 62877 *Fax:* 62345, pg 550

Imprimerie et Papeterie Commerciale, IPC (Mauritius) *Tel:* 2124190; 2127701; 2127702 *Fax:* 2083523, pg 461

IMPS Research Ltd (Papua New Guinea) *Tel:* 3213283 *Fax:* 3217360 *E-mail:* imps@online.net.pg, pg 515

IMPS SA (Belgium) *Tel:* (02) 6520220 *Fax:* (02) 6520160, pg 68

Impuls (Poland) *Tel:* (012) 422-41-80 *Fax:* (012) 422-59-47 *E-mail:* impuls@impulsoficyna.com.pl *Web Site:* www.impulsoficyna.com.pl, pg 523

Impuls-Theater-Verlag (Germany) *Tel:* (089) 8597577 *Fax:* (089) 8593044 *E-mail:* info@buschfunk.de *Web Site:* www.buschfunk.de, pg 241

Imrie & Dervis Literary Agency (United Kingdom) *Tel:* (020) 8809 3282 *Fax:* (020) 8880 2086 *E-mail:* info@imriedervis.com, pg 1140

In Dialogo (Italy) *Tel:* (02) 58391342 *Fax:* (02) 58391345 *E-mail:* indial@tin.it, pg 393

In-Tune Books (Australia) *Tel:* (02) 9974 5981 *Fax:* (02) 9974 4552 *Web Site:* www.haywardbooks.com.au, pg 26

INADES (Institut Africain pour le Developpment Economique et Social) (Cote d'Ivoire) *Tel:* 22404720 *Fax:* 22448438 *E-mail:* inades@ci.refer.org; inades@africaonline.co.ci *Web Site:* www.inades.ci.refer.org, pg 1500

INADES (Institut Africain pour le Developpment Economique et Social) (Rwanda) *Tel:* (0225) 22404720; (0225) 2244 20 59 *Fax:* (0225) 44 84 38 *E-mail:* inades@africaonline.co.ci; inades@ci.refer.org *Web Site:* www.inades.ci.refer.org, pg 550

Inbal Publishers (Israel) *Tel:* (03) 9030111 *Fax:* (03) 9030888 *E-mail:* inbalpub@internet-zahav.net, pg 368

Inbal Travel Information (Israel) *Tel:* (03) 5753032 *Fax:* (03) 5753130, pg 368

Incafo Archivo Fotografico Editorial, SL (Spain) *Tel:* (091) 4313460; (091) 5780961 *Fax:* (091) 4313589, pg 587

Incunabula Press (Australia) *Tel:* (03) 9381 1559, pg 26

Independence Educational Publishers Ltd (United Kingdom) *Tel:* (01223) 566 130 *Fax:* (01223) 566 131 *E-mail:* issues@independence.co.uk *Web Site:* www.independence.co.uk, pg 712

Independent Publishers Guild (United Kingdom) *Tel:* (01763) 247014 *Fax:* (01763) 246293 *E-mail:* info@ipg.uk.com *Web Site:* www.ipg.uk.com/, pg 1291

Independent Writers Publications Ltd (United Kingdom) *Tel:* (020) 8438 0179 *Fax:* (020) 8438 0179, pg 712

Editora Index Ltda (Brazil) *Tel:* (021) 516 2336 *Fax:* (021) 253 3507 *E-mail:* editoraindex@ax.ibase.org.br, pg 84

India Book House Pvt Ltd (India) *Tel:* (022) 2840165 *Fax:* (022) 2835099 *E-mail:* padmini@ibhindia.com, pg 336

Indian Association of Special Libraries & Information Centres (IASLIC) (India) *Tel:* (033) 2352 9651; (033) 2354 9066 *E-mail:* iaslic@vsnl.net *Web Site:* www.iaslic.org, pg 1564

Indian Association of Academic Librarians (India) *Tel:* (011) 6831717, pg 1564

Indian Book Depot (India) *Tel:* (011) 3673927; (011) 3523635 *Fax:* (011) 3552096 *E-mail:* ibdmaps@ndb.vsnl.net.in; indiabo@indiabookfair.net, pg 336

Indian Council for Cultural Relations (India) *Tel:* (011) 3370732; (011) 3378647 *Fax:* (011) 3712639 *E-mail:* iccr@vsnl.com *Web Site:* education.vsnl.com/iccr, pg 336

Indian Council of Agricultural Research (India) *Tel:* (011) 388991 (ext 496); (011) 23382306 *Fax:* (011) 387293 *E-mail:* jssamra@icar.delhi.nic.in *Web Site:* www.icar.org.in, pg 336

Indian Council of Social Science Research (ICSSR) (India) *Tel:* (011) 23385959; (011) 26717066 *Fax:* (011) 26179836 *E-mail:* info@icssr.org *Web Site:* www.icssr.org, pg 336

Indian Council of World Affairs Library (India) *Tel:* (011) 3317246 *Fax:* (011) 3317248, pg 1516

Indian Documentation Service (India) *Tel:* (0124) 6322005; (0124) 6322779 *Fax:* (0124) 6324782 *E-mail:* indoc@indiatimes.com, pg 337

Indian Institute of Advanced Study (India) *Tel:* (0177) 72303; (0177) 75139 *Fax:* (0177) 75139 *E-mail:* info@iias.org *Web Site:* www.iias.org, pg 337

Indian Institute of Management (India) *Tel:* (079) 2630 7241 *Fax:* (079) 2630 6896 *E-mail:* director@iimahd.ernet.in *Web Site:* www.iimahd.ernet.in, pg 1516

Indian Institute of Technology Madras Central Library (India) *Tel:* (044) 2578740 *Fax:* (044) 2350509 *E-mail:* libinfo@iitm.ac.in *Web Site:* www.cenlib.iitm.ac.in, pg 1516

Indian Institute of World Culture (India) *Tel:* (080) 6678581 *Web Site:* www.ultindia.org/culture.htm, pg 337

Indian Library Association (India) *Tel:* (011) 326 4748; (011) 765 1743 *E-mail:* ilanet1@nda.vsnl.net.in, pg 1564

Indian Museum (India) *Tel:* (033) 249 9902; (033) 249 9979; (033) 249 8948; (033) 249 8931 *Fax:* (033) 249 5699 *E-mail:* imbot@cal2.vsnl.net.in *Web Site:* www.indianmuseum-calcutta.org, pg 337

Indian Society for Promoting Christian Knowledge (ISPCK) (India) *Tel:* (011) 23866323 *Fax:* (011) 23865490 *E-mail:* ispck@nde.vsnl.net.in *Web Site:* ispck.org.in, pg 337

Instituto Indigenista Interamericano (Mexico) *Tel:* (05) 5595 8410; (05) 5595 4324 *Fax:* (05) 595 8410 *E-mail:* ininin@data.net.mx, pg 466

Indigo & Cote-Femmes Editions (France) *Tel:* (01) 43 79 74 79 *Fax:* (01) 43 79 46 87 *E-mail:* indigo.cote-femmes.edition@wanadoo.fr *Web Site:* www.indigo-cf.com, pg 168

PT Indira (Indonesia) *Tel:* (021) 3904290; (021) 3148868 *Fax:* (021) 3929373 *E-mail:* indirawb@mweb.co.id, pg 355

PT Indira (Indonesia) *Tel:* (021) 3148868; (021) 3904290 *Fax:* (021) 3929373 *E-mail:* indirawb@mweb.co.id, pg 1318

Indo Lingua Services Ltd (United Kingdom) *Tel:* (020) 7515 3987 *E-mail:* indolingua@compuserve.com, pg 1150

Indonesian ISBN Agency (Indonesia) *Tel:* (021) 3154864; (021) 3154870 *Fax:* (021) 3103554 *E-mail:* info@pnri.go.id *Web Site:* www.pnri.go.id, pg 1273

Indonesian PEN Centre (Indonesia) *Tel:* (093) 3905837 *Fax:* (093) 325890, pg 1401

Indra Publishing (Australia) *Tel:* (03) 9439 7555 *Fax:* (03) 9439 7555 *Web Site:* www.indra.com.au, pg 27

Indrajaya CV (Indonesia) *Tel:* (021) 3457039; (021) 3457041 *Fax:* (021) 3457039, pg 355

Indus Publishing Co (India) *Tel:* (011) 25935289; (011) 25151333 *Fax:* (011) 25922102 *E-mail:* indus@indusbooks.com *Web Site:* www.indusbooks.com, pg 338

Industria-Verlagsbuchhandlung GmbH (Germany) *Tel:* (02323) 1410 *Fax:* (02323) 141123, pg 241

Industrial Publishing House (Democratic People's Republic of Korea), pg 436

Industrial Technology Institute Information Services Centre (Sri Lanka) *Tel:* (01) 693807; (01) 693808; (01) 693809; (01) 698621; (01) 698622; (01) 698623 *Fax:* (01) 686567 *E-mail:* info@iti.lk *Web Site:* www.iti.lk, pg 1546

Industrias del Envase SA (Peru) *Tel:* (01) 574-1150 *Fax:* (01) 574-1287 *E-mail:* webmast@envase.com.pe *Web Site:* www.envase.com.pe, pg 1222

Industrie- und Handelsverlag GmbH & Co KG (Germany) *Tel:* (0511) 98489957 *Fax:* (0511) 98489952 *E-mail:* info@fhb-online.de *Web Site:* www.fhb-online.de/, pg 241

Verlag Industrielle Organisation (Switzerland) *Tel:* (01) 4667711 *Fax:* (01) 4667412 *E-mail:* info@ofv.ch *Web Site:* www.ofv.ch, pg 625

Styret for det Industrielle Rettsvern Information Department (Norway) *Tel:* (022) 38 73 00 *Fax:* (022) 38 73 01, pg 1534

Industrieschau Verlagsgesellschaft mbH (Germany) *Tel:* (06151) 38920 *Fax:* (06151) 389280 *E-mail:* info@abconline.de *Web Site:* www.abconline.de, pg 241

Industrilitteratur Vindex, Forlags AB (Sweden) *Tel:* (08) 783 81 00 *Fax:* (08) 660 59 11 *E-mail:* aestan.orstadius@industrilitteratur.se, pg 612

Info Access & Distribution (Singapore) *Tel:* 6741 8422 *Fax:* 6741 8821 *E-mail:* info.sg@igroup.net.com *Web Site:* www.igroup.net, pg 1339

Infoa (Czech Republic) *Tel:* (0583) 449 091 *Fax:* (0583) 456 810 *E-mail:* infoa@infoa.cz *Web Site:* www.infoa.cz, pg 124

Infoboek NV (Belgium) *Tel:* (014) 369292 *Fax:* (014) 369293 *E-mail:* info@infoboek.be *Web Site:* www.infoboek.com, pg 68

Informa Publishing Group Ltd (United Kingdom) *Tel:* (020) 7453 1000 *E-mail:* publishing.customers@informa.com *Web Site:* www.informa.com, pg 712

Instituto de Informacion Cientifica y Tecnologica (IDICT) (Cuba) *Tel:* (07) 862-6531; (07) 860-3411 *Fax:* (07) 862-6531 *E-mail:* andresdt@idict.cu; comercial@idict.cu *Web Site:* www.idict.cu, pg 120

Informatica Cosmos SA de CV (Mexico) *Tel:* (05) 6774868; (05) 6776043 *Fax:* (05) 6793575 *E-mail:* online@cosmos.com.mx *Web Site:* www.cosmos.com.mx, pg 466

Mediteg-Gesellschaft fuer Informatik Technik und Systeme Verlag (Germany) *Tel:* (06081) 5171 *Fax:* (06081) 56017, pg 241

Information Agents Ltd (United Kingdom) *Tel:* (020) 7837 3345 *Fax:* (020) 7837 8901 *E-mail:* eps@epsltd.com *Web Site:* www.epsltd.com, pg 1140

Informationsfoerlaget AB (Sweden) *Tel:* (08) 34 09 15 *Fax:* (08) 31 39 03 *E-mail:* red@informationsforlaget.se, pg 612

Informationsstelle Suedliches Afrika eV (ISSA) (Germany) *Tel:* (0228) 464369 *Fax:* (0228) 468177 *E-mail:* issa@comlink.org *Web Site:* www.issa-bonn.org, pg 241

Informationszentrum fuer Informationswissenschaft und -praxis (IZ) (Germany) *Tel:* (0331) 580-2210; (0331) 580-2230 *Fax:* (0331) 580-2229 *E-mail:* iz@fh-potsdam.de *Web Site:* www.fh-potsdam.de/~BIB/neu/iz, pg 1563

Informator dd (Croatia) *Tel:* (01) 4852 665; (01) 4852 668 *Fax:* (01) 4852 673 *E-mail:* informator@informator.hr *Web Site:* www.informator.hr, pg 118

Infostelle Industrieverband Deutscher Schmieden e V (Germany) *Tel:* (02331) 958828 *Fax:* (02331) 958728 *E-mail:* orders@metalform.de *Web Site:* www.metalform.de, pg 241

Infotex NV (Belgium) *Tel:* (09) 265 64 23 *Fax:* (09) 225 84 06, pg 68

INFRA-M Izdatel 'skij dom (Russian Federation) *Tel:* (095) 4857077; (095) 4855918 *Fax:* (095) 4855318 *E-mail:* books@infra-m.ru *Web Site:* www.infra-m.ru, pg 545

Editions Infrarouge (France) *Tel:* (01) 44 93 45 64 *Fax:* (01) 49 95 08 74 *E-mail:* editionsinfrarouge@libertysurf.fr; editions.infrarouge@caramail.com *Web Site:* www.chez.com/editinfrarouge, pg 168

Ingenioeren/Boger (Denmark) *Tel:* 63 15 17 00 *Fax:* 63 15 17 33 *E-mail:* info@nyttf.dk *Web Site:* www.bog.ing.dk, pg 132

Ingenioeren/Boger (Denmark) *Tel:* 63 15 17 00 *Fax:* 63 15 17 33 *Web Site:* www.bog.ing.dk, pg 1154

Ingenjoersforlaget AB (Sweden) *Tel:* (08) 796 66 90 *Fax:* (08) 22 77 44 *E-mail:* redaktionen@miljorapporten.se, pg 612

Inkilap Publishers Ltd (Turkey) *Tel:* (0212) 5140611; (0212) 5140610 *Fax:* (0212) 5140612 *Web Site:* www.inkilap.com, pg 650

Inland Publishers (United Republic of Tanzania) *Tel:* (068) 40064, pg 643

Inner Mongolia Science & Technology Publishing House (China) *Tel:* (0476) 82222 942, pg 105

Inno Vatio Verlags AG (Germany) *Tel:* (0228) 93-444-31 *Fax:* (0228) 93-444-93 *E-mail:* medien-tenor@innovatio.de *Web Site:* www.innovatio.de; www.medien-tenor.de, pg 241

Editrice Innocenti SNC (Italy) *Tel:* (0461) 236521 *Fax:* (0461) 230115, pg 393

Innodata Isogen Inc (United States) *Tel:* 201-488-1200 *Toll Free Tel:* 800-567-4784 *Fax:* 201-488-9099 *E-mail:* solutions@innodata-isogen.com *Web Site:* www.innodata-isogen.com, pg 1188

Brian Inns Booksales & Services (United Kingdom) *Tel:* (01926) 498428 *Fax:* (01926) 498428, pg 1351

Universitaetsbibliothek Innsbruck (Austria) *Tel:* (0512) 507 2401 *Fax:* (0512) 507 2893 *E-mail:* ub-hb@uibk.ac.at *Web Site:* ub.uibk.ac.at, pg 1491

Innverlag + Gatt (Austria) *Tel:* (0512) 34 53 31 *Fax:* (0512) 34 12 90 *E-mail:* innverlag@tirol.com; info@innverlag.at *Web Site:* www.innverlag.at, pg 52

Innverlag + Gatt (Austria) *Tel:* (0512) 34 53 31 *Fax:* (0512) 34 12 90 *E-mail:* info@innverlag.at *Web Site:* www.innverlag.at, pg 1300

Inprint Caribbean Ltd (Trinidad & Tobago) *Tel:* 6271569; 6231711 *Fax:* 6271451, pg 647

Editorial Inquerito Lda (Portugal) *Tel:* (021) 9211 460 *Fax:* (021) 9217 940 *E-mail:* publicidade@iol.pt, pg 532

INRA Editions (Institut National de la Recherche Agronomique) (France) *Tel:* (01) 30833406 *Fax:* (01) 30833449 *E-mail:* inra_editions@versailles.inra.fr *Web Site:* www.inra.fr/editions, pg 168

Insel Verlag (Germany) *Tel:* (069) 75601-0 *Fax:* (069) 75601-522 *Web Site:* www.suhrkamp.de, pg 241

Editions INSERM (France) *Tel:* (01) 44 23 60 82 *Fax:* (01) 44 23 60 69 *Web Site:* www.inserm.fr, pg 168

Insituto Centroamericano de Administracion de Empresas (INCAE) (Costa Rica) *Tel:* 433-9908; 433-9961; 437-2305 *Fax:* 433-9989; 433-9983 *E-mail:* incaecr@mail.incae.ac.cr *Web Site:* www.incae.ac.cr, pg 115

Inspirace (Czech Republic) *Tel:* (02) 7356615, pg 124

Editions l'Instant Durable (France) *Tel:* (04) 73 91 13 87 *Fax:* (04) 73 91 13 87 *E-mail:* art@instantdurable.com *Web Site:* www.instantdurable.com, pg 169

Instauratio Press (Australia) *Tel:* (03) 59666217 *Fax:* (03) 59666447 *E-mail:* catholic@scservnet.com, pg 27

Institucion Fernando el Catolico de la Excma Diputacion de Zaragoza (Spain) *Tel:* (0976) 28 88 78; (0976) 28 88 79 *Fax:* (0976) 28 88 69 *E-mail:* info@ifc.dpz.es *Web Site:* www.dpz.es, pg 587

Editorial Institucional y Desarrollo Humanistico SA de CV Edicion de Libros (Mexico) *Tel:* (05) 5215060; (05) 5215009, pg 466

Institut Africain de Developpement Economique et de Planification (IDEP), Bibliotheque (Senegal) *Tel:* 823 10 20 *Fax:* 822 29 64 *E-mail:* idep@sonatel.senet.net, pg 1541

Institut de Bibliotheconomie et des Sciences Documentaires (Algeria) *Tel:* (021) 94 14 40 *Fax:* (021) 94 14 40, pg 1557

Institut de Formation et de Recherche Demographiques (IFORD) (Cameroon) *Tel:* (023) 222471; (023) 231917 *Fax:* (023) 226793 *E-mail:* wyaounde@un.cm; jtsoyenk@un.cm *Web Site:* www.un.cm/iford, pg 1263

Bibliotheque de l'Institut de France (France) *Tel:* (01) 44 41 44 10 *Fax:* (01) 44 41 44 11 *E-mail:* bibliotheque@bif.univ-paris5.fr *Web Site:* www.institut-de-france.fr/bibliotheques/institut.htm, pg 1507

Institut de l'Information Scientifique et Technique (INIST) (France) *Tel:* (03) 83 50 46 00 *Fax:* (03) 83 50 46 50 *E-mail:* webmaster@inist.fr *Web Site:* www.inist.fr, pg 1507

Institut de Presse & des Sciences de l'Information (Tunisia) *Tel:* (01) 33 52 16 *Fax:* (01) 34 85 96, pg 1551

Institut de Recherche en Sciences Humaines (Niger) *Tel:* 73-51-41, pg 1533

Institut des Belles Lettres Arabes (IBLA) (Tunisia) *Tel:* (01) 560133 *Fax:* (01) 572683 *E-mail:* ibla@gnet.tn, pg 1406

Institut Fondamental d'Afrique Noire, Bibliotheque (Senegal) *Tel:* 825 00 90; 825 98 90; 825 71 24 *Fax:* 24 49 18 *E-mail:* bifan@telecomplus.sn *Web Site:* www.refer.sn/ifan, pg 1541

Bibliotheque de l'Institut Francais d'Archeologie du Proche Orient (Lebanon) *Tel:* (01) 615 844; (01) 615 844 *Fax:* (01) 615 866 *E-mail:* ifapo@lb.refer.org, pg 1524

Institut Francais de Recherche Scientifique pour le Developpement en Cooperation (French Guiana) *Tel:* 299 292 *Fax:* 319 855 *E-mail:* dir.cayenne@cayenne.ird.fr *Web Site:* www.cayenne.ird.fr, pg 1507

Institut fuer Baustoffe, Massivbau und Brandschutz/Bibliothek (Germany) *Tel:* (0531) 391 5400 *Fax:* (0531) 391 5900 *E-mail:* ibmb@tu-bs.de *Web Site:* www.ibmb.tu-bs.de, pg 241

Institut fur Oesterreichkunde (Austria) *Tel:* (01) 512-79-32 *Fax:* (01) 512-79-32 *E-mail:* loek.wirtschaftsgeschichte@univie.ac.at, pg 1396

Institut Geographique National IGN (France) *Tel:* (01) 43988000 *Fax:* (01) 43988400 *Web Site:* www.ign.fr, pg 169

Institut National Agronomique, Bibliotheque (Algeria) *Tel:* (021) 52 47 81; (021) 52 47 84 *Fax:* (021) 52 59 04, pg 1489

Institut Nauchnoy Informatsii po Obschestvennym Naukam, Rossijskoj Akademii Nauk RF (Russian Federation) *Tel:* (095) 128-88-81; (095) 128-89-30 *Fax:* (095) 420-22-61 *E-mail:* info@inion.ru *Web Site:* www.inion.ru, pg 1540

Institut Pasteur d'Algerie, Bibliotheque (Algeria) *Tel:* 21 67 25 02; 21 67 25 11; 21 67 23 44 *Fax:* 267 25 03 *E-mail:* ipa@ibnsima.ands.dz; ipabib@sante.dz *Web Site:* www.ands.dz/ipa/pageaccueil.htm, pg 1489

Institut Pedagogique National (The Democratic Republic of the Congo) *Tel:* (012) 80573, pg 1499

Institut pour la Recherche Scientifique en Afrique Centrale (IRSAC) (The Democratic Republic of the Congo), pg 1499

Institut Royal des Relations Internationales (Belgium) *Tel:* (02) 2234114 *Fax:* (02) 2234116 *E-mail:* info@irri-kiib.be *Web Site:* www.irri-kiib.be, pg 68

Institut Royal des Sciences Naturelles de Belgique, Bibliotheque (Belgium) *Tel:* (02) 627 42 11 *Fax:* (02) 627 41 13 *E-mail:* bib@naturalsciences.be *Web Site:* www.naturalsciences.be, pg 1493

Institut Scientifique (Morocco) *Tel:* (07) 77 45 48; (07) 77 45 49; (07) 77 45 50; (07) 77 45 55 *Fax:* (07) 77 45 70 *Web Site:* www.emi.ac.ma/univ-MdV/IS.html, pg 1529

Institut Teknologi Bandung (Indonesia) *Tel:* (022) 2550935 *Fax:* (022) 2550935 *E-mail:* info-center@itb.ac.id *Web Site:* www.itb.ac.id, pg 355

Perpustakaan Pusat Institut Teknologi Bandung (Indonesia) *Tel:* (022) 250 0089 *Fax:* (022) 250 0089 *E-mail:* library@itb.ac.id *Web Site:* www.lib.itb.ac.id, pg 1517

Institute of Aboriginal Development (IAD Press) (Australia) *Tel:* (08) 8951 1311 *Fax:* (08) 8952 2527 *E-mail:* ozlit@netspace.net.au *Web Site:* home.vicnet.au/~ozlit/iadpress.html, pg 27

Institute for Agricultural Research (IAR) (Nigeria) *Tel:* (069) 550571; (069) 550572; (069) 550573; (069) 550574; (069) 550681 *Fax:* (069) 50563 *E-mail:* iar.abu@kaduna.rcl.ng.com, pg 1533

Institute for Financial Affairs Inc-KINZAI (Japan) *Tel:* (03) 3358-0052 *Fax:* (03) 3358-2069, pg 419

Institute for Fiscal Studies (United Kingdom) *Tel:* (020) 7291 4800 *Fax:* (020) 7323 4780 *E-mail:* mailbox@ifs.org.uk *Web Site:* www.ifs.org.uk, pg 712

The Institute for Israeli Arabs Studies (Israel) *Tel:* (09) 7486738 *Fax:* (09) 7486341, pg 368

Institute for Palestine Studies, Publishing & Research Organization (IPS) (Lebanon) *Tel:* (01) 814175; (01) 804959 *Fax:* (01) 814193; (01) 868387 *E-mail:* ipsbrt@palestine-studies.org *Web Site:* www.palestine-studies.org, pg 446

Institute for Reformational Studies CHE (South Africa) *Tel:* (018) 299-1623 *Fax:* (018) 299-2799 *E-mail:* irsajvdw@puknet.puk.ac.za *Web Site:* www.puk.ac.za, pg 565

Institute for Research Extension and Training in Agriculture (IRETA) (Samoa) *Tel:* (0685) 22372; (0685) 21882; (0685) 21671 *Fax:* (0685) 22347; (0685) 22933 *E-mail:* uspireta@samoa.usp.ac.fj, pg 550

Institute for Social & Economic Change Library (India) *Tel:* (080) 23215468; (080) 23215519; (080) 23215592; (080) 23215468 *Fax:* (080) 23217008 *E-mail:* admin@isec.ac.in *Web Site:* www.isec.ac.in, pg 1516

The Institute for the Translation of Hebrew Literature (Israel) *Tel:* (03) 5796830 *Fax:* (03) 5796832 *E-mail:* hamachon@inter.net.il; litscene@ithl.org.il *Web Site:* www.ithl.org.il, pg 368

The Institute for the Translation of Hebrew Literature (Israel) *Tel:* (03) 579 6830 *Fax:* (03) 579 6832 *E-mail:* hamachon@inter.net.il; litscene@ithl.org.il *Web Site:* www.ithl.org.il, pg 1133

The Institute for the Translation of Hebrew Literature (Israel) *Tel:* (03) 579 6830 *Fax:* (03) 579 6832 *E-mail:* hamachon@inter.net.il *Web Site:* www.ithl.org.il, pg 1148, 1274

Institute of African Studies Library (Ghana) *Tel:* (021) 500512 *Fax:* (021) 502397 *E-mail:* asofo@ghana.com, pg 1512

Institute of African Studies, Onyeka, A (Nigeria) *Tel:* (022) 400550; (022) 400614 (ext 12444), pg 505

Institute of Arab Research & Studies Arab League Educational, Cultural & Scientific Organization Library (Egypt (Arab Republic of Egypt)) *Tel:* (02) 3551648 *Fax:* (02) 3562543, pg 1503

Institute of Development Studies (United Kingdom) *Tel:* (01273) 606261 *Fax:* (01273) 621202; (01273) 691647 *E-mail:* ids@ids.ac.uk *Web Site:* www.ids.ac.uk, pg 712

Institute of Development Studies (United Kingdom) *Tel:* (01273) 606261 *Fax:* (01273) 621202; (01273) 691647 *E-mail:* blds@ids.ac.uk *Web Site:* www.ids.ac.uk, pg 1553

Institute of Economic Affairs (United Kingdom) *Tel:* (020) 7799 8900 *Fax:* (020) 7799 2137 *E-mail:* enquiries@iea.org.uk; iea@iea.org.uk *Web Site:* www.iea.org.uk, pg 712

Institute of Economics Library (Myanmar) *Tel:* (01) 530376 *Fax:* (01) 664889 *Web Site:* www.aun.chula.ac.th/u_iey_mm.htm, pg 1530

Institute of Education Library (Myanmar) *Tel:* (01) 31345, pg 1530

Institute of Education Library, Kabul University (Afghanistan) *Tel:* 42594, pg 1489

Institute of Education, University of London (United Kingdom) *Tel:* (020) 7612 6260 *Fax:* (020) 7612 6560 *E-mail:* info@ioe.ac.uk *Web Site:* www.ioe.ac.uk/publications, pg 712

Institute of Employment Rights (United Kingdom) *Tel:* (020) 7498 6919 *Fax:* (020) 7498 9080 *E-mail:* office@ier.org.uk *Web Site:* www.ier.org.uk, pg 712

Institute of Ethiopian Studies Library (Ethiopia) *Tel:* (01) 55-05-44 *Fax:* 55-26-88 *E-mail:* ies.aau@telecom.net.et *Web Site:* www.abyssiniagateway.net, pg 1504

Institute of Financial Services (United Kingdom) *Tel:* (01227) 818 687 *Fax:* (01227) 763 788 *E-mail:* institute@ifslearning.com *Web Site:* www.ifslearning.com, pg 712

YELLOW PAGES

Institute of Food Science & Technology (United Kingdom) *Tel:* (020) 7603 6316 *Fax:* (020) 7602 9936 *E-mail:* info@ifst.org *Web Site:* www.ifst.org, pg 713

Institute of Governance (United Kingdom) *Tel:* (0131) 650 2456 *Fax:* (0131) 650 6345 *Web Site:* www.institute-of-governance.org, pg 713

Institute of Irish Studies, The Queens University of Belfast (United Kingdom) *Tel:* (028) 9027 3386 *Fax:* (028) 9043 9238 *E-mail:* iispubs@qub.ac.uk *Web Site:* www.qub.ac.uk/iis, pg 713

Institute of Islamic Culture (Pakistan) *Tel:* (042) 6305920; (042) 6363127, pg 512

Institute of Jamaica Publications (Jamaica) *Tel:* 876-929-4785; 876-929-4786 *Fax:* 876-926-8817, pg 413

Institute of Kiswahili Research (United Republic of Tanzania) *Tel:* (051) 410376 *E-mail:* IKR@udsm.ac.tz *Web Site:* www.uib.no/udsm/ucb/instiofkiswahili.html, pg 643

Institute of Linguists (United Kingdom) *Tel:* (020) 7940 3100 *Fax:* (020) 7940 3101 *E-mail:* info@iol.org.uk *Web Site:* www.iol.org.uk, pg 1150

Institute of Neohellenic Studies, Manolis Triantaphyllidis Foundation (Greece) *Tel:* (02310) 997128 *Fax:* (02310) 997122 *E-mail:* ins@phil.auth.gr, pg 308

Institute of Physics Publishing (United Kingdom) *Tel:* (0117) 929 7481 *Fax:* (0117) 929 4318 *E-mail:* custserv@iop.org *Web Site:* www.iop.org; www.iop.org/IOPP/ioppabout.html, pg 713

Institute of Printing (United Kingdom) *Tel:* (01892) 538118 *Fax:* (01892) 518028 *E-mail:* admin@instituteofprinting.org *Web Site:* www.instituteofprinting.org/, pg 1291

Institute of Public Administration (Ireland) *Tel:* (01) 240 3600 *Fax:* (01) 2698644 *E-mail:* information@ipa.ie *Web Site:* www.ipa.ie, pg 361

Institute of Public Administration Library (Saudi Arabia) *Tel:* (01) 476 1600 *Fax:* (01) 479 2136 *E-mail:* library@ipa.edu.sa *Web Site:* www.ipa.edu.sa, pg 1541

Institute of Scientific & Technical Communicators (ISTC) (United Kingdom) *Tel:* (01733) 390141 *Fax:* (01733) 390126 *E-mail:* istc@istc.org.uk *Web Site:* www.istc.org.uk, pg 1291

Institute of Southeast Asian Studies (Singapore) *Tel:* (65) 6778 0955 *Fax:* (65) 6775 6259 *E-mail:* pubsunit@iseas.edu.sg *Web Site:* bookshop.iseas.edu.sg, pg 556

Institute of Translation & Interpreting (United Kingdom) *Tel:* (01908) 325250 *Fax:* (01908) 325259 *E-mail:* info@iti.org.uk *Web Site:* www.iti.org.uk, pg 1151

Instituti Editoriali E Poligrafici Internazionali SRL (Italy) *Tel:* (050) 878066 *Fax:* (050) 878732 *E-mail:* iepi@iepi.it *Web Site:* www.iepi.it, pg 393

Institution of Chemical Engineers (United Kingdom) *Tel:* (01788) 578214 *Fax:* (01788) 560833 *E-mail:* jcressey@icheme.org.uk *Web Site:* www.icheme.org, pg 713

Institution of Electrical Engineers (United Kingdom) *Tel:* (01438) 313311 *Fax:* (01438) 742792 *E-mail:* postmaster@iee.org.uk *Web Site:* www.iee.org.uk/publish, pg 713

Biblioteca del Instituto Anglo-Mexicano de Cultura (Mexico) *Tel:* (05) 566-4500 *Fax:* (05) 566-6739 *E-mail:* biblioteca@theanglo.org.mx *Web Site:* www.theanglo.org.mx/lib.html, pg 1529

Instituto Autonomo, Biblioteca Nacional y de Servicios de Bibliotecas (Venezuela) *Tel:* (02) 5059141 *Fax:* (02) 5059159, pg 1555

Instituto Caro y Cuervo (Colombia) *Tel:* (01) 3456004 *Fax:* (01) 2170243; (01) 3422121 *E-mail:* direcciongeneral@caroycuervo.gov.co *Web Site:* www.caroycuervo.gov.co, pg 111

Instituto Caro y Cuervo (Colombia) *Tel:* (01) 3456004 *Fax:* (01) 2170243 *E-mail:* secretariagenera@caroycuervo.gov.co *Web Site:* www.caroycuervo.gov.co, pg 1398

Instituto Centroamericano de Administracion de Empresas (INCAE) Library (Nicaragua) *Tel:* (02) 65 8141; (02) 65 8149; (02) 65 8272 *Fax:* (02) 65 8617; (02) 65 8630 *E-mail:* biblioteca@mail.incae.edu.ni; incaeni@mail.incae.edu.ni *Web Site:* www.incae.ac.cr/biblioteca, pg 1533

Instituto Colombiano de Cultura Hispanica (Colombia) *Tel:* (01) 3413857 *Fax:* (01) 2811051, pg 1398

Instituto de Bibliografia del Ministerio de Educacion de la Provincia de Buenos Aires (Argentina) *Tel:* (021) 35915, pg 1557

Instituto de Estudios Economicos (Spain) *Tel:* (091) 782 05 80 *Fax:* (091) 562 36 13 *E-mail:* iee@ieemadrid.com *Web Site:* www.ieemadrid.com, pg 587

Instituto de Informacion Cientifica y Tecnologica (IDICT) (Cuba) *Tel:* (07) 862-6531; (07) 860-3411 *Fax:* (07) 862-6531 *E-mail:* andresdt@idict.cu; commercial@idict.cu *Web Site:* www.idict.cu/, pg 1500

Instituto de Investigaciones Bibliograficas (Mexico) *Tel:* (05) 6226818 *Fax:* (05) 6650951 *Web Site:* biblional.bibliog.unam.mx, pg 1567

Instituto de Investigaciones Electricas (Mexico) *Tel:* (073) 18 38 11 *Fax:* (073) 182521 *E-mail:* garroyo@iie.org.mx *Web Site:* www.iie.org.mx, pg 1529

Instituto de Literatura y Lingueistica (Cuba) *Tel:* (07) 75 485 *Fax:* (07) 338054; (07) 331325 *E-mail:* acc@ceniai.cu *Web Site:* www3.cuba.cu/ciencia/acc/, pg 1500

Instituto dos Arquivos Nacionais/Torre do Tombo (Portugal) *Tel:* (01) 7811500 *Fax:* (01) 7937230 *E-mail:* dc@iantt.pt, pg 1539

Instituto Interamericano de Cooperacion para la Agricultura (IICA) (Costa Rica) *Tel:* (0506) 2160222 *Fax:* (0506) 2160233 *E-mail:* iicahq@iica.ac.cr *Web Site:* www.iica.int, pg 1264

Instituto Nacional de Administracion Publica (Spain) *Tel:* (091) 3493115; (091) 3493241 *Fax:* (091) 3493287 *E-mail:* cati.fuente@inap.map.es *Web Site:* www.inap.map.es, pg 587

Instituto Nacional del Educacion Fisica Madrid (INEF-Madrid) (Spain) *Tel:* (091) 336 4000 *Fax:* (091) 336 4032 *E-mail:* webmaster@inef.upm.es *Web Site:* www.inef.com, pg 587

Instituto Nacional de Estadistica (Spain) *Tel:* (091) 583 91 00 *Fax:* (091) 583 91 58 *E-mail:* info@ine.es *Web Site:* www.ine.es, pg 587

Instituto Nacional de la Salud (Spain) *Tel:* (0901) 400-100 *Fax:* (091) 5964480 *E-mail:* oiac@msc.es *Web Site:* www.msc.es, pg 587

Biblioteca del Instituto Panamericano de Geografia e Historia (Mexico) *Tel:* (055) 5277 5888; (055) 5277 5791; (055) 5515 1910 *Fax:* (055) 5271 6172 *E-mail:* info@ipgh.org.mx *Web Site:* www.ipgh.org.mx, pg 1529

Instituto Portugues da Sociedade Cientifica de Goerres (Portugal) *Tel:* (021) 7265554 *Fax:* (021) 7260546 *E-mail:* mrato@reitoria.ucp.pt, pg 1404

Instituto Tecnologico y de Estdios Superiores de Monterrey Biblioteca (Mexico) *Tel:* (081) 8328-4096 *Fax:* (081) 8328-4067 *Web Site:* cib.mty.itesm.mx; biblioteca.itesm.mx, pg 1529

Instituto Vasco de Criminologia (Spain) *Tel:* (0943) 321411; (0943) 321412 *Fax:* (0943) 321272 *Web Site:* www.sc.ehu.es, pg 587

Editura Institutul European (Romania) *Tel:* (032) 230197; (032) 233731; (032) 233800 *Fax:* (032) 230-197 *E-mail:* rtvnova@mail.cccis.ro; euroedit@mail.dntis.ro, pg 540

Institutul National de Informare si Documentare (INID) (Romania) *Tel:* (01) 315 87 65 *Fax:* (01) 312 67 34 *E-mail:* inid@home.ro *Web Site:* www.inid.ro, pg 1540

Instytut Badan Literackich PAN (Poland) *Tel:* (022) 8269945; (022) 6572895 *Fax:* (022) 8269945 *E-mail:* ibadlit@ibl.waw.pl *Web Site:* www.ibl.waw.pl, pg 1404

INTERCONTINENTAL LITERARY AGENCY

Instytut Bibliograficzny (Poland) *Tel:* (022) 452-2999 *Fax:* (022) 825-5251 *E-mail:* biblnar@bn.org.pl *Web Site:* www.bn.org.pl, pg 1537

Instytut Meteorologii i Gospodarki Wodnej (Poland) *Tel:* (022) 56-94-100 *Fax:* (022) 834-54-66 *E-mail:* sekretariat@imgw.pl *Web Site:* www.imgw.pl, pg 523

Instytut Wydawniczy Pax, Inco-Veritas (Poland) *Tel:* (022) 625 23 01 *Fax:* (022) 625 68 86 *E-mail:* iwpax@com.pl *Web Site:* www.iwpax.com.pl, pg 523

INT Press (Australia) *Tel:* (03) 9326 2416 *Fax:* (03) 9326 2413 *E-mail:* sales@intpress.com.au *Web Site:* www.intpress.com.au, pg 27

Integrated Book Technology Inc (United States) *Tel:* 518-271-5117 *Fax:* 518-266-9422 *E-mail:* mail@integratedbook.com *Web Site:* www.integratedbook.com, pg 1167, 1188, 1230, 1240

Integrated Book Technology Inc (United States) *Tel:* 518-271-5117 *Fax:* 518-266-9422 *Web Site:* www.integratedbook.com, pg 1249

Intellect Ltd (United Kingdom) *Tel:* (0117) 9589910 *Fax:* (0117) 9589911 *E-mail:* mail@intellectbooks.com *Web Site:* www.intellectbooks.com, pg 713

Intellectual Publishing Co (Singapore) *Tel:* 7466025 *Fax:* 7489108, pg 556

Intellectual Publishing House (India) *Tel:* (011) 3275860, pg 338

Inter American University of Puerto Rico Library (Puerto Rico) *Tel:* (787) 878-5475 (ext 320) *Fax:* (787) 880-1624 *E-mail:* sabreu@uiprl.inter.edu, pg 1539

Inter-Cultural Book Promoters (Sri Lanka) *Tel:* 525359 *Fax:* 525359 *E-mail:* inculture@eureka.lk, pg 606

Inter-India Publications (India) *Tel:* (011) 5441120; (011) 5467082, pg 338

Inter-Medica (Argentina) *Tel:* (011) 4961-9234 *Fax:* (011) 4961-5572 *E-mail:* info@inter-medica.com.ar *Web Site:* www.inter-medica.com.ar, pg 6

Inter-Parliamentary Union (Switzerland) *Tel:* (022) 919 41 50 *Fax:* (022) 919 41 60 *E-mail:* postbox@mail.ipu.org *Web Site:* www.ipu.org, pg 1285

Inter-Varsity Press (United Kingdom) *Tel:* (0115) 978 1054 *Fax:* (0115) 942 2694 *E-mail:* sales@ivpbooks.com *Web Site:* www.ivpbooks.com, pg 713

Libreria Interacademica SA de CV (Mexico) *Tel:* (05) 265-1165 *Fax:* (05) 265-1164, pg 1327

Instituto Interamericano de Cooperacion para la Agricultura (IICA) (Costa Rica) *Tel:* (0506) 216-0222 *Fax:* (0506) 216-0233 *E-mail:* iicahq@iica.ac.cr *Web Site:* www.iica.int, pg 115

Interbook-Business AO (Russian Federation) *Tel:* (095) 2006462; (095) 956-37-52 *Fax:* (095) 956-37-52 *E-mail:* interbook@msk.tsi.ru, pg 545

Intercept Ltd (United Kingdom) *Tel:* (01264) 334748 *Fax:* (01264) 334058 *E-mail:* intercept@andover.co.uk *Web Site:* www.intercept.co.uk, pg 714

Editora Interciencia Ltda (Brazil) *Tel:* (021) 242-2861 *Fax:* (021) 242-7787, pg 84

Interconnections Reisen und Arbeiten Georg Beckmann (Germany) *Tel:* (0761) 700650 *Fax:* (0761) 700688, pg 242

Intercontinental Editora (Paraguay) *Tel:* (021) 496991; (021) 449738 *Fax:* (021) 448721 *Web Site:* www.libreriaintercontinental.com.py, pg 516

Intercontinental Literary Agency (United Kingdom) *Tel:* (020) 7379 6611 *Fax:* (020) 7379 6790 *E-mail:* ila@ila-agency.co.uk, pg 1141

Intercultural Networking Ltd (ICN) (United Kingdom) *Tel:* (0171) 628 5876 *Fax:* (0171) 628 9147 *E-mail:* icn@dircon.co.uk *Web Site:* www.users.dircon.co.uk/~icn/, pg 1151

Interculture (Sweden) *Tel:* (08) 642 78 04 *Fax:* (08) 642 35 91, pg 612

Interdigest Publishing House (Belarus) *Tel:* 331888; 333418 *Fax:* 133073; 333180, pg 62

InterEditions (France) *Tel:* (01) 40 46 35 00 *Fax:* (01) 40 46 49 95, pg 169

Les Editions Interferences (France) *Tel:* (01) 45 67 33 56 *E-mail:* interferences@editions-interferences.com *Web Site:* www.editions-interferences.com, pg 169

Interfisc Publishing (United Kingdom) *Tel:* (020) 7702 9799 *Fax:* (020) 7702 3583 *E-mail:* editor@interfisc.com *Web Site:* www.interfisc.com, pg 714

Interfrom AG Editions (Switzerland) *Tel:* (01) 2020900, pg 625

Interlivros Edicoes Ltda (Brazil) *Tel:* (021) 3913134 *Fax:* (021) 3521005 *E-mail:* interlivros@ibm.net, pg 84

Intermedia Audio, Video Book Publishing Ltd (Israel) *Tel:* (03) 5608501 *Fax:* (03) 5608513 *E-mail:* freed@inter.net.il, pg 368

Libreria Internacional Estudio (Chile) *Tel:* (041) 225 533 *Fax:* (041) 244 542, pg 1305

Ediciones Internacionales Universitarias SA (Spain) *Tel:* (091) 5193907 *Fax:* (091) 4136808 *E-mail:* eiunsa@ibernet.com *Web Site:* www.eunsa.es, pg 588

Internationaal Instituut voor Sociale Geschiedenis (Netherlands) *Tel:* (020) 6685866; (020) 6928810 *Fax:* (020) 6654181; (020) 6630349; (020) 4680505 *E-mail:* info@iisg.nl; user.service@iisg.nl *Web Site:* www.iisg.nl, pg 1531

International Bookshops (Saudi Arabia) *Tel:* (03) 4641851 *Fax:* (03) 4641851, pg 1338

International Academic Publishers (IAP) (China) *Tel:* (010) 8316677-530 *Fax:* (010) 4015664, pg 105

International African Institute (United Kingdom) *Tel:* (020) 7898 4420; (020) 7898 4435 *Fax:* (020) 7898 4419 *E-mail:* iai@soas.ac.uk; ed2@soas.ac.uk *Web Site:* www.iaionthe.net, pg 1291

International Association for Mass Communication Research (Denmark) *Tel:* (045) 9635 8080 *Fax:* (045) 9815 6864 *E-mail:* prehn@hum.auc.dk *Web Site:* www.auc.dk/fak-hum, pg 1265

International Association for the Evaluation of Educational Achievement (IEA) (Netherlands) *Tel:* (020) 6253625 *Fax:* (020) 4207136 *E-mail:* department@iea.nl *Web Site:* www.iea.nl, pg 1279

International Association of Agricultural Information Specialists (United Kingdom) *Tel:* (01865) 340054 *Web Site:* www.iaald.org, pg 1292

International Association of Law Libraries (IALL) (United States) *Tel:* 804-924-3384 *Fax:* 804-982-2232 *E-mail:* lbw@virginia.edu *Web Site:* www.iall.org, pg 1294

International Association of Literary Critics (France) *Tel:* (01) 40513300 *Fax:* (01) 43549299 *E-mail:* aicl.org@tiscalinet.it *Web Site:* www.aicl.org, pg 1268

International Association of Music Libraries, New Zealand Branch, Inc (New Zealand) *Tel:* (03) 941 7923 *Fax:* (03) 941 7848 *E-mail:* library@ccc.govt.nz *Web Site:* library.christchurch.org.nz, pg 1568

International Association of Music Libraries, Archives & Documentation Centres (IAML) (New Zealand) *Tel:* (04) 474 3039 *Fax:* 613-520-2750 *Web Site:* www.iaml.info, pg 1280

International Association of Music Libraries, Archives & Documentation Centres (New Zealand) *Tel:* (04) 474 3039 *Fax:* (04) 474 3035 *Web Site:* www.iaml.info, pg 1568

International Association of Music Libraries, Archives & Documentation Centres (UK & Ireland Branch) (United Kingdom) *Tel:* (0131) 242 8053 *Fax:* (0131) 242 8009 *Web Site:* www.iaml-uk-irl.org, pg 1573

International Association of Orientalist Librarians (Russian Federation) *Tel:* (095) 2028852 *Fax:* (095) 2029187 *E-mail:* oricen@mail.ru *Web Site:* www.orient.ru/eng/org/oricen/index.htm, pg 1282

International Association of Scholarly Publishers (IASP) (United States) *Tel:* 517-355-9543 *Fax:* 517-432-2611 *E-mail:* bohm@pilot.msu.edu, pg 1294

International Association of School Librarianship (Australia) *Fax:* (03) 9428 7612 *E-mail:* iasl@rockland.com *Web Site:* www.iasl-slo.org, pg 1260

International Association of Scientific, Technical & Medical Publishers (STM) (Netherlands) *Tel:* (070) 314 09 30 *Fax:* (070) 314 09 40 *E-mail:* info@stm-assoc.org *Web Site:* www.stm-assoc.org, pg 1279

International Association of Sound & Audiovisual Archives (Germany) *Tel:* (07221) 9293487 *Fax:* (07221) 9294199 *Web Site:* www.llgc.org.uk/iasa/, pg 1270

International Association of Technological University Libraries (IATUL) (United Kingdom) *Tel:* (0131) 449 5111 *Fax:* (0131) 451 3164 *E-mail:* iatul@qut.edu.au *Web Site:* www.iatul.org, pg 1292

International Association of Universities (France) *Tel:* (01) 45 68 48 00 *Fax:* (01) 47 34 76 05 *E-mail:* iau@unesco.org *Web Site:* www.unesco.org/iau, pg 1268

International Atomic Energy Agency (IAEA) (Austria) *Tel:* (0222) 2600-0 *Fax:* (0222) 2600-7 *E-mail:* official.mail@iaea.org; info@iaea.org *Web Site:* www.iaea.org, pg 1261

International Bee Research Association (United Kingdom) *Tel:* (02920) 372409 *Fax:* (02920) 665522 *E-mail:* mail@cardiff.ac.uk *Web Site:* www.cf.ac.uk/ibra, pg 714

International Bible Society (Sweden) *Tel:* (0513) 219 30 *Fax:* (0513) 215 01, pg 612

International Board on Books for Young People (IBBY) (Switzerland) *Tel:* (061) 272 29 17 *Fax:* (061) 272 27 57 *E-mail:* ibby@ibby.org *Web Site:* www.ibby.org, pg 1162, 1285

International Book Centre (Portugal) *Tel:* (021) 942 53 94 *Fax:* (021) 941 98 93, pg 1337

International Book Development (IBD) (United Kingdom) *Tel:* (0118) 902 1000 *Fax:* (0118) 902 1434 *E-mail:* enquiries@cfbt.com *Web Site:* www.cfbt.com, pg 1292

International Book Distributors (India) *Tel:* (0135) 2656526; (0135) 2657497; (0135) 2650949 *Fax:* (0135) 2656554 *E-mail:* ibdbooks@sancharnet.in *Web Site:* ibdbooks.com, pg 338

International Book House Pvt Ltd (India) *Tel:* (022) 22021634; (022) 22021795 *Fax:* (022) 22851109 *E-mail:* ibh@vsnl.com *Web Site:* www.intbh.com, pg 1316

International Booksellers Federation (IBF) (Belgium) *Tel:* (02) 223 49 40 *Fax:* (02) 223 49 38 *E-mail:* ibf.booksellers@skynet.be *Web Site:* www.ibf-booksellers.org, pg 1262

International Catholic Organization for Cinema & Audiovisual (OCIC) (Belgium) *Tel:* (02) 7344294 *Fax:* (02) 7343207 *E-mail:* sg@ocic.org *Web Site:* www.ocic.org, pg 1262

International Centre for Ethnic Studies (Sri Lanka) *Tel:* (08) 234892 *Fax:* (08) 234892 *E-mail:* ices@slt.lk *Web Site:* www.icescolombo.org, pg 606

International Centre for Research in Agroforestry (ICRAF) (Kenya) *Tel:* (02) 524000 *Fax:* (02) 524001 *E-mail:* icraf@cgiar.org *Web Site:* www.worldagroforestrycentre.org, pg 434

International Centre Study Preservation & Restoration of Cultural Property (ICCROM) (Italy) *Tel:* (06) 585531 *Fax:* (06) 58553349 *E-mail:* iccrom@iccrom.org *Web Site:* www.iccrom.org, pg 1274

International Chamber of Commerce (France) *Tel:* (01) 49 53 28 28 *Fax:* (01) 49 53 28 59 *E-mail:* icclib@ibnet.com; icc@iccwbo.org *Web Site:* www.iccwbo.org, pg 1268

International Commission of Jurists (Switzerland) *Tel:* (022) 979 38 00 *Fax:* (022) 979 38 01 *E-mail:* info@icj.org *Web Site:* www.icj.org, pg 1285

International Communications (United Kingdom) *Tel:* (020) 7713 7711 *Fax:* (020) 7713 7898; (020) 7713 7970 *E-mail:* icpubs@africasia.com *Web Site:* www.africasia.com, pg 714

International Community of Writers' Unions (Russian Federation) *Tel:* (095) 2916307 *Fax:* (095) 2919760, pg 1282

International Comparative Literature Association (United States) *Tel:* 416-487-6727 *Fax:* 416-487-6786 *E-mail:* icla@byu.edu *Web Site:* www.byu.edu/~icla, pg 1294

International Council on Archives (France) *Tel:* (01) 40 27 63 49; (01) 40 27 63 06; (01) 40 27 61 34 *Fax:* (01) 42 72 20 65 *E-mail:* ica@ica.org *Web Site:* www.ica.org, pg 1268

International Crops Research Institute for the Semi-Arid Tropics (ICRISAT) (India) *Tel:* (040) 3296161 *Fax:* (040) 3241239; (040) 3296182 *E-mail:* icrisat@cgnet.com *Web Site:* www.icrisat.org, pg 1273

International Culture Publishing Corp (China) *Tel:* (010) 64013415 *Fax:* (010) 64013437, pg 105

Institut International de la Marionnette (France) *Tel:* (03) 24 33 72 50 *Fax:* (03) 24 33 72 69 *E-mail:* institut@marionnette.com *Web Site:* www.marionnette.com, pg 169

The International Documentary Centre of Arab Manuscripts (Lebanon), pg 446

International Documentation Center, The University of Tokyo (Japan) *Tel:* (03) 5841-2645 (ext 22645) *Fax:* (03) 5841-2658 *E-mail:* kokusai@lib.u-tokyo.ac.jp *Web Site:* www.lib.u-tokyo.ac.jp/undepo, pg 1521

International Ediemme (Italy) *Tel:* (06) 39378788 *Fax:* (06) 6380839 *E-mail:* iscd@colosseum.it, pg 393

International Editors' Co (Argentina) *Tel:* (011) 4788-2992; (011) 4786-0888 *Fax:* (011) 4786-0888 *E-mail:* costa@lvd.com.ar, pg 1129

International Editors' Co SL (Spain) *Tel:* (093) 2158812 *Fax:* (093) 4873583 *E-mail:* ieco@es.inter.net, pg 1136

International Educational Services (Pakistan) *Tel:* (021) 732-6602 *Fax:* (021) 813-1919, pg 512

International Federation for Information Processing (IFIP) (Austria) *Tel:* (02236) 73616 *Fax:* (02236) 736169 *E-mail:* ifip@ifip.or.at *Web Site:* www.ifip.or.at, pg 1261

International Federation of Library Associations & Institutions (IFLA) (Netherlands) *Tel:* (070) 3140884 *Fax:* (070) 3834827 *E-mail:* ifla@ifla.org *Web Site:* www.ifla.org, pg 1279, 1568

International Federation of Reproduction Rights Organisations (IFRRO) (Belgium) *Tel:* (02) 551 08 99 *Fax:* (02) 551 08 95 *E-mail:* iffro@skynet.be; secretariat@ifrro.be *Web Site:* www.ifrro.org, pg 1262

International Fiction Review (Canada) *Tel:* 506-453-4636 *Fax:* 506-447-3166 *E-mail:* ifr@unb.ca *Web Site:* www.lib.unb.ca/Texts/IFR, pg 1264

International Institute for Applied Systems Analysis (IIASA) (Austria) *Tel:* (02236) 807 433 *Fax:* (02236) 71313 *E-mail:* info@iiasa.ac.at; publications@iiasa.ac.at *Web Site:* www.iiasa.ac.at, pg 52

International Institute for Children's Literature & Reading Research (UNESCO category C) (Austria) *Tel:* (01) 505 03 59; (01) 505 28 31 *Fax:* (01) 505 03 59-17; (01) 505 28 31-17 *E-mail:* office@jugendliteratur.net *Web Site:* www.jugendliteratur.net, pg 1261

International Institute for Educational Planning (IIEP) (France) *Tel:* (01) 45 03 77 00 *Fax:* (01) 40 72 83 66 *E-mail:* information@iiep.unesco.org *Web Site:* www.unesco.org/iiep, pg 1268

International Institute for Labour Studies (Switzerland) *Tel:* (022) 799 6111 *Fax:* (022) 798 8685 *E-mail:* ilo@ilo.org *Web Site:* www.ilo.org, pg 1285

International Institute for Strategic Studies (United Kingdom) *Tel:* (020) 7379 7676 *Fax:* (020) 7836 3108 *E-mail:* iiss@iiss.org *Web Site:* www.iiss.org, pg 714

International Institute of Iberoamerican Literature (United States) *Tel:* 412-624-5246; 412-624-6100 *Fax:* 412-624-0829 *E-mail:* iili+@pitt.edu *Web Site:* www.pitt.edu, pg 1294

International Institute of Islamic Thought (Pakistan) *Tel:* (051) 229-3734 *Fax:* (051) 228-0489 *E-mail:* ziansari@iiitpak.sdnpk.undp.org *Web Site:* www.iiit.org, pg 512

International Institute of Tropical Agriculture (IITA) Library (Nigeria) *Tel:* (02) 241 2626 *Fax:* (02) 241 2221 *E-mail:* IITA@cgiar.org *Web Site:* www.iita.org/info/libsrv.htm, pg 1533

The International Irrigation Management Institute (Sri Lanka) *Tel:* (011) 2787404; (011) 2784080 *Fax:* (011) 2786854 *E-mail:* iwmi@cgiar.org *Web Site:* www.cgiar.org, pg 1284

International ISBN Agency, International ISMN Agency (Germany) *Tel:* (030) 266 2498 *Fax:* (030) 2662378 *E-mail:* isbn@sbb.spk-berlin.de; ismn@sbb.spk.berlin.de *Web Site:* isbn-international.org; ismn-international.org, pg 1270

International ISMN Agency (Germany) *Tel:* (030) 266 2496; (030) 266 2498; (030) 266 2338 *Fax:* (030) 266-2378 *E-mail:* ismn@sbb.spk-berlin.de *Web Site:* ismn-international.org, pg 1270

International Labour Office (United Kingdom) *Tel:* (020) 7828 6401 *Fax:* (020) 7233 5925 *E-mail:* ipu@ilo-london.org.uk; london@ilo-london.org.uk *Web Site:* www.ilo.org/london, pg 714

International Labour Office, Bureau of Library & Information Services (Switzerland) *Tel:* (022) 799 8675 *Fax:* (022) 799 6516 *E-mail:* inform@ilo.org *Web Site:* www.ilo.org/inform, pg 1548

International Labour Organization (ILO) (Switzerland) *Tel:* (022) 799 6111 *Fax:* (022) 798 8685 *E-mail:* ilo@ilo.org *Web Site:* www.ilo.org, pg 1286

International Language & Translation School (United Kingdom) *Tel:* (020) 8882 3362 *Fax:* (020) 8882 3362, pg 1151

International Law Book Services (Malaysia) *Tel:* (03) 7727 4121; (03) 7727 4122; (03) 7727 3890; (03) 7728-3890 *Fax:* (03) 7727 3884 *E-mail:* gbc@pc.jaring.my *Web Site:* bookgold.com, pg 456

International League of Antiquarian Booksellers (ILAB) (United States) *Tel:* 800-441-0076; 612-290-0700 *Fax:* 612-290-0646 *E-mail:* info@ilab-lila.com *Web Site:* www.ilab.org, pg 1294

International Literatuur Bureau BV (Netherlands) *Tel:* (035) 6213500 *Fax:* (035) 6215771 *E-mail:* info@ilb.nu *Web Site:* www.ilb.nu, pg 1135

International Livestock Research Institute (Kenya) *Tel:* (020) 630 743 *Fax:* (020) 631 499 *E-mail:* ilri-kenya@cgiar.org *Web Site:* www.cgiar.org/ilri, pg 1275

International Map Trade Association (United Kingdom) *Tel:* 01425) 620532 *Fax:* (01425) 620532 *E-mail:* imtaeurope@compuserve.com *Web Site:* www.maptrade.org, pg 714

International Maritime Organization (IMO) (United Kingdom) *Tel:* (020) 7735 7611 *Fax:* (020) 7587 3210 *E-mail:* publications-sales@imo.org *Web Site:* www.imo.org, pg 1292

The International Molinological Society (United Kingdom) *Tel:* (070) 3460885 *Web Site:* tims.geo.tudelft.nl, pg 1292

International Monetary Fund (United States) *Tel:* 202-623-7000; 202-623-7430 *Fax:* 202-623-4661; 202-623-7201 *E-mail:* publicaffairs@imf.org *Web Site:* www.imf.org, pg 1294

International Organization for Standardization (ISO) (Switzerland) *Tel:* (022) 749 01 11 *Fax:* (022) 733 34 30 *E-mail:* central@iso.org *Web Site:* www.iso.org, pg 1286

International PEN (United Kingdom) *Tel:* (020) 7253 4308 *Fax:* (020) 7253 5711 *E-mail:* info@internatpen.org *Web Site:* www.internatpen.org, pg 1292

The International Press Agency (Pty) Ltd (South Africa) *Tel:* (021) 5311926; (021) 5318197 *Fax:* (021) 5318789 *E-mail:* inpra@iafrica.com *Web Site:* www.inpra.co.za, pg 1136

International Press Co Pte Ltd (Singapore) *Tel:* 2983800; 2952437 *Fax:* 2971668, pg 1161, 1222

International Press Co Pte Ltd (Singapore) *Tel:* 2983800 *Fax:* 2971668, pg 1237

International Publications Agency (IPA) (Saudi Arabia) *Tel:* (03) 8954925, pg 550

International Publications Service Inc (IPS) (Republic of Korea) *Tel:* (02) 2115-8800 *Fax:* (02) 2273-8048 *Web Site:* www.ipsbook.com, pg 1324

International Publishers Association (Switzerland) *Tel:* (022) 346 3018 *Fax:* (022) 347 5717 *E-mail:* secretariat@ipa-uie.org *Web Site:* www.ipa-uie.org, pg 1286

International Publishers Distributor (S) Pte Ltd (Singapore) *Tel:* 741 6933 *Fax:* 741 6922 *E-mail:* ipdmktg@sg.gbhap.com, pg 556

International Publishing & Research Company (Nigeria) *Tel:* (080) 2317-5915 *Fax:* (080) 4213 2351, pg 505

International Reading Association (United States) *Tel:* 302-731-1600 *Fax:* 302-731-1057 *Web Site:* www.reading.org, pg 1294

International Rice Research Institute (IRRI) (Philippines) *Tel:* (02) 845-0563; (02) 845-0569 *Fax:* (02) 845-0606 *E-mail:* irri@cgiar.org *Web Site:* www.irri.org, pg 519

International Road Federation (Switzerland) *Tel:* (022) 306 0260 *Fax:* (022) 306 0270 *E-mail:* info@irfnet.org *Web Site:* www.irfnet.org, pg 1286

International Scripts Ltd (United Kingdom) *Tel:* (020) 8319 8666 *Fax:* (020) 8319 0801, pg 1141

International Society for Educational Information (ISEI) (Japan) *Tel:* (03) 33581138 *Fax:* (03) 33597188 *E-mail:* kaya@isei.or.jp *Web Site:* www.isei.or.jp, pg 419

International Standard Book Numbering Agency (South Africa) *Tel:* (012) 321 8931 *Fax:* (012) 325 5984 *E-mail:* therese@statelib.pwv.gov.za *Web Site:* www.nlsa.ac.za, pg 1284

International Standards Books & Periodicals (P) Ltd (Nepal) *Tel:* (01) 212289; (01) 224005; (01) 223036 *Fax:* (01) 223036, pg 476

International Telecommunication Union (ITU) (Switzerland) *Tel:* (022) 730 5111 *Fax:* (022) 733 7256 *E-mail:* itumail@itu.int *Web Site:* www.itu.int/home/contact/index.html, pg 1286

Uitgevery International Theatre & Film Books (Netherlands) *Tel:* (020) 60 60 911 *Fax:* (020) 60 60 914 *E-mail:* info@itfb.nl *Web Site:* www.itfb.nl, pg 484

International Thomson Publishing (ITP) (Germany) *Tel:* (0228) 970240 *Fax:* (0228) 441342 *E-mail:* mitp@mitp.de *Web Site:* www.mitp.de, pg 242

International Translations Ltd (United Kingdom) *Tel:* (0161) 834 7431 *Fax:* (0161) 832 4717 *E-mail:* admin@ititranslations.co.uk; inttrans@compuserve.com, pg 1151

International Union Against Cancer (Switzerland) *Tel:* (022) 809 18 11 *Fax:* (022) 809 18 10 *E-mail:* info@uicc.org *Web Site:* www.uicc.org, pg 1286

International Union of Geological Sciences (IUGS) (Austria) *Tel:* (01) 712 56 74 (ext 180) *Fax:* (01) 712 56 74 56 *Web Site:* www.iugs.org, pg 1261

International University Press Srl (Italy) *Tel:* (06) 8380067 *Fax:* (06) 8380064, pg 393

Internationale Jugendbibliothek (Germany) *Tel:* (089) 891211-0 *Fax:* (089) 8117553 *E-mail:* bib@ijb.de *Web Site:* www.ijb.de, pg 1270, 1509

Verlag fuer Internationale Politik GmbH (Germany) *Tel:* (0228) 7290010 *Fax:* (0228) 7290013, pg 242

Edizioni Internazionali di Letteratura e Scienze (Italy) *Tel:* (06) 61905463 *Fax:* (06) 3016728, pg 393

Internos Books (United Kingdom) *Tel:* (020) 7637 4255 *Fax:* (020) 7637 4251, pg 1351

Interpet Publishing (United Kingdom) *Tel:* (01306) 881033 *Fax:* (01306) 885009 *E-mail:* publishing@interpet.co.uk, pg 714

Interpres (Bulgaria) *Tel:* (02) 517915 *Fax:* (02) 517915 *E-mail:* interpres@bis.bg; intrpres@usa.net, pg 95

Interpress (Poland) *Tel:* (022) 6214876; (022) 6289331; (022) 6289202; (022) 6282818; (022) 6291060; (022) 6282225 *Fax:* (022) 6289331; (022) 6289202; (022) 6226850 *E-mail:* paiwydaw@pol.pl, pg 523

Interpress Aussenhandels GmbH (Hungary) *Tel:* (01) 302-7525; (01) 2508267 *Fax:* (01) 302-7530, pg 1159

Interpress Aussenhandels GmbH (Hungary) *Tel:* (01) 302-7525 *Fax:* (01) 302-7530 *E-mail:* office@interpress.hu *Web Site:* www.interpress.hu, pg 1220, 1237

Interpresse A/S (Denmark) *Tel:* 39160200 *Fax:* 39272402, pg 132

Interprint Ltd - Malta (Malta) *Tel:* (021) 240169; (021) 222720 *Fax:* (021) 243780; (021) 238115 *Web Site:* www.interprintmalta.com, pg 1160, 1221

Intersentia Uitgevers NV (Belgium) *Tel:* (03) 680 15 50 *Fax:* (03) 658 71 21 *E-mail:* mail@intersentia.be *Web Site:* www.intersentia.com, pg 68

Intersistemas SA de CV (Mexico) *Tel:* (055) 1107-1903 *Fax:* (055) 1107-0196 *E-mail:* ventas@medikatalogo.com *Web Site:* www.medikatalogo.com, pg 467

Interskol Forlag AB (Sweden) *Tel:* (040) 51 01 95 *Fax:* (040) 15 06 25 *E-mail:* info@interskol.se *Web Site:* www.interskol.se, pg 612

Uitgeverij Intertaal BV (Netherlands) *Tel:* (036) 5471650 *Fax:* (036) 5471582 *E-mail:* int@intertaal.nl *Web Site:* www.intertaal.nl, pg 484

Intertrade Publications Pvt Ltd (India) *Tel:* (033) 474872; (033) 475069, pg 338

Intertrans-Verlag GmbH (Germany) *Tel:* (069) 871500 *Fax:* (069) 852894, pg 242

Intext Book Company Pty Ltd (Australia) *Tel:* (03) 9819-4500 *Fax:* (03) 9819-4511 *E-mail:* customerservice@intextbook.com.au *Web Site:* www.intextbook.com.au, pg 27

Editions Intore (Burundi) *Tel:* (02) 225167, pg 98

Intype Libra Ltd (United Kingdom) *Tel:* (020) 8947 7863 *Fax:* (020) 8947 3652 *E-mail:* intype@btconnect.com *Web Site:* www.intype.co.uk, pg 1164

Intype Libra Ltd (United Kingdom) *Tel:* (020) 8947 7863 *Fax:* (020) 8947 3652 *E-mail:* intype@btconnect.com, pg 1185, 1226, 1239

Invandrarfoerlaget (Sweden) *Tel:* (033) 13 60 70 *Fax:* (033) 13 60 75 *E-mail:* migrant@immi.se *Web Site:* www.immi.se, pg 612

El Inversionista Mexicano SA de CV (Mexico) *Tel:* (05) 5245396; (05) 5349297 *Fax:* (05) 5243794 *E-mail:* elimmbi@iserve.net.mx, pg 467

Instituto de Investigacao Cientifica Tropical (Portugal) *Tel:* (021) 361 63 40 *Fax:* (021) 363 14 60 *E-mail:* iict@iict.pt *Web Site:* www.iict.pt, pg 532

Inwardpath Publishers (Australia) *Tel:* (03) 9499 3405 *Fax:* (03) 9497 5656, pg 27

IOM COMMUNICATIONS LTD   INDUSTRY

IOM Communications Ltd (United Kingdom) *Tel:* (020) 7451 7300 *Fax:* (020) 7839 1702 *E-mail:* admin@materials.org.uk *Web Site:* www.materials.org.uk, pg 714

IOS Press BV (Netherlands) *Tel:* (020) 688 33 55 *Fax:* (020) 620 3419 *E-mail:* info@iospress.nl *Web Site:* www.iospress.nl, pg 484

IP Oslobodenje (Bosnia and Herzegovina) *Tel:* (033) 276900; (033) 468054 *E-mail:* info@oslobodjenje.com.ba *Web Site:* www.oslobodjenje.com.ba, pg 76

Iperborea (Italy) *Tel:* (02) 781458 *Fax:* (02) 798919 *E-mail:* iperborea@iol.it, pg 393

IPIS vzw (International Peace Information Service) (Belgium) *Tel:* (03) 225 00 22; (03) 225 21 96 *Fax:* (03) 231 0151 *E-mail:* info@ipisresearch.be *Web Site:* www.ipisresearch.be, pg 69

IPL - Istituto Propaganda Libraria (Italy) *Tel:* (02) 58301960 *Fax:* (02) 58301960, pg 1274

IPL Publishing Group (New Zealand) *Tel:* (04) 477 3032 *Fax:* (04) 477 3035 *E-mail:* transpress@paradise.net.nz *Web Site:* www.transpressnz.com, pg 497

IPS Copyright Agency (International Publications Service) (Republic of Korea) *Tel:* (02) 21158800 *Fax:* (02) 22646936 *E-mail:* copyright@ips-korea.com *Web Site:* www.ipsbook.com, pg 1134

IR Indo Edicions (Spain) *Tel:* (0986) 21 48 34 *Fax:* (0986) 21 11 33 *E-mail:* correo@irindo.com *Web Site:* www.irindo.com; irindo.net, pg 588

Iralka Editorial SL (Spain) *Tel:* (0943) 32 30 14 *Fax:* (0943) 32 30 22 *E-mail:* iralka@euskalnet.net *Web Site:* www.euskalnet.net/iralka, pg 588

Iranian Information Documentation Centre (Islamic Republic of Iran) *Tel:* (021) 6462548 *Fax:* (021) 6462254 *E-mail:* info@irandoc.ac.ir *Web Site:* www.irandoc.ac.ir, pg 1517

Library of the Iraq Museum (Iraq) *Tel:* (01) 8879687, pg 1518

IRD Editions (France) *Tel:* (01) 48 03 76 06 *Fax:* (01) 48 02 79 09 *E-mail:* editions@paris.ird.fr *Web Site:* www.editions.ird.fr, pg 169

Ireland Literature Exchange (Ireland) *Tel:* (01) 8727900 *Fax:* (01) 8727875 *E-mail:* info@irelandliterature.com *Web Site:* www.irelandliterature.com, pg 1148

Irfon (Tajikistan) *Tel:* (03772) 33-39-06; (03772) 33-62-54, pg 642

Irini Publishing House - Vassilis G Katsikeas SA (Greece) *Tel:* (01) 38-39-259; (01) 38-10-465 *Fax:* (01) 38-00-651; (01) 38-05-113 *E-mail:* katsikgr@hol.gr *Web Site:* www.infomedacoop.gr, pg 308

Iris Verlag AG (Switzerland) *Tel:* (031) 7473300 *Fax:* (031) 7473301 *E-mail:* polyinfo@rentsch.com *Web Site:* www.poly-laupen.ch, pg 625

Irish Academic Press (Ireland) *Tel:* (01) 668 8244 *Fax:* (01) 660 1610 *E-mail:* sales@iap.ie *Web Site:* www.iap.ie, pg 361

Irish Academy of Letters (Ireland), pg 1401

Irish Educational Publishers' Association (Ireland) *Tel:* (01) 500 9509; (01) 500 9555 (cust serv) *Fax:* (01) 500 9598; (01) 500 9596 (cust serv), pg 1273

Irish Management Institute (Ireland) *Tel:* (01) 2078400 *Fax:* (01) 2955150 *E-mail:* 3025reception@imi.ie *Web Site:* www.imi.ie, pg 361

Irish PEN Centre (Ireland), pg 1401

Irish Texts Society (Cumann Na Scribeann nGaedhilge) (Ireland) *Tel:* (01) 6616522 *Fax:* (01) 6612378 *E-mail:* shuttonseanfile@aol.com, pg 361

Irish Times Ltd (Ireland) *Tel:* (01) 6758000 *Fax:* (01) 6773282 *Web Site:* www.ireland.com, pg 361

Irish Translators' & Interpreters' Association (Ireland) *Tel:* (01) 8721302 *Fax:* (01) 8726282 *E-mail:* translation@eircom.net *Web Site:* www.translatorsassociation.ie, pg 1148

Irish YouthWork Press (Ireland) *Tel:* (010) 8729933 *Fax:* (010) 8724183 *E-mail:* info@nyf.ie *Web Site:* www.nyf.ie, pg 361

Irmaos Vitale S/A Industria e Comercio (Brazil) *Tel:* (011) 5574-7001 *Fax:* (011) 5574-7388 *E-mail:* irmaos@vitale.com.br *Web Site:* www.vitale.com.br, pg 84

Ediciones Irusa (Spain) *Tel:* (093) 2318032 *Fax:* (093) 2653670, pg 588

Isafoldarprentsmidja hf (Iceland) *Tel:* 550-5990 *Fax:* 550-5994 *E-mail:* isafold@isafold.is *Web Site:* www.isafold.is, pg 326

ISAL (Istituto Storia dell'Arte Lombarda) (Italy) *Tel:* (03) 62528118 *Fax:* (03) 62659417 *E-mail:* isalbibl@tin.it, pg 393

ISBN Agency Australia (Australia) *Tel:* (03) 9245 7385 *Fax:* (03) 9245 7393 *E-mail:* isbn.agency@thorpe.com.au *Web Site:* www.thorpe.com.au, pg 1260

ISBN Agency (International Standard Book Number National Agency) (Malawi) *Tel:* (01) 525 240; (01) 524 148; (01) 524 184 *Fax:* (01) 525 362; (01) 524 148 *E-mail:* archives@sdnp.org.mw *Web Site:* chambo.sdnp.org.mw, pg 1277

ISBN Agency - Korea (Republic of Korea) *Tel:* (02) 590 06 27; (02) 590 06 28 *Fax:* (02) 590 06 22; (02) 590 06 21 *E-mail:* ISSNKC@mail.nl.go.kr *Web Site:* www.nl.go.kr, pg 1276

ISBN Agency - Luxembourg (Luxembourg) *Tel:* 22 97 55-1 *Fax:* 47 56 72 *E-mail:* bib.nat@bi.etat.lu *Web Site:* www.bnl.lu, pg 1276

ISBN Agency - Namibia (Namibia) *Tel:* (061) 293 53 05 *Fax:* (061) 293 53 08 *Web Site:* www.isbn-international.org, pg 1278

Bureau ISBN (Netherlands) *Tel:* (0345) 475855 *Fax:* (0345) 475895 *E-mail:* isbn@centraal.boekhuis.nl *Web Site:* www.isbn.nl, pg 1279

ISBN-Kontoret Norge (Norway) *Tel:* 23 27 62 17 *Fax:* 23 27 60 10 *E-mail:* isbn-kontoret@nb.no *Web Site:* www.nb.no/html/isbn_eng.html, pg 1280

ISBN National Agency (Slovakia) *Tel:* (043) 430 1802 *Fax:* (043) 430 1802 *E-mail:* snk@snk.sk *Web Site:* www.snk.sk, pg 1283

ISCAH Fructuoso Rodriguez (Cuba) *Tel:* (07) 62936 *Fax:* (07) 330942, pg 120

Klaus Isele (Germany) *Tel:* (07746) 91116 *Fax:* (07746) 91117 *E-mail:* klaus.isele@t-online.de, pg 242

R Ishaak (Suriname) *Tel:* 031917 *Fax:* 0231917, pg 608

Ishihara Publishing Co Ltd (Japan) *Tel:* (0992) 391200 *Fax:* (0992) 391202, pg 419

Ishiyaku Publishers Inc (Japan) *Tel:* (03) 5395-7600 *Fax:* (03) 5395-7603 *E-mail:* dev-mdp@nna.so-net.ne.jp, pg 419

Editorial Isidoriana, Libreria (Spain) *Tel:* (0987) 876161 *Fax:* (0987) 876162 *E-mail:* sanisidoro@infonegocio.com, pg 588

ISIOM Verlag fur Tondokumente, Weinreb Tonarchiv (Switzerland) *Tel:* (091) 7513524 *Fax:* (091) 7516154 *E-mail:* isiom@bluewin.ch, pg 625

Isis Publishing Ltd (United Kingdom) *Tel:* (01865) 250 333 *Fax:* (01865) 790 358 *E-mail:* sales@isis-publishing.co.uk *Web Site:* www.isis-publishing.co.uk, pg 714

Isis Yayin Tic ve San Ltd (Turkey) *Tel:* (0216) 3213851; (0216) 3213847; (0216) 3213847 *Fax:* (0216) 3218666 *E-mail:* isis@turk.net, pg 650

Iskry - Publishing House Ltd spotka zoo (Poland) *Tel:* (022) 827 94 15 *Fax:* (022) 827 94 15 *E-mail:* iskry@iskry.com.pl *Web Site:* www.iskry.com.pl, pg 523

Izdatelstvo Iskusstvo (Russian Federation) *Tel:* (095) 2035872 *Fax:* (095) 2918882, pg 545

Islam International Publications Ltd (United Kingdom) *Tel:* (01252) 783155; (01252) 783823 *Fax:* (01252) 783148 *Web Site:* www.alislam.org, pg 714

Perpustakaan Islam (Indonesia) *Tel:* (0274) 2078 *Web Site:* www.perpustakaan-islam.com, pg 1517

Verlag der Islam (Germany) *Tel:* (069) 50688-651 *Fax:* (069) 50688-655, pg 242

Islamic Book Centre (Pakistan) *Tel:* (042) 6316803 *Fax:* (042) 6360955, pg 512

Islamic Foundation Publications (United Kingdom) *Tel:* (01530) 244 944; (01530) 249 230 *Fax:* (01530) 244 946; (01530) 249 656 *E-mail:* info@islamic-foundation.org.uk; publications@islamic-foundation.com *Web Site:* www.islamic-foundation.com; www.islamic-foundation.org.uk, pg 714

Islamic Publications (Pvt) Ltd (Pakistan) *Tel:* (042) 325243; (042) 3664504 *Fax:* (042) 7248676, pg 513

Islamic Publishing House (India) *Tel:* (0495) 720092; (0495) 724618 *Fax:* (0495) 724524 *E-mail:* iphcalicut@eth.net, pg 338

The Islamic Republic of Iran Parliament Library, No 1 (Ketabkhane-ye Majles-e Shora-ye Elsami, No 1) (Islamic Republic of Iran) *Tel:* (021) 3121805; (021) 3130911 *E-mail:* frelations@majlislib.com; irparlib@majlislib.com; info@majlislib.com *Web Site:* www.majlislib.org, pg 1517

The Islamic Republic of Iran Parliament Library, No 2 (Ketab-Khane-ye Majles-e Shora-ye Eslami, no 2) (Islamic Republic of Iran) *Tel:* (021) 6135335; (021) 3130919 *Fax:* (021) 3130919; (021) 3124339 *E-mail:* frelations@majlislib.com *Web Site:* www.majlislib.com, pg 1517

Islamic Research Institute (Pakistan) *Tel:* (051) 850751; (051) 850755 *Fax:* (051) 853360 *E-mail:* dg-iri@iri-iiu.sdnpd.undp.org, pg 513

Islamic Research Institute Library (Pakistan) *Tel:* (051) 9261761-5; (051) 2252816 *Web Site:* www.iiu.edu.pk, pg 1535

The Islamic Texts Society (United Kingdom) *Tel:* (01223) 314387 *Fax:* (01223) 324342 *E-mail:* info@its.org.uk *Web Site:* www.its.org.uk, pg 715

Islamic University Central Library (Saudi Arabia) *Tel:* (04) 847 4080 *Fax:* (04) 847 4560, pg 1541

Islamiyah (Indonesia) *Tel:* (061) 25421, pg 355

Island Press (Hong Kong) *Tel:* 28588176 *Fax:* 2482 9889, pg 317

Island Press Co-operative (Australia) *Tel:* (02) 4758 6635 *E-mail:* isphaw@hermes.net.au, pg 27

Islands Business International Ltd (Fiji) *Tel:* 312 040 *Fax:* 301 423 *E-mail:* 75070.2637@compuserve.com, pg 141

Isoete (France) *Tel:* (0233) 533409 *Fax:* (0233) 534731, pg 169

Isper Club (Italy) *Tel:* (011) 66 47 803 *Fax:* (011) 66 79 768 *E-mail:* segreteria.servizi@isper.org *Web Site:* www.isper.org, pg 1253

Isper SRL (Italy) *Tel:* (011) 66 47 803 *Fax:* (011) 66 70 829 *E-mail:* isper@isper.org *Web Site:* www.isper.org, pg 393

Israbook (Israel) *Tel:* (02) 5380247 *Fax:* (02) 5388423 *E-mail:* isragefen@netmedia.net.il *Web Site:* www.israelbooks.com, pg 1319

The Israel Academy of Sciences & Humanities (Israel) *Tel:* (02) 5636211 *Fax:* (02) 5666059 *E-mail:* isracado@vms.huji.ac.il, pg 368

Israel Antiquities Authority (Israel) *Tel:* (02) 5638421 *Fax:* (02) 6289066 *Web Site:* www.israntique.org.il, pg 368

Israel Book and Printing Centre (Israel) *Tel:* (03) 5142895 *Web Site:* www.expot.gov.il, pg 368

Israel Exploration Society (Israel) *Tel:* (02) 6257991 *Fax:* (02) 6247772 *E-mail:* ies@vms.huji.ac.il *Web Site:* www.hum.huji.ac.il/ies, pg 368

The Israel Institute for Occupational Safety & Hygiene (Israel) *Tel:* (03) 6875037 *Fax:* (03) 6875038 *Web Site:* www.osh.org.il, pg 368

Israel ISBN Group Agency (Israel) *Tel:* (03) 6180151 *Fax:* (03) 5798048 *E-mail:* isbn@ici.org.il; icl@icl.org.il *Web Site:* www.icl.org.il, pg 1274

Israel Librarians & Information Specialists Association (Israel) *Tel:* (02) 6589515 *Fax:* (02) 6251628 *E-mail:* icl@icl.org.il *Web Site:* www.icl.org.il, pg 1565

Israel Museum Products Ltd (Israel) *Tel:* (02) 6708883 *Fax:* (02) 6631833 *Web Site:* www.imj.org.il, pg 368

Israel Music Institute (IMI) (Israel) *Tel:* (03) 624 70 95 *Fax:* (03) 561 28 26 *E-mail:* musicinst@bezeqint.net *Web Site:* www.imi-il.org.il, pg 368

Israel Society of Libraries & Information Centers (ASMI) (Israel) *Tel:* (02) 6249421 *Fax:* (02) 6249421 *E-mail:* asmi@asmi.org.il *Web Site:* www.asmi.org.il, pg 1565

Israel State Archives (Israel) *Tel:* (02) 568 06 80 *Fax:* (02) 679 33 75, pg 1519

Israel Translators' Association (Israel) *Tel:* (09) 741 5279 *Fax:* (09) 760 2369 *Web Site:* www.ita.org.il, pg 1148

Israel Universities Press (Israel) *Tel:* (02) 6557822 *Fax:* (02) 6528962, pg 368

The Israeli Center for Libraries (Israel) *Tel:* (03) 6180151 *Fax:* (03) 5798048 *E-mail:* icl@icl.org.il *Web Site:* www.icl.org.il, pg 1565

Israeli Music Publications Ltd (Israel) *Tel:* (02) 6241377; (02) 6241378 *Fax:* (02) 62413708 *E-mail:* khanukaev@pop.isracom.net.il, pg 368

Israeli PEN Centre (Israel) *Tel:* (03) 6964937 *Fax:* (03) 6964937, pg 1401

ISSN International Centre (France) *Tel:* (01) 44 88 22 20 *Fax:* (01) 44 88 60 96; (01) 40 26 32 43 *E-mail:* issnic@issn.org *Web Site:* www.issn.org, pg 1268

ISSN Norway (Norway) *Tel:* (023) 27 61 79; (023) 27 61 81 *Fax:* (023) 27 60 50 *E-mail:* nbo@nb.no *Web Site:* www.nb.no, pg 1160

ISSN UK Centre (United Kingdom) *Tel:* (0870) 444 1500 *Fax:* (01937) 546562 *E-mail:* issn-uk@bl.uk *Web Site:* www.bl.uk/services/bibliographic/issn.html, pg 1292

Ist Patristico Augustinianum (Italy) *Tel:* (06) 680 069 *Fax:* (06) 680 06 298 *E-mail:* segr_ipa@aug.org, pg 393

Istanbul Universitesi Merkez Kuetuephanesi (Turkey) *Tel:* (0212) 511 12 19 *Fax:* (0212) 511 12 19 *E-mail:* bilgi@library.istanbul.edu.tr *Web Site:* www.istanbul.edu.tr/library, pg 1551

Istituto della Enciclopedia Italiana (Italy) *Tel:* (06) 68981 *Fax:* (06) 68982294 *Web Site:* www.treccani.it, pg 393

Istituto Lombardo Accademia di Scienze e Lettere (Italy) *Tel:* (02) 864087 *Toll Free Tel:* (02) 86461388 *E-mail:* istituto.lombardo@unimi.it *Web Site:* www.istitutolombardo.it, pg 1402

Ediciones Istmo SA (Spain) *Tel:* (091) 8061996 *Fax:* (091) 8044028, pg 588

Istytut Bibliograficzny Biblioteka Narodowa, Krajowe Biuro ISBN (Poland) *Tel:* (022) 608-2999 *Fax:* (022) 825-5251 *E-mail:* biblnar@bn.org.pl *Web Site:* www.bn.org.pl, pg 1281

IT-og Telestyrelsen (Denmark) *Tel:* 35 45 00 00 *Fax:* 35 45 00 10; 33 37 92 99 *E-mail:* itst@itst.dk *Web Site:* www.denmark.dk; www.si.dk, pg 132

Itaca (Italy) *Tel:* (02) 48009484 *Fax:* (02) 48009493, pg 393

Italian PEN Centre (Italy) *E-mail:* fmormando@planet.it, pg 1402

Istituto Italiano Edizioni Atlas (Italy) *Tel:* (035) 249711 *Fax:* (035) 216047 *E-mail:* edizioniatlas@edatlas.it *Web Site:* www.edatlas.it, pg 393

Istituto Italiano Per Il Medio Ed Estremo Oriente (ISMEO) (Italy) *Tel:* (06) 732741; (06) 732742; (06) 732743 *E-mail:* iias@let.leidenuniv.nl *Web Site:* www.iias.nl, pg 394

Itaria Shobo Ltd (Japan) *Tel:* (03) 3262-1656 *Fax:* (03) 3234-6469 *E-mail:* HQM01271@nifty.ne.jp, pg 419

Edicoes ITAU (Instituto Tecnico de Alimentacao Humana) Lda (Portugal) *Tel:* (01) 9661603 *Fax:* (01) 9661227, pg 532

ITC (United States) *Tel:* 954-623-3101 *Fax:* 954-623-3122 *E-mail:* team@inttype.com *Web Site:* www.inttype.com, pg 1188

ITD (United Kingdom) *Tel:* (01296) 27211 *Fax:* (01296) 392019, pg 1164

ITDG Publishing (United Kingdom) *Tel:* (01926) 634501 *Fax:* (01926) 634502 *E-mail:* marketing@itpubs.org.uk; itpubs@itpubs.org.uk *Web Site:* www.itdgpublishing.org.uk; www.developmentbookshop.com, pg 715

Ithemba! Publishing (South Africa) *Tel:* (011) 726 6529 *Fax:* (011) 726 6529 *E-mail:* firechildren@icon.co.za *Web Site:* www.icon.co.za/~firechildren/ithemba/ithemba.htm, pg 565

ITK Laromedel AB (Sweden) *Tel:* (08) 24 43 60 *Fax:* (08) 650 39 84, pg 612

ITpress Verlag (Germany) *Tel:* (07251) 300575 *Fax:* (07251) 14823 *E-mail:* itpress@acm.org *Web Site:* www.itpress.com, pg 242

IUCN-The World Conservation Union (United Kingdom) *Tel:* (01223) 277894 *Fax:* (01223) 277175 *E-mail:* books@iucn.org *Web Site:* www.iucn.org, pg 715

Iudicium Verlag GmbH (Germany) *Tel:* (089) 718747 *Fax:* (089) 7140039 *E-mail:* info@iudicium.de *Web Site:* www.geist.de, pg 242

Iudicium Verlag GmbH (Germany) *Tel:* (089) 718747 *Fax:* (089) 7142039 *E-mail:* info@iudicium.de *Web Site:* www.iudicium.de, pg 242

Iustus Forlag AB (Sweden) *Tel:* (018) 693091 *Fax:* (018) 693099 *E-mail:* iustus@iustus.se *Web Site:* www.iustus.se, pg 613

Iuventus (Czech Republic) *Tel:* (02) 7817314, pg 124

Ivrea (France) *Tel:* (01) 43 26 06 21 *Fax:* (01) 43 26 11 68, pg 169

Ivy Publications (South Africa) *Tel:* (012) 218931 *Fax:* (012) 3255984 *E-mail:* therese@statelib-pww.gov.za, pg 565

IWA Publishing (United Kingdom) *Tel:* (020) 7654 5500 *Fax:* (020) 7654 5555 *E-mail:* publications@iwap.co.uk *Web Site:* www.iwapublishing.com, pg 715

Iwanami Shoten, Publishers (Japan) *Tel:* (03) 5210-4115 *Fax:* (03) 3239-9619 *Web Site:* www.iwanami.co.jp, pg 419

Reisebuchverlag Iwanowski GmbH (Germany) *Tel:* (02133) 26030 *Fax:* (02133) 260333 *E-mail:* info@iwanowski.de *Web Site:* www.iwanowski.de, pg 242

Iwasaki Shoten Publishing Co Ltd (Japan) *Tel:* (03) 3812-9131 *Fax:* (03) 3816-6033 *E-mail:* ask@iwasakishoten.co.jp *Web Site:* www.iwasakishoten.co.jp, pg 419

Izdatelstvo Ja (Bulgaria) *Tel:* (046) 26166; (046) 20077, pg 95

Izdatelstvo Lettera (Bulgaria) *Tel:* (032) 600 930 *Fax:* (032) 600 940 *E-mail:* lettera@plovdiv.technolink.com; office@lettera.bg *Web Site:* www.lettera.bg, pg 95

Izdatelstvo Literatury i isskustva (Uzbekistan) *Tel:* (0371) 445172, pg 778

Editorial Iztaccihuatl SA (Mexico) *Tel:* (05) 7050938; (05) 7051063 *Fax:* (05) 5352321, pg 467

Izvestia Sovetov Narodnyh Deputatov Russian Federation (RF) (Russian Federation) *Tel:* (095) 2093738 *Fax:* (095) 2095394, pg 545

J C Palabay Enterprises (Philippines) *Tel:* (02) 9424512 *Fax:* (02) 9424513, pg 519

J Ch Mellinger Verlag GmbH (Germany) *Tel:* (0711) 543787 *Fax:* (0711) 556889 *E-mail:* mellinger@sambo.de, pg 242

J Film Process Co Ltd (Thailand) *Tel:* (02) 247-4042; (02) 248 6888 *Fax:* (02) 247-4719, pg 1162

J Film Process Co Ltd (Thailand) *Tel:* (02) 248 6888 *Fax:* (02) 247-4719, pg 1224

J Film Process Co Ltd (Thailand) *Tel:* (02) 248 6888 *Fax:* (0662) 247 4072; (0662) 246 4620, pg 1247

J K Publications (Sri Lanka) *Tel:* (01) 518954, pg 606

J M Pantelides Booksellers Ltd (Greece) *Tel:* (01) 363 9560 *Fax:* (01) 363 6453, pg 1313

Verlag J P Peter, Gebr Holstein GmbH & Co KG (Germany) *Tel:* (09861) 4 00-3 81 *Fax:* (09861) 4 00-70 *E-mail:* peter-verlag@rotabene.de *Web Site:* www.peter-verlag.de, pg 242

J Story-Scientia BVBA (Belgium) *Tel:* (09) 2255757 *Fax:* (09) 2331409 *E-mail:* bookshop@story.be *Web Site:* www.story.be, pg 1302

Uitgeverij J van In (Belgium) *Tel:* (03) 4805511 *Fax:* (03) 4807664, pg 69

Jabiru Press (Australia) *Tel:* (03) 9609 3535 *Fax:* (03) 9857 9110, pg 27

Jabotinsky Institute in Israel (Israel) *Tel:* (03) 6210611; (03) 5287320 *Fax:* (03) 5285587 *E-mail:* jabo@actcom.co.il *Web Site:* www.jabotinsky.org, pg 368

Editoriale Jaca Book SpA (Italy) *Tel:* (02) 48561520-29 *Fax:* (02) 48193361 *E-mail:* jacabook@jacabook.it *Web Site:* www.jacabook.it, pg 394

Jacana Education (South Africa) *Tel:* (011) 648 1157 *Fax:* (011) 648 5516 *E-mail:* marketing@jacana.co.za; production@jacana.co.za *Web Site:* www.jacana.co.za, pg 565

Jacaranda Designs Ltd (Kenya) *Tel:* 569736; (02) 568353 *Fax:* 740524, pg 434

Jacklin Enterprises (Pty) Ltd (South Africa) *Tel:* (011) 265 4200 *Fax:* (011) 314 2984 *E-mail:* mjacklin@jacklin.co.za *Web Site:* www.jacklin.co.za, pg 565

Gruppo Editoriale Jackson SpA (Italy) *Tel:* (02) 665261 *Fax:* (02) 66526222 *E-mail:* ordini@futura-ge.com, pg 394

JAD Publishers Ltd (Nigeria), pg 505

H I Jaffari & Co Publishers (Pakistan) *Tel:* (051) 811153, pg 513

Editions du Jaguar (France) *Tel:* (01) 44301970 *Fax:* (01) 44301979, pg 169

Jahreszeiten-Verlag GmbH (Germany) *Tel:* (040) 2717-0 *Fax:* (040) 2717-2056 *E-mail:* press@jalag.de *Web Site:* www.jalag.de, pg 242

Editions J'ai Lu (France) *Tel:* (01) 44 39 34 70 *Fax:* (01) 44 39 32 60 *E-mail:* ajasmin@jailu.com *Web Site:* www.flammarion.com, pg 169

JAI Press Ltd (United Kingdom) *Tel:* (020) 7379 8834 *Fax:* (020) 7379 8835 *Web Site:* www.jaipress.com, pg 715

Jaico Publishing House (India) *Tel:* (022) 2676702; (022) 2676802; (022) 2674501 *Fax:* (022) 2656412 *E-mail:* jaicowbd@vsnl.com *Web Site:* www.jaicobooks.com, pg 338

Jaico Publishing House (India) *Tel:* (022) 267 6702; (022) 267 6802; (022) 267 4501 *Fax:* (022) 265 6412 *E-mail:* jaicowbd@vsnl.com *Web Site:* www.jaicobooks.com, pg 1316

B Jain Publishers Overseas (India) *Tel:* (011) 2358 0800; (011) 5169 8991; (011) 2358 3100 *Fax:* (011) 2358 0471; (011) 5169 8993 *E-mail:* bjain@vsnl.com *Web Site:* www.bjainbooks.com, pg 338

B Jain Publishers Overseas (India) *Tel:* 23583100; 23581300 *Fax:* (011) 23580471 *E-mail:* bjain@vsnl.com *Web Site:* www.bjainbooks.com, pg 1316

B Jain Publishers (P) Ltd (India) *Tel:* (011) 23580800; (011) 23581100; (011) 23583100 *Fax:* (011) 23580471 *E-mail:* bjain@vsnl.com *Web Site:* www.bjainbooks.com, pg 339

Jaipur Publishing House (India) *Tel:* (0141) 319198; (0141) 319094 *E-mail:* jph@indiaresult.com, pg 339

Jamaica Archives (Jamaica) *Tel:* (876) 984-2581; (876) 984-5001 *Fax:* (876) 984-8254, pg 1521

The Jamaica Bauxite Institute (Jamaica) *Tel:* (876) 927-2073; (876) 927-2079 *Fax:* (876) 927-1159 *E-mail:* info@jbi.org.jm, pg 413

Jamaica Bureau of Standards (Jamaica) *Tel:* (876) 926-3140; (876) 926-3145 *Fax:* (876) 929-4736 *E-mail:* info@jbs.org.jm *Web Site:* www.jbs.org.jm/, pg 413

Jamaica Information Service (Jamaica) *Tel:* (876) 926-3740; (876) 926-3749 *Fax:* (876) 926-6715 *E-mail:* jis@jis.gov.jm; research@jis.gov.jm *Web Site:* www.jis.gov.jm, pg 413

Jamaica Library Association (Jamaica) *Tel:* (876) 927-1614 *Fax:* (876) 927-1614 *E-mail:* liajapresident@yahoo.com *Web Site:* www.liaja.org.jm, pg 1565

Jamaica Library Service (Jamaica) *Tel:* (876) 926-3315 *Fax:* (876) 926-3354 *E-mail:* jamlibs@cwjamaica.com *Web Site:* www.jamlib.org.jm, pg 1521

Jamaica Printing Services (Jamaica) *Tel:* 876-967-2250; 876-967-2253; 876-967-2279; 876-967-2280; 876-922-3957 *Fax:* 876-967-2225 *E-mail:* info@jps1992.com; sales@jps1992.com *Web Site:* www.jps1992.com/, pg 414

Jamaica Publishing House Ltd (Jamaica) *Tel:* (876) 922-1385; (876) 967-3866 *Fax:* (876) 922-5412 *E-mail:* jph@jol.com.jm, pg 414

James & James (Publishers) Ltd (United Kingdom) *Tel:* (020) 7482 8888 *Fax:* (020) 7482 8889 *E-mail:* jxj@jamesxjames.co.uk *Web Site:* www.jamesxjames.co.uk, pg 715

James & James (Science Publishers) Ltd (United Kingdom) *Tel:* (020) 7387 8558 *Fax:* (020) 7387 8998 *E-mail:* jxj@jxj.com *Web Site:* www.jxj.com, pg 715

James Nicholas Publishers Pty Ltd (Australia) *Tel:* (03) 9690 5955 (customer service); (03) 9696 5545 (editorial office) *Fax:* (03) 9699 2040 *E-mail:* jamesnicholaspublishers.com.au; info@jnponline.com *Web Site:* www.jamesnicholaspublishers.com.au; www.jnponline.com, pg 27

Jamrite Publications (Jamaica) *Tel:* (876) 926-1180; (876) 926-1181 *Fax:* (876) 968-4519 *E-mail:* blackolive@cwjamaica.com, pg 414

Jan Thorbecke Verlag GmbH & Co (Germany) *Tel:* (0711) 44 06-0 *Fax:* (0711) 44 06-199 *E-mail:* info@thorbecke.de *Web Site:* www.thorbecke.de, pg 243

Nakladatelstvi Jan Vasut (Czech Republic) *Tel:* (02) 22319 319 *Fax:* (02) 2481 1059 *E-mail:* vasut@mbox.vol.cz *Web Site:* www.vasut.cz, pg 124

Jandi-Sapi Editori (Italy) *Tel:* (06) 68805515; (06) 6876054 *Fax:* (06) 68218203 *E-mail:* info@jandisapi.com *Web Site:* www.jandisapi.com, pg 394

Jane Austen Society (United Kingdom) *Tel:* (01420) 83262 *Fax:* (01420) 83262 *E-mail:* museum@janeausten.demon.co.uk *Web Site:* www.janeaustensoci.freeuk.com/index.htm, pg 1408

Janeff Books (JM & MJ Books Ltd) (New Zealand) *Tel:* (070) 777783, pg 1330

Jane's Information Group (United Kingdom) *Tel:* (020) 8700 3700 *Fax:* (020) 8763 1006 *E-mail:* info.uk@janes.com *Web Site:* www.janes.com, pg 715

Jang Publishers (Pakistan) *Tel:* (042) 6367480-83 *Fax:* (042) 6361026; (042) 6362316 *E-mail:* thenewslhr@jang.group.com *Web Site:* www.jang-group.com, pg 513

Janibi Editores SA de CV (Mexico) *Tel:* (05) 6046160 *Fax:* (05) 6882848, pg 467

Jannersten Forlag AB (Sweden) *Tel:* (0226) 619 00 *Fax:* (0226) 10927 *E-mail:* bridge@jannersten.se *Web Site:* www.jannersten.com, pg 613

Editions Jannink, SARL (France) *Tel:* (01) 45 89 14 02 *Fax:* (01) 45 89 14 02 *E-mail:* jannink@noos.fr *Web Site:* www.editionsjannink.com, pg 169

Janssen Publishers CC (South Africa) *Tel:* (021) 7861548 *Fax:* (021) 7862468 *E-mail:* janssenp@iafrica.com *Web Site:* www.janssenbooks.co.za, pg 565

Janus Pannonius Tudomanyegyetem (Hungary) *Tel:* (072) 411 433 *Fax:* (072) 15738, pg 322

Janus Publishing Co Ltd (United Kingdom) *Tel:* (020) 7580 7664 *Fax:* (020) 7636 5756 *E-mail:* sales@januspublishing.co.uk *Web Site:* www.januspublishing.co.uk, pg 716

Editrice Janus SpA (Italy) *Tel:* (035) 24 71 80 *Fax:* (035) 24 70 92, pg 394

Janus Verlagsgesellschaft, Dr Norbert Meder & Co (Germany) *Tel:* (0521) 1369236 *Fax:* (0521) 1369237, pg 243

L Japadre Editore (Italy) *Tel:* (0862) 26025 *Fax:* (0862) 25587, pg 394

Japan Association of International Publications (Japan) *Tel:* (03) 3271 6901 *Fax:* (03) 3271 6920 *E-mail:* jaip@poppy.ocn.ne.jp *Web Site:* www.jaip.gr.jp, pg 1275

Japan Bible Society (Japan) *Tel:* (03) 3567-1990; (03) 3567-1987 (distribution) *Fax:* (03) 3567-4436 (administration) *E-mail:* info@bible.or.jp *Web Site:* www.bible.or.jp, pg 419

Japan Book Publishers Association (Japan) *Tel:* (03) 3268-1303 *Fax:* (03) 3268-1196 *E-mail:* rd@jbpa.or.jp *Web Site:* www.jbpa.or.jp, pg 1275

Japan Broadcast Publishing Co Ltd (Japan) *Tel:* (03) 3780-3356 *Fax:* (03) 3780-3348 *E-mail:* webmaster@npb.nhk-grp.co.jp, pg 419

Japan Electronic Publishing Association (Japan) *Tel:* (03) 3219-2958 *Fax:* (03) 3219-2940 *Web Site:* www.jepa.or.jp, pg 1275

Japan Foreign-Rights Centre (JFC) (Japan) *Tel:* (03) 59960321 *Fax:* (03) 59960323, pg 1134

Japan Industrial Publishing Co Ltd (Japan) *Tel:* (03) 3456-1827 *Fax:* (03) 3944-6826 *E-mail:* info@nikko-pb.co.jp; yktech@mx.nikko-pb.co.jp *Web Site:* www.nikko-pb.co.jp, pg 419

Japan ISBN Agency (Japan) *Tel:* (03) 326 72 301 *Fax:* (03) 326 72 304 *E-mail:* info@isbn-center.jp *Web Site:* www.isbn-center.jp, pg 1275

Japan Publications Inc (Japan) *Tel:* (03) 32958411 *Fax:* (03) 32958416, pg 419

Japan Publications Trading Co Ltd (Import & Export) (Japan) *Tel:* (03) 3292-3751 *Fax:* (03) 3292-0410 *E-mail:* jpt@jptco.co.jp *Web Site:* www.jptco.co.jp, pg 1322

The Japan Times Ltd (Japan) *Tel:* (03) 3453-2013 *Fax:* (03) 3453-8023 *E-mail:* books@japantimes.co.jp *Web Site:* bookclub.japantimes.co.jp, pg 420

Japan Travel Bureau Inc (Japan) *Tel:* (03) 5796-5525 *Fax:* (03) 5796-5529 *Web Site:* www.jtb.co.jp, pg 420

Japan UNI Agency Inc (Japan) *Tel:* (03) 32950301 *Fax:* (03) 32945173 *E-mail:* info@japanuni.co.jp, pg 1134

Japanese PEN Centre (Japan) *Tel:* (03) 34021171; (03) 34021172 *Fax:* (03) 34025951 *E-mail:* japan-pen@asahi-net.email.ne.jp, pg 1402

Jardine Wenwu Printing Co (China) *Tel:* 6617 5748 *Web Site:* www.cypdirect.com, pg 1154

Jared Publishing (Australia) *Tel:* (03) 9874 2415, pg 27

Jarrah Publications (Australia) *Tel:* (08) 9495 4569 *Fax:* (08) 9495 4569, pg 27

Jarrold Publishing (United Kingdom) *Tel:* (01603) 763300 *Fax:* (01603) 662748 *E-mail:* info@jarrold.com *Web Site:* www.jarrold-publishing.co.uk, pg 716

JASOR (Guadeloupe) *Tel:* (0590) 911848 *Fax:* (0590) 210701, pg 313

Java Books (Indonesia) *Tel:* (021) 4515351 (Hunting) *Fax:* (021) 4534987 *E-mail:* mndl@indo.net.id, pg 1318

Pejo K Javorov Publishing House (Bulgaria) *Tel:* (02) 875201; (02) 880137; (02) 876765 *Fax:* (02) 875592, pg 95

Dayawansa Jayakody & Co (Sri Lanka) *Tel:* (011) 2695773 *Fax:* (011) 2696653 *E-mail:* dayawansa@slt.lk, pg 606

Jayantilal Jamnadas, Lda (Portugal) *Tel:* (01) 4960951, pg 1337

Jaypee Brothers Medical Publishers Pvt Ltd (India) *Tel:* (011) 3272143; (011) 3282021; (011) 3272703 *Fax:* (011) 3276490 *E-mail:* jpmedpub@del2.vsnl.net.in *Web Site:* www.jpbros.20m.com, pg 339

Al Jazirah Organization for Press, Printing, Publishing (Saudi Arabia) *Tel:* (01) 4419999 *Fax:* (01) 4412536, pg 550

(JDC) Brookdale Institute of Gerontology & Adult Human Development in Israel (Israel) *Tel:* (02) 6557445 *Fax:* (02) 5635851 *E-mail:* brook@jdc.org.il *Web Site:* www.jdc.org.il/brookdale/, pg 369

JEAG (Madagascar) *Tel:* (02022) 24141 *Fax:* (02022) 20397, pg 453

Editions Jean-Claude Lattes (France) *Tel:* (01) 44417400 *Fax:* (01) 43253047 *E-mail:* jpeguillam@editions-jclattes.fr, pg 169

Jednota Ceskych Matematiku A Fysiku (Czech Republic) *Tel:* (02) 222 111 54; (02) 220 907 08; (02) 220 907 09 *E-mail:* jcmf@math.cas.cz; predseda@jcmf.cz *Web Site:* www.jcmf.cz, pg 124

Jednota Tlumocniku a Prekladatelu (Czech Republic) *Tel:* (02) 24 142 517 *Fax:* (02) 24 142 312 *E-mail:* info@jtpunion.org *Web Site:* www.jtpunion.org, pg 1147

The Richard Jefferies Society (United Kingdom) *Tel:* (01865) 735678 *Web Site:* www.treitel.org/Richard/jefferies.html, pg 1408

Jelenkor Verlag (Hungary) *Tel:* (072) 314-782; (072) 335-767 *Fax:* (072) 532-047 *E-mail:* jelenkor@mail.datanet.hu *Web Site:* www.jelenkor.com, pg 322

Jenelle Press (Australia) *Tel:* (02) 4281531 *Fax:* (02) 4284144, pg 27

Verlag Winfried Jenior (Germany) *Tel:* (0561) 7391621 *Fax:* (0561) 774148 *E-mail:* jenior@aol.com *Web Site:* www.jenior.de, pg 243

Jeong-eum Munhwasa (Republic of Korea) *Tel:* (02) 5680070 *Fax:* (02) 5650352, pg 439

Jerusalem Books Ltd (Israel) *Tel:* (02) 643-3580 *Fax:* (02) 643 3580 *E-mail:* jerbooks@netmedia.co.il *Web Site:* www.jerusalembooks.co.il, pg 1319

Jerusalem Center for Public Affairs (Israel) *Tel:* (02) 5619281 *Fax:* (02) 5619112 *E-mail:* jcenter@jcpa.org *Web Site:* www.jcpa.org, pg 369

Jerusalem City (Public) Library (Israel) *Tel:* (02) 256 785 *Fax:* (02) 255 785, pg 1519

The Jerusalem Publishing House Ltd (Israel) *Tel:* (02) 5617744 *Fax:* (02) 5634266 *E-mail:* jphgagi@netvision.net.il, pg 369

Jesuit Publications (Australia) *Tel:* (03) 9427 7311 *Fax:* (03) 9428 4450 *E-mail:* jespub@jespub.jesuit.org.au *Web Site:* www.jesuitpublications.com.au, pg 27

Jett Samm Publishing Ltd (Trinidad & Tobago) *Tel:* 637-9548 *Web Site:* jetsamm.com, pg 647

Editions du Jeu de Paume (France) *Tel:* (01) 47 03 13 25 *Fax:* (01) 42 61 26 10, pg 169

JF Printhaus (Philippines) *Tel:* (049) 800-3961 *Fax:* (049) 562-0916, pg 1222

Jiang Xi Copyright Agency (China) *Tel:* (0791) 8528405 *Fax:* (0791) 8508901 *E-mail:* jxcopyright@hotmail.com *Web Site:* www.jxbqzx.com, pg 1306

Jiangsu Juveniles & Children's Publishing House (China) *Tel:* (025) 83242938 *Fax:* (025) 83242350 *E-mail:* susao@publicl.ptt.js.en, pg 105

Jiangsu People's Publishing House (China) *Tel:* (025) 86634309 *Fax:* (025) 83379766 *Web Site:* www.book-wind.com, pg 105

Jiangsu Science & Technology Publishing House (China) *Tel:* (025) 83273033 *Fax:* (025) 83273111 *E-mail:* cnjsstph@publicl.ptt.js.cn *Web Site:* www.jskjpub.com, pg 105

Jigyungsa Ltd (Republic of Korea) *Tel:* (02) 557-6351 *Fax:* (02) 557-6352 *E-mail:* jigyung@uriel.net *Web Site:* www.jigyung.co.kr, pg 440

Jiho (Japan) *Tel:* (03) 3265-7755 *Fax:* (03) 3265-8855, pg 420

Jika Publishing (Australia) *Tel:* (03) 9467 3295 *Fax:* (03) 9467 1770 *E-mail:* jordanca@alphalink.com.au, pg 27

Editorial Jilguero, SA de CV (Mexico) *Tel:* (05) 2590939; (05) 2590814 *Fax:* (05) 5401771 *E-mail:* mexdesco@compuserve.com *Web Site:* www.mexicodesconocido.com.mx, pg 467

Jilin Science & Technology Publishing House (China) *Tel:* (0431) 5635185 *Fax:* (0431) 5635185 *E-mail:* jlkjcbs@public.ec.jl.cn, pg 105

Jillion Publishing Co (Taiwan, Province of China) *Tel:* (02) 2571-0558 *Fax:* (02) 5231891 *E-mail:* lanbri@tpts.5.seed.net.tw, pg 640

Jinan Publishing House (China) *Tel:* (0531) 6913006, pg 105

Jinno International Group (United States) *Tel:* 845-735-4666 *Fax:* 617-344-5905 *E-mail:* jinno@hotmail.com, pg 1167, 1230, 1240

Ediciones JJB (Spain) *Tel:* (041) 236928 *Fax:* (041) 226127, pg 588

JKL Publikationen GmbH (Germany) *Tel:* (030) 74104624 *Fax:* (030) 74104626 *E-mail:* info@zeitgut.com *Web Site:* www.zeitgut.com, pg 243

JL Publications (Australia) *Tel:* (03) 98860200 *Fax:* (03) 98860200 *E-mail:* jlpubs@c031.aone.net.au, pg 28

Ediciones JLA (Spain) *Tel:* (091) 3158577 *Fax:* (091) 7336239, pg 588

Editorial Joaquin Mortiz SA de CV (Mexico) *Tel:* (05) 5598781 *Fax:* (05) 5758980, pg 467

Joensuun Yliopisto (Finland) *Tel:* (013) 251 111 *Fax:* (013) 251 2050 *E-mail:* joyk@joyl.joensuun.ti *Web Site:* www.joensuu.fi/, pg 1505

Johann Wolfgang Goethe Universitat (Germany) *Tel:* (069) 798-22608; (069) 798-23590 *Fax:* (069) 798-28313 *E-mail:* hrz-verwaltung@rz.uni-frankfurt.de *Web Site:* www.rz.uni-frankfurt.de, pg 243

Johannes Berchmans Verlagsbuchhandlung GmbH (Germany) *Tel:* (089) 38185-244, pg 243

Johannes Verlag Einsiedeln, Freiburg (Germany) *Tel:* (0761) 640168 *Fax:* (0761) 640169 *E-mail:* johverlag@aol.com, pg 243

Johannesburg Art Gallery (South Africa) *Tel:* (011) 7253130; (011) 7253180 *Fax:* (011) 7206000 *Web Site:* www.saevents.co.za/gallery.htm, pg 565

Johannesburg Public Library (South Africa) *Tel:* (011) 836 3787 *Fax:* (011) 836 6607 *E-mail:* library@mj.org.za, pg 1543

Johannis (Germany) *Tel:* (07821) 5810 *Fax:* (07821) 581-26 *E-mail:* johannis-druck@t-online.de *Web Site:* www.johannis-verlag.de, pg 243

John Mackintosh Hall Library (Gibraltar) *Tel:* 78000 *Fax:* 40843, pg 1512

Johnson Publications Ltd (United Kingdom) *Tel:* (020) 7486 6757 *Fax:* (020) 7487 5436, pg 716

Johnston & Streiffert Editions (Sweden) *Tel:* (031) 826160 *Fax:* (031) 825150, pg 613

Joho Kagaku Gijutsu Kyokai (Japan) *Tel:* (03) 3813-3791 *Fax:* (03) 3813-3793 *E-mail:* infosta@infosta.or.jp *Web Site:* www.infosta.or.jp, pg 1565

Joho Shori Gakkai (Japan) *Tel:* (03) 5484-3535 *Fax:* (03) 5484-3534 *E-mail:* intl@ipsj.or.jp *Web Site:* www.ipsj.or.jp, pg 1565

Joint Publishing (HK) Co Ltd (Hong Kong) *Tel:* 2523 0105 *Fax:* 2525 8355 *E-mail:* jpchk@hk.super.net *Web Site:* www.jointpublishing.com, pg 317

Joly Editions (France) *Tel:* (01) 56 54 16 00 *Fax:* (01) 56 54 16 46 *E-mail:* loic.even@eja.fr *Web Site:* www.editions-joly.com, pg 169

Jonas Verlag fuer Kunst und Literatur GmbH (Germany) *Tel:* (06421) 25132 *Fax:* (06421) 210572 *E-mail:* jonas@jonas-verlag.de *Web Site:* www.jonas-verlag.de, pg 243

Jones & Bartlett International (United Kingdom) *Tel:* (01892) 539356 *Fax:* (01892) 614944 *E-mail:* j&b@class.co.uk *Web Site:* www.jbpub.com, pg 716

John Jones Publishing Ltd (United Kingdom) *Tel:* (01824) 707255 *Fax:* (01824) 705272 *E-mail:* johnjonespublishing.ltd@virgin.net *Web Site:* www.johnjonespublishing.ltd.uk, pg 716

Dr Werner Jopp Verlag (Germany) *Tel:* (0611) 547116 *Fax:* (0611) 542762, pg 243

Jordan Book Centre Co Ltd (Jordan) *Tel:* (06) 5151-882; (06) 5156-882; (06) 5155-882; (06) 606-882; (06) 676-882 *Fax:* (06) 5152016 *E-mail:* jbc@go.com.jo, pg 432

Jordan Book Centre Co Ltd (Jordan) *Tel:* (06) 5151882; (06) 5155882 *Fax:* (06) 5152016 *E-mail:* jbc@go.com.jo, pg 1323

Jordan Distribution Agency Co Ltd (Jordan) *Tel:* (06) 30191; (06) 4630192 *Fax:* (06) 635152 *E-mail:* jda@go.com.jo, pg 432

Jordan Distribution Agency Co Ltd (Jordan) *Tel:* (06) 4630191; (06) 4630192 *Fax:* (06) 4635152 *E-mail:* jda@go.com.jo, pg 1323

Jordan House for Publication (Jordan) *Tel:* (06) 24224 *Fax:* (06) 51062, pg 432

Jordan Library Association (Jordan) *Tel:* (06) 462 9412 *Fax:* (06) 462 9412, pg 1566

Jordan Publishing Ltd (United Kingdom) *Tel:* (0117) 923 0600 *Fax:* (0117) 925 0486 *E-mail:* customerservice@jordanpublishing.co.uk *Web Site:* www.jordanpublishing.co.uk, pg 716

Jordan University of Science & Technology Library (Jordan) *Tel:* (02) 295111 *Fax:* (02) 295123 *Web Site:* www.just.edu.jo, pg 1522

Jordanverlag AG (Switzerland) *Tel:* (01) 3023676, pg 625

Jose Alfonso Sandoval Nunez (Costa Rica) *Tel:* 2252331; 8-326-426 *E-mail:* asandova@alpha.emate.ucr.ac.cr; k_sanny@hotmail.com, pg 115

Michael Joseph Ltd (United Kingdom) *Tel:* (020) 7416 3000 *Fax:* (020) 7416 3099, pg 716

Richard Joseph Publishers Ltd (United Kingdom) *Tel:* (01805) 625750 *Fax:* (01805) 625376 *E-mail:* sheppardsdir@aol.com *Web Site:* www.sheppardsworld.com, pg 716, 1352

Joszoveg Muhely Kiado (Hungary) *Tel:* (01) 266 0393; (01) 317 3536 *Fax:* (01) 266 0393 *E-mail:* joszoveg@euroweb.hu, pg 322

Nakladatelstvi Jota spol sro (Czech Republic) *Tel:* (05) 37 014 203 *Fax:* (05) 37 014 213 *E-mail:* jota@jota.cz; books@bm.cesnet.cz *Web Site:* www.jota.cz, pg 124

Le Jour, Editeur (France) *Tel:* (01) 49591189 *Fax:* (01) 49591196 *Web Site:* www.edjour.com, pg 169

Les Editions du Journal L' Unite Maghrebine (Morocco) *Tel:* 780169 *Fax:* 780169, pg 475

Journal on Social Change (Zimbabwe) *Tel:* (04) 72-0417; (04) 70-0047 *Fax:* (04) 73-0808 *E-mail:* schange@africaonline.co.zw, pg 783

Jouvence (Italy) *Tel:* (06) 3211500 *Fax:* (06) 3202897 *E-mail:* jouvence@flashnet.it *Web Site:* www.jouvence-ed.com, pg 394

Jouvence Editions (France) *Tel:* (04) 50 43 28 60 *Fax:* (04) 50 43 29 24 *E-mail:* info@editions-jouvence.com *Web Site:* www.editions-jouvence.com, pg 170

Editions Jouvence (Switzerland) *Tel:* (022) 794 66 22 *Fax:* (022) 794 67 86 *E-mail:* info@editions-jouvence.com *Web Site:* www.editions-jouvence.com, pg 626

Joval Publications (Australia) *Tel:* (053) 674593, pg 28

Casa Editrice Dott Eugenio Jovene SpA (Italy) *Tel:* (081) 5521019; (081) 5521274; (081) 5523471 *Fax:* (081) 5520687 *E-mail:* info@jovene.it *Web Site:* www.jovene.it, pg 394

Jovis Verlag GmbH (Germany) *Tel:* (030) 2636720 *Fax:* (030) 26367272 *E-mail:* jovis@jovis.de *Web Site:* www.jovis.de, pg 243

Jowi-Verlag (Germany) *Tel:* (09353) 2921, pg 243

Joy Verlag GmbH (Germany) *Tel:* (08376) 97383 *Fax:* (08376) 8845 *E-mail:* joy_verlag@compuserve.com, pg 243

Joyas Bibliograficas SA (Spain) *Tel:* (091) 5470220, pg 588

Jozsef Attila Tudomanyegyetem Egyetemi Koenyvtar (Hungary) *Tel:* (062) 544-036 *Fax:* (062) 544-035 *E-mail:* mader@bibl.u-szeged.hu *Web Site:* www.bibl.u-szeged.hu, pg 1514

JPM Publications SA (Switzerland) *Tel:* (021) 6177561 *Fax:* (021) 6161257 *E-mail:* information@jpmguides.com *Web Site:* www.jpmguides.com, pg 626

Ediciones Jucar (Spain) *Tel:* (098) 5170921; (098) 5349684; (098) 5349684 *Fax:* (098) 55349545, pg 588

Gerald Judd Sales Ltd (United Kingdom) *Tel:* (020) 7828 8821 *Fax:* (020) 7828 0840, pg 1164

Jane Judd Literary Agency (United Kingdom) *Tel:* (020) 7607 0273 *Fax:* (020) 7607 0623, pg 1141

Juedischer Verlag GmbH (Germany) *Tel:* (069) 75601-0 *Fax:* (069) 75601-522 *Web Site:* www.suhrkamp.de, pg 243

Juegos & Co SRL (Argentina) *Tel:* (011) 4374-7903; (011) 4371-1825 *Fax:* (011) 4372-3829 *E-mail:* juegosyc@impsat1.com.ar *Web Site:* www.demente.com, pg 6

Jugend mit einer Mission Verlag (Switzerland) *Tel:* (032) 418988 *Fax:* (032) 418920, pg 626

Jugoslavijapublik (Serbia and Montenegro) *Tel:* (011) 633 266 *Fax:* (011) 622 858, pg 552

Jugoslovenska Revija (Serbia and Montenegro) *Tel:* (011) 625-829, pg 552

Jugoslovenski Bibliografsko Informacijski Institut (Serbia and Montenegro) *Tel:* (011) 687 836; (011) 687 760 *Fax:* (011) 687 760; (011) 688 840 *E-mail:* suzana@jbi.bg.ac.yu *Web Site:* www.yu-yubin.org, pg 1570

JUGOSLOVENSKI BIBLIOGRAFSKO-INFORMACIJSKI INSTITUT, YUBIN — INDUSTRY

Jugoslovenski Bibliografsko-informacijski institut, Yubin, Agencija za ISBN (Serbia and Montenegro) *Tel:* (011) 687 836; (011) 688 840 *Fax:* (011) 687 760; (011) 688 840 *E-mail:* yubin@jbi.bg.ac.yu *Web Site:* www.jbi.bg.ac.yu/, pg 1283

Julius Klinkhardt Verlagsbuchhandlung (Germany) *Tel:* (08046) 9304 *Fax:* (08046) 9306 *E-mail:* info@klinkhardt.de *Web Site:* www.klinkhardt.de, pg 243

Junfermann-Verlag (Germany) *Tel:* (05251) 1 34 40 *Fax:* (05251) 13 44 44 *E-mail:* infoteam@junfermann.de *Web Site:* www.junfermann.de, pg 243

Jung-ang Munhwa Sa (Republic of Korea) *Tel:* (02) 717-2114 *Fax:* (02) 716-1369, pg 440

Verlag Jungbrunnen - Wiener Spielzeugschachtel GesellschaftmbH (Austria) *Tel:* (01) 512-1299 *Fax:* (01) 512-1299-75 *E-mail:* office@jungbrunnen.co.at, pg 52

Editura Junimea (Romania) *Tel:* (032) 117290, pg 540

Junior Publications Ltd (New Zealand) *Tel:* (09) 620 5459 *Fax:* (09) 620 5459, pg 497

Vydavatelstvo Junior sro Slovart Print (Slovakia) *Tel:* (02) 44872378; (02) 44872379 *Fax:* (02) 44872133 *E-mail:* obchod@junior.sk *Web Site:* www.junior.sk, pg 559

Junius Verlag GmbH (Germany) *Tel:* (040) 892599 *Fax:* (040) 891224 *E-mail:* info@junius-verlag.de *Web Site:* www.junius-verlag.de, pg 244

Junius Verlags- und Vertriebs GmbH (Austria) *Tel:* (01) 4921272, pg 52

Junod Nicolas (Switzerland) *Tel:* (022) 347 02 42 *Fax:* (022) 347 02 42, pg 626

Junta de Castilla y Leon Consejeria de Educacion y Cultura (Spain) *Tel:* (0983) 411587 *Fax:* (0983) 411527 *E-mail:* publicaciones.cec@pop-in.jcyl.es *Web Site:* www.jcyl.es, pg 588

Junta de Educacao Religiosa e Publicacoes da Convencao Batista Brasileira (JUERP) (Brazil) *Tel:* (021) 2690772 *Fax:* (021) 2690296 *E-mail:* juerp@openlink.com.br *Web Site:* www.juerp.org.br, pg 84

Jupiter Verlagsgesellschaft mbH (Austria) *Tel:* (01) 21422940 *Fax:* (01) 2160720, pg 52

Juricom (Costa Rica) *Tel:* 2836942 *Fax:* 2253800 *E-mail:* juricom@sol.racsa.co.cr, pg 115

Juridica Verlag GmbH (Austria) *Tel:* (01) 533 37 47-0 *Fax:* (01) 533 37 47-196 *E-mail:* juridica@manz.at *Web Site:* www.juridica.at, pg 52

Editions Juridiques Africaines (France) *Tel:* (01) 43370401 *Fax:* (01) 43370401, pg 170

Editions Juridiques et Techniques Lamy SA (France) *Tel:* (01) 44721200 *Fax:* (01) 44721389, pg 170

Editions Juridiques Kluwer a Deurne Anvers (Belgium) *Tel:* (02) 300 3000 *Fax:* (03) 360-04 *E-mail:* custumer.kejb@wkb.be *Web Site:* www.editionskluwer.be, pg 69

Editions du Juris-Classeur (France) *Tel:* (01) 45 58 92 00 *Fax:* (01) 45 58 94 00 *E-mail:* editorial@juris-classeur.com; relations-clients@juris-classeur.com *Web Site:* www.juris-classeur.fr, pg 170

Juris Druck & Verlag AG (Switzerland) *Tel:* (01) 2117727; (01) 2117747 *Fax:* (01) 7409019 *E-mail:* juris@swissonline.ch, pg 626

Juris Editorial (Argentina) *Tel:* (0341) 4267301; (0341) 4267302 *Fax:* (0341) 4267301; (0341) 4267302 *E-mail:* editorialjuris@arnet.com.ar *Web Site:* www.editorialjuris.com, pg 6

Editions Juris Service (France) *Tel:* (04) 72 10 10 01 *Fax:* (04) 78 28 93 83 *E-mail:* info@editionsjuris.com *Web Site:* www.editionsjuris.com, pg 170

Editorial Jus SA de CV (Mexico) *Tel:* (05) 5260538; (05) 5260540 *Fax:* (05) 5290951 *E-mail:* editjus@data.net.mx, pg 467

Justus-Liebig-Universitat Giessen (Germany) *Tel:* (0641) 99-0 *Fax:* (0641) 99-12289 *E-mail:* michael.kost@admin.uni-giessen.de *Web Site:* www.uni-giessen.de, pg 244

Juta & Co (South Africa) *Fax:* (021) 797 5569 (orders only) *E-mail:* books@juta.co.za *Web Site:* www.juta.co.za, pg 565

Juta & Co Ltd (South Africa) *Tel:* (011) 217-7200 *Fax:* (011) 883-7623 *E-mail:* books@juta.co.za *Web Site:* www.tmza.co.za/juta, pg 1340

Jutta Pohl Verlag (Germany) *Tel:* (07202) 2239 *Fax:* (07202) 3879 *E-mail:* jutta@pohlverlag.de *Web Site:* www.pohl-verlag.de, pg 244

Juvenile & Children's Publishing House (China) *Tel:* (021) 62823025 *Fax:* (021) 62526963 *Web Site:* www.jcph.com, pg 105

Juventa Verlag GmbH (Germany) *Tel:* (06201) 9020-0 *Fax:* (06201) 9020-13 *E-mail:* juventa@juventa.de *Web Site:* www.juventa.de, pg 244

Libreria Juventud (Bolivia) *Tel:* (02) 2406248 *Fax:* (02) 2406248, pg 1303

Editorial Juventud Colombiana Ltda (Colombia) *Tel:* (01) 2557485; (01) 2490543 *Fax:* (01) 2557416, pg 111

Editorial Juventud SA (Spain) *Tel:* (093) 444 18 00 *Fax:* (093) 444 18 02 *E-mail:* juventud@bcn.servicom.es *Web Site:* www.editorialjuventud.es, pg 588

Juventus/Femina Publishers (South Africa) *Tel:* (012) 3284620 *Fax:* (012) 3283809, pg 565

Jyvaskylan Yliopiston Kirjasto (Finland) *Tel:* (014) 2601211 *Fax:* (014) 2603371 *E-mail:* jyk@Library.jyu.fi *Web Site:* www.fyu.fi, pg 1505

K Dictionaries Ltd (Israel) *Tel:* (03) 5468102 *Fax:* (03) 5468103 *E-mail:* kd@kdictionaries.com *Web Site:* kdictionaries.com, pg 369

K Publishing & Distributors Sdn Bhd (Malaysia) *Tel:* (03) 5501755; (03) 5501442 *Fax:* (03) 5501826, pg 456

Kaantopiiri Oy (Finland) *Tel:* (09) 622 9970 *Fax:* (09) 135 1372 *E-mail:* like@likekustannus.fi *Web Site:* www.likekustannus.fi, pg 142

Kabardino-Balkarskoye knizhnoye izdatelstvo (Russian Federation) *Tel:* 54184, pg 545

Kadena Press (Philippines) *Tel:* (02) 9217429; (02) 9213984, pg 519

Kadokawa Shoten Publishing Co Ltd (Japan) *Tel:* (03) 32388431 *Fax:* (03) 32627733 *E-mail:* K-master@kadokawa.co.jp *Web Site:* www.kadokawa.co.jp, pg 420

Library Board of Kaduna State (Nigeria) *Tel:* (062) 242590, pg 1533

Kaerntner Druck- und Verlags-GmbH (Austria) *Tel:* (0463) 5866 *Fax:* (0463) 5866-321 *E-mail:* info@kaerntner-druckerei.at *Web Site:* www.kaerntner-druckerei.at, pg 52

Kahn & Averill (United Kingdom) *Tel:* (020) 8743 3278 *Fax:* (020) 8743 3278, pg 716

Lonnie Kahn Ltd (Israel) *Tel:* (03) 9518418 *Fax:* (03) 9518415; (03) 9518416 *E-mail:* lonikahn@netvision.net.il, pg 1320

Kahurangi Cooperative (New Zealand) *Tel:* (09) 2782731, pg 497

Kaibundo Shuppan (Japan) *Tel:* (03) 3815-3291 *Fax:* (03) 3815-3953 *E-mail:* LED04737@nifty.ne.jp, pg 420

Kaigai Publications Ltd (Kaigai Shuppan Boeki Kabushiki Kaisha) (Japan) *Tel:* (03) 32924271 *Fax:* (03) 32924278 *E-mail:* admin@kaigai-pub.co.jp, pg 1322

Kailash Editions (France) *Tel:* (01) 43.29.52.52 *Fax:* (01) 46.34.03.29 *E-mail:* kailash@imaginet.fr, pg 170

Kairali Children's Book Trust (India) *Tel:* (0481) 563226; (0481) 560918 *Fax:* (0481) 564758 *Web Site:* www.dcbooks.com/kcbt.htm, pg 339

Kairalee Mudralayam (India) *Tel:* (0481) 2563114; (0481) 2301614 *Fax:* (0481) 2564758 *E-mail:* info@dcbooks.com *Web Site:* www.dcbooks.com/kairali.htm, pg 339

Editorial Kairos SA (Spain) *Tel:* (093) 430-3746 *Fax:* (093) 410-5166 *E-mail:* kairos@sendanet.es, pg 588

Kaisei-Sha Publishing Co Ltd (Japan) *Tel:* (03) 32603229 *Fax:* (03) 32603540 *E-mail:* foreign@kaiseisha.co.jp *Web Site:* www.kaiseisha.co.jp, pg 420

Kaitakusha (Japan) *Tel:* (03) 5842-8900 *Fax:* (03) 5842-5560 *E-mail:* webmaster@kaitakusha.co.jp *Web Site:* www.kaitakusha.co.jp, pg 420

Kajima Institute Publishing Co Ltd (Japan) *Tel:* (03) 5561-2550 *Fax:* (03) 5561 2560 *E-mail:* info@kajima-publishing.co.jp *Web Site:* www.kajima-publishing.co.jp, pg 420

KaJo Verlag (Germany) *Tel:* (0931) 385235 *Fax:* (0931) 385305 *E-mail:* info@verlagshaus.com *Web Site:* www.verlagshaus.com, pg 244

Kajura Publications (United Republic of Tanzania) *Tel:* (051) 866181, pg 643

Editions Kaleidoscope (France) *Tel:* (01) 45 44 07 08 *Fax:* (01) 45 44 53 71 *E-mail:* infos@editions-kaleidoscope.com *Web Site:* www.editions-kaleidoscope.com, pg 170

Kaleidoscope Publishers Ltd (Denmark) *Tel:* 33755555 *Fax:* 33755544 *E-mail:* gujbt@gyldendal.dk *Web Site:* www.kaleidoscope.publishers.dk; www.gyldendal.dk, pg 132

Kalentis & Sia (Greece) *Tel:* (0210) 36-01-551 *Fax:* (0210) 36-23-553 *E-mail:* kalendis@ath.forthnet.gr, pg 308

Kali For Women (India) *Tel:* (011) 6864497; (011) 6852530 *Fax:* (011) 6864497 *E-mail:* kaliw@del2.vsnl.net.in *Web Site:* www.kalibooks.com, pg 339

Kalich SRO (Czech Republic) *Tel:* (02) 24947505; (02) 24220296 *Fax:* (02) 24947504; (02) 24220296 *E-mail:* kalichpub@volny.cz, pg 124

Kalligram spol sro (Slovakia) *Tel:* (02) 54415028 *Fax:* (02) 54410809 *Web Site:* www.kalligram.sk, pg 559

Kallmeyer'sche Verlagsbuchhandlung GmbH (Germany) *Tel:* (0511) 4 00 04-1 75 *Fax:* (0511) 4 00 04-1 76 *E-mail:* leserservice@kallmeyer.de *Web Site:* www.kallmeyer.de, pg 244

Kalos-Verlag (Switzerland) *Tel:* (01) 3022751 *Fax:* (01) 3022751, pg 626

Kalyani Publishers (India) *Tel:* (011) 3274393; (011) 3271469, pg 339

Ilias Kambanas Publishing Organization, SA (Greece) *Tel:* (0210) 5762791 *Fax:* (0210) 5743988 *E-mail:* kambanas@internet.gr, pg 309

Kamenyar (Ukraine) *Tel:* (0322) 72-19-49 *Fax:* (0322) 72-79-22, pg 653

J Kamphausen Verlag & Distribution GmbH (Germany) *Tel:* (0521) 172875 *Fax:* (0521) 68771, pg 244

KAMS Information & Publishing Ltd (Hong Kong) *Tel:* 23889172 *Fax:* 27716403 *E-mail:* kamsinfo@hkstar.com *Web Site:* kamsinfo.com, pg 1148

Kanakis Publications & Bookshop (Greece) *Tel:* (01) 3302385 *Fax:* (01) 3811902, pg 1313

Kanda Bookshop (Japan) *Tel:* (03) 3291-7071 *Fax:* (03) 3293-8005 *E-mail:* kanda@bookshop.co.jp *Web Site:* www.bookshop.co.jp, pg 1322

Kanehara & Co Ltd (Japan) *Tel:* (03) 3811-7185; (03) 3811-7184 (sales) *Fax:* (03) 3813-0288 *Web Site:* www.kanehara-shuppan.co.jp, pg 420

Kangaroo Press (Australia) *Tel:* (02) 6541502 *Fax:* (02) 6541338, pg 28

Kanisa la Biblia Publishers (KLB) (United Republic of Tanzania) *Tel:* (026) 2354500 *Fax:* (026) 2350911, pg 643

Kanisius Verlag (Switzerland) *Tel:* (026) 425 87 40 *Fax:* (026) 425 87 38 *Web Site:* www.canisius.ch, pg 626

Kano State Library Board (Nigeria) *Tel:* (064) 645614 *Web Site:* www.library.unt.edu/nigeria/Kano/Kano.htm, pg 1533

Kansai University Press (Japan) *Tel:* (06) 6368-1171 *Fax:* (06) 6389-5162 *Web Site:* www.kansai-u.ac.jp/index.html, pg 420

Kansallisarkisto Kirjasto (Finland) *Tel:* (09) 228521 *Fax:* (09) 176302 *E-mail:* kansallisarkisto@narc.fi *Web Site:* www.narc.fi, pg 1505

Jan Kanzelsberger Praha (Czech Republic) *Tel:* (02) 22 51 42 40; (02) 22 52 02 64 *Fax:* (02) 22 51 15 73 *E-mail:* masarykova@volny.cz, pg 124

Kaos Edizioni SRL (Italy) *Tel:* (02) 39310296 *Fax:* (02) 39325749 *E-mail:* kaosedizioni@kaosedizioni.com *Web Site:* www.kaosedizioni.com, pg 394

Kapelusz Editora SA (Argentina) *Tel:* (011) 5236-5000 *Fax:* (011) 5236-5050 *E-mail:* editorial@kapelusz.com.ar *Web Site:* www.kapelusz.com.ar, pg 7

Kapelusz Ltda Editorial (Colombia) *Tel:* (01) 2442035; (01) 3350031 *Fax:* (01) 3350042, pg 111

Editorial Kapelusz Venezolana SA (Venezuela) *Tel:* (02) 517601; (02) 526281, pg 779

Kapon Editions (Greece) *Tel:* (01) 92-35-098 *Fax:* (01) 92-14-089 *Web Site:* www.homemarket.gr, pg 1313

Karachi University Library Science Alumni Association (Pakistan) *Tel:* (021) 479001 *Fax:* (021) 473226, pg 1569

Karas-Sana Oy (Finland) *Tel:* (09) 6815 5600 *Fax:* (09) 6815 5611 *E-mail:* toimitus@sana.fi *Web Site:* www.karas-sana.fi/sana, pg 142

Dionysuis P Karavias Ekdoseis (Greece) *Tel:* (01) 3620465 *Fax:* (01) 3620465, pg 309

Kardamitsa A (Greece) *Tel:* (01) 36 15 156 *Fax:* (01) 36 31 100 *E-mail:* info@kardamitsa.gr *Web Site:* kardamitsa.gr, pg 309

S Karger GmbH Verlag fuer Medizin und Naturwissenschaften (Germany) *Tel:* (0761) 45 20 70 *Fax:* (0761) 45 20 714 *E-mail:* information@karger.de *Web Site:* www.karger.com; www.karger.de, pg 244

S Karger AG, Medical & Scientific Publishers (Switzerland) *Tel:* (061) 3061111 *Fax:* (061) 3061234 *E-mail:* karger@karger.ch *Web Site:* www.karger.com, pg 626

Karisto Oy (Finland) *Tel:* (03) 63 151 *Fax:* (03) 616 1565 *E-mail:* kustannusliike@karisto.fi *Web Site:* www.karisto.fi, pg 142

Verlag Karl Baedeker GmbH (Germany) *Tel:* (0711) 4502262 *Fax:* (0711) 4502343 *E-mail:* baedeker@mairs.de, pg 244

Karl-May-Verlag Lothar Schmid GmbH (Germany) *Tel:* (0951) 98 20 60 *Fax:* (0951) 2 43 67 *E-mail:* info@karl-may.de *Web Site:* www.karl-may.de, pg 244

Karmelitanske Nakladatelstvi (Czech Republic) *Tel:* 384 420 295 *Fax:* 384 420 295 *E-mail:* vydri@karmelitanske-nakladatelstvi.cz; zasilky@kna.cz *Web Site:* www.karmelitanske-nakladatelstvi.cz; www.kna.cz, pg 124

Karnac Books Ltd (United Kingdom) *Tel:* (020) 8969 4454 *Fax:* (020) 8969 5585 *E-mail:* books@karnac.demon.co.uk *Web Site:* www.karnacbooks.com, pg 716

Karnak House (United Kingdom) *Tel:* (020) 7243 3620 *Fax:* (020) 7243 3620 *E-mail:* connection@karnakhouse.co.uk *Web Site:* www.karnakhouse.co.uk, pg 717

Karni Publishers Ltd (Israel) *Tel:* (03) 812244 *Fax:* (03) 826138 *E-mail:* info@zmora.co.il, pg 369

Karolinger Verlag GmbH & Co KG (Austria) *Tel:* (0222) 4302093 *Fax:* (0222) 4302093, pg 52

Karolinum, nakladatelstvi (Czech Republic) *Tel:* (02) 24491276 *Fax:* (02) 24212041 *E-mail:* cupress@ruk.cuni.cz; cupress@cuni.cz *Web Site:* www.cupress.cuni.cz, pg 124

The Harry Karren Institute for the Analysis of Propaganda, Yad Labanim (Israel) *Tel:* (09) 9573736 *Fax:* (09) 9546896, pg 369

Karthala Editions-Diffusion (France) *Tel:* (01) 43 31 15 59 *Fax:* (01) 45 35 27 05 *E-mail:* karthala@wanadoo.fr, pg 170

Karto + Grafik Verlagsgesellschaft (K & G Verlagsgesellschaft) (Germany) *Tel:* (069) 76 20 31 *Fax:* (069) 76 91 06 *E-mail:* kugverlag@aol.com *Web Site:* www.hildebrands.de, pg 244

Kartoen (Netherlands) *Tel:* (050) 3110505 *Fax:* (050) 3112299 *E-mail:* mondria@worldonline.nl, pg 484

Kartografie Praha (Czech Republic) *Tel:* (02) 21969411 *Fax:* (02) 21969428 *E-mail:* info@kartografie.cz *Web Site:* www.kartografie.cz, pg 124

Kartographischer Verlag Reinhard Ryborsch (Germany) *Tel:* (06104) 79039 *Fax:* (06104) 75356, pg 244

Karunaratne & Sons Ltd (Sri Lanka) *Tel:* 692295 *Fax:* 229 9860 *E-mail:* info@calcey.com *Web Site:* www.calcey.com, pg 606

Karunia CV (Indonesia) *Tel:* (031) 5344120 *Fax:* (031) 5343409, pg 355

Karya Anda, CV (Indonesia) *Tel:* (031) 5344215; (031) 522580; (031) 5315402 *Fax:* (031) 5310594, pg 355

Main Library, Kasetsart University (Thailand) *Tel:* (02) 9428615 *Fax:* (02) 5611369; (02) 9428614 *E-mail:* ospnk@ku.ac.th *Web Site:* www.lib.ku.ac.th, pg 1550

Kastaniotis Editions SA (Greece) *Tel:* (01) 3301208; (01) 3301327 *Fax:* (01) 3822530 *E-mail:* info@kastaniotis.com *Web Site:* www.kastaniotis.com, pg 309

Kastell Verlag GmbH (Germany) *Tel:* (089) 33 21 75; (089) 399742 *Fax:* (089) 340 11 78 *E-mail:* kastell-verlag@t-online.de, pg 244

Katai & Bolza Irodalmi Ugynokseg (Hungary) *Tel:* (01) 456-0313 *Fax:* (01) 215-4420 *Web Site:* www.kataibolza.hu, pg 1132

Katalis PT Bina Mitra Plaosan (Indonesia) *Tel:* (021) 7510477, pg 355

Kathakali (Bangladesh) *Tel:* (031) 619476; (031) 619006; (031) 612625, pg 1301

Katholieke Bijbelstichting (Netherlands) *Tel:* (073) 6133220 *Fax:* (073) 6910140 *Web Site:* www.willibrordbijbel.nl/kbs, pg 484

Katholieke Universiteit Leuven (Belgium) *Tel:* (016) 32 46 60; (016) 32 46 01 *Fax:* (016) 32 46 16 *E-mail:* centrale.bibliotheek@bib.kuleuven.ac.be *Web Site:* www.bib.kuleuven.ac.be, pg 1493

Verlag Katholisches Bibelwerk GmbH (Germany) *Tel:* (0711) 619200 *Fax:* (0711) 6192044 *E-mail:* verlag@bibelwerk.de *Web Site:* www.bibelwerk.de, pg 245

Katholska kirkjan a Islandi - Landakot Publishers Thorlakssjodur (Iceland) *Tel:* 555-0188, pg 326

Katolicki Uniwersytet Wydawniczo -Redakcja (Poland) *Tel:* (081) 5257151 *Fax:* (081) 541246 *E-mail:* sekret@kul.lublin.pl, pg 523

Katoptro Publications (Greece) *Tel:* (0210) 9244827; (0210) 9244852 *Fax:* (0210) 9244756 *E-mail:* info@katoptro.gr *Web Site:* www.katoptro.gr, pg 309

Katzmann Verlag KG (Germany) *Tel:* (07473) 5427 *Fax:* (07473) 5427, pg 245

Verlag Ernst Kaufmann GmbH (Germany) *Tel:* (07821) 93 90-0 *Fax:* (07821) 9390-11 *E-mail:* info@kaufmann-verlag.de *Web Site:* www.kaufmann-verlag.de, pg 245

Kauppakaari Oyj (Finland) *Tel:* (020) 442 4730 *Fax:* (020) 442 4723 *E-mail:* etunimi.sukunimi@talentum.fi *Web Site:* www.talentum.fi/kirjat, pg 142

Kavaler Publishers (Belarus) *Tel:* (0172) 2506485; (0172) 548198 *Fax:* (0172) 238041 *E-mail:* Kavaler@inbox.ru, pg 62

Kavkazskaya Biblioteka Publishing House (Russian Federation) *Tel:* (8652) 32314, pg 545

KAW Krajowa Agencja Wydawnicza (Poland) *Tel:* (022) 6578886 *Fax:* (022) 6578887 *E-mail:* kaw@univcomp.waw.pl *Web Site:* www.polska2000.pl, pg 523

Kawade Shobo Shinsha Publishers (Japan) *Tel:* (03) 3404-1201 *Fax:* (03) 3404-6386 *E-mail:* info@kawade.co.jp *Web Site:* www.kawade.co.jp, pg 420

Al-Farabi Kazakh National University (Kazakstan) *Tel:* (03272) 471691 *Fax:* (03272) 472609 *E-mail:* anurmag@kazsu.kz *Web Site:* www.kazsu.kz, pg 432

Kazakhstan Academy of Sciences (Kazakstan) *Tel:* (03272) 624871 *Fax:* (03272) 62500 *E-mail:* teta@nursat.kz *Web Site:* www.president.kz, pg 1522

Kazakhstan, Izd-Vo (Kazakstan) *Tel:* (03272) 422929; (03272) 428562 *Fax:* (03272) 422929, pg 432

Kazamashobo Co Ltd (Japan) *Tel:* (03) 3291-5729 *Fax:* (03) 3291-5757 *E-mail:* kazama@wd6.so-net.ne.jp *Web Site:* www.kazamashobo.co.jp, pg 420

Izdatelstvo Kazanskago Universiteta (Russian Federation) *Tel:* 325363 *E-mail:* kacimov@niimm.kazan.su, pg 545

Kazi Publications (Pakistan) *Tel:* (042) 7311359; (042) 7350805 *Fax:* (042) 7117606; (042) 7324003 *E-mail:* kazip@brain.net.pk; kazipublications@hotmail.com *Web Site:* www.brain.net.pk/~kazip, pg 513

KBV Verlags-und Medien - GmbH (Germany) *Tel:* (06593) 998668 *Fax:* (06593) 998701 *E-mail:* info@kbv-verlag.de *Web Site:* www.kbv-verlag.de, pg 245

KCL Language Consultancy Ltd (Hong Kong) *Tel:* (02) 8811368 *Fax:* (02) 8080389 *E-mail:* kcl@iohk.com *Web Site:* www.iohk.com/userpages/kcl, pg 1148

Ke Mong Sa Publishing Co Ltd (Republic of Korea) *Tel:* (02) 531-5535 *Fax:* (02) 531-5550, pg 440

Keats-Shelley Memorial Association (KSMA) (United Kingdom) *Tel:* (01892) 533452 *Fax:* (01892) 519142 *Web Site:* www.keats-shelley.co.uk, pg 1408

Kedros Publishers (Greece) *Tel:* (0210) 3089712 *Fax:* (0210) 3302655 *E-mail:* books@kedros.gr *Web Site:* www.kedros.gr, pg 309

Gregory Kefalas Publishing (Australia) *Tel:* (02) 9789 6049 *Fax:* (02) 97876181, pg 28

Kegan Paul International Ltd (United Kingdom) *Tel:* (020) 7580 5511 *Fax:* (020) 7436 0899 *E-mail:* books@keganpaul.com *Web Site:* www.keganpaul.com, pg 717

Keigaku Publishing Co Ltd (Japan) *Tel:* (03) 3233-3733 *Fax:* (03) 3233-3730, pg 420

Keil & Keil Literary Agency (Germany) *Tel:* (040) 27166892 *Fax:* (040) 27166896 *E-mail:* anfragen@keil-keil.com *Web Site:* www.keil-keil.com, pg 1131

Keio University School of Library & Information Science (Japan) *Tel:* (03) 3453-4511 *Fax:* (03) 5427-1578 *E-mail:* slis-office@slis.keio.ac.jp *Web Site:* www.slis.keio.ac.jp, pg 1521

Keip GmbH (Germany) *Tel:* (06021) 59 05 0 *Fax:* (06021) 59 05 42 *E-mail:* info@keip.net *Web Site:* www.keip.net, pg 245

Keisuisha Publishing Company Ltd (Japan) *Tel:* (082) 2467909 *Fax:* (082) 2467876 *E-mail:* info@keisui.co.jp *Web Site:* www.keisui.co.jp, pg 420

Verlag Walter Keller, Dornach (Switzerland) *Tel:* (061) 7015713 *Fax:* (061) 7015716 *E-mail:* info@verlag-walterkeller.ch *Web Site:* www.verlag-walterkeller.ch, pg 626

SachBuchVerlag Kellner (Germany) *Tel:* (0421) 77866 *Fax:* (0421) 704058 *E-mail:* kellner-verlag@t-online.de *Web Site:* kellner-verlag.de, pg 245

Kells Publishing Company Ltd (Ireland) *Tel:* (046) 40117; (046) 40255 *Fax:* (046) 41522, pg 361

The Frances Kelly Agency (United Kingdom) *Tel:* (020) 8549 7830 *Fax:* (020) 8547 0051, pg 1141

Kelly's (United Kingdom) *Tel:* (01342) 335862 *Fax:* (01342) 335825 *E-mail:* kellys.mktg@reedinfo.co.uk *Web Site:* www.kellysearch.com, pg 717

Martin Kelter Verlag GmbH u Co (Germany) *Tel:* (040) 68 28 95-0 *Fax:* (040) 68 28 95 50 *Web Site:* www.kelter.de, pg 245

Kemps Publishing Ltd (United Kingdom) *Tel:* (0121) 765 4144 *Fax:* (0121) 706 1408 *E-mail:* info@kempsgold.co.uk *Web Site:* www.kempsgold.co.uk, pg 717

Kempton Park Public Library (South Africa) *Tel:* (011) 9212173 *Fax:* (011) 9750921, pg 1544

Kenek Ltd (Cyprus) *Tel:* (022) 365842 *Fax:* (022) 475150, pg 121

The Kenilworth Press Ltd (United Kingdom) *Tel:* (01296) 715101 *Fax:* (01296) 715148 *E-mail:* customer.services@kenilworthpress.co.uk *Web Site:* www.kenilworthpress.co.uk, pg 717

Kenkyusha Ltd (Japan) *Tel:* (03) 3288-7777; (03) 3288-7856 *Fax:* (03) 3288-7799 *Web Site:* www.kenkyusha.co.jp, pg 421

Kennarahaskoli Islands (Iceland) *Tel:* 5633800 *Fax:* 5633914 *E-mail:* vefur@khi.is *Web Site:* www.khi.is, pg 1515

Albertine Kennedy Publishing (Ireland) *Tel:* (01) 6607090 *Fax:* (01) 6607090, pg 361

Kentro Byzantinon Erevnon (Greece) *Tel:* (031) 270941 *Fax:* (031) 228922, pg 309

Kentron Ekdoseos Ellinon Syngrafeon (Greece) *Tel:* (01) 3612541 *Fax:* (01) 3602691, pg 1400

Kenway Publications Ltd (Kenya) *Tel:* (02) 444700; (02) 445260; (02) 445261 *Fax:* (02) 448753 *E-mail:* eaep@africaonline.co.ke *Web Site:* www.eastafricanpublishers.com, pg 434

Kenya Agricultural Research Institute (Kenya) *Tel:* (02) 583301-20 *Fax:* (02) 583344 *E-mail:* resource.centre@kari.org *Web Site:* www.hridir.org, pg 1523

Kenya Energy & Environment Organisation, Kengo (Kenya) *Tel:* (020) 749747; (020) 748281 *Fax:* (020) 749382, pg 434

Kenya Library Association (Kenya) *Tel:* (02) 334244 *Fax:* (02) 336885, pg 1566

Kenya Literature Bureau (Kenya) *Tel:* (02) 608305; (02) 608806; (02) 605595; (02) 351196; (02) 351197; (02) 506158 *Fax:* (02) 605600 *E-mail:* klb@onlinekenya.com, pg 434

Kenya Literature Bureau (Kenya) *Tel:* (02) 608806; (02) 605595 *Fax:* (02) 605600 *E-mail:* klb@onlinekenya.co.ke, pg 1275

Kenya Medical Research Institute (KEMRI) (Kenya) *Tel:* (02) 722541; (02) 722672; (02) 722532 *Fax:* (02) 720030 *E-mail:* kemrilib@ken.healthnet.org *Web Site:* www.kemri.org, pg 435

Kenya Meteorological Department (Kenya) *Tel:* (02) 567880 *Fax:* (02) 576955 *E-mail:* director@lion.meteo.go.ke; imtr@lion.meteo.go.ke *Web Site:* www.meteo.go.ke, pg 435

Kenya National Archives & Documentation Service (Kenya) *Tel:* (02) 228959 *Fax:* (02) 228020 *E-mail:* knarchives@kenyaweb.com *Web Site:* www.kenyarchives.go.ke, pg 1523

Kenya National Library Service (Kenya) *Tel:* (02) 725550; (02) 725551; (02) 718177; (02) 718012; (02) 718013 *Fax:* (02) 721749 *E-mail:* knls@nbnet.co.ke *Web Site:* www.knls.or.ke, pg 1523

Kenya Polytechnic Library (Kenya) *Tel:* (02) 338231; (02) 338232 *Fax:* (02) 219689, pg 1523

Kenya Publishers Association (Kenya) *Tel:* (020) 375 2344 *Fax:* (020) 375 4076 *E-mail:* kenyapublishers@wananchi.com *Web Site:* www.kenyabooks.org, pg 1275

Kenya Quality & Productivity Institute (Kenya), pg 435

Kenya School of Law (Kenya) *Tel:* (02) 715895 *Fax:* (02) 714783, pg 1523

Kenya Technical Teachers' College Library (KTTC) (Kenya) *Tel:* (02) 520211-5 *Fax:* (02) 520037, pg 1523

The Jomo Kenyatta Foundation (Kenya) *Tel:* (02) 557222; (02) 531965 *Fax:* (02) 531966 *E-mail:* publish@jomokenyattaf.com *Web Site:* www.kenyaweb.com/education/klb.html, pg 435

Kenyatta University Library (Kenya) *Tel:* (02) 810901 *Fax:* (02) 811575 *E-mail:* info@ku.ac.ke, pg 1523

Kenyon-Deane (United Kingdom) *Tel:* (01684) 540154 *Fax:* (01684) 540154, pg 717

P Keppler Verlag GmbH & Co KG (Germany) *Tel:* (06104) 606 0 *Fax:* (06104) 606 121 *E-mail:* info@kepplermediengruppe.de *Web Site:* www.kepplermediengruppe.de, pg 245

Kepzoemueveszeti Kiado (Hungary) *Tel:* (01) 3517585; (01) 3423323, pg 322

Kerala University, Department of Publications (India) *Tel:* (0471) 306422; (0471) 305931 *Fax:* (0471) 307158 *E-mail:* unikereg@md4.vsnl.net.in *Web Site:* www.collegeskerala.com, pg 339

Kerber Verlag (Germany) *Tel:* (0521) 95008-10 *Fax:* (0521) 95008-88 *E-mail:* info@kerber-verlag.de *Web Site:* www.kerber-verlag.de, pg 245

Alexander Kerbiser KG (Austria) *Tel:* (03852) 2204 *Fax:* (03852) 5349, pg 1300

Verlag Kerle im Verlag Herder (Germany) *Tel:* (0761) 2717-0 *Fax:* (0761) 2717-350 *E-mail:* info@kerle.de *Web Site:* www.kerle.de, pg 245

Verlag Kerle im Verlag Herder & Co (Austria) *Tel:* (01) 5121413-60 *Fax:* (01) 5121413-65 *E-mail:* vertriebsbuero@herder.at, pg 53

Kernerman Publishing Ltd (Israel) *Tel:* (03) 5468102 *Fax:* (03) 5468103 *E-mail:* kd@kdictionaries.com *Web Site:* www.kdictionaries.com, pg 369

Kerryman Ltd (Ireland) *Tel:* (066) 21666 *Fax:* (066) 21608 *E-mail:* info@kerryman.ie *Web Site:* www.unison.ie/kerryman, pg 361

C Kersten & Co (Suriname) *Tel:* 471150 *Fax:* 472320 *E-mail:* kersten@sr.net *Web Site:* www.kersten.sr, pg 608

Kesaint Blanc (Indonesia) *Tel:* (021) 4204847; (021) 4204851 *Fax:* (021) 4216792 *Web Site:* www.kesaintblanc.com, pg 355

Nurcihan Kesim Literary Agency, Inc (Turkey) *Tel:* (0212) 5285797; (0212) 5111317; (0212) 5111078 *Fax:* (0212) 5285791 *E-mail:* kesim@superonline.com; contact@nurcihankesim.com *Web Site:* www.nurcihankesim.com, pg 1138

Simona Kessler International Copyright Agency Ltd (Romania) *Tel:* (021) 231 81 50 *Fax:* (021) 231 45 22, pg 1135

Keswick Books & Gifts Ltd (Kenya) *Tel:* (02) 226-047; (02) 331-692 *Fax:* (02) 728-557 *E-mail:* keswick@swiftkenya.com, pg 1324

Keter Publishing House Ltd (Israel) *Tel:* (02) 6557822 *Fax:* (02) 6528962 *E-mail:* info@keter-books.co.il *Web Site:* www.keter-books.co.il, pg 369

Keterpress Enterprises Jerusalem (Israel) *Tel:* (02) 6557822 *Fax:* (02) 6528962 *E-mail:* info@keter-books.co.il *Web Site:* www.keter-books.co.il, pg 1159

Keterpress Enterprises Jerusalem (Israel) *Tel:* (02) 6521201 *Fax:* (02) 6527956 *E-mail:* info@keter-books.co.il *Web Site:* www.keter-books.co.il, pg 1180

Keterpress Enterprises Jerusalem (Israel) *Tel:* (02) 6521201 *Fax:* (02) 6536811 *E-mail:* info@keter-books.co.il *Web Site:* www.keter-books.co.il, pg 1220

Keterpress Enterprises Jerusalem (Israel) *Tel:* (02) 655 7822 *Fax:* (02) 6536811 *E-mail:* info@keter-books.co.il *Web Site:* www.keter-books.co.il, pg 1237

Editions Ketty & Alexandre (Switzerland) *Tel:* (021) 9051111 *Fax:* (021) 9056050, pg 626

Keurbiblioteek (South Africa) *Tel:* (012) 401 0700 *Fax:* (012) 3255498 *E-mail:* lapa@atkv.org.za, pg 1255

Die Keure (Belgium) *Tel:* (050) 47 12 72 *Fax:* (050) 34 37 68 *E-mail:* info@diekeure.be *Web Site:* www.diekeure.be, pg 69

Key Language Services (United Kingdom) *Tel:* (01908) 232101 *Fax:* (01908) 232815 *E-mail:* sales@keylanguageservices.co.uk *Web Site:* www.keylanguageservices.co.uk, pg 1151

Keysersche Verlagsbuchhandlung GmbH (Germany) *Tel:* (089) 455540 *Fax:* (089) 45554111, pg 245

Keytec Typesetting Ltd (United Kingdom) *Tel:* (01308) 427580 *Fax:* (01308) 421961 *E-mail:* all@keytectype.co.uk *Web Site:* www.keytectype.co.uk, pg 1185

Keyware sarl (Luxembourg) *Tel:* 358660 *E-mail:* texthaus@webcom.com, pg 451

Khai Wah-Ferco Pte Ltd (Singapore) *Tel:* 67583313 *E-mail:* kwfppi@pacific.net.sg, pg 1161

Khanna Publishers (India) *Tel:* (011) 2912380; (011) 7224179, pg 339

Kharisma Publications Sdn Bhd (Malaysia) *Tel:* (03) 724660 *Fax:* (03) 724602, pg 456

Khartoum Polytechnic Library (Sudan) *Tel:* 78922, pg 1546

Khartoum University Press (Sudan) *Tel:* (011) 80558; (011) 81806 *Fax:* (011) 870558 *Web Site:* www.khartoumuniversity.edu, pg 608

Khayat Book and Publishing Co Sarl (Lebanon), pg 446

Izdatelstvo Khudozhestvennaya Literatura (Russian Federation) *Tel:* (095) 261-85-41 *Fax:* (095) 261-83-00, pg 545

Ki Moon Dang (Republic of Korea) *Tel:* (02) 2295-6171 *Fax:* (02) 296-8188 *E-mail:* kimoon2@chollian.net, pg 440

Vince Kiado Kft (Hungary) *Tel:* (01) 375-7288 *Fax:* (01) 202-7145 *E-mail:* hl2618vin@ella.hu, pg 322

Kibea Publishing Co *Tel:* (02) 24 10 20; (02) 925 01 52 *Fax:* (02) 925 07 48 *E-mail:* kibea@internet-bg.net; office@kibea.net *Web Site:* www.kibea.net, pg 95

Kidemus Verlag GmbH (Germany) *Tel:* (0221) 84 20 97 *Fax:* (0221) 84 20 98 *E-mail:* info@kidemus.de *Web Site:* www.kidemus.de, pg 245

Verlag Kiepenheuer & Witsch (Germany) *Tel:* (0221) 376 85-0 *Fax:* (0221) 38 85 95 *E-mail:* verlag@kiwi-koeln.de *Web Site:* www.kiwi-koeln.de, pg 245

Gustav Kiepenheuer Verlag GmbH (Germany) *Tel:* (0341) 9954600 *Fax:* (0341) 9954620 *E-mail:* info@aufbau-verlag.de *Web Site:* www.aufbau-verlag.de, pg 245

Libreria Kier (Argentina) *Tel:* (091) 5227335 *E-mail:* info@libreriakier.com *Web Site:* www.libreriakier.com, pg 1297

Editorial Kier SACIFI (Argentina) *Tel:* (011) 4811-0507 *Fax:* (011) 4811-3395 *E-mail:* ediciones@kier.com.ar *Web Site:* www.kier.com.ar, pg 7

Kierdorf Ute Verlag (Germany) *Tel:* (02267) 2888 *Fax:* (02267) 4458 *E-mail:* Kierdorfverlag@t-online.de *Web Site:* www.kierdorfverlag.de, pg 246

Kiiarat Konyvdiado (Hungary) *Tel:* (01) 388-6312 *Fax:* (01) 388-6312, pg 322

Kilda Verlag (Germany) *Tel:* (02571) 52115 *Fax:* (02571) 953269 *E-mail:* info@kildaverlag.de *Web Site:* www.kildaverlag.com, pg 246

Verlag im Kilian GmbH (Germany) *Tel:* (06421) 2 93 30 *Fax:* (06421) 16 38 94 *E-mail:* verlag@kilian.de *Web Site:* www.kilian-verlag.de, pg 246

Kilkenny People/Wellbrook Press (Ireland) *Tel:* (056) 63366 *Fax:* (056) 63388 *Web Site:* www.srhplc.com; www.kilkennypeople.ie, pg 1180

Kilkenny People/Wellbrook Press (Ireland) *Tel:* (056) 77 21015 *Fax:* (056) 77 21414 *E-mail:* info@kilkenny-people.ie *Web Site:* www.medialive.ie/press/provincial/kilkenny.html, pg 1220

Killara Press (Australia) *Tel:* (07) 5499-7717 *Fax:* (07) 4168-0244, pg 28

Kim Hup Lee Printing Co Pte Ltd (Singapore) *Tel:* 2833306 *Fax:* 2889222, pg 1161

Kima Global Publishers (South Africa) *Tel:* (021) 686-7154 *Fax:* (021) 686-9066 *E-mail:* info@kimaglobal.co.za *Web Site:* www.kimaglobal.co.za, pg 566

Kimberley Public Library (South Africa) *Tel:* (053) 8306241 *Fax:* (053) 8331954 *E-mail:* fritz@kbymun.org.za, pg 1544

Kimio Uitgeverij bv (Netherlands) *Tel:* (035) 6950760 *Fax:* (035) 6951548 *E-mail:* info@kimio.nl *Web Site:* www.kimio.nl, pg 484

Kin-No-Hoshi Sha Co Ltd (Japan) *Tel:* (03) 3861-1861 *Fax:* (03) 3861-1507 *E-mail:* gonta@kinnohoshi.co.jp *Web Site:* www.kinnohoshi.co.jp, pg 421

Kindai Kagaku Sha Co Ltd (Japan) *Tel:* (03) 3260-6160 *Fax:* (03) 3269-6060, pg 421

Kinderbuchfonds Baobab (Switzerland) *Tel:* (061) 3332727 *Fax:* (061) 3332726 *E-mail:* baobab@access.ch *Web Site:* www.baobabbooks.ch, pg 626

Kinderbuchverlag (Germany) *Tel:* (06201) 6007-0 *Fax:* (06201) 6007-310, pg 246

Kinderbuchverlag Luzern (Switzerland) *Tel:* (062) 836 86 50 *Fax:* (062) 836 86 56 *E-mail:* sauerlaender@sauerlaender.de *Web Site:* www.sauerlaender.ch, pg 626

Kindler Verlag AG (Switzerland) *Tel:* (01) 3633007, pg 626

King Abdulasiz University Library (Saudi Arabia) *Tel:* (02) 695 2068 *Fax:* (02) 640 0169 *E-mail:* library@kaau.edu.sa *Web Site:* www.kaau.edu.sa, pg 1541

King Abdulaziz Public Library (Saudi Arabia) *Tel:* (01) 4911300; (01) 4911304 *Fax:* (01) 4911949 *E-mail:* kapl@anet.net.sa, pg 1541

King Baudouin Foundation (Belgium) *Tel:* (02) 511 18 40 *Fax:* (02) 511 52 21 *E-mail:* proj@kbs-frb.be *Web Site:* www.kbs-frb.be, pg 69

King Fahad National Library (Saudi Arabia) *Web Site:* www.kfnl.gov.sa, pg 1541

King Faisal University Library (Saudi Arabia) *Tel:* (03) 8574456 *Fax:* (03) 8576748 *E-mail:* library@kfu.edu.sa *Web Site:* www.kfu.edu.sa, pg 1541

Hilda King Educational (United Kingdom) *Tel:* (01494) 813947; (01494) 817947 *Fax:* (01494) 813947 *E-mail:* hildaking@clara.co.uk; orders@hilda-king.co.uk *Web Site:* www.hildaking.clara.net, pg 717

Laurence King Publishing Ltd (United Kingdom) *Tel:* (020) 7430 8850 *Fax:* (020) 7430 8880 *E-mail:* info@laurenceking.co.uk *Web Site:* www.laurenceking.co.uk, pg 717

King Saud University (Saudi Arabia) *Tel:* (01) 4672832 *Fax:* (01) 4672894 *Web Site:* www.ksu.edu.sa, pg 550

King Saud University Library (Saudi Arabia) *Tel:* (01) 4676148 *Fax:* (01) 4676162 *Web Site:* www.ksu.edu.sa, pg 1541

Kingfisher Books (Australia) *Tel:* (03) 9819 9100 *Fax:* (03) 9819 0977, pg 28

Kingfisher Publications Plc (United Kingdom) *Tel:* (020) 7903 9999 *Fax:* (020) 7242 5009 *E-mail:* rights@kingfisherpub.com *Web Site:* www.kingfisherpub.com, pg 717

King's Fund Publishing (United Kingdom) *Tel:* (020) 7307 2400 *Fax:* (020) 7307 2801 *E-mail:* libweb@kingsfund.org.uk *Web Site:* www.kingsfund.org.uk, pg 718

Kingsclear Books (Australia) *Tel:* (02) 95574367 *Fax:* (02) 95572337 *E-mail:* kingsclear@wr.com.au *Web Site:* www.kingsclearbooks.com.au, pg 28

Jessica Kingsley Publishers (United Kingdom) *Tel:* (020) 7833 2307 *Fax:* (020) 7837 2917 *E-mail:* post@jkp.com *Web Site:* www.jkp.com, pg 718

Kingston Bookshop Ltd (Jamaica) *Tel:* 876-938-0005 *E-mail:* info@kingstonbookshop.com *Web Site:* www.kingstonbookshop.com, pg 1321

Kingstons Ltd (Zimbabwe) *Tel:* (04) 750547; (04) 750548; (04) 750549; (04) 750550 *Fax:* (04) 775533, pg 1356

Kingsway Publications (United Kingdom) *Tel:* (01323) 437700 *Fax:* (01323) 411970 *E-mail:* books@kingsway.co.uk *Web Site:* www.kingsway.co.uk, pg 718

Kinokuniya Co Ltd (Japan) *Tel:* (03) 3354-0141 *Fax:* (03) 3439-3955 *E-mail:* info@kinokuniya.co.jp *Web Site:* www.kinokuniya.co.jp, pg 1322

Kinokuniya Co Ltd (Publishing Department) (Japan) *Tel:* (03) 5469-5919 *Fax:* (03) 5469-5958 *E-mail:* publish@kinokuniya.co.jp; info@kinokuniya.co.jp *Web Site:* www.kinokuniya.co.jp, pg 421

Kinpodo (Japan) *Tel:* (075) 751-1111 *Fax:* (075) 751-6858 *E-mail:* kkinpodo@kb3.so-net.ne.jp, pg 421

Kinta CV (Indonesia) *Tel:* (021) 5494751, pg 355

KINZAI Corporation (Japan) *Tel:* (03) 33580011 *Fax:* (03) 33580036 *Web Site:* www.kinzai.or.jp, pg 421

Kipling Society (United Kingdom) *Tel:* (020) 7286 0194 *Fax:* (020) 7286 0194 *Web Site:* www.kipling.org.uk, pg 1408

Kirby Book Co Pty Ltd (Australia) *Tel:* (02) 9698 2377 *Toll Free Tel:* 800 225271 *Fax:* (02) 9698 8748, pg 1299

Peter Kirchheim Verlag (Germany) *Tel:* (089) 267474 *Fax:* (089) 2605528 *E-mail:* info@kirchheimverlag.de *Web Site:* www.kirchheimverlag.de, pg 246

Kirja-Leitzinger (Finland) *Tel:* (09) 588 3377 *Fax:* (09) 588 3373 *E-mail:* leitzinger@luukku.com, pg 142

Kirjakauppaliitto Ry (Finland) *Tel:* (09) 6859 9110; (050) 540 6451 *Fax:* (09) 6859 9119 *E-mail:* toimisto@kirjakauppaliitto.fi *Web Site:* www.kirjakauppaliitto.fi, pg 1266

Kirjallisuudentutkijain Seura (Finland) *Tel:* (09) 19122658 *Fax:* (09) 19123008 *Web Site:* www.helsinki.fi/jarj/skts, pg 1399

Kirjastus Kunst (Estonia) *Tel:* 6411764; 6411766 *Fax:* 6411762 *E-mail:* kunst.myyk@mail.ee *Web Site:* www.kirjastused.com/kunst, pg 139

Kirjatoimi (Finland) *Tel:* (03) 360 0000 *Fax:* (03) 360 0454 *E-mail:* kirjatoimi@sdafin.org, pg 142

Kirjayhtyma Oy (Finland) *Tel:* (09) 6937641 *Fax:* (09) 69376366 *E-mail:* oppimateriaauit@tammi.net, pg 142

Kirschbaum Verlag GmbH (Germany) *Tel:* (0228) 9 54 53-0 *Fax:* (0228) 9 54 53-27 *E-mail:* info@kirschbaum.de *Web Site:* www.kirschbaum.de, pg 246

Kiryat Sefer (Israel) *Tel:* (03) 5178922 *Fax:* (03) 5100227, pg 369

Kisambo Publishers Ltd (United Republic of Tanzania) *Tel:* (051) 114876; (051) 131382 *Fax:* (051) 112351, pg 643

KIT - Royal Tropical Institute Publishers (Netherlands) *Tel:* (020) 5688 272 *Fax:* (020) 5688 286 *E-mail:* publishers@kit.nl *Web Site:* www.kit.nl/publishers, pg 484

Kitab Ghar (India) *Tel:* (011) 213206, pg 339

KITLV Press Royal Institute of Linguistics & Anthropology (Netherlands) *Tel:* (071) 5272295 *Fax:* (071) 5272638 *E-mail:* kitlvpress@kitlv.nl *Web Site:* www.iias.leidenuniv.nl/institutes/kitlv, pg 484

Kitwe Public Library (Zambia) *Tel:* (02) 226162; (02) 221001; (02) 222927 *Fax:* (02) 224698, pg 1556

Kivukoni College Library (United Republic of Tanzania) *Tel:* (051) 820047, pg 1549

Kivunim-Arsan Publishing House (Israel) *Tel:* (08) 9470791 *Fax:* (08) 9469740, pg 369

Kiyi Yayinlari (Turkey) *Tel:* (0212) 245 58 45 *Fax:* (0212) 245 40 09 *E-mail:* sbeygu@ibm.net *Web Site:* www.kiyi.net, pg 650

KJK-Kerszov (Hungary) *Tel:* (01) 464-5656 *Fax:* (01) 464-5657 *E-mail:* complex@kjk-kerszov.hu *Web Site:* www.kerszov.hu, pg 322

Klages-Verlag (Germany) *Tel:* (0511) 5358936 *Fax:* (0511) 5358928 *E-mail:* kv@lsz.de, pg 246

Klaipedos Universiteto Leidykla (Lithuania) *Tel:* (06) 398890 *Fax:* (06) 398999 *E-mail:* leidykla@ku.lt *Web Site:* www.ku.lt, pg 449

Klang Withaya Publisher (Thailand) *Tel:* (02) 2224546; (02) 2219331, pg 645

Klartext Verlagsgesellschaft mbH (Germany) *Tel:* (0201) 86 206-0 *Fax:* (0201) 86 206-22 *E-mail:* info@klartext-verlag.de *Web Site:* www.klartext-verlag.de, pg 246

Klassikerforlaget (Sweden) *Tel:* (08) 457 03 00 *Fax:* (08) 457 03 34 *E-mail:* klassikerforlaget@raben.se, pg 613

Kleidarithmos, Ekdoseis (Greece) *Tel:* (01) 3832044, pg 309

Ingrid Anna Kleihues Verlags und Autorenagentur (Germany) *Tel:* (0711) 6788800 *Fax:* (0711) 6788801 *E-mail:* info@agentur-kleihues.de, pg 1131

Ingrid Klein Verlag GmbH (Germany) *Tel:* (089) 3818010 *Fax:* (089) 338704 *E-mail:* info@piper.de *Web Site:* www.piper.de, pg 246

Verlag Kleine Schritte Ursula Dahm & Co (Germany) *Tel:* (0651) 300 698 *Fax:* (0651) 300 699 *E-mail:* mail@kleine-schritte.de *Web Site:* www.kleine-schritte.de, pg 246

Kleiner Bachmann Verlag fur Kinder und Umwelt (Germany) *Tel:* (02205) 904-79 51 *Fax:* (02205) 910 855 *E-mail:* buch@kleinerbachmann.de *Web Site:* www.kleinerbachmann.de, pg 246

Unterwegs Verlag, Manfred Klemann (Germany) *Tel:* (07731) 63544 *Fax:* (07731) 62401 *E-mail:* uv@reisefuehrer.com *Web Site:* www.reisefuehrer.com, pg 246

Forlaget Klematis A/S (Denmark) *Tel:* 86175455 *Fax:* 86175959 *E-mail:* klematis@klematis.dk; production@klematis.dk *Web Site:* www.klematis.dk, pg 132

Klens Verlag GmbH (Germany) *Tel:* (0211) 944794-0 *Fax:* (0211) 944794-30 *E-mail:* info@klensverlag.de, pg 246

Verlag Klett-Cotta (Germany) *Tel:* (0711) 6672-1256 *Fax:* (0711) 6672-2031 *E-mail:* info@klett-cotta.de *Web Site:* www.klett-cotta.de, pg 246

Ernst Klett Verlag GmbH (Germany) *Tel:* (0711) 66 720 *Fax:* (0711) 66 72-20 00 *E-mail:* klett-kundenservice@klett-mail.de *Web Site:* www.klett-verlag.de, pg 247

Klett und Balmer & Co Verlag (Switzerland) *Tel:* (041) 726 28 00 *Fax:* (041) 726 28 01 *E-mail:* info@klett.ch *Web Site:* www.klett.ch, pg 626

Kley, Werner, Beteiligungs GmbH (Germany) *Tel:* (02381) 95040-0 *Fax:* (02381) 9504019, pg 247

Kliemand Verlag (Liechtenstein) *Tel:* 2321048, pg 448

Johann Kliment KG Musikverlag (Austria) *Tel:* (01) 317 51 47 *Fax:* (01) 310 08 27 *E-mail:* office@kliment.at *Web Site:* www.kliment.at, pg 53

Narodna i univerzitetska biblioteka Kliment Ohrìdski (The Former Yugoslav Republic of Macedonia) *Tel:* (02) 3115 177; (02) 3133 418 *Fax:* (02) 3226 846 *E-mail:* kliment@nubsk.edu.mk *Web Site:* www.nubsk.edu.mk, pg 1526

Editions Klincksieck (France) *Tel:* (01) 43.54.59.53 *Fax:* (01) 43.25.25.53, pg 170

Von Kloeden KG (Germany) *Tel:* (030) 887 125 18 *Fax:* (030) 887 125 19 *E-mail:* vkloeden@t-online.de *Web Site:* www.vonkloeden.de, pg 1311

Erika Klopp Verlag GmbH (Germany) *Tel:* (040) 60790907 *Fax:* (040) 60790959 *E-mail:* klopp@vsg-hamburg.de *Web Site:* www.erika-klopp.de; www.klopp.biz, pg 247

Klosterhaus-Verlagsbuchhandlung Dr Grimm KG (Germany) *Tel:* (05572) 7310 *Fax:* (05572) 999823, pg 247

Vittorio Klostermann GmbH (Germany) *Tel:* (069) 97 08 16-0 *Fax:* (069) 70 80 38 *E-mail:* verlag@klostermann.de *Web Site:* www.klostermann.de, pg 247

Walter Klugel (Austria) *Tel:* (0222) 573 03 42, pg 1300

Uitgeverij Kluitman Alkmaar BV (Netherlands) *Tel:* (072) 52 75 075 *Fax:* (072) 52 09 400 *E-mail:* webmaster@kluitman.nl *Web Site:* www.kluitman.nl, pg 484

Kluwer Academic/Plenum Publishers (United Kingdom) *Tel:* (020) 7863 3000 *Fax:* (020) 7863 3314 *E-mail:* mail@plenum.co.uk *Web Site:* www.wkap.nl, pg 718

Kluwer Academic Publishers (Netherlands) *Tel:* (078) 657 6000 *Fax:* (078) 657 6254, pg 484

Kluwer Bedrijfswetenschappen (Netherlands) *Tel:* (0570) 647111 *Fax:* (0570) 638040, pg 485

Kluwer Law International (Netherlands) *Tel:* (070) 308 1500 *Fax:* (070) 308 1515, pg 485

Kluwer Technische Boeken BV (Netherlands) *Tel:* (0570) 647111 *Fax:* (0570) 638040, pg 485

KM C (Czech Republic) *Tel:* (02) 24810704; (02) 2311156; (02) 2314289 *Fax:* (02) 24810850, pg 1251

Verlag Fritz Knapp GmbH (Germany) *Tel:* (069) 97 08 33-0 *Fax:* (069) 7 07 84 00 *E-mail:* info@kreditwesen.de *Web Site:* www.kreditwesen.de, pg 247

Horst Knapp Finanznachrichten (Austria) *Tel:* (01) 7154460-0 *Fax:* (01) 7154460-22, pg 53

Albrecht Knaus Verlag GmbH (Germany) *Tel:* (089) 9984010 *Fax:* (089) 99840144, pg 247

Knesebeck Verlag (Germany) *Tel:* (089) 264059 *Fax:* (089) 269258 *E-mail:* sekretariat@knesebeck-verlag.de *Web Site:* www.knesebeck-verlag.de, pg 247

Knesset Library (Israel) *Tel:* (02) 6753246; (02) 6496043 *Fax:* (02) 662733 *E-mail:* sifria2@netvision.net.il *Web Site:* www.knesset.gov.il, pg 1519

KNI Inc (United States) *Tel:* 714-956-7300 *Toll Free Tel:* 800-886-7301 *Fax:* 714-635-1744 *E-mail:* kni@kniinc.com *Web Site:* www.kniinc.com, pg 1167, 1230

Izdatelstvo Kniga (Russian Federation) *Tel:* (095) 2516003 *Fax:* (095) 2500489, pg 545

Knight Features (United Kingdom) *Tel:* (020) 7622 1467 *Fax:* (020) 7622 1522 *E-mail:* gaby@knightfeatures.co.uk, pg 1141

Knihkupectvi - Antikvariat Galerie (Czech Republic) *Tel:* (0417) 537 370 *Fax:* (0417) 537 370 *E-mail:* kniha.ln@antikteplice.cz; kniha.ln@worldonline.cz *Web Site:* www.antikteplice.cz/, pg 1308

Knihovna A Tiskarna Pro Nevidome (Czech Republic) *Tel:* (02) 22 21 04 92; (02) 22 21 15 23 *Fax:* (02) 22 21 04 94 *E-mail:* ktn@ktn.cz *Web Site:* www.ktn.cz, pg 124

Knihovna Narodniho muzea (Czech Republic) *Tel:* (02) 24497111 *Fax:* (02) 24497331 *E-mail:* nm@nm.cz *Web Site:* www.nm.cz, pg 1501

Izdatelstvo Knizhnaya Palata (Russian Federation) *Tel:* (095) 2889247 *Fax:* (095) 1635827, pg 546

Univerzitna Kniznica (Slovakia) *Tel:* (02) 59 804 100 *Fax:* (02) 54 434 246 *E-mail:* ukb@ulib.sk *Web Site:* www.ulib.sk, pg 1542

Tehnicka Knjiga (Serbia and Montenegro) *Tel:* (011) 468 596 *Fax:* (011) 473 442 *E-mail:* tknjiga@eunet.yu *Web Site:* www.tehknjiga.co.yu, pg 552

Knjizevni Krug Split (Croatia) *Tel:* (021) 342 226; (021) 361 081 *Fax:* (021) 342 226 *E-mail:* bratislav.lucin@public.srce.hr, pg 118

Knockabout Comics (United Kingdom) *Tel:* (020) 8969 2945 *Fax:* (020) 8968 7614 *E-mail:* knockcomic@aol.com *Web Site:* www.knockabout.com, pg 718

Doris Knop-Verlag (Germany) *Tel:* (0421) 9885030 *Fax:* (0421) 3509628, pg 247

Knossos Publications (Greece) *Tel:* (01) 3810108; (01) 3804681 *Fax:* (01) 3804681, pg 309

Knowledge Book House (Myanmar) *Tel:* (01) 290927, pg 1328

Knowledge Media International (Germany) *Tel:* (089) 4136-8433 *Fax:* (089) 4136-8411 *Web Site:* www.k-m-i.com, pg 247

Knowledge Press (China) *Tel:* (010) 68315610 *Fax:* (010) 68316510 *E-mail:* ecphtdb@public3.bta.net.cn, pg 106

Knowledge Press & Bookhouse (Myanmar) *Tel:* (01) 290927, pg 475

Verlag Knut Reim, Jugendpresseverlag (Germany) *Tel:* (040) 34 26 41 *Fax:* (040) 34 46 87, pg 247

Koala-Kustannus Oy (Finland) *Tel:* (050) 408 1590 *Fax:* (09) 6845034 *E-mail:* info@koalakustannus.fi *Web Site:* www.koalakustannus.fi, pg 143

Kobenhavns Kommunes Biblioteker (Denmark) *Tel:* 33664650 *Fax:* 33667061 *E-mail:* kkb@kkb.bib.dk *Web Site:* www.kkb.bib.dk/, pg 1502

Kobenhavns Stadsarkiv (Denmark) *Tel:* 33662370 *Fax:* 33667039 *E-mail:* stadsarkiv@kff.kk.dk *Web Site:* www.ksa.kk.dk, pg 1502

Kober Verlag Bern AG (Switzerland) *Tel:* (031) 9714687 *E-mail:* koberpress@mindspring.com *Web Site:* www.kober.com/kvb.htm, pg 626

Verlagsanstalt Alexander Koch GmbH (Germany) *Tel:* (0711) 7591-0 *Fax:* (0711) 7591-380 *Web Site:* www.koch-verlag.de, pg 247

Koch, Neff und Oetinger & Co (Germany) *Tel:* (0711) 78600 *Fax:* (0711) 78602800 *Web Site:* www.buchkatalog.de, pg 1311

Kochbuch Verlag Olga Leeb (Germany) *Tel:* (089) 58998303; (089) 583094 *Fax:* (089) 560208; (089) 58995303, pg 247

Kodansha Disney Children's Book Club (Japan) *Tel:* (03) 3946-6201 *Fax:* (03) 3944-9915 *Web Site:* www.kodansha.co.jp; www.kodanclub.com, pg 1254

Kodansha International Ltd (Japan) *Tel:* (03) 39446491 *Fax:* (03) 39446394 *E-mail:* sales@kodansha-intl.co.jp *Web Site:* www.thejapanpage.com; www.kodansha-intl.co.jp, pg 421

Kodansha Ltd (Japan) *Tel:* (03) 5395-3420 (foreign rights dept) *Fax:* (03) 3942-8017 (foreign rights dept) *Web Site:* www.kodansha.co.jp, pg 421

Kodansha Scientific Ltd (Japan) *Tel:* (03) 5395 3420 *Fax:* (03) 3942 8017, pg 421

Koehler & Amelang Verlagsgesellschaft (Germany) *Tel:* (089) 455 54-0 *Fax:* (089) 455 54-100 *E-mail:* buch@dva.de *Web Site:* www.dva.de, pg 248

Eric Koehler (France) *Tel:* (01) 49 27 06 37; (01) 44 55 37 50 *Fax:* (01) 47 03 39 86; (01) 40 20 99 74, pg 170

K F Koehler Verlag GmbH (Germany) *Tel:* (0711) 7892 130; (0711) 7892 149 *Fax:* (0711) 7892 132 *E-mail:* info@kfk.de; sabine.haegele@kfk.de *Web Site:* www.buchkatalog.de, pg 248

Verlagsgruppe Koehler/Mittler (Germany) *Tel:* (040) 7971303 *Fax:* (040) 79713324 *E-mail:* vertrieb@koehler-mittler.de *Web Site:* www.koehler-mittler.de, pg 248

Koehlers Verlagsgesellschaft mbH (Germany) *Tel:* (040) 79713-03 *Fax:* (040) 79713324 *E-mail:* vertrieb@koehler-mittler.de *Web Site:* www.koehler-mittler.de, pg 248

Koelner Universitaets-Verlag GmbH (Germany) *Tel:* (0221) 48 81-1 *Fax:* (0221) 49 81-533 *E-mail:* welcome@iwkoeln.de *Web Site:* www.iwkoeln.de, pg 248

Koenemann Verlagesellschaft mbH (Germany) *Tel:* (0221) 3799-0 *Fax:* (0221) 3799-88, pg 248

R Koenig GmbH (Germany) *Tel:* (089) 724970 *Fax:* (089) 7238813 *E-mail:* info@koenig-specials.com *Web Site:* www.koenig-specials.com, pg 248

Koenigsfurt Verlag, Evelin Buerger et Johannes Fiebig (Germany) *Tel:* (04334) 18 99 02; (04334) 18 22 010 *Fax:* (04334) 18 22 011 *E-mail:* info@koenigsfurt.com *Web Site:* www.koenigsfurt.com, pg 248

Verlag Koenigshausen und Neumann GmbH (Germany) *Tel:* (0931) 78 40-7 00 *E-mail:* info@koenigshausen-neumann.de *Web Site:* www.koenigshausen-neumann.de/, pg 248

Edition Koenigstein (Austria) *Tel:* (02243) 26046 *Fax:* (02243) 26046 *E-mail:* edition.koenigstein@aon.at *Web Site:* members.aon.at/edition_koenigstein, pg 53

Koenyveshaz Kft (Hungary) *Tel:* (01) 1311566 *Fax:* (01) 1311566, pg 322

Koepel van de Vlaamse Noord - Zuidbeweging 11.11.11 (Belgium) *Tel:* (02) 536-11-13 *Fax:* (02) 536-19-10 *E-mail:* info@11.be *Web Site:* www.11.be, pg 69

Lucy Koerner Verlag (Germany) *Tel:* (0711) 588472 *Fax:* (0711) 5789634, pg 248

Ute Koerner Literary Agent (Spain) *Tel:* (093) 4550414; (093) 4502588 *Fax:* (093) 4365548 *E-mail:* office@uklitag.com *Web Site:* www.uklitag.com, pg 1136

Verlag Valentin Koerner GmbH (Germany) *Tel:* (07221) 22423 *Fax:* (07221) 38697 *E-mail:* info@koernerverlag.de *Web Site:* www.koernerverlag.de/, pg 248

Koesel-Verlag GmbH & Co (Germany) *Tel:* (089) 17801-0 *Fax:* (089) 17801-111 *E-mail:* leserservice@koesel.de *Web Site:* www.koesel.de/, pg 248

Koesler Verlag GmbH (Germany) *Tel:* (02263) 951650 *Fax:* (02263) 951691, pg 248

Magyar Tudomanyos Akademia Koezponti Fizikai Kutato Intezet Koenyvtara (Hungary) *Tel:* (01) 1382344 (ext 44) *Fax:* (01) 1316954 *E-mail:* kolcs@sunserv.kfki.hu, pg 322

Koezponti Statisztikai Hivatal Koenyvtar es Dokumentacios Szolgalat (Hungary) *Tel:* (01) 3456105 *Fax:* (01) 3456112 *Web Site:* www.ksh.hu; www.lib.ksh.hu, pg 1514

Kogan Page Ltd (United Kingdom) *Tel:* (020) 7278 0433 *Fax:* (020) 7837 6348 *E-mail:* kpinfo@kogan-page.co.uk; kpsales@kogan-page.co.uk; orders@kogan-page.co.uk *Web Site:* www.kogan-page.co.uk, pg 718

Kogyo Chosakai Publishing Co Ltd (Japan) *Tel:* (03) 3817-4701 *Fax:* (03) 3817-4748 *E-mail:* m-order@po.iijnet.or.jp; rtb87919@mtd.biglobe.ne.jp *Web Site:* www.iijnet.or.jp/kocho, pg 421

W Kohlhammer GmbH (Germany) *Tel:* (0711) 7863-0 *Fax:* (0711) 7863-8204 *E-mail:* redaktion@kohlhammer.de *Web Site:* www.kohlhammer.de, pg 248

Koinonia Comunidade Edicoes Ltda (Editora Koinonia Ltda) (Brazil) *Tel:* (061) 322-4458 *Fax:* (061) 3228377, pg 84

Uitgeverij J H Kok BV (Netherlands) *Tel:* (038) 3392555 *Fax:* (038) 3311776 *E-mail:* algemeen@kok.nl *Web Site:* www.kok.nl, pg 485

Kok Yayincilik (Turkey) *Tel:* (0312) 4302622 *Fax:* (0312) 4350497 *E-mail:* kokbilgi@kokyayincilik.com.tr *Web Site:* www.kokyayincilik.com.tr, pg 650

Kokudo-Sha Co Ltd (Japan) *Tel:* (03) 3943-3721 *Fax:* (03) 3943-3740 *Web Site:* www.koutoku.co.jp/kokudosha, pg 421

Kokuritsu Kobunshokan (Japan) *Tel:* (03) 3214-0621 *Fax:* (03) 3212-8806 *Web Site:* www.archives.go.jp/index_e.html, pg 1521

Kokushokankokai Co Ltd (Japan) *Tel:* (03) 5970-7421 *Fax:* (03) 5970-7427 *E-mail:* info@kokusho.co.jp *Web Site:* www.kokusho.co.jp, pg 421

Kola Sanya Publishing Enterprise (Nigeria) *Tel:* (037) 432638, pg 505

Kolibri Forlag A/S (Norway) *Tel:* (022) 438778 *Fax:* (022) 447740 *E-mail:* post@kolibriforlag.no *Web Site:* www.kolibriforlag.no, pg 509

Kolibri Publishing Group (Bulgaria) *Tel:* (02) 988-87-81; (02) 955-84-81; (02) 955-91-990 *Fax:* (02) 813625 *E-mail:* colibri@inet.bg; colibry@bgnet.bg, pg 95

Kolibri-Verlag GmbH (Germany) *Tel:* (040) 2202243 *Fax:* (040) 2276368 *E-mail:* infos@kolibriverlag.de, pg 249

Kolumbus-Verlag (Switzerland) *Tel:* (064) 7711370, pg 626

Komine Shoten Co Ltd (Japan) *Tel:* (03) 3357-3521 *Fax:* (03) 3357-1027 *E-mail:* info@komineshoten.co.jp *Web Site:* www.komineshoten.co.jp, pg 421

Kommissionsverlag Leobuchhandling (Switzerland) *Tel:* (071) 222917 *Fax:* (071) 220587, pg 626

Kommunernes Skolebiblioteksforening (Denmark) *Tel:* 33111391 *Fax:* 33111390 *E-mail:* komskolbib@ksbf.dk *Web Site:* www.ksbf.dk, pg 1561

Kompass Fleischmann (Italy) *Tel:* (0461) 961240 *Fax:* (0461) 961203, pg 394

Izdatelskii Dom Kompozitor (Russian Federation) *Tel:* (095) 2092380; (095) 2094105 *Fax:* (095) 2095498 *E-mail:* music@sumail.ru, pg 546

Komputerowa Oficyna Wydawnicza Help (Poland) *Tel:* (022) 723 89 21 *Fax:* (022) 723 87 64 *E-mail:* kowhelp@pol.pl *Web Site:* www.besthelp.pl, pg 523

Wydawnictwa Komunikacji i Lacznosci Co Ltd (Poland) *Tel:* (022) 849 27 51 *Fax:* (022) 849 23 22 *E-mail:* wkl@wkl.com.pl *Web Site:* www.wkl.com.pl, pg 524

Konark Publishers Pvt Ltd (India) *Tel:* (011) 22504101; (011) 22455731; (011) 22507103 *Fax:* (011) 22507103 *E-mail:* kppl23@eth.net; konarkpublishers@hotmail.com, pg 339

Det Kongelige Bibliotek (Denmark) *Tel:* 33 47 47 47 *Fax:* 33 93 22 18 *E-mail:* kb@kb.dk *Web Site:* www.kb.dk, pg 1502

Det Kongelige Danske Videnskabernes Selskab (Denmark) *Tel:* 33435300 *Fax:* 33435301 *E-mail:* email@royalacademy.dk *Web Site:* www.royalacademy.dk, pg 1398

Konias (Czech Republic) *Tel:* (019) 28 06 90 *Fax:* (019) 28 06 90 *E-mail:* konias@literaplzen.cz, pg 124

Koninklijke Academie voor Nederlandse Taal- en Letterkunde (Belgium) *Tel:* (09) 265 93 40 *Fax:* (09) 265 93 49 *E-mail:* info@kantl.be *Web Site:* www.kantl.be, pg 1397

Koninklijke Academie voor Wetenschappen Letteren en Schone Kunsten Van Belgie (Belgium) *Tel:* (02) 550 23 23 *Fax:* (02) 550 23 25 *E-mail:* info@kvab.be *Web Site:* www.kvab.be, pg 1397

Koninklijke Bibliotheek (Netherlands) *Tel:* (070) 3140911 *Fax:* (070) 3140450 *E-mail:* info@kb.nl *Web Site:* www.kb.nl, pg 1531

Koninklijke Vermande bv (Netherlands) *Tel:* (070) 3789880 *Fax:* (070) 3789783 *E-mail:* sdu@sdu.nl *Web Site:* www.sdu.nl/uitg/vermande, pg 485

Koninklijke Vlaamse Academie van Belgie voor Wetenschappen en Kunsten (Belgium) *Tel:* (02) 550 23 23 *Fax:* (02) 550 23 25 *E-mail:* info@kvab.be *Web Site:* www.kvab.be, pg 69

Konkordia Verlag GmbH (Germany) *Tel:* (07223) 98 89-0 *Fax:* (07223) 98 89-45 *E-mail:* verlag@konkordia.de *Web Site:* www.konkordia.de, pg 249

Konkret Literatur Verlag (Germany) *Tel:* (040) 47 52 34 *Fax:* (040) 47 84 15 *E-mail:* info@konkret-literatur-verlag.de *Web Site:* www.konkret-verlage.de, pg 249

Anton H Konrad Verlag (Germany) *Tel:* (07309) 26 57 *Fax:* (07309) 60 69 *E-mail:* info@konrad-verlag.de *Web Site:* www.konrad-verlag.de/, pg 249

Konradin-Verlagsgruppe (Germany) *Tel:* (0711) 7594-0 *Fax:* (0711) 7594-390 *E-mail:* info@konradin.de *Web Site:* www.konradin.de, pg 249

Universitat Konstanz (Germany) *Tel:* (07531) 88-0 *Fax:* (07531) 88-3688 *E-mail:* Posteingang@uni-konstanz.de *Web Site:* www.uni-konstanz.de, pg 1509

Konsultace spol sro (Czech Republic) *Tel:* (02) 2310363 *Fax:* (02) 2310363, pg 125

Konsultforlaget AB (Sweden) *Tel:* (018) 55 50 80 *Fax:* (018) 55 50 81 *E-mail:* info@uppsala-publishing.se *Web Site:* www.uppsala-publishing.se, pg 613

KONTEXTverlag (Germany) *Tel:* (030) 94415444 *Fax:* (030) 94415445 *E-mail:* service@kontextverlag.de *Web Site:* www.kontextverlag.de, pg 249

Kookaburra Technical Publications Pty Ltd (Australia) *Tel:* (03) 9560 0841 *Fax:* (03) 9545 1121 *Web Site:* members.dcsi.net.au/jtboundy/hkookafo.htm, pg 28

Koolibri (Estonia) *Tel:* 651 5300 *Fax:* 651 5301 *E-mail:* koolibri@koolibri.ee *Web Site:* www.koolibri.ee, pg 139

Koorong Books Pty Ltd (Australia) *Tel:* (02) 9857 4477 *Fax:* (02) 9857 4499 *E-mail:* west_ryde@koorong.com.au; koorong@koorong.com.au *Web Site:* www.koorong.com.au, pg 1299

kopaed verlagsgmbh (Germany) *Tel:* (089) 68890098 *Fax:* (089) 6891912 *E-mail:* info@kopaed.de *Web Site:* www.kopaed.de, pg 249

Koptisch-Orthodoxes Zentrum (Germany) *Tel:* (06085) 23 17 *Fax:* (06085) 26 66 *E-mail:* jugend@kopten.de *Web Site:* www.kopten.de, pg 249

Editions Buma Kor & Co Ltd (Cameroon) *Tel:* (023) 22 48 99 *Fax:* (023) 23 29 03, pg 98

Korea Britannica Corp (Republic of Korea) *Tel:* (02) 2272-9731; (02) 2264-0924 (sales) *Fax:* (02) 2278-9983 *E-mail:* corporate@britannica.co.kr *Web Site:* www.britannica.co.kr, pg 440

Korea Development Institute Library (Republic of Korea) *Tel:* (02) 958 4266 *Fax:* (02) 958 4261 *E-mail:* library@kdi.re.kr *Web Site:* www.kdi.re.kr, pg 1523

Korea Local Authorities Foundation for International Relations (Republic of Korea) *Tel:* (02) 730 2711; (02) 2170-6098 *Fax:* (02) 737 8970; (02) 737-7903 *E-mail:* others@klafir.or.kr *Web Site:* www.klafir.or.kr/, pg 440

Korea Psychological Testing Institute (Republic of Korea) *Tel:* (02) 784-0990 *Fax:* (02) 784-0993 *E-mail:* KPIT@unitel.co.kr *Web Site:* www.kpti.com, pg 440

Korea Publications Export & Import Corporation (Democratic People's Republic of Korea) *Tel:* (02) 3818536 *Fax:* (02) 3814404, pg 1324

Korea Science and Encyclopedia Publishing House (Democratic People's Republic of Korea) *Tel:* (02) 381 8091 (Call between 18 & 21 hours Pyongyang local time, Mon, Wed & Fri only) *Fax:* (02) 381 4550 (24 hours), pg 436

Korea Textbook Co Ltd (Republic of Korea) *Tel:* (02) 465-1341 *Fax:* (02) 464-1318 *E-mail:* kpp0114@hanmail.net, pg 440

Korea University Library (Republic of Korea) *Tel:* 23 290 1499 *Fax:* 23 234 763 *E-mail:* unneu@korea.ac.kr *Web Site:* library.korea.ac.kr, pg 1523

Korea University Press (Republic of Korea) *Tel:* (02) 3290 4231 *Fax:* (02) 923 6311, pg 440

Korean Library Association (KLA) (Republic of Korea) *Tel:* (02) 5354868 *Fax:* (02) 5355616 *E-mail:* klanet@hitel.net *Web Site:* www.korla.or.kr, pg 1566

Korean PEN Centre (Republic of Korea) *Tel:* (02) 782 1337; (02) 782 1338 *Fax:* (02) 786 1090 *E-mail:* penkon2001@yahoo.co.kr, pg 1402

Korean Publishers Association (Republic of Korea) *Tel:* (02) 735-2701; (02) 735-2704 *Fax:* (02) 738-5414 *E-mail:* kpa@kpa21.or.kr *Web Site:* www.kpa21.or.kr, pg 440, 1276

Korean Publishing Research Institute (Republic of Korea) *Tel:* (02) 7399040 *Fax:* (02) 7376187 *E-mail:* p715@chollian.net, pg 1276

Korean Research & Development Library Association (KORDELA) (Republic of Korea) *Tel:* (02) 9673692 *Fax:* (02) 29634013, pg 1566

Koreaone Press Inc (Republic of Korea) *Tel:* (02) 739-1156 *Fax:* (02) 734-3512, pg 440

Koren Publishers Jerusalem Ltd (Israel) *Tel:* (02) 5660188 *Fax:* (02) 5666658 *Web Site:* www.koren-publishers.co.il, pg 369

Galerie Kornfeld & Co (Switzerland) *Tel:* (031) 381 46 73 *Fax:* (031) 382 18 91 *E-mail:* galerie@kornfeld.ch *Web Site:* www.kornfeld.ch, pg 627

Kosei Publishing Co Ltd (Japan) *Tel:* (03) 5385-2319 *Fax:* (03) 5385-2331 *Web Site:* www.kosei-shuppan.co.jp/english/, pg 421

Koseisha-Koseikaku Co Ltd (Japan) *Tel:* (03) 3359-7371 *Fax:* (03) 3359-7375 *E-mail:* koseisha@po.iijnet.or.jp *Web Site:* www.vinet.or.jp/~koseisha; www.kouseisha.com, pg 422

Kosik (Czech Republic) *Tel:* (02) 670929 *Fax:* (02) 2359403, pg 125

Verlag A F Koska (Austria) *Tel:* (0222) 5874344, pg 53

Kossodo Verlag AG (Switzerland) *Tel:* (022) 962230, pg 627

Kossuth Kiado RT (Hungary) *Tel:* (01) 3700607 *Fax:* (01) 3700602 *E-mail:* rt@kossuted.hu *Web Site:* www.kossuth.hu, pg 322

Kossuth Lajos Tudomanyegyetem Egyetemi Koenyvtar (Hungary) *Tel:* (052) 316-835; (052) 316-666; (052) 512-900 *Fax:* (052) 410-443 *E-mail:* comp@lib.unidebu.hu *Web Site:* www.lib.unidebu.hu, pg 1514

Kotuku Media Ltd (New Zealand) *Tel:* (04) 2331842 *E-mail:* kotuku.media@xtra.co.nz, pg 497

Dr Anton Kovac Slavica Verlag (Germany) *Tel:* (089) 2725612 *Fax:* (089) 2716594 *E-mail:* 101566.2450@compuserve.com, pg 249

Roman Kovar Verlag (Germany) *Tel:* (08206) 961977 *Fax:* (08206) 961978 *E-mail:* romankovar@gmx.net *Web Site:* www.kovar-verlag.com, pg 249

Kowhai Publishing Ltd (New Zealand) *Tel:* (09) 5759126 *Fax:* (09) 5753178, pg 497

Koyo Shobo (Japan) *Tel:* (075) 312-0788 *Fax:* (075) 312-7447, pg 422

KPI (Indonesia) *Tel:* (021) 361701; (021) 41701, pg 1253

KPT InfoTrader Inc (Japan) *Tel:* (06) 6479 7160 *Fax:* (06) 6479 7163 *E-mail:* osaka@infotrader.jp, pg 1322

Verlag Karl Kraemer & Co (Switzerland) *Tel:* (01) 2528454 *Fax:* (0711) 784960 (Germany) *E-mail:* info@kraemerverlag.com *Web Site:* www.kraemerverlag.com, pg 627

Karl Kraemer Verlag GmbH und Co (Germany) *Tel:* (0711) 7 84 96-0 *Fax:* (0711) 7 84 96-20 *E-mail:* info@kraemerverlag.com *Web Site:* www.kraemerverlag.com, pg 249

Reinhold Kraemer Verlag (Germany) *Tel:* (040) 4101429 *Fax:* (040) 455770 *E-mail:* info@kraemer-verlag.de *Web Site:* www.kraemer-verlag.de, pg 249

Adam Kraft Verlag (Germany) *Tel:* (0931) 385235 *Fax:* (0931) 385305 *E-mail:* info@verlagshaus.com *Web Site:* www.verlagshaus.com, pg 250

Krafthand Verlag Walter Schultz GmbH (Germany) *Tel:* (08247) 30070 *Fax:* (08247) 300770 *E-mail:* info@krafthand.de *Web Site:* www.krafthand.de, pg 250

Verlag Edition Kraftpunkt Anton Fedrigotti (Germany) *Tel:* (0821) 705011 *Fax:* (0821) 705008, pg 250

Krajowe Biuro Miedzynarodowego Numeru Ksiazki ISBN (Poland) *Tel:* (022) 608-2410; (022) 608-2433 *Fax:* (022) 608-2433 *E-mail:* bnisbn@bn.org.pl *Web Site:* www.bn.org.pl, pg 1281

Kraks Forlag AS (Denmark) *Tel:* 95 65 00 *Fax:* 95 65 55 *E-mail:* krak@krak.dk *Web Site:* www.krak.dk, pg 132

Kralica MAB (Bulgaria) *Tel:* (02) 767357 *Fax:* (02) 767357 *E-mail:* mab@slovar.org *Web Site:* www.slovar.org/mab, pg 95

Kramds-reklama Publishing & Advertising (Kazakstan) *Tel:* (03272) 453968 *Fax:* (03272) 696753, pg 432

Karin Kramer Verlag (Germany) *Tel:* (030) 6845055; (030) 6842598 *Fax:* (030) 6858577 *E-mail:* kramer@virtualitas.com *Web Site:* www.anares.org/kramer/, pg 250

Verlag Rene Kramer AG (Switzerland) *Tel:* (091) 518941, pg 627

Verlag Waldemar Kramer (Germany) *Tel:* (069) 449045 *Fax:* (069) 449064 *E-mail:* info@frankfurtbuecher.de *Web Site:* www.frankfurtbuecher.de, pg 250

Kranich-Verlag, Dres AG & H R Bosch-Gwalter (Switzerland) *Tel:* (01) 3918484 *Fax:* (01) 3920884 *E-mail:* boschag@zik.ch, pg 627

Nara Verlag Josef Krauthaeuser (Germany) *Tel:* (08166) 8530; (08166) 8531 *Fax:* (08166) 8530 *E-mail:* info@nara-verlag.de *Web Site:* www.nara-international.de; www.nara-verlag.de, pg 250

Kremayr & Scheriau Verlag (Austria) *Tel:* (01) 713 8770-10 *Fax:* (01)713 8770-20 *E-mail:* m.scheriau@kremayr-scheriau.at, pg 53

Hubert Kretschmar Leipziger Verlagsgesellschaft (Germany) *Tel:* (0341) 2210229 *Fax:* (0341) 2210226, pg 250

Verlag Hubert Kretschmer (Germany) *Tel:* (089) 1234530 *Fax:* (089) 1238638 *E-mail:* hubert.kretschmer@t-online.de *Web Site:* www.verlag-hubert-kretschmer.de, pg 250

Kreuz Verlag GmbH & Co KG (Germany) *Tel:* (0711) 788030 *Fax:* (0711) 7880310 *E-mail:* service@kreuzverlag.de *Web Site:* www.kreuzverlag.de, pg 1311

Svet Kridel (Czech Republic) *Tel:* (0166) 43475 *Fax:* (0166) 23395, pg 125

Kriebel Verlag GmbH (Germany) *Tel:* (08806) 93 60 *Fax:* (08806) 93 61 *E-mail:* info@kriebelverlag.de *Web Site:* www.kriebel-sat.de; www.kriebelverlag.de, pg 250

Antiquariat Walter Krieg Verlag (Austria) *Tel:* (01) 5121093 *Fax:* (01) 5123266, pg 1300

De Krijger (Belgium) *Tel:* (053) 808449 *Fax:* (053) 808453 *E-mail:* de.krijger@primemedia.be, pg 69

Krishnamurthy K (India) *Tel:* (044) 2434 4519 *Fax:* (044) 2434 2009 *E-mail:* ksm@md2.vsnl.net.in; service@kkbooks.com *Web Site:* www.kkbooks.com, pg 1316

Kristen Press (Papua New Guinea) *Tel:* 8522988 *Fax:* 823313, pg 515

Kristiansand Folkebibliotek (Norway) *Tel:* (038) 12 49 10 *Fax:* (038) 12 49 49 *E-mail:* kristiansand.folkebibliotek@kristiansand.kommune.no *Web Site:* www.kristiansand.kommune.no, pg 1534

Editura Kriterion SA (Romania) *Tel:* (01) 3366509 *Fax:* (01) 313 11 07 *E-mail:* krit@dnt.ro; kriterion@mail.dnt.cj.ro, pg 540

Kritiki (Greece) *Tel:* (0210) 3803730 *Fax:* (01) 3803740 *E-mail:* biblia@kritiki.gr *Web Site:* www.kritiki.gr, pg 1313

Kritiki Publishing (Greece) *Tel:* (0210) 3803730 *Fax:* (01) 3803740 *E-mail:* biblia@kritiki.gr *Web Site:* www.kritiki.gr, pg 309

Alfred Kroner Verlag (Germany) *Tel:* (0711) 6155363 *Fax:* (0711) 61553646 *E-mail:* kontak@kroener-verlag.de *Web Site:* www.kroener-verlag.de, pg 250

Krscanska sadasnjost (Croatia) *Tel:* (01) 48 28 219; (01) 48 28 222 *Fax:* (01) 48 28 227 *E-mail:* ks@zg.tel.hr *Web Site:* www.ks.hr, pg 118

Krueger Verlag GmbH (Germany) *Tel:* (069) 6062-0 *Fax:* (069) 6062-352 *Web Site:* www.krueger-verlag.de, pg 250

Krug & Schadenberg (Germany) *Tel:* (030) 61625752 *Fax:* (030) 61625751 *E-mail:* info@krugschadenberg.de *Web Site:* www.krugschadenberg.de, pg 250

'Ksiazka i Wiedza' Spotdzielnia Wydawniczo-Handlowa (Poland) *Tel:* (022) 8275401; (022) 8279416; (022) 8279416; (022) 8279423 *E-mail:* publisher@kiw.com.pl *Web Site:* www.kiw.com.pl, pg 524

Ksiaznica Publishing Ltd (Poland) *Tel:* (032) 257 22 16 *Fax:* (032) 257 22 17 *E-mail:* ksiaznica@domnet.com.pl, pg 524

Ktitor (The Former Yugoslav Republic of Macedonia) *Tel:* (092) 21903; (092) 34746 *Fax:* (092) 34746, pg 452

Kuang Fu Book Co Ltd (Taiwan, Province of China) *Tel:* (02) 2771-6622 *Fax:* (02) 7315982 *E-mail:* lolatiao@kfgroup.com.tw *Web Site:* www.kfgroup.com.tw, pg 640

Editora Kuarup Ltda (Brazil) *Tel:* (051) 361-5522 *Fax:* (051) 361-3550 *E-mail:* kuarup@conex.com.br, pg 84

Kubbealti Akademisi Kultur ve Sasat Vakfi (Turkey) *Tel:* (0212) 516 23 56 *Fax:* (0212) 517 14 60, pg 650

KUbK Publishing House (Russian Federation) *Tel:* (095) 1640910; (095) 3679473 *Fax:* (095) 1528689, pg 546

Kubon & Sagner Buchexport-Import GmbH (Germany) *Tel:* (089) 54 218-0 *Fax:* (089) 54 218-218 *E-mail:* postmaster@kubon-sagner.de *Web Site:* www.kubon-sagner.de, pg 1311

Kuemmerly & Frey (Geographischer Verlag) (Switzerland) *Tel:* (031) 9152211 *Fax:* (031) 9152210 *E-mail:* info@swissmaps.ch *Web Site:* www.swissmaps.ch, pg 627

Kuemmerly und Frey Verlags GmbH (Austria) *Tel:* (01) 545 14 45 *Fax:* (01) 545 10 80-83 *E-mail:* kuemmerly-frey@xpoint.at, pg 53

Imprimerie A Kuendig (Switzerland) *Tel:* (022) 966013, pg 627

Kugler Publications (Netherlands) *Tel:* (070) 33-00253 *Fax:* (070) 33-00254 *E-mail:* kuglerspb@wxs.nl *Web Site:* www.kuglerpublications.com, pg 485

Verlag Ernst Kuhn (Germany) *Tel:* (030) 44342230 *Fax:* (030) 4424732 *E-mail:* ernst-kuhn-verlag@t-online.de *Web Site:* www.vek.de, pg 250

Kuiseb-Verlag (Namibia) *Tel:* (061) 225372 *Fax:* (061) 226846 *E-mail:* nwg@iafrica.com.na, pg 476

Kukmin Doseo Publishing Co Ltd (Republic of Korea) *Tel:* (02) 858-2461; (02) 858-2463 *Fax:* (02) 858-2464 *E-mail:* younhlee@chollian.net, pg 440

Kukminseokwan Publishing Co Ltd (Republic of Korea) *Tel:* (02) 7107722; (02) 7107724 *Fax:* (02) 7155771, pg 440

Kultura (Hungary) *Tel:* (01) 2501194 *Fax:* (01) 2500233, pg 1220

Kultura (The Former Yugoslav Republic of Macedonia) *Tel:* (091) 111332 *Fax:* (091) 228608, pg 1325

Kultura (Serbia and Montenegro) *Tel:* (021) 780-144 *Fax:* (021) 780-291, pg 552

Kul'tura redakcionno-izdatel skij kompleks (Russian Federation) *Tel:* (095) 2481151 *Fax:* (095) 2302180, pg 546

Kulturbuch-Verlag GmbH (Germany) *Tel:* (030) 6618484 *Fax:* (030) 6617828 *E-mail:* kbvinfo@kulturbuch-verlag.de *Web Site:* www.kulturbuch-verlag.de, pg 250

Kulturstiftung der deutschen Vertriebenen (Germany) *Tel:* (0228) 915120 *Fax:* (0228) 218397 *E-mail:* kulturstiftung@t-online.de *Web Site:* www.kulturstiftung-der-deutschen-vertriebenen.de, pg 250

Kumsung Publishing Co Ltd (Republic of Korea) *Tel:* (02) 713-9651 *Fax:* (02) 704-1979; (02) 718-4362 *E-mail:* webmaster@kumsungpub.co.kr *Web Site:* www.kumsungpub.com, pg 440

Kungl Ingenjoersvetenskapsakademien (IVA) (Sweden) *Tel:* (08) 7912900 *Fax:* (08) 6115623 *E-mail:* info@iva.se *Web Site:* www.iva.se, pg 613

Kungl Tekniska Hoegskolan Biblioteket (Royal Institute of Technology Library) (Sweden) *Tel:* (08) 790 7088 *Fax:* (08) 790 7122 *E-mail:* loandept@lib.kth.se *Web Site:* www.lib.kth.se, pg 1547

Kungl Vitterhets Historie och Antikvitets Akademien (Sweden) *Tel:* (08) 440 42 80 *Fax:* (08) 440 42 90 *E-mail:* kansli@vitterhetsakad.se *Web Site:* www.vitterhetsakad.se, pg 1405

Kungliga Biblioteket (Sweden) *Tel:* (08) 463 40 00 *Fax:* (08) 463 40 04 *E-mail:* kungl.biblioteket@kb.se *Web Site:* www.kb.se, pg 1547

Kunlun Publishing House (China) *Tel:* (010) 6732721 *Fax:* (010) 62183683; (010) 66847703, pg 106

Kunnskapsforlaget ANS (Norway) *Tel:* (022) 03 66 00 *Fax:* (022) 03 66 05 *E-mail:* kundeservice@kunnskapsforlaget.no *Web Site:* www.kunnskapsforlaget.no, pg 509

Verlag der Kunst/G+B Fine Arts Verlag GmbH (Germany) *Tel:* (0351) 3360742; (0351) 3100052 *Fax:* (0351) 3105245 *E-mail:* verlag-der-kunst@t-online.de *Web Site:* www.verlag-der-kunst.de, pg 251

Verlag Antje Kunstmann GmbH (Germany) *Tel:* (089) 1211930 *Fax:* (089) 12119320 *E-mail:* info@kunstmann.de *Web Site:* www.kunstmann.de, pg 251

Kunstmuseum Liechtenstein Vaduz (Liechtenstein) *Tel:* 235 03 00 *Fax:* 235 03 29 *E-mail:* mail@kunstmuseum.li *Web Site:* www.kunstmuseum.li, pg 448

Kunstverlag Maria Laach (Germany) *Tel:* (02652) 59360 *Fax:* (02652) 59383 *E-mail:* kunstverlag@maria-laach.de *Web Site:* www.maria-laach.de, pg 251

Kunstverlag Weingarten GmbH (Germany) *Tel:* (0751) 561290 *Fax:* (0751) 5612920 *E-mail:* kunstverlag@weingarten-verlag.de *Web Site:* www.kv-weingarten.de, pg 251

Edition Kunzelmann GmbH (Switzerland) *Tel:* (01) 7103681 *Fax:* (01) 7103817 *Web Site:* www.kunzelmann.ch, pg 627

Kupar Publishers (Estonia) *Tel:* (02) 628 6173; (02) 628 6175 *Fax:* (02) 646 2076 *E-mail:* kupar@netexpress.ee, pg 139

Kuperard (United Kingdom) *Tel:* (020) 8446 2440 *Fax:* (020) 8446 2441 *E-mail:* kuperard@bravo.clara.net *Web Site:* www.kuperard.co.uk, pg 718, 1352

Kupfergraben Verlagsgesellschaft mbH (Germany) *Tel:* (030) 2622097 *Fax:* (030) 2621990, pg 251

Kurlana Publishing (Australia) *Tel:* (08) 3886619, pg 28

Kurnia Esanata (Indonesia) *Tel:* (021) 361974; (021) 3104948, pg 355

Kustannus Oy Kolibri (Finland) *Tel:* (09) 774 5310 *Fax:* (09) 701 9351 *E-mail:* susanna.frankenhaeuser@kolibrikustannus.fi, pg 143

Rakentajain Kustannus Oy (Building Publications Ltd) (Finland) *Tel:* (09) 142855 *Fax:* (09) 5032542, pg 143

Kustannus Oy Semic (Finland) *Tel:* (03) 273 8111 *Fax:* (031) 243 8287 *E-mail:* minna.alanko@egmont-kustannus.fi, pg 143

Kustannus Oy Uusi Tie (Finland) *Tel:* (019) 77 920 *Fax:* (019) 779 2300 *E-mail:* uusitie@uusitie.com *Web Site:* www.uusitie.com, pg 143

Kustannuskiila Oy (Finland) *Tel:* (017) 303 111 *Fax:* (017) 303 242 *E-mail:* anneli-siimes@savonsanomat.fi, pg 143

Kustannusosakeyhtio Tammi (Finland) *Tel:* (09) 6937 621 *Fax:* (09) 6937 6266 *E-mail:* tammi@tammi.net *Web Site:* www.tammi.net, pg 143

Kuva ja Sana (Finland) *Tel:* (09) 477 4920 *Fax:* (09) 4774 9250 *E-mail:* kuva.sana@patmos.fi, pg 143

The Kuwait Book Shop Company Ltd (Kuwait) *Tel:* 2424687; 2424266 *Fax:* 2420558 *E-mail:* kbs@ncc.moc.kw, pg 1324

Kuwait Publishing House (Kuwait) *Tel:* 2414697, pg 444

Kuwait University Library (Kuwait) *Tel:* 4813182 *Fax:* 4816095 *Web Site:* www.kuniv.edu.kw, pg 1524

Kuwait University Library (Kuwait) *Web Site:* www.kuniv.edu.kw, pg 1566

KVB Koninklijke Vereeniging van het Boekenvak (Netherlands) *Tel:* (020) 624 02 12 *Fax:* (020) 620 88 71 *E-mail:* info@kvb.nl *Web Site:* www.kvb.nl, pg 1279

KVG de Silva & Sons (Sri Lanka) *Tel:* (01) 84146 *Fax:* (01) 586598, pg 606

KVG de Silva & Sons (Sri Lanka) *Tel:* (01) 84146 *Fax:* (01) 588875, pg 1343

Kerstin Kvint Literary & Co-Production Agency (Sweden) *Tel:* (08) 107014 *Fax:* (08) 107606, pg 1137

Kwa-Zulu Natal Provincial Library Service (South Africa) *Tel:* (033) 3940241 *Fax:* (033) 3942237 *E-mail:* daviess@plho.kzntl.gov.za, pg 1544

Kwame Nkrumah University of Science & Technology Library (Ghana) *Tel:* (051) 60199; (051) 60133 *Fax:* (051) 60358 *E-mail:* ustlib@libr.ug.edu.gh, pg 1512

Kwamfori Publishing Enterprise (Ghana), pg 304

Kwangmyong Publishing Co (Republic of Korea) *Tel:* (02) 2274-1552 *Fax:* (02) 2264-3309 *E-mail:* kwangmgl@hanmail.net, pg 440

KY KE M (Cyprus) *Tel:* (022) 450302 *Fax:* (022) 463624, pg 121

Kydds Paper Plus (New Zealand) *Tel:* (07) 8957430 *Fax:* (07) 8957977 *E-mail:* kyddpp@xtra.co.nz *Web Site:* www.middle-of-everywhere.co.nz/kyddspp.htm, pg 1330

Kyi-Pwar-Ye Book House (Myanmar) *Tel:* (02) 21003, pg 475

Kynos Verlag Dr Dieter Fleig GmbH (Germany) *Tel:* (06594) 653 *Fax:* (06594) 452 *E-mail:* info@kynos-verlag.de *Web Site:* www.kynos-verlag.de, pg 251

Kyobo Book Centre Co Ltd (Republic of Korea) *Tel:* (02) 3973508; (02) 3973509 *Fax:* (02) 7350030 *E-mail:* eslee@kyobobook.co.kr *Web Site:* www.kyobobook.co.kr, pg 440

Kyobo Book Centre Co Ltd (Republic of Korea) *Tel:* (02) 397-3481; (02) 397-3482; (02) 397-3483; (02) 397-3484; (02) 397-3485 *Fax:* (02) 735-0030 *E-mail:* kyobofbd@kyobobook.co.kr, pg 1324

Kyobunkan Inc (Christian Literature Society of Japan) (Japan) *Tel:* (03) 3561-8449 *Fax:* (03) 5250-5109 *E-mail:* fbooks@kyobunkwan.co.jp *Web Site:* www.kyobunkwan.co.jp, pg 1322

Kyodo-Isho Shuppan Co Ltd (Japan) *Tel:* (03) 3818-2361 *Fax:* (03) 3818-2368 *E-mail:* kyodo-ed@fd5.so-net.ne.jp *Web Site:* www.kyodo-isho.co.jp, pg 422

Kyodo Printing Co (S'pore) Pte Ltd (Singapore) *Tel:* 6265 2955 *Fax:* 6264 4939 *E-mail:* cschong@kyodoprinting.com.sg *Web Site:* kyodosing.com, pg 1222

Kyohaksa Publishing Co Ltd (Republic of Korea) *Tel:* (02) 7174561; (02) 8592017 *Fax:* (02) 7183976, pg 440

Kyoritsu Shuppan Co Ltd (Japan) *Tel:* (03) 3947-2511 *Fax:* (03) 3944-8182 *E-mail:* general@kyoritsu-pub.co.jp *Web Site:* www.kyoritsu-pub.co.jp, pg 422

Kyoto Sangyo University Library (Japan) *Tel:* (075) 7012151 *Fax:* (075) 7051447 *E-mail:* ksu-lib@star.kyoto-su.ac.jp *Web Site:* www3.kyoto-su.ac.jp, pg 1521

Kyrenia Municipality (Cyprus) *Tel:* (022) 351460, pg 121

Kyriakidis Brothers sa (Greece) *Tel:* (031) 208 540 *Fax:* (031) 245 541 *E-mail:* info@kyriakidis.gr *Web Site:* www.kyriakidis.gr, pg 1313

Kyriakidis Vasileios (Greece) *Tel:* (01) 3607725 *E-mail:* bkyriakid@otenet.gr, pg 309

K P Kyriakou (Books - Stationery) Ltd (Cyprus) *Tel:* (025) 747555 *Fax:* (025) 747047 *E-mail:* cybooks@logos.cy.net, pg 1307

Kyungnam University Press (Republic of Korea) *Tel:* (055) 245-5000 *Fax:* (055) 246-6184 *Web Site:* www.kyungnam.ac.kr, pg 441

Kyungpook National University Central Library (Republic of Korea) *Tel:* (053) 950-6510 *Fax:* (053) 950-6533 *E-mail:* mspark@kyungpook.ac.kr *Web Site:* kudos.knu.ac.kr, pg 1524

Kyushu University Library (Japan) *Tel:* (092) 6411101; (092) 6422111 *E-mail:* w3-admin@lib.kyushu-u.ac.jp *Web Site:* www.lib.kyushu-u.ac.jp, pg 1521

L B Publishing Co (Israel) *Tel:* (02) 5664637 *Fax:* (02) 5290774 *E-mail:* editorial_lb@yahoo.com, pg 369

Laaber-Verlag (Germany) *Tel:* (09498) 2307 *Fax:* (09498) 2543 *E-mail:* info@laaber-verlag.de *Web Site:* www.laaber-verlag.de, pg 251

Editorial Labor de Venezuela SA (Venezuela) *Tel:* (02) 7811398; (02) 7815819, pg 779

Editions Labor (Belgium) *Tel:* (02) 250-06-70 *Fax:* (02) 217-71-97 *E-mail:* labor@labor.be *Web Site:* www.labor.be, pg 69

Labor et Fides SA (Switzerland) *Tel:* (022) 311 32 69 *Fax:* (022) 781 30 51 *E-mail:* contact@laboretfides.com *Web Site:* www.laboretfides.com, pg 627

Labyrint (Czech Republic) *Tel:* (02) 24 922 422 *Fax:* (02) 24 922 422 *E-mail:* labyrint@wo.cz *Web Site:* www.labyrint.net, pg 125

Labyrinth Verlag Gisela Ottmer (Germany) *Tel:* (0531) 64259 *Fax:* (0531) 681358 *E-mail:* labyrinthbraunschweig@t-online.de *Web Site:* www.frauenart.de/labyrinthbraunschweig, pg 251

LAC - Litografia Artistica Cartografica Srl (Italy) *Tel:* (055) 483 557 *Fax:* (055) 483 690 *E-mail:* info@lac-cartografia.it *Web Site:* www.lac-cartografia.it, pg 394

Editions Lacour-Olle (France) *Tel:* (04) 66 67 30 30 *Fax:* (04) 66 21 11 23 *E-mail:* c.lacour@editions-lacour.com *Web Site:* www.editions-lacour.com, pg 170

Ambro Lacus, Buch- und Bildverlag Walter A Kremnitz (Germany) *Tel:* (08152) 1332 *Fax:* (08152) 40186, pg 251

Ladomir Publishing House (Russian Federation) *Tel:* (095) 530-9833; (095) 530-8477 *Fax:* (095) 537-4742-7870, pg 546

L'Adret editions (France), pg 170

Ladybird Books Ltd (United Kingdom) *Tel:* (020) 7010 2900 *Fax:* (01509) 234672 *Web Site:* www.ladybird.co.uk, pg 719

Laertes SA de Ediciones (Spain) *Tel:* (093) 2187020; (093) 2185558 *Fax:* (093) 2174751 *E-mail:* laertes@jet.es, pg 588

Laffitte Reprints (France) *Tel:* (04) 91 59 80 40 *Fax:* (04) 91 54 25 65, pg 170

Laffont Ediciones Electronicas SA (Argentina) *Tel:* (011) 4302-8668 *Fax:* (011) 4301-2525 *E-mail:* info@laffont.com.ar *Web Site:* www.laffont.com.ar, pg 7

Editions Robert Laffont (France) *Tel:* (01) 53 67 14 00 *Fax:* (01) 53 67 14 14 *Web Site:* www.laffont.fr, pg 170

Verlag Lafite (Austria) *Tel:* (01) 5126869 *Fax:* (01) 51268699, pg 53

Editions Jacques Lafitte - Who's Who in France (France) *Tel:* (0141) 272 830 *Fax:* (0141) 272 840 *E-mail:* whoswho@whoswho.fr *Web Site:* www.whoswho.fr, pg 170

Michel Lafon Publishing (France) *Tel:* (01) 41 43 85 85 *Fax:* (01) 46 24 00 95, pg 171

Librairie Leonce Laget (France) *Tel:* (01) 43 29 90 04 *Fax:* (01) 43 26 89 68 *E-mail:* liblaget@wanadoo.fr *Web Site:* www.franceantiq.fr/slam/laget/uk.htm, pg 171

Lagos City Council Libraries (Nigeria) *Tel:* (01) 50246, pg 1533

Lahn-Verlag GmbH (Germany) *Tel:* (02832) 929-130 *Fax:* (02832) 929-139 *E-mail:* service@lahn-verlag.de *Web Site:* www.lahn-verlag.de, pg 251

Editorin Laiovento SL (Spain) *Tel:* (0981) 887570 *Fax:* (0981) 572239 *E-mail:* laiovento@laiovento.com *Web Site:* www.laiovento.com, pg 588

Francisco J Laissue Livraria (Brazil) *Tel:* (021) 509-7298, pg 84

Lake House Bookshop (Sri Lanka) *Tel:* (01) 430581; (01) 432105; (01) 430582 *Fax:* (01) 432104 *E-mail:* bookshop@sri.lanka.net, pg 1343

Lake House Investments Ltd (Sri Lanka) *Tel:* (01) 35175; (01) 33271 *Fax:* (01) 44 7848; (01) 44 9504 *E-mail:* lhl@srilanka.net, pg 606

Lake-Livraria Editora Allan Kardec (Brazil) *Tel:* (011) 229-0526; (011) 229-1227; (011) 227-1396; (011) 229-0937; (011) 229-4592; (011) 229-0514 *Fax:* (011) 229-0935; (011) 227-5714 *E-mail:* lake@lake.com.br *Web Site:* www.lake.com.br, pg 84

Lake Publishers & Enterprises Ltd (Kenya) *Tel:* (057) 42750, pg 435

Lalit Kala Akademi (India) *Tel:* (011) 23387241; (011) 23387243; (011) 23387242 *Fax:* (011) 23782485 *E-mail:* lka@lalitkala.org.in *Web Site:* www.lalitkala.org.in, pg 339

Lalli Editore SRL (Italy) *Tel:* (0577) 933305 *Fax:* (0577) 983308 *E-mail:* lalli@lallieditore.it *Web Site:* www.lallieditore.it, pg 394

Editions Lamarre SA (France) *Tel:* (01) 41 29 99 99 *Fax:* (01) 41 29 95 13, pg 171

Charles Lamb Society (United Kingdom) *Tel:* (020) 7332 1868; (020) 7332 1870 *Web Site:* users.ox.ac.uk/~scat1492/clsoc.htm, pg 1408

Lambda Edition GmbH (Germany) *Tel:* (040) 312836 *Fax:* (040) 3192096, pg 251

Lambertus Verlag GmbH (Germany) *Tel:* (0761) 368250 *Fax:* (0761) 3682533 *E-mail:* info@lambertus.de *Web Site:* www.lambertus.de, pg 251

Lammar Offset Printing Co (Hong Kong) *Tel:* 25631068 *Fax:* 28113375, pg 1218

Lamuv Verlag GmbH (Germany) *Tel:* (0551) 44024 *Fax:* (0551) 41392 *E-mail:* info@lamuv.de *Web Site:* www.lamuv.de, pg 251

Lancashire Authors' Association (United Kingdom) *Tel:* (01254) 56788 *E-mail:* laa@lancs.communigate.co.uk *Web Site:* www.communigate.co.uk/lancs/laa/index.phtml, pg 1408

Lancer Publisher's & Distributors (India) *Tel:* (011) 6867339; (011) 6854691 *Fax:* (011) 6862077 *Web Site:* www.geocites.com/TheTropics/3328/lancer.htm, pg 340

Landarc Publications (Australia) *Tel:* (03) 93801276 *Fax:* (03) 93801276 *E-mail:* carmar@bigpond.com, pg 28

Landbuch-Verlagsgesellschaft mbH (Germany) *Tel:* (0511) 27046-153 *Fax:* (0511) 27046-150 *E-mail:* info@landbuch.de *Web Site:* www.landbuch.de, pg 251

Landcare Research NZ (New Zealand) *Tel:* (03) 3256700 *Fax:* (03) 3252127 *E-mail:* mwpress@landcare.cri.nz *Web Site:* www.landcare.cri.nz/mwpress/, pg 497

Institut fuer Landes- und Stadtentwicklungsforschung des Landes Nordrhein-Westfalen (Germany) *Tel:* (0231) 90 51-0 *Fax:* (0231) 90 51-1 55 *E-mail:* webmaster@ils.nrw.de *Web Site:* www.ils.nrw.de, pg 251

Jay Landesman (United Kingdom) *Tel:* (020) 7837 7290 *Fax:* (020) 7833 1925, pg 719

Landesverband der Verleger und Buchhaendler Rheinland-Pfalz eV (Germany) *Tel:* (06131) 234035 *Fax:* (06131) 230364, pg 1270

Landmark Education Supplies Pty Ltd (Australia) *Tel:* (056) 251701, pg 1299

Lands Department, Survey & Mapping Office (Hong Kong) *Tel:* 2848 2182 *Fax:* 2521 8726, pg 318

Landsberger (Israel) *Tel:* (03) 5176330 *Fax:* (03) 5222646, pg 1320

Landsbokasafn Islands-Haskolabokasafn (Iceland) *Tel:* 525 5600 *Fax:* 525 5615 *E-mail:* lbs@bok.hi.is *Web Site:* www.bok.hi.is, pg 1515

Landy Publishing (United Kingdom) *Tel:* (01253) 895678 *Fax:* (01253) 895678 *E-mail:* bobdobson@amserve.com, pg 719

Lanfranchi (Italy) *Tel:* (02) 86465210 *Fax:* (02) 8056083 *E-mail:* info@lanfranchieditore.com *Web Site:* www.lanfranchieditore.com, pg 394

Herbert Lang & Cie AG, Buchhandlung, Antiquariat (Switzerland) *Tel:* (031) 3108484 *Fax:* (031) 3108494, pg 627

Lang Kiado (Hungary) *Tel:* (01) 301-3888 *Fax:* (01) 301-3833 *E-mail:* holding@lang.hu *Web Site:* www.lang.hu, pg 322

Peter Lang AG (Switzerland) *Tel:* (031) 306 17 17 *Fax:* (031) 306 17 27 *E-mail:* info@peterlang.com *Web Site:* www.peterlang.com, pg 627

Peter Lang GmbH Europaeischer Verlag der Wissenschaften (Germany) *Tel:* (069) 7807050 *Fax:* (069) 780705-50 *E-mail:* zentrale.frankfurt@peterlang.com *Web Site:* www.peterlang.de, pg 252

Lang Syne Publishers Ltd (United Kingdom) *E-mail:* enquiries@scottish-memories.co.uk *Web Site:* www.scottish-memories.co.uk/langsyne/, pg 719

Lange & Springer Antiquariat (Germany) *Tel:* (030) 31504196; (030) 3422011 *Fax:* (030) 3410440; (030) 31504197 *E-mail:* buchladen@lange-springer-antiquariat.de *Web Site:* www.lange-springer-antiquariat.de, pg 1311

Langenscheidt-Verlag GmbH (Austria) *Tel:* (01) 6887133 *Fax:* (01) 68014140, pg 53

Langenscheidt AG Zuerich-Zug (Switzerland) *Tel:* (01) 2115000 *Fax:* (01) 2122149, pg 627

Langenscheidt Fachverlag GmbH (Germany) *Tel:* (089) 36096-0 *Fax:* (089) 36096-222 *E-mail:* kundenservice@langenscheidt.de *Web Site:* www.langenscheidt.de, pg 252

The Langenscheidt Group (Germany) *Tel:* (089) 36096-0; (089) 36096-258 (orders) *Fax:* (089) 36096-222; (089) 36096-258 *E-mail:* kundenservice@langenscheidt.de *Web Site:* www.langenscheidt.de, pg 252

Langenscheidt-Hachette (Germany) *Tel:* (089) 360960 *Fax:* (089) 36096-222; (089) 36096-472 (general); (089) 36096-258 (orders) *E-mail:* kundenservice@langenscheidt.de *Web Site:* www.langenscheidt.de, pg 252

Langenscheidt KG (Germany) *Tel:* (089) 36096-0; (089) 36096-258 (orders) *Fax:* (089) 36096-222 *E-mail:* kundenservice@langenscheidt.de *Web Site:* www.langenscheidt.de, pg 252

Verlag Langewiesche-Brandt KG (Germany) *Tel:* (08178) 4857 *Fax:* (08178) 7388 *E-mail:* textura@langewiesche-brandt.de *Web Site:* www.langewiesche-brandt.de, pg 252

Karl Robert Langewiesche Nachfolger Hans Koester KG (Germany) *Tel:* (06174) 7333 *Fax:* (06174) 933-039 *E-mail:* info@langewiesche-verlag.de *Web Site:* www.langewiesche-verlag.de, pg 252

Ingrid Langner (Germany) *Tel:* (04123) 7780 *Fax:* (04123) 7885, pg 252

Language Book Centre (Australia) *Tel:* (02) 92671397 *Toll Free Tel:* 800 802 432 (outside Sydney & within Australia) *Fax:* (02) 92648993 *E-mail:* language@abbeys.com.au *Web Site:* www.languagebooks.com.au, pg 1299

Language Consultancy Services (United Kingdom) *Tel:* (020) 8450 5344 *Fax:* (020) 8452 9005 *E-mail:* lucifer@ladet.demon.co.uk, pg 1151

Language Publishing House (China) *Tel:* (010) 65130349; (010) 65241766, pg 106

Language Teaching Publications (United Kingdom) *Tel:* (020) 7067 2500 *Fax:* (020) 7067 2600 *E-mail:* ltp@ltpwebsite.com *Web Site:* www.ltpwebsite.com, pg 719

Langues & Mondes-L'Asiatheque (France) *Tel:* (01) 42 62 04 00 *Fax:* (01) 42 62 12 34 *E-mail:* info@asiatheque.com *Web Site:* www.asiatheque.com, pg 171

Bibliotheque Interuniversitaire des Langues Orientales (France) *Tel:* (01) 44 77 87 20 *Fax:* (01) 44 77 87 30 *E-mail:* biulo@idf.ext.jussieu.fr *Web Site:* www.univ-paris3.fr, pg 1507

Drukkerij Lannoo NV (Belgium) *Tel:* (051) 42 42 11 *Fax:* (051) 40 70 70 *E-mail:* lannoo@lannooprint.be *Web Site:* www.lannooprint.be, pg 1153, 1175, 1215

Uitgeverij Lannoo NV (Belgium) *Tel:* (051) 42 42 11 *Fax:* (051) 40 11 52 *E-mail:* lannoo@lannoo.be *Web Site:* www.lannoo.com, pg 69

Editions Fernand Lanore Sarl (France) *Tel:* (01) 43256661 *Fax:* (01) 43296981, pg 171

Lansdowne Publishing Pty Ltd (Australia) *Tel:* (02) 9240 9222 *Fax:* (02) 9241 4818 *E-mail:* sales@lanspub.com.au, pg 28

Lansman Editeur (Belgium) *Tel:* (064) 23-78-40 *Fax:* (064) 44-31-02; (064) 23-78-49 *E-mail:* info@lansman.org *Web Site:* www.lansman.org, pg 69

Lanzhou University Press (China) *Tel:* (0931) 8843000-3514 *Fax:* (0931) 8615095 *E-mail:* press@lzu.edu.cn, pg 106

Lao Dong (Labor) Publishing House (Viet Nam) *Tel:* (04) 253972, pg 780

Lao-phanit (Laos People's Democratic Republic), pg 444

LAPA Publishers (Pty) Ltd (South Africa) *Tel:* (012) 401 0700 *Fax:* (012) 3255498 *E-mail:* lapa@atkv.org.za, pg 566

Michelle Lapautre (France) *Tel:* (01) 47348241 *Fax:* (01) 47340090 *E-mail:* lapautre@club-internet.fr, pg 1130

Lappan Verlag GmbH (Germany) *Tel:* (0441) 980660 *Fax:* (0441) 9806622; (0441) 9806624; (0441) 9806634 *E-mail:* info@lappan.de *Web Site:* www.lappan.de, pg 252

Editions du Laquet (France) *Tel:* (05) 65 37 43 54 *Fax:* (05) 65 37 43 55 *E-mail:* contact@editions-dulaquet.fr *Web Site:* editions-dulaquet.fr, pg 171

Leandro Lara Editor (Spain) *Tel:* (093) 6970036; (093) 6970364 *E-mail:* leandro@covnet.com, pg 588

Larcier-Department of De Boeck & Larcier SA (Belgium) *E-mail:* deboeck.larcier@deboeck.be *Web Site:* www.larcier.be, pg 70

Hans Richter Laromedel (Sweden) *Tel:* (0152) 150 60; (0200) 11 55 30 (orders) *Fax:* (0152) 151 40; (0200) 11 55 31 (orders) *E-mail:* info@richter.d.se *Web Site:* www.richter.d.se, pg 613

Ediciones Larousse Argentina SA (Argentina) *Tel:* (011) 4865-9581; (011) 4865-9582; (011) 4865-9583 *Toll Free Tel:* 800-333-5757 *Fax:* (011) 4865-9581; (011) 4865-9582; (011) 4865-9583 *Toll Free Fax:* 800-333-5757 *E-mail:* editorial@aique.com.ar; comercial@aique.com.ar *Web Site:* www.larousse.com.ar, pg 7

Editions Larousse (France) *Tel:* (01) 44 39 44 00 *Fax:* (01) 44 39 43 43 *Web Site:* www.larousse.fr, pg 171

Larousse Editorial SA (Spain) *Tel:* (093) 2922666 *Fax:* (093) 2922162; (093) 2922163 *E-mail:* larousse@larousse.es, pg 588

Ediciones Larousse SA de CV (Mexico) *Tel:* (05) 52082005; (05) 2085677 *Fax:* (05) 2086225 *E-mail:* dbertin@larousse.com.mx *Web Site:* www.larousse.com.mx, pg 467

Larousse (Suisse) SA (Switzerland) *Tel:* (021) 335336, pg 627

Bokforlaget Robert Larson AB (Sweden) *Tel:* (08) 732 84 60 *Fax:* (08) 732 71 76 *E-mail:* info@larsonforlag.se *Web Site:* www.larsonforlag.se, pg 613

Laruffa Editore SRL (Italy) *Tel:* (0965) 814948 *Fax:* (0965) 814954 *E-mail:* laruffa@laruffaeditore.com *Web Site:* www.laruffaeditore.com, pg 394

Editrice LAS (Italy) *Tel:* (06) 87290626 *E-mail:* las@ups.urbe.it *Web Site:* www.las.ups.urbe.it, pg 394

Roger Lascelles (United Kingdom) *Tel:* (0181) 8470935 *Fax:* (0181) 5683886, pg 719

Lasser Press Mexicana SA de CV (Mexico) *Tel:* (05) 5112312; (05) 5142705 *Fax:* (05) 5112576, pg 467

Michael Lassleben Verlag und Druckerei (Germany) *Tel:* (09473) 205 *Fax:* (09473) 8357 *E-mail:* druckerei@oberpfalzverlag-lassleben.de *Web Site:* www.oberpfalzverlag-lassleben.de, pg 252

L'Association des Professionnels de l'Information et de la Documentation (ADBS) (France) *Tel:* (01) 43 72 25 25 *Fax:* (01) 43 72 30 41 *E-mail:* adbs@adbs.fr *Web Site:* www.adbs.fr, pg 1562

Lasten Keskus Oy (Finland) *Tel:* (09) 6877 450 *Fax:* (09) 6877 4545 *E-mail:* tilaukset@lastenkeskus.fi *Web Site:* www.lastenkeskus.fi, pg 143

The Latchmere Press (United Kingdom) *Tel:* (020) 7639 7282, pg 719

Latin America Bureau (United Kingdom) *Tel:* (020) 7278 2829 *Fax:* (020) 7833 0715 *E-mail:* info@lab.org.uk *Web Site:* www.lab.org.uk, pg 1292

Latina Livraria Editora (Portugal) *Tel:* (02) 2001294 *Fax:* (02) 2086053, pg 532

YELLOW PAGES — LEMBAGA DEMOGRAFI FAKULTAS EKONOMI UNIVERSITAS INDONESIA

J Latka Verlag GmbH (Germany) *Tel:* (0228) 919320 *Fax:* (0228) 9193217 *E-mail:* info@latka.de *Web Site:* www.latka.de, pg 253

Library Association of Latvia (Latvia) *Tel:* (0371) 7287620 *Fax:* (0371) 7280851 *E-mail:* lnb@lbi.lnb.lv *Web Site:* www.lnb.lv, pg 1566

Latvian Publishers Association (Latvia) *Tel:* (0371) 7282392 *Fax:* (0371) 7280549 *E-mail:* lga@gramatizdeveji.lv *Web Site:* www.gramatizdeveji.lv, pg 1276

Laumann-Polska (Poland) *Tel:* (075) 7617182 *Fax:* (075) 7617192, pg 524

Laureate Book Co Ltd (Taiwan, Province of China) *Tel:* 8862 2219 3338 *Fax:* (02) 2218-2859 *E-mail:* laureate@ms10.hinet.net, pg 640

Laurel Press (Australia) *Tel:* (03) 6239 1139 *Fax:* (03) 6239 1139, pg 28

Editions Le Laurier (France) *Tel:* (01) 45 51 55 08 *Fax:* (01) 45 51 81 83 *E-mail:* editions@lelaurier.fr *Web Site:* www.lelaurier.fr, pg 171

The Lavenham Press Ltd (United Kingdom) *Tel:* (01787) 247436; (01787) 248267 (ISDN) *Fax:* (01787) 248267 *E-mail:* lpl@lavenhamgroup.co.uk *Web Site:* www.lavenhampress.co.uk, pg 1164, 1226

Les Presses Lavigerie (Burundi) *Tel:* (02) 22368 *Fax:* (02) 220318 *E-mail:* lpl~bujumbura@cbinf.com, pg 98

Lavis Marketing (United Kingdom) *Tel:* (01865) 767575 *Fax:* (01865) 750079 *E-mail:* orders@lavismarketing.co.uk, pg 1352

Editions Lavoisier (France) *Tel:* (01) 47 40 67 00 *Fax:* (01) 47 40 67 88 *E-mail:* edition@tec-et-doc.com *Web Site:* www.tec-et-doc.com, pg 171

Editions Lavoisier (France) *Tel:* (01) 47 40 67 00 *Fax:* (01) 47 40 67 03 *E-mail:* edition@tec-et-doc.com *Web Site:* www.tec-et-doc.com/fr, pg 1310

Edizioni Lavoro SRL (Italy) *Tel:* (06) 44251174 *Fax:* (06) 44251177 *E-mail:* info@edizionilavoro.it *Web Site:* www.edizionilavoro.it, pg 394

Il Lavoro Editoriale (Italy) *Tel:* (071) 2072210 *Fax:* (071) 2083058 *E-mail:* ilepro@tin.it *Web Site:* www.illavoroeditoriale.com, pg 395

Law Book Co Information Services (Australia) *Tel:* (02) 99366444 *Fax:* (02) 98882229, pg 28

LAW Ltd (Lucas Alexander Whitley) (United Kingdom) *Tel:* (020) 7471 7900 *Fax:* (020) 7471 7910 *E-mail:* law@lawagency.co.uk, pg 1141

Law Publishers (India) *Tel:* (0532) 2622758; (0532) 2420974 *Fax:* (0532) 2622781; (0532) 2609943 *E-mail:* lawpub@vsnl.com; lawpub@sancharnet.in *Web Site:* www.law-publishers.com, pg 340

Law Publishers Association (Sri Lanka) *Tel:* (01) 330363 *Fax:* (01) 436629, pg 607

The Law Publishing House (China) *Tel:* (010) 63266796; (010) 63266790, pg 106

Lawpack Publishing Ltd (United Kingdom) *Tel:* (020) 7394 4040 *Fax:* (020) 7394 4041 *E-mail:* enquiries@lawpack.co.uk *Web Site:* www.lawpack.co.uk, pg 719

Lawrence & Wishart (United Kingdom) *Tel:* (020) 8533 2506 *Fax:* (020) 8533 7369 *E-mail:* info@lwbooks.co.uk *Web Site:* www.l-w-bks.co.uk, pg 719

Laxmi Publications Pvt Ltd (India) *Tel:* (011) 23262368; (011) 23262370 *Fax:* (011) 23262279 *E-mail:* colaxmi@hotmail.com *Web Site:* www.laxmipublications.com, pg 340

Phillip Richard Conover Lazo (Mexico) *Tel:* (05) 5482663 *Fax:* (05) 5500641 *E-mail:* mel778@latinmail.com, pg 467

Editions Universitaires LCF (France) *Tel:* (05) 56 51 51 37 *Fax:* (05) 56 51 51 37, pg 171

LCG Malmberg BV (Netherlands) *Tel:* (073) 6288811 *Fax:* (073) 6210512 *Web Site:* www.malmberg.nl, pg 485

LDA Editores Ltda (Brazil) *Tel:* (041) 362-9173 *Fax:* (041) 262-3439 *E-mail:* lda.editores@uol.com.br, pg 84

LDA-Living & Learning (Cambridge) Ltd (United Kingdom) *Tel:* (01223) 357788 *Fax:* (01223) 460557 *E-mail:* internationalsales@mcgraw-hill.com, pg 719

Le'Dory Publishing House (Israel) *Tel:* (03) 5178555, pg 369

Lea Publications Ltd (Hong Kong) *Tel:* 25-620121 *Fax:* 2565 0187, pg 318

Lead Wave Publishing Company Ltd (Taiwan, Province of China) *Tel:* (02) 23650177 *Fax:* (02) 23656407 *E-mail:* customer@liwil.com.tw *Web Site:* www.liwil.com.tw, pg 640

Learners Press Private Ltd (India) *Tel:* (011) 26387070; (011) 26386209 *Fax:* (011) 26383788 *E-mail:* info@sterlingpublishers.com *Web Site:* www.sterlingpublishers.com, pg 340

Learning Development Aids (United Kingdom) *Tel:* (01223) 365445 *Fax:* (01223) 460557 *E-mail:* ldaorders@compuserve.com, pg 719

Learning Guides (Writers & Publishers Ltd) (New Zealand) *Tel:* (04) 239 9400 *Fax:* (04) 239 9400 *E-mail:* learning.guides@xtra.co.nz, pg 497

Learning Matters Ltd (United Kingdom) *Tel:* (01392) 215560 *Fax:* (01392) 215561 *E-mail:* info@learningmatters.co.uk *Web Site:* www.learningmatters.co.uk, pg 720

Learning Media Ltd (New Zealand) *Tel:* (04) 472 5522 *Fax:* (04) 472 6444 *E-mail:* info@learningmedia.co.nz *Web Site:* www.learningmedia.co.nz; www.learningmedia.com, pg 498

Learning Together (United Kingdom) *Tel:* (028) 90402086 *Fax:* (028) 90402086 *E-mail:* info@learningtogether.co.uk *Web Site:* www.learningtogether.co.uk, pg 720

The Lebanese Library Association (Lebanon) *Tel:* (01) 350000; (01) 340460 *Fax:* (01) 351706 *Web Site:* www.aub.edu.lb, pg 1566

Lebenshilfe-Verlag Marburg, Verlag der Bundesvereinigung Lebenshilfe fuer Menschen mit geistiger Behinderung eV (Germany) *Tel:* (06421) 4 91-0 *Fax:* (06421) 4 91-1 67 *E-mail:* bundesvereinigung@lebenshilfe.de *Web Site:* www.lebenshilfe.de, pg 253

Lebensstrom eV (Germany) *Tel:* (030) 3131247 *Fax:* (030) 3121098 *E-mail:* info@lebensstrom.com *Web Site:* www.lebensstrom.com, pg 253

Gerda Leber Buch-Kunst-und Musikverlag Proscenium Edition (Austria) *Tel:* (01) 5332858; (01) 6390025, pg 53

LED - Edizioni Universitarie di Lettere Economia Diritto (Italy) *Tel:* (02) 59902055 *Fax:* (02) 55193636 *E-mail:* led@lededizioni.it *Web Site:* www.lededizioni.it, pg 395

LEDA (Las Ediciones de Arte) (Spain) *Tel:* (093) 2379389; (093) 2155273, pg 589

Lee & Lee Communications (Taiwan, Province of China) *Tel:* (02) 8228-0518 *Fax:* (02) 8228-0618 *E-mail:* service@leelee.com; culture@leelee.com *Web Site:* www.leelee.com, pg 641

Sandra Lee Agencies (Australia) *Tel:* (03) 9592 5235 *Fax:* (03) 9592 7608 *E-mail:* winston@ozonline.com.au, pg 28

Leeds University Library (United Kingdom) *Tel:* (0113) 343 5663 *Fax:* (0113) 233 5561 *E-mail:* library@library.leeds.ac.uk *Web Site:* www.leeds.ac.uk/library, pg 1553

Editions Francis Lefebvre (France) *Tel:* (01) 41 05 22 00; (08) 36 70 00 14; (01) 41 05 22 06 *Fax:* (01) 41 05 36 80, pg 171

Claude Lefrancq Editeur (Belgium) *Tel:* (02) 344-49-34 *Fax:* (02) 347-55-34 *E-mail:* claude.lefrancq@skynet.be, pg 70

Legal Action Group (United Kingdom) *Tel:* (020) 7833 2931 *Fax:* (020) 7837 6094 *E-mail:* lag@lag.org.uk *Web Site:* www.lag.org.uk, pg 720

Legal & Technical Translation Services (United Kingdom) *Tel:* (01622) 751537; (01622) 751189 *Fax:* (01622) 754431 *E-mail:* translation@ltts.co.uk *Web Site:* www.ltts.co.uk, pg 1151

Legal Resources Foundation Publications Unit (Zimbabwe) *Tel:* (04) 251170; (04) 251174 *Fax:* (04) 728213 *E-mail:* lrfhre@mweb.co.zw *Web Site:* site.mweb.co.zw/lrf, pg 783

Ediciones Legales SA (Ecuador) *Tel:* (02) 250-7729 *Fax:* (02) 250-8490 *E-mail:* edicioneslegales@corpmyl.com *Web Site:* www.edicioneslegales.com, pg 136

LEGIS - Editores SA (Colombia) *Tel:* (01) 4255255 *Fax:* (01) 4255317 *E-mail:* scliente@legis.com.co, pg 111

Legislation Direct (New Zealand) *Tel:* (04) 495 2882 *Fax:* (04) 495 2880 *E-mail:* ldorders@legislationdirect.co.nz *Web Site:* gplegislation.co.nz, pg 498

Editions Legislatives (France) *Tel:* (01) 40 92 36 36 *Fax:* (01) 46 56 00 15 *E-mail:* infocom@editions-legislatives.fr *Web Site:* www.editions-legislatives.fr, pg 171

Legprombytizdat (Russian Federation) *Tel:* (095) 2330947, pg 546

Libreria Imprenta y Litografia Lehmann SA (Costa Rica) *Tel:* 2231212, pg 115, 1307

Lehnert & Landrock Bookshop (Egypt (Arab Republic of Egypt)) *Tel:* (02) 3927606 *Fax:* (02) 3934421, pg 138

Lehnert & Landrock, Bookshop and Art Publishers (Egypt (Arab Republic of Egypt)) *Tel:* (02) 3927606; (02) 3935324 *Fax:* (02) 3934421, pg 1309

Verlag fuer Lehrmittel Poessneck GmbH (Germany) *Tel:* (03647) 425018 *Fax:* (03647) 425020, pg 253

Lehrmittelverlag des Kantons Zurich (Switzerland) *Tel:* (01) 465 85 85 *Fax:* (01) 465 85 86 *E-mail:* lehrmittelverlag@lmv.zh.ch *Web Site:* www.access.ch/lmvzh, pg 627

Leibniz Verlag (Germany) *Tel:* (06741) 1720 *Fax:* (06741) 1749 *E-mail:* reichl-verlag@telda.net, pg 253

Leibniz-Buecherwarte (Germany) *Tel:* (05042) 15 28 *Fax:* (05042) 15 28 *E-mail:* leibniz-buecherwarte@t-online.de *Web Site:* www.leibniz-buecherwarte.com, pg 253

University of Leicester (United Kingdom) *Tel:* (0116) 252 2043 *Fax:* (0116) 252 2066 *E-mail:* libdesk@le.ac.uk *Web Site:* www.le.ac.uk/library, pg 1553

Leipziger Universitaetsverlag GmbH (Germany) *Tel:* (0341) 9900440 *Fax:* (0341) 9900440 *E-mail:* info@univerlag-leipzig.de *Web Site:* www.univerlag-leipzig.de, pg 253

Leitfadenverlag Verlag Dieter Sudholt (Germany) *Tel:* (08151) 51045 *Fax:* (08151) 50357, pg 253

Anton G Leitner Verlag (AGLV) (Germany) *Tel:* (08153) 9525-22 *Fax:* (08153) 9525-24 *E-mail:* info@aglv.com *Web Site:* www.dasgedicht.de, pg 253

Editora Leitura Ltda (Brazil) *Tel:* (031) 3371-4902 *Fax:* (031) 3714902 *E-mail:* leitura@editoraleitura.com.br *Web Site:* www.editoraleitura.com.br, pg 84

Edicions de l'Eixample, SA (Spain) *Tel:* (093) 4584600 *Fax:* (093) 2076248, pg 589

Leksikografski Zavod Miroslav Krleza (Croatia) *Tel:* (01) 4800 492; (01) 4800 494 *Fax:* (01) 4800 399 *E-mail:* lzmk@lzmk.hr *Web Site:* www.lzmk.hr, pg 118

Lembaga Demografi Fakultas Ekonomi Universitas Indonesia (Indonesia) *Tel:* (021) 3900703; (021) 336434; (021) 336539 *Fax:* (021) 3102457 *E-mail:* demofeui@indo.net.id, pg 355

Verlag Otto Lembeck (Germany) *Tel:* (069) 5970988 *Fax:* (069) 5975742 *E-mail:* verlag@lembeck.de *Web Site:* www.lembeck.de, pg 253

Uitgeverij Lemma BV (Netherlands) *Tel:* (030) 2545652 *Fax:* (030) 2512496 *E-mail:* infodesk@lemma.nl *Web Site:* www.lemma.nl, pg 485

Lemniscaat (Netherlands) *Tel:* (010) 2062929 *Fax:* (010) 4141560 *E-mail:* info@lemniscaat.nl *Web Site:* www.lemniscaat.nl, pg 485

Lemos & Crane (United Kingdom) *Tel:* (020) 8348 8263 *Fax:* (020) 8347 5740 *E-mail:* admin@lemosandcrane.co.uk *Web Site:* www.lemosandcrane.co.uk, pg 720

Edicoes Manuel Lencastre (Portugal) *Tel:* 4688328, pg 532

Izdatelstvo Lenizdat (Russian Federation) *Tel:* (0812) 3111451 *Fax:* (0812) 3151295, pg 546

Lennard Publishing (United Kingdom) *Tel:* (01582) 715866 *Fax:* (01582) 715121 *E-mail:* lennard@lenqap.demon.co.uk, pg 720

Lenos Verlag (Switzerland) *Tel:* (061) 261 34 14 *Fax:* (061) 261 35 18 *E-mail:* lenos@lenos.ch *Web Site:* www.lenos.ch, pg 627

Lentz Verlag (Germany) *Tel:* (089) 290880 *Fax:* (089) 29088-144 *E-mail:* l.eggs@herbig.net *Web Site:* www.herbig.net, pg 253

Leo Paper Products Ltd (Hong Kong) *Tel:* 28841374 *Fax:* 25130698 *E-mail:* lpp@leo.com.hk *Web Site:* www.leo.com.hk, pg 1157, 1178, 1218

Leo Paper USA (United States) *Tel:* 425-646-8801 *Fax:* 425-646-8805 *E-mail:* leo@leousa.com; sales@leousa.com *Web Site:* www.leousa.com, pg 1167

Leo Paper USA (United States) *Tel:* 425-646-8801 *Fax:* 425-646-8805 *E-mail:* leo@leousa.com *Web Site:* www.leousa.com, pg 1188, 1230

Leo Reprographic Ltd (Hong Kong) *Tel:* (02) 25696293 *Fax:* (02) 25138400 *E-mail:* lrg@leo.com.hk *Web Site:* www.leo.com.hk, pg 1178

Leong Brothers (Brunei Darussalam) *Tel:* (03) 22381 *Fax:* (03) 222223, pg 92

Leonhardt & Hoier Literary Agency ApS (Denmark) *Tel:* 33132523 *Fax:* 33134992 *Web Site:* www.leonhardt-hoier.dk, pg 1130

Leonis Verlag (Switzerland) *Tel:* (01) 475565 *Fax:* (01) 262 48 81, pg 627

Uitgeverij Leopold BV (Netherlands) *Tel:* (020) 5511250 *Fax:* (020) 4204699 *E-mail:* verkoop@leopold.nl *Web Site:* www.leopold.nl, pg 485

Leopold Stocker Verlag (Austria) *Tel:* (0316) 82 16 36 *Fax:* (0316) 83 56 12 *E-mail:* stocker-verlag@stocker-verlag.com *Web Site:* www.stocker-verlag.com, pg 53

Leopold Stocker Verlag (Austria) *Tel:* (0316) 82 16 36 *Fax:* (0316) 83 56 12 *E-mail:* buecherquelle@stocker-verlag.com *Web Site:* www.buecherquelle.at, pg 1300

Dr Gisela Lermann (Germany) *Tel:* (06131) 31149 *Fax:* (06131) 387945 *Web Site:* www.lermann-verlag.de, pg 253

Lerner Ediciones (Colombia) *Tel:* (01) 2628200; (01) 2624224 *Fax:* (01) 2624459, pg 111

Editions Dominique Leroy (France) *Tel:* (03) 86 64 15 24 *Fax:* (03) 86 64 15 24 *Web Site:* www.enfer.com, pg 171

Lesotho Library Association (Lesotho) *Tel:* 340 601 *Fax:* 340 601 *E-mail:* mmc@doc.isas.nul.ls *Web Site:* www.sn.apc.org, pg 1567

Lesotho National Library Service (Lesotho) *Tel:* 322 592; 323 100 *Fax:* 323 100, pg 1525

Editions Lessius ASBL (Belgium) *Tel:* (02) 739 34 90 *Fax:* (02) 739 34 91 *E-mail:* info@editions-lessius.be *Web Site:* www.adeb.irisnet.be/annuaire/lessius.htm, pg 70

P Lethielleux Editions (France) *Tel:* (01) 44 32 05 60 *Fax:* (01) 44 32 05 61, pg 171

Letouzey et Ane Editeurs (France) *Tel:* (01) 45 48 80 14 *Fax:* (01) 45 49 03 43 *E-mail:* letouzey@tree.tr, pg 171

Editorial Letras Cubanas (Cuba) *Tel:* (07) 862-6864 *Fax:* (07) 33-8187 *E-mail:* elc@icl.cult.cu, pg 120

Letterbox Library (United Kingdom) *Tel:* (020) 7503 4801 *Fax:* (020) 7503 4800 *E-mail:* info@letterboxlibrary.com *Web Site:* www.letterboxlibrary.com, pg 720, 1257

Casa Editrice Le Lettere SRL (Italy) *Tel:* (055) 2342710 *Fax:* (055) 2346010, pg 395

Letterland International Ltd (United Kingdom) *Tel:* (01223) 262675 *Fax:* (01223) 264126 *E-mail:* info@letterland.com *Web Site:* www.letterland.com, pg 720

Lettre International Kulturzeitung (Germany) *Tel:* (030) 30870440; (030) 30870462 *Fax:* (030) 2833128 *E-mail:* lettre@lettre.de *Web Site:* www.lettre.de, pg 253

Lettres Modernes Minard (France) *Tel:* (01) 43 36 25 83 *Fax:* (02) 31 84 48 09 *E-mail:* editorat.lettresmodernes@wanadoo.fr, pg 172

Lettres Vives Editions (France) *Tel:* (04) 95 36 40 93 *Fax:* (04) 95 36 59 92 *E-mail:* lettresvives@mic.fr, pg 172

Charles Letts & Co Ltd (United Kingdom) *Tel:* (0131) 663 1971 *Fax:* (0131) 660 3225 *E-mail:* sales@letts.co.uk; diaries@letts.co.uk *Web Site:* www.letts.co.uk, pg 1164

Charles Letts & Co Ltd (United Kingdom) *Tel:* (0131) 663 1971 *Fax:* (0131) 660 3225 *E-mail:* diaries@letts.co.uk *Web Site:* www.letts.co.uk, pg 1226

Letts Educational (United Kingdom) *Tel:* (0845) 602 1937 *Fax:* (020) 8742 8390 *E-mail:* mail@lettsed.co.uk *Web Site:* www.lettsed.co.uk, pg 720

Bernard Letu Editeur (Switzerland) *Tel:* (022) 204757 *Fax:* (022) 208492, pg 627

LEU-VERLAG Wolfgang Leupelt (Germany) *Tel:* (02204) 981141 *Fax:* (02204) 981143 *E-mail:* info@leu-verlag.net *Web Site:* www.leu-verlag.net, pg 254

Leuchter-Verlag EG (Germany) *Tel:* (06150) 97360 *Fax:* (06150) 9736-36, pg 254

Verlag Gerald Leue (Germany) *Tel:* (030) 7865020 *Fax:* (030) 78913876 *E-mail:* vertrieb@leue-verlag.de *Web Site:* www.leue-verlag.de, pg 254

Leuven University Press (Belgium) *Tel:* (016) 32 53 45 *Fax:* (016) 32 53 52 *E-mail:* university.press@upers.kuleuven.ac.be; universitaire.pers@upers.kuleuven.ac.be *Web Site:* www.lup.be, pg 70

Levante Editori (Italy) *Tel:* (080) 5213778 *Fax:* (080) 5213778 *E-mail:* levanted@tin.it *Web Site:* www.levantebari.com, pg 395

Levanter Publishing & Associates (Australia) *Tel:* (02) 9371 7824, pg 29

A G Leventis Foundation (Greece) *Tel:* (0210) 6165232 *Fax:* (0210) 6165235 *E-mail:* leventcy@zenon.logos.cy.net; eleni.mariolea@leventis.net *Web Site:* www.leventisfoundation.org, pg 309

Liana Levi Editions (France) *Tel:* (01) 43 26 29 61 *Fax:* (01) 46 33 69 56, pg 172

Levrotto e Bella Libreria Editrice Universitaria SAS (Italy) *Tel:* (011) 8121205 *Fax:* (011) 8124025 *E-mail:* levrotto@ipsnet.it, pg 395

Barbara Levy Literary Agency (United Kingdom) *Tel:* (020) 7435 9046 *Fax:* (020) 7431 2063, pg 1141

The Lexicon Bookshop (United Kingdom) *Tel:* (01624) 673004 *Fax:* (01624) 661959 *E-mail:* manxbooks@lexiconbookshop.co.im *Web Site:* www.lexiconbookshop.co.im, pg 1352

LexisNexis (Singapore) *Tel:* 6733 1380 *Fax:* 6773 1719 *Web Site:* www.lexisnexis.com.sg, pg 557

LexisNexis Butterworths South Africa (South Africa) *Tel:* (031) 268 3111; (031) 268 3007 (customer service) *Fax:* (031) 268 3108; (021) 268 3109 *Toll Free Fax:* (031) 268 3102 (Marketing) *Web Site:* www.lexisnexis.co.za, pg 566

LexisNexis India (India) *Tel:* (011) 373 9614; (011) 373 9615; (011) 373 9616; (011) 332 6454 customer service; (011) 332 6455 customer service *Fax:* (011) 332 6456 *E-mail:* info@lexisnexis.co.in; customer.care@lexisnexis.co.in *Web Site:* www.lexisnexis.co.in, pg 340

Lexus Ltd (United Kingdom) *Tel:* (0141) 2215266 *Fax:* (0141) 2263139 *Web Site:* www.lexusforlanguages.co.uk, pg 1151

La Ley SA Editora e Impresora (Argentina) *Tel:* (011) 4378-4841 *Fax:* (011) 4372-0953 *E-mail:* atcliente1@laley.com.ar *Web Site:* www.la-ley.com.ar, pg 7

Leykam Buchverlagsges mbH (Austria) *Tel:* (0316) 8076-531 *Fax:* (0316) 8076-539 *E-mail:* verlag@leykam.com *Web Site:* www.leykam.com; www.leykamverlag.at, pg 53

Les Editions LGDJ-Montchrestien (France) *Tel:* (01) 56 54 16 00 *Fax:* (01) 56 54 16 49 *Web Site:* www.lgdj.fr/lgdj/accueil.php, pg 172

Lia rumantscha (Switzerland) *Tel:* (081) 258 3222 *Fax:* (081) 258 3223 *E-mail:* liarumantscha@rumantsch.ch *Web Site:* www.liarumantscha.ch, pg 627

Liang Yu Printing Factory Ltd (Hong Kong) *Tel:* 25604453; 25677563 *Fax:* 28858099 *E-mail:* liangyup@netvigator.com, pg 1218

Liaoning People's Publishing House (China) *Tel:* (024) 3864674; (024) 3863316 *Fax:* (024) 371472, pg 106

Liaoning Provincial Library (China) *Tel:* (024) 2482-2241 *Web Site:* www.lnlib.com, pg 1497

Librairie du Liban Publishers (Sal) (Lebanon) *Tel:* (09) 217 944; (09) 217945; (09) 217 946; (09) 217 735 *Fax:* (09) 217734; (09) 217 434 *E-mail:* info@ldlp.com *Web Site:* www.ldlp.com, pg 446

Librairie du Liban Publishers (Sal) (Lebanon) *Tel:* (09) 217 735; (09) 217 944; (09) 217 745; (09) 217 946 *Fax:* (09) 217 734 *E-mail:* info@ldlp.com *Web Site:* www.ldlp.com, pg 1324

Bibliotheque Nationale du Liban (Lebanon) *Tel:* (01) 862957 *Fax:* (01) 374079, pg 1525

John Libbey & Co Ltd (United Kingdom) *Tel:* (023) 8065 0208 *Fax:* (023) 8065 0259 *E-mail:* johnlibbey@aol.com, pg 720

Editions John Libbey Eurotext (France) *Tel:* (01) 46 73 06 60 *Fax:* (01) 40 84 09 99 *E-mail:* contact@john-libbey-eurotext.fr *Web Site:* www.john-libbey-eurotext.fr, pg 172

Die Libelle Verlag Ag Libellen Haus (Switzerland) *Tel:* (071) 688 35 55 *Fax:* (071) 688 35 65 *E-mail:* info@libelle.ch *Web Site:* www.libelle.ch, pg 628

Liber AB (Sweden) *Tel:* (08) 6909200 *Fax:* (08) 6909458 *E-mail:* export@liber.se; infomaster@liber.se *Web Site:* www.liber.se, pg 613

Liber Ediciones, SA (Spain) *Tel:* (0948) 177 488; (0902) 300 307 *Fax:* (0948) 176 667 *E-mail:* info@arsliber.com *Web Site:* www.arsliber.com, pg 589

Liber Hermods AB (Sweden) *Tel:* (040) 258600 *Fax:* (040) 304600 *Web Site:* www.liberhermods.se, pg 613

Liberia Editorial Minerva-Miraflores (Peru) *Tel:* (014) 4475499 *Fax:* (014) 4458583 *E-mail:* minerva@chavin-rcp-net-pe, pg 1334

Ediciones Libertarias/Prodhufi SA (Spain) *Tel:* (091) 593 33 93 *Fax:* (091) 594 16 96 *E-mail:* libertarias@libertarias.com *Web Site:* www.libertarias.com, pg 589

Libertas- Europaeisches Institut GmbH (Germany) *Tel:* (07031) 6186-80 *Fax:* (07031) 6186-86 *E-mail:* info@libertas-institut.com *Web Site:* www.libertas-institut.com, pg 254

Libertatea (Serbia and Montenegro) *Tel:* (013) 33-51; 13 346 447 *Fax:* (013) 46-447, pg 552

Liberty (United Kingdom) *Tel:* (020) 7403 3888 *Fax:* (020) 7407 5354 *E-mail:* info@liberty-human-rights.org.uk *Web Site:* www.liberty-human-rights.org.uk, pg 720

Liberty Books (Pvt) Ltd (Pakistan) *Tel:* (021) 111-311-113; (021) 5671240; (021) 5671244 *Fax:* (021) 5684319 *E-mail:* info@libertybooks.com *Web Site:* www.libertybooks.com, pg 1333

Libiosy Libres, Editorial (Colombia) *Tel:* (01) 2907145; (01) 2907862; (01) 2886188 *Fax:* (01) 2696830, pg 111

Libra Books Pty Ltd (Australia) *Tel:* (03) 6230 2656 *Fax:* (03) 6225 0900, pg 29

Libra House Ltd (Ireland) *Tel:* (01) 4542717, pg 361

Ediciones Libra, SA de CV (Mexico) *Tel:* (05) 6049926 *Fax:* (05) 6882848, pg 467

Libra Editorial SA de CV (Mexico) *Tel:* (05) 6641454; (05) 6514156 *Fax:* (05) 6641454, pg 467

Librairie Bilingue/The Bilingual Bookshop (Cameroon) *Tel:* 224899 *Fax:* 232903, pg 1304

Librairie Clairafrique (Senegal) *Tel:* (08) 222169 *Fax:* (08) 218409 *E-mail:* clairafrique@le-senegal.com *Web Site:* www.le-senegal.com/clairafrique, pg 1338

La Librairie de Madagascar (Madagascar) *Tel:* (020) 222454 *Fax:* (020) 2264395; (020) 224395, pg 1325

Librairie des Presses Universitaires (The Democratic Republic of the Congo) *Tel:* (012) 30652, pg 1307

Librairie des Presses Universitaires de Bruxelles (Belgium) *Tel:* (02) 641 1440 *Fax:* (02) 6477962 *Web Site:* www.ulb.ac.be, pg 1302

Librairie FNAC (France) *Tel:* (01) 42 70 56 90 *E-mail:* service-clientele@fnac.com *Web Site:* www.fnac.com, pg 1310

Editions Librairie-Galerie Racine (France) *Tel:* (01) 43269724 *Fax:* (01) 43269724 *E-mail:* lgr@librairie-galerie-racine.com, pg 172

Librairie Generale des PUF (France) *Tel:* (01) 44418120 *Fax:* (01) 43546481 *E-mail:* puf-lib@puf.worldnet.net, pg 1310

Librairie Internationale (Morocco) *Tel:* (07) 75 01 83 *Fax:* (07) 75 86 61 *E-mail:* Libinter@iam.net.ma, pg 1328

Librairie Kaufmann SA (Greece) *Tel:* (0210) 3236817 *Fax:* (0210) 3230320 *E-mail:* ccaldi@otenet.gr, pg 1313

Librairie la Hune (France) *Tel:* (01) 45483585, pg 1310

Librairie les Volcans (The Democratic Republic of the Congo) *Tel:* 366, pg 1307

Librairie Luginbuhl (France) *Tel:* (01) 45 51 42 58 *Fax:* (01) 45 56 07 80 *E-mail:* liblug@club-internet.fr, pg 172

Librairie Mixte Sarl (Madagascar) *Tel:* (020) 22 251-30, pg 1325.

Librairie Orientale sal (Lebanon) *Tel:* (01) 485793; (01) 485794; (01) 485795 *Fax:* (01) 485796; (01) 216021 *E-mail:* libor@cyberia.net.lb, pg 446

Librairie Scientifique et Technique Albert Blanchard (France) *Tel:* (01) 43 26 90 34 *Fax:* (01) 43 29 97 31 *E-mail:* librairie.blanchard@wanadoo.fr *Web Site:* www.blanchard75.fr, pg 172

Librairie Universitaire (Madagascar) *Tel:* (020) 24114, pg 1325

Librairie Universitaire (Rwanda) *Tel:* 530330 *Fax:* 530210 *E-mail:* biblio@nur.ac.rw *Web Site:* www.lib.nur.ac.rw, pg 1338

Libraria Universitatii (Romania) *Tel:* (064) 198 107, pg 1338

The Librarian, University College of Swaziland (Swaziland) *Tel:* 5184011 *Fax:* 5185276 *E-mail:* kwaluseni@uniswa.sz *Web Site:* www.uniswa.sz, pg 1284

Librarie Maritime Outremer (France) *Tel:* (04) 91 54 79 40 *Fax:* (04) 91 54 79 49 *E-mail:* webmaster@librairie-outremer.com *Web Site:* www.librairie-outremer.com, pg 172

Librarie Mixte (Madagascar) *Tel:* (02) 25130 *Fax:* (02) 25130, pg 453

Library & Information Association of New Zealand Aotearoa (LIANZA) (New Zealand) *Tel:* (04) 473 5834 *Fax:* (04) 499 1480 *E-mail:* office@lianza.org.nz *Web Site:* www.lianza.org.nz, pg 1568

Library & Information Association of South Africa (LIASA) (South Africa) *Tel:* (012) 481 2870; (012) 481 2875; (012) 481 2876 *Fax:* (012) 481 2873 *E-mail:* liasa@liasa.org.za *Web Site:* www.liasa.org.za, pg 1570

Library & Information Science Society (Zimbabwe) *Tel:* (04) 752311 *Fax:* (04) 720955, pg 1574

The Library Association of Bangladesh (Bangladesh) *Tel:* (02) 504269; (02) 8619408 *E-mail:* msik@icddrb.org, pg 1558

Library Association of Barbados (Barbados), pg 1558

Library Association of China (LAC) (Taiwan, Province of China) *Tel:* (02) 23312675 *Fax:* (02) 2370-0899 *E-mail:* lac@msg.ncl.edu.tw *Web Site:* www.ncl.edu.tw, pg 1571

Library Association of Cuba (Cuba) *Tel:* (07) 552244 *Fax:* (07) 662053, pg 1560

Library Association of Cyprus (Cyprus) *Tel:* (022) 404849, pg 1560

Library Association of Singapore (Singapore) *Tel:* 6749 7990 *Fax:* 6749 7480 *Web Site:* www.las.org.sg, pg 1570

Library Association of Trinidad & Tobago (Trinidad & Tobago) *Tel:* (0868) 687 0194 *E-mail:* secretary@latt.org.tt *Web Site:* www.latt.org.tt/cms/, pg 1572

Library of Australian History (Australia) *Tel:* (02) 9929 5087 *Fax:* (02) 9929 5087 *E-mail:* grdxxx@ozemail.com.au, pg 29

Library of Chinese Academy of Sciences (China) *Tel:* (010) 82626684; (010) 82626611-6720 *Fax:* (010) 62566846 *E-mail:* office@mail.las.ac.cn; information@mail.las.ac.cn *Web Site:* www.las.ac.cn, pg 1497

Library of Parliament (South Africa) *Tel:* (021) 403 2140; (021) 403 2141; (021) 403 2142 *Fax:* (021) 461 4331 *E-mail:* library@parliament.gov.za *Web Site:* www.parliament.gov.za, pg 1544

Library of the Mineral Research & Exploration General Directorate (Turkey) *Tel:* (0312) 287 34 30 *Fax:* (0312) 287 91 88 *Web Site:* www.mta.gov.tr, pg 1551

Library of the Near East School of Theology (Lebanon) *Tel:* (01) 354194; (01) 349901 *Fax:* (01) 347129 *E-mail:* nest.lib@inco.com.lb, pg 1525

Library of the People's Assembly (Egypt (Arab Republic of Egypt)) *Tel:* (02) 3540279 *Fax:* (02) 3548977, pg 1503

Library of the Press & Information Department (Afghanistan), pg 1489

Library Promotion Bureau (Pakistan) *Tel:* (021) 632-1959 *Fax:* (021) 632-1959, pg 513

Library Promotion Bureau (Pakistan) *Tel:* (021) 632-1959; (021) 6977737 *Fax:* (021) 632-1959, pg 1569

Library Service of Fiji (Fiji) *Tel:* 311224; 315 344; 315303 *Fax:* 314 994; 314 994, pg 141

Library Service of Fiji (Fiji) *Tel:* 315 344 *Fax:* 314 994, pg 1504

The Library Shop (Ireland) *Tel:* (01) 608 1171 *Fax:* (01) 6081016 *Web Site:* www.tcd.ie/library/shop/, pg 1319

Libreria Cultural Panamena SA (Panama) *Tel:* 2235628; 2236267 *Fax:* 2237280, pg 1334

Libreria Editora Ltda (Brazil) *Tel:* (011) 608-5411 *Fax:* (011) 948-1615 *E-mail:* portal@libreria.com.br; libreria@libreria.com.br *Web Site:* www.libreria.com.br, pg 85

Libreria Editrice Fiorentina (Italy) *Tel:* (055) 579921 *Fax:* (055) 579921, pg 395

Libreria Internacional SA (Paraguay) *Tel:* (021) 491 423; (021) 491 424 *Fax:* (021) 449 730, pg 1334

Libreria la Paz (Bolivia) *Tel:* (02) 353323; (02) 357109 *Fax:* (02) 391513, pg 1303

Libreria l'Universidad, Nicolas Ojeda Fierro e Hijos SRL Ltda (Peru) *Tel:* (014) 282461; (014) 282036, pg 1335

Libreria Libertad SA (Chile) *Tel:* (02) 698 8773 *Fax:* (02) 672 6314, pg 99

Libreria Nacional Ltda (Colombia) *Tel:* (01) 825829; (01) 833849; (01) 2139842; (01) 2139882 *Fax:* (01) 822404; (01) 2138404, pg 1306

Libreria Parroquial de Claveria SA Edicion Compra y Venta de Libros (Mexico) *Tel:* (05) 3967027; (05) 3967718 *Fax:* (05) 3991243, pg 467

Libreria Tecnologica Universitaria (Nicaragua) *Tel:* (02) 773026 *Fax:* (02) 670106, pg 1331

Libreria Universitaria (Chile) *Tel:* (02) 2234555; (02) 2236980 *Fax:* (02) 2099455; (02) 499455, pg 1305

Libreria Universitaria (Ecuador) *Tel:* (02) 212521, pg 1309

Libreria Universitaria (Nicaragua) *Tel:* (0311) 2612; (0311) 2613, pg 1331

Libreria y Distribuidora Lerner Ltda (Colombia) *Tel:* (01) 243 0567; (01) 334 7826 *Fax:* (01) 281 4319, pg 1306

Libresa S A (Ecuador) *Tel:* (02) 230925; (02) 525581 *Fax:* (02) 502992 *E-mail:* libresa@interactive.net.ec, pg 137

Libretto Forlag (Norway) *Tel:* (022) 443011 *Fax:* (022) 443012, pg 509

Librex (Italy) *Tel:* (02) 58302006, pg 395

Edition Libri Illustri GmbH (Germany) *Tel:* (07141) 84720 *Fax:* (07141) 875117 *E-mail:* info@libri-illustri.de *Web Site:* www.edition-libri-illustri.de, pg 254

Libri spol sro (Czech Republic) *Tel:* (02) 5161 3113; (02) 5161 2302 *Fax:* (02) 5161 1013 *E-mail:* libri@libri.cz *Web Site:* www.libri.cz, pg 125

Libris Bokforlaget (Sweden) *Tel:* (019) 208400 *Fax:* (019) 208430 *E-mail:* info@libris.se *Web Site:* www.libris.se, pg 613

Libris Emo AS (Norway) *Tel:* 63849200 *Fax:* 63849345, pg 1333

Libris Ltd (United Kingdom) *Tel:* (020) 7482 2390 *Fax:* (020) 7485 2730 *E-mail:* libris@onetel.net.uk *Web Site:* www.librislondon.co.uk, pg 720

Libro Ltd (Greece) *Tel:* (010) 7247116; (010) 7228647 *Fax:* (010) 7226648 *E-mail:* libro@hol.gr, pg 309

Librograf Editora (Argentina) *Tel:* (011) 4300-3670; (011) 4300-1466 *Fax:* (011) 4300-3670, pg 7

Librolandia del Centro SA de CV (Mexico) *Tel:* (062) 135646; (062) 170236 *Fax:* (062) 170236, pg 1327

Editorial Libros y Libres SA (Colombia) *Tel:* (01) 2907145; (01) 2907862; (01) 2886188 *Fax:* (01) 2696830 *E-mail:* edilibro@colomsat.net.co, pg 112

Libros y Revistas SA de CV (Mexico) *Tel:* (05) 5437295 *Fax:* (05) 5364622, pg 467

Libsa Editorial SA (Spain) *Tel:* (091) 657 25 80 *Fax:* (091) 657 25 83 *E-mail:* libsa@libsa.es *Web Site:* www.libsa.es, pg 589

Licap CVBA (Belgium) *Tel:* (02) 5099672 *Fax:* (02) 5099704; (02) 5099780 *E-mail:* info@licap.be, pg 1302

Licht & Licht Literary Agency (Denmark) *Tel:* 39610908 *Fax:* 39611105, pg 1130

LID Editorial Empresarial, SL (Spain) *Tel:* (091) 372 90 03 *Fax:* (091) 372 85 14 *E-mail:* info@lideditorial.com *Web Site:* www.lideditorial.com, pg 589

Editora Lidador Ltda (Brazil) *Tel:* (021) 2569-0594 *Fax:* (021) 2204-0684 *E-mail:* lidador@infolink.com.br, pg 85

Lidel Edicoes Tecnicas, Lda (Portugal) *Tel:* (021) 571288 *Fax:* (021) 577827, pg 533

Lider Verlag (Romania) *Tel:* (01) 337-33-067; (01) 3374881 *Fax:* (01) 337-48-22, pg 540

Lidhja e Shkrimtareve dhe e Artisteve toe Shqiperise (Albania) *Tel:* (042) 23843 *Fax:* (042) 23843 *E-mail:* bashan@natlib.tirana.al, pg 1259

Edition Lidiarte (Germany) *Tel:* (030) 3137420 *Fax:* (030) 3127117 *E-mail:* edition@lidiarte.de *Web Site:* www.lidiarte.de, pg 254

Ediciones Lidiun (Argentina) *Tel:* (011) 4942-9002 *Fax:* (011) 4942-9162 *E-mail:* info@ateneo.com *Web Site:* www.ateneo.com, pg 7

Lidman Production AB (Sweden) *Tel:* (08) 6633615 *Fax:* (08) 6633590 *E-mail:* lidman@canit.se, pg 613

Lidove Noviny Publishing House (Czech Republic) *Tel:* (02) 225 223 50; (02) 222 510 845 *Fax:* (02) 225 240 12; (02) 222 514 012 *E-mail:* nln@nln.cz; nln@iol.cz *Web Site:* www.nln.cz, pg 125

Hildegard Liebaug-Dartmann (Germany) *Tel:* (02225) 909343 *Fax:* (02225) 909345 *E-mail:* liebaug-dartmann@t-online.de *Web Site:* www.liebaug-dartmann.de, pg 254

Liebenzeller Mission, GmbH, Abt. Verlag (Germany) *Tel:* (07052) 17-163 *Fax:* (07052) 17-170 *E-mail:* buch@liebenzell.org *Web Site:* www.liebenzell.org/blm/index.htm, pg 254

Liechenstein PEN Centre (Liechtenstein) *Tel:* (0423) 2327271 *Fax:* (0423) 2328071 *E-mail:* info@pen-club.li, pg 1402

Liechtenstein Verlag AG (Liechtenstein) *Tel:* 2396010 *Fax:* 2396019 *E-mail:* flbooks@verlag-ag.lol.li *Web Site:* www.lol.li/verlag_ag, pg 448

Liechtenstein Verlag AG (Liechtenstein) *Tel:* (0423) 2322414 *Fax:* (0423) 2324340 *E-mail:* flbooks@verlag-ag.lol.li, pg 1134

Liechtensteinische Landesbibliothek (Liechtenstein) *Tel:* 236 63 62 *Fax:* 233 14 19 *E-mail:* info@landesbibliothek.li *Web Site:* www.lbfl.li, pg 1525

Verlag der Liechtensteinischen Akademischen Gesellschaft (Liechtenstein) *Tel:* 232 30 28 *Fax:* 233 14 49, pg 448

Lielvards Ltd (Latvia) *Tel:* (050) 71860 *Fax:* (050) 71861 *E-mail:* lielvards@lielvards.lv *Web Site:* www.lielvards.lv, pg 445

Robert Lienau GmbH & Co KG (Germany) *Tel:* (069) 9782866 *Fax:* (069) 97828689 *E-mail:* info@lienau-frankfurt.de *Web Site:* www.lienau-frankfurt.de, pg 254

Lienhard Pallast Verlag (Germany) *Tel:* (02244) 5863 *Fax:* (02244) 5863 *E-mail:* lienhard@pallast-publisher.com *Web Site:* www.pallast-publisher.com, pg 254

Liepman Agency AG (Switzerland) *Tel:* (044) 2617660 *Fax:* (044) 2610124 *E-mail:* info@liepmanagency.com, pg 1137

Le Lierre et Le Coudrier (France) *Tel:* (01) 42550027 *Fax:* (01) 42570497, pg 172

Lietus Ltd (Lithuania) *Tel:* (02) 312298; (02) 8299 35423; (02) 745720 *Fax:* (02) 312298, pg 449

Lietuvos Rasytoju Sajungos Leidykla (Lithuania) *Tel:* (05) 2628945; (05) 2628643 *Fax:* (05) 2628945 *E-mail:* info@rsleidykla.lt *Web Site:* www.rsleidykla.lt, pg 449

Life Challenge AFRICA (Kenya) *Tel:* (02) 561121; (02) 722314 *Fax:* (02) 564030 *E-mail:* lca@umsg.org, pg 435

Life Planning Foundation of Australia, Inc (Australia) *Tel:* (03) 9670 4417 *Fax:* (03) 9640 0094 *E-mail:* lifeclub@vicnet.net.au *Web Site:* www.life.org.au, pg 29

Ligue des Bibliotheques Europeennes de Recherche (LIBER) (Germany) *Tel:* (0421) 2183361 *Web Site:* www.kb.dk/guests/intl/liber, pg 1270

Ligue pour la lecture de la Bible (Belgium) *Tel:* (02) 427-92-77 *Fax:* (02) 428-82-06 *E-mail:* llb_ibb@freegates.be, pg 70

Liguori Editore SRL (Italy) *Tel:* (081) 7206111; (081) 7206202 (orders) *Fax:* (081) 7206244 *E-mail:* liguori@liguori.it *Web Site:* www.liguori.it, pg 395

Editrice Liguria SNC di Norberto Sabatelli & C (Italy) *Tel:* (019) 829917 *Fax:* (019) 8387798, pg 395

Lijnkamp Literary Agents (Netherlands) *Tel:* (020) 6207742 *Fax:* (020) 6385298 *E-mail:* info@lijnkamp.nl *Web Site:* www.lijnkamp.nl, pg 1135

LIK Izdanija (Bulgaria) *Tel:* (02) 9443181; (02) 943400; (02) 9434748 *Fax:* (02) 9434400; (02) 9434748; (02) 9443181 *E-mail:* lik@ttm.bg, pg 95

Oy LIKE Kustannus (Finland) *Tel:* (09) 622 9970 *Fax:* (09) 135 1372 *E-mail:* like@like.fi *Web Site:* www.likekustannus.fi, pg 143

Likuni Press (Malawi) *Tel:* 721135; 721388 *Fax:* 72114133, pg 1160

Lila Libreria de Mujeres (Chile) *Tel:* (02) 2361725 *Fax:* (02) 2361725, pg 1305

The Lilliput Press Ltd (Ireland) *Tel:* (01) 6711647 *Fax:* (01) 6711233 *E-mail:* info@lilliputpress.ie *Web Site:* www.lilliputpress.ie, pg 361

LIM Editrice SRL (Italy) *Tel:* (0583) 394464 *Fax:* (0583) 394469 *E-mail:* lim@lim.it *Web Site:* www.lim.it, pg 395

Editorial Lima 2000 SA (Peru) *Tel:* (01) 440-3486 *Fax:* (01) 440-3480 *E-mail:* informes@lima2000.com.pe *Web Site:* www.lima2000.com.pe, pg 517

Waldir Lima Editora (Brazil) *Tel:* (05521) 581-5000 *Fax:* (05521) 581-3586 *E-mail:* geapo@ccaa.com.br *Web Site:* www.ccaa.com.br, pg 85

Editions des Limbes d'Or FBT de R Editions (France) *Tel:* (01) 41151969 *Fax:* (01) 41151969, pg 172

Publishing House Limbus Press (Russian Federation) *Tel:* (0812) 1126547 *Fax:* (0812) 1126706 *E-mail:* limbuspr@rol.ru; limbus@limbuspress.ru *Web Site:* www.limbuspress.ru, pg 546

Liming Cultural Enterprise Co Ltd (Taiwan, Province of China) *Tel:* (02) 23821152 *Fax:* (02) 23821244, pg 641

Limmat Verlag (Switzerland) *Tel:* (01) 445 80 80 *Fax:* (01) 445 80 88 *E-mail:* mail@limmatverlag.ch *Web Site:* www.limmatverlag.ch, pg 628

Limpert Verlag (Germany) *Tel:* (06766) 903160 *Fax:* (06766) 903320 *E-mail:* vertrieb@limpert.de, pg 254

Editorial Limusa SA de CV (Mexico) *Tel:* (05) 5128503; (05) 5128050 *Fax:* (05) 512 2903 *E-mail:* limusa@noriega.com.mx *Web Site:* www.noriega.com.mx, pg 467

Lin Pai Press Company Ltd (Taiwan, Province of China) *Tel:* (02) 7765889 *Fax:* (02) 7712568, pg 641

Linardi y Risso Libreria (Uruguay) *Tel:* (02) 915 71 29; (02) 915 73 28 *Fax:* (02) 915 74 31 *E-mail:* lyrbooks@linardiyrisso.com *Web Site:* www.linardiyrisso.com/, pg 777

Libreria Linardi y Risso (Uruguay) *Tel:* (02) 915 7129; (02) 915 7328 *Fax:* (02) 915 7431 *E-mail:* lyrbooks@linardiyrisso.com *Web Site:* www.linardiyrisso.com, pg 1355

Lincoln College Centre for Resource Management (New Zealand) *Tel:* (03) 3252811 *Fax:* (03) 325156 *Web Site:* www.lincoln.ac.nz, pg 498

Frances Lincoln Ltd (United Kingdom) *Tel:* (020) 7284 4009 *Fax:* (020) 7485 0490 *E-mail:* reception@frances-lincoln.com *Web Site:* www.franceslincoln.com, pg 720

Lincoln University Bookshop (New Zealand) *Tel:* (03) 3252811 *Fax:* (03) 3252944 *E-mail:* info@lincoln.ac.nz *Web Site:* www.lincoln.ac.nz, pg 1330

Lincoln University Press (New Zealand) *Tel:* (04) 4710601 *Fax:* (04) 4710489 *E-mail:* learn@lincoln.ac.nz *Web Site:* learn.lincoln.ac.nz, pg 498

Lindau (Italy) *Tel:* (011) 6693910; (011) 6693924 *Fax:* (011) 6693929 *E-mail:* info@lindau.it *Web Site:* www.lindau.it, pg 395

J Lindauer Verlag (Germany) *Tel:* (089) 223041 *Fax:* (089) 224315 *Web Site:* www.lindauer-verlag.de, pg 254

Linde Verlag Wien GmbH (Austria) *Tel:* (01) 24630-0 *Fax:* (01) 24630-23 *E-mail:* office@lindeverlag.at; presse@lindeverlag.at *Web Site:* www.linde-verlag.at, pg 53

H Lindemanns Buchhandlung (Germany) *Tel:* (0711) 248999-0 *Fax:* (0711) 233320 *E-mail:* lindemannsbuch@t-online.de *Web Site:* www.lindemanns-buchhandlung.de, pg 254

Linden Artists Ltd (United Kingdom) *Tel:* (020) 7738 2505 *Fax:* (020) 7738 2513 *E-mail:* martyr@btinternet.com, pg 1185

Linden-Verlag (Germany) *Tel:* (0341) 5902024 *Fax:* (0341) 5904436 *E-mail:* verlag@linden-buch.de *Web Site:* www.linden-buch.de, pg 254

De Lindenboom/INOR Publikaties (Netherlands) *Tel:* (053) 5740004 *Fax:* (053) 5729296 *E-mail:* lindeboo@worldonline.nl, pg 1135

Lindhardt og Ringhof Forlag A/S (Denmark) *Tel:* 33 69 50 00 *Fax:* 33695001 *E-mail:* lr@lrforlag.dk *Web Site:* www.lrforlag.dk, pg 132

Martha Lindner Verlags-GmbH (Germany) *Tel:* (0721) 843965 *Fax:* (0721) 8303716, pg 254

Linea d'Ombra Libri (Italy) *Tel:* (0438) 412647 *Fax:* (0438) 412690 *E-mail:* info@lineadombra.it *Web Site:* www.lineadombra.it, pg 395

Linen Hall Library (United Kingdom) *Tel:* (028) 9032 1707 *Fax:* (028) 9043 8586 *E-mail:* info@linenhall.com *Web Site:* www.linenhall.com, pg 721

David Ling Publishing (New Zealand) *Tel:* (09) 4182785 *Fax:* (09) 4182785, pg 498

Ling Kee Publishing Group (Hong Kong) *Tel:* 25616151 *Fax:* 2811 1980 *Web Site:* www.lingkee.com, pg 318

Georg Lingenbrink GmbH & Co, Libri (Germany) *Tel:* 0180-53 69 800 *Fax:* (040) 853 98 300 *E-mail:* service@libri.de *Web Site:* www.libri.de, pg 1311

Linguaphone Institute Ltd (United Kingdom) *Tel:* (020) 8687 6010 *Fax:* (020) 8687 6310 *E-mail:* ads@linguaphone.co.uk (advertising); cst@linguaphone.co.uk (customer support) *Web Site:* www.linguaphone.co.uk, pg 721

Linick International Inc (United States) *Tel:* 631-924-3888 *Fax:* 631-924-3890 *E-mail:* linickgrp@att.net *Web Site:* www.lgroup.addr.com, pg 1188, 1230, 1241

Linick International Inc (United States) *Tel:* 631-924-3888 *E-mail:* linickgrp@att.net *Web Site:* www.lgroup.addr.com, pg 1249

Linking Publishing Company Ltd (Taiwan, Province of China) *Tel:* (02) 27634300 (ext 5040) *Fax:* (02) 27634590 *E-mail:* linkingp@udngroup.com.tw *Web Site:* www.udngroup.com.tw/linkingp, pg 641

Linking-Up Publishing (Australia) *Tel:* (02) 9712 5576 *Fax:* (02) 9712 1963, pg 29

YELLOW PAGES

Christoph Links Verlag - LinksDruck GmbH (Germany) *Tel:* (030) 440232-0 *Fax:* (030) 44023229 *E-mail:* mail@linksverlag.de *Web Site:* www.linksverlag.de, pg 254

Siegbert Linnemann Verlag (Germany) *Tel:* (05241) 14061 *Fax:* (05241) 26439 *E-mail:* info@linnemann-verlag.com *Web Site:* www.linnemann-verlag.com, pg 254

Lion Hudson PLC (United Kingdom) *Tel:* (01865) 302750 *Fax:* (01865) 302757 *E-mail:* international@lionhudson.com *Web Site:* www.lionhudson.com, pg 721

Lippincott Williams & Wilkins (United Kingdom) *Tel:* (020) 7981 0500 *Fax:* (020) 7981 0501 *Web Site:* www.lww.co.uk, pg 721

LISA (Livros Irradiantes SA) (Brazil) *Tel:* (011) 2563755 *Fax:* (011) 2575776 *E-mail:* lerlisalivros@ig.com.br, pg 85

George Lise-Huyghes des Etages (Martinique) *Tel:* 736819, pg 460

Lister Art Books of Southport (United Kingdom) *Tel:* (01704) 232033 *Fax:* (01704) 505926 *E-mail:* sales@laboox.demon.co.uk, pg 1352

Editora Listin Diario (Dominican Republic) *Tel:* (0809) 686-6688 *Fax:* (0809) 686-6595, pg 136

LISU (United Kingdom) *Tel:* (01509) 263171 *E-mail:* lisu@lboro.ac.uk *Web Site:* www.lboro.ac.uk/departments/dis/lisu/lisuhp.html, pg 721

LIT Verlag (Germany) *Tel:* (0251) 235091 *Fax:* (0251) 231972 *E-mail:* lit@lit-verlag.de *Web Site:* www.lit-verlag.de, pg 255

LITA Ochranna Autorska Spolocnost' Agentura (Slovakia) *Tel:* (07) 62 80 22 48 *Fax:* (07) 62 80 22 46 *E-mail:* lita@lita.sk, pg 1136

Litag Anstalt- Literarische, Medien und Kuenstler Agentur (Liechtenstein) *Tel:* (0423) 3771809 *Fax:* (0423) 3771802, pg 448

LiTec (Librairies Techniques SA) (France) *Tel:* (01) 45 58 92 70 *Fax:* (01) 45 58 94 00 *E-mail:* libraries@juris-classeur.com *Web Site:* www.lexisnexis.fr, pg 172

LITEC (Livraria Editora Tecnica) Ltda (Brazil) *Tel:* (011) 223-7872 *Fax:* (011) 222-6728 *E-mail:* litec@litec.com.br *Web Site:* www.litec.com.br, pg 1303

Litera Prima (Bulgaria) *Tel:* (02) 9731698; (02) 9745575 *E-mail:* mmihales@vmei.acad.bg, pg 95

Litera Publishing House (Romania) *Tel:* (01) 2331349; (01) 2332749 *Fax:* (01) 2231873 *E-mail:* info@litera.ro *Web Site:* www.litera-publishing.com, pg 540

Wydawnictwo Literackie (Poland) *Tel:* (012) 4225423; (012) 4232254; (012) 4231251 *Fax:* (012) 4225423 *E-mail:* redakcja@wl.interkom.pl; handel@wl.net.pl; promocja@wl.net.pl *Web Site:* www.wl.net.pl, pg 524

Literamed Publications Nigeria Ltd (Nigeria) *Tel:* (01) 4962512; (01) 4935258 *Fax:* (01) 4972217 *E-mail:* information@lanternbooks.com *Web Site:* www.lantern-books.com, pg 505

Literar-Mechana, Wahrnehmungsgesellschaft fuer Urheberrechte GmbH (Austria) *Tel:* (01) 5872161-0 *Fax:* (01) 5872161-9 *E-mail:* literar.mechana@netway.at, pg 1261

Literarischer Verein in Stuttgart eV (Germany) *Tel:* (0711) 5499710 *Fax:* (0711) 54997121, pg 1400

Literarisches Colloquium Berlin (Germany) *Tel:* (030) 8169960 *Fax:* (030) 81699619 *E-mail:* mail@lcb.de *Web Site:* www.lcb.de, pg 1400

Literas-Verlag GmbH (Austria) *Tel:* (01) 269 22 07 *Fax:* (01) 269 22 07, pg 53

Literature Academy Publishing (Republic of Korea) *Tel:* (02) 7645057 *Fax:* (02) 7458516 *E-mail:* webmaster@munhakac.co.kr *Web Site:* www.munhakac.co.kr, pg 441

Literature and Art Publishing House (Democratic People's Republic of Korea), pg 436

The Literature Bureau (Zimbabwe) *Tel:* (04) 726929; (04) 729120, pg 783

Literature Ministry Department (Hong Kong) *Tel:* 2725 8558 *Fax:* 2386 2304 *E-mail:* hkccllmd@hkstar.com, pg 1157

Lithuanian ISBN Agency (Lithuania) *Tel:* (05) 2497023 *Fax:* (05) 2496129 *E-mail:* isbnltu@lnb.lt *Web Site:* www.lnb.lt, pg 1276

Lithuanian Librarians Association (Lithuania) *Tel:* (02) 750340 *Fax:* (02) 750340 *E-mail:* lbd@vpu.lt *Web Site:* www.lbd.lt, pg 1567

Lithuanian National Museum Publishing House (Lithuania) *Tel:* (05) 262 77 74 *Fax:* (05) 261 10 23 *E-mail:* info@lnm.lt; muziejus@lnm.lt *Web Site:* www.lnm.lt, pg 449

Lithuanian Publishers' Association (Lithuania) *Tel:* (02) 332943 *Fax:* (02) 330519, pg 449

Lithuanian Publishers' Association (Lithuania) *Tel:* (05) 2617740 *Fax:* (05) 2617740 *E-mail:* lla@centras.lt *Web Site:* www.lla.lt, pg 1276

LITkom Elisabeth Falk Agentur fur Literatur und Kommunikation (Germany) *E-mail:* falk@litkom.de *Web Site:* www.litkom.de, pg 1131

Editions Lito (France) *Tel:* (01) 45161700 *Fax:* (01) 48820085 *E-mail:* annick.cabrelli@editionslito.com, pg 172

Lito Technion Ltda (Colombia) *Tel:* (01) 2443502; (01) 2443177; (01) 2441538, pg 112

Litografia Artex, SA (Costa Rica) *Tel:* 2373144 *Fax:* 2379568, pg 115

Litografia e Imprenta LIL SA (Costa Rica) *Tel:* 2350011; 2213622 *Fax:* 2407814, pg 115

Litopia Corp Ltd (United Kingdom) *Tel:* (020) 7224 1748 *Fax:* (020) 7224 1802 *E-mail:* enquiries@litopia.com *Web Site:* www.litopia.com, pg 1141

Editeurs de Litterature Biblique (Belgium) *Tel:* (02) 384-54-02; (02) 384-52-12 *Fax:* (02) 384-98-66 *E-mail:* elbpub@elbeurope.org *Web Site:* www.elbeurope.org, pg 70

Christopher Little Literary Agency (United Kingdom) *Tel:* (020) 7736 4455 *Fax:* (020) 7736 4490, pg 1141

Little Hills Press Pty Ltd (Australia) *Tel:* (02) 9838 4373 *Fax:* (02) 9838 7929 *E-mail:* lhills@bigpond.net.au *Web Site:* www.littlehills.com, pg 29

Little Red Apple Publishing (Australia) *Tel:* (02) 9430 6867 *E-mail:* littleredapple@hotmail.com, pg 29

Littlehampton Book Services Ltd (United Kingdom) *Tel:* (01903) 828500 *Fax:* (01903) 828802 *E-mail:* enquiries@lbsltd.co.uk *Web Site:* www.lbsltd.co.uk, pg 1352

The Littman Library of Jewish Civilization (United Kingdom) *Tel:* (01865) 514688 *Fax:* (01865) 514688 *E-mail:* enquiries@littman.co.uk; editorial@littman.co.uk; marketing@littman.co.uk *Web Site:* www.littman.co.uk, pg 721

Liverpool Libraries & Information Services (United Kingdom) *Tel:* (0151) 233 5829 *Fax:* (0151) 233 5886 *E-mail:* refbt.central.library@liverpool.gov.uk, pg 1553

Liverpool University Press (United Kingdom) *Tel:* (0151) 794 2233; (0151) 794 2237 *Fax:* (0151) 794 2235 *E-mail:* j.m.smith@liv.ac.uk *Web Site:* www.liverpool-unipress.co.uk, pg 722

Living Literary Agency (Italy) *Tel:* (02) 33100584 *Fax:* (02) 33100618 *E-mail:* living@galactica.it, pg 1133

Living Word Distribution (New Zealand) *Tel:* (07) 839 5607 *Fax:* (07) 834 3916 *E-mail:* livingword.ltd@xtra.co.nz, pg 1330

Livraria Alema Buecherstube Brooklin Ltda (Brazil) *Tel:* (011) 5543 3829 *Fax:* (011) 5041 4315 *E-mail:* buchlbb@uol.com.br *Web Site:* www.buchlbb.com/, pg 1304

LIVROS DO ORIENTE

Livraria Apostolado da Imprensa (Portugal) *Tel:* (0253) 22485 *Fax:* (0253) 201221, pg 533

Livraria Barata, Antonio D M Barata (Portugal) *Tel:* (021) 848 16 31 *Fax:* (021) 80 33 44, pg 1337

Livraria Buchholz, Lda (Portugal) *Tel:* (021) 3170580 *Fax:* (021) 3522634 *E-mail:* buchholz@mail.telepac.pt *Web Site:* www.buchholz.pt, pg 1337

Livraria Caravana (Portugal) *Tel:* (089) 462879 *Fax:* (089) 462871, pg 1337

Livraria Cientifica Ernesto Reichmann Ltda (Brazil) *Tel:* (011) 3255-1342; (011) 3214-3167 *Fax:* (011) 3255-7501 *E-mail:* rrr@erdl.com *Web Site:* www.ernestoreichmann.com.br, pg 1304

Livraria Cultura Editora Ltda (Brazil) *Tel:* (011) 3170-4033 *Fax:* (011) 3285-4457 *E-mail:* livros@livrariacultura.com.br, pg 1304

Livraria Dos Advogados Editora Ltda (Brazil) *Tel:* (011) 3107-3979 *Fax:* (011) 3107-6878 *E-mail:* lael@lael.com.br *Web Site:* www.lael.com.br, pg 85

Livraria Editora Infobook SA (Brazil) *Tel:* (021) 263-3807 *Fax:* (021) 263-3807, pg 85

Livraria Kosmos Editora Ltda (Brazil) *Tel:* (021) 2224-8616 *Fax:* (021) 2221-4582 *E-mail:* livro-rio@kosmos.com.br *Web Site:* www.kosmos.com.br, pg 85

Livraria Kosmos Editora Ltda (Brazil) *Tel:* (021) 224-8616 *Fax:* (021) 221-4582, pg 1263

Livraria Kosmos Editora Ltda (Brazil) *Tel:* (021) 2224-8616 *Fax:* (021) 2221-4582, pg 1304

Livraria Latina (Portugal) *Tel:* (022) 2001294 *Fax:* (022) 2086053, pg 1337

Livraria Ler, Lda (Portugal) *Tel:* (021) 60 69 96, pg 1337

Livraria Luzo-Espanhola Lda (Portugal) *Tel:* (021) 3424917, pg 533

Livraria Manuel Ferreira (Portugal) *Tel:* (022) 5363237 *Fax:* (022) 5364406 *E-mail:* livrariaferreira@hotmail.com, pg 1337

Livraria Minerva (Portugal) *Tel:* (0239) 26259 *Fax:* (0239) 717267 *E-mail:* livrariaminerva@mail.telepac.pt, pg 533

Livraria Nobel S/A (Brazil) *Tel:* (011) 3933-2822; (011) 3933-2811 *Fax:* (011) 3218-2833; (011) 3931-3988 *E-mail:* ary@editoranobel.com.br *Web Site:* www.livnobel.com.br, pg 85

Livraria Nobel S/A (Brazil) *Tel:* (011) 3706 1469 *Fax:* (011) 3218-2833 *E-mail:* ary@editoranobel.com.br *Web Site:* www.livrarianobel.com.br, pg 1304

Livraria Teorema 1-Cogitum Livrarias Lda (Portugal) *Tel:* (021) 4394912 *Fax:* (021) 4394909 *E-mail:* cogitum@ip.pt, pg 1337

Le Livre de Paris (France) *Tel:* (01) 41 23 60 00 *Fax:* (01) 41 45 34 42 *E-mail:* ldpsiege@hachette-livre.fr *Web Site:* www.livredeparis.com, pg 173

Le Livre de Poche-L G F (Librairie Generale Francaise) (France) *Tel:* (01) 43923000 *Fax:* (01) 43923590 *Web Site:* www.livredepoche.com; www.hachette.com, pg 173

Librairie Livre-Service (Morocco) *Tel:* (02) 262072 *Fax:* (02) 473089, pg 1328

Livres de France (Egypt (Arab Republic of Egypt)) *Tel:* (02) 3935512, pg 1309

Les Livres du Dragon d'Or (France) *Tel:* (01) 53 10 36 37 *Fax:* (01) 53 10 36 39 *E-mail:* dragondor@gruend.fr, pg 173

Editora Livros do Brasil Sarl (Portugal) *Tel:* (021) 3426113 *Fax:* (021) 342 84 87 *E-mail:* livbrasil@clix.pt, pg 533

Livros Do Oriente (Macau) *Tel:* 700320; 700421 *Fax:* 700423 *E-mail:* livros.macau@loriente.com *Web Site:* www.loriente.com, pg 452

Livros Horizonte Lda (Portugal) *Tel:* (021) 346 69 17 *Fax:* (021) 326921 *E-mail:* livroshorizonte@mail.telepac.pt, pg 533

Oficina de Livros Ltda (Brazil) *Tel:* (061) 386-2355 *Toll Free Tel:* 800-644-3002 *Fax:* (061) 386-9248 *E-mail:* nicanorsena2001@aol.com.br, pg 85

LK Litho (United States) *Tel:* 631-924-3888 *E-mail:* linickgrp@att.net *Web Site:* www.lgroup.addr.com, pg 1167, 1188

LK Litho (United States) *Tel:* 631-924-3888 *E-mail:* linickgrp@att.net *Web Site:* www.lgroup.addr.com/lklitho.htm, pg 1230

LK Litho (United States) *Tel:* 631-924-3888 *E-mail:* linickgrp@att.net *Web Site:* www.lgroup.addr.com, pg 1241, 1249

LKG (Leipziger Kommissions- und Grossbuchhandelsgesellschaft mbH) (Germany) *Tel:* (034206) 65135 *Fax:* (034206) 65110 *E-mail:* lkg@lkg-service.de, pg 1311

LLB France (Ligue pour la Lecture de la Bible) (France) *Tel:* (04) 75 56 02 68 *Fax:* (04) 75 56 02 97 *E-mail:* contact@llbfrance.com *Web Site:* www.llbfrance.com, pg 173

Llibres del Segle (Spain) *Tel:* (093) 795079; (093) 794023 *Fax:* (093) 210354 *E-mail:* costapau@releline.es, pg 589

Chris Lloyd Sales & Marketing Services (United Kingdom) *Tel:* (01202) 649930 *Fax:* (01202) 649950 *E-mail:* chrlloyd@globalnet.co.uk, pg 1352

LLP Ltd (United Kingdom) *Tel:* (020) 7553 1000 *Fax:* (020) 7553 1109 *E-mail:* info@lloydslist.com *Web Site:* www.lloydslist.com, pg 722

Lluvia Editores Srl (Peru) *Tel:* (01) 3326641 *Fax:* (01) 4320732 *E-mail:* lluviaeditores2002@yahoo.com, pg 517

LMH Publishing Ltd (Jamaica) *Tel:* (876) 938-0005 *Fax:* (876) 759-8752 *E-mail:* lmhbookpublishing@cwjamaica.com *Web Site:* www.lmhpublishingjamaica.com, pg 414

Vincenzo Lo Faro Editore (Italy) *Tel:* (06) 70451187 *Fax:* (06) 70451641 *Web Site:* culturitalia.uibk.ac.at, pg 395

Local Consumption Publications (Australia) *Tel:* (02) 9519-7503 *Fax:* (02) 95197503, pg 29

Editrice la Locusta (Italy) *Tel:* (0444) 324051 *E-mail:* la_locusta@yahoo.com *Web Site:* space.tin.it/io/pibeltra/lalocust.htm, pg 395

Lodenek Press (United Kingdom) *Tel:* (01208) 880850, pg 722

Wydawnictwo Lodzkie (Poland) *Tel:* (042) 6360331; (042) 6366189 *Fax:* (042) 6368524, pg 524

Loecker Verlag (Austria) *Tel:* (01) 512 02 82 *Fax:* (01) 512 02 82-22 *E-mail:* lverlag@loecker.at *Web Site:* www.loecker.at, pg 53

Uitgeverij Loempia (Belgium) *Tel:* (03) 2184292, pg 70

Loescher Editore SRL (Italy) *Tel:* (011) 5654111 *Fax:* (011) 56 25822 *E-mail:* mail@loescher.it *Web Site:* www.loescher.it, pg 396

Rainer Loessl Verlag (Germany) *Tel:* (089) 362646, pg 255

Antiquariat Oskar Loewe (Germany) *Tel:* (02361) 960813 *Fax:* (02361) 960815 *E-mail:* loewe.bochum@t-online.de *Web Site:* www.antiquariat.net/loewe, pg 255

Loewe Verlag GmbH (Germany) *Tel:* (09208) 51-0 *Fax:* (09208) 51-309 *E-mail:* presse@loewe-verlag.de *Web Site:* www.loewe-verlag.de, pg 255

Loffredo Editore Napoli SpA® (Italy) *Tel:* (081) 5937073 *Fax:* (081) 5936953 *E-mail:* info@loffredo.it *Web Site:* www.loffredo.it, pg 396

LOG-Internationale Zeitschrift fuer Literatur (Austria) *Tel:* (01) 2313433 *Fax:* (01) 2313433, pg 53

Logans University Bookshop (Pty) Ltd (South Africa) *Tel:* (031) 3076530 *Fax:* (031) 3073230, pg 1340

Logophon Verlag und Bildungsreisen GmbH (Germany) *Tel:* (06131) 71645 *Fax:* (06131) 72596 *E-mail:* verlag@logophon.de *Web Site:* www.logophon.de, pg 255

Logos (Greece) *Tel:* (01) 03823495 *Fax:* (01) 4834000 *E-mail:* amglogos@otenet.gc, pg 309

Logos Consorcio Editorial SA (Mexico), pg 468

Logos (Divine Word) Publications Inc (Philippines) *Tel:* (02) 7111323 *Fax:* (02) 7322736 *E-mail:* dwpsvd@rp1.net, pg 519

Logos Verlag GmbH (Germany) *Tel:* (05232) 960120; (05232) 960124 *Fax:* (05232) 960121, pg 255

Logos-Verlag Literatur & Layout GmbH (Germany) *Tel:* (06893) 986096 *Fax:* (06893) 986095, pg 255

Editora Logosofica (Brazil) *Tel:* (011) 8851476; (011) 8856574 *Fax:* (011) 8879480, pg 85

Loguez Ediciones (Spain) *Tel:* (0923) 138541 *Fax:* (0923) 138586 *E-mail:* loguezediciones@eresmas.com, pg 589

Ulla Lohren Literary Agency (Denmark) *Tel:* 44494515 *Fax:* 44493515 *E-mail:* ulla.litag@get2net.dk, pg 1130

Lohse Forlag (Denmark) *Tel:* 7593 4455 *Fax:* 7592 4275 *E-mail:* lohse@imh.dk *Web Site:* www.lohse.dk, pg 132

Lojas Europa-America (Portugal) *Tel:* (01) 9211461 *Fax:* (01) 9217940, pg 1337

Lokrundschau Verlag GmbH (Germany) *Tel:* (04151) 896913 *Fax:* (04151) 82889 *E-mail:* verlag@lokrundschau.de *Web Site:* www.lokrundschau.de, pg 255

Lokvangmaya Griha Pvt Ltd (India) *Tel:* (022) 4362474 *Fax:* (022) 4313220 *E-mail:* lokvang@bol.net.in, pg 340

Y Lolfa Cyf (United Kingdom) *Tel:* (01970) 832 304 *Fax:* (01970) 832 782 *E-mail:* ylolfa@ylolfa.com *Web Site:* www.ylolfa.com, pg 722

Les Editions du Lombard SA (Belgium) *Tel:* (02) 5266811 *Fax:* (02) 5204405 *E-mail:* info@lombard.be *Web Site:* www.lelombard.com, pg 70

Lomond Books (United Kingdom) *Tel:* (0131) 551 2261 *Fax:* (0131) 559 2042 *E-mail:* info@flatman.co.uk; sales@lomand-books.co.uk *Web Site:* www.lomond-books.co.uk; www.scottishbookstore.com, pg 1352

London Chamber of Commerce & Industry Examinations Board (LCCIEB) (United Kingdom) *Tel:* (020) 8309 3000 *Fax:* (020) 8302 4169 *E-mail:* custserv@lccieb.org.uk *Web Site:* www.lccieb.com, pg 722

London Independent Books (United Kingdom) *Tel:* (020) 7706 0486 *Fax:* (020) 7724 3122, pg 1141

Lonely Planet (France) *Tel:* (01) 44 32 06 20 *Fax:* (01) 46 34 72 55 *E-mail:* 100560.415@compuserve.com *Web Site:* www.lonelyplanet.fr, pg 173

Lonely Planet Publications Pty Ltd (Australia) *Tel:* (03) 8379 8000 *Fax:* (03) 8379 8111 *E-mail:* talk2us@lonelyplanet.com.au *Web Site:* www.lonelyplanet.com.au, pg 29

Lonely Planet, UK (United Kingdom) *Tel:* (020) 7841 9000 *Fax:* (020) 7841 9001 *E-mail:* go@lonelyplanet.co.uk *Web Site:* www.lonelyplanet.com, pg 722

Barry Long Books (Australia) *E-mail:* contact@barrylongbooks.com *Web Site:* www.barrylongbooks.com, pg 29

Longacre Press (New Zealand) *Tel:* (03) 4772911 *Fax:* (03) 4772911 *E-mail:* longacre.press@clear.net.nz, pg 498

Longanesi & C (Italy) *Tel:* (02) 80206310 *Fax:* (02) 72000306 *E-mail:* info@longanesi.it *Web Site:* www.longanesi.it, pg 396

Longman Italia srl (Italy) *Tel:* (02) 6739761 *Fax:* (02) 673976501 *E-mail:* longman-italia@pearsoned-ema.com *Web Site:* www.longman-elt.com, pg 396

Longman Nigeria Plc (Nigeria) *Tel:* (01) 497 89259 *Fax:* (01) 496 4370 *E-mail:* longman@infoweb.abs.net, pg 505

Longman Zimbabwe (Pvt) Ltd (Zimbabwe) *Tel:* (04) 621 661; (04) 621 667 *Fax:* (04) 621670 *E-mail:* customeralicek@longman.co.zw *Web Site:* www.pearsoned.co.uk/contactus/worldwideoffices/africa, pg 783

Angelo Longo Editore (Italy) *Tel:* (0544) 217026 *Fax:* (0544) 217554 *E-mail:* longo-ra@linknet.it *Web Site:* www.longo-editore.it, pg 396

La Longue Vue (Belgium) *Tel:* (02) 358 23 93 *Fax:* (02) 358 17 37 *E-mail:* longuevue@skynet.be, pg 70

Stefan Loose Verlag (Germany) *Tel:* (030) 6 91 37 89 *Fax:* (030) 6 93 01 71 *E-mail:* info@loose-verlag.de *Web Site:* www.loose-verlag.de, pg 255

Livraria Lopes Da Silva-Editora de M Moreira Soares Rocha Lda (Portugal) *Tel:* (02) 21678 *Fax:* (02) 2006017, pg 533

Lopez Libreros Editores S R L (Argentina) *Tel:* (011) 4963-9646, pg 7

E Lopfe-Benz AG Rorschach, Graphische Anstalt und Verlag (Switzerland) *Tel:* (071) 8440444 *Fax:* (071) 8440445, pg 628

Lorber-Verlag & Turm-Verlag Otto Zluhan (Germany) *Tel:* (07142) 940843 *Fax:* (07142) 940844 *E-mail:* info@lorber-verlag.de; bestellen@lorber-verlag.de *Web Site:* www.lorber-verlag.de, pg 255

Lorenz Books (United Kingdom) *Tel:* (020) 7401 2077 *Fax:* (020) 7633 9499 *E-mail:* bsp2b@aol.com, pg 722

Carlo Lorenzini Editore (Italy) *Tel:* (0432) 691412 *Fax:* (0432) 691412, pg 396

Lorenzo Editore (Italy) *Tel:* (011) 2485387 *Fax:* (011) 2485387, pg 396

Johannes Loriz Verlag der Kooperative Duernau (Germany) *Tel:* (07582) 93000 *Fax:* (07582) 930020 *Web Site:* www.kooperative.de, pg 255

Editorial Losada SA (Argentina) *Tel:* (011) 4373-4006; (011) 4375-5001 *Fax:* (011) 4373-4006; (011) 4375-5001 *E-mail:* administra@editoriallosada.com, pg 7

Thomas C Lothian Pty Ltd (Australia) *Tel:* (03) 9694 4900 *Fax:* (03) 9645 0705 *E-mail:* books@lothian.com.au *Web Site:* www.lothian.com.au, pg 29

Verlag an der Lottbek (Germany) *Tel:* (0241) 873434 *Fax:* (0241) 875577, pg 255

Lotu Pacifika Productions (Fiji) *Tel:* 301314 *Fax:* 301183, pg 141

Editions Loubatieres (France) *Tel:* (05) 61 72 83 53 *Fax:* (05) 61 72 83 50 *E-mail:* loubatieres@club-internet.fr, pg 173

Loughborough University (United Kingdom) *Tel:* (01509) 263171; (01509) 223052 *Fax:* (01509) 223053 *E-mail:* dis@lboro.ac.uk *Web Site:* www.lboro.ac.uk, pg 722

Lowden Publishing Co (Australia) *Tel:* (03) 9873 7202 *Fax:* (03) 9873 0542 *E-mail:* service@theruralstore.com.au *Web Site:* www.theruralstore.com.au, pg 30

Lowfield Printing Co Ltd (United Kingdom) *Tel:* (01322) 522216 *Fax:* (01322) 555362 *E-mail:* lowfield@compuserve.com, pg 1185

Lowfield Printing Co Ltd (United Kingdom) *Tel:* (01322) 522216 *E-mail:* lowfield@compuserve.com *Web Site:* www.applegate.com, pg 1226

Andrew Lownie Literary Agency Ltd (United Kingdom) *Tel:* (020) 7828 1274 *Fax:* (020) 7828 7608 *E-mail:* lownie@globalnet.co.uk *Web Site:* www.andrewlownie.co.uk, pg 1141

Edicoes Loyola SA (Brazil) *Tel:* (011) 69141922 *Fax:* (011) 61634275 *E-mail:* editorial@loyola.com.br *Web Site:* www.loyola.com.br, pg 85

Ediciones LR SA (Argentina) *Tel:* (011) 4326-3725; (011) 4326-3826, pg 7

LT Editions-Jacques Lanore (France) *Tel:* (01) 44 41 89 30 *Fax:* (01) 44 41 89 39 *E-mail:* lanore@lanore.com *Web Site:* www.lanore.com, pg 173

LTC-Livros Tecnicos e Cientificos Editora S/A (Brazil) *Tel:* (021) 2221-7106; (021) 224-5877 *Fax:* (021) 252-2732; (021) 2221-5744, pg 85

LTR Editora Ltda (Brazil) *Tel:* (011) 3667-1101 *Fax:* (011) 3825-6695 *E-mail:* ltr@ltr.com.br *Web Site:* www.ltr.com.br/web/home.asp, pg 85

Steve Lu Publishing Ltd (Hong Kong) *Tel:* 25210681 *Fax:* 28450492 *E-mail:* ltlahk@netvigator.com, pg 318

Lua Viajante-Edicao e Distribuicao de Livros e Material Audiovisual, Lda (Portugal) *Tel:* (01) 9376180 *Fax:* (01) 9381452; (01) 9377560 *E-mail:* europress@mail.telepac.pt, pg 533

Luath Press Ltd (United Kingdom) *Tel:* (0131) 225 4326 *Fax:* (0131) 225 4324 *E-mail:* sales@luath.co.uk *Web Site:* www.luath.co.uk, pg 722

Wydawnictwo Lubelskie (Poland) *Tel:* (081) 7442667, pg 524

Lubrina (Italy) *Tel:* (035) 3470139396 *Fax:* (035) 241547 *E-mail:* editorelubrina@lubrina.it *Web Site:* www.lubrina.it, pg 396

Luc vydavatelske druzstvo (Slovakia) *Tel:* (07) 65730331 *Fax:* (07) 65730331, pg 559

Edizioni de Luca SRL (Italy) *Tel:* (06) 32650712 *Fax:* (06) 32650715 *Web Site:* culturitalia.uibk.ac.at, pg 396

Lucasville Press (Australia) *Tel:* (03) 9395 1446, pg 30

Hermann Luchterhand Verlag GmbH (Germany) *Tel:* (02631) 8010 *Fax:* (02631) 801210 *E-mail:* info@luchterhand.de *Web Site:* www.luchterhand.de, pg 255

Luchterhand Literaturverlag GmbH/Verlag Volk & Welt GmbH (Germany) *Tel:* (089) 4136-0; (01805) 990505 *Fax:* (089) 21215250 *E-mail:* vertrieb.verlagsgruppe@randomhouse.de *Web Site:* www.randomhouse.de/luchterhand, pg 255

Ediciones Luciernaga (Spain) *Tel:* (093) 443 71 00 *Fax:* (093) 443 71 30 *E-mail:* correu@grup62.com *Web Site:* www.grup62.com, pg 589

Lucis Press Ltd (United Kingdom) *Tel:* (020) 7839 4512; (020) 7839 4513 *Fax:* (020) 7839 5575 *E-mail:* london@lucistrust.org *Web Site:* www.lucistrust.org, pg 723

Lucius & Lucius Verlagsgesellschaft mbH (Germany) *Tel:* (0711) 242060 *Fax:* (0711) 242088 *E-mail:* lucius@luciusverlag.com *Web Site:* www.luciusverlag.com, pg 255

Lucky Duck Publishing Ltd (United Kingdom) *Tel:* (0117) 947 5150 *Fax:* (0117) 947 5152 *E-mail:* publishing@luckyduck.co.uk *Web Site:* www.luckyduck.co.uk, pg 723

Editora Lucre Comercio e Representacoes (Brazil) *Tel:* (019) 287-8593 *Fax:* (019) 287 8593 *E-mail:* lucre@mute.net.br, pg 85

Ludowa Spoldzielnia Wydawnicza (Poland) *Tel:* (022) 6205718; (022) 6205719 *Fax:* (022) 6207277, pg 524

Gustav Luebbe Verlag (Germany) *Tel:* (02202) 121-330 *Fax:* (02202) 121-920 *E-mail:* glv@luebbe.de *Web Site:* www.luebbe.de, pg 256

Verlagsgruppe Luebbe GmbH & Co KG (Germany) *Tel:* (02202) 121-0 *Fax:* (02202) 121-920 *E-mail:* info@luebbe.de *Web Site:* www.luebbe.de, pg 256

Editorial Luis Vives (Edelvives) (Spain) *Tel:* (091) 334 48 83 *Fax:* (091) 334 48 93 *E-mail:* jmarketing@edelvives.es *Web Site:* www.grupoeditorialluisvives.com, pg 589

Lukas Verlag fur Kunst- und Geistesgeschichte (Germany) *Tel:* (030) 44049220 *Fax:* (030) 4428177 *E-mail:* lukas.verlag@t-online.de *Web Site:* www.lukasverlag.com, pg 256

Josef Lukasik A Spol sro (Czech Republic) *Tel:* (02) 471 22 19; (02) 83 22 84; (0603) 95 52 55, pg 125

Editorial Lumen SA (Spain) *Tel:* (093) 3660300 *Fax:* (093) 3660013 *E-mail:* lumen@editoriallumen.com, pg 589

Editions Lumen Vitae ASBL (Belgium) *Tel:* (02) 3490399; (02) 3490370 *Fax:* (02) 3490385 *E-mail:* international@lumenvitae.be *Web Site:* www.catho.be/lumen, pg 70

Editura Lumina (Republic of Moldova) *Tel:* (02) 246397; (02) 246398 *Fax:* (02) 246395 *E-mail:* lumina@mdl.net, pg 473

La Luna (Italy) *Tel:* (091) 345799 *Fax:* (091) 301650 *E-mail:* laluna@arcidonna.it, pg 396

Lund Humphries (United Kingdom) *Tel:* (01252) 331551 *Fax:* (01252) 344405 *E-mail:* info@lundhumphries.com *Web Site:* www.lundhumphries.com, pg 723

Lunde Forlag AS (Norway) *Tel:* (022) 00 73 50 *Fax:* (022) 00 73 73 *E-mail:* lunde@nlm.no *Web Site:* www.lunde-forlag.no, pg 509

Lunds Universitets Bibliotek (Sweden) *Tel:* (046) 222 00 00 *Fax:* (046) 222 36 82 *E-mail:* lub@lub.lu.se *Web Site:* www.lub.lu.se, pg 1547

Lundula Publishing House (Zambia) *Tel:* (01) 96758496 *E-mail:* nlundula@yahoo.com, pg 781

Luni (Italy) *Tel:* (02) 89693000 *Fax:* (02) 89693011, pg 396

Lunwerg Editores, SA (Spain) *Tel:* (093) 2015933 *Fax:* (093) 2011587 *E-mail:* lunwerg.mad@retemail.es, pg 589

Lusaka City Library (Zambia) *Tel:* (01) 227282, pg 1556

Lusatia Verlag-Dr Stuebner & Co KG (Germany) *Tel:* (03591) 532400; (03591) 532401 *Fax:* (03591) 532400 *E-mail:* lusatiaverlag@t-online.de, pg 256

Lusva Editrice (Italy) *Tel:* (02) 4985386, pg 396

Lutchman, Drs LFS (Suriname) *Tel:* 465558; 44/453419, pg 608

Luther Forlag A/S (Norway) *Tel:* (022) 33 06 08 *Fax:* (022) 42 10 00 *E-mail:* postkasse@lutherforlag.no *Web Site:* www.lutherforlag.no, pg 509

Luther-Verlag GmbH (Germany) *Tel:* (0521) 94 40-137 *Fax:* (0521) 94 40-136 *E-mail:* vertrieb@luther-verlag.de *Web Site:* www.ekvw.de/pressehaus/lv/, pg 256

Lutherische Verlagsgesellschaft mbH (Germany) *Tel:* (0431) 55779-285 *Fax:* (0431) 55779-292, pg 256

Lutherisches Verlagshaus GmbH (Germany) *Tel:* (0511) 1241-716 *Fax:* (0511) 1241-705 *E-mail:* lvh@lvh.de *Web Site:* www.lvh.de, pg 256

The Lutterworth Press (United Kingdom) *Tel:* (01223) 350865 *Fax:* (01223) 366951 *E-mail:* publishing@lutterworth.com *Web Site:* www.lutterworth.com, pg 723

Lutyens & Rubinstein (United Kingdom) *Tel:* (020) 7792 4855 *Fax:* (020) 7792 4833, pg 1141

Verlag Waldemar Lutz (Germany) *Tel:* (07621) 88812 *Fax:* (07621) 12599 *E-mail:* wlutz@lutz-die-buchhandlung.de *Web Site:* www.verlag-lutz.de, pg 256

Lux Verbi (Pty) Ltd (South Africa) *Tel:* (021) 8733851 *Fax:* (021) 8730069 *E-mail:* luxverbi.publ@kinglsey.co.za, pg 566

Luxpress VOS (Czech Republic) *Tel:* (02) 203 972 60 *Fax:* (02) 203 972 60 *E-mail:* ibs.czech@iol.cz, pg 125

Lybid (University of Kyyiv Press) (Ukraine) *Tel:* (044) 228-11-12; (044) 228-11-81 *Fax:* (044) 229-11-71, pg 653

Lybra Immagine (Italy) *Tel:* (02) 48000818 *Fax:* (02) 48012748 *E-mail:* lybra@lybra.it *Web Site:* www.lybra.it, pg 396

Lycabettus Press (Greece) *Tel:* (210) 6741 788 *Fax:* (210) 6710 666 *Web Site:* lycabettus.com, pg 309

Lyle Publications Ltd (United Kingdom) *Tel:* (01750) 23355 *Fax:* (01750) 23388 *E-mail:* lyle.publications@talk21.com, pg 723

Lyngs Bokhandel A/S (Norway) *Tel:* 73512544 *Fax:* 73512544, pg 1333

Lynx Edicions (Spain) *Tel:* (093) 594 77 10 *Fax:* (093) 592 09 69 *E-mail:* pruizolalla@hbw.com *Web Site:* www.hbw.com, pg 590

Editions Josette Lyon (France) *Tel:* (01) 40 44 81 60 *Fax:* (01) 45 42 30 99 *E-mail:* editions.josette.lyon@wanadoo.fr *Web Site:* www.editions-josette-lyon.com, pg 173

Editions Lyonnaises d'Art et d'Histoire (France) *Tel:* (04) 78 72 49 00 *Fax:* (04) 78 69 00 48 *Web Site:* www.achatlyon.com/editionslyonnaises, pg 173

Lyra Libri (Italy) *Tel:* (02) 30 241 311 *Fax:* (02) 30 241 333, pg 396

Lyra Pragensis Obecne Prospelna Spolecnost (Czech Republic) *Tel:* (02) 222 202 89 *Fax:* (02) 222 212 67 *Web Site:* lyra-pragensis.scena.cz, pg 125

Thomas Lyster Ltd (United Kingdom) *Tel:* (01695) 575112 *Fax:* (01695) 570120 *E-mail:* books@tlyster.co.uk *Web Site:* www.tlyster.co.uk, pg 723

M & M Management & Labour Consultants Ltd (Zambia) *Tel:* (01) 217218 *Fax:* (01) 224495, pg 781

M/S Motilal Banarsidass Publishing (P) Ltd (India) *Tel:* (011) 23851985; (011) 23858335; (011) 23854826; (011) 23852747 *Fax:* (011) 23850689; (011) 25797221 *E-mail:* mail@mlbd.com *Web Site:* www.mlbd.com, pg 340

Maaliyot-Institute for Research Publications (Israel) *Tel:* (02) 5353655 *Fax:* (02) 5353947 *E-mail:* ybm@virtual.co.il, pg 370

Ma'alot Publishing Company Ltd (Israel) *Tel:* (03) 5614122 *Fax:* (03) 5611996 *E-mail:* maalot@tbpai.co.il *Web Site:* www.tbpai.co.il, pg 370

Dar Al Maaref (Egypt (Arab Republic of Egypt)) *Tel:* (02) 759411; (02) 759552 *Fax:* (02) 5744999 *E-mail:* maaref@idsc.gov.eg, pg 138

El-M'aaref Editions (Tunisia) *Tel:* (03) 256235 *Fax:* (03) 256530, pg 648

Ma'ariv Book Guild (Sifriat Ma'ariv) (Israel) *Tel:* (03) 5333333 *Fax:* (03) 5333619, pg 370

Ma'ariv Book Guild (Sifriat Ma'ariv) (Israel) *Tel:* (03) 5383313 *Fax:* (03) 6343205, pg 1253

Maatschappij der Nederlandse Letterkunde (Netherlands) *Tel:* (071) 527 2801; (071) 527 2814 *Fax:* (071) 527 2836 *E-mail:* mnl@library.leidenuniv.nl *Web Site:* www.leidenuniv.nl/host/mnl, pg 1403

The MAB Cookery Book Club (Iceland) *Tel:* 5643170 *Fax:* 5643190, pg 1253

Mabrochi International Co Ltd (Nigeria) *E-mail:* mabrochiadol@yahoo.com, pg 1331

Casa Editrice Maccari (CEM) (Italy) *Tel:* (0521) 771268 *Fax:* (0521) 771268, pg 396

Ediciones Macchi (Argentina) *Tel:* (011) 4375-1195 *Fax:* (011) 4375-1870; (011) 4374-2506 *E-mail:* info@macchi.com.ar *Web Site:* www.macchi.com, pg 7

Macedonia Prima Publishing House (The Former Yugoslav Republic of Macedonia) *Tel:* (096) 37-109 *Fax:* (096) 23-172, pg 452

Macedonian PEN Centre (The Former Yugoslav Republic of Macedonia) *Tel:* (02) 130054 *Fax:* (02) 130054 *E-mail:* macedpen@unet.com.mk *Web Site:* www.pen.org.mk, pg 1402

Antonio Machado, SA (Spain) *Tel:* (091) 4681398 *Fax:* (091) 4681098 *E-mail:* editorial@visordis.es, pg 590

Machbarot Lesifrut (Israel) *Tel:* (08) 9246565 *Fax:* (08) 9251770 *E-mail:* info@zmora.co.il, pg 370

Friends of Arthur Machen (United Kingdom) *Tel:* (01633) 422520 *Fax:* (0633) 421055 *Web Site:* www.machensoc.demon.co.uk, pg 1408

MacKays of Chatham PLC (United Kingdom) *Tel:* (01634) 864 381 *Fax:* (01634) 867 742 *E-mail:* mackays@cpi-group.co.uk *Web Site:* www.cpi-group.net, pg 1226

MacLean Art (Trinidad & Tobago) *Tel:* 622 8679 *Fax:* 622 7583 *E-mail:* gml@wow.net, pg 647

MacLean Dubois Ltd (Writers & Agents) (United Kingdom) *Tel:* (0131) 445 5885 *Fax:* (0131) 445 5898 *E-mail:* info@whiskymax.co.uk, pg 1141

MacLennan & Petty Pty Ltd (Australia) *Tel:* (02) 9349 5811 *Fax:* (02) 9349 5911 *E-mail:* macpetty@zip.com.au, pg 30

Macmillan Audio Books (United Kingdom) *Tel:* (020) 7373 6070 *Fax:* (020) 7244 6379, pg 723

Macmillan Boleswa Publishers (Pty) Ltd (Swaziland) *Tel:* 84533 *Fax:* 85247 *E-mail:* macmillan@iafrica.sz *Web Site:* www.macmillansa.co.za; www.macmillan-africa.com, pg 609

Macmillan Children's Books (United Kingdom) *Tel:* (020) 7014 6124 *Fax:* (020) 7014 6142 *Web Site:* www.panmacmillan.com, pg 723

Macmillan Editores SA de CV (Mexico) *Tel:* (05) 482 2200 *Fax:* (05) 482 2203 *E-mail:* elt@macmillan.com.mx *Web Site:* www.macmillan.com.mx/, pg 468

Editorial Macmillan de Mexico SA de CV (Mexico) *Tel:* (05) 482 2200 *Fax:* (05) 482 2202 *Web Site:* www.macmillan.com.mx, pg 468

Macmillan Education (Sierra Leone) *Tel:* (022) 225683 *Fax:* (022) 229186 *E-mail:* macmillan@sierratel.sl *Web Site:* www.macmillan-africa.com, pg 554

Macmillan Education Australia (Australia) *Tel:* (03) 9825 1025 *Fax:* (03) 9825 1010 *E-mail:* mea@macmillan.com.au *Web Site:* www.macmillan.com.au, pg 30

Macmillan Heinemann ELT (Greece) *Tel:* (01) 748 2828 *Fax:* (01) 748 8735 *E-mail:* mhelt@ath.forthnet.gr *Web Site:* www.mhelt.com, pg 310

Macmillan Heinemann ELT (Italy) *Tel:* (055) 649 1289 *Fax:* (055) 649 1501 *E-mail:* mheltinfo@dada.it *Web Site:* www.mhelt.com, pg 396

Macmillan Heinemann ELT (Spain) *Tel:* (091) 517 85 40 *Fax:* (091) 517 85 54 *E-mail:* madrid@mad.heinemann.es *Web Site:* www.heinemann.es, pg 590

Macmillan Heinemann ELT (United Kingdom) *Tel:* (01865) 405700 *Fax:* (01865) 405701 *E-mail:* elt@mhelt.com *Web Site:* www.mhelt.com, pg 723

Macmillan Kenya Publishers Ltd (Kenya) *Tel:* (02) 220 012; (02) 224 485 *Fax:* (02) 212 179 *Web Site:* www.macmillan-africa.com, pg 435

Macmillan Ltd (United Kingdom) *Tel:* (020) 7833 4000 *Fax:* (020) 7843 4640 *Web Site:* www.macmillan.com, pg 723

Macmillan Publishers Australia Pty Ltd (Australia) *Tel:* (03) 9825 1000 *Fax:* (03) 9825 1015 *Web Site:* www.panmacmillan.com.au, pg 30

Macmillan Publishers (China) Ltd (Hong Kong) *Tel:* 2811 8781 *Fax:* 2811 0743 *Web Site:* www.macmillan.com.hk, pg 318

Macmillan Publishers New Zealand Ltd (New Zealand) *Tel:* (09) 414 0350; (09) 414 0356 (customer service); (09) 414 0352 (trade sales) *Fax:* (09) 414 0351 *Web Site:* www.macmillan.co.nz, pg 498

Macmillan Publishers (UK) Ltd (United Kingdom) *Tel:* (01256) 329242 *Fax:* (01256) 812558 *E-mail:* mdl@macmillan.com *Web Site:* www.macmillan.com, pg 724

Macmillan Publishers (Zambia) Ltd (Zambia) *Tel:* (01) 223 669 *Fax:* (01) 223 657; (01) 641 018 *E-mail:* macpub@zamnet.zm *Web Site:* www.macmillan-africa.com, pg 781

Macmillan Reference Ltd (United Kingdom) *Tel:* (01256) 329242 *Fax:* (01256) 812558 *E-mail:* mdl@macmillan.co.uk *Web Site:* www.macmillan.co.uk, pg 724

The Macquarie Library Pty Ltd (Australia) *Tel:* (02) 9805 9800 *Fax:* (02) 9888 2984 *E-mail:* alison@dict.mq.edu, pg 30

Macro Edizioni (Italy) *Tel:* (0547) 346290; (0547) 346317 *Fax:* (0547) 345091; (0547) 345141 *E-mail:* ordini@macroedizioni.it *Web Site:* www.macroedizioni.it, pg 397

Macula (France) *Tel:* (01) 45 48 58 70 *Fax:* (01) 45 44 45 89, pg 173

Mad Dog Design Connection Inc (Canada) *Tel:* 416-467-0090 *Fax:* 416-484-1140 *E-mail:* maddogs9@rogers.com, pg 1153

Mad SL Editorial (Spain) *Tel:* (095) 5630820 *Fax:* (095) 5630713 *E-mail:* info@mad.es *Web Site:* www.mad.es, pg 590

Madagascar Print & Press Company (Madagascar) *Tel:* (02) 22526 *Fax:* (02) 2234534 *E-mail:* roi@dts.mg, pg 453

Madan Puraskar Library (Nepal) *Tel:* (01) 5521014 *Fax:* (01) 5536390 *E-mail:* kmldxt@wlink.com.np, pg 1530

Karin Mader (Germany) *Tel:* (04208) 556 *Fax:* (04208) 3429 *E-mail:* info@mader-verlag.de *Web Site:* www.mader-verlag.de, pg 256

Madju FA (Indonesia) *Tel:* (061) 711990; (061) 710430 *Fax:* (061) 717753, pg 355

Madras Editora (Brazil) *Tel:* (011) 6959-1127 *Fax:* (011) 6959-3090 *E-mail:* editor@madras.com.br *Web Site:* www.madras.com.br, pg 86

Madras Literary Society Library (India) *Tel:* 827 9666, pg 1516

Madris (Latvia) *Tel:* 7374000; 7374700 *Fax:* 7374000 *E-mail:* madris@latnet.lv, pg 445

Maeander Verlag GmbH (Germany) *Tel:* (08727) 1657 *Fax:* (08727) 1569, pg 256

Annemarie Maeger (Germany) *Tel:* (040) 8992480 *Fax:* (040) 8904475 *E-mail:* re@a-maeger-verlag.de *Web Site:* www.a-maeger-verlag.de, pg 256

Maeil Gyeongje (Republic of Korea) *Tel:* (02) 276-0210; (02) 2760211; (02) 2760212; (02) 2760213; (02) 2760214; (02) 2760215 *Fax:* (02) 271-0463 *E-mail:* mpd@unitel.co.kv, pg 441

Ediciones Maeva (Spain) *Tel:* (091) 355 95 69 *Fax:* (091) 355 19 47 *E-mail:* maeva@infornet.es *Web Site:* www.maeva.es, pg 590

Magabala Books Aboriginal Corporation (Australia) *Tel:* (08) 9192 1991 *Fax:* (08) 9193 5254 *E-mail:* info@magabala.com *Web Site:* www.magabala.com, pg 30

Magari Publishing (New Zealand) *Tel:* (07) 3770169 *Fax:* (07) 3773134 *E-mail:* frontdesk@magari.co.nz *Web Site:* www.magari.co.nz, pg 498

Magasin du Nord A/S (Denmark) *Tel:* (03) 33 11 44 33 *Fax:* (03) 33 15 18 40 *E-mail:* kundeservice@magasinkort.dk *Web Site:* www.magasin.dk, pg 1308

Magdalenen-Verlag GmbH (Germany) *Tel:* (08024) 5051 *Fax:* (08024) 7064 *E-mail:* info@magdalenen-verlag.de *Web Site:* www.magdalenen-verlag.de, pg 256

Magenta Lithographic Consultants (Singapore) *Tel:* 2746288 *E-mail:* magenta@singaporebusinessguide.com, pg 1161

Les Editions Maghrebines, EDIMA (Morocco) *Tel:* (02) 353230; (02) 353249; (02) 351797 *Fax:* (02) 355541, pg 475

Magi Publications (United Kingdom) *Tel:* (020) 7385 6333 *Fax:* (020) 7385 7333 *E-mail:* info@littletiger.co.uk *Web Site:* www.littletigerpress.com, pg 724

Editorial Magisterio Espanol SA (Spain) *Tel:* (093) 902107007 *Fax:* (093) 6420086 *Web Site:* www.editorialcasals.com, pg 590

Magna Large Print Books (United Kingdom) *Tel:* (01729) 840 225; (01729) 840 526; (01729) 840 251 *Fax:* (01729) 840 683 *E-mail:* enquiries@ulverscroft.co.uk *Web Site:* www.ulverscroft.co.uk, pg 724

Magnard (France) *Tel:* (01) 44 08 85 85 *Fax:* (01) 44 08 49 79 *Web Site:* www.magnard.fr, pg 173

The Magnes Press (Israel) *Tel:* (02) 6586656 *Fax:* (02) 5633370 *E-mail:* magnes@vms.huji.ac.il *Web Site:* www.huji.ac.il, pg 370

Magnum Publishing House Ltd (Poland) *Tel:* (022) 6460085; (022) 8485505 *Fax:* (022) 8485505 *E-mail:* magnum@it.com.pl, pg 524

Magnus Edizioni SpA (Italy) *Tel:* (0432) 800081 *Fax:* (0432) 810071 *E-mail:* info@magnusedizioni.it *Web Site:* www.magnusedizioni.it, pg 397

Magnus Verlag (Germany) *Tel:* (02054) 5080; (02054) 5094; (02327) 292 0 *Fax:* (02054) 83762, pg 256

Magpie Books (Australia) *Tel:* (0613) 9592 9931 *Fax:* (0613) 9592 2045 *E-mail:* admin01@magpiebooks.com.au *Web Site:* www.magpiebooks.com.au, pg 30

Magpie Books (Australia) *Tel:* (03) 95929931 *Fax:* (03) 95922045 *E-mail:* admin01@magpiebooks.com.au *Web Site:* www.magpiebooks.com.au, pg 1299

Magpie Publications (Australia) *Tel:* (06) 2509442, pg 30

Magpies Magazine Pty Ltd (Australia) *Tel:* (07) 3356 4503 *Fax:* (07) 3356 4649 *E-mail:* james@magpies.net.au *Web Site:* www.magpies.net.au, pg 30

Edicions de la Magrana SA (Spain) *Tel:* (093) 2170088 *Fax:* (093) 2171174 *E-mail:* magrana@rba.es *Web Site:* www.rbalibros.com, pg 590

Magveto Koenyvkiado (Hungary) *Tel:* (01) 302 2798; (01) 302 2799 *Fax:* (01) 302 2800 *E-mail:* magveto@mail.datanet.hu, pg 322

Magwe Degree College Library (Myanmar) *Tel:* (63) 21030, pg 1530

Magyar Irodalomtoerteneti Tarsasag (Hungary) *Tel:* (01) 377819 *Fax:* (01) 3377819, pg 1401

Magyar Iroszoevetseg (Hungary) *Tel:* (01) 322-8840; (01) 322-0631 *Fax:* (01) 321-3419, pg 1272

Magyar Iroszovetseg Konyvtara (Hungary) *Tel:* (01) 322-8840; (01) 322-0631 *Fax:* (01) 321-3419, pg 1148

Magyar Kemikusok Egyesulete (Hungary) *Tel:* (01) 2016883 *Fax:* (01) 343 25 41 *E-mail:* webinfo@mtesz.hu *Web Site:* www.mtesz.hu, pg 323

Magyar Koenyvkiadok es Koenyvterjesztoek Egyesuelese (Hungary) *Tel:* (01) 343 25 40 *Fax:* (01) 343 25 41 *E-mail:* mkke@mkke.hu *Web Site:* www.mkke.hu, pg 1272

Magyar Koenyvkiadok es Koenyvterjesztoek Egyesuelese Vereinigung der Ungarischen Buchverlage & Vertriebsunternehmen (Hungary) *Tel:* (01) 343-25-40 *Fax:* (01) 343 25 41 *E-mail:* mkke@mkke.hu *Web Site:* www.mkke.hu, pg 323

Magyar Koenyvtarosok Egyesulete (Hungary) *Tel:* (01) 311 8634 *Fax:* (01) 311 8634 *E-mail:* mke@oszk.hu *Web Site:* www.mke.oszk.hu, pg 1564

Magyar Orszagos Leveltar (MOL) (Hungary) *Tel:* (01) 225-2800 *Fax:* (01) 225-2805 *E-mail:* info@natarch.hu *Web Site:* www.natarch.hu, pg 1514

Magyar Tudomanyos Akademia Irodalomtudomanyi Intezete (Hungary) *Tel:* (01) 4665938 *Fax:* (01) 3853876 *Web Site:* www.mta.hu/kutatohelyek/intezetek/iti.htm, pg 1401

Magyar Tudomanyos Akademia Koenyvtara (Hungary) *Tel:* (01) 411 6100 *Fax:* (01) 311 6954 *E-mail:* mtak@vax.mtak.hu *Web Site:* w3.mtak.hu, pg 1515

Mahajan Publishers Pvt Ltd (India) *Tel:* 78547 *Fax:* (079) 6589101 *E-mail:* mahajan2000@hotmail.com, pg 340

Mahir Marketing Services Sdn Bhd (Malaysia) *Tel:* (088) 2827372 *Fax:* (088) 718067, pg 1326

Mahir Publications Sdn Bhd (Malaysia) *Tel:* (03) 5501826; (03) 5501442; (03) 5501755 *Fax:* (03) 5501826, pg 456

Karl Mahnke, Dierk Mahnke (Germany) *Tel:* (04231) 3011-0 *Fax:* (04231) 3011-11 *E-mail:* info@mahnke-verlag.de *Web Site:* www.mahnke-verlag.de, pg 256

Maihof Verlag (Switzerland) *Tel:* (041) 767 76 80 *Fax:* (041) 767 76 77 *E-mail:* maihofdruck@logon.ch *Web Site:* www.maihofdruck.ch, pg 628

Giuseppe Maimone Editore (Italy) *Tel:* (095) 310315 *Fax:* (095) 310315 *E-mail:* maimone@maimone.it *Web Site:* www.maimone.it, pg 397

Mainstream Publishing Co (Edinburgh) Ltd (United Kingdom) *Tel:* (0131) 557 2959 *Fax:* (0131) 556 8720 *E-mail:* enquiries@mainstreampublishing.com *Web Site:* www.mainstreampublishing.com, pg 724

Mairs Geographischer Verlag (Germany) *Tel:* (0711) 45020 *Fax:* (0711) 4502340 *E-mail:* info@mairs.de *Web Site:* www.mairs.de, pg 256

Mairs Geographischer Verlag Kurt Mair GmbH & Co (Germany) *Tel:* (0711) 4502-0 *Fax:* (0711) 4502-340, pg 257

La Maison de la Bible (Switzerland) *Tel:* (021) 867 10 10 *Fax:* (021) 867 10 15 *E-mail:* info@bible.ch *Web Site:* www.bible.ch, pg 628

Maison de la Revelation (France) *Tel:* (05) 56602477 *Fax:* (05) 56931631, pg 173

Maison d'Edition de la Librairie-Imprimerie Evangelique du Togo (Togo) *Tel:* (08) 214582 *Fax:* (08) 216967 *E-mail:* ctce@cafe.tg, pg 646

Maison des Ecrivains (France) *Tel:* (01) 49546880 *Fax:* (01) 42842087 *E-mail:* courrier@maison-des-ecrivains.asso.fr *Web Site:* www.maison-des-ecrivains.asso.fr, pg 1399

Maison des Langues Vivantes-Intertaal SA (Belgium) *Tel:* (02) 5117117 *Fax:* (02) 5145820 *E-mail:* mlv.i@skynet.be *Web Site:* maison-des-langues.com, pg 1302

Editions de la Maison des Sciences de l'Homme, Paris (France) *Tel:* (01) 49 54 20 30; (01) 49 54 20 31 *Fax:* (01) 49 54 21 33 *E-mail:* public@msh-paris.fr *Web Site:* www.editions.msh-paris.fr, pg 173

La Maison du Dictionnaire (France) *Tel:* (01) 43 22 12 93 *Fax:* (01) 43 22 01 77 *E-mail:* contact@lmdd.com *Web Site:* www.lmdd.com, pg 173

Maison Tunisienne de l'Edition (Tunisia) *Tel:* (01) 345333 *Fax:* (01) 353992, pg 648

Editions Adrien Maisonneuve (France) *Tel:* (01) 43 26 19 50 *Fax:* (01) 43 54 59 54 *E-mail:* maisonneuve@maisonneuve-adrien.com *Web Site:* www.maisonneuve-adrien.com, pg 174

Maisonneuve Editeur (France) *Tel:* (01) 34 63 33 33 *Fax:* (01) 34 65 39 70, pg 174

Maisonneuve et Larose (France) *Tel:* (01) 44414930 *Fax:* (01) 43257741 *E-mail:* servedit1@wanadoo.fr, pg 174

Makedonska kniga (The Former Yugoslav Republic of Macedonia) *Tel:* (02) 224-055 *Fax:* (091) 1212 77, pg 1325

Makedonska kniga (Knigoizdatelstvo) (The Former Yugoslav Republic of Macedonia) *Tel:* (091) 116 473; (091) 3 1610; (091) 235 524 *Fax:* (091) 1212 77, pg 452

Makerere Institute of Social Research Library (Uganda) *Tel:* (041) 554582; (041) 53 28 30; (041) 53 28 37; (041) 53 28 38; (041) 53 28 39 *Fax:* (041) 53 28 21 *E-mail:* diremisr@infocom.co.ug *Web Site:* www.makerere.ac.ug/research/misr.htm, pg 1551

Makerere University Library (Uganda) *Tel:* (041) 531041 *Fax:* (041) 540374 *E-mail:* librarian@mak.ac.ug *Web Site:* www.makerere.ac.ug/mulib, pg 1552

Maklu (Belgium) *Tel:* (03) 231-29-00 *Fax:* (03) 233-26-59 *E-mail:* info@maklu.be *Web Site:* www.maklu.be, pg 70

Makron Books do Brasil Editora Ltda (Brazil) *Tel:* (011) 829-6879 *Fax:* (011) 829-8947 *E-mail:* makron@books.com.br *Web Site:* www.makron.com.br, pg 86

Makros 2000 - Plovdiv (Bulgaria) *Tel:* (032) 620770, pg 95

Makumira Lutheran Theological College Library (United Republic of Tanzania) *Tel:* (027) 255-3634; (027) 255-3635 *Fax:* (027) 255-3493 *E-mail:* library@makumira.ac.tz *Web Site:* www.makumira.ac.tz, pg 1549

MM Mal og menning (Iceland) *Tel:* 522 2000 *Fax:* 522 2022; 522 2026 *E-mail:* malogmenning@edda.is *Web Site:* www.malogmenning.is, pg 1253

Mal og menning (Iceland) *Tel:* 522 2500 *Fax:* 522 2505 *E-mail:* edda@edda.is *Web Site:* www.edda.is, pg 326

Bibliotheque Nationale Malagasy (Madagascar) *Tel:* (02) 25872 *Fax:* (02) 22-9448, pg 1526

Biblioteca Comunale Malatestiana (Italy) *Tel:* (0547) 610 892 *Fax:* (0547) 421237 *E-mail:* malatestiana@sbn.provincia.ra.it *Web Site:* www.malatestiana.it, pg 1520

The Malawi Library Association (Malawi) *Tel:* (050) 522222 *Fax:* (050) 523225, pg 1567

Malawi National Library Service (Malawi) *Tel:* 773 700 *Fax:* 771 616 *E-mail:* nls@malawi.net, pg 1526

Malaya Books Suppliers Co (Malaysia) *Tel:* (03) 7910420, pg 456

Malaya Educational Supplies Sdn Bhd (Malaysia) *Tel:* (03) 7046628 *Fax:* (03) 7046629, pg 456

The Malaya Press Sdn Bhd (Malaysia) *Tel:* (03) 5755890; (03) 5757817 *Fax:* (03) 5757194, pg 456

Malayan Law Journal Sdn Bhd (Malaysia) *Tel:* (03) 2162 2822 *Fax:* (03) 2162 3811 *Web Site:* www.mlj.com.my, pg 456

Malaysian Book Importers & Distributors Association (Malaysia) *Tel:* (03) 7193485 *Fax:* (03) 7181664, pg 1277

Malaysian Book Publishers' Association (Malaysia) *Tel:* (03) 56379044 *Fax:* (03) 56379043 *E-mail:* inquiry@cerdik.com.my *Web Site:* www.mabopa.com.my, pg 1277

The Malaysian Current Law Journal Sdn Bhd (Malaysia) *Tel:* (03) 42705400 *Fax:* (03) 42705402 *E-mail:* rahim@cljlaw.com *Web Site:* www.cljlaw.com, pg 457

Societe Malgache d'Edition (Madagascar) *Tel:* (020) 2222635 *Fax:* (020) 2222254 *E-mail:* tribune@bow.dts.mg, pg 454

Societe Malgache d'Edition (Madagascar) *Tel:* (020) 2222635 *Fax:* (020) 2222254 *E-mail:* tribune@bow.dts.mg *Web Site:* www.madagascar-tribune.com, pg 1160, 1181

Societe Malgache d'Edition (Madagascar) *Tel:* (020) 2222635 *Fax:* (020) 2222254 *E-mail:* tribune@bow.dts.mg; tribune@blanbir.mg *Web Site:* www.madagascar-tribune.com, pg 1221

Societe Malgache d'Edition (Madagascar) *Tel:* (020) 2222635 *Fax:* (020) 2222254 *E-mail:* tribune@bow.dts.mg *Web Site:* www.madagascar-tribune.com, pg 1325

Malik Sirajuddin & Sons (Pakistan) *Tel:* (042) 7657527 *Fax:* (042) 7657490 *E-mail:* sirajco@brain.net.pk, pg 513

Malliaris - Pedia (Greece) *Tel:* (02310) 262 485 *Fax:* (02310) 264 856 *E-mail:* info@malliaris.gr *Web Site:* www.malliaris.gr, pg 1314

Mallings ApS (Denmark) *Tel:* 4444 3233 *Fax:* 4444 3633 *E-mail:* carlsen@carlsen.dk, pg 132

Mallinson Rendel Publishers Ltd (New Zealand) *Tel:* (04) 802 5012 *Fax:* (04) 802 5013 *E-mail:* publisher@mallinsonrendel.co.nz *Web Site:* www.mallinsonrendel.co.nz, pg 498

Mallory International Ltd (United Kingdom) *Tel:* (01395) 239199 *Fax:* (01395) 239168 *E-mail:* sales@malloryint.co.uk *Web Site:* www.malloryint.co.uk, pg 1352

Malmoe Stadsbibliotek (Sweden) *Tel:* (040) 660 8500 *Fax:* (040) 660 8681 *E-mail:* info@mail.stadsbibliotek.org *Web Site:* www2.malmo.stadsbibliotek.org, pg 1547

Editions Maloine (France) *Tel:* (01) 43 25 60 45; (01) 43 29 54 50 *Fax:* (03) 44 23 02 27 *E-mail:* vpc@vigot.fr *Web Site:* www.vigotmaloine.fr, pg 174

Malta Library & Information Association (MaLIA) (Malta) *Tel:* 21322054 *E-mail:* mpar1@lib.um.edu.mt *Web Site:* www.malia-malta.org, pg 1567

The Malvern Press Ltd (United Kingdom) *Tel:* (020) 7249 2991 *Fax:* (020) 7254 1720 *E-mail:* admin@malvernpress.com *Web Site:* www.malvernpress.com, pg 1227, 1239

Izdatelstvo Malysh (Russian Federation) *Tel:* (095) 4430654 *Fax:* (095) 4430655, pg 546

MAM (The House of Cyprus & Cyprological Publications) (Cyprus) *Tel:* (022) 753536 *Fax:* (022) 375802 *E-mail:* mam@mam.com.cy *Web Site:* www.mam.com.cy, pg 121

MAM (The House of Cyprus & Cyprological Publications) (Cyprus) *Tel:* (022) 753536 *E-mail:* mam@mam.com.cy *Web Site:* www.mam.com.cy, pg 1307

Mambo Bookshop (Zimbabwe) *Tel:* (054) 4016; (054) 4017 *Fax:* (054) 51991 *E-mail:* mambo@icon.co.zw, pg 1356

Mambo Press (Zimbabwe) *Tel:* (054) 24016; (054) 25807; (054) 24017; (054) 28351 *Fax:* (054) 21991 *E-mail:* mambo@icon.co.zw *Web Site:* www.rutenga.com/mambo.htm, pg 783

Mamuth Comix EPE (Greece) *Tel:* (010) 3625054 *Fax:* (010) 3625055 *E-mail:* themask@athena.gr, pg 310

Manadens Bok (Sweden) *Tel:* (08) 696 85 50 *Fax:* (08) 696 83 53 *E-mail:* info@manadensbok.se *Web Site:* www.manadensbok.se, pg 1256

Management Books 2000 Ltd (United Kingdom) *Tel:* (01285) 771441 *Fax:* (01285) 771055 *E-mail:* mb.2000@virgin.net *Web Site:* www.mb2000.com, pg 724

Management Pocketbooks Ltd (United Kingdom) *Tel:* (01962) 735 573 *Fax:* (01962) 733 637 *E-mail:* sales@pocketbook.co.uk *Web Site:* www.pocketbook.co.uk, pg 724

Manama Central Library (Bahrain) *Tel:* 231105 *Fax:* 274036, pg 1492

Manchester University Press (United Kingdom) *Tel:* (0161) 275 2310 *Fax:* (0161) 274 3346 *E-mail:* mup@man.ac.uk *Web Site:* www.manchesteruniversitypress.co.uk, pg 724

Mandala Ediciones (Spain) *Tel:* (091) 5840954 *Fax:* (091) 5480326, pg 590

Mandalay University Library (Myanmar) *Tel:* (02) 21211, pg 1530

Mandrake of Oxford (United Kingdom) *Tel:* (01865) 243671 *Fax:* (01865) 432929 *E-mail:* mandrake@mandrake.uk.net *Web Site:* www.mandrake.uk.net, pg 725

Manesse Verlag GmbH (Switzerland) *Tel:* (01) 2525551 *Fax:* (01) 2625347 *E-mail:* buch@dva.de *Web Site:* www.manesse.ch, pg 628

MANEY PUBLISHING — INDUSTRY

Maney Publishing (United Kingdom) *Tel:* (0113) 249 7481 *Fax:* (0113) 248 6983 *E-mail:* maney@maney.co.uk *Web Site:* www.maney.co.uk, pg 725, 1185

Manfrini Editori (Italy) *Tel:* (0464) 839111 *Fax:* (0464) 835086, pg 397

Editions Mango (France) *Tel:* (01) 55 30 40 50 *Fax:* (01) 55 30 40 50 *E-mail:* mango@editions-mango.fr *Web Site:* www.editions-mango.fr, pg 174

Mango Publishing (United Kingdom) *Tel:* (020) 7292 9000 *Fax:* (020) 7434 1077 *E-mail:* info@mangomedia.net *Web Site:* www.mangopublishing.net, pg 725

Mangold Kinderbucher (Austria) *Tel:* (0316) 475613 *Fax:* (0316) 475613, pg 53

Manhattan Publications (Zimbabwe) *Tel:* (04) 442827; (04) 498206 *Fax:* (04) 496292 *E-mail:* nchudy@zol.co.zw, pg 784

Manhill Publication (Ghana) *Tel:* (021) 508251 *Fax:* (021) 669078, pg 304

Manholt Verlag (Germany) *Tel:* (0421) 32 35 94 *Fax:* (0421) 3 36 54 63 *E-mail:* manholtverlag@t-online.de *Web Site:* www.manholt.de, pg 257

Manifestolibri (Italy) *Tel:* (06) 588 1496 *Fax:* (06) 588 2839 *E-mail:* redazione@manifestolibri.it; book@manifestolibri.it *Web Site:* www.manifestolibri.it, pg 397

Manila City Library (Philippines) *Web Site:* www.cityofmanila.com.ph, pg 1536

Gebr Mann Verlag GmbH & Co (Germany) *Tel:* (030) 25913589 *Fax:* (030) 25913537 *E-mail:* vertrieb-kunstverlage@reimer-verlag.de, pg 257

Mannerschwarm Skript Verlag GmbH (Germany) *Tel:* (040) 4302650 *Fax:* (040) 4302932 *E-mail:* verlag@maennerschwarm.de *Web Site:* www.maennerschwarm.de, pg 257

Manohar Publishers & Distributors (India) *Tel:* (011) 23284848; (011) 23289100; (011) 23262796; (011) 23260774 *Fax:* (011) 23265162 *E-mail:* manbooks@vsnl.com; sales@manoharbooks.com *Web Site:* www.manoharbooks.com, pg 340

Editora Manole Ltda (Brazil) *Tel:* (011) 4196-6000 *Fax:* (011) 4196 6007 *E-mail:* manole@virtual-net.com.br *Web Site:* www.manole.com.br, pg 86

The Mansk Svenska Publishing Co Ltd (United Kingdom) *Tel:* (0162) 4842855 *Fax:* (0162) 844241 *E-mail:* hanneke@advsys.co.uk, pg 725

Manson Publishing Ltd (United Kingdom) *Tel:* (020) 8905 5150 *Fax:* (020) 8201 9233 *E-mail:* manson@mansonpublishing.com *Web Site:* www.mansonpublishing.com, pg 725

Editora Mantiqueira de Ciencia e Arte (Brazil) *Tel:* (0122) 621832 *Fax:* (0122) 622126, pg 86

Editora Manuais Tecnicos de Seguros Ltda (Brazil) *Tel:* (011) 8260844 *Fax:* (011) 8250833, pg 86

Biblioteca Manuel Sanguily (Cuba) *Tel:* (07) 63 3232, pg 1500

Manus Verlag (Switzerland) *Tel:* (01) 920 27 27 *Fax:* (01) 920 27 40 *E-mail:* manart@bluewin.ch *Web Site:* www.manus.ch, pg 628

Manutius Verlag (Germany) *Tel:* (06221) 163290 *Fax:* (06221) 167143 *E-mail:* order@manutius-verlag.de *Web Site:* www.manutius-verlag.de, pg 257

Manz G J Verlag und Druckerei (Germany) *Tel:* (0711) 6151790 *Fax:* (0711) 6151791, pg 257

MANZ'sche Verlags- und Universitaetsbuchhandlung GMBH (Austria) *Tel:* (01) 531 61-161 *Fax:* (01) 531 61-181 *E-mail:* verlag@manz.at *Web Site:* www.manz.at, pg 54

MANZ'sche Verlags- und Universitaetsbuchhandlung GMBH (Austria) *Tel:* (01) 531 61-161 *Fax:* (01) 531 61-181 *E-mail:* bestellen@manz.co.at *Web Site:* www.manz.at, pg 1300

Maori Publications Unit (New Zealand) *Tel:* (07) 3087254 *Fax:* (07) 3085098, pg 498

MAP-Mapping & Publishing Ltd (Israel) *Tel:* (03) 6210500 *Fax:* (03) 5257725 *E-mail:* info@mapa.co.il *Web Site:* www.mapa.co.il, pg 370

Editorial Mapfre SA (Spain) *Tel:* (091) 581 53 60 *Fax:* (091) 581 18 83 *E-mail:* edimap@mapfre.com *Web Site:* www2.mapfre.com, pg 590

Mapin Publishing Pvt Ltd (India) *Tel:* (079) 2755-1793; (079) 2755-1833 *Fax:* (079) 2755-0955 *E-mail:* info@mapinpub.com *Web Site:* www.mapinpub.com, pg 341

MapQuest (United States) *Tel:* 717-285-8500 *Fax:* 717-285-8456 *E-mail:* infomapquest@aol.com *Web Site:* www.mapquest.com; www.oneworldmapping.com, pg 1145

Maps.com (United States) *Tel:* 805-685-3100 *Toll Free Tel:* 800-929-4MAP (sales) *Fax:* 805-685-3330 *E-mail:* publishing@maps.com *Web Site:* www.maps.com, pg 1230

Maqbool Academy (Pakistan) *Tel:* (042) 7233165 *Fax:* (042) 7324164, pg 513

Marabout (Belgium) *Tel:* (04) 246 3863; (04) 4146 3815 *Fax:* (04) 246 3635, pg 71

Maracle Press Ltd (Canada) *Tel:* 905-723-3438 *Toll Free Tel:* 800-558-8604 *Fax:* 905-428-6024 *E-mail:* maracle@maraclepress.com *Web Site:* www.maraclepress.com, pg 1153, 1175, 1215

Peter Marcan Publications (United Kingdom) *Tel:* (020) 7357 0368, pg 725

Biblioteca Marcel Roche del Instituto Venezolano de Investigaciones Cientificas (Venezuela) *Tel:* (02) 5041512 *Fax:* (02) 504 14 23 *E-mail:* infoivic@ivic.ve *Web Site:* biblioteca.ivic.ve, pg 1555

Marcham Manor Press (United Kingdom) *Tel:* (01235) 848319, pg 725

Marcial Pons Librero (Spain) *Tel:* (091) 304 33 03 *Fax:* (091) 327 23 67 *E-mail:* librerias@marcialpons.es *Web Site:* www.marcialpons.es, pg 1342

Marcial Pons Ediciones Juridicas SA (Spain) *Tel:* (091) 304 33 03 *Fax:* (091) 327 23 67; (091) 7541218 *E-mail:* librerias@marcialpons.es; ediciones@marcialpons.es *Web Site:* www.marcialpons.es, pg 590

Editora Marco Zero Ltda (Brazil) *Tel:* (011) 876-2822 *Fax:* (011) 257-2744 *E-mail:* marcozero@mutecnet.com.br, pg 86

Marcombo SA (Spain) *Tel:* (093) 3180079 *Fax:* (093) 3189339 *E-mail:* marcombo.boixareu@marcombo.es *Web Site:* www.marcombo.es, pg 590, 1136

Editions Marcus (France) *Tel:* (01) 45770404 *Fax:* (01) 45759251, pg 174

Mardaga, Pierre, Editeur (Belgium) *Tel:* (04) 3684242 *Fax:* (04) 3684240, pg 71

Mardev (Australia) *Tel:* (02) 9422 2644 *Fax:* (02) 9422 2633 *E-mail:* mardevlists@reedbusiness.com.au *Web Site:* www.mardevlists.com, pg 1260

Marfiah, CV (Indonesia) *Tel:* (031) 46023, pg 355

Editorial Marfil SA (Spain) *Tel:* (096) 5523311 *Fax:* (096) 5523496 *E-mail:* editorialmarfil@editorialmarfil.com *Web Site:* www.editorialmarfil.com, pg 590

Marg Publications (India) *Tel:* (022) 2821151; (022) 2045947-8; (022) 842520 *Fax:* (022) 047102 *E-mail:* margpub@tata.com *Web Site:* www.tata.com/marg, pg 341

Margaret Hamilton Books Pty Ltd (Australia) *Tel:* (02) 4328 3555 *Toll Free Tel:* 800-021-233 *Fax:* (02) 4323 3827 *Toll Free Fax:* 800-789-948 *E-mail:* customer_service@scholastic.com.au *Web Site:* www.scholastic.com.au, pg 30

La Marge (France) *Tel:* (04) 95512367 *Fax:* (04) 95500900, pg 174

Margraf Verlag (Germany) *Tel:* (07934) 3071 *E-mail:* info@margraf-verlag.de *Web Site:* www.margraf-verlag.de, pg 257

Librairie-Editions J Marguerat (Switzerland) *Tel:* (021) 3237717 *Fax:* (021) 3126732, pg 628

Edition Marhold (Germany) *Tel:* (030) 6917073 *Fax:* (030) 6914067, pg 257

Mariadan (Czech Republic) *Tel:* (02) 41 40 83 91, pg 125

Mariani Ritti Grafiche SRL (Italy) *Tel:* (02) 58310004 *Fax:* (02) 58310408 *E-mail:* ritti@tiw.it, pg 1220

Edition Mariannepresse (Germany) *Tel:* (04864) 660 *E-mail:* quehilie@onlinehome.de, pg 257

Marican Sdn Bhd (Malaysia) *Tel:* (03) 2981133, pg 1326

Editions Marie-Noelle (France) *Tel:* (03) 81877500; (03) 84812891 *Fax:* (03) 81875669, pg 174

Casa Editrice Marietti SpA (Italy) *Tel:* (02) 67101053 *Fax:* (02) 67389081 *E-mail:* marietti1820@split.it, pg 397

Editorial Marin SA (Spain) *Tel:* (093) 8468101 *Fax:* (093) 8468107, pg 590

Aldo Marino Editore (Italy) *Tel:* (095) 438064 *Fax:* (095) 438064, pg 397

Edition Maritim GmbH (Germany) *Tel:* (040) 3396670 *Fax:* (040) 33966777 *E-mail:* mail@edition-maritim.de, pg 257

Maritime Books (United Kingdom) *Tel:* (01579) 343663 *Fax:* (01579) 346747 *E-mail:* editor@navybooks.com *Web Site:* www.navybooks.com, pg 725

Maritime Information Association (United Kingdom) *Tel:* (020) 7261 9535 *Fax:* (020) 7401 2537 *E-mail:* enq@marine-society.org *Web Site:* www.marine-society.org.uk/, pg 1292

Biblioteca Mark Twain, Centro Cultural Costarricense-Norteamericano (Costa Rica) *Tel:* 207-7574; 207-7577 *Toll Free Tel:* 800-207-7500 *Fax:* 224-1480 *E-mail:* info@cccncr.com *Web Site:* www.cccncr.com, pg 1499

Market House Books Ltd (United Kingdom) *Tel:* (01296) 484911 *Fax:* (01296) 437073 *E-mail:* information@mhbref.com *Web Site:* www.mhbref.com, pg 725

The Market Research Society (United Kingdom) *Tel:* (020) 7490 4911 *Fax:* (020) 7490 0608 *E-mail:* info@mrs.org.uk *Web Site:* www.mrs.org.uk, pg 725

Marketasia Distributors (S) Pte Ltd (Singapore) *Tel:* 67448483; 67448486 *Fax:* 67448497; 67443690 *E-mail:* marketasia@pacific.net.sg *Web Site:* www.marketasia.com.sg, pg 1339

Marketing & Wirtschaft Verlagsges, Flade & Partner mbH (Germany) *Tel:* (089) 27813417 *Fax:* (089) 2710156, pg 257

Marketing Focus (Australia) *Tel:* (08) 92571777 *Fax:* (08) 92571888 *Web Site:* www.marketingfocus.net.au, pg 30

Markono Print Media Pte Ltd (Singapore) *Tel:* 6281-1118 *Fax:* 6286-6663 *E-mail:* saleslead@markono.com.sg *Web Site:* www.markono.com.sg, pg 1161

Markono Print Media Pte Ltd (Singapore) *Tel:* 6281-1118 *Fax:* 6286-6663 *E-mail:* kinkeong@pacific.net.sg, pg 1181

Markono Print Media Pte Ltd (Singapore) *Tel:* 6281-1118 *Fax:* 6286-6663 *E-mail:* saleslead@markono.com.sg *Web Site:* www.markono.com.sg, pg 1222, 1238, 1246

Maro Verlag und Druck, Benno Kasmayr (Germany) *Tel:* (0821) 416034 *Fax:* (0821) 416036 *E-mail:* info@maroverlag.de *Web Site:* www.maroverlag.de, pg 257

Tommaso Marotta Editore Srl (Italy) *Tel:* (081) 5758060 *Fax:* (081) 418411, pg 397

Ediciones Marova SL (Spain) *Tel:* (091) 5322606 *Fax:* (091) 5225123 *E-mail:* glanzas@infornet.es, pg 590

Marque Publishing Co Pty Ltd (Australia) *Tel:* (02) 4322 4803 *Fax:* (02) 4329 1475 *E-mail:* books@marque.com.au *Web Site:* www.marque.com.au, pg 30

Marrakech Express Inc (United States) *Tel:* 727-942-2218 *Toll Free Tel:* 800-940-6566 *Fax:* 727-937-4758 *E-mail:* print@marrak.com *Web Site:* www.marrak.com, pg 1167, 1230, 1249

Marren Publishing House, Inc (Philippines) *Tel:* (02) 7115829 *Fax:* (02) 7115830, pg 519

Mars Business Associates Ltd (United Kingdom) *Tel:* (01367) 252 506 *Fax:* (01367) 252 506 *E-mail:* sales@marspub.co.uk *Web Site:* www.marspub.co.uk, pg 725

The Marsh Agency (United Kingdom) *Tel:* (020) 7399 2800 *Fax:* (020) 7399 2801 *E-mail:* enquiries@marsh-agency.co.uk *Web Site:* www.marsh-agency.co.uk, pg 1141

Tracy Marsh Publications Pty Ltd (Australia) *Tel:* (08) 8363 1248 *Fax:* (08) 8363 1352 *Web Site:* www.tracymarsh.com, pg 31

Marshall Editions Ltd (United Kingdom) *Tel:* (020) 7700 6764 *Fax:* (020) 7700 4191 *E-mail:* info@marshalleditions.com *Web Site:* www.quarto.com/group/companies/marshalleditions.htm, pg 725

Marsilio Editori SpA (Italy) *Tel:* (041) 2406511 *Fax:* (041) 5238352 *E-mail:* info@marsilioeditori.it *Web Site:* www.marsilioeditori.it, pg 397

Marston Book Services Ltd (United Kingdom) *Tel:* (01235) 465500 *Fax:* (01235) 465555 *E-mail:* trade.enquiry@marston.co.uk *Web Site:* www.marston.co.uk, pg 1352

Marston House (United Kingdom) *Tel:* (01935) 851331 *Fax:* (01935) 851372, pg 725

Marsu Productions SAM (Monaco) *Tel:* (093) 92056111 *Fax:* (093) 92057660 *E-mail:* info@marsupilami.com; marsuproductions@compuserve.com *Web Site:* www.marsupilami.com, pg 473

Martelle (France) *Tel:* (03) 22 71 54 54 *Fax:* (03) 22 92 89 33, pg 174

Horwitz Martin Education (Australia) *Tel:* (02) 9901 6100 *Fax:* (02) 9901 6166, pg 31

H F Martinez de Murguia SA (Spain) *Tel:* (091) 522 66 34; (091) 532 39 71 *Fax:* (091) 531 37 86, pg 1342

H F Martinez de Murguia SAC y E (Argentina) *Tel:* (011) 4952-1088; (011) 4952-6173 (sales) *Fax:* (011) 4952-1088 *E-mail:* info@murguia.com.ar *Web Site:* www.murguia.com.ar, pg 1297

Ediciones Martinez-Roca SA (Spain) *Tel:* (091) 423 0314 *Fax:* (091) 423 0306 *E-mail:* info@ediciones-martinez-roca.es *Web Site:* www.edicionesmartinezroca.com, pg 591

Editions de la Martiniere (France) *Tel:* (01) 40 51 52 00 *Fax:* (01) 40 51 52 05 *E-mail:* coedition@lamartiniere.fr *Web Site:* www.lamartiniere.fr, pg 174

Livraria Tavares Martins (Portugal) *Tel:* (022) 23459, pg 533

Marton Aron Kiado Publishing House (Hungary) *Tel:* (01) 3689527; (01) 3678415 *Fax:* (01) 1689869 *E-mail:* oli@hcbc.hu, pg 323

Martynas Mazvydas National Library of Lithuania (Lithuania) *Tel:* 52398687 *Fax:* 52639111 *E-mail:* leidyba@lnb.lt *Web Site:* www.lnb.lt, pg 449

Martynas Mazvydas National Library of Lithuania (Lietuvos Nacionaline Martyno Mazvydo Biblioteka) (Lithuania) *Tel:* (02) 497023 *Fax:* (02) 496129 *E-mail:* biblio@lnb.lt *Web Site:* www.lnb.lt, pg 1525

Maruzen Asia (Pte) Ltd (Singapore) *Tel:* 7751577 *Fax:* 7351678, pg 557

Maruzen Co Ltd (Japan) *Tel:* (03) 3272-0514 *Fax:* (03) 3272-0527 *E-mail:* webmaster@maruzen.co.jp *Web Site:* www.maruzen.co.jp; www.maruzen.co.jp/home-eng/index.html, pg 422

Maruzen Co Ltd (Japan) *Tel:* (03) 3275 8595 *Fax:* (03) 3274 3239 *E-mail:* media@maruzen.co.jp *Web Site:* www.maruzen.co.jp, pg 1322

Editions Marval (France) *Tel:* (01) 48 07 50 40 *Fax:* (01) 48 07 01 08 *E-mail:* info@marval.com *Web Site:* www.marval.com, pg 174

Blanche Marvin Agency (United Kingdom) *Tel:* (020) 7722 2313 *Fax:* (020) 7722 2313, pg 1141

Institut fuer Marxistische Studien und Forschungen eV (IMSF) (Germany) *Tel:* (069) 7392934, pg 257

Marymar Ediciones SA (Argentina) *Tel:* (011) 4381-9083, pg 7

Marzorati Editore SRL (Italy) *Tel:* (06) 8546146 *Fax:* (06) 8411225, pg 397

Masagung Books Pte Ltd (Singapore) *Tel:* 4683276 *Fax:* 345000, pg 557

Masagung Books Pte Ltd (Singapore) *Tel:* 4683276, pg 1339

La Mascara, SL Editorial (Spain) *Tel:* (096) 3486500 *Fax:* (096) 3487440 *E-mail:* lamascara@arrakis.es, pg 591

Maskew Miller Longman (Botswana) *Tel:* 322969 *Fax:* 322682 *E-mail:* longman@info.bw, pg 76

Maskew Miller Longman (South Africa) *Tel:* (021) 531 7750 *Fax:* (021) 531 4877 *E-mail:* firstname@mml.co.za *Web Site:* www.mml.com, pg 566

Maskew Miller Longman (South Africa) *Tel:* (021) 531 7750 *Fax:* (021) 5314049 *E-mail:* firstname@mml.co.za *Web Site:* www.mml.co.za, pg 1340

Veselin Maslesa (Bosnia and Herzegovina) *Tel:* (033) 667735; (033) 667736 *Fax:* (033) 668351; (033) 667738 *E-mail:* sapublishing@bihart.com, pg 76

Veselin Maslesa (Bosnia and Herzegovina) *Tel:* (071) 214633, pg 1303

Masmedia (Croatia) *Tel:* (01) 457-7400 *Fax:* (01) 457 7769 *E-mail:* masmedia@zg.tel.hr; mm@masmedia.hr *Web Site:* www.masmedia.hr, pg 118

Kenneth Mason Publications Ltd (United Kingdom) *Tel:* (01243) 377977; (01243) 377978 *Fax:* (01243) 379136 *E-mail:* boatswain@dial.pipex.com, pg 726

Masons Design & Print (United Kingdom) *Tel:* (01244) 674433 *Fax:* (01244) 674274 *E-mail:* sales@masonsprint.com *Web Site:* www.masonsprint.com, pg 1164

Massada Press Ltd (Israel) *Tel:* (02) 6719441 *Fax:* (02) 6719442, pg 370

Massada Publishers Ltd (Israel) *Tel:* (03) 5716659; (03) 5712702 *Fax:* (03) 5716639, pg 370

Editrice Massimo SAS di Crespi Cesare e C (Italy) *Tel:* (02) 55 21 08 00 *Fax:* (02) 55 21 13 15, pg 397

Editions Charles Massin et Cie (France) *Tel:* (01) 45 65 48 55 *Fax:* (01) 45 65 47 00 *E-mail:* info@massin.fr *Web Site:* www.massin.fr, pg 174

Masson Editeur (France) *Tel:* (01) 73 28 16 34 *Fax:* (01) 73 28 16 49 *E-mail:* infos@masson.fr *Web Site:* www.masson.fr; www.e2med.com, pg 174

Masson Editores (Mexico) *Tel:* (05) 6870933, pg 468

Masson SpA (Italy) *Tel:* (02) 574952315 *Fax:* (02) 574952-371 *E-mail:* info@masson.it *Web Site:* www.masson.it, pg 397

Masson-Williams et Wilkins (France) *Tel:* (01) 40466000 *Fax:* (01) 40466126 *E-mail:* pradel@lsicom.fr, pg 174

MAST Verlag (Romania) *Tel:* (01) 7786950 *Fax:* (01) 4104588, pg 540

Izdatelstvo Mastatskaya Litaratura (Belarus) *Tel:* (0172) 236131 *Fax:* (0172) 269112; (0172) 236184, pg 62

Master Flo Technology Inc (Canada) *Tel:* 613-636-0539 *Fax:* 613-636-0762 *E-mail:* info@mflo.com *Web Site:* www.mflo.com, pg 1245

Matar Publishing House (Israel) *Tel:* (03) 7441199 *Fax:* (03) 7441314 *E-mail:* mtriwaks@netvision.net.il, pg 370

MATEX (Bulgaria) *Tel:* (02) 430177 *E-mail:* mmk_fte@uacg.acad.bg, pg 95

Sri Ramakrishna Math (India) *Tel:* (044) 24621110 *Fax:* (044) 24934589 *E-mail:* srkmath@vsnl.com *Web Site:* www.sriramakrishnamath.org, pg 341

Matica hrvatska (Croatia) *Tel:* (01) 4878-360; (01) 4878-354; (01) 4878-362 *Fax:* (01) 4819-319 *E-mail:* matica@matica.hr *Web Site:* www.matica.hr, pg 118

Matice moravska (Czech Republic) *Tel:* (05) 4949 1511 *Fax:* (05) 4949 1520 *E-mail:* bronek@phil.muni.cz *Web Site:* www.phil.muni.cz, pg 1398

Biblioteka Matice Srpske (Serbia and Montenegro) *Tel:* (021) 420 271; (021) 528 747 *Fax:* (021) 28 574; (021) 420 271 *E-mail:* bms@bms.ns.ac.yu *Web Site:* www.bms.ns.ac.yu, pg 1542

Matrice (France) *Tel:* (01) 69 42 13 02 *Fax:* (01) 69 40 21 57, pg 174

Mats Publishers Ltd (Estonia) *Tel:* (O2) 6563589, pg 140

Mattes Verlag GmbH (Germany) *Tel:* (06221) 45930 *Fax:* (06221) 459322 *E-mail:* mattes@mattes.de *Web Site:* www.mattes.de, pg 257

Matthaes Verlag GmbH (Germany) *Tel:* (0711) 21 33-329 *Fax:* (0711) 21 33-320 *E-mail:* info@matthaes.de *Web Site:* www.matthaes.de, pg 257

Matthes und Seitz Verlag GmbH (Germany) *Tel:* (089) 1232510 *Fax:* (089) 187534, pg 258

Adam Matthew Publications (United Kingdom) *Tel:* (01672) 511921 *Fax:* (01672) 511663 *E-mail:* info@ampltd.co.uk *Web Site:* www.adam-matthew-publications.co.uk, pg 726

Matthias-Gruenewald-Verlag GmbH (Germany) *Tel:* (06131) 92860 *Fax:* (06131) 928626 *E-mail:* mail@gruenewaldverlag.de *Web Site:* members.aol.com/matthgruen, pg 258

Matthias Media (Australia) *Tel:* (02) 3100813; (02) 9663-1478 (overseas) *Toll Free Tel:* 800 814 360 *Fax:* (02) 9663-3265; (02) 9663-3265 *E-mail:* info@matthiasmedia.com.au *Web Site:* www.matthiasmedia.com.au, pg 31

Matthiesen Verlag Ingwert Paulsen Jr (Germany) *Tel:* (04841) 83520 *Fax:* (04841) 835210 *E-mail:* info@verlagsgruppe.de *Web Site:* www.verlagsgruppe.de, pg 258

Hans K Matussek Buchhandlung & Antiquariat (Germany) *Tel:* (02153) 91 64 30 *Fax:* (02153) 1 33 63 *Web Site:* www.buchkatalog.de/matussek, pg 258

Les Editions la Matze (Switzerland) *Tel:* (027) 3231652 *Fax:* (027) 3231652, pg 628

Matzker Verlag DiA (Germany) *Tel:* (0421) 6207934, pg 258

Wilhelm Maudrich KG (Austria) *Tel:* (01) 4024712 *Fax:* (01) 4085080 *E-mail:* medbook@maudrich.com *Web Site:* www.maudrich.com, pg 54

C Maurer Druck und Verlag (Germany) *Tel:* (07331) 930-0 *Fax:* (07331) 93 0-190 *Web Site:* www.maurer-online.de, pg 1176

C Maurer Druck und Verlag (Germany) *Tel:* (07331) 9300 *Web Site:* www.maurer-online.de, pg 1217

Mauritius Archives (Mauritius) *Tel:* 233-4469; 233 7341 *Fax:* 233 4299, pg 1528

Mauritius Institute Public Library (Mauritius) *Tel:* 212 06 39 *Fax:* 212 57 17, pg 1528

Mauritius Library Association (Mauritius) *Tel:* 4549550; 4549551; 4549552 *Fax:* 4549553 *E-mail:* ielts@mu.britishcouncil.org *Web Site:* www.britishcouncil.org/mauritius/, pg 1567

Mavisu International Co Ltd (Thailand) *Tel:* (02) 2711148 *Fax:* (02) 2711168, pg 1224

Mavrogianni Publications (Greece) *Tel:* (01) 3304628 *Fax:* (01) 3304628, pg 1314

Mawaddah Enterprise Sdn Bhd (Malaysia) *Tel:* (06) 7611062 *Fax:* (06) 7633062 *E-mail:* azhari@mawadah.pc.my, pg 1326

Max Schimmel Verlag (Germany) *Tel:* (0931) 27 91 400 *Fax:* (0931) 27 91 444 *E-mail:* info@schimmelverlag.de *Web Site:* www.schimmelverlag.de, pg 258

Maxdorf Ltd (Czech Republic) *Tel:* (02) 444 710 37; (02) 41 011 680; (02) 41 011 681 *Fax:* (02) 41 710 245 *E-mail:* info@maxdorf.cz *Web Site:* www.maxdorf.cz, pg 125

Maxima Laurent du Mesnil Editeur (France) *Tel:* (01) 44397400 *Fax:* (01) 45484688 *E-mail:* edition@maxima.fr *Web Site:* www.maxima.fr, pg 174

Maximilian-Gesellschaft eV (Germany) *Tel:* (0711) 5499710 *Fax:* (0711) 54997121 *E-mail:* hiersemann.hauswedell.verlage@t-online.de *Web Site:* www.maximilian-gesellschaft.de, pg 1400

Maya Publishers Pvt Ltd (India) *Tel:* (011) 6494878; (011) 6494850; (011) 649 0451; (011) 649 0959 *Fax:* (011) 6491039; (011) 686 4614 *E-mail:* surit@del2.vsnl.net.in, pg 341

Ludwig Mayer Jerusalem Ltd (Israel) *Tel:* (02) 625-2628 *Fax:* (02) 623-2640 *E-mail:* mayerbks@netvision.net.il, pg 1320

J A Mayersche Buchhandlung GmbH & Co KG Abt Verlag (Germany) *Tel:* (0241) 4777 499 *Fax:* (0241) 4777 467 *E-mail:* vertrieb@mayersche.de *Web Site:* www.mayersche.de, pg 258

J A Mayersche Buchhandlung GmbH & Co KG Abt Verlag (Germany) *Tel:* (0241) 4777 499 *Fax:* (0241) 4777 467 *E-mail:* info@mayersche.de *Web Site:* www.mayersche.de, pg 1311

Mayibuye Books (South Africa) *Tel:* (021) 9592529 *Fax:* (021) 9593411 *E-mail:* mayibuye@mweb.co.za, pg 566

Mayne Publishing (Australia) *Tel:* (07) 4697 3228 *Fax:* (07) 4697 3228 *Web Site:* www.maynepublishing.com.au, pg 31

Mayr Miesbach Druckerei und Verlag GmbH (Germany) *Tel:* (08025) 294-0 *Fax:* (08025) 294-235 *E-mail:* info@mayrmiesbach.de *Web Site:* www.mayrmiesbach.de, pg 258

Bibliotheque Mazarine (France) *Tel:* (01) 44 41 44 06 *Fax:* (01) 44 41 44 07 *Web Site:* www.bibliotheque-mazarine.fr, pg 1507

Mazenod Book Centre (Lesotho) *Tel:* 35 0224 *Fax:* 35 0010, pg 447, 1325

Mazer Publishing Services (United States) *Tel:* 937-264-2600 *Fax:* 937-264-2624 *E-mail:* info@mazer.com *Web Site:* www.mazer.com, pg 1167, 1188, 1230, 1241, 1249

Edizioni Gabriele Mazzotta SRL (Italy) *Tel:* (02) 8055803 *Fax:* (02) 8693046 *E-mail:* mazzotta@milanoweb.com, pg 397

MBA Literary Agents Ltd (United Kingdom) *Tel:* (020) 7387 2076 *Fax:* (020) 7387 2042, pg 1142

MBMS-Bibliography & Management Service (Germany) *Tel:* (02733) 7657 *Fax:* (02733) 8492, pg 1131

Yvonne McBurney (Australia) *Tel:* (02) 68873608, pg 31

McCrimmon Publishing Co Ltd (United Kingdom) *Tel:* (01702) 218956 *Fax:* (01702) 216082 *E-mail:* sales@mccrimmons.com (sales); orders@mccrimmons.com (orders); permissions@mccrimmons.com (permission-related inquiries); clipart@mccrimmons.com (clip art); accounts@mccrimmons.com-accounts *Web Site:* www.mccrimmons.com, pg 726

McGallen & Bolden Associates (Singapore) *Tel:* 63246588 *Fax:* 63246966 *E-mail:* sales@mcgallen.com *Web Site:* mcgallen.net, pg 557

McGraw-Hill Asia/India Group (Singapore) *Tel:* 6863-1580 *Fax:* 6861-9296 *Web Site:* www.asia-mcgraw-hill.com.sg, pg 557

McGraw-Hill Australia Pty Ltd (Australia) *Tel:* (02) 9900 1800; (02) 9900 1806 (customer service); (02) 9900 1802 (customer service) *Fax:* (02) 9878 8280 (customer service) *E-mail:* cservice_sydney@mcgraw-hill.com.au *Web Site:* www.mcgraw-hill.com.au, pg 31

McGraw-Hill Colombia (Colombia) *Tel:* (01) 6003800 *Fax:* (01) 6003811 *Web Site:* www.mcgraw-hill.com.co, pg 112

Editora McGraw-Hill de Portugal Lda (Portugal) *Tel:* (021) 355 3180 *Fax:* (021) 355 3189 *E-mail:* servico-clientes@mcgraw-hill.com *Web Site:* www.mcgraw-hill.pt, pg 533

McGraw-Hill de Venezuela (Venezuela) *Tel:* (02) 238 3494; (02) 761 8181; (02) 761 6992 *Fax:* (02) 238 2374; (02) 761 6993 *E-mail:* dpmail@attmail.com, pg 780

McGraw-Hill Education Europe, Middle East & Africa Group (United Kingdom) *Tel:* (016) 2850 2500 *Fax:* (016) 2877 7342 *Web Site:* www.mcgraw-hill.co.uk, pg 726

McGraw-Hill/Interamericana de Espana SAU (Spain) *Tel:* (091) 1803000 *Web Site:* www.mcgraw-hill.es, pg 591

McGraw-Hill Interamericana Editores, SA de CV (Mexico) *Tel:* 576-73-04; 576-90-44 ext 156 *E-mail:* mcgraw-hill@infosel.net.mx *Web Site:* www.mcgraw-hill.com.mx, pg 468

McGraw-Hill Intermericana del Caribe, Inc (Puerto Rico) *Tel:* (787) 751-2451; (787) 751-3451 *Fax:* (787) 764-1890 *Web Site:* www.mhschool.com/contactus/international.html, pg 537

McGraw-Hill Libri Italia SRL (Italy) *Tel:* (02) 5357181 *Fax:* (02) 5398775 *E-mail:* editor@mcgraw-hill.it, pg 398

McGraw-Hill Mexico/Latin America Group (Mexico) *Tel:* (055) 5117-1515 *Fax:* (055) 5117-1516 *Web Site:* www.mcgraw-hill.com.mx, pg 468

McGraw-Hill Publishing Company (United Kingdom) *Tel:* (01) 628 502500 *Fax:* (01) 628 635895 *Web Site:* www.mcgraw-hill.co.uk, pg 726

J M McGregor Pty Ltd (Australia) *Tel:* (02) 9135 1923, pg 31

McGregor Publishers (Namibia) *Tel:* (061) 62155 *Fax:* (061) 63059 *E-mail:* gmcgregor@unam.na, pg 476

McLaren Morris & Todd Co (Canada) *Tel:* 905-677-3592 *Fax:* 905-677-3675; 905-677-7766 *Web Site:* www.mmt.ca, pg 1153, 1215, 1235

McLeods Booksellers (New Zealand) *Tel:* (07) 3485388 *Fax:* (07) 3490288 *E-mail:* mcleods@clear.net.nz *Web Site:* www.mcleodsbooks.co.nz, pg 1330

McMillan Memorial Library (Kenya) *Tel:* (02) 21844, pg 1523

McRae Books (Italy) *Tel:* (055) 264384 *Fax:* (055) 212573, pg 398

MDC Publishers Printers Sdn Bhd (Malaysia) *Tel:* (03) 41086600 *Fax:* (03) 41081506 *E-mail:* mdcpp@mdcpp.com.my *Web Site:* www.mdcpp.com.my, pg 457

Editions MDI (La Maison des Instituteurs) (France) *Tel:* (01) 45 87 52 11 *Fax:* (01) 45 87 51 97 *E-mail:* serviceclient@mdi-editions.com; mpetit@vuef.fr *Web Site:* www.mdi-editions.com, pg 175

ME Editores, SL (Spain) *Tel:* (091) 3151008 *Fax:* (091) 3230844, pg 591

Meander Uitgeverij BV (Netherlands) *Tel:* (071) 5601040 *Fax:* (071) 5619741 *E-mail:* info@vierwindstreken.com *Web Site:* www.vierwindstreken.com, pg 485

Meandre (Switzerland) *Tel:* (026) 322174 *Fax:* (026) 323287, pg 628

Editora Meca Ltda (Brazil) *Tel:* (011) 2599049; (011) 2599034; (011) 2575346 *Fax:* (011) 2570312 *E-mail:* editora_meca@uol.com.br *Web Site:* www.editorameca.com.br, pg 86

Landesbibliothek Mecklenburg-Vorpommern (Germany) *Tel:* (0385) 558440 *Fax:* (0385) 5584424 *E-mail:* lb@lbmv.de *Web Site:* www.lbmv.de, pg 1509

Mecron Sdn Bhd (Malaysia) *Tel:* 16 280 8772 *Fax:* (03) 6251 9869 *Web Site:* www.mecronbooks.com, pg 457

Med Info Publishing Co (Hong Kong) *Tel:* 2522 2713, pg 318

Medcom Ltd (Israel) *Tel:* (03) 9343853 *Fax:* (03) 9343850, pg 370

Bibliotheque Interuniversitaire de Medecine (France) *Tel:* (01) 40461951 *Fax:* (01) 44411020 *Web Site:* www.bium.univ-paris5.fr, pg 1507

Medecine et Hygiene (Switzerland) *Tel:* (022) 702 93 11 *Fax:* (022) 702 93 55 *E-mail:* direction@medecinehygiene.dr *Web Site:* www.medhyg.ch, pg 628

Stichting Evangelische Uitgeverij H Medema (Netherlands) *Tel:* (0578) 574995 *Fax:* (0578) 573099 *E-mail:* info@medema.nl *Web Site:* www.medema.nl, pg 485

Media Centre (Malta) *Tel:* 21249005; 21223047; 21244913; 21247460; 25699113; 25699114; 25699115 *Fax:* 21246716, pg 460

Media East Press (Australia) *Tel:* (02) 9349 6683 *Fax:* (02) 9349 6683, pg 31

Media House Publications (South Africa) *Tel:* (011) 8826237 *Fax:* (011) 8829652, pg 566

Media House Publications Pty Ltd (South Africa) *Tel:* (011) 8826237 *Fax:* (011) 8829652, pg 1340

Media Institute of Southern Africa (MISA) (Namibia) *Tel:* (061) 232975 *Fax:* (061) 248016 *E-mail:* postmaster@ingrid.misa.org.na *Web Site:* www.misanet.org, pg 476

Media-Print Informationstechnologie GmbH (Germany) *Tel:* (02941) 2 72-300 *Fax:* (02941) 2 72-540 *E-mail:* kg@mediaprint.de *Web Site:* www.mediaprint.de, pg 1155

Media-Print Informationstechnologie GmbH (Germany) *Tel:* (051) 522-300 *Fax:* (051) 522-480 *E-mail:* contact@mediaprintpb.de *Web Site:* www.mediaprint.de, pg 1176

Media-Print Informationstechnologie GmbH (Germany) *Tel:* (02941) 2 72-300 *Fax:* (02941) 2 72-540 *E-mail:* kg@mediaprint.de *Web Site:* www.mediaprint.de, pg 1217

Media Research Publishing Ltd (United Kingdom) *Tel:* (01934) 644 309 *Fax:* (01934) 644 402, pg 726

Mediabank (Republic of Korea) *Tel:* (02) 7420425 *Fax:* (02) 7452174 *E-mail:* sales@mediabank.biz *Web Site:* www.mediabank.pe.kr, pg 1134

Editions Medianes (France) *Tel:* (02) 35 88 85 71 *Fax:* (02) 35 15 28 44 *E-mail:* medianesconseil@wanadoo.fr, pg 175

Mediapress GmbH (Germany) *Tel:* (02151) 79553334, pg 258

Editions Mediaspaul (France) *Tel:* (01) 45 48 71 93 *Fax:* (01) 42 22 47 46 *E-mail:* mediaspaul.com@wanadoo.fr, pg 175

Mediatheque de Saint Pierre (Reunion) *Tel:* 96 71 91 *Fax:* 25 74 10 *Web Site:* www.mediatheque-saintpierre.fr, pg 1539

Editorial Medica JIMS, SL (Spain) *Tel:* (093) 2188800 *Fax:* (093) 2188928, pg 591

Editorial Medica Panamericana SA (Argentina) *Tel:* (011) 4821-5520; (011) 4821-0175 *Fax:* (011) 4821-1214 *E-mail:* info@medicapanamericana.com *Web Site:* www.medicapanamericana.com.ar, pg 7

Libreria Medica Paris (Venezuela) *Tel:* (02) 781-6044 *Fax:* (02) 7931753, pg 1356

Medical Sciences International Ltd (Japan) *Tel:* (03) 5804-6050 *Fax:* (03) 5804-6055 *E-mail:* info@medsi.co.jp *Web Site:* www.medsi.co.jp, pg 422

Medical University - Sofia, Central Medical Library (Bulgaria) *Tel:* (02) 952 31 71 *Fax:* (02) 952 31 71 *Web Site:* www.medun.acad.bg/, pg 1496

Medical Writers Group (United Kingdom) *Tel:* (020) 7373 6642 *Fax:* (020) 7373 5768 *E-mail:* info@societyofauthors.org *Web Site:* www.societyofauthors.org, pg 1408

Editura Medicala (Romania) *Tel:* (01) 25 25 186 *Fax:* (01) 25 25 189 *E-mail:* edmedicala@fx.ro *Web Site:* www.ed-medicala.ro, pg 540

Editions Medicales et Paramedicales de Charleroi (EMPC) (Belgium) *Tel:* (071) 324689 *Fax:* (071) 324689, pg 71

Ediciones Medicas SA (Argentina) *Tel:* (011) 4384-0750 *Fax:* (011) 4384-0750 *E-mail:* emsa@havasmedimedia.com.ar, pg 7

Edizioni Medicea SRL (Italy) *Tel:* (055) 416048 *Fax:* (055) 416048 *E-mail:* edizionimedicea@tiscalinet.it *Web Site:* www.edizionimedicea.it, pg 398

Ediciones Medici SA (Spain) *Tel:* (093) 2 010 599; (093) 2 013 807; (093) 2 012 144 *Fax:* (093) 2 097 362 *E-mail:* omega@ediciones-omega.es *Web Site:* www.ediciones-medici.es; www.ediciones-omega.es, pg 591

The Medici Society Ltd (United Kingdom) *Tel:* (020) 8205 2500 *Fax:* (020) 8205 2552 *E-mail:* info@medici.co.uk *Web Site:* www.medici.co.uk, pg 726

AS Medicina (Estonia) *Tel:* (06) 567660 *Fax:* (06) 567620 *E-mail:* medicina@hot.ee *Web Site:* medicina.co.ee, pg 140

Medicina i Fizkultura EOOD (Bulgaria) *Tel:* (02) 871308; (02) 884068 *Fax:* (02) 871308, pg 95

Izdatelstvo Medicina (Russian Federation) *Tel:* (095) 9248785 *Fax:* (095) 9286003, pg 546

Medicina Koenyvkiado (Hungary) *Tel:* (01) 312-2650 *Fax:* (01) 312-2450, pg 323

Medicina Panamericana Editora Do Brasil Ltda (Brazil) *Tel:* (011) 222-0366 *Fax:* (011) 222-0542, pg 86

Bibliothecarii Medicinae Fenniae (BMF) (Finland) *Tel:* (09) 191 26645 *Fax:* (09) 191 26652 *E-mail:* etunimi.sukunimi@helsinki.fi *Web Site:* www.terkko.helsinki.fi/bmf, pg 1561

Medico International eV (Germany) *Tel:* (069) 94438-0 *Fax:* (069) 436002 *E-mail:* info@medico.de *Web Site:* www.medico.de, pg 258

Medien & Recht (Austria) *Tel:* (01) 5052766 *Fax:* (01) 5052766-15 *E-mail:* verlag@medien-recht.ccom *Web Site:* www.medien-recht.com, pg 54

Medien-Verlag Bernhard Gregor GmbH (Germany) *Tel:* (06625) 5011; (0171) 7723972 *Fax:* (06625) 919743 *E-mail:* gregor-medien@t-online.de; mail@gregor-medien.de *Web Site:* www.gregor-medien.de, pg 258

Medienbuero Muenchen (Germany) *Tel:* (089) 299975 *Fax:* (089) 299975 *E-mail:* info@medienbuero-muenchen.com *Web Site:* www.medienbuero-muenchen.com, pg 1131

Medios Publicitarios Mexicanos SA de CV Editora de Directorios de Medios (Mexico) *Tel:* (05) 523-3346; (05) 523-3342 *Fax:* (05) 523-3379 *E-mail:* suscrip@mpm.com.mx; editorial@mpm.com.mx *Web Site:* www.mpm.com.mx, pg 468

Medios y Medios, Sa de CV (Mexico) *Tel:* (05) 56-01-85-11 *Fax:* (05) 56-88-59-85 *E-mail:* mass+medios@camoapa.com.mx, pg 468

Medis, Skopje (The Former Yugoslav Republic of Macedonia) *Tel:* (091) 118-104 *Fax:* (091) 272-253 *E-mail:* medis@informa.mk *Web Site:* www.medis.com.mk, pg 452

Mediserve SRL (Italy) *Tel:* (081) 5452717 *Fax:* (081) 5462026 *E-mail:* contact@mediserve.it *Web Site:* www.mediserve.it, pg 398

Edizioni Mediterranee SRL (Italy) *Tel:* (06) 3235433 *Fax:* (06) 3236277 *E-mail:* ediz-mediterranee.com *Web Site:* www.ediz-mediterranee.com, pg 398

Editorial Mediterrania SL (Spain) *Tel:* (093) 218 34 58; (093) 237 86 65 *Fax:* (093) 237 22 10 *E-mail:* edit.med@retemail.es, pg 591

Medium-Buchmarkt (Germany) *Tel:* (0251) 46 000 *Fax:* (0251) 46 745 *E-mail:* info@mediumbooks.com *Web Site:* www.mediumbooks.com, pg 258

Medius Editions (France) *Tel:* (01) 42 79 25 21 *Fax:* (01) 42 78 25 39 *E-mail:* contact@dervy.fr, pg 175

Medizinisch-Literarische Verlagsgesellschaft mbH (Germany) *Tel:* (0581) 808-151 *Fax:* (0581) 808-158 *E-mail:* mlverlag@mlverlag.de *Web Site:* www.mlverlag.de, pg 258

Medpharm Scientific Publishers (Germany) *Tel:* (0711) 2582-0 *Fax:* (0711) 2582-290 *E-mail:* service@medpharm.de *Web Site:* www.medpharm.de, pg 258

Medsi - Editora Medica e Cientifica Ltda (Brazil) *Tel:* (021) 5694342 *Fax:* (021) 2646392, pg 86

Medusa/Selas Publishers (Greece) *Tel:* (01) 36483234 *Fax:* (01) 3648321 *E-mail:* medusa@otenet.gr *Web Site:* www.medusaselas.gr, pg 310

Wydawnictwo Medyczne Urban & Partner (Poland) *Tel:* (071) 328 54 87; (071) 328 30 68 *Fax:* (071) 328 43 91 *E-mail:* info@urbanpartner.pl *Web Site:* www.urbanpartner.pl, pg 524

Meerut Publishers' Association (India) *Tel:* (0121) 51 0688; (0121) 51 6080 *Fax:* (0121) 52 1545 *E-mail:* vrastogi@vsnl.com, pg 1273

Willem A Meeuws Publisher (United Kingdom) *Tel:* (01235) 821994 *Fax:* (01235) 821994 *E-mail:* thorntons@booknews.demon.co.uk *Web Site:* www.thorntonsbooks.co.uk, pg 726

Megatrade AG (Liechtenstein) *Tel:* 237 5252 *Fax:* 237 5253 *E-mail:* info@wanger.net *Web Site:* www.wanger.net, pg 448

Mehanograf (Croatia) *Tel:* (01) 3498-411 *Fax:* (01) 3498-414 *E-mail:* mehanograf@zg.hinet.hr *Web Site:* www.cursor.hr/pa.nsf, pg 1154

Mehta Publishers (India) *Tel:* (011) 4476924 *Fax:* (011) 4475462 *E-mail:* mopl@vsnl.com, pg 341

Mei Ka Printing & Publishing Enterprise Ltd (Hong Kong) *Tel:* 2540 1131 *Fax:* 2559 8718; 2559 7137 *E-mail:* mkpp@netvigator.com *Web Site:* www.meika-printing.com, pg 1157

Mei Ka Printing & Publishing Enterprise Ltd (Hong Kong) *Tel:* 2540 1131 *Fax:* 2559 8718; 2559 7137 *E-mail:* mkpp@netvigator.com *Web Site:* www.meika-printing.com; www.meika-printing.b2s.com, pg 1178

Mei Ka Printing & Publishing Enterprise Ltd (Hong Kong) *Tel:* 2540 1131 *Fax:* 2559 8718; 2559 7137 *E-mail:* mkpp@netvigator.com *Web Site:* www.meika-printing.com, pg 1236

Mei Ya Publications Inc (Sueling Inc) (Taiwan, Province of China) *Tel:* (02) 7037481 *Fax:* (02) 7033847, pg 1345

Meiji Shoin Co Ltd (Japan) *Tel:* (03) 5292-0117 *Fax:* (03) 5292-6182 *E-mail:* nihongol@oak.ocn.ne.jp *Web Site:* www.meijishoin.co.jp, pg 422

Buchhaus Meili AG (Switzerland) *Tel:* (052) 625 41 44 *Fax:* (052) 625 47 46 *E-mail:* info@buchhausmeili.ch *Web Site:* www.buchhausmeili.ch, pg 1344

Peter Meili & Co, Buchhandlung (Switzerland) *Tel:* (053) 254144 *Fax:* (053) 254746, pg 628

Uitgeverij Meinema (Netherlands) *Tel:* (079) 3615481 *Fax:* (079) 3615489 *E-mail:* info@boekencentrum.nl *Web Site:* www.boekencentrum.nl, pg 485

Felix Meiner Verlag GmbH (Germany) *Tel:* (040) 298756-20 *Fax:* (040) 299361-4 *E-mail:* info@meiner.de *Web Site:* www.meiner.de, pg 258

Meisenbach Verlag GmbH (Germany) *Tel:* (0951) 861-0 *Fax:* (0951) 861-158 *Web Site:* www.meisenbach.de, pg 258

Otto Meissner Verlag (Germany) *Tel:* (030) 8249558 *Fax:* (030) 8233338, pg 259

Mejikaru Furendo-sha (Japan) *Tel:* (03) 32646611 *Fax:* (03) 32616602 (distribution); (03) 32640704 (editorial affairs) *E-mail:* mfhensyu@mb.infoweb.ne.jp; mfeigyou@mb.infoweb.ne.jp; mfsoumu@mb.infoweb.ne.jp, pg 422

Mekize Nirdamim Society (Israel) *Tel:* (02) 636072, pg 1401

Melanesian Institute (Papua New Guinea) *Tel:* 732 1777 *Fax:* 732 1214, pg 515

Melantrich, akc spol (Czech Republic) *Tel:* (02) 24227258 *Fax:* (02) 24213176, pg 125

Pustaka Melayu Baru (Malaysia) *Tel:* (03) 2985281 *Fax:* (03) 2414457, pg 457

Melbourne Institute of Applied Economic & Social Research (Australia) *Tel:* (03) 8344 2100 *Fax:* (03) 8344 2111 *E-mail:* melb-inst@unimelb.edu.au *Web Site:* www.melbourneinstitute.com, pg 31

Melbourne PEN Centre (Australia) *Tel:* (03) 95097257 *Fax:* (03) 95097257 *Web Site:* www.pen.org.au, pg 1396

Melbourne University Press (Australia) *Tel:* (03) 9342 0300 *Fax:* (03) 9342 0399 *E-mail:* mup-info@unimelb.edu.au *Web Site:* www.mup.unimelb.edu.au, pg 32

Melhoramentos de Portugal Editora, Lda (Portugal) *Tel:* (021) 3963225 *Fax:* (021) 678254, pg 533

Editora Melhoramentos Ltda (Brazil) *Tel:* (011) 3874 0854 *Fax:* (011) 3874 0855 *E-mail:* blerner@melhoramentos.com.br *Web Site:* melhoramentos.com.br, pg 86

Melissa Publishing House (Greece) *Tel:* (010) 3611692 *Fax:* (010) 3600865 *E-mail:* sales@melissabooks.com *Web Site:* www.melissabooks.com, pg 310

Melissa Publishing House (Greece) *Tel:* (010) 3611692 *Fax:* (010) 3600865 *E-mail:* webmaster@melissabooks.com *Web Site:* www.melissabooks.com, pg 1314

Mellemfolkeligt Samvirke (Denmark) *Tel:* 7731 0000 *Fax:* 7731 0101 *E-mail:* ms@ms.dk *Web Site:* www.ms.dk, pg 133

Ediciones y Publicidad Melquiades (Chile) *Tel:* (02) 2731545 *Fax:* (02) 2266602, pg 99

Melrose Press Ltd (United Kingdom) *Tel:* (01353) 646600 *Fax:* (01353) 646601 *E-mail:* tradesales@melrosepress.co.uk; info@melrosepress.co.uk *Web Site:* www.melrosepress.co.uk, pg 726

Melting Pot Press (Australia) *Tel:* (02) 9211 1660 *Fax:* (02) 9211 1868 *E-mail:* books@elt.com.au, pg 32

Melway Publishing Pty Ltd (Australia) *Tel:* (03) 9585 9888 *Fax:* (03) 9585 9800 *E-mail:* melway@ausway.com *Web Site:* www.ausway.com, pg 32

Idime Verlag Inge Melzer (Germany) *Tel:* (07541) 55220 *Fax:* (07541) 55201 *E-mail:* idime@t-online.de *Web Site:* www.idime.de, pg 259

Editions Memo (France) *Tel:* (02) 40 47 98 19 *Fax:* (02) 40 47 98 21, pg 175

Editions Memoire des Arts (France) *Tel:* (04) 78 83 22 62 *Fax:* (04) 72 19 48 74, pg 175

Editions Memor (Belgium) *Tel:* (02) 644-04-43 *Fax:* (02) 644-04-43 *Web Site:* www.memor.cjb.net, pg 71

Memorias Futuras Edicoes Ltda (Brazil) *Tel:* (021) 2053549 *Fax:* (021) 2252518 *E-mail:* memorias@br.homeshopping.com.br, pg 86

Memorie Domenicane (Italy) *Tel:* (0573) 22056; (0573) 28158 *Fax:* (0573) 975808 *E-mail:* centroriviste@tiscalinet.it, pg 86

Memory/Cage Editions (Switzerland) *Tel:* (01) 281 35 65 *Fax:* (01) 281 35 66 *E-mail:* mail@memorycage.com *Web Site:* www.memorycage.com, pg 628

Mendelova zemedelska a lesnicka univerzita v Brne (Czech Republic) *Tel:* (05) 4513 1111; (05) 4513 2678 *Fax:* (05) 4513 5008 *Web Site:* www.mendelu.cz, pg 125

Sonny A Mendoza (Philippines) *Tel:* (02) 8691111, pg 519

Libreria Menendez (Panama) *Tel:* 2258996, pg 1334

Biblioteca y Casa - Museo de Menendez Pelayo (Spain) *Tel:* (042) 23 45 34 *E-mail:* xjagenjo@sarenet.es *Web Site:* www.turcantabria.com, pg 1545

Edition Axel Menges (Germany) *Tel:* (0711) 574759 *Fax:* (0711) 574784, pg 259

Editions Menges (France) *Tel:* (01) 44 55 37 50 *Fax:* (01) 40 20 99 74 *E-mail:* info@editions-menges.com *Web Site:* www.editions-menges.com, pg 175

Casa Editrice Menna di Sinisgalli Menna Giuseppina (Italy) *Tel:* (0825) 24080 *Fax:* (0825) 24080, pg 398

Menora Publishing House (The Former Yugoslav Republic of Macedonia) *Tel:* (02) 458447 *Fax:* (02) 418872 *E-mail:* menora@lotus.mpt.com.mk, pg 452

Menoshire Ltd (United Kingdom) *Tel:* (020) 85667344 *Fax:* (020) 89912439 *E-mail:* sales@menoshire.com *Web Site:* www.menoshire.com, pg 1352

Ediciones Mensajero (Spain) *Tel:* (094) 4 470 358 *Fax:* (094) 4 472 630 *E-mail:* mensajero@mensajero.com *Web Site:* www.mensajero.com, pg 591

Menschenkinder Verlag und Vertrieb GmbH (Germany) *Tel:* (0251) 932520 *Fax:* (0251) 9325290 *E-mail:* info@menschenkinder.de *Web Site:* www.menschenkinder.de, pg 259

mentis Verlag GmbH (Germany) *Tel:* (05251) 687902; (05251) 687904 *Fax:* (05251) 687905 *E-mail:* info@mentis.de *Web Site:* www.mentis.de, pg 259

Mentor Kiado (Romania) *Tel:* (0265) 256975 *Fax:* (0265) 256975, pg 540

Mentor Publications (Ireland) *Tel:* (01) 2952112 *Fax:* (01) 2952114 *E-mail:* admin@mentorbooks.ie *Web Site:* www.mentorbooks.ie, pg 362

Mentor-Verlag Dr Ramdohr KG (Germany) *Tel:* (089) 360960 *Fax:* (089) 36096-222 (general); (089) 36096-258 (orders) *E-mail:* mentor@langenscheidt.de, pg 259

Merani Publishing House (Georgia) *Tel:* (032) 996492; (032) 935396; (032) 935554; (032) 935514 *Fax:* (032) 932996, pg 190

Meravigli, Libreria Milanese (Italy) *Tel:* (02) 2157240 *Fax:* (02) 2157833, pg 398

Merbod Verlag (Austria) *Tel:* (02622) 81724 *Fax:* (02622) 817244, pg 54

Editora Mercado Aberto Ltda (Brazil) *Tel:* (051) 3337-4833 *Fax:* (051) 3337-4905 *E-mail:* mercado@mercadoaberto.com.br *Web Site:* www.mercadoaberto.com.br, pg 86

Mercametrica Ediciones SA Edicion de Libros (Mexico) *Tel:* (055) 56-61-62-93; (055) 56-61-92-86 *Fax:* (055) 56-62-33-08 *E-mail:* mercametrica@mercametrica.com *Web Site:* www.mercametrica.com.mx, pg 468

Mercantila Publishers A/S (Denmark) *Tel:* 35436222 *Fax:* 35435151 *E-mail:* info@mercantila.dk *Web Site:* www.mercantila.dk, pg 133

Mercat Press (United Kingdom) *Tel:* (0131) 225 5324 *Fax:* (0131) 226 6632 *E-mail:* enquiries@mercatpress.com *Web Site:* www.mercatpress.com, pg 726

Mercatorfonds NV (Belgium) *Tel:* (03) 2027260 *Fax:* (03) 2311319 *E-mail:* artbooks@mercatorfonds.be *Web Site:* www.mercatorfonds.be, pg 71

Merchandising Muenchen KG (Germany) *Tel:* (089) 95078600 *Fax:* (089) 95078700 *E-mail:* info.line@merchandising-muenchen.de *Web Site:* www.merchandisingmedia.com, pg 1132

Merchiston Publishing (United Kingdom) *Tel:* (0131) 455 6150 *Fax:* (0131) 455 6193, pg 727

Editions Franck Mercier (France) *Tel:* (04) 50 57 16 50 *Fax:* (01) 450579301 *E-mail:* franck@mercier.com.ch, pg 175

Mercier Press Ltd (Ireland) *Tel:* (021) 489 9858 *Fax:* (021) 489 9887 *E-mail:* books@mercierpress.ie *Web Site:* www.mercierpress.ie, pg 362

Mercure de France SA (France) *Tel:* (01) 55 42 61 90 *Fax:* (01) 43 54 49 91 *E-mail:* mercure@mercure.fr *Web Site:* www.gallimard.fr, pg 175

Mercury Press Pvt Ltd (Zimbabwe) *Tel:* (04) 75-1515; (04) 75-1084 *Fax:* (04) 73-7670, pg 784

Editora Mercuryo Ltda (Brazil) *Tel:* (011) 5531-8222 *Fax:* (011) 5093-3265 *E-mail:* diretoraeditorial@mercuryo.com.br *Web Site:* www.mercuryo.com.br, pg 86

Meresborough Books Ltd (United Kingdom) *Tel:* (01634) 371591 *Fax:* (01634) 262114 *E-mail:* shop@rainhambookshop.co.uk *Web Site:* www.rainhambookshop.co.uk, pg 727, 1352

Mergus Verlag GmbH Hans A Baensch (Germany) *Tel:* (05422) 3636 *Fax:* (05422) 1404 *E-mail:* info@mergus.de *Web Site:* www.mergus.com, pg 259

Meriberica/Liber (Portugal) *Tel:* (021) 8583849 *Fax:* (021) 8581536 *E-mail:* geral@meriberica.pt; bd@meriberica.pt; encomendar@meriberica.pt (orders) *Web Site:* www.meriberica.pt, pg 533

Meridian Books (United Kingdom) *Tel:* (016) 3554 3816 *Fax:* (016) 3555 1004 *E-mail:* jennie@countrysidebooks.co.uk, pg 727

Editura Meridiane (Romania) *Tel:* (01) 222-33-93 *Fax:* (01) 222-30-37, pg 540

Merlin Library Ltd (Malta) *Tel:* 221205; 23 44 38 *Fax:* 221135 *E-mail:* mail@merlinlibrary.com *Web Site:* www.merlinlibrary.com, pg 460

Merlin Library Ltd (Malta) *Tel:* 21 234438; 21 221202 *Fax:* 21 221135 *E-mail:* mail@merlinlibrary.com *Web Site:* www.merlinlibrary.com, pg 1327

The Merlin Press Ltd (United Kingdom) *Tel:* (020) 7836 3020 *Fax:* (020) 7497 0309 *E-mail:* info@merlinpress.co.uk *Web Site:* www.merlinpress.co.uk, pg 727

Merlin Verlag Andreas Meyer Verlags GmbH und Co KG (Germany) *Tel:* (04137) 7207 *Fax:* (04137) 7948 *E-mail:* info@merlin-verlag.de *Web Site:* www.merlin-verlag.de, pg 259

Merrell Publishers Ltd (United Kingdom) *Tel:* (020) 7403 2047 *Fax:* (020) 7407 1333 *E-mail:* mail@merrellpublishers.com; sales@merrellpublishers.com *Web Site:* www.merrellpublishers.com, pg 727

Merrion Press (United Kingdom) *Tel:* (020) 7735 7791 *Fax:* (020) 77357 059, pg 727

Merrow Publishing Co Ltd (United Kingdom) *Tel:* (01325) 351661 *Fax:* (01325) 351661, pg 727

Verlag Merseburger Berlin GmbH (Germany) *Tel:* (0561) 789809-0 *Fax:* (0561) 789809-16 *E-mail:* info@merseburger.de; order@merseburger.de *Web Site:* www.merseburger.de, pg 259

Dr Ray-Gude Mertin Literarische Agentur (Germany) *Tel:* (06172) 29842 *Fax:* (06172) 29771 *E-mail:* mertin@em.uni-frankfurt.de, pg 1132

Merve Verlag (Germany) *Tel:* (030) 784 8433 *Fax:* (030) 788 1074 *E-mail:* merve@merve.de *Web Site:* www.merve.de, pg 259

Merz & Solitude - Akademie Schloss Solitude (Germany) *Tel:* (0711) 99 619-471 *Fax:* (0711) 99 619-50 *E-mail:* mr@akademie-solitude.de *Web Site:* www.akademie-solitude.de, pg 259

Messaggero di San Antonio (Italy) *Tel:* (049) 8225000 *Fax:* (049) 8225688 *E-mail:* info@mess-s-antonio.it *Web Site:* www.mess-s-antonio.it, pg 398

Editions H Messeiller SA (Switzerland) *Tel:* (032) 7251296 *Fax:* (032) 7241937, pg 628

Messenger Publications (Ireland) *Tel:* (01) 6767 491; (01) 6767 492 *Fax:* (01) 661 16 06 *E-mail:* sales@messenger.ie *Web Site:* www.messenger.ie, pg 362

Mestska knihovna v Praze (Czech Republic) *Tel:* (02) 22113111 *Fax:* (02) 2328230 *E-mail:* informace@mlp.cz *Web Site:* www.mlp.cz, pg 1501

Editions A M Metailie (France) *Tel:* (01) 55 42 83 00 *Fax:* (01) 55 42 83 04 *E-mail:* presse@metailie.info *Web Site:* www.metailie.info, pg 175

Metallurgical Industry Press (MIP) (China) *Tel:* (010) 64013877; (010) 64015599 *Fax:* (010) 64013877, pg 106

Izdatelstvo Metallurgiya (Russian Federation) *Tel:* (095) 2025532 *Fax:* (095) 2025752, pg 546

The Methodist Publishing House (South Africa) *Tel:* (021) 4483640 *Fax:* (021) 4483716, pg 566

Methodist Publishing House (United Kingdom) *Tel:* (01733) 325002 *Fax:* (01733) 384180 *E-mail:* sales@mph.org.uk *Web Site:* www.mph.org.uk, pg 727

Methuen (United Kingdom) *Tel:* (020) 7798 1600 *Fax:* (020) 7828 2098; (020) 7233 9827 *Web Site:* www.methuen.co.uk, pg 727

Metis Yayinlari (Turkey) *Tel:* (0212) 245 45 19; (0212) 2454696 *Fax:* (0212) 2454519 *E-mail:* metis@turk.net *Web Site:* www.metisbooks.com, pg 650

Metrica Fachverlag u Versandbuchhandlung Ing Bartak (Austria) *Tel:* (01) 769 51 60 *Fax:* (01) 769 51 60, pg 54

Metro Books (United Kingdom) *Tel:* (020) 7381 0666 *Fax:* (020) 7381 6868 *E-mail:* words@blake.co.uk *Web Site:* www.blake.co.uk, pg 727

Metropolis- Verlag fur Okonomie, Gesellschaft und Politik GmbH (Germany) *Tel:* (06421) 67377 *Fax:* (06471) 681918 *E-mail:* info@metropolis-verlag.de *Web Site:* www.metropolis-verlag.de, pg 259

Metropolitan Verlag (Germany) *Tel:* (0941) 56840 *Fax:* (0941) 5684111 *E-mail:* walhalla@walhalla.de *Web Site:* www.metropolitan.de, pg 259

Mets & Schilt Uitgevers en Distributeurs (Netherlands) *Tel:* (020) 6256087 *Fax:* (020) 6270242 *E-mail:* info@metsenschilt.com *Web Site:* www.metsenschilt.com, pg 486

Karl-Heinz Metz (Germany) *Tel:* (07225) 74098 *Fax:* (07225) 74098 *E-mail:* metzverlag@aol.com *Web Site:* www.metz-verlag.de, pg 259

J B Metzlersche Verlagsbuchhandlung (Germany) *Tel:* (0711) 2194-0 *Fax:* (0711) 2194-249 *E-mail:* info@metzelerverlag.de *Web Site:* www.metzlerverlag.de, pg 260

J M Meulenhoff bv (Netherlands) *Tel:* (020) 55 33 500 *Fax:* (020) 62 58 511 *E-mail:* info@meulenhoff.nl *Web Site:* www.meulenhoff.nl, pg 486

Preubmpassling Verlag Gisela Meussling (Germany) *Tel:* (0228) 466347 *Fax:* (0228) 466347, pg 260

Mexican Academic Clearing House (MACH) (Mexico) *Tel:* (05) 674 0779; (05) 674 0567 *Fax:* (05) 673 6209 *E-mail:* hpadilla@spin.com.mx, pg 1327

Editores Mexicanos Unidos SA (Mexico) *Tel:* (05) 5218870 al 74 *Fax:* (05) 5218516 *E-mail:* editmusa@mail.internet.com.mx *Web Site:* www.editmusa.com.mx, pg 468

Meyer & Meyer Verlag (Germany) *Tel:* (0241) 95810-0 *Fax:* (0241) 95810-10 *E-mail:* verlag@m-m-sports.com *Web Site:* www.m-m-sports.com, pg 260

Peter Meyer Verlag (pmv) (Germany) *Tel:* (069) 49 44 49 *Fax:* (069) 44 51 35 *E-mail:* info@PeterMeyerVerlag.de *Web Site:* www.petermeyerverlag.de, pg 260

Ursala Meyer und Dr Manfred Duker Ein-Fach-Verlag (Germany) *Tel:* (0241) 405501 *Fax:* (0241) 400 96 67 *E-mail:* einfachverlag@gmx.de, pg 260

Izdatelstvo Mezdunarodnye Otnoshenia (Russian Federation) *Tel:* (095) 2076793 *Fax:* (095) 2002204, pg 546

Mezhdunarodnaya Kniga (Russian Federation) *Tel:* (095) 238-46-00 *Fax:* (095) 230-21-17 *E-mail:* info@mkniga.msk.su *Web Site:* www.mkniga.msk.su, pg 1338

Mezogazda Kiado (Hungary) *Tel:* (01) 4071018 *Fax:* (01) 4071787 *E-mail:* mezogazda@matavnet.hu, pg 323

Mezopotamya Publishing & Distribution (Sweden) *Tel:* (08) 774 73 54 *Fax:* (08) 7110836, pg 613

MFK Management Consultants Services (Zambia) *Tel:* (01) 223530; (01) 252934, pg 781

MG Editores Associados Ltda (Brazil) *Tel:* (011) 8890861 *Fax:* (011) 8858646, pg 86

MGM (United Kingdom) *Tel:* (020) 7262 8386, pg 727

Mi-An Knigoizdatelstvo (The Former Yugoslav Republic of Macedonia) *Tel:* (091) 252565 *E-mail:* mtimes@soros.org.mk, pg 452

Micelle Press (United Kingdom) *Tel:* (01305) 781574 *Fax:* (01305) 781574 *E-mail:* tony@wdi.co.uk *Web Site:* www.wdi.co.uk/micelle, pg 727

Editions Albin Michel (France) *Tel:* (01) 42 79 10 00 *Fax:* (01) 43 27 21 58 *Web Site:* www.albin-michel.fr, pg 175

Michelin Editions des Voyages (Belgium) *Tel:* (02) 274 45 03 *Fax:* (02) 274 43 62 *E-mail:* kontakt@viamichelin.com *Web Site:* www.viamichelin.com, pg 71

Michelin Editions des Voyages (France) *Tel:* (01) 45 66 12 34 *Fax:* (01) 45 66 11 63, pg 175

Michelin Tyre PLC, Tourism Dept, Maps & Guides Division (United Kingdom) *Tel:* (01923) 415000 *Fax:* (01923) 415250 *Web Site:* www.michelin.co.uk, pg 728

Michlol Ltd (Israel) *Tel:* (04) 8322970 *Fax:* (04) 8223854 *E-mail:* ws2@isdn.net.il, pg 1320

Microform Academic Publishers (United Kingdom) *Tel:* (01924) 825700 *Fax:* (01924) 871005 *E-mail:* info@microform.co.uk *Web Site:* www.microform.co.uk, pg 728

Microsoft Press France (France) *Tel:* (0825) 827 829 *Fax:* (01) 64 46 06 60 *E-mail:* msfrance@microsoft.com *Web Site:* www.microsoft.com/france, pg 175

Midas Printing Ltd (Hong Kong) *Tel:* 2407 6888 *Fax:* 2408 0611 *E-mail:* info@midasprinting.com *Web Site:* www.midasprinting.com, pg 1157, 1178

Midas Printing Ltd (Hong Kong) *Tel:* 24084024 *Fax:* 24065897 *Web Site:* www.midasprinting.com, pg 1219

Gertraud Middelhauve Verlag GmbH & Co KG (Germany) *Tel:* (089) 41 94 02-0 *Fax:* (089) 47 01 08-1, pg 260

Literaturbetreuung Klaus Middendorf (LKM) (Germany) *Tel:* (08232) 78463 *Fax:* (08232) 78468 *E-mail:* lkmcorp@t-online.de *Web Site:* www.lkmcorp.com, pg 1132

Middle East Book Centre (Egypt (Arab Republic of Egypt)) *Tel:* (02) 910980, pg 138

Middle East Librarians Association (United States) *Tel:* (206) 543-8407 *Fax:* (206) 685-8049 *Web Site:* www.depts.washington.edu/wsx9/melahp.html, pg 1294

Middle East Technical University Library (Turkey) *Tel:* (0312) 210 27 80; (0312) 210 27 82 *Fax:* (0312) 210 11 19 *E-mail:* lib-hot-line@metu.edu.tr *Web Site:* www.metu.edu.tr, pg 1551

Middleton Press (United Kingdom) *Tel:* (01730) 813169 *Fax:* (01730) 812601 *Web Site:* www.middletonpress.co.uk, pg 728

Midena Verlag (Germany) *Tel:* (089) 9271-0 *Fax:* (089) 9271-168 *Web Site:* www.droemer-knaur.de, pg 260

Midi Teki Publishers (Kenya) *Tel:* (02) 506993, pg 435

Midland Publishing (United Kingdom) *Tel:* (01455) 233747 *Fax:* (01455) 233737 *E-mail:* midlandbooks@compuserve.com *Web Site:* www.ianallan.com/publishing, pg 728

Midrashiat Naom, Pardess Hanna (Israel) *Tel:* (09) 5172637 *Fax:* (09) 5100594, pg 370

Migema Ediciones Ltda (Colombia) *Tel:* (01) 2873158; (01) 2858538 *Fax:* (01) 2858538; (01) 2858224 *E-mail:* emigema@cc-net.net, pg 112

Miland Publishers (Netherlands) *Tel:* (0172) 57 1461 *Fax:* (0172) 57 2231 *E-mail:* degraaf.books@wxs.nl *Web Site:* www.antiqbook.nl/degraafbooks, pg 486

Milano Libri (Italy) *Tel:* (02) 50951 *Fax:* (02) 5065361, pg 398

Nicola Milano Editore (Italy) *Tel:* (051) 239060 *Fax:* (051) 239286 *E-mail:* scuola@nicolamilano.com *Web Site:* www.nicolamilano.com, pg 398

Milanostampa/New Interlitho USA Inc (United States) *Tel:* 212-964-2430 *Fax:* 212-964-2497 *Web Site:* www.milanostampa.com, pg 1168, 1188, 1231, 1241

Milanostampa SpA (Italy) *Tel:* (0173) 746111 *Fax:* (0173) 746248; (0173) 746249 *E-mail:* info@milanostampa.com; sales@milanostampa.com *Web Site:* www.milanostampa.com, pg 1180

Milanostampa SpA (Italy) *Tel:* (0173) 746111 *Fax:* (0173) 746248; (0173) 746249 *E-mail:* milanostampa@areacom.it *Web Site:* www.milanostampa.com, pg 1220

Milanostampa SpA (Italy) *Tel:* (0173) 746111 *Fax:* (0173) 746248; (0173) 746249 *E-mail:* info@milanostampa.com *Web Site:* www.milanostampa.com, pg 1237

Milella di Lecce Spazio Vivo srl (Italy) *Tel:* (0832) 241131 *Fax:* (0832) 303057 *E-mail:* leccespaziovivo@tiscalinet.it, pg 398

Milena Verlag (Austria) *Tel:* (01) 402 59 90 *Fax:* (01) 408 88 58 *E-mail:* frauenverlag@milena-verlag.at, pg 54

Editorial Milenio Arts Grafiques Bobala, SL (Spain) *Tel:* (0973) 236 611 *Fax:* (0973) 240 795 *E-mail:* editorial.milenio@cambrescat.es *Web Site:* www.edmilenio.com, pg 591

Miles Kelly Publishing Ltd (United Kingdom) *Tel:* (01371) 811309 *Fax:* (01371) 811393 *E-mail:* info@mileskelly.net *Web Site:* www.mileskelly.net, pg 728

Editura Militara (Romania) *Tel:* (01) 3112191; (01) 6133601 *Fax:* (01) 3237822, pg 541

Militzke Verlag (Germany) *Tel:* (0341) 42643-0 *Fax:* (0341) 42643-99 *E-mail:* info@militzke.de *Web Site:* www.militzke.de, pg 260

Millbank Books Ltd (United Kingdom) *Tel:* (01279) 655233 *Fax:* (01279) 655244 *E-mail:* caw@millbank.demon.co.uk, pg 1352

Mille et Une Nuits (France) *Tel:* (01) 45 49 82 00 *Fax:* (01) 45 49 79 96 *E-mail:* info1001nuits@editions-fayard.fr *Web Site:* www.1001nuits.com, pg 175

Cathy Miller Foreign Rights Agency (United Kingdom) *Tel:* (020) 7386 5473 *Fax:* (020) 7385 1774, pg 1142

Harvey Miller Publishers (United Kingdom) *Tel:* (01235) 465500 *Fax:* (01235) 465555 *E-mail:* harvey.miller@brepols.net, pg 728

J Garnet Miller (United Kingdom) *Tel:* (01684) 540154 *Fax:* (01684) 540154, pg 728

Miller's Publications (United Kingdom) *Tel:* (01933) 273411 *Fax:* (01933) 229330, pg 728

Milliii Kuetuephane (Turkey) *Tel:* (0312) 212 62 00 *Fax:* (0312) 223 04 51 *Web Site:* www.mkutup.gov.tr, pg 1551

Mills Group (New Zealand) *Tel:* (04) 5696744 *Fax:* (04) 5697464 *Web Site:* www.millsonline.com, pg 498

Millwood Press Ltd (New Zealand) *Tel:* (04) 4735176 *Fax:* (04) 4735177, pg 498

Milton Margai Teachers' College Library (Sierra Leone) *Tel:* (022) 024305, pg 1542

Mimosa Publications Pty Ltd (Australia) *Tel:* (03) 9819 0511 *Fax:* (03) 9819 0524 *E-mail:* info@mimosa.pub.com.au, pg 32

Min-eumsa Publishing Co Ltd (Republic of Korea) *Tel:* (02) 515-2000; (02) 515-2005; (02) 515-9108 *Fax:* (02) 515-2007; (02) 3444-5185 *Web Site:* www.minumsa.com, pg 441

Min Jung Seo Rim Publishing Co (Republic of Korea) *Tel:* (02) 7036541; (02) 7036547 *Fax:* (02) 7036549 *E-mail:* editmin@minjungdic.co.kr *Web Site:* www.minjungdic.co.kr, pg 441

Librairie Minard (France) *Tel:* (02) 31844706 *Fax:* (02) 31844809, pg 176

MIND Publications (United Kingdom) *Tel:* (020) 8519 2122 *Fax:* (020) 8522 1725; (020) 8534 6399 (orders) *E-mail:* contact@mind.org.uk; publications@mind.org.uk (mail order) *Web Site:* www.mind.org.uk, pg 728

Mindanao State University - Mamitua Saber Research Center (Philippines) *Tel:* (063) 2214050; (063) 3516151; (063) 3516152; (063) 3516172; (063) 3516174; (063) 3516153; (063) 3516154; (063) 3516155; (063) 3516156 *Fax:* (063) 221405, pg 519

Libreria Editrice Minerva (Italy) *Tel:* (075) 812381 *Fax:* (075) 816564, pg 1321

Minerva (Serbia and Montenegro) *Tel:* (024) 28834; (024) 25712 *Fax:* (024) 23-208, pg 552

Minerva Associates (Publications) Pvt Ltd (India) *Tel:* (033) 2466 3783, pg 341

Editora Minerva Central (Mozambique) *Tel:* (01) 420198 *Fax:* (01) 423677 *E-mail:* minerva@sortmoz.com, pg 475

Editions Minerva (France) *Tel:* (01) 53 63 31 60 *Fax:* (01) 45 49 17 60 *Web Site:* www.lamartiniere.fr, pg 176

Editorial Minerva (Portugal) *Tel:* (021) 3220540 *Fax:* (021) 3220549, pg 533

Editura Minerva (Romania) *Tel:* (01) 3308808; (01) 3308840 *Fax:* (01) 3308808; (01) 3308840 *E-mail:* desfacere@edituraaramis.ro, pg 541

Minerva Italica SpA (Italy) *Tel:* (02) 21213643 *Fax:* (02) 21213698 *E-mail:* info@minervaitalica.it *Web Site:* www.minervaitalica.it, pg 398

Minerva KG Internationaler Fachliteratur fur Medizin und Naturwissenschaften Neue Medien (Germany) *Tel:* (06151) 9880 *Fax:* (06151) 98839 *E-mail:* minerva@minerva.de *Web Site:* www.minerva.de, pg 1311

Minerva Medica (Italy) *Tel:* (011) 67-82-82 *Fax:* (011) 67-45-02 *E-mail:* minervamedica@minervamedica.it *Web Site:* www.minervamedica.it, pg 1159, 1221

Minerva Publications (Malaysia) *Tel:* (06) 734439 *Fax:* (06) 734439, pg 457

Minerva Shobo Co Ltd (Japan) *Tel:* (075) 581-5191 *Fax:* (075) 581-0589 *E-mail:* info@minervashobo.co.jp *Web Site:* www.minervashoboco.jp, pg 422

Minerva Edition Wissen Medizinischer und Naturwissenschaftlicher Verlag und Vertieb (Germany) *Tel:* (0700) 96 389 352 *Fax:* (0700) 96 389 353 *E-mail:* info@woetzel.de *Web Site:* www.woetzel.de, pg 260

Minervaverlag Bern (Switzerland) *Tel:* (031) 3726223 *Fax:* (031) 3726223, pg 628

Mines & Geological Department Library (Kenya) *Tel:* (02) 229261; (02) 541040 *Fax:* (02) 216951, pg 1523

Ming Pao Publications Ltd (Hong Kong) *Tel:* 2595 3084 *Fax:* 2898 2646 *E-mail:* geocomm@mingpao.com *Web Site:* security.mingpao.com/books, pg 318

Uitgeverij Mingus (Netherlands) *Tel:* (0348) 42 55 07 *Fax:* (0348) 42 55 07 *E-mail:* mingus-vk@planet.nl, pg 486

Ministere de la Culture (Luxembourg) *Tel:* 478-1 *Fax:* 40-24-27, pg 451

Ministere des Affaires Etrangeres Division de L'Ecrit et des Mediatheques (France) *Tel:* (01) 43 17 53 53 *Fax:* (01) 43 17 88 83 *Web Site:* www.france.diplomatie.gouv.fr, pg 1268

Ministerie van Verkeer en Waterstaat (Netherlands) *Tel:* (070) 3517086 *Fax:* (070) 3516430 *E-mail:* venwinfo@postbus51.nl *Web Site:* www.minvenw.nl, pg 486

Ministerio da Marinha Diretoria de Hidrografia Navegacao (Brazil) *Tel:* (021) 719-2626 (ext 147) *Fax:* (021) 719-4989 *E-mail:* 01@dhm.mar.mil.sr, pg 86

Ministerio de Economia y Hacienda Secretario General Tecnica Centro de Publicaciones (Spain) *Tel:* (091) 5063740 (ext 51307) *Fax:* (091) 4682300, pg 591

Ministerio de Educacion Biblioteca Central (Venezuela) *Tel:* (02) 5628970 (ext 8149); (02) 5621767; (02) 5640025 *Fax:* (02) 5641224, pg 780

Ministerio de Educacion y Culture Centro de Publicaciones (Spain) *Tel:* (091) 453 98 00 *Fax:* (091) 453 98 00 *Web Site:* www.mec.es/mec, pg 591

Editorial del Ministerio de Educacion (Guatemala), pg 313

Ministerio de Justicia e Interior, Centro de Publicaciones (Spain) *Tel:* (091) 390 44 29; (091) 390 20 83; (091) 390 20 97 *Fax:* (091) 390 20 92 *Web Site:* www.mju.es, pg 591

Ministerio de Trabajo y Asuntos Sociales (Spain) *Tel:* (091) 3634100 *Fax:* (091) 3634327 *E-mail:* sugerir@sta.mtas.es *Web Site:* www.mtas.es/insht/index.htm, pg 591

Ministerstvo Kul 'tury RF (Russian Federation) *Tel:* 220 4560 *E-mail:* rnb@q1as.apc.org, pg 546

Ministerstvo Kultury C R, Oddeleni Tisku Oddeleni Knizi Kultury (Czech Republic) *Tel:* (02) 57 085 111 *Fax:* (02) 24 318 155 *E-mail:* minkult@mkcr.cz *Web Site:* www.mkcr.cz, pg 1265

Ministry of Agriculture & Livestock Development Marketing Library (Kenya) *Tel:* (02) 718-870 *Fax:* (02) 725-774, pg 1523

Ministry of Agriculture Library (Malaysia) *Tel:* (03) 26954215 (ext 4216, 4217or 4298) *Fax:* (03) 26932220 *E-mail:* dahlia@agri.moa.my; lht@agri.moa.my; fuziah@agri.moa.my *Web Site:* agrolink.moa.my/library, pg 1526

Ministry of Cultural Affairs (Sri Lanka) *Tel:* (01) 437328 *E-mail:* mcasec@sltnet.lk *Web Site:* www.mca.gov.lk, pg 607

Ministry of Defence Publishing House (Israel) *Tel:* (03) 6917940 *Fax:* (03) 6375509, pg 370

Ministry of Education Library (Afghanistan), pg 1489

Ministry of Education Library (Egypt (Arab Republic of Egypt)) *Tel:* (02) 516 9744 *Fax:* (02) 516 9560 *E-mail:* telecom@gega.net *Web Site:* www.emoe.org, pg 1503

Ministry of Education (Sri Lanka) *Tel:* 565141-5150, pg 607

Ministry of Education, Department of Educational Publications (Afghanistan) *Tel:* (0873) 32076 *Fax:* (0873) 15051, pg 1

Ministry of Environment & Public Health, Library Division (Malaysia) *Tel:* (082) 319614; (082) 319613 *Fax:* (082) 311216 *E-mail:* info@moeswk.gov.my *Web Site:* www.moeswk.gov.my, pg 1526

Ministry of Information (Kuwait) *Tel:* 245-1566 *Fax:* 245-9530 *E-mail:* admin@media.gov.kw *Web Site:* www.moinfo.gov.kw, pg 444

Ministry of Information & Broadcasting (India) *Tel:* (011) 3387983; (011) 3386879; (011) 3387069; (011) 3386452 *Fax:* (011) 3387341 *E-mail:* indiapub@nda.vsnl.net.in; dpd@sb.nic.in *Web Site:* mib.nic.in, pg 341

Ministry of Justice Library (Egypt (Arab Republic of Egypt)) *Tel:* (02) 20806 *Fax:* (02) 795 8103 *E-mail:* mojeb@idsc1.gov.eg, pg 1503

Minjisa Publishing Co (Republic of Korea) *Tel:* (02) 9806382 *Fax:* (02) 9861531 *E-mail:* minjisa@nownuri.net *Web Site:* www.minjisa.co.kr, pg 441

Editions Minkoff (Switzerland) *Tel:* (022) 310 46 60 *Fax:* (022) 310 28 57 *E-mail:* minkoff-editions.com *Web Site:* www.minkoff-editions.com, pg 628

Minoas SA (Greece) *Tel:* (0210) 2711222 *Fax:* (0210) 2711056 *E-mail:* info@minoas.gr *Web Site:* www.minoas.gr, pg 310

Il Minotauro (Italy) *Tel:* (06) 5591864 *Fax:* (06) 5592337 *E-mail:* ilminotauro@tin.it *Web Site:* www.ilminotauroeditore.it, pg 398

Ediciones Minotauro (Spain) *Tel:* (093) 492 8869 *Fax:* (093) 496 7041 *E-mail:* edicionesminotauro@arrakis.es *Web Site:* www.edicionesminotauro.com, pg 591

Ediciones Minotauro SA (Argentina) *Tel:* (011) 4382-4043; (011) 4382-4045 *Fax:* (011) 4383-3793 *E-mail:* sansaldi@eplaneta.com.ar *Web Site:* www.edicionesminotauro.com, pg 7

Editorial Minutiae Mexicana SA (Mexico) *Tel:* (052) 55-5535-9488 *Fax:* (052) 722-232-0662, pg 468

Izdatelstvo Mir (Russian Federation) *Tel:* (095) 286-17-83 *Fax:* (095) 288-95-22 *Web Site:* www.mir-pubs.dol.ru, pg 546

Mir Knigi Ltd (Russian Federation) *Tel:* (095) 2083879 *Fax:* (095) 7428579, pg 546

Editores Mira, SA (Spain) *Tel:* (0976) 460505 *Fax:* (0976) 460446 *E-mail:* miraeditores@ctv.es *Web Site:* www.miraeditores.com, pg 591

Mirai-Sha (Japan) *Tel:* (03) 3814-5521 *Fax:* (03) 3814-8600, pg 422

Presses Universitaires du Mirail (France) *Tel:* (0561) 503808 *Fax:* (0561) 503800 *E-mail:* pum@univ-tlse2.fr *Web Site:* www.crlmidipyrenees.asso.fr/editeurs/pum.htm, pg 176

Mirananda Publishers BV (Netherlands) *Tel:* (070) 358 59 43 *Fax:* (070) 358 68 43 *E-mail:* info@mirananda.nl *Web Site:* www.mirananda.nl, pg 486

G Miranda & Sons (Philippines) *Tel:* (02) 7121620 *Fax:* (02) 7120502, pg 1335

Miranda-Verlag Stefan Ehlert (Germany) *Tel:* (0421) 7943226 *Fax:* (0421) 7943226 *E-mail:* miranda-verlag@t-online.de *Web Site:* www.miranda-verlag.de, pg 260

Mirinae (Republic of Korea) *Tel:* (02) 2279-2669 *Fax:* (02) 2279-2665 *E-mail:* mrn@lycos.co.kr, pg 441

Mirkam Publishers (Israel) *Tel:* (06) 6900967 *Fax:* (06) 6900967, pg 370

Mirran (Netherlands) *Tel:* (013) 5169534 *Fax:* (013) 4684764 *E-mail:* info@mirran.com *Web Site:* www.mirran.com, pg 486

Mirza Book Agency (Pakistan) *Tel:* (042) 7353601 *Fax:* (042) 5763714 *E-mail:* merchant@brain.net.pk, pg 1135

Mirzaye Shirazi Library (Islamic Republic of Iran) *Tel:* (0711) 6260011 *Fax:* (0711) 6287301 *Web Site:* www.shirazu.ac.ir, pg 1517

MiS Sport IGP (Serbia and Montenegro) *Tel:* (011) 3220226; (011) 3225361, pg 552

Misgav Yerushalayim (Israel) *Tel:* (02) 5883962 *Fax:* (02) 5815460 *E-mail:* misgav@h2.hum.huji.ac.il *Web Site:* www.hum.huji.ac.il/misgav, pg 370

Instituto Misionerao Hijas De San Pablo (Colombia) *Tel:* (01) 2435885; (01) 6 71 89 74 *Fax:* (01) 670 6378, pg 112

Miskal Publishing Ltd (Israel) *Tel:* (03) 9246980 *Fax:* (03) 9246985, pg 370

Misr Bookshop (Egypt (Arab Republic of Egypt)) *Tel:* (02) 908920, pg 1309

Galeria de Arte Misrachi SA (Mexico) *Tel:* (05) 5334551 *Fax:* (05) 55257187 *E-mail:* misrachi@acnet.net, pg 469

Missio eV (Germany) *Tel:* (0241) 75 07-00 *Fax:* (0241) 75 07-336 *E-mail:* info@missio-aachen.de *Web Site:* www.missio-aachen.de, pg 260

Mission Publications of Australia (Australia) *Tel:* (02) 4759 1003 *Fax:* (02) 4759 1101 *E-mail:* missionpublaust@bigpond.com, pg 32

Editrice Missionaria Italiana (EMI) (Italy) *Tel:* (051) 326027 *Fax:* (051) 327552 *E-mail:* sermis@emi.it *Web Site:* www.emi.it, pg 398

Missionshandlung (Germany) *Tel:* (05052) 69400 *Fax:* (05052) 3082 *E-mail:* m-druckerei@t-online.de, pg 261

Pietro Missorini & Co - Libreria Commissionaria (Italy) *Tel:* (0521) 993919 *Fax:* (0521) 993929 *E-mail:* info@missorini.it *Web Site:* www.rsadvnet.it/missorini/, pg 1133

Misuzu Shobo Ltd (Japan) *Tel:* (03) 3815-9181 *Fax:* (03) 3818-8497 *E-mail:* nakagawa@msz.co.jp *Web Site:* www.msz.co.jp, pg 422

MIT Press Ltd (United Kingdom) *Tel:* (020) 7306 0603 *Fax:* (020) 7306 0604 *E-mail:* info@hup-mitpress.co.uk *Web Site:* mitpress.mit.edu, pg 728

Mita Press, Mita Industrial Co Ltd (Japan) *Tel:* (03) 3817-7200 *Fax:* (03) 3817-7207, pg 422

Mita Toshokan Joho Gakkai (Japan) *Tel:* (03) 34533920, pg 1565

Mittal Publications (India) *Tel:* (011) 5163610; (011) 5648028; (011) 3250398 *Fax:* (011) 5648725 *E-mail:* mittalp@ndf.vsnl.net.in, pg 341

Mitteldeutscher Verlag GmbH (Germany) *Tel:* (0345) 23322-0 *Fax:* (0345) 23322-66 *E-mail:* mitteldeutscher.verlag@t-online.de *Web Site:* www.buecherkisten.de, pg 261

E S Mittler und Sohn GmbH (Germany) *Tel:* (040) 7 97 13-03 *Fax:* (040) 79713324, pg 261

Mizan (Indonesia) *Tel:* (022) 7200931 *E-mail:* info@mizan.com *Web Site:* www.mizan.com, pg 355

M Mizrahi Publishers (Israel) *Tel:* (03) 6870936 *Fax:* (03) 5475399, pg 370

MK Ediciones y Publicaciones (Spain) *Tel:* (091) 4316305 *Fax:* (091) 5754978, pg 591

Mlada fronta (Czech Republic) *Tel:* (02) 25 276 281 *Fax:* (02) 25 276 278 *Web Site:* www.mf.cz, pg 125

Mlade leta Spd sro (Slovakia) *Tel:* (07) 55 56 45 12; (07) 55 56 62 82 *Fax:* (07) 21 57 14 *Web Site:* www.mlade-leta.sk, pg 559

Mladezh IK (Bulgaria) *Tel:* (02) 882137 *Fax:* (02) 876135, pg 95

Mladinska Knjiga International (Slovenia) *Tel:* (01) 2413 284; (01) 2413 288 *Fax:* (01) 4252 294 *E-mail:* intsales@mkz-lj.si *Web Site:* www.emka.si, pg 561

Mladost d d Izdavacku graficku i informaticku djelatnost (Croatia) *Tel:* (01) 215-853; (01) 229-811 *Fax:* (01) 239-5336, pg 119

Thomas Mlakar Verlag (Austria) *Tel:* (03579) 2258 *Fax:* (03579) 2258 *E-mail:* mlakar-media@gmx.at, pg 54

MM-Verlagsgesellschaft mbH (Germany) *Tel:* (07158) 940 800 *Fax:* (07158) 940 802 *E-mail:* mm@ebb.de, pg 261

mnemes - Alfieri & Ranieri Publishing (Italy) *Tel:* (091) 588813 *Fax:* (091) 588813 *E-mail:* info@mnemes.com *Web Site:* www.mnemes.com, pg 398

Moby Dick Verlag (Germany) *Tel:* (0431) 640110 *Fax:* (0431) 6401112 *E-mail:* mobybook@aol.com, pg 261

Modan Publishers Ltd (Israel) *Tel:* (08) 9221821 *Fax:* (08) 9221299 *E-mail:* modan@modan.co.il *Web Site:* www.modan.co.il, pg 370

mode information Heinz Kramer GmbH (Germany) *Tel:* (02206) 60070 *Fax:* (02206) 600717 *E-mail:* info@modeinfo.com *Web Site:* www.modeinfo.com, pg 261

Modellsport Verlag GmbH (Germany) *Tel:* (07221) 95 21-0 *Fax:* (07221) 95 21-45 *E-mail:* modellsport@modellsport.de *Web Site:* www.modellsport.de, pg 261

The Modern Book Depot (India) *Tel:* (033) 2493102; (033) 2490933 *Fax:* (033) 2497455 *E-mail:* modcal@vsnl.com, pg 1316

Modern Electronic & Computing Publishing Co Ltd (Hong Kong) *Tel:* 2342 8299 *Fax:* 2341 4247 *E-mail:* info@computertoday.com.hk *Web Site:* www.computertoday.com.hk, pg 318

Modern Guides Company (Puerto Rico) *Tel:* (787) 723-9105 *Fax:* (787) 723-4380 *E-mail:* avc1941@attglobal.net, pg 537

Modern Press (China) *Tel:* (010) 4215031-383 *Fax:* (010) 4214540, pg 106

Moderna galerija Ljubljana/Museum of Modern Art (Slovenia) *Tel:* (01) 2416 800 *Fax:* (01) 2514 120 *E-mail:* info@mg-li.si *Web Site:* www.mg-lj.si, pg 561

Editora Moderna Ltda (Brazil) *Tel:* (011) 609-0130 *Fax:* (011) 608-3055 *E-mail:* moderna@moderna.com.br *Web Site:* www.moderna.com.br, pg 86

Moderne Buchkunst und Graphie Wolfgang Tiessen (Germany) *Tel:* (06102) 53335 *Fax:* (06102) 53335, pg 261

Editions Modernes Media (France) *Tel:* (01) 44 54 90 42 *Fax:* (01) 44 54 90 47 *E-mail:* ed.mod.media@wanadoo.fr, pg 176

modo verlag GmbH (Germany) *Tel:* (0761) 2022875 *Fax:* (0761) 2022876 *E-mail:* info@modoverlag.de *Web Site:* www.modoverlag.de, pg 261

Forlaget Modtryk AMBA (Denmark) *Tel:* 8731 7600 *Fax:* 8731 7601 *E-mail:* forlaget@modtryk.dk *Web Site:* www.modtryk.dk, pg 133

Modulo Editora e Desenvolvimento Educacional Ltda (Brazil) *Tel:* (041) 2530077 *Fax:* (041) 2530103 *E-mail:* moduloed@moduloeditora.com.br *Web Site:* www.moduloeditora.com.br, pg 87

Modulverlag (Austria) *Tel:* (01) 5129892 *Fax:* (01) 5129893, pg 54

Moeck Verlag und Musikinstrumentenwerk, Inhaber Dr Hermann Moeck (Germany) *Tel:* (05141) 88 53-0 *Fax:* (05141) 88 53-42 *E-mail:* editorial@moeck-music.de *Web Site:* www.moeck-music.de, pg 261

Karl Heinrich Moeseler Verlag (Germany) *Tel:* (05331) 95970 *Fax:* (05331) 9597-20, pg 261

MOHN Media (Germany) *Tel:* (05241) 80-4 04 10 *Fax:* (05241) 2 42 82 *E-mail:* mohnmedia@bertelsmann.de *Web Site:* www.mohnmedia.de, pg 1155

MOHN Media (Germany) *Tel:* (05241) 80 56 29 *Fax:* (05241) 1 66 92, pg 1176

MOHN Media (Germany) *Tel:* (05241) 80-4 04 10 *Fax:* (05241) 2 42 82 *E-mail:* mohnmedia@bertelsmann.de *Web Site:* www.mohnmedia.de, pg 1217, 1236

Mohr Siebeck (Germany) *Tel:* (07071) 923-0 *Fax:* (07071) 5 11 04 *E-mail:* info@mohr.de *Web Site:* www.mohr.de, pg 261

Mohr-ZA Verlagsauslieferungen Ges mbH (Austria) *Tel:* (01) 5121676; (01) 5125711; (01) 5126994 *Fax:* (01) 111859, pg 1300

MOHRBOOKS AG, Literary Agency (Switzerland) *Tel:* (043) 2448626 *Fax:* (043) 2448627 *E-mail:* info@mohrbooks.com *Web Site:* www.mohrbooks.de, pg 1137

Moksha Institute of Caribbean Arts & Letters (Trinidad & Tobago) *Tel:* 6374516, pg 647

Mokslo ir enciklopedijų leidybos institutas (Lithuania) *Tel:* (02) 45 85 26; (02) 457980; (02) 458528 *Fax:* (02) 45 85 37 *E-mail:* meli@meli.lt *Web Site:* www.meli.lt, pg 449

M Moleiro Editor, SA (Spain) *Tel:* (093) 414 20 10; (0902) 11 33 79 *Fax:* (093) 201 50 62 *E-mail:* mmoleiro@moleiro.com *Web Site:* www.moleiro.com, pg 592

Editorial Molino (Spain) *Tel:* (093) 226 06 25 *Fax:* (093) 226 69 98 *E-mail:* molino@menta.net *Web Site:* www.editorialmolino.es, pg 592

Editorial Moll SL (Spain) *Tel:* (0971) 72 41 76 *Fax:* (0971) 72 62 52 *E-mail:* info@editorialmoll.es *Web Site:* www.editorialmoll.es, pg 592

Librairie Mollat (France) *Tel:* (0556) 564040 *Fax:* (0556) 564088 *E-mail:* mollat@mollat.com *Web Site:* www.mollat.com, pg 1310

Izdatelstvo Molodaya Gvardia (Russian Federation) *Tel:* (095) 9722288 *Fax:* (095) 9720582, pg 546

Mombasa Polytechnic Library (Kenya) *Tel:* (011) 492222 *Fax:* (011) 495632 *E-mail:* msapoly@africaonline.com, pg 1523

Pavla Momcilova (Czech Republic) *Tel:* (02) 726 809 19 *Fax:* (02) 726 809 19 *E-mail:* momcilova@volny.cz, pg 125

Monarch Books (United Kingdom) *Tel:* (01865) 302750 *Fax:* (01865) 302757 *E-mail:* monarch@lionhudson.com, pg 729

Monash University Library (Australia) *Tel:* (03) 9905 5054 *Fax:* (03) 9905 2610 *E-mail:* library@lib.monash.edu.au *Web Site:* www.lib.monash.edu.au, pg 1490

Library of the Monastery of St-Saviour (Basilian Missionary Order of St-Saviour) (Lebanon), pg 1525

Arnoldo Mondadori Editore SpA (Italy) *Tel:* (02) 75421 *Fax:* (02) 75422302 *Web Site:* www.mondadori.it, pg 398

Giorgio Mondadori & Associati (Italy) *Tel:* (02) 433 131 *Fax:* (02) 89125880 *E-mail:* edgmonai@tin.it, pg 399

Edizioni del Mondo Giudiziario (Italy) *Tel:* (06) 3721071 *Fax:* (06) 35350961 *E-mail:* info@mguidiziario.it *Web Site:* www.mgiudiziario.it, pg 399

Mondo SA (Editions-Verlag-Edizioni) (Switzerland) *Tel:* (021) 924 12 40 *Fax:* (021) 924 46 62 *E-mail:* info@mondo.ch *Web Site:* www.mondo.ch, pg 629

Mondolibro Editore SNC (Italy) *Tel:* (055) 2658269 *Fax:* (055) 2679522 *E-mail:* info@mondolibroeditore.com *Web Site:* www.mondolibroeditore.com, pg 399

Mondria Publishers (Netherlands) *Tel:* (050) 3110505 *Fax:* (050) 3112299 *E-mail:* post@mondria.nl, pg 486

Monduzzi Editore SpA (Italy) *Tel:* (051) 4151123 *Fax:* (051) 4151125 *Web Site:* www.monduzzi.com, pg 399

Gerard Monfort Editeur Sarl (France) *Tel:* (01) 40 27 95 54 *Fax:* (01) 40 27 95 60 *E-mail:* contact@gerard-monfort.com *Web Site:* www.gerard-monfort.com, pg 176

Mongol Knigotorg (Mongolia), pg 474

Monia Verlag (Germany) *Tel:* (06331) 41425 *Fax:* (06331) 41425, pg 261

Editions du Moniteur (France) *Tel:* (01) 40 13 33 72 *Fax:* (01) 40 41 08 87 *E-mail:* clients@editionsdumoniteur.com *Web Site:* www.editionsdumoniteur.com, pg 176

Monitor-Projectos e Edicoes, LDA (Portugal) *Tel:* (021) 849-48-93 *Fax:* (021) 793-45-51 *E-mail:* monitor@esoterica.pt, pg 533

Monitorul Oficial, Editura (Romania) *Tel:* (01) 402-2173; (01) 402-2176; (01) 411-5833 *Fax:* (01) 312-0901; (01) 312-4703; (01) 410-7736 *E-mail:* ramomrk@bx.logicnet.ro, pg 541

Edumond Le Monnier (Italy) *Tel:* (055) 64910 *Fax:* (055) 6491200 *E-mail:* monnier@tin.it, pg 399

Monograma Ediciones (Spain) *Tel:* (071) 754124; (071) 712593 *Fax:* (071) 712593 *E-mail:* totem@atlas-iap.es, pg 592

Monoline Ltd (Israel) *Tel:* (08) 9741456 *Fax:* (08) 9741454, pg 1180, 1220, 1246

Ediciones Monserrat (Ecuador) *Tel:* (02) 222 667; (02) 505 685; (02) 222 567 *Fax:* (02) 541 294 *E-mail:* edimon@uio.satnet.net, pg 1309

Ediciones Monserrate (Colombia) *Tel:* (01) 253 1347; (01) 253 3033 *Fax:* (01) 253 9517 *E-mail:* comercial@edimonserrate.com *Web Site:* www.edimonserrate.com, pg 112

Editorial Monte Carmelo (Spain) *Tel:* (0947) 25 60 61 *Fax:* (0947) 25 60 62; (0947) 273265 *E-mail:* editorial@montecarmelo.com *Web Site:* www.montecarmelo.com, pg 592

Verlag Monte Verita (Austria) *Tel:* (01) 5487080 *Fax:* (01) 5487081 *Web Site:* www.anares.org, pg 54

Editions Paul Montel (France) *Tel:* (01) 46565266, pg 176

A Monteverde y Cia SA (Uruguay) *Tel:* (02) 915 2012; (02) 915 2939; (02) 915 8748 *Fax:* (02) 915 2012 *E-mail:* monteverde@monteverde.com.uy *Web Site:* www.monteverde.com.uy/, pg 777

The Monthly Magazine for Ceramics Co, Ltd (Republic of Korea) *Tel:* (02) 583-2747 *Fax:* (02) 597-8639, pg 441

Montreal-Contacts/The Rights Agency (France) *Tel:* (01) 43 40 06 10 *Fax:* (01) 43 40 02 12, pg 1130

Moon Jin Media Co Ltd (Republic of Korea) *Tel:* (02) 3453-9800 *Fax:* (02) 3453-4001 *E-mail:* mjmedia@hitel.kol.co.kr, pg 441

Moon-Ta-Gu Books (Australia) *Tel:* (02) 6336 0317 *Fax:* (02) 6336 1319 *E-mail:* wtba@ozemail.com.au, pg 32

Moonlight Publishing (Australia) *Tel:* (03) 5447 8221 *E-mail:* moonlight@impulse.net.au, pg 32

Moonlight Publishing Ltd (United Kingdom) *Tel:* (020) 7376 0299 *Fax:* (020) 7937 8921, pg 729

Moorley's Print & Publishing Ltd (United Kingdom) *Tel:* (0115) 9320643 *Fax:* (0115) 9320643 *E-mail:* info@moorleys.co.uk *Web Site:* www.moorleys.co.uk, pg 729

Mora Ferenc Ifjusagi Koenyvkiado Rt (Hungary) *Tel:* (01) 320 4740 *Fax:* (01) 320 5328 *E-mail:* mora.kiado@elender.hu, pg 323

Ediciones Morata SL (Spain) *Tel:* (091) 448 09 26 *Fax:* (091) 448 09 25 *E-mail:* morata@edmorata.es *Web Site:* www.edmorata.es, pg 592

Editio Moravia-Moravske hudebni vydavatelstvi (Czech Republic) *Tel:* (05) 41220025 *E-mail:* emdl@vtx.cz, pg 125

Moravska Galerie v Brno (Czech Republic) *Tel:* (05) 42 211 464; (05) 42 215 753 *Fax:* (05) 42 215 758 *E-mail:* m-gal@moravska-galerie.cz *Web Site:* www.moravska-galerie.cz, pg 126

Moravska Zemska Knihovna (Czech Republic) *Tel:* (05) 41646111 *Fax:* (05) 41646100 *E-mail:* mzk@mzk.cz *Web Site:* www.mzk.cz, pg 1501

Editrice Morcelliana SpA (Italy) *Tel:* (030) 46451 *Fax:* (030) 2400605 *E-mail:* redazione@morcelliana.it *Web Site:* www.morcelliana.it, pg 399

Izdatelstvo Mordovskogo gosudar stvennogo (Russian Federation) *Tel:* 74771 *Fax:* 74771, pg 547

EDITIONS MORESSOPOULOS

Editions Moressopoulos (Greece) *Tel:* (01) 3234217 *Fax:* (01) 3232082 *E-mail:* hcp@photography.gr, pg 310

Moretti & Vitali Editori srl (Italy) *Tel:* (035) 251300 *Fax:* (035) 4329409 *E-mail:* info@morettievitali.it *Web Site:* www.morettievitali.it, pg 399

Bibliotheque Universitaire Moretus Plantin (Belgium) *Tel:* (081) 724646 *Fax:* (081) 724645 *E-mail:* infocentre@fundp.ac.be *Web Site:* www.fundp.ac.be/bump, pg 1493

Morfotiki Estia AE (Greece) *Tel:* (01) 5227830 *Fax:* (01) 5200534, pg 310

Morfotiko Idryma Ethnikis Trapezas (Greece) *Tel:* (01) 3230841; (01) 3221335 *Fax:* (01) 3245089; (01) 3227057, pg 310

Morija Sesuto Book Depot (Lesotho) *Tel:* 76204 *Fax:* 360009, pg 1325

Morikita Shuppan Co Ltd (Japan) *Tel:* (03) 3265-8341 *Fax:* (03) 3264-8709 *E-mail:* hiro@morikita.co.jp *Web Site:* www.morikita.co.jp, pg 423

Moritz Verlag (Germany) *Tel:* (069) 4305084 *Fax:* (069) 4305083 *E-mail:* MoritzVerlag@t-online.de, pg 261

Morning Glory Press (China) *Tel:* (010) 68411973; (010) 68433187 *Fax:* (010) 68412023; (010) 68485739 *E-mail:* zh@mail.cibtc.com.cn; zh1@mail.cibtc.com.cn, pg 106

Morning Star Publisher Inc (Taiwan, Province of China) *Tel:* (04) 23595820 *Fax:* (04) 23597123 *E-mail:* morning@tcts.seed.net.tw *Web Site:* www.morning-star.com.tw, pg 641

Morrigan Book Co (Ireland) *Tel:* (096) 32555 *Fax:* (096) 32555 *E-mail:* admin@atlanticisland.ie, pg 362

Morris Press Ltd (Hong Kong) *Tel:* 2563 2187; 2563 2188 *Fax:* 2565 9069 *E-mail:* crprint@netvigator.com *Web Site:* www.cgan.net/enterprise/crprint, pg 1157

Morris Press Ltd (Hong Kong) *Tel:* 25632187; 2563 2188 *Fax:* 25659069, pg 1219

William Morris Agency (UK) Ltd (United Kingdom) *Tel:* (020) 7534 6800 *Fax:* (020) 7534 6900 *Web Site:* www.wma.com, pg 1142

William Morris Society (United Kingdom) *Tel:* (020) 8741 3735 *Fax:* (020) 8748 5207 *Web Site:* www.morrissociety.org, pg 1408

Morsak Verlag (Germany) *Tel:* (08552) 4200 *Fax:* (08552) 42050 *E-mail:* info@morsak.de *Web Site:* www.morsak.de, pg 261

E J Morten (Publishers) (United Kingdom) *Tel:* (0161) 445 7629 *Fax:* (0161) 445 7629 *E-mail:* timlovat@aol.com, pg 729

Ernst G Mortensens Forlag A/S (Norway) *Tel:* 22941000 *Fax:* 22113040, pg 510

Morula Press, Business School of Botswana (Botswana) *Tel:* (0267) 353499 *Fax:* (0267) 304809, pg 76

Morus-Verlag GmbH (Germany) *Tel:* (030) 89 79 37-0 *Fax:* (030) 75 70 81 12 *E-mail:* mail@morusverlag.de *Web Site:* www.morusverlag.de, pg 262

Mosaico Editores, LDA (Portugal) *Tel:* (021) 681902 *Fax:* (021) 387-10-81 *E-mail:* mosaico@mail.telepac.pt, pg 534

Mosaik Verlag GmbH (Germany) *Tel:* (089) 4372-0; (089) 4136-0; (01805) 990505 (hot line) *Fax:* (089) 4372-2812 *E-mail:* vertrieb.verlagsgruppe@randomhouse.de *Web Site:* www.randomhouse.de/mosaik, pg 262

Mosca Hermanos (Uruguay) *Tel:* (02) 4093141; (02) 4011111 *Fax:* (02) 200 0588 *E-mail:* empresas@mosca.com.uy *Web Site:* www.mosca.com.uy/, pg 777

Moscow University Press (Russian Federation) *Tel:* (095) 2295091; (095) 2297541 *Fax:* (095) 2036671; (095) 2297541 *E-mail:* kd_mgu@df.ru, pg 547

The Moshe Dayan Center for Middle Eastern & African Studies (Israel) *Tel:* (03) 640-9646 *Fax:* (03) 641-5802 *E-mail:* dayancen@post.tau.ac.il *Web Site:* www.dayan.org, pg 371

Izdatelstvo Moskovskii Rabochii (Russian Federation) *Tel:* (095) 2210735 *Fax:* (095) 9254274, pg 547

Moss Associates Ltd (New Zealand) *Tel:* (04) 4728226 *Fax:* (04) 4728226 *E-mail:* moss@xtra.co.nz, pg 498

K & Z Mostafanejad (Australia) *Tel:* (08) 9923 3741 *Fax:* (08) 9923 3741, pg 32

Mostly Unsung (Australia) *Tel:* (03) 9555 5401 *Fax:* (03) 9555 5401 *E-mail:* milhis@alphalink.com.au, pg 32

Library of the Mosul Museum (Iraq), pg 1518

Mosul Public Library (Iraq) *Tel:* (060) 810162 *Fax:* (060) 814765, pg 1518

Motilal Banarsidass (India) *Tel:* (011) 23851985; (011) 23858335; (011) 23854826; (011) 23852747 *Fax:* (011) 23850689; (011) 25797221 *E-mail:* mlbd@vsnl.com *Web Site:* www.mlbd.com, pg 1316

Motilal Banarsidass Publishers Pvt Ltd (India) *Tel:* (011) 23911985; (011) 23918335; (011) 23974826 *Fax:* (011) 23930689; (011) 25797221 *E-mail:* mlbd@vsnl.com *Web Site:* www.mlbd.com, pg 341

Motilal (UK) Books of India (United Kingdom) *Tel:* (020) 8905 1244 *Fax:* (020) 8905 1108 *E-mail:* info@mlbduk.com *Web Site:* www.mlbduk.com, pg 729

Motilal (UK) Books of India (United Kingdom) *Tel:* (020) 8905-1244 *Fax:* (020) 8905-1108 *E-mail:* info@mlbduk.com *Web Site:* www.mlbduk.com, pg 1352

Motivate Publishing (United Arab Emirates) *Tel:* (04) 282 4060 *Fax:* (04) 282 4436 *E-mail:* motivate@emirates.net.ae *Web Site:* www.booksarabia.com, pg 654

Michael Motley Ltd (United Kingdom) *Tel:* (01684) 276390 *Fax:* (01684) 297355 *E-mail:* michael.motley@amserve.com, pg 1142

Motor Racing Publications Ltd (United Kingdom) *Tel:* (020) 8654 2711 *Fax:* (020) 8407 0339 *E-mail:* mrp.books@virgin.net *Web Site:* www.motorracingpublications.co.uk, pg 729

Motorbuch-Verlag (Germany) *Tel:* (0711) 210 80 65 *Fax:* (0711) 210 80 70 *E-mail:* versand@motorbuch.de *Web Site:* www.motorbuch-versand.de, pg 262

Motovun Book GmbH (Switzerland) *Tel:* (041) 4109515 *Fax:* (041) 4109516 *E-mail:* motovun@bluewin.ch *Web Site:* www.motovun-group-association.org, pg 629

Motovun Co Ltd, Tokyo (Japan) *Tel:* (03) 32614002 *Fax:* (03) 32641443, pg 1134

Federico Motta Editore (Italy) *Tel:* (02) 300761; (02) 30076231 *Fax:* (02) 38010046; (02) 33403275 *E-mail:* info@mottaeditore.it *Web Site:* www.mottaeditore.it, pg 399

Motta Junior Srl (Italy) *Tel:* (02) 300761; (02) 30076231 *Fax:* (02) 38010046; (02) 33403275 *E-mail:* info@mottaeditore.it *Web Site:* www.mottaeditore.it, pg 399

Mount Eagle Publications Ltd (Ireland) *Tel:* (066) 9151463 *Fax:* (066) 9151234 *Web Site:* www.brandonbooks.com, pg 362

Mountain House Press (Australia) *Tel:* (02) 6688 6318 *Fax:* (02) 6688 6318, pg 32

Mouse House Press (Australia) *Tel:* (02) 93512612 *Fax:* (02) 93512606 *E-mail:* s.juan@edfac.usyd.edu.au, pg 32

Mouseio Benaki (Greece) *Tel:* (01) 3611617; (01) 3612694 *Fax:* (01) 3622547, pg 310

Movement for Multi-Party Democracy (Zambia) *Tel:* (01) 224850; (01) 224851; (01) 224852; (01) 224853 *Fax:* (01) 224855, pg 781

Moxon Paperbacks (Ghana) *Tel:* (021) 665397, pg 304

MPG Books Ltd (United Kingdom) *Tel:* (01208) 73266; (01208) 72008 (ISDN) *Fax:* (01208) 73603 *E-mail:* print@mpg-books.co.uk *Web Site:* www.mpg-books.com, pg 1164

MPG Books Ltd (United Kingdom) *Tel:* (01208) 73266 *Fax:* (01208) 76515 *E-mail:* print@mpg-books.co.uk *Web Site:* www.mpg-books.com, pg 1227

MPG Ltd (United Kingdom) *Tel:* (01483) 757501 *Fax:* (01483) 724629 *E-mail:* print@mpgltd.co.uk, pg 1185

MPG Ltd (United Kingdom) *Tel:* (01483) 757501 *Fax:* (01483) 724629 *E-mail:* print@mpgltd.co.uk *Web Site:* www.mpgltd.co.uk, pg 1227

MPH Bookstores (S) Pte Ltd (Singapore) *Tel:* 6453 8200 *E-mail:* mphbooks@singnet.com.sg, pg 1339

MPH Distributors Sdn Bhd (Malaysia) *Tel:* (03) 2938 3800; (03) 2938 3818 *Fax:* (03) 2938 3811; (03) 2938 3817 *E-mail:* contact@mph.com.my; customerservice@mph.com.my *Web Site:* www.mphonline.com; www.mph.com, pg 1326

MQ Publications Ltd (United Kingdom) *Tel:* (020) 7359 2244 *Fax:* (020) 7359 1616 *E-mail:* mail@mqpublications.com *Web Site:* gustocreative.dsvr.co.uk/mqp-site/home.html, pg 729

Mucchi Editore SRL (Italy) *Tel:* (059) 374094 *Fax:* (059) 282628 *E-mail:* info@mucchieditore.it *Web Site:* www.mucchieditore.it, pg 399

Anaya & Mario Muchnik (Spain) *Tel:* (091) 393 86 00 *Fax:* (091) 320 91 29; (091) 742 66 31 *E-mail:* cga@anaya.es *Web Site:* www.anaya.es, pg 592

Mudgala Trust (India) *Tel:* (044) 837257, pg 342

Mudrak Publishers & Distributors (India) *Tel:* (011) 3730818; (011) 3738319; (011) 6416317, pg 342

Verlag Rudolf Muehlemann (Switzerland) *Tel:* (071) 622 53 53 *Fax:* (071) 622 30 04, pg 629

Mueller & Schindler Verlag ek (Germany) *Tel:* (0711) 233204 *Fax:* (0711) 2369977, pg 262

C F Mueller Verlag, Huethig Gmb H & Co (Germany) *Tel:* (06221) 489 395 *Fax:* (06221) 489623 *E-mail:* cfmueller@huethig.de *Web Site:* www.huethig.de, pg 262

Verlag Karl Mueller GmbH (Germany) *Tel:* (0221) 130 65-0 *Fax:* (0221) 130 65-299 *E-mail:* info@karl-mueller-verlag.de *Web Site:* www.karl-mueller-verlag.de, pg 262

Lars Mueller Publishers (Switzerland) *Tel:* (056) 4301740 *Fax:* (056) 4301741 *E-mail:* info@lars-mueller-publishers.com *Web Site:* www.lars-mueller-publishers.com, pg 629

Verlag Norbert Mueller AG & Co KG (Germany) *Tel:* (089) 5485201 *Fax:* (089) 54852192 *E-mail:* info@vnm.de *Web Site:* www.vnm.de, pg 262

Otto Mueller Verlag (Austria) *Tel:* (0662) 881974-0 *Fax:* (0662) 872387 *E-mail:* otto.muellerverlag@salzburg.co.at, pg 54

Mueller Rueschlikon Verlags AG (Switzerland) *Tel:* (041) 443040-42 *Fax:* (041) 417115, pg 629

Mueller-Speiser Wissenschaftlicher Verlag (Austria) *Tel:* (06246) 73166 *Fax:* (06246) 73166 *E-mail:* verlag@mueller-speiser.at *Web Site:* www.mueller-speiser.at, pg 54

Mueller und Steinicke Verlag (Germany) *Tel:* (089) 74 99 156 *Fax:* (089) 74 99 157 *E-mail:* info@mueller-und-steinicke.de *Web Site:* www.mueller-und-steinicke.de, pg 262

Mueszaki Koenyvkiado Ltd (Hungary) *Tel:* (01) 1557122 *E-mail:* berczis@muzakikiado.hu, pg 323

De Muiderkring BV (Netherlands) *Tel:* (0294) 450460 *Fax:* (0294) 412782, pg 486

Robert Muir Old & Rare Books (Australia) *Tel:* (08) 9386 5842 *Fax:* (08) 9386 8211 *E-mail:* books@muirbooks.com *Web Site:* www.muirbooks.com, pg 1299

YELLOW PAGES

Instituto de la Mujer (Ministerio de Trabajo y Asuntos Sociales) (Spain) *Tel:* (091) 363 80 00 *E-mail:* inmujer@mtas.es *Web Site:* www.mtas.es/mujer, pg 592

A Mukherjee & Co Pvt Ltd (India) *Tel:* (033) 2417406; (033) 2418199 *Fax:* (033) 440-8641, pg 342

Mulavon Press Pty Ltd (Australia) *Tel:* (02) 9808 3662 *Fax:* (02) 9552 1608, pg 32

Mulder Holland BV (Netherlands) *Tel:* (020) 442022; (020) 441682; (020) 824805 *Fax:* (020) 465228, pg 486

Mulini Press (Australia) *Tel:* (02) 6251 2519 *Fax:* (02) 6251 2519, pg 32

Societa Editrice Il Mulino (Italy) *Tel:* (051) 256011 *Fax:* (051) 256034 *E-mail:* info@mulino.it *Web Site:* www.mulino.it, pg 399

Muller Edition (France) *Tel:* (01) 40 90 09 65 *Fax:* (01) 47 76 33 97 *E-mail:* courrier@muller-edition.com *Web Site:* www.muller-edition.com, pg 176

Mullick Bros (Bangladesh) *Tel:* (02) 280728, pg 61

Mullick Bros (Bangladesh) *Tel:* (02) 8619125; (02) 507434 *Fax:* (02) 8610562 *E-mail:* mullick@bd.com, pg 1301

Mult es Jovo Kiado (Hungary) *Tel:* (01) 316-70-19; (01) 438-38-06; (01) 438-38-07 *Fax:* (01) 316-70-19 *E-mail:* mandj@multesjovo.hu *Web Site:* www.multesjovo.hu, pg 323

Multi-Disciplinary Research Centre Library (Namibia) *Tel:* (061) 206 3909; (061) 206 3051 *Fax:* (061) 206 3050; (061) 206 3684 *E-mail:* tgases@unam.na *Web Site:* www.unam.na, pg 476

Multi Media Kunst Verlag Dresden (Germany) *Tel:* (0351) 8041291 *Fax:* (0351) 8041291, pg 262

Multi-Media Ltd (Trinidad & Tobago) *Tel:* 6288637; 6226774 *Fax:* 6281903, pg 647

Multilingual Matters Ltd (United Kingdom) *Tel:* (01275) 876519 *Fax:* (01275) 871673 *E-mail:* info@multilingual-matters.com *Web Site:* www.multilingual-matters.com, pg 729

Multimedia Zambia (Zambia) *Tel:* (01) 253666 *Fax:* (01) 363050, pg 781

Multinova (Portugal) *Tel:* (021) 8481820 *Fax:* (021) 8483436 *E-mail:* geral@multinova.pt *Web Site:* www.multinova.pt, pg 534

Ass Italiana Sclerosi Multipla (Italy) *Tel:* (010) 27131 *Fax:* (010) 2470226, pg 400

Multiplex Medway Ltd (United Kingdom) *Tel:* (01634) 684371 *Fax:* (01634) 683840 *E-mail:* enquiries@multiplex-medway.co.uk *Web Site:* www.multiplex-medway.co.uk, pg 1185

Multiplex Medway Ltd (United Kingdom) *Tel:* (01634) 684371; (01634) 671687 (ISDN) *Fax:* (01634) 683840 *E-mail:* enquiries@multiplex-medway.co.uk *Web Site:* www.multiplex-medway.co.uk, pg 1227

Multiplex Medway Ltd (United Kingdom) *Tel:* (01634) 684371 *Fax:* (01634) 683840 *E-mail:* enquiries@multiplex-medway.co.uk *Web Site:* www.multiplex-medway.co.uk, pg 1248

Multitech Publishing Co (India) *Tel:* (022) 5118820; (022) 5154206 *Fax:* (022) 5115904, pg 342

Mun Un Dang (Republic of Korea) *Tel:* (02) 7433504; (02) 7433505 *Fax:* (02) 7450265, pg 441

Mundi-Prensa Libros SA (Spain) *Tel:* (091) 4 36 37 00 *Fax:* (091) 5 75 39 98 *E-mail:* liberia@mundiprensa.es *Web Site:* www.mundiprensa.es, pg 592

Mundi-Prensa Libros, SA (Spain) *Tel:* (091) 436 37 00 *Fax:* (091) 575 39 98 *E-mail:* libreria@mundiprensa.es *Web Site:* www.mundiprensa.com, pg 1342

Mundici - Zanetti (Italy) *Tel:* (051) 325347 *Fax:* (051) 326109, pg 400

Editora Mundo Cristao (Brazil) *Tel:* (011) 5668-1700 *Fax:* (011) 5666-4829 *E-mail:* editora@mundocristao.com.br *Web Site:* www.mundocristao.com.br, pg 87

Mundo Medico SA de CV Edicion y Distribucion de Revistas Medicas (Mexico) *Tel:* (05) 5203-8111 *Fax:* (05) 5601-0815 *E-mail:* info@grupomundomedico.com *Web Site:* www.mundomedico.com.mx, pg 469

Mundo Negro Editorial (Spain) *Tel:* (091) 4158115; (091) 4152412 *Fax:* (091) 5192550 *E-mail:* 100623.1651@compuserve.com, pg 592

Mundo Verlag GmbH (Germany) *Tel:* (0180) 9216350 *Fax:* (0180) 921635-24 *E-mail:* info@mundo-media.de *Web Site:* www.mundo-text.de, pg 262

Munhag-gwan (Republic of Korea) *Tel:* (02) 7186810 *Fax:* (02) 7062225, pg 441

Munich, Edition, Verlag, Handels-und Dienstleistungskontar GmbH (Germany) *Tel:* (089) 349830 *Fax:* (089) 349834 *E-mail:* bzit99e@benezit.de, pg 262

Municipal Library (Cyprus), pg 1501

Biblioteca Municipal de Luanda (Angola) *Tel:* (02) 392297 *Fax:* (02) 33902, pg 1489

Bibliotheque Municipale (Madagascar) *Tel:* (04) 21176, pg 1526

Bibliotheque Municipale de Nancy (France) *Tel:* (03) 83373883 *Fax:* (03) 83379182 *E-mail:* bmnancy@mairie-nancy.fr *Web Site:* www.nancy.fr, pg 1507

Munoz Moya Editor (Spain) *Tel:* (05) 5653058 *E-mail:* editorial@mmoya.com; ediextre@mmoya.com *Web Site:* www.mmoya.com, pg 592

James Munro & Co (United Kingdom) *Tel:* (0141) 429 1234 *Fax:* (0141) 420 1694 *E-mail:* enquiry@skipper.co.uk; sales@skipper.co.uk (orders) *Web Site:* www.skipper.co.uk, pg 729

Munshiram Manoharlal Publishers Pvt Ltd (India) *Tel:* (011) 3671668; (011) 3673650 *Fax:* (011) 3612745 *E-mail:* mrml@mantraonline.com *Web Site:* www.mrmlbooks.com, pg 342

Munshiram Manoharlal Publishers Pvt Ltd (India) *Tel:* (011) 7771668 *Fax:* (011) 3612745 *E-mail:* mml@mantraonline.com, pg 1316

Uitgeverij Maarten Muntinga (Netherlands) *Tel:* (020) 521 67 67 *Fax:* (020) 626 05 96 *E-mail:* info@rainbow.nl *Web Site:* www.rainbow.nl, pg 486

Munye Publishing Co (Republic of Korea) *Tel:* (02) 3935681; (02) 3935684 *Fax:* (02) 3935685, pg 441

Munzinger-Archiv GmbH Archiv fuer publizistische Arbeit (Germany) *Tel:* (0751) 76931-0 *Fax:* (0751) 65 24 24 *E-mail:* box@munzinger.de *Web Site:* www.munzinger.de, pg 262

Editorial la Muralla SA (Spain) *Tel:* (091) 415 36 87; (091) 416 13 71 *Fax:* (091) 413 59 07 *E-mail:* arcolibros@arcomuralla.com *Web Site:* www.arcomuralla.com, pg 592

Murchison's Pantheon Ltd (United Kingdom) *Tel:* 7374 2828 *Fax:* (020) 7628 6270 *E-mail:* 100450.1105@compuserve.com, pg 730

Murdoch Books (Australia) *Tel:* (02) 8220 2000 *Fax:* (02) 8220 2020 *Web Site:* www.mm.com.au, pg 32

Murdoch Books UK Ltd (United Kingdom) *Tel:* (020) 8785 5995 *Fax:* (020) 8785 5985, pg 730

Murgorski Zoze (The Former Yugoslav Republic of Macedonia) *Tel:* (091) 241340, pg 453

Les Muriers Editions (Spain) *Tel:* (0971) 484 423 *Fax:* (0971) 484 423 *Web Site:* www.lmeditions.com, pg 1136

John Murray (Publishers) Ltd (United Kingdom) *Tel:* (020) 7873 6000 *Fax:* (020) 7873 6446 *E-mail:* enquiries@johnmurrays.co.uk *Web Site:* www.madaboutbooks.co.uk, pg 730

Gruppo Ugo Mursia Editore SpA (Italy) *Tel:* (02) 67378500 *Fax:* (02) 67378605 *E-mail:* info@mursia.com *Web Site:* www.mursia.com, pg 400

Musa Editora Ltda (Brazil) *Tel:* (011) 62-2586 *Fax:* (011) 62-2586 *E-mail:* musaeditora@vol.com.br, pg 87

Giov Muscat & Co Ltd (Malta) *Tel:* 247 380 *Fax:* 240 496, pg 1327

Musee d'Art et d'Archaeologie (Madagascar) *Tel:* (02) 21047 *Fax:* (02) 28218 *E-mail:* musedar@syfed.refer.mg, pg 454

Bibliotheque du Musee de l'Homme (France) *Tel:* (01) 44 05 72 03 *Fax:* (01) 44 05 72 12 *E-mail:* bmhweb@mnhn.fr *Web Site:* www.mnhn.fr, pg 1507

Editions de la Reunion des Musees Nationaux (France) *Tel:* (01) 40 13 49 66 *Fax:* (01) 40 13 49 73 *E-mail:* editions@rmn.fr *Web Site:* www.rmn.fr, pg 176

Museo y Biblioteca Municipal (Ecuador) *Tel:* (04) 515738, pg 1503

Biblioteca del Museo Historico Nacional (Uruguay) *Tel:* (02) 95 10 51; (02) 915 33 16 *Fax:* (02) 915 68 63, pg 1555

Museo Chileno de Arte Precolombino (Chile) *Tel:* (02) 6887078; (02) 6972779 *Fax:* (02) 6972779 *E-mail:* bibmchap@ctcreuna.cl *Web Site:* www.precolombino.cl, pg 99

Museo Historico Cultural Juan Santamaria (Costa Rica) *Tel:* 441-4775; 442-1838 *Fax:* 441-6926 *E-mail:* mhcjscr@racsa.co.cr *Web Site:* www.museojuansantamaria.go.cr, pg 115

Museo storico in Trento (Italy) *Tel:* (0461) 230482 *Fax:* (0461) 237418 *E-mail:* info@museostorico.tn.it *Web Site:* www.museostorico.tn.it/editoria_ricerca, pg 400

Museu Maritimo (Macau) *Tel:* (0853) 595481; (0853) 595483 *Fax:* (0853) 512160 *E-mail:* museumaritimo@marine.gov.mo *Web Site:* www.museumaritimo.gov.mo, pg 452

Museum Meermanno-Westreenianum (Netherlands) *Tel:* (070) 3462700 *Fax:* (070) 3630350 *E-mail:* info@meermanno.nl *Web Site:* www.meermanno.nl/, pg 1531

Museum of Victoria (Australia) *Tel:* (03) 8341 7777 *Fax:* (03) 9651 6321 *Web Site:* www.museum.vic.gov.au, pg 33

Museum Tusculanum Press (Denmark) *Tel:* 35 32 91 09 *Fax:* 35 32 91 13 *E-mail:* mtp@mtp.dk *Web Site:* www.mtp.dk, pg 133

Music Book Distributors Ltd (United Kingdom) *Tel:* (0181) 559 1522 *Fax:* (0181) 559 1522, pg 1352

Music Publishers Association (United Kingdom) *Tel:* (020) 7839 7779 *Fax:* (020) 7839 7776 *E-mail:* info@mpaonline.org.uk *Web Site:* www.mpaonline.org.uk, pg 1292

Editorial Musica Moderna (Spain) *Tel:* (091) 416 91 81; (091) 415 37 78, pg 592

Musica Publishing House Ltd (Bulgaria) *Tel:* (02) 877 963; (02) 892 642 *Fax:* (02) 877 963 *E-mail:* musicaph@abv.bg *Web Site:* www.geocities.com/musicapublishinghouse, pg 95

Editions Musicales De La Schola Cantorum (Switzerland) *Tel:* (024) 485 24 80 *Fax:* (024) 485 34 60 *E-mail:* frochaux-schola@bluewin.ch; labatiaz@bluewin.ch, pg 629

Musicoteca Lda (Portugal) *Tel:* (021) 3462653 *Fax:* (021) 3476637 *E-mail:* musicoteca@mail.telepac.pt, pg 534

Musikantiquariat und Dr Hans Schneider Verlag GmbH (Germany) *Tel:* (08158) 3050; (08158) 6967 *Fax:* (08158) 7636 *E-mail:* musikbuch@aol.com; musikantiquar@aol.com, pg 262

Musikverlag Zimmermann (Germany) *Tel:* (069) 978286-6 *Fax:* (069) 978286-89 *E-mail:* info@zimmermann-frankfurt.de; lektorat@zimmermann-frankfurt.de *Web Site:* www.zimmermann-frankfurt.de, pg 262

Musimed Edicoes Musicais Importacao E Exportacao Ltda (Brazil) *Tel:* (061) 244-9799 *Fax:* (061) 226-0478 *E-mail:* cartas@musimed.com.br *Web Site:* www.musimed.com.br, pg 87

Muslim Architecture Research Program (MARP) (Switzerland) *Tel:* (02) 4711228 *Fax:* (02) 4711228, pg 629

Muster-Schmidt Verlag (Germany) *Tel:* (05551) 908420 *Fax:* (05551) 9084229 *E-mail:* info@muster-schmidt.de *Web Site:* www.muster-schmidt.de, pg 263

Musumeci SpA (Italy) *Tel:* (0165) 761216 *Fax:* (0165) 761296, pg 400

MUT Verlag (Germany) *Tel:* (04253) 566; (04253) 672 *Fax:* (04253) 16 03, pg 263

Mu'tah University Library (Jordan) *Tel:* (06) 4617860 *Fax:* (03) 371651 *E-mail:* library@mutah.edu.jo, pg 1522

Mutiara Sumber Widya PT (Indonesia) *Tel:* (021) 3909864; (021) 3909261; (021) 3909247 *Fax:* (021) 3160313, pg 356

Mutual Book Inc (Philippines) *Tel:* (02) 796050, pg 519

Muza SA (Poland) *Tel:* (022) 621-17-75; (022) 621-50-58; (022) 629-50-83 *Fax:* (022) 629-23-49 *E-mail:* muza@muza.com.pl *Web Site:* www.muza.com.pl, pg 524

Muze UK Ltd (United Kingdom) *Tel:* (0870) 7277 256 *Fax:* (0870) 7277 257 *E-mail:* colin@muze.co.uk *Web Site:* www.muze.com, pg 730

Editura Muzicala (Romania) *Tel:* (01) 3129867 *Fax:* (01) 3129867 *E-mail:* editura_muzicala@hotmail.com, pg 541

Muzicka Naklada (Croatia) *Tel:* (01) 424 099; (01) 424 019, pg 119

Polskie Wydawnictwo Muzyczne (Poland) *Tel:* (012) 4227171; (012) 4227044 *Fax:* (012) 4227171 *E-mail:* pwm@pwm.com.pl *Web Site:* www.pwm.com.pl, pg 524

Izdatelstvo Muzyka (Russian Federation) *Tel:* (095) 921-51-70 *Fax:* (095) 928-33-04 *E-mail:* muzyka@insar.ru *Web Site:* www.muzykaizd.ru, pg 547

Franco Muzzio Editore (Italy) *Tel:* (06) 3725748 *Fax:* (06) 6868696 *E-mail:* franco@muzzioeditore.it *Web Site:* www.muzzioeditore.it, pg 400

MVB Marketing- und Verlagsservice des Buchhandels GmbH (Germany) *Tel:* (069) 1306-0; (069) 1306-339 (Boersenblatt); (069) 1306-340 (Boersenblatt) *Fax:* (069) 1306-201 *E-mail:* info@mvb-online.de *Web Site:* www.mvb-online.de, pg 263

MWH London Publishers (United Kingdom) *Tel:* (020) 7263 3071 *Fax:* (020) 7281 12687 *E-mail:* info@mwht.org.uk *Web Site:* www.mwht.org.uk, pg 730

Myanmar Library Association (MLA) (Myanmar), pg 1567

Myrtos Inc (Japan) *Tel:* (03) 3288-2200 *Fax:* (03) 3288-2225 *E-mail:* pub@myrtos.co.jp *Web Site:* www.myrtos.co.jp, pg 423

Izdatelstvo Mysl (Russian Federation) *Tel:* (095) 2324248; (095) 952-5065; (095) 955-0458, pg 547

Mystetstvo Publishers (Ukraine) *Tel:* (044) 225-53-92; (044) 224-91-01 *Fax:* (044) 229-05-64, pg 653

Mzumbe University Library (United Republic of Tanzania) *Tel:* (023) 260-4380; (023) 260-4381; (023) 260-4383; (023) 260-4384 *Fax:* (023) 260-4382 *E-mail:* idm@raha.com, pg 1549

Biblioteca Nacional (Spain) *Tel:* (091) 580 7800 *Web Site:* www.bne.es; www.mec.es, pg 1545

Cia Editora Nacional (Brazil) *Tel:* (011) 2912355 *Fax:* (011) 2918214, pg 87

Biblioteca Nacional de Angola (Angola) *Tel:* (02) 322 070 *Fax:* (02) 323 979 *E-mail:* biblioteca@netangola.com, pg 1489

Instituto Nacional de Antropologia e Historia (Mexico) *Tel:* (055) 5335246; (055) 5332272; (055) 2074559; (055) 2074584 *Fax:* (055) 2074633 *E-mail:* difusion.cdifus@inah.gob.mx *Web Site:* www.inah.gob.mx, pg 469

Instituto Nacional de Ciencia y Tecnica Hidrica (INCYTH) (Argentina) *Tel:* (011) 4295-1503 *Fax:* (011) 4800094, pg 7

Instituto Nacional de Estadistica, Geographia e Informatica (Mexico) *Tel:* 449 910 5300 (ext 5021) *Fax:* 449 918 2232 *E-mail:* ventas@dgd.inegi.gob.mx *Web Site:* www.inegi.gob.mx, pg 469

Instituto Nacional de Estudos e Pesquisa (INEP) (Guinea-Bissau) *Tel:* 21 17 15; 21 44 97; 21 13 01 *Fax:* 25 11 25 *Web Site:* www.inep.gov.br, pg 314

Editorial Nacional de Salud y Seguridad Social Ednass (Costa Rica) *Tel:* 231-2214 *Fax:* 232-7451 *E-mail:* cendeiss@info.ccss.sa.cr, pg 116

Companhia Editora Nacional (Brazil) *Tel:* (011) 6099-7799 (ext 246) *Fax:* (011) 6694-5338 *Web Site:* www.ibep-nacional.com.br, pg 87

Nacionalna i Sveucilisna Knjiznica Biblioteka (Croatia) *Tel:* (01) 61 64 111 *Fax:* (01) 61 64 186 *E-mail:* nsk@nsk.hr *Web Site:* www.nsk.hr, pg 1500

Giorgio Nada Editore SRL (Italy) *Tel:* (02) 27301126 *Fax:* (02) 27301454 *E-mail:* info@giorgionadaeditore.it *Web Site:* www.giorgionadaeditore.it, pg 400

Editions Maurice Nadeau, Les Lettres Nouvelles (France) *Tel:* (01) 48 87 75 87 *Fax:* (01) 48 87 13 01, pg 176

Edito Georges Naef SA (Switzerland) *Tel:* (022) 7380502 *Fax:* (022) 7384224 *E-mail:* naef@kister.ch *Web Site:* www.kister.ch, pg 629

Nafees Academy (Pakistan), pg 513

NAG Press (United Kingdom) *Tel:* (020) 7251 2661 *Fax:* (020) 7490 4958 *E-mail:* enquire@halebooks.com *Web Site:* www.halebooks.com/n_a_g_press_files.html, pg 730

Nagai Shoten Co Ltd (Japan) *Tel:* (06) 6452-1881 *Fax:* (06) 6452-1882 *E-mail:* nagai05@gold.ocn.ne.jp, pg 423

Nagaoka Shoten Co Ltd (Japan) *Tel:* (03) 3992-5155 *Fax:* (03) 3948-3021 *E-mail:* info@nagaokashoten.co.jp, pg 423

Nagard (Italy) *Tel:* (02) 58371400 *Fax:* (02) 58304790, pg 400

Nagare Press (New Zealand) *Tel:* (06) 3572531, pg 499

Les Editions Nagel SA (Paris) (Switzerland) *Tel:* (022) 734 17 30 *Fax:* (022) 7337424 *E-mail:* info@nagel.ch *Web Site:* www.nagel.ch, pg 629

Verlag Nagel & Kimche AG, Zurich (Switzerland) *Tel:* (01) 366 66 80 *Fax:* (01) 366 66 88 *E-mail:* info@nagel-kimche.ch *Web Site:* www.nagel-kimche.ch, pg 629

Verlag Stephanie Naglschmid (Germany) *Tel:* (0711) 62 68 78 *Fax:* (0711) 61 23 23 *E-mail:* naglschmid.vsn@t-online.de *Web Site:* www.naglschmid.de, pg 263

Nahanni Publishing Ltd (New Zealand) *Tel:* (09) 419 0681 *Fax:* (09) 419 0695 *E-mail:* info@nahanni-publishing.com; sales@nahanni.co.nz (for orders) *Web Site:* www.nahanni-publishing.com, pg 499

Nai Publishers (Netherlands) *Tel:* (010) 2010133 *Fax:* (010) 2010130 *E-mail:* info@naipublishers.nl *Web Site:* www.naipublishers.nl, pg 486

Nairobi University Press (Kenya) *Tel:* (02) 334244 (ext 28581) *Fax:* (02) 336885 *E-mail:* nup@uonbi.ac.ke *Web Site:* www.uonbi.ac.ke, pg 435

Nakas Music House (Greece) *Tel:* (01) 364-711; (01) 364-716 *Fax:* (01) 2112303 *E-mail:* bookw@nakas.gr, pg 310

Nakayama Shoten Co Ltd (Japan) *Tel:* (03) 3813-1100 *Fax:* (03) 3816-1015 *Web Site:* www.nakayamashoten.co.jp, pg 423

Naklada Ljevak doo (Croatia) *Tel:* (01) 4804-000 *Fax:* (01) 4804-001 *E-mail:* naklada-ljevak@zg.hinet.hr *Web Site:* www.naklada-ljevak.hr, pg 119

Naldoza Printers (Philippines) *Tel:* (032) 261-7326 *Fax:* (032) 261-7326 *E-mail:* naldoza@ebu.skyinet.net, pg 1181, 1222

Namsgagnastofnun (Iceland) *Tel:* 5528088 *Fax:* 5624137 *E-mail:* upplysingar@nams.is *Web Site:* www.namsgagnastofnun.is, pg 326

Nanam Publications Co (Republic of Korea) *Tel:* (02) 552-8535; (02) 552-8537 *Fax:* (02) 552-0711 *E-mail:* nanamcom@soback.kornet21.net; edit@nanamcom.co.kr; post@nanamcom.co.kr *Web Site:* www.nanamcom.co.kr, pg 441

M/S Gulshan Nanda Publications (India) *Tel:* (022) 6406994 *Fax:* (022) 4303696, pg 342

Nanga (France) *Tel:* (02) 96 72 32 16 *Fax:* (02) 96 72 08 48 *E-mail:* nanga@nanga.fr; nangaw@wanadoo.fr *Web Site:* www.nanga.info, pg 176

Nanjing tushuguan (China) *Tel:* (025) 83372163 *Fax:* (025) 83372163 *E-mail:* ntbgs@sina.com *Web Site:* www.jslib.org.cn, pg 1498

Nanjing University Press (China) *Tel:* (025) 83593450; (025) 83303347 *Web Site:* press.nju.edu.cn, pg 106

Nankodo Co Ltd (Japan) *Tel:* (03) 3811-7239 *Fax:* (03) 3811-7230 *E-mail:* info@nankodo.co.jp *Web Site:* www.nankodo.co.jp, pg 423

Nankodo Co Ltd (Japan) *Tel:* (03) 3811-9957 *Fax:* (03) 3811-5031 *E-mail:* yoshohp@nankodo.co.jp *Web Site:* www.nankodo.co.jp, pg 1322

Nan'un-Do Co Ltd (Japan) *Tel:* (03) 3268-2362 *Fax:* (03) 3268-2650, pg 423

Nanzando Co Ltd (Japan) *Tel:* (03) 56897868 *Fax:* (03) 56897857 *E-mail:* info@nanzando.com *Web Site:* www.nanzando.com, pg 423

Naouka i Izkoustvo, Ltd (Bulgaria) *Tel:* (02) 9874790; (02) 9872496 *Fax:* (02) 9872496 *E-mail:* nauk_izk@sigma–bg.com, pg 95

Napier Public Library (New Zealand) *Tel:* (06) 834 4180 *Fax:* (06) 834 4138 *E-mail:* library@napier.govt.nz *Web Site:* www.napier.govt.nz/inlib.php, pg 1532

Casa Editrice Roberto Napoleone (Italy) *Tel:* (06) 3729096 *Fax:* (06) 3729103, pg 400

Naque Editora (Spain) *Tel:* (0926) 216714 *Fax:* (0926) 216714 *E-mail:* naque@naque.es *Web Site:* www.naque.es, pg 592

Narcea SA de Ediciones (Spain) *Tel:* (091) 554 64 84; (091) 554 61 02 *Fax:* (091) 554 64 87 *E-mail:* narcea@narceaediciones.es *Web Site:* www.narceaediciones.es, pg 593

Nardini Editore srl (Italy) *Tel:* (055) 238551 *Fax:* (055) 2385529 *E-mail:* info@nardinieditore.it *Web Site:* www.nardinieditore.it, pg 400

Naresh Publishers (India) *Tel:* (011) 572-3235; (011) 575-4442 *Fax:* (011) 574-6485, pg 342

Narkaling Inc (Australia) *Tel:* (08) 9274 8022 *Fax:* (08) 9274 8362 *E-mail:* info@narkaling.com.au *Web Site:* www.narkaling.com.au, pg 33

Narodna Biblioteka Srbije (Serbia and Montenegro) *Tel:* (011) 451 2429 *Fax:* (011) 451 289 *E-mail:* kovacevic@nbsbg.nbs.bg.ac.yu *Web Site:* www.nbs.bg.ac.yu, pg 552

Narodna Biblioteka Srbije (Serbia and Montenegro) *Tel:* (011) 451-242; (011) 451-281; (011) 451-287 *Fax:* (011) 451-289; (011) 452-952 *Web Site:* www.nbs.bg.ac.yu, pg 1542

Narodna i univerzitetska biblioteka Bosne i Hercegovine (Bosnia and Herzegovina) *Tel:* (071) 33 275 312 *Fax:* (071) 33 275 431 *E-mail:* nubbih@nub.ba *Web Site:* www.nub.ba, pg 1495

Narodna in Univerzitetna Knjiznica, Ljubljana (Slovenia) *Tel:* (01) 2001 110 *Fax:* (01) 4257 293 *E-mail:* info@nuk.uni-lj.si *Web Site:* www.nuk.uni-lj.si/vstop.cgi, pg 1543

Narodna Kultura (Bulgaria) *Tel:* (02) 981 4739
Fax: (02) 981 4739 *E-mail:* peepcult@internet-bg.net
Web Site: www.geocities.com/narodna_kultura, pg 96

Narodna Kultura (Bulgaria) *Tel:* (02) 9878063; (02)
9872722; (02) 9871684 *E-mail:* peepcult@internet-
bg.net *Web Site:* web.narodnakultura.hit.bg, pg 96

Narodnaya Asveta (Belarus) *Tel:* 2236131 *Fax:* 2236184
E-mail: ngpna@asveta.belpak.minsk.by, pg 62

Narodne Novine (Croatia) *Tel:* (01) 4501-310 *Fax:* (01)
4501-348; (01) 4501-349 *E-mail:* e-pretplata@nn.hr
Web Site: www.nn.hr, pg 119

Narodni agentura ISBN v CR (Czech Republic) *Tel:* (02)
21663262 *Fax:* (02) 21663261 *E-mail:* isbn@nkp.cz
Web Site: www.nkp.cz, pg 1265

Narodni filmovy archiv (Czech Republic) *Tel:* (02) 71
770 500; (02) 71 770 502-9 *Fax:* (02) 71 770 501
E-mail: nfa@nfa.cz, pg 126

Narodni knihovna Ceske republiky (Czech Republic)
Tel: (02) 21663111 *Fax:* (02) 21663267; (02)
21663277 *E-mail:* public.ur@nkp.cz *Web Site:* www.
nkp.cz, pg 1501

Narodni Knihovna CR (Czech Republic) *Tel:* (02) 2810
13 316; (02) 2810 13 317 *Fax:* (02) 216 632 61; (02)
2810 13 333 *E-mail:* sekret.ur@nkp.cz; mirosovsky.
ivo@cdh.nkp.cz *Web Site:* www.nkp.cz, pg 126

Narodni Muzeum (Czech Republic) *Tel:* (02) 24497111;
(02) 24226488 *Fax:* (02) 22246047 *E-mail:* ais@nm.
anet.cz *Web Site:* www.nm.cz, pg 126

Publishing House Narodno delo OOD (Bulgaria)
Tel: (052) 230241; (052) 288516, pg 96

Narosa Book Distributors Pvt Ltd (India)
Tel: (011) 23243224; (011) 23243415; (011)
23243416 *Fax:* (011) 23243225; (011) 23258934
E-mail: narosa@ndc.vsnl.net.in/narosadl@nda.vsnl.
net.in *Web Site:* www.narosa.com, pg 1317

Narosa Publishing House (India) *Tel:* (011) 23243224;
(011) 23243415; (011) 23243416 *Fax:* (011)
23243225; (011) 23258934 *E-mail:* narosa@ndc.vsnl.
net.in/narosadl@nda.vsnl.net.in *Web Site:* www.narosa.
com, pg 342

Narratio Theologische Uitgeverij (Netherlands)
Tel: (0183) 62 81 88 *Fax:* (0183) 64 04 96
E-mail: lvdherik@narratio.nl *Web Site:* www.narratio.
nl, pg 486

Nasa Djeca Publishing (Croatia) *Tel:* (01) 485 6056; (01)
485 6046 *Fax:* (01) 485 6613 *E-mail:* nasa-djeca@zg.
tel.hr, pg 119

Nase vojsko, nakladatelstvi a knizni obchod (Czech
Republic) *Tel:* (02) 243 130 71; (02) 243 112 04;
(02) 249 171 47 *Fax:* (02) 243 112 04 *E-mail:* info@
nasevojsko.com; info@nasevojsko.cz *Web Site:* www.
nasevojsko.com, pg 126

Nashiran-e-Quran Pvt Ltd (Pakistan) *Tel:* (042) 58581;
(042) 58581, pg 513

Perpustakaan Nasional (Indonesia) *Tel:* (021) 315-4863;
(021) 315 4864; (021) 315 4870 *Fax:* (021) 310
3554 *E-mail:* pusnas@rad.net.id; info@pnri.go.id
Web Site: www.pnri.go.id, pg 1517

Nasionale Boekhandel Ltd (South Africa) *Tel:* (021)
5911131, pg 567

Nasou Via Afrika (South Africa) *Tel:* (021) 406-3314;
(021) 406-3005 (customer service) *Fax:* (021) 406-
2922; (021) 406-3086 *E-mail:* mdewitt@nasou.com
(customer service) *Web Site:* www.nasou-viaafrika.
com, pg 567

Nasou Via Afrika (South Africa) *Tel:* (021) 406-
3314 *Fax:* (021) 406-2922; (021) 406-3086
E-mail: mdewitt@nasou.com (customer service)
Web Site: www.nasou-viaafrika.com, pg 1340

Nassau Public Library (Bahamas) *Tel:* 3224907; 85029,
pg 1492

Wydawnictwo Nasza Ksiegarnia Sp zoo (Poland)
Tel: (022) 643 93 89 *Fax:* (022) 643 70 28, pg 524

Natal Society Library (South Africa) *Tel:* (033) 345
2383 *Fax:* (033) 394 0095 *E-mail:* nsl@futurenet.co.za
Web Site: www.lawlibrary.co.za, pg 1544

Editions Fernand Nathan (France) *Tel:* (01) 45 87
50 00; (0825) 00 11 67 *Fax:* (01) 43 37 53 00
Web Site: www.nathan.fr, pg 176

Nathan International (France) *Tel:* (01) 45 87 50 00
Fax: (01) 45 87 57 57 *Web Site:* www.nathan.fr,
pg 176

National Bookseller (Guyana) *Tel:* (02) 71244 *Fax:* (02)
57309, pg 1314

National Acquisitions Group (United Kingdom)
Tel: (01782) 750462 *Fax:* (01782) 750462
E-mail: nag@btconnect.com *Web Site:* www.nag.org.
uk, pg 1292

National Agency for ISBN (India) *Tel:* (011) 2338-4687
Fax: (011) 2338 7934 *E-mail:* isbn@sb.nic.in, pg 1273

National Archives (Egypt (Arab Republic of Egypt)),
pg 1503

National Archives (Ireland) *Tel:* (01) 4072 300
Fax: (01) 4072 333 *E-mail:* mail@nationalarchives.ie
Web Site: www.nationalarchives.ie, pg 1518

National Archives (Libyan Arab Jamahiriya) *Tel:* (021)
40 166, pg 1525

National Archives of Malaysia (Malaysia) *Tel:* (03)
62010688 *Fax:* (03) 62015679 *E-mail:* query@arkib.
gov.my *Web Site:* arkib.gov.my, pg 1526

National Archives (Trinidad & Tobago) *Tel:* 625-2689
Fax: 625-2689 *E-mail:* natt@tstt.net.tt, pg 1550

National Archives & Library of Ethiopia (Ethiopia)
Tel: (01) 516532 *Fax:* (01) 526411 *E-mail:* nale@
telecom.net.et *Web Site:* www.nale.gov.et, pg 1504

National Archives Division (Thailand) *Tel:* (02) 281
1599; (02) 281 0263; (02) 281 5450 *Fax:* (02) 281
1599; (02) 281 0263; (02) 281 5450, pg 1550

National Archives of Fiji (Fiji) *Tel:* 304 144; 304 228
Fax: 307 066 *Web Site:* www.fiji.gov, pg 1504

National Archives of India (India) *Tel:* (011) 23383436
Fax: (011) 23384127 *E-mail:* archives@ren02.nic.in
Web Site: nationalarchives.nic.in, pg 1516

National Archives of Malawi (Malawi) *Tel:* 525 240; 524
148 *Fax:* 524 148; 525 362 *E-mail:* archives@sdnp.
org.mw *Web Site:* chambo.sdnp.org.mw, pg 1526

National Archives of Namibia (Namibia) *Tel:* (061)
2063874 *Fax:* (061) 2063876 *E-mail:* library@unam.
na *Web Site:* www.unam.na/ilrc/library/archives.html,
pg 1530

National Archives of Nigeria Library (Nigeria) *Tel:* (022).
415000, pg 1533

National Archives of Pakistan (Pakistan) *Tel:* (051) 920
2044 *Fax:* (051) 920 6349 *Web Site:* www.pakistan.
gov.pk, pg 1535

National Archives of Scotland (United Kingdom)
Tel: (0131) 535 1334 *Fax:* (0131) 535 1328
E-mail: publications@nas.gov.uk; enquiries@nas.gov.
uk *Web Site:* www.nas.gov.uk, pg 730

National Archives of Singapore (Singapore) *Tel:* 6332
7909 *Fax:* 3393583 *Web Site:* www.nhb.gov.sg/NAS/
nas.shtml, pg 1542

National Archives of South Africa, Orange Free State
Archives Repository, Library/Free State Provincial
Archives (South Africa) *Tel:* (051) 522 6762
Fax: (051) 522 6765 *E-mail:* fsarch@sac.fs.gov.za
Web Site: www.national.archives.gov.za, pg 1544

National Archives of Zambia (Zambia) *Tel:* (01) 254081
Fax: (01) 254080 *E-mail:* naz@zamnet.zm, pg 1556

National Archives of Zimbabwe (Zimbabwe) *Tel:* (04)
792 741 *Fax:* (04) 792 398 *E-mail:* nat.archives@gta.
gov.zw *Web Site:* www.gta.gov.zw, pg 784

National Archives of Zimbabwe (Zimbabwe) *Tel:* (04)
792741; (04) 792742; (04) 792743 *Fax:* (04) 792398
Web Site: www.gta.gov.zw/NatArchives/home.htm,
pg 1556

National Archives Repository Library (South
Africa) *Tel:* (012) 323 5300 *Fax:* (012) 323 5287
E-mail: enquiries@dac.gov.za *Web Site:* www.national.
archives.gov.za, pg 1544

National Assembly for Wales (United Kingdom)
Tel: (029) 20 825111 *Fax:* (029) 20 825350
E-mail: stats.pubs@wales.gsi.gov.uk *Web Site:* www.
wales.gov.uk, pg 730

National Assembly Library (Republic of Korea) *Tel:* (02)
788-4143 (english service available) *Fax:* (02)
7884301; (02) 7884193 *E-mail:* question@nanet.go.kr
Web Site: www.nanet.go.kr, pg 1524

National Association for the Teaching of English (NATE)
(United Kingdom) *Tel:* (0114) 255 5419 *Fax:* (0114)
255 5296 *E-mail:* info@nate.org.uk *Web Site:* www.
nate.org.uk, pg 730

National Association of Forest Industries Ltd
(Australia) *Tel:* (02) 6285 3833 *Fax:* (02) 6285 3855
E-mail: enquiries@nafi.com.au *Web Site:* www.nafi.
com.au, pg 33

Library of the National Bank (Afghanistan), pg 1489

National Bibliographic Agency (United Republic of
Tanzania) *Tel:* (051) 150048; (051) 110573 *Fax:* (022)
2151100 *E-mail:* tlsb@africaonline.co.tz; library@esrf.
or.tz, pg 1288

National Book Chamber of Belarus (Belarus) *Tel:* (172)
235839 *Fax:* (172) 235825 *E-mail:* palata@palata.
belpak.minsk.by, pg 1262

National Book Foundation (Pakistan) *Tel:* (051)
9261533; (051) 9261534 *Fax:* (051) 2264283; (051)
2264283 *E-mail:* nbf@paknet2.ptc.pk *Web Site:* nbf.
org.pk, pg 513

National Book Organization (India) *Tel:* (011) 6518378
Fax: (011) 6851795 *E-mail:* nbtindia@ndb.vsnl.net.in
Web Site: www.nbtindia.com, pg 342

National Book Store Inc (Philippines) *Tel:* (02)
6318061; (02) 6318062; (02) 6318063; (02)
6318064; (02) 6318065; (02) 6318066 *Fax:* (02)
6318079 *E-mail:* info@nationalbookstore.com.ph
Web Site: www.nationalbookstore.com.ph, pg 519

National Book Store Inc (Philippines) *Tel:* (02) 6318061
Fax: (02) 6318079 *E-mail:* info@nationalbookstore.
com.ph *Web Site:* www.nationalbookstore.com.ph,
pg 1335

National Book Trust India (India) *Tel:* (011)
6518378; (011) 23379868 *Fax:* (011) 6851795
E-mail: nbtindia@ndb.vsnl.net.in *Web Site:* www.
nbtindia.com, pg 342

National Botanical Institute (South Africa) *Tel:* (021)
799 8800 *Fax:* (021) 761 4687 *E-mail:* rpub@nbipre.
nbi.ac.za *Web Site:* www.nbi.ac.za, pg 567

National Central Library (Taiwan, Province of
China) *Tel:* (02) 2361 9132 *Fax:* (02) 382 1489
Web Site: www.ncl.edu.tw, pg 1549

Centre National de la Photographie (France)
Tel: (01) 53 76 12 31 *Fax:* (01) 53 76 12 33
E-mail: centre.national.de.la.photographie@wanadoo.fr
Web Site: www.cnp-photographie.com, pg 176

National Centre for Language & Literacy (United
Kingdom) *Tel:* (0118) 378 8820 *Fax:* (0118) 378 6801
E-mail: ncll@reading.ac.uk *Web Site:* www.ncll.org.
uk, pg 730

National Centre of Archives (Iraq) *Tel:* (01) 416 8440,
pg 1518

National Childbirth Trust Publishing (United Kingdom)
Tel: (01223) 352790 *Fax:* (01223) 460718
E-mail: bpc@bpccam.co.uk *Web Site:* www.bpccam.
co.uk, pg 730

National Children's Educational Foundation (Sri Lanka)
Tel: 578090 *Fax:* 578090, pg 607

National Council for Voluntary Organisations
(NCVO) (United Kingdom) *Tel:* (020) 7713 6161
Fax: (020) 7713 6300 *E-mail:* ncvo@ncvo-vol.org.uk
Web Site: www.ncvo-vol.org.uk, pg 730

National Council of Applied Economic Research, Publications Division (India) *Tel:* (011) 23379861; (011) 23379862; (011) 23379863; (011) 23379865; (011) 23379866; (011) 23379868 *Fax:* (011) 23370164 *E-mail:* infor@ncaer.org *Web Site:* www.ncaer.org, pg 342

National Council of Educational Research & Training, Publication Department (India) *Tel:* (011) 6851070; (011) 662708 *Fax:* (011) 6868419 *E-mail:* crc@giasdlo1.vsnl.net.in *Web Site:* ncert.nic.in, pg 343

Institut National de Recherche Pedagogique INRP (France) *Tel:* (01) 46 34 90 00 *Fax:* (01) 46 54 32 01 *Web Site:* www.inrp.fr, pg 176

Office National d'Edition de Presse et d'Imprimerie (ONEPI) (Benin) *Tel:* 300299; 301152 *Fax:* 303463, pg 75

National Defence Industry Press (China) *Tel:* (010) 68412244; (010) 6842577 *Fax:* (010) 68413125; (010) 68427707 *E-mail:* ndip@public3.bta.net.cn, pg 106

National Diet Library (Japan) *Tel:* (03) 3581-2331 *Fax:* (03) 3508-2934 *E-mail:* kokusai@ndl.go.jp *Web Site:* www.ndl.go.jp, pg 1522

National Extension College (United Kingdom) *Tel:* (01223) 400 200 *Fax:* (01223) 400 399 *E-mail:* info@nec.ac.uk *Web Site:* www.nec.ac.uk, pg 730

National Federation of Retail Newsagents (United Kingdom) *Tel:* (0207) 253 4225 *Fax:* (0207) 250 0927 *Web Site:* www.nfrn.org.uk, pg 1292

National Federation of Standard Editor's Association in Nepal (NAFSEEN) (Nepal) *Tel:* (01) 212289; (01) 223036; (01) 224005 *Fax:* (01) 223036, pg 1278

National Federation of Standard Periodicals Publishers Association of Nepal (Nepal) *Tel:* (01) 212289; (01) 223036; (01) 224005 *Fax:* (01) 223036, pg 1278

National Federation of Standard Translator's Association in Nepal (Nepal) *Tel:* (01) 212289; (01) 223036; (01) 224005 *Fax:* (01) 223036 ISB-ASS, pg 1278

National Foster Care Association (United Kingdom) *Tel:* (020) 7620 6400 *Fax:* (020) 7620 6401 *E-mail:* nfca@fostercare.org.uk, pg 731

National Foundation for Educational Research (United Kingdom) *Tel:* (01753) 574123 *Fax:* (01753) 691632 *E-mail:* enquiries@nfer.ac.uk *Web Site:* www.nfer.ac.uk, pg 731

National Free Library of Zimbabwe (Zimbabwe) *Tel:* (09) 69827; (09) 62359 *Fax:* (09) 77662, pg 1556

National Galleries of Scotland (United Kingdom) *Tel:* (0131) 624 6257; (0131) 624 6261 *Fax:* (0131) 315 2963 *E-mail:* publications@nationalgalleries.org *Web Site:* www.nationalgalleries.org, pg 731

National Gallery of Australia (Australia) *Tel:* (02) 6240 6501; (02) 6240 6502 *Fax:* (06) 6240 6427 *E-mail:* information@nga.gov.au *Web Site:* www.nga.gov.au, pg 33

National Gallery of Victoria (Australia) *Tel:* (03) 8620 2212 *Fax:* (03) 8620 2535 *E-mail:* enquiries@ngv.vic.gov.au *Web Site:* www.ngv.vic.gov.au, pg 33

National Historical Institute (Philippines) *Tel:* (02) 590646; (02) 572644 *Fax:* (02) 5250144, pg 520

National House for Publishing, Distributing & Advertising (Iraq) *Tel:* (01) 4251846, pg 357

National Information & Documentation Centre (NIDOC) (Egypt (Arab Republic of Egypt)) *Tel:* (02) 3371696, pg 1266, 1503

National Institute for Compilation & Translation (Taiwan, Province of China) *Tel:* (02) 33225558 *Fax:* (02) 33225559, pg 1149

National Institute of Adult Continuing Education (NIACE) (United Kingdom) *Tel:* (0116) 204 4200; (0116) 204 4201 *Fax:* (0116) 285-4514 *E-mail:* enquiries@niace.org.uk; niace@niace.org.uk *Web Site:* www.niace.org.uk, pg 731

National Institute of Historical & Cultural Research (Pakistan) *Tel:* (051) 218535, pg 514

National Institute of Industrial Research (NIIR) (India) *Tel:* (011) 3923955; (011) 3935654; (011) 3945886 *Fax:* (011) 3941561 *E-mail:* niir@usnl.com *Web Site:* www.niir.org, pg 343

National Institute of Public Administration Library (Zambia) *Tel:* (01) 228802 *Fax:* (01) 27213, pg 1556

National Institute of Science Communication & Information Resources (NISCAIR) (India) *Tel:* (011) 2650141 *Fax:* (011) 26862228 *E-mail:* webmaster@niscair.res.in *Web Site:* www.niscom.res.in, pg 1148

National ISBN Agency (Bulgaria) *Tel:* (02) 9882811; (02) 9882362 *Fax:* (02) 435495 *E-mail:* nl@nationallibrary.bg *Web Site:* www.nationallibrary.bg, pg 1263

National ISBN Agency (Mauritius) *Tel:* (0230) 4646761; (0230) 4643959; (0230) 4643452 *Fax:* (0230) 4643445 *E-mail:* eoibooks@intnet.mu, pg 1277

National Library (Bangladesh) *Tel:* (02) 9129992; (02) 9112733 *Fax:* (02) 9118704, pg 1261

National Library (Guyana) *Tel:* (02) 227-4053; (02) 227-4052; (02) 226-2690; (02) 227-2699 *Fax:* (02) 227-4053 *E-mail:* natlib@sdnp.org.gy *Web Site:* www.natlib.gov.gy, pg 1513

National Library (Iraq) *Tel:* (01) 416 4190, pg 1518

National Library (Myanmar) *Tel:* (01) 283332; (01) 275997 *Fax:* (01) 212367 *Web Site:* www.myanmar.com/culture/text/P001.htm, pg 1530

National Library (Namibia) *Tel:* (061) 2934203; (061) 2934204 *Fax:* (061) 229808 *E-mail:* postmstr@natlib.mec.gov.na *Web Site:* yaotto.natlib.mec.gov.na, pg 1530

National Library (Thailand) *Tel:* (02) 2810263; (02) 2815999; (02) 2815450 *Fax:* (02) 2810263; (02) 2815999; (02) 2815450 *E-mail:* suwaksin@emisc.moe.go.th *Web Site:* www.ifla.org/VI/2/p2/natlibs.htm#T, pg 1288

National Library (United Arab Emirates) *Tel:* 6215300 *Fax:* 6336059 *Web Site:* www.cultural.org.ae/E/library.htm, pg 1552

National Library & Documentation Centre (Sri Lanka) *Tel:* (01) 685198; (01) 685199; (01) 698847; (01) 685197 *Fax:* (01) 685201 *E-mail:* natlib@sltnet.lk *Web Site:* www.natlib.lk, pg 607

National Library & Documentation Centre (Sri Lanka) *Tel:* (01) 6852003; (01) 685199; (01) 698847 *Fax:* (01) 685201 *E-mail:* natlib@sltnet.lk *Web Site:* www.natlib.lk, pg 1546

National Library & Documentation Services Board (NLDSB) (Sri Lanka) *Tel:* (01) 698847 *Fax:* (01) 685201 *E-mail:* nldsb@mail.natlib.lk *Web Site:* www.natlib.lk, pg 1570

National Library & Information System Authority (NALIS) (Trinidad & Tobago) *Tel:* (0868) 623-6962; (0868) 624-4466 *Fax:* (0868) 625-6096 *E-mail:* nalis@nalis.gov.tt *Web Site:* www.nalis.gov.tt, pg 1550

National Library for the Blind (United Kingdom) *Tel:* (0161) 355 2000 *Fax:* (0161) 355 2098 *E-mail:* enquiries@nlbuk.org *Web Site:* www.nlb-online.org, pg 1553

The National Library, Government of India (India) *Tel:* (033) 2479 1381; (033) 2479 1384 *Fax:* (033) 2479 1462 *E-mail:* nldirector@rediffmail.com; nldirector@nlindia.org *Web Site:* www.nlindia.org, pg 1516

The National Library of the Islamic Republic of Iran (Islamic Republic of Iran) *Tel:* (021) 2288680 *Fax:* (021) 8088950 *E-mail:* natlibir@neda.net *Web Site:* www.nli.ir, pg 1517

National Library 'Ivan Vazov' (Bulgaria) *Tel:* (032) 62 29 15; (032) 62 50 46 *Fax:* (032) 62 47 25 *E-mail:* nbiv@plovdiv.techno-link.com *Web Site:* fobos.primasoft.bg/libplovdiv, pg 1496

National Library of Australia (Australia) *Tel:* (02) 6262 1111 *Fax:* (02) 6257 1703 *E-mail:* www@nla.gov.au *Web Site:* www.nla.gov.au, pg 33, 1557

National Library of Belarus (Belarus) *Tel:* (017) 227-54-63 *Fax:* (017) 229-24-94 *E-mail:* sol@nacbibl.minsk.by *Web Site:* kolas.bas-net.by/bla/nb.htm, pg 1493

The National Library of China (China) *Tel:* (010) 68415566 *Fax:* (010) 68419271 *E-mail:* webmaster@publicf.nlc.gov.cn *Web Site:* www.nlc.gov.cn, pg 1498

National Library of Greece (Greece) *Tel:* (0210) 3382566 *Fax:* (0210) 3382502 *Web Site:* www.nlg.gr, pg 1513

National Library of Ireland (Ireland) *Tel:* (01) 603 02 00 *Fax:* (01) 6766690 *E-mail:* info@nli.ie *Web Site:* www.nli.ie, pg 362

National Library of Ireland (Ireland) *Tel:* (01) 6030200 *Fax:* (01) 6766690 *E-mail:* info@nli.ie *Web Site:* www.nli.ie, pg 1518

National Library of Ireland Society (Ireland) *Tel:* (01) 603 02 00 *Fax:* (01) 676 66 90 *E-mail:* info@nli.ie *Web Site:* www.nli.ie, pg 1565

National Library of Izmir (Turkey) *Tel:* (0232) 4842002 *Fax:* (0232) 4821703, pg 1551

National Library of Jamaica (Jamaica) *Tel:* (876) 967-1526; (876) 967-2516; (876) 967-2494; (876) 967-2496 *Fax:* (876) 922-5567 *E-mail:* nlj@infochan.com *Web Site:* www.nlj.org.jm, pg 1521

The National Library of Korea (Republic of Korea) *Tel:* (02) 590-0513; (02) 590-0514 *Fax:* (02) 590-0608 *E-mail:* yeolram@www.nl.go.kr *Web Site:* www.nl.go.kr, pg 1524

National Library of Kuwait (Kuwait) *Tel:* 2415192 *Fax:* 2415195 *E-mail:* nccalknl@ncc.moc.kw, pg 1524

National Library of Latvia (Latvia) *Tel:* 7289 874 *Fax:* 7280 851 *E-mail:* lnb@lnb.lv *Web Site:* www.lnb.lv, pg 1524

National Library of Libya (Libyan Arab Jamahiriya) *Tel:* (061) 9097074 *Fax:* (061) 9097073 *E-mail:* nat_lib_libya@hotmail.com *Web Site:* www.nll.8m.com, pg 1525

National Library of Malaysia (Gift & Exchange Unit) (Malaysia) *Tel:* (03) 26871700 *Fax:* (03) 26927082 *E-mail:* pnmweb@www1.pnm.my *Web Site:* www.pnm.my, pg 1527

National Library of Malta (Malta) *Tel:* 21243297; 21236585; 21232691; 21245303 *Fax:* 21235992 *E-mail:* customercare.nlm@gov.mt *Web Site:* www.libraries-archives.gov.mt, pg 1527

National Library of New Zealand (Te Puna Matauranga o Aotearoa) (New Zealand) *Tel:* (04) 474 3000 *Fax:* (04) 474 3035 *E-mail:* information@natlib.govt.nz; reference@natlib.govt.nz *Web Site:* www.natlib.govt.nz, pg 1532

National Library of Nigeria-Research & Development Dept (Nigeria) *Tel:* (09) 2646773; (09) 2346774 *Fax:* (09) 2646772 *E-mail:* info@nlbn.org *Web Site:* www.nlbn.org, pg 1533

National Library of Pakistan (Pakistan) *Tel:* (051) 9214523; (051) 92026436; (051) 9206440 *Fax:* (051) 9221375 *E-mail:* nlpiba@isb.paknet.com.pk *Web Site:* www.nlp.gov.pk, pg 1535

National Library of Scotland (United Kingdom) *Tel:* (0131) 226 4531 *Fax:* (0131) 622 4803 *E-mail:* enquiries@nls.uk *Web Site:* www.nls.uk, pg 731, 1553

National Library of Somalia (Somalia) *Tel:* (01) 227 58, pg 1543

National Library of South Africa (South Africa) *Tel:* (012) 321 8931 *Fax:* (012) 325 5984 *E-mail:* andrew.malotle@nlsa.ac.za *Web Site:* www.nlsa.ac.za, pg 1544

National Library of South Africa (South Africa) *Tel:* (021) 424 6320 *Fax:* (021) 423 3359 *E-mail:* macmahon@salib.ac.za *Web Site:* www.nlsa.ac.za, pg 1544

The National Library of Thailand (Thailand) *Tel:* (02) 2810263; (02) 281 5999; (02) 281 5450 *Fax:* (02) 281 0263; (02) 281 5999; (02) 282 5450 *E-mail:* suwaksir@emisc.moe.go.th, pg 1550

National Library of the Philippines (Philippines) *Tel:* (02) 525-3196 (Filipiniana); (02) 582271 (Reference); (02) 582660 (Public Documents); (02) 525-1748 *Fax:* (02) 524-2329 *E-mail:* amb@nlp.gov.ph *Web Site:* www.nlp.gov.ph, pg 1536

National Library of Turkmenistan (Turkmenistan) *Tel:* (07) 3632 25 3254 *Fax:* (012) 257 481, pg 1551

National Library of Uganda (Uganda) *Tel:* (041) 233633 *Fax:* (041) 348625 *E-mail:* library@imul.com, pg 1552

National Library of Vietnam (Viet Nam) *Tel:* (04) 8248051 *Fax:* (04) 8253357 *E-mail:* info@nlv.gov.vn *Web Site:* www.nlv.gov.vn, pg 1555

National Library of Wales (United Kingdom) *Tel:* (01970) 632 800 *Fax:* (01970) 615 709 *E-mail:* holi@llgc.org.uk *Web Site:* www.llgc.org.uk, pg 731, 1553

National Library Service (Barbados) *Tel:* (0809) 436 6081; (0809) 426 1744; (0809) 426 3981 *Fax:* (0809) 436 1501 *E-mail:* natlib@caribsurf.com, pg 1493

National Library Service (Botswana) *Tel:* 352288; 352397 *Fax:* 301149 *E-mail:* vmaje@gov.bw, pg 76

National Library Service of Belize (Belize) *Tel:* (02) 34248; (02) 34249 *Fax:* (02) 34246 *E-mail:* nls@btl.net; leolibrary2003@yahoo.com *Web Site:* www.nlsbze.bz, pg 1494

National Museum (India) *Tel:* (011) 3018415; (011) 3019272; (011) 3019237 *E-mail:* rdchoudh@ndf.vsnl.net.in *Web Site:* www.nationalmuseumindia.org, pg 343

National Museum & Gallery (United Kingdom) *Tel:* (029) 2039 7951 *Fax:* (029) 2037 3219 *E-mail:* post@nmgw.ac.uk *Web Site:* www.nmgw.ac.uk, pg 731

National Museum Library of Sri Lanka (NMLSL) (Sri Lanka) *Tel:* (01) 692092 *Fax:* (01) 695366 *E-mail:* cnmid@sltnet.lk *Web Site:* www.mca.gov.lk, pg 1546

National Museum of History (Taiwan, Province of China) *Tel:* (02) 3610270-514 *Fax:* (02) 3610171, pg 641

National Museum of the Philippines (Philippines) *Tel:* (02) 5271275 *Fax:* (02) 5270306 *E-mail:* nmuseum@i-next.net *Web Site:* members.tripod.com/philmuseum/index; nmuseum.tripod.com/index.htm, pg 520

Department of National Museums (Sri Lanka) *Tel:* (01) 595366 *Fax:* (01) 595366, pg 607

National Palace Museum (Taiwan, Province of China) *Tel:* (02) 8821230 *Fax:* (02) 8821440 *E-mail:* service@npm.gov.tw *Web Site:* www.npm.gov.tw, pg 641

National Portrait Gallery Publications (United Kingdom) *Tel:* (020) 7306 0055 (ext 266); (020) 7312 2482 *Fax:* (020) 7306 0092 *Web Site:* www.npg.org.uk, pg 731

National Public Health Laboratory Services (Medical Department) (Kenya) *Tel:* (02) 717077 *E-mail:* healthmin@nbnet.co.ke *Web Site:* www.ministryofhealth.go.ke, pg 1523

National Publishing House (India) *Tel:* (011) 3274161; (011) 3275267, pg 343

National Records Office Library (Sudan) *Tel:* (011) 784135; (011) 784255 *Fax:* (011) 778 603, pg 1546

National Research Institute of Papua New Guinea (Papua New Guinea) *Tel:* 326 0061; 326 0079; 326 0083 *Fax:* 326 0213 *E-mail:* nri@global.net.pg *Web Site:* www.nri.org.pg, pg 515

National Scientific & Technical Information Center (NSTIC) (Kuwait) *Tel:* 4836100; 4818630 *Fax:* 4830643 *E-mail:* public_relations@safat.kisr.edu.kw *Web Site:* www.kisr.edu.kw, pg 1524

National Standards Publisher's & Bookseller's Association Nepal (NASPUBAN) (Nepal) *Tel:* (01) 212289; (01) 223036; (01) 224005 *Fax:* (01) 223036, pg 1328

National Standards Wholesaler's Distributor's & Subscriber's Association of Nepal (NASWDISAN) (Nepal) *Tel:* (01) 212289; (01) 223036; (01) 224005 *Fax:* (01) 223036, pg 1278

National Taiwan University Library (Taiwan, Province of China) *Tel:* (02) 3366-2326 *E-mail:* tul@ntu.edu.tw *Web Site:* www.lib.ntu.edu.tw, pg 1549

Library of the National Technological University of Athens (Greece) *Tel:* (0210) 772 1471 *Fax:* (0210) 772 1565 *E-mail:* pstath@softlab.ntua.gr *Web Site:* www.lib.ntua.gr, pg 1513

National Trust (United Kingdom) *Tel:* (0870) 609 5380 *Fax:* (020) 7222 5097 *Web Site:* www.nationaltrust.org.uk, pg 731

National Union of Journalists (Book Branch) (United Kingdom) *Tel:* (020) 7278 7916 *Fax:* (020) 7873 8143 *E-mail:* book_branch@hotmail.com *Web Site:* www.nujbook.org, pg 1292

National University of Ireland Galway (NUI, Galway) (Ireland) *Tel:* (091) 524809 *Fax:* (091) 522394 *Web Site:* www.nuigalway.ie, pg 1518

National University of Lesotho Library (Lesotho) *Tel:* 340601 *Fax:* 340000 *Web Site:* www.nul.ls/library, pg 1525

National University of Malaysia Library (Malaysia) *Tel:* (03) 8921 3370; (03) 8921 5057 *Fax:* (03) 8925 4890 *E-mail:* puspa@pkrisc.cc.ukm.my *Web Site:* www.ukm.my, pg 1527

National University of Singapore Library (Singapore) *Tel:* 6874-2028 *Fax:* 6777-3571 *E-mail:* clbsec@nus.edu.sg *Web Site:* www.lib.nus.edu.sg, pg 1542

National War College Library (Taiwan, Province of China) *Tel:* (02) 3619132 *Fax:* (02) 3110155, pg 1549

National Youth Agency (United Kingdom) *Tel:* (0116) 285 3700 *Fax:* (0116) 285 3777 *E-mail:* nya@nya.org.uk *Web Site:* www.nya.co.uk, pg 731

Bibliotheque Nationale (Laos People's Democratic Republic) *Tel:* (021) 212 452 *Fax:* (021) 212 408, pg 1524

Bibliotheque Nationale Populaire (Congo) *Tel:* 833485, pg 1499

Archives Nationales d'Algerie (Algeria) *Tel:* (02) 54-21-60 *Fax:* (02) 54-16-16 *Web Site:* www.archives-dgan.gov.dz, pg 1489

Archives Nationales de Madagascar (Madagascar) *Tel:* (020) 22 235 34 *E-mail:* rijandriamihamina@malagasy.com, pg 1526

Archives Nationales du Grand-Duche de luxembourg (Luxembourg) *Tel:* 4786660; 4786661 *Fax:* 474692 *E-mail:* archives.nationales@an.etat.lu *Web Site:* www.etat.lu, pg 1525

The Nationalities Publishing House (China) *Tel:* (010) 64212794; (010) 64212031, pg 106

Natoli Stefan & Oliva Literary Agency (Italy) *Tel:* (02) 70 00 16 45 *Fax:* (02) 741277 *E-mail:* natoli.oliva@tiscalinet.it, pg 1133

Natraj Prakashan, Publishers & Exporters (India), pg 343

Verlag Natur & Wissenschaft Harro Hieronimus & Dr Jurgen Schmidt (Germany) *Tel:* (0212) 819878 *Fax:* (0212) 816216 *E-mail:* info@verlagnw.de, pg 263

Bokfoerlaget Natur och Kultur (Sweden) *Tel:* (08) 4538600 *Fax:* (08) 4538790 *E-mail:* info@nok.se *Web Site:* www.nok.se, pg 613

Natur och Kultur Fakta etc (Sweden) *Tel:* (08) 4538725 *Fax:* (08) 4538798 *E-mail:* info@nok.se *Web Site:* www.nok.se, pg 614

Bokklubben Natur og Kultur (Norway) *Tel:* 22985600 *Fax:* 22985630, pg 1255

Natura-Verlag Arlesheim (Switzerland) *Tel:* (061) 717111 *Fax:* (061) 7064201, pg 629

The Natural History Museum Library (United Kingdom) *Tel:* (020) 7942 5011 *Fax:* (020) 7942 5559 *E-mail:* genlib@nhm.ac.uk *Web Site:* www.nhm.ac.uk/library, pg 1553

Natural Resources Development College Library (Zambia) *Tel:* (01) 224610 *Fax:* (01) 224639, pg 1556

NaturaViva Verlags GmbH (Germany) *Tel:* (07033) 529830 *Fax:* (07033) 529831 *E-mail:* naturaviva@t-online.de, pg 263

Naturegraph Publishers Inc (United States) *Tel:* 530-493-5353 *Toll Free Tel:* 800-390-5353 *Fax:* 530-493-5240 *E-mail:* nature@sisqtel.net *Web Site:* www.naturegraph.com, pg 1231

Nauchnaya biblioteka im M Gor'kogo Sankt-Peterburgskogo (Russian Federation) *Tel:* (0812) 328-27-41; (0812) 328-95-46 *Fax:* (0812) 328-27-41 *E-mail:* info@mail.lib.pu.ru *Web Site:* www.lib.pu.ru, pg 1540

Naucna Knjiga (Serbia and Montenegro) *Tel:* (011) 635 819; (011) 637 868; (011) 637 230 *Fax:* (011) 638 070, pg 552

Naufal Group Sarl (Lebanon) *Tel:* 354394 *Fax:* 354898, pg 447

Nauka Ltd (Japan) *Tel:* (03) 3981-5261 *Fax:* (03) 3981-5361 *E-mail:* tokyo@nauka.co.jp *Web Site:* www.nauka.co.jp, pg 1322

Nauka Publishers (Russian Federation) *Tel:* (095) 3347151 *Fax:* (095) 4202220 *E-mail:* nauka@naukaran.ru *Web Site:* www.maik.rssi.ru, pg 547

Naukova Dumka Publishers (Ukraine) *Tel:* (044) 2244068; (044) 2251042; (044) 2254170 *Fax:* (044) 2247060 *E-mail:* ndumka@ukrpost.net, pg 653

Wydawnictwa Naukowo-Techniczne (Poland) *Tel:* (022) 826-72-71 *Fax:* (022) 826-86-20 *E-mail:* wnt@pol.pl *Web Site:* www.wnt.com.pl, pg 524

Naumann & Goebel Verlagsgesellschaft mbH (Germany) *Tel:* (02236) 39990 *Fax:* (02236) 399997 *E-mail:* einstieg@aol.com; fdvemag@netcologne.de, pg 263

Ediciones Nauta Credito SA (Spain) *Tel:* (093) 4392204 *Fax:* (093) 4107314, pg 593

Edition Nautilus Verlag (Germany) *Tel:* (040) 7213536 *Fax:* (040) 7218399 *E-mail:* edition-nautilus@t-online.de *Web Site:* www.edition-nautilus.de, pg 263

Nautiska Foerlaget AB (Sweden) *Tel:* (08) 677 00 00 *Fax:* (08) 677 00 10 *E-mail:* nautiska.ab@nautiskamf.se, pg 614

Nauwelaerts Edition SA (Belgium) *Tel:* (010) 86 67 37 *Fax:* (010) 86 16 55, pg 71

Nava (Czech Republic) *Tel:* (019) 7235633; (019) 7235721; (019) 7223294; (019) 7223251; (019) 7235509 *Fax:* (019) 223143, pg 126

Navajivan Trust (India) *Tel:* (079) 27541329; (079) 27542634; (079) 27540635 *Fax:* (079) 27541329 *Web Site:* www.navajivantrust.org, pg 343

Navakarnataka Publications (P) Ltd (India) *Tel:* (080) 22203580; (080) 22203581; (080) 22203582 *Fax:* (080) 22203582 *E-mail:* nkp@bgl.vsnl.net.in *Web Site:* www.navakarnatakabooks.com, pg 1317

Instituto de Publicaciones Navales (Argentina) *Tel:* (011) 4311-0042; (011) 4311-0043 *E-mail:* ipn@web-mail.com.ar; ipn@fibertel.com.ar *Web Site:* www.centronaval.org.ar, pg 8

Navarine Publishing (Australia) *Tel:* (02) 62824602, pg 33

Navarra, Comunidad Autonoma, Servicio de Prensa, Publica Pamplona (Spain) *Tel:* (0948) 427121 *Fax:* (0948) 427123 *E-mail:* fpubli01@cfnavarra.es *Web Site:* www.cfnavarra.es/publicaciones, pg 593

Naves Internacional de Ediciones SA (Mexico) *Tel:* (05) 6690595; (05) 9180055595 *Fax:* (05) 6823728 *E-mail:* niesa@mpsnet.com.mx, pg 469

Navrang Booksellers & Publishers (India) *Tel:* (011) 5835914; (011) 5836197 *Fax:* (011) 5836113; (011) 5836761 *E-mail:* navrang@del2.vsn.net.in, pg 343

Navyug Publishers (India) *Tel:* (011) 278370, pg 343

Naya Prokash (India) *Tel:* 349566 *Fax:* (033) 5523366; (033) 5524053, pg 343

Nayiri Bookshop (Islamic Republic of Iran) *Tel:* (021) 677578; (021) 7536802; (021) 7537029 *Fax:* (021) 677578, pg 1318

Accademia Naz dei Lincei (Italy) *Tel:* (06) 680271 *Fax:* (06) 6893616 *E-mail:* pugwash@iol.it, pg 400

Istituto Nazionale di Studi Romani (Italy) *Tel:* (06) 5743442; (06) 5743445 *Fax:* (06) 5743447 *E-mail:* studiromani@studiromani.it *Web Site:* www.studiromani.it, pg 400

NBLC Vereniging van Openbare Bibliotheken (Netherlands) *Tel:* (070) 30 90 100 *Fax:* (070) 30 90 200 *E-mail:* info@debibliotheken.nl *Web Site:* www.debibliotheken.nl, pg 1568

NBN Plymbridge (United Kingdom) *Tel:* (01752) 202300 *Fax:* (01752) 202330 *E-mail:* enquiries@plymbridge.com; orders@plymbridge.com *Web Site:* www.plymbridge.com, pg 1352

Ndanda Mission Press (United Republic of Tanzania) *Fax:* (682) 623 730; (059) 510 410, pg 644

Ndola Public Library (Zambia) *Tel:* 617173, pg 1556

NDV Neue Darmstadter Verlagsanstalt (Germany) *Tel:* (02224) 3232 *Fax:* (02224) 78639 *E-mail:* ndv@ndv.info *Web Site:* www.ndv-verlag.de, pg 263

Ed Nea Acropolis (Greece) *Tel:* (01) 8231301 *Fax:* (01) 8810830, pg 310

Nea Synora Publications (Greece) *Tel:* (01) 3610589; (01) 3600398 *Fax:* (01) 3617791 *E-mail:* neasynora@otenet.gr *Web Site:* www.nea-synora.gr, pg 310

Nea Thesis - Evrotas (Greece) *Tel:* (01) 3643932 *Fax:* (01) 3617592, pg 310

Nebel Verlag GmbH (Germany) *Tel:* (08806) 9215-0 *Fax:* (08806) 9215-22, pg 263

Nebelspalter-Verlag (Switzerland) *Tel:* (071) 8440444 *Fax:* (071) 8440445, pg 629

Neckar Verlag GmbH (Germany) *Tel:* (07721) 89 87-0 *Fax:* (07721) 89 87-50 *E-mail:* service@neckar-verlag.de *Web Site:* www.neckar-verlag.de, pg 263

Nederlands Bureau voor Bibliotheekwezen en Informatieverzorging (NBBI) (Netherlands) *Tel:* (070) 3607833 *Fax:* (070) 3615011 *Web Site:* www.stb.tno.nl, pg 1568

Nederlands Instituut voor Wetenschappelijke Informatiediensten (Netherlands) *Tel:* (020) 4628600 *Fax:* (020) 6658013 *E-mail:* info@niwi.knaw.nl *Web Site:* www.niwi.knaw.nl, pg 1531

Nederlands Literair Produktie-en Vertalingen Fonds (NLPVF) (Netherlands) *Tel:* (020) 620 62 61 *Fax:* (020) 620 71 79 *E-mail:* office@nlpvf.nl *Web Site:* www.nlpvf.nl, pg 486

Nederlands Uitgeversverbond (Netherlands) *Tel:* (020) 43 09 150 *Fax:* (020) 43 09 179 *E-mail:* info@nuv.nl *Web Site:* www.nuv.nl; www.uitgeversverbond.nl, pg 1279

Nederlandsche Vereeniging van Antiquaren (Netherlands) *Tel:* (030) 231 92 86 *Fax:* (030) 234 33 62 *E-mail:* bestboek@wxs.nl *Web Site:* www.nvva.nl, pg 1279

Nederlandsche Vereeniging voor Druk- en Boekkunst (Netherlands) *Tel:* (071) 5809634, pg 1279

Nederlandse Boekenclub (Netherlands) *Tel:* (03473) 6 11 22 *Fax:* (03473) 79380 *E-mail:* service@nbc-club.nl *Web Site:* www.nbc-club.nl, pg 1254

Nederlandse Boekverkopersbond (Netherlands) *Tel:* (030) 228 79 56 *Fax:* (030) 228 45 66 *E-mail:* nbb@boekbond.nl *Web Site:* www.boekbond.nl, pg 1279

Nederlandse Lezerskring Boek en Plaat BV (Netherlands) *Tel:* (03473) 79214 *Fax:* (03473) 79380, pg 1254

Nederlandse Vereniging voor beroepsbeoefenaren in de bibliotheeck-informatie-en kennissector (NVB) (Netherlands) *Tel:* (030) 2311263 *Fax:* (030) 2311830 *E-mail:* nvbinfo@wxs.nl *Web Site:* www.nvb-online.nl, pg 1568

Izdatelstvo Nedra (Russian Federation) *Tel:* (095) 2505255 *Fax:* (095) 2502772, pg 547

Neeta Prakashan (India) *Tel:* (011) 692013 *Fax:* (011) 4636011 *E-mail:* neeta@giasdl01.vsnl.net.in, pg 343

Paul Neff Verlag KG (Austria) *Tel:* (01) 94061115 *Fax:* (01) 947641288, pg 54

Negotiate Ltd (United Kingdom) *Tel:* (0131) 445 7571; (0131) 477 7858 *Fax:* (0131) 445 7572 *E-mail:* florence@negweb.com *Web Site:* www.negotiate.co.uk, pg 732

Negotiate Ltd (United Kingdom) *Tel:* (0131) 445 7571; (0131) 477 7858 *Fax:* (0131) 445 7572 *E-mail:* gavin@negotiate.demon.co.uk *Web Site:* www.negotiate.co.uk, pg 1142

Nehanda Publishers (Zimbabwe) *Tel:* (04) 734415; (04) 727077 *Fax:* (04) 734415 *E-mail:* lenneiye@mweb.co.zw, pg 784

Nehora Press (Israel) *Tel:* (04) 6970255 *Fax:* (04) 6970255 *E-mail:* nehora@canaan.co.il *Web Site:* www.nehorapress.com, pg 371

Nehru Memorial Museum & Library (NMML) (India) *Tel:* (011) 23017587 *Fax:* (011) 23015026, pg 1516

Neil Wilson Publishing Ltd (United Kingdom) *Tel:* (0141) 221 1117 *Fax:* (0141) 221 5363 *E-mail:* info@nwp.co.uk *Web Site:* www.nwp.co.uk, pg 732

Uitgeverij H Nelissen BV (Netherlands) *Tel:* (035) 5412386 *Fax:* (035) 5423877 *E-mail:* info@nelissen.nl *Web Site:* www.nelissen.nl, pg 486

Nelles Verlag GmbH (Germany) *Tel:* (089) 357 19 40 *Fax:* (089) 357 19 430 *E-mail:* info@nelles-verlag.de *Web Site:* www.nelles-verlag.de, pg 263

Nelson Memorial Public Library (Samoa) *Tel:* (0685) 21028 *Fax:* (0685) 21028 *Web Site:* www.samoa.com, pg 1541

Nelson Price Milburn Ltd (New Zealand) *Tel:* (04) 5687179 *Fax:* (04) 5682115 *Web Site:* www.thomsonlearning.com.au/primary, pg 499

Thomas Nelson (Nigeria) Ltd (Nigeria) *Tel:* (01) 961452, pg 505

Nelson Thornes Ltd (United Kingdom) *Tel:* (01242) 267100; (01242) 267311 *Fax:* (01242) 267311 *E-mail:* export@nelsonthornes.com *Web Site:* www.nelsonthornes.com, pg 732

Nem Chand & Brothers (India) *Tel:* (01332) 72258; (01332) 72752; (01332) 74343 *Fax:* (01332) 73258, pg 343

Nemira Verlag (Romania) *Tel:* (01) 2242156 *Fax:* (01) 2241600 *E-mail:* editura@nemira.ro, pg 541

Nemzeti Tankoenyvkiado (Hungary) *Tel:* (01) 460-1800 *Fax:* (01) 460-1862 *E-mail:* public@ntk.hu *Web Site:* www.ntk.hu, pg 323

Nemzetkozi Szinhazi Intezet Magyar Kozpontja (Hungary) *Tel:* (01) 1752372 *Fax:* (01) 1751184, pg 323

Nensho-Sha (Japan) *Tel:* (06) 6771-9223 *Fax:* (06) 6771-9424, pg 423

Nepal Library Association (Nepal) *Tel:* (01) 331316 *Fax:* (01) 483720, pg 1568

Nepal National Library (Nepal) *Tel:* (01) 521132 *Web Site:* www.natlib.gov.np, pg 1530

Neptun-Verlag (Switzerland) *Tel:* (072) 727262 *E-mail:* neptun@bluewin.ch *Web Site:* www.neptunart.ch, pg 629

Editorial Nerea SA (Spain) *Tel:* (0943) 432227 *Fax:* (0943) 433379 *E-mail:* nerea@nerea.net, pg 593

NES Arnold Ltd (United Kingdom) *Tel:* (0845) 120 4525 *Fax:* (0800) 328 0001 *E-mail:* enquiries@nesarnold.co.uk *Web Site:* www.nesarnold.co.uk, pg 1164

Nestegg Books (New Zealand) *Tel:* (04) 3836645, pg 499

Net World Vision GmbH (Germany) *Tel:* (089) 290 88 0 *Fax:* (089) 290 88 160, pg 263

Neue Dimension Buch und Musikverlag (Germany), pg 264

Neue Erde Verlags GmbH (Germany) *Tel:* (0681) 372313 *Fax:* (0681) 3904102 *E-mail:* info@neueerde.de, pg 264

Verlag Neue Kritik KG (Germany) *Tel:* (069) 727576 *Fax:* (069) 726585 *E-mail:* neuekritik@compuserve.com, pg 264

Verlag Neue Musik GmbH (Germany) *Tel:* (030) 616981-0 *Fax:* (030) 616981-21 *E-mail:* vnm@verlag-neue-musik.de *Web Site:* www.verlag-neue-musik.de, pg 264

Verlag Neue Musikzeitung GmbH (Germany) *Tel:* (0941) 94 59 30 *Fax:* (0941) 94 59 350 *E-mail:* nmz@nmz.de *Web Site:* www.nmz.de, pg 264

Verlag Neue Stadt GmbH (Germany) *Tel:* (08093) 2091 *Fax:* (08093) 2096, pg 264

Verlag Neue Wirtschafts-Briefe GmbH & Co (Germany) *Tel:* (02323) 141-900 *Fax:* (02323) 141-123 *E-mail:* info@nwb.de *Web Site:* www.nwb.de, pg 264

Neue Zuercher Zeitung AG Buchverlag (Switzerland) *Tel:* (01) 2581505 *Fax:* (01) 2581399 *E-mail:* buch.bestellung@nzz.ch *Web Site:* www.nzz-buchverlag.ch, pg 629

Neuer Honos Verlag GmbH (Germany) *Tel:* (0221) 3 36 20-0 *Fax:* (0221) 3 36 20-99 *E-mail:* nhonos@netcologne.de, pg 264

Neuer ISP Verlag GmbH (Germany) *Tel:* (0721) 31 183 *Fax:* (0721) 31 250 *E-mail:* alive@sterneck.net *Web Site:* www.sterneck.net/alive/isp, pg 264

Verlag Neuer Weg (Germany) *Tel:* (0201) 2 59 15 *Fax:* (0201) 61 444 62 *E-mail:* neuerweg@neuerweg.de *Web Site:* www.neuerweg.de, pg 264

Verlag Neues Leben GmbH (Germany) *Tel:* (030) 2827148; (020) 2827020 *Fax:* (030) 28388075, pg 264

Verlag Neues Leben (Austria) *Tel:* (05579) 31 96, pg 54

Neues Literaturkontor (Germany) *Tel:* (0251) 45343 *Fax:* (0251) 40565 *E-mail:* neues-literaturkontor@t-online.de *Web Site:* www.neues-literaturkontor.de, pg 264

Edition Neues Marchen (Austria) *Tel:* (03184) 2417 *Fax:* (03183) 7400, pg 54

Neufeld-Verlag und Galerie (Austria) *Tel:* (05577) 46 57, pg 54

Wolfgang Neugebauer Verlag GmbH (Austria) *Tel:* (05522) 747 70 *Fax:* (05522) 747 70 *E-mail:* wnverlag@utanet.at, pg 54

Neuland-Verlagsgesellschaft mbH (Germany) *Tel:* (04152) 8 13 42 *Fax:* (04152) 8 13 43 *E-mail:* vertrieb@neuland.com *Web Site:* www.neuland.com, pg 264

Verlag J Neumann-Neudamm GmbH & Co KG (Germany) *Tel:* (05661) 52222 *Fax:* (05661) 6008 *E-mail:* info@neumann-neudamm.de *Web Site:* www.neumann-neudamm.de, pg 264

Neumann Verlag (Germany) *Tel:* (0711) 4507-0 *Fax:* (0711) 4507-240, pg 264

Verlag fuer Messepublikationen Thomas Neureuter KG (Germany) *Tel:* (089) 99 30 91-0 *Fax:* (089) 93 78 96 *E-mail:* info@neureuter.de *Web Site:* www.neureuter.de, pg 265

Neuthor - Verlag (Germany) *Tel:* (06061) 40 79 *Fax:* (06061) 26 46 *Web Site:* www.neuthor-verlag.de, pg 265

Dr Waltraud Neuwirth Selbstverlag (Austria) *Tel:* (01) 3207323 *Fax:* (01) 3200225 *E-mail:* waltraud.neuwith@eunet.at, pg 54

New Africa Books (Pty) Ltd (South Africa) *Tel:* (021) 67441387 *Fax:* (021) 6742920 *E-mail:* newafrica@nacp.co.za; orders@dpp.co.za (ordering) *Web Site:* www.nacp.co.za, pg 567

New Africa Publishing Company Ltd (Nigeria) *Tel:* (083) 231891, pg 505

New Aqua Press (Indonesia) *Tel:* (021) 4897566, pg 356

New Arts Graphic Reproduction Co Ltd (Hong Kong) *Tel:* 25641323; 25618161 *Fax:* 25658262 *E-mail:* newarts@writeme.com, pg 1178

New Books/Connolly Books (Ireland) *Tel:* (01) 6711943 *Fax:* (01) 6711943, pg 362

The New Bookshop (Sudan) *Tel:* (011) 774425, pg 1343

New Cavendish Books (United Kingdom) *Tel:* (020) 7229 6765 *Fax:* (020) 7792 0027 *E-mail:* sales@cavbooks.demon.co.uk *Web Site:* www.newcavendishbooks.co.uk, pg 732

New Creation Publications Ministries & Resource Centre (Australia) *Tel:* (08) 8270 1497; (08) 8270 1861 *Fax:* (08) 8270 4003 *E-mail:* ministry@newcreation.org.au *Web Site:* www.newcreation.org.au, pg 33

New Day Publishers (Philippines) *Tel:* (02) 9988046; (02) 9275982 *Fax:* (02) 9246544 *E-mail:* newday@pworld.net.ph; newdayorders@edsamail.com.ph, pg 520

New Day Readers Circle (South Africa) *Tel:* (021) 421 5540 *Fax:* (021) 419 1865 *E-mail:* luxverbi.publ@kingsley.co.za, pg 1255

New Endeavour Press (Australia) *Tel:* (02) 3182384 *Fax:* (02) 3103613, pg 33

New Era Publications Australia Pty Ltd (Australia) *Tel:* (02) 9211 0692 *Fax:* (02) 9211 0686 *E-mail:* books@newerapublications.com *Web Site:* www.newerapublications.com, pg 33

New Era Publications Deutschland GmbH (Germany) *Tel:* (04105) 68330 *Fax:* (04150) 683322 *E-mail:* buch@newerapublications.de *Web Site:* www.newerapublications.com, pg 265

New Era Publications International ApS (Denmark) *Tel:* 33736666 *Fax:* 33736633 *E-mail:* books@newerapublications.com *Web Site:* www.newerapublications.com, pg 133

New Era Publications UK Ltd (United Kingdom) *Tel:* (01342) 314 846 *Fax:* (01342) 314 857 *E-mail:* books@newerapublications.com *Web Site:* www.newerapublications.com, pg 732

New Era Publishers (Nigeria) *Tel:* (022) 715706, pg 506

New European Publications Ltd (United Kingdom) *Tel:* (020) 7582 3996 *Fax:* (020) 7582 7021, pg 732

New Generation Publishing Co Ltd (Thailand) *Tel:* (02) 216 7393 5; (02) 2150677 *Fax:* (02) 611 0400, pg 645

New Guyana Co Ltd (Guyana) *Tel:* (02) 262471, pg 314

New Holland Publishers (UK) Ltd (United Kingdom) *Tel:* (020) 7724 7773 *Fax:* (020) 7724 6184 *E-mail:* postmaster@nhpub.co.uk *Web Site:* www.newhollandpublishers.com, pg 732

New Horn Press Ltd (Nigeria) *Tel:* (02) 41 29 72, pg 506

New House Publishers Ltd (New Zealand) *Tel:* (09) 4106517 *Fax:* (09) 4106329 *E-mail:* service@newhouse.co.nz *Web Site:* www.newhouse.co.nz, pg 499

New Island Printing Co Ltd (Hong Kong) *Tel:* 2442 8282 *Fax:* 2443 9882 *E-mail:* info@newisland.com *Web Site:* www.newisland.com, pg 1157

New Light Publishers (India) *Tel:* (011) 5712137 *Fax:* (011) 5812385 *E-mail:* newlight@vsnl.net, pg 343

New Magazine Edizioni (Italy) *Tel:* (0461) 925007 *Fax:* (0461) 925007 *E-mail:* newmagazine@tin.it *Web Site:* www.newmagazine.it; www.rivistamedica.it, pg 400

New Playwrights' Network (United Kingdom) *Tel:* (01684) 540154 *Fax:* (01684) 540154, pg 732

New Times Press (China) *Tel:* (010) 68412244 *Fax:* (010) 68413125, pg 106

New Women's Press Ltd (New Zealand) *Tel:* (09) 3767150 *Fax:* (09) 3767150, pg 499

New Writers' Press (Ireland), pg 362

New Zealand Book Council (New Zealand) *Tel:* (04) 499 1569 *Fax:* (04) 499 1424 *E-mail:* admin@bookcouncil.org.nz *Web Site:* www.bookcouncil.org.nz, pg 1403

New Zealand Council for Educational Research (New Zealand) *Tel:* (04) 384 7939 *Fax:* (04) 384 7933 *Web Site:* www.nzcer.org.nz, pg 499, 1280, 1403

New Zealand Press Council (New Zealand) *Tel:* (04) 4735220 *Fax:* (04) 4711785 *E-mail:* presscouncil@asa.co.nz *Web Site:* www.presscouncil.org.nz, pg 1280

New Zealand Society of Authors (NZSA) (New Zealand) *Tel:* (09) 356 8332 *Fax:* (09) 356 8332 *E-mail:* nzsa@clear.net.nz *Web Site:* www.authors.org.nz, pg 1403

New Zealand Writers Guild (New Zealand) *Tel:* (09) 360 1408 *Fax:* (09) 360 1409 *E-mail:* info@nzwritersguild.org.nz *Web Site:* www.nzwritersguild.org.nz, pg 1403

Newark International Enterprises (Philippines) *Tel:* (02) 2432077 *Fax:* (02) 2414893, pg 520

Newman Centre Publications (Australia) *Tel:* (02) 9637 9406 *Fax:* (02) 9637 3351, pg 33

Newpro UK Ltd (United Kingdom) *Tel:* (01367) 242411 *Fax:* (01367) 241124 *E-mail:* sales@newprouk.co.uk, pg 733

Newscom Pte Ltd (Singapore) *Tel:* 6291 9861 *Fax:* 6293 1445 *E-mail:* circulation@newscom-mail.com *Web Site:* www.newscomonline.com, pg 557

Newspread International (India) *Tel:* (011) 2331402 *Fax:* (011) 2607252, pg 343

Newton & Compton Editori (Italy) *Tel:* (06) 65002553 *Fax:* (06) 65002892 *E-mail:* info@newtoncompton.com *Web Site:* www.newtoncompton.com, pg 400

Newton Publishing Company Ltd (Taiwan, Province of China) *Tel:* (02) 2706-0336 *Fax:* (02) 2707 3759 *E-mail:* newton00@mslf.hinet.net, pg 641

Next Magazine Publishing Ltd (Hong Kong) *Tel:* 2744 2733 *Fax:* 2790 7240 *E-mail:* editorial@nextmedia.com.hk *Web Site:* www.nextmedia.com.hk, pg 318

Nexus Special Interests (United Kingdom) *Tel:* (01322) 660070 *Fax:* (01322) 667633, pg 733

The NFER-NELSON Publishing Co Ltd (United Kingdom) *Tel:* (020) 8996 8444; (020) 8996 8445 (international enquiries) *Toll Free Tel:* (0845) 602 1937 (customer service) *Fax:* (020) 8996 3660 (international enquiries) *E-mail:* information@nfer-nelson.co.uk; edu&hsc@nfer-Nelson.co.uk (customer service) *Web Site:* www.nfer-nelson.co.uk, pg 733

NGM Communication (Pakistan) *Tel:* (042) 5713849 *E-mail:* ngm@shoa.net; anjeeam@yahoo.com *Web Site:* www.geocities.com/angeeam, pg 1333

Nibondh Co Ltd (Thailand) *Tel:* (02) 221-2611; (02) 221-1553 *Fax:* (02) 224-6889 *E-mail:* kongsiri@mozart.inet.co *Web Site:* www.uiowa.edu/~lawlib/vendors/nibondh.htm, pg 1345

Nicolaische Verlagsbuchhandlung Beuermann GmbH (Germany) *Tel:* (030) 253738-0 *Fax:* (030) 253738-39 *E-mail:* info@nicolai-verlag.de *Web Site:* www.nicolai-verlag.de, pg 265

Piergiorgio Nicolazzini Literary Agency (Italy) *Tel:* (02) 48713365 *Fax:* (02) 48713365 *E-mail:* info@pnla.it *Web Site:* www.pnla.it, pg 1133

Editura Niculescu (Romania) *Tel:* (01) 2242898; (01) 2220372 *Fax:* (01) 2242898; (01) 2220372 *E-mail:* edit@niculescu.ro *Web Site:* www.niculescu.ro, pg 541

Nie/Nie/Sagen-Verlag (Germany) *Tel:* (07531) 53570 *Fax:* (07531) 64496 *E-mail:* haberkern-imz@t-online.de *Web Site:* www.nie-nie-sagen-verlag.de, pg 265

Niederland-Verlag Helmut Michel (Germany) *Tel:* (07191) 3277-200 *Fax:* (07191) 3277-15 *E-mail:* micheldruck@t-online.de, pg 265

Niederosterreichisches Pressehaus Druck- und Verlagsgesellschaft mbH (Austria) *Tel:* (02742) 802-1412 *Fax:* (02742) 802-1431 *E-mail:* verlag@np-buch.at *Web Site:* www.np-buch.at, pg 54

Niedersaechsische Landesbibliothek (Germany) *Tel:* (0511) 1267-0 *Fax:* (0511) 1267-202 *E-mail:* nlb@mail.nlb-hannover.de *Web Site:* www.nlb-hannover.de, pg 1509

Niedersaechsische Staats- und Universitaetsbibliothek Goettingen (Germany) *Tel:* (0551) 395212 (Secretariat); (0551) 393079 (chemistry); (0551) 392360 (physics); (0551) 395220 (medicine) *Fax:* (0551) 395222 *E-mail:* sub@sub.uni-goettingen.de *Web Site:* www.sub.uni-goettingen.de, pg 1510

Niedieck Linder AG (Switzerland) *Tel:* (01) 3816592 *Fax:* (01) 3816513 *E-mail:* info@nlagency.ch *Web Site:* www.nlagency.ch, pg 1137

Nielsen BookData (New Zealand) *Tel:* (09) 360 3294 *Fax:* (09) 360 8853 *E-mail:* info@nielsenbookdata.co.nz *Web Site:* www.nielsenbookdata.co.nz, pg 499

Nielsen BookData (United Kingdom) *Tel:* (01438) 744100; (01483) 712244 (customer service) *Toll Free Tel:* (0870) 7778711 (customer service) *Fax:* (01438) 745578 *E-mail:* customerservices@nielsenbooknet.co.uk; helpdesk@nielsenbooknet.co.uk *Web Site:* www.whitaker.co.uk; www.nielsenbookdata.com, pg 733

C W Niemeyer Buchverlage GmbH (Germany) *Tel:* (05151) 200-312 *Fax:* (05151) 200-319 *E-mail:* info@niemeyer-buch.de *Web Site:* www.niemeyer-buch.de, pg 265

Max Niemeyer Verlag GmbH (Germany) *Tel:* (07071) 98 94 0 *Fax:* (07071) 98 94 50 *E-mail:* max@niemeyer.de; info@niemeyer.de *Web Site:* www.niemeyer.de, pg 265

Nieswand-Verlag GmbH (Germany) *Tel:* (0431) 7028 200 *Fax:* (0431) 7028 228 *E-mail:* vertrieb@nieswandverlag.de *Web Site:* www.nieswandverlag.de, pg 265

Hans-Nietsch-Verlag (Germany) *Tel:* (0761) 2966930 *Fax:* (0761) 2966960 *E-mail:* mail@nietsch.de *Web Site:* www.nietsch.de, pg 265

Nieuwe Stad Stichting (Netherlands) *Tel:* (033) 4614615 *Fax:* (033) 4635885, pg 487

Nigensha Publishing Co Ltd (Japan) *Tel:* (03) 5210-4703 *Fax:* (03) 5210-4704 *E-mail:* sales@nigensha.co.jp *Web Site:* www.nigensha.co.jp, pg 423

Nigerian Book Development Council (Nigeria) *Tel:* (01) 862269; (01) 862272, pg 1280

Nigerian Book Suppliers Ltd (Nigeria) *Tel:* (01) 22407, pg 1331

Nigerian Environmental Study Team (Nigeria) *Tel:* (02) 8102644; (02) 8105167 *Fax:* (02) 8102644 *E-mail:* nesting@nest.org.ng, pg 506

Nigerian Institute of Advanced Legal Studies (Nigeria) *Tel:* (01) 821752; (01) 821711; (01) 821753 *Fax:* (01) 497 6076; (01) 825558; (09) 234 6505, pg 506

Nigerian Institute of International Affairs (Nigeria) *Tel:* (01) 61 56 06; (01) 61 56 07; (01) 61 56 09; (01) 61 56 10 *Fax:* (01) 61 64 04; (01) 61 63 60 *E-mail:* niia@ric.nig.com, pg 506

NIGERIAN ISBN AGENCY   INDUSTRY

Nigerian ISBN Agency (Nigeria) *Tel:* (01) 5850657; (01) 5850649 *Web Site:* www.nlbn.org, pg 1280

Nigerian Library Association (Nigeria) *Tel:* (01) 2360470 *Fax:* (01) 2631716 *E-mail:* nln@nlbn.org, pg 1569

Nigerian Publishers Association (Nigeria) *Tel:* (02) 2414427 *Fax:* (02) 2413396 *E-mail:* nigpa@skannet.com; nigpa@steineng.net; nigpa@freemail.nig.com, pg 1280

Nigerian Trade Review (Nigeria) *Tel:* (01) 961147, pg 506

Verlag Arthur Niggli AG (Switzerland) *Tel:* (071) 6449111 *Fax:* (071) 6449190 *E-mail:* info@niggli.ch *Web Site:* www.niggli.ch, pg 629

Nihon Bunka Kagakusha Co Ltd (Japan) *Tel:* (03) 39463137 *Fax:* (03) 39450908, pg 423

Nihon-Bunkyo Shuppan (Japan Educational Publishing Co Ltd) (Japan) *Tel:* (06) 6692-1261 *Fax:* (06) 6606-5172; (06) 6692-8927 *E-mail:* webadmin@nichibung.co.jp *Web Site:* www.nichibun-g.co.jp, pg 423

Nihon Eibungakkai (Japan) *Tel:* (03) 32937528 *Fax:* (03) 32937539, pg 1402

Nihon Igaku Toshokan Kyokai (Japan) *Tel:* (03) 38151942 *Fax:* (03) 38151608 *E-mail:* imlajimu@nisiq.net *Web Site:* wwwsoc.nacsis.ac.jp/jmla, pg 1565

Nihon Keizai Shimbun Inc Publications Bureau (Japan) *Tel:* (03) 3270-0251 *Fax:* (03) 5201-7505 *Web Site:* www.nikkei.co.jp/pub, pg 423

Nihon Rodo Kenkyu Kiko (Japan) *Tel:* (03) 5903-6111 *Fax:* (03) 3594-1113 *E-mail:* jil@jil.go.jp *Web Site:* www.jil.go.jp, pg 423

Nihon-Shoseki Ltd (Japan) *Tel:* (06) 6386-8601 *Fax:* (06) 6386-8620 *E-mail:* nihonsho@mtci.ne.jp *Web Site:* www.nihon-shoseki.co.jp, pg 1322

Nihon Shoten Shogyo Kumiai Rengokai (Japan) *Tel:* (03) 32940388, pg 1275

Nihon Tosho Center Co Ltd (Japan) *Tel:* (03) 3945-6448 *Fax:* (02) 3945-4515 *E-mail:* info@nihontosho.co.jp *Web Site:* www.nihontosho.co.jp, pg 423

Nihon Toshokan Joho Gakkai Shi (Japan) *Tel:* (0561) 62-4111 *Fax:* (0561) 63-9308 *E-mail:* muransky@asu.aasa.ac.jp *Web Site:* www.soc.nii.ac.jp/jslis/, pg 1566

Nihon Toshokan Kyokai (Japan) *Tel:* (03) 3523-0811 *Fax:* (03) 3523-0841 *E-mail:* info@jla.or.jp *Web Site:* www.jla.or.jp, pg 1566

Nihon Vogue Co Ltd (Japan) *Tel:* (03) 5261-5081 *Fax:* (03) 3269-8760 *E-mail:* nvsales@giganet.net *Web Site:* www.tezukuritown.com, pg 424

Nijgh & Van Ditmar Amsterdam (Netherlands) *Tel:* (020) 55 11 262 *Fax:* (020) 6203509 *E-mail:* verkoop@querido.nl; info@querido.nl *Web Site:* www.querido.nl, pg 487

Nikas (Greece) *Tel:* (010) 3634686; (010) 3633754, pg 310

Nikkagiren Shuppan-Sha (JUSE Press Ltd) (Japan) *Tel:* (03) 5379-1238 *Fax:* (03) 3356-3419 *E-mail:* sales@juse-p.co.jp *Web Site:* www.juse-p.co.jp, pg 424

The Nikkan Kogyo Shimbun Ltd (Japan) *Tel:* (03) 3222-7131 *Fax:* (03) 3234-8504 *Web Site:* www.nikkan.co.jp, pg 424

Nikoklis Publishers (Cyprus) *Tel:* (022) 456544 *Fax:* (022) 360668, pg 121

Nil Editions (France) *Tel:* (01) 53 67 14 00 *Fax:* (01) 53 67 14 90 *Web Site:* www.laffont.fr; www.nil-editions.fr, pg 177

Nile & Mackenzie Ltd (United Kingdom) *Tel:* (020) 7493 0351 *Fax:* (020) 7495 0128, pg 733

The Nile Bookshop (Sudan) *Tel:* (011) 463749 *Fax:* (011) 770821 *E-mail:* mohdelhag@yahoo.com; nilebookshop@yahoo.com, pg 1343

Nilsson & Lamm BV, Algemene Import Boekhandel (Netherlands) *Tel:* (0294) 49 49 49 *Fax:* (0294) 49 44 55 *E-mail:* info@nilsson-lamm.nl *Web Site:* www.nilsson-lamm.nl, pg 1329

Nimaroo Publishers (Australia) *Tel:* (042) 292297, pg 33

Nimrod Publications (Australia) *Tel:* (02) 4957 5562; (02) 4921 5173 *Fax:* (02) 4957 5562 *E-mail:* nimrod@hunterlink.com.au, pg 33

9-12 Club (United Kingdom) *Tel:* (01993) 893456 *Fax:* (0845) 6039092, pg 1257

Nio Pobjeda - Oour Izdavacko-Publicisticka Djelatnost (Serbia and Montenegro) *Tel:* (081) 45955; (081) 44433; (081) 44474 *Fax:* (081) 52803, pg 552

Nippon Dokubungakkai (Japan) *Tel:* (03) 3813 5861 *Fax:* (03) 3813 5861 *E-mail:* e-mail@jgg.jp, pg 1402

Nippon Hikaku Bungakukai (Japan), pg 1402

Nippon Hoso Shuppan Kyokai (NHK Publishing) (Japan) *Tel:* (03) 3780-3356 *Fax:* (03) 3780-3348 *E-mail:* webmaster@npb.nhk-grp.co.jp *Web Site:* www.nhk-grp.co.jp, pg 424

Nippon Jitsugyo Publishing Co Ltd (Japan) *Tel:* (03) 3814-5161 *Fax:* (03) 3818-1881 *E-mail:* int@njg.co.jp *Web Site:* www.njg.co.jp, pg 424

Nippon Rosiya Bungakkai (Japan), pg 1402

Nippon Shuppan Hanbai Inc (Japan) *Tel:* (03) 3233-1111 *Fax:* (03) 3292-8571 *E-mail:* press@nippan.co.jp *Web Site:* www.nippan.co.jp, pg 1322

Nippon Yakugaku Toshokan Kyogikai (Japan) *Tel:* (03) 38122111 *Web Site:* wwwsoc.nii.ac.jp/jpla, pg 1566

Niro Decje Novine (Serbia and Montenegro) *Tel:* (032) 712246; (032) 712247; (032) 714970; (032) 711256; (032) 711248; (011) 3221476; (011) 342010 *Fax:* (032) 711248, pg 553

Edit Niro (Novinska-izdavacka radna organizacija) (Croatia) *Tel:* (051) 672 119; (051) 672 112 *Fax:* (051) 672 151 *E-mail:* niro-edit@ri.tel.hr, pg 119

James Nisbet & Co Ltd (United Kingdom) *Tel:* (01462) 438331 *Fax:* (01462) 431528, pg 733

Nishimura Co Ltd (Japan) *Tel:* (025) 223-2388 *Fax:* (025) 224-7165, pg 424

Nissha Printing Co Ltd (Japan) *Tel:* (075) 811-8111 *Fax:* (075) 801-8250 *E-mail:* print-info@nissha.co.jp *Web Site:* www.nissha.co.jp, pg 1221

Nistri - Lischi Editori (Italy) *Tel:* (050) 563371 *Fax:* (050) 562726 *Web Site:* www.nistri-lischi.it, pg 400

Rainar Nitzsche Verlag (Germany) *Tel:* (0631) 61305 *Fax:* (0631) 61305 *E-mail:* rainar.nitzscheverlag@t-online.de *Web Site:* home.t-online.de/home/Rainar.NitzscheVerlag/nitzscheb.htm, pg 265

Niyo Software (India) *Tel:* (020) 546 7296; (020) 400 1603 *Fax:* (020) 400 1603 *E-mail:* info@niyoindia.com *Web Site:* www.niyoindia.com, pg 343

Niyom Witthaya (Thailand) *Tel:* (02) 217661, pg 645

Librairie A-G Nizet Sarl (France) *Tel:* (02) 47 45 50 41 *Fax:* (02) 47 45 50 15 *E-mail:* librairie-a.g-nizet@wanadoo.fr, pg 177

Izdatel'stvo Nizhegorodskogo Gosudarstvennogo Univ (Russian Federation) *Tel:* (08312) 657825 *Fax:* (08312) 658592 *E-mail:* rector@nnucnit.unn.ac.ru *Web Site:* www.unn.ac.ru, pg 547

Agencia de Librerias Nizza SA (Paraguay) *Tel:* (021) 47160, pg 1334

Njala Educational Publishing Centre (Sierra Leone), pg 554

Njala University College Bookshop (Sierra Leone) *Tel:* (022) 228788 *E-mail:* nuc@sierratel.sl; nuclib@sierratel.sl *Web Site:* www.nuc-online.com, pg 1339

Njala University College Library (University of Sierra Leone) (Sierra Leone) *Tel:* (022) 228788 *E-mail:* nuc@sierratel.sl; nuclib@sierratel.sl *Web Site:* www.nuc-online.com, pg 1542

NKI Forlaget (Norway) *Tel:* (067) 58 88 00 *Fax:* (067) 53 05 00 *E-mail:* post-fj@nki.no *Web Site:* www.nki.no, pg 510

NL SH (Albania) *Tel:* (042) 34207 *Fax:* (042) 34207, pg 1

NMA Publications (Australia) *Tel:* (03) 9428 2405 *Web Site:* www.rainerlinz.net/NMA/, pg 33

NMS Enterprises Ltd - Publishing (United Kingdom) *Tel:* (0131) 247 4026 *Fax:* (0131) 247 4012 *E-mail:* publishing@nms.ac.uk *Web Site:* www.nms.ac.uk, pg 733

Nnamdi Azikiwe Library (Nigeria) *Tel:* (042) 771444 *Fax:* (042) 770644 *E-mail:* misunn@aol.com, pg 1534

The Maggie Noach Literary Agency (United Kingdom) *Tel:* (020) 8748 2926 *Fax:* (020) 8748 8057 *E-mail:* m-noach@dircon.co.uk, pg 1142

Nobel-Verlag GmbH Vertrieb Neue Medien (Germany) *Tel:* (0201) 81300 *Fax:* (0201) 8130108 *E-mail:* mplatzkoester@beleke.de *Web Site:* www.gewusst-wo.de; www.nobel.de, pg 265

Librairie F de Nobele (France) *Tel:* (01) 43 26 08 62 *Fax:* (01) 40 46 85 96 *E-mail:* librairie.f.de.nobele@wanadoo.fr, pg 177

Nobelinstituttet (Norway) *Tel:* 22 12 93 20 *Fax:* 22 12 93 10 *E-mail:* library@nobel.no *Web Site:* www.nobel.no, pg 1534

NodoLibri (Italy) *Tel:* (031) 243113 *Fax:* (031) 3306370, pg 400

Florian Noetzel Verlag (Germany) *Tel:* (04421) 4 30 03 *Fax:* (04421) 4 29 85 *E-mail:* florian.noetzel@t-online.de, pg 265

Noguer y Caralt Editores SA (Spain) *Tel:* (093) 280 13 99 *Fax:* (093) 280 19 93 *E-mail:* noguer-caralt@mx2.redestb.es, pg 593

NOI - Verlag (Austria) *Tel:* (0463) 224722 *Fax:* (0463) 224744 *E-mail:* office@noisapil.com, pg 55

Noir Sur Blanc (France) *Tel:* (01) 41 43 72 70 *Fax:* (01) 41 43 72 71 *E-mail:* noirsurblanc@noirsurblanc.com *Web Site:* www.noirsurblanc.com, pg 177

Les Editions Noir sur Blanc (Switzerland) *Tel:* (021) 8645931 *Fax:* (021) 8644026 *E-mail:* noirsurblanc@bluewin.ch, pg 629

Nolit Publishing House (Serbia and Montenegro) *Tel:* (011) 345 017; (011) 355 510 *Fax:* (011) 627 285, pg 553, 1339

Nomiki Bibliothiki (Greece) *Tel:* (01) 3600968 *Fax:* (01) 3636422 *E-mail:* legalinn@otenet.gr, pg 310

Nomos Verlagsgesellschaft mbH und Co KG (Germany) *Tel:* (07221) 2104-0 *Fax:* (07221) 210427 *E-mail:* nomos@nomos.de *Web Site:* www.nomos.de, pg 265

Non (Thailand) *Tel:* (02) 90130, pg 645

Non-Formal Education Centre (Maldive Islands) *Tel:* 325763 *Fax:* 322231, pg 459

Mavis A Noordwijk (Suriname) *Tel:* (0597) 479402, pg 608

Editorial Noray (Spain) *Tel:* (093) 280 59 66 *Fax:* (093) 280 61 90 *E-mail:* info@noray.es *Web Site:* www.noray.es, pg 593

Norbertinum (Poland) *Tel:* (081) 5333895 *Fax:* (081) 5341243 *E-mail:* norbertinum@norbertinum.com.pl *Web Site:* www.norbertinum.com.pl, pg 524

Casa Editrice Nord SRL (Italy) *Tel:* (02) 405708 *Fax:* (02) 4042207 *E-mail:* nord@fantascienza.it *Web Site:* www.nord.fantascienza.it, pg 400

Editions Nord-Sud (France) *Tel:* (01) 39 21 90 40 *Fax:* (01) 39 21 90 42 *E-mail:* nord-sud@editions-nord-sud.com *Web Site:* www.ldj.tm.fr/editeurs/editeurs/nordsud.htm, pg 177

Nord-Sued Verlag (Switzerland) *Tel:* (01) 9366868 *Fax:* (01) 9366800, pg 629

Nordan-Comunidad (Uruguay) *Tel:* (02) 305 5609 *Fax:* (02) 308 1640 *E-mail:* nordan@nordan.com.uy; pedidos@nordan.com.uy; info@nordan.com.uy *Web Site:* www.chasque.net/nordan/; www.nordan.com.uy, pg 778

Norddeutscher Verleger- und Buchhaendler-Verband eV (Germany) *Tel:* (040) 22 54 79 *Fax:* (040) 2 29 85 14, pg 1270

Nordic Council of Ministers Publications (Denmark) *Tel:* 33960200 *Fax:* 33960202 *E-mail:* nmr@nmr.dk *Web Site:* www.norden.org, pg 1266

Nordica Printing Co Ltd (Hong Kong) *Tel:* 25648444; 25648446 *Fax:* 25656445, pg 1219

Nordik/Tapals Publishers Ltd (Latvia) *Tel:* (02) 7602672; (02) 7602816 *Fax:* (02) 7602818 *E-mail:* nordik@nordik.lv *Web Site:* www.nordik.lv, pg 445

Bengt Nordin Agency (Sweden) *Tel:* (08) 57168525 *Fax:* (08) 57168524 *E-mail:* info@nordinagency.se *Web Site:* www.nordinagency.se, pg 1137

Nordiska Bokhandelns (Sweden) *Tel:* (08) 26 98 09 *Fax:* (08) 25 42 46, pg 614

Det nordjyske Landsbibliotek (Denmark) *Tel:* 99 31 44 00 *Fax:* 99 31 44 33 *E-mail:* njl@njl.dk *Web Site:* www.njl.dk, pg 1502

Norges Landbrukshogskoles Bibliotek (Norway) *Tel:* (064) 94 76 63 *Fax:* (064) 94 76 70 *E-mail:* biblutl@bibl.nlh.no *Web Site:* www.nlh.no/biblioteket, pg 1534

NORLA (Information Office for Norwegian Literature Abroad) (Norway) *Tel:* 23 27 63 50 *Fax:* 23 27 63 51 *E-mail:* firmapost@norla.no *Web Site:* www.norla.no, pg 1403

Olaf Norlis Bokhandel A/S (Norway) *Tel:* (022) 004300 *Fax:* (022) 422651 *E-mail:* info@norli.no *Web Site:* www.norli.no, pg 1333

Norma de Chile (Chile) *Tel:* (02) 236 3355 *Fax:* (02) 236 3362 *Web Site:* www.norma.com, pg 99

Editions Norma (France) *Tel:* (01) 45 48 70 96 *Fax:* (01) 45 48 05 84 *E-mail:* norma@freesurf.fr, pg 177

Ediciones Norma SA (Spain) *Tel:* (091) 6370760; (091) 6377414 *Fax:* (091) 5470133; (091) 6370760 *E-mail:* norma-capitel@normacapitel.com *Web Site:* www.norma-capitel.com, pg 593

Editorial Norma SA (Colombia) *Tel:* (02) 660 1901 *Fax:* (02) 661 5278 *Web Site:* www.norma.com, pg 112

Cesky normalizacni institut (Czech Republic) *Tel:* (02) 21 80 21 11 *Fax:* (02) 21 80 23 10 *E-mail:* info@csni.cz *Web Site:* www.csni.cz, pg 126

Wydawnictwa Normalizacyjne Alfa-Wero (Poland) *Tel:* (02) 6218750 *Fax:* (02) 6218750, pg 525

Normenausschuss Bibliotheks- und Dokumentationswesen (NABD) im DIN Deutsches Institut fuer Normung eV (Germany) *Tel:* (030) 2601-2305 *Fax:* (030) 2601-42860 *Web Site:* www.nabd.din.de, pg 1563

Norsk Bibliotekforening (Norway) *Tel:* 2324 3430 *Fax:* 2267 2368 *E-mail:* nbf@norskbibliotekforening.no *Web Site:* www.norskbibliotekforening.no, pg 1569

Norsk Bokdistribusjon (Norway) *Tel:* 66 84 90 40 *Fax:* 66 84 55 90 *E-mail:* vv@vettviten.no *Web Site:* www.vettviten.no, pg 1333

Norsk Bokreidingslag L/L (Norway) *Tel:* 55301899 *Fax:* 55320356 *E-mail:* post@bodonihus.no, pg 510

Norsk Musikkforleggerforening (Norway) *Tel:* (022) 42 50 90 *Fax:* (022) 42 55 41 *Web Site:* www.mic.no/mic.nsf, pg 1280

Norske Akademi for Sprog og Litteratur (Norway) *Tel:* 22 56 29 50 *Fax:* 22 55 37 43 *E-mail:* ordet@riksmalsforbundet.no *Web Site:* www.riksmalsforbundet.no, pg 1403

Den Norske Forfatterforening (Norway) *Tel:* 23357620; 22 42 40 77; 22 41 11 97 *Fax:* 22 42 11 07 *E-mail:* post@forfatterforeningen.no; forfatterforeningen@online.no *Web Site:* skrift.no/dnf, pg 1280

Den Norske Forleggerforening (Norway) *Tel:* 22 00 75 80 *Fax:* 22 33 38 30 *E-mail:* dnf@forleggerforeningen.no *Web Site:* www.forleggerforeningen.no, pg 1281

Det Norske Videnskaps-Akademi (Norway) *Tel:* 22121090 *Fax:* 22121099 *E-mail:* dnva@online.no *Web Site:* www.dnva.no, pg 1403

P A Norstedt & Soener AB (Sweden) *Tel:* (08) 7893000 *Fax:* (08) 214006, pg 614

Norstedts Forlag (Sweden) *Tel:* (08) 769 88 50 *Fax:* (08) 769 88 64 *E-mail:* info.norstedts@liber.se *Web Site:* www.norstedts.se, pg 614

Norstedts Juridik (Sweden) *Tel:* (08) 690 91 00 *Fax:* (08) 6909070 *Web Site:* www.njab.se, pg 614

Norstedts Ordbok (Sweden) *Tel:* (08) 7698950 *E-mail:* info.orabok@norstedtordbok.se *Web Site:* www.norstedtsordbok.se, pg 614

Editorial Norte SA (Argentina) *Tel:* (011) 4921-1440 *Fax:* (011) 4921-1440, pg 8

North Shore City Libraries (New Zealand) *Tel:* (09) 4868460 *Fax:* (09) 4868519 *Web Site:* www.shorelibraries.govt.nz, pg 1532

North York Moors National Park (United Kingdom) *Tel:* (01439) 770657 *Fax:* (01439) 770691 *E-mail:* j.renney@northyorkmoors-npa.gov.uk *Web Site:* www.northyorkmoors-npa.gov.uk, pg 733

Northcote House Publishers Ltd (United Kingdom) *Tel:* (01822) 810066 *Fax:* (01822) 810034 *E-mail:* northcote.house@virgin.net *Web Site:* www.northcotehouse.com, pg 733

Northern Caribbean University (Jamaica) *Tel:* (876) 962-2204-7 *Fax:* (876) 962-0075 *E-mail:* info@ncu.edu.jm *Web Site:* www.ncu.edu.jm, pg 1521

Northern Map Distributors (United Kingdom) *Tel:* (0114) 2582660 *Toll Free Tel:* 800 834920, pg 1352

Northern Nigerian Publishing Co Ltd (Nigeria) *Tel:* (069) 32087, pg 506

Northern Technical College Library (Zambia) *Tel:* (02) 680141 *Fax:* (02) 680423 *E-mail:* nortec@zamtel.zm, pg 1556

Northland Historical Publications Society (New Zealand) *Tel:* (09) 4028244 *Fax:* (09) 4028296, pg 499

Northwestern Publishers (United Republic of Tanzania), pg 644

W W Norton & Company Ltd (United Kingdom) *Tel:* (020) 7323 1579 *Toll Free Tel:* 800-233-4830 (orders) *Fax:* (020) 7436 4553 *Toll Free Fax:* 800-458-6515 (orders) *E-mail:* office@wwnorton.co.uk *Web Site:* www.wwnorton.co.uk, pg 734

The Norwegian Association of Literary Translators (Norway) *Tel:* 22478090 *Fax:* 22420356 *E-mail:* post@translators.no *Web Site:* skrift.no/no/english/index.asp; skrift.no/no/index.asp, pg 1149

Norwood Publishers Ltd (United Kingdom) *Tel:* (01274) 602454, pg 734

Nosangyoson Bunka Kyokai (Japan) *Tel:* (03) 35851141 *Fax:* (03) 35891387 *E-mail:* mbk@mail.ruralnet.or.jp, pg 424

Editions Mare Nostrum (France) *Tel:* (04) 68 51 17 50 *Fax:* (05) 61 41 15 43 *E-mail:* mare.nost@wanadoo.fr, pg 177

Bibliotheque Louis Notari (Monaco) *Tel:* (093) 30-95-09 *Fax:* (093) 152941, pg 1529

Editorial Noticias (Portugal) *Tel:* (021) 3552130 *Fax:* (021) 3552168; (021) 3552169 *E-mail:* geral@editorialnoticias.pt *Web Site:* www.editorialnoticias.pt, pg 534

Editorial Noticias (Portugal) *Tel:* (01) 352 2066, pg 1338

Notos (Greece) *Tel:* (01) 3636577; (01) 3629746 *Fax:* (01) 3636737, pg 310

Nour E-Sham Book Centre (Syrian Arab Republic) *Tel:* (011) 4440575 *Fax:* (011) 3324913 *E-mail:* nouresham@mail.sy, pg 1137

Nouveau Cercle Parisien du Livre (France) *Tel:* (01) 43547195 *Fax:* (01) 40518288, pg 1252

Internationale Nouvelle Acropole (Portugal) *Tel:* (021) 827097 *Web Site:* www.acropolis.org, pg 534

La Nouvelle Agence (France) *Tel:* (01) 43258560 *Fax:* (01) 43254798 *E-mail:* lnaparis@aol.com, pg 1131

Nouvelle Cite (France) *Tel:* (01) 40927085 *Fax:* (01) 40921168, pg 177

Les Nouvelles Editions Africaines du Senegal NEAS (Senegal) *Tel:* (08) 211381; (08) 221580 *Fax:* (08) 223604 *E-mail:* neas@sentoo.sn, pg 551

Librairie/Editions Nouvelles Editions Africaines du TOGO (Togo) *Tel:* 21 67 61 *Fax:* 22 10 03, pg 1345

Les Nouvelles Editions Africaines du TOGO (NEA-TOGO) (Togo) *Tel:* (228) 21 67 61 *Fax:* (228) 22 10 03 *E-mail:* ctce@cafe.tg, pg 646

Nouvelles Editions Fiduciaires (France) *Tel:* (01) 46 39 47 13; (01) 46 39 47 00 *Fax:* (01) 47 58 00 63, pg 177

Nouvelles Editions Francaises (France) *Tel:* (01) 44 74 16 00 *Fax:* (01) 44 04 98 03, pg 177

Les Nouvelles Editions Ivoiriennes (Cote d'Ivoire) *Tel:* 21 24 07 66; 21 24 08 25 *Fax:* 21 24 24 56 *E-mail:* edition@nei-ci.com *Web Site:* www.nei-ci.com, pg 117

Les Nouvelles Editions Ivoiriennes (NEI) (Cote d'Ivoire) *Tel:* 21 24 92 12; 21 24 07 66; 21 24 08 25 *Fax:* 21 24 24 56, pg 117

Nouvelles Editions Latines (France) *Tel:* (01) 43 54 77 42 *Fax:* (01) 43 29 69 81 *E-mail:* info@editions-nel.com *Web Site:* www.editions-nel.com, pg 177

Nov Covek Publishing House (Bulgaria) *Tel:* (02) 9863766 *Fax:* (02) 9863772 *E-mail:* newman@mbox.cit.bg; vogda@stratec.net, pg 96

Nov svet (New World) (The Former Yugoslav Republic of Macedonia) *Tel:* (02) 3078-662, pg 453

Editora Nova Aguilar SA (Brazil) *Tel:* (021) 537-7189; (021) 537-8275, pg 87

Editora Nova Alexandria Ltda (Brazil) *Tel:* (011) 5571-5637 *Fax:* (011) 5571-5637 *E-mail:* novaalexandria@novaalexandria.com.br *Web Site:* www.novaalexandria.com.br, pg 87

Nova Arrancada Sociedade Editora SA (Portugal) *Tel:* (021) 3468837 *Fax:* (021) 3475122 *E-mail:* novaarrancada@mail.telepac.pt, pg 534

Editora Nova Fronteira SA (Brazil) *Tel:* (021) 25 37 87 70; (021) 22 66 51 84 *Fax:* (021) 22 86 67 55 *Web Site:* www.novafronteira.com.br, pg 87

Nova Grupo Editorial SA de CV (Mexico) *Tel:* (05) 5320946 *Fax:* (05) 6050879, pg 469

Editorial Nova, SA de CV (Mexico) *Tel:* (05) 2 80 60 80 *Fax:* (05) 2 80 31 94 *E-mail:* bolind@viernes.iwm.com.mx, pg 469

Novalis Media AG (Switzerland) *Tel:* (052) 6201490 *Fax:* (052) 6201491 *E-mail:* info@novalis.ch *Web Site:* www.novalis.ch, pg 630

Novecento Editrice Srl (Italy) *Tel:* (091) 587417 *Fax:* (091) 585702 *E-mail:* novedi@mbox.vol.it, pg 401

Novello & Co Ltd (United Kingdom) *Tel:* (020) 7434 0066 *Fax:* (020) 7287-6329 *E-mail:* music@musicsales.co.uk; media@musicsales.co.uk *Web Site:* www.musicsales.co.uk; www.chesternovello.com, pg 734

Novelty Printers & Publishers (Maldive Islands) *Tel:* 318844 *Fax:* 327039 *E-mail:* novelty@dhivehinet.net.mv, pg 459

Novorg International Szervezo es Kiado kft (Hungary) *Tel:* (01) 603790; (01) 603596; (01) 602300 *Fax:* (01) 495581 *E-mail:* info@hu.inter.net, pg 323

Novosti Izdatelstvo (Russian Federation) *Tel:* (095) 265-5008 *Fax:* (095) 975-2065; (095) 230-2119; (095) 230-2667 *E-mail:* novosty@df.ru *Web Site:* www.novosty.ru, pg 547

Novus Forlag (Norway) *Tel:* 2271 7450 *Fax:* 2271 8107 *E-mail:* novus@novus.no *Web Site:* www.novus.no, pg 510

NPA (Neue Presse Agentur) (Switzerland) *Tel:* (052) 7214374, pg 1137

NPS Educational Publishers Ltd (Nigeria Publishers Services) (Nigeria) *Tel:* (02) 2316006; (803) 370-0838, pg 506

NSB Buch- und Phonoclub (Switzerland) *Tel:* (01) 3833622, pg 1256

NSW Agriculture (Australia) *Tel:* (02) 6391 3100 *Fax:* (02) 6391 3336 *E-mail:* nsw.agriculture@agric.nsw.gov.au *Web Site:* www.agric.nsw.gov.au, pg 33

NSW Writers' Centre (Australia) *Tel:* (02) 95559757 *Fax:* (02) 98181327 *E-mail:* nswwc@ozemail.com.au *Web Site:* www.nswwriterscentre.org.au, pg 1396

NTC Research (United Kingdom) *Tel:* (01491) 411000 *Fax:* (01491) 571188 *E-mail:* info@ntc.co.uk *Web Site:* www.ntc-research.com, pg 734

La Nuee Bleue - Dernieres Nouvelles d'Alsace (France) *Tel:* (03) 88 15 77 27 *Fax:* (03) 88 75 16 21 *E-mail:* nuee-bleue@sdv.fr *Web Site:* www.sdv.fr/nuee-bleue/, pg 177

Nuer Ediciones (Spain) *Tel:* (091) 674 92 21; (091) 902 118 298 *Fax:* (091) 655 71 01 *E-mail:* nuer@pasadizo.com; correo@pasadizo.com *Web Site:* www.pasadizo.com, pg 593

Editorial Nuestro Tiempo SA (Mexico) *Tel:* (05) 5503165; (05) 5503170, pg 469

Nueva Acropolis (Spain) *Tel:* (091) 5228730 *Fax:* (091) 5312952 *E-mail:* oinaes@jet.es *Web Site:* www.acropolis.org, pg 593

Editora Nueva Generacion (Chile) *Tel:* (02) 2183974 *Fax:* (02) 2182281, pg 100

Editorial Nueva Imagen SA (Mexico) *Tel:* (05) 2711980, pg 469

Editorial Nueva Nicaragua (Nicaragua) *Tel:* (02) 666520, pg 502

Editorial Nueva Sociedad (Venezuela) *Tel:* (02) 2659975; (02) 2650593 *Fax:* (02) 2673397 *E-mail:* nuso@nuevasoc.org.ve; nusoven@nuevasoc.org.ve *Web Site:* www.nuevasoc.org.ve, pg 780

Nueva Vision (Argentina) *Tel:* (011) 8631461; (011) 8635980, pg 1297

Ediciones Nueva Vision SAIC (Argentina) *Tel:* (011) 4863-1461; (011) 4863-5050 *Fax:* (011) 4863-5980 *E-mail:* ednuevavision@ciudad.com.ar, pg 8

Editorial Nuevo Continente (Honduras) *Tel:* 22-5073, pg 315

Nuova Alfa Editoriale (Italy) *Tel:* (02) 215631 *Fax:* (02) 26413121, pg 401

Nuova Coletti Editore Roma (Italy) *Tel:* (06) 8557981 *Fax:* (06) 8557981 *E-mail:* materiale.web@futura-ge.com, pg 401

Nuova Ipsa Editore srl (Italy) *Tel:* (091) 6819025 *Fax:* (091) 6816399 *E-mail:* info@nuovaipsa.it *Web Site:* www.nuovaipsa.it, pg 401

La Nuova Italia Editrice SpA (Italy) *Tel:* (02) 50951 *Fax:* (02) 50952309, pg 401

Editrice Nuovi Autori (Italy) *Tel:* (02) 89409338 *Fax:* (02) 58107048 *E-mail:* faglier@tin.it *Web Site:* www.paginegialle.it/ednuoviaut, pg 401

Nuovi Sentieri Editore (Italy) *Tel:* (0437) 590308, pg 401

Nuovo Instituto Italiano d'Arti Grafiche (Italy) *Tel:* (035) 329111 *Fax:* (035) 329346 *E-mail:* artigraf@bertelsmann.de, pg 1180

Nuovo Instituto Italiano d'Arti Grafiche (Italy) *Tel:* (035) 329111 *Fax:* (035) 329322 *E-mail:* info.niiag@arvato.it *Web Site:* artigrafiche.bergamo.it; www.arvato.it, pg 1221

Il Nuovo Melangolo (Italy) *Tel:* (010) 2514002 *Fax:* (010) 2514037 *E-mail:* info@ilmelangolo.com *Web Site:* www.ilmelangolo.com, pg 401

Nurdan YayinlariSanayi ve Ticaret Ltd Sti (Turkey) *Tel:* (0212) 522 55 04; (0212) 513 86 53 *Fax:* (0212) 512 51 86 *E-mail:* info@nurdan.com.tr *Web Site:* www.nurdan.com.tr, pg 651

Andrew Nurnberg Associates Ltd (United Kingdom) *Tel:* (020) 7417 8800 *Fax:* (020) 7417 8812 *E-mail:* all@nurnberg.co.uk, pg 1142

Nusa Indah (Indonesia) *Tel:* (0381) 21502 *Fax:* (0381) 21645; (0381) 22373, pg 356

Nusser Verlag (Germany) *Tel:* (089) 146788 *Fax:* (089) 1493206 *Web Site:* www.nusserverlag.de, pg 266

Nwamife Publishers Ltd (Nigeria) *Tel:* (042) 338454, pg 506

Bokforlaget Nya Doxa AB (Sweden) *Tel:* (0587) 104 16 *Fax:* (0587) 142 57 *E-mail:* info@nya-doxa.se *Web Site:* www.nya-doxa.se, pg 614

nymphenburger (Germany) *Tel:* (089) 2 90 88-0 *Fax:* (089) 2 90 88-1 44 *E-mail:* nymphenburger@herbig.net *Web Site:* www.herbig.net, pg 266

Nyota Publishers Ltd (United Republic of Tanzania) *Tel:* (051) 25547; (051) 25549, pg 644

Nyt Dansk Literaturselskab (Denmark) *Tel:* 4659 5520 *Fax:* 4659 5520 *E-mail:* ndl@ndl.dk *Web Site:* www.ndl.dk, pg 1398

Nyt Nordisk Forlag Arnold Busck A/S (Denmark) *Tel:* 33733575 *Fax:* 33733576 *E-mail:* nnf@nytnordiskforlag.dk *Web Site:* www.nytnordiskforlag.dk, pg 133

NZN Buchverlag AG (Switzerland) *Tel:* (01) 266 12 92 *Fax:* (01) 266 12 93 *E-mail:* nzn@nzn.ch *Web Site:* www.nzn.ch, pg 630

O Gracklauer Verlag und Bibliographische Agentur GmbH (Germany) *Tel:* (030) 825 81 39 *Fax:* (030) 826 20 39 *E-mail:* info@gracklauer.de *Web Site:* www.gracklauer.de, pg 1270

Editorial O Livro Lda (Portugal) *Tel:* (021) 7783577 *Fax:* (021) 7783536 *E-mail:* prof@editorialolivro.pt *Web Site:* www.editorialolivro.pt, pg 534

Editorial O Livro Lda (Portugal) *Tel:* (021) 778 35 77 *Fax:* (021) 778 35 36 *E-mail:* prof@editorialolivro.pt *Web Site:* www.editorialolivro.pt, pg 1338

O Neul Publishing Co (Republic of Korea) *Tel:* (02) 716-2811 *Fax:* (02) 712-7392, pg 441

Oak Tree Press (Ireland) *Tel:* (021) 431 3855 *Fax:* (021) 431 3496 *E-mail:* info@oaktreepress.com *Web Site:* www.oaktreepress.com, pg 362

Oakwood Press (United Kingdom) *Tel:* (01291) 650444 *Fax:* (01291) 650484 *E-mail:* oakwood-press@dial.pipex.com *Web Site:* www.oakwood-press.dial.pipex.com, pg 734

OASIS, Producciones Generales de Comunicacion (Spain) *Tel:* (093) 2372020 *Fax:* (093) 2177378, pg 593

Obafemi Awolowo University Library (Nigeria) *Tel:* (036) 230291 ext 2287; (036) 230290 *Fax:* (036) 230291 (ext 2287) *E-mail:* ul@libraryoauife.edu.ng, pg 1534

Obafemi Awolowo University Press Ltd (Nigeria) *Tel:* (036) 230290-9; (036) 230284, pg 506

Obdeestro Znanie (Russian Federation) *Tel:* (095) 9281531, pg 547

Obelisco Ediciones S (Spain) *Tel:* (093) 3098525 *Fax:* (093) 3098523 *E-mail:* comercial@edicionesobelisco.com; obelisco@edicionesobelisco.com *Web Site:* www.edicionesobelisco.com, pg 593

Obelisk-Verlag (Austria) *Tel:* (0512) 58 07 33 *Fax:* (0512) 58 07 33 13 *E-mail:* obelisk-verlag@utanet.at *Web Site:* www.obelisk-verlag.at, pg 55

Oberbaum Verlag GmbH (Germany) *Tel:* (030) 624 69 21 *Fax:* (030) 624 69 21, pg 266

Oberoesterreichische Landesbibliothek (Austria) *Tel:* (0732) 664071-00 *Fax:* (0732) 664071-44 *E-mail:* landesbibliothek@ooe.gv.at *Web Site:* www.landesbibliothek.at, pg 1491

Edition Objectif Lune (Luxembourg) *Tel:* 335230 *Fax:* 335230 *E-mail:* objectif.lune@cmdnet.lu, pg 451

Editora Objetiva Ltda (Brazil) *Tel:* (021) 2556-7824 *Fax:* (021) 2556-3322 *Web Site:* www.objetiva.com.br, pg 87

Obobo Books (Nigeria) *Tel:* (01) 871333; (01) 875389 *E-mail:* obw@infoweb.abs.net, pg 506

Obod (Serbia and Montenegro) *Tel:* (086) 233-331 *Fax:* (086) 233-951 *E-mail:* ipobod@cg.ju, pg 553

O'Brien Educational (Ireland) *Tel:* (01) 4923333 *Fax:* (01) 4922777 *E-mail:* books@obrien.ie *Web Site:* www.obrien.ie, pg 362

The O'Brien Press Ltd (Ireland) *Tel:* (01) 4923333 *Fax:* (01) 4922777 *E-mail:* books@obrien.ie *Web Site:* www.obrien.ie, pg 362

Observatorio Astronomico de Lisboa (Portugal) *Tel:* (021) 361 6739; (021) 361 6730 *Fax:* (021) 362 1722 *E-mail:* info@oal.ul.pt *Web Site:* www.oal.ul.pt, pg 534

Editions Obsidiane (France) *Tel:* (03) 86965218 *Fax:* (03) 86870112 *E-mail:* genevieve.bigant@wanadoo.fr, pg 177

Obunsha Co Ltd (Japan) *Tel:* (03) 3266-6487; (03) 3266-6000 *Fax:* (03) 3266-6478 *Web Site:* www.obunsha.co.jp, pg 424

Vydavatelstvo Obzor (Slovakia) *Tel:* (07) 368395; (07) 55695; (07) 57015 *Fax:* (07) 368395, pg 560

Editions Ocean (Reunion) *Tel:* 588400 *Fax:* 588410 *E-mail:* ocean@guetali.fr, pg 538

Editions de l'Ocean Indien (Mauritius) *Tel:* 4646761 *Fax:* 4643445 *E-mail:* eoibooks@intnet.mu, pg 1327

Editions de l'Ocean Indien Ltd (Mauritius) *Tel:* 4646761 *Fax:* 4643445 *E-mail:* eoibooks@intnet.mu, pg 461

Ocean Press (Australia) *Tel:* (03) 9326 4280 *Fax:* (03) 9329 5040 *E-mail:* edit@oceanpress.com.au; info@oceanbooks.com.au *Web Site:* www.oceanbooks.com.au, pg 34

Oceanida (Greece) *Tel:* (0210) 3806137 *Fax:* (0210) 3805531 *E-mail:* oceanida@internet.gr, pg 310

Ediciones Oceano Grupo SA (Spain) *Tel:* (093) 280 20 20 *Fax:* (093) 203 17 91 *E-mail:* info@oceano.com, pg 593

Oceanographic Research Institute (South Africa) *Tel:* (031) 3288222; (031) 3288238 *Fax:* (031) 3288188 *E-mail:* library@iru.org.za *Web Site:* www.ori.org.za, pg 567

Oceans Enterprises (Australia) *Tel:* (03) 5182 5108 *Fax:* (03) 5182 5823 *Web Site:* www.oceans.com.au, pg 34

OCEI (Oficina Central de Estadistica e Informatica) (Venezuela) *Tel:* (02) 782 11 33; (02) 782 12 12; (02) 782 19 45; (02) 782 10 31; (02) 793 71 91; (02) 782 11 67 *Fax:* (02) 782 97 55, pg 780

Universitetsko Izdatelstvo 'Kliment Ochridski' (Bulgaria) *Tel:* (02) 71288; (02) 71265; (02) 704271; (02) 71151 *Fax:* (02) 704271 *E-mail:* gzisha@ns.sclg.uni-sofia.bg, pg 96

Octagon Press Ltd (United Kingdom) *Tel:* (020) 8341 5971 *Fax:* (020) 8348 9392 *E-mail:* octagon@schredds.demon.co.uk *Web Site:* www.octagonpress.com, pg 734

YELLOW PAGES

OCTAVO Produzioni Editoriali Associale (Italy) *Tel:* (055) 2346022 *Fax:* (055) 2346109, pg 401

Edition Octopus & Okeanos Presse (Germany) *Tel:* (02524) 2502, pg 266

Octopus Publishing Group (United Kingdom) *Tel:* (020) 7531 8400 *Fax:* (020) 7531 8650 *Web Site:* www.octopus-publishing.co.uk, pg 734

Octopus Verlag (Switzerland) *Tel:* (081) 252 10 29 *Fax:* (081) 252 94 66, pg 630

Odense Centralbibliotek (Denmark) *Tel:* 66514301 *Fax:* 66137337 *E-mail:* tele@fynbib.dk *Web Site:* www.odensebib.dk, pg 1502

Odense Universitetsbibliotek (Denmark) *Tel:* 6550 2644 *Fax:* 6550 2601 *E-mail:* sdub@bib.sdu.dk *Web Site:* www.bib.sdu.dk, pg 1502

Odeon Book Store Lp (Thailand) *Tel:* (02) 2210742; (02) 2216567 *Fax:* (02) 2253300; (02) 2548806, pg 1345

Odeon Buch- und Phonoclub (Czech Republic) *Tel:* (02) 264100 *Fax:* (02) 24225254 *E-mail:* odeon@comp.cz, pg 1251

Odeon Store LP (Thailand) *Tel:* (02) 2210742 *Fax:* (02) 2253300, pg 645

Editions Odile Jacob (France) *Tel:* (01) 44 41 64 84 *Fax:* (01) 44 41 64 99; (01) 43 29 88 77 *Web Site:* www.odilejacob.fr, pg 177

Anne O'Donovan Pty Ltd (Australia) *Tel:* (03) 9819 5372 *Fax:* (03) 9818 6849 *E-mail:* odonovan@netspace.net.au, pg 34

Odusote Bookstores Ltd (Nigeria) *Tel:* (02) 2316451 *Fax:* (02) 2318781 *E-mail:* odubooks@infoweb.abs.net, pg 1331

Odysseas Publications Ltd (Greece) *Tel:* (01) 3624326; (01) 3625575 *Fax:* (01) 3648030, pg 311

oebv & hpt Verlagsgesellschaft mbH & Co KG (Austria) *Tel:* (01) 40136-0 *Fax:* (01) 40136-185 *E-mail:* office@oebvhpt.at *Web Site:* www.oebvhpt.at, pg 55

Oeffentliche Bibliothek der Universitaet Basel (Switzerland) *Tel:* (061) 267 3100 *Fax:* (061) 267 3103 *E-mail:* sekretariat-ub@unibas.ch *Web Site:* www.ub.unibas.ch, pg 1548

Oeko-Test Verlag GmbH & Co KG Betriebsgesellschaft (Germany) *Tel:* (069) 9 77 77-0 *Fax:* (069) 9 77 77-139 *E-mail:* oet.verlag@oekotest.de *Web Site:* www.oekotest.de, pg 266

Oekobuch Verlag & Versand GmbH (Germany) *Tel:* (07633) 50613 *Fax:* (07633) 50870 *E-mail:* oekobuch@t-online.de *Web Site:* www.oekobuch.de, pg 266

Oekotopia Verlag, Wolfgang Hoffman GmbH & Co KG (Germany) *Tel:* (0251) 48198-0 *Fax:* (0251) 48198-29 *E-mail:* info@oekotopia-verlag.de *Web Site:* www.oekotopia-verlag.de, pg 266

Oekumenischer Verlag Dr R-F Edel (Germany) *Tel:* (02351) 51547 *Fax:* (02351) 568908, pg 266

OEMF srl International (Italy) *Tel:* (02) 5749521 *Fax:* (02) 33210200 *E-mail:* info@mason.it *Web Site:* www.oemf.it, pg 401

Martina M Oepping Literary Agency (Germany) *Tel:* (069) 59790011 *Fax:* (069) 59790012 *E-mail:* litag@oepping.de *Web Site:* www.oepping.de, pg 1132

Oertel & Sporer GmbH & Co (Germany) *Tel:* (07121) 302 555; (07121) 302 552 *Fax:* (07121) 302 558, pg 266

Oertel & Sporer GmbH & Co (Germany) *Tel:* (07121) 302555 *Fax:* (07121) 302558, pg 1176, 1217

Oesch Verlag AG (Switzerland) *Tel:* (01) 305 70 60 *Fax:* (01) 305 70 66 *E-mail:* info@oeschverlag.ch *Web Site:* www.oeschverlag.ch, pg 630

Verlag Oesterreich GmbH (Austria) *Tel:* (01) 61077-0 *Fax:* (01) 61077-419 *E-mail:* office@verlagoesterreich.at *Web Site:* www.verlagoesterreich.at, pg 55

Oesterreichische Gesellschaft fuer Dokumentation und Information (OGDI) (Austria) *Tel:* (01) 31336 5107 *Fax:* (01) 31336 905107 *E-mail:* oegdi@termnet.at *Web Site:* www.oegdi.at, pg 1558

Oesterreichische Gesellschaft fuer Literatur (Austria) *Tel:* (01) 5338159 *Fax:* (01) 5334067 *E-mail:* office@ogl.at *Web Site:* www.ogl.at, pg 1396

Oesterreichische Staatsdruckerei (Austria) *Tel:* (01) 20666-302 *Fax:* (01) 20666-100 *E-mail:* zach@staatsdruckerei.at *Web Site:* www.oesd.co.at, pg 55

Oesterreichische Verlagsanstalt GmbH (Austria) *Tel:* (01) 5445641-46 *Fax:* (01) 5445641-46 *E-mail:* prepress@agens-werk.at, pg 55

Verlag der Oesterreichischen Akademie der Wissenschaften (OEAW) (Austria) *Tel:* (01) 512 9050; (01) 51581-3401 *Fax:* (01) 51581-3400 *E-mail:* verlag@oeaw.ac.at *Web Site:* verlag.oeaw.ac.at, pg 55

Verlag des Oesterreichischen Gewerkschaftsbundes GmbH (Austria) *Tel:* (01) 662 32 96 *Fax:* (01) 662 32 96-63 85 *E-mail:* office@oegbverlag.at *Web Site:* www.verlag-oegb.co.at, pg 55

Oesterreichischer Agrarverlag, Druck- und Verlags-GmbH (Austria) *Tel:* (02235) 404-440 *Fax:* (02235) 404-459 *E-mail:* buch@agrarverlag.at *Web Site:* www.agrarverlag.at, pg 55

Oesterreichischer Bundesverlag Gmbh (Austria) *Tel:* (01) 5262091-0 *Fax:* (01) 526209111 *E-mail:* oebz@oebv.co.at *Web Site:* www.oebv.at, pg 55

Oesterreichischer Gewerbeverlag GmbH (Austria) *Tel:* (01) 535 9404 *Fax:* (01) 5330768030 *E-mail:* gewerbeverlag@tbxa.telecom.at, pg 55

Oesterreichischer Jagd -und Fischerei-Verlag (Austria) *Tel:* (01) 405 16 36-39 *Fax:* (01) 405 16 36-36 *E-mail:* verlag@jagd.at *Web Site:* www.jagd.at, pg 55

Oesterreichischer Kunst und Kulturverlag (Austria) *Tel:* (01) 587 85 51 *Fax:* (01) 587 85 52 *E-mail:* office@kunstundkulturverlag.at, pg 55

Oesterreichischer Uebersetzer- und Dolmetscherverband Universitas (Austria) *Tel:* (01) 368 60 60 *Fax:* (01) 368 60 08 *E-mail:* info@universitas.org *Web Site:* www.universitas.org, pg 1147

Oesterreichisches Institut fuer Bibliotheksforschung, Dokumentations- und Informationswesen (Austria), pg 1558

Oesterreichisches Katholisches Bibelwerk (Austria) *Tel:* (02243) 2938 *Fax:* (02243) 2939, pg 55

Oesterreichisches Staatsarchiv (Austria) *Tel:* (01) 79540 100 *Fax:* (01) 79540 199 *E-mail:* gdpost@oesta.gv.at *Web Site:* www.oesta.gv.at, pg 1491

Verlag Friedrich Oetinger GmbH (Germany) *Tel:* (040) 607909-02 *Fax:* (040) 6072326 *E-mail:* oetinger@vsg-hamburg.de *Web Site:* www.oetinger.de, pg 266

Dr Oetker Verlag KG (Germany) *Tel:* (0521) 521 155-0 *Fax:* (0521) 521 155-2995 *E-mail:* presse@oetker.de *Web Site:* www.oetker-gruppe.de, pg 266

Off the Shelf Publishing (Australia) *Tel:* (02) 9560 3058 *Fax:* (02) 9564 0758 *E-mail:* offshelf@ozemail.com.au, pg 34

Verlag Offene Worte (Germany) *Tel:* (040) 79713-03 *Fax:* (040) 79713-324 *E-mail:* vertrieb@koehler-mittler.de *Web Site:* www.koehler-mittler.de, pg 266

Office des Publications Officielles des Communautes Europeennes (Luxembourg) *Tel:* 292942001 *Fax:* 292942700, pg 451

Office des Publications Officielles des Communautes Europeennes (Luxembourg) *Tel:* 2929-1 *Fax:* 292944619 *E-mail:* opoce-info-info@cec.eu.int *Web Site:* www.eur-op.eu.int, pg 1276

Office du Livre SA (Buchhaus AG) (Switzerland) *Tel:* (026) 4675111 *Fax:* (026) 4675455 *E-mail:* information@olf.ch *Web Site:* www.olf.ch, pg 630

OKKER KIADO

Office International de Documentation et Librairie (OFFILIB) (France) *Tel:* (01) 55 42 73 00 *Fax:* (01) 43 29 91 67 *E-mail:* info@offilib.com *Web Site:* www.offilib.com, pg 1310

Office International des Epizooties (France) *Tel:* (01) 44 15 18 88 *Fax:* (01) 42 67 09 87 *E-mail:* oie@oie.int *Web Site:* www.oie.int, pg 1268

Office Marocain D'Annonces-OMA (Morocco) *Tel:* (02) 234891; (02) 232342 *Fax:* (02) 234892, pg 475

Office national des Librairies Populaires (ONLP) (Congo) *Tel:* 833 485 *Fax:* 831 879, pg 1307

Office National du Tourisme (ONT) (Burundi) *Tel:* 222 023; 222 202; 229 390 *Fax:* 229 390 *E-mail:* ontbur@cbinf.com *Web Site:* www.burundi.gov.bi/tourisme.htm, pg 1496

Office of Libraries and Archives, Papua, New Guinea (Papua New Guinea) *Tel:* 3256200 *Fax:* 3251331 *E-mail:* ola@datec.com.pg *Web Site:* www.dg.com.pg/~ola, pg 1535

Office of Libraries & Archives, Papua New Guinea (Papua New Guinea) *Tel:* 325 6200 *Fax:* 325 1331 *E-mail:* ola@datec.com.pg, pg 516

The Office of Public Works, Publications Branch (OPW) (Ireland) *Tel:* (01) 6476000 *Fax:* (01) 6610747 *E-mail:* info@opw.ie *Web Site:* www.opw.ie, pg 1132

Officina Edizioni di Aldo Quinti (Italy) *Tel:* (06) 316336 *Fax:* (06) 65740514 *E-mail:* officinaedizioni@yahoo.com, pg 401

Officina Nova Konyvek (Hungary) *Tel:* (01) 557282 *Fax:* (01) 1686674, pg 323

Ediciones Offo, SA (Spain) *Tel:* (091) 5514214 *Fax:* (091) 5010699, pg 593

Offo SL (Spain) *Tel:* (01) 5514214 *Fax:* (01) 5010699, pg 1162

OGC Michele Broutta Editeur (France) *Tel:* (01) 45779371 *Fax:* (01) 40590432, pg 177

Ogunsanya Press, Publishers and Bookstores Ltd (Nigeria) *Tel:* (022) 310924, pg 506

Oguz Yayinlari (Turkey) *Tel:* (0212) 5264745; (0212) 5113418 *Fax:* (0212) 5114695, pg 651

Ohmsa (Republic of Korea) *Tel:* (02) 776-4868-9 *Fax:* (02) 779-6757 *E-mail:* ohm@ohm.co.kr *Web Site:* www.ohm.co.kr, pg 441

Ohmsha Ltd (Japan) *Tel:* (03) 3233-0641 *Fax:* (03) 3233-2426 *E-mail:* kaigaika@ohmsha.co.jp *Web Site:* www.ohmsha.co.jp, pg 424

Oidium Books (Australia) *Tel:* (052) 757045 *E-mail:* tecnilab@ozemail.com.au, pg 34

Oikos (Argentina) *Tel:* (011) 4951-9489; (011) 4951-8129 *E-mail:* postmaster@atlas.edu.ar, pg 8

Oikos-Tau SA Ediciones (Spain) *Tel:* (093) 7590791 *Fax:* (093) 7506825, pg 593

Oilfield Publications Ltd (United Kingdom) *Tel:* (01531) 634563 *Fax:* (01531) 634239; (01531) 633744 *E-mail:* opl@oilpubs.com *Web Site:* www.oilpubs.com, pg 734

Oireachtas Library (Ireland) *Tel:* (01) 618 3412 *Fax:* (01) 661 5583 *Web Site:* www.irlgov.ie/oireachtas, pg 1518

Editions de l'Oiseau-Lyre (Monaco) *Tel:* (093) 300944 *Fax:* (093) 301915 *E-mail:* oiseaulyre@monaco377.com *Web Site:* www.oiseaulyre.com, pg 473

Ediciones Ojeda (Spain) *Tel:* (093) 2370009 *Fax:* (093) 4159845 *E-mail:* lib.europa@mx3.redestb.es, pg 594

Editions Okad (Morocco) *Tel:* (07) 796970; (07) 796971; (07) 796973 *Fax:* (07) 798556 *E-mail:* okad@wanadoo.net.ma, pg 475

Okapi Centre de Diffusion (The Democratic Republic of the Congo) *Tel:* (012) 31457, pg 1307

OKKER Kiado (Hungary) *Tel:* (01) 3324587, pg 323

1729

Okoshko Ltd Publishers (Izdatelstvo) (Russian Federation) *Tel:* (095) 2450998 *Fax:* (095) 2053424, pg 547

Oktagon Verlagsgesellschaft mbH (Germany) *Tel:* (0221) 2059653-54 *Fax:* (0221) 2059660 *E-mail:* oktagon@buchhandlung-walterkoenig.de, pg 267

Forlaget Oktober A/S (Norway) *Tel:* (022) 23 35 46 20 *Fax:* (022) 23 35 46 21 *E-mail:* oktober@oktober.no *Web Site:* www.oktober.no, pg 510

Old Pond Publishing (United Kingdom) *Tel:* (01473) 238200 *Fax:* (01473) 238201 *E-mail:* info@oldpond.com *Web Site:* www.oldpond.com, pg 734

Old Vicarage Publications (United Kingdom) *Tel:* (01260) 279276 *Fax:* (01260) 298913, pg 734

Oldcastle Books Ltd (United Kingdom) *Tel:* (01582) 761264 *Fax:* (01582) 712244 *E-mail:* info@noexit.co.uk *Web Site:* www.noexit.co.uk, pg 734

Verlag Oldenbourg (Austria) *Tel:* (01) 712 62 58 *Fax:* (01) 712 62 58-19 *E-mail:* office@oldenbourg.at, pg 56

R Oldenbourg Verlag GmbH (Germany) *Tel:* (089) 45 05 10; (089) 45 05 12 04 *Fax:* (089) 45051333 (Zeitschriften); (089) 4505200 (Schulbuch); (089) 4505333 (Fachbuch), pg 267

Ole Brumm (Norway) *Tel:* 24051000 *Fax:* 24051099 *E-mail:* post@damm.no *Web Site:* www.dammbokklubb.no, pg 1255

The Oleander Press (United Kingdom) *Tel:* (01223) 357768 *E-mail:* editor@oleanderpress.com *Web Site:* oleanderpress.com, pg 735

David O'Leary Literary Agents (United Kingdom) *Tel:* (020) 7229 1623 *Fax:* (020) 7727 9624 *E-mail:* d.o'leary@virgin.net, pg 1142

Olho D'Agua Comercio e Servicos Editoriais Ltda (Brazil) *Tel:* (011) 2631287 *Fax:* (011) 2631287 *E-mail:* editora@olhodaguo.com.br, pg 87

Editoriale Olimpia SpA (Italy) *Tel:* (055) 30321 *Fax:* (055) 3032280 *E-mail:* editore@edolimpia.it; moie@edolimpia.it *Web Site:* www.edolimpia.it, pg 401

Ediciones Olimpic, SL (Spain) *Tel:* (093) 2382864 *E-mail:* edolimpic@worldonline.es, pg 594

Olion Publishers (Estonia) *Tel:* 655 0175 *Fax:* 655 0173 *E-mail:* olion@not.ee, pg 140

Edizioni Olivares (Italy) *Tel:* (02) 76001753 *Fax:* (02) 76002579 *E-mail:* olivares@edizioniolivares.com *Web Site:* www.edizioniolivares.com, pg 401

Oliveira Rocha-Comercio e Servics Ltda (Brazil) *Tel:* (011) 2845527; (011) 2886440 *Fax:* (011) 2845362; (011) 2842096 *E-mail:* dialetic@virtual.net.com.br, pg 87

Editions Olizane (Switzerland) *Tel:* (022) 328 52 52 *Fax:* (022) 328 57 96 *E-mail:* guides@olizane.ch *Web Site:* www.olizane.ch, pg 630

Olkos Editions (Greece) *Tel:* (0210) 36 21 379 *Fax:* (0210) 36 25 576 *Web Site:* www.olkos.gr, pg 1314

Ollif Publishing (Australia) *Tel:* (02) 9477-3496, pg 34

Edition Olms AG (Switzerland) *Tel:* (01) 2445030 *Fax:* (01) 2445031 *E-mail:* info@edition-olms.com *Web Site:* www.edition-olms.com, pg 630

Georg Olms Verlag AG (Germany) *Tel:* (05121) 15010 *Fax:* (05121) 150150; (05121) 32007 *E-mail:* info@olms.de *Web Site:* www.olms.de, pg 267

Leo S Olschki (Italy) *Tel:* (055) 6530684 *Fax:* (055) 6530214 *E-mail:* celso@olschki.it *Web Site:* www.olschki.it, pg 401

Nakladatelstvi Olympia AS (Czech Republic) *Tel:* (02) 224 810 146 *Fax:* (02) 222 312 137 *E-mail:* olympia@mbox.vol.cz, pg 126

O'Mahony & Co Ltd (Ireland) *Tel:* (061) 418155 *Fax:* (061) 414558 *E-mail:* info@omahonys.ie *Web Site:* www.omahonys.ie, pg 1319

Michael O'Mara Books Ltd (United Kingdom) *Tel:* (020) 7720 8643 *Fax:* (020) 7627 8953 (Editorial); (020) 7627 4900 (Foreign Sales) *E-mail:* enquiries@michaelomarabooks.com *Web Site:* www.michaelomarabooks.com, pg 735

Omdurman Islamic University (Sudan) *Tel:* 784348; 784365; 554272 *Fax:* 775253 *Web Site:* www.sudanembassy.org/contemporarylooks/umdurman.htm, pg 1546

Omega Boek BV (Netherlands) *Tel:* (020) 690 59 97 *Fax:* (020) 695 74 28 *E-mail:* info@omegaboek.nl, pg 487

Omega Distributors Ltd (New Zealand) *Tel:* (09) 2570081 *Fax:* (09) 2570082 *E-mail:* books@omegavision.co.nz *Web Site:* www.omegavision.co.nz/omega.html, pg 1330

Ediciones Omega SA (Spain) *Tel:* (093) 2010599; (093) 2013807; (093) 2012144 *Fax:* (093) 2097362 *E-mail:* omega@ediciones-omega.es *Web Site:* www.ediciones-omega.es, pg 594

Omilos Pnevmatikis Ananeoseos (Cyprus) *Tel:* (022) 775854 *Fax:* (022) 311931, pg 121

Omnibus Books (Australia) *Tel:* (08) 8363 2333 *Fax:* (08) 8363 1420 *E-mail:* omnibus@scholastic.com.au, pg 34

Editions Omnibus (France) *Tel:* (01) 44 16 05 00 *Fax:* (01) 44 16 05 05 *E-mail:* omnibus@psb-editions.com *Web Site:* www.omnibus.tm.fr, pg 177

Omnibus Press (United Kingdom) *Tel:* (020) 7434 0066 *Fax:* (020) 7287 6329 *E-mail:* music@musicsales.co.uk *Web Site:* www.musicsales.com, pg 735

Omnicon, SA (Spain) *Tel:* (091) 527 82 49 *Fax:* (091) 528 13 48 *E-mail:* omnicon@skios.es *Web Site:* www.omnicon.es, pg 594

Omnipress Praha (Czech Republic) *Tel:* (02) 61211406 *Fax:* (02) 61211856 *E-mail:* dcf.clock@omnipress.cz *Web Site:* www.omnipress.cz, pg 126

Omsons Publications (India) *Tel:* (011) 5412452 *Fax:* (011) 3289353 *E-mail:* omsons@satyam.net.in, pg 344

Omun Gak (Republic of Korea) *Tel:* (02) 3453-8278 *Fax:* (02) 508-5210, pg 441

On Stream Publications Ltd (Ireland) *Tel:* (021) 4385798 *Fax:* (021) 4385798 *E-mail:* info@onstream.ie *Web Site:* www.onstream.ie, pg 362

On The Stone (Australia) *Tel:* (02) 6334 3442 *Fax:* (02) 6334 3009 *Web Site:* www.onthestone.com.au, pg 34

Oncken Verlag KG (Germany) *Tel:* (02302) 930 93 800 *Fax:* (02302) 930 93 801 *E-mail:* info@brockhaus-verlag.de *Web Site:* www.brockhaus-verlag.de, pg 267

Ondorisha Publishers Ltd (Japan) *Tel:* (03) 3268-3108 *Fax:* (03) 3235-8695, pg 424

One Way Book Centre (New Zealand) *Tel:* (03) 64245731 *Fax:* (03) 64245731 *E-mail:* devcommchurch@hotmail.com *Web Site:* www.devonport.tco.asn.au/comm-church/oneway.htm, pg 1330

Oneindige Verhaal, t bvba (Belgium) *Tel:* (03) 7765225 *Fax:* (03) 7765225 *E-mail:* oneindigeverhaal@boekenbank.be, pg 1302

Oneworld Publications (United Kingdom) *Tel:* (01865) 310597 *Fax:* (01865) 310598 *E-mail:* info@oneworld-publications.com *Web Site:* www.oneworld.publications.com, pg 735

Ongaku No Tomo Sha Corporation (Japan) *Tel:* (03) 3235-2091 *Fax:* (03) 3235-2148 *E-mail:* home@ongakunotomo.co.jp *Web Site:* www.ongakunotomo.co.jp, pg 425

Onibon-Oje Book Club (Nigeria) *Tel:* (022) 313956, pg 1254

Onibon-Oje Publishers (Nigeria) *Tel:* (022) 313956, pg 506

ONK Agency Ltd (Turkey) *Tel:* (0212) 2498602; (0212) 2498603 *Fax:* (0212) 2525153 *E-mail:* karaca@onkagency.com *Web Site:* www.onkagency.com, pg 1138

Online Information Resources (Australia) *Tel:* (03) 6257 9177 *Fax:* (03) 6257 9030, pg 34

Onlywomen Press Ltd (United Kingdom) *Tel:* (020) 8354 0796 *Fax:* (020) 8960 2817 *E-mail:* onlywomenpress@aol.com *Web Site:* www.onlywomenpress.com, pg 735

Dr C D Ooft (Suriname) *Tel:* (0597) 499139, pg 608

Ooievaar (Netherlands) *Tel:* (020) 624 19 34 *Fax:* (020) 622 54 61 *E-mail:* pbo@pbo.nl *Web Site:* www.pbo.nl, pg 487

Op der Lay (Luxembourg) *Tel:* 83 97 42 *Fax:* 89 93 50 *E-mail:* opderlay@pt.lu *Web Site:* webplaza.pt.lu/public/opderlay; www.phi.lu, pg 451

Bokforlaget Opal AB (Sweden) *Tel:* (08) 6571990 *Fax:* (08) 6183470 *E-mail:* opal@opal.se *Web Site:* www.opal.se, pg 614

The Open Book (Australia) *Tel:* (08) 8124 0049 *Fax:* (08) 8223 4552 *E-mail:* openbook@openbook.com.au; service@openbook.com.au *Web Site:* www.openbook.com.au, pg 1299

Open Books Publishing Ltd (United Kingdom) *Tel:* (01460) 52565 *Fax:* (01460) 52565, pg 735

Open Gate Press (United Kingdom) *Tel:* (020) 7431 4391 *Fax:* (020) 7431 5129 *E-mail:* books@opengatepress.co.uk *Web Site:* www.opengatepress.co.uk, pg 735

Open University of Israel (Israel) *Tel:* (03) 6460460 *Fax:* (03) 6419279 *E-mail:* englishsite@openu.ac.il *Web Site:* www.openu.ac.il, pg 371

Open University Press (United Kingdom) *Tel:* (01628) 502500; (01628) 502720 (customer service) *Fax:* (01628) 635895 (customer service) *E-mail:* enquiries@openup.co.uk (general enqueries); emea_orders@mcgraw-hill.com (orders); emea_queries@mcgraw-hill.com (customer service) *Web Site:* mcgraw-hill.co.uk/openup, pg 736

Open University Worldwide (United Kingdom) *Tel:* (01908) 858785 *Fax:* (01908) 858787 *E-mail:* ouwenq@open.ac.uk *Web Site:* www.open.ac.uk, pg 736

Openbare Bibliotheek (Netherlands Antilles) *Tel:* (09) 434 5200 *Fax:* (09) 465 6247 *E-mail:* publiclibrary@curinfo.an *Web Site:* www.curacaopubliclibrary.an, pg 1531

Openbook Publishers (Australia) *Tel:* (08) 8223 5468 *Fax:* (08) 8223 4552 *E-mail:* openbook@peg.apc.org; service@openbook.com.au *Web Site:* www.openbook.com.au, pg 34

Opera (Greece) *Tel:* (0210) 3304546 *Fax:* (0210) 3303634 *E-mail:* opera@acci.gr, pg 311

Opera Tres Ediciones Musicales (Spain) *Tel:* (091) 542 4320 *Fax:* (091) 541 0580; (091) 680 76 26, pg 594

Editions Ophrys (France) *Tel:* (04) 92 53 85 72 *Fax:* (04) 92 51 78 65 *E-mail:* edition.ophrys@ophrys.fr; infos@ophrys.fr *Web Site:* www.ophrys-editions.com, pg 177

Opsys Operating System (France) *Tel:* (04) 76 84 34 20; (04) 76 84 34 34 *Fax:* (04) 76 84 34 21 *E-mail:* opsys@opsys.fr *Web Site:* www.opsys.fr, pg 178

Opus Book Publishing Ltd (United Kingdom) *Tel:* (01380) 871354 *Fax:* (01380) 871354 *E-mail:* opus@dmac.co.uk, pg 736

Opus Libri SRL (Italy) *Tel:* (055) 660833 *Fax:* (055) 670604 *E-mail:* opuslib@dada.it, pg 1321

Opus Publishing Ltd (United Kingdom) *Tel:* (020) 7267 1034 *Fax:* (020) 7267 6026 *E-mail:* opuspub@btconnect.com, pg 736

Opus Records & Publishing House (Slovakia) *Tel:* (02) 58247560 *Fax:* (02) 53412447 *E-mail:* opus@ba.profinet.sk, pg 560

Edicoes Ora & Labora (Portugal) *Tel:* (0252) 94 11 76 *Fax:* (0252) 87 29 47 *E-mail:* msingeverga@net.sapo.pt, pg 534

Verlag Orac im Verlag Kremayr & Scheriau (Austria) *Tel:* (01) 713 87 70 *Fax:* (01) 713 87 70-20 *E-mail:* office@kremayr-scheriau.at *Web Site:* www.kremayr-scheriau.at, pg 56

Or'am Publishers (Israel) *Tel:* (03) 5372277 *Fax:* (03) 5372281 *E-mail:* orampub@netvision.net.il *Web Site:* www.oram.co.il, pg 371

Editions de l'Orante (France) *Tel:* (01) 47 83 55 02 *Fax:* (01) 45 66 00 16, pg 178

Orbis Books (London) Ltd (United Kingdom) *Tel:* (020) 7602 5541 *Fax:* (020) 8742 7686 *E-mail:* bookshop@orbis-books.co.uk, pg 1352

Ediciones Orbis SA (Spain) *Tel:* (093) 2800512 *Fax:* (093) 2801472 *E-mail:* orbis@edorbis.es, pg 594

Orbis Verlag fur Publizistik GmbH (Germany) *Tel:* (089) 4372-0 *Fax:* (089) 4372-2674, pg 267

Orca Publishing Services Ltd (New Zealand) *Tel:* (03) 377-0370 *Fax:* (03) 377-0390 *E-mail:* info@hazard.co.nz *Web Site:* www.hazardonline.com, pg 499

Orchid Press (Suriname), pg 608

Ordfront Foerlag AB (Sweden) *Tel:* (08) 462 44 00 *Fax:* (08) 4624490 *E-mail:* forlaget@ordfront.se; info@ordfront.se *Web Site:* www.ordfront.se, pg 614

Ordnance Survey (United Kingdom) *Tel:* (08456) 05 05 05 (customer information); (023) 8079 2912 (outside Britain); (023) 8030 5030 (business enquiries) *Fax:* (023) 8079 2615 (trade customer information); (023) 8079 2615 (outside Britain) *E-mail:* customerservices@ordnancesurvey.co.uk *Web Site:* www.ordnancesurvey.co.uk, pg 736

Orell Fuessli Buchhandlungs AG (Switzerland) *Tel:* (01) 466 77 11 *Fax:* (01) 466 74 12 *E-mail:* info@ofv.ch *Web Site:* www.ofv.ch, pg 630

Orell Fuessli Buchhandlungs AG (Switzerland) *Tel:* (0848) 849 848 *Fax:* (01) 455 56 20 *E-mail:* orders@books.ch; info@ofv.ch *Web Site:* www.ofv.ch; www.books.ch, pg 1344

Oreos Verlag GmbH (Germany) *Tel:* (08021) 86 68 *Fax:* (08021) 17 50 *Web Site:* www.oreos.de, pg 267

Orfanidis Publications (Greece) *Tel:* (01) 3836925 *Fax:* (01) 3845623, pg 311

Organisation for Economic Co-operation & Development OECD (France) *Tel:* (01) 45 24 82 00 *Fax:* (01) 45 24 85 00 *E-mail:* sales@oecd.org *Web Site:* www.oecd.org/bookshop; www.sourceoecd.org, pg 178

Verlag Organisator AG (Switzerland) *Tel:* (01) 2118155 *Fax:* (01) 4010815; (01) 4928758, pg 630

Organizacao Andrei Editora Ltda (Brazil) *Tel:* (011) 223-5111 *Fax:* (011) 221-0246 *E-mail:* diretoria@editora-andrei.com.br *Web Site:* www.editora-andrei.com.br, pg 87

Izdavacka Organizacija Rad (Serbia and Montenegro) *Tel:* (011) 3239-758; (011) 3239-998 *Fax:* (011) 3230-923, pg 553

Organizacion Cultural LP SA de CV (Mexico) *Tel:* (05) 55112312; (05) 147608 *E-mail:* orgcult@mail.internet.com.mx, pg 469

Organizacion de Bienestar Estudiantil (OBE) (Venezuela) *Tel:* (02) 6054050 (ext 4200); (02) 6054050 (ext 4201); (02) 6054050 (ext 4202) *Fax:* (02) 6930638 *Web Site:* www.ucv.ve/ftproot/obe/obe.htm, pg 1356

Organization for Economic Cooperation & Development (OECD) (France) *Tel:* (01) 45 24 82 00 *Fax:* (01) 45 24 85 00 *E-mail:* news.contact@oecd.org *Web Site:* www.oecd.org, pg 1268

Organizations of Libraries, Museums & Documentation Centre of Astan Quds (Islamic Republic of Iran) *Tel:* (098511) 2216009 *Fax:* (098511) 2220845 *E-mail:* webmaster@aqlibrary.org; info@aqlibrary.org *Web Site:* www.aqlibrary.org, pg 1517

The Organizing Committee of the 11th International Zeolite Conference (Republic of Korea) *Tel:* (042) 69-8161 *Fax:* (042) 69-8170 *E-mail:* skihm@sorak.kaist.ac.kr, pg 441

Orient Book Club (India) *Tel:* (011) 2386-2267 *E-mail:* orientpbk@vsnl.com, pg 1253

Orient Paperbacks (India) *Tel:* (011) 2386-2267; (011) 2386-2201 *Fax:* (011) 2386-2935 *E-mail:* orientpbk@vsnl.com *Web Site:* www.orientpaperbacks.com, pg 344

Oriental Books (Republic of Korea) *Tel:* (02) 334-9404 *Fax:* (02) 334-6624, pg 441

Oriental Press BV (APA) (Netherlands) *Tel:* (020) 626 5544 *Fax:* (020) 528 5298 *E-mail:* info@apa-publishers.com *Web Site:* www.apa-publishers.com, pg 487

Oriental Publications (Australia) *Tel:* (08) 8212 6055 *Fax:* (08) 8410 0863 *E-mail:* oriental@dove.mtx.net.au, pg 34

Bibliotheque Orientale (Lebanon) *Tel:* (01) 202 421 *Fax:* (01) 339 287 *E-mail:* bo@usj.edu.lb *Web Site:* www.usj.edu.lb, pg 1525

Editorial Oriente (Cuba) *Tel:* (0226) 22496; (0226) 28096 *Fax:* (0226) 86111 *E-mail:* edoriente@cultstgo.cult.cu, pg 120

Ediciones del Oriente y del Mediterraneo (Spain) *Tel:* (091) 854 34 28 *Fax:* (091) 854 83 52 *E-mail:* sicamor@teleline.es *Web Site:* www.webdoce.com/orienteymediterraneo, pg 594

Origen Editorial SA (Mexico) *Tel:* (055) 50-89-12-20 *Fax:* (055) 50-89-12-30, pg 469

L'Originel - Editions Accarias (France) *Tel:* (01) 43 48 73 07 *Fax:* (01) 43 48 73 07 *E-mail:* originel-accarias@club-internet.fr, pg 178

Origo Verlag (Switzerland) *Tel:* (031) 3114480 *Fax:* (031) 3114470, pg 630

Origo Forlag (Norway) *Tel:* 22160769 *Fax:* 22164837, pg 510

Orin Books (Australia) *Tel:* (03) 9534 5680; (03) 9534 4746 *Fax:* (03) 9527 6995, pg 34

Orion Children's Books (United Kingdom) *Tel:* (020) 7240 3444 *Fax:* (020) 7240 4822 *E-mail:* info@orionbooks.co.uk *Web Site:* www.orionbooks.co.uk, pg 736

Editorial Orion (Mexico) *Tel:* (05) 5200224 *Fax:* (05) 5200224, pg 469

Editura Orion (Romania) *Tel:* (01) 3125250 *Fax:* (01) 2104636, pg 541

Orion Publishing Group Ltd (United Kingdom) *Tel:* (020) 7240 3444 *Fax:* (020) 7240 4822 *E-mail:* info@orionbooks.co.uk *Web Site:* orionbooks.co.uk, pg 736

The Orkney Press Ltd (United Kingdom) *Tel:* (01856) 874058, pg 736

Orlanda Frauenverlag (Germany) *Tel:* (030) 216-3566; (030) 216-2960 *Fax:* (030) 2153958 *E-mail:* post@orlanda.de *Web Site:* www.orlanda.de, pg 267

Ormstunga (Iceland) *Tel:* 561 0055 *Fax:* 552 4650 *E-mail:* books@ormstunga.is *Web Site:* www.ormstunga.is, pg 326

Oros Verlag (Germany) *Tel:* (02505) 947191 *Fax:* (02505) 3534, pg 267

Orpheus Books Ltd (United Kingdom) *Tel:* (01993) 774949 *Fax:* (01993) 700330 *E-mail:* info@orpheusbooks.com *Web Site:* www.orpheusbooks.com, pg 736

Orszagos Muoszaki, Informacios Koozpont es Koonyvtar (OMIKK) (Hungary) *Tel:* (01) 463-3534; (01) 463-1069 *Fax:* (01) 463-24-40 *E-mail:* kolcs@omikk.bme.hu *Web Site:* www.omikk.bme.hu, pg 1515

Orszagos Szechenyi Koenyvtar (Hungary) *Tel:* (01) 224-3788 *Fax:* (01) 202-0804; (01) 375-9984 *E-mail:* kint@oszk.hu *Web Site:* www.oszk.hu, pg 1515

Orszagos Szechenyi Konyvtar (Hungary) *Tel:* (01) 224-3700 *Fax:* (01) 202-0804 *E-mail:* isbn@oszk.hu *Web Site:* www.oszk.hu, pg 1272

Orte-Verlag (Switzerland) *Tel:* (01) 888 1556 *E-mail:* info@orteverlag.ch *Web Site:* www.orteverlag.ch, pg 630

Editorial Alfredo Ortells SL (Spain) *Tel:* (096) 347 10 00 *Fax:* (096) 347 39 10 *E-mail:* editorial@ortells.com *Web Site:* www.ortells.com, pg 594

Editora Ortiz SA (Brazil) *Tel:* (051) 225-3026 *Fax:* (051) 225-3026, pg 88

Oruem Publishing House (Republic of Korea) *Tel:* (02) 5859122; (02) 5859123 *Fax:* (02) 5847952, pg 442

OS (Organizzazioni Speciali SRL) (Italy) *Tel:* (055) 6236501 *Fax:* (055) 669446, pg 401

Osaka Oviss Inc (Japan) *Tel:* (06) 352 7090 *Fax:* (06) 352 8898 *E-mail:* ovissbk@osk.3web.ne.jp, pg 1322

Osaka Prefectural Nakanoshima Library (Japan) *Tel:* (06) 6203-0474 *Fax:* (06) 2034914 *Web Site:* www.library.pref.osaka.jp, pg 1522

Osaka University Library (Japan) *Tel:* (06) 6850-5066 *Fax:* (06) 6850-5069 *Web Site:* www.library.osaka-u.ac.jp, pg 1522

Osanna Venosa (Italy) *Tel:* (0972) 35952 *Fax:* (0972) 35723, pg 402

Osborne Books Ltd (United Kingdom) *Tel:* (01905) 748071 *Fax:* (0190) 748952 *E-mail:* books@osborne.u-net.com *Web Site:* www.osbornebooks.co.uk, pg 736

Oscar Book International (Malaysia) *Tel:* (03) 7753515; (03) 7762797 *Fax:* (03) 7762797, pg 457

Osho Verlag GmbH (Germany) *Tel:* (0221) 278 04-0 *Fax:* (0221) 278 04-66 *E-mail:* info@oshoverlag.de *Web Site:* www.oshoverlag.de, pg 267

Osimpam Educational Books (Ghana), pg 304

Osiris Kiado (Hungary) *Tel:* (01) 266-6560 *Fax:* (01) 267-0935 *E-mail:* kiado@osirismail.hu *Web Site:* www.osiriskiado.hu, pg 323

Osnova, Kharkov State University Press (Ukraine) *Tel:* (057) 224647, pg 653

Osnovy Publishers (Ukraine) *Tel:* (044) 295 25 82; (044) 295 86 36 *Fax:* (044) 295 25 82, pg 654

Osprey Publishing Ltd (United Kingdom) *Tel:* (01933) 443863 *Toll Free Tel:* 800-826-6600 *Fax:* (01865) 727017 *E-mail:* info@ospreydirect.co.uk; info@ospreydirectusa.com (USA & Canada) *Web Site:* www.ospreypublishing.com, pg 737

Ossian Publications (Ireland) *Tel:* (021) 4502040 *Fax:* (021) 4502025 *E-mail:* ossian@iol.ie *Web Site:* www.ossian.ie, pg 363

Ossolineum Zaklad Narodowy im Ossolinskich - Wydawnictwo (Poland) *Tel:* (071) 3436961 *Fax:* (071) 3448103 *E-mail:* wydawnictwo@ossolineum.pl, pg 525

Verlag des Osterr Kneippbundes GmbH (Austria) *Tel:* (03842) 21682; (03842) 21718; (03842) 24094 *Fax:* (03842) 2171832 *E-mail:* office@kneippverlag.com *Web Site:* www.kneippverlag.com, pg 56

Osterreichische Bibelgesellschaft (Austria) *Tel:* (01) 5238240 *Fax:* (01) 5238240-20 *E-mail:* bibelhaus@bibelgesellschaft.at *Web Site:* www.oesterrbibelges.at, pg 1300

Osterreichische Nationalbibliothek (Austria) *Tel:* (01) 534 10 *Fax:* (01) 534 10 280 *E-mail:* onb@onb.ac.at *Web Site:* www.onb.ac.at, pg 1492

Osterreichischer Wirtschaftsverlag Druck-und Verlagsgesellschaft mbH (Austria) *Tel:* (01) 546 64-0 *Fax:* (01) 546 64-215 *E-mail:* office@oewv.at, pg 56

OSTFALIA-VERLAG JURGEN SCHIERER INDUSTRY

Ostfalia-Verlag Jurgen Schierer (Germany) *Tel:* (05171) 41763 *Fax:* (05171) 41769 *E-mail:* juergen.schierer@t-online.de *Web Site:* www.ostfalia-verlag.de, pg 267

Ostschweiz Druck und Verlag (Switzerland) *Tel:* (071) 2922929 *Fax:* (071) 2922938, pg 630

Vydavatel'stvo Osveta (Verlag Osveta) (Slovakia) *Tel:* (043) 4134 121 *Fax:* (0842) 35036, pg 560

Osvita (Ukraine) *Tel:* (032) 297 1206 *Fax:* (032) 297 1794 *E-mail:* info@osvita.org *Web Site:* www.osvita.org, pg 654

Otago Heritage Books (New Zealand) *Tel:* (03) 477 1500 *Fax:* (03) 477 1500 *E-mail:* otagoheritagebooks@clear.net.nz, pg 499

Otava Publishing Co Ltd (Finland) *Tel:* (09) 19961 *E-mail:* etunimi.sukunimi@otava.fi *Web Site:* www.otava.fi, pg 143

OTEN (Open Training & Education Network) (Australia) *Tel:* (02) 9715 8000; (02) 9715 8222 (sales) *Fax:* (02) 9715 8111; (02) 9715 8174 (sales) *E-mail:* oten.courseinfo@tafensw.edu.au *Web Site:* www.oten.edu.au, pg 34

Otokar Kersovani (Croatia) *Tel:* (051) 338 558; (051) 338 016 *Fax:* (051) 331 690 *E-mail:* otokar-kersovani@ri.tel.hr, pg 119

Otsuki Shoten Publishers (Japan) *Tel:* (03) 3813-4651 *Fax:* (03) 3813-4656 *E-mail:* otsuki@meibun.or.jp, pg 425

Ott Verlag Thun (Switzerland) *Tel:* (033) 225 39 39 *Fax:* (033) 225 39 33 *E-mail:* info@ott-verlag.ch *Web Site:* www.ott-verlag.ch, pg 630, 1162

Otto-Friedrich Universitat Bamberg (Germany) *Tel:* (0951) 863-1021 *Fax:* (0951) 863-4021 *E-mail:* presse@uni-bamberg.de *Web Site:* www.uni-bamberg.de/zuv/presse/mitarbeiter, pg 267

Oue Eesti Raamat (Estonia) *Tel:* 658 7885; 658 7886; 658 7887; 658 7889 *Fax:* 658 7889 *E-mail:* helgi.gailit@mail.ee *Web Site:* www.eestiraamat.ee, pg 140

Ouest Editions (France) *Tel:* (02) 40 14 34 34 *Fax:* (02) 40 14 36 36, pg 178

Editions Ouest-France (France) *Tel:* (02) 99 32 58 27 *Fax:* (02) 99 32 58 30 *Web Site:* www.edilarge.com, pg 178

Oulun Yliopiston Kirjasto (Finland) *Tel:* (08) 553 1011 *Fax:* (08) 556 9135 *Web Site:* www.kirjasto.oulu.fi/, pg 1505

Editions Oum (Morocco) *Tel:* (02) 274972; (02) 220454 *Fax:* (02) 208882; (02) 950963, pg 475

Our Lady of Manaoag Publisher (Philippines) *Tel:* (02) 610214; (02) 610219 *Fax:* (06) 610219, pg 520

Outback Books - CQU Press (Australia) *Tel:* (07) 4923 2520 *Fax:* (07) 4923 2525 *E-mail:* cqupress@cqu.edu.au *Web Site:* www.outbackbooks.com, pg 34

Outdoor Press Pty Ltd (Australia) *Tel:* (03) 5790 5226 *Fax:* (03) 5790 5393 *Web Site:* www.goldexpeditions.com.au, pg 35

Outrigger Publishers (New Zealand) *Tel:* (07) 856 6981, pg 499

Outskirts Press (United States) *E-mail:* info@outskirtspress.com *Web Site:* www.outskirtspress.com, pg 1231

Editorial Oveja Negra Ltda (Colombia) *Tel:* (01) 5309678 *Fax:* (01) 2577900, pg 112

George Over Ltd (United Kingdom) *Tel:* (01788) 573621 *Fax:* (01788) 578738 *E-mail:* xuz23@dial.pinex.com, pg 1227

Overseas Printing Corporation (United States) *Tel:* 415-835-9999 *Fax:* 415-835-9899 *Web Site:* www.overseasprinting.com, pg 1168

Deborah Owen Ltd (United Kingdom) *Tel:* (020) 7987 5119; (020) 7987 5441 *Fax:* (020) 7538 4004 *E-mail:* do@deborahowen.co.uk, pg 1142

Peter Owen Ltd (United Kingdom) *Tel:* (020) 7373 5628; (020) 7370 6093 *Fax:* (020) 7373 6760 *E-mail:* admin@peterowen.com *Web Site:* www.peterowen.com, pg 737

Owl Publishing (Australia) *Tel:* (03) 95966064 *Fax:* (03) 95966942 *E-mail:* owlbooks@bigpond.com, pg 35

Oxfam (United Kingdom) *Tel:* (01865) 313744 *Fax:* (01865) 313713 *E-mail:* oxfam@oxfam.org.uk; publish@oxfam.org.uk *Web Site:* www.oxfam.org.uk, pg 737

Oxfam Community Aid Abroad (Australia) *Tel:* (03) 9289 9444 *Fax:* (03) 9419 5895 *E-mail:* enquire@caa.org.au *Web Site:* www.caa.org.au, pg 35

Oxford & IBH Publishing Co Pvt Ltd (India) *Tel:* (011) 2332 45 78; (011) 2332 05 18 *Fax:* (011) 2371 0090 *E-mail:* oxford@vsnl.com, pg 344

Oxford & IBH Publishing Co Pvt Ltd (India) *Tel:* (011) 3320518; (011) 3324578; (011) 3357791; (011) 3315310 *Fax:* (011) 3710090 *E-mail:* oxfordpubl@axcess.net.in, pg 1317

Oxford Bibliographical Society (United Kingdom) *Tel:* (01865) 277069 *Fax:* (01865) 277182 *E-mail:* membership@oxbibsoc.org.uk *Web Site:* www.oxbibsoc.org.uk, pg 1408

Oxford International Centre for Publishing Studies (United Kingdom) *Tel:* (01865) 484951 *Fax:* (01865) 484952 *E-mail:* publishing@brookes.ac.uk *Web Site:* www.brookes.ac.uk/schools/apm/publishing, pg 737

Oxford University Press (India) *Tel:* (011) 2021029; (011) 2021198; (011) 2021396 *Fax:* (011) 3732312; (011) 3360897 *E-mail:* admin.in@oup.com, pg 344

Oxford University Press (New Zealand) *Tel:* (03) 9934 9123 *Toll Free Tel:* 1300 650 616 (Australia); 0800 442 502 (New Zealand) *Fax:* (03) 9934 9100 *Toll Free Fax:* 0800-442-503 *E-mail:* cs@oup.com.au *Web Site:* www.oup.com.au, pg 499

Oxford University Press (United Republic of Tanzania) *Tel:* (051) 222 116389; (051) 222 113704 *Fax:* (051) 222 116614 *E-mail:* oxford@raha.com *Web Site:* www.oup.com, pg 644

Oxford University Press (United Kingdom) *Tel:* (01865) 556767 *Fax:* (01865) 556646 *Web Site:* www.oup.co.uk, pg 737

Oxford University Press Children's Books (United Kingdom) *Tel:* (01865) 556767 *Fax:* (01865) 267732 *E-mail:* enquiry@oup.com *Web Site:* www.oup.co.uk, pg 737

Oxford University Press Espana SA (Spain) *Tel:* (091) 6602600 *Fax:* (091) 6602626; (091) 6602629, pg 594

Oxford University Press KK (Japan) *Tel:* (03) 3459 6489 *Fax:* (03) 3459 8661 *Web Site:* www.oupjapan.co.jp, pg 425

Oxford University, Taylor Institution Library (United Kingdom) *Tel:* (01865) 2-78154; (01865) 2-78158 (book enquiries) *Fax:* (01865) 2-78165 *E-mail:* enquiries@taylib.ox.ac.uk *Web Site:* www.taylib.ox.ac.uk, pg 1553

Oxonian Press (P) Ltd (India) *Tel:* (011) 44957; (011) 3313584 *Fax:* (011) 3322639 *E-mail:* oxford.publ@axcess.net.in, pg 344

Jill Oxton Publications Pty Ltd (Australia) *Tel:* (08) 2762722 *Fax:* (08) 3743494 *E-mail:* jill@jilloxtonxstitch.com *Web Site:* www.jilloxtonxstitch.com, pg 35

Oyster Books Ltd (United Kingdom) *Tel:* (01934) 732251 *Fax:* (01934) 732123 *E-mail:* pearls@oysterbooks.co.uk, pg 737

P & R Centrum Vydavateistvi a Nakladateistvi (Czech Republic) *Tel:* (02) 542901 *Fax:* (02) 51554485 *E-mail:* olda@katapult.cz, pg 126

P P H Penta (Poland) *Tel:* (022) 834 08 43 *Fax:* (022) 8641854; (022) 8340843 *E-mail:* penta@pol.pl *Web Site:* www.penta.pl, pg 525

Pabel-Moewig Verlag KG (Germany) *Tel:* (07222) 13 0 *Fax:* (07222) 13 218 *E-mail:* kontakt@moewig.de *Web Site:* www.vpm-online.de, pg 267

Pacific Book Centre (S) Pte Ltd (Singapore) *Tel:* 6464 0111 *Fax:* 6464 0110 *E-mail:* enquiries@snpcorp.com *Web Site:* www.snp.com.sg, pg 1339

Pacific Publications (Australia) Pty Ltd (Australia) *Tel:* (02) 9464 3300 *Fax:* (02) 9464 3375 *Web Site:* pacificpubs.com.au, pg 35

Maria Pacini Fazzi Editore (Italy) *Tel:* (0583) 440188 *Fax:* (0583) 464656 *E-mail:* mpf@pacinifazzi.it *Web Site:* www.pacinifazzi.it, pg 402

Packard Publishing Ltd (United Kingdom) *Tel:* (01243) 537977 *Fax:* (01243) 537977 *E-mail:* info@packardpublishing.co.uk *Web Site:* www.packardpublishing.com, pg 737

Packer-Evans & Associates Ltd (Jamaica) *Tel:* 876-929-0531 *Fax:* 876-926-3487, pg 414

PacPress Media Pte Ltd (Singapore) *Tel:* 2768090; 2730756 *Fax:* 2730060, pg 1223

Library of the Padagogic Institute Academia (College of Education) (Cyprus) *Tel:* (022) 402-300 *Fax:* (022) 480-505 *E-mail:* webmaster@cyearn.pi.ac.cy *Web Site:* athena.pi.ac.cy/pedagogical/index.html, pg 1501

Pademelon Press (Australia) *Tel:* (02) 9634-4655 *Fax:* (02) 9680-4634 *E-mail:* info@pademelonpress.com.au *Web Site:* www.pademelonpress.com.au, pg 35

Editorial Padilla (Dominican Republic) *Tel:* 379-1550 *Fax:* 379-2631 *E-mail:* edpadilla@codetel.net.do, pg 1308

George Padmore Research Library on African Affairs (Ghana) *Tel:* (021) 228 402; (021) 223526 *Fax:* (021) 247 768, pg 1512

Biblioteca Universitaria di Padua (Italy) *Tel:* (049) 8240211; (049) 8240241 *Fax:* (049) 8762711 *E-mail:* bupd@librari.beniculturali.it *Web Site:* www.unipd.it/bibliotecauniversitaria, pg 1520

Paerangi Books (New Zealand) *Tel:* (04) 4787789, pg 500

Pagano Editore (Italy) *Tel:* (081) 5642968 *Fax:* (081) 5646694 *E-mail:* redazione@paganoeditore.com, pg 402

Page Bros Ltd (Norwich) (United Kingdom) *Tel:* (01603) 429141 *Fax:* (01603) 485126, pg 1164, 1185, 1227

Page Bros Ltd (Norwich) (United Kingdom) *Tel:* (01603) 429141 *Fax:* (01603) 485126 *E-mail:* info@pagebros.co.uk *Web Site:* www.milex.co.uk, pg 1239, 1248

Pages Editors, SL (Spain) *Tel:* (0973) 23 66 11 *Fax:* (0973) 24 07 95 *E-mail:* ed.pages.editors@cambrescat.es; editorial.milenio@cambrescat.es, pg 594

Pageworks (United States) *Tel:* 860-395-2022; 860-434-3605 *Fax:* 860-388-4353, pg 1188

Pagina da Cultura Agencia Literaria Ideias sobre Linhas Ltda (Brazil) *Tel:* (011) 31293900 *E-mail:* paginadacultura@pobox.com *Web Site:* www.pagina-da-cultura.com.br, pg 1129

Pagina Forlags AB (Sweden) *Tel:* (08) 564 218 00 *Fax:* (08) 564 218 19 *E-mail:* info@pagina.se *Web Site:* www.pagina.se, pg 614

Pagoulatos Bros (Greece) *Tel:* (01) 03818780; (01) 03801485 *Fax:* (01) 03838028 *E-mail:* pagoulatos_publ@ath.forthnet.gr, pg 311

Pagoulatos G-G P Publications (Greece) *Tel:* (0210) 3604895; (0210) 3600720 *Fax:* (0210) 3604897, pg 311

Pahl-Rugenstein Verlag Nachfolger-GmbH (Germany) *Tel:* (0228) 632306 *Fax:* (0228) 634968 *E-mail:* prv@che-chandler.com, pg 267

Paico Publishing House (India) *Tel:* (0484) 355835 *Web Site:* www.paicoindia.com, pg 344

Paideia Editrice (Italy) *Tel:* (030) 3582434 *Fax:* (030) 3582691 *E-mail:* paideiaeditrice@tin.it, pg 402

YELLOW PAGES

Editura Paideia (Romania) *Tel:* (01) 2115804; (01) 2120347 *Fax:* (01) 2120348 *E-mail:* paideia@fx.ro, pg 541

Editura Paideia (Romania) *Tel:* (01) 2104593 *Fax:* (01) 2106987 *E-mail:* paideia@fx.ro *Web Site:* www.paideia.ro, pg 1161

Ediciones Paidos Iberica SA (Spain) *Tel:* (093) 241 92 50 *Fax:* (093) 202 29 54 *E-mail:* paidos@paidos.com *Web Site:* www.paidos.com, pg 594

Editorial Paidos Mexicana, SA (Mexico) *Tel:* (05) 5795922; (05) 5795113 *Fax:* (05) 5904361 *E-mail:* epaidos@paidos.com.mx *Web Site:* www.paidos.com, pg 469

Editorial Paidos SAICF (Argentina) *Tel:* (011) 4331-2275 *Fax:* (011) 4343-0954 *E-mail:* direccion@editorialpaidos.com.ar *Web Site:* www.paidosargentina.com.ar, pg 8

Editorial Paidotribo SL (Spain) *Tel:* (093) 3233311 *Fax:* (093) 4535033 *E-mail:* paidotribo@paidotribo.com *Web Site:* www.paidotribo.com, pg 594

Editions J H Paillet et B Drouaud (France) *Tel:* 54704303, pg 178

Charles Paine Pty Ltd (Australia) *Tel:* (02) 9890 1388 *Fax:* (02) 9890 1915, pg 35

Ediciones El Pais SA (Spain) *Tel:* (091) 3301015 *Fax:* (091) 7449093 *E-mail:* elpaisaguilar@santillana.es, pg 594

Pais Vasco Servicio Central de Publicaciones (Spain) *Tel:* (0945) 01 68 66 *Fax:* (0945) 01 87 09 *E-mail:* hac-sabd@ej-gv.es *Web Site:* www.ej-gv.net/publicaciones/cpa0/SCP.htm, pg 594

El Paisaje Editorial (Spain) *Tel:* (04) 6390774, pg 594

Paiva Osakeyhtio (Finland) *Tel:* (03) 644 6110 *Fax:* (03) 612 2109 *E-mail:* paiva@paiva.fi *Web Site:* www.paiva.fi, pg 143

Pak American Commercial (Pvt) Ltd (Pakistan) *Tel:* (051) 563709 *Fax:* (051) 565190, pg 514, 1334

Pak Book Corporation (Pakistan) *Tel:* (042) 111 636 636 *Fax:* (042) 6362328 *E-mail:* pbc@brain.net.pk, pg 1334

Pakistan Institute of Development Economics (PIDE) (Pakistan) *Tel:* (051) 9206610-27 *Fax:* (051) 9210886 *E-mail:* pide@apollo.net.pk *Web Site:* www.pide.org.pk, pg 514

Pakistan Institute of Development Economics (PIDE) (Pakistan) *Tel:* (051) 9206616 *Fax:* (051) 9210886 *E-mail:* pide@pide.org.pk *Web Site:* www.pide.org.pk, pg 1535

Pakistan Institute of Nuclear Science & Technology Library, Science Information Division (Pakistan) *Tel:* (051) 452350 *Fax:* (051) 429533 *E-mail:* ctc@shell.portal.com, pg 1535

Pakistan Library Association (PLA) (Pakistan) *Tel:* (051) 921-4523; (051) 920-2544; (051) 920-2549 *Fax:* (051) 922-1375 *E-mail:* nlpiba@isb.paknet.com.pk *Web Site:* www.nlp.gov.pk, pg 1569

Pakistan Publishing House (Pakistan) *Tel:* (021) 5681457, pg 514

Pakistan Scientific & Technological Information Centre (PASTIC) (Pakistan) *Tel:* (051) 920 1340; (051) 920 1341; (051) 920 7641 *Fax:* (051) 9207211 *E-mail:* pastic@isb.pol.com.pk *Web Site:* www.psf.gov.pk/pastic, pg 1535

Pakistan Writers' Guild (Pakistan) *Tel:* 6367124, pg 1403

Pakpassak Kanphin (Laos People's Democratic Republic), pg 444

Pal Verlagsgesellschaft mbH (Germany) *Tel:* (0621) 415741 *Fax:* (0621) 415101 *E-mail:* info@palverlag.de *Web Site:* www.pal-verlag.de, pg 267

Pala-Verlag GmbH (Germany) *Tel:* (06151) 23028 *Fax:* (06151) 292713 *E-mail:* info@pala-verlag.de *Web Site:* www.pala-verlag.de, pg 268

Palabra Ediciones S A de C V (Mexico) *Tel:* (05) 5730985 *Fax:* (05) 5730985, pg 469

Ediciones Palabra SA (Spain) *Tel:* (091) 350 1179; (091) 350 7720 *Fax:* (091) 359 02 30 *E-mail:* ayuda@edicionespalabra.es *Web Site:* www.edicionespalabra.es, pg 595

Palace Press International (Hong Kong) *Tel:* 2357 9019 *Fax:* 415-532-3007 *E-mail:* palacehk@palacepress.ocm; ppihk@palacepress.com; info@palacepress.com *Web Site:* www.palacepress.com, pg 1157

Palace Press International - Corporate Headquarters (United States) *Tel:* 415-526-1370 *Fax:* 415-526-1394 *E-mail:* info@palacepress.com *Web Site:* www.palacepress.com, pg 1168

Palace Press International - Corporate Headquarters (United States) *Tel:* 415-526-1370 *Toll Free Tel:* 800-809-3792 *Fax:* 415-526-1394 *E-mail:* info@palacepress.com *Web Site:* www.palacepress.com, pg 1188, 1231, 1241, 1249

Palacio del Libro (Uruguay) *Tel:* (02) 959019 *Fax:* (02) 957543, pg 1356

Biblioteca do Palacio Nacional de Mafra (Portugal) *Tel:* (0261) 817 550 *Fax:* (0261) 811947, pg 1539

Palas Editores Lda (Portugal) *Tel:* (021) 574903 *Fax:* (021) 795-4019, pg 534

Palatina Editrice (Italy) *Tel:* (0521) 282388 *Fax:* (0521) 282388 *Web Site:* culturitalia.uibk.ac.at, pg 402

Edit Palavra Magica (Brazil) *Tel:* (016) 610-0204 *Fax:* (016) 625-4583 *E-mail:* editora@palavramagica.com.br *Web Site:* www.palavramagica.com.br, pg 88

Palazzi Verlag GmbH (Germany) *Tel:* (0421) 321100 *Fax:* (0421) 321300, pg 268

Palestinian PEN Centre (Israel) *Tel:* (02) 6262970 *Fax:* (02) 6264620 *E-mail:* palpenc@palnet.com, pg 1401

Palgrave Publishers Ltd (United Kingdom) *Tel:* (01256) 329242 *Fax:* (01256) 479476 *E-mail:* orders@palgrave.com (ordering online); catalogue@palgrave.com (catalogue requests); conferences@palgrave.com (conference & exhibition information); rights@palgrave.com (copyright & permissions); lectureservices@palgrave.com (inspection copy service); reviews@palgrave.com (review copy requests); booksellers@palgrave.com (bookseller queries) *Web Site:* www.palgrave.com, pg 737

Pallas-Akademia Editura (Romania) *Tel:* (066) 171036 *Fax:* (066) 171036 *E-mail:* pallas@nextra.ro, pg 541

Pallas Athene (United Kingdom) *Tel:* (020) 7229 2798 *Fax:* (020) 7792 1067, pg 738

Pallas Editora e Distribuidora Ltda (Brazil) *Tel:* (021) 270-0186 *Fax:* (021) 590-6996; (21) 5618007 *E-mail:* pallas@alternex.com.br *Web Site:* www.pallaseditora.com.br, pg 88

Vydavatel'stvo SFVU Pallas (Slovakia) *Tel:* (07) 296627 *Fax:* (07) 294229; (07) 292820, pg 560

Palle Fogtdal A/S (Denmark) *Tel:* 3315 3915 *Fax:* 3393 3505, pg 133

Pallottinum Wydawnictwo Stowarzyszenia Apostolstwa Katolickiego (Poland) *Tel:* (061) 867-52-33 *Fax:* (061) 867-52-38 *E-mail:* pallottinum@pallottinum.pl *Web Site:* www.pallottinum.pl, pg 525

Palm Beach Press (Australia) *Tel:* (02) 6646 1622 *Fax:* (02) 9946 1515, pg 35

Palmerston North Public Library (New Zealand) *Tel:* (06) 351 4100 *Fax:* (06) 351 4102 *E-mail:* pncl@pncc.govt.nz *Web Site:* citylibrary.pncc.govt.nz, pg 1532

Palms Press (Australia) *Tel:* (02) 4973 1236, pg 35

Palmyra Verlag (Germany) *Tel:* (06221) 165409 *Fax:* (06221) 167310 *E-mail:* palmyra-verlag@t-online.de *Web Site:* www.palmyra-verlag.de, pg 268

Fratelli Palombi SRL (Italy) *Tel:* (06) 3214150 *Fax:* (06) 3214752 *E-mail:* flli.palombi@mail.stm.it, pg 402

PANDORA PUBLISHING HOUSE

Palphot Ltd (Israel) *Tel:* (09) 9525252 *Fax:* (09) 9525277 *E-mail:* palphot@palphot.com *Web Site:* www.palphot.com, pg 1320

Joergen Paludan Forlag ApS (Denmark) *Tel:* 4975-1536 *Fax:* 4975-1537 *E-mail:* paludans.forlag@mobilixnet.dk, pg 133

G B Palumbo & C Editore SpA (Italy) *Tel:* (091) 588850 *Fax:* (091) 6111848 *E-mail:* redazione@palumboeditore.it *Web Site:* www.palumboeditore.it, pg 402

Pamatnik narodniho pisemnictvi (Czech Republic) *Tel:* (02) 20516695 *Fax:* (02) 20517277 *E-mail:* post@pamatniknarodnihopisemnictvi.cz *Web Site:* www.pamatniknarodnihopisemnictvi.cz, pg 1501

Pan African Institute for Development (PAID) (Cameroon) *Tel:* 332 28 06 *Fax:* 332 28 06 *E-mail:* info@paid-wa.org *Web Site:* www.paid-wa.org, pg 1264

Pan Agency (Sweden) *Tel:* (08) 769 87 00 *Fax:* (08) 769 88 04 *Web Site:* www.panagency.se, pg 1137

Pan Korea Book Corporation (Republic of Korea) *Tel:* (02) 733-2011; (02) 733-2018 *Fax:* (02) 736-8696 *E-mail:* info@bumhanbook.co.kr *Web Site:* www.bumhanbook.co.kr, pg 442

Pan Macmillan (United Kingdom) *Tel:* (020) 7881 8000 *Fax:* (020) 7881 8001 *Web Site:* www.panmacmillan.com, pg 738

Pan Macmillan Australia Pty Ltd (Australia) *Tel:* (02) 9285 9100 *Fax:* (02) 9285 9100 *E-mail:* pansyd@macmillan.com.au (general); panpublicity@macmillan.com.au (publicity) *Web Site:* www.panmacmillan.com.au, pg 35

Pan Malayan Publishing Co Sdn Bhd (Malaysia) *Tel:* (603) 7910420 *Fax:* (603) 92214333, pg 457

Pan Pacific Publications (S) Pte Ltd (Singapore) *Tel:* 2616288 *Fax:* 2616088 *E-mail:* ppps@pacific.net.sg, pg 557

Pan Yayincilik (Turkey) *Tel:* (0212) 2618072; (0212) 2275675 *Fax:* (0212) 2275674 *E-mail:* pan@pankitap.com *Web Site:* www.pankitap.com, pg 651

Panaf Books (United Kingdom) *Tel:* (0870) 333 1192 *E-mail:* zakakembo@yahoo.co.uk *Web Site:* www.panafbooks.com, pg 738

Editorial Panamericana (Colombia) *Tel:* (01) 360 30 77; (01) 277 01 00; (01) 3649000 (ext 213); (03) 5603831; (03) 5603832; (03) 5603833 *Fax:* (01) 2373805 *E-mail:* panaedit@panamericanaeditorial.com *Web Site:* www.panamericanaeditorial.com, pg 112

Panamericana Libreria y Papeleria SA (Colombia) *Tel:* (01) 3649000 (ext 213) *Fax:* (01) 3600885 *Web Site:* www.panamericana.com.co, pg 1306

Instituto Panamericano de Geografia e Historia (Mexico) *Tel:* (05) 2775888; (05) 5151910; (05) 2775791 *Fax:* (05) 2716172 *E-mail:* cvasi@ipgh.spin.com.mx, pg 469

Libreria Commissionaria Internazionale di Raffaele Pancaldi (Italy) *Tel:* (051) 229466 *Fax:* (051) 229466, pg 1321

Panchasheel Prakashan (India) *Tel:* (0141) 65072 *Fax:* (0141) 326554, pg 344

Pandani Press (Australia) *Tel:* (03) 6225 1956 *E-mail:* pandani@iprimus.com.au, pg 35

Pandion-Verlag, Ulrike Schmoll (Germany) *Tel:* (06761) 7142 *Fax:* (06761) 77172 *E-mail:* pandion@t-online.de; info@pandion-verlag.de *Web Site:* www.pandion-verlag.de, pg 268

Petraco-Pandora NV (Belgium) *Tel:* (03) 2338770 *Fax:* (03) 2333399, pg 71

Pandora Publishing House (Romania) *Tel:* (021) 688 6739 *Fax:* (021) 243 3739, pg 541

1733

Panem (Hungary) *Tel:* (01) 460-0273 *Fax:* (01) 460-0274 *E-mail:* panem@mail.datanet.hu *Web Site:* www.panem.hu, pg 324

Panepistimio Ioanninon (Greece) *Tel:* (026510) 97122 *Fax:* (026510) 97015 *E-mail:* intlrel@uoi.gr *Web Site:* www.uoi.gr, pg 311

Pangea Editores, Sa de CV (Mexico) *Tel:* (05) 5738684 *Fax:* (05) 5130638 *E-mail:* pangea@data.net.mx, pg 470

Franco Cosimo Panini Editore (Italy) *Tel:* (059) 343572 *Fax:* (059)344274 *E-mail:* info@fcp.it *Web Site:* www.fcp.it, pg 402

Franco Cosimo Panini Editore SpA (Italy) *Tel:* (059) 343572 *Fax:* (059) 344274 *E-mail:* info@fcp.it *Web Site:* www.fcp.it; www.francopanini.com, pg 402

Edizioni Franco Cosimo Panini (Italy) *Tel:* (059) 343572 *Fax:* (059) 344274 *E-mail:* info@fcp.it *Web Site:* www.fcp.it, pg 402

Panjab University Publication Bureau (India) *Tel:* (0172) 541782; (0172) 534373, pg 344

Pankaj Publications (India) *Tel:* (011) 3363395; (011) 3348805 *Fax:* (011) 5163525; (01) 5511684 *E-mail:* pankajbooks@hotmail.com, pg 344

Panmun Book Co Ltd (Republic of Korea) *Tel:* (02) 953-2451 (ext 5) *Fax:* (02) 953-2456 (ext 7) *E-mail:* pmbtrd2@chollian.net; pmbimp@unitel.co.kr, pg 442

Panmun Book Co Ltd (Republic of Korea) *Tel:* (02) 953-2451-5 *Fax:* (02) 953-2456-7 *E-mail:* panmunex@unitel.co.kr, pg 1324

Editions du Panorama (Switzerland) *Tel:* (032) 3581665 *Fax:* (032) 3581665, pg 630

Panorama Editorial, SA (Mexico) *Tel:* (05) 5359348; (05) 5359074; (05) 5350377 *Fax:* (05) 5359202; (05) 5351217 *E-mail:* panorama@iserve.net.mx *Web Site:* www.panoramaed.com.mx, pg 470

Panorama NIJP/ID Grigorije Bozovic (Serbia and Montenegro) *Tel:* (038) 29 090; (038) 21 156; (038) 29 866 *Fax:* (038) 29 809, pg 553

Panorama Publishing House (Russian Federation) *Tel:* (095) 2053707 *Fax:* (095) 2053708, pg 547

Panos Institute (United Kingdom) *Tel:* (020) 7278 1111 *Fax:* (020) 7278 0345 *E-mail:* info@panoslondon.org.uk *Web Site:* www.panos.org.uk, pg 738

Panstwowe Przedsiebiorstwo Wydawnictw Kartograficznych (Poland) *Tel:* (022) 6283251; (022) 6214850 *Fax:* (022) 6280236; (022) 6214850 *E-mail:* ppwk@pdsox.com, pg 525

Panstwowe Wydawnictwo Rolnicze i Lesne (Poland) *Tel:* (022) 8276338 *Fax:* (022) 8276338, pg 525

Panstwowy Instytut Wydawniczy (PIW) (Poland) *Tel:* (022) 8260201; (022) 8260202; (022) 8260203; (022) 8260204; (022) 826-02-05 *Fax:* (022) 826-15-30 *E-mail:* piw@piw.pl *Web Site:* www.piw.pl, pg 525

Panther Publishing (Malaysia) *Tel:* (03) 2749854, pg 457

D Papadimas (Greece) *Tel:* (01) 3627318 *Fax:* (0210) 3610271, pg 311

Kyr I Papadopoulos E E (Greece) *Tel:* (0210) 2816134; (0210) 2846074; (0210) 2846075 *Fax:* (0210) 2817127 *E-mail:* info@picturebooks.gr *Web Site:* www.picturebooks.gr, pg 311

Papazissis Publishers SA (Greece) *Tel:* (0210) 3838020; (0210) 3822496 *Fax:* (0210) 3809150, pg 311

Paper Art Product Ltd (Hong Kong) *Tel:* 2481 2929 *Fax:* 2489 2255 *E-mail:* paperart@netvigator.com, pg 1158, 1219

Paper Communication Printing Express Ltd (Hong Kong) *Tel:* 27864191 *Fax:* 27864498 *E-mail:* pcpe@papercom.hk, pg 1158

Paper Communication Printing Express Ltd (Hong Kong) *Tel:* 27864191 *Fax:* 27864498 *E-mail:* pcpc@papercom.hk, pg 1179

Paper Communication Printing Express Ltd (Hong Kong) *Tel:* 27864191 *Fax:* 27864498, pg 1219

Paperback Publishers Ltd (Nigeria) *Tel:* (022) 317363, pg 507

Papirus Editora (Brazil) *Tel:* (0192) 3272 4500; (0192) 3272 4534 *Fax:* (0192) 3272 7578 *E-mail:* editora@papirus.com.br *Web Site:* www.papirus.com.br/, pg 1304

Papua New Guinea Institute of Medical Research (Papua New Guinea) *Tel:* 732-2800 *Fax:* 732-1998 *E-mail:* general@pngimr.org.pg *Web Site:* www.pngimr.org.pg, pg 516

Papua New Guinea Institute of Public Administration Library (PNGIPA) (Papua New Guinea) *Tel:* 3260433; 3267345; 3267163 *Fax:* 3261654 *E-mail:* gaudichn@upng.ac.pg, pg 1535

PapyRossa Verlags GmbH & Co Kommanditgesellschaft KG (Germany) *Tel:* (0221) 44 85 45 *Fax:* (0221) 44 43 05 *E-mail:* mail@papyrossa.de *Web Site:* www.papyrossa.de, pg 268

Editions du Papyrus (France) *Tel:* (01) 48 57 27 05 *Fax:* (01) 48 57 26 79 *E-mail:* papyrus@netfly.fr *Web Site:* www.editions-papyrus.com, pg 178

Papyrus Publishing (Australia) *Tel:* (03) 5342 2394 *Fax:* (03) 5342 2423 *E-mail:* editor@papyrus.com.au *Web Site:* www.papyrus.com.au, pg 35

Parabel Place (Australia) *Tel:* (03) 9727 1894 *Fax:* (03) 9727 1857, pg 35

Edition Parabolis (Germany) *Tel:* (030) 44 65 10 65 *Fax:* (030) 444 10 85 *E-mail:* info@emz-berlin.de *Web Site:* www.emz-berlin.de, pg 268

Editions Paradigme (France) *Tel:* (02) 38 70 84 44 *Fax:* (02) 38 70 56 76 *Web Site:* paradigme.com; cpuniv.com, pg 178

Paradox Pers vzw (Belgium) *Tel:* (03) 2318873 *Fax:* (03) 2386605 *E-mail:* paradox@glo.be; paradoxpers@belgacom.be, pg 71

Paragon Prepress Inc (India) *Tel:* (011) 2622 44 51; (011) 5160 1485 *Fax:* (011) 2622 44 51 *E-mail:* information@paragonpress.com *Web Site:* www.paragonprepress.com, pg 1179

Ediciones Paraiso, SL (Spain) *Tel:* (0985) 203 789 *E-mail:* paraiso@seteas.com, pg 595

Paramount Books (Pvt) Ltd (Pakistan) *Tel:* (021) 455 0661 *Fax:* (021) 455 3772 *E-mail:* parabks@cyber.net.pk, pg 1334

Paramount Printing Co Ltd (Hong Kong) *Tel:* 2896-8688 *Fax:* 2897-8942 *E-mail:* paraprin@netvigator.cóm *Web Site:* www.paramount.com.hk, pg 1158, 1219

Paramount Sales (India) Pvt Ltd (India) *Tel:* (011) 7776821; (011) 5746485 *Fax:* (011) 5746485, pg 344

Editorial Paraninfo SA (Spain) *Tel:* (091) 4463350 *Fax:* (091) 4456218; (091) 14478892 *E-mail:* info@paraninfo.es *Web Site:* www.paraninfo.es, pg 595

Parantez Yayinlari Ltd (Turkey) *Tel:* (0212) 252 85 67 *Fax:* (0212) 252 85 67 *E-mail:* parantez@yahoo.com *Web Site:* www.geocities.com/parantez, pg 651

Paranus Verlag - Brn Neumuenster GmbH (Germany) *Tel:* (04321) 2004-500 *Fax:* (04321) 2004-411 *E-mail:* verlag@paranus.de *Web Site:* www.paranus.de, pg 268

Parapress Ltd (United Kingdom) *Tel:* (01892) 512118 *Fax:* (01892) 512118 *E-mail:* office@parapress.eclipse.co.uk *Web Site:* www.parapress.co.uk, pg 738

PARAS (United Kingdom) *Tel:* (020) 8342 9600 *Fax:* (020) 8342 9600 *E-mail:* paraspublishing@telco4u.net, pg 738

Parasol NV (Belgium) *Tel:* (03) 460 1880 *Fax:* (03) 460 1881 *E-mail:* info@parasol.be *Web Site:* www.parasol.be, pg 71

Paravia Bruno Mondadori Editori (Italy) *Tel:* (02) 748231 *Fax:* (02) 74823362 *Web Site:* www.paravia.it; www.paramond.it; langedizioni.it; edizioniscolastichebrunomondadori.it, pg 402

G B Paravia & C SpA (Italy) *Tel:* (011) 7502111 *Fax:* (011) 75021510 *E-mail:* master@paravia.it *Web Site:* www.paravia.it, pg 402

Editions Pardes (France) *Tel:* (02) 38 33 53 28 *Fax:* (02) 38 33 58 99 *Web Site:* perso.wanadoo.fr/mackadam/livre/Editeurs/pardes.htm, pg 179

Libreria General de Tomas Pardo SRL (Argentina) *Tel:* (011) 4322-0496 *Fax:* (011) 4393-6759, pg 1297

Editions Parentheses (France) *Tel:* (0495) 08 18 20 *Fax:* (0495) 08 18 24, pg 179

Parfitts Book Services (United Kingdom) *Tel:* (01985) 216371 *Fax:* (01985) 212982 *E-mail:* parfitts@cix.compulink.co.uk, pg 1352

Parimal Prakashan (India) *Tel:* (0240) 4556, pg 345

Association Paris-Musees (France) *Tel:* (01) 44 58 99 19 *Fax:* (01) 47 03 36 44, pg 179

Park Konyvkiado Kft (Park Publisher) (Hungary) *Tel:* (01) 2125534; (01) 2125535; (01) 2124363 *E-mail:* park@mail.matav.hu, pg 324

Parkett Publishers Inc (Switzerland) *Tel:* (01) 2718140 *Fax:* (01) 2724301 *E-mail:* info@parkettart.com *Web Site:* www.parkettart.com, pg 630

Parlamentni Knihovna (Czech Republic) *Tel:* (02) 57534 409 *Fax:* (02) 57534 408 *E-mail:* posta@psp.cz *Web Site:* www.psp.cz, pg 1501

Parlamento Vasco (Spain) *Tel:* (0945) 004 000 *Fax:* (0945) 146 016 *E-mail:* protocol@parlam.euskadi.net *Web Site:* parlamento.euskadi.net, pg 595

Bibliotheque du Parlement (Belgium) *Tel:* (02) 5499271 *Fax:* (02) 5499498 *E-mail:* bibliotheque@lachambre.be, pg 1493

Library of Parliament (Zimbabwe) *Tel:* (04) 729722 ext 2131 *Fax:* (04) 795548, pg 1556

Parliamentary Library (New Zealand) *Tel:* (04) 471 9611 *Fax:* (04) 471 2551 *E-mail:* intdoc@parliament.govt.nz *Web Site:* www.ps.parliament.govt.nz/library.htm, pg 1532

Editions Parole et Silence (Switzerland) *Tel:* (024) 6982301 *Fax:* (024) 6982311, pg 631

Parramon Ediciones SA (Spain) *Tel:* (093) 289 27 20 *Fax:* (093) 426 37 30 *E-mail:* sales@parramon.es *Web Site:* www.parramon.com, pg 595

Editorial Libreria Parroquial de Claveria SA de CV (Mexico) *Tel:* (05) 3991102; (05) 3994975; (05) 3995412; (05) 3995716 *Fax:* (05) 3991243, pg 470

Parry's Book Center Sdn Bhd (Malaysia) *Tel:* (03) 4079179; (03) 4087235; (03) 4079176; (03) 4087528 *Fax:* (03) 4079180 *E-mail:* haja@pop3.jaring.my, pg 1326

Parry's Press (Malaysia) *Tel:* (03) 4079179 *Fax:* (03) 4079180 *E-mail:* haja@pop.3.jaring.my, pg 457

Parsifal BVBA (Belgium) *Tel:* (050) 339516 *Fax:* (050) 333386 *E-mail:* info@parsifal.be *Web Site:* www.parsifal.be, pg 71

La Part de L'Oeil (Belgium) *Tel:* (02) 514 18 41 *Fax:* (02) 514 18 41 *E-mail:* lapartdeloeil@brunette.brucity.be, pg 71

Ediciones Partenon (Spain) *Tel:* (091) 5634450 *Fax:* (091) 5628405, pg 595

Partenon MAM Sistem (Serbia and Montenegro) *Tel:* (011) 632535; (011) 625942; (011) 633465 *Fax:* (011) 632535; (011) 2623980 *E-mail:* partenon@infosky.net, pg 553

Editorial Parthenon Communication, SL (Spain) *Tel:* (093) 7952008 *Fax:* (093) 7952008, pg 595

Parthian Books (United Kingdom) *Tel:* (2920) 341314 *Fax:* (2920) 341314 *E-mail:* parthianbooks@yahoo.co.uk *Web Site:* www.parthianbooks.co.uk, pg 738

YELLOW PAGES

Partners Training & Innovatie (Netherlands) *Tel:* (010) 4071599 *Fax:* (010) 4202227 *E-mail:* info@ced.nl *Web Site:* www.ced-groep.nl, pg 487

Editions du Parvis (Switzerland) *Tel:* (026) 915 93 93 *Fax:* (026) 915 93 99 *E-mail:* book@parvis.ch *Web Site:* www.parvis.ch, pg 631

Verlag Parzeller GmbH & Co KG (Germany) *Tel:* (0661) 280-663 *Fax:* (0661) 280-285 *E-mail:* verlag@parzeller.de *Web Site:* www.buchkatalog.de/parzeller, pg 268

Pascal Press (Australia) *Tel:* (02) 8585 4044 *Fax:* (02) 8585 4001 *E-mail:* contact@pascalpress.com.au; info@pascalpress.com.au *Web Site:* www.pascalpress.com.au, pg 36

Pascoe Publishing Pty Ltd (Australia) *Tel:* (03) 5237 9227 *Fax:* (03) 5237 6559 *Web Site:* www.bruce-pascoe.pho-online.net, pg 36

Passage, Uitgeverij (Netherlands) *Tel:* (050) 5271332 *E-mail:* info@uitgeverijpassage.nl *Web Site:* www.uitgeverijpassage.nl, pg 487

Passagen Verlag GmbH (Austria) *Tel:* (01) 513 77 61 *Fax:* (01) 512 63 27 *E-mail:* office@passagen.at *Web Site:* www.passagen.at, pg 56

Passavia Druckerei GmbH, Verlag (Germany) *Tel:* (0851) 802670 *Fax:* (0851) 802680 *E-mail:* contact@just-print-it.com *Web Site:* www.passavia.de; www.just-print-it.com, pg 268

Passavia Universitaetsverlag und -Druck GmbH (Germany) *Tel:* (0851) 700226 *Fax:* (0851) 700277, pg 268

Kevin J Passey (Australia) *Tel:* (060) 216 933 *Fax:* (060) 412 950, pg 36

Passigli Editori (Italy) *Tel:* (055) 640265 *Fax:* (055) 644627 *E-mail:* info@passiglieditori.it *Web Site:* www.passiglieditori.it, pg 402

Libreria Passim SA (Spain) *Tel:* (093) 325 03 05 *Fax:* (093) 325 03 05 *E-mail:* passim@intercom.es, pg 1342

PasTest (United Kingdom) *Tel:* (01565) 752000 *Fax:* (01565) 650264 *E-mail:* enquiries@pastest.co.uk *Web Site:* www.pastest.co.uk, pg 738

Centre de Pastoral Liturgica (Spain) *Tel:* (093) 3022235 *Fax:* (093) 3184218 *E-mail:* cpl@tsai.es *Web Site:* www.cpl.es/, pg 595

Patakis Publishers (Greece) *Tel:* (0210) 3831078; (0210) 3811850; (0210) 3650000 *Fax:* (0210) 3628950 *E-mail:* info@patakis.gr *Web Site:* www.patakis.gr, pg 311

PATCO (Indonesia) *Tel:* (031) 310021, pg 356

Patent Documentation Publishing House (China) *Tel:* (010) 62362813; (010) 2026893 *Fax:* (010) 2019307, pg 106

Paternoster Publishing (United Kingdom) *Tel:* (01228) 512512 *Fax:* (01228) 514949 *E-mail:* orderline@stl.org *Web Site:* www.paternoster-publishing.com, pg 738

Paternoster Publishing (United Kingdom) *Tel:* (01228) 512512 *Fax:* (01228) 514949 *E-mail:* info@Paternoster-Publishing.com *Web Site:* www.paternoster-publishing.com, pg 1164

Paterson Marsh Ltd (United Kingdom) *Tel:* (0207) 399 2800 *Fax:* (0207) 399 2801 *E-mail:* info@markpaterson.co.uk *Web Site:* www.patersonmarsh.co.uk, pg 1142

Pathfinder Bookshop (New Zealand) *Tel:* (09) 3790147 *Toll Free Tel:* 0800 55 44 55 *Fax:* (09) 3098167 *E-mail:* Tim@pathfinder.co.nz; Jennifer@pathfinder.co.nz *Web Site:* www.pathfinder.co.nz, pg 1330

Pathfinder London (United Kingdom) *Tel:* (020) 7261 1354 *Fax:* (020) 7261 1354 *E-mail:* pathfinderlondon@compuserve.com *Web Site:* www.pathfinderpress.com, pg 739

Editions Patino (Switzerland) *Tel:* (022) 3470211 *Fax:* (022) 7891829, pg 631

Patio, Galerie und Druckwerkstatt (Germany) *Tel:* (06150) 84566, pg 268

Patio-Livraria Inglesa (Portugal) *Tel:* (0291) 224490 *Fax:* (0291) 232077 *E-mail:* patiolivros@hotmail.com, pg 1338

Patmos, izdevnieciba (Latvia) *Tel:* (02) 7289674 *Fax:* (02) 7820437 *E-mail:* bauc@mail.bkc.lv, pg 445

Patmos Verlag GmbH & Co KG (Germany) *Tel:* (0211) 16795-0 *Fax:* (0211) 16795-75 *E-mail:* info@patmos.de *Web Site:* www.patmos.de, pg 268

Editorial Patria SA de CV (Mexico) *Tel:* (05) 6704712 *Fax:* (05) 5613218, pg 470

Editora Patria Grande (Argentina) *Tel:* (011) 4631-6446, pg 8

Libreria Patria (Mexico) *Tel:* (05) 5613446, pg 1327

Patrimonio Nacional, Real Biblioteca (Spain) *Tel:* (091) 454 87 00; (091) 454 87 32 *Fax:* (091) 454 87 21 *E-mail:* realbiblioteca@patrimonionacional.es *Web Site:* www.patrimonionacional.es, pg 1545

Izdatel'stvo Patriot (Russian Federation) *Tel:* (095) 2844904, pg 548

Editorial Patris SA (Chile) *Tel:* (02) 2351343 *Fax:* (02) 2351343 *E-mail:* edit.patris@entelchile.net *Web Site:* www.patris.cl, pg 100

Libreria Internazionale Patron (Italy) *Tel:* (051) 223208 *Fax:* (051) 223208, pg 1321

Patron Editore SrL (Italy) *Tel:* (051) 767003 *Fax:* (051) 768252, pg 402

Pattloch Verlag GmbH & Co KG (Germany) *Tel:* (089) 9271-0 *Fax:* (089) 9271-168 *E-mail:* vertrieb@droemer-knaur.de *Web Site:* www.droemer-weltbild.de, pg 268

Ediciones Paulinas (Libreria San Pablo) (Colombia) *Tel:* (01) 2444516 *Fax:* (01) 2684288, pg 1306

Paulinas (Portugal) *Tel:* (021) 848 43 55 *Fax:* (021) 847 41 51 *E-mail:* paulinas@mail.telepac.pt, pg 534

Paulinas Editorial (Brazil) *Tel:* (011) 50855199 *Fax:* (011) 50855198 *E-mail:* editora@paulinas.org.br, pg 88

Paulines Publications-Africa (Kenya) *Tel:* (020) 4447202; (020) 4447203 *Fax:* (020) 4442097 *E-mail:* publications@paulinesafrica.org *Web Site:* www.paulinesafrica.org, pg 435

Paulinus Verlag GmbH (Germany) *Tel:* (0651) 4608-112 *Fax:* (0651) 4608-221 *E-mail:* verlag@paulinus.de *Web Site:* www.paulinus.de, pg 268

Paulus Editora (Brazil) *Tel:* (011) 50843066; (011) 5757362 *Fax:* (011) 5703627 *E-mail:* dir.editorial@paulus.org.br *Web Site:* www.paulus.com.br, pg 88

Pavilion Books Ltd (United Kingdom) *Tel:* (020) 7221 2213; (020) 7314 1469 (sales) *Fax:* (020) 7221 6455; (020) 7314 1594 (sales) *E-mail:* info@chrysalisbooks.co.uk; enquiries@chrysalis.com *Web Site:* www.chrysalisbooks.co.uk/books/publisher/pavilion, pg 739

Pavilion Publishing (Brighton) Ltd (United Kingdom) *Tel:* (01273) 623222 *Fax:* (01273) 625526 *E-mail:* info@pavpub.com *Web Site:* www.pavpub.com, pg 739

Pawel Panpresse (Germany) *Tel:* (06041) 5822, pg 268

John Pawsey (United Kingdom) *Tel:* (01903) 205167 *Fax:* (01903) 205167, pg 1142

Pax Forlag A/S (Norway) *Tel:* (023) 136900 *Fax:* (023) 136919, pg 510

Editorial Pax Mexico (Mexico) *Tel:* 5688-4828; 5604-0843 *Fax:* 5605-7677 *E-mail:* editorialpax@editorialpax.com *Web Site:* www.editorialpax.com, pg 470

Payel Yayinevi (Turkey) *Tel:* (0212) 511 82 83 *Fax:* (0212) 512 43 53 *E-mail:* shemsa@ttnet.net.tr, pg 651

PEARSON EDUCATION AUSTRALIA

Payot & Rivages (France) *Tel:* (01) 44413990 *Fax:* (01) 44413969 *E-mail:* editions@payotrivages.com, pg 179

Editions Payot Lausanne (Switzerland) *Tel:* (021) 3290264 *Fax:* (021) 3290266 *E-mail:* ed.payot.nadir@bluewin.ch, pg 631

Editora Paz e Terra (Brazil) *Tel:* (011) 3337-8399 *Fax:* (011) 223-6290 *E-mail:* vendas@pazeterra.com.br *Web Site:* www.pazeterra.com.br, pg 88

Paz-Editora de Multimedia, LDA (Portugal) *Tel:* (021) 8101282 *Fax:* (021) 8101287 *E-mail:* paz@esoterica.pt, pg 534

PC Publishing (United Kingdom) *Tel:* (01953) 889900 *Fax:* (01953) 889901 *E-mail:* info@pc-publishing.com *Web Site:* www.pc-publishing.co.uk, pg 739

PCE Press (Australia) *Tel:* (07) 3252 1114 *Fax:* (07) 3852 1564 *E-mail:* webmaster@pcq.org.au *Web Site:* www.pcq.org.au, pg 36

Peace Book Co Ltd (Hong Kong) *Tel:* 2804-6687 *Fax:* 2804-6409, pg 318

Peaceful Living Publications (New Zealand) *Tel:* (071) 5718105 *Fax:* (071) 5718513 *E-mail:* books@peaceful-living.co.nz, pg 1330

Peak Technologies UK Ltd (United Kingdom) *Tel:* (01344) 290000 *Fax:* (01344) 290001 *E-mail:* info@peakeurope.com *Web Site:* www.peakeurope.com/uk, pg 1227

Peak Translations (United Kingdom) *Tel:* (01663) 732074 *Fax:* (01663) 735499 *E-mail:* info@peak-translations.co.uk *Web Site:* www.peak-translations.co.uk, pg 1151

Peake Associates Tony Peake (United Kingdom) *Tel:* (020) 7267 8033 *Fax:* (020) 7284 1876 *E-mail:* peakeassoc@aol.com *Web Site:* www.tonypeake.com, pg 1142

Pearl River Printing Co Ltd (Hong Kong) *Tel:* 2540-6114 *Fax:* 2559-7042 *E-mail:* pearlriv@sage.net *Web Site:* www.pearlriv.com, pg 1158

Maggie Pearlstine Associates Ltd (United Kingdom) *Tel:* (020) 7828 4212 *Fax:* (020) 7834 5546 *E-mail:* post@pearlstine.co.uk, pg 1142

Pearson Educacion de Argentina (Argentina) *Tel:* (011) 4309 6100 *Fax:* (011) 4309 6199, pg 8

Pearson Educacion de Colombia LTDA (Colombia) *Tel:* (0571) 420 1955 *Fax:* (0571) 420 2168, pg 112

Pearson Educacion de Mexico, SA de CV (Mexico) *Toll Free Tel:* 01 800 0054276 *Fax:* (05) 387-0700 *E-mail:* firstname.lastname@pearsoned.com *Web Site:* www.pearson.com.mx, pg 470

Pearson Educacion S A (Spain) *Tel:* (091) 5903432 *Fax:* (091) 5903448 *E-mail:* firstname.lastname@pearsoned-ema.com, pg 595

Pearson Education (Switzerland) *Tel:* 747 4747 *Fax:* 747 4777 *E-mail:* firstname.lastname@pearson.ch; mailbox@pearson.ch *Web Site:* www.pearson.ch, pg 631

Pearson Education (Taiwan, Province of China) *Tel:* (02) 2370 8168 *Fax:* (02) 2370 8169 *E-mail:* firstname@pearsoned.com.tw *Web Site:* www.pearsoned.com.tw, pg 641

Pearson Education (United Kingdom) *Tel:* (020) 7447 2000 *Fax:* (020) 7240 5771 *E-mail:* firstname.lastname@pearsoned-ema.com, pg 739

Pearson Education Asia (Philippines) *Tel:* (02) 434 5501 *Fax:* (02) 433466 *E-mail:* custserv@pearsoned.com.ph *Web Site:* www.pearsoned.com, pg 520

Pearson Education Asia Pte Ltd (Singapore) *Tel:* 3199388 *Fax:* 3199175 *E-mail:* asia@pearsoned.com.sg *Web Site:* www.pearsoned-asia.com, pg 557

Pearson Education Australia (Australia) *Tel:* (02) 9454 2200 *Fax:* (02) 9453 0089 *E-mail:* firstname.lastname@pearsoned.com.au *Web Site:* www.pearson.com.au, pg 36

PEARSON EDUCATION CHINA LTD

Pearson Education China Ltd (Hong Kong) *Tel:* (852) 3181-0000 *Fax:* (852) 2565-7440 *E-mail:* info@ilongman.com *Web Site:* www.pearsoned.com.hk, pg 318

Pearson Education Deutschland GmbH (Germany) *Tel:* (089) 46003-0 *Fax:* (089) 46003-120 *E-mail:* firstinitiallastname@pearson.de; info@pearson.de *Web Site:* www.pearsoned.de, pg 268

Pearson Education Do Brasil (Brazil) *Tel:* (011) 3611 0740 *Fax:* (011) 3611 0444 *E-mail:* firstname.lastname@pearsoned.com.br, pg 88

Pearson Education Europe, Mideast & Africa (United Kingdom) *Tel:* (01279) 62 3623 *Fax:* (01279) 41 4130 *E-mail:* firstname.lastname@pearsoned-ema.com *Web Site:* www.pearsoned.co.uk, pg 739

Pearson Education France (France) *Tel:* (01) 7274 9000 *Fax:* (01) 4804 5361 (sales); (01) 4887 7130 (finance); (01) 4205 2217 *E-mail:* infos@pearsoned.fr *Web Site:* www.pearsoneducation.fr, pg 179

Pearson Education Hellas SA (Greece) *Tel:* (01) 937 3170 *Fax:* (01) 937 3194 *Web Site:* www.pearsoneduc.com, pg 311

Pearson Education Indochina, Ltd (Thailand) *Tel:* (02) 731-7156-57; (02) 731-7150-51 (Hotline) *Fax:* (02) 731-7158 *E-mail:* cserv@pearson-indochina.com *Web Site:* www.pearson-indochina.com, pg 645

Pearson Education Japan (Japan) *Tel:* (03) 3365 9001 *Fax:* (03) 3365 9009 *E-mail:* firstname.lastname@pearsoned.co.jp; elt@pearsoned.co.jp *Web Site:* www.pearsoned.co.jp, pg 425

Pearson Education Korea Ltd (Republic of Korea) *Tel:* (02) 353 0422 *Fax:* (02) 335 0092 *E-mail:* elt@pearsoned.co.kr, pg 442

Pearson Education Malaysia Sdn Bhd (Malaysia) *Tel:* (03) 7782 0466; (03) 7782 0659; (03) 7782 0702 *Fax:* (03) 7781 8005 *E-mail:* inquiry@pearsoned.com.my *Web Site:* www.pearson.com, pg 457

Pearson Education Malaysia Sdn Bhd (Malaysia) *Tel:* (03) 77820466 *E-mail:* inquiry@personed.com.my *Web Site:* www.pearson.com, pg 1326

Pearson Education Netherlands (Netherlands) *Tel:* (020) 575-5800 *Fax:* (020) 664-5334 *E-mail:* firstname.lastname@mail.aw.nl; amsterdam@pearsoned-ema.com *Web Site:* www.pearsoneducation.nl, pg 487

Pearson Education (PENZ) (New Zealand) *Tel:* (09) 444 4968 *Fax:* (09) 444 4957 *E-mail:* firstname.lastname@pearsoned.co.nz *Web Site:* www.pearsoned.co.nz, pg 500

Pearson Education Polska Sp z oo (Poland) *Tel:* (022) 533 1533 *Toll Free Tel:* 0800 1200 76 *Fax:* (022) 533 1534 *E-mail:* office@longman.com.pl *Web Site:* www.longman.com.pl, pg 525

Pearson Education (Prentice Hall) (South Africa) *Tel:* (021) 686 6356 *Fax:* (021) 686 4590 *E-mail:* firstname@mml.co.za *Web Site:* www.pearsoned.com, pg 567

Pearson Education Turkey (Turkey) *Tel:* (0212) 288 6941 *Fax:* (0212) 267 1851 *E-mail:* firstname.lastname@pearsoned-ema.com *Web Site:* www.pearsoneduc.com, pg 651

Peartree Publications (United Kingdom) *Tel:* 01424 844274, pg 740

Pedagogika Press (Russian Federation) *Tel:* (095) 2465969 *Fax:* (095) 2465969, pg 548

Editions Pedone (France) *Tel:* (01) 43 54 05 97 *Fax:* (01) 46 34 07 60 *E-mail:* editions-pedone@wanadoo.fr *Web Site:* www.franceedition.org/Pedone, pg 179

Pedrazzini Tipografia (Switzerland) *Tel:* (091) 751 7734 *Fax:* (091) 751 5118 *E-mail:* tipedra@webshuttle.ch, pg 631

Universidad Nacional Pedro Henriquez Urena (Dominican Republic) *Tel:* (0809) 542-6888 (ext 2301-2315, 2320 & 2321) *Fax:* (0809) 566-2206; (0809) 540-3803 *E-mail:* biblioteca@unphu.edu.do *Web Site:* www.unphu.edu.do/unphu/biblioteca, pg 1502

Peepal Tree Press Ltd (United Kingdom) *Tel:* (0113) 245 1703 *Fax:* (0113) 246 8368 *E-mail:* contact@peepaltreepress.com *Web Site:* www.peepaltreepress.com, pg 740

Peeters-France (France) *Tel:* (01) 40 51 81 05 *Fax:* (01) 40 51 89 20 *Web Site:* www.peeters-leuven.be, pg 179

Uitgeverij Peeters Leuven (Belgie) (Belgium) *Tel:* (016) 23 51 70 *Fax:* (016) 22 85 00 *E-mail:* peeters@peeters-leuven.be *Web Site:* www.peeters-leuven.be, pg 71

Editoriale PEG (Italy) *Tel:* (02) 4859181 *Fax:* (02) 485918220 *E-mail:* info@millerfreeman.it, pg 402

Pegasus Publishers & Booksellers (Netherlands) *Tel:* (020) 6231138 *Fax:* (020) 6203478 *E-mail:* pegasus@pegasusboek.nl *Web Site:* www.pegasusboek.nl, pg 1329

Pehuen Editores Ltda (Chile) *Tel:* (02) 2049399 *Fax:* (02) 2049399 *E-mail:* pehuen@cmet.net, pg 100

Ediciones Peisa (Promocion Editorial Inca SA) (Peru) *Tel:* (01) 4404603; (01) 4410473 *Fax:* (01) 4425906 *E-mail:* peisa@terro.com.pe, pg 517

Peking University Library (China) *Tel:* (010) 62751051; (010) 62757223 *Fax:* (010) 62761008 *E-mail:* zxh@lib.pku.edu.cn *Web Site:* www.lib.pku.edu.cn, pg 1498

Pelanduk Publications (M) Sdn Bhd (Malaysia) *Tel:* (03) 56386573; (03) 56386885 *Fax:* (03) 56386577; (03) 56386575 *E-mail:* pelpub@tm.net.my *Web Site:* www.pelanduk.com, pg 457

Pelckmans NV, De Nederlandsche Boekhandel (Belgium) *Tel:* (03) 660 27 00 *Fax:* (03) 660 27 01 *E-mail:* uitgeverij@pelckmans.be *Web Site:* www.pelckmans.be, pg 72

Uitgeverij Pelckmans NV (Belgium) *Tel:* (03) 6602700 *Fax:* (03) 66022701 *E-mail:* uitgeverij@pelckmans.be *Web Site:* www.pelckmans.be, pg 72

Pelikan Vertriebsgesellschaft mbH & Co KG (Germany) *Tel:* (0511) 6969-0 *Fax:* (0511) 6969-212 *Web Site:* www.pelikan.de, pg 269

Pelita Masa PT (Indonesia) *Tel:* (022) 50823, pg 356

Luigi Pellegrini Editore (Italy) *Tel:* (0984) 795065 *Fax:* (0984) 792672 *E-mail:* info@pellegrinieditore.it *Web Site:* www.pellegrinieditore.it, pg 403

Pembimbing Masa PT (Indonesia) *Tel:* (021) 367645; (021) 366042, pg 356

Pembimbing Masa PT (Indonesia) *Tel:* (021) 367645, pg 1318

Pen & Sword Books Ltd (United Kingdom) *Tel:* (01226) 734555 *Fax:* (01226) 734438 *E-mail:* enquiries@pen-and-sword.co.uk *Web Site:* www.pen-and-sword.co.uk, pg 740

Congolese PEN Centre (Congo) *Tel:* 813601 *Fax:* 813601, pg 1398

English PEN Centre (United Kingdom) *Tel:* (020) 7713 0023 *Fax:* (020) 7713 0005 *E-mail:* enquiries@englishpen.org *Web Site:* www.englishpen.org, pg 1408

Galician PEN Centre (Spain) *Tel:* (081) 587750 *E-mail:* pengalicia@mundo-r.com, pg 1405

German PEN Centre (Germany) *Tel:* (06151) 23120 *Fax:* (06151) 293414 *E-mail:* pen-germany@t-online.de, pg 1400

Hong Kong PEN Centre (Chinese-Speaking) (Hong Kong), pg 1401

Mexican PEN Centre (Mexico) *Tel:* (05) 574-4882 *Fax:* (05) 264-0813 *E-mail:* maleona@hotmail.com, pg 1403

Nepal PEN Centre (Nepal) *Fax:* (01) 522346 *E-mail:* archana@icimod.org.np; grana@saligram.mos.com.np; shaligrm@mos.com.np, pg 1403

Netherlands PEN Centre (Netherlands) *Tel:* (043) 433498 *Fax:* (043) 433498, pg 1403

Norwegian PEN Centre (Norway) *Tel:* 22194551 *Fax:* 22194551 *E-mail:* PEN@norskpen.no, pg 1403

Panamanian PEN Centre (Panama) *Tel:* 263-8822 *Fax:* 263-9918, pg 1403

Philippine PEN Centre (Philippines) *Tel:* (02) 5230870 *Fax:* (02) 5255038, pg 1404

Polish PEN Centre (Poland) *Tel:* (022) 8265784; (022) 8282823 *Fax:* (022) 8265784 *E-mail:* penclub@ikp.atm.com.pl *Web Site:* www.penclub.atomnet.pl, pg 1404

Portuguese PEN Centre (Portugal) *Tel:* (021) 7573452 *Fax:* (021) 7573452 *E-mail:* penclube@mail.telepac.pt, pg 1404

Puerto Rican PEN Centre (Puerto Rico) *Tel:* (787) 724-0869 *Fax:* (787) 724-2060 *E-mail:* saturno@prtc.net, pg 1404

Romanian PEN Centre (Romania) *Tel:* (01) 3111112 *Fax:* (01) 3125854 *E-mail:* univers@rnc.ro, pg 1404

Russian PEN Centre (Russian Federation) *Tel:* (095) 2094589; (095) 2093171 *Fax:* (095) 2000293 *E-mail:* penrussian@dol.ru; penrus@aha.ru *Web Site:* www.penrussia.org, pg 1404

Senegal PEN Centre (Senegal) *Tel:* 8256700; 8258009 *Fax:* 8643375 *E-mail:* memgoree@sonatel.senet.net, pg 1404

Serbian PEN Centre (Serbia and Montenegro) *Tel:* (011) 626081 *Fax:* (011) 635979 *E-mail:* pencent@bitsyu.net, pg 1404

Slovene PEN Centre (Slovenia) *Tel:* (01) 4254847 *E-mail:* slopen@guest.arnes.si, pg 1404

Swiss German PEN Centre (Switzerland) *Tel:* (031) 3724085 *Fax:* (031) 3723032 *E-mail:* infopen@datacomm.ch, pg 1405

Swiss Italian & Reto-Romansh PEN Centre (Switzerland) *Tel:* (091) 8039325 *Fax:* (091) 8039300 *E-mail:* p.e.n.lugano@ticino.com, pg 1405

Taipei Chinese PEN Centre (Taiwan, Province of China) *Tel:* (02) 23693609 *Fax:* (02) 23699948 *E-mail:* taipen@tpts5.seed.net.tw, pg 1405

Thai PEN Centre (Thailand) *Tel:* (02) 6685147; (02) 2792621, pg 1405

Turkish PEN Centre (Turkey) *Tel:* (0212) 2526314 *Fax:* (0212) 2526315, pg 1406

Venezuelan PEN Centre (Venezuela) *Tel:* (02) 5616691; (02) 5617589; (02) 5617287 *Fax:* (02) 5718064, pg 1410

PEN Club-German Speaking Writers Abroad (Germany) *E-mail:* intpen@dircon.co.uk *Web Site:* www.oneworld.org/internatpen/centers.htm, pg 1271

PEN Club-Writers in Exile London Branch (United Kingdom) *Tel:* (020) 8340 5279, pg 1292

Pendo Verlag GmbH (Switzerland) *Tel:* (01) 3897030 *Fax:* (01) 3897035 *E-mail:* info@pendo.ch *Web Site:* www.pendo.ch, pg 631

Pendragon Verlag (Germany) *Tel:* (0521) 69689 *Fax:* (0521) 174470 *E-mail:* pendragon.verlag@t-online.de *Web Site:* www.pendragon.de, pg 269

Penerbit Fajar Bakti Sdn Bhd (Malaysia) *Tel:* (03) 7047011 *Fax:* (03) 7047024, pg 457

Penerbit Jayatinta Sdn Bhd (Malaysia) *Tel:* (03) 7764036, pg 458

Penerbit Prisma Sdn Bhd (Malaysia) *Tel:* (03) 7034393 *Fax:* (03) 7039367, pg 458

Penerbit Universiti Sains Malaysia (Malaysia) *Tel:* (04) 6533888 *Fax:* (04) 6575714 *E-mail:* penerbitusm@notes.usm.my or rashidah@usm.my *Web Site:* www.lib.usm.my/press, pg 458

Penerbitan Jaya Bakti (Malaysia) *Tel:* (03) 6219399 *Fax:* (03) 6219585, pg 458

YELLOW PAGES

Penerbitan Pelangi Sdn Bhd (Pelangi Publishing Pte Ltd) (Malaysia) *E-mail:* info@pelangibooks.com; ppsb@po.jaring.my *Web Site:* www.pelangibooks.com, pg 458

Penerbitan Tinta (Malaysia) *Tel:* (03) 4424163 *Fax:* (03) 4424640, pg 458

Penguin Books Ltd (United Kingdom) *Tel:* (020) 7416 3000 *Fax:* (020) 7416 3099; (020) 7416 3293 *Web Site:* www.penguin.com, pg 740

Penguin Books Netherlands BV (Netherlands) *Tel:* (020) 6259566 *Fax:* (020) 6258676, pg 487

Penguin Books (NZ) Ltd (New Zealand) *Tel:* (09) 415-4700; (09) 415-4702 (orders) *Fax:* (09) 415-4701; (09) 415-4703 (orders) *E-mail:* marketing@penguin.co.nz *Web Site:* www.penguin.co.nz, pg 500

Penguin Group (Australia) (Australia) *Tel:* (613) 9811 2400 *Fax:* (613) 9811 2620 *Web Site:* www.penguin.com.au, pg 36

The Penguin Group UK (United Kingdom) *Tel:* (020) 7010 3000 *E-mail:* editor@penguin.co.uk *Web Site:* www.penguin.co.uk, pg 740

Ediciones Peninsula (Spain) *Tel:* (093) 443 71 00 *Fax:* (093) 443 71 30 *E-mail:* correu@grup62.com *Web Site:* www.grup62.com, pg 595

Penki Kontinentai (Lithuania) *Fax:* (05) 2664501 *E-mail:* info@5ci.lt *Web Site:* www.5ci.lt, pg 1135

Il Pensiero Scientifico Editore SRL (Italy) *Tel:* (06) 862821 *Fax:* (06) 86282250 *E-mail:* pensiero@pensiero.it *Web Site:* www.pensiero.it, pg 403

The Pensions Management Institute (United Kingdom) *Tel:* (020) 7247 1452 *Fax:* (020) 7375 0603 *E-mail:* enquiries@pensions-pmi.org.uk *Web Site:* www.pensions-pmi.org.uk, pg 740

Pensoft Publishers (Bulgaria) *Tel:* (02) 716451 *Fax:* (02) 704508 *E-mail:* pensoft@mbox.infotel.bg; orders@pensoft.net; info@pensoft.net *Web Site:* www.pensoft.net, pg 96

Pensord Press Ltd (United Kingdom) *Tel:* (01495) 223721; (01495) 222020 (customer service) *Fax:* (01495) 220672 *E-mail:* sales@pensord.co.uk *Web Site:* www.pensord.co.uk, pg 1164

Pentalfa Ediciones (Spain) *Tel:* (0985) 985 386 *Fax:* (0985) 985 512 *E-mail:* pentalfa@helicon.es *Web Site:* www.helicon.es/pentalfa.htm, pg 595

Pentathol Publishing (United Kingdom), pg 740

Institut Penyelidikan Minyak Kelapa Sawit Malaysia (Malaysia) *Tel:* (03) 8335155; (03) 8259775 *Fax:* (03) 8259446 *E-mail:* pub@porim.gov.my, pg 458

The People's Communications Publishing House (China) *Tel:* (010) 64214479 *Fax:* (010) 64213713, pg 106

People's Education Press (China) *Tel:* (010) 6402 4555 *Fax:* (010) 6401 0370 *E-mail:* yaod@pep.com.cn (English); dongyj@pep.com.cn (Japanese) *Web Site:* www.pep.com.cn/yingwenban; www.pep.com.cn/index.htm, pg 106

People's Fine Arts Publishing House (China) *Tel:* (010) 65122375 *Fax:* (010) 65122370, pg 106

People's Literature Publishing House (China) *Tel:* (010) 65138394 *Fax:* (010) 65138394, pg 106

People's Medical Publishing House (PMPH) (China) *Tel:* (010) 67015812; (010) 67028822 *Fax:* (010) 67025429, pg 107

The People's Posts & Telecommunication Publishing House (China) *Tel:* (010) 65139968; (010) 65138129 *Fax:* (010) 65138139, pg 107

People's Publishing House (P) Ltd (India) *Tel:* (011) 529365, pg 345

People's Sports Publishing House (China) *Tel:* (010) 67117673 *Fax:* (010) 67116129 *E-mail:* cbszbs@sohu.com, pg 107

PEP Buchhandlung & No Name Photo Gallery (Switzerland) *Tel:* (061) 261 51 61 *Fax:* (061) 261 51 61 *E-mail:* pepnoname@balcab.ch *Web Site:* www.pepnoname.ch, pg 1344

The Pepin Press (Netherlands) *Tel:* (020) 420 20 21 *Fax:* (020) 420 11 52 *E-mail:* mail@pepinpress.com *Web Site:* www.pepinpress.com, pg 487

Peramiho Publications (United Republic of Tanzania) *Tel:* (054) 2730 *Fax:* (054) 2917, pg 644, 1162, 1182, 1224, 1247

Perea Ediciones (Spain) *Tel:* (026) 568261 *Fax:* (026) 586386, pg 595

Editorial Peregrino SL (Spain) *Tel:* (0926) 338 245 *Fax:* (0926) 338 042 *E-mail:* editorialperegrino@mac.com *Web Site:* www.editorialperegrino.net, pg 595

Perfect Frontier Sdn Bhd (Malaysia) *Tel:* (03) 7832926 *Fax:* (03) 7816448, pg 458

Editorial Perfils (Spain) *Tel:* (0973) 242160 *Fax:* (0973) 221670 *E-mail:* perfils@arrakis.es, pg 595

Editora Pergaminho Lda (Portugal) *Tel:* (021) 652441 *Fax:* (021) 687543 *E-mail:* pergaminho@mail.telepac.pt, pg 534

Pergamon Flexible Learning (United Kingdom) *Tel:* (01865) 310366; (01865) 388190 *Fax:* (01865) 314290 *E-mail:* bhmarketing@repp.co.uk *Web Site:* www.bh.com/pergamonfl, pg 740

Peribo Pty Ltd (Australia) *Tel:* (02) 4457 0011 *Fax:* (02) 9457 0022 *E-mail:* peribo@bigpond.com, pg 36

Periodical & Book Publishers Association (Malta) *Fax:* (507) 295 9217 *E-mail:* bookpub@cwebdesign.com *Web Site:* www.cwebdesign.com/pbpa, pg 1277

Perioodika (Estonia) *Tel:* 644 1262 *Fax:* 644 2484 *E-mail:* perioodika@hot.ee, pg 140

E Perlinger Naturprodukte Handelsgesellschaft mbH (Austria) *Tel:* (05332) 524 40 *Fax:* (05332) 516 79 *E-mail:* engelberts.naturprodukte@tirol.com, pg 56

Permanyer Publications (Spain) *Tel:* (093) 207 59 20 *Fax:* (093) 457 66 42 *E-mail:* permanyer@permanyer.com *Web Site:* www.dolor.es; www.aidsreviews.com, pg 596

Permskaja Kniga (Russian Federation) *Tel:* (03422) 324245, pg 548

Perpetuity Press (United Kingdom) *Tel:* (0116) 221 7778 *Fax:* (0116) 221 7171 *E-mail:* orders@perpetuitypress.com *Web Site:* www.perpetuitypress.com, pg 741

Editorial El Perpetuo Socorro (Spain) *Tel:* (091) 445 51 26 *Fax:* (091) 445 51 27 *E-mail:* ed-ps@planalfa.es, pg 596

Editorial Perpetuo Socorro (Spain) *Tel:* (091) 445 51 26 *Fax:* (091) 445 51 27 *E-mail:* perso@pseditorial.com *Web Site:* www.pseditorial.com, pg 596

Perpustakaan Sultanah Zanariah (Malaysia) *Tel:* (07) 5533333 *Fax:* (07) 5572555 *E-mail:* psz@utm.my *Web Site:* www.utm.my, pg 1527

Perret Edition (Switzerland) *Tel:* (01) 9972717 *Fax:* (01) 9972718, pg 631

Persatuan Perpustakaan Kebangsaan Negara Brunei Darussalam (PPKNBD) (Brunei Darussalam) *Tel:* (02) 223060 *Fax:* (02) 235472; (02) 241817, pg 1559

Persatuan Perpustakaan Malaysia (Malaysia) *Tel:* (03) 26871700 *Fax:* (03) 26927082 *E-mail:* pnmweb@www1.pnm.my *Web Site:* www.pnm.my, pg 1567

Verlag Sigrid Persen (Germany) *Tel:* (04163) 81400 *Fax:* (04163) 814050 *E-mail:* info@persen.de *Web Site:* www.persen.de, pg 269

Perskor Books (Pty) Ltd (South Africa) *Tel:* (011) 315-3647 *Fax:* (011) 315-2757 *E-mail:* vlaeberg@icon.co.za, pg 567

Editora Perspectiva (Brazil) *Tel:* (011) 8858388 *Fax:* (011) 3885-8388 *E-mail:* editora@editoraperspectiva.com.br *Web Site:* www.editoraperspectiva.com.br, pg 88

Perspectivas e Realidades, Artes Graficas, Lda (Portugal) *Tel:* (021) 3471371 *Fax:* (021) 3471372, pg 534

PHANTOM PUBLISHERS

Justus Perthes Verlag Gotha GmbH (Germany) *Tel:* (03621) 385-0 *Fax:* (03621) 385-102 *E-mail:* perthes@klett-mail.de *Web Site:* www.klett-verlag.de/klett-perthes, pg 269

Pet Plus (Bulgaria) *Tel:* (02) 9874188 *E-mail:* editor@545plus.com; petplus@bnc.bg *Web Site:* www.545plus.com, pg 96

Peter Pan Publications (Australia) *Tel:* (07) 3848 0350 *Fax:* (07) 3848 4945 *E-mail:* paramountbooks@optusnet.com.au *Web Site:* www.peterpan.ziby.net, pg 36

Verlag Sankt Peter (Austria) *Tel:* (0662) 842166-82 *Fax:* (0662) 842166-80 *E-mail:* verlag-st.peter@magnet.at *Web Site:* www.stift-stpeter.at, pg 56

C F Peters Musikverlag GmbH & Co KG (Germany) *Tel:* (069) 6300990 *Fax:* (069) 635401 *E-mail:* vertrieb@musia.de; info@musia.de *Web Site:* www.musia.de, pg 269

Jens Peters Publikationen (Germany) *Tel:* (030) 7847265 *Fax:* (030) 7883127 *E-mail:* jens.peters@usa.net *Web Site:* www.jenspeters.de, pg 269

Heinrich Petersen Hans Buchimport GmbH (Germany) *Tel:* (040) 71003-0 *Fax:* (040) 71003-141 *E-mail:* vertrieb@petersen-buchimport.com *Web Site:* www.petersen-buchimport.com, pg 1311

Petit Editora e Distribuidora Ltda (Brazil) *Tel:* (011) 698 4162; (011) 691 7165 *Fax:* (011) 292 4616 *E-mail:* petit@dialdata.com.br *Web Site:* www.petit.com.br, pg 88

Petrion Verlag (Romania) *Tel:* (01) 3103407; (01) 3152641 *Fax:* (01) 3124525; (01) 3152641 *E-mail:* petrion@stranets.ro, pg 542

Petroleum Information Publishing Co (Taiwan, Province of China) *Tel:* (02) 29996909 *Fax:* (02) 29996746 *E-mail:* pip@tptsl.seed.net.tw *Web Site:* www.oil.net.tw, pg 641

Petrony Livraria (Portugal) *Tel:* (021) 3423911 *Fax:* (021) 3431602, pg 534

Galousis P Petros (Greece) *Tel:* (01) 360 5004, pg 311

Petrozavodskij Gosudarstvennyj Universitet (Russian Federation) *Tel:* (08142) 74-28-65 *Fax:* (08142) 71-10-00 *E-mail:* lib@mainpgu.karelia.ru *Web Site:* www.karelia.ru, pg 1540

Pevsner Public Library (Israel) *Tel:* (04) 8667766; (04) 8667768 *Fax:* (04) 8666492, pg 1519

Pfaffenweiler Presse (Germany) *Tel:* (07664) 8999 *Fax:* (07664) 8999 *E-mail:* info@pfaffenweiler-presse.de *Web Site:* www.pfaffenweiler-presse.de, pg 269

Pfalzische Verlagsanstalt GmbH (Germany) *Tel:* (06341) 142-0 *Fax:* (06341) 142-265, pg 269

PFD (United Kingdom) *Tel:* (020) 7344 1000 *Fax:* (020) 7836 9539 *E-mail:* postmaster@pfd.co.uk *Web Site:* www.pfd.co.uk, pg 1143

J Pfeiffer Verlag (Germany) *Tel:* (089) 4130010, pg 269

Verlag Dr Friedrich Pfeil (Germany) *Tel:* (089) 7428270 *Fax:* (089) 7242772 *E-mail:* info@pfeil-verlag.de *Web Site:* www.pfeil-verlag.de, pg 269

Richard Pflaum Verlag GmbH & Co KG (Germany) *Tel:* (089) 12607-0 *Fax:* (089) 12607-333 *E-mail:* info@pflaum.de *Web Site:* www.pflaum.de, pg 269

Verlag Die Pforte im Rudolf Steiner Verlag (Switzerland) *Tel:* (061) 706 91 30 *Fax:* (061) 706 91 39 *E-mail:* verlag@rudolf-steiner.com *Web Site:* www.rudolf-steiner.com, pg 631

PG Medical Books (Singapore) *Tel:* 4726339 *Fax:* 4728279, pg 557

Phaidon Press Ltd (United Kingdom) *Tel:* (020) 7843 1234 *Fax:* (020) 7843 1111 *E-mail:* esales@phaidon.com *Web Site:* www.phaidon.com, pg 741

Phantom Publishers (Zimbabwe) *Tel:* (04) 737241, pg 784

PHARMACEUTICAL PRESS

Pharmaceutical Press (United Kingdom) *Tel:* (020) 7735 9141 *Fax:* (020) 7572 2509 *E-mail:* pharmpress@rpsgb.org *Web Site:* www.pharmpress.com, pg 741

Bibliotheque Interuniversitaire de Pharmacie (France) *Tel:* (01) 53 73 95 22; (01) 53 73 95 23 *Fax:* (01) 53 73 99 05 *E-mail:* piketty@pharmacie.univ_paris5.fr *Web Site:* www.biup.univ-paris5.fr, pg 1507

Pharos-Verlag, Hansrudolf Schwabe AG (Switzerland) *Tel:* (061) 541021 *Fax:* (061) 2797972, pg 631

Editions Phebus (France) *Tel:* (01) 46 33 36 36 *Fax:* (01) 43 25 67 69 *E-mail:* phebedit@wanadoo.fr *Web Site:* www.phebus-editions.com, pg 179

Pheljna Edizioni d'Arte e Suggestione (Italy) *Tel:* (0125) 234114 *Fax:* (0125) 230085, pg 403

Editions Phi (Luxembourg) *Tel:* 541382-220 *Fax:* 541387 *E-mail:* editions.phi@editpress.lu; phi@phi.lu *Web Site:* www.phi.lu, pg 451

Philip & Tacey Ltd (United Kingdom) *Tel:* (01264) 332171 *Fax:* (01264) 384808 *E-mail:* sales@philipandtacey.co.uk *Web Site:* www.philipandtacey.co.uk, pg 741

Philipp Reclam Jun Verlag GmbH (Germany) *Tel:* (07156) 163 0 *Fax:* (07156) 163 197 *E-mail:* info@reclam.de *Web Site:* www.reclam.de, pg 269

Philippine Normal College Library & Library Science Departments (Philippines) *Tel:* (02) 5270372 *Fax:* (02) 5270372, pg 1536

Philippine Baptist Mission SBC FMB Church Growth International (Philippines) *Tel:* (02) 526-0264; (02) 526-0265; (02) 526-0266; (02) 526-0267; (02) 599256; (02) 599257 *Fax:* (02) 522-4639 *E-mail:* csm@i-manila.com.ph *Web Site:* www.fsbc.org.ph, pg 520

Philippine Education Co Inc (Philippines) *Tel:* (02) 487215; (02) 487317 *E-mail:* publications@pidsnet.pids.gov.ph *Web Site:* www.pids.gov.ph, pg 520

Philippine Education Co Inc (Philippines) *Tel:* (02) 487215; (02) 487317, pg 1335

Philippine Educational Publishers' Association (Philippines) *Tel:* (02) 7124106 *Fax:* (02) 7313448; (02) 7437687 *Web Site:* nbdb.gov.ph/pubindust.htm, pg 1281

Philippine Graphic Arts Inc (Philippines) *Tel:* (02) 364-4591 *Fax:* (02) 631-9733 *E-mail:* philippinegraphicarts@yahoo.com, pg 1222

Philippine Librarians Association Inc (Philippines) *Tel:* (02) 523-00-68 *Web Site:* www.dlsu.edu.ph/library/plai, pg 1569

Philippka-Sportverlag (Germany) *Tel:* (0251) 23005-0 *Fax:* (0251) 23005-79 *E-mail:* info@philippka.de *Web Site:* www.philippka.de, pg 269

Philipps-Universitaet Marburg (Germany) *Tel:* (06421) 28-20 *Fax:* (06421) 28-22500 *E-mail:* verwaltung@ub.uni.marburg.de *Web Site:* www.uni-marburg.de, pg 270

Philip's (United Kingdom) *Tel:* (020) 7644 6900 *Fax:* (020) 7644 6987 *E-mail:* philips@philips-maps.co.uk *Web Site:* www.philips-maps.co.uk, pg 741

Phillimore & Co Ltd (United Kingdom) *Tel:* (01243) 787636 *Fax:* (01243) 787639 *E-mail:* bookshop@phillimore.co.uk *Web Site:* www.phillimore.co.uk, pg 741

Philo Press (APA) (Netherlands) *Tel:* (020) 626 5544 *Fax:* (020) 528 5298 *E-mail:* info@apa-publishers.com *Web Site:* www.apa-publishers.com, pg 487

Philograph Publications Ltd (United Kingdom) *Tel:* (01271) 345061 *Fax:* (01271) 23076, pg 741

Philopsychy Press (Hong Kong) *Tel:* 2604 4403 *Fax:* 2604 4403 *E-mail:* ppp@hkbu.edu.hk *Web Site:* www.hkbu.edu.hk, pg 318

Philosophia Verlag GmbH (Germany) *Tel:* (089) 299975 *Fax:* (089) 299975 *E-mail:* info@philosophiaverlag.com *Web Site:* www.philosophiaverlag.com, pg 270

Philosophisch-Anthroposophischer Verlag am Goetheanum (Switzerland) *Tel:* (061) 706 84 40 *Fax:* (061) 706 84 41 *E-mail:* anthrosuisse@bluewin.ch *Web Site:* www.goetheanum.ch, pg 631

Pho Thong (Popularization) Publishing House (Viet Nam), pg 780

Phoenix Education Pty Ltd (Australia) *Tel:* (02) 9809 3579; (03) 9699 8377 *Fax:* (02) 9808 1430; (03) 9699 9242 *E-mail:* service@phoenixeduc.com *Web Site:* www.phoenixeduc.com, pg 36

Phoenix Publishers Ltd (Kenya) *Tel:* (020) 223262; (020) 222309 *Fax:* (020) 339875 *E-mail:* phoenix@insightkenya.com *Web Site:* www.phoenixpublishers.co.ke, pg 435

Phongwarin Printing Company Ltd (Thailand) *Tel:* (02) 7498934-45; (02) 3994525-31; (02) 7498275-9 *Fax:* (02) 3994524; (02) 3994255 *E-mail:* somphong@phongwarin.com *Web Site:* www.phongwarin.com, pg 1162, 1182, 1224

Photoart Ltd (Hong Kong) *Tel:* 2117 1198 *Fax:* 2507 2878 *E-mail:* info@photoart.com.hk *Web Site:* www.photoart.com.hk, pg 318

Photoengraving Inc (United States) *Tel:* 813-253-3427 *Fax:* 813-253-5491 *Web Site:* www.photoengravinginc.com, pg 1189

Photolitho AG (Switzerland) *Tel:* (043) 833 70 20 *Fax:* (043) 833 70 30 *E-mail:* info@photolitho.ch *Web Site:* www.photolitho.ch, pg 1182, 1224

PHP Institute Inc (Japan) *Tel:* (03) 3239-6233 *Fax:* (03) 3239-6263, pg 425

Physica-Verlag (Germany) *Tel:* (06221) 487-0 *Fax:* (06221) 4878-177 *E-mail:* physica@springer.de *Web Site:* www.springer.de, pg 270

Piatkus Books (United Kingdom) *Tel:* (020) 7631 0710 *Fax:* (020) 7436 7137 *E-mail:* info@piatkus.co.uk *Web Site:* www.piatkus.co.uk, pg 741

Daniela Piazza Editore (Italy) *Tel:* (011) 434 27 06 *Fax:* (011) 434 24 71 *E-mail:* daniela.piazza@tiscalinet.it *Web Site:* www.danielapiazzaeditore.com, pg 403

Pica Digital Pte Ltd (Singapore) *Tel:* 67761311 *Fax:* 67793055 *E-mail:* picaosea@singnet.com.sg, pg 1182

Editions A et J Picard SA (France) *Tel:* (01) 43 26 97 78 *Fax:* (01) 43 26 42 64 *E-mail:* livres@librairie-picard.com *Web Site:* www.abebooks.com/home/libpicard/, pg 179

Picaron Editions (Netherlands) *Tel:* (020) 6201484, pg 487

Piccadilly Press (United Kingdom) *Tel:* (020) 7267 4492 *Fax:* (020) 7267 4493 *E-mail:* books@piccadillypress.co.uk *Web Site:* www.piccadillypress.co.uk, pg 742

Piccin Nuova Libraria SpA (Italy) *Tel:* (049) 655566 *Fax:* (049) 8750693 *E-mail:* info@piccinonline.com *Web Site:* www.piccinonline.com, pg 403

Pichler Verlag GmbH & Co KG (Austria) *Tel:* (01) 203 28 28-0 *Fax:* (01) 203 28 28-6875 *E-mail:* office@styriapichler.at *Web Site:* www.styriapichler.at, pg 56

Pickering & Chatto Publishers Ltd (United Kingdom) *Tel:* (020) 7405 1005 *Fax:* (020) 7405 6216 *E-mail:* info@pickeringchatto.co.uk *Web Site:* www.pickeringchatto.com, pg 742

Editions Jean Picollec (France) *Tel:* (01) 45 89 73 04 *Fax:* (01) 45 89 40 72 *E-mail:* jean.picollec@noos.fr, pg 179

Editions Philippe Picquier (France) *Tel:* (04) 90496156 *Fax:* (04) 90499614, pg 180

Picture Research Association (United Kingdom) *Tel:* (01883) 730123 *Fax:* (01883) 730144 *E-mail:* chair@picture-research.org.uk *Web Site:* www.picture-research.org.uk, pg 1292

Editorial Piedra Santa (Guatemala) *Tel:* (02) 29053 *E-mail:* piedrasanta.sal@salnet.net, pg 313

INDUSTRY

Piedra Santa Editorial (Guatemala) *Tel:* (02) 232-9053 *Fax:* (02) 232-9053 *E-mail:* piedrasanta@guate.net, pg 1314

Piedras Press, Inc (Puerto Rico) *Tel:* (809) 731-9215, pg 537

Edizioni Piemme SpA (Italy) *Tel:* (0142) 3361 *Fax:* (0142) 74223 *Web Site:* www.edizpiemme.it, pg 403

Heinz Pier (Germany) *Tel:* (02235) 3998 *Fax:* (02235) 41654, pg 270

Van Piere Boeken (Netherlands) *Tel:* (040) 244 40 45 *Fax:* (040) 246 39 49 *E-mail:* info@vanpiere.nl *Web Site:* www.vanpiere.nl, pg 1329

Pierides Foundation (Cyprus) *Tel:* (02) 444486 *Fax:* (02) 466412, pg 121

Piero Lacaita Editore (Italy) *Tel:* (099) 9711124 *Fax:* (099) 9711124, pg 403

Piero Manni srl (Italy) *Tel:* (0832) 387057 *Fax:* (0832) 387057 *E-mail:* pieromannisrl@clio.it, pg 403

Editions Pierron (France) *Tel:* (03) 87 95 10 89 *Fax:* (03) 87 95 60 95 *E-mail:* editions@pierron.fr *Web Site:* www.editions-pierron.com, pg 180

Libreria Gozzini di Pietro e Francesco Chellini (SNC) (Italy) *Tel:* (055) 212433 *Fax:* (055) 211105 *E-mail:* gozzini@gozzini.it; info@gozzini.com *Web Site:* www.gozzini.com, pg 403

Paul Pietsch Verlage GmbH & Co (Germany) *Tel:* (0711) 2 10 80-0 *Fax:* (0711) 2 10 80-82; (0711) 2 36 04-15 *E-mail:* ppv@motorbuch.de *Web Site:* www.motorbuch.de, pg 270

Pijl Boekbedrijf nv (Belgium) *Tel:* (03) 236-98-30; (03) 270-02-70 *Fax:* (03) 235-90-02 *E-mail:* booksell@innet.be, pg 1302

Pikkhanet Kanphim (Thailand) *Tel:* (02) 222850, pg 645

Pillar Publications Ltd (United Kingdom) *Tel:* (01932) 820282 *Fax:* (01932) 858035 *E-mail:* hu@bjhc.demon.co.uk, pg 1248

La Pilotta Editrice Coop RL (Italy) *Tel:* (0521) 771268 *Fax:* (0521) 771268, pg 403

Richard Pils Publication PN°1 (Austria) *Tel:* (0043) 2856 3794 *Fax:* (0043) 2856 3792 *E-mail:* verlag@bibliothekderprovinz.at *Web Site:* www.bibliothekderprovinz.at, pg 56

Pinchgut Press (Australia) *Tel:* (02) 9908-2402 *Fax:* (02) 9960-4689, pg 36

Pinevale Publications (Australia) *Tel:* (07) 93-3169, pg 36

Pinguin-Verlag, Pawlowski GmbH (Austria) *Tel:* (0512) 281183-0 *Fax:* (0512) 293243 *Web Site:* www.worldport.at, pg 56

Editora Pini Ltda (Brazil) *Tel:* (011) 224-8811 *Fax:* (011) 224-0314; (011) 224-8541 *E-mail:* construcao@pini.com.br *Web Site:* www.piniweb.com, pg 88

Pinwheel Ltd (United Kingdom) *Tel:* (020) 7586 5100 *Fax:* (020) 7483 1999 *E-mail:* sales@pinwheel.co.uk *Web Site:* www.pinwheel.co.uk, pg 742

Pion Ltd (United Kingdom) *Tel:* (020) 8459 0066 *Fax:* (020) 8451 6454 *E-mail:* sales@pion.co.uk *Web Site:* www.pion.co.uk, pg 742

Pioneer Design Studio Pty Ltd (Australia) *Tel:* (03) 9735 5505, pg 37

Pioneer Graphic Scanning (United States) *Tel:* 845-735-4666 *Fax:* 617-344-5905, pg 1168, 1189

Livraria Pioneira Editora/Enio Matheus Guazzelli e Cia Ltd (Brazil) *Tel:* (011) 858-3199 *Fax:* (011) 858-0443 *E-mail:* pioneira@virtual-net.com.br, pg 88

Piper Verlag GmbH (Germany) *Tel:* (089) 381801-0 *Fax:* (089) 338704 *E-mail:* info@piper.de *Web Site:* www.piper.de, pg 270

PIRA Intl (United Kingdom) *Tel:* (01372) 802000 *Fax:* (01372) 802238 *E-mail:* publications@pira.co.uk *Web Site:* www.piranet.com, pg 742

YELLOW PAGES

Publicaciones Piramide, SA de CV (Mexico) *Tel:* (05) 5313215 *Fax:* (05) 2725883, pg 470

Ediciones Piramide SA (Spain) *Tel:* (091) 393 89 89 *Fax:* (091) 742 36 61 *E-mail:* piramide@anaya.es *Web Site:* www.edicionespiramide.es, pg 596

Francesco Pirella Editore (Italy) *Tel:* (010) 363628 *Fax:* (010) 1782281081 *Web Site:* www.pirella.net, pg 403

Pirene Editorial, sal (Spain) *Tel:* (093) 3178682 *Fax:* (093) 3178242, pg 596

Editions Christian Pirot (France) *Tel:* (02) 47 54 54 20; (02) 70 06 87 78 *Fax:* (02) 47 51 57 96 *E-mail:* contact@friendship-first.com *Web Site:* www.friendship-first.com, pg 180

Pitagora Editrice SRL (Italy) *Tel:* (051) 530003 *Fax:* (051) 535301 *E-mail:* pited@pitagragroup.it *Web Site:* www.pitagoragroup.it, pg 403

Pitambar Publishing Co (P) Ltd (India) *Tel:* (011) 776058; (011) 776067 *Fax:* (011) 2367 6058 *E-mail:* pitambar@bol.net.in, pg 345

Pitkin Unichrome Ltd (United Kingdom) *Tel:* (01264) 409200 *Fax:* (01264) 334110 *E-mail:* enquiries@pitkin-unichrome.com *Web Site:* www.britguides.com, pg 743

Pitspopany Press (Israel) *Tel:* (02) 6233507 *Fax:* (02) 6233510 *E-mail:* pitspop@netvision.net.il *Web Site:* www.pitspopany.com, pg 371

Amilcare Pizzi SpA (Italy) *Tel:* (02) 618361 *Fax:* (02) 61836283, pg 403

Amilcare Pizzi SpA (Italy) *Tel:* (02) 618361 *Fax:* (02) 61 83 62 83 *E-mail:* info@amilcarepizzi.it, pg 1180

Amilcare Pizzi SpA (Italy) *Tel:* (02) 618361 *Fax:* (02) 61836283 *E-mail:* info@amilcarepizzi.it, pg 1221

Pizzicato Edizioni Musicali (Italy) *Tel:* (0432) 45288 *Fax:* (0432) 45288 *Web Site:* www.pizzicato.it, pg 403

PJB Reference Sevices (United Kingdom) *Tel:* (020) 8332 8970 *Fax:* (020) 8332 8937 *E-mail:* pjbreference@pjbpubs.com *Web Site:* www.pjbreference.com, pg 743

Jean-Michel Place (France) *Tel:* (01) 44 32 05 90 *Fax:* (01) 44 32 05 91 *E-mail:* place@jmplace.com *Web Site:* www.jmplace.com, pg 180

Planet (United Kingdom) *Tel:* (01970) 611255 *Fax:* (01970) 611197 *E-mail:* planet.enquiries@planetmagazine.org.uk *Web Site:* www.planetmagazine.org.uk, pg 743

Planeta SA (Chile) *Tel:* (02) 6962374 *Fax:* (02) 6957260, pg 100

Editorial Planeta Argentina SAIC (Argentina) *Tel:* (011) 4382-4045; (011) 4382-4043 *Fax:* (011) 4383-3793 *E-mail:* info@eplaneta.com.ar; lpasiusis@planeta.com.ar, pg 8

Planeta Editora, LDA (Portugal) *Tel:* (021) 397-87-56 *Fax:* (021) 395-10-26, pg 534

Editorial Planeta Mexicana SA (Mexico) *Tel:* (05) 5758585; (05) 5758019; (05) 5755320 *Fax:* (05) 5758980 *Web Site:* www.editorialplaneta.com.mx, pg 470

Planeta Publishers (Russian Federation) *Tel:* (095) 9230470 *Fax:* (095) 2005246, pg 548

Editorial Planeta SA (Spain) *Tel:* (093) 2285800 *Fax:* (093) 2177140; (093) 2177748 *E-mail:* marketing@planeta.es *Web Site:* www.editorial.planeta.es, pg 596

Editorial Planeta Venezolana (Venezuela) *Tel:* (02) 913982; (02) 924872 *Fax:* (02) 913792 *E-mail:* planeta@viptel.com *Web Site:* www.editorialplaneta.com.ve, pg 780

Planetas Kiadoi es Kereskedelmi Kft (Hungary) *Tel:* (01) 4071018 *Fax:* (01) 4071787, pg 324

Plantagenet Press (Australia) *Tel:* (09) 4304466 *Fax:* (09) 4305217 *E-mail:* 100240.3406rogergarwood@compuserve.com, pg 37

Museum Plantin-Moretus (Belgium) *Tel:* (03) 221 14 50; (03) 221 14 51 *Fax:* (03) 221 14 71 *E-mail:* museum.plantin.moretus@antwerpen.be *Web Site:* museum.antwerpen.be, pg 1494

Plantin Publishers (United Kingdom) *Tel:* (029) 2056 0333 *Fax:* (029) 2055 4909 *E-mail:* drakegroup@btinternet.com *Web Site:* www.drakeed.com/cap, pg 743

Platano Editora SA (Portugal) *Tel:* (021) 7979278 *Fax:* (021) 7954019 *E-mail:* geral@platanoeditora.pt *Web Site:* www.plantanoeditora.pt, pg 534

Platform 5 Publishing Ltd (United Kingdom) *Tel:* (0114) 255 8000 *Fax:* (0114) 255 2471 *E-mail:* platform5@platfive.freeserve.co.uk, pg 743

Plawerg Editores SA (Spain) *Tel:* (093) 414 72 26 *Fax:* (093) 209 50 01 *E-mail:* info@plawerg.es *Web Site:* www.plawerg.com, pg 596

Playbox Theatre Co (Australia) *Tel:* (03) 9685 5100 *Fax:* (03) 9685 5112 *E-mail:* playbox@netspace.net.au *Web Site:* www.playbox.com.au, pg 37

Playlab Press (Australia) *Tel:* 3236 1396 *Fax:* 3236 1026 *E-mail:* cluster@thehub.com.au, pg 37

Playmarket (New Zealand) *Tel:* (04) 3828462 *Fax:* (04) 3828461 *E-mail:* info@playmarket.org.nz *Web Site:* www.playmarket.org.nz, pg 1135

Editorial Playor SA (Spain) *Tel:* (091) 3690652 *Fax:* (091) 3694441 *E-mail:* playor@attglobal.net, pg 596

The Playwrights Publishing Co (United Kingdom) *Tel:* (01159) 313356 *E-mail:* playwrightspublishingco@yahoo.com *Web Site:* www.geocities.com/playwrightspublishingco, pg 743

Plaza y Janes Editores SA (Spain) *Tel:* (093) 3660340 *Fax:* (093) 3660105 *Web Site:* www.plaza.es, pg 596

Plaza y Valdes SA de CV (Mexico) *Tel:* (05) 5359851; (05) 5664055 *E-mail:* editorial@plazayvaldes.com.mx, pg 470

Editorial Pleamar (Argentina) *Tel:* (011) 485-6597, pg 8

Plein Chant (France) *Tel:* (05) 45 81 93 26 *Fax:* (05) 45 81 92 83 *Web Site:* www.nanga.fr, pg 1154

Plein Chant (France) *Tel:* (05) 45 81 93 26 *Fax:* (05) 45 81 92 83, pg 1216

Pleniluni Edicions (Spain) *Tel:* (093) 301 08 87 *Fax:* (093) 3174830, pg 596

Jurriaan Plesman (Australia) *Tel:* (02) 9130 6202 *Fax:* (02) 9130 6202 *E-mail:* jurplesman@hotmail.com, pg 37

Plexus Publishing Ltd (United Kingdom) *Tel:* (020) 7622 2440 *Fax:* (020) 7622 2441 *E-mail:* info@plexusuk.demon.co.uk *Web Site:* www.plexusbooks.com, pg 743

Editorial Pliegos (Spain) *Tel:* (091) 4291545 *Fax:* (091) 4291545, pg 596

Uitgeverij Ploegsma BV (Netherlands) *Tel:* (020) 5511250 *Fax:* (020) 6203504 *E-mail:* info@ploegsma.nl *Web Site:* www.ploegsma.nl, pg 487

Plon-Perrin (France) *Tel:* (01) 44 41 35 00 *Fax:* (01) 44 41 35 02, pg 180

Plough Publishing House of Bruderhof Communities in the UK (United Kingdom) *Tel:* (01580) 883 344 *Fax:* (01580) 883 317 *Toll Free Fax:* 800-018-3347 *E-mail:* contact@bruderhof.com *Web Site:* www.plough.com, pg 743

Plum Press (Australia) *Tel:* (07) 3870 2964 *Fax:* (07) 3870 2860 *E-mail:* tom@justasktom.com *Web Site:* www.justasktom.com, pg 37

Editions Plume (France) *Tel:* (01) 40 51 31 00 *Fax:* (01) 43 14 02 01, pg 180

Plurigraf SPA (Italy) *Tel:* (05) 5576841 *Fax:* (05) 55000766 *E-mail:* plurigraf@tiscalinet.it, pg 403

Bokforlaget Plus AB (Sweden) *Tel:* (08) 654 74 08, pg 614

Editorial Plus Ultra SA (Argentina) *Tel:* (011) 4374-2973; (011) 4374-5092 *Fax:* (011) 4374-2973 *E-mail:* plus_ultra@epu.virtual.ar.net, pg 8

Pluto Books Ltd (United Kingdom) *Tel:* (020) 8348 2724 *Fax:* (020) 8348 9133 *E-mail:* pluto@plutobks.demon.co.uk *Web Site:* www.plutobooks.com, pg 743

Pluto Press (United Kingdom) *Tel:* (020) 8348 2724 *Fax:* (020) 8348 9133 *E-mail:* pluto@plutobooks.com *Web Site:* www.plutobooks.com, pg 743

Pluto Press Australia Pty Ltd (Australia) *Tel:* (02) 9692 5111; (03) 9328 3811 *Fax:* (02) 9692 5192; (03) 9329 9939 *E-mail:* pluto@plutoaustralia.com *Web Site:* www.plutoaustralia.com, pg 37

pmi Verlag (Germany) *Tel:* (069) 54 80 00-0 *Fax:* (069) 54 80 00 66 *E-mail:* pmiverlag@aol.com *Web Site:* www.pmi-verlag.de, pg 270

PoChinChai Printing Co Ltd (Republic of Korea) *Tel:* (031) 955-1150; (031) 955-1151 *Fax:* (031) 943-3234 *Web Site:* www.pochinchai.com, pg 442

Pociao's Books (Germany) *Tel:* (0228) 229583 *Fax:* (0228) 219507 *E-mail:* pociao@t-online.de *Web Site:* www.sanssoleil.de, pg 1311

Max Pock, Universitaetsbuchhandlung (Austria) *Tel:* (0316) 825254-0 *Fax:* (0316) 825258; (0316) 825254-8, pg 1300

Biblioteca del Poder Legislativo (Uruguay) *Tel:* (02) 208937 *Fax:* (02) 949162, pg 1555

Podium Uitgeverij (Netherlands) *Tel:* (020) 421 38 30 *Fax:* (020) 421 37 76 *E-mail:* post@uitgeverijpodium.nl *Web Site:* www.uitgeverijpodium.nl, pg 487

Wydawnictwo Podsiedlik-Raniowski i Spolka (Poland) *Tel:* (061) 867 95 46 *Fax:* (061) 867 68 50 *E-mail:* office@priska.com.pl, pg 525

Verlag Walter Podszun Burobedarf-Bucher Abt (Germany) *Tel:* (02961) 2507 *Fax:* (02961) 2508 *E-mail:* verlag.podszun@t-online.de, pg 270

Podzun-Pallas Verlag GmbH (Germany) *Tel:* (06036) 9436 *Fax:* (06036) 6270 *Web Site:* www.podzun-pallas.de, pg 270

Poetes Presents (France) *Tel:* (02) 97529363 *Fax:* (02) 97528390, pg 1252

Poetry Society of Australia (Australia) *Tel:* (02) 423861, pg 1396

The Poetry Book Society Ltd (United Kingdom) *Tel:* (020) 8870 8403 *Fax:* (020) 8870 0865 *E-mail:* info@poetrybooks.co.uk *Web Site:* www.poetrybooks.co.uk, pg 1257

The Poetry Society Inc (United Kingdom) *Tel:* (020) 7420 9880 *Fax:* (020) 7240 4818 *E-mail:* info@poetrysociety.org.uk *Web Site:* www.poetrysociety.org.uk, pg 1408

Poeziecentrum (Belgium) *Tel:* (09) 225 22 25 *Fax:* (09) 225 90 54 *E-mail:* info@poeziecentrum.be *Web Site:* www.poeziecentrum.be, pg 72

Pohjoinen (Finland) *Tel:* (08) 5377 111 *Fax:* (08) 5377 572 *E-mail:* pohjoinen@kaleva.fi *Web Site:* www.kaleva.fi, pg 143

Point Hors Ligne Editions (France) *Tel:* (01) 43544964 *Fax:* (01) 43253032, pg 180

Les Editions du Point Veterinaire (France) *Tel:* (01) 45 17 02 25 *Fax:* (01) 42 07 93 88 *Web Site:* www.pointveterinaire.com, pg 180

Pointer Publishers (India) *Tel:* (0141) 2568159 *Fax:* (0141) 2568159 *E-mail:* info@pointerpublishers.com; pointerpub@hotmail.com *Web Site:* www.pointerpublishers.com, pg 345

Editions POL (France) *Tel:* (01) 43 54 21 20 *Fax:* (01) 43 54 11 31 *Web Site:* www.pol-editeur.fr, pg 180

The Polding Press (Australia) *Tel:* (03) 9639 0844 *Fax:* (03) 9639 0879 *E-mail:* manager@catholicbookshop.com.au *Web Site:* www.catholicbookshop.com.au, pg 37

Literatur-Agentur Axel Poldner (Germany) *Tel:* (089) 909 558 92 *Fax:* (089) 909 558 91 *E-mail:* info@poldner.de *Web Site:* www.poldner.de, pg 1132

Le Pole Nord ASBL (Belgium) *Tel:* (02) 2184576 *Fax:* (02) 2184576 *E-mail:* pole.nord@skynet.be, pg 72

Editorial Polemos SA (Argentina) *Tel:* (011) 4383-5291 *Fax:* (011) 4382-4181 *E-mail:* editorial@polemos.com.ar *Web Site:* www.polemos.com.ar, pg 8

Polestar Purnell Ltd (United Kingdom) *Tel:* (01761) 404142 *Fax:* (01761) 404191 *Web Site:* www.polestar-group.com/purnell, pg 1164

Polgar Kiado Kft (Hungary) *Tel:* (01) 1752854 *Fax:* (01) 1568358, pg 324

Police Review Publishing Company Ltd (United Kingdom) *Tel:* (020) 7440 4700 *Fax:* (020) 7405 7167; (020) 7405 7163, pg 744

The Policy Press (United Kingdom) *Tel:* (0117) 331 4054 *Fax:* (0117) 331 4093 *E-mail:* tpp-info@bristol.ac.uk *Web Site:* www.policypress.org.uk, pg 744

Policy Studies Institute (PSI) (United Kingdom) *Tel:* (020) 7468 0468 *Fax:* (020) 7388 0914 *E-mail:* website@psi.org.uk *Web Site:* www.psi.org.uk, pg 744

Polifemo, Ediciones (Spain) *Tel:* (091) 7257101 *Fax:* (091) 3556811 *E-mail:* libros@polifemo.com *Web Site:* www.polifemo.com, pg 596

Il Polifilo (Italy) *Tel:* (02) 6551549 *Fax:* (02) 6598045, pg 403

Istituto Poligrafico e Zecca Dello Stato (Italy) *Tel:* (06) 85081 *Toll Free Tel:* 800 864035 *Fax:* (06) 8508-2517 *E-mail:* infoipzs@ipzs.it *Web Site:* www.ipzs.it, pg 1159

Istituto Poligrafico e Zecca dello Stato (Italy) *Tel:* (06) 85081 *Toll Free Tel:* 800-864035 *Fax:* (06) 85082517 *E-mail:* infoipzs@ipzs.it *Web Site:* www.ipzs.it, pg 403

Il Poligrafo (Italy) *Tel:* (04) 98360887 *Fax:* (04) 98360864, pg 404

Polirom Verlag (Romania) *Tel:* (032) 214-100; (032) 214-111; (032) 217-440 *Fax:* (032) 214-100; (032) 214-111; (032) 217-440 *E-mail:* office@polirom.ro *Web Site:* www.polirom.ro, pg 542

Polish Chamber of Books (Poland) *Tel:* (022) 826 12 01 *Fax:* (022) 826 78 55 *E-mail:* pik@arspolona.com.pl *Web Site:* www.pik.org.pl, pg 1281

Polish Chamber of Books (Poland) *Tel:* (022) 8759497 *Fax:* (022) 8759496 *E-mail:* biuro@pik.org.pl *Web Site:* www.pik.org.pl, pg 1336

Polish Scientific Publishers PWN (Poland) *Tel:* (022) 6954321; (022) 6954181 *Fax:* (022) 8267163; (022) 6954288 *E-mail:* pwn@pwn.com.pl *Web Site:* www.pwn.pl, pg 525

Politechnika Krakowska im Tadeusza Kosciuszki (Poland) *Tel:* (012) 628-20-14 *Fax:* (012) 628-20-14 *E-mail:* listy@biblos.pk.edu.pl *Web Site:* www.pk.edu.pl, pg 1538

Politechnika Slaska (Poland) *Tel:* (032) 237-12-69 *Fax:* (032) 237-15-51 *E-mail:* info@bibgl.polsl.gliwice.pl *Web Site:* www.polsl.gliwice.pl/alma.mater/biblioteka.html, pg 1538

Politechnika Wroclawska/Biblioteka Glowna i OINT (Poland) *Tel:* (071) 238-27-07; (071) 320-23-05; (071) 320-23-31 *Fax:* (071) 328-29-60 *E-mail:* bg@bg.pwr.wroc.pl *Web Site:* www.bg.pwr.wroc.pl, pg 1538

Oficyna Wydawnicza Politechniki Wroclawskiej (Poland) *Tel:* (071) 320 29 94; (071) 320 38 23; (071) 328 29 40 *Fax:* (071) 328 29 40 *E-mail:* oficwyd@pwr.wroc.pl *Web Site:* wsww.pwr.wroc.pl, pg 525

Editora Politica (Cuba) *Tel:* (07) 79 8553-59 *Fax:* (07) 811024 *E-mail:* editora@ns.cc.cu; edit63@enet.cu *Web Site:* www.pcc.cu/pccweb/publicaciones/editorapolitica.php, pg 120

Library of Political and Social History (Indonesia) *Tel:* (021) 360136, pg 1517

Politikens Forlag A/S (Denmark) *Tel:* 33 47 07 07 *Fax:* 33 47 07 08 *E-mail:* politikensforlag@pol.dk *Web Site:* www.politikensforlag.dk, pg 133

Politisk Revy (Denmark) *Tel:* 33 91 41 41 *Fax:* 33 91 51 15 *E-mail:* politiskrevy@forlagene.dk *Web Site:* www.forlagene.dk/politiskrevy, pg 133

Galerie Eva Poll (Germany) *Tel:* (030) 261 70 91 *Fax:* (030) 261 70 92 *E-mail:* galerie@poll-berlin.de *Web Site:* www.germangalleries.com/poll, pg 271

Pollinger Ltd (United Kingdom) *Tel:* (020) 7404 0342 *Fax:* (020) 7242 5737 *E-mail:* info@pollingerltd.com *Web Site:* www.pollingerltd.com, pg 1143

Pollitecon Publications (Australia) *Tel:* (02) 9713 7608 *Fax:* (02) 9713 1004 *Web Site:* members.ozemail.com.au/~vbivell, pg 37

Pollner Verlag (Germany) *Tel:* (089) 3151890 *Fax:* (089) 3151890 *E-mail:* info@pollner-verlag.de *Web Site:* www.pollner-verlag.de, pg 271

Polo Publishing (United Kingdom) *Tel:* (020) 8783 1903 *Fax:* (020) 8979 9425, pg 744

Polska Fundacja Spraw Miedzynarodowych (Poland) *Tel:* (022) 827 88 88; (022) 523 90 86 *Fax:* (022) 523 90 27 *E-mail:* warecka@qdnet.pl *Web Site:* www.sprawymiedzynarodowe.pl, pg 1538

Polskie Towarzystwo Wydawcow Ksiazek (Poland) *Tel:* (022) 826 72 71 (ext 345); (022) 826 07 35 *Fax:* (022) 826 07 35, pg 1281

Wydawnictwo Polskiego Towarzystwa Wydawcow Ksiazek (Poland) *Tel:* (022) 826 72 71, Ext 345; (022) 826 07 35 *Fax:* (022) 826 07 35, pg 525

POLTE (Pancyprian Organization of Tertiary Education) (Cyprus) *Tel:* (022) 305030 *Fax:* (022) 494953, pg 121

Polyband Gesellschaft fur Bild Tontraeger mbH & Co Betriebs KG (Germany) *Tel:* (089) 420 03-0 *Fax:* (089) 420 03-42 *E-mail:* contact@polyband.de *Web Site:* www.polyband.de, pg 271

Polybooks Ltd (United Kingdom) *Tel:* (020) 7351 4995 *Fax:* (020) 7351 4995, pg 744

Polyglot Translation (China) *Tel:* (020) 8764-1878 *Fax:* (020) 8764-2003 *E-mail:* info@polyglot.com.cn *Web Site:* www.polyglot.com.cn, pg 1147

Polyglott-Verlag (Germany) *Tel:* (089) 360960 *Fax:* (089) 36096-222 (general); (089) 36096-258 (orders), pg 271

Polygon (United Kingdom) *Tel:* (0131) 668 4371 *Fax:* (0131) 668 4466 *E-mail:* info@birlinn.co.uk *Web Site:* www.birlinn.co.uk, pg 744

Polygraf Print sro (Slovakia) *Tel:* (051) 44 13 280 *Fax:* (051) 77 13 241; (051) 77 13 270 *E-mail:* polygrafprint@polygrafprint.sk, pg 560

Polygraph Verlag GmbH (Germany) *Tel:* (0521) 97044-0 *Fax:* (0521) 97044-33, pg 271

Polygraphics Trading (Philippines) *Tel:* (02) 817-9556 *Fax:* (02) 817-9564 *Web Site:* www.piap.org.ph, pg 1160

Polynesian Press (New Zealand) *Tel:* (09) 3032349 *Fax:* (09) 3779528, pg 500

Polytechnica SA (France) *Tel:* (01) 45 78 12 92 *Fax:* (01) 45 75 05 67, pg 180

Polyteknisk Boghandel & Forlag (Denmark) *Tel:* 77 42 43 44 *Fax:* 77 42 43 54 *E-mail:* forlag@poly.dtu.dk *Web Site:* www.polyteknisk.dk, pg 133

Polyteknisk Boghandel og Forlag (Denmark) *Tel:* 77 42 44 44 *Fax:* 77 42 43 54 *E-mail:* polybog@pb.dtu.dk *Web Site:* www.pf.dtu.dk/, pg 1308

Editorial Pomaire Venezuela SA (Venezuela) *Tel:* (02) 2622122; (02) 2621253 *Fax:* (02) 2616962, pg 780

Pomegranate Europe Ltd (United Kingdom) *Tel:* (01926) 430111 *Fax:* (01926) 430888 *E-mail:* sales@pomeurope.co.uk; isb@pomeurope.co.uk *Web Site:* www.pomegranate.com, pg 744

Il Pomerio (Italy) *Tel:* (0371) 420381 *Fax:* (0371) 422080, pg 404

POMORZE-Pomorskie Wydawnictwo Prasowe (Poland) *Tel:* (052) 220237; (052) 211396; (052) 210452, pg 526

Pomorze Wydawnictwo Spoldzielnia Pracy (Poland) *Tel:* (052) 220237; (052) 211396; (052) 210452, pg 526

Editions du Centre Pompidou (France) *Tel:* (01) 44 78 12 33 *Fax:* (01) 44 78 12 05 *Web Site:* www.centrepompidou.fr, pg 180

Pomurska zalozba (Slovenia) *Tel:* (069) 32-420 *Fax:* (069) 31-086, pg 561

Libreria Pons SL (Spain) *Tel:* (0976) 550 105; (0976) 350 037; (0976) 554 920 *Fax:* (0976) 356 072 *E-mail:* promedit@libreriapons-zaragoza.com; pedidos@liberiapons-zaragoza.com; admon@liberiapons-zaragoza.com *Web Site:* www.libreriapons-zaragoza.com, pg 1342

Pontificia Academia Scientiarum (Holy See (Vatican City State)) *Tel:* 0669883195 *Fax:* 0669885218 *E-mail:* academy.sciences@acdscience.va *Web Site:* www.vatican.va/roman_curia/pontifical_academies/index_it.htm, pg 314

Pontificia Universidad Catolica de Chile Sistema de Bibliotecas (Chile) *Tel:* (02) 6864616; (02) 6864762 *Fax:* (02) 6865852 *Web Site:* www.puc.cl, pg 1497

Pontificia Universidad Catolica de Chile (Chile) *Tel:* (02) 2224516 (ext 2417) *Fax:* (02) 2225515 *Web Site:* www.puc.cl, pg 100

Pontificia Universidad Catolica del Ecuador, Centro de Publicaciones (Ecuador) *Tel:* (02) 2991700; (02) 2565627 *E-mail:* wjimenez@puceuio.puce.edu.ec *Web Site:* www.puce.edu.ec, pg 137

Fondo Editorial de le Pontificia Universidad Catolica del Peru (Peru) *Tel:* (01) 3307410; (01) 3307411 *Fax:* (01) 3307405 *E-mail:* feditor@pucp.edu.pe *Web Site:* www.pucp.edu.pe, pg 1536

Pontificia Universidad Catolica Madre y Maestra (Dominican Republic) *Tel:* (809) 5801962; (809) 5350111 *Fax:* (809) 5824549; (809) 5350053 *Web Site:* www.pucmmsti.edu.do, pg 525

Pontificia Universidad Javeriana, Biblioteca General (Colombia) *Tel:* (01) 320 8320 (ext 2135); (01) 320 8320 (ext 2150); (01) 320 8320 (ext 2151) *Fax:* (01) 320 8320 (ext 2131) *E-mail:* biblioteca@javeriana.edu.co *Web Site:* www.javeriana.edu.co, pg 1498

Pontificio Istituto di Archeologia Cristiana (Italy) *Tel:* (06) 4465574; (06) 4453169 *Fax:* (06) 4469197 *E-mail:* piac@piac.it *Web Site:* www.piac.it, pg 404

Pontifico Istituto Orientale (Italy) *Tel:* (06) 447417177; (06) 4474170 *Fax:* (06) 4465576 *E-mail:* informatica@pitagoragroup.it *Web Site:* www.pio.urbe.it, pg 404

Pontiki Publications SA (Greece) *Tel:* (0210) 3609531; (0210) 3609533 *Fax:* (0210) 3645406, pg 311

Pookie Productions Ltd (United Kingdom) *Tel:* (0131) 221868 *Fax:* (0131) 221868, pg 744

Poolbeg Press Ltd (Ireland) *Tel:* (01) 832 1477 *Fax:* (01) 832 1430 *E-mail:* info@poolbeg.com *Web Site:* www.poolbeg.com, pg 363

Poplar Publishing Co Ltd (Japan) *Tel:* (03) 3357-2211 *Fax:* (03) 3359-2359 *E-mail:* henshu@poplar.co.jp *Web Site:* www.poplar.co.jp, pg 425

Popular Army Publishing House (Viet Nam), pg 780

Popular Book Depot (India) *Tel:* (022) 382 9401; (022) 382 6762, pg 1317

Popular Book Store (Philippines) *Tel:* (02) 372-2162 *Fax:* (02) 372-2050 *E-mail:* popular@pworld.net.ph, pg 1335

Biblioteca Popular Judia (Argentina) *Tel:* (011) 4961-4534 *Fax:* (011) 4963-7056 *E-mail:* cjl@mayo.com.ar, pg 8

Popular Prakashan Pvt Ltd (India) *Tel:* (022) 494 1656 *Fax:* (022) 24945294 *E-mail:* info@popularprakashan.com *Web Site:* www.popularprakashan.com, pg 345

Popular Publications (Malawi) *Tel:* 651 833 *Fax:* 651 17133 *E-mail:* mpp@malawi.net, pg 454

Editorial Popular SA (Spain) *Tel:* (091) 409 35 73 *Fax:* (091) 573 41 73 *E-mail:* epopular@infornet.es *Web Site:* www.editorialpopular.com, pg 596

Popular Science Press (China) *Tel:* (010) 62178877, pg 107

H Pordes Ltd (United Kingdom) *Tel:* (020) 8445 1273 *Fax:* (020) 8445 5510, pg 1352

Frederique Porretta (France) *Tel:* (01) 45448868 *Fax:* (01) 45446936 *E-mail:* frederique.porretta@wanadoo.fr, pg 1131

Libreria de Porrua Hermanos y Cia, SA (Mexico) *Tel:* (05) 7024574 *Fax:* (05) 7026529 *E-mail:* porrua@porrua.com *Web Site:* www.porrua.com, pg 1327

Editorial Porrua SA (Mexico) *Tel:* (05) 7024934; (05) 7024574 *Fax:* (05) 7026529, pg 470

Portal spol sro (Czech Republic) *Tel:* (02) 83028111 *Fax:* (02) 83028112 *E-mail:* naklad@portal.cz *Web Site:* www.portal.cz, pg 126

Editions La Porte (Morocco) *Tel:* (07) 709958; (07) 706476 *Fax:* (07) 709958; (07) 706478, pg 475

David Porteous Editions (United Kingdom) *Tel:* (01626) 853310 *Fax:* (01626) 853663 *E-mail:* sales@davidporteous.com *Web Site:* www.davidporteous.com, pg 744

Porthill Publishers (United Kingdom) *Tel:* (020) 89586783 *Fax:* (020) 89054516, pg 744

Editorial Portic SA (Spain) *Tel:* (093) 412 00 30 *Fax:* (093) 301 48 63 *E-mail:* hiperenciclopedia@grec.com *Web Site:* www.enciclopedia-catalana.com, pg 596

Portikus (Germany) *Tel:* (069) 219 987-60; (069) 219 987-59 *Fax:* (069) 219 987-61 *E-mail:* portikus@pop.stadt-frankfurt.de *Web Site:* www.portikus.de, pg 271

Portland Press Ltd (United Kingdom) *Tel:* (020) 7637 5873 *Fax:* (020) 7323 1136 *E-mail:* editorial@portlandpress.com *Web Site:* www.portlandpress.com, pg 745

Porto Editora Lda (Portugal) *Tel:* (02) 2005813 *Fax:* (02) 313072 *E-mail:* pe@portoeditora.pt *Web Site:* www.portoeditora.pt, pg 535

Livraria Portugal (Dias e Andrade Lda) (Portugal) *Tel:* (01) 3474982 *Fax:* (01) 3470264 *E-mail:* liv.portugal@mail.telepac.pt, pg 1338

Portugalmundo (Portugal) *Tel:* (021) 877611 *Fax:* (021) 8144746, pg 535

Instituto Portugues Oriente (Macau) *Tel:* 530227; 530243 *Fax:* 530277 *E-mail:* info@ipor.org *Web Site:* www.ipor.org, pg 452

Editorial Porvenir (Costa Rica) *Tel:* 224-8119; 224-1052; 225-3115 *Fax:* 283-8893; 224-8119 *E-mail:* porvenir@racsa.co.cr, pg 116

Possev-Verlag GmbH (Germany) *Tel:* (069) 34-12-65 *Fax:* (069) 34-38-41 *E-mail:* possev-ffm@t-online.de, pg 271

The Beatrix Potter Society (United Kingdom) *Tel:* (01625) 267880 *Fax:* (01625) 267879 *E-mail:* info@beatrixpottersociety.org.uk *Web Site:* www.beatrixpottersociety.org.uk, pg 1409

Marilyn Potts International Language Consultants (United Kingdom) *Tel:* (0191) 222 1775 *Fax:* (0191) 261 6426 *E-mail:* info@marilyn-potts.co.uk *Web Site:* www.marilyn-potts.co.uk, pg 1151

Pournaras Panagiotis (Greece) *Tel:* (031) 0270941 *Fax:* (031) 0228922 *E-mail:* pournarasbooks@the.forthnet.gr, pg 1314

Editions Pourquoi Pas (Switzerland) *Tel:* (022) 7511031, pg 631

Power Publications (Australia) *Tel:* (02) 9351 6904 *Fax:* (02) 9351 7323 *E-mail:* power.publications@arts.usyd.edu.au *Web Site:* www.power.arts.usyd.edu.au/institute, pg 37

Shelley Power Literary Agency Ltd (France) *Tel:* (01) 42383649 *Fax:* (01) 40407008, pg 1131

Neri Pozza Editore (Italy) *Tel:* (0444) 320787; (0444) 323036 *Fax:* (0444) 324613 *Web Site:* www.neripozza.it, pg 404

Edizioni Luigi Pozzi SRL (Italy) *Tel:* (06) 8553548 *Fax:* (06) 8554105, pg 404

PPC Editorial y Distribuidora, SA (Spain) *Tel:* (091) 4228800 *Fax:* (091) 4226117 *E-mail:* buzonppc@ppc-editorial.com *Web Site:* www.ppc-editorial.com, pg 596

PPC Editorial y Distribuidora, SA (Spain) *Tel:* (091) 359 23 00 *Fax:* (091) 350 54 43, pg 1343

PPP Printers Ltd (New Zealand) *Tel:* (03) 3662727 *Fax:* (03) 3654606 *Web Site:* www.scoop.co.nz, pg 1160

PPP Printers Ltd (New Zealand) *Tel:* (03) 3662727 *Fax:* (03) 3654606, pg 1181, 1221

Prabhat Prakashan (India) *Tel:* (011) 3264676; (011) 3289555; (011) 3289666 *Fax:* (011) 3253233 *E-mail:* prabhat@indianabooks.com; prabhat1@vsnl.com *Web Site:* www.indianabooks.com, pg 345

Vydavatepstvo Praca spol sro (Slovakia) *Tel:* (02) 5249 2890 *Fax:* (07) 392840; (07) 392853, pg 560

Pracha Chang & Co Ltd (Thailand), pg 645

Georg Prachner KG (Austria) *Tel:* (01) 512 85 49-0 *Fax:* (01) 512-01-58, pg 56

Georg Prachner KG (Austria) *Tel:* (01) 5128549-0 *Fax:* (01) 5120158, pg 1300

Pradeepa Publishers (Sri Lanka) *Tel:* (094) 435074; (094) 863261; (071) 735532 *Fax:* (094) 863261, pg 607

Pragma 4 (Czech Republic) *Tel:* 241 768 565; 241 768 566; 603 205 099 *Fax:* 241 768 561 *E-mail:* pragma@pragma.cz *Web Site:* www.pragma.cz, pg 126

Agamee Prakashani (Bangladesh) *Tel:* (02) 711-1332; (02) 711-0021 *Fax:* (02) 9562018; (02) 7123945 *E-mail:* agamee@bdonline.com *Web Site:* www.agameeprakashani-bd.com, pg 61

Prasan Mit (Thailand) *Tel:* (02) 3915287; (02) 3925230, pg 645

Prasenz Verlag der Jesus Bruderschaft eV (Germany) *Tel:* (06438) 81281 *Fax:* (06438) 81282 *Web Site:* www.uni-giessen.de, pg 271

Pratibha Pratishthan (India) *Tel:* (011) 3289666 Toll Free *Tel:* (011) 3253233, pg 345

Pratiche Editrice (Italy) *Tel:* (02) 29403460 *Fax:* (02) 29513061, pg 404

Wydawnictwo Prawnicze Co (Poland) *Tel:* (022) 5729500; (022) 5729507 *Fax:* (022) 5729509 *E-mail:* biuro@lexisnexis.pl *Web Site:* sklep.lexpolonica.pl, pg 526

Prazske nakladatelstvi Pluto (Czech Republic) *Tel:* (02) 249 301 89; (02) 43 25 05 *Fax:* (02) 249 301 89, pg 127

PRC Publishing Ltd (United Kingdom) *Tel:* (020) 7700 7799 *Fax:* (020) 7700 0635 *E-mail:* info@chrysalisbooks.co.uk *Web Site:* www.chrysalisbooks.co.uk/books/publisher/prc, pg 745

Le Pre-aux-clercs (France) *Tel:* (01) 44 16 05 00 *Fax:* (01) 44 16 05 05, pg 180

Pre-Textos (Spain) *Tel:* (096) 333 32 26 *Fax:* (096) 395 54 77 *E-mail:* info@pre-textos.com *Web Site:* www.pre-textos.com, pg 596

Precision Publishing Papers Ltd (United Kingdom) *Tel:* (01935) 431800; (732) 563-9292 (USA & other) *Fax:* (01935) 431805 *E-mail:* precisionpub@pppl.co.uk *Web Site:* www.hspg.com/precision, pg 1164

Izdavacko Preduzece Matice Srpske (Serbia and Montenegro) *Tel:* (021) 420 199; (021) 420 198 *Fax:* (021) 28 574; (021) 25 859 *E-mail:* bms@bms.ns.ac.yu *Web Site:* www.bms.ns.ac.yu, pg 553

Ediciones Preescolar SA (Argentina) *Tel:* (011) 4581-3182 *Fax:* (011) 4581-3182, pg 8

Premop Verlag GmbH (Germany) *Tel:* (089) 562257 *Fax:* (089) 5803214 *E-mail:* premop@mnet-online.de, pg 271

Preney Print & Litho Inc (Canada) *Tel:* 519-966-3412 *Toll Free Tel:* 877-870-4164 *Fax:* 519-966-4996 *E-mail:* contactus@preneyprint.com, pg 1175

Preney Print & Litho Inc (Canada) *Tel:* 519-966-3412 *Toll Free Tel:* 877-870-4164 *Fax:* 519-966-4996 *E-mail:* contacts@preneyprint.com *Web Site:* www.preneyprint.com, pg 1215

Editorial Prensa Espanola (Spain) *Tel:* (091) 4462616, pg 597

Prensa Medica Latinoamericana (Uruguay) *Tel:* (02) 707 91 09 *Fax:* (02) 707 91 09 *E-mail:* prensmed@adinet.com.uy, pg 778

Ediciones Cientificas La Prensa Medica Mexicana SA de CV (Mexico) *Tel:* (05) 5504500 *Fax:* (05) 6589193, pg 470

Prensas Universitarias de Zaragoza (Spain) *Tel:* (0976) 761330 *Fax:* (0976) 761063 *E-mail:* spublica@posta.unizar.es *Web Site:* wzar.unizar.es/spub/, pg 597

Prentsmidjan Oddi (Iceland) *Tel:* 5155000 *Fax:* 5155001 *E-mail:* oddi@oddi.is *Web Site:* www.oddi.is, pg 326

Prepare Inc (United States) *Tel:* 201-934-8451 *Fax:* 201-934-2992 *E-mail:* csr@emilcomp.it; prepare@optonline.net, pg 1189

PrePress Imaging Inc (United States) *Tel:* 636-940-9146 *Toll Free Tel:* 800-886-6122 *Fax:* 636-896-8107 *E-mail:* mail@ppi-stl.com *Web Site:* www.ppi-stl.com, pg 1189

Casa Editora Presbiteriana SC (Brazil) *Tel:* (011) 270-7099 *Fax:* (011) 279-1255 *E-mail:* cep@cep.org.br *Web Site:* www.cep.org.br, pg 88

Presbyterian Book Depot & Printing Press Ltd (PRESBOOK) (Cameroon) *Tel:* 332114 *Fax:* 332694, pg 1305

Presbyterian Book Depot Ltd (Ghana) *Tel:* (021) 662707 *Fax:* (021) 665594 *E-mail:* pcg@africaonline.com.gh, pg 1312

Editorial Presenca (Portugal) *Tel:* (021) 4347000 *Fax:* (021) 4346502 *E-mail:* info@editpresenca.pt *Web Site:* www.editpresenca.pt, pg 535

Presence Africaine Editions (France) *Tel:* (01) 43 54 13 74; (01) 43 54 15 88 *Fax:* (01) 43 25 96 67 *E-mail:* presaf@club-internet.fr *Web Site:* www.letissu.com, pg 180

Editorial Presencia Gitana (Spain) *Tel:* (091) 373 62 07 *Fax:* (091) 373 44 62 *E-mail:* anpregit@teleline.es, pg 597

Preses Nams (Latvia) *Tel:* (02) 7062270 *Fax:* (02) 7062344 *E-mail:* presesnams@presesnams.lv *Web Site:* www.presesnams.lv, pg 445

President Boekklub (South Africa) *Tel:* (012) 401 0700 *Fax:* (012) 3255498 *E-mail:* lapa@atkv.org.za *Web Site:* www.lapauitgewers.org.za, pg 1255

President Inc (Japan) *Tel:* (03) 32373734 *Fax:* (03) 32373746 *E-mail:* matu-pre@po.iijnet.or.jp *Web Site:* www.president.co.jp; www.president.co.jp/pre/english.html, pg 425

THE PRESS / INDUSTRY

The Press (Jamaica) *Tel:* (876) 977-2659 *Fax:* (876) 977-2660 *E-mail:* uwipress_marketing@cwjamaica.com; cuserv@cwjamaica.com (customer service & orders) *Web Site:* www.uwipress.com, pg 414

Press Agency (Kuwait) *Tel:* 432269 *Fax:* 411495, pg 444

Press & Publication Administration of the People's Republic of China (China) *Tel:* (010) 5127809 *Fax:* (010) 5127875, pg 1264

Press & Publicity Centre Ltd (United Republic of Tanzania) *Tel:* (051) 127765; (051) 122881; (051) 131078 *Fax:* (051) 113619; (051) 116749, pg 644

The Press & Publishing Engineering Society (Russian Federation) *Tel:* (095) 290-62-86; (095) 291-42-42 *Fax:* (095) 291-85-06 *E-mail:* sitsev@mail.sitek.ru *Web Site:* usea.mailru.com, pg 1282

Press for Success (Australia) *Tel:* (08) 9221 6166 *Fax:* (08) 9221 6166 *E-mail:* press4@press4success.com.au *Web Site:* www.press4success.com.au, pg 37

Press Mark Media Ltd (Hong Kong) *Tel:* 28822230 *Fax:* 2882 3949; 2882 2471 *E-mail:* magazine@todayliving.com, pg 318

Press Photo Publications (Greece) *Tel:* (0210) 8541400 *Fax:* (0210) 8541485 *E-mail:* photomag@photo.gr *Web Site:* www.photo.gr, pg 1314

Pressa Publishing House (Russian Federation) *Tel:* (095) 2573482 *Fax:* (095) 2505205, pg 548

PressArt Nakladatelstvi (Czech Republic) *Tel:* (048) 29377 *Fax:* (048) 27958, pg 127

Presse-Grosso-Bundesverband Deutscher Buch-, Zeitungs-und Zeitschriften-Grossisten eV (Germany) *Tel:* (0221) 9213370 *Fax:* (0221) 92133744 *E-mail:* bvpg@bvpg.de *Web Site:* www.pressegrosso.de, pg 1271

PIAG Presse Informations AG (Germany) *Tel:* (07221) 301 7560 *Fax:* (07221) 301 7570 *E-mail:* office@piag.de *Web Site:* www.piag.de, pg 271

Presse Verlagsgesellschaft mbH (Germany) *Tel:* (069) 97460-0 *Fax:* (069) 97460-400 *E-mail:* journal@mmg.de *Web Site:* www.journal-frankfurt.de, pg 271

Presses agronomiques de Gembloux ASBL (Belgium) *Tel:* (081) 62 22 42 *Fax:* (081) 62 22 42 *E-mail:* pressesagro@fsagx.ac.be *Web Site:* www.bib.fsagx.ac.be/presses/, pg 72

Presses de la Cite (France) *Tel:* (01) 44160500 *Fax:* (01) 44160505 *Web Site:* www.pressesdelacite.com, pg 180

Presses de la Renaissance (France) *Tel:* (01) 55 43 27 50 *Fax:* (01) 55 43 27 60 *Web Site:* www.presses-renaissance.com, pg 181

Presses de la Sorbonne Nouvelle/PSN (France) *Tel:* (01) 45874027; (01) 45874168 *Fax:* (01) 45877854; (01) 45874175 *E-mail:* n.carbon@univ-paris3.fr *Web Site:* www.univ-paris3.fr, pg 181

Presses de l'Ecole Nationale des Ponts et Chaussees (France) *Tel:* (01) 44 58 27 40 *Fax:* (01) 44582744 *Web Site:* www.enpc.fr, pg 181

Presses de Sciences Politiques (France) *Tel:* (01) 44 39 39 60 *Fax:* (01) 45 48 04 41 *Web Site:* www.sciences.po.fr, pg 181

Les Presses d'Ile-de-France Sarl (France) *Tel:* (01) 44 52 37 24 *Fax:* (01) 42 38 09 87 *E-mail:* scouts@scouts-france.fr *Web Site:* www.scouts-france.fr, pg 181

Les Presses du Management (France) *Tel:* (01) 53 00 11 71 *Fax:* (01) 53 00 10 08, pg 181

Presses Polytechniques et Universitaires Romandes, PPUR (Switzerland) *Tel:* (021) 693 41 31 *Fax:* (021) 693 40 27 *E-mail:* ppur@epfl.ch *Web Site:* www.ppur.org, pg 631

Presses Universitaires d'Afrique (Cameroon) *Tel:* (023) 22 00 30 *Fax:* (023) 22 23 25, pg 98

Presses Universitaires de Bruxelles asbl (Belgium) *Tel:* (02) 649 97 80 *Fax:* (02) 647 79 62 *E-mail:* editions@admin.ulb.ac.be *Web Site:* www.ulb.ac.be/ulb/docs/pub.html, pg 72

Presses Universitaires de Caen (France) *Tel:* (02) 31 56 62 20 *Fax:* (02) 31 56 62 25 *E-mail:* puc@mrsh.unicaen.fr *Web Site:* www.unicaen.fr/mrsh/puc, pg 181

Presses Universitaires de France (PUF) (France) *Tel:* (01) 58 10 31 00 *Fax:* (01) 58 10 31 82 *E-mail:* puf.com@puf.com *Web Site:* www.puf.com, pg 181

Presses Universitaires de Grenoble (France) *Tel:* (04) 76 82 56 51; (04) 76 82 56 52 *Fax:* (04) 76 82 78 35 *E-mail:* pug@pug.fr *Web Site:* www.pug.fr, pg 181

Presses Universitaires de Liege (Belgium) *Tel:* (041) 562218, pg 72

Presses Universitaires de Lyon (France) *Tel:* (04) 78 29 39 39 *Fax:* (04) 78 29 39 41 *Web Site:* sites.univ-lyon2.fr/pul, pg 181

Presses Universitaires de Namur ASBL (Belgium) *Tel:* (081) 72 48 84 *Fax:* (081) 72 49 12 *E-mail:* pun@fundp.ac.be *Web Site:* www.pun.be, pg 72

Presses Universitaires de Nancy (France) *Tel:* (03) 83 96 84 30 *Fax:* (03) 83 96 84 39 *E-mail:* pun@univ-nancy2.fr *Web Site:* www.univ-nancy2.fr/PUN, pg 181

Presses Universitaires de Strasbourg (France) *Tel:* (03) 88 25 97 21 *Fax:* (03) 88 35 65 23 *E-mail:* info@pu-strasourg.com *Web Site:* www.pu-strasbourg.com, pg 182

Presses Universitaires du Septentrion (France) *Tel:* (03) 20 41 66 80 *Fax:* (03) 20 41 66 90 *E-mail:* septentrion@septentrion.com *Web Site:* www.septentrion.com, pg 182

Presses Universitaires du Zaiire (PUZ) (The Democratic Republic of the Congo) *Tel:* 30652, pg 114

Pressfoto Vydavatelstvi Ceske Tiskove Kancelare (Czech Republic) *Tel:* (02) 727 700 10 *Fax:* (02) 727 700 10, pg 127

Guido Pressler Verlag (Germany) *Tel:* (02429) 1385; (02408) 929692 *Fax:* (02408) 955931 *E-mail:* info@pressler-verlag.com *Web Site:* www.pressler-verlag.com, pg 271

Prestel Verlag (Germany) *Tel:* (089) 38 17 09 0 *Fax:* (089) 33 51 75 *E-mail:* info@prestel.de *Web Site:* www.prestel.de, pg 271

Prestige Booksellers & Stationers (Kenya) *Tel:* (02) 223515 *Fax:* (02) 2246796 *E-mail:* prest@iconnect.co.ke, pg 1324

Preston Corporation Sdn Bhd (Malaysia) *Tel:* (03) 7574222 *Fax:* (03) 7573607, pg 458

Helmut Preussler Verlag (Germany) *Tel:* (0911) 95478 0 *Fax:* (0911) 542486 *E-mail:* preussler_verlag@t_online.de, pg 271

Mathew Price Ltd (United Kingdom) *Tel:* (01935) 816010 *Fax:* (01935) 816310 *E-mail:* mathewp@mathewprice.com *Web Site:* www.mathewprice.com, pg 745

Price Publishing (Australia) *Tel:* (02) 9904 9811 *E-mail:* pricesys@localnet.com.au, pg 37

Priese GmbH & Co (Germany) *Tel:* (030) 8263024 *Fax:* (030) 3249630, pg 1155, 1177

Priese GmbH & Co (Germany) *Tel:* (030) 8263024 *Fax:* (030) 8266024, pg 1217

Priese GmbH & Co (Germany) *Tel:* (030) 8263024 *Fax:* (030) 3249630, pg 1236, 1245

Priestley Consulting (Australia) *Tel:* (07) 4937179 *Fax:* (07) 54458288 *E-mail:* adpriestley@ozemail.com.au, pg 37

Prim-Ed Publishing UK Ltd (United Kingdom) *Tel:* (0870) 876 0151 *Fax:* (0870) 876 0152 *E-mail:* sales@prim-ed.com *Web Site:* www.prim-ed.com, pg 745

Primary English Teaching Association (Australia) *Tel:* (02) 9565 1277 *Fax:* (02) 9565 1070 *E-mail:* info@peta.edu.au *Web Site:* www.peta.edu.au, pg 37

Edizioni Primavera SRL (Italy) *Tel:* (055) 50621 *Fax:* (055) 5062298 *E-mail:* d.basciafarei@giunti.it, pg 404

Editora Primor Ltda (Brazil) *Tel:* (021) 4744966, pg 89

Primrose Hill Press Ltd (United Kingdom) *Tel:* (01869) 277 000 *Fax:* (01869) 277 820 *Web Site:* www.primrosehillpress.co.uk, pg 745

Principato (Italy) *Tel:* (02) 312025 *Fax:* (02) 33104295 *E-mail:* princi.red@comm2000.it, pg 404

Printafoil Ltd (United Kingdom) *Tel:* (0181) 6403074 *Fax:* (020) 8640 2136, pg 1227

Printafoil Ltd (United Kingdom) *Tel:* (01473) 721701 *Fax:* (01473) 270705 *E-mail:* printafoil@blockfoil.com *Web Site:* www.blockfoil.com, pg 1239

Printcrafters Inc (Canada) *Tel:* 204-633-7117 *Fax:* 204-694-1519 *E-mail:* info@printcraftersinc.com *Web Site:* www.printcraftersinc.com, pg 1175

Printcrafters Inc (Canada) *Tel:* 204-633-7117 *Fax:* 204-694-1519 *E-mail:* info@printcraftersinc.com, pg 1215, 1235

Printcrafters Inc (Canada) *Tel:* 204-633-7117 *Fax:* 204-694-1519 *E-mail:* info@printcraftersinc.com *Web Site:* www.printcraftersinc.com, pg 1245

EDITIONS Le Printemps (Mauritius) *Tel:* 6961017 *Fax:* 6867302 *E-mail:* elp@intnet.mu, pg 461

Printer Industria Grafica SA (Spain) *Tel:* (093) 631 01 23 *Fax:* (093) 631 02 05; (093) 631 02 06 *E-mail:* info.printer@arvato-print.es *Web Site:* www.printer-spain.com, pg 1223

Printer Portuguesa Industria Grafica Lda (Portugal) *Tel:* (01) 9216025 *Fax:* (01) 9218363 *E-mail:* lissabon.printerportuguesa@bertelsmann.de, pg 1222

Printing Corp of the Americas Inc (United States) *Tel:* 954-781-8100 *Fax:* 954-781-8421 *E-mail:* pcaprint@bellsouth.net *Web Site:* www.pcaprint.bellsouth.net, pg 1168, 1189, 1231, 1241

Printing Industry Publishing House (China) *Tel:* (010) 68218367 *Fax:* (010) 8214683 *E-mail:* capt@public3.bta.net.cn, pg 107

Printpak (Z) Ltd (Zambia) *Tel:* (01) 611001; (01) 611002; (01) 600113; (01) 612027 *Fax:* (01) 617096, pg 782

Prints India (India) *Tel:* (011) 3268645 *Fax:* (011) 3275542, pg 1317

PrintWest (Canada) *Tel:* 306-525-2304 *Toll Free Tel:* 800-236-6438 *Fax:* 306-757-2439 *E-mail:* general@printwest.com *Web Site:* www.printwest.com, pg 1153, 1175, 1235, 1245

Printworld Services Pte Ltd (Singapore) *Tel:* 7442166 *Fax:* 7460845 *E-mail:* printw@mbox2.singnet.com.sg, pg 557

Prion Books Ltd (United Kingdom) *Tel:* (020) 7482 4248 *Fax:* (020) 7482 4203 *E-mail:* books@prion.co.uk, pg 745

Priroda Publishing (Slovakia) *Tel:* (02) 5556 4672 *Fax:* (02) 5556 4669 *E-mail:* priroda@priroda.sk *Web Site:* www.priroda.sk, pg 560

Prism Press Book Publishers Ltd (United Kingdom) *Tel:* (01202) 665432 *Fax:* (01202) 666219 *E-mail:* orders@orcabookservices.co.uk, pg 745

Bokforlaget Prisma (Sweden) *Tel:* (08) 7698900 *Fax:* (08) 241276 *E-mail:* prisma@prismabok.se *Web Site:* www.prismabok.se, pg 614

Prismi - Editrice Politecnica (Italy) *Tel:* (081) 7612884 *Fax:* (081) 668339, pg 404

Priuli e Verlucca, Editori (Italy) *Tel:* (0125) 23 99 29 *Fax:* (0125) 23 00 85 *E-mail:* info@priulieverlucca.it *Web Site:* www.priulieverlucca.it, pg 404

Private Libraries Association (PLA) (United Kingdom) *Web Site:* www.the-old-school.demon.co.uk/pla.htm, pg 1292

Privredni Pregled (Serbia and Montenegro) *Tel:* (011) 625522; (011) 628477 *Fax:* (011) 3281473; (011) 3281912 *E-mail:* novinska@hotmail.com; desk@grmec.co.yu *Web Site:* www.grmec.co.yu, pg 553

Pro Juventute Verlag (Switzerland) *Tel:* (01) 2567777 *Fax:* (01) 2567778 *E-mail:* info@projuventute.ch *Web Site:* www.projuventute.ch, pg 631

Pro Media Productions (Suriname) *Tel:* 479355, pg 608

Pro Natur Verlag GmbH (Germany) *Tel:* (069) 9688610 *Fax:* (069) 96886124, pg 272

Pro Natura (Hungary) *Tel:* (01) 1317330 *Fax:* (01) 1117270, pg 324

Editions Pro Schola (Switzerland) *Tel:* (021) 323 66 55 *Fax:* (021) 323 67 77 *E-mail:* benedict@benedict-schools.com *Web Site:* www.benedict-international.com, pg 631

Proa SA (Chile) *Tel:* (02) 633 65 34; (02) 633 98 54 *Fax:* (02) 633 98 54 *E-mail:* proa@eutelchile.net, pg 100

Edicions Proa, SA (Spain) *Tel:* (093) 4120030 *Fax:* (093) 3014863 *E-mail:* enciclo.catalan@bcn.servicom.es, pg 597

Procultura SA (Colombia) *Tel:* (01) 2818254, pg 112

PRODIG (France) *Tel:* (01) 44 32 14 81; (01) 42 34 56 21 *Fax:* (01) 43 29 63 83 *E-mail:* prodig@univ-paris1.fr *Web Site:* prodig.univ-paris1.fr/umr, pg 182

Prodim SPRL (Belgium) *Tel:* (02) 640 59 70 *Fax:* (02) 640 59 91 *E-mail:* prodim.books@prodim.be *Web Site:* www.prodim.be, pg 72

Professional Book Supplies Ltd (United Kingdom) *Tel:* (01235) 861234 *Fax:* (01235) 861601 *E-mail:* probooks@aol.com, pg 745

Professional Engineering Publishing Ltd (United Kingdom) *Tel:* (01284) 763277 *Fax:* (01284) 718692 (sales) *E-mail:* orders@pepublishing.com *Web Site:* www.pepublishing.com, pg 745

Professional, Managerial & Healthcare Publications (United Kingdom) *Tel:* (01243) 576444 *Fax:* (01243) 576456 *E-mail:* admin@pmh.uk.com *Web Site:* www.pmh.uk.com, pg 746

Professional Publishing Co (Hong Kong) *Tel:* 25254623 *Fax:* 28453681, pg 1158

Profile Books Ltd (United Kingdom) *Tel:* (020) 7404 3001 *Fax:* (020) 7404 3003 *E-mail:* info@profilebooks.co.uk *Web Site:* www.profilebooks.co.uk, pg 746

Profile Publishing Ltd (New Zealand) *Tel:* (09) 6308940; (09) 3585455 *Fax:* (09) 6302307; (09) 6301046; (09) 3585462 *E-mail:* info@profile.co.nz *Web Site:* www.profile.co.nz, pg 500

Profizdat (Russian Federation) *Tel:* (095) 924-5740; (095) 924-8225 (books); (095) 924-4637 (periodicals) *Fax:* (095) 975-2329 *E-mail:* profizdat@profizdat.ru *Web Site:* www.profizdat.ru, pg 548

Progensa (Spain) *Tel:* (0954) 186 200 *Fax:* (0954) 186 111 *E-mail:* progensa@progensa.com *Web Site:* www.progensa.es, pg 597

Editorial Progreso SA de C V (Mexico) *Tel:* (05) 5477304 *Fax:* (05) 5415342 *E-mail:* editprogresosav@infosel.net.mx, pg 470

Progress Press Co Ltd (Malta) *Tel:* 21241464; 21241469; 21241411; 21241412 *Fax:* 21241171, pg 460

Progress Publishers (Russian Federation) *Tel:* (095) 2469032 *Fax:* (095) 2302403, pg 548

Progress-Verlag Dr Micolini's Witwe (Austria) *Tel:* (0316) 829508 *Fax:* (0316) 829508, pg 56

Prohazka I Kacarmazov (Bulgaria) *Tel:* (02) 654969 *Fax:* (02) 654969 *E-mail:* eto@einet.bg, pg 96

Projektion J Buch- und Musikverlag GmbH (Germany) *Tel:* (06443) 68-0 *Fax:* (06443) 68-34 *E-mail:* info@gerth.de *Web Site:* www.gerth.de, pg 272

Prolog Publishing House (Israel) *Tel:* (03) 9022904 *Fax:* (03) 9022906 *E-mail:* info@prolog.co.il *Web Site:* www.prolog.co.il, pg 371

De Prom (Netherlands) *Tel:* (035) 5482403 *Fax:* (035) 5418221 *E-mail:* info.fontein@defonteinbaarn.nl, pg 488

Promedia Verlagsges mbH (Austria) *Tel:* (01) 405 27 02 *Fax:* (01) 405 71 59 22 *E-mail:* promedia@mediashop.at *Web Site:* www.mediashop.at, pg 56

Ediciones Promesa (Costa Rica) *Tel:* 253-3759; 225-1511; 283-3033 *Fax:* 225-1286 *E-mail:* edicionespromesa@hotmail.com, pg 116

Ediciones Promesa, SA de CV (Mexico) *Tel:* (05) 5623174; (05) 3938707 *Fax:* (05) 5623174 *E-mail:* promesa@mati.net.mx; riveraluisa@hotmail.com, pg 470

Prometej Izdatelstvo (Russian Federation) *Tel:* (095) 2454495, pg 548

Prometheus (Netherlands) *Tel:* (020) 624 19 34 *Fax:* (020) 622 54 61 *E-mail:* pbo@pbo.nl *Web Site:* www.pbo.nl, pg 488

*Promilla & Publishers (India) *Tel:* (011) 668720 *Fax:* (011) 6448947, pg 345

Promociones de Mercados Turisticos SA de CV (Mexico) *Tel:* (05) 2771480; (05) 5160162; (05) 2714736 *Fax:* (05) 2725942 *E-mail:* tm@mail.internet.com.mx *Web Site:* www.travelguidemexico.com, pg 471

Editions Promoculture (Luxembourg) *Tel:* 480691 *Fax:* 400950 *E-mail:* promocul@pt.lu *Web Site:* www.promoculture.lu, pg 451

Librairie Promoculture (Luxembourg) *Tel:* 480691 *Fax:* 400950 *E-mail:* promocul@pt.lu, pg 1325

Promoedition SA (Switzerland) *Tel:* (022) 8099460 *Fax:* (022) 7811414, pg 631

Promotion Litteraire (France) *Tel:* (01) 45004210 *Fax:* (01) 45001018 *E-mail:* promolit@club-internet.fr, pg 1131

Promotional Publications Int BV (Netherlands) *Tel:* (030) 2650650 *Fax:* (030) 2620850, pg 488

Promotional Reprint Co Ltd (United Kingdom) *Tel:* (020) 7736 5666 *Fax:* (020) 7736 5777, pg 1353

Prompter Publications (Republic of Korea) *Tel:* (02) 82 2214 1794, pg 442

Pronaos, SA Ediciones (Spain) *Tel:* (091) 5418199; (091) 5412766 *Fax:* (091) 4203429; (091) 5412766 *E-mail:* pronaos@teleline.es; jaire@teleline.es, pg 597

PRONI (Public Record Office of Northern Ireland) (Ireland) *Tel:* (02890) 255905 *Fax:* (02890) 255999 *E-mail:* proni@dcalni.gov.uk *Web Site:* proni.nics.gov.uk, pg 1519

Prontaprint Asia Ltd (Hong Kong) *Tel:* 28657525 *Fax:* 28661064 *E-mail:* postmaster@pronta.com.hk, pg 1158, 1179, 1219

Prontaprint Asia Ltd (Hong Kong) *Tel:* 28657525 *Fax:* 28661064, pg 1236, 1246

Henri Proost & Co, Pvba (Belgium) *Tel:* (014) 40 08 11 *Fax:* (014) 42 87 94 *Web Site:* www.proost.be, pg 72

Propos de Campagne (France) *Tel:* (04) 92 77 03 51 *Fax:* (04) 92 77 09 36 *E-mail:* ProposdeC@aol.com *Web Site:* www.lisez.com/propos, pg 182

Propylaeen Verlag, Zweigniederlassung Berlin der Ullstein Buchverlage GmbH (Germany) *Tel:* (0302) 5913500 *Fax:* (030) 25913533, pg 272

ProQuest Information & Learning (United Kingdom) *Tel:* (01223) 215512 *Fax:* (01223) 215514 *E-mail:* marketing@proquest.co.uk *Web Site:* www.proquest.co.uk, pg 746

Proskinio Spyros Ch Marinis (Greece) *Tel:* (0210) 3648170 *Fax:* (0210) 3648033, pg 311

Prospect Media Pty Ltd (Australia) *Tel:* (02) 9349 6077 *Fax:* (02) 9439 5411 *E-mail:* prospect@prospectmedia.com.au *Web Site:* www.prospectmedia.com.au, pg 37

Prostor, nakladatelstvi sro (Czech Republic) *Tel:* (02) 224 826 688 *Fax:* (02) 242 441 694 *E-mail:* prostor@ini.cz *Web Site:* www.prostor-nakladatelstvi.cz, pg 127

Izdatelstvo Prosveshchenie (Russian Federation) *Tel:* (095) 789-30-29; (095) 789-30-40 *Fax:* (095) 200-42-66; (095) 289-33-98 *E-mail:* msamodwrova@prosv.ru *Web Site:* www.prosv.ru, pg 548

Prosveta (Serbia and Montenegro) *Tel:* (011) 629 843; (011) 631 566 *Fax:* (011) 182 581, pg 553

Prosveta (Serbia and Montenegro) *Tel:* (011) 629 843; (011) 631 566 *Fax:* (011) 182 581 *E-mail:* prosveta@eunet.yu *Web Site:* www.prosveta.co.yu, pg 1339

Editions Prosveta (France) *Tel:* (04) 94 19 33 33 *Fax:* (04) 94 19 33 34 *E-mail:* international@prosvesta.com *Web Site:* www.prosveta.com, pg 182

Prosveta-Izdavako preduzece (Serbia and Montenegro) *Tel:* (011) 629 843; (011) 631 566; (011) 625760 *Fax:* (011) 627465, pg 1255

Prosveta Publishers AS (Bulgaria) *Tel:* (02) 760651; (02) 9743696; (02) 761182 *Fax:* (02) 764451 *E-mail:* prosveta@intech.bg, pg 96

Prosvetno Delo Publishing House (The Former Yugoslav Republic of Macedonia) *Tel:* (02) 117 255; (02) 2 225 434 *Fax:* (02) 129 402; (02) 225 434 *E-mail:* prodelo@nic.mpt.com.mk *Web Site:* www.prodelo.com.mk, pg 453

Prosvjeta (Croatia) *Tel:* (01) 4872 477 *Fax:* (01) 366 5309, pg 119

Prosvjeta (Novinsko-izdavacko i Stamparsko) (Croatia) *Tel:* (043) 245 222; (043) 245 223 *Fax:* (043) 245 220, pg 119

Protestant Publications (Australia) *Tel:* (02) 9868 4591 *Fax:* (02) 9868 7953, pg 38

Proton Editora Ltda (Brazil) *Tel:* (011) 2103616; (011) 8147922; (011) 8159708 *Fax:* (011) 8159920, pg 89

Instituto Provincial de Investigaciones y Estudios Toledanos (IPIET) (Spain) *Tel:* (0925) 259367 *Fax:* (0925) 259348 *E-mail:* diputolepu@diputoledo.es, pg 597

Prozoretz Ltd Publishing House (Bulgaria) *Tel:* (02) 765171; (02) 746053 *Fax:* (02) 746053 *E-mail:* prozor@tea.bg, pg 96

Prugg Verlag (Austria) *Tel:* (02682) 2114, pg 56

Przedsiebiorstwo Wydawniczo-Handlowe Wydawnictwo Siedmiorog (Poland) *Tel:* (071) 341 68 71 *Fax:* (071) 341 68 87 *E-mail:* siedmiorog@siedmiorog.com.pl *Web Site:* www.siedmiorog.pl, pg 526

Wydawnictwa Przemyslowe WEMA (Poland) *Tel:* (022) 8275456; (022) 8272117 *Fax:* (022) 6355779, pg 526

PSAI Press (Ireland) *Tel:* (01) 6081651 *E-mail:* nconnol4@tcd.ie *Web Site:* www.politics.tcd.ie/psai, pg 363

M Psaropoulos & Co EE (Greece) *Tel:* (01) 3606808 *Fax:* (01) 3609645, pg 311

Psichogios Publications SA (Greece) *Tel:* (0210) 3302535; (0210) 3302234 *Fax:* (0210) 3640683; (0210) 3302098 *E-mail:* psicho@otenet.gr, pg 311

Psicologica Editrice (Italy) *Tel:* (06) 35453558 *Fax:* (06) 35341466 *E-mail:* ontonet@tin.it, pg 404

Bookclub Psyche (Japan) *Tel:* (03) 33290031 *Fax:* (03) 33043822, pg 1254

Psychiatrie-Verlag GmbH (Germany) *Tel:* (0228) 725340 *Fax:* (0228) 7253420 *E-mail:* verlag@psychiatrie.de *Web Site:* www.psychiatrie.de/verlag, pg 272

Psychoanalyticke Nakladatelstvi (Czech Republic) *Tel:* (02) 33340305; (02) 545 97 12; (02) 627 1855 *Fax:* (02) 312 03 05, pg 127

Psychological Corporation Ltd (United Kingdom) *Tel:* (01) 865888188 *Fax:* (01) 865314348 *E-mail:* tpc@harcourt.com *Web Site:* www.tpc-international.com, pg 746

Psychologie Verlags Union GmbH (Germany) *Tel:* (06201) 60070 *E-mail:* info@beltz.de *Web Site:* www.beltz.de, pg 272

Psychosophische Gesellschaft (Switzerland) *Tel:* (071) 59 13 01, pg 632

Psychosozial-Verlag (Germany) *Tel:* (0641) 77819 *Fax:* (0641) 77742 *E-mail:* info@psychosozial-verlag.de; bestellung@psychosozial-verlag.de *Web Site:* www.psychosozial-verlag.de, pg 272

Psykologifoerlaget AB (Sweden) *Tel:* (08) 775 09 00; (08) 775 09 10 (orders) *Fax:* (08) 775 09 20 *E-mail:* info@psykologiforlaget.se *Web Site:* www.psykologiforlaget.se, pg 614

PT Bhakti Baru (Indonesia) *Tel:* (0411) 5192 *Fax:* (0411) 7156, pg 356

PT Pradnya Paramita (Indonesia) *Tel:* (021) 8583369 *Fax:* (021) 8504944, pg 356

PT Pradnya Paramita (Indonesia) *Tel:* (021) 8583369 *Fax:* (021) 8583369, pg 1318

PT Pustaka LP3ES Indonesia (Indonesia) *Tel:* (021) 5674211; (021) 5667139; (021) 56967920 *Fax:* (021) 5683785 *Web Site:* www.lp3es.or.id, pg 356

Pt Ravishankar Shukla University Library (India) *Fax:* (0771) 234283 *E-mail:* info@rsuniversity.com *Web Site:* www.rsuniversity.com, pg 1516

PTI - Publicacoes Tecnicas Internacionais Ltda (Brazil) *Tel:* (011) 3159 2535 *Fax:* (011) 3159 2450 *E-mail:* info@pti.com.br *Web Site:* www.pti.com.br, pg 1304

Publi-Fusion (France) *Tel:* (05) 65220303 *Fax:* (05) 65220322, pg 182

Public Archives of Sierra Leone (Sierra Leone) *Tel:* (022) 229 471, pg 1542

Public Lending Right (United Kingdom) *Tel:* (01642) 604699 *Fax:* (01642) 615641 *E-mail:* registrar@plr.uk.com *Web Site:* www.plr.uk.com, pg 1293

Public Lending Right Scheme (Australia) *Tel:* (02) 6271 1650 *Toll Free Tel:* 800 672 842 (Australia only) *Fax:* (02) 6271 1651 *E-mail:* plr.mail@dcita.gov.au *Web Site:* www.dcita.gov.au, pg 1260

Public Library (Afghanistan), pg 1489

Public Library (Jordan), pg 1522

Public Library of Latakia (Syrian Arab Republic), pg 1548

Public Record Office (United Kingdom) *Tel:* (020) 8876 3444 *Fax:* (020) 8392 5286 *E-mail:* enquiry@nationalarchives.gov.uk *Web Site:* www.pro.gov.uk, pg 1554

Publicaciones Cultural SA de CV (Mexico) *Tel:* (05) 55618333; (05) 55619299 *Fax:* (05) 5615231; (05) 55614063 *E-mail:* info@patriacultural.com.mx *Web Site:* www.patriacultural.com.mx, pg 471

Publicaciones de la Universidad de Alicante (Spain) *Tel:* (0965) 909 576 *Fax:* (0965) 909 445 *E-mail:* publicaciones.ventas@ua.es *Web Site:* publicaciones.ua.es, pg 597

Publicaciones de la Universidad Pontificia Comillas-Madrid (Spain) *Tel:* (091) 542 28 00 *Fax:* (091) 734 45 70 *E-mail:* edit@pub.upco.es *Web Site:* www.upco.es, pg 597

Publicaciones Importantes SA (Mexico) *Tel:* (05) 5101884; (05) 5109489 *Fax:* (05) 5129411, pg 471

Publicaciones Lo Castillo SA (Chile) *Tel:* (02) 235 2606 *Fax:* (02) 235 2007, pg 100

Publicaciones Nuevo Extremo (Chile) *Tel:* (02) 698 1523; (02) 697 2337 *Fax:* (02) 697 2545 *E-mail:* nexxtremo@entelchile.net, pg 100

Publicaciones y Ediciones Salamandra SA (Spain) *Tel:* (093) 2151199 *Fax:* (093) 2154636 *E-mail:* emece@ran.es, pg 597

Publicacoes Dom Quixote Lda (Portugal) *Tel:* (021) 538079 *Fax:* (021) 574595, pg 535

Ediouro Publicacoes, SA (Brazil) *Tel:* (021) 5606122 *Fax:* (011) 55893300 *E-mail:* ediourolivrosp@openlink.com.br; livros@ediouro.com.br *Web Site:* www.ediouro.com.br, pg 89

Editora de Publicacoes Medicas Ltda (Brazil) *Tel:* (021) 2654047; (021) 2253516 *Fax:* (021) 2613749, pg 89

Publications & Information Directorate, CSIR (India) *Tel:* (011) 5785359; (011) 5786301 (ext 288) *Fax:* (011) 5787062, pg 345

Publications de la Fondation Temimi pour la Recherche Scientifique et L'Information (Tunisia) *Tel:* (072) 676 446; (072) 680 110 *Fax:* (072) 676 710 *E-mail:* temimi.fond.@gnet.tn *Web Site:* temimi.org (in Arabic); refer.org/6 (in French), pg 648

Publications de l'Ecole Moderne Francaise (PEMF) (France) *Tel:* (04) 92921757 *Fax:* (016) 92921804 *Web Site:* ceos.cnes.fr:1800, pg 1252

Editions Publications de l'Ecole Moderne Francaise sa (PEMF) (France) *Tel:* (04) 92 28 42 84 *Fax:* (04) 92 28 42 99, pg 182

Publications de l'Universite de Rouen (France) *Tel:* (02) 35 14 63 43 *Fax:* (02) 35 14 65 38, pg 182

Publications des Facultes Universitaires Saint Louis (Belgium) *Tel:* (02) 211 78 94 *Fax:* (02) 211 79 97 *Web Site:* www.fusl.ac.be, pg 72

Publications du Palais de Monaco (Monaco) *Tel:* 093 251831, pg 474

Publications Orientalistes de France (POF) (France) *Tel:* (04) 71 43 23 78 *Fax:* (04) 71 43 23 78 *E-mail:* sieffert@pofjapon.com *Web Site:* www.pofjapon.com, pg 182

Publik-Forum-Verlagsgesellschaft mbH (Germany) *Tel:* (06171) 70030 *Fax:* (06171) 700340, pg 272

Publishers' & Booksellers' Association of Thailand (Thailand) *Tel:* (02) 954-9560-4 *Fax:* (02) 954-9565-6 *E-mail:* info@pubat.or.th *Web Site:* www.pubat.or.th, pg 1288

Publishers Association (Russian Federation) *Tel:* (095) 2021174 *Fax:* (095) 2023989, pg 1282

The Publishers Association (United Kingdom) *Tel:* (020) 7691 9191 *Fax:* (020) 7691 9199 *E-mail:* mail@publishers.org.uk *Web Site:* www.publishers.org.uk, pg 1293

Publishers' Association for Cultural Exchange, PACE, Japan (Japan) *Tel:* (03) 32915685 *Fax:* (03) 32333645 *E-mail:* office@pace.or.jp *Web Site:* www.pace.or.jp, pg 1275

Publishers' Association of South Africa (PASA) (South Africa) *Tel:* (021) 782 7677 *Fax:* (021) 782 7679 *E-mail:* pasa@publishsa.co.za *Web Site:* www.publishsa.co.za, pg 1284

Publishers' Enterprises Group (PEG) Ltd (Malta) *Tel:* 21440083; 21448539; 21490540 *Fax:* 21488908 *E-mail:* contact@peg.com.mt *Web Site:* www.peg.com.mt, pg 460

Publishers Group South West (Ireland) (Ireland) *Tel:* (027) 73025 *Fax:* (027) 73131 *E-mail:* 73551.655@compuserve.com, pg 363

Publishers Licensing Society Ltd (United Kingdom) *Tel:* (020) 7299 7730 *Fax:* (020) 7299 7780 *E-mail:* info@pls.org.uk *Web Site:* www.pls.org.uk, pg 1293

Publishers Marketing Services Pte Ltd (Singapore) *Tel:* 62565166 *Fax:* 62530008 *E-mail:* info@pms.com.sg *Web Site:* www.pms.com.sg, pg 1339

Publishers United Pvt Ltd (Pakistan) *Tel:* (042) 7352238 *Fax:* (042) 6316015 *E-mail:* smalipub2@hotmail.com; smalipub@wol.net.pk, pg 514

Publishing Center of Belarus State University (Belarus) *Tel:* (0172) 227 18 08 *Fax:* (0172) 226 01 75 *E-mail:* pubcentre@org.bsu.unibee.by, pg 62

Publishing Council of the Academy of Sciences of the Russian Academy of Sciences (Russian Federation) *Tel:* (095) 952905 *Fax:* (095) 2379107, pg 1282

Publishing Resources Inc (Puerto Rico) *Tel:* (787) 268-8080 *Fax:* 787-774-5781 *E-mail:* publishingresources@att.net, pg 537

Publishing Resources Inc (Puerto Rico) *Tel:* 787-268-8080 *Fax:* (787) 774-5781 *E-mail:* pri@tld.net, pg 1181

Publishing Resources Inc (Puerto Rico) *Tel:* 787-268-8080 *Fax:* 787-774-5781 *E-mail:* publishingresources@worldnet.att.net, pg 1222

Publishing Resources Inc (Puerto Rico) *Tel:* (787) 727-1800 *Fax:* (0787) 727-1823 *E-mail:* pri@chevako.net, pg 1246

Publishing Services Suriname (Suriname) *Tel:* (0598) 472746; (0598) 455792 *Fax:* (0598) 410366 *E-mail:* pssmoniz@sr.net *Web Site:* www.parbo.com, pg 608

Publishing Solutions Ltd (New Zealand) *Tel:* (04) 4710582 *Fax:* (04) 4710717 *E-mail:* gen@pubsol.co.nz, pg 500

Publishing Training Centre at BookHouse (United Kingdom) *Tel:* (020) 8874 2718 *Fax:* (020) 8870 8985; (020) 7207 5915 (bookings) *E-mail:* publishing.training@bookhouse.co.uk *Web Site:* www.train4publishing.co.uk, pg 746

Publisud Editions (France) *Tel:* (01) 45 80 78 50 *Fax:* (01) 45 89 94 15 *E-mail:* publisud@compuserve.com; edipublisud@wanadoo.fr, pg 182

Publitec Publications (Lebanon) *Tel:* (01) 495401; (01) 495403 *Fax:* (01) 493330, pg 447

Publitoria Publishers (South Africa) *Tel:* (012) 3290313 *Fax:* (012) 3290306, pg 568

Pudeleco/Publicaciones de Legislacion (Ecuador) *Tel:* (02) 543273 *Fax:* (02) 2543607 *E-mail:* pudeleco@uio.satnet.net, pg 137

Pueblo y Educacion Editorial (PE) (Cuba) *Tel:* (07) 20021490 *Fax:* (07) 2040844 *E-mail:* epe@ceniai.inf.cu, pg 121

Ediciones Puerto (Puerto Rico) *Tel:* 787-721-0844 *Fax:* 787-725-0861 *E-mail:* feriapr@caribe.net, pg 537

Puffin Book Clubs (United Kingdom) *Tel:* (020) 7416 3000 *Toll Free Tel:* (0500) 454 444 *Fax:* (020) 7416 3099 *Web Site:* www.penguin.co.uk, pg 1257

Editions du Puits Fleuri (France) *Tel:* (01) 64 23 61 46 *Fax:* (01) 64 23 69 42, pg 182

Pulp Master Frank Nowatzki Verlag (Germany) *Tel:* (030) 6868292 *Fax:* (030) 6868292 *E-mail:* master@txt.de *Web Site:* www.maasmedia.de, pg 272

Pulso Ediciones, SL (Spain) *Tel:* (0935) 896 264 *Fax:* (0935) 895 077 *E-mail:* pulso@pulso.com *Web Site:* www.pulso.com, pg 597

Puma Editora Lda (Portugal) *Tel:* (021) 9425394 *Fax:* (021) 9425214, pg 535

Punjab Public Library (Pakistan) *Tel:* (042) 325487 *E-mail:* zilpk@yahoo.com, pg 1535

Punjab University Library (Pakistan) *Tel:* (042) 923 1099 *Fax:* (042) 923 1101 *E-mail:* vc@pu.edu.pk *Web Site:* www.pu.edu.pk/library.htm, pg 1535

Punktum AG (Switzerland) *Tel:* (01) 422 45 40, pg 1256

Punktum AG, Buchredaktion und Bildarchiv (Switzerland) *Tel:* (01) 422 45 40 *Fax:* (01) 422 48 13, pg 632

Il Punto D Incontro (Italy) *Tel:* (0444) 239189 *Fax:* (0444) 239266 *E-mail:* ordini@edizionilpuntodincontro.it *Web Site:* www.edizionilpuntodincontro.it, pg 404

Punto de Encuentro Ediciones (Uruguay) *Tel:* (02) 405167, pg 778

Pursuit Publishing (New Zealand) *Tel:* (09) 4385725 *Fax:* (09) 4382543 *Web Site:* www.pursuit.co.nz, pg 500

Pusat Penelitian Perkebunan Sumbawa (Indonesia) *Tel:* (0711) 312182; (0711) 361793 *Fax:* (0711) 361793, pg 356

Pushtu Toulana, Afghan Academy (Afghanistan) *Tel:* 20350, pg 1

Pustak Mahal (India) *Tel:* (011) 23276539; (011) 23272783; (011) 23272784 *Fax:* (011) 3260518 *E-mail:* pustakmahal@vsnl.net.in *Web Site:* www.pustakmahal.com, pg 345

Pustaka Cipta Sdn Bhd (Malaysia) *Tel:* (03) 2744593 *Fax:* (03) 2749588 *E-mail:* rrapc@pc.jaring.my, pg 458

Pustaka Delta Pelajaran Sdn Bhd (Malaysia) *Tel:* (03) 7570000 *Fax:* (03) 7576688, pg 458

Pustaka Nasional Pte Ltd (Singapore) *Tel:* 7454321; 7454649 *Fax:* 7452417 *E-mail:* sales@pustaka.com.sg; mohamed@pustaka.com.sg *Web Site:* www.pustaka.com.sg, pg 557

Pustaka Sistem Pelajaran Sdn Bhd (Malaysia) *Tel:* (03) 904-7558; (03) 904-7017; (03) 904-7018 *Fax:* (03) 904-7573, pg 458

Pustaka Utama Grafiti, PT (Indonesia) *Tel:* (021) 8567502 *Fax:* (021) 8582430, pg 356

Verlag Anton Pustet (Austria) *Tel:* (0662) 87 35 07-55 *Fax:* (0662) 87 35 07-79 *E-mail:* buch@verlag-anton-pustet.at *Web Site:* www.verlag-anton-pustet.at, pg 56

Verlag Friedrich Pustet GmbH & Co Kg (Germany) *Tel:* (0941) 94 24 105 *Fax:* (0941) 94 24 100 *E-mail:* buecher@pustet.de *Web Site:* www.pustet.de, pg 272

Puthigar Ltd (Bangladesh) *Tel:* (02) 231374; (02) 235333; (02) 259867, pg 1301

Verlag Harry Putz (Czech Republic) *Tel:* (048) 515 21 20; (048) 510 32 75 *Fax:* (048) 510 32 75 *E-mail:* harrputz@mbox.vol.cz, pg 127

PYC Edition (France) *Tel:* (01) 53 26 48 00 *Fax:* (01) 53 26 48 01 *E-mail:* info@pyc.fr *Web Site:* www.pyc.fr, pg 182

Pyeong-hwa Chulpansa (Republic of Korea) *Tel:* (02) 7343341; (02) 7343343 *Fax:* (02) 7392129, pg 442

Editions Pygmalion (France) *Tel:* (01) 45 67 40 77 *Fax:* (01) 47 34 51 52 *E-mail:* pygmalion@pygmalion.fr, pg 182

Pyunghwa Dang Printing Co Ltd (Republic of Korea) *Tel:* (02) 735-4011 *Fax:* (02) 734-5201 *E-mail:* comuser@hitel.kol.co.kr, pg 1180

Pyunghwa Dang Printing Co Ltd (Republic of Korea) *Tel:* (02) 735 4011 *Fax:* (02) 734 5201 *E-mail:* comuser@hitel.kol.co.kr, pg 1221

PZWL Wydawnictwo Lekarskie Ltd (Poland) *Tel:* (022) 6954033; (022) 6954497 *Fax:* (022) 6954032; (022) 6954497 *E-mail:* promocja@pzwl.pl *Web Site:* www.pzwl.pl, pg 526

Q & B Books (Zambia) *Tel:* (01) 290032; (096) 747187 *Fax:* (01) 290032 *E-mail:* qbbooks@yahoo.com, pg 1356

edition q Berlin Edition in der Quintessenz Verlags-GmbH (Germany) *Tel:* (030) 761 80-5 *Fax:* (030) 761 80-680 *E-mail:* editionq@quintessenz.de; info@quintessenz.de *Web Site:* www.quintessenz.de, pg 272

The Q Group Plc (United Kingdom) *Tel:* (01279) 719070 *Fax:* (01279) 757409 *E-mail:* marketing@qgroupplc.com; support@qgroupplc.com *Web Site:* www.qgroupplc.com, pg 1164

Qatar National Library (Qatar) *Tel:* 442 9955 *Fax:* 442 9976 *E-mail:* qanaly@qatar.net.qa, pg 1539

Qatar University Library (Qatar) *Tel:* 4852405 *Fax:* 4835092 *E-mail:* postmaster@qu.edu.qa *Web Site:* www.qu.edu.qa/english/library/libraries.htm, pg 1539

Qi Lu Press (China) *Tel:* (0531) 6910055-4920 *Fax:* (0531) 2906811, pg 107

Qingdao Publishing House (China) *Tel:* (0532) 5814611; (0532) 362524 *Fax:* (0532) 515240, pg 107

Qinghua daxue tushuguan (China) *Tel:* (010) 62782137 *Fax:* (010) 62781758 *E-mail:* tsg@mail.lib.tsinghua.edu.cn *Web Site:* www.lib.tsinghua.edu.cn, pg 1498

Quaderns Crema SA (Spain) *Tel:* (093) 4144906 *Fax:* (093) 4147107 *E-mail:* correo@acantilado.es *Web Site:* www.quadernscrema.com, pg 597

Il Quadrante SRL (Italy) *Tel:* (081) 991433 *Fax:* (081) 981672 *E-mail:* info@ilquadrante.com *Web Site:* www.ilquadrante.com, pg 404

Quadrille Publishing Ltd (United Kingdom) *Tel:* (020) 7839 7117 *Fax:* (020) 7839 7118 *Web Site:* www.quadrille.co.uk, pg 746

Quaid-i-Azam University Department of Biological Sciences (Pakistan) *Tel:* (051) 2482513 *Fax:* (051) 2482513 *E-mail:* qau@gmx.net; daud@gmx.net *Web Site:* members.tripod.com/qau, pg 514

Quaker Books (United Kingdom) *Tel:* (020) 7663 1000 *Fax:* (020) 7663 1008; (020) 7663 1001 (orders) *E-mail:* bookshop@quaker.org.uk *Web Site:* www.quaker.org.uk, pg 746

Quakers Hill Press (Australia) *Tel:* (02) 9626 6112 *Fax:* (02) 9626 9846 *E-mail:* dayp@mpx.com.au, pg 38

Qualitymark Editora Ltda (Brazil) *Tel:* (021) 3860-8422 *Fax:* (021) 3860-8424 *E-mail:* quality@qualitymark.com.br *Web Site:* www.qualitymark.com.br, pg 89

Qualum Publishing (United Kingdom) *Tel:* (020) 7431 7171 *Fax:* (020) 7681 1316 *E-mail:* info@qualum.com *Web Site:* www.qualum.com, pg 746

Quantum Colorgraphics (United States) *Tel:* 973-783-0462 *Fax:* 973-783-0637, pg 1189

Quartet Books Ltd (United Kingdom) *Tel:* (020) 7636 3992; (020) 7636 0968 *Fax:* (020) 7637 1866 *E-mail:* quartetbooks@easynet.co.uk, pg 746

Quarto Publishing plc (United Kingdom) *Tel:* (020) 7700 6700 *Fax:* (020) 7700 4191 *E-mail:* quarto@quarto.com *Web Site:* www.quarto.com, pg 746

Quartz Editions (United Kingdom) *Tel:* (020) 8951 5656 *Fax:* (020) 8904 1200 *E-mail:* quartzeditions@btconnect.com, pg 746

Edizioni Quasar di Severino Tognon SRL (Italy) *Tel:* (06) 84241993; (06) 85358444 *Fax:* (06) 85833591 *E-mail:* qn@edizioniquasar.it *Web Site:* www.edizioniquasar.it, pg 404

Quatro Elementos Editores (Portugal) *Tel:* (021) 703695, pg 535

Edizioni Quattroventi SNC (Italy) *Tel:* (0722) 2588 *Fax:* (0722) 320998, pg 404

Queen Anne Press (United Kingdom) *Tel:* (01582) 715866 *Fax:* (01582) 715121 *E-mail:* queenanne@lenqap.demon.co.uk, pg 747

Queen Victoria Museum & Art Gallery Publications (Australia) *Tel:* (03) 6323 3777 *Fax:* (03) 6323 3776 *E-mail:* library@qvmag.tas.gov.au *Web Site:* www.qvmag.tas.gov.au, pg 38

Queensland Art Gallery (Australia) *Tel:* (07) 3840 7333; (07) 3840 7303 *Fax:* (07) 3844 8865; (07) 3840 7350 *E-mail:* gallery@qag.qld.gov.au *Web Site:* www.qag.qld.gov.au, pg 38

Queensway Bookshop & Stores Ltd (Ghana) *Tel:* (021) 62707, pg 1312

Editorial Quehacer Politico SA (Mexico) *Tel:* (05) 5414245 *Fax:* (05) 5384855 *Web Site:* 148.233.5.66/qp/, pg 471

Queillerie Publishers (South Africa) *Tel:* (021) 406 3326 *Fax:* (021) 406 3111 *E-mail:* queiller@nbh.naspers.co.za, pg 568

Quell Verlag (Germany) *Tel:* (0711) 601000 *Fax:* (0711) 6010076, pg 273

Quelle Press (Germany) *Tel:* (07664) 7016 *Fax:* (07664) 60979 *E-mail:* quellepress.germany@gmx.net, pg 1132

Quelle und Meyer Verlag GmbH & Co (Germany) *Tel:* (06766) 903200 *Fax:* (06766) 903320 *E-mail:* vertrieb@quelle-meyer.de *Web Site:* www.quelle-meyer.de, pg 273

Quellen-Verlag (Switzerland) *Tel:* (071) 227 47 77 *Fax:* (071) 227 47 58, pg 1344

Quentin Books Ltd (United Kingdom) *Tel:* (01206) 825433; (01206) 825434 *Fax:* (01206) 822990, pg 747

Em Querido's Uitgeverij BV (Netherlands) *Tel:* (020) 55 11 200 *Fax:* (020) 55 11 256 *E-mail:* info@querido.nl *Web Site:* www.querido.nl, pg 488

Editrice Queriniana (Italy) *Tel:* (030) 2306925 *Fax:* (030) 2306932 *E-mail:* direzione@queriniana.it; redazione@queriniana.it *Web Site:* www.queriniana.it, pg 404

Querverlag GmbH (Germany) *Tel:* (030) 78 70 23 39; (030) 78702340 *Fax:* (030) 788 49 50 *E-mail:* mail@querverlag.de *Web Site:* www.querverlag.de, pg 273

Quesire SRL (Italy) *Tel:* (06) 68136068 *Fax:* (06) 68134167 *E-mail:* ristucciad@quesire.it *Web Site:* www.ristucciaadvisors.com, pg 404

Editorial Quetzal-Domingo Cortizo (Argentina) *Tel:* (011) 4641-5639 *E-mail:* profika@ciudad.com.ar, pg 8

Quetzal Editores (Portugal) *Tel:* (021) 3426172 *Fax:* (021) 3426173 *E-mail:* quetzal@ip.pt, pg 535

Quick Service Books Ltd (Ghana) *Tel:* (021) 224236, pg 304

Quid Juris - Sociedade Editora (Portugal) *Tel:* (021) 651946 *Fax:* (021) 3875538 *E-mail:* quidjuris@mail.telepac.pt, pg 535

Quiller Publishing Ltd (United Kingdom) *Tel:* (01939) 261616 *Fax:* (01939) 261606 *E-mail:* info@quillerbooks.com, pg 747

Quimera Editores Lda (Portugal) *Tel:* (021) 845 59 50 *Fax:* (021) 845 59 51 *E-mail:* quimera@quimera-editores.com *Web Site:* www.quimera-editores.com, pg 535

Quintessence Publishing Co Ltd (United Kingdom) *Tel:* (020) 89496087 *Fax:* (020) 83361484 *E-mail:* info@quintpub.co.uk *Web Site:* www.quintpub.co.uk, pg 747

Quintessenz Verlags-GmbH (Germany) *Tel:* (030) 761805 *Fax:* (030) 76180680 *E-mail:* info@quintessenz.de *Web Site:* www.quintessenz.de, pg 273

Quintet Publishing Ltd (United Kingdom) *Tel:* (020) 7700 2001 *Fax:* (020) 7700 5785 *E-mail:* quintet@quarto.com *Web Site:* www.quarto.com, pg 747

R & R Publications Pty Ltd (Australia) *Tel:* (03) 9381 2199 *Toll Free Tel:* 800 063 296 *Fax:* (03) 9381 2689, pg 38

R P L Books (New Zealand) *Tel:* (09) 4437448 *Fax:* (09) 4430147 *E-mail:* rplbooks@rplbooks.co.nz, pg 500

RA-MA, Libreria y Editorial Microinformatica (Spain) *Tel:* (091) 658 42 80 *Fax:* (091) 662 81 39 *E-mail:* info@ra-ma.com *Web Site:* www.ra-ma.com, pg 597

Dr Josef Raabe-Verlags GmbH (Germany) *Tel:* (030) 2129870 *Fax:* (030) 21298730 *E-mail:* w.heuse@raabe.de *Web Site:* www.raabe.de, pg 273

Rabe Verlag AG Zuerich (Switzerland) *Tel:* (01) 261 85 40 *Fax:* (01) 261 85 41, pg 632

Raben och Sjoegren Bokforlag (Sweden) *Tel:* (08) 7698800 *Fax:* (08) 7698813 *E-mail:* raben-sjogren@raben.se *Web Site:* www.raben.se, pg 614

Raben Verlag von Wittern KG (Germany) *Tel:* (089) 3594879 *Fax:* (089) 3596622, pg 273

Raboni Editora Ltda (Brazil) *Tel:* (019) 32428433 *Fax:* (019) 32428505 *E-mail:* raboni@raboni.com.br *Web Site:* www.raboni.com.br, pg 89

RAC Publishing (United Kingdom) *Tel:* (020) 8686 0088 *Fax:* (020) 8688 2882, pg 747

RACC-62 (Spain) *Tel:* (093) 443 71 00 *Fax:* (093) 443 71 30 *E-mail:* correu@grup62.com *Web Site:* www.grup62.com, pg 597

Editions Racine (Belgium) *Tel:* (02) 646 44 44 *Fax:* (02) 646 55 70 *E-mail:* info@racine.be *Web Site:* www.racine.be, pg 72

Radcliffe Medical Press Ltd (United Kingdom) *Tel:* (01235) 528820 *Fax:* (01235) 528830 *E-mail:* contact.us@radcliffemed.com *Web Site:* www.radcliffe-oxford.com, pg 747

Wydawnictwa Radia i Telewizji (Poland) *Tel:* (022) 412264, pg 526

Radiant Publishers (India) *Tel:* (011) 6435477; (011) 6482861 *Fax:* (011) 6479870 *E-mail:* rpbooksind@yahoo.com, pg 346

Radiating Books (Australia) *Tel:* (066) 536 280 *Fax:* (066) 514 970, pg 38

Radin-Repro I Roto (Croatia) *Tel:* (01) 3869 200 *Fax:* (01) 3862 673 *E-mail:* radin-repro-i-roto@zg.tel.hr *Web Site:* www.odisej.hr, pg 1154

Izdatelstvo Radio i Svyaz (Russian Federation) *Tel:* (095) 2585351, pg 548

Radius-Verlag GmbH (Germany) *Tel:* (0711) 6076666; (0172) 7126573 *Fax:* (0711) 6075555 *E-mail:* radiusverlag@freenet.de *Web Site:* www.radius.skileon.de, pg 273

Radnicka Stampa (Serbia and Montenegro) *Tel:* (011) 3230-927; (011) 3230-921; (011) 3236-259 *E-mail:* radstamp@sezampro.yu *Web Site:* www.radnickastampa.co.yu/, pg 553

Raduga Publishers (Russian Federation) *Tel:* (095) 2416815 *Fax:* (095) 2416353 *E-mail:* raduga@pol.ru *Web Site:* www.raduga.express.ru, pg 548

Robert Raeber, Buchhandlung am Schweizerhof (Switzerland) *Tel:* (041) 512371, pg 632

Raethgloben Verlagsgesellschaft mbH (Germany) *Tel:* (0341) 4511212 *Fax:* (0341) 4427537 *E-mail:* raethgloben1917@gmx.de, pg 273

Edition Raetia Srl-GmbH (Italy) *Tel:* (0471) 976904 *Fax:* (0471) 976908 *E-mail:* info@raetia.com, pg 405

Rageot Editeur (France) *Tel:* (01) 45 48 07 31 *Fax:* (01) 42 22 68 01 *E-mail:* rageotediteur@editions-hatier.fr *Web Site:* www.rageotediteur.fr, pg 182

Ragged Bears Ltd (United Kingdom) *Tel:* (01264) 772269 *Fax:* (01264) 772391 *E-mail:* books@ragged-bears.co.uk *Web Site:* www.ragged-bears.co.uk, pg 747

Rahul Publishing House (India) *Tel:* (0121) 2774518, pg 346

RAI-ERI (Italy) *Tel:* (06) 36864418 *Fax:* (06) 36822071 *E-mail:* rai-eri@rai.it *Web Site:* www.eri.rai.it, pg 405

Rainbow Book Agencies Pty Ltd (Australia) *Tel:* (03) 9481 6611 *Fax:* (03) 9481 2371 *E-mail:* rba@rainbowbooks.com.au; custserv@rainbowbooks.com.au; despatch@rainbowbooks.com.au (warehouse) *Web Site:* www.rainbowbooks.com.au, pg 38

Rainbow Grafics Intl - Baronian Books SC (Belgium) *Tel:* (02) 7348114 *Fax:* (02) 7325764, pg 72

Rainbow Graphic & Printing Co Ltd (Hong Kong) *Tel:* 27523423 *Fax:* 28974890 *E-mail:* rgarts@netvigator.com, pg 1179

Raincloud Productions (Australia) *Tel:* (02) 6251 1765, pg 38

Rainforest Publishing (Australia) *Tel:* (02) 93313004 *Fax:* (02) 93805729 *E-mail:* rod.ritchie@sfine.arts.sa.edu.au, pg 38

Rajasthan Hindi Granth Academy (India) *Tel:* (0141) 61410; (0141) 511129, pg 346

Rajendra Publishing House Pvt Ltd (India) *Tel:* (022) 6300741; (022) 6300742; (022) 6301930 *Fax:* (022) 6301940; (022) 6322146 *E-mail:* books@rajendrabooks.com *Web Site:* www.rajendrabooks.com, pg 346

Rajesh Publications (India) *Tel:* (011) 274550, pg 346

Rajkamal Prakashan Pvt Ltd (India) *Tel:* (011) 3288769; (011) 3274463 *Fax:* (011) 3278144, pg 346

Rajpal & Sons (India) *Tel:* 223904; 229174 *Fax:* (0141) 2967791, pg 346

Rake Verlag GmbH (Germany) *Tel:* (0431) 6611515 *Fax:* (0431) 6611517 *E-mail:* info@rake.de *Web Site:* www.rake.de, pg 273

Rakennusalan Kustantajat RAK (Finland) *Tel:* (09) 503 2540 *Fax:* (09) 503 2542 *E-mail:* info@sarmala.com *Web Site:* www.sarmala.com, pg 144

Rakennustieto Oy (Finland) *Tel:* (09) 549 5570 *Fax:* (09) 5495 5320 *E-mail:* rakennustieto@rakennustieto.fi *Web Site:* www.rakennustieto.fi, pg 144

Rakla (Bulgaria) *Tel:* (02) 580-569 *E-mail:* grigorit@yahoo.com, pg 96

RAM Editores (Colombia) *Tel:* (01) 2623067, pg 112

Ramakrishna Vedanta Centre (United Kingdom) *Tel:* (01628) 526464 *E-mail:* vedantauk@talk21.com *Web Site:* www.ramakrishna.org; www.vedantauk.com, pg 747

Dr Mohan Krischke Ramaswamy Edition RE (Germany) *Tel:* (0171) 8026882 *Fax:* (0171) 5311065 *E-mail:* edition.re@epost.de, pg 273

Ramboro Books Plc (United Kingdom) *Tel:* (020) 7700 7444 *Fax:* (020) 7700 4552 *E-mail:* enquiries@ramboro.co.uk, pg 747

Ramboro Books Plc (United Kingdom) *Tel:* (020) 7700 7444 *Fax:* (020) 7700 4552 *E-mail:* enquiries@ramboro.co.uk *Web Site:* www.ramborobooks.com, pg 1353

Rams Skull Press (Australia) *Tel:* (07) 4093 7474 *Fax:* (07) 4051 4484 *E-mail:* ramskull@tpg.com.au, pg 38

Editions Ramsay (France) *Tel:* (01) 53 10 02 80 *Fax:* (01) 53 10 02 88, pg 182

Ramsay Head Press (United Kingdom) *Tel:* (0131) 225 5646 *E-mail:* ramsayhead@btinternet.com, pg 747

Randall & Swift Ltd (United Kingdom) *Tel:* (020) 8553 3030 *Fax:* (020) 8559 1522, pg 1353

Ian Randle Publishers Ltd (Jamaica) *Tel:* (876) 978-0739; (876) 978-0745 *Toll Free Tel:* 866-330-5469 (orders) *Fax:* (876) 978-1156 *E-mail:* info@ianrandlepublishers.com *Web Site:* www.ianrandlepublishers.com, pg 414

Random House Australia (Australia) *Tel:* (02) 8923 9863 *Fax:* (02) 9753 3944 *E-mail:* randomhouse@randomhouse.com.au, pg 38

Random House UK Ltd (United Kingdom) *Tel:* (020) 7840 8400 *Fax:* (020) 7233 8791 *E-mail:* enquiries@randomhouse.co.uk *Web Site:* www.randomhouse.co.uk, pg 747

Rankin Publishers (Australia) *Tel:* (07) 3376 9115 *Fax:* (07) 3376 9360 *E-mail:* info@rankin.com.au *Web Site:* www.rankin.com.au, pg 39

Ransom Publishing Ltd (United Kingdom) *Tel:* (01491) 613 711 *Fax:* (01491) 613 733 *E-mail:* ransom@ransom.co.uk *Web Site:* www.ransom.co.uk, pg 748

The Arthur Ransome Society Ltd (TARS) (United Kingdom) *Tel:* (01539) 722464 *E-mail:* tarsinfo@arthur-ransome.org *Web Site:* www.arthur-ransome.org/ar, pg 1409

Grupul Editorial RAO (Romania) *Tel:* (01) 224-12-31; (01) 224-14-72; (01) 224-18-47; (01) 224-21-36 *Fax:* (01) 224-12-31; (01) 224-14-72; (01) 224-18-47; (01) 224-21-36 *E-mail:* office@raobooks.com; club@raobooks.com *Web Site:* www.raobooks.com, pg 542

RAO International Publishing Co (Romania) *Tel:* (01) 224-1002; (01) 224-1704 *Fax:* (01) 222-8059 *E-mail:* rao.b@bx.logicnet.ro, pg 542

Raphael, Editions (Switzerland) *Tel:* (021) 9215230 *Fax:* (021) 9215237, pg 632

Rapra Technology Ltd (United Kingdom) *Tel:* (01939) 250383 *Fax:* (01939) 251118 *E-mail:* publications@rapra.net *Web Site:* www.rapra.net; www.polymer-books.com, pg 748

Rara Istituto Editoriale di Bibliofilia e Reprints (Italy) *Tel:* (02) 4983264 *Fax:* (02) 4814676, pg 405

Margi Rastai Publishers (Lithuania) *Tel:* (02) 429526; (02) 427909; (02) 429527; (02) 426705 *Fax:* (02) 426705 *E-mail:* margirastai@takas.lt, pg 449

Rastogi Publications (India) *Tel:* 24142; 24688 *E-mail:* vrastogi@vsnl.com; info@indianbookmart.com, pg 346

F J Ratchford Ltd (United Kingdom) *Tel:* (0161) 4808484 *Fax:* (0161) 4803679 *E-mail:* info@fjratchford.co.uk *Web Site:* www.fjratchford.co.uk, pg 1164

Rationalisierungs-Kuratorium der Deutschen Wirtschaft eV (RKW) (Germany) *Tel:* (0211) 680010 *Fax:* (0211) 68001 68; (0211) 68001 69 *E-mail:* info@rkw-nrw.de *Web Site:* www.rkwnrw.de, pg 273

Rationalist Press Association (United Kingdom) *Tel:* (020) 7436 1151 *Fax:* (020) 7079 3588 *E-mail:* info@rationalist.org.uk *Web Site:* www.rationalist.org.uk, pg 748

Ratna Book Distributors (Pvt) Ltd (Nepal) *Tel:* (01) 223026 *E-mail:* rpb@wlink.com.np, pg 1328

Walter Rau Verlag GmbH & Co KG (Germany) *Tel:* (0211) 92 80 40 *Fax:* (0211) 28 38 27 *Web Site:* www.rau.de, pg 273

Werner Rau Verlag (Germany) *Tel:* (0711) 687 21 43 *Fax:* (0711) 68 22 47 *E-mail:* info@rau_verlag.de *Web Site:* www.rau-verlag.de, pg 273

Rauhreif Verlag (Switzerland) *Tel:* (061) 851 53 63, pg 632

Gerhard Rautenberg Druckerei und Verlag GmbH & Co KG (Germany) *Tel:* (0931) 385235 *Fax:* (0931) 385305 *E-mail:* info@verlagshaus.com *Web Site:* www.verlagshaus.com, pg 273

Rav Kook Institute (Israel) *Tel:* (02) 6526231 *Fax:* (02) 6526968, pg 371

Rav Kook Institute (Israel) *Tel:* (02) 6526231 *Fax:* (02) 6526968 *E-mail:* mosad-haravkook@neto.bezeqint.net, pg 1320

Ravan Press (Pty) Ltd (South Africa) *Tel:* (011) 4840916 *Fax:* (011) 48442631, pg 568

Ravensburger Buchverlag Otto Maier GmbH (Germany) *Tel:* (0751) 86 1717 *Fax:* (0751) 861818 *E-mail:* info@ravensburger.de *Web Site:* www.ravensburger.de, pg 274

Ravenstein Verlag GmbH (Germany) *Tel:* (06196) 609630 *Fax:* (06196) 63619 *E-mail:* g.koenig@ravenstein-verlag.de, pg 274

Ravette Publishing Ltd (United Kingdom) *Tel:* (01403) 711443 *Fax:* (01403) 711554 *E-mail:* ravettepub@aol.com, pg 748

Rawlhouse Publishing (Australia) *Tel:* (08) 9321 8951 *Fax:* (08) 9481 1914 *E-mail:* info@rawlhouse.com *Web Site:* www.rawlinsons.com, pg 39

RCS Libri SpA (Italy) *Tel:* (02) 50951 *Fax:* (02) 5065361, pg 405

RCS Rizzoli Libri SpA (Italy) *Tel:* (02) 50951 *Fax:* (02) 5065361, pg 405

RCS Rizzoli Libri SpA (Italy) *Tel:* (02) 50951 *Fax:* (02) 5065361 *Web Site:* www.rcs.it, pg 1133

RDC Agencia Literaria (Spain) *Tel:* (091) 3085585 *Fax:* (091) 3085600 *E-mail:* rdc@idecnet.com, pg 1136

Reach Publications (New Zealand) *Tel:* (09) 376 3235 *Fax:* (09) 376 3250 *E-mail:* giftedednz@xtra.co.nz, pg 500

Read-a-Book Club (Zambia) *Tel:* (01) 222324; (01) 236629 *Fax:* (01) 225073, pg 1258

Oficyna Wydawnicza Read Me (Poland) *Tel:* (022) 8706024 (ext 130) *Fax:* (022) 6771425 *E-mail:* readme@rm.com.pl *Web Site:* www.rm.com.pl, pg 526

Reader's Digest AB (Sweden) *Tel:* (08) 6334800 *Fax:* (08) 7528701 *E-mail:* kundtjanst@readersdigest.se *Web Site:* www.readersdigest.se, pg 1256

The Reader's Digest Association Ltd (United Kingdom) *Tel:* (020) 7715 8000 *Fax:* (020) 7715 8181 *Web Site:* www.readersdigest.co.uk, pg 748

Reader's Digest (Australia) Pty Ltd (Australia) *Tel:* (02) 96906935 *Fax:* (02) 96906390, pg 39

Reader's Digest Children's Books (United Kingdom) *Tel:* (01225) 312200 *Fax:* (01225) 460942, pg 748

Reader's Digest Deutschland Verlag Das Beste GmbH (Germany) *Tel:* (0711) 66020 *Fax:* (0711) 6602547 *E-mail:* verlag@readersdigest.de *Web Site:* www.readersdigest.de, pg 274

Reader's Digest SA (Belgium) *Tel:* (02) 5268111 *Fax:* (02) 5268112, pg 72

Reader's Digest Southern Africa (South Africa) *Tel:* (021) 670 6100 *Fax:* (021) 670 6200 *E-mail:* customer.sa@readersdigest.com *Web Site:* www.readersdigest.co.za, pg 568

Readers Union (United Kingdom) *Tel:* (020) 7629 8144 *Fax:* (020) 7499 9751, pg 1257

Reading University Library (United Kingdom) *Tel:* (0118) 378 8770 *Fax:* (0118) 378 6636 *E-mail:* library@reading.ac.uk *Web Site:* www.library.rdg.ac.uk, pg 1554

Readit Books (United Republic of Tanzania) *Tel:* (022) 2184077 *Fax:* (022) 2181077 *E-mail:* readit@raha.com, pg 644, 1345

Ready-Ed Publications (Australia) *Tel:* (08) 9349 6111 *Fax:* (08) 9349 7222 *E-mail:* info@readyed.com.au *Web Site:* www.readyed.com.au, pg 39

Ready Press (Philippines) *Tel:* (02) 6471163; (02) 6471227 *Fax:* (02) 6471158 *E-mail:* casper@pworld.net.ph *Web Site:* www.metro.com.sg, pg 1160

Reaktion Books Ltd (United Kingdom) *Tel:* (020) 7404 4930 *Fax:* (020) 7404 4931 *E-mail:* info@reaktionbooks.co.uk *Web Site:* www.reaktionbooks.co.uk, pg 748

Real Academia de Bones Lletres de Barcelona (Spain) *Tel:* (093) 3150010 *Fax:* (093) 3102349, pg 1405

Real Academia Sevillana de Buenas Letras (Spain) *Tel:* (09542) 21198 *Fax:* (09542) insacan@insacan.org *Web Site:* www.insacan.org, pg 1405

The Real Estate Institute of Australia (Australia) *Tel:* (02) 6282 4277 *Fax:* (02) 6285 2444 *E-mail:* reia@reiaustralia.com.au *Web Site:* www.reiaustralia.com.au, pg 39

Real Ireland Design (Ireland) *Tel:* (01) 2860799 *Fax:* (01) 2829962 *E-mail:* info@realireland.ie *Web Site:* www.realireland.ie, pg 363

Realisations pour l'Enseignement Multilingue International (REMI) (France) *Tel:* (01) 45 75 78 49 *Fax:* (01) 45 79 06 66, pg 183

Realitatea Casa de Edituri Productie Audio-Video Film (Romania) *Tel:* (01) 6117105; (01) 6517105; (01) 6332468; (01) 6143793 *Fax:* (01) 2105411 *E-mail:* leu@dnt.ro, pg 542

Realizacoes Artis (Portugal) *Tel:* (01) 363796 *Fax:* (01) 9170130, pg 535

Reardon Publishing (United Kingdom) *Tel:* (01242) 231800 *E-mail:* reardon@bigfoot.com *Web Site:* www.reardon.co.uk; www.coltswoldbookshop.com (bookshop), pg 748

Rebel Publishing House Pvt Ltd (India) *Tel:* (0212) 628562 *Fax:* (0212) 624181, pg 346

Rebo Productions BV (Netherlands) *Tel:* (0252) 431 556 *Fax:* (0252) 431 557 *E-mail:* info@rebo-publishers.com *Web Site:* www.rebo-publishers.com, pg 488

Recallmed Oy (Finland) *Tel:* (09) 8797177 *Fax:* (09) 8797088 *E-mail:* recallmed@recallmed.fi, pg 144

Verlag fuer Recht und Gesellschaft AG (Switzerland) *Tel:* (061) 726 26 26 *Fax:* (061) 726 26 27 *E-mail:* info@vrg-verlag.ch *Web Site:* www.vrg-verlag.ch, pg 632

Verlag Recht und Wirtschaft GmbH (Germany) *Tel:* (06221) 9060 *Fax:* (06221) 906259 *E-mail:* verlag@ruw.de *Web Site:* www.ruw-ruw.de, pg 274

Reclam Verlag Leipzig (Germany) *Tel:* (0341) 997170 *Fax:* (0341) 9971730 *E-mail:* info@reclam-leipzig.de *Web Site:* www.reclam.de, pg 274

RECOM Verlag (Switzerland) *Tel:* (061) 2646480 *Fax:* (061) 2616213 *Web Site:* www.recom-pcc.de, pg 632

Distribuidora Record de Servicos de Imprensa SA (Brazil) *Tel:* (021) 2585-2000 *Fax:* (021) 2580-4911 *E-mail:* record@record.com.br *Web Site:* www.record.com.br, pg 89

Red Editorial Iberoamericana Mexico SA de CV (Mexico) *Tel:* (05) 5456860; (05) 5456861 *Fax:* (05) 5619112, pg 471

The Red House Books Ltd (United Kingdom) *Tel:* (0870) 191 99 80 *Fax:* (0870) 6077720 *E-mail:* enquiries@redhouse.co.uk *Web Site:* www.redhouse.co.uk, pg 1257

Red Internacional Del Libro (Chile) *Tel:* (02) 2238100 *Fax:* (02) 2254269 *E-mail:* ril@rileditores.com *Web Site:* www.rileditores.com, pg 100

Red/Studio Redazionale (Italy) *Tel:* (02) 30 241 311 *Fax:* (02) 30 241 333, pg 405

Redcliffe Press Ltd (United Kingdom) *Tel:* (0117) 9737207 *Fax:* (0117) 9238991, pg 749

Rede Das Artes (Boccato Editores Collector's) (Brazil) *Tel:* (011) 246-5556 *Fax:* (011) 246-5556, pg 89

Redhouse Bookstore (Turkey) *Tel:* (0212) 520 7778; (0212) 520 2960; (0212) 520 0090 *Fax:* (0212) 522 1909 *E-mail:* info@redhouse.com.tr *Web Site:* www.redhouse.com.tr, pg 1346

Redhouse Press (Turkey) *Tel:* (0212) 520 7778; (0212) 520 2960; (0212) 520 0090 *Fax:* (0212) 522 1909 *E-mail:* info@redhouse.com.tr; sales@redhouse.com.tr *Web Site:* www.redhouse.com.tr, pg 651

Bokforlaget Rediviva, Facsimileforlaget (Sweden) *Tel:* (08) 25 70 07, pg 615

Redstone Press (United Kingdom) *Tel:* (020) 7352 1594 *Fax:* (020) 7352 8749 *Web Site:* www.redstonepress.co.uk, pg 749

Redwood Books Ltd (United Kingdom) *Tel:* (01225) 769979 *Fax:* (01225) 769050 *E-mail:* enquiries@redwood-books.co.uk *Web Site:* www.cpi-group.net, pg 1185

Redwood Books Ltd (United Kingdom) *Tel:* (01225) 769979 *Fax:* (01225) 769050 *E-mail:* enquiries@redwood-books.co.uk, pg 1227

Reed Business Information (United Kingdom) *Tel:* (020) 8652 3500 *Fax:* (01342) 335960 *E-mail:* webmaster@rbi.co.uk *Web Site:* www.redbusiness.com, pg 749

Reed Educational & Professional Publishing (United Kingdom) *Tel:* (01865) 311366 *Fax:* (01865) 314641 *E-mail:* reededucational@repp.co.uk *Web Site:* www.repp.com, pg 749

Reed Educational Publishing Australia (Australia) *Tel:* (03) 9245 7188 *Fax:* (03) 9245 7265 *E-mail:* admin@reededucation.com.au; customerservice@reededucation.com.au *Web Site:* www.reededucation.com.au, pg 39

Reed Elsevier Deutschland GmbH (Germany) *Tel:* (089) 898170 *Fax:* (089) 85817-102, pg 274

Reed Elsevier Group plc (United Kingdom) *Tel:* (020) 7222 8420 *Fax:* (020) 7227 5799 *Web Site:* www.reed-elsevier.com, pg 749

Reed Elsevier Nederland BV (Netherlands) *Tel:* (020) 515 9111 *Fax:* (020) 618 0325 *Web Site:* www.elsevier.com, pg 488

Reed Elsevier, South East Asia (Singapore) *Tel:* 6789 9900 *Fax:* 6789 9966 *Web Site:* www.reed-elsevier.com, pg 557

Reed for Kids (Australia) *Tel:* (03) 5516111 *Fax:* (03) 95517490, pg 39

Reed Publishing (NZ) Ltd (New Zealand) *Tel:* (09) 441 2960 *Fax:* (09) 480 4999 *E-mail:* info@reed.co.nz (customer service) *Web Site:* www.reed.co.nz, pg 500

William Reed Directories (United Kingdom) *Tel:* (01293) 613 400 *Fax:* (01293) 610 322 *E-mail:* directories@william-reed.co.uk *Web Site:* www.william-reed.co.uk, pg 749

References cf (France) *Tel:* (04) 75 27 52 59 *Fax:* (04) 75 27 52 59, pg 183

Regalia 6 Publishing House (Bulgaria) *Tel:* (02) 754111 *Fax:* (02) 566573 *E-mail:* vpruu@dir.bg, pg 96

Regenbogen Verlag (Switzerland) *Tel:* (01) 454 3033 *Fax:* (01) 454 3035 *E-mail:* info@regenbogen-verlag.ch *Web Site:* www.regenbogen-verlag.ch, pg 632

Regency House Publishing Ltd (United Kingdom) *Tel:* (014383) 14488 *Fax:* (014383) 11303 *E-mail:* regencyhouse@btclick.com, pg 749

Regency Press CP Ltd (United Kingdom) *Tel:* (020) 7404 4882 *Fax:* (020) 7404 4885 *E-mail:* info@regency.org *Web Site:* www.regency.org, pg 749

Regency Publications (India) *Tel:* (011) 5712539; (011) 5740038 *Fax:* (011) 5783571 *E-mail:* regency@satyam.net.in, pg 346

Regency Publishing (Australia) *Tel:* (08) 8348 4599 Toll Free *Tel:* 800 649 898 (ext 4599) *Fax:* (08) 8348 4400 *E-mail:* regencypublishing@regency.tafe.sa.edu.au *Web Site:* www.regencypublishing.com.au; www.tafe.sa.edu.au/institutes/regency/regency-publishing/main.htm, pg 39

REGENSBERG Druck & Verlag GmbH & Co (Germany) *Tel:* (0251) 749800 *Fax:* (0251) 7498040, pg 274

Universitatsbibliothek Regensburg (Germany) *Tel:* (0941) 943-3901; (0941) 943-3902 *Fax:* (0941) 943-3285 *Web Site:* www.bibliothek.uni-regensburg.de, pg 1510

Regent Publishing Services (United States) *Tel:* 314-631-7581 *Fax:* 314-638-5113 *E-mail:* regentstl@aol.com, pg 1168, 1189, 1231, 1241, 1249

Editora Regional de Murcia - ERM (Spain) *Tel:* (068) 280246 *Fax:* (068) 298293 *E-mail:* editora.regional@carm.es *Web Site:* www.carm.es, pg 597

Regional ISBN Agency (CARICOM) (Guyana) *Tel:* (02) 226 9280 *Fax:* (02) 226 7816 *E-mail:* carisec1@caricom.org; carisec2@caricom.org; carisec3@caricom.og *Web Site:* www.caricom.org, pg 1272

Regional ISBN Centre The ISBN Officer (Fiji) *Tel:* 3313 900 *Fax:* 3300 830 *E-mail:* mamtora_j@usp.ac.fj; library@usp.ac.fj *Web Site:* www.usp.ac.fj, pg 1266

Verlag fur Regionalgeschichte (Germany) *Tel:* (05209) 6714; (05209) 980266 *Fax:* (05209) 6519; (05209) 980277 *E-mail:* regionalgeschichte@t-online.de *Web Site:* www.regionalgeschichte.de, pg 274

Regura Verlag (Germany) *Tel:* (0711) 2269835 *Fax:* (0711) 2238829, pg 274

Ediciones Rehue Ltda (Chile) *Tel:* (02) 6344653; (02) 6341804 *Fax:* (02) 6351096, pg 100

Konrad Reich Verlag GmbH (Germany) *Tel:* (0381) 693020 *Fax:* (0381) 693021, pg 274

Reich Verlag AG (Switzerland) *Tel:* (041) 4103721 *Fax:* (041) 4103227 *Web Site:* www.terramagica.de, pg 632

Dr Ludwig Reichert Verlag (Germany) *Tel:* (0611) 461851 *Fax:* (0611) 468613 *E-mail:* info@reichert-verlag.de *Web Site:* www.reichert-verlag.de, pg 274

Reichl Verlag Der Leuchter (Germany) *Tel:* (06741) 1720 *Fax:* (06741) 1749 *E-mail:* reichl-verlag@telda.net *Web Site:* www.reichl-verlag.de, pg 274

J R Reid Printing Group Ltd (United Kingdom) *Tel:* (01698) 826000 *Fax:* (01698) 824944 *E-mail:* office@reid-print-group.co.uk *Web Site:* www.reid-print-group.co.uk, pg 1185

J R Reid Printing Group Ltd (United Kingdom) *Tel:* (01698) 826000 *Fax:* (01698) 824944 *E-mail:* clindsay@reid-print-group.co.uk *Web Site:* www.reid-print-group.co.uk, pg 1227

J R Reid Printing Group Ltd (United Kingdom) *Tel:* (01698) 826000 *Fax:* (01698) 824944 *E-mail:* info@reid-print-group.co.uk *Web Site:* www.reid-print-group.co.uk, pg 1239

Reimei-Shobo Co Ltd (Japan) *Tel:* (052) 9623045 *Fax:* (052) 9519065 *E-mail:* reimei@mui.biglobe.ne.jp *Web Site:* wwwl.biz.biglobe.ne.jp/~reimei/, pg 425

Dietrich Reimer Verlag GmbH (Germany) *Tel:* (030) 25 91 15 70 *Fax:* (030) 25 91 15 77 *E-mail:* vertrieb-kunstverlage@reimer-verlag.de *Web Site:* www.reimer-verlag.de, pg 274

Ernst Reinhardt Verlag GmbH & Co KG (Germany) *Tel:* (089) 17 80 16 0 *Fax:* (089) 17 80 16 30 *E-mail:* webmaster@reinhardt-verlag.de *Web Site:* www.reinhardt-verlag.de, pg 275

Verlag Friedrich Reinhardt AG (Switzerland) *Tel:* (061) 264 64 64 *Fax:* (061) 264 64 65 *Web Site:* www.reinhardt.ch, pg 632

E Reinhold Verlag (Germany) *Tel:* (03447) 311889 *Fax:* (03447) 375611 *E-mail:* erv@querstand.de *Web Site:* www.querstand.de, pg 275

Reinhold Schmidt Verlag (Austria) *Tel:* (02236) 72469 *Fax:* (02236) 73784, pg 56

Reise Know-How (Germany) *Tel:* (06872) 91737 *Fax:* (06872) 91738 *E-mail:* hoff-verlag@reise-know-how.com *Web Site:* www.reise-know-how.com, pg 275

Reise Know-How Verlag-Daerr GmbH (Germany) *Tel:* (0521) 946490 *Fax:* (0521) 441047 *E-mail:* info@reise-know-how.de *Web Site:* www.reise-know-how.de, pg 275

Reise Know-How Verlag Dr Hans-R Grundmann GmbH (Germany) *Tel:* (04488) 761994 *Fax:* (04488) 761030 *E-mail:* reisebuch@aol.com, pg 275

Reise Know-How Verlag Helmut Hermann (Germany) *Tel:* (07145) 8278 *Fax:* (07145) 26736 *E-mail:* rkhhermann@aol.com, pg 275

Reise Know-How Verlag Peter Rump GmbH (Germany) *Tel:* (0521) 94649-0 *Fax:* (0521) 441047 *E-mail:* info@reise-know-how.de *Web Site:* www.reise-know-how.de, pg 275

Reise Know-How Verlag Tondok (Germany) *Tel:* (089) 3514857 *Fax:* (089) 3518485 *E-mail:* rhk@tondok-verlag.de *Web Site:* www.tondok-verlag.de, pg 275

Verlagsgruppe Reise Know-How (Germany) *Tel:* (0521) 946490 *Fax:* (0521) 441047 *E-mail:* info@reise-know-how.de *Web Site:* www.reise-know-how.de, pg 275

R V Reise- und Verkehrsverlag GmbH (Germany) *Tel:* (089) 431890; (030) 254098-0 (Berlin) *Fax:* (089) 43189458; (030) 2629115 (Berlin), pg 275

C A Reitzel Boghandel & Forlag A/S (Denmark) *Tel:* 33 12 24 00 *Fax:* 33 14 02 70 *E-mail:* info@careitzel.dk *Web Site:* www.careitzel.dk, pg 134

C A Reitzel Boghandel & Forlag A/S (Denmark) *Tel:* 33 12 24 00 *Fax:* 33 14 02 70 *Web Site:* www.careitzel.dk, pg 1308

Hans Reitzel Publishers Ltd (Denmark) *Tel:* 33382800 *Fax:* 33382808 *E-mail:* hrf@hansreitzel.dk *Web Site:* www.hansreitzel.dk, pg 134

Rekha Prakashan (India) *Tel:* (011) 23279907; (011) 23279904 *Fax:* (011) 2321783 *E-mail:* rprakashan@satyam.net.in *Web Site:* www.museumoffolkandtribalart.org, pg 346

RELATE (United Kingdom) *Tel:* (01788) 573241 *Fax:* (01788) 535007 *E-mail:* enquires@relate.org.uk *Web Site:* www.relate.org.uk, pg 749

Relay Books (Ireland) *Tel:* (067) 31734 *Fax:* (067) 31734 *E-mail:* relaybooks@eiscom.net, pg 363

Reliance Publishing House (India) *Tel:* (011) 5852605; (011) 5772768; (011) 5737377 *Fax:* (011) 5786769 *E-mail:* reliance@indiatimes.com, pg 346

Remaja Rosdakarya CV (Indonesia) *Tel:* (022) 5200287, pg 356

Remzi Kitabevi (Turkey) *Tel:* (0212) 513 94 24; (0212) 513 94 25; (0212) 513 94 74; (0212) 513 94 75 *Fax:* (0212) 522 90 55 *E-mail:* post@remzi.com.tr *Web Site:* www.remzi.com.tr, pg 651

La Renaissance du Livre (Belgium) *Tel:* (069) 89 15 55 *Fax:* (069) 89 15 50 *Web Site:* www.larenaissancedulivre.com, pg 72

Les Editions Albert Rene (France) *Tel:* (01) 45 00 41 41 *Fax:* (01) 40 67 95 12 *E-mail:* rene.cominfo@editions-albert-rene.com *Web Site:* www.editions-albert-rene.com, pg 183

Library of the Renmin University of China (China) *Tel:* (010) 62511014 *Fax:* (010) 62515263; (010) 62515336 *E-mail:* rmdxxb@mail.ruc.edu.cn; leader@mail.ruc.edu.cn *Web Site:* www.ruc.edu.cn, pg 1498

Rentrop & Straton Verlagsgruppe und Wirtschaftsconsulting (Romania) *Tel:* (021) 337.4146 *Fax:* (021) 337.2211 *E-mail:* rs@rs.ro; office@rs.ro *Web Site:* www.rs.ro, pg 542

Verlag Norman Rentrop (Germany) *Tel:* (0228) 36 88 40 *Fax:* (0228) 36 58 75 *E-mail:* tt@rentrop.com *Web Site:* www.normanrentrop.de, pg 275

Editora Replicacao Lda (Portugal) *Tel:* (021) 677058 *Fax:* (021) 396 9808 *E-mail:* replic@mail.telepac.pt, pg 535

Reporter (Bulgaria) *Tel:* (02) 760834; (02) 761084; (02) 769028 *Fax:* (02) 745114 *E-mail:* reporter@techno-link.com, pg 96

Representative Church Body Library (Ireland) *Tel:* (01) 4923979 *Fax:* (01) 4924770 *E-mail:* library@ireland.anglican.org *Web Site:* www.ireland.anglican.org, pg 1519

Republicki Zavod za Unapredivanje Vaspitanja i Obrazovanja (Serbia and Montenegro) *Tel:* (011) 659322, pg 553

Res Polona (Poland) *Tel:* (042) 6363634; (042) 6374587; (042) 6374607 *Fax:* (042) 6373010 *E-mail:* info@res-polona.com.pl *Web Site:* www.res-polona.com.pl, pg 526

Resch Verlag (Austria) *Tel:* (089) 8 54 65-0 *Fax:* (089) 8 54 65-11 *E-mail:* info@resch-verlag.com *Web Site:* www.resch-verlag.com, pg 56

Research Centre for Translation (Hong Kong) *Tel:* 2609 7399; 2609 7407 *Fax:* 2603 5110; 2603 5195 *E-mail:* rct@cuhk.edu.hk *Web Site:* www.cuhk.edu.hk/rct/home.html, pg 319

Research Signpost (India) *Tel:* (0471) 2460384 *Fax:* (0471) 2573051 *E-mail:* ggcom@vsnl.com *Web Site:* www.researchsignpost.com, pg 347

Research Society of Pakistan (Pakistan) *Tel:* (042) 322542, pg 514

Research Studies Press Ltd (RSP) (United Kingdom) *Tel:* (01462) 895060 *Fax:* (01462) 892546 *E-mail:* info@research-studies-press.co.uk *Web Site:* www.research-studies-press.co.uk, pg 749

Researchco Reprints (India) *Tel:* (011) 28712565; (011) 55150446; (011) 28714057 *Fax:* (011) 28716134, pg 347

Editora Resenha Tributaria Ltda (Brazil) *Tel:* (011) 5772822 *Fax:* (011) 5772526, pg 89

Residenz Verlag GmbH (Austria) *Tel:* (0662) 641986-0 *Fax:* (0662) 643548 *E-mail:* info@residenzverlag.at *Web Site:* www.residenzverlag.at, pg 57

Resource Books Ltd (New Zealand) *Tel:* (09) 5758030 *Fax:* (09) 5758055 *E-mail:* sales@resourcebooks.co.nz *Web Site:* www.resourcebooks.co.nz, pg 500

Respublica Verlag (Germany) *Tel:* (02241) 62925; (02241) 64039 *Fax:* (02241) 53891, pg 275

Respublika (Russian Federation) *Tel:* (095) 251-7956, pg 548

Respublikanskij izdatei skij Kabinet (Kazakstan) *Tel:* (03272) 910703; (03272) 910333 *Fax:* (03272) 631207, pg 432

Retail Entertainment Data Publishing Ltd (United Kingdom) *Tel:* (020) 7566 8216 *Fax:* (020) 7566 8259 (Inquiry); (020) 7566 8316 (Editorial) *E-mail:* info@redpublishing.co.uk *Web Site:* www.redpublishing.co.uk, pg 750

Luis A Retta Libros (Uruguay) *Tel:* (02) 400-0766 *Fax:* (02) 409-0174 *E-mail:* rettalib@chasque.apc.org, pg 778

Editorial Reus SA (Spain) *Tel:* (091) 2213619; (091) 2223054 *Fax:* (091) 5312408 *E-mail:* reus@editorialreus.es *Web Site:* www.editorialreus.es, pg 598

Editora Revan Ltda (Brazil) *Tel:* (021) 25027495 *Fax:* (021) 22736873 *E-mail:* editor@revan.com.br *Web Site:* www.revan.com.br, pg 89

Ediciones Luis Revenga (Spain) *Tel:* (091) 5434646 *Fax:* (091) 5434706 *E-mail:* cuadcerv@elr.es, pg 598

Reverdito Edizioni (Italy) *Tel:* (0461) 942285 *Fax:* (0461) 946563 *E-mail:* reverditoedizioni@virgilio.it *Web Site:* www.culturitalia.uibk.ac.at, pg 405

Editorial Reverte SA (Spain) *Tel:* (093) 419 33 36; (093) 419 32 76 *Fax:* (093) 419 51 89 *E-mail:* istz0125@tsai.es; prom.reverte@teleline.es *Web Site:* www.ludosoft.net/reverte/present.htm, pg 598

Editorial Reverte Venezolana SA (Venezuela) *Tel:* (02) 572 44 68; (02) 572 66 70 *Fax:* (02) 572 25 98, pg 780

Review Publishing Co Ltd (Hong Kong) *Tel:* 2573 7121 *Fax:* 2503 1530 *E-mail:* review@feer.com *Web Site:* www.feer.com, pg 1158

Livraria Editora Revinter Ltda (Brazil) *Tel:* (021) 2563-9700 *Fax:* (021) 2563-9701 *E-mail:* livraria@revinter.com.br *Web Site:* www.revinter.com.br, pg 89

Editorial Revista Agustiniana (Spain) *Tel:* (091) 550-5000 *Fax:* (091) 550-5225 *E-mail:* revista@agustiniana.com *Web Site:* www.agustiniana.com, pg 598

Revista Penteado (Portugal) *Tel:* (021) 862963 *Fax:* (021) 870972 *E-mail:* rromano@mail.telepac.pt, pg 535

Editions Revue EPS (France) *Tel:* (01) 41 74 82 82 *Fax:* (01) 43 98 37 38 *E-mail:* revue@revue-eps.com *Web Site:* www.revue-eps.com, pg 183

Revue Espaces et Societes (France) *Tel:* (0551) 60 35 70 *Fax:* (0551) 60 49 58 *E-mail:* jjaquin@espacesetsocietes.com *Web Site:* www.espacesetsocietes.com, pg 183

Revue Noire (France) *Tel:* (01) 43 20 92 00 *Fax:* (01) 43 22 92 60 *E-mail:* redaction@revuenoire.com *Web Site:* www.revuenoire.com, pg 183

Rex Book Store Inc (Philippines) *Tel:* (02) 712-41-06; (02) 711-57-02, pg 1335

Rex Bookstores & Publishers (Philippines) *Tel:* (02) 7437688; (02) 4143512; (02) 4146774 *Fax:* (02) 7437687 *E-mail:* rex@usinc.net, pg 520

Rex Verlag (Switzerland) *Tel:* (041) 4194700 *Fax:* (041) 4194711 *E-mail:* info@rex-freizyt.ch *Web Site:* www.rex-freizyt.ch, pg 632

Libreria Universitaria Jose T Reyes (Honduras) *Tel:* 232-2110 *Fax:* 235-3361 *Web Site:* www.unah.hn, pg 1314

Reyes Publishing Inc (Philippines) *Tel:* (02) 721-8792 *Fax:* (02) 721-8782 *E-mail:* reyesbub@skyinet.net, pg 1161

Reyes Publishing Inc (Philippines) *Tel:* (02) 721-7492 *Fax:* (02) 721-8782 *E-mail:* reyesbub@skyinet.net, pg 1181

Reyes Publishing Inc (Philippines) *Tel:* (02) 721-7492 *Fax:* (02) 721-8782 *E-mail:* reyespub@skyinet.net, pg 1335

Borgarbokasafn Reykjavikur (Iceland) *Tel:* 5631717 *Fax:* 5631705 *E-mail:* borgarbokasafn@borgarbokasafn.is *Web Site:* www.borgarbokasafn.is, pg 1515

Verlagsgruppe Rhein Main GmbH & Co KG (Germany) *Tel:* (06131) 48-46-94 *Web Site:* www.main-rheiner.de, pg 275

Rhein-Trio, Edition/Editions du Fou (Switzerland) *Tel:* (061) 6831635 *Fax:* (061) 6831635 *E-mail:* rhein-trio@usa.net, pg 632

Rheinische Landesbibliothek Koblenz (Germany) *Tel:* (0261) 91500 40 *Fax:* (0261) 91500 91 *E-mail:* info@rlb.de *Web Site:* www.rlb.de, pg 1510

Verlag Rheinischer Merkur GmbH (Germany) *Tel:* (0228) 884-0 *Fax:* (0228) 88 41 70 (sales); (0228) 88 41 99 (editorial); (0228) 88 42 99 (advertising) *E-mail:* abo@merkur.de *Web Site:* www.merkur.de, pg 276

RVBG Rheinland-Verlag-und Betriebsgesellschaft des Landschaftsverbandes Rheinland mbH (Germany) *Tel:* (02234) 9854265 *Fax:* (02234) 82503, pg 276

Rheintal Handelsgesellschaft Anstalt (Liechtenstein) *Tel:* (075) 3921882; (01) 8442786 *Fax:* (075) 3923646; (01) 8442806 *E-mail:* vetsch.p@bluewin.ch, pg 448

RHJ Livros Ltda (Brazil) *Tel:* (031) 3334-1566 *Fax:* (031) 3332-5823 *Web Site:* www.editorarhj.com.br, pg 89

Rhodes University Library (South Africa) *Tel:* (046) 603 8436 *Fax:* (046) 6223487 *E-mail:* library@ru.ac.za *Web Site:* www.rhodes.ac.za/library/, pg 1544

Rhodos, International Science & Art Publishers (Denmark) *Tel:* 32543020 *Fax:* 32543022 *E-mail:* rhodos@rhodos.com *Web Site:* www.rhodos.dk, pg 134

Rhombus Verlag (Austria) *Tel:* (01) 526 61 52 *Fax:* (01) 522 87 18, pg 57

Ediciones Rialp SA (Spain) *Tel:* (091) 3260504 *Fax:* (091) 3261321 *E-mail:* ediciones@rialp.com *Web Site:* www.rialp.com/, pg 598

RIBA Publications (United Kingdom) *Tel:* (020) 7251 0791 *Fax:* (020) 7608 2375 *Web Site:* www.ribabookshop.com; www.ribac.co.uk, pg 750

RIC Publications Pty Ltd (Australia) *Tel:* (09) 9240 9888 *Fax:* (09) 9240 1513 *E-mail:* mail@ricgroup.com.au *Web Site:* www.ricgroup.com.au, pg 39

Biblioteca Riccardiana (Italy) *Tel:* (055) 212586; (055) 293385 *Fax:* (055) 211379 *E-mail:* riccardiana@riccardiana.firenze.sbn.it *Web Site:* www.riccardiana.librari.beniculturali.it, pg 1521

Franco Maria Ricci Editore (FMR) (Italy) *Tel:* (02) 414101 *Fax:* (02) 48301473 *E-mail:* ricci@fmrmagazine.it *Web Site:* www.fmrspa.it, pg 405

Riccardo Ricciardi Editore SpA (Italy) *Tel:* (01) 156561, pg 405

Edizioni del Riccio SAS di G Bernardi (Italy) *Tel:* (0571) 609338 *Fax:* (055) 716362, pg 405

Richardi Helmut Verlag GmbH (Germany) *Tel:* (069) 9708330 *Fax:* (069) 7078400 *E-mail:* kreditwesen@t-online.de, pg 276

Richards Literary Agency (New Zealand) *Tel:* (09) 479 5681 *Fax:* (09) 479 5681, pg 1135

The Richmond Publishing Co Ltd (United Kingdom) *Tel:* (01753) 643104 *Fax:* (01753) 646553 *E-mail:* rpc@richmond.co.uk, pg 750, 1353

Richters Egmont (Sweden) *Tel:* (040) 38 06 00 *Fax:* (040) 933708 *E-mail:* egmont@egmont.com *Web Site:* www.egmont.com, pg 615

Richters Forlag (Sweden) *Tel:* (040) 38 06 80 *Fax:* (040) 93 08 20 *Web Site:* www.egmontrichter.com, pg 1256

Ricordi Americana SAEC (Argentina) *Tel:* (011) 4371-9841; (011) 4371-9843 *Fax:* (011) 4372-3459 *E-mail:* ricordi@sminter.com.ar, pg 8

RICS Books (United Kingdom) *Tel:* (020) 7222 7000 (ext 698) *Fax:* (020) 7334 3851 *E-mail:* weborders@rics.org.uk *Web Site:* www.ricsbooks.com, pg 750

RICS Books (United Kingdom) *Tel:* (0870) 333 1600 *Fax:* (020) 7334 3851 *E-mail:* weborders@rics.org.uk *Web Site:* www.ricsbooks.com, pg 1353

Editora Rideel Ltda (Brazil) *Tel:* (011) 6977-8344 *Fax:* (011) 6976-7415 *E-mail:* rideel@virtual-net.com.br *Web Site:* www.rideel.com.br, pg 89

Rigodon-Verlag Norbert Wehr (Germany) *Tel:* (0201) 77 81 11; (0221) 360 21 92 *Fax:* (0201) 77 51 74; (0221) 360 21 92 *E-mail:* Schreibheft@NetCologne.de *Web Site:* www.schreibheft.de, pg 276

Rigsarkivet (Denmark) *Tel:* 33923310 *Fax:* 33153239 *E-mail:* mailbox@ra.sa.dk *Web Site:* www.sa.dk, pg 1502

Rihani Printing & Publishing House (Lebanon) *Tel:* 868384 *Fax:* 868384, pg 447

Rijksmuseum Research Library (Netherlands) *Tel:* (020) 6747047 *Fax:* (020) 6747001 *E-mail:* library@rijksmuseum.nl *Web Site:* library.rijksmuseum.nl, pg 1531

Bibliotheek der Rijksuniversiteit Groningen (Netherlands) *Tel:* (050) 363 50 20; (050) 363 3708 *Fax:* (050) 363 49 96; (050) 363 3720 *E-mail:* info@ub.rug.nl *Web Site:* www.rug.nl/bibliotheek, pg 1531

Riksarkivet (Norway) *Tel:* (022) 02 26 00 *Fax:* (022) 23 74 89 *E-mail:* riksarkivet@riksarkivaren.dep.no *Web Site:* www.riksarkivet.no; www.arkivverket.no, pg 1534

Riksarkivet (Sweden) *Tel:* (08) 737 63 50 *Fax:* (08) 737 64 74 *E-mail:* registry@riksarkivet.ra.se *Web Site:* www.ra.se, pg 1547

Riksbibliotektjenesten (Norway) *Tel:* 23 11 89 00 *Fax:* 23 11 89 01 *E-mail:* rbt@rbt.no, pg 1569

Rimbaud Verlagsgesellschaft mbH (Germany) *Tel:* (0241) 54 25 32; (0241) 9019583 *Fax:* (0241) 514117 *E-mail:* info@rimbaud.de *Web Site:* www.rimbaud.de, pg 276

RIMU Publishing Co Ltd (New Zealand) *Tel:* (07) 8555536 *Fax:* (07) 8555536, pg 500

Rinsen Book Co Ltd (Japan) *Tel:* (075) 721-7111 *Fax:* (075) 781-6168 *E-mail:* kyoto@rinsen.com *Web Site:* www.rinsen.com, pg 425

Edizioni Ripostes (Italy) *Tel:* (089) 336049 *Fax:* (089) 336049, pg 405

Riquelme y Vargas Ediciones SL (Spain) *Tel:* (053) 270066 *Fax:* (053) 270066, pg 598

Rirea Casa Editrice della Rivista Italiana di Ragioneria e di Economia Aziendale (Italy) *Tel:* (06) 8417690 *Fax:* (06) 8845732 *E-mail:* rirea_@infinito.it, pg 405

Riso-Sha (Japan) *Tel:* (047) 366-8003 *Fax:* (047) 360-7301, pg 425

Rithofundasamband Islands (Iceland) *Tel:* 5683190 *Fax:* 5683192 *E-mail:* rsi@rsi.is *Web Site:* www.rsi.is, pg 1401

Ritter Druck und Verlags KEG (Austria) *Tel:* (0463) 42631 *Fax:* (0463) 42631-77 *E-mail:* office@ritterbooks.com *Web Site:* www.ritterbooks.com, pg 57

Ritterbach Verlag GmbH (Germany) *Tel:* (02234) 18 66 0 *Fax:* (02234) 18 66 90 *E-mail:* service@ritterbach.de; coeln.ml@ritterbach.de *Web Site:* www.ritterbach.de, pg 276

Ritzau KG Verlag Zeit und Eisenbahn (Germany) *Tel:* (08196) 252 *Fax:* (08196) 1240 *E-mail:* mail@ritzau.kg.de *Web Site:* www.ritzau-kg.de, pg 276

Editori Riuniti (Italy) *Tel:* (06) 6889951 *Fax:* (06) 6868696 *Web Site:* www.editoririuniti.it, pg 405

River Press (New Zealand) *Tel:* (03) 5738383 *Fax:* (03) 5738383, pg 500

Rivers Oram Press (United Kingdom) *Tel:* (020) 7607 0823 *Fax:* (020) 7609 2776 *E-mail:* ro@riversoram.demon.co.uk, pg 750

Riverside Agency SAC (Argentina) *Tel:* (011) 4957-2336 *Fax:* (011) 4956-1985 *E-mail:* riverside@laisla.net, pg 1297

Riverside Communications (Nigeria) *Tel:* (084) 334042 *Fax:* (084) 334042 *E-mail:* isoun@aol.com; rvsdcom@aol.com, pg 507

La Riviere Creatief (Netherlands) *Tel:* (035) 5486600 *Fax:* (035) 5486675, pg 488

Yves Riviere Editeur (France) *Tel:* (01) 42 74 77 84 *Fax:* (01) 42 78 12 65 *E-mail:* yvestri@mail.club.internet.fr, pg 183

Rizal Library (Philippines) *Tel:* (02) 426-6001; 5800-5816 (Local) *Fax:* (02) 426-5961 *Web Site:* rizal.lib.admu.edu.ph, pg 1536

Libreria Rizzoli della Rizzoli Editore SpA (Italy) *Tel:* (02) 50951 *Fax:* (02) 5065361, pg 1321

RMIT Publishing (Australia) *Tel:* (03) 9925 8100 *Fax:* (03) 9925 8134 *E-mail:* info@rmitpublishing.com.au *Web Site:* www.rmitpublishing.com.au, pg 39

Road Editions (Greece) *Tel:* (0210) 3613242 *Fax:* (0210) 3614681 *E-mail:* roadsales@road.gr *Web Site:* www.road.gr, pg 1314

Roadmaster Publishing (United Kingdom) *Tel:* (01634) 862843 *Fax:* (01634) 201555 *E-mail:* susanwright@blueyonder.co.uk, pg 750

Editorial Roasa SL (Spain) *Tel:* (058) 0227846 *Fax:* (058) 132530, pg 598

Le Robert (France) *Tel:* (01) 45 87 43 00 *Fax:* (01) 45 35 76 06 *Web Site:* www.lerobert.com.fr, pg 183

Roberts Rinehart Publishers (Ireland) *Tel:* (01) 497-6860 *Fax:* (01) 497-6861 *E-mail:* books@townhouse.ie, pg 363

Tom Roberts (Pat Roberts) (Australia) *Tel:* (08) 8143 7578, pg 39

J Robinson & Co (Israel) *Tel:* (03) 5605461; (03) 5601626 *Fax:* (03) 5660439 *E-mail:* rob_book@netvision.net.il *Web Site:* www.robinson.co.il, pg 1320

The Robinswood Press Ltd (United Kingdom) *Tel:* (01384) 397475 *Fax:* (01384) 440443 *E-mail:* info@robinswoodpress.com *Web Site:* www.robinswoodpress.com, pg 750

Robson Books (United Kingdom) *Tel:* (020) 7221 2213; (020) 7314 1469 (sales) *Fax:* (020) 7221 6455; (020) 7314 1594 (sales) *E-mail:* robson@chrysalisbooks.co.uk *Web Site:* www.chrysalisbooks.co.uk/books/publisher/robson, pg 750

Laurus Robuffo Edizioni (Italy) *Tel:* (06) 5651492 *Fax:* (06) 5651233, pg 405

Livraria Roca Ltda (Brazil) *Tel:* (011) 221-8609; (011) 221-6814 *Fax:* (011) 3331-8653 *E-mail:* edroca@uol.com.br *Web Site:* www.editoraroca.com.br, pg 89

Ediciones Roca, SA (Mexico) *Tel:* (05) 5758585; (05) 2770946 *Fax:* (05) 5758980, pg 471

Ediciones La Rocca (Argentina) *Tel:* (011) 4382 8526 *Fax:* (011) 4384 5774 *E-mail:* ed-larocca@sinectis.com, pg 89

Editora Rocco Ltda (Brazil) *Tel:* (021) 2507-2000 *Fax:* (021) 2507-2244 *E-mail:* rocco@rocco.com.br *Web Site:* www.rocco.com.br, pg 89

Roce (Consultants) Ltd (Uganda) *Tel:* (041) 106010 *Fax:* (041) 321062 *Web Site:* www.rutaagi.com, pg 653

Editiones Roche (Switzerland) *Tel:* (061) 688 3611 *Fax:* (061) 688 2775 *Web Site:* www.roche.com, pg 632

Les Editions du Rocher (Monaco) *Tel:* (093) 40465400 *Fax:* (093) 43293506 *E-mail:* jpb.droits@wanadoo.fr, pg 474

Rodera-Verlag der Cardun AG (Switzerland) *Tel:* (052) 292442 *Fax:* (052) 292592, pg 632

Rodopi (Netherlands) *Tel:* (020) 6114821 *Fax:* (020) 4472979 *E-mail:* info@rodopi.nl *Web Site:* www.rodopi.nl, pg 488

Ediciones Joaquin Rodrigo (Spain) *Tel:* (091) 555 2728 *Fax:* (091) 556 4334 *E-mail:* ediciones@joaquin-rodrigo.com *Web Site:* www.joaquin-rodrigo.com, pg 598

Libreria Rodriguez SA, Dto Suscripciones (Argentina) *Tel:* (011) 4326-3725; (011) 4326-3826 *Fax:* (011) 4326-1959 *E-mail:* librerod@ssdnet.com.ar, pg 1297

Roehrig Universitaets Verlag Gmbh (Germany) *Tel:* (06894) 8 79 57 *Fax:* (06894) 87 03 30 *E-mail:* info@roehrig-verlag.de *Web Site:* www.roehrig-verlag.de, pg 276

Verlag Roeschnar (Austria) *Tel:* (0463) 740513 *Fax:* (0463) 740817 *E-mail:* roesch@eunet.at *Web Site:* members.eunet.at/roesch, pg 57

Erich Roeth-Verlag (Germany) *Tel:* (039206) 90103 *Fax:* (039206) 90103, pg 276

Roetzer Druck GmbH & Co KG (Austria) *Tel:* (02682) 2473 *Fax:* (02682) 65008 *E-mail:* roetzeredition@wellcom.at, pg 57

Rogan McIndoe Print Ltd (New Zealand) *Tel:* (03) 474 0111 *Toll Free Tel:* 800-477-0355 *Fax:* (03) 477 0116 *Web Site:* www.rogan.co.nz, pg 1160

Rogan McIndoe Print Ltd (New Zealand) *Tel:* (03) 474 0111 *Toll Free Tel:* 800-477-0355 *Fax:* (03) 474 0116 *E-mail:* quality@rogan.co.nz *Web Site:* www.rogan.co.nz, pg 1181

Rogan McIndoe Print Ltd (New Zealand) *Tel:* (03) 477 0355 *Fax:* (03) 474 0116 *E-mail:* quality@rogan.co.nz *Web Site:* www.rogan.co.nz, pg 1221

Rogan McIndoe Print Ltd (New Zealand) *Tel:* (03) 474 0111 *Toll Free Tel:* 800 477 0355 *Fax:* (03) 474 0116 *E-mail:* quality@rogan.co.nz *Web Site:* www.rogan.co.nz, pg 1237

Rogan McIndoe Print Ltd (New Zealand) *Tel:* (03) 474 0111 *Toll Free Tel:* (0800) 477 0355 *Fax:* (03) 474 0116 *E-mail:* production@rogan.co.nz *Web Site:* www.rogan.co.nz, pg 1246

Libreria Editrice Rogate (LER) (Italy) *Tel:* (06) 7023430 *Fax:* (06) 7020767, pg 406

Rogers, Coleridge & White Ltd (United Kingdom) *Tel:* (020) 7221 3717 *Fax:* (020) 7229 9084 *E-mail:* rcwlitagency@rcwlitagency.co.uk, pg 1143

Heidi Rogner (Germany) *Tel:* (02429) 2561, pg 276

Rogner und Bernhard GmbH & Co Verlags KG (Germany) *Tel:* (040) 4302110 *Fax:* (040) 4302716 *E-mail:* service@on-line.de *Web Site:* www.zweitausendeins.de, pg 276

Hans Rohr Verlag (Switzerland) *Tel:* (01) 3614846 *Fax:* (01) 3639513 *E-mail:* buchhandlung.hans.rohr@dm.krinfo.ch, pg 632

Ediciones ROL SA (Spain) *Tel:* (093) 200 80 33 *Fax:* (093) 200 27 62 *E-mail:* rol@e-rol.es *Web Site:* www.e-rol.es, pg 598

Roli Books Pvt Ltd (India) *Tel:* (011) 6462782; (011) 6442271; (011) 6460886 *Fax:* (011) 6467185 *E-mail:* roli@vsnl.com *Web Site:* rolibooks.com, pg 347

Edicoes Rolim Lda (Portugal) *Tel:* (021) 526375, pg 535

Verlag und Buchversand Wolfgang Roller (Germany) *Tel:* (06103) 71886 *Fax:* (06103) 929501 *E-mail:* greif@12move.de *Web Site:* www.verlag-roller.de, pg 276

Rolnik Publishers (Israel) *Tel:* (03) 6496663 *Fax:* (03) 6478661 *E-mail:* rolknik@attglobal.net *Web Site:* www.rolnik.com; www.bible2000.com, pg 371

Edizioni Universitarie Romane (Italy) *Tel:* (06) 491503; (06) 4940658 *Fax:* (06) 4453438 *E-mail:* eur@eurom.it *Web Site:* www.eurom.it, pg 406

Romantic Cyprus Publications (Cyprus) *Fax:* (022) 445155, pg 121

Romantic Novelists' Association (RNA) (United Kingdom) *Tel:* (01827) 714776 *Fax:* (01827) 714776 *Web Site:* www.rna-uk.org, pg 1409

Rombach GmbH Druck und Verlagshaus & Co (Germany) *Tel:* (0761) 4500 0 *Fax:* (0761) 4500 2125 *E-mail:* info@buchverlag.rombach.de *Web Site:* www.rombach.de, pg 276

Editions Rombaldi SA (France) *Tel:* (01) 41 23 65 00 *Fax:* (01) 46 45 34 42, pg 183

Romiosini Verlag (Germany) *Tel:* (0221) 5101288 *Fax:* (0221) 5101288 *E-mail:* romiosini@unisolo.de *Web Site:* www.unisolo.de/pls/romiosini/griechische_literatur, pg 276

George Ronald Publisher Ltd (United Kingdom) *Tel:* (01235) 529137 *E-mail:* sales@grbooks.com *Web Site:* www.grbooks.com, pg 750

Rondeau Giannipiero a Monaco (Monaco) *Tel:* (093) 303075 *Fax:* (093) 257047, pg 474

Rondo Verlag (Switzerland) *Tel:* (055) 246 39 37 *Fax:* (055) 246 42 93 *Web Site:* www.rondo-verlag.ch, pg 632

Rooster Books Ltd (United Kingdom) *Tel:* (01763) 242939 *Fax:* (01763) 243332 *E-mail:* rooster@solutions-for-business.co.uk *Web Site:* www.solutions-for-books.co.uk/rooster, pg 751

Roraima Publishers Ltd (Guyana) *Tel:* (02) 2-73551; (02) 2-2363; (02) 2-5057 *Fax:* (02) 62319; (02) 58844 *E-mail:* roraima-distributors@solutions2000.net, pg 314

Mercedes Ros Literary Agency (Spain) *Tel:* (093) 5401353 *Fax:* (093) 5401346 *E-mail:* info@mercedesros.com *Web Site:* www.mercedesros.com, pg 1136

Mercedes Ros Literary Agency (Spain) *Tel:* (093) 540 13 53 *Fax:* (093) 540 13 46 *E-mail:* info@mercedesros.com *Web Site:* www.mercedesros.com, pg 1223

Sean Ros Press (Ireland) *Tel:* (051) 28666, pg 363

Rosda Jaya Putra (Indonesia) *Tel:* (021) 3904984; (021) 3901692; (021) 3904985 *Fax:* (021) 3901703, pg 356

Rosebud Ediciones (Uruguay) *Tel:* (02) 771773 *Fax:* (02) 6287111 *E-mail:* zapican@adinet.com.uy, pg 778

Rosenberg e Sellier SpA (Italy) *Tel:* (011) 812 76 56 *Fax:* (011) 812 77 44, pg 1321

Rosenberg e Sellier Editori in Torino (Italy) *Tel:* (011) 8127820 *Fax:* (011) 8127808, pg 406

Rosendale Press Ltd (United Kingdom) *Tel:* (020) 7834 1123 *Fax:* (020) 7834 1240 *E-mail:* info@rosendale.demon.co.uk, pg 751

Rosenheimer Verlagshaus GmbH & Co KG (Germany) *Tel:* (08031) 2838 0 *Fax:* (08031) 2838 44 *E-mail:* info@rosenheimer.com *Web Site:* www.rosenheimer.com, pg 276

Rosenkilde & Bagger (Denmark) *Tel:* 33157044 *Fax:* 33937007 *E-mail:* r-b@rosenkilde-bagger.dk *Web Site:* www.rosenkilde-bagger.dk, pg 1

Guide Rosenwald (France) *Tel:* (01) 44 30 81 00 *Fax:* (01) 44 30 81 11 *E-mail:* info@rosenwald.com *Web Site:* www.rosenwald.com, pg 183

Rosie O'Hara German Translations (United Kingdom) *Tel:* (01667) 456 222 *Fax:* (01667) 456 222 *Web Site:* www.rosieohara.co.uk/index1.htm, pg 1151

Rosikon Press (Poland) *Tel:* (022) 7226101; (022) 7226102; (022) 7226666 *Fax:* (022) 7226667 *E-mail:* biuro@rosikonpress.com; office@rosikompress.com *Web Site:* www.rosikonpress.com, pg 526

Roskilde University Library (Denmark) *Tel:* 46742007 *Fax:* 46742233 *E-mail:* rub@ruc.dk *Web Site:* www.rub.ruc.dk, pg 1502

Louise Ross & Co, Ltd (United Kingdom) *Tel:* (0225) 44 87 86 *Fax:* (0225) 44 87 89 *E-mail:* louise.ross@btinternet.com, pg 1353

Rossato (Italy) *Tel:* (0455) 411000 *Fax:* (0455) 411550 *E-mail:* grossato@didanet.it, pg 406

Rossi, E Kdoseis Eleni Rossi-Petsiou (Greece) *Tel:* (0210) 3304440; (0210) 3301854 *Fax:* (0210) 3304410, pg 312

Rossiiskaya Knizhnaya Palata (Russian Federation) *Tel:* (095) 2911278; (095) 291-96-30 *Fax:* (095) 291-96-30; (095) 202-67-25 *E-mail:* bookchyu@postman.ru *Web Site:* www.bookchamber.ru/international, pg 1282

Rossiiskaya Nacionalnaya biblioteka (Russian Federation) *Tel:* (0812) 310-2856 *Fax:* (0812) 310-6148 *E-mail:* office@nlr.ru *Web Site:* www.nlr.ru:8101, pg 1540

Gosudarstvennaya publichnaya nauchno-tekhnicheskaya biblioteka Sibirskogo otdeleniya Rossiiskoi Akademii Nauk (Russian Federation) *Tel:* (0382) 66-18-60 *Fax:* (0382) 66-33-65 *E-mail:* root@librr.nsk.su *Web Site:* www.gpntb.ru, pg 1540

Rossijskoye avtorskoye obshestvo (Russian Federation) *Tel:* (095) 2033777; (095) 2033260 *E-mail:* rao@rao.ru *Web Site:* www.rao.ru, pg 1136

Rossipaul Kommunikation GmbH (Germany) *Tel:* (089) 17 91 06 0 *Fax:* (089) 17 91 06 22 *E-mail:* info@rossipaul.de *Web Site:* www.rossipaul.de, pg 277

Universitaet Rostock Universitaetsbibliothek (Germany) *Tel:* (0381) 4 98 22 83 *Fax:* (0381) 4 98 22 70 *E-mail:* ub-sekretariat@ub.uni-rostock.de00.de *Web Site:* www.uni-rostock.de, pg 1510

Rotedic SA (Spain) *Tel:* (091) 8031676 *Fax:* (091) 8038316 *Web Site:* www.rotedic.com, pg 1223

Roth et Sauter SA (Switzerland) *Tel:* (021) 801 75 61 *Fax:* (021) 802 32 79, pg 632

Rothschild & Bach (Netherlands) *Tel:* (020) 6389329, pg 488

RotoVision SA (United Kingdom) *Tel:* (01273) 727 268 *Fax:* (01273) 727 269 *E-mail:* sales@rotovision.com *Web Site:* www.rotovision.com, pg 751

Rotpunktverlag (Switzerland) *Tel:* (01) 2418434 *Fax:* (01) 2418474 *E-mail:* info@rotpunktverlag.ch *Web Site:* www.rotpunktverlag.ch, pg 632

Rotten-Verlags AG (Switzerland) *Tel:* (027) 948 30 32 *Fax:* (027) 948 30 33 *E-mail:* rottenverlag@mengis.ch, pg 633

Gemeentebibliotheek Rotterdam (Netherlands) *Tel:* (010) 281 61 00 *Fax:* (010) 2816181 *Web Site:* www.rotterdamnet.nl/bieb.htm, pg 1531

Editions Roudil SA (France) *Tel:* (01) 43 54 47 97 *Fax:* (01) 43 54 06 97, pg 183

Editions du Rouergue (France) *Tel:* (05) 65.77.73.70 *Fax:* (05) 65.77.73.71 *E-mail:* info@lerouergue.com *Web Site:* www.lerouergue.com, pg 183

Rough Guides Ltd (United Kingdom) *Tel:* (020) 7010 3000 *Fax:* (020) 7010 6767 *E-mail:* mail@roughguides.com *Web Site:* www.roughguides.com, pg 751

Roularta Books NV (Belgium) *Tel:* (051) 266967 *Fax:* (051) 266680 *E-mail:* info@roularta.be *Web Site:* www.roulartabooks.be, pg 72

Round Hall Sweet & Maxwell (Ireland) *Tel:* (01) 662 5301 *E-mail:* info@roundhall.ie *Web Site:* www.roundhall.ie, pg 363

Roundhouse Group (United Kingdom) *Tel:* (01237) 474 474 *Fax:* (01237) 474 774 *E-mail:* roundhouse.group@ukgateway.net *Web Site:* www.roundhouse.net, pg 751

Roundhouse Group (United Kingdom) *Tel:* (01237) 474474 *Fax:* (01237) 474774 *E-mail:* roundhouse.group@ukgateway.net *Web Site:* www.roundhouse.net, pg 1353

Routledge (United Kingdom) *Tel:* (020) 7583 9855 *Fax:* (020) 7842 2298 *E-mail:* info@routledge.co.uk *Web Site:* www.routledge.com, pg 751

RoutledgeCurzon (United Kingdom) *Tel:* (020) 7583 9855 *Fax:* (020) 7842 2298 *E-mail:* info@routledge.co.uk *Web Site:* www.routledge.com, pg 751

Antony Rowe Ltd (United Kingdom) *Tel:* (01249) 659 705 *Fax:* (01249) 448 900 *E-mail:* sales@antonyrowe.co.uk *Web Site:* www.antonyrowe.co.uk, pg 1165, 1185, 1227

Antony Rowe Ltd (United Kingdom) *Tel:* (01249) 659 705; (01249) 445 535 (ISDN) *Fax:* (01249) 448 900 *E-mail:* sales@antonyrowe.co.uk *Web Site:* www.antonyrowe.co.uk, pg 1239, 1248

Joseph Rowntree Foundation (United Kingdom) *Tel:* (01904) 629241 *Fax:* (01904) 620072 *E-mail:* julia.lewis@jrf.org.uk *Web Site:* www.jrf.org.uk, pg 752

Rowohlt Berlin Verlag GmbH (Germany) *Tel:* (030) 2853840 *Fax:* (040) 28538422 *E-mail:* info@rowohlt.de *Web Site:* www.rowohlt.de, pg 277

Rowohlt Verlag GmbH (Germany) *Tel:* (040) 72720 *Fax:* (040) 7272319 *E-mail:* info@rowohlt.de *Web Site:* www.rowohlt.de, pg 277

Elizabeth Roy Literary Agency (United Kingdom) *Tel:* (01778) 560672 *Fax:* (01778) 560672, pg 1143

Royal Book Co (Pakistan) *Tel:* (021) 5684244 *Fax:* (021) 5683706, pg 514

Royal Book Co (Pakistan) *Tel:* (021) 5684244 *Fax:* (021) 5683706 *E-mail:* royalbook@hotmail.com, pg 1334

Royal College of General Practitioners (RCGP) (United Kingdom) *Tel:* (020) 7581 3232 *Fax:* (020) 7225 3047; (020) 7584 6716 (editorial) *E-mail:* info@rcgp.org.uk *Web Site:* www.rcgp.org.uk, pg 752

Royal College of Surgeons in Ireland Library (Ireland) *Tel:* (01) 402 2100 *E-mail:* info@rcsi.ie *Web Site:* www.rcsi.ie, pg 1519

Royal Dublin Society (Ireland) *Tel:* (01) 6680866 *Fax:* (01) 6604014 *E-mail:* info@rds.ie *Web Site:* www.rds.ie, pg 363

Royal Dublin Society Library (Ireland) *Tel:* (01) 6680866; (01) 2407288 *Fax:* (01) 6604014 *E-mail:* info@rds.ie *Web Site:* www.rds.ie, pg 1519

Royal Institute of International Affairs (United Kingdom) *Tel:* (020) 7957 5700 *Fax:* (020) 7957 5710 *E-mail:* contact@riia.org *Web Site:* www.riia.org, pg 752

Royal Irish Academy (Ireland) *Tel:* (01) 6762570 *Fax:* (01) 6762346 *E-mail:* admin@ria.ie *Web Site:* www.ria.ie, pg 363

Royal Literary Fund (United Kingdom) *Tel:* (020) 7353 7150 *Fax:* (020) 7353 1350 *E-mail:* rlitfund@btconnect.com *Web Site:* www.rlf.org.uk, pg 1409

Royal Nepal Academy (Nepal) *Tel:* (01) 547714; (01) 547715; (01) 547716; (01) 547717; (01) 547718 *Fax:* (01) 547713 *E-mail:* info@ronast.org.np; ronast@mos.com.np *Web Site:* www.ronast.org.np, pg 477

Royal Scientific Society Library (Jordan) *Tel:* (06) 5344701 *Fax:* (06) 5344806 *E-mail:* kahhaleh@rss.gov.jo *Web Site:* www.rss.gov.jo, pg 1522

The Royal Society (United Kingdom) *Tel:* (020) 7839 5561 *Fax:* (020) 7930 2170 *E-mail:* info@royalsoc.ac.uk *Web Site:* www.royalsoc.ac.uk, pg 752

The Royal Society for the Encouragement of Arts, Manufactures & Commerce (RSA) (United Kingdom) *Tel:* (020) 7930 5115 *Fax:* (020) 7839 5805 *E-mail:* general@rsa.org.uk *Web Site:* www.rsa.org.uk, pg 1409

The Royal Society of Chemistry (United Kingdom) *Tel:* (020) 7437 8656 *Fax:* (020) 7437 8883 *E-mail:* sales@rsc.org *Web Site:* www.rsc.org, pg 752

Royal Society of Literature (United Kingdom) *Tel:* (020) 7845 4676 *Fax:* (020) 7845 4679 *E-mail:* info@rslit.org *Web Site:* www.rslit.org, pg 1409

Royal Society of Medicine Press Ltd (United Kingdom) *Tel:* (020) 7290 2921 *Fax:* (020) 7290 2929 *E-mail:* publishing@rsm.ac.uk *Web Site:* www.rsmpress.co.uk, pg 752

Royal Society of New South Wales (Australia) *Tel:* (02) 9887 4448 *Fax:* (02) 9887 4448 *E-mail:* info@nsw.royalsoc.org.au *Web Site:* nsw.royalsoc.org.au, pg 40

Royal Society of South Africa Library (South Africa) *Tel:* (021) 650 2543 *Fax:* (021) 650 2710 *E-mail:* roysoc@science.uct.ac.za *Web Site:* www.rssa.uct.ac.za, pg 1544

Royal Society of Victoria Inc (Australia) *Tel:* (03) 9663 5259 *Fax:* (03) 9663 2301 *E-mail:* sciencevictoria@org.au; rsvinc@vicnet.net.au *Web Site:* www.sciencevictoria.org.au, pg 40

RSVP Publishing Co Ltd (New Zealand) *Tel:* (09) 3723480 *Fax:* (09) 3728480 *E-mail:* rsvppub@iconz.co.nz *Web Site:* www.rsvp-publishing.co.nz, pg 500

Wydawnictwo RTW (Poland) *Tel:* (022) 633 70 10; (022) 663 74 74 *Fax:* (022) 633 70 10; (022) 39120123 *E-mail:* rtw@wydawrtw.media.pl, pg 526

Josep Ruaix Editor (Spain) *Tel:* (093) 820 81 36; (093) 830 02 33 *Web Site:* www.ruaix.com/, pg 598

Ruamsarn (1977) Co Ltd (Thailand) *Tel:* (02) 221-6483 *Fax:* (02) 222-2038, pg 645

Rubber Research Institute of Malaysia Library (Malaysia) *Tel:* (03) 4567033 *Fax:* (03) 4511301 *Web Site:* w3.itri.org.tw/k0000/apec/malaysia/malay-1.htm, pg 1527

Rubbettino Editore (Italy) *Tel:* (0968) 662034 *Fax:* (0968) 662035 *E-mail:* info@rubbettino.it *Web Site:* www.rubbettino.it, pg 406

The Rubicon Press (United Kingdom) *Tel:* (020) 7937 6813, pg 752

Rubin Mass Ltd (Israel) *Tel:* (02) 627-7863 *Fax:* (02) 627-7864 *E-mail:* rmass@barak.net.il *Web Site:* www.rubin-mass.com, pg 371, 1320

Libreria Rubinos - 1860 SA (Spain) *Tel:* (091) 435 22 39 *Fax:* (091) 435 32 72, pg 1343

Rueda, SL Editorial (Spain) *Tel:* (091) 619 27 79; (091) 619 25 64 *Fax:* (091) 610 28 55 *E-mail:* ed_rueda@infornet.es *Web Site:* www.editorialrueda.es, pg 598

Ruegger Verlag (Switzerland) *Tel:* (01) 4912130 *Fax:* (01) 4931176 *E-mail:* info@rueggerverlag.ch *Web Site:* www.rueggerverlag.ch, pg 633

Ruetten & Loening Berlin GmbH (Germany) *Tel:* (030) 283 94 0 *Fax:* (030) 283 94 100 *E-mail:* info@aufbau-verlag.de *Web Site:* www.aufbau-verlag.de, pg 277

Dieter Ruggeberg Verlagsbuchhandlung (Germany) *Tel:* (0202) 592811 *Fax:* (0202) 592811 *E-mail:* vrggeberg@aol.com *Web Site:* www.vbdr.de, pg 277

Rugginenti Editore (Italy) *Tel:* (02) 89501283 *Fax:* (02) 89521273 *E-mail:* info@rugginenti.com *Web Site:* www.rugginenti.com, pg 406

Ruh ve Madde Yayinlari ve Saglik Hizmetleri AS (Turkey) *Tel:* (0212) 2431814 *Fax:* (0212) 2520718 *E-mail:* bilyay@bilyay.org.tr *Web Site:* www.ruhvemadde.com, pg 651

Ruhland Verlag Gimblt (Germany) *Tel:* (069) 811768 *Fax:* (069) 811769, pg 277

Verlag an der Ruhr GmbH (Germany) *Tel:* (0208) 4395454 *Fax:* (0208) 4395439 *E-mail:* info@verlagruhr.de *Web Site:* www.verlagruhr.de, pg 277

Rumsby Scientific Publishing (Australia) *Tel:* (02) 98076184 *Fax:* (02) 98076184, pg 40

Runa Press (Ireland) *Tel:* (01) 2801869, pg 363

Rupa & Co (India) *Tel:* (011) 344821; (011) 346305 *Fax:* (011) 327 7294 *E-mail:* rupa@ndb.vsnl.net.in; del.rupaco@axcess.net.in, pg 347

Rupa & Co (India) *Tel:* (011) 3278588; (011) 3272161 *Fax:* (033) 3277294 *E-mail:* rupa@ndb.vsnl.net.in, pg 1317

Rusconi Libri Srl (Italy) *Tel:* (05) 41326306 *Fax:* (05) 41392344 *E-mail:* relazioniesterne@rusconi.it, pg 406

Ruskin Rowe Press (Australia) *Tel:* (02) 9918-8810 *Fax:* (02) 9918-8884, pg 40

The Ruskin Society of London (United Kingdom) *Tel:* (01865) 310987; (01865) 515962 *Fax:* (01865) 240448, pg 1409

Michael Russell Publishing Ltd (United Kingdom) *Tel:* (01953) 887776 *Fax:* (01953) 887762, pg 752

Russian Book Chamber (Russian Federation) *Tel:* (095) 2034653; (095) 2035608 *Fax:* (095) 2982576; (095) 2982590 *E-mail:* chamber@aha.ru *Web Site:* www.bookchamber.ru, pg 1283

Russian State Historical Archives (Russian Federation) *Tel:* (0812) 311-09-26 *Fax:* (0812) 311-22-52, pg 1540

Russkaya Kniga Izdatelstvo (Publishers) (Russian Federation) *Tel:* (095) 2053377 *Fax:* (095) 2053424, pg 548

Russkij Jazyk (Russian Federation) *Tel:* (095) 9239705 *Fax:* (095) 9288906 *Web Site:* www.russyaz.ru, pg 548

K Rustem & Bro (Cyprus) *Tel:* (022) 71041; (022) 71418; (022) 52085, pg 1308

The Rutland Press (United Kingdom) *Tel:* (0131) 229 7545 *Fax:* (0131) 228 2188 *Web Site:* www.rias.org.uk, pg 752

Rux Guru srl (Italy) *Tel:* (075) 5270257; (075) 5270258 *Fax:* (075) 5288244 *E-mail:* ruxinfo@rux-distribuzione.com *Web Site:* www.rux-distribuzione.com, pg 1321

RWS Translations Ltd (United Kingdom) *Tel:* (01753) 480200 *Fax:* (01753) 480280 *E-mail:* rwstrans@rws.com *Web Site:* www.rws.com, pg 1151

RWTH Aachen Hochschulbibliotek (Germany) *Tel:* (0241) 80-944 45 *Fax:* (0241) 80-92 273 *E-mail:* auskunft@bth.rwth-aachen.de *Web Site:* www.rwth-aachen.de; www.bth.rwth-aachen.de, pg 1510

Ryland Peters & Small Ltd (United Kingdom) *Tel:* (020) 7436 9090 *Fax:* (020) 7436 9790 *E-mail:* info@rps.co.uk *Web Site:* www.rylandpeters.com, pg 752

John Rylands University Library of Manchester (United Kingdom) *Tel:* (0161) 275 3751 (Main Library Bldg); (0161) 834 5343 (Deansgate Bldg) *Fax:* (0161) 273 7488 (Main Library Bldg); (0161) 834 5574 (Deansgate Bldg) *E-mail:* special.collections@man.ac.uk *Web Site:* rylibweb.man.ac.uk, pg 1554

Ryosho-Fukyu-Kai Co Ltd (Japan) *Tel:* (03) 3813-1251 *Fax:* (03) 3811-6490 *E-mail:* ryosho@po.iijnet.or.jp, pg 425

Simon Rysavy (Czech Republic) *Tel:* (05) 42 212 052; (05) 42 213 849 *Fax:* (05) 42 216 633 *E-mail:* info@rysavy.cz *Web Site:* www.itn.cz/rysavy-books; www.rysavy.cz, pg 127

Ryvellus Medienagentur Dopfer (Germany) *Tel:* (0681) 372313 *Fax:* (0681) 3904102, pg 277

S/A Tiesiskas informacijas cerfus (Latvia) *Tel:* (02) 7220422 *Fax:* (02) 7213854 *E-mail:* mariss@date.lv, pg 445

Livraria Sa da Costa (Portugal) *Tel:* (021) 346 07 21, pg 1338

Edicioes Joao Sa da Costa Lda (Portugal) *Tel:* (021) 8400428; (021) 571118; (021) 563603 *Fax:* (021) 534194, pg 535

Sa da Costa Livraria (Portugal) *Tel:* (021) 346 07 21; (021) 346 07 23; (021) 346 07 24; (021) 346 07 25 *Fax:* (021) 346 07 22, pg 535

Saar Publishing House (Israel) *Tel:* (03) 5445292 *Fax:* (03) 5445293, pg 371

Saara Buddhi Publication (Sri Lanka), pg 607

Saarbrucker Druckerei und Verlag GmbH (SDV) (Germany) *Tel:* (0681) 66501-0 *Fax:* (0681) 66501-10 *Web Site:* www.sdv-saar.de, pg 277

Saarlaendische Universitaets und Landesbibliothek (Germany) *Tel:* (0681) 3022070 *Fax:* (0681) 3022796 *E-mail:* sulb@sulb.uni-saarland.de *Web Site:* www.sulb.uni-saarland.de, pg 1510

Saatkorn-Verlag GmbH (Germany) *Tel:* (04131) 98 35-02 *Fax:* (04131) 98 35 505 *E-mail:* info@saatkornverlag.de *Web Site:* wwww.saatkorn-verlag.de, pg 277

SAB Schweiz Arbeitsgemeinschaft fuer die Berggebiete (Switzerland) *Tel:* (056) 411079 *Fax:* (056) 413642, pg 633

Sabah Kitaplari (Turkey) *Tel:* (0212) 5028410; (0212) 5028319, pg 651

Sabah State Library (Malaysia) *Tel:* (088) 225865 *Fax:* (088) 270714 *Web Site:* www.ssl.sabah.gov.my, pg 1527

SABDA (India) *Tel:* (0413) 2334980; (0413) 2223328 *Fax:* (0413) 2223328 *E-mail:* sabda@sriaurobindoashram.org *Web Site:* sabda.sriaurobindoashram.org, pg 347

Sabe AG Verlagsinstitut (Switzerland) *Tel:* (01) 2024477 *Fax:* (01) 2021932 *E-mail:* sabeverlag@access.ch, pg 633

Sabe U (Myanmar), pg 1328

SACEM (Societe des Auteurs Copositeurs et Editeurs de Musique) (France) *Tel:* (01) 47 15 47 15 *Fax:* (01) 47 15 47 86 *E-mail:* communication@sacem.fr *Web Site:* www.sacem.fr, pg 1269

Verlag Werner Sachon GmbH & Co (Germany) *Tel:* (08261) 999-0 *Fax:* (08261) 999 391 *E-mail:* info@sachon.de *Web Site:* www.sachon.de, pg 277

Sachse & Heinzelmann Kunst- und Buchhandlung GmbH (Germany) *Tel:* (0511) 360240 *Fax:* (0511) 324167 *E-mail:* info@sachse-heinzelmann.de *Web Site:* www.sachse-heinzelmann.de, pg 1311

Sachsenbuch Verlagsgesellschaft Mbh (Germany) *Tel:* (0341) 9784259; (0341) 9784261 *Fax:* (0341) 9784259, pg 277

Sada, Literaturno-Izdatel'skij Centr (Azerbaijan) *Tel:* (012) 927564 *Fax:* (012) 929843, pg 60

Sadan Publishing Ltd (Israel) *Tel:* (03) 6954402 *Fax:* (03) 6953122, pg 371

Sadeepa Bookshop (Sri Lanka) *Tel:* (011) 686114; (011) 694289; (011) 678043 *Fax:* (011) 683813; (011) 678044 *E-mail:* sadeepabk@itmin.com *Web Site:* www.sadeepabooks.com, pg 1343

Biblioteca Municipala Mihail Sadoveanu (Romania) *Tel:* (01) 2113625 *Fax:* (01) 2113625, pg 1540

Saechsische Landesbibliothek- Staats- und Universitaetsbibliothek Dresden (Germany) *Tel:* (0351) 4677-123 *Fax:* (0351) 4677-111 *E-mail:* direktion@slub-dresden.de *Web Site:* www.tu-dresden.de/slub, pg 1510

Saeculum IO (Romania) *Tel:* (021) 2228597 *Fax:* (021) 3452827; (021) 2228597 *E-mail:* saeculum@tcnet.ro *Web Site:* www.saeculum.ro, pg 542

Saela Shobo (Librairie Ca et La) (Japan) *Tel:* (03) 3268-4261 *Fax:* (03) 3268-4264 *E-mail:* info@saela.co.jp *Web Site:* www.saela.co.jp, pg 425

Saendig Reprint Verlag, Hans-Rainer Wohlwend (Liechtenstein) *Tel:* 232 36 27 *Fax:* 232 36 49 *E-mail:* saendig@adon.li *Web Site:* www.saendig.com, pg 448

J.C. Saez Editor (Chile) *Tel:* (02) 3260104 *E-mail:* jcsaezc@jcsaezeditor.cl *Web Site:* www.jcsaezeditor.cl, pg 100

Univerzita Pavla Jozefa Safarika (Slovakia) *Tel:* (055) 622 26 08 *Fax:* (055) 766 959 *E-mail:* sekretr@kosice.upjs.sk; rektor@kosice.upjs.sk *Web Site:* www.upjs.sk, pg 1543

Klub Saffier (South Africa) *Tel:* (011) 6736725 *Fax:* (011) 6736719, pg 1255

Sagano Shoin (Japan) *Tel:* (075) 391-7686 *Fax:* (075) 391-7321 *E-mail:* sagano@mbox.kyoto-inet.or.jp *Web Site:* www.saganoshoin.co.jp, pg 426

Ratna Sagar Pvt Ltd (India) *Tel:* (011) 7654095; (011) 7654099 *Fax:* (011) 7250787 *E-mail:* rsagar@giasdlo1.vsnl.net.in; rsagar@nda.vsnl.net.in, pg 347

Biblioteca Nazionale Sagarriga Visconti Volpi (Italy) *Tel:* (080) 5212534; (080) 5211298 *Fax:* (080) 5211298 *E-mail:* visconti@librari.beniculturali.it, pg 1521

SAGE Publications India Pvt Ltd (India) *Tel:* (011) 2649 1290 *Fax:* (011) 2649 2117 *E-mail:* sage@vsnl.com; marketing@indiasage.com; editors@indiasage.com *Web Site:* www.indiasage.com, pg 347

SAGE Publications Ltd (United Kingdom) *Tel:* (020) 7374 8500; (020) 7374 0645 (customer service) *Fax:* (020) 7374 8600 *E-mail:* info@sagepub.co.uk *Web Site:* www.sagepub.co.uk, pg 753

SAGEP Libri & Comunicazione Srl (Italy) *Tel:* (010) 593355 *Fax:* (010) 581713 *E-mail:* info@sagep.it *Web Site:* www.sagep.it, pg 406

Il Saggiatore (Italy) *Tel:* (02) 202301 *Fax:* (02) 29513061 *E-mail:* stampa@saggiatore.it *Web Site:* www.saggiatore.it, pg 406

Verlag Otto Sagner (Germany) *Tel:* (089) 54 218-0 *Fax:* (089) 54 218-218 *E-mail:* postmaster@kubon-sagner.de *Web Site:* www.kubon-sagner.de, pg 278

Sagra-D C Luzzatto Livreiros, Editores e Distribuidores Ltda (Brazil) *Tel:* (051) 3227 5222 *Fax:* (051) 3227 4438 *E-mail:* atendimento@sagra-luzzatto.com.br *Web Site:* www.sagra-luzzatto.com.br, pg 1304

Sahasrara Publications (India) *Tel:* (011) 2432617 *E-mail:* sahasrarapublications@yahoo.co.in, pg 348

Edition Sahel (Senegal) *Tel:* 212164, pg 551

Sahitya Akademi (India) *Tel:* (011) 3386626; (011) 3735297; (011) 3364207 (sales); (011) 3386629 *Fax:* (011) 3382428; (011) 3364207 *E-mail:* sesy@ndl.vsnl.net.in, pg 348

Sahitya Akademi (India) *Tel:* (011) 3386626; (011) 3386627; (011) 3386628; (011) 3386629; (011) 3387386; (011) 3386088 *Fax:* (011) 3382428 *Web Site:* www.sahitya-akademi.org, pg 1401

Sahitya Akademi Library (India) *Tel:* (011) 3386626; (011) 3387386; (011) 3386088 *Fax:* (011) 3382428 *E-mail:* secy@sahitya-akademi.org *Web Site:* www.sahitya-akademi.org, pg 1516

Sahitya Pravarthaka Co-operative Society Ltd (India) *Tel:* (0481) 4111; (0481) 4112, pg 348

SAIE Editrice SRL (Italy) *Tel:* (011) 871022 *Fax:* (011) 830826 *Web Site:* www.culturitalia.uibk.ac.at, pg 406

Saiensu-Sha Co Ltd (Japan) *Tel:* (03) 5474-8500 *Fax:* (03) 5474-8900 *E-mail:* rikei@saiensu.co.jp, pg 426

Saik Wah Press (Pte) Ltd (Singapore) *Tel:* 6292 8759 *Fax:* 6296 0638 *E-mail:* sales@saikwah.com.sg *Web Site:* www.saikwah.com.sg, pg 1161

The Sailor Publishing Co, Ltd (Japan) *Tel:* (03) 3846-2955 *Fax:* (03) 3846-0452, pg 426

Sainsbury Publishing Ltd (United Kingdom) *Tel:* (01636) 830499 *Fax:* (01636) 830175, pg 753

Saint Andrew Press (United Kingdom) *Tel:* (0131) 225 5722 *Fax:* (0131) 220 3113 *E-mail:* standrewpress@cofscotland.org.uk *Web Site:* www.churchofscotland.org.uk, pg 753

St Andrew's Biblical Theological College (Russian Federation) *Tel:* (095) 2702200 *Fax:* (095) 2707644 *E-mail:* standrews@standrews.ru *Web Site:* www.standrews.ru, pg 548

Editions Saint-Augustin (Switzerland) *Tel:* (024) 486 05 04 *Fax:* (024) 486 05 23 *E-mail:* editions@staugustin.ch, pg 633

St Clair Press (Australia) *Tel:* (02) 9818 1942 *Fax:* (02) 9418 1923 *E-mail:* stclair@australis.net.au *Web Site:* www.stclairpress.com.au, pg 40

St Clement of Ohrid National & University Library (The Former Yugoslav Republic of Macedonia) *Tel:* (02) 3115 177; (02) 3133 418 *Fax:* (02) 3226 846 *E-mail:* kliment@nubsk.edu.mk *Web Site:* www.nubsk.edu.mk, pg 453

Verlag St Gabriel (Austria) *Tel:* (02236) 803-225 *Fax:* (02236) 24483 *E-mail:* zeitschriften.stgabriel@steyler.at@steyler.at *Web Site:* www.steyler.at, pg 57

St George Books (Australia) *Tel:* (08) 9482 9051 *Fax:* (08) 9482 9043, pg 40

St George's Press (United Kingdom) *Tel:* (020) 8504 1199 *Fax:* (020) 8559 0989 *E-mail:* sgp17@aol.com *Web Site:* www.eppingforest.co.uk/stgeorgespress, pg 753

St Jerome Publishing (United Kingdom) *Tel:* (0161) 973 9856 *Fax:* (0161) 905 3498 *E-mail:* stjerome@compuserve.com *Web Site:* www.stjerome.co.uk, pg 753

St Joseph Publications (Australia) *Tel:* (02) 99297344 *Fax:* (02) 91303678; (02) 99297994 *E-mail:* sosjelt@internet-australia.com, pg 40

Saint Mary's Publishing Corp (Philippines) *Tel:* (02) 7119730; (02) 7119743 *Fax:* (02) 7350955, pg 520

Saint Michael's Mission Social Centre (Lesotho), pg 447

Editions Saint-Michel SA (France) *Tel:* (04) 75 87 10 50 *Fax:* (04) 75 87 10 61, pg 183

Saint-Paul (The Democratic Republic of the Congo), pg 114

Librairie Saint-Paul (The Democratic Republic of the Congo) *Tel:* 77726, pg 1307

Editions Saint-Paul (Luxembourg) *Tel:* 49931 *Fax:* 485876, pg 451

Editions Saint-Paul (Switzerland) *Tel:* (026) 4264111 *Fax:* (026) 4264531 *E-mail:* druckerei@st-paul.ch *Web Site:* www.st-paul.ch, pg 633

Editions Saint-Paul SA (France) *Tel:* (01) 39 67 16 00 *Fax:* (01) 30 21 41 95, pg 183

St Pauls (Republic of Korea) *Tel:* (02) 9861361; (02) 9861364 *Fax:* (02) 984-4622 *E-mail:* miari@paolo.net; felix@paolo.net; stpaul@paolo.net *Web Site:* www.paolo.net, pg 442

St Paul's Bibliographies Ltd (United Kingdom) *Tel:* (0130) 386 2258 *Fax:* (0130) 386 2660 *E-mail:* stpauls@stpaulsbib.com *Web Site:* www.oakknoll.com/spbib.html, pg 753

St Pauls Publications (Australia) *Tel:* (02) 9746 2288 *Fax:* (02) 9746 1140 *E-mail:* publications@stpauls.com.au; info@stpauls.com.au; sales@stpauls.com.au *Web Site:* www.stpauls.com.au, pg 40

St Pauls Publishing (United Kingdom) *Tel:* (020) 7978 4300 *Fax:* (020) 7978 4370 *E-mail:* editions@stpauls.org.uk *Web Site:* www.stpauls.ie, pg 753

Saint Publishing (New Zealand) *Tel:* (09) 623-2510 *Fax:* (09) 623-2890 *E-mail:* info@saintpublish.co.nz, pg 501

Bibliotheque Sainte-Genevieve (France) *Tel:* (01) 44 41 97 97 *Fax:* (01) 44 41 97 96 *E-mail:* bsgmail@univ.paris1.fr *Web Site:* www-bsg.univ-paris1.fr, pg 1507

Saints Cyril & Methodius National Library (Bulgaria) *Tel:* (02) 9882811 *Fax:* (02) 8435495 *E-mail:* nl@nationallibrary.bg *Web Site:* www.nationallibrary.bg, pg 1496

Sairaanhoitajien Koulutussaatio (Finland) *Tel:* (09) 5666788 *Fax:* (09) 531504, pg 144

Sajha Prakashan, Co-operative Publishing Organization (Nepal) *Tel:* (01) 5521118, pg 477

The Sakai Agency Inc (Japan) *Tel:* (03) 32951405 *Fax:* (03) 32954366 *E-mail:* sakai@sakaiagency.com, pg 1134

Sakartvelo Publishing House (Georgia) *Tel:* 954201; 952927, pg 190

Sakkoulas Publications SA (Greece) *Tel:* (0210) 33 87 500 *Fax:* (0210) 33 90 075 *E-mail:* info@sakkoulas.gr *Web Site:* www.sakkoulas.gr, pg 312

Salamander Books Ltd (United Kingdom) *Tel:* (020) 7314 1469 *Fax:* (020) 7314 1594 *Web Site:* www.chrysalisbooks.co.uk/books/publisher/salamander, pg 753

Salamandra Consultoria Editorial SA (Brazil) *Tel:* (021) 2406306 *Fax:* (021) 2404775; (021) 5331622 *E-mail:* salprod@openlink.com.br, pg 89

Adriano Salani Editore srl (Italy) *Tel:* (028) 0206624 *Fax:* (027) 2018806 *E-mail:* info@salani.it, pg 406

The Salariya Book Co Ltd (United Kingdom) *Tel:* (01273) 603 306 *Fax:* (01273) 693 857 *E-mail:* salariya@salariya.com *Web Site:* www.salariya.com, pg 753

Saldo Penzugyi Tanacsado es Informatikai Rt (Hungary) *Tel:* (01) 203 8213 *Fax:* (01) 203 8217 *E-mail:* kiado@saldo.datanet.hu, pg 324

Salerno Editrice SRL (Italy) *Tel:* (06) 3608201 *Fax:* (06) 3223132 *E-mail:* info@salernoeditrice.it *Web Site:* www.salernoeditrice.it, pg 406

Salesian Press/Don Bosco Sha (Japan) *Tel:* (03) 3351-7041 *Fax:* (03) 3351-5430, pg 426

Salesiana Publishers Inc (Philippines) *Tel:* (02) 8161506; (02) 889234 *Fax:* (02) 8922154, pg 521

Edicoes Salesianas (Portugal) *Tel:* (022) 565750 *Fax:* (022) 536 58 00 *E-mail:* edisal@clix.pt, pg 535

Salmon Publishing (Ireland) *Tel:* (065) 7081941 *Fax:* (065) 7081941 *E-mail:* info@salmonpoetry.com *Web Site:* www.salmonpoetry.com, pg 363

Biblioteca Municipal Dr Joaquin de Salterain (Uruguay) *Tel:* (02) 95 62 82 *Web Site:* www.mec.gub.uy/biblo.htm, pg 1555

The Saltire Society (United Kingdom) *Tel:* (0131) 556 1836 *Fax:* (0131) 557 1675 *E-mail:* saltire@saltiresociety.org.uk *Web Site:* www.saltiresociety.org.uk, pg 753

Salto Publishers (Greece) *Tel:* (031) 262854 *Fax:* (031) 285879 *E-mail:* saltos@spocrk.net.gr, pg 1314

Saltwater Publications (Australia) *Tel:* (03) 5974 1959 *Fax:* (03) 5974 1959, pg 40

Salvat Editores de Mexico (Mexico) *Tel:* (05) 2034813; (05) 2034393 *Fax:* (05) 5318773 *E-mail:* hachettemex@hachette.ex.com.mx, pg 471

Salvat Editores SA (Spain) *Tel:* (090) 2117547 *Fax:* (093) 4955710 *E-mail:* infosalvat@salvat.com *Web Site:* www.salvat.es, pg 598

Editorial Miguel A Salvatella SA (Spain) *Tel:* (093) 2189026 *Fax:* (093) 2177437 *E-mail:* editorial@salvatella.com *Web Site:* www.salvatella.com, pg 598

Salvationist Publishing & Supplies Ltd (United Kingdom) *Tel:* (020) 7367 6570; (020) 7367 6580 (mail orders) *Fax:* (020) 7367 6589 *E-mail:* mail_order@sp-s.co.uk *Web Site:* www.archive.salvationarmy.org.uk, pg 754

Editions Salvator Sarl (France) *Tel:* (01) 53 10 38 38 *Fax:* (01) 53 10 38 39 *E-mail:* salvator.editions@wanadoo.fr, pg 183

Salvioni arti grafiche SA (Switzerland) *Tel:* (091) 8211111 *Fax:* (091) 8211112, pg 633

Salvy Editeur (France) *Tel:* (01) 43 25 74 40 *Fax:* (01) 46 33 56 21, pg 183

Verlag der Salzburger Druckerei (Austria) *Tel:* (0662) 873507-56 *Fax:* (0662) 873507-62 *E-mail:* verlag@salzburger-druckerei.at, pg 57

Salzburger Kulturvereinigung (Austria) *Tel:* (0662) 845346 *Fax:* (0662) 842665 *E-mail:* kulturvereinigung@salzburg.co.at *Web Site:* www.salzburg.com/kulturvereinigung, pg 57

Salzburger Nachrichten Verlagsgesellschaft mbH & Co KG (Austria) *Tel:* (0662) 8373-0; (0662) 8373-210 *Fax:* (0662) 8373-210 *E-mail:* anzeigen@salzburg.com *Web Site:* www.salzburg.com, pg 57

Eugen Salzer-Verlag GmbH & Co KG (Germany) *Tel:* (07131) 68294 *Fax:* (07131) 171331, pg 278

Sam Woode Ltd (Ghana) *Tel:* (021) 305287 *Fax:* (021) 310482 *E-mail:* samwoode@ghana.com, pg 304

Saman Saha Madara Publishers (Sri Lanka) *Tel:* (01) 2862055 *Fax:* (01) 2868071 *E-mail:* prince@eureka.lk, pg 607

Samaya SRL (Italy) *Tel:* (0789) 750039 *Fax:* (0789) 750081 *E-mail:* info@benesseresardegna.com, pg 406

Samayawardena Printers Publishers & Booksellers (Sri Lanka) *Tel:* (01) 694682 *Fax:* (01) 698977; (01) 683525 *E-mail:* samaya@applestr.lk, pg 607

Sambandet Forlag (Norway) *Tel:* 55317963 *Fax:* 55310944 *E-mail:* vestlandskes.bokhandel@c2i.net, pg 510

Samdistribution AB (Sweden) *Tel:* (08) 696 80 00 *Fax:* (08) 696 83 73 *E-mail:* samdistribution@bok.bonnier.se *Web Site:* www.bok.bonnier.se, pg 1344

Samfundet De Nio (Sweden) *Tel:* (08) 411 15 42 *Fax:* (08) 21 19 15 *Web Site:* www.samfundetdenio.com, pg 1405

Samfundslitteratur (Denmark) *Tel:* 38153880 *Fax:* 35357822 *E-mail:* samfundslitteratur@sl.cbs.dk; slforlag@sl.cbs.dk *Web Site:* www.samfundslitteratur.dk, pg 134

Samho Music Publishing Co Ltd (Republic of Korea) *Tel:* (02) 512-3578 *Fax:* (02) 512-3594 *E-mail:* webmaster@samhomusic.com *Web Site:* www.samhomusic.com, pg 442

Samhwa Publishing Co Ltd (Republic of Korea) *Tel:* (02) 7766687 *Fax:* (02) 7732993, pg 442

Samkaleen Prakashan (India) *Tel:* (011) 3523520; (011) 3518197, pg 348

Samkwang Publishing Co (Republic of Korea) *Tel:* (02) 3237275 *Fax:* (02) 3251153, pg 442

Samlerens Bogklub (Denmark) *Tel:* 70 11 00 33 *Fax:* 70 11 01 33 *E-mail:* samlerens-bogklub@gyldendal.dk *Web Site:* www.samlerens-bogklub.dk, pg 1252

Samlerens Forlag A/S (Denmark) *Tel:* 3341 1800 *Fax:* 3341 1801 *E-mail:* samleren@samleren.dk *Web Site:* www.samleren.dk, pg 134

Verlag fuer Sammler (Austria) *Tel:* (0316) 47 22 30 *Fax:* (0316) 67 39 87 *E-mail:* ssu@literaturhaus.at *Web Site:* www.literaturhaus.at/buch/verlagsportraits/sammler.html, pg 57

Samseong Publishing Co Ltd (Republic of Korea) *Tel:* (02) 3470-6852 *Fax:* (02) 3452-2907, pg 442

Samsom BedrijfsInformatie BV (Netherlands) *Tel:* 0172 466633 *Fax:* 0172 475933 *E-mail:* info@kluwer.nl *Web Site:* www.kluwer.nl, pg 488

Samsprak Forlags AB (Sweden) *Tel:* (019) 13 24 45 *Fax:* (019) 18 72 55 *E-mail:* info@samsprak.se *Web Site:* www.samsprak.se, pg 615

San Carlos Publications (Philippines) *Tel:* (032) 253-1000 *Fax:* (032) 255-4341 *E-mail:* uscjournals@lycos.com, pg 521

Editoriale San Giusto SRL Edizioni Parnaso (Italy) *Tel:* (040) 370200 *Fax:* (040) 3728970 *E-mail:* info@edizioniparnaso.it *Web Site:* www.edizioniparnaso.it, pg 406

Edizioni San Lorenzo (Italy) *Tel:* (0522) 323140 *Fax:* (0522) 323140 *E-mail:* redazione@edizioni-sanlorenzo.it *Web Site:* www.edizioni-sanlorenzo.it, pg 407

Editrice San Marco SRL (Italy) *Tel:* (035) 940178 *Fax:* (035) 944385 *E-mail:* info@editricesanmarco.it *Web Site:* www.editricesanmarco.it, pg 407

Editorial San Martin (Spain) *Tel:* (091) 8599964 *Fax:* (091) 8599964, pg 598

San Min Book Co Ltd (Taiwan, Province of China) *Tel:* (02) 25006600 *Fax:* (02) 25064000 *E-mail:* editor@sanmin.com.tw *Web Site:* www.sanmin.com.tw, pg 641

San Pablo (Argentina) *Tel:* (011) 5555-2400; (011) 555-2401 *Fax:* (011) 5555-2425 *E-mail:* sobicain@san-pablo.com.ar *Web Site:* www.san-pablo.com.ar, pg 9

San Pablo Ediciones (Spain) *Tel:* (091) 7425113 *Fax:* (091) 7425723 *E-mail:* dir.editorial@sanpablo-ssp.es *Web Site:* www.sanpablo-ssp.es, pg 598

Libreria San Pablo (Chile) *Tel:* (02) 698 9145 *Fax:* (02) 671 6884 *E-mail:* alameda@san-pablo.cl *Web Site:* www.san-pablo.cl, pg 1305

Edizioni San Paolo SRL (Italy) *Tel:* (02) 660751 *Fax:* (02) 66075211 *E-mail:* sanpaoloedizioni@stpauls.it, pg 407

Ediciones San Pio X (Spain) *Tel:* (091) 726.28.17; (091) 355 2727 *Fax:* (091) 726.28.17 *E-mail:* espx@planalfa.es, pg 599

Simone Sanchez (French Polynesia) *Tel:* (0689) 533260, pg 190

Forlaget Sanctus (Metodistkyrkans Forlag) (Sweden) *Tel:* (08) 31 55 70 *Fax:* (08) 31 55 79, pg 615

Editions Sand et Tchou SA (France) *Tel:* (01) 44 55 37 50 *Fax:* (01) 40 20 99 74 *E-mail:* info@editions-menges.com, pg 184

Erik Sandberg (Norway) *Tel:* 22335555 *Fax:* 22413562, pg 510

Sandila Import-Export Handels-GmbH (Germany) *Tel:* (07764) 93970 *Fax:* (07764) 939739 *E-mail:* info@sandila.de *Web Site:* www.sandila.de, pg 1311

Sandpiper Books Ltd (United Kingdom) *Tel:* (020) 8767 7421 *Fax:* (020) 8682 0280 *E-mail:* enquiries@sandpiper.co.uk, pg 1353

Sandviks Bokforlag (Norway) *Tel:* (051) 44 00 00 *Fax:* (051) 44 00 99 *Web Site:* www.sandviks.com, pg 510

Lennart Sane Agency AB (Spain) *Tel:* (0952) 834180 *Fax:* (0952) 833196 *E-mail:* lennart.sane@telia.com, pg 1136

Lennart Sane Agency AB (Sweden) *Tel:* (0454) 123 56 *Fax:* (0454) 149 20 *E-mail:* lennart.sane@telia.com, pg 1137

Sane Toregard Agency (Sweden) *Tel:* (0454) 123 56 *Fax:* (0454) 149 20, pg 1137

Sang Choy International Pte Ltd (Singapore) *Tel:* (065) 6289 0829 *Fax:* (065) 6282 7673 *E-mail:* marketing@sc-international.com.sg *Web Site:* www.sc-international.com.sg, pg 1182

Editions Sang de la Terre (France) *Tel:* (01) 42 82 08 16 *Fax:* (01) 48 74 14 88 *E-mail:* editeur@sangdelaterre.com *Web Site:* www.sangdelaterre.com, pg 184

Sang-e-Meel Publications (Pakistan) *Tel:* (042) 7220100; (042) 7228143; (042) 7667970 *Fax:* (042) 7245101 *E-mail:* smp@sang-e-meel.com *Web Site:* www.sang-e-meel.com, pg 514

Sangam Books Ltd (United Kingdom) *Tel:* (020) 7377-6399 *Fax:* (020) 7375-1230 *E-mail:* goatony@aol.com, pg 754

Sangdad Publishing Company Ltd (Thailand) *Tel:* (02) 5385553; (02) 5387576 *Fax:* (02) 559-2643; (02) 5381499 *E-mail:* sangdad@asianet.co.th, pg 645

Sangster's Book Stores Ltd (Jamaica) *Tel:* (876) 922-3648; (876) 922-3640 *Toll Free Tel:* 888-269-2665 *Fax:* (876) 922-3813 *E-mail:* info@sangstersbooks.com *Web Site:* www.sangstersbooks.com, pg 1321

Sangyo-Tosho Publishing Co Ltd (Japan) *Tel:* (03) 3261-7821 *Fax:* (03) 3239-2178 *E-mail:* info@san-to.co.jp *Web Site:* www.san-to.co.jp, pg 426

Sankt-Johannis-Druckerei (Germany) *Tel:* (07821) 581-0 *Fax:* (07821) 581-26 *Web Site:* www.medienverbaende.de, pg 1155

Verlag der Sankt-Johannis-Druckerei C Schweickhardt (Germany) *Tel:* (07821) 5810 *Fax:* (07821) 58126 *E-mail:* johannis-druck@t-online.de *Web Site:* www.johannis-verlag.de, pg 278

Sankt-Peterburgskogo Gosudarstvennogo Universiteta (Russian Federation) *Tel:* (0812) 3262000 *Fax:* (0812) 2182741 *E-mail:* office@inform.pu.ru *Web Site:* www.spbu.ru, pg 1540

Sankyo Publishing Company Ltd (Japan) *Tel:* (03) 3264-5711 *Fax:* (03) 3264-5713, pg 426

Sanra Book Trust (Bulgaria) *Tel:* (02) 665124; (02) 9549481 *Fax:* (02) 9549871, pg 96

Sanseido Bookstore Ltd (Japan) *Tel:* (03) 3896 6332 *Fax:* (03) 5839 0292 *E-mail:* fbook_stock@mail.books-sanseido.co.jp *Web Site:* www.books-sanseido.co.jp, pg 1322

Sanseido Co Ltd (Japan) *Tel:* (03) 3230-9404 *Fax:* (03) 3230-9569 *Web Site:* www.sanseido-publ.co.jp/, pg 426

Sanshusha Publishing Co, Ltd (Japan) *Tel:* (03) 3842-1711 *Fax:* (03) 3845-3965 *E-mail:* info@sanshusha.co.jp *Web Site:* www.sanshusha.co.jp, pg 426

Sansoni-RCS Libri (Italy) *Tel:* (02) 50951 *Fax:* (02) 5065361 *E-mail:* sansoni@rcs.it, pg 407

Sant Jordi Asociados Agencia (Spain) *Tel:* (093) 2240107 *Fax:* (093) 2254539 *E-mail:* info@santjordi-asociados.com *Web Site:* www.santjordi-asociados.com, pg 1136

Libreria Santa Fe (Argentina) *Tel:* (011) 4824-5005; (011) 4829-2545 (virtual store) *Fax:* (011) 824-7932 *E-mail:* info@lsf.com.ar *Web Site:* www.lsf.com.ar; www.libreriasantafe.com, pg 1297

Editions du Santal (New Caledonia) *Tel:* (0687) 262533 *Fax:* (0687) 262533 *E-mail:* santal@offratel.nc, pg 493

Graficas Santamaria SA (Spain) *Tel:* (0945) 229100 *Fax:* (0945) 246393 *E-mail:* grsantamaria@sea.es; grsantamaria@graficassantamaria.com *Web Site:* www.graficassantamaria.com, pg 1162, 1182, 1223

Universidad de Santiago de Compostela (Spain) *Tel:* (0981) 593 500 *Fax:* (0981) 593 963 *E-mail:* spublic@usc.es, pg 599

Editorial Santiago Rueda (Argentina) *Tel:* (011) 4611-9174, pg 9

Editorial Santillana (Mexico) *Tel:* (05) 6887566; (05) 6888227; (05) 6888966 *Fax:* (05) 6042304 *E-mail:* mexico@santillana.com.mx *Web Site:* www.gruposantillana.com, pg 471

Grupo Santillana (Mexico) *Tel:* (05) 6888966; (05) 6887566; (05) 6888227 *Fax:* (05) 6042304 *E-mail:* mexico@santillana.com.mx *Web Site:* www.gruposantillana.com, pg 471

Editorial Santillana SA (Colombia) *Tel:* (01) 635 12 00 *Fax:* (01) 236 93 82 *E-mail:* alfaquar@latino.net.co *Web Site:* www.santillana.com.co, pg 112

Biblioteca Municipal de Santo Domingo (Dominican Republic), pg 1502

Livraria Santos Editora Comercio e Importacao Ltda (Brazil) *Tel:* (011) 574-1200 *Fax:* (011) 573-8774 *E-mail:* editorasantos@terra.com.br, pg 90

Editora Santuario (Brazil) *Tel:* (012) 3104-2000 *Fax:* (012) 565 2141 *E-mail:* vendas@redemptor.com.br *Web Site:* www.redemptor.com.br, pg 90

Santype International Ltd (United Kingdom) *Tel:* (01722) 334261 *Fax:* (01722) 333171 *E-mail:* info@santype.com *Web Site:* www.santype.com, pg 1185

Sanyo Shuppan Boeki Co Inc (Japan) *Tel:* (03) 5351-3021 *Fax:* (03) 5351-3028, pg 426

Sanyo Shuppan Boeki Co Inc (Japan) *Tel:* (03) 5351 3021 *Fax:* (03) 5351 3028 *E-mail:* ssb01@mx1.alpha-web.ne.jp, pg 1323

Sapere 2000 SRL (Italy) *Tel:* (06) 4465363 *Fax:* (06) 4465363 *E-mail:* sapere2000@flshnet.it, pg 407

Sapes Trust Ltd (Zimbabwe) *Tel:* (04) 252962; (04) 252963; (04) 252965 *Fax:* (04) 252963 *E-mail:* administrator@sapes.org.zw *Web Site:* www.sapes.co.zw, pg 784

Paul Sappl, Schulbuch- und Lehrmittelverlag (Austria) *Tel:* (05372) 64300 *Fax:* (05372) 64300-17, pg 57

Saqi Books (United Kingdom) *Tel:* (020) 7221 9347 *Fax:* (020) 7229 7492 *E-mail:* info@saqibooks.com *Web Site:* www.saqibooks.com, pg 754

Saqi Books (United Kingdom) *Tel:* (020) 7229 8543; (020) 7221 9347 *Fax:* (020) 7229 7492 *E-mail:* saqibooks@dial.pipex.com *Web Site:* www.saqibooks.com, pg 1353

Saraiva SA, Livreiros Editores (Brazil) *Tel:* (011) 861-3344 *Fax:* (011) 861-3308 *E-mail:* diretoria.editora@editorasaraiva.com.br *Web Site:* www.editorasaraiva.com.br, pg 90

Saraiva SA, Livreiros Editores (Brazil) *Tel:* (011) 3933-3300 *Fax:* (011) 3662-2062 *E-mail:* atendimento@livrariasaraiva.com.br *Web Site:* www.livrariasaraiva.com.br; www.saraiva.com.br, pg 1304

Sarasavi Book Shop Pvt Ltd (Sri Lanka) *Tel:* (01) 2852519; (01) 2820983; (01) 4304564 *Fax:* (01) 2509503; (01) 2821454 *E-mail:* sarasavi@slt.lk *Web Site:* www.sarasavi.lk, pg 1343

Saraswati Publishers & Distributors (India), pg 348

Saray Medikal Yayin Tic Ltd Sti (Turkey) *Tel:* (0232) 3394969 *Fax:* (0232) 3733700 *E-mail:* eozkarahan@novell.cs.eng.dev.edu.tr, pg 651

Sardini Editrice (Italy) *Tel:* (030) 7750430 *Fax:* (030) 7254348 *E-mail:* sardini@intelligenza.it *Web Site:* www.sardini.it, pg 407

M C Sarkar & Sons (P) Ltd (India) *Tel:* (033) 2417490, pg 348

Editions Le Sarment (France) *Tel:* (01) 45 49 82 00 *Fax:* (01) 42 22 40 17 *E-mail:* cremond@editions-fayard.fr *Web Site:* www.editions-fayard.fr, pg 184

Saros International Publishers (Nigeria) *Tel:* (084) 331763 *Fax:* (084) 331763, pg 507

Sarpay Beikman Book Club (Myanmar) *Tel:* (01) 83611, pg 1254

Sarpay Beikman Bookshop (Myanmar) *Tel:* (01) 83611; (01) 16611, pg 1328

Sarpay Beikman Public Library (Myanmar) *Tel:* (01) 83611, pg 476

Sarpay Lawka (Myanmar) *Tel:* (01) 274391; (01) 285166, pg 1328

Sarvier - Editora de Livros Medicos Ltda (Brazil) *Tel:* (011) 571-4570 *Fax:* (011) 571-3439, pg 90

Sarvodaya Vishva Lekha (Sri Lanka) *Tel:* (01) 714820; (01) 714829; (01) 731601 *Fax:* (01) 738932 *E-mail:* sarvs101@sri.lanka.net, pg 1162

Sasa Sema Publications Ltd (Kenya) *Tel:* (020) 550400; 722-200544; 734-600887 *E-mail:* sasasema@wananchi.com *Web Site:* www.sasasema.com, pg 435

Sasavona Publishers & Booksellers (South Africa) *Tel:* (011) 4032502 *Fax:* (011) 3397274, pg 568

Sassafras Verlag (Germany) *Tel:* (02151) 787770 *Fax:* (02151) 771302, pg 278

Sasta Sahitya Mandal (India) *Tel:* (011) 3310505, pg 348

Sastra Hudaya PT (Indonesia) *Tel:* (021) 3904223, pg 356

Sat Sahitya Prakashan (India) *Tel:* (011) 3276316, pg 348

Sri Satguru Publications (India) *Tel:* (011) 716497; (011) 7434930 *Fax:* (011) 7227336 *E-mail:* ibcindia@vsnl.com *Web Site:* www.indianbookscentre.com, pg 348

Satprakashan Sanchar Kendra (India) *Tel:* (0731) 475744; (0731) 475637 *Fax:* (0731) 47573 *E-mail:* sskin@sancharnet.in, pg 348

Satrap Publishing & Translation (United Kingdom) *Tel:* (020) 8748 9397 *Fax:* (020) 8748 9394 *E-mail:* satrap@btconnect.com *Web Site:* www.satrap.co.uk, pg 1151

Sattva Kunst Verlag (Germany) *Tel:* (08028) 90 68-0 *Fax:* (08028) 90 68-10; (08028) 90 68-20, pg 278

Oy Satusiivet - Sagovingar AB (Lasten Parhaat Kirjat) (Finland) *Tel:* (09) 6933267 *Fax:* (09) 6944186, pg 1309

Satyr-Verlag Dr Humbel (Switzerland) *Tel:* (01) 2810845 *Fax:* (01) 2810846, pg 633

Saudi Publishing & Distributing House (Saudi Arabia) *Tel:* (03) 8334158 *Fax:* (03) 8335520 *E-mail:* info@spdh-sa.com *Web Site:* www.spdh-sa.com, pg 550

I H Sauer Verlag GmbH (Germany) *Tel:* (06221) 9060 *Fax:* (06221) 906259 *E-mail:* sauer-verlag@ruw.de *Web Site:* www.ruw-ruw.de, pg 278

Sauerlaender AG (Switzerland) *Tel:* (062) 836 86 26 *Fax:* (062) 836 86 20 *E-mail:* sauerlaender@sauerlaender.ch *Web Site:* www.sauerlaender.ch, pg 633

Verlag Sauerlaender GmbH (Germany) *Tel:* (069) 942118-0 *Fax:* (069) 412099, pg 278

J D Sauerlaender's Verlag (Germany) *Tel:* (069) 555217 *Fax:* (069) 5964344 *E-mail:* j.d.sauerlaenders.verlag@t-online.de *Web Site:* www.sauerlaender-verlag.com, pg 278

K G Saur Verlag GmbH, A Gale/Thomson Learning Company (Germany) *Tel:* (089) 76902-0 *Fax:* (089) 76902-150 *E-mail:* saur.info@thomson.com *Web Site:* www.saur.de, pg 278

Sauramps Medical (France) *Tel:* (04) 67 63 68 80 *Fax:* (04) 67 52 59 05 *E-mail:* sauramps.medical@livres-medicaux.com *Web Site:* www.livres-medicaux.com, pg 184

Librairie Sauramps Medical (France) *Tel:* (04) 67636880 *Fax:* (04) 67525905 *E-mail:* librairie-sauramps-medical@wanadoo.fr *Web Site:* www.livres.medicaux.com, pg 1310

Editions Andre Sauret SA (Monaco) *Tel:* (093) 506794 *Fax:* (093) 307104, pg 474

Steve Savage Publishers Ltd (United Kingdom) *Tel:* (020) 7770 6083 *E-mail:* mail@savagepublishers.com *Web Site:* www.savagepublishers.com, pg 754

Savannah Editions SARL (New Caledonia) *Tel:* (0687) 252919 *Fax:* (0687) 282470, pg 493

Savannah Publications (United Kingdom) *Tel:* (020) 8244 4350 *Fax:* (020) 8244 2448 *E-mail:* savpub@dircon.co.uk *Web Site:* www.savannah-publications.com, pg 754

Savez Inzenjera i Tehnicara Jugoslavije (Serbia and Montenegro) *Tel:* (011) 3243653; (011) 3243652 *Fax:* (011) 3243652 *E-mail:* internet@eunet.yu, pg 553

Savitri Books Ltd (United Kingdom) *Tel:* (020) 7436 9932 *Fax:* (020) 7580 6330, pg 754

Savremena Administracija (Serbia and Montenegro) *Tel:* (011) 668567; (011) 661913; (011) 667436 *Fax:* (011) 667436, pg 553

Sawan Kirpal Publications (India) *Tel:* (011) 7110722; (011) 7222244 *Fax:* (011) 7210720, pg 348

SAWD Publications (United Kingdom) *Tel:* (01795) 472 262 *Fax:* (01795) 422 633 *E-mail:* wainman@sawd. demon.co.uk, pg 754

Sax-Verlag Beucha (Germany) *Tel:* (034292) 75210 *Fax:* (034292) 75220 *E-mail:* info@sax-verlag.de *Web Site:* www.sax-verlag.de, pg 278

The Dorothy L Sayers Society (United Kingdom) *Tel:* (01273) 833444 *Fax:* (01273) 835988 *E-mail:* info@sayers.org.uk *Web Site:* www.sayers.org.uk, pg 1409

The Sayle Literary Agency (United Kingdom) *Tel:* (020) 7263 8681 *Fax:* (020) 7561 0529, pg 1143

Sayrols Editorial SA de CV (Mexico) *Tel:* (05) 660-3535 *Fax:* (05) 687-4699 *E-mail:* ventas@sayrols.com.mx *Web Site:* www.sayrols.com.mx, pg 471

SB Publications (United Kingdom) *Tel:* (01323) 893498 *Fax:* (01323) 893860 *E-mail:* sales@sbpublications.swinternet.co.uk, pg 754

SBT Professional Publications (Malaysia) *Tel:* (03) 80265811; (03) 80235663 *Fax:* (03) 8023566; (03) 80265999 *E-mail:* admin@sbtpp.com *Web Site:* www.sbtpp.com, pg 458

SBW Publishers (India) *Tel:* (011) 3279603, pg 348

Scaillet, SA (Belgium) *Tel:* (071) 516335 *Fax:* (071) 511795, pg 73

Editions Scala (France) *Tel:* (01) 49 29 42 25 *Fax:* (01) 49 29 99 33 *E-mail:* editions.scala@wanadoo.fr *Web Site:* www.ldj.tm.fr/editeurs/editeurs/scala.htm, pg 184

Scala Group spa (Italy) *Tel:* (055) 623311 *Fax:* (055) 6233280 *E-mail:* info@scalagroup.com *Web Site:* www.scalagroup.it, pg 407

Scan-Globe A/S (Denmark) *Tel:* 46 18 54 00 *Fax:* 46 18 52 70 *E-mail:* info@scanglobe.dk, pg 134

Scandinavia Publishing House (Denmark) *Tel:* 35 31 03 30 *Fax:* 35 31 03 34 *E-mail:* info@scanpublishing.dk *Web Site:* www.scanpublishing.dk, pg 134

scaneg Verlag (Germany) *Tel:* (089) 759 33 36 *Fax:* (089) 759 39 14 *E-mail:* verlag@scaneg.de *Web Site:* www.scaneg.de, pg 278

Scanvik Books Import ApS (Denmark) *Tel:* 3312 7766 *Fax:* 3391 2882 *E-mail:* mail@scanvik.dk; scanvik@bog.dk *Web Site:* www.scanvik.dk, pg 1130

Scanvik Books Import ApS (Denmark) *Tel:* 3312 7766 *Fax:* 3391 2882 *E-mail:* mail@scanvik.dk *Web Site:* www.scanvik.dk, pg 1308

Lo Scarabeo Srl (Italy) *Tel:* (011) 283793; (011) 283978 *Fax:* (011) 280756 *E-mail:* info@loscarabeo.com *Web Site:* www.loscarabeo.com, pg 407

Scarthin Books (United Kingdom) *Tel:* (01629) 823272 *Fax:* (01629) 825094 *E-mail:* clare@scarthinbooks.demon.co.uk *Web Site:* www.scarthinbooks.com; www.books.co.uk, pg 754

Scena (Lithuania) *Tel:* (02) 751 828; (02) 614 145 *Fax:* (02) 610 814, pg 449

De Schaar/Geknipt Papier (Belgium) *Tel:* (09) 225 5414 *Fax:* (09) 225 9724 *E-mail:* geknipt@skynet.be, pg 73

Verlag Th Schaefer im Vicentz Verlag KG (Germany) *Tel:* (0511) 87575-075 *Fax:* (0511) 87575-079, pg 278

Verlag Anke Schaefer (Germany) *Tel:* (06439) 7870, pg 278

Schaeffer-Poeschel Verlag fuer Wirtschaft Steuern Recht (Germany) *Tel:* (0711) 2194-0 *Fax:* (0711) 2194-119 *E-mail:* info@schaeffer-poeschel.de *Web Site:* www.schaeffer-poeschel.de, pg 279

Schangrila Verlags und Vertriebs GmbH (Germany) *Tel:* (08343) 581 *Fax:* (08343) 657 *E-mail:* info@schangrila.com *Web Site:* www.schangrila.com, pg 279

Schapen Edition, H W Louis (Germany) *Tel:* (0531) 360921 *Fax:* (0531) 363190 *E-mail:* schapen.edition@t-online.de, pg 279

M & H Schaper GmbH & Co KG (Germany) *Tel:* (05181) 8009-0 *Fax:* (05181) 8009-33 *E-mail:* info@schaper-verlag.de *Web Site:* www.schaper-verlag.de, pg 279

Schattauer GmbH Verlag fuer Medizin und Naturwissenschaften (Germany) *Tel:* (0711) 2 29 87-0 *Fax:* (0711) 2 29 87-50 *E-mail:* info@schattauer.de *Web Site:* www.schattauer.de, pg 279

Guillermo Schavelzon (Argentina) *Tel:* (011) 48 13 84 20 *Fax:* (011) 48 13 28 76 *E-mail:* info@schavelzon.com, pg 1129

Schawk (Canada) *Tel:* 416-703-1445 *Fax:* 416-703-1494 *Web Site:* www.schawk.com, pg 1175, 1216

Scheffler-Verlag (Germany) *Tel:* (02330) 1743 *Fax:* (02330) 2281, pg 279

Scheltema (Netherlands) *Tel:* (020) 5231411 *Fax:* (020) 6227684 *E-mail:* scheltema@scheltema.nl; informatie@scheltema.nl *Web Site:* www.scheltema.nl, pg 1329

Schelzky & Jeep, Verlag fuer Reisen und Wissen (Germany) *Tel:* (030) 6939495 *Fax:* (030) 6914697, pg 279

Schena Editore (Italy) *Tel:* (080) 4414681 *Fax:* (080) 4426690 *E-mail:* info@schenaeditore.com *Web Site:* www.schenaeditore.it, pg 407

Dr A Schendl GmbH und Co KG (Austria) *Tel:* (01) 484 17 85-0 *Fax:* (01) 484 17 85-15 *E-mail:* info@schendl.at *Web Site:* www.schendl.at, pg 57

Renate Schenk Verlag (Germany) *Tel:* (0341) 2300825 *Fax:* (0341) 2300826 *E-mail:* schenk-verlag@t-online.de *Web Site:* www.schenk-verlag.de, pg 279

Richard Scherpe Verlag GmbH (Germany) *Tel:* (02151) 539-0 *Fax:* (02151) 505390, pg 279

Scherz Verlag AG (Switzerland) *Tel:* (031) 227337 *Fax:* (031) 3277171, pg 633

Papierfabrik Scheufelen GmbH & Co KG (Germany) *Tel:* (07026) 66-779 *Fax:* (07026) 66-719 *Web Site:* 213.174.48.47/scheufelen/, pg 1155

Chr Schibsteds Forlag A/S (Norway) *Tel:* (022) 863000 *Fax:* (022) 864150 *E-mail:* schibsted.forlag@schibsted.no *Web Site:* www.schibsted-forlag.no, pg 510

Ulrich Schiefer bahn Verlag (Germany) *Tel:* (089) 89020999 *Fax:* (089) 89020087, pg 279

Schiffahrts-Verlag (Germany) *Tel:* (040) 79713-02 *Fax:* (040) 79713-324; (040) 79713-208; (040) 79713-214 *E-mail:* r_spieckermann@hansa-online.de, pg 279

Schild-Verlag GmbH (Germany) *Tel:* (089) 8 64 1189 *Fax:* (089) 8 63 2310, pg 279

Schildts Forlags AB (Finland) *Tel:* (09) 88 70 400 *Fax:* (09) 804 32 57 *E-mail:* schildts@schildts.fi *Web Site:* www.schildts.fi, pg 144

Verlag der Schillerbuchhandlung Hans Banger OHG (Germany) *Tel:* (0221) 46014-0 *Fax:* (0221) 46014-25; (0221) 46014-26 *E-mail:* banger@banger.de *Web Site:* www.banger.de, pg 279

Schillinger Verlag GmbH (Germany) *Tel:* (0761) 33233 *Fax:* (0762) 39055 *E-mail:* schillingerverlag@t-online.de *Web Site:* schillingerverlag.de, pg 279

Paul Schiltz (Belgium) *Tel:* (087) 553271, pg 73

Karin Schindler (Brazil) *Tel:* (011) 5041-9177 *Fax:* (011) 5041-9077 *E-mail:* kschind@terra.com.br, pg 1129

Karin Schindler Representante de Direitos Autorais (Brazil) *Tel:* (011) 241-9177 *Fax:* (011) 241-9077, pg 90

Schirmer/Mosel Verlag GmbH (Germany) *Tel:* (089) 2126700 *Fax:* (089) 338695 *E-mail:* mail@schirmer-mosel.com *Web Site:* www.schirmer-mosel.com, pg 279

Schirner Verlag (Germany) *Tel:* (06151) 29 39 59 *Fax:* (06151) 29 39 87 *E-mail:* verlag@schirner.com *Web Site:* www.schirner.com, pg 280

Schlaepfer & Co AG (Switzerland) *Tel:* (071) 354 64 64 *Fax:* (071) 525126, pg 633

Schlesinger Institute (Israel) *Tel:* (02) 655-5266 *Fax:* (02) 655-5266 *E-mail:* medhal@szmc.org.il *Web Site:* www.szmc.org.il, pg 371

Agora Verlag Manfred Schlosser (Germany) *Tel:* (030) 8545372; (030) 8545915 *Fax:* (030) 8545372 *E-mail:* agora2@gmx.net, pg 280

Thomas Schlueck GmbH (Germany) *Tel:* (05131) 497560 *Fax:* (05131) 497589 *E-mail:* mail@schlueckagent.com *Web Site:* www.schlueckagent.com, pg 1132

Schmetterling Verlag Jorg Hunger und Paul Sander (Germany) *Tel:* (0711) 62 67 79 *Fax:* (0711) 62 69 92 *E-mail:* info@schmetterling-verlag.de *Web Site:* www.schmetterling-verlag.de, pg 280

Schmid Verlag GmbH (Germany) *Tel:* (0941) 21519 *Fax:* (0941) 28766 *E-mail:* info@schmid-verlag.de *Web Site:* www.schmid-verlag.de, pg 280

Verlag Dr Otto Schmidt KG (Germany) *Tel:* (0221) 9 37 38-01 *Fax:* (0221) 9 37 38 931 *E-mail:* info@ottoschmidt.de; verlag@ottoschmidt.de *Web Site:* www.otto-schmidt.de, pg 280

Erich Schmidt Verlag GmbH & Co (Germany) *Tel:* (030) 25 00 85-0 *Fax:* (030) 25 00 85-305 *E-mail:* esv@esvmedien.de *Web Site:* www.erich-schmidt-verlag.de, pg 280

Verlag Hermann Schmidt Universitatsdruckerei GmbH & Co (Germany) *Tel:* (06131) 506030 *Fax:* (06131) 506080 *E-mail:* info@typografie.de *Web Site:* www.typografie.de, pg 280

Schmidt Periodicals GmbH (Germany) *Tel:* (08064) 221 *Fax:* (08064) 557 *E-mail:* schmidt@periodicals.com *Web Site:* www.periodicals.com, pg 280

Max Schmidt-Roemhild Verlag (Germany) *Tel:* (0451) 70 31-01 *Fax:* (0451) 70 31-253 *E-mail:* msr-luebeck@t-online.de *Web Site:* www.schmidt-roemhild.de, pg 280

Wilhelm Schmitz Verlag (Germany) *Tel:* (0641) 877 3939 *Web Site:* www.wilhelm-schmitz-verlag.de, pg 280

Schneekluth Verlag (Germany) *Tel:* (089) 92710 *Fax:* (089) 9271168 *Web Site:* www.schneekluth.de, pg 280

Rudolf Schneider Verlag (Germany) *Tel:* (089) 8113466 *Fax:* (089) 8110619, pg 280

Verlag Schnell und Steiner GmbH (Germany) *Tel:* (0941) 787850 *Fax:* (0941) 7878516 *E-mail:* susvertrieb@t-online.de, pg 281

Schnellmann-Verlag (Switzerland) *Tel:* (055) 2111472 *Fax:* (055) 2111477 *Web Site:* www.dictionaries.ch, pg 633

Andreas Schnider Verlags-Atelier (Austria) *Tel:* (0316) 471302 *Fax:* (0316) 4713024 *E-mail:* bookstore@net.burger.at, pg 57

Schnitzer GmbH & Co KG (Germany) *Tel:* (07724) 9432-0 *Fax:* (07724) 9432-20, pg 281

Schocken Publishing House Ltd (Israel) *Tel:* (03) 5610130 *Fax:* (03) 5622668 *E-mail:* find@schocken.co.il, pg 371

Schoeffling & Co (Germany) *Tel:* (069) 92 07 87-0 *Fax:* (069) 92 07 87-20 *E-mail:* info@schoeffling.de *Web Site:* www.schoeffling.de, pg 281

Bibliotheque Schoelcher (Martinique) *Tel:* 702 667 *Fax:* 724 555 *E-mail:* biblio-schoelcher-dep@cg972.fr, pg 1528

Verlag fuer Schoene Wissenschaften (Switzerland) *Tel:* (061) 7013911 *Fax:* (061) 7011417 *E-mail:* schoene_wissenschaften@bluewin.ch, pg 633

Verlag Hans Schoener GmbH (Germany) *Tel:* (07232) 4007-0 *Fax:* (07232) 4007-99 *E-mail:* info@verlag-schoener.de *Web Site:* www.verlag-schoener.de, pg 281

Ferdinand Schoeningh Verlag GmbH (Germany) *Tel:* (05251) 1275 *Fax:* (05251) 127860; (05251) 127670 *E-mail:* info@schoeningh.de *Web Site:* www.schoeningh.de, pg 281

Schofield & Sims Ltd (United Kingdom) *Tel:* (01484) 607080 *Fax:* (01484) 606815 *E-mail:* post@schofieldandsims.co.uk *Web Site:* www.schofieldandsims.co.uk, pg 754

Scholastic Australia Pty Ltd (Australia) *Tel:* (02) 4328 3555 *Toll Free Tel:* 800-021-233 *Fax:* (02) 4323 3827 *Toll Free Fax:* 800-789-948 *E-mail:* customerservice@scholastic.com.au *Web Site:* www.scholastic.com.au, pg 40

Scholastic Ltd (United Kingdom) *Tel:* (01926) 887799; (01926) 813910 (warehouse) *Fax:* (01926) 883331 *E-mail:* scholastic@tens.co.uk *Web Site:* www.scholastic.co.uk, pg 754

Scholastic Publications Ltd (United Kingdom) *Tel:* (0845) 6039091; (01993) 893475 (outside UK) *Fax:* (0845) 6039092; (01993) 893424 (outside UK) *E-mail:* sbcenquiries@scholastic.co.uk *Web Site:* www.scholastic.co.uk/schoolbookclub, pg 1257

Kurt Scholl (Germany) *Tel:* (06221) 707661, pg 1312

Det Schonbergske Forlag A/S (Denmark) *Tel:* 33 73 35 85 *Fax:* 33 73 35 76 *E-mail:* Schoenberg@nytnordiskforlag.dk *Web Site:* www.nytnordiskforlag.dk, pg 134

School Library Association (United Kingdom) *Tel:* (01793) 791787 *Fax:* (01793) 791786 *E-mail:* info@sla.org.uk *Web Site:* www.sla.org.uk, pg 1573

School of Administration Library (Ghana) *Fax:* (021) 500024 *E-mail:* soa@libr.ug.edu.gh, pg 1512

School of Oriental & African Studies (United Kingdom) *Tel:* (020) 7637 2388 *Fax:* (020) 7436 3844 *E-mail:* md2@soas.ac.uk; aol@soas.ac.uk *Web Site:* www.soas.ac.uk, pg 755

School of Oriental & African Studies Library (United Kingdom) *Tel:* (020) 7637 2388 *Fax:* (020) 7436 3844 *E-mail:* libenquiry@soas.ac.uk *Web Site:* www.soas.ac.uk/library/home.html, pg 1554

School Supplies (NZ) Ltd (New Zealand) *Tel:* (09) 273 9883 *Toll Free Tel:* 800 577 700 *Fax:* (09) 273 9884 *Toll Free Fax:* 800 367 724 *E-mail:* orders@schoolsupplies.co.nz *Web Site:* www.schoolsupplies.co.nz, pg 1330

SchoolPlay Productions Ltd (United Kingdom) *Tel:* (01206) 540111 *Fax:* (01206) 766944 *E-mail:* schoolplay@inglis-house.demon.co.uk *Web Site:* www.schoolplayproductions.co.uk, pg 755

Schott Freres SA (Editeurs de Musique) (Belgium) *Tel:* (02) 5123980 *Fax:* (02) 5142845, pg 73

Schott Musik International GmbH & Co KG (Germany) *Tel:* (06131) 246-0 *Fax:* (06131) 246-211 *Web Site:* www.schott-online.com, pg 54

Schrader Verlag Paul Pietsch Verlage GmbH & Co KG (Germany) *Tel:* (0711) 210 80 12 *Fax:* (0711) 236 04 15 *Web Site:* www.paul-pietsch-verlag.de, pg 281

Verlag Silke Schreiber (Germany) *Tel:* (089) 2710180 *Fax:* (089) 2716957 *E-mail:* metzel@verlag-Silke-schreiber.de *Web Site:* www.verlag-silke-schreiber.de, pg 281

Verlag und Schriftenmission der Evangelischen Gesellschaft Wuppertal (Germany) *Tel:* (0202) 278500 *Fax:* (0202) 2785040, pg 281

Schroedel Schulbuchverlag GmbH (Germany) *Tel:* (0511) 83880 *Fax:* (0511) 8388425 *E-mail:* sco@schroedel.de *Web Site:* www.schroedel.de, pg 281

Schubert & Franzke Gesellschaft mbH (Austria) *Tel:* (02742) 78 501-0 *Fax:* (02742) 78 501-15 *E-mail:* office@schubert-franzke.com *Web Site:* map2web.cc/schubert-franzke, pg 57

A Schudel & Co AG, Verlag (Switzerland) *Tel:* (061) 671011 *Fax:* (061) 671363 *E-mail:* a.schudel@bluewin.ch, pg 633

Walther-Schuecking-Institut fuer Internationales Recht an der Universitaet Kiel (Germany) *Tel:* (0431) 880 2367 *Fax:* (0431) 880 1619 *E-mail:* fb.internat-recht@ub.uni-kiel.de *Web Site:* www.uni-kiel.de/internat-recht, pg 1510

Carl Ed Schuenemann KG (Germany) *Tel:* (0421) 369030 *Fax:* (0421) 3690339 *E-mail:* kontakt@kunstverlag.de *Web Site:* www2.schuenemann-verlag.de, pg 281

Schueren Verlag GmbH (Germany) *Tel:* (06421) 6 30 84; (06421) 6 30 85 *Fax:* (06421) 68 11 90 *E-mail:* info@schueren-verlag.de *Web Site:* www.schueren-verlag.de, pg 281

Verlag Karl Waldemar Schuetz (Germany) *Tel:* (09561) 80780 *Fax:* (09561) 807820, pg 281

Schulthess Polygraphischer Verlag AG (Switzerland) *Tel:* (01) 251 93 36 *Fax:* (01) 261 63 94 *Web Site:* www.schulthess.com, pg 633

Schultz Forlag AB (Sweden) *Fax:* (08) 641 35 36, pg 615

Schultz Information (Denmark) *Tel:* 43632300 *Fax:* 43631969 *E-mail:* schultz@schultz.dk *Web Site:* www.schultz.dk, pg 134

Schulz-Kirchner Verlag GmbH (Germany) *Tel:* (06126) 93200 *Fax:* (06126) 9320-50 *E-mail:* info@schulz-kirchner.de *Web Site:* www.schulz-kirchner.de, pg 282

Verlag R S Schulz GmbH (Germany) *Tel:* (089) 36007-0 *Fax:* (089) 36007-3310 *E-mail:* rss@rss.de *Web Site:* www.rss.de, pg 282

H O Schulze KG (Germany) *Tel:* (09571) 78010 *Fax:* (09571) 78055 *E-mail:* verkauf@schulze-kg.de *Web Site:* www.schulze-kg.de, pg 282

Theodor Schuster (Germany) *Tel:* (0491) 925900 *Fax:* (0491) 9259059 *E-mail:* buchhandlung-Schuster@t-online.de, pg 282

Schuyt & Co Uitgevers en Importeurs BV (Netherlands) *Tel:* (030) 7508273 *Fax:* (030) 7508327 *E-mail:* info@schuytco.nl *Web Site:* www.schuyt-co.nl, pg 1329

Heinrich Schwab Verlag KG (Germany) *Tel:* (05575) 20101 *Fax:* (05575) 4745 *E-mail:* heinrichschwabverlag@aon.at *Web Site:* www.heinrichschwabverlag.de, pg 282

Schwabe & Co AG (Switzerland) *Tel:* (061) 278 95 65 *Fax:* (061) 272 95 66 *E-mail:* verlag@schwabe.ch *Web Site:* www.schwabe.ch, pg 633

Schwabenverlag Aktiengesellschaft (Germany) *Tel:* (0711) 4406-0 *Fax:* (0711) 4406-177 *E-mail:* info@schwabenverlag.de *Web Site:* www.schwabenverlag.de, pg 282

Schwaneberger Verlag GmbH (Germany) *Tel:* (089) 3239302 *Fax:* (089) 3232402 *E-mail:* webmaster@michel.de *Web Site:* www.michel.de, pg 282

Otto Schwartz Fachbochhandlung GmbH (Germany) *Tel:* (0551) 31051 *Fax:* (0551) 372812 *E-mail:* schwartz.stadt@t-online.de, pg 282

Dr Wolfgang Schwarze Verlag (Germany) *Tel:* (0202) 622005; (0202) 622006 *Fax:* (0202) 63631, pg 282

Verlagsbuero Karl Schwarzer (Austria) *Tel:* (01) 548 31 15-0 *Fax:* (01) 548 31 15-39 *E-mail:* verlagsbuero@schwarzer.at *Web Site:* www.schwarzer.at, pg 57

Verlag Schweers + Wall GmbH (Germany) *Tel:* (0241) 87 22 51 *Fax:* (0241) 8 52 06 *E-mail:* schweers.wall@t-online.de, pg 282

Schweizer Buchzentrum (Switzerland) *Tel:* (062) 2092525; (062) 2092644 *Fax:* (062) 2092627; (062) 2092760 *E-mail:* info@sbz.ch *Web Site:* www.sbz.ch, pg 1247

Schweizer Buchzentrum (Switzerland) *Tel:* (062) 476161 *Fax:* (062) 465676, pg 1344

Schweizer Spiegel Verlag Mit (Switzerland) *Tel:* (01) 472195 *Fax:* (01) 7502943, pg 634

E Schweizerbart'sche Verlagsbuchhandlung (Naegele und Obermiller) (Germany) *Tel:* (0711) 3514560 *Fax:* (0711) 351456-99 *E-mail:* mail@schweizerbart.de *Web Site:* www.schweizerbart.de, pg 282

Schweizerische Bibliophilen-Gesellschaft (Switzerland), pg 1405

Schweizerische Landesbibliothek (Bibliotheque nationale suisse) (Switzerland) *Tel:* (031) 322 89 11; (031) 3228979 (Lending Dept); (031) 3228935 (Information) *Fax:* (031) 322 84 63 *E-mail:* IZ-Helvetica@slb.admin.ch *Web Site:* www.snl.ch, pg 1548

Schweizerische Stiftung fuer Alpine Forschungen (Switzerland) *Tel:* (01) 461 01 47 *Fax:* (01) 461 07 11 *E-mail:* mail@alpinfo.ch *Web Site:* www.alpineresearch.ch; www.alpinfo.ch, pg 634

Schweizerische Vereinigung fur Dokumentation (Switzerland) *Tel:* (041) 726 45 05 *Fax:* (041) 726 45 09 *E-mail:* svd-asd@hispeed.ch *Web Site:* www.svd-asd.org, pg 1571

Schweizerischer Buchhaendler- und Verleger-Verband SBVV (Switzerland) *Tel:* (01) 421 28 00 *Fax:* (01) 421 28 18 *E-mail:* sbvv@swissbooks.ch *Web Site:* www.swissbooks.ch, pg 1286

Schweizerischer Bund fuer Jugendliteratur (Switzerland) *Tel:* (041) 741 31 40 *Fax:* (041) 740 01 59 *E-mail:* sbj@bluewin.ch, pg 1405

Schweizerischer Schriftstellerinnen und Schriftsteller-Verband (Switzerland) *Tel:* (01) 3500460 *Fax:* (01) 3500461 *E-mail:* letter@ch-s.ch *Web Site:* www.ch-s.ch, pg 1405

Schweizerischer Verein fuer Schweisstechnik (Switzerland) *Tel:* (061) 233973 *Fax:* (061) 3178480, pg 634

Schweizerisches Bundesarchiv (Switzerland) *Tel:* (031) 322 89 89 *Fax:* (031) 322 78 23 *E-mail:* bundesarchiv@bar.admin.ch *Web Site:* www.bundesarchiv.ch, pg 1548

Schweizerisches Jugendschriftenwerk, SJW (Switzerland) *Tel:* (01) 462 49 40 *Fax:* (01) 462 69 13 *E-mail:* office@sjw.ch *Web Site:* www.sjw.ch, pg 634

Verlag Schweizerisches Katholisches Bibelwerk (Switzerland), pg 634

Schweizerisches Wirtschaftsarchiv (Archives Economiques Suisses) (Switzerland) *Tel:* (061) 267 32 19 *Fax:* (061) 267 32 08 *E-mail:* info-wzb@unibas.ch *Web Site:* www.ub.unibas.ch/wwz, pg 1548

Sciamed Verlag AG (Switzerland) *Tel:* (061) 231775; (061) 235366 *Fax:* (061) 2722775, pg 634

Salvatore Sciascia Editore (Italy) *Tel:* (0934) 551509 *Fax:* (0934) 551366, pg 407

Science & Technics Publishing House (Viet Nam) *Tel:* (04) 9 424 786; (04) 9 423 172; (04) 8220682; (04) 9423132; (04) 9423128; (04) 9423543; (04) 9423171 *Fax:* (04) 8 220 658 *E-mail:* nxbkhkt@hn.vnn.vn *Web Site:* www.nxbkhkt.com.vn, pg 780

Science & Technology Information Institute Department of Science & Technology (Philippines) *Tel:* (02) 837-2191 *Fax:* (02) 837-7520 *Web Site:* www.stii.dost.gov.ph, pg 1536

Science Fiction Magazine Club (Thailand) *Tel:* (02) 2330302; (02) 2356931, pg 1256

Science Press (Australia) *Tel:* (02) 9516 1122 *Fax:* (02) 9550 1915, pg 40

Science Press (China) *Tel:* (010) 6401643; (010) 64019823 *Fax:* (010) 64010642, pg 107

Science Publications Centre (Republic of Korea) *Tel:* (02) 3254015; (02) 7336719; (02) 3254017 *Fax:* (02) 3335799, pg 1324

Science Reviews Ltd (United Kingdom) *Tel:* (01727) 847322 *Fax:* (01727) 847323 *E-mail:* scilet@scilet.com *Web Site:* www.scilet.com, pg 755

Scientia Verlag und Antiquariat Schilling OHG (Germany) *Tel:* (07361) 41700 *Fax:* (07361) 45620, pg 282

Scientific and Cultural Publications (Islamic Republic of Iran) *Tel:* (021) 685475; (021) 686278, pg 357

Scientific & Technical Information Service (Belgium) *Tel:* (02) 519 56 40 *Fax:* (02) 519 56 45 *E-mail:* info@stis.fgov.be *Web Site:* www.stis.fgov.be, pg 1558

Scientific Book Agency (India) *Tel:* (033) 292915; (033) 4642206 *E-mail:* debmalya@giase101.vsnl.net.in, pg 348

Scientific Book Agency (India) *Tel:* (033) 292915; (033) 4642206; (033) 4638273 *E-mail:* psjs@cal3.usnl.net.in, pg 1317

Scientific Documentation Centre (Iraq) *Tel:* (01) 7760023, pg 1518

Scientific Library Voronezh State University (Russian Federation) *Tel:* (0732) 55-35-59 *Fax:* (0732) 208-258 *E-mail:* root@lib.vsu.ru *Web Site:* www.lib.vsu.ru, pg 1541

Scientific Publishers India (India) *Tel:* (0291) 512712; (0291) 433323 *Fax:* (0291) 512580 *E-mail:* scienti@sancharnet.in, pg 349

Scientific Research Council (Jamaica) *Tel:* 876-927-1771; 876-927-1774 *Fax:* 876-927-1990 *E-mail:* prinfo@src-jamaica.org *Web Site:* www.src-jamaica.org, pg 414

Edizioni Scientifiche Italiane (Italy) *Tel:* (081) 7645443 *Fax:* (081) 7646477 *E-mail:* info@esispa.com, pg 407

Editoriale Scienza (Italy) *Tel:* (040) 364810 *Fax:* (040) 364909 *E-mail:* info@editscienza.it *Web Site:* www.editscienza.it, pg 407

Editora Scipione Ltda (Brazil) *Tel:* (011) 2392255 *Fax:* (011) 31053526 *E-mail:* info@scipione.com.br *Web Site:* www.scipione.com.br, pg 90

SciPrint Ltd (Ireland) *Tel:* (061) 472114; (061) 472520 *Fax:* (061) 472021, pg 1180, 1237

SCM-Canterbury Press Ltd (United Kingdom) *Tel:* (020) 7359 8033 *Fax:* (020) 7359 0049 *E-mail:* admin@scm-canterburypress.co.uk *Web Site:* www.scm-canterburypress.co.uk, pg 755

SCMP Book Publishing Ltd (Hong Kong) *Tel:* 2836 6088 *Fax:* 2838 4061, pg 319

Scoop Infotex NV (Belgium) *Tel:* (09) 2056430 *Fax:* (09) 2056449 *E-mail:* scoop@infotex.be, pg 73

Scorpion Publishers (Russian Federation) *Tel:* (095) 4436991, pg 548

Scottish Book Marketing Group (United Kingdom) *Tel:* (0131) 228 6866 *Fax:* (0131) 228 3220, pg 1293

Scottish Book Trust (United Kingdom) *Tel:* (0131) 524 0160 *Fax:* (0131) 228 4293 *E-mail:* info@scottishbooktrust.com *Web Site:* www.scottishbooktrust.com, pg 1293

Scottish Braille Press (United Kingdom) *Tel:* (0131) 662 4445 *Fax:* (0131) 662 1968 *E-mail:* enquiries@scottish-braille-press.org *Web Site:* www.scottish-braille-press.org, pg 755

Scottish Braille Press (United Kingdom) *Tel:* (0131) 662 4445 *Fax:* (0131) 662 1968 *E-mail:* enquiries@scottish-braille-press.org *Web Site:* www.scottish-braille-press.org, pg 1165

Scottish Council for Research in Education (United Kingdom) *Tel:* (0131) 557 2944 *Fax:* (0131) 556 9454 *E-mail:* scre.info@scre.ac.uk; scre@scre.ac.uk *Web Site:* www.scre.ac.uk, pg 755

Scottish Cultural Press (United Kingdom) *Tel:* (0131) 660-6366 (editorial); (0131) 660-4757 (editorial); (0131) 660-4666 (orders) *E-mail:* info@scottishbooks.com *Web Site:* www.scottishbooks.com, pg 755

Scottish Executive Library & Information Services (United Kingdom) *Tel:* (0131) 244 4552 *Fax:* (0131) 244 4545 *Web Site:* www.scotland.gov.uk, pg 755

Scottish Library Association (United Kingdom) *Tel:* (01698) 458888 *Fax:* (01698) 283170 *E-mail:* slic@slainte.org.uk *Web Site:* www.slainte.org.uk, pg 1573

Scottish Newspaper Publishers' Association (United Kingdom) *Tel:* (0131) 220 4353 *Fax:* (0131) 220 4344 *E-mail:* info@snpa.org.uk *Web Site:* www.snpa.org.uk, pg 1293

Scottish PEN Centre (United Kingdom) *Tel:* (01436) 672010 *E-mail:* info@scottishpen.org *Web Site:* www.scottishpen.org, pg 1409

Scottish Poetry Library (United Kingdom) *Tel:* (031) 557 2876 *Fax:* (031) 557 8393 *E-mail:* inquiries@spl.org.uk *Web Site:* www.spl.org.uk, pg 1554

Scottish Publishers Association (United Kingdom) *Tel:* (0131) 2286866 *Fax:* (0131) 2283220 *E-mail:* info@scottishbooks.org *Web Site:* www.scottishbooks.org, pg 1293

Scottish Text Society (United Kingdom) *Tel:* (0115) 951 5922 *E-mail:* sts@arts.gla.ac.uk *Web Site:* www.scottishtextsociety.org, pg 755

Casa Editrice Marietti Scuola SpA (Italy) *Tel:* (011) 2098741; (011) 2098720 *Fax:* (011) 2098765 *E-mail:* redazione@mariettiscuola.it *Web Site:* www.mariettiscuola.it, pg 407

Ediciones Scriba SA (Spain) *Tel:* (093) 215 19 33 *Fax:* (093) 487 37 66, pg 599

SCRIPTA - Distribucion y Servicios Editoriales, SA de CV (Mexico) *Tel:* (05) 5481716 *Fax:* (05) 6161496 *E-mail:* dyse@data.net.mx, pg 471

SCRIPTA - Distribucion y Servicios Editoriales, SA de CV (Mexico) *Tel:* (05) 5481716 *Fax:* (05)5500564, pg 1327

Scripta Theofilus Palevratzis-Ashover (Greece) *Tel:* (0210) 5230382 *Fax:* (0210) 5233574, pg 312

Editions Scriptar SA (Switzerland) *Tel:* (021) 7911065 *Fax:* (021) 7914084 *E-mail:* info@jsh.ch *Web Site:* www.jsh.ch, pg 634

Scriptum (Netherlands) *Tel:* (010) 4271022 *Fax:* (010) 4736625 *E-mail:* info@scriptum.nl *Web Site:* www.scriptum.nl, pg 488

Scriptum Forlags AB (Finland) *Fax:* (06) 3242 210 *E-mail:* scriptum@svof.fi *Web Site:* www.svof.fi/scriptum, pg 144

Scripture Union (United Kingdom) *Tel:* (01908) 856000 *Fax:* (01908) 856111 *E-mail:* info@scriptureunion.org.uk *Web Site:* www.scriptureunion.org.uk, pg 756

Editura 'Scrisul Romanesc' (Romania) *Tel:* (051) 419506, pg 542

Scroll Publishers (Australia) *Tel:* (07) 5573 0835 *Fax:* (07) 5529 9155, pg 40

Editrice la Scuola SpA (Italy) *Tel:* (030) 29931 *Fax:* (030) 2993299 *Web Site:* www.lascuola.it, pg 407

Scuola Vaticana Paleografia - Scuola Vaticana di Paleografia Diplomatica e Archivistica (Holy See (Vatican City State)) *Tel:* (06) 69883595 *Fax:* (06) 69881377 *E-mail:* pagano@librs6k.vatlib.it, pg 315

SDL Agency (United Kingdom) *Tel:* (0114) 253 5353 *Toll Free Tel:* 800 917 0044 *Fax:* (0114) 253 5200 *Web Site:* www.sdl.com, pg 1151

SDU Juridische & Fiscale Uitgeverij (Netherlands) *Tel:* (070) 3789880; (070) 3789911 *Fax:* (070) 3854321; (070) 3789783; (070) 3458068 *E-mail:* sdu@sdu.nl *Web Site:* www.sdu.nl, pg 488

Sdu Uitgevers bv (Netherlands) *Tel:* (070) 378 99 11; (070) 378 98 80 *Fax:* (070) 385 43 21; (070) 378 97 83 *E-mail:* sdu@sdu.nl *Web Site:* www.sdu.nl, pg 488

SDX (Shenghuo-Dushu-Xinzhi) Joint Publishing Co (China) *Tel:* (010) 555159 *Fax:* (010) 5138378, pg 107

Se-Kwang Music Publishing Co (Republic of Korea) *Tel:* (02) 714-0046 *Fax:* (02) 719-2191, pg 442

Seagull Press (New Zealand) *Tel:* (03) 3899338, pg 501

Seanachas Press (Australia) *Tel:* (02) 6299 5434, pg 40

Search Press Ltd (United Kingdom) *Tel:* (01892) 510850 *Fax:* (01892) 515903 *E-mail:* searchpress@searchpress.com *Web Site:* www.searchpress.com, pg 756

Derek Searle Associates (United Kingdom) *Tel:* (01753) 539295 *Fax:* (01753) 551863 *E-mail:* dsapublish@aol.com, pg 1353

Universitas Sebelas Maret (Indonesia) *Tel:* (0271) 646994; (0271) 646761; (0271) 646624 *Fax:* (0271) 46655 *E-mail:* due-uns@slo.mega.net.id; pptk-uns@slo.mega.net.id *Web Site:* www.uns.ac.id, pg 356

SECAP (Ecuador) *Tel:* (02) 446248 *Fax:* (02) 448644, pg 137

Martin Secker & Warburg (United Kingdom) *Tel:* (020) 7840 8570 *Fax:* (020) 7233 6117 *E-mail:* enquiries@randomhouse.co.uk *Web Site:* www.randomhouse.co.uk, pg 756

Seckin Yayinevi (Turkey) *Tel:* (0312) 4353030 *Fax:* (0312) 4352472 *E-mail:* seckin@seckin.com.tr *Web Site:* www.seckin.com.tr, pg 651

Biblioteca de la Secretaria de Estado de Relaciones Exteriores (Dominican Republic) *Tel:* 535-6280 *Fax:* 508-6863; 533-5772 *E-mail:* cmedina018@hotmail.com *Web Site:* www.serex.gov.do, pg 1502

Secretariado Trinitario (Spain) *Tel:* (0923) 23 56 02 *Fax:* (0923) 23 56 02 *E-mail:* secretrinitario@planalfa.es *Web Site:* www.aecae.es/secretrinitario, pg 599

Secretariat of the Pacific Community Library (New Caledonia) *Tel:* 26 20 00 *Fax:* 26 38 18 *E-mail:* noumeaexternal@spc.int *Web Site:* www.spc.int/library, pg 1532

Seculo XXI Editora e Comercio de Livros (Brazil) *Tel:* (051) 3614459 *Fax:* (051) 3614459 *E-mail:* sewloxxi@poa-online.com.br, pg 90

SEDA Publications (United Kingdom) *Tel:* (0121) 415 6801 *Fax:* (0121) 415 6802 *E-mail:* office@seda.ac.uk *Web Site:* www.seda.ac.uk/publications.htm, pg 756

Sedco Publishing Ltd (Ghana) *Tel:* (021) 221332 *Fax:* (021) 220107 *E-mail:* sedco@africaonline.com.gh, pg 305

SEDIT (Societe d'Etudes et de Diffusion des Industries Thermiques et Aerauliques) (France) *Tel:* (01) 30 85 20 10 *Fax:* (01) 30 85 20 38 *E-mail:* sedit@costic.com *Web Site:* www.costic.com, pg 184

See Australia Guides P/L (Australia) *Tel:* (03) 5962 5723 *Fax:* (03) 5962 4718 *E-mail:* sag@minopher.net.au, pg 40

Editions Seghers (France) *Tel:* (01) 53 67 14 00 *Fax:* (01) 53 67 14 14 *Web Site:* www.laffont.fr/seghers, pg 184

Segment BV (Netherlands) *Tel:* (046) 43894444 *Fax:* (046) 4389401; (046) 4370161 *E-mail:* secretariant@segment.nl *Web Site:* www.segment.nl, pg 488

Edizioni Segno SRL (Italy) *Tel:* (0432) 575179 *Fax:* (0432) 575589 *E-mail:* info@edizionisegno.it *Web Site:* www.edizionisegno.it, pg 407

Segretariato Nazionale Apostolato della Preghiera (Italy) *Tel:* (06) 6976071 *Fax:* (06) 6781063 *E-mail:* adp@adp.it *Web Site:* www.adp.it, pg 408

Seibido (Japan) *Tel:* (03) 3291-2261 *Fax:* (03) 3293-5490 *E-mail:* seibido@mua.biglobe.ne.jp *Web Site:* www.seibido.co.jp, pg 426

Seibido Shuppan Company Ltd (Japan) *Tel:* (03) 3814-4351 *Fax:* (03) 3814-4355 *Web Site:* www.seibidoshuppan.co.jp, pg 426

Seibt Verlag GmbH (Germany) *Tel:* (06151) 380-140 *Fax:* (06151) 380-141 *E-mail:* info@seibt.com *Web Site:* www.seibt.de, pg 282

Seibu Time Co Ltd (Japan) *Tel:* (03) 5283-0270 *Fax:* (03) 5283-0234, pg 426

Seibundo (Japan) *Tel:* (03) 3203-9201 *Fax:* (03) 3203-9206 *E-mail:* eigyobu@seibundoh.co.jp *Web Site:* www.seibundoh.co.jp, pg 426

Seibundo Shinkosha Publishing Co Ltd (Japan) *Tel:* (03) 5800-5780 *Fax:* (03) 5800-5781 *Web Site:* www.seibundo.net, pg 426

Seibundo Shuppan (Japan) *Tel:* (06) 6211-6265 *Fax:* (06) 6211-6492, pg 426

Seishin Shobo (Japan) *Tel:* (03) 3946-5666 *Fax:* (03) 3945-8880, pg 427

Seiun-Sha (Japan) *Tel:* (03) 3947-1021 *Fax:* (03) 3947-1617 *E-mail:* greatobe@yo.rim.ur.jp, pg 427

Seiwa Shoten Co Ltd (Japan) *Tel:* (03) 3329-0033 *Fax:* (03) 5374-7186 *E-mail:* sales@seiwa-pb.co.jp *Web Site:* www.seiwa-pb.co.jp, pg 427

Seix Barral (Argentina) *Tel:* (011) 4382-4043; (011) 4382-4045; (011) 4381-8285 *Fax:* (011) 4383-3793 *E-mail:* editorial@seix-barral.es *Web Site:* www.seix-barral.es, pg 9

Editorial Seix Barral SA (Spain) *Tel:* (093) 496 7003 *Fax:* (093) 496 7004 *E-mail:* editorial@seix-barral.es *Web Site:* www.seix-barral.es, pg 599

Seizando-Shoten Publishing Co Ltd (Japan) *Tel:* (03) 3357-5861 *Fax:* (03) 3357-5867, pg 427

Seizmoloska Opservatorija (The Former Yugoslav Republic of Macedonia) *Tel:* (091) 231953 *Fax:* (091) 114042 *E-mail:* ljupco@iunona.pmf.ukim.edu.mk, pg 453

Sejong Daewang Kinyom Saophoe (Republic of Korea), pg 442

Sekai Bunka-Sha (Japan) *Tel:* (03) 3262-5111 *Fax:* (03) 3237-8446 *Web Site:* www.sekaibunka.com, pg 427

Selangor Public Library (Malaysia) *Tel:* (03) 55197667 *Fax:* (03) 55196045 *E-mail:* ppas@sel.lib.edu.my; jothi@ppas.org.my *Web Site:* www.ppas.org.my, pg 1527

Selecoes Eletronicas Editora Ltda (Brazil) *Tel:* (021) 2539268 *Fax:* (021) 2638840, pg 90

Select Books Pte Ltd (Singapore) *Tel:* 6732 1515 *Fax:* 6736 0855 *E-mail:* info@selectbooks.com.sg *Web Site:* www.selectbooks.com.sg, pg 1339

Select Publishing Pte Ltd (Singapore) *Tel:* 6732 1515 *Fax:* 6736 0855 *E-mail:* info@selectbooks.com.sg *Web Site:* www.selectbooks.com.sg, pg 557

Selecta-Catalonia Ed (Spain) *Tel:* (093) 3172331; (093) 3185183 *Fax:* (093) 3024793, pg 599

Selection du Reader's Digest SA (France) *Tel:* (01) 46748484 *Fax:* (01) 46748580 *E-mail:* serviceclients@readersdigest.tm.fr *Web Site:* www.selectionclic.com/srd/; www.rd.com/international/shared/?countryid=fr, pg 184

Editions Selection J Jacobs SA (France), pg 184

Selector SA de CV (Mexico) *Tel:* (055) 588-7272 *Fax:* (055) 761-5716 *E-mail:* info@selector.com.mx *Web Site:* www.selector.com.mx, pg 471

SELF Syndicate of French Language Authors (France) *Tel:* (01) 40600501 *Fax:* (01) 46707395, pg 1269

Selina Publishers (India) *Tel:* (011) 3280711 *Fax:* (011) 3277230, pg 349

Selinunte Editora Ltda (Brazil) *Tel:* (011) 2760318, pg 90

Sellerio Editore (Italy) *Tel:* (091) 6259475 *Fax:* (091) 6258802, pg 408

Dr Arthur L Sellier & Co KG-Walter de Gruyter GmbH & Co KG OHG (Germany) *Tel:* (030) 26005-0 *Fax:* (030) 260 05-251 *E-mail:* wdq-info@degruyter.de *Web Site:* www.degruyter.de, pg 283

Selwood Printing (United Kingdom) *Tel:* (01444) 236060 *Fax:* (01444) 245043 *E-mail:* sales@selwood.com, pg 1227

SEMAR Publishers SRL (Italy) *Tel:* (06) 6876523; (06) 6879333 *Fax:* (06) 68308601 *E-mail:* info@semarweb.com *Web Site:* www.semarweb.com, pg 408

Editions Semences Africaines (Cameroon) *Tel:* (023) 224058, pg 98

Bokforlaget Semic AB (Sweden) *Tel:* (08) 799 30 50 *Fax:* (08) 799 30 64 *E-mail:* bokforlaget@semic.se *Web Site:* www.semic.se, pg 615

Semic Bokforlaget International AB (Sweden) *Tel:* (08) 779 30 50 *Fax:* (08) 799 30 64 *E-mail:* bokforlaget@semic.se *Web Site:* www.semic.se, pg 615

Semic Junior Press (Netherlands) *Tel:* (035) 6944914 *Fax:* (035) 6944909, pg 489

Seminar on the Acquisition of Latin American Library Materials (SALALM) (United States) *Tel:* 505-277-5102 *Fax:* 505-277-0646, pg 1294

Senate Books Co Ltd (Taiwan, Province of China) *Tel:* (02) 23213054 *Fax:* (02) 23214041 *E-mail:* senatebooks@usa.net, pg 641

Sencor (United States) *Tel:* 212-947-5601 *Fax:* 212-947-5604 *E-mail:* sales@sencor.net *Web Site:* www.sencor.net, pg 1189

Send the Light Ltd (United Kingdom) *Tel:* (01228) 512 512 *Fax:* (01228) 514 949 *E-mail:* info@stl.org *Web Site:* www.stl.org, pg 1353

Senmon Toshokan Kyogikai (SENTOKYO) (Japan) *Tel:* (03) 3537-8335 *Fax:* (03) 3537-8336 *E-mail:* jsla@jsla.or.jp *Web Site:* www.jsla.or.jp, pg 1566

Senouhy Publishers (Egypt (Arab Republic of Egypt)), pg 138

Sentraldistribusjon ANS (Norway) *Tel:* (022) 98 57 10 *Fax:* (022) 98 57 20 *E-mail:* sdinfo@sd.no *Web Site:* www.sd.no, pg 1333

Seogwangsa (Republic of Korea) *Tel:* (02) 9246161; (02) 9246165 *Fax:* (02) 9224993, pg 442

Seoul International Publishing House (Republic of Korea) *Tel:* (02) 4698326; (02) 4698327, pg 443

Seoul National University Library (Republic of Korea) *Tel:* (02) 880-8070 *Fax:* (02) 878-2730 *E-mail:* kimya@plaza.snu.ac.kr *Web Site:* library.snu.ac.kr/snu, pg 1524

Seoul National University Press (Republic of Korea) *Tel:* (02) 880-5114 *Fax:* (02) 885-5272 *Web Site:* www.snu.ac.kr, pg 443

Sepia Editions (France) *Tel:* (01) 43 97 22 14 *Fax:* (01) 43 97 32 62 *E-mail:* sepia@editions-sepia.com *Web Site:* www.editions-sepia.com, pg 184

Editions de Septembre (France) *Tel:* (01) 53 68 96 20 *Fax:* (01) 53 68 96 21, pg 184

Serafin (Slovakia) *Tel:* (02) 54434359 *Fax:* (02) 54434342 *E-mail:* vydserafin@gmx.net *Web Site:* www.serafin.sk, pg 560

Ediciones del Serbal SA (Spain) *Tel:* (093) 408 08 34 *Fax:* (093) 408 07 92 *E-mail:* serbal@ed-serbal.es *Web Site:* www.ed-serbal.es, pg 599

Seren (United Kingdom) *Tel:* (01656) 663018 *Fax:* (01656) 649226 *E-mail:* general@seren-books.com *Web Site:* www.seren-books.com, pg 756

Serie-pocket-klubben (Sweden) *Tel:* (08) 7993110 *Fax:* (08) 7645764, pg 1256

Serif (United Kingdom) *Tel:* (020) 8981 3990 *Fax:* (020) 8981 3990, pg 756

Editions Le Serpent a Plumes (France) *Tel:* (01) 55 35 95 85 *Fax:* (01) 42 61 17 46 *E-mail:* contact@serpentaplumes.com, pg 184

Serpent's Tail Ltd (United Kingdom) *Tel:* (020) 7354-1949 *Fax:* (020) 7704-6467 *E-mail:* info@serpentstail.com *Web Site:* www.serpentstail.com, pg 756

Servedit (France) *Tel:* (01) 44 41 49 30 *Fax:* (01) 43 25 77 41 *E-mail:* servedit@wanadoo.fr, pg 184

Servei de Biblioteques de la UAB (Spain) *Tel:* (093) 581 1015 *Fax:* (093) 581 3219 *E-mail:* bib.utp@uab.es; s.biblioteques@uab.es *Web Site:* www.bib.uab.es; www.uab.es, pg 1545

Service Central de la Statistique et des Etudes Economiques (STATEC) (Luxembourg) *Tel:* 478-4384 *Fax:* 464289 *E-mail:* info@statec.etat.lu *Web Site:* www.statec.lu; www.statec.public.lu, pg 451

Service Central des Imprimes et des Fournitures de Bureau de l'Etat (Luxembourg) *Tel:* (00352) 4988111 *Fax:* (00352) 400881 *E-mail:* hotline@scie.etat.lu *Web Site:* www.scie.etat.lu, pg 451

Service commun de la documentation de l'Universite de Lille III (France) *Tel:* (03) 20 43 44 10 *Fax:* (03) 20 33 71 04 *Web Site:* ustl.univ-lille1.fr, pg 1507

Service de l'Information et des Archives Nationales (Rwanda) *Tel:* 76 995 *Fax:* 82 162, pg 1541

Service des Publications Scientifiques du Museum National d'Histoire Naturelle (France) *Tel:* (01) 40 79 48 38 *Fax:* (01) 40 79 38 40 *E-mail:* diff.pub@mnhn.fr *Web Site:* www.mnhn.fr/publication, pg 184

Service Hydrographique et Oceanographique de la Marine (SHOM) (France) *Tel:* (01) 44 38 41 16 *Web Site:* www.shom.fr, pg 184

Service Technique pour l'Education (France) *Tel:* (01) 45084756, pg 184

Editions Services et Informations pour Etudiants (Morocco) *Tel:* (02) 210163, pg 475

Services for Export & Language (SEL) (United Kingdom) *Tel:* (0161) 7457480 *Fax:* (0161) 2955110 *E-mail:* sales@sel-uk.com *Web Site:* www.sel-uk.com, pg 1151

Servicio a La Iglesia Catolica AC Edicion y Distribucion de Libros Religiosos (Mexico) *Tel:* (05) 6710269 *Fax:* (05) 5441675, pg 1327

Servicio de Biblioteca (Spain) *Tel:* (04) 6006125 *Fax:* (04) 6006049 *E-mail:* biblioteca.cruces@hcru.osakidetza.net *Web Site:* www.osakidetza-svs.org, pg 1545

Servicio de Publicaciones Universidad de Cadiz (Spain) *Tel:* (0956) 015268 *Fax:* (0056) 015634 *E-mail:* publicaciones@uca.es *Web Site:* www.uca.es/serv/publicaciones, pg 599

Servicio de Publicaciones Universidad de Cordoba (Spain) *Tel:* (0957) 21 81 25 *Fax:* (0957) 21 81 96; (057) 218666 (Director) *E-mail:* publicaciones@uco.es; pal1gocag@lucano.uco.es (Director) *Web Site:* www.uco.es/organiza/servicios/publica/presenta.htm, pg 599

Servicio de Publicaciones y Produccion Documental de la Universidad de Las Palmas de Gran Canaria (Spain) *Tel:* (0928) 451000; (0928) 451023 *Fax:* (0928) 451022 *E-mail:* universidad@ulpgc.es *Web Site:* www.ulpgc.es, pg 599

Servicios Especiales Maciel SA de CV (Mexico) *Tel:* 05 5435533, pg 472

Servicios Especializados y Representacionesen Comercio Exterior SA de CV (Mexico) *Tel:* (05) 7609129; (05) 7605149, pg 1327

Servire BV Uitgevers (Netherlands) *Tel:* (030) 2349211 *Fax:* (030) 2349247 *E-mail:* servire@pi.net, pg 489

Servire BV Uitgevers (Netherlands) *Tel:* (030) 2349211 *Fax:* (030) 2349247 *E-mail:* info@kosmoszk.nl *Web Site:* www.servire.nl; www.boekenwereld.com, pg 1135

Servitium (Italy) *Tel:* (035) 4398011 *Fax:* (035) 792030 *E-mail:* servitium@spm.it, pg 408

Forlaget Sesam (Denmark) *Tel:* 3330-5044; 3330-5522 *Fax:* 3391-3878 *E-mail:* aschehoug@ash.egmont.com, pg 134

Sesame Publication Co (Hong Kong) *Tel:* 2508 9920; 2508 9311 *Fax:* 2508 9603 *E-mail:* sesame01@hkstar.hk, pg 319

Setberg (Iceland) *Tel:* 5517667; 552-9150 *Fax:* 5526640, pg 326

Bokforlaget Settern AB (Sweden) *Tel:* (0435) 80470 *Fax:* (0435) 80400 *E-mail:* info@settern.se *Web Site:* www.settern.se, pg 615

Editions du Seuil (France) *Tel:* (01) 40 46 50 50 *Fax:* (01) 40 46 43 00 *E-mail:* contact@seuil.com *Web Site:* www.seuil.com, pg 184

Seven Hills Publishers (Bulgaria) *Tel:* (032) 262235 *Fax:* (032) 262235, pg 96

Klub 707 (South Africa) *Tel:* (011) 6736725 *Fax:* (011) 6736719, pg 1255

Edicoes 70 Lda (Portugal) *Tel:* (021) 319 02 40 *Fax:* (021) 319 02 49 *E-mail:* edi.70@mail.telepac.pt *Web Site:* www.edicoes70.pt, pg 535

Severn House Publishers Inc (United Kingdom) *Tel:* (0208) 7703930 *Fax:* (0208) 7703850 *E-mail:* sales@severnhouse.com *Web Site:* www.severnhouse.com, pg 756

Severnside Printers Ltd (United Kingdom) *Tel:* (0684) 594521 *Fax:* (0684) 594344, pg 1185

Severnside Printers Ltd (United Kingdom) *Tel:* (01684) 594521 *Fax:* (01684) 594344, pg 1227

Ediciones Seyer (Spain) *Tel:* (095) 2320887 *Fax:* (095) 2325511, pg 599

Sh Ghulam Ali & Sons (Pvt) Ltd (Pakistan) *Tel:* (042) 7588979; (042) 7501664 *Fax:* (042) 7583611, pg 514

Shaar Zion Library (Israel) *Tel:* 03 69101410, pg 1519

Shaibya Prakashan Bibhag (India) *Tel:* (033) 388268; (033) 2411748, pg 349

Shakai Hoken Shuppan-Sha (Japan) *Tel:* (03) 3291-9841 *Fax:* (03) 3291-9847, pg 427

Shakai Shiso-Sha (Japan) *Tel:* (03) 3813-8101 *Fax:* (03) 3813-9061, pg 427

Shakespearean Authorship Trust (United Kingdom) *Tel:* (01473) 890264; (020) 7902 1403 *Fax:* (01473) 890803 *E-mail:* info@shakespeareanauthorshiptrust.org.uk *Web Site:* www.shakespeareanauthorshiptrust.org.uk, pg 1409

Shakti Communications Ltd (United Kingdom) *Tel:* (020) 8903 5442 *Fax:* (020) 8903 4684 *E-mail:* info@shakticom.com *Web Site:* www.shakticom.com, pg 756

Shalem Press (Israel) *Tel:* (02) 566-0601 *Fax:* (02) 566-0590 *E-mail:* shalem@shalem.org.il *Web Site:* www.shalem.org.il, pg 372

Shandong Education Publishing House (China) *Tel:* (0531) 2092661; (0531) 2092663 *Fax:* (0531) 2092661 *E-mail:* sdjys@sjs.com.cn *Web Site:* www.sjs.com.cn, pg 107

Shandong Fine Arts Publishing House (China) *Tel:* (0531) 6910055 *Fax:* (021) 6911563, pg 107

Shandong Friendship Publishing House (China) *Tel:* (0531) 2060055-7302 *Fax:* (0531) 2909354 *E-mail:* friendpub@sina.com *Web Site:* www.sdpress.com.cn, pg 107

Shandong Literature & Art Publishing House (China) *Tel:* (0531) 6910055 *Fax:* (0531) 613584, pg 107

Shandong Science & Technology Press (China) *Tel:* (0531) 6915110 *Fax:* (0531) 2023898 *E-mail:* li_yujn@sina.com, pg 107

Shandong University Press (China) *Tel:* (0531) 8902601 *E-mail:* hustpub@blue.hust.edu.cn, pg 108

Shanghai Academy of Social Sciences Library (China) *Tel:* (021) 6486 2266 (ext 1305) *Fax:* (021) 6427 6018 *E-mail:* tsg@sass.stc.sh.cn *Web Site:* www.sass.stc.sh.cn, pg 1498

Shanghai Book Co Ltd (Hong Kong) *Tel:* 2548 6160, pg 319

The Shanghai Book Co (Pte) Ltd (Singapore) *Tel:* 336 0144 *Fax:* 336 0490 *E-mail:* shanghaibooks@sbg.com.sg, pg 558

Shanghai Calligraphy & Painting Publishing House (China) *Tel:* (021) 64311905 *Fax:* (021) 3207505 *E-mail:* shcpph@online.sh.cn, pg 108

Shanghai College of Traditional Chinese Medicine Press (China) *Tel:* (021) 64175039 *Fax:* (021) 64175039, pg 108

Shanghai Educational Publishing House (China) *Tel:* (021) 64 37 71 65 *Fax:* (021) 64 33 99 95 *E-mail:* wuyiyang@public2.sta.net.cn, pg 108

Shanghai Far East Publishers (China) *Tel:* (021) 62247733-661 *Fax:* (021) 62414469 *E-mail:* ydbook@ydbook.com *Web Site:* www.ydbook.com, pg 108

Shanghai Foreign Language Education Press (China) *Tel:* (021) 65425300; (021) 65422896 *Fax:* (021) 65609540 *Web Site:* www.sflep.com, pg 108

Shanghai People's Fine Arts Publishing House (China) *Tel:* (021) 54044520 *Fax:* (021) 54032331 *E-mail:* finearts@shi63.net, pg 108

Shanghai Scientific & Technical Publishers (China) *Tel:* (021) 64736055; (021) 64184881; (021) 64174349 *Fax:* (021) 64730679 *E-mail:* gjb@sstp.cn *Web Site:* www.sstp.com.cn; www.sstp.cn, pg 108

Shanghai Scientific & Technological Literature Press (China) *Tel:* (021) 64370782, pg 108

Shanghai tushuguan (China) *Tel:* (021) 64455555 *Fax:* (021) 64455001 *Web Site:* www.libnet.sh.cn, pg 1498

Sharbain's Bookshop (Jordan) *Tel:* (06) 638709 *Fax:* (06) 699119, pg 1323

Sharda Prakashan (India) *Tel:* (011) 653982, pg 349

Shaw & Sons Ltd (United Kingdom) *Tel:* (01322) 621100 *Fax:* (01322) 550553 *E-mail:* sales@shaws.co.uk *Web Site:* www.shaws.co.uk, pg 756

David Shaw & Associates Ltd (Canada) *Tel:* 416-487-2019 *Fax:* 416-486-1744 *E-mail:* djshaw@simpatico.ca, pg 1176

The Shaw Society (United Kingdom) *Tel:* (020) 86973619 *Fax:* (020) 86973619 *E-mail:* bernardshawinfo@netscape.net *Web Site:* www.sndc.demon.co.uk/shawsub.htm, pg 1409

Shearwater Associates Ltd (New Zealand) *Tel:* (04) 2399024 *Fax:* (04) 2399024, pg 501

Shearwater Press Ltd (United Kingdom) *Tel:* (01624) 627727 *Fax:* (01624) 663627, pg 757

Sheck Wah Tong Printing Press Ltd (Hong Kong) *Tel:* (852) 25628293 *Fax:* 25655431 *Web Site:* www.sheckwahtong.com, pg 1219

Sheed & Ward UK (United Kingdom) *Tel:* (020) 7922 0880 *Fax:* (020) 7922 0881 *E-mail:* info@breathemail.net *Web Site:* www.continuumbooks.com, pg 757

Sheffield Academic Press Ltd (United Kingdom) *Tel:* (01202) 665 432 *Fax:* (01202) 666 219 *E-mail:* orders@orcabookservices.co.uk *Web Site:* www.sheffieldacademicpress.com, pg 757

Sheil Land Associates Ltd (United Kingdom) *Tel:* (020) 7405 9351 *Fax:* (020) 7831 2127 *E-mail:* info@sheilland.co.uk, pg 1143

Caroline Sheldon Literary Agency (United Kingdom) *Tel:* (01938) 760205, pg 1143

Sheldon Press (United Kingdom) *Tel:* (020) 7643 0382 *Fax:* (020) 7643 0391 *E-mail:* director@sheldonpress.co.uk *Web Site:* www.sheldonpress.co.uk, pg 757

Sheldrake Press (United Kingdom) *Tel:* (020) 8675 1767; (01752) 202301 (orders); (01752) 202300 (warehouse) *Fax:* (020) 8675 7736 *E-mail:* mail@sheldrakepress.demon.co.uk *Web Site:* www.sheldrakepress.co.uk, pg 757

Shelfmark Books (United Kingdom) *Tel:* (020) 8986 4854 *Fax:* (020) 8533 5821 *E-mail:* orders@centralbooks.com, pg 757

Shepheard-Walwyn (Publishers) Ltd (United Kingdom) *Tel:* (020) 7721 7666 *Fax:* (020) 7721 7667 *E-mail:* books@shepheard-walwyn.co.uk *Web Site:* www.shepheard-walwyn.co.uk, pg 757

Sherbourne Publications (United Kingdom) *Tel:* (01691) 657 853 *Fax:* (01691) 657 853, 757

The Sheringa Book Committee (Australia) *Tel:* (086) 878750, pg 41

Sherratt & Hughes (United Kingdom) *Tel:* (01793) 695195, pg 1353

Sherwood Publishing (United Kingdom) *Tel:* (01923) 224737 *Fax:* (01923) 210648 *E-mail:* sherwood@adinternational.com *Web Site:* www.sherwoodpublishing.com, pg 757

R R Sheth & Co (India) *Tel:* (022) 2013441 *Fax:* (079) 5321732 *E-mail:* chintan@rrsheth.com *Web Site:* www.rrsheth.com, pg 349

R R Sheth & Co (India) *Tel:* (079) 5356573 *E-mail:* chintan@rrsheth.com *Web Site:* www.rrsheth.com, pg 1317

Shibil Publications (Pvt) Ltd (Pakistan) *Tel:* (021) 533414; (021) 539570; (021) 571488, pg 514

Shibun-Do (Japan) *Tel:* (03) 3268-2441 *Fax:* (03) 3268-3550, pg 427

Shiko-Sha Co Ltd (Japan) *Tel:* (03) 3400-7151 *Fax:* (03) 3400-7294, pg 427

Shiksha Bharati (India) *Tel:* (011) 386-7791, pg 349

Shimizu-Shoin (Japan) *Tel:* (03) 3260-5261 *Fax:* (03) 3260-5270, pg 427

Shin Won Agency Co (Republic of Korea) *Tel:* (031) 955-2255; (031) 955-2265; (031) 955-2266 *E-mail:* main@shinwonagency.co.kr *Web Site:* www.shinwonagency.co.kr, pg 1134

Shincho-Sha Co Ltd (Japan) *Tel:* (03) 3266 5138 *Fax:* (03) 3266 5377, pg 427

SHINE-Scottish Health Information Network (United Kingdom) *Tel:* (0131) 536 5582 *Fax:* (0131) 536 5502 *E-mail:* mdg@ednet.co.uk *Web Site:* www.shinelib.org.uk, pg 1573

Shing Lee Group Publishers (Singapore) *Tel:* 67601388 *Fax:* 67651506 *E-mail:* kongjing@shinglee.com.sg, pg 558

Shingakusha Co Ltd (Japan) *Tel:* (075) 581-6111 *Fax:* (075) 501-0514 *E-mail:* info@sing.co.jp *Web Site:* www.sing.co.jp, pg 427

Shinkenchiku-Sha Co Ltd (Japan) *Tel:* (03) 38117101 *Fax:* (03) 38128229, pg 427

Shinko Tsusho Co Ltd (Japan) *Tel:* (03) 33531751 *Fax:* (03) 33532205 *E-mail:* shinko@tokyo.e-mail.ne.jp, pg 1323

Shinkwang Publishing Co (Republic of Korea) *Tel:* (02) 9255051; (02) 9255053 *Fax:* (02) 9255054, pg 443

Shire Publications Ltd (United Kingdom) *Tel:* (01844) 344301 *Fax:* (01844) 347080 *E-mail:* shire@shirebooks.co.uk *Web Site:* www.shirebooks.co.uk, pg 757

Shirikon Publishers (Kenya), pg 436

Shiseido Booksellers Ltd (Japan) *Tel:* (075) 431 2345 *Fax:* (075) 432 6588 *E-mail:* shiseido@jd5.so-net.ne.jp *Web Site:* www.shiseido-book.co.jp, pg 1323

Shkoder Public Library (Albania), pg 1489

Shoal Bay Press Ltd (New Zealand) *Tel:* (03) 384 6057 *Fax:* (03) 384 6087 *E-mail:* ros@shoalbay.co.nz, pg 501

Akane Shobo Co Ltd (Japan) *Tel:* (03) 3263-0641 *Fax:* (03) 3263-5440 *E-mail:* mail@akaneshobo.co.jp *Web Site:* www.akaneshobo.co.jp/, pg 427

Hara Shobo (Japan) *Tel:* (03) 5212-7801 *Fax:* (03) 3230-1158 *E-mail:* toshi@harashobo.com *Web Site:* www.harashobo.com, pg 427

Shobunsha Publications Inc (Japan) *Tel:* (03) 3556-8154 *Fax:* (03) 3556-5973 *E-mail:* LEH05353@niftyserve.or.jp *Web Site:* www.mapple.co.jp, pg 427

Shogakukan Inc (Japan) *Tel:* (03) 3230-5211 *Fax:* (03) 3234-5660 *E-mail:* info@shogakukan.co.jp *Web Site:* skygarden.shogakukan.co.jp, pg 427

Shogun International Ltd (United Kingdom) *Tel:* (020) 8749 2022 *Fax:* (020) 8740 1086, pg 1353

Mitsumura Suiko Shoin (Japan) *Tel:* (075) 493-8244 *Fax:* (075) 493-6011 *E-mail:* mitsumur@mbox.kyoto-inet.or.jp *Web Site:* www.mitsumura-suiko.co.jp, pg 428

Shokabo Publishing Co Ltd (Japan) *Tel:* (03) 3262-9166 *Fax:* (03) 3262-9130 *E-mail:* shkb-01@cb3.so-net.ne.jp *Web Site:* www.shokabo.co.jp/, pg 428

Shokokusha Publishing Co Ltd (Japan) *Tel:* (03) 3359-3231 *Fax:* (03) 3357-3961, pg 428

Shorin-Sha Co ltd (Japan) *Tel:* (03) 5689-7377 *Fax:* (03) 5689-7577, pg 428

Shortland Publications Ltd (New Zealand) *Tel:* (09) 687128 *Fax:* (09) 6230143 *E-mail:* heather_peach@mcgraw-hill.com, pg 501

Shtepia Botuese Enciklopedike (Albania) *Tel:* (042) 28064 *Fax:* (042) 28064, pg 1

Shueisha Inc (Japan) *Tel:* (03) 3230-6393 *Fax:* (03) 3230-2547, pg 428

Shufu-to-Seikatsu Sha Ltd (Japan) *Tel:* (03) 3563-5124 *Fax:* (03) 3563-5005, pg 428

Shufunotomo Co Ltd (Japan) *Tel:* (03) 5280-7539 *Fax:* (03) 5280-7587 *E-mail:* international@shufunotomo.co.jp *Web Site:* www.shufunotomo.co.jp, pg 428

Shumawa Publishing House (Myanmar), pg 476

Shunjusha (Japan) *Tel:* (03) 3255-9611 *Fax:* (03) 3253-1384, pg 428

Shuppan News Co Ltd (Japan) *Tel:* (03) 3262-2076 *Fax:* (03) 3261-6817, pg 428

Oru Shuppan (Japan) *Tel:* (03) 3234-0971 *Fax:* (03) 3261-6602, pg 428

Shuter & Shooter (Pty) Ltd (South Africa) *Tel:* (033) 394 8881 *Fax:* (033) 342 7419, pg 568

Shuter & Shooter (Pty) Ltd (South Africa) *Tel:* (033) 347 6100 *Fax:* (033) 347 6120 *Web Site:* www.shuter.co.za, pg 1341

Shuttle Multimedia Inc (Taiwan, Province of China) *Tel:* (02) 87924088 *Fax:* (02) 87924089 *Web Site:* www.eduplus.com, pg 641

Shwepyidan Printing & Publishing House (Myanmar), pg 476

Shy Mau & Shy Chaur Publishing Co Ltd (Taiwan, Province of China) *Tel:* (02) 2218-3277 *Fax:* (02) 2218-3239 *E-mail:* carrol@coolbooks.com.tw *Web Site:* www.coolbooks.com.tw, pg 641

The Siam Society (Thailand) *Tel:* (02) 66164707 *Fax:* (02) 2583491 *E-mail:* info@siam-society.org *Web Site:* www.siam-society.org, pg 1406

Siamantas VA A Ouvas (Greece) *Tel:* (0210) 8824960 *Fax:* (0210) 8824960, pg 312

Sibelius-Akatemian Kirjasto (Finland) *Tel:* (09) 4054 541 *Fax:* (09) 4054 542 *E-mail:* sibakirjasto@siba.fi *Web Site:* www.siba.fi/Kirjastot, pg 1505

Sibi (Bulgaria) *Tel:* (02) 9870141 *Fax:* (02) 9875709 *E-mail:* sibi@ind.interner-bg.bg, pg 97

SIBS Publishing House Inc (Philippines) *Tel:* 687-6164 *Fax:* 687-1716 *E-mail:* sibsbook@info.com.ph; sibs@eyp.ph *Web Site:* www.sibs.com.ph, pg 521

Wydawnictwo SIC (Poland) *Tel:* (022) 8400753 *Fax:* (022) 8400753 *E-mail:* sic@sic.ksiazka.pl, pg 526

Sicania (Italy) *Tel:* (090) 2936373 *Fax:* (090) 2932461, pg 408

Sichuan Science & Technology Publishing House (China) *Tel:* (028) 664982; (028) 662 5025 *Fax:* (028) 6654063, pg 108

Sichuan University Press (China) *Tel:* (028) 583875-62529, pg 108

Edizioni Librarie Siciliane (Italy) *Tel:* (091) 8570221 *Fax:* (091) 342670, pg 408

Siciliano SA (Brazil) *Tel:* (011) 8395500; (011) 8319911 *Fax:* (011) 8328616, pg 90

J Sideris OE Ekdoseis (Greece) *Tel:* (0210) 3833434; (0210) 5140627 *Fax:* (0210) 3832294, pg 312

Michalis Sideris (Greece) *Tel:* (0210) 3301165; (0210) 03301161 (bookstore) *Fax:* (0210) 3301164, pg 312

Sidgwick & Jackson Ltd (United Kingdom) *Tel:* (020) 7881 8000 *Fax:* (020) 7881 8001, pg 757

Siebenberg-Verlag (Germany) *Tel:* (05695) 1028 *Fax:* (05695) 1027 *E-mail:* fh@huebner-books.de *Web Site:* www.huebner-books.de, pg 283

Siebert Verlag GmbH (Germany) *Tel:* (06201) 6007-0 *Fax:* (06201) 6007-310, pg 283

Siedler Verlag (Germany) *Tel:* (030) 44 38 45-0 *E-mail:* bettine.vonborries@bertelsmann.de *Web Site:* www.randomhouse.de/siedler, pg 283

Siegler & Co Verlag fuer Zeitarchive GmbH (Germany) *Tel:* (02241) 3164-0, pg 283

Georg Siemens Verlagsbuchhandlung (Germany) *Tel:* (030) 769904-0 *Fax:* (030) 769904-18 *E-mail:* gsiemensv@t-online.de, pg 283

Sierra Leone Association of Archivists, Librarians & Information Scientists (SLAALIS) (Sierra Leone) *Tel:* (022) 220758, pg 1570

Sierra Leone Library Board (Sierra Leone) *Tel:* (022) 226 993, pg 1542

Sierra Leone University Press (Sierra Leone) *Tel:* (022) 27300; (022) 23494; (022) 27399; (022) 27323, pg 554

Sifri Ltd (Israel) *Tel:* (03) 5784679, pg 372

Sifriat Poalim Ltd (Israel) *Tel:* (03) 5183143 *Fax:* (03) 5183191 *E-mail:* akantor@inter.net.il, pg 372

Siglo XXI Editores de Colombia Ltda (Colombia) *Tel:* (01) 6110787 *Fax:* (01) 6110757, pg 112

Siglo XXI de Espana Editores SA (Spain) *Tel:* (091) 562 37 23; (091) 561 77 48 *Fax:* (091) 561 58 19 *E-mail:* sigloxxi@sigloxxieditores.com *Web Site:* www.sigloxxieditores.com, pg 599

Siglo XXI Editores SA de CV (Mexico) *Tel:* (05) 6587999; (05) 6587588 *Fax:* (05) 6587599 *E-mail:* sigloxxi@inetcorp.net.mx *Web Site:* www.sigloxxi-editores.com.mx, pg 472

Sigloch Edition Helmut Sigloch GmbH & Co KG (Germany) *Tel:* (07953) 883-0 *Fax:* (07953) 883-320 *E-mail:* info@sigloch.de *Web Site:* www.sigloch.de, pg 283

Sigma (Greece) *Tel:* (0210) 3638941; (0210) 3607667 *Fax:* (0210) 3638941 *E-mail:* sigma@sigmabooks.gr *Web Site:* www.sigmabooks.gr, pg 312

Sigma Press (United Kingdom) *Tel:* (01625) 531035 *Fax:* (01625) 531035 *E-mail:* info@sigmapress.co.uk *Web Site:* www.sigmapress.co.uk, pg 758

Edition Sigma e.Kfm (Germany) *Tel:* (030) 623 23 63 *Fax:* (030) 623 93 93 *E-mail:* verlag@edition-sigma.de *Web Site:* www.edition-sigma.de, pg 283

Editorial Sigmar SACI (Argentina) *Tel:* (011) 4381-2844; (011) 4381-2241 *Fax:* (011) 4383-5633 *E-mail:* editorial@sigmar.com.ar *Web Site:* www.sigmar.com.ar, pg 9

Editions Du Signal Rene Gaillard (Switzerland) *Tel:* (021) 3290194 *Fax:* (021) 3290194, pg 634

Signament I Comunicacio, SL Signament Edicions (Spain) *Tel:* (093) 4516888 *Fax:* (093) 3234417, pg 599

Editura Signata (Romania) *Tel:* (056) 153081, pg 542

Signes du Monde (France) *Tel:* (06) 12 99 73 37 *Fax:* (0561) 575717, pg 1176, 1216

Ediciones Sigueme SA (Spain) *Tel:* (0923) 21 82 03 *Fax:* (0923) 27 05 63 *E-mail:* sigueme@ctv.es, pg 600

Uitgeverij De Sikkel NV (Belgium) *Tel:* (03) 312 86 30 *Fax:* (03) 311 77 39 *E-mail:* informatie@deboeck.be *Web Site:* www.desikkel.be, pg 73

Sila & Zivot (Bulgaria) *Tel:* (056) 20965 *E-mail:* silajivot@bse.bg, pg 97

Edicoes Silabo (Portugal) *Tel:* (021) 525880 *Fax:* (021) 314 58 80 *E-mail:* silabo@mail.telepac.pt, pg 536

Edicoes Silabo (Portugal) *Tel:* (021) 8130345 *Fax:* (021) 8166719 *E-mail:* silabo@silabo.pt *Web Site:* www.silabo.pt, pg 1161

Edicoes Silabo (Portugal) *Tel:* (021) 316 12 81 *Fax:* (021) 314 58 80 *E-mail:* silabo@mail.telepac.pt, pg 1181

Edicoes Silabo (Portugal) *Tel:* (021) 8130345 *Fax:* (021) 8166719 *E-mail:* silabo@silabo.pt *Web Site:* www.silabo.pt, pg 1222, 1246

Silberburg-Verlag Titus Haeussermann GmbH (Germany) *Tel:* (07071) 6885-0 *Fax:* (07071) 6885-20 *E-mail:* info@silberburg.de *Web Site:* www.silberburg.com, pg 283

Die Silberschnur Verlag GmbH (Germany) *Tel:* (02687) 929068 *Fax:* (02687) 929524 *E-mail:* info@silberschnur.de *Web Site:* www.silberschnur.de, pg 283

Silex Ediciones (Spain) *Tel:* (091) 356.69.09 *Fax:* (091) 361.00.75 *E-mail:* pedidosweb@silexediciones.com *Web Site:* www.silexediciones.com, pg 600

Silkroad Publishers Agency, Ltd (Thailand) *Tel:* (02) 2584798; (02) 2588266 *Fax:* (02) 6620553 *E-mail:* silkroad@ji-net.com, pg 1138

Silkworm Books (Thailand) *Tel:* (053) 4765326 *Fax:* (053) 4765326 *E-mail:* silkedit@loxinfo.co.th *Web Site:* www.silkwormbooks.com, pg 645

Silliman University Library (Philippines) *Tel:* (035) 4227208; (035) 4226002 *Fax:* (035) 4227208 *E-mail:* sulib@su.edu.ph *Web Site:* su.edu.ph, pg 1536

Siloe - Kerdore (France) *Tel:* (02) 43532601 *Fax:* (02) 43535601 *E-mail:* siloe-kerdore@wanadoo.fr, pg 185

Silsilah Publication (Philippines) *Tel:* (02) 5663, pg 521

Silva (Italy) *Tel:* (0521) 804106 *Fax:* (0521) 804406, pg 408

Editions Andre Silvaire Sarl (France) *Tel:* (01) 43 26 72 34 *Fax:* (01) 55 42 16 69, pg 185

Silvana Editoriale SpA (Italy) *Tel:* (02) 618361 *Fax:* (02) 6172464 *E-mail:* international@silvanaeditoriale.it *Web Site:* www.silvanaeditoriale.it, pg 408

Silver Link Publishing Ltd (United Kingdom) *Tel:* (01536) 330588 *Fax:* (01536) 330469 *E-mail:* sales@nostalgiacollection.com *Web Site:* www.nostalgiacollection.com, pg 758

Dorie Simmonds Agency (United Kingdom) *Tel:* (020) 7486 9228 *Fax:* (020) 7486 8228, pg 1143

Jeffrey Simmons (United Kingdom) *Tel:* (020) 7224 8917 *Fax:* (020) 7224 8918 *E-mail:* jas@london-inc.com, pg 1143

Simon & Schuster (Australia) Pty Ltd (Australia) *Tel:* (02) 9415 9900 *Fax:* (02) 9417 3188 (customer service); (02) 9417 4292 (editorial); (02) 9417 1087 (publicity) *E-mail:* cservice@simonandschuster.com.au; rights.dept@simonandschuster.com. au *Web Site:* www.simonsays.com; www.simonandschuster.com.au, pg 41

Simon & Schuster Ltd (United Kingdom) *Tel:* (020) 7316 1900 *Fax:* (020) 7316 0332 *E-mail:* firstname.surname@simonandschuster.co.uk *Web Site:* www.simonsays.co.uk, pg 758

Buchkonzept Simon KG (Germany) *Tel:* (089) 21939012 *Fax:* (089) 21939014, pg 283

Simon Stevin NV (Belgium) *Tel:* (02) 5121085; (02) 5138295 *Fax:* (02) 5117015, pg 1302

Samuel Simson Ltd (Israel) *Tel:* (03) 5181604 *Fax:* (03) 5181544 *E-mail:* sefer-lakol@mixam.co.il, pg 372

The Simul Press Inc (Japan) *Tel:* (03) 3226-2861 *Fax:* (03) 3226-2860, pg 428

Sin Min Chu Publishing Co (Hong Kong) *Tel:* (02) 2334 9327 *Fax:* (02) 76 58 471, pg 319

Sinag-Tala Publishers Inc (Philippines) *Tel:* (02) 8192681 *Fax:* (02) 8192563, pg 521

Sinai Publishing Co (Israel) *Tel:* (03) 5163672 *Fax:* (03) 5163672, pg 372

Sind University Central Library (Pakistan) *Tel:* (0221) 771188, pg 1535

Sindhi Adabi Board (Pakistan) *Tel:* (0221) 771276; (0221) 771465; (0221) 771600, pg 1403

Sindicato Nacional dos Editores de Livros (SNEL) (Brazil) *Tel:* (021) 2233-6481 *Fax:* (021) 2253-8502 *E-mail:* snel@snel.org.br *Web Site:* www.snel.org.br, pg 1263

Sing Cheong Printing Co Ltd (Hong Kong) *Tel:* 25618801; 25626317 *Fax:* 25659467 *E-mail:* info@singcheong.com.hk, pg 1158, 1219

Singapore Book Publishers' Association (Singapore) *Tel:* (065) 3447801; (065) 4407409 *Fax:* (065) 4470897 *E-mail:* twcsbpa@singnet.com.sg, pg 1283

Singapore University Press Pte Ltd (Singapore) *Tel:* 67761148; 68742382; 68742472; 68748186 *Fax:* 67740652 *E-mail:* nusbooks@nus.edu.sg *Web Site:* www.nus.edu.sg/npu, pg 558

Single X Publications (Australia) *Tel:* (08) 8127 0827, pg 41

Sinisukk (Estonia) *Tel:* 656 1872 *Fax:* 656 1872 *E-mail:* sinisukk@vorguvara.ee, pg 140

Sino Publishing House Ltd (Hong Kong) *Tel:* 2884 9963 *Fax:* 2884 9321 *E-mail:* info@sinophl.com *Web Site:* www.sinophl.com, pg 1158

Sino Publishing House Ltd (Hong Kong) *Tel:* 2884 9963 *Fax:* 2884 9321 *Web Site:* www.sinophl.com, pg 1219, 1236

Sino Publishing House Ltd (Hong Kong) *Tel:* 2884 9963 *Fax:* 2884 9321 *E-mail:* benyan@sinophl.com *Web Site:* www.sinophl.com, pg 1246

Editora Sinodal (Brazil) *Tel:* (051) 590-2366 *Fax:* (051) 590-2664 *E-mail:* editora@editorasinodal.com.br *Web Site:* www.editorasinodal.com.br, pg 90

Editora Sinodal (Brazil) *Tel:* (051) 590 2366 *Fax:* (051) 590 2664 *E-mail:* editora@editorasinodal.com.br *Web Site:* www.editorasinodal.com.br, pg 1304

Sinodalno Izdatelstvo na Balgarskata pravoslavna carkva (Bulgaria) *Tel:* (02) 875611; (02) 875245, pg 97

Sinorama Magazine Co (Taiwan, Province of China) *Tel:* (02) 2392-2256 *Fax:* (02) 2397-0655 *E-mail:* service@mail.sinorama.com.tw *Web Site:* www.sinorama.com.tw, pg 641

Editorial Sintes SA (Spain) *Tel:* (093) 3182838, pg 600

Editorial Sintesis, SA (Spain) *Tel:* (091) 593 20 98 *Fax:* (091) 445 86 96 *E-mail:* sintesis@sintesis.com *Web Site:* www.sintesis.com, pg 600

Sinwel-Buchhandlung Verlag (Switzerland) *Tel:* (031) 425205 *Fax:* (031) 3331376, pg 634

Alex Siokis & Co (Greece) *Tel:* (02310) 230257; (02310) 287016 *Fax:* (02310) 281014 *E-mail:* siokis@spark.net.gr, pg 312

SIPI (Servizio Italiano Pubblicazioni Internazionali) Srl (Italy) *Tel:* (06) 5920509 *Fax:* (06) 5924819, pg 408

SIR Publishing (New Zealand) *Tel:* (04) 472 7421 *Fax:* (04) 473 1841 *E-mail:* sirp@rsnz.govt.nz *Web Site:* www.rsnz.govt.nz/publ, pg 501

Siriraj Medical Library (Thailand) *Tel:* (02) 411 3112; (02) 419 7635; (02) 419 7637 *Fax:* (02) 412 8418 *E-mail:* silib@diamond.mahidol.ac.th *Web Site:* www.medlib.si.mahidol.ac.th, pg 1550

Equipo Sirius SA (Spain) *Tel:* (091) 710 73 49 *Fax:* (091) 705 43 04 *E-mail:* sirius@equiposirius.com *Web Site:* www.equiposirius.com, pg 600

R Sirkis Publishers Ltd (Israel) *Tel:* (03) 7510792 *Fax:* (03) 7513750 *E-mail:* sirkispb@inter.net.il, pg 372

Sirmio (Spain) *Tel:* (093) 2123808 *Fax:* (093) 4182317 *E-mail:* qcrema@mito.ibernet.com, pg 600

Ediciones Siruela SA (Spain) *Tel:* (091) 3555720; (091) 3554605; (091) 3552202 *Fax:* (091) 3552201 *E-mail:* siruela@siruela.com *Web Site:* www.siruela.com, pg 600

Sistema Bibliotecario (Honduras) *Tel:* 232-2204 *Fax:* 232-2204º *E-mail:* webmaster@biblio.unah.edu.hn *Web Site:* www.biblio.unah.edu.hn, pg 1514

Sistema de Bibliotecas y de Informacion (Argentina) *Tel:* (011) 4952-0078 *Fax:* (011) 4952-6557 *E-mail:* webmaster@sisbi.uba.ar *Web Site:* www.sisbi.uba.ar, pg 1490

Sistemas Tecnicos de Edicion SA de CV (Mexico) *Tel:* (05) 6559144; (05) 6845220 *Fax:* (05) 5739412, pg 472

Sistemas Universales, SA (Mexico) *Tel:* (05) 705-4568; (05) 705-5937 *Fax:* (05) 705-3421 *E-mail:* 73661.405@coms, pg 472

SiT Tapir Fagbokhandel (Norway) *Tel:* 73598420 *Fax:* 73598495 *E-mail:* forlag@tapir.no *Web Site:* www.campus.tapir.no, pg 1333

Sita Books & Periodicals Pvt Ltd (India) *Tel:* (022) 5555589; (022) 5973281; (022) 5973282; (022) 5973283 *Fax:* (022) 5561622 *E-mail:* ssrao@bom5.vsnl.net.in; sitabook@bom7.vsnl.net.in *Web Site:* www.sitabooks.com, pg 349

Sita-MB (Bulgaria) *Tel:* (092) 872285, pg 97

6-9 Club (United Kingdom) *Tel:* (01993) 893456 *Fax:* (01993) 6039092, pg 1257

Edicions 62 (Spain) *Tel:* (093) 4437100 *Fax:* (093) 4437130 *E-mail:* correu@grup62.com *Web Site:* www.grup62.com, pg 600

Grup 62 (Spain) *Tel:* (093) 443 71 00 *Fax:* (093) 443 71 30 *E-mail:* correu@grup62.com *Web Site:* www.grup62.com, pg 600

Sjaloom Uitgeverijen (Netherlands) *Tel:* (020) 6206263 *Fax:* (020) 4288540 *E-mail:* post@sjaloom.nl *Web Site:* www.sjaloom.nl, pg 489

Sjoestrands Foerlag (Sweden) *Tel:* (08) 29 99 32 *Fax:* (08) 98 46 45, pg 615

Skandinavia Verlag (Germany) *Tel:* (030) 8137006 *Fax:* (030) 8141029, pg 1132

SKAT (Swiss Centre for Development Cooperation in Technology & Management) (Switzerland) *Tel:* (071) 2285454 *Fax:* (071) 2285455 *E-mail:* info@skat.ch *Web Site:* www.skat.ch, pg 634

A/S Skattekartoteket (Denmark) *Tel:* 33117874 *Fax:* 33938025 *E-mail:* magnus@cddk.dk, pg 134

Skills Publishing (Australia) *Tel:* (02) 4759 2844 *Fax:* (02) 4759 3721 *E-mail:* aww@skillspublish.com.au *Web Site:* www.skillspublish.com.au, pg 41

Charles Skilton Ltd (United Kingdom) *Tel:* (020) 7351 4995 *Fax:* (020) 7351 4995, pg 758

Editions D'Art Albert Skira SA (Switzerland) *Tel:* (022) 906 80 00 *Fax:* (022) 3495535, pg 634

Skjaldborg Ltd (Iceland) *Tel:* 5882400 *Fax:* 5888994 *E-mail:* skjaldborg@skjaldborg.is, pg 326

Skolska Knjiga (Croatia) *Tel:* (01) 48 30 491; (01) 48 30 511 *Fax:* (01) 48 30 506 *E-mail:* skolska@skolskaknjiga.hr *Web Site:* www.skolskaknjiga.hr, pg 119

Skoob Russell Square (United Kingdom) *Tel:* (020) 7278 8760 *E-mail:* books@skoob.com *Web Site:* www.skoob.com, pg 758

SKT's Boghandel (Denmark) *Tel:* 44686662 *Fax:* 44686660 *E-mail:* skt@sktbooks.dk *Web Site:* www.sktbooks.dk, pg 1308

Skuggsja bokaforlag (Iceland) *Tel:* 555-0045, pg 326

'Slask' Ltd (Poland) *Tel:* (032) 258 07 56; (032) 2581812; (032) 2583222; (032) 2581910 *Fax:* (032) 2583229 *E-mail:* biuro@slaskwn.com.pl *Web Site:* www.slaskwn.com.pl, pg 526

Biblioteka Slaska (Poland) *Tel:* (032) 208 38 75 *Fax:* (032) 208 37 20 *E-mail:* bsl@bs.katowice.pl *Web Site:* www.bs.katowice.pl, pg 1538

Slatkine Reprints (Switzerland) *Tel:* (022) 3100476 *Fax:* (022) 3107101 *E-mail:* librarie@slatkine.ch *Web Site:* www.slatkine.ch, pg 634

Slavena (Bulgaria) *Tel:* (052) 602465; (052) 225935 *Fax:* (052) 225935 *E-mail:* slavena@triada.bg *Web Site:* www.slavena.net, pg 97

Privlacica Slavonska Naklada (Croatia) *Tel:* (032) 306 068; (032) 306 069; (032) 306 070 *Fax:* (032) 331735 *E-mail:* privlacica@vk.tel.hr, pg 119

Verlag Josef Otto Slezak (Austria) *Tel:* (01) 587 02 59 *Fax:* (01) 587 02 59 *E-mail:* verlag.slezak@aon.at *Web Site:* www.byronny.at/index.html, pg 57

SLG Press (United Kingdom) *Tel:* (01865) 721301 *Fax:* (01865) 790860 *E-mail:* editor@slgpress.co.uk; orders@slgpress.co.uk *Web Site:* www.slgpress.co.uk, pg 758

Slo Viet (Slovakia) *Tel:* (07) 52494886, pg 560

Slon Sociologicke Nakladatelstvi (Czech Republic) *Tel:* (02) 222 220 025 *Fax:* (02) 222 220 025 *E-mail:* redakce@slon-knihy.cz *Web Site:* www.slon-knihy.cz, pg 127

Slouch Hat Publications (Australia) *Tel:* (03) 5986-6437 *Fax:* (03) 5986-6312 *E-mail:* slouchat@surf.net.au *Web Site:* www.slouch-hat.com.au, pg 41

Slovansky Tatran, Vydavatel 'stro spoi sro (Slovakia) *Tel:* (02) 54435849 *Fax:* (02) 54435777, pg 560

Slovart Co Ltd (Slovakia) *Tel:* (02) 5479 1528 *Fax:* (02) 6541 1375 *E-mail:* slovart-expo@zutom.sk *Web Site:* www.slovart-expo.sk, pg 1339

Slovenska matica (Slovenia) *Tel:* (01) 2514 200; (01) 2514 227; (01) 4263 190 *Fax:* (01) 2514 200, pg 561

Slovenska Narodna Kniznica, Martin (Slovakia) *Tel:* (0842) 31861 *Fax:* (0842) 32993 *E-mail:* vms@esix.matica.sk, pg 560

Slovenska Narodna Kniznica, Martin (Slovakia) *Tel:* (043) 430 18 02 *Fax:* (043) 430 18 02 *E-mail:* snk@snk.sk *Web Site:* www.snk.sk, pg 1543

Slovenske pedagogicke nakladateistvo (Slovakia) *Tel:* (07) 55423892 *Fax:* (07) 55571894 *E-mail:* spn@spn.sk, pg 560

Slovensky Spisovatel Ltd as (Slovakia) *Tel:* (02) 5249 9734 *Fax:* (02) 5249 9736, pg 560

SLS Legal Publications (NI) (United Kingdom) *Tel:* (028) 9027 3451 *Fax:* (028) 9027 3376; (028) 9033 5040 *E-mail:* law-enquiries@qub.ac.uk *Web Site:* www.law.qub.ac.uk, pg 758

Sluntse Publishing House (Bulgaria) *Tel:* (02) 988 37 97 *Fax:* (02) 987 14 05 *E-mail:* info@sluntse.com *Web Site:* www.sluntse.com, pg 97

Sluzbeni List (Serbia and Montenegro) *Tel:* (011) 3060333; (011) 3060310 *Fax:* (011) 3060393, pg 553

Ediciones SM (Spain) *Tel:* (091) 4228800 *Fax:* (091) 5089927 *E-mail:* jcabrerap@ediciones-sm.com, pg 600

Small Industry Research Institute (SIRI) (India) *Tel:* (011) 23841893; (011) 2916804 *Fax:* (011) 2910805 *E-mail:* siri@ndf.vsnl.net.in; siricon@vsnl.com, pg 349

Smart & Mookerdum (Myanmar), pg 476

SMC Publishing Inc (Taiwan, Province of China) *Tel:* (02) 2362-0190 *Fax:* (02) 3623834 *Web Site:* www.smcbook.com.tw, pg 642

Koninklijke Smeets Offset (Netherlands) *Tel:* (0495) 57 09 11 *Fax:* (0495) 54 29 05 *E-mail:* rswinfo@rotosmeets.com, pg 489

Smena Publishing House (Slovakia) *Tel:* (07) 491455; (07) 497171, pg 560

Rudolf G Smend (Germany) *Tel:* (0221) 312047 *Fax:* (0221) 9 32 07 18 *E-mail:* smend@smend.de, pg 283

SMER Diffusion (Morocco) *Tel:* (07) 723725; (07) 725960 *Fax:* (07) 701643, pg 1328

Smith-Gordon & Co Ltd (United Kingdom) *Tel:* (020) 7351 7042 *Fax:* (020) 7351 1250 *E-mail:* publisher@smithgordon.com, pg 758

John Smith & Son Booksellers (United Kingdom) *Tel:* (01425) 471160 *Fax:* (01425) 471718 *Web Site:* www.johnsmith.co.uk, pg 1353

Smith Settle Ltd (United Kingdom) *Tel:* (01756) 701381 *Fax:* (01524) 251708 *E-mail:* editorial@dalesman.co.uk, pg 758

Smurfit Print (Ireland) *Tel:* (01) 202-7000 *Fax:* (01) 269-4481 *Web Site:* www.smurfit.ie, pg 1180

Smurfit Print (Ireland) *Tel:* (01) 202 7000 *Fax:* (01) 269 4481 *Web Site:* www.smurfit.ie, pg 1220

Colin Smythe Ltd (United Kingdom) *Tel:* (01753) 886000 *Fax:* (01753) 886469 *E-mail:* sales@colinsmythe.co.uk *Web Site:* www.colinsmythe.co.uk, pg 759

Snoeck-Ducaju en Zoon NV (Belgium) *Tel:* (09) 267.04.11 *Fax:* (09) 267.04.60 *E-mail:* sdz@sdz.be *Web Site:* www.sdz.be, pg 73

Snofugl Forlag (Norway) *Tel:* 72872411 *Fax:* 72871013 *E-mail:* snofugl@online.no, pg 510

Snowbooks Ltd (United Kingdom) *Tel:* (020) 7553 4473 *Fax:* (020) 7251 3130 *E-mail:* info@snowbooks.com *Web Site:* www.snowbooks.com, pg 759

SNP Best-Set Typesetter Ltd (Hong Kong) *Tel:* 2897 6033 *Fax:* 2897 5170 *E-mail:* bestset@snpcorp.com *Web Site:* www.bestset-typesetter.com, pg 1179

SNP Best-Set Typesetter Ltd (Hong Kong) *Tel:* 2897 6033 *Fax:* 2897 5170 *E-mail:* best-set-usa@email.msn.com; bestset@snpcorp.com *Web Site:* www.bestset-typesetter.com, pg 1219

SNP Best-Set Typesetter Ltd (United States) *Toll Free Tel:* 866-888-8767 *Fax:* 914-961-8212 *Web Site:* www.bestset-typesetter.com, pg 1189

SNP Leefung Holdings Ltd (Hong Kong) *Tel:* 2810 6801 *Fax:* 2810 5612 *Web Site:* www.leefung-asco.com, pg 1158

SNP Panpac Pacific Publishing Pte Ltd (Singapore) *Tel:* 6261 6288 *Fax:* 6261 6088 *Web Site:* www.snp.com/sg, pg 558

SNP SPrint Pte Ltd (Singapore) *Tel:* 6741-2500 *Fax:* 6744-7098; 6743-9661 *E-mail:* enquiries@snpcorp.com *Web Site:* www.snpcorp.com, pg 1161

SNP SPrint Pte Ltd (Singapore) *Tel:* 6826-9600 *Fax:* 6820-3341 *E-mail:* enquiries@snpcorp.com *Web Site:* www.snp-corp.com, pg 1182

SNP SPrint Pte Ltd (Singapore) *Tel:* 6741 2500 *Fax:* 6744 3770 *E-mail:* paulwong@snpcorp.com *Web Site:* www.snpcorp.com, pg 1223

SNP SPrint Pte Ltd (Singapore) *Tel:* 6741-2500 *Fax:* 6744-7098 *E-mail:* enquiries@snpcorp.com *Web Site:* www.snpcorp.com, pg 1238

SNP SPrint Pte Ltd (Singapore) *Tel:* 6741-2500 *Fax:* 6744-3770 *E-mail:* enquiries@snpcorp.com *Web Site:* www.snpcorp.com, pg 1246

SNS Foerlag (Sweden) *Tel:* (08) 507 025 00 *Fax:* (08) 507 025 15 *E-mail:* info@sns.se *Web Site:* www.sns.se, pg 615

William Snyder Publishing Associates (United Kingdom) *Tel:* (01865) 513186 *Fax:* (01865) 513186, pg 759

Sober Foerlags AB (Sweden) *Tel:* (08) 672 6000 *Fax:* (08) 672 6001, pg 615

Sobrindes Linha Grafica E Editora Ltda (Brazil) *Tel:* (061) 2247778; (061) 2247706; (061) 2247756 *Fax:* (061) 2241895 *E-mail:* linhagrafica@conectanet.com.br, pg 90

Sobun-Sha (Japan) *Tel:* (03) 3263-7101 *Fax:* (03) 3263-6789 *E-mail:* info@sobunsha.co.jp *Web Site:* www.sobunsha.co.jp, pg 428

Sociaal en Cultureel Planbureau (Netherlands) *Tel:* (070) 3407000 *Fax:* (070) 3407044 *E-mail:* info@scp.ul *Web Site:* www.scp.nl, pg 489

Social Club Books (Australia) *Tel:* (03) 9473 5555 *Fax:* (03) 9417 5574 *E-mail:* info@scb.com.au *Web Site:* www.scb.com.au, pg 41

Social Science Press (Australia) *Tel:* 800-654-831 *Fax:* 800-641-823 *E-mail:* newtext@thomsonlearning.com.au *Web Site:* www.thomsonlearning.com.au/higher/index.asp, pg 41

Social Sciences Library (Viet Nam) *Tel:* (08) 20644 *Fax:* (08) 223735, pg 1555

Sociedad Biblica Peruana Asociacion Cultural (Peru) *Tel:* (014) 4330232 *Fax:* (014) 4336389 *E-mail:* sbpac01@telemail.telematic.edu.pe, pg 1335

Biblioteca de la Sociedad Cientifica del Paraguay (Paraguay) *Tel:* (021) 24832, pg 1536

Sociedad de Bibliotecarios de Puerto Rico (Puerto Rico) *Tel:* (787) 764-0000 (ext 5205) *Fax:* (787) 764-0000 (ext 5204) *E-mail:* vtorres@upracd.upr.clu.edu *Web Site:* www.geocities.com/sociedadsbpr, pg 1570

Sociedad de Ciencias, Letras y Artes El Museo Canario (Spain) *Tel:* (0928) 336800 *Fax:* (0928) 336801 *E-mail:* info@elmuseocanario.com *Web Site:* www.elmuseocanario.com, pg 1405

Sociedad Editorial Americana (Dominican Republic) *Tel:* 689 7813 *Fax:* 688 9378, pg 136

Sociedad General de Autores de la Argentina (SGAA) (Argentina) *Tel:* (011) 4811-2582; (011) 4812-9996 *Fax:* (011) 4812-6954 *E-mail:* info@argentores.org.ar *Web Site:* www.argentores.org.ar, pg 1259

Sociedad General Espanola de Libreria SA - SGEL (Spain) *Tel:* (091) 657 69 00; (091) 657 69 12 *Fax:* (091) 657 69 28; (091) 657 69 19 *Web Site:* www.sgel.es, pg 600

Sociedade Brasileira de Cultura Inglesa - Biblioteca (Brazil) *Tel:* (071) 247-9788 *Fax:* (021) 245-3287 *E-mail:* culturainglesa@br.inter.net *Web Site:* www.culturainglesa-ba.com.br, pg 1495

Sociedade Distribuidora de Livros Ltda (Sodilivro) (Brazil) *Tel:* (021) 580-1168; (021) 580-6230 *Fax:* (021) 580-5868, pg 90

Sociedade Portuguesa de Autores (Portugal) *Tel:* (021) 3594400 *Fax:* (021) 3530257 *E-mail:* geral@spautores.pt *Web Site:* www.spautores.pt, pg 1404

Societa Dantesca Italiana (Italy) *Tel:* (055) 287134 *Fax:* (055) 211316 *E-mail:* sdi@leonet.it; sdi.biblio@leonet.it (library) *Web Site:* www.danteonline.it, pg 1402

Societa Editrice Internazionale - SEI (Italy) *Tel:* (011) 52271 *Fax:* (011) 5211320, pg 408

Societa Editrice la Goliardica Pavese SRL (Italy) *Tel:* (0382) 529570 *Fax:* (0382) 423140, pg 408

Societa Napoletana Storia Patria Napoli (Italy) *Tel:* (081) 2536340 *Fax:* (081) 2536509 *E-mail:* snsp@unina.it *Web Site:* www.storia.unina.it, pg 408

Societa Stampa Sportiva (Italy) *Tel:* (06) 5817311 *Fax:* (06) 5806526 *E-mail:* segreteria@stampasportiva.com *Web Site:* www.stampasportiva.com, pg 408

Societa Storica Catanese (Italy) *Tel:* (095) 434782, pg 408

Societa Ziaristilor din Romania (Romania) *Tel:* (01) 222 83 51; (01) 222 38 71; (01) 315 24 82 *Fax:* (01) 222 42 66 *E-mail:* szrpress@moon.rol, pg 1282

Societaets-Verlag (Germany) *Tel:* (069) 75 01-0 *Fax:* (069) 75 01-48 77 *Web Site:* www.societaets-verlag.de, pg 283

Societatea de Stiinte Filologice din Romania (SSF) (Romania) *Tel:* (021) 3123148, pg 1404

Societe Africaine d'Edition (Senegal) *Tel:* 217977; 220284, pg 551

La Societe Africaine d'Edition et de Communication (SAEC) (Guinea) *Tel:* 45 34 44 *Fax:* 45 34 44 *E-mail:* dtniane@eti-bull.net, pg 1272

Societe Belge des Auteurs, Compositeurs et Editeurs (SABAM) (Belgium) *Tel:* (02) 230 2640 *Fax:* (02) 231 1800 *E-mail:* 101641.2761@compuserve.com *Web Site:* www.sabam.be, pg 1397

Societe Cheriffienne de Distribution et de Presse Sochepress (Morocco) *Tel:* (02) 22400223 *Fax:* (02) 22404032 *E-mail:* infolivre@sochepress.co.ma, pg 1328

Societe de Langue et de Litterature Wallonnes ASBL (Belgium) *Tel:* (086) 344432 *E-mail:* sllw.be@skynet.be *Web Site:* users.skynet.be/sllw, pg 1397

Societe d'Edition d'Afrique Nouvelle (Senegal) *Tel:* (08) 211381; (08) 221580 *Fax:* (08) 223604, pg 551

Societe des Auteurs et Compositeurs Dramatiques (SACD) (France) *Tel:* (01) 40 23 44 44 *Fax:* (01) 45 26 74 28 *E-mail:* infosacd@sacd.fr *Web Site:* www.sacd.fr, pg 1399

Societe des Editions Grasset et Fasquelle (France) *Tel:* (01) 44392200 *Fax:* (01) 42226418 *E-mail:* editorial@grasset.fr *Web Site:* www.grasset.fr, pg 185

Societe des Editions Privat SA (France) *Tel:* (05) 34 31 81 81; (05) 34 31 81 88 *Fax:* (05) 34 31 64 44 *E-mail:* editionsprivat@wanadoo.fr, pg 185

Societe des Gens de Lettres de France (France) *Tel:* (01) 53 10 12 00 *Fax:* (01) 53 10 12 12 *E-mail:* depot.sgdlf@wanadoo.fr *Web Site:* www.sgdl.org, pg 1399

Societe des Libraires et Editeurs de la Suisse Romande (SLESR) (Switzerland) *Tel:* (021) 319 71 11 *Fax:* (021) 319 79 10 *E-mail:* aself@centrezational.cl *Web Site:* www.culturactif.ch/editions/asef1.htm, pg 1286

la Societe des Poetes Francais (France) *Tel:* (01) 60 29 46 06 *E-mail:* poetesfrancais@aol.com, pg 1399

Societe d'Etudes Dantesques (France) *Tel:* 497134610; 497134611 *Fax:* 497134640 *E-mail:* cum@ville-nice.fr *Web Site:* www.cum-nice.org, pg 1399

Societe d'Histoire Litteraire de la France (France) *Tel:* (01) 45872330 *Fax:* (01) 45872330 *E-mail:* srhlf@aol.com, pg 1399

Societe Ennewrasse Service Librairie et Imprimerie (Morocco) *Tel:* (077) 6413 *Fax:* (077) 6413, pg 475

Societe Francaise des Traducteurs (France) *Tel:* (01) 48 78 43 32 *Fax:* (01) 44 53 01 14 *E-mail:* sft@tiscali.fr *Web Site:* www.sft.fr, pg 1147

Societe Internationale des Bibliotheques et des Musees des Arts du Spectacle (SIBMAS) (United Kingdom) *Tel:* (020) 7943 4720 *Fax:* (020) 7943 4777 *Web Site:* www.theatrelibrary.org/sibmas/sibmas.html, pg 1293

Societe Mathematique de France - Institut Henri Poincare (France) *Tel:* (01) 44 27 67 96 *Fax:* (01) 40 46 90 96 *E-mail:* smf@dma.ens.fr *Web Site:* smf.emath.fr, pg 185

Societe Nationale d'Edition et de Diffusion (Tunisia) *Tel:* (01) 255000; (01) 261799, pg 1346

Societe Nouveaux Loisirs (France) *Tel:* (01) 49 54 42 00 *Fax:* (01) 45 44 94 03 *Web Site:* www.gallimard.fr, pg 185

Society for Editors & Proofreaders (United Kingdom) *Tel:* (020) 7736 3278 *Fax:* (020) 7736 3318 *E-mail:* administration@sfep.org.uk *Web Site:* www.sfep.org.uk, pg 1409

Society for Endocrinology (United Kingdom) *Tel:* (01454) 642200 *Fax:* (01454) 642222 *E-mail:* info@endocrinology.org; sales@endocrinology.org *Web Site:* www.endocrinology.org, pg 759

Society for Macedonian Studies (Greece) *Tel:* (031) 268710 *Fax:* (031) 971501 *E-mail:* ems@hyper.gr, pg 312

The Society for Promoting Christian Knowledge (SPCK) (United Kingdom) *Tel:* (020) 7643 0382 *Fax:* (020) 7643 0391 *E-mail:* spck@spck.org.uk *Web Site:* www.spck.org.uk, pg 759

Society for the Promotion of African, Asian & Latin American Literature (Germany) *Tel:* (069) 2102247 *Fax:* (069) 2102227 *E-mail:* litprom@book-fair.com *Web Site:* www.litprom.de, pg 1132

Society for the Study of Medieval Languages & Literature (United Kingdom) *Tel:* (01865) 276087 *Fax:* (01865) 276087 *Web Site:* www.mod-langs.ox.ac.uk/ssmll, pg 1409

Society of Archivists (United Kingdom) *Tel:* (01823) 327030 *Fax:* (01823) 371719 *E-mail:* offman@archives.org.uk *Web Site:* www.archives.org.uk, pg 1573

Society of Arts, Literature & Welfare (Bangladesh) *Web Site:* www.bjfao.gov.cn, pg 1396

Society of Authors (United Kingdom) *Tel:* (020) 7373 6642 *Fax:* (020) 7373 5768 *E-mail:* info@societyofauthors.org *Web Site:* www.societyofauthors.org/prizes.htm, pg 1165, 1293

Society of College, National & University Libraries (SCONUL) (United Kingdom) *Tel:* (020) 7387 0317 *Fax:* (020) 7383 3197 *E-mail:* info@sconul.ac.uk *Web Site:* www.sconul.ac.uk, pg 1573

The Society of County Librarians (United Kingdom) *Tel:* (0604) 20262, pg 1573

Society of Indexers (United Kingdom) *Tel:* (0114) 292 2350 *Fax:* (0114) 292 2351 *E-mail:* admin@indexers.org.uk *Web Site:* www.socind.demon.co.uk, pg 1293

The Society of Metaphysicians Ltd (United Kingdom) *Tel:* (01424) 751577 *Fax:* (01424) 751577 *E-mail:* newmeta@btinternet.com; info@metaphysicians.org.uk *Web Site:* www.newmeta.btinternet.co.uk; www.metaphysicians.org.uk; www.metaphysicalresearchgroup.org.uk, pg 759

The Society of Women Writers & Journalists (United Kingdom) *Tel:* (01379) 740550 *Fax:* (01379) 741716 *Web Site:* www.swwj.co.uk, pg 1409

Society of Women Writers NSW Inc (Australia) *Tel:* (03) 63310267 *Web Site:* www.womenwritersnsw.org, pg 1260

SocTip SA (Portugal) *Tel:* (021) 263 00 99 00 *Fax:* (021) 263 00 99 99 *E-mail:* soctip@soctip.pt *Web Site:* www.soctip.pt, pg 536

Edizioni Rosminiane Sodalitas (Italy) *Tel:* (0323) 30091 *Fax:* (0323) 31623 *E-mail:* edizioni@rosmini.it *Web Site:* www.rosmini.it/EdRosminiane.htm, pg 408

Soderstroms Forlag (Finland) *Tel:* (09) 6841 8620 *Fax:* (09) 6841 8621 *E-mail:* soderstrom@soderstrom.fi *Web Site:* www.soderstrom.fi, pg 144

Sodilivros (Portugal) *Tel:* (021) 3878902; (021) 3878903 *Fax:* (021) 3876281 *E-mail:* sodilivros@mail.telepac.pt, pg 1338

Soemwit Barwakhan (Thailand) *Tel:* (02) 214541, pg 645

Soez Yayin/Oyunajans (Turkey) *Tel:* (0212) 2806701 *Fax:* (0212) 2806803 *Web Site:* www.oyunajans.com, pg 651

Sofa (Slovakia) *Tel:* (02) 55422508 *Fax:* (02) 55422508 *E-mail:* sofa@ba.sknet.sk, pg 560

Sofia City & District State Archives (Bulgaria) *Tel:* (02) 940 01 06 *Fax:* (02) 980 14 43, pg 1496

Sofia University Kliment Ohridski Biblioteka (Bulgaria) *Tel:* (02) 9443719 *Fax:* (02) 467170 *E-mail:* lsu@libsu.uni-sofia.bg *Web Site:* www.libsu.uni-sofia.bg, pg 1496

Sofiac (Societe Francaise des Imprimeries Administratives Centrales) (France) *Tel:* (01) 40 64 42 42 *Fax:* (01) 40 64 42 40 *E-mail:* ble@berger-levrault.fr *Web Site:* www.editions.berger-levrault.fr, pg 185

Sofiprin (Czech Republic) *Tel:* (0602) 30 87 21 *Fax:* (02) 758280, pg 127

Sogang University Press (Republic of Korea) *Tel:* (02) 705-8213 *Fax:* (02) 705-0797 *E-mail:* chisook@ccs.sogang.ac.kr *Web Site:* www.sogang.ac.kr, pg 443

Sogensha Publishing Co Ltd (Japan) *Tel:* (06) 62319011 *Fax:* (06) 62333112 *E-mail:* sgse@email.msn.com *Web Site:* www.sogensha.co.jp, pg 428

Sohaksa (Republic of Korea) *Tel:* (02) 7967600 *Fax:* (02) 7968700, pg 443

Verlag SOI (Schweizerisches Ost-Institut) (Switzerland) *Tel:* (031) 431212 *Fax:* (031) 3513801, pg 634

Sojuz na drustavata za makedonski jazik i literatura (The Former Yugoslav Republic of Macedonia), pg 1402

Sokoine University of Agriculture Library (United Republic of Tanzania) *Tel:* (056) 3510; (056) 3514 *E-mail:* usa@hnettan.gri.apc.org, pg 1549

Ediciones Sol del Sur (Uruguay) *Tel:* (02) 621627, pg 778

Soldi-Verlag im Drockzentrum Harburg (Germany) *Tel:* (04181) 29 16 22 *Fax:* (04181) 29 16 23 *E-mail:* kontakt@karismaverlag.de *Web Site:* www.karismaverlag.de, pg 283

Il Sole 24 Ore Libri (Italy) *Tel:* (02) 30223944 *Fax:* (02) 3022405 *E-mail:* servizioclienti.libri@ilsole24ore.com *Web Site:* www.ilsole24ore.com, pg 408

Il Sole 24 Ore Pirola (Italy) *Tel:* (02) 30226651 *Fax:* (02) 38011205 *E-mail:* servizio.abbonamenti@ilsole24ore.com *Web Site:* www.ilsole24ore.com, pg 409

Editions du Soleil (Haiti) *Tel:* (01) 23147, pg 314

Anna Soler-Pont Literary Agecy (Spain) *Tel:* (093) 201 90 90 *Fax:* (093) 201 90 90 *E-mail:* pontas@intercom.es, pg 600

Solidaridad Publishing House (Philippines) *Tel:* (02) 586581; (02) 591241 *Fax:* (02) 525-5038, pg 521

Editions Soline (France) *Tel:* (01) 43 33 74 24 *Fax:* (01) 43 33 67 37 *E-mail:* contact@soline.fr *Web Site:* perso.wanadoo.fr/soline, pg 185

Solivros (Portugal) *Tel:* (0252) 42385, pg 536

Solum Forlag A/S (Norway) *Tel:* (022) 50 04 00 *Fax:* (022) 50 14 53 *E-mail:* solumfor@online.no *Web Site:* www.solumforlag.no, pg 510

Somaiya Publications Pvt Ltd (India) *Tel:* (022) 2048272 *Fax:* (022) 2047297 *Web Site:* www.somaiya.com, pg 349

Michael Somare Library (Papua New Guinea) *Tel:* 326 7280 *Fax:* 326 7187 *E-mail:* Library@upng.ac.pg *Web Site:* www.theatrelibrary.org, pg 1536

Somawathi Hewavitharana Fund (Sri Lanka) *Tel:* (01) 698079, pg 607

Somerset Publications (Australia) *Tel:* (07) 3425 1857 *Fax:* (07) 3425 1857 *E-mail:* info@crabbetarabian.com; crabbetarabian@hotkey.net.au *Web Site:* www.crabbetarabian.com; www.hotkey.net.au/~crabbetarabian, pg 41

Sommer & Sorensen (Denmark) *Tel:* 36153615 *Fax:* 36153616, pg 134

Somogy editions d'art (France) *Tel:* (01) 48 05 70 10 *Fax:* (01) 48 05 71 70 *E-mail:* somogy@magic.fr, pg 185

Edizioni Sonda (Italy) *Tel:* (0142) 461516 *Fax:* (0142) 461523 *E-mail:* sonda@sonda.it *Web Site:* www.sonda.it, pg 409

Sonnentanz-Verlag Roland Kron (Germany) *Tel:* (0821) 311070 *Fax:* (0821) 158979 *E-mail:* sonnentanz@t-online.de, pg 284

Sonneville Press (Uitgeverij) VTW (Belgium) *Tel:* (050) 321112, pg 73

Johannes Sonntag Verlagsbuchhandlung GmbH (Germany) *Tel:* (0711) 8931-0 *Fax:* (0711) 8931-706 *Web Site:* www.sonntag-verlag.com, pg 284

Sony Magazines Inc (Japan) *Tel:* (03) 3234-5811 *Fax:* (03) 3234-8042, pg 428

Sonzogno (Italy) *Tel:* (02) 50951 *Fax:* (02) 5065361, pg 409

Editorial Sopena Argentina SACI e I (Argentina) *Tel:* (011) 4912-2383 *Fax:* (011) 4912-2383 *E-mail:* edsopena@elsitio.net, pg 9

Ramon Sopena SA (Spain) *Tel:* (093) 3223703 *Fax:* (093) 3223703, pg 600

Sophia Book Service (Republic of Korea) *Tel:* (02) 362-2036 *Fax:* (02) 362-2036, pg 1324

Educatieve Uitgeverij Sorava (Suriname) *Tel:* 483879 *Web Site:* www.icpcredit.com, pg 608

Sorbona (Italy) *Tel:* (08) 15453443 *Fax:* (08) 15464991, pg 409

Bibliotheque de la Sorbonne (France) *Tel:* (01) 40 46 30 27 *Fax:* (01) 40 46 30 44 *E-mail:* adminst@biu.sorbonne.fr *Web Site:* www.sorbonne.fr, pg 1507

Publications de la Sorbonne (France) *Tel:* (01) 43 25 80 15 *Fax:* (01) 43 54 03 24 *E-mail:* publisor@univ-paris1.fr *Web Site:* www.univ-paris1.fr/recherche/rubrique46.html, pg 185

Association d'Editions Sorg (France) *Tel:* (01) 48252524 *Fax:* (01) 46052563, pg 186

Soryusha (Japan) *Tel:* (03) 32631471 *Fax:* (03) 32632943, pg 428

Editions SOS (Editions du Secours Catholique) (France) *Tel:* (01) 40 35 44 65 *Fax:* (01) 40 35 42 73, pg 186

Soshisha Co Ltd (Japan) *Tel:* (03) 3476-6565 *Fax:* (03) 3470-2640 *E-mail:* soshisha@magical.egg.or.jp, pg 428

Sota Graphic Arts Co Ltd (Hong Kong) *Tel:* 23421083 *Fax:* 23415426 *E-mail:* sales@goldencup.com.hk, pg 1179

Sota Graphic Arts Co Ltd (Hong Kong) *Tel:* 23421083 *Fax:* 23415426 *E-mail:* sales@goldencup.com.hk *Web Site:* www.goldencup.com.hk, pg 1219

Souffles (France) *Tel:* (01) 42 31 07 20 *Fax:* (01) 42310729, pg 186

Soundbooks (Australia) *Tel:* (03) 98247711 *Fax:* (03) 98247855 *E-mail:* audio@vicnet.com.au *Web Site:* www.soundbooks.com.au, pg 1299

Les Editions de la Source Sarl (France) *Tel:* (01) 45 25 30 07, pg 186

Sousa & Almeida Livraria (Portugal) *Tel:* (022) 2050073 *Fax:* (022) 2050073 *E-mail:* sousaealmeida@net.sapo.pt; geral@sousaealmeida.com *Web Site:* www.sousaealmeida.com, pg 536

Livraria Sousa e Almeida Lda (Portugal) *Tel:* (022) 2050073 *Fax:* (022) 2050073 *E-mail:* sousaealmeida@net.sapo.pt; geral@sousaealmeida.com *Web Site:* www.sousaealmeida.com, pg 1338

South African Booksellers' Association (South Africa) *Tel:* (021) 918 8616 *Fax:* (021) 951 4903 *E-mail:* fnel@naspers.com *Web Site:* sabooksellers.com, pg 1284

South African Extension Unit (United Republic of Tanzania) *Tel:* (051) 150314; (051) 150346 *Fax:* (051) 150346 *E-mail:* saeu@intafrica.com *Web Site:* www.saide.org.za/worldbank/courtries/tanzania/saeu.htm, pg 644

South African Institute of International Affairs (South Africa) *Tel:* (011) 339 2021 *Fax:* (011) 339 2154 *E-mail:* saiiagen@global.co.za *Web Site:* www.wits.ac.za/saiia, pg 569

South African Institute of Race Relations (South Africa) *Tel:* (011) 403-3600 *Fax:* (011) 403-3671; (011) 339-2061 *E-mail:* sairr@sairr.org.za *Web Site:* www.sairr.org.za, pg 569

South African Library for the Blind (South Africa) *Tel:* (046) 622 7226 *Fax:* (046) 622 4645 *E-mail:* blindlib@iafrica.com *Web Site:* www.blindlib.org.za, pg 1544

South Asia Publications (India) *Tel:* (011) 7241869; (011) 7235539, pg 349

South Asian Publishers Pvt Ltd (India) *Tel:* (011) 276292; (011) 276740 *E-mail:* vchigs@giasdla.vsnl.net.in, pg 350

South Australian Government-Department of Education, Employment & Training (Australia) *Tel:* (08) 8377 0399 *Fax:* (08) 8377 0341, pg 41

South China Morning Post Ltd (Hong Kong) *Tel:* 2680 8888 *Web Site:* www.scmp.com, pg 319

South China Printing Co (1988) Ltd (Hong Kong) *Tel:* 26373611 *Fax:* 26374221 *Web Site:* www.nysingtao.com, pg 1158

South China University of Science & Technology Press (China) *Tel:* (020) 87113489; (020) 87113484, pg 108

South East Asian Central Banks (SEACEN) Research & Training Centre (Malaysia) *Tel:* (03) 7958 5600 *Fax:* (03) 7957 4616 *E-mail:* info@seacen.org *Web Site:* www.seacen.org, pg 1527

South Head Press (Australia) *Tel:* (07) 5526 4670, pg 41

South Pacific Association for Commonwealth Literature & Language Studies (SPACLALS) (New Zealand) *Tel:* (07) 838-4466 *Fax:* (07) 838 4722, pg 1280

South Pacific Books Imports Ltd (New Zealand) *Tel:* (09) 649 448 1591 *Fax:* (09) 649 448 1592 *E-mail:* sales@soupacbooks.co.nz *Web Site:* www.soupacbooks.co.nz, pg 1330

University of the South Pacific (Fiji) *Tel:* (033) 13900 *Fax:* (033) 01305 *Web Site:* www.usp.ac.fj, pg 141

South Sea Books (New Zealand) *Tel:* (03) 3317630 *E-mail:* southsea@ihug.co.nz *Web Site:* www.abebooks.com/home/southsea, pg 1331

South Sea International Press Ltd (Hong Kong) *Tel:* 2897 1083 *Fax:* 2558 1473 *E-mail:* books@ssip.com.hk *Web Site:* www.ssip.com.hk, pg 1158, 1179

South Sea International Press Ltd (Hong Kong) *Tel:* 2897 1083 *Fax:* 2558 1473 *E-mail:* ssiphk@hk.super.net, pg 1219

Southeast Asian Ministers of Education Organization Regional Language Centre (SEAMEO RELC) (Thailand) *Tel:* (02) 3910144; (02) 3910554; (02) 3916413 *Fax:* (02) 3812587 *E-mail:* secretariat@seameo.org *Web Site:* www.seameo.org, pg 1288

Southeast Asian Regional Branch of the International Council on Archives (SARBICA) (Malaysia) *Tel:* (03) 651 0688 *Fax:* (03) 651 5679 *E-mail:* sarbica.sec@arkib.gov.my *Web Site:* arkib.gov.my/sarbica/index.html, pg 1277

Southern Book Publishers (Pty) Ltd (South Africa) *Tel:* (011) 3153633 *Fax:* (011) 3153810 *E-mail:* Southern@struik.co.za, pg 569

Southern Cross PR & Press Services (Australia) *Tel:* (02) 6737 5436 *Fax:* (02) 6737 5436, pg 41

Southern Press Ltd (New Zealand) *Tel:* (04) 233-1899, pg 501

Southgate Publishers (United Kingdom) *Tel:* (01363) 776888 *Fax:* (01363) 776889 *E-mail:* info@southgatepublishers.co.uk *Web Site:* www.southgatepublishers.co.uk, pg 759

Southwest China Jiaotong University Press (China) *Tel:* (028) 784160-763 *Fax:* (028) 24377 *E-mail:* swju@swjtu.edu.cn, pg 108

Southwood Press Pty Ltd (Australia) *Tel:* (02) 9560 5100 *Fax:* (02) 9550 0097 *E-mail:* info@southwoodpress.com.au *Web Site:* www.southwoodpress.com.au, pg 1215

Souvenir Press Ltd (United Kingdom) *Tel:* (01235) 400400 *Fax:* (01235) 400500 *E-mail:* orders@bookpoint.co.uk, pg 759

Sovereign World Ltd (United Kingdom) *Tel:* (01732) 850598 *Fax:* (01732) 851077 *E-mail:* sovereignworldbooks@compuserve.com *Web Site:* www.sovereign-world.org, pg 759

Izdatelstvo Sovetskii Pisatel (Russian Federation) *Tel:* (095) 209 2384; (095) 209 4105; (095) 209 1942 *Fax:* (095) 2023200, pg 548

Sovremennik Publishers Too (Russian Federation) *Tel:* (095) 9412992 *Fax:* (095) 9413544, pg 548

SP Interbuk, Russian-Slovenien jv (Russian Federation) *Tel:* (095) 9245081 *Fax:* (095) 2002281; (095) 2302403, pg 549

SPA Books Ltd (United Kingdom) *Tel:* (01293) 552727 *Fax:* (01438) 310104 *E-mail:* strongoakpress@hotmail.com, pg 759

Space Sellers Ltd (Kenya) *Tel:* (02) 555811; (02) 557517; (02) 557863 *Fax:* (02) 557815; (02) 558847 *E-mail:* sstms@africaonline.co.ke, pg 436

Spacevision Publishing (Australia) *Tel:* (03) 5127 2398, pg 41

Spala Editora Ltda (Brazil) *Tel:* (021) 542-9995 *Fax:* (021) 542-4738, pg 90

Spaniel Books (Australia) *Tel:* (02) 9360 9985 *Fax:* (02) 9331 4653 *E-mail:* spanielbooks@hotmail.com, pg 41

Vivliofilia K Ch Spanos (Greece) *Tel:* (0210) 3623917; (0210) 3614332 *Fax:* (0210) 8953076 *E-mail:* biblioph@otenet.gr, pg 312

Specialist Publications (Australia) *Tel:* (02) 9736 2191 *Fax:* (02) 9736 2663 *Web Site:* www.specialist.com.au, pg 41

SpectraComp (United States) *Tel:* 717-697-8600 *Toll Free Tel:* 800-666-2662 *Fax:* 717-691-0433 *E-mail:* info@spectracomp.com *Web Site:* www.spectracomp.com, pg 1189

Spectres Familiers (France) *Tel:* (0491) 912645 *Fax:* (0491) 909951, pg 186

Spectrum Books Ltd (Nigeria) *Tel:* (02) 2310058; (02) 2311215; (02) 2312705 *Fax:* (02) 2312705; (02) 2318502 *E-mail:* admin1@spectrumbooksonline.com *Web Site:* www.spectrumbooksonline.com, pg 507

Uitgeverij Het Spectrum BV (Netherlands) *Tel:* (030) 2650650 *Fax:* (030) 2620850 *E-mail:* het@spectrum.nl *Web Site:* www.spectrum.nl, pg 489

Spectrum Publications (Australia) *Tel:* (03) 9429 1404 *Fax:* (03) 9428 9407 *E-mail:* spectpub@ozemail.com.au *Web Site:* www.ozemail.com.au/~spectpub, pg 41

Spectrum Publications (India) *Tel:* (0361) 26381; (0361) 24791 *Fax:* (0361) 544791, pg 350

Spee Buchverlag GmbH (Germany) *Tel:* (0651) 4608121 *Fax:* (0651) 4608220, pg 284

Speechmark Publishing Ltd (United Kingdom) *Tel:* (01869) 244644 *Fax:* (01869) 320040 *E-mail:* info@speechmark.net *Web Site:* www.speechmark.net, pg 760

Speedflex Asia Ltd (Hong Kong) *Tel:* 2542 2780 *Fax:* 2542 3733 *E-mail:* info@speedflex.com.hk *Web Site:* www.speedflex.com.hk, pg 1158, 1219, 1236

Speer -Verlag (Switzerland) *Tel:* (01) 341 42 56; (01) 262 33 91 *Fax:* (01) 342 45 31, pg 634

Bokforlaget Spektra AB (Sweden) *Tel:* (035) 360 30 *Fax:* (035) 361 77, pg 615

Spektrum der Wissenschaft Verlagsgesellschaft mbH (Germany) *Tel:* (06221) 9126600 *Fax:* (06221) 9126751 *E-mail:* marketing@spektrum.com *Web Site:* www.spektrum.de, pg 284

Spektrum Forlagsaktieselskab (Denmark) *Tel:* 33 14 77 14 *Fax:* 33 14 77 91, pg 134

Spellbound Promotions (Australia) *Tel:* (066) 542133 *Fax:* (066) 541258 *E-mail:* Jodiadv@oncs.com.au, pg 42

Spellmount Ltd Publishers (United Kingdom) *Tel:* (01892) 837171 *Fax:* (01892) 837272 *E-mail:* enquiries@spellmount.com, pg 760

Spengler Editeur (France) *Tel:* (01) 49 70 15 55 *Fax:* (01) 49 70 15 50, pg 186

Sperling e Kupfer Editori SpA (Italy) *Tel:* (02) 217211 *Fax:* (02) 21721277 *Web Site:* www.sperling.it, pg 409

Libreria Internazionale Sperling e Kupfer (Italy) *Tel:* (02) 21721-1 *Fax:* (02) 21721-277 *Web Site:* www.sperling.it, pg 1321

SPES Editorial SL (Spain) *Tel:* (093) 2413505 *Fax:* (093) 2413511 *E-mail:* vox@vox.es *Web Site:* www.vox.es, pg 600

Speurwerk Stichting betreffende het Boek (Netherlands) *Tel:* (020) 625 49 27 *Fax:* (020) 620 88 71 *E-mail:* info@speurwerk.kvb.nl *Web Site:* www.speurwerk.nl, pg 1279

Sphinx Publishing Co (Egypt (Arab Republic of Egypt)) *Tel:* (02) 392 4616 *Fax:* (02) 391 8802 *E-mail:* sphinx@intouch.com, pg 138

Sphinx Verlag AG (Switzerland) *Tel:* (061) 2619292 *Fax:* (061) 2629221, pg 634

Spiegel-Verlag Rudolf Augstein GmbH & Co KG (Germany) *Tel:* (040) 3007-0 *Fax:* (040) 3007-2247 *E-mail:* spiegel@spiegel.de, pg 284

Spiess Volker Wissenschaftsverlag GmbH (Germany) *Tel:* (030) 6917073-74 *Fax:* (030) 6914067, pg 284

Spieth-Verlag Verlag fuer Symbolforschung (Germany) *Tel:* (0331) 2705199 *Fax:* (0331) 2010849, pg 284

Spinal Publications New Zealand Ltd (New Zealand) *Tel:* (04) 2937020 *Fax:* (04) 2932897 *E-mail:* enquiries@spinalpublications.co.nz *Web Site:* www.spinalpublications.co.nz, pg 501

Spindulys Printing House (Lithuania) *Tel:* (037) 226243 *Fax:* (037) 204970 *E-mail:* spaustuve@spindulys.lt *Web Site:* www.spindulys.lt, pg 1160

Spindulys Printing House (Lithuania) *Tel:* (037) 226243 *Fax:* (037) 204970 *E-mail:* spindul@kaunas.aiva.lt, pg 1180

Spindulys Printing House (Lithuania) *Tel:* (037) 226243 *Fax:* (037) 204970 *E-mail:* spaustuve@spindulys.lt *Web Site:* www.spindulys.lt, pg 1221

Spinifex Press (Australia) *Tel:* (03) 9329-6088 *Fax:* (03) 9329-9238 *E-mail:* women@spinifexpress.com.au *Web Site:* www.spinifexpress.com.au, pg 42

Spirali Edizioni (Italy) *Tel:* (02) 8054417; (02) 8053602 *Fax:* (02) 8692631 *E-mail:* redazione@spirali.com *Web Site:* www.spirali.it; www.spirali.com, pg 409

Spiridon-Verlags GmbH (Germany) *Tel:* (02104) 47260 *Fax:* (0211) 786823, pg 284

Spokesman (United Kingdom) *Tel:* (0115) 9708318; (0115) 9784504 *Fax:* (0115) 9420433 *E-mail:* elfeuro@compuserve.com *Web Site:* www.spokesmanbooks.com; www.russfound.org, pg 760

Spoleczny Instytut Wydawniczy Znak (Poland) *Tel:* (012) 4291469; (012) 4219776 *Fax:* (012) 4219814 *E-mail:* rucinska@znak.com.pl *Web Site:* www.znak.com.pl, pg 526

Spolok slovenskych spisovatel'ov (Slovakia) *Tel:* (07) 533 53 71, pg 1283

Spon Press (United Kingdom) *Tel:* (020) 7583 9855 *Fax:* (020) 7842 2298 *E-mail:* info@routledge.co.uk *Web Site:* www.sponpress.com, pg 760

Adolf Sponholtz Verlag (Germany) *Tel:* (05151) 200312 *Fax:* (05151) 200319 *Web Site:* www.niemeyer-buch.de, pg 284

Sport & Hobby Book Club (Greece) *Tel:* (01) 3234217 *Fax:* (01) 3232082 *E-mail:* hcp@photography.gr, pg 1253

Sport Publishing House Ltd (Slovakia) *Tel:* (07) 49249618 *Fax:* (07) 49249586, pg 561

Sports Turf Research Institute (STRI) (United Kingdom) *Tel:* (01274) 565131 *Fax:* (01274) 561891 *E-mail:* info@stri.co.uk *Web Site:* www.stri.co.uk, pg 760

The Sportsman's Press (United Kingdom) *Tel:* (020) 8789 0229 *Fax:* (020) 8789 0229, pg 760

Sportverlag Berlin GmbH SVB (Germany) *Tel:* (030) 8973666 *Fax:* (030) 2591-3516 *E-mail:* marketing@sportverlag-berlin.de *Web Site:* www.sportverlag-berlin.de, pg 284

Spotdzielna Anagram (Poland) *Tel:* (022) 6229324; (022) 6229326, pg 526

Editions Spratbrow (France) *Tel:* (03) 27 33 62 58; (03) 27 41 12 14 *Fax:* (03) 27 45 29 99 *E-mail:* sjbv.cdi@wanadoo.fr, pg 186

Spraymation Inc (United States) *Tel:* 954-484-9700 *Toll Free Tel:* 800-327-4985 *Fax:* 954-484-9778 *E-mail:* sales@spraymation.com *Web Site:* www.spraymation.com, pg 1231

Spriditis Publishers (Latvia) *Tel:* (02) 7286516 *Fax:* (02) 7286818, pg 445

Axel Springer Publicaciones (Spain) *Tel:* (091) 5140600 *Fax:* (091) 5140624, pg 601

Axel Springer Verlag AG (Germany) *Tel:* (040) 347-00 *Fax:* (040) 345811 *E-mail:* info@asv.de *Web Site:* www.asv.de, pg 284

Editions Springer France (France) *Tel:* (01) 5393 3647 *Fax:* (01) 53933729 *Web Site:* www.springer-paris.fr, pg 186

Springer Hungarica Kiado Kft (Hungary) *Tel:* (01) 3700599 *Fax:* (01) 3709075, pg 324

Springer Science+Business Media GmbH & Co KG (Germany) *Tel:* (06221) 487-0 *Fax:* (06221) 487-8366 *E-mail:* orders@springer.de *Web Site:* www.springer.de, pg 284

Springer Science+Business Media GmbH & Co KG, Berlin (Germany) *Tel:* (030) 82787-0; (030) 82787 5282 (press & public relations) *Fax:* (030) 8214091; (030) 82787 5707 (press & public relations) *E-mail:* press@springer-sbm.com *Web Site:* www.springer-sbm.de, pg 285

Springer-Verlag Hong Kong Ltd (Hong Kong) *Tel:* 27 23 96 98 *Fax:* 27 24 23 66, pg 319

Springer-Verlag Iberica, SA (Spain) *Tel:* (093) 4570227; (093) 4570759 *Fax:* (093) 4571502 *E-mail:* springer.bcn@springer.es, pg 601

Springer-Verlag London Ltd (United Kingdom) *Tel:* (0483) 418800; (01483) 418822 (sales) *Fax:* (01483) 415151; (01483) 415144 *E-mail:* orders@springer.de, pg 760

Springer-Verlag Tokyo (Japan) *Tel:* (03) 3812-0757 *Fax:* (03) 3812-0719 *Web Site:* www.springer-tokyo.co.jp/, pg 428

Springer-Verlag Wien (Austria) *Tel:* (01) 3302415 *Fax:* (01) 3302426 *E-mail:* books@springer.at (orders); journals@springer.at (orders) *Web Site:* www.springer.at, pg 58

Springfield Books Ltd (United Kingdom) *Tel:* (01484) 864955 *Fax:* (01484) 865443, pg 1353

SPS Verlaggsservice GmbH (Germany) *Tel:* (0261) 80706-0 *Fax:* (0261) 80706-54, pg 1312

Barbara Spurll Illustration (Canada) *Tel:* 416-594-6594 *Fax:* bspurll@yahoo.com *Web Site:* www.barbaraspurll.com, pg 1176

Spyropoulos A (Greece) *Tel:* (0210) 671 2991 *Fax:* (0210) 671 9622, pg 312

Square Dance Partners Forlag (Denmark) *Tel:* 45 83 99 83, pg 135

Square One Publications (United Kingdom) *Tel:* (01684) 593704 *Fax:* (01684) 594640, pg 760

Square Two Design Inc (United States) *Tel:* 415-437-3888 *Fax:* 415-437-3880 *E-mail:* sq2d@square2.com *Web Site:* www.square2.com, pg 1189

Sraka International (Slovenia) *Tel:* (07) 3342 274 *Fax:* (07) 3342 094, pg 1340

Arhiv Srbije (Serbia and Montenegro) *Tel:* (011) 33-70-781; (011) 33-70-782; (011) 33-70-879; (011) 33-70-880 *Fax:* (011) 33-70-246 *E-mail:* office@archives.org.yu *Web Site:* www.archives.org.yu, pg 1542

Srebaren lav (Bulgaria) *Tel:* (02) 752298, pg 97

Y Sreberk (Israel) *Tel:* (03) 6293343 *Fax:* (03) 6299297, pg 372

Sredne-Uralskoye knizhnoye izatelstve (Middle Urals Publishing House) (Russian Federation) *Tel:* (03432) 514162 *Fax:* (03432) 512859, pg 549

Sree Rama Publishers (India) *Tel:* (040) 2522609 *E-mail:* thehindu@usnl.com *Web Site:* www.hinduonnet.com, pg 350

SRHE (United Kingdom) *Tel:* (020) 7637 2766 *Fax:* (020) 7637 2781 *E-mail:* srheoffice@srhe.ac.uk *Web Site:* www.srhe.ac.uk, pg 760

Sri Lanka Association of Publishers (Sri Lanka) *Tel:* (01) 695773 *Fax:* (01) 696653, pg 1284

Sri Lanka Jama'ath-e-Islami (Sri Lanka) *Tel:* (01) 687091 *Fax:* (01) 686030, pg 607

Sri Lanka Library Association (Sri Lanka) *Tel:* (01) 2589103 *Fax:* (01) 2589103 *E-mail:* slla@operamail.com *Web Site:* www.naresa.ac.lk/slla; www.nsf.ac.lk/slla, pg 1571

Sri Satguru Publications (India) *Tel:* (011) 27126497; (011) 27434930 *Fax:* (011) 27227336 *E-mail:* ibcindia@giasdlo1.vsnl.net.in or ibcindia@ibcindia.com, pg 350

Srinakharinwirot University, Central Library (Thailand) *Tel:* (02) 2584002 (ext 160, 161, 162); (02) 2584003 (ext 160, 161, 162); (02) 6641000 (ext 5382) *Fax:* (02) 2604514; (02) 2584002 *E-mail:* library@swu.ac.th *Web Site:* www.swu.ac.th/lib, pg 1550

Srpska Knjizevna Zadruga (Serbia and Montenegro) *Tel:* (011) 330 305 *Fax:* (011) 626-224, pg 553

Biblioteka Srpske Akademije Nauka i Umetnosti (Serbia and Montenegro) *Tel:* (011) 33-42-400 *Fax:* (011) 639-120 *E-mail:* admin@bib.sanu.ac.yu *Web Site:* www.bib.sanu.ac.yu, pg 1542

L Staackmann Verlag KG (Germany) *Tel:* (08027) 337; (089) 342248 *Fax:* (08027) 816, pg 286

Staatliche Museen Kassel (Germany) *Tel:* (0561) 93 77-7 *Fax:* (0561) 93 77-6 66 *E-mail:* info@museum-kassel.de *Web Site:* www.museum-kassel.de, pg 286

Staats- und Universitaetsbibliothek Hamburg Carl von Ossietzky (Germany) *Tel:* (040) 42838 2233 *Fax:* (040) 42838-3352 *E-mail:* auskunft@sub.uni-hamburg.de *Web Site:* www.sub.uni-hamburg.de, pg 1510

Staats- und Universitatsbibliothek Bremen (Germany) *Tel:* (0421) 2182601 *Fax:* (0421) 2182614 *E-mail:* suub@suub.uni-bremen.de *Web Site:* www.suub.uni-bremen.de, pg 1510

Staatsbibliothek zu Berlin - Preusscher Kulturbesitz (Germany) *Tel:* (030) 266-0 *E-mail:* webserveradmin@sbb.spk-berlin.de *Web Site:* www.sbb.spk-berlin.de; www.staatsbibliothek-berlin.de, pg 286

Staatsbibliothek zu Berlin - Preusscher Kulturbesitz (Germany) *Tel:* (030) 266-0 *Web Site:* www.staatsbibliothek-berlin.de; www.sbb.spk-berlin.de, pg 1510

Stabenfeldt A/S (Norway) *Tel:* (051) 84 54 00 *Fax:* (051) 84 54 91 *E-mail:* int.post@stabenfeldt.no *Web Site:* www.stabenfeldt.no, pg 510

Stacey International (United Kingdom) *Tel:* (020) 7221 7166 *Fax:* (020) 7792 9288 *E-mail:* stacey-inter@btconnect.com *Web Site:* www.stacey-international.co.uk, pg 761

Stadler Verlagsgesellschaft mbH (Germany) *Tel:* (07531) 898-0 *Fax:* (07531) 898-101 *E-mail:* info@verlag-stadler.de *Web Site:* www.verlag-stadler.de, pg 286

Stadsbibliotheek (Belgium) *Tel:* (03) 206 87 10 *Fax:* (03) 206 87 75 *E-mail:* stadsbibliotheek@stad.antwerpen.be *Web Site:* stadsbibliotheek.antwerpen.be, pg 1494

Stadt Duisburg - Amt Fuer Statistik, Stadtforschung und Europaangelegenheiten (Germany) *Tel:* (0203) 283 4502 *Fax:* (0203) 288 4404 *E-mail:* amt12@stadt-duisburg.de, pg 286

Stadt Frankfurt a Main Stadt-und Universitaetsbibliothek (Germany) *Tel:* (069) 212-39-205 *Fax:* (069) 212-39-380 *E-mail:* auskunft@stub.uni-frankfurt.de *Web Site:* www.stub.uni-frankfurt.de, pg 1510

Stadt- und Universitaetsbibliothek (Germany) *Tel:* (069) 212-39-205; (069) 212-39-256; (069) 212-39-229; (069) 212-39-230; (069) 212-39-231 *Fax:* (069) 212-39-380; (069) 212-39-062 *E-mail:* direktion@uni-frankfurt.com; auskunft@stub.uni-frankfurt.de *Web Site:* www.stub.uni-frankfurt.de, pg 1510

Stadt- und Universitaetsbibliothek (Switzerland) *Tel:* (031) 3203211 *Fax:* (031) 3203299 *E-mail:* info@stub.unibe.ch *Web Site:* www.stub.unibe.ch, pg 1548

Stadtbibliothek Leipzig (Germany) *Tel:* (0341) 123 53 43 *Fax:* (0341) 123 53 05 *E-mail:* stadtbib@leipzig.de *Web Site:* www.leipzig.de/stadtbib.htm, pg 1510

Staedte-Verlag, E v Wagner und J Mitterhuber GmbH (Germany) *Tel:* (0711) 576201 *Fax:* (0711) 5762199 *E-mail:* info@staedte-verlag.de *Web Site:* www.staedte-verlag.de, pg 286

Buchhandlung Staeheli AG (Switzerland) *Tel:* (01) 2099111 *Fax:* (01) 2099112 *E-mail:* info@staehelibooks.ch *Web Site:* www.staehelibooks.ch, pg 1344

Staempfli Verlag AG (Switzerland) *Tel:* (031) 3006666 *Fax:* (031) 3006688 *E-mail:* verlag@staempfli.com *Web Site:* www.staempfli.com, pg 634

Stahlbau Zentrum Schweiz (Switzerland) *Tel:* (01) 261 89 80 *Fax:* (01) 262 09 62 *E-mail:* info@szs.ch *Web Site:* www.szs.ch, pg 634

Verlag Stahleisen GmbH (Germany) *Tel:* (0211) 6707-0 *Fax:* (0211) 6707-117 *E-mail:* stahleisen@stahleisen.de *Web Site:* www.stahleisen.de, pg 286

Stainer & Bell Ltd (United Kingdom) *Tel:* (020) 8343 3303 *Fax:* (020) 8343 3024 *E-mail:* post@stainer.co.uk *Web Site:* www.stainer.co.uk, pg 761

Verlag H Stam GmbH (Germany) *Tel:* (02203) 30290 *Fax:* (02203) 302940, pg 286

Stamford College Publishers/Authors-Publishers (Singapore) *Tel:* 3323639 *Fax:* 3323273 *E-mail:* legaldep@nlb.gov.sq.hdtsdnl@technet.sq, pg 558

Stamford Press Pte Ltd (Singapore) *Tel:* 6294 7227 *Fax:* 6294 4396; 6294 3319 *E-mail:* lynn@stamford.com.sg *Web Site:* www.stamford.com.sg, pg 1161

Stamford Press Pte Ltd (Singapore) *Tel:* 6294 7227 *Fax:* 6294 4396; 6294 3319 *E-mail:* stamfad@signet.com.sg *Web Site:* www.stamford.com.sg, pg 1182

Stamford Press Pte Ltd (Singapore) *Tel:* 6294 7227 *Fax:* 6294 4396; 6294 3319 *E-mail:* lynn@stamford.com.sg *Web Site:* www.stamford.com.sg, pg 1223

Stampa Alternativa - Nuovi Equilibri (Italy) *Tel:* (0761) 352277; (0761) 353485 *Fax:* (0761) 352751 *E-mail:* nuovi.equilibri@agora.it *Web Site:* www.stampalternativa.it, pg 409

Standaard Uitgeverij (Belgium) *Tel:* (03) 285 72 00 *Fax:* (03) 285 72 99 *E-mail:* info@standaarduitgeverij.be *Web Site:* www.standaarduitgeverij.be, pg 73

Standard Book Numbering Agency (Argentina) *Tel:* (011) 4381-8383 *Fax:* (011) 4381-9253 *E-mail:* registrolibros@editores.com *Web Site:* www.editores.com, pg 1259

STANDARD BOOK NUMBERING AGENCY / INDUSTRY

Standard Book Numbering Agency (Austria) *Tel:* (01) 512 15 35 *Fax:* (01) 512 84 82 *E-mail:* isbn@hvb.at *Web Site:* www.buecher.at, pg 1261

Standard Book Numbering Agency (Brunei Darussalam) *Tel:* (02) 382511 *Fax:* (02) 381817, pg 1263

Standard Book Numbering Agency (Chile) *Tel:* (02) 6989519; (02) 6724088 *Fax:* (02) 6989226 *E-mail:* camlibro@terra.cl; prolibro@ctcreuna.cl *Web Site:* www.camlibro.cl, pg 1264

Standard Book Numbering Agency (Colombia) *Tel:* (01) 2886188 *Fax:* (01) 2873320 *E-mail:* agenciaisbn@camlibro.com.co *Web Site:* www.camlibro.com.co, pg 1264

Standard Book Numbering Agency (Costa Rica) *Tel:* (0506) 2212436; (0506) 2212479 *Fax:* (0506) 2235510 *E-mail:* proctec@racsa.co.cr, pg 1264

Standard Book Numbering Agency (Cyprus) *Tel:* (022) 303337 *Fax:* (022) 443565 *E-mail:* antonism@ucy.ac.cy, pg 1265

Standard Book Numbering Agency (Egypt (Arab Republic of Egypt)) *Tel:* (02) 5751078; (02) 5750886; (02) 5752883 *Fax:* (02) 5765634 *E-mail:* libmang@darelkotob.org, pg 1266

Standard Book Numbering Agency (Estonia) *Tel:* (02) 630 7372 *Fax:* (02) 631 1200 *E-mail:* eraamat@nlib.ee; nlib@nlib.ee *Web Site:* www.nlib.ee, pg 1266

Standard Book Numbering Agency (Gambia) *Tel:* 226491 *Fax:* 223776 *E-mail:* national.library@ganet.gm, pg 1269

Standard Book Numbering Agency (Ghana) *Tel:* (021) 223526; (021) 228402 *Fax:* (021) 247768 *E-mail:* GeorgePadmore@Africanmail.com; Padmoreslib@yahoo.co.uk, pg 1271

Standard Book Numbering Agency (Greece) *Tel:* (01) 33 82 601; (01) 33 82 581 *Fax:* (01) 36 08 495 *E-mail:* ebe@nlg.gr *Web Site:* www.nlg.gr, pg 1272

Standard Book Numbering Agency (Islamic Republic of Iran) *Tel:* (021) 6414991 *Fax:* (021) 6415360 *E-mail:* dariushmatlabi@yahoo.com; isbn@ketab.org.ir; dmatlabi@yahoo.com *Web Site:* www.ketab.ir, pg 1273

Standard Book Numbering Agency (Kenya) *Tel:* (02) 718012; (02) 718013; (02) 725550 *Fax:* (02) 721749 *E-mail:* knls@nbnet.co.ke *Web Site:* www.knls.or.ke, pg 1275

Standard Book Numbering Agency (Latvia) *Tel:* (02) 7212668 *Fax:* (02) 7224587 *E-mail:* anitag@lbi.lnb.lv *Web Site:* www.lnb.lv/eng/centrala.htm, pg 1276

Standard Book Numbering Agency (Lesotho) *Tel:* (022) 340601; (022) 340468 *Fax:* 340000 *E-mail:* isbn@lib.nul.ls *Web Site:* www.nul.ls, pg 1276

Standard Book Numbering Agency (The Former Yugoslav Republic of Macedonia) *Tel:* (02) 3115 177; (02) 3133 418 *Fax:* (02) 3226 846 *E-mail:* kliment@nubsk.edu.mk *Web Site:* www.nubsk.edu.mk, pg 1276

Standard Book Numbering Agency (Malaysia) *Tel:* (03) 26871700 *Fax:* (03) 26927082 *E-mail:* pnmweb@www1.pnm.my *Web Site:* www.pnm.my, pg 1277

Standard Book Numbering Agency (Maldive Islands) *Tel:* 323261 *Fax:* 321201 *E-mail:* educator@dhivehinet.net.mv *Web Site:* www.moe.gov.mv, pg 1277

Standard Book Numbering Agency (Malta) *Tel:* (021) 440083; (021) 448539; (021) 490540 *Fax:* (021) 488908 *E-mail:* contact@peg.com.mt *Web Site:* www.peg.com.mt, pg 1277

Standard Book Numbering Agency (New Zealand) *Tel:* (04) 474 3074 *Fax:* (04) 474 3161 *E-mail:* isbn@natlib.govt.nz *Web Site:* www.natlib.govt.nz, pg 1280

Standard Book Numbering Agency (Pakistan) *Tel:* (051) 921 4523; (051) 920 2544; (051) 920 2549 *Fax:* (051) 922 1375 *E-mail:* nlpiba@paknet2.ptc.pk *Web Site:* www.nlp.gov.pk, pg 1281

Standard Book Numbering Agency (Papua New Guinea) *Tel:* 3256200 *Fax:* 3251331 *E-mail:* paraide@datec.com.pg *Web Site:* www.dg.com.pg/ola, pg 1281

Standard Book Numbering Agency (Portugal) *Tel:* (021) 843 51 80 *Fax:* (021) 848 93 77 *E-mail:* isbn@apel.pt *Web Site:* www.apel.pt, pg 1282

Standard Book Numbering Agency (Qatar) *Tel:* 42 9955 *Fax:* 42 9976 *E-mail:* qanali@qatar.net.qa, pg 1282

Standard Book Numbering Agency (Russian Federation) *Tel:* (095) 2034653; (095) 2035608 *Fax:* (095) 2982576; (095) 2982590 *E-mail:* chamber@aha.ru, pg 1283

Standard Book Numbering Agency (Saudi Arabia) *Tel:* (01) 464 51 97; (01) 462 48 88 (ext 224); (01) 462 48 88 (ext 601); (01) 462 48 88 (ext 238) *Fax:* (01) 464 53 41; (01) 462 27 07 *E-mail:* saudi-isbn@kfnl.gov.sa, pg 1283

Standard Book Numbering Agency (Singapore) *Tel:* 6546 7271 *Fax:* 6546 7262 *E-mail:* legaldep@nlb.gov.sg *Web Site:* www.nlb.gov.sg, pg 1283

Standard Book Numbering Agency (Slovenia) *Tel:* (01) 5861 333 *Fax:* (01) 5861 311 *E-mail:* isbn@nuk.uni-lj.si *Web Site:* www.nuk.uni-lj.si, pg 1283

Standard Book Numbering Agency (Suriname) *Tel:* 472545 *Fax:* 410563 *E-mail:* postmaster@interfundgroup.com, pg 1284

Standard Book Numbering Agency (Taiwan, Province of China) *Tel:* (02) 2361 9132 ext 701 *Fax:* (02) 2311 5330 *E-mail:* isbn@msg.ncl.edu.tw *Web Site:* www.ncl.edu.tw/isbn, pg 1288

Standard Book Numbering Agency (Thailand) *Tel:* (02) 2810263; (02) 6285196 *Fax:* (02) 2810263 *E-mail:* suwksir@emisc.moe.go.th; suwaksir@yahoo.com *Web Site:* www.isbn.org, pg 1288

Standard Book Numbering Agency (Turkey) *Tel:* (0312) 231 78 26; (0312) 231 78 29 *Fax:* (0312) 231 35 64 *E-mail:* kultur@kutuphanelergm.gov.tr *Web Site:* www.kutuphanelergm.gov.tr, pg 1288

Standard Book Numbering Agency (Uruguay) *Tel:* (02) 402 08 12; (02) 408 50 30 *Fax:* (02) 409 69 02; (02) 401 67 16 *E-mail:* bibna@adinet.com.uy, pg 1295

Standard Book Numbering Agency (Venezuela) *Tel:* (0212) 576 5650; (0212) 576 5370; (0212) 576 7120; (0212) 577 5106 *Fax:* (0212) 576 8720 *E-mail:* isbn_cenal@platino.gov.ve *Web Site:* www.bnv.bib.ve; www.cenal.gov.ve, pg 1295

Standard Book Numbering Agency (Zambia) *Tel:* (01) 292 837 (ext 1342); (01) 253 952; (01) 250 845 *Fax:* (01) 295 038 *E-mail:* library@unza.zm *Web Site:* www.unza.zm/, pg 1295

Standard Book Numbering Agency (Zimbabwe) *Tel:* (04) 792 741 *Fax:* (04) 792 398 *E-mail:* nat.archives@gta.gov.zw, pg 1295

Standard Book Numbering Agency (Botswana) (Botswana) *Tel:* 3952 397; 3952 288 *Fax:* 3957 108; 3901 149, pg 1263

Standard Book Numbering Agency (ISBN Agency-Sri Lanka) (Sri Lanka) *Tel:* (01) 698847; (01) 685198 *Fax:* (01) 685201 *E-mail:* natlib@slt.lk, pg 1284

Standard Book Numbering Agency of Iceland (Iceland) *Tel:* 525 5600 *Fax:* 525 5615 *E-mail:* lbs@bok.hi.is; isbn@bok.hi.is *Web Site:* www.bok.hi.is, pg 1273

Standard Book Numbering Agency, The National Library of the Philippines (Philippines) *Tel:* (02) 5253196; (02) 5251748 *Fax:* (02) 5242324 *E-mail:* director@nlp.gov.ph *Web Site:* www.nlp.gov.ph, pg 1281

International Standard Buchnummer GmbH (Germany) *Tel:* (069) 1306-387 *Fax:* (069) 1306-258 *E-mail:* lehr@bhv.de *Web Site:* www.german-isbn.org, pg 1271

Standards Association of Australia (Australia) *Tel:* (02) 99634231 *Fax:* (02) 9746 8450, pg 42

Standards Association of Zimbabwe (SAZ) (Zimbabwe) *Tel:* (04) 885511; (04) 885512; (04) 882021; (04) 882022 *Fax:* (04) 882020 *E-mail:* sazlabs@mall.pcl.co.zw, pg 784

Izdatelstvo Standartov (Russian Federation) *Tel:* (095) 252 0348; *Fax:* (095) 268-4724 *E-mail:* standard@online.ru, pg 549

Verlag fuer Standesamtswesen GmbH (Germany) *Tel:* (069) 40 58 94 0 *Fax:* (069) 40 58 94 99 *E-mail:* info@vfst.de *Web Site:* www.vfst.de, pg 286

Standing Conference of African Library Schools (SCALS) (Senegal) *Tel:* (08) 250530 *Fax:* (08) 255219, pg 1283

Standing Conference of African University Libraries (SCAUL) (Nigeria) *Tel:* (01) 524968 *Fax:* (01) 822644, pg 1280

Standing Conference on Library Materials on Africa (United Kingdom) *Tel:* (020) 7747 6164 *Fax:* (020) 7747 6168 *E-mail:* scolma@hotmail.com *Web Site:* www.soas.ac.uk/scolma/, pg 1293

Stanley Editorial (Spain) *Tel:* (0943) 64 04 12 *Fax:* (0943) 64 38 63 *Web Site:* www.libross.com, pg 601

Stapp Verlag Wolfgang Stapp (Germany) *Tel:* (030) 2622097 *Fax:* (030) 2621990, pg 286

Star Publications (P) Ltd (India) *Tel:* (011) 23268651; (011) 23286757; (011) 23258993; (011) 23261696 *Fax:* (011) 23273335; (011) 26481565 *Web Site:* www.starpublic.com, pg 350

Star Publications (P) Ltd (India) *Tel:* (011) 328 6757; (011) 23258993; (011) 326 1696; (011) 326 8651 *Fax:* (011) 23273335; (011) 648 1565 *E-mail:* starpub@satyam.net.in *Web Site:* www.starpublic.com, pg 1317

Star Publishers' Distributors (India) *Tel:* (011) 23286757; (011) 23268651; (011) 23261696; (011) 23258993 *Fax:* (011) 23273335; (011) 26481565 *E-mail:* starpub@satyam.net.in *Web Site:* www.starpublic.com, pg 1253

C A Starke Verlag (Germany) *Tel:* (06431) 96 15-0 *Fax:* (06431) 96 15 15 *E-mail:* starkeverlag@t-online.de *Web Site:* www.starkeverlag.de, pg 287

Harold Starke Publishers Ltd (United Kingdom) *Tel:* (01379) 388334; (020) 7588 5195 *Fax:* (01379) 388335 *E-mail:* red@eclat.force9.co.uk, pg 761

State Archives (Mongolia) *Tel:* (01) 323100, pg 1529

State Archives of the Russian Federation (Russian Federation) *Tel:* (095) 245-81-41 *Fax:* (095) 245-12-87, pg 1541

State Archives Service: Natal Archives Depot (South Africa) *Tel:* (033) 342 4712 *Fax:* (033) 394 4352, pg 1544

State Book Trading Office (Mongolia) *Tel:* (01) 22312, pg 1328

State Central Library (India) *Tel:* (040) 4600107; (040) 4615621, pg 1516

The State Library of New South Wales (Australia) *Tel:* (02) 9273 1414 *Fax:* (02) 9273 1255 *E-mail:* library@sl.nsw.gov.au *Web Site:* www.sl.nsw.gov.au, pg 1490

State Library of NSW Press (Australia) *Tel:* (02) 92731568 *Fax:* (02) 92731259 *E-mail:* helene@ilanet.slnsw.gov.au *Web Site:* www.sl.nsw.gov.au, pg 42

State Library of Queensland (Australia) *Tel:* (07) 3840 7666 *Fax:* (07) 3846 2421 *E-mail:* srlenquiries@slq.qld.gov.au *Web Site:* www.slq.qld.gov.au/, pg 1490

State Library of South Australia (Australia) *Tel:* (08) 82077200 *Toll Free Tel:* 800-182-013 *Fax:* (08) 82077247 *E-mail:* info@slsa.sa.gov.au *Web Site:* www.slsa.sa.gov.au, pg 1491

State Library of Tasmania (Australia) *Tel:* (03) 6233 7511 *Fax:* (03) 6231 0927 *E-mail:* state.library@education.tas.gov.au *Web Site:* www.statelibrary.education.tas.gov.au, pg 1491

State Library of Victoria (Australia) *Tel:* (03) 8664 7000 *Fax:* (03) 9639 2175 *E-mail:* abirkenbeil@slv.vic.gov.au *Web Site:* www.slv.vic.gov.au, pg 42

State Library of Victoria (Australia) *Tel:* (03) 8664 7000 *Fax:* (03) 9639 3673 *E-mail:* info@slv.vic.gov.au *Web Site:* www.statelibrary.vic.gov.au, pg 1491

State Library of Western Australia (Australia) *Tel:* (08) 9427 3111 *Fax:* (08) 9427 3256 *E-mail:* info@liswa.wa.gov.au *Web Site:* www.liswa.wa.gov.au, pg 1491

State Press (Mongolia), pg 474

State Printing Corp (Sri Lanka) *Tel:* (01) 503694 *Fax:* (01) 503694, pg 607

State Publishing Unit of State Print SA (Australia) *Tel:* (08) 9226 4677 *Fax:* (08) 9226 4726, pg 42

State Textbook Publishing House (Albania) *Tel:* (042) 22331 *Fax:* (042) 22331, pg 1

Statiqum Kiado es Nyomda Kft (Hungary) *Tel:* (01) 1803311 *Fax:* (01) 1688635, pg 324

Statistical Service (Ghana) *Tel:* (021) 682629 *Fax:* (021) 667069 *E-mail:* baahwadieh@yahoo.com, pg 1512

Statisticke a evidencni vydavatelstvi tiskopisu (SEVT) (Czech Republic) *Tel:* 233 551 711; 283 090 352 *Fax:* 233 543 918 *E-mail:* sevt@sevt.cz *Web Site:* www.sevt.cz, pg 127

Statistics Finland Library (Finland) *Tel:* (09) 1734 2220 *Fax:* (09) 1734 2279 *E-mail:* library@stat.fi *Web Site:* www.stat.fi/tk/kk/index_en.html, pg 1505

Statistics New Zealand (New Zealand) *Tel:* (04) 931 4600 *Fax:* (04) 931 4610 *E-mail:* info@stats.govt.nz *Web Site:* www.stats.govt.nz, pg 501

Statistics Sweden Library (Sweden) *Tel:* (08) 506 940 00 *Fax:* (08) 661 5261 *E-mail:* scb@scb.se *Web Site:* www.scb.se, pg 1547

Statistisk sentralbyras bibliotek og informasjonssenter (Norway) *Tel:* 21 09 46 42 *Fax:* 21 09 45 04 *E-mail:* biblioteket@ssb.no *Web Site:* www.ssb.no/biblioteket, pg 1534

Statni technicka knihovna (Czech Republic) *Tel:* (02) 21 663 111 *Fax:* (02) 22 221 340 *E-mail:* techlib@stk.cz *Web Site:* www.stk.cz, pg 1501

Statni Vedecka Knihovna Usti Nad Labem (Czech Republic) *Tel:* (047) 5200045; (047) 5209126 *Fax:* (047) 5200045 *E-mail:* library@svkul.cz *Web Site:* www.svkul.cz, pg 127

Statsbiblioteket (Denmark) *Tel:* 89462022 *Fax:* 89462220 *E-mail:* sb@statsbiblioteket.dk *Web Site:* www.statsbiblioteket.dk, pg 1502

Stattbuch Verlag GmbH (Germany) *Tel:* (030) 6913094; (030) 6913095 *Fax:* (030) 6943354, pg 287

Stauffenburg Verlag Brigitte Narr GmbH (Germany) *Tel:* (07071) 9730-0 *Fax:* (07071) 973030 *E-mail:* info@stauffenburg.de *Web Site:* www.stauffenburg.de, pg 287

Stedelijk Van Abbemuseum (Netherlands) *Tel:* (040) 2381000 *Fax:* (040) 2460680 *E-mail:* info@vanabbemuseum.nl *Web Site:* www.vanabbemuseum.nl, pg 489

Steidl Verlag (Germany) *Tel:* (0551) 49 60 60 *Fax:* (0551) 49 60 649 *E-mail:* mail@steidl.de *Web Site:* www.steidl.de, pg 287

Steiermaerkische Landesbibliothek (Austria) *Tel:* (0316) 8770 *Fax:* (0316) 877-22 *E-mail:* post@stmk.gv.at *Web Site:* www.verwaltung.steiermark.at, pg 1492

Steiger Verlag (Germany) *Tel:* (089) 9271-0 *Fax:* (089) 9271-68, pg 287

Steimatzky Group Ltd (Israel) *Tel:* (03) 5775777 *Fax:* (03) 5794567 *E-mail:* info@steimatzky.co.il *Web Site:* www.steimatzky.com, pg 372, 1320

Abner Stein (United Kingdom) *Tel:* (020) 7373 0456 *Fax:* (020) 7370 6316 *E-mail:* abnerstein@compuserve.com, pg 1143

Conrad Stein Verlag GmbH (Germany) *Tel:* (02384) 963912 *Fax:* (02384) 963913 *E-mail:* outdoor@tng.de *Web Site:* outdoor.tng.de, pg 287

Micheline Steinberg Associates (United Kingdom) *Tel:* (020) 7631 1310 *Fax:* (020) 7631 1146 *E-mail:* info@steinplays.com, pg 1143

J Steinbrener OHG (Austria) *Tel:* (07712) 2038 *Fax:* (07712) 2038-20 *E-mail:* steinbrener@aon.at, pg 58

Franz Steiner Verlag Wiesbaden GmbH (Germany) *Tel:* (0711) 2582 0 *Fax:* (0711) 2582 290 *E-mail:* service@steiner-verlag.de *Web Site:* www.steiner-verlag.de, pg 287

Editorial Rudolf Steiner (Spain) *Tel:* (091) 5 531 481 *Fax:* (091) 5 531 481 *E-mail:* rudolfsteiner@teleline.es, pg 601

Rudolf Steiner Press (United Kingdom) *Tel:* (01342) 824433 *Fax:* (01342) 826437 *E-mail:* office@rudolfsteinerpress.com; editorial@rudolfsteinerpress.com *Web Site:* www.rudolfsteinerpress.com, pg 761

Rudolf Steiner Verlag (Switzerland) *Tel:* (061) 706 91 30 *Fax:* (061) 706 91 39 *E-mail:* verlag@rudolf-steiner.com *Web Site:* www.rudolf-steiner.com, pg 634

Steinhart-Katzir Publishers (Israel) *Tel:* (03) 6960995 *Toll Free Tel:* 800-22-5854 *Fax:* (09) 8854771 *E-mail:* webmaster@haolam.co.il *Web Site:* www.haolam.co.il, pg 372

J F Steinkopf Verlag GmbH (Germany), pg 287

Dr Dietrich Steinkopff Verlag GmbH & Co (Germany) *Tel:* (06151) 82899-0 (bestellungen) *Fax:* (06151) 82899-40 *E-mail:* info.steinkopff@springer.de *Web Site:* www.steinkopff.springer.de, pg 287

Steintor Verlag GmbH (Germany) *Tel:* (0451) 8798849 *Fax:* (0451) 8798837 *E-mail:* info@steintor-verlag.de *Web Site:* www.steintor-verlag.de, pg 287

Steinweg-Verlag, Jurgen vomHoff (Germany) *Tel:* (0531) 2339197 *Fax:* (0531) 2336649, pg 287

Editorial Stella (Argentina) *Tel:* (011) 4374-0346 *Fax:* (011) 4374-8719 *E-mail:* admin@editorialstella.com.ar *Web Site:* www.editorialstella.com.ar, pg 9

Le Stelle Scuola (Italy) *Tel:* (02) 55181460 *Fax:* (02) 5400017, pg 409

Steltman Editions (Netherlands) *Tel:* (020) 622 8683 *Fax:* (020) 620 7588 *E-mail:* steltman@steltman.com *Web Site:* www.steltman.com, pg 489

Edition Stemmle AG (Switzerland) *Tel:* (01) 7235050 *Fax:* (01) 7235059 *E-mail:* info@editionstemmle.ch *Web Site:* www.editionstemmle.com, pg 635

Verlag Stendel (Germany) *Tel:* (07151) 956603 *Fax:* (07151) 956605 *E-mail:* info@stendel-verlag.de; verlag.stendel@t-online.de *Web Site:* www.verlag-stendel.de, pg 287

Stenlake Publishing Ltd (United Kingdom) *Tel:* (01290) 551122 *Fax:* (01290) 551122 *E-mail:* info@stenlake.co.uk *Web Site:* www.stenlake.co.uk, pg 761

Stenstroems Bokfoerlag AB (Sweden) *Tel:* (08) 6637601; (08) 662078028 *Fax:* (08) 6632201, pg 615

Frank Stenvalls Forlag (Sweden) *Tel:* (040) 127703 *Fax:* (040) 127700 *E-mail:* fstenval@algonet.se, pg 615

Stenvert Systems & Service BV (Netherlands) *Tel:* (033) 457 0199 *Fax:* (033) 457 0198 *E-mail:* info@stenvert.nl *Web Site:* www.stenvert.nl, pg 489

Stephanus Edition Verlags GmbH (Germany) *Tel:* (07556) 8331 *Fax:* (07556) 8373 *E-mail:* 0755692110@tonline.de, pg 287

Sterling Information Technologies (India) *Tel:* (011) 669560 *Fax:* (011) 26383788, pg 350

Sterling Publishers Pvt Ltd (India) *Tel:* (011) 26387070; (011) 26386209; (011) 26386165; (011) 26385677 *Fax:* (011) 26383788 *E-mail:* info@sterlingpublishers.com *Web Site:* www.sterlingpublishers.com, pg 350

Stern-Verlag Janssen & Co (Germany) *Tel:* (0211) 3881-0 *Fax:* (0211) 3881-280 *E-mail:* webmaster@buchhaus-sternverlag.de *Web Site:* www.buchsv.de, pg 288

Stern-Verlag Janssen & Co (Germany) *Tel:* (0211) 3881-0 *Fax:* (0211) 3881-200 *E-mail:* buchhaus-sternverlag@t-online.de *Web Site:* www.buchsv.de, pg 1312

Sternberg-Verlag bei Ernst Franz (Germany) *Tel:* (07123) 938922 *Fax:* (07123) 938920, pg 288

Ian Stewart Marine Publications (Australia) *Tel:* (08) 9593 1331 *Fax:* (08) 9593 1331, pg 42

Steyler Verlag (Germany) *Tel:* (02157) 120220 *Fax:* (02157) 120260 *E-mail:* verlag@steyler.de *Web Site:* www.steyler.de, pg 288

Stichting Arnhemse Openbare en Gelderse Wetenschappelijke Bibliotheek (Netherlands) *Tel:* (026) 3543111 *Fax:* (026) 4458616 *Web Site:* www.biblioarnhem.nl, pg 1531

Stichting Drukwerk in de Marge (Netherlands) *Tel:* (020) 6227748 *Fax:* (020) 6227748 *Web Site:* www.drukwerkindemarge.nl, pg 1160

Stichting Federatie van Organisaties van Bibliotheek-, Informatie-, Dokumentatiewezen (FOBID) (Netherlands) *Tel:* (070) 3090115 *Fax:* (030) 233 29 60; (070) 3090200 *E-mail:* vanwestrienen@surf.nl, pg 1568

Stichting IVIO (Netherlands) *Tel:* (0320) 229900 *Fax:* (0320) 229999 *E-mail:* info@ivio.nl *Web Site:* www.ivio.nl, pg 489

Stichting Kinderkrant Suriname (Suriname), pg 608

Stichting Kunstboek bvba (Belgium) *Tel:* (050) 461910 *Fax:* (050) 461918, pg 73

Stichting Ons Erfdeel VZW (Belgium) *Tel:* (056) 41 12 01 *Fax:* (056) 41 47 07 *E-mail:* info@onserfdeel.be *Web Site:* www.onserfdeel.be, pg 73

Stichting Volksboekwinkel (Suriname) *Tel:* 472469, pg 608

Stichting Wetenschappelijke Informatie (Suriname) *Tel:* 475232 *Fax:* 422195 *E-mail:* swin@sr.net, pg 608

Stiebner Verlag GmbH (Germany) *Tel:* (089) 1257378 *Fax:* (089) 12162282, pg 288

Stiefel Eurocart GmbH (Germany) *Tel:* (08456) 924100 *Fax:* (08456) 924134 *E-mail:* stiefel.gmbH@stiefel-online.de *Web Site:* www.stiefel-online.com, pg 288

Stiftsbibliothek (Switzerland) *Tel:* (071) 227 34 16 *Fax:* (071) 227 34 18 *E-mail:* stibi@stibi.ch *Web Site:* www.stibi.ch, pg 1548

Stiftung Buchkunst (Germany) *Tel:* (069) 1525-1800 *Fax:* (069) 1525-1805 *E-mail:* buchkunst@dbf.ddb.de *Web Site:* www.stiftung-buchkunst.de, pg 288

Stiftung Lesen (Germany) *Tel:* (06131) 2 88 90-0 *Fax:* (06131) 23 03 33 *E-mail:* mail@stiftunglesen.de *Web Site:* www.stiftunglesen.de, pg 1271

Editura Stiintifica SA (Romania) *Tel:* (01) 3351654; (01) 3367442 *Fax:* (01) 3356499, pg 542

Editura Stiintifica si Enciclopedica (Romania) *Tel:* (01) 175168, pg 542

Editions Stil (France) *Tel:* (01) 48009224; (06) 85024238 *Fax:* (01) 48009336, pg 186

Stirling Press (Australia) *Tel:* (08) 327-1166 *Fax:* (08) 9327-1166 *E-mail:* stirl@ozemail.com.au, pg 42

STM Publishers Services Pte Ltd (Singapore) *Tel:* 62864998 *Fax:* 62882116, pg 1339

Stobart Davies Ltd (United Kingdom) *Tel:* (01269) 593100 *Fax:* (01269) 596116 *E-mail:* sales@stobartdavies.com *Web Site:* www.stobartdavies.com, pg 761

Edition Gunter Stoberlein (Germany) *Tel:* (089) 8115289, pg 288

Stochastis (Greece) *Tel:* (0210) 3601956; (0210) 3610445 *Fax:* (0210) 3610445, pg 312

Editions Stock (France) *Tel:* (01) 49543655 *Fax:* (01) 49543662 *Web Site:* www.editions-stock.fr/, pg 186

Verlag Stocker-Schmid AG (Switzerland) *Tel:* (01) 7404444, pg 635

Stockholms Stadsbibliotek (Sweden) *Tel:* (08) 508 31 100 *Fax:* (08) 508 31 007 *E-mail:* info.ssb@kultur.stockholm.se *Web Site:* www.ssb.stockholm.se, pg 1547

Stockholms Universitetsbibliotek (Sweden) *Tel:* (08) 16 28 00 *Fax:* (08) 15 77 76 *Web Site:* www.sub.su.se, pg 1547

Stoeppel Verlag-Buchvertrieb KG (Germany) *Tel:* (08233) 381-186 *Fax:* (08233) 381-246 *E-mail:* service@stoeppel.de *Web Site:* www.stoeppel.de, pg 288

Stofnun Arna Magnussonar a Islandi (Iceland) *Tel:* 525-4010 *Fax:* 525-4035 *E-mail:* rosat@hi.is *Web Site:* www.am.hi.is, pg 326

Stokesby House Publications (United Kingdom) *Tel:* (01493) 750645 *Fax:* (01493) 750146 *E-mail:* stokesbyhouse@btinternet.com *Web Site:* www.stokesbyhouse.co.uk, pg 761

Stollfuss Verlag Bonn GmbH & Co KG (Germany) *Tel:* (0228) 7 24-0 *Fax:* (0228) 7 24-9 11 81 *E-mail:* info@stollfuss.de *Web Site:* www.stollfuss.de, pg 288

Stora Enso Oyj (Finland) *Tel:* (09) 2046 131 *Fax:* (09) 2046 214 71 *Web Site:* www.storaenso.com, pg 1154

Stora Familjebokklubben (Sweden) *Tel:* (08) 696 88 30 *Fax:* (08) 696 83 50 *E-mail:* medlemsservice@sfbk.bonnier.se; info@sfbk.bonnier.se *Web Site:* www.storafamiljebokklubben.se, pg 1256

Stora Romanklubben (Sweden) *Tel:* (08) 696 88 40 *Fax:* (08) 696 88 41 *E-mail:* info@srk.bonnier.se *Web Site:* www.storaromanklubben.se, pg 1256

Istituto Storico Italiano per l'Eta Moderna e Contemporanea (Italy) *Tel:* (06) 68806922 *Fax:* (06) 6875127 *E-mail:* iststor@libero.it, pg 409

Stott Brothers Ltd (United Kingdom) *Tel:* (01422) 362184 *Fax:* (01422) 353707 *E-mail:* stottbros@aol.com, pg 1227, 1239

Stott's Correspondence College (United Kingdom) *Tel:* (020) 586 4499 *Fax:* (020) 722 1068 *E-mail:* microworld@ndirect.co.uk *Web Site:* www.microworld.ndirect.co.uk, pg 761

Stowarzyszenie Bibliotekarzy Polskich (Poland) *Tel:* (022) 6082256 *Fax:* (022) 8259157 *E-mail:* biurozgsbp@wp.pl *Web Site:* ebib.oss.wroc.pl/sbp/, pg 1570

Stowarzyszenie Ksiegarzy Polskich (Poland) *Tel:* (022) 252-874; (022) 256-061 *Web Site:* www.bookweb.org/orgs/1322.html, pg 1281

Stowarzyszenie Tlumaczy Polskich (Poland) *Tel:* (022) 621 56 78; (022) 825 09 04 *Fax:* (022) 621 56 78 *E-mail:* stp-waw@interkom.pl *Web Site:* www.stp.org.pl, pg 1149

STP Distributors Pte Ltd (Singapore) *Tel:* 6213 9288 *Fax:* 6281 3991 *E-mail:* stpds@tpl.com.sg *Web Site:* www.tpl.com.sg, pg 1339

Straelener Manuskripte Verlag GmbH (Germany) *Tel:* (02834) 6588 *Fax:* (02834) 6588 *Web Site:* www.straelener-manuskripte.de, pg 288

Strandbergs Forlag (Denmark) *Tel:* 4589 4760 *Fax:* 4589 4701 *E-mail:* strandberg.publishing@get2net.dk, pg 135

Institut Pro Stredoevropskou Kulturu A Politiku (ISE) (Czech Republic) *Tel:* (02) 249 168 60 *Fax:* (02) 249 168 60 *E-mail:* panevropa@iol.cz, pg 127

Stree (India) *Tel:* (033) 2466 0812 *Fax:* (033) 2464 4614; (033) 2466 6677 *E-mail:* stree@vsnl.com *Web Site:* www.streebooks.com, pg 350

Streiffert Forlag AB (Sweden) *Tel:* (08) 661 58 80 *Fax:* (08) 783 04 33 *E-mail:* info@streiffert.se *Web Site:* www.streiffert.se, pg 615

A J G Strengholt's Boeken, Anno 1928, BV (Netherlands) *Tel:* (035) 695 84 11 *Fax:* (035) 694 61 73 *E-mail:* boeken@strengholt.nl, pg 489

Strk Publishing House (The Former Yugoslav Republic of Macedonia) *Tel:* (091) 20 53 93 *Fax:* (091) 20 53 93, pg 453

Strobel Druck & Verlag - A Strobel GmbH & Co KG (Germany) *Tel:* (02931) 89 00 0 *Fax:* (02931) 89 00 38 *E-mail:* info@a-strobel.de *Web Site:* www.ikz.de, pg 1155

Stroemberg B&T Forlag AB (Sweden) *Tel:* (08) 6201900 *Fax:* (08) 7399836 *E-mail:* bokforlaget@stromberg.se *Web Site:* www.stromberg.se, pg 616

Stroemfeld Verlag (Germany) *Tel:* (069) 955 226-0 *Fax:* (069) 955 226-22 *E-mail:* info@stroemfeld.de *Web Site:* www.stroemfeld.de, pg 288

Strom-Verlag Luzern (Switzerland) *Tel:* (041) 4408845 *Fax:* (041) 4408844 *E-mail:* pegasus.ebikon@edi.begasoft.ch, pg 635

Stromberg (Sweden) *Tel:* (08) 6201900 *Fax:* (08) 7399836 *E-mail:* bokforlaget@stromberg.se *Web Site:* www.stromberg.se, pg 616

Stroyizdat Publishing House (Russian Federation) *Tel:* (095) 2516967, pg 549

Strubes Forlag og Boghandel ApS (Denmark) *Tel:* 36721750 *Fax:* 36721752, pg 135

Strucmech Publishing (Australia) *Tel:* (03) 95989245 *Fax:* (03) 95989245, pg 42

Struik Publishers (Pty) Ltd (South Africa) *Tel:* (021) 4624360 *Fax:* (021) 462-4379; (021) 461-9378 *E-mail:* admin@struik.co.za *Web Site:* www.struik.co.za, pg 569

The Struik Publishing Group (South Africa) *Tel:* (021) 462 4360 *Fax:* (021) 462 4379 *Web Site:* www.struik.co.za, pg 1341

STS Standard Tabellen und Software Verlag GmbH (Germany) *Tel:* (089) 89517-0 *Fax:* (089) 89517290, pg 288

Boksala Studenta (The University Bookstore) (Iceland) *Tel:* (05) 700 777 *Fax:* (05) 700 778 *E-mail:* boksala@boksala.is *Web Site:* www.boksala.is, pg 1315

Studenterboghandelen ved Odense Universitet (Denmark) *Tel:* 6550 1700 *Fax:* 6550 1701 *E-mail:* studenter@boghandel.sdu.dk *Web Site:* www.boghandel.sdu.dk/, pg 1308

Studentlitteratur AB (Sweden) *Tel:* (046) 312000 *Fax:* (046) 305338 *E-mail:* info@studentlitteratur.se *Web Site:* www.studentlitteratur.se, pg 616

Studieforlaget i Goteborg Stiftelsen Kursverksamhetens Forlag (Sweden) *Tel:* (031) 106580 *Fax:* (031) 135359 *E-mail:* kursbokhandeln@folkuniversitetet.se, pg 616

Studien Verlag Gmbh (Austria) *Tel:* (0512) 395045 *Fax:* (0512) 395045-15 *E-mail:* order@studienverlag.at *Web Site:* www.studienverlag.at, pg 58

Studio Bibliografico Adelmo Polla (Italy) *Tel:* (0863) 78522 *Fax:* (0863) 78522, pg 409

Studio Editions Ltd (United Kingdom) *Tel:* (020) 7973 9690 *Fax:* (020) 7233 6057, pg 761

Studio Editoriale Programma (Italy) *Tel:* (049) 8753110 *Fax:* (049) 8755870, pg 409

Edizioni Studio Tesi SRL (Italy) *Tel:* (06) 3235433 *Fax:* (06) 3236277 *E-mail:* info@ediz-mediterranee.com *Web Site:* www.ediz-mediterranee.com, pg 409

Studio 31 (United States) *Tel:* 772-781-7195 *Fax:* 772-781-6044 *E-mail:* studio31@mindspring.com *Web Site:* www.studio31.com, pg 1189

Libreria Studium SA (Peru) *Tel:* (01) 326278; (01) 275960; (01) 325528 *Fax:* (01) 4325354, pg 517

Libreria Studium SA (Peru) *Tel:* (01) 275960; (01) 326278; (01) 325528 *Fax:* (01) 4325354, pg 1335

Edizioni Studium SRL (Italy) *Tel:* (06) 68 65 846 *Fax:* (06) 68 75 456 *E-mail:* edizionistudium@libero.it, pg 409

Sturtz Verlag GmbH (Germany) *Tel:* (0931) 385235 *Fax:* (0931) 385305 *E-mail:* info@verlagshaus.com *Web Site:* www.verlagshaus.com, pg 288

Styria Medien AG (Austria) *Tel:* (0316) 8063-1012 *Fax:* (0316) 8063-3034 *E-mail:* medien.ag@styria.com *Web Site:* www.styria.com, pg 1300

Verlag Styria (Austria) *Tel:* (0316) 8063 7601 *Fax:* (0316) 8063 7004 *E-mail:* office@styriapichler.at *Web Site:* www.verlagstyria.com, pg 58

Su Hoc (Historical) Publishing House (Viet Nam), pg 781

Su That (Truth) Publishing House (Viet Nam) *Tel:* (04) 252008, pg 781

Suaver, Javier Presa Suarez (Spain) *Tel:* (086) 439507, pg 601

Sub-Saharan Publishers (Ghana) *Tel:* (021) 228398 *E-mail:* sub-saharan@ighmail.com, pg 305

Editions Subervie (France) *Tel:* (05) 65 67 20 17 *Fax:* (05) 65 67 36 38 *E-mail:* contact@subervie.com *Web Site:* www.subervie.com, pg 186

Success Publications Pte Ltd (Singapore) *Tel:* 4432003; 4430512 *Fax:* 4453156 *E-mail:* succpub@singnet.com.sg, pg 558

SUD (France) *Tel:* (0491) 336068 *Fax:* (0491) 336068, pg 186

Sud Editions (Tunisia) *Tel:* 71 79 80 64 *Fax:* 71 79 52 60, pg 648

Editions Sud Ouest (France) *Tel:* (0556) 44 68 21 *Fax:* (0556) 44 40 83 *E-mail:* contact@editions-sudouest.com *Web Site:* www.editions-sudouest.com, pg 186

Editorial Sudamericana SA (Argentina) *Tel:* (011) 4300-5400 *Fax:* (011) 4362-7364 *E-mail:* info@edsudamericana.com.ar *Web Site:* www.edsudamericana.com.ar, pg 9

The Sudan Bookshop Ltd (Sudan) *Tel:* (011) 74123; (011) 76781, pg 1343

Sudan Literature Centre (Kenya) *Tel:* (020) 565641 *Fax:* (020) 564141 *E-mail:* across@across-sudan.org *Web Site:* www.across-sudan.org, pg 436

Sudanese Publishers' Association (Sudan) *Tel:* (0249) 11-7780031 *Fax:* (0249) 11-770358, pg 1284

Izdatelstvo Sudostroenie (Russian Federation) *Tel:* (0812) 3124479 *Fax:* (0812) 3120821, pg 549

Sueddeutsche Verlagsgesellschaft mbH (Germany) *Tel:* (089) 2183-0 *Fax:* (089) 2183-787 *E-mail:* verlag@sueddeutsche.de; redaktion@sueddeutsche.de *Web Site:* www.sueddeutsche.de, pg 288

Suedverlag GmbH (Germany) *Tel:* (07531) 9053-0 *Fax:* (07531) 9053-98 *E-mail:* willkommen@uvk.de *Web Site:* www.suedverlag.de, pg 288

Suedwest Verlag GmbH & Co KG (Germany) *Tel:* (089) 4136-0; (01805) 990505 (hotline) *Fax:* (089) 5148-2229 *E-mail:* heyne-suedwest@randomhouse.de *Web Site:* www.suedwest-verlag.de, pg 289

Suedwind - Buchwelt GmbH (Austria) *Tel:* (01) 798 83 49 *Fax:* (01) 798 83 75 *E-mail:* versand@suedwind.at *Web Site:* www.suedwind.at, pg 58

Sueleymaniye Kuetuephanesi (Turkey) *Tel:* (0212) 520 64 60 *Fax:* (0212) 520 64 62, pg 1551

Sugarco Edizioni SRL (Italy) *Tel:* (02) 4078370 *Fax:* (02) 4078493, pg 409

Suhagsa (Republic of Korea) *Tel:* (02) 584-4642 *Fax:* (02) 521-1458, pg 443

Suhrkamp Verlag (Germany) *Tel:* (069) 75601-0 *Fax:* (069) 75601-522; (069) 75601-314 *Web Site:* www.suhrkamp.de, pg 289

Suin Buch-Verlag (Germany) *Tel:* (06255) 2657 *Fax:* (06255) 9596875, pg 289

YELLOW PAGES

Suisse Romand PEN Centre (Switzerland), pg 1405

Suksapan Panit (Business Organization of Teachers Council of Thailand) (Thailand) *Tel:* (02) 811845 *Web Site:* www.suksapan.or.th, pg 645

Suksit Siam Co Ltd (Thailand) *Tel:* (02) 225-9531-2 *Fax:* (02) 222-5188 *E-mail:* sop@ffc.inet.co.th, pg 646

Suksit Siam Co Ltd (Thailand) *Tel:* (02) 225-9531-2 *Fax:* (02) 222 5188, pg 1345

Livraria Sulina Editora (Brazil) *Tel:* (051) 254765; (051) 250287 *E-mail:* sulina@sulina.com.br, pg 91

Sulina Livraria Editora (Brazil) *Tel:* (0512) 254765; (0512) 250287 *Fax:* (0512) 280734, pg 1304

Sultan Chand & Sons Pvt Ltd (India) *Tel:* (011) 3266105; (011) 3277843; (011) 3281876 *Fax:* (011) 3266357 *E-mail:* nbcnd@ndb.vsnl.net.in, pg 350

Sultan's Library (Cyprus), pg 1501

Suman Prakashan Pvt Ltd (India) *Tel:* (011) 5842253; (011) 5721750 *Fax:* (011) 5754739 *E-mail:* info@sumanprakashan.com *Web Site:* www.sumanprakashan.com, pg 351

Sumatera Utara University Press (Indonesia) *Tel:* (061) 811045 *Fax:* (061) 816264, pg 356

Sumathi Book Printing (Pvt) Ltd (Sri Lanka) *Tel:* (0941) 330-673-5 *Fax:* (0941) 449-593 *E-mail:* lakbima@isplanka.lk *Web Site:* www.sumathi.lk, pg 1162, 1182, 1224

Summer Institute of Linguistics, Australian Aborigines Branch (Australia) *Tel:* (08) 8922 5700 *Fax:* (08) 8922 5717 *E-mail:* sildarwin@taunet.net.au, pg 42

Summer Institute of Linguistics (Papua New Guinea) *Tel:* 7373544 *Fax:* 7374111 *E-mail:* png@sil.org, pg 516

Summerson Eastern Publishers Ltd (Hong Kong) *Tel:* 25408123 *Fax:* 2559 7869, pg 319

Summus Editorial Ltda (Brazil) *Tel:* (011) 38723322 *Fax:* (011) 38727476 *E-mail:* summus@summus.com.br *Web Site:* www.summus.com.br, pg 91

Sun Fung Offset Binding Co Ltd (Hong Kong) *Tel:* 25618109; 25623381; 25621925 *Fax:* 28110638 *E-mail:* sunfung@sunfung.com.hk *Web Site:* www.sunfung.com.hk, pg 1219

Sun Mui Press (Hong Kong) *Tel:* 2694 8525 *Fax:* 2610 1202 *E-mail:* auly@chevalier.net, pg 319

Uitgeverij SUN (Netherlands) *Tel:* (020) 622 61 07 *Fax:* (020) 625 33 27 *E-mail:* info@uitgeverijboom.nl *Web Site:* www.uitgeverijboom.nl, pg 489

Sun Ya Publications (HK) Ltd (Hong Kong) *Tel:* 2562 0161 *Fax:* 2565 9951 *E-mail:* info@sunya.com.hk *Web Site:* www.sunya.com.hk, pg 319

Sun Yat-Sen Library (Hong Kong) *Tel:* 23365291, pg 1514

Sun Yat-sen Library (Taiwan, Province of China) *Tel:* (02) 2758 2045 *Fax:* (02) 2729 7030, pg 1549

Sunera Publishers (Sri Lanka) *Tel:* 511527, pg 607

Sunflower Books (United Kingdom) *Tel:* (020) 7589 1862 *Fax:* (020) 7589 1862 *E-mail:* mail@sunflowerbooks.co.uk *Web Site:* www.sunflowerbooks.co.uk, pg 761

Sunny Printing (Hong Kong) Co Ltd (Hong Kong) *Tel:* 25578663 *Fax:* 28898070 *E-mail:* enquiry@sunnyprinting.com.hk *Web Site:* www.sunnyprinting.com.hk, pg 1219

Sunshine Books International Ltd (New Zealand) *Tel:* (09) 5203049 *Toll Free Fax:* 0800 85 1000 *E-mail:* orders@my-dictionary.com *Web Site:* www.my-dictionary.com, pg 501

Sunshine Multi Media Ltd, Wendy Pye Ltd (New Zealand) *Tel:* (09) 525-3575 *Fax:* (09) 525-4205 *E-mail:* admin@sunshine.co.nz *Web Site:* www.sunshine.co.nz, pg 501

Sunshine Press Ltd (Hong Kong) *Tel:* 25532386 *Fax:* 28732930 *E-mail:* spl@sunshinepress.com.hk, pg 1158, 1179

Sunshine Press Ltd (Hong Kong) *Tel:* 25530228; 25532303 *Fax:* 28732930 *E-mail:* spl@sunshinepress.com.hk, pg 1219

Suomalainen Kirjakauppa Oy (Finland) *Tel:* (09) 852 751 *Fax:* (09) 852 7980 *E-mail:* etunimi.sukunimi@suomalainenkk.fi *Web Site:* www.suomalainen.com, pg 1309

Suomalainen Tiedeakatemia (Finland) *Tel:* (09) 636800 *Fax:* (09) 660117 *E-mail:* acadsci@acadsci.fi *Web Site:* www.acadsci.fi, pg 1399

Suomalaisen Kirjallisuuden Seura (Finland) *Tel:* (09) 131231 *Fax:* (09) 1312 3219, pg 144

Suomalaisen Kirjallisuuden Seura (Finland) *Tel:* (09) 131231 *Fax:* (09) 13123220 *E-mail:* sks-fls@finlit.fi *Web Site:* www.finlit.fi, pg 1399

Suomen Kirjailijaliitto (Finland) *Tel:* (09) 445392 *Fax:* (09) 492278 *E-mail:* info@suomenkirjailijaliitto.fi *Web Site:* www.suomenkirjailijaliitto.fi, pg 1266

Suomen Kirjastoseura (Finland) *Tel:* (09) 694 1858 *Fax:* (09) 694 1859 *E-mail:* fla@fla.fi *Web Site:* www.kaapeli.fi/~fla/presentation.html, pg 1561

Suomen Kustannusyhdistys (Finland) *Tel:* (09) 22877250 *Fax:* (09) 6121226 *Web Site:* www.skyry.net, pg 1266

Suomen Matkailuliitto ry (Finland) *Tel:* (09) 622 6280 *Fax:* (09) 654 358 *E-mail:* matkailuliitto@matkailuliitto.org *Web Site:* www.matkailuliitto.org, pg 144

Suomen Pipliaseura RY (Finland) *Tel:* (09) 612 9350 *Fax:* (09) 612 935 11 *E-mail:* info@bible.fi; etunimi.sukunimi@bible.fi *Web Site:* www.bible.fi, pg 144

Suomen Tieteellinen Kirjastoseura ry (Finland) *Tel:* (017) 34 22 25 *Fax:* (017) 34 22 79 *E-mail:* meri.kuula@arcada.fi *Web Site:* pro.tsv.fi/stks, pg 1561

Super Book House (India) *Tel:* (022) 2830560 *Fax:* (022) 2834452, pg 1317

Supportive Learning Publications (United Kingdom) *Tel:* (01691) 774778 *Fax:* (01691) 774849 *E-mail:* sales@slpuk.demon.co.uk *Web Site:* www.slpuk.demon.co.uk, pg 762

Sur Casa de Estudios del Socialismo (Peru) *Tel:* (01) 4235431 *Fax:* (01) 4235431 *E-mail:* casasur@terra.com.pe *Web Site:* www.casasur.org, pg 517

Suriwong Book Centre, Ltd (Thailand) *Tel:* (053) 281052 *Fax:* (053) 271902 *E-mail:* suriwong@loxinfo.co.th, pg 1345

Suriyaban Bookstore (Thailand) *Tel:* (02) 2347991; (02) 2347992, pg 1345

Suriyaban Publishers (Thailand) *Tel:* (02) 2347991; (02) 2347992, pg 646

Surjeet Publications (India) *Tel:* (011) 3914746; (011) 3914174 *Fax:* (011) 3918475 *E-mail:* surpub@del3.vsnl.net.in, pg 351

Ediciones Suromex SA (Mexico) *Tel:* (055) 2770744; (055) 2723570; (055) 2723630; (055) 2734989 *Fax:* (055) 2710470; (055) 2719378 *E-mail:* suromex@mail.internet.com.mx *Web Site:* www.intralector.com/suromex/, pg 472

Surugadai-Shuppan Sha (Japan) *Tel:* (03) 3291-1676 *Fax:* (03) 3291-1675 *E-mail:* edit@surugadai.com *Web Site:* www.e-surugadai.com, pg 429

Susaeta Ediciones (Colombia) *Tel:* (01) 2884422; (01) 2885500 *Fax:* (01) 881472 *E-mail:* mdsusaet@medellin.impsat.net.co, pg 113

Ediciones Susaeta SA (Spain) *Tel:* (091) 3009100 *Fax:* (091) 3009110 *E-mail:* ediciones.susaeta@nexo.es, pg 601

Sussex Publications (United Kingdom) *Tel:* (020) 586 4499 *Fax:* (020) 722 1068 *E-mail:* microworld@ndirect.co.uk *Web Site:* www.microworld.ndirect.co.uk, pg 762

SVERIGES LANTBRUKSUNIVERSITETS BIBLIOTEK

Sut Phaisan (Thailand) *Tel:* (02) 4682066; (02) 4675066, pg 646

Sutton Publishing Ltd (United Kingdom) *Tel:* (01453) 731114 *Fax:* (01453) 731117 *E-mail:* sales@sutton-publishing.co.uk; editorial@sutton-publishing.co.uk; publishing@sutton-publishing.co.uk *Web Site:* www.suttonpublishing.co.uk, pg 762

Suuri Suomalainen Kirjakerho Oy (Finland) *Tel:* (09) 2705 0077; (09) 1566 830 *Fax:* (09) 145 510 *E-mail:* sskk.palaute@sskk.fi *Web Site:* www.sskk.fi, pg 1252

Suva City Library (Fiji) *Tel:* 313 433 *Fax:* 302 158, pg 1504

SV-Kauppiaskanava Oy (Finland) *Tel:* (09) 10 53010 *Fax:* (09) 10 5336238 *E-mail:* kaija.tynkkynen@k-kauppiasuitto.fi *Web Site:* www.k-kauppiasliitto.fi, pg 144

Bokklubben Svalan (Sweden) *Tel:* (08) 696 88 00 *Fax:* (08) 696 83 76 *E-mail:* medlemsservice@svalan.bonnier.se *Web Site:* www.bokklubbensvalan.se, pg 1256

Svato Zapletal (Germany) *Tel:* (040) 4390004 *Fax:* (040) 4390004, pg 289

Svaz Antikvaru CR (Czech Republic) *Tel:* (02) 22220286 *Fax:* (02) 22220286 *E-mail:* info@meissner.cz *Web Site:* www.meissner.cz, pg 1265

Svaz ceskych knihkupcu a nakladatelu (SCKN) (Czech Republic) *Tel:* (02) 24 219 944 *Fax:* (02) 24 219 942 *E-mail:* sckn@sckn.cz *Web Site:* www.sckn.cz, pg 1265

Svaz knihovniku informacnich pracovniku Ceske republiky (SKIP) (Czech Republic) *Tel:* (02) 21663111 *Fax:* (02) 21663261 *Web Site:* www.nkp.cz, pg 1560

Svensk Biblioteksforening (Sweden) *Tel:* (08) 54513230 *Fax:* (08) 54513231 *E-mail:* info@biblioteksforeningen.org *Web Site:* www.biblioteksforeningen.org, pg 1571

Svensk-Norsk Bogimport A/S (Denmark) *Tel:* 33142666 *Fax:* 33143588 *E-mail:* snb@bog.dk *Web Site:* www.snbog.dk, pg 1308

Svenska Forlaggareforeningen (Sweden) *Tel:* (08) 736 19 40 *Fax:* (08) 736 19 44 *E-mail:* info@forlaggareforeningen.se *Web Site:* www.forlaggareforeningen.se, pg 1285

Svenska alliansmissionens (SAM) foerlage (Sweden) *Tel:* (036) 71 98 70 *Fax:* (036) 71 98 20 *E-mail:* info@sam.f.se *Web Site:* www.sam.f.se, pg 616

Svenska Arbetsgivareforeningens forlag (Sweden) *Tel:* (08) 553 430 00 *Fax:* (08) 553 430 99, pg 616

Svenska Arkivsamfundet (Sweden) *Tel:* (046) 197000 *Fax:* (046) 197070 *E-mail:* info@arkivsamfundet.org *Web Site:* www.arkivsamfundet.org, pg 1571

Svenska Barnboksinstitutet (Sweden) *Tel:* (08) 54 54 20 50 *Fax:* (08) 54 54 20 54 *E-mail:* info@sbi.kb.se; biblioteket@sbi.kb.se *Web Site:* www.sbi.kb.se, pg 1547

Svenska Foerlaget liv & ledarskap ab (Sweden) *Tel:* (08) 412 27 00 *Fax:* (08) 411 41 30 *E-mail:* kundservice@svenskaforlaget.com *Web Site:* www.svenskaforlaget.com, pg 616

Svenska Institutet (Sweden) *Tel:* (08) 453 78 00 *Fax:* (08) 20 72 48 *E-mail:* si@si.se *Web Site:* www.si.se, pg 616

Svenska Litteratursaellskapet i Finland (Finland) *Tel:* (09) 618777 *Fax:* (09) 6187 7277 *E-mail:* sls@mail.sls.fi *Web Site:* www.sls.fi, pg 1399

Svenska Oesterbottens Litteraturfoerening (Finland) *Tel:* (06) 3450286, pg 144, 1399

Svepomoc (Czech Republic) *Tel:* (02) 24223446; (02) 24223450 *Fax:* (02) 24223439, pg 127

Sveriges Lantbruksuniversitets Bibliotek (Sweden) *Tel:* (018) 67 10 00 *Fax:* (018) 67 28 53 *E-mail:* infosok@bibul.slu.se *Web Site:* www.bib.slu.se, pg 1547

Svetovi (Serbia and Montenegro) *Tel:* (021) 28032; (021) 28036 *Fax:* (021) 28036; (021) 28032 *E-mail:* aum.mar@eunet.yu, pg 554

Svetra Publishing House (Bulgaria) *Tel:* (02) 62 27 39; (02) 983 45 42 *Fax:* (02) 23 49 66 *E-mail:* svetlev@cybernet.bg, pg 97

Sveucilisna tiskara doo (Croatia) *Tel:* (01) 4564430; (01) 4564428 *Fax:* (01) 4564427, pg 119

Sviesa Publishers (Lithuania) *Tel:* (0837) 409126 *Fax:* (0837) 342032 *E-mail:* mail@sviesa.lt *Web Site:* www.sviesa.lt, pg 449

Svietimo ir mokslo ministerijos Leidybos centras (Lithuania) *Tel:* (02) 617480; (02) 611060; (02) 616081 *Fax:* (02) 617480 *E-mail:* office@smmlc.elnet.lt, pg 449

Svjetlost (Bosnia and Herzegovina) *Tel:* (033) 442634; (033) 200066 *Fax:* (033) 443435 *E-mail:* ipsvjet@bih.net.ba, pg 76

Svjetlost (Bosnia and Herzegovina) *Tel:* (071) 443 419; (071) 664 535; (071) 664 066; (071) 214 578; (071) 207 352 *Fax:* (071) 443 435, pg 1303

NS Svoboda spol sro (Czech Republic) *Tel:* (02) 449 132 58; (02) 23 06 14 *Fax:* (02) 449 132 58 *E-mail:* nssvobod@centrum.cz, pg 127

Svoboda Servis GmbH (Czech Republic) *Tel:* (02) 449 132 58; (02) 230614 *Fax:* (02) 449 132 58 *E-mail:* nssvoboda@centrum.cz, pg 127

Swakopmunder Buchhandlung (Namibia) *Tel:* 402613 *Fax:* 404183, pg 1328

Swarna Hansa Foundation (Sri Lanka) *Tel:* (01) 712566 *Fax:* (01) 733649, pg 607

Swaziland College of Technology Library (Swaziland) *Tel:* (040) 42681; (040) 43539 *Fax:* (040) 44521 *E-mail:* scotlibrary@africaonline.co.sz, pg 1546

Swaziland Library Association (Swaziland) *Tel:* 404-2633 *Fax:* 404-3863 *E-mail:* sdnationalarchives@realnet.co.sz *Web Site:* www.swala.sz, pg 1571

Swaziland National Library Service (Swaziland) *Tel:* 42633 *Fax:* 43863 *E-mail:* snlssz@realnet.co.sz *Web Site:* www.library.ohiou.edu/subjects/swaziland/snls.htm, pg 1547

Swedenborg - Verlag (Switzerland) *Tel:* (01) 2515945, pg 635

Swedish-English Literary Translators' Association (SELTA) (United Kingdom) *Tel:* (020) 8641 8176 *Fax:* (020) 8641 8176 *Web Site:* www.swedishbookreview.com, pg 1151

Swedish PEN Centre (Sweden) *Tel:* (08) 453 86 80 *E-mail:* info@pensweden.org *Web Site:* www.pensweden.org, pg 1405

Sweet & Maxwell Ltd (United Kingdom) *Tel:* (020) 7393 7000; (020) 7449 1104 *Fax:* (020) 7449 1144 *E-mail:* info@routledge.co.uk, pg 762

Swets & Zeitlinger Publishers (Netherlands) *Tel:* (0252) 435111 *Fax:* (0252) 415888 *E-mail:* info@nl.swets.com *Web Site:* www.swets.nl, pg 489

Swindon Book Co Ltd (Hong Kong) *Tel:* 2366 8001 *Fax:* 2739 4978 *E-mail:* swindon@netvigator.com *Web Site:* www.swindonbooks.com, pg 1314

SWP, BV Uitgeverij (Netherlands) *Tel:* (020) 3307200 *Fax:* (020) 3308040 *E-mail:* swp@wxs.nl *Web Site:* www.swpbook.com, pg 490

Syarikat Cultural Supplies Sdn Bhd (Malaysia) *Tel:* (03) 7046628; (03) 7554103; (03) 7915728 *Fax:* (03) 7046629 *E-mail:* malian@po.jaring.my, pg 458

Sybex (France) *Tel:* (01) 55 58 40 00 *Fax:* (01) 49 65 04 10 *E-mail:* contact@sybex.fr *Web Site:* www.sybex.fr, pg 186

Sybex BV (Netherlands) *Tel:* (031) 3560 27625 *Fax:* (031) 3560 26556 *E-mail:* sybex@sybex.nl *Web Site:* www.sybex.nl, pg 490

Sybex Verlag GmbH (Germany) *Tel:* (02236) 399920-0 *Fax:* (02236) 399922-9 *E-mail:* sybex@sybex.de *Web Site:* www.sybex.de, pg 289

Syddansk Universitetsforlag (Denmark) *Tel:* 66 15 79 99 *Fax:* 66 15 81 26 *E-mail:* press@forlag.sdu.dk *Web Site:* www.universitypress.dk, pg 135

Sydney Jary Ltd (United Kingdom) *Tel:* (0117) 974-1640 *Fax:* (0117) 973-7116 *E-mail:* admin@s-jary.co.uk, pg 762

Sydney PEN Centre (Australia) *Tel:* (02) 9514 2738 *Fax:* (02) 9514 2778 *E-mail:* sydney@pen.org.au *Web Site:* www.pen.org.au, pg 1396

J G Sydy's Buchhandlung Ludwig Schubert GmbH Nachfolge KG (Austria) *Tel:* (02742) 35 31 89 *Fax:* (02742) 35 31 89; (02742) 35 31 85 *E-mail:* schubert.sydys@aon.at; info@buchhandlung-schubert.at *Web Site:* www.buchhandlung-schubert.at, pg 1301

Sygma Publishing (Botswana) *Tel:* 351371 *Fax:* 372531 *E-mail:* sygma@info.bw, pg 76

Syllogos Ekdoton Bibliopolon Athinon (Greece) *Tel:* (01) 3830029; (01) 3303268 *Fax:* (01) 3823222 *E-mail:* seva@otenet.ge, pg 1272

Syndicat des Libraires Universitaires et Techniques (France) *Tel:* (01) 43 29 88 79 *Fax:* (467) 525905, pg 1269

Syndicat National de la Librairie Ancienne et Moderne (SLAM) (France) *Tel:* (01) 43 29 46 38 *Fax:* (01) 43 25 41 63 *E-mail:* slam-livre@wanadoo.fr *Web Site:* www.slam-livre.fr, pg 1269

Syndicat National de l'Edition (France) *Tel:* (01) 4441 4050 *Fax:* (01) 4441 4077 *Web Site:* www.snedition.fr, pg 1269

Syndicat National des Auteurs et Compositeurs (France) *Tel:* (01) 48 74 96 30 *Fax:* (01) 42 81 40 21 *E-mail:* snac.fr@wanadoo.fr *Web Site:* www.snac.fr, pg 1400

Synthesis Verlag (Germany) *Tel:* (0201) 51 01 88 *Fax:* (0201) 51 10 49 *E-mail:* synthesis@synthesis-verlag.com *Web Site:* www.synthesis-verlag.com, pg 289

Systematics Studies Ltd (Trinidad & Tobago) *Tel:* (868) 645-8466 *Fax:* (868) 645-8467 *E-mail:* tobe@trinidad.net, pg 647

SystemConsult (Czech Republic) *Tel:* (040) 466 501 585 *Fax:* (040) 466 501 585 *E-mail:* system.consult@tiscali.cz *Web Site:* www.systemconsult.cz, pg 127

Systex (Australia) *Tel:* (02) 9944 2668, pg 42

Systime (Denmark) *Tel:* 70 12 11 00 *Fax:* 70 12 11 05 *E-mail:* systime@systime.dk *Web Site:* www.systime.dk, pg 135

Szabad Ter Kiado (Hungary) *Tel:* (01) 3561565; (01) 3755922 *Fax:* (01) 1560998, pg 324

Szabvanykiado (Hungary) *Tel:* (01) 1183011; (01) 1183442 *Fax:* (01) 1185125, pg 324

Szarvas Andras Cartographic Agency (Hungary) *Tel:* (01) 363 0672; (01) 221 68 30 *Fax:* (01) 363 0672; (01) 221 68 30 *E-mail:* szarvas.andras@mail.datanet.hu, pg 324

Szazadveg (Hungary) *Tel:* (01) 4795280 *Fax:* (01) 479 5290 *E-mail:* szazadveg@szazadveg.hu *Web Site:* www.szazadveg.hu, pg 324

Uniwersytet Szczecinski (Poland) *Tel:* (091) 444-23-61 *Fax:* (091) 444-23-62 *E-mail:* info@bg.univ.szczecin.pl *Web Site:* www.univ.szczecin.pl/us/biblioteka.html, pg 1538

Szepirodalmi Koenyvkiado Kiado (Hungary) *Tel:* (01) 3117293, pg 324

Wydawnictwa Szkolne i Pedagogiczne (Poland) *Tel:* (022) 8265451; (022) 8265452; (022) 8265453; (022) 8265454; (022) 8265455; (022) 5762500; (022) 5762501 *Toll Free Tel:* 800-220555 *Fax:* (022) 8279280 *E-mail:* wsip@wsip.com.pl *Web Site:* www.wsip.com.pl, pg 527

Oficyna Wydawnicza Szkoly Glownej Handlowej w Warszawie Oficyna Wydawnicza SGH (Poland) *Tel:* (022) 337 92 13; (022) 337 92 17; (022) 337 97 61; (022) 337 97 69 *Fax:* (022) 646 61 03 *E-mail:* dwz@sgh.waw.pl *Web Site:* www.sgh.waw.pl, pg 527

Magyar Eszperanto Szoevetseg (Hungary) *Tel:* (01) 1334343; (01) 1563659, pg 324

T & E Publishers (Uganda) *Tel:* (041) 542207 *Fax:* (041) 542207, pg 653

Ta Ha Publishers Ltd (United Kingdom) *Tel:* (020) 7737 7266 *Fax:* (020) 7737 7267 *E-mail:* sales@taha.co.uk *Web Site:* www.taha.co.uk, pg 762

Ta Kung Pao (HK) Ltd (Hong Kong) *Tel:* 25737213; 25757181 *Fax:* 257463316, pg 319

Edicoes Tabajara (Brazil) *Tel:* (0512) 241073; (0512) 247724, pg 91

Tabansi Press Ltd (Nigeria) *Tel:* (046) 211661; 08033243783; 08033418218, pg 507

Ediciones Tabapress, SA (Spain) *Tel:* (01) 5320876 *Fax:* (01) 5325890 *E-mail:* ediciones.tabapress@tsai.es, pg 601

Tabb House (United Kingdom) *Tel:* (01841) 532316 *Fax:* (01841) 532316 *E-mail:* tabbhouse@connexions.co.uk; books@tabb-house.fsnet.co.uk, pg 762

Les Editions de la Table Ronde (France) *Tel:* (01) 40 46 70 70 *Fax:* (01) 40 46 71 01 *E-mail:* editionslatableronde@wanadoo.fr, pg 186

Tabletop Press (Australia) *Tel:* (06) 6242 0995 *Fax:* (06) 6242 0674, pg 42

Editeurs Tacor International (France) *Tel:* (01) 39 18 29 39 *Fax:* (01) 30 82 43 90, pg 186

Tael Ltd (Estonia) *Tel:* (02) 6314162 *Fax:* (02) 6314162 *E-mail:* tael@teleport.ee, pg 140

Tafelberg Publishers Ltd (South Africa) *Tel:* (021) 406 3033 *Fax:* (021) 4242510 *E-mail:* tafelbrg@tafelberg.com *Web Site:* www.nb.co.za/tafelberg, pg 569

Tages-Anzeiger (Switzerland) *Tel:* (01) 248 44 11 *Fax:* (01) 248 44 71 *E-mail:* tamedia@tamedia.ch *Web Site:* www.tages-anzeiger.ch, pg 635

Tai Yip Co (Hong Kong) *Tel:* 2524-5963 *Fax:* 2845-3296 *E-mail:* tybook@taiyipart.com.hk *Web Site:* www.taiyipart.com.hk, pg 319

Taigh Na Teud Music Publishers (United Kingdom) *Tel:* (01471) 822528 *Fax:* (01471) 822811 *E-mail:* sales@scotlandsmusic.com *Web Site:* www.scotlandsmusic.com, pg 762

Taimeido Publishing Co Ltd (Japan) *Tel:* (03) 3291-2374 *Fax:* (03) 3291-2376 *E-mail:* taimei1@ibm.net, pg 429

Taipei Yung Chang Printing (Taiwan, Province of China) *Tel:* (02) 5932392 *Fax:* (02) 5932763, pg 1224

Taiwan Branch Library, National Central Library (Taiwan, Province of China) *Tel:* (02) 771 8528, pg 1549

Tajak Korok Muzeumok Egyesuelet (Hungary) *Tel:* (01) 303 4069 *Fax:* (01) 303 4069 *E-mail:* tkmets@elender.hu, pg 324

Takahashi Shoten Co Ltd (Japan) *Tel:* (03) 3943-4525 *Fax:* (03) 3943-4288 *Web Site:* www.takahashishoten.co.jp, pg 429

Imprimerie Takariva (Madagascar) *Tel:* 02 23856, pg 454

Take That Ltd (United Kingdom) *Tel:* (01423) 507545 *Fax:* (01423) 526035 *E-mail:* sales@takethat.co.uk *Web Site:* www.takethat.co.uk, pg 762

Edicoes Talento (Portugal) *Tel:* (021) 7154281 *Fax:* (021) 7154257, pg 536

Talento Publicacoes Editora e Grafica Ltda (Brazil) *Tel:* (011) 3816-1718 *Fax:* (011) 2823752 *E-mail:* talento@talento.com.br *Web Site:* www.talento.com.br, pg 91

Talentum Konyves es Kereskedo Kft (Hungary) *Tel:* (01) 2057077; (01) 2057138, pg 1315

Editions Tallandier (France) *Tel:* (01) 40 46 43 88 *Fax:* (01) 40 46 43 98 *Web Site:* www.tallandier.com, pg 187

Editora Taller (Dominican Republic) *Tel:* 531-7975 *Fax:* 531-7979 *E-mail:* editora.taller@codetel.net.do, pg 136

Talmudic Encyclopedia Publications (Israel) *Tel:* (02) 6423242 *Fax:* (02) 6423919, pg 372

Taltos Kiadasszervezesi Ltd (Hungary) *Tel:* (01) 1213515; (01) 1420676, pg 324

Tamagawa University Press (Japan) *Tel:* (042) 739-8935 *Fax:* (042) 739-8940 *E-mail:* tup@tamagawa.ac.jp *Web Site:* www.tamagawa.ac.jp/sisetu/up, pg 429

Tamarind Publications (Australia) *Tel:* (02) 467934 *Fax:* (02) 659515 *E-mail:* sigi@hunterlink.net.au, pg 42

Tampereen Kirjakauppa Oy (Finland) *Tel:* (03) 2128380 *Fax:* (03) 2122136 *E-mail:* trekirja@vip.fi *Web Site:* www.tampereenkirjakauppa.fi, pg 1309

Tampereen Yliopiston Kirjasto (Finland) *Tel:* (03) 215 6434 *Fax:* (03) 215 7493 *Web Site:* www.uta.fi/~kimiii, pg 1505

Tana Press Ltd & Flora Nwapa Books Ltd (Nigeria) *Tel:* (042) 338857, pg 507

Tandem Press (New Zealand) *Tel:* (09) 480-1452 *Fax:* (09) 480-1455 *E-mail:* customers@tandempress.co.nz *Web Site:* www.tandempress.co.nz, pg 501

Tangens Systemverlag GmbH (Germany) *Tel:* (040) 3985860 *Fax:* (040) 395118, pg 289

Tango Books (United Kingdom) *Tel:* (020) 8996 9970 *Fax:* (020) 8996 9977 *E-mail:* edith@tangobooks.co.uk, pg 762

Tankosha Publishing Co Ltd (Japan) *Tel:* (075) 432 5151 *Fax:* (075) 432 0275 *E-mail:* info@tankosha.co.jp *Web Site:* tankosha.topica.ne.jp, pg 429

Tantalum-Niobium International Study Center (Belgium) *Tel:* (02) 6495158 *Fax:* (02) 6496447 *E-mail:* info@tanb.org *Web Site:* www.tanb.org, pg 1262

Tanum Karl Johan A/S (Norway) *Tel:* (022) 41 11 00 *Fax:* (022) 33 32 75 *E-mail:* karl.johan@tanum.no; nettservice@tanum.no *Web Site:* www.tanum.no, pg 1333

Tanzania Library Association (United Republic of Tanzania) *Tel:* (022) 2775411 *E-mail:* tla_tanzania@yahoo.com *Web Site:* www.angelfire.com/al4/tla/, pg 1571

Tanzania Library Service (United Republic of Tanzania) *Tel:* (022) 215 09 23; (022) 215 00 48 *Fax:* (022) 215 11 00 *E-mail:* tlsb@africaonline.co.tz, pg 1288, 1549

Tanzania Library Services Board (United Republic of Tanzania) *Tel:* (022) 215 09 23; (022) 215 00 48 *E-mail:* tlsb@africaonline.co.tz, pg 644

Tanzania Publishing House (United Republic of Tanzania) *Tel:* (051) 32164, pg 644

Taoasis Verlag, Birgit Meyer (Germany) *Tel:* (05261) 2321 *Fax:* (05261) 9383-21 *E-mail:* info@taoasis.de *Web Site:* www.taoasis.de, pg 289

Tappeiner (Italy) *Tel:* (0473) 563666 *Fax:* (0473) 563689 *E-mail:* tappeiner@pass.dnet.it, pg 409

Taprobane Ltd (United Kingdom) *Tel:* (020) 8998 3024 *Fax:* (020) 8810 5415, pg 762

Tara Publishing (India) *Tel:* (044) 24401696; (044) 24912846 *Fax:* (044) 24453658 *E-mail:* mail@tarabooks.com *Web Site:* www.tarabooks.com, pg 351

DB Taraporevala Sons & Co Pvt Ltd (India) *Tel:* 2041433; 2041434, pg 351

Editions Tardy SA (France) *Tel:* (01) 45 44 38 34 *Fax:* (01) 45 49 93 92, pg 187

Tarea Asociacion de Publicaciones Educativas (Peru) *Tel:* (01) 424-0997 *Fax:* (01) 332-7404 *E-mail:* postmaster@tarea.org.pe *Web Site:* www.tarea.org.pe, pg 517

Target Publishers (Edms) Bpk (South Africa) *Tel:* (018) 4627556 *Fax:* (018) 4627557, pg 569

Taride Editions (France) *Tel:* (01) 48 78 40 74 *Fax:* (01) 48 78 40 77 *Web Site:* www.taride.com, pg 187

Tarka Publishing (Australia) *Tel:* (02) 9955 2074 *Fax:* (02) 9925 0664, pg 42

Editions Tarmeye (France) *Tel:* (0471) 650153 *Fax:* (0471) 650154, pg 187

Tarquin Publications (United Kingdom) *Tel:* (01379) 384 218 *Fax:* (01379) 384 289 *E-mail:* enquiries@tarquin-books.demon.co.uk *Web Site:* www.tarquin-books.demon.co.uk, pg 762

Ediciones Tarraco (Spain) *Tel:* (077) 233813 *Fax:* (077) 233851, pg 601

La Tartaruga Edizioni SAS (Italy) *Tel:* (02) 584501 *Fax:* (02) 58307512, pg 409

Tartu University Library (Estonia) *Tel:* (07) 375 702 *Fax:* (07) 375 701 *E-mail:* library@utlib.ee *Web Site:* www.utlib.ee, pg 1504

TASCHEN GmbH (Germany) *Tel:* (0221) 201 80 0 *Fax:* (0221) 25 49 19 *E-mail:* contact@taschen.com *Web Site:* www.taschen.com, pg 289

Taschen UK Ltd (United Kingdom) *Tel:* (020) 7437 4350 *Fax:* (020) 7437 4360 *E-mail:* contact@taschen.com *Web Site:* www.taschen.com, pg 763

Tassorello, SA (Peru) *Tel:* (01) 460-2040; (01) 460-0255 *Fax:* (01) 461-5714 *E-mail:* tassorello@terra.com.pe, pg 517

Tassotti Editore (Italy) *Tel:* (0424) 566105 *Fax:* (0424) 566205 *E-mail:* info@tassotti.it *Web Site:* www.tassotti.it, pg 409

Est-Samuel Tastet Verlag (Romania) *Tel:* (01) 6386250 *Fax:* (01) 3122012, pg 542

Tata McGraw-Hill Publishing Co Ltd (India) *Tel:* (011) 2588 2743; (011) 2588 2746; (011) 2588 9304; (011) 2588 9307 *E-mail:* info_india@mcgraw-hill.com *Web Site:* www.tatamcgrawhill.com, pg 351

Tate Publishing Ltd (United Kingdom) *Tel:* (020) 7887 8000; (020) 7887 8008 *Fax:* (020) 7887 8878 *E-mail:* tp.enquiries@tate.org.uk *Web Site:* www.tate.org.uk, pg 763

Tatran Publishing House (Slovakia) *Tel:* (07) 54435849 *Fax:* (07) 54435777, pg 1255

Edition Tau u Tau Type Druck Verlags-und Handels GmbH (Austria) *Tel:* (02625) 32000 *Fax:* (02625) 320003, pg 58

I B Tauris & Co Ltd (United Kingdom) *Tel:* (020) 7243 1225 *Fax:* (01727) 856398 *E-mail:* mail@ibtauris.com *Web Site:* www.ibtauris.com, pg 763

Taurus (South Africa) *Tel:* 7860018, pg 569

Taylor Books (New Zealand) *Tel:* (07) 5786024, pg 501

Taylor & Francis (United Kingdom) *Tel:* (01235) 828600 *Fax:* (01235) 828900 *E-mail:* info@tandf.co.uk *Web Site:* www.tandf.co.uk, pg 763

Taylor & Francis Asia Pacific (Singapore) *Tel:* 67415166 *Fax:* 67429356 *E-mail:* info@tandf.com.sg *Web Site:* www.tandf.co.uk, pg 558

Taylor & Francis Medical Books (United Kingdom) *Tel:* (020) 7842 2244 *Fax:* (020) 7842 2300, pg 763

Taylor Graham Publishing (United Kingdom) *Web Site:* www.taylorgraham.com, pg 764

Taylor Publishing Company (United States) *Tel:* 214-819-8226 *Toll Free Tel:* 800-677-2800 *Fax:* 214-630-1852 *E-mail:* info@taylorpub.com *Web Site:* www.taylorpub.com, pg 1168, 1189, 1231, 1241

TBI Publishers' Distributors (India) *Tel:* (011) 3325247 *Fax:* (011) 3325247, pg 1317

TBS-Britannica Co Ltd (Japan) *Tel:* (03) 5436-5721 *Fax:* (03) 5436-5759, pg 429

Tcherikover Publishers Ltd (Israel) *Tel:* (03) 6870621; (03) 6396099 *Toll Free Tel:* 800-828-080 *Fax:* (03) 6874729 *E-mail:* barkay@inter.net.il, pg 372

Te Waihora Press (New Zealand) *Tel:* (03) 348-8675 *Fax:* (03) 348-8675, pg 501

Te-Wi Verlag Unternehmensbereich Buch der Ziff Verlag GmbH (Germany) *Tel:* (089) 14312470 *Fax:* (089) 14312469, pg 289

TEA Ediciones SA (Spain) *Tel:* (091) 2 705 000 *Fax:* (091) 3 458 608 *E-mail:* madrid@teaediciones.com *Web Site:* www.teaediciones.com, pg 601

TEA Kirjastus (Estonia) *Tel:* 644 9253; 645 9206 *Fax:* 645 9208 *E-mail:* info@tea.ee *Web Site:* www.tea.ee, pg 140

TEA Tascabili degli Editori Associati SpA (Italy) *Tel:* (02) 80206625 *Fax:* (02) 8900844 *Web Site:* www.tealibri.it, pg 409

Teachers Book Club (United Kingdom) *Tel:* (01926) 813910 *Fax:* (01926) 817727 *E-mail:* enquiries@scholastic.co.uk *Web Site:* www.scholastic.co.uk/teach_index.html, pg 1257

Teaterforlaget Drama (Denmark) *Tel:* 70 25 11 41 *Fax:* 74 65 20 93 *E-mail:* drama@drama.dk *Web Site:* www.drama.dk, pg 135

Tech Publications Pte Ltd (Singapore) *Tel:* 2763611 *Fax:* 2763622 *E-mail:* techpub@pacific.net.sg, pg 558

Techbooks (New Zealand) *Tel:* (09) 524-0132 *Fax:* (09) 523-3769 *E-mail:* techbooks@techbooks.co.nz *Web Site:* www.techbooks.co.nz, pg 1331

Technica (Bulgaria) *Tel:* (02) 987 1283 *Fax:* (02) 987 4906 *E-mail:* technica@netel.bg; sales@technica-bg.com *Web Site:* www.technica-bg.com, pg 97

Technical Books Ltd (South Africa) *Tel:* (021) 216540 *Fax:* (021) 4216593 *E-mail:* techbkct@mweb.co.za, pg 1341

Technical Centre for Agricultural & Rural Co-operation (Netherlands) *Tel:* (0317) 467100 *Fax:* (0317) 460067 *E-mail:* cta@cta.nl *Web Site:* www.cta.nl, pg 1279

Technical Chamber of Greece (Greece) *Tel:* (0210) 3254591; (0210) 3314403 *Fax:* (0210) 3314403 *E-mail:* registry@central.tee.gr, pg 312

Library of the Technical Chamber of Greece (Greece) *Tel:* (0210) 3291701; (0210) 3245180 *Fax:* (0210) 3237525 *E-mail:* tee_lib@tee.gr *Web Site:* www.tee.gr, pg 1513

Technical University Library (Turkey) *Tel:* (0212) 285 35 96 *Fax:* (0212) 285 33 02 *E-mail:* library@papirus.library.itu.edu.tr *Web Site:* www.library.itu.edu.tr, pg 1551

Technical University of Sofia Library & Information Complex (Bulgaria) *Tel:* (02) 62 3073 *Fax:* (02) 68 5343 *E-mail:* office_tu@tu-sofia.bg *Web Site:* www.tu-sofia.bg, pg 1496

Technicka Univerzita (Slovakia) *Tel:* (045) 5206111 *Fax:* (0855) 20027, pg 561

Hochschule fur Technik Wirtschaft und Kultur Leipzig (FH) (Germany) *Tel:* (0341) 3076-0 *Fax:* (0341) 3076-6456 *E-mail:* ebert@r.htwk.leipzig.de *Web Site:* www.htwk-leipzig.de, pg 289

Instytut Techniki Budowlanej, Dzial Wydawniczo-Poligraficzny (Poland) *Tel:* (022) 8431471 *Fax:* (022) 8432931 *E-mail:* wydawnictwa_itb@pro.onet.pl *Web Site:* www.itb.pl, pg 527

Technion - Israel Institute of Technology Libraries (Israel) *Tel:* (04) 8292507 *Fax:* (04) 8295662 *E-mail:* webteam@tx.technion.ac.il *Web Site:* library.technion.ac.il, pg 1519

Editions Technip SA (France) *Tel:* (01) 45 78 33 80 *Fax:* (01) 45 75 37 11 *E-mail:* info@editionstechnip.com *Web Site:* www.editionstechnip.com, pg 187

Editions Techniques et Scientifiques SPRL (Belgium) *Tel:* (02) 6401040 *Fax:* (02) 6400739, pg 73

EDITIONS TECHNIQUES ET SCIENTIFIQUES FRANCAISES

INDUSTRY

Editions Techniques et Scientifiques Francaises (France) *Tel:* (01) 40 46 35 00 *Fax:* (01) 40 46 49 95 *E-mail:* infos@dunod.com *Web Site:* www.dunod, pg 187

Editions Techniques Specialisees (Tunisia) *Tel:* (01) 71 74 61 61; (01) 71 74 70 04 *Fax:* (01) 71 74 61 60 *E-mail:* info@pagesjaunes.com.tn, pg 648

Universitaetsbibliothek der Technischen Universitaet Wien (Austria) *Tel:* (01) 58801 44051 *Fax:* (01) 58801 44099 *E-mail:* info@mail.ub.tuwien.ac.at *Web Site:* www.ub.tuwien.ac.at, pg 1492

Technology Exchange Ltd (Hong Kong) *Tel:* 2602 6300 *Fax:* 2609 1687, pg 319

Technosdar Ltd (Israel) *Tel:* (03) 560-7418; (03) 5605951 *Fax:* (03) 5605951 *E-mail:* technos@internet-zahav.net, pg 1159

Technosdar Ltd (Israel) *Tel:* (03) 560-7418; (03) 5605951 *Fax:* (03) 5605951, pg 1180

Technosdar Ltd (Israel) *Tel:* (03) 560-7418 *Fax:* (03) 560-4932 *E-mail:* technos@zahav.net.il, pg 1220

Tecman Bible House (Singapore) *Tel:* 6338-6764 *Fax:* 6338-8236 *E-mail:* tecman@tecman.com.sg *Web Site:* www.tecman.com.sg, pg 558

Publicaciones Tecnicas Mediterraneo (Chile) *Tel:* (02) 251 62 57; (02) 233 82 72 *Fax:* (02) 231 06 94 *E-mail:* msalinero@entelchile.net, pg 100

Ediciones Tecnicas Rede, SA (Spain) *Tel:* (093) 4103097 *Fax:* (093) 4392813, pg 601

Tecniche Nuove SpA (Italy) *Tel:* (02) 390901 *Fax:* (02) 7610351 *E-mail:* info@tecnichenuove.com; vendite-libri@tecnichenuove.com *Web Site:* www.tecnichenuove.com, pg 410

Editores Tecnicos Asociados SA (Spain) *Tel:* (093) 4193336, pg 601

Editorial Tecnologica de Costa Rica (Costa Rica) *Tel:* 552-5333 ext 2297 *Fax:* 552-5354; 551-5348 *E-mail:* editec@itcr.ac.cr *Web Site:* www.itcr.ac.cr, pg 116

Instituto Tecnologico de Galicia, ITG (Spain) *Tel:* (0981) 17 32 06 *Fax:* (0981) 17 32 23 *E-mail:* itg1@itg.es *Web Site:* www.itg.es, pg 601

Editorial Tecnos SA (Spain) *Tel:* (091) 3938800; (091) 393 86 86 *Fax:* (091) 7426631 *Web Site:* www.tecnos.es, pg 601

Teduca, Tecnicas Educativas, CA (Venezuela) *Tel:* (02) 235 58 78; (02) 235 43 95; (02) 235 62 65 *Fax:* (02) 239 79 52, pg 780

Teeney Books Ltd (United Kingdom) *Tel:* (01225) 775657 *Fax:* (01225) 775676 *E-mail:* teeneybo@primex.co.uk, pg 764

Editura Tehnica (Romania) *Tel:* (01) 222-33-21 *Fax:* (01) 222-37-76, pg 542

Tehnicka Knjiga (Croatia) *Tel:* (01) 481 0818 *Fax:* (01) 481 0821, pg 119

Tehnicka Knjiga (Croatia) *Tel:* (041) 4810818 *Fax:* (041) 481 0821, pg 1307

Tehniska Zalozba Slovenije (Slovenia) *Tel:* (01) 4790211 *Fax:* (01) 4790230 *E-mail:* info@tzs.si *Web Site:* www.tzs.si, pg 1340

Otto Teich (Germany) *Tel:* (06151) 824120 *Fax:* (06151) 895656, pg 289

Editorial Teide SA (Spain) *Tel:* (093) 4398009 *Fax:* (093) 3224192 *E-mail:* info@editorialteide.es *Web Site:* www.editorialteide.es, pg 601

Teikoku-Shoin Co Ltd (Japan) *Tel:* (03) 32620834 *Fax:* (03) 32627770 *E-mail:* kenkyu@teikokushoin.co.jp *Web Site:* www.teikokushoin.co.jp, pg 429

Almerinda Teixeira (Portugal) *Tel:* (021) 2762352, pg 536

Tek Translation International SA (Spain) *Tel:* (091) 4141111 *Fax:* (091) 4144444 *E-mail:* sales@tektrans.com *Web Site:* www.tektrans.com, pg 1149

Tekmirio (Greece) *Tel:* (01) 3637912; (01) 2287548, pg 312

Teknillisen Korkeakoulun Kirjasto (Finland) *Tel:* (09) 451 4111 *Fax:* (09) 451 4132 *E-mail:* infolib@hut.fi *Web Site:* lib.hut.fi, pg 1505

Tekniska Litteratursaellskapet (Sweden) *Tel:* (08) 678 23 20 *Fax:* (08) 678 23 01 *E-mail:* kansliet@tls.se *Web Site:* www.tls.se, pg 1571

Teknografiska Institutet AB (Sweden) *Tel:* (08) 83 42 85 *Fax:* (08) 73 04 13, pg 616

Teknologisk Forlag (Norway) *Tel:* 22471100 *Fax:* 22471149, pg 510

Tel Aviv Books Ltd (Israel) *Tel:* (03) 6210500 *Fax:* (03) 5257725, pg 372

Tel Aviv University (Israel) *Tel:* (03) 6408111; (03) 6424571; (03) 6409200; (03) 6426682 *Fax:* (03) 6422404; (03) 6408355 *E-mail:* tauinfo@post.tau.ac.il *Web Site:* www.tau.ac.il, pg 372

Tel Aviv University Library (Israel) *Tel:* (03) 640-8111 *Fax:* (03) 6407833 *E-mail:* tauinfo@post.tau.ac.il *Web Site:* www.tau.ac.il, pg 1520

Telegraph Books (United Kingdom) *Tel:* (020) 7538 5000 *Fax:* (020) 7538 6064 *Web Site:* www.telegraph.co.uk, pg 764

Editorial Augusto E Pila Telena SL (Spain) *Tel:* (091) 857 28 88; (607) 25 20 82 *Fax:* (091) 857 28 80 *E-mail:* pilatena@arrakis.es *Web Site:* www.arrakis.es/~pilatena, pg 601

Telex-Verlag Jaeger & Waldmann GmbH (Germany) *Tel:* (06151) 33 02-0 *Fax:* (06151) 33 02-50 *E-mail:* jwemail@aol.com; jwdir@aol.com, pg 289

Tell Forlag (Norway) *Tel:* 66780918 *Fax:* 66900572 *E-mail:* tell@online.no *Web Site:* www.tell.no, pg 511

Telos Boeken (Netherlands) *Tel:* (020) 5241010 *Fax:* (020) 5241011 *E-mail:* info@buijten.nl *Web Site:* www.buijten.nl, pg 490

Tema Celeste (Italy) *Tel:* (02) 8065171; (02) 80651732 (subscriptions) *Fax:* (02) 80651743 *E-mail:* editorial@temaceleste.com; subscriptions@temaceleste.com *Web Site:* www.gabrius.com/default_tc.htm, pg 410

Tema Publishers Ltd (United Republic of Tanzania) *Tel:* (051) 113608 *Fax:* (051) 75422, pg 644

Ediciones Temas de Hoy, SA (Spain) *Tel:* (091) 4230318 *Fax:* (091) 4230309; (091) 5970654 *E-mail:* bnogueras@temasdehoy.es; info@temasdehoy.es *Web Site:* www.temasdehoy.es, pg 601

Tembec Paperboard Group (Canada) *Tel:* 514-871-0137 *Toll Free Tel:* 800-411-7011 *Fax:* 514-397-0896 *Web Site:* www.tembec.com, pg 1235

Libreria Temis SA (Colombia) *Tel:* (01) 341 3225 *Fax:* (01) 269 0793, pg 1307

Edition Temmen (Germany) *Tel:* (0421) 34843-0 *Fax:* (0421) 348094 *E-mail:* info@edition-temmen.de *Web Site:* www.edition-temmen.de, pg 290

Temple Lodge Publishing Ltd (United Kingdom) *Tel:* (01342) 824000 *Fax:* (01342) 826437 *E-mail:* office@templelodge.com *Web Site:* www.templelodge.com, pg 764

Tempo Publishing (M) Sdn Bhd (Malaysia) *Tel:* (03) 7570000 *Fax:* (03) 7576688; (03) 7587001, pg 458

Tempus Editores (Brazil) *Tel:* (021) 4535000 *Fax:* (021) 4426482, pg 91

TEMTO (Bulgaria) *Tel:* (02) 524-924 *E-mail:* temto@sf.icn.bg, pg 97

10/18 (France) *Tel:* (01) 44 16 05 00 *Fax:* (01) 44 16 05 03 *E-mail:* editeur@10-18.fr; commercial@10-18.fr *Web Site:* www.10-18.fr, pg 187

teNeues Verlag GmbH & Co KG (Germany) *Tel:* (02152) 916-0 *Fax:* (02152) 916-111 *E-mail:* verlag@teneues.de *Web Site:* www.teneues.com, pg 290

Tenri Central Library (Japan) *Tel:* (0743) 63-9200 *Fax:* (0743) 63-7728 *E-mail:* info@tcl.gr.jp *Web Site:* www.tcl.gr.jp, pg 1522

Editura Teora (Romania) *Tel:* (021) 2106204 *Fax:* (021) 2103828 *E-mail:* mesaj@teora.ro *Web Site:* www.teora.ro, pg 542

Teorema (Portugal) *Tel:* (021) 529988 *Fax:* (021) 352 14 80 *E-mail:* editorial.teorema@netc.pt, pg 536

Teorija Verojatnostej i ee Primenenija (Russian Federation) *Tel:* (095) 1352380; (095) 3324410 *Fax:* (095) 1135125 *E-mail:* tvp@caravan.ru, pg 549

Librairie Pierre Tequi et Editions Tequi (France) *Tel:* (01) 43.01.01.81 *Fax:* (01) 43.02.25.52 *E-mail:* pierre.tequi@wanadoo.fr *Web Site:* www.librairietequi.com, pg 187

Terania Rainforest Publishing (Australia) *Tel:* (02) 6688 6204 *Fax:* (02) 6688 6227 *E-mail:* terania@nrg.com.au, pg 43

Tercer Mundo Editores SA (Colombia) *Tel:* (01) 2551539; (01) 2550737; (01) 2551695 *Fax:* (01) 2125976 *E-mail:* tmundo@polcola.com.co, pg 113

Libreria Tercer Mundo (Colombia) *Tel:* (01) 255 1539; (01) 255 0737 *Fax:* (01) 212 5976 *E-mail:* tmundoed@polcola.com.co, pg 1307

Edizioni del Teresianum (Italy) *Tel:* (06) 585401 *Fax:* (06) 58540300, pg 410

Tern Press (United Kingdom) *Tel:* (01630) 652153, pg 764

Terra Grischuna Verlag Buch-und Zeitschriftenverlag (Switzerland) *Tel:* (081) 2867050 *Fax:* (081) 2867057 *E-mail:* info@terra-grischuna.ch *Web Site:* www.terra-grischuna.ch, pg 635

Terra Sancta Arts (Israel) *Tel:* (03) 6499520; (03) 6499525 *Fax:* (03) 6490532, pg 372

Uitgeverij Terra bv (Netherlands) *Tel:* (0575) 58 13 10 *Fax:* (0575) 52 52 42 *E-mail:* terra@terraboek.nl *Web Site:* www.terraboek.nl, pg 490

Terra-Verlag GmbH (Germany) *Tel:* (07531) 81220 *Fax:* (07531) 812299 *E-mail:* info@terra-verlag.de *Web Site:* www.terra-verlag.de, pg 290

Editorial Sal Terrae (Spain) *Tel:* (0942) 369 198 *Fax:* (0942) 369 201 *E-mail:* salterrae@salterrae.es *Web Site:* www.salterrae.es, pg 602

Terre Vivante (France) *Tel:* (04) 76 34 80 80 *Fax:* (04) 76 34 84 02 *E-mail:* infos@terrevivante.org *Web Site:* www.terrevivante.org, pg 187

Tertiary Press (Australia) *Tel:* (03) 9726 1505 *Fax:* (03) 9726 1706 *E-mail:* tertiarypress@swin.edu.au *Web Site:* www.tertiarypress.com.au, pg 43

Terveystieteiden keskuskirjasto (TERKKO) (Finland) *Tel:* (09) 191 26643 *Fax:* (09) 241 0385 *E-mail:* terkko-info@helinski.fi *Web Site:* www.terkko.helsinki.fi/, pg 1505

Tesitex, SL (Spain) *Tel:* (0923) 255115 *Fax:* (0923) 258703 *E-mail:* tesitex@tesitex.es *Web Site:* www.tesitex.es, pg 602

Tessloff Verlag Ragnar Tessloff GmbH & Co KG (Germany) *Tel:* (0911) 39906-0 *Fax:* (0911) 39906-39 *E-mail:* tessloff@osn.de *Web Site:* www.tessloff.com, pg 290

Nicola Teti e C Editore SRL (Italy) *Tel:* (02) 55015584 *Fax:* (02) 55015595 *E-mail:* teti@teti.it *Web Site:* www.teti.it, pg 410

Tetra Verlag Gmbh (Germany) *Tel:* (03304) 20 22-0 *Fax:* (03304) 20 22-20 *E-mail:* info@tetra-verlag.de *Web Site:* www.tetra-verlag.de, pg 290

Tetzlaff Verlag (Germany) *Tel:* (040) 237 14-03 *Fax:* (040) 237 14-233 *Web Site:* www.eurailpress.com, pg 290

B G Teubner Verlag (Germany) *Tel:* (0611) 78780 (0611) 7878470 *Web Site:* www.teubner.de; www.gwv-fachverlage.de, pg 290

TEV Leidykla (Lithuania) *Tel:* (02) 729318; (02) 729803 *Fax:* (02) 729804 *E-mail:* tev@tev.lt *Web Site:* www.tev.lt, pg 450

Tevan Kiado Vallalat (Hungary) *Tel:* 66441181, pg 324

Texere Publishing Ltd (United Kingdom) *Tel:* (020) 7204 3644 *Fax:* (020) 7208 6701 *Web Site:* www.etexere.com, pg 764

Editorial Texido Ltda (Chile) *Tel:* (02) 6224652 *Fax:* (02) 6224660, pg 100

edition Text & Kritik im Richard Boorberg Verlag GmbH & Co (Germany) *Tel:* (089) 43600012 *Fax:* (089) 43600019 *E-mail:* info@etk-muenchen.de *Web Site:* www.etk-muenchen.de, pg 290

Text Book Centre Ltd (Kenya) *Tel:* (02) 330340 *Fax:* (02) 225779 *E-mail:* admin@tbc.co.ke *Web Site:* www.textbook.centre.com, pg 1324

Text Books Malaysia Sdn Bhd (Malaysia) *Tel:* (074) 911181 *Fax:* (074) 911181 *E-mail:* textbook@tm.net.my, pg 459

Text Publishers Ltd Too (Russian Federation) *Tel:* (095) 156-4202 *Fax:* (095) 150-0472 *E-mail:* textpub@windoms.sitek.net, pg 549

The Text Publishing Company Pty Ltd (Australia) *Tel:* (03) 9272 4700 *Fax:* (03) 9926 4854 *E-mail:* books@textmedia.com.au *Web Site:* www.textpublishing.com.au, pg 43

Textile & Art Publications Ltd (United Kingdom) *Tel:* (020) 7499 7979 *Fax:* (020) 7409 2596 *E-mail:* post@textile-art.com *Web Site:* www.textile-art.com, pg 764

Texto Editora (Portugal) *Tel:* (021) 427 22 00 *Fax:* (021) 427 22 01 *E-mail:* info@te.pt *Web Site:* www.textoeditora.pt; www.te.pt, pg 536

Editorial Texto Ltda (Costa Rica) *Tel:* 2316643 *Fax:* 2962429, pg 116

Tf Editores (Spain) *Tel:* (091) 484 1870; (091) 484 1878 *Fax:* (091) 661 3594 *E-mail:* editorial@tfeditores.com *Web Site:* www.tfeditores.com, pg 602

TFPL (United Kingdom) *Tel:* (020) 7251 5522 *Fax:* (020) 7251 8318 *E-mail:* central@tfpl.com *Web Site:* www.tfpl.com, pg 764

Thai Library Association (Thailand) *Tel:* (02) 734-8022; (02) 734-8023 *Fax:* (02) 734-8024 *Web Site:* tla.tiac.or.th, pg 1571

Thai National Documentation Centre (TNDC) (Thailand) *Tel:* (02) 579 1121; (02) 579 1130; (02) 579 5515; (02) 579 0160 *Fax:* (02) 561 4771, pg 1550

Thai Watana Panich Co, Ltd (Thailand) *Tel:* (02) 215-0060-3 *Fax:* (02) 215-1360 *E-mail:* twpp@loxinfo.th *Web Site:* www.twppress.com, pg 646

Thai Watana Panich Press Co Ltd (Thailand) *Tel:* (02) 2150060-3 *Fax:* (02) 2152360 *E-mail:* twpp@loxinfo.co.th *Web Site:* www.twppress.com, pg 1162

Thalacker Medien GmbH Co KG (Germany) *Tel:* (0531) 38004 0 *Fax:* (0531) 38004 25 *E-mail:* info@thalackermedien.de *Web Site:* www.thalackermedien.de, pg 290

Thales Sociedad Andaluza de Educacion Matematica (Spain) *Tel:* (095) 4623658 *Fax:* (095) 4236378 *E-mail:* thales@cica.es *Web Site:* thales.cica.es, pg 602

Editions Thames & Hudson (France) *Tel:* (01) 56240450 *Fax:* (01) 56240458 *E-mail:* thameshudson@wanadoo.fr *Web Site:* www.thameshudson.fr, pg 187

Thames & Hudson (Australia) Pty Ltd (Australia) *Tel:* (03) 9646 7788 *Fax:* (03) 9646 8790 *E-mail:* thaust@thaust.com.au, pg 43

Thames & Hudson Ltd (United Kingdom) *Tel:* (020) 7845 5000 *Fax:* (020) 7845 5050 *E-mail:* sales@thameshudson.co.uk *Web Site:* www.thamesandhudson.com, pg 764

Thammasat University Libraries (Thailand) *Tel:* (02) 623-5161; (02) 623-5167 *Fax:* (02) 623-5173 *E-mail:* tulib@alpha.tu.ac.th *Web Site:* library2.tu.ac.th, pg 1550

Thanhaeuser Edition (Austria) *Tel:* (07234) 83800 *Fax:* (07234) 83800 *E-mail:* thanhaeuser@bibliotheca-selecta.de, pg 58

Tharpa Publications (United Kingdom) *Tel:* (01229) 588599 *Fax:* (01229) 483919 *E-mail:* tharpa@tharpa.com *Web Site:* www.tharpa.com, pg 764

Editorial Thassalia, SA (Spain) *Tel:* (093) 4511298 *Fax:* (093) 4511283, pg 602

Thauros Verlag GmbH (Germany) *Tel:* (08387) 2510 *Fax:* (08387) 3731 *E-mail:* thaurosverlag@t-online.de, pg 290

The Tarragon Press (United Kingdom) *Tel:* (01988) 850368 *Fax:* (01988) 850304, pg 765

Editions Theatrales (France) *Tel:* (01) 53 10 23 00 *Fax:* (01) 53 10 23 01 *E-mail:* info@editionstheatrales.fr *Web Site:* www.editionstheatrales.fr, pg 187

Konrad Theiss Verlag GmbH (Germany) *Tel:* (0711) 255 27-0 *Fax:* (0711) 255 27-17 *E-mail:* service@theiss.de *Web Site:* www.theiss.de, pg 290

Theodor (Imprimerie) (Haiti), pg 314

Theologischer Verlag und Buchhandlungen AG (Switzerland) *Tel:* (01) 299 33 55 *Fax:* (01) 299 33 58 *E-mail:* tvz@ref.ch *Web Site:* www.tvz.ref.ch, pg 635

Theoria SRL Distribuidora y Editora (Argentina) *Tel:* (011) 4381-0131 *Fax:* (011) 4381-0131 *E-mail:* edicionestheoria@ciudad.com.ar, pg 9

Theosophical Publishing House (India) *Tel:* (044) 412904 *Fax:* (044) 4901399; (044) 4902706 *E-mail:* intl-hq@ts-adyar.org *Web Site:* ts-adyar.org, pg 351

Thesen Verlag Vowinckel (Luxembourg) *Tel:* (0352) 748715 *Fax:* (0352) 26740429, pg 452

Theseus - Verlag AG (Switzerland) *Tel:* (01) 9109294 *Fax:* (01) 9108019, pg 635

Thex Editora e Distribuidora Ltda (Brazil) *Tel:* (021) 2221-4458 *Fax:* (021) 2252-9338 *E-mail:* atendimento@thexeditora.com.br *Web Site:* www.thexeditora.com.br, pg 91

Druck-und Verlagshans Thiele & Schwarz GmbH (Germany) *Tel:* (0561) 9 59 25-0 *Fax:* (0561) 9 59 25-68 *E-mail:* info@thiele-schwarz.de *Web Site:* www.thiele-schwarz.de, pg 290

Georg Thieme Verlag KG (Germany) *Tel:* (0711) 8931-0 *Fax:* (0711) 8931-298 *E-mail:* kunden.service@thieme.de *Web Site:* www.thieme.de, pg 291

ThiemeMeulenhoff (Netherlands) *Tel:* (030) 239 2 111 *Fax:* (030) 239 2 270 *E-mail:* info.bao@thiememeulenhoff.nl *Web Site:* www.thiememeulenhoff.nl, pg 490

Thien, Hans-Gunter, u Hanns Wienold (Germany) *Tel:* (0251) 3900480 *Fax:* (0251) 39004850 *E-mail:* info@dampfboot-verlag.de *Web Site:* www.dampfboot-verlag.de, pg 291

Thienemann Verlag GmbH (Germany) *Tel:* (0711) 210 55-0 *Fax:* (0711) 210 55 39 *E-mail:* info@thienemann.de *Web Site:* www.thienemann.de, pg 291

James Thin, Bookseller (United Kingdom) *Tel:* (0131) 622 8222 *Fax:* (0131) 557 8149 *E-mail:* enquiries@jthin.co.uk, pg 1353

Thin Rich Press (Australia) *Tel:* (08) 9364 4799 *Fax:* (08) 9316 3338, pg 43

The Third Wave Enterprise Co Ltd (Taiwan, Province of China) *Tel:* (02) 87803636 *Fax:* (02) 87805656 *E-mail:* AIWebmaster@acer.com.tw *Web Site:* www.acertwp.com.tw, pg 642

34 Literatura S/C Ltda (Brazil) *Tel:* (011) 3816-6777 *Fax:* (011) 3816-0078 *Web Site:* www.rattapallax.com/editora34.htm, pg 91

Thistle Press (United Kingdom) *Tel:* (01464) 821053 *Fax:* (01464) 821053 *E-mail:* info@oldmilldesign.co.uk, pg 765

Thjodsagao ehf (Iceland) *Tel:* 567-1777 *Fax:* 567-1240 *E-mail:* pbk@centrum.is, pg 326

Verlag Theodor Thoben (Germany) *Tel:* (05431) 3486 *Fax:* (05431) 3584 *E-mail:* info@buecher-thoben.de *Web Site:* www.buecher-thoben.de, pg 291

Thoemmes Press (United Kingdom) *Tel:* (0117) 929 1377 *Fax:* (0117) 922 1918 *E-mail:* info@thoemmes.com *Web Site:* www.thoemmes.com, pg 765

Hans Thoma Verlag GmbH Kunst und Buchverlag (Germany) *Tel:* (0721) 932750 *Fax:* (0721) 9327520, pg 291

Alain Thomas Editeur (France) *Tel:* (01) 45 88 28 03 *Fax:* (01) 45 88 49 24 *Web Site:* alainthomasimages.com, pg 187

Thomas Technology Solutions (UK) Ltd (United Kingdom) *Tel:* (020) 7070 7550 *Fax:* (020) 7070 7551 *E-mail:* marketing@thomastechsolutions.com *Web Site:* www.thomastechsolutions.com, pg 1185

Thomson Publications (South Africa) *Tel:* (011) 7892144 *Fax:* (011) 7893196, pg 569

Thomson Corporation (Hong Kong) *Tel:* 2533 5416 *Fax:* 2530 3588 *Web Site:* www.tfibcm.com, pg 319

Forlaget Thomson A/S (Denmark) *Tel:* 33 74 07 00 *Fax:* 33 12 16 36 *E-mail:* thomson@thomson.dk *Web Site:* www.thomson.dk, pg 135

Thomson Gale (United Kingdom) *Tel:* (01264) 342962 *Fax:* (01264) 342763 *Web Site:* www.gale.com, pg 765

Thomson Learning Japan (Japan) *Tel:* (03) 3221-1385 *Fax:* (03) 3237-1459 *E-mail:* elt@tlj.co.jp *Web Site:* www.tlj.co.jp, pg 429

M & A Thomson Litho Ltd (United Kingdom) *Tel:* (01355) 233081 *Fax:* (01355) 245 039 *E-mail:* enquiries@thomsonlitho.com *Web Site:* www.thomsonlitho.com, pg 1165

M & A Thomson Litho Ltd (United Kingdom) *Tel:* (01355) 233 081 *Fax:* (01355) 245 039 *Web Site:* www.thomsonlitho.com, pg 1185

M & A Thomson Litho Ltd (United Kingdom) *Tel:* (01355) 233081 *Fax:* (01355) 245 039 *Web Site:* www.thomsonlitho.com, pg 1227, 1239

Thomson Publications Zimbabwe (Pvt) Ltd (Zimbabwe) *Tel:* (04) 736835 *Fax:* (04) 749803 *E-mail:* tpubl@mweb.co.zw, pg 784

Thomson Publishing Services (United Kingdom) *Tel:* (01264) 332424 *Fax:* (01264) 364418, pg 1354

Thornbill Press (Australia) *Tel:* (08) 2705172, pg 43

Caroline Thornton (Australia) *Tel:* (08) 9386 1555 *Fax:* (08) 9389 5162, pg 43

Thornton's of Oxford Ltd (United Kingdom) *Tel:* (01235) 821994 *E-mail:* thorntons@booknews.demon.co.uk *Web Site:* www.thorntonsbooks.co.uk, pg 1354

Thorpe-Bowker (Australia) *Tel:* (03) 8645 0300 *Fax:* (03) 8645 0333 *E-mail:* yoursay@thorpe.com.au *Web Site:* www.thorpe.com.au, pg 43

Thoth Publications (United Kingdom) *Tel:* (01509) 210626 *Fax:* (01509) 238034 *E-mail:* enquiries@thoth.co.uk *Web Site:* www.thothpublications.com; www.thoth.co.uk, pg 765

Thoth Publishers (Netherlands) *Tel:* (035) 6944144 *Fax:* (035) 6943266 *E-mail:* thoth@euronet.nl, pg 490

Thrass (UK) Ltd (United Kingdom) *Tel:* (01829) 741413 *Fax:* (01829) 741419 *E-mail:* enquiries@thrass.demon.co.uk *Web Site:* www.thrass.co.uk, pg 765

3 Dimension World (3-D-World) (Switzerland) *Tel:* (061) 424917, pg 635

Three Sisters Publications Pty Ltd (Australia) *Tel:* (047) 588138, pg 43

3A Corporation (Japan) *Tel:* (03) 32925751 *Fax:* (03) 32925754 *E-mail:* 3ac@mail.at-m.or.jp *Web Site:* www.at-m.or.jpl~3ac, pg 429

Threshold Publishing (Australia) *Tel:* (03) 9724 9067 *Fax:* (03) 9724 9067, pg 43

Thudhammawaddy Press (Myanmar), pg 476

Thueringer Universitaets- und Landesbibliothek (Germany) *Tel:* (03641) 9-40000 *Fax:* (03641) 9-40002 *E-mail:* thulb_direktion@thulb.uni-jena.de; thulb_auskunft@thulb.uni-jena.de *Web Site:* www.uni-jena.de/thulb, pg 1510

Edi Thule Club (Italy) *Tel:* (091) 323699, pg 1253

J M Thurley Management (United Kingdom) *Tel:* (020) 8977 3176 *Fax:* (020) 8943 2678, pg 1143

Edition Thurnhof KEG (Austria) *Tel:* (02982) 629-54 *Fax:* (02982) 3333 *E-mail:* edition@thurnhof.at *Web Site:* www.thurnhof.at, pg 58

Thwe Thauk (Myanmar), pg 1328

Thymari Publications (Greece) *Tel:* (0210) 3634901; (0210) 3643015 *Fax:* (0210) 3636591 *E-mail:* thymari@thymari.gr *Web Site:* thymari.gr, pg 312

Edizioni Thyrus SRL (Italy) *Tel:* (0744) 389496 *Fax:* (0744) 388700, pg 410

Tianjin Science & Technology Publishing House (China) *Tel:* (022) 7312749 *Fax:* (022) 27312755 *E-mail:* tjstp@public.tpt.tj.on, pg 108

Istituto Editoriale Ticinese (IET) SA (Switzerland) *Tel:* (091) 8200101 *Fax:* (091) 8251874, pg 635

Tiden Norsk Forlag (Norway) *Tel:* (022) 23 32 76 60 *Fax:* (022) 23 32 76 97 *E-mail:* tiden@tiden.no *Web Site:* www.tiden.no, pg 511

Tiderne Skifter Forlag A/S (Denmark) *Tel:* 33 18 63 90 *Fax:* 33 18 63 91 *E-mail:* tiderneskifter@tiderneskifter.dk *Web Site:* www.tiderneskifter.dk, pg 135

Tien Wah Press Pte Ltd (Singapore) *Tel:* 64666222 *Fax:* 64689710, pg 1223

Tietohuollon Neuvottelukunta (Finland) *Tel:* (09) 13 41 71 *Fax:* (09) 65 67 65 *E-mail:* jylha@csc.fi, pg 1562

Tietoteos Publishing Co (Finland) *Tel:* (09) 2564475 *Fax:* (09) 8136361 *E-mail:* tt@jkttietoteos.fi *Web Site:* www.jkttietoteos.fi, pg 144

Tiger Books International PLC (United Kingdom) *Tel:* (0181) 8925577 *Fax:* (0181) 8916550 *E-mail:* gp@dial.pipex.com, pg 765

Tiger Books International PLC (United Kingdom) *Tel:* (0181) 8925577 *Fax:* (0181) 8916550, pg 1354

Tihama Bookstores (Saudi Arabia) *Tel:* (02) 6444444 *Fax:* (02) 6519277 *E-mail:* info@tihama.com *Web Site:* www.tihama.com/book/book.htm, pg 1338

Uitgeverij de Tijdstroom BV (Netherlands) *Tel:* (0342) 450867 *Fax:* (0342) 450365 *E-mail:* info@tijdstroom.nl *Web Site:* www.tijdstroom.nl, pg 490

Tilburg University Press (Netherlands) *Tel:* (013) 466 2124 *Fax:* (013) 466 2996 *E-mail:* library@kub.nl *Web Site:* www.tilburguniversity.nl, pg 490

Tilgher-Genova sas (Italy) *Tel:* (010) 839 11 40 *Fax:* (010) 870653 *E-mail:* tilgher@tilgher.it *Web Site:* www.tilgher.it, pg 410

The Tilling Society (United Kingdom) *Fax:* (01424) 813237 *E-mail:* society@tilling.org.uk *Web Site:* www.tilling.org.uk/society, pg 1409

Timber Press Inc (United Kingdom) *Tel:* (01954) 232959 *Fax:* (01954) 206040 *E-mail:* timberpressuk@btinternet.com *Web Site:* www.timberpress.com, pg 765

Timbro (Sweden) *Tel:* (08) 587 898 00 *Fax:* (08) 587 898 55 *E-mail:* info@timbro.se *Web Site:* www.timbro.se, pg 616

Time Life Australia Pty Ltd (Australia) *Tel:* (02) 1300 364 437 *Toll Free Tel:* 300 364 437 *Fax:* (02) 9957 2773 *E-mail:* tlservice@timelife.com *Web Site:* www.timelife.com.au, pg 43

Time-Life Internacional de Mexico (Mexico) *Tel:* (055) 5469000 *Fax:* (055) 5159764 *Web Site:* www.timelife.com, pg 472

Time-Life (UK) (United Kingdom) *Tel:* (020) 7911 8000 *Fax:* (020) 7911 8100 *E-mail:* email@timelife.demon.co.uk; email.uk@timewarnerbooks.co.uk *Web Site:* www.twbookmark.com; www.timewarnerbooks.co.uk, pg 765

Time Out Group Ltd (United Kingdom) *Tel:* (020) 7813 3000 *Fax:* (020) 7323 3438 *E-mail:* net@timeout.co.uk *Web Site:* www.timeout.com, pg 765

Time-Space Inc (Republic of Korea) *Tel:* (02) 2272 2381 *Fax:* (02) 2273 8900 *E-mail:* tspace@timespace.co.kr *Web Site:* www.fotato.com, pg 1134

Time Track (M) Sdn Bhd (Malaysia) *Tel:* (05) 3124329; (05) 3127541 *Fax:* (05) 2630305, pg 459

Time Warner Book Group UK (United Kingdom) *Tel:* (020) 7911 8000 *Fax:* (020) 7911 8100 *E-mail:* email.uk@twbg.co.uk *Web Site:* www.twbg.co.uk, pg 766

Times The Bookshop (Singapore) *Tel:* 6213 9288 *Fax:* 6382 2571 *E-mail:* ttb@tpl.com.sg *Web Site:* www.timesone.com.sg, pg 1339

Times Educational Co Sdn Bhd (Malaysia) *Tel:* (03) 7571766 *Fax:* (03) 7573607, pg 459

Times Graphics (Singapore) *Tel:* 6213-9288 *Fax:* 6284 4733; 6288 1186 *E-mail:* tpl@tpl.com.sg *Web Site:* www.tpl.com.sg, pg 1182

Times Media Pte Ltd (Singapore) *Tel:* 62848844 *Fax:* 62771186 *E-mail:* te@corp.tpl.com.sg *Web Site:* www.timesone.com.sg/te, pg 559

Times Printers Pte Ltd (Singapore) *Tel:* 6311-2888 *Fax:* 682-1313 *E-mail:* tp@timesprinters.com *Web Site:* www.tpl.com.sg; www.timesprinters.com, pg 1161

Times Printers Pte Ltd (Singapore) *Tel:* 6311-2888 *Fax:* 6862-1313 *E-mail:* tp@timesprinters.com; enquiry@timesprinters.com *Web Site:* www.timesprinters.com; www.tpl.com.sg, pg 1182

Times Printers Pte Ltd (Singapore) *Tel:* 862 3333 *Fax:* 862 1313 *E-mail:* tp@timesprinters.com *Web Site:* www.tpl.com.sg, pg 1223

Times Printers Pte Ltd (Singapore) *Tel:* 6311-2888 *Fax:* 6862-1313 *E-mail:* enquiry@timesprinters.com *Web Site:* www.timesprinters.com, pg 1238, 1246

Times Publishing Group (United States) *Tel:* 914-366-9888 *Fax:* 914-366-9898 *Web Site:* www.tpl.com.sg, pg 1168, 1189, 1231, 1241, 1249

Times Publishing (Hong Kong) Ltd (Hong Kong) *Tel:* 23342421 *Fax:* 27645095; 23657834 *E-mail:* admin@federalbooks.com, pg 319

Times Ringier Ltd (Hong Kong) *Tel:* 2854 4266 *Fax:* 2854 4009 *E-mail:* contact@ringierpacific.com *Web Site:* www.ringierpacific.com, pg 319

Tintamas Indonesia PT (Indonesia) *Tel:* (021) 3107148; (021) 7393701 *Fax:* (021) 3911459; (021) 3107148, pg 356

Tipografica Editora Argentina (Argentina) *Tel:* (011) 4373-2581 *Fax:* (011) 4775-2521 *E-mail:* bernardosm@sinectis.com.ar, pg 9

Tipress Dienstleistungen fur das Verlagswesen GmbH (Germany) *Tel:* (07634) 591193 *Fax:* (07634) 591192 *E-mail:* tipress@tipress.com *Web Site:* www.tipress.com, pg 291, 1132

Tir Eolas (Ireland) *Tel:* (091) 637452 *Fax:* (091) 637452 *E-mail:* info@tireolas.com *Web Site:* www.tireolas.com, pg 363

Tirant lo Blanch SL Libreriaa (Spain) *Tel:* (096) 3610048 *Fax:* (096) 3694151 *E-mail:* tlb@tirant.es *Web Site:* www.tirant.es, pg 602

Editions Tiresias Michel Reynaud (France) *Tel:* (01) 42 23 47 27 *Fax:* (01) 42 23 73 27 *E-mail:* editions.tiresias@club-internet.fr *Web Site:* www.editions-tiresias.fr.tc, pg 187

Tirian Publications (Australia) *Tel:* (02) 9908 1196 *Fax:* (02) 9907 1196 *E-mail:* Tirian@bigpond.com; infoweb@tirian.com *Web Site:* www.users.bigpond.com/tirian, pg 43

Tirion Uitgevers BV (Netherlands) *Tel:* (035) 5486600 *Fax:* (035) 5486675 *E-mail:* info@tirionuitgevers.nl *Web Site:* www.tirionuitgevers.nl, pg 490

Ramona S Tirona Memorial Library (Philippines) *Tel:* (02) 5268421 (loc 176) *Fax:* (02) 5266935, pg 1537

Tirosh Communication Ltd (Israel) *Tel:* (03) 6044959 *Fax:* (03) 6053840 *E-mail:* hgeffen@netvision.net.il, pg 372

Editrice Tirrenia Stampatori SAS (Italy) *Tel:* (011) 877010 *Fax:* (011) 8177010, pg 410

Titan Books Ltd (United Kingdom) *Tel:* (020) 7620 0200 *Fax:* (020) 7620 0032 *E-mail:* readerfeedback@titanemail.com *Web Site:* www.titanbooks.com, pg 766

Titania-Verlag Ferdinand Schroll (Germany) *Tel:* (0711) 63 81 25 *Fax:* (0711) 63 69 872, pg 291

Titles Old and Rare Books of Oxford (United Kingdom) *Tel:* (01865) 727928 *Fax:* (01865) 727928, pg 1354

Tivenan Publications (Ireland) *Tel:* (069) 62596 *Fax:* (069) 62933 *E-mail:* wellwoman@wellwoman.info *Web Site:* www.wellwoman.info, pg 364

TJ International Ltd (United Kingdom) *Tel:* (01841) 532691 *Fax:* (01841) 532862 *E-mail:* sales@tjinternational.ltd.uk *Web Site:* www.tjinternational.ltd.uk, pg 1165, 1227

TMS Development International Ltd (United Kingdom) *Tel:* (01904) 641640 *Fax:* (01904) 640076 *E-mail:* enquiry@tmsdi.com *Web Site:* www.tmsdi.com, pg 1248

To Rodakio (Greece) *Tel:* (0210) 3221700; (0210) 3221742 *Fax:* (0210) 3221700 *E-mail:* rodakio@otenet.gz, pg 312

Tobias Associates Inc (United States) *Tel:* 215-322-1500 *Toll Free Tel:* 800-877-3367 *Fax:* 215-322-1504 *E-mail:* sales@tobiasinc.com *Web Site:* www.densitometer.com, pg 1231, 1249

Tobin Music (United Kingdom) *Tel:* (01279) 726625 *E-mail:* candida@tobinmusic.co.uk *Web Site:* www.candidatobin.co.uk, pg 766

Tobler Verlag (Switzerland) *Tel:* (071) 755 6060 *Fax:* (071) 755 1254 *E-mail:* books@tobler-verlag.ch *Web Site:* www.tobler-verlag.ch, pg 635

Todariana Editrice (Italy) *Tel:* (02) 56812953 *Fax:* (02) 55213405 *E-mail:* toeurs@tin.it, pg 410

Today & Tomorrow's Printers & Publishers (India) *Tel:* (011) 5721928; (011) 5727770, pg 351

Todor Kableshkov University of Transport (Bulgaria) *Tel:* (02) 9709335; (02) 9709384; (02) 9709478 *Fax:* (02) 9709407 *E-mail:* office@vtu.bg *Web Site:* www.vtu.bg, pg 97

S Toeche-Mittler Verlag GmbH (Germany) *Tel:* (06151) 33665 *Fax:* (06151) 314048 *E-mail:* info@net-library.de *Web Site:* www.net-library.de, pg 291

Tohan Corporation (Japan) *Tel:* (03) 3269-6111 *Fax:* (03) 3235-1337, pg 1323

Toho Book Store (Japan) *Tel:* (03) 32331001 *Fax:* (03) 32950800, pg 429

Toho Shuppan (Japan) *Tel:* (03) 6779-9571 *Fax:* (06) 6779-9573 *Web Site:* www.tohoshuppan.co.jp, pg 429

Tohoku University Library (Japan) *Tel:* (022) 217 5935; (0221) 217 4844 *Fax:* (0222) 217 5949; (0222) 217846 *E-mail:* desk@library.tohoku.ac.jp *Web Site:* www.library.tohoku.ac.jp, pg 1522

Libris Toison d'Or SA (Belgium) *Tel:* (02) 5116400 *Fax:* (02) 5140961, pg 1302

YELLOW PAGES

Tokai University Press (Japan) *Tel:* (0463) 79-3921 (Sales); (0463) 79-3921 (Editorial) *Fax:* (0463) 69-5087 *E-mail:* webmaster@press.tokai.ac.jp *Web Site:* www.press.tokai.ac.jp, pg 429

Toker Yayinlari (Turkey) *Tel:* (0212) 5223309, pg 651

Tokuma Shoten Publishing Co Ltd (Japan) *Tel:* (03) 5403-4300 *Fax:* (03) 3573-8771 *E-mail:* iwabuchi@ shoten.tokuma.com *Web Site:* www.tokuma.jp, pg 429

Tokyo Kagaku Dojin Co Ltd (Japan) *Tel:* (03) 3946-5311 *Fax:* (03) 3946-5316 *E-mail:* tokyokagakudozin@a. email.ne.jp, pg 429

Tokyo Metropolitan Central Library (Japan) *Tel:* (03) 3442-8451 *Fax:* (03) 3447-8924 *Web Site:* www. library.metro.tokyo.jp/, pg 1522

Tokyo Publications Service Ltd (Japan) *Tel:* (03) 3561-9741 *Fax:* (03) 3561-9743 *E-mail:* tps@cf.mbn.or.jp *Web Site:* plaza8.mbn.or.jp/~tokyoyosho, pg 1323

Tokyo Shoseki Co Ltd (Japan) *Tel:* (03) 5390-7531 *Fax:* (03) 5390-7409 *E-mail:* home@tokyo-shoseki. co.jp *Web Site:* www.tokyo-shoseki.co.jp, pg 430

Tokyo Sogensha Co Ltd (Japan) *Tel:* (03) 3268-8201 *Fax:* (03) 3268-8230, pg 430

Tokyo Tosho Co Ltd (Japan) *Tel:* (03) 3816-2563 *Fax:* (03) 3815-7330, pg 430

Joe-Tolalu & Associates (Nigeria) *Tel:* (01) 4925078, pg 507

Toledo Creative Management (Netherlands) *Tel:* (020) 6226873 *Fax:* (020) 6276720 *E-mail:* agency@toledo-cm.nl, pg 1135

Toleranz Verlag, Nielsen Frederic W (Germany) *Tel:* (0761) 81415 *E-mail:* irenenielsen@web.de, pg 291

The Tolkien Society (United Kingdom) *Tel:* (01242) 529757 *E-mail:* membership@tolkiensociety.org *Web Site:* www.tolkiensociety.org, pg 1409

Tom Publications (Australia) *Tel:* (08) 9444 4570, pg 43

Tomar Publishing Ltd (Ireland) *Fax:* (01) 744697, pg 364

Tomo Edizioni srl (Italy) *Tel:* (081) 00920 *Fax:* (081) 00920, pg 410

Tomorrow Publications (Australia) *Tel:* (02) 4961 2115 *E-mail:* tomorrowtrading@hotmail.com, pg 44

Tomorrow Publishing House (China) *Tel:* (0531) 206 0055 *Fax:* (0531) 290 2094 *E-mail:* tomorrow@ sdpress.com *Web Site:* www.tomorrowpub.com, pg 109

Tomus Verlag GmbH (Germany) *Tel:* (08581) 910666 *Fax:* (08581) 910668 *E-mail:* info@tomus.de *Web Site:* www.tomus.de, pg 291

Toneelfonds J Janssens BVBA (Belgium) *Tel:* (03) 366 44 00 *Fax:* (03) 366 45 01 *E-mail:* info@toneelfonds. be *Web Site:* www.toneelfonds.be, pg 73, 1129

P J Tonger Musikverlag GmbH & Co (Germany) *Tel:* (0221) 935564-0 *Fax:* (0221) 935564-11 *E-mail:* musikverlag@tonger.de *Web Site:* www.tonger. de, pg 291

Uitgeverij De Toorts (Netherlands) *Tel:* (023) 5532920 *Fax:* (023) 5320635 *E-mail:* uitgeverij@toorts.nl *Web Site:* www.toorts.nl, pg 490

TOP Editions (France) *Tel:* (01) 30 14 19 30 *Fax:* (01) 34 60 31 32 *E-mail:* info@editionschiron.com *Web Site:* www.editionschiron.com, pg 188

Top Secret Collection Publishers (Russian Federation) *Tel:* (095) 2022011; (095) 2024531 *Fax:* (095) 2913885 *E-mail:* topsec@glasnet.ru, pg 549

Editura Top Suspans (Romania) *Tel:* (01) 6830924; (01) 6103359, pg 543

Topaz Publications (Ireland) *Tel:* (01) 2800460 *Fax:* (01) 2800460, pg 364

Topic Verlag GmbH (Germany) *Tel:* (08131) 97038 *Fax:* (08131) 98404, pg 1155, 1177

Topos Verlag AG (Liechtenstein) *Tel:* 3771111 *Fax:* 3771119 *E-mail:* topos@supra.net *Web Site:* www.topos.li, pg 448

Toppan Co Ltd (Japan) *Tel:* (03) 5418-2535 *Fax:* (03) 5418-2529 *E-mail:* kouhou@toppan.co.jp *Web Site:* www.toppan.co.jp, pg 430

Toppan Printing Co America Inc (United States) *Tel:* 212-489-7740 *Fax:* 212-246-3067 *Web Site:* www. ta.toppan.com, pg 1168

Toppan Printing Co (HK) Ltd (Hong Kong) *Tel:* 2475-5666; 2561-0101 *Fax:* 2475-4321 *E-mail:* info@ toppan.co.jp *Web Site:* www.toppan.co.jp, pg 1179

Toppan Printing Co (HK) Ltd (Hong Kong) *Tel:* 2561-0101 *Fax:* 24754321 *E-mail:* info@toppan.co.jp *Web Site:* www.toppan.co.jp, pg 1219

Toppan Printing Co (UK) Ltd (United Kingdom) *Tel:* (020) 7828 7292; (020) 7828 7296 *Fax:* (020) 7828 5310 *E-mail:* kawamura@toppan.co.uk; info.e@ toppan.co.jp *Web Site:* www.toppan.co.jp, pg 1165

Torch of Wisdom (Taiwan, Province of China) *Tel:* (02) 7075802 *Fax:* (02) 7085054 *E-mail:* tow@ms2.hinet. net, pg 642

Instituto Torcuato Di Tella (Argentina) *Tel:* (011) 4783-8680; (011) 4784-0084 *Fax:* (011) 4783-3061 *E-mail:* postmaster@itdtar.edu.ar *Web Site:* www.itdt. edu, pg 9

Gregorio del Toro Editor (Spain) *Tel:* (091) 3080077; (091) 3190139 *Fax:* (091) 3080187, pg 602

Toros Yayinlari Ltd Co (Turkey) *Tel:* (0212) 2444155 *Fax:* (0212) 2452858; (0212) 2444155, pg 652

Ediciones de la Torre (Spain) *Tel:* (091) 692 20 34 *Fax:* (091) 692 20 34 *E-mail:* info@ edicionesdelatorre.com *Web Site:* www. edicionesdelatorre.com, pg 602

Torremozas SL Ediciones (Spain) *Tel:* (091) 350 50 27; (091) 359 03 15 *Fax:* (091) 345 85 32 *E-mail:* ediciones@torremozas.com *Web Site:* www. torremozas.com, pg 602

Tosui Shobo Publishers (Japan) *Tel:* (03) 3261-6190 *Fax:* (03) 3261-2234, pg 430

Total Home Entertainment (United Kingdom) *Tel:* (01782) 566566 *Fax:* (01782) 565400 *E-mail:* thenews@the.co.uk, pg 1354

Totalidade Editora Ltda (Brazil) *Tel:* (011) 3064 3688 *Fax:* (011) 3081 9503 *E-mail:* totail@terra.com.br *Web Site:* www.totalidade.com.br, pg 91

Toubis M (Greece) *Tel:* (01) 9923876; (01) 9923806 *Fax:* (01) 9923 867 *E-mail:* toubis@otenet.gr, pg 312

Toucan Press (United Kingdom) *Tel:* (01481) 57017, pg 766

Toulon Uitgeverij (Belgium) *Tel:* (059) 800927, pg 73

Editions Tousch (Luxembourg) *Tel:* 452977 *Fax:* 458743, pg 452

Touzimsky & Moravec (Czech Republic) *Tel:* (02) 612 13 631; (02) 612 12 458 *Fax:* (02) 612 12 458, pg 127

Towarzystwo Literackie im Adama Mickiewicza (Poland) *Tel:* (022) 265231 (ext 279), pg 1404

Towarzystwo Naukowe w Toruniu (Poland) *Tel:* (056) 6223941 (ext 8), pg 527

Tower Books (Australia) *Tel:* (02) 9975 5566 *Fax:* (02) 9975 5599 *E-mail:* info@towerbooks.com.au *Web Site:* www.towerbooks.com.au, pg 44

Tower Books (Ireland) *Tel:* (021) 4872294 *Fax:* (021) 4872294, pg 1159

Town House & Country House (Ireland) *Tel:* (01) 4972399 *Fax:* (01) 4970927 *E-mail:* books@ townhouse.ie *Web Site:* www.irelandseye.com/cle/ publish/townhouse.html, pg 364

Towy Publishing (United Kingdom) *Tel:* (01267) 236569 *Fax:* (01267) 220444 *E-mail:* towyfairs@btopenworld. com, pg 766

TRANSLATORS ASSOCIATION

The Toyo Bunko (Japan) *Tel:* (03) 39420121 *Fax:* (03) 39420258 *E-mail:* webmaster@toyo-bunko.or.jp *Web Site:* www.toyo-bunko.or.jp/toyobunko-e, pg 1522

Toyo Keizai Shinpo-Sha (Japan) *Tel:* (03) 3246-5467 *Fax:* (03) 3270-4127 *E-mail:* tk@toyokeizai.co.jp *Web Site:* www.toyokeizai.co.jp/, pg 430

Wydawnictwo TPPR Wspolpraca (Poland) *Tel:* (022) 200301 (ext 227), pg 527

TR - Verlagsunion GmbH (Germany) *Tel:* (089) 2121 390 *Fax:* (089) 296129; (089) 296357 *E-mail:* vertrieb@tr-verlag.de *Web Site:* www.tr-verlag. de, pg 291

Trachsel - Verlag AG (Switzerland) *Tel:* (33) 6711407 *Fax:* (33) 6712449, pg 635

Tradespools Ltd (United Kingdom) *Tel:* (01373) 461475 *Fax:* (01373) 474112 *E-mail:* sales@tradespools.co.uk *Web Site:* www.tradespools.co.uk, pg 1185

Traditionell Bogenschiessen Verlag Angelika Hornig (Germany) *Tel:* (0621) 68 94 41 *Fax:* (0621) 68 94 42 *E-mail:* info@bogenschiessen.de *Web Site:* www. bogenschiessen.de, pg 292

Trainer International Editore-I Libri del Bargello (Italy) *Tel:* (055) 288162 *Fax:* (055) 218951, pg 410

Training Publications Ltd (United Kingdom) *Tel:* (01923) 243730 *Fax:* (01923) 213 144, pg 766

Giovanni Tranchida Editore (Italy) *Tel:* (02) 66802270 *Fax:* (02) 69003425 *E-mail:* tranchida@infinito.it *Web Site:* www.tranchida.it, pg 410

Trano Printy Fiahyohana Loterana Malagasy (Madagascar) *Tel:* (020) 223340; (020) 24569, pg 1325

Trano Printy Fiangonana Loterana Malagasy (TPFLM)- (Imprimerie Lutherienne) (Madagascar) *Tel:* (020) 223340 *Fax:* (020) 262643 *E-mail:* impluth@dts.mg, pg 454

Trans Tech Publications (Germany) *Tel:* (05323) 96970 *Fax:* (05323) 969796 *E-mail:* ttp@transtech-online. com *Web Site:* www.transtech-online.com, pg 292

Trans Tech Publications SA (Switzerland) *Tel:* (01) 9221022 *Fax:* (01) 9221033 *E-mail:* ttp@ttp.net *Web Site:* www.ttp.net, pg 635

TransAction Translators Ltd (United Kingdom) *Tel:* (0114) 2661103 *Fax:* (0114) 2631959 *E-mail:* transaction@transaction.co.uk *Web Site:* www. transaction.co.uk, pg 1151

Transafrica Press (Kenya) *Tel:* (020) 244724, pg 436

Transcontinental Printing Book Group (Canada) *Tel:* 514-337-8560 *Toll Free Tel:* 800-361-3599 *Fax:* 514-339-5230 *Web Site:* www.transcontinental. com; www.transcontinental-printing.com, pg 1153, 1176, 1216, 1235

Transcontinental Printing Book Group (Canada) *Tel:* 514-337-8560 *Toll Free Tel:* 800-361-3599 *Fax:* 514-339-5230 *Web Site:* www.transcontinental. com, pg 1245

Transedition ASBL (France) *Tel:* (01) 43211080 *Fax:* (01) 43211079, pg 188

Transedition Ltd (United Kingdom) *Tel:* (01865) 396700 *Fax:* (01865) 712500 *E-mail:* enquiries@transed.co.uk *Web Site:* www.translateabook.com, pg 766

Transeuropa (Italy) *Tel:* (02) 29 402156 *Fax:* (02) 20 47922, pg 410

Transeuropeennes/RCE (France) *Tel:* (01) 55 07 88 90 *Fax:* (01) 55 07 97 38 *E-mail:* te.revue@ transeuropeennes.org; contact@transeuropeennes.org *Web Site:* www.transeuropeennes.org, pg 188

Universitatea Transilvania Din Brasov Biblioteca Centrala (Romania) *Tel:* (068) 413 000 *Fax:* (068) 150 474 *E-mail:* libr@vega.unitbv.ro, pg 1540

Translators Association (United Kingdom) *Tel:* (020) 7373 6642 *Fax:* (020) 7373 5768 *E-mail:* info@ societyofauthors.org *Web Site:* www.societyofauthors. org/translators, pg 1151

Translators Association (United Kingdom) *Tel:* (020) 7373 6642 *Fax:* (020) 7373 5768 *E-mail:* info@societyofauthors.org *Web Site:* www.societyofauthors.org, pg 1409

Translators Guild (Czech Republic) *Tel:* 222 564 082 *E-mail:* info@obecprekladatelu.cz *Web Site:* www.obecprekladatelu.cz, pg 1147

Translegal AG (Switzerland) *Tel:* (033) 221622 *Fax:* (033) 2253933, pg 635

Transpareon Press (Australia) *Tel:* (02) 99874570 *Fax:* (02) 99874570, pg 44

Transport Bookman Publications Ltd (United Kingdom) *Tel:* (020) 8560 2666 *Fax:* (020) 8569 8273, pg 766

Izdatelstvo Transport (Russian Federation) *Tel:* (095) 2625964 *Fax:* (095) 2611322, pg 549

Transportation Publishing House (Democratic People's Republic of Korea), pg 436

Transpress Verlagsgesellschaft mbH (Germany) *Tel:* (0711) 210 80 65 *Fax:* (0711) 210 80 70 *E-mail:* versand@motorbuch.de *Web Site:* www.motorbuch-versand.de, pg 292

Transvaal Museum Library (South Africa) *Tel:* (012) 322 7632 *Fax:* (012) 322 7939 *Web Site:* www.nfi.org.za, pg 1544

Transworld Publishers Ltd (United Kingdom) *Tel:* (020) 8579 2652 *Fax:* (020) 8579 5479 *E-mail:* info@transworld-publishers.co.uk *Web Site:* www.booksattransworld.co.uk, pg 766

Transworld Publishers (NZ) Ltd (New Zealand) *Tel:* (09) 4156210 *Fax:* (09) 4156221, pg 502

Transworld Publishers Pty Ltd (Australia) *Tel:* (02) 9954 9966 *Fax:* (02) 9954 4562, pg 44

Transworld Research Network (India) *Tel:* (0471) 2460384 *Fax:* (0491) 2573051 *E-mail:* ggcom@vsnl.com *Web Site:* www.transworldresearch.com, pg 351

Trauner Verlag (Austria) *Tel:* (0732) 77 82 41-212 *Fax:* (0732) 77 82 41-400 *E-mail:* office@trauner.at *Web Site:* www.trauner.at, pg 58

Trautvetter & Fischer Nachf (Germany) *Tel:* (06421) 33309 *Fax:* (06421) 34959 *E-mail:* bestell@trautvetterfischerverlag.de *Web Site:* www.trautvetterfischerverlag.de, pg 292

Trea Ediciones, SL (Spain) *Tel:* (098) 5303801 *Fax:* (098) 5303717; (098) 5303712 *E-mail:* trea@trea.es, pg 602

Institut de Treball Social - Serveis Socials (Spain) *Tel:* (093) 217 26 64 *Fax:* (093) 237 36 34 *E-mail:* intressbar@intress.org *Web Site:* www.intress.org, pg 602

Tree Shade Technical Services (Kenya) *Tel:* (02) 225798; (02) 220712, pg 436

Treehouse Children's Books Ltd (United Kingdom) *Tel:* (01749) 330529 *Fax:* (01749) 330544 *E-mail:* ca.baker@virgin.net, pg 767

Trees Wolfgang Triangel Verlag (Germany) *Tel:* (0241) 6 99 00 *Fax:* (0241) 6 99 15 *E-mail:* info@triangelverlag.de *Web Site:* www.triangel-verlag.de, pg 292

Treffer-Boekklub (South Africa) *Tel:* (012) 401 0700 *Fax:* (012) 3255498 *E-mail:* lapa@atkv.org.za, pg 1255

Libreria Trejos SA, pg 1307

Michael Treloar Antiquarian Booksellers (Australia) *Tel:* (08) 82231111 *Fax:* (08) 82236599 *E-mail:* treloars@treloars.com *Web Site:* www.treloars.com, pg 1299

Trentham Books Ltd (United Kingdom) *Tel:* (01782) 745567; (01782) 844699 *Fax:* (01782) 745553 *E-mail:* tb@trentham-books.co.uk *Web Site:* www.trentham-books.co.uk, pg 767

Tres Torres Ediciones SA (Spain) *Tel:* (093) 3637450 *Fax:* (093) 3637452, pg 602

Trescher Verlag GmbH (Germany) *Tel:* (030) 2 83 24 96 *Fax:* (030) 2 81 59 94 *E-mail:* post@trescherverlag.de *Web Site:* www.trescherverlag.de, pg 292

Treves Editions Verein Zur Foerderung der Kuenstlerischen Taetigkeiten (Germany) *Tel:* (0651) 309 010 *Fax:* (0651) 300 699 *E-mail:* mail@treves.de *Web Site:* www.treves.de, pg 292

Casa Editrice Luigi Trevisini (Italy) *Tel:* (02) 5450704 *Fax:* (02) 55195782, pg 410

Publicacoes Trevo Lda (Portugal) *Tel:* (021) 9211461 *Fax:* (021) 9217940, pg 536

Lavinia Trevor Literary Agency (United Kingdom) *Tel:* (020) 8749 8481 *Fax:* (020) 8749 7377, pg 1143

Tri-Graphic Printing (Ottawa) Ltd (Canada) *Tel:* 613-731-7441 *Toll Free Tel:* 800-267-9750 *Fax:* 613-731-3741 *Web Site:* www.tri-graphic.com, pg 1154, 1176, 1216

Livraria Triangulo Ltda (Brazil) *Tel:* (011) 3231-0922; (011) 3231-0362; (011) 3231-0552 *Fax:* (011) 3231-0162 *E-mail:* livraria.triangulo@terra.com.br *Web Site:* www.livrariatriangulo.com.br, pg 1304

Trias Verlag in MVS Medizinverlage Stuttgart GmbH & Co KG (Germany) *Tel:* (0711) 8931-0 *Fax:* (0711) 8931-298 *E-mail:* kunden.service@thieme.de *Web Site:* www.thieme.de; www.medizinverlage.de, pg 292

Tribhuvan University Central Library (Nepal) *Tel:* (01) 331317; (01) 330834 *Fax:* (01) 226964 *E-mail:* tucl@healthnet.org.np *Web Site:* www.tucl.org.np, pg 1530

Editions du Tricorne (Switzerland) *Tel:* (022) 7388366 *Fax:* (022) 7319749 *E-mail:* tricorne@freesurf.ch *Web Site:* www.tricorne.org, pg 635

Trigon Press (United Kingdom) *Tel:* (0181) 7780534 *Fax:* (0181) 7767525 *E-mail:* trigon@easynet.co.uk, pg 767

Ediciones Trilce (Uruguay) *Tel:* (02) 412 77 22; (02) 412 76 62 *Fax:* (02) 412 76 62; (02) 412 77 22 *E-mail:* trilce@adinet.com.uy; infoventas@trilce.com.uy *Web Site:* www.trilce.com.uy, pg 778

Editorial Trillas SA de CV (Mexico) *Tel:* (055) 6330612; (055) 6331112 *Fax:* (055) 6330870; (055) 6342221 *E-mail:* laviga@trillas.com.mx; Trillasenvios@att.net.mx *Web Site:* www.trillas.com.mx, pg 472

Trinity College Library (United Kingdom) *Tel:* (01223) 338488 *Fax:* (01223) 338532 *E-mail:* trin-lib@lists.cam.ac.uk *Web Site:* library.trin.cam.ac.uk, pg 1554

Trinity College Library Dublin (Ireland) *Tel:* (01) 608 1665 *Fax:* (01) 608 3774 *Web Site:* www.tcd.ie/library, pg 1519

Triom Centro de Estudos Marina e Martin Hawey Editorial e Comercial Ltda (Brazil) *Tel:* (011) 3168-8380 *Fax:* (011) 3845-0966 *E-mail:* info@triom.com.br *Web Site:* www.triom.com.br, pg 91

N M Tripathi Pvt Ltd Publishers & Booksellers (India) *Tel:* (022) 22013651 *Fax:* (022) 22050048, pg 351

N M Tripathi Pvt Ltd Publishers & Booksellers (India) *Tel:* (022) 22013651; (022) 22050048, pg 1317

Ediciones Tripode (Venezuela) *Tel:* (02) 2378860; (02) 2378972 *Fax:* (02) 2377697 *E-mail:* tripode@comsis.com.ve *Web Site:* www.comsis.com.ve/tripode/, pg 780

Trito Edicions, SL (Spain) *Tel:* (093) 342 61 75 *Fax:* (093) 302 26 70 *E-mail:* info@trito.es *Web Site:* www.trito.es, pg 602

Triumph House (United Kingdom) *Tel:* (01733) 898102 *Fax:* (01733) 313524 *E-mail:* triumphhouse@forwardpress.co.uk *Web Site:* www.forwardpress.co.uk, pg 767

Editorial Trivium, SA (Spain) *Tel:* (091) 3147495 *Fax:* (091) 3153236, pg 602

Trix Corporation Sdn Bhd (Malaysia) *Tel:* (03) 253 2019 *Fax:* (03) 255 1068 *E-mail:* cpd@trix.po.my, pg 459

Trizonia (Czech Republic) *Tel:* (02) 5816502, pg 128

La Trobe University Bookshop (Australia) *Tel:* (03) 94791234 *Fax:* (03) 94702011 *E-mail:* enquiries@bookshop.latrobe.edu.au *Web Site:* www.bookshop.latrobe.edu.au, pg 1299

Troika (United Kingdom) *Tel:* (020) 7619 0800 *Fax:* (020) 7619 0801 *E-mail:* troika@sellbooks.demon.co.uk, pg 1354

Editions des Trois Collines Francois Lachenal (Switzerland) *Tel:* (022) 7561309 *Fax:* (022) 7561302, pg 635

Troll Books of Australia (Australia) *Tel:* (02) 9417 2699 *Fax:* (02) 9417 1599 *E-mail:* webmaster@troll.com *Web Site:* www.troll.com, pg 44

Marco Tropea Editore (Italy) *Tel:* (02) 202301 *Fax:* (02) 29513061 *E-mail:* stampa@saggiatore.it *Web Site:* www.saggiatore.it, pg 410

Tropical Press Sdn Bhd (Malaysia) *Tel:* (03) 22825138; (03) 22825338 *Fax:* (03) 22823526 *E-mail:* feedback@tpress.po.my, pg 459

Tropicana Press (Australia) *Tel:* (02) 9543 7728, pg 44

Tropos Zois (Greece) *Tel:* (0210) 6840156; (0210) 6858852 *Fax:* (0210) 6858851, pg 312

Editorial Troquel SA (Argentina) *Tel:* (011) 4308-3638; (011) 4308-3637 *Fax:* (011) 4941-3110 *E-mail:* info@troquel.com.ar *Web Site:* www.troquel.com.ar, pg 9

Trotman Publishing (United Kingdom) *Tel:* (0870) 900 2665 *Fax:* (020) 8486 1161 *E-mail:* sales@trotman.demon.co.uk *Web Site:* www.careers-portal.co.uk/trotmanpublishing, pg 767

Trotta SA Editorial (Spain) *Tel:* (091) 5430361 *Fax:* (091) 5431488 *E-mail:* editorial@trotta.es *Web Site:* www.trotta.es, pg 602

John Trotter Books (United Kingdom) *Tel:* (020) 8349 9484 *Fax:* (020) 8346 7430 *E-mail:* John.Trotter@bibliophile.net *Web Site:* www.bibliophile.net/John-Trotter-Books.html, pg 1354

Trotzdem-Verlags Genossenschaft eG (Germany) *Tel:* (07033) 44273 *Fax:* (07033) 45264 *E-mail:* trotzdemusf@t-online.e *Web Site:* www.trotzdem-verlag.de; www.txt.de/trotzdem, pg 292

Troubadour Press (Australia) *Tel:* (08) 8270 1861 *Fax:* (08) 8270 4003 *E-mail:* newcreat@camtech.net.au, pg 44

Mario Truant Verlag (Germany) *Tel:* (06131) 961660 *E-mail:* viva@truant.com *Web Site:* www.truant.com, pg 292

Trud - Izd kasta (Bulgaria) *Tel:* (02) 9814110; (02) 9878261; (02) 9872924 *Fax:* (02) 467565 *E-mail:* book@cybernet.bg *Web Site:* www.trud.bg, pg 97

Harry S Truman Research Institute for the Advancement for Jerusalem (Israel) *Tel:* (02) 58823000; (02) 58823001; (02) 5882315 *Fax:* (02) 5828076 *E-mail:* mstruman@pluto.mscc.huji.ac.il *Web Site:* atar.mscc.huji.ac.il/~truman, pg 372

Trumpet Publishers (Pvt) Ltd (Sri Lanka) *Tel:* (01) 447622 *Web Site:* www.lankawebdirectory.com, pg 607

Trung-Tam San Xuat Hoc-Lieu (Viet Nam), pg 781

Tryckeriforlaget AB (Sweden) *Tel:* (08) 756 74 45 *Fax:* (08) 756 03 95 *E-mail:* tidkort@tidkort.se, pg 616

Tshwane Community Library & Information Service (South Africa) *Tel:* (012) 3088837 *Fax:* (012) 3088873, pg 1544

Tsileondriaka Edition (Madagascar) *Tel:* (02) 31033; (02) 30659 *Fax:* (02) 31033, pg 454

Tsinghua University Press (China) *Tel:* (010) 62783933; (010) 62594726 *Fax:* (010) 62770278 *E-mail:* right-tup@mail.tsinghua.edu.cn, pg 109

Tsipika Edition (Madagascar) *Tel:* (02) 24595, pg 454

TSO (The Stationery Office) (United Kingdom) *Tel:* (020) 7873 8787 *E-mail:* customer.services@tso.co.uk *Web Site:* www.tso.co.uk, pg 767

TSO (The Stationery Office) (United Kingdom) *Tel:* (020) 7873 8787 *Fax:* (0870) 600 5533 (orders) *E-mail:* customer.services@tso.co.uk *Web Site:* www.tso.co.uk, pg 1143

TSO (The Stationery Office) (United Kingdom) *Tel:* (020) 7873 8787; (0870) 600 5522 (orders) *Fax:* (0870) 600 5533 (orders) *E-mail:* customer.services@tso.co.uk *Web Site:* www.theso.co.uk, pg 1354

Tsukiji Shokan Publishing Co (Japan) *Tel:* (03) 3542-3731 *Fax:* (03) 3541-5799, pg 430

Tuba Press (United Kingdom) *Tel:* (01285) 760424 *Fax:* (01285) 760766, pg 767

Tuckwell Press Ltd (United Kingdom) *Tel:* (01620) 860 164 *Fax:* (01620) 860 164 *E-mail:* customerservices@tuckwellpress.co.uk *Web Site:* www.tuckwellpress.co.uk, pg 767

Sarospataki Reformatus- Kollegium Tudomanyos Gyuejtemenyei Nagykoenyvtar (Hungary) *Tel:* 4111057, pg 1515

Tudor Australia Press (Australia) *Tel:* (08) 8332 8884, pg 44

Tuduv Verlagsgesellschaft mbH (Germany) *Tel:* (089) 280 90 95 *Fax:* (089) 280 95 28 *E-mail:* info@tuduv.de *Web Site:* www.tuduv.de, pg 292

Tuebinger Vereinigung fur Volkskunde eV (TVV) (Germany) *Tel:* (07071) 295449; (07071) 2972374 (orders) *Fax:* (07071) 295330 *E-mail:* info@tvv-verlag.de *Web Site:* www.tvv-verlag.de, pg 292

Tuerdok (Turkish Scientific & Technical Documentation Centre) (Turkey) *Tel:* (0312) 468 5300 *Fax:* (0312) 427 7489 *E-mail:* www-adm@tubitak.gov.tr *Web Site:* www.tubitak.gov.tr, pg 1551

Tuerk Editoerler Dernegi (Turkey) *Tel:* (0212) 5125602 *Fax:* (0212) 5117794, pg 1289

Tuerk Kueuephaneciler Dernegi (Turkey) *Tel:* (0312) 230 13 25 *Fax:* (0312) 232 04 53 *E-mail:* tkd-o@tr.net *Web Site:* www.kutuphaneci.org.tr, pg 1572

TUeV-Verlag GmbH (Germany) *Tel:* (0221) 806-3535 *Fax:* (0221) 806-3510 *E-mail:* tuev-verlag@de.tuv.com *Web Site:* www.tuev-verlag.de; www.qm-aktuell.de; www.mt-medizintechnik.de, pg 293

Tun Razak Library (Malaysia) *Tel:* (05) 508073, pg 1527

Library Tun Seri Lanang (Malaysia) *Tel:* (03) 89250199 *Fax:* (03) 89256067 *E-mail:* kpustaka@pkrisc.cc.ukm.my *Web Site:* www.ukm.my/library, pg 1527

Libreria Tuncho Granados G (Guatemala) *Tel:* (02) 24736; (02) 27269; (02) 21181, pg 1314

Societe Tunisienne de Diffusion (Tunisia) *Tel:* (01) 255000; (01) 261799, pg 648

Turinta-Turismo Internacional (Portugal) *Tel:* (021) 487 9420 *Fax:* (021) 487 2099 *E-mail:* info@turinta.pt *Web Site:* www.turinta.pt, pg 536

Turisticka Stampa (Serbia and Montenegro) *Tel:* (011) 750-740; (011) 759 076 *Fax:* (011) 762-236, pg 554

Turkischer Schulbuchverlag Onel Cengiz (Germany) *Tel:* (0221) 5879084; (0221) 5879085 *Fax:* (0221) 488093; (0221) 5879004, pg 293

Cyprus Turkish Public Library (Cyprus) *Tel:* (022) 83257, pg 1501

Turkish Republic - Ministry of Culture (Turkey) *Tel:* (0312) 309 08 50 *Fax:* (0312) 312-4359 *E-mail:* yayimlar@kutuphanelergm.gov.tr *Web Site:* www.kultur.gov.tr, pg 652

Izdatelstvo Turkmenistan (Turkmenistan) *Tel:* (03632) 294275, pg 652

Turnaround Publisher Services Ltd (United Kingdom) *Tel:* (020) 8829 3000 *Fax:* (020) 8881 5088 *E-mail:* enquiries@turnaround-uk.com; orders@turnaround-uk.com, pg 1243

Turnaround Publisher Services Ltd (United Kingdom) *Tel:* (020) 8829 3000 *Fax:* (020) 8881 5088 *E-mail:* enquiries@turnaround-uk.com *Web Site:* www.turnaround-uk.com, pg 1248, 1354

Alexander Turnbull Library (New Zealand) *Tel:* (04) 474 3000 *Fax:* (04) 474 3063 *E-mail:* atl@natlib.govt.nz *Web Site:* www.natlib.govt.nz, pg 1532

Jane Turnbull (United Kingdom) *Tel:* (020) 8743 9580 *Fax:* (020) 8749 6079 *E-mail:* agents@cwcom.net, pg 1144

Editorial Turner de Mexico (Mexico) *Tel:* (055) 5553 1183 *Fax:* (055) 5211 2070 *Web Site:* www.turnerlibros.com, pg 472

Turner Memorial Library (Zimbabwe) *Tel:* (0120) 63412 *Fax:* (0120) 61002, pg 1556

Turner Publicaciones (Spain) *Tel:* (091) 308 33 36 *Fax:* (091) 319 39 30 *E-mail:* turner@turnerlibros.com *Web Site:* www.turnerlibros.com, pg 602

Turris (Italy) *Tel:* (0372) 23845 *Fax:* (0372) 23845, pg 410

Tursen, SA (Spain) *Tel:* (091) 3667148 *Fax:* (091) 3653148, pg 603

Turton & Armstrong Pty Ltd Publishers (Australia) *Tel:* (02) 9489 6719 *Fax:* (02) 9489 6719 *E-mail:* turtarm@attglobal.net, pg 44

Turun Yliopiston Kirjasto (Finland) *Tel:* (02) 333 51 *Fax:* (02) 333 5050 *E-mail:* kirjasto@utu.fi *Web Site:* www.kirjasto.utu.fi, pg 1505

Turun Kansallinen Kirjakauppa Oy (Finland) *Tel:* (02) 2831000 *Fax:* (02) 2831010 *E-mail:* info@kansallinenkirjakauppa.fi *Web Site:* www.kansallinenkirjakauppa.fi, pg 1309

Edition Tusch (Austria) *Tel:* (01) 485 40 01 *Fax:* (01) 485 40 01-15 *E-mail:* citypost@cpz.at, pg 58

Tusquets Editores (Spain) *Tel:* (093) 2530400 *Fax:* (093) 4176703; (093) 4188698 (Rights & Editing) *E-mail:* general@tusquets-editores.es *Web Site:* www.tusquets-editores.com, pg 603

Ediciones Tutor SA (Spain) *Tel:* (091) 5599832 *Fax:* (091) 5410235 *E-mail:* tutor@autovia.com, pg 603

Charles E Tuttle Publishing Co Inc (Japan) *Tel:* (03) 5437-0171 *Fax:* (03) 5437-0755 *E-mail:* info@tuttlepublishing.com *Web Site:* www.tuttlepublishing.com, pg 430, 1323

Tuttle-Mori Agency Inc (Japan) *Tel:* (03) 3230-4081 *Fax:* (03) 3234-5249, pg 1134

Tuum (Estonia) *Tel:* 627 6427; (051) 41 290 *Fax:* 641 8054 *E-mail:* enelier@yahoo.com, pg 140

Bogklubben 12 Boget A/S (Denmark) *Tel:* 33695050 *Fax:* 33695051 *E-mail:* b12b@bogklubben-12-boget.dk, pg 1252

Twelveheads Press (United Kingdom) *E-mail:* sales@twelveheads.com *Web Site:* www.twelveheads.com, pg 767

Twente University Press (Netherlands) *Tel:* (053) 4899111 *Fax:* (053) 4892000 *E-mail:* info@utwente.nl *Web Site:* www.utwente.nl/tupress, pg 490

Twenty-First Century Publishers, Inc (Republic of Korea) *Tel:* (032) 429-9411 *Fax:* (032) 4299418, pg 443

Editions 24 Heures (Switzerland) *Tel:* (021) 3494500 *Fax:* (021) 3494224, pg 635

Ediciones 29 - Libros Rio Nuevo (Spain) *Tel:* (093) 675 41 35 *Fax:* (093) 590 04 40 *E-mail:* ediciones29@comunired.com *Web Site:* www.ediciones29.com, pg 603

Twin Guinep Ltd (Jamaica) *Tel:* 876-927-5390; 876-944-4324 *Fax:* 876-944-4324 *E-mail:* info@twinguinep.com; sales@twinguinep *Web Site:* www.twinguinep.com, pg 414

Two-Can Publishing Ltd (United Kingdom) *Tel:* (020) 7583 1585 *Fax:* (020) 7664-1652 *E-mail:* helpline@two-canpublishing.com; sales@creativepub.com *Web Site:* www.two-canpublishing.com, pg 768

Editorial Txertoa (Spain) *Tel:* (0943) 45 97 57 *Fax:* (0943) 46 09 41 *E-mail:* txertoa@nexo.es, pg 603

Typos (Greece) *Tel:* (01) 3819083; (01) 3819085; (01) 3619083 *Fax:* (01) 3825012, pg 313

Typotex Kft Elektronikus Kiado (Hungary) *Tel:* (01) 316-2473; (01) 316-3759 *Fax:* (01) 316-3759 *E-mail:* info@typotex.hu *Web Site:* www.typotex.hu, pg 324

Tyrolia Verlagsanstalt GmbH (Austria) *Tel:* (0512) 2233-510 *Fax:* (0512) 2233-512 *E-mail:* pgh@tyrolia.at *Web Site:* www.tyrolia.at, pg 58

Tyrolia Verlagsanstalt GmbH (Austria) *Tel:* (0512) 2233-0 *Fax:* (0512) 2233-501 *E-mail:* tyrolia@tyrolia.at *Web Site:* www.tyrolia.at, pg 1301

Tysk Bogimport ApS (Denmark) *Tel:* 7020 4990 *Fax:* 7020 4991 *E-mail:* kontakt@tyskforlaget.dk *Web Site:* www.tyskforlaget.dk, pg 1308

Tyto Alba Publishers (Lithuania) *Tel:* (02) 498 602; (02) 497 453; (02) 497 597 *Fax:* (02) 498 602 *E-mail:* tytoalba@taide.lt *Web Site:* www.tytoalba.lt, pg 450

UBS Publishers' Distributors Ltd (United Kingdom) *Tel:* (020) 8450 8667 *Fax:* (020) 8452 6612, pg 1354

UBS Publishers Distributors Ltd (India) *Tel:* (011) 273601; (011) 3266646 *Fax:* (011) 3276593; (011) 3274261 *E-mail:* ubspd@ubspd.com *Web Site:* www.ubspd.com, pg 351

UBS Publishers' Distributors Pvt Ltd (India) *Tel:* (011) 3273601; (011) 3266646 *Fax:* (011) 3276593; (011) 3274261 *E-mail:* ubspd@ubspd.com *Web Site:* www.gobookshopping.com; www.ubspd.com, pg 1317

Edizioni Ubulibri SAS (Italy) *Tel:* (02) 20241604 *Fax:* (02) 29510265 *E-mail:* edizioni@ubulibri.it, pg 410

Libreria UCA (El Salvador) *Tel:* 240011 (ext 193); 234491 *Fax:* 2731010, pg 1309

UCA Editores (El Salvador) *Tel:* 210-6600 *Fax:* 210-6655 *E-mail:* info@uca.edu.sv *Web Site:* www.uca.edu.sv, pg 138

UCL Press Ltd (United Kingdom) *Tel:* (020) 7583 9855 *Fax:* (020) 7842 2298 *E-mail:* info@tandf.co.uk *Web Site:* www.tandf.co.uk, pg 768

Universitas Udayana Library (Indonesia) *Tel:* (0361) 702772 *Fax:* (0361) 702-765 *Web Site:* www.unud.ac.id, pg 1517

Verlag Carl Ueberreuter GmbH (Austria) *Tel:* (01) 40 444-172 *Fax:* (01) 40 444-5 *E-mail:* office-v@ueberreutes.at *Web Site:* www.ueberreuter.de, pg 58

Wirtschaftsverlag Carl Ueberreuter (Germany) *Tel:* (069) 580905-80 *Fax:* (069) 580905-10 *E-mail:* info@redline-wirtschaft.de *Web Site:* www.redline-wirtschaft.de, pg 293

Uebersetzergemeinschaft Interessengemeinschaft von Uebersetzerinnen und Uebersetzern literarischer und wissenschaftlicher Werke (Austria) *Tel:* (01) 526 20 44-18 *Fax:* (01) 524 64 35 *E-mail:* ueg@literaturhaus.at *Web Site:* www.translators.at, pg 1147

UGA Editions (Uitgeverij) (Belgium) *Tel:* (056) 36 32 00 *Fax:* (056) 35 60 96 *E-mail:* publ@uga.be *Web Site:* www.uga.be, pg 73

Uganda Bookshop (Uganda) *Tel:* (041) 243756 *Fax:* (041) 245597, pg 1346

Uganda Library Association (ULA) (Uganda) *Tel:* (0141) 285001 (ext 4) *Fax:* (0141) 348625 *E-mail:* library@imul.com, pg 1572

Uganda Polytechnic Library at Uganda Technical College (Uganda) *Tel:* (041) 28 5211, pg 1552

Uganda Publishers & Booksellers Association (Uganda) *Tel:* (041) 259 163 *Fax:* (041) 251 160 *E-mail:* mbd@infocom.co.ug, pg 1289

Uglan Islenski Kiljuklubburinn (Iceland) *Tel:* 522 2020 *Fax:* 522 2022 *E-mail:* bokaklubbar@edda.is *Web Site:* www.edda.is, pg 1253

Evzen Uher, Musikverlag UHER (Czech Republic) *Tel:* (0632) 40376, pg 128

Verlag Dr Alfons Uhl (Germany) *Tel:* (09081) 87248 *Fax:* (09081) 23710, pg 293

Uitgeverij Altamira-Becht BV (Netherlands) *Tel:* (023) 54 11 190 *Fax:* (023) 52 74 404 *E-mail:* post@gottmer.nl *Web Site:* www.altamira-becht.nl, pg 490

Uitgeverij Averbode NV (Belgium) *Tel:* (013) 780 184 *Fax:* (013) 780 183 *E-mail:* educational@verbode.be *Web Site:* www.averbode.com, pg 74

Uitgeverij Contact (Netherlands) *Tel:* (020) 5249800 *Fax:* (020) 6276851 *E-mail:* businesscontact@contact-bv.nl *Web Site:* www.boekenwereld.com, pg 490

Uitgeverij De Garve (Belgium) *Tel:* (050) 400050 *Fax:* (050) 388099 *E-mail:* info@degarve.be *Web Site:* www.degarve.be, pg 74

UK International Standard Book Numbering Agency Ltd (United Kingdom) *Tel:* (01252) 742525 *Fax:* (01252) 742526 *E-mail:* isbn@whitaker.co.uk *Web Site:* www.whitaker.co.uk/isbn.htm, pg 1293

UK Serials Group-UKSG (United Kingdom) *Tel:* (01635) 254292 *Fax:* (01635) 253826 *E-mail:* uksg.admin@dial.pipex.com *Web Site:* www.uksg.org, pg 1165

Ulisse Editions (France) *Tel:* (01) 48 78 40 74 *Fax:* (01) 48 78 40 77 *Web Site:* www.ulisseditions.com, pg 188

Editora Ulisseia Lda (Portugal) *Tel:* (021) 380 1100 *Fax:* (021) 386 5397 *Web Site:* www.editorialverbo.pt, pg 536

Ullstein Heyne List GmbH & Co KG (Germany) *Tel:* (089) 51 48 0 *Fax:* (089) 51 48 2229 *Web Site:* www.ullstein.de, pg 293

Universitat Ulm (Germany) *Tel:* (0731) 502-01 *Fax:* (0731) 5022038 *E-mail:* post@uni-ulm.de *Web Site:* www.uni-ulm.de, pg 1510

Guenter Albert Ulmer Verlag (Germany) *Tel:* (07464) 98740 *Fax:* (07464) 3054 *E-mail:* info@ulmertuningen.de *Web Site:* www.ulmertuningen.de, pg 293

Verlag Eugen Ulmer GmbH & Co (Germany) *Tel:* (0711) 4507-0 *Fax:* (0711) 4507-120 *E-mail:* info@ulmer.de *Web Site:* www.ulmer.de, pg 293

Werner Ulmer & Co (Switzerland) *Tel:* (033) 432220 *Fax:* (033) 434848, pg 636

Ulrico Hoepli - Libreria Internazionale (Italy) *Tel:* (02) 864871 *Fax:* (02) 8052886; (02) 864322 (library) *E-mail:* libreria@hoepli.it *Web Site:* www.hoepli.it, pg 1321

Ulrike Helmer Verlag (Germany) *Tel:* (06174) 936060 *Fax:* (06174) 936065 *E-mail:* info@ulrike-helmer-verlag.de *Web Site:* www.ulrike-helmer-verlag.de, pg 293

Ulster Historical Foundation (United Kingdom) *Tel:* (028) 90 332288 *Fax:* (028) 90 239885 *E-mail:* enquiry@uhf.org.uk *Web Site:* www.ancestryireland.com, pg 768

Ultragraphics (Ireland) *Tel:* (01) 4599133 *Fax:* (01) 4512368, pg 1180, 1220

Ultramar Editores SA (Spain) *Tel:* (093) 3460612 *Fax:* (093) 8412334 *E-mail:* ultramar@javajan.com, pg 603

Ulverscroft Large Print Books Ltd (United Kingdom) *Tel:* (0116) 236 4325 *Fax:* (0116) 234 0205 *E-mail:* sales@ulverscroft.co.uk *Web Site:* www.ulverscroft.co.uk, pg 768

Editoriale Umbra SAS di Carnevali e (Italy) *Tel:* (0742) 357541 *Fax:* (0742) 351156 *E-mail:* editumbra@libero.it *Web Site:* www.italand.com/eu, pg 411

G Umbreit GmbH & Co KG (Germany) *Tel:* (07142) 596-0 *Fax:* (07142) 596-200 *E-mail:* info@umbreit-kg.de *Web Site:* www.umbreit-kg.de, pg 1312

Umea University Library (Sweden) *Tel:* (090) 786 5693 *Fax:* (090) 786 6677 *E-mail:* laneexp@ub.umu.se; www.bibliotekschefen@ub.umu.se *Web Site:* www.ub.umu.se, pg 1547

Umm al Qura University Library (Saudi Arabia) *Tel:* (02) 5565621 *Fax:* (02) 5501000 (ext 5562) *E-mail:* lib@uqu.edu.sa *Web Site:* www.uqu.edu.sa, pg 1541

Ummah Press (Egypt (Arab Republic of Egypt)) *Tel:* (02) 337-8556 *E-mail:* ghurabh@internetegypt.com, pg 138

Neuer Umschau Buchverlag (Germany) *Tel:* (06321) 877850 *Fax:* (06321) 877859 *E-mail:* info@umschau-buchverlag.de *Web Site:* www.umschau-buchverlag.de, pg 293

Unesco Books & Copyright Division, USBN agency (France) *Tel:* (01) 44 41 29 19 *Fax:* (01) 44 41 29 03 *E-mail:* afnil@electre.com *Web Site:* www.afnil.org; www.afnil.com, pg 1269

UNESCO Institute for Education (UIE) (Germany) *Tel:* (040) 4480410 *Fax:* (040) 4107723 *E-mail:* uie@unesco.org *Web Site:* www.unesco.org/education/uie, pg 1271

UNESCO Publishing (France) *Tel:* (01) 45 68 10 00 *Fax:* (01) 45 67 16 90 *E-mail:* publishing.promotion@unesco.org *Web Site:* www.upo.unesco.org, pg 188

Unesco Regional Office, Asia & the Pacific (Thailand) *Tel:* (02) 3910577 *Fax:* (02) 3910866 *E-mail:* bangkok@unesco.org *Web Site:* www.unescobkk.org, pg 646

Editora UNESP (Brazil) *Tel:* (011) 3242-7171 *Fax:* (011) 3242-7172 *E-mail:* feu@editora.unesp.br *Web Site:* www.editora.unesp.br, pg 91

Uni-Text Book Co (Malaysia) *Tel:* (03) 7185426, pg 459

Libreria Uniandes (Colombia) *Tel:* (01) 2824066 (ext 2197); (01) 2824066 (ext 2198) *Fax:* (01) 2841890, pg 1307

Uniao dos Escritores Angolanos (UEA) (Angola) *Tel:* (02) 323205; (02) 322421 *Fax:* (02) 323205 *E-mail:* uea@uea-angola.org *Web Site:* www.uea-angola.org, pg 1259

Unichurch Publishing (Australia) *Tel:* (02) 8267 4308 *Fax:* (02) 9267 4716 *E-mail:* insights@nsw.uca.org.au *Web Site:* www.nsw.uca.org.au/cu/publishing.htm, pg 44

Edizioni Unicopli SpA (Italy) *Tel:* (02) 42299666 *Fax:* (02) 76021612 *E-mail:* info@edizioniunicopli.it *Web Site:* www.edizioniunicopli.it, pg 411

Unicorn Books (United Kingdom) *Tel:* (020) 8420 1091 *Fax:* (020) 8428 0125 *Web Site:* www.unicornbooks.co.uk/, pg 768

Unicorn Books Ltd (Hong Kong) *Tel:* 2561 6151 *Fax:* 2811 1980, pg 320

Unicorn International Printing Co Ltd (Hong Kong) *Tel:* 2515-9810 *Fax:* 2515-9992 *E-mail:* unicorn7@netvigator.com; unicornhk@netvigator.com *Web Site:* www.unicorn88.com, pg 1158, 1219

Unieboek BV (Netherlands) *Tel:* (030) 63 77 660 *Fax:* (030) 63 77 600 *E-mail:* info@unieboek.nl *Web Site:* www.unieboek.nl, pg 490

Uniepers BV (Netherlands) *Tel:* (0294) 285111 *Fax:* (0294) 283013 *E-mail:* info@uniepers.nl *Web Site:* www.uniepers.nl, pg 491

Unigraphics (Pte) Ltd (Sri Lanka) *Tel:* (01) 694538 *Fax:* (01) 693731 *E-mail:* uni.graphics@lanka.ccom.lk, pg 607

UNILINC (Australia) *Tel:* (02) 9283 1488 *Fax:* (02) 9267 9247 *E-mail:* info@unilinc.edu.au *Web Site:* www.unilinc.edu.au, pg 1260

Unimax Macmillan Ltd (Ghana) *Tel:* (021) 227 443; (021) 223 709 *Fax:* (021) 225 215 *E-mail:* info@unimacmillan.com *Web Site:* www.macmillan-africa.com; www.unimacmillan.com, pg 305

Union de Escritores y Artistas de Cuba (Cuba) *Tel:* (07) 324551; (07) 324252; (07) 324553; (07) 553113 *Fax:* (07) 333158, pg 121

Union de Escritores y Artistas de Cuba (Cuba) *Tel:* (07) 553113 *Fax:* (07) 333158 *E-mail:* informatica@uneac.co.cu *Web Site:* www.uneac.com, pg 1265

Union des Ecrivains Tunisiens (Tunisia) *Tel:* (01) 257591 *Fax:* (01) 257807 *E-mail:* koutteb@planet.tn *Web Site:* www.alkhadra.com/ittihad-koutteb, pg 1406

Union des Libraires de France (ULF) (France) *Tel:* (01) 43 29 88 79 *Fax:* (01) 43 29 88 79, pg 1269

Union Mundial para la Naturaleza (UICN), Oficina Regional para Mesoamerica (Costa Rica) *Tel:* 241-0101 *Fax:* 240-9934 *E-mail:* correo@iucn.org *Web Site:* www.iucn.org/places/orma, pg 116

Union of Translators of Bulgaria, Magazin Panorama (Bulgaria) *Tel:* (02) 65 51 90; (02) 65 61 87, pg 1147

Union of Welsh Publishers & Booksellers (United Kingdom) *Tel:* (01559) 362371 *Fax:* (01559) 363758, pg 1293

Union of Writers of the African Peoples (Ghana) *Tel:* (021) 774944 *Fax:* (021) 774250, pg 1272

Union Press Ltd (Hong Kong) *Tel:* 2567 3762 *Fax:* 2394 5084, pg 320

Unipa A/S (Norway) *Tel:* (05) 31 84 05 *Fax:* (05) 32 42 70 *E-mail:* unipa@online.no, pg 1333

Unipress (Italy) *Tel:* (049) 8752542 *Fax:* (049) 8752542, pg 411

Unisa Press (South Africa) *Tel:* (012) 4293549 *Fax:* (012) 4293221 *E-mail:* kempg@alpha.unisa.ac.za *Web Site:* www.unisa.ac.za/dept/press/index.html, pg 569

Unistad Verspreiding CV (Belgium) *Tel:* (03) 2307725 *Fax:* (03) 2307725, pg 74

Unitas Forlag (Denmark) *Tel:* 36166481 *Fax:* 38116481 *E-mail:* forlag@unitas.dk *Web Site:* forlag.unitas.dk, pg 135

UNITAS Publishing Co Ltd (Taiwan, Province of China) *Tel:* (02) 27634300 *Fax:* (02) 27491208 *E-mail:* unitas@udngroup.com.tw *Web Site:* www.udngroup.com.tw, pg 642

United Book Suppliers (United Kingdom) *Tel:* (01232) 832362 *Fax:* (01232) 848780, pg 1354

United Christian Council Literature Bureau (Sierra Leone) *Tel:* 032462, pg 554

United Nations Library (Switzerland) *Tel:* (022) 917 41 81 *Fax:* (022) 917 04 18 *E-mail:* library@unog.ch *Web Site:* www.unog.ch/library, pg 1548

United Nations Conference on Trade and Development (UNCTAD) (Switzerland) *Tel:* (022) 917 1234; (022) 917 5809 *Fax:* (022) 907 0043 *E-mail:* info@unctad.org *Web Site:* www.unctad.org, pg 1286

United Nations Depository Library (Republic of Korea) *Tel:* 23 290 1499 *Fax:* 29 234 763 *E-mail:* unneu@korea.ac.kr *Web Site:* library.korea.ac.kr, pg 1524

United Nations Economic Commission for Africa, ECA (Ethiopia) *Tel:* (01) 51 72 00 *Fax:* (01) 51 03 65 *E-mail:* ecaweb@uneca.org *Web Site:* www.uneca.org, pg 1266

United Nations Economic Commission for Africa Library (Ethiopia) *Tel:* (01) 51 72 00 *Fax:* (01) 51 22 33; (01) 51 03 65 *E-mail:* ecaweb@uneca.org *Web Site:* www.uneca.org, pg 1504

United Nations Economic Commission for Europe (UNECE) (Switzerland) *Tel:* (022) 917 12 34 *Fax:* (022) 917 05 05 *E-mail:* info.ece@unece.org *Web Site:* www.unece.org, pg 1286

United Nations Educational, Scientific & Cultural Organization (UNESCO) (France) *Tel:* (01) 45 68 10 00 *Fax:* (01) 45 67 16 90 *E-mail:* clearing-house@unesco.org *Web Site:* www.unesco.org, pg 1269

United Nations Environment Programme (UNEP) (Kenya) *Tel:* (02) 621234 *Fax:* (02) 624489; (02) 624490 *E-mail:* eisinfo@unep.org *Web Site:* www.unep.org, pg 1275

United Nations Library, Bangkok (Thailand) *Tel:* (02) 2881360; (02) 2881341 *Fax:* (02) 2883036 *E-mail:* libref@un.org; library-escap@un.org *Web Site:* www.unescap.org/unis/lib.htm; www.unescap.org/unis/library/net08.asp, pg 1288

United Nations Publications (United States) *Tel:* 212-963-8302 *Toll Free Tel:* 800-253-9646 (orders US only) *Fax:* 212-963-3489 *E-mail:* publications@un.org *Web Site:* www.un.org/Pubs/sales.htm, pg 1294

United Nations Research Institute for Social Development (UNRISD) (Switzerland) *Tel:* (022) 917 3020 *Fax:* (022) 917 0650 *E-mail:* info@unrisd.org *Web Site:* www.unrisd.org, pg 1287

United Nations University Press (Japan) *Tel:* (03) 3499-2811 *Fax:* (03) 3406-7345 *E-mail:* mbox@hq.unu.edu *Web Site:* www.unu.edu/unupress, pg 430

United Publishers Services Ltd (Japan) *Tel:* (03) 5479-7251 *Fax:* (03) 5479-7307 *E-mail:* general@ups.co.jp, pg 1323

United States Information Service Library (Sierra Leone) *Tel:* 226481 *Fax:* 225471, pg 1542

United Theological College of the West Indies (Jamaica) *Tel:* (876) 927-2868; (876) 927-1724; (876) 977-0810 *Fax:* (876) 977-0812 *E-mail:* unitheol@cwjamaica.com *Web Site:* www.utcwi.edu.jm, pg 1521

United Writers Publications Ltd (United Kingdom) *Tel:* (01736) 365954 *Fax:* (01736) 365954 *E-mail:* info@unitedwriters.co.uk, pg 768

Uniting Education (Australia) *Tel:* (03) 9416 4262 *Fax:* (03) 9416 4264 *E-mail:* contact@unitinged.org.au *Web Site:* www.unitinged.org.au, pg 44

Uniting Education (New Zealand) *Tel:* (03) 94164262 *Fax:* (03) 94164264, pg 502

Unity Books Ltd (New Zealand) *Tel:* (04) 499 4245 *Fax:* (04) 499 4246 *E-mail:* unity.books@clear.net.nz, pg 1331

Unity Press (Australia) *Tel:* (02) 4671342 *Fax:* (02) 9736-2663, pg 44

Uniunea Scriitorilor din Romania (Romania) *Tel:* (0256) 294895 *Fax:* (0256) 294895 *Web Site:* www.infotim.ro/usrt/usrt.htm, pg 1282

Editura Univers SA (Romania) *Tel:* (01) 2244640; (01) 3104510 *Fax:* (01) 3104510 *E-mail:* univers@rnc.ro, pg 543

Universal Academy Press, Inc (Japan) *Tel:* (03) 3813-7232 *Fax:* (03) 3813-5932 *E-mail:* general@uap.co.jp *Web Site:* www.uap.co.jp, pg 430

Universal Book Shop (India) *Tel:* (0532) 603012, pg 1318

Universal Book Traders (India) *Tel:* (011) 2396 1288; (011) 2391 1966; (011) 2399 0487 *Fax:* (011) 2392 4152; (011) 2745 9023 *E-mail:* unilaw@vsnl.com *Web Site:* www.unilawbooks.com, pg 1318

Universal Business Directories, Australia Pty Ltd (New Zealand) *Tel:* (09) 526-6300 *Toll Free Tel:* 800 823-225 (New Zealand only) *Fax:* (09) 526-6313 *Toll Free Fax:* 800 329 823 (New Zealand only) *E-mail:* sales@ubd.co.nz *Web Site:* www.ubd.co.nz, pg 502

Universal Dalsi (Romania) *Tel:* (01) 3355354; (01) 3371682 *Fax:* (01) 3373566; (01) 3129709 *E-mail:* marian@kappa.ro, pg 543

Universal Edition AG (Austria) *Tel:* (01) 337 23-0 *Fax:* (01) 337 23-400 *E-mail:* office@universaledition.com *Web Site:* www.universaledition.com, pg 58

Libreria Universal (Guatemala) *Tel:* (02) 28 484, pg 1314

Universal Postal Union (UPU) (Switzerland) *Tel:* (031) 350 31 11 *Fax:* (031) 350 31 10 *E-mail:* info@upu.int *Web Site:* www.upu.int, pg 1287

Universal Press Pty Ltd (Australia) *Tel:* (02) 9857 3700 *Toll Free Tel:* 800 021 987 *Fax:* (02) 9888 9074 *Toll Free Fax:* 800 636 197 *E-mail:* unipress@unipress.com.au, pg 44

Universal Publications Agency Press (Republic of Korea) *Tel:* (02) 32-8175 *Fax:* (02) 32-8176 *E-mail:* upa@upa.co.kr *Web Site:* www.upa.co.kr, pg 443

Universal Publications Agency Press (Republic of Korea) *Tel:* (02) 3672 0044 *Fax:* (02) 3672 1222 *E-mail:* upa@upa.co.kr *Web Site:* www.upa.co.kr, pg 1134, 1324

Universidad Autonoma - Biblioteca Universitaria (Spain) *Tel:* (091) 3974399 *Fax:* (091) 3975058 *E-mail:* servicio.biblioteca@uam.es *Web Site:* www.uam.es, pg 1545

Biblioteca de la Universidad Autonoma de Santo Domingo (Dominican Republic) *Tel:* 533-1104 *Fax:* 508-7374 *E-mail:* rectoria.uasd@codetel.net.do *Web Site:* www.uasd.edu.do, pg 1502

Universidad Autonoma Tomas Frias, Div de Extension Universitaria (Bolivia) *Tel:* (062) 2-73-28; (062) 2-73-00 *Fax:* (062) 2-66-63; (062) 2-31-96 *E-mail:* rector@rect.nrp.edu.bo *Web Site:* www.unam.mx/udal/afiliacion/Bolivia/frias.htm, pg 75

Universidad Boliviana Tomas Frias, Departamento de Bibliotecas (Bolivia) *Tel:* (062) 27300 *Fax:* (062) 27329; (062) 26663, pg 1494

Biblioteca de la Universidad Catolica de Valparaiso (Chile) *Tel:* (032) 273261; (032) 273000 *Fax:* (032) 273183 *Web Site:* biblioteca.ucv.cl, pg 1497

Biblioteca de la Universidad Central de Ecuador (Ecuador) *Tel:* (02) 2234 722 *Fax:* (02) 2236 367; (02) 2521 925 *Web Site:* www.ucentral.edu.ec, pg 1503

Biblioteca Central de la Universidad Central de Venezuela (Venezuela) *Tel:* (02) 605-29-09; (02) 605-29-10 *Fax:* (02) 6622486 *Web Site:* www.ucv.ve, pg 1555

Universidad Central del Ecuador, Departamento de Publicaciones (Ecuador) *Tel:* (02) 2234 722 *Fax:* (02) 2236 367; (02) 2521 925 *Web Site:* www.ucentral.edu.ec, pg 137

Biblioteca General de la Universidad Central "Marta Abreu" de las Villas (UCLV) (Cuba) *Tel:* (0422) 81410; (0422) 81618; (0422) 8178 *Fax:* (0422) 81608; (0422) 22113 *E-mail:* luishs@dri.uclv.edu.cu, pg 1500

Universidad Centroamericana (Nicaragua) *Tel:* (02) 278-3923 *Fax:* (02) 267-0106 *E-mail:* comsj@ns.uca.edu.ni *Web Site:* www.una.edu.ni, pg 1533

Biblioteca de la Universidad Centroamericana Jose Simeon Canas (El Salvador) *Tel:* 210-6600 (ext 278) *Fax:* 210-6657 *E-mail:* ucabib.director@bib.uca.edu.sv *Web Site:* www.uca.edu.sv, pg 1502

Biblioteca de la Universidad Complutense (Spain) *Tel:* (091) 394 69 25; (091) 394 69 39 *Fax:* (091) 394 69 26 *E-mail:* bucweb@buc.ucm.es *Web Site:* www.ucm.es/BUCM, pg 1545

Universidad de los Andes, Biblioteca General, Ramon de Zubiria (Colombia) *Tel:* (01) 3394999; (01) 3394949 *Fax:* (01) 3324472 *E-mail:* sisbibli@uniandes.edu.co *Web Site:* biblioteca.uniandes.edu.co, pg 1498

Universidad de los Andes, Consejo de Publicaciones (Venezuela) *Tel:* (074) 401111 ext 1998 *Fax:* (074) 274240 ext 1998 *E-mail:* dsia@ula.ve *Web Site:* www.ula.ve, pg 780

Servicios Bibliotecarios Universidad de los Andes (Serbiula) (Venezuela) *Tel:* (0274) 2402731; (0274) 2402729 *Fax:* (0274) 2402507; (0274) 2402748 *E-mail:* adquisi@serbi.ula.ve *Web Site:* www.serbi.ula.ve, pg 1555

Universidad de Antioquia, Division Publicaciones (Colombia) *Tel:* (04) 210 50 10 *Fax:* (04) 210 50 12 *E-mail:* direccion@editorialudea.com; comunicaciones@editorialudea.com *Web Site:* www.editorialudea.com, pg 113

Universidad de Antioquia, Escuela Interamericana de Bibliotecologia, Biblioteca (Colombia) *Tel:* (04) 210 59 41 *Fax:* (04) 210 59 46 *E-mail:* bibeib@caribe.udea.edu.co *Web Site:* caribe.udea.edu.co/~bibeib/principal.htm, pg 1499

Universidad de Cantabria Biblioteca (Spain) *Tel:* (0942) 201 180 *Fax:* (0942) 201 183 *Web Site:* www.buc.unican.es, pg 1545

Biblioteca Central de la Universidad de Chile (Chile) *Tel:* (02) 6782583 *Fax:* (02) 6782574 *E-mail:* sisib@uchile.cl *Web Site:* www.uchile.cl/bibliotecas, pg 1497

Universidad de Concepcion Direccion de Bibliotecas (Chile) *Tel:* (041) 20 41 15; (041) 20 43 93 *Fax:* (041) 24 60 76 *E-mail:* info@udec.cl *Web Site:* www.bib.udec.cl, pg 1497

Universidad de Costa Rica Sistema de Bibliotecas, Documentacion e Informacion (Costa Rica) *Tel:* 253-6152; 207-5316; 207-4461 *Fax:* 204-2809 *E-mail:* marqueda@sibdi.bldt.ucr.ac.cr *Web Site:* sibdi.bldt.ucr.ac.cr/sibdi.htm, pg 1499

Biblioteca Central de la Universidad de El Salvador (El Salvador) *Tel:* 503 2250278 *Fax:* 503 2250278 *E-mail:* sb@biblio.ues.edu.sv *Web Site:* www.ues.edu.sv/biblio.html, pg 1504

Universidad de Granada (Spain) *Tel:* (0958) 243025 *Fax:* (0958) 243066 *Web Site:* www.ugr.es, pg 603

Biblioteca General, Universidad de Guayaquil (Ecuador) *Tel:* 2282440 *Fax:* 2391010 *E-mail:* zd@ug.edu.ec *Web Site:* www.ug.edu.ec, pg 1503

Editorial de la Universidad de Costa Rica (Costa Rica) *Tel:* 207-5006; 207-5837 *Fax:* 224-9367 *E-mail:* direccion@editorial.ucr.ac.cr *Web Site:* www.editorial.ucr.ac.cr, pg 116

Ediciones de la Universidad de la Frontera (Chile) *Tel:* (045) 325000 *Fax:* (045) 325116, pg 100

Universidad de la Habana, Direccion de Informacion Cientifico Tecnica (Cuba) *Tel:* (07) 78-3231 *Fax:* (07) 33-5774, pg 1500

Universidad de Las Palmas de Gran Canaria, Escuela Universitaria de Informatica (ULPGC) (Spain) *Tel:* (0928) 45-87-81; (0928) 45-87-00 *Fax:* (0928) 45-87-11 *E-mail:* organizacion@sinf.ulpgc.es, pg 603

Universidad de Lima-Fondo de Desarollo Editorial (Peru) *Tel:* (01) 437-6767 *Fax:* (01) 437-8066; (01) 435-3396 *E-mail:* fondo_ed@lima.edu.pe *Web Site:* www.ulima.edu.pe, pg 517

Universidad de los Andes Editorial (Colombia) *Tel:* (01) 3394949; (01) 3394999 *Fax:* (01) 3394949 (ext 2158) *E-mail:* infeduni@uniandes.edu.co *Web Site:* ediciones.uniandes.edu.co, pg 113

Universidad de Malaga (Spain) *Tel:* (095) 213 29 17 *Fax:* (095) 213 29 18 *E-mail:* buzon@uma.es *Web Site:* www.uma.es, pg 603

Universidad de Navarra, Ediciones SA (Spain) *Tel:* (0948) 256850 *Fax:* (0948) 256854 *E-mail:* eunsa@cin.es *Web Site:* www.eunsa.es, pg 603

Universidad de Oviedo Servicio de Publicaciones (Spain) *Tel:* (0985) 210160; (0985) 222428 *Fax:* (0985) 218352 *Web Site:* www.uniovi.es, pg 603

Universidad de Panama, Biblioteca Interamericana Simon Bolivar (Panama) *Tel:* 2636133, pg 1535

Ediciones Universidad de Salamanca (Spain) *Tel:* (0923) 294598 *Fax:* (0923) 262579 *E-mail:* eus@usal.es *Web Site:* www3.usal.es, pg 603

Biblioteca Central de la Universidad de San Carlos (Guatemala) *Tel:* (02) 460 611 *E-mail:* usacbibc@usac.edu.gt *Web Site:* www.usac.edu.gt/dependencias/biblioteca, pg 1513

Universidad de Sevilla Secretariado de Publicaciones (Spain) *Tel:* (095) 487444; (095) 487442 *Fax:* (095) 487 7443 *Web Site:* publius.cica.es, pg 603

Universidad de Valladolid Secretariado de Publicaciones e Intercambio Editorial (Spain) *Tel:* (0983) 187810 *Fax:* (0983) 187812 *E-mail:* spic@uva.es *Web Site:* www.uva.es, pg 604

Biblioteca Central de la Universidad de Zulia
(Venezuela) *Tel:* (061) 596701 *Fax:* (061) 596700
Web Site: www.serbi.luz.ve/bibcentral, pg 1555

Universidad del Pacifico Libreria (Peru) *Tel:* (01)
471-2277; (01) 472-9635 *Fax:* (01) 470-6121
E-mail: Biblioteca@up.edu.pe *Web Site:* www.up.edu.
pe/biblioteca, pg 1536

Biblioteca Central, Universidad del Salvador (Argentina)
Tel: (011) 4371-0422 *Fax:* (011) 4371-0422
E-mail: uds-bibl@salvador.edu.ar *Web Site:* www.
salvador.edu.ar, pg 1490

Editorial Universidad SRL (Argentina) *Tel:* (011)
4382-9022; (011) 4382-6850 *Fax:* (011) 4381-2005
E-mail: univers@nat.com.ar *Web Site:* www.nat.com.
ar/universidad, pg 9

Editorial Universidad Estatal a Distancia (EUNED)
(Costa Rica) *Tel:* 234-7954; 253-2121 (ext 2440)
Fax: 257-5042; 234-9138 *E-mail:* editoria@uned.ac.cr
Web Site: www.uned.ac.cr/ejecutiva/editorial/, pg 116

Universidad Externado de Colombia Biblioteca
(Colombia) *Tel:* (01) 3420288; (01) 3419900 (ext
3350); (01) 3419900 (ext 3351) *E-mail:* biblioteca@
uexternado.edu.co *Web Site:* www.uexternado.edu.
co/biblioteca/, pg 1499

Biblioteca de la Universidad Iberoamericana (Mexico)
Tel: (055) 5950 4000 *Fax:* (055) 5950 4248
E-mail: buzon@uiacia.bib.uia.mx *Web Site:* www.bib.
uia.mx, pg 1529

Biblioteca Central de la Universidad Mayor de San
Andres (Bolivia) *Tel:* (02) 440047; (02) 352232
Fax: (02) 442505 *E-mail:* rector@umsanet.edu.bo
Web Site: www.umsanet.edu.bo; www.bc.umsanet.edu.
bo, pg 1494

Universidad Mayor de San Andres, Editorial
Universitaria (Bolivia) *Tel:* (02) 359491, pg 75

Biblioteca Central de la Universidad Mayor de San
Francisco Xavier de Chuquisaca (Bolivia) *Tel:* (04)
6453308 *Fax:* (04) 6455308 *Web Site:* www.usfx.edu.
bo, pg 1495

Universidad Nacional Abierta y a Distancia (Colombia)
Tel: (01) 212 0159; (01) 346 0088 *Fax:* (01) 522 3497
E-mail: unisur12@gaitana.interred.net.co, pg 113

Universidad Nacional Autonoma de Mexico (National
University of Mexico) (Mexico) *Tel:* (05) 6226329;
(05) 6226330 *Fax:* (05) 6226328 *E-mail:* libros@
bibliounam.unam.mx, pg 472

Universidad Nacional Centro Editorial (Colombia)
Tel: (01) 2448640, pg 113

Universidad Nacional de Colombia, Biblioteca Central
(Colombia) *Tel:* (01) 2691743 *E-mail:* refer@
biblioteca.campus.unal.edu.co *Web Site:* www.unal.
edu.co, pg 1499

Biblioteca Mayor de la Universidad Nacional de
Cordoba (Argentina) *Tel:* (351) 4331072 *Fax:* (351)
4331079 *E-mail:* biblio@bmayor.unc.edu.ar
Web Site: www.bmayor.unc.edu.ar, pg 1490

Biblioteca de la Universidad Nacional de La Plata
(Argentina) *Tel:* (021) 423-6600; (021) 423-6608;
(021) 423-6607; (021) 423-6601 *Fax:* (021) 425-5004
E-mail: biblio@isis.unlp.edu.ar *Web Site:* www.unlp.
edu.ar, pg 1490

Universidad Nacional del Litoral (Argentina) *Tel:* (0342)
4571110 *Fax:* (0342) 4571110 *E-mail:* informes@unl.
edu.ar *Web Site:* www.unl.edu.ar, pg 1490

Editorial Universidad Nacional (EUNA) (Costa
Rica) *Tel:* 277-3204; 277-3825 *Fax:* 277-3204
E-mail: editoria@una.ac.cr *Web Site:* www.una.ac.
cr/euna, pg 116

Universidad Nacional Mayor de San Marcos (Peru)
Tel: (01) 428-9272; (01) 433-5922 *Fax:* (01) 428-5210
Web Site: www.unmsm.edu.pe, pg 517

Libreria y Distribuidora de la Universidad Nacional
Mayor de San Marcos (Peru) *Tel:* (01) 464-0560
Fax: (014) 464-0560 *E-mail:* libreria@unmsm.edu.pe
Web Site: www.unmsm.edu.pe, pg 1335

Universidad Nacional San Antonio Abad del Cusco
(UNSAAC) (Peru) *Tel:* (084) 222271; (084) 228661
Fax: (084) 238156 *Web Site:* www.unsaac.edu.pe,
pg 1536

Universidad para la Paz (Costa Rica) *Tel:* 205-9000;
249-1511 (ext 20) *Fax:* 249-1929 *E-mail:* info@
upeace.org *Web Site:* www.upeace.org, pg 116

Universidad Pontificia de Salamanca, Biblioteca
(Spain) *Tel:* (0923) 277 118 *Fax:* (0923) 277 118
E-mail: bibliotecario.general@upsa.es *Web Site:* www.
upsa.es/biblioteca.html, pg 1545

Universidad Technologica Metropolitana (UTEM),
Sistema de Bibliotecas (Chile) *Tel:* (02) 272-40-32
Web Site: www.bibliotecautem.cl, pg 1497

Universidad Veracruzana Direccion General
Editorial y de Publicaciones (Mexico) *Tel:* (029)
71316 *E-mail:* direditaspeedy@coacade.uv.mx
Web Site: www.uv.mx, pg 472

Universidade Agostinho Neto Biblioteca (Angola)
Tel: (02) 330 517 *Fax:* (02) 330 520 *Web Site:* www.
uan.ao, pg 1490

Universidade de Brasilia, Biblioteca Central (Brazil)
Tel: (061) 307-2417 *Fax:* (061) 274-2412
E-mail: informacoes@bce.unb.br *Web Site:* www.bce.
unb.br, pg 1495

Editora Universidade de Brasilia (Brazil) *Tel:* (061) 226-
6874 *Fax:* (061) 323-1017 *E-mail:* editora@unb.br
Web Site: www.editora.unb.br, pg 91

Universidade de Macau, Centro de Publicacoes (China)
Tel: 397 4504 *Fax:* 397 4506 *E-mail:* pub_grp@umac.
mo *Web Site:* www.umac.mo, pg 109

Editora da Universidade de Sao Paulo (Brazil) *Tel:* (011)
8184160; (011) 8138837 *Fax:* (011) 221-6988, pg 91

Sistema Integrado de Bibliotecas da Universidade de Sao
Paulo (SIBi) (Brazil) *Tel:* (011) 818-4194; (011) 818-
4197 *Fax:* (011) 815-2142 *E-mail:* dtsibi@org.usp.br
Web Site: www.usp.br/sibi, pg 1495

Universidade do Minho (Portugal) *Tel:* (0253) 604150
Fax: (0253) 604159 *E-mail:* sdum@sdum.uminho.pt
Web Site: www.sdum.uminho.pt, pg 1539

Bibliotecas da Universidade Eduardo Mondlane
(Mozambique) *Tel:* (01) 492875 *Fax:* (01) 493174
Web Site: www.uem.mz/reitoria/dsd/bibdsd.htm,
pg 1530

Biblioteca Central da Universidade Federal do Parana
(Brazil) *Tel:* (041) 360-5000 *Fax:* (041) 2627784
E-mail: webmaster@ufpr.br *Web Site:* www.ufpr.br/,
pg 1495

Centro de Ciencias da Saude da Universidade Federal do
Rio de Janeiro (Brazil) *Tel:* (021) 2562 6632; (021)
2562 6716; (021) 2562 6641 *Fax:* (021) 2270 0119
E-mail: ddbhome@sibi.ufrj.br *Web Site:* www.sibi.ufrj.
br, pg 1495

Editora Universidade Federal do Rio de Janeiro
(Brazil) *Tel:* (021) 2542-7640 *Fax:* (021) 2295-0346
E-mail: livraria@editora.ufrj.br *Web Site:* www.
editora.ufrj.br; www.ufrj.br, pg 92

Universidade Federal do Rio Grande do Sul (UFRGS),
Biblioteca Central (Brazil) *Tel:* (051) 3316-3065
Fax: (051) 3316-3984 *E-mail:* bcentral@bc.ufrgs.br
Web Site: www.biblioteca.ufrgs.br, pg 1496

Universita degli Studi di Firenze, Biblioteca di Lettre e
Filosofia (Italy) *Tel:* (055) 46 22 402 *Fax:* (055) 47
56 40 *E-mail:* bibfil@unifi.it *Web Site:* www.unifi.it,
pg 1521

Universita di Roma 'La Sapienza' (Italy) *Tel:* (06)
4456820; (06) 4474021; (06) 4991 *Fax:* (06)
4474024 *E-mail:* alessandrina@librari.beniculturali.
it *Web Site:* www.alessandrina.librari.beniculturali.it;
www.uniroma1.it, pg 1521

Universitaets-Bibliothek Osnabrueck (Germany)
Tel: (0541) 969-0 *Fax:* (0541) 969-4482 *E-mail:* aaa@
uni-osnabrueck.de *Web Site:* www.uni-osnabrueck.de,
pg 1510

Universitaets- und Landesbibliothek Muenster
(Germany) *Tel:* (0251) 83 224021 *Fax:* (0251) 83
28398 *E-mail:* sekretariat.ulb@uni-muenster.de
Web Site: www.uni-muenster.de/ULB, pg 1511

Universitaets - und Landesbibliothek Sachsen-Anhalt
(Germany) *Tel:* (0345) 55 22000 *Fax:* (0345) 55
27140 *E-mail:* direktion@bibliothek.uni-halle.de;
auskunft@bibliothek.uni-halle.de *Web Site:* www.
bibliothek.uni-halle.de, pg 1511

Universitaets- und Stadtbibliothek Koeln (Germany)
Tel: (0221) 470-2214; (0221) 470-2374; (0221) 470-
3316 *Fax:* (0221) 470-5166 *E-mail:* auskunft@ub.uni-
koeln.de; sekretariat@ub.uni-koeln.de *Web Site:* www.
ub.uni-koeln.de, pg 1511

Universitaetsbibliothek Bamberg (Germany) *Tel:* (0951)
863-1503; (0951) 863-1501 *Fax:* (0951) 863-1565
E-mail: unibibliothek.bamberg@unibib.uni-bamberg.de
Web Site: www.uni.bamberg.de/unibib, pg 1511

Universitaetsbibliothek Bochum (Germany) *Tel:* (049234)
3222350; (049234) 3222351 *Fax:* (049234) 3214736
E-mail: direktion-ub@rub.de *Web Site:* www.ub.ruhr-
uni-bochum.de, pg 1511

Universitaetsbibliothek Erlangen-Nuernberg (Germany)
Tel: (09131) 85-22160 *Fax:* (09131) 85-29309
E-mail: direktion@bib.uni-erlangen.de *Web Site:* www.
ub.uni-erlangen.de, pg 1511

Universitaetsbibliothek Freiburg (Germany) *Tel:* (0761)
2033918 *Fax:* (0761) 2033987 *E-mail:* info@ub.uni-
freiburg.de *Web Site:* www.ub.uni-freiburg.de, pg 1511

Universitaetsbibliothek Freie Universitaet Berlin
(Germany) *Tel:* (030) 838 54224; (030) 838 54273
Fax: (030) 838 53738 *E-mail:* auskunft@ub.fu-berlin.
de *Web Site:* www.ub.fu-berlin.de, pg 1511

Universitaetsbibliothek Heidelberg (Germany)
Tel: (06221) 54 2380 *Fax:* (06221) 54 2623
E-mail: ub@ub.uni-hd.de *Web Site:* www.ub.uni-
heidelberg.de, pg 1511

Universitaetsbibliothek Kaiserslautern (Germany)
Tel: (0631) 205-2241 *Fax:* (0631) 205-2355
E-mail: unibib@ub.uni-kl.de *Web Site:* www.uni-kl.
de/bibliothek, pg 1511

Universitaetsbibliothek Leipzig (Germany) *Tel:* (0341)
97 30577 *Fax:* (0341) 97 30596 *E-mail:* auskunft@
ub.uni-leipzig.de *Web Site:* www.ub.uni-leipzig.de/ubl,
pg 1511

Universitaetsbibliothek Mannheim (Germany) *Tel:* (0621)
181-2941; (0621) 181-2948; (0621) 181-2989
Fax: (0621) 181-2939 *E-mail:* biblubma@bib.uni-
mannheim.de *Web Site:* www.bib.uni-mannheim.de,
pg 1511

Universitaetsbibliothek Salzburg (Austria) *Tel:* (0662)
8044 77550 *Fax:* (0662) 8044 103 *E-mail:* info.hb@
sbg.ac.at *Web Site:* www.ubs.sbg.ac.at, pg 1492

Universitaetsbibliothek Tuebingen (Germany)
Tel: (07071) 29-72846 *Fax:* (07071) 29-3123
E-mail: info-zentrum@ub.uni-tuebingen.de
Web Site: www.uni-tuebingen.de/ub, pg 1511

Universitaetsbibliothek Wuppertal (Germany) *Tel:* (0202)
439-2705 *Fax:* (0202) 439-2695 *E-mail:* information@
bib.uni-wuppertal.de *Web Site:* www.bib.uni-wuppertal.
de, pg 1511

Universitaetsverlag Winter GmbH Heidelberg GmbH
(Germany) *Tel:* (06221) 7702-60 *Fax:* (06221) 7702-
69 *E-mail:* info@winter-verlag-hd.de *Web Site:* www.
winter-verlag-hd.de, pg 293

Bibliotheek Universitair Centrum (Belgium) *Tel:* (03)
265 37 94 *Fax:* (03) 265 36 52 *E-mail:* helpdesk@lib.
ua.ac.be *Web Site:* lib.ua.ac.be, pg 1494

Bibliotheque Universitaire de Bangui (Central African
Republic) *Tel:* 612 000 *Fax:* 61-78-90, pg 1497

Presses Universitaires de Louvain-UCL (Belgium)
Tel: (010) 47 40 30 *Fax:* (010) 47 25 31
Web Site: www.ucl.ac.be, pg 74

Editorial Universitaria Centroamericana (EDUCA) (Costa
Rica) *Tel:* 2258740 *Fax:* 2340071 *E-mail:* educacr@
sol.racsa.co.cr, pg 117

Editorial Universitaria de America Ltda (Colombia) *Tel:* (01) 2566948; (01) 3201097 *Fax:* (01) 3201097, pg 113

Livraria e Editora Universitaria de Direito Ltda (Brazil) *Tel:* (011) 3105-6374 *Fax:* (011) 3104-0317, pg 92

Editoria Universitaria de la Patagonia (Argentina) *Tel:* (02967) 428834; (02967) 424969 *E-mail:* rcesar@unpbib.edu.ar, pg 9

Libreria Universitaria de l'Universidad de El Salvador (El Salvador) *Tel:* 259427; 256604 *Fax:* 259427, pg 1309

Editorial Universitaria de la Universidad de El Salvador (El Salvador) *Tel:* 2558826 *Fax:* 254208, pg 139

Editorial Universitaria (Honduras) *Tel:* 312110, pg 315

Editorial Universitaria (Panama) *Tel:* 264-2087 *Fax:* 269-2684, pg 515

Biblioteca Central Universitaria 'Jose Antonio Arze' (Bolivia) *Tel:* (042) 232540 *E-mail:* biblioteca-c@umss.edu.bo *Web Site:* www.umss.edu.bo, pg 1495

Editorial Universitaria SA (Chile) *Tel:* (02) 487 0700 *Fax:* (02) 487 0702 *E-mail:* comunicaciones@universitaria.cl *Web Site:* www.universitaria.cl/index.pl, pg 100

Ediciones Universitarias de Valparaiso (Chile) *Tel:* (032) 273087; (02) 6332230 *Fax:* (032) 273429, pg 100

Universitas (France) *Tel:* (01) 45 67 18 38 *Fax:* (01) 45 66 50 70 *E-mail:* info@universitas.fr, pg 188

Biblioteca de la Universitat de Barcelona (Spain) *Tel:* (093) 403 45 89 *Fax:* (093) 403 45 92 *E-mail:* sbib@org.ub.es *Web Site:* www.bib.ub.es, pg 1546

Publicacions de la Universitat de Barcelona (Spain) *Tel:* (093) 402 11 00 *Fax:* (093) 403 54 46 *E-mail:* srodon@pu.ges.ub.es *Web Site:* www.ub.es, pg 604

Universitat de Valencia Servei de Publicacions (Spain) *Tel:* (096) 3864115 *Fax:* (096) 3864067 *E-mail:* publicacions@uv.es *Web Site:* www.uv.es, pg 604

Edicions de la Universitat Politecnica de Catalunya SL (Spain) *Tel:* (093) 4016 883 *Fax:* (093) 4015 885 *E-mail:* edicions-upc@upc.es *Web Site:* www.edicionsupc.es, pg 604

Universitat Wuerzburg (Germany) *Tel:* (0931) 888-5906 *Fax:* (0931) 888-5970 *E-mail:* direktion@bibliothek.uni-wuerzburg.de; information@bibliothek.uni-wuerzburg.de *Web Site:* www.bibliothek.uni-wuerzburg.de, pg 1511

Universitat Zentralbibliothek Zuerich (Switzerland) *Tel:* (01) 2683100 *Fax:* (01) 2683290 *E-mail:* zb@zb.unizh.ch *Web Site:* www-zb.unizh.ch, pg 1548

Universitatea de Medicina si Farmacie Biblioteca Centrala (Romania) *Tel:* (064) 192629 *Fax:* (064) 190832 *Web Site:* www.bib.umfcluj.ro, pg 1540

Biblioteca Universitatii Politehnica Bucuresti (Romania) *Tel:* (021) 402 3982 *Fax:* (021) 312 70 44 *Web Site:* www.library.pub.ro, pg 1540

Universitats und Landesbibliothe Darmstadt (Germany) *Tel:* (06151) 165850 *Fax:* (06151) 165897 *E-mail:* auskunft@ulb.tu-darmstadt.de *Web Site:* www.ulb.tu-darmstadt.de, pg 1511

Universitatsbibliothek Augsburg (Germany) *Tel:* (0821) 598 5320; (0821) 598 5306; (0821) 598 5305 *Fax:* (0821) 598 5354 *E-mail:* dir@bibliothek.uni-augsburg.de *Web Site:* www.bibliothek.uni-augsburg.de, pg 1511

Der Universitatsverlag Freiburg (Switzerland) *Tel:* (026) 426 43 11 *Fax:* (026) 426 43 00 *E-mail:* eduni@st-paul.ch *Web Site:* www.st-paul.ch/uni-press-FR, pg 636

Universitatsverlag Ulm GmbH (Germany) *Tel:* (0731) 15 28 60 *Fax:* (0731) 15 28 62 *E-mail:* info@uni-verlag-ulm.de *Web Site:* www.uni-verlag-ulm.de, pg 293

Presses de l'Universite du Benin (Togo) *Tel:* (228) 21 30 27 *Fax:* (228) 21 85 95 *E-mail:* cafmicro@ub.tg *Web Site:* www.ub.tg, pg 646

Editions de l'Universite de Bruxelles (Belgium) *Tel:* (02) 650 37 99 *Fax:* (02) 650 37 94 *E-mail:* editions@admin.ulb.ac.be *Web Site:* www.editions-universite-bruxelles.be, pg 74

Universite Catholique de Louvain (Belgium) *Tel:* (010) 47 21 11 *E-mail:* sceb@sceb.ucl.ac.be *Web Site:* www.ucl.ac.be, pg 1494

Universite Cheikh Anta Diop de Dakar, Bibliotheque Universitaire (Senegal) *Tel:* 825 02 79 *Fax:* 824 23 79 *Web Site:* www.bu.ucad.sn, pg 1542

Bibliotheque Centrale, Universite d'Alger (Algeria) *Tel:* (021) 63-71-01 *Fax:* (021) 63-76-29 *E-mail:* bu@univ-alger.dz *Web Site:* www.univ-alger.dz, pg 1489

Universite de Kisangani Bibliotheque Centrale (The Democratic Republic of the Congo) *Tel:* 215-2, pg 1499

Universite de la Reunion, Service Commun de la Documentation (Reunion) *Tel:* 93 83 83 *Fax:* 93 83 64 *Web Site:* www.univ-reunion.fr, pg 1539

Bibliotheque Centrale de l'Universite de Lubumbashi (The Democratic Republic of the Congo) *Tel:* (022) 22-5285 *E-mail:* unilu@unilu.net *Web Site:* www.unilu.net, pg 1499

Bibliotheque de l'Universite de Niamey (Niger) *Tel:* 74-12-73 *Fax:* 73-38-62, pg 1533

Universite de Ouagadougou (Burkina Faso) *Tel:* 30 70 64; 30 70 65 *Fax:* 30 72 42 *E-mail:* info@univ-ouaga.bf *Web Site:* www.univ-ouaga.bf, pg 1496

Universite de Toulouse-Mirail (France) *Tel:* (0561) 50 45 99 *Fax:* (0561) 50 35 20 *E-mail:* europe@univ-tlse2.fr *Web Site:* www.univ-tlse2.fr/scd.html, pg 1507

Universite de Yaounde, Bibliotheque (Cameroon) *Tel:* 222 1320 *Fax:* 222 1320 *E-mail:* rect.uyl@uycdc.uninet.cm *Web Site:* www.uninet.cm/biblio.html, pg 1497

Universite d'Oran, Bibliotheque (Algeria) *Tel:* (041) 41-69-39; (041) 41-66-44 *Fax:* (041) 41-60-21 *E-mail:* igmo@univ-oran.dz *Web Site:* www.univ-oran.dz, pg 1489

Bibliotheque de l'Universite du Benin (Togo) *Tel:* 21 30 27 *Fax:* 21 85 95 *E-mail:* cafmicro@ub.tg *Web Site:* www.ub.tg, pg 1550

Bibliotheque de l'Universite du Burundi (Burundi) *Tel:* (022) 2857, pg 1497

Librairie de l'Universite (France) *Tel:* (0476) 46 61 63 *Fax:* (0476) 46 14 59, pg 1310

Bibliotheque de l'Universite Nationale du Rwanda (Rwanda) *Tel:* 530330 *Fax:* 530210 *E-mail:* biblio@nur.ac.rw *Web Site:* www.lib.nur.ac.rw, pg 1541

Publications de l'Universite de Pau (France) *Tel:* (05) 59923347 *Fax:* (05) 59923275 *Web Site:* www.univ-pau.fr, pg 188

Bibliotheque de l'Universite Quaraouyine (Morocco), pg 1529

Universiteit Antwerpen Bibliotheek UFSIA (Belgium) *Tel:* (03) 2204996 *Fax:* (03) 2204437 *E-mail:* helpdesk@lib.ua.ac.be *Web Site:* lib.ua.ac.be, pg 1494

Bibliotheek van de Universiteit van Amsterdam (Netherlands) *Tel:* (020) 525 2301 *Fax:* (020) 525 2311 *E-mail:* secr-uba@uva.nl *Web Site:* www.uba.uva.nl, pg 1531

Universiteits-Bibliotheek, Universiteit van de Nederlandse Antillen (Netherlands Antilles) *Tel:* (09) 8684422 *Fax:* (09) 8685465 *E-mail:* bibliotheek@una.an *Web Site:* www.una.net, pg 1531

Universiteitsbibliotheek Leiden (Netherlands) *Tel:* (071) 527 2832 *Fax:* (071) 527 2836 *E-mail:* secretariaat@library.leidenuniv.nl; helpdesk@library.leidenuniv.nl *Web Site:* ub.leidenuniv.nl, pg 1531

Universiteitsbibliotheek Nijmegen (Netherlands) *Tel:* (024) 3612400 *Fax:* (024) 3615944 *E-mail:* info@ubn.kun.nl *Web Site:* www.kun.nl/ubn/, pg 1531

Universiteitsbibliotheek Utrecht (Netherlands) *Tel:* (030) 2536600; (030) 2536601; (030) 2537262 *Fax:* (030) 2538398 *E-mail:* info@library.nl; uitleen@library.uu.nl *Web Site:* www.library.uu.nl, pg 1531

Universitetsbiblioteket i Bergen (Norway) *Tel:* 55 58 25 32 *Fax:* 55 58 97 03 *E-mail:* adm@ub.uib.no *Web Site:* www.ub.uib.no, pg 1534

Universitetsbiblioteket i Oslo (Norway) *Tel:* (022) 85 50 50 *Fax:* (022) 85 90 50 *E-mail:* informasjon@uio.no *Web Site:* www.ub.uio.no, pg 1534

Universitetsbiblioteket i Trondheim (Norway) *Tel:* (073) 59 51 10 *Fax:* (073) 59 51 03 *E-mail:* ubit@ub.ntnu.no *Web Site:* www.ub.ntnu.no, pg 1534

Universitetsbogladen (Denmark) *Tel:* 3524 0444; 3532 6570 *Fax:* 3532 6571 *E-mail:* panum@unibog.dk *Web Site:* www.universitetsbogladen.dk, pg 1308

Universitetsforlaget (Norway) *Tel:* (022) 24147500 *Fax:* (022) 24147501 *E-mail:* post@universitetsforlaget.no *Web Site:* www.universitetsforlaget.no, pg 511

Universiti Putra Malaysia Library (UPM) (Malaysia) *Tel:* (03) 89468642 *Fax:* (03) 89483745 *E-mail:* lib@lib.upm.edu.my *Web Site:* www.lib.upm.edu.my, pg 1527

University Library, Universiti Sains Malaysia (Malaysia) *Tel:* (04) 6533888; (04) 6533700; (04) 6585518 *Fax:* (04) 6571526 *E-mail:* chieflib@notes.usm.my *Web Site:* www.lib.usm.my, pg 1527

Penerbit Universiti Teknologi Malaysia (Malaysia) *Tel:* (07) 521 8131; (07) 521 8180; (07) 521 8166 *Fax:* (07) 521 8174 *E-mail:* penerbit@utm.my *Web Site:* www.penerbit.utm.my, pg 459

Universities Administration Office (Myanmar), pg 476

Universities' Central Library (Myanmar) *Tel:* (01) 545 750 *Fax:* (01) 545 750 *E-mail:* ucl@mptmail.net.mm, pg 1530

University Book Shop (Auckland) Ltd (New Zealand) *Tel:* (09) 306 2700 *Fax:* (09) 306 2701 *E-mail:* campus@ubsbooks.co.nz *Web Site:* www.ubsbooks.co.nz, pg 1331

University Book Shop (Canterbury) Ltd (New Zealand) *Tel:* (03) 3667001 *Fax:* (03) 3642999 *E-mail:* info@canterbury.ac.nz *Web Site:* www.canterbury.ac.nz, pg 1331

University Book Shop Inc (Papua New Guinea) *Tel:* 326 7375 *Fax:* 326 0961, pg 1334

University Book Shop (Otago) Ltd (New Zealand) *Tel:* (03) 4776976 *Fax:* (03) 4776571 *E-mail:* ubs@unibooks.co.nz *Web Site:* www.unibooks.co.nz, pg 1331

University Booksellers Association of Nigeria (Nigeria) *Tel:* (052) 200250 (Ugbowo); (052) 200480 (Ekehuan) *Fax:* (052) 241156, pg 1280

University Bookshop (Ghana) *Tel:* (021) 500398 *Fax:* (021) 500398 *E-mail:* unibks@ug.gn.apc.org, pg 1272

University Bookshop (Ghana) *Tel:* (021) 500398 *Fax:* (021) 500774 *E-mail:* bookshop@ug.edu.gh *Web Site:* www.ghanaweb.com/GhanaHomePage/education/legon.html, pg 1312

University Bookshop (Ghana) *Tel:* (051) 60223 *Fax:* (051) 60137 *E-mail:* library@knust.edu.gh *Web Site:* www.knust.edu.gh, pg 1312

University Bookshop (Zambia) *Tel:* (01) 294690; (01) 290319 *Fax:* (01) 253952; (01) 294690, pg 1356

University Bookshop Ltd (Nigeria) *Tel:* (036) 230290, pg 1331

University Bookshop (Nigeria) Ltd (Nigeria) *Tel:* (02) 400550 (ext 1208); (02) 400550 (ext 1047); (02) 400614 (ext 1244); (02) 400614 (ext 1042), pg 1332

University Bookstore (Liberia) *Tel:* 224671, pg 1325

University Co-operative Bookshop Ltd (Australia) *Tel:* (02) 93259600 *Fax:* (02) 92123372 *E-mail:* webhelp@coop-bookshop.com.au *Web Site:* www.coop-bookshop.com.au, pg 1299

University College Cork, Boole Library (Ireland) *Tel:* (021) 4902794 *Fax:* (021) 4273428 *E-mail:* library@ucc.ie *Web Site:* booleweb.ucc.ie, pg 1519

University College Dublin Library (Ireland) *Tel:* (01) 716 7694 *Fax:* (01) 283 7667 *E-mail:* library@ucd.ie *Web Site:* www.ucd.ie/library, pg 1519

University Library (Afghanistan) *Tel:* 42594, pg 1489

University Library (Mauritius) *Tel:* 454 1041 (ext 1229) *Fax:* 454 0905 *E-mail:* int.libservice@uom.ac.mu *Web Site:* www.uom.ac.mu, pg 1528

University of Aberdeen (United Kingdom) *Tel:* (01224) 272580 *Fax:* (01224) 273956 *E-mail:* library@abdn.ac.uk *Web Site:* www.abdn.ac.uk/diss/library, pg 1554

University of Asmara Library (Eritrea) *Tel:* (01) 161926; (01) 162553 *Fax:* (01) 162236 *E-mail:* assefawa@uoa.edu.er *Web Site:* www.uoa.edu.er, pg 1504

University of Auckland Library (New Zealand) *Tel:* (09) 3737599 *Fax:* (09) 3737565 *E-mail:* library@auckland.ac.nz *Web Site:* www.library.auckland.ac.nz, pg 1532

Central Library of the University of Baghdad (Iraq) *Tel:* (01) 776 7819 *Fax:* (01) 776 3592, pg 1518

University of Bahrain Library (Bahrain) *Tel:* 17438808 *Fax:* 17449838 *E-mail:* library@admin.uob.bh *Web Site:* www.uob.edu.bh, pg 1492

University of Baluchistan Library (Pakistan) *Tel:* (081) 41770, pg 1535

Central Library of the University of Basrah (Iraq) *Tel:* (01) 8868520 *Fax:* (01) 8868520 *E-mail:* basrahyni@uruklink.net, pg 1518

The University of Birmingham (United Kingdom) *Tel:* (0121) 414 3344 *Fax:* (0121) 414 3971 *Web Site:* www.general.bham.ac.uk, pg 768

University of Botswana Library (Botswana) *Tel:* 355-0000; 355-2304 *Fax:* 395-6591 *Web Site:* www.ub.bw, pg 1495

University of Cairo Library (Egypt (Arab Republic of Egypt)) *Tel:* (02) 5729584 *Fax:* (02) 628884, pg 1503

University of Cape Coast Library (Ghana) *Tel:* (042) 60133 *Fax:* (042) 32485 *E-mail:* Ucclib@ucc.gn.apc.org, pg 1512

University of Cape Town Libraries (South Africa) *Tel:* (021) 650-3097 *Fax:* (021) 689-7568 *E-mail:* webco@uctlib.uct.ac.za *Web Site:* www.lib.uct.ac.za/, pg 1544

Library of the University of Crete (Greece) *Tel:* (02831) 077810 *Fax:* (02831) 077850 *Web Site:* www.libh.uoc.gr, pg 1513

University of Dar es Salaam Library (United Republic of Tanzania) *Tel:* (051) 43241 *Fax:* (051) 43241 *E-mail:* libdirec@udsm.ac.tz; director@libis.udsm.ac.tz *Web Site:* www.udsm.ac.tz/library, pg 1549

University of Dar Es Salaam Bookshop (United Republic of Tanzania) *Tel:* (022) 2410093; (022) 2410500 (ext 2568) *Fax:* (022) 2410137, pg 1345

University of Dschang Central Library (Cameroon) *Tel:* 451092 *Fax:* 451202; 252751, pg 1497

University of Durban-Westville Library (South Africa) *Tel:* (031) 204 4111; (031) 204 5058 *Fax:* (031) 204 4383; (031) 204 4474 *E-mail:* mmoodley@pixie.udw.ac.za, pg 569

University of Engineering & Technology Central Library (UET) (Pakistan) *Tel:* (042) 6829243 *Fax:* (042) 6822566 *E-mail:* central_library@yahoo.com *Web Site:* www.uet.edu.pk, pg 1535

University of Exeter Press (United Kingdom) *Tel:* (01392) 263066 *Fax:* (01392) 263064 *E-mail:* uep@ex.ac.uk *Web Site:* www.ex.ac.uk/uep, pg 768

University of Garyounis Library (Libyan Arab Jamahiriya) *Tel:* (061) 2220147 *Fax:* (061) 2229602 *E-mail:* info@garyounis.eu *Web Site:* www.garyounis.edu, pg 1525

University of Ghana Library (Ghana) *Tel:* (021) 502701 *Fax:* (021) 502701 *E-mail:* balme@ug.gn.apc.org *Web Site:* www.ug.edu.gh, pg 1512

University of Goroka (Papua New Guinea) *Tel:* 731 1700 *Fax:* 732 2620 *E-mail:* infouog@uoginfo.ac.pg *Web Site:* www.uog.ac.pg, pg 516

University of Haifa Library (Israel) *Tel:* (04) 257753 *Fax:* (04) 342104 *E-mail:* webmaster@lib.haifa.ac.il *Web Site:* lib.haifa.ac.il, pg 373

University of Haifa Library (Israel) *Tel:* (04) 8240289 *Fax:* (04) 8257753 *E-mail:* info@mail.uhaifa.org *Web Site:* lib.haifa.ac.il, pg 1520

University of Hertfordshire Press (United Kingdom) *Tel:* (01707) 284682 *Fax:* (01707) 284666 *E-mail:* uhpress@herts.ac.uk *Web Site:* www.herts.ac.uk/uhpress, pg 768

The University of Hong Kong, Department of Philosophy (Hong Kong) *Tel:* 28592797 *Fax:* 2559 8452 *E-mail:* fctmoore@hkuxa.hku.hk, pg 320

University of Hong Kong Libraries (Hong Kong) *Tel:* 2859 7000; 2859 2203 *Fax:* 2858 9420 *E-mail:* libadmin@hkucc.hku.hk *Web Site:* lib.hku.hk, pg 1514

University of Ibadan, Kenneth Dike Library (Nigeria) *Tel:* (02) 810 3118 *Fax:* (02) 810 3118 *E-mail:* library@kdl.ui.edu.ng, pg 1534

University of Isfahan Library (Islamic Republic of Iran) *Tel:* (0311) 684799; (0311) 792-2793 *Fax:* (0311) 275145, pg 1518

University of Jordan Bookshop (Jordan) *Tel:* (06) 843555 (ext 3339) *Fax:* (06) 836446 *E-mail:* admin@ju.edu.jo, pg 1323

University of Jordan Library (Jordan) *Tel:* 5355000 (ext 3135) *Fax:* 5355570 *E-mail:* library@ju.edu.jo *Web Site:* www.ju.edu.jo, pg 1522

University of Jos Library (Nigeria) *Tel:* (073) 610514; (073) 53724; (073) 44952 *Fax:* (073) 610514 *Web Site:* 128.255.135.155/libraries, pg 1534

University of Khartoum Bookshop (Sudan) *Tel:* (011) 80558, pg 1343

University of Khartoum Library (Sudan) *Web Site:* www.sudan.net/uk, pg 1546

University of KwaZulu-Natal Press (South Africa) *Tel:* (033) 260 5226; (033) 260 5225 *Fax:* (033) 260 5801 *E-mail:* books@ukzn.ac.za *Web Site:* www.ukznpress.co.za, pg 569

University of Lagos Bookshop (Nigeria) *Tel:* (01) 820279 *Fax:* (01) 822644, pg 1332

University of Lagos Library (Nigeria) *Tel:* (01) 41 361 *Fax:* (01) 822644 *Web Site:* www.unilag.edu/library/index.asp, pg 1534

University of Lagos Press (Nigeria) *Tel:* (01) 825048 *Fax:* (01) 825048, pg 507

University of Liberia Libraries (Liberia) *Tel:* 226 418 *Fax:* 227 033; 226 418 *Web Site:* www.hometown.aol.com/dcronteh/myhomepage/index.html, pg 1525

University of London (United Kingdom) *Tel:* (020) 7862 8000 *Fax:* (020) 7636 5874 *E-mail:* enquiries@lon.ac.uk *Web Site:* www.lon.ac.uk, pg 1354

University of London Careers Service (United Kingdom) *Tel:* (020) 7554 4500 *Fax:* (020) 7383 5876 *E-mail:* careers@lon.ac.uk *Web Site:* www.careers.lon.ac.uk, pg 768

University of London Library (United Kingdom) *Tel:* (020) 7862 8500 *Fax:* (020) 7862 8480 *E-mail:* enquiries@ull.ac.uk *Web Site:* www.ull.ac.uk, pg 1554

University of Malawi Libraries (Malawi) *Tel:* (01) 526 622; (01) 525 760 *E-mail:* university.office@unima.mw *Web Site:* www.unima.mw, pg 1526

University of Malawi, Polytechnic Library (Malawi) *Tel:* 670411 *Fax:* 670578 *Web Site:* www.poly.ac.mw, pg 1526

University of Malaya Co-operative Bookshop Ltd (Malaysia) *Tel:* (03) 756 5000; (03) 756 5425 *Fax:* (03) 755 4424, pg 1326

University of Malaya, Department of Publications (Malaysia) *Tel:* (03) 79574361 *Fax:* (03) 79574473 *E-mail:* terbit@um.edu.my *Web Site:* www.um.edu.my/umpress, pg 459

University of Malta Library (Malta) *Tel:* 3290 2316 *Fax:* 314 306 *Web Site:* www.lib.um.edu.mt, pg 1528

The University of Malta Publications Section (Malta) *Tel:* 21333903-6 *Fax:* 21336450 *Web Site:* www.um.edu.mt, pg 460

University of Malysia Library (Malaysia) *Tel:* (03) 7956 7800 *Fax:* (03) 7957 3661 *E-mail:* query.perpustakaan@um.edu.my *Web Site:* www.umlib.um.edu.my, pg 1527

University of Manila Central Library (Philippines) *Tel:* (02) 7355256 *Fax:* (02) 7355089 *E-mail:* um@univman.edu.ph *Web Site:* www.univman.edu.ph, pg 1537

University of Melbourne Baillieu Library (Australia) *Tel:* (03) 8344 5378 *Fax:* (03) 9348 1142 *Web Site:* www.lib.unimelb.edu.au/, pg 1491

Central Library of the University of Mosul (Iraq) *Tel:* (060) 810162 *Fax:* (060) 8011; (060) 8015, pg 1518

University of Mumbai Library (India) *Tel:* (022) 2652819 *Fax:* (022) 2652832 *Web Site:* www.mu.ac.in, pg 1516

The University of Nagoya Press (Japan) *Tel:* (052) 789-3678; (052) 789-3683 (interlibrary loan); (052) 789-3680 (reference) *Fax:* (052) 789-3694 *E-mail:* info@unp.nagoya-u.ac.jp *Web Site:* www.nul.nagoya-u.ac.jp, pg 430

University of Nairobi Bookshop (Kenya) *Tel:* (02) 334244 *Fax:* (02) 336885 *E-mail:* webmaster@uonbi.ac.ke *Web Site:* www.uonbi.ac.ke, pg 1324

University of Nairobi Libraries (Kenya) *Tel:* (02) 334244 *Fax:* (02) 336885 *E-mail:* jkml@uonbi.ac.ke *Web Site:* www.uonbi.ac.ke/jkml, pg 1523

University of New South Wales Library (Australia) *Tel:* (02) 9385 1000 *Web Site:* www.info.library.unsw.edu.au, pg 1491

University of New South Wales Press Ltd (Australia) *Tel:* (02) 9664 0900 *Fax:* (02) 9664 5420 *E-mail:* info.press@unsw.edu.au *Web Site:* www.unswpress.com.au, pg 44

University of Newcastle (Australia) *Tel:* (02) 4921 5000 *Web Site:* www.newcastle.edu.au, pg 45

University of Newcastle Upon Tyne (United Kingdom) *Tel:* (0191) 222 6000 *Fax:* (0191) 222 6229 *Web Site:* www.ncl.ac.uk, pg 768

University of Nigeria (Nigeria) *Tel:* (042) 771444 *Fax:* (042) 770644; (042) 771500 *E-mail:* unnlibrary@yahoo.com *Web Site:* www.unn-edu.net, pg 1534

University of Nigeria Bookshop Ltd (Nigeria) *Tel:* (042) 332077; (042) 771911, pg 1332

University of Otago Library (New Zealand) *Tel:* (03) 479 8916 *Fax:* (03) 479 8947 *E-mail:* library@otago.ac.nz; reference.central@library.otago.ac.nz *Web Site:* www.library.otago.ac.nz, pg 1532

University of Otago Press (New Zealand) *Tel:* (03) 479 8807 *Fax:* (03) 479 8385 *E-mail:* university.press@otago.ac.nz *Web Site:* www.otago.ac.nz, pg 502

University of Papua New Guinea Press (Papua New Guinea) *Tel:* 3267654 *Fax:* 3260127, pg 516

University of Peradeniya Library (Sri Lanka) *Tel:* (08) 388678 *Fax:* (08) 388678 *E-mail:* lib@mail.pdn.ac.lk *Web Site:* www.pdn.ac.lk/library/main, pg 1546

University of the Philippines Press (Philippines) *Tel:* (02) 9205301; (02) 9205302; (02) 9205303; (02) 9205304; (02) 9205305; (02) 9266642; (02) 9253243; (02) 9253244 *Fax:* (02) 9282558 *E-mail:* press@nicole.upd.edu.ph; uppress@uppress.org *Web Site:* www.upd.edu.ph, pg 521

University of Port Elizabeth Library (South Africa) *Fax:* (041) 504 2280 *E-mail:* library@upe.ac.za *Web Site:* www.upe.ac.za/library, pg 1544

University of Pretoria Academic Information Services (South Africa) *Tel:* (012) 420 2241 *Fax:* (012) 362 5100 *Web Site:* www.ais.up.ac.za, pg 1544

University of Puerto Rico, General Library, Mayaguez Campus (Puerto Rico) *Tel:* (787) 265-3810; (787) 832-4040 (ext 3810, 2151, 2155) *Fax:* (787) 265-5483 *E-mail:* library@rumlib.uprm.edu *Web Site:* www.uprm.edu/library, pg 1539

University of Puerto Rico, Library System, Rio Piedras Campus (Puerto Rico) *Tel:* (787) 764-0000 (ext 3311); (787) 764-0000 (ext 5085); (787) 764-0000 (ext 5089) *Fax:* (787) 772-1479 *Web Site:* biblioteca.uprrp.edu, pg 1539

University of Puerto Rico, Medical Sciences Campus Library (Puerto Rico) *Tel:* (787) 758-2525; (787) 751-8199 *Fax:* (787) 759-6713 *E-mail:* zgarcia@rcm.upr.edu *Web Site:* rcm-library.rcm.upr.edu, pg 1539

University of Puerto Rico Press (EDUPR) (Puerto Rico) *Tel:* (787) 758-6932; (787) 758-8345 (sales) *Fax:* (787) 753-9116, pg 537

University of Queensland Library (Australia) *Tel:* (07) 3365 6949 *Fax:* (07) 3365 1737 *E-mail:* universitylibrarian@library.uq.edu.au *Web Site:* www.library.uq.edu.au, pg 1491

University of Queensland Press (Australia) *Tel:* (07) 3365 2127; (07) 3377 7244; (07) 3365 2440 (sales) *Fax:* (07) 3365 7579 *E-mail:* uqp@uqp.uq.edu.au *Web Site:* www.uqp.uq.edu.au, pg 45

University of Rajshahi Library (Bangladesh) *Tel:* (0721) 750041; (0721) 750033 *Fax:* (0721) 750064 *E-mail:* rajcc@citechco.net *Web Site:* www.ugc.org/rajsahai_uni.htm, pg 1493

Central Library of the University of Salahaddin (Iraq) *Tel:* 00873762566859 *Fax:* 00873762566861 *Web Site:* www.salun.org, pg 1518

University of San Carlos Library System (Philippines) *Tel:* (032) 254 0432 *Fax:* (032) 254 0432 *E-mail:* direklib@usc.edu.ph *Web Site:* www.usc.edu.ph, pg 1537

University of Santo Tomas Library (Philippines) *Tel:* (02) 731-3101 *Fax:* (02) 740-9709 *E-mail:* library@ust.edu.ph *Web Site:* www.ust.edu.ph, pg 1537

University of South Africa Library (South Africa) *Tel:* (012) 4293131 *Fax:* (012) 4292925 *E-mail:* willej@alpha.unisa.ac.za, pg 1544

University of South Australia Library (Australia) *Tel:* (08) 8302 6661 *Fax:* (08) 8302 6250 *Web Site:* www.library.unisa.edu.au, pg 1491

University of Southampton (United Kingdom) *Tel:* (01703) 22180 *Fax:* (01703) 23007 *E-mail:* libenqs@soton.ac.uk *Web Site:* www.library.soton.ac.uk, pg 1554

University of Stellenbosch Library (South Africa) *Tel:* (021) 808 4385 *Fax:* (021) 808 4336 *Web Site:* www.sun.ac.za/library, pg 1544

University of Swaziland Library (Swaziland) *Tel:* (051) 84011; (051) 85108 *Fax:* (051) 85276 *E-mail:* kwaluseni@uniswa.sz *Web Site:* library.uniswa.sz, pg 1547

University of Sydney Library (Australia) *Tel:* (02) 9351 2990 *Fax:* (02) 9351 2890 *Web Site:* www.library.usyd.edu.au, pg 1491

University of Tabriz Central Library (Islamic Republic of Iran) *Tel:* (0411) 3342199 *Fax:* (0411) 3355993 *Web Site:* www.tabrizu.ac.ir/centrallibrary/lib-general.htm, pg 1518

University of Technology, Jamaica (Jamaica) *Tel:* (876) 927-1680-9 *Fax:* (876) 927-1614 *E-mail:* library@utech.edu.jm *Web Site:* www.utechjamaica.edu.jm, pg 1521

University of Technology, Sydney Library (Australia) *Tel:* 9514 2000 *E-mail:* info@uts.edu.au *Web Site:* www.uts.edu.au, pg 1491

Central Library & Documentation Centre of University of Teheran (Islamic Republic of Iran) *Tel:* (021) 6462699; (021) 6419831; (021) 6405047 *Fax:* (021) 6409348 *E-mail:* publicrel@ut.ac.ir *Web Site:* pages.ut.ac.ir/library/home.htm, pg 1518

University of Tehran Publications & Printing Organization (Islamic Republic of Iran) *Tel:* (021) 6462699; (021) 6419831; (021) 6405047 *Fax:* (021) 6409348 *Web Site:* www.ut.ac.ir, pg 357

University of the East Library (Philippines) *Tel:* (02) 7358544 *Fax:* (02) 7356976 *E-mail:* webmaster@uec.edu.ph *Web Site:* www.ue.edu.ph, pg 1537

University of the Philippines Diliman University Library (Philippines) *Tel:* (02) 920-5301 *Fax:* (02) 926-1876 *Web Site:* www.mainlib.upd.edu.ph, pg 1537

University of the South Pacific Library (Fiji) *Tel:* 3313 900 *Fax:* 3300 830 *E-mail:* library@usp.ac.fj *Web Site:* www.usp.ac.fj/library, pg 1505

University of the West Indies Library (Jamaica) (Jamaica) *Tel:* (876) 935-8294; (876) 935-8295; (876) 935-8296 *Fax:* (876) 927-1926 *E-mail:* manlibry@uwimona.edu.jm *Web Site:* www.library.uwimona.edu.jm:1104, pg 1521

University of the West Indies (Trinidad & Tobago) (Trinidad & Tobago) *Tel:* (868) 662 2002; (868) 662 3232 (ext 2132) *Fax:* 6639684 *E-mail:* infocentre@library.uwi.tt *Web Site:* www.uwi.tt, pg 647

University of the West Indies Library (Barbados) (Barbados) *Tel:* (0246) 425-1310 *Fax:* (0246) 425-1327 *E-mail:* webmaster@uwichill.edu.bb *Web Site:* www.cavehill.uwi.edu, pg 1493

University of the West Indies Library (Trinidad & Tobago) (Trinidad & Tobago) *Tel:* (0868) 662 2002 (ext 2132) *Fax:* (0868) 662-9238 *E-mail:* mainlib@library.uwi.tt *Web Site:* www.mainlib.uwi.tt, pg 1550

University of the West Indies Press (Jamaica) *Tel:* (876) 977-2659 *Fax:* (876) 977-2660 *E-mail:* cuserv@cwjamaica.com (customer service & orders); uwipress_marketing@cwjamaica.com *Web Site:* www.uwipress.com, pg 414

University of the West Indies Publishers' Association (Jamaica) *Tel:* (876) 977-2659 *Fax:* (876) 977-2660, pg 1274

University of the Western Cape Library (South Africa) *Tel:* (021) 959 2947 *Fax:* (021) 959 2659 *Web Site:* www.uwc.ac.za/library, pg 1545

University of the Witwaterstrand Library (South Africa) *Tel:* (011) 716-2400 *Fax:* (011) 403-1421 *E-mail:* 056heath@libris.wwl.wits.ac.za, pg 1545

Library of the University of Thessaloniki (Greece) *Tel:* (031) 995325; (031) 995327 *Fax:* (031) 995322 *E-mail:* syra@ipatia.ccf.auth.gr *Web Site:* www.lib.auth.gr, pg 1513

University of Tokyo Library (Japan) *Tel:* (03) 5841 2612 *Fax:* (03) 3816 4208 *E-mail:* kikaku@lib.u-tokyo.ac.jp *Web Site:* www.lib.u-tokyo.ac.jp, pg 1522

University of Tokyo Press (Japan) *Tel:* (03) 3815-7789 *Fax:* (03) 3812-6958 *Web Site:* www.u-tokyo.ac.jp, pg 430

University of Toronto Press Inc (Canada) *Tel:* 416-667-7767 *Fax:* 416-667-7803 *E-mail:* printing@utpress.utoronto.ca *Web Site:* www.utpress.utoronto.ca, pg 1154, 1176, 1216, 1235

University of Wales Press (United Kingdom) *Tel:* (029) 2049-6899 *Fax:* (029) 2049-6108 *E-mail:* press@press.wales.ac.uk *Web Site:* www.wales.ac.uk/press, pg 769

University of Western Australia Library (Australia) *Tel:* (08) 9380 1777 *Fax:* (08) 9380 1012 *E-mail:* uwalibrary@library.uwa.edu.au *Web Site:* www.library.uwa.edu.au/, pg 1491

University of Western Australia Press (Australia) *Tel:* (08) 9380 3670 *Fax:* (08) 9380 1027 *E-mail:* uwap@cyllene.uwa.edu.au *Web Site:* www.uwapress.uwa.edu.au, pg 45

University of Zambia Press (UNZA Press) (Zambia) *Tel:* (01) 213221; (01) 293058; (01) 292884; (01) 293580; (01) 219624; (01) 252514 *Fax:* (01) 253952, pg 782

University of Zambia Press (UNZA Press) (Zambia) *Tel:* (01) 290740; (01) 290409 *Fax:* (01) 253952, pg 1556

University of Zimbabwe Library (Zimbabwe) *Tel:* (04) 303211 *Fax:* (04) 335383 *E-mail:* mainlib@uzlib.uz.zw; infocentre@uzlib.uz.ac.zw *Web Site:* www.uz.ac.zw/library, pg 784

University of Zimbabwe Library (Zimbabwe) *Tel:* (04) 303211 *Fax:* (04) 335383 *E-mail:* mainlib@uzlib.uz.zw *Web Site:* uzweb.uz.ac.zw/library, pg 1556

University of Zimbabwe Publications (Zimbabwe) *Tel:* (04) 303211 (ext 1236 or 1662) *Fax:* (04) 333407 *E-mail:* uzpub@admin.uz.ac.zn *Web Site:* www.uz.ac.zw/publications/, pg 784

The University Press Ltd (Bangladesh) *Tel:* (02) 861208; (02) 255789 *Fax:* (02) 8332112 *E-mail:* upl@bangla.net; upl@bttb.net.bd, pg 61

University Presses of California, Columbia & Princeton Ltd (United Kingdom) *Tel:* (01243) 843291 *Fax:* (01243) 820250 *E-mail:* lois@upccp.demon.co.uk *Web Site:* www.ucpress.edu, pg 769

University Publishing Co (Nigeria) *Tel:* (046) 230013, pg 507

University Publishing Projects Ltd (Israel) *Tel:* (09) 745-9955 *Fax:* (09) 745-9977 *E-mail:* upp@upp.co.il *Web Site:* www.upp.co.il, pg 373

Editorial Universo SA (Peru) *Tel:* (014) 241639; (014) 233190, pg 517

Universo Editorial SA de CV Edicion de Libros Revistas y Periodicos (Mexico) *Tel:* (048) 21593, pg 473

Editorial Universo SA de CV (Mexico) *Tel:* (05) 5750711 ext 30; (05) 5750711 ext 31, pg 473

Librairie Universssitaire de la Reunion (Reunion) *Tel:* 210758, pg 1338

Univerza Ljubljana (Slovenia) *Tel:* (01) 241 85 00 *Fax:* (01) 241 86 60 *Web Site:* www.uni-lj.si, pg 1543

Univerza v Ljubljani Ekonomska Fakulteta (Slovenia) *Tel:* (061) 5892-400 *Fax:* (061) 5892-698 *E-mail:* joze.cibej@uni-lj.si *Web Site:* www.ef.uni-lj.si, pg 562

Univerzitet u Beogradu biblioteka 'Svetozar Markovic' (Serbia and Montenegro) *Tel:* (011) 3370-509 *Fax:* (011) 3370-354 *Web Site:* ns.unilib.bg.ac.yu, pg 1542

Biblioteka Uniwersytecka w Warszawie (Poland) *Tel:* (022) 5525660; (022) 5525181 *Fax:* (022) 5525181 *E-mail:* buw@uw.edu.pl *Web Site:* www.buw.uw.edu.pl, pg 1538

Biblioteka Uniwersytecka we Wroclawiu (Poland) *Tel:* (071) 3463120 *Fax:* (071) 3463166 *E-mail:* infnauk@bu.uni.wroc.pl *Web Site:* www.bu.uni.wroc.pl, pg 1538

Uniwersytet Gdanski (Poland) *Tel:* (058) 5509413 *Fax:* (058) 5515221 *E-mail:* bib@bg.univ.gda.pl; info@bg.univ.gda.pl *Web Site:* www.bg.univ.gda.pl/library/, pg 1538

Biblioteka Uniwersytecka w Torruniu (Poland) *Tel:* (056) 61 14 408 *Fax:* (056) 652 04 19 *E-mail:* sekrretariat@bu.uni.torun.pl *Web Site:* www.bu.uni.torun.pl/en, pg 1538

WYDAWNICTWA UNIWERSYTETU WARSZAWSKIEGO

Wydawnictwa Uniwersytetu Warszawskiego (Poland) *Tel:* (022) 5531318 *Fax:* (022) 5531318 *E-mail:* wuw@uw.edu.pl, pg 527

Wydawnictwo Uniwersytetu Wroclawskiego SP ZOO (Poland) *Tel:* (071) 3752809 *Fax:* (071) 3752735 *E-mail:* marketing@wuwr.com.pl *Web Site:* www.wuwr.com.pl, pg 527

UNO-Verlag GmbH (Germany) *Tel:* (0228) 94 90 2-0 *Fax:* (0228) 94 90 2-22 *E-mail:* info@uno-verlag.de *Web Site:* www.uno-verlag.de, pg 293

Unrast Verlag e V (Germany) *Tel:* (0251) 666293 *Fax:* (0251) 666120 *E-mail:* kontakt@unrast-verlag.de *Web Site:* www.unrast-verlag.de, pg 293

Editrice Uomini Nuovi (Italy) *Tel:* (0332) 723007 *Fax:* (0332) 723264 *E-mail:* libreria@eun.ch; eunitaly@eun.ch *Web Site:* www.eun.ch, pg 411

Uplands Books (United Kingdom) *Tel:* (01424) 422306 *Fax:* (01424) 719879 *E-mail:* sales@uplands-books.com, pg 769

UPM-Kymmene Ltd (Finland) *Tel:* 358 204 15111 *Fax:* 358 204 150500 *E-mail:* info@upm-kymmene.com *Web Site:* www.upm-kymmene.com, pg 1154

Upper Kabete Library (Kenya) *Tel:* (02) 334244 *Fax:* (02) 336885 *Web Site:* www.uonbi.ac.ke/jkml, pg 1523

Upplysing - Felag bokasafns- og upplysingafraeoa (Iceland) *Tel:* 553-7290; 862-8627 *Fax:* 588-9239 *E-mail:* upplysing@bokis.is *Web Site:* www.bokis.is, pg 1564

Uppsala Universitetsbibliotek (Sweden) *Tel:* (018) 471 39 00 *Web Site:* www.ub.uu.se, pg 1547

UPS Translations (United Kingdom) *Tel:* (020) 7837 8300 *Fax:* (020) 7486 3272 *E-mail:* production@upstranslations.com *Web Site:* www.upstranslations.com, pg 1152

Izdatelstvo Ural' skogo (Russian Federation) *Tel:* (03432) 515448 *Fax:* (03432) 51-54-48 *E-mail:* info@idc.e-burg-ru, pg 549

Urania Verlag mit Ravensburger Ratgebern (Germany) *Tel:* (030) 28447-112; (030) 28447-113 *Fax:* (030) 28447-123 *E-mail:* urania.ravensburger@dornier-verlage.de *Web Site:* www.urania-ravensburger.de, pg 294

Uranium Verlag Zug (Switzerland) *Tel:* (042) 217744, pg 636

Ediciones Urano, SA (Spain) *Tel:* (093) 2375 564 *Fax:* (093) 4153 796 *E-mail:* atencion@edicionesurano.com *Web Site:* www.edicionesurano.com, pg 604

Urban und Schwarzenberg GmbH (Austria) *Tel:* (01) 4052731 *Fax:* (01) 405272441, pg 59, 1301

Urban & Vogel Medien und Medizin Verlagsgesellschaft mbH & Co KG (Germany) *Tel:* (089) 4372-0 *Fax:* (089) 4372-2633 *E-mail:* verlag@urban-vogel.de *Web Site:* www.urban-vogel.de, pg 294

Urbaniana University Press (Italy) *Tel:* (06) 6988 2182 *Fax:* (06) 6988 2182 *E-mail:* uupamm@urbaniana.edu *Web Site:* www.urbaniana.edu/uup, pg 411

Urdu Academy Sind (Pakistan) *Tel:* (021) 2631485, pg 514

Urdu Science Board (Pakistan) *Tel:* (042) 5758674; (042) 878168 *Fax:* (042) 5758674, pg 1281

Urim Publications (Israel) *Tel:* (02) 679-7633 *Fax:* (02) 679-7634 *E-mail:* publisher@urimpublications.com *Web Site:* www.urimpublications.com, pg 373

Urmo SA de Ediciones (Spain) *Tel:* (094) 424 53 07 *Fax:* (094) 423 19 84 *E-mail:* urmo@infonegocio.com *Web Site:* www.urmo.com, pg 604

Urozaj (Ukraine) *Tel:* (044) 2440517, pg 654

La Urpila Editores (Uruguay) *Tel:* (02) 9085347, pg 778

Ursa ry (Finland) *Tel:* (09) 684 0400 *Fax:* (09) 6840 4040 *E-mail:* ursa@ursa.fi *Web Site:* www.ursa.fi, pg 144

Editia Uruguay (Uruguay) *Tel:* (02) 915-9633; (02) 915-9759 *Fax:* (02) 916-4419 *E-mail:* edita@adinet.com.uy *Web Site:* www.editia.com, pg 778

Usaha Baru CV (Indonesia) *Tel:* (031) 22128, pg 357

Usborne Publishing Ltd (United Kingdom) *Tel:* (020) 7430 2800 *Fax:* (020) 7430 1562; (020) 7242 0974 *E-mail:* mail@usborne.co.uk *Web Site:* www.usborne.com, pg 769

The Useful Publishing Co (Australia) *Tel:* (08) 9370 4577 *Fax:* (08) 9370 2540, pg 45

UST Publishing House (Philippines) *Tel:* (02) 7313101 *Fax:* (02) 7811473 *E-mail:* qui_test@ust.edu.ph *Web Site:* www.ust.edu.ph, pg 521

Ustav informacii a prognoz skolstva mladeze a telovychovy (Slovakia) *Tel:* (02) 6542 6521 *Fax:* (02) 6542 6521 *E-mail:* hrab@uip.sanet.sk, pg 561

Ustredna kniznica Slovenskej akademie vied (Slovakia) *Tel:* (02) 52926 321; (02) 52926 325 *Fax:* (02) 52921 733 *E-mail:* knizhorv@klemens.savba.sk *Web Site:* www.uk.sav.sk/, pg 1543

Usus Editora (Portugal) *Tel:* (021) 4535000 *Fax:* (021) 4426482, pg 536

UT Orpheus Edizioni Srl (Italy) *Tel:* (051) 226468 *Fax:* (051) 263720 *E-mail:* mail@utorpheus.com *Web Site:* www.utorpheus.com, pg 411

UTAS-Verlag fur Moderne Lernmethoden Uta Stechl (Germany) *Tel:* (08633) 1450 *Fax:* (08633) 7805, pg 294

UTB fuer Wissenschaft Uni Taschenbuecher GmbH (Germany) *Tel:* (0711) 7 82 95 55-0 *Fax:* (0711) 7 80 13 76 *E-mail:* utb@utb-stuttgart.de *Web Site:* www.utb.de, pg 294

UTET Periodici Scientifici (Italy) *Tel:* (02) 6241171 *Fax:* (02) 62411720 *E-mail:* utet@utet.it *Web Site:* www.utetperiodici.it, pg 411

UTET (Unione Tipografico-Editrice Torinese) (Italy) *Tel:* (011) 2099111 *Fax:* (011) 2099394 *E-mail:* utet@utet.it *Web Site:* www.utet.it, pg 411

Utusan Publications & Distributors Sdn Bhd (Malaysia) *Tel:* (03) 9287 7777 *Fax:* (03) 9282 7751 *E-mail:* shafina@utusan.com.my *Web Site:* www.utusangroup.com.my, pg 459

Uudet Kirjat (Finland) *Tel:* (09) 6168 3370 *E-mail:* uudetkirjat@wsoy.fi *Web Site:* www.uudetkirjat.fi, pg 1252

UVK Universitatsverlag Konstanz GmbH (Germany) *Tel:* (07531) 90530 *Fax:* (07531) 905398 *E-mail:* willkommen@uvk.de *Web Site:* www.uvk.de, pg 294

UVK Verlagsgesellschaft mbH (Germany) *Tel:* (07531) 90530 *Fax:* (07531) 905398 *E-mail:* willkommen@uvk.de *Web Site:* www.uvk.de, pg 294

UWI Publishers' Association (Jamaica) *Tel:* 876-927-1660; 876-927-1669 *Fax:* 876-977-2660 *E-mail:* helpdesk@uwimona.edu.jm, pg 414

Izdatelstvo Uzbekistan (Uzbekistan) *Tel:* (0371) 443810, pg 778

Uzima Press Ltd (Kenya) *Tel:* (020) 21239 *E-mail:* uzima@nbnet.co.ke, pg 436

V S P International Science Publishers (Netherlands) *Tel:* (030) 692 5790 *Fax:* (030) 693 2081 *E-mail:* vsppub@brill.nl *Web Site:* www.vsppub.com, pg 491

Edition Va Bene (Austria) *Tel:* (02243) 22 159; (0664) 1616356 (mobile) *Fax:* (02243) 22 159 *E-mail:* edition@vabene.at *Web Site:* www.vabene.at, pg 59

Vacation Work Publications (United Kingdom) *Tel:* (01865) 241978 *Fax:* (01865) 790885 *E-mail:* info@vacationwork.co.uk *Web Site:* www.vacationwork.co.uk, pg 769

Vaccari SRL (Italy) *Tel:* (059) 764106; (059) 771251 *Fax:* (059) 760157 *E-mail:* info@vaccari.it *Web Site:* www.vaccari.it, pg 411

Vacher Dod Publishing Ltd (United Kingdom) *Tel:* (020) 7828 7256 *Fax:* (020) 7828 7269 *E-mail:* politics@vacherdod.co.uk *Web Site:* www.vacherdod.co.uk, pg 769

Vaco NV Uitgeversmij (Suriname) *Tel:* (0597) 472545 *Fax:* (0597) 10563 *E-mail:* interf@sr.net, pg 608

Vadell Hermanos Editores CA (Venezuela) *Tel:* (02) 5723108; (02) 5778110 *Fax:* (02) 5725243 *Web Site:* www.vadellhermanos.com/, pg 780

Vaga Ltd (Lithuania) *Tel:* (02) 49 81 21 *Fax:* (02) 49 81 22 *E-mail:* info@vaga.lt *Web Site:* www.vaga.lt, pg 450

La Vague a l'ame (France) *Tel:* (04) 76470784, pg 188

Editions Vague Verte (France) *Tel:* (03) 22 30 72 50 *Fax:* (03) 22 26 58 73 *E-mail:* edlavagueverte@wanadoo.fr *Web Site:* perso.wanadoo.fr/editionslavagueverte, pg 188

Vaidelote, SIA (Latvia) *Tel:* 937943; 9552391 *Fax:* 7570828, pg 445

Imprimeur - Editeur Vaillant-Carmanne SA (Belgium) *Tel:* (011) 612452 *Fax:* (011) 612451, pg 74

Les Editions Vaillant-Miroir-Sprint Publications (France) *Tel:* (01) 42819103, pg 188

Vaka-Helgafell (Iceland) *Tel:* 522 2000 *Fax:* 522 2022 *E-mail:* vaka@edda.is *Web Site:* www.vaka.is, pg 326

Vaka-Helgafell (Iceland) *Tel:* 522 2000 *Fax:* 522 2022 *E-mail:* vaka@edda.is *Web Site:* vaka.is, pg 1315

Vakils Feffer & Simons Ltd (India) *Tel:* (022) 2611221; (022) 2619121 *Fax:* (022) 2614924; (022) 2610432, pg 352

Editura Valahia SRL (Romania) *Tel:* (097) 680948, pg 543

Valdonega SRL (Italy) *Tel:* (045) 6020444 *Fax:* (045) 6020334 *E-mail:* valdonega@valdonega.it, pg 411

Valdonega SRL (Italy) *Tel:* (045) 6020444 *Fax:* (045) 6020334 *E-mail:* valdonega@valdonega.it *Web Site:* www.valdonega.it, pg 1159

Carlos Valencia Editores (Colombia) *Tel:* (01) 2839040; (01) 3426224 *Fax:* (01) 2839235 *E-mail:* ancoraed@elancoraeditores.com, pg 113

Valeton b v (Netherlands) *Tel:* (020) 6201454 *Fax:* (020) 6279209, pg 1329

Valgus Publishers (Estonia) *Tel:* 650 5025; (050) 59 958 *Fax:* 650 5104 *E-mail:* info@kirjastusvalgus.ee, pg 140

Vallardi & Assoc (Italy) *Tel:* (02) 6555545 *Fax:* (02) 6555640, pg 411

Vallardi Industrie Grafiche (Italy) *Tel:* (02) 9370284 *Fax:* (02) 93570442, pg 411

Vallentine, Mitchell & Co Ltd (United Kingdom) *Tel:* (020) 8952 9526 *Fax:* (020) 8952 9242 *E-mail:* info@vmbooks.com *Web Site:* www.vmbooks.com, pg 769

Valmartina Editore SRL (Italy) *Tel:* (011) 2098741; (011) 2098720 *Fax:* (011) 2098765 *E-mail:* redazione@valmartina.it *Web Site:* www.valmartina.it, pg 411

Van Buuren Uitgeverij BV (Netherlands) *Tel:* (023) 5325440 *Fax:* (023) 5327017, pg 491

Van Dale Lexicografie BV (Netherlands) *Tel:* (031) 232 47 11 *Fax:* (031) 231 68 50 *E-mail:* info@vandale.nl *Web Site:* www.vandale.nl, pg 491

Editions Van de Velde (France) *Tel:* (02) 47 49 43 43 *Fax:* (02) 47 49 43 49, pg 188

Marc Van de Wiele bvba (Belgium) *Tel:* (050) 333805 *Fax:* (050) 346457, pg 74

YELLOW PAGES

Dorothea van der Koelen (Germany) *Tel:* (06131) 346 64 *Fax:* (06131) 36 90 76 *E-mail:* dvanderkoelen@xterna-net.de, pg 294

Frank P van Eck Publishers (Liechtenstein) *Tel:* (075) 3923000 *Fax:* (075) 3922277 *E-mail:* vaneck@datacomm.ch, pg 448

Van Gorcum & Comp BV (Netherlands) *Tel:* (0592) 37 95 55 *Fax:* (0592) 37 20 64 *E-mail:* assen@vgorcum.nl *Web Site:* www.vangorcum.nl, pg 491

Kelvin van Hasselt Publishing Services (United Kingdom) *Tel:* (01263) 862724 *Fax:* (01263) 862803 *E-mail:* kvhbooks@aol.com, pg 1144

Van Lear Ltd (United Kingdom) *Tel:* (020) 7385 1199 *Fax:* (020) 7385 6262 *E-mail:* evl@vanlear.co.uk, pg 1144

The Van Leer Jerusalem Institute (Israel) *Tel:* (02) 5605222 *Fax:* (02) 5619293 *E-mail:* values@vanleer.org.il *Web Site:* www.vanleer.org.il, pg 373

Van Molle Publishing (United Kingdom) *Tel:* (01239) 851482 *Fax:* (01239) 851482, pg 769

Uitgeverij G A van Oorschot bv (Netherlands) *Tel:* (020) 623 14 84 *Fax:* (020) 625 40 83 *E-mail:* verkoop@vanoorschot.nl, pg 491

Van Schaik Bookstore University Bookshop (South Africa) *Tel:* (021) 918 85 00 *Fax:* (021) 951 14 70 *E-mail:* vsblv@vanschaik.com; vsblv@vanschaiknet.com *Web Site:* www.vsonline.co.za; www.vanschaik.com, pg 1341

Van Schaik Publishers (South Africa) *Tel:* (012) 342-2765 *Fax:* (012) 430-3563 *E-mail:* vanschaik@vanschaiknet.com *Web Site:* www.vanschaiknet.com, pg 569

Uitgeverij Van Walraven BV (Netherlands) *Tel:* (035) 5482421 *Fax:* (035) 5421672, pg 491

Uitgeverij Van Wijnen (Netherlands) *Tel:* (0517) 394588 *Fax:* (0517) 397179 *E-mail:* info@uitgeverijvanwijnen.nl *Web Site:* www.uitgeverijvanwijnen.nl, pg 491

Vandenhoeck & Ruprecht (Germany) *Tel:* (0551) 5084-40 *Fax:* (0551) 5084-422 *E-mail:* info@v-r.de *Web Site:* www.v-r.de, pg 294

Vander Editions, SA (Belgium) *Tel:* (02) 7629804 *Fax:* (02) 7620662, pg 74

Vandrer mod Lysets Forlag Aps (Denmark) *Tel:* 3315 7815 *Fax:* 3315 8030 *Web Site:* www.vandrer-mod-lyset.dk, pg 135

Vanguard Books Ltd (Pakistan) *Tel:* (042) 7243779; (042) 7120776; (042) 7120781; (042) 7243783; (042) 7235767 *Fax:* (042) 7245097; (042) 73551978 *Web Site:* www.vanguardbooks.com, pg 515

Vani Prakashan (India) *Tel:* (011) 23273167 *Fax:* (011) 23275710 *E-mail:* vani-prakashan@yahoo.com, pg 352

Societa Editrice Vannini (Italy) *Tel:* (030) 313374 *Fax:* (030) 314078 *E-mail:* info@vanninieditrice.it *Web Site:* www.vanninieditrice.it, pg 411

Vantage Publishers International Ltd (Nigeria) *Tel:* (022) 415341, pg 507

Var Skola Foerlag AB (Sweden) *Tel:* (08) 662 33 51 *Fax:* (08) 6621843 *E-mail:* var.skola@pi.se, pg 616

Editorial Varazen SA (Mexico) *Tel:* (05) 5459230; (05) 5335274 *Fax:* (05) 2555172, pg 473

D & J Vardikos Vivliotechnica Hellas (Greece) *Tel:* (0210) 3631148 *Fax:* (0210) 9564354, pg 313

Fundacao Getulio Vargas (Brazil) *Tel:* (021) 2559-5542; (021) 2559-5543; (021) 2559-5544 *Toll Free Tel:* 800-217777 *Fax:* (021) 2559-5532 *E-mail:* editora@fgv.br *Web Site:* www.fgv.br, pg 92

Varlik Yayinlari AS (Turkey) *Tel:* (0212) 5226924 *Fax:* (0212) 5162005 *E-mail:* varlik@varlik.com.tr; varlik@isbank.net.tr *Web Site:* www.varlik.com.tr, pg 652

Drs F H R Oedayrajsingh Varma (Suriname), pg 608

Varsity Book Club (Nigeria) *Tel:* (046) 210013, pg 1254

VAS-Verlag fuer Akademische Schriften (Germany) *Tel:* (069) 77 93 66 *Fax:* (069) 7073967 *E-mail:* info@vas-verlag.de *Web Site:* www.vas-verlag.de, pg 294

Ladislav Vasicek (Czech Republic), pg 128

Uitgeverij Vassallucci bv (Netherlands) *Tel:* (020) 521 8322 *Fax:* (020) 623 6761 *E-mail:* info@vassallucci.nl *Web Site:* www.vassallucci.nl, pg 491

J Vassiliou Bibliopolein (Greece) *Tel:* (01) 3623382; (01) 3623480 *Fax:* (01) 3623580, pg 313

Osuuskunta Vastapaino (Finland) *Tel:* (03) 214 6246 *Fax:* (03) 214 6646 *E-mail:* vastapaino@vastapaino.fi *Web Site:* www.vastapaino.fi, pg 144

Vastu Gyan Publication (India) *Tel:* (011) 3318730, pg 352

Libreria Editrice Vaticana (Holy See (Vatican City State)) *Tel:* (06) 698-85003 *Fax:* (06) 698-84716, pg 315

Libreria Editrice Vaticana (Italy) *Tel:* (06) 69885003 *Fax:* (06) 69884716 *E-mail:* lev@publish.va *Web Site:* www.libreriaeditricevaticana.com, pg 411

Robert Vaughan Antiquarian Booksellers (United Kingdom) *Tel:* (01789) 205312, pg 1355

Ivan Vazov Publishing House (Bulgaria) *Tel:* (02) 878481; (02) 871572 *Fax:* (02) 878416, pg 97

VCH Verlags-AG (Switzerland) *Tel:* (01) 3602438 *Fax:* (01) 3602439 *E-mail:* info@wiley-vch.de *Web Site:* www.wiley-vch.de, pg 636

VCL (Netherlands) *Tel:* (038) 3328912 *Fax:* (038) 3327331, pg 1254

VCTA Publishing (Australia) *Tel:* (03) 94199622 *Fax:* (03) 94191205 *E-mail:* vcta@vcta.asn.au *Web Site:* www.vcta.asn.au, pg 45

VdA - Verband deutscher Archivarinnen und Archivare e V (Germany) *Tel:* (03643) 870-101 *Fax:* (03643) 870-164 *E-mail:* info@vda.archiv.net *Web Site:* www.vda.archiv.net, pg 1563

VDE-Verlag GmbH (Germany) *Tel:* (030) 34 80 01 0 *Fax:* (030) 341 70 93 *E-mail:* voss@vde-verlag.de *Web Site:* www.vde-verlag.de, pg 294

Vdf Hochschulverlag AG an der ETH Zurich (Switzerland) *Tel:* (01) 632 42 42 *Fax:* (01) 632 12 32 *E-mail:* verlag@vdf.ethz.ch *Web Site:* www.vdf.ethz.ch, pg 636

VDI Verlag GmbH (Germany) *Tel:* (0211) 61 88-0 *Fax:* (0211) 61 88-306 *E-mail:* info@vdi-nachrichten.com *Web Site:* www.vdi-nachrichten.com, pg 294

Editorial De Vecchi SA (Spain) *Tel:* (093) 272 46 70 *Fax:* (093) 487 74 94, pg 604

Editora Vecchi SA (Brazil) *Tel:* (021) 2444522, pg 92

VEDA (Vydavatel'stvo Slovenskej akademie vied) (Slovakia) *Tel:* (02) 63831172 *Fax:* (02) 63835391; (02) 63832254 *Web Site:* www.veda-sav.sk, pg 561

Vedecka knihovna V olomouci (Czech Republic) *Tel:* (068) 585223441 *Fax:* (068) 585225774 *E-mail:* info@vkol.cz *Web Site:* www.vkol.cz, pg 1501

Veen Bosch & Keuning Uitgevers NV (Netherlands) *Tel:* (030) 2349311 *Fax:* (030) 2349208 *E-mail:* algemeen@veenboschenkeuning.nl *Web Site:* www.veenboschenkeuning.nl, pg 491

Libreria Tecnica Vega (Venezuela) *Tel:* (02) 6221397 *Fax:* (02) 6622092, pg 1356

Vega-Publicacao e Distribuicao de Livros e Revistas, Lda (Portugal) *Tel:* (021) 789414 *Fax:* (021) 786395, pg 536

Ediciones Vega SRL (Venezuela) *Tel:* (02) 6622092; (02) 6621397, pg 780

The Vegetarian Society (United Kingdom) *Tel:* (0161) 925 2000 *Fax:* (0161) 926 9182 *E-mail:* info@vegsoc.org *Web Site:* www.vegsoc.org, pg 769

EDITORIAL VERBO SA

Veloce Publishing Ltd (United Kingdom) *Tel:* (01305) 260068 *Fax:* (01305) 268864 *E-mail:* info@veloce.co.uk *Web Site:* www.veloce.co.uk; www.velocebooks.com, pg 769

Venezuelan Library & Archives Association (Venezuela) *Tel:* (02) 5721858, pg 1574

Vents d'Ouest (France) *Tel:* (01) 41 46 11 46 *Fax:* (01) 40 93 05 58 *Web Site:* www.ventsdouest.com, pg 188

Ventura Ediciones, SA de CV (Mexico) *Tel:* (05) 2087681; (05) 5530798 *Fax:* (05) 5431173, pg 473

Venture Press Ltd (United Kingdom) *Tel:* (0121) 622 3911 *Fax:* (0121) 622 4860 *E-mail:* info@basw.co.uk, pg 769

Vera-Reyes Inc (Philippines) *Tel:* (02) 7218792 *Fax:* (02) 7218782, pg 521

Verband der Antiquare Oesterreichs (Austria) *Tel:* (01) 512 15 35 *Fax:* (01) 512 84 82 *E-mail:* sekretariat@hvb.at *Web Site:* www.antiquare.at, pg 1261

Verband der Oesterreichischen Buch-und Presse-Grossisten und der Werbenden Zeitschriftenhaendler (Austria) *Tel:* (01) 512 15 35 *Fax:* (01) 512 84 82 *E-mail:* hvb@buecher.at *Web Site:* www.buecher.at, pg 1261

Verband der Schulbuchverlage eV (Germany) *Tel:* (069) 70 30 75 *Fax:* (069) 70 79 01 69 *E-mail:* verband@vds-bildungsmedien.de *Web Site:* www.vds-bildungsmedien.de, pg 1271

Verband der Verlage- und Buchhaendlungen Berlin-Brandenburg eV (Germany) *Tel:* (030) 26 39 18 0 *Fax:* (030) 26 39 18 18 *E-mail:* verband@berliner-buchhandel.de *Web Site:* www.berliner-buchhandel.de, pg 1271

Verband der Verlage und Buchhandlungen in Nordrhein-Westfalen eV (Germany) *Tel:* (0211) 8 64 45-22 *Fax:* (0211) 32 44 97 *E-mail:* info@buchnrw.de *Web Site:* www.buchnrw.de, pg 1271

Verband der Wissenschaftlichen Gesellschaften Oesterreichs (VWGOe) (Austria) *Tel:* (01) 932166; (01) 934756 *Fax:* (01) 5262054, pg 59

Verband Deutscher Antiquare eV (Germany) *Tel:* (06435) 909147 *Fax:* (06435) 909148 *E-mail:* buch@antiquare.de *Web Site:* www.antiquare.de, pg 1271

Verband Deutscher Auskunfts und Verzichnismedien (Germany) *Tel:* (0211) 577995-0 *Fax:* (0211) 577995-44 *E-mail:* info@vdav.org *Web Site:* www.vdav.de, pg 1271

Verband deutschsprachiger Uebersetzer literarischer und wissenschaftlicher Werke eV (VDUe) (Germany) *Tel:* (030) 6956-2331 *Fax:* (030) 6956-3655 *Web Site:* www.literaturuebersetzer.de, pg 1148

Verband katholischer Verleger und Buchhaendler eV (Germany) *Tel:* (0228) 2421560 *Fax:* (0228) 2421561 *E-mail:* vkb2000@aol.com, pg 1271

Verband von selbstaendigen Verlagsvertreten Oesterreichs (Austria) *Tel:* (01) 512 15 35 *Fax:* (01) 512 84 82 *E-mail:* hvb@buecher.at *Web Site:* www.buecher.at, pg 1261

Verbandsdruckerei AG (Switzerland) *Tel:* (031) 252911, pg 636

Verbatim (United Kingdom) *Tel:* (01844) 208474 *Web Site:* www.verbatimbooks.com, pg 769

Verbinum Wydawnictwo Ksiezy Werbistow (Poland) *Tel:* (022) 6107878; (022) 8703286 *Fax:* (022) 6107775, pg 527

Editorial Verbo Divino (Spain) *Tel:* (0948) 55 65 05; (0948) 55 65 11 *Fax:* (0948) 55 45 06 *E-mail:* ventas@verbodivino.es; evd@verbodivino.es *Web Site:* www.verbodivino.es, pg 604

Editora Verbo Ltda (Brazil) *Tel:* (021) 380 1100 *Fax:* (021) 386-5397 *E-mail:* verbo@virtual-net.com.br *Web Site:* www.editorialverbo.pt, pg 92

Editorial Verbo SA (Portugal) *Tel:* (021) 380 21 31; (021) 380 11 00 *Fax:* (021) 386 11 22; (021) 386 53 97 *Web Site:* www.editorialverbo.pt, pg 536

VERBUM FOERLAG AB

Verbum Foerlag AB (Sweden) *Tel:* (08) 743 65 00 *Fax:* (08) 641 45 85 *E-mail:* info.forlag@verbum.se *Web Site:* www.verbum.se, pg 616

Verbum Forlag (Norway) *Tel:* (022) 93 27 00 *Fax:* (022) 93 27 27 *E-mail:* verbumforlag@verbumforlag.no *Web Site:* www.verbumforlag.no, pg 511

Editorial Verbum SL (Spain) *Tel:* (091) 446 88 41 *Fax:* (091) 594 45 59 *E-mail:* verbum@globalnet.es, pg 604

Livraria Verdade e Vida Editora (Portugal) *Tel:* (0249) 531417 *Fax:* (0249) 531417, pg 536

Editions Verdier (France) *Tel:* (04) 68 24 05 75; (01) 43 79 20 45 *Fax:* (04) 68 24 00 89; (01) 43 79 84 20 *E-mail:* contact@editions-verdier.fr *Web Site:* www.editions-verdier.fr, pg 188

Verein der Benediktiner zu Beuron- Beuroner Kunstverlag (Germany) *Tel:* (07466) 17-0 *Fax:* (07466) 17-107 *E-mail:* kunstverlag@erzabtei-beuron.de *Web Site:* www.erzabtei-beuron.de, pg 294

Verein der Diplom-Bibliothekare an wissenschaftlichen Bibliotheken eV (Germany) *Tel:* (0221) 5747161 *Fax:* (0221) 5747110 *Web Site:* www.bibliothek.uni-regensburg.de/vddb, pg 1563

Verein Deutscher Bibliothekar eV (VDB) (Germany) *Tel:* (030) 266-1728 *Fax:* (030) 266-1717 *E-mail:* olaf.hanann@sbb.spk-berlin.de; info@vdb_online.de *Web Site:* www.vdb-online.org, pg 1563

Verein Schweizerischer Archivarinnen und Archivare (Switzerland) *Tel:* (031) 322 89 89; (031) 322 92 85 *Web Site:* www.staluzern.ch/vsa, pg 1571

Vereinigte Fachverlage GmbH (Germany) *Tel:* (06131) 992-0 *Fax:* (06131) 992-100, pg 295

Vereinigung der Buchantiquare und Kupferstichhaendler in der Schweiz (Switzerland) *Tel:* (01) 261 57 50 *Fax:* (01) 793 19 33 *E-mail:* eos@eos.ch *Web Site:* www.vebuku.ch, pg 1287

Vereinigung des katholischen Buchandels der Schweiz (Switzerland) *Tel:* (026) 4 26 43 11 *Fax:* (026) 4 26 43 00, pg 1287

Vereinigung Oesterreichischer Bibliothekarinnen und Bibliothekare (VOEB) (Austria) *E-mail:* voeb@uibk.ac.at *Web Site:* voeb.uibk.ac.at, pg 1558

Vereinte Evangelische Mission, Abt Verlag (Germany) *Tel:* (0202) 89004 0 *Fax:* (0202) 89004 79 *E-mail:* info@vemission.org *Web Site:* www.vemission.org, pg 295

Vereniging van Religieus-Wetenschappelijke Bibliothecarissen (Belgium) *Tel:* (016) 323807 *Fax:* (016) 323862 *Web Site:* www.theo.kuleuven.ac.be/vrb, pg 1558

Javier Vergara Editor SA (Argentina) *Tel:* (011) 4343-7510; (011) 4343-7706 *Fax:* (011) 4334-0173 *E-mail:* ediciones-b-arg@ciudad.com.ar, pg 9

Javier Vergara Editor SA (Spain) *Tel:* 6163600 *Fax:* 6163708, pg 604

Javier Vergara Editor SA de CV (Mexico) *Tel:* (05) 6053374; (05) 6048283, pg 473

Editions de Vergeures (France) *Tel:* (01) 45 43 82 60 *Fax:* (01) 45 43 81 40, pg 188

Varkki Verghese (Luxembourg) *Tel:* 923121 *Fax:* 929076, pg 452

Buchhandlung Veritas (Austria) *Tel:* (0732) 776451-280 *Fax:* (0732) 776451-239 *E-mail:* veritas@veritas.at *Web Site:* www.veritas.at, pg 1301

Veritas Co Ltd (Ireland) *Tel:* (01) 878 8177 *Fax:* (01) 8786507 *E-mail:* publications@veritas.ie *Web Site:* www.veritas.ie, pg 364

Veritas Co Ltd (Ireland) *Tel:* (01) 878 8177 *Fax:* (01) 874 4913 *E-mail:* sales@veritas.ie *Web Site:* www.veritas.ie, pg 1319

Veritas Foundation Publication Centre (United Kingdom) *Tel:* (020) 8749 4957; (020) 8749 4965 *Fax:* (020) 8749 4965 *E-mail:* veritas@polish.co.uk, pg 770

Veritas Press (Australia) *Fax:* (071) 529256 *E-mail:* copytype@interworx.com.au, pg 45

Verlag Veritas Mediengesellschaft mbH (Austria) *Tel:* (0732) 776451; (0732) 776450 *Fax:* (0732) 776451-283, pg 59

Verkehrshaus der Schweiz (Switzerland) *Tel:* (041) 370444 *Fax:* (041) 3706168 *E-mail:* mail@verkehrshaus.org *Web Site:* www.verkehrshaus.ch, pg 636

Verlag Beltz & Gelberg (Germany) *Tel:* (06201) 60070 *E-mail:* info@beltz.de *Web Site:* www.beltz.de, pg 295

Verlag fuer die Frau GmbH (Germany) *Tel:* (0341) 99540 *Fax:* (0341) 9954367 *E-mail:* kuratorium.hdb@t-online.de, pg 295

Verlag fur die Rechts- und Anwaltspraxis GmbH & Co (Germany) *Tel:* (02361) 9142-0 *Fax:* (02361) 9142-35 *E-mail:* hotline@zap-verlag.de *Web Site:* www.zap-verlag.de, pg 295

Verlag fur Schweissen und Verwandte Verfahren (Germany) *Tel:* (0211) 15910 *Fax:* (0211) 1591150 *E-mail:* verlag@dvs-hg.de *Web Site:* www.dvs-verlag.de, pg 295

Verlag Moderne Industrie AG & Co KG (Germany) *Tel:* (089) 5484202 *Fax:* (089) 548428428 *E-mail:* info@mi-verlag.de *Web Site:* www.mi-verlag.de, pg 295

Verlag Anton Schroll & Co (Austria) *Tel:* (01) 5445641-46 *Fax:* (01) 544564166 *E-mail:* prepress@agenswerk.at, pg 59

Verlag und Druckkontor Kamp GmbH (Germany) *Tel:* (0234) 51617-0 *Fax:* (0234) 51617-18 *E-mail:* verlag@kamp-verlag.de *Web Site:* www.kamp-verlag.de, pg 295

Verlag und Studio fuer Hoerbuchproduktionen (Germany) *Tel:* (06421) 889-110 *Fax:* (06421) 889-1111 *E-mail:* verlag@hoerbuch.de; info@hoerbuch.de *Web Site:* www.hoerbuch.de; www.hoerbuch.com, pg 295

Verlag Wilhelm Braumuller Universitats-Verlagsbuchhandlung GmbH (Austria) *Tel:* (01) 319 11 59 *Fax:* (01) 310 28 05 *E-mail:* office@braumueller.at *Web Site:* www.braumueller.at, pg 59

Verlagsbuchhandlung AG (Switzerland) *Tel:* (061) 239723, pg 636

Verlagsgruppe Jehle-Rehm GmbH (Germany) *Tel:* (089) 54 8 52-06 *Fax:* (089) 54 8 52-82 30 *E-mail:* info@HJR-verlag.de *Web Site:* www.jehle-rehm.de, pg 295

Verlegervereinigung Rechtsinformatik eV (Germany) *Tel:* (0221) 94373-0 *Fax:* (0221) 94373-901 *E-mail:* marketing@heymanns.com *Web Site:* www.heymanns.com, pg 1271

Uitgeverij Verloren (Netherlands) *Tel:* (035) 6859856 *Fax:* (035) 6836557 *E-mail:* info@verloren.nl *Web Site:* www.verloren.nl, pg 492

Vernadsky Central Scientific Library of the National Academy of Sciences of Ukraine (Ukraine) *Tel:* (044) 285 81 64 *Fax:* (044) 264 33 98 *E-mail:* nlu@csl.freenet.kiev.ua, pg 1552

Editions Eliane Vernay (Switzerland) *Tel:* (022) 7350460 *Fax:* (022) 7350460, pg 636

Particip Verold (Iceland) *Tel:* 5688433 *Fax:* 5688142, pg 1253

Veron Editor (Spain) *Tel:* (093) 4161643 *Fax:* (093) 4161433 *E-mail:* veron@veroneditor.com, pg 604

Ediciones Versal SA (Spain) *Tel:* (093) 494 85 90 *Fax:* (093) 419 02 97 *E-mail:* cga.barcelona@cga.es *Web Site:* www.anaya.es, pg 604

Verso (United Kingdom) *Tel:* (020) 7437 3546; (020) 7434 1704; (020) 7439 8194 *Fax:* (020) 7734 0059 *E-mail:* enquiries@verso.co.uk *Web Site:* www.versobooks.com, pg 770

Versus Verlag AG (Switzerland) *Tel:* (044) 2510892 *Fax:* (044) 2626738 *E-mail:* info@versus.ch *Web Site:* www.versus.ch, pg 636

Vertice Ltda (Colombia) *Tel:* (01) 2437113, pg 113

Verulam Publishing Ltd (United Kingdom) *Tel:* (01727) 872770 *Fax:* (01727) 873866 *E-mail:* verulampub@yahoo.co.uk; sales@verulampub.demon.co.uk, pg 770

Vervuert Verlagsgesellschaft (Germany) *Tel:* (069) 597 4617 *Fax:* (069) 5978743 *E-mail:* info@iberoamericanalibros.com *Web Site:* www.ibero-americana.net, pg 295

Verwertungsgesellschaft Wort (Germany) *Tel:* (089) 5 14 12-0 *Fax:* (089) 5141258 *E-mail:* vgw@vgwort.de *Web Site:* www.vgwort.de, pg 1271

Veselka Publishers (Ukraine) *Tel:* (044) 213-95-01 *Fax:* (044) 213-33-59 *E-mail:* veskiev@iptelecom.net.ua, pg 654

Editura de Vest (Romania) *Tel:* (056) 191959 *Fax:* (056) 14212, pg 543

Vestala Verlag (Romania) *Tel:* (01) 222-8597; (01) 345-2827 *Fax:* (01) 222-8597; (01) 345-2827, pg 543

Vesti (Serbia and Montenegro) *Tel:* (031) 513261; (031) 514263 *Fax:* (031) 511941 *E-mail:* redakcija@vesti.co.yu *Web Site:* www.vesti.co.yu/onama.htm, pg 554

Vett & Viten AS (Norway) *Tel:* 66849040 *Fax:* 66845590 *E-mail:* vv@vettviten.no *Web Site:* www.vettviten.no, pg 511

Verlag Alfred Vetter (Switzerland) *Tel:* (01) 2011184, pg 636

Vexer Verlag (Switzerland) *Tel:* (071) 220986 *E-mail:* vexer@freesurf.ch, pg 636

Vianello Libri (Italy) *Tel:* (0422) 440666 *Fax:* (0422) 440645 *E-mail:* info@vianellolibri.it *Web Site:* www.vianellolibri.it, pg 411

Vibal Publishing House Inc (VPHI) (Philippines) *Tel:* (02) 712-9156; (02) 712-2722; (02) 712-9157; (02) 712-9158; (02) 712-9159 *Fax:* (02) 711-8852 *E-mail:* sales@vibalpublishing.com *Web Site:* www.vibalpublishing.com, pg 521

Vice Versa Verlag (Germany) *Tel:* (030) 61609237 *Fax:* (030) 61609238 *E-mail:* viceversa@comp.de, pg 295

Gobierno de Canarias - Viceconsejeria de Cultura y Deportes (Spain) *Tel:* (0922) 202202 *Fax:* (092) 2474165, pg 605

Editorial Vicens-Vives (Spain) *Tel:* (093) 2523700; (093) 2523703 *Fax:* (093) 2523710 *E-mail:* e@vicensvives.es *Web Site:* www.vicensvives.es, pg 605

Ediciones A Madrid Vicente (Spain) *Tel:* (091) 5336926 *Fax:* (091) 5330286 *E-mail:* amadrid@acta.es *Web Site:* www.amvediciones.com, pg 605

Vicks Lithograph & Printing Corp (United States) *Tel:* 315-736-9344 *Fax:* 315-736-1901 *Web Site:* www.vickslitho.com, pg 1168, 1231

Ed Victor Ltd (United Kingdom) *Tel:* (020) 7304 4100 *Fax:* (020) 7304 4111, pg 1144

Victoria Publishers (Lithuania) *Tel:* (02) 221915; (02) 632632; (02) 221914 *Fax:* (02) 630797, pg 450

Victoria University Press (New Zealand) *Tel:* (04) 463 6580 *Fax:* (04) 463 6581 *E-mail:* victoria-press@vuw.ac.nz *Web Site:* www.vuw.ac.nz, pg 502

Victorian Arts Centre Trust (Australia) *Tel:* (03) 9281 8000 *Fax:* (03) 9281 8282 *Web Site:* www.artscentre.net.au, pg 45

Victory Books (Papua New Guinea) *Tel:* 5421081 *Fax:* 5423030 *E-mail:* bcbes@datec.com.pg, pg 516

Victory Offset Prima PT (Indonesia) *Tel:* (021) 460-2742; (021) 460-8968; (021) 4682-0555 *Fax:* (021) 460-2740; (021) 4682-0551 *E-mail:* info@victoryoffset.com *Web Site:* www.victoryoffset.com, pg 1159, 1179

YELLOW PAGES

Victory Offset Prima PT (Indonesia) *Tel:* (021) 460-8968; (021) 460-2742; (021) 4682-0555 *Fax:* (021) 460-2740; (021) 4682-0551 *E-mail:* info@victoryoffset.com *Web Site:* www.victoryoffset.com, pg 1220

Victory Offset Prima PT (Indonesia) *Tel:* (021) 460-2742; (021) 460-8968; (021) 4682-0555 *Fax:* (021) 460-2740; (021) 4682-0551 *E-mail:* info@victoryoffset.com *Web Site:* www.victoryoffset.com, pg 1237

Editora Vida Crista Ltda (Brazil) *Tel:* (011) 6647-7788 *Toll Free Tel:* 800-11-5074 *Fax:* (011) 6647-7125 *E-mail:* editora@vidacrista.com.br *Web Site:* www.vidacrista.com.br, pg 92

Videograf II Sp z o o Zaklad Poracy Chronionej (Poland) *Tel:* (03) 2036558; (03) 2036559; (03) 2036560 *Fax:* (03) 2036558; (03) 2036559; (03) 2036560 *E-mail:* videograf@videograf.dnd.com.pl, pg 527

Vidhi (India) *Tel:* (011) 389001, pg 352

Vidura Science Publishers (Sri Lanka) *Tel:* (091) 564713, pg 607

Vidya Puri (India) *Tel:* (0671) 620637; (0671) 617260, pg 352

Vidyarthi Mithram Press (India) *Tel:* (0481) 354003; (0481) 563282; (0481) 564713; (0481) 562616 (after office hours) *Fax:* (0481) 562616, pg 352

Les Editions Vie ouvriere ASBL (Belgium) *Tel:* (02) 5125090 *Fax:* (02) 5145231, pg 74

Vieda, SIA (Latvia) *Tel:* 7249728 *Fax:* (02) 7140680, pg 445

Vienna International Centre Library (Austria) *Tel:* (01) 2600-22620 *Fax:* (01) 2600-29584 *E-mail:* iaea.library.infodesk@iaea.org *Web Site:* www.iaea.or.at, pg 1492

Vier-Tuerme GmbH Benedikt Press (Germany) *Tel:* (09324) 20292 *Fax:* (09324) 20495 *E-mail:* info@vier-tuerme.de *Web Site:* www.vier-tuerme.de, pg 1177

Vier-Tuerme GmbH Benedikt Press (Germany) *Tel:* (09324) 20214 *Fax:* (09324) 20444 *Web Site:* www.vier-tuerme.de/benedictpress, pg 1217

Vier Tuerme GmbH Verlag Klosterbetriebe (Germany) *Tel:* (09324) 20292 *Fax:* (09324) 20495 *E-mail:* info@vier-tuerme.de *Web Site:* www.vier-tuerme.de, pg 295

Friedr Vieweg & Sohn Verlag (Germany) *Tel:* (0611) 7878-0 *Fax:* (0611) 7878-470 *E-mail:* vieweg.service@bertelsmann.de *Web Site:* www.vieweg.de; www.gwv-fachverlage.de, pg 296

Editora Vigilia Ltda (Brazil) *Tel:* (031) 3372744; (031) 3372363 *Fax:* (031) 3372834, pg 92

Editions Vigot Universitaire (France) *Tel:* (01) 43 29 54 50 *Fax:* (01) 46 34 05 89 *E-mail:* vpc@vigot.fr *Web Site:* www.vigotmaloine.fr, pg 188

Vikas Publishing House Pvt Ltd (India) *Tel:* (011) 24315313; (011) 24315570; (011) 24317857 *Fax:* (011) 24310879 *E-mail:* helpline@vikaspublishing.com, pg 352

Viking (United Kingdom) *Tel:* (020) 7416 3000 *Fax:* (020) 7416 3274, pg 770

Viking Children's Books (United Kingdom) *Tel:* (020) 7416 3000 *Fax:* (020) 7416 3086, pg 770

Viking Sevenseas NZ Ltd (New Zealand) *Tel:* (04) 902-8240 *Fax:* (04) 902-8240 *E-mail:* vikings@paradise.net.nz, pg 502

Viktoria-Verlag Peter Marti (Switzerland) *Tel:* (031) 7911932 *Fax:* (031) 7912564, pg 636

Magyar Tudomanyos Akademia VilagGazdasagi Kutato Intezet (Hungary) *Tel:* (01) 1668433 *Fax:* (01) 1620661, pg 325

Editions Village Mondial (France) *Tel:* (01) 72 74 90 00 *Fax:* (01) 42 05 22 17 *E-mail:* infos@pearsoned.fr *Web Site:* www.pearsoneducation.fr, pg 189

Villamonta Publishing Services Inc (Australia) *Tel:* (03) 5229 2029 *Fax:* (03) 5222 5399 *E-mail:* villapub@ozemail.com.au, pg 45

Biblioteca Daniel Cosio Villegas El Colegio de Mexico AC (Mexico) *Tel:* (055) 5449 3000; (055) 5449 2909; (055) 5449 2936; (055) 5449 2934 *Fax:* (055) 5645 0464; (055) 5645 4584 *E-mail:* biblio@colmex.mx *Web Site:* biblio.colmex.mx, pg 1529

Villegas Editores Ltda (Colombia) *Tel:* (01) 6161788 *Fax:* (01) 6160020 *E-mail:* villedi@cable.net *Web Site:* www.villegaseditores.com, pg 113

Vilnius Art Academy Publishing House (Lithuania) *Tel:* (02) 22 30 63 *Fax:* (02) 61 99 66 *E-mail:* muziejus@vda.lt *Web Site:* vdamuziejus.mch.mii.lt, pg 450

Vilnius University Library (Lithuania) *Tel:* (085) 2687101 *Fax:* (085) 2687104 *E-mail:* mb@mb.vu.lt *Web Site:* www.mb.vu.lt, pg 1525

Editions Vilo SA (France) *Tel:* (01) 45 77 08 05 *Fax:* (01) 45 79 97 15, pg 189

Vinaches Lopez, Luisa (Spain) *Tel:* (01) 3694488 *Fax:* (01) 3694488, pg 605

Edition Vincent Klink (Germany) *Tel:* (0711) 62007211 *Fax:* (0711) 6409408 *E-mail:* edition@vincent-klink.de, pg 296

Curt R Vincentz Verlag (Germany) *Tel:* (0511) 9910000 *Fax:* (0511) 9910099 *E-mail:* info@vincentz.de *Web Site:* www.vincentz.de, pg 296

Vinciana Editrice sas (Italy) *Tel:* (02) 4982306 *Fax:* (02) 48003275 *E-mail:* info@vinciana.com *Web Site:* www.vinciana.com, pg 412

Forlaget Vindrose A/S (Denmark) *Tel:* 36153615 *Fax:* 36153616 *E-mail:* post@borgen.dk *Web Site:* www.borgen.dk, pg 135

Vine House Distribution Ltd (United Kingdom) *Tel:* (01825) 723 398 *Fax:* (01825) 724 188 *E-mail:* sales@vinehouseuk.co.uk *Web Site:* www.vinehouseuk.co.uk, pg 1355

Vinpress Sdn Bhd (Malaysia) *Tel:* (03) 7173333; (03) 7188877 *Fax:* (03) 7192942 *E-mail:* vinsoh@pc.jaring.my, pg 459

Vinten Editor (Uruguay) *Tel:* (02) 2090223 *Fax:* (02) 290223 *E-mail:* dayraq@chasque.apc.org *Web Site:* www.chasque.apc.org/dayraq/vinten, pg 778

Vipopremo Agencies (Kenya) *Tel:* (02) 227189; (02) 333882, pg 436

Virago Press (United Kingdom) *Tel:* (020) 7911 8000 *Fax:* (020) 7911 8100 *E-mail:* virago.press@timewarnerbooks.co.uk *Web Site:* www.virago.co.uk, pg 770

Viratham (Thailand) *Tel:* (02) 866848, pg 646

Virgin Publishing Ltd (United Kingdom) *Tel:* (020) 7386 3300 *Fax:* (020) 7386 3360 *E-mail:* info@virgin-books.co.uk; info@virgin-pub.co.uk *Web Site:* www.virginbooks.com, pg 770

Virlogeux Francoise-COMEDIT (Martinique) *Tel:* 683985 *Fax:* 683423, pg 460

Visalaandhra Publishing House (India) *Tel:* (040) 24744580 *Fax:* (040) 4735905, pg 1318

Edition Curt Visel (Germany) *Tel:* (08331) 2853 *Fax:* (08331) 490364 *E-mail:* info@edition-curt-visel.de *Web Site:* www.edition-curt-visel.de, pg 296

Vision Books Pvt Ltd (India) *Tel:* (011) 2386-2267; (011) 2386-2201 *Fax:* (011) 2386-2935 *E-mail:* mail@orientpaperbacks.com, pg 352

Vision Pub Co Ltd (Hong Kong) *Tel:* 23147627; 92676502 *Fax:* 29078838 *E-mail:* pcgameos@pcgame.com.hk *Web Site:* www.pcgame.com.hk, pg 320

Vision Publications (Zimbabwe), pg 784

Vision Srl (Italy) *Tel:* (06) 44292688 *Fax:* (06) 44292688 *E-mail:* info@visionpubl.com *Web Site:* www.visionpubl.com, pg 412

Visor Distribuciones, SA (Spain) *Tel:* (091) 4681248; (091) 4681011; (091) 4681102 *Fax:* (091) 4681098 *E-mail:* editorial@visordis.es *Web Site:* www.visordis.es, pg 605

Visor Libros (Spain) *Tel:* (091) 5492655 *Fax:* (091) 544 86 95 *E-mail:* visor-libros@visor-libros.com *Web Site:* www.visor-libros.com, pg 605

Vista Computer Services Ltd (United Kingdom) *Tel:* (01923) 830200 *Fax:* (01923) 238789 *E-mail:* solutions@vistacomp.com *Web Site:* www.vistacomp.com, pg 1165

Vista Point Verlag GmbH (Germany) *Tel:* (0221) 921613-0 *Fax:* (0221) 921613-14 *E-mail:* info@vistapoint.de *Web Site:* www.vistapoint.de, pg 296

Vista Productions Ltd (Hong Kong) *Tel:* 25632492 *Fax:* 25655803, pg 320

Vista Publications (Australia) *Tel:* (03) 9534 8881 *Fax:* (03) 9534 9711 *E-mail:* vistaof@mbox.com.au, pg 45

S Viswanathan (Printers & Publishers) Pvt Ltd (India) *Tel:* (044) 826 5623; (044) 826 5633 *Fax:* (044) 825 6002 *E-mail:* svprint@md2.vsnl.net.in, pg 352

Vita (Belgium) *Tel:* (09) 3842114 *Fax:* (09) 1842114, pg 74

Vita e Pensiero (Italy) *Tel:* (02) 72342335; (02) 72342259 *Fax:* (02) 72342260 *E-mail:* editvep@mi.unicatt.it *Web Site:* www.vitaepensiero.it, pg 412

Edizioni La Vita Felice (Italy) *Tel:* (02) 29 52 46 00 *Fax:* (02) 29 40 18 96 *E-mail:* lavitafelice@iol.it *Web Site:* www.lavitafelice.it, pg 412

Vitagraf (Croatia) *Tel:* (051) 215087; (051) 338489 *Toll Free Tel:* (051) 322880 *Fax:* (051) 212622 *E-mail:* vitagraf@ri.hinet.hr, pg 119

Vital Publications (Australia) *Tel:* (03) 9379-1219 *Fax:* (03) 9379-0015 *E-mail:* vitalpubs@churchesofchrist.org.au; aceditor@ozemail.com.au, pg 45

Vitalis sro (Czech Republic) *Tel:* (02) 57530732 *Fax:* (02) 57531974 *E-mail:* info@vitalis-verlag.com *Web Site:* www.vitalis-verlag.com, pg 128

Viva Books Pvt Ltd (India) *Tel:* (011) 3258325; (011) 3283121 *Fax:* (011) 3267224 *E-mail:* viva@mantraonline.com *Web Site:* www.vivagroupindia.com, pg 352

Viva Lithographers Pte Ltd (Singapore) *Tel:* 2721880 *Fax:* 2735425 *E-mail:* vivasing@singnet.com.sg *Web Site:* ifc.tp.edu.sg/Project_2000July/Viva, pg 1162

Vivalda Editori SRL (Italy) *Tel:* (011) 7720444 *Fax:* (011) 7732170 *Web Site:* www.cdavivalda.it, pg 412

Vivek Prakashan (India) *Tel:* (011) 2529649; (011) 2944014 *Fax:* (011) 6827347, pg 353

Vivere In SRL (Italy) *Tel:* (08) 06907030 *Fax:* (08) 06907026 *E-mail:* edizioniviverein@tint.it *Web Site:* www.viverein.it, pg 412

Luis Vives (Edelvives) (Spain) *Tel:* (091) 334 48 83; (091) 334 48 82 *Fax:* (091) 334 48 92 *E-mail:* dediciones@edelvives.es *Web Site:* www.grupoeditorialluisvives.com, pg 1162

Luis Vives (Edelvives) (Spain) *Tel:* (091) 334 48 83 *Fax:* (091) 334 48 92 *E-mail:* dediciones@edelvives.es *Web Site:* www.grupoeditorialluisvives.com, pg 1223

Luis Vives (Edelvives) (Spain) *Tel:* (091) 334 48 83 *Fax:* (091) 334 48 82 *E-mail:* dediciones@edelvives.es *Web Site:* www.grupoeditorialluisvives.com, pg 1247

Editions Vivez Soleil SA (Switzerland) *Tel:* (04) 50 87 27 09 *Fax:* (04) 50 87 27 13, pg 636

Viviani Editore srl (Italy) *Tel:* (06) 6872855 *Fax:* (06) 6872856, pg 412

Vivlia Publishers & Booksellers (South Africa) *Tel:* (011) 472-3912 *Fax:* (011) 472-4904 *E-mail:* vivlia@icon.co.ta, pg 570

Vivliothiki Eftychia Galeou (Greece) *Tel:* (0210) 6841191 *Fax:* (0210) 6825862, pg 313

VIZAVI EDITIONS

Vizavi Editions (Mauritius) *Tel:* 2112435 *Fax:* 2113047 *E-mail:* vizavi@intnet.mu, pg 461

Cristina Vizcaino Literary Agency (Spain) *Tel:* (091) 5944992 *E-mail:* vizcaino@infornet.es, pg 1136

Vjesnik dd (Croatia) *Tel:* (01) 61 66 666; (01) 36 41 111 *Fax:* (01) 61 61 602; (01) 61 61 650 *E-mail:* vjesnik@vjesnik.hr; vjesnik@vjesnik.com *Web Site:* www.vjesnik.hr; www.vjesnik.com, pg 1154

VJK Verlag Josef Knecht Carolusdruckerei GmbH (Germany) *Tel:* (069) 281767; (069) 281768 *Fax:* (069) 296653, pg 296

Vlaamse Boekverkopersbond (VBB) (Belgium) *Tel:* (03) 230 89 23 *Fax:* (03) 281 22 40 *E-mail:* info@boek.be *Web Site:* www.boek.be, pg 1263

Vlaamse Esperantobond VZW (Belgium) *Tel:* (03) 2343400 *Fax:* (03) 2335433 *E-mail:* esperanto@agoranet.be, pg 74

Vlaamse Uitgevers Vereniging (VUV) (Belgium) *Tel:* (03) 2308923 *Fax:* (03) 2812240 *E-mail:* info@boek.be *Web Site:* www.vbvb.be, pg 1263

Vlaamse Vereniging voor Bibliotheek- Archief-en Documentatiewezen (VVBAD) (Belgium) *Tel:* (03) 2814457 *Fax:* (03) 2188077 *E-mail:* vvbad@vvbad.be *Web Site:* www.vvbad.be, pg 1558

Vlassi (Greece) *Tel:* (0210) 3812900; (01) 3833013 *Fax:* (0210) 3827557 *Web Site:* www.vlassi.gr, pg 1314

Vlassis (Greece) *Tel:* (0210) 3812900; (0210) 3827557 *Fax:* (0210) 3827557 *E-mail:* amvlassi@otenet.gr, pg 313

Editions VM (France) *Tel:* (01) 44 41 11 11 *Fax:* (01) 44 41 11 85, pg 189

VNU Business Press Group BV (Netherlands) *Tel:* (023) 546 5666 *Fax:* (023) 546 5541 *Web Site:* www.vnubp.nl, pg 492

VNU Business Publications (United Kingdom) *Tel:* (020) 7316 9000 *Fax:* (020) 7316 9440 *Web Site:* www.vnu.co.uk, pg 770

VNU Business Publications BV (Netherlands) *Tel:* (023) 546 5666 *Fax:* (023) 546 5541 *Web Site:* www.vnubp.nl, pg 492

Vocatio Publishing House (Poland) *Tel:* (022) 648-5450 *Fax:* (022) 648-6382 *E-mail:* vocatio@vocatio.com.pl *Web Site:* www.vocatio.com.pl, pg 527

Voce della Bibbia (Italy) *Tel:* (059) 55 63 03; (059) 55 79 10 *Fax:* (059) 57 31 05 *E-mail:* bbbitaly@tin.it *Web Site:* www.vocedellabibbia.org, pg 412

Vodnar (Czech Republic) *Tel:* (02) 51563603 *Fax:* (02) 51563603 *E-mail:* naklvodnar@volny.cz *Web Site:* www.volny.cz/naklvodnar, pg 128

Voenno Izdatelstvo (Bulgaria) *Tel:* (02) 9802766; (02) 9804186; (02) 9802779 *Fax:* (02) 881568, pg 97

Verlag A Vogel (Switzerland) *Tel:* (071) 335 66 66 *Fax:* (071) 334684 *E-mail:* vavch@access.ch *Web Site:* www.verlag-avogel.ch, pg 636

Vogel Medien GmbH & Co KG (Germany) *Tel:* (0931) 418-2028 *Fax:* (0931) 418-2860 *E-mail:* info@vogel-medien.de *Web Site:* www.vogel.de, pg 296

Voggenreiter-Verlag (Germany) *Tel:* (0228) 93 575-0 *Fax:* (0228) 35 50 53 *E-mail:* info@voggenreiter.de *Web Site:* www.voggenreiter.de, pg 296

Ellen Vogt Garbe Verlag (Germany) *Tel:* (0911) 5430983 *Fax:* (0911) 5430983, pg 296

Vogt-Schild Ag, Druck und Verlag (Switzerland) *Tel:* (032) 6247111 *Fax:* (032) 6247444, pg 636

La Voix du Regard (France) *Tel:* (01) 46 70 88 69 *Fax:* (01) 46 70 88 69 *E-mail:* voixduregard@9online.fr, pg 189

Vojnoizdavacki i novinski centar (Serbia and Montenegro) *Tel:* (011) 644 188; (011) 641 159 *Fax:* (011) 645 020, pg 554

Verlag Volk & Welt GmbH (Germany) *Tel:* (089) 4372 2769 *Fax:* (089) 4372 2743, pg 296

Volk und Wissen Verlag GmbH & Co (Germany) *Tel:* (030) 201 83-502 *Fax:* (030) 2041846 *E-mail:* mail@vwv.de *Web Site:* www.vwv.de, pg 296

Verlag Deutsches Volksheimstaettenwerk GmbH (Germany) *Tel:* (0228) 7259930 *Fax:* (0228) 7259919 *E-mail:* ibn@bonn.ihk.de *Web Site:* www.ibn.ihk-bonn.de, pg 296

Voltaire Foundation Ltd (United Kingdom) *Tel:* (01865) 284600 *Fax:* (01865) 284610 *E-mail:* email@voltaire.ox.ac.uk *Web Site:* www.voltaire.ox.ac.uk, pg 771

Editorial Voluntad SA (Colombia) *Tel:* (01) 241 04 44 *Fax:* (01) 241 04 39 *E-mail:* voluntad@voluntad.com.co *Web Site:* www.voluntad.com.co, pg 113

Volvox Globator Nakladatelstvi & vydavatelstvi (Czech Republic) *Tel:* 224 236 268 *Fax:* 224 217 721 *E-mail:* volvox@volvox.cz *Web Site:* www.volvox.cz, pg 128

Dokument und Analyse Verlag Bogislaw von Randow (Germany) *Tel:* (089) 2720100 *Fax:* (089) 2720311, pg 296

Vorarlberger Verlagsanstalt Aktiengesellschaft (Austria) *Tel:* (05572) 24 6 97-0 *Fax:* (05572) 24 6 97-78 *E-mail:* office@vva.at *Web Site:* www.vva.at, pg 59

Voronezh State University Publishers (Russian Federation) *Tel:* (0732) 560481, pg 549

VOSA, SL Ediciones (Spain) *Tel:* (091) 7259430 *Fax:* (091) 7259430 *E-mail:* mauosa@terra.es, pg 605

Votobia sro (Czech Republic) *Tel:* (068) 522 46 21 *Fax:* (068) 523 18 90 *E-mail:* votobia@mbox.vol.cz, pg 128

Votsis Nikos (Greece) *Fax:* (01) 3820646 *E-mail:* mvotsis@otenet.gr, pg 1314

Votum Verlag GmbH (Germany) *Tel:* (0251) 26514-0 *Fax:* (0251) 26514-20 *E-mail:* info@votum-verlag.de *Web Site:* www.votum-verlag.de, pg 297

Vox Editura (Romania) *Tel:* (01) 2220213; (01) 2220214 *Fax:* (01) 2220213 *E-mail:* edituravox@hotmail.com, pg 543

Voyenizdat (Russian Federation) *Tel:* (095) 1950154 *Fax:* (095) 1952454, pg 549

Publicaciones Voz de Gracia (Puerto Rico) *Tel:* 809-784-4366 *Fax:* 809-261-5401 *E-mail:* vozdegra@caribe.net *Web Site:* www.cristo.org, pg 537

Vozes Editora Ltda (Brazil) *Tel:* (024) 237 5112 *Fax:* (024) 231 4676 *E-mail:* editorial@vozes.com.br *Web Site:* www.vozes.com.br, pg 92

Vremea Publishers Ltd (Romania) *Tel:* (01) 3358131 *Fax:* (01) 3110219 *E-mail:* vremea@fx.ro, pg 543

H de Vries Boeken (Netherlands) *Tel:* (023) 5319458 *Fax:* (023) 5311680 *E-mail:* boeken@vries-boeken.com *Web Site:* www.vries-boeken.com, pg 1329

C De Vries Brouwers BVBA (Belgium) *Tel:* (03) 2374180 *Fax:* (03) 2377001, pg 74

Vrije Universiteit Brussel Universiteitsbibliotheek (Belgium) *Tel:* (02) 629 21 11 *Fax:* (02) 629 22 82 *E-mail:* info@vub.ac.be *Web Site:* www.vub.ac.be, pg 1494

Librairie Philosophique J Vrin (France) *Tel:* (01) 43 54 03 47 *Fax:* (01) 43 54 48 18 *E-mail:* contact@vrin.fr *Web Site:* www.vrin.fr, pg 189

VS Verlag fur Sozialwissenschaften (Germany) *Tel:* (0611) 78780 *Fax:* (0611) 7878-470 *Web Site:* www.vs-verlag.de; www.gwv-fachverlage.de, pg 297

Vysoka skola banska - Technicka Univerzita Ostrava (Czech Republic) *Tel:* (069) 596 991 111 *Fax:* (069) 596 998 507 *Web Site:* www.vsb.cz, pg 1501

Vserossijskaja gosudarstvennaja biblioteka inostrannoj literatury im M I Rudomino (Russian Federation) *Tel:* (095) 9153621 *Fax:* (095) 9153637 *E-mail:* vgbil@libfl.ru *Web Site:* www.libfl.ru, pg 1541

Vsesoyuznii Molodejnii Knizhnii Centre (Russian Federation) *Tel:* (095) 924 7879, pg 549

Vsesoyuznoe Obyedineniye Vneshtorgizdat (Russian Federation) *Tel:* (095) 2505162 *Fax:* (095) 2539794, pg 549

VSO Books (United Kingdom) *Tel:* (020) 8780 7200 *Fax:* (020) 8780 7300 *E-mail:* enquiry@vso.org.uk *Web Site:* www.vso.org.uk, pg 1293

VTB-Travel Bookshop (Belgium) *Tel:* (03) 224 10 52 *Fax:* (03) 224 10 56 *E-mail:* info.cultuur@vtb.be *Web Site:* www.vtb.be, pg 1302

VU Boekhandel/Uitgeverij BV (Netherlands) *Tel:* (020) 64 443 55 *Fax:* (020) 646 27 19 *E-mail:* info@vuboekhandel.nl *Web Site:* www.vuboekhandel.nl, pg 492

VUB Brussels University Press (Belgium) *Tel:* (02) 629 35 90 *Fax:* (02) 629 26 94 *E-mail:* vubpress@vub.ac.be *Web Site:* www.vubpress.org, pg 74

Editorial Vuelta, SA de CV (Mexico) *Tel:* (05) 5548810; (05) 5548811 *Fax:* (05) 6580074, pg 473

Librairie Vuibert (France) *Tel:* (01) 44 08 49 00 *Fax:* (01) 44 08 49 39 *Web Site:* www.vuibert.com, pg 189

Vuk Karadzic (Serbia and Montenegro) *Tel:* (011) 423-290; (011) 424-558; (011) 424-560 *Fax:* (011) 422-012, pg 554

Vuk Karadzic (Serbia and Montenegro) *Tel:* (011) 628066; (011) 628043 *Fax:* (011) 623150, pg 1339

Ediciones Vulcano (Spain) *Tel:* (091) 500 16 49; (091) 461 44 58 *Fax:* (091) 461 44 58 *E-mail:* vulcano@vulcanoediciones.com *Web Site:* www.vulcanoediciones.com, pg 605

Vulkan-Verlag GmbH (Germany) *Tel:* (0201) 82002-0 *Fax:* (0201) 82002-40 *Web Site:* www.oldenbourg.de/vulkan-verlag, pg 297

Uitgeverij De Vuurbaak BV (Netherlands) *Tel:* (0342) 411731 *Fax:* (0342) 411731 *E-mail:* vuurbaak@nd.nl; plateau@nd.nl *Web Site:* www.vuurbaak.nl, pg 492

VVF Verlag V Florentz GmbH (Germany) *Tel:* (089) 2809095 *Fax:* (089) 2809528, pg 297

VWB-Verlag fur Wissenschaft & Bildung, Amand Aglaster (Germany) *Tel:* (030) 251 04 15 *Fax:* (030) 251 11 36 *E-mail:* 100615.1565@compuserve.com *Web Site:* www.vwb-verlag.com, pg 297

Vydavatelstvi Cesky Geologicky Ustav (Czech Republic) *Tel:* 257 089 411 *Fax:* 257 531 376 *E-mail:* sekret@cgu.cz *Web Site:* www.cgu.cz, pg 128

Vysehrad spol sro (Czech Republic) *Tel:* 224 221 703 *Fax:* 224 221 703 *E-mail:* info@ivysehrad.cz *Web Site:* www.ivysehrad.cz, pg 128

Vysoka Vojenska Skola Letecka (Slovakia) *Tel:* (095) 6512183; (095) 6333851 *Fax:* (095) 333851, pg 561

Izdatelstvo Vysshaya Shkola (Russian Federation) *Tel:* (095) 2000456 *Fax:* (095) 2090350, pg 549

Vyturys Vyturio leidykla, UAB (Lithuania) *Tel:* (02122) 027404; (02122) 622542 *Fax:* (02122) 629407 *E-mail:* vyturys@vyturys.lt *Web Site:* www.vyturys.lt, pg 450

W Ludwig Verlag GmbH (Germany) *Tel:* (089) 41360; (01805) 990505 (hotline) *E-mail:* heyne-suedwest@randomhouse.de *Web Site:* www.ludwig-verlag.de, pg 297

Verlag Die Waage (Switzerland) *Tel:* (01) 7155569; (01) 7241969 *Fax:* (01) 7153380, pg 636

M Waagmeester-Verkuyl (Suriname) *Tel:* (0597) 498356, pg 608

Uitgeverij Waanders BV (Netherlands) *Tel:* (038) 4658628 *Fax:* (038) 4655989 *E-mail:* info@waanders.nl *Web Site:* www.waanders.nl, pg 492

Wydawnictwo WAB (Poland) *Tel:* (022) 646 05 10; (022) 646 05 11; (022) 646 01 74; (022) 646 01 75 *Fax:* (022) 646 05 10; (022) 646 05 11; (022) 646 01 74; (022) 646 01 75 *E-mail:* wab@wab.com.pl *Web Site:* www.wab.com.pl, pg 527

Wachholtz Verlag GmbH (Germany) *Tel:* (04321) 250-930 *Fax:* (04321) 906-275 *E-mail:* info@wachholtz.de *Web Site:* www.wachholtz.de, pg 297

Verlag Klaus Wagenbach (Germany) *Tel:* (030) 23 51 51-0 *Fax:* (030) 2 11 61 40 *E-mail:* mail@wagenbach.de *Web Site:* www.wagenbach.de, pg 297

Friedenauer Presse Katharina Wagenbach-Wolff (Germany) *Tel:* (030) 312 99 23 *Fax:* (030) 312 99 02 *Web Site:* www.friedenauer-press.de, pg 297

Wageningen Academic Publishers (Netherlands) *Tel:* (0317) 47 65 16 *Fax:* (0317) 45 34 17 *E-mail:* info@wageningenacademic.com *Web Site:* www.wageningenacademic.com, pg 492

Universitaetsverlag Wagner GmbH (Austria) *Tel:* (0512) 597721 *Fax:* (0512) 582209 *E-mail:* mail@uvw.at, pg 59

Wagner'sche Universitaetsbuchhandlung (Austria) *Tel:* (0512) 59505-0 *Fax:* (0512) 59505-38 *E-mail:* buch@wagnersche.at *Web Site:* www.wagnersche.at, pg 1301

AB Wahlstroem & Widstrand (Sweden) *Tel:* (08) 696 84 80 *Fax:* (08) 696 83 80 *E-mail:* info@wwd.se *Web Site:* www.wwd.se, pg 616

Wahlstrom & Widstrand (Sweden) *Tel:* (08) 696 84 80 *Fax:* (08) 696 83 80 *E-mail:* info@wwd.se *Web Site:* www.wwd.se, pg 616

B Wahlstroms (Sweden) *Tel:* (08) 619 86 00 *Fax:* (08) 618 97 61 *E-mail:* info@wahlstroms.se *Web Site:* www.wahlstroms.se, pg 616

John Waite Ltd (United Kingdom) *Tel:* (1797) 344 283 *Fax:* (01892) 784156, pg 771

Wakefield Press Pty Ltd (Australia) *Tel:* (08) 8362 8800 *Fax:* (08) 8362 7592 *E-mail:* info@wakefieldpress.com.au *Web Site:* www.wakefieldpress.com.au, pg 46

Verlag im Waldgut AG (Switzerland) *Tel:* (054) 222344 *Fax:* (054) 7288927, pg 636

Walhalla Fachverlag GmbH & Co KG Praetoria (Germany) *Tel:* (0941) 5684-0 *Fax:* (0941) 5684-111 *E-mail:* walhalla@walhalla.de *Web Site:* www.walhalla.de, pg 297

Walker Books Ltd (United Kingdom) *Tel:* (01256) 329242 *Fax:* (01256) 812558; (01256) 812521 *E-mail:* enquiry@walker.co.uk *Web Site:* www.walkerbooks.co.uk, pg 771

S Walker Literary Agency (United Kingdom) *Tel:* (01234) 216229, pg 1144

Sally Walker Language Services (United Kingdom) *Tel:* (0117) 929 1594 *Fax:* (0117) 929 6033 *E-mail:* translations@sallywalker.co.uk; languages@sallywalker.co.uk *Web Site:* www.sallywalker.co.uk, pg 1152

Edgar Wallace Society (United Kingdom) *E-mail:* info@edgarwallace.org *Web Site:* www.edgarwallace.org, pg 1410

Librairie Walter (Togo), pg 1345

Walter Verlag AG (Switzerland) *Tel:* (062) 341188 *Fax:* (062) 321184 *E-mail:* info@walter-verlag.ch *Web Site:* www.walter-verlag.ch, pg 637

Verlag Mag Wanzenbock (Austria) *Tel:* (01) 7148542 *Fax:* (01) 7135814, pg 59

The Warburg Institute (United Kingdom) *Tel:* (020) 7862 8949 *Fax:* (020) 7862 8955 *E-mail:* warburg@sas.ac.uk *Web Site:* www.sas.ac.uk/warburg/, pg 771

Ward Lock Educational Co Ltd (United Kingdom) *Tel:* (01342) 318980 *Fax:* (01342) 410980 *E-mail:* wle@lingkee.com *Web Site:* www.wardlockeducational.com, pg 771

Ward Lock Ltd (United Kingdom) *Tel:* (020) 7420 5555 *Fax:* (020) 7240 7261, pg 771

Peter Ward Book Exports (United Kingdom) *Tel:* (020) 8772 3300 *Fax:* (020) 8772 3309 *E-mail:* peter@pwbookex.dircon.co.uk, pg 1144

Peter Ward Book Exports (United Kingdom) *Tel:* (020) 8772 3300 *Fax:* (020) 8772 3309 *E-mail:* pwbookex@dircon.co.uk, pg 1355

Warna Publishers (Sri Lanka), pg 607

Frederick Warne Publishers Ltd (United Kingdom) *Tel:* (020) 7010 3000 *Fax:* (020) 7010 6706, pg 771

Uwe Warnke Verlag (Germany) *Tel:* (030) 29049903 *E-mail:* warnke@snafu.de, pg 297

Wartburg Verlag GmbH (Germany) *Tel:* (03643) 24 61-44 *Fax:* (03643) 24 61-18 *E-mail:* buch@wartburgverlag.de *Web Site:* www.wartburgverlag.de, pg 297

Waruni Publishers (Sri Lanka) *Tel:* (08) 24370 *Fax:* (08) 32343, pg 607

Waseda University Library (Japan) *Tel:* (03) 32034141 *E-mail:* info@wul.waseda.ac.jp *Web Site:* www.wul.waseda.ac.jp, pg 1522

Waseda University Press (Japan) *Tel:* (03) 32031551; (03) 32031570 *Fax:* (03) 32070406; (03) 32031570 *E-mail:* info@waseda-up.co.jp *Web Site:* www.waseda-up.co.jp, pg 431

Ernst Wasmuth Verlag GmbH & Co (Germany) *Tel:* (07071) 97 55 00 *Fax:* (07071) 97 55 013 *E-mail:* info@wasmuth-verlag.de *Web Site:* www.wasmuth-verlag.de, pg 297

Water Resources and Electric Power Press (CWPP) (China) *Tel:* (010) 898031 *Fax:* (010) 68353010, pg 109

Waterkant-Uitgewers (Edms) Bpk (South Africa) *Tel:* (021) 215540 *Fax:* (021) 4191865, pg 570

The Watermark Press (Australia) *Tel:* (02) 9818 5677 *Fax:* (02) 9818 5581 *E-mail:* books@nsw.bigpond.net.au, pg 46

Waterstone & Co Ltd (United Kingdom) *Tel:* (020) 8742 3800, pg 1355

Waterville Publishing House (Ghana) *Tel:* (01) 3254591; (01) 3314403 *Fax:* (01) 3314403, pg 305

Watkiss Automation Ltd (United Kingdom) *Tel:* (01767) 682177 *Fax:* (01767) 691769 *E-mail:* info@watkiss.com; contact@watkiss.com *Web Site:* www.watkiss.com, pg 1165

Watkiss Automation Ltd (United Kingdom) *Tel:* (01767) 682177 *Fax:* (01767) 691769 *E-mail:* contact@watkiss.com *Web Site:* www.watkiss.com, pg 1185, 1227, 1239, 1248

Watson, Little Ltd (United Kingdom) *Tel:* (020) 7431 0770 *Fax:* (020) 7431 7225, pg 1144

A P Watt Ltd (United Kingdom) *Tel:* (020) 7405 6774 *Fax:* (020) 7831 2154 *E-mail:* apw@apwatt.co.uk *Web Site:* www.apwatt.co.uk, pg 771, 1144

Watthana Phanit (Thailand) *Tel:* (02) 2217225, pg 646

Watti-Kustannus Oy (Finland) *Tel:* (09) 1356878 *Fax:* (09) 1356437, pg 144

Franklin Watts Australia (Australia) *Tel:* (02) 8338 8800 *Fax:* (02) 8338 8881 *E-mail:* info@wattspub.com.au *Web Site:* www.wattspub.com.au, pg 46

The Watts Publishing Group Ltd (United Kingdom) *Tel:* (020) 7739 2929 *Fax:* (020) 7739 2181 *E-mail:* gm@wattspub.co.uk *Web Site:* www.wattspub.co.uk, pg 771

Waxmann Verlag GmbH (Germany) *Tel:* (0251) 265040 *Fax:* (0251) 2650426 *E-mail:* info@waxmann.com *Web Site:* www.waxmann.com, pg 297

WDV Wirtschaftsdienst Gesellschaft fur Medien & Kommunikation mbH & Co OHG (Germany) *Tel:* (06172) 670-0 *Fax:* (01672) 670144 *E-mail:* info@wdv.de *Web Site:* www.wdv.de, pg 298

Weather Press (Australia) *Tel:* (03) 9762-1647, pg 46

Weatherbys Allen Ltd (United Kingdom) *Tel:* (01933) 440077 (ext 351) *Fax:* (01933) 270300 *E-mail:* turfnews@weatherbys-group.com *Web Site:* www.weatherbys-allen.com, pg 772

Web Printers Sdn Bhd (Malaysia) *Tel:* (03) 7956 3577 *Fax:* (03) 7726 3563, pg 1221

Webb & Bower (Publishers) Ltd (United Kingdom) *Tel:* (01803) 835525 *Fax:* (01803) 835552, pg 772

Webcom Ltd (Canada) *Tel:* 416-496-1000 *Toll Free Tel:* 800-665-9322 *Fax:* 416-496-1537 *E-mail:* webcom@webcomlink.com *Web Site:* www.webcomlink.com, pg 1154, 1216, 1245

Weber SA d'Editions (Switzerland) *Tel:* (07) 93104541, pg 637

Weber Zucht & Co (Germany) *Tel:* (0561) 519194; (0561) 515953 *Fax:* (0561) 5102514 *E-mail:* wezuco@t-online.de, pg 298

WebsterWorld Pty Ltd (Australia) *Tel:* (02) 9939 5505 *Fax:* (02) 9939 8355 *E-mail:* webpub@websterpublishing.com *Web Site:* www.websterpublishing.com; www.websterworld.com; www.websterselearning.com, pg 46

Websters International Publishers Ltd (United Kingdom) *Tel:* (020) 7940 4700 *Fax:* (020) 7940 4701 *E-mail:* info@websters.co.uk *Web Site:* www.websters.co.uk; www.ozclarke.com, pg 772

Wegener Falkplan BV (Netherlands) *Tel:* (040) 2 642 111 *Fax:* (040) 2 410 955 *E-mail:* info@suurland.nl *Web Site:* www.suurland.nl, pg 492

Wehr & Wissen Verlagsgesellschaft mbH (Germany) *Tel:* (0228) 64830 *Fax:* (0228) 6483109 *E-mail:* 101336.245@compuserve.com; advert@moench-group.com, pg 298

Wei-Chuan Publishing Company Ltd (Taiwan, Province of China) *Tel:* (02) 27021148 *Fax:* (02) 27042729, pg 642

A Weichert Verlag GmbH & Co KG (Germany) *Tel:* (069) 942118-22 *Fax:* (069) 942118-17, pg 298

Weidler Buchverlag Berlin (Germany) *Tel:* (030) 394 86 68 *Fax:* (030) 394 86 98 *E-mail:* weidler_verlag@yahoo.de *Web Site:* www.weidler-verlag.de, pg 298

Weidlich Verlag (Germany) *Tel:* (0931) 385235 *Fax:* (0931) 385305 *E-mail:* info@verlagshaus.com *Web Site:* www.verlagshaus.com, pg 298

Weidmannsche Verlagsbuchhandlung GmbH (Germany) *Tel:* (05121) 15010 *Fax:* (05121) 150150 *E-mail:* info@olms.de *Web Site:* www.olms.de, pg 298

Fred Weidner & Daughter Printers (United States) *Tel:* 212-964-8676 *Fax:* 212-964-8677 *E-mail:* info@fwdprinters.com *Web Site:* www.fwdprinters.com, pg 1189, 1231, 1249

Weilburg Verlag (Austria) *Tel:* (02622) 29538 *Fax:* (02622) 2953822, pg 59

Weilin & Goos Oy (Finland) *Tel:* (09) 4377 603 *Fax:* (00) 4377 334 *E-mail:* asiakaspalvelu@wg.fi *Web Site:* www.wg.fi, pg 144

Galerie Lucie Weill-Seligmann (France) *Tel:* (01) 43 54 71 95 *Fax:* (01) 40 51 82 88, pg 189

Josef Weinberger Plays (United Kingdom) *Tel:* (020) 7580 2827 *Fax:* (020) 7436 9616 *E-mail:* general.info@jwmail.co.uk *Web Site:* www.josef-weinberger.com, pg 1144

Verlag W Weinmann (Germany) *Tel:* (030) 855 48 95 *Fax:* (030) 8 55 94 64 *E-mail:* info@weinmann-verlag.de *Web Site:* www.weinmann-verlag.de, pg 298

Rupertusbuchhandlung Augustin Weis und Soehne KG (Austria) *Tel:* (0662) 878733-0 *Fax:* (0662) 871661 *E-mail:* info@rupertusbuch.at, pg 1301

Dr Otfried Weise Verlag Tabula Smaragdina (Austria) *Tel:* (01) 804 2974 *Fax:* (01) 961 8287 *E-mail:* tabula@smaragdina.at *Web Site:* smaragdina.at, pg 59

Herbert Weishaupt Verlag (Austria) *Tel:* (03151) 8487 *Fax:* (03151) 84874 *E-mail:* verlag@weishaupt.at *Web Site:* www.weishaupt.at, pg 59

Weisser Ring, Gemeinnutzige Verlagsgesellschaft mbH (Germany) *Tel:* (06131) 83 03 01 *Fax:* (06131) 83 03 45 *E-mail:* info@weisser ring.de *Web Site:* www.weisser-ring.de, pg 298

Weitz Center for Development Study (Israel) *Tel:* (08) 9474111 *Fax:* (08) 9475884 *E-mail:* dsc@netvision.net.il, pg 1520

Weizmann Institute of Science Libraries (Israel) *Tel:* (08) 9343583 (WIX Central Library); (08) 9343211 (Weizmann Institute); (08) 9344176 *E-mail:* hedva.milo@weizmann.ac.il *Web Site:* www.weizmann.ac.il/WIS-library, pg 1520

Editions Weka (France) *Tel:* (01) 53 35 16 16; (01) 53 35 17 17 *Fax:* (01) 53 35 17 01 *E-mail:* infos@weka.fr *Web Site:* www.weka.fr, pg 189

WEKA Firmengruppe GmbH & Co KG (Germany) *Tel:* (08233) 23-0 *Fax:* (08233) 23-7500 *E-mail:* service@weka.de *Web Site:* www.weka.de; www.weka-group.de; www.weka-group.com, pg 298

Weka Informations Schriften Verlag AG (Switzerland) *Tel:* (01) 4328432 *Fax:* (01) 4328201, pg 637

Wellcome Library for the History & Understanding of Medicine (United Kingdom) *Tel:* (020) 7611 8722 *Fax:* (020) 7611 8369 *E-mail:* library@wellcome.ac.uk *Web Site:* library.wellcome.ac.uk, pg 1554

Wellday Ltd (Hong Kong) *Tel:* 23628489 *Fax:* 23628564, pg 320

Wellington City Libraries (New Zealand) *Tel:* (04) 801 4040 *Fax:* (04) 801 4047 *E-mail:* central@wcl.govt.nz *Web Site:* www.wcl.govt.nz, pg 1532

Wellington Lane Press Pty Ltd (Australia) *Tel:* (02) 99040962 *Fax:* (02) 99040962, pg 46

Wellington Orchid Society Publications (New Zealand) *Tel:* (04) 4783901, pg 502

Wellness Australia (Australia) *Tel:* (08) 9387 6134 *Fax:* (08) 9383 7323 *E-mail:* info@workteams.com, pg 46

H G Wells Society (United Kingdom) *Web Site:* hgwellsusa.50megs.com, pg 1410

Verlag Welsermuehl (Austria) *Tel:* (07242) 231-0 *Fax:* (07242) 23118, pg 59

Welsh Academic Press (United Kingdom) *Tel:* (029) 2056 0343 *Fax:* (029) 2056 1631 *E-mail:* post@ashley.drake.com *Web Site:* www.welsh-academic-press.co.uk, pg 772

Welsh Books Council (United Kingdom) *Tel:* (01970) 624151 *Fax:* (01970) 625385 *E-mail:* castellbrychan@wbc.org.uk *Web Site:* www.cllc.org.uk, pg 1293, 1355

Welsh Library Association (United Kingdom) *Tel:* (01970) 622174 *Fax:* (01970) 622190 *E-mail:* hle@aber.ac.uk *Web Site:* www.dil.aber.ac.uk/holi/wla/wla.htm, pg 1573

Verlagsgruppe Weltbild (Germany) *Tel:* (0821) 70 04-70 00 *Fax:* (0821) 70 04-17 90 *E-mail:* info@weltbild.com *Web Site:* www.weltbild.com, pg 298

Weltforum Verlag GmbH (Germany) *Tel:* (0228) 3682436 *Fax:* (0228) 3682436 *E-mail:* wfv@internationsafrikaforum.de, pg 299

Weltkunst Verlag GmbH (Germany) *Tel:* (089) 1269900 *Fax:* (089) 12699011 *E-mail:* info@weltkunstverlag.de *Web Site:* www.weltkunstverlag.de, pg 299

Weltrundschau Verlag AG (Switzerland) *Tel:* (041) 761 54 31 *Fax:* (041) 761 44 04 *E-mail:* wrs@bluewin.ch *Web Site:* www.wrs.ch, pg 637

Weltwoche ABC-Verlag (Switzerland) *Tel:* (01) 2078643; (01) 2078650; (01) 2078756 *Fax:* (01) 2078680 *E-mail:* order@baz.ch, pg 637

Verlag Galerie Welz Salzburg (Austria) *Tel:* (0662) 841771; (0662) 840990 *Fax:* (0662) 84177120 *E-mail:* office@galerie-welz.at *Web Site:* www.galerie-welz.at, pg 59

Wennergren-Cappelen A/S (Norway) *Tel:* (022) 35 72 50 *Fax:* (022) 33 71 04 *E-mail:* wenca@wenca.no *Web Site:* www.wenca.no, pg 1333

Wepf & Co AG (Switzerland) *Tel:* (061) 256377 *Fax:* (061) 253597 *E-mail:* wepf@dial.eunet.ch, pg 637

Wepf & Co AG (Switzerland) *Tel:* (061) 269 85 15 (Germany) *Fax:* (061) 261 35 97 (Germany) *E-mail:* wepf@dial.eunet.ch *Web Site:* www.wepf.ch, pg 1344

Wer liefert was? GmbH (Germany) *Tel:* (040) 25440-0 *Fax:* (040) 25440-100 *E-mail:* info@wlw.de *Web Site:* www.wlw.de, pg 299

Gideon S Were Press (Kenya) *Tel:* (020) 331135 *E-mail:* gswere@nbnet.co.ke, pg 436

Wereldbibliotheek (Netherlands) *Tel:* (020) 638 18 99 *Fax:* (020) 638 44 91 *E-mail:* info@wereldbibliotheek.nl *Web Site:* www.wereldbibliotheek.nl, pg 492

Wereldwijd Mediahuis VzW (Belgium) *Tel:* (02) 3-2162935 *Fax:* (02) 3-2377757 *E-mail:* wereldwijd@wereldwijd.ngonet.be, pg 74

Werner Druck AG (Switzerland) *Tel:* (061) 2710690 *Fax:* (061) 2710601 *Web Site:* www.wernerdruck.ch, pg 637

Werner Soederstrom Osakeyhtio (WSOY) (Finland) *Tel:* (09) 61 681 *Fax:* (09) 616 3566, pg 145

Werner Soederstrom Osakeyhtio (WSOY) (Finland) *Tel:* (00) 61681 *Fax:* (90) 61683566, pg 1130

Werner Verlag GmbH & Co KG (Germany) *Tel:* (0211) 3 87 98-0 *Fax:* (0211) 3 87 98-11 *E-mail:* info@werner-verlag.de, pg 299

Wespennest - Zeitschrift fuer brauchbare Texte und Bilder (Austria) *Tel:* (01) 332 66 91 *Fax:* (01) 333 29 70 *E-mail:* office@wespennest.at *Web Site:* www.wespennest.at, pg 59

Wessex Translations (United Kingdom) *Tel:* (0870) 1669 300 *Toll Free Tel:* 800 975 5900 *Fax:* (0870) 1669 299 *E-mail:* sales@wt-lm.com; info@wt-lm.com *Web Site:* www.wt-languagemanagement.com, pg 1152

West African Book Publishers Ltd (Nigeria) *Tel:* (01) 960760; (01) 960764; (01) 825020; (01) 526616 *Fax:* (01) 619835, pg 507

West Country Writers' Association (United Kingdom) *Tel:* (01395) 222749 *E-mail:* wcwa@westcountrywriters.co.uk *Web Site:* www.author.co.uk/wcwa, pg 1410

West-Friesland/Boekproject-ontwikkeling (Netherlands) *Tel:* (0229) 212625 *Fax:* (0229) 216949, pg 492

John West Publications Co Ltd (Nigeria) *Tel:* (01) 932011, pg 507, 1332

West-Pakistan Publishing Co (Pvt) Ltd (Pakistan) *Tel:* (042) 52427, pg 515, 1334

Georg Westermann Verlag GmbH (Germany) *Tel:* (0531) 708-244 *Fax:* (0531) 708-248 *E-mail:* westermann@plus.at, pg 299

Westermann Schulbuchverlag GmbH (Germany) *Tel:* (0531) 7 08-0 *Fax:* (0531) 70 82 09 *E-mail:* schulservice@westermann.de *Web Site:* www.westermann.de, pg 299

Uitgeverij Westers (Netherlands) *Tel:* (030) 2931043 *Fax:* (030) 2944586 *E-mail:* boekhandel@westers-utrecht.nl, pg 492

Verlag Westfaelisches Dampfboot (Germany) *Tel:* (0251) 3900480 *Fax:* (0251) 39004850 *E-mail:* info@dampfboot-verlag.de *Web Site:* www.dampfboot-verlag.de, pg 299

Westholsteinische Verlagsanstalt und Verlagsdruckerei Boyens & Co (Germany) *Tel:* (0481) 6886-151; (0481) 6886-152 *Fax:* (0481) 688467 *E-mail:* buchhandlung@sh-nordsee.de *Web Site:* www.sh-nordsee.de, pg 299

Westminster Abbey Library (United Kingdom) *Tel:* (020) 7654 4830 *Fax:* (020) 7654 4827 *E-mail:* library@westminster-abbey.org *Web Site:* westminster-abbey.org, pg 1554

Westview Press (United Kingdom) *Tel:* (01865) 865466 *Fax:* (01865) 862763 *E-mail:* perseus@oppuk.co.uk *Web Site:* www.westviewpress.com, pg 772

Wettergrens Bokhandel AB (Sweden) *Tel:* (031) 706 25 00 *Fax:* (031) 778 14 80 *E-mail:* info@wettergrens.se, pg 1344

Buchverlag der Druckerei Wetzikon AG (Switzerland) *Tel:* (01) 9333111 *Fax:* (01) 9323232, pg 637

Erich Wewel Verlag GmbH (Germany) *Tel:* (0906) 73-0 *Fax:* (0906) 73-1 77 *Web Site:* www.klett.de/geschaeftsbereiche/grundschule.html, pg 299

WH Trade Binders Ltd (United Kingdom) *Tel:* (01327) 704911 *Fax:* (01327) 872588 *E-mail:* wh@whtradebinders.demon.co.uk, pg 1227

Wharncliffe Publishing Ltd (United Kingdom) *Tel:* (01226) 734222 *Fax:* (01226) 734438 *E-mail:* sales@pen-and-sword.co.uk, pg 772

A H Wheeler & Co Ltd (India) *Tel:* (011) 3312629; (011) 3318537 *Fax:* (011) 3357798 *E-mail:* wheelerpub@mantraonline.com, pg 353

Which? Ltd (United Kingdom) *Tel:* (020) 7770 7000 *Fax:* (020) 7770 7485; (020) 7770 7600 *E-mail:* editor@which.net *Web Site:* www.which.net, pg 772

Whitaker Information Services (United Kingdom) *Tel:* (01252) 742525 *Fax:* (01252) 742526 *E-mail:* custserv@whitaker.co.uk *Web Site:* www.whitaker.co.uk, pg 1355

Whitcoulls Ltd (New Zealand) *Tel:* (09) 356 5410 *Fax:* (09) 356 5423 *E-mail:* feedback@whitcoulls.co.nz *Web Site:* www.whitcoulls.co.nz, pg 1331

White Cockade Publishing (United Kingdom) *Tel:* (01865) 510411 *E-mail:* mail@whitecockade.co.uk *Web Site:* www.whitecockade.co.uk, pg 772

White Eagle Publishing Trust (United Kingdom) *Tel:* (01730) 893300 *Fax:* (01730) 892235 *E-mail:* enquiries@whiteagle.org *Web Site:* www.whiteaglelodge.org, pg 772

White Lotus Co Ltd (Thailand) *Tel:* (02) 332-4915; (02) 741-6288; (02) 741-6289 *Fax:* (02) 311-4575; (02) 741-6287; (02) 741-6607 *Web Site:* thailine.com/lotus, pg 646, 1345

Whiting & Birch Ltd (United Kingdom) *Tel:* (020) 8244 2421 *Fax:* (020) 8244 2448 *E-mail:* savpub@dircon.co.uk *Web Site:* www.whitingbirch.com, pg 773

Whittet Books Ltd (United Kingdom) *Tel:* (01449) 781877 *Fax:* (01449) 781898 *Web Site:* www.whittetbooks.com, pg 773

Whittles Publishing (United Kingdom) *Tel:* (01593) 741240 *Fax:* (01593) 741360 *E-mail:* info@whittlespublishing.com *Web Site:* www.whittlespublishing.com, pg 773

Who's Who In Italy srl (Italy) *Tel:* (02) 66503753; (02) 6101627 *Fax:* (02) 6105587 *E-mail:* whoswhogc@attglobal.net *Web Site:* www.whoswho-sutter.com, pg 412

Who's Who of Southern Africa (South Africa) *Tel:* (011) 8802406 *Fax:* (011) 8802366, pg 570

WHSmith PLC (United Kingdom) *Tel:* (020) 7409 3222 *Fax:* (020) 7514 9633 *E-mail:* customer.relations@whsmith.co.uk *Web Site:* www.whsmith.co.uk, pg 1355

Whurr Publishers Ltd (United Kingdom) *Tel:* (020) 7359 5979 *Fax:* (020) 7226 5290 *E-mail:* info@whurr.co.uk *Web Site:* www.whurr.co.uk, pg 773

WI Enterprises Ltd (United Kingdom) *Tel:* (020) 7371 9300 *Fax:* (020) 7471 9300 *E-mail:* d.page@nfwi.org.uk *Web Site:* www.womens-institute.co.uk/shop/policies/about.shtml, pg 773

Wichern Verlag GmbH (Germany) *Tel:* (030) 28 87 48 10 *Fax:* (030) 28 87 48 12 *E-mail:* info@wichern.de *Web Site:* www.wichern.de, pg 299

Wichern-Verlag GmbH (Germany) *Tel:* (030) 288748-0 *Fax:* (030) 28874812 *E-mail:* 101711.1207@compuserve.com, pg 299

Herbert Wichmann Verlag (Germany) *Tel:* (06221) 4890 *Fax:* (06221) 489279 *E-mail:* wichmann@huethig.de *Web Site:* www.huethig.de, pg 299

Widjaya Penerbit (Indonesia) *Tel:* (021) 3813446, pg 357

Wiechmann-Verlag Betriebs GmbH (Germany) *Tel:* (0700) 08000035 *Fax:* (0700) 08000036, pg 300

'Wiedza Powszechna' Panstwowe Wydawnictwo (Poland) *Tel:* (022) 8277651 *Fax:* (022) 8269592; (022) 8268594, pg 527

Universitaetsbibliothek Wien (Austria) *Tel:* (01) 427715001 *Fax:* (01) 42779150 *E-mail:* aer.ub@univie.ac.at; info.ub@univie.ac.at *Web Site:* www.ub.univie.ac.at, pg 1492

Dinah Wiener Ltd (United Kingdom) *Tel:* (020) 8994 6011 *Fax:* (020) 8994 6044 *E-mail:* dinahwiener@enterprise.net, pg 1144

Wiener Dom-Verlag GmbH (Austria) *Tel:* (01) 5123503 *Fax:* (01) 5123503-30 *Web Site:* www.buchwirtschaft.at, pg 59

Wiener Stadt- und Landesarchiv (Austria) *Tel:* (01) 4000-84815 *Fax:* (01) 4000-7238 *E-mail:* post@m08.magwien.gv.at *Web Site:* www.magwien.gv.at, pg 1492

Wiener Stadt- und Landesbibliothek (Austria) *Tel:* (01) 4000-84920 *Fax:* (01) 4000-7219 *E-mail:* post@m09.magwien.gv.et *Web Site:* www.stadtbibliothek.wien.at, pg 1492

Wienerland Zeitung & Verlag (Austria) *Tel:* (02244) 3536 *Fax:* (02244) 3536-4 *E-mail:* wienerland@asn.or.at, pg 60

Wiese Verlag AG (Switzerland) *Tel:* (061) 6391315 *Fax:* (061) 6391343 *E-mail:* order@baz.ch *Web Site:* www.baz.ch, pg 637

Wieser Verlag (Austria) *Tel:* (0463) 37036 *Fax:* (0463) 37635 *E-mail:* office@wieser-verlag.com *Web Site:* www.wieser-verlag.com, pg 60

Verlag Alexander Wild (Switzerland) *Tel:* (031) 3114480 *Fax:* (031) 3114470, pg 637

Ediciones Alfred y Cia Wild Ltda (Colombia) *Tel:* (01) 6218000 *Fax:* (01) 6114338 *E-mail:* info@galeriaalfredwild.com *Web Site:* www.galeriaalfredwild.com, pg 114

Wild & Woolley (Australia) *Tel:* (02) 9337 6844 *Fax:* (02) 9337 6822 *E-mail:* pwoolley@fastbooks.com.au *Web Site:* www.booksandwriters.net, pg 46

Wild Goose Publications (United Kingdom) *Tel:* (0141) 332 6292 *Fax:* (0141) 332 1090 *E-mail:* admin@ionabooks.com *Web Site:* www.ionabooks.com, pg 773

Wild Publications Pty Ltd (Australia) *Tel:* (03) 9826-8482 *Fax:* (03) 9826-3787 *E-mail:* management@wild.com.au *Web Site:* www.wild.com.au, pg 46

Wildscape Australia (Australia) *Tel:* (07) 4093 7171 *Fax:* (07) 4093 8897, pg 46

Wileman Publications (Australia) *Tel:* (07) 312770 *E-mail:* wileman@onthenet.com.au, pg 46

Magazyn Wilenski (Lithuania) *Tel:* (05) 242 77 18 *E-mail:* magazyn@magwil.lt *Web Site:* www.magwil.lt, pg 450

Wiley Europe Ltd (United Kingdom) *Tel:* (01243) 779777 *Fax:* (01243) 775878 *E-mail:* customer@wiley.co.uk *Web Site:* www.wiley.co.uk, pg 773

John Wiley & Sons (Asia) Pte Ltd (Singapore) *Tel:* 64632400 *Fax:* 64634605; 64634604 *E-mail:* enquiry@wiley.com.sg *Web Site:* www.wiley.co.uk, pg 559

John Wiley & Sons Australia, Ltd (Australia) *Tel:* (07) 3859 9755 *Fax:* (07) 3859 9715 *E-mail:* brisbane@johnwiley.com.au *Web Site:* www.johnwiley.com.au, pg 46

Wiley-VCH Verlag GmbH (Germany) *Tel:* (06201) 606 0 *Fax:* (06201) 606 328 *E-mail:* info@wiley-vch.de *Web Site:* www.wiley-vch.de, pg 300

Wydawnictwo Wilga sp zoo (Poland) *Tel:* (022) 826-08-82; (022) 827-90-11 (ext 282) *Fax:* (022) 826-06-43 *E-mail:* wilga@wilga.com.pl, pg 527

Bridget Williams Books Ltd (New Zealand) *Tel:* (04) 4738317 *Fax:* (04) 4738417 *E-mail:* bwbooks@ihug.co.nz, pg 502

Jonathan Williams Literary Agency (Ireland) *Tel:* (01) 2803482 *Fax:* (01) 2803482, pg 1133

Wilmington Business Information Ltd (United Kingdom) *Tel:* (020) 7549 8704 *Fax:* (020) 7490 2979 *Web Site:* www.waterlow.com/signature/, pg 774

Editions Luce Wilquin (Belgium) *Tel:* (019) 69 98 13 *Fax:* (019) 69 98 13 *E-mail:* wilquin.bouquin@skynet.be *Web Site:* www.wilquin.com, pg 74

A S Wilson Inc (Australia) *Tel:* (02) 9528 8977, pg 47

Wilson & Horton Publications Ltd (New Zealand) *Tel:* (09) 360 3820 *Fax:* (09) 360 3831 *E-mail:* whpubs@listener.co.nz *Web Site:* www.wilsonandhorton.co.nz, pg 502

John Wilson Booksales (United Kingdom) *Tel:* (01844) 275927 *Fax:* (01844) 274402 *E-mail:* jw@jwbs.co.uk, pg 1248

Philip Wilson Publishers (United Kingdom) *Tel:* (020) 7033 9900 *Fax:* (020) 7033 9922 *E-mail:* sales@philip-wilson.co.uk *Web Site:* www.philip-wilson.co.uk, pg 774

Wimbledon Publishing Company Ltd (United Kingdom) *Tel:* (020) 7401 4200 *Fax:* (020) 7928 4201 *E-mail:* enquiries@wpcpress.com *Web Site:* www.wpcpress.com, pg 774

Windhoek Public Library (Namibia) *Tel:* (061) 224899 *Fax:* (061) 212169 *E-mail:* rviljoen@unam.na, pg 1530

Windhoeker Buchhandlung (Namibia) *Tel:* (061) 225216 *Fax:* (061) 225011, pg 1328

Windhorse Books (Australia) *Tel:* (02) 9519 8826 *Fax:* (02) 9519 8826 *E-mail:* books@windhorse.com.au *Web Site:* www.windhorse.com.au, pg 47

Windhorse Publications (United Kingdom) *Tel:* (0121) 449 9191 *Fax:* (0121) 449 9191 *E-mail:* info@windhorsepublications.com *Web Site:* www.windhorsepublications.com, pg 774

Windmuehle GmbH Verlag und Vertrieb von Medien (Germany) *Tel:* (040) 86 83 07 *Fax:* (040) 866 31 23 *E-mail:* info@windmuehle-verlag.de *Web Site:* www.windmuehle-verlag.de, pg 300

Windpferd Verlagsgesellschaft mbH (Germany) *Tel:* (08343) 1404 *Fax:* (08343) 1403 *E-mail:* info@windpferd.de *Web Site:* www.windpferd.de, pg 300

The Windrush Press Ltd (United Kingdom) *Tel:* (01608) 658758 *Fax:* (01608) 659345 *E-mail:* info@windrushpublishingservices.com *Web Site:* www.windrushpress.com, pg 774

Windsor Books International (United Kingdom) *Tel:* (01865) 361122 *Fax:* (01865) 361133 *E-mail:* sales@windsorbooks.co.uk *Web Site:* www.windsorbooks.co.uk, pg 774

Windward Publications (Australia) *Tel:* (02) 4464 1977 *Fax:* (02) 4464 1906 *E-mail:* sales@windward.com.au *Web Site:* www.windward.com.au, pg 47

Winetitles (Australia) *Tel:* (08) 8233 4799 *Fax:* (08) 8233 4790 *E-mail:* admin@winetitles.com.au *Web Site:* www.winetitles.com.au, pg 47

Wing King Tong Group (Hong Kong) *Tel:* 24073287; 24073309; 24074547 *Fax:* 24074130 *E-mail:* humanre@wkt-group.com *Web Site:* www.cgan.com, pg 1158

Wing King Tong Group (Hong Kong) *Tel:* 24073287; 24073309; 24074547 *Fax:* 24074130, pg 1179

Wing King Tong Group (Hong Kong) *Tel:* 24073287 *Fax:* 24074130; 24087939 *E-mail:* printing@wkt.cc; books@wkt.cc *Web Site:* www.wkt.cc, pg 1220, 1236

Rosa Winkel Verlag GmbH (Germany) *Tel:* (030) 85729295 *Fax:* (030) 85729296 *E-mail:* rosawinkel@t-online.de, pg 300

Dr Dieter Winkler (Germany) *Tel:* (0234) 9650200 *Fax:* (0234) 9650201 *E-mail:* winkler-verlag.bochum@tonline.de *Web Site:* www.winklerverlag.de, pg 300

Winklers Verlag Gebrueder Grimm (Germany) *Tel:* (06151) 87 68-0 *Fax:* (06151) 87 68-61 *E-mail:* service@winklers.de *Web Site:* www.winklers.de, pg 300

Winter & Co UK Ltd (United Kingdom) *Tel:* (01480) 377177 *Fax:* (01480) 377166 *E-mail:* sales@winteruk.com *Web Site:* www.winteruk.com, pg 1239

Berthold Winter (Germany) *Tel:* (030) 362 35 30 *Fax:* (030) 362 96 93, pg 1312

Verlag fuer Wirtschaft & Verwaltung Hubert Wingen GmbH & Co KG (Germany) *Tel:* (0201) 22 25 41; (0201) 22 25 42; (0201) 221451-52 *Fax:* (0201) 229660, pg 300

Wisby & Wilkens (Denmark) *Tel:* 7023 4622 *Fax:* 7043 4722 *E-mail:* mail@bogshop.dk *Web Site:* www.wisby-wilkens.com, www.bogshop.dk, pg 135

Wisdom Books (United Kingdom) *Tel:* (020) 8553 5020 *Fax:* (020) 8553 5122 *E-mail:* sales@wisdom-books.com *Web Site:* www.wisdom-books.com, pg 1355

Wison Verlag GmbH (Germany) *Tel:* (0221) 4722-0 *Fax:* (0221) 448911, pg 300

Verlag Wissenschaft und Politik (Germany) *Tel:* (034904) 32946 *Fax:* (034904) 32946 *E-mail:* helker.pflug@t-online.de, pg 300

Wissenschaftliche Allgemeinbibliothek der Stadt Erfurt (Germany) *Tel:* (0361) 562 48 76 *Fax:* (0361) 646 20 71, pg 1511

Wissenschaftliche Buchgesellschaft (Germany) *Tel:* (06151) 33 08-0 *Fax:* (06151) 31 41 28 *E-mail:* service@wbg-darmstadt.de *Web Site:* www.wbg-darmstadt.de, pg 300

Wissenschaftliche Buchgesellschaft (Germany) *Tel:* (06151) 3308-161 *Fax:* (06151) 3308208 *E-mail:* service@wbg-darmstadt.de, pg 1252

Wissenschaftliche Verlagsgesellschaft mbH (Germany) *Tel:* (0711) 2582-0 *Fax:* (0711) 2582-290 *E-mail:* service@wissenschaftliche-verlagsgesellschaft.de *Web Site:* www.dav-buchhandlung.de, pg 300, 1155

Wissenschaftsrat (Germany) *Tel:* (0221) 3776-0 *Fax:* (0221) 38 84 40 *E-mail:* post@wissenschaftsrat.de *Web Site:* www.wissenschaftsrat.de, pg 300

Vydavatelstvo Wist sro (Slovakia) *Tel:* (0842) 4289652 *Fax:* (0842) 4289652 *E-mail:* wist@enelux.sk, pg 561

WIT Press (United Kingdom) *Tel:* (023) 8029 3223 *Fax:* (023) 8029 2853 *E-mail:* witpress@witpress.com *Web Site:* www.witpress.com, pg 774

Witherby & Co Ltd (United Kingdom) *Tel:* (020) 7251 5341 *Fax:* (020) 7251 1296 *E-mail:* books@witherbys.co.uk *Web Site:* www.witherbys.com, pg 775, 1355

Witman Publishing Co (HK) Ltd (Hong Kong) *Tel:* 2562 6279 *Fax:* 2565 5482 *E-mail:* witmanp@hk.star.com, pg 320

Verlag Claus Wittal (Germany) *Tel:* (0611) 502907 *Fax:* (0611) 503021 *E-mail:* cw@exlibrisart.com *Web Site:* www.exlibrisart.com, pg 301

Friedrich Wittig Verlag GmbH (Germany) *Tel:* (0431) 55779 206 *Fax:* (0431) 55779 292, pg 301

Verlag Konrad Wittwer GmbH (Germany) *Tel:* (0711) 25 07 0 *Fax:* (0711) 25 07 145 *E-mail:* info@wittwer.de *Web Site:* www.wittwer.de, pg 301

Verlags -und Sortiments-Buchhandlung Konrad Wittwer GmbH & Co KG (Germany) *Tel:* (0711) 25 07 0 *Fax:* (0711) 25 07 145 *E-mail:* info@wittwer.de *Web Site:* www.wittwer.de, pg 1312

Witwatersrand University Press (South Africa) *Tel:* (011) 4845907 *Fax:* (011) 4845971 *Web Site:* www.wits.ac.za/wup.html, pg 570

Wizard Books Pty Ltd (Australia) *Tel:* (03) 5332 3435 *Fax:* (03) 5331 1488 *E-mail:* admin@wizardbooks.com.au *Web Site:* www.wizardbooks.com.au, pg 47

The Woburn Press (United Kingdom) *Tel:* (020) 8920 2100 *Fax:* (020) 8447 8548 *E-mail:* info@woburnpress.com *Web Site:* www.frankcass.com/wp, pg 775

Wochenschau Verlag, Dr Kurt Debus GmbH (Germany) *Tel:* (06196) 8 60 65 *Fax:* (06196) 8 60 60 *E-mail:* info@wochenschau-verlag.de *Web Site:* www.wochenschau-verlag.de, pg 301

Woeli Publishing Services (Ghana) *Tel:* (021) 227182; (021) 229294 *Fax:* (021) 777098; (021) 229294 *E-mail:* woeli@libr.ug.edu.gh; asempa@ghana.com, pg 305

Galerie Esther Woerdehoff (France) *Tel:* (01) 43 21 44 83 *Fax:* (01) 43 21 45 03 *E-mail:* galerie@ewgalerie.com *Web Site:* www.ewgalerie.com, pg 189

Verlagshaus Wohlfarth (Germany) *Tel:* (0203) 3 05 27-0 *Fax:* (0203) 3 05 27-820 *E-mail:* info@wohlfarth.de *Web Site:* www.wohlfarth.de, pg 301

Koninklijke Wohrmann Bv (Netherlands) *Tel:* (0575) 582121 *Fax:* (0575) 582128 *E-mail:* secretariaat@wohrmann.nl *Web Site:* www.wohrmann.nl, pg 1221

Forlaget Woldike K/S (Denmark) *Tel:* 33 73 35 85, pg 135

J E Wolfensberger AG (Switzerland) *Tel:* (01) 2857878 *Fax:* (01) 2857879 *E-mail:* prepress@wolfensberger-ag.ch *Web Site:* www.wolfensberger-ag.ch, pg 637

Wolfhound Press Ltd (Ireland) *Tel:* (01) 6764373 *Fax:* (01) 6764373 *E-mail:* websales@wolfhound.ie, pg 364

Kunstverlag Wolfrum (Austria) *Tel:* (01) 512 53 98-0 *Fax:* (01) 512 53 98-57 *E-mail:* your-welcome@wolfrum.at *Web Site:* www.wolfrum.at/html/wolfrum.htm, pg 60

Kunstverlag Wolfrum (Austria) *Tel:* (01) 5125398-0 *Fax:* (01) 5125398-57 *E-mail:* your-welcome@wolfrum.at *Web Site:* www.wolfrum.at, pg 1301

Wolf's-Verlag Berlin (Germany) *Tel:* (030) 5675190, pg 301

Wolgang Fietkau (Germany) *Tel:* (0203) 71 105 *Fax:* (0203) 71 109 *E-mail:* fietkau@fietkau.de *Web Site:* www.fietkau.de, pg 301

Wolke Verlags GmbH (Germany) *Tel:* (06192) 7243 *Fax:* (06192) 952939 *E-mail:* wolke-verlag@t-online.de *Web Site:* www.wolke-verlag.de, pg 301

The Wolsey Press (United Kingdom) *Tel:* (01473) 719377; (01473) 272616 (ISDN) *Fax:* (01473) 272115 *E-mail:* studio@wolseypress.co.uk *Web Site:* www.wolseypress.co.uk, pg 1227

Wolters Kluwer Belgie NV (Belgium) *Tel:* (015) 36 10 00, pg 74

Wolters Kluwer B.V. Juridische Boekenen Tijschriften (Netherlands) *Tel:* (0570) 647111 *Fax:* (0570) 636683, pg 492

Wolters Kluwer Espana SA (Spain) *Tel:* (091) 6020023 *Fax:* (091) 6020021 *E-mail:* pilarg@wke.es, pg 605

Wolters-Noordhoff B V (Netherlands) *Tel:* (050) 5226922 *Fax:* (050) 5277599 *E-mail:* info@wolters.nl *Web Site:* www.wolters.nl, pg 492

Wolters Plantyn Educatieve Uitgevers (Belgium) *Tel:* (03) 360 03 37 *Fax:* (03) 360 03 30 *E-mail:* klantendienst@woltersplantyn.be *Web Site:* www.woltersplantyn.be, pg 74

Women in Publishing (United Kingdom) *E-mail:* wipub@hotmail.com; info@wipub.org.uk *Web Site:* www.cyberiacafe.net/wip, pg 1293

Women's Health Advisory Service (Australia) *Tel:* (02) 4655 8855 *Fax:* (02) 4655 8699 *Web Site:* www.whas.com.au, pg 47

The Women's Press Book Club (United Kingdom) *Tel:* (020) 7636 3992 *Fax:* (020) 7637 1866 *E-mail:* sales@the-womens-press.com *Web Site:* www.the-womens-press.com, pg 1257

The Women's Press Ltd (United Kingdom) *Tel:* (020) 7636 3992 *Fax:* (020) 7637 1866 *E-mail:* sales@the-womens-press.com *Web Site:* www.the-womens-press.com, pg 775

Woodfield & Stanley Ltd (United Kingdom) *Tel:* (01484) 421467; (01484) 532401 *Fax:* (01484) 510237 *Web Site:* www.woodfield-stanley.co.uk, pg 1355

Woodhead Publishing Ltd (United Kingdom) *Tel:* (01223) 891358 *Fax:* (01223) 893694 *E-mail:* wp@woodhead-publishing.com; info@woodhead-publishing.com *Web Site:* www.woodhead-publishing.com, pg 775

Woodlands Publications (Australia) *Tel:* (02) 4969 3961 *Fax:* (02) 4962 3162 *E-mail:* woodlands@whopres.com.au *Web Site:* www.woodlandspublications.com, pg 47

Woongjin Media Corporation (Republic of Korea) *Tel:* 3281-6471 *Fax:* 3281-6473 *E-mail:* wjmhky@woongjin.co.kr *Web Site:* www.woongjin.com, pg 443

Woongjin.com Co Ltd (Republic of Korea) *Tel:* (02) 3670-1064 *Fax:* (02) 3670-1474 *E-mail:* wjmap@chollian.dacom.co.kr, pg 443

The Word Factory (United Kingdom) *Tel:* (0115) 914 5654 *Fax:* (0115) 914 5675 *E-mail:* info@thewordfactory.co.uk *Web Site:* www.thewordfactory.co.uk, pg 1165

Word of Life Press (Republic of Korea) *Tel:* (02) 738 6555 *Fax:* (02) 739 3824, pg 443

Words Work (New Zealand) *Tel:* (07) 3482953 *Fax:* (07) 3482953 *E-mail:* wordswrk@clear.net.nz, pg 502

Wordsworth Editions Ltd (United Kingdom) *Tel:* (01920) 465167 *Fax:* (01920) 462267 *E-mail:* enquiries@wordsworth-editions.com *Web Site:* www.wordsworth-editions.co.uk/distributors.htm, pg 775

Wordwright Publishing (United Kingdom) *Tel:* (020) 7284 0056 *Fax:* (020) 7284 0041 *E-mail:* wordwright@clara.co.uk, pg 775

Workaway Guides (Australia) *E-mail:* workaway@bigpond.com *Web Site:* www.users.bigpond.com/workaway, pg 47

Working People's Organization Publishing House (Democratic People's Republic of Korea), pg 437

World Affairs Press (China) *Tel:* (010) 65232695 *Fax:* (010) 5133181 *E-mail:* wap@bj.col.com.cn, pg 109

World Alliance of Reformed Churches (Switzerland) *Tel:* (022) 791 6240 *Fax:* (022) 791 6505 *E-mail:* warc@warc.ch *Web Site:* www.warc.ch, pg 1287

World Blind Union (WBU) - Union Mondiale des Aveugles (UMA) (Spain) *Tel:* (091) 5713685; (091) 5711236 *Fax:* (091) 5715777 *E-mail:* umc@once.es *Web Site:* www.once.es/wbu, pg 1284

World Book Co Ltd (Taiwan, Province of China) *Tel:* (02) 2311-0183 *Fax:* (02) 2331-7963, pg 642

The World Book Co (Pte) Ltd (Singapore) *Tel:* 3382323 *Fax:* 3371186, pg 1339

World Book Publishing (Lebanon) *Tel:* (01) 349370; (01) 743357; (01) 743358 *Fax:* (01) 351226 *E-mail:* info@wbpbooks.com *Web Site:* www.arabook.com, pg 447

World Books Publishing Corporation (China) *Tel:* (010) 64016320 *Fax:* (010) 4016320 *E-mail:* wpc@china.kw.co.cn, pg 109

World Conservation Union (IUCN) (Switzerland) *Tel:* (022) 999 0000 *Fax:* (022) 999 0002 *E-mail:* mail@iucn.org *Web Site:* www.iucn.org, pg 1287

World Council of Churches (WCC Publications) (Switzerland) *Tel:* (022) 7916379 *Fax:* (022) 7981346 *E-mail:* hs@wcc-coe.org *Web Site:* www.wcc-coe.org, pg 637

World Health Organization (WHO) (Switzerland) *Tel:* (022) 791 2111 *Fax:* (022) 791 3111 *E-mail:* publications@who.int *Web Site:* www.who.int, pg 1287

World Intellectual Property Organization (WIPO) (Switzerland) *Tel:* (022) 338 95 20 *Fax:* (022) 740 14 29 *E-mail:* info@wipo.int *Web Site:* www.wipo.org, pg 1287

World Leisure Marketing (United Kingdom) *Tel:* (01332) 573737 *Fax:* (01332) 573399 *E-mail:* office@wlmsales.co.uk, pg 1355

World Literature Project (Ghana) *Tel:* (022) 2119 *Fax:* (022) 2119, pg 305

World Meteorological Organization (Switzerland) *Tel:* (022) 730 8111 *Fax:* (022) 730 8181 *E-mail:* pubsales@gateway.wmo.ch; ipa@www.wmo.ch *Web Site:* www.wmo.ch, pg 637

World Meteorological Organization (Switzerland) *Tel:* (022) 730 8111 *Fax:* (022) 730 8181 *E-mail:* pubsales@gateway.wmo.ch *Web Site:* www.wmo.ch, pg 1288

World Microfilms Publications Ltd (United Kingdom) *Tel:* (020) 7586 4499; (0845) 606 0612 *Fax:* (020) 7722 1068 *E-mail:* microworld@ndirect.co.uk *Web Site:* www.microworld.ndirect.co.uk, pg 775

The World of Books Literaturverlag (Germany) *Tel:* (06241) 205352 *Fax:* (06241) 205352 *E-mail:* info@twobl-online.de *Web Site:* www.twobl-online.de, pg 301

World of Information (United Kingdom) *Tel:* (01799) 521150 *Fax:* (01799) 524805 *E-mail:* queries@worldinformation.com *Web Site:* www.worldinformation.com, pg 776

World of Islam Altajir Trust (United Kingdom) *Tel:* (020) 7581 3522 *Fax:* (020) 7584 1977, pg 776

World Publications Printers Pte Ltd (Singapore) *Tel:* 7449888 *Fax:* 8406118 *E-mail:* wphsin@singnet.com.sg *Web Site:* web.singnet.com.sg, pg 1223

World Scientific Publishing Co Pte Ltd (Singapore) *Tel:* 6467-5775 *Fax:* 6467-7667 *E-mail:* wspc@wspc.com.sg *Web Site:* www.worldscientific.com, pg 559

The World Society of Victimology eV (Germany) *Tel:* (02161) 186 609 *Fax:* (02161) 186 633 *Web Site:* www.world-society-victimology.de/, pg 301

World Wild Life Films (Pty) Ltd (Switzerland) *Tel:* (01) 4331444 *Fax:* (01) 4331460 *Web Site:* www.kftu.com, pg 637

Worlddidac (Switzerland) *Tel:* (031) 311 76 82 *Fax:* (031) 312 17 44 *E-mail:* info@worlddidac.org *Web Site:* www.worlddidac.org, pg 1288

Worsley Press (Australia) *Tel:* (03) 5979-1112 *Fax:* (03) 5979-1112 *E-mail:* info@worsleypress.com *Web Site:* www.worsleypress.com, pg 47

Verlag DAS WORT GmbH (Germany) *Tel:* (09391) 504135 *Fax:* (09391) 504133 *E-mail:* info@das-wort.com *Web Site:* www.das-wort.com; www.universal-spirit.cc, pg 301

Wouters Import NV (Belgium) *Tel:* (016) 233481 *Fax:* (016) 229841 *E-mail:* info@bookshop.wouters.be *Web Site:* www.wouters.be, pg 1302

WOZ Die Wochenzeitung (Switzerland) *Tel:* (01) 448 14 14 *Fax:* (01) 448 14 15 *E-mail:* woz@woz.ch *Web Site:* www.woz.ch, pg 637

Wrightbooks Pty Ltd (Australia) *Tel:* (03) 9532 7082 *Toll Free Tel:* 800 777 474 *Fax:* (03) 9532 7082 *Toll Free Fax:* 800 802 258 *E-mail:* custservice@johnwiley.com.au *Web Site:* www.wrightbooks.com.au, pg 47

Writers & Scholars International (United Kingdom) *Tel:* (020) 7278 2313 *Fax:* (020) 7278 1878 *E-mail:* natasha@indexoncensorship.org *Web Site:* www.indexonline.org/, pg 1294

YELLOW PAGES

Writers' Guild of Great Britain (United Kingdom) *Tel:* (020) 7833 0777 *Fax:* (020) 7833 4777 *E-mail:* admin@writersguild.org.uk *Web Site:* www.writersguild.org.uk, pg 1294

Writers' Publishing House (China) *Tel:* (010) 65004079; (010) 65389244 *Fax:* (010) 65930761 *E-mail:* wrtspub@public.bta.net.cn *Web Site:* www.zuojiachubanshe.com, pg 109

WRS Verlag Wirtschaft, Recht und Steuern GmbH & Co KG (Germany) *Tel:* (089) 89 517-0 *Fax:* (089) 89 517-250 *E-mail:* info@wrs.de *Web Site:* www.wrs.de, pg 301

WS Bookwell Ltd (Finland) *Tel:* (019) 21 941 *Fax:* (019) 2194 802 *Web Site:* www.bookwell.fi, pg 1154

WS Bookwell Ltd (Finland) *Tel:* (019) 21 941 *Fax:* (019) 219 4800 *E-mail:* pekka.tykkylainen@bookwell.fi *Web Site:* www.bookwell.fi, pg 1216

WS Bookwell Ltd (Finland) *Tel:* (019) 21 941 *Fax:* (019) 219 4800 *Web Site:* www.bookwell.fi, pg 1235

WTO (World Trade Organization) (Switzerland) *Tel:* (022) 739 51 11 *Fax:* (022) 731 42 06 *E-mail:* info@wto.org *Web Site:* www.wto.org, pg 1288

Wu Nan Book Co Ltd (Taiwan, Province of China) *Tel:* (02) 2705-5066 *Fax:* (02) 2706-6100 *E-mail:* wunan@wunan.com.tw *Web Site:* www.wunan.com.tw, pg 642

Wuerttembergische Bibliotheksgesellschaft (Germany) *Tel:* (0711) 212-4454; (0711) 212-4421 *Fax:* (0711) 212-4422 *E-mail:* information@wlb-stuttgart.de *Web Site:* www.wlb-stuttgart.de, pg 1563

Wuerttembergische Landesbibliothek (Germany) *Tel:* (0711) 2124424 *Fax:* (0711) 2124422 *E-mail:* direktion@wlb-stuttgart.de; information@wlb-stuttgart.de *Web Site:* www.wlb-stuttgart.de, pg 1511

Wuhan University Press (China) *Tel:* (027) 7870651; (010) 82001239 *Fax:* (027) 712661; (10) 82001248, pg 109

Das Wunderhorn Verlag GmbH (Germany) *Tel:* (06221) 402428 *Fax:* (06221) 402483 *E-mail:* info@wunderhorn.de *Web Site:* www.wunderhorn.de, pg 301

Wunderlich Verlag (Germany) *Tel:* (040) 72 72 0 *Fax:* (040) 72 72 319 *E-mail:* info@rowohlt.de *Web Site:* www.rowohlt.de, pg 301

Fachbuchverlag Armin W Wuth (Germany) *Tel:* (02306) 205247 *Fax:* (02306) 55686, pg 301

WUV/Facultas Universitaetsverlag (Austria) *Tel:* (01) 310 53 56 *Fax:* (01) 319 70 50 *E-mail:* verlage@facultas.at *Web Site:* www.wuv-verlag.at, pg 60

WUV/Service Fachverlag (Austria) *Tel:* (01) 310 53 56 *Fax:* (01) 319 70 50 *E-mail:* verlag@facultas.at *Web Site:* www.wuv-verlag.at/WUV, pg 60

Wydawn Na Sprawa' Wydawniczo-Oswiatowa Spotdzielnia Inwalidow (Poland) *Tel:* (022) 6209071 (ext 26) *Fax:* (022) 6209197, pg 528

Wyss Verlag AG Bern (Switzerland) *Tel:* (031) 253715; (031) 254425 *Fax:* (031) 3814821; (031) 254821, pg 637

Ediciones Xandro (Spain) *Tel:* (091) 5520261 *Fax:* (091) 5014145, pg 605

Xarait Libros SA (Spain) *Tel:* (091) 534 15 67 *Fax:* (091) 535 08 31, pg 605

Xenos Verlagsgesellschaft mbH (Germany) *Tel:* (040) 538093-0 *Fax:* (040) 5386000 *E-mail:* xenos.verlag@t-online.de *Web Site:* www.xenosverlag.de, pg 301

Edicions Xerais de Galicia (Spain) *Tel:* (0986) 214888 *Fax:* (0986) 201366 *E-mail:* xerais@xerais.es *Web Site:* www.xerais.es, pg 605

Xiamen University Library (China) *Tel:* (0592) 2085102 (0592) 2182360 *Fax:* (0592) 2256623 *E-mail:* xiaodh@xmu.edu.cn *Web Site:* www.xmu.edu.cn, pg 1498

Xiamen International Book Exchange Center (China) *Tel:* (0592) 5061401 *Fax:* (0592) 5061400 *E-mail:* xibc@xpublic.fz.fj.cn, pg 1306

Xiamen University Press (China) *Tel:* (0592) 2186128 *E-mail:* chbanshe@jingxian.xmu.edu.cn; xmdx@fjbook.com, pg 109

Xi'an Cartography Publishing House (China) *Tel:* (029) 7898962, pg 109

Xinhua Publishing House (China) *Tel:* (010) 3073880 *Fax:* (010) 3073880 *E-mail:* nianzh@xinhuanet.com, pg 109

Xunta de Galicia (Spain) *Tel:* (081) 544816 *Fax:* (081) 544887, pg 605

Y Cyfarwyddwr Urdd Gobaith Cymru (United Kingdom) *Tel:* (01970) 613100 *Fax:* (01970) 626120 *E-mail:* urdd@urdd.org *Web Site:* www.urdd.org, pg 776

Y Hoc Publishing House (Viet Nam) *Tel:* (04) 253274, pg 781

Yachdav, United Publishers Co Ltd (Israel) *Tel:* (03) 5614121 *Fax:* (03) 5611996 *E-mail:* maalot@tbpai.co.il *Web Site:* www.tbpai.co.il, pg 373

Yad Eliahu Kitov (Israel) *Tel:* (02) 6248868 *Fax:* (02) 6248838 *E-mail:* benarza@netvision.net.il, pg 373

Yad Izhak Ben-Zvi Press (Israel) *Tel:* (02) 5398887; (02) 5398888 *Fax:* (02) 5638310 *E-mail:* ybz@ybz.org.il *Web Site:* www.ybz.org.il, pg 373

Yad Tabenkin (Israel) *Tel:* (03) 5346268 *Fax:* (03) 5346376 *E-mail:* yadtab@inter.net.il *Web Site:* www.ic.org, pg 373

Yad Vashem - The Holocaust Martyrs' & Heroes' Remembrance Authority (Israel) *Tel:* (02) 6443400 *Fax:* (02) 6443443 *E-mail:* general.information@yadvashem.org.il *Web Site:* www.yad-vashem.org.il, pg 373

Yakuji Nippo Ltd (Japan) *Tel:* (03) 3862-2141 *Fax:* (03) 3866-8495 *E-mail:* shuppan@yakuji.co.jp *Web Site:* www.yakuji.co.jp/, pg 431

Yale University Press London (United Kingdom) *Tel:* (020) 7079 4900 *Fax:* (020) 7079 4901 *E-mail:* sales@yaleup.co.uk *Web Site:* www.yalebooks.co.uk, pg 776

Yama-Kei Publishers Co Ltd (Japan) *Tel:* (03) 3436-4055 *Fax:* (03) 34334057 *E-mail:* info@yamakei.co.jp, pg 431

Yamaguchi Shoten (Japan) *Tel:* (075) 781-6121 *Fax:* (075) 705-2003, pg 431

Yanagang Publishing (Australia) *Tel:* (03) 9870-3052 *Fax:* (03) 9876-1853 *E-mail:* gallerywithoutwalls@hotmail.com, pg 47

Julio F Yanez, Agencia Literaria S L (Spain) *Tel:* (093) 2007107; (093) 2005443 *Fax:* (093) 2094865 *E-mail:* yanezag@retemail.es, pg 1136

Eric Yang Agency (Republic of Korea) *Tel:* (02) 5923356 *Fax:* (02) 5923359 *E-mail:* info@ericyangagency.co.kr *Web Site:* www.ericyangagency.co.kr, pg 1134

Yapi-Endustri Merkezi Yayinlari-Yem Yayin (Turkey) *Tel:* (0212) 2193939 *Fax:* (0212) 2256623 *E-mail:* yem-od@yunus.mam.tubitak.gov.tr; kitap@yem.net *Web Site:* www.yem.net, pg 652

Yarmouk University Library (Jordan) *Tel:* (02) 7271100 (ext 2878) *Fax:* (02) 7271273 *E-mail:* yarmouk@yu.edu.jo *Web Site:* www.yu.edu.jo, pg 1522

Yaron Golan Publishers (Israel) *Tel:* (03) 6992867 *Fax:* (03) 6952664, pg 373

CV Yasaguna (Indonesia) *Tel:* (021) 8290422, pg 357

Roy Yates Books (United Kingdom) *Tel:* (01403) 822299 *Fax:* (01403) 823012, pg 1355

Yavneh Publishing House Ltd (Israel) *Tel:* (03) 6297856 *Fax:* (03) 6293638 *Web Site:* www.dbook.co.il, pg 373

YORVIK PUBLISHING LTD

Yavneh Publishing House Ltd (Israel) *Tel:* (03) 6297856 *Fax:* (03) 6293638, pg 1320

Yayasan Jaya Baya (Indonesia) *Tel:* (031) 41169, pg 357

Yayasan Kawanku (Indonesia) *Tel:* (021) 583100, pg 357

Yayasan Lontar (Indonesia) *Tel:* (021) 574-6880 *Fax:* (021) 572-0353 *E-mail:* lontar@attglobal.net *Web Site:* www.lontar.org, pg 357

Yayasan Obor Indonesia (Indonesia) *Tel:* (021) 3920114; (021) 31926978 *Fax:* (021) 31924488 *E-mail:* obor@ub.net.id *Web Site:* www.obor.or.id, pg 357

Kabalci Yayinevi (Turkey) *Tel:* (0212) 512 5602 *Fax:* (0212) 511 7794 *E-mail:* info@turkyaybir.com.tr *Web Site:* www.turkyaybir.org.tr/kabalci.html, pg 652

Alev Yayinlari (Turkey) *Tel:* (0212) 2921016 *Fax:* (0212) 2921017, pg 652

Yazhou Zhoukan Ltd (Hong Kong) *Tel:* 2515 5483 *Fax:* 2595 0497 *E-mail:* yzad@mingpao.com *Web Site:* www.yzzk.com, pg 320

YBM/Si-sa (Republic of Korea) *Tel:* (02) 2000-0501; (02) 2000-0330 (orders) *Fax:* (02) 2265-7573 *E-mail:* suite@ybmsisa.co.kr *Web Site:* www.ybm.co.kr; www.ybmsisa.co.kr, pg 443

Yearimdang Publishing Co (Republic of Korea) *Tel:* (02) 5661004 *Fax:* (02) 5679660 *E-mail:* webmaster@yearim.co.kr *Web Site:* www.yearim.co.kr, pg 443

Yedioth Ahronoth Books (Israel) *Tel:* (03) 768-3333 *Fax:* (03) 768-3300 *E-mail:* info@yedbooks.co.il *Web Site:* www.ybook.co.il, pg 373

Yee Wen Publishing Co Ltd (Taiwan, Province of China) *Tel:* (02) 2362-6012 *Fax:* (02) 2366-0977 *E-mail:* yeewen_us@yahoo.com, pg 642

Yeha Publishing Co (Republic of Korea) *Tel:* (02) 5535933; (02) 5535936 *Fax:* (02) 5525149, pg 443

Yetkin Printing & Publishing Co Inc (Turkey) *Tel:* (0312) 4181273; (0312) 2314234, pg 652

Yi Hsien Publishing Co Ltd (Taiwan, Province of China) *Tel:* (02) 2918-2288 *Fax:* (02) 2917-2266 *E-mail:* yihsient@ms17.hinet.net *Web Site:* www.yihsient.com.tw, pg 642

Ying Tat Co (Hong Kong) *Tel:* 25645980; 25645963; 25639981 *Fax:* 28111280 *Web Site:* www.cgan.com, pg 1158

Ying Tat Co (Hong Kong) *Tel:* 25645980; 25645963; 25639981 *Fax:* 28111280, pg 1179, 1236

Y L Peretz Publishing Co (Israel) *Tel:* (03) 5281751 *Fax:* (03) 5257983, pg 373

Yliopistopaino/Helsinki University Press (Finland) *Tel:* (09) 7010 230; (09) 7010 2360 *Fax:* (09) 7010 2370 *E-mail:* sst@yopaino.yliopistopaino.helsinki.fi *Web Site:* www.yliopistopaino.helsinki.fi, pg 145

YMCA-Press (France) *Tel:* (01) 43 54 74 46 *Fax:* (01) 43 25 34 79, pg 189

Yohan Shuppan (Japan) *Tel:* (03) 3984-0221 *Fax:* (03) 3984-0223 *E-mail:* shinsuke@yohan-pub.co.jp, pg 431

Yohan (Western Publications Distribution Agency) (Japan) *Tel:* (03) 3208-0181 *Fax:* (03) 3208-5308 *Web Site:* www.yohan.co.jp, pg 1323

Yokendo Ltd (Japan) *Tel:* (03) 3814-0911 *Fax:* (03) 3812-2615 *E-mail:* yokendo@gol.com, pg 431

Zie Yongder Co Ltd (Hong Kong) *Tel:* 29630111, pg 320

Yonsei University Library (Republic of Korea) *Tel:* (02) 2123-3486 *Fax:* (02) 393-7272 *E-mail:* ewebmaster@yonsei.ac.kr *Web Site:* www.yonsei.ac.kr; library.yonsei.ac.kr, pg 1524

Yonsei University Press (Republic of Korea) *Tel:* (02) 3926201 *Fax:* (02) 3931421 *E-mail:* ysup@bubble.yonsei.ac.kr *Web Site:* www.yonsei.ac.kr, pg 444

Yorvik Publishing Ltd (Zambia) *Tel:* (02) 311628; (02) 312852; (02) 313707 *Fax:* (02) 311628, pg 782

Yoshioka Shoten (Japan) *Tel:* (075) 781-4747 *Fax:* (075) 701-9075, pg 431

Youlhwadang Publisher (Republic of Korea) *Tel:* (031) 955-7000-5; (02) 5153143; (02) 5153142 *Fax:* (031) 955-7010 *E-mail:* yhdp@hitel.net; horang2@unitel.co.kr; webmaster@youlhwadang.co.kr *Web Site:* www.youlhwadang.co.kr, pg 444

Anglia Young Books (United Kingdom) *Tel:* (01799) 531192 *Fax:* (01799) 531192 *Web Site:* www.btinternet.com/~r.hayes, pg 776

Club of Young Readers (Slovakia) *Tel:* (02) 502 272 25 *Fax:* (02) 555 718 94 *E-mail:* spn@spn.sk *Web Site:* www.mlade-leta.sk, pg 1255

Bibliotheque Ben Youssef (Morocco) *Tel:* (04) 25465 *Web Site:* www.miniculture.gov.ma, pg 1529

Youth Cultural Publishing Co (Taiwan, Province of China) *Tel:* (02) 2311-2832 *Fax:* (02) 2311-3309 *E-mail:* youth@ms2.hinet.net *Web Site:* www.youth.com.tw, pg 642

Youval Tal Ltd (Israel) *Tel:* (02) 6248897 *Fax:* (02) 6245434, pg 1159

Yritystieto Oy - Foretagsdata AB (Finland) *Tel:* (00) 648292 *Fax:* (00) 648250, pg 145

Yuan Liou Publishing Co, Ltd (Taiwan, Province of China) *Tel:* (02) 2365-1212 *Fax:* (02) 2365 8989 *E-mail:* ylib@yuanliou.ylib.com.tw *Web Site:* www.ylib.com.tw, pg 642

Yuce Reklam Yay Dagt AS (Turkey) *Tel:* (01) 5227506 *Fax:* (01) 5163959, pg 652

Yugaku-sha Ltd (Japan) *Tel:* (03) 32333731 *Fax:* (03) 32333730, pg 431

Yuhikaku Publishing Co Ltd (Japan) *Tel:* (03) 3264-1319 *Fax:* (03) 3264-5030 *E-mail:* soumu@yuhikaku.co.jp, pg 431

Yuki Shobo (Japan) *Tel:* (03) 3203-0151 *Fax:* (03) 3203-0157, pg 431

Yunnan Provincial Library (China) *Tel:* (0871) 532 2035; (0871) 532 3851 *Web Site:* www.ynu.edu.cn, pg 1498

Yunnan University Press (China) *Tel:* (0871) 5032001; (0871) 5031057 *Fax:* (0871) 5162823 *Web Site:* www.ynup.com, pg 109

Yushodo Co Ltd (Japan) *Tel:* (03) 3357-1411 *Fax:* (03) 3351-5855 *E-mail:* ysdhp@yushodo.co.jp; antiq@yushodo.co.jp; intl@yushodo.co.jp *Web Site:* www.yushodo.co.jp, pg 1323

Yushodo Shuppan (Japan) *Tel:* (03) 3943-5791 *Fax:* (03) 3351-5855; (03) 3943-6024 *E-mail:* intl@yushodo.co.jp *Web Site:* www.yushodo.co.jp, pg 431

Editions Philateliques Yvert et Tellier (France) *Tel:* (03) 22914171 *Fax:* (03) 22912454, pg 189

Verlag Philipp von Zabern (Germany) *Tel:* (06131) 28747-0 *Fax:* (06131) 28747-44 *E-mail:* zabern@zabern.de *Web Site:* www.zabern.de, pg 302

IE Zachariadou OHG (Bucherstube) (Greece) *Tel:* (0310) 276334 *Fax:* (0310) 229936 *E-mail:* info@lillisbookstore.gr *Web Site:* www.lillisbookstore.gr, pg 1314

S J Zacharopoulos SA Publishing Co (Greece) *Tel:* (0210) 3231525; (0210) 3225011; (0210) 8142611 *Fax:* (0210) 3243814, pg 313

Zacharopoulos Z & G (Greece) *Tel:* (0210) 211 1895-7 *Fax:* (0210) 211 1897 *E-mail:* zachapub@otenet.gr, pg 313

Manrique Zago Ediciones SRL (Argentina) *Tel:* (011) 4382-8880; (011) 4501-1497; (011) 4383-2611 *Fax:* (011) 4502-7937 *E-mail:* mzago@lvd.com.ar, pg 9

Jorge Zahar Editor (Brazil) *Tel:* (021) 2240-0226 *Fax:* (021) 2262-5123 *E-mail:* jze@zahar.com.br *Web Site:* www.zahar.com.br, pg 92

Al Zahiriah (Syrian Arab Republic) *Tel:* (011) 112813, pg 1548

Zakheim Publishing House (Israel) *Tel:* (03) 5708840 *Fax:* (03) 5708850 *E-mail:* zakheim@netvision.net.il, pg 373

Zaklad Wydawnictw Statystycznych (Poland) *Tel:* (022) 6083223; (022) 608-32-10 (orders); (022) 608-38-10 (orders) *Fax:* (022) 625-9078; (022) 608-38-67 (orders), pg 528

The Zalman Shazar Center (Israel) *Tel:* (02) 5650444; (02) 5650445 *Fax:* (02) 6712388 *E-mail:* shazar@shazar.org.il *Web Site:* www.shazar.org.il, pg 374

Zalozba Mihelac d o o (Slovenia) *Tel:* (01) 4344 431 *Fax:* (01) 4344 431, pg 562

Zalozba Obzorja d d Maribor (Slovenia) *Tel:* (02) 2283116 *Fax:* (02) 2523213 *E-mail:* pivec@zalozba-obzorja.si *Web Site:* www.zalozba-obzorja.si, pg 562

Zambia Association for Research & Development (ZARD) (Zambia) *Tel:* (01) 224536; (01) 222883 *Fax:* (01) 222883 *E-mail:* zard@zamnet.zm; zard@zamtel.zm *Web Site:* www.zard.org.zm, pg 782

Zambia Catholic Bookshop (Mission Press) (Zambia) *Tel:* (02) 680456; (02) 680466 *Fax:* (02) 680484 *E-mail:* mpress@zamnet.zm, pg 1356

Zambia Educational Publishing House (Zambia) *Tel:* (01) 229490; (01) 229211 *Fax:* (01) 225073 *E-mail:* zpa@zamnet.zm, pg 782

Zambia Library Association (Zambia), pg 1574

Zambia Library Service (Zambia) *Tel:* (01) 254993 *Fax:* (01) 254993 *E-mail:* zamlibs@zamnet.zm, pg 1556

Zambia Printing Company Ltd (ZPC) (Zambia) *Tel:* (01) 227673; (01) 227674; (01) 227675 *Fax:* (01) 225026, pg 782

Zambian Ornithological Society (ZOS) (Zambia) *E-mail:* zos@zamnet.zm *Web Site:* www.fisheagle.org, pg 782

Zambon Verlag (Germany) *Tel:* (069) 779223 *Fax:* (069) 773054 *E-mail:* zambon@online.de *Web Site:* www.zambonverlag.de, pg 302

Martha Zamora Edicion de Libros (Mexico) *Tel:* (05) 2940231 *Fax:* (05) 2943856, pg 473

Silvio Zamorani editore (Italy) *Tel:* (011) 8125700 *Fax:* (011) 8126144 *E-mail:* szamora@tin.it *Web Site:* www.zamorani.com, pg 412

Zanfi-Logos (Italy) *Tel:* (059) 418810 *Fax:* (059) 418747, pg 412

Zanichelli Editore SpA (Italy) *Tel:* (051) 293111; (051) 245024 *Fax:* (051) 249782 *E-mail:* zanichelli@zanichelli.it *Web Site:* www.zanichelli.it, pg 412

Edizioni Zara (Italy) *Tel:* (0521) 489956 *Fax:* (0521) 241750, pg 412

Victor P de Zavalia SA (Argentina) *Tel:* (011) 942-1274; (011) 942-3046 *Fax:* (011) 942-5706, pg 10

Zavod za Izdavanje Udzbenika (Serbia and Montenegro) *Tel:* (021) 22068 *Fax:* (021) 22069, pg 554

Zavod za udzbenike i nastavna sredstva (Serbia and Montenegro) *Tel:* (011) 635-142; (011) 3051-900 (sales) *Fax:* (011) 2390-072 (sales) *E-mail:* prodaja@zavod.co.yu (sales) *Web Site:* www.zavod.co.yu, pg 554

Zazusy, Izd-Vo (Kazakstan) *Tel:* (03272) 422849, pg 432

Zbinden Druck und Verlag AG (Switzerland) *Tel:* (061) 2722105 *Fax:* (061) 2726722, pg 637

ZBW-Deutsche Zentralbibliothek fuer Wirtschaftswissenschaften/Bibliothek des Instituts fuer Weltwirtschaft (Germany) *Tel:* (0431) 8814-383; (0431) 8814-555 *Fax:* (0431) 8814-520 *E-mail:* info@zbw.ifw-kiel.de *Web Site:* www.zbw-kiel.de, pg 1512

Zdruzenie Zaloznikov in Knjigotrzcev Slovenije Gospodarska Zbornica Slovenije (Slovenia) *Tel:* (01) 5898 474 *Fax:* (01) 5898 100 *E-mail:* info@gzs.si *Web Site:* www.gzs.si, pg 1283

Zebra Agency (United Kingdom) *Tel:* (077193) 75575 *E-mail:* admin@zebraagency.co.uk *Web Site:* www.zebraagency.co.uk, pg 1144

Zebulon Verlag GmbH & Co KG (Germany) *Tel:* (0221) 3405620 *Fax:* (0221) 3405622 *E-mail:* zebulon-koeln@t-online.de, pg 302

Zed Books Ltd (United Kingdom) *Tel:* (020) 7837 4014; (020) 7837 0384 *Fax:* (020) 7833 3960 *E-mail:* zedbooks@zedbooks.demon.co.uk *Web Site:* zedweb.hypermart.net/zed/contact.htm, pg 776

Zeimukeiri-Kyokai (Japan) *Tel:* (03) 3953 3325 *Fax:* (03) 3565 3391 *E-mail:* katsu@zeikei.co.jp *Web Site:* www.zeikei.co.jp, pg 431

Zeitgeist Media GmbH (Germany) *Tel:* (0211) 55 62 55 *Fax:* (0211) 57 51 67 *E-mail:* info@zeitgeistmedia.de *Web Site:* www.zeitgeistverlag.de, pg 302

Verlag Zeitschrift fur Naturforschung (Germany) *Tel:* (07071) 31555 *Fax:* (07071) 360571 *E-mail:* mail@znaturforsch.com *Web Site:* www.znaturforsch.com, pg 302

Zen Now Press (Taiwan, Province of China) *Tel:* (02) 7182727 *Fax:* (02) 7174146, pg 642

Editorial Zendrera Zariquiey, SA (Spain) *Tel:* (093) 280 12 34 *Fax:* (093) 280 61 90 *E-mail:* info@editorialzendrera.com *Web Site:* www.editorialzendrera.com, pg 605

Zenemukiado Vallalat (Hungary) *Tel:* (01) 1176222 *E-mail:* musicpubl@emb.hu, pg 325

Zenkoku Kyodo Shuppan (Japan) *Tel:* (03) 3359-4811 *Fax:* (03) 3358-6174, pg 431

Zentral- und Landesbibliothek Berlin (ZLB) (Germany) *Tel:* (030) 902260; (030) 90226-401 *Fax:* (030) 90226-163 *E-mail:* info@zlb.de *Web Site:* www.zlb.de, pg 1512

Verlag Clemens Zerling (Germany) *Tel:* (08651) 602295 *Fax:* (08651) 602295, pg 302

Uitgeverij 010 (Netherlands) *Tel:* (010) 4333509 *Fax:* (010) 4529825 *E-mail:* office@010publishers.nl *Web Site:* www.010publishers.nl, pg 493

Zettner Verlag GmbH & Co KG (Germany) *Tel:* (0931) 91970 *Fax:* (0931) 960 097 *E-mail:* info@zettnerverlag.com *Web Site:* www.zettnerverlag.com, pg 302

Editorial Zeus SRL (Argentina) *Tel:* (0341) 449-5585 *Fax:* (0341) 425-4259 *E-mail:* editorialzeus@citynet.net.ar *Web Site:* www.editorial-zeus.com.ar, pg 10

Susanna Zevi Agenzia Letteraria (Italy) *Tel:* (02) 6570863; (02) 6570867 *Fax:* (02) 6570915 *E-mail:* susiz@tin.it, pg 1133

Zhejiang Education Publishing House (China) *Tel:* (0571) 5170300; (0571) 85103298 *Fax:* (0571) 5176944 *E-mail:* zjjy@zjcb.com, pg 109

ZheJiang Provincial Library (China) *Tel:* (0571) 799-9812 *Fax:* (0571) 7046263, pg 1498

Zhejiang University Press (China) *Tel:* (0571) 88273066 *Fax:* (0571) 88273066 *E-mail:* zupress@zju.edu.cn *Web Site:* www.zjupress.com, pg 109

Zhong Hua Book Co (China) *Tel:* (010) 63458226 *Fax:* (010) 63458226 *Web Site:* www.zhbc.com, pg 110

Zhongshan Library of Guangdong Province (China) *Tel:* (020) 83830676; (020) 83810164 *E-mail:* zxtxgwyh@163.net *Web Site:* www.zslib.com.cn, pg 1498

Verlag im Ziegelhaus Ulrich Gohl (Germany) *Tel:* (0711) 46 63 63 *Fax:* (0711) 46 13 41 *E-mail:* gohl@n.zgs.de, pg 302

Ziegler Druck- und Verlags-AG, Gemsberg-Verlag, Foto & Schmalfilm-Verlag (Switzerland) *Tel:* (052) 266 99 00 *Fax:* (052) 266 99 10 *Web Site:* www.zieglerdruck.ch, pg 637

Ziethen-Panorama Verlag GmbH (Germany) *Tel:* (02253) 6047 *Fax:* (02253) 6756 *E-mail:* annette@ziethen-panoramaverlag.de *Web Site:* www.ziethen-panoramaverlag.de, pg 302

Zig-Zag SA (Chile) *Tel:* (02) 335 7477 *Fax:* (02) 335 7545 *E-mail:* zigzag@rdc.cl *Web Site:* www.zigzag.cl, pg 101

Zilinska Univerzita (Slovakia) *Tel:* (089) 625919; (089) 621247 *Fax:* (089) 620023 *Web Site:* www.utc.sk, pg 561

Zimbabwe Book Publishers Association (ZBPA) (Zimbabwe) *Tel:* (04) 754256 *Fax:* (04) 754256 *E-mail:* engelbert@collegepress.co.zw, pg 1295

Zimbabwe Foundation for Education with Production (ZIMFEP) (Zimbabwe) *Tel:* (04) 755991; (04) 771833; (04) 771844; (04) 771834; (04) 771845; (04) 795679 *Fax:* (04) 749147 *E-mail:* zimfep@africaonline.co.zw, pg 784

Zimbabwe International Book Fair (Zimbabwe) *Tel:* (04) 702104; (04) 702108 *Fax:* (04) 702129 *E-mail:* execdir@zibf.org.zw *Web Site:* www.zibf.org.zw, pg 784

Zimbabwe Library Association (ZLA) (Zimbabwe) *Tel:* (04) 692741, pg 1574

Zimbabwe Publishing House (Pvt) Ltd (Zimbabwe) *Tel:* (04) 495335; (04) 497555 *Fax:* (04) 497554 *E-mail:* trade@zph.co.zw, pg 784

Zimbabwe Women Writers (Zimbabwe) *Tel:* (04) 774261 *Fax:* (04) 750282 *E-mail:* zww@telco.co.zw, pg 785

Zimbabwe Women's Bureau (Zimbabwe) *Tel:* (04) 747905; (04) 747809; (04) 747433; (263) 720575 *Fax:* (04) 747905 *E-mail:* zwbtc@africaonline.co.zw, pg 785

The Zimbabwe Writers Union (Zimbabwe) *Tel:* (054) 23284, pg 1410

Zindermans AB (Sweden) *Tel:* (031) 775 04 00 *Fax:* (031) 12 06 60, pg 617

Zip Editora Ltda (Brazil) *Tel:* (021) 2807272, pg 92

Zirkular - Verlag der Dokumentationsstelle fuer neuere oesterreichische Literatur (Austria) *Tel:* (01) 526 20 44-0 *Fax:* (01) 526 20 44-30 *E-mail:* info@literaturhaus.at *Web Site:* www.literaturhaus.at, pg 60

Zmora-Bitan, Publishers Ltd (Israel) *Tel:* (08) 9246565 *Fax:* (08) 9251770 *E-mail:* info@zmora.co.il, pg 374

Znaci Vremena, Institut Za Istrazivanje Biblije (Croatia) *Tel:* (042) 729 977 *Fax:* (042) 729 977, pg 119

Znanje d d (Croatia) *Tel:* (01) 4551500 *Fax:* (01) 4553-652 *E-mail:* znanje@zg.tel.hr, pg 119

Zoe Books Ltd (United Kingdom) *Tel:* (01962) 851318 *Fax:* (01962) 843015 *E-mail:* enquiries@zoebooks.co.uk *Web Site:* www.zoebooks.co.uk, pg 1165

Editions Zoe (Switzerland) *Tel:* (022) 309 36 06 *Fax:* (022) 309 36 03 *E-mail:* edzoe@iprolink.ch *Web Site:* www.editionszoe.ch, pg 638

Zoe Publishing Pty Ltd (Australia) *Tel:* (07) 5534 1522 *Fax:* (07) 5534 1502 *E-mail:* zoemkt@onthenet.com.au, pg 47

ZOI (Greece) *Tel:* (01) 3223560 *Fax:* (01) 3221283, pg 313

Har Zolindakis (Greece) *Tel:* (01) 3216504, pg 313

Zona Ediciones y Publications SA de CV (Mexico) *Tel:* (05) 5547438, pg 473

Zoshindo JukenKenkyusha (Japan) *Tel:* (06) 6532-1581 *Fax:* (06) 6532-1588 *E-mail:* jzoshindo@ybb.ne.jp *Web Site:* www.zoshindo.co.jp, pg 431

ZRD Trust (Zimbabwe) *Tel:* (04) 774775; (04) 744519 *Fax:* (04) 774764, pg 785

Zrinyi Kiado (Hungary) *Tel:* (01) 4595371; (01) 3339113, pg 325

ZS Verlag Zabert Sandmann GmbH (Germany) *Tel:* (089) 548 25 15-0 *Fax:* (089) 550 18 19 *E-mail:* contact@zsverlag.de *Web Site:* www.zsverlag.de, pg 302

Paul Zsolnay Verlag GmbH (Austria) *Tel:* (01) 50576610 *Fax:* (01) 505766110 *E-mail:* info@zsolnay.at *Web Site:* www.zsolnay.at, pg 60

Zuid Boekprodukties BV (Netherlands) *Tel:* (0252) 431565 *Fax:* (0252) 431567 *E-mail:* info@rebo-publishers.com *Web Site:* www.rebo-publishers.com, pg 493

Zuid En Noord VZW (Belgium) *Tel:* (011) 34 4991 *Web Site:* www.schrijversnet.nl, pg 75

Zuid-Nederlandse Uitgeverij NV/Central Uitgeverij (Belgium) *Tel:* (03) 8774400 *Fax:* (03) 8772115, pg 75

Zumpres Publishing Firm (The Former Yugoslav Republic of Macedonia) *Tel:* (091) 163-539; (091) 425-175 *Fax:* (091) 429-196; (091) 425-175 *E-mail:* zumpres@yahoo.com, pg 453

Zumstein & Cie (Switzerland) *Tel:* (031) 312 00 55 *Fax:* (031) 312 23 26 *E-mail:* post_zumstein@briefmarken.ch *Web Site:* www.zumstein-cie.ch, pg 638

Zunica (Bulgaria) *Tel:* (02) 551-977, pg 97

Zvaigzne ABC Publishers Ltd (Latvia) *Tel:* (0371) 7508799 *Fax:* (0371) 7508798 *E-mail:* foreign.rights@zvaigzne.lv *Web Site:* www.zvaigzne.lv, pg 445

Zveza bibliotekarskih drustev Slovenije (ZBDS) (Slovenia) *Tel:* (01) 20 01 193 *Fax:* (01) 42 57 293 *Web Site:* www.zbds-zveza.si, pg 1570

Zweipunkt Verlag K Kaiser KG (Germany) *Tel:* (06062) 61108 *Fax:* (06062) 63422, pg 302

Zwemmer Holdings Co Ltd (United Kingdom) *Tel:* (020) 7297 4555 *Fax:* (020) 7836 7049 *E-mail:* sales@zwemmer.com *Web Site:* www.zwemmer.com, pg 776

Zwiazek Literatow Polskich (Poland) *Tel:* (022) 8260589; (022) 8260866; (022) 8262504, pg 1281

Instytut Wydawniczy Zwiazkow Zawodowych (Poland) *Tel:* 6250765, pg 528

Uitgeverij Zwijsen BV (Netherlands) *Tel:* (013) 5838800 *Fax:* (013) 5838880 *E-mail:* klantenservice@zwijsen.nl *Web Site:* www.zwijsen.nl, pg 493

ZYC Holding Ltd (Hong Kong) *Tel:* 2963 0111, pg 320

Zyrichidi Bros (Greece) *Tel:* (031) 227915; (031) 266036 *Fax:* (031) 266036, pg 313

Notes

Notes

Notes